sav·ior, *Brit.* **sav·iour,** săv′yẽr, *n.* [O.Fr. *sauveour* (Fr. *sauveur*), < L.L. *salvator*, < *salvare*, E. *save*.] One who saves, rescues, or delivers; (*cap*), a title of God and esp. of Christ, often preceded by 'the.'

Guide word, in the right-hand column, a guide to the last entry word on the page

sa·vor·y, *Brit.* **sa·vour·y,** sā′vo·rē, *a.*— *savorier, savoriest.* Having a pleasant flavor and smell; pleasantly piquant to the taste; respectable.—*n. pl.* **sa·vor·ies.** *Brit.* a spicy dish eaten either before a meal to stimulate the appetite or afterward as a dessert.—**sa·vor·i·ly,** *adv.*—**sa·vor·i·ness,** *n.*

Qualifying label

sa·vor·y, sā′vo·rē, *n.* [M.E. *saverey*, ult. < L. *satureia*, savory.] *Bot.* any of the aromatic, menthaceous plants of the genus *Satureia*, esp. *S. hortensis*, an herb native in southern Europe and much cultivated as a seasoning. Also **sum·mer sa·vor·y.**

Homographs

saw, sa̤, *n.* [O.E. *saga, sage,* a saw = Dan. *sav,* Icel. *sŏg,* D. *zaag,* O. *sage*; same root as L. *seco,* to cut.] A hand tool or powered cutting instrument consisting of a blade, band, or disk of thin metal with a dentated or toothed edge.—*v.t.*—past *sawed,* pp. *sawed* or *sawn,* ppr. *sawing.* To cut with a saw; to form by cutting with a saw; to move through, slash, or slice as if operating a saw; as, to *saw* the air.—*v.i.* To use a saw; to cut with a saw; to be cut with a saw, as wood.—**saw·er,** *n.*—**saw·like,** *a.*

Synonym

Changing parts of speech

scab, skab, *n.* [O.E. *scaeb,* < L. *scabies,* scab, itch, < *scabo,* to scratch. Hence *shabby.*] A sort of crust formed over a sore in healing; *veter. pathol.* scabies or mange in animals, esp. in sheep. A fungous or bacterial plant disease causing crustlike spots in the affected areas. *Slang,* a non-union workman, esp. one who works in the place of a striker; a union worker who does not participate in a strike; a scoundrel or villainous fellow. *Metal.* a roughness or scale on the surface of a piece of iron or steel.—*v.i.*—*scabbed, scabbing.* To form or to have scabs; to work as a scab.

Usage labels

scal·ly·wag, skal′ē·wag″, *n.* Scalawag.

scal·y ant·eat·er, *n.* Pangolin.

Cross references

sce·nog·ra·phy, sē·nog′ra·fē, *n.* Representation or drawing according to the rules of perspective; this art applied to stage scene painting.—**sce·no·graph·ic,** sē″no·-graf′ik, sen″o·graf′ik, *a.*—**sce·no·graph·i·cal·ly,** *adv.*

Derived forms

Schmidt sys·tem, shmit′ sis′tem, *n.* An optical system used for reflecting telescopes and cameras which utilizes a spherical mirror objective and a transparent corrector plate near the focus to reduce spherical aberration.

Proper noun

schwa, shwä, *G.* shvä, *n.* [G. < Heb.] *Phon.* the indeterminate vowel sound of most syllables that are not stressed in English, as the *a* in *scholar,* the *u* in *tetanus,* the *i* and *e* in *prominent,* and the *o* in *piston*; the phonic symbol denoting that sound (ə).

sea, sē, *n.* [O.E. *sæ,* sea or lake = D. *see, zee,* Dan. *sö,* Icel. *saer,* G. *see,* Goth. *saivs.*] The continuous mass of salt water which covers the greater portion of the earth; the ocean; a segment of this that is enclosed to some degree by land; as, the North *Sea*; a name given to some large landlocked lakes; as, the Caspian *Sea*; a large wave or surge; as: A *sea* put the deck awash. Large swells or series of waves, as: A heavy *sea* was running that night. Any large quantity; as, a *sea* of difficulties; a flood; the vocation of a sailor, as: The *sea* is a hard life.—*a.*—**at sea,** aboard ship on the ocean; bewildered or perplexed; as, to be all *at sea* about the matter.—**fol·low the sea,** to make a career of seafaring.—**go to sea,** to voyage on the sea, esp. as an occupation.—**put to sea,** to set out, as a ship, onto the ocean.—**sea·most,** *a.* Located closest to the sea.

Examples of usage

Idiomatic expressions

ser·vi·ette, sẽr″vē·et′, *n.* [Fr.] *Brit., Canadian,* a table napkin.

u- tub, cūbe, bṳll; **oi-** oil; **ou-** pound.

Pronunciation key, a capsule guide

PRONUNCIATION SYMBOLS USED IN THIS DICTIONARY

(Continued)

s	seat, last, mass
sh	shark, rush
t	tea, mate, pat
th	thin
TH	then
u	tub, rough
ū	tube, cube
ṳ	bull, took
u	schwa sound, as in circus
v	victor, river, believe
w	wig
y	youth
z	zeal
zh	azure

FOREIGN

ä	Fr. ami
ch	G. ach
h	Sp. jacal — ha·käl′
N	Fr. bon
Œ	Fr. feu, G. schön
R	Fr. rouge, G. rot, It. mare, Sp. pero
V	Sp. Habana — ä·vä′nä
Y	Fr. tu, G. über

SUFFIX SOUNDS

ancy	ancē
ble	bl
ceous, cious	shus
ent	ent
esque	esk
ous	us
sion, tion	shan
tor	ta̤r, tur, to̤r, ter
ture	chẽr, chṳr

SOUTH AMERICA

LAMBERT AZIMUTHAL EQUAL-AREA PROJECTION

SCALE OF MILES
0   100   200   400   600

SCALE OF KILOMETRES
0 100 200   400   600

Capitals of Countries..............☆
International Boundaries...........
Canals ....

Copyright by C. S. HAMMOND & CO., N.Y.

Tropic of Capricorn

Cabo Frio
Niteroi
RIO DE JANEIRO
Angra dos Reis
I. S. Sebastião
Santos
SÃO PAULO
Paranaguá
Sorocaba
Juguá
Castro
Pto. Mendes
Curitiba
Joinville
Florianópolis
I. Santa Catarina
Laguna
Sa. do Mar
Pôrto Alegre
L. dos Patos
Rio Grande
L. Mirim
Pelotas
Santana do Livramento
Bagé
Caxias do Sul
Cruz Alta
Posadas
Uruguaiana
Rivera
Melo
Rocha
Villarrica
Encarnación
Corrientes
Concordia
Salto
Paysandú
Florida
MONTEVIDEO
Río de la Plata
Mercedes
C. San Antonio
Mar del Plata
Formosa
Resistencia
Reconquista
Paraná
Rosario
Pergamino
La Plata
Dolores
Quequén
Asunción
Santa Fé
Córdoba
Villa María
Río Cuarto
Mercedes
Chivilcoy
Avellaneda
BUENOS AIRES
Sta. Rosa
Tandil
Bahía Blanca
Bahía Blanca
Victorica
Gral. Acha
Salto
Jujuy
Saltao
S. Antonio
Rosario
Santiago del Estero
Catamarca
La Rioja
Chilecito
Mar Chiquita
Dulce
Tucumán
Salado
Ojos del Salado
22,539
Tinogasta
Santa María
San Luis
Mendoza
San Rafael
General Alvear
Victorica
Sta. Rosa
Colorado
Viedma
Negro
Puerto Madryn
Salina Grande
Rawson
Las Plumas
Pen. Valdés
Golfo San Matías
Camarones
Comodoro Rivadavia
Golfo San Jorge
Colonia Las Heras
Puerto Deseado
C. Tres Puntas
C. Tres Puntas
San Julián
Santa Cruz
Bahía Grande
Río Gallegos
FALKLAND ISLANDS (Br.)
Stanley
East Falkland
West Falkland
I. de los Estados (Staten I.)
Tierra del Fuego
Ushuaia
C. San Diego
Bahía Nassau
Cape Horn (Cabo de Hornos)
I. Hoste
Sta. Inés
Desolación
Strait of Magellan
Punta Arenas
I. Clarence
Pto. Natales
I. Hanover
I. Madre de Dios
I. Wellington
I. Campana
G. de Penas
C. Tres Montes
PEN. TAITAO
ARCHIPIÉLAGO de los CHONOS
Isla de Chiloé
Castro
Ancud
Pto. Montt
Valdivia
Villarrica
Temuco
Concepción
Arauco
Talcahuano
Constitución
Talca
Chillán
Santiago
Valparaíso
Viña del Mar
Los Vilos
La Serena
Coquimbo
Ovalle
San Juan
Aconcagua 22,831
Mercedario 22,211
Tupungato 21,356
San Carlos de Bariloche
Zapala
Neuquén
Norquinco
Esquel
Tecka
Gobernador Costa
Tierra del Fuego

Jachal
Copiapó
Caldera
Chañaral
Taltal
Antofagasta
Vol. Llullaillaco 22,057
Huasco
Vallenar
I. Más a Tierra
I. San Ambrosio (Chile)
I. de San Félix (Chile)
I. Más Afuera
Is. Juan Fernández (Chile)

Tropic of Capricorn

URUGUAY
PARAGUAY
ARGENTINA
CHILE
BRASIL
ATLANTIC OCEAN
PACIFIC OCEAN

MIDDLE AMERICA

BONNE PROJECTION

Copyright by C. S. HAMMOND & Co., N.Y.

SCALE OF MILES
0   200   400   600

KILOMETRES
0   200   400   600

Capitals of Countries .... ⊛
International Boundaries .... ━·━·━
Canals .... ━━━

EUROPE

LAMBERT AZIMUTHAL EQUAL-AREA PROJECTION

SCALE OF MILES

0 100 200 300 400 500 600

SCALE OF KILOMETRES

0 100 200 300 400 500 600

Capitals of Countries ⊙ International Boundaries -----
Internal Boundaries -----

Copyright by C.S.HAMMOND & CO., N.Y.

WESTERN AND CENTRAL EUROPE
CONIC PROJECTION

SCALE OF MILES
0 50 100 200 300

SCALE OF KILOMETRES
0 50 100 200 300

National Capitals
Administrative Centers
International Boundaries
Internal Boundaries
Canals

ASIA

LAMBERT AZIMUTHAL EQUAL-AREA PROJECTION

SCALE OF MILES

0   150   300   600   900   1200

SCALE OF KILOMETRES

0   300   600   900   1200

Capitals of Countries......☆
International Boundaries......
Canals......

AUSTRALIA AND THE PACIFIC OCEAN

LAMBERT AZIMUTHAL EQUAL-AREA PROJECTION

Capitals of Countries ⊗
Other Capitals ⊙

New Webster's Dictionary
of the
English Language

Based on a painting by Samuel F. B. Morse COURTESY OF THE CHICAGO PUBLIC LIBRARY

NOAH WEBSTER

New Webster's Dictionary

of the English Language

Contents

Preface

When plans were formulated for the creation of this new dictionary, the publishers decided that its emphasis, unlike that of many other dictionaries of the English language, should be on the future. It was decided to look ahead, and thus we planned this dictionary for the twenty-first century, as well as for the present.

Our work, which is completely new in content, has been designed and styled in the most modern format possible. It is set in an attractive, easy-to-read type, and it is printed on glare-free, long-life paper.

It is the latest contribution in the great tradition of English-language lexicography, a tradition that includes the works of Nathan Bailey (1721, 1730), Samuel Johnson (1755), Noah Webster (1783, 1806, and 1828), Joseph Emerson Worcester (1830), and Charles Richardson (1836-37). Our dictionary carries on it the name *Webster* in recognition of and respect for the American lexicographer, Noah Webster, whose work in the standardization of American usage and pronunciation set the guides for those of us who follow.

Based on the principle that language is essentially speech (a *living*, vibrant, constantly changing medium of expression), and that, as the language changes, so must its guidelines, our dictionary strives to bring to its users the English language in its most modern, and most accurate, form. It makes readily available to the home, to the student at school, and to the office—for reference, for formal learning, and for self-instruction—all but the most technical and the most esoteric words from our ever-expanding storehouse of knowledge, and it has been written in a style that is easily read and understood by people at all levels of intellectual development. The definitions are clear and comprehensive; the scientific and technical vocabulary is extensive, accurate, and the most modern possible; and the selection has been guided by usefulness to the reader. Within these covers are collected all of the words in common use which are essential for the vocabulary of an educated man.

But, because our dictionary is a general dictionary, intended for the general reader and not for such technicians of the English language as philologists, semanticists, and etymologists, it is not "unabridged." (An "unabridged" dictionary would contain within it all of the vocabulary thus far recorded in the long history of the English language.) Such an "unabridged" dictionary, prepared on the scale of our own general dictionary, would be unwieldy—it would not best serve the needs of the home, of the student, and of the office. Hence the one hundred thirty-five thousand entries here have been selected primarily because of their usefulness to the average dictionary user.

Our permanent editorial staff has labored for more than three years to prepare this essential tool of modern and effective communication, though the basic research for the project had been under way many years earlier. The work has been reviewed and tested by a distinguished panel of experts from a wide variety of disciplines. The panel includes not only scholars, but editors, authors, newspaper columnists, radio and television commentators, and reference librarians; it includes men and women from many walks of life who employ the English language daily in performance of their varied professional duties. These are the people who best understand and appreciate the richness and the variety of English. These are the members of our panel, and they, like us, believe we have done our job well.

In itself, this dictionary is a guide to spelling, to pronunciation, to grammar; in its etymological information it reveals to us past use and derivation, and its definitions of today's use suggest the future uses of words.

The aids to the dictionary should be used by the reader to make each excursion into this work as fruitful as possible. We urge our readers to study with especial care the *Guide to the Use of This Dictionary* which follows, as well as the *Pronunciation Guide*. Our editorial staff always welcomes any comment you may have on their work.

THE PUBLISHERS

Staff

Prepared by the publisher's editorial staff under the general supervision of

Dana F. Kellerman

ADMINISTRATIVE EDITORS

Harry E. Clarke
Lucinda R. Summers

SENIOR EDITORS

Joan Attenberg
Frances A. Bredin
Helen Dahlskog
Edith Glassner
Carol McCarthy
Margaret R. Murley
Bruce Scully

EDITORS

David Anderson
Ann Butterfield
William des Rochers
Diane Hirsch
Janice R. Pope
Joyce B. Sacks

ASSISTANT EDITORS

Gloria Ball
Adeline Becker
Charles Bliss, Jr.
Marvin Boydston
Anne Cambal
Meg Campbell
Vera Chatz
Penny Cohen
Lorain Field
Gabrielle Fitzgerald
Deborah Ann Flatley
Roberta Friedman
Joan Gladden
Harold V. Hopkins
Janice Hutchinson
Susan Weissner
James Johnson
Darryl Jordan
Roshan L. Khipple
Jacqueline Magnuson
Eileen Mather
Sandra Williamson
Ruth A. Meeron
Elliot Pine
Eduardo Schoua
Raymond Silvertrust
Jeanne Weimann

EDITORIAL ASSISTANTS

Stephen D. Beitler
Paul Cartwright
Linda Craig
Peter M. Davis
Karen Dillon
Sandra Lea Earley
Mary L. Fortney
Judith Ann Gecas
Margaret Ginn
Myrna Goldstein
Jeffrey Gordon
George R. Haithcock
Fitzgerald Higgins
Timothy Kellogg
Margaret Knapp
Mary Agnes Leonard
James Marousis
Oscar Marquis
David Muffelman
Charlotte Mullen
Gloria Olsberg
Lyman Rhoades
Margaret Rosenbloom
Valerie G. Russell
Eric D. Schlesinger
Sarah Swanson
Constance Taylor
James Winship
Larry C. Winterburn
Alice Zimbelman

ADMINISTRATIVE SUPERVISOR

Thomas J. Vadakekalam

ADMINISTRATIVE ASSISTANT

Betty P. Luhrman

OFFICE ASSISTANTS

Marie Comer
Jennifer Edwards
Pamela Edwards
Janice Elaine Ellis
Chris Gordon
Jeanne Haithcock
Patricia Saporito
Elizabeth Hass
Hope Kanner
Reah Logan
Julie McCarthy
Gail Miller
Evelyn A. O'Reilly

PRODUCTION AND DESIGN

Willard G. Smythe, *Director*
Walter Eckart, *Editorial Production Manager*
Larry Heeb, *Editorial Production Assistant*

ARTISTS

Emil C. Borcich
Charles Bozett
Eugene H. Goldberger

MANUFACTURING

Ervin J. Havers, *Vice President*
Stanley J. Brust
Edward W. Wolkowicz

Contributors and Consultants

JAMES DE T. ABAJIAN
Bibliographer, Martin Luther King Special
Collection, San Francisco Public Library

JULIA BOND
Circulation Librarian, Atlanta University
Libraries

ARNA W. BONTEMPS, L.H.D.
Author; Lecturer; Curator, Beinecke
Library, Yale University

JEAN-LOUIS BRINDAMOUR, PH.D.
General Editor, Afro-Am Press

CHARLES C. COLLINGWOOD
Chief Foreign Correspondent, CBS; Radio
and Television Commentator

ROY H. COPPERUD, PH.D.
Author; Professor of Journalism, University
of Southern California; Columnist,
Editor & Publisher

LEONARD S. DAVIDOW
Editor; Chairman, The Better-Speech Institute
of America; President, *Family Weekly Magazine*

MAXIMILIAN ELLENBOGEN, PH.D.
Author; Professor of Classical and Oriental
Languages, Queens College of The City University
of New York

KENNETH SEEMAN GINIGER
Author; Publisher; President, Laymen's
National Bible Committee, Inc.

JORY GRAHAM
Author; Columnist, *Chicago Sun-Times*

ABEL GREEN
Author; Editor, *Variety*

JAMES B. HALL, PH.D.
Author; Provost, College V, The University
of California at Santa Cruz

LOUIS G. HELLER, PH.D.
Author; Associate Professor of Classical
Languages and Hebrew, City College of The
City University of New York

PAUL HUME, D.M.
Author; Professor of Music, Georgetown University;
Music Editor, *Washington Post*

MARGARET HUNTON
Reference Librarian, The New York Public Library

BLYDEN JACKSON, PH.D.
Author; Editor; Professor of English,
Duke University

KENNETH R. JOHNSON, PH.D.
Associate Professor of Education,
University of Illinois, Chicago Circle

LYLE H. KENDALL, JR., PH.D.
Author; Professor of English, University of Texas;
Associate Editor, *American Literary Realism*

RALLA KLEPAK, J.D.
Attorney-at-Law; Reading Consultant, Division
of Vocational Rehabilitation, State of Illinois

JULIUS LESTER
Author; Editor; Folklorist; Musician

ADAM MAKKAI, PH.D.
Author; Associate Professor of Linguistics,
University of Illinois, Chicago Circle

RAVEN I. MCDAVID, JR., PH.D.
Author; Anthropologist; Professor of English,
University of Chicago

THOMAS B. MCDONOUGH, S.T.L., J.D.
Author; Editor; Former Chaplain, University of Chicago

MARGARET R. MURLEY, PH.D.
Botanist; Editor

DON CLEVELAND NORMAN, PH.B., D.D.
Author; Editor

MARIO PEI, PH.D.
Author; Professor Emeritus of Romance
Philology, Columbia University

CJ STEVENS, PH.D.
Professor of Speech and Theatre, and Chairman
of the Department, Herbert H. Lehman College
of The City University of New York

WILLIAM ALLEN SUMMERS, JR., PH.D.
Visiting Assistant Professor of Chemistry,
University of Oklahoma

MARK VAN DOREN, PH.D.
Author; Poet; Professor Emeritus of English,
Columbia University

A Historical Sketch of the English Language

By Mario Pei

Of some three thousand existing languages, large and small, English is second only to Chinese in number of speakers. It has well over 300 million native speakers, plus probably as many more who handle it in pidgin fashion or as an acquired tongue. It enjoys the widest distribution of any language on earth, appearing in numerous countries on every continent as an official tongue, and unofficially in many more. Over half of the world's scientific publications, books, newspapers, and magazines are entirely or partly in English. In international congresses and gatherings, English is used more often than any other tongue. More than half of the world's radio and television programs are in English, and it is the language most commonly used in the world's airways and seaways.

Yet around the year A.D. 1100, when the first unofficial census of English speakers (William the Conqueror's *Domesday Book*) appeared, the rough estimate was that they numbered about 1.5 million. About 1500, English seems to have had some 5 million speakers, as against, roughly, 10 million for German, 12 million for French, 8 or 9 million for Spanish and Italian. By 1700, the number of English speakers had grown to 8 million (with 2 million already on American soil). By 1900, English had taken a substantial lead over other European languages, with some 123 million (of whom only about 33 million were now on English soil), as against 80 million for German, 52 million for French, 58 million for Spanish, 54 million for Italian, 85 million for Russian. Today, the more than 300 million speakers of English (200 million of them in the United States) hold a commanding lead over the 100 million speakers of German, the 75 million of French, the 160 million of Spanish, the 60 million of Italian, the 200 million of Russian. Only Chinese, with its tremendous mass of over 700 million speakers, outstrips English.

Two factors were at work in this historical process. One was the natural population growth common to all countries, though in different degrees. The other was overseas expansion to such areas as the United States, Canada, Australia, New Zealand, and South Africa, with the concomitant absorption of millions of speakers of other languages who migrated to those areas, and whose descendants grew up in an English-speaking atmosphere. The same factor, though to a lesser degree, was operative in the case of other great colonial languages, such as Spanish, Portuguese, French, and Russian. The English language may therefore be said to have been the greatest beneficiary of British colonialism and American expansionism.

The English language had its official beginning as Anglo-Saxon, the tongue of the invaders from the European mainland North Sea coast who in the fifth century, under the mythical leadership of Hengist and Horsa, began to push back the Celtic-speaking, Romanized Britons into the mountain fastnesses of Wales and Cornwall. Racially and linguistically, the newcomers were a conglomerate of Angles, Saxons, and Jutes, speaking Germanic dialects akin to Dutch, Frisian, and Low German. For what concerns language, they formed part of a larger, West Germanic branch of the Germanic or Teutonic subgroup of Indo-European, the vast family of related languages whose other branches are Celtic, Latin-Romance, Balto-Slavic, Greek, Albanian, Armenian, and the Indo-Iranian tongues of northern India, Pakistan, and Iran. The Teutonic subgroup comprised an East Germanic branch, now extinct, whose major representative was Gothic; a North Germanic or Scandinavian branch, which survives today in Icelandic, Danish, Norwegian, and Swedish; and a West Germanic branch, whose ancient members included Old High German, Old Saxon, Old Frisian, and Anglo-Saxon, and whose modern members are German, both High and Low, Dutch-Flemish, Afrikaans, Frisian, and English.

The mixture of Low German dialects spoken by the Anglo-Saxons differed from modern English to such a degree that it cannot be read or understood by present-day English speakers without a special course of study. Like all the older members of the Indo-European family, it had a rich system of cases for nouns and adjectives, special endings for separate verb forms, a sound structure which has undergone radical transformations, and a vocabulary which is scanty by modern standards, but adequate for the needs of the Anglo-Saxon civilization at that period.

While it is true that less than a fourth of the present-day English vocabulary consists of words and roots of Anglo-Saxon origin, these nevertheless constitute that segment of today's spoken language which is basic and which has the greatest frequency of occurrence—words that appear over and over again in the flow of spoken and even written language: common connectives and adverbs such as *and, if, but, who, that, which, when, where, here, there*; articles and prepositions such as *the, a, to, for, in, by, of, with, from*; adjectives such as *hot, cold, great, small, good, bad*; nouns such as *bread, water, sea, land, world, heaven, hell*; verbs such as *be, have, ask, answer, go, come*; pronouns such as *I, me, you, he, she, it*. In a running conversational text, it is not rare to find that as many as 90 percent of the words are of Anglo-Saxon origin.

The tongue of the Anglo-Saxons, unstandardized at first, had achieved a measure of unification by the time of King Alfred in the latter part of the ninth century. It had already begun to receive contributions from other than West Germanic sources. The antipathy between Britons and Saxons was such that very few Celtic words came into the Saxon language at this period (*crag, dun, combe*, among them; most borrowings from Celtic took place at a later period: *glen, heather, clan, bard, plaid, slogan* from Scots Gaelic; *colleen, whiskey, blarney* from Irish; *eisteddfod, flannel* from Welsh). But the missionaries who converted the Anglo-Saxons to Christianity also brought to them a fairly large number of Latin and Greek words, many of religious connotation, which were added to those which the Anglo-Saxons had picked up from their contacts with the Romans while they were still on the European mainland. In this fashion, the Old English of King Alfred's period already possessed such words as *kitchen* (Latin *coquina*), kiln (Latin *culina*), street (Latin *strata*); cheese (Latin *caseus*), shrive (Latin *scribere*), mint (Latin *moneta*), minster (Latin *monasterium*), kirk or church (Greek *kyriake*). It even had such words as *persoc* (Latin *persica*), later displaced by the same Latin word in Norman-French development (*peach*).

The first major crisis in the history of the English language came with the Danish invasions at about A.D. 870. The Danes were members of the same Teutonic stock as the Anglo-Saxons, but of the Northern or Scandinavian branch. Their language, while close, was different. When King Alfred, tired of fighting and raids, offered them appeasement by granting them permission to settle in the northeastern areas of England, they accepted, and intermingled with the local Anglo-Saxons. The languages also intermingled, with the result that several West Germanic Anglo-Saxon words were replaced by North Germanic Scandinavian equivalents. Among the latter are the all-important pronouns *they, them*, replacing Anglo-Saxon *hie, hem* (the latter is said to survive in colloquial "I met 'em yesterday"); verbs such as *take, cut, get* (Anglo-Saxon used *niman, snidan, weorthan*—if these had come down into the modern language, they would probably have as their present-day forms *nim, snide, werth*—compare German *nehmen, schneiden, werden*, which were not subjected to Scandinavian influence); nouns such as *knife, leg, steak, sister*; and adjectives such as *ill, ugly, happy, low*. The verb form *are* is Scandinavian (compare Anglo-Saxon *sint, sindon*, German *sind*, but Swedish *är*). In many cases, both the Anglo-Saxon and the Danish word have come down to modern times (*no—nay; from—fro; shirt—skirt; ditch—dike; welkin—sky*). Many English place-name suffixes, such as *-by, -thorpe*, and *-dale*, are of Scandinavian origin. The Scandinavian contribution to the formation of English is large and important, but also generally unrecognized by the nonspecialist, because it has so thoroughly merged with kindred Anglo-Saxon.

The next, and last, invasion from abroad came with the Norman Conquest of 1066. Racially, the Normans were of the same breed as the Danes who had settled in northeastern England centuries before. Under very similar circumstances, these Northmen had settled at the somewhat unwilling invitation of the French kings in a province of northwestern France that was given their name, Normandy—"land of the Normans or Northmen." Just as the Danes had become thoroughly assimilated to the Anglo-Saxons, the Normans had taken over French customs and the French language. When their leader, William of Normandy, wrested control of England from Harold, last of the Saxon kings, the language his followers spoke was the Norman dialect of French.

Merging of the Old English of the Anglo-Saxons and the French of the Normans was by no means the easy process that had attended the merger of Anglo-Saxon and Danish. French, too, belonged to the great Indo-European family of languages, but it was of the Latin-Romance, not the Germanic group. For centuries the two languages remained apart: English was spoken by the Anglo-Saxon lower classes, and French by the Norman overlords and their retainers, the clergy, the scholars, and the royal court. At first the conquerors disdained the tongue of their subjects, and English, which had attained literary pretensions during the late Anglo-Saxon period, sank to an unbelievably low estate. Practically all writing was done in Latin or French. In the twelfth and thirteenth centuries there developed on English soil a flourishing literature in French, with such masterpieces as the *Lays* of Marie de France and, probably, the *Chanson de Roland*. But in the same period all that English can boast of is a few works of a religious nature, such as the continuation of the Peterborough Chronicle, the *Ormolum*, and the *Ancres Riwle* (Layamon's *Brut* is only an Anglo-Saxon paraphrase of an earlier French work by Wace).

Yet during this dark period when the English language seemed prostrate, it was not only changing and developing in the mouths of the people, but making inroads into the speech habits of the upper classes. In the course of nearly three centuries and many bitter wars fought against the French on the mainland, the upper classes were becoming convinced that their future lay in their new English possessions, not on the continent. By the middle of the thirteenth century they, too, were speaking English habitually. By the beginning of the fourteenth, the new state of linguistic affairs was fully recognized, and long before the end of that century it had become official.

But in the meantime several things had been happening to the English language. Bereft of official support and a true written standard, it had been transforming itself from Anglo-Saxon to Middle English, with the loss of many of the old flectional endings and widespread mergers among the rest (*blinda* and *blindan*, for example, merged into *blinde*, which forecasts the modern endingless *blind*). Many changes were taking place in the sound pattern, though the most far-reaching of these, the Great Vowel Shift, was to come later. Most important, perhaps, was the tremendous infiltration of French words into the vocabulary, laying the foundation for the word stock of modern English, which is more than half Latin-Romance. A vast flood of words of extremely frequent occurrence, usually monosyllabic in form, and which most people take for granted as being "English" from the beginning of time, were assimilated from the French of the Normans. Consider a list that includes *please, wait, pay, large, air, noise, play, piece, nice, poor, real, cry, catch, chase, grief, pray*. Add a few two-syllable words such as *army, money, very*, where French *armée, monnaie, verai*, or *vrai* have replaced the original Anglo-Saxon *here*, that still appears in German *Heer*, the *gild* that corresponds to German *Geld*, the *sore* of "I am sore wroth" that coincides with German *sehr*. Think of the *beef, veal, pork* (French *boeuf, veau, porc*) whose Anglo-Saxon counterparts, now differentiated as to meaning, are *ox, calf, swine*. As in the case of Danish, the intrusion into the language of a French word did not invariably displace the old Saxon form; both lived on happily together, giving rise to a rich series of synonyms (*heal—cure; lord—sire; glass—mirror; bowman—archer; wedlock—marriage; spear—lance; sorrow—grief; might—power; doom—judgment; beseech* or *bid—pray*; in each couple the first word is Saxon, the second French). But in the case of *medicine, geometry, lieutenant, uncle*, the French word effectively displaced the Saxon-derived *leechcraft, earthcraft, steadholder, eme*.

As far back as 1340, when a Kentish writer titled his poem *The Ayenbite* (Again-bite) *of Inwyt* (In-wit) rather than *The Remorse of Conscience*, there have been attempts to "purify" the language of its foreign importations, and restrict it to its original Anglo-Saxon or, at the most, Germanic content. They have never been successful.

The complete and successful marriage of Germanic and Latin-Romance is shown by the late fourteenth-century output of Chaucer, who deftly blends both vocabulary elements into a literary tongue that is substantially modern English, and can be understood by the present-day reader with a minimum of study and explanations.

But the language was still to undergo many changes before achieving its modern state. Between the Chaucerian and the Elizabethan periods, English vowel sounds were radically transformed, though little of that phonetic transformation was reflected in the spelling. Old English vowels, both long and short, were for the most part "pure" vowel sounds, without the diphthongal glide that characterizes our so-called "long" vowels of today (in the alphabet pronunciation of today, *a, e, i, o, u* are diphthongs, consisting of a basic sound preceded or followed by an on- or off-glide, with the sole possible exception of *e*, which some American linguists insist is *iy*; the others are pronounced respectively as *ey, ay, ow, yu*). The transformation was achieved in several distinct stages over a period of centuries. Anglo-Saxon *stān*, for instance, moved on to *stōn*, with the *ō* pronounced as in German *Sohn*, then diphthongized into the two sounds that are heard in the modern General American and British standard pronunciation of *stone* (American *stown*, British *stawn*). Anglo-Saxon *hūs*, first changing into *hows*, moves on to American *haws*, British *həws*. The final *-e* that had largely supplanted Anglo-Saxon endings tended to become more and more silent, even when retained in spelling. Fluctuations in plural forms were largely leveled out in favor of the now almost universal *-s* formation (but there are survivals of earlier plural-forming systems, such as *oxen, children, deer, feet, mice*; it is my own theory that this triumph of the *-s* plural, which is general in English, fairly widespread in Dutch, rare in German, practically nonexistent in Scandinavian, may in part have been due to French influence).

The fifteenth and sixteenth centuries mark the beginning of a slowing down of phonetic and grammatical changes, but also the appearance of a mass of vocabulary accretions of a learned nature, which are overwhelmingly Latin and Greek. England could not escape (nor indeed did she make the slightest attempt to escape) the pervading influence of the European Renaissance and Humanism. This meant a new flowering of classical studies and widespread pilfering of classical lexicons to round out the great European languages. Often the pilfering took place on English soil, with the coining of "aureate" and "inkhorn" terms which as often as not dropped out of the language after a brief lifespan (*assation, ataraxy, clancular, dignotion, exolution* are cases in point). Just as often the long, classical-sounding words came into English from French and Italian—languages that were closer to the source. Most of these accretions are with us today, and form an important, not to say indispensable part of our literary, scientific, and even everyday vocabulary. Try getting along without such words, unchanged from the original Latin, at least in written appearance, as *alias, alibi, extra, deficit, bonus, exit, item, agenda, propaganda*; or such Greek scientific coinages as *protein, allergy, antibiotic, hormone, cosmetic, automatic, microphone, telegraph, stratosphere*.

Modern civilization is a matter of both adaptation and give-and-take. The latter process is common to all civilized languages. It is in vain that French purists like Etiemble fulminate against the French tendency to borrow and adapt English words. The speakers of English have taken from French far more than they will ever be able to repay, for they are probably the greatest word borrowers in history. Once modern interchanges begin, there is no stopping them.

English borrowings from French include not only the thousands of words that came in with the Normans, and which had achieved full citizenship by the time of Chaucer (words such as *crown, state, court, tax, office, mayor, prince, count, peasant, treason, sermon, lesson, clerk, saint, faith, mercy, proof, fine, arrest, accuse, peace, battle, soldier, dress, robe, coat, fur, chair, closet, cellar, porch, amusement, art, beauty, color, pen, pain, joy, flower* and *flour, city, labor, river, cost, safe, seem, close, move, push, quit, easy, single, sudden, allow, carry, obey, remember, suppose*). They also include later acquisitions that may or may not retain some perceptible trace of their origin in their spelling or pronunciation (*sumptuous, brunette, ballet, champagne, dentist, patrol, syndicate, chauffeur, foyer, garage*). They even include ultramodern terms such as *discothèque* and *gogo* (French slang *à gogo* means "aplenty").

Next to French, the greatest foreign influence exerted upon English was from Italian. Here we have a wealth of musical and artistic terms (*opera, aria, piano, torso, vista, gala, cameo, cello*), some of which have strayed far beyond their original function

and meaning (*tempo, crescendo, staccato, stanza, inferno, studio, solo*). Many are disguised by reason of having used French as an intermediary, or because English speakers chose to adapt them to English sound schemes (*cash, deposit, costume, pilot, medal, lumber, escort, cartoon, laundry, manage, group, pants, concert, attack, vogue, compliment, burlesque, campaign*, even *flu* from *influenza*, *boloney* from Bologna, and *wig* from *periwig* from *perruque* from *parrucca*). While most of these acquisitions occurred in past centuries, some are fairly recent (*manifesto, zucchini, broccoli, spaghetti, ravioli, confetti, Punch* from *Punchinello* from *Pulcinella, pasta, marina, credenza*).

Spanish and Portuguese have contributed heavily to the Anglo-American vocabulary, especially in connection with contacts in the American Southwest. Here are words such as *cargo, mosquito, sherry* (from the city of Jerez in Spain), *pimento, tornado, rodeo, sombrero, stampede, bonanza, incommunicado, commando, cork, conga*. Many words from the Iberian Peninsula are disguised almost beyond recognition by adaptation to English sound patterns (*cockroach* from *cucaracha, hoosegow* from *juzgado, vamoose* from *vamos, alligator* from *el lagarto, lariat* from *la reata, pickaninny* from *pequenino*). More recent acquisitions include *aficionado* and *sangría*.

Dutch, closest of the other Germanic languages to English, has been a generous contributor, with such words as *boor, deck, drawl, boom, nap, gin, tub, scum, spool, stripe, freight, leak, pump, dock, snap, switch, toy, brandy, cookie, cole slaw, yacht*, to which may be added South African *trek* and *veld*. North Germanic Scandinavian, which helped out in the earliest formative period of English, continues with such offerings as *fjord, floe, ski, slalom, geyser*. German, which had given us *swindler, halt, plunder, sauerkraut, stroll, kindergarten, poodle, yodel, poker*, along with loan translations such as *masterpiece, homesickness, sharpshooter, standpoint, chain-smoker, mailed fist, storm and stress, superman*, continues with words not yet naturalized, such as *Weltschmerz, Blitz, ersatz, Lebensraum, Luftwaffe, Panzer, Dirndl*.

The Slavic languages, notably Russian, contributed in the past words such as *czar, vodka, steppe, pogrom*, joined more recently by *bolshevik, kulak, sputnik*, and words that Russian had previously taken from the west, such as *commissar* and *intelligentsia*. From Serbo-Croatian comes *cravat*, from Czech *robot*, from Polish *polka* and *mazurka*.

Among Oriental contributors, first place goes to the two great Semitic languages, Arabic and Hebrew. The first offers such words as *alcohol, alkali, algebra, assassin, syrup, divan, sofa, mattress, magazine, safari*, along with many medieval Persian forms that came to the west by way of Arabic: *azure, candy, check, lemon, lilac, orange, spinach, scarlet, sugar*. Persian itself supplies *bazaar, caravan, crimson, jungle, khaki, shawl, tulip, turban, van, veranda*, while from India come *loot, pundit, guru, rajah, punch* (the drink), *coolie, bungalow, calico, cot, polo, thug*.

Hebrew, with its kindred Aramaic, gives us many old words, largely religious: *camel, ebony, sapphire, seraph, cherub, rabbi, abbot*. From the modern Ivrit of Israel we get *kibbutz* and *sabra*.

The Far East gives us Chinese *tea, tycoon, kowtow, tong, yen*; Japanese *kimono, samurai, kamikaze, kabuki, judo, ju jitsu* and *karate*. Australian native languages give us *kangaroo* and *boomerang*; Polynesian tongues *aloha, lei, luau, atoll, tattoo, bamboo*. From African languages are *gorilla, guinea, voodoo, hoodoo, zebra, jazz, okra, gumbo, jumbo*, while North American Indian tongues are responsible for *moccasin, wigwam, moose, raccoon, skunk, totem, tomahawk, porgy, terrapin*, with those of Mexico contributing *chocolate, tomato* and *coyote*, those of the West Indies *mahogany, barbecue, hurricane, cannibal, maize, potato, tobacco*, those of South America *quinine, llama, pampa, jaguar, tapioca*, and the recent *lagniappe*.

It is obvious that the vocabulary of English, though firmly rooted in a Germanic-Latin-Romance-Greek base, is among the most international on earth, more so than those of most deliberately constructed "neutral" languages, including Esperanto.

English has always been a heavily dialectalized language. Our oldest Anglo-Saxon records indicate an early division into Northumbrian and Mercian, both stemming from Anglian; West Saxon, coming from the language of the Saxons; and Kentish, from that of the Jutes. By the time of the Norman conquest in 1066 the three main divisions of English—Northern, Midland, and Southern—are perceptible. These divisions continue today in British English, despite the creation of a somewhat artificial "King's English" or "Received Standard," based on the speech of the cultivated classes of London.

Greater dialectal divergences began to arise with the overseas migration of the language to the newly discovered continents of America and Australia, as well as to South Africa and New Zealand. While the English varieties of Australia, New Zealand, and South Africa continue to lean toward British pronunciation and usage, the same cannot be said of the English of the United States and Canada. The overall result is today's cleavage between the two great divisions of the English-speaking world, the British and the American.

The divergence of the American tongue from British standards began to be noticed in the eighteenth century. Even before the American Revolution, it was suggested by many that a new "American" language was developing which, in the words of Noah Webster, would eventually differ from the tongue of Britain as much as Dutch or Danish differ from German. Thanks to the growth of modern means of communication, this fortunately did not come to pass. Nevertheless, the differences are substantial. Because of a common literature and widespread literacy, these divergences show up only occasionally in writing (there are, however, a considerable number of divergent spellings, which supply almost unfailing clues to the nationality of the writer: American *labor, theater, traveled, check, curb, jewelry, connection, defense*, vs. British *labour, theatre, travelled, cheque, kerb, jewellery, connexion, defence*). In speech, the differences are most noticeable in the fields of pronunciation and vocabulary usage; for the first, consider the customary American pronunciation of *clerk, nephew, figure, schedule, lieutenant*, as against a British pronunciation which might be represented by spellings such as *clark, nevew, figger, shedule, leftenant*. Vocabulary usage tends to differ especially in certain fields; in automotive transportation, for instance, where the American will normally use *hood, wrench, gas, truck, trunk, top, windshield, directional sign, traffic circle*, the British preference is for *bonnet, spanner, petrol, lorry, boot, hood, windscreen, trafficator, traffic circus*, respectively; elsewhere we have American *corn, review, clipping, roast, eggplant, cracker, dessert, signboard, inheritance tax, radio, TV, vacation*, vs. British *maize, notice, cutting, joint, aubergine, biscuit, sweet, hoarding, death duty, wireless, telly, holiday*.

Consider also the twenty-four local dialectal varieties of Britain, and those of America, which were once thought to be three (Eastern, Southern, and Midwestern or General American), but which on closer scrutiny turn out to be at least a dozen, plus dialectal forms peculiar to large cities.

Canadian English generally coincides with American, but with a few vocabulary divergences and one or two telltale differences in pronunciation (Canadian *house, about*, where the *ou* diphthong comes closer to that of Britain that to that of most of America; *zed* instead of *zee* for the last letter of the alphabet).

South African English is rather strongly influenced by Dutch-based Afrikaans, with such constructions as *by the house* for *at* or *in the house, to trek at schimmel day* for *to start out at sunrise*, and such words as *baas, dopper, springbok, lekker, strandloper* for *boss, conservative, raw recruit, nice, beachcomber*. New Zealand English uses such expressions as *skite, up stick, be pie on, sharemilker, squatter* (*to brag, to move house, to be good at, sharecropper, large-scale farmer*), along with Maori terms (*kapai, tenakoe, paheka, mana, kiwi*, for *O.K., hello, stranger, prestige, doughboy*). Australian English, based largely on London Cockney, has gone on to evolve its own phonology and vocabulary. The latter includes *paddock* and *station* (*field* and *ranch*), *to stand treat* (*to shout*), *cooee* (*yoo-hoo*), *cow* (*awful*).

The current period of English, as of most civilized languages, is one of slow, often almost imperceptible change in sounds and grammatical forms (save insofar as such widespread slang usages as *between you and I, who did you see?, like a cigarette should* manage to take hold). But this is coupled with rapid, kaleidoscopic transformations in the vocabulary sector, due to a variety of causes, among which may be listed slangy and colloquial creativity, scientific and technological advances calling for added words to express new concepts, the proliferation of professional and trade jargons, and changed, often brand-new fields of human activity. The measure of probable future change may be gauged by glancing at some of the myriad words and expressions that have been added to the language since the turn of the century, when such terms as *motel, genocide, corny, snafu, smog, kodak, zen, astronaut, quasar*, and *feedback* would have been totally meaningless, and such other expressions as *integration, deceleration, satellite, swing, square*, and *bromide*, while in existence, would not have been recognized in their current, often slangy acceptances. To these may be added various word combinations of the type of *fringe benefit, sit-in, airlift, count-down, brain-washing, fallout, loyalty oath*, and downright slang expressions such as *scram, jerk, goof, stash, boondoggle, beatnik, schlemiel* and *schmo*.

It is more than likely that the English of a hundred years hence would sound to present-day speakers (who, of course, would not be around to hear it) like so much double-talk—recognizably English, but thoroughly incomprehensible.

It is the task of good dictionaries to keep abreast of the rising tide of words that threatens to engulf us; grant them admission where permanence is more or less assured, and reject the nonce words; to indicate those words which have become completely archaic, such as *vocular, viduous, deruncinate, begeck, yuke, pringle*; properly label as obsolescent others current in our youth, such as *drawing room, sparking light, spinney, weald* and *skiddoo*; and maintain a clear-cut distinction between what is standard and what is substandard, what is general, at least throughout an entire English-speaking country, and what is purely a localism.

In a language that does not have or want a language academy, it is the function of the dictionary not merely to record usage, but to present it discriminatingly, for the guidance of those who wish to be guided along paths of the "best" (which in effect means the most effective) usage.

Major Languages of the World

MARIO PEI, consultant

This chart classifies languages according to their geographic and linguistic affiliations. The overall arrangement is geographic,[1] but the rest of the groupings are essentially *genetic* (historical).

The languages are first grouped in *families*. In general, it is assumed that the languages in each *family* evolved from a single "proto-language" once spoken by prehistoric peoples.

The *branches* represent language-clusters that have relatively independent histories within the families. This does not mean that the histories of the *branches* are isolated from each other. Languages in separate *branches*—even in separate families—often enter into contact and influence each other.

Within the branches the languages are classified in *groups*. Wherever possible, genetic criteria are again used in establishing these. However, the *groups* sometimes represent language-clusters which exhibit typological similarities (similarities of structure)—or else simply languages spoken by peoples in the same cultural or geographic vicinity.

The chart does not attempt to classify all languages. Relatively important "specimen" languages have been selected to represent each family. Moreover, some rather large or diversified *dialectal subgroups* are listed under the heading "language." In those cases the name of the subgroup or its principal language is followed by the abbreviation "*d.*," meaning "dialects."

Many of these classifications are tentative. Even some of the "families" shown here are merely proposed groupings which appear realistic in light of current research in linguistics.

AFRICA

Macro-Khoisan Family

Branch	Group	Language
KHOISAN	HOTTENTOT	Grikwa*, Korana*, Naman *d.*, !gona*[2]
	BUSHMAN	Auen, G/ana,[2] Naron, /aba, /auni, !kung, !xong
SANDAWE		Sandawe *d.*
HATSA		Hadzapi

Niger-Kordofanian Family

Niger-Congo		
MANDE-BAMBARA-MANINKA		Bambara-Maninka-Diula *d.*, Kpelle-Mende *d.*, Malinke, Mandingo, Soninke, Susu, Vai
NON-MANDE West Atlantic		Fula, Gola, Kissi, Temne, Wolof
Gur		Baria, Dogomba, Gurma, Mossi *d.*, Senufo *d.*
Kwa	TOGO	Avatime, Togo
	EWE-AKAN	Akan, Ashanti, Ewe, Fanti, Ga, Kru *d.*, Twi
	IBO	Ibo, Nupe, Yoruba
Ijo		Ijo *d.*
Benue-Congo		Efik, Tivi
	BANTU Western Bantu	Ambo *d.*, Fang-Bulu *d.*, Herero, Kimbundu, Kongo, Lingala, Umbundu
	Eastern Bantu	Bemba, Burundi, Ganda, Kikuyu, Luba-Lulua *d.*, Makua, Nyamwezi-Sukuma *d.*, Nyanja, Nyasa, Rwanda-Rundi *d.*, Shona, Swahili, Tonga, Tutsi
	Southern (Nguni) Bantu	Ngono, Sotho *d.*, Swazi, Tswana, Xhosa, Zulu
Adamawa-Eastern (Ubangi)		Banda, Sango, Zande
Kordofanian		
		Kordofanian *d.*

Sahara-Savannah Family

SONGHAI		Songhai *d.*
SAHARAN		Saharan *d.*, Zaghawa
MABAN		Maba *d.*
MACRO-SUDANIC Central Sudanic		Bagirmi, Bongo Pygmy, Efe Pygmy, Madi, Mangbetu, Moru
Eastern Sudanic	NUBIAN	Kanuri-Tibo *d.*, Nubian *d.*, Old Nubian*
	NILOTIC West Nilotic	Acholi, Dinka, Langu, Luo, Nuer, Shilluk
	South Nilotic	Nandi, Suk
KOMAN		Gule, Koma *d.*

AFROASIA

Hamito-Semitic Family

Hamitic		
Branch	Group	Language
CHADIC		Angas, Bata *d.*, Hausa *d.*
CUSHITIC		Agau *d.*, Beja *d.*, Dankali, East Sidāmo *d.*, Galla, Saho, Somāli, West Sidāmo *d.*
LIBYCO-BERBER Libyan		Numidian*, Old Libyan*
Berber	MASMUDIC	Rif, Shilh
	SANHAJA	Kabyle, Tuareg (Tamashek), Zenet
	ZENAGA	Shawia, Zenaga
EGYPTIAN		Ancient Egyptian*, Coptic*

Semitic		
NORTHERN SEMITIC Northeastern Semitic		Akkadian*, Babylonian*
Northwestern Semitic	CANAANITE	Canaanite*, Ugaritic*
	Phoenician	Phoenician*, Punic*
	Hebraic	Ancient Hebrew*, Israeli Hebrew, Moabite*
	AMORITE	Amorite, Ancient Amorite*
	ARAMAIC Eastern Aramaic (Syriac)	Ancient Syriac*, East Neo-Aramaic, Mandaic, Neo-Aramaic, Talmudic*
	Western Aramaic	Judeo-Aramaic*, Palestinian Christian*, Palmyrene, Samaritan*, West Neo-Aramaic
ARABIC	NORTH ARABIC Literary Arabic	Ancient Arabic*, Classical Arabic
	Modern Arabic	Algerian-Tunisian *d.*, Egyptian-Sudanese *d.*, Iraqi *d.*, Maghribi, Maltese *d.*, Syrian *d.*
	SOUTH ARABIC	Himyaritic*, Minaean*, Sabaean*, South Arabic
	ETHIOPIC North Ethiopic	Geez*, Tigré, Tigrinya
	South Ethiopic	Amharic, Argobba, Gafat, Harari, Gurage *d.*

*EXTINCT

1. In some cases migrations have made precise geographic classifications impossible. For example, the Finno-Ugric languages, spoken primarily in Europe, are listed here under ASIA, since they probably originated there.

2. The symbols "!" and "/" stand for implosive click sounds.

3. The linguistic status of these families is uncertain.

4. Hindi and Urdu are literary languages. They are practically identical when spoken, and may be considered to be forms of Hindostani. Hindi is written with Sanskrit characters, whereas Perso-Arabic script is used for Urdu.

MAJOR LANGUAGES OF THE WORLD

ASIA

Dravidian Family

Branch	Group	Language
	SOUTHERN GROUP	Kanarese, Niligri d., Telugu
	Tamil-Malayalam	Malayalam, Tamil
	CENTRAL GROUP	Gondi d., Kolami, Kui
	NORTHERN GROUP	Brahui, Kurukh

Uralo-Altaic Family

Uralic

FINNO-UGRIC Ugric		Hungarian (Magyar), Ob-Ugric d., Ostyak, Vogul
Finno-Permean	PERMEAN	Votyak, Zyrian
	FINNIC	Cheremiss d., Estonian, Finnish (Suomi), Ingrian, Karelian, Lapp, Livonian, Mordvinian d., Vepsa
SAMOYEDIC		Ostyak-Samoyedic, Yenisei, Yurak

Altaic

TURKIC		Middle Turkish*, Old Turkish*
	EASTERN TURKIC Turki	Chagatai*, New Uighur, Old Uighur*, Uzbek
	Oghuz	Azerbaijani, Modern Turkish, Osmanli Turkish, Türkmen
	Kipchak	Balkar, Bashkir, Crimean Tatar (Khazar), Kazakh, Kazan' Tatar, Kipchak, Kirghiz, Noghai, Ob Turkic, Volga Turkic, West Siberian Tatar
	Sayan	Abakan d., Baraba, Oirot d.
	Yakut	Yakut
	WESTERN TURKIC (BULGARIC)	Chuvash d.
MONGOLIAN		Afghanistan Mongol, Buryat d., Dahur, Kalmuck, Khalka, Literary Mongolian, Monguor, Ordos, Tsakhar, Tunghsiang
TUNGUS-MANCHU Tungus		Evenki d., Lamut d., Negidal
Manchu		Dzürčen*, Goldi d., Manchu d., Orochi, Udehe

Japanese-Korean Family

		Japanese, Korean

Ainu Family[3]

		Ainu d.

Paleo-Siberian Family[3]

		Chukchi, Kamchatkan, Koryak

EURASIA

Caucasian Family

Branch	Group	Language
		Elamite*, Hatti*
SOUTHERN CAUCASIAN	MINGRELIAN-SVANIAN	Colchian*, Laz, Mingrelian, Svanian
	GEORGIAN	Georgian d., Imeretian
NORTHERN CAUCASIAN	ABKHAZ-ADIGEH	Abkhasian, Adigeh, Kabardinian-Circassian d.
	CHECHENIAN-INGUSH	Chechenian, Ingush
	DAGHESTAN GROUP	Andi, Avar, Darghwa, d., Dido, Kapuchi, Kuri, Lakh, Lezginian, Tabassarian

Asianic Family[3]

		Etruscan*

Basque-Iberian Family[3]

		Basque, Iberian

Indo-European Family

East Indo-European

INDO-IRANIAN Indic		Pali*, Prakrit*, Sanskrit*, Vedic Sanskrit*
	CENTRAL INDIC	Eastern Hindi d., Hindi-Urdu,[4] Hindostani[4]
	PAHARI	Pahari d.
	WESTERN INDIC	Bhili, Gujarati, Rajasthani
	NORTHERN INDIC	Lahndā, Punjabi d., Sindhi
	SOUTHERN INDIC	Marathi d.
	EASTERN INDIC	Assamese, Bengali, Bihari d., Oriya
	SINHALESE	Sinhalese d.
Dardic		Kashmiri, Khowar, Romany (Gypsy)
Iranian		Ancient Persian*, Avestan*
	EASTERN IRANIAN	Kurdish, Ossetic, Pamir d., Pashto, Saka*, Sogdian*
	WESTERN IRANIAN	Baluchi, Caspian d., Pahlavi*, Persian, Tajiki
THRACO-ILLYRIAN		Illyrian*, Phrygian*, Thracian*
ARMENIAN		Ashkharabar (Modern), Grabar (Classical)
ALBANIAN		Gheg, Tosk
BALTO-SLAVONIC Baltic	WESTERN BALTIC	Old Prussian*
	EASTERN BALTIC	Kurish*, Lettish (Latvian), Lithuanian
Slavonic	EASTERN SLAVONIC	Byelorussian, Russian, Ukranian
	WESTERN SLAVONIC	Czech, Kashubian*, Polabian*, Polish, Slovak, Slovincian*
	Sorbian	Lusatian, Wendish
	SOUTHERN SLAVONIC	Bulgarian, Macedonian, Old Church Slavic*, Serbo-Croatian, Slovene

West Indo-European

HELLENIC		Achaean*, Aeolian*, Attic*, Dorian*, Ionian*, Koinê*, Modern Greek
	Minoan	Ancient Minoan*
ITALIC Osco-Umbrian		Oscan*, Umbrian*, Venetic*
Latinian		Faliscan*, Sicel*
	OLD LATIN	Classical Latin*, Old Latin*, Vulgar Latin d.*
	ROMANCE Eastern Romance	Dalmatian* (Vegliote*), Italian, Rumanian
	Western Romance	Catalan, French, French Creole, Galician, Old French*, Portuguese, Provençal, Rhaeto-Romance d., Sardinian, Spanish
CELTIC	CONTINENTAL CELTIC	Gaulish*
	BRYTHONIC	Breton, Brythonic*, Cornish*, Middle Welsh*, Old Welsh*, Welsh
	GOIDELIC	Gaelic*, Irish Gaelic, Manx*, Middle Irish*, Old Irish*, Scotch Gaelic
GERMANIC East Germanic		Gothic*, Vandalic*
North Germanic		Danish, Faroese, Icelandic, Norwegian, Old Norse*, Swedish
West Germanic	GERMAN High German	Middle High German*, Modern German, Old High German*, Pennsylvania German, Schwyzer-Tütsch, Yiddish
	Low German	Old Saxon*, Plattdeutsch
	Franconian	Afrikaans, Dutch, Flemish, Old Low Franconian*
	ANGLO-FRISIAN Frisian	Frisian, Old Frisian*
	English	American English, British English, Middle English*, Old English*

ASIA-AUSTRONESIA

Sino-Tibetan Family

Branch	Group	Language
TIBETO-BURMESE Bhotia		Himalayan Bhotia, Tibetan Bhotia
	Lolo	Kachin, Lolo, Naga
Burmese		Burmese, Karen d.
MIAO-YAO		Miao d., Yao d.
SINO-SIAMESE Chinese		Archaic Chinese*
	Northern Chinese	Cheng-tu, East Mandarin, Kiangsi d., Modern Chinese (Kuo-yü), North Mandarin, Southwest Mandarin
	Central Chinese	Wu (Shanghai)
	Southern Chinese	Cantonese, Foochow d., Fukienese (Min), Kam-Hakka d.
Muong-Annamese		Muong d., Vietnamese
Siamese		Dioi, Lao, Li, Shan, Siamese

Austric Family

AUSTRO-ASIATIC Munda		Old Korku*
	Western Munda	Korku
	Northern Munda	Ho, Mundari, Santali
Mon-Khmer		Cambodian (Khmer), Cham, Khasi, Mon, Nicobarese
MALAYO-POLYNESIAN Western Oceanic	Malay-Indonesian	Achinese, Baba Malay, Bahasa Indonesia, Balinese, Batak, Bazaar Malay, Bugi, Dayak, Javanese, Madurese, Makasarese, Malagasy, Sundanese
	Philippine	Bikol, Chamorro, Ilokano, Palaung, Tagalog, Visayan
	Caroline	Caroline, Yapese
Eastern Oceanic	Micronesian	Guamese, Micronesian d.
	Polynesian West Polynesian	Maori, Samoan, Tonga d.
	East Polynesian	Hawaiian, Marquesan, Tahitian

Papuan Family[3]

		Arapesh, Ayamaru, Bilua, Ekari, Kate, Kiwai

Australian (Aboriginal) Family[3]

		Arandic d., Kamilaroi, Murngin, Murrawarra, Narrinyeri*

NORTH AND CENTRAL AMERICA

Eskimo-Aleut Family

Branch	Group	Language
		Aleut d., Eskimo d.

Algonkian-Wakashan Family

ALGONKIAN-RITWAN Algonkian		Algonkin, Arapaho, Blackfoot, Cheyenne, Cree, Delaware, Fox, Kickapoo, Micmac, Mohegan*, Narragansett*, Ojibwa, Penobscot, Shawnee
Ritwan		Wiyot, Yurok
WAKASHAN-SALISH		Coeur d'Alene, Kwakiutl, Nootka

Na-Dene Family

HAIDA		Haida d.
CONTINENTAL NA-DENE Tlingit		Tlingit
Athapaskan	North Athapaskan	Beaver, Chipewyan
	Pacific Athapaskan	Chasta Costa, Wailaki
	South Athapaskan	Apache d., Navaho

Penutian Family

NORTHERN PENUTIAN		Kalapuya, Klamath, Kus, Maidu, Miwok-Costanoan d., Modoc, Nez Percé, Takelma, Wallawalla, Witun, Yakonan, Yokuts d.
MEXICAN PENUTIAN Mixe-Zoque		Mixe, Zoque
Huave		Huave d.
Mayan		Huasteco, Itza, Quiché, Tabasco, Yucateco

Hokan-Siouan Family

HOKAN-COAHUILTECAN		Chumash, Coahuilteco, Esselen, Karok, Salinan, Seri, Shasta-Achumawi d., Tequistlateco, Washo d., Yana*, Yuman
IROQUOIS-CADDOAN Iroquoian		Cayuga, Cherokee, Huron, Mohawk, Oneida, Seneca, Tuscarora
Caddoan		Caddo, Pawnee, Wichita
EASTERN HOKAN-SIOUAN Siouan-Yuchi	Siouan	Catawba, Crow, Dakota, Iowa, Kansa, Omaha, Winnebago
	Yuchi	Yuchi d.
Natchez-Muskogean	Natchez	Natchez
	Muskogean	Creek, Seminole

Aztec-Tanoan Family

UTO-AZTECAN	Nahuatlan	Azteca*, Nahuatlate, Tolteca-Chichimeca d.
	Piman	Pima
	Shoshonean	Comanche, Hopi, Paiute d., Shoshone, Snake, Ute
TANOAN-KIOWA		Kiowa, Tanoan d.
ZUÑI		Zuñi

CENTRAL AND SOUTH AMERICA

Macro-Oto-Manguean Family

Branch	Group	Language
OTO-MANGUEAN		Manguean d., Mazatecan d., Otomi d., Trique
OTHER		Mixteco, Zapoteco

Tarascan Family[3]

		Tarasco

Macro-Chibchan Family

MISUMALPAN-CHIBCHAN-JIJARAN	Misumalpan	Choco, Coco, Miskito, Panamaca, Xinca
	Chibchan	Chibcha, Guanaco, Murire, Paez, San Blas. Tembe, Tunebo
	Jijaran	Jijara

Ge-Pano-Carib Family

MACRO-CARIB Cariban		Akawai, Carib, Kauishana, Taurepan
Peba-Yaguan		Peba, Witoto, Yagua
MACRO-GE Ge		Apinayé, Cayapo, Shavanté, Timbira
Other		Bororo d., Caxibo, Kaingua d., Puelche, Yamaica

Andean-Equatorial Family

ANDIAN		Araucanian d., Esmeralda, Zaparo
Quechu-Maran		Aymara d., Cuzco, Quechu d.
Jivaroan		Jivaro d.
EQUATORIAL Arawakan		Arawak, Guayupe, Guinao, Tampa, Uru
Tupi-Guarani	Guaranian	Apapocuva, Guarani, Tapirape, Taruma
	Tupian	Mundurucú, Tembe, Tupi d., Urubu
OTHER		Cayuvava, Macu, Puinave

xvi

A Guide to the Use of This Dictionary

This guide provides a detailed description with illustrative examples of the format of entries within the dictionary. It explains the various typefaces, labels, pronunciations, abbreviations, punctuation, etymologies, and symbols that appear in entries. A careful reading of the guide will help you make more effective use of the dictionary. The major divisions and subdivisions in the order in which they appear within the entry (*if* they appear, because not all appear in every entry) are as follows:

ENTRIES

I. THE ENTRY WORD

The words that make up the vocabulary are printed flush with the left margin of the column and are in boldfaced type. They are listed in alphabetical order. Guide words at the top of each page indicate the first and last entries on that page and facilitate the location of a particular word. Each entry is fully syllabicated and is followed by its pronunciation, part of speech, inflected form, etymology, and definition:

> **dic·tion·ar·y,** dik′sha·ner″ē, *n.* pl. **dic·tion·ar·ies.** [L.L. *dictionarium.*] A book containing words of a language arranged in alphabetical order, with explanations of their meanings, pronunciations, etymologies, and other information; a lexicon; a word book; any work which communicates information on an entire subject or branch of a subject, under entries or heads arranged alphabetically.

II. VARIANTS

If a word has two or more accepted spellings, the most commonly used spelling is listed first, with the others following in order of preferred use. If the pronunciation of a variant spelling is identical to an entry word, and if both spellings apply to all definitions, then the variant is listed immediately after the entry word in boldface type and is fully syllabicated:

> **dri·er, dry·er,** drī′ér, *n.*

If a foreign word is pronounced the same as an entry but is spelled differently, the variant spelling is preceded by a usage label and follows the entry word:

> **draft,** *chiefly Brit. also* **draught,** draft, dräft, *n.*

III. HOMOGRAPHS

If a word has a single spelling but two or more distinct origins or meanings, each variation is listed as a separate entry. The preferred or most common meaning is entered first. If there is no preferred meaning the order of definitions is arbitrary:

> **counter** . . . *n.* [O.Fr. *comptoer, comptoir* (Fr. *comptoir*) . . . .] A table or board
> **counter** . . . *adv.* [O.Fr. Fr. *contre* . . . .] In the opposite direction

IV. FOREIGN WORDS

Foreign words which have become assimilated into the English language or which have fairly widespread usage in the United States are listed as entries. In these entries, original spellings and pronunciations are indicated as well as any variations in spelling or pronunciation which may have occurred as a result of Anglicization. The language from which the word is taken is indicated in the etymology or by a usage label preceding the definition:

> **naïve, naive,** nä·ēv′, *a.* [Fr. *naïf,* fem. *naïve,* < L. *nativus,* native; latterly also rustic, simple.]
> **chargé d'affaires,** shär·zhā′ da·fâr′, shär′zhā da·fâr′, *Fr.* shäʀ·zhā dä·feʀ′, *n.* [Fr., lit. 'charged with affairs.']

V. SUBENTRIES

A subentry is a word, usually a grammatical variant of the entry word, that is so linguistically or semantically similar to the entry word that a separate listing does not seem appropriate. Subentries are set in boldfaced type, syllabicated, and may be followed by pronunciation, part of speech, etymology, and definition. Subentries are preceded by a dash and follow all regular definitions of a word:

di·verse, *a.* . . . Different; unlike; of sundry types or forms. — **di·verse·ly,** di·vụrs′lē, *adv.* — **di·verse·ness,** *n.* — **di·ver·si·fi·ca·tion,** *n.* The act of diversifying; the state of being diversified.

VI. SPECIAL ENTRIES

A. Abbreviations

A list of abbreviations used in definitions is located in the front of the dictionary. Common abbreviations are listed alphabetically as entries throughout the dictionary. The words represented are indicated in the etymology or the definition:

> **DDT,** *n.* [(D)ichloro-(D)iphenyl-(T)richloroethane.] The powerful insecticide
>
> **IQ, I.Q.** Abbr. for intelligence quotient.

B. Proper Adjectives

Proper adjectives are alphabetized as entries. The proper nouns from which they are derived are indicated in the etymology or, if necessary, defined:

> **Japanese** . . . *a.* Pertaining to Japan, a country consisting of four large islands and numerous small ones

C. Trademarks

Commonly used trademarks are included in the dictionary. Each trademark is identified as such in its definition:

> **Dictaphone** . . . a dictating machine. (Trademark.)

D. Proper Nouns

Proper nouns that refer to well-known objects or events are alphabetized as entries:

> **Polaris** . . . *Astron.* a star of the second magnitude
> **Lent** . . . A 40-day period of self-denial

E. Tables

The following tables are alphabetized as entries:

VII. CROSS REFERENCES

Semantic relationships between words are indicated by cross references. If two words are identical in meaning, a definition will follow the more common entry and a cross reference will follow the less common entry:

> **entomb** . . . *v.t.* . . . To deposit in a tomb
> **intomb** . . . *v.t.* Entomb.

Cross references also follow definitions of a word. If the reference refers to all definitions of an entry word, the reference is preceded by "Also":

> **Tatar** . . . *n.* A member of any of various Mongolian and other tribes . . .; a member of the descendants of these peoples . . .; any of their languages. Also *Tartar.*

If the cross reference refers to only one definition, then the reference immediately follows that definition and is preceded by "also":

relief . . . *n. Sculp., arch.* the projection or prominence of a figure . . .; also *relievo. Painting,* the appearance of projection and solidity

GUIDE TO PRONUNCIATION

Pronunciations are given for every entry. A chart explaining pronunciation symbols and sounds and suffix and consonant sounds is included in this guide. A shortened explanation of pronunciation symbols is printed on the lower margin of each page.

I. PLACEMENT OF PRONUNCIATION

The pronunciations follow the entry word. When a word has different pronunciations for different meanings, all pronunciations immediately follow the entry word and the correct pronunciation also follows the definition to which it applies:

> **slough,** slou, slö, *n.* . . . . A section of soft muddy ground or bog . . ., slö. *Fig.* a condition of degradation . . ., slou.

The pronunciation for a word may vary depending on its grammatical functions. A differing pronunciation immediately follows the dash separating the parts of speech and their definitions. The pronunciation is followed by an abbreviation describing its grammatical function:

> **del·e·gate,** del′*e·*gāt″, *v.t.* . . . To send or appoint . . . — del′*e·*git, *n.* One delegated to act for or represent

II. SYSTEM OF PRONUNCIATION

All pronunciations are in roman type, except for certain vowel sounds which are in italics and some foreign word sounds in small roman capitals:

> **char·la·tan,** shär′*la·*tan, *n.*
>
> **di·seur,** de·zụr′, *Fr.* de·zŒR′, *n.*
>
> **coif·fure,** kwä·fyụr′, *Fr.* kwȧ·fYR′, *n.*

Pronunciations begin with a lower-case letter, and are followed by a comma. The most common pronunciation is given first:

> **lev·er,** lev′ẻr, lē′vẻr, *n.*
>
> **eu·pat·rid,** ū·pa′trid, ū′*pa·*trid, *n.* pl. **eu·pat·ri·dae,** ū·pa′tri·dē.

III. SYLLABICATION AND STRESS

Due to different rules, syllabication of the entry and syllabication of pronunciation do not always agree. Syllabication in the pronunciation is indicated by a raised center dot except between syllables where stress marks are needed. The syllable having the greatest stress is followed by a primary stress mark (′). The syllable having less stress is followed by a secondary stress mark (″). One-syllable words do not have stress:

> **Le·val·loi·si·an,** lev″*a·*loi′zē·*an,* lev″*a·*loi′zhan, *a.*
>
> **rife,** rīf, *a.*

IV. VARIANT PRONUNCIATIONS

If there is more than one pronunciation for an entry or subentry, the variants follow the entry and are separated by commas:

> **lev·i·rate,** lev′ẻr·it, lev′*e·*rāt″, lē′ver·it, lē′vi·rāt″, *n.*

When a plural form, or a different part of speech, or a sub-entry derived from the entry differs significantly from the entry in pronunciation, the appropriate pronunciation immediately follows the form to which it applies and is separated from it by a comma:

clo·a·ca, klō·ā′k*a*, *n.* pl. **clo·a·cae,** klō·ā′kē.

Foreign pronunciations follow the English pronunciations, and are preceded by a foreign language label:

sched·ule, skej′öl, skej′ụl, skej′ö·*a*l, *Brit.* shed′ūl, shej′öl, *n.*

V. PRONUNCIATION OF COMPOUNDS

Multiword entries are followed by a pronunciation only if one or more of the entry words is not pronounced elsewhere:

High Mass, *n. Eccles.* a liturgical function

Cui·se·naire rod, kwiz″*e*·nâr′ rod, *n.*

Hyphenated words are considered as single words and are pronounced:

bric-a-brac, brik′*a*·brak″, *n.*

Multiword subentries are not given pronunciations:

hand, hand, *n.* . . . The extremity of the arm . . . —**at hand,** within reach . . . —**hand o·ver fist,** *slang,* rapidly

PARTS OF SPEECH

English words are traditionally classified into parts of speech which are determined by their form, meaning, and syntactic function in a sentence. A part of speech is listed for each entry in this dictionary.

I. ABBREVIATIONS FOR PARTS OF SPEECH

The part of speech is listed immediately after the pronunciation and is preceded by a comma. Parts of speech are italicized and abbreviated as follows:

n.	noun	*pron.*	pronoun
v.t.	transitive verb	*prep.*	preposition
v.i.	intransitive verb	*conj.*	conjunction
a.	adjective	*interj.*	interjection
adv.	adverb	*art.*	article

II. CHANGING PARTS OF SPEECH

If a word is more than one part of speech and its meanings are semantically different, each meaning will be listed as a separate entry. If, however, the definitions for all parts of speech are semantically similar, then the word will be defined under a single entry. The definition for each part of speech is then preceded by a dash and the italicized abbreviation of the part of speech which is to be defined:

fine . . . *a.* . . . Of the highest quality

fine . . . *n.* . . . *Law,* a pecuniary payment

grip . . . *n.* . . . The act of grasping . . . —*v.t.* To grasp or seize. . . . —*v.i.* To take firm hold

III. PARTS OF SPEECH FOR ALTERNATE FORMS

Alternate forms are listed at the end of definitions. Such forms are preceded by a dash, are in boldface type, and are fully syllabicated. The part of speech of each form is designated:

groan . . . *v.i.* . . . . To utter a deep inarticulate sound . . . —**groan·er,** *n.* —**groan·ing·ly,** *adv.*

IV. PARTS OF SPEECH FOR MULTIWORD SUBENTRIES

The part of speech is generally not given for multiword subentries or idiomatic expressions unless such information is necessary to the understanding of the meaning of the phrase. If a part of speech is listed, it is abbreviated and italicized.

INFLECTIONAL FORMS

All irregular inflected forms of nouns, pronouns, verbs, adjectives, and adverbs are listed immediately after the designated part of speech of an entry. Inflected forms are preceded by a dash and usually labeled. Labels for inflected forms are abbreviated as follows:

compar.	comparative	ppr.	present participle
intens.	intensive	pres.	present
nom.	nominative	pret.	preterit
obj.	objective	refl.	reflexive
pl.	plural	sing.	singular
poss.	possessive	subj.	subjunctive
pp.	past participle	superl.	superlative

I. DECLENSION

A. Nouns

Plurals of nouns that are not formed by adding -s or -es are printed in boldface type and are fully syllabicated. If more than one plural exists, the preferred is listed first:

nar·cis·sus . . . *n.* pl. **nar·cis·sus, nar·cis·si, nar·cis·sus·es**
cac·tus . . . *n.* pl. **cac·tus·es,** *L.* **cac·ti.**

For nouns that are plural in form but singular in function see Qualifying and Usage Labels.

B. Pronouns

When necessary, the case, number, and classification for pronouns are listed. The inflected form is then italicized and the label abbreviated:

he . . . *pron.* —sing. nom. *he,* poss. *his,* obj. *him,* intens. and refl. *himself;* pl. nom. *they,* poss. *their* or *theirs,* obj. *them*

II. CONJUGATION

Irregular constructions of principal parts of verbs are preceded by a dash and italicized. Generally only the past participle and the present participle are given:

rule . . . *v.t.* —*ruled, ruling.*

If a verb has additional irregular parts they are labeled and listed in the following order: present singular, present plural, past singular, past plural, past participle, present participle:

do . . . *v.t.* —pres. sing. *do, do* or archaic *doest* or *dost, does* or archaic *doeth* or *doth;* pres. pl. *do;* past sing. *did, did* or archaic *didst, did;* past pl. *did;* pp. *done,* ppr. *doing*

III. COMPARISON

Irregular comparative and superlative forms of adjectives and adverbs are preceded by a dash and italicized. The comparative form is listed first:

big . . . *a.* — *bigger, biggest*

little . . . *adv.* — *less, least.*

ETYMOLOGIES

Etymologies concern the derivation of an entry word and the linguistic changes it has undergone to attain its present form. The information given varies with the nature of the word itself, i.e. some words may be traced back to their Latin roots whereas others, such as acronyms, are modern creations:

> **cu·cum·ber** . . . *n.* [O.Fr. *coucombre* (Fr. *concombre*), < L. *cucumis* (*cucumer-*).]

> **DEW line,** *n.* [< (*D*)istant (*E*)arly (*W*)arning.]

The etymology follows the part of speech (or inflected forms) and immediately precedes the first definition.

I. ORIGINS AND DATES

Languages from which words are derived are abbreviated. The dates to which the abbreviations apply are as follows:

M.E.	Middle English (A.D. 1150-1475)
M.Fr.	Middle French (A.D. 1300-1500)
M.Gr.	Middle Greek (A.D. 700-1500)
M.H.G.	Middle High German (A.D. 1100-1500)
M.L.G.	Middle Low German (A.D. 1100-1500)
O.E.	Old English (A.D. 450-1150)
O.Fr.	Old French (A.D. 800-1400)
O.H.G.	Old High German (A.D. 800-1100)
O.Norse	Old Norse (A.D. 700-1300)

Other etymological abbreviations are listed in "Abbreviations Used in This Dictionary."

A word of foreign origin or a foreign spelling is labeled and italicized and followed by its English translation:

> **chic** . . . *n.* [Fr. < Gr. *schick*, due order, tact.]

Literal translations of origin words are given in the same cases. These are preceded by the abbreviation *lit.* and are in single quotes:

> **amicus curiae** . . . *n.* [L., lit. 'friend of the court.']

Cross references are indicated by either the abbreviation *cf.* or the word *compare* and refer to another etymology and definition:

> **chev·y** . . . *n.* . . . [Perhaps < Chevy Chase, title of an old English ballad: cf. O.Fr. *chevauchie*, a riding; raid.]

II. SYMBOLS

The following symbols are used in etymologies:

> < from, derived from
> = equals
> ∴ therefore

III. SPECIAL ETYMOLOGIES

The following examples illustrate the form used in special etymologies:

Acronyms

> **laser** . . . *n.* [(*l*)ight (*a*)mplification by (*s*)timulated (*e*)mission of (*r*)adiation.]

Blends

> **motel** . . . *n.* [(*mo*)tor and ho(*tel*).]

Biographical Information

> **covellite** . . . *n.* [From N. *Covelli*, who in 1839 found it in lava from Vesuvius.]

Diminutives

> **crackle** . . . *v.i.* [Dim. of crack.]

Onomatopoetic Words

> **crash** . . . *v.t.* [M.E.; imit.]

> **fizz** . . . *v.i.* [Imit.]

Non-English Origins

> **cowry, cowrie** . . . *n.* [Hind. *kaurī*.]

> **pokeweed** . . . *n.* [Of Amer. Ind. origin.]

Uncertain or Unknown Origin

> **cove** . . . *n.* [Origin obscure; first in rogues' slang.]

> **euchre** . . . *n.* [Origin uncertain.]

QUALIFYING AND USAGE LABELS

Qualifying and usage labels are used to give information about or restrict the use of some definitions. These labels introduce the definition to which they apply and are italicized. Labels apply to all definitions which follow until a period or another label intervenes.

I. QUALIFYING LABELS

Qualifying labels refer to capitalization and number. If a label gives information about capitalization, it is italicized and in parentheses. If a label gives information about number, it is italicized only.

Both kinds of labels are abbreviated:

(*cap.*)	capital	*pl.*	plural
(*l.c.*)	lower case	*sing.*	singular

> **house** . . . *n.* . . . The building in which a legislative body of government meets; (*cap.*) the body itself; as, the House of Commons . . . (*often cap.*) a family consisting of ancestors and descendants

> **jump** . . . *v.i.* . . . To spring . . . —*n.* . . . *Pl.* a physical condition

> **decretal** . . . *n.* . . . A papal decree . . . *pl.* (*cap.*) the body or collection of such decrees

II. USAGE LABELS

Usage labels either restrict the use of a word, indicate a specialized meaning, or identify a region or context in which the word is widely associated:

> **measles** . . . *n.* . . . *Med.* an infectious disease . . . *Veter. pathol.* a disease affecting swine

> **heck** . . . *interj.* . . . *Slang,* an expression of disappointment

> **ornery** . . . *a.* . . . *Colloq.* Ugly in disposition

> **ain't** . . . *Regarded as nonstandard,* is not, are not, has not, have not. *Regarded as nonstandard in all but a few U.S. dialects,* am not

Most usage labels are abbreviated and may be found in the section entitled "Abbreviations Used in This Dictionary."

When a definition of a word is altered by its context, the appropriate word or phrase is indicated:

> **open** . . . *v.i.* . . . to afford access, followed by *in* or *into;* to have an opening . . ., followed by *into, upon, toward,* or the like

Words which have a plural form but a singular function are so labeled:

> **electronics** . . . *n. pl. but sing. in constr.*

DEFINITIONS

All parts of speech of the English language except proper names are included as entries. Each entry is followed by a definition or cross reference except in the case of conjunctions which are followed by information concerning their use and function, and interjections which are followed by information concerning the context in which they are used and the mood they convey:

> **and** . . . *conj.* . . . A particle joining words and sentences
> **oh** . . . *interj.* . . . An expression of surprise

I. PLACEMENT AND STYLE OF DEFINITIONS

Definitions follow the etymology of the entry word with semicolons separating the different meanings. In some instances periods have been used between definitions, either to indicate the extent to which a usage label applies or to show a complete change of meaning. Each new part of speech, multiword subentry, or subentry is introduced with a dash:

> **lend,** lend, *v.t.—lent, lending.* [O.E. *laenan,* to lend, < *laen,* a loan, (< *lihan* = G. *leihen,* to lend); cf. D. *leenen,* Dan. *laane,* Icel. *lana,* to lend.] To grant to another for temporary use; to furnish on condition of the thing or its equivalent in kind being returned; to afford, grant, or furnish in general, as assistance.—*refl.* to accommodate; to adapt so as to be of assistance, as: He *lent* himself to the scheme.—*v.i.* To make a loan.—**lend a hand,** to assist.—**lender,** *n.*

II. ORDER OF DEFINITIONS

Definitions are listed with the preferred sense first and following senses according to common usage. Archaic definitions are listed last and labeled. If an archaic definition is necessary to the understanding of the contemporary use of a word, the archaic definition will be listed first and labeled. If a word does not have a clear preferred use, the order of definitions is arbitrary:

> **lurcher** . . . *n. Archaic,* a sneak thief; a poacher

Major parts of speech are defined first in an entry. Multiword subentries are then listed and defined. Single word subentries, which are usually grammatical variants of the entry word, are listed in alphabetical order at the end of an entry and usually are not defined:

> **pass** . . . *v.i.* . . . To go, move onward . . .—*v.t.* To go by or move past . . .—**pass a·way,** to pass out of existence . . .—**pass off,** to run off . . .—**passer,** *n.*

III. MULTIWORD SUBENTRIES

Idiomatic and compound expressions in the English language are listed as subentries under the appropriate root word. Multiword subentries are introduced with a dash, printed in boldfaced type, and otherwise treated as entries except that no pronunciation or part of speech is given for them:

> **number** . . . *v.i.* . . . To count; to be numbered or included . . .—**any number of,** many; a large amount. —**get one's number,** *slang,* to have identified hidden aspects of a person and his motives. Also **have one's number.—number one,** *(often cap.), slang,* oneself

IV. EXAMPLES

When examples are used to illustrate the meaning or proper use of a word they follow the definition to which they apply:

> **smoke** . . . *v.i.* . . . To give off or emit smoke, as in burning; to give out smoke offensively or improperly, as a stove

> **hot** . . . *a.* . . . carrying a high voltage current; as, a *hot* wire; very warm, as weather or climate

ABBREVIATIONS AND SYMBOLS

I. ABBREVIATIONS

Parts of speech, inflection labels, etymological information, qualifying labels, and some usage labels are abbreviated in this dictionary. A list of these abbreviations may be found either under the appropriate heading in this Guide, or in the section entitled "Abbreviations Used In This Dictionary." Standard chemical abbreviations are listed under "Periodic Table of the Elements" which may be found on page 705 of the dictionary. Whenever an entry word has a frequently used abbreviation, the abbreviation is listed at the end of the entry:

> **ounce** . . . *n.* A unit of weight . . . abbr. *oz.* Fluid ounce; abbr. *fl. oz.*

II. SYMBOLS

Symbols for entry words are listed at the end of the entry.

> **atomic number** . . . *n.* . . . An integer that expresses the positive charge . . . . Abbr. *at. no.;* sym. *Z.*

Pronunciation Symbols
Used in This Dictionary

′ primary accent ″ secondary accent

a	fat, band	l	like, whole, mail	z	zeal	
ā	fate, tame	m	make, pamper, palm	zh	azure	
â	fare, pair	n	name, pencil, pan			
ä	far, father	ng	sing		**FOREIGN**	
a̧	fall, ought, orb	o	not, squat, yacht	ä	Fr. ami	
a	schwa sound, as in ago	ō	note, boat	*ch*	G. ach	
b	bat, abide, bib	ö	move, groove	h	Sp. jacal—ha·käl′	
c	catch, because, idealistic	*o*	schwa sound, as in gallop	N	Fr. bon	
ch	chain	oi	oil	Œ	Fr. feu, G. schön	
d	date, ladder, road	ou	pound, now	R	Fr. rouge, G. rot, It.	
e	met, threat	p	pea, paper, lamp		mare, Sp. pero	
ē	me, feat	r	rust, narrow, latter	V	Sp. Habana—ä·vä′nä	
e̊	her, fir, urn	s	seat, last, mass	Y	Fr. tu, G. über	
e	schwa sound, as in happen	sh	shark, rush			
ēr	mere, rear	t	tea, mate, pat		**SUFFIX SOUNDS**	
f	fine, muffin, leaf	th	thin		ancy	*ancē*
g	gold, ingrate, log	TH	then		ble	bl
h	hang, behold	u	tub, rough	ceous, cious	shus	
hw	whig	ū	tube, cube		ent	*ent*
i	pin, hymn	u̧	bull, took		esque	esk
ī	pine, by	*u*	schwa sound, as in circus		ous	us
i	schwa sound, as in fossil	v	victor, river, believe	sion, tion	sh*a*n	
j	job, rigid, edge	w	wig		tor	ta̧r, tur, *tor*, te̊r
k	king, lake, clock	y	youth		ture	che̊r, ch*u*r

Abbreviations Used in This Dictionary

A

a. or *adj.*	adjective
abbr.	abbreviation
abl.	ablative
absol.	absolute
acc.	accusative
act.	active
ad.	adapted
A.D.	Anno Domini
adv.	adverb
advbl.	adverbial
aeron.	aeronautics
Afr.	African
A.Fr.	Anglo-French
Afrik.	Afrikaans
agric.	agriculture
A.L.	Anglo-Latin
alchem.	alchemy
alg.	algebra
Amer.	American
anal.	analogous, analogy
anat.	anatomy
anc.	ancient
Anglo-Ind.	Anglo-Indian
anthropol.	anthropology
antiq.	antique, antiquities, antiquity
aor.	aorist, aoristic
Apoc.	Apocalypse
appar.	apparently
art.	article
Ar.	Arabic
Aram.	Aramaic
arch.	architecture
archaeol.	archaeology
arith.	arithmetic
Armor.	Armoric
astrol.	astrology
astron.	astronomy
at. no.	atomic number
attrib.	attributive, attributively
at. wt.	atomic weight
aug.	augmentative
Aust.	Australian
aux.	auxiliary
aux. v.	auxiliary verb
avi.	aviation

B

b.	born
bact.	bacteriology
B.C.	Before Christ
b.f.	bold face
Bib.	Biblical
bibliog.	bibliography
biochem.	biochemistry
biog.	biography
biol.	biology
Bohem.	Bohemian
bot.	botany
Brazil.	Brazilian
Bret.	Breton
Brit.	British
Bulg.	Bulgarian
bus.	business

C

c.	*circa* (about)
C.	Centigrade
cap.	capital
caps.	capitals

Carib.	Caribbean
carp.	carpentry
Cath.	Catholic
Celt.	Celtic
cent.	century
ceram.	ceramics
cf.	*confer* (compare)
Ch.	Church
chem.	chemistry
chem. sym.	chemical symbol
Chin.	Chinese
Chron.	Chronicles
class.	classical
cogn.	cognate
coll.	collectively
colloq.	colloquial
com.	commerce
commerc.	commercial
comp.	composition
compar.	comparative
conch.	conchology
conj.	conjunction
conn.	connected
constr.	construction
contr.	contracted, contraction
Copt.	Coptic
Cor.	Corinthians
Corn.	Cornish
correl.	correlative
corrupt.	corruption
craniol.	craniology
craniom.	craniometry
crystal.	crystallography

D

d.	died
D.	Dutch
Dan.	Danish
dat.	dative
def.	definite
defs.	definitions
demonst.	demonstrative
deriv.	derivation
Deut.	Deuteronomy
dial.	dialect
dim.	diminutive
dist.	distinguished

E

E.	English
Eccles.	Ecclesiastes
eccles.	ecclesiastical
ecol.	ecology
econ.	economics
ed.	edition
educ.	education
e.g.	*exempli gratia* (for example)
Egypt.	Egyptian
Egyptol.	Egyptology
E.Ind.	East Indian
elect.	electricity
electron.	electronics
embryol.	embryology
Eng.	England
engin.	engineering
entom.	entomology
equiv.	equivalent
erro.	erroneous
esp.	especially
etc.	*et cetera* (and so forth)

Ex.	Exodus
ethnol.	ethnology

F

F.	Fahrenheit
facet.	facetious
fem.	feminine
feud.	feudal, feudalism
fig.	figuratively
Finn.	Finnish
Flem.	Flemish
foll.	following
fort.	fortification
Fr.	French
freq.	frequentative
Fries.	Friesian
Fris.	Frisian
fut.	future

G

G.	German
Gael.	Gaelic
galv.	galvanism
Gaul.	Gaulish
Gen.	Genesis
genit.	genitive
geog.	geography
geol.	geology
geom.	geometry
Goth.	Gothic
gov.	government
Gr.	Greek
gram.	grammar
Gr.Brit.	Great Britain
gun.	gunnery

H

Heb.	Hebrew
her.	heraldry
Hind.	Hindustani
hist.	history
horol.	horology
hort.	horticulture
Hung.	Hungarian

I

ibid.	*ibidem* (in the same book, chapter, page, etc.)
Icel.	Icelandic
ichth.	ichthyology
i.e.	*id est* (that is)
imit.	imitative
impers.	impersonal
impf.	imperfect
impv.	imperative
Ind.	Indian
indef.	indefinite
indic.	indicative
Indo-Eur.	Indo-European
inf.	infinitive
intens.	intensive
interj.	interjection
interrog.	interrogative
introd.	introduction
Ir.	Irish
iron.	ironical, ironically
irreg.	irregular, irregularly
Isa.	Isaiah
It.	Italian
ital.	italics

J

Jap.	Japanese
Jav.	Javanese
journ.	journalism

L

L.	Late, Latin
l.c.	lower case
Lett.	Lettish
L.G.	Low German
L.Gr.	Late Greek
ling.	linguistics
lit.	literal, literally
liter.	literature, literary
Lith.	Lithuanian
L.L.	Late Latin

M

mach.	machinery
Malay.	Malayan
manuf.	manufacturing
masc.	masculine
math.	mathematics
M.D.	Middle Dutch
M.E.	Middle English
mech.	mechanics
med.	medical, medicine
Med.L.	Medieval Latin
mensur.	mensuration
metal.	metallurgy
metaph.	metaphysics
meteor.	meteorology
Mex.	Mexican
M.Fr.	Middle French
M.Gr.	Middle Greek
M.H.G.	Middle High German
milit.	military
min.	mining
mineral.	mineralogy
M.L.	Middle Latin
M.L.G.	Middle Low German
mod.	modern
Mod.Fr.	Modern French
Mongol.	Mongolian
MS.	manuscript
MSS.	manuscripts
mus.	music
mythol.	mythology

N

n.	noun
N.	North
N.Amer.	North American
nat.	natural
nat. hist.	natural history
nat. order	natural order
nat. phil.	natural philosophy
nat. sc.	natural science
naut.	nautical
nav.	naval, navy
navig.	navigation
neg.	negative
neut.	neuter
N.Gr.	New Greek
N.L.	New Latin
nom.	nominative
Norm.	Norman

north. . . . northern
North.E. . Northern English
N.T. . . . New Testament
numis. . . numismatics

O

O. . . . . Old
obj. . . . . objective
obs. . . . . obsolete
obstet. . . obstetrics
O.E. . . . Old English
O.Fr. . . . Old French
O.H.G. . . Old High
   German
O.L. . . . Old Latin
O.L.G. . . Old Low
   German
ophthalm. . ophthalmology
opt. . . . . optics
orig. . . . original,
   originally
ornith. . . ornithology

P

p. or *part.* . participle
paint. . . . painting
paleon. . . paleontology
parl. . . . parliamentary
pathol. . . pathology
perf. . . . perfect
perh. . . . perhaps
Pers. . . . Persian
persp. . . . perspective
petrog. . . petrography
Pg. . . . . Portuguese
phar. . . . pharmacy
pharm. . . pharmacology
philol. . . philology
philos. . . philosophy
phon. . . . phonetic,
   phonetics
photog. . . photography
phr. . . . phrase
phren. . . phrenology

phys. . . . . physical,
   physics
physiol. . . physiology
pl. . . . . . plural
pneum. . . . pneumatics
poet. . . . . poetic
Pol. . . . . Polish
pol. econ. . . political
   economics
polit. . . . . political
poss. . . . . possessive
pp. . . . . . past participle
ppr. . . . . present
   participle
Pr. . . . . . Provençal
prep. . . . preposition
pres. . . . . present
pret. . . . . preterit
print. . . . printing
priv. . . . . privative
prob. . . . . probably
pron. . . . pronoun
prop. . . . . properly
pros. . . . . prosody
Prot. . . . . Protestant
Prov. . . . . Proverbs
provinc. . . provincial
Ps. . . . . . Psalms
psychoanal. . psychoanalysis
psychol. . . psychology
punct. . . . . punctuation

R

rail. . . . . railroad,
   railways
redupl. . . . reduplication
ref. . . . . . reference
refl. . . . . . reflexive
reg. . . . . . regular
rel. . . . . . relative
relig. . . . . religion
repr. . . . . represented
Rev. . . . . Revelation
rhet. . . . . rhetoric

Rom. . . . . Roman
Rom. antiq. . . Roman
   antiquities
Rom. Cath. Ch. Roman
   Catholic
   Church
Russ. . . . . Russian

S

S. . . . . . . South
S. Amer. . . . South
   American
Sax. . . . . . Saxon
Sc. . . . . . Scottish
Scand. . . . Scandinavian
scrip. . . . . scripture
sculp. . . . . sculpture
sing. . . . . singular
Skr., Skt. . . Sanskrit
Slav. . . . . Slavic
sociol. . . . sociology
south. . . . southern
Sp. . . . . . Spanish
specif. . . . specific,
   specifically
sp. gr. . . . specific
   gravity
spirit. . . . spiritualism
St. . . . . . saint
subj. . . . . subjunctive
superl. . . . superlative
surg. . . . . surgery
surv. . . . . surveying
Sw. . . . . . Swedish
syll. . . . . syllable
sym. . . . . symbol
syn. . . . . synonym
Syr. . . . . . Syriac

T

techn. . . . technical
teleg. . . . telegraphy
teleph. . . . telephony
term. . . . . termination

Teut. . . . . Teutonic
theatr. . . . theatrical
theol. . . . . theology
transf. . . . transference
transl. . . . translated,
   translation
trig. . . . . trigonometry
Turk. . . . . Turkish
TV . . . . . television
typog. . . . typography

U

ult. . . . . . ultimate,
   ultimately
U.S. . . . . United States
usu. . . . . . usually

V

v. . . . . . verb
var. . . . . . variant
vbl. n. . . . verbal noun
veter. . . . . veterinary
veter. pathol. . veterinary
   pathology
v. i. . . . . verb
   intransitive
V.L. . . . . Vulgar Latin
v.n. . . . . verb neuter
voc. . . . . . vocative
v. phr. . . . verb phrase
v. t. . . . . verb transitive

W

W. . . . . . Welsh
W.Gmc. . . West
   Germanic
W.Ind. . . . West Indian
W.Sax. . . . West Saxon
W.W.I . . . World War One
W.W.II . . . World War
   Two

Z

zoogeog. . . . zoogeography
zool. . . . . . zoology

New Words

1. Words that are new to the English language. 2. New uses of previously existing words. 3. Words, especially technical ones, that were once used only by specialists but are now in general use.

acetaminophen *n.* A pain- and fever-relieving drug.

acid rain, *n.* Precipitation containing sulfuric and nitric acid pollutants.

acid rock, *n.* Rock music suggestive of a psychedelic experience.

acupressure, *n.* Finger-pressure therapy; the application of finger pressure to a system of points on the body to promote the health and well-being of the recipient.

acyclovir, *n.* Experimental drug believed to prevent cold sores and genital herpes infections in transplant patients.

adenovirus, *n.* Any one of a group of viruses containing DNA; causative of respiratory diseases, possibly of malignant tumors.

aerobics, *n.* System of exercise based on increasing oxygen intake to stimulate heart and lung activity.

afterburner, *n.* Device for destroying (usually by burning) carbon wastes, e.g., from the engine of a motor vehicle to reduce air pollution.

Agent Orange, *n.* Defoliant mixture of two herbicides, 2,4-D and 2,4,5-T, containing high levels of dioxin.

AIDS or **A.I.D.S.,** *n.* Acquired immune deficiency syndrome, a severe disorder in which part of the body's immune system is damaged, making a victim vulnerable to serious infection.

aikido, *n.* Japanese method of self-defense, using the opponent's momentum to create holds, throws, and locks.

airbag, *n.* Plastic bag for automobile dashboard, designed to inflate upon collision to form a protective cushion.

alien, *n.* Intelligent extraterrestial being come to earth.

alpha helix, *n.* Single coil structure characteristic of some proteins and DNA.

amniocentesis, *n.* Process of withdrawing amniotic fluid from the uterus of a pregnant female for analysis to determine sex of the fetus or to diagnose possible fetal defects.

anabolic steroids, *n.* Group of muscle-building drugs, banned for use in competition by amateur athletes.

analog recording, *n.* Reproduction of sounds by recording sound wave vibrations.

anchorman, *n.* In television news, the prime announcer to whom each correspondent refers back. Also *anchorperson.*

angel dust, *n. Slang.* Phencyclidine hydrochloride, a highly dangerous animal tranquilizer sometimes smoked with marijuana to heighten hallucinogenic effects.

angiography, *n.* Nonsurgical technique and process for determining arrangement of blood or lymph vessels.

antiallergenic or **antiallergic,** *a.* Providing relief from the symptoms of allergy.

antianxiety, *a.* Providing relief for anxiety, e.g., an antianxiety drug.

antiballistic missile, *n.* Defensive guided missile that intercepts and destroys a ballistic missile in flight. Abbr. ABM.

anticonvulsant, *n.* Convulsion preventative or mitigator such as used in treating epileptics.

antidepressant, *n.* A drug used to relieve psychic depression.

antihypertensive, *n.* Drug effective against high blood pressure. **—antihypertensive,** *a.*

antinuclear, *a.* Opposed to development of nuclear weapons or power plants.

area code, *n.* Three-digit code designating areas of telephone subscribers. It precedes the seven-digit local number.

artificial language, *n.* A synthetic language based on a given set of specifications as to its use, e.g., for a computer.

aspartame, *n.* An artificial sugar substitute.

atomic physics, *n.* Science concerned with structure of the atom and the particles which compose it.

audiophile, *n.* High-fidelity hobbyist.

autoimmune disease, *n.* Ailment resulting from breakdown of the body's immune system so that the immune response is directed against the body's own organisms.

autonetics, *n.* Science of automatic guidance systems.

ayatollah, *n.* A Shiite Moslem spiritual leader in Iran.

bag man, *n. Slang.* One who picks up payments of illicit money. **—bag woman.**

barcode reader, *n.* Device that reads combinations of bars and numbers, e.g., on food packages.

BASIC, *n.* Acronym for Beginner's All-purpose Symbolic Instruction Code, computer language using many terms in English in its programs.

behavior therapy, *n.* Program designed to replace undesirable behavior patterns with new ones.

benchmark, *n.* A reference point for making measurements.

Beta, *a.* Referring to a type of video cassette recorder and the disks it uses.

beta-endorphin, *n.* An endorphin that acts as a potent painkiller.

biathlon, *n.* Combination cross-country skiing and rifle shooting at targets as a competitive sport.

bioavailability, *n.* The extent and rate of absorption of a dose of a given drug.

bioethics, *n.* Study of ethical problems involved in biological research, e.g., in genetics, organ transplants, artificial insemination.

biofeedback, *n.* Conditioning technique designed to control normally involuntary responses, including blood pressure and heartbeat.

biological engineering, *n.* Creation of life forms toward an objective such as creating greater crop yield in a type of plant.

biotron, *n.* Chamber with controlled climate; used in experiments on the effects of environment on organisms.

black belt, *n.* 1. In judo or karate, certification of highest proficiency. 2. One who has earned the degree.

Black English, *n.* Dialect common among some Afro-Americans.

black hole, *n.* Hypothetical area in space postulated to be a collapsed star into which matter has contracted so that it vanishes except for an intense gravitational effect.

Black Panthers, *n.* Organization of militant blacks advocating black nationalism in the U.S.

boat people, *n. Colloq.* Refugee emigrants, esp. Vietnamese, who escape their country by boat with no authorized destination.

body language, *n.* Conscious or unconscious positions, movements, or gestures that communicate one's attitudes and emotional responses to others.

bodysurf, *n.* To ride the waves horizontally without a surfboard.

bracket creep, *n.* The tendency of income tax rates to increase with inflation as taxpayers fall into higher tax brackets without an increase in real income.

Brown Power, *n.* Policy designed to provide greater influence for Mexican-Americans and other hispanics in U.S.

bump, *v.* To preempt a place, particularly on a public carrier or for an event.

buzz word, *n.* 1. Expression designed to impress the uninitiated, usually consisting of technical or esoteric terms. 2. Expression that triggers a strong emotional reaction.

cable television, *n.* System delivered by direct wire to paid subscribers. Abbr. CATV.

Byzantine, *a.* Highly complicated or involving intrigue.

call-back, *n.* Recall by a manufacturer of a defective product.

capital-intensive, *a.* Of production by a high ratio of equipment or other investment to the role of labor.

capsid, *n.* Protein shell of a virus.

cardiopulmonary resuscitation, *n.* Emergency method used to start breathing and blood circulation in a cardiac-arrest victim. Abbr. CPR.

catalytic converter, *n.* Device used in automobiles that chemically changes noxious gases to nonpolluting products.

Catch-22, *n.* Double-bind situation in which one factor invalidates or makes impossible other factors, usu. used satirically; from the novel *Catch-22,* by Joseph Heller.

catecholamine, *n.* Any of various neurotransmitter drugs or hormones, e.g., epinephrine, dopamine.

CAT scanner, *n.* X-ray device that uses computerized axial tomography to provide views of cross-sections of the body.

cave, *n.* An area shielded to protect against radioactivity in which processing is usually done by remote control.

cell, *n.* Unit of computer memory with one-word capacity.

charge nurse, *n.* Nurse assigned to the management of a ward.

charm, *n.* Hypothetical quark (the fourth).

chemotaxonomy, *n.* Classification of flora and fauna in accordance with biochemical composition.

Chicano (masc.), **Chicana** (fem.), *n.* U.S. resident of Mexican descent.

Chinese restaurant syndrome, *n.* Temporary symptoms, including headache, affecting some who have ingested monosodium glutamate.

chip, *n.* Miniaturized wafer disk of silicon on which an integrated circuit is printed.

chloracne, *n.* A disease that primarily affects skin, but in extreme cases can lead to general organ toxicity. It is caused by exposure to certain chlorinated compounds, including dioxin.

citizens band or **citizens wave band,** *n.* Radio frequencies allocated for citizen communications, widely used by drivers of motor vehicles. Abbr. CB.

clean, *a. Slang.* 1. Producing little or no radioactive residue, as a *clean* weapon. 2. Not possessing drugs. 3. Not addicted to drugs. 4. Not possessing any stolen merchandise.

clone, *v.* To grow an identical form of life asexually from a cell of an organism. **—clone,** *n.* The exact reproduction of an organism.

coliform index, *n.* A rating of the purity of water based on a count of fecal bacteria.

collapsar, *n.* A black hole.

compact disk or **compact disc,** *n.* A truly digital recording with improved fidelity, smaller than a traditional LP and played by a laser beam instead of a phonograph needle. Abbr. CD.

computerized axial tomography, *n.* A system of providing 3-dimensional X rays of areas of the body.

computer science, *n.* The study of computer hardware and software technology and operations.

conglomerate, *n.* Corporate entity consisting of several companies in a variety of industries.

console, *n.* A grouping of controls, indicators, etc., used to monitor readiness of and/or to control specific functions of a system.

consumerism, *n.* 1. The movement to promote consumer interests. 2. Promotion of growth of increased use of goods.

convection oven, *n.* Stove in which a fan circulates heated air through the oven for fast, even cooking.

cool, *a. Slang.* Restrained; utilizing understatement and underemphasis in conversation.

core, *n.* Magnetic doughnut-shaped ring for storing computer information.

corn row, *n.* Tightly braided hairstyle resembling rows of corn on each side of the head.

coronary bypass, *n.* Surgical establishment of blood supply to a part of the heart in which the arteries have been blocked or destroyed. Also *revascularization.*

cosmetic, *a.* Of something done solely for the sake of appearance.

cost-effective, *a.* Relatively beneficial for the cost involved.

counter conditioning, *n.* Substituting a desirable habit or condition for an undesirable one.

counter culture, *n.* Mores contrary to the accepted ones of the time and place.

crib death, *n.* Sudden infant death syndrome.

Taken from *The Morrow Book of New Words* by N.H. and S.K. Mager, copyright © 1982 by Sylvia K. Mager. Reprinted by permission of William Morrow and Company, Inc.

cross-dress, v. To dress in clothing traditionally appropriate to the opposite sex.

cryonics, n. System and practice of freezing deceased organisms for storage in expectation of future revival and use. —**cryonic**, a.

culture shock, n. The disorientation caused by a major change in milieu.

cursor, n. A moving device on a video screen that indicates position.

cyanoacrylate, n. Acrylic monomer used to close a wound and as an industrial adhesive.

cytomegalovirus, n. Virus that causes cell enlargement resulting in diseases of brain, kidneys, liver, lung, and salivary glands, esp. in newborn infants.

daisy-wheel printer, n. Computer printing device.

datamation, n. 1. The computer industry. 2. Automation using data processing.

citizens band or **citizens wave band**, n. Radio frequencies allocated for citizen communications, widely used by drivers of motor vehicles. Abbr. CB.

clean, a. Slang. 1. Producing little or no radioactive residue, as a clean weapon. 2. Not possessing drugs. 3. Not addicted to drugs. 4. Not possessing any stolen merchandise.

clone, v. To grow an identical form of life asexually from a cell of an organism. —**clone**, n. The exact reproduction of an organism.

coliform index, n. A rating of the purity of water based on a count of fecal bacteria.

collapsar, n. A black hole.

compact disk or **compact disc**, n. A truly digital recording with improved fidelity, smaller than a traditional LP and played by a laser beam instead of a phonograph needle. Abbr. CD.

computerized axial tomography, n. A system of providing 3-dimensional X rays of areas of the body.

computer science, n. The study of computer hardware and software technology and operations.

conglomerate, n. Corporate entity consisting of several companies in a variety of industries.

console, n. A grouping of controls, indicators, etc., used to monitor readiness of and/or to control specific functions of a system.

consumerism, n. 1. The movement to promote consumer interests. 2. Promotion of growth of increased use of goods.

convection oven, n. Stove in which a fan circulates heated air through the oven for fast, even cooking.

cool, a. Slang. Restrained; utilizing understatement and underemphasis in conversation.

core, n. Magnetic doughnut-shaped ring for storing computer information.

corn row, n. Tightly braided hairstyle resembling rows of corn on each side of the scalp.

coronary bypass, n. Surgical establishment of blood supply to a part of the heart in which the arteries have been blocked or destroyed. Also revascularization.

cosmetic, a. Of something done solely for the sake of appearance.

cost-effective, a. Relatively beneficial for the cost involved.

counter conditioning, n. Substituting a desirable habit or condition for an undesirable one.

counter culture, n. Mores contrary to the accepted ones of the time and place.

crib death, n. Sudden infant death syndrome.

cross-dress, v. To dress in clothing traditionally appropriate to the opposite sex.

cryonics, n. System and practice of freezing deceased organisms for storage in expectation of future revival and use. —**cryonic**, a.

culture shock, n. The disorientation caused by a major change in milieu.

cursor, n. A moving device on a video screen that indicates position.

cyanoacrylate, n. Acrylic monomer used to close a wound and as an industrial adhesive.

cytomegalovirus, n. Virus that causes cell enlargement resulting in diseases of brain, kidneys, liver, lung, and salivary glands, esp. in newborn infants.

daisy-wheel printer, n. Computer printing device.

datamation, n. 1. The computer industry. 2. Automation using data processing.

debug, v. 1. Remove problems in the operation of an apparatus, esp. in a computer program. 2. Remove concealed devices for monitoring telephone and room-area conversations.

deck, n. Means of storing computer information for future use, e.g., magnetic tape.

defibrillate, v. To restore twitching heart rhythm to normal.

degauss, v. To erase a magnetic tape, disk, etc.

delimiter, n. Computer symbol to mark the beginning or end of a unit of information.

delta wave, n. Brain wave during deepest period of sleep.

demographics, n. Statistical characteristics of a population.

deprogramming, n. Process of eliminating an attitudinalor thinking process inculcated by a course of intensive indoctrination, e.g., from a religious cult. —**deprogram**, v.

dermabrasion, n. Technique utilizing chemical and mechanical abrasives for removing a layer of skin in order to get rid of blemishes.

descrambler, n. Device for interpreting scrambled messages, e.g., in radio or telephone communication. —**descramble**, v.

diethylstilbestrol, n. A synthetic estrogen, once used to avoid miscarriage, sometimes used as morning-after contraceptive; held to cause cancer in offspring at maturity. Abbr. DES.

digital recording, n. Reproduction of sound fed into a computer through an amplifier, converted to numbers, and stored with recording.

dimethyl sulfoxide, n. An industrial solvent derived from wood pulp. It has been used as a pain reliever and anti-inflammatory agent. Abbr. DMSO.

dioxin, n. 2,3,7,8,-tetrachlorodibenzo-p-dioxin, a highly toxic impurity formed in some chemical manufacturing processes. Abbr. TCDD.

dirty, a. Pertaining to a bomb or nuclear weapon that purposefully leaves a larger than necessary radioactive residue.

disco, n. 1. Short for discotheque. 2. Popular music with a strong beat.

disk or **disc**, n. 1. Magnetic coated plastic record for storing computer data. 2. Grid in a phototypesetting apparatus.

display, n. Device for communicating visually, e.g., a cathode-ray tube.

distributive education, n. Schooling integrated with on-the-job training.

DNAse or **DNAase**, n. An enzyme that converts DNA to nucleotides by hydrolysis.

docudrama, n. Motion picture dramatizing a real-life situation.

dojo, n. School for training in Oriental (esp. Japanese) techniques of self-defense.

Dolby system, n. Trademark for device to eliminate noise from recordings.

domino theory, n. Political view that the fall or change of allegiance of one nation precipitates the fall of the governments of its neighbors.

dopa, n. An amino acid that is a precursor of dopamine.

dopamine, n. An amine that increases systolic and pulse pressure without affecting diastolic pressure.

double helix, n. Two intertwined coils that form the crystalline structure of DNA.

dove, n. One who advocates a peaceful solution to international conflicts. —**dovish**, a.

downer, n. Slang. 1. A depressant drug, esp. a barbiturate. 2. A depressing experience or person.

Down's syndrome, n. Mongolism, a type of congenital mental retardation.

dreadlocks, n. Long, braided hairstyle worn by Rastafarians to symbolize commitment to their faith.

drone, n. A land, sea, or air pilotless vehicle that is remotely or automatically controlled.

dump, v. To transfer computer data from an internal to an external storage.

dyslexia, n. A disorder causing impaired reading ability.

ekistics, n. Study of problems of human communities, including economics, geography, sociology, and government.

electromyograph, n. A device to record electrical voltage generated by body muscles.

embryo transfer, n. Technique of placement into the uterus of an egg extracted from the body and fertilized in a petri dish.

encounter group, n. Therapeutic group designed to increase sensitivity and physical and emotional awareness.

endoradiosonde, n. A device implanted in the body to transmit data on body functions.

endorphin, n. One of a group of morphinelike substances naturally secreted in humans and animals. They were originally found in the brain but have since been found throughout the body.

endrin, n. Toxic pesticide said to cause irreversible damage to the human central nervous system.

enhanced-radiation weapon, n. A nuclear weapon designed to minimize explosive force, and maximize radiation.

enkephalin, n. An endorphin.

environmentalist, n. One devoted to protecting the ecological balance of the earth.

Epstein-Barr virus, n. Virus associated with Burkitt's lymphoma, some human cancers, infectious mononucleosis, etc.

ergonomics, n. Study of the functions, psychology and techniques of human beings, machines, and their environments.

extended family, n. Family unit consisting of three or more generations living together.

extraterrestrial, n. One from outside the earth.

fastback, n. 1. Automobile designed with rear section sloping downward in an unbroken line. 2. The roof of such a vehicle.

fast breeder reactor, n. Nuclear plant that produces fissionable material from high-energy neutrons as a by-product in excess of the amount it uses.

fast-food, a. Of restaurants, usually part of a chain, that serve quickly prepared food.

feedback, n. Response following an action, e.g., comments after a speech, esp. when designed to correct a situation.

fence-mending, n. Restoring good political relationships.

field-ion microscope, n. Microscope that translates positive-ion electron emissions to produce an image on a fluorescent screen.

firebomb, n. An incendiary bomb.

fireflood, v. To send steam or air under pressure into an exhausted oil well to revive oil production.

firmware, n. Software and hardware component so integrated in a computer as to make function of each indistinguishable.

fish-eye lens, n. An extremely wide angle (180°) lens.

flash-forward, n. Storytelling technique of presenting future events before the contemporary story line.

flextime, n. System of optional work times that permits staggered work hours.

floor exercise, n. Competitive gymnastics event including tumbling, somersaults, handstands, ballet movement.

floppy disk, n. Flexible magnetic coated plastic disk used for storing computer data.

food processor, n. An electrified mechanical device that mixes, chops, and liquefies food.

food stamp, n. Certificate redeemable at retail food stores, issued by the goverment to low-income individuals.

format, v. To produce in a special plan, size, shape, or proportion.

freak, n. Slang. Heavy user or addict, e.g., drug freak, old-book freak.

garbage, n. Inaccurate or unsuitable computer data.

gasohol, n. Mixture of 10% ethanol and 90% gasoline for use by motor vehicles.

gene splicing, n. 1. Injection of genetic material from foreign organisms to change genetic structure of other organisms. 2. Technique of changing inherited characteristics by recombining segments of the genetic material in DNA.

genetic engineering, n. The science of alteration of genetic material to produce new traits.

gentrification, n. The redevelopment of a low-income residential area by inducing higher-income individuals to move in. —**gentrify**, v.

geoprobe, n. Satellite designed to explore the space surrounding earth.

glitch, n. A misfunction in machinery, esp. in electricity input resulting in a surge in power.

gluon, n. Hypothetical particle believed to hold

together the centers of atoms.

gofer, *n. Slang.* An assistant often sent on errands, from "go for."

granola, *n.* A breakfast or snack food, usually a rolled oat, nut, and raisin mixture.

graphic, *n.* A visual, nonalphabetical or numerical display generated by a computer.

grass, *n. Slang.* Marijuana.

graviton, *n.* Hypothetical unit of gravitational field energy.

Gray Panthers, *n.* Organization of militant older citizens seeking to improve the legal, economic, and political situation of the elderly in the U.S.

gridlock, *n.* A massive urban traffic jam in which no car can move in any direction.

groupie, *n. Slang.* 1. A follower of famous people, esp. a teenage follower of a rock 'n' roll singer. 2. A woman who follows celebrities for sexual association.

grunt, *n. Slang.* A private infantryman, esp. in Vietnam.

halfway house, *n.* Sheltered residence designed to help adjustment of institutionalized persons in the process of release, e.g., mental patients, prisoners.

hang glide, *v.* To glide in harness in a kitelike glider, usually pushing off from a hill. —**hang glider,** *n.* —**hang gliding,** *n.*

hard-core, *a.* 1. Of persons whose status is not easily changed, e.g., hard-core unemployed. 2. Of pornography, explicit.

hard drug, *n.* An addictive drug, e.g., heroin.

hard rock, *n.* Hard driving, loud rock 'n' roll music with a regular beat, usu. involving electronically amplified instruments.

Hare Krishna, *n.* Religious group dedicated to the god Krishna.

hatchback, *n.* 1. A motor vehicle with a rear sloping roof that swings open upward, to accept luggage and/or passengers. 2. The roof of such a vehicle.

hawk, *n.* A person who advocates a military or bellicose solution to a disagreement. —**hawkish,** *a.*

head shop, *n. Slang.* Outlet for drug-use accessories and associated artifacts.

health food, *n.* Special food and food supplements believed to be beneficial, esp. unsprayed, organically grown, and unprocessed foods.

health spa, *n.* A recreational hotel with facilities for weight reduction, massage, etc.

Heimlich maneuver, *n.* Procedure to assist a choking victim by forcing air into windpipes by manually pressing a victim's upper abdomen.

helicity, *n.* The spin of a particle around an axis.

herpes type II, *n.* Form of persistent viral venereal disease caused by herpes simplex virus.

high, *n. Colloq.* A state of exhilaration.

histocompatibility, *n.* Sufficient compatibility to be suitable for tissue grafting.

holistic, *a.* Of a planning approach that views a situation as a whole. —**holistically,** *adv.*

holistic medicine, *n.* Treatment of the whole organism, not just the symptoms of a disease.

hospice, *n.* A program that provides palliative and supportive care for terminally ill patients and their families.

hot-dog, *v.* To perform stunts while skiing.

hot shoe, *n.* Base on a camera for a synchronized flash attachment.

hot-wire, *v.* To start an ignition system without a key.

human diploid cell vaccine, *n.* Improved antirabies treatment.

hypothermia, *n.* The condition of having lower-than-normal temperature in the body.

informatics or **information science,** *n.* Science of obtaining and transmitting information.

infrasound, *n.* Extremely low-frequency sound.

interface, *n.* 1. Point at which two elements of a system join. 2. The method of integrating these two elements. —**interface,** *v.* To operate together.

interferon, *n.* Antibody protein produced in cells of some mammals.

International System of Units, *n.* International standards for measuring units of length, time, mass, electric current, temperature, luminosity intensity, and substance. Abbr. SI.

jetavator, *n.* Device designed to direct the exhaust of a rocket to effect change in direction of the craft.

jet lag, *n.* Fatigue, irritability, and other mental and physical symptoms resulting from air travel through several time zones.

John Birch Society, *n.* An extreme right-wing private organization formed in 1950 to combat Communism. —**Bircher** or **John Bircher,** *n.* A member.

joystick, *n.* A device used to play many video games.

junk food, *n.* Foods with limited nutritional value, used principally as snacks.

Kaposi's sarcoma, *n.* Rare form of cancer, sometimes associated with immune deficiency states.

Keogh plan, *n.* A savings program that lets self-employed individuals make tax-deductible contributions to a formal retirement plan.

kepone, *n.* A pesticide ingredient suspected of being carcinogenic.

kilohertz, *n.* Formerly called "kilocycle," unit of frequency equal to 1,000 cycles per second. Abbr. kHz.

kiwi, *n.* An egg-size fruit with sweet green pulp, native to China.

kung fu, *n.* An oriental self-defense technique.

Laetrile, *n.* Trade name for a substance derived from amygdalin; its use as a treatment for cancer is controversial.

Lamaze method, *n.* Technique of natural childbirth.

lander, *n.* Space satellite vehicle for landing on the moon or other celestial body.

laparoscope, *n.* An illuminated optical instrument for examining internal organs, piercing the body wall. —**laparoscopy,** *n.* Surgery using the laparoscope.

launder, *v.* To legitimatize illegally obtained funds by processing through a third-party business. —**laundered,** *a.*

lcd, *n.* [(l)iquid (c)rystal (d)isplay.] A display in which liquid crystal is sandwiched between pieces of glass, used in digital watches, calculators, etc.

leachate, *n.* Materials that pollute water as it seeps through solid waste.

LED, *n.* Light-emitting diode, an electronic-readout solid-state lamp used in digital clocks, etc.

Legionnaires' disease, *n.* Form of pneumonia, first recognized at a 1976 convention of the American Legion in Philadelphia, Pa.

light pen, *n.* A hand-held instrument used for making changes in the information on a cathode ray display.

limbic, *a.* Of the circumference portion of the brain.

living will, *n.* A written request to have one's life terminated at any time when only artificial means can sustain it.

load-shedding, *n.* Cutback of electric power to prevent a blackout.

logic, *n.* Principles and applications of truth tables and factors involving arithmetic computations in computers.

machine translation, *n.* Instructions translated by a computer from one computer language to another.

machismo, *n.* [Span.] Exaggerated masculinity; manly assurance. —**macho,** *a.*

macrobiotics, *n.* A Zen-influenced theory that holds that a vegetarian diet is in balance and in harmony with the cosmos.

macroinstruction or **macro,** *n.* A coded instruction that commands a sequence of computer operations.

magnetic bottle, *n.* The magnetic field that confines plasma in a thermonuclear reaction.

magnetic bubble, *n.* A small mobile region of magnetism on which great amounts of computer data may be stored magnetically.

magnetogasdynamics or **magnetoplasmadynamics,** *n.* Magnetohydrodynamics.

mainframe, *n.* The central processing unit of a computer, containing the control unit and the circuits.

mammogram, *n.* Breast X-ray, used to detect breast cancer. —**mammography,** *n.* The process.

mantra, *n.* Sacred sounds or words repeated by Hindus and Buddhists in prayer and/or meditation.

Maoism, *n.* Form of Marxism-Leninism developed by Chinese-Communist leader Mao Zedong.

martial art, *n.* Any of several Oriental techniques of self-defense, e.g., karate, judo.

megahertz, *n.* Unit of frequency equal to 1,000,000 cycles per second. Abbr. MHz.

megavitamin, *n.* Extremely large dose of a vitamin, sometimes used to treat mental or emotional illness.

melatonin, *n.* A hormone used for lightening skin color.

meltdown, *n.* The melting of the protective cases surrounding a nuclear reactor.

messenger RNA, *n.* A form of RNA carrying genetic information to the ribosome.

meter maid, *n.* Attendant who oversees meter parking, issuing tickets for violations of parking regulations.

microcircuit, *n.* Miniaturized circuit usu. produced photographically, used in computers, space equipment, etc. Also *microelectronic circuit, microminiature circuit.*

microcomputer, *n.* A small, inexpensive computer.

microdot, *n.* The photographic reproduction of a document reduced to the size of a dot.

microelectronics, *n.* The study of miniaturization of electronic components.

microfiche, *n.* A document substantially reduced (to 8 mm or smaller), usu. filed with other microfiches on a card for long-term storage.

microprobe, *n.* 1. Device used to examine a microscopic area by measuring the emissions spectrum created by radiation. 2. Device used for analyzing the chemical composition of materials by using an electron beam (laser) with optical apparatus.

microwave oven, *n.* An oven that utilizes microwaves for rapid food preparation.

mini, *n.* A very short skirt. Also *miniskirt.*

minibike, *n.* Small one-passenger motorbike with a low body and high handlebars.

minicomputer, *n.* A small computer, faster and more powerful than a microcomputer.

minipill, *n.* Oral contraceptive with a minimum of progesterone, and no estrogen.

modem, *n.* Acronym for (mo)dulator-(dem)odulator, a device that converts the form of data so that they can be transmitted by another medium, e.g., computerized data changed to electronic pulses for telephone transmission, then reconverted to computer-compatible data.

module, *n.* 1. A standardized unit that can be assembled to create a functional unit, e.g., a piece of furniture, a home. 2. A separable part of a space vehicle. —**modular,** *a.*

mole, *n.* An intelligence agent who remains inactive for a long period of time, awaiting a particular order or event to become active.

molecular biology, *n.* The science of programming the genetic system and the creation of biological chemicals in living organisms.

monoamine oxidase, *n.* An enzyme that oxidizes amines. Abbr. MAO.

monosome, *n.* An unpaired sex chromosome.

monounsaturate, *n.* An oil or fat that has one double bond per molecule.

Moog synthesizer, *n.* An electronic keyboard musical instrument with a wide range.

Moonie, *n.* A member of the Unification Church headed by Sun-Myung Moon.

moped, *n.* A two-wheeled vehicle with motor and pedal options.

motocross, *n.* Motorcycle race on a fixed course over a difficult terrain.

multimedia, *a.* Involving several media.

mutagen, *n.* Any substance that causes mutations.

Mylar, *n.* Trade name for a polyester film plastic used for insulation, balloons, etc.

myoelectric, *a.* Of the use of electric power produced by muscles to move prosthetic devices.

narc or **nark,** *n. Slang.* An official investigator of narcotics violations.

narcoanalysis, *n.* Use of drugs to facilitate questioning or analysis.

Native American, *n.* An American Indian.

negritude, *n.* 1. The state and pride of being black. 2. Pride in the cultural heritage of black people.

network, *v.* To make connections among people or groups.

neutron bomb, *n.* Enhanced-radiation weapon.

neutron star, *n.* Celestial body emitting X-rays, hypothetically conceived as nuclear particles from a collapsed star.

ninja, *n.* A Japanese mercenary or warrior who masters the art of making himself invisible by means of some artifice. Ninjas traditionally engaged in espionage activities.

nitrosamines, *n.* Carcinogenic nitrogen compounds; they can occur from combining nitrites found in bacon and other cured meats with secondary amines in the digestive process.

nonproliferation, *a.* Of a program to halt expansion

of nuclear weapon capability.

notchback, *n.* 1. A slant-roofed passenger car with a flat rear bumper. 2. The roof of such a car.

NOW account, *n.* [(N)egotiable (O)rder of (W)ithdrawal.] Interest-paying banking account that substitutes for a personal checking account.

nuclear family, *n.* Family unit consisting of husband, wife, and their children.

nucleosynthesis, *n.* Process of creating chemical elements from the nuclei or protons of hydrogen.

oncogenesis, *n.* The formation and growth of a tumor.

on-line, *a.* Of a computer system in which the central processing unit controls the operation and peripheral devices.

op-ed page, *n.* A page of a newspaper, usually placed opposite the editorial page, on which individual points of view are discussed.

open admissions, *n.* 1. A policy of admitting any high school graduate to an institution of higher learning. 2. Policy of admitting any qualified student resident in or outside a neighborhood into a public school. Also *open enrollment.*

open classroom, *n.* Educational method using an informal curriculum centered on the discussion and investigation of subjects, carried on by students under teacher guidance.

open-loop, *n.* Computer system that has no self-correcting mechanism, depending entirely on input.

open marriage, *n.* An arrangement between spouses permitting each to carry on his or her own activities (including extramarital sexual relations).

optical fiber, *n.* A glass or plastic fiber that carries light.

optical maser, *n.* A laser.

optical scanner, *n.* Photoelectric scanning device for converting characters or other images into signals acceptable by a digital computer.

orienteering, *n.* Outdoor race in which competitors find their way through unfamiliar area using a map and a compass.

orthomolecular medicine, *n.* A philosophy of medicine that holds that disease, esp. mental illness, is curable by restoring normal body chemistry.

orthotics, *n.* Branch of medicine dealing with the mechanical support of weak joints and muscles. — **orthotic,** *a.*

palimony, *n. Colloq.* Settlement payment awarded to a separated partner of an unmarried couple that has lived together.

paparazzi, *n.* Aggressive free-lance celebrity-chasing photographers.

paralegal, *n.* A paraprofessional legal assistant; one trained to assist an attorney.

paramedic, *n.* Trained medical worker capable of performing basic emergency medical functions.

paraprofessional, *n.* One trained to assist a professional, esp. in teaching, nursing, etc.

parietals, *n.* Rules regarding visitors of the opposite sex in a men's or women's dormitory.

particle board, *n.* Board made of resin-bonded bits of material.

pascal, *n.* A unit of pressure equal to a force of 1 newton per square meter.

penicillinase, *n.* An enzyme that destroys penicillin.

peripheral, *n.* An electronic or mechanical device not part of the basic processor, e.g., card reader, printer, terminal, etc.

peroxyacetyl nitrate, *n.* Toxic element in smog, created by action of sunlight on hydrocarbon exhausts from automobiles.

phagosome, *n.* Vesicle in a cell holding material captured by ameboid cells.

pheromone, *n.* Chemical substance secreted by an animal to produce a response (e.g., sexual) in others of the same species.

photocoagulation, *n.* Technique of causing tissue to coagulate under intense controlled light, e.g., in ophthalmological surgery.

picornavirus, *n.* Any of a group of small ether-resistant RNA viruses.

pita, *n.* Flat, round bread of the Middle East.

plaque, *n.* Calcified bacteria that can accumulate on teeth, leading to gum disease.

plat, *n.* Scale diagram of an area with legal identification of boundaries.

plea bargaining, *n.* Negotiation between the defense attorney in a criminal action and the prosecutor for a

reduced charge in exchange for a plea of guilty.

pod, *n.* A unit designed to detach from a spacecraft.

polychlorinated biphenyl, *n.* Any of a group of highly toxic, very persistent carcinogenic pollutants, used in plastics and as an insulator in electrical devices. Abbr. PCB.

polypropylene, *n.* A thermoplastic resin that is a moisture-resistant, hard, tough plastic.

polysorbate, *n.* Any of a group of fatty-acid esters used as emulsifying, dispersing, and solubilizing agents in production of certain foods and drugs.

polyvinyl chloride, *n.* Vinyl resin used to make a transparent flexible plastic film that releases hydrochloric acid when burned; used in food packaging. Abbr. PVC.

potassium-argon dating, *n.* Method of determining the age of geological specimens based on the measurement of radioactive decay from potassium to argon.

poxvirus, *n.* Any of a group of large, chemically complex DNA viruses that cause smallpox and other pox diseases in lower animals.

preppie or **preppy,** *n.* One who attends or has attended a preparatory school.

pro-life movement, *n.* Antiabortion political movement.

prostaglandin, *n.* Any of a group of potent compounds present in many tissues. They are important in metabolism, smooth-muscle contraction, transmission of nerve impulses, and blood-pressure control.

psychic energizer, *n.* A mental stimulant, e.g., amphetamine.

psychoactive, *a.* Of a drug or drugs that affect the mind or behavior.

psychohistory, *n.* A psychoanalytic approach to history.

psychopharmaceutical, *n.* A drug that is designed to affect one's mental condition.

psychotropic, *a.* Of a drug that modifies mental condition.

pulsar, *n.* A source in space of strong, pulsating radio waves, believed to be the core of an exploded or rotating neutron star.

punk rock, Hard rock music with heavy, insistent rhythms and nihilistic lyrics. — **punk,** *a.* Of punk rock music; of the style of dress associated with punk rock musicians and their admirers.

pusher, *n. Slang.* One who sells drugs illegally.

Quaalude, *n.* Trade name for methaqualone, a non-barbiturate sedative and hypnotic.

quark, *n.* A hypothetical subatomic nuclear particle, held to be the basic component of protons, neutrons, etc.

rabbit ears, *n. Colloq.* A V-shaped indoor television antenna.

radial, radial-ply tire, or **radial tire,** *n.* A pneumatic tire made with ply casing cords parallel at right angles to the center line and rim.

radiocarbon dating, *n.* Carbon dating.

radio galaxy, *n.* Galaxy from which radio energy emissions are detected.

radiolabel, *v.* To insert a radioactive substance into a material for identification or tracing.

radiopaque, *a.* Impenetrable by radiation.

RAM, *n.* Computer acronym for random-access memory.

ramjet, *n.* A jet-propulsion engine that depends for its operation on the air compression accomplished by the forward motion of the engine.

Rastafarian, *n.* Follower of the Jamaica-based religion that views Haile Selassi as messiah, and looks forward to the establishment of a theocratic world order and an end to white supremacy.

recycle, *v.* To process so that basic raw material may be used again.

red-line, *v.* To refuse to lend money on properties in areas that are poor financial risks.

reggae, *n.* Jamaican rock music with pulsating blues style, often with a political or religious message derived from Rastafarian beliefs.

reovirus, *n.* Acronym for respiratory enteric orphan virus, any of a group of relatively large RNA viruses that are parasitic for humans and most animals and believed to cause intestinal ailments and tumors.

rhabdovirus, *n.* Any of a group of viruses associated with animal-bite diseases, e.g., rabies.

rhinovirus, *n.* Any of the small viruses in the picor-

navirus group, associated with the common cold.

ribonuclease, *n.* Any of various enzymes present in body tissue that polymerize ribonucleic acid.

Richter scale, *n.* A logarithmic scale for measuring the magnitude of a seismic disturbance.

RNAse or **RNAase,** *n.* Ribonuclease.

robotics, *n.* The science of automated devices (robots) used to replace live workers, esp. in factories.

rolfing, *n.* Method of improving the body's structural alignment to create good physical and emotional health; developed by Ida P. Rolf.

ROM, *n.* Computer acronym for read-only memory.

RV, *n.* Recreational vehicle, e.g., a trailer.

R-value, *n.* Unit of measure of resistance to heat flow.

samizdat, *n.* [Russian, "self-publication."] Unauthorized works, clandestinely circulated to avoid legal censorship.

Saturday night special, *n. Slang.* An inexpensive, easily obtained handgun.

saxitoxin, *n.* Highly toxic substance found in red-tide algae and mollusks.

scam, *n. Slang.* An illegal operation, usu. a confidence racket, involving a sum of money.

scan, *v.* 1. To examine a body by X-ray or other radioactive material. 2. To examine stored material in a computer for a purpose. 3. To examine computer channels for input-output activity.

sci-fi, *n. Colloq.* Science fiction.

scramjet, *n.* A ramjet engine that uses a conventional method to reach the speed of sound.

seed money, *n.* Funds to initiate a business or nonprofit undertaking.

sexism, *n.* 1. The judging of human worth on the basis of gender or sex roles. 2. Prejudice or discrimination, usu. against women, based on gender.

shiatsu, *n.* Japanese massage technique using finger pressure at critical acupuncture points.

shrink-wrap, *n.* Plastic film packaging that shrinks under heat to conform to shape of contents, e.g., a book.

sick-out, *n.* A job action in which employees call in sick, esp. where a strike is not feasible.

skateboard, *n.* A short riding board mounted on roller-skate wheels.

skibob, *n.* A bicyclelike sled mounted on two short skis.

Skinner box, *n.* A device used in training animals, developed by B. F. Skinner.

skyjack, *v.* To assume control of an aircraft by force or threat of force, usu. in order to divert it from its original destination.

sky marshal, *n.* An armed federal plainclothes security guard assigned to prevent skyjackings.

slimnastics, *n.* Weight-reducing exercises.

slow virus, *n.* A virus that remains latent for many years, believed to be the causative agent in rheumatoid arthritis and in multiple sclerosis and other nervous disorders.

slumlord, *n. Colloq.* A landlord who neglects or abandons urban properties.

smart bomb, *n.* An airborne missile capable of being directed to its target by laser beams, television, or other homing device.

sociolinguistics, *n.* Study of language as determined or affected by sociocultural factors.

sodium fluoride, *n.* Chemical used as a decay inhibitor in drinking water and in dentistry.

soft-core, *a.* Of pornography, not as explicit or prurient as hard-core.

soft drug, *n.* A supposedly nonaddictive drug, e.g., marijuana.

soft rock, *n.* Sophisticated, low-keyed rock 'n' roll with a less defined rhythm than hard rock.

soft sculpture, *n.* Sculpture utilizing pliable materials, e.g., plastic, foam rubber, cloth.

sonogram, *n.* Ultrasonogram.

soup, *n.* A chemical mixture, often residual or waste product.

spark chamber, *n.* Device used to trace the path of a particle and to detect radiation.

speed, *n. Slang.* A stimulant drug, esp. an amphetamine.

sprawl, *n.* Unplanned development of open land, e.g., urban sprawl.

stagflation, *n.* Period of economic stagnation combined with inflation.

stannous fluoride, *n.* A fluoride compound used in

toothpaste.

state of the art, *n.* The highest level of technology in a field at any given time.

stereology, *n.* The study of three-dimensional objects seen in two dimensions.

stishovite, *n.* A dense polymorph of quartz created under pressure, believed of extraterrestrial origin.

stochastic, *a.* Of or involving random variables.

straight, *a. Slang.* Of one who is conventional, e.g., esp. not homosexual, a drug user, or a hippie.

street theater, *n.* Short plays or pantomine, usu. antiestablishment and presented on the street or in a park.

strip mining, *n.* Process of stripping land of its surface rock and soil to make available underlying mineral deposits.

strung out, *a. Slang.* 1. Addicted to a drug. 2. Debilitated from drug use.

subcompact, *n.* An automobile smaller than a compact car.

subtherapeutic, *a.* Of a preventive drug dosage, as in animal feed.

sudden infant death syndrome, *n.* Unexpected infant mortality that occurs during sleep. Abbr. SIDS.

suicide seat, *n. Colloq.* Seat next to the driver of a motor vehicle.

sulfonylurea, *n.* Any of a number of drugs that lessen blood sugar by increasing secretion of endogenous insulin, used in treating diabetes.

superalloy, *n.* A metal alloy with the capacity to resist high stresses, temperatures, etc.

supercluster, *n.* A large group of galaxies.

supercurrent, *n.* Electrical current running without resistance, as through a metal at or near absolute zero.

superstar, *n.* 1. A celestial body emitting great energy, e.g., a quasar. 2. A widely known personality of superior talent.

surface-to-air missile, *n.* An earth-launched guided missile with an airborne target. Acronym SAM.

surfactant, *n.* A surface-active agent.

surrogate mother, *n.* A woman who bears a child for another woman, conceiving the child by artificial insemination.

survivalist, *n.* One who intends to endure life in a postnuclear-holocaust world, often preparing by moving to a remote area, storing foodstuffs and ammunition, and acquiring combat and outdoor skills.

sushi, *n.* Japanese dish of raw fish served in thin slices.

swinger, *n. Slang.* 1. One who has many sexual partners. 2. One who is up-to-date in modern fashions and activities.

swing-wing, *n.* An aircraft in which retractable wings can be adjusted for various speeds.

synfuel, *n.* Synthetic fuel.

synthesizer, *n.* A device that creates complex entities of simple sound or frequency elements, e.g., a voice synthesizer in a computer.

tachyon, *n.* Hypothetical elementary particle characterized by speed greater than light.

tai chi or **tai chi chuan,** *n.* Chinese system of calisthenics, self-defense, and meditation that produces bodily flexibility and peace of mind.

talk show, *n.* A television or radio program in which celebrities or other persons discuss or are interviewed on subjects of interest.

target language, *n.* The language into which the language of a program is to be translated for the ongoing operation.

tax shelter, *n.* An investment that enables the taxpayer to have substantial deductions in income tax.

Tay-Sachs disease, *n.* An inherited neurological disease, leading to death by age 2.

T cell, *n.* A lymphocyte that helps to destroy viruses, fungi, and certain bacteria, and reject foreign tissue and tumors.

teenybopper, *Slang.* A teenager devoted to adolescent fads in dress, music, star worship.

teratogen, *n.* An agent that causes fetal malformation.

terminal, *n.* The instrument, usually a keyboard, that

enables data to enter or leave a computer.

test-tube baby, *n.* A child born as the result of a successful embryo transfer.

tetrahydrocannabinol, *n.* A compound derived from hemp that provides the chief intoxicant in marijuana. Abbr. THC.

thalidomide, *n.* A sedative and hypnotic drug that was found to be responsible for malformed offspring when used during pregnancy.

thermography, *n.* Technique of body-heat measurement used for early detection of cancer cells.

threatened species, *n.* A species that might become endangered within a short period of time.

time frame, *n.* A period of time.

time-sharing, *n.* Purchase of a property limited to use at a specified time only, e.g., for vacations.

T lymphocyte, *n.* T cell.

tofu, *n.* Soybean curd.

tokamak, *n.* A doughnut-shaped device in which plasma is contained by magnetic fields.

tokenism, *n.* Fulfilling legal and/or moral obligations by a nominal conformity.

total, *v. Slang.* To wreck a motor vehicle beyond repair.

towaway zone, *n.* Zone from which illegally parked vehicles may be towed away.

toxic shock syndrome, *n.* An infection *(bacterium staphylococcus aureus),* sometimes fatal, often associated with use of tampons. Abbr. TSS.

trail bike, *n.* A lightweight motorcycle designed for rough terrain.

transactinide series, *n.* Hypothetical elements following element 103 (lawrencium) in the periodic table.

transactional analysis, *n.* A form of group therapy in which subjects alternately assume roles in order to provide verbal outlets for undesired responses.

transcendental meditation, *n.* A meditation technique in which the mind is released from tension through use of a mantra.

transcribe, *v.* To carry a message from DNA to RNA.

transdermal drug, *n.* A pharmaceutical that is applied to the skin (usually by means of a small patch that is worn) rather than taken internally.

transducer, *n.* A virus that causes a change in the genetic character of a mocroorganism through action of nucleic acid.

transfer RNA, *n.* A form of RNA that combines with amino acids and messenger RNA to cause remaining amino acids to combine in a certain sequence in protein synthesis. Abbr. tRNA.

transsexual, *n.* A person who undergoes surgery to modify his or her sex organs to become physically like the opposite sex.

triage, *n.* 1. The sorting or screening of patients seeking hospital care, to determine which service is initially required and with what priority. 2. The sorting of battle or disaster casualties for those requiring immediate help, those who can wait, and those beyond help.

trichology, *n.* The study of hair. —**trichologist,** *n.*

ultrafiche, *n.* A microfilm of documents reduced to 1/90 or less normal size.

ultramicrotome, *n.* A device to cut very thin tissue sections for use in an electron microscope.

ultrasonograph, *n.* Diagnostic device utilizing ultrasonic waves to penetrate tissue. —**ultrasonogram,** *n.* The resulting record.

ultrasound, *n.* Ultrasonic sound, widely used in diathermy, medical diagnosis, cleaning, etc.

Ultrasuede, *n.* Trademark for a washable, suedelike fabric.

unisex, *a.* 1. Suitable for both men and women, e.g., clothes, hairstyles. 2. Indistinguishable as to sex.

universal product code, *n.* A 10-digit code based on ratio of printed bars to adjacent spaces, affixed to a package and readable electronically or by laser beam. It is used by retail stores for inventory control and checkout. Abbr. UPC.

upper, *n. Slang.* A stimulant drug, esp. amphetamine.

urbanology, *n.* The study of cities and their social and economic problems.

urban renewal, *n.* Rehabilitation (and rebuilding) of a decaying urban area, with or without government aid.

value-added tax, *n.* A tax based on the value added at each stage of production, designed to fall ultimately on the consumer. Abbr. VAT.

vanity plate, *n.* An automobile license plate carrying a word, name, and/or numbers selected by the owner.

varactor or **varactor diode,** *n.* A semiconductor diode in which the capacitance varies with the voltage applied.

vasoactive, *a.* Affecting the expansion or contraction of blood vessels.

vegan, *n.* A vegetarian who eats no dairy products. —**veganism,** *n.*

Velcro, *n.* Trade name for fabric created with hooked surface to adhere to other fabrics; it is used in lieu of fasteners.

velocimeter, *n.* A device to measure sound velocity in water.

vernier rocket, *n.* An auxiliary rocket used for fine adjustments in speed or direction.

VHS, *n.* Abbr. for video home system, a type of video cassette recorder.

video cassette or **video cartridge,** *n.* A videotape encased in a cartridge.

video cassette recorder, *n.* A device for recording a television program from a television set for later playback. Abbr. VCR.

videodisk or **videodisc,** *n.* A plastic disk containing a television recording.

video game, *n.* An electronic game with a visual display (often a home television screen).

virion, *n.* A complete infective viral particle.

vital signs, *n.* Basic diagnostic elements, e.g., pulse rate, respiratory rate, body temperature.

wafer, *n.* A thin polished piece of semiconductor crystal material, usu. silicon, on which circuits are fabricated, etched, or printed.

waffle, *v. Colloq.* To equivocate, esp. in decision-making.

Wankel engine, *n.* A small, light, rotary engine that utilizes a rounded triangular rotor-piston and that has only two major moving parts.

WASP or **Wasp,** *n.* Acronym for White Anglo-Saxon Protestant.

water bed, *n.* A bed whose mattress is a vinyl bag filled with water.

weak force, *n.* A force that governs the interactions of neutrinos, modifies the forces of gravity and electromagnetism, and causes radioactive decay. Also *weak interaction.*

whiffleball, *n.* A plastic ball with openings to increase air resistance, used for golf, softball, or baseball practice.

Wicca, *n.* Witchcraft. —**Wiccan,** *a.*

wind-chill factor, *n.* The effect of wind velocity in raising or lowering discomfort caused by the temperature.

wok, *n.* Convex metal Chinese cooking utensil.

women's liberation, *n.* (sometimes cap.) Feminist movement for equality of the sexes.

word processing, *n.* System of recording, storing, and retrieving typewritten data, often with visual presentation on a screen —**word processor,** *n.* The machine used.

workaholic, *n.* One who works excessively.

W particle, *n.* Hypothetical elementary particle believed to be the quantum of the weak force in nuclear interactions.

X-ray astronomy, *n.* Astronomy carried on by analysis of X-rays emitted by celestial bodies.

XYY syndrome, *n.* Congenital male disorder (of an extra Y chromosome), hypothesized to be a factor in causing social inadequacy, aggressive behavior, and low intelligence.

zap, *n. Slang.* A sudden hit or other occurrence. —*v.* To destroy suddenly.

zircalloy, *n.* An alloy of zirconium with heat- and corrosion-resistant properties.

Table of Alphabets

ARABIC			HEBREW			GREEK			RUSSIAN[3]			GERMAN			ROMAN[9]
Letter	Name	Transliteration	Letter	Name	Transliteration	Letter[2]		Name	Transliteration	Letter[2]		Transliteration	Letter[6]	Letter[7]	Transliteration	Letter[2]
ا	alif	’	א	aleph	’	A α	alpha	a	А а	a	𝔄 𝔞	A a	a	A a
ب	ba	b	ב	beth	b, v	B β	beta	b	Б б	b	𝔄 𝔞	Ä ä	ae	B b
ت	ta	t	ג	gimel	g	Γ γ	gamma	g	В в	v	𝔅 𝔟	B b	b	C c
ث	sa	th	ד	daleth	d	Δ δ	delta	d	Г г	g	ℭ 𝔠	C c	c	D d
ج	jim	j	ה	he	h	E ε	epsilon	e	Д д	d	𝔇 𝔡	D d	d	E e
ح	ha	h	ו	vav	v, w	Z ζ	zeta	z	Е е	e, ye	𝔈 𝔢	E e	e	F f
خ	kha	kh	ז	zayin	z	H η	eta	ē	Ж ж	zh	𝔉 𝔣	F f	f	G g
د	dal	d	ח	kheth	ḥ	Θ θ	theta	th	З з	z	𝔊 𝔤	G g	g	H h
ذ	zal	th	ט	teth	t	I ι	iota	i	И и	i	ℌ 𝔥	H h	h	I i
ر	ra	r	י	yod	y, j, i	K κ	kappa	k	Й й	ĭ, i, y	ℑ 𝔦	I i	i	J j
ز	za	z	כ, ך[1]	kaph	k, kh	Λ λ	lambda	l	К к	k	𝔍 𝔧	J j	j	K k
س	sin	s	ל	lamed	l	M μ	mu	m	Л л	l	𝔎 𝔨	K k	k	L l
ش	shin	sh	מ, ם[1]	mem	m	N ν	nu	n	М м	m	𝔏 𝔩	L l	l	M m
ص	sad	s	נ, ן[1]	nun	n	Ξ ξ	xi	x	Н н	n	𝔐 𝔪	M m	m	N n
ض	dad	d	ס	samekh	s	O o	omicron	o	О о	o	𝔑 𝔫	N n	n	O o
ط	ta	t	ע	ayin	‘	Π π	pi	p	П п	p	𝔒 𝔬	O o	o	P p
ظ	za	z	פ, ף[1]	pe	p, f	P ρ	rho	r, rh	Р р	r	Ö ö	Ö ö	oe	Q q
ع	ain	‘	צ, ץ[1]	tsadi	ṣ	Σ σ, ς[1]	sigma	s	С с	s	𝔓 𝔭	P p	p	R r
غ	ghain	gh	ק	koph	ḳ	T τ	tau	t	Т т	t	𝔔 𝔮	Q q	q	S s
ف	fa	f	ר	resh	r	Υ υ	upsilon	u, y	У у	u	𝔕 𝔯	R r	r	T t
ق	qaf	k	ש	sin	ś	Φ φ	phi	ph	Ф ф	f	𝔖 ſ, 𝔰[8]	S s	s	U u
ك	kaf	k	שׁ	shin	sh	X χ	chi	kh, ch	Х х	kh, x	— ß		ss	V v
ل	lam	l	ת	tav	t, th	Ψ ψ	psi	ps	Ц ц	ts, c	𝔗 𝔱	T t	t	W w
م	mim	m				Ω ω	omega	ō	Ч ч	ch, č	𝔘 𝔲	U u	u	X x
ن	nun	n							Ш ш	sh, š	Ü ü	Ü ü	ue	Y y
ه	ha	h							Щ щ	shch, šč	𝔙 𝔳	V v	v	Z z
و	waw	w							Ъ[4] ъ[4]		𝔚 𝔴	W w	w	
ي	ya	y							Ы ы	y, i	𝔛 𝔵	X x	x	
									Ь[5] ь[5]		𝔜 𝔶	Y y	y	
									Э э	e	𝔷 𝔷	Z z	z	
									Ю ю	yu				
									Я я	ya				

1. The alternative form is used only at the end of a word. 2. Upper- and lower-case. 3. Sometimes called Cyrillic. Each Slavic language (*see* World Families of Languages, page xiv) uses a different modified form of the Cyrillic alphabet. 4. A sign used to indicate the nonpalatalization of a preceding consonant. 5. A sign used to indicate the palatalization of a preceding consonant. 6. German Fraktur, upper- and lower-case. 7. Latin equivalent, upper- and lower-case. 8. The alternative form is used only at the end of a syllable. 9. Scandinavian (North Germanic) languages use the Roman alphabet with the following additional characters: Danish, Å å, Æ æ, Ø ø; Icelandic, Æ æ, Ð ð, Ö ö, Þ þ; Norwegian. Å å, Æ æ, Ø ø; Swedish, Ä ä, Å å, Ö ö.

A, a, ă, *n.* The first letter of the English alphabet and of nearly every alphabet in the world, the chief exceptions being the Old Germanic (Runic), where it stood in fourth place, and the Ethiopic, where it is the thirteenth letter.

a, ā, *a, indef. art.* [M.E. < O.E. *ān* one. AN.] Used before words beginning with consonant sounds, as opposed to *an* before vowel sounds. Used primarily before nouns in the singular; before collectives which imply a number of persons or things; as, *a* dozen, *a* few; before a proper name used as a type of character; as, *a* Napoleon, *a* Jack Dempsey; with distributive forces; as, *a* mile *a* minute, *a* hundred *a* year, where the second *a,* historically a preposition, is now felt as an indefinite article.

A, ā, *n.* A symbol denoting the first in order or quality of a series. *Mus.* the sixth note of the model or diatonic scale of C, the note sounded by the open second string of the violin.—**A-1,** ā″wun′, *a.* Superior; first-class, esp. in classification of shipping according to seaworthiness, in shipping registers.

aard·vark, ärd′värk″, *n.* [Afrik. < *aard,* earth, and *vark,* pig.] A large South African quadruped, *Orycteropus afer,* a burrowing, edentate mammal with strong claws, an extensible tongue, and large ears and tail, which feeds principally on ants and termites.

aard·wolf, ärd′wŭlf, *n.* pl. **aard·wolves.** [Afrik. < *aard* and *wolf.*] The earth wolf of South Africa, *Proteles cristatus,* a striped animal resembling the hyenas, which feeds on carrion and insects.

Aar·on's-beard, âr′onz·bērd′, *n.* [Scrip. Ps. cxxxiii. 2.] A dwarf evergreen shrub, *Hypericum calycinum,* with yellow flowers and conspicuous hairlike stamens; St.-John's-wort.

Aar·on's rod, âr′onz rod′, *n.* [Scrip. Ex. vii. 10; Num. xvii. 8.] An architectural ornament consisting of a rod with leaves sprouting on either side, or with one serpent twined about it; one of several plants with tall flowering stems, as the goldenrod.

AB, ā·bē, *n.* One of the major blood types, allowing one who possesses it to donate blood to type AB and receive blood from types A, B, AB, and O.

A.B. [< L. *Artium Baccalaureus.*] Abbr. for Bachelor of Arts, an academic degree.

a·ba, a·bä′, ä′ba, *n.* [Ar.] A fabric, usually striped, woven of goat's or camel's hair in Arabia, Syria, and neighboring countries; also, an outer garment of this fabric or silk, worn by Arabs.

a·ba·ca, ä″bä·kä′, ä″ba·kä′, *n.* [Sp. < Tagalog *abaka′.*] Native name of the Philippine plant which yields manila hemp, *Musa textilis,* or its fiber.

a·back, a·bak′, *adv.* Backward; *naut.* catching the wind against the forward side so as to urge a sailing vessel backward.—**tak·en a·back,** by surprise; unexpectedly.

ab·a·cus, ab′a·kas, a·bak′as, *n.* pl. **ab·a·cus·es, ab·a·ci,** ab′a·sī″, ab′a·kī″, a·bak′ī. [L. < Gr. *abax,* slab.] A counting frame holding beaded rods, widely used by the Chinese, who call it *swanpan,* used for making mathematical calculations; *arch.* a slab or table forming the crowning of a column and its capital.—**ab·a·cist,** ab′a·sist, *n.* One who uses an abacus.

a·baft, a·baft′, a·bäft′, *adv., prep.* [Prefix *a,* and O.E. *be-aeftan, baeftan.* AFT.] On or toward the stern, aft, or hinder part of a ship.

ab·a·lo·ne, ab″a·lō′nē, *n.* [Sp. of unknown origin.] A marine mollusk, genus *Haliotis,* a species of ear shell which furnishes lightly colored mother-of-pearl. Also *ear shell, sea ear.*

a·ban·don, a·ban′don, *v.t.* [M.E. < M.Fr.

abandoner (Fr. *abandonner*), < *a bandon,* under one's jurisdiction: *a* (L. < *ad*), to; *bandon,* proclamation, authority, < M.L. *bandum, bannum,* proclamation, = E. *ban, n.*] To give up wholly, as to another; yield or relinquish utterly; surrender without restraint; renounce; forsake or desert; also, to banish; *milit.* to bail out of, as an aircraft, and let it crash; yield, as oneself, as to personal feelings.—*n.* Abandonment to naturalness of action or manner; freedom from conventional restraint.—**a·ban·doned·ly,** a·ban′dond·lē, *adv.*

a·ban·doned, a·ban′dand, *a.* [pp. of abandon.] Forsaken; deserted; unrestrained; immoral and shameless.

a·ban·don·ee, a·ban″don·ē′, *n. Law,* one to whom a thing, as the salvage of a disabled ship, is abandoned.—**a·ban·don·er,** a·ban′don·ėr, *n.* One who abandons.

a·ban·don·ment, a·ban′don·ment, *n.* The act of abandoning, or the state of being abandoned; relinquishment; surrender; desertion; freedom from constraint; abandon.

à bas, ä bä′, *interj.* [Fr. *à* (< L. *ad.*), to; *bas,* < L.L. *bassus,* low.] Down; down with, the person or thing named.

a·base, a·bās′, *v.t.*—abased, abasing. [M.E. < Fr. *abasisser*—*a,* to, and *baisser,* to lower, < L.L. *bassus,* low. BASE.] *Archaic,* to lower or depress, as objects. To reduce or lower, as in rank; humble; degrade.—**a·base·ment,** a·bās′ment, *n.* The act of abasing; a state of depression, degradation, or humiliation.

a·bash, a·bash′, *v.t.* [M.E. < M.Fr. *esbahir, ppr. esbahissant,* < *es* = *ex,* intens., *bair, baer,* to gape.] To disconcert, confuse, or confound, as by consciousness of guilt, inferiority, etc.; make ashamed; put to confusion.

a·bash·ment, a·bash′ment, *n.* The state of being abashed; sense of shame or uneasiness.

a·bate, a·bāt′, *v.t.*—abated, abating. [M.E. < O.Fr. *abattre* < L. *ad,* to (or *ab,* from), and *battere,* for *battuere,* beat.] To bring down; reduce in amount, intensity, etc.; diminish; curtail; also, to deduct or subtract; omit. *Law,* to put down or suppress, as a nuisance; suspend or extinguish, as an action; annul, as a writ.—*v.i.* To go down; decrease; subside. *Law,* to fail; become void.—**a·bat·a·ble,** a·bāt′a·bl, *a.* Capable of being abated.—**a·bat·ed,** a·bāt′id, *a.* Beaten down, or cut away, as the background of a decorative pattern in relief.—**a·bat·er,** a·bāt′ėr, *n.* One who or that which abates.

a·bate·ment, a·bāt′ment, *n.* The act of abating, or the resulting state; reduction; decrease; mitigation; also, an amount abated; a deduction. *Law,* annulment or failure; intrusion on a freehold before the entry of the heir; also, the decrease in an assessment of taxes to be paid. *Her.* a mark of dishonor.

ab·a·tis, ab′a·tē′, ab′a·tis, a·bat′ē, a·bat′is, *n.* pl. **ab·a·tis,** ab′a·tēz, ab′a·tis″iz, a·bat′i·siz. [Fr. *abattis, abattre,* to beat down. ABATE.] *Fort.* a collection of felled trees from which the smaller branches have been cut off, and which are laid side by side with the branched ends toward assailants, forming an obstruction to their progress; a collection of felled trees interlaced with barbed wire to obstruct the enemy.

A bat·te·ry, *n. Elect.* a power source which heats the filament contained in an electron tube.

ab·at·toir, ab″a·twär′, *n.* [Fr. *abattre,* to beat or knock down. ABATE.] A public slaughterhouse.

ab·ax·i·al, ab·ak′sē·al, *a.* [Prefix *ab,* from, and *axial.*] Not in the axis; away from the axis.

abb, ab, *n.* [O.E. *ab, aweb:* see *woof.*] The woof, or yarn for the woof, in weaving; low-grade wool from the inferior parts of a fleece.

Ab·ba, ab′a, *n.* [Aram. *abba.*] Father, as in Mark xiv. 36; also, an ecclesiastical title in some Eastern churches.

ab·ba·cy, ab′a·sē, *n.* [M.E. *abbatie.*] The office, dignity, rights, and privileges of an abbot; the jurisdiction of an abbot or abbey.—**ab·ba·tial,** a·bā′shal, *a.* Belonging to or related to an abbot or abbacy.

Ab·bas·id, ab′a·sid, a·bas′id, *n.* One belonging to the line of caliphs, who from A.D. 750 to A.D. 1258 governed Bagdad and claimed to be descendants of Abbas, the uncle of Mohammad.

ab·bé, a·bā′, ab′ā, *n.* [Fr., an abbot.] In France, especially before the Revolution, one who devoted himself to divinity, or who had pursued a course of study in a theological seminary; priest; abbot; a title of respect for any ecclesiastic or member of the secular clergy of France.

ab·bess, ab′is, *n.* [M.E. < O.Fr. *abbesse* < L.L. *abbatissa.*] A female superior of an abbey of nuns, possessing, in general, the same dignity and authority as an abbot, except that she cannot exercise the spiritual functions appertaining to the priesthood.

Abbe·vill·i·an, Abbe·vil·i·an, ab·i·vil′ē·an, ab·vil′yan, ab″a·vil′·an, ab″a·vil′·yan, *a.* Referring to a Paleolithic culture in Europe, which originated during the first glacial epoch and existed for the duration of the second interglacial epoch.

ab·bey, ab′ē, *n.* pl. **ab·beys.** [M.E. < O.Fr. *abbaye,* < L.L. *abbatia,* an abbey. ABBOT.] A monastery governed by an *abbot* or a convent governed by an *abbess;* a society of persons of either sex, secluded from the world, and devoted to religion and celibacy; the buildings so occupied; also, an abbatial church.

ab·bot, ab′ot, *n.* [M.E. *abbod* < O.E. < L.L. *abbas, abbatis,* < Aram. *abba,* father.] The male head or superior of a monastery. Some abbots were mitred abbots, almost equal in rank to bishops. Laymen were sometimes abbots, enjoying the abbey revenues.

ab·bre·vi·ate, a·brē′vē·āt″, *v.t.*—abbreviated, abbreviating. [M.E. < L.L. *abbreviatus,* pp. of *abbreviare,* < L. *ad,* to, and *breviare,* shorten, < *brevis,* short, brief.] To make briefer; abridge; shorten; reduce to a briefer form, as a word or phrase, esp. by omission of a part; *milit.* pertaining to a report or written survey: reduce in length, esp. if it is being forwarded to a higher echelon.

ab·bre·vi·a·tion, a·brē″vē·ā′shan, *n.* [L.L. *abbreviatio*(n-).] Reduction in length; abridgment; also, a reduced or shortened form, esp., part of a word or phrase used as a symbol for the whole.—**ab·bre·vi·a·tor,** a·brē″vē·ā″tėr, *n.* One who abbreviates.—**ab·bre·vi·a·to·ry,** a·brē″vē·a·tōr″ē, *a.* Serving to abbreviate.

ABC, ā′bē″sē′, *n.* pl. **ABC's, ABCs.** [First three letters of the alphabet.] (*Usu. pl.*) the alphabet. The rudiments of any subject, practice, or field of knowledge.

ABC·soil, *n.* A soil in which three well-distinguished layers (horizons), A-, B-, and C-, form a contrasted profile.

ab·di·ca·ble, ab′di·ka·bl, *a.* Of or pertaining to that which one may abdicate or renounce.

ab·di·cate, ab′di·kāt″, *v.t.*—abdicated, abdicating. [L. *abdico, abdicatum*—*ab,* from, and *dico, dicatum,* to declare publicly.] To give up, renounce, lay down, relinquish, or withdraw from in a voluntary, public, or formal manner, as a throne, duties, etc.; vacate; surrender; resign; reject; disinherit. —*v.i.* To renounce or give up power voluntarily.—**ab·di·ca·tion,** ab″di·kā′-

shan, *n.* The act of abdicating an office, especially the kingly office; renunciation.—**ab·di·ca·tor**, ab′di·kā″tėr, *n.* One who abdicates.

ab·do·men, ab′do·men, ab·dō′men, *n.* [L.] That part of the human body which lies between the thorax and the pelvis, containing the stomach, liver, spleen, pancreas, kidneys, bladder, and intestines; the posterior of the three parts of a perfect insect.—**ab·dom·i·nal**, ab·dom′i·nal, *a.* Pertaining to the abdomen; on, in, or for the abdomen. —**ab·dom·i·nal·ly**, *adv.*

ab·dom·i·nous, ab·dom′i·nus, *a.* Abdominal; potbellied; possessing a large belly.

ab·duce, ab·dūs′, ab·dūs′, *v.t.—abduced, abducing.* [L. *abduco*, to lead away—*ab*, and *duco*, to lead, to draw; DUKE.] To draw or conduct away; to abduct.

ab·du·cent, ab·dō′sent, ab·dū′sent, *a.* Drawing away; pulling back; abducting.— **ab·du·cent mus·cles**, muscles which pull back certain parts of the body from the mesial line.

ab·duct, ab·dukt′, *v.t.* [L. *abductus* pp. of *abducere* < *ab*—and *ducere* to lead.] To draw or lead away; to take away surreptitiously and by force; *physiol.* to draw away from the main axis of the body or from a part of the body.

ab·duc·tion, ab·duk′shan, *n.* The act of abducting; the state of being abducted; *anat.* the action by which muscles withdraw a limb or other part from the axis of the body; *law*, the unlawful leading away of a person, as a young woman, by fraud, persuasion, or open violence; *logic*, a syllogism, the minor premise and conclusion of which are only probable.

ab·duc·tor, ab·duk′tėr, *n.* One who or that which abducts; *anat.* a muscle which moves certain parts from the axis of the body.

a·beam, a·bēm′, *adv. Naut.* in the direction of the beams, that is, at right angles to the length or keel of a ship; opposite to the side of the ship, followed by *of*; as, *abeam* of the ship.

a·be·ce·dar·i·an, ā″bē·sē·dâr′ē·an, *n.* [From the letters *a*, *b*, *c*, *d*.] One who teaches the letters of the alphabet, or a learner of the letters. An amateur in any area of learning. —*a.* Of the alphabet; in alphabetical order; elementary; rudimentary.

a·be·ce·da·ry, ā″bē·sē′da·rē, *a.* Pertaining to or formed by the letters of the alphabet; alphabetical.—*n. pl.* **a·be·ce·da·ries.** A first principle or element; rudiment; a beginner.

a·bed, a·bed′, *adv.* In bed; gone to bed; on the bed; restricted to bed.

a·bele, a·bēl′, ā′bel, *n.* [D. *abeel*, G. *albele*, L. *albus*, white.] The white poplar, specif. *Populus alba* and variations *globosa*, *nivea*, etc.

A·be·li·an group, a·bē′lē·an gröp, a·bēl′-yan, *n. Alg.* a commutative group (thus *BA*=*AB* where *A* and *B* are any two elements within the group): named after Norwegian mathematician Niels Abel.

a·bel·mosk, ā′bel·mosk″, *n.* [N.L. *Abel-moschus*, < Ar. *abu'l-misk*, father of musk.] A malvaceous plant, *Hibiscus abelmoschus*, of warm countries, cultivated for its musky seed, which is used in perfumery, flavoring of coffee, etc.

Ab·er·deen An·gus, ab′er·dēn″ ang′gus, *n.* Black hornless beef cattle of a breed originating in the two counties in Scotland after which it is named.

Ab·er·deen ter·ri·er, ab′er·dēn″ ter′ē·ėr, *n.* One of a breed of small terriers originating in Aberdeen, Scotland. Also *Scottish Terrier*.

ab·er·rance, ab·er′ans, *n.* A straying away; deviation from what is regular or normal; condition of aberration; *geom.* deviation of a curve from its circle of curvature. Also **ab·er·ran·cy.**

ab·er·rant, ab·er′ent, a·ber′ent, *a.* [L. < *ab*- and *errare*, to err, wander.] Straying from the usual or normal method or course of action; not being truthful or proper; exceptional or abnormal.—*n.* One who deviates from the accepted social behavior pattern of the group; an aberrant structure, individual, natural group, etc., esp. in regard to variable chromosome numbers.— **ab·er·rant·ly**, *adv.*

ab·er·ra·tion, ab″e·rā′shan, *n.* [L. *aberra-tio(n-)* < *aberrare*. ABERRANT.] Deviation from the right course, or from a standard or type; abnormal procedure or character; lapse from a sound mental state. *Optics*, deviation of refracted or reflected light rays from a single focus, or their convergence to different foci, due to the spherical shape of the lens or mirror, and resulting in the formation of a blurred image (spherical aberration); an analogous phenomenon depending on the different refrangibilities of the rays composing white light, and resulting in a prismatic coloring around the edge of the image (chromatic aberration). *Astron.* apparent displacement of a heavenly body, due to the motion of the earth and of light; difference between the true and the observed position of a heavenly body.— **ab·er·ra·tion·al**, ab″e·rā′shan·al, *a.*

a·bet, a·bet′, *v.t.—abetted, abetting.* [M.E. < M.Fr. *abetter*, *abeter*, to incite, to lure; *abet*, a bait—prefix *a*, and word=*bait*, to incite, set on. BAIT, BITE.] To encourage by aid, countenance, or approval, used chiefly in an illicit sense; incite; support; encourage; back up.—**a·bet·ment**, a·bet′ment, *n.* The act of abetting; aid.

a·bet·tor, **a·bet·ter**, a·bet′or, *n.* One who abets or incites; a supporter or encourager, generally of something illicit.

a·bey·ance, a·bā′ans, *n.* [M.E. < M.Fr. *abeance* < O.Fr. *abbaiaunce*, expectation, < *abbayer*, to listen with the mouth open, < *bayer*, *baer*, to gape, as in crying *bah!* ABASH.] A state of expectation or waiting, as for an occupant or holder, said of lands, honors, or dignities; a state of temporary suspension, as of a law or a rule; a period of dormancy.

a·bey·ant, a·bā′ant, *a.* Being in abeyance; temporarily inactive.

ab·hor, ab·hạr′, ab·hor′, *v.t.—abhorred, abhorring.* [M.E. < L. *abhorreo*, to shrink back—*ab*, from, and *horreo*, to feel horror. HORRIBLE.] To hate, loathe, or abominate; shrink from with horror.—**ab·hor·rence**, ab·hạr′ens, ab·hor′ens, *n.* Extreme hatred; detestation; great aversion.—**ab·hor·rer**, ab·hạr′ėr, ab·hor′ėr, *n.*

ab·hor·rent, ab·hạr′ent, ab·hor′ent, *a.* Struck with abhorrence; hating; detesting; utterly repugnant, used formerly with *from*, now with *to*.—**ab·hor·rent·ly**, ab·hạr′ent-lē, ab·hor′ent·lē, *adv.* With abhorrence.

a·bid·ance, a·bīd′ans, *n.* The act of abiding; abode; compliance, followed by *by*; as, *abidance by* laws; continuance.

a·bide, a·bīd′, *v.i.—abode* or *abided*, *abiding.* [O.E. *abidan*, *gebidan*, to abide, < *bidan*, to bide. See BIDE.] To take up one's abode; to reside.—*v.t.* To be prepared for; to await; be able to endure or sustain; remain firm under; to tolerate.—**a·bide by**, to adhere to; to maintain; to remain faithful; to remain satisfied with.—**a·bid·er**, a·bīd′ėr, *n.* One who abides.

a·bid·ing, a·bī′ding, *a.* Continuing; permanent; steadfast; as, an *abiding* faith.— **a·bid·ing·ly**, a·bī′ding·lē, *adv.* In such a manner as to continue; permanently.— **a·bid·ing·ness**, a·bī′ding·nis, *n.*

a·bil·i·ty, a·bil′i·tē *n. pl.* **a·bil·i·ties.** [M.E. < M.Fr. *habilite*, L. *habilitas*, ableness. ABLE.] The state or condition of being able; aptitude; competence; capability; power to do something, whether physical,

mental, legal, etc. *Usu. pl.* talents, or acquired proficiencies; powers of the mind; mental gifts or endowments.

ab·i·o·gen·e·sis, ab″ē·ō·jen′i·sis, *n.* [Gr. *a*, not, *bios*, life, and *genesis*, generation.] The doctrine that living matter may be produced by nonliving matter; spontaneous generation.

ab·i·og·e·nist, ab″ē·oj′e·nist, *n.* One who believes in the doctrine of abiogenesis. —**ab·i·o·ge·net·ic**, ab″ē·ō·je·net′ik, *a.* Of, pertaining to, or produced by abiogenesis.—**ab·i·o·ge·net·i·cal·ly**, ab″ē·ō-je·net′i·kal·lē, *adv.*

ab·ir·i·tant, ab·ir′i·tant, *n.* A lotion or other agent used to reduce irritation.

ab·ject, ab′jekt, ab·jekt′, *a.* [M.E. < L. *abjectus*, *abjicio*, to throw away.—*ab*, and *jacio*, to throw.] Sunk to a low condition; worthless, mean, despicable; low, groveling. —*n. Obs.* A person in an abject condition; an outcast.—**ab·jec·tion**, ab·jek′shan, *n.* A low state; meanness of spirit; abjectness; abasement.—**ab·ject·ly**, ab·jekt′lē, ab′jekt·lē, *adv.* In an abject or contemptible manner; meanly; servilely.—**ab·ject·ness**, ab·jekt′nis, *n.* The state of being abject; meanness; servility.

ab·ju·ra·tion, ab″jụ·rā′shan, *n.* The act of abjuring; a denial upon oath; a rejection or denial with solemnity; a total abandonment. —**ab·jur·a·to·ry**, ab·jụr′a·tōr″ē, *a.* Pertaining to abjuration.

ab·jure, ab·jụr′, *v.t.—abjured, abjuring.* [M.E. < L. *abjuro*, to deny upon oath—*ab*, and *juro*, to swear. JURY.] To renounce upon oath; forswear; to reject or withdraw from with solemnity; abandon, as allegiance or errors; to recant or retract; to relinquish.— **ab·jur·er**, ab·jụr′ėr, *n.* One who abjures.

ab·lac·tate, ab·lak′tāt, *v.t.—ablactated, ablactating.* [L. *ablacto*, to wean—*ab*, from, and *lac*, milk.] To wean from the breast.— **ab·lac·ta·tion**, ab″ lak·tā′shan, *n.* The weaning of a child from the breast.

ab·late, a·blāt′, *v.t.—ablated, ablating.* To withdraw or dissipate by cutting, melting, eroding, etc.—*v.i.* To be ablated; to be cut or melted and withdrawn at a high temperature. *Milit.* to carry away; specif. to carry away heat generated by aerodynamic heating.

ab·la·tion, ab·lā′shan, *n.* [L. *ablatio(n-)*, < *ablatus*, pp. of *auferre*, take away.] The act of taking away; removal, esp. as by surgery; the melting of the nose cone of a space vehicle as it reenters the atmosphere at hypersonic speeds; *geol.* a process of wearing or melting away, esp. glacial ice through erosion, melting, etc.

ab·la·tive, ab′la·tiv, *a.* [L. *ablativus*, < *ablatus*, carried away—*ab*, away, and *latus*, carried.] Taking or tending to take away, applied to a case in declension of nouns in Sanskrit, Latin, and some other languages, or to a word in that case.

ab·la·tive ab·so·lute, *n.* A Latin construction in which a noun or pronoun and its adjunct, both in the ablative case, combine to form an adverbial phrase, usually expressing an attending circumstance; as, the house *having been built.*

ab·laut, ab′laut, ab′lout, *n.* [G. < *ab*, off, and *laut*, sound.] *Philol.* in Indo-European languages, a substitution of one vowel for another in the body of a word, to indicate a corresponding modification of a use or meaning, as *bind, band, bound, bond*, esp. the change of a vowel to indicate differences in use, meaning, or tense, instead of the addition of a syllable (-*ed*), as *sink, sank, sunk.*

a·blaze, a·blāz′, *a.* In a blaze; in a state of eager excitement, anger, or desire; on fire; resplendent with bright color.

a·ble, ā′bl, *a.* [M.E. < M.Fr. *able, hable, habile,* skillful, fit; < L. *habilis,* suitable, fit; < *habeo*, to have; akin are *ability*, *habiliment*, *habit*, suffix *able*.] Having the power, means, skill, or qualification; sufficient; competent; qualified; clever; having strong or unusual powers of mind, or intellectual qualifications; gifted; vigorous; active.—**a·bly**, ā′blē, *adv*. In an able manner; with ability.

a·ble-bod·ied, ā′bl-bod′ēd, *a*. Having a sound, strong body; having strength sufficient for work, often applied to a seaman who is well skilled in seamanship, and classed in the ship's books as A.B.

ab·le·gate, ab′le·gāt, *n*. [L. *ablegatus*, pp. of *ablegare*, send away, < *ab*, from, and *legare*, send as legate.] A papal envoy to a newly appointed dignitary.

a·bloom, a·blöm′, *a*., *adv*. In a blooming state.

ab·lu·ent, ab′lö·ent, *a*. [L. *abluens, abluentis*, ppr. of *abluo*, to wash off—*ab*, from, and *luo*, to wash.] Washing clean; cleansing by water or liquids.—*n*. That which washes or carries off impurities; a detergent.

ab·lu·tion, ab·lö′shan, a·blö′shan, *n*. The act of washing; cleansing or purification by a liquid, usually water; specifically, a washing of the body as a part of religious rites.—**ab·lu·tion·ar·y**, ab·lö′shan·âr″ē, a·blö′shan·âr″ē, *a*. Pertaining to ablution.

ab·ne·gate, ab′na·gāt″, *v.t.*—abnegated, abnegating. [L. *abnego, abnegatum—ab*, from, and *nego*, to deny. NEGATIVE, DENY.] To deny; to refuse; to renounce; to relinquish; to surrender.

ab·ne·ga·tion, ab″ne·gā′shan, *n*. [L. *abnegatio*.] The act of abnegating; relinquishing of rights; denial; renunciation.—**ab·ne·ga·tor**, *n*. One who abnegates, denies, or renounces.

ab·nor·mal, ab·nar′mal, *a*. [Fr. < L. *abnormis—ab*, from, and *norma*, a rule. NORMAL.] Not conformed or conforming to rule; deviating from a type or standard; irregular; unnatural; contrary to system or law. Unusually large; as, an *abnormal* margin of profit.

ab·nor·mal·i·ty, ab″nar·mal′i·tē, *n*. pl. **ab·nor·mal·i·ties**. The state or quality of being abnormal; deviation from a standard, rule, or type; irregularity; peculiarity; that which is abnormal. Also **ab·nor·mi·ty**, ab·nar′mi·tē, pl. **ab·nor·mi·ties**.

a·board, a·bōrd′, a·bärd′, *adv*. On board; alongside; within a ship, plane, or other passenger vehicle; *baseball slang*, on base.— *prep*. On board; into; as, to go *aboard* a ship.—**all a·board!** A warning signal to passengers that the vehicle is about to depart.

a·bode, a·bōd′, *n*. [M.E. *abod* < *abiden*, abide.] Residence or place of residence; home; a place where a person abides; a dwelling; habitation.

a·bol·ish, a·bol′ish, *v.t.* [M.E. < M.Fr. *abolir*; L. *abolere*, to annul, abolish—*ab*, from, and *oleo*, to grow. ADULT.] To do away with; to nullify; to destroy; to efface or obliterate; to make void; to annul; to put out of existence; to suppress; to annihilate; to extinguish; to put an end to, as laws, customs, or conditions of existence.— **a·bol·ish·a·ble**, a·bol′ish·a·bl, *a*. Capable of being abolished.—**a·bol·ish·er**, a·bol′ish·ėr, *n*. One who or that which abolishes. —**a·bol·ish·ment**, a·bol′ish·ment, *n*. Abolition.

ab·o·li·tion, ab″o·lish′an, *n*. The act of abolishing, or the state of being abolished; the destruction of some recognized abuse; annihilation; elimination.

ab·o·li·tion·ism, ab″o·lish′a·niz″um, *n*. The principles or policies which foster abolition.—**ab·o·li·tion·ist**, ab″o·lish′an·ist, *n*. A person who favors the abolition of something, applied especially to those in

the 19th century who favored the abolition of slavery in the United States.

ab·o·ma·sum, ab″o·mā′sum, *n*. pl. **ab·o·ma·sa**, ab″o·mā′sa. [L. prefix *ab*, from, and *omasum*.] The fourth or real stomach of ruminating animals, lying next to the omasum, or third stomach. Also **ab·o·ma·sus**, pl. **ab·o·ma·si**, ab″o·ma′sī.—**ab·o·ma·sal**, ab″o·mā′sal, *a*.

A-bomb, *n*. The atomic bomb; as, *A-bomb* squadron, *A-bomb* warhead. See *atomic bomb*.

a·bom·i·na·ble, a·bom′i·na·bl, *a*. Deserving or liable to be abominated; detestable; repugnant; loathsome; odious in the utmost degree; execrable.—**a·bom·i·na·ble·ness**, a·bom′i·na·bl·nis, *n*. The quality or state of being abominable, detestable, or odious.—**a·bom·i·na·bly**, a·bom′i·na·blē, *adv*. In an abominable or abhorrent manner.

A·bom·i·na·ble Snow·man, *n*. A huge hirsute mammal, which has features similar to those of man and supposedly exists in the Himalayas. Also *yeti*.

a·bom·i·nate, a·bom′i·nāt, *v.t.*—abominated, abominating. [L. *abominor, abominatus*, to deprecate, as an ill omen—*ab*, from, and *omen*, an omen.] To hate extremely; to abhor; to detest; to loathe.

a·bom·i·na·tion, a·bom″i·nā′shan, *n*. The act of abominating or state of being abominated; detestation; extreme aversion; that which is abominated or abominable; hence, hateful or shameful vice.

ab·o·ral, ab·ōr′al, *a*. *Anat., zool.* in a direction away from the mouth.

ab·o·rig·i·nal, ab″o·rij′i·nal, *a*. [L. *ab*, from, and *origo*, origin.] Inhabiting a country from the earliest known times; as, *aboriginal* tribes.—*n*. An original inhabitant; one of an aboriginal race.—**ab·o·rig·i·nal·ly**, ab″o·rij′i·nal·lē, *adv*. In, or of, first origin; originally; from the very first.

ab·o·rig·i·ne, ab″o·rij′i·nē, *n*. [L.] One of the first inhabitants of a country especially as opposed to foreign invaders or colonists; *pl.* the original animals and flowers of a region.

a·born·ing, a·bar′ning, *adv*. In the process of birth; previous to completion or fulfillment.—*a*. Being conceived; being realized or fulfilled, as: The 17th century was *aborning*.

a·bort, a·bart′, *v.t., v.i.* To cut short or break off an action, operation, or procedure with an aircraft, space vehicle, or the like, esp. because of equipment failure; as, to *abort* a mission, the launching was *aborted*. —*n*. An aircraft, space vehicle, or the like that aborts; an act or instance of aborting.

a·bort, a·bart′, *v.i.* [L. *aborior, abortus*, to miscarry—*ab*, and *orior, ortus*, to arise. ORIENT.] To miscarry in giving birth; to give birth or produce the fetus before it is viable; to appear in a rudimentary or undeveloped state.

a·bor·ti·fa·cient, a·bar″ti·fā′shant, *n*. Something employed in producing an abortion, usually referring to a drug inducing abortion.

a·bor·tion, a·bar′shan, *n*. The act of miscarrying, or producing young before the natural time, or before the fetus is at a viable stage; the product of untimely birth; a misshapen being; a monster; anything which fails before it is matured or perfect, as a design.

a·bor·tion·ist, a·bar′sha·nist, *n*. One who induces abortions, esp. illegal or unauthorized abortions.

a·bor·tive, a·bar′tiv, *a*. Brought forth in an immature state; rudimentary; imperfectly formed or developed. *Fig.* in reference to projects and programs, failed or gone awry; not brought to completion or to a successful issue; coming to naught.—**a·bor·tive,**

a·bar′tiv, *n*. A drug causing or thought to cause abortion.—**a·bor·tive·ly**, a·bar′tiv·lē, *adv*. In an abortive manner; immaturely.—**a·bor·tive·ness**, a·bar′tiv·nis, *n*. The state of being abortive.

ABO Sys·tem, ā·bē·ō sis′tem, *n*. The basic human blood system which functions as an allelic group to form the four common blood types, A, B, AB, and O.

a·bound, a·bound′, *v.i.* [M.E. < M.Fr. *abonder*, from L. *abundare*, to overflow—*ab*, and *unda*, a wave. UNDULATE, WATER.] To be in great plenty; be very prevalent; have or possess in great quantity; to be filled to capacity; be copiously supplied, often followed by *with* or *in*; as, lakes which *abound with* fish.

a·bout, a·bout′, *prep*. [O.E. *âbûtan, onbûtan*, about, around—prefixes *a, on*, on, and *butan*, without. BUT.] Around; on the outside or surface of; in a circle surrounding; round (two yards *about* the stem); near to in place, time, size, number, quantity, etc.; near to in action; on the point of, followed by the infinitive (to be *about to speak*); concerned in; engaged in (what is he *about?*); concerning; relating to; respecting; in control of (keeping your wits *about* you).—*adv*. Around the outside; in circuit; in a circle; near to in number, time, place, quality, or degree (*about* as high); here and there; around; in one place and another; in different directions.—**bring a·bout**, to cause to happen; to effect or accomplish.—**come a·bout**, to come to pass; to happen.—**go a·bout**, to prepare to do.—**turn a·bout**, alternately; in rotation.

a·bout-face, a·bout′fās″, a·bout′ fās′, *n*. A complete reversal of opinion or direction; *milit.* a command or order to reverse the direction of march.—*v.i.* To alter one's position so as to face the opposite direction; to reverse one's opinion completely.

a·bout-ship, a·bout′ship′, *v.i.* To change a ship's course.

a·bove, a·buv′, *prep*. [O.E. *âbûfan*, above: a triple compound of *â*, on, at, *be*, by, and *ûfan*, upward, akin to E. *over*, L. *super*, Gr. *hyper*, above.] In or to a higher place than; superior to in any respect; too high for (*above* mean actions); more in number, quantity, or degree than; in excess of (*above* a ton.—*adv*. In or to a higher place; overhead; before, in rank or order, especially in a book or writing (what has been said *above*); *archaic*, besides.—*n*. Heaven; the aforesaid, as: From the *above* you will learn.—*a*. Preceding; foregoing.—**a·bove all**, before everything else; before every other consideration.

a·bove·board, a·buv′bōrd″, a·buv′bärd″, *adv*. [Lit. 'above the table,' not with hands below the table.] Within sight; without tricks, dishonesty, or disguise.—*a*.

a·bove·ground, a·buv′ground″, *a*. Located above the ground.

ab·ra·ca·dab·ra, ab″ra·ka·dab′ra, *n*. [L.] A word of Eastern origin used in incantations: when written on paper so as to form a triangle, the first line contained the word in full, the one below it omitted the last letter, and so on each time until only one letter remained; worn as an amulet, it was supposed to be an antidote against certain diseases. Any charm supposedly used as a magic formula or spell. Jargon; gibberish.

a·bra·dant, a·brād′ant, *n*. A material for grinding, polishing, etc., such as emery, sand, or glass.—*a*. Having an abrasive quality.

a·brade, a·brād′, *v.t.*—abraded, abrading. [L. *abrado*, to scrape off—*ab*, away, and *rado*, to scrape, whence *raze, razor*, etc.] To rub or wear down, primarily through friction; to erode; to irritate; to rub or grate off.

a·bran·chi·ate, ă·brang′kē·it, ă·brang′-kē·āt″, *a.* [Gr. *a*, without, and *branchia*, gills.] Devoid of branchiae or gills.

a·bra·sion, *a*·brā′zhan, *n.* [L. *abrasio* < *abradere* < *ab*, away, *radere*, to scrape.] The act of abrading, wearing, or rubbing off; an injury of the skin by abrading of the outer layer; any scraped area.

a·bra·sive, *a*·brā′siv, *a*·brā′ziv, *a.* Serving to abrade.—*n.* An abradant; a substance employed in grinding or abrading.

ab·re·act, ab″rē·akt′, *v.t. Psychol.* to relieve (repressed emotion), as by discussing it; to relieve or cure through abreaction.—**ab·re·ac·tion,** ab″rē·ak′shan, *n.* Relief of a past disagreeable experience by reliving it.

a·breast, *a*·brest′, *adv., a.* Side by side; as, to march four *abreast*; up to a level or standard; as, to keep *abreast* of science; equivalent in progress.

a·bri, *a*·brē′, ä·brē′, *n.* [Fr.] A shelter, or place of refuge, esp. in military use.

a·bridge, *a*·brij′, *v.t.—abridged, abridging.* [M.E. < M.Fr. *abreger*, < L. *abbreviare*, to shorten. ABBREVIATE.] To make shorter while preserving the essential contents; to curtail; to epitomize; to shorten by using fewer words; to condense; to lessen; to diminish; to deprive or cut off from, followed by *of*; as, to *abridge* one of his rights.—**a·bridg·er,** *a*·brij′ėr, *n.* One who, or that which, abridges.—**a·bridg·a·ble, a·bridge·a·ble,** *a.*

a·bridg·ment, a·bridge·ment, *a*·brij′ment, *n.* The act of abridging or state of being abridged; that which is abridged; condensation; digest; an epitome; a summary, as of a book; an abstract.

a·broach, *a*·brōch′, *a., adv.* Tapped; in a position for letting out liquor: said of a cask; broached. Astir; circulating.

a·broad, *a*·brạd′, *adv.* At large; without being confined to narrow limits; with expansion; as, to spread its branches *abroad*; in circulation; about; out of doors; beyond or out of the walls of a house or other enclosure; beyond the bounds of a country; in foreign countries; in error; astray.

ab·ro·gate, ab′ro·gāt″, *v.t.—abrogated, abrogating.* [L. *abrogo*, to repeal—*ab*, from, and *rogo*, to ask, propose as a law.] To repeal; to make void; to annul by an authoritative act.—**ab·ro·ga·ble,** ab′ro·ga·bl, *a.* Capable of being abrogated.—**ab·ro·ga·tion,** ab″ro·gā′shan, *n.* The act of abrogating; repeal by authority.—**ab·ro·ga·tive,** ab′ro·gā″tiv, *a.* Capable of abrogating; tending to abrogate.

ab·rupt, *a*·brupt′, *a.* [L. *abruptus,* < *abrumpo*, to break off—*ab*, off, from, and *rumpo, rumptum*, to break, whence *rupture,* etc.] Steep; craggy (of rocks, precipices, etc.); sudden; brusque; without notice to prepare the mind for the event (an *abrupt* entrance); disconnected; having sudden transitions (an *abrupt* style).—**ab·rupt·ly,** *a*·brupt′lē, *adv.* In an abrupt manner; suddenly; without any notice or warning; precipitously.—**ab·rupt·ness,** *a*·brupt′nis, *n.* The state or quality of being abrupt; precipitousness; suddenness; unceremonious haste or vehemence.

ab·rup·tion, *a*·brup′shan, *n.* A sudden and violent breaking off.

ab·scess, ab′ses, *n.* [L. *abscessus,* < *abscedere*, to separate, to gather into an abscess—*abs*, away, and *cedo, cessum*, to go, whence *cession, cede,* etc.] *Pathol.* a collection of purulent matter in the tissue of a body organ or part, with pain, heat, and swelling.—**ab·scessed,** *a.*

ab·scind, ab·sind′, *v.t.* [L. *abscindo, abscissum*, to cut off—*ab*, from, and *scindo,* to cut.] To cut off; to sever.

ab·scise, ab·sīz′, *v.i.—abscised, abscising. Bot.* to become detached by abscission, as a flower from a plant.

ab·scis·sa, ab·sis′*a*, *n.* pl. **ab·scis·sas, ab·scis·sae,** ab·sis′ē. Any part of the diameter or transverse axis of a conic section, as an ellipse, intercepted between the vertex and a line at right angles to the axis; the *x*-coordinate of a point.

ab·scis·sion, ab·sizh′an, ab·sish′an, *n.* The act of cutting off; severance; removal, especially suddenly; the natural detachment of leaves, flowers, etc., from plants; an abrupt termination in the middle of a sentence or phrase, usually for rhetorical effect.

ab·scond, ab·skond′, *v.i.* [L. *abscondo,* to hide—*abs*, from, and *condo*, to hide.] To withdraw or absent oneself in a private manner; run away, often with stolen valuables, in order to avoid a legal process; decamp.—**ab·scond·er,** ab·skond′ėr, *n.* One who absconds.

ab·seil, äp′zil, *n.* [G. *abeil, abseilen,* the verb < *ab-*, down, and *seil,* rope.] *Mountain climbing,* a means of descending from a steep cliff by securing a line at the peak.—*v.i.* To descend in this manner.

ab·sence, ab′sens, *n.* [L. *absentia,* < *absens, absentis,* absent, ppr. of *absum,* to be absent —*ab* or *abs,* away, and *sum, esse,* to be.] The state of being absent: opposite of *presence;* the state of being at a distance in place; the state of being wanting; nonexistence within a certain sphere (*absence* of evidence).

ab·sent, ab′sent, *a.* Not present; away; not attentive; wanting; lacking; nonexistent. —**ab·sent·ly,** ab′sent·lē, *adv.* In an absent or inattentive manner.

ab·sent, ab·sent′, *v.t.* To keep away intentionally; as, to *absent* oneself.—**ab·sent·er,** ab·sent′ėr, *n.* One who absents himself.

ab·sen·tee, ab·sen·tē′, *n.* One who is absent; one who absents himself from his own duty or habitat: often applied to landlords who, deriving their income from one area, reside in another.

ab·sen·tee bal·lot, *n.* The ballot used by a voter who is absent from his state or district on election day.

ab·sen·tee·ism, ab·sen·tē′iz″um, *n.* The high rate of absence where regular attendance is expected.

ab·sen·tee vot·er, *n.* A person qualified to vote who fulfills his duty by mail because of necessary absence from his voting district on election day.

ab·sent-mind·ed, ab′sent-mīn′did, *a.* Preoccupied; forgetful; inattentive.—**ab·sent-mind·ed·ly,** *adv.*—**ab·sent-mind·ed·ness,** *n.*

ab·sent with·out leave, *a.* Of a member of the armed services or any other person subject to military law: gone or absent from his place of duty without permission or authorization, and without the intention of deserting. Also *AWOL*.

ab·sinthe, ab′sinth, *n.* [Fr. < L. *absinthium,* wormwood.] A popular French liqueur or cordial consisting of brandy flavored with wormwood. The common wormwood, *Artemisia absinthium.*—**ab·sin·thi·al,** ab·sin′thē·al, *a.* Like wormwood.

ab·so·lute, ab′so·lōt,″ *a.* [M.E. < L. *absolutus.* ABSOLVE.] Free from restriction or limitation; unconditioned or unconditional; unqualified; perfect; pure; as, *absolute* alcohol, (ethyl alcohol containing not more than one per cent by weight of water); thorough; positive; independent; arbitrary or despotic; as, an *absolute* monarchy; viewed independently; not comparative or relative; self-existent; ultimate. *Gram.* syntactically independent; forming an element in a sentence but not grammatically connected with it; as, the ablative *absolute* in Latin; of an adjective, having its noun understood, not expressed; of a transitive verb, used without its object being expressed. *Phys.* independent, or accepted as independent, of arbitrary standards; as, the *absolute* zero of temperature, *absolute* units; based on an absolute zero or unit; as, *absolute* temperature, *absolute* velocity or pressure; of or pertaining to absolute units. —*n.* Something absolute. *Metaph.* with *the*, that which is unconditioned or nonrelative; the ultimate ground of all things; God.—**ab·so·lute·ly,** ab′so·lōt″lē, ab″so·lōt′lē, *adv.*—**ab·so·lute·ness,** ab′so·lōt″nis, ab″so·lōt′nis, *n.*

ab·so·lute ceil·ing, *n.* The greatest altitude above sea level at which aircraft may continue normal horizontal flight.

ab·so·lute pitch, *n. Mus.* the exact position of a tone in a standard scale in terms of vibrations per second. The ability to recognize the pitch of a tone, or to sing a particular note without having heard it; also *perfect pitch*.

ab·so·lute scale, *n. Phys.* any temperature scale which is based on absolute zero.

ab·so·lute sys·tem of u·nits, *n.* A system of units based on certain units (esp. those of mass, length, and time) of invariable value which are taken as fundamental, as contrasted with any system of units based partly on some arbitrary unit, as of gravitation, the value of which varies with latitude, altitude, or the like.

ab·so·lute tem·per·a·ture, *n.* Temperature measured from the absolute zero, esp. on a scale depending upon certain thermodynamic principles.

ab·so·lute u·nit, *n.* Any of the units in an absolute system of units.

ab·so·lute val·ue, *n. Math.* The numerical magnitude of a real number quantity, regardless of sign. The positive expression of the distance of a value (from the origin), written as $|x|$ (the absolute value of x). The positive root of the sum of the squares of a complex number, written as $|a+bi| = \sqrt{a^2 - b^2}$ (the absolute value of a plus bi).

ab·so·lute ze·ro, *n.* The lowest possible temperature which the nature of matter admits, or that temperature at which the particles whose motion constitutes heat would be at rest: being a hypothetical point $-273.16°$ C. or $-459.7°$ F.

ab·so·lu·tion, ab″sa·lō′shan, *n.* [L. *absolutio(n-),* < *absolvere:* see *absolve.*] The act of absolving, or the state of being absolved; release; discharge; forgiveness; remission, as of sin or of punishment for a sin; the formula declaring this remission; also, a form of prayer for pardon, as over the dead in the burial service, esp. in the Roman Catholic Church.

ab·so·lut·ism, ab′so·lō″tiz″um, *n.* The principle or the exercise of absolute power in government; *metaph.* the doctrine of an absolute or nonrelative being. The quality of certainty; positivism.—**ab·so·lut·ist,** ab′so·lōt″ist, *n.* An advocate of absolutism.—**ab·so·lu·tis·tic,** ab″so·lō·tis′tik, *a.*

ab·sol·u·to·ry, ab·sol′ū·tōr″ē, ab·sol′-ū·tạr″ē, *a.* In an absolving manner; having or possessing the capacity to absolve.

ab·solve, ab·zolv′, ab·solv′, *v.t.—absolved, absolving.* [L. *absolvo, absolutum,* to set free —*ab*, from, and *solvo,* to loose. SOLVE.] To set free or release from some duty, obligation, or responsibility (to *absolve* a person *from* a promise); to liberate from the consequences or penalties arising from actions; acquit; to forgive or grant remission of sins to (with *from*).—**ab·solv·a·ble,** ab·zolv′-*a*·bl, ab·solv′*a*·bl, *a.* Capable of being absolved.—**ab·solv·er,** ab·zolv′ėr, ab·solv′ėr, *n.* One who absolves.

ab·so·nant, ab′so·nant, *a.* [L. *ab*, from, and *sonas* (*sonant*), pp. of *sonare,* sound.] Discordant; dissonant; contrary; abhorrent; incongruous: often followed by *from* or *to.*

---

ab·sorb, ab·sarb′, ab·zȧrb′, *v.t.* [L. *absorbeo*—*ab*, from, and *sorbeo*, to suck in.] To drink in; suck up; incorporate; imbibe, as a sponge; take in by capillarity; swallow up; engross or engage complete attention or energies; to assimilate.—**ab·sorb·a·bil·i·ty**, ab·sarb″a·bil′i·tē, ab·zȧrb″a·bil′i·tē, *n.* The state or quality of being absorbable.—**ab·sorb·a·ble**, ab·sarb′a·bl, ab·zȧrb′a·bl, *a.* Capable of being absorbed or imbibed.

ab·sorb·en·cy, ab·sarb′en·sē, ab·zȧrb′en·sē, *n.* The state or quality of being absorbent.

ab·sorb·ent, ab·sar′bent, ab·zȧr′bent, *n.* Anything which absorbs; a vessel in an animal body which takes nutritive matter into the system; a substance applied to a wound to stanch or arrest the flow of blood; a liquid utilized in separating gases or explosive materials in the manufacture of gas and the refining of petroleum.—*a.* Capable of absorbing fluids, light rays, etc.; performing the function of absorption.

ab·sorb·ing, ab·sar′bing, ab·zȧr′bing, *a.* Exceptionally interesting; engrossing.

ab·sorp·tion, ab·sarp′shan, ab·zȧrp′shan, *n.* The act or process of absorbing; state of being absorbed or engrossed; assimilation; incorporation; *phys.* the process wherein radiant energy is absorbed and converted into other forms of energy. In general, the assimilation of one substance by another.—**ab·sorp·tive**, ab″sarp′tiv, ab″zȧrp′tiv, *a.* Having the power to absorb or imbibe.—**ab·sorp·tiv·i·ty**, ab″sarp·tiv′i·tē, ab″zȧrp·tiv′i·tē, *n.* The power or capacity of absorption.

ab·stain, ab·stān′, *v.i.* [M.E. < M.Fr. *abstener*, < L. *abstineo*, to keep from—*abs*, from, and *teneo*, to hold, whence *contain*, *tenant*, *tenacious*, etc.] To forbear or refrain from an action voluntarily; to withhold.—**ab·stain·er**, ab·stān′ẽr, *n.* One who abstains; specifically, one who abstains from the use of intoxicating liquors.

ab·ste·mi·ous, ab·stē′mē·us, *a.* [L. *abstemius*—*abs-*, and root seen in *temetum*, strong drink, *temulentus*, drunken; Skt. *tim*, to be wet.] Temperate in diet; refraining from a free use of food and strong drinks; temperate; devoted to or spent in abstemiousness or abstinence; as, an *abstemious* life; very moderate and plain; very sparing; as, an *abstemious* diet.—**ab·ste·mi·ous·ly**, ab·stē′mē·us·lē, *adv.* In an abstemious manner.—**ab·ste·mi·ous·ness**, *n.*

ab·sten·tion, ab·sten′shan, *n.* The act of holding off or abstaining; abstinence.

ab·sterge, ab·stẽrj′, *v.t.*—*absterged*, *absterging*. [L. *abstergeo*, to wipe off.—*abs*, and *tergeo*, *tersum*, to wipe, whence *terse*.] To wipe, or make clean by wiping; to wash away; to purge.—**ab·ster·gent**, ab·stẽr′jent, *a.* Having cleaning or purgative properties.—**ab·ster·gent**, *n.* Whatever aids in cleansing; a detergent.

ab·sti·nence, ab′sti·nans, *n.* [M.E. < O.Fr. < L. *abstinentia*.] The act or practice of voluntarily refraining from the use of anything within our reach, esp. from some bodily indulgence; partaking sparingly of food or drink.—**ab·sti·nent**, ab′sti·nent, *a.* Practicing abstinence.—**ab·sti·nent·ly**, ab′sti·nent·lē, *adv.* In an abstinent manner.

ab·stract, ab·strakt′, *v.t.* [< L. *abstraho*, *abstractum*, to draw away—*abs*, and *traho*, *tractum*, to draw, seen also in *trace*, *contract*, *detract*, *retract*, etc.] To draw or take away; to remove; to withdraw; to purloin; to take away mentally; consider separately; epitomize or reduce to a summary.—**ab·stract·er**, ab·strak′tẽr, *n.* One who abstracts.

ab·stract, ab′strakt, ab·strakt′, *a.* Considered or thought of in itself; not concrete; considered and treated apart from any particular object; as, *abstract* mathematics, *abstract* logic; hard to understand; based on theory; not practical or applied. *Gram., logic, abstract nouns* or *terms* are names of qualities, in opposition to *concrete*, which are names of things.—*n.* A summary or epitome containing the substance; a bare or brief statement of facts detailed elsewhere; *pharm.* a powder made from a drug by mixing a solid extract with milk sugar, making the final product twice as strong as the original.

ab·stract·ed, ab·strak′tid, *a.* Absent in mind; absorbed in thought; inattentive.—**ab·stract·ed·ly**, ab·strak′tid·lē, *adv.* In an abstracted or absent manner.—**ab·stract·ed·ness**, ab·strak′tid·nis, *n.*

ab·strac·tion, ab·strak′shan, *n.* The act of abstracting or separating; the act of withdrawing; the act of considering separately what is united in a complex object; something abstract; an idea or notion of an abstract character; an impractical or unrealistic idea; absence of mind; the state of being entirely engrossed in thought; *art*, an artistic composition intended to suggest an idea or emotion without imitating recognizable objects.

ab·strac·tive, ab·strak′tiv, *a.* Having the power or quality of abstracting.—**ab·strac·tive·ly**, ab·strak′tiv·lē, *adv.* In an abstractive manner.

ab·stric·tion, ab·strik′shan, *n.* [L. *ab*, from, and *stringo*, *strictum*, to bind.] *Bot.* a method of spore formation in which successive portions of the sporophore are cut off through the growth of septa; abjunction.

ab·struse, ab·strös′, *a.* [L. *abstrusus*, pp. of *abstrudo*, to thrust away.] Remote from ordinary minds or notions; difficult to be comprehended or understood; esoteric; profound; recondite.—**ab·struse·ly**, ab·strös′lē, *adv.* In an abstruse manner; profoundly; with terms or notions remote from such as are obvious.—**ab·struse·ness**, ab·strös′nis, *n.* The quality of being abstruse.

ab·surd, ab·surd′, ab·zurd′, *a.* [L. *absurdus*—*ab*, and *surdus*, deaf, insensible. SURD.] Inconsistent with reason or common sense; ridiculous; nonsensical; unsound; preposterous; illogical; contradictory; untrue.—**ab·surd·i·ty**, ab·sur′di·tē, ab·zur′di·tē, *n.* pl. **ab·surd·i·ties**. The state or quality of being absurd; that which is absurd; an absurd action, statement, etc.—**ab·surd·ly**, ab·surd′lē, ab·zurd′lē, *adv.* In an absurd manner.—**ab·surd·ness**, ab·surd′nis, ab·zurd′nis, *n.* The quality of being absurd.

ab·surd·ist, ab·surd′ist, ab·zurd′ist, *a.* Relating to, or incorporated with, the Theatre of the Absurd.—*n.* A person, article, etc., which supports the Theatre of the Absurd; a playwright who uses this technique.

a·bu·li·a, a·bū′lē·a, *n.* [N.L. < Gr. *a*- and *bulia*, to will.] *Psychol.* a form of mental derangement in which volition is impaired or lost; inordinate lack of decisiveness.—**a·bu·lic**, a·bū′lik, *a.*

a·bun·dance, a·bun′dans, *n.* [M.E. < M.Fr. < L. *abundantia*, abundance, < *abundo*, to abound. ABOUND] A fullness; great to overflowing; sufficiency; wealth; profusion; copiousness.

a·bun·dant, a·bun′dant, *a.* Plentiful; ample; rich in supply; sufficient; abounding; overflowing.—**a·bun·dant·ly**, a·bun′dant·lē, *adv.* In a plentiful or sufficient degree; amply; plentifully.

a·buse, a·būz′, *v.t.*—*abused*, *abusing*. [M.E. < M.Fr. *abuser*; L. *abutor*, *abusus*—*ab*, and *utor*, to use. USE.] To misuse; to put to a wrong or bad use; to do wrong to; injure; dishonor; violate; ravish; to cheat.

a·buse, a·būs′, *n.* Improper treatment or employment; improper use or application; misuse; a corrupt practice or custom; as, the *abuses* of government; injury; scurrilous or contumelious language.—**a·bus·er**, a·būz′ẽr, a·būs′ẽr, *n.* One who abuses, in speech or behavior.

a·bu·sive, a·bū′siv, *a.* Practicing abuse; offering harsh words or ill-treatment; scurrilous; coarse; opprobrious; insulting.—**a·bu·sive·ly**, a·bū′siv·lē, *adv.* In an abusive manner.—**a·bu·sive·ness**, a·bū′siv·nis, *n.* The quality of being abusive; rudeness of language.

a·but, a·but′, *v.t.*—*abutted*, *abutting*. [M.E. < O.Fr. *abouter*, to meet at the end, to border on—*a*, at, and *bout*, end. BUTT.] To be contiguous to; to join at a border or boundary.—*v.i.* To form a point or line of contact, used with *on*, *upon*, *against*, as: Their home *abuts against* the beach.

a·bu·ti·lon, a·būt′i·lon″, *n.* [N.L. *Abutilon*; < Ar.] Any plant of the malvaceous genus *Abutilon*, which includes species cultivated for their bell-shaped flowers and variegated leaves; flowering maple, *A. megapotamicum*, an ornamental plant whose leaves resemble those of maples.

a·but·ment, a·but′ment, *n.* The condition of abutting; the part abutting; junction; the solid part of a pier or wall against which an arch abuts or from which it springs.

a·but·tal, a·but′al, *n.* The abutting part of a piece of land; state of abutting or bordering on.

a·bysm, a·biz′um, *n.* [M.E. *abime* < O.Fr. *abisme*, a superl. form < L. *abyssus*: see ABYSS.] An abyss.

a·bys·mal, a·biz′mal, *a.* Pertaining to an abyss; profound; immeasurable.

a·byss, a·bis′, *n.* [M.E. < L. *abyssus* < Gr. *abyssos*, bottomless—*a*, not, and *byssos*, bottom.] A bottomless gulf; anything profound and unfathomable; hell, literally or figuratively.—**a·byss·al**, a·bis′al, *a.* Relating to or like an abyss; pertaining to the deeper parts of the sea.

Ab·ys·sin·i·an, ab″e·sin′ē·an, *a.* Belonging to Abyssinia, now Ethiopia, or its inhabitants.—*n.* A native or inhabitant of Abyssinia; a member of the Abyssinian Church.

a·ca·cia, a·kā′sha, *n.* [L. *acacia*, Gr. *akakia*, < *ake*, a point.] Any of the ornamental trees and shrubs of the genus *Acacia*, belonging to the legume family, some species of which produce catechu, and some exude gum arabic.—**a·ca·cia tree**, a name sometimes applied to the black locust tree, *Robinia pseudoacacia*.

Ac·a·deme, ak″a·dēm′, *n.* [< L. *Academia*: see *academy*.] The Academy of Athens. (*l.c.*) any place for instruction; an academy; environment of an institution of higher learning; one who prefers the atmosphere of a college or university.

ac·a·dem·ic, ak″a·dem′ik, *a.* Pertaining to a school, particularly of higher education; relating to liberal or classical studies, rather than vocational; theoretical; having no practical value; learned, but lacking in practical application of knowledge; conforming to rules or traditions; conventional; as, *academic* art.—*n.* A student or faculty member of a college or university.

ac·a·dem·i·cal, ak″a·dem′i·kal, *n.* A member of an academy; *pl.* the costume proper to the officers and students of a school or college.—**ac·a·dem·i·cal·ly**, ak″a·dem′i·kal·lē, *adv.* In an academical manner.

ac·a·dem·ic free·dom, *n.* Freedom to teach or study a subject without fear of reprisal or hindrance.

a·cad·e·mi·cian, a·kad″e·mish′an, ak″a·de·mish′an, *n.* One who belongs to a society established to promote interest in arts, sciences, etc.

ac·a·dem·i·cism, ak″a·dem′i·siz″um, *n.* The system or mode of teaching at an academy; an academical mannerism or traditionalism, as in literature.

a·cad·e·my, *a*·kad′*e*·mē, *n.* pl. **a·cad·- e·mies.** [L. *academia*, Gr. *academeia*, the Academy, from the hero *Academus*, to whom the ground originally belonged which formed the garden in which Plato taught.] A school holding a rank between a college and an elementary school; a seminary of learning of the higher class; a college or school that primarily teaches military subjects, but also educates undergradu- ates, who upon graduation rank as officers and enter into the armed forces; an association for the promotion of literature, science, or art, established sometimes by government, and sometimes by the volun- tary union of private individuals, the members of which are called *academicians.* The Academy of Plato was the philosoph- ical school founded by that Greek phi- losopher.

A·ca·di·an, *a*·kā′dē·*a*n, *a.* Belonging to Acadia, a former name of Nova Scotia.—*n.* A native or inhabitant of Acadia; also, a person who is a descendant of an Acadian and resides in Louisiana.

ac·a·jou, ak′*a*·zhö, *n.* [Fr. < Brazilian name.] The cashew tree, or its fruit; also, a gum or resin from the bark.

a·can·tha, *a*·kan′tha, *n.* [Gr. *akantha*, a spine or thorn.] A prickle of a plant; a spine of an animal; one of the acute processes of the vertebrae of animals.—**ac·an·tha·- ceous,** ak·an·thā′shus, *a.* Armed with prickles, as a plant from the family *Acan- thaceae.*—**a·can·thine,** *a*·kan′thin, *a.* Per- taining to or resembling the plant acanthus; prickly.—**a·can·tho·ceph·a·lan,** *a*·kan″- tha·sef′*a*·lan, *a.* [Gr. *akantha*, thorn, *kophale*, head.] *Zool.* having spines or hooks on the head, as certain intestinal worms (the Acanthocephala), which are thus attached within the bodies of animals. —**a·can·thous,** *a*·kan′thus, *a.* Spiny.

a·can·thoid, *a*·kan′thoid, *a.* Having the shape of a spine; spiny; spinous; prickly.

ac·an·thop·ter·yg·i·an, ak″an·thop″te·- rij′ē·an, *a.* Of or pertaining to the order *Acanthopterygii.*—*n.* An acanthopterygian fish; a fish with spinelike fins, such as the bass.

a·can·thus, *a*·kan′thus, *n.* pl. **a·can·- thus·es, a·can·thi,** *a*·kan′thī. [< Gr. *akanthos*, bear's foot.] Any of a genus of plants of the Mediterranean region having large spiny leaves; an architectural orna- ment used in capitals of the Corinthian and Composite orders, and resembling some- what the foliage of the acanthus plant.

a cap·pel·la, ä″ka·pel′a, *a.* [< It. *a cappella*, in chapel style.] *Mus.* In the style of chapel music; without instrumental accompaniment.

ac·a·ri·a·sis, ak″a·rī′a·sis, *n.* [N.L.] A skin disease caused by mites.

ac·a·rid, ak′a·rid, *n.* [< Gr. *akarēs*, too short to be cut, small.] One of the *Acaridae*, a division of the *Arachnida*, including mites and ticks, in all of which the mouth is formed for sucking.—**a·car·i·cide,** *a*·kar′- i·sīd″, ak′ar·i·sīd″, *n.* A substance that destroys mites.

ac·a·roid, ak′a·roid″, *a.* Bearing a resem- blance to an acarus or mite.

ac·a·roid res·in, ak′a·roid″, *n.* A red or yellow resin that exudes from the grass trees, used in varnishes.

a·car·pel·ous, a·car·pel·lous, ā·kär′pe·- lus, *a.* [< Gr.] *Bot.* lacking carpels.

a·car·pous, ā·kär′pus, *a.* [Gr. *akarpos*, unfruitful—*a*, not, and *karpos*, fruit.] *Bot.* Not producing fruit; sterile; barren.

ac·a·rus, ak′a·rus, *n.* pl. **ac·a·ri,** ak′a·rī″. [N.L. < Gr. *akari*, a kind of mite, < *akarē*, short, tiny.] Any member of the genus *Acarus*; a mite.

a·cat·a·lec·tic, ā·kat″a·lek′tik, *a., n.* [Gr. *akatalektos.*] Having the complete number of syllables (an *acatalectic* verse).

a·cau·date, ā·kä′dāt, *a.* Having no tail; not caudate. Also **a·cau·dal.**

ac·au·les·cent, ak″a·les′ent, *a. Bot.* Not caulescent; stemless; without visible stem. Also **a·cau·line,** ā·ka′lin, **a·cau·lose,** ā·ka′lōs, **a·cau·lous,** ā·ka′lus.—**ac·au·- les·cence,** ak″a·les′ens, *n.*

ac·cede, ak·sēd′, *v.i.*—*acceded, acceding.* [M.E. < L. *accedo*—*ad*, to, and *cedo*, to move, to give place. CEDE.] To agree or assent, as to a proposition, or to terms proposed by another; to give approval; to become a party to by agreeing to terms; to join or be added; to succeed to, as of an heir; come to by inheritance: said especially of a sovereign.

ac·ce·le·ran·do, ak·sel′*e*·rän′dō, *a., adv.* [It.] *Mus.* gradually increasing in speed.

ac·cel·er·ate, ak·sel′a·rāt″, *v.t.*—*acceler- ated, accelerating.* [L. *accelero, acceleratum*, to hasten—*ad*, to, and *celer*, swift. CELERITY.] To make quicker; quicken; to cause to move or advance faster; hasten; add to the velocity of; bring about or help to bring about more speedily.—*v.i.*

ac·cel·er·a·tion, ak·sel″a·rā′·shan, *n.* The act of accelerating or state of being accelerated; increase in speed; *avi.* rate of velocity increase, which is usually recorded in G's; *educ.* the increase in scope of a course of study to meet the needs of students who learn readily.

ac·cel·er·a·tion of grav·i·ty, *n.* Acceler- ation of a falling body due to gravity, which is a little more than 32 feet per second squared at sea level and which varies with latitude and altitude.

ac·cel·er·a·tor, ak·sel′e·rā″tor, *n.* One who or that which accelerates; a hastener; a device for opening or closing the throttle in an automobile; *chem.* a catalyst; *phys.* any device that increases the speed of charged particles; *anat.* any nerve or muscle that speeds up a movement.—**ac·cel·er·a·to- ry,** ak·sel′e·ra·tō″rē, *a.* Accelerating or tending to accelerate.—**ac·cel·er·a·tive,** ak·sel′e·rā″tiv, ak·sel′ĕr·a·tiv, *a.* Tending to accelerate; adding to velocity.

ac·cel·er·om·e·ter, ak·sel″e·rom′i·tĕr, *n.* An instrument used to measure and record the acceleration of aircraft speed.

ac·cent, ak′sent, *n.* [M.Fr. < L. *accentus*, < *ad*, to, and *canere*, sing.] A special effort of utterance making one syllable more promi- nent than others, as by a change of pitch or by stress of voice; stress; a mark indicating stress or some other distinction in pronun- ciation or value; a letter or type bearing such marks as á, à, ê, ē; stress in verse, music, etc.; manner of utterance; *pl.* words as spoken; *math.* a mark, or one of a number of marks, placed after a letter or figure to distinguish similar algebraic magnitudes which differ in value, as in *a*′, *a*″, *a*‴, etc. (called *a prime, a second, a third*, etc., respectively), or to indicate a particular unit or measure, as feet (′) or inches (″) (5′3″, for example, meaning 5 feet, 3 inches), or as minutes (′) or seconds (″) of time or of a degree (18′25″, for example, meaning 18 minutes, 25 seconds). A method of pro- nunciation characteristic of a certain group or locality; *mus.* stress given to particular notes which as a feature of rhythm regularly recur.—ak′sent, ak·sent′, *v.t.* [Fr. *accenter.*] To pronounce with an accent or stress; mark with an accent; accentuate; empha- size; also, to utter.

ac·cen·tu·al, ak·sen′chö·al, *a.* Pertaining to accent; rhythmical.—**ac·cen·tu·al verse,** a verse in which accentuation is the basis of the rhythm.—**ac·cen·tu·al·ly,** ak·sen′- chö·al·ē, *adv.*

ac·cen·tu·ate, ak·sen′chö·āt″, *v.t.*—*ac- centuated, accentuating.* [M.L. *accentuatus*, pp. of *accentuare*, < L. *accentus*, E. *accent.*]

To mark with an accent; emphasize; to make a portion of (something) more prominent or pronounced; accent.—**ac·- cen·tu·a·tion,** ak·sen″chö·ā′shan, *n.* Meth- od of accenting; distinction by emphasis; that which is accentuated by pronunciation or accent marks.

ac·cept, ak·sept′, *v.t.* [M.E. *accepten* < M.Fr. *accepter* < L. *acceptare* < *acceptus*, pp. of *accipere*, take to oneself, < *ad*, to, and *capere*, take.] To take (something offered); receive with favor or acquiescence; accede, or assent to; to respond to in an affirmative manner; to receive formally, as into a college or club; also, to receive as to meaning; understand; *com.* to acknowledge, by signature, as calling for payment, and thus to agree to pay, as a draft. To assume responsibility for.—*v.i.* To accept a gift, proposal, invitation, suggestion, etc.—**ac·- cept·er, ac·cep·tor,** ak·sep′tĕr, *n.* One who accepts, specifically in reference to a bill of exchange.

ac·cept·a·ble, ak·sep′ta·bl, *a.* Capable or worthy of being accepted; satisfactory; suitable; meeting minimum requirements; merely adequate. *Milit.* of an action or the price paid for the action: considered to be within the limits of affordable cost.—**ac·cept·a·bil·i·ty, ac·cept·a·ble·ness,** ak·sep″ta·bil′i·tē, *n.*—**ac·cept·a·bly,** ak·- sep′ta·blē, *adv.*

ac·cept·ance, ak·sep′tans, *n.* The act of accepting, or the state of being accepted; favorable reception; favor; approval; belief; assent; agreement to terms, whether ex- pressly or by some act constituting a virtual acknowledgment, as of a contract. *Com.* an engagement to pay [an order, draft, or bill of exchange when it becomes due, as by the person on whom it is drawn; also, an order, draft, etc., which a person has accepted as calling for payment and has thus promised to pay; as, a trade *acceptance.*

ac·cept·ant, ak·sep′tant, *a.* Receptive.

ac·cep·ta·tion, ak″sep·tā′shan, *n.* [< L.L. *acceptatio(n-).*] The act of accepting or receiving; kind or favorable reception; the meaning or sense in which a word or expression is understood, or generally received; assent; belief; conviction.

ac·cept·ed, ak·sep′tid, *a.* Commonly ap- proved; generally thought of as normal or right; conventional; valid; proper.—**ac·- cept·ed·ly,** ak·sep′tid·lē, *adv.*

ac·cep·tive, ak·sep′tiv, *a.* Willing to receive or accept; receptive.

ac·cess, ak′ses, *n.* [L. *accessus*, < *accedo*, to come near, to approach. ACCEDE.] A coming to; near approach; admittance; the state of being approachable; the means or way of approach; passage allowing communica- tion; accession; *theol.* one's approach to God by means of Jesus Christ. An emo- tional fit or outburst.

ac·ces·si·bil·i·ty, ak·ses″i·bil′i·tē, *n.* The condition or quality of being accessible or of admitting approach; *milit.* the state of an object which causes it to be obtainable or reachable, as: the *accessibility* of a target. The capability of an aircraft which enables it to reach a destination; its capability to take off and to land at various locations.

ac·ces·si·ble, ak·ses′i·bl, *a.* Able to be attained or approached; easy of access; open to the influence of.

ac·ces·sion, ak·sesh′an, *n.* [L. *accessio(n-)*, < *accedere*: see *accede.*] The act of acceding; attainment to an office, right or dignity; adhesion or assent; addition or increase; something added; *law*, addition to property by growth or improvement; *internat. law,* an agreement between states or acceptance of a treaty. *Med.* the onset of disease; an attack.—*v.t.* To enter in an accession book. —**ac·ces·sion book,** a blank book in which the titles of books received by a library are entered, with all necessary details.—**ac·ces·sion num·ber**, the number given to a volume when it is entered in an accession book.

ac·ces·so·ri·al, ak″si·sōr′ē·al, ak″si·sạr′ē·al, a. Pertaining to an accessory.

ac·ces·so·ry, **ac·ces·sa·ry**, ak·ses′o·rē, ak·ses′a·rē, a. [L. *accessorius*, < *accessus*, *accedo*. ACCEDE.] Contributing; aiding in producing some effect, or acting in subordination to the principal agent; contributing to a general effect; belonging to something else as principal; accompanying. —*n*. pl. **ac·ces·so·ries**. One who aids or countenances a crime; that which belongs to something else, as its principal; that which contributes to the effect of something more important; an accompaniment.— **ac·ces·so·ri·ly**, ak·ses′a·ri·lē, adv. In the manner of an accessory; supplementary; not as principal but as a subordinate agent. —**ac·ces·so·ri·ness**, ak·ses′a·rē·nes, n. The state of being accessory, or of being or acting in a secondary character.

ac·ces·so·ry fruit, n. A fruit (pear) which contains one or more ripened ovaries and tissues of some other floral section, such as the receptacle or calyx.

ac·ciac·ca·tu·ra, ä·chä″ka·tür′a, n. [It., < *acciaccare*, crush.] *Mus.* a short grace note one half-step below, and struck at the same time as, a principal note; also, a short appoggiatura. *Phon.* the unemphatic first sound in a rising diphthong.

ac·ci·dence, ak′si·dens, n. [< L. *accidentia*, inflections of words, nonessential qualities, pl. of *accidens*, n.] That part of grammar which treats the inflection of words, or the declension of nouns, adjectives, etc., and the conjugation of verbs; a small book containing the rudiments of grammar; the elementary parts of a subject; rudiments.

ac·ci·dent, ak′si·dent, n. [L. *accidens*, *accident-*, falling chance,—*ad*, and *cado*, to fall, whence *case*, *cadence*, *casual*, *decadence*, etc.] Chance or what happens by chance; an event that happens when quite unlooked for; an unforeseen and undesigned injury to a person; unexpected happening; casualty; mishap; a property or quality of a thing which is not essential to it nor is it one of its invariable signs (as whiteness in paper); *philos.* an event or entity which depends upon the existence of something else; *geol.* the small irregularity of a surface, the cause of which is not apparent.

ac·ci·den·tal, ak″si·den′tal, a. Happening by chance or accident; unexpected; casual; fortuitous; nonessential; not necessarily belonging; adventitious.—n. A casualty; a property not essential; *mus.* a note or tone which does not occur in the scale of the key in which the piece is composed.—**ac·ci·den·tal·ly**, ak″si·den′tal·lē, adv. In an accidental manner; not intentionally; by chance; fortuitously; not essentially.

ac·cip·i·ter, ak·sip′i·tẽr, n. [L. hawk.] Any bird of the genus *Accipiter*, which comprises short-winged, long-tailed hawks of small or moderate size, as the European sparrow-hawk; a raptorial bird; a bird of prey; *surg.* a bandage applied to the nose.— **ac·cip·i·tral**, ak·sip′i·tral, a.—**ac·cip·i·trine**, ak·sip′i·trin, ak·sip′i·trīn″, a.

ac·claim, a·klām′, v.t. [L. *acclamo*—*ac* for *ad*, and *clamo*, to cry out, whence *claim*, *clamor*, etc.] To applaud; to acknowledge; to announce; to declare or salute by acclamation.—n. A shout of joy; acclamation; loud applause; approval or welcome.

ac·cla·ma·tion, ak″la·mā′shan, n. [< L. *aclamatio(n-)* < *acclamatus*, pp. of *acclamo*.] A shout or other demonstration of applause made by a multitude, indicating joy, hearty assent, approbation, or good wishes; act of acclaiming; an oral vote, often unanimous,

showing acceptance.—**ac·clam·a·to·ry**, a·klam′a·tạr″ē, a·klam′a·tō″rē, a. Expressing joy or applause by acclamation; expressing public acknowledgment of approval.

ac·cli·mate, a·klī′mit, ak′li·māt′, v.t., v.i.—*acclimated*, *acclimating*. [Fr. *acclimater*, to acclimate. CLIMATE.] To adapt or become adapted to a foreign or unfamiliar environment.

ac·cli·ma·tion, ak″li·mā′shan, n. The act or process of acclimatizing; the state of being acclimatized; *physiol.* adjustments of the body, both structural and functional, when exposed to a change in climate or environment.

ac·cli·ma·tize, a·klī′ma·tīz″, v.t., v.i.—*acclimatized*, *acclimatizing*. To acclimate.— **ac·cli·ma·ti·za·tion**, n.

ac·cliv·i·ty, a·kliv′i·tē, n. pl. **ac·cliv·i·ties**. [< L. *acclivitas*, an acclivity—*ac* for *ad*, to, and *clivus*, a slope, < root *cli* seen in *clino*, *inclino*, to incline, Gr. *klino*, to bend, incline; akin E. to *lean*.] A slope or inclination of the earth, as the side of a hill, considered as ascending, in opposition to *declivity*; an ascent.—**ac·cliv·i·tous**, **ac·cli·vous**, a·kliv′i·tus, a·klī′vus, a. Rising, as a hill with a slope; sloping upwards.

ac·co·lade, ak″a·lād′, ak″o·lād′, ak′a·lād″, ak′a·lād″, n. [Fr. < It. *accollata*, < *accollare*, embrace, < L. *ad*, to, and *collum*, neck.] An embrace, a kiss, or, later, a tap on the shoulder with the flat of a sword, given in conferring knighthood; any honor, award or commendable notice. *Mus.* a brace joining several staves; *arch.* a curved molding above an arched opening.

ac·com·mo·date, a·kom′a·dāt″, v.t.— *accommodated*, *accommodating*. [L. *accommodo*, to apply or suit—*ac* for *ad*, to, and *commodo*, to profit or help, < *con*, with, and *modus*, measure, proportion, limit, or manner. MODE.] To make suitable, correspondent, or consistent; to fit; adapt; conform; adjust; reconcile, with *to* after the object; to supply or furnish with required conveniences, with *with* after the object; as, *accommodate* a friend *with* money. To do a favor for; oblige; to have or make room for.—v.i. To act conformably; agree.

ac·com·mo·dat·ing, a·kom′a·dā″ting, a. Obliging; yielding to the desires of others; willing to alter principles or convictions to comply with circumstances; disposed to comply and to oblige another.

ac·com·mo·da·tion, a·kom″a·dā′shan, n. The act of accommodating; adjustment; adaptation; adjustment of differences; reconciliation; anything which supplies a want, as in respect of ease, refreshment, and the like; a convenience; a loan of money; willingness to help others. *Usu. pl.* lodgings.

ac·com·mo·da·tion bill, n. Bill of exchange, not given like a genuine bill of exchange in payment of a debt, but merely intended to accommodate the drawer, enabling him to obtain credit or to raise money.

ac·com·mo·da·tion lad·der, n. A ladder hung over the side of a ship, usually at the gangway, to facilitate ascending from, or descending to, smaller boats.

ac·com·mo·da·tive, a·kom′a·dā″tiv, a. Furnishing accommodation; disposed to accommodate; adaptive.

ac·com·pa·ni·ment, a·kum′pa·ni·ment, a·kump′ni·ment, n. Something that attends as a circumstance, or which is added by way of ornament to the principal thing, or for the sake of symmetry; anything that accompanies something else. The subordinate part or parts performed by instruments accompanying a voice, or several voices, or a principal instrument.

ac·com·pa·nist, a·kum′pa·nist, a·kump′nist, n. The performer in music who plays or sings the accompaniment.

ac·com·pa·ny, a·kum′pa·nē, v.t.— *accompanied*, *accompanying*. [M.E. < M.Fr. *accompagnier*, to accompany—*ac* for *ad*, to, and *compagnon*, a companion. COMPANION.] To go with or attend as a companion or associate; to go together; to be associated or connected with; to play a subordinate musical part to, as to a singer or other performer of a musical composition.

ac·com·plice, a·kom′plis, n. [< Incorrect division of M.E. *a complice* < M.Fr. *complice* < L. *complex*, *complicis*, confederate, participant—*con*, with, and *plico*, to fold, *plica*, a fold, a stem which appears also in E. *comply*, *ply*, *triple*, etc. PLY, etc.] An associate or confederate, especially in a crime; a partner or partaker in guilt, usually a subordinate.

ac·com·plish, a·kom′plish, v.t. [M.E. *accomplisshen* < M.F. *accompliss-*, stem of *accomplir*, to finish—prefix *ac* for *ad*, to, and L. *compleo*, to complete. COMPLETE.] To complete; to finish entirely; to execute; to carry out; to fulfill or bring to pass; to succeed in doing; *milit.* to complete (a mission or operation); to attain (an objective); to make out a form or statement.—**ac·com·plish·a·ble**, a·kom′plish·a·bl, a. Capable of accomplishment.—**ac·com·plish·er**, a·kom′plish·ẽr, n.

ac·com·plished, a·kom′plisht, a. Perfected; finished; consummated; trained; skilled; proficient; having the attainments and graces regarded as necessary for cultivated or fashionable society.

ac·com·plish·ment, a·kom′plish·ment, n. The act of accomplishing or carrying into effect; fulfillment; attainment; achievement, esp. such as belongs to fashionable society; that which has been accomplished.

ac·cord, a·kạrd′, n. [M.E. < O.Fr. *acorder* < L. *ac-* for *ad-*, to, and *cor*, *cordis*, the heart, formed like L. *concors*, *discors*, E. *concord*, *discord*.] Agreement; harmony of minds; as, to do a thing with one *accord*; just correspondence of things; concord; harmony of sound; a formal act of agreement between governments; as, the Geneva *accords* of 1954; voluntary or spontaneous impulse or act; as, *of my, of his, of its, of their own accord.*—v.t. To grant; to give; to concede; as, to *accord* due praise.—v.i. To be in correspondence or harmony.

ac·cord·ance, a·kạr′dans, n. The state of being in accord; agreement with a person; conformity with a thing; as, in *accordance* with his wishes; the act of granting.

ac·cord·ant, a·kạr′dant, a. Corresponding; consonant; agreeable; of the same mind; conformable.—**ac·cord·ant·ly**, a·kạr′dant·lē, adv. In accordance or agreement.

ac·cord·ing, a·kạr′ding, a. Agreeing; agreeable; in harmony.—**ac·cord·ing to**, agreeable to; in accordance with; as, *according to* what he says.

ac·cord·ing·ly, a·kạr′ding·lē, adv. Agreeably; suitably; in a manner conformable; consequently; therefore; in due course.

ac·cor·di·on, a·kạr′dē·an, n. [< G. *akkordion* < *akkord*, chord and *ion* (see *melodion*).] A portable, keyed, bellowslike wind instrument sounded by means of metallic reeds.—a. Having folds like the bellows of an accordion.—**ac·cor·di·on·ist**, a·kạr′dē·an·ist, n. A player on the accordion.

ac·cost, a·kạst′, a·kost′, v.t. [Fr. *accoster*, L.L. *accostare*, be or put side by side—*ac* for *ad*, to, and L. *costa* (Fr. *côte*), a rib, a side. COAST.] To speak first to; to address before being addressed; to solicit for immoral purposes: said of prostitutes.

ac·couche·ment, a·kōsh′mänt, n. [Fr. *accoucher*, to be brought to bed; to deliver. COUCH.] Confinement; childbirth.

ac·cou·cheur, ä·kō·shŒR′, n. [Fr. obstetrician—*ac* for *ad*, and *coucher*, to lie or lay down. COUCH.] A surgeon who attends women in childbirth; obstetrician.—ac··cou·cheuse, ä·kö·shœz′, n. A midwife.

ac·count, a·kount′, v.t. [M.E. accounten < M.Fr. accompter < a- (L. ad-) and compter (L. computo) count.] To deem; to consider; to credit or impute to.—v.i. To render an account or statement of particulars: used with to or for; to furnish an explanation: with for.

ac·count, a·kount′, n. A reckoning, enumeration, or computation; a list of debits and credits, or charges; a statement of things bought or sold, of payments, services, etc.; an explanatory statement of particulars, facts, or events; narrative; relation; description; reason or consideration; ground (on all accounts); profit; advantage (to turn to account); regard; behalf; sake (trouble incurred on one's account). Stock market, the operations on the stock exchange performed during the period before the ordinary settlement day; the record of a customer's transactions with and through a stockbroker.

ac·count·a·bil·i·ty, a·koun″ta·bil′i·tē, n. The state of being accountable, answerable, liable, or responsible.

ac·count·a·ble, a·koun′ta·bl, a. Liable to pay or make good in case of loss; responsible for a trust; liable to be called to account; explicable.—ac·count·a·ble·ness, a·koun′ta·bl·nis, n. The state of being accountable; accountability.—ac·count·a·bly, a·koun′ta·blē, adv. In an accountable manner.

ac·count·an·cy, a·koun′tan·sē, n. The work or practice of an accountant; the maintaining or inspecting of commercial accounts.

ac·count·ant, a·koun′tant, n. One who makes the keeping or examination of accounts his profession; an officer in a public office who has charge of the accounts.—ac·count·ant·ship, a·koun′tant·ship, n. The office or employment of an accountant. See certified public accountant.

ac·count ex·ec·u·tive, n. The administrator of a client's account in a service business such as advertising.

ac·count·ing, a·koun′ting, n. The theory and system of setting up, maintaining, and auditing the books of a firm; the art of analyzing the financial position and operating results of a business concern from a study of its sales, purchases, etc; a statement of credits and debits.

ac·cou·ter, ac·cou·tre, a·kö′tėr, v.t.—accoutred, accoutring. [Fr. accoutrer—prefix ac for ad, to, and couture, a seam, < L. consutura, a stitching together, < con, together, and suo, sutum, to sew.] To equip or furnish with personal trappings; especially, to array in a military dress and arms; to equip for military service.

ac·cou·ter·ment, Brit. ac·cou·tre·ment, a·kö′tėr·ment, n. The act of accoutering; an item, esp. an accessory, of dress or equipment; usu. pl. trappings or equipment, esp. that issued to a soldier, excluding his weapons and clothes.

ac·cred·it, a·kred′it, v.t. [Fr. accréditer, to accredit—L. ad, to, and credere, to trust.] To attribute to; give credit to; to acknowledge the merits of (an educational institute); to certify as coming up to a set standard; to believe (a story); to confer credit or authority on; to send with credentials, as an envoy.—ac·cred·i·ta·tion, n.

ac·cres·cent, a·kres′ent, a. [< L. accrescens (-ent-), ppr. of accrescere: ACCRETE.] Growing; increasing; bot. growing larger after flowering.—ac·cres·cence, a·kres′ens, n. Act of increasing; gradual growth or increase; accretion.

ac·crete, a·krēt′, v.i.—accreted, accreting. [< L. accretus, pp. of accrescere, < ad, to and crescere, grow.] To grow together; adhere; with to.—v.t. To add as by growth.—a. Accreted; grown together.—ac·cre·tion, a·krē′shan, n. [L. accretio(n-).] Growth in size or extent; increase by natural growth or by gradual external addition; adhesion or gradual addition of new matter or parts; a whole which results from such growth and accumulation; also, something adhering or gradually added; an accession; law, increase of property by external accessions, as of land by alluvium; pathol. the growing together of parts normally separate.—ac·cre·tive, a·krē′tiv, a.

ac·croach, a·krōch′, v.t. [O.Fr. acrochier (Fr. accrocher), < a (<L. ad), to, and croc, hook.] To take to oneself, as power, etc.; usurp.—ac·croach·ment, n.

ac·cru·al, a·krö′al, n. Act or process of accruing; accretion; something accrued.

ac·crue, a·krö′, v.i.—accrued, accruing. [M.E. acreuen, prob. < M.Fr. acreue, growth < L. accrescere—ac for ad, to, and cresco, to grow, seen also in crescent, decrease, increase.] To be gained or obtained; to proceed, arise, or spring; as, a profit or a loss accruing from a commercial transaction; to result as a natural growth or addition.

ac·cul·tur·a·tion, a·kul″cha·rā′shan, n. [L. ad, to, and cultura, culture.] The adoption by one cultural group of the culture of another. The process of conditioning a child to cultural traits or social patterns. Ling. the process of acquiring an understanding of a foreign culture to strengthen facility with language skills.—ac·cul·tur·ate, a·kul′cha·rāt″, v.t., v.i.—acculturated, acculturating.

ac·cum·bent, a·kum′bent, a. [L. accumbens, ppr. of accumbere < ad, to, and cumbere, to lie down.] Leaning or reclining; lying against anything.—ac·cum·ben·cy, a·kum′ben·sē, n. State of being accumbent.

ac·cum·u·late, a·kū′mya·lāt″, v.t.—accumulated, accumulating. [L. accumulo, accumulatum, to heap up—ad, to, and cumulus, a heap.] To heap or pile up; to amass; to collect or bring together.—v.i. To grow to be extensive in number or quantity; to increase greatly.

ac·cum·u·la·tion, a·kū″mya·lā′shan, n. The act of accumulating; a collecting or being heaped up; that which has accumulated; a mass that has been collected; growth by continuous increases.

ac·cu·mu·la·tive, a·kū″mya·lā″tiv, a··kyö′mya·la·tiv, a. Causing an accumulation; cumulative; heaping up.—ac·cu·mu·la·tive·ly, a·kū′mya·lā″tiv·lē, a·kū′mya·la·tiv·lē, adv. In an accumulative manner; in heaps.

ac·cum·u·la·tor, a·kū″mya·lā″tor, n. One who or that which accumulates; a contrivance, such as a spring, that by being coiled up serves as a store of force or energy; any of the various machines that accumulate totals such as an adding machine, cash register, or computer; Brit. a storage cell or battery. A pressurized reservoir which stores fluid at approximately the working pressure of the hydraulic or pneumatic system in which it will be used; a vessel for storing fluid which is ready to flash into steam.

ac·cu·ra·cy, ak′yur·a·sē, n. The condition or quality of being accurate; extreme precision or exactness; exact conformity to truth, or to a rule or model; correctness. Also ac·cu·rate·ness.

ac·cu·rate, ak′yur·it, a. [L. accuratus, prepared with care—ac for ad, to, and cura, care. CURE.] In exact conformity to truth, or to a standard or rule, or to a model; free from error or defect; exact; precise; strictly correct; adhering to exactness.—ac·cu·rate·ly, ak′yur·it·lē, adv.

ac·curse, a·kurs′, v.t.—accursed, accursing.

[Prefix ac for ad, or O.E. â, intens., and curse.] To call down curses on; to curse.

ac·curs·ed, ac·curst, a·kur′sid, a·kurst′, a. Lying under a curse; blasted; ruined; cursed; damnable; detestable; abominable.—ac·curs·ed·ly, a·kur′sid·lē, adv.—ac·curs·ed·ness, n.

ac·cu·sal, a·kū′zal, n. Accusation.

ac·cu·sa·tion, ak″ū·zā′shan, n. The act of accusing; that of which one is accused; a charge brought against one.

ac·cu·sa·tive, a·kū′za·tiv, a. [M.E. < O.Fr. < L. accusativus.] Gram. in such inflected languages as Latin, German, and Russian, referring to an objective case, the most general function being the direct object of a verb.—n.

ac·cu·sa·to·ry, a·kū′za·tôr″ē, a·kū′za·tar″ē, a. Accusing; containing an accusation; as, an accusatory libel. Also ac·cu·sa·to·ri·al.

ac·cuse, a·kūz′, v.t.—accused, accusing. [M.E. < O.Fr. < L. accuso, to call to account, blame, indict—ad, to, and causa, cause, process. CAUSE.] To charge with a crime, offense, or fault, with of; as, to accuse him of lying; to blame.—v.i. To make an accusation.—ac·cus·er, a·kūz′ėr, n. One who accuses; one who formally brings a charge.—ac·cus·ing·ly, adv.

ac·cused, a·kūzd′, n. A person or persons charged with a crime; a defendant in a court of law.

ac·cus·tom, a·kus′tom, v.t. [M.E. < M.Fr. acoustumer, to accustom—ac for L. ad, to, and O.Fr. coustume, custom. CUSTOM.] To familiarize by use or habit; to habituate or inure.

ac·cus·tomed, a·kus′tomd, a. Often practiced; customary; habitual; usual, characteristic; wonted; familiar; as, in their accustomed manner.

ac·cus·tom·i·za·tion, a·kus″tom·i·zā′shan, n. The process of learning to live comfortably, or with a minimum of discomfort, in an extreme or new environment.

ace, ās, n. [M.E. < O.Fr. as, ace at dice or cards < L. as, a unit, a pound, a foot, etc., < Doric Gr. as, ais, Attic Gr. heis, one.] A unit; a single pip on a card or die, or the card or face of a die so marked; a trifle or insignificant quantity or distance (within an ace of it); a particle; the ace in certain card games counting as ten; an expert; a champion; one proficient in a particular field of endeavor. Milit. slang, the name given to a combat pilot officially credited with shooting down five or more enemy planes.—a. Excellent; expert; outstanding; first in quality.

ace, ās, v.t.—aced, acing. In tennis, badminton, handball, etc. to gain a point against one's opponent by scoring on a shot that an opponent fails to touch. In golf, to make a hole in one.

a·ce·di·a, a·sē′dē·a, n. [L.L. acēdia < Gr. akēdiā, a- not, and kedos, care.] A condition of lethargy and apathy; loss of interest in living.

a·cel·lu·lar, ā·sel′ū·lar, a. Not composed of cells.

a·cen·tric, ā·sen′trik, a. [Prefix a, neg., and centre.] Not centric; away from a center; having no center.

a·ceph·a·lous, ā·sef′a·lus, a. Without a head; headless; without a governing head or chief.

a·ce·quia, a·sā′kya, ä·se′kyä, n. [Sp. < Ar.] An irrigating canal or ditch.

ac·er·ate, as′e·rāt″, as′er·it, a. [<L. acer, sharp.] Bot. Needle-shaped; sharp and pointed. Also acerose.

a·cerb, a·surb′, a. [L. acerbus, unripe, harsh, sour, < acer, sharp; same root as in acid.] Sour, bitter, and harsh to the taste; sarcastic; critical; sour with astringency and roughness.

ac·er·bate, as′ĕr·bāt″, v.t.—acerbated, acerbating. [L. acerbatus, pp. of acerbare, < acerbus, E. acerb.] To sour; exasperate; embitter, irritate.—a·sur′bit, a. Acerbated; embittered.

a·cer·bi·ty, a·sur′bi·tē, n. Sourness, with roughness or astringency of taste; poignancy or severity; painfulness; sharpness; harshness or severity of temper; sourness.

ac·er·ose, as′e·rōs, a. Acerate.

a·ce·rous, ā·sēr′us, a. [Gr.] Zool. having no horns, tentacles, or antennae.

a·cer·vate, a·sur′vit, a·sur′vāt, a. [L. acervo, to heap up, < acervus, a heap.] Bot. growing in heaps or in compact bunches.— **a·cer′vate·ly,** adv.

a·ces·cent, a·ses′ent, a. [L. acescens (-ent-), ppr. of acescere, become sour, < acere, be sour.] Turning sour; slightly sour; acidulous.—**a·ces·cence, a·ces·cen·cy,** a·ses′ens, a·ses′en·sē, n.

ac·e·tab·u·lum, as″i·tab′yu·lum, n. pl. **ac·e·tab·u·la,** as″i·tab′yu·la. [L. vinegar cruet, a cup-shaped vessel, < L. acetum, vinegar. ACID.] The cavity which receives the head of the thigh bone; the socket in which the leg of an insect is inserted; the cuplike sucker with which the arms of the cuttlefish are provided; in ancient Rome, a small cup used at the table for holding vinegar or sauce.—**ac·e·tab·u·lar,** as″i·tab′yu·lar, a.

ac·e·tal, as′i·tal″, n. [acetic and alcohol.] Chem. a liquid formed by the imperfect oxidation of alcohol.

ac·et·al·de·hyde, as″i·tal′de·hid″, n. A water-soluble and colorless liquid, CH_3CHO, which evaporates rapidly and has a pungent odor; used mainly in organic synthesis and in silvering mirrors.

ac·et·am·ide, as″i·tam′id, as″i·tam′id, a·set′e·mid″, a·set′e·mid, n. Chem. the amide, C_2H_5NO, of acetic acid: a white crystalline solid, employed mainly in organic synthesis.

ac·et·an·i·lide, as″i·tan′i·lid″, as″i·tan′i·lid, n. A substance, C_8H_9NO, formed by the action of glacial acetic acid upon analine: used as a remedy for fever, headache, rheumatism, etc.

ac·e·tate, as′i·tāt″, n. A salt formed by the union of acetic acid with a base; a product made from cellulose acetate, for example, acetate rayon; a clear, plastic covering placed over artwork as a protective device.

a·ce·tic, a·sē′tik, a·set′ik, a. [L. acetum, vinegar.] Having the properties of vinegar; sour.—**a·ce·tous, ac·e·tose,** as′i·tus, as′i·tōs″, a. Having a sour taste; having the character of vinegar; acid; causing or connected with acetification.

a·ce·tic ac·id, n. An acid, CH_3COOH, often prepared by the oxidation of alcohol (acetous fermentation), and with water forming the chief ingredient of vinegar.

a·cet·i·fi·ca·tion, a·set″i·fi·kā′shan, n. The act of acetifying or making acetous or sour; the process of becoming acetous; the operation of making vinegar.

a·cet·i·fi·er, a·set′i·fī″ĕr, n. An apparatus used in making vinegar.

a·cet·i·fy, a·set′i·fī″, v.t.—acetified, acetifying. To convert into acid or vinegar.—v.i. To become acid; to be converted into vinegar.

ac·e·tom·e·ter, ac·e·tim·e·ter, as″i·tom′i·tĕr, as″i·tim′i·tĕr, n. An instrument for determining the strength or purity of acetic acid in solution.

ac·e·tone, as′i·tōn″, n. [acetic and ketone.] A volatile chemical compound, $(CH_3)_2CO$, used as a solvent for paints and varnishes, fats, rubber, and plastic; also used in organic synthesis.—**ac·e·ton·ic,** as″i·ton′ik, a.

ac·e·to·phe·net·i·din, as″i·tō·fe·net′i·din, a·sē″tō·fe·net′i·din, n. A solid crystalline compound, $C_{10}H_{13}NO_2$, used in medicine to relieve pain or to check fever.

a·ce·tyl, a·sēt′el, a·set′el, as′i·tel, a. Chem. pertaining to the acetyl group (the univalent group, CH_3CO, appearing in acetic acid, $CH_3CO·OH$).—n. The radical derived from acetic acid, CH_3CO.—**ac·e·tyl·ic,** as″i·til′ik, a.

a·cet·y·late, a·set′i·lāt″, v.t.—acetylated, acetylating. To introduce an acetyl group into(a compound).

a·ce·tyl·cho·line, a·sēt′el·kō′lēn, a·sēt″el·kō′lin, a·sēt′el·kol′ēn, a·sēt′el·kol′in, as″i·til·ko′lēn, as″i·til·ko′lin, as″i·til·kol′-ēn, as″i·til·kol′in, n. A chemical compound, $C_7H_{17}NO_3$, liberated from nerve endings, involved in transmission of nerve impulses; in commercial form, a compound which is useful in initiating peristalsis and decreasing blood pressure.

a·cet·y·lene, a·set′e·lēn″, a·set′e·lin, n. [acetyl- and -ene.] A flammable gas, HC—CH, made with calcium carbide and water: used as a fuel in welding and in organic synthesis.

a·ce·tyl·sal·i·cyl·ic ac·id, a·sēt′el·sal″-i·sil′ik, a·set″el·sal′i·sil′ik, n. Aspirin.

ache, āk, n. [M.E. aken < O.E. ace, aece, ece, ache, pain; acan, to ache; akin to Icel. aka, to drive, press hard; cogn. L. ago, to drive.] Pain, or continued dull pain, in opposition to sudden twinges or spasmodic pain; a continued gnawing pain (toothache or earache); feeling of distress (heartache); a feeling of eagerness or yearning.

ache, āk, v.i.—ached, aching. To suffer from an ache or pain; to be distressed; to feel eager; to long; to feel sympathetic toward someone or something.

a·chene, ā·kēn′, n. [Gr.] Bot. a small dry carpel, containing a single seed, which does not open when ripe.

Ach·e·ron, ak′e·ron″, n. [L. < Gr. Acherōn.] Gr. and Rom. myth. a river in Hades, over which the souls of the dead were ferried by Charon; hence, the lower world; hell.

a·chiev·a·ble, a·chēv′a·bl, a. Capable of being achieved or performed; attainable.

a·chieve, a·chēv′, v.t.—achieved, achieving. [M.E. < M.Fr. achever, to finish—a, to, and O.Fr. cheve, the head or end. CHIEF.] To perform or execute; to accomplish; to finish or carry on to a final and successful close; to obtain or bring about; to attain, as by effort.—**a·chiev·er,** a·chēv′ĕr, n. One who achieves or accomplishes.

a·chieve·ment, a·chēv′ment, n. The act of achieving or performing; accomplishment; an exploit; a great or heroic deed; a feat.

Ach·il·le·an, ak″i·lē′an, a. Of or pertaining to Achilles, the Greek legendary hero in the war against Troy.

A·chil·les, a·kil′ēz, n. In Homer's Iliad, mythical Greek hero of the Trojan War, who was killed when wounded by Paris in his only vulnerable spot, his heel.

A·chil·les heel, n. The point of weakness that is most vulnerable or susceptible.

A·chil·les ten·don, n. Anat. the tendon that joins the heelbone and the muscles of the calf.

a·chlam·y·date, ā·klam′i·dāt″, ā·klam′-i·dit, a. [< Gr. a, not, and chlamys, chlamy-dos, a cloak.] Zool. not possessing a mantle or pallium, as certain mollusks.

ach·la·myd·e·ous, ak″la·mid′ē·us, a. Bot. having neither calyx nor corolla, the flowers being without floral envelope.

a·chlor·hy·dri·a, ā″klōr·hi′drē·a, ā″klar·-hi′drē·a, n. The absence of hydrochloric acid from gastric juices.

a·chon·dro·pla·sia, ā·kon″dro·plā′zha, ā·kon″dro·plā′zhē·a, ā·kon″dro·plā′zē·a, n. Med. defective development of cartilage causing dwarfism.

ach·ro·mat·ic, ak″ro·mat′ik, a. [< Gr. a, not, and chrōma, chrōmatos, color.] Destitute of color; free from chromatic aberration; transmitting light without

decomposing it into its primary colors; as, an achromatic lens or telescope; containing achromatin; mus. having no changes in key or accidentals.

ach·ro·ma·tic·i·ty, ak″rō·ma·tis′i·tē, ā·krō′ma·tis′i·tē, n. The state of being achromatic; want of color. Also **a·chro·ma·tism,** ā·krō′ma·tiz″um.—**a·chro·ma·tize,** ā·krō′ma·tīz″, v.t. To deprive of color; to render achromatic.

a·chro·ma·tin, ā·krō′ma·tin, n. Biol. that portion in the nucleus of a cell which is unstainable.

a·chro·ma·tous, ā·krō′ma·tus, a. Having no color; of a lighter color than is usual or normal.

a·cic·u·la, a·sik′yu·la, n. pl. **a·cic·u·lae,** a·sik′yu·lē″. [L. dim. of acus, a needle. ACID.] The spine or prickle of an animal or plant; a needlelike crystal.—**a·cic·u·lar,** a·sik′yu·lar, a. Having the shape of a needle; having aciculae; having sharp points like needles; needle-shaped.—**a·cic·u·lar·ly,** a·sik′yu·lar·lē, adv. In an acicular manner.

ac·id, as′id, a. [< L. acidus, sour, < root ac-, a point, seen in acus, a needle; acuo, to sharpen; acer, sharp; aceo, to be sour; acetum, vinegar; giving such English words as acrid, acumen, acute, ague, eager, etc.] Sour, sharp, or biting to the taste; not sweet; not alkaline; sour, sharp, or biting in disposition or manner; having an abnormal concentration of acid.

ac·id, as′id, n. Chem. a compound containing hydrogen as an essential constituent and which possesses a sour taste, changes blue vegetable colors to red, neutralizes alkalis, and combines with bases to form salts. A sour substance; figuratively, something sour or ill-natured, such as a remark or a piece of writing; informally, the hallucinogenic drug LSD-25 (lysergic acid diethylamide).

Ac·i·dan·the·ra, as″i·dan′thĕr·a, n. [N.L. < Gr. akid (sing. of akis) needle and N.L.—anthera.] A summer-blooming, bulbous genus of African herbs belonging to the iris family Irideceae, and characterized by sword-shaped leaves, long-tubed flowers, and flowers in long, loose, leafy spikes.

ac·id-fast, as′id·fast″, as′id·fäst″, a. Not easily decolorized by acids when stained, as the tubercle bacillus.

ac·id head, ac·id·head, n. Slang, in the language of users of hallucinogenic drugs, one who occasionally or habitually takes LSD for its hallucinogenic effect.

a·cid·ic, a·sid′ik, a. Chem. Pertaining to acid; containing a large amount of an acid constituent.

a·cid·i·fi·a·ble, a·sid′i·fī″a·bl, a. Capable of being acidified or converted into an acid.

a·cid·i·fi·ca·tion, a·sid″i·fi·kā′shan, n. The act or process of acidifying.

a·cid·i·fi·er, a·sid′i·fī″ĕr, n. That which acidifies; any chemical producing an acid effect.

a·cid·i·fy, a·sid′i·fī″, v.i., v.t.—acidified, acidifying. To make acid; to convert into an acid; to turn sour.

ac·i·dim·e·ter, as″i·dim′i·tĕr, n. Chem. an instrument used for measuring the amount of acid in a particular weight or volume of a solution or other mixture.

a·cid·i·ty, a·sid′i·tē, n. The quality of being acid or sour; sourness; tartness.

ac·i·do·phile, as′i·dō·fīl″, a·sid′o·fīl″, n. Biol. a tissue, organism, cell, or substance which shows an affinity toward an acidic environment.

ac·i·do·phil·ic, as″i·dō·fil′ik, a·sid″o·fil′-ik, a. Biol. Having the quality of being easy to stain with acid; thriving or flourishing in an acid environment. Also **ac·i·doph·i·lus.**

ac·i·doph·i·lus milk, as″i·dof′i·lus, *n.* [N.L.] A milk which has acidophilic bacteria added to it, used for medical purposes.

ac·i·do·sis, as″i·dō′sis, *n.* Abnormally high concentration of acid in the blood and body tissues.

ac·id test, *n.* [From a test utilizing nitric acid to ascertain the gold content of jewelry.] A crucial or conclusive test.

ac·id trip, *n. Slang,* a prolonged state of heightened perception and distorted sensations induced by the hallucinogenic drug LSD.

a·cid·u·late, a·sij′u·lāt′, a·sid′ye·lāt″, *v.t.* —*acidulated, acidulating.* [< L. *acidulus,* slightly sour.] To make acid in a moderate degree; to embitter.—**a·cid·u·la·tion,** *n.*

a·cid·u·lent, a·sij′u·lent, a·sid′ye·lent, *a.* Somewhat acid or sour; acidulous; tart; peevish.

a·cid·u·lous, a·sij′u·lus, a·sid′ye·lus, *a.* Slightly sour in manner or taste; sharp; caustic; acidulent; subacid, as cream of tartar, oranges, etc.

ac·i·er·ate, as′ē·a·rāt, *v.t.*—*acierated, acierating.* [Fr. *acierer,* < *acier,* steel.] To convert (iron) into steel.

ac·i·form, as′i·fąrm″, *a.* [< L. *acus,* needle, and *form.*] Sharp; needle-shaped; acicular.

ac·i·na·ceous, as″i·nā′shus, *a.* [< L. *acinus,* a grapestone or kernel.] Full of kernels or seeds.—**ac·i·nar·i·ous,** as″i·nâr′ē·us, *a.* Covered with little spherical stalked vesicles resembling grape seeds, as some algae.— **a·cin·i·form,** a·sin′i·fąrm″, *a.* Having the form of grapes, or being in clusters like grapes.

ac·i·nac·i·form, as″i·nas′i·fąrm″, *a.* [L. *acinaces,* < Gr. *akinakēs,* a scimitar.] Formed like or resembling a scimitar; as, an *acinaciform* leaf.

ac·i·nose, ac·i·nous, as′i·nōs″, as′i·nus, *a.* Consisting of acini.

ac·i·nus, as′i·nus, *n.* pl. **ac·i·ni,** as′i·nī″. [< L. berry, grape, grapestone.] *Bot.* a drupelet; a grape seed. *Anat.* a minute lobule; the smallest saccular subdivision of a gland.

ack-ack, ak′ak″, *n.* [From pronunciation of AA, antiaircraft, by British radio operators.] An antiaircraft gun; antiaircraft artillery; antiaircraft fire.

ac·knowl·edge, ak·nol′ij, *v.t.*—*acknowledged, acknowledging.* [Prefix *a,* on, and *knowledge.*] To own or recognize by avowal or by some act; to express thanks or appreciation for; to show gratitude for; to assent to the truth or claims of; to admit to be; to own or confess to; to avow receiving.— **ac·knowl·edge·a·ble,—ac·knowl·edg·er,** ak·nol′ij·ėr, *n.* One who acknowledges.

ac·knowl·edg·ment, ac·knowl·edge·ment, ak·nol′ij·ment, *n.* The act of acknowledging or owning up to; recognition; avowal; confession; expression of thanks; something given or done in return for a favor; a receipt for money received. *Law,* a formal declaration by a person stating the fact that he executed a legal document; a public recognition of an illegitimate child by his father. The message received from the originator of a communication that his communication has reached its destination and is understood.

a·clin·ic, ā·klin′ik, *a.* [< Gr. *aklines,* not bending, < *a-,* not and *klinein,* incline.] Free from inclination or dip of the magnetic needle: applied to an imaginary line near the earth's equator.—**a·clin·ic line,** the magnetic equator.

ac·me, ak′mē, *n.* [Gr. *akmē,* a point. Root *ak-.* ACID.] The top or highest point; summit; the furthest point attained; maturity or perfection; the height or crisis of a disease; climax.

ac·ne, ak′nē, *n.* [Gr. *aknē,* eruption on the face, M.S. var. of *akmē,* lit., point. ACME.]

An eruption of hard, inflamed tubercles or pimples on the face, especially during adolescence; an inflammatory disease of the skin, arising from the obstruction of the sebaceous glands.

a·cock, a·kok′, *adv.* In a cocked position.— **a·cock·bill,** a·kok′bil″, *adv. Naut.* with bills or ends cocked or turned upward, as an anchor hanging ready to be dropped, or as yards tilted at an angle with the deck.

ac·o·lyte, ak′o·līt″, *n.* [M.E. *acolite* < O.Fr. < M.L. *acoluthus* < Gr. *akolouthos,* following, < *a-* (denoting association) and *keleuthos,* path.] An attendant; *Rom. Cath. Ch.* one of a minor order of clergy, who attends during service on the superior orders; a lay attendant so employed; an altar boy; a follower.

ac·o·nite, ak′a·nīt″, *n.* [< L. *aconitum,* Gr. *akoniton,* a poisonous plant, like monkshood.] Any plant of the genus *Aconitum,* both poisonous and medicinal species. Also *aconitum, wolfsbane.*

a·co·ni·tum, ak″a·nī′tum, *n.* Aconite.

a·corn, ā′kąrn, ā′kern, *n.* [M.E. *akern* < O.E. *æceren, æcern,* an acorn; Goth. *akram,* fruit; Icel. *akarn,* Dan. *agern,* M.H.G. *ackeran,* (collective) acorns; the word originally meant simply fruit, fruit of the field, being allied to *acre.*] The fruit of the oak, a one-celled, one-seeded, oval nut, which grows in a permanent cup; a knop or finial in the shape of an acorn, as on a piece of furniture.

a·corn tube, *n. Elect.* an acorn-shaped vacuum tube used primarily in ultrahigh-frequency electronic devices.

a·cos·mism, å·koz′miz·um, *n.* [< Gr. *a-,* not, and *kósmos,* world.] *Philos.* denial of the existence of a physical universe.—**a·cos·mist,** å·koz′mist, *n.*

a·cot·y·le·don, å″kot″e·lēd′on, å·kot″e· lēd′on, *n.* [< Gr. *a,* not, and *kotylēdōn,* any cup-shaped cavity, < *kotylē,* a hollow.] *Bot.* A plant whose seeds, called spores, are not furnished with cotyledons or seed lobes; thus a plant belonging to a group lower than the seed plants.—**a·cot·y·le·don·ous,** å″kot″e·led′o·nus, *a.*

a·cous·tic, a·kö′stik, *a.* [< Gr. *akoustikos,* < *akouo,* to hear.] Pertaining to the sense or organs of hearing, or to the science of acoustics; intended for the control of sound, as *acoustic* tile. Also **a·cous·ti·cal.** —*n.* A remedy for deafness or imperfect hearing.—**a·cous·ti·cal·ly,** a·kö′sti·kal· lē, *adv.* In relation to or in a manner adapted to acoustics.

a·cous·tic mine, *n.* A mine exploded in water by the sound of the propeller, engines, etc., of a ship.

a·cous·tics, a·kö′stiks, a·kou′stiks, *n.* The science of sound, of the cause, nature, and phenomena of the vibrations of elastic bodies which affect the organ of hearing; the properties determining audibility or fidelity of sound in an auditorium, etc.— **ac·ous·ti·cian,** ak″ų·stish′an, *n.* An expert in acoustics.

a·cous·tic ve·loc·i·ty, *n.* The velocity of sound waves, or similar waves, in a given environment.

ac·quaint, a·kwānt′, *v.t.* [M.E. *aquainten, acointen* < O.Fr. *accointer* < M.L. *accognitare,* to make known, < L. *ad,* to, and *cognitus,* known, < *cognosco, cognitum,* to know; same root as in *know.*] To make to know; to make aware of; to apprise; to make familiar; to bring into social contact; inform: usually followed by *with;* as, *acquaint* a person *with* facts.

ac·quaint·ance, a·kwān′tans, *n.* A state of being acquainted, or of having more or less intimate knowledge; personal knowledge; familiarity, followed by *with;* a person known to one; the whole body of those with whom one is acquainted.—**ac·quaint·-**

ance·ship, a·kwān′tans·ship″, *n.* State of being acquainted.

ac·quaint·ed, a·kwān′tid, *a.* Knowing; being acquainted with, but not close or intimate.

ac·quest, a·kwest′, *n.* [Fr. *acquest* (now *acquet*) prob. < L. *acquisitus,* pp. of *acquirire, acquire.*] Acquirement; an acquisition; *civil law,* property acquired other than by succession.

ac·qui·esce, ak″wē·es′, *v.i.*—*acquiesced, acquiescing.* [Fr. *acquiescer,* L. *acquiescere,* to rest, to acquiesce—*ad,* to, and *quiescere,* to be quiet. QUIET.] To rest satisfied, or apparently satisfied, or to rest without opposition and discontent; to assent quietly; to agree; to yield (to).

ac·qui·es·cence, ak″wē·es′ens, *n.* The act of acquiescing or giving a quiet, passive assent; a yielding; *law,* neglect of legal action for such a time as to imply the abandonment of a right.

ac·qui·es·cent, ak″wē·es′ent, *a.* Disposed to acquiesce; disposed to agree or submit without protest; quietly assenting.—**ac·qui·es·cent·ly,** ak″wē·es′ent·lē, *adv.*

ac·quir·a·ble, a·kwi er′a·bl, *a.* Capable of being acquired.

ac·quire, a·kwiẽr′, *v.t.*—*acquired, acquiring.* [M.E. *acqueren* < M.F. < L. *acquiro,* to get— *ad,* to and *quaero,* to look or search for. QUEST.] To get or gain; to achieve possession of, often through unspecified manner or means. To gain for oneself through one's own action.—**ac·quir·er,** a·kwiẽr′ẽr, *n.* A person who acquires.

ac·quired char·ac·ter, *n.* A biological change that results from use or environment rather than from heredity.

ac·quire·ment, a·kwi er′ ment, *n.* The act of acquiring, or of making acquisition; that which is acquired; attainment, especially personal attainment (as contrasted with a natural *gift* or *endowment*).

ac·qui·si·tion, ak″wi·zish′an, *n.* The act of acquiring; the thing acquired or gained: generally applied to material gains; *space,* the location process of the orbit of a satellite or trajectory of a space probe in order that tracking or telemetry data be found.

ac·quis·i·tive, a·kwiz′i·tiv, *a.* Disposed to make acquisitions; having a propensity to acquire property, knowledge, etc.

ac·quis·i·tive·ly, a·kwiz′i·tiv·lē, *adv.* In an acquisitive manner; by way of acquisition.

ac·quis·i·tive·ness, a·kwiz′i·tiv·nis, *n.* Quality of being acquisitive.

ac·quit, a·kwit′, *v.t.*—*acquitted, acquitting.* [M.E. < O.Fr. *aquiter,* to discharge, to set at rest with respect to a claim.—L. *ad,* to, and *quietus,* at rest, quiet. QUIET.] To release or discharge from an obligation, accusation, or the like; to settle; to pronounce not guilty, with *of* before the charge. To behave; to bear or conduct (oneself).

ac·quit·tal, a·kwit′al, *n.* The act of acquitting; settlement of an obligation or a debt; a judicial setting free from the charge of an offense.

ac·quit·tance, a·kwit′ans, *n.* An acquitting or discharging from a debt or any other liability; the writing which is evidence of such a discharge.

a·cre, ā′kẽr, *n.* [O.E. *acer, æcer,* a field—D. *akker,* Icel. *akr,* Dan. *ager,* G. *acker,* Goth. *akrs,* arable land, a field; L. *ager,* Gr. *agros,* Skt. *ajra,* a field. From root, *ag, ak,* as in L. *ago.* Icel. *aka,* to drive; the word probably meaning originally the place to or over which cattle were driven; a pasture. *Acorn* is from this root.] A definite quantity of land, the United States and British statute acre containing 160 square rods, 4,840 square yards, or 43,560 square feet. *Pl.* lands; estate. *Pl., colloq.* any great amount or broad expanse.

---

a·cre·age, ā′kẽr·ij, *n.* The number of acres in a piece of land; acres taken collectively.

a·cre-foot, ā′kẽr·fu̇t′, *n.* The amount of water (43,560 cubic feet) that would cover one acre to a depth of one foot.

a·cre-inch, ā′kẽr·inch′, *n.* One-twelfth of an acre-foot, or 3,630 cubic feet.

ac·rid, ak′rid, *a.* [< L. *acer, acris,* sharp: with *id,* < the common L. adjective termination *-idus.* ACID.] Sharp or biting to the taste or smell; pungent; bitter; virulent; bitter, as in temper or disposition; caustic. —**a·crid·i·ty, ac·rid·ness,** a·krid′i·tē, ak′rid·nis, *n.*—**ac·rid·ly,** ak′rid·lē, *adv.*

ac·ri·dine, ak′ri·dēn′, ak′ri·din, *n.* A colorless crystalline compound, $C_{13}H_9N$, obtained from coal tar, used to make certain drugs and dyes.

ac·ri·fla·vine, ak″ri·flā′vin, ak″ri·flā′vēn, *n. Chem.* an acridine derivative existing as a granular solid, $C_{14}H_{14}N_3Cl$, usually found in mixture with proflavine, differing from it in molecular structure by a methyl group: used chiefly in medicine as an antiseptic.

ac·ri·mo·ni·ous, ak″ri·mō′nē·us, *a.* Abounding in acrimony; severe; bitter; virulent; caustic; stinging.—**ac·ri·mo·ni·ous·ly,** ak″ri·mō′nē·us·lē, *adv.*—**ac·ri·mo·ni·ous·ness,** ak″ri·mō′nē·us·nis, *n.*

ac·ri·mo·ny, ak′ri·mō″nē, *n.* [L. *acrimonia,* < *acris,* sharp.] Acridity; pungency; sharpness or severity of temper; bitterness of expression; acerbity; asperity.

a·crit·i·cal, ā·krit′i·kal, *a. Med.* Not critical; providing no warning of a crisis.

ac·ro·bat, ak′ro·bat″, *n.* [Gr. *akrobatos* < *akros,* high, and *baino,* to go.] A high-wire dancer; one who practices vaulting, tumbling, somersaults, trapeze and trampoline gymnastics, etc.; one who exhibits an agile performance of gymnastic skills. One who easily makes sudden alterations in his relationships or opinions.—**ac·ro·bat·ic,** ak″ro·bat′ik, *a.*

ac·ro·bat·ics, ak″ro·bat′iks, *n. pl., sing. or pl. in constr.* The activities of an acrobat; gymnastics; acts of physical skill and strength performed with great ease and agility.

ac·ro·car·pous, ak″ro·kär′pus, *a.* [N.L. < Gr. *akros,* highest, and *karpos,* fruit.] *Bot.* applied to mosses whose fruit terminates the growth of a primary axis.

ac·ro·dont, ak′ro·dont″, *a.* Possessing rootless teeth joined to the ridges of the upper and lower jaws.—*n.* Any animal possessing such teeth.

a·crod·ro·mous, a·krod′ro·mus, *a.* [Gr. *acron,* end, top, and *dromos,* < *dramein,* run.] *Bot.* running to a point: said of a nervation with the nerves terminating in, or curving inward to, the point of a leaf. Also **ac·ro·drome,** ak′ro·drōm″.

ac·ro·gen, ak′ro·jen, *n.* [Gr. *akros,* high, on the top, and root *gen,* to produce.] A plant (as a moss, fern, horsetail) increasing by extension of the stem or axis of growth at the top.

a·crog·e·nous, a·kroj′e·nus, *a.* Increasing by growth at the summit, as the tree ferns; pertaining to the acrogens.

a·cro·le·in, a·krō′lē·in, *n. Chem.* the volatile liquid aldehyde, CH_2CHCHO, having an acrid odor, obtained by the dehydration of glycerol in the distillation of fats or the oxidation of allyl alcohol: used chiefly in organic synthesis.

ac·ro·lith, ak′ro·lith, *n.* [Gr. *akrólithos,* with ends made of stone, < *ákros,* at the end, and *lithos,* stone.] A sculptured figure having only the head and extremities made of stone or marble.—**ac·ro·lith·ic,** ak″ro·lith′ik, *a.*

ac·ro·meg·a·ly, ak″ro·meg′a·lē, *n.* [Gr. *akros,* an extremity; *megale,* large.] A rare glandular disease, associated with overgrowth of bone, especially in the jaws, hands, and feet.—**ac·ro·me·gal·ic,** ak″rō·me·gal′ik, *a.* Referring to or suffering from acromegaly.—*n.* A person afflicted with acromegaly.

a·cro·mi·on, a·krō′mē·an, *n. pl.* **a·cro·mi·a,** a·krō′mē·a. [*acro-* and Gr. *omos,* shoulder.] *Anat.* the outward end of the spine of the scapula or shoulder blade.—**a·cro·mi·al,** a·krō′mē·al, *a.*

a·cron·i·cal, a·kron′i·kal, *a.* [Gr. *akros,* extreme, and *nyx,* night.] Occurring at sunset or nightfall: said of the rising or setting of a star, as distinguished from *cosmical.*—**a·cron·i·cal·ly,** a·kron′i·kal·ē, *adv.* In an acronical manner.

ac·ro·nym, ak′ro·nim, *n.* [*acro-* and Gr. *onoma,* name.] A word formed from the initial syllables or letters of other words, as *radar* from 'radio detecting and ranging'; an acrostic.

a·crop·e·tal, a·krop′i·tal, *a.* [Gr. *akron,* top, and L. *petere,* seek.] *Bot.* developing from the base toward the apex.

ac·ro·pho·bi·a, ak″ro·fō′bē·a, *n.* [Gr. *akron,* a height; *phobos,* fear.] A pathological dread of high places.

a·crop·o·lis, a·krop′o·lis, *n.* [Gr. *akros,* high, and *polis,* a city.] The citadel or highest part of an ancient Grecian city, usu. situated on an eminence commanding and fortifying the town.

ac·ro·spire, ak′ro·spīr″, *n.* [Gr. *akros,* highest, and *speira,* a spire or spiral line.] The first leaf which rises above the ground when grain germinates; the rudimentary stem or first leaf which appears in malted grain.

ac·ro·spore, ak′ro·spōr″, *n.* [Gr. *akros,* at the end, and *spora,* seed, E. *spore.*] *Bot.* a spore borne at the end of a sporophore, as in fungi.

a·cross, a·kràs′, a·kros′, *adv.* [Prefix *a-,* and *cross.*] From side to side: opposed to *along;* on or at the other side; athwart; intersecting; transversely; passing over at any angle; crosswise.—*prep.*—*a.* Crossed.

a·cross-the-board, a·kràs′тHe·bōrd′, a·kràs′тHe·bȧrd′, a·kros′тHe·bōrd′, a·kros′тHe·bȧrd′, *a.* Referring to a radio or TV program that comes on at the same time Monday through Friday; pertaining to a racing bet in which equivalent amounts of money are bet on the same horse to win, place, and show; pertaining to and including all members or categories.

a·cros·tic, a·krȧ′stik, a·kros′tik, *n.* [Gr. *akrostichis,* an acrostic—*akros,* extreme, and *stichos,* order or verse.] A composition or verse in which the first, or the first and last, or certain other letters of the lines, taken in order, form a name, title, motto, etc., or other word, phrase, or the alphabet; acronym.—*a.*—**a·cros·ti·cal·ly,** a·krȧs′ti·kal·ē, *adv.* In the manner of an acrostic.

ac·ro·tism, ak′ro·tiz″um, *n.* [Gr. *a,* not, and *krotos,* a beating.] An absence or weakness of the pulse.

ac·ry·late, ak′re·lāt″, ak′re·lit, *n. Chem.* an ester or salt coming from an acrylic acid.

a·cryl·ic, a·kril′ik, *a.* Pertaining to the acid $CH_2=CHCO_2H$, obtained from acrolein, or its derivatives.

a·cryl·ic ac·id, *n. Chem.* $CH_2=CHCO_2H$, a colorless, destructive liquid with a bitter smell, most frequently obtained by the oxidation of acrolein: most important in the formation of acrylic resins.

a·cryl·ic fi·ber, *n.* One of the group of synthetic textile fibers obtained from a compound of acetylene and hydrogen cyanide.

a·cryl·ic res·in, *n.* Thermoplastic resin from polymerization of acrylic or methacrylic acid esters, used for transparent airplane parts, lenses, dentures.

ac·ry·lo·ni·trile, ak″re·lō′ni′tril, ak″re·lō′ni′trēl, ak″re·lō′ni·tril, *n. Chem.* $CH_2=CHCN$, a colorless, volatile, combustible liquid mainly used in the polymerization of acrylic fibers, synthetic rubber, and plastics.

act, akt, *v.i.* [M.E. < L. *ago, actum,* to exert power, to put in motion, to do; Gr. *agō* to lead; allied to Icel. *aka,* to drive, and to E. *acre* (which see).] To exert power; to produce effects; to be in action or motion; to carry into effect a purpose or determination of the mind; to behave, demean, or conduct oneself; to perform, as an actor; to substitute for; as, to *act* as captain.—*v.t.* To transact; to do or perform; to represent as real; to perform on or as on the stage; to play; hence, to feign or counterfeit.—**act as,** to serve as; perform the duties or function of.—**act on,** to obey or act in accordance with; to affect. —**act out,** to perform or demonstrate; *psychol.* to express openly subconscious emotions.—**act up,** to be wantonly disorderly or insubordinate.—**act·a·ble,** akt′a·bl, *a.* Capable of being acted or performed; practically possible.—**act·a·bil·i·ty,** *n.*

act, akt, *n.* That which is being done or which has been done; a deed; an exploit; the exertion of power; the effect of which power exerted is the cause; a state of reality or real existence, as opposed to a possibility; actuality; a part or division of a play, generally subdivided into smaller portions called scenes; a decree, edict, or law, especially one proceeding from a legislative body.—**caught in the act,** discovered or apprehended during a surreptitious action.—**get in·to the act,** to join or participate in an activity normally restricted to others.—**put on an act,** to pretend.

ACTH, *n. Biochem.* initials for *adrenocorticotropic hormone,* a pituitary hormone that stimulates the cortex of the adrenal glands. *Phar.* a material which is obtained from the pituitary glands of animals.

ac·tin, ak′tin, *n.* A protein important in contraction of muscles.

act·ing, ak′ting, *a.* Performing temporarily the duty, service, or functions of another person.—*n.* A playing on the stage or in front of cameras.

ac·tin·i·a, ak·tin′·ē·a, *n. pl.* **ac·tin·i·ae,** ak·tin′ē·ē. [Gr. *aktis, aktinos,* a ray; their tentacles being raylike.] A sea anemone; a polyp having the mouth surrounded by tentacles in concentric circles, which when spread resemble the petals of a brightly colored flower.

ac·tin·ic, ak·tin′ik, *a.* [Gr. *aktis, aktinos,* a ray.] Pertaining to rays, esp. to the chemical rays of the sun; dealing with, or relating to, actinism.—**ac·ti·nol·o·gy,** ak″ti·nol′o·jē, *n.* The science which investigates the power of sunlight to cause photochemical reaction.

ac·tin·ic ray, *n. Phys.* a ray of light which is composed of short wavelengths, is found in the ultraviolet and violet areas of the spectrum, and causes photochemical changes.

ac·ti·nide se·ries, ak′ti·nīd″, *n. Chem.* a group of radioactive elements which contains the elements from actinium, number 89, to lawrencium, number 103.

ac·tin·i·form, ak·tin′i·fȧrm″, *a.* Bearing a resemblance to an actinia; having its radiate form; rayed.

ac·tin·ism, ak′ti·niz″um, *n.* The radiation of heat or light; the property of the chemical part of the sun's rays, which, as seen in photography, produces chemical combinations and decompositions.

ac·tin·i·um, ak·tin′ē·um, *n. Chem.* a radioactive element, an isotope of mesothorium, discovered in pitchblende. Sym. Ac, at. no. 89. See Periodic Table of Elements.

ac·tin·o·graph, ak·tin′o·graf″, ak·tin′o·gräf″, *n.* An instrument for measuring and registering the variations of actinic or chemical influence in the solar rays.

ac·ti·noid, ak″ti·noid″, *a*. Resembling a ray or rays; radiated.

ac·tin·o·lite, ak·tin′o·līt″, *n*. *Mineral*. a vibrant green or gray-green amphibole which appears in crystals or in clumps. —**ac·tin·o·lit·ic**, ak″ti·no·lit′ik, *a*. Like or pertaining to actinolite.

ac·ti·nom·e·ter, ak″ti·nom′i·tėr, *n*. An instrument for measuring the intensity of the sun's actinic rays, most often by the photochemical effect; exposure meter.— **ac·ti·no·met·ric**, ak″ti·nō·me′trik, *a*. Of or belonging to the actinometer or its use.

ac·ti·no·mor·phic, ak″ti·nō·mạr′fik, *a*. Having radial symmetry; of certain flowers, as the buttercup, divisible vertically into similar halves by each of a number of planes.

ac·ti·no·my·cete, ak″ti·nō·mī·sēt′, *n*. *Bact*. a member of the order *Antinomycetales*, which contains rod-shaped or filamentous bacteria.

ac·ti·no·my·cin, ak″ti·nō·mīs′in, *n*. One of the yellow-red or red polypeptide antibiotics separated from soil bacteria.

ac·ti·non, ak′ti·non″, *n*. A radioactive, gaseous, inert element, which exists for only a few seconds, and is isotopic with radon.

ac·ti·no·u·ra·ni·um, ak″ti·nō·yụ·rā′nē·um, *n*. An isotope of uranium with an atomic mass of 235.

ac·ti·no·zo·an, ak″ti·no·zō′an, *n*. Any of a class of marine coelenterates, *Anthozoa*.— *a*. Pertaining to an actinozoan.

ac·tion, ak′shan, *n*. [L. *actio*. ACT.] The state or manner of acting or being active, as opposed to *rest*; activity; an act or thing done; the performance of a function; a deed; exertion; an exploit; a battle or engagement; the mechanism or movement of a compound instrument, or the like; agency; operation; procedure; impulse; the connected series of events on which the interest of a drama or a work of fiction depends; gesture or gesticulation; a suit or process at law; the effect that one thing has upon another; *physiol*. an alteration in tissues, organs, etc., which results in the occurrence of a function. *Milit*. a military mission or operation; a war maneuver or activity; the procedure of completing what is necessary to satisfy an administrative or operational purpose.

ac·tion·a·ble, ak′sha·na·bl, *a*. Furnishing ground for an action at law.—**ac·tion·a·bly**, ak′sha·na·blē, *adv*. In an actionable manner.

ac·ti·vate, ak′ti·vāt″, *v.t.*—*activated, activating*. To make active; to organize. *Phys*. to render radioactive; to speed up a reaction by applying a catalyst. *Milit*. to render a constituted unit active by sending members to it; to establish an operating entity.—*v.i*. To become active.—**ac·ti·va·tor**, *n*.

ac·ti·vat·ed car·bon, *n*. A powdered or granular carbon that is employed mainly for purification by adsorption and is obtained through the processes of carbonization and chemical activation.

ac·ti·va·tion, ak″ti·vā′shan, *n*. The act of activating.

ac·tive, ak′tiv, *a*. [M.E. < M.Fr. *actif, active*; L. *activus*. ACT.] Having the power or property of acting; having power to exert influence: as opposed to *passive*; producing results; effective; performing actions quickly; quick; nimble; brisk; agile; engaged constantly in action; busy; assiduous; accompanied or characterized by action, work, or by the performance of business; as, *active* demand for goods; actually proceeding; as, *active* warfare. *Gram*. denoting a verb form or voice in which the subject performs the action ('broke' in 'He broke the glass.'): opposed to *passive*. Serving in the armed forces; as, *active* duty; participating; as *active* member; vigorous.— **ac·tive·ly**, ak′tiv·lē, *adv*.—**ac·tive·ness**, *n*.

ac·tive du·ty, *n*. Regular full-time duty with a branch of the military service.

ac·tive sat·el·lite, *n*. A satellite which receives, amplifies, and then retransmits microwave signals (telephone, television, etc.), as Telstar.

ac·tiv·ism, ak′ti·viz″um, *n*. *Philos*. a theory that the active, creative mind is the source of all reality; *polit*. the doctrine of originative activity and decisiveness—**ac·tiv·ist**, *n., a*.

ac·tiv·i·ty, ak·tiv′i·tē, *n. pl*. **ac·tiv·i·ties**. The state or quality of being active; the active faculty; active force; nimbleness; agility; liveliness; briskness. A natural or normal process; a specific action, pursuit, or sphere of actions; as, an extracurricular *activity*; *milit*. the work executed in completing a mission or task.

act of God, *n*. *Insurance, law*, a direct occurrence which no one can predict or prevent, as a tornado, earthquake, or other natural disaster.

ac·to·my·o·sin, ak″to·mī′o·sin, *n*. A contractile complex which consists of actin and myosin, and is related to adenosine triphosphate in muscular contractions.

ac·tor, ak′tor, *n*. One who acts or performs; one who represents a character or acts a part in a play, motion picture, or other dramatic performance.—**ac·tress**, ak″tris, *n*. A female actor.

Acts of the A·pos·tles, *n*. A book of the New Testament, credited to Luke and recounting the origin of the Christian church.

ac·tu·al, ak′chö·al, *a*. Acting or existing truly and objectively; real; effectively operative; effectual: opposed to potential or nominal; now existing; present; current.— *n*. Something actual or real. A movie or television presentation based on true incidents; a documentary.—**ac·tu·al·ness**, ak′chö·al·nis, *n*. The quality of being actual.

ac·tu·al·i·ty, ak″chö·al′i·tē, *n. pl*. **ac·tu·al·i·ties**. The state of being actual; that which is real or actual.

ac·tu·al·i·za·tion, ak″chö·al·i·zā′shan, *n*. A making real or actual; a realization.

ac·tu·al·ize, ak″chö·a·līz″, *v.t.*—*actualized, actualizing*. To make actual; to realize.

ac·tu·al·ly, ak″chö·a·lē, *adv*. In fact; in reality; really; with active manifestation.

ac·tu·ar·y, ak″chö·er″ē, *n. pl*. **ac·tu·ar·ies**. [L. *actuarius*, a clerk, a registrar, < *acta*, records, acts.] A registrar or clerk; an official in a joint-stock company, particularly an insurance company, whose duty is to compute insurance and annuity premiums, risks, and dividends.—**ac·tu·ar·i·al**, ak″chö·âr′ē·al, *a*. Of or pertaining to an actuary or to his business.

ac·tu·ate, ak′chö·āt″, *v.t.*—*actuated, actuating*. [< act.] To put into action; to move or incite to action; to impel; to begin (a process).—**ac·tu·a·tion**, ak″chö·ā′shan, *n*. The state of being put into action; an impulse; an actuating force.

ac·tu·a·tor, ak′chö·ā″tėr, *n*. One who or that which actuates or puts in action.

ac·u·ate, ak′yö·it, ak′yö·āt, *a*. [M.E. < L. *acus*, needle.] Needle-shaped; pointed; sharp.

a·cu·i·ty, a·kū′i·tē, *n*. [M.Fr. *acuite*, < M.L. *acuitas*, < L. *acuere*, sharpen.] Sharpness; acuteness; keen sense of perception.

a·cu·le·ate, a·kū′lē·it, a·kū′lē·āt″, *a*. [L. *aculeus*, a spine, a prickle, dim. of *acus*, a needle. ACID.] *Bot*. having prickles or sharp points; *zool*. having a sting. Also **a·cu·le·at·ed**, a·kyö′lē·it″id, a·kyö′lē·āt″id.

a·cu·le·us, a·kū′lē·us, *n. pl*. **a·cu·le·i**, a·kū′lē·ī″. [N.L. < L. dim. of *acus*, needle.] *Zool*. the sting of a wasp, bee; *bot*. a prickle.

a·cu·men, a·kū′men, ak′yu·men, *n*. [L. *acumen*, < *acuo*, to sharpen. ACID.] Quickness of perception; mental acuteness or penetration, esp. in practical affairs; keenness of insight; sagacity.

a·cu·mi·nate, a·kū′mi·nit, a·kyö′mi·nāt″, *a*. [L. *acuminatus*, sharpened.] Pointed; acute; tapered to a point.

a·cu·mi·nate, a·kū′mi·nāt″, *v.t.*—*acuminated, acuminating*. To render sharp or keen.—*v.i*. To taper to a point.—**a·cu·mi·na·tion**, a·kū″mi·nā′shun, *n*. Act of acuminating or sharpening; a pointed extremity; a sharp point or jag.

ac·u·punc·ture, ak′ū·pungk″chur, *n*. [L. *acus*, a needle, and *punctura*, a pricking. PUNCTURE.] First used by the Chinese, a surgical operation resorted to in certain complaints, as in headaches, neuralgia, rheumatism, etc.: the insertion of a delicate needle or set of needles into the body in order to draw off fluids or relieve pain.

a·cute, a·kūt′, *a*. [L. *acutus*, sharp-pointed, < *acuo*, to sharpen < root, *ac, ak*, a point. ACID.] Sharp at the end; ending in a sharp point: opposed to *blunt* or *obtuse*; intellectually sharp; perceiving minute distinctions; characterized by the use of minute distinctions; having keenness of insight: opposed to *dull* or *stupid*; having nice or quick sensibility; susceptible of slight impressions; as, *acute* hearing; keen; crucial; sharp: said of pain, high in pitch: said of sound; shrill; *med*. a term applied to a disease which is attended with more or less violent symptoms, and comes speedily to a crisis. Requiring immediate, serious attention; *geom*. less than a right angle, that is, less than 90°.—**a·cute·ly**, a·kūt′lē, *adv*. In an acute manner; sharply; keenly; with nice discrimination.—**a·cute·ness**, a·kūt′nis, *n*. The quality of being acute; sharpness; keenness; sagacity; acumen.

a·cy·clic, ā·sī′klik, ā·sik′lik, *a*. *Bot*. not cyclic; not arranged in whorls. *Chem*. pertaining to a compound with an open-chain structure.

ad, ad, *n*. *Colloq*. advertisement.

a·dac·ty·lous, ā·dak′te·lus, *a*. [Gr. *a-*, no, and *dactyl*, finger, toe.] Without fingers or toes.

ad·age, ad′ij, *n*. [Fr. *adage*, L. *adagium*, a proverb.] A proverb; an old saying which has obtained credit by long use and general understanding; maxim.

a·da·gio, a·dä′jō, a·dä′zhē·o″, *a., adv*. [It.] *Mus*. Slow; slowly, leisurely, and with grace.—*n*. A slow movement in music or ballet.

Ad·am, ad′am, *n*. The name of the first man: Gen. ii. 7. *Fig*. the frailty inherent in human nature, used esp. in the phrase *the old Adam*, as: He had a lot of *the old Adam* in him.—**A·dam·ic**, a·dam′ik, *a*.

ad·am-and-eve, ad′am·an·ēv″, *n*. The puttyroot plant; an orchid with yellow-brown flowers and a single leaf at its base.

ad·a·mant, ad′a·mant, ad′a·mant″, *n*. [L. *adamas, adamantis*, Gr. *adamas*, the hardest iron or steel, anything inflexibly hard; impenetrable, lit. 'the unconquerable.'—Gr. *a*, not, and *damao*, to tame. TAME, DIAMOND.] Any substance of impenetrable hardness: chiefly a rhetorical or poetical word. Formerly it sometimes meant the diamond, sometimes loadstone, from confusion with L. *adamantem* through the loving-attractive quality. —*a*. Utterly unyielding in opinion or ideas in spite of all urgings.—**ad·a·man·tean, ad·a·man·tine**, ad″a·man′tīn, ad″a·man′tēn, ad″a·man′tin, *a*. Made of or resembling adamant; impenetrable.— **ad·a·mant·ly**, *adv*. Unyielding.

Ad·am's ap·ple, *n*. The prominence on the fore part of the throat of the thyroid cartilage, predominant in men; also, the crape jasmine, a showy, sweet-smelling shrub.

Ad·am's nee·dle, *n.* The popular name of the plants otherwise called yucca, cultivated for ornament.

a·dapt, *a·*dapt', *v.t.* [L. *adapto—ad,* to, and *apto,* to fit. APT.] To make suitable; to make to correspond; to fit or suit; to proportion; to adjust; to conform.—*v.i.* To become adapted, as to environment.

a·dapt·a·bil·i·ty, *a·*dap"ta·bil'i·tē, *n.* Capability of being adapted.

a·dapt·a·ble, *a·*dap'ta·bl, *a.* Capable of being adapted; able to adjust oneself without difficulty to new, unfamiliar, or unexpected conditions.—**a·dapt·a·ble·ness,** *a·*dap'ta·bl·nis, *n.*

ad·ap·ta·tion, ad"ap·tā'shan, *n.* The act of adapting or making suitable; adjustment; the state of being suitable or fit; that which is adapted; *biol.* a change, as of an organism's structure, to conform to environment. *Sociol.* a slow modifying of a society's or an individual's behavior to adjust to cultural conditions; also *adaption.*

a·dapt·er, *a·*dap'tėr, *n.* One who or that which adapts; a connecting device enabling parts to be fitted together; as a threaded bushing used to adapt a fuse to a projectile; an accessory to change a machine to a new or modified use.

a·dap·tion, *a·*dap'shan, *n.* See *adaptation.*

a·dap·tive, *a·*dap'tiv, *a.* Tending to adapt.

ad·ax·i·al, ad·ak'sē·al, *adj. Bot.* toward or facing the axis, as the upper side of a leaf stalk.

add, ad, *v.t.* [L. *addo,* to add—*ad,* to, and *do,* to put, to place, to give.] To set or put together to become a larger number; to join or unite; to put into one sum; to annex; subjoin; say further.—*v.i.* To be or serve as an addition (with *to*); also, to perform the arithmetical operation of addition.—**add·a·ble, add·i·ble,** ad'a·bl, *a.* Capable of being added.

ad·dax, ad'aks, *n.* A species of large antelope with spiral horns which inhabits Africa and Arabia.

ad·dend, ad'end, *n.* [Short for *addendum.*] *Math.* a number or quantity which is added to a preceding or consequent quantity in forming a sum.

ad·den·dum, *a·*den'dum, *n. pl.* **ad·den·da,** *a·*den'da. [< L. neut. of *addendus,* gerundive of *addere,* add.] An addition; an appendix to a book or literary work; something which is added; *mach.* part of a gear tooth that projects beyond the pitch circle.

ad·der, ad'ėr, *n.* [M.E. *addre, addere,* by loss of initial *n* < O.E. *nædre, næddre,* by incorrect interpretation of *a nædre* as an *ædre.* O. and Prov. E. *nedder,* Icel. *nadr.* Goth. *nadrs,* G. *natter.*] A variety of venomous serpents, as the common viper, found in America and Europe.

add·er, ad'ėr, *n.* A person who adds; a machine used for adding.

ad·der's-tongue, ad'ėrz·tung", *n.* A fern of the genus *Ophioglossum,* having a spike somewhat suggestive of a snake's tongue; an American dogtooth violet.

ad·dict, *a·*dikt', *v.t.* [L. *addicere, addictum,* to assign, surrender—*ad,* to, and *dico,* to fix, determine.] To apply habitually; to habituate: generally with a reflexive pronoun, and with an undesirable connotation, followed by *to;* as, to *addict oneself to* narcotics.—**ad·dict·ed,** *a·*dik'tid, *a.* Habitually practicing; given to; devoted; habituated, followed by *to.*

ad·dict, ad'ikt, *n.* One who is addicted to a practice or a habit, esp. to narcotics.

ad·dic·tion, *a·*dik'shan, *n.* The state of being addicted or given up to a practice; the state of being strongly devoted; habitual, compulsive use of narcotics.

ad·dic·tive, *a·*dik'tiv, *a.* Causing addiction

or characterized by addiction; as, an *addictive* drug.

ad·dic·tive, *a·*dik'tiv, *n.* One of a class of drugs which are habit-forming in nature, as: An *addictive* was administered.

Ad·di·so·ni·an, ad"i·sō'nē·an, *a.* Pertaining to or characteristic of the English author Joseph Addison (1672–1719) or his style of writing.—*n.* A student of the writings of Addison.

Ad·di·son's dis·ease, ad'i·sunz. [From T. Addison (1793–1860), English physician who first described it.] *Pathol.* a disease characterized by asthenia, digestive disturbances, and usu. a brownish coloration of the skin due to disturbance of function of the suprarenal glands.

ad·di·tion, *a·*dish'an, *n.* The act or process of adding; the uniting of two or more numbers in one sum; the rule or branch of arithmetic which treats of adding numbers to determine the total; an increase; something added; *U.S.* a room, wing, etc. added to a building, or adjacent land added to real estate already owned.

ad·di·tion·al, *a·*dish'a·nal, *a.* Supplementary; more; added; extra.—**ad·di·tion·al·ly,** *a·*dish'a·nal·ē, *adv.*

ad·di·tive, ad'i·tiv, *a.* Additional; helping to increase; showing or relating to addition; cumulative.—*n.* A substance added in small amounts to another, for the improvement of desirable qualities or as a preservative for food. Specifically, a substance added to a propellant to achieve some purpose, such as a more even rate of combustion.

ad·dle, ad'el, *a.* [M.E. *adel,* filth < O.E. *adela;* Sw. *adel* (seen in *ko adel,* cow urine), urine; Sc. *addle,* putrid water, urine.] Confused; disoriented; mixed up mentally. Rotten, putrid: applied to eggs.—*v.t. addled, addling.* To confuse—*v.i.* To become confused; of eggs, to spoil.—**ad·dle·brained,** ad'l·brānd, *a.* Muddled; confused; witless. Also **ad·dle·head·ed, ad·dle·pat·ed.**

ad·dress, *a·*dres', *v.t.* [M.E. *addressen* < M.Fr. *adresser* < *a-* (< L. *ad-,* to) and *dresser,* arrange. DRESS.] To direct or aim (words); to pronounce; to apply to by words or writings; to accost; to speak to; to direct in writing; to write an address on; to court or make suit to. To direct (information) to a certain location in an electronic computer. —*v.i.* To make preparations.—**to ad·dress one·self to,** to speak to; apply oneself to a task.

ad·dress, *a·*dres', ad'res, *n.* The act of turning one's attention and conversation to a person; a speaking to; any speech or writing in which one person or set of persons communicates with another person or set of persons; manner of speaking to another; a person's bearing in conversation; courtship (in this sense generally in the plural); direction of a letter as it appears on the envelope; the place or the name of the place where a person may be reached.

ad·dress, *a·*dres', ad'res, *n. Computers,* a location, in the memory of a computer, in which data is kept, to which data is sent, or from which data is drawn; any part of an instruction to a computer that specifies, by name, label, or number, the location of data to be operated on in that instruction.

ad·dress·ee, ad"re·sē', *a·*dre·sē', *n.* One who is addressed; one to whom a letter is addressed.

ad·duce, *a·*dōs', *a·*dūs', *v.t.—adduced, adducing.* [L. *adduco,* to lead or bring to— *ad,* to, and *duco,* to lead. DUKE.] To cite; to name or instance as authority or evidence; to bring to notice as bearing on a subject.— **ad·duc·er,** *a·*dōs'ėr, *a·*dūs'ėr, *n.* One who adduces.—**ad·duc·i·ble,** *a·*dōs'i·bl, *a·*dūs'i·bl, *a.* Capable of being adduced.

ad·du·cent, *a·*dō'sent, *a·*dū'sent, *a.* [L. *adducent,* stem of *adducens,* leading to, ppr.

of *adducere.*] Bringing forward or together (an *adducent* muscle).

ad·duct, *a·*dukt', *v.t.* [L. *adductus,* pp. of *adducere:* ADDUCE.] *Anat.* to draw (one's limb) toward the body's main axis.

ad·duc·tion, *a·*duk'shan, *n.* The act of adducing; *anat.* the action by which a part of the body is drawn toward the bodily axis.—**ad·duc·tive,** *a·*duk'tiv, *a.*

a·de·lan·ta·do, ad"e·län·tä'dō, *n.* [Sp.] Formerly, in Spanish use, the governor of a province; any of the early explorers or colonists in Spanish America.

a·demp·tion, *a·*demp'shan, *n. Law,* the act of revoking a legacy.

ad·e·nine, ad'e·nin, ad'e·nēn", ad'e·nīn", *n. Chem.* one of the purine bases, C_5H_3-N_4NH_2, a white, crystalline alkaloid, obtained from tea, glandular organs, or from uric acid: used chiefly in medicine.

ad·e·no·car·ci·no·ma, ad'e·nō·kär"si·nō'ma, *n. Pathol.* a malignant tumor which appears in glandular epithelium.

ad·e·noid, ad'e·noid", *n. Usu. pl., pathol.* an enlarged mass of lymphoid tissue in the upper pharynx, hindering nasal breathing. —*a.* Of glands or adenoids. Also **ad·e·noi·dal.**—**ad·e·nol·o·gy,** ad'e·nol'o·jē, *n.* The science or study of the glands.

ad·e·no·ma, ad"e·nō'ma, *n. pl.* **ad·e·no·mas,** ad·e·no·ma·ta, ad"e·nō'ma·ta. [N.L.] *Pathol.* A benign tumor originating in a gland; a tumor of glandlike structure. —**ad·e·nom·a·tous,** ad"e·nōm'a·tus, *a.*—**ad·e·nop·a·thy,** ad"e·nop'a·thē, *n.* Disease of glands.—**ad·e·no·path·ic,** ad"e·nō·path'ik, *a.*—**ad·e·not·o·my,** ad"e·not'o·mē, *n.* Dissection or incision of a gland.

a·den·o·sine, *a·*den'o·sēn", *a·*den'o·sin, *n. Chem.* a crystalline nucleoside, $C_{10}H_{13}$-N_5O_4, derived from the nucleic acid of yeast, which upon undergoing hydrolysis yields adenine and ribose.

a·den·o·sine di·phos·phate, *n.* A coenzyme important to the transfer of energy through the cell during glycolysis: found in all living cells. Abbr. *ADP.*

a·den·o·sine tri·phos·phate, *n.* A nucleotide that occurs in all cells. It represents the reserve energy of muscle and is important to many biochemical processes that produce or require energy. Abbr. *ATP.*

a·dept, ad'ept, *a·*dept', *n.* [L. *adeptus,* pp. of *adipisci,* to obtain. Alchemists who were reputed to have obtained the philosopher's stone were termed *adepts;* hence *adept,* a proficient.] One fully skilled or well versed in any art; a trained expert; a proficient.

a·dept, *a·*dept', *a.* Well-skilled; proficient. —**a·dept·ly,** *a·*dept'lē, *adv.*—**a·dept·ness,** *a·*dept'nis, *n.*

ad·e·qua·cy, ad'e·kwa·sē, *n.* The state of being adequate; sufficiency for a particular purpose.

ad·e·quate, ad'e·kwit, *a.* [L. *adaequatus,* made equal, pp. of *adaequare—ad,* to, and *aequus,* equal.] Equal; proportionate; exactly correspondent; suitable; fully sufficient; barely suitable or sufficient. *Law,* reasonably sufficient.—**ad·e·quate·ly,** ad'e·kwit·lē, *adv.* In an adequate manner; sufficiently.— **ad·e·quate·ness,** ad'e·kwit·nis, *n.* The state of being adequate; sufficiency.

ad eun·dem, ad" ē·an'dem, *adv., a.* [L. *ad eundem gradum,* to the same rank.] In, to, or of the same rank, used primarily in the bestowing of honorary academic degrees.

ad·here, ad·hēr', *v.i.—adhered, adhering.* [L. *adhaerere—ad,* to, and *haerere,* to stick, whence *hesitate.*] To stick together; to cling; to become closely joined or united; to be fixed in attachment or devotion, usu. followed by *to;* as, to *adhere to* a belief.

ad·her·ence, ad·hēr'ens, *n.* The quality or state of adhering; fidelity; steady attachment.

---

ad·her·end, ad·hēr'end, ad"hi·rend', n. [*adhere* and *-end* (gerundive suffix < L. *-endus*).] *Chem.* a substance or surface which is held to another by an adhesive.

ad·her·ent, ad·hēr'ent, a. [M.E. < M.Fr. or M.L. < L. *adhaerent-*, ppr. of *adhaerere*.] Sticking fast to something; clinging; attached; *gram.* modifying and standing before a noun. *Bot.* adnate; congenitally attached.—**ad·her·ent·ly**, ad·hēr'ent·lē, *adv.* In an adherent manner.

ad·her·ent, ad·hēr'ent, n. One who adheres; one who follows a leader, party, cause or profession; a follower or partisan.

ad·he·sion, ad·hē'zhan, n. [L. *adhaesio*, < *adhaerere*, to adhere.] The act or state of adhering, or being united and attached; a sticking together of the surface of bodies; close connection or association; steady attachment of the mind or feelings; assent; concurrence; as, *adhesion* to a treaty. *Surg.* a growth of scar tissue resulting from an incision. *Bot.* the union of usually separate parts.

ad·he·sive, ad·hē'siv, n. A substance used to make one object adhere to another, as mucilage or glue.

ad·he·sive, ad·hē'siv, a. Sticky; gummy; tenacious.—**ad·he·sive·ly**, ad·hē'siv·lē, *adv.* In an adhesive manner.—**ad·he·sive·ness**, ad·hē'siv·nis, n. The state or quality of being adhesive.

ad·he·sive tape, n. Tape with a gummy substance on one side and having various uses, such as holding a bandage in place.

ad hoc, ad hok', a., adv. [L.] For this particular purpose; without wider application or prior justification; as, an *ad hoc* explanation.

ad hoc com·mit·tee, n. A committee that is established for one specific reason or occasion.

ad ho·mi·nem, ad hō'mi·nem", a. [L., to the man.] Appealing to a person's prejudices and personal feelings rather than his intellect and reason; attacking the character or background of an opponent in order to discredit or instead of answering his argument.

ad·i·a·bat·ic, ad"ē·a·bat'ik, ā"dī·a·bat'ik, a. [Gr. *a*, not, *diabainō*, pass through.] Of physical changes without gain or loss of heat.—**ad·i·a·bat·ic curve**, curve showing relation between the volume and the pressure of a fluid which changes its volume without gain or loss of heat.

ad·i·aph·o·ra, ad·ē·af'o·ra, n. pl. [N.L. < Gr. *adiaphora*, neut. pl. *adiaphoros*, indifferent, < *a-* not, and *diaphoros*, different < *diapherein*, differ.] Things morally indifferent; matters that have no moral merit or demerit; nonessentials in faith or conduct.—**ad·i·aph·or·ism**, ad"ē·af'o·rizm, n. Indifferentism; religious tolerance.—**ad·i·aph·o·rous**, ad"ē·af'or·us, a. Indifferent or nonessential, esp. morally; neutral.

ad·i·a·ther·ma·nous, ad"ē·a·thér'ma·nus, a. *Phys.* not diathermanous; impermeable by radiant heat.—**ad·i·a·ther·man·cy**, ad"ē·a·thér'man·sē, n.

a·dieu, a·dō', a·dū', interj. [Fr. *à*, to, and *Dieu*, God, It. *addio*, Span. *a dios*, all forms of L. *ad*, to, and *Deus*, God.] *Lit.* to God: an ellipsis for I commend you to God. Farewell; good-by: an expression of kind wishes at the parting of friends.—n. pl. **a·dieus, a·dieux**, a·dōz', a·dūz'.

ad in·fi·ni·tum, ad in"fi·nī'tum, a. [L.] Endless.—*adv.*

a·di·os, ä"dē·ōs', ad"ē·ōs', interj. [Sp.] Adieu; good-by; farewell.

ad·i·pose, ad'i·pōs", a. [< L. *adeps, adipis*, fat.] Fatty; consisting of or resembling fat.—n. Fat; animal fat stored in the cells of adipose tissue; the fat on the kidneys.—**ad·i·pos·i·ty**, ad"i·po'si·tē, n. Obesity.

ad·i·pose tis·sue, n. Animal tissue in which fat is stored, made up of connective tissue composing the fat of meat.

ad·it, ad'it, n. [L. *aditus*—*ad*, to, and *ire, itum*, to go.] Approach; entrance; access; passage; a more or less horizontal passage into a mine.

ad·ja·cen·cy, a·jā'sen·sē, n. pl. **ad·ja·cen·cies**. The state of being adjacent; contiguity; a radio or television announcement or broadcast which immediately precedes or follows another.

ad·ja·cent, a·jā'sent, a. [L. *adjacens, adjacentis*, pp. of *adjacere*, to lie contiguous.—*ad*, to, and *jacere*, to lie.] Lying near or close; bordering upon; neighboring; adjoining.—**ad·ja·cent·ly**, a·jā'sent·lē, *adv.*

ad·jec·ti·val, aj"ik·tī'val, a. Belonging to or like an adjective; having the import of an adjective.—**ad·jec·ti·val·ly, ad·jec·tive·ly**, aj"ik·tī'va·lē, aj'ik·tiv·lē, *adv.* By way of, or as, an adjective.

ad·jec·tive, aj'ik·tiv, n. [M.E., < M.Fr. *adjectif* < L. *adjectivum, adjectivus*, added.—*ad*, to, and *jacere*, to throw.] *Gram.* a word used with a noun to express a quality of the thing named, or something attributed to it, or to specify or describe a thing as distinct from something else, and so to limit and define it.—a. Dependent; additional; functioning as an adjective; adjectival; not standing alone; relevant to dyes which require a mordant that makes them permanent.

ad·join, a·join', v.t. [M.E. *adjoinen* < M.Fr. *adjoindre*; L. *adjungo*—*ad*, to, and *jungo*, to join. JOIN.] To join or add; to be adjacent to; to unite; to annex or append.—v.i. To lie or be next or in contact; to be contiguous.

ad·join·ing, a·joi'ning, a. Adjacent; contiguous; neighboring; in the closest relative position to.

ad·journ, a·jurn', v.t. [M.E. < M.Fr. *ajourner*, O.Fr. *ajorner, adjorner*—prefix *a, ad*, to, and O.Fr. *jorn* (now *jour*), a day, L. *diurnus*, diurnal, < *dies*, a day. DIURNAL; JOURNEY.] To put off or defer to another day or until a later period; to suspend the meeting of, as of a public or private body, to a future day; to postpone to a future meeting of the same body.—v.i. To cease sitting and carrying on business for a time; to suspend proceedings.

ad·journ·ment, a·jurn'ment, n. The act of adjourning; the period during which a legislature or other public body adjourns its sittings.

ad·judge, a·juj', v.t.—*adjudged, adjudging*. [M.E. < M.Fr. *ajugier* < L. *adjudicare* < *ad-* and *judicare*, to judge. JUDGE.] To declare or pronounce formally by law; to award judicially; to sentence or condemn; to adjudicate upon; to settle; to rule upon.

ad·ju·di·cate, a·jö'di·kāt", v.t.—*adjudicated, adjudicating*. [L. *adjudico*, to give sentence—*ad*, to, and *judico*, to judge. JUDGE.] To adjudge; to award judicially.—v.i. To sit in judgment; to give a judicial decision.—**ad·ju·di·ca·tor**, a·jö'di·kā"tor, n. One who adjudicates.

ad·ju·di·ca·tion, a·jö'di·kā'shan, n. The act of adjudicating; the act or process of trying and determining judicially; a decree, judgment or decision of a court.

ad·junct, aj'ungkt, a. [L. *adjunctus*, pp. of *adjungere*: ADJOIN.] Joined to a thing or person, esp. subordinately; associated; auxiliary.—**ad·junc·tive**, a·jungk'tiv, a. Forming an adjunct.—**ad·junct·ly**, aj·ungkt'lē, *adv.*

ad·junct, aj'ungkt, n. Something joined, annexed, or pertaining; an accompaniment; an accessory; also, a subordinate colleague; an associate or assistant; *gram.* a qualifying word, phrase, etc., depending on a particular member of a sentence.

ad·junc·tion, a·jungk'shan, n. [L. *adjunc-*

tio, < *adjungere*.] The act of adjoining; addition.

ad·ju·ra·tion, aj"u·rā'shan, n. The act of adjuring; an earnest request; a solemn oath.—**ad·jur·a·to·ry**, a·jur'a·tōr"ē, a.·jur'a·tąr"ē, a. Containing an adjuration, or characterized by adjurations.

ad·jure, a·jur', v.t.—*adjured, adjuring*. [M.E. < L. *adjuro*.—*ad*, to, and *juro*, to swear.] To charge, bind, command, or entreat earnestly and solemnly, as with an oath.—**ad·jur·er**, a·jur'ér, n. One who adjures.

ad·just, a·just', v.t. [Fr. *ajuster*, L.L. *adjuxtare*, to bring together—*ad*, and *juxta*.] To harmonize; to make correspondent; to fix; to put in order; to regulate or reduce to a system; settle or bring to a satisfactory state, so that parties are agreed on the result. *Milit.* to correct the sight of (a gun) for accurate aim.—v.i. To conform oneself; to adapt.

ad·just, a·just', v.t. *Insurance*, to decide the amount paid in settlement of (a claim).—**ad·jus·tor**, a·just'ér, n. One who adjusts insurance claims.

ad·just·a·ble, a·just'a·bl, a. Capable of being adjusted or regulated for a specific purpose; *aeron.* an aircraft component subject to being set or fixed in two or more positions; as, an *adjustable* wing.

ad·just·er, ad·jus·tor, a·just'ér, n. One who or that which adjusts.

ad·just·ment, a·just'ment, n. The act of adjusting; adaptation to a need; the means of adjusting, such as with a dial or lever; the settlement of a disputed claim; a change, as in cost, to satisfy specific conditions.

ad·ju·tan·cy, aj'u·tan·sē, n. The office held by an adjutant.

ad·ju·tant, aj'u·tant, n. [L. *adjutans*, ppr. of *adjuto*, to assist—*ad*, and *juvo, jutum*, to help.] *Milit.* an officer whose duty is to assist a commanding officer by receiving and communicating orders. An assistant.

ad·ju·tant bird, n. A very large wading bird allied to the storks, a native of the warmer parts of India, which feeds on carrion; also **ad·ju·tant crane, ad·ju·tant stork**.

ad·ju·tant gen·er·al, n. pl. **ad·ju·tants gen·er·al**. *Milit.* the chief administrative officer of the U.S. Army or of a major military unit.

ad·ju·vant, aj'u·vant, n. An assistant; *med.* a substance added to a prescription to aid the operation of the principal ingredient or basis.—a. Auxiliary; helping.

Ad·le·ri·an, ad·lér'ē·an, a. Pertaining to Alfred Adler or his doctrines in psychiatry and psychology.—**Ad·le·ri·an psy·chol·o·gy**, n. An approach to psychology based on the hypothesis that behavior is governed by an effort to compensate for inferiority or deficiency.

ad lib, ad lib', ad'lib', adv. [L. *ad libitum*.] Without restriction or limit.—n. Something ad-libbed.—**ad-lib**, a. Improvised; spoken without preparation.—v.t.—*ad-libbed, ad-libbing*. To improvise; to deliver spontaneously.—v.i. To speak or act without preparation.

ad lib·i·tum, ad lib'i·tum, adv. *Mus.* As one wishes: a direction to the performer, opposed to *obbligato*.

ad·man, ad'man", ad'man , n. pl. **ad·men**. One whose business is to compose, design, or solicit advertisements; also, advertising man.—**ad·wom·an**, ad'wum"an, n.

ad·meas·ure, ad·mezh'ér, v.t.—*admeasured, admeasuring*. [M.E. < M.Fr. < *a-* and *mesurer*, measure. MEASURE.] To ascertain the dimensions, size, or capacity of; to measure; to apportion; *naut.* to ascertain by measurements the dimensions and capacity of a (vessel.)

ad·meas·ure·ment, ad·mezh′ur·ment, *n.* The act of admeasuring; apportionment; the measure of a thing, or dimensions ascertained.

ad·min·is·ter, ad·min′i·stėr, *v.t.* [M.E. < M.Fr. < L. *administro*—*ad,* to, and *ministro,* to serve. MINISTER.] To manage or conduct as chief agent or directing and controlling official; to direct or superintend the execution of, as of laws; to afford, give, furnish, or supply; to give, as a dose of medicine; to dispense or distribute; to tender, as an oath; *law,* to manage, as the estate of a deceased person, collecting debts, paying legacies, etc.—*v.i.* To contribute assistance; to bring aid or supplies: with *to*; as, to *administer to* one's necessities; *law,* to perform the office of administrator.—**ad·min·is·tra·ble,** ad·-min′i·stra·bl, *a.*

ad·min·is·trate, ad·min′i·strāt″, *v.t.*—*administrated, administrating.* To administer.

ad·min·is·tra·tion, ad·min″i·strā′shan, *n.* The act of administering; direction; management; government of public affairs; the executive functions of government; the persons, collectively, who are entrusted with such functions, and their period of being in office; the executive; *law,* the management of the estate of a deceased person, consisting of collecting debts, paying debts and legacies, and distributing the property among the heirs.

ad·min·is·tra·tive, ad·min′i·strā″tiv, ad·min′i·stra·tiv, *a.* Pertaining to or resulting from administration or management.

ad·min·is·tra·tive coun·ty, *n.* A local administrative district in Britain, as opposed to the older county.

ad·min·is·tra·tor, ad·min′i·strā″tor, *n.* One who administers, or who directs, manages, distributes, or dispenses; one who has charge of the goods and estate of a person dying without a will.—**ad·min·is·tra·tor·ship,** ad·min′i·strā″tor·ship″, *n.* The office of an administrator.—**ad·min·is·tra·trix,** ad·min″i·strā′triks, ad″min·-i·strā′triks, *n.* A female administrator.

ad·mi·ra·ble, ad″mer·a·bl, *a.* Worthy of admiration, reverence, respect, or affection; most excellent.—**ad·mi·ra·ble·ness,** ad″-mer·a·bl·nis, *n.*—**ad·mi·ra·bly,** ad″mer·a·blē, *adv.* In an admirable manner; excellently; exceedingly well.

ad·mi·ral, ad″mir·al, *n.* [M.E. *amiral,* Fr. *amiral,* < Ar. *amir, emir,* a prince, chief, with the Ar. article suffixed.] Commander in chief of a fleet; highest rank of naval officer; high rank of naval officer: in U.S. Navy grades are fleet admiral, admiral, vice admiral, and rear admiral. Either of two species of butterflies, *Vanessa atalanta,* or red admiral, and *Limenitis camilla,* or white admiral.

ad·mi·ral of the fleet, *n.* The officer holding the highest rank in the British Navy.

ad·mi·ral·ty, ad″mir·al·tē, *n.* pl. **ad·-mi·ral·ties.** Jurisdiction of an admiral; *Brit.* department of state having charge of naval affairs. Court concerned with maritime problems.—**the Ad·mi·ral·ty,** official building of British commission for naval affairs in London.

ad·mi·ra·tion, ad″mi·rā′shan, *n.* Wonder mingled with pleasing emotions, as approbation, esteem, love, or veneration; an emotion excited by something beautiful or excellent.

ad·mire, ad·mīer′, *v.t.*—*admired, admiring.* [M.Fr. *admirer,* L. *admiror*—*ad,* and *miror,* to wonder.] To regard with wonder mingled with approbation, esteem, reverence, or affection; to take pleasure in the excellence or beauty of; to look on or contemplate with pleasure.—*v.i.* To feel or express admiration.—**ad·mir·er,** ad·mīer′-

ėr, *n.* One who admires; one who esteems greatly; one who openly shows his admiration of a woman; a lover.—**ad·mir·ing·ly,** ad·mīer′ing·lē, *adv.* In an admiring manner; with admiration.

ad·mis·si·bil·i·ty, ad·mis′i·bil″i·tē, *n.* The quality of being admissible.

ad·mis·si·ble, ad·mis′i·bl, *a.* [Fr. *admissible,* L.L. *admissibilis,* from *admitto, admissum,* to admit.] Capable of being admitted, allowed; deserving; conceded.—**ad·mis·si·bly,** ad·mis′i·blē, *adv.* In an admissible manner; so as to be admitted.

ad·mis·sion, ad·mish′an, *n.* [L. *admissio.*] The act of admitting; power or permission to enter; a fee charged for entrance; entrance; access; power to approach; the granting of an argument or position not fully proved; a point or statement admitted; acknowledgment; confession of a charge, error, or crime; an acknowledgment of the veracity of a statement or thing.—**ad·mis·sive,** ad·mis′iv, *a.* Having the nature of an admission.

ad·mit, ad·mit′, *v.t.*—*admitted, admitting.* [M.E. < L. *admitto*—*ad,* and *mitto, missum,* to send, seen also in *commit, submit, mission,* etc.] To allow to enter; to grant entrance to; to give right of entrance to; to give access to a society, corporation, place, privileges, etc.; to grant in argument; to accept as true; to permit, grant, or allow, or to be capable of; to acknowledge; to own; to confess.—*v.i.* To give warrant or allowance; to grant opportunity; to afford possibility; to permit: with *of,* as: The words do not *admit* of this interpretation.—**ad·mit·ted·ly,** ad·mit′id·lē, *adv.* By admission, acknowledgment, or concession.

ad·mit·tance, ad·mit′ans, *n.* The act of admitting; permission to enter; entrance; *elect.* the measure of the capacity of a circuit to carry an alternating current.

ad·mix, ad·miks′, *v.t.* [M.E. *admixt* < L. *admixtus.*] To mingle with something else; to blend.

ad·mix·ture, ad·miks′cher, *n.* The act of mingling or mixing; that which is formed by mingling; any ingredient which is added to a mixture.

ad·mon·ish, ad·mon′ish, *v.t.* [M.E. *ad-monissen, admonesten, amonesten,* M.Fr. *amonester,* to admonish—prefix, *a, ad,* and L.L. *monestum,* for L. *monitum,* pp. of *moneo,* to warn. MONITION.] To warn or notify of a fault; to reprove with mildness; to counsel against wrong practices; to caution, advise, or exhort; to instruct or direct; to remind; to recall or urge to duty.—**ad·mon·ish·er,** ad·mon′ish·ėr, *n.* One who admonishes; also **ad·mon·i·tor.**

ad·mo·ni·tion, ad″mo·nish′an, *n.* The act of admonishing; counsel or advice; a warning; gentle reproof; instruction in duties; caution; direction.

ad·mon·i·to·ry, ad·mon′i·tōr″ē, ad·-mon′i·tạr″ē, *a.* Containing admonition; tending or serving to admonish; expressing a warning.

ad·nate, ad′nāt, *a.* [L. *adnatus*—*ad,* to, and *natus,* grown.] Growing congenitally attached: chiefly in botany.—**ad·na·tion,** ad·nā′shan, *n.* The state of existing in an adnate condition.

ad nau·se·am, ad nạ′shē·um, *adv.* [L.] Sickeningly; to the point of being sickening.

a·do, a·dö′, *n.* [M.E. *at do.* AT. DO.] Bustle; fuss; trouble; labor; difficulty; turmoil.

a·do·be, a·dō′bē, *n.* [Sp. < Ar. *at-tub,* brick.] A sun-dried brick, or the clay used in making this type of brick; a house, wall, etc., that is made of sun-dried brick.

ad·o·les·cence, ad″o·les′ans, *n.* [L. *ado-lescentia*—*ad,* and *olesco,* to grow.] The state of growing: applied almost exclusively to the young of the human race; youth, or the

period of life between childhood and the full development of the body, or from puberty to full maturity.

ad·o·les·cent, ad″o·les′ent, *a.* Growing up; characteristic of adolescence; advancing from childhood to manhood or womanhood.—*n.* One who is in his teens and is in his adolescence.

A·do·nai, ä″dō·nī′, ä″dō·noi′, *n.* [Heb. *adonai,* lit. 'my lords,' < *adon,* lord.] A Hebrew name of God, reverentially used in reading as a substitute for the "ineffable name," Heb. JHVH, commonly rendered in English by *Jehovah.* Also, Christ, the Second Person of the Blessed Trinity.

A·don·ic, a·don′ik, a·don′ik, *a.* [Fr. *adonique.*] Of or pertaining to Adonis, a beautiful youth of Greek mythology; *pros.* noting a verse consisting of a dactyl and a spondee or trochee, said to have been so designated because of its use in songs at the festival of Adonis.—*n.* An Adonic verse or line.

a·dopt, a·dopt′, *v.t.* [L. *adopto*—*ad,* and *opto,* to desire or choose. OPTION.] To take into one's family and treat as one's own child, esp. legally; to take to oneself by choice or approval, as policies, principles, opinions, a course of conduct, etc.—**a·dopt·a·ble,** a·dopt′a·bl, *a.* Capable of, fit for, or worthy of being adopted.—**a·dopt·er,** a·dopt′ėr, *n.* One who adopts.

a·dop·tion, a·dop′shan, *n.* [L. *adoptio.*] The act of adopting, or the state of being adopted.

a·dop·tion·ism, a·dop′shan·izm, *n.* (*Often cap.*) the belief that Jesus Christ became the son of God through adoption, and was not born as such.

a·dop·tive, a·dop′tiv, *a.* Constituted by adoption; adopting or adopted; assumed.—**a·dop·tive·ly,** *adv.*

a·dor·a·bil·i·ty, a·dōr″a·bil′i·tē, a·dạr″-a·bil′i·tē, *n.* Quality of being adorable.

a·dor·a·ble, a·dōr′a·bl, a·dạr′a·bl, *a.* Demanding adoration; worthy of being adored; exquisitely charming; delightful; lovable.—**a·dor·a·ble·ness,** a·dōr′a·bl·nis, a·dạr′a·bl·nis, *n.*—**a·dor·a·bly,** a·dōr′a·blē, a·dạr′a·blē, *adv.* In a manner worthy of adoration.

ad·o·ra·tion, ad″o·rā′shan, *n.* The act of adoring; the act of paying honor and reverence, as to a divine being; worship addressed to a deity; the highest degree of love, as of a man for a woman.

a·dore, a·dōr′, a·dạr′, *v.t.*—*adored, adoring.* [M.Fr. < L. *adoro,* to pray, to adore—*ad,* to, and *oro,* to ask. ORACLE.] To worship with profound reverence; to honor or to pay divine honor to; to regard with the utmost devotion, esteem, love, and respect; to love in the highest degree, as a man and a woman. —**a·dor·er,** a·dōr′ėr, a·dạr′ėr, *n.* One who adores; one who worships or honors as divine; a lover.—**a·dor·ing·ly,** *adv.*

a·dorn, a·dạrn′, *v.t.* [M.E. < L. *adorno*—*ad,* to, and *orno,* to deck or beautify.] To deck or decorate; to add to the attractiveness of by dress or ornaments; to set off to advantage.

a·dorn·ment, a·dạrn′ment, *n.* An ornament or decoration, as jewelry; the act of adorning.

ad·re·nal, a·drē′nal, *a.* [L. *ad,* near, and *renes,* kidney.] On or near the kidney; pertaining to a product of the adrenal gland.—*n.* An adrenal gland.

ad·re·nal gland, a·drē′nal, *n.* A small endocrine gland, consisting of a cortex and medulla, attached to the kidney.

a·dren·a·line, a·dren′a·lin, a·dren′a·lēn″, *n.* Epinephrine, a hormone secreted by the medulla of the adrenal gland.—**A·dren·a·lin, a·dren·a·lin,** a·dren′a·lin, *n.* A drug used as a heart stimulant, muscle relaxant, etc. (Trademark.)

---

a- fat, fāte, fär, fâre, fạll;   **e-** met, mē, mēre, hėr;   **i-** pin, pīne;   **o-** not, nōte, möve;   **u-** tub, cūbe, bụll;   **oi-** oil;   **ou-** pound.

ad·ren·er·gic, ad″re·nĕr′jik, *a. Med.* liberated or activated by adrenaline or a similar substance.

a·dre·no·cor·ti·co·trop·ic, a·drē′nŏ·kar″ti·kō·trop′ik, *a.* Affecting the adrenal cortex. Also **a·dre·no·cor·ti·co·troph·ic,** a·drē′nŏ·kar″ti·kō·trof′ik.—**ad·re·no·cor·ti·co·trop·ic hor·mone,** *n.* ACTH.

a·drift, a·drift′, *a.* or *adv.* [Prefix *a*, on, and *drift*, a driving or floating. DRIVE.] Floating at random; moving without direction; at the mercy of winds and currents; swayed by any chance impulse; at sea; at a loss; lacking guidance.

a·droit, a·droit′, *a.* [Fr. *adroit*, dexterous—*a*, to, and *droit*, right, as opposed to left (cf. *dexterous*, < L. *dexter*, right); < L. *directus*, straight, direct.] Expert; nimble; active in the use of the hand, and, figuratively, in the exercise of the mental faculties; ingenious; ready in invention or execution.—**a·droit·ly,** a·droit′lē, *adv.*—**a·droit·ness,** a·droit′nis, *n.*

ad·sci·ti·tious, ad″si·tish′us, *a.* [L. *adscitus*, pp. of *adsciscere*, accept, take, < *ad*, to, and *sciscere*, learn, approve, < *scire*, know.] Derived from without; adventitious; extrinsic.—**ad·sci·ti·tious·ly,** ad″si·tish′us·lē, *adv.*

ad·script, ad′skript, *a.* [L. *adscisco*, to enroll—*ad*, to, and *scribo*, to write.] Written to the right of and in line with another letter or symbol: distinguished from *subscript*.—*n.* An adscript character.

ad·sorb, ad·sarb′, ad·zarb′, *v.t.* To collect, as molecules of gases, dissolved substances, or liquids, in a thin layer on a surface.

ad·sorb·ate, ad·sar′bāt, ad·sar′bit, ad·zar′bāt, ad·zar′bit, *n.* The adsorbed substance in the process of adsorption.

ad·sor·bent, ad·sarb′ent, ad·zarb′ent, *a.* Having the ability or tendency to adsorb; adsorbing.

ad·sorp·tion, ad·sarp′shan, ad·zarp′shan, *n.* Adhesion of a thin layer of liquid or gas to the surface of solid bodies or liquids, in which adhesion the solid does not combine chemically with the adsorbed substance; the adhesion of molecules to a surface, as distinguished from *absorption*.

ad·u·lar·i·a, aj″u·lâr′ē·a, *n.* [It. < Fr. *Adula*, mountains in Switzerland where fine specimens are found.] A very pure, limpid, translucent variety of the common feldspar; also *moonstone.*

ad·u·la·tion, aj″u·lā′shan, *n.* [L. *adulatio, adulationis,* a fawning, *adulor, adulatus,* to flatter.] Servile flattery; praise in excess, or beyond what is merited; high compliment. —**ad·u·late,** aj′u·lāt″, *v.t.*—*adulated, adulating.* To show feigned devotion to; to flatter servilely or excessively.—**ad·u·la·tor,** aj′u·lā″tor, *n.*—**ad·u·la·to·ry,** aj′u·la·tŏr″ē, aj′u·la·tar″ē, *a.*

a·dult, a·dult′, ad′ult, *a.* [L. *adultus,* pp. of *adolescere,* grow up. ADOLESCENCE.] Grown-up; full-grown; mature; suitable for an adult.—*n.* A person who is grown-up or of legal age; a full-grown animal or plant.

a·dul·ter·ant, a·dul′tĕr·ant, *a.* The thing that adulterates.—*a.*

a·dul·ter·ate, a·dul′te·rāt″, *v.t.*—*adulterated, adulterating.* [L. *adultero,* from *adulter,* mixed, an adulterer—*ad,* to, and *alter,* other.] To debase or deteriorate by an admixture of foreign or baser materials.—**a·dul·ter·a·tor,** a·dul′te·rā″tĕr, *n.*

a·dul·ter·ate, a·dul′te·rāt″, a·dul′te·rit, *a.* Adulterated or adulterous; being adulterated in form, or manner, etc.

a·dul·ter·a·tion, a·dul″te·rā′shan, *n.* The act of adulterating, or the state of being adulterated; an adulterated substance, product, or condition.

a·dul·ter·er, a·dul′tĕr·ĕr, *n.* A person guilty of adultery.

a·dul·ter·ess, a·dul′ter·is, a·dul′tris, *n.* A woman guilty of adultery.

a·dul·ter·ine, a·dul′tĕr·in, a·dul′te·rēn″, a·dul′te·rīn″, *a.* Born of or involving adultery; adulterated; impure; spurious.

a·dul·ter·ous, a·dul′ter·us, *a.* Guilty of adultery; pertaining to adultery; illicit.— **a·dul·ter·ous·ly,** a·dul′ter·us·lē, *adv.*

a·dul·ter·y, a·dul′te·rē, *n.* [L. *adulterium,* < *adulter,* an adulterer. ADULTERATE.] Voluntary sexual intercourse by a married person with one who is not his or her spouse.

ad·um·brate, ad·um′brāt, ad′um·brāt″, *v.t.*—*adumbrated, adumbrating.* [L. *adumbro,* to shade—*ad,* and *umbra,* a shade.] To give a faint shadow or brief outline of; to overshadow; shade or obscure partially; to vaguely foreshadow.—**ad·um·bra·tion,** ad″um·brā′shan, *n.* The act of adumbrating or foreshadowing; a faint or imperfect representation of a thing.—**ad·um·bra·tive,** ad·um′bra·tiv, ad′um·brā″tiv, *a.*—**ad·um·bra·tive·ly,** ad·um′bra·tiv·lē, *adv.*

a·dust, a·dust′, *a.* [M.E. < L. *adustus,* burned—*ad,* to, and *uro, ustum,* to burn.] Burned; scorched; parched; looking as if burned or scorched; dusty. Gloomy in mood or appearance.

ad·va·lo·rem, ad va·lōr′um, ad va·lar′um. [L.] According to value: a phrase used, often adjectively, for duties or charges representing a fixed percentage of the certified value of goods.

ad·vance, ad·vans′, ad·väns′, *v.t.*—*advanced, advancing.* [M.E. < O.Fr. *avancer,* < *avant,* forward (whence also E. *van*), < *abante,* < *before,* in front—*ab,* and *ante,* before.] To bring forward; to move further in front; to promote; to raise to a higher rank; to forward or further; to move forward or place later in time; to encourage the progress of; to hasten or place earlier in time; to enhance (price); to accelerate the growth of; to offer or propose; to bring to view or notice, as something one is prepared to abide by; to allege; to supply beforehand; to furnish on credit, or before goods are delivered, or work done.—*v.i.* To move or go forward; to proceed; to make progress; to grow better, greater, wiser, or older; to rise in rank, office, or consequence.—*a.* Placed before; furnished or completed ahead of time or beforehand.— **ad·vanced,** ad·vanst′, ad·vänst′, *a.* Being in advance; having gone beyond an initial or elementary stage; progressive.

ad·vance, ad·vans′, ad·väns′, *n.* A moving forward; gradual progression; improvement; advancement; promotion; a proposal; a first step toward; addition to price; rise in price; a giving beforehand; that which is given beforehand, especially money.—**in ad·vance,** in front, before; beforehand; before an equivalent is received.

ad·vance·ment, ad·vans′ment, *n.* The act of advancing; the state of being advanced; the act of promoting; improvement; furtherance.

ad·van·tage, ad·van′taj, *n.* [M.E. *avauntage, avantage,* < M.Fr. *avant,* before, forward, < L.L. *abante.* ADVANCE.] A favorable factor or circumstance affording superiority; a favorable position; a benefit; *tennis,* the first point won after deuce.—**to ad·van·tage,** so as to bring about a favorable or desired result or impression.

ad·van·tage, ad·van′tij, *v.t.*—*advantaged, advantaging.* To bring advantage to; to be of service to; to benefit; to promote; help; to yield profit or gain to.

ad·van·ta·geous, ad″van·tā′jus, *a.* Being of advantage; profitable; useful; furnishing convenience; beneficial.—**ad·van·ta·geous·ly,** ad″van·tā′jus·lē, *adv.* In an advantageous manner; profitably.—**ad·van·ta·geous·ness,** ad″van·tā′jus·nis, *n.*

ad·vec·tion, ad·vek′shan, *n.* [L. *advectio(n-),* < *advehere,* carry to, < *ad,* to, and *vehere,* carry.] The transference of heat or other properties of the atmosphere by the horizontal motion of a mass of air; the horizontal movement of the air in the atmosphere.

ad·vene, ad·vēn′, *v.i.* [L. *advenio,* to come to—*ad,* to, and *venio,* to come. VENTURE.] To accede or become added to; to become a part, though not essential.

ad·vent, ad′vent, *n.* [L. *adventus,* n., < *advenire:* ADVENE.] Coming or arrival; (*sometimes cap.*), *eccles.,* the coming of Christ into the world; (*cap.*) a season (including four Sundays) preceding Christmas, commemorative of Christ's coming.

Ad·vent·ism, ad′ven″tiz′um, *n.* The belief or doctrine that the expected second coming of Christ is near at hand.—**Ad·vent·ist,** ad′ven·tist, ad·ven′tist, *n.* A member of any of certain Christian denominations which maintain that the expected second coming of Christ is near at hand; also called **Sec·ond Ad·vent·ist.**

ad·ven·ti·ti·a, ad″ven·tish′ē·a, ad″ven·tish′a, *n.* An external connective tissue which covers an organ.

ad·ven·ti·tious, ad″ven·tish′us, *a.* [L. *adventicius,* < *advenire:* ADVENE.] Coming from without; foreign; extraneous; extrinsic; accidentally or casually present; *bot., zool.* appearing in an abnormal or unusual position or place, as a root.— **ad·ven·ti·tious·ly,** ad″ven·tish′us·lē, *adv.* —**ad·ven·ti·tious·ness,** ad″ven·tish′us·nis, *n.*

ad·ven·tive, ad·ven′tiv, *a.* [L. *adventus,* pp. of *advenire:* ADVENE.] Extraneous; adventitious; *bot., zool.* not indigenous, or not thoroughly naturalized, as exotic plants or animals.

ad·ven·ture, ad·ven′chur, *n.* [M.E. < O.Fr. *adventure,* Fr. *aventure,* L.L. *adventura, aventura,* < L. *adventurus,* about to arrive, fut. part. of *advenio,* to arrive. ADVENE.] An exciting experience; a hazardous enterprise; a bold and dangerous undertaking of uncertain outcome; a commercial speculation; a remarkable occurrence in one's personal history; a noteworthy event or experience in one's life.—**ad·ven·tur·ism,** ad·ven′chur·iz″um, *n.* Behavior in defiance of accepted procedures or practices.

ad·ven·ture, ad·ven′chur, *v.t.*—*adventured, adventuring.* To risk or hazard; to venture on; to attempt.—*v.i.*

ad·ven·tur·er, ad·ven′chur·ĕr, *n.* One who engages in an adventure or speculation; one who attempts or takes part in bold, novel, or extraordinary enterprises; one who lives by underhand means, or by a system of imposition; an unscrupulous rogue.

ad·ven·ture·some, ad·ven′chur·sum, *a.* Inclined toward taking risks; daring; bold.

ad·ven·tur·ess, ad·ven′chur·es, *n.* A female adventurer; a woman who seeks wealth or social position by questionable means.

ad·ven·tur·ous, ad·ven′chur·us, *a.* Liking or seeking adventure; courageous; enterprising; full of hazard; attended with risk. —**ad·ven·tur·ous·ly,** ad·ven′chur·us·lē, *adv.* In an adventurous manner; rashly; boldly.—**ad·ven·tur·ous·ness,** ad·ven′chur·us·nis, *n.*

ad·verb, ad′vurb, *n.* [M.Fr. < L. *adverbium*—*ad,* to, and *verbum,* a word, a verb.] *Gram.* an indeclinable part of speech, modifying verbs, adjectives, or other adverbs for the purpose of limiting or extending their signification: this part of speech usually expresses time, place, manner, condition, cause, result, degree, means, etc.

ad·ver·bi·al, ad·vŭr′bē·al, *a.* Pertaining to or having the character or structure of an adverb.—**ad·ver·bi·al·ly,** ad·vŭr′bē·al·ē, *adv.* In the manner or with the force or character of an adverb.

ad·ver·bum, ad vŭr′bum, *adv.* Exactly word for word; verbatim; in the same words.

ad·ver·sar·y, ad′ver·ser″ē, *n. pl.* **ad·ver·sar·ies.** [L. *adversarius.* ADVERSE.] An enemy, a foe, or a person having hostility for another person or group of people; a group or a person who is an opponent of or works against some other group or person; an antagonist; (*cap.*) the devil.

ad·ver·sa·tive, ad·vŭr′sa·tiv, *a.* Expressing difference, contrariety, or opposition (an *adversative* conjunction).—*n.* A word denoting contrariety or opposition.—**ad·ver·sa·tive·ly,** *adv.*

ad·verse, ad′vŭrs, ad·vŭrs′, *a.* [L. *adversus,* opposite—*ad,* to, and *versus,* turned, < *verto,* to turn.] Acting in a contrary direction; counteracting; opposing (*adverse* winds); hostile; inimical (*adverse* criticism); unfortunate; calamitous; unprosperous (*adverse* circumstances).—**ad·verse·ly,** ad″vŭrs′lē, *adv.* In an adverse manner.—**ad·verse·ness,** ad″vŭrs′nis, *n.* The state or quality of being adverse.

ad·ver·si·ty, ad·vŭr′si·tē, *n. pl.* **ad·ver·si·ties.** An event, or series of events, which oppose success or desire; misfortune; calamity; affliction; misery; distress; state of unhappiness.

ad·vert, ad·vŭrt′, *v.i.* [L. *advertere*—*ad,* to, and *vertere,* to turn.] To turn the mind or attention; to regard, observe, or notice; to refer or allude: followed by *to.*

ad·vert·ence, ad·vŭr′tens, *n.* Attention; notice; regard; heedfulness. Also **ad·vert·en·cy.**

ad·vert·ent, ad·vŭr′tent, *a.* Attentive; heedful.—**ad·vert·ent·ly,** ad·vŭr′tent·lē, *adv.* In an advertent manner.

ad·ver·tise, ad′ver·tīz, *v.t.*—*advertised, advertising.* [M.E. < M.Fr. < *avertir, avertissant,* to warn, inform, < L. *adverto,* to turn toward—*ad* and *verto,* to turn.] To inform or give notice; to call attention to; to make public, especially by printed or broadcast notice; make known the desirability of in order to sell.—*v.i.* To bring to public attention by means of advertising.—**ad·ver·tis·er,** ad′ver·tīz″ėr, *n.*

ad·ver·tise·ment, ad″ver·tīz′ment, ad·vŭr′tis·ment, *n.* A notice or message intended to make the advantages and desirable qualities of a product or service known to the public, especially a paid notice, printed in a newspaper or magazine or broadcast by radio or television; the act of advertising.

ad·ver·tis·ing, ad′ver·tī″zing, *n.* The attracting of public attention to a product, service, etc., esp. by means of paid announcements, broadcasts or printed material; the business concerned with planning, writing, designing, and scheduling advertisements; advertisements.

ad·vice, ad·vīs′, *n.* [M.E. < O.Fr. *advis,* opinion, counsel—L. *ad,* to, and *visum,* what is seen or judged proper. VISION.] An opinion recommended, or offered, as worthy to be followed; counsel; suggestion; information; report; notice; intelligence; a notification in respect to a business transaction; a diplomatic or political official report.

ad·vis·a·bil·i·ty, ad·vī″za·bil′i·tē, *n.* The quality of being advisable.

ad·vis·a·ble, ad·vī′za·bl, *a.* Proper to be advised; expedient; proper to be done or practiced; open to advice.—**ad·vis·a·ble·ness,** ad·vī′za·bl·nis, *n.* The quality of being advisable or expedient.—**ad·vis·a·bly,** ad·vī′za·blē, *adv.* With advice; wisely; prudently.

ad·vise, ad·vīz′, *v.t.*—*advised, advising.* [O.Fr. *aviser.* ADVICE.] To give counsel to; to counsel; to give information to; to inform; to give notice to; to acquaint.—*v.i.* To consider, to reflect; to take counsel.—**ad·vis·er,** **ad·vi·sor,** ad·vī′zėr, *n.* One who gives advice or admonition; a counselor.

ad·vised, ad·vīzd′, *a.* Cautious; prudent; thoughtfully considered; informed; done, formed, or taken with advice or deliberation (an *advised* act).—**ad·vis·ed·ly,** ad·vī′zid·lē, *adv.* With deliberation or advice; heedfully; purposely; by design.—**ad·vis·ed·ness,** ad·vī′zid·nis, *n.* The state of being advised; prudent procedure; caution.

ad·vise·ment, ad·vīz′ment, *n.* Consultation; careful consideration; as, to take under *advisement.*

ad·vi·so·ry, ad·vī′zo·rē, *a.* Having power to advise; containing advice.

ad·vo·ca·cy, ad′vo·ka·sē, *n. pl.* **ad·vo·ca·cies.** The act of advocating; a pleading for; intercession; espousal; defense.

ad·vo·cate, ad′vo·kit, ad′vo·kāt″, *n.* [M.E. < M.Fr. < L. *advocatus,* one summoned to aid—*ad,* to, and *voco, vocatum,* to call. VOICE, VOCAL.] One who pleads the cause of another in a court of law; one who defends, vindicates, or espouses a cause by argument; a pleader in favor of something; intercessor.

ad·vo·cate, ad′vo·kāt″, *v.t.*—*advocated, advocating.* To plead in favor of, as of a cause, policy, etc.; to defend by argument before a public tribunal; to recommend publicly; to support or vindicate.—**ad·vo·ca·tion,** ad″vo·kā′shan, *n.* The act of advocating; the act of summoning; a pleading for.

ad·y·na·mi·a, ad″e·nā′mē·a, *n.* [Gr. *a,* not, and *dynamis,* power.] Weakness; want of strength occasioned by disease; a deficiency of vital power.—**ad·y·nam·ic,** ad″e·nam′ik, ā″dī·nam′ik, *a.* Weak; destitute of strength.

ad·y·tum, ad′i·tum, *n. pl.* **ad·y·ta,** ad′i·ta. [L. *adytum,* Gr. *adyton,* lit. a place not to be entered—*a,* not, and *dyō,* to enter.] An innermost sanctuary or shrine; in ancient temples, the sanctuary which only priests were permitted to enter; the chancel or altar end of a church; a private room or a sanctum.

adz, adze, adz, *n.* [M.E. *adese, adse* < O.E. *adese,* an adze.] An instrument of the ax type used for chipping the surface of timber, the cutting edge being at right angles to the handle.—*v.t.* To chip or shape with an adz.

ad·zu·ki bean, ad·zŏ′kē bēn, *n.* [Jap. *adzuki.*] An annual, bushy bean, *Phaseolus angularis,* cultivated in Japan; the seeds, which are used for flour.

AEA, A.E.A., *n. Brit.* Atomic Energy Authority.

a·e·des, ā·ē′dēz, *n.* [< Gr. *aedes,* unpleasant < *a-,* not, and *edos,* pleasure.] A mosquito, *Aëdes aegypti,* that carries yellow fever; also *yellow-fever mosquito.* Any mosquito of the genus *Aëdes.*

ae·dile, ē′dil, *n.* [L. *aedilis,* < *aedes,* a building.] In ancient Rome, a magistrate in charge of buildings, streets, markets, games, etc.—**ae·dile·ship,** ē′dil·ship″, *n.*

Ae·ge·an, i·jē′an, *a.* [L. *Ægaeus,* < Gr. *Aiuaios.*] Pertaining to the Aegean Sea, an arm of the Mediterranean lying east of Greece; esp., noting or pertaining to the civilization which preceded the historic Hellenic period, and which flourished in various islands in, and lands adjacent to, the Aegean Sea, as Crete, Argolis, etc.

ae·gis, ē′jis, *n.* [Gr. *aigis,* goatskin.] *Gr. mythol.* the shield of Zeus. In later times, a kind of breastplate, part of the armor of Pallas Athena; hence, anything that pro-

tects or shields; a protecting power or influence.

A·e·ne·o·lith·ic, ā·ē″nē·ō·lith′ik, *a.* Pertaining to a period earlier than the Bronze Age, when copper was used by prehistoric man.

Ae·o·li·an, ē·ō′lē·an, *a.* Pertaining to Aeolus, the Greek god of the winds. (*l.c.*) pertaining to the wind; sounded by the wind or by air, as a musical instrument; borne by or due to the wind.

ae·o·li·an harp, *n.* A box with an opening over which are stretched strings of equal length which produce sound when wind blows over them.

ae·o·lo·trop·ic, ē″o·lō·trop′ik, *a.* [Gr. *aiolos,* varied, *tropē,* a turn.] Applied to bodies unequally elastic in different directions: opposed to *isotropic.*

ae·on, ē′on, ē′on, *n.* [L. < Gr. *aion,* age.] A period of time of indefinite or interminable length; an age; *geol.* the largest unit of geologic time, consisting of two or more eras. Also *eon.*

ae·o·ni·an, ē·ō′nē·an, *a.* Eternal; lasting forever.

aer·ate, âr′āt, ā′e·rāt″, *v.t.*—*aerated, aerating.* [L. *aer,* air. AIR.] To combine with carbon dioxide or other gas, or with air; to expose (something) to the effects of air. *Physiol.* to supply, as the blood, with oxygen, as in the process of respiration; oxygenate; expose to air.—**aer·a·tion,** âr′ā·shan, ā·e·rā′shan, *n.* The act or operation of aerating.

aer·a·tor, âr′ā·tor, ā′e·rā″tor, *n.* A blower; an apparatus for making carbonated beverages; a fumigating device to keep moisture out of wheat or other grain in bins.

aer·i·al, âr′ē·al, ā·ēr′ē·al, *a.* [L. *aerius* < Gr. *aerios* < *aer.*] Belonging or pertaining to the air or atmosphere; inhabiting or frequenting the air; pertaining to aircraft; produced by or in the air; unsubstantial; visionary; reaching far into the air; high; lofty; possessed of a light and graceful beauty; growing in the air, such as certain roots.—âr′ē·al, *n.* Antenna; object which receives radiated waves as a unit within the receiver or as an antenna.—**aer·i·al·ly,** âr′ē·al·ē, ā·ēr′ē·a·lē, *adv.* In an aerial manner.

aer·i·al bomb, *n. Milit.* a bomb constructed to be dropped from an aircraft, usu. detonated by a timing device or upon contact.

aer·i·al com·bat, *n. Milit.* combat in the air between the aircraft of battling forces.

aer·i·al en·gi·neer, *n. Milit.* a flight engineer, usually of enlisted rank.

aer·i·al·ist, âr′ē·a·list, ā·ēr′ē·a·list, *n.* An acrobat who performs on a high wire, trapeze, etc., usually in a circus.

aer·i·al lad·der, *n.* A ladder that may be extended to reach heights, as on a fire department's truck.

aer·i·al mine, *n. Milit.* a mine constructed to be dropped from an aircraft, usually into water. An early World War II bomb, usu. dropped by parachute.

aer·ie, aer·y, eyr·ie, âr′ē, ēr′ē, *n.* [M.L. *aerea* < L. *area.*] The nest of a bird of prey, as of an eagle or hawk; a lofty dwelling of any large bird; any elevated house or dwelling.

aer·if·er·ous, â·rif′er·us, *a.* Conveying or containing air.

aer·i·fi·ca·tion, âr″i·fi·kā′shan, ā·ēr″i·fi·kā′shan, *n.* The act of aerifying or combining with air.

aer·i·form, âr′i·fârm″, *a.* Having the form or nature of air; unreal; gaseous; lacking material substance.

aer·i·fy, âr′i·fī″, ā·ēr′i·fī″, *v.t.*—*aerified, aerifying.* To infuse air into; to fill with air, or to combine with air; to change into an aeriform state; to aerate.

aer·o, âr′ō, *a.* Pertaining to the air, aircraft, or the flying of aircraft.

aer·o·bal·lis·tics, âr″ō·ba·lis′tiks, *n. pl., sing. or pl. in constr.* The ballistics of projectiles fired, dropped, or launched from aircraft.

aer·o·bat·ics, âr″ō·bat′iks, *n. pl., sing. or pl. in constr.* [Gr. *aēr*, air, and (*a ro-*) *-batics*, see *acrobat.*] *Sing.* the art or the act of performing feats, as loops or rolls, with airplanes or gliders; stunt flying. *Pl.* such feats, as executed in a dogfight during combat or in exhibition flying.—**aer·o·bat·ic**, âr″o·bat′ik, *a.*

aer·obe, âr′ōb, *n.* [Gr. *aēr*, air, *bios*, life.] A microorganism whose existence requires the presence of air or free oxygen, as opposed to *anaerobe.*—**aer·o·bic**, â·rō′bik, *a.* Requiring air or free oxygen in order to live and thrive: caused by the presence of aerobes.

aer·o·bi·o·sis, âr″ō·bī·ō′sis, *n.* Life in an atmosphere of air or oxygen.

aer·o·bi·um, â·rō′bē·um, *n. pl.* **aer·o·bi·a**, â·rō′bē·a. [N.L. < Gr. (*aēr-*), air, and *bios*, life.] An aerobe.

aer·o·drome, âr′ō·drōm″, *n.* [< Gr. *aēr* (*aer*), air and *dromos*, a running, course.] *Brit.* an airdrome.

aer·o·dy·nam·ics, âr″ō·dī·nam′iks, *n. pl. sing. or pl. in constr.* [< Gr. *aēr*, and *dynamis*, force, power.] That field of dynamics which pertains to the motion of air and other gaseous fluids, and to the forces acting on bodies in motion relative to such environment.—**aer·o·dy·nam·ic**, *a.*—**aer·o·dy·nam·i·cist**, âr″ō·dī·nam′i·sist, *n.*

aer·o·dyne, âr′o·dīn″, *n.* [< *aerodynamics.*] A heavier-than-air aircraft, as the conventional airplane, glider, or helicopter.

aer·o·em·bo·lism, âr″ō·em′bo·lizm, *n.* [*aëro-* and *embolism.*] The occlusion of blood vessels by nitrogen gas bubbles which form when the body undergoes a rapid decrease in air pressure, as in high-altitude flying.

aer·o·em·phy·se·ma, âr″ō·em″fi·sē′ma, âr″ō·em″fi·zē′ma, *n.* An altitude decompression sickness caused by the formation of gas bubbles in the connective tissues of the body, as in high-altitude flying.

aer·o·gram, âr′o·gram, *n.* [< *aëro-* and *-gram.*] An airmail or wireless message; a sheet of airmail stationery designed to carry a written message at special postal rates and which folds to form its own envelope. Also **aer·o·gramme.**

aer·og·ra·pher, â·rog′ra·fèr, *n.* A U.S. Navy officer who studies and forecasts weather conditions.

aer·og·ra·phy, â·rog′ra·fē, *n.* Description of the air or atmosphere; meteorology.

aer·o·lite, âr′o·līt″, *n.* [Gr. *aēr*, air, and *lithos*, a stone.] A meteoric stone; a meteorite. Also **aer·o·lith.**—**aer·o·lit·ic**, âr″o·lit′ik, *a.* Relating to aerolites.

aer·o·log·i·cal, âr″o·loj′i·kal, *a.* Pertaining to aerology. Also **aer·o·log·ic.**

aer·ol·o·gist, âr·ol′o·jist, *n.* One who is versed in aerology.

aer·ol·o·gy, â·rol′o·jē, *n.* [Gr. *aēr, aeros*, air, *logos*, description, *gnōsis*, knowledge.] That branch of physics which treats of the air, its constituent parts, properties, and phenomena; *meteor.* the study of the atmosphere at high altitudes.

aer·o·me·chan·ic, âr″ō·me·kan′ik, *n.* A mechanic in aviation.—*a.* Pertaining to, or referring to, aeromechanics.

aer·o·me·chan·ics, âr″ō·me·kan′iks, *n. pl., sing. or pl. in constr.* [Gr. *aēr*, and *mechanikos, mechane*, a machine.] The study of air and other gases in motion or equilibrium, or of solid bodies immersed in gases.—**aer·o·me·chan·ic**, **aer·o·me·chan·i·cal**, *a.*

aer·o·med·i·cal, âr″o·med′i·kal, *a.* Per-

taining to the science of aviation medicine and its practice.

aer·o·med·i·cine, âr″o·med′i·sin, *n.* That branch of medicine concerned with the disorders which may result from or occur during flying.

aer·o·me·te·or·o·graph, âr″omē′tē·or·o·graf″, âr″o·mē′tē·or·o·gräf″, âr″o·mē″tē·ər′o·graf″, âr″o·mē″tē·or′o·graf″, *n.* A meteorograph used in aircraft.

aer·om·e·ter, â·rom′i·tèr, *n.* [Gr. *aēr*, air, and *metron*, measure.] An instrument for weighing air, or for ascertaining the density and weight of air and gases.

aer·o·met·ric, âr″o·met′rik, *a.* Pertaining to aerometry.—**aer·om·e·try**, â·rom′i·trē, *n.* The science of measuring the weight or density of air and gases.

aer·o·naut, âr′o·not″, âr′o·nat″, *n.* [Gr. *aēr*, air, and *nautes*, a sailor, from *naus*, a ship.] An aerial navigator of a lighter-than-air craft; a balloonist.

aer·o·naut·ic, âr′o·na′tik, âr″o·not′ik, *a.* Pertaining to aeronautics. Also **aer·o·nau·ti·cal.**

aer·o·nau·ti·cal en·gi·neer, *n.* An engineer who is competent in the design and building of aircraft and components of aircraft.

aer·o·naut·ics, âr″o·na′tiks, âr″o·not′iks, *n. pl. but sing. in constr.* The science, art, or business of designing, manufacturing, and operating aircraft.

aer·o·neu·ro·sis, âr″ō·nu̵·rō′sis, âr″ō·nyu̵·rō′sis, *n.* A psychoneurotic condition occurring in airmen and aviators resulting from nervous tension, worry, or fatigue, characterized by mild depression, abdominal pains, insomnia and nervous irritability.

ae·ron·o·my, â·ron′o·mē, *n.* The study of physical and chemical phenomena in the upper regions of the atmosphere.

aer·o·pause, âr′o·paz″, *n.* [Gr. *aēr*, air, and *pausis*, stop.] A region of indeterminate limits in the upper atmosphere, considered as a boundary or transition region between the denser portion of the atmosphere and space.

aer·o·phore, âr′o·fōr″, âr′o·far″, *n.* [Gr. *aēr* (*aer-*), *pherō*, to bring.] A portable apparatus for purifying air; an apparatus which forces air into the lungs, as in the treatment of asphyxia.

aer·o·plane, âr′o·plān″, *n.* [Gr. *aēr*, air, and E. *plane.*] *Brit.* airplane.

aer·o·scep·sis, âr″ō·skep′sis, *n.* [N.L. < Gr. *aēr*, air, and *skepsis*, viewing, perception.] *Zool.* sensitivity to the conditions of the atmosphere, as odors. Also **aer·o·scep·sy**, âr′o·skep″sē.

aer·o·sol, âr′o·sōl, âr′o·sal″, âr′o·sol″, *n.* [*acro-* and *-sol.*] *Physical chem.* a suspension of fine particles, solid or liquid, in a gas producing a smoke or fog. A liquid substance under pressure with an inert gas within a metal container, the substance being released through a valve; the container.

aer·o·sol·ize, âr′o·sōl·īz″, âr′o·sal·īz″, âr′o·sol·īz″, *v.t.*—**aerosolized, aerosolizing.** To scatter or disperse in an aerosol-like manner.

aer·o·sol bomb, *n.* A small container having a device to release an aerosol, esp. a spray of insecticidal or germicidal liquid.

aer·o·space, âr′o·spās″, *n.* The atmosphere of the earth and the space immediately beyond it taken as a whole. Earth's envelope of air and space above it; the two considered as a single realm for activity in the flight of air vehicles and in the launching, guidance, and control of ballistic missiles, earth satellites, dirigible space vehicles, and the like.—*a.* Pertaining to aerospace, esp. to the manufacture of vehicles which operate in aerospace, as missiles, rockets, and satellites.

aer·o·sphere, âr′o·sfēr″, *n.* The body of air above the earth's atmosphere where flight by manned aircraft is possible.

aer·o·stat, âr′o·stat″, *n.* [Fr. *aerostat*, a balloon—Gr. *aēr*, air, and *statos*, standing, < *histemi*, to stand.] Any aircraft that derives its buoyancy or lift from a lighter-than-air gas contained within its envelope, as balloons and dirigibles.—**aer·o·stat·ic**, **aer·o·stat·i·cal**, âr″o·stat′ik, âr″o·stat′i·kal, *a.*

aer·o·stat·ics, âr″o·stat′iks, *n. pl. but sing. in constr.* A branch of physics concerned with the equilibrium of solid bodies immersed in gaseous fluids and with the equilibrium of gaseous fluids.

aer·o·sta·tion, âr″o·stā′shan, *n.* The science or art of flying or operating aerostats, as distinguished from aviation.

aer·o·ther·mo·dy·nam·ics, âr″ō·thur″mō·dī·nam′iks, *n. pl. but sing. in constr.* The study of aerodynamic phenomena at sufficiently high velocities that thermodynamic properties of the gas are important.—**aer·o·ther·mo·dy·nam·ic**, *a.*

aer·o·train, är′a·trān, *n.* A train which runs at high speed, utilizing the monorail and air-cushion principles.

aer·y, âr′ē, ēr′ē, *n. pl.* **aer·ies.** Aerie.

aer·y, âr′ē, ā′e·rē, *a.* *Poet.* Airy; breezy; ethereal; aerial.

Aes·cu·la·pi·an, es″kū·lā′pē·an, *a.* *Med.* Of or pertaining to Aesculapius, the ancient healing god; referring to the art of healing.—*n.* A physician.

aes·thete, es′thēt, *n.* [< *aesthetic.*] One devoted to the principles or doctrines of aesthetics; a lover of the beautiful.

aes·thet·ic, es·thet·ic, es·thet′ik, *a.* [Gr. *aisthētikos*, < *aisthanomai*, to perceive by the senses.] Pertaining to the study of taste or beauty; pertaining to the sense of the beautiful. Also **aes·thet·i·cal**, **es·thet·i·cal.**—**aes·thet·i·cal·ly**, **es·thet·i·cal·ly**, es·thet′ik·lē, *adv.*

aes·thet·i·cism, **es·thet·i·cism**, es·thet′i·sizm, *n.* The principles or doctrines of aesthetics.

aes·thet·ics, **es·thet·ics**, es·thet′iks, *n. pl., sing. or pl. in constr.* The theory of the fine arts and the philosophy of the mind and emotions in relation to it; that branch of philosophy which deals with the beautiful; the doctrines of taste.

aes·ti·val, **es·ti·val**, es′ti·val, e·stī′val, *a.* [M.E. *estival* < L. *aestivalis* < *aestas*, summer. EDIFY.] Relating to summer.

aes·ti·vate, **es·ti·vate**, es′ti·vāt″, *v.i.*—*aestivated, aestivating, estivated, estivating.* *Biol.* to spend the summer in an inactive condition.—**aes·ti·va·tion**, **es·ti·va·tion**, es″ti·vā′shan, *n.*

ae·thri·o·scope, ē′thrē·o·skōp″, eth′rē·o·skōp″, *n.* [Gr. *aithria*, open sky, and *skopein*, view.] An instrument for measuring minute variations of temperature due to different conditions of the sky.

ae·ti·ol·o·gy, **e·ti·ol·o·gy**, ē″tē·ol′o·jē, ē″tē·ol′o·jē, *n. pl.* **ae·ti·ol·o·gies**, **e·ti·ol·o·gies.** [L.L. *aetiologia*, < Gr. *aitiol·ogia*, < *aitia*, cause, *legein*, speak.] The assigning of a cause; a theory of the cause of a phenomenon, as disease; the science of causes.—**ae·ti·o·log·i·cal**, **e·ti·o·log·i·cal**, *a.*

a·far, a·fär′, *adv.* At a distance in place; to or from a distance: often with *from* preceding, or *off* following, or both.

a·feard, **a·feared**, a·fērd′, *a.* [O.E. *āfǣred*, pp. of *āfǣran*, affect with fear.] *Brit. and southern U.S. dial.* Frightened; afraid.

af·fa·bil·i·ty, af″a·bil′i·tē, *n.* The quality of being affable or sociable. Also **af·fa·ble·ness.**

af·fa·ble, af′a·bl, *a.* [M.Fr. < L. *affabilis*, affable—*af* for *ad*, to, *fari*, to speak.] Easy of conversation; admitting others to free conversation without reserve; courteous; complaisant; of easy manners; cordial; pleasant.—**af·fa·bly**, af′a·blē, *adv.*

af·fair, *a·*fâr′, *n.* [M.E. < M.Fr. *affaire* < L. *facere*, to make, to do.] Business of any kind; that which is done, or is to be done; an event provoking public scandal or controversy; a happening or social gathering; *pl.* public or pecuniary concerns; as, to put one's *affairs* in order. A brief amorous relationship, usually illicit.

af·fect, *a·*fekt′, *v.t.* [L. *affecto*, to desire, to strive after, freq. of *afficio*, *affectum*, to affect the mind or body—*af* for *ad*, to, and *facio*, to do.] To act upon; to produce an effect or change upon; to influence; to move or touch by exciting the feelings; to aspire to; to follow after habitually or gravitate toward; make a show of; to assume the appearance of; to pretend.—**af·fect·ed·-ness,** *a·*fek′tid·nis, *n.*

af·fect, af′ekt, *a·*fekt′, *n. Psychol.* Emotion or feeling, as distinguished from *cognition* and *volition*; an emotion with accompanying physical movements.

af·fec·ta·tion, af″ek·tā′shan, *n.* [L. *affectatio.*] An attempt to assume or exhibit what is not natural or real; false pretense, especially of what is praiseworthy or uncommon; artificial appearance or show.

af·fect·ed, *a·*fek′tid, *a.* Inclined or disposed; given to affectation; assuming or pretending to possess what is not natural or real; assumed artificially; moved with feeling; deeply touched; acted upon, as by disease.—**af·fect·ed·ly,** *a·*fek′tid·lē, *adv.* In an affected or assumed manner; with affectation.

af·fect·ing, *a·*fek′ting, *a.* Having power to excite emotion; suited to affect; pathetic.—**af·fect·ing·ly,** *a·*fek′ting·lē, *adv.* In an affecting or impressive manner.

af·fec·tion, *a·*fek′shan, *n.* [M.E. < M.Fr. < L. *affectio*, *affectionis*, the being affected or touched. AFFECT.] The state of having one's feelings affected in some way; bent or disposition of mind; sentiment; a fond feeling or attachment for another; devotion; love; the act of affecting or acting upon; the state of being affected; a property or attribute inseparable from its object; any particular modification, as an attribute or detraction of the body; as, a gouty *affection.*

af·fec·tion·al, *a·*fek′sha·nal, *a.* Pertaining to or implying the affections.

af·fec·tion·ate, *a·*fek′sha·nit, *a.* Having great love or affection; warmly attached; fond; kind; loving; proceeding from affection; tender.—**af·fec·tion·ate·ly,** *a·*fek′sha·nit·lē, *adv.* In an affectionate manner; fondly; tenderly; kindly.—**af·fec·tion·ate·ness,** *a·*fek′sha·nit·nis, *n.* The quality of being affectionate; fondness; affection.

af·fec·tive, *a·*fek′tiv, *a.* [M.Fr. *affectif*, < M.L. *affectivus*, < L. *afficere.*] Expressing feeling or emotion; pertaining to the affections; *psych.* pertaining to emotion rather than thought.

af·fen·pin·scher, af″en·pin′sher, *n.* [G. < *affe*, monkey and *pinscher*, a hunting dog.] A breed of small dog having stiff red, black, or gray coat, pointed ears, and shaggy hairs about the nose, eyes, and chin.

af·fer·ent, af′er·ent, *a.* [L. *afferens*, *afferentis*, ppr. of *affero*—*af* for *ad*, to, and *fero*, to carry.] *Physiol.* leading or conducting inward toward a center point, as certain nerves and veins: opposed to *efferent.*

af·fet·tuo·so, *a·*fech″ö·ō′sō, *a.* [It.] *Mus.* tender; affecting.—*adv. Mus.* with emotion: an instruction to the performer.—*n. Mus.* a movement or composition which is tender and affecting in character.

af·fi·ance, *a·*fī′ans, *v.t.*—*affianced, affiancing.* To betroth; to bind by promise of marriage.

af·fi·ant, *a·*fī′ant, *n.* [M.Fr., ppr. of *affier.*] *Law.* One who makes an affidavit; deponent.

af·fi·da·vit, af″i·dā′vit, *n.* [3rd pers. sing. perf. ind. of L.L. *affido*, to pledge one's faith—L. *af* for *ad*, to, and *fides*, faith.] A written declaration under oath; a statement of facts in writing signed by the party, and sworn to or confirmed by declaration before an authorized magistrate.

af·fil·i·ate, *a·*fil′ē·āt′, *v.t.*—*affiliated, affiliating.* [M.L. *affiliatus*, pp. of *affiliare*, < L. *ad*, to, and *filius*, son.] To take or bring into relationship, as by adoption or formal association; to associate, as oneself, followed by *with*; in an institution, to receive as members or to incorporate, as other bodies or branches; *law*, to fix the paternity of, with *upon.*—*v.i.* To associate oneself.—*a·*fil′ē·it, *n.* An affiliated person, group, or company.

af·fil·i·a·tion, *a·*fil″ē·ā′shan, *n.* [M.L. *affiliatio(n-).*] The act of affiliating, or the state of being affiliated; association; alliance; relationship.

af·fine, *a·*fīn′, *a·*fīn′, af′īn, *n.* [M.Fr. < L.] A relative by marriage.—**af·fi·nal,** *a·*fīn′al, *a.* Pertaining to marriage.—**af·fined,** *a·*-fīnd′, *a.* Closely related; joined.

af·fine, *a·*fīn′, *a·*fīn′, af′īn, *a. Math.* Maintaining finiteness by assigning finite values to finite quantities; referring to an interpretation which graphs finite points to finite points and parallel lines to parallel lines.

af·fin·i·tive, *a·*fin′i·tiv, *a.* Characterized by affinity; closely related or associated.

af·fin·i·ty, *a·*fin′i·tē, *n.* pl. **af·fin·i·ties.** [M.E. < L. *affinitas*, < *affinis*, adjacent, related—*af* for *ad*, to, and *finis*, boundary.] The relation contracted by marriage: distinguished from *consanguinity*; relation, connection, or alliance in general, as of languages or sounds; similarity in kind or nature; a natural attraction; the recipient of such a feeling of attraction; *chem.* that force by which bodies of dissimilar nature unite in certain specific proportions to form a compound, different in its nature from any of its constituents.

af·firm, *a·*furm′, *v.t.* [M.E. < M.Fr. < L. *affirmo*—*af* for *ad*, to, and *firmo*, to make firm.] To assert positively; to tell with confidence; to aver; declare; allege: opposed to *deny*; to confirm or ratify.—*v.i.* To make a solemn assertion or declaration; to make a legal affirmation.—**af·firm·a·ble,** *a·*-furm′a·bl, *a.* Capable of being affirmed, asserted, or declared.—**af·firm·a·bly,** *a·*-furm′a·blē, *adv.* In a way capable of affirmation.—**af·firm·ance,** *a·*fur′mans, *n.* Confirmation; ratification; affirmation.—**af·firm·ant,** *a·*fur′mant, *n.* One who affirms or asserts; one who makes affirmation instead of an oath. Also **af·firm·er.**

af·fir·ma·tion, af″ir·mā′shan, *n.* The act of affirming or asserting as true; that which is asserted; averment; confirmation; ratification; a solemn declaration made in lieu of an oath by one who has scruples about taking the oath.

af·firm·a·tive, *a·*fur′ma·tiv, *n.* A word or phrase expressing assent or affirmation or answering a question affirmatively; the opposite of a negative; *debate*, that side of a debated question which maintains the truth of the affirmative proposition.

af·firm·a·tive, *a·*fur′ma·tiv, *a.* Affirming or asserting: opposed to *negative.*—**af·firm·-a·tive·ly,** *a·*fur′ma·tiv·lē, *adv.* In an affirmative manner; positively.

af·fix, *a·*fiks′, *v.t.* [L. *affigo*, *affixum*—*af* for *ad*, to, and *figo*, *fixum*, to fix.] To subjoin, annex, unite, or add in writing at the close or end of a document; attach or append, as one's signature; to fasten or stick, as one thing to another.

af·fix, af′iks, *n.* A syllable or letter added to the beginning or the end of a word, base or root, producing a derivative; a prefix or suffix; infix; anything appended.

af·fla·tus, *a·*flā′tus, *n.* [L. < *afflare*, to blow on.] A creative inspiration, as that of the poet; divine communication of knowledge.

af·flict, *a·*flikt′, *v.t.* [M.E. < L. *afflicto*, intens. of *affligo*, to dash down—*af* for *ad*, to, and *fligo*, to strike.] To give, as pain which is continued or of some permanence, to the body or mind; to humble; to trouble; to grieve; to harass; to torment; to distress.—**af·flict·er,** *a·*flikt′ér, *n.* One who afflicts.

af·flic·tion, *a·*flik′shan, *n.* The state of being afflicted; a state of acute pain or distress of body or mind; the cause of this.

af·flic·tive, *a·*flik′tiv, *a.* Painful; distressing.—**af·flic·tive·ly,** *a·*flik′tiv·lē, *adv.*

af·flu·ence, af′lö·ens, *n.* [M.E. < M.Fr. < L. *affluentia*, < *affluo*, to flow to—*ad*, to, and *fluo*, to flow. FLUENT.] A flowing to or concourse; afflux; an abundant supply, as of worldly goods; wealth.

af·flu·ent, af′lö·ent, *a.* Flowing to; wealthy; abundant.—**af·flu·ent·ly,** af′lö·ent·lē, *adv.*

af·flu·ent, af′lö·ent, *n.* A tributary stream.

af·flux, af′luks, *n.* [< L. *affluo*, *affluxum.* AFFLUENCE.] The act of flowing to; a flowing to, or that which flows to, as a crowd of people or a stream of blood.

af·ford, *a·*fōrd′, *a·*fard′, *v.t.* [M.E. *aforth*, to afford, < prefix *a*, and *forth*; O.E. *forthian*, to further.] To give forth; to yield, supply, or produce, as a profit; to grant or confer, as consolation or gratification; to buy, sell, or expend, from having a sufficiency of means; to spare without much loss; to be able to bear the expense of, preceded by *can*, *could*, *may*, *might.*

af·for·est, *a·*far′ist, *a·*for′ist, *v.t.* [M.L. < L. *af-* for *ad-*, to, and *forest.*] To convert, as land, into a forest.—**af·for·est·a·-tion,** *a·*far″is·tā′shan, *a·*for″is·tā′shan, *n.* The act of converting land into a forest; the land afforested.

af·fran·chise, *a·*fran′chīz, *v.t.*—*affran-chised, affranchising.* [M.Fr. < *af-*, and *franchise.*] To make free; to liberate from servitude; to grant full citizenship and the right to vote. Also *enfranchise.*

af·fray, *a·*frā′, *n.* [M.E. *afray*, *affray* < M.F. *esfrei*, *effray*, *affray*, *effroyer*, Fr. *effrayer*, to frighten; < L.L. *extrediare*—L. *ex.*, intens, and O.H.G. *fridu*, G. *friede*, peace. AFRAID.] A public fight; fray; altercation; brawl.

af·freight, *a·*frāt′, *v.t.* [Fr. *affréter*, < *à* (< L. *ad*), to, and *fréter*, let by charter, akin to E. *freight.*] To hire, as a ship, for the transportation of goods or freight.—**af·-freight·er,** *a·*frāt′ér, *n.*—**af·freight·ment,** *a·*frāt′ment, *n.*

af·fri·cate, af′ri·kit, *n.* [L. *affricatus*, pp. of *affricare*, rub on or against, < *ad*, to, and *fricare*, rub.] *Phon.* an intimate combination of a stop with an immediately following spirant or fricative in the same position of the vocal organs, as *ch* in *teach* or the *g* in *gentle.*

af·fri·ca·tion, af″ri·kā′shan, *n. Phon.* The process of converting, as a stop sound, to an affricate; the resulting change, as *pf* in German.

af·fright, *a·*frīt′, *v.t.* [O.E. *āfyrhtian*, *āfyrhtan*—prefix *a*, intens., and *fyrhtan*, to frighten. FRIGHT.] To impress with sudden fear or terror; to frighten suddenly or unexpectedly.—*n.* Sudden fright.

af·front, *a·*frunt′, *v.t.* [M.E. < M.Fr. *afronter*, to encounter face to face—*af* for *ad*, to, and L. *frons*, *frontis*, front, face.] To offend by an open manifestation of disrespect; to insult; to confront defiantly.—**af·front·er,** *a·*frunt′ér, *n.* One who affronts.

af·front, *a·*frunt′, *n.* An open manifestation of disrespect or contumely; an outrage to the feelings; an insult; anything producing a feeling of shame or disgrace.

---

a- fat, fāte, fär, fâre, fall; **e-** met, mē, mēre, hėr; **i-** pin, pīne; **o-** not, nōte, möve; **u-** tub, cūbe, bull; **oi-** oil; **ou-** pound.

af·fuse, a·fūz', *v.t.*—*affused, affusing.* [L. *affundo, affusum*—*af* for *ad*, to, and *fundo, fusum*, to pour out.] To pour upon; to sprinkle, as with a liquid.

af·fu·sion, a·fū'zhan, *n.* The act of pouring or sprinkling liquid upon, as for baptism.

Af·ghan, af'gan, af'gan, *n.* A native of Afghanistan; a language of Aryan affinity, spoken in Afghanistan; (*l.c.*) a blanket or covering of knitted or crocheted wool.—*a.* Pertaining to Afghanistan.

Af·ghan hound, af'gan, af'gan, *n.* A breed of hunting dog indigenous to the Near East, with a long, silky topknot, silky hair, and a narrow head.

a·fi·cio·na·do, a·fish"yi·nä'dō, *n.* [Sp. pp. of *aficionar*, inspire affection < *afición*, affection < L. *affectio(n)*-.] An enthusiastic devotee.

a·field, a·fēld', *adv.* To the field; in the field; abroad; away from home; astray; beyond the field of one's experience or knowledge.

a·fire, a·fīr', *a., adv.* On fire.

a·flame, a·flām', *a., adv.* Flaming; glowing; blazing.

a·float, a·flōt', *a., adv.* Borne on the water; floating; at sea; flooded; drifting; passing from one person to another in circulation, as a rumor; unhampered by difficulties.

a·foot, a·fut', *a., adv.* On foot; borne by the feet; walking; in progress; in a state of being planned, as a plan or plot.

a·fore, a·fōr', a·far', *adv., prep., conj.* [Prefix *a*, at, and *fore*; O.E. *onforan*.] *Dial.* before in time or place.

a·fore·said, a·fōr'sed", a·far'sed", *a.* Mentioned previously in the same writing or discourse. Also **a·fore·men·tioned**, a·fōr'men"shand, a·far'men"shand.

a·fore·thought, a·fōr'that, a·far'that, *a.* Thought of beforehand; premeditated.—*n.* Premeditation.

a·foul, a·foul', *a., adv.* In or into an entanglement or a collision; fouled, tangled.

a·foul of, *prep.* In or into conflict or entanglement with; as, to run or fall *afoul of* the law.

a·fraid, a·frād', *a.* [M.E. *affrayd, afrayde*, pp. of *affray*. AFFRAY.] Impressed with fear or apprehension; reluctant; fearful. *Colloq.* inclined to think: to soften an otherwise unpleasant remark, as: I'm *afraid* you'll have to wait.

af·reet, **af·rit**, a·frēt', af'rēt, *n. Arabian mythol.* a powerful evil genie or demon.

a·fresh, a·fresh', *adv.* Anew; again; after a pause.

Af·ri·can, af'ri·kan, *a.* Pertaining to Africa or its peoples.—*n.* A native or inhabitant of Africa; a person belonging to one of the peoples of Africa.

Af·ri·can·der, **Af·ri·kan·der**, af"ri·kan'dèr, *n.* [Afrik. *Afrikaander*.] One born in South Africa but of European, esp. Dutch, descent; also *Afrikaner*. A breed of southern African cattle resistant to high temperatures.—**Af·ri·can·der·ism**, af"ri·kan'de·rizm, *n.* A word, expression, usage, or the like, peculiar to or originating among the Africanders.

Af·ri·can·ist, af'ri·ka·nist, *n.* One who specializes in the study of African cultures or languages.

Af·ri·can vi·o·let, *n.* A popular house plant, *Saintpaulia ionantha*, with pink, violet, or white flowers and velvety leaves.

Af·ri·kaans, af"ri·käns', af"ri·känz', *n.* A language spoken in South Africa, derived from the speech of 17th century Dutch settlers.

Af·ri·ka·ner, af"ri·kä'nèr, af"ri·kan'èr, *n.* [Afrik. < L. *africanus*.] Africander.

Af·ro-, af'rō. A form of the L. *Afer*, African, used in combination, as in *Afro-*

Asian (African and Asian, Asian of African descent), *Afro-European.*

Af·ro-A·mer·i·can, af"rō·a·mer'i·kan, *a.* Relating to Americans of African, usu. Negroid, descent.

Af·ro-A·si·at·ic, af"rō·ā"zhē·at'ik, af"rō·ā"shē·at'ik, *a.* Pertaining to a family of languages spoken throughout parts of southwestern Asia and northern Africa, including the Egyptian, Semitic, Chad, Berber, and Cushitic subfamilies.

aft, aft, äft, *a., adv.* [M.E. *afte*, back < O.E. *æft, eft*, after, behind; Goth. *afta*; < O.E. *af, æf*, Goth. *af*, E. *of, off.*] *Naut.* a word used to denote position at or near, or direction toward, the stern of a ship or aircraft.

af·ter, af'tèr, äf'tèr, *a.* [O.E. *æfter*, a compar. < *af*, E. *of, off, -ter* being the compar. syllable, seen as *-ther* in *whether, hither*, as *-der* in *under*. OF.] Later in time; subsequent; succeeding; as, an *after* period of life: in this sense often combined with the following noun.

af·ter, af'tèr, äf'tèr, *conj.* Subsequent to the time that or when; as, *after* the others arrived.

af·ter, af'tèr, äf'tèr, *adv.* Later in time; afterward; behind; succeeding; in pursuit.

af·ter, af'tèr, äf'tèr, *prep.* Behind in place; later in time; in pursuit of; in search of; with or in desire for; in imitation of, or in imitation of the style of; as, *after* a model; according to; in conformity with; in proportion to; as, *after* our desserts; below in rank or excellence; next to; concerning; as, inquire *after*; having the name of; as, named *after* her mother.—**af·ter all**, at last; upon the whole; at the most; notwithstanding.

af·ter·birth, af'tèr·burth", äf'tèr·burth", *n.* The placenta and fetal membranes which are expelled from the uterus after the birth of a child. Also *secundines.*

af·ter·bod·y, af'tèr·bod"ē, äf'tèr·bod"ē, *n. Aerospace.* A companion body that follows a satellite; a section of a rocket or spacecraft that enters the atmosphere unprotected behind the nose cone or other body that is protected for entry; the afterpart of a vehicle.

af·ter·brain, af'tèr·brān", äf'tèr·brān", *n.* The myelencephalon.

af·ter·burn·er, af'tèr·bur"nèr, äf'tèr·bur"nèr, *n. Aeron.* an auxiliary combustion chamber within, or attached to, the tail pipe of certain jet engines, in which hot unused oxygen of exhaust gases from fuel already burned is used to burn a second fuel and thus augment the density and temperature of the exhaust gases as they leave the tailpipe, with consequent increase in thrust.

af·ter·care, af'tèr·kâr", äf'tèr·kâr", *n. Med.* the treatment and care required by a convalescent patient.

af·ter·clap, af'tèr·klap", äf'tèr·klap", *n.* A startling repercussion following an affair assumed to be finished.

af·ter·damp, af'tèr·damp", äf'tèr·damp", *n.* Chokedamp or toxic carbonic acid, found in coal mines after an explosion of firedamp.

af·ter·deck, af'tèr·dek", äf'tèr·dek", *n. Naut.* the section of a deck that is abaft the middle of a ship.

af·ter·ef·fect, af'tèr·i·fekt", äf'tèr·i·fekt", *n.* A delayed effect; *med.* a result appearing after the immediate effect, as of a drug.

af·ter·glow, af'tèr·glō", äf'tèr·glō", *n.* A broad, high arch of radiance or glow seen occasionally in the western sky above the highest clouds in deepening twilight, caused by the scattering effect of fine particles of dust suspended in the upper atmosphere; a secondary glow, as in heated metal before it becomes incandescent; pleasing recollection of a former experience; phosphorescence.

af·ter·im·age, af'tèr·im"ij, äf'tèr·im"ij, *n.* The image or sense impression which remains after the stimulus disappears.

af·ter·life, af'tèr·līf", äf'tèr·līf", *n.* Life following death; a future or subsequent period in a person's life.

af·ter·math, af'tèr·math", äf'tèr·math", *n.* [*after* and *math* (crop, mowing).] Consequence, result; a second mowing of grass from the same land in the same season.

af·ter·most, af'tèr·mōst", äf'tèr·mōst", *a.* [O.E. *æftemest*, a double superlative, *mest* being < *ma* and *st*, superlative suffixes.] Hindmost: opposed to *foremost. Naut.* farthest aft; also *aftmost.*

af·ter·noon, af'tèr·nön", äf'tèr·nön", *n.* The part of the day which follows noon, between noon and evening; *fig.* the latter part of something.—*a.*

af·ter·noons, *adv.* Every afternoon; on any afternoon; repeatedly in the afternoon.

af·ter·piece, af'tèr·pēs", äf'tèr·pēs", *n.* A short dramatic entertainment performed after the principal performance.

af·ter·shaft, af'tèr·shaft", äf'tèr·shäft", *n.* A bird feather that arises from the side of another feather.

af·ter·taste, af'tèr·tāst", äf'tèr·tāst", *n.* A taste which succeeds eating or drinking; the feeling which remains after an experience.

af·ter·thought, af'tèr·that", äf'tèr·that", *n.* Reflection after an act; some consideration that occurs to one's mind too late or after the performance of the act to which it refers; later explanation.

af·ter·time, af'tèr·tīm", äf'tèr·tīm", *n.* Succeeding time: more commonly in the plural; the future.

af·ter·ward, **af·ter·wards**, af'tèr·ward, äf'tèr·ward, af'tèr·wards, äf'tèr·wards, *adv.* [O.E. *æfterweard.* (The *-s* is the sign of the old adverbial genitive.) WARD.] In later or subsequent time.

af·ter·world, af'tèr·wurld", äf'tèr·wurld", *n.* The world assumed to be the place of existence after death.

aft·most, aft'mōst, aft'most, äft'mōst, äft'most, *a. Naut.* Farthest aft; aftermost.

a·ga, **a·gha**, ä'ga, *n.* [Turk. *aghā.*] In Turkey, a chief; a commander; a title of respect, as for age.

a·gain, a·gen', a·gān', *adv.* [O.E. *ongegn, ongeân*, again; *geân*, against. AGAINST.] A second time; once more; on another occasion; on the other hand; moreover; besides; further; in return; back to the original condition, place, or position; in answer; in addition.

a·gainst, a·genst', a·gänst', *prep.* [M.E. *agayns, ongaenes.* O.E. *ongeân*, against. The *es* is an adverbial or genitive termination and the *t* has been added, like that in *amidst, betwixt.* O.E. *geân*, again or against, is the same as *gain* in *gainsay*; G. *gegen*, against.] Opposite in place, often preceded by *over*; in opposition to; counter to; contrary to; adverse or hostile to; as, *against* law or opinion; toward or upon; in contact with; bearing or resting upon; as, to lean *against* the wall.

a·gam·ete, ā·gam'ēt, ā"ga·mēt', *n. Biol.* an asexual reproductive cell which produces an organism without uniting with another cell.

a·gam·ic, a·gam'ik, *a.* [Gr. *a*, not, and *gamos*, marriage.] Asexual. Also **ag·a·mous**, ag'a·mas.

ag·a·mo·gen·e·sis, ag"a·mō·jen'i·sis, *n.* [Gr. *a*, not, *gamos*, marriage, and *genesis*, production.] The production of young without the congress of the sexes, asexually.—**ag·a·mo·ge·net·ic**, ag"a·mō·je·net'ik, *a.*

a·ga·pe, ä·gä'pā, ä'ga·pā", ag'a·pā", *n.* [Gr. *agapē*, love.] Among the primitive Christians a love feast or feast of charity; brotherly love of one Christian for another.

a·gape, *a·*gāp′, *a·*gap′, *a.,* *adv.* Gaping as with wonder; having the mouth open, as with surprise or expectation.

a·gar-a·gar, ä′gär-ä′gär, ag′ar·ag′ar, *n.* [Malay.] A gelatinous product derived from certain Asiatic seaweeds, used as a medium in bacteria culture, as a purgative, or a stabilizer in certain foods. Also **a·gar.**

ag·a·ric, ag′a·rik, a·gar′ik, *n.* [L. < Gr. *agarikon.*] Any of various species of fungi of the family *Agaricaceae,* including the common mushroom, *Agaricus campestri,* cultivated for its edibility.

ag·ate, ag′it, *n.* [M.Fr. *agate,* < L. *achates,* so called because found near a river of that name in Sicily.] A semi-pellucid mineral, consisting of bands or layers of various colors blended together, the base generally being chalcedony, and this mixed with jasper, amethyst, quartz, opal, etc.; a size of type, about 5½ point; a playing marble made of or resembling agate.

ag·ate line, *n.* A unit of measurement in advertising, that is 1/14 inch in depth and one column wide.

ag·ate·ware, ag′it·wâr″, *n.* A type of pottery or enamelware dappled so as to look like agate.

a·ga·ve, a·gā′vē, a·gä′vē, *n.* [N.L. < Gr. *agave* fem. of *agavos,* noble.] Any plant of the American (chiefly Mexican) amaryllis family, genus *Agave,* species of which yield useful fibers (sisal hemp, etc.), a fermented beverage (pulque), a distilled spirit (mescal), or a soap substitute (amole): also cultivated for ornament, as the century plant which lives ten to seventy years before flowering.

a·gaze, a·gāz′, *a.* Gazing; staring.

age, āj, *n.* [M.E. < O.Fr. *eage,* L.L. *aetaticum,* < L. *eatas, aetatis,* abbrev. of *aevitas,* < *aevum,* an age. EVER.] A period of time representing the whole or part of the duration of any individual thing or being; the time during which an individual has lived; the latter part of life; the state of being old; old people collectively; as, *age* versus youth; life expectancy; as, the *age* of the fruit fly; legal maturity, or the age when certain rights are granted; as, to be under *age*; *colloq.* a long or protracted period; as, not to have been there in an *age.* A historical epoch; as, the Victorian *Age*; an epoch having a particular character; as, an *age* of expansion; the people who live in a particular period or generation; as, *ages* yet unborn.

age, āj, *v.i.*—*aged, aging, aged, ageing.* To grow old; to assume the appearance of old age.—*v.t.* To give the character of age or ripeness to; as, to *age* wine.

a·ged, ā′jid, ājd, *a.* Of advanced age; very old; brought to full development; pertaining to old age, ā′jid. Of the age of, ājd.—**a·ged·ly,** ā′jid·lē, *adv.*—**a·ged·ness,** ā′jid·nis, *n.*

age·less, āj′lis, *a.* To be exempt from age; never old or outdated.

age·long, āj′lang″, āj′long′, *a.* Lasting as long as an age.

a·gen·cy, ā′jen·sē, *n.* pl. **a·gen·cies.** [M.L. *agentia.* AGENT.] The state of being in action or of exerting power; instrumentality; means; the office or business of an agent or factor; an organization or company that offers its services; a governmental division.

a·gen·da, a·jen′da, *n.* pl. *but sing.* in *constr.* [L. things to be done.] Memoranda; list or program of things to be done or acted upon.

a·gene, ā′jēn, *n.* Commercially produced nitrogen trichloride. (Trademark.)

a·gen·e·sis, ā·jen′i·sis, *n. Med.* A lack or an imperfect development, as of a body part; sterility.

a·gent, ā′jent, *n.* [M.E. < Med. < *agens, agentis,* acting. ACT.] One who or that which acts; an active power or cause; a body or substance that causes a certain action to begin; a person entrusted with the business of another.

a·gen·tial, ā·jen′shal, *a.* Pertaining to an agent or agency.

a·gent of·fi·cer, *n. Milit.* an army officer selected to allocate funds.

a·gent pro·vo·ca·teur, a·zhon prō·vō·ka·têr′, *n.* pl. **a·gents pro·vo·ca·teurs.** [Fr. provocatory agent.] Any secret agent employed to incite persons to some action, for the purpose of rendering them liable to punishment.

age-old, āj′ōld′, *a.* Ancient; having been in existence for ages.

ag·er·a·tum, aj″e·rā′tum, a·jer′a·tum, *n.* [N.L. < Gr. *ageration,* kind of plant, < *a-* and *geras,* old age.] One of the tropical American composite plants of the aster family, genus *Ageratum,* as *A. conyzoides,* a garden annual with small, dense, blue or white flowerheads; any of the blue-flowered composite plants.

ag·glom·er·ate, a·glom′e·rāt″, *v.t.*—*agglomerated, agglomerating.* [L. *agglomeratus,* pp. of *agglomerare,* < *ad,* to, and *glomerare,* form into a ball, < *glomus,* ball.] To collect or gather into a mass.—*v.i.* To cluster together.—*a.*glom′er·it, a·glom′er·rāt″, *n.* An agglomerate mass or formation, as of angular volcanic fragments.—*a.* Massed or packed together; *bot.* densely clustered.

ag·glom·er·a·tion, a·glom′e·rā′shan, *n.* The act of agglomerating; agglomerated state; an indiscriminately formed mass.—**ag·glom·er·a·tive,** a·glom′e·rā″tiv, a·glom′er·e·tiv, *a.* Tending to agglomerate.

ag·glu·ti·nant, a·glöt′i·nant, *a.* Uniting as glue; tending to cause adhesion.—*n.* Any viscous substance which agglutinates or unites other substances.

ag·glu·ti·nate, a·glöt′i·nāt″, *v.t.*—*agglutinated, agglutinating.* [L. *agglutino—ad,* and *glutino,* < *gluten,* glue. GLUE.] To unite or cause to adhere, as with glue or other viscous substance; to glue together; to combine; to attach.—*v.i.* To unite or adhere in a cluster.—*a.*glöt′i·nit, a·glöt′i·nāt, *a.* United as by glue; joined.

ag·glu·ti·na·tion, a·glöt′i·nā′shan, *n.* The act or the state of agglutinating; adhesion of parts; *ling.* word formation in which the morphemes retain an independence of meaning and form rather than fusing or blending with combining elements; *biol.* the clumping together of bacteria or other cells because of the introduction of an antibody.

ag·glu·ti·na·tive, a·glö′tin·ā″tiv, a·glö′tin·a·tiv, *a.* Tending or having power to agglutinate; *ling.* characterized by agglutination.

ag·grade, a·grād′, *v.t.*—*aggraded, aggrading.* [L. *ad,* to, and *gradus,* E. grade.] *Geol.* to raise the grade or level of a river valley, etc., as by the depositing of detritus: opposed to *degrade.*—**ag·gra·da·tion,** ag·rā·dā′shon, *n.*

ag·gran·dize, ag′ran·dīz″, a·gran′dīz, *v.t.*—*aggrandized, aggrandizing.* [Fr. *agrandir*—L. prefix *a* for *ad,* to, and *grandis,* grand.] To make great or greater: especially to make greater in power, wealth, rank, or honor; to make something appear greater; to exaggerate; to promote; to exalt; to elevate; to extend; to enlarge.—**ag·gran·dize·ment,** a·gran′diz·ment, *n.* The act of aggrandizing; the act of increasing one's own power, rank, or honor; advancement.—**ag·gran·diz·er,** ag′ran·dīz″ẽr, *n.* One who aggrandizes.

ag·gra·vate, ag′ra·vāt″, *v.t.*—*aggravated, aggravating.* [L. *aggravo—ad,* to, and *gravis,* heavy. GRAVE, GRIEF.] To make worse, more severe, or less tolerable; to make more enormous, or less excusable; to intensify; to exaggerate; to provoke; to irritate; to tease; to annoy.—**ag·gra·vat·ing,** ag′ra·vāt″ing, *a.* Provoking; annoying.—**ag·gra·vat·ing·ly,** ag′ra·vāt″ing·lē, *adv.* In an aggravating manner.

ag·gra·va·tion, ag″ra·vā′shan, *n.* The act of aggravating or making worse; provocation; irritation; source of annoyance.

ag·gre·gate, ag′re·gāt″, *v.t.*—*aggregated, aggregating.* [M.E. < L. *aggrego, aggregatum*—*ad,* and *grex, gregis,* a herd or band.] To bring together; to collect into a sum, mass, or body; to amount to; to form a sum of.

ag·gre·gate, ag′re·git, ag′re·gāt″, *n.* A sum, mass, or assemblage of particulars; a whole or total; the small particles which make up soil; *geol.* a combination of mineral substances which can be separated by mechanical means, as sandstone.—**in the ag·gre·gate,** taken altogether; considered as a whole; collectively.—**ag·gre·gate·ly,** ag′re·git·lē, ag′re·gāt″lē, *adv.* Collectively; taken in a sum or mass.

ag·gre·gate, ag′re·git, ag′re·gāt″, *a.* Formed by the conjunction or collection of particulars into a whole mass or sum; total; *bot.* pertaining to or characterized by a cluster of florets or carpels.

ag·gre·ga·tion, ag″re·gā′shan, *n.* The act or the state of aggregating; an aggregate; *biol.* a group of organisms living closely together but not as integrated as a society.

ag·gre·ga·tive, ag′re·gā″tiv, *a.* Tending to aggregate; collective.

ag·gress, a·gres′, *v.i.* [L. *aggredior, aggressus—ad,* and *gradior,* to go.] To make a first attack; to commit the first act of hostility or offense.—*v.t.* To attack.

ag·gres·sion, a·gresh′an, *n.* The first attack or act of hostility; the first act leading to a war or controversy; an encroachment or inroad; offensive action. *Psych.* inwardly or outwardly directed hostility.

ag·gres·sive, a·gres′iv, *a.* Characterized by aggression; tending to agress; offensive, as contrasted with *defensive*; taking the initiative boldly forward.—**ag·gres·sive·ness,** a·gres′iv·nis, *n.* The quality of being aggressive.

ag·gres·sor, a·gres′ẽr, *n.* The person who aggresses; an assaulter; an invader.

ag·grieve, a·grēv′, *v.t.*—*aggrieved, aggrieving.* [M.E. < M.Fr. *agrever,* to weigh down, *grever,* to oppress, < L. *gravis,* heavy, whence also *grief, grave,* etc.] To give pain or sorrow to; to afflict; to grieve; to oppress or injure in one's rights; to trouble sorely.

ag·grieved, a·grēvd′, *a.* Injured or wronged; *law,* deprived of legal rights. Unhappy; worried; bothered.

a·ghast, a·gast′, a·gäst′, *a.* [A participial form < M.E. *agastern, agesten,* to terrify—prefix *a.* intens., and O.E. *gaestan,* to terrify; allied to Goth. *gaisjan; usgaisjan,* to terrify.] Struck with amazement or consternation; stupefied with sudden fright or horror.

ag·ile, aj′il, *a.* [M.Fr. *agile,* < L. *agilis,* < *ago.* ACT.] Nimble; spry; quick and light in movement; of the mind or intelligence, alert, active.—**ag·ile·ly,** aj′il·ē, *adv.* In an agile or nimble manner.

a·gil·i·ty, a·jil′i·tē, *n.* The state or quality of being agile; nimbleness; briskness; activity; intellectual acuity. Also **ag·ile·ness,** ag′il·nis.

ag·i·o, aj′ē·ō″, *n.* [It.] The difference in value between one sort of money and another, especially between paper money and metallic coin; a premium paid for exchanging currencies.

ag·i·o·tage, aj′ē·a·tij, *n.* The business of one who deals in foreign exchange.

---

ag·i·tate, aj′i·tāt″, *v.t.*—*agitated*, *agitating*. [L. *agito*, *agitatum*, freq. < *ago*. ACT.] To move or force into violent irregular action; to shake or move briskly; to perturb; to discuss; debate; arouse public attention to, as by speeches, pamphlets, etc.—*v.i.* To engage in agitation.—**ag·i·tat·ed·ly**, aj′i·tāt″id·lē, *adv.*—**ag·i·ta·tive**, aj′i·tā″tiv, *a.*

ag·i·ta·tion, aj″i·tā′shan, *n.* The act of agitating, or state of being agitated; perturbation of mind or feelings; bodily disturbance; commotion. Persistent urging of a cause, esp. political or social, before the public.

a·gi·ta·to, aj″i·tä′tō, *a.* [It.] *Mus.* In a hurried or restless style or movement; agitated.—*adv.*

ag·i·ta·tor, aj′i·tā″tor, *n.* One who or that which agitates, arouses, or stirs up public discontent; a mixing device.

a·gleam, a·glēm′, *a.* Gleaming; bright, shiny.

ag·let, ag′lit, *n.* [M.E. *aglet* < M.Fr. *aiguillette*, diminutive of *aiguille*, a needle; L. *acus*, a needle.] A metal tag at the end of a shoelace; a similar ornamentation on clothing. Also *aiglet*.

a·gley, a·glē′, a·glī′, *adv.* [Sc., lit. squintingly < *a*- and *gley*, to squint.] *Chiefly Sc.* Off the right track; awry; wrong.

a·glim·mer, a·glim′ẽr, *adj.* In a shining state; glimmering.

a·glit·ter, a·glit′ẽr, *adj.* In a glittering state.

a·glow, a·glō′, *a.* In a glow; glowing; *fig.* excited.

ag·nail, ag′nāl, *n.* [M.E. corn on the foot < O.E. *angnægl* = *ange*, pain, and *nægl*, nail.] A hangnail; inflammation of a fingernail or toenail.

ag·nate, ag′nāt, *n.* [L. *agnatus*, *ad*, and *nasci*, *natus*, to be born.] Any male relation on the father's side.—*a.* Related or akin on the father's side.—**ag·nat·ic**, ag·nat′ik, *a.* Pertaining to descent by the male line, of ancestors.—**ag·na·tion**, ag·nā′shan, *n.* Relation by the father's side only or descent in the male line.

ag·no·men, ag·nō′men, *n.* pl. **ag·nom·i·na**, ag·nom′e·na. [L.—*ag* for *ad*, to, and *nomen*, a name.] An additional name or epithet conferred on a person, especially used in reference to the ancient Romans; a nickname.

ag·nos·tic, ag·nos′tik, *n.* [Gr. *agnostos*, unknowing, unknown; < *a*, not, and stem of *gignōskō*, to know. Same root as *know*.] A person who disclaims any knowledge of God or of the origin of the universe or of anything but material phenomena, holding that with regard to such matters, nothing can be known; *philos.* one who doubts or denies that ultimate knowledge in some area of study is possible.—*a.* Pertaining to the agnostics or their doctrines; maintaining the uncertainty of all claims of knowledge. —**ag·nos·ti·cism**, ag·nos′ti·sizm, *n.* The doctrines or belief of agnostics.

Ag·nus De·i, ag′nus dē′ī, ä′nyös de′ē, *n.* [LL., "Lamb of God": see John, i. 29.] *Eccles.* a figure of a lamb as emblematic of Christ.

a·go, a·gō′, *a.*, *adv.* [M.E. *agon*, *ago*, pp. of *agon*, pass away < O.E. *âgân*, gone by—*â*, away, *gân*, to go.] Past; gone; preceding the present time; as, a year *ago*.

a·gog, a·gog′, *a.*, *adv.* [M.Fr. *en gogues*, lively, merry, lit. in mirth.] In eager excitement; highly excited by eagerness, anticipation, or curiosity.

ag·on, ag′ōn, ag′on, *n.* pl. **ag·ons**, **a·go·nes**, a·gō′nēz. [Gr. *agon*, struggle.] In ancient Greece, a competition in which awards were given to those who excelled in different categories, such as painting, athletics, drama, etc.; in ancient Greek drama, an organized discussion; *liter.* struggle, esp. the struggle that exists between the hero and his adversary.

ag·o·nal, ag′o·nal, *a.* Relating to or characteristic of agony.

a·gon·ic, ā·gon′ik, *a.* [Gr. *a*, not, and *gōnia*, an angle.] Not forming an angle.

a·gon·ic lines, *n.* An imaginary line on the earth's surface, joining places having no magnetic declination and at which the magnetic needle points to the true north as well as magnetic north.

ag·o·nist, ag′on·ist, *n.* [L.L. *agonista*, competitor, < Gr. *agonistes* < *agonizesthai*: see *agonize*.] A contender in public games; a combatant. A person who is struggling with inner conflicts. *Physiol.* a contracting muscle which is controlled by another opposing muscle.

ag·o·nize, ag′o·nīz″, *v.i.*—*agonized*, *agonizing*. To be in agony or extreme pain; put forth excessive effort; strain.—*v.t.* To distress with extreme pain; to torture.

ag·o·nized, ag′o·nīzd″, *a.* Marked by suffering or exhibiting agony.

ag·o·niz·ing, ag′o·nī″zing, *a.* Bringing about agony or acute suffering.

ag·o·ny, ag′o·nē, *n.* pl. **ag·o·nies**. [Gr. *agōnia*, struggle, anguish, < *agōn*, a contest or struggle, < *agō*, to lead, to bring together.] Extreme bodily or mental pain; intense suffering; anguish; torment. The struggle, frequently unconscious, that precedes natural death.

ag·o·ny col·umn, *n.* *Colloq.* a newspaper column comprised of advertisements by people searching for lost relatives, possessions, etc.

ag·o·ra·pho·bi·a, ag″or·a·fō′bē·a, *n.* [L. < Gr. *agora*, a marketplace, N.L. *phobia*, fear.] Morbid fear of open spaces.

a·graffe, **a·grafe**, a·graf′, *n.* [Fr. *agrafe*, O.Fr. *agrape*, < *a*, to, and *grape*, hook: GRAPE.] An ornamental clasp for hooking together parts of clothing, etc.; a device for preventing vibration in a piano-string; a small cramp iron used by a builder.

a·gran·u·lo·cyte, a·gran″ū·lō′sīt, *n.* A leukocyte that does not have cytoplasmic granules.

a·gran·u·lo·cy·to·sis, a·gran″yu·lō·sī″tō′sis, *n.* A serious, destructive blood disease distinguished by a decrease of the leukocytes.

ag·ra·pha, ag′ra·fa, *n. pl.* [N.L. Gr. *agrapha*, neut. pl. of *agraphos*, unwritten, *a*-, not, and *graphein*, write.] Sayings ascribed to Jesus which have been preserved in the writings of early Christians and in the parts of the New Testament not including the Canonical Gospels.

a·graph·i·a, a·graf′ē·a, *n.* [Gr. *a*, not, and *graphein*, to write.] A form of aphasia; a cerebral disorder, in which the patient is unable to express ideas by written signs.

a·grar·i·an, a·grâr′ē·an, *a.* [L. *agrarius* < *ager*, a field. ACRE.] Relating to lands, or the division of lands, especially public lands; rural; growing wild in fields; pertaining to farmers or their organizations and interests.

a·grar·i·an, a·grâr′ē·an, *n.* One in favor of an equal division of landed property and the progress of farmers' organizations and movements.

a·grar·i·an·ism, a·grâr′ē·a·nizm, *n.* The doctrine and movement advocating equal division of lands and property, and any innovations or proposals which would improve the economic status of the farmer.

a·gree, a·grē′, *v.i.*—*agreed*, *agreeing*. [M.E. *agreen* < M.Fr. *agreer*—*a*-, to, and *gre* < O.Fr. *gret*, good-will, favor, < L. *gratus*, pleasant, whence *gratitude*, *grateful*, etc.] To be of one mind; to harmonize in opinion; to live in concord or without contention; to come to an arrangement or understanding; to arrive at a settlement; to be consistent; not to contradict or be repugnant; to tally; to match; to corre-

spond; to suit; to be accommodated or adapted, followed by *with*, as: Food *agrees* *with* a person. *Gram.* to correspond in number, case, gender, or person.

a·gree·a·bil·i·ty, a·grē″a·bil′i·tē, *n.* Agreeableness.

a·gree·a·ble, a·grē′a·bl, *a.* Suitable; conformable; correspondent; pleasing, either to the mind or senses (*agreeable* manners, *agreeable* to the taste); willing or ready to agree or consent.—**a·gree·a·ble·ness**, a·grē′a·bl·nis, *n.* The state or quality of being agreeable.—**a·gree·a·bly**, a·grē′a·blē, *adv.* In an agreeable manner; suitably; consistently; conformably; in a manner to give pleasure; pleasingly.

a·gree·ment, a·grē′ment, *n.* The state of agreeing or being agreed; harmony; conformity; union of opinions or sentiments; bargain; compact; contract; *gram.* correspondence, as in gender, case, or number.

a·gré·ment, ä″grä·mänt′, *n.* pl. **a·gré·ments**. [Fr.] Official approval by a government of an envoy who has been proposed by a foreign government.

a·gres·tic, a·gres′tik, *a.* [L. *agrestis*, < *ager*, a field.] Rural; rustic; uncouth.

ag·ri·cul·tur·al, ag″ri·kul′chur·al, *a.* Pertaining to, connected with, or engaged in agriculture.

ag·ri·cul·ture, ag′ri·kul″chur, *n.* [Fr. < L. *agricultura*—*ager*, a field, and *cultura*, cultivation. ACRE and CULTURE.] The cultivation of the ground; the raising of crops and feeding of cattle or other livestock; husbandry; tillage; farming; agronomy.— **ag·ri·cul·tur·ist**, **ag·ri·cul·tur·al·ist**, ag″ri·kul′chur·ist, ag″ri·kul′chur·al·ist, *n.*

ag·ri·mo·ny, ag′ri·mō″nē, *n.* pl. **ag·ri·mo·nies**. [M.E. < M.Fr. *aigremoine* < L. *argemonia* (by metathesis) *agrimonia* < Gr. *argemōnē*, poppy.] One of several N. American plants of the genus *Agrimonia*, having small yellow flowers, pinnate leaves, and small fruits with hooked bristles.

ag·ri·ol·o·gy, ag″rē·ol′o·jē, *n.* [Gr. *agrios*, pertaining to a wild state, and *logos*, a discourse.] The comparative study of human customs, especially of the customs of man in a civilization of lesser development.— **ag·ri·ol·o·gist**, ag″rē·ol′o·jist, *n.* A student of agriology.

ag·ro·bi·o·log·ic, ag″rō·bī·o·loj′ik, *a.* Of or pertaining to agrobiology.

ag·ro·bi·ol·o·gy, ag″rō·biäl′o·jē, *n.* The science of plant nutrition and life as related to the production of crops.

ag·ro·log·ic, ag″ro·loj′ik, *a.* Of or pertaining to agrology.

a·grol·o·gist, a·grol′o·jist, *n.* One who specializes in the science of agrology.

a·grol·o·gy, a·grol′o·jē, *n.* [< Gr. *agros*, field.] The study of soils, esp. in relation to the production of crops.

a·gron·o·my, a·gron′o·mē, *n.* [Probably < Fr. < Gr. *agros*, field, and -nomy < Gr. *nomos*, law.] Agriculture; management of farms; science of crop production.—**ag·ro·nom·ic**, **ag·ro·nom·i·cal**, ag″ro·nom′ik, ag″ro·nom′i·kal, *a.* Relating to agronomy.—**a·gron·o·mist**, a·gron′o·mist, *n.* One who studies agronomy.

ag·ro·tech·ny, ag′ro·tek·nē, *n.* [< Gr. *agros*, field, and *techne*, art.] The branch of agricultural science that deals with the conversion of raw farm products into manufactured commodities, as in dairying, canning, etc.

a·ground, a·ground′, *a.*, *adv.* On the ground; run ashore; stranded.

a·gue, ā′gū, *n.* [M.E. < M.Fr. *ague*, < M.L. (*febris*, fever) *acuta*, prop. fem. of L. *acutus*, acute.] An intermittent malarial fever with periodic chills; a fit or attack of shivering; a chill.—*v.t.*—*agued*, *aguing*. To affect as with ague.—**a·gu·ish**, ā′gū·ish, *a.* Of or

like ague; conducive or subject to ague.—
a·gu·ish·ly, ä′gū·ish·lē, *adv.*

ah, ä, *interj.* [M.E. *a*, comp. G. *ach*, L. *ah*, Skt. *â*, *âh*, ah.] An exclamation expressive of pain, surprise, pity, compassion, complaint, contempt, dislike, joy, exultation, etc., according to the manner of utterance.

a·ha, ä·hä′, *interj.* [M.E. comp. G. *aha*, Skt. *ahô*, *ahaha*.] An exclamation expressing triumph, contempt, derision, surprise, etc.

a·head, a·hed′, *adv.* Headlong; in or to the front; in advance; before; upward in position; further on.

a·hem, a·hem′, *interj.* An utterance designed to attract attention, express doubt, or serve as a warning.

a·him·sa, a·him′sä, a·hing′sä, *n.* [< Skt.] *Jainism, Hinduism* and *Buddhism*, the religious principle which rejects any use of violence.

A ho·ri·zon, *n.* The uppermost layer in the soil profile, often called surface soil or topsoil, in which organic matter is most plentiful.

a·hoy, a·hoi′, *interj.* [Longer form of *hoy!*] A word used chiefly at sea in hailing.

aid, ād, *v.t.* [M.E. < M.Fr. *aider*, < L. *adjutare*, freq. of *adjuvo, adjutum*, to help—*ad*, to, and *juvo, jutum*, to help.] To help; to facilitate; to come to the support or relief of; to succor.

aid, ād, *n.* Support; assistance; the person or thing that aids or yields assistance; an auxiliary.—**aid·er**, ād′er, *n.* One who aids; an assistant.—**for·eign aid**, any assistance granted by one nation to another for political, social, or economic purposes.

aide, ād, *n.* [Fr.] A person acting as an official assistant to a superior; subordinate; aide-de-camp.

aide-de-camp, ād′de·kamp′, *n.* pl. **aides-de-camp**, ādz′de·kamp′. [Fr. lit. 'field assistant.'] *Milit.* an officer whose duty is to receive and communicate the orders of a general officer, and to act as his secretary.

aid·man, ād′man, ād′män, *n.* pl. **aid·men.** *Milit.* a medical corpsman in the army assigned to a field unit.

aid sta·tion, *n. Milit.* a medical installation in a forward or isolated area where emergency or minor treatment, sorting, and classification of sick and wounded battle casualties are performed.

ai·glet, ā′glit, *n.* Aglet.

ai·grette, ā′gret, ā·gret′, *n.* [Fr. *aigrette*, O.Fr. *aigrete*, < *aigron-hairon*, E. *heron*.] The small white egret or heron of Europe; also a tuft or plume of heron or other feathers used as a head ornament, in millinery, etc.; a jeweled or other head-ornament of similar form.

ai·guille, ā·gwēl′, ā′gwēl, *n.* [Fr. a needle.] The needlelike points or tops of rocks and mountain masses, or sharp-pointed masses of ice on glaciers; also a drill for blasting holes.

ai·guil·lette, ā″gwi·let′, *n.* [Fr. *aiguillette*, see AIGUILLE.] A metal tag; *milit.* a metal-tipped, three-strand braided cord worn around the left shoulder of a service uniform by attachés and aides.

ail, āl, *v.t.* [M.E. *eylen*, O.E. *eglian*, to feel pain; to ail; *eglan*, to give pain; *egle*, trouble, grief; comp. Goth. *aglo*, affliction, Sw. *agg*, a prick.] To affect with pain or uneasiness, either of body or mind; to trouble, as: What *ails* her?—*v.i.* To be in pain, ill health, or trouble.—**ail·ing**, ā′ling, *a.*

ai·lan·thus, ā·lan′thus, *n.* pl. **ai·lan·thus·es.** [< Amboinese *ai lanto*, tree of heaven.] An Asiatic tree of the genus *Ailanthus*, with ill-scented green flowers; the tree of heaven, widely grown in cities.

ai·ler·on, ā′le·ron″, *n.* [Fr. < *aile*, wing, and *-eron*, a diminutive.] *Aeron.* a control surface set into or near the trailing edge of an airplane wing, extending, when in the wing, toward the tip and usually within the contour of the wing, used to control the rolling movements of the airplane. A wing wall, as that of a church aisle.

ail·ment, āl′ment, *n.* Disease; physical disorder.

aim, ām, *v.i.* [M.E. < M.Fr. *esmer, aesmer*— L. *ad*, to, and *aestimare*, to estimate.] To direct a missile toward an object; to direct the mind or intention; to make an attempt; to endeavor, followed by *at.*—*v.t.* To level, as an object or remark, followed by *at*; to intend, followed by an infinitive, as: We *aim* to finish today. *Milit.* to point, as a fighter plane, so that its guns may be brought to bear upon a target; to point, as a gun, so that its missile is expected to strike a target; to drop, as a bomb or mine.

aim, ām, *n.* The pointing or directing of a missile; the target intended to be hit, or object intended to be affected; the mark; a purpose; design; scheme.

aim·less, ām′lis, *a.* Without aim; purposeless; futile.—**aim·less·ly**, ām′lis·lē, *adv.*

ain't, ānt. [Variation of *amn't*, contraction of *am* and *not.*] *Regarded as nonstandard*, is not; are not; has not; have not. *Regarded as nonstandard in all but a few U.S. dialects*, am not. Although the use of *ain't* is considered acceptable in some varieties of spoken English, it is so widely regarded as a mark of illiteracy that it should generally be avoided. *Ain't* is never acceptable in written English.

air, âr, *n.* [M.E. < O.Fr. *air*, L. *aër*, < Gr. *aēr*, air.] A heterogeneous mixture of tasteless, odorless, colorless, and invisible gases surrounding the earth, consisting of 78.03% nitrogen, 20.99% oxygen, 0.94% argon, 0.03% carbon dioxide, 0.01% hydrogen, and traces of krypton, neon, helium, and xenon; that which we breathe and which is essential to all plant and animal life; air in motion. *Mus.* a tune; the principal melody part in a harmonized piece of music. Mien, manner of a person or thing; as, an *air* of importance; semblance; an affected manner.

air, âr, *v.t.* To expose to, put out in, the air; to let air into; to ventilate; as, to *air* a room; to state publicly; as, to *air* one's views.

air al·ert, *n. Milit.* A state of alertness on the part of an aircrew for meeting an air attack, or for engaging in some other air action, marked by getting airplanes into the air ready for immediate response to orders; the signal for this kind of action.

air base, *n. Milit.* In the U.S. Air Force, an establishment comprising an airfield, its installations, facilities, personnel, and activities for the flight, operation, maintenance, and supply of aircraft and air organizations; a similar installation belonging to any other air force; the base of operations for aircraft: in a restricted sense, only the physical installation.

air blad·der, *n.* A sac filled with air located under the backbone of most fish, and responsible for their buoyancy, which regulates hydrostatic pressure in many higher fish. Also **air sac.**

air·borne, âr′bōrn″, âr′bȯrn″, *a.* Supported entirely by aerodynamic forces; flying; having risen from the ground; unmoored and floating in air; aloft; transported through or by the air.

air brake, *n.* A mechanical brake operated by compressed air which acts on a piston; an aircraft speed brake.

air·brush, âr′brush, *n.* A device attached to a compressed-air hose, for the spraying of paint.

air·burst, âr′burst″, *n.* An explosion occurring in the air, usually of a bomb, shell, or the like.

air car·ri·er, *n.* An organization, esp. a civil one, in the business of air transportation; an aircraft that carries cargo, mail, or passengers.

air cas·tle, *n.* A daydream; an unrealizable scheme.

air cham·ber, *n.* Any cavity or compartment filled with air.

air coach, *n.* The more economical and less elegant class of passenger transportation offered by certain airlines.

air com·mand, *n. Milit.* a unit of command comprising two or more air forces.

air con·di·tion, *v.t.* To regulate the quality, temperature, etc. of air indoors.

air con·di·tion·er, *n.* A ventilating device used esp. for cooling purposes.

air con·di·tion·ing, *n.* The process of regulating the quality, temperature, humidity, and circulation of air in a space enclosure.

air con·trol·man, *n.* A U.S. Navy petty officer who is coordinator of air traffic.

air-cooled, âr′kōld, *a.* Cooled by air, as in an automobile engine.

air cor·ri·dor, *n. Milit.* a passage in the air for aircraft, esp. such a passage either leading through a system of anti-aircraft defenses or established by international agreement.

air·craft, âr′kraft″, âr′kräft″, *n.* pl. **air-craft.** *Aeron.* any machine or craft designed to go through the air (including, in some instances, outer space), given lift by its own buoyancy (as with airships), or by dynamic reaction of air particles over and about its surfaces, or by reaction to a jet stream or other fluid jet.

air·craft car·ri·er, *n.* A ship designed to carry naval airplanes, with special decks for taking off and landing.

air·crew, âr′krö″, *n.* The group of persons responsible for the flying of an aircraft.

air cur·rent, *n.* A stream of air moving in any direction other than horizontal, esp. in the vertical.

air de·fense, *n. Milit.* Defense system against attack by enemy aircraft or guided missiles; the sum total of all measures undertaken for this purpose; an organization or activity providing this defense.

air drill, *n.* A device for drilling, powered by compressed air.

air·drome, âr′drōm″, *n.* An airfield; a hangar; a landing field for airplanes; airport; aerodrome.

air·drop, âr′drop″, *v.t.*—*airdropped, airdropping. Milit.* to release troops or equipment from an aircraft in flight.—*n.* An instance of airdropping.

air-dry, âr′drī″, *a.* So dry that no moisture is removed upon exposure to air.—*v.t.*— *airdried, airdrying.* To dry through exposure to air.

air duct, *n.* A tube, especially used in mines, through which fresh air is pumped in, and impure air expelled.

Aire·dale ter·ri·er, âr′dāl, *n.* [From *Airedale* in Yorkshire, England.] A large, heavy type of terrier with a rough brown or tan coat which is black or grizzled over the back.

air-en·gine, âr′en″jin, *n.* An engine driven by heated or compressed air.

air ex·press, *n.* A system for the prompt transportation of goods by air; the goods transported by this method.

air·field, âr′fēld″, *n.* A landing field equipped with runways for airplanes; an airport.

air fleet, *n. Milit.* a grouping of aircraft, esp. under the direction of a single commanding officer; as, the 7th *Air Fleet.*

air·flow, âr′flō″, *n.* A flow or movement of air caused by a vehicle in motion.

air·foil, âr′foil″, *n.* Wing, rudder, or any aircraft surface designed to control an airplane by reacting to a moving air stream.

air force, *n. Milit.* the organization of personnel, equipment, and installations for carrying out military operations in the air; (*cap.*) a numbered or named air force as, the 7th Air Force, the U.S. Air Force, etc. The amount of power exerted in or from the air; any of the forces exerted upon an object in flight as, drag, gravity, thrust, etc. or the sum of these forces; aerodynamic force.

air·frame, âr′frām″, *n.* The structural components of an airplane without the engines.

air freight, *n.* Air cargo; air express; a system or service for the transport of this air cargo.

air gauge, *n.* An instrument for measuring air pressure.

air·glow, âr′glō″, *n.* A radiant emission from the upper atmosphere that appears at night over the middle and low latitudes.

air gun, *n.* A firearm operated by compressed air; a hand tool operated by compressed air.

air·head, âr′hed, *n. Milit.* an area within enemy territory, or within friendly territory which is threatened, or territory that is not readily accessible by surface movement, held or seized to insure continuous supply of troops and material by air.

air hole, *n.* A hole made to allow air to pass in or out; a natural outlet in the ice covering a pond or river; an air pocket.

air·i·ly, âr′i·lē, *adv.* In an airy, breezy manner; in a light, gay manner; jauntily.

air·ing, âr′ing, *n.* An exposure to air; as, to give clothes an *airing*; a short walk or drive out of doors; an exposure to public notice.

air jack·et, *n.* An inflatable jacket (life jacket) rendering the wearer buoyant in water; also, an envelope of enclosed air about part of a machine, as for checking radiation of heat.

air lane, *n.* A particular route through the air traversed by aircraft; airway.

air launch, *v.t.* To launch from an aircraft in the air; as, to *air launch* a guided missile.

air·lift, air lift, âr′lift″, *n.* A supply line operated by aircraft.—*v.t.* To transport by air, esp. to a beleagured place or situation.

air·line, âr′līn″, *n.* An established system of aerial transportation, esp. a commercial system, together with its equipment, holdings, and facilities; the company owning or operating such a system; a great circle route between two points.

air·lin·er, air lin·er, âr′līn″nėr, *n.* A commerical transport airplane used by an airline.

air lock, *n.* An airtight area at the entrance of a pressure chamber for the purpose of regulation; an impediment, as in a water pipe or pump, caused by an air bubble.

air·mail, air-mail, âr′māl″, *n.* Mail service by airplane; mail so transmitted.—*v.t.* To send by airmail.—*a.* Of, or relating to airmail; as, an *airmail* stamp.

air·man, âr′man, *n.* pl. **airmen.** A civilian aviator; an enlisted man or woman of any Air Force rank below staff sergeant.

air·man ba·sic, *n.* An enlisted man in the Air Force, who is of the lowest rank.

air·man·ship, âr′man·ship″, *n.* The art or skill of piloting or navigating aircraft.

air mar·shal, *n Brit. milit.* a commissioned officer in the air force of a rank above an air vice-marshal and below an air chief marshal. Abbr. *A.M.*

air mass, *n.* A large body of air over a wide area, having uniform moisture and temperature conditions throughout in a horizontal direction.

Air Med·al, *n. Milit.* a decoration presented to U.S. Air Force personnel for meritorious achievement while in aerial flight.

air mile, *n.* A nautical mile by air.

air·mind·ed, âr′mīn″did, *a.* Interested in and approving of air travel or things aeronautic.

air·plane, âr′plān″, *n. Aeron.* In a broad sense, any heavier-than-air craft supported by the dynamic reaction of air flowing over fixed or rotating plane surfaces (as distinguished from aerostats), including the piston-driven and jet airplane, the glider, helicopter, gyroplane, and the winged guided missile; in a restricted sense, a power-driven aircraft having a fixed wing or an adjustable fixed wing; any winged aircraft, including the helicopter, exclusive of the glider and the winged guided missile; a landplane as distinguished from a seaplane.

air plant, *n. Bot.* A general name for plants that grow upon others and derive all their food from the atmosphere, as many orchids; an epiphyte.

air pock·et, *n.* An airspace marked by strong, vertical current flow which, when entered or encountered by an aircraft, causes the craft suddenly to rise or drop, esp. to drop, as if into a pocket.

air po·lice, *n.* (*Often cap.*) the organized police in the Air Force or Air National Guard reponsible for maintaining law and order.

air·port, âr′pōrt″, âr″pårt″, *n.* An airfield on land or water, with a hangar or hangars, for the landing, take-off, and servicing of aircraft that receive or discharge passengers or cargo.

air·post, âr′pōst, *n.* A mail service by airplane; airmail.

air pow·er, *n.* That power which arises from man's ability to fly in a vehicle or to cause a vehicle to go through the air or through space; *milit.* this power as it exists in a particular nation, as determined by the development of military, commercial, and private aviation.

air pres·sure, *n.* Either the static or dynamic pressure of air, or both, esp., that of the atmosphere; atmospheric pressure; *milit.* force or pressure brought to bear through air power.

air pump, *n.* A machine for the purpose of compressing air, or of exhausting air from a vessel to create a vacuum.

air raid, *n.* An attack by enemy aircraft against a target on the ground, as a city or airfield.

air ri·fle, *n.* A rifle that uses compressed air to propel bullets, pellets, etc.

air route, *n.* An established route followed by commercial aircraft.

air sac, *n.* A sac containing air; one of certain air-filled cavities in birds, fish, etc.

air scoop, *n.* A device or part mounted on an aircraft and open toward the front for taking in air during flight, also used to furnish additional air to an automobile engine.

air·screw, âr′skrō″, *n. Brit.* an aircraft propeller.

air shaft, *n.* A passage for admitting fresh air into a mine or tunnel; a passage in a building which affords ventilation and light.

air·ship, âr′ship″, *n.* A machine for navigating the air, capable of being steered, supported by gas bags and propelled by an engine or engines; a dirigible.

air·sick·ness, âr′sik″nis, *n.* A sickness or disorder sometimes affecting persons aboard an aircraft in flight, caused by the motions of the aircraft and the altitude, characterized esp. by nausea and vertigo.—**air·sick,** âr′sik, *a.*

air-slaked, âr′slākt″, *a.* Slaked by moist air, as lime.

air sleeve, *n.* Windsock; a cloth device tapered to be caught by the wind, showing the wind direction.

air·space, âr′spās″, *n.* Space in the air, or space above a particular surface of the earth, esp. such space above a nation, considered to be under the jurisdiction of that nation.

air·speed, âr′spēd″, *n.* The speed of an aircraft relative to the surrounding air rather than relative to the ground.

air spring, *n.* Any device for resisting sudden pressure by means of the elasticity of air.

air·stream, âr′strēm″, *n.* A current of air; airflow.

air·strip, âr′strip″, *n.* A runway for airplanes.

air ter·mi·nal, *n.* An airport, city, or other geographical place considered to mark a place where commercial aircraft are landed and serviced; an airline terminal.

air·tight, âr′tīt″, *a.* Impermeable to air; hermetically sealed; providing no opening for attack or challenge; as, an *airtight* alibi.

air-to-air, âr′tö-âr′, âr′to-âr′, *adv.* Between or among aircraft in flight.—*a.* Used or occurring between or among aircraft in the air; as, an *air-to-air* missile.

air-ves·sel, *n.* A vessel containing or conducting air; an air chamber; a respiratory duct.

air·wave, âr′wāv″, *n.* The medium by which radio and television broadcasts are transmitted.

air·way, âr′wā″, *n.* A path or route in the air designated by proper authority to be suitable for air traffic; a passage for air currents, as provided in a mine.

air·wor·thy, âr′wur″ṮHē, *a.* Fit, well adapted, or safe for service in the air, as an airplane or airship.—**air·wor·thi·ness,** *n.*

air·y, âr′ē, *a.*—**airier, airiest.** Consisting of or having the character of air; unsubstantial; exposed to air; gay and sprightly; light in movement; lively; affected.—**air·i·ness,** âr′ē·nis, ar′i·nis, *n.* The state or condition of being airy.

aisle, īl. *n.* [M.E. *ile* < M.Fr. *aile,* a wing, an aisle; L. *ala,* a wing; the *s* does not properly belong to the word.] A lateral division of a cathedral or other church, separated from the central part, called the nave, by pillars or piers; any passageway between rows of seats.—**aisled,** īld, *a.* Furnished with aisles.

aitch·bone, āch′bōn, *n.* [M.E. *hach-boon, ach-boon* < *nachebon* (by loss of initial *n* as in *apron*), < M.Fr. *nache,* L.L. *naticae,* L. *nates,* the rump.] The rumpbone of an ox; a section of beef which contains this bone. Also **edge·bone** (by false etymology).

a·jar, *a*·jär′, *a., adv.* [M.E. *achra, onchar,* lit. 'on the turn'—prefix *a,* on, *jar, char,* O.E. *cerre,* a turn, seen also in *chare, char*-woman.] Neither quite open nor shut; partly opened: said of a door; not in harmony with; in discord with.

ak·va·vit, äk′vä·vēt″, *n.* [Sw., Dan., Norw. *akvavit* < M.L. *aqua vitae,* lit. water of life.] A dry, colorless Scandinavian spirit resembling gin, made from neutral spirits which have been redistilled and flavored with caraway seeds. Also *aquavit.*

a·kim·bo, *a*·kim′bō, *a., adv.* [M.E. *kenebowe,* in a sharp bend.] With the elbow pointing outwards and the hand resting on the hip: said of the arm.

a·kin, *a*·kin′, *a.* Related by blood; allied by nature; partaking of the same properties.

à la, ä′lä, ä′la, *prep.* [Fr.] According to or in the mode, manner, or style of: used esp. in reference to cooking; as, beef *à la* Burgundy, or to literary style; as, a short story *à la* O. Henry.

a·la, ä′la, *n.* pl. **a·lae,** ä′lē. [L. wing.] A wing; an anatomical appendage resembling a wing; a winglike part, process, or expansion, as of a bone, a shell, a seed, a stem, etc.; one of the two side petals of a papilionaceous flower; in ancient Rome, a small room in the house which opened into a larger room or courtyard area.

---

ch- chain, G. na*ch*t;   **th-** THen, thin;   **w-** wig, hw as sound in whig;   **z-** zh as in azure, zeal.   *Italicized vowel* indicates schwa sound.

al·a·bas·ter, al′a·bas″tẻr, al′a·bä″stẻr, n. [L. *alabaster,* Gr. *alabastros,* from Alabastron, a village in Egypt where it was obtained.] A hard, translucent marblelike mineral of which there are two well-known varieties, the gypseous and the calcareous, often used for ornamental pieces.—**al·a·-bas·trine,** al′a·bas′trin, a. Of or pertaining to alabaster.

à la carte, ä″la·kärt′, al″a·kärt′, Fr. ä lä kärt′, a. [Fr.] According to the bill of fare; with a stated price for each dish.

a·lack, a·lak′, interj. [M.E. *alacke.*] Archaic, an exclamation expressive of sorrow or regret.—**a·lack·a·day,** a·lak′a·dā″, interj. [Comp, *Well-a-day!*] An exclamation uttered to express regret or sorrow.

a·lac·ri·ty, a·lak′ri·tē, n. [L. *alacritas,* < *alacer, alacris,* cheerful.] A cheerful readiness or promptitude to do some act; cheerful willingness; briskness.

al·a·mo, al′a·mō″, ä′la·mō″, n. [Sp. *álamo.*] In Spanish use, a poplar; in the southwestern U.S., a cottonwood.

al·a·mode, al′a·mōd″, n. [Fr. *à la mode,* after the fashion.] A delicate, glossy fabric used for scarves.

a·larm, a·lärm′, n. [M.E. *alarme* < M.Fr. *alarme,* alarm, < It. *all'arme*—L. *ad illa arma,* to arms.] A summons to arms; an outcry or other notice of approaching danger; a tumult; a disturbance; a sudden fear or painful suspense excited by an apprehension of danger; apprehension; a mechanical contrivance for awakening persons from sleep or rousing their attention.

a·larm, a·lärm′, v.t. To call to arms for defense; to give notice of danger to; to rouse to vigilance; to disturb with terror; to distress; to fill with anxiety by the prospect of evil.—**a·larm·ing,** a·lärm′ing, a. Calculated to rouse alarm; causing apprehension.—**a·larm·ing·ly,** a·lärm′ing·lē, adv. In an alarming manner.

a·larm clock, n. A clock equipped with a bell or buzzer that can be set to sound at a desired time, so as to awaken a sleeper.

a·larm·ism, a·lär′miz″um, n. The tendency or habit to raise alarm with no sufficient reason.

a·larm·ist, a·lär′mist, n. One who excites alarm; one who is prone to take alarm, and to circulate and exaggerate any sort of bad news; one who tends to raise alarm with no sufficient reason.—a.

a·larm re·ac·tion, n. Physiol. The first stage of the adaptation syndrome wherein the body exhibits shock in response to stress; a patterned muscular movement repeated by birds when disturbed.

a·lar·um, a·lar′um, a·lär′um, n. [M.E. *alarom.*] Archaic, alarm.

a·las, a·las′, a·läs′, interj. [O.Fr. *alas,* < interj. *a, ah,* L. *lassus,* weary.] An exclamation expressive of sorrow, grief, pity, concern, or apprehension of evil.

A·las·kan, a·las′kan, a. Of or pertaining to Alaska, the 49th state, extending northwest from Canada and admitted to the U.S. January 3, 1959.—n. A native or resident of Alaska.

A·las·kan mal·a·mute, n. A large, strong dog of Alaskan breed, having a coarse, thick coat of gray or black-and-white fur; used esp. to pull sleds.

A·las·ka Stan·dard Time, n. The standard time in the central Alaskan time zone, two hours behind Pacific Standard Time.

a·late, ā′lāt, a. [L. *alatus,* < *ala,* wing.] Having wings; winged; having alae or winglike parts. Also, **a·lar,** ā′lar; **a·lat·ed,** ā′lā·ted.—**a·la·tion,** ā·lā′shan, n. Alate condition or form; manner of formation or disposition of the wings, as in insects.

alb, alb, n. [L. *alba,* white (*vestis,* garment, understood).] A clerical vestment worn by priests; a long robe of white linen bound with a girdle, worn under the chasuble and over the cassock.

al·ba·core, al′ba·kōr″, al′ba·kar″, n. [Pg. *albacor* < Ar. *al-bakurah,* the tuna.] A large, long-finned oceanic fish, *Thunnus germo,* prized for its edible flesh, the chief source of canned tuna; any of several tunalike fishes.

Al·ba·ni·an, al·bā′nē·an, al·bān′yan, a. Relating to the language, customs and people of Albania, a Balkan republic of southeastern Europe located between Yugoslavia and Greece.—n. A native or inhabitant of Albania; the Indo-European language of the Albanian people.

al·ba·ta, al·bā′ta, n. [< L. *albus,* white.] An alloy consisting of a combination of nickel, zinc, tin, and copper, often with antimony and silver. Also *German silver.*

al·ba·tross, al′ba·tras″, al′ba·tros″, n. [< Sp. and Pg. *alcatraz,* a pelican, the -b- possibly coming from association with L. *alba,* white (the bird's color).] Any of various large aquatic birds of the family *Diomedeidae,* including the largest sea birds.

al·be·do, al·bē′dō, n. [L.L. whiteness, < L. *albus,* white.] Astron. the measurement of light rays upon a planet or satellite, with emphasis on rays emitted and received.

al·be·it, al·bē′it, conj. [M.E. *al be it,* although it be.] Although, notwithstanding, even if.

al·ber·type, al′bẻr·tīp″, n. [From J. *Albert,* the inventor: and *-type.*] A method of printing in ink from a gelatin photographic plate; a print so made; collotype.

al·bes·cent, al·bes′ent, a. [L. *albescere,* to grow white, to begin to whiten < *albus,* white.] Becoming white or rather whitish; moderately white; of a pale, hoary aspect.

Al·bi·gen·ses, al″bi·jen′sēz, n. pl. A sect of religious reformers in the 12th century, who were ruthlessly persecuted: so called from *Albi,* a town of Languedoc in France, where they resided.

al·bin·ic, al·bin′ik, a. Of or pertaining to albinism.

al·bi·nism, al′bi·niz″um, n. The condition or state of being an albino; lack of pigment; inability to produce pigment.

al·bi·no, al·bī′nō, n. pl. **al·bi·nos,** al·bī′-nōz. [Pg. < Sp. *albo* < L. *albus,* white.] A person of abnormally pale, milky complexion, with light hair and pink eyes due to a deficiency in pigmentation; an animal or plant characterized by a lack of normal pigmentation.

Al·bi·on, al′bē·on, n. [L. < Celtic.] Poet. one of the ancient names of England.

al·bite, al′bit, n. [L. *albus,* white.] A name given to feldspar with an alkali of soda instead of potash, light in color and found in alkali rocks.

al·bum, al′bum, n. [L. < *albus,* white.] A book, originally blank, for autographs, pieces of poetry or prose, photographs, memorabilia, etc.; one or more phonograph records contained in one jacket and classified as to performer, composer, or composition; the container itself.

al·bu·men, al·bū′men, n. [< L. *alb(us),* white, and *-u-* (connective) and suffix *-men,* cf. *omen, numen, nomen.*] The white, or clear viscous part of an egg; *bot.* nutritive matter surrounding the embryo in a seed. *Biochem.* a member of a class of proteins which are water-soluble, and are found in the juices and tissues of animals and vegetables, and which contain sulfur, oxygen, hydrogen, carbon, and nitrogen; also **al·bu·min.**—**al·bu·men·ize,** al·bū′ me·niz″, v.t.—**albumenized,** *albumenizing.* To convert into or to cover or impregnate with albumen. Also **al·bu·men·ise.**

al·bu·min·oid, al·bū′mi·noid″, n. A substance resembling albumen; a simple protein found in horny or cartilaginous tissues; protein.—a. Having the characteristics of albumen or albumin.

al·bu·mi·nous, al·bū′mi·nus, a. Pertaining to or having the properties of albumen or albumin, applied to plants whose seeds have a store of albumen, as grain, palms, etc. Also **al·bu·mi·nose,** al·bū′mi·nōs″.

al·bu·mi·nu·ri·a, al·bū″mi·nur′ē·a, al·bū″ mi·nyur′ē·a, n. [*Albumen* and Gr. *ouron,* urine.] *Pathol.* a condition in which the urine contains albumen, often indicating a diseased state of the kidneys.

al·bu·mose, al′byu·mōs″, n. Any of the compounds formed by the action of enzymatic protein hydrolysis.

al·bur·num, al·bur′num, n. [L. *alburnum,* sapwood, < *albus,* white.] The white and softer part of the wood of exogenous plants between the inner bark and the heartwood; the sapwood.

al·cai·de, al·kī′dē, n. [Sp. and Pg. < Ar. *al-qā'id,* the chief.] In Spain, Portugal, southwestern U.S., etc., a commander of a fortress; a jailer or prison warden. Also **al·cayde.**

al·cal·de, al·kal′dē, n. [Sp. and Pg. < Ar. *al quādī,* the judge.] In Spain, Portugal, southwestern U.S., etc., a mayor having both judicial and administrative powers. Also **al·cade.**

al·ca·zar, al′ka·zär″, al·kaz′ẻr, n. [Sp. *alcázar,* < Ar. *al,* the, and *qaçr,* castle.] A castle or palace of the Spanish Moors; hence, a name sometimes given to a public building in the Moorish style.

al·che·mist, al′ke·mist, n. One who practices alchemy.

al·che·my, al′ke·mē, n. [M.E. *alkamie, alquemie* < M.Fr. or M.L.; M.Fr. *alquemie* < M.L. *alchymia,* < Ar. *al,* the, and *kīmiā',* prob. < L.Gr. *chemeia,* for *chumeia,* fusion (of metals), < Gr. *chein,* pour, melt, smelt.] Medieval chemistry, an art which sought in particular to transmute baser metals into gold, also to find a universal solvent (alkahest) and an elixir of life; hence, any magical power or process of transmutation; formerly, a mixed metal resembling brass.

al·co·hol, al′ko·hal″, al′ko·hol″, n. [< M.L. < O.Sp. < Ar. *al,* the, and *kuhul,* powdered antimony.] A colorless, inflammable volatile liquid; the intoxicating principle of liquors formed from certain sugars (esp. glucose) by fermentation, and now usually prepared from grain by treating this with malt and causing the maltose and dextrin so formed to ferment by the addition of yeast; hence, any alcoholic liquor. *Chem.* any of a class of chemical compounds derived from hydrocarbons by replacing one or more of the hydrogen atoms with an equal number of hydroxyl radicals; term for ethyl alcohol (ethanol, C_2H_5OH), the alcohol of commerce and medicine.

al·co·hol·ic, al″ko·ha′lik, al″ko·hol′ik, a. Pertaining to alcohol, or partaking of its qualities.—n. An habitual drunkard.

al·co·hol·ism, al′ko·ha·liz″um, al′ko·ho·-liz″um, n. The condition of habitual drunkards who are poisoned by alcohol.

al·co·hol·ize, Brit. **al·co·hol·ise,** al′ko·-ho·liz″, al″ko·ha·liz″, v.t.—alcoholized, alcoholising, alcoholised, alcoholising.* To convert into alcohol; to rectify (spirit) till it is wholly purified; to make drunk or put under the influence of alcohol.

al·co·hol·om·e·ter, al″ko·ha·lom′i·tẻr, al″ko·ho·lom′i·tẻr, n. [Fr.] An instrument for determining the quantity of pure alcohol in any liquid.—**al·co·hol·om·e·try,** n. The determination of the percentage of absolute alcohol in a liquid.

al·cove, al′kōv, n. [Fr. *alcove,* Sp. *alcoba*— Ar. *al,* the, and *kubbeh,* an alcove, a little chamber.] A wide and deep recess in a room, intended for the reception of a bed or chairs, etc.; any natural recess, as: The child hid the brooch in the *alcove.*

al·de·hyde, al′de·hīd″, *n.* [*al*, first syllable of *alcohol*, and *dehyd*, the first two of *dehydrogenatus*, deprived of hydrogen.] *Chem.* A transparent colorless liquid produced by the oxidation of pure alcohol; one of a class of highly reactive organic compounds containing the group -CHO, derived from alcohol by the abstraction of two atoms of hydrogen, and converted into acids by the addition of one atom of oxygen.

al·der, al′dẽr, *n.* [M.E. *allor* (the *d* being a more modern insertion), O.E. *alor, alr*; Icel. *ölr*, G. *eller*; allied to L. *alnus*, an alder.] The popular name of plants of the genus *Alnus*, *Alnus glutinosa* being the common alder, usually growing in moist, cool regions.

al·der·man, al′dẽr·man, *n.* pl. **al·der·men,** al′dẽr·men. [O.E. *aldormann, ealdormann*, < *aldor*, chief, elder, and *mann*, man.] One of a body of municipal officers, ranking below the mayor, with powers (executive, judicial, or legislative) varying according to locality.—**al·der·man·ic,** al′dẽr·man′ik, *a.* Of or befitting an alderman.

Al·der·ney, al′dẽr·nē, *n.* pl. **Alderneys.** One of a breed of small cattle, usually fawn-colored, originating on the island of Alderney, in the English Channel, and noted for their milk.

Al·dine, al′dīn, al′dēn, *a.* Proceeding from the printing press of Aldus Manutius, of Venice, and his family, from 1490 to 1597.

Al·dine type, *n.* Italic type designed by the printer for his 1501 edition of Virgil.

ale, āl, *n.* [O.E. *ealu*, Dan. Sw. and Icel. *öl*, ale.] A liquor, which contains approximately 6 percent alcohol, made by fermentation from an infusion of malt.

a·le·a·to·ry, ā′lē·a·tōr″ē, ā′lē·a·tạr″ē, *a.* [L. *alea*, a die, chance.] Pertaining to chance or contingency; depending on a contingency; *mus.*, *art*, using chance in the selection of notes or design.

a·lee, a·lē′, *adv.* *Naut.* On the lee side; in the side opposite to that on which the wind strikes: opposed to *aweather.*

ale·house, āl′hous″, *n.* A place where beer and ale are sold for drinking on the premises; a tavern.

Al·e·man·nic, al″e·man′ik, *n.* The High German dialects spoken in Switzerland, Alsace and southwestern Germany.—*a.*

a·lem·bic, a·lem′bik, *n.* [M.E. < M.L. *alembicum*; < Ar. *al*, the, *ambik*, an alembic, from Gr. *ambix*, a cup.] A chemical vessel formerly used in distillation, usually made of glass or copper; an instrument which refines by a process resembling distillation.

a·leph-null, ä′lef′nul″, ä′lif·nul″, *n.* *Math.* The smallest infinite nonordinal number; the cardinal number aggregate of all positive integers. Also **a·leph-ze·ro.**

a·lert, a·lụrt′, *a.* [It. *all'erta*, to the watchtower, the lookout—*erta*, fem. pp. of L. *erigere*, erect.] Active in vigilance; nimble; on or upon the alert; on watch; on guard; on lookout; guarding against surprise or danger.—**a·lert·ness,** a·lụrt′nis, *n.* The state or quality of being alert.

a·lert, a·lụrt′, *n.* A warning of imminent danger; the time span during which the alert is in effect.

a·lert, a·lụrt′, *v.t.* To declare the possibility of danger to; to warn.

al·eu·rone, al′ū·rōn″, a·lụr′ōn, *n.* [Gr. *aleuron*, fine flour.] Albuminoid granules found in seeds of cereals.

Al·eut, a·lōt′, al′ē·ōt″, *n.* A native or inhabitant of the Aleutian Islands, esp. one belonging to a division of the Eskimo; the language.—**Al·eu·tian,** a·lö′shan, *a.* Pertaining to the northwestern area of Alaska and to the Aleutian Islands, their people, or their language.

ale·wife, āl′wīf, *n.* pl. **ale·wives.** A small N. American fish resembling the shad and herring, found in coastal waters of the Atlantic Ocean, as: At the end of spring, Chicago's beaches are infested with *alewives*. A woman who manages an alehouse.

al·ex·an·der, al″ig·zan′dẽr, al″ig·zän′dẽr, *n.* A cocktail made with crème de cacao, sweet cream, and brandy or gin.

Al·ex·an·dri·an, al″ig·zan′drē·an, al″ig·zän′drē·an, *a.* Pertaining to Alexandria in Egypt, more especially to ancient Alexandria.

al·ex·an·drine, al″ig·zan′drin, al″ig·zan′drēn, al″ig·zän′drin, al″ig·zän′drēn, *n.* (*Sometimes cap.*) a kind of verse consisting of twelve syllables in English poetry, or in French of twelve and thirteen in alternate couplets: so called from a poem written in French on the life of Alexander the Great. —*a.*

al·ex·an·drite, al″ig·zan′drīt, al″ig·zän′drīt, *n.* [From *Alexander II* of Russia.] A variety of chrysoberyl appearing dark-green by daylight and red by artificial light or by daylight: used as a gem.

a·lex·i·a, a·lek′sē·a, *n.* [N.L. < Gr. *a*-priv. and *lexis*, a speaking, < *legein*, speak.] *Pathol.* a cerebral disorder marked by inability to read, or to read aloud.

a·lex·in, a·lek′sin, *n.* [Gr. *alexein*, ward off.] *Physiol.*, *chem.* any of certain substances present in normal blood-serum which are capable of destroying bacteria.

a·lex·i·phar·mic, a·lek″si·fär′mik, *a.* [Gr. *alexo*, to ward off, *pharmakon*, a drug, remedy, poison.] Acting as a means of warding off disease or the effects of poison; acting as a remedy.—*n.* A remedy; an antidote.

al·fa, al′fa, *n.* A code word in communications to represent the letter A.

al·fal·fa, al·fal′fa, *n.* [Sp. < Ar. *al fasfasah*, the alfalfa.] A common name in the United States for the fodder plant lucerne, *Medicago sativa*, having purplish-blue flowers and widely grown as food for horses and cattle.

al·fi·le·ri·a, al·fil″e·rē′a, *n.* [Amer. Sp. < Sp. *alfiler*, pin < Ar. *al khilāl* the thorn.] The pingrass, *Erodium cicutarium*, a weed of the geranium family native in Europe but naturalized elsewhere, and valued as a forage plant. Also *Western U.S.* **al·fil·a·ri·a,** al·fil″a·rē′a.

al·for·ja, al·fạr′ja, *n.* [Sp. < Ar. *al khurj*.] In the American West, a leather pouch or saddlebag.

al·fres·co, al·fres′kō, *a.* [It., "in the fresh."] In the open air; out of doors; as, an *alfresco* dinner.—*adv.*

al·ga, al′ga, *n.* pl. **al·gae,** al′jē. [L.] One of many plants of a subdivision of thallophytes found for the most part in both salt and fresh water, including pondscums, kelps and some seaweeds; a seaweed.

al·gar·ro·ba, al·ga·ro·ba, al″ga·rō′ba, *n.* [Sp. < Ar. *al*, the, and *kharrūbah*, carob.] The carob (fruit or tree); also, the mesquite, *Prosopis glandulosa*, or its sweet, beanlike pods; also, a large tree, *Hymenæa courbaril*, of the West Indies.

al·ge·bra, al′je·bra, *n.* [Sp. *algebra*, from Ar. *al-jabr*, the putting together of broken things, reduction of fractions to whole numbers, < Ar. *jabara*, to bind together, to consolidate.] That branch of mathematical analysis in which signs are employed to denote arithmetical operations, and letters are used to represent numbers and quantities; treatise or textbook treating this subject.—**al·ge·bra·ist,** al′ja·brā′ist, *n.* One versed in the science of algebra.

al·ge·bra·ic, al″je·brā′ik, *a.* Pertaining to algebra. Also **al·ge·bra·i·cal.—al·ge·bra·i·cal·ly,** al″je·brā′i·ka·lē, *adv.* By algebraic process.

al·ge·bra·ic num·ber, *n.* *Alg.* the root obtained from an algebraic equation having rational coefficients.

Al·ge·ri·an, al·jēr′ē·an, *a.* Of or relating to the characteristics of the inhabitants of Algeria, a republic on the Mediterranean coast of northwest Africa, under French control until 1962.—*n.* A native or inhabitant of Algeria.

Al·ge·rine, al″je·rēn′, *a.* Algerian.—*n.* A native or inhabitant of Algiers or Algeria, esp. one of the indigenous Berber or Arab inhabitants.

al·gid, al′jid, *a.* [L. *algidus*, cold, *algeo*, to be cold.] Cold; chilly.—**al·gid·i·ty, al·gid·ness,** al·jid′i·tē, al′jid·nes, *n.* The state of being algid; chilliness; coldness.

al·gin, al′jin, *n.* *Chem.* any of many colloidal, hydrophilic substances found in or obtained from marine brown algae.

al·go·lag·ni·a, al″go·lag′nē·a, *n.* [N.L. < *algo-* pain, and Gr. *lagneia*, lust.] *Psych.* The abnormal sexual pleasure experienced by inflicting or enduring pain; sadism or masochism.

al·gol·o·gy, al·gol′o·jē, *n.* [L. *alga*, seaweed: see *-logy.*] The part of botany that treats of algae.—**al·gol′o·gist,** al·gol′o·jist, *n.*

al·gom·e·ter, al·gom′i·tẽr, *n.* [Gr. *algos*, pain, and *meter.*] A device for determining sensitiveness to pain due to pressure.—**al·go·met·ric,** al″go·me′trik, *a.*

Al·gon·ki·an, al·gong′kē·an, *a.* Algonquian; *geol.* noting or pertaining to a geological era or period, or a group or system of rocks, immediately preceding the Cambrian in North America.—*n.* *Geol.* the Algonkian period or system.

Al·gon·qui·an, al·gong′kē·an, al·gong′-kwē·an, *a.* Belonging to or constituting a linguistic stock of North American Indians formerly extending from Labrador and the northern half of the U.S. eastern coast westward to the Rocky Mountains, and including the Algonquin, Cheyenne, Cree, Delaware, Micmac, Mohican, Ojibwa, Shawnee, and many other tribes.—*n.* A person belonging to an Algonquian tribe. Also **Al·gon·quin,** *Algonkian,* **Al·gon·kin.**

al·go·pho·bi·a, al″go·fō′bē·a, *n.* An extreme dread or fear of pain.

al·go·rism, al′go·riz″um, *n.* [M.E. < M.L. *algorism*, < Ar. *al-Khowārazmi*, "the native of *Khwārazm* (Khiva)," Abu Ja'far Mohammed ben Musa, an Arabian mathematician.] The Arabic system of arithmetical notation (with the figures 1, 2, 3, etc.); hence, arithmetic; also, any method of computation, esp. with a special notation; algorithm.

al·go·ri·thm, al′gō·riTH″um, *n.* [Var. of *algorism.*] *Math.* a number of rules, which are to be followed in a prescribed order, for solving a specific type of problem; see *algorism.*—**al·go·rith·mic,** al″ga·rith′mik, al″gō·rith′mik, *a.* Pertaining to or involving algorithms.

a·li·as, ā′lē·as, *adv.* [L., otherwise.] Otherwise known by the name of: used especially of persons who assume names other than their own; as, John Smith *alias* Thomas Jones.—*n.* pl. **a·li·as·es,** ā′lē·a·siz. An adopted or feigned name.

al·i·bi, al′i·bī″, *n.* [L., elsewhere.] *Law*, a plea which avers that the accused was in another place at the time of the commission of the offense, and therefore cannot be guilty. Any evidence of innocence.

al·i·bi, al′i·bī″, *v.i.* To provide an excuse.—*v.t.* To clear from accusation or blame by plausible proof of innocence.

al·i·dade, al′i·dād″, n. [M.E. < M.L. < Ar. al-'idādah.] A movable arm passing over a graduated circle and carrying a vernier or an index, attached to instruments for measuring angles; the telescope and attachments of a surveyor's instrument.

al·ien, āl′yen, ā′lē·en, a. [M.E. < O.Fr. < L. alienus, alien, < alius, another.] Not belonging to the same country, land or government; residing in a foreign country without possessing the rights and privileges of citizenship; foreign; different in nature; estranged; adverse, often followed by to or from.

al·ien, āl′yen, ā′lē·en, n. A foreigner; one born in or belonging to another country; one who is not a citizen or entitled to the privileges of a citizen.

al·ien·a·bil·i·ty, āl′ye·na·bil′i·tē, ā″lē-·e·na·bil′i·tē, n. The state or quality of being alienable.

al·ien·a·ble, āl′ye·na·bl, ā′lē·e·na·bl, a. Capable of being sold or transferred to another.

al·ien·age, āl′ye·nij, ā′lē·e·nij, n. The state of being an alien; an alien's legal status.

al·ien·ate, āl′ye·nāt″, ā′lē·e·nāt″, v.t.—alienated, alienating. [M.E. < L. alieno, alienatum, to alienate.] To cause to be withdrawn, as affection; to make indifferent or averse, where love or friendship before existed; to estrange, followed by from; law, to transfer, as title, property, or other right, to another.—**al·ien·a·tor,** āl′ye·nā″tẻr, ā′lē·e·nā″tẻr, n. One who alienates.

al·ien·a·tion, āl″ya·nā′shan, n. [M.E. < L. alienatio.] The act of alienation or the state of being alienated; estrangement of the affections of another person's spouse; law, the giving over of the control of the title of property from one person to another. Psych. legal insanity; mental sickness.—**al·ien·ee,** āl″ye·nē′, ā′lē·e·nē′, n. One to whom the title of property is transferred.

al·ien·ism, āl′ye·niz″um, ā′lē·e·niz″um, n. The state of being an alien; alienage; the scientific study and treatment of mental alienation or insanity.

al·ien·ist, āl′ye·nist, ā′lē·e·nist, n. One who studies or practices the psychiatric treatment of mental diseases.

al·i·form, al′i·fẹrm″, ā′li·fẹrm″, a. [L. ala, wing, and forma, shape.] Wing-shaped or winglike.

a·light, a·līt′, v.i.—alighted, alighting, alit, alighting. [O.E. âlihtan, gelihtan, to alight or light. See LIGHT in this sense.] To get down or descend, as from horseback or an airplane; to settle or lodge, as a bird on a tree; to happen upon: followed by on.

a·light, a·līt′, a., adv. [O.E. alīhtan < lihtan to light.] Lighted, illuminated; kindled; made to burn by having a light applied.

a·lign, a·līn′, v.t. [Fr. aligner, to align—a, to, and ligne, L. linea, a line.] To lay out or regulate by a line; to form in line, as troops. —v.i. To ally oneself, as to a party or a cause. Also **a·line.**

a·lign·ment, a·line·ment, a·lin′ment, n. The act of aligning; an adjusting of electronic or mechanical parts to a line or to each other; the line of adjustment; the groundplan of a railway or other road, in distinction from the gradients or profile; a row of things; the act of aligning oneself to a party or a cause.

a·like, a·līk′, a. [M.E. alyke, alik, ilik < ilich < O.E. gelíc, onlíc. LIKE.] Having resemblance or similitude; without difference.

a·like, a·līk′, adv. In the same manner, form or degree; equally; resembling exactly; in common, as: All have erred alike.

al·i·ment, al′i·ment, n. [M.E. < L. alimentum, nourishment—alo, to nourish.] That which nourishes; food; nutriment.—al′i·ment″, v.t. To nourish or sustain.

al·i·ment·al, al″i·ment′al, a. Of or pertaining to aliment; supplying food; having the quality of nourishing.—**al·i·ment·al·ly,** adv. In an alimental manner.

al·i·men·ta·ry, al″i·men′ta·rē, a. Pertaining to aliment or food; having the quality of nourishing; nutritive.

al·imen·ta·ry ca·nal, n. Anat. The canal from the mouth to the anus through which food passes; digestive tract.

al·i·men·ta·tion, al″i·men·tā′shan, n. The act or power of affording nutriment; the state of being nourished or maintained; increase in the volume of a glacial mass through the addition of ice and snow.

al·i·mo·ny, al′i·mō″nē, n. [L. alimonia, sustenance.] A monetary allowance made by a man for the support of a woman divorced or legally separated from him.

al·i·phat·ic, al″i·fat′ik, a. [Gr. aleiphar, oil.] Of or pertaining to fat; chem. designating organic compounds which have only an open chain formed by carbon atoms.

al·i·quant, al′i·kwant, a. [L. aliquantum, somewhat.] Arith. applied to a number which does not divide into another number without a remainder, as: 7 is an aliquant part of 20.

al·i·quot, al′i·kwat, a. Referring to a number which can be divided into another without a remainder, as: 7 is an aliquot part of 21.

a·li·tur·gi·cal, ā″li·tẹr·ji′kal, a. Eccles. Not liturgical; having no connection with the official services of the church, esp. noting certain days on which the eucharistic service is not to be celebrated. Also **a·li·tur·gic,** ā″li·tẹr′jik.

a·li·un·de, ā″lē·un′dē, adv. [L. < alius, other, and unde, whence.] From another source.

a·live, a·līv′, a. [O.E. on līfe. LIVE.] Having life; living; not dead; in a state of action; aware; existent in force or operation; as, to keep an agitation alive; full of alacrity; sprightly; as, alive with excitement; easily impressed; sensitive to; susceptible; as, alive to the beauties of nature.

a·liz·a·rin, a·liz′ẻr·in, n. [Fr. < Sp. < Ar. al'asārah, the juice.] A coloring matter orig. obtained from madder and yielding red pigment, but now made synthetically.

al·ka·hest, al·ca·hest, al′ka·hest″, n. [Prob. coined by Paracelsus.] The universal solvent sought by the alchemists.—**al·ka·hes·tic,** al″ka·hes′tik, a.

al·ka·les·cent, al″ka·les′ent, a. [See -escent.] Tending to become alkaline; slightly alkaline.—**al·ka·les·cence, al·ka·les·cen·cy,** al″ka·les′ens, al″ka·les′en·sē, n. The quality or condition of being alkaline.

al·ka·li, al′ka·lī″, n. pl. **al·ka·lies,** or **al·ka·lis,** al′ka·līz″. [M.E. alkaly < M.Fr. alcali, < Ar. al, the, and qalī, saltwort ashes, < qalay, roast.] Orig. the soda derived from the ashes of plants; now, any of various compounds, the hydroxides of sodium, potassium, lithium, rubidium, and caesium (the alkali metals), and of ammonium, which neutralize acids to form salts and turn red litmus paper blue; any of various other more or less active bases, as calcium hydroxide; any of various other compounds, as the carbonates of sodium and potassium; a soluble mineral salt, or a mixture of soluble salts, occurring in soils.—**al·ka·lif·er·ous,** al″ka·lif′e·rus, a. [See -ferous.] Yielding an alkali.—**al·ka·li·fy,** al′ka·li·fī, v.t., v.i.—alkalified, alkalifying. [See -fy.] To convert into or become an alkali.—**al·ka·lig·e·nous,** al″ka·lij′e·nus, a. Generating an alkali.

al·ka·li flat, n. A sterile plain at the bottom of an undrained basin, containing an excess of alkali in its soil.

al·ka·li met·al, n. Any metal, such as potassium, sodium, or francium, having an alkali for an hydroxide.

al·ka·lim·e·ter, al″ka·lim′i·tẻr, n. An instrument for ascertaining the strength of alkali in a mixture or solution.—**al·ka·lim·e·try,** al″ka·lim′i·trē, n. The procedure of determining the amount of real alkali in an alkaline mixture or solution.

al·ka·line, al′ka·lin″, al′ka·lin, a. Having the properties of an alkali.—**al·ka·lin·i·ty,** al″ka·lin′i·tē, n. The state of being alkaline; the quality which constitutes an alkali.—**al·ka·lin·ize,** al′ka·li·nīz, v.t.—alkalinized, alkalinizing. To make alkaline.

al·ka·line earths, n. Oxide of barium, strontium, calcium, and sometimes magnesium.

al·ka·li soil, n. Any of various soils in poorly drained or arid regions, containing an unusually large amount of soluble mineral salts (chiefly of sodium) which during dry weather appear on the surface in the form of a usually white crust or powder.

al·ka·lize, al′ka·līz″, v.t.—alkalized, alkalizing. Alkalinize.—**al·ka·liz·a·ble,** a.—**al·ka·li·za·tion,** al″ka·li·zā′shan, n.—**al·ka·liz·er,** al′ka·līz″ẻr, n.

al·ka·loid, al′ka·loid, n. A term applied to a class of nitrogenized compounds found in living plants, and containing their active principles, such as morphine, quinine, aconitine, caffeine, etc.—a. Relating to or containing alkali.—**al·ka·loi·dal,** a.

al·ka·lo·sis, al″ka·lō′sis, n. Pathol. a condition wherein the concentration of alkali in the body is higher than normal.

al·ka·net, al′ka·net″, n. [M.E., < O.E. alcaneta, dim. of alcana, alcanna, from Ar. al-hinna, henna.] A plant, Alkanna tinctoria, the root of which yields a red dye.

Al·ko·ran, al″kō·rän′, al″kō·ran′, al″ka-·rän′, al″ka·ran′, n. [Ar.—al, the, qurân, book.] The book which contains the religious and moral code of the Mohammedans, and by which all their transactions, civil, legal, military, etc., are regulated; the Koran.

al·kyd res·in, al′kid, n. Any of a group of sticky resins made from phthalic acid, (or more commonly, phthalic anhydride), and glycerol, used primarily in adhesives and paints which are noted for their flexibility, gloss, and satisfactory weathering properties.

all, al, a. [M.E. all < O.E. eal (sing.), ealle (pl.); Icel. allr, Goth. alls, G. all, all. Common to all the Teutonic tongues; also in Celtic.] Every one of; the whole number or quantity of, used before an article or adjective; belonging to the; as, all the men; during the whole, used with nouns of time; as, all day, or all night.—**all-** A combining form which means exclusively or entirely; as, all-powerful; also, totally inclusive, used attributively; as, all-expense-paid; totally inclusive, used as the object of an action; as, all-seeing.

all, al, n. The whole number; the entire thing; the aggregate; the total.—**above all,** firstly.—**at all,** in the least degree; to the least extent; under any circumstances.—**in all,** everything reckoned or taken into account.

all, al, adv. Wholly; completely; entirely; altogether; quite; as, all alone.—**all but,** nearly; almost; not quite.—**all one,** the same thing in effect; quite the same.

al·la bre·ve, ä′la brev′ā, It. äl′ lä bre′ve, a. [It. lit. 'according to the short (time)!] Mus. in duple or cut time; with normal or marked tempo values halved, thus to be executed twice as fast.—n. A passage, work, etc., to be played in this manner; the musical symbol representing this.

Al·lah, al′a, ä′la, n. The Arabic name of the Supreme Being.

all-A·mer·i·can, äl″*a*·mer′i·kan, *a.* Made up exclusively of Americans; wholly within the United States; chosen, at a certain time, as the best in any field in the U.S., esp. sports.—*n.* The player or performer selected for an all-American team.

al·lan·to·ic, al″an·tō′ik, *a.* Pertaining to or contained in the allantois. Also **al·-lan·toid·al**, al″an·toid′al.

al·lan·to·is, *a*·lan′tō·is, *a*·lan′tois, *n.* [N.L. < Gr. *allantoeides* < *allas, allantos*, a sausage, and *eidos*, form. *Allantoeides* was mistaken for a plural (cf. *heroides*, heroes) and the singular *allantois* was created on the pattern of *herois*, hero.] *Zool.* a sac developed from the posterior end of the abdominal cavity in birds, reptiles, and certain mammals.

al·lar·gan·do, ä″lär·gän′dō, *a.* [It. widening < *allargare* < *al* < L. *ad* and *largere*, to widen.] *Mus.* becoming broader while the volume stays the same or increases.

all-a·round, ạl′a·round″, *a.* Capable of doing things well in different fields; versatile. Also **all-round**.

al·lay, *a*·lā′, *v.t.*—*allayed, allaying.* [M.E. *aleggen, alayen* < O.E. *ālecgan*, to lay down, suppress, tranquilize, < prefix *a*, and *lecgan* to lay. LAY.] To make quiet; to pacify or appease (a tumult); to abate, mitigate, or subdue; to relieve or alleviate (grief, thirst). —**al·lay·er**, *a*·lā′ẽr, *n.* One who or that which allays.

all but, *adv.* Almost; nearly.

all clear, *n.* The signal that danger is no longer present.

al·le·ga·tion, al″e·gā′shan, *n.* The act of alleging; affirmation; declaration; that which is affirmed or asserted.

al·lege, *a*·lej′, *v.t.*—*alleged, alleging.* [M.E. *alleggen* < O.Fr. *alleguer* < L. *allegare*, dispatch, cite < *ad-* and *legare*, depute.] To assert; to pronounce with positiveness; to declare; to produce, as an argument, plea, or excuse; to quote.

al·lege·a·ble, *a*·lej′a·bl, *a.* Capable of being alleged or affirmed.

al·leged, *a*·lejd′, *a.* Asserted; declared to be true or as specified; doubtful; supposed.— **al·leg·ed·ly**, *a*·lej′id·lē, *adv.*

Al·le·ghe·ny spurge, al″e·gā′nē spụrj′, *n.* A low herb or subshrub, *Pachysandra procumbens*, that has purplish or white flowers and is cultivated as a ground cover.

al·le·giance, *a*·lē′jans, *n.* [M.E. *alegeaunce*, for *legeaunce*, < M.Fr. *ligeance*, < *lige*, liege.] The obligation of loyalty of a subject or citizen to his sovereign or government; duty owed to a sovereign or state; hence, in general, fidelity; devotion.

al·le·giant, *a*·lē′jant, *a.* Loyal.—*n.* One who owes allegiance.

al·le·gor·ic, al″e·gạr′ik, al″e·gor′ik, *a.* Pertaining to allegory; in the manner of allegory. Also **al·le·gor·i·cal**, al″e·gạr′i·kal, al″e·gor′i·kal.—**al·le·gor·i·cal·ly**, al″e·gạr′i·ka·lē, al″e·gor′i·ka·lē, *adv.* In an allegorical manner; by way of allegory.

al·le·go·rist, al′e·gōr″ist, al′e·gạr″ist, al′e·gor·ist, *n.* One who allegorizes; a writer of allegory. Also **al·le·go·riz·er**, al′e·go·-rīz″ẽr.

al·le·gor·i·za·tion, al″e·gạr″i·zā′shan, *n.* The act of turning into allegory; allegorical explanation or interpretation.

al·le·go·rize, al′e·go·rīz″, *v.t.*—*allegorized, allegorizing.* To turn into allegory; to narrate in allegory; to explain in an allegorical sense.—*v.i.* To use allegory.

al·le·go·ry, al′e·gōr″ē, al′e·gạr″ē, *n.* pl. **al·le·go·ries.** [M.E. *allegorie* < L. *allegoria* < Gr. *allegoria* < *allegorein*, to speak figuratively—*allos*, other, and *ago-reuō*, to speak, from *agora*, a forum, an oration.] A figurative discourse, in which the principal subject is depicted by another subject resembling it in its properties and

circumstances; a symbolic representation; a narrative in which abstract ideas are personified; a sustained metaphor.

al·le·gret·to, al″e·gret′ō, *a., adv.* [It. dim. of *allegro*.] *Mus.* more rapidly than andante, but not as quick as allegro.—*n.* pl. **al·le·gret·tos.** A musical composition or movement in such tempo.

al·le·gro, *a*·lā′grō, *a*·leg′rō, *a., adv.* [It. < L. *alacer*, lively, brisk.] *Mus.* Brisk; rapid; more rapid than allegretto but slower than presto.—*n.* pl. **al·le·gros.** An allegro movement.

al·lele, *a*·lēl′, *n.* [G. *allel*, short for *allelomorph*.] *Genetics*, either a dominant or recessive member of any pair of alternative characters, as tallness and shortness, which are present as genes and segregate at the time of sex cell production. See *Mendelism.* —**al·lel·ic**, *a*·lē′lik, *a.*—**al·lel·ism**, *a*·lē′liz″um, *n.*

al·le·lo·morph, *a*·lē′lo·mạrf″, *a*·lel′o·mạrf″, *n.* [Gr. *allelon*, of one another, and *morph*, form.] Allele.—**al·le·lo·mor·phic**, *a*·lē″lo·mạr′fik, *a*·lel″o·mạr′fik, *a.*—**al·le·lo·mor·phism**, *a*·lē″lo·mạr′fiz″um, *a*·lel″o·mạr′fiz″um, *n.*

al·le·lu·ia, al″e·lö′ya, *interj.* [M.E. < L.L. < Gr. < Heb. *halelûyâh*, praise to Jah—*halal*, to praise, and *Yâhweh*, Jehovah.] Praise Jehovah: a word used to denote pious joy and exultation, chiefly in hymns and anthems.—*n.* A song of praise. Also *halleluiah, hallelujah.*

al·le·mande, al′e·mand″, al′e·mänd″, al″e·mand′, al″e·mänd″, *n.* [Fr. fem of (*danse*) *allemande*, German (dance).] A slow, duple-time court dance of the 17th and 18th centuries, developed in France from a German folk dance; also, a triple-meter German folk dance. Music for the allemande; a piece of music based on the allemande rhythm; a movement in the classical suite, based on the allemande rhythm and occurring after the prelude.

al·ler·gen, al′ẽr·jen″, *n.* [Gr. *allos*, other, *ergon*, work, and *gen*, to produce.] Any substance that induces allergy.—**al·ler·gen·ic**, *a.*

al·ler·gic, *a*·lụr′jik, *a.* Pertaining to or affected with allergy. Extremely sensitive.

al·ler·gist, al′ẽr·jist, *n.* A medical specialist in the field of treating allergies.

al·ler·gy, al′ẽr·jē, *n.* pl. **al·ler·gies.** [Gr. *allos*, other, and *ergon*, work.] Excess sensitivity producing a bodily reaction to certain substances, as food, pollen, drugs, or heat or cold, which are harmless to most persons: common allergies are hay fever, hives, and asthma.

al·le·thrin, al′e·thrin, *n.* A synthetic insecticide, yellow in color, $C_{19}H_{26}O_3$, which is usually used in household aerosols.

al·le·vi·ate, *a*·lē″vē·āt″, *v.t.*—*alleviated, alleviating.* [L.L. *alleviare, alleviatus*, L. *allevare, allevatus*—*ad*, to, and *levo*, to ease, < *levis*, light. LEVITY.] To make light, in a figurative sense; to lessen, relieve, or make easier to be endured (sorrow, pain, distress).—**al·le·vi·a·tion**, *a*·lē″vē·ā′shan, *n.* The act of alleviating; that which lessens, mitigates, or makes more tolerable.—**al·le·vi·a·tor**, *a*·lē″vē·ā″tor, *n.* One who or that which alleviates.

al·le·vi·a·tive, *a*·lē″vē·ā″tiv, *a*·lē″vē·a·-tiv, *a.* Tending to alleviate; mitigative. Also **al·le·vi·a·to·ry**, *a*·lē″vē·a·tōr″ē.

al·ley, al′ē, *n.* pl. **al·leys**, al′ēz. [M.E. < M.Fr. *alee* (Fr. *allée*), < *aler* (Fr. *aller*), go.] A narrow passageway or street between rows of houses; a long narrow enclosure with a wood floor for bowling or tenpins.

al·ley, al′ē, *n.* pl. **al·leys**, al′ēz. [Abbr. of *alabaster*.] A choice playing marble, white or colored.

al·ley·way, al′ē·wā″, *n.* An alley, as between houses; a narrow passage.

All Fools' Day, *n.* The first day of April; April Fool's Day.

all fours, *n.* A game of cards, so called from the four chances to score of which it consists.—**on all fours**, of a quadruped, having all four feet on the ground; of a person, being down on the hands and knees, esp. when crawling.

all hail, *interj.* All health: a phrase of salutation.

All·hal·lows, ạl′hal′ōz, *n.* All Saints' Day.

all·heal, ạl′hēl″, *n.* Any of several plants, esp. common wild valerian, so called from its medicinal virtues; a selfheal.

al·li·a·ble, *a*·lī′a·bl, *a.* Capable of being allied.

al·li·a·ceous, al″ē·ā′shus, *a.* [L. *allium*, garlic.] Pertaining to garlic and allied plants; having the properties of garlic or onion.

al·li·ance, *a*·lī′ans, *n.* [O.Fr. *alliance*.] The state of being allied or connected; the relation or union between families, contracted by marriage; a union between nations, contracted by compact, treaty, or league; any union or connection of interests; a compact or treaty; the persons or parties allied.

al·lied, *a*·līd′, al′īd, *a.* [See *ally, v.t.*] United by agreement, kinship, or other ties; associated; joined; connected; related; (*cap.*) of the Allies of the World Wars; as, the *Allied* navies.

al·li·ga·tor, al′i·gā″tor, *n.* [A corruption of Sp. *el lagarto*, lit. the lizard—*el*, the, and *lagarto*, a lizard, from assumed L.L. *lacertuso* whence E. *lizard.*] Either of two large reptiles, genus *Alligator*, found in southeastern U.S. and in China, differing from the true crocodiles in having a shorter and flatter head, in having cavities or pits in the upper jaw, into which the long canine teeth of the under jaw fit, and in having the feet much less webbed; leather fashioned from the hide of an alligator.

al·li·ga·tor pear,*n.* [Said to be a corruption of *avocado pear.*] The fruit of the avocado, a tree found in the West Indies and tropical America.

al·li·ga·tor snap·per, *n.* A snapping turtle, *Macroclemys temmincki*, found in the rivers of the Gulf States of America, a ravenous animal which may reach a weight of 150 pounds and a length of five feet.

al·lit·er·ate, *a*·lit′e·rāt″, *v.i.*—*alliterated, alliterating.* [Back-formation < *alliteration.*] To have the same initial letter or sound; also, to use alliteration.—*v.t.* To compose or arrange with alliteration.—**al·lit·er·a·tor**, *a*·lit′e·rā″tor, *n.* One who uses alliteration.

al·lit·er·a·tion, *a*·lit″e·rā′shan, *n.* [*ad-* and L. *littera*, letter.] Constant or frequent repetition of the same initial letter or sound, as in verse.

al·lit·er·a·tive, *a*·lit′e·rā″tiv, *a*·lit′-ẽr·a·tiv, *a.* Pertaining to or characterized by alliteration.—**al·lit·er·a·tive·ly**, *a*·lit′e·rā″tiv·lē, *a*·lit′ẽr·a·tiv·lē, *adv.*— **al·lit·er·a·tive·ness**, *a*·lit′e·rā″tiv·nis, *a*·lit′ẽr·a·tiv·nis, *n.*

al·li·um, al′ē·um, *n.* Any bulb plant, genus *Allium*, of the lily family, such as garlic or onion, with a strong odor.

al·lo, al′ō, *a.* Related to; equal to; isomeric.

al·lo·ca·ble, al′o·ka·bl, *a.* Able to be allocated. Also **al·lo·cat·a·ble**, al′o·kāt″-a·bl.

al·lo·cate, al′o·kāt″, *v.t.*—*allocated, allocating.* [< M.L. *allocatus*, pp. of *allocare* < *ad*, to, and *loco, locatum*, to place, < *locus*, a place.] To assign or allot to a person or persons; to set apart, as resources for a particular purpose; to apportion or distribute, as shares in a corporation or the like.— **al·lo·ca·tion**, al″o·kā′shan, *n.* The act of allocating, allotting, or assigning; allotment; assignment; apportionment.

---

ch- chain, G. na*ch*t;   **th-** THen, thin;   **w-** wig, hw as sound in whig;   **z-** zh as in azure, zeal.   *Italicized vowel* indicates schwa sound.

al·lo·chro·mat·ic, al″o·kro·mat′ik, al″o·krō·mat′ik, a. [Gr. allos, other, and chroma (chromat-), color.] Exhibiting variety of color, as a gem.

al·lo·cu·tion, al″o·kū′shan, n. [L. allocutio —ad, to, and loqui, to speak.] A speaking to; an address, especially a formal, authoritative, or official address.

al·lo·di·um, a·lō′dē·um, n. pl. **al·lo·di·a,** a·lō′dē·a. [L.L. allodium, of G. or Scand. origin; all, all, od, estate. Cf. Icel. odal, Dan. and Sw. odel, a patrimonial estate.] Real estate held in absolute independence, without being subject to any rent, service, or acknowledgment to a superior.—**al·lo·di·al,** a·lō′dē·al, a.

al·log·a·mous, a·log′a·mus, a. Bot. having the property of reproduction by means of cross-fertilization.

al·log·a·my, a·log′a·mē, n. [< Gr. allos, other, and gamos, marriage.] Bot. Fecundation of the ovules of one flower by pollen from another, on the same or another plant; cross-fertilization: opposed to autogamy.

al·lo·graph, al′o·graf″, al′o·gräf″, n. [< Gr. allos, other, and graphein, write.] A writing made by one person on behalf of another: opposed to autograph. A variant or alternative of a letter of an alphabet, such as A or a.

al·lom·er·ism, a·lom′e·riz″um, n. [< Gr. allos, other, and meros, part.] Variability in chemical constitution without change in crystalline form.—**al·lom·er·ous,** a·lom′e·rus, a.

al·lom·e·try, a·lom′i·trē, n. The increase in size of one part of an organism related to the growth of the whole.—**al·lo·met·ric,** al″o·me′trik, a. Of or pertaining to allometry.

al·lo·morph, al′o·marf″, n. [Gr. allos, other, and morphē, form.] A variety, as of a mineral, differing in form but not in chemical constitution. Ling. a variant or alternative form of a meaningful unit, such as the -s in dogs (pronounced z), the -es in matches, the -s in books, the -en in oxen, all allomorphs of the morpheme which has the basic meaning of "plural."—**al·lo·mor·phic,** al″o·mar′fik, a.—**al·lo·mor·phism,** al″o·mar′fiz″um, n. Variability in form without change in chemical constitution.

al·lo·nym, al′o·nim, n. [Fr. allonyme < Gr. all(os), other, and onyma, name.] The name of another person assumed by an author; a work thus published under another's name. —**al·lon·y·mous,** a·lon′o·mus, a.

al·lo·path, al′o·path″, n. [See allopathy.] An allopathist; a person who practices allopathy.

al·lop·a·thy, a·lop′a·thē, n. [Gr. allos, other, and pathos, morbid condition.] The method of treating disease by the use of agents producing effects different from those of the disease treated: opposed to homeopathy.—**al·lo·path·ic,** al·o·path′ik, a. Pertaining to allopathy.—**al·lo·path·i·cal·ly,** a″lo·path′i·ka·lē, adv. In a manner conformable to allopathy.—**al·lop·a·thist,** a·lop′a·thist, n. One who practices allopathy.

al·lo·pat·ric, al″o·pa′trik, a. [< Gr. all(os) and patra, fatherland < patēr, father.] Ecology, occurring in, or originating in different geographical regions.

al·lo·phane, al′o·fān″, n. [Gr. allophanes, appearing otherwise < all(os) and phan-, stem of phainesthai, appear.] A mineral which is a pale blue, green, or brown color, and is an amorphous hydrous silicate of aluminum.

al·lo·phone, al′o·fōn″, n. [< Gr. all(os), other, and phone, sound, voice.] Ling. a speech sound constituting a variant of the same phoneme.

all-or-none, al′or·nun′, a. Denoting either a complete response or operation or none at all.

al·lot, a·lot′, v.t.—allotted, allotting. [M.E. allotten < O.Fr. alloter, to divide, part—al for ad, to, and lotir, to cast lots for, from lot, a share, which itself is a Teutonic word—O.E. hlot. LOT.] To distribute or parcel out in parts or portions or as by lot; to divide; to assign; to make allotment; to set apart; to destine.

al·lot·ment, a·lot′ment, n. The act of allotting; that which is allotted; a share, part, or portion granted or distributed; a place or piece of ground appropriated.—**al·lot·ment sys·tem,** the system of allotting small portions of land to farm laborers or others. Milit. the system whereby a portion of the pay of a member of the armed forces is paid to an allottee; an authorization of personnel to a command or other unit.

al·lo·trope, al′o·trōp″, n. [< allotropy.] One of two or more existing forms of a chemical element: charcoal, graphite, and the diamond are allotropes of carbon.—**al·lo·trop·ic, al·lo·trop·i·cal,** al″o·trop′ik, al″o·trop′i·kal,a. Pertaining to or characterized by allotropy.—**al·lo·trop·i·cal·ly,** al″o·trop′i·kal·ē, adv.

al·lot·ro·py, a·lo′tro·pē, n. [< Gr. all(os), and tropos, turn, way, guise. See trope.] A property of certain chemical elements, as carbon, sulfur, and phosphorus, existing in two or more distinct forms. Also **al·lot·ro·pism,** a·lo′tro·piz″um.

al·lot·ta·ble, a·lot′a·bl, a. Capable of being allotted; able to be allotted.

al·lot·tee, a·lot·ē′, n. One to whom something is allotted.

all-out, al′out′, a. Milit. conducted with all possible energy and available resources, as an assault, offensive, war or the like. Complete; total; as, all-out assistance.

all-o·ver, al′ō″vėr, n. A decorated fabric covered by pattern or design over the entire surface.—al′ō′vėr, a.

al·low, a·lou′, v.t. [M.E. allowen < M.Fr. allouer, to grant, settle, place < L.L. allocare—ad, to, and locare, to place. (ALLOCATE.) O.Fr. allouer, to approve or praise, < L. ad, and laudare, to praise, < laus, laudis, praise, has also influenced the meaning.] To grant, give, or make over; to assign; as, to allow him $300 a year; to admit; to own or acknowledge; as, allow a claim; to abate or deduct; to set apart; as, allow so much for loss; to grant permission to; to permit; to sanction.—v.i. To concede; to make abatement or concession; to make provision, followed by for.

al·low·a·ble, a·lou′a·bl, a. Proper to be or capable of being allowed or permitted; not forbidden; permissible.—**al·low·a·bly,** a·lou′a·blē, adv. In an allowable manner; with propriety.

al·low·ance, a·lou′ans, n. Permission; license; sanction; a quantity allowed or granted, esp. money; a deduction or abatement; tolerance. Milit. a monetary amount paid an individual in lieu of furnished quarters, subsistence, a railroad ticket, or the like.—v.t.—allowanced, allowancing. To put on an allowance.

al·low·ed·ly, a·lou′id·lē, adv. Admittedly; with permission.

al·loy, al′oi, a·loi′, n. [M.Fr. aloi < O.Fr. aley < aleier, combine < L. alligare, bind, with possible confusion of Fr. aloi; legal standard of coin, a, according, and loi, law.] A baser metal mixed with a finer; a substance that has metallic properties and is composed of two or more chemical elements of which at least one is an elemental metal; any metallic compound; fig. evil mixed with good.

al·loy, a·loi′, v.t. To reduce the purity of (a metal) by mixing with it a portion of less valuable metal; to reduce, abate, or impair by mixture.

all right, a. Correct; satisfactory; acceptable; agreeable; safe; well.

all right, adv. Satisfactorily; acceptably; certainly; used alone as a term of assent: yes; okay.

all-round, al′round′, a. Complete; knowledgeable in many fields or departments; useful for a variety of tasks. Also all-around.

All Saints' Day, n. A church festival held on November 1 in honor of the saints.

all·seed, al′sēd″, n. Any of various many-seeded plants, as a goosefoot, Chenopodium polyspermum, and the knotgrass, Polygonum aviculare.

All Souls' Day, n. A day of prayer on November 2nd in the Roman Catholic Church and certain Anglican Churches, when prayers are offered for the dead.

all·spice, al′spis″, n. A spice of a mildly pungent taste, the fruit of a West Indian tree, so called from being regarded as combining many different flavors; pimento.

all told, adv. Counting everything; in all.

al·lude, a·lōd′, v.i.—alluded, alluding. [L. alludere, to play upon, to allude—ad, and ludere, to play.] To refer to something not directly mentioned; to hint at by remote suggestions, followed by to.

all-up weight, al′up wāt′, n. Avi. the gross weight of an aircraft when in the air, including passengers, cargo, crew, and fuel.

al·lure, a·lur′, v.t.—allured, alluring. [M.E. aluren < M.Fr. alurer < O.Fr. a- (< L. ad-) and lurer, lure. LURE.] To tempt by the offer of some good, real or apparent; to draw or try to draw by some proposed pleasure or advantage; to entice, decoy, tempt, charm, attract.—n. Charm; appeal.—**al·lure·ment,** a·lur′ment, n. The act of alluring, or that which allures.—**al·lur·er,** a·lur′ėr, n. —**al·lur·ing,** a·lur′ing, a. Inviting; having the quality of attracting or tempting. —**al·lur·ing·ly,** a·lur′ing·lē, adv.

al·lu·sion, a·lō′zhan, n. [L.L. allusio(n)- < allusus, pp. of alludere.] The act of alluding; a reference to something not explicitly mentioned; an indirect or incidental suggestion; an implied reference; a hint.

al·lu·sive, a·lō′siv, a. Having allusion or reference to something not fully expressed; containing allusions.—**al·lu·sive·ly,** a·lō′siv·lē, adv. In an allusive manner; by way of allusion.—**al·lu·sive·ness,** n.

al·lu·vi·al, a·lō′vē·al, n. Soil deposited by running water, esp. gold-bearing soil.

al·lu·vi·al, a·lō′vē·al, a. Of or pertaining to alluvium.

al·lu·vi·al fan, n. Phys. geog. a fan-shaped alluvial deposit formed by a stream when its velocity is reduced as it issues from a ravine into a plain.

al·lu·vi·on, a·lō′vē·on, n. [L. alluvio (n)-, < alluere, wash against, < ad, to, and lavere, wash.] The wash of water against a shore; overflow or flood; also, matter washed along and deposited; law, addition to land resulting from deposits made thereon by water.

al·lu·vi·um, a·lō′vē·um, n. pl. **al·lu·vi·ums, al·lu·vi·a,** a·lō′vē·a. [L.L., neut. of alluvius, alluvial, < L. alluere: see alluvion.] A deposit of sand, mud, etc., formed by flowing water; geol. the sedimentary matter deposited thus within recent times, esp. in the valleys of large rivers.

al·ly, a·lī′, v.t.—allied, allying. [M.E. allien < O.Fr. alier < Fr. allier, to join, to unite, s'allier, to confederate or become allied < L. ad, to, and ligare, to bind, whence league, ligament.] To unite by marriage, treaty, league, or confederacy; to connect by formal agreement; to bind together or connect, as by friendship or pursuits.—v.i. To form an alliance.

al·ly, al′ī, a·lī′, n. pl. **al·lies.** A prince or state united to another by treaty or league:

a confederate; supporter; auxiliary; helper; one who helps another achieve a particular goal; *milit.* a nation joined with another nation or other nations for the purpose of prosecuting a war against a common enemy, esp. a member of the coalition that fought against Germany in either World War I or World War II.

Al·ma·gest, al′ma·jest″, *n.* [M.E. *almageste* < M.Fr. < M.L. < Ar. *alamajisti,* < *al,* the, and Gr. *megiste,* fem. of *megistos,* greatest, superl. of *megas,* great.] The famous Greek work on astronomy by the Alexandrian astronomer Ptolemy, second century A.D.; (*l.c.*) any of various great medieval works, as on astrology or alchemy.

al·ma ma·ter, äl′ma mä′tẽr, al′ma mä′tẽr, al′ma mä′tẽr, *n.* [L., benign mother, fostering mother.] A term applied by students to the school, college, or university where they have been educated.

al·ma·nac, ạl′ma·nak″, *n.* [M.E. *almenak* < M.L. *almanac*(*h*) < Sp. *almanaque,* Ar. *al-manakh,* the almanac, calendar, probably < a root meaning to reckon; Heb. *manah.*] A table, book, or publication, generally annual, comprising a calendar of days, weeks, and months, with the times of the rising of the sun and moon, changes of the moon, eclipses, stated festivals of churches, etc., for a certain year or years.

al·man·dine, al′man·dẽn″, al′man·dĩn″, al′man·din, *n.* [M.E. *alabandine,* Fr. *almandine* < L.L. *alamandina, alavandina, alabandina,* a gem brought from *Alabanda,* a city in Asia Minor.] A name given to the deep red or violet varieties of the garnet. Also *almandite.*

al·man·dite, al′man·dĩt″, *n.* Almandine.

al·might·y, ạl·mĩ′tẽ, *a.* [M.E. < O.E. *ealmihtig, aelmihtig* < *eal-, ael-,* all and *mihtig,* mighty. ALL. MIGHTY.] Possessing all power; omnipotent; being of unlimited might.— **the Al·might·y,** the omnipotent God.

al·mond, ä′mond, am′ond, *n.* [M.E. *almande* < M.Fr. *alemandle* < L.L. *amandula,* var. of L. *amygdala* < Gr. *amygdalē,* almond.] The nutlike stone or kernel of the fruit of the almond tree, *Prunus amygdalus,* of warm regions; the tree itself; also, something almond-shaped.—**al·mond-eyed,** ä′mond·ĩd″, am′ond·ĩd″, *a.* Having almond-shaped eyes.—**al·mond-shaped,** ä′mond·shäpt″, am′omd·shäpt″, *a.* Of a long or narrow oval shape, tending to a point at the ends.

al·mon·er, al′mo·nẽr, ä′mo·nẽr, *n.* [M.E. *almoiner* < O.Fr. *almosnier,* < *almosne* < L.L. *eleemosyna,* alms. ALMS.] A dispenser of alms or charity; more especially an officer who directs or carries out the distribution of charitable doles in connection with religious communities, hospitals, or almshouses, or on behalf of some superior.

al·most, ạl′mōst, ạl·mōst′, *adv.* [M.E. < O.E. *almæst, ealmæst* < *al-, eal-* all, and *mæst,* most. ALL. MOST.] Nearly; well-nigh; for the greatest part.

alms, ämz, *n.* pl. **alms.** [M.E. *almesse, almes* < O.E. *almes, aelmesse,* < L.L. *eleemosyna,* alms, < Gr. *eleēmosynē,* pity.] Anything given gratuitously to relieve the poor; a charitable dole; charity.—**alms·giv·er,** ämz′giv″ẽr, *n.* One who gives alms.—**alms·giv·ing,** *n.* The giving of alms.

alms·house, ämz′hous″, *n.* A house for the poor, maintained at the public expense or, as in Great Britain, by private endowment.

alms·man, ämz′man, *n.* pl. **alms·men.** A person supported by charity or by public provision; one who receives alms; *archaic,* one who gives alms.

al·ni·co, al′ni·kō″, *n.* [< *al*uminum, *ni*ckel, *co*balt.] A strong permanent-magnet alloy of aluminum, iron, nickel, and other elements.

al·oe, al′ō, *n.* [M.E. < L. < Gr. *aloē,* dried juice of aloe leaves.] Any plant of the liliaceous genus *Aloe,* chiefly African, various species of which yield a purgative drug, aloin, and a fiber; also, the century plant, American aloe.

a·loft, a·loft′, a·lạft′, *adv.* [M.E. < Icel. *à lopt,* in (the) air. LOFT.] On high; in the air; high above the ground; *naut.* on the higher yards, masts, or rigging.

a·lo·ha, a·lō′a, ä·lō′hä, *interj.* [< Hawaiian *aloha,* love.] A Hawaiian expression of greeting or farewell.—*n.* A greeting.

a·lone, a·lōn′, *a.* [M.E. *al one,* "all (wholly) one."] Apart from others; unaccompanied or unaided; solitary; to the exclusion of all others or all else.—**a·lone·ness,** a·lōn′nis, *n.*

a·lone, a·lōn′, *adv.* Only; exclusively; solely; merely; without help.

a·long, a·long′, a·lạng′, *adv.* [O.E. *andlang, anlong*—prefix *and, an* (in answer) against, and *lang,* long.] By the length; lengthwise; in line with the length; as, stretched *along;* in line or with progressive motion; onward; as, walk *along;* in company; together: followed by *with;* from one to another; on hand.

a·long, a·long′, a·lạng′, *prep.* By the length of, as distinguished from *across;* in a longitudinal direction over or near; in accord with; during.

a·long·shore, a·long′shōr, a·long′shạr, a·lạng′shōr, a·lạng′shạr, *adv.* By the shore or coast; lengthwise and near the shore.

a·long·side, a·long′sĩd″, a·lạng′sĩd″, *adv.* Along or by the side; close to the side; beside each other; as, to lie *alongside.*—**a·long·side,** a·lạng′sĩd″, a·long′sĩd″, *prep.* Beside; by the side of; parallel to.

a·loof, a·lōf′, *adv.* [Orig. naut.: *a-,* to, and *loof,* windward. LUFF.] At a distance; intentionally apart from others, as from want of sympathy, favor, or involvement; as, to stand, hold, or keep *aloof.*—*a.* Uninvolved; reserved.—**a·loof·ly,** a·lōf′lē, *adv.*—**a·loof·ness,** a·lōf′nis, *n.*

al·o·pe·ci·a, al″o·pē′shē·a, *n.* [L. *alopecia,* Gr. *alòpekia, alòpex,* a fox, because foxes are said to be subject to this disease.] Loss of hair, as from disease; baldness.

a·loud, a·loud′, *adv.* In an audible tone; not whispered; by means of the speaking voice.

a·low, a·lō′, *adv.* In a low place, or a lower part of a vessel; below: opposed to *aloft.*

alp, alp, *n.* [< the *Alps,* mountains in Central Europe.] A high mountain; one of the Alps.

al·pac·a, al·pak′a, *n.* [Peruvian *alpaco.*] A ruminant mammal, genus *Lama,* a native of the South American Andes, valued for its long, soft, and silky wool which is woven into fabrics of great beauty; a fabric manufactured from the wool of the alpaca; an imitation of this fabric.

al·pen·glow, al′pen·glō″, *n.* [< G. *Alpenglühen.*] A reddish glow often seen on the summits of mountains before sunrise and after sunset.

al·pen·horn, al′pen·hạrn, *n.* [G. *Alpen,* the Alps, and *horn,* a horn.] A very long, powerful, nearly straight horn, but curving slightly and widening toward its extremity, used on the Alps to convey signals. Also **alp·horn.**

al·pen·stock, al′pen·stok″, *n.* [G. *Alpen,* the Alps, and *stock,* a stick.] A strong stick shod with iron, pointed at the end, used in mountain climbing.

al·pes·trine, al·pes′trin, *a.* [M.L. *alpestris,* mountainous < L. *Alpes,* the Alps.] Pertaining to mountain regions; *bot.* growing on mountains near the timber line; subalpine.

al·pha, al′fa, *n.* [M.E. < L. < Gr. < Heb. *aleph.*] The first letter in the Greek alphabet; *fig.* the first or beginning.

al·pha and o·me·ga, *n.* The first and last letters of the Greek alphabet; *fig.* the beginning and the end.

al·pha·bet, al′fa·bet″, *n.* [M.E. *alphabete* < L. < Gr. *alphabetos* < *alpha* and *beta,* A and B.] The letters of a language arranged in the customary order; any series of elementary signs or symbols used for a similar purpose; hence, first elements; simplest rudiments.

al·pha·bet·ic, al″fa·bet′ik, *a.* Pertaining to an alphabet; furnished with an alphabet; expressed with an alphabet; in the order of the letters of the alphabet. Also **al·pha·bet·i·cal.**—**al·pha·bet·i·cal·ly,** *adv.* In an alphabetical manner; in the customary order of the letters.

al·pha·bet·i·za·tion, al″fa·bet″i·zā′shan, *n.* The act of putting in an alphabetical order or expressing with an alphabet; the act of furnishing with an alphabet.

al·pha·bet·ize, al′fa·bi·tĩz″, *v.t.*—*alphabetized, alphabetizing.* To arrange alphabetically.

al·pha de·cay, *n. Phys.* the radioactive transformation of a nuclide by alpha particle emission. Also **al·pha dis·in·te·gra·tion.**

al·pha i·ron, *n. Metal.* An allotropic form of iron which has stability below the same temperature (910°C.) as beta iron, but differs from beta iron in that it is magnetic: both are common varieties of ferrite. Also *ferrite.*

al·pha·mer·ic, al″fa·mer′ik, *a.* Alphanumeric.

al·pha·nu·mer·ic, al″fa·nö·mer′ik, al″fa·nū·mer′ik, *a.* [< *alpha*bet and *numeric.*] *Computer,* consisting of both numbers and letters; as, an *alphanumeric* set of characters. Also **alphameric.**

al·pha par·ti·cle, *n. Phys.* a subatomic particle, having an atomic weight of 4 and a positive charge equal to 2 electronic charges (essentially a helium nucleus), which is given off from the nuclei of certain atoms during radioactive disintegration.

al·pha ray, *n. Phys.* a flow of helium nuclei.

Al·pine, al′pĩn, al′pin, *a.* Of, pertaining to, or connected with the Alps; (*l.c.*) resembling an alp.

al·pin·ism, al′pi·niz″um, *n.* (*Sometimes cap.*) the practice of mountain climbing. —**al·pin·ist,** *n.*

al·read·y, ạl·red′ē, *adv.* [M.E. *already,* wholly ready < *al,* all, and *redy,* ready. ALL READY.] Before the present time; previously; so soon before some specified time; previously; so soon.

Al·sa·tian, al·sā′shan, *a.* Pertaining to Alsace or to Alsatia or Whitefriars (precinct in London), a former sanctuary for debtors and criminals.

al·sike, al′sik, al′sĩk, ạl′sĩk, ạl′sik, *n.* [< *Alsike,* in Sweden.] A European clover, *Trifolium hybridum,* with whitish or pink flowers, much grown in the U.S. for forage.

al·so, ạl′sō, *adv.* [*All* and *so;* O.E. *eall-swā, ealswā, alswā,* < *eall, eal,* all quite, and *swā,* so. *As* is contracted from this word.] In like manner; likewise; as well; in addition; too.

also-ran, ạl′sō·ran″, *n.* A person or any contestant who fails to achieve success, used esp. in reference to the loser of an election, horse race, or other contest.

Al·ta·ic, al·tā′ik, *a.* Pertaining to the Altai, a vast range of mountains in Eastern Asia, or to a family of languages which includes Hungarian, Finnish, Turkish, etc. Also **Al·ta·ian,** al·tā′an.—*n.* A European and Asian language family consisting of the Mongolian, Tungusic, Turkic, and Korean subfamilies.

al·tar, ạl′tẽr, *n.* [M.E. < O.E. *alter, altar* < L. *altare,* a root seen in L. *altus,* high.] An elevated place on which sacrifices were offered to a deity or ancestor, or on which incense was burned; a table in a church for the celebration of the Eucharist.

al·tar boy, *n.* One who assists the principal celebrant in a religious ceremony; an acolyte.

---

ch- chain, G. na*ch*t;   **th-** THen, thin;   **w-** wig, hw as sound in whig;   **z-** zh as in azure, zeal.   *Italicized vowel* indicates schwa sound.

al·tar call, *n.* A general appeal made by an evangelist to participators in the worship to come to the front of the church and publicly commit themselves to Jesus Christ.

al·tar·piece, ạl'tér·pēs", *n.* A painting or piece of sculpture placed behind or above an altar in a church for the purpose of decoration.

al·tar rail, *n.* The rail in front of the altar separating the body of the church from the sanctuary.

al·tar stone, *n.* A stone slab on an altar of worship; *Rom. Cath. Ch.* a stone which contains precious relics of martyrs.

alt·az·i·muth, al·taz'i·muth, *n.* [< *altitude* and *azimuth.*] An astronomical instrument for determining the altitude and azimuth of heavenly bodies, consisting of a vertical circle and attached telescope, the two having both a vertical and a horizontal motion; also, several other instruments which are mounted in a similar manner.

al·ter, ạl'tér, *v.t.* [M.E. *alteren* < M.Fr. *alteren* < M.L. *alterare,* to change, < L. *alter,* another of two.] To make over or different; to make some change in; to modify; to vary in some degree, without an entire change.—*v.i.* To become, in some respects, different; to vary; to change, as one's personality.—**al·ter·a·bil·i·ty,** ạl"tér·a·bil'i·tē, *n.* The quality of being susceptible of alteration.—**al·ter·a·ble,** ạl'tér·a·bl, *a.* Capable of being altered, varied, or made different.—**al·ter·a·ble·ness,** ạl'tér·a·bl·nis, *n.* The quality of being alterable.—**al·ter·a·bly,** ạl'tér·a·blē, *adv.* In an alterable manner; so as to be altered or varied.

al·ter·ant, ạl'tér·ant, *n.* That which produces alteration; that which alters.

al·ter·a·tion, ạl'te·rā'shan, *n.* The act of altering; the state of being altered; also, the change made.

al·ter·a·tive, ạl'te·rā"tiv, *a.* Causing alteration; having the power to alter.

al·ter·cate, ạl'tér·kāt, ạl'tér·kāt, *v.i.* [< L. *altercatus,* pp. of *altercari,* to wrangle, < *alter,* another. ALTER.] To contend in words; to dispute; to wrangle.

al·ter·ca·tion, ạl'tér·kā'shan, ạl"tér·kā'shan, *n.* The act of altercating; vigorous contention in words; heated argument or dispute; a wrangle.

al·ter e·go, *n.* [L., lit. 'other I.'] Close friend; second self; an exact substitute.

al·ter·nate, ạl'tér·nāt", ạl'tér·nāt", *v.t.*—*alternated, alternating.* [L. *alternatus,* pp. of *alternare* < *alternus,* alternate, < *alter.*] To perform by turns; cause to take turns; interchange successively, one with another. —*v.i.* To succeed by turns; take turns; change about by turns between points, states, actions.

al·ter·nate, ạl'tér·nit, ạl'tér·nit, *n.* Something that alternates; an official substitute, as at a political convention.—**al·ter·nate·ly,** ạl'tér·nit·lē, *adv.* In an alternate manner.—**al·ter·nate·ness,** ạl'tér·nit·nis, ạl'tér·nit·nis, *n.*—**al·ter·nat·ing·ly,** ạl'tér·nāt"ing·lē, ạl'tér·nāt"ing·lē, *adv.*

al·ter·nate, ạl'tér·nit, ạl'tér·nit, *a.* Forming or having an alternating series; succeeding by turns; recurring as one of an alternating series; appearing in turn or as every other; *bot.* of leaves, as placed singly and at different heights on the axis, first on one side and then on the other, or at definite angular distances from one another; *geom.* noting two non-adjacent angles made by the crossing of two lines by a third line, both angles being either interior or exterior, and one being on one side of the third line and the other on the other side.

al·ter·nat·ing cur·rent, *n. Elect.* A current that reverses direction in cycles. Abbr. *AC.*

al·ter·na·tion, ạl'tér·nā'shan, ạl"tér·nā'-shan, *n.* [L. *alternatio(n-).*] The act of alternating; the state of being alternate; appearance, occurrence, or change by turns.

al·ter·na·tion of gen·er·a·tions, *n. Bot.* The occurrence of alternating sporophyte and gametophyte reproductive phases in the life cycle of a plant; the alternation of asexual and sexual reproduction. Compare *metagenesis.*

al·ter·na·tive, ạl·tŭr'na·tiv, ạl·tŭr'na·tiv, *n.* A choice between two things, so that if one is taken the other must be left; a possibility of one of two things, so that if one thing is false the other must be true.—**al·ter·na·tive·ly,** ạl·tŭr'na·tiv·lē, ạl·tŭr'na·tiv·lē, *adv.* In an alternative manner. —**al·ter·na·tive·ness,** ạl·tŭr'na·tiv·nis, ạl·tŭr'na·tiv·nis, *n.*

al·ter·na·tive, ạl·tŭr'na·tiv, ạl·tŭr'na·tiv, *a.* Offering a choice or possibility of one of two things.

al·ter·na·tor, ạl'tér·nā"tér, ạl'tér·nā"tér, *n.* An electric generator used in the production of alternating current.

al·the·a, al·thē'a, *n.* [L. *althæa,* < Gr. *althaia,* wild mallow.] Any plant of the malvaceous genus *Althaea,* as the hollyhock, *Althaea rosea,* or the marshmallow, *Althaea officinalis*; also, a malvaceous flowering garden shrub, *Hibiscus syriacus,* the rose of Sharon.

alt·horn, alt'harn", *n.* [G. < *alt,* alto, and *horn.*] The tenor saxhorn, often substituted for the French horn in bands.

al·though, ạl·thō', *conj.* [M.E. *although* < *all,* if, even, and *though.*] Grant all this; be it so; supposed that; even though; admit all that.

al·tim·e·ter, al·tim'i·tér, ạl'ti·mē"tér, *n.* [< L. *altus,* high, and E. *-meter* < Gr. *metron,* measure.] An instrument for determining altitudes by geometrical principles, as a quadrant; an instrument, as an aneroid barometer, that measures height by registering changes in atmospheric pressure.—**al·tim·e·try,** al·tim'i·trē, *n.* The science of ascertaining altitudes.

al·ti·pla·no, ạl"ti·plä'nō, *n.* [Amer. Sp., < L. *altus* and *planum,* plain.] A high plateau.

al·ti·tude, al'ti·tūd", al'ti·tōd", *n.* [L. *altitudo,* height, depth < *altus,* high (whence *exalt, haughty.*)] Height; amount of space to a point above from one below; measure of elevation; a high location or area; a high position or rank.

al·to, al'tō, *n.* [It. < L. *altus,* high, being above the tenor.] *Mus.* Contralto; the deepest voice among women and boys, and the highest among men, a special voice above the tenor; a singer in this voice; in a family of musical instruments, the second highest instrument.—*a.* Pertaining to this voice.

al·to·cu·mu·lus, ạl"tō·kū'mū·lus, *n.* [< L. *alt(us),* high and *-o-* and *cumulus.*] A cloud, a form of cumulus of great altitude, appearing in fleecy clumps or globular masses variously grouped.

al·to·geth·er, ạl"to·geth'ér, *adv.* [M.E. *altogedere,* "all together."] Wholly; entirely; completely; quite.—*n.* A whole.—**in the al·to·geth·er,** *colloq.* in the nude.

al·to·ri·lie·vo, äl'tạ·Rē·lye'vạ, *n.* pl. **al·ti·ri·lie·vi,** äl'tē·Rē·lye've.** *It.* High relief; sculpture in which the figures stand out prominently from the background; sculpture in high relief.

al·to·stra·tus, ạl"tō·strā'tus, *n.* [L. *alt(us),* high and *-o-* and *stratus*: STRATUS.] A comparatively high, veillike or sheetlike cloud that is similar to the cirrostratus, and located from 8,000 to 20,000 feet.

al·tri·cial, al·trish'al, *a.* [< L. *altric-,* stem of *altrix,* one who nourishes (fem.) < *altus,* pp. of *alere,* nourish.] Immature and helpless at hatching, and requiring parental help and care.

al·tru·ism, al'trö·iz"um, *n.* [Fr. *altruisme* < O.Fr. or It. *autrui,* others, < L. *alter,* another.] Devotion to others or to humanity, as opposed to *selfishness.*—**al·tru·ist,** al'trö·ist, *n.* One who practices altruism.—**al·tru·is·tic,** al"trö·is'tik, *a.* Pertaining to altruism; regardful of others.

al·u·la, al'yū·la, *n.* pl. **al·u·lae.** [N.L. dim. of L. *ala,* wing.] *Ornith.* the tuft of small, bastard feathers which grow upon the first digit of a bird's wing. Also *bastard wing.*

al·um, al'um, *n.* [M.E. < M.Fr. *alum* < L. *alumen.*] A general name for a class of double sulfates containing aluminum and such metals as potassium, ammonium, and iron. Common or potash alum is used in medicine as an astringent and a styptic; in dyeing, as a mordant; in tanning, for restoring the cohesion of skins.

a·lu·mi·na, a·lö'mi·na, *n.* [< *alumin-,* stem of L. *alumen,* alum.] The natural or synthetic oxide of aluminum, the most abundant of the earth's elements, occurring naturally as corundum and as bauxite, a major source of aluminum.

a·lu·mi·nate, a·lö'mi·nāt, *n. Chem.* a salt formed from aluminum hydroxide when it acts as a weak acid.

a·lu·mi·nif·er·ous, a·lö"mi·nif'ér·us, *a.* [< L. *alumin-* and *-fer* (< L. *ferre,* bear).] Containing alum, alumina, or aluminum.

al·u·min·i·um, al"ū·min'ē·um, *n. Chiefly Brit.* aluminum.

a·lu·mi·nize, a·lö'mi·nīz", *v.t.*—*aluminized, aluminizing.* To cover or treat with aluminum.

a·lu·mi·no·sil·i·cate, a·lö"mi·nō·sil'i·-kit, a·lö"mi·nō·sil'i·kāt", *n.* Any combination of aluminate and silicate occurring either in nature or synthetically, as feldspar or zeolite.

a·lu·mi·nous, a·lö'mi·nus, *a.* Pertaining to or containing alum or alumina.

a·lu·mi·num, a·lö'mi·num, *n. Chem.* an oxidation-resistant white metal with a bluish tinge, and a luster somewhat resembling, but far inferior to, that of silver. Sym. Al, at. no. 13, at. wt. 26.9815. See Periodic Table of Elements.

a·lu·mi·num sul·fate, *n. Chem.* a white salt, $Al_2(SO_4)_3$, existing in crystalline form: used chiefly in water purification.

a·lum·na, a·lum'na, *n.* pl. **a·lum·nae,** a·lum'nē. Fem. of *alumnus*; a female graduate of an educational institution.

a·lum·nus, a·lum'nus, *n.* pl. **a·lum·ni,** a·lum'nī. [L. a disciple, < *alere,* to nourish.] Formerly a pupil, now a graduate of an educational institution, such as a college or university.

al·um·root, al'um·rōt", al'um·rụt", *n.* Any of several N. American plants of the genus *Heuchera,* with astringent roots, esp. *H. americana*; the root.

A·lun·dum, a·lun'dum, *n.* Abrasive and refractory material made by fusing alumina. (Trademark.)

al·u·nite, al'ū·nīt", *n.* [Fr. < *alun,* alum.] *Chem.* a mineral, a hydrous sulfate of potassium and aluminum, $K(AlO)_3(SO_4)_2$·$3H_2O$, occurring in finely granular masses or sometimes in crystals.

al·ve·o·lar, al·vē'o·lér, *a.* Containing sockets, hollow cells, or pits; pertaining to sockets, specifically the sockets of the teeth; *ling.* spoken with the tongue near or touching the alveolar ridge.

al·ve·o·late, al·vē'o·lāt", al·vē'o·lit, *a.* Deeply pitted, so as to resemble a honeycomb.

al·ve·o·lus, al·vē'o·lus, *n.* pl. **al·ve·o·li,** al·vē'o·lī. [L. a small hollow, dim. of *alveus,* hollow, cavity < *alvus,* belly.] A cell, pit, or small cavity, as in a honeycomb or in a fossil; the socket of a tooth; a terminal air sac deep within the lungs.

al·ways, ạl'wāz, ạl'wĕz, *adv.* [M.E. *alwayes* < O.E. *ealne weg,* all the way < *eal,* all and *weg,* way. ALL, WAY.] Perpetually; uninterruptedly; forever; continually; as, *always* the same; as often as occasion recurs; as, *always* late; if necessary.

Al·yce clo·ver, al'ĭs, *n. Bot.* the biennial or annual herb *Alysicarpus vaginalis,* of the legume family, *Leguminosae,* grown as a forage plant, esp. for permanent pasture and hay.

a·lys·sum, *a*·lis'*u*m, *n.* [N.L. < Gr. *alysson,* plant believed to cure rabies < *a-* and *lyssa,* rabies.] Any of the herbs, genus *Alyssum,* bearing small yellow or white racemose flowers with hairy leaves.—**sweet a·lys·sum,** a garden plant with small white flowers.

a.m. [< L. *ante meridiem.*] Before 12:00 noon and after 12:00 midnight; also *A.M.*

A.M. See *Amplitude Modulation.*

am, am. [O.E. *eom, eam, am;* akin Goth. *im,* Icel. *em,* Lith. *esmi,* Ir. *am,* Gr. *eimi,* L. *sum,* Skt. *asmi.* IS. BE.] The first person singular of the present indicative of the verb *to be.*

a·mah, ä'm*a*, am'*a*, *n.* [Pg. *ama.*] In India, China, etc., a nurse or maid; female servant.

a·mal·gam, *a*·mal'g*a*m, *n.* [M.E. < M.Fr. < M.L. *amalgama* < Gr. *malagma,* poultice, < *malacos,* soft.] An alloy of mercury with another metal or metals; *fig.* a mixture or combination.—**a·mal·gam·a·ble,** *a*·mal'g*a*m·*a*·bl, *a.* Capable of being amalgamated.

a·mal·gam·ate, *a*·mal'g*a*·māt", *v.t.*—*a* malgamated, amalgamating. To form into an amalgam; combine; unite.—*v.i* To form an amalgam; blend; coalesce.

a·mal·gam·a·tion, *a*·mal"g*a*·mā'shan, *n.* The act of amalgamating, or the resulting state; combination; union; fusion; *metal.* extraction of the precious metals from their ores by treatment with mercury; *com.* the merging of two or more corporations.—**a·mal·gam·a·tive,** *a*·mal'g*a*·mā"tiv, *a.* Tending to amalgamate.—**a·mal·gam·a·tor,** *a*·mal'g*a*·mā"tor, *n.*

a·man·u·en·sis, *a*·man'ū·en'sis, *n.* pl. **a·man·u·en·ses,** *a*·man'ū·en'sēz. [L. *a,* by, and *manus,* the hand.] A person whose employment is to write what another dictates, or to copy what has been written by another; secretary.

am·a·ranth, am'*a*·ranth", *n.* [L. < Gr. *amarantos,* unfading < *a,* not, and *marainō,* to wither.] A poetical name loosely used to signify a flower supposed never to fade; a color inclining to purple.

am·a·ran·thine, am"*a*·ran'thin, am"*a*·ran'thin, *a.* Belonging to, consisting of, or resembling amaranth; never fading; undying; of a purplish color.

am·a·relle, am'*a*·rel", *n.* [G. < M.L. < L. *amarus,* bitter.] Any variety of *Prunus Cerasus,* the sour cherry, which differs from the morello by its colorless juice.

am·a·ryl·lis, am"*a*·ril'is, *n.* [L. < Gr. *Amaryllis.*] A bulbous plant, *Amaryllis belladonna,* the belladonna lily, with large, lilylike, normally rose-colored flowers; any of several related plants once referred to the genus *Amaryllis.*

a·mass, *a*·mas', *v.t.* [M.Fr. *amasser—a,* to, and *masse,* L. *massa,* a mass.] To collect into a heap; to gather a great quantity or number of; to accumulate.—**a·mass·ment,** *a*·mas'ment, *n.* The act of amassing.

am·a·teur, am'*a*·chur", am'*a*·tyur", am"*a*·tur', *n.* [Fr. < L. *amator,* lover, < *amare,* love.] One who cultivates any art or pursuit for the enjoyment of it, instead of professionally or for gain, sometimes implying desultory action or crude results; a devotee. —*a.* Of or being an amateur; lacking the talent or polish of a professional.—**am·a·teur·ism,** am'*a*·chu·riz"um, am'*a*·tyu·riz"um, am"*a*·tur'iz·um, *n.* The practice or character of an amateur.

am·a·teur·ish, am"*a*·chur'ish, am"*a*·tyur'ish, am"*a*·tur'ish, *a.* Of or being an amateur; suggestive of an amateur, as wanting the skill, finish, or other faculties of a professional.—**am·a·teur·ish·ly,** am"*a*·chur'ish·lē, am"*a*·tyur'ish·lē, am"*a*·tur'ish·lē, *adv.*—**am·a·teur·ish·ness,** am"*a*·chur'ish·nis, am"*a*·tyur'ish·nis, am"*a*·tur'ish·nis, *n.*

A·ma·ti, ä·mä'tē, *n.* A violin made by the Amati family of Cremona, Italy, in the 16th and 17th centuries.

am·a·tive, am'*a*·tiv, *a.* [M.L. < L. *amo, amare,* to love.] Full of love; inclined to love; amorous; amatory.—**am·a·tive·ness,** am'*a*·tiv·nis, *n.* That propensity which impels to sexual passion.—**am·a·to·ri·al,** am'*a*·tōr"ē·al, am'*a*·tạr"ē·al, *a.* Pertaining to love; amatory.—**am·a·to·ry,** am'*a*·tōr"ē, am'*a*·tạr"ē, *a.* Pertaining to or producing love; expressive of love, as verses or sighs.

am·a·tol, am'*a*·tol", am'*a*·tạl", am'*a*·tōl", *n.* [*am(monia)* and *(trinitro)tol(uene).*] An explosive consisting of ammonium nitrate and TNT, or trinitrotoluene.

am·au·ro·sis, am"ạ·rō'sis, *n.* [N.L. < Gr. *amaurōsis,* < *amauros,* obscure.] A partial or complete loss of sight from loss of power in the optic nerve or retina, without any visible defect in the eye except an immovable pupil. —**am·au·rot·ic,** am"ạ·rot'ik, *a.* Pertaining to or affected with amaurosis.

a·maze, *a*·māz', *v.t.*—*amazed, amazing.* [O.E. *amasian.*] To confound with sudden surprise or wonder; to confuse utterly; to astound; to astonish; to bewilder; to surprise.—**a·maz·ed·ly,** *a*·mā'zid·lē, *adv.* With amazement.—**a·maz·ed·ness,** *a*·mā'zid·nis, *n.* The state of being amazed; amazement.—**a·maz·ing,** *a*·mā'zing, *a.* Very wonderful; exciting astonishment; as, *amazing* grace.—**a·maz·ing·ly,** *a*·mā'zing·lē, *adv.* In an amazing manner or degree.

a·maze, *a*·māz', *n. Poetic,* wonder.

a·maze·ment, *a*·māz'ment, *n.* The state of being amazed or astounded; astonishment.

Am·a·zon, am'*a*·zon", am'*a*·zon, *n.* [M.E. < L. < Gr. *Amazōn;* origin uncertain. The name of the river *Amazon* refers to female warriors seen in its vicinity.] The largest river, in volume of water, in the world, located in South America; one of a race of female warriors said in Greek legend to dwell near the Black Sea. (*Often l.c.*) a very tall, strong woman; a virago.

Am·a·zo·ni·an, am"*a*·zō'nē·an, *a.* Of, like, or befitting an Amazon, female warrior of Greek mythology; warlike; aggressive; also, pertaining to the Amazon river.

am·a·zon·ite, am'*a*·zo·nīt", *n.* [From the river *Amazon.*] A beautiful semi-precious green variety of microcline found near the Amazon River and in other parts of the world. Also *Amazon stone.*

Am·a·zon stone, *n.* See *amazonite.*

am·bas·sa·dor, am·bas'*a*·dor, *n.* [M.E. < Fr. *ambassadeur,* < *ambassade,* an embassy, < L. *ambactus,* a vassal, a dependent, < a Teutonic word = Goth. *ambaht,* O.E. *ambiht, ambeht,* a servant, < prefix and *(the an* in *answer),* and a root allied to Skt. *bhaj,* to serve or honor.] A minister of the highest rank employed by one prince or state at the court of another to transact state affairs; a messenger; intermediary; authorized envoy; official representative; as, the *ambassador* to France.—**am·bas·sa·do·ri·al,** am·bas"a·dōr'ē·al, am·bas"a·dạr'ē·al, *a.* Belonging to an ambassador.

am·bas·sa·dress, am·bas'*a*·dris, *n.* The wife of an ambassador; a female ambassador.

am·ber, am'bėr, *n.* [M.E. < M.Fr. *ambre,* It. *ambra,* Sp. *ambar,* < Ar. *ambar,* ambergris, from its resemblance to this.] A hard, pale-yellow, and sometimes reddish or brownish fossil resin of extinct pine trees, used for ornamental pieces; the pale yellow to brownish color of amber.

am·ber, am'bėr, *a.* Of or like amber; of the color of this resin.

am·ber·gris, am'bėr·grēs", am'bėr·gris, *n.* [M.E. < M.Fr. *ambre gris (gris,* gray), gray amber.] A solid, opaque, waxy, ash-colored substance used in perfumery; a morbid secretion, probably from the sperm whale.

am·bi·dex·trous, am"bi·dek'strus, *a.* [L. < *ambi-,* both, and *dexter,* skillful.] Having the faculty of using both hands with equal ease and facility; double-dealing; versatile.

am·bi·ence, am'bē·ens, *n.* The surrounding mood, atmosphere, or environment.

am·bi·ent, am'bē·ent, *a.* [L. *ambiens, ambientis—amb,* around, and *iens,* ppr. of *ire,* to go.] Surrounding; encompassing on all sides: applied to fluids or diffusible substances; as, the *ambient* air.

am·big·u·ous, am·big'ū·us, *a.* [L. *ambiguus,* < *ambigo,* to go about < *ambi,* about, and *ago,* to drive.] Doubtful or uncertain; likely to be interpreted two ways; equivocal; indefinite.—**am·big·u·ous·ly,** am·big'ū·us·lē, *adv.* In an ambiguous manner; with doubtful meaning.—**am·big·u·ous·ness,** am·big'ū·us·nis, *n.*

am·bi·gu·i·ty, am"bi·gū'i·tē, *n.* The state or quality of being ambiguous or obscure; doubtfulness or uncertainty, particularly of signification.

am·bit, am'bit, *n.* [M.E. < L. *ambitus,* a circuit. AMBIENT.] Compass or circuit; circumference; scope; sphere; bounds; range; extent; limits.

am·bi·tion, am·bish'an. *n.* [M.E. < L. *ambitio, ambitionis,* the going about of candidates for office in Rome, hence flattery, ambition < *amb,* around, round about, and *eo, itum,* to go, < L., Gr., and Skt. root *i,* to go.] An eager and sometimes inordinate desire for honor, power, fame, or whatever confers distinction; aspiration toward an object; desire to distinguish oneself among others; determination to progress in one's business or other career.

am·bi·tion, am·bish'an, *v.t.* To seek after ambitiously; to desire.

am·bi·tious, am·bish'us, *a.* [L. *ambitiosus.*] Possessing ambition; eagerly or inordinately desirous of power, honor, fame, office, superiority, or distinction; strongly desirous, followed by *of* or *after;* springing from, indicating, or characterized by ambition; showy; pretentious; as, an *ambitious* ornament; requiring unusual effort; as, an *ambitious* undertaking.—**am·bi·tious·ly,** am·bish'us·lē, *adv.*—**am·bi·tious·ness,** am·bish'us·nis, *n.* Ambition.

am·biv·a·lence, am·biv'a·lens, *n.* [L. *ambi-,* both, and *valere,* to be strong.] Coexistence of contradictory feelings about a particular person, object, or action.

am·bi·ver·sion, am"bi·vur'shan, am"bi·vur'zhan, *n. Psychol.* the state of being an ambivert.

am·bi·vert, am'bi·vurt", *n.* [L. *ambi-,* on both sides, and *vertere,* to turn.] *Psychol.* a person possessing characteristics of both the introvert and the extrovert.

am·ble, am'bl, *v.i.*—*ambled, ambling.* [M.E. < M.Fr. *ambler,* to amble, < L. *ambulare,* to walk, < *amb,* about.] To move by lifting both legs on each side alternately: said of horses, etc.; hence, to move easily and gently at an unhurried pace; to saunter.

am·ble, am'bl, *n.* Easy motion; gentle pace; the pace of a horse or like animal when ambling.—**am·bler,** am'blėr, *n.* One who ambles.

am·blyg·o·nite, am·blig'o·nīt", *n.* [G. < Gr. < *amblys,* blunt, and *gōnia,* angle.] A whitish mineral, Li(AlF)PO₄, occurring in crystals of different pale shades, composed of basic lithium aluminum phosphate; a source of lithium.

---

ch- chain, G. na**ch**t; **th-** THen, thin; **w-** wig, hw as sound in whig; **z-** zh as in azure, zeal. *Italicized vowel* indicates schwa sound.

am·bly·o·pi·a, am″blē·ō′pē·a, *n.* [< Gr. *amblys,* dull, and *ōps, ōpos,* the eye.] Dullness or dimness of eyesight without any apparent defect in the organs; the first stage in amaurosis.

am·boi·na wood, am·boi′na wụd, *n.* [*Amboyna,* one of the Molucca Islands.] A beautifully mottled and curled wood employed in cabinet work; also **am·boy·na wood.**

am·broid, am′broid, *n.* Amber in large masses, produced from small fragments with the aid of heat and pressure.

am·bro·sia, am·brō′zha, *n.* [L. < Gr. *ambrosia,* < *ambrotos,* immortal < *a,* not, and same root as L. *mors,* death, E. *murder.*] The fabled food of the ancient Greek gods, which conferred immortality on those who partook of it; hence, anything pleasing to the taste or smell, as a perfumed draught, unguent, or the like; a dessert made of sweet orange segments and shredded coconut.—**am·bro·si·al,** am·brō′zhal, *a.* Of or pertaining to ambrosia; anointed or fragrant with ambrosia; delicious; fragrant.—**am·bro·si·al·ly,** am·brō′zhal·ē, *adv.* In an ambrosial manner; with an ambrosial odor.

am·bu·lac·rum, am″bū·lak′rum, am″bū·lā′krum, *n. pl.* **am·bu·lac·ra,** am″bū·lak′ra, am″bū·lā′kra. [N.L. < L. *ambulacrum,* an alley < *ambulare* to walk.] *Biol.* the perforated spaces or avenues through which are protruded the tube feet, by means of which locomotion is effected in the sea urchins, etc. —**am·bu·lac·ral,** am″bū·lak′ral, *a.* Pertaining to ambulacra.

am·bu·lance, am′bū·lans, *n.* [Fr. *ambulate.*] A vehicle fitted with suitable appliances for conveying the injured and sick; also a mobile hospital unit which accompanies an army in the field.

am·bu·lance chas·er, *n. Slang,* a lawyer or his agent who encourages and incites accident victims to sue for injuries suffered.

am·bu·lant, am′bū·lant, *a.* Moving from place to place; ambulatory.

am·bu·late, am′bū·lāt, *v.i.*—*ambulated, ambulating.* [L. *ambulo, ambulatum,* to go about. AMBLE.] To walk; travel; move about.

am·bu·la·to·ry, am′bū·la·tōr″ē, am″bū·la·tạr″ē, *a.* Having the power or faculty of walking; adapted for walking; pertaining to a walk; accustomed to move from place to place; not stationary; as, an *ambulatory* court; movable.

am·bu·la·to·ry, am′bū·la·tōr″ē, am″bū·la·tạr″ē, *n.* Any sheltered part of a building intended as a passageway for walking.

am·bus·cade, am″bū·skād′, *n.* [M.Fr. *embuscade,* < It. *imboscata,* < M.L. *imboscata,* < *imboscare.* AMBUSH.] An ambush; a trap; also, a place of ambush; also, a force lying in ambush.—*v.i.*—*ambuscaded, ambuscading.* To lie in ambush.—*v.t.* To conceal in ambush; also, to attack from ambush.— **am·bus·cad·er,** am″bū·skād′ér, *n.* One who ambushes.

am·bush, am′bụsh, *v.t.* [M.E. < O.Fr. *embuschier,* < M.L. *imboscare,* < *in,* in, and *boscus,* wood.] To station troops, etc., in concealment to await and attack, as an enemy, by surprise; conceal in or as in ambush; also, to attack from ambush; waylay.—*v.i.* To lie in or as in ambush.

am·bush, am′bụsh, *n.* An arrangement of troops or other persons in concealment for the purpose of attacking by surprise; the position or station of the attacking force, or the force itself.—**am·bush·er,** am′bụsh·ér, *n.*—**am·bush·ment,** am′bụsh·ment, *n.* The act or position of ambushing; an ambush.

a·me·ba, *n.* See *amoeba.*

a·mel·io·rate, a·mēl′yu·rāt″, *v.t.*—*ameliorated, ameliorating.* [Fr. *améliorer,* < L. *ad,* to, and *melioro, melioratum,* to make better, < *melior,* better.] To make better; to improve; to meliorate.—*v.i.* To grow better;

to meliorate.—**a·mel·io·ra·ble,** a·mēl′yėr·a·bl, *a.*Capable of being ameliorated.— **a·mel·io·ra·tion,** a·mēl′yo·rā′shan, *n.* The act of ameliorating; improvement; melioration.—**a·mel·ior·a·tive,** a·mēl′yū·rā″·tiv, *a.* Producing, or having a tendency to produce, amelioration.—**a·mel·io·ra·tor,** a·mēl′yu·rā″tor, *n.*

a·men, ā′men′, ä′men′, *adv., interj.* [O.E. < L. < Gr. *amēn,* < Heb. *āmēn,* firm or true, truth, truly, < *āman,* strengthen, confirm.] Truly; verily: esp. used as a solemn expression of concurrence, or a concluding formula, as after a prayer.—*n.* An utterance of amen; an expression of concurrence; a concluding word or act.

a·me·na·bil·i·ty, a·mē″na·bil′i·tē, a·men″a·bil′i·tē, *n.* The state of being amenable.

a·me·na·ble, a·mē′na·bl, a·men′a·bl, *a.* [M.E. < M.Fr. *amener,* to bring or lead to.] Liable to be called to account; responsible; ready to yield or submit, as to advice; submissive; agreeable.—**a·me·na·ble·ness,** a·mē′na·bl·nis, a·men′a·bl·nis, *n.*—**a·me·na·bly,** a·mē′na·blē, a·men′ablē, *adv.* In an amenable manner.

a·mend, a·mend′, *v.t.* [M.E. < O.Fr. *amender,* < *emender,* to correct, < L. *emendo,* to free from faults < *e-,* out, out of, and *menda,* a fault. MEND.] To make better, or change for the better; to alter, as a bill, constitution, motion, etc., by formal procedure; to correct; to improve; to reform; to alter or modify an order, plan, or the like.—*v.i.* To grow or become better by reformation or rectifying something wrong in manners or morals.—**a·mend·a·ble,** a·mend′a·bl, *a.* Capable of being amended or corrected. —**a·mend·er,** a·mend′ér, *n.* One who amends.

a·mend·a·to·ry, a·men′da·tōr″ē, a·men′·da·tạr″ē, *a.* Capable of amending; corrective.

a·mend·ment, a·mend′ment, *n.* The act of amending, or changing for the better, in any way; improvement; correction; the act of becoming better, or state of having become better; an alteration proposed to be made in the draft of a legislative bill, or in the terms of any motion under discussion before a meeting; (*cap.*) any of the additions to the U.S. Constitution.

a·mends, a·mendz′, *n. pl.* Compensation for a loss or injury; recompense; satisfaction; equivalent.

a·men·i·ty, a·men′i·tē, a·mē′ni·tē, *n.* [M.E. < L. *amaenitas, amaenus,* pleasant.] The quality of being pleasant or agreeable, in respect of situation, prospect, climate, etc., as also of temper, disposition, or manners.—**a·men·i·ties,** *n. pl.* Agreeable features, circumstances, ways; civilities.

a·men·or·rhe·a, ā·men″o·rē′a, *n.* [N.L. < Gr. *a,* not, *mén,* month, *rheo,* to flow.] *Med.* a morbid or unnatural suppression of menstruation.

a·men·tia, ā·men′sha, *n.* [N.L. < L., want of reason < *a,* from, and *mens, mentis,* mind.] Imbecility of mind; idiocy. or dotage; deficiency of. mental capacity.

a·merce, a·mụrs′, *v.t.*—*amerced, amercing.* [M.E. < A.Fr. *amercié,* fined at the mercy of the court < *a,* at, and *merci,* mercy.] To punish by a pecuniary penalty, the amount of which is left to the discretion of the court; hence, to punish by deprivation of any kind; to fine.—**a·merce·a·ble,** a·mụrs′a·bl, *a.* Liable to amercement.— **a·merce·ment,** a·mụrs′ment, *n.* The act of amercing; a fine imposed on an offender at the discretion of the court.—**a·merc·er,** a·mụrs′ér, *n.* One who amerces.

A·mer·i·can, a·mer′i·kan, *a.* [From *Americus* Vespucius (Amerigo Vespucci), 1451–1512, Italian merchant and adventurer.] Of or pertaining to either continent of America;

often, of or pertaining to the U.S.; also, noting or pertaining to the so-called "red" race, characterized by a reddish or brownish skin, dark eyes, black hair, and prominent cheek-bones, and embracing the aborigines of N. and S. America (sometimes excluding the Eskimos), known as American Indians.

A·mer·i·can, a·mer′i·kan, *n.* A native or inhabitant of America; orig. a member of the aboriginal American (Indian) race; later, a person born or resident in America, esp. a citizen of the U.S.

A·mer·i·ca·na, a·mer″i·kan′a, a·mer″i··kä′na, a·mer″i·kā′na, *n. pl.* Books, papers, etc., relating to America, esp. to its history and geography.

A·mer·i·can cheese, *n.* A type of mild cheddar cheese made in the U.S.; a cheddar-type processed cheese.

A·mer·i·can ea·gle, *n.* The bald eagle. See *eagle.*

A·mer·i·can Eng·lish, *n.* The English language as it is written and spoken in the U.S., as distinct from the English of Britain, Australia, Canada, etc.; official language of the U.S.

A·mer·i·can In·di·an, *n.* Any of the aboriginal peoples inhabiting N. and S. America, excluding the Eskimo.

A·mer·i·can·ism, a·mer′i·ka·niz″um, *n.* American sympathies, nationality, or citizenship; an American trait or usage; a word or idiom considered to have originated in, or gained currency from American use; loyalty to policies and traditions of the U.S.

A·mer·i·can·ist, a·mer′i·ka·nist, *n.* One who specializes in the study of the American Indian's customs or languages; anyone who studies American geography, history, etc. in detail; one who supports American policy.

A·mer·i·can i·vy, *n.* Virginia creeper.

A·mer·i·can·ize, a·mer′i·ka·nīz″, *v.t., v.i.*—*Americanized, Americanizing.* To make or become American; conform to the American character or type.—**A·mer·i·can·i·za·tion,** a·mer′i·ka·nī·zā′shan, *n.*

A·mer·i·can plan, *n.* That method of conducting a hotel according to which a fixed charge per day covers room and meals. Compare *European plan.*

A·mer·i·can sa·ble, *n.* A pine marten, *Martes americana,* or its pelt.

A·mer·i·can sad·dle horse, *n.* One of a breed of horses, three-gaited or five-gaited, bred mainly in Kentucky.

A·mer·i·can Stand·ard Ver·sion, *n.* A 1901 revision of the authorized King James version of the Bible.

am·er·i·ci·um, am″e·rish′ē·um, *n.* A radioactive element produced by the bombardment of uranium and plutonium with high-energy helium ions. Sym. Am, at. no. 95, at. wt. 243. See Periodic Table of Elements.

Am·er·ind, am′e·rind, *n.* [< *Amer(ican)* and *Ind(ian).*] An American Indian or Eskimo; one of the indigenous languages spoken by the American Indian.—**Am·er·in·di·an,** am″e·rin′dē·an, *a., n.*—**Am·er·in·dic,** am″e·rin′dik, *a.*

a·met·a·bol·ic, ā″met·a·bol′ik, *a. Zool.* undergoing little, or lacking, metamorphosis. Also **a·me·tab·o·lous.**—**a·me·tab·o·lism,** ā″me·tab′a·liz″um, *n.*

am·e·thyst, am′i·thist, *n.* [M.E. *amatiste* < O.Fr. < L. *amethystus* < Gr. *amethystos* < *a-,* not, and *methyein,* to inebriate, from its supposed power of preventing or curing intoxication.] A violet-blue or purple variety of quartz which is wrought into various articles of jewelry.—**am·e·thys·tine,** am″i·this′tin, am″i·this′tīn, *a.* Pertaining to, composed of, or resembling amethyst.

am·e·tro·pi·a, am″i·trō′pē·a, *n.* [N.L. < Gr. *ametros,* without measure, disproportionate, and *ops,* eye.] *Pathol.* an abnormal condition of the eye with respect to refraction of light, as in myopia, etc.—**am·e·trop·ic**, am″i·trop′ik, *a.*

Am·har·ic, am·har′ik, äm·här′ik, *a.* Pertaining to the Semitic language which is the official and court language of Ethiopia.—*n.* The official language of Ethiopia.

a·mi, ä·mē′, *n.* pl. **a·mis.** [Fr. < L. *amicus.*] *French.* A friend; *slang*, on the European continent, an American.

a·mi·a·ble, ä′mē·a·bl, *a.* [M.E. < M.Fr. < L.L. *amicabilis* < *amicus*, friend < *amare*, to love.] Possessing agreeable qualities; having a kindly and attractive disposition; pleasing; friendly; good-natured.—**a·mi·a·bil·i·ty**, **a·mi·a·ble·ness**, *n.* The quality of being amiable or lovable; sweetness of temper.—**a·mi·a·bly**, *adv.* In an amiable, genial, or cooperative manner.

am·i·an·thus, am″ē·an′thus, *n.* [< L. *amiantus* < Gr. *amiantos* < *a-*, not, and *miainō*, to pollute or vitiate; so called from its incombustibility.] Flexible asbestos, earth flax, or mountain flax; an incombustible mineral composed of delicate filaments, very flexible, and somewhat elastic, often long and resembling threads of silk.

am·i·ca·bil·i·ty, am″i·ka·bil′i·tē, *n.* Quality of being amicable.

am·i·ca·ble, am′i·ka·bl, *a.* [M.E. < L.L. *amicabilis*, < *amicus*, a friend, < *amare*, to love.] Characterized by or exhibiting friendship, peaceableness, or harmony; friendly; peaceable; harmonious in social or mutual transactions.—**am·i·ca·bly**, *adv.* In an amicable or friendly manner; with harmony.—**am·i·ca·ble·ness**, *n.*

am·ice, am′is, *n.* [M.E. *amis, amyce* < M.Fr. *amis* (pl. of *amit*) < M.L. *amictus*, cloak, < pp. of *amicire*, wrap around < *am(b)-*, around, and *-ject(us)*, pp. of *jacere*, throw.] An oblong embroidered piece or strip of fine linen, falling down the shoulders like a cape, worn partly under the alb by priests during the service of the Mass.

a·mi·cro·nu·cle·ate, ā″mī·krō·nō′clē·it, ā″mī·krō·nū′clē·it, *adj. Biol.* not having a micronucleus.

a·mi·cus cu·ri·ae, a·mī′kus kūr′ē·ē″, *n.* pl. **a·mi·ci cu·ri·ae**, a·mī′kī kūr′ē·ē″. [L., lit. 'friend of the court.'] *Law*, a bystander who is asked for or volunteers information on some matter of law as a help to a court.

a·mid, a·mid′, *prep.* [< *a-*, on, in, and *mid, midst.* M.E. *amidde, amiddes* (the latter a genetive form); O.E. *on-middan*; the *t* has been tacked on as in *against.*] In the midst or middle of; surrounded or encompassed by; mingled with; among; during. Also *amidst.*

am·ide, am′īd, am′id, *n.* [< *ammonia.*] Any chemical compound derived from ammonia by the substitution of acid or acyl groups for the atoms of hydrogen.

am·i·dol, am′i·dōl″, am′i·dạl″, am′i·dol″, *n.* [G., < *Amidol*, trade name.] *Chem.* a salt, $C_6H_8N_2O·2HCl$, derived from a phenol, and used chiefly as a developer in photography.

a·mid·ships, a·mid′ships, *adv. Naut.* in or toward the middle of a ship or aircraft, or the part midway between stem and stern. Also **a·mid·ship.**—*a.* In the middle line, lengthwise, of a ship or aircraft. Also **a·mid·ship.**

a·midst, a·midst′, *prep.* Amid.

a·mi·go, a·mē′gō, ä·mē′gō, *Sp.* ä·mē′gạ, *n.* [Sp. < L. *amicus.*] *Sp.* a friend.

a·mine, a·mēn′, am′in, *n.* [< *ammonia.*] *Chem.* any of the derivative compounds of ammonia in which the hydrogen atoms are replaced by one or more organic hydrocarbon radicals.—**a·min·ic**, a·mē′nik, a·min′ik, *a.* Denoting the presence of an NH_2 group.—**a·min·i·ty**, *n.*

a·mi·no, a·mē′nō, am′i·nō, *a. Chem.*

Denoting the presence of, or relation to, the univalent group NH_2; denoting the presence of an amine.

a·mi·no ac·id, *n. Chem.* an organic compound containing the amino group NH_2 and at least one carboxyl group, these acids forming the basic constituents of proteins.

a·mi·no·ben·zo·ic ac·id, a·mē′nō·ben·zō′ik, am′i·nō·ben·zō′ik, a·mē″nō·ben·zō′ik, am″i·nō·ben·zō′ik, *n. Chem.* any one of the three crystalline isomer derivatives of benzoic acid with the formula $H_2NC_6H_4-COOH$, esp. the para-derivative, para-amino benzoic acid, which is a growth factor of the vitamin B complex.

a·mi·no ni·tro·gen, *n. Chem.* the nitrogen in the amino radical NH_2.

a·mi·no·py·rine, a·mē″nō·pī′rēn, am″i·nō·pī′rēn, *n. Pharm.* a drug used as a fever preventative and pain reliever which exists as a white, crystalline solid, $C_{13}H_{17}N_3O$. Also **a·mi·do·py·rine.**

a·mir, a·mēr′, *n.* [Ar. *amīr*, < *amara*, command.] In Mohammedan countries, a commander or ruler; a chieftain; a title sometimes applied to Turkish officials. Also *emir.*

A·mish, ä′mish, am′ish, *a.* Pertaining to Jakob Ammann (Amman, or Amen), a Swiss Mennonite of the 17th century, or to his followers or their sect.—*n. pl.* The Amish Mennonites.

a·miss, a·mis′, *adv.* In a faulty manner; improperly; astray.—*a.* At fault; wrong; improper.

am·i·to·sis, am″i·tō′sis, *n.* [N.L.: *a-* and *mitosis.*] *Biol.* the direct method of cell division, characterized by simple cleavage of the nucleus, without the formation of chromosomes. Compare *mitosis.*—**am·i·tot·ic**, am″i·tot′ik, *a.* Pertaining to or characterized by amitosis.—**am·i·tot·i·cal·ly**, am″i·tot′i·ka·lē, *adv.*

am·i·ty, am′i·tē, *n.* [M.E. *amite* < M.Fr. *amité* (Fr. *amitié*) < M.L. *amicitas*, friendship; L. *amicus*, a friend, < *amo*, to love.] Friendship; harmony; good understanding, especially between nations.

am·me·ter, am′mē″tèr, *n.* [< *am(pere)-* and *-meter.*] An instrument which measures electric current in amperes.

am·mine, am′ēn, a·mēn′, *n. Chem.* A compound in which ammonia molecules are present in a coordinate linkage complex or bonded to a metal ion; an ammino compound.

am·min·o, a·mē′nō, am′i·nō, a·mē′nō, *a. Chem.* about, pertaining to, or being an ammine, or ammine in nature.

am·mo, am′ō, *n.* Short form for ammunition.

am·mo·nia, a·mōn′ya, a·mō′nē·a, *n.* [N.L. < L. (*sal*)*ammoniacum* < Gr. *ammoniakon*, of Ammon (Egyptian god; the salt and gum resin (see *ammoniac*) were said to have been prepared near the temple of Ammon, in Libya).] The volatile alkali, a colorless, pungent, suffocating gas, NH_3, a compound of nitrogen and hydrogen, very soluble in water and thus forming ammonia water or aqueous ammonia; hence, loosely, ammonia water.—**am·mon·ic**, a·mon′ik, a·mō′nik, *a.* Pertaining to ammonia.

am·mo·ni·ac, a·mō′nē·ak″, *n.* [M.E. < L. < Gr. *ammoniakon.* See *ammonia.*] An exudation of an umbelliferous plant (the Persian herb, *Dorema ammoniacum*) with a fetid smell, used as an antispasmodic and expectorant, and in plasters. Also *gum ammoniac.*

am·mo·ni·a·cal, am″o·nī′a·kal, *a.* Pertaining to ammonia, or possessing its properties.

am·mo·ni·ate, a·mō′nē·āt″, *v.t.*—**ammoniated, ammoniating.** To mix or impregnate with ammonia.—*n.* Any of a number of compounds which contain ammonia.—**am·mo·ni·at·ed**, a·mō′nē·ā·tid, *a.*

---

am·mon·i·fy, a·mon′i·fī″, a·mō′ni·fī″, *v.t.*—**ammonified, ammonifying.** To combine or impregnate with ammonia; form into ammonia or ammonium compounds.—*v.i.* To become ammonified; produce ammonification.—**am·mon·i·fi·ca·tion**, a·mon″i·fi·kā′shan, a·mō″ni·fi·kā′shan, *n.* The act of combining or impregnating with ammonia; the result of this process.

am·mo·ni·um, a·mō′nē·um, *n.* [N.L. *ammoniac.*] *Chem.* a radical, NH_4, which plays the part of a metal in the compounds (ammonium salts) formed when ammonia reacts with acids.

am·mo·ni·um chlo·ride, *n. Chem., pharm.* a white salt, NH_4Cl, existing as a volatile, crystalline powder, used chiefly in dry cells and as an expectorant. Also **sal am·mo·ni·ac.**

am·mo·ni·um hy·drox·ide, *n. Chem.* the weak base NH_4OH occurring only in the solution made of ammonia gas and water, used as a household cleaner and in smelling salts.

am·mo·ni·um ni·trate, *n. Chem.* the salt NH_4NO_3 existing as a water-soluble, crystalline powder, used for fertilizers and explosives.

am·mo·ni·um sul·fate, *n. Chem.* the salt $(NH_4)_2SO_4$ existing as a water-soluble, crystalline solid, used chiefly as a fertilizer.

am·mu·ni·tion, am″ū·nish′an, *n.* [Fr. *amunition* (obsolete) < *la munition* (wrongly interpreted as *l'amunition*) < L. *munitio(n-)*, defense < *munire*, to fortify.] Generically, certain composite objects or substances which are used in the process of inflicting damage to game or an actual enemy; cartridges, shells, or other projectiles for guns, as distinguished from bombs, mines, or grenades.

am·ne·sia, am·nē′zha, *n.* [N.L. < Gr. *amnesia*, variant of *amnestia*, oblivion.] *Pathol.* loss of memory partially or completely.—**am·ne·sic**, am·nē′sik, am·nē′zik, *a.*—**am·nes·tic**, am·nes′tik, *a.*

am·nes·ty, am′ni·stē, *n.* pl. **am·nes·ties.** [L. *amnestia*, < Gr. *amnestia*, oblivion.] An act of forgiving; forgetting of offenses; a general pardon of the offenses of subjects against the government, or the proclamation of such pardon.—*v.t.*—**amnestied, amnestying.** To grant an amnesty to; to pardon.

am·ni·on, am′nē·on, *n.* pl. **am·ni·ons, am·ni·a**, am′nē·a. [N.L. < Gr. *amnion*, inner fetal membrane < *amn(os)*, lamb, and *-ion* (diminutive suffix).] The innermost membrane surrounding the fetus of mammals, birds, and reptiles; a similar membrane enclosing the embryos of various invertebrates.—**am·ni·on·ic, am·ni·ot·ic**, am″nē·on′ic, am″nē·ot′ic, *a.*

a·moe·ba, a·mē′ba, *n.* pl. **a·moe·bae**, a·moe′bas, a·mē′bē. [N.L., < Gr. *amoibē*, change, < *ameibein*, change.] *Biol.* a member of a genus of protozoa, a one-celled semi-fluid animal that feeds and moves by means of pseudopodia. Also **a·me·ba.**

a·moe·bic, a·mē′bik, *a.* [< *amoeba.*] Of, pertaining to, or resembling an amoeba; characterized by or due to the presence of amoebae, as certain diseases.—**a·moe·bi·cide**, a·mē′bi·sīd″, *n.* An agent that destroys amoebae.—**a·moe·bi·form**, a·mē′bi·farm, *a.* Amoeba-like; varying in form like an amoeba.

a·moe·bic dys·en·ter·y, *n. Med.* a form of dysentery, characterized by ulceration of the intestinal tract, caused by the amoeba, *Endamoeba hystolytical.* Also **a·me·bic dys·en·ter·y.**

a·moe·boid, a·me·boid, a·mē′boid, *a.* Of or pertaining to or resembling the amoeba.

a·mok, a·muk′, a·mok′, *n., a., adv.* Amuck.

---

a·mo·le, *a·mō′lä*, *n.* [Sp., < Mex. Indian *amolli*, soap.] The root of any of various plants, as Mexican species of *Agave*, used as a substitute for soap; any plant so used.

a·mong, *a·mung′*, *prep.* [M.E. *amonge*, *amonges, amongest,* O.E. *amang, onmang, ongemonge < on,* in, and *gemonge,* crowd, < *ge-* and *mengan,* to mingle; the *es* being an adverbial genitive termination, and the *t* tacked on, as in *amidst.* MINGLE.] Mixed or mingled with (implying a number); in or into the midst of; in or into the number of; by the combined action of.

a·mongst, *a·mungst′*, *prep.* Among.

a·mon·til·la·do, *a·mon″ti·lä′dō*, *n.* [Sp. < *a,* to, and *Montilla* (city in Spain which produces the wine).] A dry kind of Spanish sherry, light in color with a sweet taste.

a·mor·al, *ā·mạr′al*, *a·mạr′al*, *ā·mor′al*, *a·mor′al,* *a.* Lacking, or indifferent to, moral responsibility; independent of moral distinctions.

am·o·ret·to, *am″o·ret′ō*, *n.* pl. **am·o·ret·ti,** *am″o·ret′ē.* [It. < *amor,* love.] Cupid.

a·mo·ri·no, *ä″mạ·Rē′nạ*, *n.* pl. **a·mo·ri·ni,** *ä″mạ·Rē′nē.* Cupid.

am·o·rist, *am′o·rist*, *n.* [L. *amor,* love.] One devoted to love or love-making; a gallant.—**am·o·ris·tic,** *am″o·ris′tik, a.*

am·o·rous, *am′ėr·us, a.* [M.E. < M.Fr. *amoureux,* < M.L. *amorosus < amor,* love.] Inclined to love persons of the opposite sex; having a propensity to love, or to sexual enjoyment; loving; fond; pertaining or relating to love; produced by love; indicating love; enamored, followed by *of.*—**am·o·rous·ly,** *am′or·us·lē, adv.* In an amorous manner; fondly, lovingly.—**am·o·rous·ness,** *am′or·us·nis, n.*

a·mor·phism, *a·mạr′fiz″um, n.* Amorphous condition; absence of definite form or crystalline structure.

a·mor·phous, *a·mạr′fus, a.* [Gr. *amorphos < a-,* neg., and *morphē,* form.] Having no determinate form; of irregular shape; not having the regular forms exhibited by the crystals of minerals; being without crystallization; formless; shapeless; indeterminate; unorganized; characterless.

am·or·tize, *am′ėr·tīz″, a·mạr′tīz, v.t.*—*amortized, amortizing.* [M.E. *amortissen* < L.L. *amortisare,* to sell in mort-*main* < M.Fr. *amortiss-,* stem of *amortir* < L. *ad-,* to, and *mors, mortis,* death.] To liquidate, as a mortgage; to extinguish, as a debt, by means of regular payments into a sinking fund.—**am·or·ti·za·tion,** *am″ėr·ti·zā′shan, n.*

a·mount, *a·mount′, v.i.* [M.E. *amounten* < O.Fr. *amonter,* to advance, increase < *amont,* upwards < L. *mons, montis,* a hill.] To total by an accumulation of particulars; to come in the aggregate or whole; to result in; to be tantamount or equivalent: followed by *to.*

a·mount, *a·mount′, n.* The sum total of two or more particular sums or quantities; the aggregate; the effect, substance, or result; money, as principal plus the interest earned.

a·mour, *a·mụr′, n.* [Fr. < L. *amor,* love.] A love intrigue or affair, usually illicit; an affair of gallantry.

am·pe·lop·sis, *am″pe·lop′sis, n.* [N.L. < Gr. *ampelos,* vine, and *opsis,* appearance.] Any plant, genus *Ampelopsis,* comprising climbing woody vines or shrubs, as the pepper-vine; also, some allied plants, as the Japanese ivy or the Virginia creeper.

am·per·age, *am′pėr·ij, am·pēr′ij, n.* The strength of an electric current measured in amperes.

am·pere, *am′pēr, am·pēr′, n.* [< A. M. *Ampère* (1775-1836), French physicist.] *Elect.* the unit of current strength, the current produced by an electromotive force of one volt acting through a resistance of one ohm.

am·pere-hour, *am′pėr·our′, am′pēr·ou″ėr,* *n. Elect.* the quantity of electricity (3,600 coulombs) transferred by a current of one ampere in one hour: used as a unit.

am·pere-turn, *am′pėr·tųrn″, n. Elect.* One complete turn or convolution of a conducting coil, through which one ampere of current passes; the magnetomotive force produced by one ampere passing through one complete turn or convolution of a coil.

am·per·sand, *am′pėr·sand″, am″pėr·sand′, n.* [*and, per se,* and *and.*] The character *&,* symbol for *and.*

am·phet·a·mine, *am·fet′a·mēn″, am·fet′a·min, n.* [*alpha-methyl-phenethyl,* and *amine.*] A compound, ($C_9H_{13}N$), used as a drug in the treatment of colds, hay fever, depression, and in cases of obesity.

am·phib·i·a, *am·fib′ē·a, n. pl.* [N.L. neut. pl. of *amphibius,* < Gr. *amphibios,* < *amphi-* on both sides, double, and *bios,* mode of life.] The various cold-blooded vertebrates adapted to live in water and on land; *(cap.)* the class of vertebrates, including the frogs, newts, and salamanders, having gills in larval form, and developing into lung-breathing adults.—**am·phib·i·an,** *am·fib′ē·an, a.* Belonging to amphibia, or to the class *Amphibia.*—*n.* An amphibian animal; an amphibious plant; sea plane; hydroplane.

am·phi·bi·ot·ic, *am″fi·bī·ot′ik, a.* Pertaining to life that lives in water in the larval state.

am·phib·i·ous, *am·fib′ē·us, a.* Able to live on land or water; able to function on land or water; as, an *amphibious* craft; *milit.* referring to an assault landing on a shore by combined land and naval forces.

am·phi·bole, *am′fi·bōl″, n.* [Fr. < Gr. *amphibolos,* ambiguous: see *amphibolous.*] A silicate mineral of varying composition, usually consisting of a silicate of calcium, magnesium, and one or more other metals, and having numerous varieties, including tremolite, common hornblende, etc.; a source of asbestos.

am·phi·bol·ic, *am″fi·bol″ik, a.* Doubtful; equivocal.

am·phib·o·lite, *am·fib′o·līt″, n.* [< *amphibole.*] A metamorphic rock consisting essentially of amphibole or hornblende.

am·phi·bol·o·gy, *am″fi·bol′o·jē, n. pl.* **am·phi·bol·o·gies.** [Gr. *amphibologia—amphi-,* in two ways, *ballō,* to throw, and *logos,* discourse.] A phrase or discourse susceptible of more than one interpretation; and hence, a phrase of uncertain meaning; ambiguity resulting from grammatical construction.—**am·phib·o·log·i·cal,** *am·fib″o·loj′i·kal, a.* Of or pertaining to amphibology; of doubtful meaning.

am·phib·o·lous, *am·fib′o·lus, a.* [L.L. *amphibolus,* < Gr. *amphibolos,* ambiguous, < *amphi-,* on both sides, and *ballein,* throw.] Ambiguous, as in meaning; equivocal; characterized by amphibology.—**am·phib·o·ly,** *n. pl.* **am·phib·o·lies.** [L. *amphibolia,* < Gr. *amphibolia.*] Amphibolous character or speech; ambiguity; ambiguous phrase.

am·phi·brach, *am′fi·brak″, n.* [Gr. *amphi-,* on both sides, and *brachys,* short.] *Pros.* a metrical foot of three syllables, the middle one long, the first and last short, or the middle syllable accented and the first and last unaccented.

am·phi·car·pous, *am″fi·kär′pus, a.* [Gr. *amphi* and *carpos,* fruit.] *Bot.* bearing two classes of fruit, differing in form or in time of ripening.

am·phi·dip·loid, *am″fi·dip′loid, a. Biol.* having two sets of diploid chromosomes, one set from each parent of an interspecific hybrid.—*n.* Any interspecific hybrid with two diploid sets of chromosomes.

am·phi·go·ry, *am′fi·gōr″ē, am′fi·gạr″ē, n. pl.* **am·phi·go·ries.** [Fr. *amphigouri.*] A meaningless rigmarole; a nonsensical par-ody; a meaningless composition, etc.—**am·phi·gor·ic,** *a.*

am·phim·a·cer, *am·fim′a·sėr, n.* [Gr. *amphimakros,* long on both sides, < *amphi-* and *makros,* long.] *Pros.* a metrical foot of three syllables, the middle one short and the others long.

am·phi·mic·tic, *am″fa·mik′tik, a.* [< Gr. *amphi-* and *miktos,* mixed < *mignynai,* to mix.] *Biol.* being capable of interbreeding to produce fertile offspring.

am·phi·mix·is, *am″fi·mik′sis, n. pl.* **am·phi·mix·es,** *am″fi·mik′sēz.* [Gr. *amphi-* and *mixis,* a mixing, < *mignynai,* to mix.] *Biol.* the combining or coming together of the germ cells in sexual reproduction; *genetics,* the combining of genetic information from the parental organisms; *psychol.* a combination of genital and anal eroticism.

am·phi·pod, *am′fi·pod″, n.* [Gr. *amphi-,* on both sides, and *pod-,* stem of *pous,* a foot.] One of an order *Amphipoda,* of small crustaceous animals common in fresh and salt water, including the sand flea, possessing two sets of limbs, one used for jumping, the other for swimming.

am·phip·ro·style, *am·fip′ro·stīl″, am″fi·prō′stil, a.* [L. *amphiprostylos,* Gr. *amphiprostylos.*] *Arch.* having a pillared portico at the front and rear only, as a temple.—*n.* An amphiprostyle building.

am·phi·sty·lar, *am″fi·stī′lėr, a. Arch.* referring to a building, esp. a temple, which has columns on both sides or at both ends.

am·phi·the·a·ter, *am′fi·thē″a·tėr, n.* [Gr. *amphitheatron—amphi-,* on both sides, and *theatron,* theater.] A structure of an oval form, having a central area encompassed with rows of seats, rising higher as they recede from the center, on which people sit to view a sports event or other spectacle or performance; a similarly arranged room in which medical students may watch surgery; a large auditorium; arena; anything, as a natural hollow among hills, resembling an amphitheater in form.—**am·phi·the·at·ric,** **am·phi·the·at·ri·cal,** *am″fi·thē·a′trik, am″fi·thē·a′tri·kal, a.* Pertaining to or resembling an amphitheater; exhibited in an amphitheater.—**am·phi·the·at·ri·cal·ly,** *adv.*

am·phit·ro·pous, *am·fi′tro·pus, adj.* [< Gr. *amphi-* and *-trop- < trope,* a turning.] *Bot.* pertaining to an ovule which has been inverted so that the funicular attachment is in the middle of one side.

am·pho·ra, *am′for·a, n. pl.* **am·pho·rae,** **am·pho·ras,** *am′fo·rē″.* [L. *amphora,* Gr. *amphiphoreus, amphoreus—amphi,* on both sides, and *phoreō,* to carry from its two handles.] Among the Greeks and Romans, a vessel, usually tall and narrow, with two handles or ears and a narrow neck, used for holding wine, oil, honey, and the like.

am·pho·ter·ic, *am″fo·ter′ik, a.* [< Gr. *amphoteros,* either of two.] *Chem.* Able to react or function as an acid or base; having or showing the characteristics of both a base and an acid.

am·ple, *am′pel, a.—ampler, amplest.* [Fr. *ample* < L. *amplus.*] Large in dimensions; of great size, extent, capacity, or bulk; wide; spacious; extended (*ample* room); fully sufficient for some purpose intended; abundant; copious; liberal; plentiful (an *ample* supply, *ample* justice).—**am·ple·ness,** *n.* The state of being ample; largeness; sufficiency; abundance.

am·pli·dyne, *am′pli·din″, n.* [< *amplifier* and *-dyn-,* < Gr. *dynamis,* power.] A direct current generator, with a rotating armature and a high degree of positive feedback, used to regulate a large power output by magnifying the power applied to the field winding, with the amplified power utilized in the operation of an attached direct-current motor.

a- fat, fāte, fär, fâre, fạll;   **e-** met, mē, mēre, hėr;   **i-** pin, pīne;   **o-** not, nōte, möve;   **u-** tub, cūbe, bụll;   **oi-** oil;   **ou-** pound.

am·pli·fi·ca·tion, am″pli·fi·kā′shan, *n.* The act of amplifying; an enlargement; extension; diffusive description or discussion.—**am·pli·fi·ca·to·ry,** am·plif′i·ka·tōr″ē, am·plif′i·ka·tar″ē, *a.* Serving or tending to amplify, enlarge, or extend, as a narrative.

am·pli·fi·er, am′pli·fī″ēr, *n.* That which amplifies or enlarges; *electron.* a device for increasing the power or strength of electric waves or impulses, commonly including one or more vacuum tubes or transistors.

am·pli·fy, am′pli·fī″, *v.t.*—*amplified, amplifying.* [M.E. *amplifien* < M.Fr. *amplifier* < L. *amplificare* < *amplus.*] To make more ample, larger, more extended, more copious, and the like; to increase; to explain in greater detail.—*v.i.* To grow or become ample or more ample; to be diffuse in argument or description; to elaborate, often followed by *on.*

am·pli·tude, am′pli·tŏd″, am′pli·tūd″, *n.* [L. *amplitudo.*] State of being ample; largeness of dimensions; abundance; extent of surface or space; greatness; *astron.* an arc of the horizon intercepted between the east or west point and the center of the sun or star at its rising or setting; *phys.* the extent of a vibration; *elect.* the maximum variation or departure from the average of an alternating current; *electron.* the greatest value of an alternating radio wave or the like in one direction, measured from zero during one oscillation.

am·pli·tude mod·u·la·tion, *n. Electron.* a system of radio transmission in which the amplitude of the carrier wave is modulated (contrasted with frequency modulation).—*a.* Referring to a broadcasting station or network using this system. Abbr. *AM.*

am·ply, am′plē, *adv.* In an ample manner; largely; sufficiently; copiously.

am·poule, am′pūl, *n.* See *ampul.*

am·pul, am′pūl, *n.* [M.E. *ampulle* < O.E. *ampulle* < L. *ampulla.*] *Med.* a small, bulbous, hermetically sealed vessel which holds a solution for hypodermic injection. Also *ampoule, ampule.*

am·pule, am′pūl, *n.* See *ampul.*

am·pul·la, am·pul′a, am·pul′a, *n.* pl. **am·pul·lae,** am·pul′lē. [L.] A more or less globular bottle, used by the Romans for holding oil; a vessel for holding the consecrated oil used in various church rites and at the coronation of kings; *bot.* a hollow flask-shaped leaf; *anat.* a dilated section of a duct or canal.—**am·pul·la·ceous,** am″pu·lā′shus, *a.* Of or pertaining to or like an ampulla.

am·pu·tate, am′pū·tāt″, *v.t.*—*amputated, amputating.* [L. *amputatus,* pp. of *amputare,* < *am-, amb-,* around, and *putare,* to lop, prune.] To cut off, as a limb or other member, by a surgical operation; to remove all or part of by cutting.—**am·pu·ta·tion,** am″pū·tā′shan, *n.*

am·pu·tee, am″pū·tē′, *n.* One who has had one or more limbs, or parts of limbs, amputated.

am·trac, am·track, am′trak″, *n.* [< *amphibious* and *tractor*.] *Milit.* an amphibious, flat-bottomed, armored vehicle, propelled on land or water by caterpillar tracks with extended side fins.

a·muck, a·muk′, *n.* [Malay or Javanese *amok,* furious attack, charge.] A furious, reckless onset comparable to a psychic disturbance observed in the Eastern Archipelago of Asia, in which the afflicted rush about frantically, attacking everyone. Also *amok.*—*adv.*—**run a·muck,** to go berserk; to act in a frenzied manner.

am·u·let, am′ū·lit, *n.* [L. *amuletum.*] Something worn or carried upon the person, intended to act as a charm or preservative against evils or mischief, such as disease and witchcraft.

a·muse, a·mūz′, *v.t.*—*amused, amusing.* [Fr. *amuser,* to amuse, to divert.] To entertain or occupy pleasantly, as with humor; to divert.—**a·mus·a·ble,** a·mūz′a·bl, *a.* Capable of being amused.

a·muse·ment, a·mūz′ment, *n.* The act of amusing, or state of being amused; a slight amount of mirth or tendency toward merriment; that which amuses; entertainment; sport; pastime.

a·muse·ment park, *n.* A commercially operated park containing various recreational facilities, such as roller coasters, ferris wheels, and merry-go-rounds.

a·mus·ing, a·mū′zing, *a.* Giving amusement; pleasing; diverting; causing mirth.—**a·mus·ing·ly,** a·mū′zing·lē, *adv.* In an amusing manner.

a·mu·sive, a·mū′ziv, *a.* Providing amusement, or inciting mirth.

a·myg·da·la·ceous, a·mig″da·lā′shus, *a.* [L. *amygdalaceus,* almondlike.] Belonging to the almond family of plants, which includes the almond, peach, plum, cherry, etc.

a·myg·da·late, a·mig′da·lit, a·mig′da·lāt″, *a.* [< L. *amygdalus,* an almond.] Of or pertaining to almonds; resembling almonds.—**a·myg·da·line,** a·mig′da·lin, a·mig′da·līn″, *a.* Pertaining to, resembling, or made of almonds. *Anat.* of or relating to a tonsil.

a·myg·da·lin, a·mig′da·lin, *n.* [< L. *amygdala.*] *Chem.* a white glycosidic powder, $C_6H_5CHCNOC_{12}H_{21}O_{10}$, obtained from bitter almonds, chiefly used medically as an expectorant.

a·myg·da·loid, a·mig′da·loid″, *n.* [L. *amygdalus,* almond, and *-oid.*] A term applied to igneous rock, especially trap, containing round or almond-shaped vesicles or cavities partly or wholly filled with crystalline nodules of various minerals.—*a.* Resembling an amygdaloid; almond-shaped.—**a·myg·da·loid·al,** a·mig′da·loid″al, *a.* Pertaining to an amygdaloid.

am·yl, am′il, *n.* [Gr. *amylon,* starch.] *Chem.* a univalent hydrocarbon radical, C_5H_{11}, existing in several isomeric modifications, compounds of which occur in fusel oil and fruit essences.

am·y·la·ceous, am″i·lā′shus, *a.* Pertaining to starch, or the farinaceous part of grain; resembling starch.

am·yl al·co·hol, am′il al·co·hol, *n. Chem.* a liquid (C_5H_{11}-OH) consisting of alcohol obtained from fusel oil or from fermentation of starches, used chiefly as a solvent.

am·yl·ase, am′e·lās″, *n.* [< Gr. *amylon,* starch.] Any of the enzymes that convert starch into sugar, as in saliva and germinating seeds.

am·y·loid, am′e·loid″, *n.* A semigelatinous food substance, analogous to starch. *Pathol.* a hard material formed in tissues in certain diseases.

am·y·loid, am′e·loid″, *a.* Resembling or being of the nature of amylum; starchy.

am·y·lol·y·sis, am″e·lol′i·sis, *n.* [N.L. < L. *amylum,* starch, and Gr. *lysis,* a loosing or decomposition.] The conversion of starch into sugar, esp. by enzymes.—**am·y·lo·lyt·ic,** am″e·lō·lit′ik, *a.*

am·y·lop·sin, am″e·lop′sin, *n.* [L. *amylum,* starch, and *-psin,* as in *trypsin, pepsin.*] *Chem.* an enzyme of the pancreatic juice, capable of converting starch into sugar.

am·y·lose, am′i·lōs, *n.* [L. *amylum,* starch.] *Chem.* any of a group of carbohydrates, as starch, cellulose, etc., having the formula $C_6H_{10}O_5$, or some multiple thereof.

am·y·lum, am′i·lum, *n.* [L. starch, < Gr. *amylon,* fine flour, prepared otherwise than by the usual grinding.] Starch.

a·my·o·to·ni·a, ā″mī·o·tō′nē·a, ā·mī″o·tō′nē·a, *n.* [N.L.] A lack of muscle tone.

an, a, an, a, *indef. art.* [O.E. *án,* one, an, the former being the original, the latter a developed meaning; the same word as *one.*

one.] A word used before nouns in the singular number to denote an individual as one among more belonging to the same class, and not marking singleness like *one,* nor pointing to something known and definite like *the.* In such phrases as "once *an* hour," "a dollar *an* ounce," *an* has a distributive force, being equivalent to *each, every.* The form *a* is used before consonants (including the name sound of *u* as in *unit, European=yu);* *an* is used before words beginning with a vowel sound, or sometimes before *h,* usu. silent, when the accent falls on any syllable except the first; as, *an inn, an historian, an heir.*

an·a, an′a, *adv.* [Gr. *ana,* prep., at the rate of (so much) each.] In equal quantities; of each: used in medical prescriptions, with reference to ingredients. Sym. *āā.*

a·na, ā′na, ä′na, *n.* [The neuter plural termination of Latin adjectives in *-anus,* often forming an affix to the names of eminent men to denote a collection of their memorable sayings—thus *Scaligeriana, Johnsoniana.*] A collection of notable sayings, information, or anecdotes.

an·a·bap·tism, an·a·bap′tiz″um, *n.* [L.Gr. *anabaptismos,* < *anabaptizein,* baptize again, < Gr. *ana-,* again, and *baptizein,* E. *baptize.*] A second baptism; (*cap.*) the doctrine or practices of the Anabaptists.—**An·a·bap·tist,** *n.* A member of any of various sects arising in Germany, Switzerland, etc., early in the 16th century, who denied the validity of infant baptism and required the baptism of adults on entrance into communion: also applied, more or less opprobriously, to members of later sects or religious bodies holding the same doctrine.

a·nab·a·sis, a·nab′a·sis, *n.* pl. **a·nab·a·ses,** a·nab′a·sēz″. [Gr. < *ana-,* up, and *basis,* a going, < *bainein,* to go.] A going up; an expedition from the coast inland; also a military expedition; (*cap.*) the expedition of Cyrus the Younger against Persia in 401 B.C. described by Xenophon.

an·a·bat·ic, an″a·bat′ik, *a.* [< Gr. *anabatos,* going up, < *anabainein.*] *Meteor.* Rising; lifting; referring to the direction of wind blowing upwards from the horizontal plane of the earth's surface.

an·a·bi·o·sis, an″a·bī·ō′sis, *n.* [N.L. < Gr. *anabiosis,* a return to life, < *anabioun,* to return to life; < *ana-,* again; and *bios,* life.] A return to life from death or from a state resembling death.

a·nab·o·lism, a·nab′o·liz″um, *n.* [< Gr. *ana-,* upward, and *-bolism,* as in *metabolism.*] Constructive metabolism: opposed to *catabolism.*—**an·a·bol·ic,** *a.*

a·nab·o·lite, a·nab′o·līt″, *n. Biol.* a complex substance synthesized from a simpler form by constructive metabolism.

a·nach·ro·nism, a·nak′ro·niz″um, *n.* [Gr. *anachronismos < anachronesthai,* to be an anachronism, < *anachronizein,* to be late, < *ana-,* implying inversion, error, and *chronos,* time.] An error in computing historical time; error in chronological order; any error which implies the misplacing, usually earlier, of persons or events in time; anything foreign to or out of keeping with a specified epoch.—**a·nach·ro·nis·tic, a·nach·ro·nis·ti·cal, a·nach·ro·nous,** a·nak′ro·nis′tik, a·nak′ro·nis′ti·kal, a·nak′ro·nus, *a.*

an·a·cli·nal, an″a·klīn′al, *a.* [Gr. *ana-, klinein,* to lean (something) upon, < *ana-,* against, and *klinein,* incline.] *Geol.* transverse to the dip, as a valley. Compare *cataclinal.*

an·a·co·lu·thic, an″a·ko·lö′thik, *a.* Lacking grammatical sequence; containing an anacoluthon.

an·a·co·lu·thon, an″a·ko·lö′thon, *n.* [L.L. < Gr. *anakolouthos,* wanting sequence— neg. *an-,* and *akolouthos,* following < *ha-, a-*

together, and *keleuthos*, path.] *Gram.* lack of sequence in a sentence, owing to the latter member of it belonging to a different grammatical construction from the preceding; as, "He that curseth father or mother, let him die the death." (Mat. xv. 4.)

an·a·con·da, an″*a*·kon′da, *n.* [Probably < Singhalese *henakandayā*, a slender green snake.] A large, heavy, nonvenomous serpent, *Eunectes murinus*, found in S. America, growing to a length of over 20 feet, and crushing its prey within its coils; any large boa snake.

an·a·cous·tic zone, an″*a*·kös′tik zōn, *n. Phys.* the region above an altitude of about 100 miles where the distance between the air molecules is greater than the wavelength of sound, and sound waves can no longer be propagated.

A·nac·re·on·tic, *a*·nak″rē·on′tik, *a.* [L. *Anacreonticus* < *Anacreont-* (stem of *Anacreon*) < Gr.] Of or resembling the poetry of Anacreon, Greek poet; relating to the praise of love and wine; convivial.

an·a·cru·sis, an″*a*·krö′sis, *n. pl.* **an·a·cru·ses,** an″*a*·krö′sēz. [N.L. < Gr. *anakrousis*, striking up < *anakrouein*, to begin a song < *ana-*, up, and *krouein*, to strike, beat.] One or more unstressed syllables at the beginning of a verse not included in the metrical pattern; an upbeat note or notes in music which precede the first downbeat.

an·a·dem, an′*a*·dem″, *n.* [L. *anadema* < Gr. *anadēma*, a head-band or fillet < *anadein*, to wreathe < *ana-*, up, and *dein*, to bind.] A head band, fillet, garland, or wreath: primarily used in poetic reference.

an·a·di·plo·sis, an″*a*·di·plō′sis, *n.* [L. < Gr. *anadip losis*, < *anadiploun*, double.] *Rhet.* repetition in the first part of one clause or sentence of a prominent word in the latter part of the preceding clause or sentence, often with extended or changed meaning.

a·nad·ro·mous, *a*·nad′ro·mus, *a.* [Gr. *anadromos*, running upward < *anadramein*, to run.] Passing upstream from the sea into fresh waters at stated seasons to spawn, as the salmon. Compare *catadromous*.

an·aer·obe, an·âr′ōb, *n.* [Gr. *a, an-*, without, *aer*, air, and *bios*, life.] A microorganism that lives without air or free oxygen.—**an·aer·o·bic,** an″â·rō′bik, an″*a*·rō′bik, *a.*

an·aes·the·sia, an″is·thē′zha, *n.* Anesthesia.—**an·aes·thet·ic,** an″is·thet′ik, *a., n.* Anesthetic.

an·a·glyph, an′*a*·glif, *n.* [L.L. *anaglyphos*, embossed < Gr. *anaglyphein*, embossed work < *ana*, up, and *glyphein*, to engrave.] An ornament in low relief, chased or embossed; *opt.* a picture in two colors which, when viewed through glasses of corresponding colors, produces an illusion of depth, or three-dimensional effect.—**an·a·glyph·ic,** an″*a*·glif′ik, *a.*

an·a·go·ge, an·a·go·gy, an″*a*·gō′jē, an′*a*·gō″jē, *n.* [L.L. < Gr. *anagōgē*, reference < *anagein*, to refer < *ana-*, upward, and *agein*, to lead.] The spiritual meaning or application of words; a mysterious or allegorical interpretation, esp. of the Scripture.—**an·a·gog·ic, an·a·gog·i·cal,** an″*a*·goj′ik, an″*a*·goj′i·kal, *a.* Of or pertaining to anagoge; mysterious; elevated; spiritual.—**an·a·gog·i·cal·ly,** an″*a*·goj′i·kal·ē, *adv.*

an·a·gram, an′*a*·gram″, *n.* [L. *anagramma* < Gr. *anagrammatizein*, to transpose letters < *ana-*, up, again, and *gramma*, a letter.] A transposition of the letters of a word or sentence to form a new word or sentence; a game in which the objective is the formation of new words through the transposition of letters; the new word that is formed thereby.—**an·a·gram·mat·ic, an·a·gram·mat·i·cal,** an″*a*·gra·mat′ik, an″*a*·gra·mat′i·kal, *a.*

a·na·gram·ma·tize, an″*a*·gram′*a*·tīz″, *v.t.*—*anagrammatized, anagrammatizing.* To transpose, as the letters of a word, so as to form an anagram.—*v.i.* To make anagrams.

a·nal, ān′al, *a.* [L. *anus*, the ring.] Pertaining to or situated near the anus.—**a·nal·ly,** *adv.*

a·nal·cime, *a*·nal′sim, *a*·nal′sēm, *a*·nal′sim, *n.* [Fr. < Gr. *analkimos*, weak < *an-*, not, and *alkimos*, strong, < *alkē*, strength.] A mineral of frequent occurrence in traprocks, especially in the cavities of amygdaloids, in either crystal or mass form. Also **a·nal·cite,** *a*·nal′sīt, an′al·sīt″.

an·a·lects, an′*a*·lekts″, *n. pl.* [Gr. neut. pl. of *analektos*, select < *ana*, up-, and *legein*, to gather.] Extracts or small pieces selected from different authors and combined. Also **an·a·lec·ta,** an″*a*·lek′ta.

an·a·lem·ma, an″*a*·lem′a, *n. pl.* **an·a·lem·mas, an·a·lem·ma·ta,** an″*a*·lem′*a*·ta. [L. sundial < Gr. *analēmma*, sundial.] A figure-eight-shaped graduated scale which shows the declination of the sun and the equation of time for each day of the year.

an·a·lep·tic, an″*a*·lep′tik, *a.* [Gr. *analeptikos* < *analambanein*, take up, restore.] Invigorating; giving strength after disease; awakening, especially from drug stupor.—*n.* An analeptic remedy; a restorative.

an·al·ge·si·a, an″al·jē′zē·a, an″al·jē′sē·a, *n.* [N.L. < Gr. *analgesia, an-* no, and *algesis*, sense of pain < *algein*, feel pain < *algos*, pain.] *Med.* absence of sensibility to pain while retaining consciousness.—**an·al·ge·sic,** an″al·jē′zik, an″al·jē′sik, *a., n.*—**an·al·get·ic,** an″al·jed′ik, *a. Med.* pertaining to or causing analgesia.—*n.* A remedy that removes pain.

an·a·log, an′*a*·lag, an′*a*·log, *a. Computer,* pertaining to continuous physical variables such as distance, voltage, or rotation, as opposed to numerical quantities. Also *analogue.*

an·a·log com·put·er, *n. Computer.* A computer which calculates by using physical analogs, such as quantities of electrical resistance, of the variables of a given problem and provides solutions in a graphic representation, such as an oscilloscope pattern; a computer with a physical system in which the analysis of a problem is mirrored by the varying behavior of the physical system itself, simulating the problem in all its infinite variations. Also *analogue computer.*

an·a·log·i·cal, an″*a*·loj′i·kal, *a.* Having analogy; analogous; used by way of analogy; expressing or implying analogy.—**an·a·log·i·cal·ly,** an″*a*·loj′i·kal·ē, *adv.*

a·nal·o·gist, *a*·nal′o·jist, *n.* One who adheres to and reasons by analogy.

a·nal·o·gize, *a*·nal′o·jīz″, *v.t., v.i.*—*analogized, analogizing.* To explain or reason by analogy; to consider, as a question, with regard to its analogy to something else.

a·nal·o·gous, *a*·nal′o·gus, *a.* Having analogy; bearing some resemblance in the midst of differences (followed by *to* or *with*); comparable.—**a·nal·o·gous·ly,** *a*·nal′o·gus·lē, *adv.*

an·a·logue, an′*a*·lag″, an′*a*·log″, *n.* [< Fr. < Gr. *analogon*, neut. of *analogos*. See *analogy*.] Something resembling or having analogy with something else; something similar. *Biol.* an organ which is, with respect to an organ in another plant or animal, similar in function but different in origin and structure.

an·a·logue com·put·er, *n.* See *analog computer.*

a·nal·o·gy, *a*·nal′o·jē, *n. pl.* **a·nal·o·gies.** [L. *analogia* < Gr. *ana-*, according to, and *logos*, ratio, proportion.] An agreement or likeness between things in some circumstances or effects; conformity; parallelism; likeness.

an·al·pha·bet, an·al′fa·bet, *n.* [Gr. *analphabetos*, not knowing one's a-b-c, < *an-* not, and *alpha*, alpha (a), and *beta* (b).] A totally illiterate person.—**an·al·pha·bet·ic,** an″al·fa·bet′ik, an·al″fa·bet′ik, *a.*

a·nal·y·sand, *a*·nal′i·sand″, *a*·nal′i·zand″, *n.* One who undergoes psychoanalysis.

a·nal·y·sis, *a*·nal′i·sis, *n. pl.* **a·nal·y·ses,** *a*·nal′i·sēz. [N.L. < Gr. *analyein*, to break up < *ana-*, implying distribution, and *lysis*, a loosing, resolving, < *lyein*, to loosen.] The resolution of a compound object into its constituent elements or component parts: opposed to *synthesis*; a consideration of anything in its separate parts and their relation to each other; a statement of this; the process of subjecting to chemical tests to determine ingredients; psychoanalysis.

a·nal·y·sis si·tus, *n.* [N.L., lit. 'analysis of the situation.'] Topology.

an·a·lyst, an′*a*·list, *n.* One who analyzes or is versed in analysis; psychoanalyst.

an·a·lyt·ic, an″*a*·lit′ik, *a.* [L.L. *analyticus* < Gr. *analytikos* < *analyein*.] Pertaining to analysis or analytics; often using analysis: opposed to *synthetic.* Also **an·a·lyt·i·cal.**—**an·a·lyt·i·cal·ly,** an″*a*·lit′i·kal·ē, *adv.* In an analytical manner; in the manner of analysis.

an·a·lyt·ic ge·om·e·try, *n.* The branch of geometry wherein procedures of algebraic reasoning are applied, using symbols referring to coordinates.

an·a·lyt·ics, an″*a*·lit′iks, *n. pl. but sing. in constr.* The branch of logic concerned with analysis.

an·a·lyz·a·ble, an′*a*·liz″a·bl, *a.* Capable of being analyzed.

an·a·ly·za·tion, an″*a*·li·zā′shan, *n.* The act of analyzing.

an·a·lyze, an′*a*·līz″, *v.t.*—*analyzed, analyzing.* [< *analysis*, by back-formation.] To resolve into its elements; to determine the essential features of; to study critically; to separate, as a compound subject, into its parts or propositions; psychoanalyze.—**an·a·lyz·er,** an′*a*·liz″ér, *n.* One who or that which analyzes.

an·am·ne·sis, an″am·nē′sis, *n. pl.* **an·am·ne·ses,** an″am·nē′sēz. [N.L. < Gr. *anamnēsis* < *anamimnēskein* < *ana-*, back, and *mimnēskein*, to remember (with reduplicated form of the root *-mne-*, remember).] The recalling of things past; recollection; reminiscence; *med.* the original history of the case of a psychiatric or medical patient.—**an·am·nes·tic,** an″am·nes′tik, *a.*—**an·am·nes·ti·cal·ly,** *adv.*

an·a·mor·phic, an″*a*·mar′fik, *a.* [N.L. < Gr. *ana-*, incorrect, and *-morph-*, form, and *-ic.*] *Opt.* having or causing unequal magnification of an image in each of two directions which are perpendicular to each other.

An·a·ni·as, an″*a*·nī′as, *n.* [< *Ananias*, in Acts, v. 1-10, who was struck dead for lying.] A liar.

an·a·pest, an·a·paest, an′*a*·pest″, *n.* [L. *anapaestus*, < Gr. *anapaistos*, lit, struck back < *ana-*, back, and *paiein*, strike.] A poetical foot consisting of three syllables, the first two short or unaccented, the last long or accented; a line of verse in this style.—**an·a·pes·tic, an·a·paes·tic,** an″*a*·pes′tik, *a.* Pertaining to an anapest; consisting of anapests.

an·a·phase, an′*a*·fāz″, *n.* The stage in mitosis in which the chromosome halves move away from each other toward opposite ends of the cell.

a·naph·o·ra, *a*·naf′or·a, *n.* [L. < Gr. *anaphora* < *anapherein*, bring up, < *ana-*, up, and *pherein*, bear.] *Rhet.* repetition of the same word or words at the beginning of two or more successive verses, clauses, or sentences, primarily for a poetic effect.

an·aph·ro·dis·i·ac, an·af″ro·diz′ē·ak″, *n.* [N.L. < Gr. neg. *an-*, and *aphrodisiakos*,

---

a- fat, fāte, fär, fâre, fạll;   **e-** met, mē, mēre, hėr;   **i-** pin, pīne;   **o-** not, nōte, mōve;   **u-** tub, cūbe, bụll;   **oi-** oil;   **ou-** pound.

venereal.] A substance capable of dulling or reducing sexual appetite.—**an·aph·ro·dis·i·a**, an·af″ro·diz′ē·a, n. The impairment of sexual desire.

an·a·phy·lax·is, an″a·fi·lak′sis, n. [N.L. < Gr. *ana-*, back, against, and *-phylaxis* (as in *prophylaxis*) < *phylassein*, to guard.] *Pathol.* increased susceptibility to the action of a foreign protein as the result of a first injection of the substance, such as penicillin.—**an·a·phy·lac·tic**, an″a·fi·lak′tik, a. Pertaining to, affected by anaphylaxis.—**an·a·phy·lac·toid**, an″a·fi·lak′toid, a. Having the characteristics of anaphylaxis.

an·a·plas·ty, an′a·plas″tē, n. [Gr. < *anaplastos*, remolded.] Plastic surgery.—**an·a·plas·tic**, an″a·plas′tik, a. Of or pertaining to anaplasty.

an·ap·tot·ic, an″ap·tot′ik, a. [Gr. *ana-*, back, again, and *aptotos*, indeclinable: see *aptote*.] *Philol.* designating a language, such as English, which has a tendency to lose, or has already lost, the use of inflections.

an·arch, an′ärk, n. [< *anarchy*.] One who excites disorder or revolt in a state; an advocate of anarchy or anarchism.

an·ar·chic, an·är′kik, a. Of or pertaining to anarchy or anarchism; in a state of anarchy or confusion; lawless. Also **an·ar·chi·cal**, an·är′ki·kal.

an·ar·chism, an′ar·kiz″um, n. The doctrine of the abolition of formal government and free action for the individual, land and other resources being common property; the active support of anarchistic principles.

an·ar·chist, an′ar·kist, n. One who advocates violent revolution against the established order as a prerequisite of freedom.—**an·ar·chis·tic**, a.

an·ar·chy, an′ar·kē, n. [M.L. *anarchia*, lawlessness < Gr. *anarchos*, rulerless < *an-*, no, and *archos*, ruler.] Lack of government; a state of society when there is no law or supreme power; uncontrolled political confusion and disorder.

an·ar·thri·a, an·är′thrē·a, n. [N.L. < Gr. *anarthros*, inarticulate < *an-*, no, and *arthron*, joint.] Loss of the ability to articulate words.

an·a·sar·ca, an″a·sär′ka, n. [Gr. *ana-*, up, and *sarx* (*sarc-*), flesh.] *Pathol.* dropsy, of considerable extent, in the subcutaneous connective tissue.—**an·a·sar·cous**, an″a·sär′kus, a.

an·as·tig·mat, a·nas′tig·mat″, n. [G. < *anastigmatisch*, anastigmatic.] A system of lenses in which astigmatic defects are overcome.

an·as·tig·mat·ic, an″a·stig·mat′ik, a·nas″tig·mat′ik, a. Not astigmatic: applied esp. to a lens, or a system of lenses, in which astigmatic defects are overcome.

a·nas·to·mose, a·nas′to·mōz″, v.i.—*anastomosed, anastomosing*. [< *anastomosis*.] *Anat., bot.* To unite or run into each other; to communicate with each other by minute branches or ramifications, as the arteries and veins.

a·nas·to·mo·sis, a·nas″to·mō′sis, n. pl. **a·nas·to·mo·ses**. [L.L. < Gr. *anastomosis* < *anastomoun*, to provide with an outlet < *ana-*, up, and *stoma*, mouth, opening.] The joining of streams; *anat.* union of vessels such as arteries and veins.—**a·nas·to·mot·ic**, a·nas″to·mot′ik, a. Pertaining to anastomosis.

a·nas·tro·phe, a·nas′tro·fē, n. [M.L. < Gr. *anastrophe*, a turning-back < *anastrephein*, to turn back < *ana-*, back, *strephein*, to turn.] An inversion of the natural order of words, primarily for the purpose of achieving rhetorical effect.

an·a·tase, an′a·tāz″, n. [Fr. < Gr. *anastasis*, extension < *anatenein*, extend.] A titanium dioxide, TiO_2, in the form of tetragonal crystals, used as a white pigment.

a·nath·e·ma, a·nath′a·ma, n. pl. **a·nath·e·mas**. [L.L. < Gr. *anathema*, a curse or thing devoted to evil, < *anatithēmi*, to

dedicate < *ana-*, up, and *tithēmi*, to place.] A curse, denunciation or condemnation pronounced with religious solemnity by ecclesiastical authority, and accompanied by excommunication; execration generally; curse; the person or object denounced or detested.

a·nath·e·ma·tize, a·nath′e·ma·tiz″, v.t.—*anathematized, anathematizing*. To pronounce an anathema against; to ban; to curse.—v.i. To pronounce anathemas; to curse.—**a·nath·e·mat·iz·a·tion**, a·nath″e·ma·ti·zā′shan, n.

an·a·tom·ic, an″a·tom′ik, a. Belonging to anatomy or dissection. Also **an·a·tom·i·cal**, an″a·tom′i·kal.—**an·at·om·i·cal·ly**, an″a·tom′i·kal·ē, adv.

a·nat·o·mist, a·nat′o·mist, n. One who is skilled in dissection, or in the doctrine and principles of anatomy.

a·nat·o·mize, a·nat′o·miz″, v.t.—*anatomized, anatomizing*. To cut up or dissect for the purpose of displaying or examining the structure of. *Fig.* to lay open or expose minutely; to analyze (to *anatomize* an argument).—**a·nat·o·mi·za·tion**, a·nat″o·mi·zā′shan, n. The act of anatomizing.

a·nat·o·my, a·nat′o·mē, n. pl. **a·nat·o·mies**. [L.L. *anatomia*, dissection < Gr. *anatomē* < *anatemnein*, dissect < *ana-*, up, and *tomē*, a cutting.] The art of dissecting or artificially separating the different parts of an organized body, to discover their situation, structure, and function; the science which treats of the internal structure of organized bodies, as elucidated by dissection; the act of taking something to pieces for the purpose of examining in detail (the anatomy of a discourse); physique. *Colloq.* a skeleton; a human body.

a·nat·ro·pous, a·na′tro·pus, a. [Gr. *ana-*, up, and *tropos* < *trepein*, turn.] *Bot.* of an ovule, inverted at an early stage of growth, so that the micropyle is turned toward the funiculus, the chalaza being situated at the opposite end.

an·ces·tor, an′ses·tèr, n. [M.E. *ancestre* < O.Fr. *ancestre*, *ancessor* (Fr. *ancêtre*, an ancestor) < L. *antecessor*, a predecessor < *ante-*, before, and *cedere*, *cessum*, to go. CEDE.] One from whom a person descends, either by the father or mother, esp. one more remote than a grandparent; a progenitor; a forefather; one from whom an inheritance is derived.—**an·ces·tress**, an′ses·tris, n. A female ancestor.

an·ces·tral, an·ses′tral, a. Pertaining to or stemming from an ancestor.

an·ces·try, an′ses·trē, n. pl. **an·ces·tries**. A series of ancestors; lineage; honorable descent; high birth; *fig.* the history of the development of an idea or object.

an·chor, ang′kėr, n. [M.E. *anere* < O.E. *ancor*, < L. *ancora*, Gr. *angkyra*, an anchor < a root meaning crooked, bent, seen in L. *angulus*, a corner, E. *ankle*, *angle*.] An iron implement, consisting usually of a straight bar called the shank, at the upper end of which is a transverse piece called the stock, and of two curved arms at the lower end of the shank, each of which terminates in a triangular plate called a fluke, and used for holding a ship or other vessel at rest in comparatively shallow water; something serving a purpose analogous to that of a ship's anchor. *Fig.* that which gives stability or security; that on which we place dependence for safety.—**at an·chor**, floating attached to an anchor; anchored.

an·chor, ang′kėr, v.t. To hold, as a ship, at rest by lowering the anchor; to place at anchor. *Fig.* to fix or fasten on; to fix in a stable condition.—v.i. To cast anchor; to become anchored.

an·chor·age, ang′kėr·ij, n. The act of anchoring; state of being anchored; a place where a ship can anchor; a duty imposed on ships for anchoring in a harbor.

an·cho·ress, ang′kèr·is, n. A female anchoret.

an·cho·ret, ang′kèr·it, ang′kè·ret″, n. [M.E. < L.L. *anchorita* < L. *anachoreta* < Gr. *anachorētēs* < *anachōrein*, to withdraw < *ana-*, back, and *chōrein*, to retire, < *chōros*, a place.] A hermit; a recluse; one who retires from society to avoid the temptations of the world and devote himself to religious duties. Also **an·cho·rite**, ang′kè·rīt″.—**an·cho·ret·ic**, ang″kè·ret′ik, a. Pertaining to a hermit, or his mode of life.

an·chor ring, n. *Geom.* torus.

an·cho·vy, an′chō·vē, an′chō·vē, an·chō′vē, n. pl. **an·cho·vies**. [Pg. and Sp. *anchova*, an anchovy.] A small fish belonging to the herring family, *Engraulidae*, and used for food.

an·cien ré·gime, on·sē′an rā·jēm′, n. [Fr.] The ancient or old system of government, esp. the political and social system of France before the Revolution of 1789.

an·cient, ān′shent, a. [M.E. *ancien* < Fr. < Vulgar L. (assumed) *antianus*, < L. *prep. ante*, before.] Having happened or existed in former times, usually at a great distance of time; associated with, or bearing marks of, the times of long ago (*ancient* authors); of long standing; having lasted from a remote period; of great age; old (an *ancient* city); *poet.* having lived long (an *ancient* man).—**an·cient·ly**, ān′shent·lē, adv. In old times; in times long past.—**an·cient·ness**, ān′shent·nis, n. Antiquity.

an·cient, ān′shent, n. A person who lived in an early period of history; a very old man; an elder or person of influence; a classical writer.

an·cil·lar·y, an′si·ler″ē, a. [L. *ancillaris*, relating to maid-servants < *ancilla*, a maidservant.] Subservient; aiding; auxiliary; subordinate.—**an·cil·la**, an·sil′a, n. An aid; an accessory.

an·cip·i·tal, an·sip′i·tal, a. [< L. *ancipit-*, (stem of *anceps*, two-headed, ambiguous) < *an-* for *amb-*, on both sides, and *caput*, the head.] *Bot.* two-edged.

an·con, ang′kon, n. pl. **an·co·nes**, ang·kō′nēz. [L. < Gr. *ankōn*, elbow.] *Anat.* the upper end of the ulna or elbow; *arch.* a console, cantilever, bracket, or other stone projection designed for support.

an·cy·los·to·mi·a·sis, an″si·los″to·mī′a·sis, n. [N.L. < *Ancylostoma*, genus of hookworms, < Gr. *agcylos*, bent, hooked, and *stoma*, mouth.] Hookworm disease.

and, and, and, conj. [M.E. < O.E. *and*, D. *en*, *ende*, G. *und*, O.H.G. *anti*, all signifying and; Icel. *enda*, and yet, and if.] A particle joining words and sentences, and expressing the relations of connection or addition; sometimes used to introduce interrogative and other clauses. Sym. & (ampersand).

an·da·lu·site, an″da·lö′sīt, n. [< *Andalusia*, division of southern Spain.] A mineral, Al_2SiO_5, found in various colors, consisting of a silicate of aluminum.

an·dan·te, an·dan′tē, än·dän′tā, It. än·dän′te, a., adv. [It. pp. of *andare*, walk.] *Mus.* proceeding with a moderate, even, slow movement.

an·dan·ti·no, an″dan·tē′nō, än″dän·tē′nō, a., adv. [It. dim. of *andante*.] *Mus.* of a movement played somewhat quicker than andante.—n.

An·de·an, an·dē′an, an′dē·an, a. Pertaining to the Andes, the great mountain chain of South America.

an·des·ite, an′di·zīt″, n. [< G. *andesit* < *Andes* (Mountains).] A widespread igneous rock occurring in various colors and resembling trachyte.

and·i·ron, and′ī·ėrn, n. [M.E. *andiren*, *aundirn*, *aundire*, O.Fr. *andier*; origin unknown.] A horizontal iron bar raised on short legs, with an upright standard at one end, used to support pieces of wood when burning on an open hearth, one being placed on each side.

an·dra·dite, an′dra·dīt″, n. [From José B. Andrada e Silva (d. 1838), Brazilian geologist.] A garnet, $Ca_3Fe_2(SiO_4)_3$, occurring in yellow, green, brown, or black crystals.

an·dro·gen, an′dro·jen, n. [< Gr. andr-, stem of anēr, a man, and -gen-, stem connoting bringing forth, genesis, hydrogen.] A substance, as androsterone, which promotes the development of secondary male sex characteristics.

an·drog·y·nous, an·droj′i·nus, a. [L. androgynus, hermaphrodites, < Gr. androgynos < andr- (stem of anēr), a man, and gȳnē, woman.] Having two sexes; being male and female; hermaphrodital; having staminate and pistillate flowers in the same cluster; having or partaking of the mental and physical characteristics of both sexes. Also **an·drog·y·nal**, an·droj′i·nal.—**an·drog·y·ny**, an·droj′i·nē, n.

an·dros·ter·one, an·dros′te·rōn″, n. [< andr-, sterol, -one.] A male sex hormone ($C_{19}H_{30}O_2$) found in urine of the human male.

an·ec·dote, an′ik·dōt″, n. [Fr. < Gr. anekdota (neut. pl.), unpublished items < anekdotos, not published < a-, neg., < ekdidonai, publish < ek, out, and didonai, to give.] A short story, narrating a detached incident or fact of an interesting nature; a biographical incident; a single passage of private life.—**an·ec·dot·age**, an′ik·dō″tij, n. The garrulity of dotage, or old age; tendency to tell stories, anecdotes.—**an·ec·dot·ic, an·ec·do·tal, an·ec·dot·i·cal**, an″ik·dot′ik, an″ik·dōt′al, an′ik·dōt″al, an″ik·dot′i·kal, a. Pertaining to anecdotes; consisting of or of the nature of anecdotes. —**an·ec·dot·ist**, an′ik·dō″tist, n. One who tells or collects anecdotes.

an·e·cho·ic, an″e·kō′ik, a. Pertaining to a room, studio, etc., characterized as being free from echoes and having an unusually low reverberation level.

a·nele, a·nēl′, v.t.—aneled, aneling. [M.E. anelen < an, on, and elen, to anoint < ele, oil < O.E. œl < L. oleum.] Archaic, to anoint, as in extreme unction.

an·e·lec·tric, an″i·lek′trik, a. [Gr. an-, not, and E. electric.] Elect. having no electric properties; incapable of obtaining an electric charge when exposed to friction; nonelectric.—n. A nonelectric material; a conductor.

a·ne·mi·a, a·nae·mi·a, a·nē′mē·a, n. [N.L. < Gr. anaimia, bloodlessness < an-, no, and haima, blood.] Med. A deficiency of the hemoglobin, resulting in a lack of energy and vitality; a state of the system marked by a deficiency in certain constituents of the blood.—**a·ne·mic, a·nē′mik**, a. Pertaining to or affected with anemia. Deficient in vitality or vigor.—**a·ne·mi·cal·ly**, a·nē′mi·ka·lē, adv.

a·nem·o·chore, a·nem′o·kōr, a·nem′o·kar, n. A seed or plant dispersed by the wind.

a·nem·o·graph, a·nem′o·graf, a·nem′o·gräf″, n. [< Gr. anemos, the wind.] An instrument for measuring and recording the force and direction of the wind; a recording anemometer.

an·e·mol·o·gy, an″e·mol′o·jē, n. The study of the wind and related phenomena.

an·e·mom·e·ter, an″e·mom′i·tėr, n. An instrument for measuring force and velocity of the wind.

an·e·mom·e·try, an″e·mom′i·trē, n. The process of determining the pressure or force of the wind by an anemometer.

a·nem·o·ne, a·nem′o·nē″, n. [Gr. anemōnē, the wind-flower, lit. 'daughter of the wind' < anemos, the wind, and -ōnē, fem. patronymic suffix.] Any plant of the genus Anemone, having divided or lobed leaves and colorful flowers lacking petals, specif. Anemone quinquefolia, a spring flower with slender stem and delicate whitish blossoms.

an·e·moph·i·lous, an″e·mof′i·lus, a. [< Gr. anemos, wind, philos, loving.] Bot. having the pollen conveyed and fertilization effected by the wind.

a·nem·o·scope, a·nem′o·skōp″, n. [< Gr. anemos, wind, and skopeein, to view.] A device which shows the direction of the wind; a weathercock; a wind vane.

an·e·mo·sis, an″e·mō′sis, n. pl. **an·e·mo·ses**, an″e·mō′sēs. [N.L. < Gr. anemos, wind.] A condition of the wood of some trees, in which the annual layers are separated from one another: supposed by some to be due to the action of strong winds upon the trunk; wind shake.

a·nent, a·nent′, prep. [M.E. anent, anen, < O.E. on efn, on emn, alongside, on a level, near, lit. on even. The t, as in ancient, is superfluous.] About; respecting; regarding; concerning.

an·er·oid, an′e·roid″, a. [< Gr. a, not, nēros, moisture, and eidos, form.] Able to function without fluid.

an·er·oid ba·rom·e·ter, n. A barometer the action of which depends on the pressure of the atmosphere on a circular metallic box exhausted of air, hermetically sealed, and having a slightly elastic top, the vacuum serving the purpose of the column of mercury in the ordinary barometer.

an·es·the·si·a, an″is·thē′zha, n. [N.L. < Gr. anaisthēsia < an-, not, and aisthēsis, perception < aisthanesthae, perceive.] Diminished or lost sense of feeling; an artificially produced state of insensibility, especially to the sense of pain.

an·es·the·si·ol·o·gist, an″is·thē″zē·ol′o·jist, n. Med. a physician specializing in anesthesiology.

an·es·the·si·ol·o·gy, an″is·thē″zē·ol′o·jē, n. Med. the science of the administration of anesthetics.

an·es·thet·ic, an″is·thet′ik, a. Of or belonging to anesthesia; having the power to deprive of feeling or sensation.—n. A substance which has the power of depriving of feeling or sensation, as chloroform when its vapor is inhaled.—**an·es·thet·i·cal·ly**, an″is·thet′i·kal·ē, adv.

an·es·the·tist, an·aes·the·tist, a·nes′thi·tist, n. One who administers anesthetics.

an·es·the·tize, a·nes′thi·tīz″, v.t.—anesthetized, anesthetizing. To bring under the influence of an anesthetic agent; to render insensible to the feeling of pain.

an·e·thole, an′a·thōl″, n. A crystalline compound, $C_{10}H_{12}O$, obtained from Fennel oils and anise, and used in perfumery and medicine.

an·eu·rysm, an·eu·rism, an′yu·riz″um, n. [Gr. aneurysma, < aneurynein, to dilate, < ana-, up, and eurynein, widen, < eurys, wide.] Pathol. a localized dilatation of an artery, due to the pressure of the blood acting on a part weakened by disease or injury.—**an·eu·rys·mal, an·eu·ris·mal**, an″yu·riz′mal, a.

a·new, a·nō′, a·nū′, adv. [M.E. of (= from) newe, onew, < O.E. of nīwe.] Again; once more; in a new form; afresh.

an·frac·tu·os·i·ty, an·frak″chō·os′i·tē, n. pl. **an·frac·tu·os·i·ties**, an·frak″chō·os′i·tēz. An anfractuous state; sinuosity; a winding, or winding passage; a complex thinking process; anat. one of the sulci or fissures separating the convolutions of the brain.

an·frac·tu·ous, an·frak′chō·us, a. [< L.L. anfractuosus < anfractus, a coil or bend < an- (= ambi-), around, and frangere, break.] Characterized by winding; sinuous; tortuous; circuitous. Bot. sinuous or twisted, as anthers.

an·ga·ry, ang′ga·rē, n. [L.L. angaria,

service to a lord < angareia, compulsory public service < angaros, a courier (< Persian).] International law, the right of a belligerent, during time of war, to seize or destroy property of neutrals, subject to payment of full compensation.

an·gel, ān′jel, n. [M.E. < O.Fr. angele or O.E. engel, < L.L. angelus, < Gr. angelos, messenger.] A messenger, esp. of God; theol. one of a class of spiritual beings, attendants of God, conventionally represented in human form with wings. In general, a spirit, good or bad; also, a person of heavenly virtues or charms; colloq. a financial backer of a theatrical enterprise or political campaign.

an·gel, ān′jel, n. Aeron. a type of confusion reflector having the reflecting material often suspended from parachutes or balloons to give delayed descent; a measure of altitude equivalent to 1,000 ft.

an·gel·fish, ān′jel·fish″, n. Any of the beautifully colored warm-water fish of the family Chaetodontidae, having an extraordinarily narrow body; scalare.

an·gel food cake, n. A kind of delicate white sweet cake, made with the whites of many eggs but without shortening.

an·gel·ic, an·jel′ik, a. Resembling or belonging to, or having the nature of angels; also **an·gel·i·cal**, an·jel′i·kal.—**an·gel·i·cal·ly**, an·jel′i·kal·ē, adv. In an angelic manner.

an·gel·i·ca, an·jel′i·ka, n. [N.L. < M.L. herba angelica.] Any plant of the genus Angelica, tall umbelliferous plants found in both hemispheres, specif. Angelica archangelica, cultivated in Europe for its aromatic scent and its roots.

an·gel shark, n. Any of the Atlantic sharks of the family Squatinidae, thought to be the evolutionary link between the rays and sharks because of their large winglike pectoral fins.

An·ge·lus, an′je·lus, n. Rom. Cath. Ch. A solemn devotion in memory of the Incarnation; the bell tolled to indicate the time when the Angelus is to be recited.

an·ger, ang′gėr, n. [M.E., grief, anger < O.N. < angr, grief, sorrow, angra, to grieve, annoy; Dan. anger, sorrow; same root as in O.E. ange, vexed, narrow, G. egne, narrow; L. angere, to trouble, angor, vexation, Gr. angchein, to choke.] A violent, revengeful passion or emotion, excited by a real or supposed injury to oneself or others; passion; ire; choler; rage; wrath. Anger is more general and expresses a less strong feeling than wrath and rage, both of which imply a certain outward manifestation, and the latter, violence and want of self-command.

an·ger, ang′gėr, v.t. To excite to anger; to rouse resentment in; to make angry; to exasperate.—v.i. To become roused with anger.

An·ge·vin, an′je·vin, an′je·vin, a. [Fr. < O.Fr. < M.L. andegavinus, of Andegavia (Angou).] Of or pertaining to Anjou, a former western province of France.—n. A resident of Anjou or a member of its royal house, the Plantagenets.

an·gi·na, an·jī′na, n. [L. angina, quinsy < angere, constrict, distress.] Pathol. Any inflammatory affection of the throat or fauces, as quinsy, croup, mumps, etc., marked by attacks of severe pain; a disease accompanied by spasms of severe pain. See angina pectoris.—**an·gi·nal**, an·jīn′al, an′ji·nal, a. Pertaining to angina.—**an·gi·nose**, an′ji·nōs″, an·jī′nōs, a.—**an·gi·nous**, an·jī′nus, a.

an·gi·na pec·to·ris, an·jī′na pek′to·ris, n. [N.L., lit. angina of the chest.] Pathol. a disease characterized by paroxysms of acute pain in the chest, with sense of suffocation, associated usually with morbid conditions of the heart or arteries, caused by ischemia of the heart muscle.

---

a- fat, fāte, fär, fâre, fạll; **e-** met, mē, mēre, hėr; **i-** pin, pīne; **o-** not, nōte, möve; **u-** tub, cūbe, bụll; **oi-** oil; **ou-** pound.

an·gi·o·car·pous, an″jē·o·kär′pus, *a.* [< Gr. *angio-*, and *karpos*, fruit.] *Bot.* having a fruit whose seed vessels are enclosed within a covering that does not form a part of themselves, as the acorn.

an·gi·ol·o·gy, an″jē·ol′o·jē, *n.* The branch of anatomy that treats of the blood vessels and lymphatics.

an·gi·o·ma, an″jē·ō′ma, *n.* pl. **an·gi·o·mas,** or **an·gi·o·ma·ta,** or an″jē·ō′mas, an″jē·ō′ma·ta. *Pathol.* a tumor consisting chiefly of dilated or newly formed blood or lymph vessels.—**an·gi·om·a·tous,** an″jē·om′a·tus, an″jē·ō′ma·tus, *a.*

an·gi·o·sperm, an″jē·o·spµrm″, *n.* [< N.L. *angio-* and Gr. *sperma*, seed.] *Bot.* a plant which has its seed enclosed in a seed vessel. —**an·gi·o·sper·mous,** an″jē·o·spµr″mus, *q. Bot.* having seeds enclosed in a seed vessel.

an·gle, ang′gl, *n.* [M.E. < M.Fr. *angle* < L. *angulus*, corner.] A recess or part within two or more sides diverging from a common point or line. *Geom.* the space within lines (straight or curved) or planes so diverging, or the figure formed; as, a right *angle*; the amount of divergence of two lines, measured by the intercepted arc of a circle whose center is the meeting point of the lines.

an·gle, ang′gl, *v.t.*—*angled, angling.* To move or bend in angles; to place at an angle or angles.—**an·gled,** ang′gld, *a.* Having an angle or angles.

an·gle, ang′gl, *v.i.*—*angled, angling.* To fish with hook and line; hence, to seek (*for*) by any artful means of catching or obtaining; to move on an angle; to slant in a particular direction, as: The street *angled* to the left.

An·gle·doz·er, ang′gl·dō″zėr, *n.* A bulldozer with the blade mounted at an angle in order to push earth, snow, etc., to one side. (Trademark.)

an·gle i·ron, *n.* A bar of iron in the form of an angle, esp. a rolled iron or steel bar with an L-shaped cross-section, used in iron constructions.

an·gle of at·tack, *n. Aeron.* the acute angle between the chord of an airfoil, and a line representing the undisturbed relative airflow.

an·gle of in·ci·dence, *n. Geom., phys.* the angle at which a material, body, or radiation (as a ray of light) strikes a surface, as measured from the moving material to a line perpendicular to the surface at the impact point (the normal).

an·gle of re·flec·tion, *n. Geom., phys.* the angle between the normal of a surface at the point of reflection, and a reflected ray of light or the like.

an·gle of re·frac·tion, *n. Phys., opt.* the angle between a refracted ray of light, or the like, and a normal to the interface between two media at the point of refraction.

an·gler, ang′glėr, *n.* One who angles; a fisherman with hook and line; also, a fish, *Lophius piscatorius,* of the coasts of Europe and America, which is said to attract small fish, its prey, by the movement of filaments attached to its head and mouth; also, any of various fishes with a modified free dorsal spine above the mouth.

an·gle·worm, ang′gl·wµrm″, *n.* An earthworm.

An·gli·can, ang′gli·kan, *a.* [M.L. *anglicanus* < *anglicus*, English.] English; pertaining to the English Church.—**An·gli·can Church,** the Church of England and related churches, sometimes including the Episcopal churches of the United States and Canada.—*n.* A member of the Anglican Church.

An·gli·can·ism, ang′gli·ka·niz″um, *n.* The principles of or adherence to the Church of England.

An·gli·cism, ang′gli·siz″um, *n.* The quality or characteristics of being English; an English idiom in another language; loyalty

to culture and customs of England; *U.S.* a British idiom.

An·gli·cist, ang′gli·sist, *n.* A specialist in the study of the English language, esp. the history and structure of the language.

An·gli·cize, ang′gli·sīz″, *v.t.*—*anglicized, anglicizing.* To make English; to render conformable to the English idiom or to English analogies, esp. a borrowed foreign word. Also **An·gli·fy.**—**An·gli·ci·za·tion,** ang·gli·si·zā′shan, *n.* Method or effect of being Anglicized or of Anglicizing.

an·gling, ang′gling, *n.* The act or sport of fishing with a rod and line; rod fishing.

An·glo-Cath·o·lic, *n.* A member of the Church of England who lays stress on the claim that his church is historically a part of the Catholic Church.—*a.*—**An·glo-Ca·thol·i·cism,** *n.* The principles or doctrines of the Anglo-Catholics, including their emphasis on Catholic liturgy.

An·glo-French, *n.* The French language of England from the Norman Conquest (1066) until the end of the medieval period.—*a.*

An·glo·ma·ni·a, ang″glo·mā′nē·a, ang″glo·mān′ya, *n.* [Gr. *mania*, madness.] An excessive or undue attachment to, respect for, or imitation of Englishmen or English institutions and customs by a foreigner.

An·glo-Nor·man, *n.* One of the Normans who lived in England during the period 1066–1154 or after the Conquest (1066) or one of their descendants, their literature, their languages.—*a.* Referring to this period.

An·glo·phile, ang′glo·fīl″, ang′glo·fil, *n.* A person who admires or sympathizes with England and English views, policy, things, etc.: opposed to *Anglophobe.*

An·glo·phobe, ang′glo·fōb″, *n.* A person who is hostile toward England and anything which is English. Compare *Anglophile.*

An·glo·pho·bi·a, ang″glo·fō′bē·a, *n.* [Gr. *phobos,* fear.] An excessive hatred or dread of English people, customs, or institutions.

An·glo-Sax·on, *n.* [ANGLES, SAXONS.] A member of the nation formed by the Angles, Saxons, and other early Teutonic settlers in Britain, or one of their descendants; one belonging to the English race; the language of the Anglo-Saxons, or Old English; plain language; words considered crude or vulgar.—*a.* Pertaining to the Anglo-Saxons or to Old English.

an·go·ra, ang·gōr′a, ang·gar′a, an·gōr′a, an·gar′a, *n.* A light cloth, made from the wool or long silky hair of the Angora goat, a native animal of Asia Minor.

An·go·ra cat, *n.* A long-haired variety of the domestic cat, orig. from Angora. See *angora.*

An·go·ra goat, *n.* A variety of goat, orig. from Angora, extensively reared for its long, silky hair or wool.

An·go·ra rab·bit, *n.* A European breed of white rabbit raised primarily for its long silky hair.

An·go·ra wool, *n.* The hair of the Angora goat or the Angora rabbit; mohair.

an·gos·tu·ra bark, ang″go·stµr′a, ang″go·stūr′a, *n.* [From *Angostura,* town in Venezuela.] The bitter aromatic bark of a South American rutaceous tree of the genus *Galipea,* with tonic properties.

An·gos·tu·ra bit·ters, *n.* A bitter tonic prepared from angostura bark. (Trademark.)

an·gri·ly, ang′gri·lē, *adv.* In an angry manner.

an·gri·ness, ang′grē·nis, *n.* The state of being angry.

an·gry, ang′grē, *a.* Feeling resentment; provoked; showing anger; caused by anger; raging; wrathful; tumultuous.

angst, ängkst, *n.* [Dan.] Anguish; feeling of dread.

ang·strom u·nit, ang′strom, *n.* [From A. J. *Angstrom,* 1814–1874, Sw. physicist.] One tenth of a millimicron or one hun-

dred-millionth of a centimeter; a unit used to express the length of light waves.

an·guish, ang′gwish, *n.* [M.E. *anguisse, angwisshe* < O.Fr. *angoisse* < L. *angustia,* a strait, perplexity, from *angustus,* narrow; root *ang-* as in O.E. *eng,* E. *anger.*] Extreme pain or distress, either of body or mind; any keen affection of the emotions or feelings.

an·guish, ang′gwish, *v.t.* To cause acute distress.—*v.i.* To suffer intensely.

an·gu·lar, ang′gū·lėr, *a.* [< M.Fr. *angulaire* < L. *angularis.*] Having an angle or angles; having corners; pointed; consisting of or forming an angle; bony.—**an·gu·lar mo·tion,** the motion or velocity of a body or a point moving circularly. Also **an·gu·lar ve·loc·i·ty.**

an·gu·lar·i·ty, ang″gū·lar′i·tē, *n.* The quality of being angular.—**an·gu·lar·ly,** ang′gū·lėr·lē, *adv.* In an angular manner.—**an·gu·lar·ness,** ang′gū·lėr·nis, *n.* The quality of being angular.

an·gu·late, ang′gū·lit, ang′gū·lāt″, *a.* Angled; cornered.—**an·gu·lat·ed,** ang′gū·lāt″id, *a.*

an·gu·la·tion, ang″gū·lā′shan, *n.* The state of being angulated; that which is angulated; the measurement of the degrees of angles; an angular shape or formation.

An·gus, ang′gus, *n.* Aberdeen Angus.

an·hy·dride, an·hī′drīd, an·hī′drid, *n.* One of a class of oxygen compounds derived from other more complex compounds by removing water.

an·hy·drite, an·hī′drīt, *n.* [G. *anhydrit* < Gr. *anydros.*] Anhydrous sulfate of calcium, $CaSO_4$, a mineral resembling a coarse-grained granite and used as a substitute for gypsum in cement.

an·hy·drous, an·hī′drus, *a.* [Gr. *anydros,* dry < neg. *an-,* and *hydōr,* water.] Destitute of water; *chem.* destitute of the water of crystallization.

a·ni, ä′nē, *n.* [Sp. or Pg. < Tupi (Brazilian Indian).] Any of certain black birds of the cuckoo family constituting the genus *Crotophagus,* inhabiting the warmer parts of America.

an·i·line, an′i·lin, an′i·līn″, *n.* [Gr. *anilin < anil,* indigo < Fr. < Pg. < Ar. *an-nil,* the indigo plant < Skt. *nīlī < nīla,* dark blue.] A substance, $C_6H_5NH_2$, available from indigo and other organic substances, synthetically obtained from nitrobenzene used in dyes, varnish, drugs, and resins.

an·i·line dye, *n. Chem.* any of the synthetic dyes obtained from aniline, usually from coal tar.

an·i·mad·ver·sion, an″i·mad·vµr′shan, an″i·mad·vµr′zhan, *n.* [< L. *animadversio(n-) < animadversus,* pp. of *animadvertere.*] The act of one who animadverts; a remark by way of criticism or censure; stricture; blame.

an·i·mad·vert, an″i·mad·vµrt′, *v.i.* [L. *animadvertere < animus,* mind, and *advertere,* to turn to.] *Obs.* to perceive or take cognizance. To make remarks by way of criticism; to pass strictures or criticisms, followed by *on, upon.*

an·i·mal, an′i·mal, *n.* [L. *animal,* a living being, < *anima,* air, breath, life, the soul.] A living being characterized by having sensation and voluntary motion; an inferior or irrational being, in contradistinction to man; also, often popularly used to signify a quadruped.—*a.* Belonging or relating to animals; as, *animal* functions; pertaining to the merely sentient part of a living being, as distinguished from the intellectual or spiritual part; as, *animal* passions; of or pertaining to, or consisting of the flesh of animals.

an·i·mal·cu·lar, an″i·mal′kū·lėr, *a.* Pertaining to or resembling animalcules.—**an·i·mal·cu·lum,** an″i·mal′kū·lum, *n.*

pl. **an·i·mal·cu·la,** an″i·mal′kū·la. An animalcule.

an·i·mal·cule, an″i·mal′kūl, *n.* [L.L. *animalculum*, dim. of L. *animal*, an animal.] A minute animal, especially one that is microscopic or invisible to the naked eye.

an·i·mal heat, *n.* Heat formed in the body of living animals by metabolic activity.

an·i·mal hus·band·ry, *n.* That branch of agriculture pertaining to the care and breeding of domestic animals.

an·i·mal·ism, an′i·ma·liz″um,*n.* The characteristics of being an animal; the state of being actuated by sensual appetites only; sensuality; a theory that man is without a spiritual nature.—**an·i·mal·ist,** an′i·ma·list, *n.* One adhering to the theories of animalism.

an·i·mal·i·ty, an″i·mal′i·tē, *n.* The state of being an animal; the traits of an animal; the animal world; the animal nature in man, as opposed to the spiritual.

an·i·mal·i·za·tion, an″i·mal·i·zā′shan, *n.* The act of animalizing; the condition of being animalized.

an·i·mal·ize, an′i·ma·liz″, *v.t.*—*animalized, animalizing.* To give animal life to; to convert into animal matter; to bring under the sway of animal appetites; sensualize; brutalize.

an·i·mal mag·net·ism, *n.* Any force or power in certain individuals said to give them the ability to induce hypnosis; allure for persons of the opposite sex because of one's physical characteristics.

an·i·mal spir·its, *n. pl.* Vigor, exuberance resulting from physical well-being and energy.

an·i·mate, an′i·māt″, *v.t.*—*animated, animating.* [L. *animatus*, animated, pp. of *animare*, to fill with breath. ANIMAL.] To give natural life to; to quicken; to make alive; to give life, spirit, or liveliness to; to heighten the powers or effect of; to stimulate or incite; to inspirit; rouse.—**an·i·mate,** an′i·mit, *a.* Alive; possessing animal life.—**an·i·mat·ed,** an′i·mā″tid, *a.* Lively; vigorous; full of spirit; as, an *animated* discourse.—**an·i·mat·ing,** an′i·mā″ting, *a.* Giving life; infusing spirit; enlivening; rousing.—**an·i·mat·ing·ly,** an′i·mā″ting·lē, *adv.* So as to animate.—**an·i·ma·tor,** *n.* One who animates; one who draws animated cartoons.

an·i·mat·ed car·toon, *n.* A motion picture formed by a series of drawings suggesting motion, when filmed, by the slight changes made from one drawing to the next.

an·i·ma·tion, an″i·mā′shan, *n.* The act of animating or state of being animated; state of having life; liveliness; briskness; vivacity.

a·ni·ma·to, ä″ni·mä′tō, an″i·mä′tō, *a.* [< It.] *Mus.* In an animated manner; animated.—*adv.*

an·i·mé, an′i·mā″, an′i·mē″, *n.* [Fr. < Sp., Pg. < Tupi *anim*, resin.] A resin exuded from a large tropical American tree, *Hymenaea courbaril*, from which varnish, lacquers, and flavorings are produced; copal.

an·i·mism, an′i·miz″um, *n.* [L. *anima*, the soul.] The old hypothesis of a force (*Anima mundi*, soul of the world) immaterial but inseparable from matter, and giving to matter its form and movements; the attribution of spirit or soul to inanimate things.—**an·i·mist,** an′i·mist, *n.* One who holds to or believes in animism.—**an·i·mis·tic,** an″i·mist′ik, *a.* Pertaining to, or founded on, animism.

an·i·mos·i·ty, an″i·mos′i·tē, *n.* [M.E. *animosite* < M.Fr. *animosite* < L.L. *animositas*, < *animosus*, full of courage, ardent, < *animus*, the mind, courage, pride.] Rancorous feeling; bitter and active enmity; ill will.

an·i·mus, an′o·mus, *n.* [L. spirit, temper.] Intention; purpose; spirit; temper; espe-

cially, hostile spirit or angry temper; antagonism.

an·i·on, an′i″on, *n.* [Gr. *ana-*, upward, and *iŏn*, going.] *Physical chem.* The element of an electrolyte which collects at the positive pole or anode in electrolysis; a negatively charged ion.

an·i·on·ic, an″i·on′ik, *a. Chem.* about or referring to anions.

an·ise, an′is, *n.* [M.E. *anis* < O.Fr. < L. < Gr. *anīson.*] An annual umbelliferous plant, *Pimpinella anisum*, the seeds of which have an aromatic smell and a pleasant warm taste, and are employed in the manufacture of liqueurs.

an·i·seed, an′i·sēd″, an′is·sēd″, *n.* [M.E. *annes sede.* ANISE. SEED.] The seed of the anise which has a licorice-like taste, and is used in cooking.

an·i·sette, an″i·set′, an″i·zet′, an′i·set″,an′-i·zet″,*n.* [Fr.] A liqueur flavored with anise.

an·i·sog·a·mous, an″i·sog′a·mus, *a. Biol.* carrying on a type of reproduction characterized by the fusion of individuals differing in size or by dissimilar gametes.

an·i·so·met·ric, an·i″so·me′trik, an″i·so·me′trik, *a.* [Fr. < *an-* and *isometric.*] Not isometric; of unequal measurement: applied to crystals developed dissimilarly in the three axial directions.

an·i·so·trop·ic, an·i″so·trop′ik, an″i·so·trop′ik, *a.* [< *an-* and *isotropic.* ISOTROPIC.] Applied to bodies which vary in size in different directions; aelotropic.

an·ker·ite, ang′ke·rīt″, *n.* [< M. J. *Anker*, of Austria.] A mineral, Ca(Fe, Mg, Mn)-$(CO_3)_2$, closely related to dolomite in composition, but containing relatively large quantities of iron.

ankh, angk, *n.* [Egypt.] *Egypt. art*, a cross with a loop at the top, used as a symbol of generation or enduring life.

an·kle, ang′kl, *n.* [M.E. *ankel* < O.E. *ancleow*, O. Fris. *ankel*, Dan. and Sw. *ankel*, G. *enkel*; < a root *ang*, meaning crooked. ANCHOR.] The joint which connects the foot with the leg.

an·kle·bone, ang′kl·bōn″, *n.* The talus.

an·klet, ang′klit, *n.* An ornament, support, or protection for the ankle; a sock that comes just above the ankle.

an·ky·lose, an·chy·lose, ang′ki·lōs″, *v.t.*—*ankylosed, ankylosing, anchylosed, anchylosing.* [< *ankylosis.*] To affect with ankylosis; to grow together.—*v.i.* To become ankylosed.

an·ky·lo·sis, an·chy·lo·sis, ang″ki·lō′sis, *n.* [Gr. < *angkylos*, crooked.] Stiffness and immovability of a joint, due to a disease or as a result of surgery; morbid adhesion of the articular ends of contiguous bones.—**an·ky·lot·ic,** ang″ki·lot′ik, *a.* Pertaining to ankylosis.

an·la·ge, än′lä·ge, *n.* pl. **an·la·gen,** än′lä·gen, **an·la·ges,** än′lä·ges. [G. < *an-*, on, and *lage*, position. LAY.] *Biol.* the initial accumulation of cells in a growing organ or part. The initial step in any development.

an·nal·ist, an′a·list, *n.* A writer of annals; a chronicler.—**an·nal·is·tic,** an″a·lis′tik, *a.* Pertaining or peculiar to an annalist.

an·nals, an′alz, *n. pl.* [L. *annales* (*libri*, books, understood), *annalis*, pertaining to a year, < *annus*, a year.] A history or relation of events in chronological order, each event being recorded under the year in which it happened.

An·na·mese, an″a·mēz′, an″a·mēs′, *n. pl.* **An·na·mese.** A Mongolian people mainly occupying the eastern coast of Viet Nam, once the French protectorate Annam; the largest ethnic group of Vietnamese people; the language spoken by the Annamese.—*a.*

an·nat·to, a·nat′ō, a·nä′tō, *n.* [Carib.] A small tropical American tree, *Bixa orellama*, the seeds of which yield an orange-red dyestuff; the dyestuff so produced.

an·neal, a·nēl′, *v.t.* [O.E. *anaelan, onaelan*, to set on fire, to anneal < *an-* or *on-*, on, and *aelan*, to kindle.] To heat, as glass or iron vessels, in an oven or furnace, and then cool slowly, for the purpose of rendering less brittle; to temper by a gradually diminishing heat; to heat in order to fix colors; to bake; to toughen.

an·ne·lid, an′e·lid, *n.* [L. *annellus*, a little ring, and Gr. *eidos*, form.] A segmented worm of the phylum *Annelida*, of annulose animals, so called because their bodies are formed of a great number of small rings, as in the earthworm. Also **an·nel·i·dan,** a·nel′i·dan.—*a.*

an·nex, a·neks′, *v.t.* [M.E. < M.L. *annecto*, *annexum*, to bind to < *ad-*, to, and *necto*, *nexum*, to bind.] To unite at the end; to subjoin; to unite, as a smaller thing to a greater; to incorporate; to attach; to connect, especially as a consequence; as, to *annex* a penalty.

an·nex, an′eks, *n.* Something annexed; an addition, supplement, added condition, or stipulation.—**an·nex·a·tion,** an″ek·sā′shan, an″ek·sā·shan, *n.* The act of annexing; what is annexed; addition; union.—**an·nex·a·tion·ist,** an″ek·sā′shan·ist, *n.* One favorable to annexation, as of a portion of one country to another.

an·ni·hi·late, a·nī′i·lāt″, *v.t.*—*annihilated, annihilating.* [L. *annihilo* < *ad-*, to, and *nihil*, nothing.] To reduce to nothing; to destroy the existence of; to cause to cease to be; to annul; to cancel; to destroy the form or peculiar distinctive properties of.—**an·ni·hi·la·tion,** a·nī′i·lā′shan, *n.* The act of annihilating or the state of being annihilated; destruction.—**an·ni·hi·la·tor,** a·nī′i·lā″tor, *n.* One who, or that which, annihilates.

an·ni·ver·sa·ry, an·i·vur′sa·rē, *a.* [M.E. < L. *anniversarius* < *annus*, a year, and *verto*, *versum*, to turn.] Returning with the year at a stated time; annual; yearly.—*n.* pl. **an·ni·ver·sa·ries.** A stated day on which some event is annually celebrated; the annual celebration in honor of an event; as, a wedding *anniversary.*

an·no Dom·i·ni, an′ō dom′i·nī, an′ō dom′i·nē″, ä′nō dom′i·nī″, ä′nō dom′i·nē″. [M.L.] In the year of the Lord, *i.e.*, of the Christian era. Abbr. *A.D.*

an·no he·gi·rae, an′ō hi·ji′rē, an′ō hej′i·rē″, ä′nō hi·ji′rē, ä′nō hej′i·rē″, *adv.* (*Sometimes cap.*) In the year of the Hegira, A.D. 662; within the Muslim era, said of a date or period of time. Abbr. *A.H.* Also **an·no he·ji·rae.**

an·no·tate, an′ō·tāt″, *v.t.*—*annotated, annotating.* [L. *annoto, annotatum—ad*, to, and *noto*, to note.] To comment upon; to make remarks on by notes.—*v.i.* To act as an annotator; to make annotations or notes (with *on*).—**an·no·ta·tor,** an′ō·tā″tor, *n.* A writer of annotations or notes; a commentator.

an·no·ta·tion, an″ō·tā′shan, *n.* The act of annotating or making notes on; a critical note on some passage of a book.

an·nounce, a·nouns′, *v.t.*—*announced, announcing.* [M.E. < M.Fr. *annoncer*, < L. *annuncio—ad*, and *nuncio*, to tell, from *nuncius*, a messenger.] To publish; to proclaim; to make known in advance; to give notice or first notice of; to serve as announcer of.

an·nounce·ment, a·nouns′ment, *n.* The act of announcing or giving notice; proclamation; publication; a formal declaration of some event.

an·nounc·er, a·noun′sēr, *n.* One who announces, esp. a person who introduces programs, etc., on television and radio; a proclaimer.

an·noy, a·noi′, *v.t.* [M.E. < O.Fr. *anoier*, < *anoi*, annoyance, vexation, from L. *in odio*, in hatred, common in such phrases as *est* *mihi in odio,* 'it is hateful to me.' ODIUM.] To torment or disturb, especially by continued or repeated acts; to tease, vex, pester, or molest.—*n.* Molestation; annoyance (chiefly a poetical word).

an·noy·ance, *a*·noi'*ans, n.* The act of annoying, the state of being annoyed; that which annoys; a nuisance; a source of trouble.

an·noy·er, *a*·noi'ẽr, *n.* One who annoys.

an·noy·ing, *a*·noi'ing, *a.* Vexatious; troublesome.

an·nu·al, an'ū·*al, a.* [M.E. < L.L. *annualis,* < L. *annus,* a year.] Returning every year; coming yearly; lasting or continuing only one year or one yearly season; performed in a year; reckoned by the year.—*n.* A plant that grows from seed, flowers, and perishes in the course of the same season; a literary production published annually; a yearbook. —**an·nu·al·ly,** an'ū·*al·ē, adv.* Yearly; returning every year; year by year.

an·nu·al ring, *n. Bot.* the yearly growth of wood about the stem of a woody plant.

an·nu·i·tant, *a*·nö'i·*tant, a*·nū'i·*tant, n.* One receiving an annuity.

an·nu·i·ty, *a*·nö'i·tē, *a*·nū'i·tē, *n.* [M.E. < M.Fr. *annuité,* < L. *annus,* a year.] A yearly payment of money which a person receives for life or for a term of years; also, the right to receive or the obligation to make such payments.

an·nul, *a*·nul', *v.t.*—*annulled, annulling.* [M.E. < M.Fr. *annuller,* < L. *ad nullum,* to nothing.] To reduce to nothing or annihilate; to make void; to nullify; to abrogate; to abolish; cancel, as laws, decrees, compacts.

an·nu·lar, an'yu·lẽr, *a.* [L. *annularis,* < *annulus, anulus,* dim. of *anus,* a ring, akin to *annus,* a year. ANNUAL.] Having the form of a ring; pertaining to a ring.—**an·nu·lar·i·ty,** an'yu·lar'i·tē, *n.*—**an·nu·lar·ly,** an'yu·lẽr·lē, *adv.* In the manner of a ring.

an·nu·lar e·clipse, *n. Astron.* an eclipse in· which an outer ring of the sun is not covered by the moon.

an·nu·lar lig·a·ment, *n. Anat.* a ring-shaped ligament.

an·nu·late, an'yu·lāt″, an'yu·lat, *a.* Furnished with rings, or circles like rings, as the body of a worm; having bands. Also **an·nu·lat·ed,** an'yu·lāt″id.

an·nu·la·tion, an″yu·lā'shan, *n.* A circular or ringlike formation.

an·nu·let, an'yu·lit, *n.* [M.Fr., a dim. of *anel* < L. *annulus,* a ring.] A little ring or ringlike body; *arch.* a ring around a pillar or column.

an·nul·ment, *a*·nul'ment, *n.* The act of annulling; the state of being annulled; a judicial declaration stating that a marriage is invalid.

an·nu·lose, an'yu·lōs″, *a.* [N.L. ANNULUS. -OSE.] Furnished with rings; having a body composed of rings; pertaining or relating to animals forming a subkingdom which embraces the worms, leeches, crabs, spiders, insects.

an·nu·lus, an'ū·lus, *n.* pl. **an·nu·li,** an·nu·lus·es, an'ū·li″. [L. prop. *anulus,* dim. of *anus,* ring.] A ring; a ringlike structure, part, band, or space.

an·nun·ci·ate, *a*·nun'sē·āt″, *a*·nun'shē·- āt″, *v.t.*—*annunciated, annunciating.* To bring tidings of; to announce.

an·nun·ci·a·tion, *a*·nun″sē·ā'shan, *a*- nun″shē·ā'shan, *n.* [M.E. < L. ANNOUNCE.] The act of announcing; announcement. (*Cap.*) the tidings brought by the angel to Mary of the Incarnation of Christ; the church festival in memory of this announcement, falling on March 25.

an·nun·ci·a·tor, *a*·nun'sē·ā″tor, *a*·nun'- shē·ā″tor, *n.* One who announces; an electrical indicator.

a·no·ci·as·so·ci·a·tion, *a*·nō'sē·*a*·sō″- sē·ā'shan, *a*·nō'sē·*a*·sō″shē·ā'shan, *n.* [<

a- and L. *nocere,* harm, and E. *association.*] A method of treatment before, during, and after a surgical operation, for preventing shock and other harmful effects: consisting principally in a combination of general and local anesthesia (whereby the brain is entirely cut off from the field of operation), and in shielding the patient from alarming mental impressions. Also *anociation.*

an·ode, an'ōd, *n.* [< Gr. *anodes,* the way up < *ana*- and *hodos,* way.] The positive pole or electrode in a battery, vacuum tube, etc. Often called the "plate": opposed to *cathode.*—**an·od·ic,** an·od'ik, *a.*—**an·od·**i·cal·ly, an·od'i·kal·ē, *adv.*

an·o·dize, an'o·dīz″, *v.t.*—*anodized, anodizing.* To coat, as a metal, with a protective film by subjecting it to electrolytic action.

an·o·dyne, an'o·dīn″, *n.* [L. *anodynos* < Gr. *anōdynos* < neg. *an*-, and *odynē,* pain.] Any medicine which allays pain; anything which diminishes distress.—*a.* Assuaging pain; relieving.

a·noint, *a*·noint', *v.t.* [M.E. *anointen, enointen;* O.Fr. *enoindre,* part. *enoint,* < L. *inungere* < *in*-, in, on, and *ungere,* to anoint. UNGUENT.] To pour oil upon; to smear or rub with oil or unctuous substances; to consecrate in a sacred rite by unction, or the use of oil.—**a·noint·er,** *a*·noint'ẽr, *n.* One who anoints.—**a·noint·ment,** *a*·noint'- ment, *n.* The act of anointing.

a·nom·a·lis·tic, *a*·nom″*a*·lis'tik, *a.* Pertaining to an anomaly.

a·nom·a·lis·tic year, *n.* The period of one revolution of the earth about the sun from perihelion to perihelion; 365 days, 6 hours, 13 minutes, 53.0 seconds in 1900, and increasing at the rate of 0.26 second per century.

a·nom·a·lous, *a*·nom'*a*·lus, *a.* [L. *anomalus,* Gr. *anomalos* < *a*- and *homalos,* even, < *homos,* same.] Forming an anomaly; deviating from a general rule, method, or analogy; irregular; peculiar; abnormal.— **a·nom·a·lous·ly,** *a*·nom'*a*·lus·lē, *adv.*— **a·nom·a·lous·ness,** *a*·nom'*a*·lus·nis, *n.*

a·nom·a·ly, *a*·nom'*a*·lē, *n.* [Fr. *anomalie;* L. *anomalia,* Gr. *anomalia,* inequality, neg. prefix *an,* and *homalos,* equal, similar, < *homos,* the same. SAME.] Deviation from common rule; something abnormal; irregularity; an inconsistency. *Astron.* the distance of a planet from its perihelion, measured in degrees; also, the angle measuring apparent irregularities in the motion of a planet. *Meteor.* the difference between the local mean value of a meteorological element at some latitude and the mean value of that element for that latitude. Compare *meteorological elements.*—**a·nom·**a·lism, *a*·nom'*a*·liz″um, *n.* An anomaly; a deviation from rule.

an·o·mie, an·o·my, an'o·mē″, *n. Sociol.* A state of society or of an individual in which social and behavioral norms are weak, nonexistent or in a process of change; lawlessness; society in which standards have weakened, or disappeared entirely.

an·o·nym, an'o·nim, *n.* An assumed or false name. A person who remains anonymous.

an·o·nym·i·ty, an″o·nim'i·tē, *n.* The condition or state of being anonymous; a person who is anonymous.

a·non·y·mous, *a*·non'i·mus, *a.* [L.L. *anonymus* < Gr. *anōnymos* < neg. *an*-, and *onyma,* name. NAME.] Wanting a name; without any name acknowledged as that of author, contributor, and the like; lacking individuality.—**a·non·y·mous·ly,** *a*·non'i- mus·lē, *adv.* In an anonymous manner; without a name.—**a·non·y·mous·ness,** *a*·non'i·mus·nis, *n.* The state of being anonymous.

a·noph·e·les, *a*·nof'e·lēz″, *n.* [N.L. < Gr. *anopheles,* useless, < *an*-, no, and *ophelos,*

advantage.] A mosquito of the genus *Anopheles,* which, when infected with the organisms causing malaria, may transmit the disease to human beings by biting.

a·no·rak, ä'no·räk, *n.* [Greenland Eskimo *anoraq.*] A hooded jacket; parka.

an·o·rex·i·a, an″o·rek'sē·*a, n.* [N.L. < Gr. < *a*-, no, and *orexis,* appetite, longing < *oregein,* to reach after.] *Med.* A pathological loss of appetite; specif. *anorexia nervosa,* a loss of appetite accompanied by psychotic symptoms.

an·os·mi·a, an·oz'mē·*a,* an·os'mē·*a, n.* [N.L. < Gr. < neg. *an*-, and *osmē,* smell.] *Med.* a deficiency or loss of the sense of smell.

an·oth·er, *a*·nuTH'ẽr, *a.* [M.E. < *an,* indefinite art., and *other.*] Not the same; different; being one more, in addition to a former number; any other.

an·oth·er, *a*·nuTH'ẽr, *pron.* One more; one that is distinct from a present one; one that is of an unspecified group. Often used without a noun, as a substitute for the name of a person or thing and much used in opposition to *one,* as: *One* went *one* way, *another another.* Also frequently used with *one* in a reciprocal sense, as: "Love *one another.*" Any other; some other.

an·ox·e·mi·a, an″ok·sē'mē·*a, n.* [Gr. *an*-, no, *ox(ygen),* and Gr. *haima* (whence *-emia,* cf. *anemia),* blood.] *Med.* A condition characterized by an abnormally low tension of oxygen in arterial blood; hypoxemia.

an·ox·i·a, an·ok'sē·*a, a*·nok'sē·*a, n.* [< Gr. *an*-, *ox(ygen),* and *-ia(sis).*] Insufficient oxygen supply in the body tissues; the complications that result from a lack of oxygen.

an·schluss, än'shlus, *n.* [G.] Joining; union; specif. [*cap.*], the political union of Austria with Germany in 1938.

an·ser·ine, an'se·rīn″, an'se·rin, *a.* [L. *anserinus,* < *anser,* a goose.] Relating to or resembling a goose, or the skin of a goose: applied to the skin when roughened by cold or disease; foolish, silly. Also *anserous.*

an·swer, an'sẽr, än'sẽr, *v.t.* [M.E. < O.E. *andswerian,* to answer < *and*-, against (= *a in along,* L. *ante*-, before, Gr. *anti*-, against), and *swerian,* to swear.] To speak or write in return to; to reply to; to refute; to say or do in reply; to act in compliance with, or in fulfillment or satisfaction of; to render account to or for; to be security for; to be equivalent or adequate to; to serve; to suit.—*v.i.* To reply; to speak or write by way of return; to respond to some call; to be fit or suitable.—**an·swer for,** to be accountable for; to guarantee.—**an·swer to,** to be known by; to correspond to, in the way of resemblance, fitness, or correlation.

an·swer, an'sẽr, än'sẽr, *n.* [M.E. < O.E. *andswaru.*] A reply; a response; that which is said, written, or done, in return to a call, question, argument, challenge, allegation, petition, prayer, or address; the result of an arithmetical or mathematical operation; a solution; something done in return for, or in consequence of, something else; *law,* a counterstatement of facts in a course of pleadings. A reply to a charge; a defense.

an·swer·a·ble, an'sẽr·*a*·bl, än'sẽr·*a*·bl, *a.* Capable of being answered; obliged to give an account; responsible.—**an·swer·a·ble·ness,** an'sẽr·*a*·bl·nis, än'sẽr·*a*·bl·nis, *n.* The quality of being answerable.—**an·swer·a·bly,** an'sẽr·*a*·blē, än'sẽr·*a*·blē, *adv.*

ant, ant, *n.* [M.E. *ante, emete, am(e)te,* < O.E. *æmette.*] An emmet; a hymenopterous insect of the family *Formicidea,* living in communities which consist of males, females, and neuters; the name is also given to the neuropterous insects more correctly called termites.

an·ta, an′ta, *n.* pl. **an·tae,** an′tē. [Probably < L. *antae*, pilasters (akin to *ante*, before).] *Arch.* a square or rectangular pier or pillar, formed by thickening a wall at its extremity.

ant·ac·id, ant·as′id, *n.* [*Anti*, against, and *acid*.] An alkali, or a remedy for acidity in the stomach.—*a.* Counteracting or preventing acidity.

an·tag·o·nism, an·tag′o·niz″um, *n.* Character of being an antagonist or antagonistic; an opposing force; counteraction or contrariety of things or principles; a feeling of hostility; *physiol.* opposition to the action of a substance on living tissues or cells.

an·tag·o·nist, an·tag′o·nist, *n.* [L.L. *antagonista* < Gr. *antagonistēs*, adversary < *antagonizesthai*, contend against. See *antagonize*.] One who contends with another; an opponent; a competitor; an adversary; a drug that counteracts the action of another one; a muscle that counteracts another muscle.—*a.* Counteracting; opposing (said of muscles).

an·tag·o·nis·tic, an·tag″o·nis′tik, *a.* Contending against; acting in opposition; hostile; opposing.—*n.* A muscle whose action counteracts that of another.—**an·tag·o·nis·ti·cal·ly,** an·tag″o·nis′ti·kal·ē, *adv.*

an·tag·o·nize, an·tag′o·nīz″, *v.t.*—*antagonized, antagonizing.* [< Gr. *antagonizesthai*, contend with < *anti*-, against, and *agonizestha*: struggle < *agon*, contest.] To contend against; to act in opposition; to cause to become unfriendly or hostile.—*v.i.* To render antagonistic; to provoke resentment.

ant·al·ka·li, ant·al′ka·lī″, *n.* [*Anti*-, against, and *alkali*.] A substance which neutralizes an alkali.—**ant·al·ka·line,** ant·al′ka·līn″, ant·al′ka·lin, *a.* Having the property of neutralizing or preventing alkalies.

ant·arc·tic, ant·ärk′tik, ant·är′tik, *a.* [M.E. *antartik* < L. *antarcticus*, Gr. *antarktikos* < *anti*-, against, and *arktos*, the north. ARCTIC.] *Often cap.* Opposite to the northern or arctic pole; relating to the southern pole or to the region near it, and applied to a circle parallel to the equator and distant from the pole 23° 28′.

ant·arc·tic cir·cle, *n. Often cap. A and C.* an imaginary line drawn so that it is circling the earth and parallel to the equator, at 23° 28′ N. of the South Pole.

ant bear, *n.* A kind of large anteater, *Myrmecophaga jubata,* of S. America. Also **great ant·eat·er,** aardvark.

ant cow, *n.* An aphid or plant louse from which ants obtain honeydew. Also **ant cat·tle.**

an·te, an′tē, *n.* [Cf. L. *ante*, before.] *Poker.* a stake put into the pool by each player before being dealt cards. A payment; a share of the expenses.—*v.i., v.t.*—*anted* or *anteed, anteing.*

ant·eat·er, ant′ē″tèr, *n.* A quadruped that eats ants, especially an edentate animal, genus *Myrmecophaga,* which feeds on ants and other insects, catching them by thrusting among them the long tongue covered with a viscid saliva.

an·te·bel·lum, an″tē·bel′um, *a.* [L.] Before the war, often meaning the U.S. Civil War.

an·te·cede, an″ti·sēd′, *v.t.*—*anteceded, anteceding.* [L. *antecedere*, to go before < *ante*-, before, and *cedere*, to go. CEDE.] To go before in time; to precede.

an·te·ced·ence, an″ti·sēd′ans, *n.* The act or state of going before in time; precedence; priority.

an·te·ced·ent, an″ti·sēd′ent, *n.* [M.E. < M.L. *antecedent*-, stem of *antecedens,* that which goes before < ppr. of *antecedere,* to go before.] One who or that which goes before in time or place; *gram.* the noun to which a relative or other pronoun refers. A predecessor. *Pl.* the earlier events of a man's life; previous course, conduct, or avowed principles; ancestors.

an·te·ced·ent, an″ti·sēd′ent, *a.* Going before; prior; anterior; preceding.

an·te·ced·ent·ly, an″ti·sēd′ent·lē, *adv.* Previously; at a time preceding.

an·te·ces·sor, an″ti·ses′or, *n.* [M.E. *antecessour* < L. *antecessor,* one who goes before < *antecedere.* See *antecede.*] One who goes before; a leader; predecessor.

an·te·cham·ber, an′tē·chām″bėr, *n.* [M.Fr. *antichambre* < It. *anticamera* < *anti*- (< L. *ante*-, before) and *camera,* chamber.] A chamber or room leading to another room or apartment; also *anteroom.*

an·te·choir, an′tē·kwīr″, *n.* A space, more or less enclosed, in front of the choir of a church.

an·te·date, an′ti·dāt″, *n.* [*ante*-, before, and *date.*] Prior date; a date antecedent to another.

an·te·date, an′ti·dāt″, an″ti·dāt′, *v.t.*—*antedated, antedating.* To date before the true time or beforehand; to give an earlier date than the real one to; to precede, as: England *antedates* the U.S.

an·te·di·lu·vi·an, an″tē·di·lö′vē·an, *a.* [L. *ante*-, before, and *diluvium,* a flood.] Existing, happening, or relating to what happened before the deluge; antiquated.—*n.* One who lived before the deluge.

an·te·flex·ion, an″tē·flek′shan, *n.* [L. *ante*-, before, and *flexio(n)*-, a bending.] *Pathol.* a bending forward, esp. of the body of the uterus; cf. *retroflexion.*

an·te·lope, an′te·lōp″, *n.* pl. **an·te·lopes, an·te·lope.** [M.E. *antelop, antelope* < O.Fr. < L. *anthalopus* < Gr. *antholops,* fabulous beast.] One of many species of ruminant mammals of the family *Bovidae* resembling the deer in general appearance, but essentially different in nature from them, having hollow, unbranched horns that are not deciduous; leather from the hide of this animal.

an·te me·rid·i·em, *n.* [L.] Before noon: used in specifying the hour of the day, usu. in the abbreviated form *A.M.,* as, 10 *A.M.* (or *a.m.*).—**an·te·me·rid·i·an,** *a.*

an·te-mor·tem, an′tē·mạr′tem, *a.* [L. *ante mortem,* before death.] Previous to death: as, an *ante-mortem* statement; cf. *post-mortem.*

an·te·mun·dane, an″tē·mun′dān, *a.* [L. *ante*-, before, and *mundus,* world.] Being before the creation of the world.

an·ten·na, an·ten′a, *n.* pl. **an·ten·nae,** an·ten·nas, an·ten′ē. [L. *antenna,* a sailyard.] One of the hornlike filaments that project from the head in insects, crustacea, and myriapods, and are considered as organs of touch and hearing; a feeler; pl. **an·ten·nae.** *Radio, TV,* the device through which electromagnetic waves are transmitted and intercepted; pl. **an·ten·nas.**

an·ten·nule, an·ten′ūl, *n. Zool.* a small antenna.

an·te·pen·di·um, an″ti·pen′dē·um, *n.* pl. **an·te·pen·di·a,** an″ti·pen′dē·a. [M.L. < L. *ante*-, before, and *pendere,* to hang.] The hanging with which the front of an altar, pulpit, or lectern is covered.

an·te·pe·nult, an″tē·pē′nult, an″tē·pi·nult′, *n.* [L. *ante*-, before, *pene,* almost, and *ultimus,* last.] The second syllable from the last in a word.—**an·te·pe·nul·ti·mate,** an″tē·pi·nul′ti·mit, *a.*

an·te·ri·or, an·tēr′ē·or, *a.* [L. a comparative < *ante,* before.] Before in time; prior; earlier; antecedent; before in place; in front: opposed to posterior.—**an·te·ri·or·i·ty,** an·tēr″ē·ar′i·tē, an·tēr″ē·or′i·tē, *n.*—**an·te·ri·or·ly,** an·tēr′ē·or·lē, *adv.*

an·te·room, an′tē·rōm″, an′tē·rụm″, *n.* A room leading into a chief apartment; an adjoining waiting room.

an·te·type, an′tē·tīp″, *n.* An earlier type or form; a prototype.

an·te·vert, an″tē·vụrt′, *v.t.* [L. *ante*-, before, and *vertere,* turn.] *Pathol.* To turn forward; displace (the uterus) as by tipping forward. Cf. *retrovert.*—**an·te·ver·sion,** an″tē·vụr′zhan, an″tē·vụr′shan, *n.*

ant·he·li·on, ant·hē′lē·on, an·thē′lē·on, *n.* pl. **ant·he·li·a,** ant·hē′lē·a. [Gr. < *anti*-, opposite to, and *hēlios,* the sun.] A luminous ring, or rings, caused by the diffraction of light, seen in alpine and polar regions opposite the sun when rising or setting.

an·them, an′them, *n.* [M.E. *antempne, antemne, antefne,* etc., O.E. *antefen,* an anthem; < L.L. *antiphona,* < Gr. *antiphōnon,* an antiphon < *anti*-, against, and *phōne,* sound, the voice.] A hymn sung in alternate parts; in modern usage, a piece of sacred music set to words taken from the Bible; a song of praise, gladness, or patriotism; as, the national *anthem.*

an·ther, an′thėr, *n.* [N.L. < Gr. *anthēros,* flowery, < *anthos,* a flower.] The essential part of the stamen of a plant containing the pollen or fertilizing dust.

an·ther·id·i·um, an″the·rid′ē·um, *n.* pl. **an·ther·id·i·a,** an″the·rid′ē·a. [N.L. < *anthera:* see *anther.*] *Bot.* the male reproductive organ in ferns, mosses, etc., containing male gametes. Also **an·ther·id,** an′the·rid. —**an·ther·id·i·al,** an″the·rid′ē·al, *a.* Pertaining to or of an antheridium.

an·the·sis, an·thē′sis, *n.* [N.L. < Gr. < *antheo,* to bloom, < *anthos,* a flower.] *Bot.* The period necessary for flowers to expand; expansion into a flower.

ant hill, *n.* A mound or hillock of earth, leaves, etc., formed by a colony of ants for, or in the process of, constructing their habitation.

an·tho·cy·a·nin, an″tho·sī′a·nin, *n.* [Gr. *anthos* a flower, and *kyanos,* blue.] Any of the blue, purple, or red water-soluble pigments of plants.

an·tho·di·um, an·thō′dē·um, *n.* pl. **an·tho·di·a,** an·thō′dē·a. [N.L. < Gr. *an, thōd(es),* flowerlike, and L. *-ium,* suffix -ium.] *Bot.* the head or involucre of a flower, esp. in composite plants.

an·thol·o·gist, an·thol′o·jist, *n.* One who compiles an anthology.

an·thol·o·gize, an·thol′o·jīz″, *v.i.*—*anthologized, anthologizing.* To compile an anthology.—*v.t.* To put into an anthology.

an·thol·o·gy, an·thol′o·jē, *n.* pl. **an·thol·o·gies.** [N.L. < Gr. < *anthos,* flower, and *logia* < *legein,* to gather. LEGEND.] A collection of literary selections or passages, usu. centered about a theme; as, an *anthology* of contemporary American drama.

an·tho·phore, an′tho·fōr″, an′tho·fạr″, *n.* [Gr. *anthophorous,* flower-bearing < *anthos,* a flower, and *pherein,* to bear.] *Bot.* a columnar process arising from the bottom of the calyx, as in the pink family of cultivated annuals or perennials, and having at its apex the petals, stamens, and pistil.

an·tho·tax·y, an′tho·tak″sē, *n.* [N.L. < Gr. *antho(s),* flower, and *-taxy* < *taxis,* a combining, putting in order < *tassein,* to put in order.] *Bot.* the arrangement of flowers on the axis of growth; inflorescence.

an·tho·zo·an, an″tho·zō′an, *n.* [N.L. < Gr. *anthos,* flower, and *zoon,* animal.] Any marine coelenterate of the class *Anthozoa,* as corals and sea anemones, a class of marine animals corresponding inexactly to the actinozoan.—*a.*

an·thra·cene, an′thra·sēn″, *n.* [ANTHRACITE.] A hydrocarbon, $C_6H_4(CH_2)C_6H_4$, obtained from coal tar, used for furnishing alizarine and anthraquinone, and measuring radioactive substances.

an·thra·cite, an′thra·sīt″, *n.* [< L. *anthracites,* bloodstone < Gr. *anthrakites,* lit. coal-like < *anthrak*- (stem of *anthrax*), coal.] Glance or blind coal, a nonbituminous coal of a shining luster, approaching metallic, which burns without smoke, with a weak or no flame, and with intense heat.—**an·thra·cit·ic,** an″thra·sit′ik, *a.*

an·thrax, an'thraks, *n.* pl. **an·thra·ces,** an'-thra·sēz. [M.E. *antrax* < L. *anthrax* < Gr., coal, carbuncle.] *Med.* A carbuncle; a malignant ulcer; a malignant infectious disease of certain warm-blooded animals which may be transmitted to man, due to *Bacillus anthracis* in the blood.

an·throp·ic, an·throp'ik, *a.* [Gr. *anthrō-pikos,* < *anthrōpos,* man.] Pertaining to man, or to the time of mankind's living on earth. Also **an·throp·i·cal.**

an·thro·po·cen·tric, an"thro·pō·sen'trik, *a.* Regarding man as the central fact of the universe; interpreting everything in terms of man and his values.

an·thro·po·gen·e·sis, an"thro·pō·jen'i·sis, *n.* [Gr. *anthrōpo-* and L. *genesis.*] The genesis or development of the human race, esp. as a subject of scientific study.

an·thro·po·gen·ic, an"thro·pō·jen'ik, *a.* About or referring to anthropogenesis; referring to or involving the genesis of man.

an·thro·pog·ra·phy, an"thro·pog'ra·fē, *n.* The branch of anthropology that de-scribes the varieties of mankind and their geographical distribution, physical charac-teristics, and customs.

an·thro·poid, an'thro·poid', *a.* [Gr. *an-thropoeides* < *anthrōpos,* a man, and *eidos,* resemblance.] Resembling man.—*n.* Any of the larger apes.

an·thro·pol·a·try, an"thro·pol'o·trē, *n.* [Gr. *anthropolatreia,* < *anthropos,* man, and *latreia,* worship.] The worship of a human being as divine.—**an·thro·pol·at·ric,** an"-thro·pol'a·trik, *a.*

an·thro·po·log·ic, an"thro·po·loj'ik, *a.* Pertaining to anthropology; also **an·thro·po·log·i·cal.**

an·thro·pol·o·gist, an"thro·pol'o·jist, *n.* One who specializes in anthropology.

an·thro·pol·o·gy, an"thro·pol'o·jē, *n.* [N.L. *anthropologia* < Gr. *anthropos,* a man, and *logos,* discourse.] The science of man and mankind, including the study of the physical and mental constitution of man, his cultural development, social conditions, as exhibited both in the present and the past.

an·thro·po·met·ric, an"thro·po·me'trik, an"thro·pō·me'trik, *a.* About or referring to anthropometry.

an·thro·pom·e·try, an"thro·pom'i·trē, *n.* [< Gr. *anthrōpos,* a man, and *metron,* measure.] The comparative measurement and study of the human body.

an·thro·po·mor·phic, an"thro·po·mor'-fik, an"thro·pō·mor'fik, *a.* [L.L. < Gr. *anthropomorphos,* having a human form, < *anthropos,* man, and *morphe,* form.] Ascrib-ing human form or attributes to beings or things not human, esp. to a deity; charac-terized by or involving such ascription.— **an·thro·po·mor·phi·cal·ly,** an"thro·po·-mor'fi·kal·ē, an"thro·pō·mor'fi·kal·ē, *adv.*

an·thro·po·mor·phize, an"thro·po·mor'-fīz, an"thro·pō·mor'fīz, *v.t.*—*anthropo-morphized, anthropomorphizing.* To ascribe human characteristics to.—**an·thro·po·-mor·phism,** an"thro·po·mor'fiz"um, an"-thro·pō·mor'fiz"um, *n.* Anthropomorphic conception or representation, as of a deity. —**an·thro·po·mor·phist,** an"thro·po·-mor' fist, an"thro·pō·mor'fist, *n.*

an·thro·pop·a·thy, an"thro·pop'a·thē, *n.* [M.L. or Gr. *anthrōpopatheia,* humanity, the possession of human feelings < *an-thrōpos,* man, and *pothein,* suffer.] Ascrip-tion of human passions or feelings to beings not human, esp. to God.—**an·thro·pop·-a·thism,** an"thro·pop'a·thiz"um, *n.*—**an·-thro·po·path·ic,** an"thro·po·path'ik, *a.* —**an·thro·po·path·i·cal·ly,** *adv.*

an·thro·poph·a·gi, an"thro·pof'a·jī, *n.* pl. [L., pl. of *anthropophagus,* < Gr. *anthro-pophagos,* man-eating, < *anthrōpos,* man, and *phagein,* eat.] Man-eaters; cannibals.—**an·-**

thro·po·phag·ic, an·thro·po·phag·i·cal, an"thro·po·faj'ik, an"thro·po·faj'i·kal, *a.* Pertaining to or practicing anthropophagy.

an·thro·poph·a·gism, an"thro·pof'a·jiz"-um, *n.* Anthropophagy.—**an·thro·poph·a·-gist, an·thro·poph·a·gite,** an"thro·pof'-a·jist, an"thro·pof'a·jīt, *n.* A man-eater; a cannibal.

an·thro·poph·a·gous, an"thro·pof'a·gus, *a.* Man-eating.—**an·thro·poph·a·gy,** *n.*

an·thro·pos·o·phy, an"thro·pos'a·fē, *n.* [< Gr. *anthrōpo-,* man, and *-sophy* (< *sophia,* knowledge).] *Philos.* a spiritualist doctrine founded by the Austrian social philosopher Rudolf Steiner (1861–1925) which explains life in terms of man's inner nature and presupposes the possibility of constant improvement in his nature.

an·thu·ri·um, an·thyur'ē·um, *n.* [N.L. < Gr. *anthos,* flower, and *oura,* tail.] Any plant of the tropical American araceous genus *Anthurium,* including species cultivated in greenhouses, some for the showy, often richly-colored spathes out of which the fleshy flower spikes rise, others for the handsomely veined or colored foliage.

an·ti, an'ti, an'tē, *n.* pl. **an·tis,** an'tīz, an'tēz. [Shortening of some compound of *anti-*.] *Colloq.* one who is opposed to some course, measure, policy, or party.

an·ti·air·craft, an"tē·âr'kraft", an"-tē·âr'kräft", an"tī·âr'kraft", an"tī·âr'kräft, *a. Milit.* used to strike against airborne air-craft, including surface guns, missile launchers, ballistic and guided missiles. Directed from the surface against airborne aircraft, including fire, shells, guided missiles, ballistic missiles. Abbr. *AA.*—*n.*

an·ti·ar, an'tē·är", *n.* [Javanese.] The upas tree. The milky juice which exudes from wounds made in the upas tree, and which is one of the most acrid and virulent vegetable poisons; also *antiarin.*

an·ti·art, an"tē·ärt', *n.* A type of art which does not follow artistic and esthetic standards.

an·ti·bi·o·sis, an"tē·bī·ō'sis, an"tī·bī·ō'-sis, *n.* [N.L. < Gr.] *Biol.* a relationship between two organisms which is harmful to one, as parasitism.

an·ti·bi·ot·ic, an"ti·bī·ot'ik, an"tī·bē·ot'-ik, an"tē·bē·ot'ik, an"tē·bī·ot'ik, an"tī·bē·-ot'ik, an"tī·bī·ot'ik, *n. Biochem.* any member of the group of chemical com-pounds produced by fungi and other micro-organisms which, in diluted solution, inhibit or destroy bacteria: used in the treatment of infectious diseases, and includ-ing penicillin and the "mycin" drugs.—*a.* Pertaining to antibiotics.—**an·ti·bi·ot·i·-cal·ly,** an"tī·bī·ot'i·kal·ē, *adv.*

an·ti·bod·y, an'ti·bod"ē, an'tē·bod"ē, *n.* pl. **an·ti·bod·ies,** an'ti·bod"ēz, an'tē·-bod"ēz. *Pathol.* any of various substances existing in the blood or developed in im-munization which counteract toxins or bacterial poisons in the system.

an·tic, an'tik, *a.* [L. *antiquus,* ancient. The modern sense of this word is derived < the grotesque figures seen in the antique sculpture of the Middle Ages. ANTIQUE.] Odd; fanciful; grotesque; fantastic (tricks, postures).—*n.* A buffoon or merry-andrew; a grotesque or fantastic figure; an absurd or ridiculous gesture; an odd gesticula-tion; a piece of buffoonery; a caper; a playful trick.—**an·tic·ly,** an'tik·lē, *adv.* In an antic manner.

an·ti·cat·a·lyst, an"tē·kat'a·list, an"tī·-kat'a·list, *n. Chem.* something which in-hibits a reaction to a catalyst.

an·ti·cath·ode, an"tē·kath'ōd, an"tī·kath'-ōd, *n.* The plate, often of platinum, opposite to the cathode in a vacuum tube, on which the cathode rays impinge, thus producing x-rays.

an·ti·christ, an'ti·krīst", *n.* [M.E. *anticrist* < L.L. *Antichristos* < Gr. < *anti-* and *Chris-*

tos.] An opponent of Christ; a person or power antagonistic to Christ.—**an·ti·-chris·tian,** an"tē·kris'chan, an"tī·kris'-chan, *a.* Opposite to or opposing the Christian religion.

an·tic·i·pant, an·tis'i·pant, *a.* Anticipat-ing; anticipative; expectant.

an·tic·i·pate, an·tis'i·pāt, *v.t.*—*antici-pated, anticipating.* [L. *anticipatus,* to *take* beforehand < *ante,* before, and *capio,* to take.] To be before in doing something; to prevent or preclude by prior action; to fore-stall; to realize beforehand; to foretaste or foresee; to look forward to; to expect.—*v.i.* To treat of something, as in a narrative, before the expected or planned time.

an·tic·i·pa·tion, an·tis'i·pā'shan, *n.* The act of anticipating; expectation; foretaste; realization beforehand; previous notion; preconceived opinion. *Mus.* a tone intro-duced ahead of its harmony.

an·tic·i·pa·tive, an·tis'i·pā"tiv, an·-tis'i·pa·tiv, *a.* Anticipating or tending to anticipate; containing anticipation.—**an·-tic·i·pa·tive·ly,** an·tis'i·pā"tiv·lē, *adv.* By anticipation.—**an·tic·i·pa·tor,** an·-tis'i·pā"tor, *n.* One who anticipates.

an·tic·i·pa·to·ry, an·tis'i·pa·tōr"ē, an·-tis'i·pa·tar"ē, *a.* Anticipative; exhibiting anticipation.

an·ti·clas·tic, an"tē·klas'tik, an"tī·klas'tik, *a.* [Gr. *anti-,* opposite to, and *klastos,* adj. < *klan,* break, deflect.] Noting or pertaining to a surface, such as that of a saddle, which is curved convexly in its length and concavely in its breadth, or vice versa: opposed to *synclastic.*

an·ti·cler·i·cal, an"tē·kler'i·kal, an"tī·-kler'i·kal, *a.* Opposed to the influence of the church and clergy in public affairs.—**an·-ti·cler·i·cal·ism,** *n.*

an·ti·cli·mac·tic, an"tē·klī·mak'tik, *a.* Concerning the nature of an anticlimax.

an·ti·cli·max, an"tī·klī'maks, *n.* An ex-pressed passage, written or vocal, in which the ideas first increase in force, and then terminate in something less important and striking: opposed to *climax.* An abrupt descent from the important to the trivial.

an·ti·cli·nal, an"tī·klīn'al, *a.* [Gr. *anti-,* against, and *klinein,* incline.] *Geol.* Inclining downward on both sides from a median line or axis, as an upward fold of rock strata; pertaining to such a fold.—**an·ti·cline,** an'tī·klīn", *n.* An anticlinal fold of stratified rock. Cf. *syncline.*

an·ti·co·ag·u·lant, an"tē·kō·ag'u·lant, an"tī·kō·ag'u·lant, *n. Med.* any agent which prevents coagulation, esp. of the blood.—*a.* Inhibiting or preventing coagulation; also **an·ti·co·ag·u·la·tive.**

an·ti·cy·clone, an"tī·sī'klōn, *n.* A meteoro-logical phenomenon consisting of a region of high barometric pressure, the pressure being greatest in the center, with light winds flowing outward from the center and not inward as in the cyclone.

an·ti·dot·al, an"tī·dōt'al, *a.* Having the qualities of an antidote; serving as an anti-dote.

an·ti·dote, an'tī·dōt", *n.* [M.E. < L. *anti-dotum,* < Gr. *antidoton,* an antidote < *anti-,* against, and *dotos,* given, < *didōnai,* to give.] A medicine or remedy to counteract the effects of poison, or of anything noxious taken into the stomach; *fig.* anything that prevents or counteracts evil.

an·ti·en·zyme, an"tē·en'zīm, an"tī·en'-zīm, *n. Biochem.* A substance which retards, inhibits, or prevents enzymatic action; a chemical substance (an antibody) produced by an organism to inhibit or counteract a foreign enzyme's effect.

an·ti·fe·brile, an"tē·fē'bril, an"tē·feb'ril, an"tī·fē'bril, an"tī·feb'ril, *a.* Having the quality of abating fever; opposing or tend-ing to cure fever; antipyretic.

an·ti·fed·er·al, an″tē·fed′ėr·al, an″tĭ·fed′-ėr·al, *a.* Opposed to or opposing federalism or a federal constitution.—**an·ti·fed·er·al·ism,** an″tē·fed′ėr·al·iz″um, an″tĭ·fed′-ėr·al·iz″um, *n.* Opposition to federalism.

an·ti·fed·er·al·ist, an″tē·fed′ra·list, an″tē·fed′ra·list, an″tē·fed′ra·list, an″tĭ·fed′ra·list, *n.* One who is averse to federalism. (*Cap.*), *U.S. Hist.* a person who belonged to or supported the Antifederal party; an opponent of the adoption in 1787-1788 of the U.S. Constitution.

an·ti·foul·ing, an″tē·fou′ling, an″tĭ·fou′-ling, *a. Naut.* of a coating, having the quality of preventing the fouling (by barnacles, algae, etc.) of underwater surfaces.

an·ti·freeze, an′tĭ·frēz″, an″tē·frēz″, *n.* A substance having a low freezing point: used in the radiator of an internal-combustion engine to prevent freezing of the cooling system during cold weather.

an·ti·gen, an″tĭ·jen, an″tĭ·jen″, *n.* [< Gr. *anti-*, against, and *gen*, to form.] A substance that gives rise to an antibody when introduced into blood or tissue.

an·ti·he·ro, an″tē·hēr″ō, an″tĭ·hēr″ō, *n.* A protagonist in literature or drama who does not possess the conventional qualities of a hero, such as courage or righteousness.

an·ti·his·ta·mine, an″tĭ·his′ta·mēn″, an″tĭ·his′ta·min, *n. Med.* any of a number of compounds that inactivate histamine in the body, used mainly for the treatment of allergies and colds.

an·ti·im·pe·ri·al·ism, an″tē·im·pēr′ē·a·liz″um, an″tĭ·im·pēr′ē·a·liz″um, *n.* Opposition to imperialism or the spirit and methods of empire, esp. as in the acquisition and government of dependencies.—**an·ti·im·pe·ri·al·ist,** *n.*—**an·ti·im·pe·ri·al·is·tic,** *a.*

an·ti·knock, an′tĭ·nok″, an″tē·nok″, *n.* A substance which, when added to an internal-combustion engine fuel, reduces the rate of combustion, allows a higher compression ratio, and eliminates detonation in the combustion process.

an·ti·le·gom·e·na, an″tĭ·le·gom′e·na, *n. pl.* [N.L., < Gr. *antilegomena, antilegein,* speak against.] Certain books of the New Testament (Hebrews, James, Jude, 2 Peter, 2 and 3 John, and Revelation) whose inspiration was not universally acknowledged in the early church.

an·ti·log, an′tĭ·läg″, *n.* Antilogarithm.

an·ti·log·a·rithm, an″tĭ·la̱′ga·riTH″um, an″tĭ·log′a·riTH″um, *n. Math.* the number corresponding to a logarithm.

an·ti·ma·cas·sar, an″tĭ·ma·kas′ar, *n.* [Gr. *anti-*, against, and E. *macassar*, oil.] A covering for furniture, made of open cotton or worsted work, to protect the back and arms from being soiled.

an·ti·mag·net·ic, an″tē·mag·net′ik, an″tĭ·mag·net′ik, *a.* Not subject to magnetization; having parts composed of alloys which are resistant to magnetism; as, an *antimagnetic* precision instrument.

an·ti·ma·lar·i·al, an″tē·ma·lâr′ē·al, an″-tĭ·ma·lâr′ē·al, *a.* Preventing malaria or its growth.—*n.* Any such agent.

an·ti·mat·ter, an″tē·mat″ėr, an′tĭ·mat″ėr, *n.* Matter consisting of antiparticles.

an·ti·mere, an′tĭ·mēr″, *n.* [Gr. *anti-*, opposite, *meros*, part.] *Biol.* one of two or more corresponding parts on opposite sides of animals.

an·ti·mi·cro·bi·al, an″tē·mĭ·krō′bē·al, an″tĭ·mĭ·krō′bē·al, *a.* Destroying or retarding the growth of microbes.—*n.*

an·ti·mis·sile, an″tē·mis′il, an″tĭ·mis′il, *a.* Designed for use in the defense against enemy missiles.—**an·ti·mis·sile mis·sile,** an explosive missile launched to intercept and destroy an enemy missile in flight.

an·ti·mon·ic, an′tĭ·mō′nik, an″tĭ·mon′ik, *a.* Of or containing antimony; as, *antimonic*

acid.—**an·ti·mo·ni·ous,** an″tĭ·mō′nē·us, *a.* Containing antimony in larger proportion than a corresponding antimonic compound; as, *antimonious* acid.

an·ti·mo·ny, an′tĭ·mō″nē, *n.* [M.E. < M.L. *antimonium*; origin doubtful.] A metallic element, brittle, lustrous, and white in color, used chiefly in alloys and (in compounds) in medicine and pigments. Sym. Sb (stibium), at. no. 51. See Periodic Table of Elements.—**an·ti·mo·nial,** an″tĭ·mō′nē·al, *a.* Pertaining to antimony, or partaking of its qualities; composed of or containing antimony.—*n.* A preparation of antimony; a medicine in which antimony is a principal ingredient.

an·ti·neu·tri·no, an″tē·nö·trē′nō, an″tē·-nü·trē′nō, an″tĭ·nö·trē′nō, an″tĭ·nü·trē′nō, *n. Phys.* a hypothetical subatomic particle having the same relation to the neutrino as the positron has to the electron, having near zero mass, no electric charge, a spin opposite in direction to that of the neutrino, and thought to be given off in the process of radioactive decay.

an·ti·neu·tron, an″tē·nü′tron, an″tē·nö′-tron, an″tĭ·nü′tron, an″tĭ·nö′tron, *n. Phys.* a hypothetical particle of mass equal to that of the neutron, without electric charge, and with a magnetic moment opposite to that of the neutron.

ant·ing, an′ting, *n.* The dropping or rubbing of ants amongst the feathers to kill parasites, practiced by certain types of birds.

an·ti·node, an′tĭ·nōd, *n. Phys.* a point, line, or plane in a vibrating body at which the amplitude of vibration is greatest, situated halfway between two adjacent nodes.

an·ti·no·mi·an, an″tĭ·nō′mē·an, *a.* Opposed to law; pertaining to the Antinomians. —*n.* (*Cap.*) one who maintains that, under the gospel dispensation, the moral law is of no use or obligation, faith being the only essential to salvation.—**an·ti·no·mi·an·ism,** an″tĭ·nō′mē·an·iz″um, *n.*

an·tin·o·my, an·tin′o·mē, *n. pl.* **an·tin·o·mies.** Opposition between laws or principles; a contradiction.

an·ti·nu·cle·on, an″tē·nö′klē·on″, an″tĭ·-nö′klē·on″, *n. Phys.* a particle in the nucleus of an atom having the same mass as the nucleon, but with differing electric charge and direction of magnetic moment.

an·ti·ox·i·dant, an″tē·ok′si·dant, an″tĭ·-ok′si·dant, *n.* A substance added to rubber that inhibits its deterioration; any substance inhibiting oxidation.

an·ti·par·ti·cle, an″tē·pär′ti·kal, an″tĭ·-pär′ti·kal, *n. Phys.* A subatomic particle, such as an antineutron or antiproton, which is found in radioactive decay and has a charge and magnetic moment opposite to its corresponding particle, such as neutron, proton, or neutrino.

an·ti·pas·to, an″tĭ·pä′stō, an″tĭ·pas′tō, *n.* [It. < L. *ante-* and *pasto* < L. *pastus*, food.] An Italian appetizer course, usu. of fish, meat, olives, etc.

an·ti·pa·thy, an·tip′a·thē, *n. pl.* **an·tip·a·thies.** [L. *antipathia* < Gr. *antipatheia* < *anti*, against, and *pathos*, feeling. PATHOS.] Natural aversion; instinctive contrariety or opposition in feeling; an aversion felt at the presence of an object; repugnance; contrariety in nature: commonly with *to* before the object.—**an·ti·pa·thet·ic,** an·ti·pa·thet′ik, *a.*—**an·ti·pa·thet·i·cal·ly,** an·ti·pa·thet′i·klē, *adv.*

an·ti·pe·ri·od·ic, an″tē·pēr″ē·od′ik, an″-tĭ·pēr″ē·od′ik, *a. Med.* efficacious against periodic diseases, as intermittent fever.—*n.*

an·ti·per·son·nel, an″tē·pur″so·nel′, an″-tĭ·pur″so·nel′, *a. Milit.* used to destroy or obstruct individuals rather than matériel.

an·ti·phlo·gis·tic, an″tē·flō·jis′tik, an″tĭ·-flō·jis′tik, *a.* Counteracting inflammation,

or an excited state of the system.—*n.* A medicine which checks inflammation.

an·ti·phon, an′tĭ·fon″, *n.* [M.L. *antiphona*, responsive singing < Gr. *antiphona*, neut. pl. of *antiphonos*, sounding in answer < *anti*, in response to, and *phōnē*, voice. ANTHEM.] The answer of one choir or one portion of a congregation to another when an anthem or psalm is sung alternately; a short versicle sung before and after the psalms.—**an·tiph·o·ny,** an·tif′o·nē, *n.* Alternate singing.

an·tiph·o·nal, an·tif′o·nal, *n.* [M.L. *antiphonarium*.] A book of antiphons or anthems; also **an·tiph·o·nar·y,** an·tif′o·-nėr″ē, pl. **an·tiph·o·nar·ies.**—*a.* Pertaining to antiphony or alternate singing; responsive; also **an·ti·phon·ic,** an″tĭ·fon′ik.

an·tiph·ra·sis, an·tif′ra·sis, *n.* [L. < Gr. *antiphrazein*, to speak the opposite.] *Rhet.* the use of words in a sense opposite to the proper meaning.—**an·ti·phras·tic,** an″tĭ·-fras′tik, *a.*

an·tip·o·dal, an·tip′o·dal, *a.* Belonging to the antipodes; on the opposite side of the globe; in general, diametrically opposite.

an·ti·pode, an′tĭ·pōd″, *n.* Anything exactly opposite to something else; that point on the earth 180° from a given place.

an·tip·o·des, an·tip′o·dēz″, *n. pl.* [M.E. < L. < Gr. *antipodes* < *antipod-* (stem of *antipous*), with feet opposite.] Those on the opposite side of the globe; the region directly on the opposite side of the globe. *Fig.* anything diametrically opposite or opposed to another; a contrary.

an·ti·pope, an′tĭ·pōp″, *n.* [< M.Fr. *antipape* < M.L. *antipapa*.] One who usurps the papal power in opposition to the pope; a pretender to the papacy.

an·ti·pov·er·ty, an″tē·pov′ėr·tē, an″tĭ·-pov′ėr·tē, *a.* Designed to relieve or attack poverty: used esp. of a program or organization in economically depressed areas.

an·ti·pro·ton, an″tē·prō″ton, an″tĭ·prō″-ton, *n. Phys.* a hypothetical particle with mass equal to that of a proton but carrying a negative charge, postulated as existing in the nuclei of hypothetical inverted atoms.

an·ti·py·ret·ic, an″tē·pī·ret′ik, an″tĭ·pī·-ret′ik, *n.* [< Gr. *anti-*, against, and *pyretos*, fever.] *Med.* a remedy efficacious against fever.

an·ti·py·rine, an·ti·py·rin, an″tē·pī′rin, an″tĭ·pī′rin, *n.* A white, crystalline powder used to reduce fever or relieve pain.

an·ti·quar·i·an, an″tĭ·kwer′ē·an, *a.* [L. *antiquarius*, of antiquity (< *antiquus*, old) and *-an*.] Pertaining to antiquaries or to antiquity; relating to rare books.—*n.* An antiquary.—**an·ti·quar·i·an·ism,** an″tĭ·-kwâr′ē·an·iz″um, *n.*

an·ti·quar·y, an′tĭ·kwer″ē, *n. pl.* **an·ti·quar·ies.** [L. *antiquarius*, < *antiquus*, old, ancient, from *ante-*, before.] One devoted to the study of ancient times through their relics; one versed in antiquity.

an·ti·quate, an′tĭ·kwāt″, *v.t.*—*antiquated, antiquating.* [L.L. *antiquatus*, pp. of *antiquāre*, < *antiquus*.] To make outdated by substituting something new or more practical; to make (something) appear to be an antique.

an·ti·quat·ed, an′tĭ·kwā″tid, *a.* Grown old-fashioned; obsolete; out of use; aged; behind the times.

an·tique, an·tēk′, *a.* [Fr. < L. *antiquus*, ancient. ANTIC.] Having existed in ancient times; belonging to or having come down from antiquity; ancient (an *antique* statue); having the characteristics of an earlier day; of old fashion (an *antique* robe); denoting a rough, uncoated paper.—*n.* Anything very old, usually 100 yrs.; a term applied to the relics or objects of ancient art.—*v.t.* To cause something to appear as if an antique; to emboss, as paper or fabric.—**an·tique·ly,**

an·tēk′lē, *adv.*—**an·tique·ness**, an·tēk′-nis, *n.*

an·tiq·ui·ty, an·tik′wi·tē, *n. pl.* **an·tiq·-ui·ties**. [L. *antiquitas* < *antiquus*, ancient.] The quality of being ancient; ancientness; great age; ancient times; former ages, esp. prior to the Middle Ages; the people of ancient times. *Pl.* the remains of ancient times; institutions, customs, etc., belonging to ancient nations.

an·tir·rhi·num, an″ti·rī′num, *n.* [N.L. < L. snapdragon < Gr. *anti-*, like (from *anti*, equivalent to, against) and *rhis* (stem *rhin-*) a nose. The flowers of most of the species bear a resemblance to the snout of some animal.] Any of the herbaceous plants of the genus *Antirrhinum*, in the figwort family, as the snapdragon.

an·ti·scor·bu·tic, an″tē·skạr·bū′tik, an″tī·skạr·bū′tik, *a. Med.* counteracting scurvy or a scorbutic tendency.—*n.* A remedy for or a preventive of scurvy.

an·ti-Sem·i·tism, an″tē·sem′i·tiz″um, an″tī·sem′i·tiz″um, *n.* Hostility or discrimination against Jews.

an·ti·sep·sis, an″ti·sep′sis, *n.* [Gr. *anti-*, against, and *septos*, putrid, < *sepein*, to putrefy.] The inhibition or destruction of microorganisms; prevention of sepsis.

an·ti·sep·tic, an″ti·sep′tik, *a.* [< *anti-*, against, and Gr. *sēptikos*, putrefying.] Pertaining to or effecting antisepsis; devoid of germs; especially clean; sometimes used in a derogatory sense to mean stark, uninteresting, or lacking feeling.— **an·ti·sep·ti·cal·ly**, an″ti·sep′tik·lē, *adv.* —**an·ti·sep·ti·cize**, an″ti·sep′ti·sīz, *v.t.*— *antisepticized, antisepticizing.* To treat with antiseptics.

an·ti·sep·tic, an″ti·sep′tik, *n.* An agent that inhibits the growth of microorganisms.

an·ti·se·rum, an″ti·sēr′um, *n.* A serum inclusive of antibodies acquired from the blood of an animal and used for injection into other animals to provide against a certain disease.

an·ti·slav·er·y, an″tē·slā′ve·rē, an″tē·slāv′rē, an″tī·slā′ve·rē, an″tī·slāv′rē, *a.* Against or opposed to slavery.—*n.* Resistance or opposition to slavery.

an·ti·so·cial, an″tē·sō′shal, an″tī·sō′shal, *a.* Opposed or averse to social intercourse or relations; opposed to social order, or to the principles on which society is constituted; hostile toward other people; antagonistic.

an·tis·tro·phe, an·tis′tro·fē, *n.* The part of an ancient Greek choral ode answering a previous strophe, sung by the chorus when returning from left to right; *pros.* the second of two metrically corresponding systems in a lyric poem.—**an·ti·stroph·ic**, an″ti·strof′ik, *a.*

an·ti·tank, an″tē·tangk, an″tī·tangk, *a.* Used, or designed to be used, to attack or destroy a tank or other armored vehicle; pertaining to actions against tanks.

an·tith·e·sis, an·tith′i·sis, *n. pl.* **an·tith·e·ses**, an·tith′i·sēz. [L. < Gr. *antithesis* < *anti-*, against, and *thesis*, a setting, < *tithēnai*, to place.] Opposition; contrast. *Rhet.* a figure by which contraries are opposed to contraries; a contrast or opposition of words or sentiments, as: The prodigal *robs his heir*, the miser *robs himself*.

an·ti·thet·i·cal, an″ti·thet′i·kal, *a.* Pertaining to or characterized by antithesis; opposed. Also **an·ti·thet·ic**.—**an·ti·thet·i·cal·ly**, an″ti·thet′i·kal·ē, *adv.* In an antithetical manner.

an·ti·thy·roid, an″ti·thī′roid, *a.* Capable of preventing overactivity of the thyroid.

an·ti·tox·ic, an″ti·tok′sik, an″tē·tok′sik, *a.* Counteracting poisons or toxic influences; pertaining to or serving as an antitoxin.

an·ti·tox·in, an″ti·tok′sin, an″tē·tok′sin, *n.* A substance formed in the body, capable of counteracting a specific toxin or infective agency; the antibody formed in immunization with a given toxin: used in treating certain infectious diseases or in producing immunity against them.

an·ti·trades, an′ti·trādz″, *n. pl.* The tropical winds blowing above a trade wind and in the opposite direction.

an·ti·trust, an′tē·trust″, an″tī·trust″, *a.* Referring to governmental or legal barriers against monopoly by large business combinations, as a means of limiting concentration of economic power and encouraging competition.

an·ti·tus·sive, an″ti·tus′iv, an″tī·tus′iv, *a.* Apt to control, or capable of controlling or counteracting a cough.

an·ti·type, an′ti·tīp″, *n.* [L. < Gr.] That which is correlative to a type; that which is prefigured or represented by a type.— **an·ti·typ·i·cal**, an″ti·tip′i·kal, *a.*

an·ti·ven·in, an″tē·ven′in, an″tī·ven′in, *n.* [Gr. *anti-*, against, and L. *venenum*, poison.] An antitoxin produced in the blood by repeated injections of venom, as of snakes; also, the antitoxic serum obtained from such blood. Also **an·ti·ven·ene**, an″tī·ve·nēn′, an″tē·ve·nēn′.

an·ti·vi·ta·min, an″ti·vī′ta·min, *n.* A material that makes a vitamin powerless either by changing it into a mixture of different composition or by rendering it unavailable through mixture with it.

an·ti·viv·i·sec·tion·ist, an″tē·viv·i·sek′-shan·ist, an″tī·viv·i·sek′shan·ist, *n.* One who is opposed to scientific experimentation on living animals.

ant·ler, ant′lẽr, *n.* [M.E. *aunteler* < O.Fr. *antoillier, entoillier*; < L. *ante-* and *oculus* eye.] A branch of the horn of a deer, particularly of a stag; a bony horn, usu. branched, of animals in the deer family.— **ant·lered**, ant′lẽrd, *a.* Having antlers.

an·to·no·ma·sia, an″to·no·mā′zha, *n.* [L. < Gr. *antonomasia*, < *antonomazein*, call instead, < *ant*, instead of, and *onomazein*, call, < *onoma*, name.] *Rhet.* the use of some epithet or appellative, as *His Highness*, instead of a person's name, or the use of a proper name out of its original application, as a *Shylock*.—**an·to·no·mas·tic**, an″to·nō·mas′tik, *a.*

an·to·nym, an′to·nim, *n.* A word that is opposite in meaning to another: the opposite of a *synonym*.

an·trorse, an·trạrs′, *a.* [N.L. < L. *ante-*, before, and *orsus*, turned.] *Bot.* forward or upward in direction.

an·trum, an′trum, *n. pl.* **an·tra**, an′tra. [Gr. *antron*, cave.] Chamber or cavern. *Anat.* cavity in a hollow organ; a sinus, esp. the maxillary antrum.

an·u·re·sis, an″ū·rē′sis, *n. Med.* inability to bring about the act of urination.— **an·u·ret·ic**, an″ū·ret′ik, *adj.*

an·u·ri·a, a·nūr′ē·a, a·nụr′ē·a, *n. Med.* The total suppression of urine; failure to urinate due to lack of urine.

an·u·rous, an′ūr·us, a·nūr′us, *a. Zool.* without a tail.

a·nus, ā′nus, *n.* [L., ring, anus.] *Anat.* the lower orifice of the alimentary canal.

an·vil, an′vil, *n.* [M.E. *anfilt, anvelt* < O.E. *anfealt*, < *anfilt, an-*, on, and *fealdan*, to fold.] An iron block with a smooth, usually steel face, and often a projecting horn, on which metals are hammered and shaped. The incus, a small bone of the ear.

anx·i·e·ty, ang·zī′i·tē, *n. pl.* **anx·i·e·ties**. [L. *anxietas*, < *anxius*, solicitous, < *ango*, to vex. ANGER.] Pain or uneasiness of mind respecting some event, future or uncertain; concern; solicitude; care; disquietude.

anx·ious, angk′shus, ang′shus, *a.* [L. *anxius*, akin to ANGER.] Full of anxiety or uneasiness concerning something in the future or unknown; being in painful suspense; attended with or proceeding from solicitude or uneasiness, often followed by *for, about, on account of.* Desirous; eager.—**anx·-ious·ly**, angk′shus·lē, *adv.*—**anx·ious·ness**, angk′shus·nis, *n.*

an·y, en′ē, *a.* [O.E. *ǣnig*, < *ǎn*, one.] One; a or an; quantitatively, some, whether little or much; few or many; as, *any* money, *any* eggs: in affirmative sentences, often practically equivalent to *every* or *all*, as: *Any* child knows that.

an·y, en′ē, *pron.* Any person or persons; any individual, instance, or number (of several or more possible); also, any quantity or part; *Eng. dial.* either (of two).

an·y, en′ē, *adv.* In any degree; to any extent; at all.

an·y·bod·y, en′ē·bod″ē, en′ē·bud″ē, *pron.* Any person; anyone. Anyone of importance, as: Everybody who is *anybody* was present. —*n. pl.* **an·y·bod·ies**.

an·y·how, en′ē·hou″, *adv.* In any way whatever; howsoever; in any case; at all events; carelessly; haphazardly.

an·y·more, en′ē·mōr′, *adv.* Now; contemporaneously; at this time (usually used negatively).

an·y·one, en′ē·wun″, en′ē·wun, *pron.* Any person; anybody.

an·y·place, en′ē·plās″, *adv.* In any location; in any place.

an·y·thing, en′ē·thing″, *n., pron.* Any thing, whatever it may be; a thing of any kind; something, no matter what.—*adv. Archaic.* At all; to any degree; to any extent.

an·y·thing but, *adv.* In no respect; not at all.

an·y·way, en′ē·wā″, *adv.* In any way; anyhow; to any extent; also, conjunctively, in any case; at all events.

an·y·ways, en′ē·wāz″, *adv. Dial.* anyway.

an·y·where, en′ē·hwãr″, en′ē·wãr″, *adv.* In, at, or to any place; at all; to any degree or extent.—*n.*

an·y·wise, en′ē·wīz″, *adv.* In any way, respect, or degree; at all.

An·zac, an′zak, *n.* The Australian and New Zealand Army Corps: name taken from the initial letters; an Australian or New Zealander, particularly a soldier.

a·o·rist, ā′o·rist, *n.* [Gr. *aoristos*, indefinite < *a-*, not, and *horos*, limit.] *Gram.* a tense of Greek verbs which expresses past time indefinitely, or denotes an activity without implying its completion.—**a·o·ris·tic**, ā″o·ris′tik, *a.*

a·or·ta, ā·ạr′ta, *n.* [N.L. < Gr. *aortē*, < *aeirō*, to lift, to heave.] *Anat.* the great artery or trunk of the arterial system, proceeding from the left ventricle of the heart, and giving origin to all the arteries except the pulmonary.—**a·or·tal**, **a·or·tic**, ā·ạr′tal, ā·ạr′tik, *a.* Pertaining to the aorta.

a·pace, a·pās′, *adv.* [M.E. *a pas(e)*, at a (good) pace.] With a quick pace; fast; speedily; with haste.

a·pache, a·pash′, a·päsh′, *n.* [American Indian tribe.] A French street ruffian or desperado.

ap·a·go·ge, ap·a·gō′jē, *n.* [N.L. < Gr. *apagoge*, < *apagein*, lead off, < *apo*, from, and *agein*, lead.] *Logic*, demonstration of a proposition by showing the impossibility or absurdity of the contrary.—**ap·a·gog·ic**, **ap·a·gog·i·cal**, ap·a·goj′ik, ap·a·goj′i·kal, *a.*

ap·a·nage, ap′a·nij, *n.* See *appanage.*

a·pa·re·jo, ap″a·rā′ō, ap″a·rā′hō, ä″pa·rā′ō, ä″pa·rā′hō, *n. pl.* **a·pa·re·jos**. *Sp.-Amer.* A canvas or stuffed-leather packsaddle.

a·part, a·pärt′, *adv.* [M.E. < M.Fr. *à part*, aside, separate < *à*, < L. *ad-*, to, and *part* = E. *part*, side.] Separately; in a state of separation; distinct or away from others; at some distance. Into pieces.—**a·part·ness**, a·pärt′nis, *n.* The condition of being separate.

a·part, *a·*pärt′, *a.* Isolated; in a class by itself; as, a world *apart*.

a·part from, *prep.* Aside from; besides.

a·part·heid, *a·*pärt′hāt, *a·*pärt′hīt, *n.* [Afrik. lit. separateness < *apart* and -*heit*, -*hood*.] The governmental policy of separation of the racial groups and discrimination against nonwhites, as practiced in the Republic of South Africa; racial segregation.

a·part·ment, *a·*pärt′ment, *n.* [Fr. *appartement*.] A room in a building; a division in a house separated from others by partitions; a suite, or set, of rooms comprising a dwelling unit.

a·part·ment build·ing, *n.* A building divided into rooms and groups of rooms which are rented as apartments. Also **a·part·ment house.**

ap·a·thet·ic, ap″*a·*thet′ik, *a.* Affected with or proceeding from apathy; devoid of feeling; insensible; displaying no emotion; indifferent. Also **ap·a·thet·i·cal,** ap″*a·*thet′i·kal.

ap·a·thy, ap′*a·*thē, *n.* pl. **ap·a·thies.** [L. *apathia,* Gr. *apatheia* < *apathēs,* without feeling < *a,* no, and *pathos,* suffering.] Want of feeling; privation of passion, emotion, or excitement; insensibility; indifference.

ap·a·tite, ap′*a·*tīt″, *n.* [G. *apatit* < Gr. *apatē,* deceit, from having been mistaken for other minerals.] Calcium fluorophosphate, $Ca_5FP_3O_{12}$, consisting chiefly of phosphate of lime, used as a fertilizer; any of several calcium phosphate minerals, which are found in phosphate rock, bones, and teeth.

ape, āp, *n.* [M.E. < O.E. *apa,* Icel. *api,* D. *aap,* Dan. *abe,* G. *affe,* O.H.G. *affo,* Ir. and Gael. *apa:* an initial velar has been lost, seen in Gr. *kēpos,* Skt. *kapi,* an ape.] One of a family, *Pongidae,* of large quadrumanous animals, having the teeth of the same number and form as in man, and possessing neither tails nor cheek pouches; *fig.* one who imitates servilely.—*v.t.*—*aped, aping.* To imitate servilely; to mimic.—**ap·ish,** ā′pish, *a.* Having the qualities of an ape; inclined to imitate superiors.—**ap·ish·ly,** *adv.*—**ap·ish·ness,** *n.*

a·peak, *a·*pēk′, *adv.* [< *a-,* on, and *peak.*] On the point; in a posture to pierce; vertically; *naut.* perpendicularly, or inclining to the perpendicular: said of the anchor or yards.—*a.*

ape-man, āp′man, *n.* pl. **ape-men.** A primate, representative of the transition between true man, *Homo sapiens,* and the higher apes. Also, a human thought to have been brought up by apes.

a·per·cu, A·peR′SY′, *n.* pl. **a·per·çus,** *a·*pâr′sö′. [Fr., perceived < *apercevoir,* perceive.] A glimpse; a hasty glance; a rapid survey; an outline or summary; an immediate impression.

a·per·i·ent, *a·*pēr′ē·ent, *a.* [L. *aperient-,* stem of *aperiens,* opening, ppr. of *aperire,* to open.] *Med.* Gently purgative; having the quality of opening; laxative.—*n.* A medicine which gently opens the bowels; a laxative.

a·pe·ri·od·ic, ā″pēr·ē·od′ik, *a.* Not periodic, as a fever; of irregular occurrence; *phys.* noting, pertaining to, or having an index needle or other moving part which comes to a stop with little or no recoil or oscillation.

a·pé·ri·tif, ä·per″i·tēf′, *a·*per″i·tēf′, *n.* [Fr., orig. *aperient,* opening (the bowels) < M.Fr. *adj. aperitif,* aperient < M.L. *aperitivus, adj.* < *aperīre,* open: see *aperient.*] A kind or a portion of alcoholic liquor (cordial, bitters, etc.) taken before a meal to stimulate the appetite.

ap·er·ture, ap′ẽr·chẽr, *n.* [M.E. < L. *apertura,* < *aperīre, apertum,* to open.] An opening; a mouth, hole, entrance, gap, cleft, etc.; a passage; a perforation; the diameter of the exposed part of the object glass of a telescope or other optical instrument; the opening in the front of a camera through which light rays pass when a picture is taken.

ap·er·y, ā′pe·rē, *n.* pl. **ap·er·ies,** ā·pe·rēz. Apish behavior or mimicry; an apish trick.

a·pet·al·ous, ā·pet′*a·*lus, *a.* [Gr. *a-,* neg., and *petalon,* a petal.] *Bot.* having no petals.—**a·pet·a·lous·ness,** ā·pet′*a·*lus·nis, *n.*

a·pex, ā′peks, *n.* pl. **a·pi·ces,** **a·pex·es,** ap′i·sēz″, ā′pi·sēz″. [L. *apex,* pl. *apices.*] The tip, point, summit, or climax of anything.

a·phaer·e·sis, a·pher·e·sis, *a·*fer′i·sis, *n.* [L.L. < Gr. *aphairesis,* a taking away < *aphairein,* to take away < *apo-,* from, and *haireō,* to take.] *Gram.* the taking of a letter or syllable from the beginning of a word, as *possum* from *opossum; med.* the removal of anything noxious; *surg.* amputation.

aph·a·nite, af′*a·*nīt″, *n.* [Gr. *aphanes,* indistinct < *a-,* not, and *phainein,* to bring to light.] Fine-grained igneous rock whose separate grains cannot be detected by the naked eye.—**aph·a·nit·ic,** af″*a·*nit′ik, *a.* Pertaining or similar to aphanite.

a·pha·sia, *a·*fā′zha, *n.* [N.L. < Gr. *a-,* not, *phasis,* speech.] Loss of the faculty of speech, or of connecting words and ideas, resulting from damage to brain tissue, while the speech organs and general intelligence remain unaffected.

a·phe·li·on, *a·*fē′lē·on, *a·*fēl′yon, ap·hē′lē·on, *n.* pl. **a·phe·li·a,** *a·*fē′lē·*a, a·*fēl′ya, ap·hē′lē·*a.* [N.L. < Gr. *apo-,* from, and *hēlios,* the sun.] That point of a planet's or comet's orbit which is most distant from the sun: opposed to *perihelion.*

a·phe·mi·a, *a·*fē′mē·*a, n.* [N.L. < Gr. *a-* priv. and *pheme,* voice.] *Pathol.* motor aphasia, esp. a form marked by inability to express ideas in spoken words.—**a·phem·ic,** *a·*fēm′ik, *a.*

aph·e·sis, af′i·sis, *n.* [N.L. < Gr. *aphesis,* a letting go < *apo-* and *hienai,* to send.] Loss of a short unaccented syllable or vowel at the beginning of a word, as *squire* for *esquire.*—**a·phet·ic,** *a·*fet′ik, *a.*

a·phid, ā′fid, af′id, *n.* [Back formation from *aphides,* pl. of *aphis.* APHIS.] A homopterous insect of the family *Aphidae.* The aphids are small insects, some of them wingless; they are very numerous and destructive, almost every species of plant supporting a different variety; a plant louse.—**a·phid·i·an,** *a·*fid′ē·an, *a.* Pertaining to the aphids.

a·phis, ā′fis, af′is, *n.* pl. **a·phi·des,** af′i·dēz″. [N.L.], coined by Linnaeus, perhaps < Gr. *aphysso* to draw or drink up liquids.] An aphid; a plant louse.

a·phis-li·on, ā′fis·lī″an, af′is·lī″an, *n.* Any of various insect larvae, as those of the lacewings, that prey on plant lice or aphids; also the adult insects. Also **a·phid-li·on.**

a·phis-sug·ar, ā′fis·shug′ar, *n.* Honeydew secreted by plant lice.

a·pho·ni·a, ā·fō′nē·*a, n.* [N.L. < Gr. < *a-,* not, and *phōnē,* voice.] A loss of voice; dumbness; speechless.—**a·phon·ic,** ā·fon′·ik, *a.* Destitute of voice.

aph·o·rism, af′o·riz″um, *n.* [M.L. < Gr. *aphorismos,* < *aphorizō,* to mark out, to define < *apo-,* from, and *horos,* a boundary.] A precept or principle expressed in a few words; a brief sentence containing some important truth; a maxim. *Aphorism* is the brief statement of a doctrine. *Axiom,* a statement claiming to be considered as a self-evident truth. *Maxim,* a formula referring rather to practical than to abstract truth; a rule of conduct. *Apophthegm,* a terse sententious saying.—**aph·o·rist,** af′o·rist, *n.* A writer of aphorisms.—**aph·o·ris·tic,** af″o·ris′tik, *a.* Pertaining to, resembling, or containing aphorisms; in the form of an aphorism.—**aph·o·ris·ti·cal·ly,** af″o·ris′ti·kal·ē, *adv.* In the form or manner of aphorisms.

aph·o·rize, af′o·riz″, *v.i.*—*aphorized, aphorizing.* To make aphorisms.

a·pho·tic, ā·fō′tik, *a.* Dark; without light.

aph·ro·dis·i·ac, af″ro·diz′ē·ak″, *a.* [Gr. *aphrodisios, aphrodisiakos,* < *Aphrodite,* goddess of love.] Exciting sexual desire.—*n.* Food or a medicine exciting sexual desire.

Aph·ro·di·te, af″ro·dī′tē, *n.* [Gr. *Aphroditē.*] The Greek goddess of love and beauty, identified by the Romans with Venus.

a·phyl·lous, ā·fil′us, *a.* [Gr. < *a-,* neg., and *phyllon,* a leaf.] *Bot.* destitute of leaves.

a·pi·an, ā′pē·an, *a.* [L. *apianus* < *apis,* bee.] Of or concerning bees.

a·pi·ar·i·an, ā″pē·âr′ē·an, *a.* Relating to bees.—*n.* A beekeeper; an apiarist.

a·pi·a·rist, ā′pē·*a·*rist, *n.* One who keeps bees.

a·pi·a·ry, ā′pē·er″ē, *n.* pl. **a·pi·ar·ies.** [L. *apiarium,* < *apis,* a bee.] The place where bees are kept for their honey; a stand or shed for bees.

ap·i·cal, ap′i·kal, ā′pi·kal, *a.* [L. *apex,* an apex, a sharp point or peak.] Relating to the apex or top; belonging to the pointed end of a cone-shaped body; *phon.* spoken mainly with the help of the tip of the tongue.

a·pic·u·late, *a·*pik′yu·lit, *a·*pik′yu·lāt, *a.* [N.L. dim. of L. *apex.*] *Bot.* tipped with a short and abrupt point.

a·pi·cul·ture, ā′pi·kul″chẽr, *n.* [L. *apis,* bee, and *cultura,* culture.] The rearing of bees; beekeeping, esp. for commercial purposes.—**a·pi·cul·tur·al,** ā″pi·kul·tur′al, *a.*—**a·pi·cul·tur·ist,** ā″pi′·kul′chẽr·ist, *n.* A beekeeper.

a·piece, *a·*pēs′, *adv.* To each, as the share of each, as: Two dollars *apiece* was their reward. Each by itself; by the individual.

ap·ish, ā′pish, *a.* Of, like, or befitting an ape; senselessly imitative; foolishly affected; ridiculous.—**ap·ish·ly,** ā′pish·lē, *adv.*—**ap·ish·ness,** ā′pish·nis, *n.*

a·piv·or·ous, ā·piv′or·us, *a.* [L. *apis,* bee and *vorare,* devour.] Feeding on bees, as certain birds.

a·pla·cen·tal, ā″pla·sen′tal, ap″la·sen′tal, *a.* Applied to those mammals in which the young are destitute of a placenta, as the kangaroo or duck mole.

ap·la·nat·ic, ap″la·nat′ik, *a.* [Gr. *a-,* not, and *planao,* to wander. PLANET.] *Optics,* corrective of the defect by which rays of light diverge and do not come to a focus; as, an *aplanatic* lens.

a·pla·sia, *a·*plā′zha, *n.* [N.L. < Gr. *a-* priv. and *plassein,* form.] Congenital absence or defective development of a tissue or organ.—**a·plas·tic,** ā·plas′tik, *a.* Characterized by aplasia.

ap·lite, ap′līt, *n.* A fine-grained granite, mostly containing quartz and feldspar. Also **hap·lite.**

a·plomb, *a·*plom′, *a·*plum′, *n.* [Fr. *a plomb,* the state of being perpendicular, or true to the plumb line.] Self-possession springing from perfect self-confidence; assurance; poise.

a·poc·a·lypse, *a·*pok′*a·*lips, *n.* [M.E. < L. < Gr. *apocalypsis,* < *apocalyptein,* uncover, < *apo-,* from, and *calyptein,* cover.] A revelation; esp., any of a class of writings (apocalyptic literature), Jewish and Christian, which appeared from about 200 B.C. to 350 A.D., assuming to make revelation of the ultimate divine purpose; *(cap.)* the book of Revelation, the last book of the New Testament.—**a·poc·a·lyp·tic,** *a·*pok″*a·*lip′tik, *a.* Pertaining to or of the nature of an apocalypse; affording a revelation; esp., pertaining to the Apocalypse, or book of Revelation.—*n.* Apocalyptic writing or literature.—**a·poc·a·lyp·ti·cal,** *a·*pok″*a·*lip′ti·kal, *a.* Apocalyptic.

ap·o·chro·mat·ic, ap″*o*·krō·mat′ik, ap″-ō·kro·mat′ik, *a. Optics,* corrected for spherical and chromatic aberration.

a·poc·o·pe, a·pok′o·pē, *n.* [L. < Gr. *apokopē,* a cutting off.] Omission of the last letter or syllable of a word, as *th'* for *the.*—**a·poc·o·pate,** a·pok′o·pāt, *v.t.*—*apocopated, apocopating.* To cut off or drop the last letter or syllable of.

A·poc·ry·pha, a·pok′ra·fa, *n.* [M.E. < L. < Gr. *apokryphos,* hidden, spurious < *apo-,* away, and *krypto,* to conceal. CRYPT.] The collective name of 14 books, not considered canonical, which are included in the Old Testament in the Vulgate and Septuagint versions, but not in Protestant or Jewish editions; (*l.c.*) any writings of doubtful origin or authenticity.

a·poc·ry·phal, a·pok′ri·fal, *a.* (*Cap.*) pertaining to the Apocrypha. Not canonical; of uncertain authority or credit; fictitious. —**a·poc·ry·phal·ly,** a·pok′ri·fal·ē, *adv.* In an apocryphal manner; equivocally; doubtfully.—**a·poc·ry·phal·ness,** a·pok′ri·fal·nis, *n.*

ap·o·dal, ap′o·dal, *a.* Having no feet; said of fishes, having no ventral fins, as the eel, swordfish, etc.

ap·o·dic·tic, ap′o·dik′tik, *a.* [L. < Gr. *apodeiktikos* < *apo-,* forth, and *deiknynai,* to show.] Demonstrable; evident beyond contradiction. Also **ap·o·dic·ti·cal,** ap″o·dik′ti·kal.—**ap·o·dic·ti·cal·ly,** ap″o·dik′ti·kal·ē, *adv.*

ap·o·en·zyme, ap″ō·en′zīm, *n. Biochem.* a protein, which, in combination with a co-enzyme, forms an enzymatically active system, and determines the substrate specificity of the system.

a·pog·a·my, a·pog′a·mē, *n.* [Gr. *apo-,* from, and *gamos,* marriage.] *Bot.* reproduction by processes other than fertilization. *Zool.* mating or pairing at random; interbreeding of all varieties.

ap·o·gee, ap′o·jē, *n.* [L. < Gr. < *apo-,* from, and *gē,* the earth.] That point in the orbit of a planet or other heavenly body which is at the greatest distance from the earth, as opposed to *perigee;* properly, this particular point of the moon's orbit; the farthest point away; the highest attainment.

ap·o·graph, ap′o·graf″, ap′o·gräf″, *n.* [L. < Gr. *apographon, apographein,* write off.] A copy or transcript, as of a manuscript.

a·polit·i·cal, ā·po·lit′i·kal, ä·po·lit′i·kal, *a.* Having repugnance for, or disinterest in, politics, with no involvement. Having no importance politically.

A·pol·lo, a·pol′ō, *n.* [L. < Gr. *Apollon.*] A Greek and Roman deity, the god of light, health and healing, music, poetry, prophecy, etc., represented as the highest type of youthful manly beauty; a well-formed, handsome young man. A spacecraft equipped to carry a three-man crew into space and land on the moon.

Ap·ol·lo·ni·an, ap″o·lō′nē·an, *a.* About, referring to, or resembling the Greek god Apollo; well-balanced in character; harmonious.

A·pol·lyon, a·pol′yon, *n.* [Gr. < *apollūmi,* to destroy.] The Devil; the destroying angel from hell.

a·pol·o·get·ic, a·pol″o·jet′ik, *a.* Of or pertaining to or containing apology; defending by words or arguments; regretful. Also **a·pol·o·get·i·cal,** a·pol″o·jet′i·kal.—**a·pol·o·get·i·cal·ly,** a·pol″o·jet′i·kal·ē, *adv.* In an apologetic manner; by way of apology.

a·pol·o·get·ics, a·pol″o·jet′iks, *n. pl. but sing. in constr.* That branch of theology by which Christians are enabled scientifically to justify and defend the precepts of their faith, and to answer its opponents.

a·pol·o·gist, a·pol′o·jist, *n.* One who makes a defense of a cause; one who apologizes in speech or writing. Also **a·pol·o·giz·er,** a·pol′o·jīz″ĕr.

a·pol·o·gize, a·pol′o·jīz″, *v.i.*—*apologized, apologizing.* To make an apology. To offer an excuse for some injustice.

ap·o·logue, ap′o·lâg″, ap′o·log″, *n.* [Fr. < L. < Gr. *apologos,* an apologue, a fable.] A moral fable; a fictitious account intended to convey useful truths, such as the fables of Aesop; an allegory.

a·pol·o·gy, a·pol′o·jē, *n. pl.* **a·pol·o·gies.** [M.Fr. < L. < Gr. *apologia,* a speech in defense.] Something said or written in defense; justification; vindication; an acknowledgment, usu. accompanied by an expression of regret, for some improper remark or act; *colloq.* a poor substitute or makeshift.

ap·o·mor·phine, ap″o·mạr′fēn, ap″o·mạr′fin, *n. Chem.* an artificial crystalline alkaloid, $C_{17}H_{17}NO_2$, prepared from morphine: used in the form of the hydrochloride as an emetic and expectorant.

ap·o·neu·ro·sis, ap″o·nụ·rō′sis, *n. pl.* **ap·o·neu·ro·ses,** ap″o·nụ·rō′sēz. [N.L. < Gr. *aponeurosis* < *apo-,* from, and *neuron,* a nerve, because formerly supposed to be an expansion of a nerve or nerves.] A white, shining, and very resistant membrane, composed of interlaced fibers, found surrounding the voluntary muscles, large arteries, and other parts of the body, and formed by the expansion of a tendon.—**ap·o·neu·rot·ic,** ap″o·nụ·rot′ik, *a.* Relating to the aponeuroses.

ap·o·pemp·tic, ap″o·pemp′tik, *a.* [Gr. *apopempticos,* < *apopempein,* send away.] Pertaining to sending away; valedictory.

a·poph·a·sis, a·pof′a·sis, *n.* [L.L. < Gr. *apophasis,* denial, < *apophanai,* deny.] *Rhet.* denial of an intention to speak of something which is at the same time hinted or insinuated.

a·poph·y·sis, a·pof′i·sis, *n. pl.* **a·poph·y·ses,** a·pof′i·sēz″. [N.L. < Gr. < *apo-,* from, and *physis,* growth.] *Anat.* A prominence; an outgrowth; a projecting part of a bone.—**ap·o·phys·e·al,** ap″o·fiz′ē·al, *a.*

ap·o·plec·tic, ap″o·plek′tik, *a.* Pertaining to or consisting in apoplexy; predisposed to apoplexy. Also **ap·o·plec·ti·cal,** ap″o·plek′ti·kal.—*n.* A person affected with apoplexy.

ap·o·plex·y, ap′o·plek″sē, *n.* [M.E. < L.L. < Gr. *apoplexia.*] *Pathol.* abolition or sudden diminution of sensation and voluntary motion, resulting from congestion or rupture of a blood vessel of the brain.

a·port, a·pōrt′, a·pạrt′, *adv., a. Naut.* To port; to the left.

ap·o·se·mat·ic, ap″o·se·mat′ik, *a.* [Gr. *apo-,* and *sēma,* sign.] *Zool.* Of an obvious nature; in the nature of a warning.

ap·o·si·o·pe·sis, ap″o·sī″o·pē′sis, *n. pl.* **ap·o·si·o·pe·ses.** [L.L. < Gr. < *apo-,* from, and *siopaein,* to be silent.] *Rhet.* sudden stopping short and leaving a thought or statement unfinished for the sake of effect.

a·pos·ta·sy, a·pos′ta·sē, *n. pl.* **a·pos·ta·sies.** [M.E. < L.L. < Gr. *apostasia,* a revolt, a defection < *apo-,* from, and root *sta,* to stand.] An abandonment of what one has professed; a total desertion or departure from one's faith, principles, or party.

a·pos·tate, a·pos′tāt, a·pos′tit, *n.* One who has forsaken his faith, principles, or party. —*a.* False, traitorous.

a·pos·ta·tize, a·pos′ta·tīz″, *v.i.*—*apostatized, apostatizing.* To commit apostasy; to abandon principles, religious faith, or party; to defect.

a pos·te·ri·o·ri, ā″po·stēr″ē·ôr′ī, ā″po·stēr″ē·ạr′ī, ā″po·stēr″ē·ôr′ē, ạr′ē, *a.* [L. *posterior,* after.] Founded on observation of effects, consequences, or facts; from effect to cause; inductive: opposed to *a priori.*

a·pos·tle, a·pos′el, *n.* [O.E. *apostol* < L.L < Gr. *apostolos, lit.* one sent forth, a messenger < *apo-,* forth, and *stellō,* to send.] One of the Twelve Disciples of Christ, who were commissioned to preach the gospel; one regarded as having a similar mission. A person who advocates a large moral reformation or new practices. A high ecclesiastical office in some sects; a member of the Mormon 12-man administration.—**a·pos·tle·ship,** a·pos′el·ship″, *n.*

A·pos·tles′ Creed, *n.* A traditional Christian creed originally attributed to the Twelve Apostles.

a·pos·to·late, a·pos′to·lāt″, a·pos′to·lit, *n.* The dignity, mission, or office of an apostle; the dignity or office of the pope, the holder of the apostolic see.

ap·os·tol·ic, ap″o·stol′ik, *a.* Pertaining or relating to or characteristic of an apostle, more especially of the Twelve Apostles; according to the doctrines of the Apostles; proceeding from an apostle. Also **ap·os·tol·i·cal,** ap″o·stol′i·kal.—**Ap·os·tol·ic see,** the see of the bishop of Rome, as directly founded by the apostle Peter.—**ap·os·tol·ic suc·ces·sion,** the uninterrupted succession of popes, and, through them, of bishops in the church by regular ordination from the first Apostles down to the present day.

ap·os·tol·ic del·e·gate, *n.* A papal representative to a country having no steady diplomatic relationships with the Vatican.

Ap·os·tol·ic Fa·thers, *n. pl.* A group of church fathers of the first or second century A.D. who were reported to have known or been familiar with one of the Apostles.

a·pos·tro·phe, a·pos′tro·fē, *n.* [L.L. < Gr. *apostrophos,* elision < *apostrephein* < *apo-* and *strephein,* to turn away.] The sign (') which indicates the omission of a letter or letters from a word, as in *don't,* the possessive case in nouns, or the plural of numerals or letters, as in *the three R's.* A direct address to a person not present, or to a thing personified for purposes of rhetoric.

a·poth·e·car·ies′ meas·ure, *n.* The system of units used in the U.S. in compounding and dispensing liquid drugs.

a·poth·e·car·ies′ weight, *n.* A system of weights used in compounding and dispensing drugs. The grain, ounce, and pound are the same as in troy weight, the grain alone being the same as in avoirdupois weight.

a·poth·e·car·y, a·poth′e·ker″ē, *n. pl.* **a·poth·e·car·ies,** a·poth′e·ker″ēz. [M.E. < M.L. < L. *apotheca,* storehouse, < Gr. *apothece,* < *apo-,* from, and *tithenai,* put, set.] One who prepares and sells drugs or medicines; a pharmacist, a druggist; a pharmacy.

ap·o·thegm, ap·o·phthegm, ap′o·them″, *n.* [Gr. *apo-,* from, and *phtegma,* word.] A short, pithy, and instructive saying; a sententious precept or maxim.—**ap·o·theg·mat·ic, ap·o·theg·mat·i·cal,** ap″o·theg·mat′ik, ap″o·theg·mat′i·kal, *a.* Pertaining to or having the character of an apothegm; containing or using apothegms; sententious.—**ap·o·theg·mat·ize,** ap″o·theg′ma·tīz, *v.i.* To utter apothegms.—**ap·o·theg·ma·tist,** ap″o·theg′ma·tist, *n.*

ap·o·them, ap′o·them″, *n.* [N.L. < Gr.] *Geom.* a perpendicular from the center of a regular polygon to one of its sides.

a·poth·e·o·sis, a·poth″ē·ō′sis, ap″o·thē′o·sis, *n. pl.* **a·poth·e·o·ses.** [L.L. < Gr. *apo-,* and *theos,* God.] Deification; the placing or ranking of a person among deities; the glorification of a person.—**a·poth·e·o·size,** a·poth′ē·o·sīz″, ap″o·thē′o·sīz″, *v.t.* To exalt to the dignity of a deity; to deify.

Ap·pa·la·chi·an, ap·a·lach′ē·an, ap″a·lā′chē·an, ap″a·lā′chan, *a.* [< the *Apalachi* Indians.] Noting or pertaining to a system of mountains in eastern North America, extending from Cape Gaspé, in the province of Quebec, to northern Alabama, and divided into many ranges bearing separate names. Esp. in the U.S., the areas within its borders.

ap·pall, ap·pal, a·pạl', v.t.—appalled, appalling. [M.E. < M.Fr. < O.Fr. appalir, to make pale, < ap- for ad-, and palle, pale, < L. pallidus, pallid.] To impress with overpowering fear; to confound with terror; to dismay.—**ap·pall·ing**, a·pạl'ing, a.—**ap·pall·ing·ly**, a·pạl'ing·lē, adv.

ap·pa·nage, ap'a·nij, n. [Fr. appanage, apanage, < O.Fr. apaner, L.L. apanare, to furnish with bread < L. ad-, to, and panis, bread.] An allowance to the younger branches of a sovereign house out of the revenues of the country, generally together with a grant of public domains; whatever belongs or falls to one from rank or station in life. A natural endowment or attribute; also apanage.

ap·pa·rat·us, ap"a·rat'us, ap"a·rā'tus, n. pl. **ap·pa·rat·us, ap·pa·rat·us, ap"a·rat'us·ez, ap·pa·rā'tus·ez**. [L. < apparare, to prepare < ad-, and paro, to make ready.] Things provided as means to some end; a collection or combination of articles or materials for the accomplishment of some purpose, operation, or experiment; the organization of a group or movement, often political and conspiratorial; physiol. a collection of organs all ministering to the same function.

ap·par·el, a·par'el, n. [M.E. < O.Fr. apareillier to fit < L. apparare < a-, to, and parare, to fit.] Clothing; vesture; garments; dress; external array. Naut. the masts, sails, furniture, etc., of a ship.

ap·par·el, a·par'el, v.t.—appareled, appareling. To dress or clothe; to cover, as with garments; to adorn.

ap·par·ent, a·par'ent, a·pâr'ent, a. [M.E. < O.Fr. < L. apparens, apparentis, < apparēre. APPEAR.] Visible to the eye; within sight or view; appearing to the eye or to the judgment; seeming, often in distinction to real; obvious; plain; capable of being understood; evident: in the latter sense now used only as a predicate.—**heir ap·par·ent**, the heir who is certain to inherit if he survives the present holder; one who has a claim.—**ap·par·ent·ly**, a·par'ent·lē, a·pâr'ent·lē, adv. Openly; evidently; seemingly; in appearance.—**ap·par·ent·ness**, a·par'ent·nis, a·pâr'ent·nis, n.

ap·pa·ri·tion, ap"a·rish'an, n. [M.E. L.L. < L. apparēre. APPEAR.] The act of appearing; manifestation; appearance; the thing appearing, especially a ghost; a specter; a visible spirit.—**ap·pa·ri·tion·al**, ap"a·rish'a·nal, a.

ap·par·i·tor, a·par'i·tor, n. [L. < apparitus < apparēre, to attend. APPEAR.] A messenger or officer of a magistrate or court.

ap·peal, a·pēl', v.i.[M.E. < M.Fr. appeler, < L. appellare, to call, address, appeal to.] To call, as for aid, mercy, sympathy, and the like; to refer to another person or authority for a decision or vindication; law, to refer to a higher judge or court for a final settlement.—v.t. Law, to remove (a case) from an inferior to a superior judge or court; archaic, to charge with a crime. To accuse.—n. A call for sympathy, mercy, aid, and the like; a supplication; an entreaty; law, the removal of a case or suit from an inferior to a superior court. A challenge; a reference to another for proof or decision; recourse; as, an appeal to arms; attraction. —**ap·peal·a·ble**, a·pēl'a·bl, a. Liable to be appealed; removable to a higher tribunal for decision.—**ap·peal·er**, a·pēl'ėr, n. One who appeals; an appellant.

ap·pear, a·pēr', v.i. [M.E. < O.Fr. apparoir < L. appārēre show oneself.] To

come in sight; to become visible to the eye; to stand in the presence of one; to be obvious; to perform publicly; to be clear or made clear by evidence; to seem; to look like.

ap·pear·ance, a·pēr'ans, n. The act of appearing or coming into sight; a coming into the presence of a person or persons; the thing seen; a phenomenon; an apparition; external show; semblance, in opposition to reality or substance; mien; build and carriage; figure; law, the coming into court of a party to a legal action, or his lawyer.

ap·peas·a·ble, a·pēz'a·bl, a. Capable of being appeased.

ap·pease, a·pēz', v.t.—appeased, appeasing. [M.E. < O.Fr. apaisier, to pacify < a-, < L. ad-, to, and pais < L. pax, pacis, peace.] To make quiet; to still; to assuage, as hunger; to tranquilize; to calm or pacify (a person, anger); to seek peace by yielding to the terms of (an adversary).—**ap·pease·ment**, a·pēz'ment, n. Act of appeasing; appeased state.— **ap·peas·er**, a·pēz'ėr, n. One who appeases.

ap·pel·lant, a·pel'ant, n. One who appeals, as from a judicial verdict; one who removes a case to a higher tribunal.

ap·pel·late, a·pel'it, a. Relating to appeals; having cognizance of appeals; law, having the authority to hear and decide appeals from the decisions of a lower court.

ap·pel·la·tion, ap"e·lā'shan, n. [L. appel-lātiō, < appellāre, to address, accost, appeal to.] The word by which a thing or person is known; name; title.

ap·pel·la·tive, a·pel'a·tiv, a. Referring to a common noun; serving as an appellation; name-giving or marking out; denominative. —n. An appellation; a descriptive name; gram. a common noun.

ap·pel·lee, ap"e·lē', n. Law, one against whom an appeal is brought.

ap·pend, a·pend', v.t. [L. appendere < ad-, to, and pendere, to hang. PENDANT.] To hang on or attach; to add, as accessory or adjunct to a thing; to subjoin; to annex.

ap·pen·dage, a·pen'dij, n. Something appended or attached to a greater thing; a subordinate part.

ap·pend·ant, a·pen'dant, a. Hanging to; rightfully belonging to; annexed; attached as an appendage.—n.

ap·pen·dec·to·my, ap"en·dek'to·mē, n. [N.L. < appendix (vermiformis) and -ectomy.] Surg. excision of the vermiform appendix; also **ap·pen·di·cec·to·my**, a·pen"di·sek'to·mē.

ap·pen·di·ci·tis, a·pen"di·sī'tis, n. [N.L. < appendix and -itis.] Inflammation of the vermiform appendix, a small hollow blind process attached to the cecum in man and some animals.

ap·pen·dic·u·lar, ap"en·dik'ū·lar, a. Relating to an appendage or limb; as, appendicular skeleton.

ap·pen·dix, a·pen'diks, n. pl. **ap·pen·dix·es, ap·pen·di·ces**, a·pen'di·sēz". [L. appendix, appendicis, < appendere. APPEND.] Something appended or added; an addition appended to a book relating, but not essential, to the main work; anat. an appendage, process, or projecting part esp. the vermiform appendix.

ap·per·ceive, ap"ėr·sēv', v.t.—apperceived, apperceiving. [M.E. < O.Fr. aperceivre, < L. ad-, to, and percipere, perceive.] To perceive. Psychol. to be conscious of perceiving; comprehend.

ap·per·cep·tion, ap"ėr·sep'shan, n. Perception; apprehension. Psychol. conscious perception; a voluntary mental activity accompanied with self-consciousness; also, the assimilation of a new perception or idea by a group or mass of ideas already present in the mind.—**ap·per·cep·tive**, ap"ėr·sep'tiv, a. Pertaining to apperception.— **ap·per·cep·tive·ly**, ap"ėr·sep'tiv·lē, adv.

ap·per·tain, ap"ėr·tān', v.i. [M.E. < O.Fr. apertenir < L. ad-, and pertinēre, to pertain.] To belong or pertain: with to.

ap·pe·tence, ap'i·tens, n. [L. appetentia, < appetens, appetentis, ppr. of appetere, < ad-, and petere, to desire. PETITION.] Desire; inclination; propensity; strong natural craving or tendency; appetite. Also **ap·pe·ten·cy**, ap'i·ten·sē.

ap·pe·tite, ap'i·tīt", n. [M.E. < M.Fr. < L. appetitus, < appetere < ad- and petere, to desire.] The natural desire for pleasure or good; taste; inclination; preference; a desire to supply a bodily want or craving; a desire for food or drink; eagerness or longing.—**ap·pe·ti·tive**, ap'i·tī"tiv, a. Relating to appetite.

ap·pe·tiz·er, ap'i·tī"zėr, n. A food or drink served before a meal to whet the appetite.

ap·pe·tiz·ing, ap'i·tī"zing, a. Whetting the appetite; appealing or tempting to the appetite.

ap·plaud, a·plạd', v.t. [L. applaudere, applausum < ad-, and plaudere, to make a noise by clapping the hands.] To show approbation of by clapping the hands, acclamation, or other significant sign; to praise highly; to extol.—v.i. To give praise; to express approbation; to give approval.

ap·plause, a·plạz', n. [M.L. applausus, a clashing noise < L., pp. of applaudere.] Praise loudly expressed; approbation expressed by clapping the hands or shouting; commendation; approval.—**ap·plau·sive**, a·plạ'siv, a·plạ'ziv, a. Applauding; containing applause.

ap·ple, ap'l, n. [M.E. < O.E., aeppel, aepl, a word common to the Teutonic, Celtic, Slavonic, and Lithuanian tongues; root unknown.] A fleshy, red or yellow fruit of the apple tree, Malus pumila, or the tree itself; also, a name popularly given to various exotic fruits or trees having little or nothing in common with the apple, as the pineapple, etc.—**ap·ple of one's eye**, a precious object or person.

ap·ple·jack, ap'pl·jak", n. A brandy product distilled from apple cider; a beverage that is taken from the liquid center of a container of frozen cider.

ap·ple-pie, ap'l·pī", a. Perfect or excellent; as, in apple-pie order.

Ap·ple·ton lay·er, ap'pl·ton lā'ėr, n. [After the British physicist, Sir E. V. Appleton.] F layer.

ap·pli·ance, a·plī'ans, n. The act of applying; the thing applied; a device, esp. an electrical or gas-operated household device as a toaster, refrigerator, etc.; an application.

ap·pli·ca·bil·i·ty, ap"li·ka·bil'i·tē, n. pl. **ap·pli·ca·bil·i·ties**. The quality of being applicable.

ap·pli·ca·ble, ap'li·ka·bl, a·plik'a·bl, a. [< L. applic(āre), to apply.] Capable of being applied; fit to be applied; having relevance.—**ap·pli·ca·ble·ness**, ap'li·ka·bl·nis, n. The state or quality of being applicable.—**ap·pli·ca·bly**, ap'li·ka·blē, adv.

ap·pli·cant, ap'li·kant, n. [< L. applicant-, stem of applicans, applying, ppr. of applicāre, to apply.] One who applies; a petitioner; a candidate.

ap·pli·ca·tion, ap·li·kā'shan, n. [M.E. applicacioun < L. applicatio(n-), inclination < applicatus, applied, pp. of applicare, to apply.] The act of applying or putting to use; the thing applied; the act of requesting or soliciting; close study; attention; the testing of something theoretical by applying it in practice; a form asking for admission, employment, etc.

ap·pli·ca·tive, ap'li·kā"tiv, a·plik'a·tiv, a. Having an application; pertaining to that which may be applied. Also **ap·pli·ca·to·ry**.

---

a- fat, fãte, fär, fâre, fạll; e- met, mē, mēre, hėr; i- pin, pīne; o- not, nōte, mōve; u- tub, cūbe, bụll; oi- oil; ou- pound.

ap·pli·ca·tor, ap'li·kā"tor, n. Any device for applying medicine, cosmetics, chemicals, etc.

ap·plied, a·plīd', a. Put or affixed to something (as, *applied* ornaments in needle-work); also, put to practical use, as a science when its laws are employed and exemplified in dealing with concrete phenomena (distinguished from *abstract, theoretical,* or *pure*).

ap·pli·er, a·plī'ér, n. One who applies.

ap·pli·qué, ap"li·kā', a. [Fr., pp. of *appliquer,* to put on < L. *applicāre,* to apply.] Applied; formed with ornamentation of one material sewed or otherwise applied to another.—n. Work so formed.

ap·pli·qué, ap"li·kā', v.t.—*appliquéd, appliquéing.* To sew an appliqué to (a background); to apply or form as in appliqué work.

ap·ply, a·plī', v.t.—*applied, applying.* [M.E. *applien* < O.Fr. *applier,* < L. *applicare,* to fasten to < *ad-,* to, and *plicāre,* to fold. PLY.] To lay on (the hand to a table); to put or place on another thing; to use or employ for a particular purpose or in a particular case (a remedy, a sum of money); to put, refer, or use as suitable or relative to some person or thing (a proverb, etc.); to engage and employ with attention; to occupy (the mind).—v.i. To suit; to agree; to have some connection, agreement, analogy, or reference; to make request; to solicit; to have recourse with a view to gain something; followed by *to.*

ap·point, a·point', v.t. [M.E. *appointen* < O.Fr. *apointier* (Fr. *appointer*) to arrange.] To assign authoritatively to a particular use, task, or office; allot; designate; also, to equip or provide with requisites or accessories (now only in *appointed,* pp.).—**ap·point·a·ble,** a·point'a·bl, a.—**ap·point·er,** n.

ap·point·ee, a·poin·tē', a·"poin·tē', n. A person appointed; a beneficiary under a legal appointment.—**ap·poin·tor,** a·poin'tèr, n.

ap·poin·tive, a·poin'tiv, a. Pertaining to, subject to, or dependent on appointment.

ap·point·ment, a·point'ment, n. [M.E. *appoyntement* < M.F. *appointement.*] The act of appointing; ordainment, or an ordinance; designation to office, or the office; assignment, as, in law, of the use of an estate created under a preceding deed or will; engagement, as for a meeting; *usu. pl.* equipment, or a requisite or accessory of equipment.

ap·por·tion, a·pōr'shan, a·par'shan, v.t. [M.Fr. *apportionner* < a- < L. *ad-,* and *portionner,* to portion.] To divide and assign in just proportion according to a definite rule; to distribute in proper shares; to allot.

ap·por·tion·ment, a·pōr'shan·ment, n. The act of apportioning. The apportioning of elective districts or the number of members in any legislative body, esp. the number of members in the U.S. House of Representatives.

ap·pose, a·pōz', v.t.—*apposed, apposing.* [M.Fr. *apposer,* to set before, < a- < L. *ad-,* to, and *poser,* put, but associated with derivatives of L. *apponere:* see *apposite, apposition.*] To put, as a thing to another thing, usu. used with *to;* apply; also, to place next, as one thing to another; place side by side, as two things.—**ap·pos·a·ble,** a·pōz'a·bl, a.

ap·po·site, ap'o·zit, a·poz'it, a. [L. *appositus,* set or put to, pp. of *apponere, appositum* < *ad,-* and *pono,* to place or put.] Suitable; fit; appropriate; relevant; very applicable; well adapted: said of answers, arguments, etc.—**ap·po·site·ly,** ap'o·zit·-lē, adv. In an apposite manner; suitably; fitly.—**ap·po·site·ness,** ap'o·zit·nis, n. The state or quality of being apposite; fitness.

ap·po·si·tion, ap"o·zish'an, n. The act of adding layer upon layer; addition; a setting to; the act of bringing into juxtaposition; *gram.* the relationship between two nouns or noun phrases which are immediately adjacent in a sentence, the second being set off by commas, and which refer to the same object or person, as *Cicero, the orator,* was there.—**ap·po·si·tion·al,** ap"o·zish'a·nal, a. Pertaining to apposition.

ap·pos·i·tive, a·poz'i·tiv, a. Placed in apposition. *Gram.* of an adjectival phrase or adjective, coming right after the noun it modifies.—n. A word in apposition.

ap·prais·al, a·prā'zal, n. Evaluation; price set by an appraiser.

ap·praise, a·prāz', v.t.—*appraised, appraising.* [M.E. *appreisen* < M.Fr. *apprisier,* to appraise. PRAISE, PRICE, PRECIOUS.] To set a price upon; to estimate the value of under the direction of a competent authority; to estimate generally.—**ap·-praise·ment,** a·prāz'ment, n. The act of appraising; the value fixed; the valuation.—**ap·prais·er,** a·prāz'ér, n. One who appraises; a person licensed and sworn to estimate and fix the value of goods and estate.

ap·pre·ci·a·ble, a·prē'shē·a·bl, a·prē'sha·bl, a. Capable of being appreciated or estimated; sufficiently great to be capable of estimation or of being measured.—**ap·-pre·ci·a·bly,** adv. To a degree that may be appreciated or estimated; perceptibly.

ap·pre·ci·ate, a·prē'shē·āt", v.t.—*appreciated, appreciating.* [< L.L. *appretiatus,* valued, pp. of *appretiāre* < *ad-* and *pretium,* price.] To be grateful for; to regard highly; to esteem or value properly; to set a just price, value, or estimate on.—v.i. To rise in value; to become of more value.—**ap·pre·ci·a·to·ry,** a·prē'shē·a·tōr"ē, a·prē'shē-a·tar"ē, a·prē'sha·tōr"ē, a·prē'sha·tar"ē, a. Pertaining to appreciation.

ap·pre·ci·a·tion, a·prē"shē·ā'shan, n. The act of appreciating; the act of valuing or estimating. An increase in value or worth; gratitude; awareness of esthetic value.

ap·pre·ci·a·tive, a·prē'sha·tiv, a·prē'-shē·ā"tiv, a. Capable of appreciating; manifesting due appreciation.

ap·pre·hend, ap"ri·hend', v.t. [M.E. *apprehenden* < L. *apprehendere,* to seize < *ad-,* and *prehendere,* to take or seize, *prae,* before, and *hendere* (not used), to seize.] To take or seize (a person); to arrest; to take or lay hold of by the mind; to become cognizant of; to understand; to entertain suspicion or fear of; to anticipate; to dread or be apprehensive of.—v.i. To form a conception; to conceive; to believe or be of opinion without positive certainty; to be apprehensive; to be in fear of a future evil.—**ap·pre·hen·si·ble,** ap"ri·hen'si·bl, a. Capable of being apprehended or conceived.

ap·pre·hen·sion, ap"ri·hen'shan, n. [M.E. < L.L. *apprensio(n-),* a seizing < *apprehensus,* pp. of *apprehendere,* to seize.] The act of apprehending; a seizing or arresting by legal process; the operation of the mind in contemplating ideas, or merely taking them into the mind; opinion; belief; the power of perceiving and understanding; distrust or fear at the prospect of future evil, accompanied with uneasiness of mind.

ap·pre·hen·sive, ap"ri·hen'siv, a. Inclined to believe, fear, or dread; anticipating or in expectation of evil; as, *apprehensive* of evil, *apprehensive* for our lives.—**ap·-pre·hen·sive·ly,** ap"ri·hen'siv·lē, adv. In an apprehensive manner.—**ap·pre·hen·-sive·ness,** ap"ri·hen'siv·nis, n. The character of being apprehensive.

ap·pren·tice, a·pren'tis, n. [M.E. *aprentis* < M.Fr. < O.Fr *aprend-* (stem of *aprendre,* to learn) < L. *apprehendere, apprendere,* to seize, to apprehend, and -*if* (< L. *ivus*). APPREHEND.] One bound, often by legal document, to learn some art, trade, or profession; a learner in any subject; one not well versed in a subject.—**ap·pren·tice·-ship,** a·pren'tis·ship', n. The state or condition of an apprentice; the term during which one is an apprentice.

ap·pren·tice, a·pren'tis, v.t.—*apprenticed, apprenticing.* To make an apprentice of; to put under the care of a skilled master, for the purpose of learning a trade or profession.

ap·pressed, a·prest', a. [L. *appressus,* pp. of *apprimere,* press to < *ad-,* to, and *premere,* press.] Pressed close, as leaves to a stem, or as folds of strata.

ap·prise, ap·prize, a·priz', v.t.—*apprised, apprising, apprized, apprizing.* [Fr. *appris, apprise,* informed, pp. of *apprendre,* to inform, to learn, < L. *apprehendere.* APPREHEND.] To give notice, verbal or written; to inform, with *of.*

ap·prize, ap·prise, a·priz', v.t.—*apprized, apprizing, apprised, apprising.* [M.E. *apprisen* < M.Fr. *apprisier* < a- (< L. *ad-*), and *prisier,* to appraise.] Appraise.—**ap·prize·ment,** n.—**ap·priz·er,** n.

ap·proach, a·prōch', v.i. [M.E. *approchen* < O.Fr. *approchier* < L.L. *appropiare,* to approach < L. *ad-,* to, and *prope,* near. PROPINQUITY.] To come or go near in place or time; to draw near; to advance nearer.—v.t. To come or draw near to, either literally or figuratively; to come near to, so as to be compared with; to approximate; to make a proposition to. To set about.—n. The act of approaching or drawing near an object or a given point; a coming or advancing near; access; a passage or avenue by which buildings are approached; the course to or the drawing near to a landing field, bombing target, or airborne target.

ap·proach·a·bil·i·ty, a·prō"cha·bil'i·tē, n. The condition or quality of being approachable.

ap·proach·a·ble, a·prō'cha·bl, a. Capable of being approached; accessible.

ap·pro·bate, ap'ro·bāt', v.t.—*approbated, approbating.* [M.E. *approbaten* < L. *approbat(us),* approved, pp. of *approbare,* to approve.] To express satisfaction with; to express approval of; to approve.

ap·pro·ba·tion, ap"ro·bā'shan, n. [L. *approbatio < approbatus.* APPROBATE.] The act of approving; approval; sanction; praise.—**ap·pro·ba·tive,** ap'ro·bā"tiv, a·prō'ba·tiv, a. Approving; implying approbation.

ap·pro·pri·a·ble, a·prō'prē·a·bl, a. Capable of being appropriated, set apart, or assigned to a particular use.

ap·pro·pri·ate, a·prō'prē·āt", v.t.—*appropriated, appropriating.* [M.E. *appropriaten* < L.L. *appropriatus,* pp. of *appropriare,* to make one's own < *ad-,* to, *proprius,* one's own. PROPER, PROPRIETY.] To claim or take to oneself in exclusion of others; to claim or use, without proper permission, as by an exclusive right; to set apart for or assign to a particular purpose; to provide (funds or money), esp. by an act of Congress.—a·prō'prē·it, a. Set apart for a particular use or person; hence, belonging or peculiar to; suitable; fit; proper.—**ap·pro·pri·ate·-ly,** a·prō'prē·it·lē, adv. In an appropriate manner.—**ap·pro·pri·ate·ness,** a·prō'prē·it·nis, n.—**ap·pro·pri·a·tor,** n.

ap·pro·pri·a·tion, a·prō"prē·ā'shan, n. The act of appropriating; application to a special use or purpose; anything appropriated or set apart; official permission to spend funds for a certain purpose; the money so approved.

ap·pro·pri·a·tive, a·prō'prē·ā"tiv, a·-prō'prē·a·tiv, a. Appropriating; making appropriation.

ap·prov·a·ble, a·prōv'a·bl, a. Capable of being approved.

ap·prov·al, a·prō'val, n. The act of approving; approbation; commendation; sanction; ratification.

ap·prove, a·prōv′, v.t.—approved, approving. [M.E. approven < Fr. approuver, approver, < L. approbare, to approve, to find good < ad-, to and probare, to try, test, prove, from probus, good.] To admit the propriety or excellence of; to think or judge well or favorably of; to find to be satisfactory; to give official sanction to (a proposal, plan, request, or the like); obs. to show to be real or true (to approve one's bravery).—v.i. To be pleased; to feel or express approbation; to think or judge well or favorably: followed by of.—**ap·prov·er,** a·prōv′ẽr, n. One who approves.—**ap·prov·ing·ly,** a·prōv′ing·lē, adv. In an approving manner.

ap·prox·i·mate, a·prok′si·māt″, v.t.—approximated, approximating. [< L.L. approximat(us), pp. of approximare, to bring or come near < ad- and proximare, to come near < proximus, nearest. PROXIMATE, APPROACH.] To come or bring near; to estimate; to cause to approach (especially said of amount, state, or degree).—v.i. To come near; to approach.—a·prok′si·mit, a. Being near in state, place, or quantity; approaching; nearly equal or like.—**ap·prox·i·mate·ly,** a·prok′si·mit·lē, adv. In an approximate manner; by approximation.
ap·prox·i·ma·tion, a·prok″si·mā′shan, n. The act of approximating; an approximate estimate or amount; approach; proximity.

ap·pulse, a·puls′, n. [< L. appulsus, < appellere, drive to, < ad-, to, and pellere, drive.] A driving upon; approach; impact. Astron. the approach or act of impact of two heavenly bodies.—**ap·pul·sion,** a·pul′shan, n.—**ap·pul·sive,** a·pul′siv, a. Driving upon; impinging.

ap·pur·te·nance, a·pur′te·nans, n. [M.E. < M.Fr. < a- and -purtenance, a belonging. APPURTENANT, APPERTAIN.] That which appertains, belongs, or is subordinate to something else; an adjunct; an appendage. A right or feature belonging to a property and passing with it if the property is sold.
ap·pur·te·nant, a·pur′te·nant, a. [M.E. apertenant < M.Fr. < O.Fr., ppr. of apartenir, to belong.] Appertaining or belonging; law, having the effect of a legal accompaniment.—n.

a·prax·i·a, a·prak′sē·a, ā·prak′sē·a, n. [N.L. < Gr. a-, no, and praxis, action < prassein, to do.] Med. a voluntary movement disorder consisting of almost complete inability to execute purposeful, coordinated movement although muscular power, sensitivity and general coordination have not atrophied.—**a·prax·ic,** a.

ap·ri·cot, ap′ri·kot″, ā′pri·kot″, n. [M.E. apricock, < Fr. abricot, Sp. albarcoque, < Ar. alburqūq, < al, the article, and burqūq, apricot < L.Gr. praikokkion, < L. praecox, praeoquus (short for persicum praecox, early ripening peach. PRECOCIOUS.] A roundish fruit of the tree, Prunus armeniaca, similar in flavor to the peach or plum; also the tree; a pinkish-yellow or light orange color.

A·pril, ā′pril, n. [M.E. < O.Fr. avrill and L. Aprilis, the month in which the earth opens for the growth of plants < aperio, to open.] The fourth month of the year, containing 30 days.
A·pril fool, n. One who is sportively imposed upon by others on April 1, as by being sent on some absurd errand.—**A·pril Fool's Day,** n. April 1.

a pri·o·ri, ā″prī·ôr′ī, ā″prī·ar′ī, ā″prē·ar′-ē, ā″prē·ôr′ē, ā″prē·ôr′ē, ā″prē·ar′ē, a., adv. [L., lit., 'from something prior or going before.'] Applied to a mode of reasoning by which we proceed from the cause to the effect, as opposed to a posteriori reasoning, by which we proceed from the effect to the cause; applied to knowledge independent of or prior to all experience.

a·pron, ā′pron, n. [M.E. napron, Fr. naperon, diminutive of nape, nappe, a tablecloth, etc. (whence E. napkin), nappe being another form of mappe, E. map. Apron, like adder, auger, has lost the initial n.] A piece of cloth or leather worn to keep the clothes clean or protect them from injury; a covering for the front part of a body; any shielding piece or part; a paved area at an airport where airplanes take on and discharge passengers; geol. a sand or gravel deposit projecting forward from a moraine. The part of a stage which extends beyond the proscenium arch and the front curtain; the forestage.—v.t. To put an apron on; to furnish with an apron.

ap·ro·pos, ap″ro·pō′, a. [Fr., lit., à, to, according to, and propos, purpose < L. propositum, a thing proposed.] Opportune; seasonable; to the purpose; as, an apropos remark; pertinent.—adv.
ap·ro·pos of, prep. With relation to, concerning, pertaining to.

apse, aps, n. [< M.L. apsis < L.] A portion of any building forming a termination or projection semicircular or polygonal in plan, and having a dome or vaulted roof; esp. such a structure at the end of a church.

ap·sis, ap′sis, n. pl. **ap·si·des,** ap′si·dēz″. [N.L. apsis (stem apsid-) < L. apsis, arch, orbit < Gr. hapsis (stem hapsid-) < haptein, to fasten.] Arch. an apse; astron. either of the two points in the orbit of a heavenly body or satellite which mark its greatest and its least distance from the center of attraction.

apt, apt, a. [M.E. < L. aptus, fitted, fit, pp. of apere, to fasten.] Fit; suitable; apposite; pertinent; intelligent; quick to learn; appropriate; having a tendency; liable; inclined; disposed; ready; prompt.—**apt·ly,** apt′lē, adv. In an apt or suitable manner; justly; pertinently; readily; quickly; cleverly.—**apt·ness,** apt′nis, n. The state or quality of being apt; fitness; tendency; quickness of apprehension; readiness in learning.

ap·ter·al, ap′tẽr·al, a. Zool. apterous; class. arch. having no columns along the sides.
ap·ter·ous, ap′tẽr·us, a. [Gr. apteros, without wings.] Zool. wingless, as certain insects; bot. without winglike parts or expansions.
ap·ter·yx, ap′te·riks, n. [N.L. < Gr. a-, not, and pteryx, a wing.] A bird peculiar to but now nearly extinct in New Zealand, having no tail and very short rudimentary wings. Also kiwi.

ap·ti·tude, ap′ti·tōd″, ap′ti·tūd″, n. [M.E. < L. aptitudo.] The state or quality of being apt; a natural ability; disposition; tendency; fitness; suitableness; readiness in learning; intelligence.

aq·ua, ak′wa, ä′kwa, n. pl. **aq·uae,** **aq·uas,** ak′wē, ä′kwē. [L. Water.] Water; a liquid; a solution: esp. used in pharmacy.

aq·ua·board, ak′wa·bärd, ak′wa·bôrd, ä′kwa·bärd, n. A surfboard used to teach water skiing; a surfboard equipped with handles.

aq·ua·cade, ak′wa·kād″, ä′kwa·kād″, n. [Orig. used for a 1937 water show in Cleveland, O. (< aqua and (caval)cade).] Water show with musical accompaniment including exhibitions of swimming, diving, and acrobatics.

aq·ua for·tis, ak′wa fạr′tis, n. [N.L. < L., lit. 'strong water.'] Nitric acid.

aq·ua·lung, ak′wa·lung″, ä′kwa·lung″, n. A device to permit breathing under water, consisting of a watertight face mask and cylinders of compressed air.

aq·ua·ma·rine, ak″wa·ma·rēn′, ä″kwa·ma·rēn′, n. [L. aqua, water, and marinus, pertaining to the sea.] The finest beryl, so-called from its bluish or sea-green tint; also the bluish-green color.

aq·ua·naut, ak′wa·nạt″, ak′wa·not″, ä′kwa·nạt″, n. A diver who stays underwater for long periods of time to test living and working conditions in an underwater environment.

aq·ua·plane, ak′wa·plān″, ä′kwa·plān″, n. A board on which a person stands as it is pulled over the water by a speedboat.—v.i. —aquaplaned, aquaplaning. To ride an aquaplane.

aq·ua pu·ra, ak′wa pū′ra, n. [L.] Pure water; distilled water.

aq·ua re·gi·a, ak′wa rē′jē·a, n. [N.L., lit., 'royal water' (with allusion to its power to dissolve gold).] A mixture of one part of nitric acid and three to four parts of hydrochloric acid, employed mainly to dissolve metals, esp. gold or platinum.

aq·ua·relle, ak″wa·rel′, ä″kwa·rel′, n. [Fr. obsolete It. acquarella < L. aqua, water.] Watercolor painting; a painting in watercolor.

a·quar·ist, a·kwär′ist, a·kwer′ist, n. A keeper of an aquarium.

a·quar·i·um, a·kwär′ē·um, n. pl. **a·quar·i·ums,** **a·quar·i·a.** [L. aquarium, watering-place for cattle < aquarius, pertaining to water < aqua, water.] A case, vessel, tank, or the like, in which aquatic plants and animals are kept; a place containing a collection of such vessels or tanks for public exhibition.

A·quar·i·us, a·kwär′ē·us, n. [L.] The Waterbearer, a zodiacal constellation located between Capricornus and Pisces. The eleventh sign of the Zodiac, which the sun enters about January 15.

a·quat·ic, a·kwat′ik, a·kwot′ik, a. [M.E. < L. aquaticus < aqua, water.] Pertaining to water; living in or frequenting water.—n. A plant which grows in water; pl. sports or exercises practiced on or in water, as rowing or swimming.

aq·ua·tint, ak′wa·tint″, ä′kwa·tint″, n. [< It. aqua tinta, tinted water.] A method of etching on copper by which a beautiful effect is produced, resembling a fine drawing in watercolors or India ink; the etching so produced.

aq·ua·vit, ä′kwa·vēt″, ak′wa·vēt″, n. [Sw., Dan., and Norw. akvavit < M.L. aqua vitae, lit. 'water of life.'] A clear, dry Scandinavian liquor, somewhat like gin, made from redistilled spirits and caraway flavoring. Also akvavit.

aq·ua vi·tae, ak′wa vī′tē, n. [M.L., lit., 'water of life.'] Alcohol; spirituous liquor, as brandy or whiskey.

aq·ue·duct, ak′wi·dukt″, n. [L. aquaeductus < aquae ductus, a drawing-off of water < aqua, water, and ducere, lead.] A conduit or channel for conveying water from one place to another; a structure for conveying water for the supply of a town.

a·que·ous, ā′kwē·us, ak′wē·us, a. [M.L. aqueus < L. aqua, water.] Of, like, or containing water; watery; of rocks, formed of matter deposited from water.—**a·que·ous·ly,** ad·v. —**a·que·ous·ness,** n.
a·que·ous hu·mor, n. Anat. the watery fluid which fills the anterior and posterior chambers of the eye between the crystalline lens and the cornea.

aq·ui·cul·ture, ak′wi·kul′chẽr, n. [< L. aqua, water, and E. -culture.] Cultivation of the natural inhabitants of water; fishbreeding; hydroponics.—**aq·ui·cul·tur·al,** ak″wi·kul′chẽr·al, a.

aq·ui·fer, ak′wi·fẽr, n. [N.L. < L. aqua, water, and fer- (< ferre, to bear).] Geol. a stratum of permeable rock, sand, etc., which contains water, esp. one which acts as a water source for a well or the like.—**a·quif·er·ous,** a·kwif′ẽr·us, a.

aq·ui·le·gi·a, ak′wi·lē′jē·a, ä″kwi·lē′jē·a, n. [N.L.] Bot. A plant of the genus Aquilegia, which includes the columbines.

---

a- fat, fāte, fär, fâre, fạll;   **e-** met, mē, mēre, hẽr;   **i-** pin, pīne;   **o-** not, nōte, mõve;   **u-** tub, cūbe, bụll;   **oi-** oil;   **ou-** pound.

aq·ui·line, ak'wi·līn″, ak'wi·lin, *a.* [L. *aquilinus,* < *aquila,* an eagle.] Of or belonging to the eagle; resembling an eagle's beak; curving; hooked.

Ar·ab, ar'ab, *n.* [L. *Arabs* < Gr. *Araps,* Ar. '*Arab.*'] A native of Arabia, or a member of the Arabic race (now widespread in Asia and Africa, and formerly in southern Europe); an Arabian horse; (*sometimes l.c.*) a wanderer or outcast, esp. a child of the streets (commonly in 'street Arab').—**A·ra·bi·an, Ar·a·bic,** *a.*rä′bē·an, ar′a·bik, *a.*

ar·a·besque, ar″a·besk′, *n.* [Fr., Arabian < It. *arabesc* < *Arab* and *-esco,* -ish.] Ornamentation in which flowers, foliage, fruits, geometrical figures, etc. (in strict Mohammedan use, no animals), are combined in an intricate pattern. A ballet position in which the artist, standing on one leg, extends the body and one arm forward while the other arm and leg reach backward in the same horizontal plane.

A·ra·bi·an, *a*·rä′bē·an, *a.* [L. *Arabius.*] Pertaining to Arabia or the Arabs.—*n.* An Arab.

A·ra·bi·an, *a*·rä′bē·an, *n.* A breed of fast, spirited horses of the Arabs.—*a.*

A·ra·bi·an cof·fee, *n.* An African small evergreen tree or large shrub grown in warm regions for its seeds from which coffee is made.

Ar·a·bic, ar′a·bik, *a.* [L. *Arabicus.*] Belonging to or derived from Arabia or the Arabians; as, *Arabic* architecture, *Arabic* numerals or figures (the characters 1, 2, 3, 4, 5, 6, 7, 8, 9, 0).

Ar·a·bic, ar′a·bik, *n.* The language of the Arabians, a Semitic dialect which has contributed largely to many Oriental and other languages and is spoken in Arabia, Lebanon, Jordan, Egypt, Iraq, Syria, and in sections of North Africa.

ar·a·bic·a cof·fee, ar′a·bik″a ka′fē, *n.* (*Often cap.*) a beverage produced from Arabian coffee.

ar·a·bil·i·ty, ar″a·bil′i·tē, *n.* The condition of being arable.

Ar·ab·ist, ar′a·bist, *n.* One versed in the Arabic language, literature, or learning.

ar·a·ble, ar′a·bl, *a.* [< M.Fr. < L. *arabilis,* < *arare,* plow.] Fit for plowing or tilling.—*n.* Arable land.

a·ra·ceous, *a*·rä′shus, *a.* [See *arum.*] Belonging to the *Araceae,* or arum family of plants, which includes the arums, skunk-cabbage, sweet-flag, calla lily, taro, etc.

a·rach·nid, *a*·rak′nid, *n.* [< Gr. *arachnē,* a spider.] Any member of a class, *Arachnida,* of wingless arthropods with segmented bodies including spiders, mites, and scorpions.—**a·rach·ni·dan,** *a*·rak′ni·dan, *n.* One of the Arachnida.

a·rach·noid, *a*·rak′noid, *a.* [< Gr. *arachnē,* spider, spider's web.] Resembling a spider's web; resembling an arachnid; *anat.* applied to a semitransparent, thin membrane which is spread over the brain and pia mater; *bot.* having hair that gives an appearance of being covered with cobweb; *zool.* spiderlike.—*n.* The arachnoid membrane; an arachnoid.

a·rag·o·nite, *a*·rag′o·nīt″, ar′a·go·nīt″, *n.* [From *Aragon,* division of northeastern Spain.] A mineral, $CaCO_3$, consisting of calcium carbonate, chemically identical with calcite but differing in its orthorhombic crystallization, greater hardness and specific gravity, less marked cleavage, etc.

Ar·a·ma·ic, ar·a·mā′ik, *a.* Pertaining to the Biblical country of Aram (Syria and Mesopotamia), or to a language or group of dialects spoken there and in neighboring regions.—*n.* The Aramaic language, or group of dialects, belonging to the Semitic family and including the Syriac and the dialect spoken in Palestine at the time of Christ.

Ar·a·me·an, Ar·a·mae·an, ar″a·mē′an, ar″a·mē′an, *a.* [L. *Aramaeus,* < Gr. *Aramaios* < Heb. '*Arām',* Aram (ancient name for Syria).] Of or pertaining to Aram or its language; Aramaic.—*n.* A Semite of the division associated with Aram; also, the Aramaic language.

a·ra·ne·id, *a*·rä′nē·id, *n.* [N.L. *Araneida,* pl. < L. *aranea,* spider, spider's web.] An arachnid of the order *Araneida;* a spider.—**ar·a·ne·i·dan,** ar·a·nē′i·dan, *a., n.*

ar·a·ne·i·form, ar″a·nē′i·farm″, *a.* [L. *aranea,* spider.] Spiderlike.

a·ra·ne·ose, *a*·rä′nē·ōs″, *a.* [L. *araneosus,* < *aranea,* spider's web: cf. *araneid.*] Cobweblike; arachnoid. Also **a·ra·ne·ous,** *a*·rä′nē·us.

A·rap·a·ho, A·rap·a·hoe, *a*·rap′a·hō″, *n.* pl. **A·rap·a·ho, A·rap·a·hos, A·rap·a·hoe, A·rap·a·hoes.** A subgroup of the Algonquian plains Indians who inhabited the area from southern Saskatchewan and Manitoba to New Mexico and Texas; the Algonquian language of the Arapaho; a member of the group of Arapaho.

Ar·a·wak, ar′a·wäk″, ar′a·wak″, *n.* A subgroup of the Arawakan Indians now inhabiting the northeast coast of South America; a member of the Arawaks; the language of the Arawaks.

Ar·a·wak·an, ar″a·wä′kan, ar″a·wak′an, *n.* A group of Indians formerly inhabiting territory from Florida to Chile, now basically South American; a member of this group; the family of languages spoken by the Arawakan peoples.—*a.*

ar·ba·list, ar·ba·lest, är′ba·list, *n.* [M.E. *arblast* < O.E. < O.Fr. *arbaleste,* < L.L. *arcubalistta* < L. *arcus,* a bow, and *ballista, balista,* an engine to throw stones.] A kind of powerful crossbow used during the Middle Ages.—**ar·ba·list·er,** är′ba·lis″tẽr, *n.* A crossbowman.

ar·bi·ter, är′bi·tẽr, *n.* [M.E. *arbitre* < M.Fr. < L. an arbiter, umpire, judge.] A person appointed or chosen by parties in controversy to decide their differences; one who judges and determines without control; one whose power of deciding and governing is absolute; an arbitrator.

ar·bi·tra·ble, är′bi·tra·bl, *a.* Subject to arbitrative determination.

ar·bi·trage, är″bi·träzh′, *n.* [M.E. *arbitrage,* arbitration < M.Fr. < O.Fr. < *arbitrer,* to render judgment < L. *arbitrari,* to think.] *Finance.* The calculation of the best mode by which advantage may be taken of differences in the value of money, stocks, etc., in different places at the same time; the dealing in bills of exchange, stocks, etc., for the purpose of making profit by such calculations; simultaneous buying and selling of stocks, etc., in order to make a profit by the difference in prices.

ar·bi·tral, är′bi·tral, *a.* Pertaining to an arbiter or to arbitration.

ar·bit·ra·ment, är·bi′tra·ment, *n.* [M.E. < M.Fr. *arbitrement* < *arbitrer.*] Determination; decision; settlement; award (the *arbitrament* of the sword); arbitration; the power of absolute decision.

ar·bi·trar·i·ly, är′bi·trer″i·lē, är″bi·trâr′-i·lē, *adv.* In an arbitrary manner; capriciously.

ar·bi·trar·i·ness, är′bi·trer″ē·nis, *n.* The quality of being arbitrary.

ar·bi·trar·y, är′bi·trer″ē, *a.* [M.E. < L. *arbitrarius,* uncertain, depending on an arbiter's decision.] Given, adjudged, or done according to one's will or discretion; exercised according to one's will or discretion; decided by an arbiter rather than by law; capricious; despotic; imperious; tyrannical; uncontrolled; *math.* undetermined, having no specific value.

ar·bi·trate, är′bi·trāt″, *v.i.—arbitrated, arbitrating.*[L. *arbitratus,* decided, pp. of *ar-*

bitrari, to think.] To act as an arbiter or umpire; to hear and decide in a dispute, as labor negotiations.—*v.t.* To hear and decide on; determine.

ar·bi·tra·tion, är″bi·trā′shan, *n.* [M.E. < L. *arbitratio(n)-* < *arbitratus.* ARBITRATE.] The act of arbitrating; the hearing and determination of a cause between parties in controversy, by a person or persons chosen by the parties. *International law,* the settlement of international disputes through the application of judicial methods.

ar·bi·tra·tor, är′bi·trā″tor, *n.* One who arbitrates; an arbiter.

ar·bour, *Brit.* **ar·bour,** är′bor, *n.*[M.E. *erber,* *herber,* plot of grass < O.Fr. *herbier,* plot of grass < *herbe,* grass.] A tree- or vine-shaded nook, often framed by a latticework entwined with climbing shrubs or vines.—**ar·bor·ous,** är′bor·us, *a.*

ar·bor, är′bor, *n.* [L. *arbor,* a tree, shaft.] The principal spindle or axis of a machine, communicating motion to the other moving parts or supporting a rotating cutting tool.

ar·bo·ra·ceous, är″bo·rā′shus, *a.* [N.L. *arboraceus* < L. *arbor,* tree.] Treelike; arboreal.

Ar·bor Day, *n.* [L. *arbor,* tree.] A day publicly appointed or observed in individual States of the U.S. for the planting of trees: varying in date according to the State, and being in some States a legal holiday.

ar·bo·re·al, är·bôr′ē·al, är·bar′ē·al, *a.* [L. *arboreus,* pertaining to a tree < *arbor,* tree.] Pertaining to trees; living on or among trees; having the character of a tree.—**ar·bo·re·al·ly,** *adv.*

ar·bo·re·ous, är·bôr′ē·us, *a.* Characterized by a plentiful quantity of trees; living in an area surrounded by trees.

ar·bo·res·cence, är″bo·res′ens, *n.* [< L. *arborescent-,* stem of *arborescens,* growing into a tree < *arborescere,* to grow into a tree.] The state of being arborescent; an arborescent form or growth.

ar·bo·res·cent, är″bo·res′ent, *a.* [L. *arborescens,* ppr. of *arborescere,* to grow to a tree.] Resembling a tree. *Bot.* partaking of the nature and habits of a tree; dendritic.

ar·bo·re·tum, är″bo·rē′tum, *n.* pl. **ar·bo·re·tums,** är·bo·re·ta, är″bo·rē′ta. [N.L. < L. *arboretum,* a place grown with trees.] A place in which a collection of different trees and shrubs is cultivated for scientific, educational, or decorative purposes.

ar·bor·i·cul·ture, är′bor·i·kul″chẽr, *n.* [< L. *arbor,* a tree, and *-culture* (< L. *cultura*), as in *agriculture.*] The cultivation of trees; the art of planting, dressing, and managing trees and shrubs, esp. for ornamentation.—**ar·bor·i·cul·tur·ist,** är″bor·i·kul′chẽr·ist, *n.*

ar·bor·i·za·tion, är″bor·i·zā′shan, *n.* A mineral, fossil, or other body with a treelike form; the formation of an object in the figure of a tree.

ar·bor·vi·tae, är′bor·vī′tē, *n.* [L. *lit.,* 'tree of life.'] A common name of certain coniferous trees. A treelike arrangement which appears in the medullary substance of the brain when the cerebellum is cut vertically; also **ar·bor vi·tae.**

ar·bu·tus, är·bū′tus, *n.* [L. the strawberry-tree.] The generic name of an evergreen tree or shrub, with bright red or yellow berries; also, a trailing plant, the trailing arbutus, with fragrant pink flowers.

arc, ärk, *n.* [M.E. *ark* < M.Fr. *arc,* < L. *arcus,* bow, arch, arc.] Something bow-shaped, as a rainbow; an architectural arch; *geom.* any part of a circle or other curved line; *astron.* the part of a circle representing the apparent course of a heavenly body either above or below the horizon; *elect.* the luminous bridge formed by the passage of a current across a gap between two conductors or terminals, due to the incandescence of the conducting vapors.—*v.i.*—*arcked, arcking, arced, arcing. Elect.* to form an arc.

ar·cade, är·kād′, *n.* [Fr. < It. *arcata* < M.L. *arcata* < L. *arcus.* ARC.] A series of arches supported on piers or pillars; an arched, roofed, or covered passageway, sometimes lined with shops; an arched building or passageway in a building.

ar·ca·di·a, är·kā′dē·a, *n.* [From *Arcadia*, a mountainous district in ancient Greece, proverbial for the contented pastoral simplicity of its people.] Any region (real or ideal) characterized by pastoral simplicity, innocence, and contentment.

Ar·ca·di·an, är·kā′dē·an, *a.* Pertaining to, or of, Arcadia. (*l.c.*) simple; rustic.—*n.* A native of Arcadia. The dialect of ancient Greek spoken in Arcadia. (*l.c.*) one who leads a quiet, uncomplicated life.

ar·cane, är·kān′, *a.* [L. *arcanus* < *arcere*, keep, shut up. ARK.] Hidden; secret; obscure.

ar·ca·num, är·kā′num, *n.* pl. **ar·ca·na**, är·kā′na. [L., neut of *arcanus*, secret.] A secret; a mystery, esp. one of the great secrets that the alchemists sought to discover; hence, a sovereign remedy.

arch, ärch, *n.* [M.E. *arche* < O.Fr. < (assumed) V.L. < *arca* < L. *arcus*, a bow, arch, arc.] A structure composed of separate wedge-shaped pieces, arranged on a curved line, so as to retain their position by mutual pressure; a covering, or structure, of a bow shape; a doorway with a curved head; a vault.

arch, ärch, *a.* [M.E. *arche* < O.E. *arce*, O.Fr. *arch* < L.L. *arch* < L. < Gr. < *archein* to begin, rule.] Cunning, sly, shrewd; waggish; mischievously saucy; roguish. Most important, chief; as, *arch* criminal.

arch, ärch, *v.t.* To furnish, cover, or span with an arch; also, to curve like an arch.—*v.i.* To form an arch; to follow an archlike course; as, a bridge *arching* over the river.

Ar·chae·an, Ar·che·an, är·kē′an, *a.* [Gr. *archaios*, ancient.] *Geol.* applied to the oldest rocks of the earth's crust, crystalline in character, and embracing granite, syenite, gneiss.—*n.* The Archaeozoic Era.

ar·chae·o·log·i·cal, ar·che·o·log·i·cal, är″kē·o·loj′i·kal, *a.* Pertaining to archaeology.

ar·chae·ol·o·gist, ar·che·ol·o·gist, är″kē·ol′o·jist, *n.* One skilled in archaeology.

ar·chae·ol·o·gy, ar·che·ol·o·gy, är″kē·ol′o·jē, *n.* [Gr. *archaiologia* < *archaio*, ancient, and *logos*, discourse.] The science of antiquities, especially prehistoric antiquities, which investigates the history of peoples by the remains belonging to the earlier periods of their existence.

ar·chae·op·ter·yx, är″kē·op′te·riks, *n.* [N.L. < Gr. *archaios*, ancient, and *pteryx*, wing.] A fossil bird of the extinct genus *Archaeopteryx*, about the size of a crow, having two claws representing the thumb and forefinger projecting from the wing, and about twenty tail vertebrae prolonged as in mammals; the oldest known avian type.

ar·chae·or·nis, är″kē·ar′nis, *n.* [N.L. < *archae-* (< Gr. *archaios*, ancient) and Gr. *ornis*, bird.] *Ornith.* An extinct genus of bird dating back to the upper Jurassic period; the toothed bird believed to be the evolutionary link between modern birds and reptiles.

Ar·chae·o·zo·ic, Ar·che·o·zo·ic, är″kē·o·zō′ik, *a.* [Gr. *archaios*, ancient, and *zoe*, life.] *Geol.* noting or pertaining to the division of Archaean time characterized (supposedly) by the presence of organic life.

ar·cha·ic, är·kā′ik, *a.* [Gr. *archaikos*, old-fashioned, < *archaios*, ancient.] Old fashioned; antiquated; marked by characteristics of an earlier period in time; not com-

monly used during the present time, as words; surviving from a previous, usually more primitive period, esp. an evolutionary stage; (*cap.*) of a style of the fine arts developed in Greece between the 7th and 5th centuries B.C.

ar·cha·ic smile, *n. Fine arts*, an expression resembling a smile similar to expressions found in ancient Greek sculpture.

ar·cha·ism, är′kē·iz″um, är′kā·iz″um, *n.* [N.L. < Gr. *archaismos* < *archaios*, ancient.] An ancient word or idiom; antiquity of style or use; the survival of something from the past.—**ar·cha·ist**, *n.*—**ar·cha·is·tic**, *a.*

ar·cha·ize, är′kē·īz″, är′kā·īz″, *v.i.*—*archaized, archaizing.* [Gr. *archaizein*, to imitate the language of ancient authors.] To use archaisms; affect archaism.—*v.t.* To render archaic; give an archaic appearance or quality to.

arch·an·gel, ärk·ān″jel, *n.* [M.E. < O.Fr. *archangele* or L.L. *archangelus* < Gr. *archangelos* < *arch*, chief, and *angelos*, angel.] An angel of the highest order in the celestial hierarchy.—**arch·an·gel·ic**, ärk″an·jel′ik, *a.*

arch·bish·op, ärch′bish′op, *n.* [M.E. < O.E. *arcebiscop* < L.L. *archiepiscopus* < Gr. *archiepiskopos* < *arch*(i)-, main, chief, and *episkopos*, bishop.] A bishop who has the supervision of other bishops (the sees of whom form his province), and also exercises episcopal authority in his own diocese.

arch·bish·op·ric, ärch″bish′op·rik, *n.* The jurisdiction, office, or see of an archbishop.

arch·dea·con, ärch′dē′kon, *n.* [M.E. < O.E. < L.L. < Gr. < *arch*(i)-, main, chief, and *diakonos*, deacon.] In England, an ecclesiastical dignitary, next in rank below a bishop, who has jurisdiction either over a part of, or over the whole, diocese.—**arch·dea·con·ate**, ärch″dē′kon·at, *n.* The office, jurisdiction, or residence of an archdeacon. Also **arch·dea·con·ry, arch·dea·con·ship.**

arch·di·o·cese, ärch′dī′o·sēs, *n.* The diocese of an archbishop.—**arch·di·oc·e·san**, ärch″dī·os′i·san, *a.*

arch·du·cal, ärch′dö′kal, ärch′dū′kal, *a.* [Fr. *archiducal* < *archiduc*.] Pertaining to an archduke or archduchy.

arch·duch·ess, ärch′duch′is, *n.* [Fr. *archiduchesse*.] The wife of an archduke. A woman who has a rank equal to that of an archduke.

arch·duch·y, ärch′duch′ē, *n.* pl. **arch·duch·ies.** [Fr. *archiduché*.] The territory or rank of an archduke or archduchess.

arch·duke, ärch′dūk′, ärch′dök′, *n.* [M.Fr. *archeduc*.] A prince belonging to the imperial family of the Austrian empire; any ruling prince.

Ar·che·an, *a.* Archaean.

arched, ärcht, *a.* Having an arch or arches; curved like an arch.

arch·en·e·my, ärch′en′e·mē, *n.* pl. **arch·en·e·mies.** A principal enemy; Satan.

Ar·che·o·zo·ic, *a.* Archaeozoic.

arch·er, är′chėr, *n.* [M.E. < O.Fr. *archer*, < L.L. *arcarius, arcuarius*, of a bow < *arcus*, a bow. ARCH.] One who uses, or is skilled in the use of, the bow and arrow; a bowman.

ar·cher·y, är′che·rē, *n.* [M.E. *archerye* < M.Fr. *archerie*.] The practice, art, or skill of shooting with a bow and arrow. The equipment used by the archer.

ar·che·typ·al, är′ki·tī″pal, *a.* Of or pertaining to an archetype. Also **ar·che·typ·i·cal**, är″ki·tip′i·kal.

ar·che·type, är′ki·tīp″, *n.* [L. *archetypum*, < Gr. *archetypon* < *archein*, beginning, and *typos*, form.] A model or first form; the original pattern after which a thing is made, or to which it corresponds.

arch·fiend, ärch′fēnd′, *n.* A chief fiend; with *the*, Satan.

ar·chi·di·ac·o·nal, är″ki·di·ak′a·nal, *a.* Pertaining to an archdeacon.

ar·chi·e·pis·co·pate, är″kē·e·pis′ko·pit, är″kē·e·pis′ko·pāt″, *n.* The dignity, office, or province of an archbishop.—**ar·chi·e·pis·co·pal**, är″kē·i·pis′ko·pal, *a.*

ar·chil, är′kil, *n.* [M.E. *orchell*.] A violet, mauve, or purple coloring matter obtained from lichens; the plant which yields this dye. Also **or·chil**, ar′kil, ar′chil.

ar·chi·mage, är′ki·māj″, *n.* [N.L. *archimagus*, < Gr. *archimagos*, chief mage.] A chief or great magician. Also **ar·chi·ma·gus**, är″ki·mā′gus, pl. **ar·chi·ma·gi**, är″ki·mā′jī.

ar·chi·man·drite, är″ki·man′drīt, *n.* [L.L. *archimandrites* < Gr. *arch*(i)-, chief, *mandra*, a monastery.] *Greek Ch.* an abbot, or abbot general, who has the superintendence of other abbots and convents.

Ar·chi·me·de·an, är″ki·mē′dē·an, är″ki·mi·dē′an, *a.* Pertaining to Archimedes, the Greek physicist.—**Ar·chi·me·de·an screw**, an instrument for raising water, formed by winding a flexible tube around a cylinder in the form of a screw, being placed in an inclined position, and the lower end immersed in water; by causing the screw to revolve, the water is raised to the upper end.

ar·chi·pel·a·go, är″ki·pel′a·gō″, *n.* pl. **ar·chi·pel·a·goes, ar·chi·pel·a·gos.** [< It. *arcipelago* < Gr. *arch*(i)-, chief, and *pelagos*, the sea. Originally the Aegean Sea, which is studded with a number of small islands.] Any water space interspersed with many islands; a group of many islands.—**ar·chi·pe·lag·ic**, är″ki·pe·laj′ik, *a.*

ar·chi·tect, är′ki·tekt″, *n.* [M.Fr. *architecte*, L. *architectus*, < Gr. *architektōn*, master builder < *arch*(i)-, chief, and *tektōn*, a workman.] A person skilled in the art and science of building; one who makes it his occupation to form plans and designs of buildings, and superintend their erection; a planner or designer of anything.

ar·chi·tec·ton·ic, är″ki·tek·ton′ik, *a.* [L. *architectonicus* < Gr. ARCHITECT.] Pertaining to architecture or architects skilled in architecture; resembling architecture, usually in regard to organization; as, a novel's *architectonic* structure.—**ar·chi·tec·ton·i·cal·ly**, *adv.*

ar·chi·tec·ton·ics, är″ki·tek·ton′iks, *n. pl. but sing. in constr.* The science of architecture.

ar·chi·tec·tur·al, är″ki·tek′chėr·al, *a.* Pertaining to architecture or the art of building; abiding by the rules and principles of architecture; containing the qualities of architecture.

ar·chi·tec·ture, är′ki·tek″chėr, *n.* [L. *architectura*.] The art or science of building; that branch of the fine arts which has for its object the production of edifices, areas, communities, and sometimes furnishings and decorations pleasing to a cultivated and artistic taste; construction; the character or style of the above; as, the *architecture* of Rome; the product of architecture; the structure of anything; as, the *architecture* of a play.

ar·chi·trave, är′ki·trāv, *n.* [Fr. < It. *architrave* < *archi*-, chief, and *trave* < L. *trabs*, beam.] *Arch.* The lowest division of an entablature, resting immediately on the columns; also, a band of moldings or other ornamentation about a (properly rectangular) door or other opening.

ar·chi·val, är·kī′val, *a.* Pertaining to or contained in archives or records.

ar·chive, är′kīv, *n.* [L.L. *archivum*, a place for keeping public records < Gr. *archeion*, a government building, < *archē*, rule, government.] A record or document preserved in evidence of something: almost always in plural, and signifying documents or records relating to the affairs of a family, corporation, community, or nation; *usu. pl.* the location of such records; *sing.* any extensive collection of data.

ar·chi·vist, är′ki·vist, *n.* The custodian of archives or records.

ar·chi·volt, är′ki·vōlt″, *n.* [< It. *archivolto,* appar. for *arcovolto* (= O.Fr. *arvolt, arcvol*), arch, < *arco,* arch, and *volto,* turned, arched.] *Arch.* a band of moldings or other ornamentation about an arched opening: corresponding to the architrave of a rectangular opening.

arch·ly, ärch′lē, *adv.* In an arch or roguish manner.

arch·ness, ärch′nis, *n.* The state of being arch.

ar·chon, är′kon, *n.* [Gr. *archōn,* ppr. of *archein,* to rule.] One of the chief magistrates of ancient Athens chosen to superintend civil and religious concerns; any magistrate or ruler.

arch·way, ärch′wā″, *n.* A passage under an arch.

ar·ci·form, är′si·fårm″, *a.* [L. *arcus,* bow, and E. *-i-* and *-form.*] Bow-shaped; arched.

arc lamp, *n.* A form of lamp employing an electric arc. Also **arc light.**

arc·tic, ärk′tik, *a.* [M.E. *artik* < L. *arcticus* < Gr. *arktikos,* < *arktos,* a bear, the northern constellation Ursa Major.] Northern; (*often cap.*) surrounding or lying near the North Pole. Of, from, or like the arctic regions; as, *arctic* air; cold, frigid.—**the Arc·tic,** the region within the Arctic Circle.

arc·tic, ärk′tik, *n.* A waterproof overshoe made of rubber reaching to or above the ankle.

arc·tic cir·cle, *n.* (*Often cap.*) an imaginary circle drawn on the earth, its borders parallel to the equator and located about 23° 27′ south of the North Pole.

ar·cu·ate, är′kū·it, är′kū·āt″, *a.* [L. *arcuatus,* pp. of *arcuare,* to bend like a bow < *arcus,* a bow.] Bent or curved in the form of a bow.

ar·den·cy, är′den·sē, *n.* The quality of being ardent; warmth; ardor; eagerness; fervor; intensity.

ar·dent, är′dent, *a.* [M.E. < M.Fr. < L. *ardens, ardentis,* pp. of *ardēre,* to burn, to be eager.] Burning; causing a sensation of burning; warm: applied to the passions and affections; vehement; passionate; eager; fervent; fervid; zealous—**ar·dent spir·its,** distilled liquors.—**ar·dent·ly,** är′dent·lē, *adv.*

ar·dor, *Brit.* **ar·dour,** är′dèr, *n.* [M.E. < L. *ardor* < *ardere,* to burn.] Heat in a literal sense; warmth or heat, as of the passions and affections; eagerness.

ar·du·ous, är′jū·us, *a.* [L. *arduus,* laborious, steep.] Steep, and therefore difficult of ascent; hard to climb; attended with great labor; difficult; hard, as a task or employment. Energetic; vigorous.—**ar·du·ous·ly,** är′jū·us·lē, *adv.*—**ar·du·ous·ness,** är′jū·us·nis, *n.*

are, är. [M.E. < O. Northumbrian *aron, arn,* we (you, they) are; the O.E. form proper is *sind* or *sindon.*] The present tense plural and the second person singular of the verb *to be.*

are, âr, är, *n.* [< L. *area.*] A unit of measure for area, equivalent to 100 square meters or 119.6 square yards.

ar·e·a, âr′ē·a, *n.* [L. *arae,* a threshing floor, then any level open piece of land.] Any plane surface within boundaries, as the floor of a hall, etc.; a geographical region; a space reserved for a particular function; as, a residential *area* of a city; a space sunk below the general surface of the ground in front of the windows in the basement of a building; a yard; contents of the surface of any space; a surface, as given in square inches, feet, yards, etc.; field of study or inquiry; a section of the cerebral cortex that has a specific function; the range or scope of an operation, concept, or activity.—**ar·e·al,** âr′ē·al, *a.* Pertaining to an area.

ar·e·a·way, âr′ē·a·wā″, *n.* A sunken area forming a passageway to a basement, or a space for air and light in front of a basement window.

a·re·na, a·rē′na, *n.* [L. *arena,* lit. 'sand, a sandy place.'] The enclosed space (usually covered with sand) in the central part of the Roman amphitheater; hence, the scene or theater of a contest of any kind.

ar·e·na·ceous, ar″e·nā′shus, *a.* Abounding with sand; having the properties of sand; sandy; granular.

a·re·na the·a·ter, *n.* A theater arranged so that the entire stage is encircled by the audience; also *theater-in-the-round.*

ar·e·nose, ar′e·nōs″,*a.* [L. *arenosus* < *arena,* sand.] Full of sand; sandy.

aren't, ärnt, är′ent. Contraction of are not.

ar·e·o·graph·ic, ar″ē·o·graf′ik, *a.* *Aerospace,* referring to positions on Mars measured in latitude from Mars' equator and in longitude from a reference meridian.

a·re·o·la, a·rē′o·la, *n.* pl. **a·re·o·lae,** a·re·o·las, a·rē′o·lē. [N.L. < L., dim. of *area.*] A small area or space; a small interstice; the colored circle or halo surrounding the nipple or surrounding a pustule.—**ar·e·o·la·tion,** âr″ē·o·lā′shan, *n.* Any small space or spot differing from the rest of a surface in color, texture, etc.

ar·e·ole, âr′ē·ōl″, *n.* Areola.

ar·e·ol·o·gy, âr″ē·ol′o·jē, *n.* The scientific investigation of the planet Mars itself, not including its orbital motion and the like.

ar·e·thu·sa, ar″e·thö′za, *n.* [< *Class. Myth.* the nymph *Arethusa.*] *Bot.* a genus of low, terrestrial, bog orchids.

ar·gent, är′jent, *n.* [M.E. < M.Fr. < L. *argentum,* silver: cogn. Gr. *argyros,* silver, *argos,* white; Ir. *arg,* white, *airgiod,* silver, money.] *Her.* the white color in coats of arms, intended to represent silver, etc.—*a.* Resembling silver; bright like silver; silvery.

ar·gen·tic, är·jen′tik, *a.* Pertaining to, like, or containing silver.

ar·gen·tif·er·ous, är″jen·tif′ér·us, *a.* Producing or containing silver; as, *argentiferous* ore.

ar·gen·tine, är′jen·tin, är′jen·tīn″, *n.* A white metal having the appearance of silver.—*a.* Silvery.

Ar·gen·tine, är′jen·tēn″, är′jen·tīn″, *a.* Of or pertaining to the culture and residents of Argentina, a country in South America situated between the Andes and the Atlantic.—*n.* A native or inhabitant of Argentina.

ar·gen·tite, är′jen·tīt″, *n.* Sulfide of silver, Ag_2S, a valuable ore of that metal.

ar·gen·tous, är·jen′tus, *a.* [L. *argentum,* silver.] Containing univalent silver, in larger proportion than a corresponding argentic compound.

ar·gen·tum, är·jen′tum, *n.* [L.] *Chem.* silver.

ar·gil, är′jil, *n.* [L. *argilla,* white clay < Gr. *argillos* < *argos,* white.] Clay or potter's earth; sometimes, pure clay or alumina.—**ar·gil·la·ceous,** *a.*

ar·gil·lite, är′ji·līt″, *n.* Clay-slate; any compact sedimentary rock made up mainly of clay; clay stone.

ar·gi·nine, är′ji·nīn″, *n.* [< G. *arginin.*] *Biochem.* an amino acid, $C_6H_{14}O_2N_4$, essential in the makeup of proteins in both plants and animals, present in the sperm of some fish (salmon, herring, etc.).

ar·gon, är′gon, *n.* [Gr. *argos,* inert < *a-,* no, and *ergon,* work.] A colorless, odorless, gaseous element that is chemically inactive and is used in electric bulbs and electron tubes. Sym. Ar, at. no. 18. See Periodic Table of Elements.

Ar·go·naut, är′go·nạt″, *n.* [< L. *Argonautes* < Gr. < *Argō,* and *nautēs,* a sailor.] One of the persons who, in the Greek legend, sailed with Jason in the ship Argo in quest of the Golden Fleece. (*l.c.*) a kind of cuttlefish, the paper nautilus or paper sailor of the Mediterranean, the female having a boatlike shell in which its eggs are received; an adventurer who is involved in a search.—**Ar·go·nau·tic,** är″go·nạ′tik, *a.*

ar·go·sy, är′go·sē, *n.* pl. **ar·go·sies.** [< *ragusy* < It. *Ragusea* (ship) of Ragusa (now Dubrovnik, Yugoslavia).] A large merchantman or other ship, especially if richly laden. *Poet.* a fleet of ships; a bountiful supply.

ar·got, är′gō, är′got, *n.* [Fr., origin unknown.] The peculiar language or jargon of thieves and vagabonds; thieves' cant; hence, the cant, jargon, or specialized vocabulary of any class or group; slang.—**ar·got·ic,** är·got′ik, *a.*

ar·gu·a·ble, är′gū·a·bl, *a.* Questionable; capable of being argued.

ar·gue, är′gū, *v.i.*—argued, arguing. [M.E. *arguen* < M.Fr. *arguer,* to accuse (< L. *argutare,* to prate) or L. *arguere,* to show, argue, to make clear.] To offer reasons to support or overthrow a proposition, opinion, or measure; to reason; to discuss; to debate; to dispute.—*v.t.* To debate or discuss; as, *argue* a cause in court; to prove, show, or evince; to cause to be inferred; as, conduct which *argued* suspicion; to convince through argument.—**ar·gu·er,** är′gū·ér, *n.*

ar·gu·ment, är′gya·ment, *n.* [M.E. < M.Fr. < L. *argumentum,* proof, theme, subject matter < *arguere,* ARGUE.] The subject of a discourse or writing; an abstract or summary of a book or section of a book; a reason offered for or against something; a debate, controversy, or discussion; a process of reasoning. A verbal altercation.

ar·gu·ment, är′gya·ment, *n.* *Math.* an independent variable upon which the value of a mathematical expression depends; *computer,* the object of a search, which, if found, may govern the execution of subsequent instructions to the computer.

ar·gu·men·ta·tion, är″gya·men·tā′shan, *n.* The act of arguing, discussing, or debating; reasoning.

ar·gu·men·ta·tive, är″gya·men′ta·tiv, *a.* Consisting of argument; addicted to argument, disputing, or debating. Partial to debate and discussion.—**ar·gu·men·ta·tive·ly,** är″gya·men′ta·tiv·lē, *adv.*—**ar·gu·men·ta·tive·ness,** är″gya·men′ta·tiv·nis, *n.*

ar·gu·men·tum, är″gya·ment′um, *n.* pl. **ar·gu·men·ta,** är″gyu·ment′a. [L., argument.] An argument presented by a coherent series of reasons.

Ar·gus, är′gus, *n.* A being in Greek mythology having a hundred watchful eyes; hence, any watchful person. (*l.c.*) a species of pheasant, genus *Argusianus* or *Rheinardia,* having its plumage marked with eyelike spots.

Ar·gus-eyed, är′gus·īd″, *a.* Vigilant; watchful; extremely observant.

ar·gyle, ar·gyll, är′gīl, *n.* [< *Argyle,* branch of the Scottish clan of Campbell, from whose tartan the design came.] (*Often cap.*) A pattern of different-colored diamonds on a single-colored background used in knitting; a sock knit in that pattern.

Ar·hat, är′hat, *n.* [Skt. < *arhati,* he deserves.] A Buddhist monk who is greatly respected for achieving Nirvana.

a·ri·a, ä′rē·a, âr′ē·a, *n.* [It. lit. 'atmospheric air' < L. *aer.*] A song; an air; a tune; an intricate melody for a single voice and accompaniment, as in an opera.

Ar·i·an, âr′ē·an, ar′ē·an, *n.* One maintaining the doctrines of *Arius* (fourth century A.D.), who held Christ to be a created being inferior to God.—*a.* Pertaining to these doctrines.—**Ar·i·an·ism**, âr′ē·a-·niz″um, ar′ē·a·niz″um, n.

a·ri·bo·fla·vin·o·sis, ā″rī·bo·flā″vi·nō′-sis, n. Med. a state brought about by a deficiency of riboflavin (vitamin B$_2$ or G) in the diet, in which irritation of the mucous membrane of the mouth and discoloration of the tongue may be found.

ar·id, ar′id, a. [L. aridus.] Dry; exhausted of moisture; parched with heat; unimaginative; lifeless.—**a·rid·i·ty**, a·rid′i·tē, n. The state of being arid; dryness; want of interest.

Ar·ies, âr′ēz, âr′ē·ēz″, n. [L. aries, a ram.] The Ram, a northern constellation located between Taurus and Pisces; the first of the twelve signs in the zodiac.

a·right, a·rīt′, adv. [M.E. < O.E. ariht < a and riht, right.] In a right way or form; properly; correctly; rightly.

ar·il, ar′il, n. [Probably < N.L. arillus, raisin, seed < L. arere, to be dry.] An extra covering or appendage of the seed of some plants, as the nutmeg, outside the true seed coats, falling off spontaneously.

a·ri·o·so, är″ē·ō′sō, ar″ē·ō′sō, adv. [It. < aria.] Mus. in the manner of an aria: a musical direction.—n.

a·rise, a·rīz′, v.i.—past arose, pp. arisen, ppr. arising. To move to a higher place; to mount; to ascend; to come into view; to appear; to get out of bed, or quit a sitting or lying posture; to spring; to originate; to start into action; to rise.

a·ris·ta, a·ris′ta, n. pl. **a·ris·tae**, a·ris′tē. [N.L. < L., beard of grain.] Bot. An awn or beard; a bristlelike appendage.—**a·ris·tate**, a·ris′tāt, a.

ar·is·toc·ra·cy, ar″i·stok′ra·sē, n. pl. **ar·is·toc·ra·cies**. [L.L. aristocratia < Gr. aristokratia < aristos, best, and -kratia, -cracy < kratos, rule.] Government by the nobility or persons of rank in the state; the nobility or chief persons in a state; a superior group or class; as, the intellectual aristocracy.

a·ris·to·crat, a·ris′to·krat″, ar′i·sto·krat″, n. [< aristocratic.] A member of the aristocracy; one who favors an aristocracy; one who apes the aristocracy.

a·ris·to·crat·ic, a·ris″to·krat′ik, a. [< M.Fr. or M.L. < Gr. aristocratikos. ARISTOCRACY.] Pertaining or belonging to the aristocracy or to the rule of aristocrats; resembling the aristocracy. Also **a·ris·to·crat·i·cal**.—**a·ris·to·crat·i·cal·ly**, a·ris″to·krat′i·kal·ē, adv.

Ar·is·to·te·lian, ar″i·sto·tēl′yan, ar″i·sta·tē′lē·an, a·ris″to·tēl′yan, a·ris″to·tē′lē·an, a. Pertaining to Aristotle (born 384 B.C.), the celebrated Greek philosopher and founder of the Peripatetic school.—n. A follower of Aristotle; a Peripatetic.—**Ar·is·to·te·lian·ism**, n.

a·rith·me·tic, a·rith′me·tik, n. [L. arithmetica < Gr. arithmētikē, of numbers < arithmos, number.] The science of numbers or the art of computation by figures or numerals.—ar″ith·met′ik, a. Pertaining to arithmetic; according to the rules or methods used in arithmetic. Also **ar·ith·met·i·cal**.—**ar·ith·met·i·cal·ly**, ar″ith·met′i·kal·ē, adv. By the rules or methods of arithmetic.—**a·rith·me·ti·cian**, a·rith′mi·tish′an, ar″ith·mi·tish′an, n. One skilled in arithmetic.

ar·ith·met·ic mean, n. A quantity formed by adding several numbers together in any order and dividing the result by the number of addends. (The arithmetic mean of 3, 7, 9, 11, and 15 is 9.)

ar·ith·met·ic pro·gres·sion, n. A series of numbers showing increase or decrease by a constant quantity, as 2, 4, 6, 8, etc. 9, 7, 5, 3; compare geometric progression.

ark, ärk, n. [M.E. < O.E. arc, < L. arca, a chest.] Scrip. the repository of the covenant

or tablets of the law; the large floating vessel in which Noah and his family were preserved during the deluge. A place of safety; the place in a synagogue for the Torah.

arm, ärm, n. [M.E. < O.E. arm, earm = Goth. arms, Icel. armr, Gr., Fris., D., Dan., and Sw. arm; cogn. with L. armus, the shoulder; Gr. armos, a fitting, < arariskein, to fit.] The limb of the human body which extends from the shoulder to the hand; an anterior limb; anything projecting from a main body, as a branch of a tree; a narrow inlet of waters from the sea; a support, as part of a chair, for comfort; a branch of the national defense.

arm, ärm, n. [M.E. armen < O.Fr. < L. arma, arms.] A weapon; a branch of a military service. Pl. war; the military profession; armor; armorial bearings.

arm, ärm, v.t. [M.E. armen < O.Fr. armer < L. armare, to arm < arma, weapons.] To furnish or equip with arms or weapons; to cover or provide with whatever will add strength, force, or security; to fortify.—v.i. To provide oneself with arms; to take arms.—**arm·er**, är′mėr, n.

ar·ma·da, är·mä′da, är·mā′da, n. [Sp. < M.L. armata, fleet < armatus, armed < armare, to arm.] A fleet of armed ships; a squadron. (Cap.) the Spanish fleet assembled to act against England in the reign of Queen Elizabeth I, 1588 A.D.

ar·ma·dil·lo, är″ma·dil′ō, n. pl. **ar·ma·dil·los**. [Sp. dim. of armado, one who is armed, so called from its bony shell.] A mammal peculiar to warm regions of N. and S. America, covered with a hard bony shell divided into small separate plates like a coat of mail.

Ar·ma·ged·don, är″ma·ged′on, n. [Possibly from Plain of Megiddo.] The scene of the final conflict of nations, Rev. xvi. 16; any decisive conflict; a conflict between good and evil.

ar·ma·ment, är′ma·ment, n. [L. armamenta (pl.), armaments.] A nation's military forces equipped for war; a land force or a naval force; armor and combat equipment; preparation for combat.

ar·ma·men·tar·i·um, är″ma·men·târ′-ē·um, n. pl. **ar·ma·men·tar·i·a**, är″-ma·men·târ′ē·a. [L., arsenal, armory < armamenta.] An equipment of implements, appliances, or the like, esp., the equipment of instruments, drugs, therapeutic resources, etc., at the command of a physician.

ar·ma·ture, är′ma·chėr, n. [L. armatura, arms, equipment < armatus. ARM.] A piece of iron connecting two poles of a magnet; the part of a dynamo or generator which consists primarily of coils or wire around a core of iron; armor; anything serving as a defense, as the prickles and spines of plants.

arm·chair, ärm′châr″, n. A chair with arms to support the elbows and arms.

arm·chair, a. Pertaining to a person who partakes vicariously of experiences as sports, travel, etc.; also referring to one who offers suggestions for the solution of a problem for which he has no responsibility and scant experience.

armed, ärmd, a. Having arms; as, long-armed. Bearing weapons; fortified.

armed forc·es, n. pl. The combined naval, military, and air forces of a nation or group of allied nations.

Ar·me·ni·an, är·mē′nē·an, är·mēn′yan, a. Of Armenia, an ancient country in Western Asia, now a region comprising a U.S.S.R. republic and parts of Turkey and Iran; of the people of Armenia or their Indo-European language.—n. A native of Armenia; the Indo-European language of the Armenians, derived from the Aramaic alphabet.

arm·ful, ärm′fụl″, n. pl. **arm·fuls**. As much as the arms can hold; that which is em-

braced by the arms; a large quantity; as, an armful of sticks.

arm·hole, ärm′hōl″, n. An opening for the arm in an article of clothing.

ar·mi·ger, är′mi·jėr, n. [L. < arma, arms, and genere, bear.] An armor-bearer to a knight; a squire; also, one entitled to armorial bearings.—**ar·mig·er·ous**, är·mij′ėr·us, a. Entitled to armorial bearings.

ar·mil·la·ry sphere, är′mi·ler″ē sfēr, är·mil′a·rē, n. Astron. an arrangement of rings, intended to show the relative positions of the principal circles of the heavens.

Ar·min·i·an, är·min′ē·an, n. A member of the Protestant sect who follows the teaching of Arminius, a Dutch theologian (died 1609), chiefly opposed to the Calvinistic doctrine of predestination.

ar·mi·stice, är′mi·stis, n. [Fr. < N.L. < L. arma, and stitium < sistere, to stop.] A suspension of military operations by mutual agreement among the belligerent parties.

Ar·mi·stice Day, n. Veterans Day; Nov. 11, observed in commemoration of the day, Nov. 11, 1918, on which the armistice asked by Germany and granted by the Allies went into effect, at the close of World War I.

arm·let, ärm′lit, n. A little arm or armlike part, as of the sea; also, an ornamental band for the upper arm.

ar·moire, ärm·wär′, n. [Fr.] A large cupboard, closet, or wardrobe.

ar·mor, Brit. **ar·mour**, är′mor, n. [M.E. armure, O.Fr. armeure, < L. armatura, armor, < armare, to arm.] Defensive arms; any covering worn to protect the body in battle, sports, etc.; the steel covering intended as a protection for an airplane, tank, or warship; heavy protective coating on wire or hose.

ar·mor·clad, Brit. **ar·mour·clad**, är′mor·klad″, a. Encased in or covered with armor for protection.

ar·mored, Brit. **ar·moured**, är′mord, a. Milit. of vehicles and other equipment, protected by armor. Of a military force, provided with tanks and other armored equipment.

ar·mor·er, Brit. **ar·mour·er**, är′mor·ėr, n. A maker or manufacturer of armor or arms, or one who keeps them in repair; one who has the care of arms and armor.

ar·mo·ri·al, Brit. **ar·mour·i·al**, är·mōr′ē·al, a. Belonging to armor, or to the arms or escutcheon of a family.

Ar·mor·ic, är·mor′ik, är·mor′ik, a. [Celt, ar-, upon, and mor, the sea.] Pertaining to the northwestern part of France, formerly called Armorica, now Brittany. Also **Ar·mor·i·can**, är·mor′i·kan, är·mor′i·kan.—n. The language of the Celtic inhabitants of Brittany, allied to the Welsh; Breton.

ar·mor·y, Brit. **ar·mour·y**, är′mo·rē, n. pl. **ar·mor·ies**, **ar·mour·ies**. A repository for arms and instruments of war, a collection of arms; a place where military reserves are trained.

arm·pit, ärm′pit″, n. The hollow under the shoulder or upper arm; axilla.

ar·my, är′mē, n. pl. **ar·mies**. [M.E. < M.Fr. armée, an armed force or army < M.L. armata. ARMADA.] A collection or body of persons in regiments, brigades, or similar divisions under proper officers, exclusive of the navy and air force; a unit of a military land force; as, the 5th Army; a host; a vast multitude; a great number.

ar·my ant, n. Any ant of the suborder Dorylinae, traveling in large groups and usually establishing temporary nests.

ar·my·worm, n. The caterpillar of a noctuid moth, Pseudaletia unipuncta, so called from its marching in compact and enormous bodies, devouring green things.

ar·ni·ca, är′ni·ka, n. [N.L.] A composite plant, genus Arnica, otherwise called mountain tobacco. The roots yield tannin.

---

a- fat, fāte, fär, fâre, fạll;   e- met, mē, mėre, hėr;   i- pin, pīne;   o- not, nōte, mŏve;   u- tub, cūbe, bụll;   oi- oil;   ou- pound.

and a tincture of the dried flower heads is used as an application to wounds and bruises.

ar·oid, ar'oid, âr'oid, *a.* [N.L. < *arum.*] Arumlike; araceous.—*n.* Any araceous plant.—**a·roi·de·ous,** a·roi'dē·us, *a.*

a·ro·ma, a·rō'ma, *n.* [M.E. *aromat,* spice < O.Fr. < L. < Gr. *arōma,* spice, sweet herb.] An agreeable odor; fragrance; perfume; bouquet; a distinctive characteristic; flavor.

ar·o·mat·ic, ar"o·mat'ik, *a.* Giving out an aroma; fragrant; sweet-scented; odoriferous; also **ar·o·mat·i·cal,** ar"o·mat'i·kal. *Chem.* pertaining to a compound containing an unsaturated ring of carbon atoms.

ar·o·mat·ic, ar"o·mat'ik, *n.* A plant, drug, or medicine which yields a fragrant smell, and often a warm, pungent taste.

a·ro·ma·tize, a·rō'ma·tīz", *v.t.—aroma-tized, aromatizing.* To impregnate with aroma; to render fragrant; to perfume.

a·round, a·round', *adv.* [M.E. < *a-* and *round.*] In a round, circle, or circuit; circularly or spherically about; on every side; as, a dense mist lay *around;* here and there, throughout or about; as, to travel *around* from place to place; somewhere about or near; as, to wait *around* for.

a·round, a·round', *prep.* In a direction that turns about; so as to encircle or encompass; on all sides of. *Colloq.* here and there in; as, to roam *around* the country; somewhere in or near; as, to stay *around* the house.

a·rouse, a·rouz', *v.t.—aroused, arousing.* [*a-,* and *rouse.*] To excite into action; to stir or put in motion or exertion; to rouse; to animate; to awaken; to provoke.—*v.i.* To awaken oneself or become aroused.

ar·peg·gi·o, är·pej'ē·ō", är·pej'ō, *n.* pl. **ar·peg·gi·os.** [It. < *arpa,* a harp.] *Mus.* The distinct sound of notes of a chord, heard when the notes are struck in rapid succession; a chord executed in arpeggio.

ar·pent, är'pent, *n.* [M.Fr. < L.L. *arepennis;* < Celtic.] An old French land-measure, varying in extent but averaging .85 acre (still used in Louisiana and Quebec); also, in Quebec, a linear measure equal to about 12 rods.

ar·que·bus, är'kwe·bus, *n.* pl. **ar·que·bus·es.** [Fr. *arquebuse,* corrupted < D. *haakbus,* a gun fired from a rest, < *haak,* a hook, a forked rest, and *bus,* a gun = E. *hagbut, hackbut.*] An old-fashioned hand gun fired from a rest. Also *harquebus.*

ar·rack, ar'ak, *n.* [Ar. *araq,* juice, spirits, from *araqa,* to sweat.] A spirituous liquor distilled in the East and Middle East, from rice, the juice of the coconut and other palms, etc.

ar·raign, a·rān', *v.t.* [M.E. < M.Fr. *ar-raigner, aresner,* to arraign < O.Fr. *a-* (< L. *ad-*), to, and *raisnier,* speak < L. *ratio, rationis,* account, a pleading in a suit. REASON.] To call or set at the bar of a court of justice to answer an indictment; to call before the bar of reason or taste; to accuse or charge; to censure publicly; to impeach. —**ar·raign·ment,** a·rān'ment, *n.* The act of arraigning.

ar·range, a·rānj', *v.t.—arranged, arranging.* [M.E. *arangen* < M.Fr. *arangier* < O.Fr. *a-* (< L. *ad-*), and *rengier,* to set in a row.] To put in proper order; to dispose or set out; to give a certain collocation to; to adjust; to settle; to come to an agreement or understanding regarding; to prepare; to adapt, as a musical score.—*v.i.* To make or come to terms; to come to a settlement or agreement.—**ar·rang·er,** a·rānj'ĕr, *n.*

ar·range·ment, a·rānj'ment, *n.* The act of arranging; disposition in suitable form; that which is arranged; a preparatory measure. *Usu. pl.* preparations. Settlement; adjustment; adaptation, as of a musical score.

ar·rant, ar'ant, *a.* [A form of *errant,* wan-

dering, hence vagrant, vagabond, thorough, in a bad sense.] Notorious; evil.—**ar·rant·-ly,** ar'ant·lē, *adv.*

ar·ras, ar'as, *n.* [From *Arras,* in France, where this article was manufactured.] Tapestry; wall hangings, consisting of woven fabric ornamented with figures; *theater,* a loosely-hung curtain that forms the backdrop of a stage.

ar·ray, a·rā', *n.* [M.E. < O.Fr. *arrai,* order, arrangement, dress—prefix *ar-* (L. *ad,* to), and (assumed) *rai,* order, from the Teutonic root seen in E. *ready.*] A collection or assemblage of men or things disposed in regular order, as an army in order of battle. Raiment; dress; apparel.

ar·ray, a·rā', *v.t.* To place or dispose in order, as troops for battle; to marshal; to deck or dress; to attire.

ar·rear, a·rēr', *n.* [M.E. < M.Fr. *arrière,* behind < L. *ad-,* to, and *retro,* behind.] *Usu. pl.* The state of being behind in completing one's obligations; a debt; that which remains unpaid or undone when the due time is past.

ar·rear·age, a·rēr'ij, *n.* The state of being in arrears; a debt or liability that is overdue.

ar·rest, a·rest', *v.t.* [M.E. < M.Fr. *ar-rester* < L. < *ad-,* to, and *restare,* to remain. REST.] To check or hinder the motion or action of; to stop; to seize or apprehend by virtue of a warrant from authority; to seize and fix (attention); to engage; to secure; to catch.

ar·rest, a·rest', *n.* The act of arresting; seizure; apprehension; stoppage; stay; restraint.—**ar·rest·er, ar·res·tor,** a·rest'ĕr, a·rest'or, *n.* One that arrests.—**ar·rest·ment,** a·rest'ment, *n.* The act of arresting; detention; arrest.

ar·rest·ing, a·res'ting, *a.* Attracting attention; impressive; eye-catching.

ar·rhyth·mi·a, a·riTH'mē·a, *n.* [N.L. < Gr. < *a-,* neg. and *rhythmes, rhythm.*] Absence or disturbance of rhythm, as, for example, in heartbeat.

ar·rhyth·mic, a·riTH'mik, *a.* [N.L. < Gr. *a-* and *rhythmos.*] Without regularity or rhythm.

ar·ris, ar'is, *n.* [M.Fr. *areste,* an arris.] The line in which two meeting surfaces of a body form an angle, as between two channels on a Doric column.

ar·ri·val, a·rī'val, *n.* The act of arriving; a coming to or reaching of some goal; attainment; the person or thing which arrives.

ar·rive, a·rīv', *v.i.—arrived, arriving.* [M.E. < O.Fr. *arriver,* < L.L. *adripare,* to come to shore < L. *ad-,* to, and *ripa* (Fr. *rive*), the shore or bank.] To come to a certain place or point; to get to a destination; to reach a point or stage; to attain a certain result or state, followed by *at;* as, to *arrive at* an answer.

ar·ri·vé, ar"ē·vā', *n.* [Fr. < *arriver,* to arrive.] A person who has climbed swiftly to a position of status or wealth.

ar·ri·viste, ar"ē·vēst', *n.* [Fr. < *arriver* to arrive.] An individual who has achieved success through dubious means; a forward person.

ar·ro·gance, ar'o·gans, *n.* [M.E. < L. *arrogantia* < *arrogare* < *ad-,* to, and *rogare,* to ask or desire.] The character of being arrogant; the disposition to make exorbitant claims of rank, dignity, or estimation; the pride which exalts one's own importance; pride with contempt of others; presumption; haughtiness; disdain.

ar·ro·gant, ar'o·gant, *a.* [M.E. < L. AR-ROGANCE.] Making exorbitant claims on account of one's rank, power, worth; presumptuous; haughty; overbearing; proud and assuming.—**ar·ro·gant·ly,** ar'o·gant·-lē, *adv.* In an arrogant manner.

ar·ro·gate, ar'o·gāt", *v.t.—arrogated, arro-gating.* [M.E. < L. ARROGANCE.] To claim or

demand unduly or presumptuously; to lay claim to in an overbearing manner. To attribute (something) to another presumptuously.—**ar·ro·ga·tion,** ar"o·gā'shan, *n.* The act of arrogating; the claiming of superior consideration or privileges.

ar·ron·disse·ment, a·ron'dis·ment, är"on·dēs'ment, *n.* [Fr.] In France, the largest administrative division of a department.

ar·row, ar'ō, *n.* [M.E. *arewe* < O.E. *arwe, earh.*] A slender missile weapon consisting of a long slender shaft with a sharp, pointed head, used for shooting from a bow; a mark similar in form to show direction, often painted on signs or buildings; anything resembling an arrow. (*Cap.*), *astron.* the northern constellation Sagitta.

ar·row·head, ar'ō·hed', *n.* The head or tip of an arrow, typically of an elongated triangular shape with the base or short side often having a reentrant angle; any mark having the shape of an arrowhead; also, any plant of the aquatic genus *Sagittaria,* species of which have arrow-headed leaves. —**ar·row·head·ed,** *a.*

ar·row·root, ar'ō·rōt", *n.* A tropical American plant, *Maranta arundinacea,* or some other species, whose rhizomes yield a nutritious starch much used in food preparations; the starch itself, or a similar starch from some other plant; a food preparation made of such starch.

ar·row·wood, ar'ō·wụd", *n.* Any of several shrubs and small trees, as the wahoo, *Euonymus atropurpureus,* and certain viburnums, with tough, straight shoots, formerly used for making arrows.

ar·roy·o, a·roi'ō, *n.* pl. **ar·roy·os,** a·roi'-ōz. [Sp.] *Southwestern U.S.* A watercourse; also, the dry bed of a stream; a gully.

ar·se·nal, är'se·nal, *n.* [It. *arsenale* < Ar. *dār sinā'ah,* lit. 'house of handwork.'] A repository or magazine of arms and military stores for land or naval service; a public establishment where military equipment is manufactured or stored.

ar·se·nate, är'se·nāt, är'se·nit, *n. Chem.* a salt of arsenic acid.

ar·se·nic, är'se·nik, *n.* [M.E. < L. < Gr. *arsenikon,* arsenic by folk etymology of *arsen-,* male, and *-ikes, -ic* < Syriac *zarniq,* arsenic.] An element, a grayish-white substance having a metallic luster and forming poisonous compounds. Sym. As, at. no. 33. See Periodic Table of Elements. Arsenic trioxide, As_2O_3, a white or transparent, highly poisonous substance used in medicine and in industry.

ar·sen·ic, är·sen'ik, *a.* Of, concerned with, or partially composed of arsenic, particularly in the pentavalent state.

ar·sen·i·cal, är·sen'i·kal, *a.* Of or pertaining to arsenic; containing arsenic. Also **ar·se·ni·ous.**

ar·se·nide, är'se·nīd", är'se·nid, *n. Chem.* a binary compound of arsenic and a positively charged group (as a metal) wherein the arsenic is not bonded to oxygen.

ar·se·nite, är'se·nīt", *n.* A salt or ester of an acid containing arsenic with a trivalent element.

ar·se·no·py·rite, är"se·nō·pī'rīt, är·sen'-o·pī'rit, *n.* [*Arsenic* and *pyrite.*] A silver-white or steel-gray mineral, a compound of iron, arsenic, and sulfur, FeAsS, occurring in orthorhombic crystals or in masses or grains: an important ore of arsenic. Also *mispickel.*

ar·sine, är·sēn', är'sēn, är'sin, *n.* [N.L. < *arsenic.*] *Chem.* AsH_3, a colorless, inflammable, highly poisonous gas, with a fetid garliclike odor.

ar·sis, är'sis, *n.* pl. **ar·ses,** är'sēs. [Gr. *arsis* < *airein,* to elevate.] *Mus.* the unaccented portion of a measure; upbeat. *Pros.* a greater stress or force on a syllable; originally, the unstressed syllable.

---

ar·son, är′son, *n.* [O.Fr. < L. *ardēre*, to burn.] The malicious burning of property.
—ar·son·ist, *n.*

art, ärt, *n.* [M.E. < O.Fr. < L. *ars, artis,* art. ARM.] The use or employment of things to answer some special purpose; the employment of means to accomplish some end: opposed to *nature*; a system of rules to facilitate the performance of certain actions; skill in applying such rules: opposed to *science*; as, the *art* of building or of engraving, the fine *arts*; one of the fine arts or the fine arts collectively, that is, those that appeal to the taste or sense of beauty, as painting, sculpture, music; the profession of a painter or sculptor; the special skill required by those who practice these arts; artistic faculty; skill knack; artfulness; cunning; duplicity. *Pl.* liberal arts.

art, ärt. [O.E. *eart.*] *Archaic, poet.* second person sing., present tense, of *be.*

ar·te·mis·i·a, är″te·miz′ē·a, är″te·mizh′ē·a, *n.* [N.L. < L. < Gr.] *Hort.* Wormwood; the genus of composite plants found in the drier portions of the Northern Hemisphere; specif. *Artemisia tridentata,* the western sage brush.

ar·te·ri·al, är·tēr′ē·al, *a.* Pertaining to an artery or to the oxygenated blood contained in the arteries. Pertaining to through traffic on a street or highway.—*n.* A street or highway with through-traffic facilities.

ar·te·ri·al·ize, är·tēr′ē·a·līz″, *v.t.—arterialized, arterializing.* To change venous blood to arterial blood by oxygenation.

ar·te·ri·og·ra·phy, är·tēr′ē·äg′ra·fē, *n.* [N.L.] *Med.* The visualization of an artery or arterial system by x-ray after the injection of a radiopaque medium; a description of the pulse (sphygmography) or arteries.

ar·te·ri·o·la, är·tēr′ē·ō′la, *n.* Arteriole.

ar·te·ri·ole, är·tēr′ē·ōl′, *n.* [N.L. < *artery* and *-ola,* dim.] *Anat.* A small, muscular walled artery approx. 0.2 mm in diameter; a terminal (end) artery feeding into the capillaries. Also *arteriola.*—**ar·te·ri·o·lar,** är·tēr′ē·ō·lar, *a.*

ar·te·ri·o·scle·ro·sis, är·tēr″ē·ō·skle·rō′sis, *n.* [N.L. < Gr. *arteria,* artery, and *scleros,* hard.] A disease in which thickening of the walls of arteries impedes circulation of the blood.

ar·te·ri·o·ve·nous, är·tēr″ē·ō·vē′nus, *a.* [N.L. < *arterio-* and *venous.*] Relating to the veins and arteries; also, connecting them.

ar·te·ri·tis, är·te·rī′tis, *n.* [N.L.] *Pathol.* inflammation of an artery.

ar·ter·y, är′te·rē, *n. pl.* **ar·ter·ies.** [M.E. < L. *arteria* < Gr. *artēria.*] One of a system of cylindrical vessels or tubes, which convey the blood from the heart to all parts of the body, to be brought back again by the veins. *Fig.* a main channel, as for transportation or communication.

ar·te·sian, är·tē′zhun, *a.* [Fr. *artésien,* pertaining to *Artois.*] Of or pertaining to a kind of well formed by a perpendicular boring into the ground, often of great depth, through which water rises to the surface of the soil by subterranean pressure, producing a constant flow or stream.

art·ful, ärt′ful, *a.* Cunning; sly; devious; crafty; skillful; ingenious.—**art·ful·ly,** ärt′ful·ē, *adv.* In an artful manner; cunningly; craftily.—**art·ful·ness,** ärt′ful·nis, *n.* The quality of being artful.

ar·thral·gia, är·thral′je, *n.* [N.L. < Gr. *arthron,* joint, and *algos,* pain.] *Pathol.* pain, esp. neuralgic pain, in a joint.—**ar·thral·gic,** är·thral′jik, *a.*

ar·thrit·ic, är·thrit′ik, *a.* Pertaining to or affected by arthritis.—*n.*—**ar·thrit·i·cal·ly,** är·thrit′i·kal·ē, *adv.*

ar·thri·tis, är·thrī′tis, *n.* [L. < Gr. < *arthron,* a joint.] Any inflammation of the joints; the gout.

ar·thro·mere, är′thro·mēr″, *n.* [N.L.] *Zool., anat.* one of the segmented parts of an articulate or jointed animal, esp. an invertebrate.

ar·thro·pod, är′thro·pod″, *n.* [N.L. < Gr. *arthron,* joint, and *poùs, podos,* foot.] Any member of the *Arthropoda,* a phylum of invertebrates with segmented bodies and jointed limbs: included are myriapods, arachnids, crustaceans, and insects.—**ar·throp·o·dal, ar·throp·o·dan, ar·throp·o·dous,** är·throp′o·dal, är·throp′o·dan, är·throp′o·dus, *a.*

ar·thro·sis, är·thrō′sis, *n. pl.* **ar·thro·ses,** är·thrō′sēz. [N.L. < Gr. *arthrōsis, arthrōyn,* fasten by a joint, < *arthron,* a joint.] *Anat.* an articulation or suture of two bones or cartilages.

ar·thro·spore, är′thro·spōr″, är′thro·spạr″, *n.* [N.L. < *arthro-,* < Gk., *arthros,* joint and *spore.*] *Bact.* an isolated vegetative cell which has passed into a resting state: occurring in species of bacteria, and not regarded as a true spore.—**ar·thro·spo·rous,** är″thro·spōr′us, är″thro·spạr′us, *a.*

Ar·thu·ri·an, är·thụr′ē·an, *a.* Of or pertaining to Arthur, a legendary king of ancient Britain, who, with his knights, formed the subject of a great body of romantic literature.

ar·ti·ad, är′tē·ad″, *n.* [< Gr. *artios,* even.] *Chem., obs.* an element whose atomic number is even: opposed to *perissad.*

ar·ti·choke, är′ti·chōk, *n.* [It. *articiocco* < Ar. *al pharshûf* the artichoke.] A composite plant somewhat resembling a thistle, cultivated in gardens for the thick and fleshy flower head, used as a cooked vegetable. See *Jerusalem artichoke.*

ar·ti·cle, är′ti·kal, *n.* [M.E. < O.Fr. < L. *articulus,* a joint, division, part, or member, dim. of *artus,* a joint.] A single clause, item, point, or particular; a point of faith, doctrine, or duty; a provision of a contract or treaty, as of the Charter of the United Nations; a prose contribution to a newspaper, magazine, or other periodical; a particular commodity or substance; a part of speech used before nouns to limit or define their application: in English, *a* or *an* and *the.*

ar·ti·cle, är′ti·kal, *v.t.—articled, articling.* To draw up under distinct heads or particulars; to bind, as an apprentice; to indenture.

ar·tic·u·lar, är·tik′yu·lẽr, *a.* [M.E. < L. *articularis.*] Belonging to the joints or to a joint.

ar·tic·u·late, är·tik′yu·lit, *a.* [N.L. < L. *articulatus,* jointed, distinct.] Jointed; formed with joints (an *articulate* animal); formed by the distinct and intelligent movement of the organs of speech; pronounced distinctly; expressed clearly; distinct (*articulate* speech or utterance); pertaining to one who speaks with ease or facility of vocabulary.—**ar·tic·u·late·ly,** är·tik′yu·lit·lē, *adv.* In an articulate manner; with distinct utterance.—**ar·tic·u·late·ness,** är·tik′yu·lit·nis, *n.* The quality of being articulate.

ar·tic·u·late, är·tik′yu·lāt″, *v.t.—articulated, articulating.* To joint; to unite by means of a joint; to utter by intelligent and appropriate movement of the vocal organs; to enunciate, pronounce, or speak clearly.—*v.i.* To utter articulate sounds; to utter distinct syllables or words.—**ar·tic·u·la·tor,** är·tik′yu·lā″tor, *n.* One who articulates.

ar·tic·u·la·tion, är·tik″yu·lā′shan, *n.* The act or manner of articulating or being articulated; a joining or juncture, as of the bones; a joint; a part between two joints.

ar·tic·u·la·to·ry, är·tik′yu·la·tōr″ē, *a.* Of or concerned with articulation.

ar·ti·fact, ar·te·fact, är′ti·fakt″, *n.* [L. *arte,* by art or skill, and *factum < facere,* to do.] Any man-made object, esp. a simple ornament or tool; an artificial product of some external source or agency; *biol.* any unnatural change in structure or tissue.

ar·ti·fice, är′ti·fis, *n.* [M.Fr. < L. *artificium < ars, artis,* art, and *facio < facere,* to do, to make.] Artful, skillful, or ingenious contrivance; a crafty device; a clever trick; shift; stratagem; deception; cunning; guile; fraud.

ar·tif·i·cer, är·tif′i·sẽr, *n.* A skillful or artistic worker; a maker or contriver; a mechanic or handicraftsman.

ar·ti·fi·cial, är″ti·fish′al, *a.* Made or contrived by art, or by human skill and labor; feigned; simulated; fictitious; assumed; affected; stilted; not genuine or natural.—**ar·ti·fi·ci·al·i·ty,** är″ti·fish″ē·al′i·tē, *n. pl.* **ar·ti·fi·ci·al·i·ties.** The quality of being artificial; an artificial trait.—**ar·ti·fi·cial·ly,** är″ti·fish′a·lē, *adv.* In an artificial manner; by human skill and contrivance.—**ar·ti·fi·cial·ness,** är″ti·fish′al·nis, *n.*

ar·ti·fi·cial ho·ri·zon, *n. Aeron.* The line on a flight indicator of an airplane designed to show pitching and banking movements of the plane; the flight indicator itself.

ar·ti·fi·cial in·tel·li·gence, *n.* The ability of a computer to perform tasks characteristic of human intelligence, such as learning from experience and reasoning.

ar·ti·fi·cial res·pi·ra·tion, *n.* A method by which air is rhythmically forced into and out of the lungs of a person whose respiration has ceased.

ar·til·ler·ist, är·til′e·rist, *n.* A person skilled in gunnery; artilleryman.—**ar·til·ler·y·man,** är·til′e·rē·man, *n.* A soldier engaged in the management of large guns.

ar·til·ler·y, är·til′e·rē, *n.* [M.E. < M.Fr. *artillerie,* < *artiller,* to work with art, to fortify, < L. *ars, artis,* art.] Formerly offensive weapons of war in general, whether large or small; now, cannon; great guns; ordnance; ordnance and its equipment both in men and materiel; the men and officers that manage the guns; the science of the use and management of great guns; a branch of an army using such guns.

art·i·ly, ärt′i·lē, *adv.* In an artistic or arty manner.

art·i·ness, ärt′ē·nis, *n.* The quality of being arty.

ar·ti·o·dac·tyl, är″tē·ō·dak′til, *n.* [Gr. *artios,* even-numbered, and *daktylos,* a toe.] A hoofed mammal in which the number of toes is even, as the ox and other ruminants, the pig, etc.

ar·ti·san, är′ti·zan, *n.* [Fr. *artisan* < It. *artigiano* < L.L. *artitianus,* < *ars, artis,* art.] One skilled in any art or trade; a handicraftsman; a mechanic.

art·ist, är′tist, *n.* [M.Fr. *artiste* < M.L. *artista* < L. *ars, artis,* art.] One skilled in an art or profession, especially, one who professes and practices one of the fine arts, as painting, sculpture, engraving, and architecture; specifically, and most frequently, a painter. An adept entertainer.

ar·tiste, är·tēst′, *n.* One [Fr.] who is unusually skillful in an art, as a singer, a dancer, or a chef.

ar·tis·tic, är·tis′tik, *a.* Pertaining to art or artists; trained in art; satisfying the aesthetic standards of art; conformable to or characterized by art. Showing taste or sensitivity. Exhibiting skill in execution.—**ar·tis·ti·cal·ly,** är·tis′ti·kal·ē, *adv.* In an artistic manner.

art·ist·ry, är′ti·strē, *n.* High quality of workmanship; artistic ability.

art·less, ärt′lis, *a.* Devoid of art, skill, or cunning; crude; ingenuous; natural; simple.—**art·less·ly,** ärt′lis·lē, *adv.* In an artless manner; naturally; simply.—**art·less·ness,** ärt′lis·nis, *n.*

art·y, är′tē, *a.*—*artier, artiest.* Imitative of art, esp. garish, crude, or showy; trying to be artistic.

ar·um, âr′um, *n.* [L.] Any plant of the genus *Arum* in the family *Araceae,* the arum family, bearing flowers in a large spathe; any related plant, as the calla lily.

a·run·di·na·ceous, a·run″di·nā′shus, *a.* [L. < *arundo,* a reed.] Pertaining to reeds; resembling a reed.

Ar·y·an, âr′ē·an, âr′yan, ar′ē·an, ar′yan, *n.* [Skt. *ârya,* noble, eminent.] *Ethnol.* a descendant of speakers of early Indo-European languages. In Nazi ideology, a non-Jewish Caucasian of Nordic extraction. *Ling.* Indo-European; Indo-Iranian.—*a.*

ar·y·te·noid, ar″i·tē′noid, a·rit′e·noid″, *a.* [N.L. < Gr. *arytainoeidēs* < *arytaina,* ladle, cup, and *eidos,* form.] *Anat.* Ladle-shaped, hence, pertaining to or being the two cartilages of the larynx, to which are attached the vocal cords; relating to muscles and glands adjoining the larynx.—*n.* An arytenoid cartilage.—**ar·y·te·noi·dal,** ar″i-ta·noid′al, a·rit″a′noid′al, *a.*

as, az, *adv.* [M.E. *als, alse, also,* < O.E. *alswā, ealswā,* all so, quite so, quite as, as. ALSO.] To such a degree or extent: the antecedent in the correlation *as . . . as* (as good as gold), the consequent being sometimes omitted (this is *as* good); for example: in the style or manner.—**as well as,** as much or as truly as; just as; as also; as, to give facts *as well as* opinions; good *as well as* beautiful; hence, elliptically, *as well,* equally; also; too; as, beautiful, and good *as well.*

as, az, *conj.* The consequent in the correlations *as . . . as, so . . . as, such . . . as, same . . . as,* etc., noting degree, extent, manner, etc. (as good *as* gold, in the same way *as* before), or in the correlations *so as, such as,* noting purpose or result (with infinitive: to listen so *as* to hear, such *as* to please); also (without antecedent), in the degree, manner, etc., of or that (to be good *as* gold, to rank *as* major, do *as* we do); also, when or while; since; for instance; even or just, now chiefly in the phrase *as yet.*—**as if,** as it would be if; also **as though.**—**as it were,** so to speak.

as, az, *prep.* Like; in the role or capacity of, as: He works *as* a salesman.

as, as, *n. pl.* **as·ses,** as′iz. A Roman weight of 12 oz.; also, a Roman copper or bronze coin, weighing ½ oz.

as·a·fet·i·da, as·a·foet·i·da, as″a·fet′i·da, *n.* [M.E. < M.L. < *asa* (< Per. *azā,* mastic) and L. *fetida, foetida,* fetid.] A gum-resin with a strong garliclike odor, from the roots of several plants of Persia and Afghanistan, of the genus *Ferula:* used in medicine as an antispasmodic.

as·bes·tos, as·bes·tus, as·bes′tus, az·-bes′tus, *n.* [M.E. *albestron* < L. < Gr. *asbestos,* inextinguishable < *a-,* neg., and *sbennynai,* to extinguish, and *-tos.*] A fibrous variety of hornblende having fine, elastic, flexible filaments, which are incombustible, and are made into fireproof cloth, paper, etc.; the mineral chrysotile used in the same way; the material made from asbestos.—**as·bes·tine,** as·bes′tin, az·bes′tin, *a.*

as·cend, a·send′, *v.i.* [M.E. < L. *ascendere* < *ad-,* to, and *scandere,* climb.] To climb or go upward (opposed to *descend*); rise to a higher point or degree; slope or tend upward; go toward the source or beginning; go back in time.—*v.t.* To climb; mount; go up; go toward the source of (a river).—**as·cend·a·ble, as·cend·i·ble,** *a.*

as·cend·ance, as·cend·ence, a·sen′dans, *n.* Ascendancy.—**as·cend·an·cy, as·cend·en·cy,** a·sen′dan·sē, *n.* The state of being in the ascendant; dominance.

as·cend·ant, as·cend·ent, a·sen′dant, *a.* [M.E. < L. *ascendēns (-ent-) < ascendere.*] Ascending; rising, esp. above the horizon or toward the zenith; superior; dominant.

as·cend·ant, a·sen′dant, *n.* An ancestor (opposed to *descendant*). *Astrol.* the point of the ecliptic or the degree of the zodiac rising above the horizon at a specific time; the horoscope; hence, fig. 'the ascendant,' the position of dominance or controlling influence; superiority; predominance.

as·cend·er, a·sen′dėr, *n.* The portion of a letter of the lower case which extends above the x-height. A letter in the lower case that has a portion which extends above the x-height, for example: *d.* One who ascends.

as·cend·ing, a·sen′ding, *a.* Rising; tending upward; *bot.* growing or directed upward, esp. obliquely or in a curve from the base.

as·cen·sion, a·sen′shan, *n.* [M.E. < L. *ascensio(n-).*] The act of ascending; ascent; *astron.* the rising of a star or point above the horizon on the celestial sphere; *eccles.,* (*cap.*) the bodily passing of Christ from earth to heaven, Luke, xxiv. 51.

as·cen·sion·al, a·sen′shan·al, *a.* Referring or pertaining to ascent or ascension.

As·cen·sion Day, *n.* The day on which Christ's Ascension into Heaven is annually commemorated, the fortieth day after Easter.

as·cent, a·sent′, *n.* [< *ascend.*] The act of rising; motion upward; advancement; rise; the way by which one ascends; acclivity; an upward slope; the act of proceeding from an inferior to a superior degree, from particulars to generals, or the like.

as·cer·tain, as″ėr·tān′, *v.t.* [M.E. < M.Fr. < O.Fr. *acertener* < a- for *ad-,* to, and *certener* < *certain* < L. *certus,* sure. CERTAIN.] To make certain; to make sure or find out by trial or examination; to establish; to determine with certainty.—**as·cer·tain·a·ble,** as″ėr·tān′a·bl, *a.* Capable of being ascertained.—**as·cer·tain·ment,** as″ėr·tān′ment, *n.* The act of ascertaining.

as·cet·ic, a·set′ik, *a.* [Gr. *askētikos,* exercised, disciplined, < *askein,* to exercise.] Excessively strict or rigid in devotions or mortifications; severe; austere; rigorous.—*n.* One who retires from the world and devotes himself to a strictly devout life; one who practices excessive rigor and self-denial; a hermit; a recluse.—**as·cet·i·cism,** a·set′i·siz″um, *n.*

as·cid·i·an, a·sid′ē·an, *n.* [N.L. < Gr. *askidion,* dim. of *askos,* bag, wineskin.] One of a class, *Ascidiacea,* of marine animals; a sea squirt; a tunicate.

as·cle·pi·ad, a·sklē′pē·ad, *n.* [N.L. < Gr., after ASCLEPIUS.] *Bot.* any plant of the milkweed family.

as·co·carp, as′ko·kärp″, *n.* [N.L. < Gr. *askos* and *carpos,* fruit. ASCUS.] *Bot.* in certain higher fungi, one of the spherical, saucer-shaped, or cup-shaped bodies enclosing the asci, spores, and paraphyses.

as·co·go·ni·um, as″ko·gō′nē·um, *n. pl.* **as·co·go·ni·a,** as″ko·gō′nē·a. [N.L. < *ascus* and *gonium.*] *Bot.* the female sexual organ in the gametophyte of some higher fungi.—**as·co·go·ni·al,** as″ko·gō′nē·al, *a.*

as·co·my·cete, as″ko·mī·sēt′, *n.* Any of the *Ascomycetes,* a class of fungi characterized by formation of spores within an ascus and including yeasts and certain mildews and molds.—**as·co·my·ce·tous,** as″ko·mī·sē′-tus, *a.*

a·scor·bic ac·id, ā·skạr′bik as′id, a·-skạr′bik, *n.* [N.L. < a- neg., and *scorbutus,* scurvy. SCORBUTIC.] The antiscorbutic vitamin, $C_6H_8O_6$, vitamin C, abundant in citrus fruits, tomatoes, and green vegetables and also produced synthetically.

as·cot, as′kot, *n.* [< *Ascot* Heath, a racetrack in England.] A wide neck scarf that is looped and knotted under the chin with the ends crossing each other.

a·scrib·a·ble, a·skrīb′a·bl, *a.* Capable of being ascribed or attributed.

as·cribe, a·skrīb′, *v.t.*—*ascribed, ascribing.* [M.E. < L. *ascrībere* < *ad-,* to, and *scrībere,* to write. SCRIBE.] To attribute, impute, or refer, as to a cause; to credit; to assign; to set down; to attribute, as a quality or appurtenance.

as·crip·tion, a·skrip′shan, *n.* The act of ascribing.

as·cus, as′kus, *n. pl.* **as·ci,** as′ī. [N.L. < Gr. *askos,* a bladder, a leather bottle.] *Bot.* one of the little membranous bags or cells in ascomycetes in which the sexual spores are developed.

as·dic, az′dik, *n.* [(*A*)nti-(*S*)ubmarine (*D*)etection (*I*)nvestigation (*C*)ommittee.] Sonar.

a·sep·sis, a·sep′sis, ā·sep′sis, *n.* [N.L. < Gr. *a-,* without, and *sepsis,* putrefaction.] Absence of microorganisms; prevention of sepsis.

a·sep·tic, a·sep′tik, ā·sep′tik, *a.* [N.L.] Free or freed from septic material; free from germs causing disease; also, without warmth or feeling.

a·sex·u·al, ā·sek′shö·al, *a.* [N.L. < a-, neg. and *sexual.*] *Biol.* Not sexual; having no distinctive sex organs, or having imperfect organs; performed without the union of males and females or without sexual differentiation; produced without sexual differentiation or action.—**a·sex·u·al·ly,** ā·sek′shö·al·ē, *adv.* In an asexual manner.

a·sex·u·al gen·er·a·tion, *n. Biol.* the generation of an organism (which undergoes alternation of generations) in which asexual reproduction takes place.

a·sex·u·al re·pro·duc·tion, *n. Biol.* reproduction without union (of germ cells), as fission, spore formation, etc.

as for, *prep.* Concerning.

ash, ash, *n.* [O.E. *æsc, asce.*] What remains of a completely burned material; the dust or powdery substance to which a body is reduced by the action of fire: generally used in the plural; incombustible residue. *Pl.* the remains of a human body when cremated; remains; ruins.

ash, ash, *n.* [O.E. *aesc* = Icel. *askr.* Sw. and Dan. *ask,* D. *esh,* G. *esche.*] A well-known oleaceous tree of the genus *Fraxinus,* cultivated extensively for its hard and tough timber; the timber of this tree.

a·shamed, a·shāmd′, *a.* [M.E. < O.E. < *āscamian* < *ā-,* perfective, and *scamian,* to shame.] Affected or touched by shame; feeling shame or guilt; exhibiting shame (an *ashamed* look); deterred by fearing shame or ridicule.—**a·sham·ed·ly,** a·shām′id·lē, *adv.* In a shamefaced manner.

ash·can, ash′kan″, *n.* A metal refuse container; *navy slang,* a depth charge.

ash·en, ash′en, *a.* Pertaining to or like the ash tree; made of ash timber. Pale; ash-colored; of ashes.

Ash·ke·naz·i, äsh″ke·nä′zē, *n. pl.* **Ash·-ke·naz·im,** äsh″ke·nä′zim. [Heb. < *Ashkenaz,* a descendant of Japheth (Gen. x. 3), a people descended from him, and *-i,* indicating membership.] One of the Central and Eastern European Jews and their descendants, as distinguished from the Sephardim or Spanish-Portuguese Jews and their descendants, the two groups differing from each other in liturgy and in pronunciation of Hebrew, but not in doctrine.—**Ash·ke·naz·ic,** äsh″ke·nä′zik, *a.*

ash·lar, ash·ler, ash′lėr, *n.* [M.E. *asheler* < M.Fr. < O.Fr. *aisselle, aissil,* a shingle, < L. *assula,* a small board, a chip or splinter.] Squared building stone; a facing made of squared stones on the front of buildings; hewn stone for such facing.

a·shore, a·shōr′, a·shạr′, *adv.* On the shore, bank, or beach; on the land adjacent to water; to the shore.

Ash Wed·nes·day, *n.* The first day of Lent.

ash·y, ash′ē, *a.*—*ashier, ashiest.* Composed of or resembling ashes; lifeless and pale.

A·sian, ā′zhan, ā′shan, *a.* Pertaining to Asia or its inhabitants.

A·sian chol·er·a, *n. Pathol.* cholera.

A·sian in·flu·en·za, *n. Pathol.* a variant epidemic form of influenza, probably originating in China. Also **A·sian flu.**

A·si·at·ic, ā″zhē·at′ik, ā″shē·at′ik, ā″zē··at′ik, *a.* Belonging to Asia or its inhabitants. —*n.* A native of Asia.

a·side, a·sīd′, *n. Theater,* the lines of an actor intended only for the audience, and supposedly not heard by others on the stage. A digression from the main theme, as a parenthetical remark.

a·side, a·sīd′, *adv.* On or to one side; to or at a short distance off; apart; away from some normal direction; out of one's thoughts, consideration, or regard; away; off; as, to lay cares *aside;* in reserve; as, to set something *aside;* in a separate place.

a·side from, *prep.* Besides; excluding.

as if, *conj.* That; as one would if; as it would be if.

as·i·nine, as′i·nīn″, *a.* [L. *asininus,* < *asinus,* an ass.] Belonging to or having the qualities of an ass; absurdly stupid or obstinate; silly.

ask, ask, äsk, *v.t.* [O.E. *ascian, acsian, axian,* = Dan. *æske,* D. *eischen,* O.Fris. *askia,* O.G. *eiscôn.*] To request; to seek to obtain by words; to petition (with *of* before the person); to require, expect or claim; to demand; to interrogate or inquire of; to question; to inquire concerning; to seek to be informed about (to *ask* the way); to invite.—*v.i.* To make a request or petition (with *for* before an object); to inquire or seek by request (often followed by *after*).—

ask·er, ask′ėr, äsk′ėr, *n.* One who asks; a questioner, inquirer, petitioner.

a·skance, a·skans′, *adv.* [M.E. *ascaunce,* etymology doubtful.] Sideways; obliquely; out of one corner of the eye. With mistrust or suspicion. Also **a·skant,** a·skant′.

a·skew, a·skū′, *adv., a.* In an oblique or skew position; obliquely; awry.

a·slant, a·slant′, a·slänt′, *adv.* At a slant; slantingly; obliquely.—*prep.* Slantingly across; athwart.

a·sleep, a·slēp′, *a., adv.* In or into a state of sleep; at rest; in a dormant state; sleeping.

a·slope, a·slōp′, *a., adv.* Sloping; diagonally; deflected from the perpendicular.

a·so·cial, ā·sō′shal, *a.* Withdrawn; avoiding the company of others; selfish.

as of, *prep.* During; at or on a specific date, time, etc.; from.

a·so·ma·tous, ā·sō′ma·tus, *a·sō′ma·tus, a.* [L.L. < Gr. *asomatos,* < *a-,* neg., and *soma,* body.] Without a body; incorporeal.

asp, asp, *n.* [M.E. *aspis* < L. < Gr. *aspis,* an asp.] A deadly species of viper, esp. the Egyptian cobra; also, a species of viper found on the continent of Europe.—**asp·ish,** as′pish, *a.*

as·par·a·gin, as·par·a·gine, a·spar′a··jin, *a·spar′a·jēn″, n.* [Fr. < L. < Gr. ASPARAGUS.] *Biochem.* an amino acid, $NH_2COCH_2CH(NH_2)COOH$, which occurs in rhombic crystals and may be found in asparagus, marshmallow, belladonna, and several other plants.

as·par·a·gus, a·spar′a·gus, *n.* [N.L. < L. < Gr. *asparagos* < *spargan,* to swell.] A perennial herb of the lily family cultivated in gardens for its edible young shoots; the shoots of this plant.

as·par·tic ac·id, a·spär′tik, as′id, *n.* [N.L. < L. *asparagus.*] *Biochem.* the acidic amino acid, $COOHCHNH_2CH_2COOH$, occurring as a product of hydrolysis in proteins. Also

a·mi·no·suc·cin·ic ac·id, as·par·a··gin·ic ac·id, as·par·a·gic ac·id.

as·pect, as′pekt, *n.* [M.E. < L. *aspectus,* < *aspicere,* < to look on < *ad-,* to, and *specere,* to see or look.] Look; view; appearance to the eye or the mind (to present a subject in its true *aspect);* countenance; look or particular appearance of the face; mien; air (a severe *aspect);* view commanded; feature; prospect; outlook (a house with a southern *aspect); astrol.* the apparent position of one planet with respect to another.

as·pect ra·tio, *n. Television,* the ratio of the width to the height of an image.

as·pen, as′pen, *n.* [O.E. *aspen, æspe,* the aspen = D. *esp,* Icel. *ösp,* Sw. and Dan. *asp,* G. *espe,* the aspen tree.] A species of poplar that has become proverbial for the trembling of its leaves, which move with the slightest impulse of the air. Also **asp.**

as·per·ges, a·spur′jēz, *n.* [L., 2nd pers. sing. fut. of *aspergere,* to sprinkle.] *Rom. Cath. Ch.* the rite of sprinkling the altar, clergy, and people with holy water before High Mass on Sundays; *(cap.)* the anthem beginning "Asperges," sung while the priest performs this rite.

as·per·gil·lo·sis, as″pėr·ji·lō′sis, *n.* pl. **as·per·gil·lo·ses.** *Med.* the condition characterized by the presence of *Aspergillus* in tissues or on a mucous surface; *veter. med.* infection of the lungs and air sacs of birds by the mold *Aspergillus fumigatus.*

as·per·gil·lus, as″pėr·jil′us, *n.* pl. **as··per·gil·li.** [N.L. < *aspergillum.*] *Bot.* a fungus of the genus *Aspergillus,* family *Aspergillacae,* class *Ascomycetes,* with branched radiate sporophores.

as·per·i·fo·li·ate, as″pėr·i·fō′lē·āt, *a.* [N.L. < L. *asper,* rough, and *folium,* leaf.] *Bot.* having rough leaves.

as·per·i·ty, a·sper′i·tē, *n.* pl. **as·per·i··ties.** [M.E. < O.Fr. < L. *asperitas,* from *asper,* rough.] The quality or state of being rough; roughness or harshness to the touch, taste, hearing, or feelings; tartness; crabbedness; severity; acrimony.

as·perse, a·spurs′, *v.t.*—*aspersed, aspersing.* [L. *aspergere, aspersus* < *ad-,* and *spargere,* to scatter or sprinkle.] To sprinkle; to bespatter with foul reports or false and injurious charges; to slander or calumniate.

as·per·sion, a·spur′zhan, a·spur′shan, *n.* A sprinkling, as of water; the spread of calumnious reports or charges; calumny; a damaging criticism. The act of defamation, or a defamatory statement.

as·phalt, as′falt, as′falt, *n.* [M.E. < L.L. < Gr. *asphaltos,* < *asphalizein,* to make firm.] The most common variety of bitumen; mineral pitch; a black or brown substance which melts readily and has a strong pitchy odor; a mixture of asphalt or bitumen and sand or other substances, used for pavements, floors, the lining of tanks, etc.— **as·phalt rock** or **stone,** a dark-colored bituminous limestone.—**as·phal·tic,** as··falt′ik, as·falt′ ik, *a.* Pertaining to or containing asphalt; bituminous.

as·phal·tite, as·fal′tīt, as·fal′tīt, as′fal··tīt″, *n.* A form of subterranean native asphalt.

a·spher·ic, ā·sfer′ik, *a. Opt.* not truly spherical. Also **a·spher·i·cal,** ā·sfer′i·kal.

as·pho·del, as′fo·del″, *n.* [L. *asphodelus,* < Gr. *asphodelos.*] Any of various liliaceous plants of the genera *Asphodelus* and *Asphodeline,* native to southern Europe, with white or yellow flowers; also, any of various other perennial plants, as the daffodil.

as·phyx·i·a, as·fik′sē·a, *n.* [N.L. < Gr. *asphyxia* < *a-,* not, and *sphyxis,* the pulse, < *sphyzein,* to throb.] Lack of oxygen or an excess of carbon dioxide in the system resulting in suspended animation or loss of consciousness, caused by interrupted respiration, particularly from suffocation or

drowning, or the inhalation of irrespirable gases.

as·phyx·i·ate, as·fik′sē·āt″, *v.t.*—*asphyxiated, asphyxiating.* To bring to a state of asphyxia; to cause asphyxia in. To kill or cause unconsciousness by halting normal breathing through gas, choking, etc.—*v.i.* To become asphyxiated.—**as·phyx·i·a··tion,** as·fik″sē·ā′shan, *n.*

as·pic, as′pik, *n.* [Fr. origin unknown.] A dish consisting of a clear, savory meat, fish or tomato jelly.

as·pi·dis·tra, as″pi·dis′tra, *n.* [N.L. < Gr. *aspid-, aspis,* shield.] The herb *Aspidistra elatoir,* also called cast-iron-plant because of its resistance to heat, cold, dust, etc.

as·pir·ant, a·spīr′ant, as′pir·ant, *n.* One who aspires or seeks with eagerness; a candidate.

as·pir·ant, a·spīr′ant, as′pir·ant, *a.* Aspiring.

as·pi·rate, as′pi·rāt″, *v.t.*—*aspirated, aspirating.* *Phon.* to pronounce with a breathing or audible emission of breath; to pronounce with such a sound as the letter *h* in the word *horse. Med.* to remove fluid from a body; to inhale fluid into the lungs.

as·pi·rate, as′pir·it, *n. Phon.* An aspirated sound like that of *h;* the letter *h* itself, or any mark of aspiration.

as·pi·ra·tion, as″pi·rā′shan, *n.* The act of aspirating; *phon.* an aspirated sound in pronunciation. The act of aspiring or of ardently desiring; an ardent wish or desire chiefly after what is great and good; *med.* the removal of fluid from the body.— **as·pir·a·to·ry,** a·spīr′a·tōr″ē, a·spīr′a··tạr″ē, *a.* Pertaining to breathing; suited to the inhaling of air.

as·pi·ra·tor, as′pi·rā″tor, *n.* A device that uses suction to move air, liquids, or granular substances.

as·pire, a·spīr′, *v.i.*—*aspired, aspiring.* [M.E. < M.Fr. < L. *aspirare,* to breathe < *ad-,* to, and *spirare,* to breathe, to endeavor after (in *expire, respire,* etc.). SPIRIT.] To desire with eagerness; to aim at something elevated or above one; to be ambitious, followed by *to* or *after;* to ascend; to tower; to point upward; to soar.—**as·pir·er,** a·spīr′-ėr, *n.*

as·pi·rin, as′pi·rin, as′prin, *n.* [< G. trademark < *A(cetyl), Spir(säure)* salicylic acid, and *-in.*] *Pharm.* a white crystalline derivative of salicylic acid, $C_9H_8O_4$, used to relieve pain and reduce fever; a tablet made of this.

as·por·ta·tion, as″por·tā′shan, *n.* [M.E. < L. *asportatio* < *asportare,* to carry off.] A carrying away; specifically, the felonious removal of goods from the place where they were deposited.

as re·gards, *prep.* Concerning.

ass, as, *n.* [O.E. *assa,* a male ass, *assen,* the female, also *esol, asal* = Goth. *asilus,* D. *ezel,* G. *esel.* Icel. *asni, asna,* Dan. *asen,* Lith. *asilas,* Gael. *asal,* W. *asyn,* L. *asinus;* ultimate origin unknown.] A type of quadruped, *Equus asinus,* of the horse family, used as a beast of burden. A dull, stupid fellow; a dolt; a blockhead.

as·sa·fet·i·da, as″a·fet′i·da, *n.* Asafetida.

as·sa·gai, as·se·gai, as′a·gī, *n.* [Pg. *azagaia* < Ar. *alzagâya* < *al,* the, and *zagaya,* a Berber word for a kind of weapon.] An instrument of warfare among the Kaffirs; a throwing spear; a species of javelin. A South African cornaceous tree which provides the wood for such spears.

as·sail, a·sāl′, *v.t.* [M.E. < O.Fr. *asaillir* < L. *assilire,* to leap or rush upon < *ad-,* to, and *salire,* to leap, to rise. ASSAULT.] To fall upon with violence; to set upon; assault; attack, with actual weapons or with arguments, censure, abuse, criticism, entreaties, or the like; to make an impact upon. *Assail* is not so strong as *assault,* which implies more violence, and is more frequently used in a figurative sense.—**as·sail·a·ble**, *a·-sāl′a·bl*, *a*. Capable of being assailed.— **as·sail·ant**, *a·sāl′ant*, *n*. One who assails, attacks, or assaults.

as·sas·sin, *a·sas′in*, *n*. [M.L. < Ar. *hashsā-shīn*, *hashishin*, one who murders when infuriated by *hashish*, a maddening drink made from hemp.] One who kills, esp. one who kills for money or because of fanatical beliefs; a murderer, esp. of a high-ranking political figure. (*Cap.*) one of a secret Muslim sect in Palestine at the time of the Crusades whose members terrorized Christians.

as·sas·si·nate, *a·sas′i·nāt*, *v.t.—assassinated, assassinating.* To kill by surprise or secret assault; to murder by sudden violence. To destroy treacherously.—**as·sas·si·na·tion**, *a·sas″i·nā′shan*, *n*. The act of assassinating; a killing or murdering by surprise or secret assault.—**as·sas·si·na·tor**, *a·sas′-i·nā′tor*, *n*.

as·sault, *a·salt′*, *n*. [M.E. *asuat* < O.Fr. *assault*, < L.L. *assaltus*, < L. *ad-*, to, and *saltus* < *salire*, to leap. Assail, insult, result, etc., are akin.] An attack or violent onset, physical or verbal; *law*, a threat or attempt to injure a person without doing the injury: compare *battery*. A sudden and vigorous attack on a fortified defense.

as·sault, *a·salt′*, *v.t.* To fall upon by violence or with a hostile intention; to fall on with force; to assail; to rape.—**as·sault·er**, *a·sal′tèr*, *n*. One who assaults.

as·sault boat, *n*. *Milit.* a small, lightweight boat used for amphibious troop landings on beaches and for crossing rivers and lakes. Also *storm boat*.

as·say, *a·sā′*, *as′ā*, *n*. [M.E. < O.Fr. *assai*, *essay*, a trial, examination, *essayer*, to test, from L. *exagium*, Gr. *exagion*, a weighing < *ex-*, out, *agere*, to bring. *Essay* is derived from the same word.] The trial of the purity, weight, value, etc., of metals, especially gold and silver, their ores and alloys; analysis of a material to determine its composition; the material to be analyzed; the results of the analysis.

as·say, *a·sā′*, *v.t.* To make an assay of; to examine by trial; to test the purity or metallic constituents of.—*v.i.* To have a measurable content of precious metal as shown by an assay.—**as·say·er**, *a·sā′èr*, *n*.

as·se·gai, *as′e·gī″*, *n*. Assagai.

as·sem·blage, *a·sem′blij*, *n*. The act of assembling, or state of being assembled; a collection of individuals or of particular things; a gathering or company.

as·sem·ble, *a·sem′bl*, *v.t.—assembled, assembling.* [M.E. < O.Fr. *assembler*, < L.L. *assimulare*, to assemble < L. *ad-*, to, and *simul*, together; akin, *similar*, *simulate*, *assimilate*, etc.; same root as E. *same*.] To collect into one place or body; to bring or call together; to convene; to fit together, as pieces of mechanism.—*v.i.* To meet or come together; to gather; to congregate; to convene.—**as·sem·bler**, *a·sem′blèr*, *n*.

as·sem·bly, *a·sem′blē*, *n*. pl. **as·sem·blies**. [See *assemble*.] A company or collection of human beings in the same place, usually for the same purpose; the name given to the legislative body or one of the divisions of it in various states. The fitting together of intricate machinery; a collection of machine parts; a component part, itself made of assembled pieces.

as·sem·bly line, *n*. Production line along which successive operations are performed until the final product is completed.

as·sem·bly·man, *a·sem′blē·man*, *n*. pl. **as·sem·bly·men.** Member of a legislative assembly.

as·sent, *a·sent′*, *n*. [M.E. < O.Fr. *assent* < L. < *ad-*, and *sentire*, to think (also in *consent*, *dissent*, *sense*, etc.).] Consent;

concurrence; acquiescence; agreement to a proposal; accord; agreement; approval.— **roy·al as·sent**, the approbation given by the British sovereign in Parliament to a bill which has passed both houses, after which it becomes law.

as·sent, *a·sent′*, *v.i.* To express an agreement of the mind to what is alleged or proposed; to concur; to acquiesce.— **as·sent·er**, *a·sen′tèr*, *n*. One who assents.

as·sen·ta·tion, *as″en·tā′shan*, *n*. [M.E. < L. *assentatio*, flattery; < *assentor*, to assent from interested motives, to flatter.] Ready agreement in order to flatter; adulation.

as·sert, *a·surt′*, *v.t.* [L. *asserere*, *assertum* < *ad-*, to, and *serere*, to join, connect, bind. SERIES.] To vindicate a claim or title to; to affirm positively; to asseverate; to aver; *refl.* to come forward and assume one's rights, claims, etc.—**as·sert·or, as·sert·er**, *a·surt′or*, *n*.

as·ser·tion, *a·sur′shan*, *n*. The act of affirming; the maintaining of a claim; a positive declaration or averment; an affirmation.

as·ser·tive, *a·sur′tiv*, *a*. Positive; affirming confidently; peremptory; declaratory. Also **as·ser·to·ry**, *a·sur′to·rē*.—**as·ser·tive·ly**, *a·sur′tiv·lē*, *adv*. In an assertive manner; affirmatively.—**as·ser·tive·ness**, *a·sur′tiv-nis*, *n*.

as·sess, *a·ses′*, *v.t.* [M.E. < L.L. *assessāre*, < L. *assidēre*, to sit beside, and hence to act as assessor < *ad-*, to, and *sedēre*, to sit; akin, *assiduous*, *reside*, *sedentary*, etc.] To set a certain sum, as a tax, upon; to determine the value of, as property, for the purpose of being taxed; to settle or determine the amount of, as of damages; to evaluate the quality or worth of.—**as·sess·a·ble**, *a·ses′-a·bl*, *a*. Capable of being assessed; liable to be assessed.—**as·sess·a·bly**, *a·ses′a·blē*, *adv*.

as·sess·ment, *a·ses′ment*, *n*. The act of assessing; appraisal; a valuation of property, profits, or income, for the purpose of taxation; a tax or specific sum charged on a person or property.

as·ses·sor, *a·ses′or*, *n*. One appointed to make assessments, esp. of real estate, as a basis for taxes.

as·set, *as′et*, *n*. [Back formation < the sing. *assets*, enough to pay < M.E. < Anglo-French *asetz* < O.Fr. *assez*, enough, < L. *ad-*, to, and *satis*, enough.] An article of goods or property available for the payment of a person's obligations or debts: generally used in the plural; any portion of the entire effects belonging to a person; *pl.* items that can be converted into cash. An advantage.

as·sev·er·ate, *a·sev′e·rāt″*, *v.t.—asseverated, asseverating.* [L. *asseverare*, *asseveratum* < *ad-*, to, and *severus*, serious, severe.] To affirm or aver positively, or with solemnity.—**as·sev·er·a·tion**, *a·sev″e·rā′shan*, *n*.

as·sib·i·late, *a·sib′i·lāt″*, *v.t.—assibilated, assibilating.* [L. *assībilātus*, pp. of *assībilāre*, to hiss at.] *Phon.* To give a hissing sound to; make sibilant.

as·si·du·i·ty, *as″i·dö′i·tē, as″i·dū′i·tē*, *n*. pl. **as·si·du·i·ties.** The quality of being assiduous; constant or diligent application to any business or enterprise; diligence; industry.

as·sid·u·ous, *a·sij′ö·us*, *a*. [L. *assiduus*, < *assidēre*, to sit close < *ad-*, and *sedēre*, to sit. ASSESS.] Constant in application; attentive; industrious; devoted; persevering; unremitting; performed with constant diligence or attention.—**as·sid·u·ous·ly**, *a·sij′ö·us·lē*, *adv*. In an assiduous manner.— **as·sid·u·ous·ness**, *a·sij′ö·us·nis*, *n*.

as·sign, *a·sīn′*, *v.t.* [M.E. < O.Fr. *assigner* < L. *assignare*, < *ad-*, and *signare*, to allot, mark out, < *signum*, a mark (whence *sign*, *consign*, etc.).] To mark out as a portion

allotted; to apportion; to allot; to fix or specify; *law*, to transfer or make over to another.

as·sign, *a·sīn′*, *n*. A person to whom property or an interest is transferred; an assignee.

as·sign·a·bil·i·ty, *a·sī″na·bil′i·tē*, *n*. Condition, state, or quality of being assignable.

as·sign·a·ble, *a·sīn′a·bl*, *a*. Capable of being assigned or attributed.—**as·sign·a·bly**, *a·sīn′a·blē*, *adv*.

as·sig·na·tion, *as″ig·nā′shan*, *n*. The act of assigning or allotting; the act of fixing or specifying; a making over by transfer of title; an appointment of time and place for meeting: chiefly of illicit love meetings.

as·sign·ee, *a·sī·nē′, as″i·nē′*, *n*. A person to whom an assignment is made; a person appointed or deputed to perform some act or business, or enjoy some right.

as·sign·er, as·sign·or, *a·sīn′èr, a·sīn′or*, *n*. One who assigns or appoints.

as·sign·ment, *a·sīn′ment*, *n*. The act of assigning, fixing, or specifying; the writing by which an interest is transferred. A position to which one is appointed. Work assigned; as, a homework *assignment*.

as·sim·i·la·bil·i·ty, *a·sim″i·la·bil′i·tē*, *n*. The quality of being assimilable.

as·sim·i·la·ble, *a·sim′i·la·bl*, *a*. Capable of being assimilated.

as·sim·i·late, *a·sim′i·lāt″*, *v.t.—assimilated, assimilating.* [M.L. < L. *assimulare*.] To make alike; to cause to resemble; to absorb and incorporate, as food, into the system; to incorporate with organic tissues; to adapt, esp. socially or culturally; to liken or compare.—*v.i.* To become similar; to harmonize; to become incorporated with the body; to adjust; to perform the act of converting food into the substance of the body.

as·sim·i·late, *a·sim′i·lāt″, a·sim′i·lat*, *n*. Something that is taken in, absorbed, or assimilated.—**as·sim·i·la·tor**, *a·sim′i-lā·tor*, *n*.

as·sim·i·la·tion, *a·sim″i·lā′shan*, *n*. The act or process of assimilating or being assimilated; the process by which animals and plants convert and absorb nutriment so that it becomes part of the substances composing them. *Phon.* the act of joining adjacent sounds into one sound, as in *kub′erd* for *cupboard*.

as·sim·i·la·tive, *a·sim′i·lā″tiv, a·sim′i-la·tiv*, *a*. Having the power of assimilating; tending to assimilate; producing assimilation. Also **as·sim·i·la·to·ry**, *a·sim′i·la-tor″ē, a·sim′i·la·tar″ē*.

as·sist, *a·sist′*, *v.i.* [M.Fr. *assister* < L. *assistere* < *ad-*, to, and *sistere*, to stand.] To give aid; to take part in any performance. —*v.t.* To take part in or with; aid; help; be associated with as assistant.

as·sist, *a·sist′*, *n*. An act of assisting, as in making a goal in hockey or an out in baseball.

as·sist·ance, *a·sis′tans*, *n*. The act of assisting; the aid or help provided.

as·sist·ant, *a·sis′tant*, *a*. Assisting; auxiliary; associated with a superior in some office or work.—*n*. A helper; an aid; an auxiliary; one who assists a superior in some office or work.

as·size, *a·sīz′*, *n*. [M.E. < O.Fr. *assise*, *assizes*, *assise*, a fixed rate, a tax, < L. *assidēre*, to sit beside, assist. ASSESS.] (*Usu. pl.*) the periodical sessions of court in English counties for the purpose of trying criminal and certain other cases before a jury. An ordinance; a decree; an assessment; formerly, an ordinance which fixed the weight, measure, and price of articles (hence the word *size*).

as·so·ci·a·ble, *a·sō′shē·a·bl, a·sō′sha·bl, a·sō′sē·a·bl*, *a*. Capable of being associated, linked, or connected.

---

as·so·ci·ate, *a·sō'shē·āt", a·sō'sē·āt", v.t.* —associated, associating. [M.E.] < L. *associare, associatum < ad-,* to, and *sociare < socius,* a companion. SOCIAL.] To adopt as a partner, companion, and the like; to join or connect intimately (things together); to unite; to combine. *v.i.* To unite in company; to join in a confederacy or association with others.

as·so·ci·ate, *a·sō'shē·it, a·sō'sē·it, a··sō'shē·āt", a·sō'sē·āt", a.* Joined in interest, object, office, etc.; combined; joined with another or others; having subordinate rank or privileges; as, an *associate* professor.

as·so·ci·ate, *a·sō'shē·it, a·sō'sē·it, a··sō'shē·āt", a·sō'sē·āt", n.* A companion; a mate; a fellow; a partner; a confederate; an accomplice; an ally.

as·so·ci·a·tion, *a·sō'sē·ā'shan, a·sō'·shē·ā'shan, n.* The act of associating or state of being associated; connection; union; a society, the members of which are united by mutual interests or for a common purpose; *philos.* the tendency which one idea or feeling has to recall another; *ecology,* a grouping of organisms living together under uniform conditions and having a uniform distinctive aspect.—**as·so·ci·a··tion·al,** *a.*

as·so·ci·a·tion foot·ball, *n.* Soccer.

as·so·ci·a·tive, *a·sō'shē·ā"tiv, a·sō'sē·ā"·tiv, a·sō'sha·tiv, a.* Capable of associating; tending to associate or unite; leading to association. *Math., logic,* having an equality when elements are regrouped without change in order, as: $(a+b)+c=a+(b+c)$; referring to this property: *associative* law of addition.—**as·so·ci·a·tive·ly,** *a·sō'shē··ā"tiv·lē, a·sō'sē·ā"tiv·lē, a·sō'sha·tiv·lē, adv.*

as·so·nance, *as'o·nans, n.* [Fr. < L. *assonare.*] Resemblance of sounds; *pros.* a species of imperfect rhyme which consists of using the same vowel sound with different consonants following.—**as·so·nant,** *as'o·· nant, a.* Having a resemblance of sounds; *pros.* rhyming only so far as the vowels are concerned.

as soon as, *conj.* Immediately following the time that; immediately at the time that.

as·sort, *a·sạrt', v.t.* [M.Fr. *assortir,* to sort, to assort < *as-* for L. *ad-,* to, and *sors, sortis,* a lot. SORT.] To separate and distribute into sorts, classes, or kinds; to furnish with a suitable variety of goods (to *assort* a cargo); to adapt or suit.—*v.i.* To agree; to suit together; to associate; to keep company.— **as·sort·a·tive,** *a.*—**as·sort·er,** *n.*

as·sort·ed, *a·sạrt'id, a.* Made up of various selected types, sorts, etc.; as, *assorted* chocolates; fitted or matched; as, a curiously *assorted* couple.

as·sort·ment, *a·sạrt'ment, n.* The act of assorting; classification; a mixed collection of things assorted.

as·suage, *a·swāj', v.t.*—assuaged, assuaging. [M.E. < O.Fr. *assouager, assouagier,* < L. *ad-,* to, and *suavis,* sweet.] To allay, mitigate, ease, or lessen pain or grief; to moderate; to appease or pacify passion or tumult.—**as·suage·ment,** *a·swāj'ment, n.*

as·sua·sive, *a·swā'siv, a.* [Appar. a mixture of *assuage* and *persuasive.*] Soothing; alleviative.—*n.* A soothing remedy.

as·sume, *a·sōm', v.t.*—assumed, assuming. [M.E. < L. *assumere < ad-,* to, and *sumere,* to take, also seen in *consume, presume, sumptuous,* etc.] To take upon oneself; to take on; to appear in (*assume* a figure or shape); to appropriate; to take for granted; suppose as a fact; to pretend to possess; to put on; as, to *assume* a wise air; *law,* to undertake or promise.—*v.i.* To be arrogant; to claim more than is due.

as·sum·ing, *a·sōm'ing, a.* Putting on airs of superiority; haughty; arrogant; presumptuous; overbearing.

as·sump·sit, *a·sump'sit, n.* [N.L. he undertook < *assumere,* to undertake.] *Law.* An action to recover damages for breach of a simple contract or a promise not under seal; also, an actionable promise.

as·sump·tion, *a·sump'shan, n.* [L. *assumptio < L. < assumere.* ASSUME.] The act of assuming; a taking upon oneself; a taking possession of; the act of taking for granted; supposition; arrogance; the thing supposed; a postulate or proposition assumed on the future course of events; (*cap.*) a church festival celebrated August 15 in honor of the miraculous ascent to heaven of the Virgin Mary's body after death.

as·sump·tive, *a·sump'tiv, a.* Capable of being assumed; assumed; taken for granted; presumptuous.

as·sur·ance, *a·shụr'ans, n.* The act of assuring; a pledge furnishing ground of full confidence; firm persuasion; certain expectation; undoubting steadiness; intrepidity; excess of boldness; impudence; laudable confidence; self-reliance; courage; firmness; *Brit.* insurance.

as·sure, *a·shụr', v.t.*—assured, assuring. [M.E. < M.Fr. < M.L. *assecurare < L. ad-,* to, and *securus,* secure.] To make (a person) sure or certain; to convince (to *assure* a person of a thing); to declare or affirm solemnly to; to confirm; to ensure; to secure (to *assure* success to a person); insure; *N.T.* to embolden or make confident.

as·sured, *a·shụrd', a.* Certain, convinced; guaranteed; not doubting or doubtful; bold to excess; confident; having life or goods insured (in this sense often a noun, sing. or pl.).—**as·sur·ed·ly,** *a·shụr'id·lē, adv.* Certainly; indubitably.—**as·sur·ed·ness,** *a·· shụr'ed·nes, n.* The state of being assured; certainty; full confidence.

as·sured, *a·shụrd', n.* pl. **as·sured, as··sureds.** *Insurance.* The party insured; the party in whose favor an insurance policy stands.

as·sur·er, *a·shụr'ér, n.* One who assures; *specif.* an insurance underwriter.

as·sur·gent, *a·sụr'jent, a.* [L. *assurgens, assurgentis,* ppr. of *assurgere < ad-,* to, and *surgere,* to rise, SURGE.] Rising or directed upward.

As·syr·i·an, *a·sir'ē·an, a.* Pertaining or relating to Assyria, an ancient Asian land, to its inhabitants or their language.—*n.* A native or inhabitant of Assyria; the language of the Assyrians.

As·syr·i·ol·o·gy, *a·sir''ē·ol'o·jē, n.* [See *-logy.*] The science or study of Assyrian antiquities.—**As·syr·i·ol·o·gist,** *a·sir''ē·· ol'o·jist, n.*

a·stat·ic, *ā·stat'ik, a.* [Gr. *a-,* not, and root *-sta-,* to stand.] Unstable; unsteady; having no tendency to take a definite position, as a magnetic needle whose directive power has been neutralized; *phys.* being without polarity.—**a·stat·i·cal·ly,** *ā·stat'i·kal·ē, adv.* In an astatic manner.—**a·stat·i··cism,** *a·stat'i·siz"um, n.*

as·ta·tine, *as'ta·tēn, as'ta·tin, n.* [Gr. *astatos,* unstable.] *Chem.* an unstable element belonging to the halogen family and produced by bombardment of bismuth with alpha particles. Sym. At, at. no. 85. See Periodic Table of Elements.

as·ter, *as'tér, n.* [N.L. < L. < Gr. *astēr,* a star.] A large genus of composite plants, with ray and tubular flowers, or only tubular flowers, which somewhat resemble stars.

a·ste·ri·a, *a·stēr'ē·a, n.* [L. < Gr. *asterios,* starry < *aster,* star.] A gem stone, as a sapphire, which when cut as a cabochon shows a starlike luminous figure. See *asterism.*

as·te·ri·at·ed, *a·stēr'ē·ā"tid, a.* Exhibiting asterism, as a sapphire.

as·ter·isk, *as'te·risk, n.* [L. < Gr. *asteriskos,* a little star < *aster,* star.] A figure resembling a star, thus *, used in printing and writing, as a reference to a note or to fill the space where something is omitted.

as·ter·isk, *as'te·risk, v.t.* To note with an asterisk; to star.

as·ter·ism, *as'te·riz"um, n.* [Gr. *asterismos, < asterizein,* mark with stars, < *aster, star.*] A group of stars; also, three asterisks placed before a passage to direct attention to it; rarely, a single asterisk; also, a property of some crystallized minerals of showing a starlike luminous figure in reflected or transmitted light, as in sapphire.

a·stern, *a·stụrn', adv.* In, at, or toward the stern of a ship; behind a ship; backward; with the stern foremost.

a·ster·nal, *ā·stụr'nal, a. Anat.* Not connected to the sternum or breastbone; without a sternum; not sternal.

as·ter·oid, *as'te·roid", n.* [Gr. < *aster,* a star, and *eidos,* form.] One of the small planets that revolve about the sun mainly between the orbits of Mars and Jupiter, more accurately called *planetoids.* A starfish.

as·ter·oid, *as'te·roid", a.* Resembling a star; pertaining to the asteroids, or to starfish. Also **as·ter·oi·dal,** *as''te·roid'al.*

as·the·ni·a, *as·thē'nē·a, as''the·nī'a, n.* [N.L. < Gr. *astheneia < a-,* not, and *sthenos,* strength.] Debility; want of strength.

as·then·ic, *as·then'ik, a.* Characterized by asthenia or debility; weak; frail; slight in build.

asth·ma, *az'ma, as'ma, n.* [M.E. < M.L. < Gr. *asthma,* short-drawn breath.] A chronic, paroxysmal disorder of respiration, characterized by difficulty in breathing.—**asth··mat·ic,** *az·mat'ik, as·mat'ik, a.* Pertaining to asthma; affected by asthma.—*n.* A person troubled with asthma.

as though, *conj.* As if.

as·tig·mat·ic, *as''tig·mat'ik, a.* [N.L. < Gr. *a-,* priv., and *stigma (stigmat-),* prick, spot.] Pertaining to or exhibiting astigmatism.—**as·tig·mat·i·cal·ly,** *as''tig·mat'i·· kal·ē, adv.*—**a·stig·ma·tism,** *a·stig'ma·· tiz"um, n.* A defect of the eye or of a lens whereby rays of light from an external point fail to converge to a focus, thus giving rise to imperfect vision or images.

a·stir, *a·stụr', adv., a.* On the move; stirring.

as to, *prep.* About; respecting; according to.

a·sto·ma·tal, *ā·stäm'at·al, ā·stō'mat·al, a. Bot.* having no stomata.

a·stom·a·tous, *ā·stom'a·tus, ā·stō'ma··tus, a.* [< Gr. *a-,* without, and *stoma,* a mouth.] *Zool., bot.* without a mouth, stoma, or stomata.

as·ton·ish, *a·ston'ish, v.t.* [M.E. *astonien* < O.Fr. *estoner < L.L. extonare < ex-* and *tonare,* thunder.] To strike or impress with wonder, surprise, or admiration; to surprise; to amaze.—**as·ton·ish·ing,** *a·ston'· i·shing, a.* Calculated to astonish; amazing; wonderful; surprising.—**as·ton·ish·ing·ly,** *a·ston'i·shing·lē, adv.*

as·ton·ish·ment, *a·ston'ish·ment, n.* The state or feeling of being astonished; amazement; great surprise; *O.T.* a cause or matter of astonishment.

as·tound, *a·stound', v.t.* [For old *astoune,* O.E. *astunian,* with *d* added, as in *sound, expound.*] To astonish; to strike dumb with amazement; to shock with wonder.— **as·tound·ing,** *a·stoun'ding, a.* Amazing; calculated to astound; causing terror; astonishing.

a·strad·dle, *a·strad'l, adv.* Straddling; with one leg on either side; astride.—*a.*

as·tra·gal, *as'tra·gal, n.* [L. < Gr. *astra-galos,* the hipbone, a molding.] *Arch.* a narrow, convex molding, often in beaded form.

a·strag·a·lus, *a·strag'a·lus, n. Anat.* In the higher vertebrates, a bone proximal to the tarsus; in man, the talus, or ankle bone.

---

a- fat, fāte, fär, fâre, fạll;   **e-** met, mē, mēre, hér;   **i-** pin, pīne;   **o-** not, nōte, mōve;   **u-** tub, cūbe, bụll;   **oi-** oil;   **ou-** pound.

as·tra·khan, as′tra·kan, as′tra·kan″, n. [From *Astrakhan* in the U.S.S.R.] Closely curled fur of young lambs from Astrakhan; a rough kind of cloth with a curled pile resembling Astrakhan. Also **as·tra·chan.**

as·tral, as′tral, a. [L.L. *astralis* < L. *astrum* < Gr. *astron*, a star.] Belonging to the stars; starry; *theosophy*, noting the second (astral) body of an individual, composed of a supersensible substance which pervades all space and survives the individual after death.—**as·tral·ly**, as′tral·ē, adv.

a·stray, a·strā′, adv., a. [M.E. < M.Fr. < *estraier*, to stray.] Having strayed; out of the right way or proper place; off the correct path; into error.

a·stride, a·strīd′, adv. With one leg on each side; with the legs wide apart.

a·stride, a·strīd′, prep. Above with a leg on either side of; as, *astride* a horse; bestriding; straddling; lying on both sides of; stretching over or across.

as·trin·gen·cy, a·strin′jen·sē, n. The quality of being astringent.

as·trin·gent, a·strin′jent, a. [L. < *astringere* < *ad-*, to, and *stringere*, to draw.] Stern; severe; terse. *Med.* contracting; styptic; contracting the organic tissues and canals of the body, and thereby checking or diminishing bleeding or excessive discharges.

as·trin·gent, a·strin′jent, n. An astringent substance, as alum, catechu, etc.

as·tro·dome, as′tro·dōm″, n. [N.L. < *astro-* and *dome*.] A transparent dome in the fuselage or body of an aircraft or spacecraft intended primarily to permit taking celestial observations in navigating. Also, an enclosed, climate-controlled arena for sporting events and other entertainment.

as·tro·dy·nam·ics, as″trō·dī·nam′iks, n. pl. [N.L. < *astro-* and *dynamics*.] The practical application of celestial mechanics, astroballistics, propulsion theory, and allied fields to the problem of planning and directing the trajectories of space vehicles.

as·tro·gate, as′tro·gāt″, v.t.—*astrogated, astrogating. Aeron.* to navigate in interplanetary space by means of celestial navigation.—**as·tro·ga·tion**, as″tro·gā′shan, n. The act of astrogating.—**as·tro·ga·tor**, as′tro·gā″tor, n. One who astrogates.

as·tro·labe, as′tro·lāb″, n. [M.E.<M.L.< Gr. < *astēr*, a star, and *-lab-* < *lambánein*, to take.] An instrument formerly used for taking the altitude of the sun or stars at sea, now superseded by the quadrant and sextant. An instrument designed for very accurate celestial altitude measurements, as in survey work.

as·trol·o·ger, a·strol′o·jėr, n. One who practices astrology.

as·tro·log·ic, a″stro·loj′ik, a. Pertaining to astrology. Also **as·tro·log·i·cal.—as·tro·log·i·cal·ly**, a″stro·loj′i·kal·ē, adv. In an astrological manner.

as·trol·o·gy, a·strol′o·jē, n. [M.E. < L. < *astēr*, a star, and *logos*, discourse, theory.] A system which is concerned with the supposed effect and influence of celestial bodies on human affairs.

as·trom·e·try, a·strom′i·trē, n. The branch of astronomy dealing with the geometrical relations of the celestial bodies and their real and apparent motions.

as·tro·naut, as′tro·nạt″, n. [< Fr. *astronaute*; *astro*, astronomy, and *naut*, nautical.] A person who rides in a space vehicle; a traveler in interplanetary space. Specifically, one of the test pilots selected to participate in United States programs for manned space flight.

as·tro·nau·tics, as″tro·nạ′tiks, n. pl. but sing. in constr. [< Fr. *astronautique*; *astro*, astronomy, and *naut*, nautical.] The art, skill, or activity of operating spacecraft; the science of space flight.—**as·tro·nau·ti·cal**, as″tro·nạ′ti·kal, a.—**as·tro·nau·ti·cal·ly**, as″tro·nạ′ti·kal·ē, adv.

as·tro·nav·i·ga·tion, as″trō·nav″i·gā′shan, n. The plotting and directing of the movement of a spacecraft from within the craft by means of observations on celestial bodies. Also *celestial navigation.*

as·tron·o·mer, a·stron′o·mėr, n. One who is versed in astronomy; one who observes celestial bodies.

as·tro·nom·ic, as″tro·nom′ik, a. Pertaining to astronomy. Enormous; exceedingly large. Also **as·tro·nom·i·cal**, as″tro·nom′i·kal. —**as·tro·nom·i·cal·ly**, as″tro·nom′i-kal·ē, adv. According to the principles of astronomy.

as·tro·nom·i·cal u·nit, n. A basic measurement of astronomy; the mean distance between the earth and the sun; 149,599,000 kilometers (approx. 93,000,000 miles).

as·tron·o·my, a·stron′o·mē, n. [M.E. < L. < Gr.] The science that treats of the location, magnitudes, motions, nature, and constitution of celestial bodies and structures.

as·tro·pho·tog·ra·phy, as″trō·fo·tog′ra-fē, n. Photography of the heavenly bodies, as for astronomic purposes.—**as·tro·pho·to·graph·ic**, as″trō·fō″to·graf′ik, a.

as·tro·phys·i·cist, as″trō·fiz′i·sist, n. *Phys.* one who is learned in, or who specializes in, astrophysics.

as·tro·phys·ics, as″trō·fiz′iks, n. pl. but sing. in constr. A branch of astronomy that treats of the chemical composition and physical properties of celestial bodies such as luminosity, size, mass, density, and temperature.

as·tute, a·stōt′, a·stūt′, a. [L. *astūtus*, < *astus*, craft, subtlety.] Of a shrewd and penetrating turn; cunning; sagacious; keen. —**as·tute·ly**, a·stōt′lē, a·stūt′lē, adv. In an astute manner; shrewdly; sharply; cunningly.—**as·tute·ness**, a·stōt′nis, a·stūt′-nis, n. The quality of being astute; cunning.

a·sun·der, a·sun′dėr, adv., a. [O.E. *on sundrum*.] Apart; into parts or pieces; separately.

as well as, prep. In addition to.

as yet, adv. Up to now; up to the present or a specified time.

a·sy·lum, a·sī′lum, n. [L. *asylum* < Gr. *asylon* < *a-*, not, and *sylon*, right of seizure.] A sanctuary or place of refuge; any place of retreat and security; an institution for receiving and maintaining persons suffering from certain bodily defects or mental maladies; a refuge for the destitute.

a·sym·me·try, ā·sim′i·trē, n. [Gr. < *a-*, neg., and *symmetria*, symmetry.] The lack of symmetry or proportion between the parts of a whole.—**a·sym·met·ric**, **a·sym·met·ri·cal**, ā″si·me′trik, ā″si·me′tri·kal, a. Not having symmetry; inharmonious; not reconcilable.—**a·sym·met·ri·cal·ly**, ā′si-me′tri·kal·ē, adv.

a·symp·to·mat·ic, ā·simp″to·mat′ik, a. [N.L.] Lacking any evidence of disease.— **a·symp·tom·at·i·cal·ly**, ā·simp″to·mat′-i·kal·ē, adv.

as·ymp·tote, as′im·tōt″, n. [Gr. *asymptōtos*, not falling together < *a-*, not, *syn-*, with, and *piptein*, to fall.] *Math.* a line which approaches nearer and nearer to some curve, but though infinitely extended would never meet it.—**as·ymp·tot·ic**, as·im·tot′ik, a. Belonging to or having the character of an asymptote. Also **as·ymp·tot·i·cal**, as·im-tot′ik·al.—**as·ymp·tot·i·cal·ly**, as·im-tot′ik·al·li, adv. In an asymptotic manner.

a·syn·chro·nism, ā·sing′kro·niz″um, ā-sin′kro·niz″um, n. [N.L.] Want of synchronism, or coincidence in time.

a·syn·chro·nous, ā·sing′kro·nus, ā·sin′-kro·nus, a. Not synchronous; not happening at the same time.

as·yn·det·ic, as′in·det′ik, a. Pertaining to or characterized by the use of asyndeton.— **as·yn·det·i·cal·ly**, as″in·det′i·kal·ē, adv.

a·syn·de·ton, a·sin′di·ton″, a·sin′di·ton, n. [Gr. *asyndetos*, < *a-*, not, *syn-*, together, *dein*, to bind.] A figure of speech in which conjunctions are omitted, as, *veni, vidi, vici*: I came, I saw, I conquered.

at, at, prep. [O.E. *æt*, Goth. O.S. Icel. *at*, Dan. *ad*, O.H.G. *az*; allied to L. *ad*, to, Skt. *adhi*, upon.] Denoting coincidence or contiguity: in time (*at* first); in space (*at* home, *at* church); in occupation or condition (*at* work, *at* prayer); in degree or condition (*at* best, *at* the worst); in effect, as coincident with the cause (*at* the sight); in relation, as existing between two objects (*at* your command); in value (*at* a dollar a head); also, direction toward (fire *at* the target).—*at large*, at liberty; unconfined; also, generally; as a whole (the country *at large*).

At·a·brine, at′a·brin, at′a·brēn″, n. *Pharm.* quinacrine, used in the treatment of malaria. (Trademark.)

at·a·cam·ite, at″a·kam′īt, a·tak′a·mīt″, n. [< *Atacama*, province of Chile.] A mineral, $CU_2CI(OH)_3$, a basic chloride of copper, occurring commonly in small green prismatic crystals.

at·a·ghan, at′a·gan, n. Yataghan.

at all, adv. In any manner or respect; to the smallest extent; under any circumstances; esp. negative; as, not *at all* well.

at·a·man, at′a·man, n. pl. **at·a·mans.** [Russ.] A chief of Cossacks.

at·a·mas·co, at·a·mas′kō, n. [N. Amer. Ind.] A plant of the amaryllis family, *Atamosco atamasco*, of the southeastern U.S., bearing a single white lilylike flower; also, any species of this genus. Also **at·a·mas·co lil·y.**

at·a·rac·tic, at′a·rak′tik, n. [Gr. *ataraktos*, without confusion < *a-*, neg., and *tarassein*, to disturb.] A drug that decreases anxiety or tension; a tranquilizer.—a. Tranquilizing.

a·tav·ic, a·tav′ik, a. [Fr. < L. *atavus*, remote ancestor.] Of, or pertaining to, remote ancestors. Also **at·a·vis·tic.**

at·a·vism, at′a·viz″um, n. [Fr. < L. *atavus*, an ancestor.] The resemblance of offspring to a remote ancestor; the return or reversion among animals to the original type; *med.* the recurrence of any peculiarity or disease of an ancestor.—**at·a·vist**, at′a·vist, n.— **at·a·vis·tic**, at″a·vis′tik, a.—**at·a·vis·ti·cal·ly**, at″a·vis′ti·kal·ē, adv.

a·tax·i·a, a·tak′sē·a, n. [Gr. *a-*, not, and *taxis*, order.] Want of order; disturbance; *med.* irregularity in the functions of the muscles or in the crisis and paroxysms of disease.—**a·tax·ic**, a·tak′sik, a. Irregular; disorderly; characterized by irregularity.

at·e·lec·ta·sis, at″e·lek′ta·sis, n. pl. **at·e·lec·ta·ses**, at″e·lek′ta·sēs. [N.L. < Gr. *atelēs*, incomplete, and *ektasis*, extension.] *Pathol.* Partial collapse of the lung; failure of the lung to expand completely, esp. at birth.

at·el·ier, at′el·yā″, n. [Fr. a workshop < O.Fr. *astele*, chip of wood < L.L. *astella*.] A workshop; specifically, the workroom of sculptors and painters.

a tem·po, ä tem′pō, adv., a. *Mus.* a direction to resume the original speed; in time.

Ath·a·pas·can, ath″a·pas′kan, a. [N. Amer. Ind.] Belonging to or constituting a linguistic stock of North American Indians extending from Alaska to Hudson Bay and southward to Mexico, and including the Apache, Navajo, and other tribes. Also **Ath·a·pas·kan, Ath·a·bas·can,** and **Ath·a·bas·kan.**

a·the·ism, ā′thē·iz″um, n. [M.E. < Gr. *atheos*, an atheist < *a-*, not, and *theos*, God.] The disbelief in the existence of a God or Supreme Being.

a·the·ist, ā′thē·ist, n. One who professes atheism or disbelief in God.—**a·the·is·tic**

a·the·is·ti·cal, ā″thē·is′tik, ā″thē·is′ti·kal, *a.* Pertaining to, implying, or containing atheism; disbelieving the existence of a God. —**a·the·is·ti·cal·ly,** ā″thē·is′ti·kal·ē, *adv.*

ath·el·ing, ath′e·ling, *n.* [O.E. *ætheling,* < *æthele,* noble = G. *edel,* noble.] In Anglo-Saxon times, a prince; one of the royal family; a nobleman.

ath·e·nae·um, ath·e·ne·um, ath″e·nē′-um, *n.* [L. < Gr. *Athēnē,* the goddess of wisdom.] An institution for the encouragement of literature and art, where books, periodicals, etc., are kept for the use of the members.

A·the·ni·an, a·thē′nē·an, *a.* Pertaining to the city of Athens, in Greece.—*n.* A native or citizen of Athens.

ath·er·o·ma, ath″e·rō′ma,*n.*pl.**ath·er·o·-mas, ath·er·o·ma·ta.** [N.L. < L. < Gr. < *athare,* gruel.] *Pathol.* A condition in which there is a deposit of lipids (fats) within the inner walls of an artery, often causing arteriosclerosis; a sebaceous cyst.

ath·er·o·scle·ro·sis, ath″e·rō·skle·rō′sis, *n.* [N.L.] *Pathol.* A disease in which an artery is dangerously narrowed by lipid deposits in the inner walls; one of the three types of arteriosclerosis—**ath·er·o·scle·rot·ic,** ath″e·rō·skle·rōt′ik, *a.*

ath·e·to·sis, ath″i·tō′sis, *n.* [N.L. < Gr. *athetos,* without position or place, < *a-,* neg., and *tithenai,* to set.] *Pathol.* a condition in which the hands and feet continually perform involuntary, slow, irregular movements, most frequently in children.

a·thirst, a·thurst′, *a.* [O.E. *ofthyrst* < *of,* from, and *thyrstan,* to thirst.] Thirsty; wanting drink; having a keen appetite or desire, followed by *for.*

ath·lete, ath′lēt, *n.* [M.E. < L. < Gr. *athlētēs,* < *athlon,* a contest.] One trained to exercises or games of agility and strength.

ath·lete's foot, *n. Pathol.* ringworm of the feet, a contagious disease caused by a fungus which grows in wet or damp areas.

ath·let·ic, ath·let′ik, *a.* Pertaining to athletes or such exercises as are practiced by athletes; strong; robust; active; vigorous.

ath·let·ics, ath·let′iks, *n. pl., sing. or pl. in constr.* Athletic exercises; sports such as tennis, rowing, boxing, etc.—**ath·let·i·cal·ly,** ath·let′i·kal·ē, *adv.* In an athletic manner.—**ath·let·i·cism,** ath·let′i·siz″um, *n.*

ath·o·dyd, ath′o·did, *n.* [*a*(ero)-*th*(erm)*ody*-(namic) *d*(uct).] *Aeron.* a ramjet, a jet which utilizes no mechanical compresser but the motion of the aircraft to force air into the combustion chamber and produce thrust.

at-home, at-hōm′, *n.* A reception of visitors during certain hours for which a hostess or host has been announced to be "at home."

ath·ro·cyte, ath′ro·sit″, *n.* [N.L. < Gr. *athroos,* together, and *-cyte.*] *Biol.* a cell which has the ability to ingest foreign matter and store it, in granular form, in its cytoplasm.—**ath·ro·cy·to·sis,** ath″ro·sī·-tō′sis, *n.*

a·thwart, a·thwart′, *prep.* Across; from side to side of; *naut.* across the line of a ship's course.

a·thwart, a·thwart′, *adv.* In a manner to cross and perplex; in an opposing manner; *naut.* obliquely across, as the direction of another ship.

a·tilt, a·tilt′, *a., adv.* At a tilt; tilted; with lance inclined, as in a joust.

At·lan·te·an, at″lan·tē′an, at″lan·tē′an, *a.* Pertaining to Atlantis or the Titan Atlas.

at·lan·tes, at·lan′tēz, *n. pl., sing.* **at·las,** at′las. [Gr., pl. of *Atlas.*] Sculptured figures or half figures of men used in the place of columns or pilasters in buildings, supporting or seeming to support some mass above them.

At·lan·tic, at·lan′tik, *a.* Pertaining to or descended from Atlas; pertaining to that division of the ocean which lies between Europe and Africa on the east and America on the west (named from *Mt. Atlas*); pertaining to the Atlas mountains.

At·lan·tis, at·lan′tis, *n.* [L. < Gr.] A mythical island in the Atlantic Ocean, first mentioned by Plato: archaeologists suggested in 1967 that the true Atlantis may be an island off the coast of Greece.

At·las, at′las, *n.* [Gr. *Atlas.*] One of the Titans, who, according to legend, bore the earth on his shoulders; a person greatly burdened down. (*l.c.*), *anat.* the first vertebra of the neck (so named because it supports the head).

at·las, at′las, *n. pl.* **at·las·es.** A collection of maps in a volume; a volume of plates or tables illustrative or explanatory of some subject; any of the atlantes.

At·las, *n.* A long-range ballistic missile built for the U.S. Air Force.

at·mol·y·sis, at·mol′i·sis, *n. pl.* **at·mol·-y·ses.** Separation of mixed gases by partial diffusion through a porous substance.

at·mom·e·ter, at·mom′i·tẽr, *n.* An instrument for measuring evaporation.—**at·mo·met·ric,** at·mo·met′rik, *a.*—**at·mom·e·try,** *n.*

at·mos·phere, at′mos·fẽr″, *n.* [N.L. < Gr. *atmos,* vapor, and *sphaira,* a sphere.] The whole mass of aeriform fluid surrounding or comprising any planet or other celestial body; any similar gaseous envelope or medium, esp. around a celestial body; the amount of pressure of a column of the atmosphere on a square inch (=14.69 lbs.); *fig.* pervading influence, aura, environment; as, to live in an *atmosphere* of doubt.

at·mos·pher·ic, at″mos·fer′ik, *a.* Pertaining to, existing in, or consisting of the atmosphere; hazy, caused, produced, or operated on by the atmosphere; mood-producing; as, *atmospheric* music. Also **at·mos·pher·i·cal.**—**at·mos·pher·i·cal·-ly,** at″mos·fer′i·kal·ē, *adv.*

at·mos·pher·ic pres·sure, *n.* The pressure at any point in an atmosphere due solely to the weight of the atmospheric gases above the point concerned.

at·mos·pher·ics, at″mos·fer′iks, *n. pl.* The interference in radio reception caused by electromagnetic radiations originating, principally, in the irregular surges of electrical charge in thunderstorm lightning discharges.

at·oll, at′al, at′ol, at′ōl, a·tal′, a·tol′, a·tōl′, *n.* [Name in the Maldive group.] A coral island, consisting of a strip or ring of coral surrounding a central lagoon or lake: such islands are very common in the Pacific Ocean.

at·om, at′om, *n.* [L. *atomus,* Gr. *atomos,* an atom, lit. what is indivisible < *a-,* not, and *temnein,* to cut.] *Chem., phys.* the smallest particle of an element which can enter into a chemical combination: it is composed of subatomic particles (protons, neutrons, electrons) whose number and arrangement characterize the element; a group of these particles making up the smallest quantity of a radical, as a carboxyl *atom;* the atom as the nucleus of the fission bomb, hence the power of the atom, esp. destructive or constructive power. A minute quantity.

a·tom·ic, a·tom′ik, *a.* Pertaining to atoms; consisting of atoms; extremely minute; powered by or utilizing atomic energy; *chem.* existing as free atoms. Also **a·tom·i·cal,** a·tom′ik·al.—**a·tom·i·cal·ly,** a·tom′i·-kal·ē, *adv.*—**a·tom·ist,** at′om·ist, *n.* An adherent of the atomic philosophy or theory.

a·tom·ic bomb, *n.* A bomb whose explosive power is derived from the splitting (fission) of nuclei of atoms (plutonium, uranium) by bombardment with neutrons to release atomic energy. Also **at·om bomb.**—*v.t.* To bomb with such a weapon.

a·tom·ic clock, *n.* A very precise electric clock governed by the sound vibration frequency of atoms or molecules of certain substances.

a·tom·ic cock·tail, *n. Slang,* a suspension of radioactive isotopes in liquid administered orally for the treatment of cancer.

a·tom·ic en·er·gy, *n.* Energy obtained from changes within the nucleus of an atom, by fission of a heavy nucleus or by fusion of light nuclei into heavier ones with loss of mass.

at·o·mic·i·ty, at″o·mis′i·tē, *n. Chem.* the number of electrons in a molecule of a gas, atoms in a molecule of an element, hydroxyl groups in an alcohol or base, carboxyl or other groups in an acid; valence or combining power of a substance. *Philos.* the quality of being atomic.

a·tom·ic mass, *n. Chem.* the mass of any type of atom, usually expressed in atomic mass units.

a·tom·ic mass u·nit, *n. Phys.* a unit of a mass used to express the mass of atomic and subatomic particles: 1/12 the mass of a carbon atom (isotope 12). Abbr. *amu.*

a·tom·ic num·ber, *n.* An integer that expresses the positive charge of the nucleus in multiples of the electronic charge; the number of electrons outside the nucleus of a neutral (un-ionized) atom and the number of protons in the nucleus. Abbr. *at. no.;* sym. *Z.*

a·tom·ic phil·os·o·phy, *n.* A system of philosophy which teaches that atoms, by virtue of their own properties, brought all things into being without the aid of a Creator.

a·tom·ic pile, *n. Phys.* a nuclear reactor.

a·tom·ics, a·tom′iks, *n. pl. but sing. in constr.* That branch of physics which is concerned with the atom or the energy it produces.

a·tom·ic the·o·ry, *n.* The theory that all matter is composed of atoms; the theory that all chemical combinations take place in a definite manner between the ultimate particles or atoms of bodies; any of the theories of the structure of the atom.

a·tom·ic weight, *n. Chem.* the mass of an atom of any element according to a standard of comparison, hydrogen being assigned the atomic weight 1, though usually based on carbon (12) or oxygen (16). Abbr. *at. wt.*

a·tom·ic weight u·nit, *n. Phys.* 1/16 the weighted mean of the masses of the neutral atoms of oxygen of isotopic composition.

at·om·ism, at′o·miz″um, *n.* The doctrine of atoms; the philosophy which supports the theory that matter is composed of minute, finite and indivisible elements; *psychol.* that which reduces all psychological phenomena to simple elements.

at·om·is·tic, at″o·mis′tik, *a.* Pertaining to atomism; relating to atoms; characterized by individualism or atomism.

at·om·ize, at′o·mīz″, *v.t.*—*atomized, atomizing.* To reduce to atoms, hence reduction to small particles; to convert (something) into a spray, dust, etc.; to subject to an atomic attack or devastation.

at·om·iz·er, at′o·mī″zẽr, *n.* One who or that which atomizes or reduces to atoms; an apparatus for reducing a liquid into spray for disinfecting, cooling, perfuming, etc.

a·tom smash·er, *n. Phys.* a particle accelerator. See *accelerator.*

at·o·my, at′o·mē, *n. pl.* **at·o·mies.** *Archaic.* An atom; a minute creature.

a·ton·al, ā·tōn′al, *a.* Absence of tonality.—**a·ton·al·is·tic,** ā·tōn″a·lis′tik, *a.*—**a·to·nal·i·ty,** ā″tō·nal′i·tē, *n. Mus.* a system of composition in which the tones and chords are not related to a central keynote.—**a·ton·-al·ly,** ā·tōn′a·lē, *adv.*

a·tone, a·tōn′, *v.i.*—*atoned, atoning.* [M.E. *atonen* < *at,* and *on,* one.] To make

---

reparation, amends, or satisfaction, as for an offense or a crime.—*v.t.* To expiate; to answer or make satisfaction for.

a·tone·ment, *a·tōn′ment, n.* The act of atoning, reconciling, or making reparation; reconciliation after enmity or controversy; specifically, the reconciliation of God with man through Christ; satisfaction; expiation.—**a·ton·er**, *a·tōn′ẽr, n.* One who makes atonement.

a·ton·ic, *a·ton′ik, ā·ton′ik, a. Med.* characterized by atony.

at·o·ny, *at′o·nē, n.* [Gr. *atonia* < *a-*, not, *tonos*, tone.] *Med.* A want of tone; flaccidity; defect of muscular power; debility.—**at·o·nic·i·ty**, *at·o·nis′i·tē, n.*

a·top, *a·top′, adv.* On or at the top.—*prep.* On the top of.

a·tri·o·ven·tric·u·lar, *ā″trē·ō·ven·trik′·yū·lar, a.* [N.L. < *atrio-* < L. *atrium*, heart, and VENTRICULAR.] *Anat.* relating or referring to both the ventricles and atria (auricles) of the heart.

a·trip, *a·trip′, a. Naut.* Of an anchor loosed from the bottom by a cable; of sails turned from horizontal to vertical position.

a·tri·um, *ā′trē·um, n.* pl. **a·tri·a**, **a·tri·ums**, *ā′trē·a.* [L.] The entrance hall and usually the most splendid apartment of an ancient Roman house; a central open area at the core of a house; *zool.* the chamber into which the intestine opens in ascidians. *Anat.* either of the two receiving chambers of the heart; the auricles.—**a·tri·al**, *ā′trē·al, a.*

a·tro·cious, *a·trō′shus, a.* [L. *atrox, atrocis*, fierce, cruel < *atr-*, black, and *-oc-*, eye.] Extremely heinous, criminal, or cruel; enormously or outrageously wicked; enormous; abominable; horrible.—**a·tro·cious·ly**, *a·trō′shus·lē, adv.* In an atrocious manner.—**a·tro·cious·ness**, *a·trō′shus·nis, n.* The quality of being atrocious.

a·troc·i·ty, *a·tros′i·tē, n.* pl. **a·troc·i·ties.** The state or quality of being atrocious; enormous wickedness or cruelty; a specific act, object, or situation of extreme heinousness or cruelty.

a·troph·ic, *a·trof′ik, a.* Pertaining to or characterized by atrophy.

at·ro·phy, *a′tro·fē, n.* pl. **at·ro·phies.** [L.L. *atrophia* < Gr. *atrophia* < *a-*, neg., and *trephein*, nourish.] A wasting away of the body or of an organ or part, as from defective nutrition or other causes; degeneration.—*v.t.*—*atrophied, atrophying.* To affect with atrophy.—*v.i.* To undergo atrophy.

at·ro·pine, *a′tro·pēn″, n.* [G. < N.L. *belladonna*, < Gr. *atropos* < *a-*, neg., and *tropos* < *trepein*, to burn.] *Pharm.* a very poisonous alkaloid, $C_{17}H_{23}NO_3$, obtained from the deadly nightshade (*Atropa belladonna*), used esp. to dilate the pupil of the eye and alleviate spasms. Also **at·ro·pin**, *a′tro·pin.*

at·tac·ca, *a·tä′ka, impv.* [It. impv. of *attaccare*: see *attack*.] *Mus.* attack, or begin, at once: a direction at the end of a movement to proceed with the following movement immediately.

at·tach, *a·tach′, v.t.* [M.E. < M.Fr. *attacher* < O.Fr. < *a-* (< L. *ad-*), and *tachier*, to tack.] To make to adhere; to tie, bind, or fasten; to connect or associate; to attribute; to seize by lawful authority, as in case of debt.—*v.i.* To be attached or connected, joined or bound up with (with *to*), to belong (with *to*), as: Interest *attaches to* a subject.—**at·tach·a·ble**, *a·tach′a·bl, a.* Capable of being attached.

at·ta·ché, *at″a·shā′, n.* [Fr.] One attached to an embassy or legation of his country in a foreign nation.

at·ta·ché case, *n.* A light-weight brief case, or suitcase, usually used as a carrier for business papers.

at·tached, *a·tacht′, a.* Joined; cemented; bound; containing a wall that is also connected to another structure; as, an *attached* garage. *Zool.* fixed to the foundation permanently; connected by the substratum.

at·tach·ment, *a·tach′ment, n.* The act of attaching; the process in which two particles collide and adhere to form a single complex particle, as the formation of a negative ion from electron attachment to an atom or molecule; the state of being attached; close adherence or affection; any passion or liking which binds one person to another or to a place, etc.; love; regard; that which attaches one object to another; the object attached; an adjunct, esp. to a machine or electrical device; *law*, a taking of a person or goods by legal means to secure a debt.

at·tack, *a·tak′, v.t.* [M.Fr. *attaquer* < It. *attaccare*, to attack.] To assault; to fall upon with force or violence; to criticize violently; to assail; to endeavor to injure by act, speech, or writing; to seize, as a disease.—*v.i.* To make an attack or onset; to begin an assault.

at·tack, *a·tak′, n.* A falling on, with force or violence, or with calumny or satire; an onset; an assault; a seizure by a disease.

at·tain, *a·tān′, v.t.* [M.E. < O.Fr. *ataindre* < L. *attingere* < *ad-*, to, and *tangere*, to touch.] To reach by effort; to achieve or accomplish; acquire, gain: said of an end or object; to come to; to arrive at; to reach: said of a place.—*v.i.* To reach; to come or arrive: followed by *to*.—**at·tain·a·ble**, *a·tān′a·bl, a.* Capable of being attained, reached, achieved, or accomplished.—**at·tain·a·bil·i·ty**, *a·tān″a·bil′i·tē, a·tān′a·bl·nis, n.*

at·tain·der, *a·tān′dẽr, n.* [M.E. < O.Fr. *atteindre, attaindre*, to touch or reach, as with law; to attaint, < L. *attingere.* ATTAIN, *v.t.*] *Obs.* The act or legal process of subjecting a person to the consequences of judgment of death pronounced in respect of treason or felony; forfeiture of civil privileges.

at·tain·ment, *a·tān′ment, n.* The act of attaining; that which is attained; an acquisition; an acquirement.

at·taint, *a·tānt′, v.t.* [M.E. < M.Fr. *ataint*, pp. of *ataindre*.] *Law*, to affect with attainder; *obs.* to find guilty of a crime, as of felony or treason, involving forfeiture of civil privileges. To disgrace.

at·tar, *at′ar, n.* [Pers. < Ar. *atr*, perfume.] A perfume or oil from flowers. Also **at·ar**, **ath·ar**, *otto*, **ot·tar**.—**at·tar** or **ot·to of ros·es**, an essential oil made from various species of roses, which forms a valuable perfume.

at·tempt, *a·tempt′, v.t.* [L. *attemptare*.] To make an effort to effect; to endeavor to perform; to undertake; to try; to attack; as, to *attempt* someone's life.

at·tempt, *a·tempt′, n.* An essay, trial, or endeavor; an effort to gain a point; an attack, onset, or assault.—**at·tempt·a·ble**, *a·tempt′a·bl, a.* Capable of being attempted.

at·tend, *a·tend′, v.t.* [M.E. < O.Fr. *atendre* < L. *attendere*, to turn one's mind to, to turn to < *ad-*, to, and *tendere*, to stretch. TEND.] To accompany or be present with, as a companion or servant; to be present at or in for some purpose (church, a concert, etc.); to accompany or follow in immediate sequence, especially from a causal connection (a cold *attended* with fever).—*v.i.* To pay regard or heed; to be present, in pursuance of duty; to act as an attendant; to be concomitant: by itself or followed by *on* or *upon*.

at·tend·ance, *a·ten′dans, n.* The act of attending or attending on; the act of waiting on or serving; service; ministry; the persons attending for any purpose; the number of persons attending; the number of times persons are present.

at·tend·ant, *a·ten′dant, a.* Accompanying; being present or in attendance upon; connected with, or immediately following.

at·tend·ant, *a·ten′dant, n.* One who attends or accompanies another; an usher; one who belongs to a person's retinue; a follower; one who is present or regularly present; that which accompanies or is consequent on.

at·ten·tion, *a·ten′shan, n.* [M.E. < L. *attentio, attentionis*, < *attendere.* ATTEND.] The act of attending or heeding; the application of the ear to sounds, or of the mind to objects presented to its contemplation; heedfulness; observation; an act of civility or courtesy; formal posture of a soldier, or the command to assume the prescribed position.—**at·ten·tion·al**, *a·ten′shan·al, a.*

at·ten·tive, *a·ten′tiv, a.* Paying or giving attention; heedful; intent; observant; regarding with care; mindful; habitually heedful or mindful.—**at·tent·ive·ly**, *a·ten′tiv·lē, adv.* In an attentive manner.—**at·ten·tive·ness**, *a·ten′tiv·nis, n.* The state of being attentive; attention.

at·ten·u·ate, *a·ten′ū·āt″, v.t.*—*attenuated, attenuating.* [L. *attenuatus*, pp. of *attenuare*, < *ad-*, to, and *tenuare*, to make thin, < *tenuis*, thin.] To make thin; make slender or fine; reduce in density; dilute; to weaken; lower; reduce.—*v.i.* To become thin, slight, or weak.

at·ten·u·ate, *a·ten′ū·it, a·ten′ū·āt″, a.* Attenuated; thin; *bot.* tapering to a narrow extremity.—**at·ten·u·a·tion**, *a·ten″ū·ā′·shan, n.* The act of attenuating, or the resulting state; reduction in thickness, density, strength, etc.; dilution; weakening.

at·test, *a·test′, v.t.* [M.Fr. *attester* < L. *attestor* < *ad-*, and *testor*, to witness. TESTAMENT, DETEST.] To bear witness to; to certify; to affirm to be true or genuine; to declare the truth of; to manifest, as one's joy, etc.—*v.i.* To bear witness (usually followed by *to*).—**at·tes·ta·tion**, *at″e·stā′shan, n.* The act of attesting; a solemn declaration, verbal or written, in support of a fact; evidence; testimony.—**at·test·er**, *a·test′ẽr, n.*

at·tic, *at′ik, n.* [Fr. < L. *Atticus.*] *Arch.* A low story erected over a principal; an apartment in the uppermost part of a house, with windows in the cornice or the roof; a garret.

At·tic, *at′ik, a.* [L. *Atticus* < Gr. *Attikos*.] Pertaining to Attica, in Greece, or to its principal city, Athens; marked by the qualities characteristic of the Athenians, as refinement, delicacy, simplicity.—**At·tic wit**, **At·tic salt**, a delicate wit for which the Athenians were famous.—*n.* The dialect spoken in Attica or Athens; the chief literary and most elegant language of ancient Greece.—**At·ti·cism**, **at·ti·cism**, *at′i·siz″·um, n.* A characteristic of Athenian customs, styles, or language; a predilection for Athenian customs.

at·tire, *a·tīr′, v.t.*—*attired, attiring.* [M.E. < O.Fr. *atirier*, to array, < *at-* (L. *ad-*,) to, and *tire*, rank, = G. *zier*, ornament, O.E. *tīr*, splendor, Dan. *ziir*, ornament.] To dress; to deck; to array; to adorn with elegant or splendid garments.

at·tire, *a·tīr′, n.* Dress; clothes; garb; apparel. *Her.* the horns of a deer.

at·ti·tude, *at′i·tōd″, at′i·tūd″, n.* [Fr. < It. *attitudine*, fitness, posture, < L.L. *aptitudo*, fitness, L. *aptus*, fit. APT.] Posture or position of a person; manner, emotion, or actions toward an object or person; *aeron.* the aspect that an aircraft presents at any given moment, as determined by its inclinations around its three axes.

at·ti·tu·di·nize, *at″i·tōd′i·nīz″, at″i·tūd′·i·nīz, v.i.*—*attitudinized, attitudinizing.* To assume affected attitudes, airs, or postures.

at·torn, *a·t̲u̲rn′, v.t.* [M.E. < M.Fr. < O.Fr. *atorner*, transfer, appoint.] *Law.* Turn over to another; transfer.—*v.i. Law.* To transfer homage and service to a new feudal lord; acknowledge the relation of a tenant to a new landlord.

at·tor·ney, *a·t̲u̲r′nē, n.* pl. **at·tor·neys.** [M.E. < O.Fr. *attorné,* pp. of *atorner,* to transfer < *a-* (< L. *ad-*), to, and *torner,* to turn. TURN.] A legal agent who represents a client in legal affairs; a lawyer; one who is legally appointed or admitted in the place of another to transact any business for him. —**let·ter** or **pow·er of at·tor·ney,** a formal instrument by which one person authorizes another to act for him.—**at·tor·ney·ship,** *n.*

At·tor·ney Gen·er·al, *n.* Head of the Federal Department of Justice. (*l.c.*) the chief officer and legal representative of a Federal judicial district; also legal adviser to the state legislature.

at·tract, *a·trakt′, v.t.* [M.E. < L. *attrahere, attractum* < *ad-*, to, and *trahere,* to draw, whence *tract, treat, trace,* etc.] To draw to or toward, either in a physical or mental sense; to cause to draw near or close to by some influence; to invite or allure; to entice; to win.—*v.i.* To possess or exert the power of attraction; to be attractive or winning.— **at·tract·a·ble,** *a·trakt′a·bl, a.* Capable of being attracted; subject to attraction.— **at·tract·or,** *a·trak′tor, n.* One who or that which attracts.

at·trac·tion, *a·trak′shan, n.* The act, power, or property of attracting; *physics,* a force by which all particles of matter are attracted or drawn toward each other. Allurement; enticement; that which attracts; a charm.

at·trac·tive, *a·trak′tiv, a.* Having the quality of attracting; having the power of charming or alluring; inviting; engaging; enticing.—**at·trac·tive·ly,** *a·trak′tiv·lē, adv.* In an attractive manner.—**at·trac·tive·ness,** *a·trak′tiv·nis, n.* The quality of being attractive or engaging.

at·tri·bute, *a·trib′yŏt, v.t.*—*attributed, attributing.* [M.E. < L. *attribuere, attributum* < *ad-,* and *tribuere,* to assign.] To ascribe; to impute; to consider as belonging or as due to a person or thing; to assign; to credit; to assume to be caused by, or created by, a person or thing.

at·tri·bute, *a′tri·būt″, n.* Any property, quality, or characteristic that can be ascribed to a person or thing; *fine arts,* a symbol of office or character added to any figure: thus the eagle is the *attribute* of Jupiter.—**at·tri·but·a·ble,** *a·trib′yŭt·a·bl, a.* Capable of being, or liable to be, attributed; ascribable; imputable.

at·tri·bu·tion, *a″tri·bū′shan, n.* The act of attributing; that which is ascribed; attribute.

at·trib·u·tive, *a·trib′yŭ·tiv, a.* Pertaining to or expressing an attribute; *gram.* coming before the noun it qualifies.—*n. Gram.* A word expressive of an attribute; a noun which modifies or qualifies a noun immediately adjacent; as, a *university* graduate.—**at·trib·u·tive·ly,** *a·trib′yŭ·tiv·lē, adv. Gram.* In an attributive manner; used before the noun.

at·trit·ed, *a·trīt′id, a.* Worn by attrition.

at·tri·tion, *a·trish′an, n.* [L.L. *attritio*(*n-*) < *atterere* < *ad-,* to, and *terere,* to rub.] A rubbing against; a wearing down or away by friction or, figuratively, by constant abuse and heckling; abrasion; a gradual reduction of labor force, office staff, school enrollment, etc., by voluntary withdrawal of members. *Theol.* remorse for one's sins prompted by a base motive; imperfect contrition; see *contrition.*—**at·tri·tion·al,** *a·trish′a·nal,* **at·tri·tive,** *a·trī′tiv, a.* Showing attrition. —**at·tri·tus,** *a·trī′tus, n.* Material worn into particles by attrition.

at·tune, *a·tūn′, a·tön′, v.t.*—*attuned, attuning.* To tune or put in tune; to adjust, as one sound to another; to make accordant; *fig.* to arrange fittingly; to bring into harmony. concord, or agreement.

a·typ·i·cal, *ā·tip′i·kal, a.* Not typic or typical; not conforming to the type; irregular; abnormal. Also **a·typ·ic.**—**a·typ·i·cal·ly,** *ā·tip′i·kal·ē, adv.*

au·ber·gine, *ō′bĕr·zhĕn″, ō′bĕr·jĕn″, ō′-ber·zhĕn″, ō′ber·jĕn″, n.* [Fr. < Catalan < Ar. *al bādhinān,* the eggplant.] The fruit of the eggplant, or the plant; also, a dark-purple color, like that of the fruit.

au·burn, *a′burn, a.* [M.E. *auborne,* blond, < M.Fr. < M.L. *alburnus* < L. *albus,* white.] Reddish-brown: usually applied to hair.— *n.* An auburn color.

Au·bus·son car·pet, *ō′bu·saN″ kär′pit, n.* A choice kind of tapestry carpet made in one piece by hand at Aubusson, France, in elegant designs (usually with a central medallion) and fine material and coloring.

au cou·rant, *ō kö·räN′, a.* [Fr.] Up-to-date; aware of current happenings.

auc·tion, *ak′shan, n.* [L. *auctio, augēre, auctum,* to increase (from the rising in successive bids); = Icel. *auka,* Goth. *aukan,* AUGMENT, AUXILIARY.] A public sale of property to the highest bidder; the bidding in certain card games; as, *auction* bridge.

auc·tion, *ak′shan, v.t.* To sell by auction.

auc·tion bridge, *n.* A card game which preceded contract bridge in popularity, differing principally in that all tricks taken in excess of the bid contract also counted toward game.

auc·tion·eer, *ak″sha·nēr′ n.* One whose business it is to sell things by auction.

auc·to·ri·al, *ak·tōr′ē·al, ak·tar′ē·al, ouk′-tōr″ē·al, ouk′tar″ē·al, a.* [L. *auctor.* AUTHOR.] Of or concerning an author; by an author.

au·da·cious, *a·dā′shus, a.* [M.Fr. < L. *audax, audacis,* < *audēre,* to dare.] Over-bold or daring; bold in wickedness; insolent; imprudent; shameless; unrestrained; unabashed.—**au·da·cious·ly,** *a·dā′shus·lē, adv.* In an audacious manner.

au·dac·i·ty, *a·das′i·tē, n.* The quality of being audacious; boldness; impudence; effrontery; insolence. Also **au·da·cious·ness,** *a·dā′shus·nis.*

au·di·ble, *a′di·bl, a.* [L.L. *audibilis* < *audire,* to hear.] Capable of being heard; perceivable by the ear; loud enough to be heard.—**au·di·bly,** *a′di·blē, adv.* In an audible manner.

au·di·bil·i·ty, *a·di·bil′i·tē, n.* The quality of being audible. Also **au·di·ble·ness,** *a′di·bl·nis.*

au·di·ence, *a′dē·ens, n.* [M.E. < M.Fr. < L. *audientia* < *audire,* to hear.] The act of listening; a hearing; liberty or opportunity of being heard before a person or assembly; an assembly of hearers; a group of spectators at some public event.

au·dile, *a′dil, a′dīl, n.* [L. *audire,* hear.] *Psychol.* one in whose mind auditory images are especially distinct rather than visual or motor images.

au·di·o, *a′dē·ō″, a.* [L.] Relating to audible sound waves and the reproduction, transmission, and reception of sound; auditory.

au·di·o, *a′dē·ō″, n.* [L.] *Television,* the sound portion of a script, production, etc.; the equipment which deals with audible frequency reception: opposed to *video.*

au·di·o-fre·quen·cy, *a″dē·ō·frē′kwen·sē, a. Elec.* Pertaining to a frequency corresponding to audible frequencies of sound waves, that is, from 20 to 20,000 cycles per second.

au·di·om·e·ter, *a″dē·om′i·tĕr, n.* [N.L.] An instrument for testing the power of hear-

ing.—**au·di·om·e·try,** *a″dē·om′i·trē, n.*— **au·di·o·met·ric,** *a″dē·o·me′trik, a.*

au·di·o-vis·u·al, *a″dē·ō·vizh′ō·al, a.* Of, or pertaining to, sight and hearing, as certain methods of teaching and learning with the aid of moving pictures, charts, phonographs, etc.

au·dit, *a′dit, n.* [M.E. < L. *audit,* he hears, or *auditus,* a hearing, < *audire,* to hear. AUDIBLE.] An examination into accounts or dealings with money or property by proper officers, or persons appointed for that purpose; hence, a calling to account; an examination of one's actions.

au·dit, *a′dit, v.t.* To make audit of; to examine, as an account or accounts. To enroll in, as a course of study, without the purpose of earning credit for the course.

au·di·tion, *a·dish′an, n.* [L. *auditio,* a hearing < *audire,* to hear.] The act or sense of hearing; a hearing. A trial performance to evaluate an entertainer's abilities.

au·di·tion, *a·dish′an, v.t.* To give a trial hearing or test audience to, as a singer, musician, or other artist seeking a professional appointment.—*v.i.* To perform as a trial.

au·di·tive, *a′di·tiv, a.* Relating to hearing or to the sense or organs of hearing; auditory.

au·dit·or, *a′di·tor, n.* [L.] A hearer; a listener; a person appointed and authorized to audit or examine an account or accounts. One who attends a class but who does not participate for credit.

au·di·to·ri·um, *a″di·tōr′ē·um, n.* [L.] In an opera house, public hall, etc., the space allotted to the audience; a building, hall, or large room used for public gatherings.

au·di·to·ry, *a′di·tōr″ē, a′di·tar″ē, a.* [L. *auditorius.*] Relating to hearing or to the sense or organs of hearing.

au·di·to·ry nerve, *n. Anat.* The nerve of hearing, *nervus vestibulocochlearis,* going from the organs of hearing and the semicircular canals to the brain; the 8th cranial nerve. Also **a·cous·tic nerve.**

au fait, *ō fe′, a.* [Fr.] Well-versed; informed; competent; experienced.

au·gend, *a′jend, a·jend′, n.* [L. < *augere,* to increase.] *Math.* a number to which an addend is added.

au·ger, *a′gĕr, n.* [< M.E. *nauger,* initial *n* having been lost (as in *adder, apron*), < O.E. *nafe-gār, nafugâr,* from *nafu, nafa,* the nave of a wheel; and *gār,* a sharp-pointed thing, a dart or javelin. NAVE, GORE, to pierce.] An instrument for boring holes in wood; any instrument on the same plan used for boring into the soil, etc.

aught, *at, n.* [< *a naught.*] A cipher; zero. Also *ought.*

aught, *at, adv.* [O.E. *āwiht, ōwiht,* "ever a whit," < *ō, ā,* ever, and *wiht,* thing, E. *whit*: cf. *ought.*] In any respect; in any degree; at all.

au·gite, *a′jīt, n.* [L. < Gr. *augē,* brightness.] The name given to a class of minerals, greenish black, pitch or velvet black, or leek green in color, and consisting of silicates of lime, calcium, magnesium, and iron, with aluminum in the darker varieties.—**au·git·ic,** *a·jit′ik, a.* Of or resembling augite.

aug·ment, *ag·ment′, v.t.* [M.E. < M.Fr. *augmenter* < L. *augmento* < *augmentum,* increase, < *augēre,* to increase. AUCTION.] To increase; to enlarge in size or extent; to swell; to make bigger.—*v.i.* To increase; to grow larger.—**aug·ment·a·ble,** *a.*—**aug·ment·er,** *n.*

aug·ment, *ag′ment, n. Gram.* an increase at the beginning of certain inflectional forms of a verb, as the *e* prefixed in certain tenses of the Greek verb, and the *ge* in the past participle of the German verb.

aug·men·ta·tion, *ag″men·tā′shan, n.* The act of augmenting; the act of adding to or enlarging; the state or condition of being made larger; increase; enlargement; accession; the thing added by way of enlargement; addition.

aug·ment·a·tive, ag·men′ta·tiv, a. Having the quality or power of augmenting.—n. Gram. an affix intensifying, or increasing the size of, a word.

aug·ment·ed, ag·ment′id, a. Made greater; mus. increased by a semitone over the major or perfect interval.

au grat·in, ō grät′in, ō grat′in, a. [Fr., lit. 'with the burnt scrapings from the pan.'] Cooked until browned with a coating of grated cheese or butter and crumbs.

au·gur, a′gẽr, n. [L. augur, origin unknown.] Among the ancient Romans, a functionary whose duty was to derive signs concerning future events from the flight or other actions of birds, from certain appearances in quadrupeds, from lightning and other unusual occurrences; hence, one who foretells future events by omens; a soothsayer; a prophet.

au·gur, a′gẽr, v.i. To guess; to conjecture, as from signs or omens; to be a sign; to bode (to augur well or ill for a project).— v.t. To guess or conjecture; to predict; to anticipate: said of persons; to betoken; to forebode: said of things.

au·gu·ry, a′gyu·rẽ, n. pl. au·gu·ries. The art or practice of divination; that from which a prediction is drawn; an omen; a prognostication.

au·gust, a·gust′, a. [L. augustus, < augēre, to increase, the same word as the name Augustus. AUGMENT, AUCTION.] Grand; magnificent; majestic; impressing awe; inspiring reverence.—**au·gust·ly,** a·gust′lẽ, adv. In an august manner.—**au·gust·ness,** a·gust′nis, n. The quality of being august.

Au·gust, a′gust, n. [O.E. < L. Augustus, from the Roman Emperor Augustus.] The eighth month of the year, containing thirty-one days.

Au·gus·tan, a·gus′tan, a. Pertaining to the Emperor Augustus, as, the Augustan Age, which was the most brilliant period in Roman literature; hence, any brilliant period in the literary history of other countries, esp. the neo-classical period in England.

Au·gus·tin·i·an, a″gu·stin′ē·an, a. Pertaining to St. Augustine (354–430), bishop of Hippo in northern Africa, to his doctrines, or to any religious order following his rule.— n. One who adopts the views or doctrines of St. Augustine; also, a member of any of several religious orders deriving their name and rule from St. Augustine.—**Au·gus·tin·i·an·ism,** a″gu·stin′ē·a·niz″um, n.

au jus, ō·zhōs′, ō·jös′, a. [Fr., lit., 'with juice.'] Served with the natural juices obtained from meat during cooking.

auk, ąk, n. [Dan. alke, Icel. alka, álka, an auk.] The name of several swimming birds of the family Alcidae found in the colder parts of the Northern Hemisphere, having their legs placed so far back as to cause them to stand nearly upright, and with very short wings more useful for swimming and diving than for flight.

auk·let, ąk′lit, n. Any of various small auks of the North Pacific coasts.

au lait, ō lā′, a. [Fr.] With milk.

auld, ąld, a. Scottish form of old.—**auld lang syne** ("old long since"), old times, esp. as fondly remembered.

au na·tu·rel, ō nä·tö·rel′, a. [Fr.] In a natural state; nude; plainly cooked.

aunt, änt, ant, n. [M.E. < O.Fr. ante < L. amita.] A sister of one's father or mother; an uncle's wife; a familiar term applied to any elderly woman.—**aunt·y,** **aunt·ie,** an′tē, än′tē, n. Familiar diminutive of aunt.

au·ra, ąr′a, n. pl. au·ras, au·rae, ąur′ē.

[M.E. < L. aura, a breath of air < Gr. < aēr, air.] An air; a subtle influence or quality emanating from or surrounding a person or object; an effluvium or odor; an exhalation; pathol. a feeling or sensation which precedes an attack of some kind, such as hysteria or epilepsy.

au·ral, ąr′al, a. [L. auris, the ear.] Relating to the ear (aural surgery).—**au·ri·form,** ąr′i·farm″, a. Ear-shaped; having the form of the human ear.—**au·ral·ly,** ąr′al·ē, adv.

au·re·ate, ąr′ē·it, ąr′ē·āt″, a. [M.E. < M.L. aureatus < L. aureus, golden.] Golden; gilded; brilliant.

au·re·ole, ąr′ē·ōl″, n. [M.E. < L. aureolus, dim. of aureus, golden, < aurum, gold.] Painting, an illumination surrounding a holy person, as Christ, a saint, etc.; anything resembling an aureole; a halo; an encircling ring of light; astron. a corona. Also **au·re·o·la,** a·rē′o·la.

Au·re·o·my·cin, ąr″ē·ō·mī′sin, n. Pharm. An antibiotic isolated from the fungus Streptomyces aureofaciens, and effective against certain diseases. (Trademark.)

au re·voir, ō″ re·vwär′, interj. [Fr.] Goodby for now; farewell until we meet again.

au·ric, ąr′ik, a. [L. aurum, gold.] Chem. of or containing gold, esp. in its highest valence. Compare aurous.—**au·ric ac·id,** chem. a hydroxide of gold, which behaves as a weak acid and forms salts.

au·ri·cle, ąr′i·kal, n. [L. auricula, dim. < auris, the ear.] The external ear, or that part which is prominent from the head; either of the two cavities in the mammalian heart, placed above the two ventricles, and resembling in shape the external ear.

au·ric·u·la, a·rik′yu·la, n. [L.] A garden flower of the primrose family, found native in the Swiss Alps.

au·ric·u·lar, a·rik′yu·lẽr, a. Pertaining to the ear or the sense of hearing, or to an auricle; confided to one's ear, especially privately confided to the ear of a priest (auricular confession). Related to one of the auricles of the heart.

au·ric·u·late, a·rik′yu·lit, a·rik′yu·lāt″, a. Shaped like the ear; having ears or some kind of expansions resembling ears; eared, as a leaf.

au·rif·er·ous, a·rif′ẽr·us, a. [L. aurifer < aurum, gold, and -fer, producing.] Yielding or producing gold; containing gold.

au·ro·ra, a·rōr′a, a·rạr′a, a·rōr″a, a·rạr′a, n. [M.E. < L. the goddess of morning, the dawn; same root as L. uro, to burn, aurum, gold.] The sporadic radiant emission of light from the upper atmosphere over middle and high latitudes.—**au·ro·ral,** a·rōr′al, a·rạr′al, a. Belonging to or resembling the dawn; belonging to or resembling the polar lights; roseate; rosy.

au·ro·ra aus·tral·is, n. [N.L. < aurora, and australis, southern.] The aurora of the Southern Hemisphere,

au·ro·ra bor·e·al·is, n. [N.L. < aurora and borealis, northern.] The northern lights or streamers; a luminous meteoric phenomenon of varying brilliancy seen in the northern heavens at night, and in greatest magnificence in the arctic regions, believed to be electric in origin. Also **au·ro·ra po·lar·is,** northern lights.

au·rous, ąr′us, a. [N.L. < L. aurum, gold.] Chem. of or containing gold, esp. in its univalence.

au·rum, ąr′um, n. [L.] Gold. Abbr. Au.

aus·cul·tate, a′skul·tāt″, v.t.—auscultated, auscultating. Med. to examine by listening to the sounds of the viscera by ausculation.— v.i.

aus·cul·ta·tion, a″skul·tā′shan, n. [L. auscultatio, a listening, < auscultare, to listen, < auris, the ear.] Med. a method of distinguishing the state of the internal parts of the body, particularly of the chest, by

observing the sounds arising there either through the application of the ear or the stethoscope.—**aus·cul·ta·tor,** ąs′kul·tāt··ẽr, n. One who practices auscultation.— **aus·cul·ta·to·ry,** a·skul′ta·tōr″ē, a·skul′-ta·tạr″ē, a. Pertaining to auscultation.

aus·pice, a′spis, n. pl. **aus·pic·es.** [L. auspicium, < auspex, an augur < avis, a bird, and specere, to view.] An augury from birds; an omen or sign in general. Usu. pl. support; protection; favorable influence.

aus·pi·cious, a·spish′us, a. Having omens of success, or favorable appearances; propitious; favorable; prosperous; happy. —**aus·pi·cious·ly,** a·spish′us·lē, adv.— **aus·pi·cious·ness,** a·spish′us·nis, n.

aus·ten·ite, a′ste·nīt″, n. [< Sir Roberts-Austen, a metallurgist and suffix-ite.] Metal. The solid solution of iron carbide (Fe_3C) or cementite in gamma iron; an allotropic form of iron which is stable at higher temperatures (910°C. to 1400°C.) than ferrite (910°C.); gamma iron: used as a primary building material in the construction of carbon steel.

aus·tere, a·stẽr′, a. [M.E. < M.Fr. < L. austerus < Gr. austēros, harsh.] Harsh; tart; sour to the taste; severe; grave; sober; severely simple; limited; rigid; rigorous; stern.—**aus·tere·ly,** a·stẽr′lē, adv.

aus·ter·i·ty, a·ster′i·tē, n. pl. **aus·ter·i·ties.** The state or quality of being austere; severity; rigor; strictness; harshness. Also **aus·tere·ness.**

aus·tral, a′stral, a. [L. australis < auster, the south wind, or south.] Southern; lying or being in the south.

Aus·tra·la·sian, a″stra·lā′zhan, a′stra-lā′shan, a. [< Australasia < Fr. Australasie < L. australis, southern, and Asia, Asia.] Of or pertaining to Australasia, a division of Oceania comprising Australia, Papua, Tasmania, New Zealand, and neighboring islands.—n. A native or inhabitant of Australasia.

Aus·tral·ian, a·strāl′yan, a. Of or pertaining to the people, languages, and culture of Australia, a continent southeast of Asia between the Indian and Pacific Oceans; geog. of a geographical division including Australia, New Guinea, Tasmania, New Zealand, Polynesia, and adjacent islands.— n. A native or inhabitant of Australia; an Australian aborigine; the speech of the aborigines of Australia containing elements of more than a hundred languages.

Aus·tral·ian bal·lot, n. A type of secret ballot containing the names of all the nominated candidates for public offices, distributed at the polling place, and marked in seclusion by qualified voters.

aus·tra·lite, ąs′tra·līt, n. Geol. a round lump of a natural glass form (tektite) which is found primarily in Australia, although its origin is unknown.

Aus·tra·loid, a′stra·loid″, a. Of or pertaining to an ethnic group encompassing the Australian aborigines and other peoples native to southern Asia and the South Pacific.

aus·tra·lo·pith·e·cine, a·strā″lō·pith′i·sin, a·strā″lō·pith′i·sin, ä·strā″lō·pi·thē′-sin, a·strā″lō·pi·thē′sin, n. [N.L. < L. australis, southern, and Gr. pithēkos, ape.] Any hominid of the extinct genus Australopithecus of the Pleistocene epoch with dentition similar to the human.—a.

Aus·tral·orp, a′stra·larp″, n. [Australian and Orpington.] A domestic breed of black Australian chickens raised for egg production.

Aus·tri·an, a′strē·an, a. Of or pertaining to the people, language, or culture of Austria, formerly an empire, now a republic of central Europe.—n. A native or inhabitant of Austria; the German dialect of Austria.

Aus·tro·a·si·at·ic, a″strō·ā″zhē·at′ik, a″strō·ā″shē·at′ik, a. Of or pertaining to a family of languages once widely spoken in southeast Asia and India.

Aus·tro·ne·sian, a″strō-nē′zhan, a″strō-nē′shan, a. Of or relating to the Austronesian family of languages native to most Pacific islands. Also **Ma·lay·o·Pol·y·ne·sian.**

au·ta·coid, a′ta-koid″, n. [N.L. < auto-, Gr. akos, remedy, and -oid.] Physiol. a substance, which is introduced into either the blood system or the lymphatic system by an organ, which will affect an organic process elsewhere in the body.—**au·ta·coi·dal,** a′ta-koid″al, a.

au·tar·chy, a′tär.kē, n. pl. **au·tar·chies.** [Gr. < autos, self, and archos, ruler.] Absolute or autocratic rule; despotism.—**au·tarch,** n.—**au·tar·chic, au·tar·chi·cal,** a.

au·tar·ky, a′tär·kē, n. pl. **au·tar·kies.** [Gr. autarkeia, sufficiency < auto, self, and arkein, to suffice.] Economic self-sufficiency; an economically independent area.—**au·tar·kic,** a.tär′kik, a.

aut·e·col·o·gy, a″te·kol′o·jē, n. [N.L.] That branch of ecology which deals with the individual organism.—**aut·ec·o·log·i·cal,** a.—**aut·ec·o·log·i·cal·ly,** adv.

au·then·tic, a·then′tik, a. [M.E. < M.Fr. < L.L. authenticus < Gr. authentikos, original, genuine, < authentēs, one who does anything with his own hand.] Being what it purports to be; not false or fictitious; genuine; valid; verified; authoritative; reliable.—**au·then·tic·al·ly,** a·then′ti·kal·ē, adv.

au·then·ti·cate, a·then′ti·kāt″, v.t.—authenticated, authenticating. To render or prove authentic; to give authority to by proof, attestation, etc.; to determine as genuine.—**au·then·ti·ca·tion,** a·then″ti·kā′shan, n. The act of authenticating; the giving of proof of authority.—**au·then·tic·i·ty,** a″·then·ti′si·tē, a″thin·tis′i·tē, n. The quality of being authentic; the quality of being genuine; genuineness.—**au·then·ti·ca·tor,** a·then′ti·kā″tor, n.

au·thor, a′thor, n. [M.E. < L. auctor, improperly written autor, author, < augēre, auctum, to increase, to produce. AUGMENT.] The originator or creator of anything; the original writer or composer of a literary work.—v.t. To write or create (something).—**au·thor·ess,** a′thor·is, n. A female author.

au·thor·i·tar·i·an, a·thar′i·târ′ē·an, a·thor′i·târ′ē·an, a. Favoring the principle of authority as opposed to that of individual freedom; favoring unquestioning submission to authority.—n. One who favors submission to authority.—**au·thor·i·tar·i·an·ism,** a·thar′i·târ′ē·a·niz″um, a·thor′i·târ′ē·a·niz″um, n.

au·thor·i·ta·tive, a·thor′i·tā″tiv, a·thar′i·tā″tiv, a. Having authority; having the sanction or appearance of authority; positive; peremptory; dictatorial.—**au·thor·i·ta·tive·ly,** a·thor′i·tā·tiv·li, adv.—**au·thor·i·ta·tive·ness,** a·thor′i·tā″tiv·nis, a·thar′i·tā″tiv·nis, n.

au·thor·i·ty, a·thar′i·tē, a·thor′i·tē, n. pl. **au·thor·i·ties.** [M.E. < O.Fr. authorite < L. auctor, author.] Power or right to command or act; dominion; control; a person or persons exercising power or command: generally in the plural (the civil authorities); government or governmental agency; a reference source or expert in a field to support a fact, opinion, action, etc. (a person's authority for a statement); a ruling; proof; justification; credit or credibility (a work of no authority); assurance (to speak with authority).

au·thor·i·za·tion, a″thor·i·zā′shan, n. The act of authorizing; a sanction.

au·thor·ize, a′tho·rīz″, v.t.—authorized, authorizing. To give authority, warrant, or legal power to; to give a right to act to; to empower; to make legal; to establish by authority or by usage or public opinion (an authorized idiom); to warrant; to sanction; to justify.—**au·thor·iz·er,** a′tho·rīz″ėr, n.

Au·thor·ized Ver·sion, n. The King James version of the Bible published in 1611 A.D.

au·thor·ship, a′thor·ship″, n. The character or state of being an author; the source from which a work proceeds.

au·tism, a′tiz″um, n. [N.L. < L.] Psychol. the tendency to escape reality through daydreams or fantasy to satisfy self-desires.—**au·tis·tic,** a·tis′tik, a.

au·to, a′tō, n. Shortened form of automobile.

au·to·bahn, ou′tō·bän″, n. pl. **au·to·bahns,** ou′tō·bahn·en, ou′tō·bäns″, ou′tō·bä″nen. [G.] A German superhighway.

au·to·bi·og·ra·pher, a″tō·bi·og′ra·fėr, n. One who writes an autobiography.

au·to·bi·o·graph·i·cal, a″tō·bi″o·graf′i·kal, a. Pertaining to, consisting of, or containing autobiography. Also **au·to·bi·o·graph·ic,** a″tō·bi″o·graf′ik.—**au·to·bi·o·graph·i·cal·ly,** a″tō·bi″o·graf′i·kal·ē, adv.

au·to·bi·og·ra·phy, a″tō·bi·og′ra·fē, a″·tō·bē·og′ra·fē, n. pl. **au·to·bi·og·ra·phies.** [Gr. autos, self, and E. biography.] Biography or memoirs of a person's life written by himself.

au·to·bus, a′to·bus″, n. pl. **au·to·bus·es,** au·to·bus·ses. See omnibus.

au·toch·thon, a·tok′thon, n. pl. **au·toch·thon·es,** a·tok′tho·nēz. [Gr. autochthōn < autos, self, and chthōn, the earth.] One of the primitive inhabitants of a country; an aboriginal inhabitant; that which is original to a particular country.

au·to·clave, a′to·klāv″, n. [Fr. < Gr. auto, self, and L. clavism, key.] Airtight vessel for sterilizing, cooking, etc., by high-pressure steam; pressure cooker.—v.t. To sterilize in an autoclave; to cause to experience the effects of an autoclave.

au·toc·ra·cy, a·tok′ra·sē, n. pl. **au·toc·ra·cies.** Supreme power invested in a single person; the government or power of an absolute monarch.

au·to·crat, a′tō·krat″, n. [Gr. autokratēs, ruling by oneself.] An absolute sovereign; a monarch who governs without being subject to restriction, hence, one who is invested with or assumes unlimited authority in any relation.

au·to·crat·ic, a″tō·krat′ik, a. Pertaining to autocracy; absolute; despotic; holding unlimited powers of government. Also **au·to·crat·i·cal,** a″tō·krat′i·kal.—**au·to·crat·i·cal·ly,** a″tō·krat′i·kal·ē, adv.

au·to·da·fé, a″tō·da·fā′, n. pl. **au·tos·da·fé,** a″tōz·da·fā′. [Pg.] A public ceremony, formerly held by the courts of the Inquisition in Spain and Portugal and their dependencies at the execution of heretics condemned to the stake.

au·to·di·dact, a′tō·di·dakt″, n. [Gr. autodidaktos, self-taught.] One who is self-taught.—**au·to·di·dac·tic,** a″tō·di·dak′tik, a.

au·to·dyne, a′to·dīn″, n. [N.L.] Electron. a heterodyne circuit in which the auxiliary current is generated in the device used for rectification.

au·toe·cious, a·tē′shus, a. [Gr. autus, self, and oikos, house.] Bot. passing through all stages of growth on the same host, as certain parasitic fungi.—**au·toe·cism,** a·tē′siz·um, n.

au·to·e·rot·ic, a″tō·i·rot′ik, a. Psychol. of or pertaining to autoerotism.—**au·to·e·rot·i·cal·ly,** a″tō·i·rot′i·kal·ē, adv.

au·to·er·o·tism, a″tō·er′o·tiz″um, n. Psychol. Sexual gratification within or by oneself, usually by masturbation; sexual arousal without perceivable external stimulation.

au·tog·a·mous, a·tog′a·mus, a. Bot. pertaining to or reproduced by autogamy.

au·tog·a·my, a·tog′a·mē, n. [N.L. < Gr. autos, self, and gamos, marriage.] Bot. Fecundation of the ovules of a flower by its own pollen; self-fertilization: opposed to allogamy.

au·to·gen·e·sis, a″tō·jen′i·sis, n. [N.L.] Self-production; spontaneous generation; abiogenesis. Also **au·to·gen·y.**—**au·to·ge·net·ic,** a″tō·je·net′ik, a. Pertaining to autogenesis; self-generated.—**au·to·ge·net·i·cal·ly,** a″tō·je·net′i·kal·ē, adv.

au·to·gen·ic, a″tō·jen′ik, a. Autogenous.

au·tog·en·ous, a·toj′e·nus, a. [Gr. < autos, self, and -gen-, to generate.] Self-produced; self-generated; produced independently.

au·to·gi·ro, a″to·ji′rō, n. pl. **au·to·gi·ros,** a″to·ji′rōs. A form of airplane with an unpowered revolving rotor on an upright axis projecting above the fuselage, which lifts the machine and allows it to ascend and descend almost vertically, and a conventional propeller for forward motion. Also **au·to·gy·ro.**

au·to·graph, a′to·graf″, a′tō·gräf″, n. [L. < Gr. < autos, self, and graphein, to write.] A person's own handwriting; an original manuscript or signature.

au·to·graph, a′to·graf″, a′to·gräf″, v.t. To write in one's own hand; to write one's signature on or in; to reproduce, as in the original writing or form.

au·to·graph·ic, a′to·graf′ik, a. Pertaining to autographic writing, reproducing the original writing or form; self-recording, as an instrument; recorded by such an instrument, as a record.—**au·to·graph·i·cal·ly,** a″to·graf′i·kal·ē, adv.

au·to·harp, a′tō·härp″, n. A musical instrument of the zither class, having across the strings bars with dampers, each of which, when pressed down, renders all strings mute except those of a particular chord.

au·to·hyp·no·sis, a″tō·hip·nō′sis, n. [N.L.] Self-induced hypnosis.—**au·to·hyp·no·tism,** a′tō·hip′nō·tiz″um, n.—**au·to·hyp·not·ic,** a″tō·hip·not′ik, a.

au·to·in·fec·tion, a″tō·in·fek′shan, n. Pathol. infection of the body from within.

au·to·in·oc·u·la·tion, a″tō·i·nok″yu·lā′shan, n. Pathol. inoculation or vaccination of a healthy part with virus from a diseased part of the same body.

au·to·in·tox·i·ca·tion, a″tō·in·tok″si·kā′shan, n. Pathol. poisoning from toxic substances formed within the body.

au·to·ki·ne·sis, a″tō·ki·nē′sis, n. [N.L. < Gr. autokinesis < autokinein, move of itself.] Voluntary or spontaneous motion.—**au·to·ki·net·ic,** a″tō·ki·net′ik, a″tō·ki·net′ik, a. Self-moving; automatic.

au·to·ki·net·ic il·lu·sion, n. The illusion of a fixed object or light moving when gazed at steadily. Also **au·to·ki·net·ic ef·fect.**

au·tol·o·gous, a·täl′o·gus, a. [N.L. < auto- and Gr. logos, relation, and suffix -ous.] Grafted, transplanted, or relocated within the same body; as, an autologous transplant.

au·tol·y·sate, a·tol′i·sāt″, n. Biochem. a product resulting from autolysis.

au·to·ly·sin, a″t′o·li′sin, a·tol′i·sin, n. Biochem. any agent or substance which produces autolysis.

au·tol·y·sis, a·tol′i·sis, n. [N.L. < Gr.] Physiol. digestion or disintegration of tissue by ferments generated in its cells.—**au·to·lyt·ic,** at″o·lit′ik, a.

au·to·mat, a′to·mat, n. [G.] An automatic apparatus for serving articles of food to customers upon the dropping of suitable coins or tokens into a slot; a restaurant using such apparatus.

au·to·mate, a′to·māt″, v.t.—automated, automating. To control by automation; to change or convert to automation; to automatize.—v.i.

au·to·mat·ic, a″to·mat′ik, a. [Gr. automatos, self-moving.] Predominantly or completely involuntary or reflexive; spontaneous; self-controlling; physiol. acting independently of volition, as certain involuntary muscular actions. In firearms, using the recoil force to eject the used cartridge shell, insert a new cartridge, and fire it; mech.

---

a- fat, fāte, fär, fâre, fạll; **e-** met, mē, mēre, hėr; **i-** pin, pīne; **o-** not, nōte, möve; **u-** tub, cūbe, bụll; **oi-** oil; **ou-** pound.

designed to function without human control or regulation.—**au·to·mat·i·cal·ly,** ạ″to-mat′i·kal·ē, *adv.*—**au·to·mat·ic,** *n.* An apparatus that operates automatically; an automatic firearm.

au·to·ma·tic·i·ty, ạ″to·ma·tis′i·tē, *n.* The condition of being automatic.

au·to·mat·ic com·pu·ter, *n.* A computer which can automatically perform a comprehensive sequence of operations.

au·to·mat·ic con·trol, *n.* Control of devices and equipment, including aerospace vehicles, by electronic or other automatic means.

au·to·mat·ic gun, *n.* A rifle, pistol, or other firearm that after the first shot fires others in rapid succession.

au·to·mat·ic pi·lot, *n. Aeron.* Equipment which automatically stabilizes the pitch, roll, and yaw axes of an aircraft or other vehicle; an electronic mechanism that automatically adjusts the control surfaces of an aircraft to hold it on its course and maintain stability.

au·to·ma·tion, ạ″to·mā′shan, *n.* The technique of making an industrial machine, process, or system operate automatically; the use of electronic devices for controlling processes or systems.

au·tom·a·tism, ạ·tom′·a·tiz″um, *n.* Automatic action; *philos.* the theory which regards man's actions as automatic, the conscious mind having no control in life activities; *physiol.* the involuntary functioning of an organ or organic process without conscious neural stimulation, as the heart. *Psychol.* performance of actions without conscious volition, as sleepwalking; the doctrine, of the Surrealists esp., which allows the mind to express itself through uncontrolled, uncensored images.

au·tom·a·ti·za·tion, ạ·tom″a·tī·zā′shan, *n.* Automation.

au·tom·a·tize, ạ·tom′a·tīz, *v.t.*—*automatized, automatizing.* To render automatic.

au·tom·a·ton, ạ·tom′a·ton″, ạ·tom′a·ton, *n.* pl. **au·tom·a·tons, au·tom·a·ta,** ạ·tom′a·tonz, ạ·tom′a·ta. That which is self-moving; a self-acting machine; a mechanical contrivance which imitates the arbitrary or voluntary motions of living beings; a robot; a person who acts mechanically.

au·to·mo·bile, ạ″to·mo·bēl′, ạ′to·mo-bēl″, ạ′to·mō′bēl, ạ′to·mo·bil, *a.* Self-moving; automotive.

au·to·mo·bile, ạ″to·mo·bēl′, ạ′to·mo-bēl″, ạ″to·mō′bēl, ạto·mo·bil, *n.* [Fr. < Gr. *autos,* self, and L. *mobilis,* movable.] A four-wheeled vehicle, esp. a car for passengers, carrying its own propelling mechanism, usu. an internal-combustion engine; a motorcar.—**au·to·mo·bil·ist,** ạ″to·mo-bē′list, ạ′to·mō′bi·list, *n.*

au·to·mo·tive, ạ·to·mō′tiv, *a.* Self-moving or self-propelled, as a vehicle; carrying its own source of motive power.

au·to·nom·ic, ạ″to·nom′ik, *a.* Of or pertaining to autonomy; spontaneous; acting without volition, as reflexes; of or relating to the autonomic nervous system.—**au·to-nom·i·cal·ly,** ạ″to·nom′i·kal·ē, *adv.*

au·to·nom·ic ner·vous sys·tem, *n. Physiol.* that part of the nervous system which innervates the blood vessels, heart, viscera, smooth muscles, and glands, and regulates involuntary actions.

au·ton·o·mist, ạ·ton′o·mist, *n.* An advocate of autonomy.

au·ton·o·mous, ạ·ton′o·mus, *a.* [Gr. *autonomos < autos,* self, and *nomos,* law.] Self-governing; independent; subject to its own laws only; also, pertaining to an autonomy; *biol.* existing as an independent organism and not as a mere form or state of development of an organism; *bot.* spontaneous; as, *autonomous* movements.—**au·ton·o·mous·ly,** ạ·ton′o·mus·lē, *adv.*

au·ton·o·my, ạ·ton′o·mē, *n.* pl. **au·ton-o·mies,** ạ·ton′o·mēz. [Gr. *autonomia, < autonomos.*] The condition of being autonomous; self-government, or the right of self-government; independence; a self-governing community.

au·to·phyte, ạ′to·fīt″, *n. Bot.* any plant capable of synthesizing its food from basic inorganic matter.

au·to·pi·lot, ạ′tō·pī′lot, *n.* An automatic pilot.

au·to·plas·ty, ạ′to·plas″tē, *n.* [Gr. *auto-plastos,* self-formed < *autos,* self, and *plas-sein,* form.] *Surg.* the repairing of lesions with tissue from another part of the patient's body.—**au·to·plas·tic,** *a.*

au·top·sy, ạ′top·sē, ạ′top·sē, *n.* pl. **au-top·sies.** [Gr. *autopsia, < autos,* self, and *op-,* see, as in *opsis,* sight, *opticos,* E. *optic.*] Dissection and inspection of a body after death, as for determination of the cause of death; a post-mortem examination.—**au-top·sic, au·top·si·cal,** ạ·top′sik, ạ·top′si-kal, *a.*—**au·top·si·cal·ly,** ạ·top′si·kal·ē, *adv.*

au·to·ra·di·o·graph, ạ″to·rā′dē·o·graf″, ạ″to·rā′dē·o·gräf″, *n.* A picture or image produced on a photographic film or plate revealing the presence of radioactive material in a substance which has been placed in contact with the film. Also *radioautograph.*

au·to·sex·ing, ạ′tō·sek″sing, *a. Biol.* displaying differential sex characteristics at birth or hatching.

au·to·so·mal, ạ″to·sō′mal, *a. Genetics,* of or pertaining to an autosome.

au·to·some, ạ′to·sōm″, *n. Genetics,* any chromosome that is not a sex chromosome.

au·to·sug·ges·tion, ạ″tō·sug·jes′chan, *n. Psychol.* suggestion by the mind to itself of ideas that operate to produce actual or physical effects.

au·to·tel·ic, ạ″to·tel′ik, *a. Philos.* having a subconscious, unreasoning instinct for existence.

au·tot·o·mize, ạ·tot′o·miz″, *v.i. Zool.* to experience autotomy.—*v.t.* To effect autotomy.

au·tot·o·my, ạ·tot′o·mē, *n.* pl. **au·tot-o·mies.** [N.L.] *Zool.* a reflex separation of a damaged or trapped appendage from the body, as claws by crabs; self-performed surgery.—**au·to·tom·ic,** ạ″to·täm′ik, *a.*

au·to·tox·e·mi·a, au·to·tox·ae·mi·a, ạ″tō·tok·sē′mē·a, *n.* Autointoxication.

au·to·tox·in, ạ″to·tok′sin, *n. Pathol.* a toxic or poisonous principle formed within the body and acting against it.—**au·to-tox·ic,** ạ″to·tok′sik, *a.*—**au·to·tox·is,** ạ″-to·tok′sis, *n.*

au·to·trans·form·er, ạ″tō·trans·fạr′mẻr, *n. Elect.* a transformer in which parts of the primary and secondary coils may be used interchangeably.

au·to·trans·plant, ạ″to·trans·plant″, *n. Surg.* tissue taken from one part of a body and grafted onto another part of the same body.

au·to·troph, ạ′to·trof″, ạ′to·trạf″, *n. Biol.* a microorganism capable of producing carbon exclusively from carbon dioxide; an autotrophic organism.

au·to·troph·ic, ạ″to·trof′ik, *a.* [N.L. < *auto-* and *-troph.*] *Biol.* needing only inorganic materials for metabolic synthesis, as most plants and certain protozoans and bacteria.

au·to·truck, ạ′to·truk″, *n.* An automobile truck.

au·to·type, ạ′to·tīp″, *n.* [Gr. *autos,* self, *typos,* a stamp.] A photographic process using a carbon pigment; a picture produced by the process.

au·tumn, ạ′tum, *n.* [M.E. < L. *autumnus,* for *auctumnus,* the season of increase, < *augēre, < auctum,* to increase.] The third

season of the year, or the season between summer and winter, beginning at the autumnal equinox, about September 22, and ending at the winter solstice, December 21. Also *fall.*—**au·tum·nal,** ạ·tum′nal, *a.* Belonging to autumn; produced or gathered in autumn; *fig.* belonging to the period past the middle stage of life.

au·tum·nal e·qui·nox, *n.* That point of intersection on the celestial sphere of the ecliptic and the celestial equator occupied by the sun as it changes from north to south declination, on or about September 22.

au·tumn cro·cus, *n. Bot.* any of several autumn blooming liliaceous herbs of the genus *Colchicum* bearing white, purple, or pink flowers.

au·tun·ite, ạt′un·īt″, ō·tun′it, *n.* A light yellow, fluorescent, crystalline mineral, $Ca(UO_2)_2(PO_4)_2 \cdot 10H_2O$, occurring in almost square tabular form.

aux·e·sis, ag·zē′sis, ak·sē′sis, *n.* [N.L. < Gr. *auxesis < auxein,* increase.] *Biol.* growth, esp. that due to a cell increasing in size.

aux·il·ia·ry, ag·zil′ya·rē, ag·zil′a·rē, *a.* [L. *auxiliarius < auxilium,* aid, < *auxein,* increase.] Helping or aiding; giving support; subsidiary or additional; as, *auxiliary* power; supplementary; serving in reserve.

aux·il·ia·ry, ag·zil′ya·rē, ag·zil′a·rē, *n.* pl. **aux·il·ia·ries,** ag·zil′ya·rēz. A helper or aid; a confederate; a group which is subordinate to another organization; as, the ladies' *auxiliary* of a men's club; *usu. pl.* an ally, as in war. A tug, supply-ship, or the like, as distinguished from fighting craft, as in the U.S. Navy (naval *auxiliary*); a sailing vessel carrying auxiliary power; *gram.* a verb, as *have, will, be, may, do,* etc., which indicates tense, person, voice, and mood, and is used with participial forms of main verbs; *math.* a quantity introduced to facilitate an operation.

aux·il·ia·ry land·ing gear, *n.* That part or parts of an airplane's landing gear, as an outboard wheel, which is intended to stabilize the craft on the surface but which bears no significant part of the weight.

aux·il·ia·ry po·wer u·nit, *n.* A power unit carried on an aircraft or spacecraft which can be used in addition to the main sources of power for the craft.

aux·in, ak′sin, *n.* [N.L. < Gr. *auxein,* to increase.] A substance or hormone which regulates plant growth, specif. the growth of roots, buds, and fruit.

a·vail, a·vāl′, *v.t.* [M.E. < O.Fr. *valeir,* to be worth, < L. *valēre,* to be strong, and *a-* for L. *ad-*.] To assist or profit; to benefit.—*v.i.* To be of use, benefit, or advantage; to answer a purpose.—**a·vail one·self of,** to turn to one's profit or advantage; to take advantage of.

a·vail, a·vāl′, *n.* Effective use in accomplishing one's goal, as: Argument was of no *avail.*

a·vail·a·bil·i·ty, a·vā″la·bil′i·tē, *n.* State of being available; validity; an available person or thing.

a·vail·able, a·vā′la·bl, *a.* [M.E.] Capable of being used; attainable; accessible; having efficacy; valid.—**a·vail·a·ble·ness,** a·vā′la·bl·nis, *n.*—**a·vail·a·bly,** *adv.*

av·a·lanche, av′a·lanch″, *n.* [Fr. < *la valanche,* the avalanche.] A vast body of snow, ice, rock, or earth sliding down a mountain or over a precipice.

av·a·lanche, av′a·lanch″, av′a·länch″, *n. Phys., chem.* the cumulative process in which charged particles accelerated by an electric field produce additional charged particles through collision with neutral gas molecules or atoms.

av·a·lanche, av′a·lanch″, av′a·länch″, *v.i.* —*avalanched, avalanching.* To descend or come down in, or as if in, an avalanche.

a·vant-garde, *a·*vänt″gärd′, *a·*vant″gärd′, *n.* [Fr., VANGUARD.] The innovating, progressive people in any field, esp. artists or writers, who first utilize unorthodox or revolutionary concepts or techniques.—*a.* Belonging or pertaining to the avant-garde.

av·a·rice, av′ar·is, *n.* [M.E. < O.Fr. < L. *avaritia* < *avarus*, greedy, < *avēre*, to covet.] An inordinate desire to gain and possess wealth; covetousness; cupidity.

a·va·ri·cious, av″a·rish′us, *a.* Characterized by avarice; miserly; covetous.—**av·a·ri·cious·ly,** av″a·rish′us·lē, *adv.*—**av·a·ri·cious·ness,** av″a·rish′us·nis, *n.*

a·vast, *a·*vast′, *a·*väst′, *interj.* [< D. *houd vast,* hold fast, stop.] *Naut.* the order to stop, hold, cease, or stay in any operation: sometimes used colloquially, without reference to ships.

av·a·tar, av″a·tär′, *n.* [Skt. *avatāra* < *ava,* down, and root *tri,* to go.] The incarnation of the Hindu deities, or their appearance in some manifest shape upon earth; a manifestation, as in a person, of some principle, theory, etc.

a·ve, ä′vā, ä′vē, *interj.* [L. < *avēre,* to be well.] Hail! farewell! God bless you! (*cap.*). The shortened form of Ave Maria, the prayer.

a·vel·lan, *a·*vel′an, av′e·lan, *a.* [L., filbert, < *Abella,* ancient town in Italy.] *Her.* having the form of a cross, the arms of which are shaped like filberts.

A·ve Ma·ri·a, ä′vā ma·rē′a, *n.* [L., Hail, Mary!—the first words of Gabriel's salutation to the Virgin Mary.] Title of the Latin version of the Hail Mary, a prayer to the Virgin used in the Roman Catholic Church in recitation of the rosary and in other devotions.

a·venge, *a·*venj′, *v.t.*—avenged, avenging. [M.E. < O.Fr. *avengier* < *vengier* < *a-*, and L. *vindicare,* to avenge, vindicate.] To vindicate by inflicting pain or evil on the wrongdoer; to deal punishment for (injury done); to gain satisfaction by inflicting pain or punishment on the injuring party.— *v.i.* To take vengeance.—**a·veng·er,** *a·*venj′ėr, *n.*

av·ens, av′inz, *n.* pl. **av·ens.** [M.E. < O.Fr. < M.L. *avencia,* a kind of clover.] The popular name of several species of rosaceous plants, of the genus *Geum,* growing wild, having red, yellow, or white flowers.

a·ven·tu·rine, a·ven·tu·rin, *a·*ven′chu-rin, *n.* [Fr. *aventure,* chance.] A variety of artificial gem consisting of glass, oxide of copper, and oxide of iron: a compound discovered accidentally; also, any of the varieties of minerals, esp. feldspar or quartz, containing spangles of mica, hematite, or other minerals.

av·e·nue, av′e·nū″, av′e·nö″, *n.* [Fr. < *avenir,* to arrive, < L. *advenire.*] A passage; a way or opening for entrance; a wide, straight roadway or street; an alley or walk planted on each side with trees; *fig.* means of access or attainment, as: He found the *avenue* to wealth.

a·ver, *a·*vụr′, *v.t.*—averred, averring. [M.E. < M.Fr. *averer,* < L. < *ad-,* to, and *verus,* true.] To affirm with confidence; to declare in a positive or peremptory manner; to assert.

av·er·age, av′ėr·ij, av′rij, *n.* [M.E. < M.Fr. *avarie,* Sp. *averia,* damage sustained by goods at sea; < Ar. *avär,* defect, flaw, modified by the influence of L.L. *averagium,* the carriage of goods by *averia* or draft cattle, a contribution toward loss of things carried; from O.Fr. *aver,* a work horse, from L. *havere,* to have.] A sum or quantity intermediate to a number of different sums or quantities; a mean or medial amount; a general estimate based on comparison of a number of diverse cases; a medium; *marine law,* a contribution falling on the owners of a ship's freight and cargo, in proportion to their several interests, to make good a loss that has been sustained.

av·er·age, av′ėr·ij, av′rij, *v.t.*—averaged, averaging. To find the average of; to reduce to a mean sum or quantity; to have as an average or mean as: Trees *average* 50 feet in height.—*v.i.* To purchase or sell securities to maintain a more favorable average price for all one's holdings; to be averaged, as: The gains *averaged* 20 percent.

av·er·age, av′ėr·ij, av′rij, *a.* Exhibiting a mean proportion or mean quality; forming an average; medium; not extreme; typical; ordinary; estimated in accordance with the rules of average.

av·er·age de·vi·a·tion, *n. Statistics,* the average arithmetic mean of the deviations, taken without regard to sign, from some fixed value, usually the arithmetic mean of the data.

a·ver·ment, *a·*vụr′ment, *n.* The act of averring; affirmation; a positive assertion or declaration.

a·verse, *a·*vụrs′, *a.* [L. *aversus,* turned from, < *avertere.*] Turned away from; opposed; having a feeling of repugnance; averted; unwilling; having repugnance: now regularly followed by *to.*—**a·verse·ly,** *a·*vụrs′lē, *adv.*—**a·verse·ness,** *n.*

a·ver·sion, *a·*vụr′zhan, *n.* Opposition or repugnance; dislike; disinclination; reluctance; hatred: sometimes used with *to.*

a·vert, *a·*vụrt′, *v.t.* [L. *averto, aversum,* to turn away < *a-*, from, and *vertere, versum,* to turn, whence *verse, convert, converse, diverse,* etc.] To turn or direct away from; to turn or to cause to turn off or away (the eyes, calamity, etc.); to prevent.

A·ves, ä′vēz, *n. pl.* [L., pl. of *avis,* bird.] *Zool.* the class of vertebrates comprising birds.

av·gas, av′gas″, *n.* [< aviation gasoline.] *Avi. slang,* gasoline used for airplanes.

a·vi·an, ä′vē·an, *a.* [L. *avis,* a bird.] Pertaining to birds.

a·vi·a·rist, ä′vē·a·rist, ä′vē·er″ist, *n.* One who maintains a cage, house, or enclosure in which birds are kept.

a·vi·ar·y, ä′vē·er″ē, *n.* pl. **a·vi·ar·ies.** [L. *aviarium* < *avis,* bird.] A building or enclosure for the breeding, rearing, and keeping of birds.

a·vi·ate, ä′vē·āt″, av′ē·āt″, *v.i.*—aviated, aviating. To navigate an aircraft.

a·vi·a·tion, ä″vē·ā′shan, av″ē·ā′shan, *n.* [Fr. < L. *avis,* bird.] Aerial navigation by machines heavier than air; military aircraft; the design and manufacture of airplanes.

a·vi·a·tor, ä′vē·ā″tor, av′ē·ā″tor, *n.* One who engages in aviation; a pilot of an airplane.—**a·vi·a·trix,** ä″vē·ā′triks, av″ē·ā′-triks, *n.* A female aviator.

a·vi·cul·ture, ä′vi·kul″chur, *n.* [N.L. < L. *avis* and E. *culture.*] The breeding and rearing of birds.

av·id, av′id, *a.* [L. *avidus,* < *avēre,* to desire. AVARICE.] Eager; enthusiastic; keen; greedy: with *for.*—**av·id·ly,** av′id·lē, *adv.*

av·i·din, av′i·din, *a·*vid′in, *n.* [< avid (because it greedily consumes biotin) and (prote)in.] *Biochem.* a protein that neutralizes biotin, found in egg-white.

a·vid·i·ty, *a·*vid′i·tē, *n.* Greediness; strong appetite; eagerness; intenseness of desire.

a·vi·fau·na, ä′vi·fa″na, *n.* [N.L. < L. *avis* and N.L. *fauna.*] A collective name for the birds of a period or district.

av·i·ga·tion, av″i·gā′shon, *n.* [< avi- and navigation.] Aerial navigation.

a·vi·on·ic, ä″vē·on′ik, av″ē·on′ik, *a.* Relating to the field of avionics.

a·vi·on·ics, ä″vē·on′iks, av″ē·on′iks, *n. pl.* [< aviation electr*onics.*] The invention and application of electronic and electrical devices for use in airplanes, missiles, and spacecraft; the devices and systems developed in this field.

a·vir·u·lent, ä·vir′yu·lent, ä·vir′u·lent, *a.* [N.L.] *Pathol.* Being without virulence; nonpathogenic.

a·vi·ta·min·o·sis, ä·vī″ta·mi·nō′sis, ä″-vi·tam″i·nō′sis, *n.* A disease caused by vitaminic deficiency.

av·o·ca·do, av″o·kä′dō, ä′va·kä′dō, *n.* pl. **av·o·ca·dos.** [Corrupted from Mexican *aguacate* < Nahuatl *ahuscatl.*] The edible, dark green or purple fruit of a small tree of the laurel family, common in tropical America and the West Indies; also *alligator pear.* The avocado tree.

av·o·ca·tion, av″o·kā′shan, *n.* [L. < *avocare,* to call away.] A chosen spare-time occupation or hobby; a person's regular job or occupation.—**av·o·ca·tion·al,** av″o·kā′-shan·al, *a.*

av·o·cet, av′o·set″, *n.* Avoset.

a·void, *a·*void′, *v.t.* [M.E. < A.Fr. < *a-* and *voider,* to empty.] *Law,* to make void; to annul. To shun; to keep away from; to eschew; to evade; to elude (expense, danger, bad company).—**a·void·a·ble,** *a·*void′a·bl, *a.* That which may be vacated or annulled; capable of being avoided, shunned, or escaped from.—**a·void·a·bly,** *adv.*

a·void·ance, *a·*void′ans, *n.* The act of annulling or making void; the act of avoiding or shunning.

av·oir·du·pois, av″or·du·poiz′, *n.* [O.Fr. *avoir du pois,* to have weight < L. *habēre,* to have, *pensum,* something weighed out. POISE.] A system of weight of which 1 lb. contains 16 oz., an ounce weighing 16 drams, in distinction to troy weight, which has only 12 oz.: the system by which commodities in general are weighed in the U.S.

a·vo·set, a·vo·cet, av′o·set″, *n.* [Fr. *avocette* < It. *avocetta.*] A wading bird with very long legs, feathers variegated with black and white, and a long slender bill bent upward toward the tip.

a·vouch, *a·*vouch′, *v.t.* [M.E. < M.Fr. < L. *advocare.* ADVOCATE.] To affirm openly; to avow; to vouch for; to maintain, vindicate, or justify, as a statement; to admit; to guarantee; to substantiate.—**a·vouch·ment,** *a·*vouch′ment, *n.*

a·vow, *a·*vou′, *v.t.* [M.E. < O.Fr. *avouer* < *a-* (< L. *ad-,* to), and *vouer,* to vow.] To declare openly, with a view to justify, maintain, or defend, as sentiments; to acknowledge; to confess; to own.—**a·vow·er,** *a·*vou′ėr, *n.* One who avows, owns, or asserts.

a·vow·al, *a·*vou′al, *n.* An open declaration; frank acknowledgment.

a·vowed, *a·*voud′, *a.* Declared; acknowledged; open; as, an *avowed* enemy.—**a·vow·ed·ly,** *a·*vou′id·lē, *adv.* In an avowed or open manner.

a·vulse, *a·*vuls′, *v.t.* To separate or detach forcibly, as the flesh of a wound.

a·vul·sion, *a·*vul′shan, *n.* [L. *avulsio* < *avellere* < *a-*, away, and *vellere, vulsum,* to pull.] A pulling or tearing asunder or off, as by surgery. *Law,* the removal of land by action of water during a flood or a change in the water course; the land so removed.

a·vun·cu·lar, *a·*vung′kyu·lėr, *a.* [L. *avunculus,* an uncle.] Of or pertaining to an uncle.

a·wait, *a·*wāt′, *v.t.* [M.E. < O.Fr. < *a-* (< L. *ad-*) and *waiter,* to wait.] To wait for; to look for or expect; to be in store for; to be ready for, as: A reward *awaits* him.—*v.i.*

a·wake, *a·*wāk′, *a.* [O.E. *awacen,* pp. of *awacan.*] Not sleeping; alert; in a state of vigilance or action.

a·wake, *a·*wāk′, *v.t.*—awoke, awaking, awaked, awaking. [O.E. *āwacan,* pret. *āwóc,* also *awacnian,* to awake. WAKE.] To rouse from sleep or from a state resembling sleep; to put into action; make aware of,

a·wak·en, *a·wā'ken, v.i.* [O.E. *āwacnan, awacnian,* to awake (intrans.).] To become awake; to awake.—*v.t.* To rouse from sleep; to awake.—**a·wak·en·ing,** *a·wā'ke·ning, n.* Act of awaking from sleep; a revival of religion; any arousal or realization.—*a.*

a·ward, *a·wȧrd', v.t.* [M.E. < A.Fr. *awarder,* to have under ward, to inspect, to pronounce as to the sufficiency of. WARD.] To adjudge; to assign judicially or by sentence, as an arbitrator pronouncing upon the rights of parties; to give as due; to bestow as a prize.

a·ward, *a·wȧrd', n.* Judgment; decision; the decision of arbitrators on points submitted to them; a prize.—**a·ward·er,** *a·wȧrd'ẽr, n.* One who awards or makes an award.—**a·ward·a·ble,** *a·wȧrd'a·bl, a.*

a·ware, *a·wâr', a.* [O.E. *gewær,* wary, cautious; G. *gewahr,* aware. WARE, WARY.] Apprised; cognizant; informed; conscious: followed by *of.* (Sometimes used attributively.)—**a·ware·ness,** *a·wâr'nis, n.*

a·wash, *a·wosh', a·wȧsh', a., adv.* At such a level as to be washed by the waves or tide; washed over; washed about, as by waves on the shore.

a·way, *a·wā', a.* Not present at a place; afar; *sports,* on an opponent's grounds; not at home; as, an *away* game; *golf,* pertaining to the ball lying farthest from the cup; *baseball,* out; as, one *away* in the 7th inning.

a·way, *a·wā', adv.* [O.E. *onweg* < *on-,* on, and *weg,* way.] At a distance; apart; in another place; to a distance (to go *away*); on the way. It is often used elliptically (whither *away* so fast?). With many verbs it conveys a notion of using up or consuming (to squander *away,* to idle or loiter *away*); it has also merely an intensive force (eat *away,* laugh *away*).

awe, *a, n.* [M.E. *aghe, eghe,* O.E. *ege,* fear, dread; Icel. *agi,* awe, terror; Goth. *agis,* fear; allied to Gael. *agh,* fear; Gr. *achos,* anguish—from root seen in *anguish, anger,* etc. ANGER.] Dread or great fear; fear mingled with admiration or reverence; reverential fear; feeling inspired by something sublime.

awe, *a, v.t.*—**awed, awing.** To strike with awe; to deter by fear, reverence, or respect.

a·wea·ry, *a·wē'rē, a. Poet.* weary.

a·weath·er, *a·weTH'ẽr, a., adv.* On or to the weather side of a ship: opposed to *alee.*

a·weigh, *a·wā', a. Naut.* raised just enough to be clear of the ground and hanging perpendicularly: said of an anchor.

awe·less, aw·less, *a'lis, a.* Devoid of awe; wanting the power of inspiring reverence or awe; fearless.

awe·some, *a'sum, a.* Inspiring awe; as, an *awesome* display of talent; awful; characterized by awe.—**awe·some·ly,** *a'sum·lē, adv.*—**awe·some·ness,** *a'sum·nis, n.*

awe·strick·en, *a'strik"en, a.* Struck or impressed with awe. Also **awe-struck,** *a'struk".*

aw·ful, *a'ful, a.* Dreadful; unpleasant; ugly; objectionable. Striking or inspiring with awe; filling with dread, or dread mingled with profound reverence; proceeding from awe.

aw·ful·ly, *a'ful·lē, adv.* In an awful manner; in a manner to fill with awe. *Colloq.* terribly; excessively; extremely.

aw·ful·ness, *a'ful·nis, n.* The quality of being awful, or of striking with awe, reverence, or terror.

a·while, *a·hwīl', a·wīl', adv.* [O.E. *āne hwīle,* a while.] For a space of time; for some time.

a·whirl, *a·hwŭrl', a·wŭrl', a.* In a whirl; spinning.—*a.*

awk·ward, *ak'ward, a.* [M.E. < O.E. *awk, awke,* wrong, backward, reverse (= Icel. *öfigr, öfugr,* Sw. *afvig,* turned the wrong

way, from *af* = E. *off*) and *-ward.*] Wanting dexterity in the use of the hands or of instruments; bungling; clumsy; ungraceful in manners; inconvenient; uncouth; unmanageable; hazardous; embarrassing.—**awk·ward·ly,** *ak'ward·lē, adv.*—**awk·ward·ness,** *ak'ward·nis, n.*

awl, *al, n.* [O.E. *awul, ael, ál* (= Icel. *alr,* G. *ahle*).] A pointed instrument for piercing small holes in leather, wood, etc.

awn, *an, n.* [O.E. < O.N. *ögn* = Icel. *ögn,* Dan. *avne,* Sw. *agne,* chaff, husk; akin to Gr. *achnē,* chaff.] The bristle or beard of corn or grass, or any similar bristlelike appendage.—**awned,** *and, a.* Having awns. —**awn·less,** *an'lis, a.* Without an awn.

awn·ing, *a'ning, n.* A canvas-covered frame or similar structure that shelters a window, deck, or the like from sun and rain.

AWOL, A.W.O.L., *ā'wal, n.* [*Absent without leave.*] (*Sometimes l.c.*), *milit. slang,* any official personnel who are absent without leave; the situation of being absent without leave.—*a., adv.* In the position of being absent without leave.

a·wry, *a·rī', a., adv.* [M.E. WRY.] Turned or twisted toward one side; crooked; amiss; off course.

ax, axe, *aks, n. pl.* **ax·es.** [O.E. *ax, æcx,* Icel. *ox,* Dan. *oxe,* D. *aakse,* G. *ax, axt; =* Gr. *axinē,* L. *ascia* for *acsia,* an axe.] An instrument, consisting of a head, with an arching edge of steel in the plane of the sweep of the tool, attached to a handle, and used for hewing timber and chopping wood.—**get the ax,** *slang,* to be suddenly rejected or dismissed, as from a job or school.

ax, axe, *aks, v.t.*—**axed, axing.** To cut, shape, or dress with an ax. *Slang.* To discharge, as an employee; to fire; to remove.

ax·i·al, *ak'sē·al, a.* Pertaining to an axis.— **ax·i·al·ly,** *ak'sē·a·lē, adv.* According to or in line with the axis.

ax·i·al skel·e·ton, *n. Anat.* the segment of the human skeleton which includes the head and trunk.

ax·il, *ak'sil, n.* [L. *axilla,* armpit.] *Bot.* the angle between the upper side of a leaf or stem and the supporting stem or branch.

ax·il·la, *ak·sil'a, n. pl.* **ax·il·lae,** *ak·sil'ē.* [L. armpit.] *Anat.* the armpit; the corresponding region under a bird's wing. *Bot.* an axil.

ax·il·lar, *ak'si·lar, a.* Axillary.—*n. Usu. pl.* the underwing coverts of a bird, growing from the axilla.

ax·il·lar·y, *ak'si·ler"ē, n. pl.* **ax·il·lar·ies,** *ak'si·ler'ēz.* An axillar.

ax·il·lar·y, *ak'si·ler"ē, a.* Pertaining to the axilla or axil; situated in or growing from the axil of a plant.

ax·i·ol·o·gy, *ak'sē·ol'o·jē, n.* [Gr. *axios,* worthy, and *-logy.*] *Philos.* the study of values and value judgments, their nature, types, etc., esp. in ethics, aesthetics, and religion.—**ax·i·o·log·i·cal,** *ak"sē·o·loj'i·kal, a.* About or pertaining to axiology.

ax·i·om, *ak'sē·um, n.* [M.E. < L. < Gr. *axiōma* < *axioein,* to consider worthy.] A self-evident truth or proposition; a proposition whose truth is so evident at first sight that no process of reasoning or demonstration can make it plainer; an established principle in some art or science; a principle universally received.

ax·i·o·mat·ic, *ak"sē·o·mat'ik, a.* Pertaining to, consisting of, or having the character of an axiom; self-evident; obvious. Also **ax·i·o·mat·i·cal,** *ak"sē·o·mat'i·kal.*— **ax·i·o·mat·i·cal·ly,** *ak"sē·o·mat'i·kal·ē, adv.*

ax·is, *ak'sis, n. pl.* **ax·es,** *ak'sēz.* [L.] A straight line, real or imaginary, that passes through a body and about which the body may, or actually does, revolve; a hypothetical line in reference to which a body is symmetrical; the pivotal vertebra of the neck

on which the head turns; (*cap.*) the alliance of Germany, Italy, and Japan during World War II.

ax·is cyl·in·der, *n. Anat.* the central, conducting part of a nerve fiber.

ax·ite, *ak'sit, n. Anat.* An axon; any of an axon's terminal branches.

ax·le, *ak'sel, n.* [M.E. *axel-,* in *axeltre* < O.N. *öxultrē,* axletree; akin to O.E. *eaxl,* shoulder, L. *axis,* Gr. *axon,* axle, axis.] The pin, bar, shaft, or the like, on which, or together with which, a wheel or wheels rotate; either end (spindle) of an axletree or the like; the whole (fixed) axletree, or a similar bar connecting and turning with two opposite wheels of a vehicle.

ax·le·tree, *ak'sel·trē", n.* [M.E. *axeltre,* O.N. *öxultrē.*] A bar fixed crosswise under the body of a vehicle, with a rounded spindle at each end upon which a wheel rotates.

ax·man, axe·man, *aks'man, n. pl.* **ax-men, axe·men,** *aks'men.* One who wields an ax, as in lumbering or, formerly, in battle.

Ax·min·ster, *aks'min"stẽr, n.* A kind of carpet with a finely tufted, velvet-like pile, orig. made by hand at Axminster, England.

ax·o·lotl, *ak'so·lot"el, n.* [Nahuatl, water doll.] A remarkable member of the tailed amphibians found in Mexican lakes, possessing four limbs resembling those of a frog, and usually having throughout life both lungs and gills, but sometimes losing the latter.

ax·om·e·ter, *ak·som'e·tẽr, n.* [N.L.] An optician's measuring device used in adjusting frames of spectacles to the centers of the eyes.

ax·on, *ak'son, n.* [N.L. < Gr. *axōn,* axis.] *Anat.* a long, single, nerve cell process which carries transmitted nerve impulses away from the body of the cell. Also **ax·one,** **neu·rite,** *ak'sōn, nŭr'it, nūr'it.*—**ax·on·al,** *ax·on·ic,* **ax·son·al,** ak·son'ik, *a.*

ax·o·no·met·ric pro·jec·tion, *ak"so·nō·me'trik pro·jek'shan, n.* [< Gr. *axōn, -o-,* and *-metric.*] *Drafting,* a projection in which a three-dimensional object is represented by an exact scale drawing which appears as an optical distortion of curves and diagonals.

ay, aye, *ā, adv.* [M.E. *ai, ei* < O.N. = O.E. *ā,* ever.] *Poet.* Ever; always.

a·yah, *ä'ya, n.* [< Hindi < Pg. *aia,* maid, < L. *avia,* grandmother.] In India, a native maid or governess.

aye, ay, *ī, interj.* [M.E. *yie.* YEA.] Yes; yea; a sound or expression of assent or affirmation; truly; certainly; indeed.

aye, ay, *ī, n.* The expression of assent in parliamentary procedure; hence, an affirmative vote.—**the ayes have it,** the affirmative votes are in a majority.

Ay·ma·ra, *ī"mä·rä', n. pl.* **Ay·ma·ras,** *ī"mä·räz'.* [Sp.] An Indian people, inhabiting Peru and Bolivia, and their language.

Ayr·shire, *âr'shẽr, âr'shẽr, n.* One of a hardy breed of dairy cattle of medium size and usually of a white and brown color, originating in Ayrshire, Scotland.

a·zal·ea, *a·zāl'ya, n.* [N.L. < Gr. *azaleos,* dry, from inhabiting dry localities.] Any of certain flowering plants of the genus *Rhododendron* in the heath family, many of which are cultivated in various hybrid forms for their profuse, showy blooms.

az·i·muth, *az'i·muth, n.* [M.E. < M.Fr. < Ar. *as-sumūt,* pl. of *as-samt,* a way, a path. *Zenith* has the same origin.] *Avi.* bearing in the horizontal plane, usually expressed as an angle, and in air navigation measured clockwise from true north, grid north, or magnetic north, from 0° to 360°. In celestial navigation, the angle at the zenith measured clockwise from true north to the vertical circle passing through the body. A certain star or aircraft may be said to have an *azimuth* angle of 35°, meaning that the star or aircraft on a

horizontal plane is bearing 35° clockwise from true north as seen by the observer.—
az·i·muth·al, az″i·muth′al, *a.*

az·i·muth·al e·qui·dis·tant pro·jec·-tion, *n. Cartography,* a map projection centered at a given point so that a straight line from the center to any other point is representative of the shortest distance between those two points.

az·o, az′ō, *a.* [AZOTE.] *Chem.* That contains nitrogen, often used in combining form.

az·o dye, *n. Chem.* any of a large class of versatile dyes composed of one or more azo groups and having the azo radical N=N.

a·zo·ic, a·zō′ik, ā·zō′ik, *a.* [Gr. *a-,* not, and *zōē,* life.] *Geol.* Destitute of any vestige of organic life, as applied to ancient rocks in which no fossils have been found; pertaining to the period of geologic time prior to the first appearance of life on earth.

a·zon·al, ā·zōn′al, *a.* Not separated into zones. Pertaining to soil distinguished by a lack of thoroughly developed horizons.

a·zon·ic, ā·zon′ik, *a.* [Gr. *azonicos.*] Not confined to any particular zone or region; not local.

az·ote, az′ōt, a·zōt′, *n.* [Fr. < Gr.] *Chem.* nitrogen.

az·o·te·mi·a, az″o·tē′mē·a, *n.* [N.L.] *Pathol.* usually a symptom of uremic poisoning, a large accumulation of nitrogenous waste in the blood resulting from a kidney malfunction.

az·oth, az′oth, *n.* [M.E. < Ar. *al,* the, and *zāūq,* mercury.] *Alchem.* mercury, as the assumed first principle of all metals.

a·zot·ic, a·zot′ik, *a.* Of or pertaining to azote; nitric.

az·o·tu·ri·a, az″o·tyụr′ē·a, *n.* [N.L.] An overabundance of urea in the urine; an excess of other nitrogenous substances in the urine.

Az·tec, az′tek, *n.* [Sp.] A member of an Indian people dominant in central Mexico at the time of the Spanish invasion (1519); also, their language, still spoken by Mexican Indians; Nahuatl.—*a.* Of or pertaining to the Aztecs or their language; also **Az·tec·-an,** az′tek·an.

az·ure, azh′ur, ā′zhur, *a.* [M.E. < O.Fr. *azur* < L.L. *azurrum, lazurum,* etc., < Ar. *laz-werd,* blue.] Resembling the clear blue color of the sky; sky blue.—*n.* The blue color of the sky; a name common to several sky-colored or blue pigments, as ultramarine or smalt; the sky or vault of heaven.

az·ur·ite, azh′u·rīt″, *n.* A blue mineral, an ore of copper, $Cu_3(CO_3)_2(OH)_2$, composed chiefly of hydrous carbonate and sometimes used as a semiprecious gem.

az·y·gous, az′i·gus, *a.* [Gr. *azygos* < *a-,* not and *zygon,* a yoke.] *Biol.* Not one of a pair; single: applied to certain muscles, etc.

az·ym, az·yme, az′im, *n.* [L.L. *azymus* < Gr. *azymos,* unleavened.] A cake of unleavened bread, used in the Eucharistic service.

B

B, b, bē, *n.* The second letter and the first consonant in the English alphabet; *mus.* the seventh note of the model diatonic scale or scale of C. A ranking on a scale with A representing excellence and B representing above average performance.

baa, bä, ba, *n.* [Imitation of the sound.] Bleating of a sheep.—*v.i.—baaed, baaing.*

ba·bas·su, bä″ba·sö′, *n.* [Pg. *babaçú,* perhaps < Tupi.] The tall palm, *Orbignya martiana,* cultivated in northeastern Brazil for the oil its nuts yield.

bab·bitt, bab′it, *n.* Babbitt metal.

Bab·bitt, bab′it, *n.* [From the protagonist of

the novel of the same name by Sinclair Lewis.] A seemingly self-satisfied businessman who readily conforms to the norms and ideals of middle-class society.

Bab·bitt met·al, *n.* [From the name of the inventor.] An alloy of copper, tin, and antimony used for lining bearings.

bab·ble, bab′bl, *v.i.—babbled, babbling.* [< *ba,* a sound uttered by an infant; D. and G. *babbeln,* Icel. *babbla,* Dan. *bable,* Fr. *babiller.*] To utter words imperfectly or indistinctly; to talk idly or irrationally; to make a continuous murmuring sound; to prate; to tell secrets.—*v.t.* To utter idly or irrationally.—*n.* Idle talk; senseless prattle; murmur, as of a stream.—**bab·bler,** bab′lẽr, *n.*

babe, bāb, *n.* [< Celtic; W. Ir. and Gael. *baban,* Gael. and Ir. *bab,* child, infant.] An infant; a young child of either sex; a very young animal; *colloq.* a childish person; *slang,* a pretty girl or woman.

Ba·bel, bā′bel, bab′l, *n.* [Heb. *Bābel,* Babylon.] An ancient city of Shinar where, according to Gen. xi. 4–9, the building of a tower intended to reach to heaven was begun and a confounding of the language of the people took place. (*Usu. l.c.*), *fig.* a scene of noise and confusion; a confusion of sounds.

ba·biche, ba·bēsh′, *n.* [Fr. Canadian < Algonquin Indian.] *Canada.* A thong or lacing made from animal skin; rawhide.

Ba·bin·ski re·flex, *a.* A normal reflex action in children up to one year of age in which the large toe extends upwards and the other toes bend down when the sole of the foot is stroked. Also **Ba·bin·ski sign.**

ba·boon, ba·bön′, *n.* [Fr. *babouin.*] Any of certain primates of Africa and Asia of the genus *Papio* or *Cynocephalus,* having elongated muzzles like a dog. *Slang,* a crude person with little intelligence.

ba·bu, bä′bö, *n.* [Hind. *bābū.*] *Anglo-Indian,* any native of India with a smattering of English speech and culture.—**ba·bu·ism,** bä′bö·iz″um, *n.* The superficial English culture and English speech of babus.

ba·bush·ka, ba·bụsh′ka, ba·bösh′ka, *n.* [Russ. *babushka,* grandmother.] A woman's headpiece made by folding a kerchief into a triangle and worn with two corners tied under the chin.

ba·by, bā′bē, *n. pl.* **ba·bies.** [Dim. of *babe.*] A very young child; an infant; a newborn animal; the youngest member of a group; one who acts in a childish manner. *Slang,* one's sweetheart; a pretty woman or girl. A person or thing.—*a.*—**ba·by·hood,** bā′-bē·hụd, *n.*—**ba·by·ish,** bā′bē·ish, *a.*

ba·by, bā′bē, *v.t.—babied, babying.* To care for meticulously; to pamper.

ba·by bon·us, *n. Canada slang,* the Family Allowance, a welfare program in which assistance is based on the number of children in a family.

ba·by farm, *n.* A place providing for the care and attention of babies for a fee.

Bab·y·lo·ni·an, bab″i·lō″nyan, bab″i·lō′-nē·an, *a.* Of or pertaining to Babylon, an ancient city of western Asia on the river Euphrates, noted for its luxury and wickedness; sybaritic; luxurious.

ba·by's-breath, bā′bēz·breth″, *n.* A tall herb, *Gypsophila paniculata,* bearing numerous small, fragrant, white or pink flowers. Also **ba·bies'-breath.**

ba·by-sit, bā′bē·sit″, *v.i.—baby-sat, baby-sitting.* To assume the responsibility and care for a child or children during the absence of the parents, usu. for a fee.—**ba·by-sit·ter,** bā′bē·sit″ẽr, *n.*

bac·ca, bak′a, *n. pl.* **bac·cae,** bak′ē. [L.] *Bot.* A berry, a one-celled fruit, with several naked seeds immersed in a pulpy mass.

bac·cate, bak′āt, *a. Bot.* Having a pulpy texture like a berry; bearing berries;

berried.—**bac·cif·er·ous,** bak·sif′ẽr·us, *a.* [L. *bacca,* and *ferre,* to bear.] Bearing or producing berries.—**bac·civ·or·ous,** bak·-siv′or·us, *a.* [L. *bacca,* and *vorāre,* to devour.] Eating or subsisting on berries.

bac·ca·lau·re·ate, bak″a·lạr′ē·it, *n.* [L.L. *baccalaureatus,* < *baccalaureus.*] The degree of Bachelor of Arts; a part of commencement exercises in schools and universities, in which the sermon is addressed to the graduating class.

bac·ca·rat, bä′ka·rä″, bak′a·rä″, bä″ka·rä′, bak″a·rä′, *n.* [Fr.] A game of cards played by any number of players betting against a banker.

bac·cha·nal, bä″ka·näl′, bak′a·nal, bak″-a·nal′, *a.* [L. *bacchanalis,* < *Bacchus,* the god of wine.] Revelling in or characterized by intemperate drinking; riotous; noisy. Also **bac·cha·na·li·an,** bak″a·nā′lē·an, bak″a·näl′yan.—*n.* A votary of *Bacchus;* a drunken feast.

Bac·cha·na·li·a, bak″·a·nā′lē·a, bak″a·-näl′ya, *n. pl., sing. or pl. in constr.* [L.] Feasts or festive rites in honor of Bacchus; a drunken orgy.

bac·chant, bak′ant, *n.* [L. *bacchans,* ppr. of *bacchari,* to celebrate the feast of Bacchus.] A priest of Bacchus; a bacchanal.

bac·chan·te, ba·kan′tē, ba·kant′, bak′ant, *n.* [Fr. *bacchante.*] A priestess of Bacchus, or one who joined in the feasts of Bacchus; one in a state of Bacchanal frenzy; a female bacchanal.

Bac·chus, bak′us, *n.* [L. < Gr. *Bakchos.*] *Mythol.* In ancient Greece and Rome, the god of wine; Dionysus.

bach, bach, *v.i.* [Short for *bachelor.*] *Slang,* to live by oneself as does a bachelor, usu. used in the expression *to bach it.*

bach·e·lor, bach′e·lor, bach′lor, *n.* [O.Fr. *bacheler, bachilier,* Fr. *bachelier,* < L.L. *baccalarius,* the owner of a small farm or a herd of cows, a vassal, < *bacca,* for L. *vacca,* a cow.] Formerly, a young man in the first or probationary stage of knighthood; hence, a man who has not been married; a male seal without a mate; one who has taken the undergraduate degree below that of Master or Doctor in Arts, Science, or other subjects at a college or university.—**bach·e·lor·hood, bach·e·lor·ship,** *n.*

bach·e·lor's but·ton, *n.* Any of a type of plant having a relatively small round flower or flower head which resembles a button, esp. the cornflower.

bac·il·lar·y, bas′i·ler″ē, *a.* Relating to a bacilli; rod-shaped; made up of small rods.

ba·cil·lus, ba·sil′us, *n. pl.* **ba·cil·li,** ba·sil′ī. [L. a little rod.] Any rod-shaped bacteria that produces spores in the presence of free oxygen; a bacterium.

bac·i·tra·cin, bas″i·trā′sin, *n.* [L.L. *baci(llus),* rod, and *Trace,* a patient having such an infection, and *-in.*] An antibiotic effective against bacterial infections.

back, bak, *n.* [O.E. *bac,* Icel. Sw. and L.G. *bak.*] The posterior part of the trunk; the region of the spine; the hinder part of the body in man and the upper in other animals; that which is behind or furthest from the face or front; the rear; as, the *back* of a house; that which is behind or in the furthest distance; the part which comes behind in the ordinary movements or use of a thing; as, the *back* of the hand, a fork, a spade, etc.; a reserve or secondary resource; a position and the player holding this position in some games such as football; a support or second; *pl.* among leather dealers, the thickest and best tanned hides.—**be·hind one's back,** in secret, or when one is absent.

back, *v.i.* To move or go back; to move in a reverse direction; to move with the back foremost—*v.t.* To furnish with a back or backing; to support; to second or strengthen by aid (often with *up*); to bet or wager in favor of; to write something on the back of; to endorse; to put backward; to cause to move backwards or recede. —**backed**, bakt, *a.*

back, bak, *a.* Belonging to the back; lying in the rear; remote; in a backward direction: chiefly in compound words; being behind schedule in payment of a debt; originating at an earlier time; as, *back* issues of a newspaper.

back, bak, *adv.* To or toward a former place, state, or condition; not advancing; in a state of restraint or hindrance; as, to keep *back*; toward times or things past; as, to look *back*; again; in return; as, to give *back*; away from contact; by reverse movement; in withdrawal from an undertaking or engagement; as, to draw *back*.

back·ache, bak′āk″, *n.* A pain or discomfort generally located in the small of the back and often caused by muscle stress.

back·bench·er, bak′ben″chėr, *n.* Any member of a British legislature who is not one of the party leaders.

back·bite, bak′bīt″, *v.t.*—past *backbit*, pp. *backbitten* or colloq. *backbit*, ppr. *backbiting*. To censure, slander, or speak evil of, in the absence of the person traduced.—*v.i.* To speak evil of one who is absent.—**back·bit·er**, bak′bīt″ėr, *n.*

back·board, bak′bōrd″, bak′bȧrd″, *n. Basketball*, the board to which the basket is attached.

back·bone, bak′bōn″, *n.* The bone of the back; the spine; the vertebral column; the bound edge of a book. *Fig.* firmness; the sturdiest part of something; decisive character; reolution; courage; fortitude; perseverence. *Colloq.* nerve, as: He has a lot of *backbone*.

back con·ces·sions, *n. pl. Canada*, esp. Ontario and Quebec, rural areas as distinguished from the cities.

back·cross, bak′krȧs″, bak′kros″, *v.t.* To interbreed, as a first-generation hybrid with a plant which is the parent, or is similar to the parent of the hybrid.—*n.* The act of backcrossing.

back door, *n.* A door in the back part of a building; a secretive or illicit method or relationship.—**back-door**, *a.* Secretive; illicit.

back·down, bak′doun″, *n.* The abandoning of an attempt or pretension.—*v.i.*

back·drop, bak′drop″, *n.* A cloth or curtain hung to serve as the background of a stage setting; the setting for an event.

back·er, bak′ėr, *n.* One who supports or aids another, esp. financially; one who bets in favor of a particular party in a contest.

back·fill, bak′fil″, *n. Building*, earth, stone, or rubbish used to fill excavations around completed foundations.

back·fire, bak′fīėr″, *n.* A fire intentionally set to bare the path of an advancing fire (such as a prairie fire) in order to deplete the supply of fuel to the approaching fire; a premature explosion in the cylinder of an internal-combustion engine; an action that achieves an unexpected result opposite to its intended purpose.—*v.i.*—*backfired*, *backfiring*.

back for·ma·tion, *n.* Formation of a word from one that has the appearance of being its derivative, as of *greed* from *greedy*, *orate* from *oration*, *typewrite* from *typewriter*; a word so formed.

back·gam·mon, bak′gam″on, bak′gam′on, *n.* A game played by two persons upon a table or board made for the purpose, with pieces, dice boxes, and dice; a victory in this game.

back·ground, bak′ground″, *n.* The part of a picture represented as farthest from the spectator; the ground behind another

object or representation; the combination of happenings or conditions which existed previous to an event or phenomenon. *Fig.* a situation little seen or noticed; a state of being out of view (to keep a fact in the *background*).

back·ground, bak′ground″, *n.* The set of influences and environmental development, such as training, education, or experience, affecting an individual's personality; information preceding the consideration of an event and helpful to a better interpretation of the problem.

back·ground mu·sic, *n.* Music that is played to influence the mood of an audience during a play, movie, television or radio program, or other such production; music played, usually in public places, to soothe listeners while they are engaged in some form of activity.

back·hand, bak′hand″, *n.* The hand turned backward in making a stroke, as in tennis; the position or play to the left of a right-handed player and to the right of a left-handed player; handwriting in which the upward slope of the letters is to the left.

back·hand, bak′hand″, *adv.* By means of a backhand.—*v.t.* To strike, attain, or accomplish with a backhand.

back·hand·ed, bak′han″did, *a.* With the back of the hand; as, a *backhanded* blow; done or effected with the hand turned backward, or with the back of the hand in the direction of the stroke; marked by a backward slope, as handwriting; awkward; being the opposite in meaning; as, a *backhanded* compliment; indirect; insincere; of a rope, twisted in the opposite way from the usual or right-handed method.—**back·hand·er**, bak′han″dėr, *n. Colloq.* a backhanded blow or stroke.

back haul, *n.* The return trip of an airplane or other vehicle, when carrying cargo; excessive and unnecessary re-routing or double-handling of cargo.

back·ing, bak′ing, *n.* The back part of a thing; something placed at or attached to the back of anything to support or strengthen it; aid or support of any kind; supporters or backers collectively.

back·lash, bak′lash″, *n.* The backward striking motion of a badly fitted machine part that results from changes in velocity; any sudden, forceful, or violent reaction; *sociol.* reaction against an innovation as the establishment of private schools for white students to circumvent laws which dictate the racial integration of public schools. A tangle in fishing line which is wound around a casting reel.

back·log, bak′lȧg″, bak′log″, *n.* An accumulated volume of stock, work, business, etc., awaiting processing or held in reserve; a large log located at the back of a hearth fire.—*v.t.*—*backlogged*, *backlogging*. To hold in reserve or accumulate.

back mat·ter, *n.* The parts of a book following the text (index, appendix, etc.).

back of, *prep.* Behind.

back off, *v.i.* To retreat, as from a dangerous or challenging situation.

back or·der, *n.* An order set aside to be completed or filled in the future because goods are temporarily unavailable.

back pay, *n.* Wages due an employee representing the difference between a previously existing rate and a higher rate granted retroactively; wages due an employee.

back·ped·al, bak′ped″al, *v.i.*—*backpedaled*, *backpedaling*, Brit. *backpedalled*, *backpedalling*. To move the pedals of a bicycle, etc., backward, or press down upon a pedal as it rises in order to retard speed; *fig.* to step backward, as in boxing. To retreat from a position or argument.

back·rest, bak′rest″, *n.* An object used to rest one's back; as, the *backrest* of a chair.

back·saw, bak′sȧ″, *n.* A rigid metal saw with a reinforcing rib along its back.

back·scat·ter, bak′skat″ėr, *n.* The deflection or scattering of radiation opposite to the direction in which the rays were originally traveling; the rays (as x-rays) so deflected. Also **back·scat·ter·ing**, bak′skat″ėr·ing.

back·set, bak′set″, *n.* A reverse; an eddy or counter-current; setback.

back·side, bak′sīd″, *n.* The back part of anything; the side opposite to the front; the posterior or rump.

back·sight, bak′sīt″, *n. Surv.* a sight or reading taken in a backward direction or toward a previous station.

back·slap, bak′slap″, *v.t.* To express a gushing benevolent interest in the welfare of, as a person.—*v.i.* To express effusive friendliness toward another or others.—**back·slap·per**, *n.*—**back·slap·ping**, *a.*, *n.*

back·slide, bak′slīd″, *v.i.*—past *backslid*, pp. *backslid* or *backslidden*, ppr. *backsliding*. To slide back; to fall off or turn away from religion or morality; to apostatize.—**back·slid·er**, bak′slīd·ėr, *n.*

back·spin, bak′spin″, *n.* A reverse rotation on a projected object, as a ball.

back·stage, bak′stāj′, *adv.* Behind the stage area in a theater, esp. in the dressing rooms; at the rear area of the stage. —*a.* Pertaining to or taking place in the backstage area; pertaining to the personal lives of professional entertainers.

back·stairs, bak′stârz′, *n.* A stair or stairs in the back part of a house; private stairs.— *a.* Of or pertaining to backstairs, hence, indirect; underhand; secret; as, *backstairs* gossip. Also **back·stair**, bak′stâr′.

back·stay, bak′stā″, *n.* A long rope or stay, extending from the top of a mast backward to the side of a ship to assist the shrouds in supporting the mast; a supporting device in a machine.

back·stitch, bak′stich″, *n.* Stitching or a stitch in which the thread doubles back each time on the preceding stitch.—**back·stitch**, bak′stich″, *v.i.*, *v.t.*

back·stop, bak′stop″, *n. Baseball.* A barrier located behind a playing area to keep the ball from rolling away, as a wire screen; *colloq.* the catcher. An object intended to impede regressive motion.—*v.t.*—*backstopped*, *backstopping*. To support; reinforce.

back·stretch, bak′strech″, *n.* That part of a race track furthest across the infield from the grandstand and opposite the homestretch.

back·stroke, bak′strōk″, *n.* A stroke or blow in return; a recoil; *swimming*, a stroke executed on the back, similar to an inverted crawl, but requiring more leg action.

back·swept, bak′swept″, *a.* Inclined toward the back.

back·swim·mer, bak′swim″ėr, *n.* An insect of the family *Notonectidae*, that propels itself through water by swimming on its back.

back·sword, bak′sōrd″, bak′sȧrd″, *n.* A sword with only one sharp edge; a cudgel with a basket hilt, used like a sword or foil in fencing; a backswordman.

back talk, *n.* An impudent or disrespectful reply.

back·track, bak′trak″, *v.i.* To retrace one's steps; to reverse one's position, attitude, or course of action.

backup, bak′up″, *n.* An item kept available to replace another item if it fails to perform satisfactorily; cessation of movement due to an obstacle; as, a *backup* of cars at the toll gate.—*a.* Pertaining to a person or object available as a replacement; as, a *backup* crew for a space mission.

back up, *v.t. Slang*, to give support to; to verify; as, to *back up* testimony. To cause a delay; as, to *back up* traffic; to move in reverse.

back·ward, bak'ward, *adv*. Toward the back, rear, or past; with the back foremost; in the reverse of the usual or right way; retrogressively. Also **back·wards**, bak'-wards.

back·ward, bak'ward, *a*. Directed toward the back or the past; reversed or in reverse; returning; behind in time or progress; late; dull; not quick of apprehension; slow; reluctant; bashful.—**back·ward·ly**, bak'-ward·lē, *adv*.

back·ward·ness, bak'wụrd·ṅes, *n*. Slow mental development or retardation that is not due to lack of intelligence; the characteristic of a slow learner.

back·wash, bak'wosh", bak'wạsh", *n*. The water thrown back by a boat's motor, oars, paddle wheels, or the like; the results or consequence of an event.

back·wa·ter, bak'wạtẻr, bak'wot"ẻr, *n*. Water turned or held back, as by a dam; ebbtide; backwash; *fig*. a place which is out of touch with the world, isolated, or opposed to any change.

back·woods, bak'wụdz", *n. pl., sing. or pl. in constr*. Woody or forest districts of a country situated back or away from the more thickly settled parts; a culturally unadvanced area.—*a*. Unsophisticated; related to the backwoods.—**back·woods·-man**, *n*.

ba·con, bā'kon, *n*. [O.Fr. *bacon* < Teut. and akin to E. *back*.] The back and sides of the hog salted, dried, and usu. smoked, and eaten.

Ba·co·ni·an, bā·kō'en·an, *a*. Of or pertaining to Francis Bacon (1561–1626), English philosopher and statesman, or his doctrines; as, the *Baconian* method in science.—**Ba·co·ni·an the·ory**, the theory that Bacon wrote the plays usu. attributed to Shakespeare.

ba·con·y, bā'ko·nē, *a*. Brit. fatty.

bac·ter·i·a, bak·tēr'ē·a, *n. pl.* Bacterium.

bac·te·ri·al, bak'tēr'ē·al, *a*. Of, pertaining to, or caused by bacteria; of the nature of or consisting of bacteria.—**bac·ter·ic**, bak'-tēr'ik, *a*.—**bac·te·ri·al·ly**, *adv*.

bac·te·ri·ci·dal, bak'tēr"*i*·sīd'al, *a*. Capable of killing bacteria.—**bac·te·ri·ci·-dal·ly**, *adv*.

bac·te·ri·cide, bak·tēr'i·sīd", *n*. Anything capable of destroying bacteria.

bac·te·rin, bak'te·rin, *n*. A vaccinal preparation of killed or weakened bacteria.

bac·te·ri·o·log·ic, bak·tēr"ē·o·loj'ik, *a*. Pertaining to or concerned with bacteriology.—**bac·te·ri·o·log·i·cal**, bak·tēr"ē·o·loj'i·kal, *a*.—**bac·te·ri·o·log·i·cal·ly**, bak·tēr"ē·o·loj'i·kal·lē, bak·tēr"ē·o·loj'i·-ka·lē, *adv*.

bac·te·ri·ol·o·gy, bak·tēr"ē·ol'o·jē, *n*. The study of bacteria and the part they play in medicine, agriculture, and industry; bacterial life processes.—**bac·te·ri·ol·o·-gist**, bak·tēr"ē·ol'o·jist, *n*.

bac·te·ri·ol·y·sis, bak·tēr"ē·ol'i·sis, *n*. The process of dissolution or destruction of bacteria.—**bac·te·ri·o·lyt·ic**, bak·tēr"-ē·o·lit'ik, *a*.

bac·te·ri·o·phage, bak·tēr'ē·o·fāj", *n*. Any of a group of viruses that effect bacteriolysis on specific viruses found in sewage or body products.—**bac·te·ri·o·-phag·ic**, bak·te·ri·oph·a·gous, bak·tēr"-ē·o·faj'ik, bak·tēr"ē·af'o·gus, *a*.—**bac·te·-ri·oph·a·gy**, bak·tēr"ē·äf'a·jē, *n*.

bac·te·ri·os·co·py, bak·tēr"ē·os'ka·pē, *n*. Microscopic investigation of bacteria.—**bac·te·ri·o·scop·ic**, bak·tēr"ē·o·skop'ik, *a*.—**bac·te·ri·os·co·pist**, bak·tēr"ē·os'-ko·pist, *n*.

bac·te·ri·o·sta·sis, bak·tēr"ē·o·stā'sis, *n*. Prevention of the growth of bacteria without killing them.—**bac·te·ri·o·stat**, *n*. A substance used for bacteriostasis.

bac·te·ri·um, bak·tēr'ē·um, *n. pl.*

bac·te·ri·a, bak·tēr'ē·a. [N.L. < Gr. *baktērion*, a stick.] Any of the microscopic organisms of the class *Schizomycetes*, having round, spiral, or rod-shaped bodies, which occur in soil, water, organic matter such as sewage, and in animal tissues: typhoid or pneumonia bacteria are disease-producing while others are useful in bringing about fermentation in many industrial processes.

bac·te·ri·za·tion, bak·te·ri·zā'shan, *n*. The condition of being bacterized; the process of bacterizing.

bac·ter·ize, bak'te·rīz", *v.t.*—*bacterized, bacterizing*. To expose to the decomposing effects of bacteria.

bac·ter·oid, bak'te·roid", *n*. A rod-shaped bacterium present in the tubercles on the roots of nitrogen producing plants.—**bac·-te·roi·dal**, bak'te·roid"al, *a*. Similar to or resembling bacteria.

ba·cu·li·form, ba·kū'li·farm", *a*. Rod-shaped or rectilinear.

bad, bad, *a*.—*worse, worst*. [Perhaps of Celtic origin; cf. Corn. *bad*, Gael. *baodh, baoth*, vain, foolish, etc.] The opposite of good; wanting good qualities, physical or moral; not coming up to a certain type of standard or the average of individuals of the particular class; wicked, unprincipled, depraved, immoral, vicious; pernicious, debasing or corrupting (influence, habits); ill or infirm (health); unwholesome or noxious (air, climate, food); defective or insufficient (work, crop); infertile or sterile (soil); unfortunate or unhappy (result, marriage); incompetent (workman).—**bad·ly**, bad'lē, *adv*. In a bad manner; not well; unskillfully.

bad, bad, *n*. That which is bad; the state of being bad.—**go to the bad**, to fall into bad company, bad ways, or bad circumstances; to fall into vicious habits and ruin one's life.—**bad·ness**, bad'nis, *n*. The state of being bad; want of good qualities, physical or moral.

bad blood, *n*. Malevolence; virulence; hostile relationship, as: There was *bad blood* between them.

bad·der·locks, bad'ẻr·loks", *n*. [Formerly *Balderlocks*, perhaps < *Balder*, Scandinavian god, and *locks* (of hair).] A seaweed found on the shores of the north of Europe, the midrib of which is edible.

badge, baj, *n*. [L.L. *bagia*, a sign, probably < O.E. *beag*, Icel. *baugr*, a bracelet, ring, garland.] A mark, sign, token, or cognizance worn to show the relation of the wearer to any person, occupation, or order.—*v.t.*—*badged, badging*. To mark or distinguish with a badge or as with a badge.

badg·er, baj'ẻr, *n*. [Perhaps < *badge*, with allusion to the stripes on the head.] Any of various burrowing carnivorous mammals of the family *Mustelidæ*, as *Meles vulgaris*, a European species about two feet long, with gray fur, and with black and white stripes on the head, and *Taxidea americana*, a similar American species; any of certain other animals, as in Australia a wombat. —*v.t.* To harass, as if baiting a badger; worry; torment; pester; tease.

bad·i·nage, bad'i·näzh", bad'i·nij, *n*. [Fr. < *badin*, facetious. M.L. *batare*, gape.] Light or playful discourse.—*v.t.*—*badinaged, badinaging*. To tease without malice.

bad·land, bad'land", *n. pl.* **bad·lands**, bad'landz". *Usu. pl.* a highly eroded, inhospitable area characterized by scanty vegetation and many intricate rock formations.

bad·min·ton, bad'min·ton, *n*. [< a residence of the Dukes of Beaufort.] An outdoor game, similar to lawn tennis, but played with shuttlecocks and light rackets with a high net dividing the court.

Bae·de·ker, bā'de·kẻr, *n*. Any of the series of European guidebooks originally published for the benefit of travelers by Karl Baedeker,

1801–1859, a noted German publisher; a traveler's guidebook.

baf·fle, baf'fl, *v.t.*—*baffled, baffling*. [Origin unknown.] To elude; to foil, bewilder, or perplex; to deflect flow of a gas, liquid, sound, etc.; to frustrate; to defeat; to thwart; to prevent interference or exchange of, as sound waves.—**baf·fler**, baf'lẻr, *n*. —**baf·fling·ly**, baf'ling·lē, *adv*.

baf·fle, baf'fl, *n*. A plate or screen or other contrivance that deflects or regulates flow of a gas, liquid, etc. Any partition or boxlike enclosure used to prevent sound waves from interfering with each other, as in a loudspeaker.

bag, bag, *n*. [M.E. *bagge*: cf. Icel. *baggi*, bag, bundle, and O.Fr. *bagues*, baggage.] A receptacle of leather, cloth, paper, etc., capable of being closed at the mouth; a sack; a pouch; a valise or other portable receptacle for carrying articles as in traveling; a purse or moneybag; the contents of a bag or pouch; a sportsman's take of game, etc.; any of various measures of capacity; something resembling or suggesting a bag; a sac, as in an animal body; an udder; a baggy part; *coal-mining*, a cavity filled with gas or water; *baseball*, a square canvas base-marker; *slang*, an unpleasant, often untidy female.—**in the bag**, certain; completely successful.

bag, bag, *v.i.*—*bagged, bagging*. To swell or bulge; hang loosely like an empty bag.—*v.t.* To cause to swell or bulge; distend; to put into a bag, as killed game; kill or catch, as in hunting; *colloq*. to catch, seize, or steal.

ba·gasse, ba·gas', *n*. [Fr. < Sp. *bagazo*, refuse from crushed fruit < L. *bacca*, berry.] The sugarcane or sugar beets in dry, crushed state after the juice has been extracted; paper made from bagasse.

bag·a·telle, bag"a·tel', *n*. [Fr. < It. *bagattella*, dim. < *baga*, berry < L. *bacca*.] A trifle; a thing of no importance; a short and light musical composition, usually for the piano; a game played on a board having holes into which balls are driven by being struck with a cue.

ba·gel, bā'gel, *n*. [Yiddish < O.H.G. *boug*, ring.] A leavened hard roll, glazed and shaped like a doughnut, often served with cream cheese and lox.

bag·ful, bag'ful, *n. pl.* **bag·fuls**. A quantity sufficient to fill a bag; a sizable amount.

bag·gage, bag'ij, *n*. [Fr. *bagage*, baggage, O.Fr. *bague*, a bundle. BAG.] Luggage; things required for a journey; the transportable equipment of an army, or other body of men on the move; extraneous, unnecessary items.

bag·gage, bag'ij, *n*. [Fr. *bagasse*, It. *bagascia*, Sp. *bagazo*, a strumpet.] A low undignified woman; a vivacious young woman; *archaic*, a wanton.

bag·gat·a·way, ba·gat'a·wä", *n. Canada*, the game played by Indians, from which modern lacrosse was derived.

bag·ging, bag'ing, *n*. The cloth, such as hemp, or other materials for bags.

bag·gy, bag'ē, *a*.—*baggier, baggiest*. Having the appearance of a bag; loose; puffy, as eyes.

bag·man, bag'man, *n. pl.* **bag·men**, bag'men. A person who collects or distributes bribes or payoff money; *Brit.* a tramp.

bagn·io, ban'yō, bän'yō, *n. pl.* **bagn·ios**, ban'yōz. [It. *bango*, < L. *balneum*, bath.] A bath or bathing house; a house of prostitution; a brothel.

bag·pipe, bag'pīp", *n*. A musical wind instrument consisting of a leather bag which receives the air from the mouth or from a bellows, and of pipes into which the air is pressed from the bag by the performer's elbow.—**bag·pip·er**, bag'pīp"ẻr, *n*.

ba·guette, ba·get', *n*. [Fr.] A molding; a narrow, rectangularly cut gem.

---

a- fat, fāte, fär, fâre, fạll; **e-** met, mē, mēre, hẻr; **i-** pin, pīne; **o-** not, nōte, mŏve; **u-** tub, cūbe, bụll; **oi-** oil; **ou-** pound.

bag·worm, bag′wụrm″, *n.* The larva of a lepidopterous insect, *Thyridopteryx ephemeraeformis*, of the northern U.S.: so called from the silken bag which it constructs and carries about for protection.

bah, bä, ba, *interj.* An exclamation expressing contempt, disdain, disgust, or incredulity.

Ba·ha'i Faith, bạ·hä′ē fāth, *n.* [Ar. Baha′-u′llah, glory of God.] An independent world religion, founded in 1863 in Iran, which declares that religious truth revolves around a belief in the oneness of God, the oneness of religion, and the oneness of mankind.— **Ba·ha·i**, bạ·hä′ē, *n.* pl. **Ba·ha·is**. A follower of Bahaism.—**Ba·ha·ist**, bạ·hä′ist, *n., a.*

bail, bāl, *v.t.* [Fr. *baille*, a bucket, < L. *bajulus*, porter.] To free (a boat) of water with a bucket or other utensil, usually used with *out.*—*v.i.* To free of water; to parachute from an airplane, usu. used with *out.*

bail, bāl, *v.t.* [O.Fr. *bailler*, to bail, to guard, from L. *bajulus*, a bearer, later a tutor or governor. Hence *bailiff.*] To liberate from arrest and imprisonment, upon security that the person liberated shall appear and answer in court; to help in a predicament by supplying financial aid.

bail, bāl, *n.* [O.Fr. *baille*, a palisade, < L. *baculum*, a rod or staff.] *Cricket*, a little stick laid on the tops of the stumps.

bail, bāl, *n.* The person or persons who procure the release of a prisoner from custody by becoming surety for his appearance in court; the security given for the release, as: We were his *bail*.

bail, bāl, *n.* The hinged bar on a typewriter which holds paper against the platen; *fishing*, the wire device by which one controls the line on a spinning reel; the hoop-shaped handle of a kettle or pail.

bail·a·ble, bā′lạ·bl, *a.* Capable of being admitted to bail; admitting of bail; as, a *bailable* offense.

bail bond, *n.* A bond, money or property, given to insure due appearance of one who is bailed.

bail·ee, bā″lē′, *n. Law*, one to whom goods are committed in bailment for storage or use.

bail·ey, bā′lē, *n.* pl. **bail·eys**, bā′lēz. The wall of defense about the outer court of a feudal castle, or any one of several circuits of walls surrounding the keep; the outer court, or any court between the circuits of walls.

bail·iff, bā′lif, *n.* [O.Fr. *baillif, bailli, baillir, bailler*, to hold, to govern, < L. *bajulare*, to bear, < *bajulus*, a porter. BAIL, to liberate.] A civil officer or functionary; a sheriff's deputy; a court officer who executes writs, processes, distraints, and arrests, and who also acts as a messenger or usher in court; *chiefly Brit.* the overseer of an estate or farm.

bail·i·wick, bā′li·wik, *n.* [-*wick* < O.E. *wic*, dwelling, station < L. *vicus*, a village.] The precincts in which a bailiff has jurisdiction; the bailiff's office; a person's area of influence or authority.

bail·ment, bāl′ment, *n.* The act of placing goods in the possession of a bailee; the freeing of an arrested person.

bail·out, bāl′out″, *n.* The action of bailing out of an aircraft.

bails·man, bālz′man, *n.* pl. **bails·men**, bālz′men. *Law*, a person who gives bail or security for another, usually for a fee.

Bai·ly's beads, bā′lēz bēdz, *n.* [From F. *Baily*, a British astronomer.] The belt of bright sunlight shining through mountains on the moon's surface that is seen just before and just after a total eclipse of the sun.

bain-ma·rie, ban″ma·rē′, *n.* pl. **bains-ma·rie**. [Fr. earlier *bain de marie*, 'bath of Mary' (perhaps with allusion to the gentle heat).] A vessel containing hot water, in which another vessel is placed to heat its contents; a double boiler; a steam table.

bait, bāt, *v.t.* [< Icel. *beita*, to make to eat, to feed, to bait a hook—a causative of *bita*, E. *bite*.] To furnish with a piece of flesh or other substance which acts as a lure to fish or other animals; as, to *bait* a hook; to lure or entice; to captivate; to provoke and harass, esp. by dogs, as a bull, badger, or bear; to annoy; to persecute. To give food and drink to an animal when traveling.

bait, bāt, *n.* Any substance used as a lure to catch fish or other animals, or to poison pests; an allurement; enticement.

baize, bāz, *n.* [Formerly a plural < Fr. *baies*, plural of *baie*, bay-colored < L. *badius*.] A thick woolen fabric with a nap, now usually green and used as the billiard table cover on which balls are rolled.

bake, bāk, *v.t.*—*baked, baking.* [O.E. *bacan.*] To cook (food) by dry heat in a closed place, as an oven; harden bricks, pottery, etc., by heat.—*v.i.* To bake bread, etc.; to become baked.

Ba·ke·lite, bā′ke·līt″, bāk′līt″, *n.* [From L. H. *Baekeland*, a Belgian-American chemist and inventor.] A hard, non-inflammable synthetic material produced by the action of formaldehyde on phenol under pressure. (Trademark.)

bak·er, bā′kėr, *n.* One whose occupation is to bake food; a small portable oven.

bak·er's doz·en, *n.* Thirteen, the extra one serving to protect against faulty merchandise or a short count.

bak·ers' yeast, *n.* A variety of yeast used for leavening breadstuff.

bak·er·y, bā′ka·rē, *n.* pl. **bak·er·ies**. A place for baking or selling bread and cakes. A store which sells baked products; also *bakeshop*.

bake·shop, bāk′shop″, *n.* See *bakery.*

bak·ing pow·der, *n.* A mixture of baking soda and an acid substance, used as a leavening agent.

bak·ing so·da, *n.* Sodium bicarbonate.

bak·shish, bak′shēsh, *n.* [Pers. < *bakkshidan*, to give.] A present or gratuity of money: used in Arabic countries.

bal·a·lai·ka, bal″a·lī·ka, *n.* [Russ.] A musical instrument of the guitar kind, with a triangular body, of ancient Slavic origin.

bal·ance, bal′ans, *n.* [O.Fr. *balance*, < L.L. *bilanx* having two scales < L. *bi-* two and *lanx*, scale.] An instrument for weighing, typically a bar poised or swaying on a central support according to the weights borne in scales suspended at the ends; hence, power to decide as by a balance; authoritative control; (*cap.*) the zodiacal constellation of sign Libra. Either one of the scales of a balance; a contrivance, now usually a balance wheel, for regulating the beat of a watch or clock; a condition in which the counteracting weights in a balance are equal; a state of equilibrium or equipoise; equal distribution of weight, amount, etc.; harmonious arrangement or adjustment, esp. in design; equanimity or mental stability; composure; something used to produce equilibrium; a weight put into one scale of a balance to offset that in the other; a counterpoise; the turn of the balance; the preponderating weight, as of public opinion; an act of balancing; comparison as to weight, amount, importance, etc.; estimate; an adjustment of accounts; the excess of either side, debit or credit, of an account over the other; the remainder or the rest; equality between the totals of the two sides of an account; a balancing movement in dancing.— **bal·ance·a·ble**, bal′ans·a·bl, *a.* Capable of being balanced.

bal·ance, bal′ans, *v.t.*—*balanced, balancing.* To weigh in or as in a balance; ponder over, as a matter; compare, as two or more things, as to relative weight, value, importance, etc.; bring to or hold in equilibrium; poise; adjust evenly; sway like a balance; to be proportionate to; furnish or be a counterpoise for; counterbalance or offset; use as a counterpoise; set off one against another; reckon up, adjust, or settle, as accounts.— *v.i.* To be in equilibrium; be even; move to and fro, esp. in dancing; sway; waver; reckon or adjust accounts.

bal·ance of pay·ments, *n.* A comparison of a nation's income from, and payments to, other nations, including gold movements due to foreign exchange differences, investments made in other countries, and receipts and payments for goods and services.

bal·ance of pow·er, *n.* An equilibrium of power among or between nations or coalitions of nations so that one nation or a coalition cannot endanger or impinge upon the sovereignty of any other.

bal·ance of trade, *n.* The difference in amount or value between the exports and the imports of a country, said to be favorable or unfavorable according as the exports are greater or less than the imports.

bal·anc·er, bal′an·sėr, *n.* One who or that which balances; an organ of an insect useful in balancing the body; a tumbler or acrobat.

bal·ance sheet, *n.* An itemized statement showing the financial condition of a corporation as of a specific date; a statement in which assets and liabilities plus capital should balance or equal each other.

bal·ance wheel, *n.* A wheel for regulating motion; a wheel in a watch or chronometer which regulates the beat; a flywheel, as of an engine.

bal·as, bal′as, bā′las, *n.* [< O.Fr., < Ar. *balakhsh*, < *Balakhshān*, in Central Asia.] A variety of spinel ruby, of a pale rose-red color, sometimes inclining to orange.

bal·a·ta, bal′a·ta, *n.* [South Amer. Indian.] A water-resistant gum obtained from a S. American tree similar to gutta percha which is used for golf balls and belts for machinery; the tree from which the gum is obtained.

bal·brig·gan, bal·brig′an, *a.* Referring to cotton hosiery made at Balbriggan, Ireland, and hence applied also to machine-knit garments of similar fabric or appearance made elsewhere.—*n.*

bal·co·ny, bal′ko·nē, *n.* pl. **bal·co·nies**. [It. *balcone*, < *balco*, a scaffold, < O.H.G. *balko*, G. *balken* = E. *balk*, a beam.] A platform projecting from the upper wall of a building, supported by columns, pillars, or brackets, and encompassed with a balustrade or railing; a projecting gallery in the interior of a building, as of a theater.

bald, bạld, *a.* [M.E. *balled*, lit. 'marked with a white spot'; of Celtic origin, comp. Armor. *bal*, a white mark on an animal's face; Ir. and Gael. *bal*, a spot.] Destitute of hair, especially on the top and back of the head; having white on the face, said of animals; destitute of the natural or usual covering; destitute of appropriate ornament; unadorned, said of style or language; unconcealed; *bot.* destitute of beard or awn.—**bald·ly**, bạld′lē, *adv.* Nakedly; meanly; inelegantly.—**bald·ness**, bạld′nis, *n.* The state or quality of being bald.

bal·da·chin, **bal·da·quin**, bal′da·kin, bạl′da·kin, *n.* [Fr. < It. *baldacchino*, < *Baldacco*, Italian form of *Bagdad*, where the cloth was manufactured.] A canopy or covering; a canopy on four poles held over an important person or object; a canopy on four columns over an altar; a canopy over a throne; an ornate fabric woven with gold or silver threads.

bald eagle, *n.* The white-headed eagle of North America.

bal·der·dash, bạl'dèr·dash", *n.* [W. *baldor-dus,* prattling, *baldordd,* prattle.] Senseless prate; a jargon of words; noisy nonsense.

bald-faced, bạld'fāst", *a.* Having a white face or white on the face: said of animals. Brashly outright; as, a *bald-faced* lie.

bald·head, bạld'hed", *n.* A person bald on the head; a member of a certain breed of domestic widgeons. Also **bald·pate.**

bald prai·rie, *n. Canada,* the treeless parts of the western prairie; also **go·pher ranch.** A worked-out farm.

bal·dric, bạl'drik, *n.* [M.E. *baudric, baldric,* etc., O.Fr. *baudric,* from O.G. *balderich,* from *balz,* a belt. BELT.] A broad belt, stretching from the right or left shoulder diagonally across the body, either as an ornament or to suspend a sword or horn.

bale, bāl, *n.* [O.Fr. *bale,* the same word as *ball,* meaning originally a round package.] A bundle or package of goods, as cotton or hay, usually bound with cord or wire. A number of turtles.

bale, bāl, *v.t.—baled, baling.* To make up into a bale or bundle.

ba·leen, ba·lēn', *n.* [L. *balæna,* a whale.] The whalebone used for commercial purposes.

bale·fire, bāl'fīr", *n.* [M.E. *bale* < Icel. *bal,* flame, a funeral pyre.] A signal fire; an alarm fire; a bonfire.

bale·ful, bāl'fu̇l, *a.* Destructive; calamitous; deadly; foreboding; portending evil. **bale·ful·ly,** bāl'fu̇l·lē, *adv.—bale·ful·ness,** bāl'fu̇l·nis, *n.*

balk, bạk, *n.* [O.E. *balca,* ridge = G. *balken,* beam: akin *balcony.*] A ridge, as between furrows; a strip left unplowed; a miss, slip, or failure; an illegal deceptive motion of a baseball pitcher, as if to pitch; a thin place in a coal-bed; a check or hindrance; a large beam or timber; *billiards,* any of the eight panels or compartments lying between the cushion of the table and the balk-lines.

balk, bạk, *v.t.* To miss; to evade or shirk; to hinder, thwart, or foil; disappoint.—*v.i.* To stop, as at an obstacle; of horses, to stop short and stubbornly refuse to go on.— **balk·er,** bạk'ėr, *n.* One who balks.

bal·kan·ize, bạl'ka·nīz", *v.t.—balkanized, balkanizing.* [< the *Balkan* states, examples of this process.] (*Sometimes cap.*) to partition, as an area, into various small, politically ineffective divisions which often display hostility among themselves.— **bal·kan·i·za·tion,** bạl'ka·ni·zā'shan, *n.*

balk·line, bạk'lin", *n.* Billiards, a straight line drawn across the table near one end, behind which the cue balls are placed in beginning a game; any of four lines, each parallel with one side of the cushion, which divide the table into a large central panel or compartment and eight smaller compartments (balks) lying between this and the cushion. *Track sports,* starting line.

balk·y, bạ̧'kē, *a.—balkier, balkiest.* Given to balking, as a horse or mule.

ball, bạl, *n.* [M.E. *bal,* prob. < Icel. *böllr.*] A spherical body; a sphere; a globe; a round or roundish body, of different materials and sizes, for use in various games, as baseball, football, tennis, or golf; such a ball in play or action, as tossed, thrown, struck, etc.; as, a low *ball,* a high *ball,* a curved *ball;* a baseball pitched too high or too low or not over the plate, and not struck at by the batter; a game played with a ball, esp. baseball. A solid projectile, originally spherical but now also conical or cylindrical, for cannon or smaller weapons, as distinguished from a *shell;* projectiles, esp. bullets, collectively; any globular or rounded mass; as, a meat*ball* or a *ball* of fire; a globular mass made by winding thread, twine, yarn, etc.; a bolus, or quantity of medicine in the form of a large pill; any rounded protuberant part of a

thing, esp. of the human body, as on the palm of the hand at the base of the thumb or on the sole of the foot at the base of the great toe. *Astron.* a planetary or celestial body, esp. the earth. **—car·ry the ball,** *colloq.* to assume leadership or responsibility.—**get on the ball,** to become knowledgeable, efficient, or alert.—**get the ball roll·ing,** *colloq.* to initiate activity.— **have a ball,** to enjoy a good time without restrictions or reservations.—**have a lot on the ball,** *slang,* to be exceptionally capable.— **on the ball,** *slang.* Alert; able; knowledgeable.—**play ball,** to start a baseball game; to continue a game or any other activity; *colloq.* to cooperate or comply with.

ball, bạl, *v.t.* To make into a ball; round out. *Slang,* to ruin by blundering; to confuse, with *up.—v.i.* To form or gather into a ball.

ball, bạl, *n.* [Fr. *bal,* L.L. *ballare,* to dance, to shake, < Gr. *ballizein,* to dance.] A social assembly of persons of both sexes for the purpose of dancing.

bal·lad, bạl'ad, *n.* [O.Fr. < Pr. *ballada,* dancing-song < *ballar,* to dance, < L.L. *ballare,* dance.] Any light, simple song, esp. one of sentimental or romantic character, having two or more stanzas, all sung to the same melody; a simple, often crude, narrative poem, of popular origin, composed in short stanzas, esp. one of romantic character and adapted for singing; any poem written in similar style.

bal·lade, bạl·läd', *n.* [Fr. BALLAD.] A poem consisting commonly of 3 stanzas of 8 or 10 lines each, followed by an envoy of 4 or 5 lines, the last line of each stanza and of the envoy being the same, and the same rhyme sounds recurring throughout. *Mus.* an ornate romantic arrangement for a ballad.

bal·lad·ry, bạl'a·drē, *n.* Ballad poetry.

ball-and-sock·et joint, bạl'an·sok'it joint, *n.* A natural or an artificial joint formed by a ball or knob working in a socket, and permitting, to a certain degree, rotary movement in every direction.

bal·last, bạl'ast, *n.* [Danish *ballast,* ballast, lit., 'worthless load.'] Heavy matter, as stone, sand, or iron carried in the bottom of a ship or other vessel, to prevent it from being readily overturned: a vessel is said to be in *ballast* when she sails without a cargo. Sand carried in bags in the car of a balloon to steady it, and enable the aeronaut to lighten the balloon by throwing part of it out; material filling up the space between the rails on a railroad in order to make it firm and solid; *fig.* that which confers steadiness on a person.

bal·last, bạl'ast, *v.t.* To place ballast in or on, as a ship or a railroad track; *fig.* to steady. To counterbalance.

ball bear·ing, *n.* A bearing in which the shaft or journal turns upon a number of steel balls running in an annular track; any of the steel balls so used.

ball cock, *n.* A kind of self-acting stop cock opened and shut by means of a hollow sphere or ball of metal floating on the surface of a liquid, and attached to the end of a lever connected with the cock.

bal·le·ri·na, bạl"e·rē'na, *n.* [It. < *ballare,* dance < L.L.] A female ballet dancer.

bal·let, ba·lā', bạl'ā, *n.* [Fr. *ballet,* It. *balletto < ballo < ballare,* dance. BALL.] A classical dance, more or less elaborate, in which several persons take part and create a certain expression by particular movements; a theatrical representation, in which a story is told by gesture, accompanied by dancing, scenery, etc.; a professional dancing company; the music used in a ballet performance.

bal·let·o·mane, ba·let'ō·mān", ba·let'o-mān", *n.* [Fr.] A devotee of the ballet.—

bal·let·o·ma·ni·a, ba·let"o·mā'nē·a, *n.* Inordinate interest in and enjoyment of ballet.

ball·flow·er, bạl'flou"èr, *n. Arch.* an ornament resembling a ball placed in a circular flower, the three (or rarely four) petals of which form a cup around it: usually inserted in a hollow molding.

bal·lis·ta, ba·lis'ta, *n.* pl. **bal·lis·tae,** ba·lis'tē. [L., from Gr. *ballein,* to throw.] A military engine used by the ancients for discharging heavy stones or other missiles.

bal·lis·tic, ba·lis'tik, *a.* [< L. *ballista.*] Pertaining to the throwing of missiles or projectiles, or to the science of ballistics.— **bal·lis·ti·cal·ly,** *adv.*

bal·lis·tic mis·sile, *n. Milit.* any missile controlled in the upward part of its trajectory, but becoming a free-falling body, subject to ballistic reactions, in the descent from its apex.

bal·lis·tics, ba·lis'tiks, *n. pl., but sing. in constr.* The study of the behavior of missiles or projectiles in flight; the art or science of designing projectiles so as to give them efficient motion and flight behavior; the examination of bullets and firearms to determine the source of a bullet.

ball light·ning, *n.* A relatively rare form of lightning, consisting of a reddish, luminous ball, approximately one foot in diameter, which may move rapidly along solid objects or remain floating in midair.

bal·lo·net, bạl"o net', *n.* [Fr., dim. < *ballon,* balloon.] A gasbag which is located in the interior of a balloon or airship and which can be changed in volume to regulate the shape and buoyancy of the vessel.

bal·loon, ba·lön', *n.* [Fr. *ballon,* an aug. of *balle,* a ball. BALL.] A large bag or hollow body usually made of a light fabric, filled with heated air or a gas lighter than air causing it to rise and float in the atmosphere, and often fitted with a basket or gondola for carrying passengers or scientific equipment. A brightly colored rubber bag used as a toy which can be inflated and sealed to form many three-dimensional figures, often filled with a gas lighter than air for buoyancy. A balloon-shaped outline in a cartoon or drawing which contains words spoken by characters in the cartoon.—**bal·loon·ist,** ba·lön'ist, *n.* One who manages or ascends in a balloon; an aeronaut.

bal·loon, ba·lön', *v.t.* To fill with air or inflate.—*v.i.* To go aloft in a balloon; to expand; to grow rapidly.

bal·loon sail, *n. Naut.* A relatively large lightweight sail used on yachts during a light wind.

bal·loon tire, *n.* An automobile tire containing air at low pressure to absorb the shock of bumpy areas in the road.

bal·loon vine, *n.* A tropical variation of *Cardiospermum halicacabum,* possessing large, balloon-like pods.

bal·lot, bạl'ot, *n.* A paper, ball, etc., used to cast a vote in a secret election; action or system of voting by marking a ballot or using a voting machine; the whole number of votes cast or recorded; the right to vote. **—bal·lot box,** *n.* The container for voters' ballots; the system of voting by secret ballot.—**bal·lot·er,** bạl'ot·ėr, *n.*

bal·lot, bạl'ot, *v.t.—balloted, balloting.* To vote on by ballot; to select by drawing lots. *—v.i.* To vote by ballot; to draw lots (*for*).

bal·lotte·ment, ba·lot'ment, *n.* [Fr. < *ballotter,* toss as a ball, < *ballotte,* dim. of *balle,* ball.] *Med.* A method of diagnosing pregnancy, in which a sudden shock is imparted to the fetus, as through the uterine wall, causing it to move suddenly upward and fall back again against the examining finger; a similar method to determine the incidence of a floating kidney.

ball-peen ham·mer, bạl'pēn" ham'ẽr, *n.* A hammer with a hemispherical head used for beating metal.

ball·point pen, bạl'point" pen, *n.* A pen with a tiny steel ball as a writing point, inked by rotating against a cartridge of ink.

ball·room, bạl'rŏm", *n.* A large room for balls or dancing.

bal·lute, ba·lŏt', *n.* [Ball(oon) and (parach)-ute.] A cross between a balloon and a parachute, used to brake the free fall of observation rockets from the upper atmosphere.

ball valve, *n.* A valve in which the fluid pressure exerted on a ball operates to lift this ball, permitting the fluid to pass through the opening while gravity lowers the ball and closes off the flow when the pressure is removed.

bal·ly·hoo, bal'ē·hŏ", *n.* [Akin Ballyhooly, an Irish town.] *Slang.* An exaggerated, clamorous attempt to win customers or advance any cause; blatant advertising or publicity; in general clamor or outcry. *v.i., v.t.*—*ballyhooed, ballyhooing. Slang,* to use, offer, or advertise by ballyhoo.

bal·ly·rag, bal'ē·rag", *v.t.* Bullyrag.

balm, bäm, *n.* [O.Fr. *basme, baume* < L. *balsamum* < Gr. *balsamon,* balsam.] Any of various oily, fragrant, resinous substances, often of medicinal value, exuding from certain plants, esp. tropical trees of the genus *Commiphora;* a plant or tree yielding such a substance; any of various aromatic plants, esp. of the genus *Melissa;* an aromatic or fragrant ointment; *fig.* anything that heals, soothes, or mitigates.

balm·i·ly, bäm'i·lē, *adv.* In a balmy manner.

balm·i·ness, bäm'ē·nis, *n.* The state or quality of being balmy.

balm of Gil·e·ad, *n.* An oleoresin obtained from a tree or shrub, *Commiphora meccanensis,* and esteemed in the East for its fragrance and medicinal properties; a variety of the balsam poplar, *Populus tacamahaca;* the balsam fir, *Abies balsamea.*

bal·mor·al, bal·mạr'al, bal·mor'al, *n.* [< *Balmoral* Castle in Aberdeenshire, Scotland.] (*Sometimes cap.*) A kind of laced shoe; a kind of brimless Scotch cap with a flat top projecting around the head, known also as a tam-o'-shanter, and worn in the U.S. by curling enthusiasts and others.

balm·y, bä'mē, *a.*—*balmier, balmiest.* Having the qualities of balm; aromatic; fragrant; healing; soothing; assuaging; mild; as, *balmy* weather; refreshing. *Slang,* silly, crazy, or foolish.

bal·ne·ol·o·gy, bal'nē·ol'o·jē, *n.* [< L. *balneum,* bath and Gr. *logia,* discourse.] *Med.* the study of the effects of baths employed in therapy.

ba·lo·ney, ba·lō'nē, *n.* [Alteration of *bologna.*] *Slang.* Nonsense; insincerity.—*interj.* Not so! *Colloq.* bologna sausage. Also *boloney.*—*a.*

bal·sa, bạl'sa, bäl'sa, *n.* A tree of the *Bombacaceae* family, *Ochroma lagopus,* of tropical America, which has an exceedingly light wood which is used for making toy airplanes, life preservers and rafts; a raft made of balsa wood; a life raft.

bal·sam, bạl'sam, *n.* [L. *balsamum* < Gr. *balsamon.*] Any of various fragrant exudations from certain trees, as the balm of Gilead, and the 'balsam of Peru' yielded by a leguminous tree, *Toluifera pereirae,* of Central America. Balm; an oleoresin; any of certain transparent turpentines, as 'Canada balsam' obtained from the balsam fir, *Abies balsamea,* and used for mounting objects for the microscope. A plant or tree yielding a balsam; the balsam fir; any of various plants of the genus *Impatiens,* as *I. balsamina,* a common garden annual. Any aromatic ointment, whether for cere-

monial or for medicinal use; any healing or soothing agent or agency; as, the *balsam* of tender words.

bal·sam·ic, bạl·sam'ik, bal·sam'ik, *a.* Of, like, or containing balsam; balmy; fragrant; soothing; healing.—**bal·sam·i·cal·ly,** *adv.*

bal·sam of Pe·ru, *n.* Balsam from a leguminous tree of central America used in the manufacture of chocolate, medicine, and perfumes.

bal·sam of To·lu, *n.* A medicinal preparation obtained from a tropical American evergreen, *Myroxylon balsamum,* used primarily in cough syrups and perfumes.

Bal·tic, bạl'tik, *a.* Noting, pertaining to, or situated on the sea which separates Sweden from Germany, Poland, and Russia; pertaining to a group or branch of the Indo-European languages.

Bal·to-Slav·ic, bạl'tō·slä'vik, bạl'tō·slav'-ik, *n.* A mixture of the Indo-European languages which includes the Baltic and Slavic groups.

Ba·lu·chi, ba·lŏ'chē, *n.* A member of the nomadic, warlike, Indo-Iranian people of Baluchistan; the language of these people.

bal·us·ter, bal'u·stẽr, *n.* [Fr. *balustre,* L. *balaustium,* Gr. *balaustion,* wild pomegranate flower with vase-shaped calyx.] *Arch.* one of the small pillars forming the support for the rail of a balustrade.

bal·us·trade, bal'u·strād", bal'u·strād', *n.* [Fr. *balustrade.*] A row of small columns or balusters, joined by a rail, serving as an enclosure for altars, balconies, staircases, and terraces, or used as an ornament.

bam·bi·no, bam·bē'nō, *n. pl.* **bam·bi·ni, bam·bi·nos,** bam·bē'nē. [It., dim. of *bambo,* child.] A child or baby; an image of the infant Jesus.

bam·boo, bam·bŏ', *n.* [Malay, *bambu.*] A woody tropical plant of the grass family; the hollow, jointed stem of this plant, used for building, for furniture, and for fishing poles.

bam·boo cur·tain, *n.* A barrier created by strict censorship, restricted travel, and official secrecy in Communist-controlled areas of the Orient. Compare *iron curtain.*

bam·boo·zle, bam·bŏ'zl, *v.t.*—*bamboozled, bamboozling.* [Origin uncertain.] To impose or practice upon; to hoax; to humbug; to —*v.i.*—**bam·boo·zler,** bam·bŏ'zlẽr, *n.*

ban, ban, *v.t.*—*banned, banning.* [O.E. *ban, gebann,* interdict, proclamation, edict; D. *ban,* excommunication; Icel. and Sw. *bann,* proclamation; Dan. *band,* a ban, *bande,* to curse.] To prohibit; to interdict; to bar the sale of (a book), holding of (a meeting), or showing of (play, movie or television).

ban, ban, *n.* A public proclamation or edict; in feudal times, the summons of the sovereign's vassals for military service; *pl.* a proclamation or notice of an intended marriage (*banns*). A malediction, curse, or execration, esp. a formal ecclesiastical denunciation; an authoritative prohibition or interdiction; censure; *fig.* informal denunciation or prohibition, as by public opinion.

ba·nal, bān'al, ba·nal', ba·näl', ban'al, *a.* [O.Fr. *ban,* summoning of the king's vassals.] Hackneyed, commonplace, or trite.—**ba·nal·i·ty,** ba·nal'·i·tē, *n.*

ba·nan·a, ba·nan'a, *n.* [Sp., from the native name.] A herbaceous plant, genus *Musca,* closely allied to the plantain, and extensively cultivated in tropical countries for its soft pulpy fruit; the fruit of this plant. —**top ba·nan·a,** *slang.* Orig. the leading comedian in a burlesque show; an important man in an organization or group.

ba·nan·a oil, *n.* A colorless, sweet-smelling liquid, amyl acetate, used as a solvent and as an artificial fruit flavoring.

band, band, *n.* A company or group of

persons and sometimes animals or things united by some common bond, esp. a body of armed men; a company of soldiers; a body of instrumental musicians consisting of wind and percussion instruments only.

band, band, *n.* [Fr. *bande,* ultimately Teut.] That which binds together; a bond or means of attachment in general; something which restrains morally or spiritually; an obligation; a fetter or similar fastening; a narrow strip or ribbon-shaped ligature, tie, or connection; a division of a long-playing record; a fillet; a border or strip on an article of dress; the linen ornament about the neck of a clergyman.

band, band, *n. Elect.* A given segment of the electromagnetic spectrum; a range of frequencies within two definite limits; a group of different carrier frequencies designated for the same purpose; as, the FM *band* on a radio.

band, band, *v.t.* To bind or tie up with a band; to mark with a band; to unite in a troop, company, or confederacy.—*v.i.* To associate or unite for some common purpose.

band·age, ban'dij, *n.* [Fr. < O.Fr. *bander,* to bind < *bande,* flat strip < Teut.] A strip of cloth or gauze used in dressing and binding up wounds, restraining hemorrhages, etc.

band·age, ban'dij, *v.t.*—*bandaged, bandaging.* To dress, as a wound; to apply a bandage to.

ban·dan·a, ban·dan·na, ban·dan'a, *n.* [Hind. *bâdhnû.*] A large, colorfully printed kerchief.

ban·deau, ban·dō', ban'dō, *n. pl.* **ban·deaux,** ban·dōz', ban'dōz. [Fr. dim. of O.Fr. *bande,* band.] A band worn about or on the head; a fillet; a circular band of stiff material for fastening in or under a woman's hat to fit it to the head; a brassiere.

ban·de·role, ban'de·rōl, *n.* [Fr. *banderole,* It. *banderuola,* a little banner, from *bandiera,* a banner.] A little flag or streamer affixed to a mast; a pennon; a funeral banner. *Arch.* a stone band with inscription.

ban·di·coot, ban'di·kŏt", *n.* [Telugu *pandikokku.*] A very large East Indian rat, *Nesokia bandicota;* any of various ratlike marsupials (family *Peramelidae*) of Australia and nearby regions.

ban·dit, ban'dit, *n. pl.* **ban·dits, ban·dit·ti,** ban·dit'ē. [It. *bandito,* pp. of *bandire,* L.L. *bannire,* to banish. BAN, BANISH.] An outlaw; a robber; a highwayman.—**ban·dit·ry,** ban'di·trē, *n.*

band·mas·ter, band'mas"tẽr, band'mä"stẽr, *n.* The conductor and trainer of a band of musicians.

ban·do·leer, ban"do·lēr', *n.* [Fr. *bandouliere* < Sp. *bando,* a sash.] A shoulder belt carrying cartridges.

ban·dore, ban·dōr', ban·dạr', ban'dōr, ban'dạr, *n.* [Fr. < It. *pandora,* L. *pandura,* Gr. *pandoura,* a musical instrument ascribed to *Pan.*] A musical stringed instrument resembling a lute or a guitar. Also **ban·du·ra, ban·du·ria.**

band·saw, band'sạ, *n.* A saw consisting of a long flexible belt of steel revolving on pulleys.

band shell, *n.* A bandstand with an acoustically resonant structure resembling a huge concave seashell at its rear, in which concerts are performed.

bands·man, bandz'man, *n. pl.* **bands·men.** A player in a band of musicians.

band·stand, band'stand", *n.* A raised platform, indoor or outdoor, for orchestras or bands.

band·wag·on, band'wag"on, *n.* A wagon carrying a band of music, as at the head of a procession or parade; hence, a figurative wagon of this kind humorously conceived as leading some movement or organized effort, as in a political campaign, and advancing confidently or triumphantly toward expected victory; as, to climb aboard the Republican *bandwagon.*

band·width, band´width, band´with″, *n. Electron.* The range of frequencies within a band; the number of cycles per second between the limits of a frequency band; as, a *bandwidth* of six megacycles.

ban·dy, ban´dē, *a.* Bent, bowed, especially having a bend or crook outwards: said of a person's legs.—**ban·dy·leg·ged**, ban´dē··leg″id, ban´dē·legd″, *a.* Having bandy or crooked legs; bowlegged.

ban·dy, ban´dē, *v.t.*—*bandied, bandying.* To bat back and forth, as a ball in play; toss from one to another; to exchange contentiously; to give and receive reciprocally (words, compliments); to banter or tease.

bane, bān, *n.* [O.E. *bana*, slayer; destruction, death, bane; Icel. *bani*, Dan. and Sw. *bane*, O.H.G. *bana*.] Any fatal cause of mischief, injury, or destruction; ruin; curse; deadly poison.

bane·ber·ry, bān´ber″ē, bān´be·rē, *n. pl.* **bane·ber·ries.** Any plant of the genus *Actaea*, comprising herbs which bear nauseous poisonous berries; the berry itself.

bane·ful, bān´fụl, *a.* Destructive; pernicious.—**bane·ful·ly**, bān´fụl·lē, *adv.* In a baneful manner.—**bane·ful·ness**, bān´fụl··nis, *n.*

bang, bang, *v.t.* [Akin Icel. *bang*, a knocking; G. *bängel*, a club, the clapper of a bell; D. *bangel*, a bell.] To beat, as with a club or cudgel; to thump; to cudgel; to beat or handle roughly or with violence; to bring a loud noise from or by, as in slamming a door, and the like.—*v.i.* To resound with a loud noise; to produce a loud noise; to thump violently.

bang, bang, *n.* A loud, sudden sound; a heavy blow; a sudden spurt of energy; *slang*, a thrill; *pl.* hair that is cut to cover the forehead when brushed forward.

bang, bang, *adv.* With a bang; suddenly and loudly; abruptly.

ban·ga·lore tor·pe·do, bang″ga·lōr´ tạr··pē´dō, *n.* [From *Bangalore*, city in India.] A metal tube containing explosive material and a firing mechanism for severing barbed wire, detonating mines, etc.

bang·kok, bang´kok, *n.* [From *Bangkok*, capital of Thailand, where the straw also grows.] A hat of fine straw constructed in the Philippines; the straw itself.

ban·gle, bang´gel, *n.* [Hind. *banglī*.] A bracelet in the form of a ring, without a clasp; an ornamental anklet.

Bang's Dis·ease, *n.* [From B. *Bang*, a Danish biologist.] In cattle, an infectious abortion caused by the bacterium *Brucella abortus.*

ban·ish, ban´ish, *v.t.* [O.Fr. *baniss-*, ppr. stem of *bannir* < Teut. O.H.G. *bannan*, to proclaim. BAN. Akin PERISH.] To condemn to exile; to send (a person) from a country as a punishment; to drive away; to exile; to cast from the mind (thoughts, care, business).—**ban·ish·er**, ban´ish·ẽr, *n.* —**ban·ish·ment**, ban´ish·ment, *n.*

ban·is·ter, **ban·nis·ter**, ban´i·stẽr, *n.* [Form of *baluster.*] A baluster; an upright in a stair rail; a handrail.

ban·jo, ban´jō, *n.* A musical instrument having five or six strings, a body like a tambourine, and a neck like a guitar.

bank, bangk, *n.* [M.E. *banke*, probably < Icel. *bakki*, ridge.] A mound or heap of earth; a mass of clouds or fog; any steep acclivity, as one rising from a river, the sea, or forming the side of a ravine; the rising ground in the sea, esp. from the continental shelf; a shoal; the face of coal at which miners are working.

bank, bangk, *n.* An establishment which trades in money; an establishment for the

deposit, custody, remittance, and issue of money; the office in which the transactions of a banking company are conducted; the funds of a gaming establishment; a fund in certain card games.

bank, bangk, *v.i.* To deposit money in a bank; to operate a bank.

bank, bangk, *n.* [O.Fr. *banc*, bench; < Teut. source of E. *bench.*] A bench, platform, or table; a tier or row of objects; as, a *bank* of elevators; a row of keys as on an organ or typewriter; *journ.* part of a headline.

bank, bangk, *v.i.* To incline an aircraft laterally, usually when making a turn, to prevent skidding; to turn an aircraft—*v.t.* Of aircraft or persons within, to incline laterally, to turn.—*n.*

bank, bangk, *v.i.* To border with or like a bank; embank; to raise in a bank; heap (*up*); to cover (a fire) with ashes, so that it will burn long and slowly; *billiards*, to drive (a ball) to the bank or cushion; *pool*, to pocket (the object ball) by driving it against the bank. When building a roadway, to incline the surface laterally, inner side downward around a curve.—*v.i.* To border (*on*); rise in or form banks, as clouds or snow; form a slope or acclivity.

bank·a·ble, bang´ka·bl, *a.* Accepted at or receivable by a bank.

bank ac·cep·tance, *n.* A draft which is accepted or acknowledged by the bank on which it is drawn.

bank draft, *n.* A bill of exchange drawn by a bank on another bank.

bank·er, bang´kẽr, *n.* One who conducts a banking business dealing with the custody, receipt and transmission of money, bills of exchange, and loans; the dealer responsible for keeping the funds in a gambling game.

bank·er, bangk´ẽr, *n.* An American maritime term for a vessel or fisherman employed in cod fishery on the Newfoundland banks.

bank·er's bill of ex·change, *n.* A bill of exchange drawn on a domestic or foreign bank, as opposed to being drawn on the account of an individual or business firm.

bank hol·i·day, *n. Brit.* a legal holiday; *U.S.* a period in which banks are closed to control banking practices or currency.

bank·ing, bangk´ing, *n.* The business or profession of a banker; the system followed by banks in carrying on their business.

bank mon·ey, *n.* Checks and drafts used as a medium of exchange, as opposed to the use of currency.

bank note, *n.* A promissory note issued by a bank and payable on demand.

bank on, *v.t.* To rely on, as something or someone; to be confident of, as a person's reliability.

bank pa·per, *n.* Bills, acceptances, drafts, or other commercial paper that may be discounted by a bank.

bank·roll, bank´rōl, *n.* An available sum of money; the money that one possesses. *Slang*, financing or backing, as for a theatrical production or other speculative enterprise.—*v.t. Slang*, to finance.

bank run, *n.* Excessive withdrawal of bank deposits because of the presence or threat of unfavorable economic conditions.

bank·rupt, bangk´rupt, *n.* [Fr. *banqueroute*, < It. *bancarotta*, bankruptcy, < *banca*, bench, bank, and *rotta*, pp. fem. of *rompere*, < L. *rumpere*, break.] A business or a person who, upon his own petition or that of his creditors, is adjudged insolvent by a court, and whose property is administered for and divided among his creditors, under a system of bankruptcy laws; in popular usage, any insolvent debtor; one who is destitute or hopelessly in debt; one unable to satisfy any just claims made upon him.

bank·rupt, bangk´rupt, *a.* Subject to, or under, legal process because of insolvency; unable to pay one's debts; insolvent. *Fig.*

at the end of one's resources; bereft or destitute; wanting.

bank·rupt, bangk´rupt, *v.t.* To make bankrupt; to deplete; to impoverish.

bank·rupt·cy, bangk´rupt·sē, bangk´rup-·sē, *n. pl.* **bank·rupt·cies.** The state of being or the fact of becoming bankrupt; *fig.* utter failure, wreck, or ruin.

bank·si·a, bangk´sē·a, *n.* [N.L., from Sir Joseph Banks (1743-1820), English naturalist.] Any plant of the Australasian genus *Sirmuellera* (formerly *Banksia*), comprising shrubs and trees with leathery leaves and dense cylindrical heads of flowers.

ban·ner, ban´ẽr, *n.* [O.Fr. < Teut. akin to Goth. *bandwo*, sign, token.] A piece of cloth attached by one side to the upper part of a pole or staff, formerly used as the standard of a sovereign, lord, or knight, and serving as a rallying point in battle; the flag of a country, army, troop, etc.; an ensign bearing some device or motto attached by its upper edge to a pole and borne in processions; anything displayed as a profession; type running the width of the page; *bot.* a vexillum.

ban·ner, ban´ẽr, *a.* Leading or foremost in some respect, esp. in excellence; as, the *banner* county of the country in the production of cotton.

ban·ner·ol, ban´e·rōl, *n.* Banderole.

ban·nis·ter, ban´i·stẽr, *n.* Banister.

ban·nock, ban´ak, *n. Canada*, a round, flat cake baked of a dough composed of unleavened, flour, salt, and water. *Sc., Brit.* an unleavened cake of oatmeal baked at an open fire, and generally on an iron plate.

banns, banz, *n. pl.* [See *ban.*] An announcement of a proposed marriage, made in a church or other prescribed place.

ban·quet, bang´kwit, *n.* [Fr. *banquet* < It. *banchetto*, dim. of *banco*, bench. BANK.] An elegant feast; a rich entertainment of meat and drink; *fig.* something especially delicious or enjoyable.

ban·quet, bang´kwit, *v.t.* To treat with a feast or rich entertainment.—*v.i.* To feast; to regale oneself.—**ban·quet·er**, *n.*

ban·quette, bang·ket´, *n.* [Fr. < It. *banchetta*.] A little raised way or bank running along the inside of a parapet, on which soldiers stand; an embankment; a sidewalk; the footway of a bridge when raised above the roadway; a long upholstered bench or sofa.

ban·shee, ban´shē, ban·shē´, *n.* [Ir. *bean-sīth* < *bean*, *ban*, woman, and *sīth*, fairy.] A female spirit possessed of a weird and ghostly wail, believed in Ireland and Scotland to attach herself to a particular house, and to appear before the death of one of the family.

ban·tam, ban´tam, *n.* [Prob. from Bantam, in W. Java, where the breed may have originated.] A tiny domestic fowl of any or varied breeds, characterized by its small size and feathered shanks; a small person of quarrelsome nature; *Brit.* a small car. An early model of jeep.

ban·tam·weight, ban´tam·wāt″, *n.* A boxer who is classed over 112 but no heavier than 118 lbs.

ban·ter, ban´tẽr, *v.t.* [Origin unknown.] To address humorous raillery to; to attack with jokes or jests; to make fun of; to rally.—*v.i.* to speak cleverly or teasingly.—**ban·ter·er**, ban´tẽr·ẽr, *n.* One who banters.—**ban·ter·ing·ly**, ban´tẽr·ing·lē, *adv.*

ban·ter, ban´tẽr, *n.* A joking or jesting; humorous and good-natured raillery; pleasantry.

bant·ing·ism, ban´ting·iz″um, *n.* [From Wm. *Banting*, a 19th century cabinetmaker of London who first followed and recommended the diet.] (*Often cap.*) a method of reducing weight consisting of limiting the diet to lean meat, fish, and dry toast.

bant·ling, bant'ling, *n.* A young child: a term carrying with it a shade of contempt.

ban·yan, ban·ian, ban'yan, *n.* An Indian tree of the fig genus, *Ficus benghalensis*, remarkable for its horizontal branches sending down shoots which take root when they reach the ground and form secondary trunks, which in their turn send out branches; the tree in this manner spreading over a large area.—**ban·ia,** ban'ya, *n.* A Hindu trader whose wares were displayed under the protective cover of banyan trees.

ban·zai, bän·zī', bän'zī, *interj.* [Jap. 'ten thousand years.'] A Japanese complimentary salutation in honor of the emperor; patriotic shout used by attacking Japanese troops.

ba·o·bab, bā'ō·bab″, bä'ō·bab″, *n.* [The name in Senegal.] A large African tree, genus *Adamsonia*, esp. *A. digitata*, usually from 40 to 70 feet high, and often 30 feet in diameter, having an oblong pulpy fruit called monkey bread.

bap·tism, bap'tiz″um, *n.* [Gr. *baptisma* < *baptizein*, immerse < *baptein*, dip in water.] A sacramental, ritual, or religious ceremony signifying spiritual rebirth, admission, or purification, usu. accomplished by immersion in water or application of water; *fig.* any experience which initiates or sanctifies.—**bap·tis·mal,** bap·tiz'mal, *a.* —**bap·tis·mal·ly,** *adv.*

bap·tist, bap'tist, *n.* [O.Fr. *baptiste* < L.L. *baptista,* < Gr. *Baptistēs*.] One who baptizes; as, John the *Baptist*; (*cap.*) a member of a Christian denomination which maintains that baptism, usually implying immersion, can be administered only upon a personal profession of Christian faith.—*a.* (*cap.*) Of or pertaining to Baptists.

bap·tis·ter·y, bap'ti·ste·rē, bap'ti·strē, *n.* pl. **bap·tis·ter·ies.** A building or a portion of a building in which the rite of baptism is administered.

bap·tize, *Brit.* **bap·tise,** bap·tīz', bap'tīz, *v.t., v.i.*—*baptized, baptizing.* [Gr. *baptizein*. BAPTISM.] To administer the sacrament of baptism to; to purify or purge spiritually; to dedicate; to christen.

bar, bär, *n.* [O.Fr. *barre*, < Vulgar Latin *barra*; origin unknown.] A relatively long and evenly-shaped piece of some solid substance; esp. such a piece of wood or metal used as a guard or obstruction, or for some mechanical purpose; as, a crow*bar*; any barrier or obstruction; a bank of sand, etc., in water; a railing enclosing the space occupied by counsel in a court of justice; the legal profession; the place in court where prisoners are stationed; any tribunal; a counter or a place where liquor is served to customers; a band or stripe; *her.* a stripe, properly horizontal, crossing the field. *Mus.* a vertical line marking off a measure on the staff; also, the measure. *Pl., veter.* a toothless space in the mouth of a horse between the molar and canine teeth, in which the bit is fitted.

bar, bär, *n.* [Gr. *baros*, weight.] *Phys.* A unit of pressure expressing a centimeter-gram-second relationship; a unit of pressure equal to one million dynes per square centimeter. Formerly called microbar or barye.

bar, bär, *v.t.*—*barred, barring.* To provide, fasten, or obstruct with a bar or bars; shut in or out by or as by bars; to block, as someone's way, as with a barrier; prevent or hinder, as access; debar, as a person or an action; exclude or except; to mark with bars, stripes, or bands.

bar, bär, *prep.* Barring; except; as, *bar* none.

barb, bärb, *n.* [O.Fr. *barbe*, < L. *barba*, beard.] A beard-like growth or part; one of the side processes of a feather; a point projecting backward from a main point, as of a fishhook or an arrowhead; a sharply

critical remark; *usu. pl., veter.* a small protuberance under the tongue in horses and cattle, esp. when inflamed and swollen.

barb, bärb, *v.t.* To furnish with a barb or barbs, as a fishhook; to clip, as a coin.

barb, bärb, *n.* A horse of the Barbary breed, remarkable for speed, endurance, and docility; a breed of pigeons somewhat related to the carrier pigeons.

bar·bar·i·an, bär·bâr'ē·an, *n.* [L. *barbarus*, < Gr. *barbaros*, one whose language is unintelligible, a foreigner.] A foreigner; a man in his rude savage state; an uncivilized person; a cruel, savage, brutal man; one destitute of pity or humanity.—*a.*

bar·bar·ic, bär·bar'ik, *a.* Of, pertaining to, or characteristic of, a barbarian; uncivilized; savage; wild; ornate, without being in accordance with sound taste.

bar·ba·rism, bär'bar·iz″um, *n.* An uncivilized state; want of civilization; rudeness of manners; an act of barbarity, cruelty, or brutality; an outrage; an offense against purity of style or language; any form of speech contrary to correct idiom.

bar·bar·i·ty, bär·bar'i·tē, *n.* pl. **bar·bar·i·ties.** The state of being barbarous; barbarousness; savageness; ferociousness; inhumanity; a barbarous act.

bar·ba·ri·za·tion, bär″bar·i·zā'shan, *n.* The act or process of rendering barbarous or of becoming barbarous.

bar·ba·rize, bär'ba·rīz, *v.i.*—*barbarized, barbarizing.* To use barbarisms of speech; also, to become barbarous.—*v.t.* To render barbarous; esp. to debase (language, etc.) by departure from recognized classical standards.

bar·ba·rous, bär'ba·rus, *a.* Unacquainted with arts and civilization; uncivilized; rude and ignorant; pertaining to or characteristic of barbarians; adapted to the taste of barbarians; barbaric; cruel; fierce; merciless; ferocious; inhuman.—**bar·ba·rous·ly,** bär'ba·rus·lē, *adv.* Savagely; cruelly; ferociously; inhumanly.—**bar·ba·rous·ness,** bar'ba·rus·nis, *n.*

Bar·ba·ry ape, bär'ba·rē ãp′, *n.* [From *Barbary* Coast, North Africa, where they originated.] A tailless, easily-tamed monkey, *Macaca sylvana*, inhabiting Gibraltar and the northern area of Africa.

bar·bate, bär'bāt, *a.* [L. *barbatus* < *barba*, beard.] *Zool., bot.* Bearded; tufted or furnished with hairs.

bar·be·cue, bär'be·kū″, *n.* [Sp. *barbacoa*, framework of sticks set upon posts < Arawak.] A metal grill placed over hot coals or another heat source, where meats, fish, fowl, and vegetables are roasted or broiled; a movable fireplace with a rack or a spit; *West Indies*, a wooden framework on which meat or fish is dried or cured over a fire; a lamb, pig, or other large animal cooked whole or split over an open fire. Pieces of meat, fowl, fish, or vegetables cooked in a barbecue sauce.—*v.t.*—*barbecued, barbecuing.* To broil or roast (food) outdoors on a rack or spit over hot coals or another heat source; to prepare in a well-seasoned sauce.

barbed, bärbd, *a.* Furnished with a barb or barbs, as a fishhook or an arrowhead; made with sharp points at intervals; as, *barbed* wire.

barbed wire, *n.* Strands of wire twisted together and having sharp-pointed barbs projecting at even and short intervals, used for fencing livestock. Also **barb·wire.**

bar·bel, bär'bel″, *n.* [O.Fr. *barbel* < Vulgar Latin *barbellus*, a barbel (the fish) < L. *barba*, a beard.] A fresh-water fish, genus *Barbus*, having four beardlike appendages on its upper jaw; a vermiform process appended to the mouth of certain fishes, serving as an organ of touch.

bar·bell, bär'bel″, *n.* A device used in

weight lifting consisting of a bar with various-sized weights that may be attached to, or detached from, the ends of the bar.

bar·bel·late, bär'be·lāt, *a.* [N.L. *barbella*, dim. of L. *barbula*, dim. of *barba*, beard.] *Bot.* having short, bristly, stiff hairs.

bar·ber, bär'bêr, *n.* [Norm. Fr. *barbour* < *barbe*, < L. *barba*, a beard.] One whose occupation is to shave beards or to cut and dress hair.—**bar·ber chair,** an adjustable chair specially designed for use in barber shops.

bar·ber, bär'bêr, *v.t.* To shave or trim and dress the hair and beard of (men).—*v.i.* To act as a barber.

bar·ber·ry, bär'ber″ē, bär'be·rē, *n.* pl. **bar·ber·ries.** [M.L.] A shrubby plant bearing small acid and astringent red berries, common in hedges.

bar·ber's itch, *n. Pathol.* a type of ringworm infecting the face and neck. Also **tin·e·a bar·bae.**

bar·bet, bär'bit, *a.* [Fr. *barbet*, ultimately < L. *barba*, a beard.] One of a group of tropical birds of the family *Capitonidae* having a large conical beak with tufts of stiff bristles at the base.

bar·bette, bär·bet', *n.* A platform or mound of earth within a fortification, from which guns may be fired over the parapet instead of through embrasures; an armored structure on a warship, protecting a gun platform.

bar·bi·cel, bär'bi·sel, *n.* [N.L. *barbicella*, dim. of L. *barba*, beard.] One of the minute processes fringing the barbules of certain feathers.

bar·bi·tal, bär'bi·tal″, bär'bi·tạl″, *n.* A drug, $C_8H_{12}N_2O_3$, containing barbituric acid, used as a hypnotic and often given in the form of its soluble sodium salt.

bar·bi·tu·rate, bär·bich'u·rāt″, bär·bich'ur·it, bär″bi·tyụr'āt, bär″bi·tyụr'it, *n. Chem.* A derivative of barbituric acid; any of a group of drugs used as sedatives or hypnotics.

bar·bi·tur·ic ac·id, bär″bi·tyụr'ik as'id, bär″bi·tur'ik, *n.* [N.L. *barbata*, bearded (lichen) and *uric* (acid).] A crystalline substance, $C_4H_4N_2O_3$, that is the basis for many sedative and hypnotic drugs.

bar·bule, bär'būl, *n.* [L. *barbula*, dim. of *barba*, beard.] A little barb; one of the small processes fringing the barbs of a feather.

bar·ca·role, bar·ca·rolle, bär'ka·rōl″, *n.* [Fr. < It. *barcarolo*, a boatman < *barca*, a boat or barge < L. BARK.] A simple song or melody with a beat which suggests a rowing rhythm, sung by Venetian gondoliers; a piece of instrumental music composed in imitation of such a song.

bar chart, *n.* A bar graph.

bard, bärd, *n.* [Gael. and Ir. *bard*, W. *bardd*.] An ancient Celtic poet and singer; a minstrel; in general, any poet; (*cap.*) Shakespeare, the *Bard* of Avon.

bard, bärd, *n.* [Fr. *barde* < Sp. *barda*; perhaps < Ar.] Any of various pieces of defensive armor for a horse, or an ornamental covering, as of velvet, representing such a piece; *pl.* armor of metal plates, formerly worn by men-at-arms.

bard, bärd, *v.t.* To furnish with bards; to cover (meat for roasting) with strips of bacon.

bare, bâr, *a.*—*barer, barest.* [O.E. *bær.* Cf. Icel. *ber,* Sw., Dan. *bar,* D. *bāar,* G. *bar, baar*.] Naked; without covering; laid to open view; detected; no longer concealed; poor; destitute; indigent; ill-supplied; empty; unfurnished; unprovided: often followed by *of*; as, *bare of* money; threadbare; much worn.—**bare·ness,** bâr'nis, *n.* The state of being bare; want of clothing or covering; nakedness; deficiency of appropriate covering, ornament, and the like; poverty; indigence.

bare, bâr, *v.t.*—*bared, baring*. To strip off the covering from; to make naked.—**bare·ly**, bâr′lē, *adv*. In a bare manner; nakedly; poorly; without decoration; scarcely; hardly.

bare·back, bâr′bak″, *a., adv*. With the back of an animal unsaddled, esp. a horse; on a horse's bare back, as a circus performer.

bare·faced, bâr′fāst′, *a*. Having the face uncovered; hence undisguised; beardless; unreserved; shameless; impudent; audacious *barefaced* robbery .—**bare·fac·ed·ly**, bâr″fā′sid·lē, bâr″fāst′lē, *adv*. In a barefaced manner; openly; shamelessly; impudently.—**bare·fac·ed·ness**, bâr″fā′sid·nis, bâr″fāst′nis, *n*. Effrontery; assurance.

bare·foot, bâr′fut″, *a*. With the feet bare; without shoes or stockings.—*adv*. Also **bare·foot·ed**, bâr′fut″id.

bare·hand·ed, bâr′han″did, *a*. With hands uncovered; with empty hands; without a tool, weapon, or other aid.

bare·head·ed, bâr′hed″id, *a., adv*. Without covering on the head.—**bare·head·ed·ness**, bâr″hed′id·nis, *n*.

bar·fly, bâr′flī″, *n. Slang*, one who spends time drinking alcoholic beverages at bars.

bar·gain, bär′gin, *n*. [O.Fr. *bargaine*, L.L. *barcania*, a bargain, traffic; believed to be < L.L. *barca*, a bark.] A contract or agreement between two or more parties; a compact settling that something shall be done, sold, transferred, etc.; the thing purchased or stipulated for; what is obtained by an agreement; something bought or sold at a low price.

bar·gain, bär′gin, *v.i*. To make a bargain or agreement; to make an agreement about the transfer of property; to dicker or haggle over a price at which something is to be bought or sold.—*v.t*. To sell; to transfer for a consideration, followed by *away*.—**bar·gain·er**, bär′gin·ẽr, *n*.

bar·gain·ing a·gent, *n*. In collective bargaining, the union chosen by a group of employees to represent them in labor contract negotiations and certified as such by the National Labor Relations Board; one who acts in behalf of another or in behalf of a group in negotiations of a contract or agreement.

barge, bärj, *n*. [O.Fr. *barge*, < M.L. *barga*, variant of L.L. *barca*, bark.] Formerly, any of various seagoing sailing-vessels; now, a comparatively large, usually flat-bottomed boat towed by a tug, used for transporting freight; a two-decked boat towed by another boat, used esp. for pleasure excursions; a vessel of state, used in pageants, etc.; a large, elegantly finished rowing boat for the use of a naval flag officer; a long, narrow racing boat, somewhat wider and stronger than a shell; a large wagon or omnibus used for picnics, etc.—*v.t*.—*barged, barging*. To carry or transport by barge.—*v.i*. To move recklessly, without forethought; to intrude, followed by *in*; to move clumsily; to interrupt; to offer unrequested aid or advice.

barge·board, bärj′bōrd″, *n*. [Akin M.L. *bargus*, kind of gallows.] *Arch*. a board, often ornamental, placed along the projecting sloping edge of a gable roof, usually concealing or taking the place of a rafter.

bar·gee, bär·jē′, *n*. One of the crew of a barge or canal boat.

barge·man, bärj′man, *n. pl*. **barge·men**. The man who manages a barge; a deck hand on a barge.

bar·ghest, bär′gest, *n*. [Origin obscure: cf. *ghost*.] A local specter or goblin, often in the form of a monstrous dog, believed to portend misfortune or death.

bar graph, *n*. A graphic representation of statistics by means of bars of various, proportionate lengths. Also *bar chart*.

bar·ic, bar′ik, *a*. Of or containing barium.

bar·ie, bar′ē, *n*. [Fr. *barie* < Gr. *bareia*, fem. of *Barys*, heavy.] *Phys*. microbar, a measurement used in acoustics.

bar·ite, bâr′īt, bar′īt, *n*. Native barium sulfate, BaSO₄; chief source of barium.

bar·i·tone, bar′i·tōn″, *a*. [It. *baritono* < Gr. *barytonos* < *barys*, heavy, and *tonos*, tone.] Ranging between tenor and bass; having a voice ranging between tenor and bass.—*n*. A male voice or voice part, the compass of which falls between the bass and the tenor; a person with a voice of this quality; a deep-toned brass instrument.

bar·i·um, bâr′ē·um, bar′ē·um, *n*. [< *bary*(ta) and (sod)*ium*.] *Chem*. an element of the alkaline-earth series, a whitish malleable metal occurring in combination: used in alloys and pyrotechnics. Sym. Ba, at. no. 56. See Periodic Table of Elements.

bar·i·um sul·fate, *n. Chem*. an insoluble, colorless, crystalline compound, BaSO₄, used chiefly in medicine, as a pigment, and as a substance impenetrable to x-rays.

bark, bärk, *v.i*. [O.E. *beorcan*.] To emit the cry of a dog, or a similar sound; to speak in an abrupt, severe, or reprimanding tone.—*n*. The sound made by the domestic dog.

bark, bärk, *n*. [Icel. *börkr* = Sw. and Dan. *bark*.] The external covering of the woody stems or roots of plants (sometimes restricted to the rough outer part, but usually including the corky tissues and the phloem or inner bark); *phar*. cinchona (Peruvian bark); *tanning*, tanbark.—*v.t*. To strip off the bark of; remove a circle of bark from; scrape off the dead bark of; scrape or rub off the skin from; to cover or enclose with, or as with, bark; incrust; to treat with an infusion of bark; tan.

bark, bärk, *n*. Barque.

bark bee·tle, *n*. Any of the small beetles constituting the family *Scolytidae*, nearly all of which make burrows between the bark and the wood of woody plants.

bar·keep·er, bär′kē″pẽr, *n*. One who owns or tends a bar where liquor is served; also **bar·keep**.

bar·ken·tine, bar·kan·tine, bär′ken·tēn″, *n*. [< *bark*, after *brigantine*.] A three-masted vessel with the foremast square-rigged and the mainmast and mizzenmast fore-and-aft rigged.

bark·er, bär′kẽr, *n*. An animal that barks; a person who clamors unreasonably; a person stationed before a carnival, sideshow, etc., to persuade passersby to enter; one who removes bark from trees.

bark·y, bär′kē, *a*.—*barkier, barkiest*. Covered with or resembling bark.

bar·ley, bär′lē, *n. pl*. **bar·leys**. [O.E. *bærlic*, appar. < *bere*, barley.] A widely distributed cereal plant of the genus *Hordeum*; its grain or seed, variously used as food for men and animals, and esp. in the making of beer, ale, and whiskey.

bar·ley·corn, bär′lē·kärn″, *n*. Barley, or a grain of barley; *John Barleycorn*, as personifying barley used in making malt liquor, or malt liquor itself; an old measure equal to the third part of an inch.

barm, bärm, *n*. [O.E. *beorma* = Sw. *bärma*, Dan. *bärme*, L.G. *barme*, G. *bärme*, barm; from root of *brew*.] Yeast formed on malt liquors during fermentation.

bar·maid, bär′mād″, *n*. A maid or woman who serves at a bar or other place of refreshment.

bar·man, bär′man, *n*. Bartender.

bar mitz·vah, bär mits′va, *n*. [Heb., son of the commandment.] A Jewish ceremony held in recognition of the adulthood of a boy who has had his thirteenth birthday and has undergone a prescribed course of study of Judaism; the boy that the ceremony is for.—**bas mitz·vah**, bäs mits′va, *n*. The

corresponding ceremony held for a thirteen-year-old Jewish girl; the girl.

barm·y, bär′mē, *a*.—*barmier, barmiest*. Containing or consisting of barm; fermenting; frothy, as beer. *Slang*, balmy; silly.

barn, bärn, *n*. [O.E. *berern* < *bere*, barley, and *ern*, a storehouse.] A covered building for storing grain, hay, etc., and farm machinery, and for housing domestic animals.—*v.t*. To store in a barn.

bar·na·cle, bär′na·kl, *n*. [Fr. *bernacle*, perhaps ultimately < L. *perna*, kind of shellfish.] A wild goose, *Bernicla* or *Branta leucopsis*, chiefly of northern Europe; also **bar·na·cle goose**. Any of certain crustaceans of the order *Cirripedia* which attach themselves to ships' bottoms, and the acorn barnacles found incrusting rocks along seacoasts; *fig*. a thing or person that clings tenaciously.

barn dance, *n*. A festive party featuring square dances and lively hillbilly music played on fiddles.

barn·storm·er, bärn′stẏrm″ẽr, *n*. One of a troupe of actors playing in makeshift theatres of small country towns, usu. on one-night engagements; one who makes brief stops in his tour of towns, as a politician, speaker, or entertainer; *avi*. one who participates in airplane joy-riding, stunt flying, or exhibition flying as in circuses and the like.—**barn·storm·ing**, bärn′stẏrm″ing, *n*.

barn·yard, bärn′yärd″, *n*. The area adjacent to and immediately surrounding a barn.

bar·o·don·tal·gi·a, bâr″ō·dän·tal′gē·a, *n*. [< Gr. *baros*, weight, and Eng. *odontalgia*.] *Med*. The practice of dentistry concerned with disorders resulting from decreased barometric pressure, or other factors peculiar to aviation; the pain accompanying these disorders.

bar·o·gram, bar′o·gram″, *n. Meteor*. a tracing of atmospheric pressure changes that have been recorded by a barograph.

bar·o·graph, bar′o·graf″, bar′o·gräf″, *n*. A self-registering barometric instrument for recording variations in the pressure of the atmosphere.

ba·rom·et·er, ba·rom′i·tẽr, *n*. [< Gr. *baros*, weight, and *metron*, measure.] An instrument for measuring the weight or pressure of the atmosphere, and thereby indicating probable weather changes; *fig*. something which registers change in intensity, rate, etc.; as, a *barometer* of public opinion.—**bar·o·met·ric, bar·o·met·ric·al**, bar″o·me′trik, bar″o·me′tri·kal, *a*. Pertaining or relating to the barometer; made by a barometer.—**bar·o·met·ric·al·ly**, bar″o·me′tri·kal·ē, *adv*.

bar·o·met·ric grad·i·ent, *n. Meteor*. the rate at which the atmospheric pressure changes from one point to another.

bar·o·met·ric pres·sure, *n. Meteor*. a unit of measurement expressing density of atmosphere at any given point; atmospheric pressure; the measurement of air pressure (mass × gravitational acceleration) at any given point by a barometer. The barometer measures variations in air pressure from points above and below a standard pressure or atmosphere equal to the pressure exerted by a vertical column of mercury, 29.53 inches, at sea level.

bar·on, bar′on, *n*. [O.Fr. *baron*, < Teut.] In Great Britain, a title or degree of nobility; one who holds the lowest rank in the peerage; a title of certain judges or officers; as, *barons* of the exchequer; the judges of the court of exchequer; a man of great power or influence in a particular field; as, a *baron* of finance.—**bar·on of beef**, a sirloin cut of double thickness.

bar·on·age, bar′o·nij, *n*. The whole body of barons or peers; the dignity or condition of a baron.

---

a- fat, fāte, fär, fâre, fạll;　**e-** met, mē, mēre, hẽr;　**i-** pin, pīne;　**o-** not, nōte, mōve;　**u-** tub, cūbe, bụll;　**oi-** oil;　**ou-** pound.

bar·on·ess, bar′o·nis, *n.* A baron's wife or widow; a holder of the title in her own right.

bar·on·et, bar′o·nit, bar′o·net″, *n.* [Dim. of *baron.*] One who possesses a hereditary rank or degree of honor next below a baron, and therefore not a member of the peerage, but superior to a knight's except those of the garter.

bar·on·et·age, bar′o·nit·ij, bar′o·net″ij, *n.* The baronets as a body; the dignity of a baronet.

bar·on·et·cy, bar′o·nit·sē, bar′o·net″sē, *n.* pl. **bar·on·et·cies.** The title or dignity of a baronet.

ba·rong, bä·rong′, bä·rạng′, *n.* [Philippine.] A large, broad-bladed knife used by the Moros.

ba·ro·ni·al, ba·rō′nē·al, *a.* Pertaining to a baron or a barony; stately, ample.

bar·o·ny, bar′o·nē, *n.* pl. **bar·o·nies,** bar′o·nēz. [O.Fr. *baronie* < *baron.* BARON.] The domain of a baron; in Ireland, a division of a county; in Scotland, any large freehold estate; the rank or dignity of a baron.

ba·roque, ba·rōk′, *a.* [Fr. < Pg. *barroco.*] Irregular in shape, as some pearls; artistically irregular, incongruous, or fantastic, as a style of architectural and other decoration of the 17th and 18th centuries; tastelessly odd; bizarre; grotesque.

bar·o·tal·gi·a, bâr′ō·tal′gē·a, *n.* [< Gr. *baros,* weight and Eng. *otalgia.*] *Med.* an ailment of the middle ear resulting from high altitude flying without a pressurized cabin.

ba·rouche, ba·rōsh′, *n.* [G. *barutsche,* < It. *biroccio,* < Vulgar L. *birotium,* two-wheeled, < L. *bi-,* two, and *rota,* wheel.] A four-wheeled carriage with a seat in front for the driver, and seats inside for two couples, the forward one facing backward and the rear one forward, and with a falling or folding top over the back seat.

barque, bärk, *n.* [Fr. *barque,* L.L. *barca,* a barque, through a dim. form *barica,* < Gr. *baris,* a skiff. *Barge* is a form of this word.] *Poet.* a sailing vessel of any kind; *naut.* a three-masted vessel with only fore-and-aft sails on the mizzenmast, the other two masts being square rigged. Also *bark.*—**bar·quen·tine,** bär′ken·tēn″, *n.* [From *barque,* in imitation of *brigantine.*] A three-masted vessel square rigged in the foremast and fore-and-aft rigged in the main and mizzenmasts.

bar·rack, bar′ak, *n.* [Fr. *baraque,* < It. *baracca* < Sp. *barraca,* probably < *barro,* clay.] *Usu. pl.* A building or range of buildings for lodging soldiers, esp. in garrison; also, a large, plain building or a collection of huts or cabins, in which large numbers of men are lodged.

bar·rack, bar′ak, *v.t., v.i.* To lodge in barracks.

bar·ra·cu·da, bar″a·kö′da, *n.* pl. **bar·ra·cu·da, bar·ra·cu·das.** [Sp.; origin uncertain.] A large voracious, carnivorous fish, *Sphyraena barracuda,* of West Indian and neighbouring seas.

bar·rage, bär′ij, ba·räzh′, *Brit.* bar′äzh, *n.* [Fr. *barrage,* < *barrer,* to bar < *barre,* a bar.] The act of barring; the formation of an artificial obstruction in a watercourse to increase the depth of the water, facilitate irrigation, etc.; the obstruction or bar thus formed. *Milit.* the formation of a barrier of artillery fire to prevent the enemy from advancing, and at the same time to enable troops behind it to operate more safely, or to cut off the enemy's retreat in one or more directions; the artillery fire so formed; see *barrage balloon.*

bar·rage, ba·räzh′, *Brit.* bar′äzh, *v.t.*—*barraged, barraging.* To subject to a barrage.

bar·rage bal·loon, *n.* A balloon used in coordination with other balloons in strategic

military areas as a station for suspension of wires or nets to protect the areas from low-flying enemy aircraft.

bar·ra·mun·da, bar″a·mun′da, *n.* pl. **bar·ra·mun·das, bar·ra·mun·da.** [Native Australian.] A dipnoan fish, *Neoceratodus forsteri,* of rivers of Australia. Also **bar·ra·mun·di,** bar″a·mun′dē, pl. **bar·ra·mun·dis, bar·ra·mun·dies.**

bar·ran·ca, ba·rang′ka, *n.* [Sp.; origin uncertain.] A deep gully or ravine.

bar·ra·tor, bar′a·tor, *n.* [O.Fr. *barateur,* a cheater, *barate,* deceit. BARTER.] One who frequently incites suits at law; an encourager of litigation; the master or one of the crew of a ship who commits any fraud in the management of the ship or cargo, by which the owner, freighters, or insurers are injured; one who deals in ecclesiastical preferments or offices of state.—**bar·ra·trous,** bar′a·trus, *a.* Characterized by or tainted with barratry.—**bar·ra·trous·ly,** bar′a·trus·lē, adv.

bar·ra·try, bar′a·trē, *n.* pl. **bar·ra·tries.** The act or practice of a barrator; the inciting and encouraging of lawsuits and quarrels; fraud by a shipmaster or crew to the injury of the owners, freighters, or insurers, as by stealing, sinking, or deserting the ship; dealing in ecclesiastical preferments or offices of state.

barre, bär, *n.* [Fr. lit., *bar.*] A waist-high bar attached to the walls of a ballet school, used for body support while practicing.

barred, bärd, *a.* Having bars; as, a five-*barred* gate; *ornith.* having stripes or bands in different colors.

bar·rel, bar′el, *n.* [O.Fr. *baril;* origin uncertain.] A wooden vessel, approximately cylindrical, with slightly bulging sides made of staves hooped together, and with flat, parallel ends; a cask; the quantity which such a vessel of some standard size can hold (as $31\frac{1}{2}$ gallons of liquid or 196 pounds of flour); any vessel, case, or part similar in form; a cylinder or drum; the firing tube of a gun.—**o·ver a bar·rel,** in a helpless position; in the power of a creditor or the like.

bar·rel, bar′el, *v.t.*—*barreled, barreling, barrelled, barrelling.* To put in a barrel.—*v.i. Slang,* to proceed at great speed.

bar·rel chair, *n. Furniture.* A high-backed, heavily upholstered easy chair; tub chair.

bar·rel·ful, bar′el·fụl, *n.* pl. **bar·rel·fuls,** bar′al·fụlz. An unusually large quantity; the amount that may be contained in a barrel.

bar·rel or·gan, *n.* A musical instrument in which air from a bellows is admitted to a set of pipes by means of a revolving barrel-like mechanism; a hand organ.

bar·rel roll, *n. Aeron.* a maneuver of a flying aircraft which involves a complete revolution about the longitudinal axis.—*v.i.* To perform such a maneuver.

bar·ren, bar′en, *a.* [O.Fr. *baraigne, brehaine, brehaigne,* sterile, possibly from Armor. *brec'han,* sterile.] Incapable of producing its kind; not prolific: applied to animals and vegetables; unproductive; unfruitful; sterile, applied to land. *Fig.* not producing or leading to anything; as, *barren* of ideas; unsuggestive; uninstructive.

bar·ren, bar′en, *n.* A bare or unproductive tract of land.—**bar·ren·ly,** bar′en·lē, adv. Unfruitfully.—**bar·ren·ness,** bar′en·nis, *n.* The state or quality of being barren; sterility; want of fertility, instructiveness, interest, or the like.

Bar·ren Ground, *n.* A bare, treeless region of northern Canada, west of Hudson Bay. Also **Bar·ren Lands.**

bar·rette, ba·ret′, *n.* [Fr. *barrette,* dim. of *barre,* bar.] A clasp for holding a woman's hair up or back.

bar·ri·cade, bar′i·kād″, bar″i·kād′, *n.*

[Fr. < Pr. *barricada,* barricade of earth-filled casks < *barrica,* cask.] A temporary fortification made of trees, earth, stones, or anything that will obstruct the progress of an enemy or serve for defense or security against his shot; a fence around or along the side of a space to be kept clear; any barrier or obstruction.

bar·ri·cade, bar′i·kād″, *v.t.*—*barricaded, barricading.* To stop up, or block off, by a barricade; to erect a barricade across; to obstruct.

bar·ri·er, bar′ē·ėr, *n.* [O.Fr. *barrière,* a barrier, < *barre,* a bar. BAR.] A fence; a railing; any obstruction natural or man-made; a hindrance to approach, attack, or progress; something in the way; an obstacle; a limit or boundary of any kind; a line of separation.

bar·ri·er, bar′ē·ėr, *n. Psychol.* A state of mind described as a mental block; an obstacle or fear which serves to restrict a person's actions or thoughts.

bar·ri·er reef, *n.* A coral reef rising from a great depth to the level of low tide, encircling an island like a barrier, or running parallel to a coast, with a navigable channel inside; as, the Great *Barrier Reef* on the northeast coast of Australia.

bar·ring, bär′ing, *prep.* Excluding from consideration; excepting, as: *Barring* accidents, it will be ready on time.

bar·ri·o, bär′ē·ō, *n.* pl. **bar·ri·os.** [Sp. < Ar. *barri* exterior; outside.] In Spain and countries colonized by Spain, one of the divisions into which a town or city, together with the contiguous rural territory, is divided. In the U.S., a section of a city in which Puerto Rican and other Spanish-speaking people live.

bar·ris·ter, bar′i·stėr, *n.* [< *bar.*] *Brit.* a counselor or advocate admitted to plead at the bar of the higher courts of law in protection and defense of clients, as distinguished from solicitor; *U.S. colloq.* a lawyer.

bar·room, bär′rö̇m″, bär′rụm, *n.* A place devoted exclusively to the serving of alcoholic beverages; a bar, taproom, tavern, or pub.

bar·row, bar′ō, *n.* [M.E. *barewe.*] A flat, rectangular frame with projecting shafts at each end for handles, used by two or more persons for carrying a load; a hand-barrow; another boxlike type has flaring sides supported in front by a wheel with shafts at the rear by which one man may push it; a wheelbarrow; *Brit.* a pushcart or handcart. The load carried on or in a barrow. *Archaeol.* a mound of earth or stone above graves.

bar·row, bar′ō, *n.* [O.E. *bearg, bearh.*] The castrated male of swine.

bar sin·is·ter, *n.* A heraldic insignia supposedly denoting bastardy; the quality or state of being illegitimate.

bar·ten·der, bär′ten″dėr, *n.* A barkeeper; one who prepares and serves alcoholic beverages at a bar.

bar·ter, bär′tėr, *v.i.* [O.Fr. *barater* (= It. *barattare*), exchange, barter, cheat: cf. *barrator.*] To trade by exchanging commodities, rather than by the use of money.—*v.t.* To exchange in trade, as one commodity for another; to trade; to foolishly or dishonorably bargain away, as: He *bartered* away his pride for a job.—**bar·ter,** *n.*—**bar·ter·er,** *n.*

bar·ti·zan, bär′ti·zan, *n.* [Alteration of *bratticing.*] A small turret projecting from the top of a tower or wall, for the purpose of lookout or defense.

bar·ton, bär′ton, *n. Brit.* a farmyard.

bar·y·on, bar′ē·on″, *n.* [< Gr. *barys,* heavy and *-on,* as in *proton.*] *Phys.* any of the heavier subatomic particles having masses greater than a neutron. Also *hyperon.*

ba·ry·ta, ba·rī′ta, n. [N.L. < Gr. barytēs, weight.] Chem. any one of several compounds of barium: calcined baryta, caustic baryta, baryta water, baryta yellow.—**ba·ryt·ic,** ba·ri′tik, a. Of or containing baryta.

ba·sal, bā′sal, bā′zal, a. Of or pertaining to a base; situated at the base; fundamental; basic.—**bas·i·lar, bas·i·lar·y,** bas′i·lar, bas′i·ler′ē, a.

ba·sal met·a·bol·ic rate, n. Physiol. A measurement of an organism's basal metabolism; the measurement of the rate at which energy is produced by an organism at rest and, preferably fasting, as measured by the oxygen intake and heat discharge. Abbr. B.M.R.

ba·sal me·tab·o·lism, n. Physiol. the amount of energy required by a person to maintain minimum vital functions.

ba·salt, ba·salt′, bas′alt, bā′salt, n. [L. basaltes.] Any of various heavy, dark-colored, basic rocks of volcanic origin, containing various constituents (such as plagioclase, augite, olivine, and magnetite), occurring in porphyritic and coarse or fine crystalline forms, and sometimes displaying a remarkable columnar structure.—**ba·sal·tic,** ba·sal′tik, a. Of or like basalt.

bas·cule, bas′kŭl, n. [Fr., seesaw < battre, bump and cul, buttocks.] A structure in bridges by which one portion balances another.—**bas·cule bridge,** a kind of drawbridge in which the roadway may be raised at will and kept in an upright position by means of weights.

base, bās, n. [O.Fr. base, < L. basis: BASIS.] The bottom of anything, considered as its support; that on which a thing stands or rests; a fundamental principle or groundwork; the principal element or ingredient of anything, considered as its fundamental part; the stem of a word; that from which a commencement, as of action or reckoning, is made; sports, a starting point or a goal; baseball, any of the four corners of the diamond. Arch. the lowest member of a wall, monument, or the like; that part of a column on which the shaft rests. Biol. the part of an organ nearest its point of attachment; the point of attachment. Geom. the line or surface forming that part of a figure on which it is supposed to stand; fort. the imaginary line drawn from the salient angle of one bastion to that of the next. Math. the number which serves as a fundamental number for a logarithmic or other system; a radix. Surv. an accurately determined line forming one side of a triangle or serving as the starting point for a system of triangles; also base line. Milit. a fortified or more or less protected tract or place from which military operations proceed or from which supplies are obtained. Chem. a compound which reacts with an acid to form a salt, as oxides and hydroxides of metals.—**off base,** slang, mistaken; baseball, not in contact with a base, as a runner.

base, bās, a.—**baser, basest.** [O.Fr. bas, < M.L. bassus, short, low.] Of illegitimate birth; morally low; without dignity of sentiment; mean-spirited; selfish; cowardly; befitting or characteristic of an inferior person or thing; abject; unworthy; menial; coarse in quality; common, poor, or shabby; not classical or refined, as language; of little comparative value; as, base metals; worthless; debased or counterfeit, as coin.

base, bās, v.t.—**based, basing.** To make or form a base or foundation for; place or establish on a base or basis.

base·ball, bās′bal″, n. The national American game or sport played with bat and ball, four bases at the points of the diamond marking the course each player takes in scoring a run, played by two teams of nine players each; a horsehide-covered ball used in the game.

base·board, bās′bōrd″, bās′bård″, n. A strip of board located at the base of a wall and covering the joint of the wall and the floor; a board which forms the base of something.

base·born, bās′barn, a. Of low or humble birth; of base origin; illegitimate.

base·burn·er, bās′bur″nér, n. A stove or furnace with a self-acting fuel hopper over the fire chamber.

base hit, n. Baseball, a hit which enables the batter to reach base safely without an error and without forcing out another base runner.

base·less, bās′lis, a. Without a base; without grounds or foundation; as, a baseless rumor.

base lev·el, n. Geol. the lowest level to which a stream can erode its valley, as the level of the sea or of a lake.

base line, n. Any line or specified quantity used as a point of reference; baseball, the path between bases which base runners must follow in advancing from any base to the next; tennis, the boundary line parallel to the net at each end of the court.

base·man, bās′man, n. pl. **base·men.** Baseball, a player stationed on defense at first, second, or third base.

base·ment, bās′ment, n. A base or foundation; the lowest division of the wall of a building; the area partly or wholly below ground level.

base met·al, n. A metal or alloy of relatively inferior value as compared with the noble metals, gold and silver; the chief component of an alloy; the metal upon which another metal is overlaid.

Ba·sen·ji, ba·sen′jē, n. A terrierlike dog of African origin that rarely barks, has a reddish brown coat and curled tail.

base pay, n. Wages as determined by the amount earned during a given work period exclusive of bonuses, overtime, etc.

base rate, n. The rate of pay for a stated output or period of labor.

base run·ner, n. Baseball, a player of the offensive team when on base or while advancing toward another base.

bash, bash, v.t. [Scand., Dan. bask, a slap, baske, to slap.] Slang. To beat violently; to knock out of shape.—n. Slang. A powerful blow; a lively, lavish party.

ba·shaw, ba·sha′, n. [Pers. bâshâ, pâshâh.] A pasha.

bash·ful, bash′ful, a. [< (a) bash and -ful.] Easily put to confusion; modest to excess; diffident; shy; self-conscious.—**bash·ful·ly,** adv. In a bashful manner; very modestly.—**bash·ful·ness,** n.

ba·sic, bā′sik, a. Of, pertaining to, or forming a base; fundamental. Chem. pertaining to, of the nature of, or containing a base; alkaline; not having all of the hydroxyls of the base replaced by the acid radical, or having the metal or its equivalent united partly to the acid radical and partly to oxygen; as, a basic chloride, salt, etc. Geol. of rocks, having a relatively small amount of the acid element or constituent (silicon or silica); metal. noting, pertaining to, or made by a steel-making process in which the furnace is lined with a basic or non-siliceous material, principally lime and magnesia.—**ba·si·cal·ly,** adv.

ba·sic, bā′sik, n. Something which is fundamental; milit. an airman or soldier in basic training.

Ba·sic Eng·lish, n. A system of English speech devised by C. K. Ogden, with a vocabulary reduced to 850 essential words.

ba·sic·i·ty, bā·sis′i·tē, n. Chem. the state of being a base; the power of an acid to unite with one or more atoms of a base.

ba·sic skills, n. pl. A term used in education to denote those skills in any given field which must be acquired as fundamental to further learning.

ba·sic slag, n. The slag used in the making of basic steel and useful afterward as a fertilizer because of its high oxide content.

ba·sid·i·o·my·ce·tous, ba·sid″ē·ō·mī·sē′tus, a. [N.L. Basidiomycetes, pl. < basidium and Gr. mykes, myketos, fungus.] Bot. belonging or pertaining to the Basidiomycetes, a large group of fungi including the mushrooms.—**ba·sid·i·o·my·cete,** ba·sid″ē·ō·mī·sēt′, n. A division of fungi.

ba·sid·i·um, ba·sid′ē·um, n. pl. **ba·sid·i·a,** ba·sid′ē·a. [N.L. < Gr. basis, base and a dim. suffix.] Bot. the cell on a basidiomycete to which the sexual spores of some fungi are attached.

ba·si·fixed, bā′si·fikst″, a. Bot. attached at the base, as an anther.

ba·si·fy, bā′si·fī, v.t.—**basified, basifying.** Chem. To cause to become alkaline; to convert into a base.

bas·il, baz′il, n. [O.Fr. basile, < Gr. basilikos, royal, < basileus, a king.] A plant of the genus Ocinum, a native of India, cultivated in Europe as an aromatic potherb, and used for flavoring foods.

Ba·sil·i·an, ba·zil′ē·an, ba·zil′yan, ba·sil′ē·an, ba·sil′yan, a. Of, pertaining to, instituted by, or named for St. Basil, 329-379 A.D., a Greek father of the Christian church.—n. A member of a religious order deriving its name and rule from St. Basil.

ba·sil·i·ca, ba·sil′i·ka, n. [L. < Gr. basilikē, royal (colonnade or porch) < basileus, a king.] An ancient Roman building, rectangular in shape, with a middle and two side aisles divided by columns, and an apse at one end, used as a court room or assembly hall; a structure in this style or design, used as a Christian church. Rom. Cath. Ch. any of numerous ancient churches in Rome; a church which has been granted ceremonial rights and privileges by the Pope.

bas·i·lisk, bas′i·lisk, baz′i·lisk, n. [L. basiliscus, < Gr. basiliskos, kind of serpent, dim. of basileus, king.] A fabled creature (serpent, lizard, or dragon) said by the ancients to kill by its breath or look; zool. a tropical American lizard of the genus Basiliscus, of the iguana family, with an erectile crest along the back and a dilatable membranous pouch on the head.

ba·sin, bā′sin, n. [O.Fr. bacin < L.L. bacchinon. BACK.] A vessel or dish of some size, usually circular, rather broad and not very deep, used to hold water for washing, and for various other purposes; the amount held by such a vessel; any reservoir for water, natural or artificial; the whole tract of country drained by a river and its tributaries. Geol. an aggregate of strata dipping toward a common axis or center; a depressed area of strata or deposits lying in older rocks. A sheltered area of a shoreline where boats may be anchored; as, a yacht basin; bot. the depression in a pome opposite the point at which the stem meets the fruit.

ba·sip·e·tal, bā·sip′i·tl, a. [L. basis, base, and petere, seek.] Bot. developing from the apex toward the base.

ba·sis, bā′sis, n. pl. **ba·ses,** bā′sēz. [L. basis, < Gr. basis, a stepping, step, base, < bainein, go.] The bottom or base of anything, or that on which it stands or rests; hence, that by which anything is sustained, or upon which it is established; a foundation or support; a groundwork or fundamental principle; the principal constituent; a fundamental ingredient.

bask, bask, bäsk, v.i. [Formerly to bathe, a word of Scandinavian origin = Icel. batha sik, to bathe oneself—sik being the reflexive pronoun.] To lie in warmth; to be exposed to a genial atmosphere; to be at

---

a- fat, fāte, fär, fâre, fall;   **e-** met, mē, mēre, hèr;   **i-** pin, pīne;   **o-** not, nōte, mŏve;   **u-** tub, cūbe, bull;   **oi-** oil;   **ou-** pound.

ease and thriving under benign influences; to partake of pleasant surroundings.

bas·ket, bas′kit, bä′skit, *n*. [M.E.; origin unknown.] A vessel or receptacle made of straw, rushes, thin strips of wood, or other flexible material, woven together; any object which is similar in shape or is employed for the same purpose; the contents of such a vessel, or as much as it will hold; a protection of wickerwork for the handle of a sword; the car suspended beneath a balloon, for passengers, etc.; *basketball*, either of the two basketlike goals, or a score: two points for a field goal, one point for a foul shot.

bas·ket·ball, bas′kit·bal, bä′skit·bal, *n*. A game played, usually indoors, between two teams of five players, with an inflated ball, the object being to throw the ball into elevated basketlike goals placed at opposite ends of the court; also, the ball used.

bas·ket hilt, *n*. A basketlike hilt of a sword, etc., as of narrow plates of steel, serving to cover and protect the hand.

bas·ket·ry, bas′ki·trē, bä′ski·trē, *n*. Basketwork; baskets in general; the procedure, skill, or craft of basket making.

bas·ket stitch, *n*. A stitch in embroidery in which the threads are interlaced as in basketry.

bas·ket weave, *n*. A textile woven to resemble the surface of a basket.

ba·so·phil, bā′sa·fil, *n. Biol.* a tissue or cell having a natural inclination for basic stains. Also **ba·so·phile,** bā′sa·fīl″, bā′sa·fil.—**ba·so·phil·ic,** bā″sa·fil′ik, *a*.

Basque, bask, *n*. [Fr. < L. *Vascones*, inhabitants of the Pyrenees.] A language of unknown affinities spoken in parts of France and Spain on both sides of the Pyrenees at the angle of the Bay of Biscay, supposed to represent the tongue of the ancient Iberians, the primitive inhabitants of Spain; an inhabitant of the western Pyrenees; (*l.c.*) a bodice for women which is tight-fitting.—*a*. Pertaining to the people or language of Biscay.

bas-re·lief, bä″ri·lēf′, bas″ri·lēf′, bas′ri·lēf″, bä′ri·lēf″, *n*. [Fr. *bas*, It. *basso*, low, and *relief*, It. *rilievo*, relief.] A sculpture in low relief; a mode of sculpturing figures on a flat surface, the figures being raised above the surface, but not so much as in high relief.

bass, bās, *n*. [It. *basso*, deep, low. BASE.] *Mus.* The lowest part in the harmony of a musical composition, whether vocal or instrumental; the lowest male voice; a person with such a voice; a deep-toned musical instrument; as, a *bass* fiddle.

bass, bās, *a. Mus.* Low; deep; grave.

bass, bas, *n.* pl. **bass, bass·es.** [Variant of *barse*, O.E. *baers*, perch.] Any of various North American fish of the families *Serranidae* and *Centrarchidae*; the European perch, *Perca fluviatilis*, some of them of considerable size and used as food.

bass, bas, *n*. [Same as *bast*, the *t* being dropped. BAST.] The American linden or basswood tree.

bass clef, bās klef, *n. Mus.* on a staff, a reversed, elongated C with two dots to the right of it, one above and one below the fourth or F line, a symbol which indicates that notes on that staff are below middle C. Also *F clef.*

bass drum, bās drum, *n*. A large drum having two heads and producing a deep sound when struck.

bas·set, bas′sit, *n*. [Fr. *basset*, dim. of *bas*, low.] A dog with short crooked legs and a long body, used for hunting. Also **bas·set hound.**

bas·set, bas′it, *v.i. Geol.* To incline upward, so as to appear at the surface; to crop out.—*n*.

bass fid·dle, bās fid′el, *n*. The largest, lowest-pitched of the violin-type musical instruments. Also **bass vi·ol,** *double bass.*

bass horn, bās horn, *n*. A tuba.

bas·si·net, bas″a·net′, bas′a·net″, *n*. [Fr. BASINET.] A basket made of wicker, plastic, etc., with a covering or hood over one end, used as an infant's bed; a perambulator of similar construction.

bas·so, bas′ō, bäs′ō, *n*. pl. **bas·sos,** *It.* **bas·si,** bas′ē, bäs′ē. [It.] A singer of bass parts, esp. operatic.

bas·soon, ba·sön′, ba·sön′, *n*. [Fr. *basson* < It. *bassone*, aug. of *basso*, low.] A musical wind instrument of the double feed order, blown with a bent metal mouthpiece, and holed and keyed like the clarinet; the bass among woodwind instruments.

bas·so pro·fun·do, bas′ō prō·fun′dō, bäs′ō prō·fun′dō, *n*. pl. **bas·so pro·fun·dos,** bas′ō prō·fun′dōz, bäs′o prō·fun′dōz. [It. deep bass.] *Mus.* the lowest bass voice or singer.

bass·wood, bas′wud, *n*. A linden, esp. *Tilia americana*; the wood of such a tree.

bast, bast, *n*. [O.E. *bæst* = Icel., Sw., D., Dan., and G. *bast*, bark.] The inner bark of exogenous trees, consisting of several layers of fibers; phloem; rope or matting of this.

bas·tard, bas′tard, *n*. [O.Fr. *bastard*, < *bast*, a packsaddle, with the common termination -*ard* added; referring to the old locution *fils de bast*, son of a packsaddle, old saddles being often used by way of beds or to serve as pillows.] A child begotten and born out of wedlock; an illegitimate child; what is spurious or inferior in quality. *Slang*, a low, cruel person; one who is intensely disliked.—**bas·tard·ly,** bas′tard·lē, *a*. Bastard; spurious.

bas·tard, bas′tard, *a*. Begotten and born out of lawful matrimony; illegitimate; spurious; not genuine; false; adulterate; impure; of unusual shape; not of the first or usual order or character.

bas·tard·ize, bas′tar·dīz″,*v.t.*—*bastardized, bastardizing.* To make or prove to be a bastard; to debase.

bas·tard wing, *n. Ornith.* A group of stiff feathers attached to the bone of a bird's wing that represents the thumb; the alula.

bas·tard·y, bas′terd·ē, *n*. The state of being a bastard, or begotten and born out of lawful wedlock; the act of begetting an illegitimate child.

baste, bāst, *v.t.*—*basted, basting.* [O.Fr. *bastir*, lit. to sew with *bast*.′ BAST.] To sew with long stitches, and usually to keep parts together temporarily; to sew slightly.

baste, bāst, *v.t.*—*basted, basting.* [O.Fr. *basser*, dampen.] To drip fat, pan drippings, etc. as upon meat, to moisten it while cooking.

bas·tille, bas·tile, ba·stēl′, *n*. [Fr. *bastille*, a fortress, O.Pr. *bastida*, tower < L.L. *bastire*, build.] Any tower, prison, or fortification; (*cap.*) an old fortress in Paris used as a prison, demolished by the enraged populace in 1789.

Bas·tille Day, *n*. The French national holiday which annually commemorates the fall of the Bastille on July 14, 1789.

bas·ti·na·do, bas·ti·nä′dō, *n*. pl. **bas·ti·na·does.** [Sp. *bastonada*, from *baston*, a stick, a baton.] A sound beating with a stick or cudgel; a mode of punishment in oriental countries, esp. Mohammedan, by beating the soles of the feet or the buttocks with a rod; a stick; a cudgel.—*v.t.*—*bastinadoed, bastinadoing.* To beat, esp. on the soles of the feet.

bast·ing, bā′sting, *n*. The long stitches by which pieces of garments are temporarily sewn to each other; the action of basting; the thread used in basting.

bas·ti·on, bas′chan, bas′tē·on, *n*. [Fr. *bastion*, variant of *bastillon*, dim. of *bastille*.

BASTILLE.] *Fort.* a huge mass of earth, faced with sod, brick, or stones, standing out with an angular form from the rampart at the angles of a fortification. A fortified location; a stronghold.—**bas·ti·oned,** *a*.

bat, bat, *n*. [Alteration of M.E. *bakke.* Akin. Dan. *bakke* (in *aften-bakke*, a bat, lit. evening-bird), the word having lost an *l*, seen in Icel. *lethrblaka*, "leather-flapper," a bat, from *blaka*, to flutter.] One of a group of mammals of the order *Chiroptera*, possessing a pair of leathery wings which extend between the fore and the posterior limbs, the former being specially modified for flying, the bones of the forefeet being extremely elongated.

bat, bat, *n*. [O.E. *batt*.] A heavy stick or club; a piece of wood used in driving the ball in baseball and similar games; a batsman; a turn at bat; a piece of a brick; a brickbat; a heavy blow; *slang*, a wild spree.

bat, bat, *v.t.*—*batted, batting.* [Var. of *bate.*] To wink or blink the eyes; to blink repeatedly.—**not bat an eye,** *colloq.* to remain calm without change of expression despite sudden surprise or danger.

bat, bat, *v.i.*—*batted, batting. Baseball*, to take one's turn at bat or swing one.

batch, bach. [M.E. variant of O.E. *bacar*, bake.] The quantity baked at one time; any quantity of a thing made at once; a number of individuals or articles similar to each other.—*v.t., v.i.* To prepare by the batch.

bate, bāt, *v.t.*—*bated, bating.* [Short for *abate.*] To abate, lessen, or reduce; as, to *bate* one's breath; to diminish.

ba·teau, bat·teau, ba·tō′, *n*. pl. **ba·teaux, bat·teaux,** ba·tōz′. [Fr.] A light, broad, and flat-bottomed boat used in the U.S. and Canada; the pontoon of a floating bridge.—**ba·teau neck·line,** a neckline cut along the collarbone.

bate·ment light, bāt′ment līt, *n. Arch.* a section of a window having vertical sides and a curved or inclined bottom.

bat·fish, bat′fish, *n*. pl. **bat·fish, bat·fish·es.** Any of the flat-bodied marine fishes (thought to resemble the bat) constituting the family *Ogcocephalidae*, as *Ogcocephalus vespertilio*, which is common along the southern Atlantic coast of the U.S.; any of various other fishes, as the flying-gurnard, *Dactylopterus volitans*; a stingray, *Myliobatis californicus*, found in the ocean near California.

bat·fowl·ing, bat′foul″ing, *n*. A mode of catching birds at night by means of a light and nets, wherein the roused birds fly toward the light and are entangled in the nets.

bath, bath, bäth, *n*. pl. **baths.** [O.E. *baeth* = G. *bad.*] An immersion of the body in, or an exposure of it to, the action of water, other liquid, or vapor, for cleansing, refreshment, or medical treatment; water or other agent prepared for this purpose; a vessel for containing this; as, a *bath*tub; a room with equipment for bathing; *often pl.* a building containing rooms or apartments fitted for bathing, esp. with reference to one of the elaborate bathing establishments of the ancients; *usu. pl.* a town or place visited for medical treatment by bathing. A preparation, as an acid solution, in which something is immersed; the vessel containing such a preparation; a device for heating or cooling something by means of a surrounding medium such as sand or water; the mass of molten metal in a metallurgical furnace; the state of being immersed, or covered with a substance, as: He was in a *bath* of mud.

Bath brick, *n*. [English town of *Bath*, in Somersetshire.] A preparation of siliceous earth in the form of a brick, used for cleaning knives, and polishing metals.

---

ch- chain, G. na*ch*t;   **th-** THen, thin;   **w-** wig, hw as sound in whig;   **z-** zh as in azure, zeal.   *Italicized vowel* indicates schwa sound.

83

bath chair — **bawdy**

bath chair, *n.* A small hooded chair having wheels, used by invalids; any wheelchair.

bathe, bāth, *v.t.*—*bathed, bathing.* [O.E. *bathian.* Cogn. Icel. *batha,* Dan. *bade,* D. and G. *baden.* BATH.] To subject to a bath; to immerse in water for pleasure, health, or cleanliness; to wash, moisten, or suffuse with any liquid; to immerse in or surround with anything analogous to water; to go for a swim.—*v.i.* To take a bath; to be or lie in a bath; to be in water or in other liquid; to be immersed or surrounded as if with water. —*n.* Brit. act of bathing, as in a lake.— **bath·er,** *n.* One who bathes.

bath·house, bath'hous", *n.* A house or building fitted up for bathing; a structure, as at the seaside, serving as a dressing room for bathers or containing a number of such rooms; a building for bathing equipped with medical baths, and sometimes a swimming pool.

bath·o·lith, bath' o·lith, *n.* [Gr. *bathos,* depth, and *lithos,* stone.] *Geol.* A great mass of deep-seated, intrusive igneous rock, which may be exposed by erosion. Also **bath·o·lite,** bath' o·līt".—**bath·o·lit·ic, bath·o·lith·ic,** bath"o·lit'ik, bath"o·lith'ik, *a.*

ba·thom·e·ter, ba·thom'i·tėr, *n.* [Gr. *bathos,* depth, and *metron,* a measure.] An apparatus for determining depths of water.

ba·thos, bā'thos, *n.* [Gr. *bathos,* < *bathys,* deep.] A ludicrous descent from the elevated to the commonplace in writing or speech; over-exaggerated pathos; extreme sentimentality.

bath·robe, bath'rōb", bäth'rōb", *n.* A long, loose garment for wear in going to and from a bath, and as leisure wear in the home.

bath·room, bath'rōm", *n.* A room for bathing and usually containing a wash basin and a toilet.

bath·tub, bath'tub", bäth'tub", *n.* A tub to bathe in, esp. an elongated one forming a permanent fixture in a bathroom.

ba·thym·e·try, ba·thim'i·trē, *n.* [Gr.] The science of measuring depths, esp. in the sea; the facts learned from such measurement.—**ba·thym·e·ter,** *n.*—**bath·y·met·ric,** bath"i'me'trik, *a.*

bath·y·scaphe, bath·y·scaph, bath'i·skāf", bath'i·skaf", *n.* [Gr. *bathys,* deep, and *skaphē,* bowl; tub.] A submersible deep-sea exploratory craft using gasoline for buoyancy and lead or iron pellets for ballast, and having a habitable watertight chamber fitted with scientific devices.

bath·y·sphere, bath'i·sfēr", *n.* [Gr.] A diving sphere used for observation of deep-sea life.

bath·y·ther·mo·graph, bath"i·thur'mo·graf", bath"i·thur'mo·gräf", *n.* [Gr.] A device to locate the depth in water at which the temperature changes radically.

ba·tik, ba·tēk', bat'ik, *n.* [Malay *bātik,* Javanese *batik.*] A process of executing designs on a fabric, employed orig. in the Dutch East Indies, by covering with melted wax the portions forming the pattern, and dyeing the uncovered portions, the wax being then removed; fabric so decorated.

ba·tiste, ba·tēst', ba·tēst', *n.* [Fr. *batiste.*] A fine, sheer fabric of natural or synthetic fibers.

bat·man, bat'man, *n. pl.* **bat·men.** [Fr. *bât,* a packsaddle.] In the British army, a person assigned to an officer as an orderly.

bat·on, ba·ton', ba·ton', bat'n, *n.* [Fr. *bâton,* O.Fr. *baston* < L.L. *bastum,* stick.] A staff, club, or truncheon, esp. as a mark of office or authority. *Mus.* the wand used by a conductor for beating time; the stick used by a band's drum major. *Her.* a small band, of one-fourth the breadth of the bend sinister and extending in the same diagonal direction, but cut off at each end so as not to reach the edge of the field, borne in England as a mark of bastardy; *track,* the hollow cylinder passed from runner to runner in a relay race.

ba·tra·chi·a, ba·trā'kē·a, *n. pl.* [N.L. < Gr. *batrachos,* a frog.] Froglike animals; a group of amphibious animals, otherwise known as the tailless amphibia; frogs and toads.—**ba·tra·chi·an,** ba·trā'kē·an, *a.*

bat·ra·choid, bat'ra·koid, *a.* Froglike, as various amphibious vertebrates.

bats·man, bats'man, *n. pl.* **bats·men.** The player who wields the bat in cricket.

bat·tal·ion, ba·tal'yan, *n.* [Fr. *bataillon,* < It. *battaglione,* aug. of *battaglia,* a battle or body of soldiers, L. *battuere,* strike. BATTLE.] An army or marine unit consisting of a headquarters and two or more companies or batteries; a body of troops organized for united action; any large group or force; as, a *battalion* of ants.

bat·ten, bat'n, *n.* [Fr. *bâton,* a stick.] A long piece of wood from 1 inch to 7 inches broad, and from ½ inch to 2½ inches thick, used for flooring or as a support, or used to seal or reinforce something; a plank. *Naut.* one of the slips of wood used to keep a tarpaulin close over a hatchway; *weaving,* the movable bar for holding and positioning the reed in a loom.

bat·ten, bat'n, *v.t.* To fasten with battens; as, to *batten* down the hatches.

bat·ter, bat'ėr, *v.t.* [Fr. *battre,* It. *battere,* < L.L. *batere,* a form of L. *batuere,* to beat, whence also *battle.*] To beat with successive blows; to beat with violence, so as to bruise or dent; to assail by a battering ram or ordnance; to wear or impair, as by beating, long service, or the like.—*v.i.* To make attacks, as by a battering ram or artillery; to deal repeated blows.

bat·ter, bat'ėr, *n.* A mixture of several ingredients, as flour, eggs, shortening, etc., beaten together with some liquid into a paste, and used in baking; *arch.* form in which the face of a wall or other structure recedes and slopes upward; *baseball,* player who bats, or who is taking his turn at bat; *print.* term given to damaged surface of type face.

bat·ter·ing ram, *n.* An ancient engine of war used to beat down the walls of besieged places, consisting of a large beam, with a head of iron somewhat resembling the head of a ram, whence its name.

bat·ter·y, bat'e·rē, *n. pl.* **bat·ter·ies,** bat'e·rēz. [Fr. *batterie* < O.Fr. *battre,* beat < L. *battuere,* strike, beat.] The act of beating or battering; *law,* an unlawful attack upon another by beating or wounding, or even by touching in a menacing manner. *Milit.* two or more pieces of artillery used for combined action; a tactical unit of artillery, usually consisting of four guns together with the artillerymen, equipment, etc.; a group of guns on, or the whole armament of, a warship; a parapet or fortification equipped with artillery; an artillery unit corresponding to a company of infantry. *Mech.* a set or series of similar machines, parts, or the like, as a group of boilers. *Elect.* a dry cell; a device for generating and storing electricity consisting of one or more cells, connected in series. *Baseball,* the pitcher and catcher together. *Mus.* the percussion section. Any group or series of related things, as a group of tests.

bat·ting, bat'ing, *n.* Cotton wool in rolls or sheets, used as stuffing or lining; *baseball,* the act of swinging a bat.

bat·ting av·er·age, *n. Baseball,* a percentage which measures a batter's score over a period of time: determined by dividing the number of hits by the number of times at bat; *slang,* a record of achievement.

bat·tle, bat'l, *n.* [Fr. *bataille,* < L.L. *batalia, batualia,* a fight; from L. *battuere,* to beat, to fence. BATTER.] A fight or encounter between the forces of enemy nations or opposing armies; an engagement, more especially a general engagement between large bodies of troops, planes, or warships; a combat, conflict, or struggle.—**give bat·tle,** to attack.—**join bat·tle,** to meet in hostile encounter.

bat·tle, bat'l, *v.i.*—*battled, battling.* To join in battle; to contend; to struggle; to strive or exert oneself.—*v.t.* To struggle against.

bat·tle-ax, bat·tle-axe, bat'l aks", *n.* An ax formerly used as a weapon of war; *slang,* a woman with a bad temper or domineering nature, esp. a wife.

bat·tle cry, *n.* A cry or shout of troops rushing into or engaged in battle; any campaign slogan.

bat·tle·dore, bat'l·dōr", *n.* [Probably < O.Pr. *batedor,* a beater, < *battre,* to beat < L. *battuere.*] An instrument with a handle and a flat board or palm, used to strike a ball or shuttlecock; a racket; the game played with such a racket, the forerunner of badminton.—*v.t., v.i.*—*battledored, battledoring.* To discuss; to cause to fly back and forth, as an idea or plan; to bat about.

bat·tle fa·tigue, *n.* A neurosis suffered by soldiers after prolonged combat duty and exposure to danger, rendering them incapable of further fighting. Also **com·bat fa·tigue, shell shock.**

bat·tle·field, bat'l·fēld", *n.* The field or scene of a land battle.

bat·tle·ment, bat'l·ment, *n.* [Perhaps < O.Fr. *bastille,* a fortress, *bastiller,* to fortify, to embattle, modified by the influence of E. *battle.*] A notched or indented parapet of a castle, originally for defense, afterward for ornament. Also **em·bat·tle·ment.**

bat·tle roy·al, *n.* A common brawl in which there are more than two adversaries; a free-for-all.

bat·tle·ship, bat'l·ship", *n.* A vessel of war; one of a class of warships comprising those which are the largest and most heavily armored, and are equipped with the most powerful guns.

bat·tue, ba·tö', ba·tü', *n.* [Fr. < *battre,* to beat.] A kind of sport in which game is driven by a body of beaters from under cover into a limited area where the animals may be easily shot; a group of hunters who use this method of hunting.

bat·ty, bat'ē, *a.*—*battier, battiest.* Pertaining to or resembling a bat. *Slang,* insane; mad.

bau·ble, ba̧'bl, *n.* [O.Fr. *babole,* a toy or baby-thing; from same Celtic root as *babe.*] A short stick with a fool's head, formerly carried by the fools attached to great houses; a trifling piece of finery; something showy without real value; a gewgaw; a trifle.

baulk, ba̧k. See *balk.*

baux·ite, bak'sit, bō'zīt, *n.* [Fr. < Les Baux, in southern France.] A mineral consisting essentially of a hydrated aluminum oxide, used as a source of alum and aluminum.

Ba·va·ri·an, ba·vâr'ē·an, *a.* Of or pertaining to Bavaria, in southern Germany; as, the *Bavarian* Alps.—*n.* A native or inhabitant of Bavaria.—**Ba·va·ri·an cream,** a dessert, variously made, of whipped cream combined with chopped fruit or a custard or other ingredients, and stiffened with gelatin.

baw·bee, ba̧·bē', *n.* [< the laird *Sillebawby,* master of a 16th Century mint.] An old Scottish coin of little value. *Fig.* anything of insignificant value; a trifle.

bawd, ba̧d, *n.* [O.Fr. *baud,* bold, wanton, < G. *bald* = E. *bold.*] A person who keeps a house of prostitution or acts as a go-between in illicit relations; a prostitute.

baw·dy, ba̧'dē, *a.*—*bawdier, bawdiest.* Obscene; suggestive.

a- fat, fāte, fär, fâre, fạll;   **e-** met, mē, mēre, hėr;   **i-** pin, pīne;   **o-** not, nōte, mȯve;   **u-** tub, cūbe, bu̧ll;   **oi-** oil;   **ou-** pound.

bawl, bạl, *v.i.* [A word imitative of sound; akin, *bell, bellow*; L. *balo*, to bleat.] To cry out with a loud full sound; to weep loudly, as a child; to make vehement or clamorous outcries; to shout.—*v.t.* To proclaim by outcry; to shout out; to sell by shouting.— **bawl out**, *colloq.* To reprimand strongly; to scold angrily.—**bawl·er**, *n.*

bawl, bạl, *n.* A vehement cry or clamor; a period of loud weeping.

bay, bā, *n.* [O.Fr. *baee* (Fr. *baie*) an opening, < *baer*, < L.L. *badare*, gape.] *Arch.* a compartment of a structure as marked off by beams or pillars; a wing of a building; a bay window. A compartment in a barn, as for hay; the section on a ship used as a hospital; any of several compartments in an airplane; as, a bomb *bay*.

bay, bā, *n.* [Fr. *baie*, L.L. *baia*, a bay; of uncertain origin.] A rather wide recess in the shore of a sea or lake; the expanse of water between two capes or headlands; a gulf; any recess or land formation resembling a bay.

bay, bā, *n.* A horse of reddish-brown color; the color of a bay horse.—*a.* Reddish-brown, as a horse.

bay, bā, *n.* [Fr. *baie*, L. *bacca*, a berry.] The laurel tree, *Laurus nobilis*, or sweet bay; any of various related trees or shrubs; a garland or crown bestowed as a prize for victory or excellence, consisting of leaves of the laurel; *usu. pl.* fame or renown.

bay, bā, *n.* [O.Fr. *abai, abbai*, a barking, *abbayer*, to bark; akin Fr. *bayer*, to gape, or to stand gaping. ABASH.] The bark of a dog, esp. a deep-toned bark or howl; the situation of being cornered and forced to fight. —*v.i.* To bark with a deep sound, as a hound.—*v.t.* To bark at; to hold at bay.

ba·ya·dere, bī′a·dēr″, bī′a·der″, *n.* [Fr. *bayadère*, < Pg. *bailadeira*, < *bailar*, dance.] An East Indian dancing girl.—*a.* Of stripes on fabrics, running crosswise; transverse; of fabrics, having such stripes.

bay ant·ler, *n.* [For *bes-antler*, < O.Fr. *bes-* (< L. *bis*, twice) and E. *antler*.] The second branch from the base of a stag's horn.

Bay·ard, bā′ẽrd, *n.* A heroic and chivalrous man: after the French knight; a magical horse: from medieval fables.

bay·ber·ry, bā′ber″ē, bā′be·rē, *n.* pl. **bay·ber·ries.** Any of certain shrubs or trees of the genus *Myrica*, as *M. carolinensis*, a shrub common on seacoasts, and *M. cerifera* (see *wax-myrtle*); the berry of such a plant; a West Indian tree, *Pimenta acris*, whose leaves yield oil used in making bay rum.

bay leaf, *n.* The leaf of the bay tree, dried for use as a flavoring in cooking.

bay·on·et, bā′o·nit, bā′o·net″, bā′o·net″, *n.* [Fr. *baïonnette*, < *Bayonne* in France, because bayonets are said to have been first made there.] A short sword or dagger, made so that it may be fixed upon the muzzle of a rifle.—*v.t.*—*bayoneted, bayoneting, bayonetted, bayonetting*. To stab with a bayonet; to compel or drive by threat of a bayonet.

bay·ou, bī′ö, bī′ō, *n.* pl. **bay·ous.** [Louisiana Fr. < Choctau *bayuk*, a small stream.] An arm or outlet of a lake, river, etc.; an extent of sluggish water.

bay rum, *n.* A fragrant liquid originally obtained from the leaves of the bayberry and used for cosmetic and medicinal purposes.

bay salt, *n.* Coarse-grained salt, esp. that obtained by evaporation of seawater.

bay win·dow, *n.* The window of an alcove which extends beyond the exterior wall line of an edifice; *slang*, a protruding abdomen or paunch.

bay·wood, bā′wụd,*n.* A variety of mahogany native to some parts of Mexico.

ba·zaar, ba·zar, ba·zär′, *n.* [Pers. *bâzâr*.] In the Orient, a place where goods are offered for sale, usually consisting of small shops or stalls in a narrow street or series of streets; a series of adjacent shops or stalls in a European town; a sale of miscellaneous articles in furtherance of some charitable or other purpose; a fancy fair; a department store.

ba·zoo·ka, ba·zö′ka, *n.* A simple metal wind instrument producing a coarse sound; a hand-carried rocket gun which launches projectiles of great penetrating power.

B bat·ter·y, *n. Electron.* a battery designed to furnish positive voltage to a vacuum tube.

B com·plex, *n.* See *vitamin B complex.*

bdel·li·um, del′ē·um, del′ē·yum, *n.* [L. *bdellium*, Gr. *bdellion*, < Heb.] An aromatic gum resin of plants (genus *Commiphora*) brought chiefly from Africa and India, used as a perfume.

be, bē, *v.i.*—pres. sing. *am, are* or archaic *art, is*; pres. pl. *are*; past sing. *was, were* or archaic *wast* or *wert, was*; past pl. *were*; subj. pres. *be*; subj. past *were*; pp. *been*; ppr. *being*. [O.E. *bēon*, inf. (akin to G. *bin*, am, L. *fui*, I was, Gr. *phyesthai*, come into being, Skt. *bhū-*, become). A defective verb, with parts supplied from three unconnected stems, *am, is, was*.] To exist; have reality; live; to occupy a position; take place; occur; remain as before; as, he *is* no more; it was not to *be*; think what might have *been*; the wedding *was* last week; let it *be*. *Copula*, a link connecting a subject with predicative or qualifying words in assertive, interrogative, and imperative sentences, or serving to form infinitive and participial phrases; as, you *are* late; he *is* much to blame; *is* he here? he *is* (here); do *be* still; *be* it so; try to *be* just; the art of *being* agreeable. *Auxiliary*, used with the present participle of a principal verb to form a continuous present tense (as, I *am* waiting), or with the past participle of transitive verbs to form the passive voice (as, the date *was* fixed; it must *be* done), and formerly with the past participle of intransitive verbs to form the perfect tense (as, he *is* come); also used with an infinitive to express futurity (as, he *is* to start later).

beach, bēch, *n.* [Origin unknown.] The loose water-worn pebbles of the seashore or other water's edge; that part of the shore of the sea, or of a large river or a lake, which is washed by the tide or waves.

beach, bēch, *v.t., v.i.* To run or haul up, as a vessel, on the beach; run a boat ashore.

beach·comb·er, bēch′kō″mẽr, *n.* One who earns a living by collecting redeemable wreckage along ocean beaches; a beachfront vagrant; a long wave that rolls in from the ocean onto the beach.

beach flea, *n.* A small hopping crustacean, family *Talitridae*, found on beaches.

beach·head, bēch′hed″, *n. Milit.* a seashore area taken and held by the attacking force in an amphibious invasion; the occupying force on this area. A new, significant development or innovative advance in knowledge or technology.

bea·con, bē′kan, *n.* [O.E. *bēcn, bēacen*, a beacon; hence *beck, beckon*.] Any signal that serves to guide or orient, as a fire, a lighthouse, a radio beacon, etc.; a movable or stationary apparatus that sends out light, radio, or radar beams to guide or orient ships or aircraft; a beacon transmitter or a beacon station.

bea·con, bē′kan, *v.t.* To light up by a beacon; to illuminate; to signal; to supply with beacons.—*v.i.* To serve as a beacon.

bead, bēd, *n.* [M.E. *bede*, < O.E. *bed-gebed*, prayer, akin to *biddan*, ask: see *bid*.] One of the small, perforated, usually round or roundish objects threaded on a string to form a chaplet or rosary to keep count of

prayers; a similar object used with others for ornament, as in a necklace; a small globule or drop, as of liquid; a bubble of foam; one of the bubbles in an effervescing liquor; the foam or head formed by these; a small projecting piece of metal near the muzzle of a firearm, serving as a sight; as, to draw a *bead* on; a glass globule for trying the strength of alcoholic spirits; *chem., mineral.* a globule of borax or of some other flux, supported on a platinum wire, with which a small amount of some other substance is heated in a flame as a test for its constituents. *Arch.* a small globular ornament, esp. one of a series in a line or row; a narrow convex molding, usually more or less semicircular in section.— **bead·like,** *a.*

bead, bēd, *v.t.* To furnish or adorn with beads or beading.—*v.i.* To form beads.

bead·ed, bē′did, *a.* Adorned with or having beads; formed into or like beads.

bead·ing, bēd′ing, *n.* Narrow openwork trimming, as of lace or embroidery, through which ribbon may be run; beadwork. *Arch.* the beads ornamenting an object; a narrow convex molding.

bea·dle, bē′dl, *n.* [O.Fr. *bedel* < Teut.] A messenger or crier of a court; a parish officer whose business is to punish petty offenders; a church officer with various subordinate duties; an official who leads processions; the macebearer.

bead·roll, bēd′rōl″, *n.* A list of persons for whom prayers are to be said; hence, any list or catalogue; the rosary.

beads·man, bēdz′man, *n.* pl. **beads·men.** One employed to pray for another; *archaic*, one who resides in a poorhouse.

bead·work, bēd′wụrk, *n.* Ornamental work made of or with beads; *arch.* beading.

bead·y, bē′dē, *a.*—*beadier, beadiest*. Consisting of or containing beads; beadlike, as *beady*-eyed; small, round, and bright; bead-covered.

bea·gle, bē′gl, *n.* [M.E. *begle*; origin unknown.] One of a breed of small hounds with short legs and drooping ears, used in hunting hares. *Fig.* one who scents out or hunts down; a spy or detective.

beak, bēk, *n.* [O.Fr. *bec*, < L. *beccus* < the Celtic—Armor. *bek, beg*, Ir. and Gael. *bec*, a beak.] The bill of a bird; anything in some way resembling a bird's bill; the bill-like mouth of some fishes, reptiles, etc.; the proboscis; a pointed piece of wood fortified with brass, fastened to the prow of ancient galleys, and intended to pierce the vessels of an enemy. *Brit.* a justice of the peace; a schoolmaster. *Arch.* a slightly projected molding ending in an arris; *slang*, someone's nose.—**beaked,** bēkd, *a.* Having a beak or something resembling a beak.

beak·er, bē′ker, *n.* [Icel. *bikarr* < Vulgar L. *bicarium*; hence *pitcher*.] A large drinking-vessel with a wide mouth; also, an open-mouthed vessel of glass, etc., often with a lip for pouring, used chiefly in scientific experiments; the contents of such a vessel.

beak-i·ron, bēk′i″ẽrn, *n.* [Alteration of obs. *bickern* < Fr. *bigorne* < L. *bicornis*, two-horned.] The horn or tapering end of an anvil; an anvil with such a horn.

beam, bēm, *n.* [O.E. *bēam*, a beam, post, tree, ray of light. Akin. G. *baum*, a tree.] A straight, heavy piece of timber, iron, or the like serving for support or consolation, esp. a horizontal timber; *engin.* an inflexible structure supported at its ends and exposed to pressure perpendicular to its length. The part of a scale which supports the weighing tray(s); the cylindrical part of a loom around which the warp is wound. *Naut.* the width of a vessel; the shaft of an anchor; the boom; spar. A ray of light, specif. a collection of parallel rays (x-rays) or particles (electrons); the angle or range of effective use at which a microphone functions best. *Aeron.* a constant unidirectional radio signal transmitted along a narrow course as a guide for pilots; any such course; the direction extending from the side of an airplane at right angles to the plane of symmetry. The primary extension of a deer's antler; a glimmer or possibility; as, a *beam* of faith.—**on the beam**, *colloq.* Correct; alert; on the right track.

beam, bēm, *v.t.* To emit, as light or radio signals, in the form of rays or beams.—*v.i.* To emit rays of light, radio signals, or beams; to give out radiance; to shine; to smile enthusiastically.

beam·y, bē′mē, *a.*—*beamier, beamiest.* Like a beam; heavy or massive; emitting beams or rays of light; radiant. *Zool.* possessing antlers.—**beam·i·ly**, *adv.*—**beam·i·ness**, *n.*

bean, bēn, *n.* [O.E. *bēan* = Icel. *baun*, Sw. *bōna*, Dan. *bonne*, D. *boon*, G. *bohne*.] Any of several kinds of edible leguminous seeds, esp. of the genus *Phaseolus*, contained in a bivalve pod; any plant producing them, as the common bean, cultivated as food for men and animals; any of several seeds or plants which are similar to beans; a small lump found on the upper mandible of waterfowl. *Slang*, the top of the head; the mind. *Brit. slang*, a coin.—*v.t. Slang*, to strike on the head, esp. with a pitched ball.

bean ca·per, *n.* A small tree, *Zygophyllum fabago*, growing in warm climates, the flowerbuds of which are used as capers.

bean·ie, bean·y, bē′nē, *n. pl.* **bean·ies.** A skullcap worn by children, freshman college students, and initiates into organizations.

bear, bâr, *n. pl.* **bears, bear.** [O.E. *bera* = G. *bär*.] Any of the plantigrade, carnivorous or omnivorous mammals of the family *Ursidae*, esp. of the genus *Ursus*, having massive bodies, long shaggy hair, short limbs, and almost rudimentary tails; any of various animals resembling the bear; as, the ant-*bear*; *fig.* a rough, gruff, or surly person; *astron.*, either of two northern constellations, Ursa Major ("Great Bear") and Ursa Minor ("Little Bear").

bear, bâr, *v.t.*—*bore* or archaic *bare, borne, bearing.* [O.E. *beran*, akin to G. *gebären*, bring forth, L. *ferre*, Gr. *pherein*, Skt. *bhar-, bear*.] To hold up or support; to carry, fetch, or bring; to press against or push back; to afford, as testimony; sustain or undergo, without giving way; to endure, as pain or loss; to stand, as annoyance; meet or accept, as expense; to have, as a name, aspect, marks, traces, or the like; to entertain, as malice or ill will; to wield or exercise, as influence; to deport or conduct, as oneself; to bring forth or produce, as young or fruit.—*v.i.* To suffer or endure; to hold, or remain firm, as under pressure, often with *up*; be patient, followed by *with*; to press or use force, with *down, on*, or *against*; have an effect, reference, or bearing, followed by *on*; tend in course or direction; move or go; be situated, as: The land *bore* due west from the ship.—**bear down**, to exert pressure; to apply oneself diligently; to strive; to attempt to overtake, often with hostility.—**bear in mind**, to remember; to take into account.—**bear out**, to give support or countenance to, as a person or thing; to uphold, corroborate, establish, justify.—**bear up**, to have fortitude; to be firm; to keep up one's spirits and physical strength under trying circumstances.—**bear with**, to tolerate; to be indulgent; to forbear.

bear, bâr, *n. Stock market*, one who sells stocks short (which he does not own at the time of sale) hoping to cover or replace them later at a lower price and thereby profit from the transaction: opposite of *bull.*

bear·a·ble, bâr′a·bl, *a.* Capable of being

borne, endured, or tolerated.—**bear·a·bly**, *adv.* In a bearable manner.

bear·bait·ing, bâr′bā″ting, *n.* The former sport, now prohibited, of attacking chained bears with dogs.

bear·ber·ry, bâr′ber″ē, bâr′be·rē, *n. pl.* **bear·ber·ries.** A creeping or trailing evergreen shrub of the heath family, *Arctostaphylos uva-ursi*, growing in cooler areas in parts of the northern hemisphere, having red berrylike drupes, the bright green leaves used as an astringent and tonic.

bear·cat, bâr′kat, *n.* A panda, *Ailurus fulgens*, of the Himalayas; *colloq.* an esp. fierce or forceful person.

beard, bērd, *n.* [O.E. *beard*, a beard = D. *baard*, G. *bart*; L. *barba*, W. and Armor. *barf*, beard.] The hair that grows on the chin, lips, and adjacent parts of the face of male adults; anything resembling this; a hairy, bristly, or threadlike appendage of various kinds, such as the filaments by which some shellfish attach themselves to foreign bodies, etc.; the awn on the ears of grain; a barb, as of an arrow. *Print.* the sloping part of a type which divides the face from the shoulder of the body.—**beard·ed**, *a.* Having a beard in any of the senses of that word.—**beard·less**, *a.* Without a beard; hence, of persons of the male sex, young; not having arrived at manhood.

beard, bērd, *v.t.* To take by the beard; to oppose face to face; to set at defiance; to challenge boldly; to provide a beard for.

bear·er, bâr′ėr, *n.* One who or that which bears, sustains, supports, carries, conveys, etc.; a plant which produces fruit; person in possession of a bank check or other instrument redeemable for payment in money; *Anglo-Indian*, a native male employed as servant in a home.

bear·grass, bâr′gras, *n.* Any of several American plants of the genus *Yucca*, having grasslike foliage; any of certain similar plants.

bear·ing, bâr′ing, *n.* The act of a person or thing that bears; a product of bearing, as a crop; carriage or deportment; reference or relation (with *on*); aspect; *often pl.* direction or relative position. A supporting part, as in a structure; a part resting on a support, or spanning the distance between supports; *mach.* a part in which a journal, pivot, or the like, turns or moves; *her.* any single charge or device on a coat of arms.

bear·ing, bâr′ing, *n.* The horizontal direction of an object or point, usually measured clockwise from a reference line or direction through 360°.

bear·ing rein, *n.* The rein by which the head of a horse is held up in driving; checkrein.

bear·ish, bâr′ish, *a.* Resembling a bear; rude; violent in conduct; surly. *Com.* tending toward, or predictive of, a decline in prices or unfavorable prospects in the national economy.

Bé·ar·naise, ber·nāz′, *Fr.* bā·ar·nez′, *n.* [Fr. *Béarn*, a district of southwest France.] (*Sometimes l.c.*) A sauce similar to Hollandaise, made with egg yolks, butter, vinegar or lemon juice, shallots, pepper, tarragon, and chervil. Also, **Bé·ar·naise sauce.**

bear·skin, bâr′skin″, *n.* The skin of a bear; a coarse, shaggy woolen cloth for overcoats; a tall black fur hat worn by soldiers.

beast, bēst, *n.* [O.Fr. *beste*, < L. *bestia*, a beast.] Any four-footed animal, as distinguished from birds, insects, fishes, and man. A brutal man; a filthy disgusting person.

beast·li·ness, bēst′lē·nes, *n.* The state or quality of being beastly; brutality; filthiness.

beast·ly, bēst′lē, *a.*—*beastlier, beastliest.* Like a beast; brutish; brutal; filthy; contrary to the nature and dignity of man; *Brit. colloq.* nasty.—*adv. Brit., colloq.* Very; to a great degree; outrageously.

beat, bēt, *v.t.*—*beaten, beating.* [O.E. *bēatan* = Icel. *bauta, bjata*, O.H.G. *bōzan*, to beat; akin *butt, abut, beetle* (a mallet).] To strike repeatedly; to lay repeated blows upon; to knock, rap, or dash against often; to pound; to stir with vigor; to strike for the purpose of producing sound, as a drum; to report a news event in advance of, as other media; to shape by hammer; *hunting*, to bustle about noisily in order to drive game toward the gunner; to overcome, vanquish, or conquer, as in a battle, contest, competition; to surpass or excel; to be too difficult for; to be beyond the power or skill of; to baffle; to fatigue utterly; to prostrate; to flutter, as wings. —**beat a·bout**, to search by various means or ways.—**beat a re·treat**, to give a signal to retreat; to retreat or withdraw.—**beat a·round the bush**, *colloq.* to evade telling the truth or bad news by talking around a subject.—**beat back**, to compel to retire or return.—**beat down**, to dash down by beating or battering, as a wall; to lay flat; to cause to lower a price by importunity or argument; to lessen the price or value of; to depress or crush.—**beat off**, to repel or drive back.—**beat out**, to extend by hammering.—**beat up**, to attack suddenly and viciously.—**beat time**, to regulate tempo in music by the motion of the hand or the sound of a metronome.

beat, bēt, *v.i.* To strike or knock repeatedly; to move with pulsation; to throb, as the pulse, heart, etc.; to dash or fall with force or violence, as a storm, flood, etc.; to summon or signal by beating a drum; *phys.* to cause a beat or beats; *naut.* to make progress against the direction of the wind by sailing in a zigzag.

beat, bēt, *n.* A blow struck in a series; the rhythmic emphasis in music; the limited area patrolled by a policeman; news published prior to general dissemination.

beat·en, bēt′n, *a.* Made smooth by beating or treading; worn by use; conquered; vanquished; exhausted; baffled; stirred briskly, as food.

beat·er, bē′tėr, *n.* One who or that which beats; an instrument for pounding, stirring, or pulverizing substances; the striking part in various machines; *hunting*, one who drives game from brush.

beat gen·er·a·tion, *n.* A term applied to the young bohemian nonconformists of the early 1950's, including the beatniks.

be·a·tif·ic, bē″a·tif′ik, *a.* [L.L. *beatificus*, < L. *beatus*, blessed, happy, and *facere*, make.] Blessing or making happy; imparting bliss; serenely happy in appearance.

be·at·i·fy, bē·at′i·fī″, *v.t.*—*beatified, beatifying.* [L.L. *beatificare* < *beatus*, blessed, and *facere*, make.] To make happy. *Rom. Cath. Ch.* to declare by public decree that a person is to be revered as "blessed," has attained the second degree of sanctity, and is entitled to public religious honor; a preparatory step to canonization.—**be·at·i·fi·ca·tion**, bē·at″i·fi·kā′shan, *n.*

beat·ing, bē′ting, *n. Phys.* a wave phenomenon in which two or more periodic quantities of different frequencies produce a resultant having pulsations of amplitude.

be·at·i·tude, bē·at′i·tōd″, bē·at′·i·tūd″, *n.* [L. *beatitudo*, < *beatus*, happy.] Blessedness; felicity of the highest kind; consummate bliss.—**the Be·at·i·tudes**, the declarations of blessedness made by Jesus in the Sermon on the Mount.

beat·nik, bēt′nik, *n.* [From *beat* (or *beatific*), and -*nik*, a suffix meaning "person, individual" in Yiddish.] *Colloq.* A person who lives a nonconformist life; a member of the beat generation; one who disregards conventional behavior and dress and is preoccupied with avant-garde philosophizing and self-expression.

---

a- fat, fāte, fär, fâre, fall;   **e-** met, mē, mēre, hėr;   **i-** pin, pīne;   **o-** not, nōte, mōve;   **u-** tub, cūbe, bull;   **oi-** oil;   **ou-** pound.

beau, bō, *n.* pl. **beaux,** bōz. [Fr. *beau,* O.Fr. *bel,* < L. *bellus,* beautiful.] A fop; a dandy; a man who attends or is suitor to a lady; a male sweetheart or lover.—*v.t.* To escort, as a lady, to a social event.

Beau·fort scale, bō″fėrt skāl, *n.* [From Sir Francis *Beaufort,* 1774–1857, the inventor.] A scale for indicating wind force, ranging from force 0 (calm) to force 12 (hurricane) and sometimes to force 17.

beau geste, bō″ zhest′, *n.* pl. **beaux gestes,** bō″ zhest′. [Fr. lit., 'beautiful gesture.'] A fine or generous gesture; a magnanimous gesture, often only for appearance's sake.

beau i·de·al, *n.* pl. **beau i·de·als.** [Fr. *beau idéal,* beautiful ideal.] A conception of any object in its perfect typical form; a model of excellence in the mind or fancy.

beau monde, bō″ mond′, *Fr.* bō·mąNd′, *n.* pl. **beau mondes, beaux mondes,** bō mąNdz′. [Fr. *beau monde,* fine world.] The fashionable world and high society; people of distinguished family, wealth, fame, fashion, and gaiety.

beau·te·ous, bū′tē·us, *a.* Possessing beauty; beautiful.—**beau·te·ous·ly,** *adv.*

beau·ti·cian, bū·tish′an, *n.* One whose business is to improve the appearance of women's hair, nails, and complexion.

beau·ti·fi·ca·tion, bū″ti·fi·kā′shon, *n.* The act of beautifying or rendering beautiful; decoration; adornment; embellishment.

beau·ti·fi·er, bū′ti-fī-ėr, *n.* One who or that which beautifies.

beau·ti·ful, bū′ti·ful, *a.* Having the qualities that constitute beauty; highly pleasing to the eye, the ear, or the mind; as, a *beautiful* scene, melody, poem, character (but not a *beautiful* taste or smell); beauteous; lovely; handsome; fair; charming; comely; the best of a particular kind.—**beau·ti·ful·ly,** bū′ti·fųl·li, *adv.*—**beau·ti·ful·ness,** bū′ti·fųl·nes, *n.*

beau·ti·fy, bū′ti·fī″, *v.t.*—*beautified, beautifying.* To make or render beautiful; to adorn; to deck; to decorate.

beau·ty, bū′tē, *n.* pl. **beau·ties.** [O.Fr. *biauté,* L.L. *bellitas, bellitatis,* beauty, < L. *bellus,* beautiful.] An assemblage of perfections through which an object is rendered pleasing to the eye; those qualities in the aggregate that give pleasure to the aesthetic sense; any quality that delights the eye, ear, or mind; loveliness; elegance; grace; a particular grace or ornament; that which is beautiful; a beautiful person, especially a beautiful woman; a beautiful object; an advantage; as, the *beauty* of a method; something excellent; as, that catch was a *beauty:* sometimes ironical; as, that error was a *beauty.*

beau·ty shop, *n.* An establishment where a woman may receive a hairdress, manicure, and other beauty treatments. Also, **beau·ty par·lor, beau·ty sa·lon.**

beaux arts, bō zär′, *Fr.* bō zar′, *n. pl.* [Fr. lit., 'fine arts.'] The fine arts, as painting and sculpture.

beaux arts, *a.* Marked by formalism and the free adaptation of architectural forms popular in France from the 16th to 18th century, combined in a symmetrical but elaborate and showy manner; relating to the teaching methods, principles, and architecture of the École des Beaux Arts, often used disparagingly to indicate an excessive formalism which disregards logical planning, economy, and certain structural truths.

bea·ver, bē′vėr, *n.* [O.E. *beofer* = D. *bever,* Dan. *bæver,* Sw. *bäfver,* Icel. *bjórr,* G. *biber,* L. *fiber.*] A rodent quadruped valued for its fur, about two feet long, living in streams and lakes, now found in considerable numbers only in North America, and generally living in colonies; beaver fur; a hat or cap made of beaver fur; man-made fabric which simulates real fur; (*cap.*) one

who resides in Oregon, the "Beaver State."

bea·ver, bē′vėr, *n.* [O.Fr. *baviere,* a child's bib, a beaver, *bave,* slaver.] *Armor.* The face-guard of a helmet; a visor.

be·bop, bē′bop″, *n.* [Imitative.] Jazz style characterized by dissonance, complex rhythms, and experimental instrumentation permitting more freedom for, and putting more emphasis on, the soloist.

be·calm, bē·käm′, *v.t.* To render calm, still, or quiet, as the sea, wind, passions, etc.; to keep from motion for want of wind, as a ship; to delay, as a person, by a calm.

be·cause, bē·kąz′, bē·koz′, bē·kuz′, *conj.* [*Be* for *by,* and *cause;* M.E. *bicause, bycause* = by or for the cause that.] By cause, or by the cause that; on this account that; for the cause or reason next explained, as: He fled *because* (as the reason given) he was afraid.

be·cause of, *prep.* On account of; as a result of.

bec·ca·fi·co, bek″a·fē′kō, *n.* pl. **bec·ca·fi·cos, bec·ca·fi·coes.** [It., lit. 'fig-pecker.'] A small bird resembling the nightingale, esp. the European garden warbler, *Sylvia hortensis,* which is regarded as a table delicacy.

bech·a·mel, bā′sha·mel″, *n.* [Named after L. *Béchamel,* steward in the service of Louis XIV.] A white sauce, seasoned occasionally with onion and nutmeg.

bêche·de·mer, besh″de·mâr′, *n.* pl. **bêch·es-de-mer, bêche-de-mer.** [Fr., spade of (the) sea.] A trepang; sea cucumber; a jargon used in Melanesia.

beck, bek, *n.* [Short for *beckon.*] A beckoning gesture; as, to be at one's *beck* and call; summons or command; *chiefly Sc.* a nod, bow, or curtsy.

beck·et, bek′it, *n.* [Origin unknown.] *Naut.* Any of various contrivances for holding spars, etc., in position, as a short rope with a knot at one end; a kind of bracket.

beck·et bend, bek′it, *n. Naut.* See *sheet bend.*

beck·on, bek′n, *v.i.* [O.E. *beácnian, bécnian,* to beckon, < *beácn, bécn,* a beacon.] To make a sign or signal to another by a motion of the hand or finger, etc., intended as a hint or intimation; to lure.—*v.t.* To make a significant sign to; to direct by making signs, as: *Beckon* him to us.

be·cloud, bē·kloud′, *v.t.* To darken; to obscure; to cause confusion about.

be·come, bē·kum′, *v.i.*—past *became,* pp. *become,* ppr. *becoming.* [O.E. *becuman, bicuman,* to arrive, happen, turn out < prefix *be* = by, and *cuman,* to come, to happen.] To pass from one state to another; to come into existence; to change, grow, or develop into.—*v.t.* To suit or to be suitable to, as: Anger *becomes* him not. To befit; to accord with, in character or circumstances; to be worthy of, or proper to; to grace or suit as regards outward appearance, as: The dress *becomes* her.—**be·come of** (usually as a question with *what is* preceding), to be the fate of; to be the end of; to be the final or subsequent condition.

be·com·ing, bē·kum′ing, *a.* Suitable; proper; appropriate; befitting; seemly; tending to have an attractive effect.—**be·com·ing·ly,** bē·kum′ing·lē, *adv.*

Bec·que·rel rays, bek″e·rel′, *n. pl.* [Named after *Becquerel,* French physicist.] Formerly, the rays from a radioactive substance.

bed, bed, *n.* [O.E. *bedd* = D. *bed* = G. *bett* = Goth. *badi,* bed.] That upon which or within which a person reposes or sleeps; the use of a bed for the night; the bed as the place of conjugal union; the bed as the place of childbirth; any resting-place; *fig.* the grave; the resting-place of an animal; something resembling a bed in form or position; a plot or piece of ground in a garden, usually raised somewhat, in which plants, esp. flowers, are grown; an extended

mass of anything on or within the earth; a layer or stratum; a layer of shellfish covering a tract of the bottom of the sea; as, an oyster *bed;* the bottom of a body of water; that on which anything rests; the gravel, broken stone, etc., upon which the rails of a railroad are laid; *print.* the level surface in a printing press on which the form of type is laid; *mach.* etc., a piece or part forming a foundation. *Building,* a layer of cement or mortar in which a stone or brick is embedded, or against which it bears; either of the horizontal surfaces of a stone in position; the under surface of a brick, shingle, slate, or tile in position. *Sports,* the canvas surface on a trampoline; the hard surface of a billiard table; the floor of a bowling alley.

bed, bed, *v.t.*—*bedded, bedding.* To provide with a bed; put to bed; plant in, or as in a bed; lay flat, or in a bed or layer; to take to bed; embed, as in a substance.—*v.i.* To go to bed; share a bed; lie or rest on something; *geol.* form a compact layer.

be·daub, bē·dąb′, *v.t.* To daub over; to soil with anything thick, slimy, and dirty. To ornament to excess.

be·daz·zle, bē·daz′l, *v.t.*—*bedazzled, bedazzling.* To dazzle completely; blind or confuse by dazzling; to impress in a forceful manner, making oblivious any faults.—**be·daz·zle·ment,** bē·da′zel·ment, *n.*

bed bolt, *n.* A bolt for fastening something, as a machine, to its bed or foundation.

bed·bug, bed′bug″, *n.* A small, flat, wingless, bloodsucking hemipterous insect, *Cimex lectularius,* that infests houses and esp. beds.

bed·clothes, bed′klōz, bed′klōTHz″, *n. pl.* Blankets, sheets, coverlets, etc., for beds; bedding.

bed·ding, bed′ing, *n.* Bedclothes; material used as a bed for animals; a foundation; the lowest layer; *geol.* placement of rocks in strata.

bed·ding, bed′ing, *a. Hort.* suitable for culture in open-air beds; as, to transplant *bedding* plants.

be·deck, bē·dek′, *v.t.* To deck out; decorate showily; adorn; ornament.

bed·e·gar, bed·e·guar, bed′e·gär″, *n.* [Fr. *bédegar, bédeguar,* < Pers. *bādāwar,* windbrought.] A spongy excrescence or gall on rosebushes, esp. on the sweet-brier, caused by various gallflies, as *Rhodites rosæ.*

be·dev·il, bē·dev′l, *v.t.*—*bedeviled, bedeviling,* Brit. *bedevilled, bedevilling.* To treat diabolically; torment maliciously; to possess as with a devil; bewitch; to confound; muddle; to hamper constantly; spoil.—**be·dev·il·ment,** *n.*

be·dew, bē·dō′, bē·dū′, *v.t.* To wet with or as with dew.

bed·fast, bed′fast″, bed′fäst″, *a.* Confined to bed; bedridden.

bed·fel·low, bed′fel″ō, *n.* One who occupies the same bed with another; bedmate; a collaborator.

Bed·ford cord, bed′ford, kąrd, *n.* [From *Bedford,* town in England.] A thick woolen or cotton fabric with heavy lengthwise ribs separated only by narrow lines of depression.

be·diz·en, bē·diz′n, bē·dī′zn, *v.t.* To deck out with clothes or finery; dress or adorn gaudily.—**be·diz·en·ment,** *n.*

bed·lam, bed′lam, *n.* [Alteration of *Bethlehem.*] (*Cap.*) the hospital of St. Mary of Bethlehem, founded in 1247 in London as a priory, later an insane asylum. (*l.c.*) any madhouse; wild uproar and confusion.

bed·lam·ite, bed′la·mīt″, *n., a.* Lunatic.

bed lin·en, *n.* Sheets, pillow cases, etc., for beds.

Bed·ling·ton ter·ri·er, bed′ling·tan ter′ē·ėr, *n.* [Named after *Bedlington,* town in England.] One of an English breed of terriers with a light build, a fleecy coat, and a head resembling that of a lamb.

bed mold·ing, *n. Arch.* The molding, or series of moldings, between the corona and the frieze of an entablature; any molding under a projection.

Bed·ou·in, Bed·u·in, bed′ö·in, bed′win, *n. pl.* **Bed·ou·in, Bed·ou·ins.** [O.Fr. *beduin,* < Ar. *badawin,* pl. of *badawīy,* dweller in the desert, < *badw,* desert.] An Arab of the desert, in Asia or Africa; a nomadic Arab; a nomad; wanderer.—*a.* Characteristic of or related to the Bedouin.

bed·pan, bed′pan″, *n.* A necessary utensil for urination or defecation by bedriddden persons.

bed·plate, bed′plāt″, *n.* The soleplate or foundation plate of an engine or machine. Also **base plate.**

bed·post, bed′pōst, *n.* One of the vertical posts forming part of the framework of a bed. *Pl., bowling slang,* a condition in bowling when a split occurs and the seven and ten pins are left standing.

be·drab·ble, bē·drab′l, *v.t.*—*bedrabbled, bedrabbling.* To render all wet and muddy; bedraggle.

be·drag·gle, bē·drag′l, *v.t.*—*bedraggled, bedraggling.* To soil by drawing along on damp ground or mud; to soak.

bed·rid·den, bed′rid′n, *a.* [O.E. *bedrida, bedreda,* bed rider.] Confined, permanently or for a very long period, to one's bed, as by sickness. Also **bed·rid.**

bed·rock, bed′rok′, *n.* Underlying rock; rocky or solid foundation; lowest layer or stratum. A firm basis; a set of basic principles.—*a.*

bed·roll, bed′rōl″, *n.* Bedding that is rolled up for easy transportation, and is mainly used for sleeping out-of-doors.

bed·room, bed′rōm, bed′rụm, *n.* A sleeping room or bedchamber.—*a.* Pertaining to or intended for use in bedrooms; concerned with matters of sex; as, a *bedroom* joke.

bed·room sub·urb, *n.* A suburb with little or no industry, and populated mainly by the families of men who commute daily to jobs in the city. Also **dor·mi·to·ry sub·urb.**

bed·side, bed′sīd″, *n.* The side of a bed, esp. as the place of one in attendance on the sick.—*a.* At a bedside; as, a *bedside* table.— **bed·side man·ner,** the attitude and approach of the physician toward his patient.

bed·sore, bed′sōr″, bed′sạr, *n.* A sore liable to occur on bedridden persons on the parts of the body subjected to most pressure.—*a.* Afflicted with skin irritation caused by prolonged illness in bed.

bed·spread, bed′spred″, *n.* An outer bedcover, usually decorative.

bed·spring, bed′spring″, *n.* A spring for the support of the mattress on a bed.

bed·stead, bed′sted″, bed′stid, *n.* A framework to support a bed.

bed·straw, bed′strạ, *n.* [< its former use as mattress stuffing.] A herbaceous perennial plant, genus *Galium,* formerly used as mattress stuffing.

bed·tick, bed′tik″, *n.* A tick or stout linen or cotton bag containing the feathers or other mattress material of a bed.

bed·time, bed′tīm, *n.* The time to go to bed; the usual hour of retiring to rest.

bee, bē, *n.* [O.E. *bēo,* akin to G. *biene,* bee.] Any of various hymenopterous insects of the genus *Apis,* esp. *A. mellifica* (the common honey-bee), producing honey and wax, and forming highly organized colonies; any of various similar (social or solitary) insects of other genera; a figure or representation of a bee (used as a decorative emblem by Napoleon); *chiefly U.S.* a social gathering for joint work or amusement; as, a husking *bee.*—**a bee in one's bon·net,** a

craze, mad notion, nagging awareness, or tormenting desire for something.

bee·balm, bē′bäm″, *n.* The perennial North American mint, *Monarda didyma.* Also *Oswego Tea.*

bee·bread, bē′bred″, *n.* A bitter brownish substance, consisting of pollen, or pollen and honey, stored up by bees as food for their young.

beech, bēch, *n.* [O.E. *bēce,* also *bōc* (cf. *buckwheat*), akin to G. *buche* and L. *fagus,* beech, Gr. *phēgos,* oak.] Any tree of the genus *Fagus,* of temperate regions, having a smooth gray bark, and bearing small edible triangular nuts. The wood of such a tree; also **beech·wood.** Any of various similar trees.

beech·drops, bēch′drops″, *n., sing. or pl. in constr.* An annual plant, *Epifagus virginiana,* which belongs to the broomrape family, lacks green foliage, and is parasitic on the roots of the beech.

bee-eat·er, bē′ē″tẻr, *n.* Any member of the family *Meropidae,* comprising Old World, insectivorous birds with a long, slender bill, a swallowlike flight, and brilliant plumage.

beef, bēf, *n. pl.* **beefs, beeves,** bēvz. [O.Fr. *boef,* < L. *bos* (*bov-*), akin to Gr. *boûs,* Skt. *go,* bull or cow, O.E. *cū,* E. *cow.*] Any animal, esp. an adult, of the genus *Bos,* whether a steer, bull, or cow; the flesh of such an animal used as food. *Colloq.* brawn or muscularity; strength; flesh of a human; a person's weight. *Slang,* a complaint.—*v.i. Slang.* To complain; protest.—**beef up,** to add vigor or strength to; reinforce; as, to *beef up* an army before battle.

beef cat·tle, *n.* Cattle reared especially for table meat, distinguished by quick growth and solid build.

beef·eat·er, bēf′ē″tẻr, *n.* An eater of beef; a yeoman of the royal guard of England, a body of men who attend the sovereign at state banquets and on other occasions; a similarly attired guard at the Tower of London. *Slang,* any Englishman; any person who is well fed.

bee fly, *n. pl.* **bee flies.** A fly which more or less resembles a bee, esp. a fly of the family *Bombyliidae.*

beef·steak, bēf′stāk″, *n.* A steak or slice of hindquarter of beef for broiling.

beef·steak fun·gus, *n.* A scarlet mass of edible spore fungus, *Fistulina hepatica,* found growing on dead trees. Also **beef·steak mush·room.**

beef·wood, bēf′wụd, *n.* Any of several hard, reddish woods used chiefly in making furniture; any of various common Australian trees of the genus *Casuarina,* yielding this wood.

beef·y, bē′fē, *a.*—*beefier, beefiest.* Fleshy; brawny; solid; heavy; of or similar to beef.

bee gum, *n. Southern and western U.S.* A gum tree, hollowed as by decay, in which bees live or from which hives are made; hence, a beehive.

bee·hive, bē′hīv″, *n.* A hive or receptacle, usu. dome-shaped, serving as a habitation for bees; a natural habitat for bees; any busy, crowded location.—*a.* Similar to an artificial beehive; as, a *beehive* hat or hairdo.

bee·keep·er, bē′kē″pẻr, *n.* A person who raises bees as a means of livelihood.

bee kill·er, *n.* Any of the large, voracious, insectivorous dipterous flies constituting the family *Asilidae,* which attack honeybees on the wing and kill them; robber fly.

bee·line, bē′līn″, *n.* The direct line or shortest distance between two places.— **make a bee·line for,** hurry directly to.

Be·el·ze·bub, bē·el′ze·bub″, *n.* [Heb. *baal = zebub,* lit. lord of the flies, and *zebub,* a fly.] A god of the Philistines; in the New Testament, the prince of devils; Satan; in *Paradise Lost* by Milton, a fallen angel who ranks second only to Satan.

bee plant, *n.* Any plant which is especially useful in furnishing nectar to bees, as several species of clover, genus *Trifolium,* or the figwort, genus *Scrophularia.*

beer, bēr, *n.* [O.E. *bēor* = G. *bier.*] An alcoholic beverage made by fermentation from cereals, usually malted barley, and flavored with hops, etc., in a broad sense including ale, but in a restricted sense distinguished from ale as being of lighter alcoholic content; a serving of beer, in glass, can, or bottle. Any of various beverages made from roots, molasses, sugar, or yeast, etc.—**beer gar·den,** a garden or place where beer is sold and served at tables.

beer·y, bēr′ē, *a.*—*beerier, beeriest.* Of, like, or abounding in beer; affected by or suggestive of beer.

beest·ings, bē′stingz, *n. pl. but sing. in constr.* [O.E. *bȳsting,* < *bēost,* beestings.] The first milk given by a mammal, esp. a cow, after parturition. Also **beast·ings.**

bees·wax, bēz′waks, *n.* The wax secreted by bees, of which they construct their honeycomb.—*v.t.* To rub, polish, or treat with beeswax.

beet, bēt, *n.* [O.E. *bēte,* < L. *beta.*] Any of various biennial plants of the genus *Beta,* whose varieties include the common red beet, *B. vulgaris,* which has a thick, fleshy edible root, and the sugar-beet, *B. saccharifera;* the root of this plant; the leaves of the plant used in a salad or as a cooked vegetable.

bee·tle, bēt′l, *n.* [O.E. *bitula,* < *bītan,* bite.] Any insect of the order *Coleoptera,* with hard outer wing covers meeting in a straight line down the back, as the Colorado *beetle,* the potato *beetle;* popularly, any of various insects more or less resembling a beetle.

bee·tle, bēt′l, *n.* [O.E. *bīetel,* < *bēatan,* beat.] A heavy hammering or ramming instrument, usually of wood, used to drive wedges, force down paving stones, consolidate earth, etc.; a mallet for mashing or pounding; a machine which gives fabrics a gleaming finish.—*v.t.*—*beetled, beetling.*

bee·tle, bēt′l, *v.i.*—*beetled, beetling.* [M.E. *bitel,* sharp, hence prominent, < O.E. *bitan,* to bite.] To be prominent, as a cliff or battlement; to hang or extend out in a threatening manner; to overhang; to jut.— *a.*—**bee·tle-browed,** bēt′l-broud″, *a.* Having prominent brows; frowning; sullen.

beet leaf·hop·per, *n.* A destructive insect, *Circulifer tenellus,* that transmits a virus disease to sugar beets and other crops and ornamental plants in the western U.S.

bee tree, *n.* The basswood or American linden, *Tilia americana,* whose flowers are rich in honey; a hollow tree occupied by bees.

be·fall, bi·fạl′, *v.t.*—past *befell,* pp. *befallen,* ppr. *befalling.* [O.E. *befeallan.*] To happen to; to occur to.—*v.i.* To happen for no discernible reason; to come to pass.

be·fit, bi·fit′, *v.t.*—*befitted, befitting.* To be fitting for; to be appropriate for; to suit; to be suitable or proper to.—**be·fit·ting,** *a.*

be·fog, bi·fog′, bi·fạg′, *v.t.*—*befogged, befogging.* To obscure in fog; hence, to confuse; to becloud.

be·fool, bi·fōl′, *v.t.* To fool; to deceive; to make a fool of; to delude or lead into error.

be·fore, bi·fōr′, bi·fạr′, *adv.* [O.E. *beforan.*] In front; in advance; ahead. In time preceding; previously; prior to; earlier or sooner.

be·fore, bi·fōr′, bi·fạr′, *prep.* In front of; in advance of; ahead of; at a time preceding that of; previous to; earlier than; in precedence of, as in order or rank; in preference to; rather than; under order of; confronted by; under the influence of; in the presence or sight of.—**be·fore the mast,** *naut.* as a common sailor (the crew of a ship being berthed forward of the foremast).—**be·fore the wind**, *naut.* in the direction in which the wind blows; hence, *fig.* in prosperous circumstances; out of debt or difficulty.

be·fore, bi·fōr′, bi·fạr′, *conj.* Previous to the time when, as: I will phone *before* we leave. Sooner than; rather than.

be·fore·hand, bi·fōr′hand″, bi·fạr′hand″, *adv.* In advance; at a time prior to.

be·foul, bi·foul′, *v.t.* To make foul; sully; to soil.

be·friend, bi·frend′, *v.t.* To act as a friend to; to make friends with; to aid, benefit, or assist.

be·fud·dle, bi·fud′l, *v.t.*—*befuddled, befuddling.* To fuddle, or render stupid with intoxicating liquor; bemuse with drink; to confuse.

beg, beg, *v.t.*—*begged, begging.* [Norm. Fr. *begger.* BEGGAR.] To ask or supplicate in charity; to ask for earnestly (alms); to ask earnestly (a person); to beseech; to implore; to entreat or supplicate with humility; to take for granted; to assume without proof; to avoid or evade.—*v.i.* To ask alms or charity; to live by asking alms.—**beg off**, to avoid the performance of one's duty.—**beg the ques·tion**, to use an argument that assumes as true the subject under discussion.—**go beg·ging**, to remain unused, unaccepted, or unsold, as: Tickets for the event *went begging*, due to lack of interest.

be·get, bi·get′, *v.t.*—*past begot* or archaic *begat*, pp. *begotten* or *begot*, ppr. *begetting*. [O.E. *begitan, bigitan.*] To procreate, as a father or sire; to produce, as an effect; to cause to exist; to generate.—**be·get·ter**, bē·get′ẻr, *n.*

beg·gar, beg′ẻr, *n.* [Apparently < O.Fr. *begard*, Beghard, a name said to have been assumed by numerous mendicants in the 13th century.] One who begs alms, or lives by begging; a mendicant; a penniless person; a wretch or rogue (often playfully). —**beg·gar·dom, beg·gar·hood,** *n.* The class or fraternity of beggars.

beg·gar, beg′ẻr, *v.t.* To reduce to begging; impoverish; hence, to exhaust the resources of; as, to *beggar* description; to deprive wholly (*of*).

beg·gar·ly, beg′ẻr·lē, *a.* Like or befitting a beggar; wretchedly poor; inadequate, as: He contributed a *beggarly* five dollars.

beg·gar's-lice, beg′ẻrz·līs″, *n. pl.* The burrs or prickly or adhesive fruit of various plants, so called because they stick to the clothing; *sing.* any of these plants. Also **beg·gar-lice**, beg′ẻr·līs″.

be·gin, bi·gin′, *v.i.*—*past began*, pp. *begun*, ppr. *beginning*. [O.E. *beginnan*, to begin—prefix *be*, and *ginnan*, to begin.] To take rise; to originate; to commence; to do the first act; to enter upon something new; to start one's existence; to take the first step.—*v.t.* To do the first act of; to enter on; to commence.—**be·gin·ner**, bi·gin′ẻr, *n.* A person who begins or originates; the agent who is the cause; one who first enters upon any art, science, or business; a young practitioner; a novice; a tyro.

be·gin·ning, bi·gin′ing, *n.* The first cause; origin; the first state; commencement; entrance into being; that from which a greater thing proceeds or grows.—**be·gin·nings**, bi·gin′ingz, *n. pl.* Origin; initial stage.

be·gone, bi·gạn′, *v.i.* [< *be gone*.] Be gone; go away; depart: used interjectionally, as an imperative, and hence sometimes for other verb forms, as: He charged them to *begone*.

be·go·ni·a, bi·gōn′ya, bi·gō′nē·a, *n.* [N.L., *Begonia*, named after M. *Bégon*, French patron of science.] Any plant of the tropical genus *Begonia*, including species much cultivated for their handsome, often varicolored leaves and waxy flowers.

be·grime, bi·grīm′, *v.t.*—*begrimed, begriming.* To dirty; to make grimy.

be·grudge, bi·gruj′, *v.t.*—*begrudged, begrudging.* To grudge; be reluctant to give, concede, grant, or allow (something); to resent the good fortune or pleasure of; to have or take little or no pleasure in.

be·guile, bi·gīl′, *v.t.*—*beguiled, beguiling.* To practice guile upon; to delude; to deceive; to cheat; to trick; to dupe; to impose on by artifice or craft; to dispel or render unfelt by diverting the mind (cares); to while away (time).—**be·guile·ment**, bi·gīl′mẹnt, *n.* The act or state of beguiling. —**be·guil·er**, bi·gīl′ẻr, *n.*

be·guine, bi·gēn′, *n.* [< West Indian Fr. *béguin*, flirtation.] A social dance based on vigorous Latin American music: in South America, a bolero tempo, in Santa Lucia and Martinique, similar to the rumba.

be·gum, bē′gum, *n.* [Urdu, *begam*.] In India, a Muslim lady of high social status.

be·half, bi·haf′, bi·häf′, *n.* Interest; profit; support; defense; often in such phrases as in or on *behalf* of, in my, his, some person's *behalf*.

be·have, bi·hāv′, *v.t.*—*behaved, behaving.* To conduct, as oneself, properly.—*v.i.* To act in a certain manner; to conduct oneself in conformity with proper, acceptable standards.

be·hav·ior, *Brit.* **be·hav·iour**, bi·hāv′yẻr, *n.* Manner of behaving or acting; conduct; deportment; mode or course of action; sometimes, proper deportment. *Psychol.* the aggregate of observable actions or activities of the individual as matter for psychological study; see *behaviorism.*—**be·hav·ior·al**, *a.*—**be·hav·ior·al·ly**, *adv.*

be·hav·ior·al sci·ence, *n.* Any of the sciences which deal with observation of the behavior and habits of man and the lower animals in various physical and social environments, including psychology, sociology, and social anthropology.

be·hav·ior·ism, bi·hāv′yo·riz″um, *n.* *Psychol.* a theory or method of psychological procedure that regards objective facts of behavior or activity, in the broadest sense, of both man and animals, as the proper matter for study.—**be·hav·ior·ist**, bi·hāv′yo·rist, *n.* An advocate of behaviorism; one who follows the method of behaviorism. —**be·hav·ior·is·tic**, bi·hāv″yo·rist′ik, *a.* Pertaining to behaviorist or behaviorism. —**be·hav·ior·is·ti·cal·ly**, *adv.*

be·head, bi·hed′, *v.t.* [M.E. *bihefden* < *be-* priv. and O.E. *hēafod*, head.] To cut off the head of; decapitate; execute (a condemned person) by decapitation.—**be·head·al**, bi·hed′l, *n.* Beheading; execution by beheading.

be·he·moth, bi·hē′moth, bē′e·moth, *n.* [Heb.] An animal described in Job xl. 15–24, and which some suppose to be an elephant, a hippopotamus, or a crocodile; *colloq.* any huge or grotesque animal or thing.

be·hest, bi·hest′, *n.* [O.E. *behaes*, promise.] A command; an urgent request.

be·hind, bi·hīnd′, *prep.* [O.E. *behindan*, behind.] On the side opposite the front or nearest part of, or opposite to that which fronts a person; at the back of; in support of; toward the back or back part of; remaining after; later in point of time than; beyond; farther back than; in the position of making less progress than; in an inferior position to.

be·hind, bi·hīnd′, *adv.* At the back; in or toward the rear; out of sight; not exhibited; remaining; toward the back part; backward; slow; remaining after one's departure.

be·hind, bi·hīnd′, *n.* The backside (as of a person); *slang*, buttocks.

be·hind·hand, bi·hīnd′hand″, *adv., a.* In a state in which means are not adequate to the supply of wants; in arrear; in a state of

being behind the times; not sufficiently advanced; not equally advanced with another; tardy.

be·hind the eight ball, *advbl. phr. Slang.* In a losing or unlucky position; in a situation that one cannot resolve successfully.

be·hold, bi·hōld′, *v.t.*—*beheld, beholding.* [O.E. *behealdan*—prefix *be*, and *healdan*, to hold.] To look at with attention; to observe; to see.—*v.i.* To look, in this sense chiefly in the imperative, and used interjectionally to call attention.—**be·hold·er**, *n.*

be·hold·en, bi·hōl′dn, *a.* Held or bound by obligation; indebted; obligated.

be·hoof, bi·hōf′, *n. pl.* **be·hooves**, bi·hōvz′. [O.E. *behóf* = D. *behoef*, G. *behuf*.] That which is advantageous to a person; behalf; benefit: always in such phrases as in *behoof* of.

be·hoove, *Brit.* **be·hove**, bi·hōv′, bi·hōv′, *v.t.*—*behooved, behooving.* [O.E. *behófian*, from the noun.] To be fit or meet for, with respect to necessity, duty, or convenience; to be worthwhile; to be necessary for: used impersonally, as: It *behooves* us.—*v.i.* To be proper, necessary, or fit.

beige, bāzh, *n.* [Fr. *beige*, O.Fr. *bege*, neutral color.] A light brownish-gray color like that of unbleached, undyed wool.—*a.*

be·ing, bē′ing, *n.* Existence, whether real or only in the mind; essence; life; that which has life; a person; a creature.

be·jew·el, bi·jō′el, *v.t.*—*bejeweled, bejeweling, bejewelled, bejewelling.* To adorn with or as with jewels.

bel, bel, *n.* [After A. G. *Bell*, American scientist and inventor.] *Radio, teleph., acoustics*, a unit of measurement of power ratios; a unit equivalent to 10 decibels.

be·la·bor, *Brit.* **be·la·bour**, bi·lā′bẻr, *v.t.* To beat soundly; to deal blows to; to argue (an issue) for an unnecessary length of time.

be·lat·ed, bi·lā′ted, *a.* Being subsequent to the appointed time; detained; delayed.— **be·lat·ed·ly**, bi·lā′ted·lē, *adv.*—**be·lat·ed·ness**, bi·lā′ted·nes, *n.*

be·lay, bi·lā′, *v.t.*—*belayed, belaying.* [M.E. *beleggen* < O.E. *belecgan.*] *Naut.* to fasten, as a rope, by winding around a pin or the like. —*n.* In mountain climbing, any rock, shrub, or imbedded pick secure enough to serve as a hold for a rope.—**be·lay there!**, *naut.* make fast the rope; *fig.* stop!

be·lay·ing pin, *n. Naut.* a small, rounded piece of metal or wood fitted into a pin rail for use in belaying a rope and for securing any running gear.

bel can·to, bel′ kan′tō, *It.* bel kän′tạ, *n.* [It. lit., '*fine singing*.'] Singing of a type originating with 17th and 18th century Italian opera singers, marked by pure, rich, even tones and vocal agility.

belch, belch, *v.t.* [O.E. *bealcian*, to belch.] To throw out or eject with violence, as from the stomach through the mouth, or from a deep hollow place; to cast forth (a volcano *belches* flames or ashes).—*v.i.* To involuntarily eject wind from the stomach in a noisy manner; to issue out in a violent spasm, as with eructation.—*n.* The act of one who or that which belches; eructation; a violent eruption of smoke, flame, or gas.

bel·dam, bel·dame, bel′dam, bel′dãm, *n.* [Fr. *belle*, fine, handsome, and *dame*, lady.] It was at one time applied respectfully to elderly females.] An old woman in general, especially an ugly old woman; a hag.

be·lea·guer, bi·lē′gẻr, *v.t.* [D. *belegeren*.] To besiege; to surround with an army so as to preclude escape; to blockade; to harass.

bel·fry, bel′frē, *n. pl.* **bel·fries**. [O.Fr. *berfrei, berfroi* < Teut., = M.H.G. *bercvrit*, O.H.G. *bergan*, protect, and *fridu*, peace, shelter.] A bell tower, generally one attached to a church or other building; that part of a steeple or other structure in which a bell is hung; a wooden tower, generally movable, used in medieval siege operations as a shelter for troops and as an engine of attack; *slang*, the head, or the intelligence.

Bel·gian, bel′jan, bel′jē·an, *a.* [L. *Belgium,* country of the Belgæ. BELGIC.] Of or pertaining to Belgium, a small country of Europe, bordering on France, Germany, and Holland, formerly part of the Netherlands but established as an independent kingdom in 1830.—*n.* A native or inhabitant of Belgium; a breed of very large, powerful, often chestnut-colored horses.—**Bel·gian mar·ble,** a dull-red marble marked with blue and white, obtained from Belgium.

Bel·gian hare, *n.* One of a breed of domestic rabbits of dark red or mahogany color notable for its large size.

Bel·gian sheep·dog, *n.* A hardy sheepherding dog developed in Belgium, generally black or gray in color. Also *Groenendael.*

Bel·gic, bel′jik, *a.* [L. *Belgicus,* < *Belgæ.*] Of or pertaining to the Belgæ, an ancient warlike people of northern Gaul, probably of mixed Celtic and Teutonic stock; of or pertaining to Belgium; Belgian.

Bel·gra·vi·an, bel·grā′vē·an, *a.* Belonging to Belgravia, an aristocratic portion of London; aristocratic; fashionable.—*n.* An inhabitant of Belgravia; a member of the newly rich.

Be·lial, bē′lē·al, bēl′yal, *n.* [Heb. *b'liya'al,* worthlessness.] The spirit of evil personified; the devil; Satan; in Milton's *Paradise Lost,* one of the fallen angels.

be·lie, bi·lī′, *v.t.*—**belied, belying.** [O.E. *beléogan.*] To report falsely; to distort the truth of; to contradict, as: Calm bearing *belied* his fear.—**be·li·er,** bi·lī′ėr, *n.*

be·lief, bi·lēf′, *n.* An assent of the mind to the truth of a declaration, proposition, or alleged fact, on the ground of evidence, distinct from personal knowledge; faith, or a firm persuasion of the truths of religious tenets; the thing believed; the object of belief; the body of tenets held by the professors of any faith; a creed; confidence; as, *belief* in the future.

be·liev·a·ble, bi·lēv′a·bl, *a.* Capable of being believed; credible.—**be·liev·a·bly,** bi·lēv′a·blē, *adv.*

be·lieve, bi·lēv′, *v.i.*—**believed, believing.** [Middle Eng. *beliven,* for O.E. *geliefan* = G. *glauben,* believe: cf. *belief.*] To be convinced of the truth, dependability, or existence of something without demonstrable evidence; to have confidence (*in*); trust, rely on through faith.—*v.t.* To have belief in; credit; accept on the basis of credibility.—**be·liev·er,** bi·lēv′ėr, *n.* One who believes; an adherent of some religious faith.—**be·liev·ing·ly,** bi·lē′ving·lē″, *adv.*

be·lit·tle, bi·lit′l, *v.t.*—**belittled, belittling.** To make little or less important; decry; depreciate; disparage.—**be·lit·tle·ment,** bi·lit′l·ment, *n.*—**be·lit·tler,** bi·lit′lėr, *n.*

bell, bel, *n.* [M.E. *belle* < O.E. *bellan,* to roar.] A hollow metallic object, generally cup-shaped, which gives forth a clear, musical, ringing sound on being struck; the tones made by this instrument; anything in the form of a bell; the large open end of a funnel or musical wind instrument; a percussion instrument with metal bars or tubes, a glockenspiel, which gives forth bell-like sounds when played with hammers. The corolla of a flower; the body of a jellyfish; *arch.* the underlying section of the capital of a foliated column; *naut.* a unit of nautical time, which is measured in half-hour units over a four-hour period and indicated by a stroke of a ship's bell for each unit.—**ring a bell,** to remind one of something; recall something to one's mind; jog one's memory.

bell, bel, *v.t.* To put a bell on; to affix a bell to.

bell, bel, *v.i.* [O.E. *bellan,* Icel. *belja,* to bellow. BELLOW.] To roar; to bellow, as a deer in rutting-time; to take the shape of a bell; *bot.* to produce bell-shaped flowers.

bel·la·don·na, bel″a·don′a, *n.* [It. 'fair lady.'] A poisonous plant, *Atropa belladonna,* from the leaves and root of which atropine is derived. Also **dead·ly night·shade.**

bel·la·don·na lil·y, *n.* An African bulbous plant, *Amaryllis belladonna,* with a heavy fragrance and tremendous flowers, either white or rose colored.

bell·bird, bel′bŭrd″, *n.* A name for various birds of the southern hemisphere whose notes resemble the sound of a bell.

bell·boy, bel′boi″, *n.* In a hotel, an employee (usually uniformed) who serves guests by escorting them to their rooms, carrying luggage, bringing beverages, or running errands. Also *bellman.*

bell buoy, bel bō′ē, bel boi, *n.* A buoy on which is fixed a bell, which rings as a warning to approaching boats.

belle, bel, *n.* [Fr. fem. of *beau.*] A woman or girl who is especially admired for her beauty; a recognized or reigning beauty.

belles let·tres, bel·le′tra, *n. pl.* [Fr. lit. 'fine letters.'] Polite or elegant literature, a term including rhetoric, poetry, history, criticism, and the languages in which the literature is written.

bell·flow·er, bel′flou″ėr, *n.* A common name of plants of the genus *Campanula,* from the shape of the flower.

bell glass, *n.* A bell-shaped glass vessel or cover, for protecting delicate instruments or bric-à-brac, or for holding gases in chemical operations. Also *bell jar.*

bell·hop, bel′hop″, *n.* A bellboy.

bel·li·cose, bel′i·kōs″, *a.* [L. *bellicosus,* < *bellum,* war.] Inclined to war; warlike; hostile; pugnacious.—**bel·li·cose·ly,** *adv.*—**bel·li·cos·i·ty,** bel″i·kos′i·tē, *n.*

bel·lied, bel′ēd, *a.* Having a belly, used in combination; as, big-*bellied.*

bel·lig·er·ence, be·lij′ėr·ens, *n.* The act of carrying on war; warfare; warlike nature.

bel·lig·er·en·cy, be·lij′ėr·en·sē, *n.* The state of being involved in a war as a legally recognized belligerent.

bel·lig·er·ent, be·lij′ėr·ent, *a.* [Fr. *belligerant,* < L. *belligerans* (-ant-), ppr. of *belligerare,* wage war, < *bellum,* war, and *gerere,* bear, wage.] Waging war; warlike; actively hostile; bellicose; pertaining to belligerents.—*n.* A nation, power, or person engaged in war; a combatant.—**bel·lig·er·ent·ly,** be·lij′ėr·ent·lē, *adv.*

bell jar, *n.* See *bell glass.*

bell·man, bel′man, *n.* pl. **bell·men,** bel′men. A man who carries or rings a bell, esp. a town crier or watchman; bellboy.

bell met·al, *n.* A variety of bronze; an alloy of about 80 percent copper and about 20 percent tin, of which bells are made.

bell·mouthed, bel′mouᵺd″, bel′mouᵀᴴt″, *a.* Flaring at the mouth in the form of a bell.

bel·low, bel′ō, *v.i., v.t.* [O.E. *bylgean.*] To cry as a bull, cow, or deer; roar; shout; bawl.—*n.* The act or sound of bellowing.—**bel·low·er,** bel′ō·ėr, *n.*

bel·lows, bel′ōz, bel′as, *n. pl., sing. or pl. in constr.* [Origin. pl. < O.E. *belg,* bag (*blǣst-belg,* 'blast-bag,' bellows).] An instrument or machine for producing a strong current of air, as for blowing a fire or sounding a musical instrument, consisting essentially of an air-chamber which can be alternately expanded to draw in air through a valve and contracted to expel the air through a tube; anything resembling or suggesting this, as the expansile part of a photographic camera; the lungs.

bell pep·per, *n.* The bell-shaped fruit of a variety of sweet pepper, *Capsicum frutescens,* used for pickling and as a vegetable.

bell pull, *n.* A handle, cord, or cloth pull used to sound a doorbell, call servants, etc.

bell·weth·er, bel′weth″ėr, *n.* A wether or sheep which leads the flock, with a bell on his neck; one who takes the lead; a trend indicator.

bell·wort, bel′wŭrt, *n.* Bellflower; a plant of the genus *Uvularia,* bearing a delicate, slenderly bell-shaped, yellow flower.

bel·ly, bel′ē, *n. pl.* **bel·lies.** [O.E. *boelg, belg, boelig,* bag = Icel. *belgr,* D. *balg,* Dan. *boelg,* G. *balg,* the belly; akin to *bulge*; comp. Gael. and Ir. *bolg, balg,* the belly, a bag, bellows. *Bellows* is a plural form of this word.] That part of the human body which extends from the breast to the thighs, containing the bowels; the abdomen; the womb; any bulging surface; the corresponding part of other animals; the section of a muscle which is fleshy; the part of anything which resembles the human belly in protuberance or cavity; *music,* the bulging part of an instrument such as the violin.

bel·ly, bel′ē, *v.t.*—**bellied, bellying.** To fill; to swell out.—*v.i.* To swell and become protuberant like the belly.

bel·ly·ache, bel′ē·āk″, *n.* Pain in the abdomen.—*v.i.*—**bellyached, bellyaching.** *Slang.* To complain; to grumble.

bel·ly·band, bel′ē·band″, *n.* A band that goes round the belly of a horse as part of its harness; girth. *Naut.* a piece of canvas attached to a sail as a reinforcement.

bel·ly·but·ton, bel′ē·but″on, *n. Colloq.* navel.

bel·ly-land·ing, bel′ē·land″ing, *n.* The landing of an airplane on its fuselage without benefit of landing gear.—**bel·ly-land,** bel′ē·land″, *v.i., v.t.*

bel·ly laugh, *n.* A loud, boisterous, and uninhibited laugh.

be·long, bi·lang′, bi·long′, *v.i.* [Prefix *be,* and O.E. *long,* to belong (to extend in length to), from the adjective *long*; akin. D. and G. *belangen,* to concern, from *lang,* long.] To be the property of; to appertain; to be the concern or affair; to be appendant or connected; to be suitable; to possess certain qualifications; to be due; to have a settled residence; to be domiciled; to be a native of a place; to have original residence: in all senses often followed by *to, in,* or *among.*

be·long·ing, bi·lang′ing, bi·long′ing, *n.* That which belongs to one, used generally in plural: qualities, endowments, property, possessions, appendages.

Be·lo·rus·sian, byel″a·rush′an, bel″a·rush′an, *n.* A native of the western region of the U.S.S.R.; a White Russian; the Slavic language of the Belorussians. Also **Bie·lo·rus·sian, Bye·lo·rus·sian.**

be·loved, bi·luv′id, bi·luvd′, *a.* Loved; greatly loved; dear to the heart.—*n.* One who is greatly loved.

be·low, bi·lō′, *prep.* Under in place; beneath; not so high as; inferior to in rank or excellence.

be·low, bi·lō′, *adv.* In a lower place, with respect to any object; on a lower level; beneath; in a lower or inferior position on the earth, as opposed to the heavens; in hell, or the regions of the dead; further down on a page or on the following page; in a court of inferior jurisdiction. *Theatr.* downstage.

be·low, bi·lō′, *n.* That which is placed lower or follows, as on a page, as: Check the *below.*—*a.* Placed lower on a page or subsequent page.

be·low par, *a. Stock market,* priced below the face value, as a security. Of inferior quality.

be·low the line, *a., adv. Accounting,* showing a nonrecurring or extraordinary item of income or expense in an income statement; *bridge,* in scoring, denoting points earned toward game, other points including honors and sets being shown above the line.

belt, belt, *n.* [O.E., *belt* = Dan. *bælte,* Icel. *belti,* a belt, a girdle, from L. *balteus,* a belt. Akin Ir. and Gael. *balt,* a border, a welt.]

A girdle; a band, usually of leather, worn around the waist to support a skirt or trousers; anything resembling a belt; a strip; a stripe; a band; a band passing around two wheels, and communicating motion from one to the other; an area having certain homogeneous characteristics; as, the corn belt.—**be·low the belt**, unfairly.—**belt·ed**, *a.*

belt, belt, *n. Slang*, a blow, esp. a punch struck with clenched fist.—*v.t. Slang*, to beat severely.

belt, belt, *v.t.* To encircle; to surround as with a belt; to furnish with a belt; to fasten with a belt; to strike or whip with a belt.

Bel·tane, bel'tān, *n.* [Gael. and Ir.] May 1 in the ancient Scottish calendar; May Day; an ancient Celtic festival celebrated with bonfires, in Scotland on May Day, in Ireland on June 21.

belt·ing, belt'ing, *n.* Belts taken generally; the material of which the belts are made; *slang*, a beating.

belt line rail·road, *n.* A railroad shuttle system surrounding a main terminal point and engaged in transporting cars between train lines.

Belts·ville Small White, belts'vil smạl hwit, *n.* A small white turkey developed by the Department of Agriculture in Beltsville, Maryland.

belt·way, belt'wā, *n.* A highway that bypasses a city or congested area by going around it; also **belt·line**.

be·lu·ga, be·lō′ga, *n.* [Rus. *bieluga*, from *bielyi*, white.] A white sturgeon, *Acipenser huso*, of the Black and Caspian seas, a source of caviar; a dolphin, *Delphinapterus leucas*, of arctic waters, white when adult.

bel·ve·dere, bel′vi·dēr′, bel″vi·dēr′, *n.* [It., lit. 'a beautiful view'—*bello, bel*, beautiful, and *vedere*, to see.] A building, or an open structure on the top of a building, with a commanding view; *Canadian*, a scenic lookout along a highway; (*cap.*) a palace used as an art gallery in Rome. A cigar, similar to the corona.

be·ma, bē′ma, *n. pl.* **be·ma·ta**, bē′ma·ta. [Gr. *bema*, < *bainein*, go.] *Eastern Ch.* The enclosed space surrounding the altar; the sanctuary or chancel. *Judaism*, the dais from which services are conducted.

be·mire, bi·mīr′, *v.t.—bemired, bemiring.* To drag or stall in the mire; to soil, as by passing through mud; to sink in mud.

be·moan, bi·mōn′, *v.t.* To moan or mourn for; to lament; to bewail; to express sorrow for.—*v.i.* To mourn.

be·mock, bi·mok′, *v.t.* To mock; to jeer at; deride; delude mockingly.

be·mud·dle, bi·mud′l, *v.t.—bemuddled, bemuddling.* To muddle; to confuse.

be·muse, bi·mūz′, *v.t.—bemused, bemusing.* To confuse or stupefy, as with drink; to bemuddle; bewilder.

be·mused, bi·mūzd′, *a.* Engrossed; sunk in reverie; muddled; preoccupied; stupefied.—**be·mus·ed·ly**, *adv.*

ben, ben, *n.* A tree of India, *Moringa oleifera*, having seeds or nuts that yield a fine lubricating oil, oil of ben, used in making cosmetics and fine lubricating oils; the seed of the tree.

bench, bench, *n.* [O.E. *benc*; from a Teut. source whence also E. *bank.*] A long seat, as for several persons; the seat on which judges sit in court; the office or dignity of a judge; a court of justice; the body of persons sitting as judges; a seat occupied by persons in their official capacity, the office or dignity of those occupying it, or the persons themselves; as, the episcopal *bench*; the work table of a carpenter or other mechanic; a platform on which animals are placed for exhibition, as at a dog-show; *geol.* a raised, level tract of land, as between a river and

hills; *sports*, the strength and number of substitutes on a team.

bench, bench, *v.t.* To furnish with benches; to seat or place on a bench. To show; put on exhibition; *sports*, to prevent, as someone, from participating in a team game; *min.* to excavate or work, as a mine or quarry, by cutting away in benches.—*v.i.* To form a bench, as soil.

bench·er, ben′chẽr, *n. Brit.* One who sits on a bench, as a magistrate, a senior member of the bar, or a member of Parliament.

bench mark, *n. Surv.* a mark cut into some durable material, as stone, to serve as a guide in a line of levels for the determination of altitudes over any region.

bench pen·al·ty, *n. Hockey*, a penalty against a team for a minor infraction, requiring the removal of one of its players from the ice for two minutes. Also **bench mi·nor.**

bench show, *n.* An exhibition of animals, as dogs, arranged on benches, where awards are made for physical merits.

bench war·rant, *n. Law*, a warrant issued by a presiding judge or a court against a person charged with some offense.

bend, bend, *v.t.—bent* or archaic *bended, bending.* [O.E. *bendan*, bind, bend (a bow) = Icel. *benda*, bend; from the same Teut. source as E. *bend.*] To strain, as a bow, into a state of tension; render curved or angular; flex; crook; force into a different or particular shape, as by pressure; cause to bow or yield; as, to *bend* a man to one's will; bow the head; turn in a particular direction; incline; direct or apply, as the mind or efforts; to fasten; *in the passive*, to be determined or resolved (usually with *on*); *naut.* to fasten.—*v.i.* To become curved, crooked, or bent; stoop, or assume a bent posture; bow in submission or reverence; yield or submit; turn or incline in a particular direction; be directed; direct one's energies; as, to *bend* to a task.

bend, bend, *n.* A bending, or a bent condition; an inclination of the body; a turning in a particular direction; inclination; a bent thing or part; a curve or flexure; a crook; *pl., naut.* the wales of a ship.

bend, bend, *n.* [M.E. < O.E. *bend*, band and M.E. *bende*, band.] The half of a trimmed hide of sole-leather; *her.* a diagonal band; *naut.* a knot by which a rope is fastened to another rope or to something else.

Ben Day proc·ess, ben′dā′, *n.* [From Ben Day (1838–1916) New York printer.] *Print.* a photoengraving technique for reproducing gradations and tones in an illustration by applying a fine pattern of dots, stipples, or other markings to original negatives or plates. Also **Ben·day proc·ess.**

bend dex·ter, *n. Her.* the regular bend on an escutcheon which extends diagonally from dexter chief to sinister base.

bend·er, ben′dẽr, *n.* One who or that which bends, as a pair of pliers; *Brit. slang*, a sixpence; *U.S. slang*, a drinking spree.

bends, bendz, *n. pl. Colloq.* Pains in the extremities, abdomen, and chest caused by aeroemphysema and in some instances by aeroembolism resulting from the reduction of ambient air pressure; caisson disease.

bend si·nis·ter, *n. Her.* a diagonal band extending from the sinister chief to the dexter base.

be·neath, bi·nēth′, *prep.* [O.E. *beneoth, beneothan*—prefix *be*, and *neothan*, below. NETHER.] Under; lower in place than something which rests above; lower than in rank, dignity, or excellence; below the level of; subject to the control or dictates of.

be·neath, bi·nēth′, *adv.* In or to a lower place; below; underneath.

ben·e·dict, ben′i·dikt, *n.* A sportive name for a newly married man, especially one who has long been a bachelor: from one of the

characters in Shakespeare's *Much Ado About Nothing.* Also **ben·e·dick**, ben′i·dik.

Ben·e·dic·tine, ben″i·dik′tēn, *a.* Pertaining to the monks of St. Benedict.—ben″i·dik′tin, ben″i·dik′tēn, ben″i·dik′tin, *n.* A Blackmonk; a member of the order of monks founded at Monte Cassino about the year 530 by St. Benedict, and wearing a loose black gown with large wide sleeves, and a cowl on the head; also an order of nuns who follow the rule of St. Benedict and are devoted to a life of scholarship and the study of the liturgy. A trade name for a liqueur made orig. by Benedictine monks, ben″i·dik′tēn.

ben·e·dic·tion, ben″i·dik′shạn, *n.* [L.] The act of invoking a blessing; blessing, prayer, or kind wishes uttered in favor of any person or thing; a solemn or affectionate invocation of happiness.

ben·e·dic·to·ry, ben″i·dik′to·rē, *a.* Giving a blessing; expressing a benediction or wishes for good.

Ben·e·dic·tus, ben″i·dik′tus, *n.* [L., blessed—"Blessed be the Lord God of Israel", etc.] The song of Zacharias in Luke i, used in the service of the Roman Catholic Church and introduced with English words into the morning prayer of the English Church.

ben·e·fac·tion, ben′e·fak″shạn, *n.* [L. *benefactio*, < *benefacio*, to do good to one. BENEFICE.] The act of conferring a benefit; a benefit conferred, especially a charitable donation.

ben·e·fac·tor, ben′e·fak″tor, ben″e·fak′tor, *n.* [LL. < L. *benefacere.*] One who confers a benefit; a kindly helper; one who makes a benefaction, as to a charitable or religious institution; one who makes a bequest or endowment.

ben·e·fac·tress, ben′e·fak″tris, ben″e·fak′tris, *n.* A female benefactor.

be·nef·ic, be·nef′ik, *a.* [L. *beneficus.*] Beneficent; benign; *astrol.* of good or favorable influence.

ben·e·fice, ben′e·fis, *n.* [O.Fr. *benefice* (Fr. *bénéfice*), < L. *beneficium*, benefit, favor.] An ecclesiastical post or position, appointment to which includes an endowment of property or income.—*v.t.—beneficed, beneficing.* To appoint to a benefice and its endowment.

be·nef·i·cence, be·nef′i·sens, *n.* [L. *beneficentia.*] The practice of doing good; active goodness, kindness, or charity.

be·nef·i·cent, be·nef′i·sent, *a.* Performing, or causing to be done, acts of kindness and charity; doing good.—**be·nef·i·cent·ly**, be·nef′i·sent·lē, *adv.*

ben·e·fi·cial, ben″e·fish′ạl, *a.* Contributing to a valuable end; conferring benefit; advantageous; useful; profitable; helpful.—**ben·e·fi·cial·ly**, ben″e·fish′ạl·ē, *adv.*

ben·e·fi·ci·ar·y, ben″e·fish′ē·er″ē, ben″e·fish′a·rē, *n. pl.* **ben·e·fi·ci·ar·ies.** One named in a conveyance to receive the property, benefits, or grants provided by insurance, a trust fund, etc. *Eccles.* one who holds a benefice.

ben·e·fit, ben′e·fit, *n.* [O.Fr., Fr. *bienfait*, < L. *benefactum*, prop. pp. neut. of *benefacere.*] Good done or received; a kindness or favor; anything that is for the good of a person or thing; advantage or profit; a theatrical performance or other public entertainment given to raise money for a particular cause.

ben·e·fit, ben′e·fit, *v.t.—benefited, benefiting.* To do good to; be of benefit, advantage, or service to.—*v.i.* To derive benefit.—**ben·e·fit·er**, ben′e·fit″ẽr, *n.*

ben·e·fit of cler·gy, *n.* The privilege of exemption from trial before a secular court and of appearing instead before an ecclesiastical one, formerly accorded to the clergy; the sanction of the church.

---

ch- chain, G. na*ch*t;   **th-** THen, thin;   **w-** wig, hw as sound in whig;   **z-** zh as in azure, zeal.   *Italicized vowel* indicates schwa sound.

ben·e·fit so·ci·e·ty, n. An association of persons formed for the purpose of creating a fund, as by dues or assessments, for the assistance of members in sickness, etc., and of their families in case of death.

Ben·e·lux, ben'e·luks", n. The union of Belgium, the Netherlands, and Luxembourg bound by economic ties.

be·nev·o·lence, be·nev'o·lens, n. [L. benevolentia—bene, well, and volens, volentis, ppr. of volo, to will or wish.] The disposition to do good; the love of mankind, accompanied with a desire to promote its happiness; good will; kindness; charitableness; an act of kindness; a contribution or tax illegally exacted by certain kings of England. **—be·nev·o·lent,** be·nev'o·lent, a.—**be·nev·o·lent·ly,** be·nev'o·lent·lē, adv.

ben·ga·line, beng'ga·lēn", n. [Fr.] A fabric, usu. of silk, rayon, or cotton, having narrow transverse cords similar to poplin.

Ben·gal light, ben·gal līt, beng·al, ben'gal, beng'al, n. A species of fireworks used as signals by night or illumination, producing a steady and vivid blue-colored fire.

be·night, bi·nīt', v.t. To surround with the darkness of night or ignorance.—**be·night·ed,** bi·nī'tid, a. Overtaken by night. Fig. involved in moral darkness; ignorant; unenlightened.

be·nign, bi·nīn', a. [L. benignus for benigenus, kind-hearted—benus for bonus, good, and genus, kind, race.] Of a kind disposition; gracious; favorable; healthful; kind; as, a benign sovereign; proceeding from or expressive of gentleness, kindness, or benignity; salutary; as, benign influences. Med. mild; not malignant; not severe or violent.—**be·nig·ni·ty,** bi·nig'ni·tē, n. pl. **be·nig·ni·ties.**—**be·nign·ly,** adv.

be·nig·nan·cy, bi·nig'nan·sē, n. pl. **be·nig·nan·cies.** The condition of being benevolent, gentle, mild; also, a gracious action or favor.

be·nig·nant, bi·nig'nant, a. Kind; gracious; favorable; beneficial; benign: frequently, like benign, used of the kindness of superiors.—**be·nig·nant·ly,** adv.

ben·i·son, ben'i·zen, ben'i·sen, n. [O.Fr. beneiçon, < L. benedictio, a benediction. Benediction is thus the same word.] A blessing uttered by a person; a benediction.

ben·ja·min, ben'ja·min, n. [Corruption of benjoin, earlier form of benzoin.] The resin benzoin.—**ben·ja·min-bush,** ben'ja·min-bush", n. The spice-bush.

ben·ne, ben'ē, n. [Malay.] Sesame, an East Indian annual herbaceous plant, from the seeds of which a valuable, edible oil is expressed.

ben·net, ben'it, n. An avens of the genus Geum, as the herb bennet, having yellow flowers and an aromatic, tonic, and astringent root.

bent, bent, n. A condition of being curved from an original straightness, as a bow; flexure; turn; inclination; disposition; natural tendency; leaning or interest of the mind.

bent, bent, a. Deviated from a straight, even, or level condition; as, a bent axle, a bent finger. Resolved or determined, followed by on; as, bent on going to college.

bent, bent, n. [M.E. akin to G. binse.] Any stiff, wiry grass or grasslike plant, such as grows on waste ground or sandy shores; a grassy tract; a perennial grass, genus Agrostis, suitable for smooth, velvety lawns.

ben·thal, ben'thal, a. Of or pertaining to depths of the sea of a thousand fathoms and more.

Ben·tham·ism, ben'tha·miz"um, ben'ta-·miz"um, n. The doctrine according to Jeremy Bentham, England, 1748–1832, by which man's actions are regulated purely by utilitarian considerations; profit-and-loss morality, wherein actions are considered good if they produce pleasure and bad if they produce pain.

ben·thos, ben'thos, n. Biol. the aggregate of all organisms which live under water either in the depths or near the shore; compare plankton and nekton. The bottom of the sea, esp. the deepest parts.—**ben·thon·ic,** ben·thon'ik, ben'-thik, a. Pertaining to the ocean depths.

ben·ton·ite, ben'to·nīt, n. [Named for Fort Benton, Montana.] A rock consisting mainly of the clay minerals montmorillonite and beidellite, formed from the decomposition of volcanic ash, capable of absorbing large quantities of water, and capable of being activated by acid: used as an emulsifier in drugs and as a carrier for chemicals.

be·numb, bi·num', v.t. [NUMB.] To make numb or torpid, as by cold; to deprive of sensation; to stupefy; to render inactive; to drug, deaden, or paralyze.

ben·zal·de·hyde, ben·zal'de·hīd", n. [For benzoic aldehyde.] Chem. an aldehyde, C_6H_5CHO, in oil of bitter almonds.

Ben·ze·drine, ben'zi·drēn", ben'zi·drin, n. A drug used to stimulate the central nervous system, etc.; amphetamine. (Trademark.)

ben·zene, ben'zēn, ben·zēn', n. Fuel oil; diesel oil. Chem. a clear, colorless, aromatic liquid, the simplest aromatic hydrocarbon extracted from coal tar, C_6H_6: used as a solvent and intermediate in manufacturing organic chemicals; also benzol.

ben·zene nu·cle·us, n. Benzene ring.

ben·zene ring, n. Chem. A ring of six carbon atoms assumed to be present in the molecule of benzene or a benzene derivative; the graphic representation of these six carbon atoms or of benzene, in the form of a hexagon. Also benzene nucleus.

ben·zi·dine, ben'zi·dēn", ben'zi·din, n. Chem. a crystalline hydrocarbon, $C_{12}H_{12}N_2$, usually derived from nitrobenzene, used chiefly in the manufacture of dyes and in the detection of blood.

ben·zine, ben'zēn, ben·zēn', n. The essential and principal ingredient of gasoline, the remaining 0.5% of which is anti-knock additives; white gas, sometimes used as a solvent; chem. a liquid mixture of aliphatic hydrocarbons constituting the lighter and more volatile fraction of petroleum from which it is obtained by fractional distillation.

ben·zo·ate, ben'zō·āt, n. Chem. a salt or ester of benzoic acid.—**ben·zo·at·ed,** ben'zō·a·tid, a. Mixed or treated with benzoic acid or with benzoin.

ben·zo·ate of so·da, n. Chem. a water-soluble powder, C_6H_5COONa, used in medicine and as a food preservative. Also sodium benzoate.

ben·zo·caine, ben'zō·kān", n. [N.L. < benzoin and -caine.] Pharm. the crystalline ester, $C_9H_{11}NO_2$, employed, usually in an ointment, as a local anesthetic.

ben·zo·ic ac·id, n. [N.L. < benzoin.] Chem. the crystalline compound, C_6H_5COOH, occurring naturally, as in resins such as benzoin, or synthesized, and primarily used as a preservative, as a germicide, and in manufacturing certain chemical compounds. —**ben·zo·ic,** ben·zō'ik, a. Of or from benzoin or benzoic acid.

ben·zo·in, ben'zōin, ben'zoin, ben·zō·in, ben'zō·in, n. [Of Ar. origin = Fr. benjoin, Pg. beijoim.] A resin from a tree of Sumatra or Java, chiefly used in medicine, cosmetics, perfumes, and in incense; also benjamin, **ben·zo·in gum, gum ben·ja·min.** Any shrub of the genus Lindera; chem. a compound, $C_{14}H_{12}O_2$, used as an antiseptic.

ben·zol, ben'zōl, ben'zal, ben'zol, n. Benzene.

ben·zo·phe·none, ben"zō·fi·nōn', n. [N.L. < benzoin, phen-, benzene, and -one.] Chem. the crystalline ketone, $C_{13}H_{10}O$, primarily used in manufacturing perfumes.

ben·zo·yl, ben'zō·il, n. Chem. a univalent radical, C_6H_5CO, present in benzoic acid and allied compounds.

ben·zyl, ben'zil, n. Chem. An organic, monovalent radical, $C_6H_5CH_2$.

be·queath, bi·kwēth', bi·kwēth', v.t. [O.E. becwethan—prefix be, and cwethan, to say. QUOTH.] To give or leave by will; to devise by testament; to hand down; to transmit.

be·quest, bi·kwest', n. The act of bequeathing or leaving by will; something left by will; a legacy.

be·rate, bi·rāt', v.t.—berated, berating. To chide vehemently; to admonish; to scold.

ber·ceuse, ber·suz', n. [Fr.] A cradlesong or lullaby; a piece of instrumental music of similar tranquil character.

bere, bēr, n. [O.E. bere, barley. BARLEY.] North. Eng., a species of barley.

be·reave, bi·rēv', v.t.—bereaved or bereft, bereaving. [Prefix be, and reave; O.E. bereafian. REAVE.] To deprive of someone loved or something that is prized, usually followed by of.—**be·reave·ment,** bi·rēv'ment, n. The act of bereaving; state of being bereaved; deprivation, particularly the loss by death.

Ber·e·ni·ce's Hair, ber·e·nī'sēz har, n. Astron. the constellation Coma Berenices.

be·ret, be·rā', ber'ā, n. [Fr.] A soft, visorless, cloth cap with a broad, flat crown.

berg, burg, n. [O.E. and G. berg, a hill.] A large mass or mountain, as of ice; an iceberg.

ber·ga·mot, bur'ga·mot", n. [Fr. bergamote, It. bergamotta, from Bergamo, in Italy.] A variety of pear; the tree Citrus bergamia; a citrus fruit, the rind of which yields a fragrant oil; an essence or perfume from the fruit; any of various mints, as Monarda fistulosa, from which an essence similar to bergamot is derived.

ber·i·ber·i, ber'ē·ber'ē, n. [Singhalese.] Pathol. a form of multiple neuritis caused by a lack of vitamin B_1, characterized by loss of muscular power, emaciation, and exhaustion.

Ber·ing time, bēr'ing tīm, ber'ing, bar'ing, n. The civil time of the zone established by the 165th meridian, passing through western Alaska.

Berke·lei·an, Berke·ley·an, burk·lē'an, burk'lē·an, Brit. bärk·lē'an, bärk'lē·an, a. Pertaining to the philosophy of the Irish bishop, George Berkeley, esp. in respect to its denial of the reality of the material world.—n. An advocate of this philosophy. —**Berke·lei·an·ism,** n.

ber·ke·li·um, ber·kē'lē·um, n. [From Berkeley, Calif., where it was discovered.] Synthetic radioactive element first produced by helium-ion bombardment of americium 241. Sym. Bk, at. no. 97. See Periodic Table of Elements.

Berk·shire, burk'shēr, burk'shir, Brit. bärk'sher, bärk'shir. n. A county in southern England; also **Berks,** burks, Brit. bärks. A breed of black and white hogs of medium size.

ber·lin, bur·lin', bur'lin, n. A four-wheeled carriage of the chariot kind, first made at Berlin.

Ber·lin wool, n. A kind of fine dyed wool used for tapestry, knitting, etc.

berm, burm, n. [Fr. berme < Teut., and perhaps akin to E. brim.] A narrow space or ledge at the edge of a road; fort. a space of ground of varying width, sometimes left between the moat and the base of the parapet. The nearly level section of a beach, formed by material deposited and shaped by the movement of waves.

Ber·mu·da grass, ber·mū'da gras, n. A creeping grass native to southern Europe and grown in other warm areas, particularly India, southern U.S., and the Caribbean islands, for pastures, lawns, etc. Also Ba·ha·ma grass, dev·il grass, scutch grass, ba·hä′ma gras, ba·hä′ma gräs, ba·hä′ma.

Ber·mu·da rig, *n.* A rig of three-cornered sails used on a yacht. Also *Marconi rig.*

Ber·mu·das, bẽr·mū′daz, *n.* Shorts extending to just above the knee, worn by men and women. Also **Ber·mu·da shorts.**

Ber·nese moun·tain dog, bẽr′nēz moun′tin dᶏg, bẽr′nēz moun′tin dog, *n.* A Swiss breed of large dogs of black coat with brown and white markings, formerly used as draft animals in the Bernese Alps.

ber·ret·ta, be·ret′a, *n.* [It.] Biretta.

ber·ried, ber′ēd, *a.* Having berries; covered with berries; of lobsters, etc., having eggs.

ber·ry, ber′ē, *n.* pl. **ber·ries.** [O.E. *berie,* a berry; Icel. *ber,* Sw. and D. *bär,* G. *beere,* Goth. *basi;* root seen in Skt. *bhas,* to eat.] A succulent or pulpy fruit, containing many seeds, and usually small, such as the gooseberry or strawberry; certain dried seeds as grain, coffee; what resembles a berry, as one of the eggs of the lobster; the rose hip.— **ber·ry·less,** *a.*—**ber·ry·like,** *a.*

ber·ry, ber′ē, *v.i.*—*berried, berrying.* To bear or produce berries; to pick berries.

ber·sa·glie·re, ber″sal·yâr′ē,n. pl. **ber·sa·glie·ri,** ber″sal·yâr′ē. [It. sharpshooter, < *bersaglio,* mark, target.] One of a class of riflemen or sharpshooters in the Italian army.

ber·seem, bẽr·sēm′, *n.* [Egyptian Ar. *barsîm.*] An Egyptian clover, *Trifolium alexandrinum,* cultivated as a forage plant in Egypt, southwest U.S., and elsewhere.

ber·serk, bẽr·sụrk′, bẽr·zụrk′, *a.* [< *berserker.*] Violent; frenzied; in an uncontrolled rage.—*adv.* Into a violent frenzy; as, to go *berserk.*—*n.* One who is berserk.

ber·serk·er, bẽr·sụr′kẽr, bẽr·zụr′kẽr, *n.* [Icel. *berserkr,* lit. 'bearsark,' or bear-shirt.] A kind of wild warrior or champion of heathen times in Scandinavia, a person of extreme violence and fury.

berth, bụrth, *n.* [Origin uncertain; prob. < *bear.*] Searoom for a vessel; *often fig.* a space allowed for convenience or safety; as, to give one a wide *berth.* A station for a vessel at anchor or at a wharf; a sleeping place or bunk in a ship, railroad car, etc.; in general, a place, position, or situation; a post of employment on vessels.

berth, bụrth, *v.t.* To place (a boat) in, or assign to, a berth; provide with a berth or berths.—*v.i.* To have or occupy a berth.

ber·tha, bụr′tha, *n.* [Fr. *berthe,* < *Berthe,* Bertha, a modest Frankish queen of the 8th century.] A kind of collar or trimming, as of lace, worn by women about the shoulders, as at the top of a low-necked dress.

berth·age, bụr′thij, *n.* Accommodation for berthing a vessel; berth dues, the charge for this accommodation.

Ber·til·lon sys·tem, bụr′ti·lon sis′tem, *Fr.* ber·tē·yan′ sis′tem, *n.* [From the inventor, A. *Bertillon,* French criminologist (1853–1914).] A system of identifying persons, as criminals, by a record of individual measurements and physical peculiarities.

ber·yl, ber′il, *n.* [O.Fr. *beril* (Fr. *béryl*), < L. *beryllus,* < Gr. *beryllos.*] A mineral, $Be_3Al_2Si_6O_{18}$, a silicate of aluminum and beryllium, occurring in various colors, esp. green, and in both opaque and transparent varieties, including the emerald and aquamarine; a clear, pale bluish green; seagreen.—**ber·yl·line,** ber′i·lin″, *a.*

be·ryl·li·um, bi·ril′ē·um, *n.* A hard, steelgray, bivalent, light metallic element (formerly *glucinum*) always occurring in combination, used mainly in copper alloys, in contacts, and in springs. Sym. Be, at. no. 4, at. wt. 9.0122. See Periodic Table of Elements.

be·seech, bi·sēch′, *v.t.*—*besought* or *beseeched, beseeching.* [M.E. *bisechen,* var. of *biseken,* < *bi-* (E. *be-*) and *seken,* seek.] To beg eagerly for; entreat; to supplicate or implore (a person).—**be·seech·er,** *n.*—**be·seech·ing·ly,** *adv.*

be·set, bi·set′, *v.t.*—*beset, besetting.* [O.E. *besettan.*] To set, stud, or surround with something; also, to surround as in a siege or attack; hem in; besiege; attack on all sides; assail.—**be·set·ment,** bi·set′ment, *n.* The act of besetting, or the state of being beset; something that besets.

be·set·ting, bi·set′ing, *a.* Habitually attacking or assailing; as, a *besetting* sin (Heb. xii. 1).

be·show, bi·shō′, *n.* [N. Amer. Ind.] An acanthopterygian food fish, *Anoplopoma fimbria,* of the western coast of North America; a sablefish.

be·side, bi·sīd′, *prep.* At the side of, as a person or thing; near to; apart from; not connected with; as, *beside* the present subject.—**be be·side one·self,** to be out of one's wits or senses.

be·sides, bi·sīdz′, *adv.* Along the side of; moreover; over and above; not included in the number, or in what has been mentioned. Also, less common, **be·side,** bi·sīd′.

be·sides, bi·sīdz′, *prep.* Over and above; separate or distinct from; in addition to.

be·siege, bi·sēj′, *v.t.*—*besieged, besieging.* To lay siege to; beset or surround with armed forces for the purpose of compelling to surrender; to importune; to beset; to harass; as, *besieged* with applications.—**be·sieg·er,** bi·sēj′ẽr, *n.* One who besieges.

be·smear, bi·smir′, *v.t.* To smear all over; to bedaub; to overspread with some viscous, glutinous, or soft substance that adheres; to foul; to soil.

be·smirch, bi·smụrch′, *v.t.* To sully; to tarnish.

bes·om, bē′zum, *n.* [O.E. *besema, besma,* a besom = D. *bezem,* G. *besem, besen:* root unknown.] A broom; a brush of twigs or other materials for sweeping.

be·sot, bi·sot′, *v.t.*—*besotted, besotting.* To make mentally dull, as with drink; to infatuate; to stupefy; to make stupid, or senseless.—**be·sot·ted,** bi·sot′ed, *a.*

be·spat·ter, bi·spat′ẽr, *v.t.* To soil by spattering; *fig.* to asperse with slander or reproach.

be·speak, bi·spēk′, *v.t.*—*past bespoke,* pp. *bespoke* or *bespoken,* ppr. *bespeaking.* To speak beforehand for something wanted; to order or engage against a future time; to betoken; to indicate by outward appearance; as, action that *bespoke* a kind heart.

be·sprin·kle, bi·spring′kl, *v.t.*—*besprinkled, besprinkling.* To sprinkle over, as with salt; to cover by scattering or being scattered over.

Bes·se·mer proc·ess, bes′e·mẽr pros′es, *n.* [From Sir H. *Bessemer* (1813–1898), English inventor.] A process of removing carbon and other constituents from molten iron in steel-making, by means of a blast of air.

Bes·se·mer steel, *n.* Steel made directly from molten pig iron by driving through it currents of air so as to oxidize and carry off the carbon and impurities, the proper quantity of carbon for making steel being then introduced.

best, best, *a., irreg. superl. of good.* [O.E. *betest, betst, best,* serving as the superl. of *gód, good* = D. and G. *best,* Dan. *beste,* Icel. *bestr,* Sw. *bästa.* The root is *bat, bet,* seen also in *better,* Goth. *batista, best.* BETTER.] Having good qualities or attainments in the highest degree; possessing the highest advantages.

best, best, *adv.* In the highest degree; in the most desirable way; most excellently.

best, best, *n.* Highest possible state of excellence; all that one can do, or show in oneself: often used in this sense with the possessive pronouns *my, thy, his, their,* etc. —**at best,** considered or looked at in the most favorable light.—**make the best of,** to use to the best advantage; to put up with as well as one can.

best, best, *v.t.* To defeat; to outdo, as: He *bested* his opponent.

best bid, *n. Stock market,* the highest bid at a given moment, which determines the market quoted for a stock.

bes·tial, bes′chal, best′yal, *a.* [L. *bestialis,* from *bestia,* a beast.] Belonging to a beast or to the class of beasts; animal; having the qualities of a beast; incapable of intelligent judgment; brutal; brutish, carnal.—**bes·tial·ize,** bes′ti·al·īz, *v.t.*—*bestialized, bestializing.* To make like a beast; to bring or reduce to the condition of a beast.— **bes·tial·ly,** bes′chal·lē, best′yal·lē, *adv.*

bes·tial·i·ty, bes″chē·al′i·tē, bes″tē·al′i·tē, *n.* pl. **bes·tial·i·ties.** The quality of a beast; beastliness; beastly behavior.

bes·ti·a·ry, bes′chē·er″ē, bes′tē·er″ē, *n.* pl. **bes·ti·a·ries.** [M.L. *bestiarium,* prop. neut. of L. *bestiarius,* pertaining to beasts, < *bestia,* E. *beast.*] A treatise or allegory on beasts or animals, such as those written in the Middle Ages.

be·stir, bi·stẽr′, *v.t.*—*bestirred, bestirring.* To stir; to put into brisk or vigorous action: usually reflexive.

best man, *n.* The right-hand man or chief attendant of the bridegroom at a wedding.

be·stow, bi·stō′, *v.t.* To stow away; to deposit; to lodge; to place (often reflexive); to give; to confer; to impart: followed by *on* or *upon* before the recipient.—**be·stow·al,** bē·stō′al, *n.* The act of bestowing.

be·strew, bi·strō′, *v.t.* To scatter over; to strew.

be·stride, bi·strīd′, *v.t.*—*past bestrid* or *bestrode,* pp. *bestrid, bestridden,* ppr. *bestriding.* To stride over; to stand or sit on with the legs on either side.

best sel·ler, *n.* Any item of sale, esp. a book, which is considered the most popular in its category for a given period of time because of demand.

bet, bet, *n.* A wager; that which is laid, staked, or pledged on the result of any uncertain question or event; the terms on which a bet is laid.

bet, bet, *v.t., v.i.*—*bet* or *betted, betting.* [A contraction of *abet,* to encourage, back up.] To lay or stake in wagering; to take or pledge something upon the result of a contest; to wager.

be·ta, bā′ta, bē′ta, *n.* [Gk. *beta,* < Heb. *beth,* second letter of alphabet.] The second letter of the Greek alphabet; the second of any series, esp. in scientific classification. *Chem.* the second of two or more isomeric compounds; the second of two or more positions, in a compound, of an atom or group; *astron.* a star of the second order of brightness in any given constellation.

be·ta de·cay, *n.* Radioactive transformation of a nuclide in which the atomic number changes by plus or minus 1 with the emission of a beta particle, and the mass number remains unchanged. Also *beta disintegration.*

be·ta dis·in·te·gra·tion, *n.* Beta decay.

be·ta·ine, bē′ta·ēn″, bē′ta·in, bi·tā′ēn, bi·tā′in, *n. Chem., pharm.* a clear, sweettasting, water-soluble alkaloid, $(CH_3)NCH_2$-COO, from beets or synthesized from glycine used in medicine in hydrochloride form.

be·ta i·ron, *n. Metal.* an allotropic form of iron which is stable below the same temperature (910°C) as alpha iron, and differs from alpha iron in that it is not magnetic.

betake   93   **biaural**

be·take, bi·tāk´, v.t.—past betook, pp. be-taken, ppr. betaking. With the reflexive pronouns, to cause to go, as: He will betake himself to the meeting.

be·ta par·ti·cle, n. Phys. a high-speed electron or positron ejected from the atomic nucleus during radioactive disintegration.

be·ta ray, n. Phys. a stream of high-speed electrons or positrons occurring in radioactive disintegration.

be·ta·tron, bā´ta·tron″, bē´ta·tron, n. Phys. a device for the high-speed acceleration of electrons to form a beam of beta rays.

be·tel, bēt´l, n. [Pg. from Dravidian name.] An East Indian pepper plant, Piper betle, the leaves of which are chewed in Southeast Asia with the betel nut and lime.

Be·tel·geuse, bēt´al·jöz″, bēt´al·jœz″, n. Astron. a red star of first magnitude in the constellation Orion.

be·tel palm, n. The palm of southeastern Asia, Areca cathecu, that bears the areca nut or betel nut.

bête noire, bāt″nwär´, n. pl. bêtes noires, bāt″nwär´. [Fr. black beast.] A bugbear; an object of one's special dread or aversion.

beth·el, beth´el, n. [Heb. bēth-ēl, 'house of God.'] A hallowed spot, or a pillar or structure marking it; Brit. a dissenters' chapel or meeting house. A church or chapel for seamen, often one afloat in a harbor.

be·tide, bi·tīd´, v.t.—past betided, pp. betid, ppr. betiding. [O.E. tidan, to happen. TIDE.] To happen to; to befall; to come to.—v.i. To come to pass; to happen.

bê·tise, be·tēz´, n. [Fr. < bête, beast.] Stupidity; also, a stupid thing; a foolish act or speech.

be·to·ken, bi·tō´ken, v.t. To be or serve as a token of; to foreshow.

bet·o·ny, bet´e·nē, n. pl. bet·o·nies. [M.E. betone (Fr. bétoine), < L. betonica, vettonica.] A plant, Stachys officinalis, of the mint family, with spikes of purple flowers, formerly used in medicine and dyeing; also, any of various similar plants.

be·tray, bi·trā´, v.t. [Prefix be, and O.Fr. traïr, Fr. trahir, to betray, < L. tradere, to give up or over. TRADITION.] To deliver into the hands of an enemy by treachery in violation of trust; to violate by fraud or unfaithfulness; as, to betray a cause or trust; to play false to; to reveal or disclose (secrets, designs); to let appear or be seen inadvertently; as, to betray ignorance.—**be·tray·al**, bi·trā´al, n. Act of betraying. —**be·tray·er**, bi·trā´ér, n. A traitor.

be·troth, bi·trōTH´, bi·trᴀth´, v.t. To contract to (anyone) in agreement to a future marriage; to affiance. Bib. to pledge one's troth to.

be·troth·al, bi·trō´THal, bi·trᴀ´thal, n. The act of betrothing; engagement; a mutual agreement to marry. Also **be·troth·ment**, bi·trōTH´ment, bi·trᴀth´ment.

be·trothed, bi·trōTHd´, bi·trᴀtht´, n. A person promised in marriage.

bet·ter, bet´ér, a., compar. of good. [O.E. betera, betra, with corresponding forms in the other Teutonic languages. BEST.] Having good qualities in a greater degree than another; superior in excellence; of a higher quality; preferable, in regard to use, fitness, or the like; improved in health. —**be bet·ter off**, to be in improved or in superior circumstances.

bet·ter, bet´ér, adv., compar. of well. In a more excellent or superior manner; more correctly or fully; in a higher or greater degree; more completely; with greater advantage; more, in extent or amount; as, better than a mile.

bet·ter, bet´ér, n. Something or someone of greater excellence; a superior; one who has a claim to precedence: generally in the plural, and with possessive pronouns.—**the**

bet·ter, a state of improvement: generally in adverbial phrase for the better; as, to alter a thing for the better; advantage; superiority; victory; as, to have or get the better of.

bet·ter, bet´ér, v.t. To make better; to improve; to ameliorate; to increase the good qualities of, as soil; to advance the interest or worldly position of; to surpass; to exceed; to improve on, as a previous effort.—v.i. To grow better; to become better; to improve.

bet·ter·ment, bet´ér·ment, n. A making better; improvement; value added to property from public improvements.

bet·tor, **bet·ter**, bet´ér, n. One who lays bets or wagers.

bet·u·la·ceous, bech″ṳ·lā´shas, a. [L. betula, birch.] Belonging to the Betulaceae, a family of trees and shrubs including the birch, alder, hornbeam, etc.

be·tween, bi·twēn´, prep. [O.E. betwēonum, < be, by, and twēonum, akin to twā, E. two.] In the space separating two points, objects, etc.; in the interval of time separating; intermediate to in degree, amount, character, etc.; as, between zero and 32°, between $5 and $6, between pink and red; connecting; as, a link between parts, relation between ideas; involving, concerning, or as to both of; as, war between states, comparison or choice between things; by joint action or possession of, as: They did it between them. They own the land between them: strictly referring to two objects, but sometimes used (for among) of more than two.

be·tween, bi·twēn´, adv. In the intervening space or time; in an intermediate position or relation.

be·tween·brain, bi·twēn´brān″, n. The diencephalon.

be·tween·times, bi·twēn´tīmz″, adv. Between periods of activity; betweenwhiles.

be·tween·whiles, bi·twēn´hwilz″, adv. Betweentimes.

be·twixt, bi·twikst´, prep. [O.E. betweox, betweohs.] Between; passing between; from one to another.

bev·a·tron, bev´a·tron″, n. [< (b)illion (e)lectron (v)olts and elec(tron).] A large accelerator of the synchrotron type which yields particles having kinetic energies of a billion or more electron volts.

bev·el, bev´el, n. [O.Fr. bevel; origin unknown.] The obliquity or inclination of one surface of a solid body to another surface of the same body; an instrument for drawing or measuring angles.

bev·el, bev´el, v.t.—beveled, beveling, Brit. bevelled, bevelling. To cut to a bevel.—v.i. To slant or incline on to a bevel angle.

bev·el gear, n. A species of toothed wheels in which the axis or shaft of the driving wheel forms an angle with the axis or shaft of the wheel driven.

bev·er·age, bev´ér·ij, bev´rij, n. [O.Fr. beuvrage, from boivre, bevre, L. bibere, to drink.] Drink; liquor or nonalcoholic liquid for drinking; libation.

bev·y, bev´ē, n. pl. bev·ies. [Perhaps of similar origin with beverage, and originally a drinking company, or animals collected at a watering place.] A flock of birds, esp. quail; a company of females; a group of roebuck.

be·wail, bi·wāl´, v.t. To wail or weep aloud for; to lament.—v.i. To express grief.

be·ware, bi·wâr´, v.i. To be wary or cautious; to be suspicious of danger; to take care: now used only in imperative and infinitive, with of before the noun denoting what is to be avoided.

be·wil·der, bi·wil´dér, v.t. [Prefix be, and old wilder, to lead astray. WILD.] To lead into complete perplexity or confusion; to perplex; to puzzle; to confuse.—**be·wil·der·ing·ly**, bi·wil´dér·ing·lē, adv. So as to bewilder.—**be·wil·der·ment**, bi·wil´-dér·ment, n.

be·witch, bi·wich´, v.t. To subject to the influence of witchcraft; to cast a charm or spell over; to please to such a degree as to take away the power of resistance.—**be·witch·er**, bi·wich´ér, n. One who bewitches or fascinates.—**be·witch·er·y**, bi·wich´-ér·ē, n.—**be·witch·ing**, bi·wich´ing, a. Having power to bewitch or to control by pleasing.—**be·witch·ing·ly**, adv.

be·witch·ment, bi·wich´ment, n. Fascination; the power of charming; magic spell.

bey, bā, n. [Turk. beg, pron. as bey.] A governor of a town or district in the Ottoman Empire.

be·yond, bē·ond´, bi·yond´, adv. [O.E. begeondan, < be, by, and geondan, beyond, < geond, across, through, beyond.] On or to the farther side; farther away.

be·yond, bē·ond´, bi·yond´, prep. On or to the farther side of; farther away than; further on than; later than; past; outside the limit of; out of reach of; above or surpassing; more than; in addition to.

be·yond, bē·ond´, bi·yond´, n. That which lies beyond, in space or time; heaven; the hereafter; as, the great beyond.

bez·ant, bez´ant, be·zant´, n. [O.Fr. besant, < L. Byzantius, Byzantine.] Arch. an ornament in the form of a flat disk, often one of a number in close succession or overlapping.

bez·el, bez´el, n. [A form of basil, Fr. biseau, a slope. BASIL.] The part of a finger ring which surrounds and holds fast the stone; the groove in which the glass of a watch is set; the sloping end of the blade of a cutting tool, as a chisel.

be·zique, be·zēk´, n. [Fr. bésigue, bésy; origin uncertain.] A game of cards played with two packs, 64 cards, from which all the cards having from two to six spots have been removed; the combination of the queen of spades and the jack of diamonds in this game.

be·zoar, bē´zōr, bē´zar, n. [O.Fr. bezoar, < Pers. pādzahr—pād, dispelling, and zahr, poison.] A name for certain concretions found in the intestines of some animals, especially ruminants, formerly (and still in some places) supposed to be magical and an antidote to poison.

bhak·ti, buk´tē, n. [Skt., devotion.] Hinduism. Devotion to a deity to attain salvation; at a more mundane level, worship of God or a god involving an arduous course of ritualistic penances, fasts, and scriptural recitations to beget certain worldly comforts, or get divine cure of certain diseases.

bhang, bang, n. [Hind. < Skt. bhangā, hemp.] The Indian hemp plant; see hemp. A preparation of the leaves and capsules, used in India for smoking or swallowing, as a narcotic and intoxicant. See hashish.

bhees·ty, **bhees·tie**, bē´stē, n. pl. bhees·-ties. [Pers. bihishtī, < bihisht, paradise.] In India, a water carrier.

B-ho·ri·zon, bē″ho·rī´zon, n. Geol. a soil layer beneath the A-horizon in a soil profile.

bi·an·gu·lar, bī·ang´yu·lér, a. Having two angles or corners.

bi·an·nu·al, bī·an´ū·al, a. Having a frequency of twice a year.

bi·as, bī´as, n. [Fr. biais, slant, slope: hence, inclination to one side.] That which causes the mind to incline toward a particular object or course; inclination; bent; prejudice; a direction diagonal to the woven grain of fabric; the quantity or direction of statistical variation from true value.

bi·as, bī´as, a. Oblique; diagonal; running diagonally to the texture of a fabric.

bi·as, bī´as, adv. Diagonally.

bi·as, bī´as, v.t.—biased, biasing, biassed, biassing. To give a bias or particular direction to; to prejudice.

bi·au·ral, bī´ar´al, bī´ar´al, a. Hearing with both ears; binaural.

a- fat, fāte, fär, fâre, fᴀll;   **e-** met, mē, mēre, hėr;   **i-** pin, pīne;   **o-** not, nōte, möve;   **u-** tub, cūbe, bṳll;   **oi-** oil;   **ou-** pound.

bi·au·ric·u·lar, bī″ạ·rik′ya·lėr, *a.* Having two auricles; pertaining to the two ears.

bi·au·ric·u·late, bī″ạ·rik′ya·lit, bī″ạ·rik′ya·lāt, *a.* Anat. having two earlike parts.

bi·ax·i·al, bī·ak′sē·al, *a.* Having two axes; of a crystal, having two lines or directions in which no double refraction occurs.— **bi·ax·i·al·ly,** bī·ak′sē·al·lē, *adv.*

bib, bib, *n.* [< M.E. *bibben,* poss. < mod. of L. *bibere,* drink.] A cloth, or article of clothing, worn under the chin by a child, esp. while eating, to protect the clothing; the upper part of an apron or overalls.

bi·ba·sic, bī·bā′sik, *a. Chem.* dibasic.

bib·ber, bib′ėr, *n.* [< L. *bibere,* drink.] A tippler; a man given to drinking.

bib·cock, bib′kok, *n.* A cock or faucet having a nozzle bent downward.

bi·be·lot, bib′lō, *Fr.* bēb·e·lō′, *n. pl.* **bi·be·lots.** [Fr. lit. 'curio, trinket.'] Any small object of curiosity, beauty, or rarity.

Bi·ble, bī′bl, *n.* [O.Fr. Fr. *Bible,* < L.L. *biblia,* < Gr. *biblia,* pl. of *biblion,* dim. of *byblos,* book, papyrus bark.] The collection of sacred writings of the Christian religion, comprising the Scriptures of the Old and the New Testaments; formerly the Old Testament as distinct from the New Testament; the Old Testament in the form received by the Jews ("Hebrew Bible"); a copy of the Scriptures; a particular version or edition of the Scriptures; (*often cap.*) the sacred writings of any religion; (*l.c.*) any book accepted as an authority.—**Bi·ble Chris·tian,** a Christian according to the Scriptural standard; a Fundamentalist; also, one of a religious sect founded in 1816 by William O'Bryan, a Methodist preacher in Cornwall, England.—**Breech·es Bi·ble,** the Geneva Bible, so called because in Gen. iii. 7 occurs the expression "made themselves *breeches* [Authorized and Revised Versions *aprons*]."—**Ge·ne·va Bi·ble,** an English Bible issued by several English divines at Geneva in 1560.—**Gu·ten·berg Bi·ble,** an edition of the Vulgate printed at Mainz before 1456, ascribed to Gutenberg and others.—**Maz·a·rin Bi·ble,** the Gutenberg Bible, the first known copy of which was discovered in the library of Cardinal Mazarin (1602–61).—**Trea·cle Bi·ble,** an English Bible of the year 1568, in which Jer. viii. 22 reads, "Is there no *tryacle* [Authorized and Revised Versions *balm*] in Gilead?"—**Vin·e·gar Bi·ble,** an English Bible printed at Oxford in 1717, with the heading to Luke, xx. as the "Parable of the *Vinegar* [instead of *Vineyard*]."—**Wick·ed Bi·ble,** a Bible printed in 1631, in which the word *not* is omitted from the commandment "Thou shalt not commit adultery" (Ex. xx. 14); also **Dev·il's Bi·ble.**

Bi·ble belt, *n.* An area of southern and midwestern U.S. where fundamentalist interpretation of the Bible prevails, a term first used by H. L. Mencken.

Bib·li·cal, bib′li·kal, *a.* [< M.L. *biblicus.*] (*Sometimes l.c.*) Of, pertaining to, or contained in the Bible; in accordance with the teachings of the Bible.—**Bib·li·cal·ly,** *adv.*

Bib·li·cism, bib′li·siz″um, *n.* A literal interpretation of the words of the Bible.

Bib·li·cist, bib′li·sist, *n.* One who accepts the Bible literally; a biblical scholar.

bib·li·o·film, bib′lē·a·film″, *n.* A microfilm used to photograph valuable printed material or much-used books in libraries.

bib·li·og·ra·pher, bib·lē·og′ra·fėr, *n.* [< Gk. *bibliográphos.*] One versed in bibliography; one who composes or compiles the history of books.

bib·li·o·graph·ic, bib′lē·ō·graf″ik, *a.* Pertaining to bibliography. Also **bib·li·o·graph·i·cal,** bib′lē·ō·graf″ik·al.

bib·li·og·ra·phy, bib·lē·og′ra·fē, *n. pl.* **bib·li·og·ra·phies.** [Gr. *biblion,* a book

and *grapho,* to write.] A history or description of books or manuscripts, with notices of the different editions, the times when they were printed, etc.; a list of source materials which have been consulted in the process of writing a book or paper; a list of a certain author's works.

bib·li·ol·a·ter, bib″lē·ol′a·tėr, *n.* One who is devoted to a literal interpretation of the words of the Bible.

bib·li·ol·a·try, bib″lē·ol′a·trē, *n.* [Gr. *biblion,* a book, and *latreia,* worship.] Worship or homage paid to books; excessive reverence for the Scriptures literally interpreted.

bib·li·o·man·cy, bib′lē·ō·man″sē, *n.* [Gr. *biblion,* a book, and *manteia,* divination.] Divination performed by means of a book; divination by means of the Bible, consisting in selecting passages of Scripture at random and drawing from them indications concerning future things.

bib·li·o·ma·ni·a, bib″lē·ō·mā′nē·a, bib″lē·ō·mān′ya, *n.* [Gr. *biblion,* a book, and *mania,* madness.] Book-madness; a rage for possessing rare and curious books.—**bib·li·o·ma·ni·ac,** *n.*—**bib·li·o·ma·ni·a·cal,** bib″lē·ō·ma·nī′a·kal, *a.*

bib·lio·phile, bib′lē·o·fīl″, bib′lē·o·fil, *n.* [Gr. *biblion,* book, and *phileō,* to love.] A lover of books; a book collector.—**bib·li·oph·i·lism,** bib·lē·of′il·iz″um, *n.* Love of bibliography or of books.—**bib·li·oph·i·list,** bib″lē·of′a·list, *n.* A bibliophile.

bib·li·o·the·ca, bib″lē·a·thē′ka, *n.* [L., < Gr. *biblion,* a book, and *thēkē,* a repository.] A library; a collection or list of books.

bib·li·ot·ics, bib″lē·ot′iks, *n. pl., sing. or pl. in constr.* The scientific analysis of writing materials and documents to authenticate authorship.—**bib·li·ot·ic,** *a.*

Bib·list, bī′blist, bib′list, *n.* One conversant with the Bible; one who makes the Bible the sole rule of faith.

bib·u·lous, bib′ya·les, *a.* [L. *bibulus.*] Having the quality of imbibing fluids; absorbent; spongy; addicted to drinking intoxicants; pertaining to the drinking of intoxicants; as, *bibulous* propensities.

bi·cam·er·al, bī·kam′er·al, *a.* [L. prefix *bi,* twice, and *camera,* a chamber.] Pertaining to or consisting of two legislative bodies.

bi·cap·su·lar, bī·kap′sa·lėr, *a. Bot.* Having two capsules: also, having a two-celled capsule.

bi·car·bo·nate, bī·kär′ba·nit, bī·kär′ba·nāt″, *n.* A carbonate in which one half of the hydrogen of the carbonic acid is replaced by a metal or its equivalent; an acid carbonate—**bi·car·bo·nate of so·da,** *n.* Sodium bicarbonate.

bice, bīs, *n.* [< M.E. *bis* < O.Fr. *bis,* dark-colored.] A name given to two colors used in painting, one blue, the other green, and both made from native carbonates of copper.

bi·cen·te·nar·y, bī″sen·ten′a·rē, bī·sen′ta·ner″ē, *n. pl.* **bi·cen·te·nar·ies.** The period of two hundred years; the commemoration of an event that happened two hundred years before.—*a.* Relating to a bicentenary; occurring once in two hundred years.

bi·cen·ten·ni·al, bī″sen·ten′ē·al, *n.* A two-hundredth anniversary.—*a.* Relating to a two-hundred year period.

bi·cen·tric, bī·sen′trik, *a. Biol.* Having two centers of origin; an animal or plant having two bases of distribution.

bi·ceph·a·lous, bī·sef′a·lus, *a.* [L. *bi-,* two, and Gr. *cephale,* head.] Having two heads; dicephalous.

bi·ceps, bī′seps, *n. pl.* [L. *bi,* double, and *caput,* the head.] A muscle having two heads or origins; the name of two muscles, one of the upper arm, the other of the thigh.

bi·chlo·ride, bī·klōr′īd, bī·klôr′id, bī-

klär·id, *n.* A compound in which two atoms of chlorine are combined with another element or radical; an abbreviation for 'bichloride of mercury,' or corrosive sublimate.

bi·chro·mate, bī·krō′māt, *n. Chem.* A salt of a theoretical acid, $H_2Cr_2O_7$, containing two atoms of chromium; as, *bichromate* of potassium; an abbreviation for 'bichromate of potassium.'

bi·cip·i·tal, bī·sip′i·tal, *a.* Having two heads; two-headed; pertaining to the biceps.

bick·er, bik′er, *n.* A fight, especially a confused controversy; a contention; a dispute.

bick·er, bik′er, *v.i.* [M.E. *biker(en).*] To skirmish; to quarrel; to wrangle; to contend in words; to scold. To run rapidly; to rush; to move quickly with some noise, as a stream. To quiver; to flicker; to make a confused noise; to clatter.

bi·col·or, *Brit.* **bi·col·our,** bī′kul·or, *a.* [L.] Of two colors. Also **bi·col·ored,** *Brit.* **bi·col·oured.**

bi·con·cave, bī·kon′kāv, bī″kon·kāv′, *a.* Hollow or concave on both sides.

bi·con·vex, bī·kon′veks, bī″kon·veks′, *a.* Convex on both sides, as a lens.

bi·corn, bī′kạrn, *a.* Having two horns or antlers; crescent-shaped. Also **bi·corn·u·ate,** bī′kạr·nū·wat.

bi·cul·tur·al, bī·kul′chur·al, *a.* Possessing or combining two distinct cultures.

bi·cus·pid, bī·kus′pid, *a.* Having two cusps or points, as certain teeth.—*n.* One of eight human bicuspid teeth, located four each in pairs behind the canine teeth in the upper and lower jaws; a premolar.—**bi·cus·pi·date, bi·cus·pi·dal,** bī·kus′pi·dāt, bī·kus′pi·dl, *a.*

bi·cy·cle, bī′si·kl, *n.* [Fr. *bicycle,* < L. *bi-,* two, and Gr. *cyclos,* circle, wheel.] A vehicle with two wheels, one in front of the other, and a saddlelike seat for the rider, steered by a handlebar and driven by pedals or a motor: in some forms carrying more than one rider.

bi·cy·cle, bī′si·kl, *v.i.*—**bicycled, bicycling.** To ride a bicycle.—**bi·cy·clist,** *n.*

bi·cy·clic, bī·sī′klik, bī·sik′lik, *a.* An arrangement of two cycles or circles; *bot.* a flower having petals in two whorls; *chem.* structure or substance having two rings, as naphthalene.

bi·cy·lin·dri·cal, bī″sa·lin′dri·kl, *a.* Pertaining to two cylindrical surfaces with axes usually parallel.

bid, bid, *v.t.*—past *bid* or *bade,* pp. *bid, bidden,* ppr. *bidding.* [< O.E. *biddán,* to pray, ask, declare, command = Icel. *bidja,* G. *bitten,* Goth. *bidjan,* to ask, to pray; influenced by O.E. *beódan,* to offer, to bid = Goth. *biudan,* G. *bieten,* to offer, command.] To ask, request, or invite; to pray; to wish; to say to by way of greeting or benediction; as, to *bid* good-day, farewell; to command; to order or direct; to summon or enjoin, as: *Bid* him come. To offer; to propose, as a price at an auction.—**bid·der,** bid′er, *n.* One who bids or offers a price.

bid, bid, *n.* An offer of a price, especially at an auction; an act of bidding; an invitation; an effort to achieve some goal. *Cards,* an announcement of a certain number of points or tricks one will achieve; the amount of a bid or contract.

bid·da·ble, bid′a·bl, *a.* Of enough value to be bid upon; as, a *biddable* hand of cards in the game of bridge; tractable; easily obedient.—**bid·da·bil·i·ty,** *n.*

bid·dy, bid′ē, *n. pl.* **bid·dies.** [Dim. of *Bridget.*] A servant girl or cleaning woman; a fuss-budget. A hen; a young chicken.

bide, bīd, *v.i.*—*bided, biding.* [O.E. *bīdan* = Icel. *bida,* D. *beiden,* Goth. *beidan.* Hence *abide.*] To be or remain in a place or state;

to dwell; to abide.—*v.t. Archaic*, to endure; to suffer; to bear. To wait for: chiefly in the phrase, *to bide one's time.*

bi·den·tate, bī·den′tāt, *a.* [L.] Having two teeth, or processes like teeth.

bid·ri, bid′rē, *n.* [Hind. *bidrī*, < *Bidar*, town in Hyderabad, south-central India.] An alloy of copper, lead, zinc, etc., formerly used for making various articles inlaid with gold or silver.

bi·en·ni·al, bī·en′ē·el, *a.* [L. *biennium*, a space of two years—prefix *bi*, twice, *annus*, a year.] Happening or taking place once in two years; lasting for two years. *Bot.* continuing for two years and then perishing; taking two years to produce flowers and fruit.—*n.* A biennial event; *bot.* a biennial plant.—**bi·en·ni·al·ly**, *adv.* Once in two years; at the return of two years.

bi·en·ni·um, bī·en′ē·um, *n. pl.* **bi·en·ni·ums, bi·en·ni·a**, bī·en′ē·a. A period of two years.

bier, bēr, *n.* [< M.E. *bere* < O.E. *bær* = G. *bahre*.] A framework on which a corpse or the coffin is laid before burial or carried to the grave; the coffin and framework.

biff, bif, *v.t.* [Imit.] *Colloq.* to strike with a smart blow; to punch.—*n. Colloq.* a punch.

bi·fid, bī′fid, *a.* [L. *bifidus*—prefix *bi*, twice, *findo, fidi*, to split.] Cleft or divided into two parts; forked. *Bot.* divided half-way down into two parts; opening with a cleft.

bi·fi·lar, bī·fī′lar, *a.* Furnished or fitted with two filaments or threads.—*n.* A form of micrometer in which measurements are made by means of two very fine filaments. —**bi·fi·lar·ly**, bī·fī′lar·lē, *adv.*

bi·flag·el·late, bī·flaj′a·lāt″, bī·flaj′a·lit, *a. Biol.* possessing two whiplike projections or flagella.

bi·fo·cal, bī·fō′kal, *a.* Having two foci.— **bi·fo·cals**, *n. pl.* Eyeglasses with bifocal lenses.—**bi·fo·cal lens**, a lens with two parts: one for near and one for distant vision.

bi·fo·li·ate, bī·fō′lē·it, bī·fō′lē·āt″, *a. Bot.* having two leaves.

bi·form, bī′fɑrm, *a.* [L. *biformis*, double-formed.] Combining two forms, as some crystals; combining the characteristics of two individual forms, as a unicorn. Also **bi·formed**, bī′fɑrmed.

bi·fur·cate, bī′fer·kāt, bī·fur′kāt, *v.t., v.i.* —*bifurcated, bifurcating.* [M.L. *bifurcatus*, two-forked.] To divide or fork into two branches.—*a.* Forked; divided into two branches.

bi·fur·ca·tion, bī′fer·kā′ shan, *n.* A forking or division into two branches; the point of division.

big, big, *a.*—*bigger, biggest.* [Origin uncertain.] Having size; great; filled; important; large; bulky; great with young; pregnant; *fig.* full of something important. Teeming; distended; full, as with grief or passion; tumid; generous or kind; haughty in air or mien; pompous; proud.

big, big, *adv.* To a great extent, amount, or degree; *colloq.* finely or prosperously, as: Things are going over *big.* Pretentiously or boastfully; as, to talk *big.*—**go o·ver big**, to attain popularity; to be successful, as in entertainment.

big·a·mist, big′a·mist, *n.* One who has committed bigamy.

big·a·mous, big′a·mas, *a.* Of or pertaining to bigamy; guilty of bigamy.

big·a·my, big′a·mē, *n. pl.* **big·a·mies**. [< L. *bi*, twice, and Gr. *gamos*, marriage.] The crime of entering into marriage with another person while still legally married to a person from whom no valid divorce has been obtained.

big·ar·reau, big′a·rō, *n. pl.* **big·ar·reaus, big·ar·reaux**, big′a·rōz, big′a·rō. [Fr. *bigarrer*, variegate.] A kind of large heart-

shaped cherry of light color with sweet flavor and firm flesh; the tree which bears this fruit. Also **big·a·roon**, big″e·rön′.

Big Ben, *n.* The bell of the clock of the tower of Parliament in London, England.

big board, *n.* A name by which the New York Stock Exchange, the largest securities market in the United States, is known.

big broth·er, *n.* A man or youth who acts as sponsor or counselor for a young person, often within the membership of an organized group. (*Cap.*) the ominous figure which represents the all-seeing rule of heads or leaders of an authoritarian state.

bi·ge·ner·ic, bī″ja·ner′ik, *a.* Pertaining to two genera.

big·eye, big′ī″, *n.* Either of two varieties of food fish, reddish to silver in coloring, found in the tropical waters of the Pacific and in the Caribbean.

big game, *n. Hunting*, the larger wild animals and fish prized as trophies by sportsmen.

big·head, big′hed″, *n. Veter. pathol.* a disease of horses, sheep, etc., characterized by enlargement or swelling of the head. *colloq.* conceit.

big-heart·ed, big′här′tid, *a.* Kind; compassionate; generous.

big·horn, big′harn″, *n.* A large and very wild species of sheep, *Ovis montana* or *canadensis*, with curving horns, found in the western mountains of N. America; the Rocky Mountain sheep.

bight, bīt, *n.* [< M.E. < O.E. *byht*, a bend, < *būgan*, bow.] A bend or bending; an angle, as in the human or animal body; esp. the loop or bent part of a rope; the part of a rope between the ends; an indentation or recess, as in the shore of the sea or a river; hence, the space between two headlands; a bay, esp. a slightly receding bay between comparatively distant headlands.

big league, *n.* Major league.—**big-league**, big′lēg′, *a.* Of or on the highest level in any field.

big·mouthed, big′moutHd″, *a.* Having a big mouth; *fig.* pertaining to a person who talks loudly and indiscreetly.

big·no·ni·a, big·nō′nē·a, *n.* [N.L. named for J. *Bignon*, librarian to Louis XV.] Any plant of the genus *Bignonia*, which comprises climbing shrubs, American, Japanese, and mostly tropical, including species much cultivated in gardens and greenhouses for their showy trumpet-shaped flowers.

big·ot, big′ot, *n.* [Origin uncertain.] A person obstinately and unreasonably wedded to a particular religious creed, opinion, or practice; a person blindly attached to any opinion, system, or party, and bitterly intolerant of those who believe differently.— **big·ot·ed**, *a.*—**big·ot·ed·ly**, *adv.*

big·ot·ry, big′a·trē, *n. pl.* **big·ot·ries**. The tenets or actions of a bigot; obstinate or blind attachment to a particular creed or to certain tenets; unreasoning zeal; intolerance.

big shot, *n. Slang.* An important or influential person; one who is famous or very successful.—*a.* Influential, successful.

big-time, big′tīm′, *a. Slang*, pertaining to an endeavor of the highest quality or rank of its kind; as, a comedian from the *big-time* vaudeville era.—**big time**, *n.*

big top, *n.* The principal or largest tent of a circus; a circus.

big tree, *n.* An extremely tall and large tree, a species of sequoia, *Sequoia giganteum*, of California.

big wheel, *n. Slang.* An influential person; one who is successful or important; a big shot.

bi·jou, bē′zhū, bē·zhū′, *n. pl.* **bijoux**, bē′zhōz, bē·zhō′. [Fr. < Breton *bizou*, finger-ring.] A jewel; *fig.* something small and choice.

bi·ju·gous, bī′jö·gus, bī′jū·gus, *a.* [L. *bijugus*—*bi*, two, *jugum*, a yoke.] *Bot.* having two pairs of leaflets. Also **bi·ju·gate**, bī′jö·gāt, bī′jö·git.

bike, bīk, *n. Colloq.* a bicycle.—*v.i.* To bicycle.

bi·ki·ni, bi·kē′nē, *n.* [Fr. < *Bikini*, an atoll in the Marshall Islands.] A woman's very scanty two-piece bathing suit.

bi·la·bi·al, bī·lā′bē·l, *a.* Referring to a speech sound produced when the lips are close or touching, as in the sounds of *b*, *p*, or *m* and the semivowel *w*.—*n.* A speech sound so produced.

bi·la·bi·ate, bī·lā′bē·āt″, bī·lā′bē·it, *a.* [L. *bi*, twice, and *labium*, a lip.] *Bot.* applied to a corolla having two lips, as of mint.

bi·lan·der, bil′an·dẽr, bī′lan·dẽr, *n.* [D. *bijlander*—*bij*, by, near, and *land*, land.] A small merchant vessel with two masts, used chiefly in the Dutch canals.

bi·lat·er·al, bī·lat′er·al, *a.* [N.L. *bilateralis*, < L. *bi-*, two, and *latus* (*later-*), side.] Pertaining to or affecting two or both sides; disposed on opposite sides of an axis; two-sided; of a contract, binding the parties to mutual obligations.—**bi·lat·er·al·ism**, *n.*—**bi·lat·er·al·ly**, *adv.*—**bi·lat·er·al·ness**, *n.*

bil·ber·ry, bil′ber″ē, *n. pl.* **bil·ber·ries**, bil′ber″ēz. [Prob. < Scand., Dan. *böllebær.*] The edible fruit, whortleberry, of the shrub *Vaccinium myrtillus*; the shrub itself.

bile, bil, *n.* [Fr. *bile*, < L. *bilis*.] A bitter, viscid, yellow or greenish alkaline liquid secreted by the liver and aiding in digestion. *Fig.* ill humor; anger.

bile ac·id, *n.* An acid found in bile which promotes the digestion of fats, and aids in the absorption of many water-insoluble, organic substances.

bile duct, *n.* The tube through which the liver secretion passes as it leaves the gall bladder.

bilge, bilj, *n.* [Var. of *bulge*.] The protuberant part of a cask; the breadth of a ship's bottom, or that part of her floor which approaches to horizontal. *Slang*, foolish talk; drivel.

bilge keel, *n.* A keellike projection extending longitudinally along the turn of a ship's bilge on either side of the hull to retard rolling.

bilge wa·ter, *n.* A water which enters a ship and lies upon her bilge or bottom.

bil·i·ar·y, bil′ē·er″ē, *a.* Pertaining to the bile-conveying passages, or containing bile.

bi·lin·e·ar, bī·lin′ē·ẽr, *a.* Of, pertaining to, or involving two lines.

bi·lin·gual, bī·ling′gwal, *a.* [L. *bilinguis*—*bi*, double, and *lingua*, a tongue, a language.] Containing, or expressed in, two different languages; capable of speaking two languages, often with equal proficiency.

bil·ious, bil′yus, *a.* [L. *biliosus*.] Suffering from, caused by, or attended with disorder of the liver or bile; *fig.* choleric, peevish, or testy.—**bil·ious·ly**, *adv.*—**bil·ious·ness**, *n.*

bi·li·ru·bin, bil″a·rū′ban, bī·la·rū′ban, *n.* [< L. *bilis*. bile, and *rubeus*, red.] A reddish,-yellow pigment of urine, blood, or bile.

bi·li·ver·din, bil″a·vard′an, bī·la·vard′an, *n.* [< L. *bilis*, bile, and O.Fr. *verd*, green.] A greenish pigment found in bile.

bilk, bilk, *v.t.* [Origin uncertain.] To defraud, cheat, elude, disappoint.—**bilk·er**, bilk′er, *n.* A swindler.

bill, bil, *n.* [A.Fr. *bille*, < A.L. *billa*, for M.L. *bulla*, writing, document.] A formal written or printed declaration, as a statement of particulars; a written or printed public notice or advertisement, as a handbill, placard, or poster; an account of money due or claimed, in full or as monthly payments, for goods supplied or services rendered; a bank note or other like piece of paper money; *slang*, $100. A bill of exchange; a draft of a proposed statute, presented to a legislature for adoption; *law*, a written statement, usually of complaint, presented to a court.

bill, bil, *v.t.* To enter in a bill; charge in a bill; to announce by bill or public notice; to post, as bills, throughout a town, etc.

bill, bil, *n.* [O.E. *bile.*] The horny sheath enveloping the jaws of a bird; a similar structure in other animals, as the turtle; a beak; also, a beaklike projection; a narrow promontory; the point of the fluke of an anchor.—*v.i.* Of birds, to join bills, as if caressing.

bill, bil, *n.* [< M.E. < O.E. *bil, bill,* a bill, a sword, etc.; D. and G. *bille,* a pick; Dan. *biil,* D. *bijl,* G. *beil,* a hatchet; root in Skt. *bhil,* to split.] A cutting instrument hook-shaped toward the point, or with a concave cutting edge, used in pruning, etc.; a bill-hook.

bil·la·bong, bil′a·bong″, *n.* [Native Australian.] A branch of a river flowing away from the main stream, in some cases returning to it lower down; a stream which is dry except during the rainy season.

bill·board, bil′bōrd″, *n.* A board, fence, or other construction on which large, printed advertisements are affixed.

billed, bild, *a.* Having a bill or beak.

bil·let, bil′it, *n.* [< M.E. *billette* < O.Fr. *bille,* a writing; hence, an order.] *Milit.* nonmilitary quarters for a soldier; a directive to provide such quarters. *Naut.* sleeping accommodations assigned to a crew member of a ship.

bil·let, bil′it, *v.t.* To quarter or place in lodgings, as soldiers in private houses.—*v.i.* To be quartered; to lodge soldiers.

bil·let, bil it, *n.* [O.Fr. Fr. *billette,* dim. of *bille,* log.] A thick stick of wood, esp. one for fuel; a bar or slab of iron or steel, esp. when obtained from an ingot by forging, etc.; *arch.* one of a series of short cylindrical rods forming part of a molding.

bil·let-doux, bil′ē·dö′, bil′ā·dö′, *n.* pl. **bil·lets-doux,** bil′ē·döz′, bil′ā·döz′. [Fr., lit. 'sweet billet or note.'] A love note or short love letter.

bill·fish, bil′fish″, *n.* pl. **bill·fish, bill·fishes.** One of various fishes with a long beak or snout, as the gar or the sword fish.

bill·fold, bil′fōld″, *n.* A folding case carried in the pocket, for holding credit cards, personal documents, and paper money; wallet.

bill·head, bil′hed″, *n.* A heading, usually containing one's name and address, printed on a form used for billing charges; a form with the heading.

bill·hook, bil′huk″, *n.* An instrument with a blade curving inward at the tip, for pruning or cutting.

bil·liard, bil′yard, *a.* Pertaining to billiards. —*n. Colloq.* a carom or shot in billiards in which the cue ball hits the two other balls consecutively.

bil·liards, bil′yardz, *n. pl., sing. or pl. in constr.* [Fr. *billard,* the game of billiards, a billiard cue, from *bille,* a piece of wood.] A game played on a long rectangular, cloth-covered table, without pockets, with three ivory balls: scores are made by the use of a cue to cause one ball to strike the other two. —**pock·et bil·liards,** a game played on the same kind of table but having six pockets and fifteen numbered balls and one cue ball, the object being to drive the numbered balls into pockets with the cue ball.

bil·lings·gate, bil′ingz·gāt″, *n.* [< a fish-market of this name in London, notorious for the use of foul language.] Profane or abusive language; ribaldry.

bil·lion, bil′yon, *n.* [Fr., contr. < L. *bis,* twice, and *million.*] A thousand millions in

the U.S. and France; a million millions in Great Britain and Germany.—**bil·lion·aire,** bil″ya·nâr′, *n.* The owner of a billion dollars, francs, pounds, etc.—**bil·lionth,** *a.* Being the final unit in a series of a billion; referring to one of a billion identical parts. —*n.* The billionth unit in a series; the billionth part.

bill of cred·it, *n. U.S. hist.* a paper issued by a State, and based on its own credit, to be circulated as money: forbidden by the Constitution.

bill of ex·change, *n.* An order in writing to pay a certain sum in money to a specified person or to his order.

bill of fare, *n.* A list of the dishes served at a meal, or of those that may be ordered, as at a restaurant.

bill of goods, *n.* An order or shipment of saleable items; *slang,* an argument, a business deal, etc., esp. if undesirable, unwanted, or of doubtful authenticity, as: He sold me a *bill of goods.*

bill of health, *n.* A certificate signed by consuls or other authorities as to the health of a ship's company at the time of her clearing any port.—**clean bill of health,** *colloq.* A good report; a declaration of qualifications or suitability.

bill of lad·ing, *n.* A written receipt given by a carrier for goods delivered to the carrier for transportation.

bill of rights, *n.* A formal statement of the fundamental rights of the people of a nation; (*cap.*) the first ten amendments to the Constitution of the United States.

bill of sale, *n.* A formal instrument for the conveyance or transfer of personal property.

bil·lon, bil′on, *n.* [Fr. and O.Fr. *billon,* debased metal, ingot, < *bille,* log.] An alloy used in coinage, consisting of gold or silver with a preponderant admixture of some base metal, esp. an alloy of silver with copper or the like in very large proportion, used for coins of small denomination; any coin made from such an alloy.

bil·low, bil′ō, *n.* [Icel. *bylgja,* Dan. *bölge,* Sw. *bölja,* a swell, a billow, from root of *bulge, belly, bellows.*] A great wave or surge of the sea; a wavelike mass, as of flame.— **bil·low·y,** *a.*—billowier, billowiest.

bil·low, bil′ō, *v.i.* To swell; to rise and roll in large waves or surges.

bill·post·er, bil′pōs″tėr, *n.* One whose business it is to post up bills or advertisements in public places. Also **bill·stick·er.**

bil·ly, bil′ē, *n.* pl. **bil·lies.** [Fr. < *Billy,* for *William,* man's name.] A bludgeon, as one for carrying in the pocket; a policeman's club; in the Australian bush, a tin kettle or pot for cooking or making tea.

bil·ly·cock, bil′ē·kok, *n. Brit.* A derby hat; any round, low-crowned felt hat worn by men.

bil·ly goat, *n.* [From the man's name.] A male goat.

bi·lo·bate, bī·lō′bāt, *a.* Divided into two lobes; as, a *bilobate* leaf. Also **bi·lo·bat·ed,** bi·lobed, bī′lōbd″.

bi·loc·u·lar, bī·lok′ya·lar, *a.* [L. *bi,* twice, and *loculus,* a cell, < *locus,* a place.] Divided into two cells or small compartments. Also **bi·loc·u·late,** bī·lok′ū·lāt.

bil·tong, bil′tong″, *n.* [S.Afr. D.] Lean meat in strips dried in the open air.

bi·man·u·al, bī·man′ū·al, *a.* Involving the use of both hands.—**bi·man·u·al·ly,** *adv.*

bi·mes·ter, bī·mes′tėr, bī′mes·tėr, *n.* A period of time covering two months.— **bi·mes·tri·al,** bī·mes′trē·al, *a.*

bi·met·al·lism, bī·met′al·iz″um, *n.* That system of currency which recognizes coins of two metals, as silver and gold, as legal tender to any amount; the policy or doctrine which maintains this standard.—**bi·met·**

al·list, *n.* One who favors bimetallism.— **bi·me·tal·lic,** bī″me·tal′ik, *a.*

bi·mil·le·nar·y, bī″mi·len′a·rē, *n.* A period of time covering 2,000 years; the anniversary which observes the completion of a 2,000-year period. Also **bi·mil·len·ial,** bī″mi·len′ē·al.—*a.*—**bi·mil·len·nium,** *n.* pl. **bi·mil·len·niums, bi·mil·len·nia.**

bi·mod·al, bī·mōd′al, *a. Statistics,* containing two statistical modes; of a frequency distribution with two modes or two items in a series whose values occur most frequently, or, if arranged in groups, two classes with the largest number of items.

bi·mo·lec·u·lar, bī″mo·lek′ū·lėr, *a. Chem.* having to do with, or formed by, two molecules.

bi·month·ly, bī·munth′lē, *n.* pl. **bi·month·lies.** A bimonthly publication.

bi·month·ly, bī·munth′lē, *a.* Occurring every two months. *Colloq.* twice a month.

bi·mo·tored, bī·mō′tord, *a.* Possessing two motors.

bin, bin, *n.* [< M.E. < O.E. *bin, binn,* a bin, a hutch; D. *ben,* G. *benne, binne,* a basket.] A box or enclosed place used as a repository for any commodity; one of the subdivisions of a cellar, for such as grain, coal, or wine.

bi·na·ry, bī′na·rē, *a. Computer,* pertaining to a quality in a thing, a system, or a situation, that carries possibilities of making a choice between two alternatives.—*n.* pl. **bi·na·ries.** A numerical system based on units of two; anything having only two principal elements.

bi·na·ry code, *n. Computer,* a system of numerical calculations employing only two characters.

bi·na·ry dig·it, *n. Computer,* bit.

bi·na·ry sys·tem, *n. Computer,* a numeration system with base 2 (contrasted with our common system of base 10) in which all numbers are expressed by 0 or 1 or a combination of these digits: used in digital computers.

bi·nate, bī′nāt, *a. Bot.* being double or in couples; growing in pairs.

bin·au·ral, bī·nar′al, bin·ar′al, *a.* Having two ears; also, of, with, or for both ears; as, *binaural* sound, sound that is transmitted over two channels simultaneously and received through earphones.

bin·au·ral broad·cast·ing, *n.* Radio broadcasting via both FM and AM microphones, so arranged that pickup on FM and AM receivers provides a stereophonic effect.

bind, bīnd, *v.t.*—*bound, binding.* [< M.E. O.E. *bindan,* pret. *band,* pp. *bunden* = Icel. Sw. *binda,* Dan. *binde,* D. and G. *binden,* same root as Skt. *bandh,* to bind.] To tie or confine with a cord, or anything that is flexible; to fasten or encircle, as with a band or ligature; to put a ligature or bandage on; to put in bonds or fetters; to hold in, confine, constrict, or restrain; to make cohere; to engage by a promise, agreement, vow, law, duty, or any other moral or legal tie; to form a border on, or strengthen by a border; to sew together and cover (a book); *law,* to place under legal obligation. To indenture (a person) as an apprentice; *pathol.* to constipate.—*v.i.* To exercise an obligatory influence; to be obligatory; to tie up; to hinder free movement, as tight clothing; to exercise a restraining force; become compact; to tie sheaves up; to grow hard or stiff (of soil); to jam.

bind, bīnd, *n.* That which binds; the process of binding; the condition of being bound by limiting circumstances; as, in a *bind*; a location where binding takes place; *mus.* a brace, tie, or slur.

bind·er, bīnd′ėr, *n.* A person who binds; one whose occupation is to bind books; a machine that binds sheaves; anything that binds, as a cord, rope, or band; a bandage;

that which causes cohesion of elements in a mixture; an agreement granting insurance coverage until a policy is issued; a receipt which assures the right to buy real estate on agreed terms.

bind·er·y, bīn′da·rē, bīn′drē, *n. pl.* **bind·- er·ies.** A place where books are bound within covers.

bind·ing, bīn′ding, *n.* The act of one who binds; anything which binds; the cover of a book, with the sewing and accompanying work; something that secures the edges of cloth; a set of ski fastenings used to secure the boot onto the ski.—**bind·ing·ly,** *adv.* In a binding manner; so as to bind.— **bind·ing·ness,** *n.*

bind·ing, bīn′ding, *a.* Serving to bind; having power to bind or oblige; obligatory; making fast; astringent.

bind·ing en·er·gy, *n. Physics,* the energy needed to separate a particle or other entity from a system; the energy required to disperse a molecule, atom, or nucleus completely into its constituent particles against the forces of cohesion. Also **sep·a·ra·tion en·er·gy.**

Bi·net test, bi·nā′ test′, *n.* [From A. *Binet* and T. *Simon,* 19th–20th century French psychologists.] A test for determining the relative development of intelligence, consisting of a series of questions and tasks graded with reference to the ability of the normal person to deal with them at successive ages. Also **Bi·net Si·mon test,** bi·nā′- sī′man test′, *Stanford-Binet test.*

binge, binj, *n. Slang.* A spree; a fit or spell of anything.

bin·go, bing′gō, *n.* A game similar to lotto, often played simultaneously by large groups, the winner being the first contestant to cover a line of five numbered spaces on his card as selected by chance and announced by the game's caller.

bin·na·cle, bin′a·kal, *n.* [Formerly, *bittacle,* < Fr. *habitacle,* a little house.] A case on the deck of a vessel, near the helm, containing the compass and lights by which it can be read at night.

bi·noc·u·lar, bi·nok′ū·lẽr, bī·nok′ū·lẽr, *a.* Pertaining to or employing both eyes; suited for the simultaneous use of both eyes, as certain telescopes, etc.—*n. Usu. pl.* A binocular optical instrument, as a field glass.—**bi·noc·u·lar·i·ty,** bī·nok′ū·lar′i·- tē, *n.*—**bi·noc·u·lar·ly,** *adv.*

bi·no·mi·al, bī·nō′mē·al, *a.* [M.L. *binomius,* < L. *binominis.*] *Math.* consisting of or pertaining to two terms connected by the sign + or −.

bi·no·mi·al, bī·nō′mē·al, *a.* Having or using two names, as of genus and species.

bi·no·mi·al dis·tri·bu·tion, *n. Math.* a frequency distribution based on the inherent probability of the binomial expansion.

bi·no·mi·al ex·pan·sion, *Math.* the multiplicative expansion given by the binomial theorem.

bi·no·mi·al no·men·cla·ture, *n. Bot., zool.* the scientific system of naming and classifying animals and plants by giving, in order, their generic and specific terms, as: *Felis leo* (the lion) and *Felis tigris* (the tiger), two animals of the same genus (*Felis*) but different species; the present system was first standardized by Linnaeus in the mid-18th century and forms part of the International Rules of Nomenclature. Also *binomial.*

bi·no·mi·al the·or·em, *n.* A celebrated theorem by Sir Isaac Newton, for raising a binomial to any power, or for extracting any root of it, expressed by: $(x + y)^n =$

$$x^n + nx^{n-1}y + \frac{n(n-1)}{2!}x^{n-2}y^2 +$$

$$\frac{n(n-1)(n-2)}{3!}x^{n-3}y^3 + \cdots + y^n.$$

bi·nu·cle·ar, bī·nö′klē·är, bī·nū′klē·är, *a.* Having two nuclei. Also **bi·nu·cle·ate,** bī·nö′klē·āt″, bī·nū′klē·āt″.

bio·as·say, bī″ō·a·sā′, bī″ō·as′ā, *n. Biol.* quantitative determination or estimate of the biological activity or potency of a substance, such as a hormone, by observation of its action on a test organism.—bī″ō·a·- sā′, *v.t.* To do a bioassay on.

bio·as·tro·nau·tics, bī″ō·as″trō·nạ′tiks, *n. pl. but sing. in constr.* The study of the biological, behavioral, and medical effects of air flight and space travel on plant and animal life; space medicine.

bi·o·cat·a·lyst, bī″ō·kat′a·list, *n.* A biochemical catalyst; a substance that accelerates or modifies a physiological process, such as a hormone.

bio·chem·is·try, bī″ō·kem′i·strē, *n.* The science that studies the chemical processes of plant and animal life.—**bio·chem·ist,** *n.* —**bio·chem·i·cal,** *a.*

bi·o·cide, bī′o·sīd″, *n.* Destruction of living organisms by such unphysiologic effects of civilization as pollution, nuclear fallout, and pesticides; a pesticide.—**bi·o·cid·al,** *a.*

bi·o·cli·ma·tol·o·gy, bī″ō·klī″ma·tol′o·jē, *n.* The study of the relations of climate and life, particularly the effects of climate on the health and activity of living things.— **bi·o·cli·mat·ic,** bī″ō·klī·mat′ik, *a.*

bi·o·com·mu·ni·ca·tion, bī″ō·ko·mū″- ni·kā′shan, *n.* The exchange of information as alarms, threats, mating calls, etc., between biological units of the same species, usually by means of visual or auditory signals.

bi·o·dy·nam·ics, bī″ō·dī·nam′iks, *n. pl., sing. or pl. in constr.* The branch of biology that treats of vital force, energy, or action of living organisms: opposed to *biostatics.*— **bi·o·dy·nam·ic, bi·o·dy·nam·i·cal,** *a.*

bi·o·e·col·o·gy, bī″ō·i·kol′o·jē, *n.* Branch of science dealing with the interaction of plants and animals with their environment.

bi·o·en·er·get·ics, bī″ō·en″ẽr·jet′iks, *n. pl., sing. or pl. in constr.* A branch of biology dealing with energy transformations in life processes and the application of fundamental rules of thermodynamics to living systems.

bi·o·en·gi·neer·ing, bī″ō·en″ji·nẽr′ing, *n.* Use of principles of engineering in the study and direction of processes and products of biology.

bi·o·gen·e·sis, bī″ō·jen′i·sis, *n.* The development of living matter from preexisting matter, as opposed to *abiogenesis;* the history of the life development of organized existences.—**bio·ge·net·ic,** bī″ō·je·net′ik, *a.*

bi·o·ge·og·ra·phy, bī″ō·jē·og′ra·fē, *n.* The branch of biology that treats of the geographical distribution of living things. —**bi·o·ge·o·graph·ic, bi·o·ge·o·graph·- i·cal,** bī″ō·gē″o·graf′ik, *a.*

bi·o·graph, bī′o·graf″, *n.* A kind of cinematograph; also *bioscope.*

bi·og·ra·pher, bī·og′ra·fer, bē·og′ra·fer, *n.* A person who writes biography; a writer of accounts of the lives of others.

bi·o·graph·i·cal, bī″o·graf′i·kal, *a.* Pertaining to biography; containing biography; of, or relating to an individual's life. Also **bi·o·graph·ic,** bī″o·graf′ik.—**bi·o·graph·- i·cal·ly,** *adv.*

bi·og·ra·phy, bī·og′ra·fē, bē·og′ra·fē, *n. pl.* **bi·og·ra·phies.** The history of the life and character of another person; a life history of an object, as of a coin; biographical writings in general, or as a department of literature.

bi·o·in·stru·ment, bī″ō·in′stru·ment, *n.* An apparatus fastened to the body to record physiological information.

bi·o·log·i·cal, bī″o·loj′i·kal, *a.* Pertaining to biology or life; dealing with applied biology. Also **bi·o·log·ic.**—*n. Pharm.* a

biochemical product, as a vaccine, serum, or antitoxin. Also **bi·o·log·ic.**

bi·o·log·i·cal bat·ter·y, *n.* A means of producing electrical current by utilizing a sea-water solution containing bacteria.

bi·o·log·i·cal clock, *n.* A mechanism located internally in living organisms which commands the rhythmic cycles of diverse involuntary activities.

bi·o·log·i·cal con·trol, *n.* Attack on pests and parasites by interfering with their relationship to their environment, as by the introduction of their natural enemies.

bi·o·log·i·cal e·lec·tric·i·ty, *n.* The electricity which is created by living beings and cells.

bi·o·log·i·cal war·fare, *n.* Warfare using bacteria or viruses or their products against men, domestic animals, or food plants.

bi·ol·o·gism, bī·ol′o·jiz″um, *n.* A doctrine constructed from the biological point of view; adherence to such a point of view, esp. preoccupation with biological explanations of social phenomena.—**bi·o·lo·gis·tic,** *a.* Of or relating to a biologism.

bi·ol·o·gist, bī·ol′o·jist, *n.* One skilled in or one who studies biology.

bi·ol·o·gy, bī·ol′o·jē, *n.* The science of life, or which treats generally of the life of animals and plants, including their morphology, physiology, origin, development, and distribution; the lives of plants and animals in a certain region; the biological phenomena relating to an organism or group.

bi·o·lu·mi·nes·cence, bī″ō·lö″mi·nes′- ens, *n.* The emission of light from living organisms, such as fireflies.

bi·o·mass, bī′ō·mas″, *n. Biol.* the amount of living matter in any given habitat usually measured by the weight of organisms per unit area or by the volume of organisms per unit volume of habitat.

bi·o·me·chan·ics, bī″ō·me·kan′iks, *n. pl., sing. or pl. in constr.* The observation of how living organisms function, esp. in situations of unexpected violence, or continuing tension.

bi·o·med·i·cine, bī″ō·med′i·sin, *n.* A field of medical science concerned with the ability of a human being to live and act in abnormal environments.—**bi·o·med·i·cal,** bī″ō·med′i·kal, *a.*

bi·om·e·try, bī·om′i·trē, *n.* The measurement of life; the calculation of the probable duration of human life; also, the branch of biological science concerned with quantitative statistics of the properties and phenomena of living things. Also **bi·o·met·rics,** bī·ō·met′triks, *n. pl., sing. or pl. in constr.*

bi·o·nom·ics, bī″ō·nom′iks, *n. pl., sing. or pl. in constr.* That branch of biology which treats of the relations between organisms and their environment; ecology.—**bi·o·- nom·ic, bi·o·nom·i·cal,** *a.*—**bi·on·o·- mist,** bī·on′o·mist, *n.*

bi·on·o·my, bī·on′o·mē, *n.* The science of the natural laws of living organisms and the interrelation of these organisms to their environment; ecology.

bi·o·phys·ics, bī″ō·fiz′iks, *n. pl., sing. or pl. in constr.* The study of living things using the methods and principles of physics.—**bi·o·phys·i·cal,** *a.*—**bi·o·phys·i·- cist,** *n.*

bi·o·pol·y·mer, bī″ō·pol′i·mẽr, *n.* A polymeric material, such as a protein, produced in a living system.

bi·op·sy, bī′op·sē, *n. pl.* **bi·op·sies.** The examination of tissue from a living subject for diagnostic purposes.

bi·o·rhy·thm, bī″ō·rith′um, *n.* An essential rhythm that begins or governs a biological process.

bi·o·sat·el·lite, bī″ō·sat′e·līt″, *n.* An artificial satellite designed to contain and support men, animals, or other living material in outer space, and which possesses means for safe return to the earth with information on the effects of extraterrestrial conditions on live organisms.

bi·o·sci·ence, bī″ō·sī′ans, n. Biology.

bi·o·scope, bī′ō·skōp″, n. An early moving-picture projector of about 1900.

bi·o·sphere, bī′o·sfēr″, n. The earth, water, and region of the atmosphere that supports plant and animal life.

bi·o·stat·ics, bī·ō·stat′iks, n. pl. but sing. in constr. The branch of biology that treats of the structure of organisms in relation to their functions: opposed to biodynamics.—**bi·o·stat·ic, bi·o·stat·i·cal,** a.

bi·o·syn·the·sis, bī″ō·sin′thi·sis, n. The synthesis of a chemical within and by a living organism.

bi·o·ta, bī·ō′ta, n. [N.L., < Gr. bio(s), life.] The animal and plant life of a given region or period.

bi·o·tech·nol·o·gy, bī″ō·tek·nol′o·jē, n. Aerospace, the application of engineering and technological principles to the life sciences.

bi·o·tel·em·e·try, bī″ō·te·lem′i·trē, n. Aerospace, the remote measuring and evaluation of life functions, as in spacecraft and artificial satellites.

bi·ot·ic, bī·ot′ik, a. Pertaining to life; vital. Also **bi·ot·i·cal.**

bi·ot·ic po·ten·tial, n. Biol. the capacity of a species of animals or plants to survive and reproduce, usually described as the number that could be produced under optimum conditions.

bi·o·tin, bī′o·tin, n. Biochem. A crystalline growth vitamin, $C_{10}H_{16}O_3N_2S$, of the vitamin B complex, vital in the prevention of animal death due to an excess of egg white in the diet; also, vitamin H.

bi·o·tite, bī′o·tīt″, n. [Named for J. B. Biot, French physicist, 1774–1862.] A black, dark brown, or green mica containing magnesium, aluminum, iron, and potassium; an important part of crystalline rocks.—**bi·o·tit·ic,** bī″o·tit′ik, a.

bi·o·tron, bī′o·tron, n. A test chamber used for biological research, esp. for observation of the effect of variations in environment on living organisms.

bi·o·type, bī′o·tīp″, n. Biol. a group of organisms or individuals having many of the same or similar genetic traits and physiological characteristics.—**bi·o·typ·ic,** bī″o·tip′ik, a.

bi·o·vu·lar, bī″ō·vū·lèr′, a. Originating from two ova, such as fraternal twins.

bi·pack, bī′pak″, n. Photog. a film having two superimposed layers, each with an emulsion sensitive to a different color, used in color photography.

bip·ar·ous, bip′ėr·us, a. [L. bi, twice, and pario, to bear.] Bringing forth two at a birth. Bot. bearing two axes or branches.

bi·par·ti·san, bī·pär′ti·zan, a. Of or pertaining to two parties or two divergent viewpoints cooperating to further a single purpose, as the Democratic and Republican parties, legislators, or government executives.

bi·par·tite, bī·pär′tīt, a. Having two parts; bot. divided into two parts nearly to the base, as a leaf; law, being in two corresponding parts, as a contract.—**bi·par·ti·tion,** bī″pär·tish′an, n.

bi·ped, bī′ped, n. [L. bipes.] An animal having two feet, as man.—**bi·ped·al,** bī′ped·al, a. Having two feet.

bi·pet·al·ous, bī·pet′a·lus, a. Bot. having two petals.

bi·phen·yl, bī·fen′l, bī·fēn′l, n. Chem. a colorless, crystalline hydrocarbon derived from coal tar; used in lacquer and for preserving citrus fruits. Also diphenyl.

bi·plane, bī′plān″, n. An early type of airplane with two supporting wings, one above the other.

bi·pod, bī′pod, n. A stand supported by two legs.

bi·po·lar, bī·pō′lar, a. Having two poles, as the Arctic and the Antarctic; pertaining to or found at both poles.—**bi·po·lar·i·ty,** bī″pō·lar′i·tē, n.

bi·pro·pel·lant, bī″pro·pel′ant, n. A rocket propellant composed of fuel and oxidizer fed separately to the combustion chamber.

bi·quad·rat·ic, bī″kwo·drat′ik, n. [L. bi, double, twice, and quadratus, squared.] Math. The fourth power, arising from the multiplication of a square by itself; the square of the square.—a. Pertaining to this power.

bi·ra·cial, bī·rā′shal, a. Pertaining to or consisting of a combination of people of two races, as white and Negro.

bi·ra·di·al, bī·rā′dē·al, a. Having both radial and bilateral symmetry.

bi·ra·mose, bī·rā′mōs, bī″ra·mōs′, a. Having, or consisting of, two branches. Also **bi·ra·mous,** bī·rā′mus.

birch, bûrch, n. [M.E. birche, birch tree < O.E. birce < Skt. bhūrja, kind of birch.] A graceful tree of the genus Betula having small leaves, slender, often drooping branches, and a smooth, multi-layered, whitish bark.

birch·bark, bûrch′bärk″, n. A light canoe made of bark from the birch tree.

birch·en, bûr′chen, a. Made of birch; consisting of birch.

bird, bûrd, n. [O.E. bridd, young bird.] Any of the Aves, a class of warm-blooded vertebrates having a body more or less completely covered with feathers, and the forelimbs so modified as to form wings by means of which most species fly in the air; among sportsmen, any of various game-birds, as a partridge; also, a clay pigeon. Brit. slang, a young girl.

bird, bûrd, v.i. To watch, catch, or shoot birds.

bird·bath, bûrd′bath″, bûrd′bäth″, n. An ornamental basin placed outdoors to be filled with water in which birds may bathe.

bird·brain, bûrd′brān″, n. Colloq. a scatterbrain.—**bird·brained,** a.

bird·cage, bûrd′kāj″, n. A cage for a bird.

bird call, n. The call or cry of a bird, or a sound in imitation of it; also, an instrument for imitating the call.

bird col·o·nel, n. Slang, a full colonel of the U.S. Army. Also chicken colonel.

bird dog, n. Any of several breeds of dogs, capable of being trained to hunt birds.

bir·der, bûr′dèr, n. One who has a special or commercial interest in observing, hunting, or raising birds. Also **bird watch·er.**

bird·house, bûrd′hous″, n. pl. **bird·hous·es.** A box used outdoors to attract and shelter birds, often styled to resemble a miniature dwelling; an aviary.

bird·ie, bûr′dē, n. Sports, in golf, a score based on one stroke under par on a hole. A small bird.

bird·lime, bûrd′līm″, n. A viscous substance smeared on twigs to catch small birds.—v.t.—birdlimed, birdliming. To smear or catch with or as with birdlime.

bird louse, n. An insect parasitic on birds.

bird·man, bûrd′man″, bûrd′man, n. pl. **bird·men.** One who raises, hunts, or studies birds; an ornithologist; colloq. an aviator.

bird of par·a·dise, n. Any bird of the family Paradiseidae, of New Guinea, etc., noted for magnificent plumage, as Paradisea apoda, one of the most beautiful species.

bird of pas·sage, n. A migratory bird; often used figuratively to refer to a migratory or footloose person.

bird of prey, n. Any of a group of predaceous, flesh-eating birds comprising the eagles, hawks, vultures, owls, etc.

bird pep·per, n. A variety of red pepper, producing pods which are used as condiments or gastric stimulants.

bird·seed, bûrd′sēd″, n. A seed mixture used to feed small birds in cages, or to attract wild birds.

bird's-eye, bûrdz′ī″, a. Seen comprehensively, as by a bird flying above; as, a bird's-eye view; hence, general, not entering into details; having markings or spots resembling birds' eyes; as, bird's-eye maple. —n.

bird's-foot, bûrdz′fut″, n. pl. **bird's-foots.** Any of various plants whose leaves, flowers, or pods resemble or suggest the claw of a bird, esp. plants of the genus Ornithopus, which have clawlike pods.

bird's-foot tre·foil, n. A forage plant of the bean family, U.S. and European, the pods of which spread to resemble a crow's foot.

bird's nest, n. The nest of a bird; the nest of swifts of the genus Collocalia, consisting largely of inspissated saliva of birds, used esp. by the Chinese in soup; one of various plants, as the wild carrot.—**bird's-nest,** bûrdz′nest, v.i. To search for birds' nests.

bird·wom·an, bûrd′wum″an, n. pl. **bird·wom·en.** Slang, an aviatress.

bi·re·frin·gence, bī″ri·frin′jens, n. The double refraction of light to form two unequal rays.—**bi·re·frin·gent,** a.

bi·reme, bī′rēm, n. [< L. bi, two, and remus, an oar.] An ancient Greek or Roman galley with two banks or tiers of oars.

bi·ret·ta, bi·ret′a, n. [It. berretta, < M.L. birretum, < L. birrus, cloak.] A stiff, square cap with three (or four) upright projecting pieces extending from the center of the top to the edge, worn by Roman Catholic ecclesiastics. Also berretta, **bir·ret·ta.**

birl, bûrl, v.t. [Origin uncertain.] Brit. to spin; to tread on, as a floating log, and make turn rapidly; to pour, as a drink, or supply, as a person, with drink.—v.i. Carouse; colloq. to gamble or dispose of money without reservation. To move by whirling.

bir·ne, bir′na, n. [< G. lit. pear.] Boule.

birr, bur, n. [Imitative of the sound.] A whirring noise; strength; vigor; emphatic speech.—v.i. To move with a whirring sound.

birth, bûrth, n. [< M.E. byrth(e) < beran, to bear; Goth. gabaurths, G. geburt.] The act or process of being born; the occasion of an individual's coming into life; the act of bearing or bringing forth; parturition; the condition in which a person is born; lineage; extraction; descent; that which is born or produced; origin; beginning.

birth cer·ti·fi·cate, n. An official copy of the record of one's birth with pertinent information such as names of parents, place, and date of birth.

birth con·trol, n. The prevention or the regulation of conception through the use of drugs or devices.

birth·day, bûrth′dā, n. The day on which any person is born, or the anniversary of the day; day or time of origin.

birth·mark, bûrth′märk″, n. Some congenital mark on a person's body; nevus.

birth·place, bûrth′plās″, n. The place of one's birth; place of origin.

birth rate, n. The ratio of the number of births in a given time and population to the total population (usually expressed in terms of the number of births per one thousand of population).

birth·right, bûrth′rīt″, n. Any right or privilege to which a person is entitled by birth; right of primogeniture.

birth·root, bûrth′rōt″, bûrth′rut″, n. A North American plant, Trillium erectum, the roots of which are esteemed as astringent, tonic, and antiseptic.

birth·stone, bûrth′stōn″, n. A stone of precious or semi-precious quality traditionally associated with a certain month or sign of the zodiac, and popularly regarded as a token of good luck for the wearer who was born in that time period.

birth trau·ma, *n.* Severe emotional stress experienced by a child at birth, considered in psychoanalytic theory a likely source of neuroses in later years.

birth-wort, burth′wurt, *n,* A plant, *Aristolochia clematitis,* native to Europe, reputed in folk medicine to have properties which facilitate childbirth.

bis, bis, *adv.* [L. *bis,* twice.] Twice; a second time: used esp. to direct or request a repetition, as of a piece of music.

bis·cuit, bis′kit, *n.* [< L. *bis,* twice, and *cuit.* pp. to cook.] Bread baked in small pieces from dough leavened with soda, yeast, or baking powder; *Brit.* a kind of unraised bread, plain or fancy, formed into flat cakes, and baked hard: commonly called *cracker* in the United States. A cookie; a light brown color. *Ceram.* porcelain or earthenware after being first fired, and before the application of the glazing and embellishments; also *bisque.*

bise, bēz, *n.* [M.E. < O.Fr. < O.H.G. *bīsa,* north wind.] A dry, cold north or northeast wind in southeastern France, Switzerland, and adjoining regions.

bi·sect, bī·sekt′, bī′sekt, *v.t.* To divide into two parts; esp. into two equal parts, as a line, etc.; to intersect.—*v.i.* To fork, as in a road.

bi·sec·tion, bī·sek′shən, *n.* The act of bisecting; the division of a line, angle, etc., into two equal parts.

bi·sec·tor, bī·sek′tėr, bī′sek·tér, *n. Geom.* A straight line or plane surface that bisects an angle or a line segment; that which bisects.

bi·ser·rate, bī·ser′āt, *a. Bot.* doubly serrate; notched like a saw, with the teeth also notched, as certain leaves; *zool.* serrate on both sides, as some antennae.

bi·sex·u·al, bī·sek′shö·al, *a.* Having the organs of both sexes in one individual; of two sexes; hermaphrodite; *bot.* having both stamen and pistil within the same envelope. *Psychiatry,* to be responsive sexually to either sex.—*n.*

bish·op, bish′op, *n.* [O.E. *biscop,* a bishop, < Gr. *episcopos,* an overseer—*epi,* over, and *skopeō,* to look.] A member of the highest order of the ministry; a prelate having the spiritual direction and government of a diocese, the oversight of the clergy within it, and with whom rests the power of ordination, confirmation, and consecration; a piece in the game of chess; *Brit.* a hot drink made with a base of port wine.

bish·op·ric, bish′op·rik, *n.* [*bishop* and O.E. suffix *-ric(e),* realm.] The office or dignity of a bishop; the district over which the jurisdiction of a bishop extends; a diocese.

bis·muth, biz′muth, *n.* [G., now *wismut,* earlier *wissmuth;* origin unknown.] *Chem.* A brittle metallic element, having compounds used in medicine. Sym. Bi, at no. 83. See Periodic Table of Elements.

bis·muth·ic, biz·mū′thik, bis·muth′ik, *a.* Of or pertaining to bismuth; containing bismuth, esp. in the pentavalent state. Also **bis·muth·al,** biz·mu′thal.—**bis·muth·ous,** biz′mu·thus, *a.* Containing bismuth, esp. in the trivalent state.

bi·son, bī′son, bī′zon, *n.* [L. *bison,* Gr. *bisōn,* a name borrowed from the ancient Germans.] Either of two bovine quadrupeds, the European bison or wisent, and the American bison, usually called the buffalo, having short, rounded horns, and on the shoulders a large fleshy hump.

bisque, bisk, *n.* [< Fr.] A thick, rich soup made of shell-fish or game stewed long and slowly; any smooth, creamy soup; as, *bisque* of tomato or asparagus; a kind of ice-cream containing powdered macaroons.

bisque, bisk, *n.* [< Fr.] A point, extra turn, or handicap, allowed to a player to equalize the odds in tennis and other games; reduction of a golf score by one or more strokes.

bisque, bisk, *n.* [For *biscuit.*] *Ceram.* Biscuit ware; a white unglazed porcelain used for statuettes and other ceramics; a pinkish-tan color.

bis·sex·tile, bī·seks′til, bi·seks′til, *a.* [L.L. *bissextilis,* < L. *bissextus,* the intercalary day of the Julian calendar, lit. 'twice sixth' (the sixth day before the calends of March being reckoned twice every fourth year).] Containing or noting the intercalary or extra day of leap year.—*n.* A leap year.

bi·sta·ble, bī·stā′bl, *a.* The quality of remaining indefinitely in either of two stable states.

bis·ter, bis·tre, bis′tėr, *n.* [Fr. *bistre;* origin unknown.] A dark-brown pigment, often used in drawing, which is prepared from the soot of wood, esp. that of the beech; also, the color of this.—**bis·tered, bis·tred,** *a.*

bis·tort, bis′tȧrt, *n.* [L. *bistorta—bis,* twice, and *tortus,* twisted.] A perennial plant, *Polygonum bistorta,* with twisted roots which can be used as astringents. Also *snakeweed.*

bis·tou·ry, bis′to·rē, *n.* pl. **bis·tou·ries.** [Fr. *bistouri;* origin unknown.] A small, narrow surgical knife, as for minor incisions.

bis·tro, bis′trō, *Fr.* bē·strō′, *n.* pl. **bis·tros,** bis′trōz, *Fr.* bē·strō′. [< Fr.] A small nightclub or café of intimate, unpretentious club atmosphere.—**bis·tro·ic,** *a.*

bi·sul·cate, bī·sul′kāt, *a.* [L. *bi,* double, and *sulcus,* a furrow.] Cloven-footed, or having two-hoofed digits, as oxen or swine.

bi·sul·fide, bī·sul′fīd, bī·sul′fid, *n. Chem.* A disulfide; a compound in which each molecule contains two atoms of sulphur.

bi·sul·fite, bī·sul′fīt, *n.* A salt of sulfurous acid, in which one half of the hydrogen of the acid is replaced by a metal.

bit, bit, *n.* [< O.E. *bita,* bit, morsel, < *bītan,* E. *bite, v.*] A piece bitten off; a small piece or quantity of anything. *Colloq.* a small measure or degree; a short time. A small coin as, a threepenny-*bit;* a Spanish or Mexican silver coin worth 12½ cents, formerly current in parts of the U.S.; *slang,* multiples of 12½ cents; as, two *bits,* twenty-five cents.

bit, bit, *n.* A small part in a theatrical performance; somewhat; as, a *bit* of an inconvenience; *slang,* a term in prison.

bit, bit, *n.* The biting, cutting, or penetrating part of various tools; the movable boring or drilling part (in many forms) used in a carpenter's brace, a drilling machine, or the like; the part of a key which enters the lock; the metallic mouthpiece of a bridle; hence, anything that curbs or restrains. The cutting edge of an ax or plane.

bit, bit, *n.* [Shortened form of bi(nary) (digi)t.] *Computer,* a digit in the binary system which uses only combinations of o and 1 to denote all numbers; a unit of information in a computer language using two characters.

bit, bit, *v.t.*—**bitted, bitting.** To put a bit in the mouth of, as a horse; to put a bit on, as a key.

bi·tar·trate, bī·tär′trāt, *n. Chem.* an acid salt; a tartrate in which one of the two hydrogen atoms in tartaric acid is replaced by a monovalent metal or positive group; as, sodium bitartrate, $NaHC_4H_4O_6$.

bitch, bich, *n.* [< M.E. *biche, bicche.*] The female of the dog, or of other, esp. canine, animals, as the wolf and fox: sometimes applied opprobriously to a woman.

bitch, bich, *v.i. Slang.* To complain; to gripe; to nag.—*v.t. Slang.* To spoil; to botch.

bite, bīt, *v.t.*—past bit, pp. bit, bitten, ppr. biting. [< M.E. *biten* < Icel. *bíta,* D. *bijten,* Goth. *beitan,* G. *beiszen;* akin L. *findo, fidi,* Skt. *bhid,* to split.] To cut, break, penetrate, or seize with the teeth; to cause a sharp or smarting pain in, as: Pepper *bites* the mouth. To pinch or nip as with frost; to blast or blight; to grip or catch into or on, so as to act with effect (as an anchor, a file, etc.); to corrode or eat into, as by acid.—*v.i.* To have a habit of biting; to seize a bait with the mouth; to grip or catch into another object, so as to act on it with effect (the anchor *bites*).—**bite the dust,** *slang.* To die, esp. in a western gunfight; to fail; to meet defeat.

bite, bit, *n.* The seizure of anything by the teeth or with the mouth; a snack; a wound made by the mouth; catch or hold of one object on another; *slang,* a request for a loan of a sum of money, usu. used in the phrase *put the bite on.*

bit·ing, bit′ing, *a.* Sharp; severe; cutting; pungent; sarcastic.—**bit·ing·ly,** *adv.* In a biting manner; sarcastically.

bit·ing midge, *n.* A blood-sucking gnat; a punkie.

bit·stock, bit′stok″, *n.* The stock or handle by which a boring bit is held and rotated; a brace.

bitt, bit, *n.* [< Icel. *biti,* a crossbeam or girder.] *Naut.* a piece of wood or frame secured to the deck, on which to make fast the mooring lines.—*v.t.* To secure a ship's cables to, as a bitt.

bit·ter, bit′ėr, *a.* [< M.E. < O.E. *biter,* < *bitan,* to bite, from causing the tongue to smart = D., G., Dan., and Sw. *bitter,* Icel. *bitr.*] Having the harsh taste characteristic of aloes, quinine, wormwood, etc.; painful to the mind or body; unpleasant to accept; hard to bear, distressful; mournful or pitiable; expressing intense grief; as, a *bitter* cry; stinging; causing pain or smart, as cold; harsh or cutting, as words; cruel; characterized by intense animosity; as, a *bitter* enemy.—**bit·ter·ish,** *a.*—**bit·ter·ly,** *adv.*—**bit·ter·ness,** *n.*

bit·ter, bit′ėr, *n.* That which is bitter; bitterness; *pl., Brit.* a very dry ale.

bit·ter, bit′ėr, *v.t.* To make bitter; embitter.

bit·ter, bit′ėr, *adv.* Bitterly; exceedingly; as, a *bitter* cold winter.

bit·ter end, *n.* The last and direst extremity; the termination of an uncomfortable situation; *naut.* the inboard end of a ship's anchor rope or cable.—**to the bit·ter end,** characterized by unyielding perseverance until a conclusion is reached.

bit·tern, bit′ėrn, *n.* [O.E. *bitore, bittor, bittour;* Fr. *butor,* Sp. *bitor;* origin uncertain.] A name given to several wading birds of the heron family, esp. *Botaurus lentiginosus,* the American bittern, or *Ixobrychus exilis,* the least bittern, known for the singular booming or drumming noise they make.

bit·tern, bit′ėrn, *n.* [Var. of *bittering.*] A bitter, oily liquid that remains in salt-making after the salt has crystallized out of seawater or brine, used as a source of bromides, iodides, etc. Also **bit·ter·ing.**

bit·ter·nut, bit′ėr·nut″, *n.* A species of hickory, *Carya cordiformis,* growing in moist woods of eastern and southern U.S.

bit·ter prin·ci·ple, *n. Chem.* any one of hundreds of natural compounds, extracted from plants, all of which have a bitter taste, and which do not have chemical classification in common.

bit·ter·root, bit′ėr·röt, bit′ėr·rут″, *n.* A plant, *Lewisia rediviva,* allied to the portulaca, having fleshy roots and handsome pink flowers, growing in the mountains of Idaho, Montana, etc.; also, the dogbane, *Apocynum androsaemifolium.*

bit·ters, bit′ėrz, *n. pl.* [See *bitter.*] Bitter

medicinal substances in general, as quinine, gentian, etc.; also, a liquid, usually alcoholic, impregnated with a bitter medicine, as gentian, quassia, etc., used as a stomachic, tonic, or the like, often used to flavor mixed drinks.

bit·ter·sweet, bit′ẽr·swēt″, bit′ẽr·swēt′, *n.* The weedy nightshade, *Solanum dulcamara*, a climbing or trailing plant with scarlet berries.—bit′ẽr·swēt′, *a.* Something that is both bitter and sweet at the same time; as, a *bittersweet* experience.—**climb·ing bit·ter·sweet**, a climbing plant, *Celastrus scandens*, with orange capsules opening to expose red-coated seeds.

bit·ter·weed, bit′ẽr·wēd″, *n.* Any of various plants containing a bitter principle, as the ragweed or sneezeweed.

bit·ter wood, *n.* A West Indian tree, *Picrasma excelsum*, producing Jamaica quassia; quassia wood.

bit·ter·wort, bit′ẽr·wûrt, *n.* A name for various species of gentian.

bi·tu·men, bi·tŏ′men, bi·tū′men, bich′u·men, *n.* [L.] Any of various mineral substances of a resinous nature and highly inflammable, as asphalt, maltha, naphtha, petroleum, etc., consisting mainly of hydrocarbons; the hydrocarbon constituents of such a substance, as distinguished from the earthy matter and other impurities it contains.—**bi·tu·mi·nize**, bi·tŏ′mi·nīz″, bi·tū′mi·nīz″, *v.t.*—bituminized, bituminizing. To convert into or treat with bitumen.

bi·tu·mi·nous, bi·tŏ′mi·nus, bi·tū′mi·nus, *a.* [L. *bituminosus*.] Of, like, or containing bitumen.

bi·tu·mi·nous coal, *n.* An impure coal containing volatile hydrocarbons, which burns with a smoky flame; soft coal.

bi·tu·mi·nous shale, *n.* A finely stratified fissile rock (shale) containing hydrocarbons or bituminous material, which, if present in sufficient quantities, yield oil or gas on distillation; oil shale.

bi·va·lence, bi·vā′lens, biv′a·lens, *n. Chem.* the quality of being bivalent.

bi·va·lent, bi·vā′lent, biv′a·lent, *a. Chem.* Having a valence of two; combining with two atoms of a monovalent element or radical.

bi·valve, bī′valv″, *n.* [L. prefix *bi*, double, and *valva*, a valve.] An animal of the molluscous class, having two valves, or a shell consisting of two parts joined by an elastic hinge and opened and closed by muscles, as the oyster, clam, mussel, etc.; *bot.* a pericarp in which the seedcase opens or splits into two parts.

bi·valve, bī′valv″, *a.* Having two valves: said especially of the shells of mollusks. Also **bi·val·vu·lar**, bī·val′vū·lar.

bi·var·i·ate, bī·vâr′ē·it, bī·vâr′ē·āt″, *a.* Of, pertaining to, or having two variables.

biv·ou·ac, biv′ŏ·ak″, biv′wak, *n.* [Fr. *bivouac*, *bivac*, < G. *beiwache*; lit. 'by-' or 'near-watch.'] A temporary encampment of soldiers in the open, usu. without tents, each remaining dressed and with his weapons by him; a similar encampment of travelers, hunters, etc.; the place used for such encampment.—*v.i.*—bivouacked, bivouacking. To encamp in bivouac; to pass the night in the open air without tents or covering.

bi·week·ly, bī·wēk′lē, *a.* Occurring or appearing every two weeks; as, *biweekly* magazine. *Colloq.* occurring twice a week; *semiweekly.*—*n. pl.* **bi·week·lies.** A publication issued biweekly.—*adv.*

bi·year·ly, bī·yẽr′lē, *a.* Occurring once in two years; biennial; biannual.—*adv.*

bi·zarre, bi·zär′, *a.* [< Fr. < Sp. *bizarro*, brave, gallant; possibly < Basque *bizar*, beard: hence *he-man*.] Strikingly singular in appearance, style, or general character; whimsically strange; odd; fantastic; involving marked incongruities.—**bi·zarre·ly**, *adv.*—**bi·zarre·ness**, *n.*

bi·zarre, bi·zär′, *n. Bot.* a flower showing striped coloring that is atypical.

bi·zon·al, bī′zōn′al, *a.* Pertaining to two combined zones or areas.

blab, blab, *n.* Idle chatter; one who blabs; a telltale. Also **blab·ber**, blab′ẽr.

blab, blab, *v.t.*—blabbed, blabbing. [Allied to L.G. *blabben*, Dan. *blabbre*, G. *plappern*, to gabble; Gael. *blabaran*, a stutterer; *blubber-lipped*, *blob*, etc.] To utter or tell in a thoughtless or unnecessary manner what ought to be kept secret; to let out (secrets). —*v.i.* To talk rapidly, incoherently, or excessively; to chatter; also **blab·ber**, blab′ẽr. To tattle.

blab·ber·mouth, blab′ẽr·mouth″, *n. pl.* **blab·ber·mouths**, blab′ẽr·mouTHz″. Someone given to indiscreet chatter; a tattletale; a babbler.

black, blak, *a.* [< M.E. *blak* < O.E. *blæc* = O.H.G. *blah-*, *blach-*, = Icel. *blakkr*.] Of the darkest possible color or hue, like soot or coal; absorbing all light, or incapable of reflecting it; of an extremely dark color; noting or pertaining to a dark-skinned race, esp. Negro; soiled or stained; characterized by the absence of light; involved or enveloped in darkness; dismal or gloomy; boding ill; sullen and forbidding; destitute of moral light or goodness; evil or wicked; causing or marked by ruin or desolation; calamitous or disastrous; deadly, malignant, or baneful; indicating censure, disgrace, or liability to punishment.

black, blak, *n.* The darkest color, opposite of white, and belonging to objects that absorb light; a black dye or pigment; black attire, esp. signifying mourning; something black, as soot; a member of a dark-colored race.

black, blak, *v.t.* To make black; put a black color on; clean and polish (shoes, etc.) with blacking; blacken; stain, sully, or defame.—*v.i.* To become black.

black·a·moor, blak′a·mụr″, *n.* [*Black* and *Moor*, in the old sense of black man or Negro, formerly written also *blackmoor*.] A Negro; a dark-skinned human being.

black-and-blue, blak′an·blō′, *a.* Of a dark, livid color from a bruise, as on the human body.

black and white, *n.* Writing or print; monochromatic artwork rendered in black and white.

black-and-white, blak′an·hwīt′, blak′an·wīt′, *a.* Concerning an evaluation in terms of two absolutes only, as in a doctrine of morality, as: Dickensian characters are *black-and-white*, either all-good or all-bad.

black art, *n.* Black magic.

black·ball, blak′bạl, *n.* An adverse vote esp. against an applicant or candidate; formerly, a black ball deposited in a ballot box in which a white ball signified a vote of approval.—*v.t.* To cast a vote against; reject or exclude by adverse vote.

black bass, *n.* An American freshwater game fish of the genus *Micropterus*, which comprises two species, the large-mouthed, *M. salmoides*, and the small-mouthed, *M. dolomieu*.

black·ber·ry, blak′ber″ē, blak′be·rē, *n. pl.* **black·ber·ries.** The juicy, edible fruit, black or very dark purple when ripe, of certain species of the genus *Rubus*; the plant.

black·bird, blak′bụrd″, *n.* A bird of the thrush family, the male being characterized by its black plumage, yellow bill, and rich mellow note; any of the several North American birds of the family *Icteridae*.

black·board, blak′bōrd″, *n.* A dark, smooth hard surface, as of wood painted black, or of slate, etc., for writing or drawing on with chalk or crayons.

black bod·y, *n. Aerospace*, a hypothetical body or surface that completely absorbs without reflection all radiant energy falling upon it.

black book, *n.* A blacklist; a book of political character, so called either from the color of its binding or from the nature of its contents, as the book compiled under Henry VIII of England containing official reports concerning abuses in the monasteries; a book containing the names of persons liable to censure or punishment; any small book in which a man lists the names, addresses, and telephone numbers of the women he dates.—**in (one's) black book**, to be in disfavor with one.

black box, *n.* In engineering design, a component whose energy output is a function of the input; *colloq., aeron.* any unit, usually an electronic device such as an amplifier, which can be mounted in a spacecraft as a single package.

black cal·la, *n.* A perennial herb, *Arum palaestinum*, grown in Jordan and Israel as an ornamental, having flowers similar to the calla lily, but with a blackish purple spathe; Solomon's lily.

black·cap, blak′kap″, *n.* A European bird of the warbler family, noted for the sweetness of its song, and so called from its black tufted crown; a species of raspberry having black fruit, native to North America; black raspberry.

black-capped, blak′kapt″, *a.* Of birds, having black feathers on top of the head.

black·cock, blak′kok″, *n.* A bird of the grouse family, so called from the glossy black plumage of the male; the heath cock or male black grouse.

black crap·pie, *n.* A black-and-silver mottled sunfish of Mississippi River tributary waters and most eastern states.

black·damp, blak′damp″, *n.* A mixture of carbon dioxide and nitrogen occurring as a mine gas and incapable of supporting life or flame. Also **choke·damp**.

Black Death, *n.* The bubonic plague which first visited Europe in epidemic form during the fourteenth century, characterized by black spots all over the skin.

black dia·mond, *n.* Carbonado; deep black hematite.—**black dia·monds**, *n. pl.* Coal.

black·en, blak′en, *v.t.* To make black; to polish with blacking; to sully; to stain; to defame; to vilify; to slander.—*v.i.* To become black or dark.

black eye, *n.* An eye with a black or blackish-brown iris; an eye with the surrounding flesh or skin discolored by a blow or bruise. *Slang*, a bad reputation; dishonor, as: Slums give a *black eye* to the city.

black-eyed pea, blak′īd″ pē′, *n.* Cowpea.

black-eyed Su·san, blak′īd″ sō′zan, *n.* Any of several plants having flowers or heads with a dark center, as the cone flower or yellow daisy, *Rudbeckia hirta*.

black·fin, blak′fin″, *n.* A whitefish, *Argyrosomus nigripinnis*, of certain northern lakes of the U.S., popularly considered a food fish; any of certain other whitefishes.

black·fish, blak′fish, *n. pl.* **black·fish**, **black·fish·es.** Any of various dark-colored fishes, as the tautog, *Tautoga onitis*, or the sea bass, *Centropristes striatus*, or a small fresh-water food fish, *Dallia pectoralis*, of Alaska and Siberia, notable for its ability to revive after having been long frozen.

black flag, *n.* The flag formerly flown by pirates bearing the mark of a white skull and cross bones on black background; see *blackjack*. A flag formerly used by a vessel to indicate that there was cholera on board.

black fly, *n. pl.* **black flies.** Any of several small, black-bodied flies, genus *Simulium*, whose bite is very painful, esp. *S. venustum* of the wooded regions of the northern U.S. and Canada.

Black·foot, blak′fụt, *n. pl.* **Black·feet**, **Black·foot.** A member of a tribe or the language of North American Indians (the Blackfeet) of Algonquian stock.

Black Fri·ar, *n.* A Dominican friar, named after the distinctive black mantle worn.

Black Fri·day, *n.* Any of various Fridays on which disastrous events occurred, as, in the U.S., Sept. 24, 1869, and Sept. 19, 1873, marked by financial panics.

black grouse, *n.* European and western Asian gamebird, *Lyrurus tetrix,* the plumage of which is black on the male and spotted on the female.

black·guard, blag'ärd, blag'erd, *n.* [Formerly a name given to the scullions and lowest menials connected with a great household, who attended to the pots, coals, etc.] A man of coarse and offensive manners; a fellow of low character; a scoundrel.

black·guard, blag'ärd, blag'erd, *v.t.* To revile in low or scurrilous language.

black gum, *n.* The tupelo (tree), *Nyssa sylvatica.*

Black Hand, *n.* A lawless European society, *La Mano Nera;* in the U.S., a secret society organized for purposes of blackmail, extortion, and deeds of violence.

black haw, *n.* A shrub or small tree, *Viburnum prunifolium,* of North America, bearing cymes of small white flowers and black drupes; a similar shrub or small tree, *V. lentago.*

black·head, blak'hed", *n.* A comedo, or skin blemish consisting of a blackish fatty secretion in a follicle. Any of several birds having a black head, as the scaup, *Æthyia* (or *Aythya*) *marila.* A malignant, infectious disease of turkeys, peacocks, etc., attacking esp. the intestines and liver.

black·heart, blak'härt", *n. Hort.* a kind of cherry bearing a somewhat heart-shaped fruit with a nearly black skin; *plant pathol.,* a disease in plants which causes internal tissues to darken.

black-heart·ed, blak'här"tid, *a.* Having a wicked, heartless, or malignant disposition.

black hu·mor, *n.* A type of fictional writing which contains distorted or morbidly humorous plots and descriptions.

black·ing, blak'ing, *n.* A preparation used to color an object black.

black, in the, *a., adv. Colloq.* operating a business profitably, as opposed to *in the red,* at a loss.

black·jack, blak'jak", *n.* The flag or ensign of a pirate; a small leather-covered club or billy weighted at the head; a card game.

black·jack, blak'jak", *v.t.* To compel, as a person, by striking with a blackjack or by other threat.

black knot, *n.* A fungus disease attacking plum and cherry trees, characterized by black nodules on the branches.

black lead, *n.* Amorphous graphite; plumbago.

black·leg, blak'leg", *n.* [Origin uncertain.] *Veter. pathol.* a disease of cattle, often fatal, characterized by gangrenous swelling of the upper parts of the leg; also *black quarter. Plant pathol.* a disease of cabbage and similar plants, characterized by dry, black lesions on the stem, caused by a fungus; a disease of potatoes, characterized by wet, black lesions on the stem, caused by a bacterium. *Brit. colloq.* a strikebreaker.—*v.t.*—*blacklegged, blacklegging.* To betray, as a cause, or deceive, as a person.

black let·ter, *n.* The heavy-faced ornate type characteristic of early English (and other) printed books: also adapted for modern use.—*a.* Printed in black letter.

black light, *n. Theatr.* a type of spotlight utilizing invisible ultraviolet or infrared light to give either a luminous effect to specially treated costumes, props, and the like, or to reduce the colors on stage for a black and white, film-like, effect. An ultraviolet or infrared light.

black·light trap, *n.* A trap using blacklight to attract and trap certain insects.

black·list, blak'list", *n.* A written or unwritten list, usually privately circulated, which names those in disfavor; a list circulated among employers enumerating persons whose affiliations or bad character makes them undesirable as employees; a list compiled by a labor union to prevent dealings with employers known for unfair labor practices.—*v.t.* To place, as someone, on a blacklist.

black·ly, blak'lē, *adv.* In a black manner; with a black appearance; darkly; gloomily; wickedly.

black mag·ic, *n.* Witchcraft; sorcery used with evil intentions. Also *black art.*

black·mail, blak'māl", *n.* [-*mail* < Icel. *mál,* stipulation, agreement, *mæla,* to stipulate.] Money or an equivalent, anciently paid, in the north of England and in Scotland, to robbers and bandits for protection from pillage; the act of demanding payment by means of intimidation; extortion of money or equivalent from a person by threats of public accusation, exposure, or censure; any extorted payment.—*v.t.*

Black Ma·ri·a, blak"ma·ri'a, *n. Colloq.* A vehicle used by the police for the transportation of prisoners; a name applied by soldiers to an explosive artillery shell that produces heavy black smoke.

black mar·ket, *n.* Trade in violation of official prices or quantities; the place where prohibited trade is conducted.—*a.*

black-mar·ket, blak'mär"kit, *v.t., v.i.* To sell or engage in illicit trade in a black market.

Black Mus·lim, *n.* A member of a Negro sect, principally U.S., believing in the Islamic religion and in the total disassociation of races.

black·ness, blak'nis, *n.* The state or quality of being black; black color; darkness; gloominess; somberness; sullen or severe aspect.

black·out, blak'out", *n.* A period of darkness, usu. as an air raid precaution; the extinguishing of stage lights to end a scene or play; censorship; a temporary loss of vision or consciousness, such as an aviator experiences from a sudden dive; a loss of memory; the halting of a communications medium, due to a strike, catastrophe, etc.

black out, *v.i.* To become engulfed in darkness; to suffer a transient loss of vision, memory, or consciousness; to turn out all lights, usu. as a precaution against air raids.—*v.t.* To cause to black out; to ban.

black perch, *n.* Any of several gamefish of dark color, such as a bass.

black·poll, blak'pōl", *n.* [Black and M.E. *polle,* (hair of the) head.] A North American warbler, *Dendroica striata,* the adult male of which has the top of the head black.

Black Pope, *n.* A nickname for the general, or head, of the Society of Jesus: a disparaging allusion to his supposed power and to the color of the Jesuit habit.

black quar·ter, *n.* See *blackleg.*

Black Rod, *n.* The chief gentleman usher of the Lord Chamberlain's department of the English royal household, usher of the Order of the Garter, whose principal duty is attendance on the House of Lords, in which he is responsible for the maintenance of order, named for the black rod he carries.

black rot, *n.* A fungous or bacterial plant disease which causes decay and dark discoloration of fruits and vegetables.

black sheep, *n.* A person viewed as a disgrace or embarrassment by the other members of his family or group.

Black Shirt, *n.* [Named for the black shirt of the uniform.] A member of Italy's Fascist party, under Mussolini.

black·smith, blak'smith", *n.* One who works in iron and makes iron utensils; an ironsmith: opposed to a *whitesmith* or *tinsmith;* a person who shoes horses.

black·snake, blak'snāk", *n.* Any of various snakes of a black or very dark color; esp. in the U.S., a nonvenomous serpent, *Coluber constrictor,* sometimes attaining a length of 5 to 6 feet, and possessing great strength and agility. A heavy, tapering, flexible whip of braided rawhide or leather.

black spruce, *n.* A spruce tree of North America, *Picea mariana,* with blue-green foliage and light, soft wood.

black·thorn, blak'thärn", *n.* A much-branched, thorny European shrub, *Prunus spinosa,* bearing white flowers which appear before the leaves, and small, plumlike fruits; also *sloe.* A walking stick or cudgel made from the stem of this shrub.

black tie, *n.* Men's semiformal evening attire; a tuxedo, worn with a black bow tie.

black·top, blak'top", *n.* Asphalt, or a similar bituminous material, for paving roads, etc.; a surface so paved.—**black·top,** *v.t.*—*blacktopped, blacktopping.*

black vom·it, *n.* A dark-colored substance, consisting chiefly of altered blood, vomited in some cases of yellow fever; the disease itself.

black wal·nut, *n.* A tree, *Juglans nigra,* of North America, cultivated as an ornamental shade tree and for its timber; the edible, oily nut of this tree; the hard, dark brown wood of this tree, used in furniture.

black·wa·ter fe·ver, *n.* An acute form of malaria occurring in tropical and semi-tropical regions, characterized by febrile paroxysms and bloody urine.

black whale, *n.* A black dolphinlike cetacean of the genus *Globicephalus.*

black wid·ow spi·der, *n.* The female of an American spider, *Latrodectus mactans,* with a poisonous bite, and so named because of its glossy black body and habit of devouring its mate.

blad·der, blad'ẽr, *n.* [M.E. < O.E. *blædre,* bladder, blister, = G. *blatter,* blister; < the Teut. source of E. *blow.*] A distensible sac with muscular and membranous walls, serving as a receptacle for the urine secreted by the kidneys; any similar sac or receptacle as, gall-*bladder;* a vesicle, blister, etc., filled with fluid or air. *Fig.* anything inflated; a pretentious person. The air-filled container within a football, basketball, etc.; *bot.* a sac or the like containing air, as in certain seaweed.

blad·der kelp, *n.* Any of various brown algae, esp. the common rockweed used in preparing commercial kelp.

blad·der·nose, blad'ẽr·nōz", *n.* A large seal, *Cystophora cristata,* of the northern Atlantic, the male of which has a large, distensible, hoodlike sac upon the head.

blad·der·nut, blad'ẽr·nut", *n.* The bladder-like fruit capsule of any shrub or small tree of the genus *Staphylea,* as *S. trifolia* of the eastern U.S.; the shrub or tree itself.

blad·der·worm, *n.* The bladderlike encysted larva of a tapeworm.

blad·der·wort, blad'ẽr·wurt", *n.* Any of various herbs of the genus *Uticularia,* some species of which float free in water by means of small bladders on the leaves, and others root in mud.

blad·der wrack, *n.* A common rockweed of the genus *Fucus,* used in preparing kelp.

blad·der·y, blad'ẽr·ē, *a.* Of the nature of or like a bladder; thin, inflated, and hollow; containing bladders or vesicles.

blade, blād, *n.* [M.E. < O.E. *blæd* = G. *blatt;* < the Teut. source of E. *blow.*] *Bot.* the leaf of a grass plant or cereal; the broad part of a leaf, as distinguished from the stalk. A thin, flat part of something as of an oar; the flat cutting part of a weapon or tool; the bottom running edge of ice skates; *phon.* the front flat part of the tongue. A dashing fellow.

blade, blād, *n.* The part of a rotating fan or propeller arm which has an airfoil shape in order to move air as it turns. A vane, as in a turbine wheel.

blain, blān, *n.* [< M.E. < O.E. *blegen* = D. *blein,* Dan. *blegn, a* blain, a blister; probably < root of to *blow,* and allied to *bladder.*] *Pathol.* A pustule; a blister; an inflammatory swelling.

blam·a·ble, blame·a·ble, blā'ma·bl, *a.* Deserving of blame; culpable; reprehensible. Also **blame·ful.**

blame, blām, *v.t.*—*blamed, blaming.* [Fr. *blâmer,* O.Fr. *blasmer* < L.L. *blasphemare,* < Gr. *blasphemein,* to calumniate. Also *blaspheme.*] To place the responsibility on, as a person or thing, for a mistake or fault; to express disapproval of; to find fault with; to censure; to condemn. (In such phrases as "he is *to blame,*" *to blame* has the passive meaning; as, "a house to let," etc.).

blame, blām, *n.* An expression of disapprobation for something deemed to be wrong; imputation of a fault; censure; reproach; reprehension; that which is deserving of censure, as: The *blame* is yours.

blame·less, blām'les, *a.* Not deserving blame or censure; irreproachable; guiltless. —**blame·less·ly,** blām'les·lē, *adv.*— **blame·less·ness,** blām'les·nes, *n.*

blame·wor·thy, blām'wur"thē, *a.* Deserving blame; censurable; culpable; reprehensible.—**blame·wor·thi·ness,** blām'wur"thē·nes, *n.*

blanc fixe, blängk' fēks, *n.* [Fr. fixed white.] A white powder, barium sulfate, used as a base in paint and as a filler in various manufactured materials.

blanch, blanch, blänch, *v.t.* [< O.Fr. < Fr. *blanchir,* < *blanc,* white: see *blank.*] To make white, esp. by depriving of color; bleach; whiten; give a white luster to, as metals, as by means of acids; cover, as sheet-iron, with a thin coating of tin; to make pale, as with sickness, fear, cold, etc.; to give a fair appearance to; palliate; *cookery,* to remove skins from, as almonds, by immersion in hot water; to scald, as meat, by short, rapid boiling.—*v.i.* To become white; bleach; turn pale.— **blanch·er,** blanch'ēr, blänch'ēr, *n.*

blanc-mange, bla mänj', bla mänzh', *n.* [Fr. *blanc,* white, and *manger,* food.] *Cookery,* a dessert of the consistency of a jelly, composed of milk, egg-white, and flavoring substances mixed with a thickening agent such as cornstarch or gelatine.

bland, bland, *a.* [L. *blandus.*] Smooth, suave, or agreeable, as persons or their speech, manner, etc.; soft, gentle, or balmy, as air; mild, as medicines; indifferent, casual.—**bland·ly,** bland'lē, *adv.* —**bland·ness,** bland'nes, *n.*

blan·dish, blan'dish, *v.t.* [O.Fr. *blandir, blandissant,* L. *blandior,* to flatter, < *blandus,* bland.] To caress, soothe, cajole, or flatter.—*v.i.* To fawn; to use flattery.— **blan·dish·er,** blan'dish·ēr, *n.* One who blandishes; one who flatters with soft words.—**blan·dish·ment,** blan'dish·ment, *n. Usu. pl.* words or actions expressive of affection or kindness, and tending to win the heart; artful caresses. Flattering attention; cajolery; endearment.

blank, blangk, *a.* [O.Fr. Fr. *blanc* (fem. *blanche*), white, < O.H.G. *blanch,* bright, shining.] White or pale; of paper, etc., left white, or free from marks; not filled out, as a check or ballot; empty or unoccupied; without contents; void or bare; unrelieved or unbroken by ornament or opening, as a wall; lacking some usual or completing feature; as, a *blank* window, door, etc., one having the usual casings,

etc., but no opening; void of interest, results, etc.; showing no attention, interest, or emotion, as a person's face or look; disconcerted or nonplussed; complete, utter, or unmitigated; as, *blank* stupidity.— **blank·ly,** blangk'lē, *adv.*—**blank·ness,** blangk'nes, *n.*

blank, blangk, *n.* The white spot in the center of a target; anything aimed at; something left blank, or not written on, filled in, etc.; a written or printed form with blank spaces to be filled in; any of these spaces; a provisional word printed in italics in a bill before a legislature; a dash put in place of an omitted word or letter; any space from which something is omitted or absent; a void; a mere form without substance; anything insignificant; a lottery ticket which does not win a prize; a piece of metal prepared to be formed into some finished object by a further operation, such as a coin or key.

blank, blangk, *v.t.* To make white; make blank or void; render void of result, etc.; keep, as an opponent, from scoring in a game; punch, as a piece of flat stock, with a die, used with *out.*

blank check, *n.* A bank check, signed but with the amount not specified; carte blanche; authority without limitation.

blank en·dorse·ment, *n.* The signing of a negotiable instrument without any qualifications; a check or note which does not name a payee in the assigning or endorsing signature and is payable to bearer.

blan·ket, blang'kit, *n.* [O.Fr. *blankete,* dim. of *blanc,* white.] A large rectangular piece of soft, loosely woven fabric, usually wool, serving as a bed-covering, a covering for a horse, etc.; a similar piece of cloth, etc., for various other uses; *fig.* a layer that covers; as, with a *blanket* of snow.

blan·ket, blang'kit, *v.t.* To cover with or as with a blanket; *naut.,* to take the wind out of the sails of (a vessel) by passing to windward of it; *radio,* to prevent the reception of (a radio signal) by interfering with a stronger signal.

blan·ket, blang'kit, *a.* Covering or intended to cover a group or class of things, conditions, contingencies, etc.; as, a *blanket* mortgage; a *blanket* indictment.

blan·ket-flow·er, blang'kit-flou"ēr, *n.* Any plant of the genus *Gaillardia,* of western N. America having bright yellow or purple-red flowers. Also *gaillardia.*

blan·ket stitch, *n.* Sewing stitches of variable space and loop used for decorative finish to edges of thick material; button hole stitches on thick material.

blank verse, *n.* Unrhymed verse as used in some of the old English dramas and epics, as well as in contemporary poetry.

blan·quette, blän·ket', *n.* [Fr., dim. of *blanc,* white.] A stew or fricassee with a white sauce, usually served with onions and mushrooms.

blare, blâr, *v.i.*—*blared, blaring.* [Probably an imitative word; akin. D. *blaren,* L.G. *blarren, blaren,* G. *blarren, blärren,* to bellow, bleat, blare.] To give forth a loud sound like a trumpet; to give out a brazen sound; to bellow.—*v.t.* To sound loudly; to proclaim noisily.

blare, blâr, *n.* Sound like that of a trumpet; noise; roar; bright glare of color or light; fanfare; pomp and show.

blar·ney, blär'nē, *n.* [< Castle *Blarney,* near Cork, in Ireland, in the wall of which is a stone said to endow anyone who kisses it with skill in the use of flattery.] *Colloq.* excessively complimentary language; gross flattery; smooth, deceitful talk.—*v.t. Colloq.* To talk over by soft delusive speeches; to flatter; to humbug with talk.

bla·sé, blä·zā', blä'zā; Fr. bla·zā', *a.* [Fr. (fem. *blasée*), pp. of *blaser,* exhaust, satiate.]

Satiated with enjoyment; having one's capacity for pleasure or interest blunted or exhausted by experience, or as a result of overindulgence; used up.

blas·pheme, blas·fēm', blas'fēm, *v.t.*— *blasphemed, blaspheming.* [L.L. *blasphemare,* < Gr. *blasphemein,* blaspheme, < *blasphemos,* speaking evil.] To speak impiously or irreverently of, as God or sacred things; in general, to speak evil of; calumniate.—*v.i.* To utter impious words; to talk profanely; also, to utter abusive words.—**blas·phem·er,** blas·fē'mēr, *n.* One who blasphemes.— **blas·phem·ous,** blas'fa·mus, *a.* Containing or exhibiting blasphemy.—**blas·phem·y,** blas'fa·mē, *n. pl.* **blas·phem·ies.** The language of one who blasphemes; the act of blaspheming; the act of claiming the powers of the deity.

blast, blast, bläst, *n.* [O.E. *blæst* = O.H.G. *blāst* = Icel. *blāstr;* akin to E. *blaze* and *blow.*] A blowing or gust of wind; a forcible stream of air, steam, etc.; the rush of gases outside a great gun upon its discharge, sometimes affecting the operation of neighboring guns; the blowing of a trumpet, etc.; the sound produced by this, or some similar sound; any pernicious or destructive influence on animals or plants; a blight; a curse; the product of a blight; a bud which never blossoms; blasted state or condition. The act of rending rock, etc., or an attempt to do this, by an explosive; the charge of explosive used for this. *Metal.* a current of air forced into a furnace to accelerate combustion; the operation of a blast-furnace with such a current, as: A furnace in *blast* when in operation, and out of *blast* when stopped.

blast, blast, bläst, *v.i.* To blow on a trumpet or the like; boast or brag.—*v.t.* To blow, as a trumpet; confound or stun as by a loud blast; blow or breathe on injuriously or destructively; cause to shrivel or wither; arrest in growth; blight; ruin or destroy, as hopes, happiness, or reputation; strike with the wrath of heaven; curse; rend or attempt to rend, as rock, by an explosive.

blast·ed, blas'tid, blä'stid, *a.* Affected with a blast or blight, or other destructive influence; withered or shriveled; blighted; damned: a euphemism.

blas·te·ma, bla·stē'ma, *n. pl.* **blas·te·ma·ta,** bla·stē'ma·ta, [N.L., < Gr. *blastema,* sprout.] *Embryol.* the mass of undifferentiated cells from which an organ or part of the body is evolved during embryonic development, or during the beginning stage of regeneration of missing body parts of certain animals such as salamanders.

blast fur·nace, *n.* A furnace in which ores are smelted by the aid of a blast of air.

blas·to·cyst, blas'ta·sist, *n. Embryol.* the blastula characteristic of mammals, having a knob of cells at one side which develops into the embryo, the remainder developing into the placenta.

blas·to·disk, blas·to·disc, blas'ta·disk", *n. Embryol.* the embryo-forming part of a fertilized egg, which usually appears as a very small disk on the surface of the egg yolk.

blast off, *v.i.* To take off, usu. rapidly, as a rocket.

blast-off, blast'af", blast'of", bläst'af", bläst'of", *n. Aerospace,* the launching of a rocket from a pad or stand, the blast effects being caused by rapid combustion of fuel as the rocket starts to move upward.

blas·to·gen·e·sis, blas"ta·jen'i·sis, *n. Biol.* Reproduction by germination; the theory of the transmission of hereditary characteristics by genes.

blas·to·my·cete, blas"ta·mī'sēt", *n.* A yeastlike fungus capable of causing disease.

blas·tu·la, blas′chụ·la, n. pl. **blas·tu·las**, blas′chụ·las, **blas·tu·lae**, blas′chụ·lē, [< Gr. *blastos*, a germ.] *Embryol.* the stage in embryonic development of animals at the end of or immediately following the stage of cleavage of the ovum, consisting of a ball made up of a single layer of cells enclosing a fluid-filled cavity.

blat, blat, *v.i.*—*blatted*, *blatting*. [Imit.] *Colloq.* To cry, as a calf; to bleat, as a sheep; give forth a harsh sound; talk loudly and senselessly or indiscreetly.—*v.t. Colloq.* To utter loudly and indiscreetly; blurt out.

bla·tan·cy, blā′tan·sē, n. The quality or state of being offensively loud or clamorous; something blatant.

bla·tant, blāt′ant, *a.* [Appar. coined by Spenser: cf. L. *blatire*, babble, and E. *bleat.*] Clamorous; loud-mouthed; vulgar; noisy; loud; brazenly obvious; as, a *blatant* lie.—**bla·tant·ly**, blāt′ant·lē, *adv.*

blath·er, blath′ẻr, n. [< O.N. *blathr* < *blathra*, talk unintelligibly.] Voluble, foolish talk; nonsensical talk; bluster. Also *blether.*—*v.i.*, *v.t.* To speak foolishly. Also *blether.*

blath·er·skite, blath′ẻr·skīt″, n. One given to voluble, empty talk; one who habitually indulges in empty bluster.

blaze, blāz, n. [M.E. < O.E. *blæse*, a blaze, a torch, < root of *blow*; akin Icel. *blys*, Dan. *blus*, a torch; akin to *blast.*] The stream of light and heat from any object when burning; a flame; brilliant sunlight; effulgence; brilliance; a sudden bursting out; an active or violent display; as, a *blaze* of wrath. *Pl.*, *slang*, hell, as: Go to blazes!

blaze, blāz, n. [Possibly < Icel. *blesi* or D. *bles* = G. *blässe*, blaze on a horse's head.] A white spot on the face of a horse, cow, etc.; a mark made on a tree, as by removing a piece of the bark, to indicate a boundary or a path in a forest; a path or trail indicated by such marks.

blaze, blāz, *v.t.*—*blazed*, *blazing*. To mark, as a tree, with a blaze; indicate, as a spot, trail, etc., by blazes; to lead, as a pioneer, in some field of action or knowledge.

blaze, blāz, *v.t.*—*blazed*, *blazing*. [M.E. < O.E. *blaesan*, to blow = Icel. *blása*, Dan. *blæse*, G. *blasen*, to blow, to sound as a trumpet. BLAST, BLOW.] To make known to all; to noise or bruit abroad; to proclaim; to display with fanfare.—*v.i.* to be aglow with zeal; to burn with emotion; to flare up; to burst out; to fire away, as with a gun.

bla·zer, blā′zẻr, n. That which blazes; a bright-colored jacket or short coat, often with an insignia and worn by members of a school, team, or club.

blaz·ing star, n. Any of the several plants known for their peculiar clusters of flowers as *Aletris farinosa* of the lily family or *Liatris squarrosa* of the perennial composite family.

bleach, blēch, *v.t.* [< M.E. < O.E. *blæcan* = G. *bleichen* = *bleikja*; akin to E. *bleak.*] To make white or whiter, as linen by exposure to sunlight or by chemical agents; deprive of color; make lighter in color; blanch.—*v.i.* To become white; whiten; become pale or colorless.

bleach, blēch, n. The act of bleaching; the color achieved by bleaching; any agent used for bleaching.

bleach·er, blē′chẻr, n. A chemical or apparatus used for bleaching; one whose occupation is to whiten or bleach.

bleach·ers, blē′chẻrz, *n. pl.* Seats or grandstand, usually uncovered and of low price, for spectators at baseball or other sporting events.

bleach·ing pow·der, n. A powder used for bleaching; esp., chloride of lime.

bleak, blēk, *a.* [O.E. *blaec* = Icel. *bleiker*, D. *bleek*, G. *bleich*, pale, pallid, white; allied

to O.E. *blican*, Icel. *blikja*, G. *blicken*, to shine, to gleam, E. to *blink.*] Exposed to cold and winds, as situation or tract of land; desolate; ungenial; cheerless; dreary; cold; chill, as *bleak* winds.—**bleak·ish**, blēk′ish, *a.* Moderately bleak.—**bleak·ly**, blēk′lē, *adv.* In a bleak manner; coldly.—**bleak·ness**, blēk′nes, n. State of being bleak; coldness; desolation.

bleak, blēk, n. [So called from the *bleak* or pale color of its scales.] A European river fish of the genus *Alburnus*, with silver-colored scales, the pigment of which is used in making imitation pearls.

blear, blēr, *a.* [M.E. *blere*; origin uncertain.] Dim from a watery discharge or other superficial affection, as the eyes; dim, misty, or indistinct.—**blear-eyed**, **blear-y-eyed**, *a.* Having blear eyes; affected with watery or sore eyes; dim-sighted; *fig.* having the mental vision dimmed; dull of perception.

blear, blēr, *v.t.* To make, as eyes, sore so that sight is indistinct; to affect with soreness of eyes; to make rheumy and dim; *fig.* to hoodwink, to deceive.

blear·y, blēr′ē, *a.*—*blearier*, *bleariest.* Blurred, sore, said of vision, as from fatigue or lack of sleep or exposure to glare; dim, foggy, unclearly defined; tired.

bleat, blēt, *v.i.* [M.E. < O.E. *blaetan* = D. *bleaten*, *bleeten*, L.G. *blaten*, *bleten*, to bleat, probably an imitative word.] To utter the cry of a sheep or a similar cry; to talk in a bleating way, as to whine; to sputter.

bleat, blēt, n. The cry of a sheep, goat, or calf; a sound resembling this cry; complaining or idle talk.—**bleat·er**, blēt′ẻr, n. One who bleats; a sheep.

bleb, bleb, n. [Prob. related to *blob.*] A blister or pustule; a bubble, as in water or glass; a small vesicular body.—**bleb·by**, bleb′ē, *a.* Full of blebs.

bleed, blēd, *v.i.*—*bled*, *bleeding.* [< M.E. < O.E. *blédan*, < *blód*, blood = D. *blœden*, Icel. *bloetha*, Dan. *blóde*, to bleed.] To lose blood; to be drained of blood; to let sap or other moisture flow from itself; to trickle or flow, as from an incision; to sacrifice blood, as in battle; to sympathize, as: My heart *bleeds* for him. To allow printed matter to run off a sheet, either intentionally or by accidentally trimming border edges too close; to run together, said of dyes or paint; to pay out money or have it extorted.—*v.t.* To take blood from by opening a vein; to emit, as: A tree *bleeds* sap; to extort or extract money from; to cause, as a printed design, to run off the edge of a sheet; to cut off part of, as a text or illustration, by trimming margin too close.

bleed, blēd, n. A page having printed matter, such as an illustration, that runs off the edges of the page after trimming; the part so trimmed.

bleed, blēd, *v.i.* To let a fluid, such as air or liquid oxygen, escape slowly from a pipe, tank, or the like.

bleed·er, blē′dẻr, n. A person predisposed to bleeding; hemophiliac; a person who draws blood from another with remedial intent.

bleed·ing heart, n. Any of various plants of the genus *Dicentra*, esp. *D. spectabilis*, a common garden plant with racemes of red heart-shaped flowers.

bleep, blēp, n. [Imitative.] A sharp, short sound issued as a signal; beep.—*v.i.* To emit such a sound.

blem·ish, blem′ish, *v.t.* [O.Fr. *blemir*, *blemissant*, to spot, to beat one blue, < Icel. *bláman*, the livid color of a wound, < *blár*, blue, livid.] To injure or impair; to mar or make defective; to deface; to sully; to tarnish, as reputation or character; to defame.

blem·ish, blem′ish, n. A noticeable defect, flaw, or imperfection, usually of the skin; something that mars beauty, completeness, perfection, or reputation; a blot or stain.

blench, blench, *v.i.* [< M.E. < O.E. *blencan*, deceive; perhaps akin to E. *blink.*] To draw back or flinch, as in fear; to become pale.—*v.t.* To whiten; blanch.

blend, blend, *v.t.*—*blended* or *blent*, *blending.* [M.E. *blenden*, appar. < Icel. *blanda* = O.E. *blandan*, mix.] To mix or mingle; mix thoroughly or intimately; combine so that the things mixed or the line of division cannot be distinguished; mix, as different sorts of a commodity, in order to produce a particular kind or quality;—*v.i.* To become mixed or mingled; unite in a uniform or harmonious whole; pass or shade imperceptibly, as colors into one another.

blend, blend, n. A mixture, as of liquids, colors, etc.; a mixture of spirits as in blended whiskey; parts of several words arranged to form a new word.

blende, blend, n. [G., < *blenden*, blind, deceive.] Any of several native sulfides, with a non-metallic luster; as, manganese-*blende*, a sulfide of manganese; sphalerite.

blend·ed whis·key, n. A mixture of two or more whiskeys, or of whiskey and neutral spirits, that includes at least 20 per cent by volume of 100 proof straight whiskey.

blend·er, blen′dẻr, n. That which blends; an appliance with motorized base, mixing blades, and receptacle for edible ingredients, used to mix drinks, purée foods, grate carrots or the like.

blend·ing in·her·it·ance, n. *Genetics*, the combining of contrasting characteristics of the parents in the offspring.

blen·ny, blen′ē, n. pl. **blen·nies**, blen′ēz. [L. *blennius*, < Gr. *blennos*, blenny, orig. slime.] Any of various fishes of the genus *Blennius*, and allied genera, with an elongated tapering body.

bles·bok, bles′bok″, n. [S. Afr. D. "blaze buck."] A large South African antelope, *Bubalis* (or *Damaliscus*) *albifrons*, having a blaze or white spot on the face. Also **bles·-buck.**

bless, bles, *v.t.*—*blessed* or *blest*, *blessing.* [< M.E. < O.E. *bletsian*, *bledsian*, to bless, < *blód*, blood; originally perhaps to consecrate by sprinkling blood.] To invoke the divine favor on; to express a wish for the good fortune or happiness of; to bestow happiness, prosperity, or good things of any kind upon; as, to *bless* with peace and plenty; to make and pronounce holy; to extol for excellencies; as, to *bless* the Lord; to esteem or account happy: with the reflexive pronoun, as: *Bless me! Bless you!* Expressions of surprise, as: *Bless my soul!*

bless·ed, bles′id, blest, *a.* [pp. of *bless.*] Favored with blessings; enjoying spiritual blessings and the favor of God; fraught with or imparting blessings; holy.—**bless·ed·ly**, bles′id·lē, *adv.*—**bless·ed·ness**, bles′id·nes, n.

Bless·ed Sac·ra·ment, n. The Eucharist: one of the reverential terms used by Roman Catholics to suggest the holiness of the Sacrament; Communion.

bless·ing, bles′ing, n. The act of one who blesses; a prayer or solemn wish imploring happiness upon another; a benediction; the act of pronouncing a benediction or blessing, as at meals; that which promotes temporal prosperity and welfare or secures immortal felicity; any good thing falling to one's lot; a mercy.

bleth·er, bleTH′ẻr, *v.i.*, *v.t.*, n. Blather.

blight, blīt, n. [Origin unknown.] Some influence, usually hidden or not conspicuous that destroys plants, arrests their growth, etc.; smut, mildew, or other fungous plant-disease; any insect which infects or destroys plants; any malignant influence of obscure or mysterious origin; anything which withers hope, blasts prospects, or checks prosperity; a blighting or being blighted.

blight, blīt, *v.t.* To affect with blight; to cause to wither or decay; to frustrate.—*v.i.* To injure as blight does.

blight·y, blī'tē, *n.* pl. **blight·ies,** blī'tēz. [Hind. *bilaiti,* used in India to signify England, or Europe, < Ar. *wilāyat,* province, government.] *Brit. army slang.* England, or home, esp. as the destination of soldiers when wounded or on furlough; a wound, furlough, or the like, that takes a soldier away from the front.

blimp, blimp, *n.* [Origin uncertain.] A small, non-rigid balloon used chiefly for military observation. *Slang,* a fat person. *Motion pictures,* a soundproof booth in which camera sounds are separated from the microphone.

blin, blin, *n.* pl. **blin·i, blin·is,** blin'ē, blin'ēz. Variation of *blintze.*

blind, blīnd, *a.* [< O.E. < M.E.; D., Icel., Sw., Dan., G. *blind;* originally meaning turbid or cloudy, and allied to blend, to mix.] Destitute of the sense of sight; not having sight; not having the faculty of discernment; not based on reason or evidence; not easily discernible; as *blind* paths; heedless; as *blind* wrath; without openings for admitting light; as a *blind* window; closed at one end; having no outlet; as a *blind* alley; *slang,* drunk.— **blind·ly,** blīnd'lē, *adv.* In a blind manner; without sight or understanding; without examination; recklessly.—**blind·ness,** *n.*

blind, blīnd, *a. Aeron.* of or pertaining to the navigation of an aircraft under conditions of limited or obstructed visibility with the aid of instruments, radio, or electronic equipment; as, *blind* flight, one in which the pilot cannot see the ground or landing field.

blind, blīnd, *v.t.* To make physically unable to see; to take away from, as a person, the ability to reason or judge objectively; to dazzle; to obscure to the eye or mind.

blind, blīnd, *n.* Something to hinder sight, to intercept a view, or keep out light; a place to hide oneself from view, as a duck *blind;* a false identity or activity to keep secret the true purpose of a society, club, or political organization.

blind as a bat, *a.* Having poor vision; almost blind.

blind date, *n.* A social engagement between two persons of opposite sex who have not previously met.

blind·er, blīn'dėr, *n.* One who or that which blinds; a blinker on a horse's bridle; an obstruction to sight or discernment; an impediment to clear thinking.

blind fish, *n.* Any of several small fishes with rudimentary, functionless eyes, found in the ocean depths, and in subterranean streams, as *Amblyopsis spelæus,* of the Mammoth Cave, in Kentucky.

blind·fold, blīnd'fōld″, *v.t.* To cover the eyes of; to hinder from seeing by binding something round the eyes; to interfere with, as another's understanding.

blind·fold, blīnd'fōld″, *n.* A cloth or other covering, placed over the eyes to block vision.—**blind·fold·ed,** *a.*

blind·ing, blīn'ding, *a.* Making blind; preventing from seeing clearly; depriving of reason or understanding.—**blind·ing·ly,** blīn'ding·lē, *adv.* In a blinding manner; so as to blind; as, a *blinding* rain.

blind·man's buff, *n.* A game in which one person is blindfolded and tries to catch another member of the group and tell who it is. Also **blind·man's bluff.**

blind spot, *n. Anat.* the point in the retina that is insensitive to light. A subject about which one is ignorant or biased; a point on which one is unable to use correct judgment; an area where radio signals or broadcasts are poorly received.

blind·stitch, blīnd'stich″, *v.t., v.i.* To sew with stitches that do not show on the right side of the material.

blind·sto·ry, blīnd'stōr″ē, *n.* pl. **blind·sto·ries.** *Arch.* a story without windows or windowlike openings, esp. the triforium of a medieval church, having no exterior windows.

blind ti·ger, *n. Slang,* a place where intoxicating liquors are sold surreptitiously without a license. Also **blind pig.**

blink, blingk, *v.i.* [M.E. *blinken* < *blenken,* to blench, = D. and G. *blinken,* Sw. *blinka,* Dan. *blinke.*] To wink, esp. rapidly and repeatedly; look with winking or half-shut eyes; glance with unsteady or dim vision; cast a glance; take a peep; to gaze with wonder or curiosity; to look with sudden disillusionment; to look evasively or with indifference; to shine unsteadily or dimly; twinkle.—*v.t.* To cause to blink; to see dimly; to shut the eyes to; evade.

blink, blingk, *n.* The act of blinking; a glance of the eye; a glimpse; a gleam; the gleam or glimmer reflected from ice in the Arctic regions.—**on the blink.** *Slang,* not in proper working condition.

blink·er, bling'kėr, *n.* One who blinks; a leather flap placed on either side of a horse's head, to prevent him from seeing sideways or backward; also *blinder.* A light that flashes as a warning, or as a coded signal.— *v.t.* To equip with blinkers.

blintze, blintz, *n.* [Yiddish < Russ. *blinets,* dim. of *blin,* pancake.] A kind of pancake, usually with a filling of fruit or cheese, believed to be of Jewish origin.

blip, blip, *n.* [Slang origin.] A spot of light or deflection of the trace on a radarscope, loran indicator, or the like, caused by the received signal, as from a reflecting object.

bliss, blis, *n.* [M.E. *blisse* < O.E. *blis, bliss, bliths,* joy, alacrity, exultation, < *blithe, blithe.*] The highest degree of happiness; blessedness; felicity: often specifically heavenly felicity.

bliss·ful, blis'ful, *a.* Full of, abounding in, enjoying, or conferring bliss.—**bliss·ful·ly,** blis'ful·lē, *adv.* In a blissful manner.— **bliss·ful·ness,** blis'ful·nes, *n.*

blis·ter, blis'tėr, *n.* [M.E. < Scand. Connected with *blast,* to blow or puff, < same root as to *blow,* akin G. *blase,* a blister, a bladder.] A thin vesicle on the skin, containing watery matter or serum, as from an injury; a pustule; an elevation made by the separation of an external film or skin, as on plants; a plant disease that causes blisterlike elevations on leaves; a bubble left in paint on a smooth surface; an emulsion bubble left on a photo film in course of its processing; something applied to the skin to raise a blister; a vesicatory.— **blis·ter·y,** blis'tėr·rē, *a.* Full of blisters.

blis·ter, blis'tėr, *v.t.* To raise a blister or blisters on; to reprimand in very harsh language; to punish severely, esp. by lashing with a whip.—*v.i.* To raise in blisters or become blistered.

blis·ter bee·tle, *n.* A beetle which produces a secretion used in medical practice to raise a blister on the skin; the Spanish fly; the secretion. Also *cantharis.*

blis·ter cop·per, *n.* A form of metallic copper in which cavities or blisters have been left by gases in the process of its solidification.

blis·ter·ing, blis'tėr·ing, *n.* Bubbles in painted finish caused by moisture or resin vaporizing under the surface.

blis·ter rust, *n.* A pine tree disease that manifests itself in the form of blisterlike elevations on the external surface of the trunk and is caused by rust fungus.

blis·ter steel, *n.* See *blister copper.*

blithe, blīTH, blīth, *a.* [O.E. *blithe, blithe.*] Gay; merry; joyous; sprightly; mirthful; swayed by joy of the moment without thought of the future.—**blithe·ly,** blīTH'lē, blīth'lē, *adv.* In a blithe, gay, or joyful manner.

blith·er, blīTH'ėr, *v.i., v.t.* [< *blather.*] To blather; to chatter nonsensically.

blithe·some, blīTH'sum, blīth'sum, blīTH'-sam, blīth'sam, *a.* Full of blitheness or gaiety; gay; merry; cheerful.—**blithe·some·ly,** blīTH'sum·lē, blīth'sum·lē, blīTH'sam·lē, blīth'sam·lē, *adv.*

blitz, blits, *n.* [G. lit. *lightning.*] Any preponderant effort; as, a *blitz* of advertising designed to saturate a market area; sudden or surprise warfare.—*v.t.* In gin rummy, to win before an opponent scores any points; to attack by blitz.

blitz·krieg, blits'krēg″, *n.* [G. *blitz,* lightning, and *krieg,* war.] A technique of warfare developed by German strategists in World War II, consisting of swift attacks designed to pierce the enemy's lines, disrupt his communications and supply systems, and separate his forces so that they can be destroyed piecemeal; an unanticipated, annihilating air raid. Also **blitz.**—*v.t.*

bliz·zard, bliz'ard, *n.* [Origin obscure; perhaps ult. < *blaze.*] A violent storm of wind with dry, driving snow and intense cold.

bloat, blōt, *n.* [M.E. *blout,* soft, puffy < Icel. *blautr.*] A person who, or a thing that is bloated; a disease of the digestive system of domestic animals brought about by eating wet forage and resulting in a swollen rumen; *slang,* a drunkard.—*a.* Puffy.

bloat, blōt, *v.t.* To cause to expand or swell with air or water; to cause to swell with conceit; to cure, as herrings, in salt water.— *v.i.* To become swollen; to dilate.

bloat·er, blō'tėr, *n.* A herring or mackerel slightly salted and partially smoke-dried, but not split open. A whitefish, *Argyrosomus prognathus,* of the Great Lakes; also **bloat·er white·fish.**

blob, blob, *n.* [Also in form *bleb,* and allied to *blab, blubber.*] A small globe of liquid; a dewdrop; a blister; a bubble; a thing of undefined shape.

blob, blob, *v.t.*—**blobbed, blobbing.** To stain with spots or blobs.

bloc, blok, *n.* [Fr. *block* or *lump.*] An association of groups or nations united, sometimes by treaty, to further their joint interests; legislators banded together, despite opposing political allegiances, to promote a common interest; as, the farm *bloc* in the U.S. Congress.

block, blok, *n.* [< M.E. *blok,* log, stump < M.Fr. *bloc.*] *Mach.* a frame on which one or more grooved pulleys are mounted and to which a hook is attached, used for transmitting power or for lifting and pulling heavy objects, by means of ropes or chains passing around the pulleys. Also *block and tackle.*

block, blok, *v.t.* To hinder passage from or to; to obstruct; to oppose or interfere successfully, as in football or boxing; to mold, shape, or stretch, as material, on a block.—**block out,** to begin to reduce to required shape; to set or support on blocks; to set, as type, so that all lines are flush at the left and right; *psychiatry,* to forget or mentally keep back; *monetary,* to limit by government edict the free exchange of foreign-held funds or currency.

block, blok, *n.* A solid mass of wood, stone, or the like, usually with one or more plane faces; a hollow building unit; a cubical toy often furnished to children in sets for play-building; a solid mass of wood, etc., used for a particular purpose, as one on which meat is chopped, a slave placed for sale, goods auctioned, or a condemned person beheaded; a mold or piece on which something is shaped or kept in shape; the mold on which a hat is formed; a wooden head for a wig; an object, with a design cut on the surface, used for printing; *slang*, the human head; blockhead.

block, blok, *n.* A mass of wood, stone, or other solid material forming an obstruction; an obstacle or hindrance; a stoppage, as of traffic on a road; *sports*, stopping an opponent's play, as in football or basketball; *psychiatry*, a cessation of thought or memory, caused by emotional stress.

block, blok, *n.* Any compact or connected mass; a large building divided into separate houses, shops, etc.; a connected mass of buildings; a portion of a city or town, usually bordered by four neighboring and intersecting streets; the length of one side of this; a quantity, portion, or section taken as a unit or dealt with at one time; as, a *block* of tickets; one of the short divisions into which a railroad is divided for signaling purposes.

block, blok, *n.* A liberal amount of stock, varying from 1,000 shares for high-priced stocks and 5,000 shares of stocks relatively lower in price.

block·ade, blo·kād′, *n.* [< *block*, *v.*] The shutting up of a place, esp. a port, harbor, or line of coast, by hostile ships or troops, to prevent ingress or egress; a blockading force; any obstruction of passage.

block·ade, blo·kād′, *v.t.—blockaded, blockading.* To subject to a blockade by warlike means; to block up; to obstruct.—**block·ad·er,** *n.*

block·ade-run·ner, blo·kād′run″ẽr, *n.* A ship or person that goes through a blockade.

block·age, blok′ij, *n.* The state of being blocked or obstructed; emotional or physical obstruction.

block and tack·le, *n.* A set of pulleys and rope used for lifting or hauling heavy objects.

block·bust·er, blok′bus″tẽr, *n. Colloq.* A large-scale demolition bomb; someone or something overwhelmingly effective.

block·bust·ing, blok′bus″ting, *n.* A practice of unscrupulous real estate agents who induce panic selling of homes at prices below value by exploiting racial prejudice in a neighborhood.—**block·bust·er,** *n.*

block di·a·gram, *n. Computer,* a diagram of a system, instrument, computer, or program in which selected portions are represented by annotated boxes and interconnecting lines.

block·er, blok′ẽr, *n.* One who or that which blocks; a tool or machine for some process of blocking.

block·head, blok′hed″, *n.* A stupid fellow; a dolt; a person slow or deficient in understanding.

block·house, blok′hous″, *n. Milit.* formerly a strong building of one or more stories, so named because constructed chiefly of logs or beams of timber, having loopholes for musketry. Any reinforced building used for protection against enemy troops.

block·house, blok′hous″, *n. Aerospace,* a reinforced concrete structure often built underground or half underground and sometimes dome-shaped to provide protection against blast, heat, or explosions during rocket launchings or related activities; specifically, such a structure at a launch site that houses electronic control instruments used in launching a rocket; the activity in such a structure.

block·ish, blok′ish, *a.* Like a block; stupid; dull; deficient in understanding; wooden.—**block·ish·ly,** blok′ish·lē, *adv.*

block let·ter, *n.* A letter or type face in sans serif.

block plane, *n.* A small plane used in carpentry to cut across the wood grain.

block sig·nal, *n.* A stationary railroad signal at the beginning of specified track sections, to direct entering trains.

block sys·tem, *n.* The system of working the traffic on a railroad, according to which the line is divided into short sections, and no train is allowed to enter upon any one section until it is signalled wholly clear, so that between two successive trains there is an interval of time as well as one of space. *Geol.* a system of mountain ranges consisting of fault blocks.

block tin, *n.* Tin cast into ingots or blocks; pure tin, as against tin plate.

block·y, blok′ē, *a.* Similar to a block in form or bulk; stocky, chunky; marked by blocks or patches of unequally distributed light and shade, as a photograph.

bloke, blōk, *n.* [Origin unknown.] *Slang, chiefly Brit.* A man; a fellow.

blond, blonde, blond, *a.* [M.E. < M.Fr. *blond, blonde,* a word of Teutonic origin; cf. D. and G. *blond,* fair, flaxen; O.E. *blonden,* grayish or grizzled; allied to *blend.*] Of a fair color of hair or complexion.—*n.* A person, esp. a woman, with blond hair.

blood, blud, *n.* [< M.E. < O.E. *blōd* = D. *bloed* = G. *blut* = Icel. *blōdh* = Goth. *blōth,* blood.] The fluid that circulates in the arteries and veins or principal vascular system of the vertebrates, in man being of a red color and consisting of a pale yellow plasma containing semisolid corpuscles, some red and some white; the vital fluid as shed from a wound; gore; bloodshed or murder; juice or sap, as of plants; the physical nature; temper or state of mind; as, to act in cold *blood*; the blood of a family or race looked upon as a distinctive attribute of its members; birth, parentage, kinship, or breed, esp. good birth or breed; lineage; royal lineage; as, a prince of the *blood*; family, race; offspring; a spirited or dashing fellow; new vitality.

blood, blud, *v.t.* To draw blood from; bleed; stain with blood; to expose, as hounds, to a first taste or sight of the prey's blood.

blood bank, *n.* An institution for storing and processing blood or blood plasma; blood or plasma so stored.

blood bath, *n.* Wholesale killing; a massacre.

blood broth·er, *n.* One whose relationship to another is that of a brother from birth; one whose ties to another are strong bonds of friendship.

blood cell, *n.* A basic, structural unit of the blood. Also *blood corpuscle.*

blood clot, *n.* The jelly-like mass formed as liquid blood congeals when blood vessels are injured.

blood cor·pus·cle, *n.* A cell circulating in the blood. A red cell or corpuscle; also *erythrocite.* A white cell or corpuscle; also *leukocyte.*

blood count, *n.* Determination of the number and proportion of red and white cells in a specific volume of blood.

blood-curd·ling, blud′kurd″ling, *a.* Frightening; terrifying enough to congeal the blood.

blood·ed, blud′id, *a.* Of good blood or breed, as thoroughbred horses or cattle.

blood feud, *n.* A feud involving bloodshed between families.

blood group, *n.* One of several classifications into which human blood can be divided, based on the proportion of specific antigens. Also *blood type.*

blood·guilt, blud′gilt″, *n.* Guilt induced by murder, or the shedding of blood as in war.—**blood·guilt·i·ness,** *n.*—**blood·guilt·y,** *a.*

blood heat, *n.* The normal temperature, about 98.6° F., of human blood.

blood·hound, blud′hound″, *n.* One of a breed of medium to large, powerful dogs with a very acute sense of smell, used for tracking game, human fugitives, etc.; *fig.* a relentless pursuer.

blood·i·ly, blud′i·lē, *adv.* In a bloody manner; cruelly.

blood·i·ness, blud′ē·nes, *n.* The state of being bloody; disposition to shed blood; murderousness.

blood·less, blud′lis, *a.* Without blood; drained of blood; dead; without shedding of blood or slaughter; as, a *bloodless* victory; without spirit or activity.—**blood·less·ly,** blud′lis·lē, *adv.* In a bloodless manner; without bloodshed.—**blood·less·ness,** blud′lis·nes, *n.*

blood·let·ting, blud′let″ing, *n.* The act of letting blood or bleeding, as by opening a vein, as a remedial measure; phlebotomy.

blood·line, *n.* The pedigree, esp. of animals.

blood·mo·bile, blud′mo·bēl″, *n.* A motor vehicle equipped to receive donations of human blood.

blood mon·ey, *n.* Money paid to procure or to compensate for the killing of a person.

blood plas·ma, *n.* The clear almost colorless fluid of the blood when separated from blood corpuscles by centrifuging: used in blood transfusions since it clots as easily as whole blood.

blood plate·let, *n.* A minute circular or oval body found in vertebrate blood, necessary for blood clotting.

blood·poi·son·ing, *n. Pathol.* A diseased condition of the blood due to the presence of toxic matter or microorganisms; toxemia; septicemia; pyemia.

blood pres·sure, *n.* The pressure exerted by the blood against the inner walls of the blood vessels, varying in different parts of the body, with exertion, excitement, strength of the heart, age, or health.

blood·red, *a.* Of the deep red color of blood; red with blood.

blood re·la·tion, *n.* One related by birth; a kinsman. Also **blood rel·a·tive.**

blood sau·sage, *n.* A sausage dark in color because of its high blood content. Also **blood pud·ding, black pud·ding.**

blood se·rum, *n.* The yellowish clear liquid remaining after all solid constituents of the blood have been removed.

blood·shed, blud′shed″, *n.* The shedding or spilling of blood; slaughter; waste of life.

blood·shot, blud′shot″, *a.* Red and inflamed because of excessively dilated capillaries: said of the eye.

blood·stained, blud′stānd″, *a.* Stained with blood; guilty of killing.

blood·stone, blud′stōn″, *n.* A greenish kind of quartz with small blood-like spots of red jasper scattered through it; a kind of hematite. See *heliotrope.*

blood·stream, blud′strēm″, *n.* The blood flowing through the circulatory system.

blood·suck·er, blud′suk″ẽr, *n.* Any animal that sucks blood, as a leech, a fly, etc. A hard niggardly man; *fig.* an extortioner.

blood sug·ar, *n.* Glucose supplied by the liver circulating in the blood of vertebrates.

blood test, *n.* The test of a blood sample to determine such qualities as blood type, or such quantities as sugar content.

blood·thirst·y, blud′thur″stē, *a.* Sadistic; anxious to shed blood; murderous.—**blood·thirst·i·ly,** blud′thur″sta·lē, *adv.*

blood type, *n.* Blood group.

blood ves·sel, *n.* Any of the vessels of the body, arteries, veins, capillaries, through which the blood circulates.

blood·worm, blud′wurm, *n.* Any of the red-colored worms, living in shallow water and mud, frequently used for bait.

blood·y, blud′ē, *a.*—**bloodier, bloodiest.** [< O.E. *blōdig.*] Of, like, or composed of blood; stained with blood; bleeding; blood-red; seeking or involving bloodshed; bloodthirsty; sanguinary; *low slang, chiefly*

Brit., a vague term of vituperation often used merely for emphasis.

blood·y, blŭd′ē, *v.t.*—**bloodied, bloodying.** To stain with blood.

blood·y Ma·ry, *n.* An alcoholic drink usually made with tomato juice and vodka.

bloom, blōm, *n.* [M.E. < Scand., cf. *blóm,* Sw. *blomma,* Dan. *blomme,* Goth. *bloma,* D. *bloem,* G. *blume,* a flower. BLOW. BLOSSOM.] A blossom; the flower of a plant; the act or state of blossoming; fullness of life and vigor; a period of high success; a flourishing condition; the delicate rose hue on the cheek indicative of youth and health; a glow; a flush; a superficial coating or appearance upon certain things, as the powdery coating upon certain fruits; surface coating formed by minerals on certain materials.

bloom, blōm, *n.* [O.E. *blōma.*] A roughly prepared oblong mass of wrought iron, usually made by squeezing or hammering one of the ball-like pasty masses of iron obtained by puddling; any of various other masses of iron or steel, esp. a thick bar of steel obtained by hammering or rolling an ingot.

bloom, blōm, *v.i.* To produce or yield blossoms; to blossom; to flower; to show the beauty of youth; to glow.—*v.t.* To impart a radiance to.

bloom·er, blō′mėr, *n.* One who attains mastery of skills and attitudes corresponding to his potential; as, a child who is a late *bloomer.*

bloom·ers, blō′mėrz, *n. pl.* Loose trousers gathered at the knee, formerly worn by women as part of gymnasium, riding, bathing, or other like dress; lady's or girl's undergarment of similar style, worn with a very short skirt.

bloom·er·y, blō′me·rē, *n. pl.* **bloom·er·ies.** The first furnace through which iron passes after it is melted from the ore.

bloom·ing, blō′ming, *a.* Blossoming; flourishing; glowing with youthful freshness and vigor. *Slang, chiefly Brit.,* a vague intensive or expletive; as, a *blooming* idiot.—**bloom·ing·ly,** *adv.*

Blooms·bury, blōmz′ba·rē, blōmz′brē *n.* An area of residence in London where academic and artistic interests are emphasized, known as an intellectual center.

bloom·y, blō′mē, *a.* Full of bloom or blossoms; flowery; having freshness or vigor as of youth; having a delicate powdery appearance, as fresh fruit.

bloop·er, blōō′pėr, *n. Slang.* An embarrassing public blunder, as by a radio or television announcer; *baseball,* a weakly hit ball too short to be caught by an outfielder.

blos·som, blos′om, *n.* [< M.E. < O.E. *blóstma,* a blossom.] The flower of a plant, consisting of one or more colored leaflets, generally of more delicate texture than the leaves; the bloom; blooming state or period, as: The plant is in *blossom.*

blos·som, blos′om, *v.i.* To put forth blossoms or flowers; to bloom; to flourish.

blot, blot, *n.* [M.E. cf. Icel. *blettur,* blot.] A spot or stain, as of ink, or mud; a disfiguring stain or mark; a blemish; a stain upon character or reputation; a striking out, obliterating, or erasing, as in a writing.

blot, blot, *v.t.*—**blotted, blotting.** To spot, stain, or bespatter, as with ink or mud; to detract from a person's reputation; cancel; efface; obscure or eclipse; paint coarsely, or daub; dry with blotting paper or the like. —*v.i.* To make blots; to become blotted or stained.

blotch, bloch, *n.* [Origin obscure: cf. *blot* and *botch.*] An inflamed eruption or discolored patch on the skin; any large irregular spot or blot.—*v.t.* To cover or mark with blotches.—**blotch·y,** bloch′ē, *a.* Covered with blotches; blotched.

blot draw·ing, *n.* The art of creating a composition by allowing a few blots of ink or color to fall at random on a sheet of paper and then folding the paper to spread the ink.

blot out, *v.t.* To obliterate or obscure; to annihilate or destroy; to make unimportant.

blot·ter, blot′ėr, *n.* One who or that which blots; something used to absorb superfluous ink, as a piece of blotting paper; a book in which transactions or occurrences, as sales, arrests, etc., are recorded as they take place.

blot·ting pa·per, *n.* A porous, unsized paper, used to absorb excess ink.

blouse, blous, blouz, *n.* [Fr.] A woman's loose, light-weight garment extending to the waist or below, worn over or tucked into a skirt or slacks; the jacket of the U.S. Army service uniform; a loose-fitting garment resembling a smock, sometimes belted, worn by European peasants and workmen. —*v.i., v.t.* To hang or cause to hang in a loose full manner.

blow, blō, *v.i.*—past **blew,** pp. **blown,** ppr. **blowing.** [< M.E. < O.E. *bláwan;* allied to G. *blähen,* to blow, Icel. *blása,* Goth. *blésan,* G. *blasen,* to blow, to blow a wind instrument; also E. to *blow,* to *bloom, bladder, blast,* etc., and L. *flo, flare,* to breathe or blow.] To make a current of air, as with the mouth, a bellows, etc.; to constitute or form a current of air; to move, as the motion of wind or air; to pant; to puff; to breathe hard or quick; to give out sound by being blown, as a horn or trumpet; to burst or explode; *colloq.* to boast; to brag. *Slang,* to spend money unnecessarily; to depart from a place; to lose a chance of winning by one's own mistake. —*v.t.* To throw or drive a current of air upon; to drive by a current of air; to sound by the breath, as a wind instrument; to form by inflation, as to *blow* a glass bottle; to swell by injecting air into; to put out of breath by fatigue; to scatter or shatter by explosives; as, to *blow* a building to pieces.

blow, blō, *n.* A gale of wind; a blast of air; the breathing or spouting of a whale; the act of producing a stream of air through the mouth, nose, or by using an instrument. *Metal.* A process of forcing air through a converter in the refining of metal; the amount of metal refined in this process.

blow, blō, *v.i.* To bloom or to flower.

blow, blō, *n.* [< M.E. < O.E. *blówan,* to bloom or blossom; D. *bloeijen,* G. *blühen;* allied to the other verb *to blow,* and to L. *florere,* to bloom.] A mass of blossoms; the state or condition of blossoming or flowering; bloom.

blow, blō, *n.* [Akin to O.D. *blauwen,* to strike; D. *blouwen,* to beat flax; G. *bleuen,* to cudgel; and perhaps also with *blue.* BLUE.] A stroke with the hand or fist, or a weapon; a knock; an act of hostility; a sudden calamity; a sudden or severe evil; mischief or damage received.—*At a blow,* by one single action; at one effort; suddenly.

blow a cork, *Slang.* To lose one's temper.

blow a fuse, *Slang.* To blow one's emotional circuit; to become excessively angry.

blow·by, blō′bī″, *n. pl.* **blow·bies,** blō′bīz″, *n. Auto.* Leakage of gases from the crankcase; a method or device to eliminate exhaust fumes.

blow-by-blow, *a.* Minutely detailed; as, a *blow-by-blow* description.—*adv.* In minute detail.

blow·er, blō′ėr, *n.* One who or that which blows; a machine for forcing air into a furnace, building, mine, etc.; *slang,* a braggart.

blow·fish, blō′fish″, *n.* Any of various fishes capable of inflating their bodies into a globular shape. See *puffer.*

blow·fly, blō′flī″, *n.* pl. **blow·flies,** blō′flīz. Any of various two-winged flies which deposit their eggs or larvæ on flesh, meat, or in wounds.

blow·gun, blō′gun″, *n.* A long pipe or tube through which darts or pellets are blown by the breath.

blow·hard, blō′härd″, *n. Slang.* A boaster; a braggart.

blow·hole, blō′hōl″, *n.* Either of two nostrils or spiracles, or a single one, at the top of the head in whales and other cetaceans, through which they breathe; any hole for the passage or escape of air; a hole in the ice to which whales, etc., come to breathe; *metal.* a defect in a casting, due to the imprisonment of a bubble of air or gas.

blow in, *v.i. Slang,* to arrive suddenly or unexpectedly.

blow·ing, blō′ing, *n.* The noise that results from a forcible expulsion of gas or air; blow molding.

blow mold·ing, *n.* A process of making hollowware in which a substance, as molten glass or plastic resin, is forced against a mold by pressurized air.

blown, blōn, *a.* [pp. of *blow.*] Carried or driven by the wind; swollen or puffed up or out; inflated, as the stomach of cattle; put out of breath; fatigued; exhausted; stale, as from exposure to air; flyblown; tainted; unsavory; shaped with a blowtube; as, *blown* glass; no longer usable; as, a *blown* fuse.

blown, blōn, *a. Hort.* Fully opened; as, a full *blown* blossom; in bloom.

blow one's top, *slang,* to depart from rational behavior, as in anger.

blow out, *v.i.* To become extinguished by a sudden rush of air; to subside.

blow·out, blō′out″, *n. Geol.* A saucer-shaped hollow formed in sand or light soil by wind erosion; the accumulation of the displaced sand or soil if it attains some height. Also **blow·out dune.**

blow·out, blō′out″, *n.* A rupture of the casing of an automobile tire with the consequent bursting of the inner tube; a sudden or violent escape of air, steam, or the like; the explosive melting of an electric fuse; *slang,* a lavish social event.

blow o·ver, *v.i.* To calm down; to cease without ill consequence, as: The scandal *blew over.*

blow·pipe, blō′pīp″, *n.* A tube through which a stream of air or gas is forced into a flame to concentrate and increase its heating action; the glassmaker's long metal tube, used in gathering and blowing molten glass; also *blowtube, blowgun. Med.* a tubular implement for inspecting or cleaning a body cavity.

blows·y, blou′zē, *a.* Blowzy.

blow·torch, blō′tọrch″, *n.* A small portable apparatus which gives an extremely hot acetylene flame intensified by a blast, used for soldering and the like.

blow·tube, blō′tōb″, blō′tūb″, *n.* A blowgun; a blowpipe; a long iron tube used in glassblowing to blow the semifluid glass into the required shape or size.

blow·up, blō′up″, *n.* An explosion; an intense disagreement and loss of temper, esp. that which causes alienation; an enlarged photograph.

blow up, *v.t.* To explode; to inflate; to enlarge beyond truthful bounds. To enlarge, as a photograph.—*v.i.* To arise, as a storm; *colloq.* to have a violent outburst of temper.

blow·y, blō′ē, *a.* Windy; easily blown about.

blowz·y, blou′zē, *a.* [Origin uncertain.] Redfaced; stout; coarse-looking; untidy.

blub·ber, blub′ėr, *n.* [A lengthened form of *blub, blob, bleb;* perhaps < same root as that of *blow, bladder.*] The fat of whales and other large sea mammals, from which oil is obtained; an overabundance of body fat; the act of sobbing uncontrollably.

blub·ber, blub'ẽr, *a.* Puffy, swelled; as *blubber* cheeks.

blub·ber, blub'ẽr, *v.i.* To weep, especially in such a manner as to swell the cheeks or disfigure the face.—*v.t.* To disfigure with weeping; to utter, esp. indistinctly while sobbing.

blub·ber·y, blub'a·rē, *a.* Abounding in or resembling blubber; fat, as a cetacean; swollen.

blu·cher, blö'kẽr, blö'chẽr, *n.* [Named for German Field Marshal von *Blücher.*] A strong leather half boot or shoe.

bludg·eon, bluj'an, *n.* [Origin unknown.] A short, heavy club or weapon, with one end loaded, or thicker and heavier than the other.—*v.t.* To beat; to coerce.

blue, blö, *a.*—*bluer, bluest.* [O.Fr. *blou, blau* (Fr. *bleu*); < Teut; O.H.G. *blāo,* G. *blau.*] Of a color like or approaching that of the clear sky; azure; cerulean; livid, as from cold or a bruise. *Fig.* low in spirits; dismal or unpromising; as, a *blue* outlook. Strict or rigid, as in morals. Of women, learned or pedantic; see *bluestocking.* Connoting the flames of hell, as irreverence; *slang,* risqué; indecent.

blue, blö, *n.* The hue between green and violet in the spectrum; azure; a blue dye or pigment; bluing; something blue, as the sky or the sea; a member of a company, party, army, etc., wearing or having blue as its distinctive color; a bluestocking; a small blue-winged butterfly of the *Lycænidae* family.—**out of the blue,** as if from nowhere; totally unexpected.

blue, blö, *v.t.*—*blued, bluing.* To make blue; tinge with bluing; in washing clothes, to use bluing to retain or restore whiteness.

blue ba·by, *n.* An infant with a bluish color from congenital heart disease or defective lungs.

Blue·beard, blö'bẽrd", *n.* Personage in medieval tale; (*l.c.*) *fig.* a wife-murderer.

blue·bell, blö'bel", *n.* Any of various plants with blue, bell-shaped flowers, as the harebell, *Campanula rotundifolia* ("bluebell of Scotland"), or a liliaceous plant, *Scilla nonscripta,* of England, or the blue jasmine; a North American spreading herb, *Polemonium reptans*; the lungwort, *Mertensia virginica,* of the U.S.

blue·ber·ry, blö'ber"ē, *n. pl.* **blue·ber·ries,** blö'ber"ēz. The edible berry, usually bluish in color, of any of various shrubs of the genus *Vaccinium,* or any of these shrubs.

blue·bird, blö'bụrd", *n.* Any bird of the genus *Sialia,* comprising small N. American passerine song-birds whose prevailing color is blue, esp. *S. sialis* of the eastern U.S. which appears early in the spring.

blue blood, *n.* [Sp. *sangre azul.*] Supposed superiority because of noble or royal heritage; a person of aristocratic family.—**blue-blood·ed,** *a.*

blue·bon·net, blö'bon"it, *n.* A broad, flat cap of blue woolen, formerly much worn in Scotland; a person wearing such a bonnet; a Scotsman; the cornflower, *Centaurea cyanus*; an annual lupine with blue flowers, esp. the State flower of Texas, *Lupinus subcarnosus.*

blue book, *n.* A register of socially prominent persons; a British parliamentary or other official publication, bound in a blue cover; an official register of persons holding U.S. government offices; a blank book with a blue cover, for replies to questions at a school examination.

blue·bot·tle, blö'bot"al, *n.* The cornflower, *Centaurea cyanus*; any of various plants with blue flowers; also, any of several species of large blowflies with a blue abdomen.

blue cat, *n.* A large bluish catfish of the Mississippi valley, often weighing over 100 lbs. and an important food fish.

blue cheese, *n.* [Fr. *fromage bleu.*] A cheese resembling Roquefort, usually made of cow's milk and veined with greenish blue mold.

blue chip, *n. Stock market,* the listed securities of a major company noted for its superior management, financial stability, and successful record of growth and earnings. *Poker,* a blue poker chip of highest value; *fig.* a thing of superior quality, value, or reputation.—*a.*

blue·coat, blö'kōt", *n.* A person who wears a blue coat, esp. as part of a uniform or livery; a policeman; a Union Army soldier in the Civil War.

blue-col·lar, blö'kol"ẽr, *a.* Of or pertaining to the wage-earning class who wear work clothes as distinguished from white dress shirts.

blue crab, *n.* An edible crab, found along the Atlantic and Gulf coasts of North America.

blue dev·ils, *n.* A colloquial phrase for dejection, hypochondria, or lowness of spirits, often called simply *the blues.*

blue·fin tu·na, *n.* A giant variety of the tuna, *Thunnus thynnus.*

blue·fish, blö'fish", *n.* Any of certain American fishes, one of them a food fish allied to the mackerel, common on the Atlantic coast.

blue flag, *n.* The common blue iris, *Iris versicolor,* grown throughout the eastern U.S.

blue gal·ax·y, *n.* A body of stars developing outside the Milky Way system, and less mature than the normal galaxies of that system.

blue·gill, blö'gil", *n.* A large fresh-water sunfish, *Lepomis pallidus,* of the Mississippi valley, much used for food and sport.

blue·grass, blö'gras", *n.* A name of several grasses, more especially a grass of Kentucky, highly valued for pasturage and hay.

blue-green al·ga, blö'grēn al'ga, *n.* Any of the algae *Myxophyceae,* usually bluish-green because of presence of blue pigments and chlorophyll.

blue gum, *n.* A tree, *Eucalyptus globulus,* yielding the drug eucalyptol, used chiefly in the treatment of nose and throat disorders: sometimes planted in malarious locations.

blue·jack, blö'jak", *n.* A small oak, *Quercus cinerea* or *brevifolia,* of the southern U.S.

blue·jack·et, blö'jak"it, *n.* In the naval service, a sailor, often as distinguished from a marine.

blue jay, *n.* A North American bird, *Cyanocitta cristata,* the crest and back of which are blue.

blue jeans, *n.* Casual pants, customarily of blue denim; dungarees.

blue laws, *n. pl.* Severe or puritanic laws, especially those forbidding any entertainment or business on the Sabbath: from an alleged code said to have been adopted in the colonies of New England.

blue mold, *n.* A fungus *Penicillium* that creates a fuzzy blue-green growth on cheese, bread and other foodstuffs; a disease that decays apples and citrus fruits.

blue moon, *n.* A considerable lapse of time, as: I see her once in a *blue moon.*

blue·nose, blö'nōz", *n.* A native of Nova Scotia; an advocate of puritanism.

blue note, *n.* A deliberately flatted note, usually of the third or seventh step on the scale, and distinguishing jazz and blues music.

blue-pen·cil, blö'pen'sal, *v.t.* To alter or cancel with a pencil that makes a blue mark, as in editing a manuscript.

blue pike, *n.* A variety of walleye, *Strizotedion vitreum glaucum,* known for its long snout and prominent eyes.

blue·point, blö'point", *n.* A small oyster suitable for serving raw, orig. one from near Blue Point, south shore of Long Island, New York.

blue point, *n.* A Siamese cat with a cream-colored body and blue-gray extremities.

blue·print, blö'print", *n.* A photographic printing method using sensitized paper for the reproduction of engineering drawings, and consisting of white lines on a blue ground; the print itself; a plan or outline.

blue rac·er, *n.* A bluish green, harmless variety of U.S. blacksnake, *Coluber constrictor,* found from Ohio to Texas.

blue rib·bon, *n.* A piece of blue ribbon signifying the highest award, as first prize; the broad, dark-blue ribbon worn by members of the Order of the Garter.

blue-rib·bon ju·ry, *n.* A jury selected by the court to try cases involving special legal points, therefore requiring the jurors to have special qualifications.

blues, blöz, *n. pl.* A style of jazz developed from a song of melancholy character and slow tempo written in characteristic key; a passing spell of mental depression; the blue uniform of U.S. Naval officers and men.

blue-sky, blö'ski", *a. Investment.* Financially unsound or questionable; purely speculative.

blue-sky law, *n.* A law designed to prevent the sale of fraudulent securities.

blue·stem, blö'stem", *n. Hort.* a grass grown in Western U.S., so called because of the bluish color of its leaf sheaths; a fungus disease of raspberries, so named because of the blue discoloration it causes.

blue·stock·ing, blö'stok"ing, *n.* A woman having literary or intellectual tastes: orig. applied to certain ladies of London who used to meet, about 1750, in plain dress, some of them wearing blue stockings, for literary or intellectual discussions and entertainment.—**blue·stock·ing·ism,** *n.*

blue stone, *Chem.* blue vitriol.

blue·stone, blö'stōn", *n.* A bluish sandstone used for building purposes.

blue streak, *n.* An exceedingly fast moving body; a rapid flow of speech.

blu·et, blö'it, *n.* [Fr. *bluet, bleuet,* dim. of *bleu,* blue.] Any of various plants with blue flowers, as the cornflower, *Centaurea cyanus*; *often pl.* any of various species of houstonia, esp. *Houstonia cærulea.*

blue vit·ri·ol, *n. Chem.* sulfate of copper, a compound occurring in large, transparent, deep-blue triclinic crystals.

blue·weed, blö'wēd", *n.* A bristly weed, *Echium vulgare,* of the borage family, with showy blue flowers, a native of Europe naturalized in the U.S.

bluff, *a.* [Origin obscure; obs. D. *blaf,* flat, broad, as a face.] Presenting a steep, nearly perpendicular front, as a cliff; pompous or surly; rough and hearty, plain and frank, broad and full.

bluff, bluf, *v.t.* [Origin unknown.] *Poker,* to deceive by a show of confidence in the strength of one's cards; *fig.* to mislead or daunt by putting on a bold pretense.—*v.i.* To make a show of strength and confidence in order to mislead.

bluff, bluf, *n.* The act of bluffing; a bold pretense of strong resources for the purpose of daunting or deceiving or testing an opponent; one who bluffs; a cliff.

blu·ing, blö'ing, *n.* [Pres. part. *to blue* as noun.] A chemical used in laundering to offset the yellow tinge of linen or cotton, and to give them a white or bluish tinge.

blun·der, blun'dẽr, *v.t.* [M.E. *blundren, blondren*; perhaps akin to *blend.*] To do clumsily and wrong; bungle; to blurt out.—*v.i.* To move or proceed blindly and clumsily; flounder; to make a stupid or gross mistake; to move without direction or guidance; bungle; stumble.

blun·der, blun'dẽr, *n.* A mistake through precipitance or mental confusion; a gross and stupid mistake.—**blun·der·er,** blun'dẽr·ẽr, *n.* One who is apt to blunder or to make gross mistakes.—**blun·der·ing·ly,** blun'dẽr·ing·lē, *adv.*

blun·der·buss, blun'dẽr·bus", *n.* [D. *don-derbus,* "thunder box."] An obsolete short gun with a large bore and funnel-shaped muzzle.

blunt, blunt, *a.* [M.E., akin to G. *bludde,* a dull or blunt knife; Dan. *blunde,* Sw. and Icel. *blunda,* to doze, E. *blunder.*] Having a thick edge or end, as an instrument; dull; not sharp; dull in understanding; slow of discernment; abrupt in address; plain; unceremonious.—**blunt·ly,** blunt'lē, *adv.*—**blunt·ness,** blunt'nis, *n.*

blunt, blunt, *v.t.* To make blunt; to dull the edge or point of, by making it thicker; to impair the force, keenness, or susceptibility of.—*v.i.* To become blunt.

blur, blur, *v.t.*—*blurred, blurring.* [Origin uncertain; perhaps connected with *blear.*] To obscure or sully as by smearing with ink; stain or blemish; obscure by making confused in form or outline; render indistinct; dim the perception or suscepti-bility of; make dull or insensible to impres-sion.—*v.i.* To make blurs; to become blurred.

blur, blur, *n.* A smudge or smear, such as that made by brushing writing before it is dry; a blot; a stain; also, a blurred con-dition; indistinctness; something lacking distinct outlines.—**blur·ry,** *a.*

blurb, blurb, *n.* A short, laudatory announce-ment or advertisement, such as on a book jacket.

blurt, blurt, *v.t.* [Perhaps imitative of abrupt sound made by the lips.] To utter suddenly or inadvertently; to divulge unadvisedly, with *out.*

blush, blush, *v.i.* [M.E. *blusshen* < O.E. *blyscan,* allied to Dan. *blusse,* to blaze, to blush, D. *blos,* a blush, *blozen,* to blush; akin *blaze, blow.*] To redden in the face, as from a sense of guilt, shame, confusion, or modesty; to feel embarrassment, used with *at* or *for;* to show by a blush; to flush; to exhibit a red or rosy color; to bloom.

blush, blush, *n.* The suffusion of the cheeks or the face with a red color through con-fusion, shame, diffidence, or the like; a red or reddish color; a rosy tint.—**at first blush,** at the first review or consideration of a matter.—**blush·ful,** blush'fụl, *a.*—**blush·ing·ly,** blush'ing·lē, *adv.*

blus·ter, blus'tẽr, *v.i.* [M.E., perhaps < M.L.G. *blüsteren,* to blow.] To roar and be tumultuous, as wind; to be boisterous; to be loud, noisy, or swaggering; to bully; to make loud, empty threats.—*v.t.* To utter or effect in a blustering manner or with noise and violence, with *out;* as, to *bluster* one's way *out* of an argument.

blus·ter, blus'tẽr, *n.* A violent blast of wind; a gust; noisy talk; swaggering; boisterousness.—**blus·ter·er,** blus'tẽr·ẽr, *n.*—**blus·ter·ing·ly,** blus'tẽr·ing·lē, *adv.*—**blus·ter·ous,** blus'tẽr·us, —**blus·ter·y,** blus'tẽr·ē, *a.*

bo·a, bō'a, *n.* [N.L. < L. *boa,* a water snake.] Any of various large, nonvenomous tropical serpents of the family *Boidae,* with vestigial posterior legs and powerful coils for crushing prey, as *Boa constrictor,* a common tropical American species. A long, snake-shaped stole of silk, fur, feathers, worn by women around their necks.

BOAC, B.O.A.C., British Overseas Aircraft Corporation.

boar, bōr, bạr, *n.* [O.E. *bār.*] The uncas-trated male of swine, wild or tame; a wild old-world species of swine, *Sus scrofa* the wild boar, the supposed original of most of the domestic hogs.

board, bōrd, bạrd, *n.* [< M.E. < O.E. *bord,* board, plank, and *bord,* side: two orig. distinct Teut. words.] A piece of timber sawed thin, and of considerable length and breadth compared with the thickness; a flat slab or surface used for a specific purpose; as, a black-*board,* bulletin *board,* or ironing *board;* a tablet or frame on which games are played; as, a chess *board;* a kind of thick, stiff paper, such as the pasteboard covers of a book; a table, esp. on which to serve food; daily meals, esp. as provided for pay; the condition of one boarding in another's house; a table at which a council is held; a body of persons directing some activity; as a *board* of trade, a school *board;* the border or edge of any-thing. *Pl.* the stage of a theater; the wooden enclosure around an ice hockey or skating rink.—**by the board,** over the ship's side; overboard.—**on board,** on a ship, plane, or other conveyance; aboard.

board, bōrd, bạrd, *v.t.* To cover or close with boards; furnish with food, or with food and lodging, esp. for pay; *naut.* to come up alongside of (a ship), as to attack or to go on board; go on board of or enter (a ship, train, etc.).—*v.i.* To take one's meals, or be supplied with food and lodging, in another's house at a fixed price; *ice hockey,* to fling an opponent against the sides of the rink while bodychecking.—**board·er,** *n.* One who boards; esp., one who has his meals; esp., one who has his meals, or both meals and lodging, in the house of another for pay.

board, *n. Econ.* The trading room of a stock exchange; a corporation's board of directors.

board foot, *n.* A unit of measure equal to the cubic contents of a board one foot square and one inch thick (144 cubic inches), used in measuring logs and lumber.

board·ing·house, *n.* A house where meals, or meals and lodging, are furnished for pay.

board·ing school, *n.* A school in which pupils are boarded and lodged as well as taught, as distinguished from *day school.*

board meas·ure, *n.* A system of cubic measure in which the unit is the board foot.

board of di·rec·tors, *n.* A group of persons responsible for the top-level management of a corporation.

board of trade, *n.* An organization of bank-ers, merchants, etc., for promoting their business interests. (*Cap.*) a governmental department of Great Britain that aids commerce and industry.

board rule, *n.* A rule or measuring device having scales for measuring board feet without calculation.

board·walk, bōrd'wạk", *n.* A walk or promenade, usually constructed of boards or planks, esp. one along a beach.

boart, bạrt, *n.* Bort.

boast, bōst, *v.i.* [Probably of Celtic origin; akin W. *bost,* a boast, *bostio,* to boast. Corn. *bostye,* to boast.] To speak in praise of one-self or one's belongings, followed by *of;* to use exulting, pompous, or pretentious language; to brag; to exult; to glory; to vaunt; to bluster.—*v.t.* To display in osten-tatious language; to speak of with pride, vanity, or exultation; to take pride in possessing; to magnify or exalt, as strength, genius, wealth, or status.—**boas·ter,** *n.*

boast, bōst, *n.* A statement expressive of ostentation, pride, or vanity; a brag; the cause of boasting.—**boast·ful,** bōst'fụl, *a.* —**boast·ful·ly,** bōst'fụl·lē, *adv.*—**boast·ful·ness,** bōst'fụl·nis, *n.*—**boast·ing·ly,** bōst'ing·lē, *adv.*

boat, bōt, *n.* [< O.E. *bát* = Icel. *bátr,* D.L.G. and G. *boot,* a boat. Ir. W. *bad.* Gael. *bata.*] A small open vessel or water-craft moved by oars, paddles, sail or engine; any waterborne vessel, from lifeboat to cruiser; a dish shaped like a boat; as, gravy*boat.*—**in the same boat,** having to cope with the same situation.—**miss the boat,** to lose one's opportunity; to fail.

boat, bōt, *v.t.* To place or transport in a boat.—*v.i.* To go by boat.

boat·el, bot·el, bō·tel', *n.* [U.S. origin: by analogy to *hotel.*] A hotel by the side of a river, lake, or sea, for those who travel in their own boats, and equipped with a landing pier for the boats. See *marina.*

boat·er, bō'tẽr, *n.* A person who boats for enjoyment; a flat-brimmed straw hat with a ribbon band.

boat hook, *n.* An iron hook with a point on the back, fixed to a long pole, to pull or push a boat.

boat·house, bōt'hous", *n.* A house or shed, usu. along the water, for sheltering boats.

boat·man, bōt'man, *n.* A man who manages or works on boats.

boat·swain, bō'san, bōt'swän", *n.* [< M.E. *bote-swayn.*] A warrant officer on a warship, or a subordinate officer on a merchant vessel, in charge of the hull, rigging, anchors, cables, etc.

boat train, *n.* A train that transports passengers to or from a port.

bob, bob, *n.* [Perhaps imitative or suggestive of abrupt, jerky motion; in some of its senses allied to Gael. *babag, baban,* a tassel.] The weight at the end of a pendulum, plumb line, etc.; a short jerking action or motion; *Brit. colloq.* a shilling. A style of short haircut formerly popular with women and children; a float for a fishing line; shortened tail of a horse.

bob, bob, *v.t.*—*bobbed, bobbing.* To move down and up quickly or suddenly, once or several times in succession; to curtsy. To cut short the hair of women or children.—*v.i.* To grab at hanging or floating objects with the teeth; as, to *bob* for apples.

bob, bob, *n.* Bobsled.

bob·ber, bob'ẽr, *n.* One who or that which bobs; a fishing float; rider on a bobsled.

bob·bin, bob'in, *n.* [Fr. *bobine.*] A reel, cylinder, or spool upon which yarn or thread is wound, for use in spinning, weaving, machine-sewing, etc.; a reel on which wire is wound in certain electrical devices.

bob·bi·net, bob"i·net', bob'i·net, *n.* A machine-made cotton netting, with hexag-onal mesh.

bob·ble, bob'al, *v.i.*—*bobbled, bobbling.* [Var. of *bob.*] To move with a continual bobbing.—*n.* A bobbing movement; a mistake; an error; *baseball,* a misplay.

bob·by, bob'ē, *n. pl.* **bob·bies,** bob'ēz. [From *Bobby,* for Robert, here Sir Robert Peel, 1788–1850, who improved the police system of London.] *Brit. slang,* a policeman.

bob·by pin, *n.* A flat, metal hair pin with a springlike action which clasps and holds the hair in place.

bob·by socks, bob·by sox, *n. pl.* White cotton mid-calf length socks or cuffed anklets, a distinctive feature of teenage girls' apparel during the 1940's.—**bob·by·sox·er, bob·by-sock·er,** *n.*

bob·cat, bob'kat", *n.* A common N. Amer. wildcat, *Lynx rufus,* having a rusty brown coat with black spots.

bob·cat, bob'kat", *n.* The first rank in cub scouting before becoming a wolf.

bo·bèche, bō·besh', *n.* [Fr.] A disk or shallow cup of glass, etc., with a central hole, placed at the base of a candle to catch melted wax.

bob·o·link, bob'a·lingk", *n.* [Imitation of bird's call, resembling *Bob o' Lincoln.*] American migratory songbird known in southern U.S. as the reedbird or ricebird.

bob·sled, bob'sled", *n.* Two short sleds having steering wheel and brake, coupled in tandem, used in racing down a steeply-

ch- chain, G. na*cht;* **th-** THen, thin; **w-** wig, hw as sound in whig; **z-** zh as in azure, zeal. *Italicized vowel* indicates schwa sound.

banked open chute; a sled formed of two short sleds coupled in tandem; either one of the sleds thus coupled.—*v.i.* To ride on a bobsled.—**bob·sled·ding,** *n.* The act of riding a bobsled for fun or in competition.

bob·tail, bob'tāl", *n.* A naturally short tail or one that is docked; an animal having such a tail; a thing curtailed; the rabble; as, ragtag and *bobtail*.—*a.* Cut short or abbreviated.—*v.t.* To cut or dock the tail of.

bob·white, bob'hwit', *n.* [Imitation of its call.] The common N. American quail, *Colinus virginianus*, with mottled reddish-brown, black, and white plumage.

bo·cac·cio, bō·kä'chō, *n.* [< It. *boccaccio*, ugly mouth.] A large, brown, big-mouth variety of rockfish found in California waters and used locally as a market fish.

bo·cage, bō·käzh', *n.* [Fr. *boscage*.] Tapestry, a decorative design of branches and leaves.

boc·cie, boch'ē, *It.* ba'chē, *n. pl. but sing. in constr.* [It. *bocce* pl. of *bac·cia*, ball, < (assumed) *I battia*, boss.] An Italian type of lawn bowling, played on a narrow court. Also **boc·ci, boc·ce, boc·cia.**

boche, bosh, bäsh, *n.* [Fr. origin uncertain; possibly a shortened form of Fr. *caboche* head, pate, noddle, < L. *caput*, head.] (*Also cap.*) A term applied colloquially and more or less opprobriously to a German: first used during the German invasion of France in 1914.—*a.* Of or pertaining to a Boche; characteristic of the Boches.

bock beer, *n.* [G. *bockbier*, for *Eimbecker bier*, beer of Eimbeck, or Einbeck, in Prussia.] A strong, dark beer, commonly drunk in the spring. Also **bock.**

bode, bōd, *v.t.*—*boded, boding.* [< O.E. *bodian*, to announce, to proclaim, < *bod*, an edict, a message; Icel. *botha*, to proclaim; to bode.] To portend; to presage; to be the omen of.—*v.i.* To promise good or ill.—**bode·ment,** bōd'ment, *n.* An omen; a portent.

bode, bōd, past tense of bide.

bo·de·ga, bō·dā'·ga, *n.* [Span. winecellar.] A winecellar; wineshop; storehouse for wine; grocery store.

Bo·dhi·satt·va, bō"di·sat'wa, *n.* [Skt. *bodhi*, enlightenment, and *sattva*, existence.] *Buddhism*, one who has attained the degree of enlightenment to become a Buddha but who refuses to become one with the Universal Spirit in order to serve humanity.

bod·ice, bod'is, *n.* [From *bodies*, pl. of *body*.] A woman's laced outer garment covering the waist and bust, common in peasant dress; the part of a woman's dress between and including the neck or shoulders and the waist, excluding the sleeves.

bod·ied, bod'ēd, *a.* Having a body; used in combination with an adjective to indicate a specific kind of body; as, full-*bodied*.

bod·i·less, bod'ē·lis, *a.* Having no body or material form; incorporeal.

bod·i·ly, bod'i·lē, *adv.* Entirely; completely; as, to remove a thing *bodily*.

bod·i·ly, bod'i·lē, *a.* Of or belonging to the body; not mental or spiritual; corporeal.

bod·ing, bō'ding, *n.* [M.E. *bodynge, bodunge,* < O.E. *bodung,* < *bodian,* to announce, < *boda,* emissary.] A portent; an omen. Also *foreboding.*—*a.* Portentous; ominous.—**bod·ing·ly,** *adv.*

bod·kin, bod'kin, *n.* [M.E. *boydekyn*; origin unknown.] A dagger; a small pointed instrument for piercing holes in cloth, etc.; a blunt needlelike instrument for drawing tape, cord, etc., through a loop, hem, or the like; a long pin-shaped instrument used by women to fasten up the hair; a printer's tool for picking out letters in making corrections in type already set.

Bo·do·ni, ba·dō'nē, ba·da'nē, *n.* [From Giambattista *Bodoni*, 1740–1813, Italian printer.] A type face based on designs by Bodoni.

bod·y, bod'ē, *n.* [< M.E. < O.E. *bodig*, body.] The physical structure or material substance of man or any animal; a dead organism; a corpse; a mass; a separate and complete portion of matter; as, a *body* of water. *Geom.* a figure having length, breadth, and depth; a solid. *Colloq.* a person.

bod·y, bod'ē, *n.* The main part of a human or animal as distinguished from the head and limbs; the torso; the main portion; as, the *body* of a document, as distinguished from the preface and appendices; *naut.* the hull of a ship; *aeron.* a plane fuselage.

bod·y, bod'ē, *n.* A group of persons as an entity; an organized or collective whole; as, student *body*.

bod·y, bod'ē, *n.* Consistency; as, a paint with *body*; density or firmness, as: This cloth has *body*. Fullness or richness, esp. in flavor, as: The wine has *body*.

bod·y, bod'ē, *v.t.*—*bodied, bodying.* To embody; to give physical reality or existence to (a thing or an idea); to give strength or substance to (something); specif. to increase the viscosity of (an oil).

bod·y cor·por·ate, *n.* A legally incorporated group of persons; a corporation.

bod·y·guard, bod'ē·gärd", *n.* The guard who protects or defends one's person.

bod·y me·chan·ics, *n.* A term for the mechanical functioning of the movable parts of the body, and related to the bodily functions that are considered mechanical.

bod·y pol·i·tic, *n.* A people as forming a political body under an organized government.

Boer, bōr, bar, *n.* [D. *boer*, peasant, countryman, = E. *boor*.] A South African Dutch colonist or farmer; an inhabitant of either of the former Dutch republics of South Africa.—*a.* Of or pertaining to the Boers; as, the *Boer* War.

bog, bog, bag, *n.* [Ir. and Gael. *bog*, soft.] A place of wet, spongy ground, with soil composed mainly of decayed vegetable matter; a quagmire; a marsh; boggy soil.—**bog·gy,** bog'ē, bag'ē, *a.*

bog, bog, bag, *v.t., v.i.*—*bogged, bogging.* To sink or stick in or as in a bog, often followed by *down*; as, to start to bog *down*.

bo·gey, bo·gy, bō'gē, *n.* [W. *bwg, bwgan,* a hobgoblin, scarecrow, *bug*-bear.] A hobgoblin; a fearsome specter; any object of dread. Also **bo·gey man, bo·gle, bo·gie.**

bo·gey, bo·gie, bō'gē, *n. Golf,* one stroke over par on a hole.—*v.t.*

bo·gey, bō'gē, *n. Milit.* an unidentified aircraft.

bog·gle, bog'l, *v.i.*—*boggled, boggling.* [Prob. connected with *bogey*, Prov. E. *bogle*, a goblin.] To doubt; to hesitate; to stop, as if afraid to proceed or as if impeded by unforeseen difficulties; to waver; to shrink; to shilly-shally.—*v.t.* To amaze; to shock.—**bog·gler,** bog'lėr, *n.* A doubter; a timorous man; a waverer; an inconstant person.

bo·gie, bō'gē, *n.* [Origin unknown.] A low, strongly built truck or cart; a pivoted truck for carrying one end of a locomotive or of a railroad-carriage; a supporting roller of an endless steel belt, as on a tank tread.

bo·gus, bō'gas, *a.* [Origin uncertain; possibly < *bogey*, applied to early counterfeiting equipment.] Counterfeit; spurious; sham; pretended.—*n. Print.* printed matter set by union rules, duplicating the text for which type was set by another publisher.

bo·hea, bō·hē', *n.* [< Chin. dial. *Bui* < Mandarin *Wui*, hilly territory where tea is grown.] An inferior kind of black tea.

bo·he·mi·a, bō·hē'mē·a, *n.* (*Often cap.*) a community of people, esp. artists or writers, who lead an unconventional life.—**bo·he·mi·an,** bō·hē'mē·an, *a., n.* (*Often cap.*) Unconventional; one who adopts a bohemian way of life.

Bo·he·mi·an Breth·ren, *n. pl.* A Christian association formed by Hussites in Bohemia in the 15th century, remnants of which formed the Moravian Church in 1722.

Bohr at·om, bōr at'om, bar at'om, *n.* [Named for Danish physicist, Niels *Bohr*.] *Physics,* a model of the structure of the hydrogen atom containing a positive nucleus encircled by a negatively charged electron traveling in any of a number of circular or elliptical orbits.

Bohr the·o·ry, bōr thē'o·rē, bär thē'o·rē, *n. Physics,* a quantum theory based on the Bohr model of the atom, stating that the possible orbits of the electrons are at different energy levels and that when an electron moves to a different orbit there is a corresponding absorption of energy if the move is from a lower energy state to a higher one and an emission of radiation when the opposite occurs.

bo·hunk, bō'hungk, *n.* [*Bo*(hemian) and *Hung*(arian), devoicing the *g*.] *U.S. slang,* an unskilled immigrant laborer, esp. one from east central Europe (an insulting term).

boil, boil, *n.* [< O.E. *býle* = G. *beule*.] A painful suppurating inflammatory sore forming a central core, caused by microbic infection; a furuncle.

boil, boil, *v.i.* [< O.Fr. *buillir* (Fr. *bouillir*), < L. *bullire*, < *bulla*, bubble.] To bubble up and emit vapor, as a liquid under the action of heat; to reach a boiling point, as: Water *boils* at 212°F. or 100°C. To undergo cooking or other treatment in liquid so heated; to hold a boiling liquid, as: The pot is *boiling*. To move in commotion or agitation; seethe; be violently agitated or incensed.—*v.t.* To cause (liquid) to boil or come to a boiling point; to cook or treat in a boiling liquid; to separate (salt, sugar, etc.) in solution by means of boiling off the liquid.—**boil down,** to reduce the amount by boiling; condense; abstract.—**boil a·way,** to evaporate through boiling.—**boil o·ver,** to flow over the brim while boiling; to let loose a simmering rage or passion.

boil, boil, *n.* The act or state of boiling; the condition of being at the boiling point.

boiled oil, *n. Chem.* any oil with the drying properties improved through chemical processing.

boil·er, boil'ėr, *n.* A person who boils something; a vessel, generally a large vessel of iron, copper, etc., in which anything is boiled in great quantities; a strong metallic vessel, usually of wrought iron or steel plates riveted together, in which steam is generated for driving engines or other purposes.

boil·er·mak·er, boil'lėr·mā"kėr, *n.* One who makes or repairs boilers and other heavy metal items; *slang,* a shot of whiskey with a beer chaser.

boil·ing point, *n. Phys., chem.* The degree of heat at which a fluid is converted into vapor with ebullition, as water at 212°F., and mercury at 675°, at sea level; the temperature at which a liquid begins to boil.

bois·ter·ous, boi'stėr·us, boi'strus, *a.* [Probably < W. *bwystus*, brutal, ferocious, *bwyst*, wildness, ferocity; perhaps connected with *boast*.] Violent; stormy; turbulent; furious; tumultuous; noisy; wild.—**bois·ter·ous·ly,** *adv.*—**bois·ter·ous·ness,** *n.*

bo·la, bō'la, *n.* [Sp. lit. *ball*.] A weapon used by hunters, warriors, and cowboys (esp. by South American Indians) consisting of a cord with weighted balls fastened at the ends, thrown with special skill at cattle and other animals to shackle and catch them. Also **bo·las,** bō'laz.

bold, bōld, *a.* [< M.E. < O.E. *beald, bald,* bold, courageous = Icel. *ballr,* D. *bout,*

O.H.G. *bald*, bold.] Daring; courageous; brave; intrepid; fearless; exhibiting courage in execution; executed with courage and spirit, as a deed; rude; forward; impudent; overstepping usual bounds; presuming upon sympathy or forbearance; showing liberty or license; striking to the eye; markedly conspicuous; steep; abrupt; prominent.—**bold·ly**, bōld′lē, *adv*. In a bold manner; courageously; abruptly.— **bold·ness**, bōld′nes, *n*. The quality of being bold, in all the senses of the word; courage; bravery; confidence; assurance; forwardness; steepness; abruptness.

bold·face, bōld′fās″, *n*. Print. thick-lined type used for emphasis and conspicuousness in display.

bold·faced, bōld′fāst″, *a*. Impudent; bold in behavior or demeanor.

bole, bōl, *n*. [< Icel. *bolr*, *bulr*, Dan. *bul*, trunk, stem of a tree; probably of same root as *bowl*, *bulge*, etc.] The body or stem of a tree.

bo·le·ro, ba·lâr′o, bō·lâr′ō, *Sp*. bạ·le′rạ, *n*. pl. **bo·le·ros**, ba·lâr′oz, bō·lâr′oz, *Sp*. bạ·le′rạs. [Sp.] A lively Spanish dance, or the music for it; a short jacket ending above or at the waist-line.

bo·let·us, bō·lē′tus, *n*. pl. **bo·le·tus·es**, **bo·le·ti**. [< L. < Gr. *bōletīs*, type of mushroom.] Any of the fungi of the genus *Boletus*, widespread in the U.S.

bo·lide, bō′līd, bō′lid, *n*. [Fr. *bolide*, < L. *bolis* (*bolid-*), < Gr. *bolis* (*bolid-*), missile, < *ballein*, throw.] *Astron.*, a large meteor, esp. one that explodes.

Bo·liv·i·an, bō·liv′ē·an, bō·liv′ē·an, *Sp*. bạ·lē′vyän, *a*. Pertaining to the customs and people of Bolivia, an inland country of west central South America.—*n*. A native or inhabitant of Bolivia.

boll, bōl, *n*. [M.E. < *bolle*, bowl.] *Bot.* the pod or capsule of a plant, as of flax or cotton.—*v.i*. To produce seed vessels.

bol·lix, bol′iks, *v.t*. [Var. of *ballocks*.] To bungle; to throw (something) into a state of confusion. Also **bol·ix**, **bol·lox**.

boll wee·vil, *n*. A weevil, *Anthonomus grandis*, the larva of which feeds on cotton bolls.

boll·worm, bōl′wụrm″, *n*. The larva of a moth destructive to the bolls of cotton and to other plants; the corn earworm.

bo·lo, bō′lō, *n*. [Dial. word of Philippine Islands.] A large, heavy knife with a single edge, resembling a machete.

bo·lo·gna, ba·lō′nē, ba·lō′na, ba·lōn′ya, *n*. [Named for *Bologna*, Italy.] A large sausage made of beef, veal, and pork, chopped fine, and enclosed in a skin. Also **bo·lo·gna sau·sage**.

bo·lo·graph, bō′la·graf″, bō′la·gräf″, *n*. A record of thermal radiation made by a bolometer.—**bo·lo·graph·ic**, *a*.

bo·lom·e·ter, bō·lom′i·tẻr, *n*. [Gr. *bolē*, a throw, ray, and *-meter*.] *Phys.* an extremely sensitive thermometer which uses metallic resistance to measure minute amounts of radiation: may be used instead of a spectroscope to detect and measure the intensity of infrared spectral bands.—**bo·lo·met·ric**, bō″la′me′-trik, *a*.—**bo·lo·met·ri·cal·ly**, *adv*.

bo·lo·ney, ba·lō′nē, *n*. See *baloney*.

Bol·she·vism, bōl′sha·viz″um, bol′shạ-·viz″um, *n*. [< Russ. akin to *bolshoi*, big, and noun suffix *-v(ik)*, and *-ism*.] The doctrines, methods, procedures, or dialectics of Russian communism; (*l.c.*) any ultraradical socialist doctrine. Also **Bol·she·vik·ism**.

Bol·she·vist, bōl′she·vist, bol′she·vist, *n*. A follower of Bolshevism; a member of the party which seized power in Russia during the 1917–1918 revolution.

bol·ster, bōl′stẻr, *n*. [< M.E. < O.E. *bolstre*.] A long pillow used on a bed or couch; something resembling a bolster in form or application, as a pad used to prevent pressure; a cushioned or padded part of a saddle; the part of a cutting tool which joins the end of the handle; a support placed horizontally on a post to lessen or prevent sag in the span of a beam or girder. **bol·ster**, bōl′stẻr, *v.t*. To furnish or support with a bolster, pillow, or any soft pad; to pad; to stuff; to support, generally followed by *up*; as, to *bolster up* one's courage.— **bol·ster·er**, bōl′stẻr·ẻr, *n*.

bolt, bōlt, *n*. [< M.E. < O.E. *bolt*, an arrow, a bolt; Dan. *bolt*, a bolt, an iron peg, a fetter, G. *bolz*, *bolzen*, an arrow, a bolt, or large nail.] An arrow; a thunderbolt; a stroke of lightning; a stout metallic pin used for holding objects together, frequently screwthreaded at one extremity to receive a nut; a movable bar for fastening a door, gate, window sash, or the like; especially that portion of a lock which is protruded from or retracted within the case by the action of the key; an iron to fasten the legs of a prisoner; a sudden withdrawal from a cause, movement, meeting, etc.; a roll of fabric as it comes from the loom.—**a bolt from the blue**, a sudden, wholly unanticipated event.

bolt, bōlt, *v.t*. To fasten or secure with a bolt or iron pin, as a door, a plank, fetters, etc.; to swallow hurriedly or without chewing; to utter impulsively; to roll into bolts, as of fabric; to sieve, as flour; to withdraw suddenly, as from a political party.

bolt, bōlt, *v.i*. To shoot forth suddenly; to spring out with speed and suddenness; to start forth like a bolt; to run out of the regular path; to start and run off.

bolt, bōlt, *adv*. Like a bolt; suddenly; as straight as a bolt; as, seated *bolt* upright.

bolt·er, bōl′tẻr, *n*. One who or that which bolts; in *U.S. politics*, one who bolts from a party. A horse given to running away.

bolt·er, bōl′tẻr, *n*. One who operates a machine for bolting; a sieve or apparatus for bolting flour.

bo·lus, bō′las, *n*. pl. **bo·lus·es**. [< L. *bolus*, a bit, a morsel, a lump, Gr. *bōlos*, a clod, a lump.] *Phar.* a soft round mass of anything medicinal to be swallowed at once, larger and less solid than an ordinary pill. Any small rounded lump, as of chewed food.

bomb, bom, *n*. [< Fr. *bombe*, < It. *bomba*, bomb, < L. *bombus*, < Gr. *bombos*, a booming sound.] A hollow projectile filled with a bursting charge, and exploded by means of a fuse, by impact, or otherwise; a shell; any similar missile or device; as, a dynamite *bomb*; a round lump of lava ejected from a volcano; a vessel lined with lead, containing radioactive material; a device to scatter crowds. *Slang*, a failure.

bomb, bom, *v.t*. To drop bombs upon, as from an airplane; bombard; to shell.

bom·bard, bom·bärd′, *v.t*. To attack with bombs; to fire shells at or into; to shell: sometimes used somewhat loosely for to assault with artillery of any kind; *fig.* to assail relentlessly.—**bom·bard·ment**, bom·bärd′ment, *n*.[< L. *bomb*(*us*), booming noise, and *-ard*.] The act of bombarding; the act of throwing shells and shot into an enemy position.

bom·bar·dier, bom″bẻr·dẻr′, *n*. A crew member on a bomber plane who aims and releases aerial bombs.

bom·bar·dier, bom″bar·dẻr′, *n*. (*Sometimes cap.*) in Canada, a type of snowmobile named after its inventor, Armand *Bombardier*, of Quebec.

bom·bar·don, bom·bär′dan, bom′bẻr·dan, *n*. [Fr., ultimately < L. *bombus*, a booming sound.] A large-sized and gravetoned brass musical instrument; a bass tuba; bass stop of an organ.

bom·bast, bom′bast, *n*. [Originally padding made of cotton, of same origin as *bom-* *basine.*] High-sounding words; inflated or boastful language; fustian; words too big and high-sounding for the occasion.— **bom·bas·tic**, bom·bas′tik, *a*. Characterized by bombast; high-sounding; turgid; inflated.—**bom·bas·ti·cal·ly**, *adv*.

bom·ba·zine, bom″ba·zēn′, bom′ba·zēn″, *n*. [O.Fr. *bombasin*, < L. *bombycinus*, of silk, < *bombyx*, silk: see *bombast*.] A fine twilled fabric with a silk warp and worsted filling, sometimes dyed black for mourning apparel. Also **bom·ba·sine**.

bomb bay, *n*. The compartment on the underside of a warplane in which bombs are carried and from which they are dropped.

bombe, bom, bomb, *n*. [Fr. lit., *ball*: from its shape.] A frozen ball-shaped confection made from a combination of ice creams, mousses, or ices.

bomb·er, bom′ẻr, *n*. A plane or person that drops bombs.

bom·bi·nate, bom′bi·nāt, *v.i*.—*bombinated bombinating*. [L.L. *bombinatus*, pp. of *bombinare*, < L. *bombus*, a booming or humming sound.] To hum; buzz; drone.— **bom·bi·na·tion**, bom′bi·nā·shan, *n*.

bomb·proof, bom′prōf″, *a*. Secure against the force of bombs; capable of resisting the shock or explosion of shells.

bomb·shell, bom′shel″, *n*. A spherical shell; a bomb; a person, thing, or event that causes an unexpected sensation.

bomb·sight, bom′sīt″, *n*. A device which enables a bombardier to determine the point in space at which bombs must be released from an aircraft to hit a target.

bo·na·ci, bō″na·sē′, *n*. [< Sp. *bonasi*, kind of fish.] A black grouper, *Mycteroperca bonaci*; any of several related salt-water fish.

bo·na fide, bō′na fīd″, bō″na fī′dē, *a*. [L.] With good faith; without fraud or deception; authentic; genuine.

bo·nan·za, ba·nan′za, bō·nan′za, *n*. [Sp. good sea; hence, good luck < L. *bonus*, good.] A rich mass of ore, as found in mining; hence, any rich source of profit; *stock market*, an unusually profitable investment or speculation.

Bo·na·part·ist, bō′na·pär″tist, *n*. [Named for *Bonapart*(*e*) and *-ist*.] One attached to the policy or the dynasty of the Bonapartes; one in favor of the claims of the Bonaparte family to the throne of France; a supporter of a military dictatorship, purportedly backed by a popular mandate.— *a*.—**Bo·na·part·ism**, bō′na·pär″tiz·um, *n*.

bon·bon, bon′bon″, *n*. [Fr., good-good.] A sweetmeat or sugarplum; a piece of confectionery; any dainty or delicacy; a fondant centered candy, coated with either chocolate or fondant, and sometimes filled with nuts or fruit; anything overly sweet or satiating.

bond, bond, *n*. Anything that binds, confines, or holds together, as a cord, a chain, a rope; a shackle or fetter; a link or tie; a material which unites components, as adhesive or glue; a tie of affection or loyalty; an obligation imposing moral duty, as a vow or a promise; *law*, a legal instrument, under seal, binding the maker, and usually his heirs, to some specific action; *finance*, an interest-bearing certificate issued by a government or corporation promising payment of principal at a certain time; *commerce*, the state of goods in bond while stored in a bonded warehouse until duties or taxes are paid on them; *insurance*, a policy covering financial losses caused by default or accident; *masonry*, *carp.*, the overlapping of brick or timber to form a compact mass; the brick or timber that form the support; *chem.* the combining of atoms in a molecule. *Elect.* see *bonding*.

bond, bond, *v.t*. To bind or join firmly together, as bricks, for solidity of construction; to put under bonds; put (goods) in bond; issue bonds on, or mortgage, as a railroad; convert into bonds, as a debt.—*v.i.* To solidify with the use of a bond or binder.—**bond·er,** bond′ĕr, *n.* One who bonds; one who deposits goods in a bonded warehouse; one of the stones which reach a considerable distance into or entirely through a wall for the purpose of binding it together.

bond·age, bon′dij, *n.* Slavery or involuntary servitude; thralldom; captivity; imprisonment; restraint of a person's liberty by compulsion.

bond·ed, bon′did, *a.* Subject to or secured by bonds; placed in bond, as goods; designed to hold goods in bond, as a warehouse.

bond·er·ize, bän′de·rīz″, *v.t.* To coat, as metal, with a chemical base for a protective finish.

bond·hold·er, bond′hōl″dĕr, *n.* A person who owns or holds a bond showing he lent money to a government or a corporation.

bond·ing, bon′ding, *n. Aeron.* a system of connections or contacts which ensure that the metal parts of an aircraft form a continuous electrical unit, thus preventing the arcing of static electricity.

bond·maid, bond′mād″, *n.* A female slave, or one bound to service without wages.

bond·man, bond′man, *n. pl.* **bond·men.** [Dan. *bonde,* pl. *bonder,* yeoman, peasant. Same as O.E. *bonda,* a householder, the *band* of *husband.*] Serf, with mistaken meaning of one bound by bond; a man slave, or one bound to service without wages. Also *bondsman,* bondz′man, *bondsmen.*

bond pa·per, *n.* A superior grade of rag pulp white paper treated to resist penetration of ink or moisture, and used frequently for documents and stationery.

bond ser·vant, *n.* A slave; a bondman or bondwoman.

bonds·man, bondz′man, *n. pl.* **bonds·men.** *Law,* one who assumes responsibility for another by posting a bond.

bond·stone, bond′stōn″, *n.* A stone which extends through the wall of a structure for bonding it together.

bone, bōn, *n.* [M.E. *boon* < O.E. *bān,* bone; G. *Bein,* leg.] The hard, porous material which forms the skeletons of vertebrate animals; a separate part of the skeleton of a vertebrate; various hard animal substances or structures resembling bone, such as ivory, whalebone, etc.—**bones,** *n. pl.* The complete skeleton of a body. *U.S.,* a simple rhythm instrument made of wood or bone clappers and used in minstrel shows; the end man in a minstrel show who traditionally played the bones; *slang,* dice.

bone, bōn, *n.* A thin strip of plastic, wire, or other stiffening material, previously whalebone, inserted in corsets, petticoats, etc.

bone, bōn, *v.t.*—*boned, boning.* To remove the bones from fowl or meat; to stiffen (a garment) with stays; to put bone meal on land.

bone, bōn, *v.i. Slang.* To study intensively and hastily; to cram. Also **bone-up.**

bone ash, *n.* Ash residue obtained from bones calcined in air, used in making china and ceramics and as fertilizer. Also **bone earth.**

bone black, *n.* A black carbonaceous substance or residue, obtained by calcining finely ground bones in airtight vessels, and used as a pigment, decolorizing agent. Also **bone·black, an·i·mal char·coal.**

bone chi·na, *n.* A fine, partially transparent white china, usually made with bone ash.

boned, bōnd, *a.* Having the bones removed; supported with stays, as a corset; fertilized with bone, as *boned* land.

bone·fish, bōn′fish″, *n.* A game fish, *Albula vulpes,* with many small bones, found in shallow, warm seas.

bone·head, bōn′hed″, *n. Colloq.* a stupid, stubborn person.

bone meal, *n.* Ground bones used as feed or fertilizer.

bon·er, bō′nĕr, *n. Slang.* A mistake; a silly blunder.—**to pull a bon·er,** to make a mistake, usually careless or foolish.

bone·set, bōn′set″, *n.* [< *bone* and *set;* from its supposed medicinal virtue.] One of several herbs of the genus *Eupatorium,* esp. *E. perfoliatum,* formerly used in medicine as a perspiration producing agent. Also *thoroughwort.*

bon·fire, bon′fī″ĕr, *n.* [Formerly, a fire for burning bones.] Any fire built in the open air, as to burn rubbish or to celebrate.

bong, bäng, bang, *n.* [Imitation of sound.] A reverberating sound, as of a large bell.—*v.t., v.i.* To make such a sound; ring.

bon·go, bong′gō, bang′gō, *n. pl.* **bon·gos, bon·goes.** [Sp. Amer.] One of a pair of small, connected drums, played by the hands, esp. used in Caribbean music.

bon·ho·mie, bon′·a·mē″, *n.* [Fr., < *bonhomme,* "good man."] Good nature; unaffected affability.

bon·i·face, bon′a·fās″, *n.* [From *Boniface,* the jolly landlord in Farquhar's play, "The Beaux' Stratagem."] The proprietor of any inn, hotel, or restaurant.

bo·ni·to, ba·nē′tō, *n. pl.* **bo·ni·to, bo·ni·tos.** [Sp.] Any of various sea fishes, esp. of the mackerel family, as *Sarda sarda,* a food fish of Atlantic waters; one of several related species of the Pacific coastal waters, esp. the skipjack, *S. chiliensis.*

bon mot, ban mō′, *n.* [Fr. *bon,* good, and *mot,* a word.] A witticism; a witty repartee.

bonne, ban, *n.* [Fr. fem. of *bon,* good; see *bonny.*] A maid-servant; a child's nurse.

bon·net, bon′it, *n.* [M.E. *bonet* < M.Fr. < M.L. *abonnis.*] A headdress formerly worn generally by women, now chiefly as part of a uniform or nun's habit; a child's outdoor head covering commonly fitting down over the hair and often tied on with strings; an American Indian's feather headdress; any of various sheltering devices over ventilators, valve chambers, and hydrants. *Brit.* an automobile hood.

bon·ny, bon·nie, bon′ē, *a.* [M.E. *bonie* < O.Fr. *bon,* good.] Handsome; beautiful; fair or pleasant to look upon; pretty; lively; healthy; joyful; fine. Of places, serene; peaceful.

bon·sai, bōn′si, bon′sī, *n. pl.* **bon·sai.** [Jap.] A potted tree or shrub-like plant which has been dwarfed by special methods of culture; the art of such culture.

bon·spiel, bon′spēl, bon′spal, *n.* [Dan. *bondespil* < *bonde,* league, and *spil,* G. *spiel,* a game.] Esp. in Scotland or Canada, a match or tournament in the game of curling.

bon ton, bon′ton′, *n.* [Fr. good tone.] High style or fashion; good breeding; fashionable society.

bo·nus, bō′nas, *n. pl.* **bo·nus·es.** A sum given or paid over and above what is required, as, a sum paid to an employee in addition to his stated wages in recognition of successful efforts; a grant made by the government to a war veteran; an extra dividend paid to stockholders out of excess profits; a premium paid by a company for a loan, charter, or other privilege; an additional item given gratuitously, as: The child was given dessert as a *bonus* for eating his entire meal.

bon vi·vant, ban vē·vän′, *n. pl.* **bons vi·vants,** ban vē·vän′. [Fr. (fem. *bonne vivante*), "good liver."] One who lives well or luxuriously; one fond of good food and drink, and of good living generally.

bon voy·age, bon voi·äzh′, Fr. ban vwä·yäzh′, *n.* [Fr.] A good trip: used as a goodbye or farewell.

bon·y, bō′nē, *a.*—*bonier, boniest.* Pertaining to, consisting of, or resembling bone; having prominent bones.

bon·y lab·y·rinth, *n.* The cavity in the temporal bone that contains the intricate passageways of the ear.

boo, bö, *interj., n.* An exclamation used to express contempt, disapprobation, etc., or to frighten.—**boo,** *v.i.*—*booed, booing.* To cry "boo"; hoot.—*v.t.* To cry "boo" at; hoot.

boob, böb, *n.* [Possibly related to Sp. *bobo* < L. *balbus,* stuttering, hence: simple-minded.] A simple-minded person who is appallingly gullible and subject to ridicule.

boo-boo, bö-bö, *n.* [Baby talk.] *Slang.* Blunder; a minor injury.

boo·by, bö′bē, *n. pl.* **boo·bies,** bö′bēz. [Prob. < Sp. *bobo,* fool, also the bird *booby.*] A stupid person; a dunce; a clumsy fool; a boob. Any of the small gannets, birds native to tropical lands and islands.

boo·by hatch, *n. Slang,* an insane asylum. *Naut.* a small hatch opening from the weather deck of a vessel to the interior of the hull.

boo·by trap, *n.* An explosive camouflaged in such a way as to appear harmless; any trap laid for the unwary person.—*v.t.* To set a trap for, as the unwary.

boo·dle, böd′al, *n.* [D. *boedel,* goods, lumber.] Goods fraudulently obtained; gain made by cheating or bribery in public office; lot, crowd, or pack of people.

boo·gey·man, bug′ē·man″, *n.* See *bogey.*

boog·ie-woog·ie, bug′ē wug′ē, bö′gē wö′gē, *n. Mus.* A blues style using melodic variations over a persistent bass rhythm, esp. for piano; a dance to this rhythm.

boo·hoo, bö′hö′, *interj.* and *n.* A word imitating the sound of noisy weeping.—**boo-hoo,** *v.i.*—*boohooed, boohooing.* To cry or weep noisily.

book, buk, *n.* [< M.E. < O.E. *boc* = G. *buch,* book, = Goth. *bōka,* letter of the alphabet, pl. *writing, book.*] A writing or document; a written or printed work of some length, as a treatise or other literary composition, esp. on sheets fastened or bound together; a volume; *cap.* the Bible. A libretto; a division of a literary work, esp. one of the larger divisions; a record of bets, as on a horse-race; any collection of sheets fastened or bound together; a number of sheets bound together and used for making entries, as of commercial transactions; a pile or package of leaves, as of tobacco; a trick at cards, or a number of cards forming a set; *bridge,* six tricks taken by one side.

book, buk, *v.t.* To enter in a book or list; record; register; to put down for a place, passage, etc.; issue a ticket to, or obtain one for (a person); to engage (a place, passage, etc.) in due manner; to enter (a theatrical company, a lecturer, etc.) for an engagement, or for the engagements of a tour; to enter on a police register the official charge against (a suspect).—*v.i.* To register one's name; engage a place, passage, etc.; make an engagement or engagements, as for public exhibition or appearance.

book, buk, *a.* Having to do with books; as, a *book* fair; according to books of account; as, *book* value.

book·bind·ing, buk′bīn″ding, *n.* The act or practice of binding books; or of sewing and trimming the sheets, and covering them with leather or other material.—**book·-bind·er,** *n.* A person or firm engaged in bookbinding.

book·case, buk′kās″, *n.* An upright case with shelves for holding books.

book end, *n.* A support, often ornamental and of considerable weight, for placing at the end of a row of books in order to keep the volumes upright: used in pairs.

book·ie, buk′ē, *n. Colloq.* in horse-racing, a bookmaker.

book·ish, bụk′ish, *a.* Given to reading or study; more acquainted with books than with the world; pertaining to, contained in, or learned from books; theoretical.—**book·ish·ness,** bụk′ish·nes, *n.* Addiction to books; fondness for study.

book·keep·er, bụk′kē″pėr, *n.* One who keeps accounts; a person who has the charge of entering or recording business transactions.—**book·keep·ing,** bụk′kē″ping, *n.* The art of recording transactions by keeping accounts in a book or set of books in such a manner as to give a permanent business record.

book·let, bụk′lit, *n.* A little book; esp. a small unbound, often paper-covered book of printed matter.

book louse, *n.* Any wingless insect that lives in and often ruins old books and papers.

book·mak·er, bụk′mā″kėr, *n.* One who writes and publishes books, especially, a printer or binder of books; in betting phraseology, a person, generally a professional gambler, who accepts bets on horse racing and other sport events.

book·man, bụk′man , bụk′man″, *n.* pl. **book·men,** bụk′man, bụk′men″. [M.E. *bokeman.*] Someone interested or versed in books; a scholar or student; a person concerned with the publishing or selling of books.

book·mark, bụk′mark″, *n.* A ribbon or the like placed between the pages of a book to mark a place; a bookplate.

book-match, bụk′mach″, *v.t.* To match a design, as sheets of wood veneer, so that one mirrors the grain of another.

book·mo·bile, bụk′mo·bēl″, *n.* A truck or trailer equipped as for a travelling library.

book of ac·count, *n.* A book or records used for recording business transactions.

Book of Com·mon Pray·er, *n.* The service book of the Anglican churches.

Book of the Dead, *n.* Among the ancient Egyptians, a collection of religious texts, etc., for the guidance of the soul on its journey to the next world, a copy of which, in whole or in part, was placed with the mummy in the tomb.

book·plate, bụk′plāt″, *n.* An identifying label bearing the owner's name or crest or some other device, for pasting in a book.

book re·view, *n.* A critical analysis or examination of a recently published book; an oral or written analysis of a book by a student or discussion group; a magazine or newspaper section devoted to the discussion of current books.

book re·view·er, *n.* A member of a magazine or newspaper staff who makes an evaluation of current books.

book·sell·er, bụk′sel″ėr, *n.* One whose business is to sell books.—**book·sell·ing,** *n.*

book shelf, bụk′shelf″, *n.* A shelf for holding books; a personal collection of books.

book·stall, bụk′stall″, *n.* A stand where second-hand books are usually sold; *Brit.* a newsstand.

book val·ue, *n.* The net worth of a business, esp. of the capital stock, as shown in the official company accounting.

book·worm, bụk′wụrm″, *n. Colloq.* a person who is dedicated to books and scholarly pursuits. An insect which feeds on books, *specif.* of the order *Corrodentia;* the book louse.

Bool·e·an al·ge·bra, bō′lē·an al′ja·bra, *n.* [Named for English mathematician of the 18th century, George *Boole,* and *-an.*] The algebraic analysis of logic used notably in the planning of digital computers.

boom, bȯm, *n.* [D. *boom,* tree, beam.] A long pole or spar used to extend the foot of certain sails; a strong spar or beam projecting from the mast of a derrick, for

supporting or guiding the weights to be lifted; an upright spar in water for marking a channel, etc.; a chain or cable or a series of connected floating timbers or the like, serving to obstruct navigation, to confine floating timber, etc.; the area thus shut off; a projecting beam on an airplane to connect the tail surfaces to the main body; a movable beam used to manipulate a camera or microphone.—**low·er the boom,** *slang.* To punish; to discipline.

boom, bȯm, *n.* A deep hollow noise, as the roar of waves or the sound of distant guns: applied also to the cry of the bittern and the buzz of the beetle; a time of sudden increase in prices, wages, and general prosperity; a rise in political popularity. See *sonic boom.*

boom, bȯm, *v.i.* [M.E. *bombon, bummyn,* cf. G. *bummen,* imit.] To make a deep, prolonged, resonant sound; to make a rumbling, humming, or droning noise; to move with a resounding rush or great impetus; to develop rapidly as a business; to grow and increase in population, as a city.—*v.t.* to give forth with a booming sound; to promote an enterprise or a candidate for office.

boo·me·rang, bō′ma·rang″, *n.* [Native Australian name.] A bent or curved piece of hard wood used as a missile by the native Australians, which can be so thrown as to return to the thrower; a statement, plan, etc. which recoils on the originator; a mobile stand or arm for supporting lights or microphones in a radio, television, or movie studio.—*v.i.*

boom·let, bȯm′lit, *n.* A boom of short duration, especially as applying to an increase of activity in the business world.

boon, bȯn, *n.* [M.E. < O.N., *bōn,* petition.] A favor sought or granted; a great privilege; a blessing.

boon, bȯn, *a.* [M.E. < M.Fr. < L. *bonus,* good.] Gay; jovial; merry; as, a *boon* companion.

boon·dog·gle, bȯn′dog″al, *n.* [Orig. coined as U.S. slang.] A useless article produced with little skill; any labor of doubtful practical value, esp. that paid for with government grants or undertaken by a government agency.—*v.i.*

boor, bụr, *n.* [D. *boer,* peasant, cf. O.E. *gebur,* farmer.] A countryman; a peasant; a rustic; one who is rude or insensitive in manners.

boor·ish, bụr′ish, *a.* Like a boor; awkward; rude; rustic.—**boor·ish·ly,** bụr′ish·lē, *adv.* —**boor·ish·ness,** bụr′ish·nes, *n.*

boost, bȯst, *v.t.* [Origin obscure.] To lift by shoving up from behind; push up; *fig.* to advance or aid.—**boost,** bȯst, *n.*

boost·er, bȯst′ėr, *n.* One who boosts; a supporter; *aeron.* a propulsion unit that supplies extra thrust at the take-off of a space vehicle, missile, or aircraft, and is detached when the vehicle is in flight; *elect.* a device for regulating or modifying circuit voltage.

boost·er rock·et, *n.* A rocket motor, either solid or liquid, that assists the normal propulsive system or sustainer engine of a rocket or aeronautical vehicle in some phase of its flight; a rocket used to set a vehicle in motion before another engine takes over; also called **launch ve·hi·cle.**

boot, bȯt, *n.* [M.E. *bote* < M.Fr.] A sheath of leather, rubber, or plastic material to cover the foot and leg; any protective covering that resembles a sheath; a sharp kick; a recruit taking basic training in the armed services.—*Brit.* luggage compartment or trunk of an automobile; *baseball,* an error on an infield play.—*v.t.* To put boots on; to kick, *slang,* to dismiss or drive out forcibly; *baseball,* to make an error.

boot, bȯt, *n.* [O.E. *bōt,* reparation, amends.] Profit; gain; advantage; that which is given to supply the deficiency of value in one of the things exchanged.—**to boot,** in addition to; over and above; into the bargain.

boot, bȯt, *n. Slang.* Abrupt dismissal, as: He was given the *boot;* a pleased or excited feeling, as: I get a *boot* out of skiing.

boot·black, bȯt′blak″, *n.* One whose business it is to black or polish boots or shoes.

boot camp, *n.* A basic training camp for recruits in the armed services.

boot·ed, bō′tid, *a.* Equipped with boots, as for riding; *ornith.* of the tarsus of certain birds, covered with a continuous horny, bootlike sheath; with feathers on shanks and toes, characteristic of certain pigeons and fowl.

boot·ee, bō·tē′, bō′tē, *n.* A baby's knitted sock; a half-boot for women.

Bo·ö·tes, bō·ō′tēz, *n.* [L. < Gr. *boōtēs,* herdsman, < *bous,* an ox or cow.] A northern constellation behind Ursa Major, called the Herdsman, containing the bright star Arcturus.

booth, bȯth, bȯTH, *n.* [M.E. *bothe,* < Scand., cf. Icel. *búth,* Dan. and Sw. *bod,* G. *bude,* a booth; allied to Gael. *buth,* Slav. *bauda, buda,* Lith. *buda,* a booth, a hut.] A covered stall at a trade show, exposition, or polling place; a closed stall for privacy when telephoning; a partially enclosed seating accommodation in a restaurant; an enclosed area to protect certain activities from interference from the surroundings; as, a broadcasting *booth* in a public place.

boot·jack, bȯt′jak″, *n.* A v-shaped instrument for drawing off boots.

boot·lace, bȯt′lās″, *n.* A strong cord used to fasten boots.

boot·leg, bȯt′leg″, *n.* That part of a boot which covers the leg; merchandise, esp. liquor, that is manufactured, transported, or sold illegally.—*v.t.*—*bootlegged, bootlegging.* To circumvent legal prohibition, avoid payment of taxes, etc.—*v.i.* To practice bootlegging.—**boot·leg·ger,** *n.*

boot·leg con·tract, *n.* An agreement between labor and management, arrived at through collective bargaining, which seeks to evade the union's statutory security limitations.

boot·less, bȯt′les, *a.* Without profit or advantage; useless.—**boot·less·ly,** bȯt′les·lē,** *adv.* In a bootless or unprofitable manner.—**boot·less·ness,** bȯt′les·nes, *n.*

boot·lick, bȯt′lik″, *v.t., v.i.* To be servile; to toady.—**boot·lick·er,** bȯt′lik″ėr, *n.* One who curries favor in a servile manner.

boots, bȯts, *n. Brit.* a servant, as at a hotel, who blacks or polishes boots, etc.

boot·strap, bȯt′strap″, *n.* A leather or cloth loop sewn at the top of a boot to assist in pulling it on.

boot tree, *n.* A shoe tree; a device for blocking or stretching boots or shoes.

boo·ty, bō′tē, *n. pl.* **boot·ies.** [M.E. *buty* < M.L.G., cf. Icel. *byii,* Dan. *bytte,* exchange, barter, booty.] Spoil taken from an enemy in war; that which is seized by violence and robbery; plunder; pillage; any prize or gain.

booze, bōz, *n.* [M.E. *bous* < *bousen,* tipple, < M.D.] Any alcoholic drink; hard liquor; a drinking spree.—*v.t., v.i.* To drink excessively.—**booz·y,** *a.*—**boozier, booziest.**

booz·er, bōz′ėr, *n.* One who drinks to excess; a drunkard.

bop, bop, *n.* [Possibly, var. of *bob.*] A form of jazz characterized by extreme changes in rhythmic pattern and often accompanied by nonsensical lyrics. Also *bebop.*

bop, bop, *v.t.*—*bopped, bopping. Slang,* to strike as with the fist or a club.—*n.* A blow.

bo·ra, bōr′a, bạr′a, *n.* [It., for *borea,* north wind, < L. *boreas.* BOREAS.] A violent, dry, cold wind blowing from the north or northeast across the Adriatic Sea.

bo·ra, bōr′a, bạr′a, *n.* [Australian *bŭr, bŏr,* a circle.] An initiation rite of the Australian aborigines in which boys achieve tribal status of men.

bo·rac·ic, bō·ras′ik, ba·ras′ik, bạ·ras′ik, *a.* [M.L. *borac-,* borax.] Of, pertaining to, or produced from borax.—**bo·rac·ic ac·id,** a compound of boron with oxygen and hydrogen.

bor·age, bur′ij, bạr′ij, bōr′ij, *n.* [M.E. < M.Fr. < M.L. *borrago,* prob. < *burra,* wool.] A plant, *Borago officinalis,* native of southern Europe, with hairy leaves and stems and blue flowers, used in salads, in flavoring beverages, and sometimes medicinally; also, any of various allied or similar plants.—**bor·age·wort,** bur′ij·wėrt, bạr′ij·wėrt, bōr′ij·wėrt, *n.* Any plant of the borage family.

bo·rate, bōr′āt, bōr′it, bạr′āt, bạr′it, *n. Chem.* a salt of boric acid.—**bo·rat·ed,** *a.*

bo·rax, bōr′aks, bōr′aks, bạr′aks, bạr′aks, *n.* [M.L., < Ar. *būraq,* < Pers. *būrah.*] A white crystalline salt, sodium tetraborate, $Na_2B_4O_7 \cdot 10H_2O$, occurring in nature or prepared artificially: used as a flux, antiseptic, cleansing agent, water softener, and as a preservative.

Bor·deaux, bạr·dō′, *n.* A seaport in southwestern France; any red or white wine produced in the French Bordeaux region; any of various dyestuffs that produce a vinous red color.

Bor·deaux mix·ture, *n. Hort.* a fungicide consisting of a mixture of copper sulfate, lime, and water.

bor·del·lo, bạr·del′o, *n. pl.* **bor·del·los.** [< It.] A brothel.

bor·der, bạr′dėr, *n.* [M.E. < M.Fr. < O.Fr. *bordure, bord, border,* to border < G., cf. O.E. *bord.* BOARD.] The outer part or edge of anything, as of a garment, piece of cloth, a country, etc.; margin; verge; brink; boundary; confine; frontier.—**bor·dered,** *a.*

bor·der, bạr′dėr, *v.i.* To have the edge or boundary adjoining; to be contiguous or adjacent; to approach; to come near: with *on* or *upon.*—*v.t.* To make a border to; to adorn with a border of ornaments; to form a border to; to touch at the edge or end; to be contiguous to; to limit.

bor·der·ing, bạr′dėr·ing, *n.* Material for or used as a border; a border or edging.

bor·der·land, bạr′dėr·land″, *n.* Land forming a border or frontier; debatable or undefined area or condition; as, *borderland* between life and death.

bor·der·line, bạr′dėr·lin″, *a.* Located near a boundary line; of uncertain classification; not quite meeting established requirements; bordering on the obscene.

bor·der line, *n.* A dividing line; a line or area of separation, as between categories or conditions; a line denoting a boundary, as between two countries.

Bor·der States, *n. pl.* Southern states such as Delaware, Maryland, West Virginia, Kentucky, Missouri, and Oklahoma which bordered states of the Confederacy but remained in the Union; the states bordering on Canada; small European countries bordering the Soviet Union.

Bor·der ter·ri·er, *n.* A small British terrier with a thick, wiry coat.

bor·dure, bōr′dŭr, *n.* [M.E. *bordure,* edge.] *Her.* the border of a shield, surrounding the field of a coat of arms.

bore, bōr, bạr, *v.t.*—*bored, boring.* [< M.E. < O.E. *borian* = G. *bohren;* akin to L. *forare,* piece.] To pierce with or as if by a rotary cutting tool, such as an auger or drill; to form or construct by hollowing out, such as a tunnel, mine, well, or passage; in machine work, to cut a hole to an exact diameter; to make one's way or to force an opening.—*v.i.* To make a hole by piercing; to admit of being drilled, as: This pine board *bores* readily; to push forward or to force a passage.

bore, bōr, bạr, *v.t.*—*bored, boring.* To weary by tedious repetition, by dullness, or by unwelcome attentions, etc.

bore, bōr, bạr, *n.* [Origin unknown.] A cause of ennui or tedium, as: The movie was a *bore;* a dull, tiresome, or uncongenial person.

bore, bōr, bạr, *n.* A hole made by or as by boring; the cylindrical cavity of a tube, as a gun-barrel; the caliber or internal diameter of a tube; a tunnel.

bore, bōr, bạr, *n.* [Prob. < Icel. *bāra,* wave, billow.] A high, abrupt tide which rushes inland with great violence.

bo·re·al, bōr′ē·al, bạr′ē·al, *a.* [M.E. < L. *borealis,* < *boreas,* the north wind.] Northern; pertaining to the north or the north wind.

bore·dom, bōr′dạm, bạr′dạm, *n.* The state of being bored.

bor·er, bōr′ėr, bạr′ėr, *n.* One who or that which bores; a term sometimes applied to certain worms, insects, mollusks, and fishes, which penetrate foreign bodies.

bo·ric, bōr′ik, bạr′ik, *a.* Pertaining to or containing boron.

bo·ric ac·id, *n.* An acid derived from boron trioxide, especially a white crystalline acid, H_3BO_3, occurring in nature or prepared from borax, and used as a weak antiseptic.

bo·ride, bōr′īd, bạr′īd, *n. Chem.* a compound of boron with a positive element or radical.

bor·ing, bōr′ing, bạr′ing, *a.* That which is tedious, tiresome, causes boredom.—**bor·ing·ly,** *adv.*

bor·ing, bōr′ing, bạr′ing, *n.* The act or process of piercing or making a hole; the hole made, or a chip, fragment, etc. produced by such action or process. *pl.* chips resulting from boring.

born, bạrn, *a.* [M.E. < O.E. *boren,* pp. of *beram,* to bear.] Brought into being or existence by birth; of the locale of one's birth; as, American-*born* musician; possessing innate characteristics from birth; as, a *born* poet.

borne, bōrn, bạrn, pp. of *bear,* to carry, etc.

bor·ne·ol, bạr′nē·ōl″, bạr′nē·al″, bạr′nē·ol″, *n.* [N.L. < *Borneo* and *-ol.*] A crystalline cyclic alcohol, $C_{10}H_{17}OH$, obtained from the trunk of *Dryobalanops aromatica,* a large tree of Borneo, Sumatra, etc., or secured by the reduction of camphor: its esters are used in the manufacture of synthetic camphor and in perfumery.

born·ite, bạr′nīt, *n.* [Named for I. von *Born* (1742–1791), Austrian mineralogist.] Copper iron sulfide, Cu_5FeS_4, a metallic reddish-brown mineral which shows purple tarnish on exposure; a valuable ore of copper. Also **pea·cock ore.**

bo·ron, bōr′on, bạr′on, *n.* [< M.L. *borax.*] *Chem.* A trivalent metalloid element found in nature only as a compound or in combination, as borax, boric acid, etc., obtained in either an amorphous or crystalline form when reduced from its compounds and used in metallurgy and nucleonics.

bo·ro·sil·i·cate, bōr″a·sil′a·kit, bōr″a·sil′a·kāt, bạr″a·sil′a·kit, bạr″a·sil′a·kāt, *n. Chem.* a double salt consisting of boric and silicic acids.

bor·ough, bur′ō, bur′ō, *n.* [O.E. *burg, burg,* castle, fortified place, town, = Icel. *borg,* G. *burg,* castle, = L.L. *burgus,* castle, later town, = F. *bourg,* town; all < Teut., prob. < the source of O.E. *beorgan,* protect.] An incorporated municipality smaller than a city; one of the five administrative divisions of the city of New York; *Brit.* an urban community incorporated by royal charter; as, municipal *borough;* a constituency represented by a member of Parliament; as, parliamentary *borough.*

bor·ough-Eng·lish, bur′ō·ing′glish, bur′ō·ing′glish, *n. Law,* an old rule of descent of estates to the youngest son instead of to the eldest, or, if the deceased left no son, to the youngest brother.

bor·row, bor′ō, bạr′ō, *v.t.* [< M.E. < O.E. *borgian,* properly to take on security, < *borg, borh,* security, < *beorgan,* to protect; G. and D. *borgen,* to borrow.] To obtain, as something on loan, trust, or credit, with the intention of returning same or an equivalent; to adopt from another source for one's own use, as, words or ideas; to derive, appropriate, imitate; *math.* in subtraction, to regroup by sets of ten the components of the minuend; *naut.* to sail close to the wind or to sail close to the shore; *golf,* to putt to the right or left of the cup, compensating for the slant of the green.—**bor·row trou·ble,** to worry needlessly; to seek out difficulties; to be pessimistic.—**bor·row·er,** *n.*

borsch, borscht, bạrsh, bạrsht, *n.* [Russ. *borshtsh.*] A Russian soup containing beets and usually cabbage, served hot or cold, often with sour cream.

bor·stal, bạr′stal, *n.* [< *Borstal,* village of Kent, England.] In England, a school for the rehabilitation of delinquent boys.

bort, bạrt, *n.* [Origin unknown.] Diamonds too coarse for ornamental setting, or small fragments of gem diamonds, used, when reduced to a powder, for polishing and grinding.

bor·zoi, bạr′zoi, *n.* [Russ., swift.] The Russian wolfhound.

bos·cage, bos′kij, *n.* [O.Fr. *boscage,* < the German. BUSH.] A mass of growing trees or shrubs; woods; groves or thickets; sylvan foliage.

bosh, bosh, *n.* [Turk., empty, useless.] Nonsense; absurdity; trash. Often used as an interjection, in disbelief.

bosk, bosk, *n.* [M.E. *bosk,* var. of *busk,* bush: BUSH.] A thicket; a small wood; *provinc. Eng.* a bush.—**bos·kage,** bos′kij, *n. Boscage.*

bos·ket, bos·quet, bos′kit, *n.* [Fr. *bosquet,* < It. *boschetto,* dim. of *bosco,* wood: BUSH.] A grove; a thicket.

bos·om, buz′am, *n.* [< M.E. < O.E. *bos(u)m.*] The breast of a woman; the part of a garment which covers the breast; the breast as the seat of thought or emotion; something similar to the breast, as a broad or sustaining surface, a hollow interior, an inmost recess, etc.; familiar inner circle.

bos·om, buz′am, *v.t.* To take to the bosom; embrace; to enclose in the bosom; to conceal in the bosom.

bos·om, buz′am, *a.* Of, or pertaining to, or worn on the bosom; cherished in the bosom; intimate or confidential; as, a *bosom* friend.

bos·omed, buz′amd, bō′zamd, *a.* Having a certain type of bosom; as, full-*bosomed;* placed in the bosom for concealment.

bos·om·y, buz′a·mē, bō′za·mē, *a.* Having a full bosom (said of a woman).

bos·son, bō′son, *n.* [Named for S. N. *Bose,* Indian physicist of the 20th century.] A term in quantum statistics for atomic and sub-atomic particles classified according to their energy levels; particles classified according to the Bose-Einstein statistics, in which two or more particles may occupy the same energy level.

boss, bạs, bos, *n.* [< D. *baas,* master.] A foreman or superintendent; a manager or employer of workmen; one who makes decisions, exerts authority, or dominates; a politician who controls the machinery of his party, including votes, political appointments, or legislative measures.

boss, bȧs, bos, n. [< M.E. < O.Fr.; It. *bozza*, projecting part.] A protuberant part; a raised circular projection; stud; a raised ornamentation shaped from the same material as the object it ornaments, as a decorative knob or stud on a shield; *arch.* an ornamental projecting block or rounded mass set at the intersection of ribs or groins in a vaulted structure. A stone left unfinished and set in place for later carving; a domelike mass or outcrop of eruptive rock laid bare by erosion; a soft pad used in ceramics and glassmaking.

boss, bȧs, bos, n. One of several pieces of brass or other metal set into the cover of a book at the edges or corners to protect or decorate.

boss, bȧs, bos, n. *Mech.* the enlarged part of a shaft.

boss, bȧs, bos, v.t. To be master of or over; control; manage; direct; to domineer or command in a high-handed manner.—v.i. To act as a boss.

boss, bȧs, bos, v.t. To furnish or ornament with bosses; emboss; to treat, as the surface of porcelain, with a boss (soft pad).

bos·sa no·va, bos′a nō′va, n. A type of music of Brazilian origin with rhythm similar to the samba; the dance accompanied by this music.

boss·i·ness, bȧ′sē·nes, bos′ē·nes, n. The quality or state of being bossy or domineering.

boss·ism, bȧ′siz·am, bos′izm, n. Control by bosses, esp. political bosses.

boss·y, bȧ′sē, bos′ē, n. *Colloq.* A cow or calf.

boss·y, bȧ′sē, bos′ē, a.—*bossier, bossiest. Colloq.* given to acting like a boss; domineering.

Bos·ton bag, n. A carrying bag held together by two handles at the top.

Bos·ton cream pie, n. A layer cake having a filling of cream or custard between layers.

Bos·ton fern, n. A variety of sword fern, the fronds of which are long and drooping.

Bos·ton i·vy, n. An oriental vine of trilobed leaves, used widely in the U.S.

Bos·ton ter·ri·er, n. An American breed of small short-haired terriers, having a brindled or black and white coat. Also called *Boston bull.*

bo·sun, bō′sən, n. A boatswain. Also **bos'n, bo's'n, bo'sun.**

bo·tan·ic, ba·tan′ik, a. Pertaining to botany; relating to plants in general. Also **bo·tan·i·cal.—bo·tan·i·cal·ly**, ba·tan′i·kal·lē, adv. In a botanical manner; after the manner of a botanist; according to a system of botany.

bo·tan·i·cal, ba·tan′i·kal, n. *Pharm.* a drug made from the roots, leaves, or stems of a plant.

bot·a·nist, bot′a·nist, n. One skilled in botany; one versed in the knowledge of plants or vegetables, their structure, and generic and specific differences.

bot·a·nize, bot′a·niz, v.i.—*botanized, botanizing.* To seek plants for botanical study; study plants botanically.—v.t. To explore botanically.—**bot·a·niz·er**, n.

bot·a·ny, bot′a·nē, n. [Gr. *botaneia*, < *botane*, a plant.] A division of biology which treats of the plant kingdom, dealing with the forms, structure, tissues, functions, and classifications of plants, their distribution over the face of the globe, and their condition at various geological epochs; the plant life of a particular region; a botanical study.

botch, boch, n. [O.E. *bocche, botche*, a sore, a swelling, O.Fr. *boce*, a boss, a botch, a boil, a parallel form of boss; akin O.D. *butse*, a boil, a swelling.] A swelling on the skin;

a large ulcerous sore; a boil or blotch; a patch, or the part of a garment patched or mended in a clumsy manner; a patchwork or hodgepodge; a part in any work bungled or ill-finished.

botch, boch, v.t. To mend or patch in a clumsy manner; to perform, construct, or express in a bungling manner.—**botch·er**, boch′ẽr, n. One who botches; a clumsy workman at mending; a mender of old clothes; a bungler.—**botch·er·y**, boch′ẽr·ē, n. pl. **botch·er·ies.** A botching, or that which is done by botching; clumsy workmanship.—**botch·y**, boch′ē, a.—*botchier, botchiest.* Marked with botches; full of botches; ineptly done.

bo·tel, bō·tel′, n. See *boatel.*

both, bōth, a. [M.E. *bōthe, bāthe*, < O.E. *bā.*] Two considered together; one and the other.

both, bōth, conj. Equally; alike, as: He was *both* surprised and pleased.

both, bōth, pron. The two considered together; the one and the other.

both·er, boTH′ẽr, n. [Possible var. of *pother.*] The state of annoyance; worry; trouble; something that bothers; someone who vexes; *interj.*, a mild exclamation of annoyance. Effort or inconvenience; as: It's too much *bother* to move all the desks. Needless disturbance about trivial things, as: Why all the *bother* over the new novel ?

both·er, boTH′ẽr, v.t. To annoy; irk; harass by noise or by trifling offenses; confuse or puzzle; bring about minor discomfort; disturb; impose upon; cause to be anxious. —v.i. To cause annoyance or trouble; to trouble oneself; to make an effort to do something; to experience slight anxiety.

both·er·a·tion, boTH·ẽr·ā′shon, n. The act of bothering, or state of being bothered; sometimes used interjectionally to indicate annoyance, vexation; perplexity.

both·er·some, boTH′ẽr·sum″, a. Causing bother; troublesome; annoying; vexing.

bot·o·pho·bi·a, bot″ō·fō′bē·a, n. Fear of underground places such as basements, tunnels, subways, and caves.

bo tree, bō′trē, n. [Singhalese *bo*, < Skt. *bodhi*, wisdom.] The pipal or sacred fig-tree, *Ficus religiosa*, of India, under which the founder of Buddhism is said to have attained the enlightenment which made him the Buddha. Also **bod·hi tree**, bō′dē trē.

bott, bot, bot, n. [Gael, *botus*, a bott, *boithag*, a maggot.] The larvae of several species of gadfly found under the hides or in other parts of animals.—**bot·fly**, n. pl. **bot·flies.** A fly that produces botts.

bot·tle, bot′al, n. A vessel, commonly of glass or plastic, with a neck or mouth that may be closed with a stopper, for holding liquids; the amount of liquid held by such a vessel; with *the*, strong drink; bottled formula for infants instead of mother's milk. —**bot·tle·ful**, n.

bot·tle, bot′al, v.t.—*bottled, bottling.* To put into bottles. *Fig.* to store or shut within, usu. with *up*; to enclose, with *up.*

bot·tle club, n. A private club whose members supply their own alcoholic drinks.

bot·tled gas, n. A flammable gaseous paraffin hydrocarbon, as propane, in pressurized containers, used for cooking and as heating fuel in rural areas.

bot·tle-fed, bot′al·fed″, a. Of an infant, fed a formula from a bottle; not breast-fed.

bot·tle-neck, bot′al·nek″, n. A constricted area, esp. in a flow of traffic; an impediment to progress.—v.i. To slow or bring to a standstill a flow, such as traffic.—a. Narrow.

bot·tle-nosed dol·phin, bot′l·nozd″ dol′-fin, n. Any of several dolphins having a bottle-shaped nose, found in warm seas.

bot·tom, bot′am, n. [O.E. *botm* = G. *boden.*] The lowest or undermost part; the foot, base, or foundation; the underlying

ground, as beneath water. *Usu. pl.* low land adjacent to a river; grounds or sediment. The part of the body on which one sits; the seat of a chair; *naut.* the part of a ship below the wales.—a. Lowest; undermost; underlying; fundamental.

bot·tom, bot′am, v.t. To furnish with a bottom; to base or found (*on* or *upon*); to get to the bottom of; fathom.—v.i. To be based; rest; to reach the bottom.—**bot·tom·ed**, a. Having a bottom; as, a flat-bottomed boat.

bot·tom·less, bot′am·lis, a. Without a bottom; baseless; fathomless; immeasurably deep.

bot·tom·most, bot′om·mōst″, Brit. bot′-om·most, a. *superl.* Located at the bottom; lowest.

bot·tom out, n. *Stock market*, the gradual stabilizing of stock market prices after a lengthy decline. Opposite of *top out.*

bot·tom round, n. A cut of beef taken above the upper leg and below the rump.

bot·tom·ry, bot′am·rē, n. pl. **bot·tom·ries.** A contract, in the nature of a mortgage, by which the owner of a ship borrows money to make a voyage, pledging the ship as security for the money.

bot·u·lin, **bot·u·line**, boch′a·lin, n. [L. *botulus*, sausage.] A neurotoxin sometimes found in improperly canned meats and vegetables.

bot·u·li·nus, boch″a·lī′nas, n. [N.L., < L. *botulus*, sausage.] The bacterium *Clostridium botulinum*, which forms the toxin causing botulism.—**bot·u·li·nal**, boch″a·lī′nal, a. Pertaining to or resulting from botulinus.

bot·u·lism, boch′a·liz″am, n. [L. *botulus*, sausage.] A form of poisoning produced by eating spoiled food, and due to a toxin formed by the growth of *Clostridium botulinum.*

bou·clé, bō·klā′, n. [Fr., pp. of *boucler*, curl.] A fabric made of a yarn having small curly loops; the yarn itself.

bou·doir, bō′dwär, bō′dwȧr, n. [Fr., "place to sulk in," < *bouder*, pout, sulk.] A lady's retiring room or private sitting room.

bouf·fant, bō·fänt′, Fr. bō·fäN′, a. [Fr. (fem. *bouffante*), ppr. of *bouffer*, swell, puff.] Puffed out; full, as sleeves, draperies, or coiffure.—n. A type of coiffure in which the hair is arranged in the form of a puff.

bouffe, bōf, n. [< Fr., farcical.] Opéra bouffe; farcical opera.

bou·gain·vil·lae·a, bō″gan·vil′ē·a, bō″-gan·vil′ya, n. [N.L.; named from L. A. de *Bougainville* (1729–1811), French navigator.] Any plant of the genus *Bougainvillæa*, shrubs with small flowers subtended by large colored bracts (red, purple, etc.), species of which are cultivated for ornament. Also **bou·gain·vil·le·a.**

bough, bou, n. [O.E. *bōg, bōh*, shoulder, bough, = D. *boeg*, L.G. *bug*, Icel. *bōgr*, shoulder, bow of a ship = G. *bug*, shoulder; akin to Gr. *pēchys*, Skt. *bāhu*, forearm.] A branch of a tree, esp. one of the larger or main branches; *archaic*, the gallows.—**boughed**, a. Having boughs; shaded with boughs.—**bough·pot**, bou′pot″, bō′pot″, n. A pot or other vessel for holding boughs or flowers for ornament; a flower pot; a bouquet.

bought, bȧt, pret. and pp. of *buy.*—**bought·en**, bȧt′an, a. *Northern U.S. dial.* bought or purchased, esp. as opposed to *home-made.*

bou·gie, bō′jē, bōzhē′, bō′zhē, n. [Fr. *Bougie*, a town in Algeria from which wax was obtained.] A slender, flexible instrument for dilating or opening passages of the body; a pencil of medicated paraffin or other readily melting substance for introduction into the body; a suppository; a wax candle.

bouil·la·baisse, bōl″ya·bās′, bōl′ya·bās″, *n.* [Fr. < Pr.] A kind of stew or chowder made of several kinds of fish and vegetables.

bouil·lon, bul′yon, bul′yan, *Fr.* bōl·yaN′, *n.* [Fr., < *bouillir: bouilli.*] A clear, thin broth made by boiling meat long and slowly with seasonings.

bouil·lon cube, *n.* A commercially made portion of bouillon in dehydrated form.

boul·der, bōl′dẽr, *n.* [Short for *boulder-stone,* M.E. *bulder ston:* cf. Sw. *bullersten.*] A large, detached rock rounded by the action of weather and water.

boul·der, bōl′dẽr, *v.t.* To make into boulders; to wear smooth, as an emery wheel, by abrading with flint pebbles.

boul·der clay, *n.* A stiff, tenacious, non-stratified clay containing boulders, deposited during the glacial epoch.

boule, bōl, *n.* A mineral, usually a synthetic gem, synthesized in the Verneuil furnace; also *birne.*

boule, boulle, bōl, *n.* See *buhl.*

boul·e·vard, bul′a·värd, bō′la·värd, *n.* [Fr. *boulevard,* O.Fr. *boulvert, bolvercq, bolluwercq;* < Teut., from the same source as E. *bulwark.*] A broad, handsome avenue of a city.

bou·le·var·dier, bul′a·vär·dẽr′, bō″la·vär·dẽr′, *Fr.* bōl·a·vaR·dyä′, *n.* [Fr.] One who frequents the boulevards; man about town.

bounce, bouns, *v.i.*—*bounced, bouncing.* [M.E. *bunsen:* cf. D. *bonzen,* bounce, knock, L.G. *bunsen,* knock.] To strike a surface and rebound; to move with a springing step; to spring or bound back suddenly, as an object which has been dropped or thrown; *colloq.* of a bank check, to be returned as worthless.—*v.t.* To cause to spring back; *colloq.* to dismiss from employment; to expel, or eject by force, as: The nightclub owner *bounced* the drunk. *Brit. slang,* to gain by bluff or loud talk; to bully.

bounce, bouns, *n.* A bound or rebound; the capacity to spring or leap; a sudden leap; verve, vivacity, high spirits; expulsion, dismissal; the quality of resilience; variance in magnitude of target echoes on a radar scope; *Brit. slang,* bluff; bluster.

bounce·a·ble, bouns′a·bl, *a.* That which may be bounced, as a ball; *Brit. slang,* inclined to bluster or exaggerate.

bounce back, *v.i.* To recover rapidly from shock, illness, or defeat.

boun·cer, bouns′ẽr, *n.* One who or that which bounces; something big of its kind; a large, strong, vigorous person; *slang,* one employed in a public place to eject disorderly or obnoxious persons. *Brit. slang,* a barefaced liar or a braggart.

bounc·ing, bouns′ing, *a.* Big; stout, strong, or vigorous.—**bounc·ing·ly,** bouns′sing·lē, *adv.*

bounc·y, bouns′ē, *a.*—*bouncier, bounciest. Colloq.* resilient; springy; buoyant; exuberant.

bound, bound, *n.* [O.Fr. *bodne, bonne,* a bound, limit (Fr. *borne*), < L.L. *bodina, bonna,* a boundary, < Armor. *boden,* a cluster of trees serving as a boundary.] That which defines or circumscribes; the external or limiting line of any object or of space; that which restrains; as, to set *bounds* to ambition.

bound, bound, *v.i.* [Fr. *bondir,* to leap, O.Fr. to ring, to echo; < L.L. *bombitare,* to resound < L. *bombus,* a humming. BOMB.] To leap; to jump; to move forward by leaps; to rebound; to spring, as: He *bounded* from his chair; to adjoin or abut, as: The park area *bounds* his property.

bound, bound, *v.t.* To set bounds or limits; to act as a bound or limit; to limit; to terminate; to restrain or confine; to circumscribe; to name the boundaries of; to cause to bound.

bound, bound, *n.* A leap; a spring; a jump; a rebound.

bound, bound, *a.* Secured by or as if by a band; tied; in bonds; contained within a cover, as a book; constipated; costive; constrained or obliged; under obligation, legally or morally; destined or sure, as: It is *bound* to happen; determined or resolved, as: He is *bound* to go. Joined in chemical or physical combination.

bound, bound, *a.* [Later form of *boun, a.,* prob. regarded also as pp. of *bind.*] Ready or intending to go; having set out, as: The plane is *bound* for Los Angeles.

bound, bound, *a. Math.* having a specific initial point as well as magnitude and direction.

bound·a·ry, boun′da·rē, boun′drē, *n.* pl. **bound·a·ries.** [< bound.] Something that indicates bounds or limits; a limiting line or bound; *cricket,* a hit that sends the ball across the field boundary line and counts as four runs for the batsman.

bound·a·ry lay·er, *n. Aeron.* a thin layer of air, next to a moving airfoil, usually a few thousandths of an inch thick, whose characteristics are distinguishable from the main air flow: these characteristics must be considered and controlled for efficient functioning of the airfoil.

bound·ed, boun′did, *a.* Having bounds or limits; *math.* having a range with an upper bound and lower bound; used mathematically to describe the variations of a function; employed in a sequence having the absolute value of each term less than or equal to some specified positive number, so restricted that every member of the respective set is contained within a specified region which has at least the highest or lowest value.

bound·en, boun′dan, *a.* [An old participle of *bind.*] Obliged or beholden; compulsory; obligatory; as, our *bounden* duty.

bound·er, boun′dẽr, *n.* An ill-bred person; a cad. [*Colloq.,* orig. Eng.]

bound·less, bound′lis, *a.* Without bounds; unlimited; vast; infinite.—**bound·less·ly,** *adv.*—**bound·less·ness,** *n.*

boun·te·ous, boun′tē·as, *a.* Disposed to give freely; bountiful; liberal; generous; munificent; abundant; plentiful.—**boun·te·ous·ly,** boun′tē·as·lē, *adv.* In a bounteous manner; liberally.—**boun·te·ous·ness,** boun′tē·as·nes, *n.*

boun·tied, boun′tēd, *a.* Having the advantage of a bounty; recompensed or rewarded by bounty.

boun·ti·ful, boun′ti·fal, *a.* Liberal in bestowing gifts, favors, or bounties; munificent; generous; abundant; lavish; unremitted.—**boun·ti·ful·ly,** boun′ti·ful·lē, *adv.* In a bountiful manner; liberally.—**boun·ti·ful·ness,** boun′ti·ful·nes, *n.*

boun·ty, boun′tē, *n.* pl. **boun·ties,** boun′tēz. [O.Fr. *bonte* (Fr. *bonte*), < L. *bonitas,* < *bonus,* good.] Liberality; generosity; munificence; a benevolent gift; a premium or reward, esp. one offered by a government; a bountiful yield, esp. of a crop; a payment to promote the capture of criminals or the destruction of predatory animals.

boun·ty hunt·er, *n.* One who hunts for the reward or bounty offered for capturing or killing criminals or certain animals.

boun·ty jump·er, *n. U.S. hist.* one who, during the Civil War, enlisted as a soldier for the sake of the bounty offered, and then deserted.

bou·quet, bō·kā′, bō·kā′, *n.* [Fr., *bouquet,* bunch, clump of trees, thicket, grove, O.Fr. *boquet, bosquet,* little wood, dim. of *bosc,* wood. BUSH.] A nosegay; a bunch of flowers fastened together; an arrangement of flowers in a container; a compliment; a distinct aroma of fine wines and liqueurs; a scent implying delicate fragrance; something resembling a bunch of flowers, as a cluster of precious stones or a burst of fireworks.

bou·quet gar·ni, bō·kā′ gär·nē′, *n.* Several herbs, such as bay leaf, parsley, and thyme, tied together and used during cooking to enhance the taste of soups and stews.

bour·bon, bur′bon, *Fr.* bōr·baN′, *n.* [*Bourbon* County, Kentucky.] A whiskey made from malt, corn, and rye that has been aged in charred oak barrels.

Bour·bon, bur′ban, *Fr.* bōr·baN′, *n.* [From seigniory of *Bourbon,* with castle at Bourbon-l'Archambault, in central France.] A member of the last royal family of France, or of any of its branches, as the former royal family of Spain; hence, an extreme conservative, or one devoted to ideas suited only to past conditions, as in U.S. politics (applied esp. to certain Southern Democrats); a reactionary.—**Bour·bon·ism,** *n.* Adherence to the Bourbons; extreme conservatism, as in U.S. politics.

bour·don, bur′dan, bōr′dan, bar′dan, *n.* [Fr. BURDEN.] *Mus.* the drone pipe of a bagpipe; the bell of a carillon of the lowest pitch; the pipe organ stop an octave below written pitch.

bourg, burg, *n.* [The French form of *borough, burgh.*] A town, esp. one in proximity to a castle.

bour·geois, bur·zhwä′, bur′zhwä, *Fr.* bōr·-zhwä′, *n.* pl. **bour·geois.** [Fr. *bourgeois* (fem. *bourgeoise*), O.Fr. *burgeis,* citizen. see *burgess.*] In France and elsewhere, a member of the middle (esp. the mercantile) class of the people.

bour·geois, bur·zhwä′, bur′zhwä, *Fr.* bōr·-zhwä′, *a.* Middle-class; common; wanting in refinement or elegance.

bour·geoise, bur′zhwäz, bur·zhwäz′, *Fr.* bōr·zhwäz′, *n.* [pl. of Fr. *bourgeois.*] A social order dominated by middle-class citizens; a woman of that class.

bour·geoi·sie, bur″zhwä·zē′, *n.* pl. **bour·geoi·sie.** [Fr.] The bourgeois class; a member of that class.

bour·geon, bur·geon, bur′jan, *n.* [Fr. *bourgeon,* a bud.] A bud.—*v.i.* To sprout; to put forth buds.

bourn, bourne, bōrn, bärn, burn, *n.* [Var. of *burn.*] A small stream; a brook; a burn.

bour·rée, bur·rā′, *Fr.* bō·Rā′, *n.* A lively French dance from the 17th century, usually in double time; music for that dance or employing its characteristic rhythmic form, frequently found as part of the classical suite.

bourse, burs, *n.* [Fr., < M.L. *bursa,* purse: BURSA.] An exchange where merchants transact business with one another; a stock exchange, as that of Paris.

bout, bout, *n.* [Older form *bought;* same word as Dan. *bugt,* a bend, a bight; closely akin to E. *bight,* and verb to *bow.*] A spell of anything; a going and returning, as in plowing, reaping, etc.; as much as is performed at one time; a set-to; a contest, esp. a boxing contest.

bou·tique, bō·tēk′, *n.* [Fr.] A retail shop, usu. small, and specializing in fashionable clothes and accessories for women.

bou·ton·niere, bōt″o·nēr′, bōt″o·nyâr′, *n.* [Fr., buttonhole, < *bouton,* button.] A buttonhole flower or bouquet.

Bou·vier des Flan·dres, *Fr.* bō·vyä′ dā flän′dRa, *n.* [Fr. lit., Cowherd of Flanders.] One of a breed of powerfully built Belgian dogs with a tousled wiry coat varying in color from brindle to black, used primarily for police work and herding.

bo·vine, bō′vin, bō′vin, bō′vēn, *a.* [L.L. *bovinus,* < L. *bos* (*bov-*), ox.] Of the ox kind; oxlike; hence, stolid; dull.—*n.* A bovine animal.

bow, bō, *n.* [O.E. *boga* = G. *bogen;* akin to E. *bow.*] A bend or curve; something curved or arc-shaped; as, a rain*bow,* an ox*bow,* a saddlebow; a strip of flexible wood or other material bent by a string stretched between its ends, used for shooting arrows; a bowman or archer; an implement, orig. curved but now almost straight, with horsehairs stretched upon it, for playing a violin or the like; a single stroke of such an implement; a knot made by looping and tying ribbon or string for decoration.

bow, bou, *n*. [< L.G. or Scand., orig. meaning "shoulder," = E. *bough*.] The forward part of a ship, beginning where the sides curve inward, and terminating where they close or unite in the stem; the bow oar of a racing shell's crew.—**bow·chas·er,** *n*. A gun at the bow of a ship, for firing at vessels pursued.

bow, bou, *n*. An inclination of the head or body as in respect, salutation, submission, gratitude, shame, reverence, or assent.

bow, bou, *v.i.* [O.E. *būgan* = G. *biegen*, bend; prob. akin to L. *fugere*, Gr. *pheugein*, flee, Skt. *bhuj*, bend.] To bend or stoop; bend the head or body, as in respect or worship; incline the head in salutation; yield or submit.—*v.t.* To cause to bend; incline; express by an inclination of the head; cause to stoop, or yield.—**bow out,** to withdraw.—**bow and scrape,** to be overly polite.—**bow to fate,** to submit to the inevitable.—**make a bow,** to stand for recognition.—**take a bow,** to be presented publicly for the first time.

bow, bō, *v.t.* To bend or bring into a curved form; curve; to play a stringed instrument with a bow.—*v.i.* To be curved.

bow, bō, *n. Opt.* The frame for lenses of eyeglasses; the curved section of the frame resting on the wearer's ear.

Bow bells, bō' belz", *n. pl.* The bells of St. Mary-le-Bow Church, London, the range of the sound of which is popularly supposed to limit the birthplace of the cockney.

bow com·pass, bō' kum'pas, *n*. Any of various forms of compasses for drawing small circles, arcs, etc., as one having the legs joined by a bow-shaped piece.

bowd·ler·ize, bōd'la·rīz', boud'la·rīz", *v.t.* —*bowdlerized, bowdlerizing.* [From Thomas Bowdler, who in 1818 issued an edition of Shakespeare in which "those words and expressions are omitted which cannot with propriety be read aloud in a family."] To delete parts of texts prudishly deemed immoral.—**bowd·ler·ism,** bōd'la·rizm", boud'la·rizm", *n.*—**bowd·ler·i·za·tion,** *n.*

bow·el, bou'al, boul, *n.* [O.Fr. *boel*, < L. *botellus*, a small sausage, an intestine.] Part of the intestines, *usu. pl.*; the interior part of anything (the *bowels* of the earth).— *v.t.*—*boweled, boweling.* To take out the bowels of; to eviscerate.

bow·er, bou'ẽr, *n.* [O.E. *būr*, a chamber, < *búan* to dwell; Icel. *búr*, a chamber, < *búa*, to live; akin *boor*, *bound* (ready).] A shelter made with boughs or twining plants; an arbor; a shady recess; a retreat; *poet.* a woman's private apartment; *naut.* an anchor carried at a ship's bow.

bow·er, bou'ẽr, *v.t.* To enfold; to shelter in or as in a bower.

bow·er·y, bou'a·rē, bou'rē, *n. pl.* **bow·er·ies.** A farm or country seat settled by Dutch colonists in New York or South Africa.—**the Bow·er·y,** an area in New York City notorious for cheap hotels, saloons, and homeless derelicts.

bow·fin, bō'fin", *n.* A North American freshwater ganoid fish, *Amia calva*, not valued for sport or food.

bow front, bō' frunt", *a. Furniture*, having a convex front; bombé; swellfront.

bow hand, bō' hand", *n. Archery*, the hand, that holds the bow, usually the left hand; *mus.* the hand that draws the bow.

bow·head, bō'hed", *n.* A whalebone whale of the genus, *Balaena mysticetus*, native to the arctic seas. Ranging in size to 60 feet long, this whale has an extremely large head which comprises more than 30 percent of its total length.

bow·ie knife, bō'ē, bō'ē, *n. pl.* **bow·ie knives.** [From James *Bowie* (1796–1836), American pioneer, whose knife became famous.] A heavy sheath-knife having a long single-edged blade.

bow·ing, bō'ing, *n.* The act of playing a stringed instrument; the manner or style of the musician playing.

bow·knot, bō'not, *n.* A decorative looped slipknot, with two loops and two ends.

bowl, bōl, *n.* [Var. of *boll* (O.E. *bolla*).] A vessel of greater width than depth, usually hemispherical or nearly so, for holding liquids; the contents of a bowl; a toilet receptacle; a rounded hollow part, as of a spoon or tobacco pipe; any bowl-shaped formation or structure; a stadium with a bowllike interior, as for athletic contests.

bowl, bōl, *n.* [O.Fr. < Fr. *boule*, ball, < L. *bulla*, bubble.] A ball or bowl; one of the biased or weighted balls used in the game of bowls; one of the balls, having little or no bias, used in playing ninepins, tenpins, or lawn bowling; the disk sometimes used in playing skittles; also, a cast or delivery of the ball in bowling.

bowl, bōl, *v.i.* To play at bowling; roll a bowl or ball; move along smoothly and rapidly, as a carriage; *cricket*, to deliver the ball to be played by the batsman.—*v.t.* To cause (a ball, hoop, etc.) to roll; carry or convey as in a wheeled vehicle; knock or strike (*over* or *down*) as by the ball in bowling; to score at bowling; *cricket*, with *out*, to retire the batsman.—**bowl o·ver,** *v.t.* to greatly surprise.

bowl·der, bōl'dẽr, *n.* See *boulder.*

bow·leg, bō'leg", *n.* Outward curvature of the legs, causing a separation of the knees when the ankles are in contact; a leg so curved.—**bow·leg·ged,** bō'legd, bō'leg"id, *a.*

bowl·er, bō'lẽr, *n.* One who bowls; *chiefly Brit.* a derby hat.

bow·line, bō'lin, bō'lin", *n.* A knot used to make a loop that cannot slip; *naut.* a rope fastened near the middle of the perpendicular edge of the square sails, and used to keep the weather edge of the sails tight forward toward the bow.

bowl·ing, bō'ling, *n.* A game in which heavy balls are rolled down a lawn or an indoor alley at a set of pins; ninepins; tenpins. See *boccie, candlepins, duckpins.*

bowl·ing al·ley, *n.* A long narrow lane used for bowling; an enclosed place or building having such lanes.

bowl·ing green, *n.* A smooth, closely mowed lawn used for bowling.

bowls, bōlz, *n. Brit.* an outdoor game where players roll biased or weighted balls as near as possible to a stationary ball; sometimes, skittles, ninepins, or tenpins.

bow·man, bō'man, *n. pl.* **bow·men.** An archer; a soldier armed with a bow.

bow·man, bou'man, *n. pl.* **bow·men.** The oarsman who sits nearest the bow of a boat; logger in the front of a boat who directs floating logs with a cant hook.

bow net, bō'net, *n.* A cylindrical wickerwork trap with a funnel-shaped opening for catching lobsters; a net fastened to a wooden bow which springs shut on captured birds when triggered from a blind.

bow pen, bō'pen, *n.* A bow compass with a pen at the end of one leg. Similarly **bow pen·cil.**

bow saw, bō' sạ", *n.* A saw with a light bow-shaped frame holding a narrow blade in tension.

bowse, bous, bouz, *n., v.t., v.i.* See *carouse.*

bow·sprit, bou'sprit, bō'sprit, *n.* The large spar or boom projecting over the bow of a vessel used for extending smaller sail.

bow·string, bō'string", *n.* The string of a bow usually waxed or sized for use in archery or music; a string used, as by the Turks, for strangling offenders.—**bow·string,** *v.t.* To strangle with a bowstring; garrote.

bow·string hemp, *n.* An herb of the lily family, genus *Sanseviera*, perennial with narrow, white or yellowish white flowers and hemplike fibers; its tough leaf fiber used in cordage, bow strings, and cloth.

bow tie, bō' tī', *n.* A short necktie tied with a bow at the collar.

bow win·dow, bō'win'dō, *n.* A rounded bay window.

bow wow, bou' wou", *interj.* [Imit.] A word representing the bark of a dog.—*n.* A dog; (a child's word.)—**bow wow,** *v.i.* To bark.

bow·yer, bō'yẽr, *n.* A maker or seller of bows; an archer.

box, boks, *n.* [O.E. *box*, < L. *buxus*, box-tree (see *box*), perhaps through L. *buxum*, boxwood, something made of boxwood: cf. also M.L. *buxis*, box, for L. *pyxis*, E. *pyx*.] A case or receptacle, as of metal, wood, or pasteboard, in many forms and sizes; a chest; the quantity contained in a box; also, a case or package containing a present or presents, as at Christmas; that which is contained in such a case; a compartment or enclosure, as one for the separate accommodation of persons, as a seating compartment in a theater; a small shelter; as, a sentry *box*; the driver's seat on a coach; a space in a newspaper, etc., set off as by enclosing lines, in which news or other matter is featured, summarized, or the like, *mach.* an enclosing, protecting, or hollow part; a casing; a chamber; a bush; a socket; *baseball*, the space where the pitcher stands to deliver the ball; any of the spaces where the coaches, batter, and catcher stand. *Brit.* a shooting box, a small cabin used while hunting.

box, boks, *n.* [O.E. *box*, < L. *buxus* = Gr. *puxos*.] An evergreen shrub or small tree of the genus *Buxus*, esp. *B. sempervirens*, much used for ornamental borders and hedges, and yielding a hard, durable wood; the wood itself (see *boxwood*); any of various other shrubs or trees, esp. species of eucalyptus.

box, boks, *v.t.* To strike with the fist or hand.—*v.i.* To fight with the fists; to be in a boxing match.

box, boks, *v.t.* To enclose, as in a box; to confine; to form (something) to the shape of a box; to boxhaul; to mix (paint or the like) by pouring back and forth from one container to another.—**box the com·pass,** to repeat or go over the points of the compass in order; to make a complete turn.

box calf, *n.* A chrome-tanned calfskin with square markings produced by graining.

box cam·er·a, *n.* A simple box-shaped camera, usually with a fixed lens and shutter.

box·car, boks'kär", *n.* An enclosed and covered freight car.

box coat, *n.* A coachman's overcoat; an overcoat with a cape; an outer coat with a straight, unfitted back.

box el·der, *n.* A North American maple, *Acer negundo*, cultivated for shade.

box·er, bok'sẽr, *n.* A breed of short-haired, medium-sized, pug-faced dogs.

box·er, bok'sẽr, *n.* One who boxes; a pugilist.

Box·er, bok'sẽr, *n.* A member of a Chinese association which in 1900 rose up against foreigners and native Christians, in the northern provinces of China, and besieged the legations at Pekin until the uprising was suppressed by foreign military forces.

box·ful, boks'ful, *n. pl.* **box·fuls.** A quantity sufficient to fill a box.

box·ing, bok'sing, *n.* Fist fighting with or without padded gloves, practiced as a sport.

box·ing, bok'sing, *n.* The act of one who boxes something; a putting into or furnishing with a box; material for boxes or casings; a structure or work of boxes; a box-like enclosure; a casing.

Box·ing Day, *n.* [From gift boxes formerly distributed to employees on this day.] *Brit.* and parts of *Canada,* December 26, a legal holiday.

box·ing glove, *n.* A large padded glove used for boxing.

box kite, *n.* A kite consisting of a light frame in the form of a box, covered with cloth or the like with the exception of the ends and a space about the middle.

box la·crosse, *n. Canada,* a variety of lacrosse played with seven players on a team.

box of·fice, *n.* In a theater, or other place where the public is admitted to a paid performance, the office in which tickets are sold.—*a.* Pertaining to the box office; having the qualities that attract the public to a paid performance.

box pleat, box plait, *n.* A double pleat, with the material folded under at each side.—*v.t.* To arrange in box pleats.

box score, *n.* The play-by-play record of a game of baseball, basketball, etc., often including the names and team positions of all participants; the printed sheet used by a spectator to record a box score during the progress of a game.

box seat, *n.* A seat in a box of an auditorium such as an opera house or theater.

box spring, *n.* A bedspring encased in padded upholstery.

box stall, *n.* A stall used as an enclosure for a large animal such as a horse.

box·thorn, boks'thạrn″, *n.* Any of the deciduous or evergreen plants, genus *Lycium,* species of which are cultivated for their ornamental foliage, flowers, and berries. Also *matrimony vine.*

box·wood, boks'wụd, *n.* The hard, fine-grained, compact wood of the box, genus *Buxus,* much used for wood-engravers' blocks, musical and mathematical instruments, etc.; the tree or shrub itself; any of various shrubs or trees with a hard, compact wood, as *Cornus florida,* the flowering dogwood of the U.S.

boy, boi, *n.* [Fris. *boi, boy,* a boy; allied to D. *boef,* G. *bube,* Sw. *bue,* a boy.] A male child from birth to the age of puberty; a lad; a man wanting in vigor, experience, judgment; a familiar term applied in addressing or speaking of grown persons, especially one's associates; as, to go out with the *boys;* in compounds, sometimes applied to grown men without implying youth or contempt; as, a bell*boy,* bus*boy;* a young male servant. —**boy·hood,** boi'hụd, *n.* The state of being a boy or of immature age.—**boy·ish,** boi'ish, *a.* Belonging to a boy; pertaining to boyhood; in a disparaging sense: childish, trifling; puerile.—**boy·ish·ly,** boi'ish·lē, *adv.*—**boy·ish·ness,** boi'ish·nes, *n.*

boy·cott, boi'kot, *v.t.* [From Capt. *Boycott,* an English land agent in Ireland, the first prominent victim of the system in 1880.] To combine in refusing to work for, or deal with, in order to intimidate or coerce; to refuse to buy from or use the services of.

boy·cott, boi'kot, *n.* An instance of or the process of boycotting.

boy friend, *n. Colloq.* a male companion of a girl or woman, esp. one whose company is preferred.

boy scout, *n.* A member of an organization of boys (Boy Scouts), founded in England in 1908 by Lieut.-Gen. Sir Robert S. S. Baden-Powell.

boy·sen·ber·ry, boi'zan·ber″ē, *n.* pl. **boy·sen·ber·ries.** A large edible berry with a flavor resembling raspberry, developed from crossing the blackberry, loganberry, and raspberry.

---

bra, brä, *n. Colloq.* a brassiere.

brace, brās, *n.* [O.Fr. *brace,* the two arms (as outstretched or embracing), < L. *bracchia,* pl. of *bracchium,* arm.] Something that holds parts together or in place, as a clasp or clamp; *pl.* suspenders. An appliance for supporting a weak back, round shoulders, etc.; a device for producing or regulating tension in a drum; the character {or} for connecting written or printed lines, staves in music, etc.; a pair or couple; anything that imparts rigidity or steadiness; a device for holding and turning tools for boring or drilling; *arch., carp.* a piece of timber, metal, etc., as across an angle, for strengthening or supporting a framework or the like.

brace, brās, *v.t.*—*braced, bracing.* To furnish, fasten, or strengthen with or as with a brace; encompass, clasp, or gird; make tight, as the skin of a drum; increase the tension of; give firmness to; bring to greater vigor, etc., often used with *up;* fix firmly; make steady; connect (lines, etc.) with a brace, in writing or printing.—*v.i.* To acquire vigor; rouse one's strength or energy.

brace·let, brās'lit, *n.* [O.Fr. Fr. *bracelet,* dim. of O.Fr. *bracel,* < L. *bracchiale,* armlet, < *bracchium,* arm.] An ornamental band or circlet for the wrist or arm; *colloq.* a handcuff.—**brace·let·ed,** *a.*

brac·er, brā'sėr, *n.* One who or that which braces; a tonic or stimulating drink; a guard or protector for the arm or wrist.

bra·ces, brā'sez, *n. pl. Orthodontics,* connecting wires attached to teeth to correct irregularities; *Brit.* suspenders.

bra·chi·al, brā'kē·al, brak'ē·al, *a.* [L. *brachialis.*] Belonging to the arm, esp. the upper arm or brachium; armlike, as an appendage.

bra·chi·ate, brā'kē·it, brā'kē·āt″, brak'ē·it, brak'ē·āt″, *a.* [L. *brachiatus.*] *Zool.* having brachia or armlike appendages, as a crinoid; *bot.* having widely spreading branches in alternate pairs.

bra·chi·ate, brā'kē·āt″, brak'ē·āt, *v.i.* To progress by swinging from one branch to another by the arms, as monkeys.

brach·i·o·pod, brā'kē·a·pod″, brak'ē·a·pod″, *n.* [N.L. *brachiopoda,* pl., < Gr. *brachion,* arm, and *poys, pod,* foot.] One of the *Brachiopoda,* a class of mollusklike animals with a pair of armlike appendages, one on each side of the mouth.

bra·chi·um, brā'kē·um, brak'ē·um, *n.* pl. **bra·chi·a,** brā'kē·a, brak'ē·a. [L., prop. *bracchium,* = Gr. *brachion,* arm.] The upper arm, from the shoulder to the elbow; the corresponding part of any forelimb, as in the wing of a bird; an armlike part, appendage, or process.

brach·y·ce·phal·ic, brak″ē·sa·fal'ik, *a.* [Gr. *brachus,* short, and *cephalē,* head.] Short-headed; having a breadth of skull at least four-fifths as great as the length from front to back: opposed to *dolichocephalic.* Also **brach·y·ceph·a·lous,** brak″ē·sef'a·las.—**brach·y·ceph·a·ly,** brak″ē·sef'a·lē, *n.*

brach·y·cra·ni·al, brak″ē·krā'nē·al, *a.* Short-skulled or broad-skulled.

brach·y·dac·ty·lous, brak″ē·dak'ti·lus, *a. Med.* having fingers and toes shorter than normal.

brach·y·u·ran, brak″ē·yụr'an, *a.* [N.L. *brachyura,* pl., < Gr. *brachys,* short, and *oyra,* tail.] Belonging or pertaining to the Brachyura, a group of stalk-eyed decapod crustaceans including the common crabs.

brac·ing, brā'sing, *n.* The act of one who or that which braces; a brace, or braces collectively.—**bra·cing,** *a.* That braces. Strengthening.—**bra·cing·ly,** *adv.*—**bra·cing·ness,** *n.*

---

brack·en, brak'an, *n.* [M.E. *braken;* prob. < Scand.] A large fern, esp. *Pteris aquilina (Pteridium aquilinum);* such ferns collectively. also **brake,** brāk, *n.*

brack·et, brak'it, *n.* [Earlier *bragget:* cf. Sp. *bragueta,* ult. < L. *bracæ,* breeches.] A projection from the face of a wall, to support a statue, pier, etc.; a corbel; a shelf-like support to be attached to a wall; any projecting support, as for a shelf; a projecting fixture for gas or electricity; one of two marks, [ ], used in writing or printing to enclose parenthetic matter, interpolations, etc.; a brace for connecting lines.

brack·et, brak'it, *v.t.* To support with a bracket; enclose in brackets; couple with a brace; associate or mention together.— **brack·et·ing,** *n.* A series of brackets or bracketlike supports.

brack·et fun·gus, *n.* A higher fungus of a type which includes mushrooms, puff balls, and rusts.

brack·ish, brak'ish, *a.* Slightly salt, as water; having a saltish or briny flavor; unpleasant.—**brack·ish·ness,** *n.*

bract, brakt, *n.* [L. *bractea,* a thin plate of metal.] *Bot.* a modified leaf differing from other leaves in shape or color, and generally situated on the peduncle near the flower.— **brac·te·ate,** brak'tē·it, brak'tē·āt″, *a.*

brac·te·o·late, brak'tē·a·lit, brak'tē·a·lāt″, *a.* Having bracteoles.

brac·te·ole, brak'tē·ōl″, *n.* [L. *bracteola,* dim. of *bractea.*] *Bot.* a small or secondary bract, as on a pedicel. Also **bract·let.**

brad, brad, *n.* [M.E. *brad, brod:* cf. Icel. *broddr,* spike.] A thin, flat, usually small nail of uniform thickness, but tapering in width, having instead of a head a slight projection at the top on one side; also, a wire nail with a small deep head; also, a small, flat wedge-shaped piece of tinplate or the like, as for holding glass in a sash.— *v.t.*—*bradded, bradding.* To attach with brads.

brad·awl, brad'al, *n.* An awl to make holes for brads or other nails.

brad·y·car·di·a, brad'i·kär'dē·a, *n.* [N.L. Gr. *cardia,* heart.] Abnormally slow heart action.

brad·y·ki·ne·sia, brad'i·ki·nē'zha, brad″i·kī·nē'zha, *n.* Exaggerated slowness of movement. Also **brad·y·ki·ne·sis.** — **brad·e·ki·net·ic,** *a.*

brad·yp·noe·a, brad″ip·nē'a, *n.* [N.L. Gr. *pnein,* blow, breathe.] Slow or labored breathing.

brae, brā, brē, *n.* [Icel. *brá,* eyelid, akin to G. *braue,* eyebrow.] *Sc.* A sloping bank; declivity.

brag, brag, *v.i.*—*bragged, bragging.* [< Celtic; W. *bragiaw,* Ir. *braghaim,* to boast; Gael. *bragaireachd,* boasting; Armor. *braga,* to make a display; from root of *break.*] To use boastful language; to speak vaingloriously; to boast; to vaunt; to swagger; to bluster.—*v.t.* To boast about, as: He *bragged* that he was first to finish.

brag, brag, *n.* A boast or boasting; a vaunt; the thing boasted of.

brag·ga·do·ci·o, brag″·a·dō'shē·ō″, *n.* [< *Braggadochio,* a boastful character in Spenser's "Faerie Queene," from the verb to *brag.*] A boasting fellow; a braggart; empty boasting; brag.

brag·gart, brag'art, *n.* [*Brag,* and suffix *-art, -ard.*] A boaster; a vain fellow.—*a.* Boastful; vainly ostentatious.

Brah·ma, brä'ma, *n.* [Skt. *bráhma,* neut., worship, prayer, the impersonal divinity, *brahmá,* masc., worshiper, priest, the divinity as personified.] *Hindu religion.* The highest object of philosophic contemplation; the impersonal and absolute divinity; later, the divinity personified, or conceived as a god, combined as Creator into a Trinity with Vishnu as Preserver and Siva as Destroyer.

Brah·man, brä′man, n. pl. **Brah·mans.** Among the Hindus, a member of the sacred or sacerdotal caste, who claim to have proceeded from the mouth of Brahma, one of the deities of the Hindu Trinity, and who are noted for their many religious observances, their abstemiousness, and their theological learning. Also **Brah·min.** —**Brah·man·ic, Brah·man·i·cal,** a. Of or pertaining to the Brahmans or their doctrines and worship.

Brah·man·ism, brä′ma·niz″um, n. The religion or doctrines of the Brahmans; the socio-religious system of the Hindus, with the Brahmans as the highest caste. Also **Brah·min·ism.**

braid, brād, v.t. [O.E. bredan, bregdan, to weave, to braid; Icel. bregtha, to braid, bragth, a sudden movement; O.H.G. brettan, to braid.] To weave or intertwine, as hair or thread, by forming three or more strands into one; to plait.—**braid·er,** n.

braid, brād, n. A sort of narrow textile band formed by plaiting or weaving several strands of silk, cotton, wool, etc., together; a plait or plaited tress of hair; slang, naval officers.

braid·ing, brā′ding, n. Braid, or trimming made of braid collectively.

brail, brāl, n. [O.Fr. braiel, cincture, orig. for holding up the breeches, < L. bracæ, breeches.] Naut. one of the ropes sometimes fitted to a sail, by which it may be gathered up, as against the mast and gaff, preparatory to or instead of furling. A leather binding placed on the wings of a hawk to prevent flight; a dip net for hauling fish from a trap on to a boat.

braille, brāl, n. [< Louis Braille (1809–52), the French inventor.] A system of writing or printing for the blind, in which combinations of raised dots or points are used to represent letters.

braille writ·er, n. A machine for writing braille for the blind, similar to a typewriter.

brain, brān, n. [O.E. brægen = L.G. brägen = D. brein.] The soft, convoluted mass of grayish and whitish nerve substance, filling the cranium of man and other vertebrates, which governs or coordinates mental and physical motions; this organ considered as the center of sensation, and the seat of thought, memory, etc.; sometimes pl. intellectual power. In many invertebrates, a part of the nervous system more or less corresponding to the brain of vertebrates.

brain, brān, n. A mechanical device that serves to perform functions of the human brain for command, guidance, or computation; as, the brain of a guided missile.

brain, brān, v.t. To dash out the brains of; to strike or beat severely about the head.

brain case, n. The bony cranium or skull that surrounds the brain.

brain child, n. An original creation or design of one's imagination, as a literary or musical composition in which the creator feels an emotional proprietary interest.

brain drain, n. A deficiency of professional help caused by the emigration of such workers to more profitable employment abroad.

brain·less, brān′les, a. Without understanding or judgment; silly; stupid.

brain·pan, brān′pan″, n. The skull; the cranium.

brain·pow·er, brān′pou″ĕr, n. Mental capacity, esp. in the sense of superior, collective ability.

brain·sick, brān′sik″, a. Crazy; deranged.

brain·storm, brān′starm″, n. A sudden inspiration, esp. one which leads to creativity; the collective inspiration of a group intensively seeking the solution to a problem or a course of action.

brain·storm·ing, brān′star″ming, n. Colloq. a group technique for stimulating creative thinking.

brain trust, n. A group of experts made up largely of professors and specialists who act as consultants to high public officials. (Originated with the New Deal era.)

brain·wash, brān′wosh″, brän′wạsh″, v.t. To subject (someone) to the techniques of brainwashing.

brain·wash·ing, brān′wosh″ing, brän′wạ″-shing, n. Systematic indoctrination by psychological manipulation to undermine or change political beliefs, sometimes supplemented by the administration of drugs or by physical coercion. Also called brainwash.

brain wave, n. An electric impulse given off by tissues of the brain. Colloq. a brain-storm; inspiration.

brain·y, brā′nē, a.—brainier, brainiest. Provided with brains; intellectual.

braise, brāz, v.t.—braised, braising. [Fr. braiser, < braise, hot charcoal, live coals; < Teut.] To brown (meat) in a small amount of fat, then simmer gently in its own juice or a little added liquid in a covered skillet.

brake, brāk, n. A mechanical device which decelerates or stops the motion of a wheel or vehicle by means of friction; a device for breaking up flax or hemp by separating the fibers; a machine for bending sheet metal.

brake, brāk, v.t.—braked, braking. To arrest the motion of (a wheel, motor, motor vehicle, etc.) as by a brake; to break up (flax, etc.) with a brake.

brake, brāk, n. [Cf. M.L.G. brake, bushes.] A place overgrown with bushes, shrubs, or brambles, or with cane; a thicket.

brake·man, brāk′man, n. pl. **brake·men,** brāk′men. A man who operates brakes, as on a railroad. Also Brit. **brakes·man.**

bram·ble, bram′bl, n. [O.E. bremel, brembel, < stem bram, brem (seen also in broom), el being simply a termination and b inserted as in number, etc., akin L.G. brummel-beere, Dan. brambär, G. brombeere, Sw. brombär, a blackberry.] A prickly trailing shrub of the rose family growing in hedges and waste places, and bearing a black berry somewhat like a raspberry; the berry itself.—**bram·bly,** bram′blē, a.—bramblier, brambliest.

bran, bran, n. [A Celtic word = W. Ir. Gael. bran, bran, chaff; Armor. brenn, bran, whence O.Fr. bren.] The outer coat of wheat, rye, or other farinaceous grain, separated from the flour by grinding.

branch, branch, bränch, n. [O.Fr. Fr. branche, < L.L. branca, paw, claw.] An arm-like part diverging from a main stem or axis, as of a tree or any ramifying system; a limb, offshoot, or ramification; an extension; a subdivision or department; a local operating division of a business house, library, or the like; a line of family descent; a tributary stream.—a. Forming a branch; of or pertaining to a branch.

branch, branch, bränch, v.i. To put forth branches; spread in branches, or ramify; issue or diverge as a branch from a main stem (with from, out, off, etc.).—v.t. To divide as into branches; to adorn with branches or sprays, as in needlework.—**branch·ed,** a. Having branches; as, many-branched.

branch, branch, bränch, n. Milit. Any of the three U.S. military services; any of the functional activities of the Air Force; as, air defense branch; second level of specialization in Headquarters U.S.A.F.

bran·chi·ae, brang′kē·ē″, n. pl. [L., < Gr. branchia, pl., gills (branchion, sing., fin).] The respiratory organs or gills of fishes; the gill-like organs of other animals.—**bran·chi·al,** a. Of, pertaining to, or resembling branchiae or gills.

Bran·chi·o·pod·a, brang′kē·o·pod″a, n. [Gr. branchia, gills, and pous, podos, a foot.] An order of crustaceous animals, so called because their branchiae, or gills, are

situated on the feet, as in the water fleas and brine shrimps.

branch of·fice, n. Another office of the same business or industry located in outer areas, domestic or foreign, from the parent firm.

brand, brand, n. A piece of wood burning or partly burned; a sword; an instrument used to brand cattle; as, a branding iron; a mark made by burning with a hot iron or by other means to indicate the quality or manufacture, as a trademark; a class of goods made by a certain manufacturer; a mark made on cattle, horses, or sheep to indicate the owner, or on criminals; a mark of infamy; a stigma; bot. a plant disease which destroys leaves, giving them a burnt appearance.

brand, brand, v.t. To burn or impress a mark upon with a hot iron, or to distinguish by a similar mark; to fix a mark of infamy upon; to stigmatize as infamous; to mark permanently.—**brand·er,** brand′ĕr, n.

bran·died, bran′dĕd, a. Prepared with or preserved in brandy.

bran·dish, bran′dish, v.t. [O.Fr. Fr. brandir (brandiss-), < brand, sword; < Teut.] To shake or wave (a weapon, etc.) threateningly; flourish; to display pompously or militantly. —**bran·dish,** n. A wave or flourish, as of a weapon.—**bran·dish·er,** n.

brand·ling, brand′ling, n. A young salmon, or parr.

brand-new, brand′nö′, brand′nụ′, a. Quite new; unused.

bran·dy, bran′dē, n. pl. **bran·dies,** bran′-dēz [Earlier brandywine, < D. brandewijn, "burnt or distilled wine."] An ardent alcoholic liquor distilled from wine, or from the fermented juice of the grape, apple, peach, etc.

bran·dy, bran′dē, v.t.—brandied, brandying. To mix, flavor, or preserve with brandy; supply or refresh with brandy.

bran·ni·gan, bran′i·gan, n. Colloq. A dispute; a noisy quarrel; a drunken spree.

brant, brant, n. [Cf. Icel. brandgās, Dan. brandgaas, "brand goose," applied to various wildfowl, appar. with reference to the coloring.] Any of several species of small, dark-colored geese of the genus Branta, esp. B. bernicla, breeding in high northern latitudes and migrating south in the autumn. Also **brant goose,** Brit. brent.

brash, brash, a. Hasty; rash; impudent.

brash, brash, n. [< Fr. brèche, a breach, broken stuff, breccia.] A confused heap of loose, broken, or angular fragments of rocks; naut. small fragments of crushed ice, collected by winds or currents, near the shore. A pile of boughs of trees.

bra·sier, bra·zier, brā′zhĕr, n. [< brass or braze.] An artificer who works in brass.

brass, bras, bräs, n. [O.E. bræs.] A durable, malleable, and ductile yellow alloy, consisting essentially of copper and zinc; anything made of it, as a memorial tablet; a brass musical instrument, or such instruments collectively in a band or orchestra; colloq. effrontery or impudence; mach. a bronze shell used with another of the same to line a bearing; slang, military officers, esp. those of high rank; any officials or authoritative persons.—a. Made of brass; brazen; brassy; brass colored; using musical instruments made of brass; as, a brass band.

bras·sage, bras′ij, brä′sij, n. [Fr., < brasser, stir (melted metal).] A charge made to an individual for coining money from his gold or silver. See seigniorage.

bras·sard, bras′ärd, n. [Fr., < bras, arm.] A piece of armor which protects the arm; a band worn around the arm above the elbow as a badge. Also **bras·sart.**

brass band, n. A band which uses only brass instruments.

brass·bound, bras′bound′, bräs′bound′, *a.* Having a border made of brass or a similar metal; reinforced by brass; ruled by tradition; unchanging.

bras·se·rie, bras″a·rē′, *n. pl.* **bras·se·ries.** [Fr., < *brasser*, brew, stir.] A restaurant serving simple fare; an inn; a beer garden.

brass hat, *n. Slang,* an officer of high rank in the armed forces; a person in authority.

bras·si·ca, bras′a·ka, *n.* [< L. cabbage.] A plant of the genus *Brassica,* which includes the cabbage, cauliflower, radish, and turnip.—**bras·si·ca·ceous,** bras″i·kā′shus, *a.* Allied to or resembling the cabbage.

brass·ie, bras′ē, brä′sē, *n.* A golf club the wooden head of which has a brass plate, used for hitting long shots from the fairway.

bras·siere, bra·zēr′, *n.* [Fr. *brassière* (obs.), bodice < *bras*, arm.] An undergarment worn by women to support the breasts. Also **bra.**

brass knuck·les, *n.* A weapon fashioned of a metal strip with four holes, worn over the knuckles.

brass tacks, *n. Colloq.* fundamental facts of a situation; as, to get down to *brass tacks.*

brass·y, bras′ē, brä′sē, *a.*—**brassier, brassiest.** Of or like brass; brazen or impudent; cheap or showy; loud, harsh, metallic.—**brass·i·ly,** *adv.*—**brass·i·ness,** *n.*

brat, brat, *n.* A child: now used only in contempt or irritation; an annoying, spoiled, or ill-mannered child; ragamuffin.—**brat·tish, brat·ty,** *a.*

brat·tice, brat′is, *n.* [O.Fr. *bretesche,* a bartizan; probably < G. *bret,* a board, a plank.] A partition which divides a mining shaft into two chambers, serving as the upcast and downcast shafts for ventilation, or placed across a gallery to keep back noxious gases, or prevent the escape of water; a fence put round dangerous machinery.—*v.t.* To line with planks or cloth, as in a mine.

bra·va·do, bra·vä′dō, *n. pl.* **bra·va·does, bra·va·dos.** [Sp. *bravado, bravata,* < It. *bravata,* < *bravare,* brave, defy, < *bravo,* E. brave, a.] Ostentatious boldness; swaggering defiance; a bold show of indifference.—**bra·va·do,** *v.i.*—**bravadoed, bravadoing.** To act or talk with bravado.

brave, brāv, *a.* [Fr. *brave,* brave, gay, proud, braggart; Sp. and It. *bravo,* brave, courageous; perhaps from the Celtic; akin Armor. *brao, brav,* gaily dressed, fine, handsome; also O.Sw. *braf,* good.] Courageous; audacious; dauntless; bold; daring; intrepid; high-spirited; valiant; fearless; making a fine display in bearing, dress, or appearance generally.—**brave·ness,** *n.*

brave, brāv, *v.t.*—**braved, braving.** To encounter with courage and fortitude, or without being moved; to defy; to dare.—**brave·ly,** brāv′li, *adv.* In a brave manner; courageously; gallantly.

brave, brāv, *n.* A brave, bold, or daring person; a North American Indian warrior.

brav·er·y, brā′va·rē, brāv′rē, *n. pl.* **brav·er·ies.** The quality of being brave; courage; undaunted spirit, intrepidity; gallantry; valor; heroism.

bra·vo, brä′vō, brä·vō′, *interj.* [It., prop. *adj.* (fem *brava*): see *brave.*] Fine! Excellent! Well done!—*n. pl.* **bra·vos,** brä′vōz, brä·voz′. A cry of "bravo!"—*v.t., v.i.*—**bravoed, bravoing.**

bra·vo, brä′vō, brä·vo′, *n. pl.* **bra·voes, bra·vos.** [It., < *bravo, adj.*: see *brave.*] A daring villain; a murderous bully; a professional assassin.

Bra·vo, brä′vō, brä·vō′, *n. Communications,* a code word for the letter b.

bra·vu·ra, brä·vōō′ra, bra·vūr′a, *n. pl.* **bra·vu·ras.** [It.] Display of daring; show of brilliant performance; dash; *mus.* a florid passage or piece, requiring great skill and spirit in the performer.—*a. Mus.* spirited; dashing.

brawl, brạl, *v.i.* [Perhaps < W. *brawl,* a boast, *broliaw,* to boast, *bragal,* to vociferate; or akin to D. *brallen,* to boast, Dan. *bralle,* to jabber, to prate, *brölle,* to roar.] To quarrel or fight noisily; to be clamorous or loud; to make the noise of rushing water, as: The brook *brawls* through a rocky narrows.—**brawl·er,** brạl′ér, *n.* One who or that which brawls; a habitual fighter.

brawl, brạl, *n.* A noisy quarrel; loud angry contention; an uproar, row, or squabble; *colloq.* a loud, disorderly, and usually drunken party.

brawn, brän, *n.*[O.Fr. *braon*; < Teut. (cf. G. *braten,* roast meat).] Firm, well-developed muscular tissue; muscular strength; manpower; *Brit.* pork, esp. boiled and pickled.

brawn·i·ness, brạ′nē·nes, *n.* The quality of being brawny; strength; hardiness.

brawn·y, brạ′nē, *a.*—**brawnier, brawniest.** Having large strong muscles; strong.

bray, brā, *v.i.* [Fr. *braire,* to bray; L.L. *bragire, bragare,* to bray, < Celtic root seen in *brag.*] To utter a harsh cry: said especially of the ass; to make a loud, harsh, disagreeable sound.—*v.t.* To utter with a loud harsh sound, sometimes with *out.*—*n.* The harsh sound or roar of mules and donkeys.

bray, brā, *v.t.* [O.Fr. *brayer* (Fr. *broyer*), to pound, < G. *brechen,* to break.] To pound, beat, or grind small, especially in a mortar.

bray·er, brā′ér, *n. Printing,* an instrument employed for spreading ink.

braze, brāz, *v.t.*—**brazed, brazing.** [Fr. *braser,* to braze, < the Scandinavian. BRASS.] To solder with hard alloy; to cover or ornament with brass; to join (metals) by flowing a thin-layer, capillary thickness, of nonferrous filler metal into the space between them.

bra·zen, brā′zan, *a.* Made of brass; from brass often serving as a type of strength or impenetrability, extremely strong; impenetrable; pertaining to brass; proceeding from brass; as, a *brazen* sound; impudent; having a front like brass.—**bra·zen·ly,** *adv.*—**bra·zen·ness,** *n.* Appearance like brass; brassiness; impudence.—**bra·zen·face,** *n.* An impudent person; one remarkable for effrontery.—**bra·zen-faced,** *a.*

bra·zen, brā′zan, *v.t.* To behave with insolence or effrontery, with an indefinite *it.* —**bra·zen out,** to defiantly persevere in treating with effrontery, with an indefinite *it,* or a noun like *matter, affair, business.*

bra·zier, brā′zhér, *n.* [Fr. *brasier, braiser,* < *braise,* embers, live coals; same origin as *braze, brass.*] An open pan for burning wood or coal used for heating a room; a similar pan used for cooking food in which a grill holds the food above the embers. Also **bra·sier.**

bra·zil, bra·zil′, *n.* [Pg. *brasil,* < *braza,* a live coal, the name being given to the wood from its color, and the country being called after the wood.] A very heavy wood of a red color, esp. of the genus *Caesalpinia,* growing in Brazil and other tropical countries, yielding a red dye; also *brazil-wood.*

Bra·zil·ian, bra·zil′yan, *a.* [< *Brazil,* orig. (Pg.) *terra de brasil,* "land of brazil (dyewood)."] Of, pertaining to, or characteristic of the culture and people of Brazil, the largest country in South America, covering nearly half the continent. In 1960 its capital was moved from Rio de Janeiro to the newly built city of Brasilia.—*n.* An inhabitant or citizen of Brazil.

Bra·zil nut, *n.* The triangular edible seed of the tree *Bertholletia excelsa,* of Brazil and other countries; the tree.

bra·zil·wood, bra·zil′wụd, *n.* See *brazil.*

breach, brēch, *n.* [Partly < O.E. *bryce,* < *brecan,* E. break, partly < O.Fr. *breche* (Fr. *brchèe*), < the same ult. (Teut.) source.] The act or the result of breaking; a break or rupture; a rift, fissure, or gap; infraction or violation, as of the peace, of faith, or trust; severance of friendly relations; an irruption, inroad, or assault.

breach, brēch, *v.t.* To make a breach or opening in; to break (a contract or law).—*v.i.* Of a whale, to spring from the water.

breach of prom·ise, *n. Law,* violation of one's solemnly given word of honor, especially of an engagement to marry.

bread, bred, *n.* [O.E. *brēad* = D. *brood* = G. *brot* = Icel. *braudh.*] A kind of food made of flour or meal, milk or water, etc., mixed into a dough or batter, with or without yeast or the like, and baked; food; sustenance; livelihood.

bread, bred, *v.t. Cookery,* to cover or dress with bread crumbs before final cooking.

bread and but·ter, *n.* Bread spread with butter: commonly taken as typical of plain, wholesome food, or as representing the material essentials of life; a principal, sustaining source of business profit.—**bread-and-but·ter,** *a.*—**bread-and-but·ter let·ter,** a written expression of appreciation for hospitality.

bread·bas·ket, bred′bas″kit, bred′bä″skit, *n.* A basket for holding or carrying bread; a tray for holding bread at the table. *Slang,* the stomach; the abdomen.

bread·board, bred′bõrd″, bred′bạrd″, *n.* A board on which bread dough is manipulated or sliced; a board on which electric or electronic circuits may be assembled for easy examination and alteration.

bread·board mod·el, *n.* An uncased assembly of an instrument or other piece of equipment, such as a radio set, having its parts laid out on a flat surface and connected together so as to permit a check or demonstration of its operation.

bread·fruit, bred′frõt″, *n.* A large, round starchy fruit yielded by the tree, *Artocarpus communis,* of the Pacific islands, used for food; the tree bearing this fruit.

bread line, *n.* A line of needy persons assembled to receive bread and sometimes other food given gratuitously as a form of charity.

bread·root, bred′rõt″, *n.* The edible farinaceous root of *Psoralea esculenta,* a plant of central North America.

bread-stick, bred′stik″, *n.* A long, slender, cylindrical piece of bread dough baked until dry and crisp.

bread·stuff, bred′stuf″, *n.* Grain, flour, or meal for making bread; any of various kinds of bread.

breadth, bredth, bretth, *n.* [O.E. *brede* with *th* added, < O.E. *braedu,* breadth, < *braid,* broad; compare *length, width.*] The measure or extent of any plane surface from side to side; width; largeness of mind; liberality; wide intellectual grasp; *fine arts,* an impression of largeness, freedom, and space produced by bold or simple touches and strokes.

breadth·ways, bredth′wāz″, *adv.* In the direction of the breadth. Also **breadth·wise.**

bread·win·ner, bred′win″ér, *n.* One in the family who works for the support of himself and his dependents.

break, brāk, *v.t.*—**broke, broken, breaking.** [O.E. *brecan* = D. and L.G. *breken* = G. *brechen* = Goth. *brikan,* break; akin to L. *frangere,* break.] To divide into parts violently by a blow or pull; reduce to pieces or fragments, shatter; crush; burst; infringe or violate, as to *break* a contract; dissolve or annul: often with *off*; to end a meeting or gathering by dispersing; make a rupture or opening in the surface of; crack; bruise or abrade; to dig or plow; to interrupt or destroy the continuity or uniformity of, as to *break* step; discontinue abruptly;

destroy the completeness of a whole by taking out a part; make a way through; penetrate; to solve; discover the key to a cipher system; make one's way out of; as, *break* jail; to better or exceed; as, *break* a record; to make known in speech or writing; as, to *break* the news; ruin financially or make bankrupt; impair or weaken in strength, spirit, force, or effect; to show the faulty logic of; as, *break* an alibi; to open the action of a gun or revolver; train to obedience or discipline; tame; accustom to or habituate to a method or procedure, often with *in*; to train away from a habit or practice, with *of*; *elect.* to render a circuit incomplete and so stop the flow of current; *boxing*, to separate fighters from a clinch.

break, brăk, *v.i.* To become broken; become separated into parts or fragments, esp. suddenly and violently; burst; fall apart; part and disperse; crack; burst open, as a boil; to become inoperative due to damage or excessive wear; become suddenly discontinuous or interrupted; change suddenly or abruptly, as in sound, movement, or direction; free oneself or escape suddenly, as from restraint, often with *away*; force a way, often with *in* or *through*; come or arrive suddenly; to dawn, as day; give way or fail under strain, often with *down*; become bankrupt; become detached, often with *off*; to sever relations, used with *with*; break ranks or fall into disorder; rise above the surface of the water; to decrease suddenly, as prices; *mus.* to change from one register to another; *sports*, to part after a clinch in boxing.

break, brăk, *n.* A breaking; a fracture, rupture, or shattering; an opening made by breaking; a gap; an interruption of continuity; a suspension or stoppage; a severance of relations; an abrupt or marked change, as in sound or direction; a breaking forth or away, as from restraint; a sudden emergence; dawn (of day); *pocket billiards*, an opening shot to scatter the balls. A sudden drop in prices; *colloq.* a breach of etiquette; opportunity; luck, good or bad; a short time of rest from work, usually for refreshments. *Elect.* the rendering of a circuit incomplete; the discontinuance of the current when a circuit is rendered incomplete. *Mus.* the place where the musical register changes.

break·a·ble, brăk′a·bl, *a.* Capable of being broken.

break·age, brā′kij, *n.* The act of breaking; a break; damage or loss by breaking; allowance made for this; *naut.* the leaving of empty space in stowing a ship's hold. Odd cents not paid to winning pari-mutuel bettors.

break·a·way, brăk′a·wā″, *n.* A breaking away; a start, as of competitors in a contest; *Australia*, a stampede of sheep, cattle, etc.; an animal which breaks away from a herd or flock. *Theater*, theatrical property or scenery constructed to break in a prearranged manner.—*a.*

break·bone fe·ver, brăk′bōn″ fē′vėr, *n.* Dengue.

break·down, brăk′doun″, *n.* A breaking down; a collapse; an analysis, as of a total; a noisy, rapid dance.

break down, *v.t.* To collapse; to make inoperative; to separate into component parts; to analyze.—*v.i.*—**ner·vous break·down,** *psychol.* an incapacitating emotional illness representing a mental, physical, or nervous disorder.

break·er, brā′kėr, *n.* One who or that which breaks; a wave that breaks or dashes into foam; a device for opening an electric circuit; a structure in which coal is broken into sizes for the market; a strip of fabric under the tread of an automobile tire for added strength and protection.

break·er, brā′kėr, *n.* [Sp. *barrica*, cask.] A small water cask for use in a boat.

break e·ven, *v.i.* To operate an enterprise or business with balancing profit and loss.

break-e·ven point, brăk′ēven point, *n.* The level of a business at which its income equals expense, showing neither profit nor loss.

break·fast, brek′fast, *n.* [M.E. *brekefast, brekfast.*] The first meal of the day, with which the fast of the night is broken; a morning meal.—**break·fast,** *v.i.* To take breakfast.—*v.t.* To supply with breakfast.

break in, *v.t.* To teach(beginners)in a new job or sport; to ease the stiffness of(a new article); to familiarize(a person)with a novel situation.

break in, *v.i.* To enter using force; to intrude upon a conversation; to begin an activity; to acquire experience in new work.

break·ing point, *n.* The point of stress at which a material or a person gives way; the point at which a situation becomes unendurable.

break·neck, brăk′nek, *a.* Endangering the neck or life; headlong; precipitous; as, at *breakneck* speed.

break-off phe·nom·e·non, brăk′af fi·nom′e·non″, *n.* The feeling which sometimes occurs during high-altitude flight of being totally detached from the earth and human society.

break·out, brăk′out″, *n.* A forceful breaking from restraint, sometimes an escape; public evidence of group feelings or activity; process in well-drilling of disassembling equipment.

break out, *v.t.* To take from storage aboard ship; to ready for use; to pull up from bottom, as an anchor; to fly unfurled, as a flag.

break out, *v.i.* To have a skin eruption indicating a specific disease; to release from an inhibition; to erupt with speech or laughter.

break·through, brăk′thrö″, *n.* A sudden enlightenment in the solution of a problem or discovery of a new technique; the penetration of a barrier or defensive line, as in warfare.

break·up, brăk′up″, *n.* A disruption; a dissolution of connection; a separation of a mass into parts; a disintegration; a disbandment.

break·wa·ter, brăk′wạ″tėr, brăk′wot″ėr, *n.* Any structure or contrivance serving to break the force of waves and protect a harbor or anything exposed to the waves.

bream, brēm, *n.* [Fr. *brème*, O.Fr. *bresme*, < O.H.G. *brahsema*, G. *bressem*, the bream.] Any of several fresh-water soft-finned fishes belonging to the carp family. Any of certain spiny-finned sea fishes resembling the perch.

breast, brest, *n.* [O.E. *brēost*, akin to G. *brust*.] Either of the two soft protuberances on the thorax in females, containing the milk-secreting organs; the analogous rudimentary organ in males; the front of the thorax in either sex; the bosom; the chest; the bosom as the seat of thoughts and feelings; any surface or part resembling or likened to the human breast.—**to make a clean breast of,** to make full confession of.

breast, brest, *v.t.* To meet or oppose with the breast; to face; advance against; stem.

breast·bone, brest′bōn″, *n.* The bone of the breast; the sternum.

breast drill, *n.* A hand-held drill with a plate against which the operator leans his chest when drilling.

breast·pin, brest′pin″, *n.* An ornamental pin worn on the breast or at the throat; a brooch.

breast·plate, brest′plāt″, *n.* A piece of armor for the breast; a plate which receives the butt-end of a boring-tool and against which

the breast is set in working; the under shell of a tortoise.

breast stroke, *n.* A swimming stroke executed prone in which the arms are moved forward and backward in unison, while making a frog-like kick.

breast wall, brest′wâl″, *n.* A retaining wall.

breast·work, brest′wurk″, *n.* *Fort.* a hastily constructed work thrown up breast high for defense; the parapet of a building.

breath, breth, *n.* [O.E. *brēath*, odor, exhalation, akin to G. *brodem*, exhalation, vapor, steam.] The air inhaled and exhaled in respiration; respiration, esp. as necessary to life; power of breathing freely; as, out of *breath*; time to breathe; pause or respite; a single respiration; the brief time required for it; an instant; something generated by breathing, as the condensed moisture seen on a cold day; an odorous exhalation, or the air impregnated by it; a light current of air; a triviality; an utterance; a whisper; a hint; *phon.* voiceless expiration of air, producing a hiss, puff, or the like.—**un·der one's breath,** in a low voice or a whisper.—**in the same breath,** at the same time, as: She criticized and praised him *in the same breath*.—**to save one's breath,** refrain from useless debate.

breath·a·lyz·er, breth′a·lī″zėr, *n.* A British device used in analyzing a person's breath to determine the fact or extent of intoxication.

breathe, brēTH, *v.i.*—breathed, breathing. [M.E. *brethen*, < *breth*, E. *breath*.] Inhale and exhale air, or respire; live or exist; exhale air from the lungs; pause, as for breath; take a rest; emit audible breath or sound; exhale an odor or fragrance; blow lightly, as air.—*v.t.* Inhale and exhale in respiration; to exhale, or emit by expiration; inject by breathing, or infuse. Give utterance to; whisper; express or manifest; as, language *breathing* the eloquence of truth; allow to rest, as to recover breath; exercise briskly; put out of breath; tire or exhaust; blow into or cause to sound by the breath; *phon.* to utter with the breath and not with the voice.—**breathe free·ly,** to be free from worry; also **breathe eas·y, breathe eas·i·ly.**—**not breathe a word** or **syl·la·ble,** to keep a secret.

breathed, bretht, brēTHd, *a.* Endowed with breath. *Philol.* uttered with breath not voice; surd or mute.

breath·er, brē′THėr, *n.* One who or that which breathes; a pause, as for breath; a vent in a hermetically sealed enclosure; a contrivance which supplies air for breathing to a submarine or other submerged environment.

breath·ing, brē′THing, *n.* The act of one who or that which breathes; respiration; a single breath; the short time required for it; a pause, as for breath; physical exercise, as stimulating breathing; utterance or words; aspiration or longing; gentle blowing, as of wind; *gram.* the marks used in Greek to indicate the use of or the omission of the *h*-sound.

breath·less, breth′lis, *a.* Being out of breath; spent with labor or violent action; without breath; panting; dead; incapable of breathing, as with wonder or admiration; holding the breath, as from fright; still; musty; close.—**breath·less·ness,** breth′lis·-nes, *n.*

breath·tak·ing, breth′tā″king, *a.* Having a shock effect that checks breathing momentarily; causing extreme pleasure, awe, excitement; thrilling.—**breath·tak·ing·ly,** *adv.*

breath·y, breth′ē, *a.*—breathier, breathiest. Vocal sounds, esp. singing, characterized by a conspicuous use of the breath; *phon.* uttered with audible breath.

brec·ci·a, brech′ē·a, *n.* [It., a breach, a breccia.] *Geol.* an aggregate composed of angular fragments of the same rock or of different rocks united by a matrix or cement.

breech, brēch, n. [A singular developed from a plural. BREECHES.] The lower part of the body behind; the posterior or buttocks; the hinder part of anything: the large thick end of a cannon or other firearm; the lower part of a pulley block.—v.t. To put into breeches; to fit or furnish with a breech; to fasten by a breeching.

breech birth, n. See breech delivery.

breech·block, brēch'blok, n. A movable piece of metal which closes the breech end of the barrel in certain firearms.

breech·cloth, brēch'klạth″, brēch'kloth″, n. A cloth worn about the breech, as by uncivilized peoples; a loin cloth. Also **breech·clout.**

breech de·liv·er·y, n. Delivery of a fetus when the breech or buttocks, or the feet appear first in the birth canal; also called breech birth.

breech·es, brich'iz, n. pl. [A double plural, < O.E. bréc, breeches, pl. of bróc, as feet is the pl. of foot = Fris. brôck, pl. brêk, breeches; D. broek, breeches; Dan. brog, breeches, the breeching of a gun; Icel. brók, pl. brœkr, breeches; Ir. brog, Gael. briogais, Armor. brœges—breeches.] Short trousers fitting snugly just below the knees; called knee breeches when referring to the type worn by men in the 17th to 19th centuries, decorated with buckles or bows at the knee. See riding breeches, jodhpur, pants.

breech·es bu·oy, n. Naut. a life-saving device consisting of a beltlike buoy from which hangs a support for the body resembling a pair of breeches, which travels on a rope, and is used to carry persons ashore or to another vessel.

breech·ing, brē'ching, brich'ing, n. The part of a harness which passes around a horse's breech, giving the horse reverse power; a rope securing a cannon to a ship's side, for checking the recoil; the breech of a gun, or its mechanism; a metal casing at the end of boilers to direct the smoke from the flues to the smokestack; a metal piece serving to connect two pipes or hoses, or to divide one pipe or hose into two sections.

breech·load·er, brēch'lō″dėr, n. A cannon or smaller firearm loaded at the breech instead of the muzzle.—**breech-load·ing,** a. Receiving the charge at the breech instead of the muzzle: applied to firearms.

breed, brēd, v.t.—bred, breeding. [M.E. brēdan, < brod, E. brood.] To produce (offspring); procreate; to raise, as cattle; to procure by the mating of parents, as: They breed white rats for the laboratory. To improve or develop (wanted characteristics) through selective mating (of animals) or controlled pollination (of plants); to engender or cause, as: War breeds destruction. To be the native place or source of, as: Swamps breed mosquitoes. To bring up, rear or train.—v.i. To generate offspring; reproduce, as: Some animals breed several times a year. To be engendered or produced; grow; develop; to originate, as: Homosexuality breeds in prisons. To procure the birth of young, as in raising stock.

breed, brēd, n. The progeny or race from particular parents or stock; lineage; strain; in domestic animals or cultivated plants, a group or variety distinguished by particular characteristics, developed and maintained in existence through the agency of man; kind or sort in a general sense.—**breeder,** n.

breed·ing, brē'ding, n. The act of a person or thing that breeds; nurture or training; the results of training as shown in behavior; manners, esp. good manners; physics, production of new fissionable material, as in a pile, at a faster rate than the original element used in the chain reaction is consumed.

breeze, brēz, n. [Fr. brise, Sp. brisa, a breeze.] A wind, generally a light or not very strong wind; a gentle current of air; colloq. an easy task.

breeze, brēz, v.i. To blow a breeze; to move easily, quickly, in a carefree manner; as, breeze in or out.

breeze, brēz, v.t. To hurry or move something; as, a horse around a track, or an actor through his part.

breeze·way, brēz'wā″, n. A roofed passageway with open sides joining two buildings, as a garage to the house.

breez·i·ness, brē'zē·nes, n. The quality of abounding in breeze; sprightliness; freshness; extroversion.

breez·y, brēz'ē, a.—breezier, breeziest. Fanned with gentle winds or breezes; subject to frequent breezes; vivacious; airy; sprightly; brisk, fresh; informal.

breg·ma, breg'ma, n. [Gr. bregma, front of the head.] Craniol. the point of junction of the sagittal and coronal sutures of the skull.—**breg·mat·ic,** **breg·mate,** breg·mat'ik, breg'māt, a.

brems·strah·lung, brem'shträ″lang, n. [G. "braking radiation."] Atomic Physics, an X-radiation caused by the collision of an atomic nucleus with an atomic particle such as a beta particle.

brems·strah·lung ef·fect, n. The emission of electromagnetic radiation as a consequence of the acceleration of charged elementary particles, such as electrons, under the influence of the attractive or repulsive force fields of atomic nuclei near which the charged particle moves.

brent, brent, n. See brant.

breth·ren, breTH'rin, n. Plural of brother; now usually denoting spiritual brotherhood.

Brethren, breTH'rin, n. pl. Members of a Protestant sect of German origin, practicing simplicity of living. Also called Dunkards.

Bret·on, bret'on, Fr. brä·tôn′, n. [Fr.: see Briton.] A native of Brittany, a former province in northwestern France; the language of Brittany, a dialect of Celtic.—a. Of or pertaining to Brittany, the Bretons, or their language.

Bret·ton Woods Con·fer·ence, bret'on wụdz′ kon′fėr·ens. A conference called on the invitation of President Roosevelt at Bretton Woods, N.H., in July 1944, with representatives of 44 nations, to deal with international monetary and financial problems; source of the International Monetary Fund and World Bank.

breve, brēv, brev, n. [Var. of brief.] A writ, as one issued by a court of law; a mark placed over a vowel to show that it is short, as in ŭ; pros. a mark ˘ indicating an unstressed syllable. Mus. the longest modern note (rarely used), equivalent to two semibreves or whole-notes.

bre·vet, bra·vet′, brev'it, n. [O.Fr., dim. of bref: see brief.] A patent conferring a privilege or rank; esp., a commission promoting a military officer to a higher rank without increase of pay.—a. Conferred or appointed by brevet.

bre·vet, brä·vet′, brev'it, v.t.—brevetted, brevetting. To appoint, honor, or promote by brevet.

bre·vi·a·ry, brē'vē·er″ē, brev'ē·ėr″ē, n. pl. **bre·vi·a·ries.** [L. breviarium, abridgment, prop. neut. of breviarius, abridged, < brevis, short.] A summary; a compendium; a book of daily offices of the Roman Catholic Church, to be read by those in major orders; any similar books used in other churches.

bre·vier, bra·vēr′, n. [G. brevier, Fr. breviaire: so called from being originally used in printing breviaries.] A printing type in size between bourgeois and minion, approximately 8-point.

brev·i·pen·nate, brev″e·pen′āt, a. [L.] Ornith. having short wings.

brev·i·ros·trate, brev″e·ros′trāt, a. [L.] Ornith. having a short beak or bill.

brev·i·ty, brev'i·tē, n. [L. brevitas, from brevis, short. BRIEF.] The state or character of being brief; shortness; conciseness; terseness.

brew, brö, v.t. [O.E. breówan, to brew; D. brouwen, Icel. brugga, Dan. brygge, G. brauen, to brew; akin broth.] To prepare, as beer, ale, or other similar liquor from malt or other materials, by steeping, boiling, and fermentation; to mingle; to mix; to prepare a hot beverage, as tea or coffee, by steeping a solid in boiling water; to concoct, as a bowl of punch or a philter; to contrive; to plot.—v.i. To perform the business of brewing or making beer; to be mixing, forming, or collecting; as, a storm brews.

brew, brö, n. The mixture formed by brewing; that which is brewed; a mixture of uncommon ingredients; as, a witch's brew.

brew·age, brö'ij, n. A fermented beverage prepared in any way.

brew·er, brö'ėr, n. One who brews; one whose occupation is to brew malt liquors.

brew·er's yeast, n. A yeast, Saccharomyces, suitable for use as a ferment in the making of malt liquors; also used as a source of B-complex vitamins.

brew·er·y, brö'a·rē, brur'ē, n. pl. **brew·er·ies.** An establishment and apparatus for brewing malt liquors.

brew·ing, brö'ing, n. The act or process of making ale, or other fermented liquor; the quantity brewed at a time.

bri·ar, brī'ėr, n. A plant having a thorny stem; a tree heath of France and Corsica whose root wood is used to make tobacco pipes; a pipe made from this root wood.—**bri·ar·y,** brī'ėr·ē, a. See brier, briery.

bri·ard, brē·är′, n. One of an old French breed of large, strong dogs having long, somewhat wavy coats, often trained for herding sheep.

brib·a·ble, brīb'a·bl, a. Capable of being bribed; liable to be bribed.

bribe, brīb, n. [Fr. bribe, Pr. Fr. brife, broken victuals, such as are given to beggars, something given away; from root seen in Armor. breva, to break; W. briw, a fragment.] A price, reward, gift, or favor bestowed or promised with a view to corrupt judgment or conduct.

bribe, brīb, v.t.—bribed, bribing. To induce to a certain course of action, especially a wrong course, by the gift or offer of something valued; to gain over by a bribe.—v.i. To practice bribery; to give a bribe to a person.—**brib·er,** brīb·ėr, n.

brib·er·y, brī'ba·rē, n. pl. **bri·ber·ies.** The act or practice of offering, giving, or taking a bribe or bribes.

bric-a-brac, brik'a·brak″, n. [Fr.] Miscellaneous articles of antiquarian interest or decorative value, such as are used for ornament about a room; knickknacks.

brick, brik, n. [O.Fr. brike, bricque (Fr. brique), brick; prob. < Teut., and perhaps akin to E. break.] A block of clay, usually rectangular, hardened by drying in the sun or by burning in a kiln, and used for building, paving, etc.; such blocks collectively; as, a house of brick; the material used in making bricks; blocks used for building which are made from another material; as, a concrete brick; block shaped objects; as, a brick of ice-cream. Colloq. a good fellow; a magnanimous person.

brick, brik, v.t. To lay, line, wall, enclose, pave, fill in, or build with brick.

brick·bat, brik'bat″, n. A piece or fragment of a brick or other solid substance, particularly when used as a projectile; an unflattering remark.

---

a- fat, fāte, fär, fâre, fạll;   e- met, mē, mēre, hėr;   i- pin, pīne;   o- not, nōte, möve;   u- tub, cūbe, bụll;   oi- oil;   ou- pound.

brick·kiln, brik′kil″, brik′kiln″, n. A kiln or furnace in which bricks are baked or burned.

brick·lay·er, brik′lā″ẽr, n. One whose occupation is to build with bricks.—**brick·-lay·ing**, brik′lā″ing, n.

brick red, n. A yellowish or brownish red.

brick·work, brik′wŭrk″, n. Masonry consisting of bricks.

brick·yard, brik′yärd″, n. A place where bricks are made, stocked, or sold.

brid·al, brīd′al, a. [O.E. brȳdealo, "bride ale."] Of or pertaining to a bride or a wedding; nuptial.

brid·al wreath, n. A rosaceous shrub, Spiræa hypericifolia, bearing long sprays of small white flowers, much cultivated for ornament; a shrub, Francoa ramosa, a native of Chile, with dense racemes of white flowers.

bride, brīd, n. [O.E. brȳd, brīd; cogn. D. bruid, Icel. brúthr, Dan. brud, Goth. bruths, G. braut—a bride.] A woman newly married, or on the eve of being married.

bride·groom, brīd′grŏm″, n. [O.E. brȳd-guma, from bryd, a bride, and guma, a man —D. bruidegom, Icel. brúthgumi, Dan. brudgom, G. bräutigam.] A man newly married, or just about to be married.

brides·maid, brīdz′mād″, n. A woman or girl who attends or accompanies the bride at a wedding.

bride·well, brīd′wel″, brid′wal, n. [From a former penal workhouse near St. Bride's (Bridget's) Well, in London.] Colloq. a house of correction for vagrants and disorderly persons; a jail.

bridge, brij, n. [O.E. brycg = G. brücke.] A structure spanning a river, chasm, road, or the like, and affording passage; any structure or part similar in form or use; a link between two activities, subjects, periods of time, etc.; anat. the ridge or upper line of the nose; the curved bow joining the lenses in a pair of eyeglasses, and resting on the bridge of the nose; a thin wooden arch raising the strings of a musical instrument above the sounding board; metal. a ridge or wall-like projection of firebrick or the like, at each end of the hearth in a metallurgical furnace; naut. a raised platform from side to side of a ship above the rail, for the officers or pilot; dentistry, a mounting for artificial teeth, secured to adjoining teeth; billiards, pool, a notched piece of wood with a long handle, or a position of the hand, for supporting the striking end of a cue; elect. an apparatus for measuring frequencies, capacitances, impedances, or inductances, by using known values to find an unknown value; music, a passage leading from one section of a composition to another.—to burn one's bridges (behind one). To sever all possible ways of turning back.

bridge, brij, n. [Origin uncertain.] A card game for four players, derived from whist. —**auc·tion bridge**, a variety of bridge in which the players bid for the privilege of declaring the trump.—**con·tract bridge**, a modification of auction bridge.

bridge, brij, v.t.—bridged, bridging. To make a bridge over; span; to make (a way) by a bridge.

bridge·board, brij′bŏrd″, brij′bàrd″, n. A notched board at the side of a wooden stair, supporting the treads and risers.

bridge·head, brij′hed″, n. A defensive work covering or protecting the end of a bridge toward the enemy; a position won by advance troops in enemy territory.

bridge·work, brij′wŭrk″, n. Dentistry, the fitting in of artificial teeth with bridges or sustaining devices.

bridg·ing, brij′ing, n. Arch. a piece of wood or an arrangement of pieces fixed between floor or roof timbers to keep them in place.

bri·dle, brīd′al, n. [O.E. brídel = D. breidel.] The part of the harness of a horse, etc., about the head, consisting usually of headstall, bit, and reins, and used to restrain and guide the animal; anything that restrains or curbs; any of various devices or parts resembling a horse's bridle in form or use; a bridling, or drawing up the head, as in disdain.

bri·dle, brīd′al, v.t.—bridled, bridling. To put a bridle on; to restrain, guide, or govern; to check, curb, or control.—v.i. To hold the head up and backward; to assume a lofty manner so as to assert one's dignity or express indignation at its being offended; to toss the head.

bri·dle path, n. A path or road used only for riding horseback.

bri·doon, bri·dŏn′, n. [Fr. bridon, < bride, a bridle.] A light snaffle or bit of a bridle in addition to the principal bit, and having a separate rein. Also **bra·doon**.

Brie cheese, brē′chĕz′, n. [From Brie, district east of Paris, France.] A soft, salted, white cream cheese using bacteria or mold for ripening.

brief, brēf, n. A short or concise writing or statement; a summary; a synopsis; an abridgment; an outline following certain rules to cover all points on one side of a controversy; an official letter or mandate, as a letter from the Pope less formal than a papal bull.

brief, brēf, n. Law, a case at law; a writ calling one to whom it is issued to follow certain action.—trial brief, a memorandum or concise statement of client's case prepared for guidance of counsel or consideration of the court in a trial at law.—hold a brief for, to advocate, endorse or defend by argument.—brief of title, an abstract of all documents relating to title to real property.

brief, brēf, n. Very short, snug underpants for men or women: usually in plural.

brief, brēf, v.t. To summarize or make a written abstract; to instruct; as, to brief an airplane crew; law, to furnish a memorandum, concisely stated, of (a client's case); Brit. to retain as counsel in a suit.

brief, brēf, a. [O.Fr. brief, bref (Fr. bref) < L. brevis, short, breve, a summary, M.L. letter, brief.] Short, esp. in duration; lasting or occupying but a short time; fleeting; short-lived; ephemeral; transitory; concise or succinct; using few words; abrupt or curt. —brief·ly, adv.—brief·ness, n.

brief case, n. A flat, rectangular, often expansible leather case with two or more lengthwise compartments, used for carrying briefs, documents, manuscripts, and business or other papers.

brief·ing, brē′fing, n. [Air Force, specif.] The instruction or lecture given to an aircrew or air passengers before a flight, regarding procedures to be followed, route, weather conditions, target, destination, enemy activity, or any other subject pertinent to the flight or mission; any similar instruction concerning procedures and particulars.

brief·less, brēf′lis, a. Having no brief, as a lawyer without clients.

bri·er, brī′ẽr, n. [O.E. brēr, brær.] A prickly plant or shrub, esp. the sweetbrier or the greenbrier; a mass of these.—**bri·er·y**, a.

bri·er, brī′ẽr, n. [Fr. bruyère, heath; < Celtic.] The white heath, Erica arborea, of France and Corsica, whose woody root is used for making tobacco pipes; a pipe made of this woody root. Also **briar**.—**bri·er·root**, n.—**bri·er·wood**, n.

brig, brig, n. The prison on a warship; slang, guardhouse.

brig, brig, n. [Short for brigantine.] A two-masted vessel square-rigged on both masts. —**her·ma·phro·dite brig**. See under hermaphrodite.

bri·gade, bri·gād′, v.t.—brigaded, brigading. To form into a brigade; to put together a (group); to combine.

bri·gade, bri·gād′, n. [Fr. brigade, < It. brigata, troop, < brigare, strive, contend, < briga, strife.] A large body of troops, esp. a unit of organization in an army, varying in different countries, but commonly consisting of two or more regiments; any body of individuals organized for a special purpose; as, a fire-brigade.

brig·a·dier, brig″a·dēr′, n. [Fr.] An officer in command of a brigade; a brigadier general; Brit. an army officer with a rank between colonel and major general.

brig·a·dier gen·er·al, n. An officer in command of a brigade or engaged in other duties, in the U.S. ranking next below a major-general.

brig·and, brig′and, n. [O.Fr. Fr. brigand, < It. brigante, < brigare: BRIGADE.] A plundering marauder; a bandit, esp. one of a gang of outlaws.—**brig·and·age**, brig′an·daj, n. The practice of brigands; plundering. —**brig·and·ism**, brig′and·izm, n.

brig·an·dine, brig′an·dēn″, n. [Fr. brigandine, < brigand, in old sense of foot soldier. BRIGAND.] Body armor composed of overlapping iron scales or small thin iron plates sewed upon canvas, linen, or leather, and covered over with similar materials.

brig·an·tine, brig′an·tēn″, brig′an·tin″, n. [Fr. brigantin, < It. brigantino, a pirate vessel, < brigante, a pirate. BRIGAND. Brig. is an abbrev. of this word.] A square-rigged, two-masted vessel which differs from a brig in not having a square mainsail.

bright, brit, a. [O.E. bryht, beorht, = O.H.G. beraht = Icel. bjartr = Goth. bairhts, bright: cf. Skt. bhrāj-, shine.] Radiating or reflecting light; luminous; shining; filled with light; vivid or brilliant, as color; clear or translucent, as liquids; radiant or splendid; illustrious or glorious, as an era; quick-witted or intelligent, as a person; characterized by happiness or gladness; favorable or auspicious.—bright, bright·ly, adv.—bright·ness, n.

bright·en, brīt′n, v.t. To make bright or brighter; to shed light on; to make to shine; to cheer; to make gay or cheerful; to heighten the splendor of; to add luster to; to make acute or witty; to sharpen the faculties of.—v.i. To grow bright or more bright; to clear up; to become less dark or gloomy.

Bright's dis·ease, n. [From R. Bright, English physician, who described it in 1827.] Kidney degeneration accompanied by imperfect uric acid elimination and high blood pressure. See nephritis.

bright work, n. A glossy or plated metalwork on an appliance, automobile or ship; the polished, varnished woodwork on a ship.

brill, bril, n. [Probably < Corn. brithĕl, mackerel, pl. brithelli, brilli, < brith, streaked, variegated.] A kind of European flatfish resembling the turbot, but inferior to it both in size and quality.

bril·liance, bril′yans, bril′yans, n. Great brightness; splendor; luster; striking achievement, talent, or ability.

bril·lian·cy, bril′yan·sē, n. A specific example of brilliance, frequently used as plural; as, in the brilliancies of a musical score.

bril·liant, bril′yant, a. [Fr. brillant, ppr. of briller, < It. brillare, shine, sparkle, < L. beryllus, E. beryl.] Shining brightly; sparkling; glittering; lustrous; vivid or intense, as color; splendid or distinguished, as an assemblage; striking or illustrious, as an achievement; characterized by or showing unusual mental keenness or cleverness; extremely favorable, as prospects.—**bril·liant·ly**, adv.—**bril·liant·ness**, n.

bril·liant, bril′yant, n. A diamond (or other gem) of a particular cut, typically shaped like two pyramids united at their bases, the top one cut off near the base and the bottom one close to the apex, with many facets on the slopes; a very small printing type, about 3½ point.

bril·lian·tine, bril'yan·tēn", n. [Fr. *brillantine.*] A dress fabric woven of cotton with mohair or worsted, resembling alpaca; a toilet preparation which adds gloss to the hair.

Brill's dis·ease, n. [Nathan E. Brill (1859–1925) Amer. physician.] An infectious disease considered to be a relatively mild form of typhus.

brim, brim, n. [O.E. *brim,* the surf, the sea = Icel. *brim,* the surf; akin Dan. *braemme,* G. *bräme,* the edge, border; < root seen in L. *fremere,* to roar, Skt. *bhram,* to whirl, *bhrimi,* a whirlpool, *brim* being thus the part where the surf roars or rages.] The upper edge of anything hollow, as a cup; a projecting edge, border, or rim, as of a hat; an edge or margin.—**brim·ful,** brim'fụl, a. Full to the top; completely full.

brim, brim, v.t.—*brimmed, brimming.* To fill to the brim, upper edge, or top.—v.i. To be full to the brim; to be full to overflowing.—**brim o·ver,** to run over the brim; to be so full as to overflow.

brim·mer, brim'ẽr, n. A cup, bowl, or glass full to the top.

brim·stone, brim'stōn", n. [O.E. *bremstone, brenston,* Sc. *brunstane, brunstane;* lit. *burnstone* or *burning-stone,* akin Icel. *brennisteinn,* brimstone.] Sulfur.

brin·dle, brin'dl, a. Brindled; variegated; tawny with darker markings.—n. A brindled coloring; a brindled animal.

brindled, brin'dld, a. [Var. of *brinded.*] Tan or gray with darker, irregular flecks or streaks; variegated; dappled. Also **brin·ded.**

brine, brīn, n. [O.E. *bryne,* brine, so called from its burning taste = O.E. *bryne,* a burning. BURN.] Water saturated or strongly impregnated with salt, like the water of the ocean; salt water; hence used for tears, and for the sea or ocean. *Chem.* any saline solution.

brine, brīn, v.t.—*brined, brining.* To steep in brine.

Bri·nell hard·ness, bri·nel' härd'nis, n. *Metal.* the resistance of a metal to indentation as measured by a standardized test originated by Johann A. *Brinell.*

Bri·nell num·ber, bri·nel' num'bẽr, n. *Metal.* the number indicating the Brinell hardness of a metal.

bring, bring, v.t.—*brought, bringing.* [O.E. *bringan, brang, brungen,* later *brengan, brohte, broht* = D. *brengen,* Goth. *briggan* (pron. *bringan*), G. *bringen;* same root as *bear,* to carry.] To bear or convey from a distant to a nearer place, or to a person; to fetch; to carry; to procure; to conduct or attend in going; to accompany; to change in state or condition; as, *bring* to nought; to persuade; as, *bring* to reason, to terms.

bring a·bout, v.t. To effect; to accomplish; to cause to happen.

bring down, v.t. To cause to come down; to lower; to humiliate; to abase; to shoot, as game.

bring forth, v.t. To produce, as young or fruit; to beget; to cause.

bring for·ward, v.t. To present for consideration; as, to *bring forward* proposals.

bring in, v.t. To introduce; to supply; to yield, as profit or income.

bring off, v.t. To clear from condemnation; to have success, as: He *brought off* the performance well.

bring on, v.t. To cause to begin; as, to *bring on* an attack; to originate; as, to *bring on* a headache.

bring out, v.t. To emphasize; to reveal; to publish; to introduce, as a new model car.

bring to, v.t. *Naut.* to check the course of a ship by the sails counteracting each other.

bring to light, v.t. To reveal.

bring to mind, v.t. To recall what has been forgotten or out of thought.

bring to pass, v.t. To effect; to cause to happen.

bring up, v.t. To nurse, feed, and tend; to rear; to educate; to introduce to notice; as, *to bring up* a subject; to cause to advance near (troops); to cause to stop (a horse); to pull up.

brink, bringk, n. [A Scandinavian word; Dan. and Sw. *brink,* a hill, declivity; allied to W. *bryncyn,* a hillock, < *bryn,* a hill.] The edge, margin, or border of a steep place, as a precipice, or of the bank of a river; verge; *fig.* a situation extremely close to danger or success; as, the *brink* of war, the *brink* of a discovery.

brink·man·ship, bringk'man·ship", n. Term used to describe U.S. foreign policy of the 1950's which was willing to go to the edge of hostilities short of actual involvement in war.

brin·y, brī'nē, a. Consisting of or resembling brine; salty.—**brin·i·ness,** n.

bri·o, brē'ạ, n. [It.] Animation; lively spirit.

bri·oche, brē'ōsh, brē'osh, n. [Fr.] A small breakfast roll baked with yeast, containing large amounts of eggs and butter.

bri·o·lette, brē"a·let', Fr. brē·ạ·let', n. [Fr.] A pear-shaped precious stone whose surface is cut by triangular facets.

bri·o·ny, brī'a·nē, n. See *bryony.*

bri·quette, bri·quet, bri·ket', n. [Fr. *briquette,* dim. of *brique,* brick.] A molded block of compacted charcoal for fuel; a similar block of some other combustible.

bri·quette, bri·quet, bri·ket', v.t.—*briquetted, briquetting.* To mold coal dust, etc., into briquettes.

bri·sance, bri·zäns', Fr. brē·zäns', n. The shattering or crushing effect of the sudden release of energy, as in an explosion of nuclear fission or nitroglycerine.

brisk, brisk, a. [Origin uncertain: cf. W. *brysg,* quick.] Quick and active; lively; smart; vigorous; spirited; sprightly; of liquors, effervescing; piquant; bracing; sharp in demeanor.—**brisk·ly,** adv.— **brisk·ness,** n.

brisk, brisk, v.t. To make brisk; vitalize; enliven.—v.i. To become brisk or lively.

bris·ket, bris'kit, n. [M.E. *brusket:* cf. O.Fr. *bruschet, brichet* (Fr. *brechet*).] The breast of an animal, or the part of the breast lying next to the ribs; *Brit. dial.* human chest.

bris·ling, brist·ling, bris'ling, n. [Norw.] A small herring, *Clupea sprattus,* found in shoals on the Atlantic coast of Europe, that resembles and is processed like a sardine.

bris·tle, bris'al, n. [M.E. *bristil,* < O.E. *byrst* = G. *borste* = Icel. *burst,* bristle.] One of the short, stiff, coarse hairs of certain animals, esp. hogs, used extensively in making brushes, etc.; any similar short, stiff hair or hairlike appendage; factory-made hair used in brushes; the stiff hair of a plant.—**bris·tly, bris·tle·like,** a.

bris·tle, bris'al, v.i.—*bristled, bristling.* To stand or rise stiffly, like bristles; to erect the bristles, as an irritated animal (sometimes with *up,* and often *fig.,* of persons); to be thickly set with something suggestive of bristles; be rough; to be visibly roused or stirred (*with*); to assume a self-assertive disposition.—v.t. To erect like bristles; to furnish with a bristle or bristles; make bristly; to rouse or perturb.

bris·tle·tail, bris'al·tāl", n. Any of various wingless insects of the order *Thysanura,* having long, bristlelike caudal appendages; the silverfish.

Bris·tol board, n. [From the city of *Bristol,* England.] A fine kind of pasteboard, smooth, and sometimes glazed on the surface for artwork or printing.

brit, britt, brit, n. [Origin obscure.] A young herring of the common kind; the young of various other marine animals, mostly crustaceans and pteropods, consumed by whales.

Bri·tan·ni·a, bri·tan'ē·a, bri·tan'ya, n. [L., < *Britanni* (later *Britones*), the ancient Britons.] The ancient Roman name for Great Britain; Britain, Great Britain, the United Kingdom, or, in a broader sense, the British Empire; a feminine personification of either, as on stamps or coins.— **Bri·tan·nic,** a. [L. *Britannicus.*] British.

bri·tan·nia met·al, n. A white alloy resembling pewter, composed of tin, copper, and antimony, and/or bismuth, with small amounts of zinc.

britch·es, brich'iz, n. pl. *Colloq.* trousers; breeches.

Brit·i·cism, brit'i·siz"am, n. A word, phrase, or idiom peculiar to the British rather than to English-speaking people generally.

Brit·ish, brit'ish, a. [O.E. *Bryttisc,* < *Bryttas, Brettas,* pl., Britons; < Celtic.] Of or pertaining to Great Britain, the British Commonwealth, or its inhabitants; of or pertaining to the ancient Britons.—n. The British people, taken collectively; the ancient British tongue; British English.

Brit·ish Eng·lish, n. The English language as Englishmen speak and write it, having features which make it distinct from American English, Australian English, and others.

Brit·ish·er, brit'i·shẽr, n. A British native or subject.

Brit·ish ther·mal u·nit (BTU), n. The heat necessary to raise the temperature of one pound of water one degree Fahrenheit at or near its point of maximum density.

Brit·on, brit'on, n. [O.Fr. *Breton* (usually, as in Fr., meaning a Breton: see *Breton*), < L. *Brito(n-), Britto(n-),* one of the people inhabiting Britain; < Celtic (cf. *British*).] One of the Celtic people who in early times occupied the southern part of Britain; a native or inhabitant of Great Britain, or of the British Empire, esp. an Englishman.

brits·ka, britz·ka, britzs'ka, brits'ka, n. [Pol. *bryczka,* dim. of *bryka,* freight-wagon.] An open carriage with a calash top and space for reclining.

Brit·ta·ny span·iel, n. A large, agile dog of a French breed, a cross between the spaniel of Brittany and the game pointer.

brit·tle, brit'l, a. [M.E. *britel,* < O.E. *brēotan,* break.] Hard, but breaking readily, with a comparatively smooth fracture, as glass; fragile. Unstable; as, a *brittle* relationship. Dry, sharp; as, a *brittle* tone. Shallow, cold; as, a *brittle* personality.—**brit·tleness,** n.

brit·tle, brit'l, n. A caramelized-sugar candy, usually containing nuts, poured in thin sheets while hot and hardening when cool.

brit·tle star, n. Any of several Ophiuroids, so-called from their fragility. Also **ser·pent star.**

brit·ton·ic, bri·ton'ik, a. Of, relating to, or characteristic of the Celtic people who inhabited Britain previous to the Anglo-Saxon invaders; relating to the Celtic languages that include Breton, Cornish, and Welsh. Also **bry·thon·ic.**

Brix scale, n. [Adolph F. Brix, German scientist.] A hydrometer scale so graduated that its readings indicate the weight of sugar per volume of sugar solutions at a specified temperature.

broach, brōch, n. [O.Fr. Fr. *broche,* < M.L. *broca, brocca,* sharp stake or instrument: cf. L. *broccus, brocchus,* projecting, as teeth.] Any of various pointed instruments; a spear; a spit for roasting meat; any of various tools or drills for boring or widening holes; a reamer; a gimlet for tapping casks; a tool for dressing stone. A brooch.

broach, brōch, *v.t.* To mention or suggest, as a subject, for the first time; to pierce with a spit; to tap, as a cask; draw off, as liquor, by tapping; break into in order to take something out; to expand, as a hole, with a broach or boring tool; to shape, as a stone, with a broach.—*v.i.* To rise above the surface from below, as a fish or submarine; *naut.* to veer a ship windward in order to be broadside to the wind.

broad, brad, *a.* [O.E. *brād* = D. *breed* = G. *breit* = Icel. *breidhr* = Goth. *braids*, broad.] Of great breadth; wide; of great extent; large; of extensive range or scope; as, *broad* principles; not limited or narrow; as, *broad* views; liberal; as, the *Broad* Church party in the Church of England; main or general; as, the *broad* outlines of a subject; unrestricted or full; as, *broad* daylight; unrestrained; as, *broad* farce; evident, plain; as, a *broad* hint; blunt; bold; plain-spoken; crude, unpolished, as speech; strongly dialectal, as pronunciation; indelicate or indecent, as a story; *art*, marked by breadth; *phon.* marked by an open vowel sound as the *a* in mawkish.—**broad·ness**, *n.*

broad, brad, *n.* The broad part of anything; as, the *broad* of the hand; a gold coin, equal to twenty shillings, issued by James I of England; *slang*, a woman.

broad, brad, *adv.* Fully; widely; plainly. Also **broad·ly.**

broad ar·row, *n.* A barbed arrow head; *Brit.* a stamp resembling the barbed head of an arrow put upon government-owned stores by the British Board of Ordnance.

broad·ax, brad′aks″, *n.* A large ax with a broad blade, as a battle-ax, or an ax for hewing timber.

broad·band, brad′band″, *a. Electronics*, of, having, or responding to a wide band of broadcasting frequencies.

broad bean, *n.* A large flat bean used chiefly for fodder in parts of Europe.

broad·bill, brad′bil″, *n.* Any of various birds with a broad bill, as the scaup, shoveler, and spoonbill; any of numerous colorful, flat-billed birds of the family *Eurylaimidae.*—**broad-billed**, *a.*

broad·brim, brad′brim″, *n.* A hat with a broad brim, like those worn by Quakers; (*cap.*), *colloq.* a Friend or Quaker.

broad·cast, brad′kast″, brad′käst″, *v.t.*—*broadcasted* or *broadcast, broadcasting.* To cast or scatter abroad over an area, as seed in sowing; *fig.* to spread or disseminate widely; as, to *broadcast* seditious principles; specif.,to send, as messages, etc., by radio or television.—*v.i.* To scatter or disseminate something broadcast; to talk or act on a radio or television program; to assume the cost of a radio or television program.—

broad·cast·er, *n.* One who or that which broadcasts; an apparatus or association that broadcasts radio or television messages, speeches, etc.

broad·cast, brad′ kast″, brad′käst″, *n.* An audio and visual image sent by radio or television; a particular radio or television program; a method of sowing or scattering seed over a large area.

broad·cast, brad′kast″, brad′käst″, *a., adv.* Cast abroad or all over an area, as seed sown thus rather than in drills or rows; *fig.* widely spread or disseminated; as, *broadcast* discontent; programs sent broadcast, as television or radio messages, music, or drama.

Broad Church, *n.* A section of the Church of England holding moderate or flexible views on doctrine, ritual, and membership.

broad·cloth, brad′klath″, brad′kloth″, *n.* A fine cloth woven about twice the usual breadth on a large loom; a wool or worsted fabric closely woven in a plain or twill pattern having a sheen; any closely woven

fabric, as silk, cotton, or rayon, having a smooth surface.

broad·en, brad′n, *v.t.* To make broad or broader; to increase the width of; to render more comprehensive, extensive, or open.—*v.i.* To become broad or broader.

broad gauge, *n.* A railroad gauge that is wider than the standard gauge of 56½ inches.

broad hatch·et, *n.* A short-handled hatchet with a broad cutting edge and a rectangular hammering surface opposite the blade.

broad jump, *n.* A jump for distance either from a stationary position or with a running start; a field event in track and field athletics. Also **long jump.**

broad·leaf, brad′lēf″, *n.* A tree, *Terminalia latifolia*, native to Jamaica whose wood is used for lumber; any variety of tobacco plants with broad leaves used for making cigars.

broad-leaved, brad′lēvd″, *a.* Having broad leaves, as maple or oak, as distinguished from the needlelike leaves of evergreen trees.

broad·loom, brad′lōm″, *a.* Of or pertaining to carpets woven on a wide loom.

broad-mind·ed, brad′mīn′did, *a.* Characterized by mental breadth; free from prejudice or bigotry; liberal; tolerant.—**broad-mind·ed·ness**, *n.*

broad seal, *n.* A great or official seal, as of a state or nation.

broad·side, brad′sīd″, *n.* The whole side of a ship above the water-line from the bow to the quarter; any broad surface or side, as of a house, etc.; all the guns that can be fired on one side of a ship, or their simultaneous discharge; *fig.* any comprehensive attack. A sheet of paper of large size, printed on one side only, as for advertising.

broad·side, brad′sīd″, *adv.* With the broader side facing out or foremost; without specific direction.

broad-spec·trum, brad′spek′trum, *a.* Pertaining to antibiotics which effectively combat a large variety of organisms.

broad·sword, brad′sōrd″, brad′sard″, *n.* A sword with a broad, flat cutting blade.

broad·tail, brad′tāl″, *n.* The skin or fur of the young of the Persian breed of sheep, killed when a few days old, before the wool has had time to develop beyond a flat, wavy state, in which it resembles moiré silk.

broad·way, brad′wā″, *n.* A broad road or highway, often the proper name of a street; (*cap.*) the theater district on or near the street Broadway in New York City, esp. as the heart of the commercial or legitimate theater in the U.S.

broad·wife, brad′wīf″, *n. Hist.* a female slave, in the slaveholding states of the U.S., whose husband belonged to a different master.

brob, brob, *n.* [Cf. *brad*.] A wedge-shaped spike driven in beside an abutting timber to keep it from slipping.

Brob·ding·nag·i·an, brob″ding·nag′ē·an, *a.* Of or befitting the region of Brobdingnag, in Swift's *Gulliver's Travels*, where everything was of enormous size; enormous; gigantic.—*n.* A giant; a gigantic person.

bro·cade, brō·kād′, *n.* [Sp. *brocado* = It. *broccato*, < M.L. *brocare*, interweave with gold or silver, < *broca*: see *broach*.] Material woven in an elaborate pattern, esp. that with an over-all, raised design, orig. formed by interweaving threads of gold or silver.

bro·cade, brō·kād′, *v.t.*—*brocaded, brocading.* To weave with a design or figure.—**bro·cad·ed**, *a.* Woven into a brocade.

bro·ca·tel, bro·ca·telle, brok″a·tel′, brō″ka·tel′, *n.* [Fr. *brocatelle*, < It. *broccatello*, dim. of *broccato*, = E. *brocade*.] A stiff fabric, used esp. for upholstery, similar to brocade, but with a more highly raised over-all pattern. An ornamental marble with variegated coloring, from Italy and Spain.

broc·co·li, broc·o·li, brok′a·lē, *n.* [It., pl.

of *broccolo*, sprout.] A variety of cabbage resembling the cauliflower; a branching cauliflower having florets at the tip of each branch.

bro·chette, brō·shet′, *Fr.* bra·shet′, *n.* [Fr., dim. of *broche*, spit: see *broach*.] A skewer for use in cookery.—**en bro·chette**, broiled on a skewer or a small spit.

bro·chure, brō·shur′, *n.* [Fr., < *brocher*, stitch.] A pamphlet; a booklet of salient facts on a subject.

brock, brok, *n.* A European badger; *Brit. dial.* a contemptible fellow.

brock·et, brok′it, *n.* [O.Fr. *brocart*, < *broque*, var. of *broche*, broach, tine.] The male red deer in the second year, with the first growth of straight, spike-like horns; any of various small South and Central American deer of the genus *Mazama*, with straight, unbranched horns.

bro·gan, brō′gan, *n.* [Ir. and Gael, *brōgan*, < *brōg*, E. brogue.] A coarse, stout shoe.

brogue, brōg, *n.* [Ir. and Gael, *brōg*.] A rude shoe, commonly of untanned hide, worn, esp. formerly, in Ireland and Scotland; in recent use, a strongly made, comfortable type of ordinary shoe, often with decorative perforations on the vamp and upper.

brogue, brōg, *n.* [Origin unknown.] A dialectal, esp. Irish, mode of pronunciation; an Irish accent in the pronunciation of English.

broil, broil, *v.t.* [O.Fr. *bruiller, bruller, brusler* (Fr. *brûler*), burn.] To cook by exposure to a clear fire, as on a gridiron; grill; to scorch; make very hot.—*v.i.* To be exposed to great or distressing heat; *fig.* to burn as with impatience.

broil, broil, *n.* [Fr. *brouiller*, to jumble or mix up, to throw into bustle or confusion; origin doubtful.] A tumult; a noisy quarrel; discord; a brawl.

broil, broil, *n.* A broiling; something broiled.

broil·er, broi′lẽr, *n.* One who or that which broils; a device for broiling meat, etc.; a fowl for broiling.

broke, brōk, *a. Slang.* Destitute; penniless; without money; in a state of bankruptcy.

bro·ken, brō′ken, *a.* [See *break*.] That has been subjected to breaking; violently separated into parts; in pieces or fragments; burst; infringed or violated; interrupted or disconnected; uneven or irregular; fragmentary or incomplete; changing direction abruptly, as a line; imperfectly spoken, as language; destroyed, overwhelmed, or ruined; weakened in strength or spirit; reduced to submission; tamed.

bro·ken-down, brō′ken·doun′, *a.* Shattered or collapsed; ruined; having given way, as in health.

bro·ken-heart·ed, brō′ken·här′tid, *a.* Having the spirits quite crushed by grief or despair.

bro·ken lot, *n. Stock market.* Odd lot.

bro·ken wind, *n. Vet. pathol.* a disease in horses, characterized by a difficult expiration of the air from the lungs, and often accompanied by an enlargement of the lungs and heart.—**bro·ken-wind·ed**, *a.*

bro·ker, brō′kẽr, *n.* [O.E. *brocour*, O.Fr. *brokeor*, orig. broacher (of casks), tapster (hence retailer); akin to E. *broach*.] A middleman or agent; one who buys and sells stocks, bonds, or other property, on commission; a pawnbroker; formerly, one who acted for both families in the arrangement of a marriage of their children.

bro·ker·age, brō′kẽr·ij, *n.* The business, service, or commission of a broker.

bro·mate, brō′māt, *n. Chem.* a salt of bromic acid.—*v.t.*—*bromated, bromating.* To combine or treat with bromine; to brominate.

brome·grass, brōm′gras″, *n.* [N.L. *Bromus* < Gr. *bromos*, kind of oats.] Any grass of the genus *Bromus*, esp. that which is used for pasture or for hay.

bro·mic, brō′mik, *a.* Of or containing bromine, esp. with a valence of five; as, *bromic* acid, $HBrO_3$.

bro·mic ac·id, *n. Chem.* an unstable, strongly oxidizing acid, $HBrO_3$, occurring only in solution or in a salt: used as an oxidizing agent in the manufacture of medicines and dyes.

bro·mide, brō′mīd, brō′mid, *n. Chem.* a compound of bromine with an element or radical; a salt of hydrobromic acid (HBr), esp. any of certain salts; as, potassium *bromide,* strontium *bromide,* etc., that act as cerebral and cardiac depressants and are used in medicine as sedatives and hypnotics. *Colloq.* a platitudinous statement; a person who is tiresome and commonplace.—**bro·mid·ic,** brō·mid′ik, *a.* Pertaining or proper to, or being a bromide.

bro·min·ate, brō′ma·nāt″, *v.t.*—*brominated,* *brominating.* To combine with bromine; to bromate.

bro·mine, brō′mēn, *n.* [Gr. *bromos,* stench.] *Chem.* an element; a dark reddish corrosive and toxic liquid, which gives off an irritating vapor, and which resembles chlorine and iodine in chemical properties: obtained from sea water and used principally for the manufacture of gasoline anti-knock compounds. Sym. Br, at. no. 35. See Periodic Table of Elements. Also **bro·min,** brō′min.

bro·min·ism, brō′ma·niz″um, *n.* A morbid condition due to excessive use of bromides. Also **bro·mism,** brō′miz·um.

bronc, brongk, *n.* Bronco.

bron·chi, brong′ki, *n.* Plural of *bronchus.*

bron·chi·a, brong′kē·a, *n. pl.* [L.L. < Gr. *bronchia,* pl., < *bronchos,* windpipe.] *Anat.* the ramifications of the bronchi or two main branches of the trachea through which air reaches the lungs.—**bron·chi·al,** brong′-kē·al, *a.* Pertaining to the bronchia or the bronchi.—**bron·chi·al tubes,** the bronchi, or the bronchi and their ramifications.

bron·chi·al asth·ma, *n. Pathol.* a respiratory disorder characterized by inflammation of the bronchi and causing difficulty in breathing.

bron·chi·ec·ta·sis, brong′kē·ek′ta·sis, *n. Pathol.* an inflamed condition of the bronchial tubes, producing paroxysms of coughing and difficult breathing.

bron·chi·ole, brong′kē·ōl″, *n. Physiol.* a tiny branch of a bronchus.

bron·chi·ol·i·tis, brong″kē·ōl·i′tis, *n. Pathol.* an inflammation of the bronchioles.

bron·chi·tis, brong·ki′tis, *n.* [The term. *-itis* signifies inflammation.] *Pathol.* an inflammation of the lining membrane of the bronchi or bronchia.—**bron·chit·ic,** brong·kit′ik, *a.* Having bronchitis.

bron·cho·pneu·mo·ni·a, brong″kō·nö··mōn′ya, brong″kō·nö·mō′nē·a, brong″-kō·nŭ·mōn′ya, brong″kō·nŭ·mō′nē·a, brong″kō·na·mōn′ya, *n. Pathol.* inflammation of the bronchia and lungs: a form of pneumonia.

bron·cho·scope, brong′ka·skōp″, *n. Med.* an instrument used to examine the trachea.

bron·chus, brong′kus, *n. pl.* **bron·chi,** brong′ki. [N.L. < Gr. *bronchos,* windpipe.] *Anat.* either of the two main branches of the trachea, or any of their ramifications.

bron·co, brong′kō, *n. pl.* **bron·cos,** brong′-kōz. [Sp., rough, rude.] A partly broken range horse or mustang of the western U.S. Also *bronc.*—**bron·co·bust·er,** brong′kō··bus″tẽr, *n.* One who breaks broncos to the saddle.—**bron·co grass,** *n.* A Mediterranean bromegrass, *Bromus maximum gussoni,* introduced into California.

bron·to·saur, bron′ta·sạr, *n.* [N.L.] Any of the herbivorous dinosaurs of the North American genus *Brontosaurus,* which attained a height of 12 feet and length of 60 feet or over.

Bronx cheer, *n.* A vulgar noise signifying disgust or scorn, which originated in the Bronx, a borough of New York City.

bronze, bronz, *n.* [Fr. < It. *bronzo,* said to be < L. *Brundisium,* It. *Brindisi,* town in southeastern Italy.] A durable alloy, consisting basically of copper and tin; something made of bronze, as a statue or other work of art; a lustrous metallic brown coloring substance; a lustrous brown color.

bronze, bronz, *v.t.*—*bronzed, bronzing.* To give the appearance or color of bronze to; make brown, as by exposure to the sun.—*v.i.* To take on a bronze color.

Bronze Age, *n.* The age in the history of mankind, between the Stone and Iron Ages, marked by the use of bronze implements.

Bronze Star, *n. Milit.* a decoration awarded by the U.S. Armed Forces for heroism or commendable service, with the exception of achievements performed by means of aircraft.

brooch, brōch, brōch, *n.* [A form of *broach.*] An ornamental pin or clasp used for fastening the dress or for ornamentation.

brood, brōd, *n.* [O.E. *brōd* = D. *broed* = G. *brut:* cf. *breed.*] A family of offspring or young; a number of young creatures produced or hatched at one time; a hatch, as of birds; breed or kind.—*a.* For breeding.

brood, brōd, *v.i.* To sit as a bird over eggs to be hatched; rest fixedly; meditate with morbid persistence, with *on* or *over.*—*v.t.* To sit as a bird over (eggs or young); incubate; cherish, as a bird her young.—**brood·er,** *n.*—**brood·ing·ly,** *adv.*—**brood·y,** *a.*—**brood·i·ness,** *n.*

brook, brụk, *n.* [O.E. *brōc,* stream, = G. *bruch,* marsh.] A small natural stream of water, as that found in woods or meadows.

brook, brụk, *v.t.* [O.E. *brúcan,* to use, enjoy = D. *gebruiken,* Icel. *bruka,* Goth. *brukjan,* to use; allied to L. *frui,* to enjoy (whence *fruition.*)] To bear; to endure; to support: usually in negative or interrogative sentences, as: They cannot *brook* restraint.

brook·ite, brụk′īt, *n.* [Named for the English mineralogist, H. J. *Brooke,* 1771–1857.] The mineral titanium dioxide, TiO_2.

brook·lime, brụk′līm″, *n.* [M.E. *brokelemke,* < *broke,* brook, and O.E. *hleomoc,* a kind of plant.] An old-world plant, *Veronica beccabunga,* with small racemose flowers, growing on the edge of brooks, etc.; an allied species, *V. americana,* of America; the watercress, *Roripa nasturtium.*

brook trout, *n.* A fish, *Salvelinus fontinalis,* the common speckled trout of eastern North America. Also **speck·led trout.**

brook·weed, brụk′wēd″, *n.* Either of two plants, *Samolus valerandi,* of the Old World, and *S. floribundus,* of North America, both bearing small white flowers.

broom, brōm, brụm, *n.* [O.E. *brōm;* akin to E. *bramble.*] Any of the shrubby fabaceous plants of the genus *Cytisus,* esp. *C.* (or *Genista*) *scoparius,* common in western Europe, which grows on uncultivated ground and has long, slender branches bearing small leaves and yellow flowers; any of various allied or other plants of the genera *Genista* and *Spartium.* A sweeping implement having a brush of twigs, straw, or plant stems attached to a stick or handle, originally made with twigs of the broom plant.

broom, brōm, brụm, *v.t.* To sweep, or sweep away, as with a broom.

broom·corn, brōm′kạrn″, brụm′kạrn″, *n.* A kind of grass, genus *Sorghum,* with long, stiff, branched flower clusters, used for making brooms.

broom·rape, brōm′rāp″, brụm′rāp″, *n.* Any of various parasitic herbs, esp. of the genus

Orobanche, living on the roots of broom and other plants.

broom·stick, brōm′stik″, *n.* The stick or handle of a broom; the fabled means of the flight of witches.

broth, brạth, broth, *n.* [O.E. *broth* = O.H.G. *brod* = Icel. *brodh;* < the root of E. *brew:* cf. *brewis.*] The liquor from boiled meat, fish, vegetables; thin soup.

broth·el, broth′l, brọth′l, bra′thal, bra′THal, *n.* [O.E. *brothel,* a wretch, < *brothen,* ruined, destroyed, < *breóthan,* to destroy.] A house appropriated to the purposes of prostitution.

broth·er, brŭTH′ẽr, brŭTH′ụr, *n. pl.* **broth·ers, breth·ren,** breTH′ren. [O.E. *brōthor* = D. *broeder* = G. *bruder* = Icel. *brōdhir* = Goth. *brōthar;* akin to L. *frater,* brother, Gr. *frater,* clansman, Skt. *bhratar,* brother.] A male relative, a son of the same parents or parent; a male member of the same tribe, nationality, fraternal order, or profession; a fellowman; a male member of a religious order; a monk; a lay member of a religious order not preparing for holy orders or not yet ready for them.—*a.* Being a brother; related by brotherhood.—*v.t.* To treat or address as a brother; admit to or join in brotherhood.

broth·er·hood, brŭTH′ẽr·hụd″, *n.* The state of being a brother or brotherly; a group of men of the same class, profession, or occupation; a fraternal or trade organization.

broth·er-in-law, brŭTH′ẽr·in·lạ″, *n. pl.* **broth·ers-in-law.** The brother of one's husband or wife; a sister's husband.

broth·er·li·ness, brŭTH′ẽr·lē·nes, *n.* State of being brotherly.

broth·er·ly, brŭTH′ẽr·lē, *a.* Characteristic of, or befitting brothers; as, *brotherly* love.

brough·am, brō′am, brōm, brō′am, *n.* [After the first Lord *Brougham.*] A one-horse closed carriage, either two- or four-wheeled, adapted to carry either two or four persons, and having a high perch on the outside front for the driver.

brou·ha·ha, brō·hä′hä, brō″hä·hä′, *n.* A public uproar brought about by some sensational event; the episode which is the cause of general confusion, esp. one of minor importance.

brow, brou, *n.* [O.E. *brū,* akin to Icel. *brún,* Gr. *ophrus,* Skt. *bhrū,* eyebrow.] The ridge or prominence over the eye; the eyebrow; the forehead; the countenance. The edge of a steep place; the upper part of a slope.

brow·beat, brou′bēt″, *v.t.;* past *browbeat,* pp. *browbeat* or *browbeaten,* ppr. *browbeating.* To intimidate by overbearing looks or words; bully.—**brow·beat·er,** *n.*

brown, broun, *a.* [O.E. *brun* = Icel. *brúnn,* Dan. *bruun,* Sw. *brun,* D. *bruin,* G. *braun,* brown; lit. of a *burnt* color, < root of *burn,* *bronze,* etc.] Of a dark or dusky color, inclining to redness.—**brown·ish,** broun′-ish, *a.* Somewhat brown.

brown, broun, *n.* A dark color between red and yellow, and resulting from a mixture of red, black, and yellow.

brown, broun, *v.i., v.t.* To become or cause to become brown by various methods, as painting, sunning, scorching.

brown al·ga, *n.* Any of a class, *Phaeophycae,* of marine algae containing a brown pigment in addition to chlorophyll.

brown bet·ty, *n.* A baked dessert made of apple or other fruit slices or pieces, bread crumbs, spices, and a sweetener, usually brown sugar or molasses.

brown bread, *n.* Any bread made of flour darker in color than the bolted wheat flour, esp. whole wheat bread; a dark-brown baked or steamed bread made of corn meal and rye meal, or wheat flour, sweetened with molasses.

---

a- fat, fāte, fär, fâre, fạll;   **e-** met, mē, mēre, hẽr;   **i-** pin, pīne;   **o-** not, nōte, mŏve;   **u-** tub, cūbe, bụll;   **oi-** oil;   **ou-** pound.

brown coal, *n.* Lignite.

brown-eyed Su·san, broun'ĭd sō'zan, *n.* A dark-centered coneflower, *Rudbeckia triloba,* grown as a garden flower in southern and eastern U.S.

Brown·i·an move·ment, brou'nē·an mŏv'ment, *n.* [Named for Robert Brown, British botanist who observed it in 1827.] The constant erratic motion of minute particles suspended in a liquid or gas, due to their being struck by the moving molecules of the liquid or gas, cited as proof that gases and liquids consist of molecules in rapid motion. Also **Brown·i·an mo·tion.**

brown·ie, brou'nē, *n.* A merry, elfin creature believed in Scottish folklore to do household tasks secretly at night; a small, square cake or cookie, usually chocolate, containing nuts; (*cap.*) a member of the junior section (approximately 7 to 10 years of age) of the Girl Scouts.

brown·out, broun'out", *n.* A reduction of the use of electric power, especially the curtailment of display lighting, as a precaution against air attack in time of war.

Brown Shirt, *n.* (*Sometimes l.c.*) a Nazi, esp. a storm trooper of the Nazi Party.

brown·stone, broun'stōn", *n.* A reddish-brown variety of sandstone, extensively used as a building material; a building, esp. a house within a row, with a brownstone front.

brown stud·y, *n.* A state of mental abstraction or meditation; a reverie.

brown su·gar, *n.* Unrefined or partially refined sugar.

Brown Swiss, *n.* A breed of brown dairy cattle, originally from Switzerland.

brown trout, *n.* A food fish, *Salmo trutta,* found in the fresh-water streams of Europe. Also *salmon trout.*

browse, brouz, *v.t.—browsed, browsing.* [Cf. O.Fr. *brouster* (Fr. *brouter*).] Of cattle, deer, to eat, as tender shoots of shrubs and trees; to pasture on; graze.—*v.i.* To leisurely inspect merchandise in a store without serious intention of purchasing; to look at random through several books to decide what one wants to read. To feed upon growing grass or other vegetation, as cattle.

browse, brouz, *n.* [Appar. < O.Fr. *broust* (Fr. *brout*), young shoot, < Teut.] Tender shoots of shrubs or other plants, such as cattle eat; green food for cattle, deer, and other animals; the act of browsing.

bru·cel·lo·sis, brō"sa·lō'sis, *n. Pathol.* any of a variety of infectious diseases caused by a parasitic bacteria (genus *Brucella*), causing abortions in animals and remittent fever in man. Also *Bang's disease, undulant fever, Malta fever.*

bru·cine, brō'sēn, *n.* [< James *Bruce* (1730–94), Scottish explorer of Africa.] A bitter, poisonous alkaloid ($C_{23}H_{26}N_2O_4$) obtained from the nux vomica tree, *Strychnos nuxvomica,* and from other species of the same genus, resembling strychnine in action but less powerful: used in denaturing alcohol. Also **bru·cin,** brō'sin.

bru·cite, brō'sīt, *n.* [< A. *Bruce,* American mineralogist.] A mineral consisting of magnesium hydroxide, usually found in thin foliated plates of white or greenish color and pearly luster.

bru·in, brō'in, *n.* [The bear's name in the celebrated fable, *Reynard the Fox;* < D. *bruin,* brown.] A bear, usu. a brown bear.

bruise, brōz, *v.t.—bruised, bruising.* [Partly < O.E. *brȳsan,* crush, bruise, partly < O.Fr. *bruisier, brisier* (Fr. *briser*), break.] To injure by a blow or by pressure without laceration; contuse; to discolor, as the skin, as a result of a blow; to batter or dent; to crush fine; *fig.* to crush to injure, as the feelings.—*v.i.* To become bruised.

bruise, brōz, *n.* An injury due to bruising;

a contusion; a discoloration of the skin due to bruising.

bruis·er, brō'zėr, *n. Slang.* A pugilist; a big, heavily-built man.

bruit, brōt, *v.t.* [O.Fr. Fr. *bruit,* < *bruire,* make a noise.] To noise abroad; report; rumor; spread the fame of.—*n. Pathol.* any sound heard within the body, as by means of a stethoscope.

Bru·maire, brY·mer', *n.* [Fr. *brumaire,* < *brume,* fog: see *brume.*] In the calendar of the first French republic, the second month of the year, extending from October 22 to November 20.

bru·mal, brō'mal, *a.* Belonging to winter; misty; foggy.

brume, brōm, *n.* [Fr. *brume,* fog, < L. *bruma,* winter, winter solstice, lit. "shortest day," < *brevis,* short.] Fog, mist.— **bru·mous,** brō'mus, *a.*

brum·ma·gem, brum'a·jam, *a.* [For *Birmingham,* manufacturing city in England.] Of a cheap, showy make or kind; sham.—*n.* Any cheaply made, showy article; a sham.

brunch, brunch, *n.* A meal that combines breakfast with lunch, taken too late to be called a breakfast, and too early for a lunch.

bru·ni·zem, brō" na zem', *n.* [Origin not known.] A dark-colored soil found in some of the areas in the Mississippi Valley.

bru·nette, bru·net, brō·net', *a.* [Fr., dim. of *brun,* brown; < Teut. Cf. *brown.*] Dark or brownish; brown or black-haired.—*n.* A person having dark complexion, hair, and eyes.

brunt, brunt, *n.* [M.E.; origin unknown.] The shock or force of an attack; the main stress, force, or violence.

brush, brush, *n.* [O.Fr. *broisse, brosse* (Fr. *brosse*); prob. < Teut. (cf. G. *borste,* bristle).] An instrument of various forms, consisting of bristles, hair, or the like, set in or attached to a handle or stock, used for removing dirt or dust, polishing, smoothing, applying moisture or paint, etc.; something resembling or suggesting this, as the bushy tail of an animal, esp. of the fox; a drum-stick with a soft bushy end used for light beats on a drum in jazz; an agricultural contrivance made of small trees, etc., used instead of a harrow for drawing over the ground to cover grain, etc., after sowing; one of the pieces of carbon, copper, or the like, in a dynamo or motor, which are in contact with the commutator and connect it with the outside circuit or external current; a kind of electric discharge accompanied by diverging rays of pale-blue light; the art or skill of a painter of pictures; a brushing, or an application of a brush; a graze or abrasion, as on a horse's leg.

brush, brush, *n.* A swift passage, as a quick ride across country; a hostile collision; a brief but smart encounter.

brush, brush, *v.t.* To pass a brush over, as for removing dirt or smoothing the surface; brighten, polish, or improve by or as by the use of a brush, with *up;* wet or paint lightly with a brush, with *over;* strike or graze lightly, as in passing; injure by grazing; move or sweep away or along with or as with a brush; apply with or as with a brush.

brush, brush, *v.i.* To use a brush; refresh or revive one's acquaintance with some subject, with *up;* pass over or touch against something lightly like a brush; move quickly or in haste; make off or be gone with a rush.— **brush·er,** *n.*—**brush-tongued,** brush'tungd', *a.* Having a tongue with long papillae on it, as of certain parrots.

brush dis·charge, *n.* A discharge of low-intensity electric current with dimly luminous circuit ends.

brushed, brusht, *a.* With a hairy finish, as on suede.

brush-fire war, brush'fĭer'wạr, *n.* War on a small scale and restricted to a narrow region.

brush-off, brush'ạf", brush'of", *n. Slang.* Snub; a quick, firm dismissal.

brush off, *v.t. Slang.* To reject rudely and suddenly; dismiss brusquely; have no more to do with.

brush·wood, brush'wụd", *n.* Densely growing bushes, shrubs, etc.; brush; broken or lopped branches.

brush·work, brush'wụrk", *n.* Any work requiring the use of a brush; the technique characteristic of an artist with respect to his use of brush strokes, as in painting with oils.

brush·y, brush'ē, *a.* Overgrown with or consisting of brush or brushwood; resembling a brush; shaggy.

brusque, brusk, brusk, *Brit.* brụsk, *a.* [Fr. *brusque,* < It. *brusco,* brusque, sharp, sour.] Abrupt in manner; blunt; rude.—**brusque·ness,** brusk'nes, *n.*—**brusque·ly,** *adv.*

brus·que·rie, brus'ka·rē, *Brit.* brụs'ka·rē, Fr. brYs·ka·Rē', *n.* [Fr.] Brusqueness; abruptness of manner.

Brus·sels car·pet, brus'elz kär'pit, *n.* A carpet having a heavy linen foundation web enclosing worsted yarns of different colors, which are raised in loops to form the patterns.

Brus·sels lace, brus'elz lās', *n.* [Named for for its point of origin.] A rich, heavy lace of bobbin or needlepoint variety, orig. handmade but now made by machine, usu. in a floral pattern, as Brussels rose point.

Brus·sels sprout, brus'elz sprout'. *Usu. pl.* a kind of cabbage originating in Belgium, *Brassica oleracea gemmifera,* having small edible heads or sprouts along the stalk, which resemble miniature cabbages.

brut, brōt, *a.* [F., < L. *brutus:* see *brute.*] Not sweet; very dry: applying to wines, esp. champagne, having less than 1.5% sugar by volume.

bru·tal, brōt'al, *a.* [M.L. *brutalis.*] Characteristic of, or resembling brutes; irrational or unreasoning; rude, coarse, or unrefined; inhuman, savage, or cruel; gross or sensual.

bru·tal·ism, brōt'al·izm, *n.* An architectural style characterized by plain, large structural parts usually made of concrete.

bru·tal·i·ty, brō·tal'i·tē, *n. pl.* **bru·tal·i·ties.** The quality of being brutal; inhumanity; savageness; gross cruelty; insensibility to pity or shame; a savage, shameless, or inhuman act.

bru·tal·ize, brōt'a·līz", *v.t.—brutalized, brutalizing.* To make brutal, inhuman, insensitive; to treat as a brute or in a brutal manner.—*v.i.* To become brutal.—**bru·tal·i·za·tion,** *n.*

brute, brōt, *a.* [L. *brutus,* heavy, dull, stupid, irrational.] Not possessing reason or understanding; as, *brute* beasts; pertaining to instincts, qualities or actions characteristic of animals as distinguished from man; lacking sensibility or refined feeling; rough or rude; crude or unpolished; savage; not endowed or associated with sense or sensation; senseless; unconscious; merely physical; lacking life and soul.—*n.* A brute creature; an animal as distinguished from man, esp. one of the larger quadrupeds; the animal nature in man; a person resembling an animal in want of intelligence or in some other quality, as cruelty or sensuality: often, a general term of contempt.

brut·ish, brō'tish, *a.* Of or pertaining to brutes or lower animals; brutelike; irrational; uncultured; unfeeling; sensual.— **brut·ish·ly,** *adv.*—**brut·ish·ness,** *n.*

bry·ol·o·gy, brĭ·ol′a·jē, *n.* [Gr. *bryon*, moss, and *logos*, discourse.] The science of mosses, their structure, affinities, classification, etc.—**bry·o·log·i·cal**, brī″a·log′i·kal, *a.*—**bry·o·l·gist**, brī″ol′a·jist, *n.*

bry·o·ny, **bri·o·ny**, brī′a·nē, *n.* [L., *bryony* < Gr. *bryonia*, < *bryein*, swell.] Any plant or vine of the old-world genus *Bryonia*, in the gourd family, having red or black berries, an acrid juice, and roots having emetic and purgative properties.

bry·o·phyte, brī′a·fīt″, *n.* [N.L. *Bryophyta*, pl., < Gr. *bryon*, moss, plant.] Any of the *Bryophyta*, a primary division or group of plants comprising the true mosses and liverworts.—**bry·o·phyt·ic**, brī″a·fit′ik, *a.*

bry·o·zo·an, brī·o·zō′an, *n.* Polyzoan.

Bryth·on, brith′an, *n.* A Celt who speaks a language of the Brythonic division; a Briton.

Bry·thon·ic, bri·thon′ik, *n.* One of the two main divisions of the Celtic language (the other being Gaelic), including Welsh, Breton, and Cornish.—*a.* Concerning the Brythons or their language.

bub, bub, *n.* [Appar. a corruption of *brother.*] *Slang.* A term used in familiar address; buddy; boy; brother.

bu·ba·line, bū′ba·lin, bū′ba·līn″, *a.* [L. *bubalinus*, < *bubalus*, buffalo, African antelope: see *buffalo.*] Pertaining to or resembling the buffalo; belonging or pertaining to a genus, *Alcelaphus*, of antelopes, esp. *A. boselaphus*, of N. Africa.

bub·ble, bub′l, *v.i.*—*bubbled, bubbling.* [< M.L.G. *bubbeln*, Dan. *boble*, bubble; imit. of sound.] To emit light explosive sounds caused by the formation and bursting of vesicles or globules of air or gas, as boiling water, to make any similar sound, as a gurgle; form bubbles; to rise in bubbles, as gas through a liquid, or water from a spring; to arise or issue like bubbles; of a person, to be in a state of animation, gaiety, or excitement.—*v.t.* To cause to bubble; to form bubbles in, as liquids.—**bub·bly**, *a.*—**bub·bling·ly**, *adv.*

bub·ble, bub′l, *n.* A thin vesicle of water or other liquid inflated with air or gas; a small globule of air or gas in or rising through a liquid, as in a carbonated beverage; a globule of air or gas, or a globular vacuum in a solid substance cooled from fusion, as glass; anything wanting firmness, permanence, substance, or reality; a false show; a vain project; sometimes a delusive commercial scheme; a financial fraud; the act, process, or sound of bubbling; a globular shelter; a dome.

bub·ble and squeak, *n. Brit.* beef and cabbage fried or boiled together, occasionally with potatoes as an added ingredient.

bub·ble cham·ber, *n. Phys.* an apparatus for studying the behavior of atomic particles; a chamber connected to an accelerator, containing a superheated liquid, through which high-speed sub-atomic particles are sent, disturbing the liquid and forming paths of bubbles which are photographed and studied.

bub·ble gum, *n.* A thick chewing gum which can be blown into bubbles.

bub·bler, bub′lêr, *n.* A drinking fountain which causes water to spout upward; *chem.* a device by which a liquid passes over a perforated plate while a gas bubbles through the perforations.

bub·ble top, *n.* A protective, clear plastic top used on official automobiles.

bu·bo, bū′bō, *n. pl.* **bu·boes**, bū′bōz. [M.L. *bubo(n)-*, < Gr. *boubōn*, groin, swelling in the groin.] *Pathol.* an inflammatory swelling of a lymphatic gland, esp. when in the groin or armpit.

bu·bon·ic plague, bū·bon′ik plāg″, bö·bon′ik, *n. Pathol.* an epidemic disease caused by infection from rodents and fleas and characterized by the formation of buboes.

buc·cal, buk′al, *a.* [L. *bucca*, cheek, mouth.] Of or pertaining to the cheek; pertaining to the sides of the mouth or to the mouth; oral.—**buc·cal·ly**, *adv.*

buc·ca·neer, buk″a·nēr′, *n.* [Fr. *boucanier*, *lit. barbecuer*, originally a hunter in the West Indies who smoked the flesh of the animals, and turned to piracy in the 17th century, < *boucaner*, to smoke meat, < *boucan*, a place for smoking meat, a Carib word.] A pirate; a sea robber, esp. one of the piratical adventurers, English and French, who preyed on the Spanish ships and colonies in America in the 17th and 18th centuries; an unprincipled adventurer in politics and business.

buc·ci·na·tor, buk′sa·nā″têr, *n.* [L., trumpeter, < *buccinare*, blow a trumpet, < *buccina*: see *buccinal.*] *Anat.* a thin, flat muscle forming the wall of the cheek, assisting in movement of the mouth as required for smiling and blowing.—**buc·ci·na·to·ry**, buk′sa·na·tōr″ē, buk′sa·-na·tar″ē, buk″sa·nā′ta·rē, *a.*

buck, buk, *n.* [O.E. *bucca*, he-goat, *buc*, male deer, = D. *bok* = G. *bock.*] The male of the deer, goat, antelope, rabbit, or the hare. A gay or dashing fellow; a dandy or fop; a male person.—*a. Milit. slang*, an enlisted man of the lowest rank.

buck, buk, *v.i.* Of a horse, to try to unseat a rider by leaping with arched back and landing with stiffened forelegs. *Colloq.* to resist obstinately; of a vehicle, to move jerkily.—*v.t.* To throw by bucking. *Colloq.* to resist; in football, to charge into, as the opposing line.—**buck up**, to be encouraged.

buck, buk, *n. Slang*, an American dollar: short for buckskin, used by N. American Indians as a standard of value.

buck, buk, *n.* A sawbuck: a kind of leather-covered frame in the shape of a sawhorse, used by gymnasts in vaulting exercises.

buck, buk, *n.* In certain card games, an article, as a penknife, passed from one player to another to indicate whose turn it is to deal or to ante for all the players.—**to pass the buck**, *slang*, to pass a burden, as responsibility or blame, to another.

buck and wing, *n.* A tap dance resembling the clog, characterized by intricate hopping and heel-clicking.

buck·a·roo, buck·e·roo, buk″a·rö′, *n.* A cowboy of Western U.S. Also **buck·-ay·ro**, ba·kâr′ō.

buck bean, *n.* A plant, *Menyanthes trifoliata*, with white or purplish flowers, growing in bogs.

buck·board, buk′bōrd″, buk′bärd″, *n.* A four-wheeled carriage in which a long flexible board or frame is fastened to the axle without the use of springs.

buck·et, buk′it, *n.* [Appar. > O.Fr. *buket*, pail, tub.] A cylindrical container for scooping up or holding liquids or solids; a compartment on the circumference of a water wheel; the flat-board of a paddlewheel; a scoop of a dredging machine; one of the scoops or cups attached to the endless chain or belt in some conveyers or elevators; the amount a bucket will hold.

buck·et, buk′it, *v.t.*—*bucketed, bucketing.* To draw up or carry in buckets; to ride hard, as a horse; to handle irregularly, as securities in a bucket shop.

buck·et bri·gade, *n.* A human chain formed to extinguish a fire by passing buckets of water swiftly from one person to the next.

buck·et seat, *n.* A low, individual seat, with a slightly rounded back, used in automobiles and airplanes.

buck·et shop, *n.* A fraudulent brokerage establishment which fails to execute orders placed on margin by customers, taking a profit when market fluctuations prove contrary to the customer's interest.

buck·eye, buk′ī, *n.* A tree or shrub, genus *Æsculus*, allied to the horse chestnut; *(cap.)* an inhabitant of Ohio.

buck fe·ver, *n. Colloq.* nervousness suffered by a novice hunter at his first glimpse of game.

buck·hound, buk′hound″, *n.* A hound for hunting deer and other game: similar to the staghound, but smaller.

buck·le, buk′l, *n.* [O.Fr. *bucle*, *boucle*, buckle, boss of a shield, Fr. *boucle*, buckle, ring, curl, < L. *buccula*, dim. of *bucca*, cheek, mouth.] A clasp consisting of a rectangular or curved rim with a tongue and catch, used for fastening together two loose ends, as of a belt or strap; a clasplike ornament used to adorn garments, handbags, shoes; the condition of being curled or bent, esp. of metal, wood, or linoleum.

buck·le, buk′l, *v.t.*—*buckled, buckling.* To fasten with a buckle, with *up*; to join together.—*v.i.* To warp or curl due to heat or weight.—**buck·le down**, to apply oneself vigorously.—**buck·le un·der**, to yield unwillingly to the insistence of another or the force of circumstances.

buck·ler, buk′lêr, *n.* [O.Fr. *boucler* (Fr. *bouclier*), shield, orig. one with a boss, < *boucle*, boss: see *buckle.*] A small, usually round shield, generally clasped by the hand only, but sometimes strapped to the arm; any means of defense; a protection; *naut.* a piece of wood or metal fitted to stop the holes for the hawsers or similar openings in a ship; *zool.* a plate or protective covering on parts of the body of various animals.—*v.t.* To shield.

buck·o, buk′ō, *n. pl.* **buck·oes**, buk′ōz. [See *buck.*] A blusterer or bully; one who domineers roughly or brutally over subordinates; *Ir.* a young lad.

buck pas·ser, *n.* One who passes blame or responsibility to someone else.—**buck·pas·sing**, buk′pas·ing, *n.*

buck·ra, buk′ra, *n.* [W. African word meaning master.] *Dial.* a white man: a term used by Negroes in Southern U.S.

buck·ram, buk′ram, *n.* [O.Fr. *boquerant* (Fr. *bougran*); origin uncertain.] A coarse linen or cotton fabric sized with glue or gum, used for stiffening garments, binding books, etc.; a stiff, formal, or haughty manner; stiffness.—*a.* Made of buckram or resembling buckram, hence, stiff, precise, formal.

buck·ram, buk′ram, *v.t.* To stiffen with or as with buckram.

buck·saw, buk′sạ″, *n.* A saw consisting of a blade set across an upright frame or bow, used with both hands in cutting wood on a sawbuck or sawhorse.

buck·shee, buk′shē, buk″shē′, *n. Brit.* Something extra, esp. an extra portion of rations; something free; a gift; a bonus.

buck·shot, buk′shot″, *n.* A coarse leaden pellet used as a projectile for killing game.

buck·skin, buk′skin″, *n.* The skin of a buck or deer; a strong, soft leather, yellowish or grayish in color, now usu. from sheepskin; *pl.* breeches or other clothing made of buckskin.

buck·tail, buk′tāl″, *n.* A fisherman's artificial lure made of hair from the tail of a deer or a like material.

buck the trend, *v.i.* To act contrary to indicated or popular expectations, as to sell securities in a bull, or rising, market.

buck·thorn, buk′thạrn″, *n.* A shrub, plant, or small tree of the genus *Rhamnus*, grown in Europe and the U.S., most common of which are *R. cathartica*, used as a hedge plant and yielding a yellow dye, and *R. purshiana*, a tree yielding a laxative substance, cascara sagarada; the tree, *Bumelia lycioides*, common in southern U.S.

buck·tooth, buk′töth″, *n. pl.* **buck·teeth**, buk′tēth″. A projecting front tooth.—**buck·toothed**, *a.*

buck·wheat, buk′hwēt″, buk′wēt″, n. [< O.E. *bōc*, beech, also D. *boekweit*, G. *buchweizen*, buckwheat, lit. "beech wheat," from its beechnut-shaped seed.] An herb, *Fagopyrum fagopyrum*, cultivated for its triangular seeds, which are used as a food for animals, and made into a dark flour used for making pancakes; the seeds or the flour.

bu·col·ic, bū·kol′ik, a. [L. *bucolicus*, < Gr. *boukolikos, boukolos*, herdsman, < *bous*, ox.] Of or pertaining to herdsmen or shepherds; pastoral; rustic; rural; countrified.

bu·col·ic, bū·kol′ik, n. A pastoral poem. *Archaic*, a rustic; a countrified person; a bumpkin.

bud, bud, n. [Reduced form of *buddy.*] *Colloq.* One's brother; (*cap.*) a familiar name for any small boy or any man, regardless of his actual name.

bud, bud, n. [M.E. *budde*; origin uncertain.] An undeveloped or rudimentary stem or branch of a plant; a small axillary or terminal protuberance on a plant, containing rudimentary foliage (leaf-bud), the rudimentary inflorescence (flowerbud), or both (mixed bud); a leaf or flower not wholly expanded. In certain animals of low organization, a prominence which develops into a new individual, sometimes permanently attached to the parent organism and sometimes becoming detached; a gemma; any small rounded organ as, a tactile *bud* or a gustatory *bud*; *fig.* anything in an immature or undeveloped state; a child or young person; a young lady just introduced into society. The state of budding, or putting forth buds.

bud, bud, v.i.—*budded, budding*. To put forth or produce buds, as a plant; to push out from the parent like a bud; to begin to grow or develop; of birds, to eat buds.—*v.t.* To cause to bud; to produce by means of buds; *hort.* to graft by inserting a bud of one plant into the stem of another.

Bud·dha, bud′a, bŏ′da, n. [Skt. 'wise, enlightened.' 'The Enlightened One,' a title applied to any one of a series of deified teachers, esp. to the founder of Buddhism, a great religious teacher, variously known as Siddhartha, Gautama (Gotama), or Sakyamuni, who is believed to have flourished in India about the 6th century B.C., regarded by his followers as the last of the Buddhas possessing perfect enlightenment and wisdom.

Bud·dha·hood, bud′a·hud″, bŏ′da·hud, n. A state of enlightenment attained or sought to be attained through a regulated course of introspection and moral action, in accordance with the teachings of Buddhism.

Bud·dhism, bud′iz·am, bŏ′diz·am, n. [*Buddha*, < Skt. *buddh*; pp. < Skt. *budh*, to awake, the Enlightened, known otherwise as Sakyamuni Gautama: the sacred name of the founder of the system, who appears to have lived in the 6th century B.C.] The religious system founded by Buddha, one of the most prominent doctrines of which is that nirvana, or an absolute release from the chain of births and deaths, is the chief good: Buddhism prevails in China, Japan, Kashmir, Tibet, Burma, Ceylon, etc.—**Bud·dhist,** n. A worshipper of Buddha; one who adheres to the system of Buddhism.—**Bud·dhis·tic,** a.

bud·dle, bud′al, bud′al, n. [Origin unknown.] A flat, sloping trough for separating the metalliferous portion of an ore from the earthy or valueless part by means of running water.—*v.t.—buddled, buddling*. To treat, as ore, in a buddle.

bud·dle·ia, bud·lē′a, bud′lē·a, n. A large shrub of tropical origin with large clusters of violet or yellow flowers, popularly cultivated in ornamental landscaping.

bud·dy, bud·die, bud′ē, n. pl. **bud·dies.** [< *bud.*] *Colloq.* A comrade or pal; one of a couple joined in the buddy system; an unceremonious form of address used when a person's name is unknown; a child's term for brother.

budge, buj, n. [O.Fr. *bouge*, L. *bulga*, a leather bag, from a Gallic word seen in Ir. and Gael. *balg, bolg*, a bag; akin *bellows, belly*.] Lambskin with the wool dressed outward, formerly used as an ornamental border for scholastic habits.

budge, buj, v.i. [Fr. *bouger*, to stir, to move = Pr. *bolegar*, to be agitated, It. *bolicare*, to bubble, < L. *bullire*, to boil. BOIL.] To move slightly: usually with a negative; to stir; to flinch; to take oneself off.

bud·ger·i·gar, buj′a·rē·gär″, n. A small parakeet native to Australia, popularly bred as a pet. Also **bud·ger·i·gah, bud·gie.**

budg·et, buj′it, n. [O.E. *boget, bouget*, < Fr. *bougette*, dim. of *bouge*, a leather bag. BUDGE, *n*.] A financial statement of estimated income and expenditures covering a specified future period of time; a plan for financing operations, based on such a statement; as, the President's annual *budget* message to Congress; the needed or allotted money for a definite purpose.—**budg·et·ar·y,** buj′i·ter″ē, a.

budg·et, buj′it, v.t. To provide for in a budget; to confine to a budget; to plan the utilization of, as: Students must learn to *budget* their time.—*v.i.* To plan a budget; to limit expenditures, as: We're *budgeting* in order to buy a house.

budg·et·eer, buj′i·tēr′, n. One who makes up or follows a budget. Also **bud·get·er,** buj′it·ēr.

bud scale, n. One of the leaves resembling scales that form the external covering of a plant bud.

bud sport, n. A plant exhibiting an unusual deviation from the normal as a result of mutation in the bud.

buff, buf, n. [Appar. for earlier *buffle*, < Fr. *buffle*, buffalo.] A kind of thick leather originally made of buffalo skin but later also of other skins, having a fuzzy surface, and used for making belts or pouches, and formerly worn in place of light armor; hence, military attire; a buffcoat; *colloq.* the bare skin. A buff stick or buff wheel; the color of leather, a light brown. *Colloq.* a well-informed enthusiast.

buff, buf, a. Made of buff leather; of the color buff, a pale brown.

buff, buf, v.t. To impart to (something) a fuzzy surface like that of buff leather; to polish with a buff; to make buff in color.

buf·fa·lo, buf′a·lō, n. pl. **buf·fa·loes, buf·fa·los.** [< Sp. *búfalo*, Fr. *buffle*, L. *bubalus, bufalus*, < Gr. *boubalos* from *bous*, an ox.] A wild, ruminant mammal of the ox family somewhat larger than the common ox and with stouter limbs: in North America, it is called the *bison*, while in India it is named *water buffalo*, in Africa, the *Cape buffalo*. A buffalo robe; a buffalo fish.

buf·fa·lo, buf′a·lō″, v.t.—*buffaloed, buffaloing. Colloq.* to render completely helpless as by sudden and disconcerting action.

buf·fa·lo ber·ry, n. The edible red or yellowish berry of either of two shrubs, *Shepherdia argentea* and *S. canadensis*, of the oleaster family of the U.S. and Canada; either of these shrubs.

buf·fa·lo bug, n. The carpet beetle, the larvae of which feed on wool fibers.

buf·fa·lo fish, n. Any of several large North American fresh-water fishes of the sucker family *Catostomidae*.

buf·fa·lo grass, n. A species of short grass growing on the prairies of North America.

buf·fa·lo robe, n. The skin of an American bison, prepared with the hair on, used as a lap robe.

buff·er, buf′ẽr, n. An apparatus, as at the end of a railroad car, for deadening the force of a concussion; anything serving to deaden or sustain a shock; *chem.* a substance added to neutralize both acids and bases in solution; *econ.* reserve moneys or securities to protect from financial ruin.

buff·er, buf′ẽr, n. One who or that which buffs or polishes.

buf·fer, buf′ẽr, v.t. To shield or cushion; *chem.* to add a partially neutralizing material, as to a solution or substance.

buf·fer state, n. A smaller neutral state lying between possibly rival larger states.

buf·fet, buf′it, n. [O.Fr. *buffet*, dim. of *buffe*, a blow: see *buff*.] A blow, as with the fist; a cuff; an adverse stroke.

buf·fet, buf′it, v.t.—*buffeted, buffeting*. To strike as with the fist; beat; to struggle against repeatedly; batter.—*v.i.* To deal blows; fight; struggle.

buf·fet, ba·fā′, bu·fā′, *Brit.* buf′it, n. [Fr. *buffet*; origin unknown.] A sideboard or cabinet for holding china, silverware, and table linen; a counter, bar, or the like, at which lunch or refreshments are served in restaurants; refreshments set out on a buffet or table so that guests may serve themselves.—**buf·fet car,** a railroad car with a small compartment equipped for preparing light meals for serving to passengers.

buff·ing wheel, n. A wheel covered with cloth or leather, used in polishing metal; also **buff wheel.**

buf·fle·head, buf′al·hed″, n. A North American diving duck, *Bucephala albeola*, the male of which has a remarkable fullness of feathers on the head.

buf·fo, bŏ′fō, *It.* bŏf′fa, n. pl. **buf·fi, buf·fos,** bŏf′fē. [It.] A male opera singer, usually a bass, whose speciality is comic parts.

buf·foon, ba·fōn′, n. [Fr. *bouffon*, < It. *buffone*, jester, < *buffa*, a jest.] One who makes a practice of amusing others by tricks, odd gestures and postures, jokes, etc.; a clown; a jester; hence, one given to coarse or undignified joking.—**buf·foon·er·y,** n. pl. **buf·foon·er·ies.—buf·foon·ish,** a.

buff stick, n. A small stick covered with leather or the like, used in polishing, as fingernails.

bug, bug, n. [Origin unknown.] *Entom.* a hemipterous insect, also called *true bug*, with a piercing, sucking mouthpiece; popularly, any of various insects or similar crawling invertebrates, esp. those regarded as most abominable; as, bedbug or cockroach; *slang*, a failing in a machine or the like, esp. one that appears unexpectedly; *colloq.* a disease-causing microbe, as a germ or virus. *Slang*, an exaggerated zeal for something, as a hobby; a fad or craze; a person with an avid or obsessive interest; as, a motorcycle *bug*; a miniature microphone, concealed so as to secretly record conversations; warning system installed in homes and offices for protection.

bug, bug, n. Any type of compact sports car, usually a two-seater; a small lunar exploration vehicle carried in a larger craft and released to carry two crew members short distances.

bug, bug, v.t.—*bugged, bugging. Slang*. To plant a hidden device on or within, as a phone; to install a warning system against intruders in, as a house.

bug, bug, v.t.—*bugged, bugging. Slang*. To pester; plague; perplex; harass with annoying persistence.—*v.i.* To be prominent, as eyes.

bug·a·boo, bug′a·bō, n. An imaginary object of fright; real or imaginary reason for concern; a bogeyman; a bugbear.

bug·bane, bug′bān, n. Any of various tall, erect herbs, of the crowfoot family, bearing long white flowers which are supposed to drive away bugs or insects.

bug·bear, bug'bâr", *n. Archaic,* an imaginary being supposed to devour naughty children. Anything arousing terror, esp. groundless terror.

bug-eyed, bug'īd, *a. Slang,* with eyes seemingly popping out of the head; bulge-eyed.

bug·ger, bug'ėr, *n.* [Fr. *bougre,* < M.L. *Bulgarus,* a Bulgarian, a heretic; certain Bulgarian heretics being charged with this crime.] One guilty of the crime of bestiality or sodomy; a despicable person, a rascal, a little fellow: often used abusively or playfully without reference to its meaning.— **bug·ger·y,** *n.* The crime of bestiality or sodomy.

bug·gy, bug'ē, *a.—buggier, buggiest.* Infested with bugs. *Slang,* crazy; ludicrous.

bug·gy, bug'ē, *n. pl.* **bug·gies.** [Origin obscure: cf. *bogie.*] A light one-horse carriage, four-wheeled in the U.S. and two-wheeled in England; a baby carriage; a small cart for short hauls; *slang,* an old or run-down car.

bug·house, bug'hous", *n. Slang,* an asylum for the insane.—*a.* Crazy; demented.

bu·gle, bū'gal, *n.* [O.Fr. *bugle,* < L. *buculus,* dim. of *bos,* ox.] A brass or copper wind instrument, shorter than a trumpet, curved in shape, used mainly by the military for signalling and in bands.—**bu·gle corps,** *n.*

bu·gle, bū'gal, *n.* [Fr. *bugle,* < L.L. *bugula,* kind of plant.] Any plant of the genus *Ajuga,* or mint family, esp. *A. reptans,* a low blue-flowered herb.

bu·gle, bū'gal, *n.* [Origin unknown.] A tubular glass bead, with hollow stem, used for ornamenting women's apparel.

bu·gle, bū'gal, *v.i.—bugled, bugling.* To sound a bugle.—*v.t.* To sound forth as a bugle does; to call by bugle.—**bu·gler,** *n.*

bu·gle·weed, bū'gal·wēd, *n.* An herb, *Lycopus virginicus,* known for its medicinal properties; an herb of the genus *Ajuga,* in the mint family, widely used in rock gardens.

bu·gloss, bū'glos, bū'glạs, *n.* [L. *buglossus,* Gr. *bouglōssos—bous,* an ox, and *glōssa,* tongue.] Any plant of the genus *Anchusa,* esp. *A. officinalis,* with narrow oblong leaves and deep purple flowers, a common weed, and so called from the shape and roughness of its leaves; oxtongue.

bug·seed, bug'sēd", *n.* An annual herb, *Corispermum hyssopifolium,* of the goosefoot variety with flat, oval seeds.

buhl, boule, boulle, böl, *n.* [A form of Fr. *boulle* or *boule* < A. *Boulle,* French cabinet maker.] In cabinet making, a method developed in the reign of Louis XIV for inlaying wood with tortoiseshell, or white or yellow metal.

buhr, burr, bụr, *n.* Burrstone; a ridge made on metal or wood by a drilling or cutting tool.

buhr·stone, bụr'stōn", *n.* Burrstone.

build, bild, *v.t.—built* (archaic *builded*), *building.* [O.E. *byldan* (in pp. *gebyld*), < *bold,* dwelling, house.] To construct or erect, as a house; to form by uniting materials into a regular structure; to fashion; to make; to establish by gradual means; to raise as on a support or foundation.—*v.i.* To erect a dwelling or other edifice; to progress toward a goal.

build, bild, *n.* Style or manner of construction; physique.

build·er, bil'dėr, *n.* One who builds or who contracts for craftsmen to construct an edifice; a chemical agent which increases the cleaning power of detergents.

build·er's knot, *n.* A knot consisting of two opposite half hitches, used to fasten a small rope to a larger one or a rope to a spar.

build in, *v.t.* In home-building, to include provision for a special feature or function; as, to *build in* cabinets.

build·ing, bil'ding, *n.* The act of one who builds; a structure, usually with a roof and four walls, generally intended for use as a working or dwelling place.

build·up, bild'up", *n.* An accumulation of materials for a future need; a concerted effort to enhance the image of a person or thing.

build up, *v.t.* To enhance the reputation or popularity of, as by support of a political candidate, publicity given a theatrical performer, or the like.

built-in, bilt'in", *a.* Constructed to be part of or permanently attached to a larger structure, as: The kitchen has a *built-in* dishwasher. Having inherent or natural characteristics, as: Her gentle manner displayed *built-in* sensitivity.—*n.* Built-in furnishing or appliance.

built-up, bilt'up', *a.* Constructed of various layers fastened together; densely covered with dwelling units.

bulb, bulb, *n.* [L. *bulbus,* a bulbous root.] A subterranean leaf bud, consisting of imbricated scales or concentric coats of leaves on a short stem base encircling one or more buds capable of developing into new plants, emitting roots from its base, and producing a stem from its center, as in the onion, lily, or hyacinth; a plant developing from a bulb; any protuberance or expansion at the end of a stalk or long and slender body, as in the tube of a thermometer; the glass globe surrounding the filament of an incandescent lamp; the bulb at the end of a syringe tube; the pneumatic bulb chiefly used to control the shutter of a camera.—*v.i.* To project or be protuberant: with *out.*—**bul·ba·ceous,** bul·bā'shus, *a.*

bul·bar, bul'bėr, bul'bär, *a.* Pertaining to a bulb, esp. to the medulla oblongata.

bul·bil, bul'bil, *n. Bot.* A separable bulb formed on certain flowering plants; a small axillary bulb.—**bulb·if·er·ous,** bul·bif'ėr·us, *a.* Producing bulbs.

bul·bous, bul'bus, *a.* Having or pertaining to bulbs or a bulb; growing from bulbs; resembling a bulb in shape; swelling out.

bul·bul, bul'bul, *n.* [Pers.] An Asiatic songbird, a kind of nightingale, much referred to in Persian and Urdu poetry. Any of several Old World tropical birds of the family *Pycnonotidae.*

Bul·gar, bul'gėr, bul'gär, *n.* One of an ancient Finnic race, living along the Volga, the Don, etc.; one of a people, now partly Slavic in blood and wholly so in language, derived from this race and forming the bulk of the population of Bulgaria, a country in southeastern Europe.

Bul·gar·i·an, bul·gâr'ē·an, bul·gâr'ē·an, *a.* Of or pertaining to the Bulgars or Bulgaria, a republic of Southeast Europe in the Balkans on the Black Sea.—*n.* A native or inhabitant of Bulgaria; esp., a Slavic Bulgar; the language of the Slavic Bulgars.

bulge, bulj, *n.* [O.Fr. *boulge,* also *bouge,* < L. *bulga,* bag; < Celtic.] A rounded protuberance; a swelling; a hump; the swirl made by a fish rising to the surface; *slang,* the advantage; as, to get, or have, the *bulge* on one.

bulge, bulj, *v.t.—bulged, bulging.* To make protuberant.—*v.i.* To form a protuberance; swell out; bend outward.

bul·gy, bul'jē, *a.—bulgier, bulgiest.* Bulging; swollen.

bu·lim·i·a, bū·lim'ē·a, *n.* [N.L., < Gr. *boulimia,* < *bous,* ox, and *limos,* hunger.] *Pathol.* Abnormally voracious appetite; a disease marked by constant and insatiable hunger.—**bu·lim·ic,** *a.*

bulk, bulk, *n.* [M.E. *bolke,* heap; prob. < Scand. (cf. Icel. *būlki,* heap, cargo).] A large mass; main body or greater part;

volume; unpackaged goods or cargo; a food which aids the normal process of digestion by forming a fibrous residue.

bulk, bulk, *v.i.* To be of great volume or size; to increase; to expand.—*v.t.* To cause to expand or bulge.

bulk·head, bulk'hed", *n.* A horizontal or inclined door leading from the outside of a house to the cellar; one of the upright partitions dividing a ship into water-tight compartments to prevent sinking; a resisting partition or wall.—**bulk·head·ed,** *a.*

bulk·y, bul'kē, *a.—bulkier, bulkiest.* Of great bulk or size; large; massive; unwieldy or clumsy.—**bulk·i·ly,** *adv.*—**bulk·i·ness,** *n.*

bulk·y col·or, *n.* A color partially transparent, envisioned as filling a space in three dimensions.

bull, bul, *n.* [M.L. *bulla,* seal, writing furnished with a seal, document: see *bulla.*] A bulla or seal; a formal papal document having a bulla or leaden seal attached; an official letter or edict.

bull, bul, *n.* [M.E. *bule, bole* (cf. Icel. *boli*); appar. < an unrecorded O.E. form implied in the dim. *bulluc,* E. *bullock.*] The male of a bovine animal, esp. of the domestic species *Bos taurus;* the male of various other animals, as the elephant, whale, etc.; *slang,* a policeman or detective; *(cap.)* the zodiacal constellation or sign Taurus.

bull, bul, *n.* [Origin obscure.] A ludicrous blunder in language, involving a contradiction in terms: commonly regarded as esp. characteristic of the Irish, and often called *Irish bull. Slang,* bragging talk; a gross exaggeration.

bull, bul, *n.* A business optimist; *stock market,* one who buys or holds commodities and securities in anticipation of uptrending prices; as opposed to *bear.*

bull, bul, *v.t. Stock Market,* to endeavor to raise the price of (stocks) in the stock exchange; to operate in (the market) for a rise in price. To push or force (one's way.)

bull, bul, *a.* Male, or of large size; characteristic of a bull, as coarse, loud, obstinate, used in composition; as, *bulrush,* etc.; increasing; as, a *bull* market.

bul·la, bul'a, bul'a, *n. pl.* **bul·lae,** bul'ē, bul'ē. [L. *bulla,* bubble, round object, M.L. seal, document.] A seal attached to an official document, as a papal bull; any ornament of rounded form, esp. if suspended; *pathol.* a vesicle or elevation of the epidermis containing a watery fluid; *anat.* an inflated portion of the bony external meatus of the ear.

bul·lace, bul'is, *n.* [M.E. *bolace,* < O.Fr. *beloce,* wild plum.] A species of European plum, *Prunus domestica insititia.*

bul·late, bul'āt, bul'it, bul'āt, bul'it, *a.* [L. *bullatus,* < *bulla:* see *bulla.*] Having blister-like projections or elevations, as a leaf; blistered or puckered.

bull-bait·ing, bul'bā"ting, *n.* The action or practice of baiting bulls with dogs: a sport formerly popular in England, but now prohibited.

bull bat, *n.* Any of various American goatsuckers, related to the whippoorwill; nighthawk.

bull·dog, bul'dag", bul'dog", *n.* A medium-sized, short-haired, muscular variety of dog, with a large head and prominent lower jaw, originally bred in England for bullbaiting; also called English bulldog. A pistol or revolver, esp. a short-barreled revolver of large caliber; a proctor's assistant at an English university.

bull·dog, bul'dog", bul'dag", *v.t.* To force to the ground, as a steer, by seizing his horns and twisting his neck. *Football,* to aggressively pursue and halt, as the ball carrier.

bull·dog, bụl'dǎg", bụl'dǒg", *a.* Like or characteristic of a bulldog; as, *bulldog* courage or tenacity.

bull·doze, bụl'dōz", *v.t.*—bulldozed, bulldozing. [Origin uncertain.] To clear off, as an area, by pushing with a bulldozer or in the manner of a bulldozer; to bully.

bull·doz·er, bụl'dō"zẽr, *n.* A powerful machine driven by a tractor with a blunt blade at the front end, used for moving earth; one who bulldozes.

bul·let, bụl'it, *n.* [Fr. *boulet*, a dim. < *boule*, a ball, < L. *bulla*, a bubble, a boss, a seal. Akin *bullion*, *bulletin*, to *boil*, a papal *bull*.] A projectile generally of lead designed to be discharged from small arms, as rifles or pistols; a small ball.

bul·le·tin, bụl'i·tan, bụl'i·tin, *n.* [Fr., < It. *bullettino*, < *bulletta*, dim. of *bulla*, *bolla*, < M.L. *bulla*, writing, document.] A brief account or statement concerning current matters of public interest, issued from an authoritative source; a periodical publication, as of a learned society.

bul·le·tin, bụl'i·tan, bụl'i·tin, *v.t.*—bulletined, bulletining. To make known by a bulletin.

bul·let·proof, bụl'it·prŏf", *a.* Capable of resisting the force of a bullet.

bull fid·dle, *n.* Double bass.

bull·fight, bụl'fīt", *n.* A combat between men and a bull or bulls in an enclosed arena: a popular spectator sport, esp. in Spain and Mexico.—**bull·fight·er**, *n.*—**bull·fight·ing**, *n.*

bull·finch, bụl'finch, *n.* A European bird, *Pyrrhula pyrrhula*, with a short, stout bill, valued as a cage bird; any of various similar birds, as the grosbeak.

bull·finch, bụl'finch", *n.* [Possibly for *bull fence* (as if for confining bulls).] *Brit.* a hedge high enough to impede hunters on horseback.

bull·frog, bụl'frŏg", bụl'frǎg", *n.* A large frog, esp. *Rana catesbiana*, living in marshy places, having a loud bass voice which resembles the bellowing of a bull.

bull·head, bụl'hed", *n.* A name given to several species of fish with wide and flattened heads, as the catfish, an obstinately stupid person.

bull·head·ed, bụl'hed'id, *a.* Headstrong; obstinate; opinionated.

bull horn, *n.* An electronic megaphone: a loudspeaker of high power, used on naval vessels, by police, at outdoor meetings, etc.

bul·lion, bụl'yan, *n.* [A.Fr. *bullion*, mint, appar. < O.Fr. *bouillon*, a boiling (< M.L. *bullio(n-)*, < L. *bullire*, boil), in part confused with O.Fr. *billon*, debased metal.] Gold or silver in the mass; uncoined or unmanufactured gold or silver in the form of bars or ingots considered only with reference to metallic value; a cordlike trimming made of twisted gold or silver wire, or a trimming of cord covered with gold or silver thread, used to ornament uniforms, etc.—**bul·lion·ism**, *n.* The doctrine or system of an exclusively metallic currency, or a metallic currency combined with a convertible paper currency.—**bul·lion·ist**, *n.*

bull·ish, bụl'ish, *a.* Of, pertaining to, or resembling a bull. *Stock Market*, aiming at, or tending to, a rise in price.

bull·mas·tiff, bụl'mas'tif, bụl'mä'stif, *n.* An English breed of dog produced by crossing the bulldog and the mastiff.

Bull Moose, *n.* A name popularly applied to the Progressive Party formed by Theodore Roosevelt; in the campaign for the U.S. presidency in 1912, a supporter of Theodore Roosevelt.

bull-neck, bụl'nek, *n.* A thick neck like that of a bull.—**bull-necked**, *a.*

bull·ock, bụl'ok, *n.* [O.E. *bulluca*, dim. of *bull*.] An ox or castrated bull; a steer.

bull pen, *n.* A pen for a bull or bulls; *colloq.* an enclosure or place in which persons, as prisoners or suspects, are temporarily confined; *baseball*, an area on the playing field where relief pitchers warm up during a game.

bull·pout, bụl'pout", *n.* [*bull*head and *pout*.] The dark bullhead or a related freshwater catfish.

bull ring, *n.* A circular arena for bullfights; a ring passed through the nose of a bull, used in controlling him; a T-section ring that supports and separates two split piston rings.

bull-roar·er, bụl'rōr"ẽr, bụl'rǎr"ẽr, *n.* A wooden slat attached at one end to a string by means of which it is whirled rapidly in the air, causing a roaring sound: used as a toy, and in some tribal rites.

bull ses·sion, *n.* *Slang*, an informal group discussion.

bull's-eye, bụlz'ī, *n.* The central division of a target, or a shot that hits it; something essential or critical; a remark or action which is especially relevant; a round, hard lump of candy; a thick disk or lenslike piece of glass inserted in a deck or the like to admit light; a plano-convex lens; a small lantern fitted with a convex lens to concentrate the light; a small circular opening or window; *naut.* an oval or circular sheaveless wooden block having a groove around it and a hole in the center through which to reeve a rope. *Meteor.* the eye of a storm; a small, dark cloud with a red center which precedes a storm.

bull·snake, bụl'snāk," *n.* Any of several large, nonvenomous snakes, genus *Pituophis*, found widely on the N. American continent, feeding chiefly on rodents, as the gopher snake.

bull·ter·ri·er, bụl"ter'ē·ẽr, *n.* One of a breed of dogs produced by crossing the bulldog and the terrier, exhibiting the courage of the former and the activity of the latter.

bull tongue, *n.* A plow with a vertically placed blade, used in the cultivation of cotton.

bull·whip, bụl'hwip", bụl'wip", *n.* A whip with a long plaited lash of rawhide and a short handle. Also **bull·whack**, bụl'hwak.

bul·ly, bụl'ē, *n. pl.* **bul·lies**. [< root of *bull*, *bellow*; originally the first element in compounds such as *bully-rock*, *bully-Jack*, and other old terms; akin Sw. *bullerbas*, a noisy person, < *bullra*, to make a noise.] A blustering, quarrelsome, overbearing fellow, more distinguished for insolence than for courage, a swaggerer; one who domineers or browbeats; *archaic*, a hired thug.

bul·ly, bụl'ē, *a. Colloq.* good; excellent; first-rate: often used as an expletive, as: *Bully* for you!

bul·ly, bũl'ē, *n.* [Fr. *bouilli*, boiled meat, prop. pp. of *bouillir*, boil.] Canned or pickled beef. Also **bul·ly beef**.

bul·ly, bụl'ē, *v.t.*—bullied, bullying. To act the bully toward; to overbear with bluster or menace.—*v.i.* To be loudly arrogant and overbearing; to be noisy and quarrelsome.

bul·ly·rag, bụl'ē·rag", *v.t.*—bullyragged, bullyragging. [Origin uncertain; cf. *bully* and *rag*.] To bully; tease. Also **bal·ly·rag**, bal'ē·rag".—*ballyragged, ballyragging*.

bul·ly tree, *n.* [< *balata*.] Any of various trees of tropical America, as *Manilkara bidentata* of Guiana, which yields gum balata.

bul·rush, bụl'rush", *n.* [M.E. *bulrysche*.] Any of various large rushes or rush like plants, as *Scirpus lacustris*, a tall perennial from which mats are made; any of various rushes of the genus *Juncus*; in Biblical use, the papyrus, *Cyperus papyrus*, the pressed fibers of which served in the earliest form of paper-making.

bul·wark, bụl'wẽrk, *n.* [Lit. a *work* built of the *boles* or trunks of trees, < Dan. *bulwerk*, D. *bolwerk*, G. *bollwerk*, rampart; hence by corruption Fr. *boulevard*.] A wall or reinforcement serving as a firm shelter against injury or danger, as a protecting barricade, a bastion, or military fortification; any moral or spiritual strength which fosters support in times of stress, strain, or doubt, as: Freedom of speech is a *bulwark* against oppression. A person of strong support, as: The older son was a real *bulwark* in that family.—*v.t.* To shield, shelter, or protect; to make secure by reinforcement.

bum, bum, *n.* A loafer, one who prefers charity to work; a person who wanders from job to job earning just enough to survive; an inebriate; a person, very devoted to a sport, who earns or sponges enough to eke out a living and spends most of his time on the sport; as, a ski *bum*.—**on the bum**, *slang*. Out of order; living like a tramp.—**bum's rush**, *slang*, coerced expulsion, as a disorderly customer from a tavern.

bum, bum, *n. Slang*, a drinking spree.

bum, bum, *n.* [Origin obscure.] *Brit. slang*, the buttocks.

bum, bum, *v.i. Colloq.* to live off others; to live by begging; to live idly; to travel without expense to oneself, by begging or stealing food and lodging.—*v.t. Colloq.* to appropriate, as an item, with no intention of repayment.

bum, bum, *a. Slang*, of poor quality; inferior; very unsatisfactory; in poor physical condition; as, a *bum* leg.—**bum steer**, *slang*, erroneous or misguiding advice.

bum·bail·iff, bum"bā'lif, *n.* Contemptuous term for a bailiff or underbailiff employed in serving writs or making arrests.

bum·ble, bum'bl, *v.i.*—bumbled, bumbling. To hum; buzz.

bum·ble, bum'bl, *v.i.*—bumbled, bumbling. To blunder; to talk in a halting, stuttering manner; to walk clumsily; to stumble.—*v.t.* To bungle; to botch up, as something.

bum·ble·bee, bum'bl·bē", *n.* Any of various large, hairy social bees of the genus *Bombus*.

bum·boat, bum'bōt", *n.* [D. *bumboot*, a wide fishing-boat, < *bum*, a tree, and *boot*, a boat.] A boat for carrying provisions to a ship at a distance from shore, or from vessel to vessel lying off shore.

bum·kin, bum'kin, *n. Naut.* a short boom, projecting from a ship's hull, used to extend a sail. Also **bump·kin**, bump'kin, **boom·kin**, bōm'kin.

bum·mer, bum'ẽr, *n.* One who lives by begging; a looter, esp. a Civil War soldier who plundered; in a quarry or mine, the man in charge of the conveyors.

bump, bump, *v.t.* [Imit.] To strike heavily against; to cause a knock or collide; to dislocate, followed by *off*; to displace, as a person, from his job through right of seniority; to increase the price of.—*v.i.* To knock heavily into something: often with *into* or *against*; to go or move with a jolt or jolts; *slang*, to dance by thrusting forward the pelvis; as, to *bump* and grind.—**bump in·to**, *colloq.* to meet by chance.—**bump off**, *slang*, to kill; murder.

bump, bump, *n.* A sudden heavy blow; a jolt experienced in air travel caused by changing air currents; *phren.* one of the natural protuberances on the surface of the skull. A sudden rise on a surface; as, a *bump* in a road. *Slang*, a dance movement common to stripteasers.

bump·er, bum'pẽr, *n.* [Corrupted < older *bumbard*, *bombard*.] A cup or glass filled to the brim; something well or completely filled; a device for absorbing shock in a collision, especially a bar across the end of an automobile; something very large; one that bumps; a type of fish, *Chlorosombus chrysurus*, found off the southern U.S. Coast. —*a.* Something unusually plentiful; as, a *bumper* crop.

bump·er, bum′pėr, *v.t.* To fill to the brim; to drink a toast to.—*v.i.* To drink a toast.

bump·kin, bump′kin, *n.* [For *bumkin*, a short boom, a bumpkin being a blockish fellow, a blockhead.] An awkward, clumsy rustic; a country lout.

bump·tious, bump′shus, *a.* [For *bumpish*, < *bump*, apt to strike against or come in contact with others.] Offensively self-assertive; disposed to quarrel; arrogant; blunt.—**bump·tious·ness**, *n.*

bump·y, bum′pē, *a. bumpier, bumpiest.* Having bumps or protuberances; causing bumps or jolts; characterized by bumps or the like, as the air or the weather.— **bump·i·ly**, *adv.*—**bump·i·ness**, *n.*

bun, bun, *n.* [M.E. *bunne*; origin uncertain.] A kind of cake or bread-roll, variously shaped; a bun-shaped knot of hair; *slang*, an inebriated state; as, having a *bun* on.

Bu·na, bō′na, bū′na, *n.* [Prob. < butadiene.] A synthetic rubber made by copolymerizing butadiene and another material. (Trademark.)

bunch, bunch, *n.* [M.E. *bunche*: origin uncertain.] A cluster of things growing or held together; a collected mass. *Colloq.* an assemblage of people. A lump, protuberance, or hump.

bunch, bunch, *v.i.* To form a bunch; swell out; cluster.—*v.t.* To form into a bunch; gather into groups.

bun·co, bung′kō, *n.* Bunko.

bund, bund, *n.* [Hind. *band.*] In India, China, Japan, etc., an embankment forming a promenade and driveway along a waterfront.

bund, bụnd, *G.* bụnt, *n.* [G., < *binden*, bind.] In German usage, a league, society, or association; (*cap.*) a pre-World War II organization in the U.S. which supported the Nazi regime in Germany.

Bun·des·rat, Bun·des·rath, bụn′das-rät″, *n.* [G., < *bund*, league, and *rat, rath*, council.] The upper house of the Federal Republic of Germany and of the Swiss and Austrian governments, to which members are appointed by the state governments.

bun·dle, bun′dl, *n.* A number of things bound, bagged, or fastened together; as, a *bundle* of straw, a *bundle* of laundry; a package or parcel, especially when wrapped for carrying; a roll, as a quantity of paper rolled together; a collection of traits or qualities considered together, as: She is a *bundle* of inconsistencies. *Bot.* an aggregation of strands of specialized tissue; as, vascular *bundle*, the conducting tissue in higher plants; *anat.* a group of fibers, as nerves or muscles; *slang*, a large amount of money.

bun·dle, bun′dl, *v.t.*—*bundled, bundling.* To tie together or bind into a roll or bundle, usually with *up*; to wrap warmly, with *off*; to send away unceremoniously.—*v.i.* To depart hurriedly; to practice bundling.

bun·dling, bun′dling, *n.* A courting custom in Wales and early New England of sweethearts sharing a bed while fully clothed.— *v.i.* To practice bundling.

bung, bung, *n.* [Allied to D. *bom*, O.D. *bonne*, a bung; Ir. *buinne*, a tap, W. *bwng*, a bung-hole.] A large cork or stopper for closing the opening in a cask; spigot; bunghole.

bung, bung, *v.t.* To stop with a bung; to plug; to cork. *Slang*, to maul; to bruise; commonly followed by *up*. *Brit. slang*, to throw, heave, or toss, as rocks.

bun·ga·low, bung′ga·lō″, *n.* [Hind. *baṅglā*, lit. "of Bengal."] In India, a one-story house with a low-peaked roof and a

veranda; in the U.S., a cottage or small house with a low-sweeping roof.

bung·hole, bung′hōl, *n.* The hole in a barrel or cask through which it is filled, then closed by a bung, cork, or plug.

bun·gle, bung′gl, *n.* A clumsy or unskillful performance or piece of work; a botch; a blunder.—**bun·gler**, *n.*—**bung·le·some**, *a.* Bungling; clumsy; unskillful.—**bun·gling·ly**, *adv.*

bun·gle, bung′gl, *v.t.*—*bungled, bungling.* [Origin uncertain.] To do, make, or mend clumsily or unskillfully; spoil by unskillful workmanship; mishandle, botch.—*v.i.* To work or act clumsily or unskillfully.

bun·ion, bun·yon, bun′yan, *n.* A knob on the side of the ball of the great toe resulting from chronic inflammation of the bursa.

bunk, bungk, *n.* [Origin uncertain: cf. *bank*.] A raised recess, case, or frame serving for a bed, as in a ship or a dormitory, often one of two or more arranged one above another; *colloq.* any sleeping-place, esp. one that is not very comfortable. A piece of timber across a sled, car, or truck, for sustaining the weight of logs; a car or truck used in logging.

bunk, bungk, *n.* [Abbr. of *bunkum*: see *buncombe*.] *Slang*. Claptrap; humbug, mere pretense.—*v.t. Slang*. To humbug; delude.

bunk, bungk, *v.i.* To occupy a bunk; to sleep, esp. in rough quarters.—*v.t.* To place, as logs, on a bunk.

bunk·er, bung′kėr, *n.* A large bin or receptacle for coal, esp. on board ship; *golf*, a sandy hollow or other rough place on the course, often artificial; *milit.* a dug-out fortification or trench, usually in a battle zone or other area exposed to bombardment or gunfire, used as a shield and as a vantage point for firing at the enemy.

bunk·er, bung′kėr, *v.t.* To load, as coal, into a steamer's bunkers for its own use; *golf*, to drive, as a ball, into a bunker.

bunk·house, bungk′hous″, *n.* A roughly constructed building serving as sleeping quarters for temporary work crews, such as in construction, lumbering, or farm work.

bun·ko, bun·co, bung′kō, *n.* [Perhaps < Sp. *banca*, bank.] *Slang*. A swindle; any game, or scheme in which a person is victimized.—*v.t. Slang*, to cheat or swindle. —**bun·ko steer·er**, *slang*, one who lures another to a rendezvous in order to cheat him.

bun·kum, bun·combe, bung′kam, *n.* [< a Congressional representative's phrase, "talking for *Buncombe*" (county of North Carolina).] Speech-making intended merely to please political constituents; insincere talk; claptrap; humbug.

bun·ny, bun′ē, *n. pl.* **bun·nies.** [Ir. and Gael. *bun*, root, stump; lit.'the short-tailed animal?] A pet name for a young rabbit or a child.

Bun·sen bur·ner, bun′san bụr′nėr, *G.* bụn′zan, *n.* A small gas burner invented by a German chemist, R. W. Bunsen (1811-99), with which a very hot, practically non-luminous flame is obtained by allowing air to enter at the base and mix with the gas.

bunt, bunt, *n.* [Origin uncertain.] A disease of wheat which destroys the kernels, due to the parasitic fungus *Tilletiatritici*; the fungus itself.—**bunt·ed**, *a.* Of wheat, affected with bunt.

bunt, bunt, *n. Naut.* the bellying part of a square sail.

bunt, bunt, *v.t., v.i.* [Cf. *butt*.] To strike with the head or horns, as a goat does; push; *baseball*, to tap the ball with the bat so that it goes only a short distance.—*n.*

bun·ting, bun′ting, *n.* [O.E. *bunting*, *bounting, buntel*, Sc. *buntlin*; origin unknown.] Any of a number of small birds closely related to finches and sparrows, as the indigo *bunting*.

bun·ting, bun′ting, *n.* [Origin uncertain.] A lightweight woolen or cotton fabric used for flags, banners, and decorations; *naut.* collectively, a ship's flags.

bun·ting, bun′ting, *n.* A type of hooded sleeping bag for babies.

bun·ya-bun·ya, bun′ya-bun′ya, *n.* [Native Australian.] A large pinaceous tree, *Araucaria bidwillii*, of Australia, having strong, durable wood, and bearing edible seeds.

bun·yip, bun′yip, *n.* [Native Australian.] *Aust.* A fabulous animal of native tradition, usually described as of amphibious character and large size; hence, an imposter; a humbug.—*a. Aust.* Fake; phony.

bu·oy, bō′ē, boi, *v.t.* To mark with a buoy or buoys; to support; keep afloat; bear up or sustain, as hope or courage; to refloat, as a sunken ship; raise or elevate.

bu·oy, bō′ē, boi, *n.* [M.D. *boeye* (D. *boei*), buoy, fetter, or O.Fr. *boyee, bouee* (Fr. *bouée*), buoy, = O.Fr. *boie, buie*, bond, fetter, < L. *boia*, collar.] An upright spar, sheet-iron can, or other floating device, fixed in a certain place to indicate the position of a rock or other object beneath the water, or to mark a channel or the like; a buoyant object used to keep a person afloat.

buoy·an·cy, boi′an·sē, bō′yan·sē, *n.* The power to float or rise in a fluid; relative lightness; the power of a fluid to support a body so that it floats; the upward pressure exerted upon a body by the fluid in which it is immersed, which is equivalent to the weight of the fluid which the body displaces, tendency to rise, as in the price of stocks; elasticity of spirit; cheerfulness; hopefulness.

buoy·ant, boi′ant, bō′yant, *a.* Having the quality of floating or rising in a fluid; capable of keeping a body afloat, as a fluid; not easily depressed; cheerful; hopeful.— **buoy·ant·ly**, *adv.*

Bur·ber·ry, bụr′ba·rē, bụr′ber″ē, *n. pl.* **Bur·ber·ries.** [Maker's name.] An overcoat or raincoat made of material specially treated by the Burberry process to be waterproof; the fabric itself. (Trademark.)

bur·ble, bụr′bl, *n.* A gentle, bubbling flow; a bubbling speech pattern; in aeronautics, a separation or turbulence in the airflow around a streamlined body, such as a wing, causing a loss of lift and increase in drag.

bur·bot, bụr′bat, *n. pl.* **bur·bots, bur·bot.** [O.Fr. *borbote, barbote*, appar. < L. *barba*, beard.] A freshwater fish, *Lota maculosa*, of North America, with an elongated body, a depressed head, and two barbels on the nose and one on the chin; a similar European species, *Lota lota.* Also *eelpout, ling.*

bur·den, bụr′dan, *n.* [O.E. *byrthen*, < the root of E. *bear*.] That which is carried; a load; a responsibility or obligation; something borne with labor or difficulty; anything grievous, wearisome, or oppressive; a heavy lot or fate; an encumbrance; a load considered as a measure of quantity; the carrying capacity of a ship; the weight of a ship's cargo; the carrying of loads; as, a beast of *burden*; *accounting*, overhead.

bur·den, bụr′dan, *n.* [M.E. *burdoun*, < O.Fr. (also Fr.) *bourdon*, a humming, the drone of a bagpipe; origin uncertain. Later E. senses show association with *burden*.] The refrain or recurring chorus of a song; something often repeated or much dwelt upon; the principal idea; the gist.

bur·den, bụr′dan, *v.t.* To load; to lay a heavy load on; to encumber with weight; to oppress with anything grievous; to surcharge.

bur·den of proof, *Law*, the obligation resting upon one of the parties to an action to establish an alleged fact by proof. The duty to verify one's position in a dispute.

bur·den·some, bur′dan·sum, *a.* Weighing like a heavy burden; heavy or hard to bear; oppressive; causing mental as well as physical strain; onerous.—**bur·den·some··ly,** *adv.*—**bur·den·some·ness,** *n.*

bur·dock, bur′dok, *n.* A plant of the genus *Arctium,* esp. *A. lappa,* a coarse, broad-leaved weed with prickly heads or burs which stick to the clothing.

bu·reau, bur′ō, *n.* pl. **bu·reaus, bu·reaux,** bur′ōz. [Fr. *bureau,* desk, office, O.Fr. *burel,* cloth-covered table, kind of woolen cloth, dim. of *bure,* coarse woolen cloth, perhaps < L. *burrus,* red.] A commercial agency for transacting business, giving out and exchanging information, making contacts and coordinating activities; *govt.* a department of government, a subdivision of such a department, or a specialized administrative unit for the transaction of public business.

bu·reau, bur′ō, *n.* pl. **bu·reaus, bu·reaux,** bur′ōz. [Fr. *bureau,* desk, office, O.Fr. *burel,* cloth-covered table, kind of woolen cloth, dim. of *bure,* coarse woolen cloth, perhaps < L. *burrus,* red.] *Brit.* a desk or writing table with a slant top and drawers for papers. *U.S.* a chest of drawers, often with a mirror at the top, for holding clothing; a dresser.

bu·reauc·ra·cy, bū·rok′ra·sē, *n.* pl. **bu·reau·cra·cies.** *Govt.* Government by bureaus; the concentration of power in administrative bureaus; a body of officials administering government bureaus; excessive red tape and inflexibility.

bu·reau·crat, bū′ra·krat″, *n.* A member of a bureaucracy; an official of a bureau, esp. one given to excessive formalism.—**bu··reau·crat·ic,** *a.*

bu·rette, bū·ret′, *n.* [Fr., cruet, dim. of *buire,* vessel for wine, etc.] *Chem.* a graduated glass tube, commonly having a stopcock at the bottom, used for measuring, or measuring out, small quantities of liquid.

burg, burg, *n.* [O.E.: see *borough.*] A fortress or fortified town of early and medieval times; *colloq.* a town or city.

burg·age, bur′gij, *n.* *Law,* in England, a tenure whereby burgesses, citizens, or townsmen held their lands or tenements of the king or other lord for a yearly rent; in Scotland, that tenure by which the property in royal burghs was held under the crown, proprietors being liable to the nominal service of watching and warding.

bur·gee, bur′jē, *n.* [Origin unknown.] A three-cornered or swallow-tailed pennant used as a distinguishing flag on merchant ships and yachts.

bur·geon, bur′jan, *n.* [M.E. *burjon,* < O.Fr. *burjon* (Fr. *bourgeon*); origin unknown.] A bud or sprout; a sudden growth or expansion.—*v.i.* To bud; sprout; grow forth. —*v.t.* To put forth, as buds.

burg·er, bur′gèr, *n.* A hamburger.

bur·gess, bur′jis, *n.* [O.Fr. *burgeis* (Fr. *bourgeois*), < M.L. *burgensis,* < L.L. of an English borough; formerly, a representative of a borough, corporate town, or university in the British Parliament; a representative in the popular branch of the colonial legislatures of Virginia and Maryland.—**bur·gess·ship,** *n.*

burgh, burg, *Scot.* bur′ō, bur′a, *n.* [Var. of *borough.*] A borough: now applied only to chartered towns in Scotland.—**burgh·al,** bur′gal, *a.* Pertaining to a burgh.

burgh·er, bur′gèr, *n.* [= D. *burger* = G. *bürger.*] An inhabitant of a borough; a citizen.

bur·glar, bur′glèr, *n.* [A.L. *burglator* (later *burgulator*), for *burgator,* > L.L. *burgus,* castle: see *borough,* and cf. O.E. *burh-bryce,* a breaking into a castle or dwelling.] One who breaks into a house with intent to commit a robbery; one guilty of burglary.

bur·glar·i·ous, bèr·glâr′ē·us, *a.* Pertaining to, involving or given to burglary.—**bur·glar·i·ous·ly,** *adv.*

bur·glar·ize, bur′gla·rīz″, *v.t.*—*burglarized, burglarizing.* To commit burglary upon.—*v.i.* To commit a burglary; to rob.

bur·gla·ry, bur′gla·rē, *n.* pl. **bur·gla·ries.** The crime of breaking into the house of another at night with felonious intent, sometimes extended by statute to cover the breaking and entering of any of various buildings, by night or day.

bur·gle, bur′gl, *v.i., v.t.*—*burgled, burgling.* [Backformation from *burglar.*] *Colloq.* to burglarize.

bur·go·mas·ter, bur′ga·mas″tèr, *n.* [D. *burgemeester* = E. *borough-master.*] The chief magistrate of a municipal town in various countries of Europe, corresponding to *mayor* in England and the United States; a large Arctic gull, *Larus hyperboreous.*

bur·goo, bur′gö, bur·gö′, *n.* [Origin unknown.] Traditionally a thick oatmeal gruel used by seamen; *dial.* a hearty, highly seasoned stew, combining several kinds of meats and vegetables, an outdoor gathering where this is served.

bur·grave, bur′grāv, *n.* [L.L. *burggravius,* < G. *burggraf—burg,* a town, and *graf,* a count, an earl.] *G. hist.* the appointed governor of a town, or, later, an hereditary lord of a town or castle and its adjacent lands.

bur·gun·dy, bur′gan·dē, *n.* A reddish wine color.—*a.* Wine-colored.

Bur·gun·dy, bur′gan·dē, *n.* pl. **Bur··gun·dies.** (*Often l.c.*) Wine, of many varieties, red and white, mostly still, full, and dry, produced in Burgundy, in eastern France; some similar wine made elsewhere.

bur·i·al, ber′ē·al, *n.* The act or ceremony of burying, especially the act of burying a deceased person; sepulture; interment.

bu·rin, bur′in, *n.* [Fr. prob. < Teut., and akin to E. *bore.*] An engraver's tool of tempered steel with a shaft beveled to a sharp point and used for cutting furrows in metal; a similar tool used by marble-workers.—**bu·rin·ist,** *n.* An engraver.

burke, burk, *v.t.*—*burked, burking.* [< the name of an Irishman who first committed the crime, in 1829, in Edinburgh.] To murder by suffocation so as to leave the body unmarked with the view to selling the dead body for dissection; to suppress, as to shelve a parliamentary bill; to get rid of by some indirect maneuver.

burl, burl, *n.* [O.Fr. *bourle,* dim. of *bourre,* hair or wool.] A wartlike growth on a tree; a veneer made from wood with burls in it.

burl, burl, *v.t.* To remove burls from; to finish, as cloth, by removing loose threads and knots.

bur·lap, bur′lap, *n.* [Origin obscure.] A coarse plain-woven fabric of flax, jute or hemp, used for sacking or wrappings, wall coverings, in making linoleum, and in upholstering furniture.

burled, burld, *a.* Having the grain distorted due to burls, said of wood.

bur·lesque, bèr·lesk′, *a.* [Fr. *burlesque,* < It. *burlesco,* ridiculous, < *burlare,* to ridicule, *burla,* mockery.] Tending to excite laughter by ludicrous images, or by a contrast between the subject and the manner of treating it; of or pertaining to theatrical burlesque.

bur·lesque, bèr·lesk′, *n.* That kind of literary composition which exhibits a contrast between the lofty subject and the manner of treating it so as to excite laughter or ridicule; travesty; caricature; a kind of dramatic extravaganza with skits, bawdy humor, and striptease acts in it; a ludicrous or debasing caricature of any kind.

bur·lesque, bèr·lesk′, *v.t.*—*burlesqued, burlesquing.* To imitate grotesquely; ridicule by

burlesque; caricature; travesty.—*v.i.* To use burlesque.—**bur·les·quer,** *n.*

bur·ley, bur′lē, *n.* [Appar. < *Burley,* proper name.] An American variety of fine-textured, air-cured tobacco grown esp. in Kentucky and southern Ohio.

bur·ly, bur′lē, *a.*—*burlier, burliest.* [Of same origin as *bur, burr,* Ir. and Gael. *borr,* a knob.] Great in bodily size; bulky; lusty; forceful; abrupt.—**bur·li·ly,** *adv.*—**bur·li·ness,** *n.*

bur mar·i·gold, *n.* Any of various herbs of the genus *Bidens,* esp. those with conspicuous yellow flowers or thorny fruits.

Bur·mese jade, *n.* *Jewelry,* an expensive piece of jade known for its superior quality: an authentic jade without imperfections. Also **Bur·ma jade.**

Bur·mese bèr·mēz′, bèr·mēs′, *a.* Pertaining to the natives and principal language of Burma, an independent republic in southeast Asia, located between China and India.—*n.* A resident of Burma; the Sino-Tibetan language of Burma.

Bur·mese cat, *n.* A breed of cat similar to the Siamese but of a darker brown color, with orange eyes rather than blue.

burn, burn, *n. Brit.* a streamlet or brook.

burn, burn, *v.i.*—*burned* or *burnt, burning.* [O.E. *beornan,* v.i., *bærnan,* v.t.; akin to G. *brennen,* Icel. *brinna, brenna,* Goth. *brinnan, brannjan,* burn.] Of fire, to be active or aglow; of a furnace, or fireplace, to contain fire; of fuel, etc., to be on fire, or in process of consumption by fire; to be fierce or vehement, as passion; be inflamed with passion, desire, etc., as a person; to be or become very hot; feel excess of heat; be affected with a sensation of heat; to flame, or give light, as a candle, lamp, or the sun; glow like fire; to undergo destruction, injury, or change from exposure to fire or heat; become charred, singed, scorched, etc.; become discolored by the effect of fire or heat, as the skin on exposure to the sun; suffer death by fire; to make a way by or as by burning, used with *into. Chem.* to undergo combustion; oxidize.—*v.t.* To consume or destroy by fire; set on fire, or consign to the flames; make a burnt-offering of; put to death by fire; to exhaust; to ruin; to infuriate, madden; keep alight, as a candle or lamp; inflame with passion, desire, etc.; expose to the action of fire or heat as, to *burn* clay; produce or make by means of fire; injure or change by fire or heat; char, singe, scorch, etc.; change the color of by fire or heat; wound or hurt by contact with fire or with something very hot; cauterize, as a wound; brand with a hot iron; produce an effect or a sensation like that of fire or heat on something. *Chem.* to cause to undergo combustion; oxidize.—**burn·ing,** *a.*—**burn·ing·ly,** *adv.*

burn, burn, *n.* The act or effect of burning; an injury or wound caused by burning; a mark made by burning; a burnt place; a sunburn; brand.—**a slow burn,** *Slang.* Indignation; gradually building anger.—**burn·a·ble,** *a.*

burn·er, bur′nèr, *n.* A worker whose occupation involves the use of heat to process a product, as in a brick kiln; a device on a stove or furnace containing the fuel and from which the flame issues.

burn·er, bur′nèr, *n. Aeron.* A combustion chamber or can, in a jet engine; a fuel-injection nozzle in the combustion chamber of a jet engine.

bur·net, bèr·net′, bur′nit, *n.* [O.Fr. *burnet, brunet,* dim. of *brun,* brown.] Any of several plants of the genus *Sanguisorba,* esp. *S. minor,* an erect herb whose leaves are used for salad.

burn·ing bush, *n.* Any of various plants, esp. the strawberrybush, *Euonymus americanus,* or the wahoo, *E. atropurpureus.*

burn·ing ghat, *n.* [Eng. *burning* and Hindi *ghat*, a place along a riverbank, usually with stairs descending to the water.] *Hinduism*, a place by the river, usually with a raised platform and stairs descending to the water, used for cremating Hindu dead in India.

burn·ing glass, *n.* A lens used to produce heat or ignite substances by bringing the direct rays of the sun to a focus.

burn·ing point, *n. Phys.* the lowest degree of heat at which the oil in a heating pan would begin to burn if a flame were applied.

bur·nish, bur̆′nish, *v.t.* [O.Fr. *burnir*, *burnissant*, to polish, < *brun*, O.H.G. *brun*, brown, BROWN.] To shine or buff; to polish or brighten (a surface) by rubbing to a luster; to refine; to make smooth.—*v.i.* To grow bright; to become glossy; *engraving*, to darken the halftone area of a printing plate by rubbing it with a tool.

bur·nish, bur̆′nish, *n.* Gloss; brightness; luster.—**bur·nish·er**, bur̆′nish·ėr, *n.*

bur·noose, **bur·nous**, bėr·nōs′, bur̆′nōs, *n.* [Fr., < Ar. *burnus*.] A hooded mantle or cloak worn by Arabs.

burn·out, burn′out″, *n. Aerospace*, the act of, or moment of, complete rocket fuel depletion. The over-heating and resulting breakdown of an electrical or mechanical device, usually resulting in damage to or destruction of the part.

burn·sides, burn′sīdz″, *n. pl.* [Named for Gen. A. E. *Burnside*, 1824–81.] A style of beard consisting of side-whiskers and a mustache, the chin being clean-shaven.

burnt, burnt, *a.* Affected by, scorched, or darkened as by burning. *Paint.* pertaining to colors of earth pigments; as, *burnt* umber; pertaining to colors of deep hue; as, *burnt* orange.

burnt of·fer·ing, *n.* An offering burnt upon an altar in sacrifice to a deity. Lev. VI.9.

burn-up, burn′up″, *n. Aerospace*, the heating of a rocket produced by air resistance.

burp, burp, *n. Colloq.* a noisy emission of gas from stomach to mouth; belch; eructation.—*v.i., v.t.*

burp gun, *n.* A submachine gun.

burr, **bur**, bur̆, *n.* [M.E. *burre* = Dan. *borre*.] A rough or prickly seed-vessel, receptacle, husk, or flower-head, as of the chestnut; a herb bearing such burrs, as the burdock; a weed that bears burrs; something that adheres like a burr; something producing a choking sensation in the throat; a rough ridge, edge, or protuberance on any object; any of various tools and mechanical devices, as a triangular chisel, a small circular saw or a dentist's drill; burrstone, commonly spelled *buhrstone*. A guttural or rough pronunciation of the letter *r* characteristic of the speech of Scotland; any rough or dialectal pronunciation; a whirring noise.

burr, **bur**, bur̆, *v.i.* To speak with a burr; to make a whirring sound.—*v.t.* To pronounce, as the letter *r*, with a burr. To form into a rough edge; to remove burrs from.

bur·ro, bur̆′ō, bur̆′ō, *n. pl.* **bur·ros.** A small donkey, used as a pack animal.

bur·row, bur̆′ō, *n.* [M.E. *borow*: cf. O.E. *beorg*, *beorh*, shelter.] A hole in the ground made by an animal, as a rabbit or a fox, for refuge and habitation; any similar habitation or place of retreat.—*v.i.* To make a burrow for habitation; work a way into or under something; lodge in or as in a burrow; hide oneself.—*v.t.* To make a burrow or burrows in; construct by burrowing; *reflex.* hide, as in a burrow.—**bur·row·er**, *n.*

burr·stone, **bur·stone**, **buhr·stone**, bur̆′stŏn′, *n.* A name given to certain siliceous rocks whose dressed surfaces present a burr or keen-cutting texture, much used for millstones; a millstone made from this rock. Also *buhr*, *burr*.

bur·ry, bur̆′ē, *a.*—**burrier**, **burriest.** Full of burs; burlike; prickly; characterized by a burr, as speech.

bur·sa, bur̆′sa, *n. pl.* **bur·sae**, bur̆′sē. [M.L., bag, purse, < Gr. *bursa*, skin, hide.] *Anat.* and *zool.* a pouch, sac, or vesicle; esp. a sac containing synovia, called *synovial bursa*, to facilitate motion, as between a tendon and a bone.—**bur·sal**, *a.*

bur·sar, bur̆′sėr, bur̆′sär, *n.* [M.L. *bursarius*, < *bursa*, purse: see *bursa*.] A treasurer, esp. of a college.—**bur·sa·ri·al**, bur̆·sâr′ē·al, *a.*—**bur·sar·ship**, *n.*

bur·sa·ry, bur̆′sa·rē, *n. pl.* **bur·sa·ries.** [M.L. *bursaria*.] A treasury, esp. of a college.

burse, burs, *n.* [Fr. *bourse*, a purse, bursary, exchange, < L.L. *bursa*, a purse, a skin, leather. PURSE.] A purse to hold something valuable; *eccles.* a special cloth case in which the communion corporal is carried.

bur·seed, bur̆′sēd, *n. Bot.* A European stickseed (*Lappula echinata*) that has been naturalized in North America.

bur·si·form, bur̆′sa·färm″, *a.* Pouch-shaped; saccate.

bur·si·tis, bėr·sī′tis, *n.* [< *bursa* and Gr. -*itis*, inflammation.] *Pathol.* inflammation of a bursa.

burst, burst, *v.i.*—**burst** (also, chiefly prov., **bursted**), **bursting.** [O.E. *berstan* = G. *bersten*.] To break or be broken suddenly, as from impact, tension or expansion of contents; explode; fly open suddenly, as a door; be extremely full, as if ready to break open; break or give way, or be on the verge of giving way, from violent pain or emotion; make a sudden display of activity or emotion; as, to *burst* into speech or tears; issue forth suddenly and forcibly from or as from confinement; become visible, audible or evident suddenly and clearly; spring forth, as a plant; force a way or passage; come or go suddenly and violently.—*v.t.* To cause to burst; break suddenly and violently; shatter; disrupt; cause or suffer the rupture of; as, to *burst* a blood vessel; force open, as a door.

burst, burst, *n.* Continuous fire from an automatic weapon, as from an aircraft machine gun, sometimes described as *long* or *short*; the explosion of a shell, as of an antiaircraft shell.

burst, burst, *n.* The act of bursting, or the resulting state; a sudden disruption; an explosion; a sudden display of activity or energy; a sudden and violent issuing forth; an outburst; a sudden opening to sight or view; a sudden expression or manifestation of emotion.—**burst·er**, *n.*—**burst·ing-charge**, *n. Ordnance*, the charge of explosive required for bursting a shell or the like.

bur·weed, bur̆′wēd″, *n.* Any of various plants having a burlike fruit, as the cockle-bur or burdock.

bur·y, ber̆′ē, *v.t.*—**buried**, **burying.** [O.E. *byrgan*, prob. akin to *beorgan*, protect. *Borough*.] To deposit in a grave or tomb, as a dead body; inter; entomb; consign, as a corpse, to any final resting place, as the sea; in general, to put underground; cover up with earth or other material; cover over so as to conceal from view; *fig.* to consign to oblivion; abandon, or forget, as: They *buried* their differences. Consign to obscurity or retirement; as, to *bury* oneself in solitude or in a monastery; absorb or engross; as, to *bury* oneself in work.—**bur·y·ing ground**, a plot of ground appropriated to the burial of the dead; a graveyard; a cemetery.—**bur·y one's head in the sand**, to shun reality; to withdraw from the obvious.

bus, bus, *n. pl.* **buses**, **busses.** [Abbr. of *omnibus*.] A motor driven vehicle, large or small, for public transportation, usually operated on a time schedule and following a set route; *slang*, an automobile or airplane.

A hand-pushed cart as that used to carry china and silverware in a restaurant.

bus, bus, *v.t.* To transport or convey by bus.—*v.i.* To travel by bus; to work as a busboy or bus girl.

bus bar, *n. Elect.* A connecting bar or tube, usually uninsulated, used as an electrical conductor where three or more circuits join to distribute them to outgoing feeders, as in electronic computers.

bus·boy, bus′boi″, *n.* An employee in a restaurant who removes the used dishes, silverware and linens, and resets the table with clean service; a waiter's assistant.

bus·by, buz′bē, *n. pl.* **bus·bies**, buz′bēz. [Prob. < proper name, *Busby*.] A tall fur hat with a bag, usually of the color of regimental facings, hanging from the top over the right side, worn by hussars, artillerymen, and engineers in the British army in full-dress uniform; a bearskin worn by British guardsmen.

bush, bush, *n.* Bushing.

bush, bush, *n.* [M.E. *busch*, *busk*, = D. *bosch* = G. *busch* = O.Fr. *bosc*, Fr. *bois*, = It. *bosco*, < M.L. *boscus*, *buscus*, a wood: origin uncertain.] A low shrub with many branches, which usually arise from or near the ground; a small clump of shrubs appearing as a single plant; thicket; undergrowth; something resembling or suggesting this, as a thick, shaggy head of hair; a fox's tail; a branch, esp. of ivy, hung outside a tavern as a sign that wine was sold; uncleared or untilled country sparsely populated, as in Australia; the country as opposed to the towns; *Canadian*, a small wooded lot, as a farm with trees left standing.

bush, bush, *v.t.* To cover with bushes; protect with bushes set round about; support with bushes; mark the course of, as a road, by planting bushes; use a harrow constructed with bushes, on, as land; cover, as seeds,with such a harrow.—*v.i.* To become bushy; branch or spread like a bush.

bush, bush, *v.t.* To line with a bush or bushing.

bush ba·by, *n.* Any of several small African lemurs of the genus *Galago*.

bush bean, *n.* A variety of kidney bean, *Phaseolus vulgaris humilis*, low-growing, bushy and not inclined to vine.

bush·buck, bush′buk″, *n.* A small antelope, *Tragelaphus scriptus*, found in wooded and bushy areas of South Africa having spirally twisted horns, a reddish body, and streaked with harnesslike white markings; any of several related species. Also **bosch·bok**, bosh′bok.

bush clo·ver, *n.* Any plant of the fabaceous genus *Lespedeza*, allied to the clover.

bushed, busht, *a.* Covered with bushes; lost in the bush; hence, bewildered. *Colloq.* exhausted; worn out.

bush·el, bush′l, *n.* [O.Fr. *boissiel* (Fr. *boisseau*), dim. < M.L. *buxta*, for *buxis*, box: see *box*.] A dry measure containing 4 pecks, equivalent in the U.S. to 2,150.42 cubic inches and in Great Britain to 2219.36 cubic inches; a vessel of this capacity; *colloq.* an indefinitely large quantity.

bush·el, bush′l, *v.t., v.i.*—**busheled**, **busheling**, **bushelled**, **bushelling.** [Origin uncertain.] To do low-grade work; to alter or repair, as garments.—**bush·el·er**, **bush·el·ler**, **bush·el·man**, *n.* A tailor's assistant who does altering or repairing.

bu·shi·do, bō′shē·da, *n.* [Valuing honor over life, Jap. "military knight way."] The code of moral principles which the knights and warriors of feudal Japan were required to put into practice in all the circumstances and relations of life.

bush·ing, bush′ing, *n. Elect.* a lining for a hole used to guard passing conductors from short circuit or abrasion; *mach.* a removable metal tube or cylinder mounted in an opening, used to reduce the opening's size or serve as a guide and/or protector from abrasion.

bush league, n. Baseball slang, a professional sports league of a minor rank, usually a training and proving ground for promising players to go on to the major leagues.—a. Slang. Mediocre; amateurish.

bush lea·guer, n. Baseball slang, a player belonging to a minor league. Slang, an incompetent performer; a smalltime operator.

bush line, n. Canada, an airline organized to fly freight and passengers over the forests of northern Canada.

bush·man, bush'man, n. pl. **bush·men.** A woodsman; a settler in the bush or forest districts of a new country, as Australia; (cap.) an aborigine living near the Cape of Good Hope, Africa.

bush·mas·ter, bush'mas"tèr, bush'mäs"tèr, n. A viper, Lachesis mutus, of tropical America which is the largest New World venomous snake.

bush pi·lot, n. Canada, an aviator who regularly flies to the northern bush country.

bush·rang·er, bush'rān"jèr, n. One who lives in the woods; in Australia, a criminal, often an escaped convict, who lives by preying on wayfarers and robbing isolated dwellings in the bush; also bushwhacker.

bush tit, n. Titmouse of the genus Psaltriparus, found in western N. America, which builds long, hanging nests.

bush·whack, bush'hwak", bush'wak", v.i. To hack one's way through dense underbrush; to fight as a partisan.—v.t. To attack from ambush, as a bushwhacker.

bush·whack·er, bush'hwak"èr, bush'wak"èr, n. One accustomed to go about in bush country; a Confederate guerrilla in the American Civil War (a term used by the Federal forces); any guerrilla; a scythe for cutting bushes.—**bush·whack·ing,** n.

bush·y, bush'ē, a.—bushier, bushiest. Full of bushes; resembling a bush; thick and spreading, like a bush; shaggy, as hair.—**bush·i·ness,** bush'ē·nes, n.

bus·i·ly, biz'a·lē, adv. In a busy manner.

busi·ness, biz'nes, biz'nis, n. [Akin busyness.] Commercial activity engaged in as means of livelihood; a trade, profession, line, or occupation; a particular field of endeavor; a role or function extended over a considerable period of time; a task, assignment or chore extended over a limited period of time; something felt to be one's own affair, personal concern, responsibility or duty. Econ. activities of a person, partnership or corporation involved in commerce, manufacturing, or performing a service; transactions of those engaged in purchase or sale of commodities for a profit; a profit-seeking commercial or industrial enterprise; a firm, factory, or store; a building or locale where commercial or industrial work takes place. Theatr. the gestures and movements used by actors to help create atmosphere and interpret a part.—**get down to busi·ness,** to pay attention to serious matters and apply oneself.—**give (some·one) the busi·ness,** slang. To deal with severely; to harm, damage, disable, or destroy; to doublecross, cheat, or defraud.—**have no busi·ness,** to have no authority (to do something).—**mean busi·ness,** colloq. To resolve to do something; to accomplish with great purpose.—**mind one's own busi·ness,** to concern oneself with one's own affairs; to restrain oneself from meddling into other people's private matters.

busi·ness cy·cle, n. A sequence of regularly recurring periods of economic prosperity, recession, depression, and recovery.

busi·ness·like, biz'nis·līk", a. Suitable for, befitting, or conforming with the methods of business or trade; methodical; systematic.

busi·ness·man, biz'nis·man", n. pl. **busi·ness·men.** A man who is active in industry or commerce, esp. as an executive or entrepreneur.—**busi·ness·wom·an,** biz'nes·wu"man, n. pl. **busi·ness·wom·en.**

busk, busk, v.t. [Icel. būask, refl. of būa, make ready.] Chiefly Sc. To prepare; get ready; equip; dress.

busk, busk, n. [Fr. busc: origin uncertain.] A strip of wood, steel, whalebone, or other stiffening material placed in the front of a corset for support; dial. the whole corset.

busk, busk, n. [Gr. puskita, fast, fasting.] A Creek Indian festival, observed when the first corn became eatable, and celebrating the start of a new year.

bus·kin, bus'kin, n. [Appar. < O.Fr. bouzequin, brosequin, Fr. brodequin: cf. M.D. broseken, Sp. borcegui, It. borzacchino.] A half-boot, reaching halfway to the knee or higher and laced to the ankle; specif., the cothurnus of ancient Greek and Roman tragic actors, sometimes taken as a symbol of tragedy; pl., eccles. gold-threaded stockings belonging to a bishop's vestments; a bishop's sandals.—**bus·kined,** a. Wearing buskins; esp. wearing the buskins of tragedy; of or pertaining to tragedy; lofty or elevated, as language.

bus·man's hol·i·day, Colloq. a holiday spent by choice in an activity closely resembling one's daily occupation, as a bus driver taking a trip in his own car.

buss, bus, n. A hearty kiss.—v.t. To smack.

bust, bust, n. [Fr. buste, < It. busto.] The chest or breast; the bosom; the human head, shoulders, and breast, sometimes with the upper arms, as represented in sculpture.

bust, bust, n. Slang. A failure or flop; an economic recession or depression; a drinking bout or spree; a punch or blow to the face.

bust, bust, v.t. Slang. To burst: substandard; to cause financial ruin to; to discipline or break, as an animal; to strike suddenly; to arrest; milit. to lower in grade or rank.—v.i. To burst: substandard; to lack funds.

bus·tard, bus'tèrd, n. [O.Fr. bistarde, < L. avis tarda, "slow bird."] Any of various old-world birds of the family Otididæ allied to both the cranes and the plovers.

bus·tee, bus'tē, n. [< Hind. basti, a small inhabited area.] A small inhabited area in India having its own individuality, and distinct from other areas with reference to location, caste, or profession of its residents: usually inhabited by people from low-income groups.

bus·ter, bus'tèr, n. Colloq. one who or that which busts, bursts, or breaks up; as, a broncobuster, a trustbuster. Slang, something very big, striking, or remarkable of its kind; a big, dashing fellow; a bender; colloq. a small boy. Aust. a destructive southern wind; also **south·er·ly bus·ter.**

bus·tic, bus'tik, n. [Origin uncertain.] A tree, Dipholis salicifolia, of southern Florida and the West Indies, having a heavy, hard, close-grained wood.

bus·tle, bus'al, v.i.—bustled, bustling. [Cf. Icel. bustla, splash about, bustle.] To move or act with a great show of energy; stir about energetically; be in a busy commotion; to hasten.—v.t. To cause to bustle; force, drive, etc., by bustling.—**bus·tler,** n.—**bus·tling,** a.—**bus·tling·ly,** adv.

bus·tle, bus'al, n. [Origin unknown.] A gathering of material at the back of a skirt below the waist; a pad or wire framework worn about 1880 beneath the skirt of a woman's dress, expanding and supporting it behind.

bus·tle, bus'al, n. Activity with noise and agitation; stir; hurry-scurry; tumult.

bus·y, biz'ē, a.—busier, busiest. [O.E. bisig = D. bezig = L.G. besig.] Actively or attentively engaged; closely occupied; employed or in use; as, a busy telephone; having much business; constantly or habitually occupied; in constant motion or activity; full of or indicating activity or business; as, a busy season, a busy street; pursued or carried on energetically; as, a busy trade; officious; meddlesome; prying. Fussily ornamental; as, wallpaper with a busy pattern.

bus·y, biz'ē, v.t.—busied, busying. [O.E. bisgian.] Usu. refl. to keep engaged, active, or occupied.

bus·y·bod·y, biz'ē·bod"ē, n. pl. **bus·y·bod·ies.** A prying person who concerns himself with the affairs of others; a meddler.

bus·y·ness, biz'ē·nis, biz'ē·nes, n. The state or quality of being busy.

but, but, conj. Except or save; as, right but for one thing; anywhere but in America; unless; except that: often used with that, as: Nothing would do but that I should come in. On the contrary; nevertheless; as, famous but humble; without the circumstance that, as: It never rains but it pours. Otherwise; as, I cannot but hope. That; as, no question but he will win; that . . . not; as, not so fine a student but she could improve; were it not that, as: I would come in but that it is impossible. Unless, as: But he be dead he will hear you. Than, as: He no sooner left but he returned.

but, but, adv. [O.E. būtan, outside, < be, by, and outside, < ūt, out.] Only or merely; as: He is but a boy. Colloq. very; exceedingly; as, to leave but fast.

but, but, pron. But who; but that: as, No one but has his troubles.

but, but, prep. With the exception of; as: No one replied but me. Except; save; as: She talked of nothing but her new home.

but, but, n. An objection; as: He must go; no ifs or buts about it. Sc. the outer room of a house or the kitchen of a cottage.

bu·ta·di·ene, bū"ta·dī'ēn, n. Chem. a flammable colorless hydrocarbon gas, C_4H_6, that polymerizes readily, used chiefly in making synthetic rubber; also bivinyl.

bu·tane, bū'tān, bū·tān', n. Chem. a colorless flammable aliphatic hydrocarbon gas, C_4H_{10}, obtained from petroleum or natural gas, used principally for making a butadiene and as a fuel, also used as a refrigerant or a solvent.

bu·ta·nol, būt'a·nōl", būt'a·nąl", būt'a·nol, n. Butyl alcohol.

butch·er, buch'èr, n. [O.Fr. bochier (Fr. boucher), < boc, buc, he-goat; < Teut., and akin to E. buck.] One who slaughters animals, or dresses their flesh, for food or for market; one who deals in meat; formerly, a candy and fruit seller on a train. One guilty of killing indiscriminately or brutally; colloq. an unskillful or bungling worker.

butch·er, buch'èr, v.t. To slaughter, as animals, or dress, as meat, for market; to murder indiscriminately or brutally; colloq. to treat bunglingly, or spoil by bad work.—**butch·er·er,** n.

butch·er·bird, buch'èr·burd", n. Any of various shrikes of the genus Lanius, so-named because they impale their prey upon thorns; any bird of the genus Cracticus, found in Australia.

butch·er's-broom, buch'èrz·brōm", buch'èrz·brum", n. A stiff, spiny shrub, Ruscus aculeatus, belonging to the lily family, often made into brooms for sweeping butchers' blocks.

butch·er·y, buch'a·rē, n. pl. **butch·er·ies.** [O.Fr., Fr. boucherie.] Chiefly Brit., a slaughterhouse or butcher's shop; the trade or business of a butcher; the act of butchering animals for food; brutal slaughter; carnage.

bu·tene, bū′tēn, *n.* Normal butylene.

bu·te·o, bū′tē·ō″, *n.* Any of a genus, *Buteo,* of hawks that fly and circle at great height.

but·ler, but′lėr, *n.* [O.Fr. *butiller,* < M.L. *buticularius,* < *buticlua:* see *bottle.*] A manservant having charge of the wines and liquors in a household; the head male servant of a household.—**but·ler·ship,** *n.*—**but·ler·y,** *n.* pl. **but·ler·ies.** A butler's room or pantry; a buttery; a room where provisions, wines, and liquors are kept.

but·ler's pan·try, *n.* A room between a kitchen and a dining room equipped with a sink, counters for serving, and cabinets for storing glassware, china, and silver; a butlery.

butt, but, *n.* [O.Fr. *but,* goal, mark, *bout,* end, extremity, < *buter, bouter:* see *butt.* With later E. senses cf. Fr. *pied bot,* clubfoot, D. *bot,* blunt, G. *butt,* Dan. *but,* short and thick, stumpy.] Backstop of a target for archery practice; an erection on which this is placed; a mound or embankment to receive shots fired in rifle or gunnery practice or experiments; *pl.* a range for archery, rifle, or gunnery practice. An object of ridicule, scorn, or abuse. The end or extremity of anything, esp. the thicker, larger, or blunt end, as of a rifle, fishing-rod, whip handle, arrow, etc.; also **butt end.** An unused stub, as of a cigar; the trunk of a tree, esp. just above the root; the base of a leaf-stalk; *colloq.* a buttock or the buttocks. The end of a plank, timber, or plate, which exactly meets another endwise in a ship's side or bottom; the joint between two such pieces; a joint where two ends meet squarely; a hinge for a door or the like, secured to the butting parts instead of the adjacent sides; the thicker or hinder part of a hide or skin; the thick leather made from this.

butt, but, *v.t.* [O.Fr. *buter, bouter,* strike thrust, abut, touch < Teut.] To strike, thrust, or push, esp. with the head or horns. —*v.i.* To strike or push with head first; to pitch forward; to jut or project.

butt, but, *n.* A thrust or push with the head or horns.

butt, but, *v.t.* To place (a timber, etc.) with its end against something; join (planks, etc.) end to end; to cut off the rough ends of (boards, etc.).—*v.i.* To join at the end; abut, be contiguous; fit together end to end.

butt, but, *n.* [O.Fr. *botte, bote* (Fr. *botte*), = It. *botte,* < M.L. *butta, buttis,* vessel, cask.] A large cask, esp. for wine or ale; a measure of capacity equivalent to 108 imperial gallons; any cask or barrel.

butte, būt, *n.* [Fr. *butte,* hill, O.Fr. *bute,* mound bearing a butt to shoot at, fem. of *but:* see *butt.*] *Western U.S., Canada,* a conspicuous isolated hill or mountain rising abruptly.

but·ter, but′ėr, *n.* [O.E. *butere,* < L. *butyrum,* < Gr. *bouturon;* origin uncertain.] The fatty portion of milk, separating as a soft whitish or yellowish solid when milk or cream is agitated or churned, and processed for the table or cookery; any of various substances of similar consistency, as various metallic chlorides, and certain vegetable oils solid at ordinary temperatures; a soft, edible spread; as, peanut *butter,* apple *butter; fig.* gross flattery.

but·ter, but′ėr, *v.t.* To spread with butter; put butter on or in.—**but·ter up,** *colloq.* to flatter with the intent of gaining special considerations; wheedle.

but·ter-and-eggs, but′ėr·an·egz′, *n.* Any of certain plants whose flowers are of two shades of yellow, as the toadflax, *Linaria vulgaris.*

but·ter·ball, but′ėr·bạl″, *n.* A bufflehead; *colloq.* a plump person.

but·ter bean, *n.* A lima bean, especially in southern U.S.; a wax bean.

but·ter clam, *n.* Either of two big, flavorful clams, *Saxidomus ruttallii* and *S. giganteus,* found on the Pacific coast of N. America.

but·ter·cup, but′ėr·kup″, *n.* Any plant of the genus *Ranunculus,* typically with yellow cup-shaped flowers.

but·ter·fat, but′ėr·fat″, *n.* The fatty component of milk extracted to make butter, composed of glycerides, mainly butyrin, olein, or the liquid part of the fat, and palmitin.

but·ter·fin·gered, but′ėr·fing″gėrd, *a.* Apt to let things slip or fall through the fingers; careless; clumsy.—**but·ter·fin·gers,** *n.*

but·ter·fish, but′ėr·fish, *n.* Any of various fishes with a smooth, slippery coating; a small silvery food fish, *Poronotus triacanthus,* of the Atlantic coast of America.

but·ter·fly, but′ėr·flī, *n.* pl. **but·ter·flies.** [O.E. *buttorfleoge,* D. *botervlieg,* G. *butterfliege,* "butter fly"; perhaps originally used of a butter-colored (yellow) species.] Any of a group of diurnal lepidopterous insects, characterized by club-shaped antennae, a slender body with broad wings, often beautifully colored and patterned; anything that resembles a butterfly; a pretty, fragile creature; a showily dressed, trifling or giddy person.

but·ter·fly bush, *n.* A variety of shrub, *Buddleia,* having clusters of showy flowers that attract butterflies.

but·ter·fly fish, *n.* Any of various fishes suggestive of a butterfly in their brilliant coloring or in having winglike fins; as, the ocellated blenny, *Blennius ocellaris,* or any of the tropical marine fishes constituting the family *Chaetodontidae.*

but·ter·fly valve, *n.* A kind of clack valve, in which there are two lidlike semicircular flaps hinged to a common crosspiece; a valve in a pipe, consisting of a disk which turns on one of its diameters.

but·ter·fly weed, *n.* Either of two North American milkweeds, *Asclepias tuberosa* and *A. decumbens,* bearing orange-colored flowers; a prairie plant of western North America having scarlet flowers, *Gaura coccinea.*

but·ter·milk, but′ėr·milk″, *n.* [= D. *botermelk* = G. *buttermilch.*] The more or less acidulous liquid remaining after butter has been churned from milk.

but·ter·nut, but′ėr nut″, *n.* The souari nut; the American tree of the walnut family, *Juglans cinerea;* the edible nut of this tree; its wood, used in cabinetmaking; yellowish-brown homespun cloth dyed with butternut extract; a Confederate soldier of the Civil War.—**but·ter·nuts,** *n.* Trousers made of homespun cloth dyed with butternut.

but·ter·scotch, but′ėr·skoch, *n.* A hard candy deriving its flavor primarily from butter and brown sugar.—*a.* Having the flavor of this mixture.

but·ter tree, *n.* A tropical tree, native to Africa and Asia, with seeds which yield a butterlike oil.

but·ter·weed, but′ėr·wēd″, *n.* Any of various wild plants with yellow flowers; the horseweed, *Leptilon canadense;* a ragwort, *Senecio lobatus* and *S. galbellus.*

but·ter·wort, but′ėr·wụrt″, *n.* Any plant of the genus *Pinguicula,* comprising small herbs whose broad, flat leaves secrete a sticky substance which catches small insects.

but·ter·y, but′a·rē, *n.* pl. **but·ter·ies,** but′a·rēz. [O.Fr. *boterie* (cf. *boutier,* butler), < *bote, botte,* cask: see *butt.*] *Chiefly Brit.* a room in which wines and liquors are kept; a pantry; in some English colleges, a place where liquors, fruit, and other food or drink are kept for sale to students.

but·ter·y, but′a·rē, *a.* Of the nature of or resembling butter in consistency or appearance; containing or covered with butter; given to gross flattery.

butt hinge, *n.* A common door hinge: when the door is shut, the two halves are folded together, one half is on the frame of the door opening, and the other on the hanging stile or door itself.

butt joint, *n.* A joint between two pieces of wood or metal which meet or butt together without overlapping at this joining point.

but·tock, but′ak, *n. Usu. pl.* Either of the two fleshy protuberances forming the lower and back part of the human trunk; similarly in animals, the rump; *naut.* the convex aftermost portion of a ship's body above the water line.

but·ton, but′on, *n.* [O.Fr. *butun, boton* (Fr. *bouton*), akin to *buter, bouter,* thrust: see *butt.*] A knob, stud, or disk with holes or a shank for sewing or attaching to a garment, used generally for securing one part to another by passing through a buttonhole or a loop, but often merely for ornament; any of various objects of similar shape or function, as the knob fixed to the point of a fencing foil, or the knob or disk pressed to ring an electric bell; a bud or other protuberant part of a plant; a young or undeveloped mushroom; *metal.* in assaying, a small lump of metal found at the bottom of a crucible or cupel after fusion.—**not have all one's but·tons,** *slang,* to be abnormal or eccentric.—**on the but·ton,** *colloq.* exactly right.—**turn but·ton,** a piece of wood or metal, turning on a nail or screw fixed through its center, used to fasten a door, window, etc.

but·ton, but′on, *v.t.* To fasten with a button or buttons; to furnish with a button or buttons.—*v.i.* To be capable of being buttoned, as: His coat *buttons* in front.—**but·ton one's lip,** *slang,* remain silent.

but·ton·ball, but′on·bal, *n.* Buttonwood.

but·ton·bush, but′on·bụsh, *n.* A North American shrub, *Cephalanthus occidentalis,* with globular flower heads.

but·ton·hole, but′on·hōl″, *n.* The hole, loop, or slit through which a button is passed and fastened.

but·ton·hole, but′on·hōl″, *v.t.*—**buttonholed, buttonholing.** To sew with the buttonhole stitch; to insert buttonholes in; to seize by the buttonhole and detain in conversation.—**but·ton·hol·er, but·an·hol·er,** *n.*

but·ton·hole stitch, *n. Sewing,* a continuous looping stitch used to strengthen buttonhole edges; *embroidery,* a decorative stitch.

but·ton snake·root, *n.* A composite plant of the genus *Liatris,* which has a spiky rose-purple flower head; a bristly, coarse herb, *Eryngium yuccifolium,* of the carrot family.

but·ton·wood, but′an·wụd″, *n.* A tall, massive plane tree, *Platanus occidentalis,* yielding a useful timber, so called from its small pendulous fruit. Also *buttonball.*

but·ton·y, but′a·nē, *a.* Buttonlike; having many buttons.

but·tress, bu′tris, *n.* [O.Fr. *bouterez,* pl. of *bouteret,* adj. and *n.* (applied to arches and pillars), < *bouter,* thrust, abut: see *butt.*] *Arch.* a structure built against or projecting from a wall or building for the purpose of giving it stability; something resembling such a structure in use or appearance; a prop or support.

but·tress, bu′tris, *v.t.* To support by a buttress; to prop up; *fig.* to uphold or strengthen (a person, an argument, etc.), as: *Buttress* your opinions with facts.

butt shaft, *n.* A blunt or barbless arrow.

butt·stock, but′stok″, *n.* The firearm stock situated in back of the breech mechanism.

butt weld, *n.* A weld formed by joining the flattened ends of two pieces of metal at a white heat; a welded butt joint.

bu·tyl, bū′til, būt′l, *n.* [< *but(yric)* and -*yl.*] *Chem.* a univalent hydrocarbon radical, C_4H_9.

---

a- fat, fāte, fär, fâre, fạll;   e- met, mē, mēre, hėr;   i- pin, pīne;   o- not, nōte, mŏve;   u- tub, cūbe, bụll;   oi- oil;   ou- pound.

Bu·tyl, bū′til, būt′l, *n.* A synthetic rubber containing little butadiene, used esp. for inner tubes of tires due to its low permeability to gases. (Trademark.)

bu·tyl al·co·hol, *n. Chem.* any one of several chemically related forms of alcohol containing the butyl radical, used for manufacturing lacquers, perfumes, fruit essences, and other organic compounds. Also *butanol.*

bu·tyl·ene, būt′a·lēn″, *n. Chem.* any of three gaseous isomeric hydrocarbons, C_4H_8, belonging to the ethylene series. Also *butene.*—*a.* Containing a butylene group.

bu·tyr·a·ceous, bū″ta·rā′shus, *a.* [< L. *butyrum*, butter.] Having the qualities of butter; resembling butter.

bu·tyr·al·de·hyde, bū″ta·ral′da·hīd″, *n. Chem.* an aldehyde, C_3H_7CHO, used in resins for making safety glass.

bu·ty·rate, bū′ta·rāt″, *n. Chem.* the ester or salt of butyric acid.

but·tyr·ic, bū·tir′ik, *a. Chem.* Of or pertaining to butyric acid.

bu·ty·ric ac·id, *n. Chem.* an isomeric fatty acid, C_3H_7COOH, found in butter in glyceride form, obtained by oxidation of butyl alcohol and used as a basic material for manufacturing flavorings and some plastics.

bu·ty·rin, bū′tér·in, *n. Chem.* a yellowish liquid fat present in butter, formed from glycerin and butyric acid.

bux·om, buk′som, *a.* [O.E. *būhsom*, compliant, obedient, < *būgan*, to bend, to *bow.*] Amply proportioned, esp. full-bosomed, said of a woman. *Archaic,* cheerful; lively; *archaic,* submissive.—**bux·om·ly**, *adv.* In a buxom manner; briskly; vigorously.—**bux·om·ness**, *n.*

buy, bī, *n.* Something purchased or to be purchased. *Colloq.* a bargain.—**buy·a·ble**, *a.*

buy, bī, *v.t.*—*bought, buying.* To acquire possession of, esp. by paying money; purchase; hire; bribe. *Slang,* to accept (a statement) as true; accept (a plan, proposition) as agreeable, as: I will *buy* that suggestion.—*v.i.* To make a purchase or purchases.—**buy on right**, to buy on a 100% cash basis, as merchandise: opposed to *on credit,* or securities, as opposed to *on margin.*

buy·er, bī′ér, *n.* One who buys; a purchaser; the head of a department in a retail store; one employed to· make purchases of equipment or supplies.

buy off, *v.t.* To obtain release from, as a responsibility, by a payment; to get rid of, as opposition or intervention, by a bribe.

buy out, *v.t.* To purchase the share or shares of, as a person, in a commercial concern.

buzz, buz, *v.i.* [Imitative.] To make a continuous humming sound such as that of bees; to speak in a low humming tone; make an indistinct murmuring sound, as a number of people talking together; be filled with such a sound, as a place; be uttered with a murmur, as words; fly or hover with or as with such a sound; to move about busily.—*v.t.* To utter or express in a murmur or whisper; spread with busy talk; to cause to buzz; to call or signal with a buzzer; to fly, as a plane, quickly over an area at a very low altitude; *slang,* to telephone.—**buzz off** or **buzz a·long**, *slang,* to go; to depart, esp. from a social gathering.

buzz, buz, *n.* A continuous humming sound such as that of bees; a confused humming sound, as of a number of people busily engaged in conversation; the sound of bustling activity; hence, a state of activity or excitement; a report or rumor; *slang,* a phone call. A summons conveyed by buzzer; a signal by flying a plane low. *Brit.* a large bushy wig; a burr; a fuzzy fly used in fishing.

buz·zard, buz′érd, *n.* [O.Fr. *busart* (Fr. *busard*), < *buse,* buzzard, < L. *buteo,* kind of hawk.] Any of various sluggish, heavily built birds, genus *Buteo,* of the hawk family; the turkey buzzard. *Slang,* a cantankerous old man; a humorous form of address between young men.

buzz bomb, *n.* An aerial projectile which steers itself, launched mainly against England by the Germans during World War II; robot bomb; guided missile.

buzz·er, buz′ér, *n.* One who or that which buzzes; a device, esp. an electrical one, for making a buzzing noise as a signal.

buzz saw, *n.* A small circular power saw, named for the sound it makes.

by, bī, *prep.* [O.E. *bī, be,* = G. *bei,* by, near; perhaps akin to L. *ambi-,* Gr. *amphi-,* about, Skt. *abhi,* to.] Beside or near; in the direction of; as, east *by* south; not later than; as, *by* six o'clock; through the means of, or efficacy of; begot or born of; with the witness of; according to; as, to learn *by* rote; in relation to; to the amount or extent of; separately with; as, two *by* two; combined with in multiplication or measuring relative dimensions; as, four feet *by* six feet.

by, bī, *adv.* Near, or at hand; as, close *by*; past, in place or time; as, days gone *by*; aside or away; as, to put or lay a thing *by*.

by, bye, bī, *a.* Situated to one side or in an out-of-the-way place; hence, secondary to the main point.

by, bye, bī, *n.* In sporting use, commonly spelled *bye.* Something aside from the main course or consideration; a sportsman in a tournament who is without an opponent; *golf,* the holes of a stipulated course remaining to be played after the match is finished; *cricket,* a run made on a ball not struck by the batsman and missed by the wicket keeper.

by and by, *adv.* Before long; after a while.

by and large, *adv.* In every aspect; on the whole; in general.

by-blow, bī′blō″, *n.* A side or accidental blow.—**bye-blow**, *Brit.* an illegitimate child.

by-e·lec·tion, bī′i·lek″shan, *n. Brit., Canadian,* a special local election to replace a Member of Parliament or of the Legislative Assembly.

by·gone, bī′gän″, bī′gon″, *a.* Past; former; departed; out of date.—*n.* That which is past.

by·law, bī′la̲, *n.* A standing rule of an organized group, created for the regulation of its internal organization and the governing of its members. *Brit.* a local law or ordinance enacted by a municipality or other community.

by-line, bī′lin″, *n. Journalism,* the author's name printed with a news story, column, or feature article in a newspaper or magazine.

by-name, bī′nām″, *n.* A secondary name or appellation; a cognomen or surname; a nickname.

by-pass, bī′pas″, bī′päs″, *n.* A detour; a secondary route or passage which avoids congested or obstructed areas; a secondary pipe or other channel for conducting a fluid around an obstruction and back to the main passage; *elect.* a shunt.

by-pass, bī′pas″, bī′päs″, *v.t.* To take a secondary route around; to avoid, as an obstacle; to intentionally ignore or sidestep, as a superior's feelings or decisions on a matter.

by-past, bī′past″, bī′päst″, *a.* Bygone; past.

by-path, bī′path″, bī′päth″, *n.* A path, road, street, or way which is secondary to a main road or street; a lesser, private, or obscure way. Also **by-street.**

by-play, bī′plā″, *n.* Action or speech carried on aside while the main action proceeds, esp. on the stage; something apart from the main purpose.

by-prod·uct, bī′prod″ukt, *n.* A secondary product; something obtained, as in a manufacturing process, in addition to the principal product or material; a minor and often unforeseen and inadvertent consequence.

byre, bīr, *n.* [A Scandinavian word = E. *bower.*] *Brit.* a cow barn.

by-road, bī′rōd″, *n.* A side road; a road other than the main or usual road.

By·ron·ic, bī·ron′ik, *a.* Of or pertaining to Lord Byron, 1788–1824, the English poet; possessing the characteristics of Byron or his poetry; gloomy; ardent; sentimental.—**By·ron·i·cal·ly**, *adv.*—**By·ron·ism**, bī′ron·iz″um, *n.*

bys·sus, bis′as, *n.* pl. **bys·si**, bis′ī. [L., < Gr. *byssos.*] Among the ancients, a fine yellowish flax, or the linen made from it, as the Egyptian mummy-cloth; later, also, cotton or silk; *zool.* a collection of silky filaments by which certain mollusks, like mussels, attach themselves to rocks.

by·stand·er, bī′stan″dér, *n.* An onlooker or spectator; one present but taking no part in what is going on.

byte, bīt, *n. Computer,* a sequence of binary digits operated upon as a unit and almost always shorter than a word.

by the by, *adv.* By the side, rather than the main way or course; aside from the main point or subject; incidentally speaking.

by the way, *adv.* Incidentally: used as an aside, in passing.

by·way, bī′wā″, *n.* A way other than the highway; a by-road; an unfrequented, secluded, or obscure road; a little-known field of research.

by·word, bī′wᵤrd″, *n.* [O.E. *biword.*] A proverb or proverbial saying; a person or thing that becomes proverbial as a type; esp., an object of derision or contempt; a nickname, esp. one of scorn.

Byz·an·tine, biz′an·tēn″, biz′an·tīn″, bi·-zan′tin, *n.* A native or inhabitant of Byzantium or Constantinople, esp. as the capital of the Byzantine Empire. Also **By·zan·ti·an**, bi·zan′shan.

Byz·an·tine, biz′an·tēn″, biz′an·tīn″, bi·-zan′tin, *a.* Of or pertaining to Byzantium, an ancient city, afterward Constantinople, which became the capital of the Eastern Roman Empire; noting or pertaining to the Eastern Empire after the fall of the Western Empire in A.D. 476; characteristic of a style of art developed in Byzantium; *arch.* noting or pertaining to a style developed from the classical under the Eastern or Byzantine Empire, characterized by the round arch, the cross, the circle, the dome supported on pendentives, and rich mosaic decoration. *Relig.* concerning the Eastern Orthodox Church; as, the *Byzantine* rite. Also **By·zan·ti·an**, bi·zan′shan.

C

C, c, sē, the third letter in the English alphabet and the second of the consonants, originally having the sound of *k,* now having also the sharp sound of *s* (before *e, i,* and *y*). (Cap.) *mus.* the name of the first or key note of the modern normal scale, answering to the *do* of the Italians and the *ut* of the French. The third in a series; in school grading systems, a mark usually indicating average or mediocre work; the Roman numeral for 100. (*l.c.*) abbr. for *calorie*; *math.* the cardinal number of the set of all real numbers; circa, about.

CAA, C.A.A., *n.* Abbr. for Civil Aeronautics Administration.

Caa·ba, kä′ba, kä′a·ba, *n.* Kaaba.

CAB, C.A.B., *n.* Abbr. for Civil Aeronautics Board.

cab, kab, *n.* [Fr. lit. *leap of a goat* (from the supposed lightness of movement) < It. *caprio*, goat < L. *caper*, goat.] A passenger automobile available for public hire, usually equipped with a meter which registers the fare; a taxicab; a horse-drawn vehicle, such as the hansom, available for public hire to convey passengers; in a locomotive, the roofed compartment for the engineer; in a truck, the roofed compartment for the driver.

ca·bal, ka·bal′, *n.* [< L. *cabbal(a)* < Heb. *qabbālāh*, tradition; lit. something received.] A number of persons secretly united in some intrigue, as to promote a private view or to usurp authority; the artifices and plots of such persons; intrigue.—*v.i. caballed, caballing.* To form a cabal; to intrigue.

cab·a·la, kab′a·la, ka·bä′la, *n.* [M.L. *cabbala.*] A system of esoteric theosophy based on a mystical interpretation of the scriptures, which was developed among Jewish rabbis during the 6th century A.D. and originally handed down by oral tradition, being adopted by certain Christian mystics in the Middle Ages; hence any occult or secret doctrine or science. Also **cab·ba·la, kab·a·la, kab·ba·la.**—**cab·a·lism,** kab′a·liz″um, *n.*—**cab·a·list,** kab′a·list, *n.*—**cab·a·lis·tic,** kab′a·lis′tik, *a.* Also **cab·a·lis·ti·cal, ca·ba·lic,** ka·bal′ik.—**cab·a·lis·ti·cal·ly,** *adv.*

ca·bal·le·ro, kab″al·yâr′ō, kab″a·lâr′ō, *Sp.* kä″vä·lye′Rą, *n.* *pl.* **ca·bal·le·ros.** [Sp. lit., 'horseman.'] A Spanish gentleman; in southwestern U.S., a horseman; an escort.

ca·ba·na, ka·ban′a, ka·ban′ya, ka·bä′na, ka·bän′ya, *n.* [< Sp. *cabaña*, cabin < L.L. *capanna*, hut.] A cabin or very small house, as at a summer resort; a bathhouse, on a beach or beside a swimming pool.

ca·bane, ka·ban′, *n.* [< Fr. < M.Fr. *caban(a)*, cabin < L.L. *capanna*, hut.] A framework of struts attached to the top of the fuselage of early airplanes for supporting a wing.

cab·a·ret, kab″a·rā′, kab′a·ret″, *n.* [Fr. < O.Fr. < probable irreg. L.L. *camera*, chamber.] A tavern; a restaurant providing entertainment; a floor show provided by the restaurant or night club.

cab·bage, kab′ij, *n.* [< Fr. *caboche*, great head < L. *caput*, head with augmentative suffix.] Any of various cultivated varieties of the cruciferous plant,*Brassica oleracea,* esp. one of the ordinary varieties with short stem and leaves formed into a compact, edible head, but in a wider sense including also such plants as the cauliflower, Brussels sprouts, kale, etc.; the head of the ordinary cabbage; any of various similar plants; also, the terminal bud of certain palms.—*v.i.*—*cabbaged, cabbaging.* To form a head like a cabbage.

cab·bage, kab′ij, *n. Brit.* something purloined, as a customer's cloth by a tailor.

cab·bage, kab′ij, *n. Slang,* paper money.

cab·bage but·ter·fly, *n.* A white or whitish butterfly, *Pieris rapae,* of the family *Pieridae,* the larvae of which feed on cabbage leaves.

cab·bage palm, *n.* Any palm, as *Sabal palmetto,* having an edible leaf bud.

cab·bage pal·met·to, *n.* A variety of cabbage palm, *Sabal palmetto,* which grows in the coastal areas of southern U.S.

cab·bage rose, *n.* A rose, *Rosa centifolia,* with a large, round, compact, pink flower.

cab·bage·town, kab′ij·toun, *n. Canada,* a run-down urban slum area.

cab·bage tree, *n.* Any of several palm trees with large terminal leaf buds which are eaten like cabbage, as *Livistona australis* or *L. inermis,*of Australasia, *Inodes palmetto,*of the southern U.S., or *Oreodoxa oleracea,* of the West Indies; any of certain other

trees and plants, as the Australasian tree, *Nuytsia floribunda,*or the tropical American tree,*Vouacapoua americana.*

cab·bage·worm, kab′ij·wurm″, *n.* A caterpillar, esp. of the genus *Pieris,* that feeds on cabbage leaves.

cab·ba·la, kab′a·la, ka·bä′la, *n.* Cabala.

cab·by, kab′ē, *n. pl.* **cab·bies.** *Colloq.* cab driver.

ca·ber, kä′bėr, *n.* [< Gael. *cabar*, rafter.] *Sc.* a pole or young tree trunk, esp. one used for tossing as a trial of strength in the Highland exercise or game, 'tossing the caber.'

cab·in, kab′·in, *n.* [O.Fr. *cabane,* < M.L. *capanna.*] A small rude house; a hut; any small room or enclosed space; a temporary room or cell; a room in a plane or ship for officers or passengers; in a passenger ship, a section for the use of passengers, sometimes called first class or second class according to the quality of accommodations; passenger space in a cable car or aerial tramway; a forerunner of a motel room or apartment.

cab·in, kab′in, *v.t.* To confine in a limited space.—*v.i.* To live in a cabin.

cab·in boy, *n.* A boy employed to wait on officers and passengers of a ship.

cab·in class, *n.* A type of accommodations for passengers on some ships, costing less and providing fewer luxuries than first class.

cab·i·net, kab′i·nit, *n.* [Fr. dim. of *cabane,* cabin.] A piece of furniture consisting of a chest or box, with drawers and doors; a cupboard with shelves and doors; a console, esp. one which houses a television or radio receiving set; the select council of an executive government. (*Often cap.*) the collective body of ministers who direct the government of a nation or country, so called from the apartment in which the meetings were originally held.—*a.* Relating to a political cabinet; private; confidential; appropriate by virtue of beauty or value for a cabinet, or by virtue of size for a small, private room; of, relating to, or suitable for use or in cabinetmaking.

cab·i·net·mak·er, kab′i·nit·mā″kėr, *n.* A man whose occupation is making furniture. —**cab·i·net·mak·ing,** *n.*

cab·i·net·work, kab′i·nit·wurk″, *n.* Woodwork of fine quality, such as in furniture construction or shelving.

cab·in pres·sure, *n.* The air pressure in an aircraft cabin.

ca·ble, kä′bl, *n.* [O.Fr. *cable* (Fr. *cable*). M.L. *capulum,* halter, < L. *capere*, take.] A thick, strong rope of hemp, more than 10 inches in circumference; a thick wire rope; the rope or chain used to hold a vessel at anchor or for supporting the roadway of a suspension bridge; an electrical conductor composed of a number of separately insulated wires twisted together; an electrical line under water for dispatching telegraph messages; a cablegram; cable length; something designed with a twist characteristic of a cable.

ca·ble, kä′bl, *v.t.*—*cabled, cabling.* To furnish with a cable; fasten with or as with a cable; to transmit by underwater telegraph cable.—*v.i.* To send a message by underwater telegraph cable.

ca·ble car, *n.* A car used to transport passengers on a cable railroad or cableway.

ca·ble·gram, kä′bl·gram″, *n.* A telegram sent overseas by underwater cable.

ca·ble-laid, kä′bl·lād″, *a.* Pertaining to a pattern of rope formed by three ropes of three strands each, laid together with a left-handed twist. Also *hawser-laid.*

ca·ble length, *n.* A nautical unit of length, figured as either 100 or 120 fathoms, or 608 feet in England, 720 feet in the U.S. Also **ca·ble's length.**

ca·ble rail·road, *n.* A railroad used esp. to ascend steep grades, on which the cars

are pulled by gripping an endless moving cable laid under the roadway and powered by a stationary motor.

ca·ble-stitch, *n.* A stitch used in knitting resulting in a raised, twisted, cablelike pattern.

ca·ble·way, kä′bl·wā″, *n.* A conveying apparatus for passengers or materials in which one or two wire cables suspended between two structures serves as an overhead track along which carriers are pulled.

ca·bob, ka·bob′, *n.* [Fr.] Kabob.

cab·o·chon, kab′a·shon″, *Fr.* ka·bą·shąn′, *n.* [< Fr. *caboche*, head.] A precious stone of convex rounded form which has been polished but not cut into facets; a small motif resembling this, used as ornamentation on certain period furniture.

ca·boo·dle, ka·böd′l, *n.* [*ca*-(?) and < D. *boedel,* stock, lot.] *Slang,* the whole lot, pack, or crowd.

ca·boose, ka·bös′, *n.* [prob. < D. *kabuis,* cook's cabin.] The last car of a freight train, used chiefly by the crew; *Brit.* a ship's galley, esp. a deckhouse where cooking is done.

cab·o·tage, kab′a·tij, *Fr.* ka·bą·tazh′, *n.* [Fr. deriv. of *caboter,* to sail along the coast, prob. < Sp. *cabo,* cape, promontory, < L. *caput*, head.] Coastwise navigation; *avi.* the carrying of cargo or passengers within the borders of a given nation, as restricted by law.

ca·bret·ta, ka·bret′a, *n.* [< Sp. *cabra,* goat.] A sheepskin of especially tough quality used in the making of shoes and gloves.

ca·bril·la, ka·bril′a, *n.* [Sp. *cabra,* goat and dim. suffix -*illa.*] Any of several sea basses, esp. *Epinephelus analogus.*

cab·ri·ole, kab′rē·ōl, *Fr.* ka·bRē·ąl′, *n.* [See *cabriolet;* from resemblance to the leg of a leaping goat.] A gracefully curving form of furniture leg, often terminating in an animal's paw or other ornamental finish, used for chairs and other articles of furniture, and found in Queen Anne and Chippendale design; a ballet leap.

cab·ri·o·let, kab′rē·o·lā′, *n.* [Fr. lit. *light caper,* < resemblance to light movement.] Orig., a light, hooded one-horse carriage with two wheels and a single seat; a cab; a type of automobile somewhat like a convertible, with a folding top.

cab·stand, kab′stand″, *n.* A place where taxicabs wait for public hire.

ca'can·ny, kä·kan′ē, ką·kan′ē, *n. Brit. slang,* a deliberate slack in production pace or output by workers as a form of protest.

ca·ca·o, ka·kā′ō, ka·kä′ō, *n.* [Sp. < Nahuatl, *cacahuatl,* seed of the cacao.] A small evergreen tree, *Theobroma cacao,* a native of tropical America, cultivated for its seeds, which are used in making cocoa and chocolate; the seeds of this tree.

ca·ca·o but·ter, *n.* Cocoa butter.

cach·a·lot, kash′a·lot″, kash′a·lō″, *n.* [Prob. < dial. Fr., origin uncertain.] The sperm whale, having a head of enormous size, containing a large receptacle filled with spermaceti: sperm oil and ambergris are obtained from this animal.

cache, kash, *n.* [< Fr. deriv. of *cache(r),* hide.] A hiding place, esp. one in the ground, for hiding a store of provisions; the provisions or other items so hidden.

cache, kash, *v.t.*—*cached, caching.* To put in a cache; conceal or hide away.

cache·pot, kash′pot″, kash′pō″, *n.* [< Fr. *cache(r),* hide, and pot.] An ornamental plant holder of tublike form, large enough to hold and conceal a flower pot.

ca·chet, ka shā′, kash′ā, *Fr.* ka shé′, *n.* [< Fr. *cache(r),* hide and suffix -*et.*] A seal, as on a letter; characteristic mark conveying prestige; a message or design on an envelope marking a philatelic or postal event; a slogan forming part of a postal cancellation; *phar.* a hollow wafer for enclosing an ill-tasting medicine.

cach·o·long, kash′ō·long, *n.* [Possibly from native Mongolian name in Kalmuck.] A variety of opal, usually milky white.

ca·chou, ka·shö′, ka·shö′, *n.* [Fr., < Malay *kāccu,* catechu.] Catechu; a pill or pastille for sweetening the breath.

ca·chu·cha, ka·chö′cha, *n.* [Sp. Andalusian dance; origin uncertain.] A lively Spanish solo dance in three-quarter time, similar to the bolero; a piece of music for it.

ca·cique, ka·sēk′, *n.* [Sp. Amer. tribal leader.] A native Indian chief of Mexico or the West Indies; a local head politician in Spain and South America; any of various tropical American orioles.

cack·le, kak′l, *v.i.*—**cackled, cackling.** [D. and L.G. *kakelen,* Sw. *kackla,* Dan. *kagle*; of imitative origin.] To utter a shrill noisy cry such as that often made by a goose or a hen after laying an egg; to laugh with a broken noise, like the cackling of a goose; as, an evil *cackling* witch; to giggle; to prate; to prattle; to tattle.—*n.* The broken cry of a goose or hen; idle talk; silly prattle.—**cack·ler,** kak′lêr, *n.*

cac·o·ë·thes, kak″ō·ē′thēz, *n.* [L., < Gr. *kakoethes,* < *kakos,* bad and *ethos,* habit.] A strong compulsion; mania; a bad habit, as of incessant talking.

cac·o·gen·e·sis, kak″a·jen′a·sis, *n.* [< Gr. *kakó(s),* bad, and (*eu*)*genics.*] The degeneration of a race, esp. as caused by the breeding of members having inferior hereditary qualities.

ca·cog·ra·phy, ka·kog′ra·fē, *n.* [< Gr. *kakos,* bad, and *graphy* < Gr. *graphein,* mark, draw, write.] Bad handwriting, as opposed to *calligraphy*; bad spelling, as opposed to *orthography.*—**ca·cog·ra·pher,** *n.*—**cac·o·graph·ic, cac·o·graph·i·cal,** kak″o·graf′ik, *a.*

ca·col·o·gy, ka·kol′o·jē, ka·kol′o·je, *n.* [*caco* < Gr. *kakos,* bad, and *logy* < Gr. *logos,* speaking.] Bad choice of words; faulty diction; bad pronunciation.

cac·o·mis·tle, cac·o·mix·l, kak′o·mis″l, *n.* [Mex.] A carnivorous animal, *Bassariscus astutus,* of Mexico and the southwestern U.S., resembling the racoon but slenderer and with a sharper snout and longer tail; its fur. Also **ring-tailed cat.**

ca·coph·o·nist, kak″a·fon′ist, *n.* [From *cacophony.*] A composer or an admirer of music marked by dissonances.

ca·coph·o·nous, ka·kof′o·nus, *a.* [Gr. *kakophonos* < *kakos,* bad, and *phone,* sound.] Harsh-sounding; discordant.—**ca·coph·o·nous·ly,** *adv.*

ca·coph·o·ny, ka·kof′a·nē, *n.* pl. **ca·coph·o·nies.** [Gr. *kakophonia,* < *kakophonos.*] Dissonance; harsh sound; an inharmonious combination of sounds; *mus.* the recurrent use of discord.

cac·ta·ceous, kak·tā′shus, *a.* Belonging to the *Cactaceæ,* or cactus family of plants.

cac·toid, kak′toid, *a.* Resembling the cactus.

cac·tus, kak′tus, *n.* pl. **cac·tus·es, cac·ti,** kak′tī. [L. < Gr. *kaktos,* kind of prickly plant.] Any of various fleshy-stemmed plants of the family *Cactaceæ,* usually leafless and spiny, and often producing showy flowers, chiefly natives of hot and dry regions.

ca·cu·mi·nal, ka·kū′mi·nl, *a.* [L. *cacumen* (*cacumin-*), top.] *Phonetics,* pertaining to a sound produced by the tip of the tongue curled back to a point of contact with the hard palate.—*n.* A cacuminal sound.

cad, kad, *n.* [Prob. short for *caddie.*] An ungentlemanly person, esp. in his behavior toward women; a bounder; *Brit.* at Oxford University, formerly a townsman.

ca·das·tre, ca·das·ter, ka·das′tër, *n.* [Fr. *cadastre,* a survey and valuation of property, < L.L. *capitastrum,* register for a poll tax, < L. *caput,* the head.] An official register or survey of the worth, amount, and proprietorship of an area's real estate, used in assessing taxes.—**ca·das·tral,** *a.*

ca·dav·er, ka·dav′ėr, ka·dā′vėr, *n.* [L. *cadāver,* corpse < *cadere,* to fall, perish.] A dead body, esp. of a human being used for dissection; a corpse.—**ca·dav·er·ic,** *a.*

ca·dav·er·ous, ka·dav′ėr·us, *a.* Pertaining to a dead body; esp. having the appearance or color of a dead human body; pale; wan; ghastly; emaciated.—**ca·dav·er·ous·ly,** *adv.*—**ca·dav·er·ous·ness,** *n.*

cad·die, cad·dy, kad′ē, *n.* [< cadet.] A person paid to carry clubs and otherwise assist a golfer; *Scot.* one who does odd jobs, as an errand boy. A small conveyance for wheeling items not easily carried by hand.—*v.i.* To serve as a caddie.

cad·dis, cad·dice, kad′is, kä′dis, *n.* [M.E. *cadas,* cotton wool.] A coarse woolen fabric; worsted yarn; worsted ribbon or binding.

cad·dis, cad·dice, kad′is, kä′dis, *n.* Caddis-worm.

cad·dis·fly, kad′is·flī″, *n.* pl. **cad·dis·flies.** Any of various mothlike insects of the order *Trichoptera,* with four membranous, more or less hairy wings: a term usually applied to the adult insect in contradistinction to the caddisworm.

cad·dish, kad′ish, *a.* Unprincipled; like a cad; ungentlemanly.—**cad·dish·ly,** *adv.*—**cad·dish·ness,** *n.*

cad·dis·worm, kad′is·wụrm″, *n.* The caddisfly's aquatic larvae, used as fishing bait, that build and inhabit silky cases covered with sand or plant debris.

cad·dy, kad′ē, *n.* pl. **cad·dies.** [= *catty.*] A small box, can, or chest for keeping small items; esp. one for holding tea.

cade, kād, *n.* [Fr. < Provençal.] A big, bushy juniper, *Juniperus oxycedrus,* of the Mediterranean region, whose wood yields a brown oily liquid ('oil of cade') used in the treatment of skin maladies.

cade, kād, *a.* [Origin unknown.] Of an animal's offspring, abandoned by the mother and brought up by human beings; as, a cade lamb.

ca·delle, ka·del′, *n.* A black beetle, *Tenebroides mauritanicus,* that feeds on stored grain.

ca·dence, kād′ens, *n.* [L.L. *cadentia,* a falling, < L. *cado,* to fall. *Chance* is the same word.] A smooth, rhythmic succession of words or sounds, as in oratory or poetry; the measure, tempo, or beat of a rhythmical movement, as in marching; the general tone or modulation of the voice in reading or reciting; a falling intonation of the voice. *Mus.* a short progression of notes or chords signifying the close of a musical passage or phrase; a cadenza.

ca·dent, kād′ant, *a.* Having cadence.—**ca·denced,** *a.*

ca·den·za, ka·den′za, *n.* [It.] *Mus.* a flourish or elaborate passage for exhibiting a soloist's musical skill, brought in toward the close of an aria or a movement in a concerto.

ca·det, ka·det′, *n.* [Fr. *cadet,* O.Fr. *capdet,* chief, < L.L. *capitettum,* dim. of L. *caput,* the head; lit. little head or chief.] A student in training for the rank of an officer in the army or navy service academies: a cadet of the U.S. Naval Academy at Annapolis is officially called a *midshipman.* A junior male member of a noble family; the younger or youngest son; *slang,* a pimp.—**ca·det·ship,** ka·det′ship, *n.* The state of being a cadet; the rank or office of cadet.

cadge, kaj, *v.t.*—**cadged, cadging.** [Perhaps < noun *cadger.*] To obtain, as meals, drinks, or the like, at another's expense

with no intention of repaying.—*v.i.* To profit by imposing on another's hospitality or generosity; to sponge; to beg.

cadg·er, kaj′ėr, *n.* [Possibly < O.Fr. *cagier,* one who carried about catches or other birds in a *cage* for sale.] One who sponges or imposes upon others.

Cad·me·an, kad·mē′an, *a.* [< L. *Cadmēus* < Gr. *Kadmeios.*] Relating to Cadmus, a legendary prince of ancient Greece credited with the founding of Thebes, and with the introduction of the 16 simple letters of the Greek alphabet, thence called *Cadmean* letters.—**Cad·me·an vic·to·ry,** a victory in which the victors suffer as much as the vanquished.

cad·mi·um, kad′mē·um, *n.* [N.L. < L. *cadmia,* < Gr. *kadmeia,* calamin (with which cadmium is usually associated).] *Chem.* A white, ductile metallic element resembling tin in appearance: used in the manufacture of certain alloys, in plating of metals and metal wires for rust-proofing, in the nickel-cadmium storage battery, as a barrier in the control of atomic fission, and in miscellaneous manufactured products. Sym. Cd, at. no. 48. See Periodic Table of Elements.—**cad·mic,** *a.*

ca·dre, ka′dra, *milit.* kad′rē, *n.* [Fr., frame, < L. *quadrum,* a square.] A specially trained group of key personnel who can capably assume direction and training of others. *Milit.* framework of a regiment; a nucleus of officers.

ca·du·ce·us, ka·dö′sē·us, *n.* pl. **ca·du·ce·i,** ka·dö′sē·ī.″[L. < Gr. *kerukeion,* < *kerux,* herald.] The emblem of the medical profession and the insignia of the U.S. Army medical corps; *mythol.* the wand borne by Mercury, or Hermes, as a messenger of the gods.—**ca·du·ce·an,** *a.*

ca·du·ci·ty, ka·dö′si·tē, ka·dū′si·tē, *n.* [See *caducous.*] Tendency to fall; frailty; the infirmity of old age; senility.

ca·du·cous, ka·dö′kus, ka·dū′kus, *a.* [L. *caducus,* perishable < *cad(ere)* to fall and *ūcus,* adjectival suffix.] Having a tendency to fall quickly: specifically applied to organs of animals and plants that drop off early or easily, such as branchiae or floral envelopes; perishable.

cae·no·gen·e·sis, sē″na·jen′i·sis, sen″a·jen′i·sis, *n.* Cenogenesis.

caes·al·pin·i·a·ceous, sez″al·pin″ē·ā′shus, ses″al·pin″ē·ā′shus, *a.* [N.L. *Cæsalpinia,* the typical genus; named for Andrea Cesalpino (1519–1603), Italian botanist.] Belonging to the *Caesalpiniaceae,* a family of leguminous plants including the cassia and senna plants, honey locust, Judas tree, carob, copaiba, logwood, and tamarind.

Cae·sar, sē′zėr, *n.* [Gaius Julius Caesar, 100–44 B.C., Roman general, statesman, and historian.] The title of the emperor of Rome from Augustus to Hadrian, later applied to the heirs presumptive; any emperor or despot.—**Cae·sar·e·an, Cae·sar·i·an,** sē·zâ′rē·an, *a.* Of or pertaining to Caesar.

cae·sar·e·an op·er·a·tion, *n. Surg.* the operation by which a fetus is taken from the uterus by cutting through the walls of the abdomen and uterus, said to have been performed at the birth of Julius Caesar. Also **cae·sar·e·an sec·tion.**

Cae·sar·ism, sē′za·riz″am, *n.* Absolute government; imperialism.—**Cae·sar·ist,** *n.*

caes·pi·tose, *a.* Cespitose.

cae·su·ra, si·zhụr′a, siz·yụr′a, *n.* pl. **cae·su·ras, cae·su·rae,** si·zhụr′ē, siz·yụr′ē. [L. *caesura,* a cutting, < *caedere, caesum,* to cut.] A pause or division in a verse; a separation, by the ending of a word or by a pause in the sense, of syllables rhythmically connected.

ca·fard, ka̲·faʀ′, *n.* [Fr. lit. *cockroach, hypocrite.* Origin uncertain.] *Colloq.* a condition of extreme morbid depression with indifference to or repugnance for surroundings and duties and a feeling of insurmountable fatigue, esp. among soldiers and among Caucasians who live in the tropics; one suffering from this condition.

ca·fé, ca·fe, ka·fā´, ka·fā´, *Fr.* kä·fā´, *n. pl.* **ca·fés,** *Fr.* kä·fā´. [Fr., lit. coffee < It. *caffè* < Turk. *kahve* < Ar. *qahwah*.] A coffeehouse; a restaurant; a barroom, tavern, or night club; coffee.

ca·fé au lait, kaf´ä·ō·lā´, ka·fā´ō·lā´, *Fr.* kä·fā´ō·le´, *n.* [Fr. lit. coffee with milk.] Coffee with milk; a deep brownish cream-color.

ca·fé noir, kä·fā´nwär´, *n.* [Fr. lit. black coffee.] Black coffee, without milk or cream.

caf·e·te·ri·a, kaf″i·tēr´ē·a, *n.* [Sp. lit. place where coffee is sold.] A kind of restaurant in which the patrons wait on themselves, carrying the food to small tables where it is eaten.

caf·feine, ka·fēn´, kaf´ēn, kaf´ē·in, *n.* A slightly bitter alkaloid used as a stimulant and diuretic, and found in coffee, tea, etc., which, when taken in large doses, is poisonous.

caf·tan, kaf´tan, käf·tän´, *n.* [Turk. *qaftān.*] A long, flowing garment with full-length sleeves cinched at the waist by a girdle, worn in Near East countries. Also **kaf·tan.** —**caf·taned,** *a.* Wearing a caftan.

cage, kāj, *n.* [Fr. *cage,* < L. *cavea,* enclosure, < *cavus,* hollow.] A boxlike receptacle or enclosure with openwork of wires or bars for confining birds or other animals; a prison or place of confinement; a lockup. *Fig.* anything that confines or imprisons; something suggestive of a cage in structure or purpose. An enclosing, confining, or protecting framework; the car or enclosed platform of an elevator; *baseball,* a movable backstop for batting practice; *basketball,* the basket; *hockey,* the goal framework; *mining,* a shaft elevator.

cage, kāj, *v.t.*—**caged, caging.** To confine in, or as in, a cage.

cag·er, kā´jer, *n. Colloq.* a basketball player; *mining,* a machine used to transfer cars on or off a cage.

cage·y, kā´jē, *a.*—**cagier, cagiest.** *Slang.* artful; cunning; cautious.—**ca·gey·ness, ca·gi·ness,** *n.*—**ca·gi·ly,** *adv.*

ca·hier, kä·yā´, *n.* [Fr. *notebook* < M.Fr. *quaier,* quire.] A number of sheets of paper or leaves of a book placed together, as for binding; a report of the proceedings of any body, as a legislature. *Fr.* a notebook or journal; a paperback book.

ca·hoot, ka·hōt´, *n.* [Possibly < Fr. *cahute,* hut, cabin.] *Slang,* partnership or league; collusion or conspiracy: used in sing. or pl. and commonly after *in.*

cai·man, cay·man, kā´man, *n. pl.* **cai·mans, cay·mans.** Any of several crocodilians, similar to alligators, found in Central and South America.

ca·ïque, kä·ēk´, *n.* [< Fr. < Turk. *kāïk.*] A long, narrow skiff or rowboat used on the Bosporus; a Levantine sailing vessel.

cairn, kârn, *n.* [< Gael. Ir. W. *carn,* a heap of stones.] In Scotland and Wales, a heap of stones, erected as a monument, tombstone or landmark. Also **carn.**—**cairned, cairn·y,** *a.*

cairn·gorm, kârn´gärm, *n.* [Named for Scottish mountain *Cairngorm.*] A variety of crystallized quartz, ranging in color from yellow to deep brown, used as a gem stone, obtained from Scotland's Cairngorm mountain. Also **Cairn·gorm stone, smok·y quartz.**

cairn ter·ri·er, *n.* A small, short-legged Scottish terrier with a shaggy, rough coat.

cais·son, kā´san, kā´son, *n.* [Fr. *caisson,* earlier *casson,* < It. *cassone,* aug. of *cassa,*

< L. *capsa,* box.] A watertight casing or chamber used in underwater construction; a boatlike float used as a dock gate; a float, sometimes called a camel, used in raising sunken vessels; a structure used to render a damaged hull watertight. *Milit.* an explosive-filled box used as a mine; an ammunition chest; a vehicle for carrying ammunition.

cais·son dis·ease, *n. Pathol.* a painfully paralyzing, sometimes fatal sickness resulting from a too rapid lowering of air pressure, as in the change from the compressed air of a caisson or diving bell to surface air pressure, which causes dissolved nitrogen to be released as bubbles in the blood and tissues; the bends.

cai·tiff, kā´tif, *n.* [O.Fr. *caitif,* < L. *captivus,* E. *captive.*] A wretched or miserable person; a base or vile person.—*a.* Base; cowardly; despicable; wicked.

caj·e·put, caj·a·put, caj·u·put, kaj´i·put, kaj´i·put, *n.* [Malay *kâyû,* a tree, and *putih,* white.] An East Indian tree, *Melaleuca leucadendron,* yielding an aromatic oil used medicinally as a stimulant, antispasmodic, sudorific and in the treatment of certain skin disorders; California laurel. Also **kaj·e·put.**

ca·jole, ka·jōl´, *v.t.*—**cajoled, cajoling.** [Fr. *cajoler;* origin uncertain.] To persuade by deliberate flattery; wheedle; coax; to deceive by false promises.—**ca·jole·ment,** *n.*—**ca·jol·er,** *n.*—**ca·jol·er·y,** *n. pl.* **ca·jol·er·ies.**—**ca·jol·ing·ly,** *adv.*

Ca·jun, kā´jan, *n.* [*Dial.* < Acadian.] One of the Louisiana descendants of the Acadian French; a person of mixed white, Indian, and Negro ancestry in southwest Alabama and adjoining sections of Mississippi; the Acadian dialect. Also **Ca·jan** or **Ca·jin.**

cake, kāk, *n.* [M.E. *cake, kake,* prob. from Scand.: cf. Icel. and Sw. *kaka,* Dan. *kage,* cake, akin to D. *koek,* G. *kuchen.*] A sweet foodstuff similar to bread, prepared by baking dough or batter into a definite form, sometimes coated with an icing; as, a layer *cake,* a fruit *cake;* a flat, thin mass of bread, esp. unleavened bread; a pancake or griddle-cake; a shaped or molded mass of other food prepared by baking or frying; as, fish *cake,* meat *cake;* any shaped, molded, or compressed mass; as, a *cake* of soap or ice.—**take the cake,** *colloq.* to deserve recognition for being unusual: usu. satirical, as: His stinginess *takes the cake!*

cake, kāk, *v.t.*—**caked, caking.** To form into a cake or compact mass.—*v.i.* To become formed into a cake, crust, or compact mass.

cakes and ale, *n. Brit. colloq.* the good things and enjoyments of life; material pleasures.

cake·walk, kāk´wak″, *n.* Formerly, a promenade or march of American Negro origin, in which couples walked, to musical accompaniment, in competition before judges and an audience, the performers of the most graceful, original, or complicated steps receiving cakes as prizes; a form of dance derived from this promenade; the music for this dance.—*v.i.* To walk in or as in a cakewalk; to dance the cakewalk.—**cake·walk·er,** *n.*

Cal·a·bar bean, kal´a·bär″ bēn, kal´a·bär″ bēn, *n.* [From *Calabar,* region on the west coast of Africa.] The violently poisonous seed of an African climbing plant, *Physostigma venenosum,* a source of physostigmine, used medically, esp. in the form of its salicylate, in the treatment of an eye disease and also used, in its natural state, by natives in witchcraft trials.

cal·a·bash, kal´a·bash″, *n.* [Fr. *calebasse,* < Sp. *calabaza,* gourd, pumpkin; perhaps ult. < Pers.] Any of various gourds, esp. the fruit of the bottle gourd, *Lageneria vulgaris;* any of the plants bearing them; the fruit of the tree, *Crescentia cujete,* of tropical America, or the tree itself; the dried hollow

shell of the calabash used as a vessel or otherwise; a bottle, kettle, tobacco-pipe bowl, or the like, made from the shell of a calabash.

cal·a·ba·zil·la, kal″a·ba·zē´a, *n.* [Mex. Sp., dim. of Sp. *calabaza:* see calabash.] A wild squash, *Cucurbita foetidissima,* of Mexico and the southwestern U.S., with a fruit whose pulp while unripe is used as a substitute for soap, and with an exceedingly large root which is macerated for use as a medicinal remedy.

cal·a·boose, kal´a·bōs″, kal″a·bōs´, *n.* [Sp. *calabozo,* dungeon.] *Colloq.* A lockup; a jail.

ca·la·di·um, ka·lā´dē·um, *n.* [N.L. genus name < Malay.] Any of several tropical plants of the family *Araceae,* genus *Caladium,* having large, showy leaves of variegated colors and cultivated as a pot plant for its handsome foliage. Also **el·e·phant's ear.**

cal·a·man·der, kal´a·man″der, *n.* [Supposed to be a corruption of *Coromandel.*] A variety of extremely hard wood obtained from the East Indian tree, *Diospyros quaesita,* being black-striped hazel-brown in color, related to ebony and resembling rosewood: used in cabinet work.

cal·a·mine, kal´a·mīn″, kal´a·min, *n.* [L.L. *calamina,* < L. *cadmia* (d being changed into l), calamine.] A pink, water-insoluble powder, consisting of zinc oxide and a small amount of ferric oxide, used in lotions and ointments to treat skin disorders; an alloy of zinc, lead, and tin formerly used for coating iron to prevent oxidation; *mineral.* hemimorphite; *Brit.* smithsonite.

cal·a·mint, kal´a·mint, *n.* [Gr. *kalaminthe, kalaminthos.*] Any of several plants of the genus *Satureja,* in the mint family, esp. *S. calamintha,* native to Europe and Asia. Also **bas·il thyme.**

ca·lam·i·tous, ka·lam´i·tus, *a.* [Fr. *calamiteux,* L. *calamitosus.*] Producing or resulting from calamity; making wretched; distressful; disastrous; miserable; baleful.—**ca·lam·i·tous·ly,** *adv.* In a calamitous manner.—**ca·lam·i·tous·ness,** *n.*

ca·lam·i·ty, ka·lam´i·tē, *n. pl.* **ca·lam·i·ties.** [L. *calamitas, calamitatis.*] Any great misfortune or cause of misery; a disaster accompanied with extensive evils; misfortune; mishap; affliction; adversity.

cal·a·mon·din, kal´a·mun″din, *n.* A citrus tree, *Citrus mitis,* native to the Philippines; the fruit of this tree which resembles the mandarin orange.

cal·a·mus, kal´a·mus, *n. pl.* **cal·a·mi,** kal´a·mī. [L., < Gr. *kalamos,* reed.] A reed or cane; the sweet flag, *Acorus calamus,* or its aromatic root; any palm of the genus *Calamus,* yielding rattan or canes. The quill of a feather.

ca·lan·do, kä·län´dō″, *a., adv.* [It.] *Music,* becoming gradually slower and softer; diminishing.

cal·ca·ne·us, kal·kā´nē·us, *n. pl.* **cal·ca·ne·i,** kal·kā´nē·ī″. *Anat.* the largest bone of the tarsus; the bone which in man forms the heel. Also **cal·ca·ne·um.**—**cal·ca·ne·al, cal·ca·ne·an,** *a.*

cal·car, kal´kär, *n. pl.* **cal·car·i·a,** kal·kâr´ē·a. [L. *calcar,* a spur; < *calx, calcis,* the heel.] *Biol.* A spurlike process on the leg of a bird; a hollow projection from the base of a petal.—**cal·ca·rate,** kal´ka·rāt″, *a. Biol.* having a spur, as the foot of a pheasant or the corolla of a larkspur.

cal·car, kal´kär, *n. pl.* **cal·car·i·a,** kal·kâr´ē·a. [L. *calcaria,* a limekiln, from *calx,* lime.] A kind of oven or reverberating furnace, used in glassworks for the calcination of sand and salt of potash, and converting them into frit.

cal·car·e·ous, kal·kâr´ē·us, *a.* [L. *calcarius,* < *calx,* lime.] Partaking of the nature of, having the qualities of, or containing calcium carbonate.

cal·ce·i·form, kal'sē·a·fạrm″, kal·sē′a·fạrm″, a. [L. *calceus*, a shoe, and *-form*.] *Bot.* having the form of a shoe or slipper, as the petals of certain orchids.

cal·ce·o·late, kal'sē·a·lāt″, a. Calceiform.

cal·ces, kal'sēz, n. Plural of *calx.*

cal·cic, kal'sik, a. [L. *calx, calcis*, lime.] Of or pertaining to lime; containing calcium.

cal·cif·er·ol, kal·sif′a·rōl″, kal·sif′a·rạl″, kal·sif′a·rol″, n. *Biochem.* vitamin D_2, a crystalline, fat-soluble compound, $C_{28}H_{43}$-OH, occurring naturally in milk and fish-liver oils.

cal·cif·er·ous, kal·sif′ẽr·us, a. [L. *calx*, and *fero*, to produce.] Producing or possessing calcium carbonate, esp. calcite.

cal·cif·ic, kal·sif′ik, a. Forming salts of calcium, esp. calcium carbonate; calcifying or calcified.

cal·ci·fi·ca·tion, kal'si·fi·kā″shan, n. The process of changing a substance through the deposition of lime.

cal·ci·fuge, kal'si·fūj″, n. A plant which cannot thrive in limestone or in soil saturated with lime.

cal·ci·fy, kal'si·fī″, v.i.—*calcified, calcifying.* [L. *calx*, and *facio*, to make.] To be gradually changed into a stony condition by the deposition or secretion of calcium salts.—*v.t.* To make stony by depositing calcium salts.

cal·ci·mine, kal'si·mīn″, n. [< L. *calx*.] A white or light-colored wash composed of whiting, glue, and water, used to paint walls or ceilings, but which cannot withstand washing.—*v.t.—calcimined, calcimining.* To coat with calcimine.

cal·cine, kal'sīn, kal'sin, v.t.—*calcined, calcining.* [Fr. *calciner*, < L. *calx*.] To reduce to a powder or to a friable state by the action of heat; to free from volatile matter by the action of heat, as limestone from carbonic acid, iron ore from sulfur; to oxidize or reduce to a metallic calx.—*v.i.* To be converted into a powder or friable substance by the action of heat.—**cal·ci·na·tion,** kal'si·nā″shon, n.

cal·cite, kal'sīt, n. The mineral, $CaCO_3$, calcium carbonate, which is found in a number of crystal forms including limestone, marble, chalk, and Iceland spar.

cal·ci·um, kal'sē·um, n. [N.L., < L. *calx*, lime.] *Chem.* a bivalent alkaline earth element used in the manufacture of metals and alloys, being a moderately soft whitish crystal in pure form, found in nature only in compounds such as limestone or chalk and an essential ingredient of bones, teeth, and shells. Sym. Ca, at. no. 20. See Periodic Table of Elements.

cal·ci·um car·bide, n. *Chem.* a compound, CaC_2, derived from pulverized limestone and coal in an electric furnace, that readily reacts with water to form acetylene gas and used in manufacturing and as a dehydrating agent.

cal·ci·um car·bon·ate, n. *Chem.* a colorless crystal or gray powder, $CaCO_3$, occurring naturally in calcite, chalk, limestone, marble, and other forms: used as a pigment, as an antacid, in dentifrices, as baking powder, and in making lime and Portland cement.

cal·ci·um chlo·ride, n. *Chem.* a white, absorbent, lumpy, or crystalline salt, $CaCl_2$, derived from calcium carbonate: used as a drying agent or preservative and for road treatment, such as dustproofing and thawing snow and ice.

cal·ci·um cy·an·a·mide, n. *Chem.* a gray-black lumpy solid, $CaCN_2$, derived from calcium carbide plus nitrogen: used primarily as a fertilizer and weed-killer

and as an intermediate in the manufacture of nitrogen compounds.

cal·ci·um cyc·la·mate, kal'sē·um sik′-la·māt″, sī′kla·māt″, n. *Chem.* a white crystalline powder, $(C_6H_{11}NHSO_3)_2Ca$--$2H_2O$, sometimes used as an artificial sweetener having 30 times the sweetening power of sucrose: related to sodium cyclamate, the calcium form used in sodium-restricted diets.

cal·ci·um hy·drox·ide, n. *Chem.* a strong alkali, $Ca(OH)_2$; in powder form called *calcium hydrate*; in solution called *lime-water*: used in mortar, plaster, and cement.

cal·ci·um light, n. A brilliant white light produced by heating lime to incandescence in an oxyhydrogen or other hot flame; limelight.

cal·ci·um phos·phate, n. *Chem.* any of several forms of combined calcium and phosphorus: used in combination as a fertilizer and in animal feed, in pure form in baking powder, in ceramics, enamels, and milk glass, and as a polishing agent in dentifrices.

calc·sin·ter, kalk'sin″tẽr, n. [L. *calx*, lime, and G. *sinter*, a stalactite.] A stalactite of calcite; travertine; tufa.

calc-spar, kalk'spär″, n. Calcite.

calc-tu·fa, kalk'tō″fa, n. An alluvial formation of calcium carbonate. Also **calc-tuff,** kalk'tuf.

cal·cu·la·bil·i·ty, kal″kū·la·bil′i·tē, n. The quality of being determinable by calculation or computation.

cal·cu·la·ble, kal'kū·la·bl, a. Capable of being calculated or ascertained by calculation.—**cal·cu·la·ble·ness,** n.—**cal·cu·la·bly,** adv.

cal·cu·late, kal'kū·lāt, v.t.—*calculated, calculating.* [L.L. *calculatus*, pp. of *calculare*, < L. *calculus*, pebble, stone used in counting, reckoning.] To ascertain by mathematical methods; compute; reckon; to estimate by common-sense judgment, as distinguished from mathematical methods; to plan in advance or think out; to adapt or fit for a purpose, chiefly as pp., as, *calculated* to excite. *Colloq.* to intend; to think or guess.—*v.i.* To make a computation.—**cal·cu·late on,** count or rely upon.

cal·cu·lat·ed, kal'kū·lā″tid, a. Determined by a mathematical process; initiated after evaluating the prospects of failure; as, a *calculated* risk; carefully planned; deliberately contrived.—**cal·cu·lat·ed·ly,** adv.

cal·cu·lat·ing, kal'kū·lā″ting, a. Able to perform arithmetical calculations; as, a *calculating* machine; given to forethought and careful analysis; selfishly and coldly scheming.

cal·cu·la·tion, kal″kū·lā′shan, n. [L.L. *calculatio(n-).*] Either the act or the result of mathematical calculating; computation; an estimate or forecast based on the various facts and circumstances in a case; careful advance planning; cold-hearted scheming.—**cal·cu·la·tive,** a.

cal·cu·la·tor, kal'kū·lā″tẽr, n. One who calculates; a machine which does mathematical computations; a person who operates such a machine; a set of tables used to speed computations.

cal·cu·lous, kal'kū·lus, a. Hard like a pebble; gritty; *pathol.* pertaining to, caused by, or affected with a calculus or calculi.

cal·cu·lus, kal'kū·lus, n. pl. **cal·cu·lus·es, cal·cu·li,** kal'kū·lī″. [L. pebble, stone used in counting.] *Math.* the study of variations of functions, using a specialized set of algebraic symbols and a systematic method of computation, usually subdivided into *calculus of variations, differential* and *integral calculus. Pathol.* a stonelike mass sometimes formed in the gall bladder, kidneys, or other organs or ducts of the body.

cal·de·ra, kal·der′a, *Sp.* käl·de′Rä, n. pl. **cal·de·ras.** [Sp. < L. *caldaria*, kettle, prop. fem. of *caldarius*, serving to heat.] A large bowllike cavity or crater produced by violent volcanic action, as when the upper part of a cone is blown off; a volcanic crater which has been enlarged by subterranean disruptive forces.

cal·dron, kạl'dron, n. Cauldron.

ca·lèche, kä·lesh′, n. pl. **ca·lèches,** kä·lesh′. In Quebec, Canada, a two-wheeled, horse-drawn vehicle accommodating two passengers and having a position for the driver in the front. Also **ca·lash,** ka·lash′.

cal·e·fa·cient, kal″e·fā′shant, a. [L. *calefacio*, to make warm, < *caleo*, to be warm, and *facio*, to make.] Warming; heating.—*n.* That which warms or heats; *med.* a substance which excites a degree of warmth in the part to which it is applied, as mustard or pepper.—**cal·e·fac·tion,** kal″e·fak′shạn, n. The act or operation of warming or heating; the state of being heated.—**cal·e·fac·tive, cal·e·fac·to·ry,** kal″e·fak′tiv, kal″e·fak′ta·rē, a.

cal·e·fac·to·ry, kal″e·fak′ta·rē, n. pl. **cal·e·fac·to·ries.** A heated sitting room in a monastery.

cal·en·dar, kal'an·dẽr, n. [L. *calendarium*, an account book, a calendar, from *calendae*, the first day of each month, the calends; root in *calo*, Gr. *kalein*, to call.] A register of the year, in which the months, weeks, and days are set down in order; an orderly table or enumeration of persons or things, as a list of criminal causes which stand for trial; a list; a catalogue; a register.—*v.t.* To enter or write in a calendar; to register.

cal·en·der, kal'an·dẽr, n. [Fr. *calandre*, L.L. *calendra*, a calender, < L. *cylindrus*, Gr. *kylindros*, a cylinder.] A machine consisting of two or more cylinders revolving so nearly in contact with each other that cloth or paper passing through between them is smoothed and glazed by their pressure.—*v.t.* To press or finish in a calender.—**cal·en·der·er,** kal'an·dẽr·ẽr, n.

ca·len·dri·cal, ka·len′dri·kal, a. Having to do with a calendar or calendar units.

cal·ends, kal·ends, kal'endz, n. pl. [L. *calendæ, kalendæ.*] The first day of the month in the Roman calendar.—**on the Greek cal·ends,** on a day that will never arrive, since the Greeks had no calends; never.

ca·len·du·la, ka·len′ja·la, n. [N.L. < L. *calendæ*, calends; so called as flowering almost every month of the year.] Any plant of the genus *Calendula*, esp. *C. officinalis*, a common marigold; the dried florets of this plant, used in medicine to promote healing.

cal·en·ture, kal'an·chẽr, kal'an·chụr″, n. [Fr. *calenture*, Sp. *calentura*, heat, a calenture, < *calentar*, to heat, < L. *caleo*, to be hot.] *Pathol.* a kind of delirium caused in the tropics by exposure to excessive heat.

ca·les·cence, ka·les′ans, n. [< L. *calesco*, to grow warm, incept. of *caleo*, to be hot.] Growing warmth; growing heat.

calf, kaf, käf, n. pl. **calves,** kavz, kävz. [O.E. *cealf* < G. *kalb*.] The young of the cow or of other bovine animals; the young of certain other animals, as the elephant, seal, whale; a small island lying near a large one; a mass of ice detached from a glacier, iceberg, or floe; *colloq.* an awkward, silly, boy or young man. Calfskin leather.

calf, kaf, käf, n. pl. **calves,** kavz, kävz. [Icel. *kálfi*, the calf of the leg.] The fleshy back part of the human leg below the knee.

calf love, n. Transitory affection or passion of a boy or a girl for a person of the opposite sex. Also *puppy love.*

calf's-foot jel·ly, kafs'fụt jel′ē, käfs'fụt, n. A jelly made from the gelatine obtained from a boiling a calf's foot and adding flavoring, as wine.

calf·skin, kaf′skin″, käf′skin″, *n.* The skin or hide of a calf, or leather made from it.

Cal·ga·ry red·eye, kal′ga·rē red′ī, *n. Canadian slang,* esp. in Alberta, a beverage composed of beer and tomato juice.

Cal·i·ban, kal′i·ban″, *n.* [< *Caliban,* "a savage and deformed slave" in Shakespeare's play, "The Tempest."] A man of low, bestial nature, esp. one who is monstrous in appearance.

cal·i·ber, cal·i·bre, kal′i·bėr, *n.* [Fr. *calibre,* possibly < Ar. *kâlib,* < *kâlab,* a mold.] The diameter of a body, as of a column or a bullet; esp. the diameter of the bore of a firearm. *Fig.* the compass or capacity of mind or ability; degree of worth or excellence; as, a person of high *caliber.*

cal·i·brate, kal′i·brāt″, *v.t.*—*calibrated, calibrating.* To ascertain the caliber of; to check and rectify the scale of, as any measuring instrument; to determine the range of.—**cal·i·bra·tion,** kal″i·brā′shan, *n.* The act or process of calibrating, especially of ascertaining the caliber of a thermometer tube, to graduate it to a scale of degrees.

cal·i·ces, kal′i·sēz″, *n.* Plural of *calix.*

ca·li·che, ka·lē′chē, *n.* [Amer. Sp. use of Sp. *caliche,* pebble, flake of lime, < L. *calx,* lime.] Any of various mineral deposits, as native Chile saltpeter, containing 48% to 75% of nitrate of sodium.

cal·i·co, kal′i·kō, *n. pl.* **cal·i·coes, cal·i·cos.** [< *Calicut,* city in southwestern India.] Orig., cotton cloth imported from India; *U.S.,* a cotton cloth with a pattern printed on one side; *Brit.,* a plain white cotton cloth.—*a.* Made of calico; resembling printed calico, as a horse or other animal marked with patches of different colors.

cal·i·co bass, *n.* A valuable fresh-water food fish, *Pomoxis sparoides,* of the eastern and central parts of the U.S.; the black crappie, a related species.

cal·i·co bush, *n.* The mountain laurel, *Kalmia latifolia.* Also **cal·i·co tree.**

cal·i·co print·ing, *n.* The process used in printing patterns of fast color on cotton cloth, such as calico.

ca·lic·u·lus, ka·lik′ya·lus, *n. pl.* **ca·lic·u·li,** ka·lik′ya·lī. A small cuplike object.

Cal·i·for·nia lau·rel, *n.* An evergreen, *Umbellularia californica,* with aromatic leaves, belonging to the laurel family and native to the west coastal area of the U.S.

Cal·i·for·nia pop·py, *n.* A plant, *Eschscholtzia californica,* of the poppy family, widely cultivated for its showy orange-yellow flowers: the State flower of California.

Cal·i·for·nia rose·bay, *n.* The pink rhododendron of the western coast of the U.S.: the State flower of Washington.

cal·i·for·nite, kal·a·fȧr′nit, *n.* [From *California.*] A mineral, a compact variety of vesuvianite, resembling jade.

cal·i·for·ni·um, kal″a·fȧr′nē·um, *n.* [From *California,* the university and state where first identified.] *Chem.* a radioactive synthetic element. Sym. Cf, at. no. 98. See Periodic Table of Elements.

cal·i·pash, kal′i·pash″, kal″i·pash′, *n.* A greenish substance just under the upper shell of a turtle that is gelatinous and regarded as a delicacy in the form of turtle soup. Also **cal·li·pash..**

cal·i·per, cal·li·per, kal′i·pėr, *n.* [Corruption of *caliber.*] Usually *pl.,* an instrument, commonly having two legs and resembling a pair of compasses, for measuring outside and inside diameters, the thickness of objects, etc.—*v.t.* To measure by means of calipers.—**cal·i·per rule,** a rule having a graduated slide with a projecting foot, used as calipers for measuring outside diameters.

ca·liph, ca·lif, ka·liph, ka·lif, kha·lif, kā′lif, kal′if, *n.* [Fr. *calife,* < Ar. *khalifa,* successor, < *khalafa,* to succeed.] A title given to the acknowledged successors of Mohammed, regarded among Mohammedans as being vested with supreme dignity and power in all matters relating to religion and civil policy.

cal·iph·ate, cal·if·ate, kal′i·fāt″, kal′i·fit, kā′li·fāt″, kā′li·fit, *n.* The office or dignity of a caliph; the government of a caliph.

cal·is·then·ics, kal″is·then′iks, *n. pl. but sing. in constr.* [Gr. *kalos,* beautiful, and *sthenos,* strength.] The art or practice of taking exercise for health, strength, or grace of movement.—**cal·is·then·ic,** kal″is·then′ik, *a.*

ca·lix, kā′liks, kal′iks, *n. pl.* **cal·i·ces,** kal′i·sēz″. [L., cup: cf. *chalice* and *calyx.*] A cuplike part or organ; *bot.* a calyx; *R. Cath. Ch.,* a chalice.

calk, kȧk, *n.* A projection on a horseshoe to prevent slipping; a similar device on the heel or sole of a shoe.—*v.t.* To fit, as a horseshoe, with calks; to injure with a calk.

call, kȧl, *v.t.* [O.E. *ceallian* = Icel. *kalla.*] To utter in a loud voice; read, as a roll or list, in a loud tone; announce or proclaim; attract the attention of; rouse from sleep; to evaluate inexactly, as: I'd *call* that a full load. Reckon, consider, or evaluate; as, to *call* a thing a success; to telephone; to reprimand, as: The boss *called* her on her absenteeism.

call, kȧl, *v.t.* To command or request to come; summon; to attract or lure, as wild birds, or other animals by a particular cry or sound; to call for, as: The judge *called* the next case. To demand payment or fulfillment of, as a loan; to require presentation for the redemption of, as a bond; to name, as: Call him Spike. To give an order for; as, to *call* a strike; *poker,* to require, as a player, to show his hand, after equaling his bet. *Sports,* to terminate, as a game, because of darkness or bad weather; of an umpire, to rule on, as a contested play; as, to *call* a player safe. *Pocket billiards,* to foretell, as a shot.—**call it quits,** *colloq.* To cease activities temporarily, as: The workmen *called it quits* for the day. To give up trying to attain a certain goal, as: They *called it quits* when their efforts to compromise were unsuccessful. To end a relationship, such as a friendship, marriage, or business partnership.

call, kȧl, *v.t.* To bid, as by divine command, as: Joan of Arc was *called* to lead the French armies. Invoke or appeal to, as: "I *call* heaven and earth to witness against you. . ." Deut. iv. 26; convoke or convene, as a meeting or assembly; summon to an office or duty; invite to a pastorate; to prophesy; to designate as something specified; to cause to remember, as: That song *calls* an event to mind.

call, kȧl, *v.i.* To speak loudly, as to attract attention; shout; cry; to make a demand; to make a short visit; to stop at a place on some errand or business; to make a request, as for a trump in card games; *poker,* to demand a showing of hands.

call, kȧl, *n.* The act of calling; a roll call; a cry or shout; a summons or bidding, as: I'm answering your *call.* A request or invitation, as to become pastor of a church; an inner drive to take up a particular occupation; a vocation; the allure of a particular place; a communication by telephone; a short visit; a stop at a place on some business; *poker,* a demand for a showing of hands.

call, kȧl, *n.* The cry of a bird or other animal; an instrument for imitating this sound; a note blown on a horn to encourage the hounds; a summons or signal sounded upon a bugle; a whistle for sounding a signal; a demand or claim, as for the repayment of money; the call to duty; a request, as: We have many *calls* for this record. An instruction in a square dance; *sports,* a decision made by a referee; *stock market,* the privilege of buying a certain amount of stock, at a specified price, within a fixed time.

cal·la, kal′a, *n.* [L.] A plant, *Calla palustris,* growing in cold marshes of Europe and North America, with heart-shaped leaves, an open white spathe, and red berries; a familiar plant of the allied genus *Aroides* (or *Richardia*) native in Africa, esp. *A. aethiopicum,* calla lily, which has a large white spathe enclosing a yellow spadix.

call·a·ble, kȧ′la·bl, *a.* Capable of being called; subject to call or summons; subject to payment on demand, as money loaned; subject to redemption upon notice.

call board, kȧl′bȯrd′, kȧl′bȧrd″, *n.* A bulletin board hung in a theater on which notifications of rehearsals or changes in cast are posted.

call·boy, kȧl′boi, *n.* A boy whose duty it is to call actors on to the stage at the proper moment; a bellboy.

call down, *v.t.* To reprehend; to beg to descend.—*n.* A sharp reprimand.

call·er, kȧ′lėr, *n.* One who calls; someone making a brief visit; the person who announces directions at a square dance.

cal·let, kal′it, *n.* [Origin uncertain.] *Brit.* A prostitute; a scold; a shrew.

call for, *v.t.* To fetch; demand; send for.

call girl, *n.* A prostitute who can be contacted by telephone for an assignation.

call house, *n.* A house or apartment which call girls use to receive phone calls or to keep appointments.

cal·lig·ra·pher, ka·lig′ra·fėr, *n.* One who does beautiful handwriting; a fine penman; a transcriber of manuscripts. Also **cal·lig·ra·phist,** ka·lig′ra·fist.

cal·lig·ra·phy, ka·lig′ra·fē, *n.* [Gr. *kalligraphia.*] Beautiful handwriting; fine penmanship; in general, handwriting; penmanship.—**cal·li·graph·ic,** kal″i·graf′ik, *a.*

call·ing, kȧ′ling, *n.* A vocation; profession; trade; usual occupation or employment. Collectively, persons following any profession; state of being divinely called; an impelling inner force; a summons; a convening, as of Congress.

call·ing card, *n.* A small card printed or engraved with a person's or a couple's name and used to give notice of a visit or to identify the source of a gift.

cal·li·o·pe, ka·lī′o·pē, kal′ē·ōp″, *n.* [L. < Gr. *kalliope,* < *kalos,* beautiful, and *ops,* voice.] A harsh musical instrument consisting of a series of steam whistles played by keys; (*cap.*) the Muse of eloquence and heroic poetry.

cal·li·op·sis, kal″ē·op′sis, *n.* An annual plant of the genus *Coreopsis.*

Cal·lis·to, ka·lis′tō, *n. Astron.* a large satellite, one of the twelve satellites of Jupiter; *mythol.* an Arcadian nymph, loved by Zeus, transformed into a bear by his jealous wife, and set as the constellation Great Bear (Ursa Major) by Zeus.

call loan, *n.* A stock market loan, used to finance purchases of securities, which may be terminated at any time by the lender or borrower; also *demand loan.*

call mar·ket, *n.* The market for making call loans.

call mon·ey, *n.* Money loaned on call or available for call loans.

call num·ber, *n. Library Science,* a classification number usually combining letters and numerals to designate subject and author, indicating the shelf location of a book in a library.

---

a- fat, fāte, fär, fâre, fȧll; **e-** met, mē, mēre, hėr; **i-** pin, pīne; **o-** not, nōte, mŏve; **u-** tub, cūbe, bull; **oi-** oil; **ou-** pound.

call off, *v.t.* To summon or take away; distract; to cancel, as that which has been planned; to speak or read out loud; as, to *call off* a list of names.

cal·lose, kal'ōs, *n. Bot.* an occasional carbohydrate or periodic component of plant cell walls, as on sieve plates, where it forms the callus.—*a.* Having callosities, as a leaf.

cal·los·i·ty, ka·los'i·tē, *n. pl.* **cal·los·i·ties.** [L. *callositas.*] The condition of being callous or hardened; abnormal hardness and thickness of skin and other tissues; a hardened thickening; any part of a plant unusually hard; *fig.* insensibility.

cal·lous, kal'us, *a.* [L. *callosus,* < *callum, callus,* hard skin.] Hard, as skin; indurated, as portions of the skin exposed to friction; *fig.* hardened in mind or feelings; unfeeling. —*v.t., v.i.* To make or come to be callous or hard.—**cal·loused,** kal'ust, *a.* Made callous; hardened.—**cal·lous·ly,** *adv.*—**cal·lous·ness,** *n.*

cal·low, kal'ō, *a.* Bald, unfledged, as birds. Lacking maturity or judgment; very young; unsophisticated; inexperienced.

call rate, *n.* The interest which is charged on a loan repayable on demand.

call sign, *n.* A sign used as a radio signal by aircraft to identify themselves to friendly forces.

call to quar·ters, *n.* A blowing of a bugle, often just before taps, to summon soldiers back to their quarters.

call-up, kal'up", *n.* An official notice to appear for active military duty; the total number of men ordered to report for military duty during a specified time.

call up, *v.t.* To telephone; to put up for discussion; to select for service in the armed forces; as, to *call up* the army reserves.

cal·lus, kal'us, *n. pl.* **cal·lus·es.** [L.] A hardened or thickened portion of the skin; a callosity; a hard excrescence on a plant; the substance or tissue which forms over the wounds of plants, protecting the inner tissues and causing healing; a new growth of osseous matter at the ends of a fractured bone, serving to unite them.—*v.t.* To cause a callus to form on.—*v.i.* To form a callus, as on the cut surface of a plant.

calm, käm, *n.* [O.Fr. Fr. *calme,* prob. (as if orig. "heat of the day," hence "time for resting, quiet") < L.L. *cauma,* < Gr. *kauma,* burning heat, < *kaiein,* burn.] Freedom from motion or disturbance; stillness; absence of wind; hence, freedom from agitation, excitement, or passion; tranquillity; serenity.

calm, käm, *a.* Without motion; still; not windy; undisturbed; tranquil; free from excitement or passion.—**calm·ly,** *adv.*— **calm·ness,** *n.*

calm, käm, *v.i.* To become calm; to relax; to abate, usu. used with *down.*—*v.t.* To make calm; to quiet; to settle or soothe.

cal·ma·tive, kal'ma·tiv, kä'ma·tiv, *a.* Sedative, soothing.—*n.* A tranquilizer.

cal·o·mel, kal'o·mel", kal'o·mel, *n. Pharm.* mercurous chloride, Hg_2Cl_2, a white, tasteless solid used as a purgative.

cal·o·res·cence, kal·o·res'ens, *n.* [L.] *Phys.* the change of infrared light (heat) into visible light rays, the change occurring indirectly following sufficient absorption of heat by a body.

ca·lor·ic, ka·lar'ik, ka·lor'ik, *n.* [L. *calor,* heat.] *Chem., phys.* an obsolete term referring to the hypothetical fluid to which heat and combustion were attributed.

ca·lor·ic, ka·lar'ik, ka·lor'ik, *a.* Of or pertaining to heat or calories.

cal·o·rie, cal·o·ry, kal'a·rē, *n. pl.* **cal·o·ries.** [Fr. *calorie,* < L. *calor,* heat, < *calere,* be hot.] *Phys.* the quantity of heat necessary, at normal atmospheric pressure, to raise the temperature of one gram of water one degree centigrade. Also **gram cal·o·rie, small cal·or·ie.** *Phys.* a quantity of heat equal to 1000 gram calories; also **ki·lo·cal·o·rie, large cal·o·rie.** *Physiol.* a unit of food measurement, having an energy-producing value of one large calorie.

cal·o·rif·ic, kal·a·rif'ik, *a.* Capable of producing heat; causing heat; heating.

cal·o·rim·e·ter, kal·o·rim'i·tėr, *n.* Any of several apparatus for measuring quantities of heat absorbed or produced by a body.—**cal·o·ri·met·ric,** kal'ėr·o·me'trik, ka·lar"o·me'trik, *a.* Of or belonging to the use of the calorimeter.—**cal·o·rim·e·try,** kal·o·rim'i·trē, *n.* The process of using the calorimeter.

cal·o·ry, kal'a·rē, *n. pl.* **cal·o·ries.** Calorie.

ca·lotte, ka·lot', *n.* [Fr. *calotte,* a skull-cap, dim. of *cale.* CAUL.] A skullcap worn by ecclesiastics; a zucchetto. *Arch.* a small dome; a metal covering on a cupola or spire.

cal·trop, cal·trap, kal'trop, *n.* [O.E. *coltræppe, calcatrippe,* spiny plant, appar. < L. *calx,* heel, and M.L. *trappa,* trap.] *Bot.* any of various plants having spiny heads or fruit, as the star thistle, *Centaurea calcitrapa; milit.* an iron ball with four projecting spikes so disposed that when the ball is placed on the ground one of them always points upward: formerly used to obstruct the passage of horses or advancing infantry. Also **cal·throp.**

cal·u·met, kal'ya·met", kal'ya·met', *n.* [Fr. < L. *calamus,* reed.] A long, ornamented tobacco pipe used by the North American Indians on ceremonial occasions, esp. in token of peace.

ca·lum·ni·ate, ka·lum'nē·āt", *v.t.*—**ca·lumniated, calumniating.** [L. *calumniatus,* pp. of *calumniari,* < *calumnia:* see *calumny.*] To assail with calumny; make malicious false statements concerning; slander; traduce. —**ca·lum·ni·a·tion,** ka·lum"nē·ā'shan, *n.* —**ca·lum·ni·a·tor,** n.—**ca·lum·ni·a·to·ry,** ka·lum"nē·a·tōr'ē, *a.*

ca·lum·ni·ous, ka·lum'nē·us, *a.* [L.L. *calumniosus.*] Of the nature of, involving, or using calumny; slanderous; defamatory.— **ca·lum·ni·ous·ly,** *adv.*

cal·um·ny, kal'am·nē, *n. pl.* **cal·um·nies.** [L. *calumnia,* < *calvi,* intrigue against.] A malicious false statement tending to defame; slander; a slanderous report.

cal·va·dos, kal"va·dōs', kal"va·dos', kal'va·dōs", kal'va·dos", *n.* A brandy, distilled from apple cider, of the type that originated in the department of Calvados, of the province of Normandy, in France.

Cal·va·ry, kal'va·rē, *n. pl.* **Cal·va·ries.** [L. *calvaria,* skull, < *calvus,* bald, used to render the Aramaic name, lit. "skull," whence E. *Golgotha.*] Golgotha, the place where Christ was crucified. Luke, xxiii. 33. *(l.c.)* a sculptured representation of the Crucifixion, erected in the open air or in a church or chapel; an experience of acute agony, usu. mental.

calve, kav, käv, *v.i.*—**calved, calving.** [O.E. *cealfian,* < *cealf,* calf.] To give birth to a calf; of a glacier or iceberg, to give off a detached piece.—*v.t.* To give birth to, as a calf; bring forth; give off.

Cal·vin·ism, kal'vi·niz"am, *n.* The theological teachings of John Calvin emphasizing the sovereignty of God, predestination, and original sin.—**Cal·vin·ist,** *n.* A follower of John Calvin; one who accepts Calvinism.

calx, kalks, *n. pl.* **calx·es, cal·ces,** kal'sēz. [L., small stone, lime.] Lime; *metal.* the oxide or ashy substance which remains after metals or minerals have been thoroughly burned or roasted; refuse glass for remelting.

cal·y·cle, kal'i·kl, *n.* [L. *calyculus,* dim. of *calyx,* calyx.] *Bot.* a set of bracts resembling an outer calyx.—**ca·lyc·u·lar,** ka·lik'ū·lar, *a.*—**ca·lyc·u·late,** ka·lik'ū·lāt', ka·lik'yū·lit, *a.*

ca·lyp·so, ka·lip'sō, *n. pl.* **ca·lyp·sos.** A type of music of the West Indies characterized by jazzlike rhythms and having satirical, often improvised, lyrics.

ca·lyp·tra, ka·lip'tra, *n.* [N.L. < Gr. *kalyptra,* veil, < *kalyptein,* cover.] *Bot.* A hoodlike part connected with the organs of fructification in flowering plants; the hood which caps the spore case in true mosses.

ca·lyx, kā'liks, kal'iks, *n. pl.* **ca·lyx·es, cal·y·ces,** kal'i·sēz, kā'li·sēz. [L. < Gr. *kalyx,* covering, husk, calyx, < *kalyptein,* cover.] *Bot.* the external, usually green, envelope of a flower; the sepals; *anat.* and *zool.* a cuplike part.—**ca·ly·ci·form,** ka·lis'i·fạrm, *a.* Having the form of a calyx; also **cal·y·cine.**

cam, kam, *n.* [Cf. D. and Dan. *kam,* G. *kamm,* comb, crest, cog, etc.] *Mach.* a device for converting regular rotary motion into irregular rotary or reciprocating motion, commonly consisting of an oval, heart-shaped, or other specially-shaped flat piece, or eccentric disc, fastened on and revolving with a shaft, and engaging with other mechanisms.

ca·ma·ra·de·rie, kä"ma·rä'de·rē, *n.* [Fr.] Comradeship; friendly fellowship.

cam·a·ril·la, kam"a·ril'a, Sp. kä"mä·-Rē'lyä, kä"mä·Rē'yä, *n.* [Sp., a small room, a dim. of *camara,* L. *camera, camara,* a vault. CHAMBER.] A company of private and perhaps secret counselors or advisers; a cabal; a clique.

cam·ass, cam·as, kam'as, *n.* [N. Amer. Ind.] Any of various plants of the liliaceous genus *Camassia,* esp. *C. quamash,* a species of western North America, with sweet, edible bulbs.

cam·ber, kam'bėr, *v.t., v.i.* [Fr. *cambrer,* < L. *camerare,* < *camera,* arch.] To arch slightly; bend or curve upward in the middle.

cam·ber, kam'bėr, *n.* A slight arching or convexity above, as of a ship's deck; a slightly arching piece of timber; *aeron.* the curve of an airfoil section.

cam·bist, kam'bist, *n.* [Fr. *cambiste,* < It. *cambista,* < *cambio,* < M.L. *cambium,* exchange.] One versed in the science of monetary exchange; a dealer in bills of exchange; a manual giving the moneys, weights, and measures of different countries with their equivalents.—**cam·bist·ry,** *n.*

cam·bi·um, kam'bē·um, *n. pl.* **cam·bi·ums, cam·bi·a,** kam'bē·a. [M.L., exchange, < L. *cambire,* exchange, barter: cf. *change.*] *Bot.* a layer of soft cellular tissue or meristem between the bark and wood, or xylem, in trees and shrubs, from which new bark and wood originate.

Cam·bo·di·an, kam·bō'dē·an, *a.* Characteristic of the culture and people of Cambodia, a constitutional monarchy in southwest Asia, situated south of Thailand on the Gulf of Siam.—*n.* A native or inhabitant of Cambodia.

cam·boose, kam·bōs', *n. Canada,* the living quarters for the loggers or shantymen in a logging camp.

Cam·bri·an, kam'brē·an, *a.* [M.L.] Pertaining to Cambria, or Wales; noting or pertaining to a geological period or a system of rocks preceding the Silurian and constituting the earliest principal division of the Paleozoic.—*n.* A Welshman; *geol.* the Cambrian period or system.

cam·bric, kām'brik, *n.* [Flem. *Kameryk,* for Fr. *Cambrai,* town in northern France.] A fine, thin linen or cotton fabric.

cam·bric tea, *n.* A mixture of hot water and milk, with sugar and, sometimes, a little tea.

Cam·bridge cock·pit, *n. Aeron.* a mock-up of an airplane cockpit containing apparatus to measure one's ability to use controls duplicating those of an airplane.

came, kăm, n. [Origin uncertain.] A slender grooved bar of lead for holding together the pieces of glass in windows of latticework or stained glass.

cam·el, kăm′el, n. [L. *camelus,* < Gr. *kamēlos,* < Semitic.] Either of two large ruminant quadrupeds of the genus *Camelus:* *C. dromedarius,* the Arabian camel, or dromedary, with one hump, and *C. bactrianus,* the Bactrian camel with two humps, used as beasts of burden. A buoyant water-tight structure placed under, or at the side, as of a ship, to raise it.

cam·el back, n. The rubber strip for recapping and retreading tires; the back of a chair with a hump like that of a camel.

cam·el·eer, kăm′a·lēr′, n. A camel driver; a soldier on a camel.

ca·mel·lia, ka·mēl′ya, ka·mē′lē·a, n. [N.L.; named for G. J. *Kamel,* Moravian Jesuit missionary.] A plant, *Thea* or *Camellia japonica,* native in Asia with glossy evergreen leaves and white or pink waxy, roselike flowers, familiar in cultivation, and popularly used in corsages.

ca·mel·o·pard, ka·mel′o·pärd, n. [L.L. *camelopardus,* L. *camelopardalis,* < Gr. *kamēlopardalis,* < *kamēlos,* camel, and *pardalis,* pard.] *Archaic,* a giraffe; *astron.* (*cap.*) the nothern constellation Camelopardalis.

cam·el's hair, kăm′elz·hâr″, n. The hair of the camel, used for cloth of a typically tan color and some paintbrushes; the cloth made of camel's hair, or of a substitute. Also **cam·el hair,** kăm′el·hâr″.

Ca·mem·bert cheese, kăm′em·bâr chēz′, n. [< *Camembert,* a village in Normandy, France.] A rich, soft, unpressed cheese characterized by a distinct flavor and odor produced by the presence of a mold.

cam·e·o, kăm′ē·ō″, n. pl. **cam·e·os.** [It. *cammeo* = Fr. *camaïeu;* origin uncertain.] An engraving in relief upon a gem or stone, esp. when differently colored layers of the stone are utilized to produce a background of one hue and a design of another; a gem or stone, so engraved; the art of engraving small figures in relief.

cam·e·o, kăm′ē·ō″, n. A brief but vivid literary vignette or theatrical role, the latter often devised to display the talents of a particular performer.

cam·er·a, kăm′er·a, kăm′ra, n. pl. **cam·er·as, cam·er·ae,** kăm′er·a·rē″. [L. a vault, a chamber, < Gr. *kamara,* anything arched. CHAMBER.] An apparatus that takes photographs by means of a lightproof enclosure fitted with a lens that focuses an external image, admitted through a shutter-controlled aperture, on light-sensitive film or plates; the device in a television transmitting system in which images to be televised are formed by means of an optical lens and then translated into electrical signals in an electron tube; a camera obscura; pl. **cam·er·as.** A chamber, esp. a judge's private chambers; pl. **cam·er·ae.—in cam·er·a,** *law,* in the privacy of a judge's chamber or office; secretly.

cam·er·al, kăm′er·al, a. [G. *kameral;* M.L. *cameralis,* < *camera,* chamber, treasury: see *camera.*] Pertaining to public finances or revenue; pertaining to a judicial or legislative chamber.

cam·er·a·lism, kăm′er·a·liz″am, n. The economic mercantilism of 17th- and 18th-century Europe advocating policies which strengthened the position of the ruler; mercantilistic principle which emphasizes monetary wealth in economic policy.— **cam·er·al·ist,** n.—**cam·er·al·is·tic,** a.— **cam·er·al·is·tics,** n. The science of public finance.

cam·er·a lu·ci·da, kăm′er·a lö′si·da,

kăm′ra lö′si·da, n. An optical instrument employing a prism or mirrors and often a microscope through which the image of an external object is projected onto a sheet of paper so that an outline may be traced.

cam·er·a·man, kăm′er·a·man″, kăm′er-·a·man, kăm′ra·man″, kăm′ra·man, n. pl. **cam·er·a·men.** A man who operates a photographic camera, esp. a moving-picture camera.

cam·er·a ob·scu·ra, kăm′er·a ob·skūr′a, kăm′ra ob·skūr′a, n. [N.L., "dark chamber."] A darkened boxlike device in which images of external objects, received through an aperture, as with a convex lens, are exhibited in their natural colors on a surface arranged to receive them: used for sketching or exhibition purposes.

cam·er·len·go, kăm″ēr·leng′gō, n. *Rom. Cath. Ch.* the cardinal who heads the papal treasury. Also **cam·er·lin·go.**

ca·mi·no re·al, kä·mē′nō Re·äl′, n. [Sp. lit. royal road.] Highway; main road.

cam·i·on, kăm′ē·an, Fr. kä·myaN′, n. [Fr. origin uncertain.] A strongly built cart or wagon for transporting heavy loads; a truck, as for carrying military supplies.

ca·mise, ka·mēz′, ka·mēs′, n. [Ar. *qamīs.*] A loose shirt, smock, or tunic.

cam·i·sole, kăm′i·sōl″, n. [Fr., < It. *camiciola,* dim. of *camicia.*] A sleeveless underbodice, usually frilly and decorative, worn by women; a short dressing gown or negligee for women.

cam·let, kăm′lit, n. [Fr. *camelot,* prob. < Ar. *khamlat,* < *khaml,* nap.] A rich fabric, apparently orig. made of goat's hair, formerly in use; a durable waterproof cloth used for cloaks.

cam·o·mile, cham·o·mile, kăm′a·mīl, kăm′a·mēl″, n. [O.Fr. Fr. *camomille,* < L. *chamomilla, chamæmelon,* < Gr. *chamaimēlon,* < *chamai,* on the ground, and *mēlon,* apple.] Any plant of the genus *Anthemis,* esp. *A. nobilis* (the common camomile of Europe and of gardens elsewhere), an herb with strongly scented foliage and flowers that are used medicinally; any of various allied plants, as *Matricaria chamomilla,* German camomile.

Ca·mor·ra, ka·mar′a, ka·mor′a, It. kä-·maR′Rä, n. [It.] A Neapolitan secret society first publicly known about 1820, which developed into a powerful political organization, and has been associated with blackmail and robbery; (*l.c.*) some similar society or group.—**Ca·mor·rism,** n. The practices of the Camorra.—**Ca·mor·rist,** n.

cam·ou·flage, kăm′a·fläzh″, n. [Fr., < *camoufler,* disguise, make up under a false semblance, < It. *camuffare,* muffle up, disguise.] The act of disguising or concealing military troops or equipment as by the use of paint, smoke screens, or branches; the material used for such a disguise; a pretense, disguise, manner, or plan intended as a false front.

cam·ou·flage, kăm′a·fläzh″, v.t.—*camouflaged, camouflaging.* To disguise or conceal. —v.i. To practice camouflage; wear a disguise.—**cam·ou·flag·er,** n. One who practices camouflage. Also **cam·ou·fleur,** kăm′o·flur′, Fr. kä·mö·flœR′.

camp, kamp, n. [Fr., < It. *campo,* < L. *campus,* plain, field.] A place where an army or other similar body of persons is lodged; the barracks, etc., collectively, or the persons sheltered; a body of troops, etc., camping and moving together; a temporary shelter used while fishing, hunting, etc.; an encamping, or camping out; a recreation area for group living, usually in the country, equipped with facilities for sports and handicrafts; as, a summer *camp* for children; a town, newly settled and usually temporary, in a mining or lumbering area; a group of persons

devoted to defending a theory or ideology; as, a political *camp.*—**day camp,** a summer camp where children are cared for only in the day.

camp, kamp, v.t. To lodge in a camp; shelter.—v.i. To establish a camp; sojourn in a camp; take up temporary quarters; live temporarily in a tent or tents or in rude places of shelter, as for pleasure and recreation, often with *out.*

camp, kamp, n. The aesthetic view that something banal, vulgar, pretentious, or distastefully extravagant can be enjoyed for its artistic style; something that appeals to persons holding this view; delight in extravagant affectation, esp. when applied to trivia; ironic or amused admiration of something formerly considered lowbrow, as old comic books.

cam·paign, kam·pān′, n. [Fr. *campagne,* < It. *campagna,* < M.L. *campania,* < L. *campus,* plain.] The military operations of an army in the field during one season or enterprise; any course of aggressive action, as that intended to influence voters in an election.—v.i. To serve in or go on a campaign.—**cam·paign·er,** n.

cam·paign rib·bon, n. A distinctively colored strip of cloth or narrow, ribbon-covered bar worn on the left breast of a military uniform to indicate campaigns participated in or medals won.

cam·pa·ni·le, kăm′pa·nē′lē, n. pl. **cam-·pa·ni·les, cam·pa·ni·li,** kăm′pa·nē′lē. [It. *campanile* < It. and L.L. *campana,* a bell.] *Arch.* a clock or bell tower, a term applied especially to detached buildings in some parts of Italy erected for the purpose of containing bells, and frequently forming part of a church complex: the Leaning Tower of Pisa is a *campanile.*

cam·pa·nol·o·gy, kăm″pa·nol′o·jē, n. [L.L. *campana,* a bell, and Gr. *logos,* discourse.] The art or principles of bell ringing or bell casting; the study of this art. —**cam·pa·nol·o·gist,** kăm″pa·nol′o·jist, n. One skilled in the art of bell ringing or bell casting.

cam·pan·u·la, kam·pan′ū·la, n. pl. **cam-·pan·u·las.** [M.L., dim. of *campana,* bell.] *Bot.* any plant of the genus *Campanula,* as the harebell or the Canterbury bell; a bell-flower.—**cam·pan·u·la·ceous,** kam·pan″-ya·lā′shus, a. *Bot.* belonging to the *Campanulaceae,* or campanula family of plants.

cam·pan·u·late, kam·pan′ya·lit, kam-·pan′ya·lāt″, a. [N.L. *campanulatus,* < M.L. *campanula:* CAMPANULA.] Bell-shaped, usually as a description of flower petals.

Camp·bell·ite, kăm′ba·līt″, kăm′a·līt″, n. [From Alexander *Campbell* (1788–1866), founder of the body.] A member of the body of Christians known as Disciples of Christ.

camp·er, kam′pêr, n. A person who lives in a tent, or lodge, or outdoors in a vacation area, usually during the summer season; a boy or girl who attends summer camp; a person who takes part in a work-camp program or a camp meeting; a vehicle used for recreational purposes equipped with accommodations for sleeping and eating.

cam·pes·tral, kam·pes′tral, a. [L. *campester,* < *campus,* field.] Pertaining to the fields or to a country setting. Also **cam-·pes·tri·an, cam·pes·trine.**

camp·fire, kamp′fīr″, n. A fire in a camp for warmth or cooking; a social gathering or reunion of soldiers or scouts.

camp·fire girl, n. A girl who is a member of Camp Fire Girls, Inc., an organization dedicated to the principles of good character, citizenship, and health.

camp fol·low·er, n. One who follows a camp or an army without being officially connected with it, as a prostitute; one who

cam·phene, kam´fēn, n. *Chem.* any of several camphor-related terpenes, esp. a colorless, crystalline substance, $C_{10}H_{16}$, found in certain essential oils and used chiefly as a camphor substitute or an intermediate in synthetic camphor.

cam·phine, cam·phene, kam´fēn, kam·fēn´, n. [< *camphor*.] A purified oil of turpentine or a mixture of oil of turpentine and alcohol, formerly burned in lamps.

cam·phol, kam´fol, kam´fạl, kam´fōl, n. [< *camphor*.] *Chem.* borneol.—**cam·phol·ic,** kam·fol´ik, a.

cam·phor, kam´fẽr, n. [Fr. *camphre*, < M.L. *camphora*, < Ar. *kāfūr*.] A whitish, translucent, volatile, and aromatic crystalline substance, obtained chiefly from the tree *Cinnamomum camphora*, the camphor tree, used in medicine, and as an irritant and stimulant.—**cam·pho·ra·ceous,** a.

cam·pho·rate, kam´fạ·rāt, v.t.—*camphorated, camphorating*. To impregnate with camphor.—n. *Chem.* a salt of camphoric acid.—**cam·phor·ic,** kam´fạr·ik, a. Of, containing, or derived from camphor; as, *camphoric* acid, a dibasic crystalline acid obtained by the oxidation of camphor.—**cam·phor·ous,** a. Camphorlike.

cam·phor glass, n. A milky-white glass resembling gum camphor in color.

cam·phor ice, n. An ointment composed chiefly of camphor, white wax, spermaceti, and castor oil, used for chapped or blemished skin.

cam·phor tree, n. A lauraceous tree, *Cinnamomum camphora*, of Japan, China, etc., yielding the camphor of commerce; any of various similar trees, as *Dryobalanops aromatica* of Borneo, which yields borneol.

cam·pim·e·ter, kam·pim´i·tẽr, n. [L. *campus*, field, and *-meter*.] An apparatus for measuring range of color sensitivity of the retina, and other visual properties.

cam·pi·on, kam´pē·on, n. [Origin uncertain.] Any of certain plants of the pink family, as *Lychnis coronaria*, the rose campion, a cultivated plant with crimson flowers.

camp meet·ing, n. A religious meeting, usually lasting for some days, held in an encampment formed for the purpose.

cam·po, kam´pō, käm´pō, n. pl. **cam·pos.** A wide grassy plain of South America.

cam·pong, n. Kampong.

camp·o·ree, kam˝po·rē´, n. A camp gathering of boy or girl scouts from a given region or area, as differentiated from the larger national or international meeting called a jamboree.

cam·po san·to, käm´pạ sän´tạ, n. [Sp. and It., holy ground.] A burial ground; a cemetery.

camp·stool, kamp´stōl, n. A light folding seat.

cam·pus, kam´pus, n. pl. **cam·pus·es.** [L., field.] The grounds or yard of an American college or other school; the educational environment as identified with the institution of higher learning.

cam·pus, kam´pus, v.t. Slang, to discipline, as a student, by denying certain privileges, often that of leaving the campus.

camp·y, kam´pē, a.—*campier, campiest.* Appealing to, or having the characteristics of camp; amusingly affected or theatrical, esp. when applied to trivia; effeminate, of a man.

cam·shaft, kam´shaft˝, kam´shäft˝, n. *Mach.* the shaft on which a cam is mounted to give motion to other mechanisms.

can, kan, aux. v.—past could. [O.E. *cann, can,* 1st and 3rd pers. sing. pres. ind. (past *cūthe*) of *unnan* = G. *können* = Icel. *kunna,* know, be able, = Goth. *kunnan,* know. KEN and KNOW.] To know how to, as: He *can* drive. To have the ability, power, right, qualifications or means to; to have the needed resolve to, as: He *can* accept his failure. To be allowed by conscience, as: I *can* forgive him. To be likely through circumstances, as: I *could* shout for joy. To be liable to, as: He *can* be sued for that. To be constructed or made to, as: It *can* hold two gallons. *Colloq.* to be permitted, as: You *can* leave now.

can, kan, v.t.—*canned, canning.* To put or preserve in a can. *Colloq.* to sink, as a golf putt, into the cup; to register, as sound, on tapes or discs. *Slang,* to expel or dismiss, as from employment; to end or stop, as: *Can* the uproar!

can, kan, n. [O.E. *canne* = G. *kanne,* can, pot, mug.] A vessel for holding or carrying liquids, now commonly one of tinned steel or aluminum; a drinking vessel; a container made of tin in which perishable foods or other products are hermetically sealed for preservation. *Slang,* a bathroom or toilet; a jail; the buttocks; *milit. slang,* a depth charge; a naval destroyer.

can, kan, n. *Aeron.* any one of the individual combustion chambers in a turbojet engine.

Ca·naan, kā´nan, n. The region, included in ancient Palestine, lying between the Jordan, the Dead Sea, and Mediterranean; the land promised by God to Abraham (Gen. xii.); *fig.* any land of promise; heaven.—**Ca·naan·ite,** kā´na·nīt˝, n. A Semitic inhabitant of the land of Canaan, which comprised ancient Palestine and Phoenicia.

ca·ña·da, kan·yä´dạ, kan·yad´a, n. [Sp.] A deep, narrow valley; in western U.S., a riverbed which is dry.

Can·a·da bal·sam, n. A fluid resin mixed with a volatile oil, obtained from the balsam fir tree, used as a transparent cement, esp. when mounting specimens on microscope slides.

Can·a·da goose, n. A large, wild goose, *Branta canadensis,* native to North America, marked by its black head and neck, white throat, and brownish-gray feathered body.

Can·a·da grouse, n. See grouse.

Can·a·da hemp, n. Indian hemp.

Can·a·da jay, n. A nonmigratory N. American bird, *Perisoreus canadensis,* with black and gray feathers, but not crested. Also **lum·ber·jack, whis·ky-jack, ven·i·son hawk, moose·bird,** and **camp rob·ber.**

Can·a·da rice, n. A plant growing in deep water in Canada and northern U.S., the seeds of which provided much of the food of American Indians, and is used as feed by flocks of waterfowl.

Can·a·da rob·in, n. The cedar bird.

Can·a·da this·tle, n. A European thistle, *Cirsium arvense,* having small purple and white flower heads, naturalized in North America and now a troublesome weed.

Ca·na·di·an, ka·nā´dē·an, a. Relating to the people and country of Canada, the largest unit of the British Commonwealth of Nations, located in North America and sharing its southern border with the U.S.—n. A native or resident of Canada; the languages characteristic of various provinces in Canada.

Ca·na·di·an ba·con, n. A boneless loin of cured, smoked pork which has the flavor of ham.

Ca·na·di·an French, n. The French language as spoken by Canadians, esp. in the province of Quebec; the natives of the French-speaking areas of Canada, descended from the French settlers.—a. Pertaining to Canadians of French descent and their language.

Ca·na·di·an Shield, n. *Geol.* a large area of pre-Cambrian granite, lying north of the Great Lakes in Canada, and noted for its rich deposits of gold, nickel, and iron ore; also **Lau·ren·tian Shield.**

ca·nai·gre, ka·nī´grē, n. [Mex. Sp.] A species of dock, *Rumex hymenosepalus,* of the southwestern U.S., whose root yields tannin.

ca·naille, ka·nāl´, Fr. kä·nä´ya, n. [Fr., < It. *canaglia,* a pack of dogs, < L. *canis,* a dog.] Riffraff; rabble; a mob.

ca·nal, ka·nal´, n. [Fr. *canal,* < L. *canalis,* a channel, < the same root as Skt. *khan,* to dig.] An artificial watercourse, particularly one constructed for the passage of boats or ships; *arch.* a channel; a groove or a flute; *anat.* any cylindrical or tubular cavity in the body through which solids, liquids, or certain organs pass; a duct; *zool.* a groove observed in different parts of certain univalve shells; *astron.* any of the long, faint, narrow markings on the surface of the planet Mars.

ca·nal, ka·nal´, v.t.—*canalled, canalling, canaled, canaling.* To make a canal through; furnish with a canal or canals.

ca·nal boat, n. A long, narrow boat or barge, either self-propelled or towed, used on canals.

can·a·lic·u·late, kan˝a·lik´ya·lit, a. [L., dim. of *canalis,* pipe, groove, channel.] Channeled; furrowed; grooved. Also **can·a·lic·u·lat·ed,** kan˝a·lik´ū·lāt·id.

can·a·lic·u·lus, kan˝a·lik´ya·lus, n. pl. **can·a·lic·u·li,** kan˝a·lik´ya·lī. [L., dim. of *canalis,* pipe, groove, channel.] *Anat., zool.* a tubular or canal-like passage or channel, as in a bone.—**can·a·lic·u·lar,** a.

ca·nal·i·za·tion, ka·nal˝i·zā´shan, n. The act of canalizing; a system of channels.

ca·nal·ize, ka·nal´īz, kan´a·līz˝, v.t.—*canalized, canalizing.* To make a canal; to convert into a canal; to furnish with a system of canals; to direct into channels or furnish with an outlet.

can·a·pé, kan·a·pā´, kan´a·pē, Fr. kä·nä·pā´, n. [Fr., = E. *canopy.*] A thin small piece of toast, bread, or a cracker covered with fish, meat, cheese, or other seasoned preparation; in furniture, an 18th-century French style of sofa and chairs; in a game of bridge, a procedure of bidding short suits before long suits.

ca·nard, ka·närd´, Fr. kä·när´, n. [Fr., lit. 'duck.'] A fabricated story or report circulated as true; a hoax; *cooking,* a duck.

ca·nard, ka·närd´, Fr. kä·när´, n. *Aeron.* an airplane having its horizontal stabilizers and elevators forward of the wing.

ca·nar·y, ka·nâr´ē, n. pl. **ca·nar·ies.** A small singing bird often kept as a pet, native to the Canary Islands, belonging to the finch family, usually yellow in color but with variation in size, form, and color; a sweet white wine made in the Canary Islands; an old dance introduced from the Canary Islands into Europe. *Slang,* an informer; a woman singer with a dance band.

ca·nar·y yel·low, n. A light and clear shade of yellow.

ca·nas·ta, ka·nas´ta, n. A popular card game which originated in Argentina, named from the small wicker basket (Sp. *canasta*) Argentinians used to hold the cards.

can·can, kan´kan, Fr. käN·käN´, n. [Fr.] A dance of French origin, performed by women entertainers, marked by high kicking, usually while holding up the front of a full ruffled skirt and which came into vogue about 1830 at the public dance halls of Paris.

can·cel, kan´sel, v.t.—*canceled, canceling, cancelled, cancelling.* [O.Fr. Fr. *canceller,* < L. *cancellare* (pp. *cancellatus*), < *cancelli,* pl., bars, lattice.] To strike out, obliterate, or delete by drawing a line or lines through; to destroy the validity of; to annul; to suppress or omit as some portion of a printed work; to deface, mark, or perforate so as to invalidate for use, as a postage stamp, check or ticket; *math.* to eliminate by striking out a factor common to both terms of a fraction or from both sides of an equation; *accounting*, to close, as an account by paying or crediting outstanding charges.—*v.i.* to counterbalance; to compensate for one another; to neutralize each other's strength.

can·cel, kan′sel, *n.* A canceling; a canceled part. *Print.* an omission, deletion, or suppression of a written passage or page; a new slip or leaf substituted in place of omitted or deleted material.—**can·cel·a··ble, can·cel·la·ble,** *a.*—**can·cel·er, can··cel·ler,** *n.*

can·cel·late, kan′sa·lāt″, kan′sa·lit, *a.* [L. *cancellatus*, pp.] Marked with crossing lines, like latticework; reticulated; *anat.* of spongy or porous structure. Also **can··cel·lat·ed,** kan′sa·lā″tid.

can·cel·la·tion, kan″sa·lā′shan, *n.* The act of canceling, making void, or invalidating, as the calling off of an arrangement, or an accommodation released; the result of canceling, as the actual marks on something made when item is canceled; the termination of an insurance policy by insurer or insured.

can·cer, kan′ser, *n.* [L. *cancer* (*cancr-*), a crab, the Crab, also the tumor < Gr. *karkinos*, Skt. *karkata*, crab.] *Pathol.* a malignant growth or tumor, esp. originating in the epithelium, and characterized by abnormal cellular growth which spreads to other areas. An evil likened to a malignant, corrosive sore; (*Cap.*) *astron.* the Crab, a northern zodiacal constellation; (*Cap.*) *astrol.* the fourth sign of the Zodiac.—**cer·ous,** *a.* Cancerlike; affected with cancer.

can·cer·ate, kan′sa·rāt″, *v.i.*—*cancerated, cancerating.* [L. *canceratus*, cancerous.] To become cancerous.—**can·cer·a·tion,** kan″sa·rā′shan, *n.*

can·cri·zans, kang′kri·zanz, kan′kri·zanz, *a.* [M.L. ppr. of *cancrizare*, go backward like a crab; < L. *cancer*, a crab, the Crab, also a tumor.] Going or moving backward, like a crab; *mus.* designating a canon in which the theme or subject is repeated backward instead of forward.

can·croid, kang′kroid, *a.* Resembling a crab; *pathol.* resembling a cancer, as certain tumors.—*n. Pathol.* a form of cancer of the skin.

can·de·la·brum, kan″de·lä′brum, *n. pl.* **can·de·la·bra, can·de·la·brums,** kan″·de·lä′bra. [L., < *candela*, a candle.] A branched, highly ornamental candlestick.

can·dent, kan′dent, *a.* [L. *candens, candentis*, < *candeo*. to be white or hot. CANDID.] *Archaic.* Heated to whiteness; glowing with white heat.

can·des·cence, kan·des′ens, *n.* [L. *candesco*, incept. of *candeo*.] *Rare.* A state of glowing; incandescence.

can·des·cent, kan·des′ent, *a.* [L. *candescens* (*-ent-*), ppr. of *candescere*, begin to glow, < *candēre*, shine.] *Rare.* Glowing; incandescent.

can·did, kan′did, *a.* [L. *candidus*, white, fair, clear, sincere, candid, < *candēre*, shine.] Frank; outspoken; open and sincere; honest; impartial; straightforward; informal, spontaneous, or unposed; as, in a *candid* photograph.—**can·did·ly,** *adv.*—**can·did·ness,** *n.*

can·di·da·cy, kan′di·da·sē, *n. pl.* **can··di·da·cies,** The state of being, or act of standing as, a candidate. Also *Brit.* **can··di·da·ture.**

can·di·date, kan′di·dāt″, kan′di·dit, *n.* [L. *candidatus*, clad in white, as a Roman candidate for office, < *candidus*, white.] One who seeks or is proposed for an appointment, office, or honor; an aspirant; a person who seems likely to reach a certain end.

can·did cam·er·a, *n.* A small camera of hand size with powerful lens and quick shutter that permits the photographing of unposed pictures.

can·died, kan′dēd, *a.* Preserved; cooked in sugar; glazed. *Fig.* honeyed, flattering.

Can·di·ot, kan′dē·ot″, *n.* A native or inhabitant of Candia, or Crete; a Cretan. Also **Can·di·ote,** kan·dē·ōt, *a.* Cretan.

can·dle, kan′dl, *n.* [O.E. *candel*, < L. *candela*, < *candēre*, shine.] A solid cylinder of tallow or wax enclosing a wick, which is burned to give light; something candlelike in form or purpose, which gives light, fumigates, or medicates. *Optics*, an international standard unit for measuring light intensity; also **new can·dle** or **can·de·la.**—**not hold a can·dle to,** not bear comparison with or approach in excellence.

can·dle, kan′dl, *v.t.*—*candled, candling.* To examine, as eggs for freshness, by holding between the eye and a lighted candle or any bright light.

can·dle·ber·ry, kan′dl·ber″ē, *n.* The wax myrtle *Myrica cerifera*; the berry of the wax myrtle, used in making candles. A Polynesian tree, *Aleurites moluccana*; also **can·dle·nut.**

can·dle·fish, kan′dl·fish″, *n. pl.* **can·dle··fish, can·dle·fish·es.** An edible fish, *Thaleichthys pacificus*, of the northwestern coast of North America, allied to the smelt, with flesh so oily that when the fish is dried and supplied with a wick it may be used as a candle. Also *eulachon.*

can·dle-foot, *n.* A foot-candle.

can·dle ice, *n. Canada*, the candlelike shapes assumed by river or lake ice as it thaws. Also **can·dled ice.**

can·dle·light, kan′dl·līt″, *n.* The light of a candle; subdued artificial light; the time, twilight, at which candles are lighted.—**can·dle·light·ing,** *n.*

Can·dle·mas, kan′dl·mas, kan′dl·mas″, *n.* [O.E. *candelmæsse.*] An ecclesiastical festival, February 2, in honor of the presentation of the infant Christ in the Temple and the purification of the Virgin Mary, celebrated by lighted candles.

can·dle·pin, kan′dl·pin″, *n.* A gently tapered bowling pin resembling a slender candle.—**can·dle·pins,** *n. pl. but sing. in constr.* A variation of bowling in which candlepins are used, played chiefly in northeastern U.S.

can·dle·pow·er, *n.* The illuminating power of a standard candle: used as a unit of measurement of light.

can·dle·stick, kan′dl·stik″, *n.* An object which has an opening or spike for holding a candle in position for burning.

can·dle·wick, kan′dl·wik″, *n.* The wick of a candle.—**can·dle·wick·ing,** *n.* Loosely twisted cotton embroidery yarn like the thread used in candles as wicks; the embroidery which uses tufts of this yarn, most commonly on muslin bedspreads. Also *candlewick.*

can·dle·wood, kan′dl·wụd″, *n.* Any resinous wood used for torches, or as a substitute for candles; any of various trees or shrubs yielding such wood.

can·dor, *Brit.* **can·dour,** kan′dėr, *n.* [L., < *candēre*, shine.] Quality of being open, frank, or straightforward; impartiality; judging without prejudice.

can·dy, kan′dē, *n. pl.* **can·dies.** [It. *candi*, candy < Ar. *gandi*, made of sugar, < *gand*, sugar.] A confection made by boiling sugar syrup to a solid state, adding flavoring or nuts, and forming into attractive shapes; a sweet morsel in many varieties such as taffy, fudge, caramels or bonbons; a piece of such confection.

can·dy, kan′dē, *v.t.*—*candied, candying.* To cover or saturate with sugar, usu. by cooking in a heavy syrup, as in making glazed carrots; to crystallize into sugar; to render agreeable; sweeten.—*v.i.* To become coated with or crystallized into sugar.

can·dy strip·er, *n. Colloq.* a young, female volunteer aid at a hospital, so called from her pink or red and white striped uniform.

can·dy·tuft, kan′dē·tuft″, *n.* [< *Candia*, the ancient Crete.] A tufted annual and perennial flower of the mustard family, genus *Ibersis*, brought from the island of Candia.

cane, kān, *n.* [Old spelling also *canne*, < L. *canna*, Gr. *kanna*, a reed.] The stem of some palms, grasses, and other plants such as the bamboo and sugarcane; a walking stick; a rod used to administer beatings; split rattan, used for casual furniture.

cane, kān, *v.t.*—*caned, caning.* To beat with a cane, or walking stick; to furnish or build with cane, as chairs.

cane·brake, kān′brāk, *n.* A dense growth of cane.

ca·nel·la, ka·nel′a, *n.* [M.L., cinnamon, < L. *canna*, E. *cane*.] The cinnamonlike bark of a West Indian tree, *Canella winterana*, used as a condiment and in medicine.—**can·el··la·ceous,** *a.* Belonging to the *Canellaceae*, a family of trees including the genus *Canella*.

can·er, kā′nėr, *n.* One who weaves cane, especially for chair seats and backs.

ca·nes·cent, ka·nes′ent, *a.* [L. *canescens, canescentis*, ppr. of *canesco*, to grow white, < *caneo*, to be white.] Growing white or hoary; *bot.* having a whitish covering.

cane sug·ar, *n.* Sugar obtained from the sugar cane; sucrose.

Ca·nic·u·la, ka·nik′ya·la, *n.* [L., dim. of *canis*, dog.] The dog star, Sirius.—**ca··nic·u·lar,** *a.* Of or pertaining to the dog star or its rising, as, the *canicular* days, the dog days; pertaining to the dog days.—**can·i·cule,** kan′i·kūl, *n.* [Fr.] The dog days.

ca·nine, kā′nīn, ka·nīn′, *a.* [L. *caninus*, < *canis*, dog.] *a.* Of or like a dog; pertaining to or characteristic of dogs; as, *canine* madness; *anat., zool.* pertaining to the four pointed teeth, esp. prominent in dogs, situated one on each side of each jaw, next to the incisors.

ca·nine, kā′nīn, ka·nīn′, *n.* A dog; any animal of the dog family, *Canidæ*; a canine tooth.—**ca·nin·i·ty,** ka·nin′i·tē, *n.* Canine nature.

Ca·nis Ma·jor, kā′nis mā′jėr. [L., "greater dog."] The Great Dog, a southern constellation following Orion, and containing Sirius, the dog star, the brightest of the fixed stars.

Ca·nis Mi·nor, kā′nis mī′nėr. [L., "lesser dog."] The Little Dog, a constellation south of Gemini, separated from Canis Major by the Milky Way, containing the bright star Procyon.

can·is·ter, kan′i·stėr, *n.* [L. *canistrum*, Gr. *kanastron*, < *kanna*, a reed.] A small box or case of tin, plastic, or the like, for tea, coffee, or other dry materials. *Milit.* a case containing shot which bursts on being discharged; case shot.

can·ker, kang′kėr, *n.* [< L. *cancer*, properly pronounced *canker*, a crab, a cancer.] A kind of cancerous, gangrenous, or ulcerous sore or disease, whether in animals or plants; an eating, corroding, or other noxious agency producing ulceration, gangrene, rot, decay, and the like; anything that insidiously or persistently destroys, corrupts, or irritates, as care, trouble, annoyance, grief or pain.—**Can·ker rose,** a dog rose, *Rosa Canina*.

can·ker, kang′kėr, *v.t.* To infect with canker either literally or figuratively; to eat into, corrode, or corrupt; to render crabbed or ill-natured.—*v.i.* To grow corrupt; to be infected with canker or some poisonous or pernicious influence; to be or become malignant.—**can·ker·ous,** kang′kėr·us.

can·ker sore, *n.* An ulcerated sore of the lips or membranous lining of the mouth.

can·ker·worm, kang′kẽr·wụrm″, *n.* A worm or larva destructive to trees or plants.

can·na, kan′a, *n.* [O.Fr. *cane* (Fr. *canne*), < L. *canna*, < Gr. *kanna*, reed.] Any plant of the tropical genus *Canna*, family *Cannaceae*, various species of which are cultivated for their large leaves and showy flowers.

can·na·bin, kan′a·bin, *n.* A poisonous resin extracted from Indian hemp.—**can·na·bism,** *n.* The morbid condition produced by excessive chewing or smoking of Indian hemp.

can·na·bis, kan′a·bis, *n.* [< Gr. *kannabis*, hemp.] The tops and leaves of Indian hemp used as a narcotic or intoxicant. Also *hashish, hasheesh.*

canned, kand, *a.* Preserved in a can or glass jar; in a metal container, as a completed movie film; recorded on tape ready for use on radio or television; prepared in advance; as, a *canned* speech. *Slang,* drunk; dismissed from employment.

can·nel coal, kan′el kōl″, *n.* A glistening grayish-black, hard, bituminous coal, so called because it burns with a bright flame like a candle.

can·nel·lo·ni, kan″e·lō′nē, *n. pl.* [It.] *Cooking,* hollow rolls of pasta, usually filled with minced and seasoned meat or cheese, and baked in a tomato or cream sauce.

can·ner, kan′ẽr, *n.* One who cans meat, fish, fruit, or the like, for preservation.

can·ner·y, kan′e·rē, *n. pl.* **can·ner·ies.** An establishment for canning or preserving meat, fish, or fruit in tins or glass jars hermetically sealed.

can·ni·bal, kan′i·bal, *n.* [Sp. *Canibal*, for *Caribal*, < *Caribe*, Carib.] A human being, esp. a savage, who eats human flesh; any animal that eats its own kind.—*a.* Pertaining to or characteristic of cannibals; given to cannibalism.—**can·ni·bal·ism,** *n.* The practice of eating one's own kind.—**can·ni·bal·is·tic,** *a.*

can·ni·bal·ize, kan′i·ba·līz″, *v.t.*—*cannibalized, cannibalizing.* To subject to cannibalism; to remove, as component parts, from one unit for use in the completion or repair of another unit, as: The mechanic *cannibalized* one motor to repair the other.—*v.i.*

can·ni·kin, kan′i·kin, *n.* [Dim. of *can.*] A little can; a cup; a small wooden bucket.

can·ni·ly, kan′i·lē, *adv.* In a canny manner.—**can·ni·ness,** *n.*

can·non, kan′on, *n. pl.* **can·nons** or, esp. collectively, **can·non.** [O.Fr. Fr. *canon*, < It. *cannone*, aug. of *canna*, tube, < L. *canna*, < Gr. *kanna*, reed.] A mounted gun for firing explosive shells; a piece of ordnance or artillery; a gun, howitzer, or mortar; *mech.* a hollow cylinder fitted over a shaft and capable of revolving independently; *zool.* the cannon bone. *Slang,* a revolver; a pickpocket. The metal loop of a bell by which it is hung; a part of a horse's bit; *Brit.* in billiards, a carom.

can·non, kan′on, *v.i.* To discharge cannon. *Brit.* to make a carom in billiards; strike and rebound; collide violently.

can·non·ade, kan″a·nād′, *n.* A continued discharge of cannon, esp. during an attack.

can·non·ade, kan″a·nād′, *v.t., v.i.*—*cannonaded, cannonading.* To attack with or discharge cannon.

can·non·ball, kan′an·bạl″, *n.* A round missile or solid projectile shot from a cannon; a fast express train; *tennis,* a hard serve with little or no arc.—*a. Swimming,* of a dive, made from a curled up position with the arms pressing the knees against the chest.—*v.i.* To move with great speed or force like a cannonball. Also **can·non ball.**

can·non bone, *n. Zool.* in hoofed quadrupeds, the bone extending from the knee or hock joint to the fetlock joint.

can·non·eer, kan″a·nēr′, *n.* An artillery gunner.

can·non fod·der, *n. Colloq.* soldiers, in reference to the expendability of their lives for the purpose of accomplishing a military objective in war.

can·non·ry, kan′an·rē, *n. pl.* **can·non·ries.** The act of discharging cannon; artillery.

can·not, kan′ot, ka·not′, ka·not′, *aux. v.* A common form of *can not.*

can·nu·la, kan′ya·la, *n. pl.* **can·nu·las, can·nu·lae.** [L. dim of *canna*, < G *kanna*, reed.] *Surg.* a small tube of metal or the like which draws off fluid or injects medicine into the body; also **can·u·la.**

can·nu·lar, kan′ya·lẽr, *a.* Tubular.—**can·nu·late, can·nu·lat·ed,** *a.* Hollow or tubular; as, a *cannulated* needle, a surgeon's hollow needle.

can·ny, kan′ē, *a.*—*cannier, canniest.* Knowing, sagacious; shrewd, astute; skilled or expert; frugal or thrifty.

ca·noe, ka·nö′, *n.* [Sp. *canoa;* prob. < Carib.] A slender, open boat, propelled by paddles, formed of a light framework covered with bark, skins, or canvas, or made of dug-out logs, orig. used by Indians of North and South America and favored by hunters and fishermen for easy portage.—**ca·noe·ist,** *n.* One who paddles a canoe; one skilled in canoeing.

ca·noe, ka·nö′, *v.i.*—*canoed, canoeing.* To paddle a canoe; to travel by canoe.—*v.t.* To carry in a canoe.

ca·noe tilt·ing, *n.* A sport involving tilting by contestants in canoes.

can·on, kan′on, *n.* [L., *rule,* canon, < Gr. *kanōn,* straight rod, rule, standard.] An ecclesiastical rule or law enacted by a church council; the body of ecclesiastical law; a general rule or law; a fundamental principle; a standard or criterion; the books of the Bible, Holy Scripture, recognized by the Christian church as genuine and inspired; any recognized set of sacred books; that part of the mass between the Sanctus and the Lord's Prayer; a catalogue or list of the saints acknowledged by the church. *Print.* 48-point printing type. *Mus.* a composition in which the different participants begin the same melody one after another at regular intervals, at the same or at a different pitch.

can·on, kan′on, *n.* [O.Fr. *canone* (Fr. *chanoine*), < L.L. *canonicus, n.* earlier *adj.* < *kanonikos,* < *kanōn,* rule.] *Eccles.* one of a group of clergymen attached to a cathedral or collegiate church; a member or 'canon regular' of certain Roman Catholic religious orders.

ca·ñon, kan′yan, *n.* Canyon.

can·on·ess, kan′a·nis, *n.* [Fem. of *canon.*] *Eccles.* a member of a community of women living under a rule, but not under a vow.

ca·non·ic, ka·non′ik, *a.* [L. *canonicus,* < Gr. *kanonikos,* < *kanōn,* rule, E. *canon.*] Pertaining to a musical canon; pertaining to one living under a religious rule.

ca·non·i·cal, ka·non′i·kal, *a.* Pertaining to, established by, or conforming to a canon or canons; authorized, recognized, or accepted; pertaining to a clergyman who is a canon.—**can·o·nic·i·ty,** kan″o·nis′i·tē, *n.*

can·on·i·cal, ka·non′i·kal, *n. Math.* the simplest and most convenient form of an equation, coordinate, etc.

ca·non·i·cal hours, *n. pl. Eccles.* certain periods of the day set apart for prayer and devotion, namely, matins with lauds, prime, terce, sext, nones, vespers, and compline; *Brit.* the hours between 8 A.M. and 3 P.M. during which marriages may legally take place in parish churches.

ca·non·i·cals, ka·non′i·kalz, *n. pl.* The articles of dress prescribed by canon for the clergy when officiating.

can·on·ist, kan′a·nist, *n.* One versed in canon law.—**can·on·is·tic, can·on·is·ti·cal,** *a.*

can·on·i·za·tion, kan′a·ni·zā″shan, *n.* The process of canonizing; the process of being raised to sainthood.

can·on·ize, kan′a·nīz″, *v.t.*—*canonized, canonizing.* [M.L. *canonizare.*] To place in the catalogue of the saints; to glorify; to include in the canon law.

can·on law, *n.* The body of laws made by a church for its own direction, esp. within the Roman Catholic Church.

can·on reg·u·lar, *n. pl.* **can·ons reg·u·lar.** A priest in one of various Roman Catholic religious institutions living in a community, usu. under Augustinian rule.

can·on·ry, kan′on·rē, *n. pl.* **can·on·ries.** The office or benefice of a canon. Also **can·on·ship.**

Ca·no·pic, ka·nō′pik, *a.* Of or from Canopus, an ancient city of Egypt; relating to a kind of vase used to hold the entrails of embalmed bodies: hence applied also to vases used elsewhere to hold the ashes of the dead.

Ca·no·pus, ka·nō′pus, *n. Astron.* a star in the Carina constellation and the second brightest star in the heavens.

can·o·py, kan′o·pē, *n. pl.* **can·o·pies,** kan′o·pēz. [O.Fr. *canape* (Fr. *canapé*), < L. *conopeum,* < Gr. *kōnopiōn* mosquito net, < *kōnōps* gnat, mosquito.] A covering suspended or supported over a throne or bed, or held over an exalted person or sacred object; hence, an overhanging protection or shelter; often, the sky; *arch.* an ornamental rooflike projection or covering; *aeron.* the transparent cover over the pilot's seat in an airplane; part of a parachute.

can·o·py, kan′o·pē, *v.t.*—*canopied, canopying.* To cover with, or as with, a canopy.

ca·no·rous, ka·nōr′us, ka·nạr′us, *a.* [L. *canorus,* < *canor,* song, melody, < *canere,* sing.] Melodious; musical.—**ca·no·rous·ly,** *adv.*—**ca·no·rous·ness,** *n.*

cant, kant, *n.* The thoughtless reiteration of trite, conventional sentiments, as statements feigning enthusiasm for high ideals; whining or singsong speech, as of beggars; the secret jargon spoken by special groups, as gypsies; the phraseology peculiar to a particular class, party, or profession; affected or insincere use of religious phraseology.

cant, kant, *v.i.* [Prob. < L. *cantare,* sing, declaim in a singing tone, < *canere,* sing.] To speak in the whining or singsong tone of a beggar; beg; to talk in cant, esp. to affect religious phraseology in a hypocritical manner.—*v.t.* To say in some conventional phraseology, or in hypocritical phrases.—**cant·er,** *n.*

cant, kant, *n.* [Prob. < O.Fr. *cant,* < M.L. *cantus,* corner, side.] A salient angle; an oblique line or surface, as one formed by cutting off the corner of a square or cube; an oblique or slanting face of anything; a slanting or tilted position; an inclination; a sudden movement tending to tilt a thing; a sudden pitch or toss.—*a.* Slanting; having oblique corners or sides.

cant, kant, *v.t.* To bevel; to give a slanting surface to; to put in an oblique position; tilt; turn over; to throw with a sudden jerk.—*v.i.* To take or have an inclined position; tilt; turn.

cant, känt, *a. Brit. dial.* Spirited; robust.

can't, kant, känt. *Colloq.* contraction of *can not.*

can·ta·bi·le, kän·tä′bi·lā″, kän·tä′bē·lä″, kan·tä′bi·lā″, kan·tä′bē·lä″, *It.* kän·tä′bē·le″, *a.* [It., < L.L. *cantabilis,* that may be sung, < *cantare,* sing.] *Mus.* songlike and flowing in style.—*n.* A cantabile-style passage or piece.

Can·ta·brig·i·an, kan″ta·brij′e·an, *a.* [M.L. *Cantabrigia,* Cambridge.] Of or pertaining to Cambridge, England, or Cambridge University; of or pertaining to Cambridge, Massachusetts, or Harvard University.—*n.* A native or inhabitant of Cambridge, England; a member or graduate of Cambridge University. Abbr. *cantab.*

can·ta·loup, can·ta·loupe, kan′ta·lōp″, *n.* [Fr., *cantaloup;* from *Cantalupo,* a former estate of the Pope near Rome.] A small, ribbed, delicately flavored variety of melon, *Cucumis melo cantalupensis,* having a sweet, orange-colored flesh.

can·tan·ker·ous, kan·tang′kėr·us, *a.* [Akin O.E. *contek, contak,* debate, strife.] Ill-natured; cross; waspish; contentious; disputatious.—**can·tan·ker·ous·ly,** *adv.*—**can·tan·ker·ous·ness,** *n.*

can·ta·ta, kan·tä′ta, *n.* [It., < *cantare,* < L. *cantare,* sing.] *Mus.* a choral composition, either sacred and resembling a short oratorio, or secular, as a lyric drama set to music but not to be acted; orig. a metrical narrative set to recitative, or alternate recitative and air, usually for a single voice, accompanied by one or more instruments.

can·ta·trice, *It.* kän″tä·trē′che, *Fr.* kän·-tä·trēs′, *n. pl. It.* **can·ta·tri·ci,** *Fr.* **can·-ta·trices,** kän″tä·trē·chē, kän″tä·trēs′. [Fr. and It., < L. *cantatrix.*] A female singer, esp. one who performs professionally.

can·teen, kan·tēn′, *n.* [Fr. *cantine,* < It. *cantina,* cellar, wine-cellar.] A place in a military camp or reservation for the sale, under military control, of food, drink, and commodities and sometimes for furnishing entertainment and recreational facilities for the benefit of military persons; a small vessel or flask, as of tin, used by soldiers and others for carrying water or other liquids for drinking; a box or chest containing table utensils; a recreation and refreshment room for servicemen maintained by civilians.

can·ter, kan′tėr, *n.* [An abbrev. of *Canterbury Gallop,* the gallop of pilgrims in olden times riding to Canterbury.] A horse's gait, easier and slower than a gallop.—*v.i.* To move at a canter or ride on a horse at a canter.—*v.t.* To cause to go, as a horse, at a moderate gallop.

can·ter·bur·y, kan′tėr·ber″ē, *n. pl.* **can·-ter·bur·ies.** [From *Canterbury,* city in southeastern England.] A stand with divisions for holding music and papers; a serving tray with divisions for dishes or cutlery.

Can·ter·bur·y bell, *n.* A plant, *Campanula trachelium,* with bell-shaped flowers, so named because found about Canterbury, England; some other species of *Campanula,* esp. *C. medium,* much cultivated for its showy flowers.

can·thar·is, kan·thar′is, *n. pl.* **can·thar·-i·des,** kan·thar′i·dēz″. [L., *pl.* of *cantharis,* < Gr. *kantharis,* a blistering fly.] A substance obtained from dried and crushed blister beetles of the genus *Cantharis,* and used in medicine, esp. externally for raising blisters and formerly as a stimulant.—**can·thar·i·dism,** *n.* A morbid state due to the use of cantharides.—**can·thar·i·dize,** *v.t.*—*cantharidized, cantharidizing.* To treat with cantharides.

cant hook, *n.* A wooden lever with a movable iron hook near the lower end, used for grasping and canting or turning over logs.

can·thus, kan′thus, *n. pl.* **can·thi,** kan′thī. [N.L., < Gr. *kanthos.*] *Anat.* the angle or corner on each side of the eye, formed by the junction of the upper and lower lids.

can·ti·cle, kan′ti·kl, *n.* [L. *canticulum,* a little song, < *canto,* to sing. CANT.] A song, especially an unmetrical hymn taken from Scripture, arranged for chanting, and used in a church service.

can·ti·lev·er, kan′ti·lev″ėr, kan′ti·lē″vėr, *n.* A beam or member projecting beyond a single support at one end; either of two beams projecting toward each other from piers to be joined to form the span of a cantilever bridge; a bracket for supporting a balcony, heavy shelf, or cornice; *aeron.* a type of wing support requiring no external bracing.—*v.t.* To build in the style of a cantilever.—*v.i.* To jut out or project as a cantilever. Also **can·ta·lev·er.**

can·til·late, kan′ti·lāt″, *v.t., v.i.*—*cantillated, cantillating.* [L. *cantillatus,* pp. of *cantillare,* dim. of *cantare,* sing.] To recite in musical tones; chant or intone, as in a liturgical text.—**can·til·la·tion,** *n.*

can·ti·na, kan·tē′na, *Sp.* kän·tē′nä, *n. Southwestern U.S.* A saloon; a pouch or bag hung on a saddle.

can·tle, kan′tl, *n.* [O.Fr. *cantel,* cornerpiece, dim. of *cant.* CANT, an angle.] A corner; a fragment; a piece; the protuberant afterpart or hind bow of a saddle.

can·to, kan′tō, *n. pl.* **can·tos.** [It. *canto,* a song; L. *cantus.* CHANT, CANT.] A part or division of a long poem.

can·ton, kan′ton, kan′ton, kan·ton′, *n.* [Fr., < It. *cantone,* aug. of *canto,* < M.L. *cantus,* corner, E. *cant.*] A small territorial district; one of the states of the Swiss confederation; a subdivision of an arrondissement in France.—*v.t.* To divide into parts or portions; divide into cantons or territorial districts; to allot quarters to, as soldiers.—*v.i.* of soldiers and sailors, to occupy quarters.

Can·ton crepe, *n.* A soft, pebbly dress cloth of silk or rayon, more full-bodied than crepe de Chine.

Can·ton·ese, kan″ton·ēz′, kan″ton·ēs′, *a.* Of or pertaining to Canton, China, its inhabitants, or their dialect.—*n.* A native or inhabitant of Canton; the Chinese dialect spoken in and around Canton.

Can·ton flan·nel, *n.* A soft, warm cotton fabric napped just on the face, used for undergarments, nightwear, and baby clothes. Also **cot·ton flan·nel.**

can·ton·ment, kan·ton′ment, kan·tōn′-ment, *Brit.* kan·tön′ment, *n.* Temporary military quarters, esp. winter or training quarters; the housing of troops in such quarters; *India,* a military post.

can·tor, kan′tėr, kan′tạr, *n.* [L. *cantor,* singer.] *Eccles.* a leader of the singing in a cathedral or other church; a precentor; *Judaism,* the synagogue official who helps lead the liturgy, singing or chanting the solo parts.

can·tus, kan′tus, *n. pl.* **can·tus.** A kind of church song; a song or melody, esp. the main part in a polyphonic composition.

can·tus fir·mus, kan′tus fėr′mus, *n. Mus.* the fixed or basic melody against which a counterpoint is set.

Ca·nuck, Ca·nuk, ka·nuk′, *n.* A French Canadian, usually a disparaging term.

ca·nu·lar, kan′ū·lėr, *a.* Cannular.

can·u·late, kan′ū·lāt″, kan′ū·lit, *a.* Cannulate.

can·vas, kan′vas, *n.* [O.Fr. Fr. *canevas,* L. *cannabis,* hemp.] A closely woven, heavy cloth of hemp, flax, or cotton, used for tents and sails; sailcloth; sails collectively; a tent or tents collectively; a piece of canvas for a particular purpose, as to receive an oil painting; an oil painting; any of various other fabrics, as of cotton or linen, with a coarse, open weave, used in sportswear or as an embroidery surface; *boxing or wrestling,* the arena floor.—**un·der can·vas,** in tents, esp. military or circus tents.

can·vas·back, kan′vas·bak″, *n.* A North American wild duck, *Æthyia (Aythya) vallisneria,* named for the white back of the male, and esteemed for the delicacy of its meat.

can·vass, kan′vas, *v.t.* [< *canvas.*] To discuss or examine carefully; to ask for opinions, votes, or subscriptions from, as persons to groups, as in an election campaign.—*v.i.* To go about engaging in discussion or debate.—*n.* The act of canvassing; an investigation by inquiry; a soliciting of votes, orders, etc.—**can·vass·er,** *n.*

can·yon, kan′yun, *n.* [Sp. *cañon,* a canon, a tube, a canyon.] A narrow valley with steep sides, formed by erosion. Also *cañon.*

can·zo·ne, kän·tsạ′ne, *n. pl.* **can·zo·ni,** kän·tsạ′nē. [It., < L. *cantio(n-),* song. CHANSON.] A form of lyric poem, of Provençal origin, developed esp. by the Italians; a short song from the period of the troubadours.

can·zo·net, kan″zo·net′, *n.* [It. *canzonetta.*] *Mus.* a little or short song, esp. one that is gay and lighthearted.

caou·tchouc, kou′chụk, kou·chök′, *n.* [A South American word.] Rubber; natural rubber, sometimes called India rubber; gum elastic.

C.A.P., *n.* Abbr. for Civil Air Patrol.

cap, kap, *n.* [O.E. *cæppe,* < M.L. *cappa, capa,* cap, hooded cloak, cape; origin uncertain.] A covering for the head, esp. one fitting closely and made of softer material than a hat, and having little or no brim; a special headdress denoting rank, occupation, etc.; any object, part, or piece resembling a cap for the head in shape, use, or position; a caplike covering or top; a percussioncap; in general, the topmost part; the acme; one of several large sizes of writing paper, as foolscap.—**set one's cap for,** to seek to win a man as a husband.—**with cap in hand,** in a supplicating manner; with humility.

cap, kap, *v.t.*—*capped, capping.* To put a cap on; to cover with a cap or as with a cap; to cover the top or end of; to place a cap on the head of, when conferring official distinction, admitting to professional honors, etc.; to complete; to consummate; to crown; to follow up with something more remarkable than what has previously been done or said.—**cap the cli·max,** to transcend what was thought to be the limit or culmination.

ca·pa·bil·i·ty, kā″pa·bil′i·tē, *n. pl.* **ca·pa·-bil·i·ties.** The quality of being capable; capacity; ability; quality of admitting of certain treatment; *usu. pl.,* properties or faculties capable of being developed or used.

ca·pa·ble, kā′pa·bl, *a.* [Fr. *capable,* capable, able, sufficient, L.L. *capabilis,* < L. *capio,* to take, which appears also in *captious, captive.*] Able to receive; open to influences; impressible; susceptible; admitting, with *of;* as, *capable of* pain; having sufficient power, skill, ability, with *of;* able; competent; fit; duly qualified; as, a *capable* instructor.—**ca·pa·ble·ness,** *n.*—**ca·pa·-bly,** *adv.*

ca·pa·cious, ka·pā′shus, *a.* [L. *capax, capacis,* able to take in or contain, spacious, capable, < *capio,* to take. CAPABLE.] Capable of containing much, either in a physical or mental sense; large; wide; spacious; extensive; comprehensive.—**ca·-pa·cious·ly,** *adv.*—**ca·pa·cious·ness,** *n.*

ca·pac·i·tance, ka·pas′i·tans, *n. Elect.* The property of a system of conductors and insulators which permits them to store an electrical charge when a difference of potential exists between the conductors; the measure of this property as the ratio of the charge on either of a pair of conductors to the potential difference between them. Sym. *C.*

ca·pac·i·tate, ka·pas′i·tāt″, *v.t.*—*capacitated, capacitating.* To make capable; to enable; to qualify.

ca·pa·ci·tive, ka·pas′i·tiv, *a. Elect.* pertaining to capacitance; as, a *capacitive* coupling, a coupling which joins circuits by means of a condenser.—**ca·pa·ci·tive·-ly,** *adv.*

ca·pac·i·tor, ka·pas'i·tẽr, *n. Elect.* a condenser.

ca·pac·i·ty, ka·pas'i·tē, *n.* pl. **ca·pac·i·ties**. [L. *capacitas*, < *capax*, capacious.] The power of receiving or containing; specifically, the power of containing a certain quantity exactly; cubic contents; the extent or comprehensiveness of the mind; the power of receiving ideas or knowledge; the receptive faculty; active power; ability; as, a man with the *capacity* of judging; ability in a moral or legal sense; legal qualification; as, to attend a meeting in the *capacity* of an elector; character; as, to give advice in the *capacity* of a friend; maximum possible output or production. *Electrostatics*, the maximum or rated load of a machine or apparatus; capacitance.

cap-a-pie, kap"a·pē', *adv.* [O.Fr., lit. head to foot.] From head to foot; all over.

ca·par·i·son, ka·par'i·san, *n.* [O.Fr. *caparasson* < Sp. *caparazón*, a cover for a saddle, aug. of *capa*, a cover.] A highly decorative cloth or covering for a horse, esp. a horse of state; ornamental trappings.—*v.t.* To cover, as a horse, with caparison; to adorn with rich dress.

cape, kāp, *n.* [Fr. *cap*, It. *capo*, a cape, < L. *caput*, the head.] A piece of land jutting into the sea or a lake beyond the rest of the coast line; a headland; a promontory.—**the Cape**, Cape of Good Hope; Cape Cod.

cape, kāp, *n.* [Fr. *cape*, < M.L. *capa*: see *cap*.] A sleeveless garment fitting closely around the neck and falling loosely from the shoulders: worn separately or attached to a coat.—**caped**, *a.*

Cape Cod, *a., n. Arch.* a compact wooden house having a gabled roof and large central chimney, evolved from a New England design of the 18th and early 19th centuries.

cap·e·lin, kap'a·lin, *n.* [Fr. *capelan*, *caplan*.] A small edible fish, *Mallotus villosus*, allied to the smelt: much used as bait for cod. Also **cap·lin**, *capling*.

Ca·pel·la, ka·pel'a, *n.* A brilliant yellow star of the first magnitude, the brightest in the constellation Auriga.

ca·per, kā'pẽr, *n.* A frolicsome leap or spring; a capricious action; a prank or wild escapade; *slang*, an illegal act.—*v.i.* To leap or skip about in a playful manner; to prance or gambol.—**cut a ca·per**, to play tricks; to act in a frolicsome way.

ca·per, kā'pẽr, *n.* [L. *capparis*, < Gr. *cap* and *paris*.] A shrub, *Capparis spinosa*, of Mediterranean regions, or its flower bud, which is pickled and used as a condiment.

cap·er·cail·lie, kap"ẽr·kāl'yē, *n.* [Gael. *capullcoille*.] The wood grouse, *Tetrao urogallus*, the largest of this type of game bird in northern Europe. Also **cap·er·cail·zie**, kap"ẽr·kal'zē.

cape·skin, kāp'skin, *n.* A leather made from the skins of goats of the Cape district of South Africa of which gloves are frequently made; leather of similar appearance made from the skins of various sheep or lambs by special tanning processes.

Ca·pe·tian, ka·pē'shan, *a.* Pertaining to the dynasty of the Capets, founded about the close of the tenth century, when Hugh Capet ascended the French throne.

ca·pi·as, kā'pē·as, kap'ē·as, *n.* [L., you may take.] *Law*, a writ authorizing the act of taking a person or possessions into custody.

cap·il·lar·i·ty, kap"i·lar'i·tē, *n.* The state of being capillary; the attraction and repulsion of molecules on the surface of a liquid in contact with a solid, as the walls of its container, which results in the rise or fall of a liquid when in narrow tubes or fibers, or in the wetting of a solid by a liquid, as in blotting action. Also *capillary action*.

cap·il·lar·y, kap'i·ler"ē, *a.* [L. *capillaris*, < *capillus*, hair.] Of or pertaining to hair; resembling a hair; very slender; having a very small bore; pertaining to or occurring in, or as in, a tube of fine bore; as, *capillary action; anat.* pertaining to a capillary or capillaries.—**cap·il·la·ceous**, kap"i·lā'shus, *a.* Hairlike; capillary.

cap·il·lar·y, kap'i·ler"ē, *n.* pl. **cap·il·lar·ies**. A tube with a very small bore; *anat.* one of the minute blood vessels between the terminations of the arteries and the beginnings of the veins.

cap·il·lar·y at·trac·tion, *n.* The apparent attraction between a liquid and a solid in capillarity: distinguished from **cap·il·lar·y re·pul·sion**.

cap·il·lar·y ac·tion, *n.* Capillarity.

cap·il·lar·y wa·ter, *n.* Water remaining in the soil after gravitational water is drained from it, that moves by capillary action and remains as a coating around soil granules.

cap·i·tal, kap'i·tal, *a.* [O.Fr. Fr. *capital*, < L. *capitalis*, pertaining to the head or to life, chief (as n., M.L. *capitale*, wealth, stock), < *caput*, head.] Pertaining to the head or top; involving the loss of life; as, *capital* punishment; fatal or serious, as an error; of or pertaining to large size letters regularly used at the beginning of a sentence, or as the first letter of a proper name; of the official seat of government of a country or state; in general, principal; highly important; excellent or first-rate, as: what a *capital* idea! Pertaining to financial capital; as, *capital* stock.

cap·i·tal, kap'i·tal, *n.* A capital letter; the city or town which is the official seat of government in a country or state.

cap·i·tal, kap'i·tal, *n.* [L. *capitellum*, dim. of *caput*, head.] *Arch.* the head, or uppermost part, of a column or pillar.

cap·i·tal, kap'i·tal, *n.* Any form of wealth employed for the production of more wealth; the wealth thus employed by a business or industrial or commercial enterprise, which can be in the form of manufactured goods, money, stocks or bonds, or relatively permanent assets as machinery or buildings; *accounting*, an excess of assets over liabilities.

cap·i·tal ac·count, *n.* An account showing an individual's or shareholder's financial interest in a business; a statement of capital assets of a business.

cap·i·tal as·sets, *n. pl.* Business assets which are of a fixed, permanent nature and not ordinarily bought and sold.

cap·i·tal ex·pen·di·ture, *n.* An expenditure involving long-term improvements in an industrial enterprise, as construction of a new factory or housing for workers.

cap·i·tal gain, *n.* Gain or gains from the sale of capital assets.

cap·i·tal in·vest·ment, *n.* Long-term investment in such physical assets of a business as machinery, tools, real estate, etc., with the expectation of profit.

cap·i·tal·ism, kap'i·ta·liz"um, *Brit.* ka·pit'a·liz"um, *n.* Possession of capital; *pol. econ.* a system under which the production and distribution of goods and services are privately managed; free enterprise.—**cap·i·tal·is·tic**, kap"i·ta·lis'tik, *Brit.* ka·pit"a·lis'tik, *a.* Of or pertaining to capitalism.

cap·i·tal·ist, kap'i·ta·list, *Brit.* ka·pit'a·list, *n.* One who has capital, esp. a person who has extensive wealth employed in business enterprises.

cap·i·tal·i·za·tion, kap"i·ta·li·zā'shan, *Brit.* ka·pit"a·li·zā'shan, *n.* The act of capitalizing; the capital stock of a corporation; the act of converting certain assets into stocks; the act of estimating present worth of future payments.

cap·i·tal·ize, kap'i·ta·līz, *Brit.* ka·pit'a·liz, *v.t.*—*capitalized, capitalizing.* To write or print in capital letters, or with an initial capital. *Finance*, to convert into or use as capital; furnish with capital; convert, as a periodical payment, into an equivalent capital or lump sum; to fix, as the capital of a corporation, at a certain sum for the purpose of issuing shares of stock accordingly. To use, as a talent or a favorable situation, to one's advantage, with *on*.

cap·i·tal lev·y, *n.* A levy on capital assets apart from the income tax.

cap·i·tal·ly, kap'i·ta·lē, *adv.* In an excellent, commendable way.

cap·i·tal pun·ish·ment, *n.* The death penalty for a convicted criminal.

cap·i·tal ship, *n.* A battleship belonging to the category of the largest in size and armed with first-rate weapons.

cap·i·tal stock, *n. Stock market*, the total shares of stock representing the capital of a corporation.

cap·i·tate, kap'i·tāt, *a.* [L. *capitatus*, < *caput*, head.] *Bot.* having or forming a head; headed; *zool.* with an enlarged or headlike end.

cap·i·ta·tion, kap"i·tā'shan, *n.* [L.L. *capitatio(n-)*, < L. *caput*, head.] The act of counting or assessing by the head; a poll tax; a tax, fee or payment fixed on a per capita basis.

Cap·i·tol, kap'i·tol, *n.* [L. *Capitolium*, < *caput*, head.] In the U.S., the edifice occupied by Congress at Washington, D.C. (*Often l.c.*) a statehouse; any building housing the center of a state government. The ancient temple of Jupiter at Rome, situated on a summit of the Capitoline Hill.

ca·pit·u·lar, ka·pich'u·lẽr, *n.* A member of an ecclesiastical or cathedral chapter; a law or canon of an ecclesiastical chapter.—*a.* Pertaining to an ecclesiastical chapter; *bot.* capitate.

ca·pit·u·lar·y, ka·pich'u·ler"ē, *n.* pl. **ca·pit·u·lar·ies**. *Usu. pl.* civil or ecclesiastical ordinances, esp. those of the Frankish kings. A member of a chapter, esp. an ecclesiastical chapter.—*a.* Belonging or pertaining to a chapter, esp. an ecclesiastical chapter.

ca·pit·u·late, ka·pich'u·lāt", *v.i.*—*capitulated, capitulating.* [L.L. *capitulo, capitulatum*, to arrange in heads or chapters, < L. *capitulum*, a chapter, dim. of *caput*, the head.] To give way under pressure; to yield or acquiesce; to surrender either unconditionally or by stipulated terms.—**ca·pit·u·lant**, *n.*—**ca·pit·u·la·tor**, *n.*—**ca·pit·u·la·tor·y**, *a.*

ca·pit·u·la·tion, ka·pich"u·lā'shan, *n.* The act of capitulating or yielding under pressure; the document embodying terms of surrender; a summary or enumeration of the main parts of a subject. *Often pl.* A treaty or agreement in which a country extends extra-territorial rights or privileges to citizens of another country, esp. those immunities formerly granted to European visitors by sultans of the Ottoman empire.

ca·pit·u·lum, ka·pich'u·lum, *n.* pl. **ca·pit·u·la**, ka·pich'u·la. [L., small head, capital of column, chapter, dim. of *caput*, head.] *Anat.* the head of a bone; *bot.* a close head of sessile flowers; a flower head.

cap·ling, kap'ling, *n.* Capelin.

ca·pon, kā'pon, kā'pon, *n.* [L. *capo*, Gr. *kapōn*, a capon, < a root seen in Gr. *keptō*, to cut.] A male chicken or rooster castrated for the purpose of improving the flesh for eating.—**ca·pon·ize**, kā'pon·iz", *v.t.*—*caponized, caponizing.* To make into a capon.

ca·pon·ette, kā"pa·net', *n.* A chemically castrated fowl.

ca·pote, ka·pōt', *Fr.* kä·pạt', *n.* [Fr., M.L. *capa*, E. *cape*.] A long cloak with a hood; a close-fitting caplike bonnet worn by women and children; a bull-fighter's cape; a movable top or hood on a vehicle such as a buggy.

capped, kapt, *a.* Wearing or having a cap; as, white-*capped*.

cap·per, kap'ẽr, *n.* One who or that which caps. *Slang,* a stool pigeon among gamblers; a by-bidder or decoy at an auction.

cap·ping, kap'ing, *n.* The act of one who or that which caps; that with which something is capped; *mining,* overburden.

cap·ric a·cid, kap'rik as'id, *n. Chem.* a malodorous fatty acid, $C_{10}H_{20}O_2$, found naturally in oils as a glyceride and used in making esters for perfumes and artificial flavorings and as an organic intermediate.

ca·pric·ci·o, ka·prē'chē·ō", *It.* kä·prēt'chō, *n.* [It., a caprice.] A caprice; a whim; a musical piece which is free and fanciful in form.

ca·price, ka·prēs', *n.* [Fr. *caprice,* < It. *capriccio:* see *capriccio*.] A sudden change of mind without apparent or adequate motive; a whim; mere fancy; susceptibility to varying or freakish impulses; something produced by whim or impulse; *mus.* a capriccio.

ca·pri·cious, ka·prish'us, *a.* Characterized by caprice; apt to change opinions unpredictably; fickle; subject to change or irregularity.—**ca·pri·cious·ly,** *adv.*—**ca·pri·cious·ness,** *n.*

Cap·ri·corn, kap'ri·kạrn", *n.* [L. *Capricornus,* < *caper,* goat, and *cornu,* horn.] *Astron.* a zodiacal constellation between Sagittarius and Aquarius. *Astrol.* the tenth sign of the zodiac. Also **Cap·ri·cor·nus,** kap"ri·kạr'nus.

cap·ri·fi·ca·tion, kap'ri·fi·kā"shan, *n.* [L. *caprificatio,* < *caprificus,* the wild figtree—*caper,* a goat, and *ficus,* a fig, < goats feeding on it.] A method of artificial pollination of figs, whereby flowering branches of the wild fig are hung in the trees, attracting the fig wasps who transfer the pollen to the edible figs.

cap·ri·fig, kap'ri·fig", *n.* [L. *caprificus,* < *caper,* goat, and *ficus,* fig.] The uncultivated form of the common fig, *Ficus carica,* bearing an inedible fruit; the wild fig.

cap·rine, kap'rīn", *a.* Goatlike.

cap·ri·ole, kap'rē·ōl", *n.* [O.Fr. *capriole,* now *cabriole,* lit. a goat leap, < L. *capriolus,* a wild goat < *caper,* a goat.] *Ballet.* a caper or leap; a spring or in-place leap given by a horse in dressage exhibitions.—*v.i.*—**caprioled, caprioling.** To execute a capriole.

ca·pro·ic ac·id, ka·prō'ik as'id, *n. Chem.* a fatty acid, $C_6H_{12}O_2$, with the odor of limburger cheese, present in milk and some natural oils, used in analytic chemistry and in the manufacture of rubber, varnishes, resins, and pharmaceuticals.

ca·pryl·ic ac·id, *n. Chem.* a fatty acid, $C_{14}H_{16}O_2$, derived from coconut oil, used for synthetic dyes, perfumes and flavorings, and in antiseptics and fungicides.

cap·sa·i·sin, kap·sā'i·sin, *n. Chem.* an alkaloid compound, $C_{18}H_{27}NO_3$, which is a strong irritant and the active principle in capsicum.

Cap·si·an, kap'sē·an, *a.* Pertaining to or of a stage of civilization of the Paleolithic period in southern Europe or northern regions of Africa.

cap·si·cum, kap'sa·kum, *n.* [< L. *capsa,* a box, < the shape of the fruit.] The generic name of some South American and Asiatic plants, many species of which are cultivated for their pods which, when dried and prepared, are used in cookery as condiments and hot peppers, and in medicine as irritants and stimulants.

cap·size, kap'sīz, kap·sīz', *v.i., v.t.*—**capsized, capsizing.** [Origin unknown.] To upset or overturn, as a boat.

cap·stan, kap'stan, *n.* [Fr. and Pr. *cabestan,* prob. < L. *capistrare,* tie with a halter, <

capistrum, halter, < *capere,* hold.] A device resembling a windlass but having a vertical axis, commonly turned by a bar or lever, as for raising weights.

cap·stone, kap'stōn", *n.* A capping or finishing stone of a structure.

cap·su·lar, kap'sa·lẽr, *a.* Of, pertaining to, in, or of the nature of a capsule. Also **cap·su·la·ry.**

cap·su·late, kap'sa·lāt", *a.* Enclosed in or formed into a capsule. Also **cap·su·lat·ed,** kap'sa·lā"tid.—**cap·su·la·tion,** kap"sa·lā'shan, *n.* Enclosure in a capsule.

cap·sule, kap'sul, *n.* [L. *capsula,* dim. of *capsa,* box, E. *case.*] A small case, envelope, or covering; a thin metal covering for the mouth of a corked bottle; *med.* a gelatinous case enclosing a dose of medicine; *anat.* and *zool.* a membranous sac or integument; *bot.* a dry fruit or seed vessel, composed of two or more carpels; the theca of mosses; *chem.* a small shallow vessel, as of porcelain.

cap·sule, kap'sul, *n. Aeron.* A small, sealed pressurized cabin with an internal environment which will support life in a man or animal during extremely high altitude flight, space flight, or emergency escape; see *ejection capsule.* A container carried on a rocket or spacecraft holding instruments intended to be recovered after a flight.

cap·sule, kap'sul, *a.* Very brief; summarized; small; miniature.

cap·tain, kap'tan, kap'tin, *n.* [Fr. *capitaine,* O.Fr. *capitain,* < L.L. *capitanus,* < L. *caput,* the head.] One who is at the head of or has authority over others; a chief; a leader; a commander, esp. in military affairs, as the military officer who commands a company; an officer in the navy commanding a ship of war; the commander or master of a merchant vessel; one who leads a team in sports; an airplane pilot.—**cap·tain·cy,** *n.* The rank, post, or commission of a captain.—**cap·tain·ship,** *n.* The condition or post of a captain or chief commander; skill in military affairs.

cap·tain, kap'tan, kap'tin, *v.t.* To lead or command, as a team, group, or ship.

cap·tion, kap'shan, *n.* [L. *captio(n-),* < *capere,* take.] That part of a legal document which states time, place, etc., of execution or performance; a heading or title, as of a chapter or article; description accompanying a picture, photograph, or illustration.—*v.t.* To write or provide a caption for.

cap·tious, kap'shus, *a.* [L. *captiosus,* < *captio(n-):* see *caption.*] Apt to ensnare or perplex, as in argument; apt to notice and make much of unimportant faults or defects; faultfinding; proceeding from a faultfinding or caviling disposition.—**cap·tious·ly,** *adv.*—**cap·tious·ness,** *n.*

cap·ti·vate, kap'ti·vāt", *v.t.*—**captivated, captivating.** [L.L. *captivatus,* pp. of *captivare,* < L. *captivus:* CAPTIVE.] To capture as by beauty or excellence; charm. *Obs.* to subjugate.—**cap·ti·vat·ing·ly,** *adv.*—**cap·ti·va·tion,** *n.*—**cap·ti·va·tor,** *n.*

cap·tive, kap'tiv, *a.* [L. *captivus,* < *capere,* take.] Made or held prisoner, as in war; kept in confinement or restraint; enslaved as by love or other passion; captivated.—*n.* A prisoner; *com.* a corporation controlled by another, called *parent company,* and operated for the latter's benefit.—**captive au·di·ence,** persons who cannot escape from hearing or seeing whatever is being broadcast, the fact of the message being unconnected with their reasons for being where they are.—**cap·tive bal·loon,** a balloon held in a particular station, as for observation purposes.

cap·tiv·i·ty, kap·tiv'i·tē, *n. pl.* **cap·tiv·i·ties.** The state or period of being captive.

cap·tor, kap'tor, *n.* [L., < *capere,* take.] One who takes or captures.

cap·ture, kap'cher, *n.* [L. *captura,* < *capere,* take.] The act of taking as by force or stratagem; that which is so taken; a prize.

cap·ture, kap'cher, *v.t.*—**captured, capturing.** To take by force or stratagem; win.—**cap·tur·er,** *n.*

cap·ture, kap'cher, *n. Nuclear physics,* the coalescence of an atomic nucleus and an additional elementary particle, esp. a neutron.—*v.t.* Of an atomic system, to acquire, as an additional particle.

cap·ture in·tel·li·gence, *n.* Military information gleaned from the examination of captured enemy documents and material, and from the interrogation of enemy prisoners of war, deserters, and civilians.

ca·puche, ka·pōsh', ka·pōch', *n.* [Fr. *capuche, capuce,* < It. *capuccio,* hood, cowl, < M.L. *capa,* E. *cape.*] A hood or cowl, esp. the long, pointed cowl of the Capuchins.

Cap·u·chin, kap'u·chin, kap'u·shin, *n.* [Fr. *capuchin,* now *capucin,* < It. *cappuccino* < *cappuccio:* CAPUCHE.] One of an order of Franciscan friars, a reformed branch of the Observants, wearing a long, pointed cowl. (*l.c.*) a hooded cloak for women; a variety of pigeon with a hoodlike tuft of feathers on the back of the head; a tropical American monkey, *Cebus capucinus,* so called from the cowlike appearance of the hair of the head, or any monkey of the same genus.

cap·y·ba·ra, cap·i·ba·ra, kap"i·bär'a, *n.* [The native Brazilian name.] 'A rodent quadruped, *Hydrochoerus capybara,* abounding in rivers of South America, feeding on vegetables and fish, over three feet in length, tailless, with a large head and blunted muzzle, and toes imperfectly webbed: the largest of all rodents.

car, kär, *n.* [O.Fr. *car, char* (Fr. *char*), < L. *carrus,* kind of two-wheeled vehicle for carrying loads; < Celtic.] An automobile; a vehicle running on rails; the part of a balloon, elevator, or the like, for carrying passengers; *Brit. dial.* a wheeled vehicle; *poet.* a chariot, as of war or triumph.

ca·ra·ba·o, kär"a·bä'ō, *n. pl.* **ca·ra·ba·os.** [Philippine Sp.] In the Philippine Islands, the water buffalo.

car·a·bi·neer, car·a·bi·nier, kär"a·bi·nēr', *n.* [Fr. *carabinier* (= It. *carabiniere*), < *carabine:* see *carbine.*] A soldier equipped with a carbine.

ca·ra·ca·ra, kär"a·kär'a, *n.* [S. Amer. name; imit. of its cry.] Any of certain vulturelike birds of the falcon family, subfamily *Polyborinae,* of the warmer parts of America.

car·ack, car·rack, kar'ak, *n.* [O.Fr. *carrake* (Fr. *caraque*), < M.L. *carraca;* origin uncertain.] A large, armed merchant vessel, esp. Spanish or Portuguese, of the 15th and 16th centuries.

car·a·cole, kar'a·kōl", *n.* [Fr. *caracole,* < Sp. *caracol,* snail, winding staircase, wheeling movement.] A spiral staircase; a half turn executed by a trained saddle horse.—*v.i.*—**caracoled, caracoling.** To execute caracoles; wheel; prance.

car·a·cul, kar'a·kul, *n.* [Russ.] The skin of the very young of certain Asiatic or Russian sheep, dressed as a fur, resembling astrakhan, but with a flatter, looser curl.

ca·rafe, ka·raf', ka·räf', *n.* [Fr.] A glass water bottle or decanter.

car·a·mel, kar'a·mel, kar'a·mel", *n.* [Fr. *caramel,* < Sp. *caramelo.*] Burnt sugar, used for coloring and flavoring food; a kind of chewy candy, commonly in small blocks, made from sugar, butter, milk, and flavoring.—**car·a·mel·ize,** kar'a·ma·līz, kär'ma·līz, *v.t., v.i.*—**caramelized, caramelizing.** [= Fr. *caraméliser.*] To convert or be converted into caramel.—**car·a·mel·i·za·tion,** *n.*

ca·ran·gid, ka·ran'jid, *n.* [N.L. *Caranx,* the typical genus (cf. Sp. *carangue,* a West Indian flatfish).] Any of the fishes belonging to or resembling the *Carangidae,* a family which includes the cavally, pompano and pilotfish.—*a.* Belonging to this family.

car·a·pace, kar'a·pās", *n.* [Fr., < Sp. *carapacho.*] The hard, bony covering or shield on all or part of an animal's back, as a turtle's shell; a hard protective surface.

car·at, kar'at, *n.* [Fr. *carat,* Ar. *qirrât,* *carat,* < Gr. *keration,* lit. 'a little horn', also the seed of the carob tree, used for a weight, a carat.] A standard unit, 200 milligrams, for weighing precious stones. See *karat.*

car·a·van, kar'a·van", *n.* [Fr. *caravane,* < Sp. *caravana,* Ar. *qairawân,* Pers. *kârwân,* a caravan.] A company of travelers who journey together through hostile territory so that they may travel with greater security; a group of vehicles or pack of animals traveling in a file; a large closed vehicle used for conveying traveling exhibitions. *Brit.* living quarters on wheels.

car·a·van·sa·ry, kar"a·van'sa·rē, *n. pl.* **car·a·van·sa·ries.** In the Near East, an inn, usually enclosing a large courtyard, for the overnight lodging of caravans; also **car·a·van·se·rai,** kar"a·van'sa·rī", kar"a·van'sa·rā".

car·a·vel, kar'a·vel", *n.* [Sp. and It. *caravela,* a caravel, dim. of L. *carabus,* Gr. *karabos,* a light ship, a boat, also a crab.] A small galley-rigged ship formerly used by the Spanish and Portuguese; a small fishing vessel. Also **car·vel,** kär'vel.

car·a·way, kar'a·wā", *n.* [Sp. *al-carahweya,* < Ar. *karwiyâ, karawiyâ,* caraway; probaby < Gr. *karon,* L. *careum,* caraway.] A biennial plant, *Carum Carvi,* with a tapered root like a parsnip, the seeds of which are used to flavor various foods.

car·ba·mate, kär'ba·māt", kär·bam'āt, *n. Chem.* a salt of carbamic acid.

car·bam·ic, kär·bam'ik, *a.* [< *carbonic* and *amide.*] *Chem.* noting or pertaining to an organic acid, NH$_2$COOH, not occurring in the free state, but known in the form of salts, esp. that of ammonium.

car·bam·ide, kär·bam'īd, kär·bam'id, kär'ba·mīd", kär'ba·mid, *n. Chem.* urea.

carb·an·i·on, kär·ban'ī'on, kär·ban'ī"on, *n. Chem.* a negatively charged organic ion such as H$_3$C−, having one additional electron more than the corresponding free radical: a short-lived ion that is an important intermediate in organic synthesis, found together with carboniums.

car·ba·zole, kär'ba·zōl", *n. Chem.* a white, crystalline, cyclic, organic compound, (C$_6$H$_4$)$_2$NH, derived from coal tar, used in the manufacture of dyes, explosives, insecticides and lubricants.

car·bide, kär'bid, kär'bīd, *n.* A compound of carbon with a metal; a carburet; a hard cutting tip for a tool, made of a mixture of powdered carbides of heavy metals.

car·bine, kär'bīn, kär'bēn, *n.* [Fr. *carabine,* a carabine; O.Fr. *carabin, calabrin,* a musketeer, < *calabre,* an engine of war, < L.L. *chadabula,* an engine for throwing stones, < Gr. *katabolē,* a throwing down— *kata,* down, and *ballo,* to throw.] A gun or firearm commonly used by cavalry, shorter in the barrel than the infantry musket or rifle; a lightweight automatic military rifle. Also **car·a·bine,** kar'a·bīn".

car·bi·nol, kär'bi·nōl", kär'bi·nạl", kär'bi·nol", *n. Chem.* methyl alcohol, CH$_3$OH; any compound of similar molecular structure, such as isopropyl alcohol, which may be called dimethylcarbinol.

car·bo·cy·clic com·pound, kär"bō·sī'klik kom'pound, *n. Chem.* any one of several organic compounds containing a ring formation made up of carbon atoms, as benzene.

car·bo·hy·drate, kär"bō·hī'drāt, kär"ba·-hī'drāt, *n.* [L. *carbo,* charcoal, Gr. *hydōr,* water.] A chemical compound made of carbon, hydrogen, and oxygen, the two latter being commonly in the same proportion as in water (H$_2$O); one member of several groups of compounds including simple sugars such as glucose, double sugars such as sucrose, and polymers such as starch and cellulose, especially one of the edible carbohydrates, one of the major sources of food for humans and animals.

car·bo·late, kär'bo·lāt, *n. Chem.* a salt of carbolic acid.—**car·bo·lat·ed,** kär'bo·lā"-tid, *a.* Containing carbolic acid.

car·bol·ic ac·id, kär·bol'ik as'id, *n. Chem.* phenol.

car·bon, kär'bon, *n.* [Fr. *carbone,* < L. *carbo(n)-,* coal, charcoal.] *Chem.* a widely distributed element which forms organic compounds, which occurs in a pure state as the diamond and as graphite, and in an impure state as charcoal; sym. C, at. no. 6. See Periodic Table of Elements. A rod or plate composed in part of carbon, used in arc lamps and batteries; a piece of carbon paper; a carbon copy.

car·bon 13, *n.* A rare carbon isotope used in cancer research and tracer studies.

car·bon 14, *n. Chem.* radioactive carbon with the mass number 14, used as an analytical research tool, especially in the dating of geological and archaeological material.

car·bo·na·do, kär"bo·nā'dō, *n. pl.* **car·bo·na·does, car·bo·na·dos.** [Sp. *carbonada,* < L. *carbo(n)-,* coal.] A piece of meat, fowl, or fish scored and broiled.—*v.t.*—**carbonadoed,** *carbonadoing.* To score and broil.

car·bo·na·do, kär"bo·nä'dō, *n. pl.* **car·bo·na·does, car·bo·na·dos.** [Pg., < *carbone,* carbon.] An opaque, dark-colored, massive form of diamond, found chiefly in Brazil, and used for drills; black diamond.

Car·bo·na·ri, kär"bo·närē, *It.* kär"ba·-nä'rē, *n. pl.* Members of a secret revolutionary society who took their name from the charcoal burners of Italy, among whom many were obliged to take refuge, and with whom they identified themselves: active in early 19th century Spain, France, and Italy.

car·bo·nate, kär'bo·nāt", kär'bo·nit, *n. Chem.* a salt of carbonic acid.

car·bo·nate, kär'bo·nāt", *v.t.*—*carbonated, carbonating.* To form into a carbonate; charge or impregnate with carbonic acid gas or carbon dioxide.—**car·bo·na·tion,** kär"ba·nä'shan, *n.*

car·bon bi·sul·fide, *n.* Carbon disulfide.

car·bon black, *n. Chem.* any of several finely divided forms of carbon derived from incomplete combustion of natural gas or petroleum: used in strengthening natural and synthetic rubber, and in inks.

car·bon cop·y, *n.* A copy of anything typed or written, made by using carbon paper; a nearly exact duplicate of a particular person or thing.

car·bon cy·cle, *n. Chem.* the process by which carbon dioxide in the air is absorbed by plants and converted into plant carbohydrates, which are eaten by animals and, through decomposition, are reconverted to carbon dioxide and returned to the air. *Phys.* a process by which the sun and other stars theoretically derive their energy; a series of nuclear reactions and transformations of carbon, hydrogen, and nitrogen resulting in the formation of helium, the release of sub-atomic particles, and the regeneration of carbon.

car·bon dat·ing, *n. Geol.* process by which the age of archeological and geological specimens can be determined through the measurement of carbon 14 content.

car·bon di·ox·ide, *n. Chem.* a heavy, colorless, odorless, noncombustible gas, CO$_2$, present in the atmosphere and formed during respiration: used principally in the manufacture of effervescent drinks and as a refrigerant; in solid form called *dry ice.* Also *carbonic-acid gas.*

car·bon di·sul·fide, *n. Chem.* a clear, colorless or yellowish, highly flammable and poisonous liquid, CS$_2$: used to manufacture viscose rayon, cellophane, and carbon tetrachloride, and used in various solvents and pesticides.

car·bon fin, *n. Aerospace,* a jet vane made of carbon and placed directly in the jet stream of a rocket.

car·bon·ic, kär·bon'ik, *a. Chem.* of or containing carbon; as, *carbonic* acid, H$_2$CO$_3$, *carbonic*-acid gas (carbon dioxide).

car·bon·ic ac·id, *n. Chem.* a weak acid, H$_2$CO$_3$, that reacts with bases to form carbonates, and that readily decomposes into water plus carbon dioxide.

car·bon·ic-ac·id gas, *n.* Carbon dioxide.

car·bon·if·er·ous, kär"ba·nif'ẽr·us, *a.* [L. *carbo(n)-,* coal, and *ferre,* bear.] Coalbearing; (*cap.*) noting or pertaining to the Carboniferous geological period.—*n.* (*cap.*) The Carboniferous geological period or system following the Devonian and preceding the Permian periods.

car·bo·ni·um, kär·bō'nē·um, *n. Chem.* a positively charged and highly reactive organic ion having one electron less than the corresponding free radical and behaving in chemical reaction as if the positive charge were located on the carbon atom: a short-lived ion that is an important intermediate in organic synthesis, found together with carbanions.

car·bon·ize, kär'bo·nīz", *v.t.*—*carbonized, carbonizing.* To convert into carbon, as by partial combustion; cover with carbon; combine with carbon.—**car·bon·i·za·tion,** *n.*—**car·bon·iz·er,** *n.*

car·bon mon·ox·ide, *n. Chem.* a colorless, odorless, very poisonous gas, CO, which burns with a pale-blue flame, and is formed when carbon burns with an insufficient supply of air: used principally in organic synthesis and metallurgy.

car·bon·ous, kär'ba·nus, *a. Chem.* of, like, or containing carbon. Also **car·bo·na·ceous,** kär"bo·nā'shus.

car·bon pa·per, *n.* Paper faced with a preparation of carbon or other material, used between two sheets of plain paper in order to reproduce upon the lower sheet that which is typed or written upon the upper sheet.

car·bon proc·ess, *n.* Photographic printing on paper coated with sensitized gelatin containing carbon or other pigment.

car·bon tet·ra·chlo·ride, *n. Chem.* a colorless, nonflammable liquid which is poisonous and gives off heavy vapors, CCl$_4$: used as a refrigerant, cleaning fluid, fire extinguisher, and solvent.

car·bon·yl, kär'ba·nil, *n. Chem.* a bivalent radical, CO, composed of one atom of carbon and one of oxygen; a metal combined with a CO group; as, nickel *carbonyl.*

car·bo·run·dum, kär"bo·run'dum, *n.* (*Often cap.*) a silicon carbide type of abrasive. (Trademark.)

car·box·yl, kär·bok'sil, *n. Chem.* a univalent radical or group containing carbon, oxygen, and hydrogen (COOH), present in organic acids.

car·box·yl·ate, kär·bok'si·lāt", *n. Chem.* salt of carboxylic acid.—*v.t.*—*carboxylated, carboxylating.* To combine carboxyl or carbon dioxide, with as a compound, with the resulting formation of carboxylic acid.—**car·box·yl·a·tion,** *n.*

car·boy, kär'boi, *n.* [Pers. *karabä,* a large vessel for containing wine.] A large, strong, glass bottle, protected by an outside covering, and used for corrosive liquids.

---

car·bun·cle, kär′bung·kl, *n.* [L. *carbunculus*, a little coal, < *carbo*, a coal.] A painful local inflammation of tissues, esp. of the back of the neck and trunk, characterized by hardness, having a tendency to spread like a boil; a red garnet cut without facets.—**car·bun·cled**, *a.* Afflicted with carbuncles.—**car·bun·cu·lar**, kär·bung′kū·lėr, *a.* Belonging to a carbuncle; resembling a carbuncle; inflamed.

car·bu·ret, kär′bu·rāt′, kär′bū·ret″, *n.* [< *carbon.*] *Chem.* a carbide.—*v.t.*—*carbureted, carbureting,* Brit. *carburetted, carburetting.* To combine with carbon; impregnate or mix with hydrocarbons.—**car·bu·ret·ant**, *n.* A hydrocarbon used for carbureting.

car·bu·re·tion, kär″ba·rā′shan, kär″bū·resh′an, *n.* The act of carbureting; the process of impregnating air with volatile hydrocarbons in an internal combustion engine.

car·bu·re·tor, kär′ba·rā″tėr, kär′bū·ret″er, *n.* A device which mixes vaporized fuel with air in order to provide explosive power for an internal combustion engine.

car·bu·rize, kär′ba·rīz″, kär′bū·rīz″, *v.t.*—*carburized carburizing,* Brit. *carburised, carburising.* [Fr. *carbure,* a carbide, < *carbone,* E. *carbon.*] To combine with carbon.—**car·bu·ri·za·tion**, Brit. **car·bu·ri·sa·tion**, *n.*

car·ca·jou, kär′ka·jö″, kär′ka·zhö″, *n.* [Fr. *carcajou,* from native name.] An American name for the wolverine, and erroneously for the badger and lynx.

car·ca·net, kär′ka·net″, kär′ka·nit, *n.* [Fr. *carcan,* a carcanet, < Armor. *kerchen,* the neck or bosom.] A necklace, collar, or headband of jewels.

car·cass, Brit. **car·case**, kär′kas, *n.* [A.Fr. *carcois* (O.Fr. *charcois*), also Fr. *carcasse* (< It. *carcassa*); ult. origin uncertain.] The dead body of an animal or (now only in contempt) of a human being; a living body, now chiefly in contempt or ridicule; anything from which the vital principle is gone; the decaying remains of anything; as, "a very dangerous flat . . . where the *carcases* of many a tall ship lie buried": Shakespeare's "Merchant of Venice," iii. 1. 6; an unfinished framework or skeleton, as of a house or ship; a case containing combustibles, used as a missile, and intended to set fire to buildings, etc.; underlying structure of a balloon tire, either new or when worn, to be recapped for further use; the covering and bladder, or the covering alone, of an inflatable ball.

car·cin·o·gen, kär·sin′o·jen, *n.* [Gr. *karkinos,* crab.] *Pathol.* a substance that produces cancer.

car·ci·no·ma, kär″si·nō′ma, *n.* pl. **car·ci·no·mas, car·ci·no·ma·ta**, kär″si·nō′ma·ta. [L., < Gr. *karkinoma, karkinoun,* affect with cancer, *karkinos,* crab, cancer.] *Pathol.* a malignant epithelial tumor that spreads and often recurs after excision; a cancer.—**car·ci·nom·a·tous**, kär″si·nom′a·tas, *a.*

car·ci·no·ma·to·sis, kär″si·nō·ma·tō′sis, *n.* A state in which numerous carcinomas, which have been disseminated from a primary source, grow in the body at the same time.

card, kärd, *n.* [O.Fr. Fr. *carte* < L. *charta:* see *chart.*] One of a set of pieces of card or cardboard printed with marks or figures used in playing various games. *Pl.* a game or games played with such a set; card-playing. A piece of stiff paper or thin pasteboard, usually rectangular, for various uses; a small sheet of stiff paper for bearing a note or message; as, a postal *card;* a piece of thin cardboard or heavy paper bearing an invitation, or serving as a ticket; a piece of cardboard with some elaborate ornamentation bearing complimentary greetings; as, a Christmas *card;* a piece of thin cardboard bearing the name, or name and address, of the person presenting it, used in making a call; as, a visiting *card;* announcing the nature and place of a person's business; as, a business *card;* a chart, map, plan, or the circular piece of paper on which the 32 points indicating direction are marked on a compass; a short published notice or advertisement, as in a newspaper; a program of events, as at the races.—**in the cards,** likely to occur; impending, as: Defeat was *in the cards.*

card, kärd, *v.t.* To provide with a card; to fasten on a card; to list or record on a card.

card, kärd, *n.* [O.Fr. Fr. *carde,* teazel, wool-card, < L. *carduus,* thistle.] A wire-toothed brush or some similar implement, as used in disentangling and combing out fibers of wool or flax, preparatory to spinning; a kind of currycomb.

card, kärd, *v.t., v.i.* To comb or open wool, flax, or hemp with a card.—**card·er**, kär′dėr, *n.* One who cards; the machine employed in carding.

card, kärd, *n. Slang.* An amusing person, usually with uninhibited behavior; a wit or a joker; a professional gambler, usually a cardplayer; a portion of a narcotic drug.

car·da·mom, kär′da·mum, *n.* [L. *cardamomum,* Gr. *kardamōmon.*] The aromatic capsule of various plants of the ginger family, employed in medicine as well as an ingredient in sauces and curries; the plant.

card·board, kärd′bōrd″, kärd′bąrd″, *n.* A stiff, moderately thick kind of paper or paste-board.—*a.* Made of, or as of cardboard.

card cat·a·logue, *n.* A catalogue in which each entry is made on a separate card, the cards being arranged in order, alphabetically or otherwise, in boxes or drawers; a file of cards listing books in a library or collection.

car·di·ac, kär′dē·ak″, *a.* [L. *cardiacus,* Gr. *kardiakos,* < *kardia,* the heart.] Pertaining to the heart; exciting action in the heart through the medium of the stomach. Also **car·di·a·cal**, kär·dī′a·kal.—**car·di·ac**, *n.* A person with a heart disease; a medicine which excites action in the heart and animates the spirits.—**car·di·al·gi·a**, kär″dē·al′jē·a, *n.* [Gr. *algos,* pain.] *Med.* Heartburn; pain in the heart.

car·di·gan, kär′digan, *n.* [< the seventh Earl of Cardigan (1797–1868).] A close-fitting, collarless, knitted, woolen jacket which opens down the center front. Also **car·di·gan jack·et.**

Car·di·gan, kär′di·gan, *n.* One of the Welsh corgi, a long-tailed, round-eared dog.

car·di·nal, kär′di·nal, *n.* An ecclesiastical prince of the Roman Catholic Church, next in rank to the Pope, and a member of the College of Cardinals. *Ornith.* a North American finch, *Richmondena cardinalis,* the male bird having brilliant red plumage and a prominent crest on the head; also *redbird.*

car·di·nal, kär′di·nal, *a.* [L. *cardinalis,* < *cardo,* a hinge.] Chief, principal, pre-eminent; fundamental; basic; pertaining to cardinal red.

car·di·nal·ate, kär′di·na·lāt″, *n.* The office, rank, or dignity of a cardinal.—**car·di·nal·ship**, *n.*

car·di·nal flow·er, *n.* The name commonly given to a species of lobelia because of its large, intensely red flowers.

car·di·nal·i·ty, kärd″in·al′it·ē, *n. Math.* Property of being presentable in terms of cardinal numbers in a finite set; essential constituents in a mathematical set.

car·di·nal num·ber, *n.* The number *one, two,* or *three,* etc., as distinct from the ordinal number *first, second,* or *third,* etc.; a numeral which indicates the number of units in a group, but does not indicate the order in which they are arranged.

car·di·nal points, *n. pl.* The four main points of a compass: north and south, east and west.

car·din·al vir·tues, *n. pl.* Plato's four natural virtues: justice, prudence, temperance, and fortitude; plus the three theological virtues: faith, hope, and charity.

car·di·o·gram, kär′dē·o·gram″, *n.* The record of a heart's action made by a cardiograph. Also **e·lec·tro·car·di·o·gram.**

car·di·o·graph, kär′dē·o·graf″, *n.* [Gr. *kardia,* heart, and *graphō,* to write.] An instrument tracing and recording the action of the heart.—**car·di·og·ra·phy**, kär·dē·og′ra·fē, *n.*

car·di·oid, kär′dē·oid, *n.* [Gr. *kardioeides,* heart-shaped.] *Math.* a somewhat heart-shaped mathematical curve, being the path of a point on the circumference of a circle which rolls on another circle of equal size.

car·di·ol·o·gy, kär″dē·ol′o·jē, *n. Med.* the science of the heart, including the study of its diseases and functions.—**car·di·ol·o·gist**, kär″dē·ol′o·jist, *n.* A specialist in cardiology.

car·di·o·vas·cu·lar, kär″dē·ō·vas′kū·lėr, *a. Med.* having reference to or involving the heart and blood vessels.

car·di·tis, kär·dī′tis, *n.* [N.L., < Gr. *kardia,* heart.] *Pathol.* inflammation of the muscles of the heart.

car·doon, kär·dön′, *n.* [Fr. *cardon,* < L. *carduus,* thistle.] A perennial plant, *Cynara cardunculus,* native in Mediterranean regions, related to the artichoke and eaten as a vegetable.

card·sharp, kärd′shärp″, *n.* One who cheats in playing cards; one who makes it a trade to fleece the unwary in games of cards.

care, kâr, *v.i.*—*cared, caring.* [O.E. *carian, cearian.*] To be concerned or solicitous; have thought or regard; to be concerned so as to feel or express objection, with a negative, as: I don't *care* if I do. To be inclined to. Have an inclination or liking for, have a fondness or affection for, to make provision or look out for; with *for.*

care, kâr, *n.* [O.E. *caru, cearu,* = Goth. *kara.*] Grief; distress; anxiety, concern, or solicitude; serious attention; heed; caution; watchful oversight; charge; an object of concern or attention.

ca·reen, ka·rēn′, *v.t.* [Fr. *carener,* < *carène,* the side and keel of a ship, L. *carina,* a keel.] To heave or bring, as a ship, to lie on one side for caulking, repairing, or cleaning; to repair or clean, as a boat, in this position.

ca·reen, ka·rēn′, *v.i.* To incline to one side, as a ship under a press of sail, or a motor car turning a corner on two wheels; to teeter from side to side; lurch.

ca·reer, ka·rēr′, *n.* [Fr. *carrière,* O.Fr. *cariere,* road, race-course, course, career, < L. *carrus,* a car. CAR.] A person's profession; one's life's work; a swift and steady course; full speed; progress.—*v.i.* To move or run very rapidly.

ca·reer·ism, ka·rēr′iz·um, *n.* Giving one's all to one's career, even at the sacrifice of moral principles and familial responsibility.—**ca·reer·ist**, *n.*

care·free, kâr′frē″, *a.* Free of care; without anxiety; happy-go-lucky.

care·ful, kâr′ful, *a.* [O.E. *carful.*] Warily, prudent, and cautious; deeply concerned about; painstaking in execution.—**care·ful·ly**, *adv.*—**care·ful·ness**, *n.*

care·less, kâr′lis, *a.* [O.E. *carlēas.*] Showing no care; being heedless; lacking in attention; inaccurate; lacking in consideration.—**care·less·ly**, *adv.*—**care·less·ness**, *n.*

ca·ress, ka·res′, *n.* [Fr. *caresse,* < It. *carezza,* < L. *carus,* dear.] An act of endearment; an expression of affection by touch, such as a kiss or a pat.

ca·ress, ka·res′, *v.t.* To show affection by bestowing caresses or patting, or fondling.—

ca·ress·er, *n.*—**ca·ress·ing·ly**, *adv.*—**ca·res·sive**, *a.* Caressing.

car·et, kar'it, *n.* [L., there is lacking.] A mark (‸) placed in written or printed matter to show where something must be inserted.

care·tak·er, kâr'tā″kẽr, *n.* One who takes care of the maintenance or security of a building, etc.; a person who temporarily fills the official role of another; as, a *caretaker* comptroller. *Brit.* a janitor.

care·worn, kâr'wôrn″, kâr'wŏrn″, *a.* Showing marks of care or anxiety; drained by fatigue due to prolonged overwork.

car·fare, kär'fâr′, *n.* Fare charged a passenger on a public vehicle, such as a bus.

car·go, kär'gō, *n.* pl. **car·goes** or **car·gos**, kär'gōz. [Sp., < *cargar*, load, = E. *charge*, *v.*] The lading or freight of a ship, airplane, or vehicle; load.

car·hop, kär'hop″, *n.* An employee who carries food to customers in their cars at drive-in eating establishments.

Car·ib, kar'ib, *n.* pl. **Car·ibs, Car·ib**. [Sp. *Caribe*: cf. *cannibal*.] A member of an Indian people of north-eastern South America, formerly dominant through the Lesser Antilles; the language of the Caribs.

Ca·ri·ban, kar'a·ban, ka·rē'ban, *n.* A *Carib*; the Carib stock of peoples or their language.—*a.* Of or pertaining to the Cariban people.

Car·ib·be·an, kar″i·bē'an, ka·rib'ē·an, *a.* Of or pertaining to the Caribs, or the Lesser Antilles, or the Caribbean Sea, the sea between the Lesser Antilles and South and Central America.

ca·ri·be, ka·rē'bē, *Sp.* kä·rē've, *n.* pl. **ca·ri·bes**. See *piranha*.

car·i·bou, kar'i·bö″, *n.* pl. **car·i·bous, car·i·bou**. [Canadian Fr., of Indian origin.] Any of several North American species or varieties of reindeer.

Car·i·bou Es·ki·mo, kar'i·bö″ es'ki·mō″, *n. Canada,* a group of Eskimos who live in Northern Canada, and depend on caribou for their food.

car·i·ca·ture, kar'a·ka·chẽr, kar'a·ka·chŭr″, *n.* [It. *caricatura*, an overloaded representation, < *caricare*, to load. CHARGE.] A representation, pictorial or descriptive, in which peculiarities or defects of a person or thing are ridiculously exaggerated, while a general likeness is retained; the art or act of producing caricatures; an absurdly incompetent copy or imitation of something or someone.—**car·i·ca·tur·ist**, *n.*

car·i·ca·ture, kar'a·ka·chẽr, kar'a·ka·chŭr″, *v.t.*—*caricatured, caricaturing.* To make or do a caricature of; to represent in a ridiculous and exaggerated fashion.

car·ies, kâr'ēz, kâr'ē·ēz″, *n.* pl. **car·ies**. [L.] Decay, as of bone or teeth, or plant tissue.—**ca·ri·ous**, kâr'ē·us, *a.* Affected with caries; decayed.—**ca·ri·os·i·ty, car·i·ous·ness**,*n.*

car·il·lon, kar'i·lon, kar'i·lon, *Brit.* ka·ril'yan, *Fr.* kä·rē·yạn′, *n.* [Fr., chime of (orig. four) bells, < L. *quattuor*, four.] A set of stationary bells arranged for playing melodies, sounded by manual action or by machinery; a melody played on such bells; a musical instrument, or an attachment to one, to imitate a peal of bells.—*v.i.* **carillonned, carillonning.**—**car·il·lon·neur**, kar″i·lo·nụr′, *Brit.* ka·ril'ya·nẽr, *n.* One who plays a carillon.

car·i·o·ca, kar″ē·ō'ka, *n.* A South American dance and its accompanying music; (*cap.*) a resident of or a person born in Rio de Janeiro, Brazil.

car·i·ole, car·ri·ole, kar'ē·ōl″, *n.* [Fr. *carriole*, < It. *carriuola*, < L. *carrus*, E. *car*.] A small open carriage; a covered cart.

Car·list, kär'list, *n.* A supporter of the claims of Don Carlos or of his family to the throne of Spain; a partisan of Charles X of France and his line.—**Car·lism**, *n.* The set of principles of the Carlists.

car·load, kär'lōd″, *n.* The load carried in a car, esp. a freight car; the minimum number of tons needed to ship at reduced carload rates.

Car·lo·vin·gi·an, kär″lo·vin'jē·an, *a., n.* See *Carolingian*.

car·ma·gnole, kär″man·yōl′, *n.* [Fr. *Carmagnole*, in Piedmont.] A revolutionary dance and song in France during 1789–93 Revolution; the costume worn by the French revolutionists.

Car·mel·ite, kär'ma·līt″, *n.* A mendicant friar or a nun of the Roman Catholic Order of Our Lady of Mount Carmel.—*a.* Pertaining to the Carmelite Order.

car·min·a·tive, kär·min'a·tiv, kär'ma·nā″tiv, *a.* [Fr. *carminatif*, < L. *carminare* (pp.-*atus*), card (wool).] Expelling wind from the body; relieving flatulence.—*n.* A carminative medicine.

car·mine, kär'min, kär'mīn, *n.* [Sp. *carmin*, < *carmesino*, carmine, crimson, < *carmes*, kermes.] The pure coloring matter or principle of cochineal; a red or crimson pigment made from cochineal.—*a.*

car·nage, kär'nij, *n.* [Fr. *carnage*, slaughter, < L.L. *carnaticum*, < L. *caro, carnis*, flesh.] Slaughter; great destruction of men; butchery; massacre.

car·nal, kär'nal, *a.* [L. *carnalis*, carnal, < *caro, carnis*, flesh.] Pertaining to the body, its passions and appetites; not spiritual; fleshly; sensual; lustful; impure.—**car·nal·i·ty**, kär·nal'i·tē, *n.* The state of being carnal; want of spirituality; fleshliness; fleshly lust or desire, or the indulgence of such lust; sensuality.—**car·nal·ly**, kär'nal·lē, *adv.* In a carnal manner; according to the flesh; not spiritually; sensually.

car·nal·lite, kär'na·līt″, *n.* [From R. von *Carnall*, 1804–74, Prussian mining official.] A mineral composed of a hydrous potassium-magnesium chloride, $KMgCl_3 \cdot 6H_2O$, which provides a valuable source of potassium.

car·nas·si·al, kär·nas'ē·al, *a.* [Fr. *carnassier*, flesh-eating, < L. *caro* (*carn-*), flesh.] *Zool.* noting or pertaining to teeth adapted for cutting and tearing flesh, esp. the last upper premolar or the first lower molar teeth in a typically carnivorous dentition.—*n.* A carnassial tooth.

car·na·tion, kär·nā'shan, *n.* [Fr. *carnation*, < L. *caro* (*carn-*), flesh.] Flesh-color; pink; sometimes, red; any of numerous cultivated varieties of the clove pink, *Dianthus caryophyllus*, with fragrant flowers of various colors.—*a.* Carnation-colored.

car·nau·ba wax, kär·nou'ba waks, *n.* The wax obtained from the carnauba, the Brazilian wax palm, greenish-yellow in color, used as a base in polishes and in phonograph disks.

Car·ne·gie u nit, *n.* The credit granted in a secondary school for the completion of one school year of study in an academic subject.

car·nel·ian, kär·nēl'yan, *n.* [More correctly *cornelian*, < Fr. *cornaline*, a carnelian, < L. *carnis*, flesh, < its fleshlike color.] A variety of chalcedony, of a deep red, flesh-red, or pale reddish color, used for jewelry. Also *cornelian*.

car·ni·val, kär'ni·val, *n.* [It. *carnevale*, prob. < L. *caro* (*carn-*), flesh, and *levare*, lighten, take away.] The season immediately preceding Lent, observed in Italy and elsewhere with merrymaking and revelry; the festivity of this season; in general, a large, usually public merrymaking; a travelling show with amusements such as side shows and rides; an entertainment.

car·ni·vore, kär'ni·vŏr″, kär'ni·vạr″, *n.* [Fr. *carnivore*, flesh-eating, < L. *carnivorus*: see *carnivorous*.] A flesh-eating animal or plant, esp. one of the *Carnivora*, an order of mammals, chiefly flesh-eating, including the cats, dogs, bears, seals, and others.

car·niv·o·rous, kär·niv'ẽr·us, *a.* [L. *carnivorus*.] Flesh-eating, as certain animals; pertaining to the carnivores which are mammals; of plants, digesting such animal matter as insects.—**car·niv·o·rous·ly**, *adv.*—**car·niv·o·rous·ness**, *n.*

car·no·tite, kär'no·tīt″, *n.* [< A. *Carnot*, a 19th century French inspector-general of mines.] A mineral, a yellow, earthy hydrous vanadate containing uranium, potassium, and radioactive substances, occurring in Colorado.

car·ny, kär'nē, *n.* pl. **car·nies**. *Slang,* one who is employed in a carnival. Also **car·ney**, **car·nie**.

car·ob, kar'ob, *n.* [O.Fr. *carobe*, < Ar. *kharrûb*, bean-pods.] A tree, *Ceratonia siliqua*, growing in the countries skirting the Mediterranean, the pods of which, known as locust beans, contain a sweet nutritious pulp; the pod of this tree, the pulp of which is eaten by men and animals.

car·ol, kar'ŏl, *n.* [O.Fr. *carole*, a kind of dance, a Christmas song or carol; < the Celtic: Armor. *koroll*, a dance; W. *carol*, a carol, a song.] A song, esp. one expressive of joy; a religious song or ballad in celebration of Christmas.—*v.i.*—*caroled, caroling, Brit. carolled, carolling.* To sing in joy or festivity, as Christmas carols.—*v.t.* To praise or celebrate in song.—**car·ol·er**, *Brit.* **car·ol·ler**, *n.*

Car·o·line, kar'a·lin, kar'a·līn″, *a.* [M.L. *Carolinus*, < *Carolus*, Charles.] Of or pertaining to some person named Charles, esp. Charles the Great (Charlemagne), Charles I, or Charles II of England. Also *Carolinian*.

Car·o·lin·gi·an, kar″a·lin'jē·an, *a.* [M.L. *Carolingi*, pl., the Carolingian dynasty, < O.H.G.*Karling*, patronymic deriv. < Karl, Charles (Charles Martel, or perhaps Charlemagne).] Belonging to the Frankish dynasty which succeeded the Merovingian dynasty in A.D. 751, and which reigned in France until A.D. 987 and in Germany until A.D. 911; pertaining to the culture of the Carolingian period.—*n.* A member of the Carolingian house, or a ruler in that dynasty. Also *Carlovingian, Carolinian*.

Car·o·lin·i·an, kar″a·lin'ē·an, *a.* [In part, < M.L. *Carolinus* (see *Caroline*); in part, < *Carolina* (North and South), named < Charles (*M.L. Carolus*) II, of England.] Of or pertaining to some person named Charles, as Charles the Great, Charlemagne; Caroline; Carolingian; of or pertaining to the two States of North and South Carolina or either one of them.—*n.* A native or inhabitant of either North or South Carolina.

car·om, kar'om, *n.* [Origin uncertain.] *Billiards,* a shot in which the ball struck with the cue is made to hit two balls in succession; a movement, as of a ball, striking and rebounding.—*v.i. Billiards,* to make a carom; to strike, esp. obliquely, and rebound.

car·o·tene, kar'o·tēn″, *n.* [L. *carota*, carrot, and -*ene*.] *Chem.* the orange or red hydrocarbon pigment, $C_{40}H_{56}$, found in some vegetables and animal fats, capable of being converted into vitamin A.

ca·rot·e·noid, ca·rot·i·noid, ka·rot'e·noid″, *n. Biochem.* one of the several yellow and red colored pigments found in plants, and also in the fatty tissues of animals.—*a.*

ca·rot·id, ka·rot'id, *a.* [Gr. pl. *karōtides*, the carotids, said to be < *karos*, a deep sleep, because the ancients believed that sleep was caused by an increased flow of blood to the head through these arteries, or by the compression of these arteries.] Of or pertaining to the two great arteries, one on either side of the neck, which convey the blood from the aorta to the head and brain.—*n.* One of these arteries.

ca·rous·al, ka·rou′zal, *n.* A noisy, drunken revel.

ca·rouse, ka·rouz′, *n.* [Fr. (obs.) *carous* (now *carrousse*), < G. *gar aus*, "quite out."] A drinking bout; a carousal; *obs.* the drinking down of a full draft of liquor.

ca·rouse, ka·rouz′, *v.i.*—*caroused, carousing.* To go on a drinking spree; to drink heavily and often.—**ca·rous·er**, *n.*

car·ou·sel, car·rou·sel, kar″a·sel′, kar″a·zel′, kar′a·sel′, kar′a·zel″, *n.* [Fr. < It. *carosello*; origin uncertain.] A merry-go-round; a medieval tournament in which the horsemen performed in skillful turns; *Canada*, the revolving circular platform at an airport onto which baggage of arriving passengers is delivered from a central chute.

carp, kärp, *n.* pl. **carp, carps.** [Same as D. *karper*, Dan. *karpe*, Sw. *karp*, a carp.] A soft-finned, fresh-water fish, *Cyprinus carpio*, found in sluggish waters and ponds, indigenous to China, but introduced into Europe, where it is prized for its food value, and into America, where it has become so numerous as to be a pest; any of the fish of the family *Cyprinidae*, as minnows and goldfish.

carp, kärp, *v.i.* [Formerly to speak, tell, from Icel. *karpa*, to boast; its modern sense being due to L. *carpo*, to seize, catch, pick.] To censure, cavil, or find fault, particularly without reason or petulantly: used absolutely or followed by *at.*—**carp·er**, kärp′ér, *n.* One who carps; a caviller.—**carp·ing**, kärp′ing, *a.* Cavilling; captious; censorious; ill-natured; petulant.—**carp·ing·ly**, kärp′ing·lē, *adv.* In a carping manner; captiously.

car·pal, kär′pal, *n. Anat.* a carpale.—*a. Anat.* pertaining to any bone in the wrist.—**car·pal joint**, *n. Anat.* in man, the joint of the carpus or wrist; a corresponding joint in other vertebrates.—*a.*

car·pa·le, kär·pā′lē, *n.* pl. **car·pa·li·a.** [N.L., neut. of *carpalis*, E. carpal.] *Anat.* any bone of the carpus or wrist. Also *carpal.*

car·pel, kär′pel, *n.* [N.L. *carpellum*, < Gr. *karpos*, fruit.] *Bot.* a simple pistil, or a single member of a compound pistil: regarded as a modified leaf.—**car·pel·lar·y**, *a.* Pertaining to or of the nature of a carpel.—**car·pel·late**, *a.* Having carpels.

car·pen·ter, kär′pen·tér, *n.* [O.Fr. *carpentier* (M.Fr. *charpentier*); L.L. *carpentarius*, a carpenter, < L. *carpentum*, a chariot.] One who builds or works with wood, and who shapes and fabricates lumber.—**car·pen·try**, kär′pen·trē, *n.* The application of the trade of a carpenter.

car·pen·ter bee, *n.* Any of the solitary bees, family *Xylocopidae*, so called from their excavating nests in sound wood.

car·pet, kär′pit, *n.* [O.Fr. *carpite*, a carpet, < It. and L.L. *carpita*, a woolly cloth, < *carpere*, to tease wool, L. *carpo*, to pluck.] A thick fabric used for covering floors, stairs; a covering resembling a carpet; as, a *carpet* of moss; any device or system of devices, electronic in nature, which when airborne are used to jam radar.—*v.t.* To cover with, or as with a carpet; to spread with carpets.—**be on the car·pet**, to be the subject of censure.

car·pet·bag, kär′pit·bag″, *n.* A traveling bag made of the same material as carpets, in common use in the U.S. in the 19th century.

car·pet·bag, kär′pit·bag″, *v.i.*—*carpet-bagged, carpetbagging.* To act as a carpet-bagger by taking up residence for the purpose of gaining political advantage.—*a.*

car·pet·bag·ger, kär′pit·bag″er, *n.* One who carries a carpetbag; *derogatory*, one who establishes residence for the purpose of gaining private advantage, esp. election to public office or the promotion of usually questionable commercial ventures. *U.S. Hist.* a post-Civil War Northerner in the

South, said to arrive carrying all his possessions in a carpetbag, who exploited the chaotic social and political conditions of the Reconstruction, often by the acquisition and subsequent abuse of public office; an itinerant banker and promoter of the Old West who carried his money around in a carpetbag.

car·pet bee·tle, *n.* Any of the small beetles of the family *Dermistidae*, which attack and damage animal fibers, particularly woolens; any household beetle having similar habits.

car·pet·ing, kär′pit·ing, *n.* Cloth for carpets; carpets in general.

car·pet weed, *n.* A North American plant, *Mollugo verticillata*, which forms a dense mat on the ground as it grows.

car·pol·o·gy, kär·pol′o·jē, *n.* [Gr. *karpos*, fruit, *logos*, discourse.] The division of botany relating to the structure of seeds and seed vessels.—**car·pol·o·gist**, *n.*

car·port, kär′pōrt″, *n.* An auto shelter with a roof and open sides, usually attached to the house.

carp·suck·er, kärp′suk″er, *n.* Any of several North American carp-like fresh-water fishes of the genus *Carpiodes*, subfamily *Ictiobinæ*. Also *buffalo fish.*

car·pus, kär′pus, *n.* pl. **car·pi.** [L., the wrist.] *Anat.* the part of the skeleton between forearm and hand; the wrist; the wrist bones collectively.—*a.*

car·ra·geen, car·ra·gheen, kar′a·gēn″, *n.* [< *Carragheen*, or *Carrigeen*, in southern Ireland.] A seaweed, *Chondrus crispus*, of the Atlantic coasts of Europe and North America; Irish moss.—**car·ra·gee·nan**, kar′a·gē·nan, *n.* A complex gelatinous carbohydrate extract of carrageen, used in foods as an emulsifier.

car·rel, car·rell, kar′al, *n.* A small recessed area or alcove, as among library stacks, used for individual study. Also *cubicle, stall.*

car·riage, kar′ij, *n.* [O.Fr. *cariage*, < *carier*, < M.L. *carricare*, convey by wagon, < L. *carrus*, kind of two-wheeled vehicle for carrying loads.] The act of carrying; conveyance; commercial transportation, or its cost; a means of carrying; a wheeled vehicle for conveying persons; a wheeled passenger vehicle drawn by horses, esp. one designed with a view to comfort and elegance; a wheeled support, as for a cannon; a part, as of a machine, designed for carrying something; bearing or mien.—**car·riage·way**, *n. Brit.* a way or road specifically for automobiles.

car·riage trade, *n.* The wealthy clientele of a store or designer's shop; the elite class of patrons of a theater.

car·ri·er, kar′ē·ér, *n.* One who or that which carries; a person or an association of persons that undertakes to convey goods or people for hire; as, a common *carrier*; one that undertakes to convey goods or passengers for hire as a public calling, inviting employment by the public generally; a carrier pigeon; *mach.* a mechanism by which something is carried or moved; *chem.* a catalytic agent which brings about a transfer of an element or group of atoms from one compound to another; *med.* a person carrying bacteria which he can transmit to others although immune to their effects himself.

car·ri·er air·craft, *n.* An aircraft based on, and operating from, an aircraft carrier; an aircraft used as a carrier for another air-craft.

car·ri·er bag, *n. Brit.* See *shopping bag.*

car·ri·er pi·geon, *n.* A pigeon trained to fly home from a distance and carry written messages; a homing pigeon; a large-wattled pigeon.

car·ri·er plane, *n.* An airplane with wheeled takeoff and landing gear designed

for use on an aircraft carrier, distinguished from a landplane or seaplane.

car·ri·ole, kar′ē·ōl″, *n.* See *cariole.*

car·ri·on, kar′ē·on, *n.* [O.Fr. *caroigne*, < L.L. *caronia*, < L. *caro, carnis*, flesh.] The dead and putrefying body or flesh of animals; flesh so corrupted as to be unfit for food.—*a.* Pertaining to carrion; feeding on carrion.—**car·ri·on crow**, *n.* The common crow, so called because it feeds on carrion.

car·ron·ade, kar″o·nād′, *n.* [< *Carron* in Scotland, where it was first made.] A short piece of ordnance of limited range formerly used in the navy.

car·ron oil, *n.* [< its use at the *Carron* iron-works in Scotland.] An ointment composed of equal parts of limewater and olive oil, used as a treatment for burns and scalds.

car·rot, kar′ot, *n.* [Fr. *carotte*; L.L. *carota*.] A plant having a long edible root of an orange color, much used as a culinary vegetable and for feeding cattle.

car·rot-top, kar′ot·top″, *n. Slang*, a red-haired person.

car·rot·y, kar′o·tē, *a.* Like a carrot in color; reddish yellow.

car·ry, kar′ē, *v.t.*—*carried, carrying.* [O.E. *carie* < O.Fr. *carier*, to convey in a car, < O.Fr. *car*, a cart or car.] To bear, convey, or transport an object; to drive, drag, or fetch; as, to *carry* off a prisoner; to sway by emotion: usu. with *away*; to capture; as, to *carry* a fortress; to transfer from one spot to another; to channel the course of; to have on one's person; to possess as a characteristic; to bear, as oneself, in a specified manner, as: She *carries* herself gracefully. To bear the weight of; to bring to fruition, as a crop; to sing relatively on pitch; as, to *carry* a tune; to stock merchandise, as: Our store *carries* exotic foods. To extend or continue in time or space or degree; to win a victory; appear in print; to keep on one's ledgers; *golf*, to advance with one stroke; *southern dial.* to escort; *sailing*, to hoist, as a sail.

car·ry, kar′ē, *n.* pl. **car·ries**, kar′ēz. A carrying; land separating navigable waters, over which a canoe or boat must be carried; a portage; range of a gun; the distance travelled by a golf ball before it lands; *football*, a single offensive running play by a ball carrier, as: The fullback gained seven yards on his first *carry.*

car·ry, kar′ē, *v.t.*—*carried, carrying. Stock market.* To provide the unpaid balance on a customer's margined security; to keep a position in commodities or securities pending an anticipated rise in price.

car·ry·all, kar′ē·əl″, *n.* [In part, an altered form of *cariole*; in part, < *carry* and *all.*] A light, covered, four-wheeled one-horse carriage that seats four people; an enclosed automobile or bus with seats for passengers arranged lengthwise and facing each other.

car·ry·all, kar′ē·əl″, *n.* A spacious case or bag.

car·ry a lot of weight, *slang*, to have a great deal of influence because of money, reputation, etc.

car·ry a torch, *slang*, to be morose and melancholy because of rejection by one's sweetheart: usu. followed by *for.*

car·ry·ing charge, *n.* The amount charged over the regular price on a purchase paid for in installments.

car·ry·ing place, *n. Canada*, a portage.

car·ry off—To kill or cause to die; to win, as an award; to do with success; to face with effrontery; to kidnap.

car·ry on—To manage or prosecute; to continue to pursue, as in the face of adversity; *colloq.* to conduct oneself in a foolish, immature, or overly emotional way.

car·ry out—To continue to the end; to accomplish; to finish; to execute a plan or an undertaking.

car·ry o·ver, *v.i.—carried over, carrying over*. To retain or remain beyond the usual time limit, as merchandise left for another selling season; to postpone; *bookkeeping*, to transfer a sum to the following column, page, or book; *accounting*, to assign a loss or unused credit to the gross income of a future tax period. To continue into another activity or time period.—**car·ry-o·ver**, kar′ē·ō′vér, *n.* Something carried over to a new period or account, as a stock of grain, goods, or credit.

car·sick·ness, kär′sik″nis, *n.* Nausea caused by motion, esp. when riding in a car.—**car·sick**, *a.*

cart, kärt, *n.* [Prob. < Icel. *kartr*, cart, = O.E. *craet*, chariot.] A heavy two-wheeled vehicle, commonly without springs, for the conveyance of heavy goods; a light two-wheeled vehicle with springs, used for pleasure or business; any small vehicle moved by hand.—**cart be·fore the horse**, something in an improper, or illogical order.—**car·ter**, *n.*—**cart·ful**, *n.*

cart, kärt, *v.t.* To convey in or as in a cart.—*v.i.* To drive or use a cart.

cart·age, kär′tij, *n.* The act or the cost of carting.

carte blanche, kart′blänch′, *n. pl.* **cart·es blanch·es**, karts′blänch′. [Fr., white paper.] A blank paper authenticated with a signature, and entrusted to a person to write in his own conditions; unrestricted authority to make decisions.

car·tel, kär·tel′, kär′tal, *n.* [Fr., < L. *chartula*, dim. of *charta*, paper, a paper.] An organization, often international, which controls commercial policy for companies engaging in the same area of production; an agreement between warring states, usually providing for the exchange of prisoners; a combination of various political groups uniting in a common cause.

Car·te·sian, kär·tē′zhan, *a.* Pertaining to the philosopher and mathematician, René Descartes, or to his philosophy.—*n.* One who adopts the philosophy of Descartes.—**Car·te·sian·ism**, *n.* The philosophy of Descartes.

Car·te·sian co·or·din·ates, *n. Math.* the location of a point described by its distances from each of two intersecting straight-line axes, measured parallel to the other axis.—**rec·tang·u·lar Car·te·sian co·or·din·ate**, *n. Math.* the location of a point described by its distances from each of three planes mutually perpendicular, measured along a line parallel to the other two planes. —**Car·te·sian co·or·din·ate sys·tem**, *n. Math.* A gridlike system of coordinates, used to graphically plot or describe the curve of an equation, or to describe the shape of a solid.

Car·tha·gin·i·an peace, *n.* A peace settled on extremely harsh terms, as in the Punic or Carthaginian wars when the Romans destroyed the city of Carthage.

Car·thu·sian, kär·thö′zhan, *n.* A member of an austere, contemplative religious order founded by St. Bruno in 1086, under Benedictine rule, so called from *Chartreuse*, in France, the place of their institution; pupil of the Charterhouse School, founded on the site of the London monastery.—*a.*

car·ti·lage, kär′ti·lij, kärt′lij, *n.* [Fr. *cartilage*, L. *cartilago*.] An elastic tissue composing most of the skeleton in embryos and young vertebrates, then converting for the most part into bone in mature higher vertebrates; gristle.

car·ti·lag·i·nous, kär″ti·laj′i·nus, *a.* Resembling a cartilage; gristly; consisting of cartilage; having a skeletal cartilage only, and not true bones, as do fish.

car·to·gram, kär′to·gram″, *n.* A map which gives simplified statistical information through use of shading or dots.

car·tog·ra·pher, kär·tog′ra·fèr, *n.* One who prepares or publishes maps or charts; a maker of maps or charts.

car·tog·ra·phy, kär·tog′ra·fē, *n.* [E. *chart*, L. *charta*, paper, and Gr. *graphē*, writing, description.] The art or practice of drawing maps or charts.—**car·to·graph·ic, car·to·graph·i·cal**, kär″to·graf′ik, kär″to·graf′i·kl, *a.* Pertaining to cartography.—**car·to·graph·i·cal·ly**, *adv.* In a cartographic manner; by cartography.

car·ton, kär′ton, *n.* [Fr. *carton*. See *cartoon*.] A box made of thin pasteboard; a white disk within the bull's-eye of a target; a shot which strikes this.

car·toon, kär·tön′, *n.* [Fr. *carton*, pasteboard, a cartoon, < It. *cartone* (same sense), aug. of *carta*, L. *charta*, paper.] A caricature, often satirical, representing important events in politics or important public figures; the comic strips; a pictorial design drawn on strong paper as a study for a picture intended to be painted in the same size, and more especially for a picture to be painted in fresco. See *animated cartoon.* —*v.t., v.i.*—**car·toon·ist**, *n.*

car·touche, car·touch, kär·tösh′, *n.* [Fr. *cartouche*, O.Fr. *cartoche*, < It. *cartoccio*, a cartridge, a roll of paper, < *carta*, L. *charta*, paper.] A gun cartridge having a paper case; a box for cartridges; an oval or oblong figure containing a royal name as in Egyptian monuments; *arch.* a sculptured ornament in the form of a scroll unrolled for inscriptions or emblems.

car·tridge, kär′trij, *n.* [Corruption of *cartouche.*] A tube of pasteboard or metal for holding a charge of powder, a bullet or the shot for a firearm; a case containing an explosive charge for blasting; a replaceable or refillable container holding liquid or other materials made for use inside a larger container; as, a *cartridge* pen; a roll of unexposed film for a camera; a small removable container in a record player holding the mechanism and needle; a pointed metal cylinder attachment to a plow pulled through the soil to form a drainage passage.

car·tridge pa·per, *n.* A durable, strong paper used for making cartridges; an inexpensive drawing paper; a paper with a rough finish used for printing by offset lithography.

car·tu·lar·y, kär′chu·ler″ē, *n. pl.* **car·tu·lar·ies**. [Fr. *cartulaire*, L.L. *cartularius*, < *chartula*, dim. of L. *charta*, paper.] A record or register of title deeds and other documents; the keeper of such a record or archives.

cart·wheel, kärt′hwēl″, kärt′wēl″, *n.* Wheel of a cart; an acrobatic trick executed by flipping the body laterally, thus resembling a turning wheel; a wide-brimmed, shallow-crowned hat; *colloq.* any large coin, esp. the U.S. silver dollar.

car·un·cle, kar′ung·kel, ka·rung′kel, *n.* [L. *caruncula*, dim. < *caro*, flesh.] A small fleshy excrescence; a fleshy excrescence on the head of a fowl, as a wattle or the like; *bot.* a protuberance surrounding the hilum of a seed.—**ca·run·cu·lar, ca·run·cu·lous**, ka·rung′kū·lèr, ka·rung′kū·lus, *a.* Pertaining to or in the form of a caruncle.—**ca·run·cu·late, ca·run·cul·at·ed**, *a.* Having a fleshy excrescence.

car·va·crol, kär′va·krạl″, kär′va·krōl″, *n. Chem.* a thick, colorless oil, $(CH_3)_2CHC_6H_3$-$(CH_3)(OH)$, usually derived from thyme or origanum oil: used in perfume and as a mint-flavored antiseptic.

carve, kärv, *v.t.—carved, carving.* [O.E. *ceorfan* = D. *kerven*, Icel. *kyrfa*, to carve; Dan. *karve*, G. *kerven*, to notch or indent; same root as *grave*.] To cut, as some solid material, in order to produce the representation of an object or decorative design; to make or shape by cutting; to form by cutting or hewing; to cut into, hew, or slash; to cut into small pieces or slices, as meat at table.—*v.i.* To exercise the trade of a carver; to engrave or cut figures; to cut up meat at table.—**carv·er**, kär′vèr, *n.* One who carves, as one who cuts ivory, wood, or the like, in a decorative way; one who cuts meat for use at table; a large knife for carving.

car·vel, kär′vel, *n.* Caravel.

car·vel-built, kär′vel·bilt″, *a. Naut.* pertaining to a ship or boat in which the planks are all flush and not overlapping, as in clinker-built boats.

carv·ing, kär′ving, *n.* A branch of sculpture usually limited to works in wood or ivory; the device or figure carved.

car·y·at·id, kar″ē·at′id, *n. pl.* **car·y·at·ids, car·y·at·i·des**, kar″·ē·at′i·dēz″. [L. < Gr. *Karyatis*, name of a priestess of Diana.] *Arch.* a figure of a woman dressed in long robes, serving to support entablatures.

car·y·op·sis, kar″ē·op′sis, *n. pl.* **car·y·op·ses, car·y·op·sid·es**, kar″ē·op′sēz, kar″ē·op′si·dēz″. [Gr. *karyon*, a nut, and *opsis*, an appearance.] *Bot.* A small, one-seeded, dry, indehiscent fruit, in which the seed adheres to the thin pericarp throughout, as in wheat and other grains; the typical fruit of all grasses and grains.

ca·sa, kä′sa, kä′sä, *n.* [Sp. lit. house.] A house, esp. in southwestern U.S.

ca·sa·ba, cas·sa·ba, ka·sä′ba, *n.* [< *Kassaba*, now Turgutlu, a town in Turkey.] A sweet, edible, winter melon with a yellow, netted skin. Also **ca·sa·ba me·lon**.

Cas·a·no·va, kaz″a·nō′va, kas″a·nō′va, *It.* kä″sä·nạ′vä, *n.* [< Giovanni Jacopo *Casanova* de Seingault (1725–98), It. adventurer and author.] A man who has the reputation of being an unscrupulous lover of many women; a Don Juan.

Cas·bah, Kas·bah, kaz′ba, kaz′bä, käz′ba, käz′bä, *n.* The old native quarter in cities of Arabic population, esp. in Algiers; in N. Africa, the portion of the city surrounding the fortress.

cas·ca·bel, kas′ka·bel″, *n.* [Sp., little bell, knob at the end of a cannon.] A knob-shaped projection at the rear of the breech of a muzzle-loading cannon; the rear part of the breech; a small, perforated bell which contains a loose pellet.

cas·cade, kas·kād′, *n.* [Fr. *cascade*, < It. *cascata*, < *cascare*, fall.] A small waterfall over a precipice or other declivity; one in a series of such falls; an arrangement of lace or other drapable material, in folds falling one over another in a zigzag fashion; something resembling a waterfall, as certain firework displays; *electronics*, consecutive stages, in which each stage is dependent on the ones before and/or after, as in a relay system.

cas·cade, kas·kād′, *v.i.—cascaded, cascading.* To fall in or like a cascade; to form in a cascade.

cas·ca·ra, kas·kār′a, *n.* Shortened form of *cascara sagrada.*

cas·ca·ra buck·thorn, *n.* A buckthorn, *Rhamnus purshiana*, of the Pacific coast of the U.S., yielding cascara sagrada.

cas·ca·ra sa·gra·da, kas·kār′a sa·grä′da, kas·kâr′a sa·grä′da, kas·kâr′a sa·grad′a, *n.* [Sp. *cáscara sagrada*, "sacred bark."] The dried bark of a cascara buckthorn, used as a cathartic or laxative.

cas·ca·ril·la, kas″ka·ril′a, *n.* [Sp., dim. of *cáscara*, bark.] The bitter aromatic bark of a West Indian shrub, *Croton eluteria*, used as a tonic; the shrub itself.

case, kās, *n.* [O.Fr. Fr. *cas*, L. *casus* < *cadere*, fall.] An instance of the occurrence or existence of something; an instance of disease or other condition requiring medical or surgical treatment, or the patient exhibiting it; *colloq.* a person viewed as an instance of some peculiarity, as: He's a *case*. The actual facts or state of things, as: That is not the *case*. A situation, condition, or plight, or a person involved in such; as, a poverty *case*; a state of things involving a question for discussion or decision; a circumstance calling for investigation or action, as by the police. *Law*, a suit or action at law, a cause; the presentation of facts or evidence on which a party to a lawsuit relies for success. A statement of facts in support of an argument; a question of moral conduct; as, a *case* of conscience. *Gram.* one of the set of forms of a noun, pronoun, or adjective, that expresses the various syntactical relations in which it may stand to other words in a sentence; a particular relation of this kind, whether in an inflected or other language; such forms or relations collectively.—**in any case,** in any event; at all events; anyhow.—**in case,** in the event that.—**in no case,** under no circumstances.

case, kās, *n.* [O.Fr. *casse,* < L. *capsa,* box, receptacle, < *capere,* hold.] A receptacle or box for containing or enclosing something; a sheath, outer covering, or protective part; as, a sword *case,* a watch *case;* a box with its contents; a quantity contained in a box; the enclosing frame or framework of a door, window, or stairs; a set; as, a *case* of instruments; *bookbinding,* the cover and backbone of a book, ready to be bound to the sewn pages; *print.* a tray, as of wood, divided into compartments for holding types for the use of the compositor, usually arranged in a set of two, the *upper case* for capital letters, and the *lower case* for small letters. The skull cavity of the sperm whale, containing spermaceti.

case, kās, *v.t.*—*cased, casing.* To put or enclose in a case; encase; *U.S. slang,* to survey or investigate in preparation for an intended robbery or other crime. To line with reinforcing material; as, to *case* a well; to fuse, as glass, onto another, differently colored, layer of glass.

ca·se·ate, kā'sē·āt″, *v.i.*—*caseated, caseating.* [L. *caseus,* cheese.] To become like cheese: said esp. of degenerating animal tissue.

ca·se·a·tion, kā″sē·ā′shan, *n. Pathol.* the deterioration, as of tubercular tissue, into a soft, crumbly, cheeselike substance; *biochem.* the separation of casein from coagulating milk, to form cheese or curd.

case bay, *n. Carp.* Any division of a roof, except that adjoining the end wall or gable, comprising two principal rafters with the purlins or the like between them; a corresponding division of a floor, comprising two girders and the intervening joists.

case·book, kās′bụk″, *n.* A book containing detailed records of cases that contain material and typify situations which are used for references, lectures, and instruction in law, psychology, sociology, and medicine.

case·hard·en, kās′här″den, *v.t.* To harden (steel or an alloy) on the surface only, by heat-treating and combination with other materials such as carbon; *fig.* to render insensible to external impressions or influences.—**case·hard·ened,** *a.*

case his·to·ry, *n.* A factual record of an individual's or family's personal history for use esp. in sociological, medical, or psychiatric analyses.

ca·sein, kā′sēn, kā′sē·in, kā·sēn′, *n. Biochem.* a white amorphous phosphoprotein formed when milk is curdled by rennet, constituting the basic ingredient of cheese and some plastics or, when precipitated from coagulating milk by acids, used in making paints and glues.

ca·sein·o·gen, kā·sē′no·jen, kā″sē·in′a··jen, *n. Biochem.* the principal protein of

milk, which in the presence of rennet is converted into casein.

case knife, *n.* A long knife kept in a case or sheath; a large table knife.

case law, *n.* Law made by decided cases that serve as precedents, as opposed to law enacted by a legislature.

case·mate, kās′māt″, *n.* [Fr. *casemate,* < It. *casamatta;* origin uncertain.] A vault in a rampart, or an armored enclosure in a warship, with embrasures for artillery firing.—**case·mat·ed,** *a.*

case·ment, kās′ment, *n.* [Prob. < *case.*] A window sash opening by swinging on hinges, which are generally attached to the upright side of its frame; a window with such sashes; *poetic,* any window. A casing or covering.—**case·ment·ed,** *a.*

ca·se·ous, kā′sē·us, *a.* [L. *caseus,* cheese.] Of or like cheese; *pathol.* cheesy; as, *caseous* degeneration, pertaining to a morbid process in which tissues are converted into a thick, cheeselike mass.

case rec·ord, *n.* Information gathered about an individual or group of individuals to serve as an organized record for use as a psychological biography in social work, psychiatry, medicine, and sociology.

case shot, *n.* A collection of small projectiles in a case, to be fired from a cannon; canister; shrapnel.

case sys·tem, *n.* An inductive method of teaching law based upon the study of reported cases rather than of textbooks and commentaries.

case·work·er, kās′wụr″kėr, *n.* An investigator who interviews handicapped or maladjusted persons and needy families for the purpose of providing aid from government or private social agencies.—**case·work,** *n.*

case·worm, kās′wụrm″, *n.* A caddisworm, so called from the case which it constructs to protect its body.

cash, kash, *n.* [Fr. *casse,* < It. *cassa,* < L. *capsa,* box.] Money, esp. ready money; money, or an equivalent, as a check, paid at the time of making a purchase.—*v.t.* To give or obtain cash for (a check).

cash, kash, *n. pl.* **cash.** [E. Ind. (Dravidian).] Any of various coins of small value of India or China.

cash·book, kash′bụk″, *n.* A book in which is kept a register or account of money received and paid.

cash·ew, kash′ō, ka·shō′, *n.* [For *acajou.*] A tree, *Anacardium occidentale,* native to tropical America, which bears a small, edible, kidney-shaped nut, "cashew nut," on an edible, fleshy receptacle of the shape and size of a pear, "cashew apple," and which has a medicinal bark that yields the gum, acajou, "cashew gum."

cash flow, *n. Com.* Reported net income of a corporation plus amounts charged off for depreciation, depletion, or amortization; extraordinary charges to reserves which are bookkeeping deductions.

cash·ier, ka·shēr′, *v.t.* [D. *casseren,* < Fr. *casser,* break, discharge, annul, < L. *quassare,* shake, break, and L.L. *cassare,* annul.] To dismiss from a position of command or trust, esp. with ignominy.

cash·ier, ka·shēr′, *n.* [Fr. *caissier* < *caisse,* cash box, = *casse,* E. *cash.*] One who has charge of cash or money; one who superintends monetary transactions, as in a bank.

cash·ier's check, *n.* A check drawn by a bank upon its own funds and signed by its cashier.

cash in, *v.t.* To turn in and receive cash for, as gambling chips.—*v.i.* To retire or withdraw from a business venture; used with *on,* to turn to one's advantage or monetary gain; as, to *cash in on* another's gullibility.

cash i·tems, *n. pl. Finance,* government bonds, securities, bank deposits, and the

like, considered equivalent to cash in a corporate statement.

cash·mere, kazh′mẽr, kash′mẽr, *n.* [From *Cashmere (Kashmir),* native state in northern India.] The fine, soft under-wool of a breed of goats of Kashmir and Tibet; a costly kind of shawl woven in characteristic patterns and colors, made of this wool; a fine, soft woolen dress fabric with a twilled face; a fine yarn of this wool alone or blended to use in knit fabrics.

cash reg·is·ter, *n.* A manual or electric device for retailers, recording the amount of cash received, adding it, showing total amounts, and usually providing a money drawer.

cas·i·mere, cas·i·mire, kas′i·mẽr″, *n.* See cassimere.

cas·ing, kā′sing, *n.* A protective or confining covering; a supporting frame as used around a door or window; the outer covering of a pneumatic tire; a thin tubular membrane for encasing processed meats.

ca·si·no, ka·sē′nō, *n. pl.* **ca·si·nos,** ka··sē′nōz. [It., dim. of *casa,* house, < L. *casa,* cottage.] A large room or building for meetings, amusements, dancing, and esp. gambling; a country house or lodge in Italy. A kind of card game in which the ten of diamonds, called "big casino," and the two of spades, called "little casino," have special counting value; also *cassino.*

cask, kask, käsk, *n.* [Appar. < Sp. *casco,* skull, helmet, cask for wine, etc. = Fr. *casque,* helmet.] A barrel-shaped vessel made of staves, headings, and hoops for holding liquids, often one larger and stronger than an ordinary barrel; the quantity such a vessel holds; a casque; hogshead; keg.

cas·ket, kas′kit, kä′skit, *n.* [In form a dim. of *cask,* but in meaning < Fr. *cassette,* a coffer or casket, dim. of *casse,* a box.] *U.S.* a coffin for burial of a corpse. A small chest or box for jewels.—*v.t.* To put in a casket.

Cas·lon, kaz′lon, *n. Print.* an old-style type modeled after the types of the English type-founder, William Caslon (1692–1766).

casque, kask, *n.* [Fr. < Sp. *casco,* a helmet.] A helmet commonly used in medieval periods; *zool.* an anatomic structure on the head suggesting a helmet.

cas·sa·ba mel·on, ka·sä′ba mel′on, *n.* See casaba.

Cas·san·dra, ka·san′dra, *n.* [< the prophetess *Cassandra,* of ancient Troy, who was fated never to be believed, although her prophecies came true.] One who prophesies or warns of coming evil.

cas·sa·tion, ka·sā′shan, ka·sä′shan, *n. Mus.* An 18th-century instrumental suite for open-air performance in several movements and divertimento style; serenade.

cas·sa·va, ka·sä′va, *n.* [Pg. *cassave,* Sp. *casabe, cazabe,* < Haitian name *kasabi.*] A slender erect shrub, genus *Manihot,* belonging to the spurge family, extensively cultivated in tropical America and the West Indies; the nutritious starch obtained from the root, and formed into cakes, as cassava bread, and into tapioca; the nutritious starch obtained from the roots of cassava.

cas·se·role, kas′e·rōl″, *n.* [Fr., *casse,* pan.] A stewpan; a dish in which food is cooked and served; the food prepared in such a utensil; a dishlike mold of rice, mashed potatoes, or the like, served with a filling of meat and vegetables; a small dish with a handle, used in chemical laboratories.—*v.t.*—*casseroled, casseroling.* To cook in a casserole.

cas·sette, ka·set′, ka·set′, *n.* [Fr. < It. *cassetta,* dim. of *cassa,* box.] A type of tape cartridge; *photog.* a plate holder or film holder of a camera.

cas·sia, kash′a, kas′ē·a, *n.* [L. *cassia,* Gr. *kasia, kassia,* < the Hebrew or Phoenician name.] A tropical leguminous plant, genus

Cassia, of many species, consisting of trees, shrubs, or herbs, the leaflets of several of which constitute the drug called senna, while the pulp from the legumes of another species is used as a purgative.—**cas·sia bark**, *n.* Bark from the tree, *Cinnamomum cassia*, providing a coarse type of cinnamon.

cas·si·mere, kas′i·mēr″, *n.* [cashmere, Kashmir.] A plain or twilled woolen cloth, used esp. for men's wear. Also *casimere*, *casimire*.

cas·si·no, ka·sē′nō, *n.* See *casino*.

Cas·si·o·pe·ia, Cas·si·o·pe·a, kas″ē-o·pē′a, *n. Astron.* a constellation in the northern hemisphere with five of its stars forming a kind of W.—**Cas·si·o·pe·ian, Cas·si·o·pe·an**, *a.*

Cas·si·o·pe·ia's Chair, *n.* [From *Cassiopeia*, of classical mythology, wife of the Ethiopian king Cepheus and mother of Andromeda: placed among the stars after death.] *Astron.* a group of stars forming the most conspicuous part of the constellation Cassiopeia and supposed to resemble a chair.

cas·sit·er·ite, ka·sit′a·rīt″, *n.* [Gr. *Kassiteros*, tin.] Native dioxide of tin, SnO_2, the chief source of the metal.

cas·sock, kas′ok, *n.* [Fr. *casaque*, < It. *casacca*; origin uncertain.] Any of various long outer garments formerly worn by soldiers, horsemen, and others; a long, close-fitting garment worn by ecclesiastics and others engaged in church functions; the clerical office, esp. in the Church of England; a clergyman.—**cas·socked**, *a.* Wearing a cassock.

cas·so·war·y, kas′o·wer″ē, *n. pl.* **cas·so·war·ies**. [Malay *kasuwari*.] Any of several large, three-toed, flightless ratite birds constituting the genus *Casuarius*, of Australasian regions, resembling the ostrich but smaller.

cast, kast, käst, *v.t.*—**cast**, **casting**. [M.E. *casten*, < Scand.: cf. Icel. and Sw. *kasta*, Dan. *kaste*, cast.] To throw; fling or hurl, often used with *away*, *off*, *out*; direct, as the eye or glance; cause, as light, to fall upon something or in a certain direction; throw out, as a fishing line or anchor; to throw down; throw (a beast) on its back or side; throw to the ground, as in wrestling; defeat in a lawsuit; to throw off or away; part with, or lose; shed or drop, as hair or fruit, esp. prematurely; bring forth (young), esp. abortively; send off (a swarm), as bees do; throw or set aside; discard or reject; dismiss or disband; throw forth, as from within; emit or eject; vomit; throw up, as earth, with a shovel; to put or place, esp. hastily or forcibly; deposit, as a vote; bestow or confer; to dispose or arrange. *Theatr.* allot the parts of, as a play, to the actors; assign (a part) to an actor. *Metal.* to form, as molten metal, into a particular shape by pouring into a mold, or produce (an object or article) by such a process. Stereotype or electrotype; to compute or calculate; add, as a column of figures; calculate astrologically, as a horoscope; forecast; to ponder or consider; contrive, devise, or plan; to turn or twist; warp; bring (a boat) round; *archaic*, tip (a scale or balance); to let go or let loose, as a vessel, from a mooring, with *loose* or *off*. —*v.i.* To throw; receive form in a mold; calculate or add; conjecture or forecast; consider; plan or scheme; look about one mentally, as for an excuse, usually with *about*; search this way and that, as for a lost scent in hunting, often with *about*; warp, as timber. *Naut.* to turn, esp. so as to get the head of the boat away from the wind; tack; to loosen a vessel from a mooring, with *off*.

cast, kast, käst, *n.* The act of casting; that which is cast; the distance to which a thing may be cast or thrown; a throw of dice; a stroke of fortune; fortune or lot;

disposition or arrangement. *Theatr.* the assignment of parts in a play to the actors; the actors to whom the parts in a play are assigned. *Metal.* the act of casting or founding; the quantity of metal cast at one time; something shaped in a mold while in a fluid or plastic state; a casting; a reproduction or copy, as of a statue, made in a mold; an impression or mold made from a thing; hence, mold or stamp. Form or appearance; sort, kind, or style; bent or tendency; a permanent twist or turn; as, to have a *cast* in one's eye; a warp; a slight tinge of some color; hue; shade; a dash or trace; a small amount; computation or calculation; addition; a conjecture or forecast.

cast·a·net, kas″ta·net′, *n.* [Sp. *castañeta*, < L. *castanea*, a chestnut, from resembling that fruit.] One of a pair of small concave pieces of ivory or hard wood, shaped like spoons, fastened to the thumb, and clicked with the middle finger in certain Spanish dances.

cast·a·way, kast′a·wā″, *n.* One who or that which is cast away or shipwrecked; one ruined in fortune or character.—*a.* Thrown away; rejected; useless; abandoned.

caste, kast, käst, *n.* [Fr. *caste*, Pg. *casta*, breed, race, caste.] One of the classes or distinct hereditary orders of social distinction into which the Hindus are divided according to the religious law of Brahmanism; a class or order of the same kind prevailing in other countries; a rank or order of society; social position; in social insects, a set of similar individuals, as the "workers" in ants and bees.

cas·tel·lan, kas′te·lan, ka·stel′an, *n.* A governor of a castle; the warden of a fort.

cas·tel·lat·ed, kas′te·lā″tid, *a. Arch.* Furnished with turrets and battlements like a castle; built in the style of a castle.

cast·er, kas′tėr, kä′stėr, *n.* A small wheel attached by a vertical pivot to the legs of a chair, sofa, or table, to facilitate their being moved without lifting; a small cruet or bottle for holding condiments for the table. Also **cas·tor**.

cast·er, kas′tėr, kä′stėr, *n.* One who or that which casts, as, printing type by a machine; specifically, one who makes castings; a founder.

cas·ti·gate, kas′ti·gāt″, *v.t.*—**castigated**, **castigating**. [L. *castigatus*, pp. of *castigare*, < *castus*, pure, and *agere*, drive, do.] To censure, chasten, or punish in order to correct; criticize severely; to emend, as a text.—**cas·ti·ga·tion**, *n.*—**cas·ti·ga·tor**, *n.*—**cas·ti·ga·to·ry**, kas′ti·ga·tor″ē, *a.* Serving to castigate; corrective; punitive.

Cas·tile soap, *n.* A kind of fine, hard, white or mottled soap, originally from Castile, Spain.

Cas·til·ian, ka·stil′yan, *n.* An inhabitant or native of Castile, in Spain; the language of Castile, the accepted literary and cultivated spoken form of the Spanish language.—*a.* Pertaining to Castile.

cast·ing, kas′ting, kä′sting, *n.* The act of one who casts; that which is cast, especially, something cast or formed in a mold; *metal.* something formed of cast metal.

cast·ing vote, *n.* A deciding vote cast by a president or chairman when the other votes are equally divided.

cast·i·ron, kast′ī′ėrn, käst′ī′ėrn, *n.* A hard, brittle, impure form of iron obtained by remelting pig-iron with limestone and running it into molds; pig-iron.—*a.* Made of castiron; resembling castiron. *Fig.* inflexible or unyielding; strong, rugged.

cas·tle, kas′el, kä′sel, *n.* [O.Fr. *castel* (also *chastel*, Fr. *château*), < L. *castellum*, fortress, castle, dim. of *castrum*, fortified place, *castra*, pl., camp.] A building, or series of connected buildings, fortified for

defense against an enemy; a fortified residence, as of a prince in feudal times; hence, a large and stately residence, as of a great noble or a person of great wealth; a tower, esp. one for defense; *chess*, rook.

cas·tle, kas′el, kä′sel, *v.t.*—**castled**, **castling**. *Chess*, to move (the king) two squares toward either rook and place that rook on the square passed over by the king.—*v.i.*

cas·tled, kas′eld, kä′seld, *a.* Having a castle or castles; built like a castle; castellated.

cas·tle in the air, *n.* A visionary project; an impracticable scheme. Also **cas·tle in Spain**.

cast on, *v.t.* To form, as a series of loops of yarn, over the knitting needle preparatory to the process of knitting.

cas·tor, kas′tėr, kä′stėr, *n.* [L., < Gr. *kastor*.] A beaver; a beaver hat, or some similar hat. A substance of a strong penetrating smell, secreted by special glands of the beaver, and used in medicine and perfumery; also **cas·tor·e·um**. A heavy woolen cloth for overcoats; a soft-finished glove leather, usually gray in color.

Cas·tor, kas′tėr, kä′stėr, *n. Astron.* one of the two bright northerly stars in the Gemini constellation; *Gr. mythol.* one of the twin sons of Leda.

cas·tor bean, *n.* The seed of the castor-oil plant, *Ricinus communis*.

cas·tor oil, *n.* A viscid oil obtained from the castor bean, used as a cathartic or lubricant.

cas·tor-oil plant, *n.* A tall plant, *Ricinus communis*, native in India but widely naturalized, yielding the castor bean and castor oil: sometimes cultivated as a foliage plant.

cas·trate, kas′trāt, *v.t.*—**castrated**, **castrating**. [L. *castro*, *castratum*, to castrate.] To deprive of the testicles; to geld; to deprive of ovaries; to spay; to take the vigor or strength from; to emasculate; to remove something from; to expurgate.—*n.* A man, as a eunuch, or male animal, as an ox, that has been castrated.—**cas·tra·tion**, *n.*—**cas·tra·tor**, *n.*

cas·u·al, kazh′ö·al, *a.* [O.Fr. Fr. *casuel*, < L.L. *casualis*, < L. *casus*, chance, E. *case*.] Happening by chance; accidental; fortuitous; occurring or coming irregularly; occasional; incidental; uncertain; indefinite; without design; unpremeditated; off hand; without plan or method; careless; concerned with what is occasional and not regular; as, a *casual* laborer; one who does odd jobs; informal; as, *casual* clothing.—**cas·u·al·ly**, *adv.*—**cas·u·al·ness**, *n.*

cas·u·al, kazh′ö·al, *n.* Something casual; a soldier who for the time being is separated from his regiment or other body, as one who has been wounded or is absent on furlough; a casual laborer; one who receives occasional public aid.

cas·u·al·ism, kazh′ö·a·liz″um, *n.* A state of things in which chance prevails; the doctrine that all things exist or are governed by chance or accident.—**cas·u·al·ist**, *n.* One who believes in the doctrine of casualism.

cas·u·al·ty, kazh′ö·al·tē, *n. pl.* **cas·u·al·ties**. Chance or accident; contingency; a mishap; an unfortunate chance or accident, esp. one involving bodily injury or death; *milit.* a man lost through any cause, as death, wounds, capture, or desertion.

cas·u·al·ty in·sur·ance, *n.* Insurance against loss or damage due to accident, as automobile, liability, burglary, explosion, but excluding life, marine, and fire insurance.

cas·u·ist, kazh′ö·ist, *n.* [Fr. *casuiste*, < L. *casus*, E. *case*.] One who studies and resolves cases of conscience or conduct; hence, an oversubtle or disingenuous reasoner upon such matters.—**cas·u·is·tic**, **cas·u·is·ti·cal**, *a.* Pertaining to casuists or casuistry; hence, sophistical.—**cas·u·is·ti·cal·ly**, *adv.*

casuistry

cas·u·ist·ry, kazh'ö·i·strē, *n.* pl. **cas·u·ist·ries.** The science or art of the casuist; the application of general ethical principles to particular cases of conscience or conduct; hence, oversubtle or quibbling reasoning or teaching upon such matters.—**cas·u·is·tics,** *n.* Casuistry.

ca·sus bel·li, kä'sụs bel'lē, *Brit.* kā'sus bel'ī, *n.* [L.] Occasion of war; a ground or reason for declaring war.

cat, kat, *n.* [O.E. *catt, catte,* akin to G. *katze,* Fr. *chat,* L.L. *cattus.*] A small, domesticated mammal, *Felis catus,* of various breeds, valued as a pet and for killing mice and rats; the fur of this cat; any member of the family *Felidae,* as the lion, tiger, cheetah, domesticated cat; one like a cat in behavior or appearance; as, a *cat* burglar, a pole*cat*; a person, usually a woman, known for speaking disparagingly or maliciously of others; the ship's tackle used to raise the anchor to the cathead; a whip called cat-o'-nine tails; a catboat; a catfish; as, channel *cat*; a ballgame, the name of which changes with the number of batters; as, one old *cat*, two old *cat*; *Brit.* the game called tipcat and the wooden piece used in this game; *slang,* a tractor with a caterpillar tread; *slang,* a jazz musician or one who is very fond of jazz; *slang,* a person, a fellow.—**let the cat out of the bag,** to disclose a secret, usually inadvertently.

cat, kat, *v.t.*—*catted, catting.* To raise, as an anchor, to the cathead of a ship; to whip with a cat-o'-nine tails.

CAT, *n.* [(*C*)lear-(*A*)ir (*T*)urbulence.] *Avi.* the turbulence encountered in cloudless air as differentiated from storm turbulence, and constituting a hazard to aircraft because of difficulty of early detection.

ca·tab·a·sis, ka·tab·a·sis, ka·tab'a·sis, *n.* pl. **ca·tab·a·ses.** [L.L., < Gr. *katabasis,* < *katabainein,* go down, < *kata,* down, and *bainein,* go.] A going down or back; a retreat, esp. military. See *anabasis.*

ca·tab·o·lism, ka·tab'o·liz"um, *n.* [Gr. *katabolē,* a throwing down, < *kataballein,* throw down, < *kata,* down, and *ballein,* throw.] *Biol.* In living organisms, a breaking down of more complex molecules into simpler ones, accompanied by an energy release; descending or destructive metabolism: opposed to *anabolism.*—**cat·a·bol·ic,** kat"a·bol'ik, *a.* Pertaining to catabolism.—**cat·a·bol·i·cal·ly,** *adv.*—**ca·tab·o·lize,** ka·tab'o·līz, *v.t.* To expose to catabolism.—*v.i.* To be subjected to catabolism.

cat·a·chre·sis, kat"a·krē'sis, *n.* [L., < Gr. *katachrēsis,* < *katachrēsthai,* misuse, < *kata,* against, and *chrēsthai,* use.] Misuse or strained use of words, as in an inconsistent metaphor; misuse of word elements, as in a perverted word form.—**cat·a·chres·tic,** *a.* [Gr. *katachrēstikos.*] Pertaining to or involving catachresis.—**cat·a·chres·ti·cal·ly,** *adv.*

cat·a·cli·nal, kat"a·klin'al, *a.* [Gr. *kata,* down, and *klinein,* incline.] *Geol.* descending with the dip of the surrounding strata, as a valley.

cat·a·clysm, kat'a·kliz"um, *n.* [L. *cataclysmos,* < Gr. *kataklysmos,* < *kataklyzein,* inundate, < *kata,* down, and *klyzein,* wash.] An extensive overflowing of water; a deluge; a flood; a sudden and violent physical action producing changes in the earth's surface; *fig.* any violent upheaval, esp. one of a social or political nature.—**cat·a·clys·mal,** *a.* Cataclysmic.—**cat·a·clys·mic,** *a.* Of, pertaining to, or resulting from a cataclysm; of the nature of, or having the effect of, a cataclysm.—**cat·a·clys·mi·cal·ly,** *adv.*

cat·a·comb, kat'a·kōm", *n.* [It. *catacomba,* < L.L. *catacumbas;* origin uncertain.] *Usu. pl.* a subterranean burial place, esp. one con-

sisting of galleries with excavated recesses for tombs.

ca·tad·ro·mous, ka·tad'ro·mus, *a.* [Gr. *kata,* down, and *dromos,* < *dramein,* run.] Of fresh-water fishes, going down a river to the sea to spawn. See *anadromous.*

cat·a·falque, kat'a·falk", kat'a·fạk", *n.* [Fr. < It. *catafalco;* akin to E. *scaffold.*] A raised structure on which the body of a deceased personage lies or is carried in state; a similar structure used at services for the dead when the remains are not present.

Cat·a·lan, kat'a·lan", kat'a·lan, kat"a·lan', kat"a·lan', *a.* Of Catalonia, formerly a province, now a division comprising several provinces in northeastern Spain, or of its inhabitants or language.—*n.* A native or inhabitant of Catalonia; the (Romance) dialect spoken in Catalonia, etc., closely related to Provençal.

cat·a·lase, kat'a·lās", *n. Chem.* an enzyme, occurring naturally in the blood, which decomposes hydrogen peroxide; when extracted from animal tissues or molds it is used in food preservation and for removing residual hydrogen peroxide in bleaching processes.—**cat·a·lat·ic,** *a.*

cat·a·lec·tic, kat"a·lek'tik, *a. Poet.* metrically incomplete; truncated; lacking one or more unaccented syllables in the final foot.—*n.*

cat·a·lep·sy, kat'a·lep"sē, *n.* [Gr. *katalēpsis,* a seizing, < *katalambanō,* to seize.] A nervous affection characterized by a temporary suspension of the senses and volition with rigidity of the muscles; trance.—**cat·a·lep·tic,** kat·a·lep'tik, *a.*

cat·a·log, cat·a·logue, kat'a·lạg, kat'a·log, *n.* [Fr. < L.L. *catalogus,* < Gr. *katalogos,* < *katalegein,* reckon, enroll, < *kata,* down, and *legein,* pick, reckon, tell.] A list or register, esp. a list arranged in alphabetical or other methodical order; a systematic arrangement of enumerated items giving descriptive details; a book or pamphlet containing such a list; the material in such a list.—*v.t.* To enter in a catalog.—*v.i.* To work on a catalog.—**cat·a·log·er, cat·a·log·ist,** *n.*—**cat·a·log·i·cal, cat·a·lo·gis·tic,** *a.*

ca·tal·pa, ka·tal'pa, *n.* [N. Amer. Ind.] A hardy, ornamental tree of the genus *Catalpa* found in Asia and North America and noted for its heart-shaped leaves, showy clusters of flowers, and long, slender pods.

ca·tal·y·sis, ka·tal'i·sis, *n.* pl. **ca·tal·y·ses,** ka·tal'i·sēz. [N.L. < Gr. *katalysis,* < *katalyein,* dissolve, < *kata,* down, and *lyein,* loose.] *Chem.* the causing or accelerating of a chemical change by the addition of a catalytic agent which is not permanently affected by the reaction. A change occurring between persons or among social forces initiated by a catalytic agent, such as a controversial book.—**cat·a·lyt·ic,** kat"a·lit'ik, *a.* [Gr. *katalytikos.*] Pertaining to or causing catalysis.—**cat·a·lyt·i·cal·ly,** *adv.*

cat·a·lyst, kat'a·list, *n. Chem.* in catalysis, the substance which causes the chemical change. A catalytic agent; that which causes or changes interactions between persons or events without itself being changed.

cat·a·lyze, kat'a·līz", *v.t.*—*catalyzed, catalyzing.* To act upon by catalysis.

cat·a·ma·ran, kat"a·ma·ran', *n.* [E. Ind. (Dravidian).] A narrow float or sailing raft made of several logs or pieces of wood lashed together; any craft with twin parallel hulls; *colloq.* a quarrelsome woman.

cat·a·mite, kat'a·mīt", *n.* A boy kept for pederasty.

cat·am·ne·sis, kat"am·nē'sis, *n.* pl. **cat·am·ne·ses,** kat"am·nē'sēs. *Med.* a patient's medical history taken during, or after recovery from, an illness. Compare *anamnesis.*

cat·a·mount, kat'a·mount", *n.* Short for *catamountain;* a wild animal of the cat family, as the cougar or lynx.

cat·a·moun·tain, kat"a·moun'tan, kat"a·moun'tin, *n.* The cat of the mountain; any of various wild cats, as the North American puma, the European wildcat, or the leopard; same as *catamount* or *cat-o'-mountain.*

cat·a·plane, kat'a·plān", *n.* An airplane designed to be launched by a catapult.

cat·a·pla·sia, kat"a·plā'zha, kat"a·plā'zhē·a, kat"a·plā'zē·a, *n. Biol.* a change in cells or tissues in which they revert to an earlier or more primitive stage.—**cat·a·plas·tic,** *a.*

cat·a·plasm, kat'a·plaz"am, *n.* [Gr. *kataplasma,* < *kataplasso,* to anoint or to spread as a plaster.] *Med.* a poultice.

cat·a·plex·y, kat'a·plek"sē, *n.* A sudden, temporary loss of muscle power caused by emotional shock; sudden prostration; a form of hypnotic sleep.—**cat·a·plec·tic,** *a.*

cat·a·pult, kat'a·pult", kat'a·pụlt", *n.* [L. *catapulta,* < Gr. *katapeltēs*—*kata,* against, and *pallō,* to brandish, hurl.] An ancient military instrument for hurling missiles; a device for launching an airplane at flying speed, usually from the deck of a ship; *Brit.* a slingshot.

cat·a·pult, kat'a·pult", kat'a·pụlt", *v.t.* To shoot, hurl, or launch from, or as if from, a catapult.—*v.i.* To become catapulted.

cat·a·ract, kat'a·rakt", *n.* [L. *cataracta,* Gr. *katarraktēs,* < *kata,* down, and *rhēgnymi,* to break.] A great fall of water over a precipice; a waterfall; any furious rush or downpour of water; *ophthalm.* a disease of the eye consisting of opacity of the crystalline lens or its capsule, which impairs or destroys vision.—**cat·a·rac·tal,** *a.*

ca·tarrh, ka·tär', *n.* [L. *catarrhus,* < Gr. *katarroos,* < *katarrein,* flow down, < *kata,* down, and *rein,* flow.] *Pathol.* inflammation of a mucous membrane, esp. of the respiratory tract, accompanied by exaggerated secretions.—**ca·tarrh·al,** *a.*—**ca·tarrh·al·ly,** *adv.*

ca·tas·ta·sis, ka·tas'ta·sis, *n.* pl. **ca·tas·ta·ses.** [N.L. < Gr. *katastasis,* appointment, settlement, condition, < *kathistanai,* set down, < *kata,* down, and *istanai,* cause to stand.] The part of a drama, preceding the catastrophe, in which the action is at its height; the climax of a play.

ca·tas·tro·phe, ka·tas'tro·fē, *n.* [L.L., < Gr. *katastrophe,* < *katastrephein,* overturn, < *kata,* down, and *strephein,* turn.] A widespread, disastrous event; any overwhelming misfortune or failure; a sudden violent disturbance, esp. of the earth's surface; a final event or conclusion; the turning point in a drama which introduces the conclusion.—**cat·as·troph·ic,** kat·ạs·trof'ik, *a.*—**cat·as·troph·i·cal·ly,** *adv.*

ca·tas·tro·phism, ka·tas'tro·fiz"am, *n. Geol.* a formerly held theory explaining the major geological changes of the earth as a result of sudden, violent physical upheavals rather than the now accepted concept of uniform, gradual change.

cat·a·to·ni·a, kat"a·tō'nē·a, *n.* A state of suspended animation with loss of voluntary motion; catalepsy; *psychiatry,* any of several schizophrenic syndromes where the patient exhibits muscular rigidity and phases of stupor alternating with periods of agitation.—**cat·a·ton·ic,** *a., n.*

ca·taw·ba, ka·tạ'ba, *n.* A variety of grape cultivated in Ohio and New York; a white wine, either still or sparkling, made from the grape; a Siouan Indian people of North or South Carolina.—*a.* Dark, purplish-red in color.

cat·bird, kat'bụrd", *n.* A black-capped, dark gray American songbird, *Dumetella carolinensis,* related to the mockingbird;

a- fat, fāte, fär, fåre, fạll;　**e-** met, mē, mēre, hėr;　**i-** pin, pīne;　**o-** not, nōte, möve;　**u-** tub, cūbe, bụll;　**oi-** oil;　**ou-** pound.

Australia, any of several birds, genus *Ailuroedus,* issuing a mewing call.

cat block, *n. Naut.* a heavy pulley block with hook, used in hoisting an anchor.

cat·boat, kat′bōt″, *n. Naut.* a broad-beamed, light draft sailboat, usually with centerboard, having a single mast set well forward and carrying one large sail extended by a long boom and gaff.

cat bri·er, *n.* Any of several plants belonging to the genus *smilax,* as the greenbrier.

cat·call, kat′kȧl″, *n.* A shrill, mewing call or whistle indicating disapproval, contempt, or derision; a device for producing such a sound.—*v.t.* To indicate disapproval by sounding catcalls.—*v.i.* To sound catcalls.

catch, kach, *v.t.*—*caught, catching.* [O.Fr. *cachier* (also *chacier,* Fr. *chasser*), < L. *captāre,* strive to take, freq. of *capere,* take.] To capture, seize, or take captive, esp. after pursuit; to snare or entrap; as, to *catch* a fish; to come upon suddenly, surprise or detect, as: They *caught* him cheating. To grasp or snatch, as: She *caught* the youngster by the collar. To grip or entangle, as: The barbed wire *caught* his trousers. To intercept and grab; as, to *catch* a ball; to overtake (something) in motion, or to be in time to reach; as, to *catch* a plane; to hold or retain; as, a barrel to *catch* rain; to check or restrain abruptly; as, to *catch* one's breath; to touch, reach, or hit, as: The blow *caught* his rib cage. To incur or contract; as, to *catch* the mumps; to be affected by, as: The leaves *caught* fire. To fasten with or as with a catch; to grasp by the senses or intellect; to obtain, as: He *catches* votes with wild promises. To understand; as, to *catch* a person's meaning; to captivate or attract, as: Her smile *caught* his fancy. To get, usually briefly, as: He *caught* sight of his friend.

catch, kach, *v.i.* To become gripped or entangled; to take hold; become fastened; *baseball,* to play the catcher's position. Usually with *up,* to overtake something moving; to equal or pass a norm, usually after a delay; to overtake or complete by a surge of effort.

catch, kach, *n.* The act of catching; anything that catches, as a device for fastening something or for checking motion; that which is caught, as a quantity of fish; anything worth catching; an acquisition; a matrimonial prize; a fragment, as of a song; *mus.* a round, esp. one in which the words are so arranged as to produce ludicrous effects. A game in which a ball is thrown from one player to another; *sports,* a grasp of a batted or thrown ball before it touches ground; *colloq.* something with a trick or drawback to it.

catch·all, kach′ȧl″, *n.* A bag, basket, or other receptacle for odds and ends.

catch-as-catch-can, kach′az·kach′kan′, *n.* A style of wrestling where attacking below the waist is permitted.—*adv.* Living, working, or performing without any prior plan or thought.

catch ba·sin, *n.* A receptacle or filter placed at the entrance of a drain or sewer to retain matter that might clog the system.

catch crop, *n.* A fast-growing crop raised between main crops, or as a substitute for a main crop failure.

catch·er, kach′er, *n.* One who or that which catches; *baseball,* the player who stands behind the bat or home base to catch the pitched ball.

catch·fly, kach′flī″, *n. pl.* **catch·flies.** Any of various plants, esp. of the genera *Lychnis* and *Silene,* having a viscid secretion on stem and calyx in which small insects are sometimes caught.

catch·ing, kach′ing, *a.* Infectious; attractive; captivating.

catch·ment, kach′ment, *n.* The act of catching water; a receptacle or drainage

system that catches water, as a reservoir; the water that is caught in such a receptacle.

catch·ment ba·sin, *n. Phys. geog., Brit.* An area drained by a river or river system.

catch on, *v.i.* To understand or comprehend; to become popular.

catch·pen·ny, kach′pen″ē, *n. pl.* **catch·pen·nies.** Anything of little value or use, made merely for quick sale.—*a.* Made merely to sell, regardless of permanent value or usefulness.

catch·pole, catch·poll, kach′pōl, *n.* [M.L. *cacepollus,* Fr. *chacepol,* a chaser of fowls, L. *pullus.*] A sheriff's deputy or bailiff whose duty is to arrest, esp. for debt.

catch·up, kach′up, kech′up, *n.* See ketchup.

catch·weight, kach′wāt″, *n. Sports,* esp. wrestling, the chance or optional weight of a contestant, as contrasted with a weight fixed by agreement.

catch·word, kach′wurd″, *n.* An often repeated word or phrase that becomes symbolic of an idea, group, or product, as, a political or advertising slogan. *Printing,* a word at the head of a page or column which identifies the first or last item on the page; in older books, the first word of a page printed at the bottom of the preceding page. An actor's cue.

catch·y, kach′ē, *a.*—*catchier, catchiest.* Attractive and easily recalled; as, a *catchy* tune; tricky or deceptive; as, a *catchy* sales premium; fitful or irregular; as, a *catchy* wind.

cat dis·tem·per, *n.* An acute viral disease of cats, characterized by fever, diarrhea, and deterioration of white blood cells.

cat·e·che·sis, kat″a·kē′sis, *n. pl.* **cat·e·che·ses.** Oral instruction of Christian converts prior to baptism or confirmation.

cat·e·chet·ic, kat″a·ket′ik, *a.* [CATECHIZE.] Relating to the method of teaching through questions and answers, including catechism instruction. Also **cat·e·chet·i·cal.**

cat·e·chism, kat′a·kiz″um, *n.* [L.L. *catechismus,* < Gr. *katēchizein:* see *catechize.*] Catechetic instruction; a book containing a comprehensive summary of the principles of a religious creed, esp. as maintained by a particular Church, in the form of questions and answers; a similar book of instruction in other subjects; a series of formal questions put to candidates.—**cat·e·chis·mal,** kat′a·kiz″mal, *a.*

cat·e·chist, kat′a·kist, *n.* One appointed to instruct catechumens in the principles of Christianity.—**cat·e·chis·tic, cat·e·chis·ti·cal,** *a.*—**cat·e·chis·ti·cal·ly,** *adv.*

cat·e·chize, kat′a·kīz″, *v.t.*—*catechized, catechizing.* [L.L. *catechizare,* < Gr. *katēchizein,* for *katechein,* resound, teach orally, < *kata,* down, and *ēchein,* sound.] To instruct orally by means of questions and answers, esp. in Christian doctrine; to question searchingly with reference to belief.—**cat·e·chi·za·tion,** *n.*—**cat·e·chiz·er,** *n.*

cat·e·chu, kat′a·chö, kat′a·kū″, *n.* [N.L. < Malay, *kāchu.*] Any of several dry, earthy, or resinous astringent substances prepared from the wood of various tropical Asiatic plants and used for medicine, dyeing, or tanning; cutch; cachou.—**cat·e·chu·ic,** *a.*

cat·e·chu·men, kat″a·kū′men, *n.* [Gr. *katēchoumenos,* instructed. CATECHIZE.] A person who is receiving instruction in the basic rudiments of Christianity before admission to church membership; a person under instruction in the fundamentals of any subject.

cat·e·gor·i·cal, kat″a·gar′i·kal, kat″a·gor′i·kal, *a.* [Gr. *kategorikos,* accusatory, affirmative, categorical, < *kateforein:* CATEGORY.] Positive, as a proposition or statement; unqualified, unequivocal, absolute, or unconditional; of or pertaining to a category.—**cat·e·gor·i·cal syl·lo·gism,**

logic, a syllogism consisting only of categorical propositions, or such as do not involve a condition or hypothesis.—**cat·e·gor·i·cal·ly,** *adv.*

cat·e·gor·i·cal im·per·a·tive, Kant's moral law that one is unconditionally bound to do oneself that which one would rule others to do under the same circumstances.

cat·e·go·rize, kat′a·go·rīz″, *v.t.*—*categorized, categorizing.* To classify; arrange into groups; to describe by titling; characterize.—**cat·e·go·ri·za·tion,** *n.*

cat·e·go·ry, kat′a·gōr″ē, kat′a·gȧr″ē, *n. pl.* **cat·e·go·ries.** [L.L. *categoria,* < Gr. *kategoria,* < *kategorein,* accuse, assert, predicate, < *kata,* against, and *agoreuein,* speak, < *agora,* assembly.] *Logic,* any of the fundamental concepts into which any known fact must conform. Any general or comprehensive division in classification; a class; group.

ca·te·na, ka·tē′na, *n. pl.* **ca·te·næ,** ka·tē′nē. [L., chain.] A chain or connected series, esp. of extracts from the writings of the fathers of the church.

cat·e·na·ry, kat′e·ner″ē, *Brit.* ka·tē′na·rē, *n. pl.* **cat·e·na·ries.** [L. *catenarius.*] *Math.* the curve of a flexible cord or chain hanging freely from two points not in the same vertical line.—*a.* Pertaining to or resembling a catenary.

cat·e·nate, kat′e·nāt″, *v.t.*—*catenated, catenating.* To connect in a series of links or ties; to concatenate.—**cat·e·na·tion,** *n.*

ca·ten·u·late, ka·ten′ū·lāt, *a.* [L. *catenula,* dim. of *catena,* chain.] Chain-like in form or appearance.

ca·ter, kā′tẽr, *v.i.* [< obs. *cater,* a caterer, O.Fr. *acateur, acator,* < *acater,* L.L. *acceptare,* to buy, < L. *ad,* to, and L. *captare,* intens. of *capere,* to take.] To provide what is desired for use, pleasure, or entertainment; to give special attention; as, to *cater* to a sick person; to purvey food, provisions, amusement, etc.: followed by *for.*—*v.t.* To provide food and provisions for; as, to *cater* a dinner.

ca·ter·er, kā′tẽr·ẽr, *n.* One who caters; a provider or purveyor of food and provisions; one who provides for any want or desire.—**ca·ter·ess,** *n.* A woman who caters; a female provider.

cat·er·pil·lar, kat′a·pil″er, kat′ẽr·pil″er, *n.* The wormlike larva of a butterfly or moth or similar larva of other insects, as the sawfly; a vehicle, as a tank, which has the wheels mounted inside an endless metal belt on each side, thus making it suitable for traversing rough or soft ground; (*cap.*) Caterpillar tractor. (Trademark.)

Cat·er·pil·lar Club, *n.* An unofficial club for aircrewmen who have parachuted from a damaged or disabled aircraft.

cat·er·waul, kat′ẽr·wȧl″, *v.i.* [< *cat,* and *waul,* in imitation of the sound made by a cat; O.E. *caterwawe.*] To utter noisy, disagreeable cries, said of a cat during rutting time; to make any similar howl or screech; to engage in noisy argument.—*n.* The cat's cry during rutting period; any loud, catlike cry.

cat·fish, kat′fish″, *n. pl.* **cat·fish, cat·fish·es** [So named because its head resembles a cat's head.] Any scaleless fish as a bullhead or channel cat, of the large order *Ostariophysi,* suborder *Siluroidea,* found principally in fresh waters and noted for their large heads and long barbels, or feelers.

cat·gut, kat′gut″, *n.* The intestines of sheep or other animals, dried and twisted, used as strings for musical instruments.

Cath·a·rine wheel, *n.* See *Catherine wheel.*

ca·thar·sis, ka·thär′sis, *n. pl.* **ca·thar·ses.** [N.L. < Gr. *katharsis,* < *kathairein,* cleanse. < *katharos,* pure.] *Med.* purgation; emotional release provided by an artistic or theatrical experience, such as the Greek dramas of Aeschylus; the elimination of repressed feelings through such psychoanalytic techniques as free association.

ca·thar·tic, ka·thär′tik, *a.* [Gr. *kathartikos.*] *Med.* Pertaining to evacuating the bowels; purgative.—*n.* A purgative.

Ca·thay, ka·thā′, *n.* [< Tatar.] A poetic name for China.

cat·head, kat′hed″, *n. Naut.* a strong beam projecting over a ship's bow to which the anchor is secured.

ca·the·dra, ka·thē′dra, kath′a·dra, *n.* [L. *cathedra,* a teacher's or professor's chair, a bishop's chair, Gr. *kathedra,* a chair or seat—*kata,* down, and *hedra,* a seat.] The throne or seat of a bishop in the cathedral or episcopal church of his diocese.

ca·the·dral, ka·thē′dral, *n.* [M.L. *cathedralis,* < L. *cathedra,* < Gr. *kata,* down, and *ezesthai,* sit.] The principal church of a diocese which contains the bishop's throne; an important church in a non-episcopal denomination.—*a.* Relating to a bishop's seat or throne.—**ca·the·draled,** *a.* Having a cathedral; cathedrallike.

Cath·er·ine wheel, *n.* [< St. *Catherine* of Alexandria, who was condemned to torture on the wheel.] Orig. a wheel with projecting spikes used for torture; a firework which revolves like a wheel while burning; a pinwheel.

cath·e·ter, kath′i·tėr, *n.* [Gr. *kathetēr,* < *kathiēmi,* to thrust in—*kata,* down, and *hiēmi,* to send.] *Surg.* A hollow tube inserted into the body to allow the withdrawal or injection of fluids, usually inserted through the urethra into the bladder to draw off urine when natural discharge is arrested.—**cath·e·ter·ize,** *v.t.* —**cath·e·ter·iz·a·tion,** *n.*

ca·thex·is, ka·thek′sis, *n.* The channeling of psychic energy in an object.

cath·ode, kath′ōd, *n.* [Gr. *kata,* down, and *hodos,* a way.] *Chem.* and *phys.* the negative terminal of an electroplating cell; the positive terminal of a storage battery, from which positively charged electric current leaves; in an electron tube, the electron-emitting electrode.

cath·ode ray, *n.* A stream of electrons projected from cathode to anode in a vacuum tube.

cath·ode ray tube, *n.* A special type of vacuum tube which utilizes a stream of cathode rays projected onto a fluorescent screen, which fluoresces at the impact of the electrons; used in variant forms as a television picture tube and as an oscilloscope.

cath·o·lic, kath′o·lik, kath′lik, *a.* [L. *catholicus,* < Gr. *katholikos,* universal, < *kata,* according to, and *holos,* whole.] Universal in extent; general; encompassing all; involving the interests or sympathies of all; broad-minded; liberal; *eccles.* of or pertaining to the whole Christian body or church; (*cap.*) noting or pertaining to the Church of Rome, the Roman Catholic Church; noting or pertaining to the Western Church; chiefly among Anglicans, noting or pertaining to the Christian body held to represent the ancient undivided Christian church.

Cath·o·lic, kath′o·lik, kath′lik, *n.* A member of a Catholic church, esp. of the Roman Catholic Church.

ca·thol·i·cate, ka·thol′i·kāt″, *n.* The diocese, jurisdiction, or seat of power of a catholicos.

Ca·thol·i·cism, ka·thol′i·sizm, *n.* The faith, system and practice of a Catholic church, esp. the Roman Catholic Church; (*l.c.*) the state of being catholic or universal.

cath·o·lic·i·ty, kath″o·lis′·i·tē, *n.* The state or quality of being catholic or universal; broadmindedness.—**ca·thol·i·cize,**

ka·thol′i·sīz, *v.i.* To make or become catholic or universal; (*cap.*) to cause another to become a Catholic, esp. a Roman Catholic.

ca·thol·i·con, ka·thol′i·kon, *n.* [Gr. *katholikon iama,* universal remedy.] A remedy for all diseases; a panacea.

ca·thol·i·cos, ka·thol′i·kus, ka·thol′i-kos″, *n.* pl. **ca·thol·i·coses, cath·ol·i·coi,** ka·thol′i·koi″. A prelate of a non-Greek Eastern church, such as the Armenian Church.

cat·i·on, kat′ī″on, kat′i·on, *n.* [Gr. *kation,* ppr. neut. of *katienai,* go down, < *kata,* down, and *ienai,* go.] *Physical chem.* the product liberated at the cathode during electrolysis; an electropositive ion.

cat·i·on·ic, kat′ī·on″ik, *a.* Relating to, or containing, cations; used especially to describe a type of synthetic detergent having outstanding germicidal action.

cat·kin, kat′kin, *n.* The ament or spikelike blossom of the willow, birch, or hazel, resembling a cat's tail.—**cat·kin·ate,** *a.*

cat·mint, kat′mint″, *n.* See *catnip.*

cat·nap, kat′nap″, *n.* A short, light nap or doze.—*v.i.* To take a brief nap; to doze.

cat·nip, kat′nip, *n.* [< *cat* and obs. or prov. *nep, nip,* < L. *nepeta,* catmint.] A mint plant, *Nepeta cataria,* with strongly scented leaves of which cats are fond; same as *catmint.*

cat-o'-nine-tails, kat″o·nin′tālz″, *n.* [Named for marks it makes similar to a cat's scratches.] A whip consisting generally of nine pieces of knotted cord on a handle, used to flog offenders on the bare back.

ca·top·tric, ka·top′trik, *a.* [Gr. *katoptrikos,* < *katoptron,* a mirror—*kata,* against, and *optomai,* to see.] Pertaining to incident and reflected light; pertaining to catoptrics.— **ca·top·trics,** ka·top′triks, *n. pl.* That branch of optics which explains the properties of incident and reflected light, and particularly that which is reflected from mirrors or polished bodies.—**ca·top·tri·cal·ly,** *adv.*

cat rig, *n. Naut.* the rig of a catboat; a rig consisting of a single mast set well forward and carrying one large sail extended by a long boom and gaff.—**cat-rigged,** *a.* Rigged like a catboat.

cats and dogs, *n.pl. Slang.* Low-cost, speculative stocks of doubtful value; miscellaneous leftovers or odd pieces, as unsold merchandise.—*adv. Slang,* intensely or very heavily; as, to rain *cats and dogs.*

cat's cra·dle, *n.* A children's game in which a string, looped over the fingers of both hands of one child, is passed to the hands of another to form a different design.

cat's-eye, kats′ī″, *n.* A hard, semi-transparent variety of quartz having an opalescent radiation or reflection of colors like a cat's eye; a metal or glass light reflector used on bicycles and road markers to pinpoint their location at night.

cat's-foot, kats′fu̟t″, *n.* pl. **cat's-feet.** The herb called ground ivy; the plant *Antennaria neodioica* or any other of the *Antennaria* genus.

cat's-paw, cats-paw, kats′pạ″, *n.* A person used by another as a tool or dupe, taken from the story of the monkey who used a cat's paw to pull chestnuts from a fire; *naut.* a light breeze which ruffles a small surface of water during a calm.

cat·sup, kat′sup, kech′up, kach′up, *n.* See *ketchup.*

cat swing, cat train, *n. Canada,* a group of sleds pulled by a caterpillar tractor, used for hauling loads over frozen muskeg in winter.

cat·tail, kat′tāl″, *n.* A tall, reedlike marsh plant, *Typha latifolia,* with flowers in long, dense cylindrical spikes; any of several other plants of the same genus; an ament or catkin. Also **reed mace.**

cat·ta·lo, cat·a·lo, kat′a·lō, *n.* pl. **cat·ta-·loes, cat·ta·los.** A hardy hybrid developed by breeding domesticated cattle and the American buffalo.

cat·ti·ness, kat′ē·nes, *n.* The trait or characteristic of being catty; spitefulness.

cat·tle, kat′al, *n.* [O.Fr. *catel,* < M.L. *capitale,* for *capitale,* wealth, stock.] Domesticated four-legged bovine animals, including cows, bulls, and steers; *slang,* a disparaging term for human beings.

cat·tle·man, kat′al·man, kat′al·man″, *n.* pl. **cat·tle·men.** A man engaged in rearing or tending cattle.

cat·tle·ya, kat′lē·a, kat·lē′a, kat·lā′a, *n.* [From William *Cattley,* an Eng. botanist.] Any of a genus of tropical American orchids characterized by a hooded flower that encloses the column.

cat·ty, kat′ē, *n.* pl. **cat·ties.** A unit of weight equivalent to approximately 1⅓ pounds, used in China and southeast Asia.

cat·ty, kat′ē, *a.*—**cattier, cattiest.** Having any of a cat's characteristics; cutting; derisive; as, a *catty* remark; prone to make such remarks.—**cat·ti·ly,** kat′i·lē, *adv.* In a catty way.

cat·ty-cor·ner, cat·ty-cor·nered, kat′ē·-kạr″ner, kat′ē·kạr″nėrd, *a., adv. Colloq.* diagonal, placed or running diagonally. Also **kit·ty-cor·ner, kit·ty-cor·nered, cat·er-cor·ner, cat·er-cor·nered.**

cat·walk, kat′wạk″, *n.* Any very narrow path, as alongside a bridge, along the roof of a railroad freight car, or over or around an otherwise impassable area.

Cau·ca·sian, kạ·kā′·zhan, kạ·kā′shan, kạ·kazh′an, kạ·kash′an, *a.* Of or pertaining to the Caucasus, a range of mountains between Europe and Asia, extending from the Black Sea to the Caspian Sea; pertaining to the white race as characterized by physical features.—*n.* A native of the Caucasus; a member of the Caucasian race. —**Cau·ca·soid,** *a., n.*

cau·cus, kạ′kus, *n.* pl. **cau·cus·es.** [Prob. < N. Amer. Ind.] In the U.S., a meeting of a group of members of a political party to nominate candidates, elect delegates to a convention; a meeting of the members of a legislative body who belong to the same party to determine upon action in that body. *Brit.* a committee or organization within a political party exercising a certain control over its affairs or action.

cau·cus, kạ′kus, *v.i.*—**caucused, caucusing.** To hold or meet in a caucus.

cau·dad, kạ′dad, *adv.* [L. *cauda,* tail, and *-ad,* < L. *ad,* to, toward.] *Anat.* toward the tail or posterior end of the body.

cau·dal, kạd′al, *a.* [N.L. *caudalis* < L. *cauda,* tail.] *Anat., zool.* Of, at, or near the tail; taillike.

cau·dal an·es·the·sia, *n.* Insensibility to pain in the lower portion of the body, caused by injection of an anesthetic drug into the caudal, or sacral, part of the spinal canal. Also **cau·dal an·al·ge·sia.**

cau·date, kạ′dāt, *a.* [N.L. *caudatus,* < L. *cauda,* tail.] Having a tail or tail-like appendage. Also **cau·dat·ed.**—**cau·da·tion,** *n.* Caudate condition.

cau·dex, kạ′deks, *n.* L. pl. **cau·di·ces,** kạ′di·sēz, E. pl. **cau·dex·es,** kạ′deks·ez. [L.] *Bot.* the perennial base of a plant, including roots and stem, which sends up new growth every year, as a palm or tree fern.

cau·dil·lo, kạ·dēl′yō, kạ·dē′ō, *Sp.* kou-THē′lya, kou·THē′ya, *n.* A Spanish or Latin-American leader or head of state with personal military backing.

cau·dle, kạd′al, *n.* [O.Fr. *caudel, chaudel,* a dim. form < L.L. *calidum, caldum,* a kind of hot drink, < L. *calidus,* warm.] A kind of warm drink made of spiced and sugared wine or ale to which eggs, gruel, or bread are sometimes added, given to sick persons

---

a- fat, fāte, fär, fâre, fạll;   e- met, mē, mėre, hėr;   i- pin, pīne;   o- not, nōte, mōve;   u- tub, cūbe, bu̟ll;   oi- oil;   ou- pound.

or women in childbed.—**cau·dle cup,** n. A vessel or cup with two handles and a top.

caul, kạl, n. [< O.Fr. *cale*, a kind of little cap; < the Celtic; comp. Ir. *calla*, Gael. *call*, a veil, a hood.] A kind of net head covering formerly worn by females; the net facing in the hinder part of a woman's cap or hat; a membrane investing some part of the intestines; the omentum; a portion of the amnion or membrane enveloping the fetus, sometimes encompassing the head of a child when born.

caul·dron, cal·dron, kạl'dron, n. A large metal kettle or boiler.

cau·li·flow·er, kạ'li·flou"er, kạ'lē·flou"er, kol'a·flou"er, kol'ē·flou"er, n. [Earlier *coleflory*: modified form (after E. *cole* or L. *caulis* and E. *flower*) < Fr. *chou fleuri* (now *chou-fleur*), "flowered cabbage."] A plant related to the cabbage family, used as a vegetable, characterized by a compact, fleshy head of white flowers.

cau·li·flow·er ear, n. An external ear which has become misshapen through injury from battering blows, and on which excessive scar tissue has formed.

caulk, calk, kạk, v.t. [O.Fr. *caliquer*, < L. *calcare*, tread, press, < *calx*, heel.] To fill the seams of, as a ship or boat, with oakum or other substance to prevent leaking; fill or close the seams or crevices of, as a tank, window, boiler, etc., in order to make water-tight, air-tight, steam-tight, or the like; to fill or close, as a seam or joint. —**caulk·er,** kạ'kẽr, n. One who caulks ships, etc. Also **calk·er.**

caus·al, kạ'zal, a. [L. *causalis*.] Relating to a cause or causes; implying, containing, involving, or expressing a cause or causes; causative.—n. A verb signifying to make to do something, as *fell*, to make to fall.— **caus·al·ly,** kạ'zal·lē, adv. In a causal manner; by tracing effects to causes; by acting as a cause.

cau·sal·i·ty, kạ·zal'i·tē, n. pl. **cau·sal·i·ties.** The state of being causal; the fact of acting as a cause; the action or power of a cause, in producing its effect; the doctrine or principle that every effect implies the operation or presence of a cause.

cau·sa·tion, kạ·zā'shan, n. The act or agency of causing or producing an effect; the doctrine as to the connection of causes and effects.

caus·a·tive, kạ'za·tiv, a. Effective as a cause or agent: often followed by *of; gram.* expressing a cause or reason; causal.—n. A word expressing a cause.—**caus·a·tive·ly,** kạ'za·tiv·lē, adv. In a causative manner.— **caus·a·tive·ness, caus·a·tiv·i·ty,** n.

cause, kạz, n. [Fr. *cause*, L. *causa*, a cause.] That which produces an effect; that which brings about a change; that from which anything proceeds, and without which it would not exist; the reason or motive that urges, moves, or impels the mind to act or decide; an ideal or goal which an individual or a party upholds and works for; any subject of question or debate; case; interest; matter; affair; that object or side of a question to which the efforts of a person or party are directed; *law*, a suit or action in court; any legal process which a party institutes to obtain his demand, or by which he seeks his right.—**cause·less,** kạz'les, a. Having no cause or producing agent; self-originated; uncreated; without just ground, reason, or motive.

cause, kạz, v.t.—*caused, causing.* To be the cause of; to effect by agency; to bring about; to be the occasion of; to produce.— **caus·er,** n. One who or that which causes.

cause cé·lè·bre, kạz'se·leb're, kạz'se·leb're, Fr. kōz sā·leb're, n. A legal case or other controversy that attracts public attention and excites feelings; a famous controversy.

cau·se·rie, kō"za·rē', Fr. kōz·a·rē', n. [Fr., < *causer*, talk, < L. *causari*, plead, < *causa*, E. *cause*.] A talk or chat; an informal discourse or written article.

cause·way, kạz'wā', n. [Original spelling *causey*, < O.Fr. *caucis* (Mod.Fr. *chaussée*), < L.L. *calciata* (*via*, understood), a road in making which lime or mortar is used, < L. *calx, calcis*, lime (whence *chalk, calcareous*).] A road or path raised above the natural level of the ground by stones, earth, timber, serving as a passage over wet or marshy ground; a raised and paved roadway.—v.t. To provide a causeway for; to pave, as a road.

cau·sey, kạ'zē, n. pl. **cau·seys.** Brit. a causeway.

caus·tic, kạ'stik, a. [L. *causticus*, < Gr. *kaustikos*, < *kaiein*, burn.] Capable of burning, corroding, or destroying animal tissue; as, *caustic* soda, sodium hydroxide; *caustic* potash, potassium hydroxide; *fig.* severely critical or sarcastic.—n. A caustic substance; as, sodium hydroxide, *caustic* soda.—**caus·ti·cal·ly,** adv.—**caus·tic·i·ty,** n. Caustic quality; corrosiveness; pungent taste; severe sarcasm.

caus·tic, kạ'stik, n. *Optics,* a curve to which all light rays originating from a single point and reflected by a concave surface, are tangent.—**caus·tic sur·face, caus·tic curve,** a curve formed by a plane section of such a surface.—a. Referring to a caustic.

caus·tic so·da, n. *Chem.* sodium hydroxide.

cau·ter·i·za·tion, kạ"ta·rī"zā·shan, n. *Surg.* the act or the effect of cauterizing.

cau·ter·ize, kạ'ta·rīz", v.t.—*cauterized, cauterizing.* [L.L. *cauterizo*, < Gr. *kautēriazō*, < *kautērion, kautēr*, a burning or branding iron, < *kaiō*, to burn.] To burn or sear with fire, a hot iron, or with caustics for beneficial purposes; to treat with cautery.

cau·ter·y, kạ'ta·rē, n. pl. **cau·ter·ies.** [L. *cauterium*, Gr. *kautērion*.] A burning or searing, as of diseased tissue, by a hot iron or by caustic substances; the instrument or chemical agent employed in cauterizing.

cau·tion, kạ'shan, n. [L. *cautio*, < *caveo, cautum*, to be on one's guard, beware.] Prudence in regard to danger; wariness; watchfulness, forethought, or vigilance; a measure taken for security; a warning or admonition. *Slang*, a person or thing that astonishes.

cau·tion, kạ'shan, v.t. To give notice of danger to; to warn; to exhort to take heed. —*v.i.* to advise or warn.

cau·tion·ar·y, kạ'sha·ner"ē, a. Containing caution, or warning to avoid danger.

cau·tious, kạ'shus, a. Possessing or exhibiting caution; prudent; circumspect; wary; watchful; vigilant; careful.—**cau·tious·ly,** adv.—**cau·tious·ness,** n.

cav·al·cade, kav"al·kād', kav'al·kād", n. [Fr., < It. *cavalcata*, < L. *caballus*, horse.] A procession of persons on horseback or in horse-drawn carriages; a file of vehicles or ships; a parade.—**cav·al·cade,** v.i.— *cavalcaded, cavalcading.* To ride in a cavalcade.

cav·a·lier, kav"a·lēr', kav'a·lēr", n. [Fr. < It. *cavaliere*, < M.L. *caballarius*, < L. *caballus*, horse.] A knight; one having the spirit or bearing of a knight; a courtly gentleman; a gallant; a man attending or escorting a woman, or acting as her partner in dancing; (*cap.*) an adherent of Charles I of England in his contest with Parliament.

cav·a·lier, kav"a·lēr', kav'a·lēr", a. Offhand or unceremonious; haughty, disdainful, or supercilious; *obs.* knightly or gallant; (*cap.*) of or pertaining to the supporters of Charles I; of or pertaining to the 17th Century Cavalier poets in England. —**cav·a·lier,** v.i. To play the cavalier;

be haughty or domineering.—**cav·a·lier·ly,** adv.—**cav·a·lier·ness,** n.

ca·val·la, ka·val'a, n. pl. **ca·val·la, ca·val·las.** See *cavally*.

ca·val·ly, ka·val'ē, n. pl. **ca·val·lies.** [Sp. *caballa*, L. *caballus*, horse.] Any of various fishes of the genus *Carangus*, esp. *C. hippos*, a food fish of both coasts of tropical America, on the Atlantic coast found north to Cape Cod; the cero fish, a mackerellike fish.

cav·al·ry, kav'al·rē, n. pl. **cav·al·ries.** [Fr. *cavalerie*, It. *cavalleria*, < *cavaliere*: see *cavalier*.] Mounted soldiers collectively; that part of a military force whose troops formerly served on horseback; horsemen, horses, collectively; *obs.* horsemanship, esp. of a knight.—**cav·al·ry·man,** n. pl. **cav·al·ry·men.**

ca·vate, kā'vāt, a. [L. *cavatus*, pp. of *cavare*, hollow out, < *cavus*, hollow.] Hollowed out; having the appearance of a cave, as a class of prehistoric dwellings.

cav·a·ti·na, kav"a·tē'na, It. kä"vä·tē'nä, n. pl. **cav·a·ti·ne.** [It.] *Mus.* a simple song or melody, properly one without a second part and a repeat; a short, simple air played on an instrument.

cave, kāv, n. [O.Fr. Fr. *cave*, < L. *cavus*, hollow.] A hollow in the earth, esp. one opening more or less horizontally into a hill or mountain; a cavern; a cellar, formed naturally, or dug in the earth and utilized for safety or storing; *Brit.* a secession, or a group of seceders, from a political party on some special question.

cave, kāv, v.t.—*caved, caving.* To hollow out; to cause to fall in.

cave, kāv, v.i. To fall or sink in, as ground; *colloq.* to give in, yield, submit, or collapse.

ca·ve·at, kā'vē·at", n. [L., "let him beware."] A legal notice to a judicial officer to suspend a certain proceeding until the notifier is given a hearing; an explanation to save misunderstanding; *U.S.* patent laws, a description of an invention filed to prevent the issuance of a patent for the same invention to another without notice; in general, a warning or caution.—**ca·ve·a·tor,** n. One who enters a caveat.

ca·ve·at emp·tor, kā'vē·at" emp'tạr, *Lat.* kä'we·ät" emp'tōr, n. [L., let the buyer beware.] A commercial principle indicating that, if there is no warranty, a buyer makes a purchase at his own risk.

cave dwell·er, n. A person, such as one of a prehistoric race, living in caves; *colloq.* a person residing, often in an apartment, in a city.

cave-in, kāv'in", n. The action of collapsing or falling in; the location where the ground has fallen in.

cave man, n. One who dwells in caves; a name given to the earliest races of prehistoric man which dwelt in natural caves; *slang*, a man whose manner with women is rough and unrefined.

cav·ern, kav'ẽrn, n. [L. *caverna*, < *cavus*, hollow. CAVE.] A deep hollow place in the earth; a cave.

cav·ern, kav'ern, v.t. To put or enclose in or as in a cavern; to hollow out in the form of a cavern.

cav·ern·ous, kav'ẽr·nus, a. [L. *cavernosus*.] Containing caverns; of or like a cavern; full of or containing small cavities or interstices; porous.—**cav·er·nous·ly,** adv.

ca·vet·to, ka·vet'ō, It. kä·vet'tạ, n. pl. **ca·vet·tos, ca·vet·ti.** [It. dim. < *cavo*, < L. *cavus*, hollow.] *Arch.* a concave molding, as in a cornice, with the curve usually a quarter circle.

cav·i·ar, cav·i·are, kav'ē·är", kav"ē·är', n. [Fr. *caviar*, Turk. *haviâr*.] The roe of certain large fish, as the sturgeon, prepared and salted.—**cav·i·ar to the gen·er·al,** a delicacy beyond the reach of most; a reasoning beyond the popular grasp.

---

ch- chain, G. na*ch*t;   **th-** THen, thin;   **w-** wig, hw as sound in whig;   **z-** zh as in azure, zeal.   *Italicized vowel* indicates schwa sound.

cav·il, kav′il, *v.i.*—*caviled, caviling,* and *Brit. cavilled, cavilling.* [O.Fr. *caviller,* L. *cavillor,* to cavil, *cavilla,* a quibble, trick, shuffle.] To raise captious and frivolous objections; to find fault without good reason: frequently followed by *at.*—*v.t.* To oppose by finding trivial faults.—*n.* A captious or frivolous objection; captious or specious argument.—**cav·il·er,** *Brit.* **cav·il·ler,** kav′il·ẽr, *n.*

cav·i·ty, kav′i·tē, *n.* pl. **cav·i·ties.** [Fr. *cavité,* L. *cavitas,* < L. *cavus,* hollow. CAVE.] A hollow place; a hollow; a void or empty space in a body; an opening; a hollow part of the human body, the hollowness being pathological, as a dental *cavity,* or natural.

ca·vort, ka·vạrt′, *v.i.* [Cf. *curvet.*] *Colloq.* to prance or caper about.—**ca·vort·er,** *n.*

ca·vy, kā′vē, *n.* pl. **ca·vies.** [S. Amer.] Any of various short-tailed South American rodents constituting the genus *Cavia* or the family *Caviidae,* esp. the domesticated guinea pig; any of several allied rodents.

caw, kạ, *v.i.* [Imitative of the sound; akin Sc. *kae,* D. *kaauw,* Dan. *kaa,* a jackdaw.] To cry like a crow, rook, or raven, or to utter a similar harsh, strident cry.—*n.* The cry of the rook or crow.

cay, kā, *n.* [Sp. *cayo,* a rock, a shoal, an islet.] An islet; a range or reef of sand or coral lying near the surface of the water; term used especially in the West Indies and sometimes written *Key* or *key.*

cay·enne, kī·en′, kā·en′, *n.* [< *Cayenne,* in French Guiana.] A hot, biting condiment composed of the ground pods and seeds of hot peppers; red pepper.

cay·man, kā′man, *n.* pl. **cay·mans.** [Prob. from Carib.] Any of several tropical American crocodilians constituting the genus *Caiman,* which are fundamentally similar to the alligator.

Ca·yu·ga, kā·ū′ga, kī·ū′ga, *n.* pl. **Ca·yu·ga, Ca·yu·gas.** The Iroquois Indians, a N. Amer. tribe formerly residing around Lake Cayuga in New York State; one of this tribe; the language spoken by the Iroquois people.

cay·use, kī·ūs′, kī′ōs, *n.* [< the *Cayuse* Indians of Oregon.] A small range horse; an Indian pony.

C bat·ter·y, *n. Elect.* a battery for maintaining constant voltage within a device, usually in a vacuum tube.

C clef, *n. Mus.* a movable notation which places middle C on the first, third, or fourth lines of the staff. See *bass clef, treble clef.*

CCTV, abbr. for closed-circuit television.

cease, sēs, *v.i.*—*ceased, ceasing.* [Fr. *cesser,* L. *cesso, cessare,* to cease, a freq. < *cedere,* to yield, to cede. CEDE.] To stop moving, acting, or speaking; to leave off; to give over; to desist: followed by *from* before a noun; to come to an end; to terminate. —*v.t.* To put a stop to; put an end to; desist from.

cease, sēs, *n.* End; cessation.

cease-fire, sēs′fī·er, *n.* A truce; an armistice; *milit.* an order to stop firing.

cease·less, sēs′lis, *a.* Without a stop or pause; incessant; continual; without intermission; enduring forever; endless.—**cease·less·ly,** *adv.*—**cease·less·ness,** *n.*

ce·cro·pi·a, si·krō′pē·a, *n.* [N.L. < *Cecrops,* legendary king of Attica.] A large silkworm moth, *Samia cecropia,* of the eastern U.S., whose larva feeds on the leaves of many trees.

ce·cum, cae·cum, sē′kum, *n.* pl. **ce·ca, cae·ca,** sē′ka. [L. *caecus,* blind.] *Anat., zool.* a sac or cavity with an opening only at one end, esp. the *intestinum cecum,* or "blind gut" in humans, at the beginning of the large intestine.—**ce·cal, cae·cal,** sē′kal, *a.* Of, belonging to, or having the form of a cecum.

ce·dar, sē′dẽr, *n.* [O.Fr. *cedre* (Fr. *cèdre*), <

L. *cedrus,* < Gr. *kedros.*] Any of the old-world pinaceous trees constituting the genus *Cedrus,* as *C. libani,* "cedar of Lebanon," a stately tree native in Asia Minor; any of various junipers, as *Juniperus virginiana,* "red cedar," an American tree with a fragrant reddish wood used for making pencils; any of various other pinaceous trees, as *Chamæcyparis thyoides,* a species of the swamps of the eastern U.S., and *Thuja occidentalis,* the arbor vitae, both called "white cedar"; any of various non-pinaceous tropical trees, as *Cedrela odorata,* "Spanish cedar," a timber tree whose wood is used for cigar boxes; the wood of any such tree, noted for its durability and fragrance.

ce·darn, sē′darn, *a. Liter.* of or pertaining to cedars; made of cedar wood.

ce·dar wax·wing, *n. Bombycilla cedorum,* a North American bird with chiefly light brown plumage which often feeds on juniper (cedar) berries. Also **ce·dar bird.**

cede, sēd, *v.t.*—*ceded, ceding.* [L. *cedere* (pp. *cessus*), go, withdraw, yield, grant.] To yield or formally resign and surrender to another, usually by treaty.

ce·dil·la, si·dil′a, *n.* [Sp. *cedilla,* now *zedilla,* the mark (orig. a *z* written after *c*), < L. *zeta,* < Gr. *zeta,* the letter *z.*] A mark placed under *c* before *a, o,* or *u,* as in *façade,* to show that it has the sound of *s*; also used in Turkish and Rumanian to render variations of the *s* sound.

ced·u·la, sej′u·la, *n.* [Sp. *cédula,* = E. *schedule.*] In Spanish-speaking countries, any of various orders, certificates, or the like; a type of security issued by some South and Central American governments and banks; *Philippine Islands,* a personal registration tax certificate, or the tax itself.

cei·ba, sā′ba, sī′ba, Sp. thā′vä, sā′vä, *n.* [< Sp. < Arawak.] A silk-cotton tree, *Ceiba pentandra,* from which comes kapok fiber; kapok.

ceil, sēl, *v.t.* [O.E. *seile,* a canopy, < Fr. *ciel,* It. *cielo,* a canopy, heaven, < L. *cælum,* heaven, same root as Gr. *koilos,* hollow, and E. *hollow.*] To overlay or cover (the inner roof of a room or building); to provide with a ceiling.

ceil·ing, sē′ling, *n.* The overhead inner lining of a room; the height above ground at which objects of prominence on the ground can be spotted; the maximum altitude an airplane can reach under certain conditions; the topmost limit legally set on wages or prices.—**hit the ceil·ing,** *slang.* To lose one's temper; to become furious, as: When he saw the dent in the fender, he *hit the ceiling.*

ceil·ing un·lim·it·ed, *n.* A cloudless or almost cloudless sky; perfect flying weather.

ceil·ing ze·ro, *n.* The atmospheric condition when a cloud ceiling is at a height of 50 feet or lower.

ceil·om·e·ter, sē·lom′i·tẽr, si·lom′i·tẽr, *n. Meteor.* a device for measuring and recording the height of a cloud ceiling, using a beam of light reflected from the cloud base and computation of the height by triangulation.

cel·a·don, sel′a·don″, sel′a·don, *n.* A pale-green color, used in Chinese porcelains; porcelains of this color.

cel·an·dine, sel′an·dīn″, *n.* [O.Fr. *celidoine,* Fr. *chelidoine,* < L. *chelidonium,* Gr. *chelidonian,* swallow-wort, *chelidon,* a swallow.] A herbaceous perennial which emits a bright orange-colored juice when its stems or leaves are crushed. This juice, an acrid and powerful irritant, finds many applications in medicine as a diuretic, purgative and fungicide. Any plant of the genus *Chelidonium,* belonging to the poppy family.

Cel·a·nese, sel′a·nēz″, sel″a·nēz′, *n.* A trademarked name for a type of rayon material made of a series of polyvinyl acetate emulsions.

cel·e·brant, sel′e·brant, *n.* One who celebrates, esp. the officiating priest in the celebration of the Eucharist.

cel·e·brate, sel′e·brāt″, *v.t.*—*celebrated, celebrating.* [L. *celebratus,* pp. of *celebrare,* < *celeber,* frequented, famous.] To perform with appropriate rites and ceremonies; solemnize; to commemorate an event with ceremonies or festivities; to sound the praises of; extol; to make known publicly; proclaim. To perform (a religious ceremony); to observe (a festival) or commemorate (an event) with ceremonies or festivities.—**cel·e·bra·tion,** *n.* [L. *celebratio(n-).*] The act of celebrating; that which is done to celebrate anything.—**cel·e·bra·tor,** *n.*

cel·e·brat·ed, sel′e·brā″tid, *a.* Famous; renowned; well-known.

ce·leb·ri·ty, se·leb′ri·tē, *n.* pl. **ce·leb·ri·ties,** se·leb′ri·tēz. [L. *celebritas,* < *celeber:* see *celebrate.*] A celebrated or famous person; the state of being celebrated, extolled or talked about; fame; renown.

ce·ler·i·ac, se·ler′ē·ak″, se·lēr′ē·ak″, *n.* [See *celery.*] A variety of celery, *Apium gravelens rapaceum,* producing an edible turnip-like root.

ce·ler·i·ty, se·ler′i·tē, *n.* [L. *celeritas,* < *celer,* swift.] Swiftness; speed.

cel·er·y, sel′e·rē, *n.* [Fr. *céleri,* It. *seleri,* < Gr. *selinon,* parsley.] A plant, *Apium groveolens,* indigenous to marshy places and long cultivated as a vegetable whose stalks are eaten raw or cooked, and sometimes used as a seasoning.

ce·les·ta, se·les′ta, *n.* [Fr. *célesta,* < L. *cælestis,* heavenly: CELESTIAL.] A musical instrument with a keyboard, the tones of which are produced by blows of hammers upon steel plates.

ce·les·tial, se·les′chel, *a.* [O.Fr. *celestial,* < L. *cælestis,* < *cælum,* sky, heaven.] Of or pertaining to the sky or visible heaven; of or pertaining to the spiritual or invisible heaven; heavenly; divine; (*cap.*) of or pertaining to the former Chinese or *Celestial* Empire or to the Chinese people. —**ce·les·ti·al·i·ty,** *n.*—**ce·les·tial·ly,** *adv.*

ce·les·tial, se·les′chel, *n.* An inhabitant of heaven; (*cap.*) *obs.* a Chinese.

ce·les·tial bod·y, *n.* Any body of matter in the universe, as a planet, star, or comet, which is classifiable as a unit for study in the science of astronomy.

ce·les·tial e·qua·tor, *n.* The great circle of the celestial sphere, assumed to be the extension of the plane of the earth's equator.

ce·les·tial globe, *n.* A globe portraying the celestial bodies.

ce·les·tial mar·riage, *n.* A marriage that is solemnized for eternity in a Mormon temple.

ce·les·tial me·chan·ics, *n.* The study of the influence of gravitational fields on the motions of celestial bodies. Also **dy·nam·i·cal as·tron·o·my.**

ce·les·tial nav·i·ga·tion, *n.* A means of navigation by which a geographical location is determined by reference to the position of celestial bodies. Also **as·tro·nav·i·ga·tion, ce·lo·nav·i·ga·tion.**

ce·les·tial pole, *n.* Each of two points on the celestial sphere where it is intersected by the earth's axis and around which the stars appear to revolve.

ce·les·tial sphere, *n.* The concept of the visible sky as one half of an imaginary sphere in which the celestial bodies supposedly lie.

ce·li·ac, cœ·li·ac, sē′lē·ak″, *a.* [L. *cœliacus,* < Gr. *koiliakos,* < *koilia,* belly, < *koilos,* hollow.] *Anat.* pertaining to the cavity of the abdomen.

---

a- fat, fāte, fär, fåre, fạll;   **e-** met, mē, mẽre, hẽr;   **i-** pin, pīne;   **o-** not, nōte, mōve;   **u-** tub, cūbe, bụll;   **oi-** oil;   **ou-** pound.

ce·li·ac dis·ease, *n. Pathol.* a disease common to the tropics, characterized by anemia, sore tongue, and gastrointestinal disturbance; a dietary deficiency disease occurring in children.

cel·i·ba·cy, sel'*a*·ba·sē, *Brit.* sa·lib'*a*·sē, *n.* [L. *cælibatus*, a single life, celibacy, < *cælebs*, unmarried.] The state of being celibate or unmarried; abstention from coitus; avowed abstention from marriage.

cel·i·bate, sel'*a*·bit, sel'*a*·bāt", *n.* One who adheres to or practices celibacy.—*a.* Pertaining to celibacy.

cell, sel, *n.* [L. *cella*, a cell, a small room, a hut, same root as *celare*, whence *concelare*, to conceal. Hole and hollow are from the same root.] A small room in a prison where persons charged or convicted of crimes are confined; a single, small room used by one person in a convent or monastery; a small place of residence such as a cave or hermitage; a small group of people making up a single basic unit within a larger organization; as, a Communist *cell*; *eccles.* a small religious house which depends on a larger religious house, as a convent or monastery. *Biol.* the basic unit of structure and function of all living things made up of a small mass of protoplasm, which contains a nucleus and cytoplasmic material, surrounded by semipermeable membrane in animals and a cell wall in plants; a tiny cavity or interstice as in plant or animal tissue. *Entom.* one of the membranous areas into which the wing of an insect is divided by veins; *bot.* the cavity of an ovary that bears seeds. *Elect.* a device which generates electricity, made up of electrodes placed in contact with an electrolyte, forming the whole or part of a voltaic battery; a single unit in a device used with radiation, for varying the intensity of an electrical current or for converting radiant energy into electrical energy. *Phys., chem.* a device consisting of the electrolyte, its container and the electrodes, which is used for producing electrolysis; *aeron.* the container or bag of gas in a balloon or airship. A part of the atmosphere that behaves as a unit despite varying conditions.

cel·la, sel'*a*, *n.* pl. cellae. [L.] *Arch.* the enclosed chamber of an ancient Greek or Roman temple, as distinct from the porticoes and other rooms, which held the image of the Deity.

cel·lar, sel'er, *n.* [L. *cellarium.* CELL.] A room in a house or other building, either wholly or partly underground, used for storage purposes; basement; the lowest standing or classification, esp. applied to athletic competition.

cel·lar·age, sel'er·ij, *n.* The space occupied by cellars; cellars collectively; charge for storage in a cellar.

cel·lar·er, sel'er·ēr, *n.* An officer in a monastery who is in charge of the cellar; a butler; one who keeps wine or spirit cellars; a spirit dealer.

cel·lar·ette, cel·lar·et, sel"*a*·ret', *n.* [Dim. of *cellar.*] A cabinet for holding bottles of liquors or wines.

cell·block, sel'blok", *n.* A prison subdivision made up of a number of cells.

cell di·vi·sion, *n. Biol.* the division of both the cytoplasm and nucleus of a cell into two, in the process of reproduction.

cel·list, 'cel·list, chel'ist, *n.* One who plays the cello; short form of *violoncellist.*

cell mem·brane, *n. Biol.* the thin semipermeable membrane enclosing the protoplasmic material of a cell.

cel·lo, 'cel·lo, chel'ō, *n.* pl. **cel·los, 'cel·los.** Shortened form of *violoncello,* a four-stringed instrument, having a range from two octaves below middle C to more than one octave above middle C,

played using a bow and held upright between the player's knees.

cel·lo·phane, sel'*o*·fān", *n.* [< *cell(ulose)* and Gr. *phainein,* show.] Regenerated cellulose, a strong, transparent, flexible film, which may be modified by additives for different degrees of moisture resistance and heatsealing ability, produced from wood pulp by the viscose process, and used for protective wrapping.

cel·lu·lar, sel'ya·lēr, *a.* Pertaining to or characterized by having cells; containing compartments or cavities; having a porous body.

cel·lu·lase, sel'ya·lās", *n. Chem.* an enzyme that hydrolyzes and depolymerizes cellulosic polysaccharides, including cellulose; obtained from the fungus, *Aspergillus niger,* and used in medicine, septic systems, brewing, and in the extraction of oils.

cel·lu·late, sel'ya·lāt", *a.* Having cellular structure; also **cel·lu·lat·ed.**—*v.t.*—*cellulated, cellulating.* To form into cells.— **cel·lu·la·tion,** *n.* Cell formation.

cel·lule, sel'ūl, *n.* [L. *cellula,* dim. of *cella.*] A little cell.

cel·lu·li·tis, sel"ya·lī'tis, *n.* [N.L.] *Pathol.* inflammation of cellular tissue.

Cel·lu·loid, sel'ya·loid", *n.* [< cellulose.] A highly inflammable, solid substance consisting essentially of soluble guncotton and camphor, formerly in wide use in toilet articles, as combs and brushes, and to make photographic film. (Trademark.) —*a.* (*l.c.*) Referring to the early years of the movie industry; as, the *celluloid* era.

cel·lu·lose, sel'ya·lōs", *n.* [Fr. < L. *cellula:* CELLULE.] A carbohydrate, a stable polymer of glucose, the chief constituent of the cell walls of plants, forming an essential part of wood, cotton, hemp, paper, and all vegetable tissues.

cel·lu·lose ac·e·tate, *n. Chem.* any one of several types of thermoplastic cellulose resins, non-flammable substitute for nitrocellulose, formed by the action of acetic or other acids on cellulose, and used for the manufacture of acetate fiber, lacquers, photographic film and transparent sheeting.

cel·lu·lose ni·trate, *n. Chem.* see *nitrocellulose.*

cel·lu·lo·sic, sel"ya·lō'sik, *n.* A cellulose compound such as cellophane.—*a.* Relating to or made of cellulose.

cell wall, *n. Biol.* the definite boundary or rigid permeable wall, formed by the protoplasm, which surrounds a biological cell, esp. a plant cell.

ce·lom, sē'lom, *n.* See *coelom.*

ce·lo·nav·i·ga·tion, sē"lō·nav"*i*·gā'shan, sel'ō·nav"*i*·gā"shan, *n.* Celestial navigation.

Cel·si·us ther·mom·e·ter, sel'sē·*us* thēr·mom'i·tēr, sel'shē-*us* thēr·mom'i·tēr, *n.* [From Anders *Celsius* (1701–44) Swedish astronomer, who introduced it.] The centigrade thermometer.

celt, selt, *n.* [L.L. *celtis,* chisel.] *Archaeol.* a prehistoric metal or stone implement resembling a chisel or ax blade.

Celt, selt, kelt, *n.* [L. *Celtæ,* Gr. *Keltoi, Keltai,* connected with W. *celt,* a covert or shade; Gael. *ceiltach,* an inhabitant of the forest.] One of a distinct group of early Indo-European peoples who inhabited many parts of ancient Europe. The Celts now remaining as a distinctive group and speaking a distinctive language are the Bretons, Welsh, Scottish Highlanders, Cornish, and a portion of the Irish. The word with its derivatives is frequently written with an initial K, as *Kelt, Keltic.*

Celt·ic, sel'tik, kel'tik, *n.* The language or group of dialects spoken by the Celts.—

Celt·i·cism, sel'ti·sizm, kel'ti·sizm, *n.* The manners and customs of the Celts; a Celtic expression or mode of expression.—

Celt·i·cist, sel'ti·sist, kel'ti·sist, *n.* A specialist in Celtic culture and languages.

Celt·ic, sel'tik, kel'tik, *a.* Pertaining to the Celts, or to their language.

Celt·ic cross, *n.* A Latin cross with an added circle around the intersection of the shaft and crossbar.

cem·ba·lo, chem'ba·lō", *n.* pl. **cem·ba·li, cem·ba·los,** chem'ba·lē", chem'ba·lōz. Harpsichord; figured bass from which the part of a harpsichord accompanist is devised.

ce·ment, si·ment', *n.* [O.Fr. *cement,* L. *cæmentum,* chips of stone made into cement, contr. < *cædimentum,* < *cædo,* to cut.] A fine gray powder, consisting chiefly of alumina, lime, iron oxide, and silica burned together, then pulverized, which forms a hard mass when mixed with water, used as an ingredient of mortar and concrete; any sticky substance which is capable of uniting bodies in close cohesion after drying; *fig.* bond of union; that which unites persons firmly together; *dentistry,* an adhesive substance used in dental work.— **ce·men·ti·tious,** sē"men·tish'us, *a.* Having the characteristics of a cement.

ce·ment, si·ment', *v.t.* To unite by cement or other matter that produces cohesion of bodies; to overspread with cement; *fig.* to unite firmly or closely.—*v.i.* To become cemented; to unite or become solid; to unite and cohere.

ce·men·ta·tion, sē"men·tā'shan, sē"men-·tā'shan, sem"en·tā'shan, *n.* The heating of a solid, immersed in a powdered substance, to change it to a new material, as in the conversion of iron into steel by heating the iron in a mass of ground charcoal.—**ce·ment·er,** *n.* The person or thing that cements.

ce·ment·ite, si·men'tit, *n. Chem.* a hard, brittle carbide of iron, Fe_3C, occurring in ordinary steel containing more than 0.85% carbon.

ce·men·tum, si·men'tum, *n.* The layer of bony tissue forming the outer surface over the root of the tooth within the gum.

cem·e·ter·y, sem'i·ter"ē, *n.* pl. **cem·e·ter·ies.** [L. *coemeterium,* a burying place, < Gr. *koimētērion,* a sleeping place, afterward a burying place, < *koimaō,* to sleep.] A place set apart for interment; a graveyard; a burial ground.

cen·a·cle, sen'*a*·kel, *n.* [L. *cenaculum,* < *cena,* dinner, supper.] A dining room; esp. the 'upper room' in which the Last Supper was eaten. Mark xiv. 15; Luke xxii. 12.

ce·no·bite, sē'no·bīt", sen'o·bīt", *n.* [L. *cænobita,* < Gr. *koinobios,* living in common, < *koinos,* common, and *bios,* life.] One of a religious order living in a convent or in community, in opposition to an anchorite or hermit, who lives in solitude.—**ce·no·bit·ic, ce·no·bit·i·cal,** *a.* Living in community, as men belonging to a convent.—**ce·no·bit·ism,** *n.* The state of being a cenobite; the principles or practice of a cenobite.

ce·nog·a·my, coe·nog·a·my, sē·nog'*a*·-mē, *n.* [Gr. *koinos,* common, and *gamos,* marriage.] The practice of having husbands or wives in common, as among some primitive tribes.

cen·o·gen·e·sis, sē"no·jen'i·sis, sen"o·-jen'i·sis. *n.* [Gr. *kainos,* new, and *genesis,* genesis.] *Biol.* the introduction of new characters in the development of an individual, absent from early phylogeny of the species: opposed to *palingenesis.*—**ce·no·ge·net·ic,** sē"no·je·net'ik, *a.*

cen·o·taph, sen'o·taf", sen'o·täf", *n.* [Gr. *kenotaphion—kenos,* empty, and *taphos,* a tomb.] A sepulchral monument erected to one who is buried elsewhere.

Ce·no·zo·ic, sē"no·zō'ik, sen"o·zō'ik, *a.* [Gr.] *Geol.* pertaining to the geologic era from the Tertiary period to the present, characterized by evolutionary changes of birds and mammals, and higher flowering plants, but no marked changes in invertebrates; pertaining to rocks whose fossils represent Cenozoic forms of life. See *Paleozoic, Mesozoic.*—*n.* The Cenozoic era or group.

cense, sens, *v.t.*—*censed, censing.* [Fr. *encenser.* INCENSE.] To perfume with incense.—*v.i.* To scatter incense.

cen·ser, sen'sẽr, *n.* [A shortened form for *incenser*; Fr. *encensoir.*] A vase or pan in which incense is burned; esp. a covered vessel for burning and wafting incense in a religious ceremony.

cen·sor, sen'sẽr, *n.* [L., < *censere*, tax, rate, judge, think.] Either of two ancient Roman officials who kept the register or census of the citizens, and also supervised manners and morals; hence, anyone who exercises supervision of manners and morals; esp. an official charged with examining books, plays, and news accounts, and empowered to prohibit them or suppress parts if deemed objectionable on moral, political, military, or other grounds; one who censures; an adverse critic; one given to faultfinding; *psychol.* the psychic force which excludes from the conscious mind unacceptable feelings, ideas and impulses. —**cen·so·ri·al**, *a.* Pertaining to a censor.

cen·sor, sen'sẽr, *v.t.* To examine, pass upon, or revise as a censor does; esp. to suppress, as parts of letters or press dispatches, before permitting them to be transmitted to their destination, as for military reasons in time of war.

cen·so·ri·ous, sen·sōr'ē·us, sen·sạr'ē·us, *a.* [L. *censorius.*] Addicted to censure; severely critical; faultfinding; carping.— **cen·so·ri·ous·ly**, *adv.*—**cen·so·ri·ous·ness**, *n.*

cen·sor·ship, sen'sẽr·ship″, *n.* The process of censoring; the authority of a censor; the term of office of a Roman censor. *Psychol.* the process of repressing from the consciousness those impulses which will be upsetting to it.

cen·sur·a·ble, sen'shur·a·bl, *a.* Worthy of censure.—**cen·sur·a·ble·ness**, *n.*—**cen·sur·a·bly**, *adv.*

cen·sure, sen'shur, *n.* [L. *censura*, < *censere*, tax, rate, judge, think.] A criticizing, esp. adversely; civil or military expression of disapproval; condemnation; a hostile criticism; *eccles.* a penalty imposed upon an offender, as a public rebuke or a suspension from office.

cen·sure, sen'shur, *v.t.*—*censured, censuring.* Criticize, esp. adversely; pass adverse judgment on; express disapprobation of; find fault with; condemn; *eccles.* to discipline by public rebuke.—*v.i.* To give censure, adverse criticism, or blame.— **cen·sur·er**, *n.*

cen·sus, sen'sus, *n.* pl. **cen·sus·es.** [L. < *censere*, tax, rate, judge, think.] In ancient Rome, the registration of citizens and their property, for purposes of taxation; in modern times, an official enumeration of inhabitants, with details of age, sex, or pursuits.—**cen·sus**, *v.t.*—*censused, censusing.* To take a census of; enumerate in a census.

cent, sent, *n.* [Contr. of L. *centum*, a hundred.] A hundred, commonly used with *per*; as, ten *per cent*, that is in the proportion of ten to the hundred; in various countries a coin equal to the hundredth part of the monetary unit; in the United States the hundredth part of the dollar.

cen·tal, sen'tal, *n.* A weight of 100 lbs.—*a.* Pertaining to or consisting of a hundred; reckoned or proceeding by the hundred.

cen·tare, sen'târ, *Fr.* sän·tär′, *n.* A square meter; *centiare.*

cen·taur, sen'tạr, *n.* [L. *centaurus*; Gr. *kentauros*, lit. bull-pricker; the Centaurs

probably represented some race that hunted wild cattle and lived almost constantly on horseback.] *Greek mythol.* a member of a race of fabulous beings supposed to be half man and half horse.

Cen·tau·rus, sen·tạr'us, *n.* A constellation in the southern hemisphere.

cen·tau·ry, sen'tạ·rē, *n.* [L. *centaurea*, Gr. *kentaurion*, after the *Centaur* Cheiron, who was said to have cured a wound in his foot.] The popular name of various plants. Common centaury is an annual herb of the gentian family in high repute among the old herbalists for its medicinal properties.

cen·te·nar·i·an, sen″te·nâr'ē·an, *n.* A person 100 years old or over.—*a.* Pertaining to a centenary or centenarian.

cen·te·na·ry, sen'te·ner″ē, *Brit.* sen·ten'a·rē, sen·tē′na·rē, *n.* pl. **cen·te·nar·ies.** [L. *centenarius*, consisting of a hundred, relating to a hundred < *centum*, a hundred.] The period or age of 100 years; a century; the commemoration of an event which occurred 100 years before; centennial.—*a.* Relating to or consisting of 100 years; pertaining to the end of a 100-year span.

cen·ten·ni·al, sen·ten′·ēal, *a.* [L. *centum*, and *annus*, a year.] Concerning or marking the end of a 100-year period; pertaining to the observance of a hundredth anniversary; lasting or aged 100 years.—*n.* A hundredth anniversary or its commemoration.—**cen·ten·ni·al·ly**, *adv.*

cen·ter, *Brit.* **cen·tre**, sen'tẽr, *n.* [O.Fr. Fr. *centre*, < L. *centrum*, < Gr. *kentron*, sharp point, center, < *kentein*, prick.] *Geom.* a point at an average distance from all exterior angles, points, or lines of a geometric figure or body. A point, pivot, or axis around which something rotates or revolves, as the hub of a wheel; the core; as, the *center* of the earth; the middle section of anything; as, soft-*centered* chocolates; the nucleus of an object or idea; a place in which an interest, activity, or purpose is centered; as, a civic *center*, an art *center*, a shipping *center*, a shopping *center*; a source or place where forces, influences, or effects originate; as, a *center* of propaganda; an area of concentrated population; *sports*, a player in the middle position in the team's playing formation; *physiol.* a group of nerve cells controlling a common organic process; as, optical *center*. *Milit.* the middle element of an army formation between two wings; a group of activities under an individual and an overall commander; as, medical *center*, separation *center*. The moderate point of view in areas such as politics, economics, sociology, or religion; the advocates of such views; middle-of-the-roaders; (*sometimes cap.*) legislators and other political figures holding moderate views, and sometimes occupying seats in the center of the legislative chambers. *Mech.* one of two tapering metal rods of a lathe or grinding machine supporting the object worked on, and about which the object revolves.

cen·ter, *Brit.* **cen·tre**, sen'tẽr, *v.t.*—*centered, centred, centering, centring.* To place in or on a center; collect at a center, or concentrate; determine or mark the center of; adjust, shape, or modify, as an object or part, so that its axis or the like is in a central or normal position.—*v.i.* To be at or come to a center; concentrate.

cen·ter bit, *n.* A carpenter's bit with a sharp, projecting central point and two cutting wings, used for boring holes.

cen·ter·board, sen'tẽr·bōrd″, sen'tẽr·bạrd″, *n. Naut.* a wooden or metal slab pivoted or arranged so that it can be lowered through a fore-and-aft slot (having above it a vertical water-tight casing in the bottom of a sailboat, in order to increase

the draft and so prevent a drifting to leeward.

cen·ter field, *n. Baseball*, roughly the center one-third of the outfield, beyond second base and between left field and right field.— **cen·ter field·er**, *n.* The defensive player stationed between the two other outfielders.

cen·ter of gra·vi·ty, *n.* That point on a body, freely acted upon by the earth's gravity, about which the body is in equilibrium in all positions.

cen·ter of mass, *n. Phys.* the point on a body which behaves as if all the mass of the body were concentrated there. Also *center of gravity*, **cen·ter of in·er·tia.**

cen·ter·piece, sen'tẽr·pēs″, *n.* An ornament intended to be placed in the middle or center of something, as of a table.

cen·ter punch, *n.* A short steel bar with a conical point used for centering drill bits.— **cen·ter·punch**, *v.t.* To stamp with a center punch.

cen·tes·i·mal, sen·tes'i·mal, *a.* [L. *centesimus*, hundredth.] Hundredth; pertaining to division into 100 parts or to instruments, as certain thermometers or gauges, which are so marked.—**cen·tes·i·mal·ly**, *adv.*

cen·ti·are, **cen·tare**, sen'tē·âr′, *Fr.* sän·tyaR′, sen'târ, *Fr.* sän taR, *n.* [Fr. CENTI-.] *Metric system*, a surface measure equal to one-hundredth of an are, or one square meter.

cen·ti·grade, sen'ti·grād″, *a.* [Fr., < L. *centum*, hundred, and *gradus*, step, degree.] Divided into 100 degrees, as a scale; specif. noting or pertaining to a thermometer which is divided into 100 degrees from the freezing point of water, or 0°, to the boiling point of water, or 100°; abbreviated *C.* Also *Celsius.*

cen·ti·gram, *Brit.* **cen·ti·gramme**, sen'ti·gram″, *n.* [Fr. *centigramme* < L. *centum*, hundred.] *Metric system*, a unit of weight equal to one hundredth of a gram, or 0.1543 grain.

cen·tile, sen'tīl, sen'til, *n. Statistics*, a scale of comparison arrived at by placing all the cases in order from lowest to highest, then dividing them into 100 ranks with the lowest as the first centile, and so on.

cen·tile rank, *n. Statistics*, a derived score showing what percent of a total distribution is below a certain score.

cen·ti·li·ter, *Brit.* **cen·ti·li·tre**, sen'ti·lē″tẽr, *n.* [Fr. *centilitre* < L. *centum*, hundred.] *Metric system*, a unit of capacity equal to one hundredth of a liter, 0.6102 cubic inch, or 0.338 U.S. fluid ounce.

cen·til·lion, sen·til'yan, *n.* In the U.S. and France, a cardinal number represented by one followed by 303 zeros, and, in Great Britain and Germany by 600 zeros.

cen·ti·me·ter, sen'ti·mē″tẽr, *n.* [Fr. *centimètre*, < L. *centum*, a hundred, and Gr. *metron*, measure.] A measure of length, the hundredth part of a meter; slightly more than 0.39 of an inch.

cen·ti·me·ter-gram-sec·ond, sen'ti·mē″tẽr·gram'sek′ond, *a.* Of or pertaining to a system of units which has as its principal units of length, mass, and time, the centimeter, gram, and mean solar second respectively.

cen·ti·pede, sen'ti·pēd″, *n.* [L. *centipeda*, < *centum*, hundred, and *pes(ped-)*, foot.] An arthropod of the *Chilopoda* class whose elongated, flat, wormlike body is divided into many segments, each of which bears a single pair of legs, of which the frontmost pair are clawlike and function as poison jaws which paralyze prey.

Cent·ner, sent'nẽr, *n.* [G., < L. *centenarius*, < *centum*, a hundred.] A name in several European countries for a weight nearly equivalent to a hundredweight.

cen·to, sen'tō, *n.* pl. **cen·tos**, sen'tōz. [L., patchwork.] A literary or musical composition made up of bits from various sources.

---

cen·trad, sen′trad, *adv.* [L. *centrum,* center: -AD.] *Anat., zool.* toward the center.

cen·tral, sen′tral, *a.* [L. *centralis,* < *centrum,* center.] Of, pertaining to, or forming the center; in, at, or near the center; dispersed more or less evenly, as if from a center; as, *central* air-conditioning; principal, chief, or dominant; in a middle position between extremes; *anat.* of, pertaining to, or originating within the central nervous system (the brain and spinal cord); *phon.* of vowels, pronounced with the tongue placed somewhere between the front and back of the mouth.—*n.* A telephone systems office where connections are made between two different lines.—**cen·-tral·ly,** *adv.*

Cen·tral In·tel·li·gence A·gen·cy, C.I.A., *n.* In the U.S., a bureau of the federal government in charge of the coordination of intelligence activities, established in 1947 under the National Security Council.

cen·tral·ism, sen′tra·liz″um, *n.* Centralization, or a centralizing system; the principle of centralization, esp. the concentration of authority within an organization such as a political system.

cen·tral·i·ty, sen·tral′i·tē, *n.* Central position or character.

cen·tral·i·za·tion, sen″tra·li·zā′shan, *n.* The act of centralizing, or the fact of being centralized; the concentration of administrative power in a central government; the concentration of authority within or among any groups or organizations.

cen·tral·ize, sen′tra·liz″, *v.t.*—*centralized, centralizing.* To draw to or toward a center; concentrate authority, esp. in an organization such as a political system.—*v.i.* To come together at a center.—**cen·tral·iz·er,** *n.*

cen·tral pro·cess·ing u·nit, *n. Computer.* of a system, the unit that controls the interpretation and execution of instructions.

Cen·tral Stan·dard Time, *n. Sometimes l.c.* the standard time of the sixth time zone west of the Greenwich meridian, covering the central U.S. between approximately 82.5 degrees and 97.5 degrees west longitude, which is six hours earlier than Greenwich time. Abbr. **CST, C.S.T., c.s.t.**

cen·tre, sen′tèr, *n. Brit.* see *center.*

cen·tric, sen′trik, *a.* [Gr. *kentrikos,* < *kentron,* center.] Pertaining to or situated at the center; central; *physiol.* pertaining to or originating at a nerve center. Also **cen·tri·cal.**—**cen·tri·cal·ly,** *adv.*—**cen·-tri·ci·ty,** sen·tris′i·tē, *n.* Centric state.

cen·trif·u·gal, sen·trif′ū·gal, sen·trif′u·-gal, *a.* [L. *centrum,* a center, and *fugio,* to flee.] Tending to move away from the center; acting by or depending on centrifugal force.—*n.* A centrifuge.

cen·trif·u·gal force, *n.* The inertia of a body moving in a circle; the force acting upon a body moving in a circle which causes the body to move in a tangent to the circle or which, acting in opposition to the centripetal force, keeps the body moving at a constant distance from the center of the circle.

cen·trif·u·ga·tion, sen·trif″ū·gā′shan, *n.* The act or process of centrifuging.

cen·tri·fuge, sen′tri·fūj″, *n.* A device that rotates at high speed and by the resulting centrifugal force separates substances having components of different densities.—*v.t.* To subject to centrifugal action in a machine for that purpose.

cen·tri·fuge, sen′tri·fūj″, *n. Aeron.* a machine for inducing artificial gravity, used to test the ability of flying personnel, animal subjects, and equipment to withstand the above-normal gravitational forces which might be encountered in high-performance aircraft, rockets, and spacecraft flights.

cen·trip·e·tal, sen·trip′i·tal, *a.* [L. *centrum,* a center, and *peto,* to seek.] Tending or progressing toward a center; pertaining to centripetal force.

cen·trip·e·tal force, *n.* The force acting upon a body moving in a circle which causes the body to move toward the center of the circle, or which, acting in opposition to the inertia of the body, keeps the body moving at a constant distance from the center of the circle.

Cen·trist, sen′trist, *n.* (*Sometimes l.c.*) in continental Europe, a member of a political party of the Center; (*l.c.*) a politically moderate thinker.

cen·tro·bar·ic, sen″tro·bar′ik, *a.* [Gr. *baros,* weight.] Pertaining to the center of gravity; possessing a center of gravity.

cen·troid, sen′troid, *n.* Center of mass; intersecting point of medians of a triangle.

cen·tro·sphere, sen′tro·sfēr″, *n. Geol.* the dense material in the central part of the earth.

cen·trum, sen′trum, *n.* pl. **cen·trums, cen·tra.** [L. CENTER.] A center; *anat.* the body of a vertebra.

cen·tum, ken′tum, ken′tum, *a.* Of or pertaining to those languages of the Indo-European group including Hellenic, Italic, Celtic, and Germanic subfamilies, Cuneiform Hittite, and Tocharian, in which there is definite preservation of the Proto-Indo-European labiovelars showing an historical development of velar articulations, as the sound K or KH from Proto-Indo-European palatal phonemes. See *satem.*

cen·tum, sen′tum, *n.* One hundred.

cen·tu·ple, sen′tu·pal, sen′tū·pal, *a.* [L. *centuplus*—*centum,* a hundred, and root of *plica,* a fold.] Multiplied or increased a hundredfold.—*v.t.*—*centupled, centupling.* To multiply a hundredfold.

cen·tu·pli·cate, sen·tū′pli·kāt″, *v.t.*—*centuplicated, centuplicating.* [L. *centuplicatus,* pp. of *centuplicare,* < *centuplex,* hundredfold, < *centum,* hundred, and *-plex.*] To make a hundred times as great; centuple.—*a.* Hundredfold; centuple.—*n.* A hundredfold number or quantity.—**cen·tu·pli·ca·tion,** *n.*

cen·tu·ri·on, sen·tu′ri·on, *n.* [L. *centurio,* < *centum,* a hundred.] In ancient Rome, a military officer who commanded a century or company of infantry consisting of a hundred men.

cen·tu·ry, sen′cha·rē, *n.* pl. **cen·tu·ries.** [L. *centuria,* < *centum,* a hundred.] An aggregate of a hundred; anything consisting of a hundred in number; a period of a hundred years; often such a period reckoned from the birth of Christ; a subdivision or company in the ancient Roman army consisting of 100 men; one of the electoral divisions of the ancient Roman people, each division having one vote.—**cen·tu·ri·al,** *a.* Pertaining to a century.

cen·tu·ry plant, *n. Agave americana,* an ornamental plant which after 15 to 30 years blooms once and then dies, mistakenly supposed to blossom once a century.

ceorl, che′arl, *n.* [O.E. .CHURL.] In old English times, a freeman of the lowest rank; a churl.

ceph·a·lad, sef′a·lad″, *adv.* [Gr. *kephalē,* head: -AD.] *Anat.* toward the head: opposed to *caudad.*

ceph·a·lal·gia, sef″a·lal′ja, sef″a·lal′jē·a, *n.* [L. < Gr. *kephalē,* head, and *algos,* pain.] Headache.—**ceph·a·lal·gic,** *a.* Pertaining to or affected with headache.

ce·phal·ic, se·fal′ik, *a.* [L. *cephalicus,* < Gr. *kephalikos,* < *kephalē,* head.] Of or pertaining to the head; situated or directed toward the head.

ce·phal·ic in·dex, *n. Craniom.* the ratio of the greatest breadth of skull to the greatest

length from front to back, multiplied by 100.

ceph·a·li·za·tion, sef″a·li·zā′shan, *n.* [Gr. *kephalē,* head.] *Biol.* a tendency in the development of animals to localization of important organs or parts in or near the head.

ceph·a·lom·e·try, sef″a·lom′i·trē, *n.* The science of measuring the head or skull.— **ceph·a·lom·e·ter,** sef″a·lom′i·ter, *n.* An instrument for measuring the head or skull; a craniometer.

ceph·a·lo·pod, sef′a·lo·pod″, *n.* Any member of the class *Cephalopoda,* a class of mollusks, which includes the octopus, cuttlefish, and chambered nautilus, characterized by prehensile tentacles which surround the mouth.

ceph·a·lo·tho·rax, sef″a·lō·thōr′aks, sef″-a·lō·thar′aks, *n.* The anterior division of the body in crustaceans, spiders, scorpions, etc., which consists of the fused head and thorax.

Ce·phe·id var·i·a·ble, sē′fē·id vâr′ē·a·bl, sef′ē·id vâr′ē·a·bl, *n.* Any of a class of pulsating stars whose brightness periodically varies as a result of alternate contractions and expansions in volume.

Ce·phe·us, sē′fē·us, sē′fūs, *n. Class. myth.* an Ethiopian king, the husband of Cassiopeia and the father of Andromeda, placed among the stars after his death; a northern constellation between Draco and Cassiopeia.

ce·ra·ceous, se·rā′shus, *a.* [L. *cera,* wax.] Of the nature of wax; waxy.

ce·ram·al, se·ram′al, *n.* See *cermet.*

ce·ram·ic, se·ram′ik, *a.* [Gr. *ceramikos,* < *ceramos,* potters' clay, pottery.] Pertaining to pottery, earthenware, porcelain, or similar products made of fired clay, or to their manufacture.

ce·ram·ics, se·ram′iks, *n.* The art of shaping and baking clay articles, as pottery, earthenware, porcelain; *pl.* pieces or specimens of such an art.

cer·a·mist, ser′a·mist, *n.* One who works in the art, technology, or manufacture of ceramics.

ce·rar·gy·rite, se·rär′jē·rīt″, *n.* [Gr. *keras,* horn, and *argyros,* silver.] Native chloride of silver, AgCl, a white, yellowish, or grayish mineral, darkening on exposure to light, presenting somewhat the appearance of horn, and forming an important ore of silver; hornsilver.

ce·rate, sēr′āt, *n. Pharm.* a thick ointment composed of oils mixed with wax, resin, etc., and medicinal ingredients.

Cer·ber·us, sur′ber·us, *n.* [L.] *Class. myth.* the three-headed watchdog of the infernal regions; hence, any watchful and dreaded guardian.—**Cer·be·re·an,** sėr·bēr′ē·an, *a.*

cer·car·i·a, sėr·kâr′ē·a, *n.* pl. **cer·ca·ri·ae,** sėr·kâ′ri·ē. [N.L. < Gr. *cerkos,* tail.] *Zool.* a larval stage of worms, characterized by an oval or discoidal body ending in a tail-like appendage.—**cer·ca·ri·an,** *a., n.*

cere, sēr, *n. Ornith.* a fleshy, wax-like skin growth, containing the nostrils, located at the base of the bill of a bird.

cere, sēr, *v.t.*—*cered, cering.* To envelop, as a corpse, in cerecloth.

ce·re·al, sēr′ē·al, *n.* A plant of the grass family, which produces a starchy, edible grain, as wheat, oats, barley, rice, rye, or corn; the grain itself; a breakfast food processed from such a grain.

ce·re·al, sēr′ē·al, *a.* [< *Ceres,* the goddess of corn.] Pertaining to edible grain, or to plants producing it.

cer·e·bel·lum, ser″e·bel′um, *n.* [L. dim. of *cerebrum,* the brain.] *Anat.* a large section of the brain, coordinating center for voluntary movements, equilibrium and posture, composed of a central lobe and two lateral lobes, and located posterior to and underlying the cerebrum.—**cer·e·- bel·lar,** *a.*

cer·e·bral, cer·e·bric, ser′e·bral, se·rē′bral, ser′e·brik, se·reb′rik, se·rē′brik, *a.* Pertaining to the cerebrum or brain; expressing an appeal to or use of the intellect.—*n.* A cerebral consonant.

cer·e·bral ac·ci·dent, *n.* A sudden injury occurring inside the cerebrum, as a hemorrhage.

cer·e·bral hem·i·sphere, *n.* Either of the two convoluted halves into which the cerebrum is divided.

cer·e·bral pal·sy, *n.* Paralysis, due to brain damage prior to birth or during delivery, and marked by a lack of muscular coordination, spasms, and difficulties in speech.

cer·e·brate, ser′e·brāt″, *v.i.* To have or exhibit brain action; to think.—**cer·e·- bra·tion,** *n.*

cer·e·bro·spi·nal, ser″e·brō·spīn′al, se·- rē″brō·spin′al, *a.* Of or pertaining to the brain and spinal cord, or to these coupled with the spinal and cranial nerves.—**cer·e·bro·spi·nal flu·id,** *n.* A serumlike liquid in the lateral ventricles of the brain.

cer·e·bro·spi·nal men·in·gi·tis, men″- in·jit′is, *n.* [Gr. *meninx, meningos,* a membrane, *-itis,* inflammation.] *Pathol.* an acute bacterial disease, involving inflammation of the membranes covering the brain and spinal cord, and outwardly manifested by fever and sometimes red spots on the skin.

cer·e·brum, ser′e·brum, se·rē′brum, *n.* [L.] The main, anterior part of the brain of vertebrate animals, divided into halves, or cerebral hemispheres, and, in man, considered the center of conscious and voluntary processes.

cere·cloth, sēr′klath″, sēr′kloth″, *n.* [Earlier *cered cloth*: CERE, *v.*] Cloth waterproofed with wax, used esp. for wrapping the dead; a winding sheet.

cere·ment, sēr′ment, *n.* [CERE, *v.*] A cerecloth for wrapping a corpse; any burial clothing; usually *pl.*

cer·e·mo·ni·al, ser″e·mō′nē·al, *n.* A system of rites; ceremonies or formalities to be observed on some particular occasion.—**cer·e·mo·ni·al·ism,** ser·e·mō′ni·al·izm, *n.* Adherence to or fondness for ceremony.—**cer·e·mo·ni·al·ly,** *adv.* In a ceremonial manner; according to rites and formalities.—**cer·e·mo·ni·al·ness,** *n.*

cer·e·mo·ni·al, ser″e·mō′nē·al, *a.* [L. *cærimonialis.*] Relating to ceremonies or external forms or rites; ritual.

cer·e·mo·ni·ous, ser″e·mō′nē·us, *a.* Full of ceremony; accompanied with rites; according to prescribed or customary formalities or punctilios; formally respectful or polite; observant of conventional forms; fond of using ceremony.—**cer·e·mo·ni·ous·ly,** *adv.* In a ceremonious manner; formally; with due forms.—**cer·e·mo·ni·ous·ness,** *n.* The quality of being ceremonious; the practice of much ceremony; formality.

cer·e·mo·ny, ser′e·mō″nē, *n. pl.* **cer·e·mo·nies.** [Fr. *cérémonie,* < L. *cærimonia,* a rite or ceremony, veneration, sanctity; probably < same root as Skt. *kri, kar,* to do.] A religious or other rite or observance; solemn or formal display of performance; a solemnity; a usage of politeness, or such usages collectively; formality; punctilio; punctiliousness; mere conventional form.—**mas·ter of cer·e·mo·nies,** a person who regulates the forms to be observed by the company or attendants on a public occasion.

Ce·res, sēr′ēz, *n. Mythol.* a Roman goddess watching over the growth of grain and other plants, associated with the Greek goddess Demeter; *astron.* the largest of the asteroids, and the first to be discovered.

ce·re·us, sēr′ē·us, *n. pl.* **ce·re·us·es.** [L., wax candle, < *cera,* wax.] Any plant of the cactaceous genus *Cereus,* of the warmer part of America, as *C. giganteus,* sometimes growing to a height of 50 or 60 feet, or *C. grandiflorus,* "night-blooming cereus," bearing fragrant flowers opening at night.

ce·rif·er·ous, si·rif′er·us, *a.* [L.] Producing wax.

ce·rise, se·rēs′, se·rez′, *n., a.* [Fr., a cherry.] Cherry-red.

ce·rite, sēr′īt, *n.* A rare mineral, of a pale rose-red color, from which cerium was first obtained.

ce·ri·um, sēr′ē·um, *n.* [< the planet *Ceres.*] *Chem.* sym. Ce, at. no. 58; a ductile, metallic element of the rare-earth series; used for ignition devices, and as a reducing agent and catalyst.—**ce·ric,** sēr′ik, ser′ik, *a.* Of or containing cerium. See *cerous.*

cer·met, ce·ram·al, sur′met, se·ram′al, *n.* An extremely strong heat-resistant ceramic composition, made by bonding a metal and a ceramic substance, used in situations involving great heat and stress, such as in rocket motors, nuclear reactors, and turbojet engines.

CERN, *n.* [Fr. *(C)onseil (E)uropeen pour la (R)echerche (N)ucleaire.*] An international body, the European Council for Nuclear Research, having its headquarters in Geneva.

cer·nu·ous, surn′ū·us, sur′nō·us, *a.* [L. *cernuus.*] *Bot.* drooping; pendulous.

ce·ro, sēr′ō, *n. pl.* **ce·ro, ce·ros.** [Sp. *sierra,* saw.] Either of two large fishes of the mackerel family, *Scomberomorus cavalla* and *S. regalis,* found chiefly in tropical western Atlantic waters.

ce·ro·plas·tic, sēr″o·plas′tik, ser″o·plas′tik, *a.* [Gr. *kēros,* wax, and *plastikē (techné),* the art of the modeler or carver.] Pertaining to the art of modeling in wax; modeled in wax.—*n.* The art of modeling in wax.

ce·rous, sēr′us, *a.* Containing cerium, in larger proportion than a corresponding ceric compound.

cer·tain, ser′tan, *a.* [Fr. *certain,* as if < L. adjective *certanus,* formed < *certus,* certain, by adding suffix *-anus. Certus* is connected with *cerno, certum,* to distinguish, *discern.*] Sure; undoubtedly true; established as a fact; undoubtedly existing or impending, as death or danger; capable of being counted on or depended on; unfailing; infallible; of things, as, a *certain* sign; of persons, as, he is *certain* to be there, you are *certain* to find him; assured in mind; free from doubt; having no doubt or suspicion regarding, often used with *of;* stated; fixed; determinate; definite; as, a *certain* rate; not specifically named; as, a *certain* person, a *certain* pleasure in something.—**for cer·tain,** without question; certainly.—**cer·tain·ly,** *adv.* Without doubt or question; in truth and fact; without fail; assuredly; of a certainty.

cer·tain, ser′tan, *pron., pl.* in *constr.* Certain beings, as: *Certain* of the zoo animals were born in captivity.

cer·tain·ty, ser′tan·tē, *n. pl.* **cer·tain·ties.** The fact or state of being certain; exemption from failure to happen or produce the natural result; a fact or truth certainly established; that which cannot be questioned; full assurance of mind; exemption from or absence of doubt.

cer·tif·i·cate, ser·tif′i·kit, *n.* [Fr. *certificat.*] A written testimony to the truth of a certain fact or facts; a testimonial; an attestation; a legally authenticated voucher or testimony of certain facts; sometimes, a kind of license.

cer·tif·i·cate, ser·tif′i·kāt″, *v.t.* To give a certificate to, as to one who has passed an examination; to attest or certify by certificate.—**cer·ti·fi·ca·tion,** sur″ti·fi·kā′shan, ser·tif″i·kā′shan, *n.* The act of certifying.

cer·ti·fied check, *n.* A check certified as good for payment by the bank upon which it is drawn, as an attestation to the fact that it is backed by sufficient funds in the drawer's account.

cer·ti·fied mail, *n.* First-class mail accompanied by a receipt to be signed by the addressee and returned to the sender to prove that the mail was delivered.

cer·ti·fied milk, *n.* Milk processed in dairies in accordance with the health regulations of a state or municipal authority.

cer·ti·fied pub·lic ac·count·ant, *n.* A public accountant who fulfills the state government requirements for proficiency in the profession, and is granted a certificate to that effect. Also *CPA.*

cer·ti·fy, ser′ti·fī″, *v.t.*—*certified, certifying.* [Fr. *certifier,* < L.L. *certifico,* to certify—L. *certus,* certain, and *facio,* to make.] To assure or make certain; to give certain information *to;* to give certain information *of;* to make clear or definite; to testify to in writing; to make known or establish as a fact; to attest or confirm as true or genuine.—*v.i.*—**cer·ti·fi·a·ble,** ser″ti·fī′a·bl, *a.* Capable of being certified; *Brit.* treated as a lunatic.—**cer·ti·fi·a·bly,** ser″ti·fī′a·blē, *adv.*—**cer·ti·fi·er,** *n.*

cer·ti·o·ra·ri, ser″shē·o·râr′ē, *n.* [L., "to be informed," lit. "made more certain."] *Law,* a writ issuing from a superior court to call up the record of a proceeding in an inferior court for trial or review in the superior one.

cer·ti·tude, ser′ti·tōd″, ser′ti·tūd″, *n.* [L.L. *certitudo.*] Certainty; state of feeling certain.

ce·ru·le·an, se·rō′lē·an, *a.* [L. *cæruleus,* azure, for *cæluleus,* sky-colored, < *cælum,* the sky.] Sky-colored; azure; blue.

ce·ru·men, si·rō′men, *n.* [N.L. < L. *cera,* wax.] Earwax.—**ce·ru·mi·nous,** *a.*

ce·ruse, sēr′ös, si·rōs′, *n.* [Fr., < L. *cerussa,* white lead, < *cera,* wax.] *Chem.* white lead, composed of hydroxide and carbonate of lead, used in painting and cosmetics.—*v.t.* To wash with ceruse; to apply ceruse to as a cosmetic.

ce·rus·site, sēr′u·sīt″, si·rus′īt, *n.* [L. *cerussa,* white lead.] A mineral consisting of carbonate of lead, in orthorhombic crystals or massive or fibrous, with an adamantine luster, and forming an important ore of lead.

cer·ve·lat, ser′ve·lat″, ser′ve·lä″, ser″ve·lat″, ser″ve·lä″, *n.* [Fr. *cervelat,* now *cervelas,* < It. *cervellata,* kind of sausage containing hogs' brains, < *cervello,* brain, < L. *cerebellum.*] A kind of highly seasoned, dry sausage, orig. made of brains but now usually of young pork salted; *Brit.* saveloy.

cer·vi·cal, ser′vi·kal, *a.* [L. *cervix, cervicis,* the neck.] *Anat.* belonging to the neck; pertaining to the narrow lower part of the uterus.

cer·vi·ci·tis, ser″vi·sī′tis, *n.* Inflammation of the lower, necklike part of the uterus.

cer·vine, ser′vin, ser′vin, *a.* [L. *cervinus,* < *cervus,* deer.] Pertaining to deer; deerlike; of a deep tawny color.

cer·vix, ser′viks, *n. pl.* **cer·vix·es, cer·vi·ces,** ser·vī′sēz, sur′vi·sēz″. [L.] *Anat.* the neck, esp. the back of the neck; any necklike part, esp. the narrow lower part of the uterus.

Ce·sar·e·an, Ce·sar·i·an, si·zâr′ē·an, si·zä′ri·an, *n.* See *Caesarean.*

ce·si·um, cae·si·um, sē′zē·um, *n. Chem.* sym. Cs, at. no. 55; a rare soft metal of the alkali group of elements, the most electropositive element known, used principally in photoelectric cells.

ce·si·um 137, sē′zē·um, *n. Chem.* cesium of mass number 137, a radioactive variant of the element cesium having a half-life of 30 years.

ces·pi·tose, caes·pi·tose, ses′pi·tōs″, *a.* [L. *caespes, cespitis,* turf.] *Bot.* pertaining to turf; matted; growing in tufts.

cess, ses, *v.t.* [Shortened < assess.] *Brit.* to impose a tax; to assess.—*n. Brit.* a rate or tax; assessment.

cess, ses, *n. Brit., Ir. colloq.* luck; as, bad *cess* to you.

ces·sa·tion, se·sā′shan, *n.* [L. *cessatio,* < *cesso,* < *cedo, cessum,* to cease.] A ceasing; a stop; a rest; the act of discontinuing motion or action of any kind, whether temporary or final.

ces·sion, sesh′on, *n.* [L. *cessio,* < L. *cedo, cessum.* CEDE.] The act of ceding, yielding, or surrendering, as of territory, property, or rights; a giving up, resignation, or surrender; the thing ceded or surrendered.

cess·pipe, ses′pīp″, *n.* A pipe for carrying off drainage from a cesspool, sink, etc.

cess·pit, ses′pit″, *n.* A receptacle for the disposal of refuse and filth.

cess·pool, ses′pōl″, *n.* [Origin uncertain.] A cistern, well, or pit for retaining the sediment of a drain or for receiving sewerage; *fig.* any place of moral corruption.

c'est la guerre, sā·lä·ger′. [Fr. That's war.] That's the way things happen.

ces·tode, ses′tōd, *a.* [N.L. *Cestoda,* pl., < Gr. *cestos,* girdle.] Belonging to the *Cestoda,* a class or group of internally parasitic flatworms, including the tapeworms.—*n.*

ces·toid, ses′toid, *a.* [L. *cestus,* a girdle, < their shape.] *Zool.* ribbon-shaped, as tapeworms.

ces·tus, ses′tus, *n. pl.* **ces·tus.** [L. *caestus,* < *caedere,* cut, strike.] *Rom.* a hand-covering made of strips of leather, sometimes loaded with metal, worn by gladiators.

ces·tus, ses′tus, *n. pl.* **ces·ti,** ses′tī. [L. < Gr. *cestos,* girdle, lit. "stitched," < *kentein,* prick, stitch.] In ancient Rome, a belt or girdle; esp. the girdle of Aphrodite or Venus, said to be decorated with everything that might awaken desire.

ce·su·ra, sa·zhụr′a, sa·zụr′a, siz·ụr′a, *n. pl.* **ce·sur·as, ce·su·rae.** See *caesura.*

ce·ta·cean, si·tā′shan, *n.* [L. *cetus,* Gr. *kēto,* any large sea monster, a whale.] A marine mammal of the order *Cetacea* including whales, dolphins, and porpoises.—**ce·ta·cean, ce·ta·ceous,** si·tā′shus, *a.* Pertaining to the whale; belonging to the *Cetacea.*—**ce·tol·o·gy,** sē·tol′o·jē, *n.* The science or study of whales.

ce·tane, sē′tān, *n. Chem.* a colorless, oily liquid, $C_{16}H_{34}$, used as an additive to improve diesel fuel.

ce·tane num·ber, *n. Chem.* a diesel fuel rating similar to the octane number rating for gasoline; the amount by volume of cetane which must be added to basic diesel fuel to achieve specified performance characteristics on a scale in which basic diesel fuel has a rating of 0 and cetane 100.

Ce·tus, sē′tus, *n.* The constellation the Whale, situated at the celestial equator south of Aries and Pisces and between Aquarius and Eridanus.

ce·vi·tam·ic ac·id, sē′vī·tam′ik as′id, sē″vī·tam′ik as′id, *n. Biochemistry,* ascorbic acid; vitamin C.

Cey·lo·nese, sē″lo·nēz′, sē″lo·nēs′, *a.* Pertaining to the culture, language, and people of Ceylon, an island republic in the Indian Ocean just off the southeastern coast of India.—*n. pl.* **Cey·lon·ese.** An inhabitant of Ceylon; the language of Ceylon.

Cha·blis, shab′·lē, shä·blē′, *n. pl.* **Cha·blis,** sha·blēz. [From Chablis, town in north central France.] A dry French white wine of the Burgundy class.

cha·bouk, cha·buk, chä′bụk, *n.* [Hind. *chabuk,* a horsewhip.] A long whip used in the Orient for corporal punishment.

cha-cha, chä′chä″, *n.* A ballroom dance of Latin-American origin noted for its fast 1-2, 1-2-3 beat.—*v.i.* To do this dance. Also called **cha-cha-cha.**

chac·ma, chak′ma, *n.* A large baboon, *Papio comatus,* found in South Africa.

Chad, chad, *n.* A branch of 'a language spoken in west central Africa.

chafe, chāf, *v.t.*—*chafed, chafing.* [O.E. *chaufe,* Fr. *chauffer,* O.Fr. *chaufer,* to warm, < L. *calefacere,* to warm, < *caleo,* to grow warm, and *facere,* to make.] To excite heat (in some part of the body) by friction; to stimulate to warmth by rubbing; to excite the passions of; to inflame; to anger; to excite violent action in; to fret and wear by rubbing.—*v.i.* To be excited or heated; to rage; to fret; to rage or boil, as the sea; to be fretted and worn by rubbing.

chafe, chāf, *n.* A state of being angry or annoyed; fret, irritation, or heat; skin soreness caused by rubbing.

chaf·er, chā′fėr, *n.* [O.E. *caefor,* a chafer: D. *kever,* G. *käfer,* a beetle.] A beetle: esp. applied to such as are destructive to plants; as, cock-*chafer,* rose-*chafer,* bark-*chafer. Brit.* any scarabaeid bettle.

chaff, chaf, chäf, *n.* [O.E. *ceaf* = D. *kaf,* G. *kaff,* chaff.] The husks of corn and grasses, but more commonly restricted to the husks when separated from the corn by thrashing, sifting, or winnowing; straw or hay cut up for food for cattle; worthless matter, esp. that which is light and apt to be driven by the wind; refuse.—**chaff·y,** chaf′ē, *a.* Like chaff; full of chaff; light; frivolous; worthless.

chaff, chaf, chäf, *v.t., v.i.* [A corruption of chafe, to irritate or annoy.] To tease; to banter; to jest.—*n.* Banter; good-natured teasing.—**chaf·fer,** *n.*

chaff, chaf, chäf, *n. Milit.* narrow metal strips of various lengths which, dropped from aircraft, create false signals on radarscopes.

chaf·fer, chā′fėr, *v.i.* [M.E. *chapfare, chaffare,* bargaining, merchandise < chap, O.E. *ceap,* a bargain, and *fare,* procedure; journey, O.E. *faru,* a journey. Akin *cheap, cheapen.* CHEAP.] To bargain or haggle; to exchange chitchat.—*v.t.* To bandy (words); to haggle for.—*n.* A bargaining or haggling over price.—**chaff·er·er,** *n.*

chaf·finch, chaf′inch, *n.* [Perhaps < its note; comp. *chiff-chaff,* the name of a British bird, < its cry.] A European bird of the finch family, popular as a pet.

chaf·ing dish, chā′fing dish, *n.* A vessel to hold charcoal, etc., for heating anything placed over it; an apparatus consisting of a metal dish with a lamp or heating appliance beneath it, for cooking food or keeping it hot at the table.

cha·grin, sha·grin′, *n.* [Fr. < O.Fr. *chagrin,* troubled, vexed; origin unknown. Fr. *chagrin,* shagreen, is appar. a later and different word.] A feeling of vexation, disappointment, or humiliation; mortification.

cha·grin, sha·grin′, *v.t.*—*chagrined, chagrining.* To affect with chagrin; mortify.

chain, chān, *n.* [Fr. *chaine,* O.Fr. *chaene, cadene,* < L. *catena,* a chain.] A series of links or rings connected or fitted into one another, usually of metal, and used for various purposes; *fig.* that which binds, restrains, confines; a bond; a fetter; bondage; a series of things linked together; a series, line, or range of things connected or following in succession; as, a *chain* of causes or events; *weaving,* the warp threads

of a web, so called because they form a long series of links or loops. *Pl., naut.* strong links or plates of iron bolted to a ship's sides, and forming part of the attachments of the shrouds. *Surv.* a measuring instrument, generally consisting of 100 links, and having a total length of 66 feet; a group of similar places of business under one management, as, a hotel *chain;* a number of atoms of the same element that are united; a measure of 10 yards used by officials in football to determine a first down.

chain, chān, *v.t.* To fasten, bind, restrain, or fetter with a chain or chains; to put in chains; to connect; to hold in control; to unite firmly; to link; *surv.* to measure a distance on the ground.

chain gang, *n.* A group of convicts chained together while working outdoors.

chain let·ter, *n.* A letter sent to a number of persons who are asked to send copies to a specified number of other persons for some supposed advantage.

chain mail, *n.* Flexible armor of linked metal rings.

chain of com·mand, *n.* The succession of administrative or military ranks or positions from superior to subordinate through which command is exercised, orders are issued, or reports or requests are processed. Also **line of au·thor·i·ty.**

chain pump, *n.* A pump equipped with an endless chain mounted with disks or buckets that raise the liquid within a cylinder by passing rapidly in the direction of the desired flow.

chain re·ac·tion, *n.* Any series of events each of which is initiated by a preceding one. *Chem.* and *phys.* a reaction between particles which is started artificially by added energy, and continues by sustaining itself. Products of the initial reaction cause additional reactions to occur, such as many types of polymerization in chemistry and nuclear fission in physics.—**chain-re·act,** *v.i.*

chain saw, *n.* A power saw with teeth on a continuous band or chain.

chain-smoke, chān′smōk″, *v.i., v.t.*—*chain-smoked, chain-smoking.* To smoke cigars or cigarettes in rapid succession; to light one cigarette from another.—**chain-smok·er,** *n.* An excessively heavy smoker.

chain stitch, *n.* An ornamental stitch consisting of threads or cords linked together in the form of a chain, sewn either by hand or machine.

chain store, *n.* One of a group of stores owned and operated by one owner or company.

chair, châr, *n.* [O.Fr. *chaiere* (Fr. *chaire*), L. *cathedra.*] A seat with a back, and often arms, usually for one person; one of the suspended seats on a chair lift; a seat of office or authority, or the office itself; the person occupying the seat or office, esp. the chairman of a meeting; a sedan chair; a chaise; *Brit.* a metal block or clutch to support and secure a rail in a railroad.

chair, châr, *v.t.* To place or seat in a chair; install in a chair of office; esp. *Brit.,* to place in a chair and carry aloft, as in triumph; to preside over, as a meeting.

chair car, *n.* A railroad passenger car fitted with chairs, instead of double seats.

chair·man, châr′man, *n.* The presiding officer of an assembly, association, or company, committee or public meeting; the administrative head of a department in a university or college; one whose business is to carry a sedan chair.—**chair·man·ship,** châr′man·ship″, *n.* The office of a chairman or presiding officer of a meeting.—**chair·wom·an,** *n.*

chair·man, châr′man, *v.t.*—*chairmaned, chairmaning, chairmanned, chairmanning.* To preside as chairman of a group, meeting, or committee.

ch- chain, G. na*ch*t;   **th-** THen, thin;   **w-** wig, hw as sound in whig;   **z-** zh as in azure, zeal.   *Italicized vowel* indicates schwa sound.

chair·warm·er, châr'wạr"mėr, *n. Slang,* an idle person.

chaise, shāz, *n.* [Fr. *chaise,* chair, chaise, var. of *chaire*: CHAIR.] A light open carriage, usually with a hood, esp. a one-horse, two-wheeled carriage for two persons; a post chaise.

chaise longue, shāz"lạng', chāz"lạng', *Fr.* shez long', *n. pl.* **chaise longues, chais·es longues.** [Fr., "long chair."] A kind of reclining-chair with an elongated seat.

chal·ced·o·ny, kal·sed'o·nē, kal'se·dō"nē, *n. pl.* **chal·ced·o·nies.** [L. *chalcedonius,* < Gr. *chalkedon*; appar. named < *Chalcedon,* town in Asia Minor.] A translucent variety of quartz in various colors, often milky or grayish.

chal·co·cite, kal'ko·sīt, *n.* [Gr. *chalkos,* copper.] Cu₂S, native sulfide of copper, a mineral of a dark-gray to black color with a metallic luster, occurring in masses or in crystals, and forming an important ore of copper.

chal·co·py·rite, kal"ko·pī'rīt, kal"ko·pēr'īt, *n. Chem.* native sulfide of copper and iron, CuFeS₂, a yellow mineral with a metallic luster, occurring in masses and in crystals, and forming an important ore of copper.

Chal·da·ic, kal·dā'ik, *a.* [L. *Chaldaicus.*] Pertaining to ancient Chaldea (southern Babylonia).—*n.* The Semitic language of Chaldea.

Chal·de·an, kal·dē'an, *a.* [L. *Chaldaeus.*] Of or belonging to ancient Chaldea (southern Babylonia); pertaining to astrology or occult learning.—*n.* An inhabitant of Chaldea; one of an ancient Semitic people that formed the dominant element in Babylonia and were celebrated as warriors, astrologers, magicians, etc.; hence, one versed in astrology or occult learning; an astrologer, soothsayer, or seer.

Chal·dee, kal·dē', kal'dē, *n.* Ancient language of Palestinian and Babylonian Jews; Aramaic vernacular found in some original passages of the Bible, as in Daniel, Ezra, and Jeremiah.

chal·dron, chạl'dron, *n.* [O.Fr. *chauderon,* kettle, = E. *caldron.*] An English dry measure for coal, coke, or lime, equal to 32 or 36 bushels, but varying with commodity and locality.

chal·et, sha·lā', shal'ā, *Fr.* shä·lā', *n.* [Fr. Swiss.] A Swiss house, usually wooden, with wide eaves at front and sides; any cottage or villa built in this style; a herdsman's hut in the Swiss mountains.

chal·ice, chal'is, *n.* [Fr. *calice,* < L. *calix, calicis,* a cup or goblet.] A drinking cup or goblet; the cup used to administer the wine in the celebration of the Lord's Supper; a flower bearing a cup-like blossom.

chalk, chạk, *n.* [O.E. *cealc,* < *calx,* lime.] A soft limestone, usually white or yellowish, consisting chiefly of the shells of foraminifers; a chalk-like substance; a prepared piece of marking chalk; a mark made with chalk; a record of credit given.—**chalk·y,** *a.*

chalk, chạk, *v.t.* To treat, mix, or rub with chalk; whiten or make pale with chalk; to mark, write, or draw with chalk.—*v.i.* To become powdery, as a painted surface exposed to weather.

chalk·stone, chạk'stōn", *n. Pathol.* a chalk-like concretion in the tissues or small joints of person affected with gout; tophus.

chalk up, *v.t.* To credit or attribute to, as: He *chalked up* his failure to insufficient study time. To accomplish or score; as, to *chalk up* another touchdown; *billiards,* to apply chalk to, as the tip of one's cue.

chal·lenge, chal'inj, *n.* A calling into question; a demand for an explanation or justification; an invitation or summons to engage in a contest of skill, strength, etc., or to compete in a sport; a call to fight, as a duel, to answer an insult or provocation; a

difficulty in a job or activity that proves stimulating or enjoyably inciting; a sentry's demand for a countersign or proof of identity; *law,* a formal exception taken to the qualifications or impartiality of a juror or jury; the questioning of the validity of a vote or of the legal qualifications of a voter.

chal·lenge, chal'inj, *v.t.*—**challenged, challenging.** To address a challenge to; to call to a contest; to summon to fight, or to a duel; to demand the countersign or password from: said of a sentry; to claim as due, to demand as a right; *law,* to demand the removal of (one) from among the prospective jurors; to question the legal qualifications of; to object to; to take exception to; to call in question, as a statement.—*v.i.* To make, issue, or present a challenge; to take legal exception or objection.—**chal·leng·er,** *n.*—**chal·lenge·a·ble,** chal'len·ja·bl, *a.* Capable of being challenged or called to account.

chal·lis, chal·lie, shal'ē, *n.* [Origin uncertain.] A lightweight fabric of wool, cotton and wool, or rayon usually in a small floral print.

chal·one, kal'ōn, *n. Physiol.* a secretion of endocrine origin which inhibits bodily activity.

cha·lu·meau, shal"ū·mō', *Fr.* shäl·ū·mō', *n. pl.* **cha·lu·meaux,** shal"ū·mōz', *Fr.* shäl·ū·mō'. The lowest register of the clarinet; the 17th century woodwind instrument which was the forerunner of the clarinet.

cha·lyb·e·ate, ka·lib'ē·it, ka·lib'ē·āt", *a.* [< Gr. *chalyps, chalybos,* steel.] Impregnated with iron: applied to medicines containing iron, and esp. to springs and waters impregnated with iron, or holding iron in solution.—*n.* Any water or medicine which contains iron.

cham·ber, chām'bėr, *n.* [Fr. *chambre,* < L. *camera,* Gr. *kamara,* a vault or arched roof.] A room, usually private, esp. a bedroom; a room where professional men, as lawyers, conduct their business; the room in which judges sit for the disposing of matters not heard in court; a hall or place where an assembly, association or body of men meets; a legislative, judicial, or similar body, esp. either of the houses of a bicameral legislature; a council or board; as, a *chamber* of commerce; a hollow or cavity in a thing, esp. when of definite form and use; in firearms, that part of a gun which holds the charge or a receptacle in the cylinder of a revolver for a cartridge.—**cham·bered,** *a.*

cham·ber, chām'bėr, *v.t.* To shut up in, or as in, a chamber.

cham·ber·lain, chām'bėr·lin, *n.* [O.Fr. *chamberlain,* < O.H.G. *chamarling, chamarlinc—chamar,* chamber, and suffix *-ling.*] A person charged with the direction and management of a chamber; an officer charged with the direction and management of the private apartments of a monarch or nobleman; the treasurer of a city or corporation.

cham·ber·maid, chām'bėr·mād", *n.* A woman who has the general care of bedrooms, making the beds and cleaning.

cham·ber mu·sic, *n.* Music suited for performance in a small room: commonly applied to concerted music for a small group of solo instruments.

cham·ber of com·merce, *n.* An organization of businessmen and merchants who meet together in an effort to protect, promote, and regulate commercial and industrial interests in their area.

cham·ber pot, *n.* A vessel for urine and other wastes, used in bedrooms.

cham·bray, sham'brā, *n.* [Cf. *cambric.*] A fine variety of gingham, commonly woven with a colored warp and white filling threads, thus giving the plain color a frosted appearance.

cha·me·le·on, ka·mē'lē·on, ka·mēl'yan, *n.* [L. *chamæleon,* Gr. *chamaileon,* < *chamai,* on the ground, and *leon,* lion.] Any of a group of old-world lizards, esp. of the genus *Chamæleon,* noted chiefly for the ability to change color to match their surroundings, which is accomplished by a quick change in the size and shape of color cells in their granular skin. They are also noted for a laterally compressed body, independently movable eyeballs, extensible tongue the length of the body, and a prehensile tail.—*a.* Fickle, changeable.—**cha·me·le·on·ic,** *a.*

cham·fer, cham'fėr, *n.* [Fr. *chanfrein,* a chamfer.] A small gutter or furrow cut in wood or other hard material; a bevel or slope; the corner of anything originally right-angled cut aslope equally on the two sides which form it.

cham·fer, cham'fėr, *v.t.* To cut a chamfer in or on; to flute; to channel; to cut or grind so as to form a bevel.

cham·ois, sham'ē, *Fr.* shä·mwä', *n. pl.* **cham·ois, cham·oix,** sham'ēz, *Fr.* shä·mwä'. [Fr.] A species of goatlike antelope inhabiting high, inaccessible mountains in Europe and Western Asia, about the size of a well-grown goat, and extremely agile; a kind of soft leather made from various skins dressed with fish oil, so called because first prepared from the skin of the chamois. Also **cham·my,** *shammy.*

cham·o·mile, kam'o·mīl", kam'o·mēl", *n.* See *camomile.*

Cha·mor·ro, cha·mạr'ō, *Sp.* chä·mạr'ṛa, *n. pl.* **Cha·mor·ros.** A member of the native race of Guam and the Mariana or Ladrone Islands in the Pacific Ocean east of the Philippines, of Micronesian (Malayo-Polynesian) stock with strong Filipino and Spanish admixture; the language of this race.—*a.* Of or pertaining to the Chamorros or their language.

champ, champ, *v.t.* [Origin uncertain; perhaps < Scand.] To crush with the teeth and chew vigorously or noisily; munch; to bite upon repeatedly, esp. impatiently, as a horse upon its bit; *Sc.* crush, mash, or trample.—*v.i.* To make a chewing or biting movement with the jaws and teeth.—*n.* An act of champing.

champ, champ, *n. Slang,* a champion, esp. a boxing or other sports champion.

cham·pagne, sham·pān', *n.* [From *Champagne,* a former province in northeastern France.] An effervescent wine, usually white, made in Champagne, France, or elsewhere; the color of champagne, a pale yellow.

cham·paign, sham·pān', *n.* [O.Fr. *champaigne,* < *champ,* L. *campus,* a field. CAMPAIGN.] A flat open expanse of country. —*a.* Level; open; having the character of a plain.

cham·per·ty, cham'pėr·tē, *n.* [O.Fr. *champart,* share of the produce of land, < L. *campus,* field, and *pars* (*part-*), part.] *Law,* an illegal proceeding whereby a party not otherwise concerned in a suit aids a plaintiff or defendant in consideration of a share of any proceeds of the litigation in case of success.—**cham·per·tor,** *n.*—**cham·per·tous,** *a.*

cham·pi·gnon, sham·pin'yan, *Brit.* cham·pin'yan, *Fr.* sham·pē·nyan', *n.* [Fr., ult. < L. *campus,* field.] The common edible mushroom.

cham·pi·on, cham'pē·an, *n.* [Fr. *champion,* L.L. *campio, campionis,* a champion, < L. *campus,* a field, later a combat, duel.] One who fights for a cause; one who engages in single combat in the cause of another; one who wins first place or prize in competition; one whose supremacy or superiority is acknowledged by public contest; anything awarded first place in a competitive exhibition.

---

a- fat, fāte, fär, fâre, fạll;   **e-** met, mē, mēre, hėr;   **i-** pin, pīne;   **o-** not, nōte, mōve;   **u-** tub, cūbe, bụll;   **oi-** oil;   **ou-** pound.

cham·pi·on, cham′pē·an, *v.t.* To challenge to a fight; to protect; to defend, support. or uphold (a cause or a person).

cham·pi·on·ship, cham′pē·an·ship″, *n.* The distinction of being a champion; support or maintenance of a cause.

champ·le·vé, shäN·le·vā′, *a.* [Fr., pp. of *champlever,* < *champ,* field, ground, and *lever,* raise, remove.] Of enameled work, having the metal ground cut out or depressed in places to receive the enamel.—*n.* pl. **champ·le·vés,** shäN·le·vā′, shäN·le·vāz′. Champlevé work, or the process of producing it.

chance, chans, chäns, *n.* [Fr. *chance,* chance, hazard, L.L. *cadentia,* a falling (E. *cadence*), L. *cadere,* to fall; in allusion to the falling of the dice.] An event occurring without apparent cause or control; kismet, fate; a purposeless cause of unexpected happenings; luck, fortune, accident; a possible or probable occurrence; contingency; an unusual and unexpected event; fortuity; an opportunity or opening; a risk, hazard, gamble; a ticket in a raffle or lottery.—**by chance,** without forethought or plan.—**on the chance,** with some hope.— **on the off chance,** with very slight hope.

chance, chans, chäns, *v.i.*—*chanced, chancing.* To happen.—*v.t.* To put under the influence of chance; to risk.—**to chance up·on,** to find unexpectedly.—*a.* Happening by chance; as, a *chance* acquaintance; casual.

chance·ful, chans′ful, *a.* Full of chances or accidents; hazardous.

chan·cel, chan′sel, chän′sel, *n.* [O.Fr. *chancel,* < M.L. *cancellus,* chancel, < L. *cancelli,* pl., bars, lattice.] That part of a church usually on a higher level than the nave and set apart by steps and a railing inside of which are located the altar or communion table, the pulpit, and lectern.

chan·cel·le·ry, chan′se·le·rē, chan′sle·rē, chän′se·le·rē, chän′sle·rē, *n.* pl. **chan·cel·le·ries.** [O.Fr. *chancelerie* (Fr. *chancellerie*), < *chancelier.*] The position, court, or department of a chancellor; the official residence or office of the chancellor; the office and official personnel attached to an embassy, or consulate.

chan·cel·lor, chan′se·lėr, chan′slėr, chän′se·lėr, chän′slėr, *n.* [O.Fr. Fr. *chancelier,* < L.L. *cancellarius,* orig. an officer stationed at the bars enclosing a tribunal, < L. *cancelli,* bars, lattice.] *U.S.* the judge, or presiding judge, in a court of equity or chancery; the chief administrative position in certain universities, or the university officer of high rank in charge of a special administrative function; the chief executive officer of higher education system in some states; a Roman Catholic priest appointed by the bishop of a diocese to aid him in legal matters and hold his consistory courts; a lay member of an Anglican diocese who is legal officer and advisor; the chief minister of state in some European countries; the chief secretary of an embassy. *Brit.* the highest judicial officer of the crown in Great Britain called Lord High *Chancellor;* the honorary, non-resident, titular head of a university.

Chan·cel·lor of the Ex·cheq·uer, *n.* Minister of finance in the British cabinet charged with management of national revenue and expenditure; foremost official of the treasury.

chance-med·ley, chans′med″lē, chäns′-med″lē, *n.* [A.Fr. *chance medlee,* "mixed chance."] *Law,* a sudden, violent altercation; unpremeditated homicide, possibly in self-defense; haphazardness; heedless or chance action.

chan·cer·y, chan′se·rē, chän′se·rē, *n.* pl. **chan·cer·ies.** [Modified < older chancery, < Fr. *chancellerie.* CHANCELLOR.] A court of equity as distinguished from a court

of common law; judicial equity; office of public records; a chancellor's court, or office, or the building in which he has his office; the office of an embassy; *Brit. (cap.)* since 1873 one of the five divisions of the High Court of Justice; *law,* in chancery, pending in a court of chancery; in litigation, under the supervision of the court; as, a ward in *chancery;* the governing office in a diocese; *R. Cath. Ch.* that division of the Curia Romana responsible for issuing bulls establishing new dioceses; *sports,* a hold in wrestling that pinions the opponent's head or encircles the neck; stranglehold.

chan·cre, shang′kėr, *n.* [Fr. < L. *cancer,* crab, cancer.] *Pathol.* the initial lesion of syphilis.—**chan·croid,** shang′kroid, *n.* A soft, local venereal sore.—**chan·crous,** *a.* Of or like a chancre.

chanc·y, chan′sē, chän′sē, *a.*—*chancier, chanciest.* Dependent on chance; uncertain; risky.

chan·de·lier, shan″de·lėr′, *n.* [Fr. CHAN-DLER.] A branched support for a number of lights, often suspended from a ceiling.

chan·delle, shan·del′, *Fr.* shäN·del′, *n.* [Fr., candle, in reference to the perpendicular flight path of the maneuver.] *Avi.* an abrupt, steep, climbing turn in which an airplane's momentum provides additional acceleration for the climb, executed in order to simultaneously change direction and gain altitude.—*v.t.* To perform a chandelle.

chan·dler, chand′lėr, chänd′lėr, *n.* [Fr. *chandelier,* a dealer in candles, < L. *candela,* a candle.] One who makes or sells candles and soap; a dealer who handles provisions, supplies, or equipment of a particular type; as, ship-*chandler;* a person who sells groceries and the like.

chan·dler·y, chand′le·rē, chänd′le·rē, *n.* pl. **chan·dler·ies.** The commodities sold by a chandler; a chandler's warehouse or business; a storeroom for candles.

change, chānj, *v.t.*—*changed, changing.* [Fr. *changer,* to change, < L.L. *cambiare,* < *cambire,* to change, to barter.] To cause to turn or pass from one state to another; to vary in form or essence; to alter or make different; to alter the site or route; to substitute another thing or things for; as, to *change* clothes; to shift; to give or procure another kind of money for; as, to *change* a dollar; to give away for a money equivalent of a different kind; to exchange; as, to *change* places with a person; to place fresh linen on; as, to *change* a bed or baby.— *v.i.* To suffer change; to be altered; to undergo variation; to be partially or wholly transformed; to move to a lower range of the voice. To change one's mode of transportation; to begin a new revolution, or to pass from one phase to another, as the moon.—**to change hands,** to be transferred from one owner to another.—**chang·er,** *n.*

change, chānj, *n.* Any variation or alteration in form, state, quality, or essence; a passing from one state, form, or place to another; a succession of one thing in the place of another; as, *change* of seasons; the passing from one phase of the moon to another; alteration in the order of a series; permutation; that which makes a variety or may be substituted for another; as, two *changes* of clothes; small units of money, which may be given for larger amounts; small coins; the balance of a sum of money returned when the price of goods is deducted; a place where merchants and others meet to transact business; in this sense an abbreviation for *Exchange,* and often written *Change; mus.* the order in which bells are rung.

change·a·ble, chān′ja·bl, *a.* Liable to change; subject to alteration; fickle; inconsistent; unstable; alterable, as a color that changes as the light shifts.—**change·a·-**

ble·ness, change·a·bil·i·ty, chān″ja·bil′i·tē, *n.*—**change·a·bly,** *adv.*

change·ful, chānj′ful, *a.* Erratic; inconstant; mutable; fickle; uncertain; subject to alteration.—**change·ful·ly,** *adv.*—**change·ful·ness,** *n.*

change·less, chānj′lis, *a.* Constant; without variation; steadfast.—**change·less·ly,** *adv.*—**change·less·ness,** *n.*

change·ling, chānj′ling, *n.* [< *change* and *-ling.*] A child secretly substituted for another; a strange, stupid, or ugly child supposedly left by fairies in place of a beautiful child.

change off, *v.i.* To exchange duties or to alternate working hours with someone.

change of heart, *n.* A revised opinion; an entirely new decision.

change of life, *n.* Menopause.

change ring·ing, *n.* The art of ringing changes on a peal of bells in a regularly varying order to produce all possible sequences.

chan·nel, chan′el, *n.* [O.Fr. *chanel,* < L. *canalis,* E. *canal.*] The bed of a stream or waterway; the part of a waterway which is navigable; a wide strait, as between a continent and an island; a means of passing, conveying, or transmitting, as *channels* of trade; an artificial course for water or liquids; a tubular passage for liquids or fluids. *Arch.* a flute in a column. *Radio, television,* and *telegraphy,* a broadcasting band; *computer,* a one way path for electrical transmission of information between two or more points.

chan·nel, chan′el, *n.* [Corruption of *chain-wale.*] *Naut.* one of the horizontal planks or ledges attached to the outside of a ship, nearly abreast of a mast, to give more spread to the shrouds.

chan·nel, chan′el, *v.t.*—*channeled, channeling, Brit. channelled, channelling.* To form a channel in; groove; to excavate as a channel; to convey through a channel; to guide in a certain course; as, to *channel* one's ambition.

chan·nel·ize, chan′e·līz″, *v.t., v.i.* To channel.—**chan·nel·i·za·tion,** *n.* The act of channeling.

chan·son, shan′son, *Fr.* shäN·sąn′, *n.* [Fr. < L. *cantio(n-),* < *canere,* sing.] A song with French lyrics, sung in any of a variety of styles.

chan·son de geste, shäN·sąn de zhest′, *n.* [Fr., "song of deed."] One of a class of old French epic poems narrating heroic exploits; as, the "Chanson de Roland."

chant, chant, chänt, *v.t.* [O.Fr. Fr. *chanter,* < L. *cantare,* freq. of *canere,* sing.] To sing; to celebrate in song; to sing to a chant, or in the manner of a chant, esp. in the church service; intone.—*v.i.* To sing; to sing a chant.

chant, chant, chänt, *n.* A song; singing; a short, repetitive melody used in liturgical singing, characterized by single notes to which are assigned as many syllables as required; a psalm, canticle, or the like chanted or for chanting; any monotonous song; a monotonous or singing intonation of the voice in speaking.

chant·er, chan′tėr, chän′tėr, *n.* One who chants; a singer; a chorister; a precentor; the finger-pipe of a bagpipe, on which the melody is played; the hedge-sparrow, *Accentor modularis.*

chan·te·relle, shan″te·rel′, chan″te·rel′, *n.* [Fr. < *chanter,* sing, < L. *cantare,* sing.] The highest string of some stringed musical instruments, as the violin or guitar.

chan·te·relle, shan″te·rel′, chan″te·rel′, *n.* [Fr., perhaps < O.Fr. *chanterelle,* a small bell, from its shape, < *chanter,* to sing.] An English edible mushroom.

chan·teuse, shan·tös′, *Fr.* shäN·tœz′, *n.* pl. **chan·teus·es.** A professional female vocalist, esp. one who performs in cabarets or nightclubs.

chan·tey, chan·ty, shan'tē, chan'tē, n. pl. **chant·eys, chant·ies,** (-tiz). [Prob. < Fr. *chanter*, sing: see *chant*.] A sailors' song, esp. one sung in rhythm with their work by sailors hauling or heaving together.

chan·ti·cleer, chan'ti·klēr", n. [O.Fr. *chantecler*, < *chanter*, sing, and *cler*, clear.] A rooster; the cock in the medieval epic poem, "*Reynard the Fox.*"

chan·try, chan'trē, chän'trē, n. pl. **chan·-tries.** [O.Fr. *chanterie*, < *chanter*, sing. CHANT.] An endowment for the singing or saying of mass for the souls of the founders or of persons named by them; the priests, or the chapel or the like, so endowed; a chapel attached to a church, used for minor services.

Cha·nu·kah, chä'nṳ·kä", chä'na·ka, hä'-nṳ·kä", hä'na·ka, n. See *Hanukkah.*

cha·os, kā'os, n. [L. < Gr. *chaos*, empty space, abyss, akin to *chainen*, yawn.] The infinity of space or formless matter supposed to precede the existence of the ordered universe; any assemblage of elements wholly without organization or order; utter confusion or disorder.—**cha·ot·ic,** a. In utter confusion or disorder.

chap, chap, v.t.—*chapped, chapping.* [M.E. var. of *chop*.] To split; crack; make rough, esp. the skin.—v.i. To become chapped, as the skin.—n. A crack in the skin.

chap, chap, n. [Short for *chapman*.] *Colloq.* a man or a boy; a fellow; *Brit. slang,* a customer.

chap, chap, n. *Brit.* see *fellow.*

cha·pa·re·jos, cha·pa·ra·jos, shap"a·-rā'ōs, *Sp.* chä"pä·re'has, n. pl. [Mex. Sp.] Protective leather breeches worn by horsemen, esp. cowboys; also called *chaps.*

chap·ar·ral, chap"a·ral', n. [Sp., < *chaparro*, evergreen oak.] A close growth of low evergreen oaks; any dense thicket.

chap·ar·ral cock, n. A terrestrial bird of the cuckoo family, *Geococcyx californianus,* of the southwestern U.S.; also called *roadrunner.*—**chap·ar·ral hen,** n. The female of the chaparral cock.

chap·ar·ral pea, n. A thorny, leguminous bush, *Pickeringia montana,* which is found in dense thickets in western U.S.

chap·book, chap'bṳk", n. A small book or tract which contains popular stories, fairy tales, ballads, or songs.

cha·peau, sha·pō', *Fr.* shä·pō', n. pl. **cha·peaux,** sha·pōz, *Fr.* shä·pō'. [Fr. *chapeau,* O.Fr. *chapel,* < M.L. *capellus* dim. of *capa, cappa,* E. *cap.*] A hat.

chap·el, chap'el, n. [O.Fr. *chapele* (Fr. *chapelle*), < M.L. *capella,* sanctuary for relics, orig. cloak (as that of St. Martin, preserved as a relic), dim. of *capa, cappa,* E. *cape, cap.*] A private or subordinate place of prayer or worship; an oratory; a part of or addition to a church, separately dedicated, devoted to special services; a room or building for worship, in or connected with a royal palace, a castle, or a college; a separate place of public worship dependent on the church of a parish; an independent place of worship, usually small, specially authorized or devoted to special services; a place of worship of a religious body outside of an established church, as for dissenting Protestant churches in England; religious service in a chapel; a choir or orchestra of a chapel; a printing-house, or the body of printers belonging to it.

chap·e·ron, chap·er·one, shap'e·rōn", n. [O.Fr. Fr. *chaperon,* hood, < *chape.*] An older woman or married woman who, for the sake of propriety, attends a young unmarried woman in public or to mixed gatherings; an older person who supervises a party of young unmarried persons of both sexes.—v.t., v.i.—**chap·e·ron·age,** shap'e·rō"nij, n. The attendance of a chaperon.

chap·fall·en, chap'fạ"len, a. Having the lower jaw depressed, from exhaustion, humiliation, or dejection; chagrined; dispirited. Also **chop·fall·en.**

chap·i·ter, chap'i·tēr, n. [< O.Fr. *chapitel,* < L.L. *capitellum,* L. *capitulum,* dim. of *caput,* a head; *chapter* is the same word.] *Arch.* the upper part or capital of a column or pillar.

chap·lain, chap'lin, n. [Fr. *chapelain;* L.L. *capellanus,* < *capella,* a chapel. CHAPEL.] An ecclesiastic who performs divine service in a chapel; more generally, an ecclesiastic who officiates in an army, garrison, ship, college, prison, or other institution.—**chap·lain·cy, chap·lain·ship,** n. The office or post of a chaplain.

chap·let, chap'lit, n. [O.Fr. Fr. *chapelet,* dim. of O.Fr. *chapel,* head-dress.] A wreath or garland for the head; a string of beads; a string of beads for counting prayers, one third of the length of a rosary; the prayers so counted; anything resembling a string of beads; *arch.* a small molding carved into beads or the like; *foundrywork,* a metal form to hold the core in place in a mold.—**chap·let·ed,** a. Adorned with a chaplet or garland.

chaps, chaps, shaps, n. [< Mexican Sp. *chaparreras,* < *chaparro,* evergreen oak.] Widely flared leather leggings worn by cowboys as extra protection when riding through brush and thorns. See *chaparejos.*

chap·ter, chap·tēr, n. [Fr. *chapitre,* formerly *chapitle, capitel,* < L. *capitulum,* dim. of *caput,* the head, whence also *capital, cattle,* etc.] A division of a book or treatise; an important division in a series of events, often marked by a significant event or a turning point; a local branch of a college fraternity, sorority, or other society or organization. *Eccles.* the council of a bishop, consisting of the canons or prebends and other clergymen attached to a collegiate or cathedral church, and presided over by a dean; the meeting of certain religious orders and societies.

chap·ter house, n. The building in which a chapter of a fraternity, council, or other organization meets; *eccles.* in a cathedral, space provided for meetings of the chapter.

cha·que·ta, chä·ke'tä, n. [Sp. jacket.] A jacket, esp. one made of leather and worn by cowboys of western U.S.

char, chär, v.t.—*charred, charring.* [Appar. detached from *charcoal.*] To burn or reduce to charcoal; to burn slightly; scorch.—v.i. To become charred.—n. Charcoal; a charred substance.

char, charr, chär, n. [It. and Gael. *cear,* red; from its having a red belly.] A name given to at least two species of the salmon family, inhabiting lakes in parts of northern Europe.

char, chare, chär, châr, n. [< O.E. *cerr, cyrr,* a turn, time, occasion; *cerran, cyrran,* to turn=D. *keeren,* G. *kehren,* to turn, move, or change. Hence *charcoal.*] A single job or piece of work; household work; *Brit.* a charwoman.—v.i. To work at others' houses by the day; to do small jobs.

char·a·banc, shar'a·bang", shar'a·bangk", *Fr.* shä·rä·bän', n. [Fr. *char à bancs,* "car with benches."] *Brit.* a large motor bus with transverse seats, used for sightseeing.

char·a·cin, kar'a·sin, n. A member of the family of fresh-water fishes, *Characidae,* found in Africa and South America, which are valued for their varied forms and bright colors for use in aquariums.

char·ac·ter, kar'ik·tēr, n. [L. < Gr. *charakter,* < *charassein,* make sharp, engrave.] A significant mark made by cutting, stamping, or drawing; a symbol as used in writing or printing, esp. one employed in recording speech, as a letter of the alphabet; writing or printing, or a style of writing or printing; the system of symbols employed in writing a particular language; as, the Greek *character; computer,* a symbol representing information in coded form for use in a computer; a distinguishing mark or feature; a characteristic; the aggregate of characteristics or distinguishing features of a thing; peculiar quality; moral constitution, as of a person or a people; often, strongly developed moral quality; reputation; often, good repute; an account of the qualities or peculiarities of a person or thing, esp. a formal statement from an employer concerning the qualities and habits of a former servant or employee; status or capacity; a person considered as exhibiting certain qualities; one of the persons represented in a drama or novel; hence, a part or role; *colloq.* a person of marked peculiarities.—**in char·ac·ter,** in conformity to one's normal situation or personality; *theater,* in a manner appropriate to the role portrayed in a performance; status or capacity.—**out of char·ac·ter,** at variance with one's usual characteristics or a dramatic role.—**char·ac·ter·less,** a.

char·ac·ter, kar'ik·tēr, v.t. To portray; describe.

char·ac·ter·is·tic, kar"ik·te·ris'tik, a. [Gr. *charakteristikos.*] Pertaining to, constituting, or indicating the character or peculiar quality; typical; distinctive.—**char·ac·-ter·is·ti·cal·ly,** adv.

char·ac·ter·is·tic, kar"ik·te·ris'tik, n. A distinguishing feature or quality; *math.* the integral part of a logarithm.

char·ac·ter·i·za·tion, *Brit.* **char·ac·-ter·i·sa·tion,** kar"ik·tēr·i·zā'shan, n. The act of characterizing; portrayal; description; often, the creation of fictitious characters.

char·ac·ter·ize, kar'ik·te·rīz", v.t.—*characterized, characterizing.* [Gr. *charakter-izein.*] To portray; describe the character or peculiar quality of; to mark or distinguish as a characteristic; be a characteristic of; to give character to.—**char·ac·ter·iz·er,** n.

cha·rade, sha·rād', *Brit.* sha·räd', n. [Fr.] A word or phrase depicted, usually by pantomime, in a guessing game; a thin pretense or make-believe, as: His interest in art was a mere *charade.* pl. the parlor game in which words or phrases are acted out, to be guessed within a specified time by the players.

char·coal, chär'kōl", n. [Origin uncertain; appar. a much older word than *char.*] The carbonaceous material obtained by the imperfect combustion of wood or other organic substances, utilized as a fuel and for artistic purposes; a very dark-gray color. *Art,* a charcoal, a drawing made with a pencil of charcoal.—**char·coal burn·er,** n. A person employed in the manufacture of charcoal by burning wood; a stove or other device in which charcoal is burned.

char·coal grill, n. A grill for outdoor use employing charcoal as fuel.—v.t. To cook steak, other meats, or fish over a charcoal fire.

chard, chärd, n. [Fr. *charde,* < L. *carduus,* a thistle or artichoke.] A kind of beet, *Beta bulgaris cicla,* with thick stalks and large tender green leaves which are used as a vegetable. Also called *Swiss chard.*

chare, chär, n., v. See CHAR.

charge, chärj, v.t.—*charged, charging.* [O.Fr. *chargier, charger* (Fr. *charger*), < M.L. *carricare,* < L. *carrus,* E. *car.*] To load or fill up to the required amount, as of gunpowder or electricity; to fill water or air with other matter in a state of diffusion or solution, as: The air was *charged* with pollen. To load or burden with emotion, as: The air was *charged* with excitement. To impose a task or responsibility on; to instruct or command authoritatively, as: The judge *charged* the jury. To accuse explicitly or formally, as: The police *charged* him with bribery. To impute as a fault, as: He *charged* the accident to low visibility. To register a debt or liability, as: The government *charged* the taxes against his estate. To impose or ask a price, as: He was *charged* one dollar. To defer payment until a bill is rendered by the creditor; to attack violently, as: The tanks *charged* the barricade.—*v.i.* To demand a payment; to make a *charge* to one's debit; to require payment for a service; to make a *charge*, as to attack; to issue a command; as, to *charge* a dog to halt.

charge, chärj, *n.* [O.Fr. Fr. *charge.*] A load or burden; the amount or quantity which an apparatus is intended to hold at one time; a quantity of explosive powder to be detonated at one time; as, a *charge* of dynamite; a duty or responsibility entrusted to one; as, to have *charge* of funds; the care, safekeeping, and support of another; as, a public *charge*; a parish or congregation committed to the care of a pastor; a command or official instruction, as: The jury receives its *charge* from the judge. An accusation or indictment; as, arrested on the *charge* of theft; the expense or cost of something; as, improvements made at one's personal *charge*; a sum or fixed price; as, a *charge* of admission; a monetary. burden; tax, lieu, or expense; as, a *charge* against an inheritance tax; a record of debit; as, a *charge* account; a liability to pay debits; as, to make a *charge* for expenses; an accumulation or store of force; as, a *charge* of memory; an impetuous onset or attack; as, a military *charge*. *Slang,* an intense feeling of amusement, as: The audience got a big *charge* out of the clowns. *Her.* a figure or device, a bearing.

charge·a·ble, chär′ja·bl, *a.* That may be charged; as, *chargeable* duty on imports; liable to be charged, as with a crime; qualified to become a public charge; financially burdensome.

charge ac·count, *n.* A credit arrangement whereby a customer may make immediate purchases and delay payment to the creditor until a later specified date.

charge-a-plate, chärj′a·plāt″, *n.* An embossed address plate used to identify a customer having a charge account; also called **charge plate.**

char·gé d'af·faires, shär·zhā′ da·fâr′, shär′zhā da·fâr′, *Fr.* shär·zhā dä·feR′, *n.* pl. **char·gés d'af·faires.** [Fr., lit. "charged with affairs."] A subordinate official left in charge of diplomatic business during the temporary absence of the ambassador or minister; a diplomatic representative accredited to a state to which a diplomat of higher rank is not appointed.

charge of quar·ters, *n.* A noncommissioned officer responsible during off-duty hours for the care and policing of a given area for a given period of time; the responsibility of this activity.

charg·er, chär′jer, *n.* One who or that which charges; a horse suitable for riding in battle; a war-horse; *elect.* an appliance for charging storage batteries.

charg·er, chär′jer, *n.* [M.E. *chargeour.*] *Archaic,* a large platter or shallow dish. Mark vi. 25, 28.

char·i·ly, châr′i·lē, *adv.* In a chary manner; carefully; sparingly.—**char·i·ness,** *n.*

char·i·ot, char′ē·ot, *n.* [O.Fr. Fr. *chariot,* < *char.* CAR.] A two-wheeled horse-drawn vehicle used by the ancients in war, racing, and processions; a stately car or carriage; a light four-wheeled pleasure carriage.

char·i·ot, char′ē·ot, *v.t.* To convey in a chariot.—*v.i.* To ride in or drive a chariot.

char·i·ot·eer, char″ē·o·tēr′, *n.* One who drives a chariot; (*cap.*) *astron.* the constellation Auriga.

cha·ris·ma, char·ism, ka·riz′ma, kar′iz·-um, *n.* pl. **cha·ris·ma·ta, char·isms.** [Gr. *charisma,* < *charizesthai,* show favor, < *charis,* grace.] *Theol.* a special gift or power divinely conferred, as the gift of prophecy. A personal aura or leadership quality endowing its possessor with the capacity for inspiring popular enthusiasm and support.

char·i·ta·ble, char′i·ta·bl, *a.* Pertaining to or characterized by charity; full of good will or tenderness; benevolent and kind; liberal in benefactions to the poor and in relieving them in distress; pertaining to almsgiving or relief to the poor; lenient in judging of others; not harsh; favorable.—**char·i·ta·ble·ness,** *n.* The quality of being charitable.—**char·i·ta·bly,** *adv.* In a charitable manner.

char·i·ty, char′i·tē, *n.* pl. **char·i·ties.** [O.Fr. *charite* (Fr. *charité*), < L. *caritas,* dearness, love, < *carus,* dear, loving.] Christian love; love for one's fellowmen; goodwill to others; leniency in judging others or their actions; almsgiving; the private or public relief of the poor; a charitable act or work; a charitable bequest, foundation, or institution.

cha·riv·a·ri, sha·riv″a·rē′, shiv″a·rē′, shä″ri·vä′rē, *n.* [Fr. origin obscure.] A mock serenade or concert of discordant noises made with kettles, pans, or horns, being addressed in jest to a newly married couple. Also **chiv·a·ree, shiv·a·ree.**

char·kha, char·ka, chär′ka, *n.* A spinning wheel for cotton used chiefly in homes in India and the East Indies.

char·la·tan, shär′la·tan, *n.* [Fr. *charlatan,* < It. *ciarlatano,* < *ciarlare,* chatter.] One who pretends to more knowledge or skill than he possesses, esp. in medicine; a quack; a pretentious impostor.—**char·la·tan·ic,** shär″la·tan′ik, *a.*—**char·la·tan·ism,** *n.* The practices of a charlatan. Also **char·la·tan·ry.**

Charles's Wain, *n.* [O.E. *Carles waen,* Carl's wagon; with reference to Charlemagne.] *Astron.* the seven brightest stars in the constellation Ursa Major, bearing a resemblance to a wain or wagon; the Big Dipper.

Charles·ton, chärlz′ton, chärl′ston, *n.* A vigorous ballroom dance popular in the jazz era of the 1920's and named after Charleston, S.C.

char·ley horse, char·lie horse, *n.* [< *Charley, Charlie,* for *Charles,* man's name.] *Slang,* cramping pain in the muscle of an arm or leg, usually caused by overexertion in athletics.

Char·lie, chär′lē, *n.* A communications code word to designate the letter C.

char·lock, chär lok, *n.* [O.E. cerlic.] The wild mustard, *Brassica arvensis,* a yellow flowering weed, troublesome in grainfields; any of various other brassicaceous plants, as the herb *Raphanus raphanistrum,* jointed charlock.

char·lotte, shär′lot, *n.* [Fr. < *Charlotte,* woman's name.] A sweet dish, hot or cold, of many varieties, commonly made by lining a mold with cake or bread and filling with fruit or a cream, custard, or gelatin preparation.—**char·lotte russe,** shär′lot rös′. [Fr. "Russian charlotte."] A mold of sponge cake filled with whipped cream.

charm, chärm, *n.* [Fr. *charme,* a charm, an enchantment, < L. *carmen,* a song, a verse, a charm.] An utterance of words believed to have magic powers; an amulet; a trinket worn on a bracelet or watch-chain; a quality which exerts an irresistible power to please and attract; fascination; attraction; allurement.

charm, chärm, *v.t.* To fascinate; to enchant; to give exquisite pleasure to; to subdue, attract, or appease through the use of

personal charm; to control by incantation or supernatural influence; to make invulnerable with charms.—*v.i.* To be pleasing; to act as a charm or spell.

charm·er, chär′mer, *n.* One who charms, fascinates, enchants, allures, or attracts.

char·meuse, shär·möz′, *Fr.* shär·mœz′, *n.* [Formerly a trademark < Fr. fem. of *charmeur,* one who charms.] A soft, flexible variety of satin.

char·nel, chär′nel, *a.* [Fr. *charnel,* O.Fr. *carnel,* carnal, < L. *carnalis,* from *caro, carnis,* flesh.] Containing dead bodies; deathlike.—*n.* A place, sometimes under or near a church, where dead bodies or the bones of the dead are deposited. Also **char·nel house.**

Char·on, kâr′on, kar′on, *n.* [L. < Gr. *Charon.*] *Class. mythol.* the ferryman who conveyed the souls of the dead across the river Styx.

char·qui, chär′kē, *n.* [The Chilian name, of which the term *jerked* beef is a corruption.] Jerked beef; beef cut into strips of about an inch thick and dried by exposure to the sun.—**char·quid,** *a.*

charr, chär, *n.* pl. **charrs.** A kind of fish, the char.

chart, chärt, *n.* [L. *charta,* paper, a leaf of paper. *Card* is the same word.] A sheet of any kind on which information is exhibited in a methodical or tabulated form; specifically, a marine map, indicating the coasts, islands, rocks, and soundings, to regulate the courses of ships; a graph.

chart, chärt, *v.t.* To delineate, as on a chart; to map out; to plan.

char·ta·ceous, kär·tā′shus, *a. Bot.* papery, resembling paper: applied to the paper-like texture of leaves or bark.

char·ter, chär′ter, *n.* [O.Fr. *chartre,* < L. *chartarius,* < *charta,* paper.] A writing given as evidence of a grant or contract; any deed or instrument executed with form and solemnity bestowing or granting powers, rights, and privileges; privilege; immunity; exemption.

char·ter, chär′ter, *v.t.* To hire, as a ship, by charter or contract; to establish; to grant; to privilege.

char·tered ac·count·ant, *n. Brit.* A member of the institute of accountants in Great Britain, holding a Royal Charter. *Abbr.* C.A.

char·tered bank, *n. Canada,* a privately owned bank chartered by Parliament and operating within the provisions of the Bank Act.

Chart·ism, chär′tiz·um, *n.* The principles or movement of a party of political reformers, chiefly working-men, active in England from 1838 to 1848: so called from the "People's Charter," the document which contained their principles and demands.—**Chart·ist,** *n.*

char·tist, chär′tist, *n.* One who plots stock market prices on a chart and speculates on basis of the information; a cartographer.

char·tog·ra·pher, kär·tog′ra·fer, *n.* See *cartographer.*

char·tog·ra·phy, kär·tog′ra·fē, *n.*—**char·to·gra·phic,** kär·to·graf′ik, *a.* See *cartography.*

Char·treuse, shär·tröz′, *Fr.* shär·trœz′, *n.* [Fr.] A Carthusian monastery; *l.c.* an aromatic liqueur, green, yellow, or white, made by the Carthusian monks, orig. at the monastery of La Grande Chartreuse, near Grenoble, France; a clear, light green color with a yellowish tinge.

char·tu·lary, kär′chu·ler″ē, *n.* See *cartulary.*

char·wom·an, chär′wum″an, *n.* [< O.E. *cerr, cyrr,* a turn, time, occasion; < *cerran, cyrran,* to turn = D. *keeren,* G. *kehren,* turn, move, or change.] A woman employed by the day on odd jobs about a house.

char·y, châr′ē, *a.*—*charier*, *chariest*. [O.E. *cearig*, full of care, sad, < *cearu*, *caru*, care.] Careful; cautious; frugal; sparing: with *of* before an object.

Cha·ryb·dis, ka·rib′dis, *n.* [L. < Gr.] A whirlpool in the Strait of Messina, near the south coast of Italy, represented in Greek mythology as a female monster, daughter of Gaea and Poseidon. See *Scylla.*

chase, chās, *v.t.*—*chased*, *chasing.* [O.Fr. *chacier*, Fr. *chasser*, chase, = *cachier*, E. *catch.*] To pursue with intent to capture or kill, as game; hunt; to pursue in order to seize or overtake; follow persistently; to drive by pursuing; put to flight.—*v.i.* To hunt; follow in pursuit; *colloq.* run or hasten.—**go chase your·self**, *imper.*, *slang*, an order to leave; go away; beat it; get lost.

chase, chās, *n.* [O.Fr. *chace*, Fr. *chasse.*] The act of chasing; pursuit; esp. the occupation or sport of hunting wild animals, "the chase"; an object of pursuit, as a hunted animal; a body of persons pursuing game; *Brit.* an unenclosed tract of privately owned land reserved for animals to be hunted as game.

chase, chās, *v.t.*—*chased*, *chasing.* [Appar. < *enchase.*] To ornament, as metal, by engraving or embossing; to cut in making a screw.

chase, chās, *n.* [Fr. *châsse*, O.Fr. *chasse*, *casse.*] A rectangular iron frame in which composed type to print from or make plates from is secured; a lengthened hollow; a groove, furrow, or trench; the bore of a gun, or the part containing the bore.

chas·er, chā′sèr, *n.* One who or that which chases metal; a tool used in cutting screw-threads.—**chas·ing**, *n.* The act or work of one who chases metal; the design executed.

chas·er, chā′sèr, *n.* A German pursuit plane of World War II; a ship's gun at the bow or stern; *colloq.* a mild beverage, as water, taken after a drink of liquor.

chasm, kaz′um, *n.* [Gr. *chasma*, < root *cha*, as in *chaos.*] A gaping or yawning opening, as in the earth; an abyss; a wide and deep cleft; a fissure; a void space; a rift in a personal relationship; a wide difference of views or outlook.—**chasm·y**, **chas·mal**, **chas·mic**, **chasmed**, *a.*

chas·seur, sha·sųr′, *Fr.* shä·sœ̇r′, *n.* [Fr. a huntsman.] One of a body of French soldiers trained for rapid movement.

chas·sis, shas′ē, shas′is, chas′ē, *n.* [Fr.] The framework which supports the body of an automobile; the frame and working parts, as contrasted with the body or cabinet, as a television *chassis*; *slang*, the human body, esp. the female torso.

chaste, chāst, *a.* [Fr. *chaste*, < L. *castus*, chaste.] Not having indulged in premarital or extramarital sexual intercourse; virtuous; free from obscenity or impurity in thought and language; as applied to literary style, free from barbarous words and phrases, affected or extravagant expressions, or the like; in art, free from excessive ornament or affectation, not gaudy.—**chaste·ly**, *adv.*

chas·ten, chā′san, *v.t.* [Earlier *chasten*, M.E. *chasten*, *chastien*, < O.Fr. *chastier*, (Fr. *châtier*), < L. *castigare.* CASTIGATE.] To inflict suffering upon for purposes of moral improvement; discipline or subdue, as by adversity; to restrain, moderate, or temper; make chaste in style; to remove excessive ornamentation.—**chas·ten·er**, *n.*

chas·tise, chas·tīz′, *v.t.*—*chastised*, *chastising.* [Same word as *chasten*, but with a different verbal termination; O.E. *chastie*, *chasty*, < O.Fr. *chastier.* CHASTEN.] To punish by physical means, such as flogging; to castigate.—**chas·tise·ment**, chas′tiz-·ment, chas·tiz′ment, *n.*—**chas·tis·er**, *n.*

chas·ti·ty, chas′ti·tē, *n.* The quality of being chaste.

chas·u·ble, chaz′ū·bl, chaz′u·bl, chas′ū·bl, chas′u·bl, *n.* [O.Fr. Fr. *chasuble*, < M.L. *casubula*, for *casula*, cloak, dim. of L. *casa*, house.] *Eccles.* a sleeveless outer vestment worn by the celebrant at mass or the Eucharist, often richly decorated.

chat, chat, *v.i.*—*chatted*, *chatting.* [An abbreviated form of *chatter.*] To talk casually or in a familiar manner.

chat, chat, *n.* Familiar conversation; also, any of several birds, as *Icteria virens*, "yellow-breasted chat," of the U.S., so-called from their chattering cries.

châ·teau, shä·tō′, *n.* pl. **châ·teaus**, **châ·-teaux**, shä·tōz, *Fr.* shä·tō′. [Fr. *château*, O.Fr. *chastel*, a castle, < L. *castellum.* CASTLE.] A French castle; a country estate; a vineyard estate in France.

chat·e·lain, shat′a·lān″, *Fr.* shät·a·laN′, *n.* The keeper of a castle; castellan.

chat·e·laine, shat′a·lān, *Fr.* shät·a·len′, *n.* [Fr. *chatelaine*, fem. of *chatelain.*] The mistress of a castle; a device for holding keys, sewing implements, and trinkets; a lapel pin with a draped chain.

cha·toy·ant, sha·toi′ant, *a.* [Fr., pp. of *chatoyer*, to change luster like the eye of a cat, < *chat*, a cat.] Having a changeable, undulating luster or color, like that of a cat's eye in the dark.—**cha·toy·ance**, **cha·toy·ancy**, *n.*

cha·toy·ant, sha·toi′ant, *n.* Any gem, such as the cat's-eye, which is cut in a cabochon and reflects a single band of light.

chat·tel, chat′el, *n.* [O.Fr. *chatel*, also *catel.* CATTLE.] A movable possession; any article of property other than real estate, or a freehold.

chat·tel mort·gage, *n.* A conditional conveyance, subject to repayment of a loan, of personal property as distinct from real property.

chat·ter, chat′er, *v.i.* [M.E.; imit.] To utter a succession of quick, inarticulate speech-like sounds, as a magpie or a monkey; to talk rapidly and to little purpose; prate; to make a rapid clicking noise by striking together, as the teeth from cold; to vibrate in cutting, as a tool, so as to form a series of nicks or notches.—*v.t.* To utter rapidly or idly; to cause to chatter.—**chat·ter**, *n.* The act or sound of chattering; idle conversation.

chat·ter·box, chat′er·boks″, *n.* One who chatters or talks incessantly.

chat·ter·er, chat′ér·er, *n.* The popular name for those passerine birds possessing an incessant speech-like cry; one who chatters.

chat·ter mark, *n.* A mark left by a tool that chatters; *geol.* one of a series of irregular gouges made on surfaces over which a glacier passes, by the abrasion of rock fragments in the lower portion of the ice.

chat·ty, chat′ē, *a.*—*chattier*, *chattiest.* Given to or full of chat or familiar talk; conversational; as, a *chatty* woman; a *chatty* writing style.—**chat·ti·ness**, *n.*—**chat·ti·ly**, *adv.*

Chau·ce·ri·an, cha·sēr′ē·an, *a.* Of, pertaining to, or characteristic of the 14th century English poet Geoffrey Chaucer, his writings, or the Middle English dialect in which he wrote.—*n.* A specialist in Chaucerian literature.

Chau·cer·i·an stan·za, *n.* See *rhyme royal.*

chauf·feur, shō′fèr, shō·fųr′, *n.* [Fr. stoker, < *chauffer*, heat. CHAFE.] One who is hired to drive an automobile.

chauf·feur, shō′fèr, shō·fųr′, *v.i.* To hold a position as chauffeur, as: He *chauffeured* to earn extra money.—*v.t.* To drive, as an automobile used for transportation of another person.

chaus·sure, shō·syr′, *n.* [Fr. < *chausser*, to shoe, < L. *calceare.* CALCEATE.] A foot-covering, as a shoe, boot, or slipper.

Chau·tau·qua, sha·tạ′kwa, *a.* Noting or pertaining to Chautauqua, New York, or the educational system which originated there in the 19th century consisting of summer lectures, home study, and concerts; (*l.c.*) pertaining to any similar program.—*n.*—**chau·tau·quan**, *n.* a Chautauqua lecturer or entertainer.—**Chau·tau·quan**, *a.*

chau·vin, shō′vin″, *n.* [From N. *Chauvin*, an enthusiastic military adherent of Napoleon.] Anyone possessed by an absurdly exaggerated enthusiasm for a cause, esp. bellicose patriotism or military zeal.—**chau·vin·ism**, *n.* The sentiments of a chauvin; absurdly exaggerated patriotism, military zeal, or enthusiasm for a cause.—**chau·vin·ist**, *n.*—**chau·vin·is·tic**, *a.*

chaw, chạ, *v.t. Colloq.* to chew, esp. tobacco. —*n. Colloq.* a chew.

cheap, chēp, *a.* [< O.E. *cēap* "bargain, market, trade."] Priced low; costing little labor or trouble to obtain; shoddy, inferior; as, *cheap* goods; yielding little satisfaction; of money, obtainable at a low interest rate; stingy; *Brit.* offered at a reduced price; *slang*, unrefined; reputedly promiscuous.— **cheap**, **cheap·ly**, *adv.*—**cheap·ness**, *n.*

cheap·en, chē′pen, *v.t.* To make cheap, lower the price of, lower the value or estimation of; belittle; vulgarize.—*v.i.* To become cheap.—**cheap·en·er**, *n.*

cheap·skate, chēp′skāt″, *n. Colloq.* a stingy person; a person who avoids paying his share of expenses.

cheat, chēt, *v.t.* [Abbrev. of *escheat*, to act like an escheater, who held an office giving opportunities of fraud. ESCHEAT.] To deceive and defraud; to trick; as, to *cheat* a person *of* or *out* of something; to mislead.— *v.i.* To act dishonestly; to practice fraud or trickery; *slang*, to be unfaithful to one's mate.

cheat, chēt, *n.* A deception; a person who cheats; the fraudulent obtaining of someone else's property. One of several grasses, esp. chess, *Bromus secalinus.*

check, *Brit.* **cheque**, chek, *interj.*, *n.* [Fr. *échec*, O.Fr. *eschec*, a check, a check at chess, < Pers. *shāh*, king, the chief piece at chess.] *Chess*, *interj.* warning that opponent's king is vulnerable to direct attack; *colloq.* all right; certainly; I understand you; I will accomplish it.—*n.* The act of suddenly stopping or restraining; a hindrance; an examination or control to evaluate honesty, accuracy, or quality of performance; a measure to prevent errors or dishonesty; a written order for money drawn on a bank; a bill for food or beverages in a restaurant; a mark put against names or items on going over a list; a ticket for articles or baggage that has been checked; a pattern on cloth resembling the squares of a chessboard; one of those squares; a small crack in paint. *Hockey*, a halt by a player in the progress of an opposing player.

check, chek, *v.t.* To stop or moderate the motion of; to restrain in action; to hinder; to investigate or inquire into; to examine for correctness, safety, or completeness; to leave or accept, as an item, temporarily in a checkroom; to deliver, as baggage, for shipment; to designate with a check mark to indicate an item has been looked over; to decorate with a pattern of squares.—*v.i.* To withdraw money from a checking account; to agree detail for detail. *Poker*, to give up the privilege of starting the betting in a round. *Chess*, to place an opponent's king under direct attack. *Hunting*, to stop dogs when they lose the scent. *Hockey*, to halt the progress of the player carrying the puck.

check·book, chek′bụk″, *n.* A book containing blank bank checks.

check·er, *Brit.* **cheq·uer,** chek'ẽr, *n.* [O.Fr. *eschequier,* Mod.Fr. *echiquier,* a chessboard, an echequer, < O.Fr. *eschecs,* chess.] A small red or black circular piece made of plastic or wood manipulated by the players in a checkers game; one of the divisions of a pattern that consists of squares; the pattern itself. *Pl. but sing. in constr.* A game played by two people, each moving his twelve men on a checkerboard; *Brit.* draughts.

check·er, chek'ẽr, *v.t.* To mark with little squares, like a chessboard, by lines or stripes of different colors; to mark with different colors; *fig.* to variegate with different qualities, scenes, or events; to diversify; to impart variety to; as, events that *checker* one's career.

check·er, chek'ẽr, *n.* A person or object that checks; a person who checks coats and hats or baggage; someone who works as a cashier in a supermarket or a cafeteria.

check·er·ber·ry, chek'ẽr·ber"ē, *n.* pl. **check·er·ber·ries.** The red fruit of the American wintergreen, *Gaultheria procumbens;* the plant itself; the partridgeberry, *Mitchella repens.*

check·er·bloom, chek'ẽr·blôm", *n.* A mallow; an herb with purple flowers, *Sidalcea malvaeflora,* which grows in western U.S.

check·er·board, *Brit.* **cheq·uer·board,** chek'ẽr·bôrd", chek'ẽr·bạrd", *n.* A board with sixty-four squares of two alternating colors on which checkers, chess, or draughts are played.

check·ing ac·count, *n.* A bank account established by a depositor for the specified purpose of drawing checks against it.

check list, *n.* An alphabetical or systematic list of names of persons or things, intended for purposes of reference, registration, comparison, verification or identification; as, a *check list* of the birds of a region; a *check list* of voters.

check·mate, chek'māt", *n.* [Pers. *shāh māt,* the king is dead (*shāh,* the king, *māt,* he is dead).] *Chess,* the position of a king when he is in check and cannot release himself, which brings the game to a close; the act of putting the king in this position; hence, defeat.

check·mate, chek'māt", *v.t.—checkmated, checkmating.* To put in check, as an opponent's king in chess playing, so that he cannot be released; hence, to defeat; to thwart; to frustrate.—*interj. Chess,* a word used by a player to tell his opponent that he has trapped his king and won the game.

check·off, chek'ạf", chek'of", *n.* A system by which the employer collects union dues by deducting them from union members' pay.

check·out, chek'out", *n.* A test of readiness for use; instruction or training given to enable one to operate a machine, as an aircraft. The process of itemizing, charging, and bundling purchases for a customer, as at a supermarket; the counter where the check-out is performed; also **check-out count·er.** The person who performs the check-out; also *checker.*

check out, *v.i.* To test for readiness for use; to instruct in the operation of a machine; to itemize, charge, and bundle customer's purchases; to present one's selections to a checker; to settle one's bill at a hotel or hospital and depart.—**check-out time,** *n.* The time established before which one must have vacated a hotel or hospital room in order not to be billed for another day.—*v.t.* To test or instruct; to requisition in accordance with established regulations, as: She *checked out* three books at the library.

check·point, chek'point", *n.* A place where traffic is stopped for inspection and clearance; a known geographical location used by a flier to determine his position.

check·rein, chek'rān", *n.* A short rein attached to the saddle of a harness to prevent a horse from lowering its head; a short rein joining the bit of one of a span or pair of horses to the driving rein of the other.

check·room, chek'rôm", chek'rụm", *n.* A room where clothing, luggage, or packages are left for safekeeping for a limited time.

check·row, chek'rō", *n.* One of a number of rows of trees or plants, esp. corn, in which adjacent trees or plants are placed at a distance apart equal to the distance between adjacent rows, the result being two series of rows intersecting at right angles, facilitating cultivation between the rows.—**check·row,** *v.t.* To plant in checkrows; plant, as corn, with a checkrower.—**check·row·er,** *n.* An attachment fitted to a corn planter to cause the seed to drop at the regular intervals requisite to form checkrows.

checks and bal·anc·es, *n.* A system used in the U.S. federal government to insure that power is shared equally by the executive, legislative, and judicial branches: each branch can check the power of either of the others by amending or voiding certain of their acts.

check·up, chek'up", *n.* An examination or test, as of an auto; a physical examination.

check valve, *n.* A one-way valve that automatically prevents a reverse flow of fluid.

Ched·dar, ched'ẽr, *n.* [From the village of Cheddar in Somersetshire, England, where this cheese was originally made.] Any of several smooth, firm-textured standard cheeses varying in taste from pungent to mild, and in color from dark yellow to white. Also **Ched·dar cheese.**

che·der, chä'dẽr, *n.* See *heder.*

chee·cha·ko, chē·chä'kō, *n. Canada,* a newcomer or tenderfoot.

cheek, chēk, *n.* [O.E. *cēace* = D. *kaak.*] Either side of the face below the eye and above the lower jawbone; something resembling the human cheek in form or position, as either of two parts forming corresponding sides of anything, as the *cheeks* of a vise, a lathe, or a door. *Slang,* impudence or effrontery; a buttock.—**cheek by jowl,** side by side; in close intimacy.

cheek·bone, chēk'bōn", *n.* Bone or bony prominence below the outer angle of the eye; the zygomatic bone.

cheek·y, chē'kē, *a.—cheekier, cheekiest. Slang,* bold; impudent; insolent.—**cheek·i·ly,** *adv.*—**cheek·i·ness,** *n.*

cheep, chēp, *v.i., v.t.* [Imitative.] To make a small, shrill noise, as a small or young bird; to chirp; to squeak.—*n.* A chirp; a squeak.

cheer, chēr, *n.* [O.E. *chere,* face, look, mien, < O.Fr. *chere, chiere,* face, countenance, < L.L. *cara,* the face < Gr. *kara,* the head.] Gaiety or gladness of feeling or spirits; something which promotes good spirits; as, a message of *cheer;* food and other provisions for a feast; a shout of acclamation, as from an audience expressing approval; a shout of encouragement or acclamation in a prescribed form, as a chant or poem used by spectators at an athletic game.

cheer, chēr, *v.t.* To gladden; to encourage, comfort, or make hopeful, as: Her presence *cheered* him in his dark moment. To express confidence or approval of with shouts or chants, often with *on;* as, to *cheer* the team *on;* to express approval or give recognition of by shouting.—*v.i.* To grow cheerful or joyous, often used with *up;* to utter a cheer or shout of acclamation or joy. —**cheer·ly,** chēr'lē, *adv.* Cheerily, heartily.

cheer·ful, chēr'fụl, *a.* Having good spirits; promoting or causing cheerfulness, as: Bright pictures make a room *cheerful.* Willing; as, *cheerful* cooperation.—**cheer·ful·ly,** *adv.*—**cheer·ful·ness,** *n.*

cheer·i·o, chēr'ē·ō", chēr"ē·ō', *interj., n.* pl. **cheer·i·os.** *Brit.* an expression used at parting, similar to good-bye; sometimes a greeting or expression used as a toast. Also **cheer·o.**

cheer·lead·er, chēr'lē"dẽr, *n.* A person who initiates and directs, frequently with prescribed motions and gymnastic routines, the formalized cheers by spectators at athletic events or school rallies.—**cheer·lead·ing,** *n.*

cheer·less, chēr'lis, *a.* Without joy, gladness, or comfort; gloomy; destitute of anything to enliven or animate the spirits.—**cheer·less·ly,** *adv.*—**cheer·less·ness,** *n.*

cheer·y, chēr'ē, *a.—cheerier, cheeriest.* Showing cheerfulness or good spirits; blithe; gay; sprightly; promoting cheerfulness.—**cheer·i·ly,** chēr'i·lē, *adv.* In a cheery manner.—**cheer·i·ness,** *n.*

cheese, chēz, *n.* [O.E. *cēse,* < L. *caseus.*] The curd of milk separated from the whey and prepared in many varieties as food; a mass or cake of this substance of definite shape or size; something of similar shape or consistency.

cheese·burg·er, chēz'bur"gẽr, *n.* A hamburger with a slice of cheese melted on top of the meat.

cheese cake, *n.* A rich cake- or pie-shaped, custardlike dessert containing cottage and/or cream cheese, sugar, and eggs.

cheese·cake, chēz'kāk", *n. Slang,* photographs featuring the legs and body of an attractive girl.

cheese·cloth, chēz'klạth", chēz'kloth", *n.* A coarse, lightweight cotton fabric of open texture, orig. used for wrapping cheeses.

cheese·par·ing, chēz'pâr"ing, *n.* The cheese rind, or a bit of it; *fig.* niggardly economy; something of little or no value.—*a.* Parsimonious.

chees·y, chē'zē, *a.—cheesier, cheesiest.* Of or like cheese; *slang,* of inferior material or poor quality; cheap.—**chees·i·ness,** *n.*

chee·tah, *Brit.* **che·tah,** chē'ta, *n.* [Hind. *chītā.*] *Acinonyx jubatus,* a cat of southern Asia and Africa, which resembles the leopard but has certain doglike characteristics, and which is the fastest animal in the world, often trained for hunting antelope or similar swift game.

chef, shef, *n.* [Fr. CHIEF.] A male head cook who is in charge of a kitchen; a cook.

chef-d'œu·vre, she·dœ'vRa, *n.,* pl. **chefs-d'œu·vre.** [Fr., "chief of work."] A masterpiece; a fine work of literature, art, or music.

che·la, kē'la, *n.* pl. **che·lae,** kē'lē. [Gr. *chēlē,* a claw.] One of the prehensile claws possessed by certain arachnids and crustaceans, as the crab and lobster.

che·late, kē'lāt, *a.* Furnished with chelae. Also **che·lif·er·ous.**—**che·late,** *n. Chem.* compound in which a central metallic ion is joined by ordinary or coordinate bonds to two or more nonmetallic atoms of the same molecule, so that one or more heterocyclic rings are formed with the central ion as part of each ring.—**che·li·form,** kē'li·fạrm, *a.* Having the form of a chela or prehensile claw.

che·late, kē'lāt, *v.t., v.i.—chelated, chelating. Chem.* to join to form a chelate structure.

Chel·le·an, Chel·li·an, shel'ē·an, *a.* Relating to Chelles, France, where relics of an early lower Paleolithic culture were unearthed; characterized by bifacial stone axes.

che·lo·ni·an, ki·lō'nē·an, *a.* [Gr. *chelōnē,* a tortoise.] Designating animals of the tortoise family, order *Chelonia.*—*n.* A tortoise or turtle.

chem·i·cal, kem'i·kal, *n.* A substance produced by or used in a chemical process.

chem·i·cal, kem'i·kal, *a.* Of, pertaining to, or concerned with the science or processes of

chemistry.— **chem·ic**, kem′ik, *a.*—**chem·-
i·cal·ly**, *adv.*

chem·i·cal en·gi·neer·ing, *n.* A branch of
chemistry that deals with the industrial uses
of chemistry.

chem·i·cal war·fare, *n.* Warfare using asphyxiating, poisonous, and corrosive gases
and oil flames.

chem·i·lum·i·nes·cence, kem″i·lŏo′mi·-
nes′ans, *n. Chem.* light produced during
chemical reactions at low temperatures.

che·min de fer, she·man′de·fâr, *Fr.*
she·mand·a·fer′, *n.* [Fr. lit. railroad.] A
card game similar to baccarat.

che·mise, she·mēz′, *n.* [Fr., < L.L.
camisia, shirt.] A woman's loose-fitting,
shirtlike undergarment; a short slip.

chem·ism, kem′iz·um, *n.* Chemical action.

chem·i·sorp·tion, kem″ē·sorp′shan, *n.*
Adsorption during a reaction between
chemicals.—**chem·i·sorb**, kem″i·sarb″,
kem′i·zarb″, *v.t.* To take in by chemisorption.

chem·ist, kem′ist, *n.* [For *alchemist*.] *Obs.*
an alchemist. One versed in chemistry or
professionally engaged in chemical operations; *Brit.* a druggist.

chem·is·try, kem′i·strē, *n. pl.* **chem·is·-
tries**. The science that investigates the
composition and interaction of existing compounds and elements and studies synthesizing of natural and artificial compounds.

che·mo·au·to·tro·phic, kem″ō·a″to·-
trof′ ik, *a. Biol.* being an autotrophic organism which oxidizes energy from an inorganic
compound.—**che·mo·au·to·tro·phi·cal·-
ly**, *adv.*—**che·mo·au·tot·ro·phy**, *n.*

chem·o·pro·phy·lax·is, kem″ō·prō″fa·-
lak′sis, kem″ō·prof″a·lak′sis, kē″mō·prō″-
fa·lak′sis, kē″mō·prof″a·lak′sis, *n. Med.* the
prevention of disease by chemical drugs or
agents.—**chem·o·pro·phy·lac·tic**, *a.*

chem·o·re·cep·tion, kem″ō·ri·sep′shan,
kē″mō·ri·sep′shan, *n. Biol.* the physiological response of a sense organ to the
reception of chemical stimuli.—**chem·o·-
re·cep·tor**, *n.*

chem·os·mo·sis, kem″oz·mō′sis, kem″os·-
mō′sis, kē″moz·mō′sis, kē″mos·mō′sis, *n.*
Chemical action between substances occurring through an intervening membrane.—
chem·os·mot·ic, *a.*

chem·o·sphere, kem′o·sfēr″, kē″mo·sfēr″,
n. A layer of atmosphere, generally considered as starting 20 miles above the
earth's surface and extending to 50 miles,
characterized by marked photochemical
activity.

chem·o·syn·the·sis, kem″o·sin′thi·sis,
kē″mo·sin′thi·sis, *n.* The process by which
organic compounds are formed from
inorganic components by energy derived
from chemical reactions.

chem·o·tax·is, kem″o·tak′sis, kē″mo·tak′-
sis, *n. Biol.* the movement of a cell or
organism toward or away from a chemical
stimulus.—**chem·o·tac·tic**, *a.*—**che·mo·-
tac·ti·cal·ly**, *adv.*

chem·o·ther·a·py, kem″o·ther′a·pē, kē″-
mo·ther′a·pē, *n. Med.* treatment of disease
with chemicals. Also **chem·o·ther·a·peu·-
tics**.—**chem·o·ther·a·peu·tic**, *a.*

che·mot·ro·pism, ki·mo′tro·piz″um, *n.*
Biol. the turning or bending of a plant or
other organism toward or away from a
chemical stimulus; *zool.* sometimes used
interchangeably with *chemotaxis*.

chem·ur·gy, kem′u·jē, *n.* [< *chemistry* and
-*ergos*, working.] A branch of applied
chemistry that utilizes organic raw materials
esp. farm products, for industry.—**chem·-
ur·gic, chem·ur·gi·cal**, *a.*

che·nille, she·nēl′, *n.* [Fr., a caterpillar.]
A tufted cord or yarn of wool, cotton, silk, or
rayon used in embroidery or fringes; a pile-
face fabric made with a filling of such yarn,
used for curtains, rugs, and bedspreads.

che·no·pod, kē′no·pod″, ken′o·pod″, *n.*
[N.L. *Chenopodium*, < Gr. *chēn*, goose, and
poys, pod-, foot.] Any plant of the genus
Chenopodium or the goosefoot family, as
Chenopodiaceæ.—**che·no·po·di·a·ceous**, *a.*
Belonging to the *Chenopodiaceæ*, or goosefoot
family of plants, which includes the beet,
mangelwurzel, spinach, orach, and many
species peculiar to saline, alkaline, or
desert regions.

cheque, chek, *n.* British preferred form of
check in the sense of a written order
directing a bank to pay money.

cheq·uer, chek′ĕr, *n. pl.* **cheq·uers**. *Brit.*
See *checker*.

cher·ish, cher′ish, *v.t.* [O.Fr. *cherir,
cherissant* (Fr. *chérir*), to hold dear, < *cher,*
L. *carus*, dear, whence also *caress*.] To hold
as dear; to treat with tenderness and
affection; to nurture, foster, or harbor
lovingly; to encourage or harbor in the
mind, as ideas, hopes, or ideals.—**cher·ish·-
ing·ly**, *adv.* In an affectionate or cherishing
manner.

cher·no·zem, cher′no·zem″, *n.* [Russ. black
earth.] A very black soil, rich in humus and
carbonates, found in cool or temperate
climates with a somewhat low humidity.

Cher·o·kee, cher′o·kē″, cher″o·kē′, *n.* A
North American Indian tribe of Iroquoian
people who originally lived in the southern
Alleghenies, but now are centered in
Oklahoma; a member of this people; the
language of the Cherokee people.

Cher·o·kee rose, *n.* A smooth-stemmed,
climbing white rose, *Rosa laevigata*,
originally found in China, but now cultivated in southern U.S.

che·root, she·rŏot′, *n.* [Tamil *curuṭṭu*, a
roll.] A cigar which has both ends cut off
square.

cher·ry, cher′ē, *n. pl.* **cher·ries**. [O.E.
cheri, chiri, < Fr. *cerise,* L. *cerasus,* < Gr.
kerasos, a cherry.] The fruit produced by
any of numerous trees and shrubs, genus
Prunus, of the rose family, consisting of a
smooth-skinned, pulpy drupe containing a
single, smooth seed; the tree itself; the
wood of this tree; any of various fruits or
plants similar to the cherry, as cherry
tomato.—*a.* Bright red or cerise in color.

cher·ry lau·rel, *n.* An evergreen shrub
bearing clusters of white blossoms and
black shiny fruit: *Prunus caroliniana*,
cultivated in southeastern U.S.; *Prunus
laurocerasus*, cultivated in Europe.

cher·ry plum, *n.* A kind of Asiatic plum,
Prunus cerasifera, used in Europe as a
budding stock for domestic varieties.

cher·ry·stone, cher′ē·stōn, *n.* A small
quahog or thick-shelled clam; the pit or
seed of the cherry fruit.

cher·so·nese, kur′so·nēz″, *n.* [Gr. *chers-
onēsos—chersos,* land, and *nēsos,* an isle.] A
peninsula.

chert, churt, *n.* [Probably Celtic; comp. Ir.
ceart, a pebble.] *Mineral.* a compact
siliceous rock composed of chalcedonic or
opaline silica, either alone or in combination; *geol.* insoluble residue composed
mainly of cryptocrystalline quartz or
chalcedony silica.—**cher·ty**, *a.* Like chert
rock or *flint*, which is a variety of chert.

cher·ub, cher′ub, *n. pl.* **cher·ubs;** Hebrew
pl. **cher·u·bim**, cher′ub·im. [Heb. *kerūbh*.]
A winged, celestial figure regarded as a
guardian of a sacred place and a servant of
God; *pl.* the second highest order of
angels, generally represented as beautiful,
winged children. A beautiful or innocent
person, esp. a child; a person having an
innocent face, generally chubby and rosy.—
che·ru·bic, che·rŏob′ik, *a.* Pertaining to or
resembling cherubs; angelic.

cher·vil, chur′vil, *n.* [O.E. *cerfille,* < L.
chærophyllum, < Gr. *chairephyllon—chairō,*
to rejoice, and *phyllon,* leaf, < their

agreeable odor.] A garden or pot herb,
Anthriscus cerefolium, of the parsley family,
having aromatic leaves used in soups and
salads; any of several plants of the same
genus, generally wild.

Chesh·ire cat, *n.* A fictitious cat with a
broad, toothy grin created by Lewis
Carroll in *Alice's Adventures in Wonderland.*—**grin like a Chesh·ire cat**, to smile
enigmatically.

Chesh·ire cheese, *n.* [From *Cheshire*,
county in western England.] A hard, deep-
colored cheese, similar to cheddar, made
from unskimmed milk.

chess, ches, *n.* [O.Fr. *esches, eschecs,* pl.
CHECK.] A game in which each of two
players use 16 pieces or *chessmen* to move
offensively and defensively across a checkerboard of 64 squares with the object of
immobilizing the opponent's prize chessman, the king, in a maneuver called
checkmate.—**chess·board**, *n.*—**chess·man**,
n. pl. **chess·men**. One of the pieces used in
the game of chess.

chess, ches, *n. pl.* **chess, chess·es**. [Origin
uncertain.] One of the transverse parallel
planks which form the roadbed of a
pontoon bridge.

chest, chest. *n.* That part of the body
enclosed by the ribs and breastbone,
extending from neck to abdomen; the
thorax.—**chest·ed**, *a.* Pertaining to the
chest of the body; as, *broad-chested*.

chest, chest, *n.* [O.E. *cest,* < L. *cista,* < Gr.
cistē, box.] A well-constructed, box-like
container with a lid, for storing or shipping
articles of value; as, a sea *chest*, jewelry
chest.—**chest of draw·ers**, a piece of furniture consisting of a set of sliding drawers
fitted into a frame.

ches·ter·field, ches′tĕr·fēld″, *n.* [Named
< the fourth Earl of Chesterfield. CHESTER-
FIELDIAN.] A single or double-breasted
semifitted overcoat of medium length with
velvet collar and fly front; a style of sofa
design with upright armrests at both ends.

Ches·ter·field·i·an, ches″tĕr·fēl′dē·an, *a.*
Of, pertaining to, or suggestive of the
fourth Earl of Chesterfield, whose letters
to his son contain directions as to manners
and etiquette; elegant; urbane.

Ches·ter White, *n.* An American breed of
large, white hogs developed in Chester
county, Pennsylvania.

chest·nut, ches′nut″, ches′nut, *n.* [For *ches-
tennut*, O.E. *chestrine, chesteyne,* < O.Fr.
chastaigne, < L. *castanea,* the chestnut tree,
< Gr. *kastanon,* < *Castana* in Pontus, where
this tree abounded.] The edible nut of a tree,
genus *Castanea*, of the beech family; the
tree itself or its timber; various other
plants resembling the chestnut, as *horse
chestnut*; a reddish-brown hue or color; a
reddish-brown horse having mane and tail
of the same color; a callosity on the inner
side of the leg of a horse. *Colloq.* an old
joke; something made stale by repetition.—
a. Reddish-brown; of, or relating to, a
chestnut.

chest·nut blight, *n.* A fungus-caused
disease characterized by bark lesions, and
attacking chestnut trees, esp. American
chestnuts.

che·tah, chē′ta, *n.* See *cheetah*.

che·val glass, she·val′ glas″, she·val′ gläs″,
n. A looking-glass, mounted in a frame
that may be tilted, and large enough to
reflect the whole figure.

chev·a·lier, shev″a′·lēr′, *Fr.* shev″äl·yä, *n.*
[Fr., < *cheval,* a horse. CAVALRY, CAVALIER.]
A horseman; a cavalier; a member of
certain orders of knighthood or national
merit, as the Legion of Honor.

cheve·lure, shĕv′·lur′, *n.* [Fr., < L.
capillatura, < *capillus,* hair.] A head of
hair; *astron.* a nebulous envelope, as the
coma of a comet.

Chev·i·ot, chev′ē·ot, chē′vē·ot, *n.* A sheep of a breed valued for their thick wool, so called from the Cheviot Hills between England and Scotland. (*l.c.*) a rough-finished twilled woolen cloth; a soft-finished cotton shirting, shev′ē·ot.

chev·ron, shev′ron, *n. Milit.* a V-shaped insignia worn on the sleeve by non-commissioned officers, policemen, and other uniformed men, to indicate rank, class, and service; *arch.* a variety of fret ornament; a zigzag molding.

chev·y, chiv·y, chiv·vy, chiv·ey, chev′ē, chiv′ē, chiv′ē, *n. pl.* **chev·ies.** [Perhaps < Chevy Chase, title of an old English ballad: cf. O.Fr. *chevauchie,* a riding; raid.] A hunting cry; a hunt, chase, or pursuit; the game of prisoners' base.—**chev·y,** *v.t.*—*chevied, chevying.* To chase.—*v.i. Brit.* to race; scamper.

chew, chö, *v.t.* [O.E. *cēowan,* akin to G. *kauen.*] To crush or grind with the teeth; masticate; *fig.* to meditate on; consider deliberately.—*v.i.* To perform the act of crushing or grinding with the teeth; *colloq.* use tobacco for chewing; *fig.* to meditate.

chew, chö, *n.* The act of chewing; that which is chewed; a portion of tobacco, for chewing; *slang,* a chaw.—**chew·er,** *n.*

chew·ing gum, *n.* A preparation of chicle or some similar natural or synthetic gum, sweetened and flavored, for chewing.

che·wink, chi·wingk′, *n.* [Imit. of its note.] The towhee, a bird, *Pipilo erythrophthalmus,* of the finch family, common in eastern North America.

chew out, *v.t. Slang,* to scold severely; berate.

chew the fat, *v.i. Slang,* to chat about trivial matters.

Chey·enne, shī·en′, shī·an′, *n.* A North American Indian tribe, formerly of Wyoming, Nebraska, and the Dakotas, now of Montana and Oklahoma; one of a tribe of Algonquin linguistic stock; the language of the Cheyenne Indians.

chi, kī, *n.* The twenty-second letter of the Greek alphabet, written as *ch* in English.

Chi·an·ti, kē·än′tē, kē·an′tē, *It.* kyän′tē, *n.* [< *Chianti* Mountains, in Tuscany.] A dry, usually red, Italian wine.

chi·a·ro·scu·ro, chi·a·roo·o·scu·ro, kē·-är″o·skur′ō, kē·är″o·ō·ō·skur′ō, *n.* [It.], lit. clear-obscure; < L. *clarus,* clear, and *obscurus,* obscure; Fr. *clair-obscur.*] The treatment and distribution of light and shade in a piece of artwork; a painting, sketch, or woodcut using only light and shade; an artist's way of using light and shade.—**chi·a·ro·scu·rist,** *n.*

Chib·chan, chib′chan, *a.* Of or pertaining to a family of S. American languages native to Colombia, Central America, and Ecuador.—**Chib·chan,** *n.*

chic, shēk, shik, *n.* [Fr. < Gr. *schick,* due order, tact.] Fashion know-how; easy elegance and tasteful, distinctive style: said esp. of a woman and her clothing.—*a.* Smart; sophisticated; exceptionally stylish.

chi·ca·lo·te, chē″kä·lạ′te, *n.* [Sp.] A prickly, white-flowered, poppy plant, *Argemone platyceras,* of Mexico and the southwestern U.S.

chi·cane, shi·kān′, *v.i.*—*chicaned, chicaning.* [Fr. *chicaner;* origin unknown.] To use chicanery.—*v.t.* To quibble over; cavil at; to overreach or trick by chicanery.—*n.* Chicanery; *card playing,* a hand without trumps.—**chi·can·er,** *n.*

chi·can·er·y, shi·kā′ne·rē, *n. pl.* **chi·can·er·ies.** Trickery, as in law, by quibbling or sophistry; a quibble or subterfuge used to mislead, trick, or delude.

chi·chi, shē′shē′, *a.* Elegant or stylish in a showy, pretentious way; affectedly delicate or artistic.

chick, chik, *n.* A young chicken, esp. one recently hatched; a young bird. A baby. *Slang,* a young woman; as, a cute *chick.*

chick·a·dee, chik′a·dē″, *n.* [Imit.] A small crestless North American bird, *Parus atricapillus,* of the titmouse family with black, white, and gray feathers.

chick·a·ree, chik′a·rē″, *n.* [Imit. of its cry.] The red squirrel, *Sciurur hudsonicus,* of North America.

Chick·a·saw, chik′a·sạ″, *n.* A member of a warlike North American tribe of Muskogean Indians who lived along and east of the Mississippi River, but now reside mostly in Oklahoma.

chicken, chik′en, chik′in, *n.* [O.E. *cicen, cycen,* a chicken; cog. L.G. *kiken,* küken, Prov. G. *küchen.*] The common barnyard fowl, *Gallus gallus,* and particularly its young; the edible meat of this fowl; any of several other species of birds or their young; a person, esp. a female, of tender years: mainly used in the phrase, she's no *chicken;* a coward.

chick·en, chik′en, chik′in, *a.* Having no more courage than a chicken; timid; cowardly; made of or with chicken; as, *chicken* potpie; *milit. slang,* sticking to the rules to the point of being mean and petty.

chick·en colo·nel, *n. Milit. slang,* a full colonel, as opposed to a lieutenant colonel.

chick·en feed, *n. Slang,* a negligible sum of money; small change, as pennies.

chick·en hawk, *n.* Popularly, a hawk that preys, or is said to prey, on domestic fowl; esp. *Cooper's hawk.*

chick·en-heart·ed, chik′en·här′tid, chik′-in·här′tid, *a. Colloq.* cowardly, fearful.

chick·en-liv·ered, chik′en·liv′ẽrd, chik′-in·liv′ẽrd, *a. Colloq.* cowardly, fearful.

chick·en out, *v.i. Slang,* to surrender or back out because of a loss of nerve.

chick·en pox, *n.* An acute, contagious, eruptive disease generally appearing in children.

chick·en snake, *n.* Any of several large colubrid snakes, genus *Elaphe,* of North America, whose food consists mainly of birds and small mammals. Also *rat snake.*

chick·en switch, *n. Aeron. slang,* a mechanical device used by an astronaut to eject the capsule he rides in if the rocket malfunctions. Also **e·gads but·ton.**

chick·pea, chik′pē″, *n.* [Earlier *chich pea.*] A fabaceous Asiatic plant, *Cicer arietinum,* bearing edible pealike seeds; the seed of this plant, used for food in southern Europe and Latin America. Also **gar·ban·zo.**

chick·weed, chik′wēd″, *n.* Any of several weedy plants of the pink family, esp. a common Old World stitchwort, *Stellaria media,* whose seeds and leaves are enjoyed by birds as food.

chic·le, chik′el, *n.* [Mex.] Elastic gum from the latex of the sapodilla tree, usual base of chewing gum.

chi·co, chē′kō, *n. pl.* **chi·cos.** The greasewood, a shrub used for fuel in western U.S.

chic·o·ry, chik′o·rē, *n. pl.* **chic·o·ries.** [Fr. *chicorée,* L. *cichorium,* < Gr. *kichōrion,* chicory.] A perennial, blue-flowered composite herb, *Cichorium intybus,* with leaves used in salads, and its fleshy tapering root, when dried, roasted, and ground, used for mixing with coffee or as a coffee substitute.

chide, chīd, *v.t.*—past *chided* or *chid,* pp. *chided, chid,* or *chidden,* ppr. *chiding.* [O.E. *cīdan,* to chide.] To scold; to reprove; to rebuke; as, to *chide* an employee for being late.—*v.i.* To scold; to find fault.

chief, chēf, *a.* [O.Fr. *chef,* chief (Fr. *chef*), the head, top, chief; < L. *caput,* the head, whence also *capital, cattle, captain,* etc.] Highest in office, authority, or rank; principal or most eminent; most important; at the head; leading; main.

chief, chēf, *n.* The person highest in authority; the head or leader; as, *chief* of police; *slang,* boss.

chief jus·tice, *n.* The presiding judge of a court.—**Chief Jus·tice of the U.S.,** *n.* The judge who presides over the U.S. Supreme Court.

chief·ly, chēf′lē, *adv.* Principally; above all; for the most part; mostly.

chief mas·ter ser·geant, *n.* A non-commissioned officer of the highest rank in the Air Force.

Chief of Staff, *n. U.S.,* a member of the Joint Chiefs of Staff; the senior officer of the Air Force or the Army. (*l.c.*) the senior staff officer in command of a major unit of a U.S. military branch.

chief of state, *n.* The formal or symbolic head of a country as distinguished from the head of government.

chief pet·ty of·fi·cer, *n.* In the U.S. Navy and Coast Guard, the officer who ranks below senior petty officer and above petty officer first class.

chief·tain, chēf′tan, chēf′tin, *n.* [O.Fr. *chevetaine, chieftaine,* etc.; < L.L. *capitanus* < *caput,* the head; really the same word as *captain.*] A leader or commander, esp. of guerrilla forces; a chief, as of an Amer. Indian tribe; the head of a clan or family.—**chief·tain·cy, chief·tain·ship,** *n.* The rank and dignity or office of a chieftain.

chif·fon, shi·fon′, shif′on, *n.* [Fr. < *chiffe,* rag.] Any bit of feminine finery, as of ribbon or lace; a soft, plain-woven, very thin, transparent fabric.—*a.* Of, like, or made of chiffon; *cooking,* pertaining to a light frothy texture, as in foods containing whipped egg whites.

chif·fo·nier, shif″o·nēr′, *n.* [Fr. *chiffonnier,* < *chiffon.*] A cabinet with drawers; a case of drawers, high in proportion to its width.

chig·ger, chig′ẽr, *n.* See *chigoe.*

chi·gnon, shēn′yon, shēn·yun′, *Fr.* shē-nyạn′, *n.* [Fr., the nape of the neck, a chignon.] A large roll, knot, or twist of hair worn at the back of the head.

chig·oe, chig′ō, *n.* [Of West Indian or South American origin.] An insect closely resembling the common flea, but of more minute size, also found in the West Indies and South America, which burrows beneath the skin and, becoming distended with eggs, produces a troublesome ulcer. Also *chigger.*

Chi·hua·hua, chi·wä′wä, chi·wä′wa, *n.* [Mexican Sp. < *Chihuahua,* Mexico.] A very small dog of ancient Mexican breed.

chil·blain, chil′blān″, *n.* [Chill, cold, and *blain.*] *Pathol.* a blain or inflamed sore on the hands or feet produced by cold.—*v.t.* To afflict with chilblains; to produce chilblains on.

child, chīld, *n. pl.* **chil·dren,** chil′dren, chil′drin. [O.E. *cild,* a child, pl. *cildru,* afterward *cildre, childre,* to which *n* or *en,* another plural termination, was added. The root is the same as that of *kin, kind,* etc., G. *kind,* a child.] A son or a daughter, esp. of an age between infancy and youth; a male or female descendant of the next generation; a very young person of either sex; one of crude or immature knowledge, experience, judgment, or attainments.—**child's play,** trivial matter of any kind; anything easily accomplished or surmounted.—**with child,** pregnant.

child·bear·ing, chīld′bâr″ing, *n.* The act of producing or bringing forth children; parturition.

child·bed, chīld′bed″, *n.* The state of a woman in childbirth or labor.

child·bed fe·ver, *n.* An infection of the mother occurring at childbirth; puerperal fever.

child·birth, chīld′bụrth″, *n.* The act of bringing forth a child; parturition; labor.

Chil·der·mas, chĭl′dẽr·mas, n. [M.E. *chyldermasse,* < O.E. *cildra,* children, and *mæsse,* mass.] Holy Innocents' Day, December 28.

child·hood, chīld′hụd, n. The state of being a child; the time in which a person is classed as a child.

child·ish, chīl′dish, a. Of or belonging to a child or to childhood; like a child, or what is proper to childhood; trifling, puerile, ignorant, silly, weak.—**child·ish·ly,** adv.

child la·bor law, n. A law, state or federal, establishing conditions for employment of children, including minimum age, hours, and health and safety standards; the federal law passed in 1938 setting 16 as the minimum legal age for full-time employment in commerce, mining, manufacturing, or transportation.

child·like, chīld′līk″, a. Resembling a child or that which belongs to children; meek; submissive; innocent; artless; dutiful.

Chil·e·an, chĭl′ē·an, Sp. chē′le·an, a. Relating to the language, traditions, and people of Chile, a republic on the southwest coast of S. America.—n. A native or inhabitant of Chile; the Spanish language as characteristically spoken in Chile.

Chil·e salt·pe·ter, n. Sodium nitrate, NaNO₃, in its natural form, used in fertilizers.

chil·i, chil·li, chil·e, chĭl′ē, n. pl. **chil·ies, chil·lies, chil·es.** [Mex.] The pod of species of capsicum, esp. *Capsicum annuum;* a Spanish-American dish of beans and meat flavored with chili powder; hot pepper.—**chil·i sauce,** a condiment made of tomatoes cooked with chili, spices, and other seasoning ingredients, often packed and sold commercially.

chil·i·ad, kĭl′ē·ad″, n. [Gr. *chilias,* < *chilioi,* thousand.] A thousand; a period of a thousand years.

chil·i con car·ne, chĭl′ē kon kär′nē, Sp. chē′lē kạn kär′ne, n. A modification of a Mexican dish popular in the U.S., consisting of ground meat, chopped peppers, chili powder, and kidney beans.

chill, chil, n. [O.E. *ciele,* coldness; akin to E. *cool, cold.*] Coldness, esp. a moderate but penetrating coldness, as in the air; a sensation of cold, usually with shivering; the cold stage, as of ague; *fig.* a depressing influence or sensation; absence of enthusiasm; a metal mold for making chilled castings.

chill, chil, v.i. To become cold; be seized with a chill; *metal.* to harden, esp. on the surface, by sudden cooling.—v.t. To affect with cold; make chilly; *fig.* to depress or dispirit; *metal.* to cool suddenly, so as to harden; esp. to harden, as cast iron or steel, on the surface by casting in a metal mold.—**chill·er,** n. A person who or a thing that chills; *writers' slang,* a horror story, film, or dramatic performance.—**chill·ing·ly,** adv.

chill, chil, a. Cold; tending to cause shivering; depressingly affected by cold; shivering with cold; not warm or hearty; as, a *chill* reception; repressed or deadened.

chill·y, chĭl′ē, a.—*chillier, chilliest.* Producing a sensation of cold; so cold as to cause shivering; feeling a sensation of cold; sensitive to cold; *fig.* without warmth of feeling.—adv.—**chill·i·ly,** chĭl′i·lē, adv.—**chill·i·ness,** n.

Chil·tern Hun·dreds, n. pl. Brit. a strictly nominal office as steward of certain lands in south central England, granted by the crown to House of Commons members as a legal way to resign their seats.

chime, chīm, n. [O.E. *chimbe, chymbe,* a cymbal, a shortening of *chymbale,* < L. *cymbalum,* a cymbal.] The harmonious sound of bells or musical instruments; a set of bells, properly five or more, tuned to a musical scale, and struck by hammers; any harmonious musical sound, as that of bells.

chime, chīm, v.i. To sound in consonance, rhythm, or harmony; to give out harmonious sounds; hence, to accord; to agree; to suit; to harmonize; to express agreement, often with *in with;* as, to *chime in with* one's personal opinions.—v.t. To cause to sound harmoniously, as a set of bells.—**chim·er,** chīm′ẽr, n. One who or that which chimes.

chime, chimb, chīm, n. [D. *kim,* Sw. *kim, kimb,* the edge of a cask, G. *kimme,* edge, brim.] The edge or brim of a cask or tub, formed by the ends of the staves projecting beyond the head. Also **chine.**

chime in, v.i. To break into a conversation, usually in an unwelcome manner; to harmonize in singing; to be compatible.

chi·me·ra, chi·mae·ra, ki·mēr′a, ki-mẽr′a, n. pl. **chi·me·ras.** [L. *chimaera,* < Gr. *chimaira,* lit. "she-goat."] (*cap.* or *l.c.*) A mythological fire-breathing monster, commonly represented with a lion's head, a goat's body, and a serpent's tail; (*l.c.*) a grotesque monster, as in decorative art; *fig.* a horrible or unreal creature of the imagination; a phantom; a vain or idle fancy.

chi·mer·ic, ki·mer′ik, ki·mẽr′ik, kī·mer′ik, kī·mẽr′ik, a. Pertaining to or of the nature of a chimera; unreal; imaginary; given to entertaining chimeras; wildly fanciful. Also **chi·mer·i·cal,**—**chi·mer·i·cal·ly,** adv.—**chi·mer·i·cal·ness,** n.

chim·ney, chim′nē, n. [Fr. *cheminée,* L.L. *caminata,* a chimney, < L. *caminus,* a furnace, a flue, < Gr. *kaminos,* an oven.] A construction, generally of stone or brick, containing a passage by which the smoke of a fire or furnace escapes to the open air; a chimney stack; a flue; the funnel of a steam engine; a tall glass to surround the flame of a lamp to protect it and promote combustion; any chimney-like structure.

chim·ney piece, n. The ornamental construction around the open recess constituting the fireplace in a room.

chim·ney pot, n. A pipe of earthenware or sheet metal placed on the top of chimneys to carry off smoke.

chim·ney sweep, n. One whose occupation is to clean chimneys of soot.

chim·pan·zee, chim″pan·zē′, chim·pan′zē, n. [W. Afr.] An anthropoid ape, *Pan troglodytes,* of equatorial Africa, smaller and less ferocious than the gorilla. Also **chimp.**

chin, chin, n. [O.E. *cin* = G. *kinn;* akin to L. *gena,* cheek, Gr. *genus,* jaw.] The lower extremity of the face, below the mouth; the point of the under jaw.

chin, chin, v.t.—*chinned, chinning.* To bring up to the chin, as a violin; to bring one's chin up to a horizontal bar on which one is hanging by the hands by lifting the body by the arms; *slang,* to talk.

chi·na, chī′na, n. A species of earthenware made in *China,* or in imitation of that made there, and so called from the country; porcelain. Also *chinaware.*

Chi·na as·ter, n. The common name of a hardy and free-flowering composite plant, having flowers in a wide variety of colors.

chi·na·ber·ry, chī′na·ber″ē, n. pl. **chi·na·ber·ries,** chī′na·ber″ēz. The china tree or its fruit; a soapberry, *Sapindus saponaria,* of Mexico, the West Indies, and the southern U.S.; any similar ornamental tree.

Chi·na rose, n. The name given to a number of varieties of garden rose, natives of China. Also **Ben·gal rose.**

Chi·na·town, chī′na·toun, n. The Chinese quarter in a city.

chi·na·ware, chī′na·wâr″, n. Ware or vessels made of china or porcelain.

chinch, chinch, n. [Sp. *chinche,* < L. *cimex,* bug.] The bedbug; a fetid American hemipterous insect of the genus *Blissus,* destructive to wheat, esp. *B. leucopterus.* Also **chinch bug.**

chin·chil·la, chin·chil′a, n. [Sp.] A genus of rodent animals peculiar to the South American continent, one species of which produces a fine pearly-gray fur; the fur of the chinchilla; a heavy woolen twill fabric used for coats.

chine, chīn, n. [Fr. *échine,* O.Fr. *eschine,* the spine.] The backbone or spine of an animal; a piece of the backbone of an animal, with the adjoining parts, cut for cooking.—v.t. To cut through the backbone of, or into chine pieces.

chine, chīn, n. Brit. a gully or course worn in a rocky bed by a brook, stream, or other running water.

Chi·nese, chī·nēz′, chī·nēs′, a. Characteristic of the varied customs, traditions, peoples, and dialects of China.—n. A native or inhabitant of China; the unique logographic script, consisting of intricate brush-stroke characters written in vertical columns from right to left; any of several languages spoken in China.

Chi·nese cab·bage, n. A lettuce-like plant, native of China, having a long head of light green leaves. Also **pe-tsai.**

Chi·nese lan·tern, n. A lantern made of colored paper used in decorative illumination. Also **Jap·a·nese lan·tern.**

Chi·nese puz·zle, n. A complicated puzzle; a situation that is very perplexing.

Chi·nese Wall, n. A system of walls around China, the original construction of which dates to the third century B.C., built as protection against the Mongolian and Manchurian nomads. Also **Great Wall of Chi·na.**

Chi·nese white, n. The white oxide of zinc used in water colors.

Ch'ing, ching, ching, n. The dynasty established in China in 1644 by a conquering Mongolian people and lasting until 1912. Also **Man·chu dy·nas·ty.**

chink, chingk, n. [Akin to O.E. *chine,* a chink, a fissure, *cīnan,* to gape.] A narrow aperture; a cleft, rent, or fissure of greater length than breadth; a cranny, gap, or crack.—v.t. To cause to open or part and form a fissure; to make chinks in; to fill up chinks in.—v.i. To crack; to open.

chink, chingk, v.i. [Imitative; comp. *jingle.*] To make a small sharp metallic sound.—v.t. To cause to sound as by shaking coins or small pieces of metal.—n. A short, sharp, clear, metallic sound; *slang,* coin, cash.

chi·no, chē′nō, n. pl. **chi·nos.** A material of heavy cotton twill often used for military uniforms; usu. pl., a pair of slacks or trousers made of chino material.

chi·noi·se·rie, shĕn·woz″e·rē′, shĕn·woz′-e·rē, n. [Fr.] A form of Chinese art and ornamentation characterized by intricate patterns and motifs; an object decorated with this type of Chinese ornamentation.

Chi·nook, shi·nụk′, shi·nŏk′, chi·nụk′, chi·nŏk′, n. A member of Indian tribes of the Columbia River region of western North America; (*l.c.*) a warm, moist southwest wind on the Pacific coast, referred to as a "wet chinook"; a warm, dry wind coming down the slopes of the Rocky Mountains or, in Canada, over Alberta into Saskatchewan.

Chi·nook·an, shi·nụk′an, shi·nŏ′kan, chi·nụk′an, chi·nŏ′kan, n. A language of the Chinook people.

Chi·nook jar·gon, Chi·nook Jar·gon, n. *Canada,* a common language of Indians and traders on the Pacific coast combining French and English with Chinookan and Nootka.

chin·qua·pin, chin·ka·pin, ching′ka·pin, n. [Of Amer. Indian origin.] The dwarf chestnut of the U.S. yielding edible nuts; an American tree allied to the oak.

chintz, chints, n. [Hind. chint, Pers. chinz, spotted, stained.] Cotton cloth or calico from India, printed in bright colors, and generally glazed.

chintz·y, chint'sē, a.—chintzier, chintziest. Decorated with a printed, glazed cotton fabric; colloq. cheap, shoddy, stingy.

chip, chip, v.t.—chipped, chipping. [M.E.; akin to chop.] To cut away with a chisel or ax; to shape or produce by cutting away pieces; to disfigure by breaking off fragments; to bet by using chips in a game; Brit. to banter, taunt, or criticize harshly.—v.i. To break off in small pieces; golf, to play a chip shot.

chip, chip, n. A small piece of wood separated by chopping, cutting, or breaking; a small cut piece of food, as a potato chip; a very thin slice of food, as a potato chip; a counter, made of ivory or plastic, used as a token in certain card games; anything trivial or worthless; something dried up or without flavor; a piece of dried dung often used as fuel in some countries; a mark made by chipping.

chip in, v.t. Slang, to give money with others into a fund for a common purpose.

chip·munk, chip'mungk, n. The popular name of the ground squirrel, a rodent animal very common in the United States.

chipped beef, n. A smoked dried beef, sliced very thin and often served in a cream sauce.

Chip·pen·dale, chip'en·dāl″, a. Pertaining to a type of English furniture characterized by graceful lines and ornate decoration in the style of Thomas Chippendale, an 18th-century furniture designer.

chip·per, chip'ẽr, a. [Probably < North. E. kipper, lively.] Cheerful; sprightly.

Chip·pe·wa, chip'e·wä″, chip'e·wä″, chip'-e·wa, n. A large tribe of North American Indians from the Lake Superior region.

chip·py, chip·pie, chip'ē, n. pl. chip·pies. The chipping sparrow Spizella passerina, usually found in urban areas of N. Amer.; a chipmunk; slang, a woman of loose morals.

chips, chipz, n. Brit. See French fries.

chips are down, the, slang, signifying an urgent, potentially disastrous situation which forces the essentials or basic realities of life to become paramount; signifying a situation in which prevarication and evasion are impossible and one's true character, feelings, or position are revealed.

chips, cash in one's, slang, to pass away; to die.

chip shot, n. Golf, a short approach shot that raises the ball into the air so it will roll when it lands on the green.

chips, in the, slang, wealthy; affluent.

chi·rog·ra·pher, kī·rog'ra·fẽr, n. [Gr. cheir, the hand, graphō, to write.] One who exercises or studies the art of writing.

chi·rog·ra·phy, kī·rog'ra·fē, n. The art of writing; handwriting.—**chi·ro·graph·ic, chi·ro·graph·i·cal**, a. Of or relating to the art of handwriting.

chi·ro·man·cy, kī'ro·man″sē, n. [Gr. cheir, the hand, and manteia, divination.] Divination by the hand; the art or practice of foretelling one's fortune by inspecting the lines of his hand; palmistry.—**chi·ro·man·cer**, kī'ro·man″sẽr, n. One who practices chiromancy.

chi·rop·o·dist, ki·rop'o·dist, ki·rop'o·dist, n. [Gr. cheir, the hand, and pous, podos, the foot.] One who treats ailments and irregularities of the feet; podiatrist.—**chi·rop·o·dy**, n. Science dealing with the treatment of foot ailments and irregularities; podiatry.

chi·ro·prac·tic, kī″ro·prak'tik, n. [Gr. cheir, hand, and praktike, practical science.] A system of therapeutics based upon the theory that disease is caused by interference with nerve function, the method being to restore normal condition by adjusting body structures, esp. the spinal column; also, a chiropractor.—**chi·ro·prac·tor**, n. One who practises chiropractic.

chi·rop·ter, kī·rop'tẽr, n. [N.L. Chiroptera, pl., < Gr. cheir, hand, and pteron, wing.] One of the Chiroptera, an order of mammals having the forelimbs modified as wings; a bat.—**chi·rop·ter·an**, a., n.—**chi·rop·ter·ous**, a.

chirp, chụrp, v.i. [Akin to G. zirpen, tschirpen, schirpen, to chirp, chirrup being a lengthened form; the same root is in D. kirren, to coo, L. garrio, to chatter.] To make a short sharp shrill sound, as is done by small birds or certain insects, as crickets or locusts; to utter a similar sound; to talk quickly and in a shrill manner.—v.t. To utter with a short shrill sound.—n. A short, shrill note of certain birds or insects.

chirr, chụr, v.i. [Imit.] To make a vibrant trilling sound, as a grasshopper or cicada; to make some similar sound.—n. The sound of chirring.

chir·rup, chẽr'up, chụr'up, v.i.—chirruped, chirruping. [A lengthened form of chirp.] To chirp.—v.t. To speak with a chirp.—n. A chirp.

chis·el, chiz'el, n. [O.Fr. chisel, cisel, (Fr. ciseau), < L. caedere, cut.] A metal tool for cutting or shaping wood or stone that has at its extremity a cutting edge transverse to the axis.

chis·el, chiz'el, v.t.—chiseled, chiselled, chiseling, chiselling. To cut or shape with a chisel; slang, to cheat; get by cheating or trickery; get by unfair methods.—v.i. To work with a chisel; slang, to use trickery; cut in unfairly; take mean advantage.—**chis·el·er, chis·el·ler**, n. One who chisels, as a stone carver; slang, a cheater or swindler; a mean or petty profit seeker.

chis·eled, chis·elled, chiz'eld, a. Cut or shaped with a chisel; clear-cut.

chit, chit, n. [Hind.] A short note or memo, esp. a voucher for a small amount owed; a piece of paper entitling the bearer to reimbursement for money spent, as: He worked overtime and put in a chit for his dinner bill. Milit. an informal request, voucher, or receipt.

chit, chit, n. [Cf. kit, kitten.] Slang, a young person, esp. a girl: used in contempt.

chit·chat, chit'chat″, n. [Varied redupl. of chat.] Small talk on one subject or another; gossip.—v.i. To carry on a light conversation; to gossip.

chi·tin, kī'tin, n. [Gr. chitōn, a tunic.] The horny organic substance which forms the wing covers and integuments of insects and the carapaces of crustacea.—**chi·tin·ous**, kī'tin·us, a. Consisting of, or having the nature of, chitin.

chi·ton, kīt'n, kī'ton, n. [Gr. chiton, a tunic.] Gr. an ancient garment for both sexes, usually worn next to the skin; zool. any of a group of sluggish, limpet-like mollusks of the class Amphineura, which adhere to rocks.

chit·ter, chit'ẽr, v.i. To chirp; to twitter like the birds; Brit. dial. to shiver, esp. because of the cold.

chit·ter·ling, chit·ling, chit·lin, chit'ẽr·ling, chit'lin, n. pl. chit·ter·lings, chit·lings, chit·lins. Cooking, part of the small intestines of pigs, fried for food; generally used in the plural.

chiv·al·ric, shiv'al·rik, shi·val'rik, a. Pertaining to chivalry; knightly; chivalrous.

chiv·al·rous, shiv'al·rus, a. [O.Fr. chevalereus, < chevalier, E. chevalier.] Knightly; of knightly spirit or virtues; nobly gallant, courteous, considerate, or helpful; worthy of the age of chivalry.—**chiv·al·rous·ly**, adv.—**chiv·al·rous·ness**, n.

chiv·al·ry, shiv'al·rē, n. pl. chiv·al·ries. [O.Fr. Fr. chevalerie, < chevalier, E. chevalier.] The medieval institution of knighthood as bound by a special code of honor and duty; the position, character, spirit, or virtues proper to a knight, as valor, magnanimity, courtesy, or helpfulness; noble gallantry; knights collectively; hence, gallant warriors or gentlemen.

chi·var·ee, shi·va·rē′, n. See charivari.

chive, chīv, n. [O.Fr. chive, cive (Fr. cive), < L. cæpa, onion.] A small perennial bulbous plant, Allium schœnoprasum, related to the leek and onion, with long, slender leaves which are used as a seasoning in cooking; chiefly used in pl.

chiv·y, chiv·vy, chiv'ē, n. pl. chiv·ies, chiv·vies. Same as chevy.—**chiv·y**, v.t.—chivied, chivying. Brit. to chase; to torment; tease; chaff.—v.i. Brit. to race; scamper.

chlo·ral, klō'ral, n. A colorless mobile liquid first prepared from chlorine and alcohol; a white crystalline substance ("chloral hydrate") formed by combining liquid chloral with water, and used as a hypnotic and anesthetic.

chlo·ral·ose, klōr'a·lōs″, klōr'a·lōz″, n. Chem. a crystalline compound, $C_8H_{11}Cl_3O_6$, made by combining chloral with dextrose: used in medicine as a hypnotic.

chlo·rate, klōr'āt, klōr'it, n. Chem. a salt of chloric acid.

chlor·dane, chlor·dan, klōr'dān, klōr'dan, n. Chem. a colorless, odorless, viscous liquid, $C_{10}H_6Cl_8$, used as an insecticide.

chlo·rel·la, klo·rel'a, n. Any fresh-water, unicellular alga of the genus Chlorella, potentially a cheap source of protein and B vitamins.

chlo·ric, klōr'ik, a. Pertaining to or containing chlorine; as, chloric acid $HClO_3·7H_2O$.

chlo·ride, klōr'īd, klōr'id, n. Chem. a compound of chlorine with an element or radical; a salt of hydrochloric acid.—**chlo·rid·ic**, klo·rid'ik, a.

chlo·ride of lime, n. Chem. a white powder used in bleaching and disinfecting, made by treating slaked lime with chlorine, and regarded, when dry, as calcium oxychloride, $CaOCl_2$.

chlo·ri·dize, klōr'i·dīz″, v.t.—chloridized, chloridizing. To convert into a chloride; esp. to roast (a silver ore) with salt in order to convert the silver into chloride; to treat with a chloride.

chlo·ri·nate, klōr'i·nāt″, v.t.—chlorinated, chlorinating. To combine or treat with chlorine; to treat, as gold ore, with chlorine gas in order that the gold may be removed as a soluble chloride; to disinfect, as water, by means of chlorine.—**chlo·ri·na·tion**, n.—**chlo·ri·na·tor**, n.

chlo·rine, klōr'ēn, klōr'in, n. [Gr. khloros, greenish-yellow, green.] Chem. sym. Cl, at. no. 17, a greenish-yellow gaseous element, highly irritating to the organs of respiration, occurring naturally combined in table salt; used in the manufacture of chemicals not containing chlorine, and in the manufacture of chemicals containing chlorine including solvents, pesticides such as DDT, plastics and fibers, and refrigerants. Also used in water and sewage treatment and textile bleaching.

chlo·rite, klōr'īt, n. [Gr. chlōritis, kind of green stone, < chloros, green.] A name for a group of minerals, hydrous silicates of aluminum, ferrous iron, and magnesium, most of which are green.—**chlo·rit·ic**, klō·rit'ik, a. Pertaining to or containing chlorite.—**chlo·ri·toid**, klō'ri·toid, n. A mineral, a native silicate of aluminum, ferrous iron, and magnesium, having a dark-green color and occurring usually in brittle laminae, and resembling mica.

chlo·rite, klōr'īt, n. Chem. a salt of chlorous acid.—**chlo·rit·ic**, a.

chlo·ro·ben·zene, klŏr″*o*·ben′zĕn, klŏr″-*o*·ben·zĕn′, *n. Chem.* a clear, colorless, volatile and flammable liquid, C_6H_5Cl, derived from chlorination of benzene; used in the manufacture of phenol, DDT, and as a solvent or intermediate in organic synthesis.

chlo·ro·form, klŏr′*i*·fąrm″, *n.* [*Chlor-*, < *chloride* or *chlorine*, and *-form*, < *formic* acid, < chemical connection.] A volatile, colorless liquid of an agreeable, fragrant taste and smell, prepared by distilling together a mixture of alcohol, water, and chloride of lime, or as a by-product of the chlorination of methane: used in refrigerants, propellants, plastics, dyes, and as an anesthetic.

chlo·ro·form, klŏr′*i*·fąrm″, *v.t.* To put under the influence of chloroform; to treat with chloroform.

chlo·ro·phyll, klŏr′*a*·fil, *n.* [Gr. *chlōros*, green, and *phyllon*, a leaf.] The green coloring matter of plants and leaves, which is used by plants to manufacture carbohydrates: several chemically different variations of chlorophyll exist.

chlo·ro·pic·rin, klŏr″*o*·pik′rin, klŏr″*o*·-pī′krin, *n. Chem.* a slightly oily, colorless, poisonous liquid used in poison gas, the manufacture of dyes, and as a soil fumigant.

chlo·ro·plast, klŏr′*o*·plast″, *n.* [Gr. *chlōros*, green, and *plastos*, formed.] *Bot.* a plastid containing chlorophyll, found in most algae and higher plants. The structure in green plants in which photosynthesis occurs.

chlo·ro·sis, kla·rō′sis, *n.* [N.L., < Gr. *chlōros*, green.] *Bot.* loss of the normal green color in a plant, from lack of iron in the soil or other causes, exclusive of lack of sunlight.—**chlo·rot·ic,** *a.*

chlo·rous, klŏr′us, *a.* Pertaining to chlorine; containing chlorine, esp. in a larger proportion than a corresponding chloric compound; as, *chlorous* acid, $HClO_2$.

chlor·pro·pa·mide, klŏr′·prō′·pa″mĭd, *n.* A compound which lowers blood sugar, used to treat mild diabetes.

chlor·tet·ra·cy·cline, klŏr″·te″tra·si′klĭn, *n. Chem.* an antibiotic, $C_{22}H_{23}ClN_2O_8$, having a wide antimicrobial spectrum, and also used as an animal feed supplement.

chock, chok, *n.* [Cf. O.Fr. *chouque, chocque* (Fr. *souche*), stump, stock.] A block or wedge of wood for filling in a space, esp. for preventing movement, as of a wheel or a cask. *Naut.* a block placed under a boat when stowed on a vessel's deck; a metal casting or block of wood, attached to a deck, with a recess, commonly between two short horn-like arms which curve together but do not meet, through which a hawser or cable passes.

chock, chok, *v.t.* To furnish with or secure by a chock or chocks; to place, as a boat, upon chocks.

chock, chok, *adv.* As close or tight as possible.

chock-a-block, chok′a·blok′, *adv. Naut.* with the blocks drawn close together, as when a tackle is hauled to the utmost; *fig.* in a jammed or crowded condition.

chock-full, chok′fŭl′, *a.* As full as possible; crammed. Also **choke-full, chuck-full.**

choc·o·late, chą′ko·lĭt, chok′o·lĭt, chąk′lĭt, chok′lĭt, *n.* [Sp. *chocolate*; Mex. *chocolatl—choco*, cocoa, and *latl*, water.] A cake, powder, or syrup composed of the kernels of the cacao nut roasted, ground, and combined with sugar; a beverage made by dissolving chocolate in boiling water or milk; a candy made of chocolate or dipped in chocolate.—*a.* Made of chocolate; as, *chocolate* ice cream; having the flavor or color of chocolate; of a dark brown color.

choc·o·late tree, *n.* The cacao, *Theobroma cacao*, which is grown for its seeds.

Choc·taw, chok′tą, *n.* pl. **Choc·taw, Choc·taws.** One of the tribes of North American Indians from the Muskogean linguistic group; a member of the tribe; the language spoken by members of the tribe.

choice, chois, *n.* [O.Fr. *chois*, a choice, < *choisir*, to choose; < German. CHOOSE.] The act or power of choosing; a selecting or separating from two or more things that which is preferred; selection; election; option; preference; the person or thing chosen; the best part of anything.

choice, chois, *a.* Carefully selected; worthy of being preferred; select; precious.—**choice·ly,** *adv.* In a choice manner or degree.—**choice·ness,** *n.* The quality of being choice or select; excellence.

choir, kwir, *n.* [O.Fr. *chœur*, L. *chorus*, Gr. *choros*, a dance in a ring, a band; same word as *chorus, quire*.] A group of singers, esp. in a church; a band of singers and dancers; the part of a church appropriated for the choir; in a cruciform church, the part eastward of the crossing.

choir, kwir, *v.t., v.i.* To sing in company.

choir, kwir, *a.* Of or pertaining to a group in a religious order qualified to chant the divine office.

choir·boy, kwir′boi″, *n.* A boy who sings as one of the members of a choir, esp. of a church choir.

choir loft, *n.* A gallery in a church, reserved for the choir.

choir·mas·ter, kwir′mas″tĕr, kwir′mä″ster, *n.* The director or conductor of a choir.

choke, chōk′, *v.t.*—*choked, choking.* [M.E. *choken, cheken*: cf. O.E. *acēocian*, choke.] To stop the breath of, by stricture of or obstruction in the windpipe; strangle; stifle; suffocate; to stop, as the breath or utterance, by or as by strangling or stifling; to check the growth, progress, or action of; suppress, as a feeling or emotion; to stop by filling; obstruct; clog; congest; to fill chock-full; to restrict the air supply to the carburetor of an engine to help starting. —*v.i.* To suffer strangling or suffocation; to be obstructed or clogged.

choke, chōk, *n.* The act or sound of choking; a narrowing, as of the bore of a gun; *auto mechanics*, a mechanism in car engines which restricts the supply of air to the carburetor as a help in starting.

choke·ber·ry, chok′ber″ē, chok′be·rē, *n.* pl. **choke·ber·ries.** The astringent berrylike fruit of shrubs of the North American genus *Aronia*, esp. *A. arbutifolia*; a plant bearing this fruit.

choke·cher·ry, chok′cher″ē, *n.* pl. **choke·-cher·ries.** Any of several species of cherry, esp. *Prunus virginiana* of North America, which bear an astringent fruit; the fruit itself.

choke coil, *n. Elect.* a coil of large inductance, which, when interposed in an electric circuit, allows steady currents to pass freely, but chokes off or greatly weakens all rapid fluctuations.

choke·damp, chok′damp″, *n. Coal-mining.* A heavy gas consisting essentially of carbon dioxide, which accumulates at the bottom of undisturbed workings and can cause choking; black-damp.

chok·er, chō′kĕr, *n.* One who or that which chokes; a short, jewelled necklace; a high, close-fitting collar.

chok·y, chō′kē, *a.*—*chokier, chokiest.* Tending to choke or suffocate one.

chol·e·cys·tec·to·my, kol″i·si·stek′to·mē, kō″li·si·stek′to·mē, *n.* pl. **chol·e·-cys·tec·to·mies.** *Med.* surgical removal of the gall bladder.

chol·er, kol′ĕr, *n.* [O.Fr. *cholere* (Fr. *colère*), choler, anger, L. *cholera*, a bilious ailment, < Gr. *cholera* < *cholē*, bile, anger.] Anger, wrath, irascibility, formerly believed to be caused by an excess of bile.

chol·er·a, kol′ĕr·a, *n.* [L. bile, a bilious complaint. CHOLER.] Any of several acute infectious diseases of men and domestic animals, characterized by severe intestinal disturbances.

chol·er·ic, kol′ĕr·ik, ko·ler′ik, *a.* Easily irritated; irascible; inclined to anger; quick-tempered.

cho·les·te·rol, ka·les′te·rōl″, ka·les′te·rąl″, ka·les′te·rol″, *n.* [Gr. *cholē*, bile, and *stereos*, solid.] A fat-soluble alcohol, $C_{27}H_{45}OH$, present in body cells and animal fats and tissues; a form of this compound used in making ointments and pharmaceuticals.

cho·lic ac·id, kō′lik as′id, kol′ik as′id, *n.* A crystalline acid, $C_{24}H_{40}O_5$, found combined with the amino acids, glycine and taurine, in bile: its commercial form, derived from beef bile, is used in biochemical research and the manufacture of drugs.

cho·line, kō′lēn, kol′ēn, kol′in, *n.* A basic substance, $C_5H_{15}NO_2$, widely distributed in animal and plant organisms which is a member of the vitamin-B complex and essential to the function of the liver.

chol·la, chōl′yä, chōl′ya, *Sp.* chą′yä, *n.* [Mex.] Any of several spiny, treelike cactuses of the genus *Opuntia*, esp. *O. fulgida*, of southwestern U.S and Mexico.

chon·drite, kon′drit, *n.* [See *chondrule*.] Meteoric stone containing crystalline spherules or chondri.—**chon·drit·ic,** kon-drit′ik, *a.*

chon·drule, kon′drŏl, *n.* [Gr. *chrondus*, grit, grain, cartilage.] One of the spherules of crystalline matter found in certain meteorites. Also **chon·drus.**

choose, chōz, *v.t.*—past *chose, chosen, choosing.* [O.E. *cēosan* = G. *kiesen* = Goth. *kiusan*; akin to L. *gestus, gustare*, a tasting, Gr. *geuesthai*, taste, Skt. *jush-*, relish.] To select from a number, or in preference to another or others, or to something else; to prefer and decide, or think fit.—*v.i.* To make a choice; to be disposed to; to decide in a game who will have first choice of players or positions.

choos·y, chō′zē, *a.*—*choosier, choosiest.* Particular in one's choice; hard to please; fussy; selective.

chop, chop, *v.t.*—*chopped, chopping.* [M.E. = D. and L.G. *kappen*, Dan. *kappe*, Sw. *kappa*, cut.] To cut with a quick, heavy blow of an ax, or with a succession of blows; to make by so cutting; to cut in pieces by repeated strokes; mince.—*v.i.* To take away the influence, power, or amount of, used with *down*; to hack with an ax; move suddenly or violently.

chop, chop, *n.* A cutting blow; a slice of mutton, veal, or pork, usually one containing a rib; material that has been chopped; a short, irregular, broken motion of waves; the mark made by an ax; a short, downward stroke of the racquet that gives backspin to a tennis ball.

chop, chop, *v.i.*—*chopped, chopping.* [Akin to *cheap* and *chapman*.] To turn, shift, or change suddenly, as the wind.

chop, chop, *n.* [Hind. *chhāp*, impression, stamp.] In India and China, an official stamp or seal, or a permit or clearance; a mark or brand on goods; a kind or brand of goods; *colloq.* a grade or quality.

chop-house, chop′hous″, *n.* An eating-house making a specialty of chops and steaks.

chop·per, chop′ĕr, *n.* A short ax with a large blade, as a butcher's cleaver; any device for regularly interrupting an electric current or beam of light; *slang,* a helicopter.

chop·pi·ness, chop′ē·nes, *n.* The state of being irregular or variable in quality or style, as a piece of literature; the surface of water being broken by short irregular waves.

chop·py, chop′ē, *a.*—**choppier, choppiest.** Shifting or changing suddenly or irregularly, as the wind; disjointed; incoherent; showing short broken waves, as on a body of water.

chop·stick, chop′stik, *n.* One of two small sticks of wood or ivory, used by the Chinese and Japanese for conveying food to the mouth.

chop su·ey, chop′sŏ′ē, *n.* [Chinese.] A mixed dish served in the U.S. in Chinese restaurants, consisting of fowl or other meat cut into bits with onions, bean sprouts, green peppers, water chestnuts, mushrooms, or other vegetables and seasoning, in a gravy or sauce: commonly eaten with rice.

cho·ra·gus, ko·rā′gus, kō·rä′gus, *n.* [Gr. *choragos—choros,* a chorus, and *agō,* to lead.] The leader of a chorus or of a theatrical representation in ancient Greece; the person who had to provide at his own expense the choruses for dramatic representations and religious festivals; any choral or theatrical conductor.—**cho·ra·gic,** ko·raj′ik, ko·rā′jik, *a.* Pertaining to or connected with a choragus.

cho·ral, kōr′al, *a.* [M.L. *choralis,* < L. *chorus.*] Of or pertaining to a chorus or a choir; sung by or adapted for a chorus or choir.—*n.* A chorale.—**cho·ral·ly,** *adv.*

cho·rale, ko·ral′, ko·räl′, kō·ral′, kō·räl′, *n.* [G.] A choral composition; a hymn tune, esp. a simple sacred tune having a plain melody, a strong harmony, and a stately rhythm.—**cho·ral·ist,** *n.* One who sings in a chorus or a choir; a composer of choral music.

cho·rale pre·lude, *n.* A composition for an organ, usually made up of two interwoven melodies, and based on a chorale or other hymn.

cho·ral speak·ing, *n.* Recitation of passages by a group, such as a chorus or ensemble.

chord, kård, *n.* [Earlier *cord,* for *accord.*] Accord; *mus.* a combination of three or more tones in harmonic relation, sounded simultaneously.—*v.i., v.t.*

chord, kård, *n.* [L. *chorda,* cord, string, < Gr. *chorde,* gut, string of a musical instrument.] *Archaic,* a string of a musical instrument; *fig.* a feeling or emotion. *Geom.* the part of a straight line between two of its intersections with a curve; a straight line joining the extremities of an arc of a circle; *engin.* a main horizontal member of a bridge-truss; *anat.* a cord.

chord·al, kår′dal, *a. Mus.* in reference to a chord; pertaining to music which is characterized by harmony rather than by counterpoint.

chor·date, kår′dāt, *n.* Any of the large primary subdivisions in the animal kingdom called *Chordata,* including the true vertebrate and those having at least an embryonic backbone or notochord.

chord or·gan, *n.* An electric organ which produces pre-set chords played by push buttons.

chore, chōr, chår, *n.* [An alteration of E. *chare,* an odd job.] A task; a duty; a small odd job.

cho·re·a, ko·rē′a, kō·rē′a, ka·rē′a, *n.* [Gr. *choreia,* a dance.] *Med.* St. Vitus' dance; convulsive motions of the limbs, and strange and involuntary gesticulations.

cho·re·o·graph·ic, kōr′ē·o·graf′ik, *a.* Pertaining to choreography.

cho·re·og·ra·phy, kōr′ē·og′ra·fē, *n.* [Gr. *choreia,* dance, and *graphy, graphein,* to write.] The art of designing and arranging ballet and other dance compositions.— **cho·re·og·ra·pher,** *n.*—**cho·re·o·graph,** *v.t., v.i.*

cho·ri·amb, kōr′ē·amb″, *n.* [Gr. *choreios,* a trochee, and *iambos,* iambus.] In poetry, a foot consisting of four syllables,

the first two forming a trochee and the second two an iambus. Also **cho·ri·amb·us.**

cho·ric, kōr′ik, *a.* Pertaining to a chorus; arranged for choral singing.

cho·ri·o·al·lan·to·is, kōr″ē·ō·a·lan′tō·is, kōr″ē·ō·a·lan′tois, *n. Zool.* a very vascular membrane formed in the fetal tissue of birds, reptiles, and some mammals, and used, as in the hen's egg, as a living culture medium for viruses and tissues. Also **cho·ri·o·al·lan·to·ic mem·brane.**

cho·ri·on, kōr′ē·on″, *n.* [N.L., < Gr. *chorion,* chorion, membrane.] *Anat.* the very vascular outer membrane enveloping a fetus of the higher vertebrates, enclosing the amnion.

chor·is·ter, kor′i·stėr, *n.* A singer in a choir; esp. a male singer in a church choir; a choir boy; a choir leader; *fig.* one of a flock of birds that sing; as, feathered *choristers.*

C hor·i·zon, *n. Geol.* in a cross-section of layers of soil, the layer above bedrock and beneath the B horizon, consisting largely of disintegrated rock.

cho·rog·raph·ic, kōr″o·graf′ik, *a.* Pertaining to chorography; descriptive of particular regions or countries.—**cho·ro·graph·i·cal,** *a.*—**cho·ro·graph·i·cal·ly,** *adv.*

cho·rog·ra·phy, ko·rog′ra·fē, kō·rog′ra·fē, *n.* [Gr. *chōros,* a place or region, and *graphō,* to describe.] The art or practice of making maps of, or of describing, particular regions, countries, or districts.— **cho·rog·ra·pher,** *n.*

cho·roid, kōr′oid, kår′oid, *n. Anat.* the middle coat of the eye.—*a.* Pertaining to the choroid; resembling the chorion and corium. Also **cho·ri·oid,** kōr′ē·oid″, kår′ē·oid.

chor·tle, chår′tl, *v.i.*—**chortled, chortling.** To chuckle or utter with glee.

cho·rus, kōr′us, *n.* [L. *chorus,* < Gr. *choros,* a dance in a ring, a chorus.] Originally a band of dancers accompanied by their own singing or that of others; the performers in a Greek play who were supposed to behold what passed in the acts, and sing their sentiments between the acts; the song between the acts; now, usually, verses of a song in which the company joins the singer, or the singing of the company with the singer; a dancing and singing ensemble of girls, men, or both in a musical comedy, night club, or other variety show; a union or chiming of voices in general; as a *chorus* of laughter or ridicule; *mus.* a composition in parts sung by many voices; the whole body of vocalists other than soloists, whether in an oratorio, opera, or concert.

cho·rus, kōr′us, *v.t.* To sing or join in the chorus of; to exclaim or call out in concert.

cho·rus boy, cho·rus girl, *n.* One who sings or dances as a member of the chorus in a musical entertainment.

chose, shōz, *n.* [Fr. thing, < L. *causa,* E. cause.] *Law,* a thing; an item of personal property.—**chose in ac·tion,** an incorporeal right enforceable by legal action, as a franchise.

chos·en, chō′zen, *a.* [CHOOSE.] Selected from a number; preferred; *theol.* elect. —**the chos·en peo·ple,** the Israelites; the Jews.

chow, chou, *n. U.S. army slang,* food.

chow chow, chow, *n.* A breed of dog, originating in China, of medium size with a broad muzzle and head, a thick coat of brown, black, or red hair, and a black tongue and mouth.

chow-chow, chou′chou″, *n.* A Chinese term for any food mixture, particularly a preserve

of mixed fruits and spices; mixed pickles; relish with mustard sauce.

chow·der, chou′dėr, *n.* [Prob. < Fr. *chaudière,* caldron.] A kind of thick soup or stew made of clams or fish with potatoes, onions, and other ingredients and seasoning.

chow hall, *n. Slang,* a large dining room, esp. a military mess hall, where meals are served to members of a group.

chow hound, *n. Slang,* one who has gluttonous eating habits.

chow line, *n. Slang,* the members of a group, such as soldiers or students, waiting in line to be served food in cafeteria style.

chow mein, chou″mān′, *n.* A Chinese-American stew usually served over a bed of fried noodles and consisting of pieces of meat and a variety of vegetables which are cooked so as to retain a certain amount of crispness.

chres·tom·a·thy, kres·tom′a·thē, *n. pl.* **chres·tom·a·thies.** [Gr. *chrēstomatheia,* < *chrēstos,* useful and *manthanein,* learn.] A book of extracts from a foreign language, intended to be used in acquiring the language; a book of extracts from one author.

chrism, kriz′am, *n.* [O.E. *crisma,* < L.L. *chrisma,* < Gr. *chrisma,* unguent, unction, < *chriein,* rub, anoint.] *Eccles.* a consecrated oil used by certain churches in the rites of baptism, confirmation, etc.; a sacramental anointing; the rite of confirmation, esp. as administered in the Greek Church; extreme unction.

chris·om, kriz′om, *n.* [Var. of *chrism.*] A white cloth or robe formerly put on a child at baptism, and also at burial if the child died soon after baptism.

Christ, krist, *n.* [L. *Christus,* Gr. *Christos,* lit. anointed, < *chriein,* to anoint.] One anointed as ruler; the appellation given to Jesus of Nazareth by the Christian world as the one fulfilling the prophecy in the Old Testament of a deliverer, a Messiah; first used as a title, *Jesus the Christ,* later as a proper name, *Jesus Christ;* an ideal type of person who resembles Jesus Christ.

christ·cross, kris′krås″, kris′krós″, *n. Brit. dial.* the signature mark made by an illiterate in place of his name.

chris·ten, kris′n, *v.t.* [O.E. *cristnian,* < *cristen,* < L. *christianus,* Christian.] To receive into the Christian church by baptism; baptize; to give a name to at baptism; hence, to name and dedicate; to name generally.

Chris·ten·dom, kris′en·dom, *n.* [O.E. *cristendōm—cristen,* Christian.] The territories, countries, or regions chiefly inhabited by Christians or those who profess to believe in the Christian religion; the whole body of Christians.

chris·ten·ing, kris′e·ning, kris′ning, *n.* The Christian ceremony of baptising and naming a child; the formal public ceremony of naming and dedicating a new ship; the ceremony of giving recognition or a name to anything new or recently completed.

Chris·tian, kris′chan, *n.* [L. *christianus,* < *Christus,* Christ.] One who believes, professes to believe, or who is assumed to believe, in the religion of Christ and whose behavior exemplifies His teachings; one who belongs to a Christian church; the given name for a boy.—*a.* Pertaining to Christ or to Christianity; *colloq.* humane; not brutal; respectable.

Chris·tian Broth·er, *n.* A member of the Roman Catholic order of brothers founded in 1680 and dedicated to teaching in primary and secondary schools.

Chris·tian e·ra, Chris·tian per·i·od, *n.* The period from the birth of Christ to the present time.

chris·ti·a·ni·a, kris″chē·an′e·a, kris·tyä′-nē·ä, *n. Skiing,* (often cap.) a turn usually made at high speed in order to stop, check speed, or alter direction, by shifting the weight of the body forward and sliding into the turn while keeping the skis parallel; commonly a **par·al·lel chris·tie** or **chris·ty.**

Chris·ti·an·i·ty, kris′chē·an′i·tē, *n. pl.* **Chris·ti·an·i·ties.** The religion of Christians, including the Eastern Orthodox, Roman Catholic, and Protestant church faiths; the system of doctrines and precepts taught by Christ; conformity with the precepts of the Christian religion.

Chris·tian·ize, kris′cha·nīz″, *v.t.—Christianized, Christianizing.* To make Christian; to convert to Christianity.—**Chris·tian·i·za·tion,** *n.*

Chris·tian name, *n.* The name given at baptism, as distinguished from the family name.

Chris·tian Re·formed, *a.* Having reference to an American Protestant Church which broke away from the Dutch Reformed Church in 1875.

Chris·tian Sci·ence, *n.* A system of religious teaching based on the Scriptures, the most notable application of which is the treatment of disease by mental and spiritual means: founded about 1866 by Mary Baker Eddy.—**Chris·tian Sci·en·tist,** *n.*

Christ·like, krĭst′lĭk″, *a.* Of or like Christ; showing the spirit of Christ. Also **Christ·ly.** —**Christ·like·ness, Christ·li·ness,** *n.*

Christ·mas, kris′m*a*s, *n.* [Christ, and *mass,* O.E. *mæsse,* a holy day or feast.] The festival of the Christian church observed annually on the 25th day of December, in memory of the birth of Christ; Christmas day.

Christ·mas·tide, kris′m*a*s·tĭd, *n.* The season of Christmas, esp. in England, from Christmas Eve until Epiphany, January 6.

Christ·mas tree, *n.* An evergreen tree or facsimile, set up at Christmas, and customarily decorated with ornaments and lights. *Slang,* the intricate assembly of pipes, valves and gauges on an oil well; the lighted derrick of an oil well; the panel in the control room of a submarine.

Chris·tol·o·gy, kri·stol′o·jē, *n.* The branch of theology which treats of Christ and His works; a doctrine concerning the person of Christ and His works.

Chris·toph·a·ny, kri·stof′o·nē, *n. pl.* **Chris·toph·a·nies.** An appearance of Christ to men after his death.

chro·ma, krō′ma, *n.* [Gr. *chrōma,* color.] The purity of a color, or the degree of its freedom from white or gray; the intensity of distinctive hue; the intensity or saturation of a color.

chro·mate, krō′māt, *n. Chem.,* a salt of chromic acid.

chro·mat·ic, krō·mat′ik, kro·mat′ik, *a.* [Gr. *chrōmatikos < chrōma,* color.] Of or pertaining to color or colors; *mus.* involving a modification of the diatonic scale by the use of semitones; progressing by semitones, and not by the regular intervals of the diatonic scale; indicating chords or harmony in a given composition which are not in the diatonic scale used in that composition.—**chro·mat·i·cal·ly,** *adv.*

chro·ma·tic ab·er·ra·tion, *n.* Aberration brought about by dissimilarities in refraction of the colored rays of the spectrum.

chro·ma·tic·i·ty, krō″ma·tis′i·tē, *n.* The condition of being chromatic; the character of a color ascertained from its dominant wavelength and its purity combined.

chro·mat·ics, krō·mat′iks, kro·mat′iks, *n.* The science of colors; that part of optics which treats of the properties of colors; the section of colorimetry which treats saturation and hue.

chro·ma·tic scale, *n. Mus.* a scale made up of thirteen successive semitones, that is, the eight diatonic tones and the five intermediate tones.

chro·ma·tid, krō′ma·tid, *n. Biol.* one of a pair of chromosomal strands which are formed when a chromosome duplicates during cell reproduction.

chro·ma·tin, krō′ma·tin, *n. Biol.* the constituent of a chromosome which is believed to carry the genes and which stains deeply with basic dyes.—**chro·ma·tin·ic,** *a.*

chro·ma·tism, krō′ma·tiz″am, *n.* [Gr. *chromatismos,* coloring, < *chromatizein,* to color, < *chroma,* color.] Abnormal coloration, as of the normally green parts of plants; *chromatic aberration.*

chro·ma·tog·ra·phy, krō″ma·tog′ra·fē, *n. Chem.* separation of closely related compounds by a method in which the compounds in solution are separately adsorbed in colored layers of an adsorbent to facilitate the analysis of mixtures.—**chro·ma·to·graph·ic,** *a.*

chro·ma·tol·o·gy, *n.* The doctrine of, or a treatise on, colors.

chro·ma·to·phore, krō′ma·to·fōr″, krō·mat′o·fōr″, kro·mat′o·fōr″, *n. Zool.* a colored mass of protoplasm; a pigment-bearing body or cell, as one of those which through contraction and expansion produce a temporary change in color in cuttlefish or chameleons; *bot.* one of the plastids in plant-cells.—**chro·ma·to·phor·ic,** *a.*

chrome, krōm, *n.* [Fr., < Gr. *chrōma,* color.] Chromium, esp. as the source of various pigments, as chrome-green, chrome-orange, chrome-yellow; finished metallic accessories on an automobile which are plated with chromium.

chrome, krōm, *v.t.—chromed, chroming. Dyeing,* to process by immersing in a solution of bichromate of potassium. To plate with a chromium compound; to use a chromium compound in treating leather.

chrome al·um, *n. Chem.* a dark-violet double sulfate of chromium and potassium or ammonium used in dyeing and tanning.

chro·mic, krō′mik, *a.* Of or containing chromium, esp. when trivalent.

chro·mic ac·id, *n.* An acid, H_2CrO_4, known in the form of chromates or salts and in solution.

chro·mi·nance, krō′mi·nans, *n. Color TV,* the measured difference in color intensity between a color and an equally bright reference color of the same hue.

chro·mite, krō′mīt, *n.* A mineral, $FeCr_2O_4$, containing chromium and ion oxides; *chem.* a salt containing bivalent chromium.

chro·mi·um, krō′mē·um, *n.* [N.L., for Fr. and E. *chrome.*] *Chem.* sym. Cr, at. no. 24; a lustrous, hard, metallic element occurring in compounds, resistant to corrosion, and widely used for making alloys and in electroplating.

chro·mo, krō′mō, *n. pl.* **chro·mos,** krō′mōz. Shortened form of *chromolithographic.*

chro·mo·gen, krō′mo·jen, *n. Chem.* a compound which, although not itself a dye, is capable of being converted into one, owing to its color-forming atomic groups.—**chro·mo·gen·ic,** *a.* Pertaining to chromogen or a chromogen; also, producing color; of bacteria, forming some characteristic color or pigment.

chro·mo·lith·o·graph, krō″mo·lith′o·graf″, krō″mō·lith′o·gräf″, *n.* A picture printed in colors by means of the lithographic process.

chro·mo·li·thog·ra·phy, krō″mō·li·thog′ra·fē, *n.* A method of reproducing colored pictures by lithography.—**chro·mo·lith·o·graph·ic,** *a.*—**chro·mo·li·thog·ra·pher,** *n.*

chro·mo·ne·ma, krō″mo·nē′ma, *n. Genetics,* the coiled, threadlike core of a chromatid considered to be the carrier of the genes.

chro·mo·phil, chro·ma·to·phil, krō′mo·fil, krō″mat′o·fil, *a. Biol.* staining easily with dyes, as cells or tissues.

chro·mo·phore, krō′mo·fōr″, *n. Chem.* a chemical group which when found in an aromatic or other compound gives color to the compound.

chro·mo·plast, krō′mo·plast″, *n. Bot.* a plastid, or mass of protoplasm, containing coloring matter other than chlorophyl.

chro·mo·pro·tein, krō″mo·prō′tēn, krō″mo·prōt′ē·in, *n. Biochem.* a protein compound, as hemoglobin, made up of a protein combined with a pigment or a carotenoid.

chro·mo·so·mal, krō″mo·sō′mal, *a. Biol.* of or pertaining to chromosomes.—**chro·mo·som·al·ly,** *adv.*

chro·mo·some, krō′mo·sōm″, *n. Biol.* one of the rod or thread-shaped bodies containing chromatin which carry the genes and are present, in a fixed number for each species, in all the cell nuclei of plants and animals.—**chro·mo·so·mic,** *a.*

chro·mo·sphere, krō′mo·sfēr″, *n.* [Gr. *chrōma,* color, and *sphaira,* a sphere.] *Astron.* a gaseous layer surrounding the sun above the photosphere, consisting primarily of hydrogen, which gives it a reddish color; a similar layer surrounding any star.—**chro·mo·spher·ic,** krō″mo·sfēr′ik, *a.* Pertaining to a chromosphere.

chro·mous, krō′mus, *a. Chem.* of or pertaining to chromium, esp. in referring to compounds in which chromium has a valence of two. See *chromic.*

chron·ic, kron′ik, *a.* [Gr. *chronikos, < chronos,* time, duration.] Long-lasting or recurring frequently over a long period of time; of a disease or ailment of long duration or repeated occurrences, as differentiated from *acute*; as, *chronic* arthritis; ever-present or constant, esp. of a worrisome or annoying situation; as, *chronic* tardiness; repeated, continuous, or habitual in manner or acts; as, a *chronic* complainer.—**chro·nic,** *n.*—**chron·i·cal,** *a.*—**chron·i·cal·ly,** *adv.* —**chro·nic·i·ty,** *n.*

chron·i·cle, kron′i·kal, *n.* [Fr. *chronique,* a chronicle.] A usually detailed record of facts or events set down in the order of time with no attempt made to evaluate or interpret. *Pl.* (*cap.*) the title of two books of the Old Testament consisting mainly of the annals of the kingdom of Judah.—*v.t.—chronicled, chronicling.* To record in a chronicle or in the style of a chronicle.—**chron·i·cler,** *n.* A writer of a chronicle.

chron·i·cle play, *n.* A drama consisting of a series of short, historic episodes in chronological order.

chron·o·gram, kron′o·gram″, *n.* [< Gr.] A word or words in which a date is expressed in boldface by the Roman numeral letters occurring therein; a record of time provided by a chronograph.—**chron·o·gram·matic, chron·o·gram·mat·i·cal,** *a.*

chron·o·graph, kron′o·graf″, kron′o·gräf″, *n.* [Gr. *chronos* and *graph, < Gr. graphein,* mark, draw, write.] An astronomical or other instrument for recording the exact instant of occurrences, or for measuring small intervals of time.—**chron·o·graph·ic,** kron′o·graf′ik, *a.*

chron·o·log·ic, kron″o·loj′ik, *a.* Relating to chronology; containing an account of events in the order of time; according to the order of time. Also **chron·o·log·i·cal.** —**chron·o·log·i·cal·ly,** *adv.* In a chronological manner.

---

chro·nol·o·gist, chro·nol·o·ger, kro·-nol′o·jist, kro·nol′o·jẽr, *n.* One versed in chronology; a person who investigates the dates of past events and transactions.

chro·nol·o·gy, kro·nol′o·jē, *n. pl.* **chro·nol·o·gies.** [Gr. *chronologia—chronos,* time, and *logos,* discourse or doctrine.] The science of ascertaining the true periods or years when past events or transactions took place, and arranging them in their proper order according to their dates; an arrangement according to time sequence; a history reference work organized according to the time sequence of past events.

chro·nom·e·ter, kro·nom′i·tẽr, *n.* Any instrument that measures time, as a clock, watch, or dial; specifically, a highly precise timepiece used in conjunction with observation of heavenly bodies, to determine longitude at sea, or employed whenever exact time measurement is necessary.—**chron·o·met·ric, chron·o·met·ri·cal,** *a.*

chro·nom·e·try, kro·nom′i·trē, *n.* The art of measuring time; the measuring of time by periods or divisions.

chron·o·scope, kron′o·skōp″, krō′no·-skōp″, *n.* An instrument for measuring the duration of extremely short-lived phenomena; more especially, the name given to instruments of various forms for measuring the velocity of projectiles.

chrys·a·lis, kris′a·lis, *n. pl.* **chrys·a·lis·es, chry·sal·i·des.** [Gr. *chrysallis,* a grub, < *chrysos,* gold, < its golden color.] The form which butterflies, moths, and most other similar insects assume when they change from the state of larva or caterpillar and before they arrive at their winged or perfect state; a pupa. Also **chrys·a·lid.**

chry·san·the·mum, kri·san′the·mum, *n.* [L., < Gr. *chrysanthemon,* < *chrysos,* gold, and *anthemon,* flower.] Any of the perennial asteraceous plants constituting the genus *Chrysanthemum,* as *C. leucanthemum,* the oxeye daisy; more commonly, any of many cultivated varieties of *C. sinense,* a native of China, and of other species of *Chrysanthemum,* notable for the diversity of color, shape, and size of their autumnal flowers; the flower of such a plant.

chrys·o·ber·yl, kris′o·ber″il, *n.* [L. *chrysoberyllus,* < Gr. *chrysobēryllos,* < *chrysos,* gold, and *beryllos,* beryl.] A native mineral, commonly of a yellow or greenish color, sometimes used as a gem.

chrys·o·lite, kris′o·līt″, *n.* [O.Fr. *crisolite* (Fr. *chrysolithe*), < L. *chrysolithos,* < Gr. *chrysolithos,* < *chrysos,* gold, and *lithos,* stone.] A native silicate of magnesium and iron, varying from yellow to green, in some forms used as a gem; olivine.

chrys·o·prase, kris′o·prāz″, *n.* [Gr. *prason,* a leek.] A translucent mineral of an apple-green color; a variety of chalcedony esteemed as a gem.

chtho·ni·an, thō′nē·an, *a.* [Gr. *chthonios,* < *chthon,* earth.] Dwelling in or beneath the surface of the earth; noting or pertaining to the deities or spirits of the underworld. Also **chthon·ic,** thon′ik.

chub, chub, *n. pl.* **chubs** or, esp. collectively, **chub.** [M.E. *chubbe;* origin unknown.] A common fish, *Leuciscus cephalus,* of Europe; the allied *Semotilus atromaculatus* of America, sometimes used as bait in angling.

chub·by, chub′ē, *a.*—**chubbier, chubbiest.** [Akin to E. *chump;* Sw. dial. *kubbug,* plump, *kubb,* a lump, a block.] Having a round plump face or plump body; round and fat; plump—**chub·bi·ness,** *n.*

chuck, chuk, *v.t.* [A modification of *shock.* Fr. *choquer,* and formerly written *chock.*] To strike, tap, or give a gentle blow; to throw, with quick motion, a short distance; to pitch; to discard; *slang,* to be done with or to quit, as: He *chucked* his job.—*n.* A

slight blow or tap under the chin; a toss; a short throw.

chuck, chuk, *n.* [Prob. var. of *chock.*] Cut of beef between the neck and the shoulder blade; *slang,* food; *mech.* a clamp, block, or the like, as on a drill or lathe, for holding a boring tool or work while being shaped.

chuck, chuk, *n.* [Imit.] A clucking sound made by a hen and some other birds, or a sound resembling that.—*v.i.*

chuck-full, chuk′ful′, *a.* See *chock-full.*

chuck·hole, chuk′hōl″, *n.* A pothole or rut in a street or road.

chuck·le, chuk′ul, *v.i.*—**chuckled, chuckling.** [Imit. CHUCK.] To laugh in an easy, amused manner, with a degree of satisfaction; laugh to oneself; to cluck, as a fowl.—**chuck·le,** *n.* A quiet, amused laugh.

chuck wag·on, *n.* A wagon that carries food and cooking equipment to ranch hands or field workers, esp. western U.S.

chuck-will's-wid·ow, chuk′wilz·wid′ō, *n.* [Imit. of its note.] A goatsucker, *Caprimulgus carolinensis,* of the southern U.S., resembling the whippoorwill, but larger.

chug, chug, *n.* [Imit.] A short, dull, cough-like noise, as from an old or malfunctioning engine.—*v.i.* To make such a sound, as: The Model T *chugged* along.

chu·kar, chu·kär′, *n.* A partridge of Asiatic and European origin, *Alectoris chukar,* now established as a game bird in the western U.S. Also **chu·kar par·tridge.**

chuk·ka, chuk′a, *n.* An ankle-high boot often made of suede, and laced through pairs of eyelets. Also **chuk·ka boot.**

chuk·ker, chuk·kar, chuk′ẽr, chu·kär′, *n.* [Hind. *chakar.*] One of the periods of play in the game of polo.

chum, chum, *n.* [Perhaps an abbrev. of *chamber-fellow;* or of *chimney-fellow.*] A close companion; a bosom friend; an intimate; a roommate, often in school or college.—*v.i.* To be someone's chum.

chum, chum, *n.* [Origin unknown.] A fish bait, consisting usually of pieces of fish, used for baiting hooks and also thrown into the water in large quantities to attract other fish.—**chum,** *v.i.*—**chummed, chumming.** To fish with chum.

chum·my, chum′ē, *a.*—**chummier, chummiest.** *Colloq.* friendly, familiar, or sociable.—**chum·mi·ly,** *adv.*—**chum·mi·ness,** *n.*

chump, chump, *n.* [Same as Icel. *kumbr,* a log, akin to *kubba,* to chop, and therefore allied to E. *chop, chub, chubby.*] A short, thick, heavy piece of wood; a blockhead; *colloq.* a dolt; an ignoramus.

chunk, chungk, *n.* [Prob. var. of *chuck.*] A thick mass or lump of anything, as wood, bread, or meat; *colloq.* a thick-set and strong person or beast.—**chunk·y,** chungk′ē, *a.* Stout; stocky.

church, church, *n.* [O.E. *circe, cirice,* = G. *kirche,* prob. < L.Gr. *kyriakon,* "Lord's house," < Gr. *kyrios,* lord.] An edifice for public, esp. Christian, worship; the whole body of believers in Christ; any division of this body professing the same creed and acknowledging the same ecclesiastical authority; a Christian denomination; that part of the whole Christian body, or of a particular denomination, belonging to the same city, country, nation; a body of Christians worshiping in a particular edifice or constituting one congregation; the ecclesiastical organization as distinguished from the state; the clerical order or profession; public worship of God in a church; church service; by extension, a place of public worship of a non-Christian religion; any non-Christian religious society or organization; as, the Mohammedan *church.*

church, church, *a.* Of or referring to a church; *Brit.* of or relating to the established church.

church, church, *v.t.* To conduct or bring to church for special services; to perform a church service of thanksgiving.

church·go·er, church′gō″er, *n.* One who goes to church, esp. habitually or frequently.—**church·go·ing,** *n., a.*

church·ly, church′lē, *a.* Of, pertaining to, or appropriate for the church or a church; ecclesiastical.—**church·li·ness,** *n.*—**church·less,** *a.* Without a church; not belonging to or attending any church.

church·man, church′man, *n. pl.* **church·men.** An ecclesiastic; a clergyman; an adherent of the church; often, a member of an established or national church.—**church·man·ly,** *a.* Of or befitting a churchman.—**church·man·ship,** *n.*

Church of Eng·land, *n.* The national church of England, as established by law.

church·war·den, church′wär″den, *n.* A lay officer in an Anglican church whose duties include the management of the church property and legal representation of the parish; a lay officer in the Protestant Episcopal church who manages the temporal affairs of the parish. A clay tobacco-pipe with a very long stem.

church·wom·an, church′wum″an, *n. pl.* **church·wom·en.** A female member of a church, esp. of an Anglican church.

church·y, chur′chē, *a.*—**churchier, churchiest.** Pertaining to or suggestive of a church or the church; excessively devoted to a church or to church forms.

church·yard, church′yärd″, *n.* The yard or ground adjoining a church, often used as a graveyard.

churl, churl, *n.* [O.E. *ceorl,* a countryman of the lowest rank; Icel. Dan. Sw. *karl,* a man, a male; G. *kerl,* a fellow.] A rustic; a peasant; a rude, surly, selfish, or rough-tempered man.

churl·ish, chur′lish, *a.* Like or pertaining to a churl; rude; surly; uncivil; selfish; avaricious; hard to work or work with; as, *churlish* soil.—**churl·ish·ly,** *adv.* In a churlish manner.—**churl·ish·ness,** *n.*

churn, chern, *n.* [*cyrn,* Sc. *kirn,* Icel. *kirna,* Dan. *kierne,* a churn.] A vessel in which cream or milk is agitated in order to separate the fatty parts to make butter.

churn, chern, *v.t.* To stir or agitate (milk or cream) in order to make into butter; to make, as butter, by the agitation of milk or cream; to shake or agitate with violence or continued motion, as: The storm *churned* the waves.—*v.i.* To move in an agitated manner, as: The water *churned* around the rocks.

churr, chur, *n.* A noise made by some birds and insects, such as a partridge.—*v.i.* To make a whirring noise.

chur·ri·gue·resque, chur″ē·gu·resk′, *a.* Of or pertaining to a Spanish baroque architectural style in Spain and its colonies in the seventeenth and eighteenth centuries, characterized by flamboyant surface detailing.

chute, shŏt, *n.* [Fr. *cheoir,* to fall, < L. *cadere,* fall.] A waterfall; a steep descent, as in a river; a rapid; an inclined channel, trough, or shaft, for conveying water, or floating objects, grain, or coal, to a lower level; a steep slope for tobogganing.—**chute,** *v.t.*—*chuted, chuting.* To send down a chute.—*v.i.* To go down by means of a chute.

chute, shŏt, *n.* A parachute.—*v.i.* To descend from the air by means of a parachute.—*v.i.* To drop supplies or equipment from the air by parachute.

chut·ney, chut′nē, *n.* An East Indian condiment compounded of citrus fruit, raisins, and spices, cooked with sour herbs and cayenne to a jamlike consistency.

chyme, kīm, *n.* [L.L. *chymus,* < Gr. *chymos,* juice, < *chein,* pour.] The semi-liquid mass into which food is converted

by gastric secretion during digestion.—
chy·mi·fy, kī′mi·fī, *v.t., v.i.—chymified, chymifying.* To convert or be converted into chyme.—**chy·mi·fi·ca·tion,** *n.*

C.I.A., *n.* See *Central Intelligence Agency.*

ci·bo·ri·um, si·bōr′ē·um, si·bär′ē·um, *n.* pl. **ci·bo·ri·a,** si·bōr′e·a̧. [M.L. *ciborium,* canopy, L. drinking-cup, < Gr. *kiborion,* cup, seed-vessel of the Egyptian bean.] A permanent canopy placed over an altar; a baldachin; a vessel or receptacle for containing the consecrated bread of the Eucharist, having the form of a chalice with a dome-shaped cover.

ci·ca·da, si·kā′da̧, *n.* pl. **ci·ca·dae,** ci·ca′dē, si·kā·dē, si·kā′daz. [L.] The popular and generic name of certain insects, the males of which have on each side of the body an organ with which they can make considerable noise; cicala.

ci·ca·la, si·kä′la̧, *It.* chi·kä′la̧, *n.* See *cicada.*

cic·a·trix, sik′a·triks, si·kā′triks, *n.* pl. **cic·a·tri·ces,** sik″a·trī′sēz. *Med.* a scar; *bot.* a scar left on the branch by a fallen leaf. Also **cic·a·trice.—cic·a·tri·cal, ci·cat·ri·cose,** *a.*

cic·a·trize, sik′a·trīz″, *v.t.—cicatrized, cicatrizing.* To induce the formation of a cicatrice on; to heal.—*v.i.* To become healed, leaving a scar; to skin over. Also **cic·a·trise.—cic·a·tri·za·tion,** *n.*

cic·e·ly, sis′e·lē, *n.* [L. *seselis,* Gr. *seseli.*] Popular name applied to several plants, *sweet cicely,* or sweet chevril, being an aromatic plant with fine, fernlike foliage.

cic·e·ro·ne, sis″e·rō′nē, *It.* pron. chē··chä·rō′nä, *n.* [It., < *Cicero,* the Roman orator.] A name given by the Italians to the guides who show travelers the antiquities of the country; hence, a guide.

Cic·e·ro·ni·an, sis″e·rō′nē·an, *a.* Resembling the style of Cicero; eloquent.

ci·der, *Brit. variation,* **cy·der,** sī′dèr, *n.* [Fr. *cidre,* < L. *sicera,* Gr. *sikera,* strong drink, < Heb. *shēkār,* to intoxicate.] A fermented, slightly alcoholic drink prepared from apple juice.

ci·gar, si·gär′, *n.* [= Fr. *cigare,* < Sp. *cigarro.*] A small, shaped roll of tobacco leaves prepared for smoking.

cig·a·rette, cig·a·ret, sig″a·ret′, sig′a·ret″, *n.* [Fr., dim. of *cigare.* CIGAR.] A roll of finely cut tobacco for smoking, usually enclosed in thin paper.—**cig·a·rette-bee·tle,** *n.* A widely distributed beetle, *Lasioderma serricorne,* destructive to dried tobacco, cigars, and cigarettes.

cil·i·a, sil′ē·a, *n.* pl. [L. *cilium,* an eyelash.] The hairs which grow from the margin of the eyelids; eyelashes; hairs or bristles situated on the margin of a vegetable body; small, generally microscopic, hairlike vibratile processes which project from animal membranes, and usually have important functions.—*Sing., seldom used,* **cil·i·um,** sil′ē·um, *n.—***cil·i·ate,** cil·i·a·ted,** *a.*

cil·i·ar·y, sil′ē·er″ē, *a.* Belonging to the eyelids or eyelashes; pertaining to or performed by vibratile cilia; as, *ciliary* motion.

cil·ice, sil′is, *n.* [Fr., < L. *cilicium,* < Gr. *kilikion,* coarse cloth made of (orig. Cilician) goat's hair.] Haircloth; an undergarment or shirt of haircloth formerly worn by certain monks; a hair shirt.

ci·mex, sī′meks, *n.* pl. **cim·i·ces,** sim′i·sēz″. [L., bug.] The bedbug of the genus *Cimex.*

Cim·me·ri·an, si·mēr′ē·an, *n.* One of a mythical people described as dwelling where the sun never shines, and perpetual darkness reigns.—*a.* Pertaining to the *Cimerii* or *Cimmerians;* very dark.

cinch, sinch, *n.* [Sp. *cincha,* < M.L. *cincia,* girdle, < L. *cingere,* gird.] A strong girth for a saddle or pack horse; a firm hold or

grip on anything; *slang,* something sure or easy; a variety of the card game *all fours.*

cinch, sinch, *v.t.* To gird with a cinch; gird or bind firmly; *slang,* to seize on or make sure of; in the game of cinch, to protect (a trick) by playing a trump higher than the five.

cin·cho·na, sin·kō′na̧, *n.* [N.L., < the Countess of *Chinchón* (1576–1639), wife of a Spanish viceroy of Peru.] Any of the trees or shrubs constituting the genus *Cinchona,* as *C. calisaya,* native in the Andes, and cultivated there and elsewhere for their bark, which yields quinine and other alkaloids.

cin·cho·nine, sin′ko·nēn″, sin′ko·nin″, *n.* An alkaloid obtained from the bark of several species of cinchona, along with quinine, and one of the medicinal active principles of this bark, being valuable to reduce fever.

cin·chon·ism, sin′ko·niz″um, *n.* A disturbed condition of the body characterized by dizziness, ear ringing, temporary deafness, and headache, the result of overdoses of cinchona or quinine.

cinc·ture, singk′chèr, *n.* [L. *cinctura,* < *cingo, cinctum,* to gird, seen also in *precinct, succinct.*] A belt, girdle, or something similar; that which rings, encircles, or encloses; enclosure.

cin·der, sin′dèr, *n.* [O.E. *sinder* = G. *sinter,* dross of iron, E. *sinter.*] The dross of iron; slag; a burned-out or partially burned piece of coal, wood, or other substance (often in pl.); pl., any residue of combustion; ashes.—*v.t.* To reduce to cinders.

cin·der·el·la, sin″da̧·rel′a̧, *n.* A person, place, or thing of unrecognized worth, in a lowly position and suddenly elevated to high position and fame; from the fairly tale, *Cinderella.*

cine, sin′ē, sin′ā, *n.* A motion picture; a motion picture theater.

cin·e·ma, sin′a·ma, *n.* pl. **cin·e·mas,** sin′a·maz. [Short for *cinematograph.*] A motion-picture theater; a motion picture; with *the,* motion pictures collectively, as an art form.—*Chiefly Brit.* **cin·e·mat·ic,** sin″a·mat′ik, *a.*

cin·e·mat·o·graph, sin″e·mat′o·graf″, sin″e·mat′o·gräf″, *n.* [Fr. *cinématographe,* < Gr. *kinema,* motion, and *graphein,* draw, write.] An apparatus for projecting on a screen in rapid succession a series of photographs of moving objects so as to give the impression of continuous motion; the apparatus for taking the photographs.—*v.t.* To reproduce by a cinematograph.—**cin·e·ma·tog·ra·pher,** *n.* A motion picture cameraman or projectionist.

cin·e·ma·tog·ra·phy, sin″e·ma·tog′ra·fē, *n.* The art of photographing motion pictures.—**cin·e·mat·o·graph·ic,** *a.*

cin·e·ol, sin′ē·ōl″, si′nē·a̧l″, sin′ē·ol″, *n.* [N.L. *cina,* wormseed.] Eucalyptol; a colorless oil, $C_{10}H_{18}O$, with a camphor odor and pungent taste, derived from eucalyptus oil and used in medicine and in perfumery.

Cin·e·ra·ma, sin″a·ram′a, sin·a·rä′ma, *n.* A motion picture which gives the illusion of being three-dimensional: a three-lens camera, a curved cycloramic screen, three projectors, and dimensional sound are employed to produce the illusion. (Trademark.)

cin·e·rar·i·a, sin″a·râr′ē·a, *n.* [CINERARY (with reference to the soft white down on the leaves).] Any variety of the asteraceous plant *Senecio cruentus,* a native of the Canary Islands, with heart-shaped leaves and clusters of flowers with white, blue, purple, red, or variegated rays.

cin·e·rar·i·um, sin″a·râr′ē·um, *n.* pl. **cin·e·rar·i·a,** sin″a·râr′ē·a. [L.] A place for depositing the ashes of the dead after cremation.—**cin·e·rar·y,** sin′e·rer″ē, *a.*

cin·e·ra·tion, sin′e·rā″shan, *n.* [Cf. M.L. *cineratus,* reduced to ashes, also E. *incinerate.*] The reduction of anything to ashes, as by burning.—**cin·e·ra·tor,** *n.* A furnace for cineration; an incinerator.

ci·ne·re·ous, si·nēr′ē·us, *a.* [L. *cineraceus, cinereus,* < *cinis, cineris,* ashes.] Like ashes: having the color of the ashes of wood.—**cin·er·i·tious,** sin·e·ri′shus, *a.* [L. *cineritius.*] Having the color or consistency of ashes; ash-gray; *anat.* a term applied to the exterior or cortical part of the brain.

cin·gu·lum, sing′gū·lum, *n.* pl. **cin·gu·la,** sing′gū·la. [L., girdle, < *cingere,* gird.] *Zool.* a belt, zone, or girdle-like part.—**cin·gu·late, cin·gu·lat·ed, cin·gu·lar,** *a.*

cin·na·bar, sin′a·bär″, *n.* [L. *cinnabaris,* Gr. *kinnabari,* a word of Eastern origin; Pers. *quinbâr.*] Red mercuric sulfide, HgS, a heavy, crystallized mineral, the chief ore of mercury; red sulfide of mercury, which, when sublimed and used as a pigment, is called vermilion; the color vermilion.

cin·nam·ic, si·nam′ik, sin′a·mik, *a.* Pertaining to or obtained from cinnamon.

cin·na·mon, sin′a·mon, *n.* [L. *cinnamomum;* < Gr. *kinnamōmon,* through Phœn. < Heb. *qinnāmōn.*] Inner bark of a tree of the laurel family, genus *Cinnamonum,* native to tropical Asia, used as a spice or in medicine as a cordial or carminative; the tree having this bark; a reddish or yellowish brown.

cin·na·mon stone, *n.* A garnet that is yellow to brown in color; essonite.

cin·quain, sing·kān′, sing′kān, *n.* Any five line stanza; a poem made up of five normally unrhymed lines, having two, four, six, eight, and two syllables respectively; any group of five.

cinque, singk, *n.* [Fr., L. *quinque,* five.] A five in dice or cards.

cin·que·cen·to, ching″kwi·chen′tō, *n.* [It., five hundred, short for *mille cinquecento,* one thousand five hundred.] The 16th century, with reference to Italy, and esp. to the Italian art or literature of that period.—**cin·que·cen·tist,** ching″kwi·chen′tist, *n.* A 16th century Italian writer or artist.

cinque·foil, singk′foil″, *n.* [L. *folium,* a leaf.] *Arch.* an ornament somewhat resembling five leaves about a common center, often seen in apertures of circular windows; the name of various plants of the rose family, genus *Potentilla,* having leaves with five lobes; *her.* a five-bladed clover.

ci·on, si′on, *n.* Scion; a cutting, esp. one made for grafting or planting.

ci·pher, sī′fèr, *n.* [O.Fr. *cifre,* Mod.Fr. *chiffre,* It. *cifra,* Ar. *ṣifr,* naught, < Ar. *ṣifr,* zero.] The numerical character or figure 0 or nothing; any numerical character; an Arabic numeral; the Arabic numerical system as a whole; some person or thing of no consequence; a monogram or literal device formed of the intertwined initials of a name; a kind of secret writing which follows a prearranged system and is used to conceal the meaning of a message; a communication written in code; a key to a code.

ci·pher, sī′fèr, *v.i.* To use figures; to practice arithmetic.—*v.t.* To figure mathematically; to write in occult or secret characters.

cip·o·lin, sip′o·lin, *n.* [Fr., < It. *cipollino* (so called from its layered structure), < *cipolla,* < L. *cæpa,* onion.] A variety of marble with alternate white and greenish zones and a laminated structure.—*It.* **ci·pol·li·no.**

cir·ca, sur′ka, *adv., prep.* [L.] About; used esp. in giving approximate dates, and often abbreviated: c., ca., cir., circ.; as, c. 1550.

cir·ca·di·an rhythm, sèr″ka·dē′an riTH′um, *n. Biol.* rhythmic changes that occur in a plant or animal during a period of 24 hours

a- fat, fāte, fär, fâre, fa̧ll;   **e-** met, mē, mēre, hèr;   **i-** pin, pīne;   **o-** not, nōte, mōve;   **u-** tub, cūbe, bu̧ll;   **oi-** oil;   **ou-** pound.

when it is isolated from any daily environmental changes. Also *diurnal rhythm*.

Cir·cas·sian, sẻr·kash′an, sẻr·kash′ē·an, *n.* A native or inhabitant of Circassia; one of the native Caucasian race of Circassia, noted for physical beauty and courage; their language.—*a.* Of or pertaining to Circassia, a region on the northern slope of the Caucasus Mountains, and bordering on the Black Sea.

Cir·cas·sian wal·nut, *n.* A kind of walnut, a variety of *Juglans regia*, native in the Old World, whose light-brown wood is used as a veneer in making furniture.

cir·ci·nate, sǔr′si·nāt″, *a.* [< L. *circinus*, a compass, a circle, < *circus*, a circle.] *Bot.* curled up at the end, as the fronds of certain young ferns, and resembling a shepherd's crook.

cir·cle, sǔr′kl, *n.* [L. *circulus*, dim. of *circus*, a circle.] *Math.* a plane figure formed by a single curved line, called its *circumference*, every point of which is equally distant from a point within it, called the *center*, that distance being called the *radius*; the line bounding such a figure. A thing in circular form, as a ring, halo, or diadem; a tier of seats in a theater or the like, usually arranged in the form of a section of a circle; a group of persons or things forming a ring; as, a *circle* of dancers. A cycle; a series of actions or a process which returns to its starting point and may continue to repeat the entire cycle, sometimes used with *full*, as: Fashions have come *full circle*. An area or sphere of influence; a coterie; as, one's *circle* of friends; a group having a common tie; as, the family *circle*, a sewing *circle*. *Logic*, a type of fallacious argument wherein the conclusion is assumed in the premise; also *vicious circle*. *Geog.* a parallel of latitude on the earth's surface such as the equator, or *great circle*.

cir·cle, sǔr′kl, *v.t.*—*circled, circling*. To encircle; to surround; to enclose; to move around; to revolve around.—*v.i.* To move circularly; to circulate; to revolve.

cir·clet, sǔr′klit, *n.* A little circle; a ring; a circular ornament, esp. one for the head.

cir·cuit, sǔr′kit, *n.* [O.Fr. Fr. *circuit*, < L. *circuitus*, < *circuire, circumire*, go around.] The act of going or moving around; a circular journey; a round; a roundabout journey or course; a periodical journey from place to place to perform certain duties, as of judges to hold court or of ministers to preach; the persons making such a journey; the route followed, places visited, or district covered by such a journey; the line going around or bounding any area or object; the distance around an area or object; the space within a boundary line; *elect.* the complete path of an electric current, usu. including the generating apparatus; sometimes, a distinct portion of such a path; *computer*, a two-way communication system composed of related "Go" and "Return" channels. A theater chain in which productions are shown in turn; a league.

cir·cuit, sǔr′kit, *v.t.* To go or move around; make the circuit of.—*v.i.* To go or move in a circuit.

cir·cuit break·er, *n. Elect.* a safety device consisting of an automatic or manually controlled switching mechanism for interrupting a circuit, usually activated by the occurrence of abnormal current flow.

cir·cu·i·tous, sẻr·kū′i·tus, *a.* [M.L. *circuitosus*.] Roundabout; not direct.—**cir·cu·i·tous·ly,** *adv.*—**cir·cu·i·tous·ness,** *n.*

cir·cuit rid·er, *n.* An itinerant minister, traditionally a Methodist one, who traveled from place to place to preach along a circuit of churches.

cir·cuit·ry, sǔr′ki·trē, *n. Elect.* a plan or arrangement of an electric circuit; the parts which make up a circuit.

cir·cu·i·ty, sẻr·kū′i·tē, *n.* pl. **cir·cu·i·ties.** Circuitous quality; roundabout character; a circuitous course or proceeding.

cir·cu·lar, sǔr′kū·lẻr, *a.* [L. *circularis*.] In the form of a circle; round; circumscribed by a circle; passing over or forming a circle, circuit, or round; addressed to a number of persons; intended for general circulation; roundabout; devious, indirect; of or pertaining to a circle.—**cir·cu·lar·i·ty,** sẻr·kū·lar′i·tē, *n.*

cir·cu·lar, sǔr′kū·lẻr, *n.* A letter, notice, or advertisement usually in the form of a printed leaflet for distribution to publicize or promote an event or a business.

cir·cu·lar·ize, sǔr′kū·la·rīz″, *v.t.*—*circularized, circularizing*. To send circulars to; to ply with circulars.—**cir·cu·lar·i·za·tion,** *n.*—**cir·cu·lar·iz·er,** *n.*

cir·cu·lar meas·ure, *n.* The measure of an angle in radians in a measurement system for circles.

cir·cu·lar sys·tem, *n. Aeron.* a system for controlling guided missiles by sending out a signal from the missile to two radio stations and timing the echoes to keep on course.

cir·cu·lar ve·lo·city, *n. Aerospace*, the critical speed at which a satellite will move in a circular orbit.

cir·cu·late, sǔr′kū·lāt″, *v.i.*—*circulated, circulating*. [L. *circulo, circulatum*.] To move in a circle; to move around and return to the same point: to flow in the veins or channels of an organism; to pass from one person or place to another; to be diffused; to be sold or distributed among many people.—*v.t.* To cause to pass from place to place or from person to person; to spread.

cir·cu·la·ting dec·i·mal, *n.* See *repeating decimal*.

cir·cu·lat·ing li·brar·y, *n.* A library where the books circulate among its members.

cir·cu·la·tion, sǔr′kū·lā′shan, *n.* The act or circulating, moving, or flowing in a course which brings the moving body back to the point where its motion began; the continuous movement of blood through the vessels of the body maintained by the pumping action of the heart; recurrence in a certain order or series; the act of passing from place to place or from person to person; the extent and amount of distribution of periodicals; currency, coins, notes, and bills in use as money; number of books and other library materials in use.—**cir·cu·la·tive, cir·cu·la·to·ry,** *a.*

cir·cu·la·tor, sǔr′kū·lā″tẻr, *n.* One who moves from place to place; a scandalmonger; one who carries tales; any mechanism for circulating liquids.

cir·cum·am·bi·ent, sǔr″kum·am′bē·ent, *a.* [L. *circum*, around, and *ambio*, to go about.] Surrounding; encompassing; enclosing or being on all sides, as the air about the earth.—**cir·cum·am·bi·en·cy,** *n.*

cir·cum·cise, sǔr′kum·sīz″, *v.t.*—*circumcised, circumcising*. [L. *circumcisus*, pp. of *circumcidere*, cut around, < *circum*, around, and *cædere*, cut.] To cut off the foreskin of (males), esp. as a religious rite; perform an analogous operation on (females); *fig.* to purify spiritually.—**cir·cum·cis·er,** sǔr′kum·sī·zẻr, *n.*

cir·cum·ci·sion, sǔr″kum·sizh′on, *n.* [L.L. *circumcisio(n-)*.] The act or the rite of circumcising; *fig.* spiritual purification; the Jews, as the circumcised people of the Bible; those spiritually purified; (*cap.*) a church festival in honor of the circumcision of Christ, observed on Jan. 1.

cir·cum·fer·ence, sẻr·kum′fẻr·ens, *n.* [L. *circumferentia*, < *circumferre*, carry around, < *circum*, around, and *ferre*, bear.] The line that bounds a circle; the bounding line

or perimeter of any regular plane, curvilinear figure; the length of such a line; the encompassing boundary of any figure; distance around; the space within a bounding line.—**cir·cum·fer·en·tial,** *a.* Of or pertaining to the circumference.—**cir·cum·fer·en·tial·ly,** *adv.*

cir·cum·flex, sǔr′kum·fleks″, *n.* A mark ^ or ˆ or ˜, originally Greek, to indicate a rising-falling tone; later, in other languages, to mark a long vowel, contraction, or particular quality of vowel sound.—*a.* Pronounced with the quality, pitch, or stress indicated by a circumflex mark; marked with the circumflex accent; winding or bending around.—*v.t.* To mark with a circumflex; pronounce as so marked; to bend around.

cir·cum·flu·ent, sẻr·kum′flō·ent, *a.* [L. *circumfluens (-ent-)*, ppr. of *circumfluere*, < *circum*, around, and *fluere*, flow.] Flowing around; encompassing; surrounded as by water or in the manner of a fluid. Also **cir·cum·flu·ous.**—**cir·cum·flu·ence,** *n.*

cir·cum·fuse, sẻr″kum·fūz′, *v.t.*—*circumfused, circumfusing*. [L. *circumfusus*, pp. of *circumfundere*, < *circum*, around, and *fundere*, pour.] To pour around; diffuse; to surround, as with a fluid; suffuse.—**cir·cum·fu·sion,** *n.*

cir·cum·gy·ra·tion, sẻr″kym·ji·rā′shan, *n.* A revolution or movement in a circular course.

cir·cum·ja·cent, sẻr″kum·jā′sent, *a.* [L. *circumjacens*—*circum*, round, and *jaceo*, to lie.] Lying round; bordering on every side.

cir·cum·lo·cu·tion, sẻr″kum·lō·kū′shan, *n.* [L. *circum*, round, and *locutio*, a speaking, *loquor*, to speak.] The use of more words than necessary to express an idea; a deliberately round-about, evasive way of speaking; a phrase or passage with these characteristics.—**cir·cum·lo·cu·tion·al, cir·cum·lo·cu·tious, cir·cum·lo·cu·to·ry,** sẻr″kum·lok′ū·tor″ē, sẻr″kum·lok′ū·tar″ē, *a.*

cir·cum·lu·nar, sǔr″cum·lö′nẻr, *a.* Moving about or surrounding the moon; *aerospace*, pertaining to a trip or mission in which a space vehicle circles the moon.

cir·cum·nav·i·gate, sǔr″kum·nav′i·gāt″, *v.t.*—*circumnavigated, circumnavigating*. [L. *circumnavigo*—*circum*, round, and *navigo*, to sail, < *navis*, a ship.] To sail around; to travel around, as an island or the globe, by water.—**cir·cum·nav·i·ga·ble,** sǔr″kum·nav′i·ga·bl, *a.*—**cir·cum·nav·i·ga·tion,** *n.*—**cir·cum·nav·i·ga·tor,** *n.* One who circumnavigates, generally applied to one who has sailed around the globe.

cir·cum·po·lar, sǔr″kum·pō′lẻr, *a.* Surrounding either pole of the earth or of the heavens.

cir·cum·scribe, sǔr″kum·skrīb′, sǔr′kum·skrīb″, *v.t.*—*circumscribed, circumscribing*. [L. *circumscribere* (pp. *circumscriptus*), < *circum*, around, and *scribere*, write, draw.] To draw a line around; encircle or surround; enclose within bounds; limit or confine, esp. narrowly; mark off or define; *geom.* to draw a figure around (another figure) so as to touch as many points as possible without intersecting; to enclose another figure in this manner.—**cir·cum·scrib·a·ble,** *a.*—**cir·cum·scrib·er,** *n.*—**cir·cum·scrip·tion,** *n.* The act of circumscribing; a circular inscription, as on a coin or seal.—**cir·cum·scrip·tive,** *a.* Circumscribing; circumscribed or limited.

cir·cum·spect, sǔr′kum·spekt″, *a.* [L. *circumspectus*—*circum*, round, and *specio*, to look.] Examining carefully all the circumstances that may affect a determination; wary; vigilant; prudent; cautious.—**cir·cum·spec·tion,** *n.*—**cir·cum·spec·tive,** *a.*—**cir·cum·spect·ly,** *adv.*

cir·cum·stance, sur′kum·stans″, *Brit.* sur′-kum·stans, *n.* [L. *circumstantia*, < *circumstare*, stand around, < *circum*, around, and *stare*, stand.] A condition, with respect to time, place, manner, agent, etc., which accompanies, determines, or modifies a fact or event; *usu. pl.*, the existing condition or state of affairs surrounding and affecting an agent; as, forced by *circumstances* to do a thing; *pl.* the condition or state of a person with respect to material welfare; as, in reduced *circumstances*. An unessential accompaniment of any fact or event; a matter of secondary importance; an accessory matter; a particular or detail; an incident or occurrence, as: His arrival was a fortunate *circumstance*. Detailed or circuitous narration; specification of particulars; ceremonious accompaniment or display; as, with pomp and *circumstance*.—**cir·cum·stance**, *v.t.*—*circumstanced*, *circumstancing*. To place in particular circumstances or relations.

cir·cum·stan·tial, sur″kum·stan′shal, *a.* [L. *circumstantia*.] Of, pertaining to, or derived from circumstances; based on or derived from other than absolute evidence; pertaining to conditions of material welfare; of the nature of a circumstance or non-essential accompaniment; secondary; incidental; dealing with or giving circumstances or details; detailed; particular; marked by ceremony or pomp.—**cir·cum·stan·tial·ness**, *n.*—**cir·cum·stan·tial·ly**, *a.*

cir·cum·stan·tial ev·i·dence, *n.* Evidence from various more or less relevant circumstances from which inferences can be made to prove the facts in a case, as distinguished from direct testimony.

cir·cum·stan·ti·ate, sur″kum·stan′shē·āt, *v.t.*—*circumstantiated*, *circumstantiating*. To confirm by circumstances; to describe circumstantially or in full detail.—**cir·cum·stan·ti·al·i·ty**, *n.* pl. **cir·cum·stan·ti·al·i·ties**. The quality of being circumstantial; minuteness; fullness of detail.

cir·cum·val·late, sur″kum·val′āt, *v.t.*—*circumvallated*, *circumvallating*. [L. *circum*, round, and *vallum*, a rampart.] To surround with or as if with a rampart.—*a.* Surrounded as by a rampart.—**cir·cum·val·la·tion**, *n.*

cir·cum·vent, sur″kum·vent′, sur″kum·vent″, *v.t.* [L. *circumvenio*, *circumventum*—*circum*, about, and *venio*, to come.] To encircle or enclose by crafty maneuver; to trick into a trap; to detour or go around; to gain advantage over by artfulness, stratagem, or deception; to avoid, as defeat or embarrassment, by cunning; to outwit.—**cir·cum·ven·tion**, *n.*—**cir·cum·ven·tive**, ser·kum·vent′iv, *a.*—**cir·cum·ven·tor**, *n.*

cir·cum·vo·lu·tion, sur″kum·vo·lō′shan, *n.* The act of rolling or turning around an axis; a single complete turn; a winding or folding about something; one of the folds of anything so wound; a winding in a sinuous course; a sinuosity; *fig.* a roundabout course or procedure.

cir·cum·volve, sur″kum·volv′, *v.t.*, *v.i.*—*circumvolved*, *circumvolving*. [L. *circumvolvere* (pp. *circumvolutus*), roll around, < *circum*, around, and *volvere*, roll.] To revolve; to wind about.

cir·cus, sur′kus, *n.* pl. **cir·cus·es**. [L., circle, ring, circus, = Gr. *kirkos*, *krikos*, ring.] A grand-scale entertainment, commonly held in one or more huge tents, usually with performing rings surrounded by tiers of seats for spectators, and featuring thrilling and extraordinary feats of bodily skill, trained animal acts, colorful parades, and clowns; a company of such performers, esp. a traveling one, along with related personnel, the animals, cages, tents, vans, and equipment. *Ancient Rome*, a large, usually oblong or oval, roofless enclosure,

surrounded by tiers of seats rising one above another, for chariot races or public games; a circular arena surrounded by tiers of seats or public entertainment held in such. Something suggestive of the Roman circus, as a natural amphitheater or a circular range of houses; *Brit.* an open space esp. circular, at a street intersection; as, Piccadilly *Circus*. A flying circus; any public spectacle; a boisterous event; someone or something hilariously funny.

cirque, surk, *n.* [Fr., < L. *circus*.] A circular space, esp. a natural amphitheater, as in mountains; *poetic*, a circle or ring of any kind. A circus.

cir·rho·sis, si·rō′sis, *n.* [Gr. *kirrhos*, orange-tawny, from the appearance of the diseased liver.] A disease consisting of diminution and deformity of the liver, often seen in alcoholics.—**cir·rhot·ic**, si·rot′ik, *a.* Affected with or having the character of cirrhosis.

cir·ri·ped, sir′i·ped″, *n.* [L. *cirrus*, and *pes*, *pedis*, the foot.] *Zool.* a marine crustacean of the order *Cirripedia*, such as the barnacle, which has thin, bristly, modified feet for gathering food and which becomes parasitic as an adult.—*a.* Of or pertaining to the *Cirripedia*; having fringelike feet or legs.

cir·ro·cu·mu·lus, sir″ō·kū′mū·lus, *n.* A cloud of high altitude, consisting of small fleecy balls or wisps which are often arranged in rows.

cir·rose, **cir·rous**, sēr′rōs, si·rōs′, sir′us, *a.* *Bot.*, *zool.* having a cirrus; resembling cirri or coiling like them; *meteor.* of or pertaining to cirrus clouds. Also **cir·rhose**, **cir·rhous**.

cir·ro·stra·tus, sir″ō·strā′tus, sir″ō·-strat′us, *n.* *Meteor.* a whitish veillike cloud or haze of minute ice crystals, with a 20,000 to 40,000 ft. altitude, which causes the illusion of halos around the sun and moon.

cir·rus, sir′us, *n.* pl. **cir·ri**, sir′ī. [L., curl, tuft, fringe.] *Bot.* a tendril; *zool.* a filament or slender appendage serving as a barbel, tentacle, foot, arm, etc. *Meteor.* a variety of cloud having a thin fleecy or filamentous appearance, normally occurring at altitudes of 20,000 to 40,000 ft. and consisting of minute ice crystals; pl. **cir·rus**.

cis·al·pine, sis·al′pin, sis·al′pin, *a.* [L. *cis*, on this side, and *Alpes*, Alps; on this side of the Alps, with regard to Rome.] Pertaining to the area south of the Alps.

cis·co, sis′kō, *n.* pl. **cis·coes**, **cis·cos**. [N. Amer. Ind.] Any of several species of whitefish of the genus *Coregonus* or *Leucichthys*, found esp. in the Great Lakes, as the lake herring.

cist, sist, kist, *n.* [W. *cist* < L. *cista*.] A prehistoric tomb or coffin made of stone. Also **kist**.

cis·ta·ceous, si·stā′shus, *a. Bot.* belonging to the *Cistaceæ*, or rockrose family of plants.

cis·tern, sis′tērn, *n.* [L. *cisterna*, < *cista*, chest.] An artificial reservoir or receptacle for holding water or other liquor. *Anat.* a space containing lymph; a sac. Also **cis·tern·a**.

cis·tron, sis′tron, *n. Genetics*, the smallest functional unit of genetic substance, considered equivalent to a gene in molecular biology.

cit·a·del, sit′a·del, sit′a·del″, *n.* [Fr. *citadelle*. Same origin as *city*.] A fortress or castle in or near a city, intended to keep the inhabitants in subjection, or, in case of a siege, to form a final point of defense.

ci·ta·tion, si·tā′shan, *n.* A summons; an official call or notice given to a person to appear, as in a court; the act of citing a passage from a book or person; the passage or words quoted; quotation; *milit.* honorable mention of a soldier or military unit for an unusual accomplishment.

cite, sit, *v.t.*—*cited*, *citing*. [Fr. *citer*, < L. *cito*, *citare*, freq. of *cieo*, to call, to summon;

seen also in *excite*, *incite*, *recite*.] To call upon officially or authoritatively to appear in court; to summon or rouse to action; to quote, as a passage, author, or book; to bring forward or refer to in support, proof, or confirmation; as, to *cite* an authority; *milit.* to mention in a report, as for courageous conduct.—**cit·a·ble**, **cite·a·ble**, *a.*

cith·a·ra, sith′ēr·a, *n.* [L. < Gr. *kithara*, whence *gittern*, *guitar*.] An ancient Greek stringed instrument resembling the more modern cittern or guitar.; also **cith·er**, **cith·ern**.

cit·i·fied, sit′i·fīd″, *a.* Marked by city ways or fashions, as: "This boy was well dressed .... He had a *citified* air about him": Mark Twain's Tom Sawyer.

cit·i·fy, sit′i·fī″, *v.t.*—*citified*, *citifying*. To cause to adopt city ways or fashions.

cit·i·zen, sit′i·zen, *n.* [A.Fr. *citezein*, O.Fr. *citeain* (Fr. *citoyen*), < L. *civitas*, E. *city*.] A native or naturalized, as opposed to alien, member of a state or nation, owing allegiance to its government and entitled to its protection; an inhabitant of a city or town, esp. one entitled to its privileges or franchises; sometimes, a civilian.

cit·i·zen·ry, sit′i·zen·rē, sit′i·sen·rē, *n.* pl. **cit·i·zen·ries**. Citizens as a group; civilians as opposed to soldiers.

cit·i·zen·ship, sit′i·zen·ship″, sit′i·sen-ship″, *n.* The state or principles of a citizen; the manner in which a person responds to his duties as a member of a community.

cit·ral, si′tral, *n.* [< *citr(us)* and *al(dehyde)*.] *Chem.* a liquid aldehyde with a strong lemonlike odor, obtained from the oils of lemon or orange, or synthetically, and used in perfumery or flavoring.

cit·rate, sit′rāt, *n. Chem.* a salt of citric acid.

cit·ric, si′trik, *a.* [CITRUS]. Pertaining to or derived from lemons, citrons, and similar fruits, or a substance chemically produced; as, *citric* acid.

cit·ric a·cid, *n.* The acid derived from lemons and similar fruits or obtained by the fermentation of carbohydrates, and used to flavor foods, beverages, and pharmaceuticals and to condition water.

cit·ri·cul·ture, si′tri·kul′chēr, *n.* The cultivation of fruits of the citric variety, such as grapefruit, oranges, lemons, and limes.

cit·rine, si′trēn, si′trin, si′trin, *a.* [L. *citrinus*, < *citrus*, a lemon or citron.] Like a citron or lemon; of a lemon color; yellow or greenish-yellow.—*n.* Lemon color; a yellow pellucid variety of quartz resembling topaz.

cit·ron, si′tran, *n.* [Fr. *citron*, < L. *citreum*, < *citrus*, the lemon or citron.] A pale yellow thick-skinned fruit resembling the lemon in shape and texture, but larger and less acid, borne by a semi-tropical tree, *citrus medica*; the tree itself; the candied or preserved rind of the fruit, used esp. in fruitcake; a round, hard-fleshed variety of watermelon, *citron melon*, used for pickles and preserves.

cit·ron·el·la, si″tra·nel′a, *n.* [Named from its citron-like odor.] A fragrant grass, *Cymbopogan nardus*, of southern Asia, cultivated as the source of an oil used in making insect repellant, liniment, perfume, and soap.

cit·ron·el·lal, si″tro·nel′al, *n. Chem.* a colorless liquid, $C_9H_{17}CHO$, obtained primarily from citronella oil and lemon grass, and characterized by an intense lemonlike odor, used mainly in the perfuming of soaps and as a flavoring agent.—*a.*

cit·ron wood, *n.* The wood of the citron, a variety of *Citrus medica*; the wood of the sandarac, *Callitris quadrivalvis*.

cit·rus, sit′rus, *n.* pl. **cit·rus**, **cit·rus·es**. [L. citron tree < Gr. *citrea*, the tree, *citrion*, *citron*, the fruit.] The genus of trees and shrubs of the rue family grown in warm regions for their large, pulpy fruit which includes grapefruit, lemons, oranges, citron and lime.—**cit·rus**, *a.* Pertaining to the genus of trees and shrubs of the rue family, esp. the fruit of such plants.

cit·tern, sit′ern, *n.* An ancient wire-stringed instrument, somewhat resembling a lute with its pear-shaped sound box but having a flat back. Also **cith·er, cith·ern**, sith′er, sith′ern.

cit·y, sit′ē, *n.* pl. **cit·ies**. [Fr. *cité*, < L. *civitas, civitatis*, a city, state, < *civis*, a citizen, whence also *civil*.] In a general sense, a large and important population center; *U.S.* an incorporated town governed by a mayor and aldermen; *Brit.* a town corporate that is or has been the seat of a bishop. The inhabitants of a city collectively. —**the Cit·y**, the center of business and finance in London, England, located within its ancient boundaries.—*a.* Pertaining to a city.

cit·y coun·cil, *n.* That authoritative body of a municipality with administrative and legislative power, composed of members elected by the citizens.

cit·y ed·i·tor, *n. U.S.* On a newspaper, the editor responsible for local news coverage; *Brit.* the financial editor of a newspaper.

cit·y man·ag·er, *n.* Generally, a skilled administrator engaged by the city council to supervise the management of the city's government.

cit·y slick·er, *n.* A shrewd, sly city dweller who dresses like a dandy and is distrusted and often regarded as a swindler by rural people.

cit·y-state, sit′ē-stāt″, *n.* A state comprised of an autonomous city and its surrounding dependent territories.

civ·et, siv′it, *n.* [Fr. *civette*, It. *zibetto*, < Ar. *zabād*, the substance civet.] A greasy, strong-smelling substance taken from an anterior gland of the civet cats, used as a fixative in perfumery; a civet cat or its fur.

civ·et cat, *n.* Any of several carnivorous mammals of the family *Viverridae*, native to Africa and southern Asia, esp. *Civettictis civetta*, the source of most commercial civet.

civ·ic, siv′ik, *a.* [L. *civicus*, < *civis*, a citizen; whence also *city*.] Pertaining to a city, a citizen, or citizenship; relating to civil affairs or honors.

civ·ics, siv′iks, *n.* The political science of the rights and duties of citizens, and of civic affairs.

civ·ies, civ·vies, siv′ēz, *n. pl.* [< *civilian* (*clothes* or *dress*).] *Slang*, civilian clothes as opposed to military uniform; mufti.

civ·il, siv′il, *a.* [L. *civilis*, < *civis*.] Relating to the community, or to the policy and government of a state; pertaining to, consisting of, or proper to citizens; as, *civil* duties; of or pertaining to a private person or to individual liberty; as, *civil* rights; happening between citizens; as, *civil* war; not ecclesiastical or military. *Law*, of, pertaining to, or derived from civil law; relating to individual rights of citizens, esp. to legal proceeding in defense of such rights: opposed to *criminal*. Exhibiting some refinement of manners; civilized; courteous; well-bred; affable; polite.

Civ·il Aer·o·naut·ics Ad·min·is·tra·tion, C.A.A., CAA, *n.* A federal organization created in 1940 which develops and maintains airway navigation aids, establishes traffic control and procedures, sets up standards for aircraft, airline operation procedures, and flight crew proficiency, conducts research to improve aircraft, and disseminates technical information.

Civ·il Aer·o·naut·ics Board, CAB, C.A.B., *n.* A board within the framework of the Department of Commerce with jurisdiction over certification, rates, safety standards, and the investigation of aircraft accidents.

Civ·il Air Pa·trol, CAP, C.A.P., *n.* A volunteer civilian organization operating as an auxiliary of the U.S. Air Force.

civ·il air·way, *n.* An airway designated and approved by the Civil Aeronautics Administration as suitable for interstate, overseas, or foreign air commerce.

civ·il a·vi·a·tion, *n.* Aviation engaged in by commercial or private concerns as distinguished from military aviation.

civ·il death, *n. Law*, status of a living person who has lost or been stripped of his civil rights, at times the result of conviction for a felony or life imprisonment.

civ·il de·fense, *n.* Plans for protection and relief organized by civilians and civilian authority to preserve life and property in the event of natural disaster, sabotage, or enemy attack.

civ·il dis·o·be·di·ence, *n.* Noncompliance with the laws or demands of a governing body for the purpose of bringing about concessions or modifications by focusing attention on those demands considered unreasonable or inequable: often a group action, as a march, or less spectacularly, a deliberate nonpayment of taxes.

civ·il en·gi·neer, *n.* An engineer skilled in the design, construction, and maintenance of aqueducts, bridges, canals, harbors, roads, and related public works.—**civ·il en·gi·neer·ing**, *n.*

ci·vil·ian, si·vil′yen, *n.* One whose pursuits are those of civil not military life; one versed in Roman or civil law.—*a.* Relating to, administered, or formed by a civilian or group of civilians.

ci·vil·i·ty, si·vil′i·tē, *n.* pl. **ci·vil·i·ties.** [L. *civilitas*, < *civilis*.] Politeness, or an act of politeness; courtesy; kind attention or expression.

civ·i·li·za·tion, siv″i·li·zā′shan, *n.* The state of human society marked by a high level of intellectual, technological, cultural, and social development; the people who have reached this advanced state; comforts made possible by such a high level of development; the act of civilizing or becoming civilized; the culture particular to a definite time, place, or group; as, Roman *civilization*; in general, populated areas as distinguished from wilderness.

civ·i·lize, siv′i·līz″, *v.t.*—*civilized, civilizing.* [Fr. *civiliser*, formerly also *civilizer*.] To bring out of a savage state; to introduce order and civic organization among; to refine and enlighten; to elevate in social life.

civ·il law, *n.* That division of law of a particular state, city, or country dealing with the interpretation and preservation of private and civil rights; the system of jurisprudence whose juridical principles have been derived from the Justinian treatises of Roman Law and which forms the basis of the law of European countries.

civ·il lib·er·ties, *n. pl.* Those political guarantees a person is legally free to practice without government interference; *U.S.* those rights which are safeguarded by the Bill of Rights and include the rights to assemble, organize, speak, and worship.

civ·il·ly, siv′il·lē, *adv.* Politely; courteously; in a well-bred manner.

civ·il mar·riage, *n.* That ceremony in which couples are united in wedlock by an authorized official other than a clergyman.

civ·il rights, *n. pl.* (*Often cap.*) Those powers and privileges, not connected with the organization or administration of government, to which an individual is lawfully entitled by virtue of his citizenship; as, in the U.S., trial by jury, freedom of contract, the right to own property, and other rights safeguarded by the 13th and 14th Amendments to the Constitution and various pursuant acts of Congress.

civ·il serv·ant, *n.* A government employee; member of the civil service.

civ·il serv·ice, *n.* The branches of the public service in which the nonmilitary employees of a government are engaged; a system of appointing government employees determined by competitive examination instead of political patronage.

civ·il war, *n.* A war between the people of the same state or country.

clab·ber, klab′er, *n.* Milk which has turned sour and thick or curdled.—*v.i.* Of milk, to become thick in souring.

clack, klak, *v.i.* [An imitative word; akin Fr. *claque*, a clap or clack; D. *klakken*, to clap; E. *clap, crack.*] To make a sudden sharp noise, as by striking or cracking; to rattle; to utter sounds or words rapidly and continually, or with sharpness and abruptness; to prattle or chatter.—*v.t.* To cause to make a sharp, short sound; to clap; to utter without thought; to blab.

clack, klak, *n.* A sharp, abrupt sound, continually repeated; continual talk; prattle.—**clack·er**, *n.* One who or that which clacks; *Brit.* a rattle which frightens birds.

clack valve, *n.* A valve in pumps with a single flap, hinged at one edge, permitting flow of fluid in one direction only.

Clac·to·ni·an, klak·tō′nē·an, *a.* [< Clacton, England.] Characteristic of, or pertaining to the second period of Stone Age culture in England, marked by the development of tools made from stone flakes.

clad, klad, *a.* Clothed; decked; adorned.

clad, klad, *v.t.*—*clad, cladding.* To cover (a metal) with another metal to provide a protective coating; sheathe; clothe.

clad·ding, klad′ing, *n.* The method of bonding metals together to protect the inner metal from corrosion.

clad·ode, klad′ōd, *n.* [Gr. *klados*, branch, and -*ode*.] *Bot.* a leaflike flattened branch, such as butcher's-broom. Also **cla·do·di·um**, kla·dō′dē·um, pl. **cla·do·di·a.**

clad·o·phyl, clad·o·phyll, klad′o·fil, *n.* [Gr. *klados*, branch, and *phyllon*, leaf.] A cladode.

claim, klām, *v.t.* [O.Fr. *claimer*, < L. *clamo, clamare*, to shout.] To ask or seek to obtain by virtue of authority, right, or supposed right; to assert a right to; to demand as due; require; to assert against a possible doubt or contradiction; maintain.

claim, klām, *n.* A demand of a right or supposed right; an assertion which is open to challenge; a right to claim or demand; a just title to anything; the thing claimed or demanded, esp. a piece of public land staked out.—**claim·a·ble**, *a.*—**claim·ant, claim·er**, *n.*

claim·ing race, *n.* A type of horse race designed to assure close competition by providing that any participating horse is liable to purchase at a fixed price by a person entering a claim before the race, the claiming privilege being usually restricted to the owners of other participating horses.

clair de lune, klâr″d·lön′, klâr″de·lön′, *n.* A pale blue or greenish blue color; a very pale bluish glaze used on Chinese porcelain.

clair·voy·ance, klâr·voi′ans, *n.* [Fr. *clair*, clear, and *voyant*, seeing, ppr. of *voir* (L. *videre*, to see.] A power attributed to persons in the mesmeric state, by which the person, called a clairvoyant, discerns objects concealed from sight and tells what is happening at a distance; intuitive knowledge.

clair·voy·ant, klâr·voi′ant, *n.* A man or woman who is said to see things not present to the senses.—*a.*

clam, klam, *n.* [O.E. *clamm*, band, bond.] A clamp; a vise; *pl.* pincers or tongs for various uses.

clam, klam, *n.* [< the clamping capacity of the shells. CLAMP.] The popular name of certain bivalvular shellfish, of several genera and many species; the edible flesh of a mollusk, used as food; *colloq.* a close-mouthed person.—*v.i.*—*clammed, clamming.* To dig for clams.

cla·mant, klā′ment, *a.* Clamorous; pressing; urgent; crying.—**cla·mant·ly,** *adv.*

clam·a·to·ri·al, klam″*a*·tōr′ē·al, klam″*a*·tar′ē·al, *a.* [N.L. *Clamatores,* pl. of L. *clamator,* one who cries out; < *clamare.*] Of or pertaining to the *Clamatores,* a large group of passerine birds, containing those with relatively simple vocal organs and little power of song, as the flycatchers.

clam·bake, klam′bāk″, *n. U.S.* an entertainment or picnic at the seashore at which the baking of clams, usually on hot stones under seaweed, is a main feature; *slang,* a party or social gathering, esp. one that is loud or raucous.

clam·ber, klam′bėr, *v.i., v.t.* [M.E. *clambren.*] To climb, using both feet and hands; climb with effort or difficulty.—**clam·ber,** *n.* A clambering.—**clam·ber·er,** *n.*

clam·my, klam′ē, *a.*—**clammier, clammiest.** Soft and damp; cool and moist.—**clam·mi·ly,** klam′i·lē, *adv.*—**clam·mi·ness,** klam′ē·nes, *n.*

clam·or, *Brit.* **clam·our,** klam′ėr, *n.* [L. *clamor,* an outcry, < *clamo,* to cry out, whence E. *claim.*] A loud outcry or outcries by one or more persons; a forceful complaint or urgent demand; a popular expression of support or protest; any loud and continued noise; a din.

clam·or, *Brit.* **clam·our,** klam′ėr, *v.t.* To utter in a loud voice; to shout; to prevail upon by clamor.—*v.i.* To make a clamor; to utter loud sounds or outcries; to make insistent complaints or demands.

clam·or·ous, klam′ėr·us, *a.* Making a clamor or outcry; noisy; vociferous.—**clam·or·ous·ly,** *adv.*—**clam·or·ous·ness,** *n.*

clamp, klamp, *n.* [Most closely connected with L.G. and D. *klamp,* Dan. *klampe,* G. *klampe,* a clamp; < root seen in E. *climb, clamber, clem* (to pinch with hunger), *clam.*] Any of several types of rigid devices that can hold objects or parts of an object together to support, strengthen, or bind them permanently, or temporarily while another type of bonding, as by gluing, is accomplished; one type of instrument which holds things between two opposing sides that can be moved together or apart to accommodate different sized objects; a vise.

clamp, klamp, *v.t.* To fasten with clamps; to fix a clamp on; to impose by decree; as, to *clamp* further restrictions on foreign trade.—*v.i.* To tread heavily.

clamp, klamp, *n.* [Imitative; akin *clank, clink.*] A heavy footstep or tread; a stomp.

clamp down, *v.t.* To impose or increase, as restrictions; *naut.* to swab, as the boat deck, by spraying it with water.—*v.i.* To become suddenly restrictive.

clamp·er, klam′pėr, kläm′pėr, *n.* A clamp; an iron frame with sharp prongs, fastened to the sole of the shoe to prevent slipping on ice.

clam·shell, klam′shel″, *n.* The shell of a clam; a dredging bucket composed of two hinged, jaw-like pieces.

clam·shell door, *n.* A cargo-loading door on the underside of an airplane, consisting of two curved panels that swing apart lengthwise like a clamshell.

clam up, *v.i. Slang.* To stop talking; to refuse to divulge information.

clan, klan, *n.* [Gael. and Ir. *clann,* family, tribe.] A number of families or households, esp. in the Scottish Highlands, claiming succession from a common progenitor and recognizing a common hereditary chief; any group of related persons; a family; a clique, sect, society, or body of persons closely united by some common interest or pursuit; among certain primitive peoples, a tribal sub-group claiming kinship and a common, frequently mythical, ancestor.

clan·des·tine, klan·des′tin, *a.* [L. *clandestinus,* < *clan,* in secret.] Secret; private; hidden from public view, usually for the purpose of deception or evil design.—**clan·des·tine·ly,** *adv.*—**clan·des·tine·ness,** *n.*

clang, klang, *n.* [Imitative of sound, and akin to *clank, clink, clack;* G. *klingen,* to sound; Dan. Sw. G. *klang,* D. *klank,* a sound; L. *clangor,* Gr. *klanggē.*] A loud, reverberating, metallic sound.

clang, klang, *v.i.* To give out a clang; to travel making such sounds, as: The fire engine *clanged* through the town.—*v.t.* To cause to sound with a clang.

clang·or, *Brit.* **clang·our,** klang′ėr, klang′gėr, *n.* [Directly < L. *clangor.*] A sharp, hard, ringing sound as of a trumpet or bell, or esp. a series of clangs; a din.—**clang·or·ous,** *a.*—**clang·or·ous·ly,** *adv.*

clang·or, *Brit.* **clang·our,** klang′ėr, klang′gėr, *v.i.* To make a clangor; to clang.

clank, klangk, *n.* [CLANG.] A short, loud, sharp, metallic sound, generally expressing a less resounding sound than *clang,* and a deeper and stronger sound than *clink.*

clank, klangk, *v.t.* To cause to sound with a clank.—*v.i.* To sound with or give out a clank.

clan·nish, klan′ish, *a.* Displaying the characteristics of a clan; imbued with the feelings, sentiments, and prejudices peculiar to a clan; limiting one's associations to a small group of similar background or status; having a narrow view of other groups or individuals belonging to other groups.—**clan·nish·ly,** *adv.*—**clan·nish·ness,** *n.*

clans·man, klanz′man, *n.* pl. **clans·men.** A member of a clan.

clap, klap, *v.t.*—*clapped,* or *clapt, clapping.* [Same as Icel. and Sw. *klappa,* Dan. *klappe,* D. and L.G. *klappen,* to clap, to pat; perhaps imitative of sound.] To strike (two objects) against each other producing a sharp, percussive sound; to strike (the palms of one's hands) together to produce a sharp sound, either to gain attention or to express approval, as applause; to administer a light, friendly slap to, in greeting or approval; to put or place hastily and vigorously, similar to clamp; to improvise hastily.—*v.i.* To make a sharp, percussive sound; to move abruptly and noisily; to applaud.

clap, klap, *n.* A loud, percussive noise; as, the *clap* of horses' hooves; the instrumentality making such a noise, as a thunder *clap;* the sound made by striking one's hands together, as applause; an unexpected blow; a light, friendly slap; *slang,* gonorrhea.

clap·board, klab′ord, klap′bōrd″, klap′-bärd″, *n.* [For obs. *clapholt,* < L.G. *klappholt* = G. *klappholz,* clapboards.] Orig. a size of oak board used for making barrel staves and wainscoting; in the U.S., a long, thin board, thicker along one edge than along the other, used in covering the outer walls of buildings, with the thick edge of each board overlapping the thin edge of the board below it; a similar roofing board.—*v.t.* To cover with clapboards.

clap·per, klap′ėr, *n.* One who or that which makes a clapping noise; the tongue of a bell; *colloq.* the human tongue, esp. that of a talkative person. One of a pair of flat objects, such as sticks or bones, struck together to produce musical rhythms.

clap·trap, klap′trap″, *n.* Pretentiousness or bombastic nonsense, esp. in language; any artifice or expedient used to impress the public; a flashy display without substance or meaning, as: The play was witty, but full of *claptrap.*—*a.* Showy; shoddy or cheap in nature; of poor quality or technique, as: The house had *claptrap* construction.

claque, klak, *n.* [Fr. < *claquer,* to clap the hands, to applaud.] A group paid to attend and applaud a performance; any group that offers praise or flattery out of self-seeking motives; a company of sycophants.

clar·a·bel·la, klar″*a*·bel′*a,* klar″ä·bel′*a, n.* An 8-foot organ stop with open wooden pipes, giving a soft sweet tone.

clar·en·don, klar′en·don, *n.* [< *Clarendon,* proper name.] A condensed form of printing type, like roman in outline but with thicker lines.

clar·et, klar′it, *n.* [O.Fr. *claret,* Fr. *clairet,* somewhat clear, light-colored, dim. of *cler,* < L. *clarus,* E. *clear.*] A general name for red table wines from the Bordeaux wine district of France; the general name for similar red wines produced elsewhere; as, California *claret;* a deep, purplish-red color.—*a.* Purplish-red.—**clar·et cup,** *n.* An iced beverage made of claret and carbonated water with lemon juice, brandy or other spirits, sugar, and fruits.

clar·i·fy, klar′i·fī″, *v.t.*—*clarified, clarifying.* [O.Fr. Fr. *clarifier,* < L.L. *clarificare,* < L. *clarus,* clear, bright, and *facere,* make.] To make clear and transparent; to render free of impurities; *chem.* to remove suspended particles from (a medium), as a liquid. To rid of obscurities, ambiguities or confusion, as: The President *clarified* his foreign policy.—*v.i.* To become clear.—**clar·i·fi·er,** *n.* One who or that which clarifies.—**clar·i·fi·ca·tion,** *n.*

clar·i·net, clar·i·o·net, klar″i′net′, klar″-ē·o·net′, *n.* [Fr. *clarinette,* < It. *clarinetto,* dim. of *clarino,* clarion.] A single-reed woodwind instrument in the shape of a cylindrical tube with a flaring end.—**clar·i·net·ist, clar·i·net·tist,** *n.*

clar·i·on, klar′ē·on, *n.* [L.L. *clario, clarionis,* a clarion, Fr. *clarion,* < L. *clarus,* clear, < its clear sound.] A medieval trumpet which produced clear, shrill tones; the sound produced by this instrument; any similar sound.—*a.* Clear, shrill, and very loud.

clar·i·ty, klar′i·tē, *n.* [L. *claritas,* < *clarus,* E. *clear.*] The state or quality of being clear as perceived by the eye; brightness or luster; pellucidity; the state or quality of being clear as perceived by the mind; a state free of ambiguity or confusion.

clark·i·a, klär′kē·*a, n.* A flowering annual herb of the evening primrose family, genus *Clarkia,* found in western U.S.

cla·ro, klär′ō, *n.* [Sp., < L. *clarus,* E. *clear.*] A light-colored and usually mild cigar.—*a.* Light-colored, as a cigar.

clar·y, klâr′ē, *n.* pl. **clar·ies.** [M.L. *sclareia;* origin unknown.] Any of several species of aromatic herbs of the genus *Salvia,* esp. *Salvia sclarea,* which is cultivated as a potherb and for ornamentation.

clash, klash, *v.i.* [Appar. imit.] To make a loud, harsh noise; collide, esp. noisily; to come into conflict; disagree; esp. followed by *with,* to oppose physically in sport or battle; of certain colors in combination, to be unpleasant or offensive to the viewer.—*v.t.* To strike with a resounding collision.

clash, klash, *n.* A harsh, frequently metallic sound, as of a collision; a collision, esp. a noisy one; a conflict; skirmish; opposition, as of views or interests.—**clash·er,** *n.*

clasp, klasp, *n.* [By metathesis for M.E. *clapse,* to clasp, *claps,* a clasp: allied to M.E. *clip,* to embrace, in the same way as *grasp,* to *grip,* and *gripe.*] A catch, hook, or other device for holding things or parts of a thing together; a grasp; a close embrace; a bar or other small metal device that, affixed to the ribbon of a military medal, indicates the campaign or service for which the medal was awarded, or that it has been awarded an additional time.

clasp, klasp, *v.t.* To fasten together with or as with a clasp; to encircle with the arms and hold tightly; to embrace; to seize firmly in or with the hand.

clasp·er, klas′pėr, *n.* That which or one who clasps. *Zool.* the copulatory organs of certain fishes; modified structures on certain male insects or crustaceans used to clasp the female during copulation.

clasp knife, *n.* A knife with a blade or blades folding into the handle; a pocket-knife; a large knife with a single blade which when open may be secured in place by a catch.

class, klas, kläs, *n.* [Fr. *classe,* < L. *classis,* class of people, etc., army, fleet.] Any division of society according to status; caste; social rank, esp. high rank; a number of pupils in a school, or of students in a college, pursuing the same studies, ranked together or graduated in the same year; the assembly of such a body; *slang,* excellence or merit, as: That girl has *class.* Any division of persons or things according to rank or grade; a number of persons or things regarded as forming one body through the possession of common attributes; a kind or sort; a zoological or botanical group or category ranking below a phylum, and above an order; *eccles.* a classis; in the early Methodist Ch., one of several small companies, each composed of about twelve members under a leader, into which each society or congregation is divided.

class, klas, kläs, *v.t.* To arrange in classes; to place or rate as to class; to classify.—*v.i.* To be classed; take or have a place in a particular class.—**class·a·ble,** *a.* That may be classed.

class con·flict, *n.* Class struggle.

class con·scious, *a.* Aware of one's class membership, esp. contrasting one's own class with other classes.

class day, *n.* In U.S. colleges and schools, a day during the commencement season on which the members of the graduating class celebrate the completion of their course with literary and other exercises.

class dia·lect, *n.* A dialect within a speech community prevalent among speakers from a certain social class, as opposed to a *regional* dialect.

clas·sic, klas′ik, *a.* [= Fr. *classique,* < L. *classicus,* pertaining to a class, of the first or highest class, < *classis.*] Of the first or highest class or rank; serving as a standard, model, or guide; of, pertaining to, or characteristic of Greek and Roman antiquity, esp. with reference to literature and art; in the style of the ancient Greek and Roman literature or art; classical; hence, of literary or historical renown. *Fashion,* conforming to an established standard; basic; as, a *classic* dress.

clas·sic, klas′ik, *n.* An author or a literary production of the first rank, esp. in Greek or Latin; something regarded as a nearly perfect example or model; a traditionally significant thing or event; *pl.* the literature of ancient Greece and Rome.

clas·si·cal, klas′i·kal, *a.* Classic; esp. in accordance with ancient Greek and Roman models in literature or art, or with later systems of principles modeled upon them; marked by classicism; pertaining to the ancient classics; *eccles.* pertaining to a classis.—**clas·si·cal·ly,** klas′i·kal·lē, *adv.*

clas·si·cal col·lege, *n. Canada,* an educational institution in French Canada at the secondary school and college levels offering

an eight-year course, chiefly in the classics and liberal arts.

clas·si·cism, klas′i·siz″um, *n.* The principles of classic literature or art, or adherence to them; the classical style in literature or art, characterized esp. by attention to form with the general effect of regularity, simplicity, and restraint; a classical idiom or form; classical scholarship or learning.—**clas·si·cal·ism,** klas′i·ka·liz″um, *n.*

clas·si·cist, klas′i·sist, *n.* A classical scholar; one who advocates the study of the ancient classics; an adherent of classicism in literature or art.—**clas·si·cis·tic,** *a.*

clas·si·cize, klas′i·siz″, *v.t., v.i.—classicized, classicizing.* To cause to conform to the classic style; to affect or use a classic style or form.

clas·si·fi·ca·tion, klas″i·fi·kā′shan, *n.* The act of classifying or forming into a class or classes, so as to bring together those beings or things which most resemble each other, and to separate those that differ; distribution into sets, sorts, or ranks; the product or the act of classifying; a group into which things may be or are classified.—**clas·si·fi·ca·to·ry,** kla·sif′i·ka·tōr″ē, kla·sif′i·ka-tar″ē, klas′i·fi·kā″tor·ē, *a.*

clas·si·fied, klas′i·fīd″, *a.* Arranged or grouped in classes; confidential; secret; as, an official document *classified* for national security reasons.—*n.* The part of a publication containing classified ads.

clas·si·fied ad, *n.* An advertisement published in a special section of a newspaper or magazine, listed according to type such as For Sale, or Help Wanted. Also *want ad.*

clas·si·fy, klas′i·fī″, *v.t.—classified, classifying.* [L. *classis,* a class, and *facio,* to make.] To arrange in a class or classes; to arrange in sets or ranks according to some method founded on common characteristics in the objects so arranged.—**clas·si·fi·er,** *n.* One who classifies; a device that separates the constituents of a substance, such as ore.—**clas·si·fi·a·ble,** *a.*

clas·sis, klas′is, *n.* pl. **clas·ses,** klas′ēz. [L.] *Eccles.* in certain Reformed churches, a body of authority corresponding to the governing presbytery in Presbyterian churches; formerly, a presbytery.

class·mate, klas′māt″, kläs′māt″, *n.* A member of the same class in a school or college.

class·room, klas′rōm″, klas′rum″, kläs′rōm, kläs′rum″, *n.* A room in which classes are held.

class strug·gle, *n.* Economic or social conflict among different classes of people due to differing backgrounds, interests, or economic status; *Marxism,* the struggle for power between workers and capitalists.

class·y, klas′ē, *a.—classier, classiest. Slang,* of high class, rank, or grade; stylish; fine.

clas·tic, klas′tik, *a.* [Gr. *klastos,* broken, < *klan,* break.] *Biol.* breaking up or dividing into fragments or parts; pertaining to such division; noting or pertaining to an anatomical model made up of detachable pieces; *geol.* noting or pertaining to rocks composed of pieces from older rocks; fragmental.

clath·rate, klath′rāt, *a.* [L. *clathratus,* < *clathri,* lattice, < Gr. *kleithron,* a bar.] *Biol.* Resembling a lattice; divided or marked like latticework.

clat·ter, klat′er, *v.i.* [< the sound. O.E. *clatrung,* a clattering, a rattle; D. *klater,* a rattle; *klateren,* to rattle.] To make rattling sounds as when hard bodies are struck rapidly together; to move or go with such a sound; to prattle or chatter noisily.—*v.t.* To cause to clatter.

clat·ter, klat′er, *n.* A rapid succession of abrupt, sharp, rattling sounds; tumultuous and confused noise; loud, noisy chatter.—**clat·ter·er,** *n.* One who clatters; a babbler.

clause, klaz, *n.* [Fr. *clause,* < L.L. *clausa,* for L. *clausula,* a conclusion, a clause, < *claudo, clausum,* to close, whence *close, exclude.*] A member of a compound or complex sentence containing both a subject and its predicate; a distinct part of a contract, will, agreement, charter, commission, or the like; a distinct stipulation, condition, proviso.—**claus·al,** *a.* Relating to a clause or clauses.

claus·tral, kla′stral, *a.* [L.L. *claustralis,* < L. *claustrum,* an enclosure, a cloister, < *claudo,* to shut.] Cloistral; cloister-like; secluded.

claus·tro·pho·bi·a, kla″stro·fō′bē·a, *n.* [L. *claustrum,* an enclosure, Gr. *phōbos,* fear.] *Psychiatry,* morbid fear of narrow spaces or closed rooms.

cla·ve, klä′vä, *n.* [Sp. *clave,* keystone < L. *clav(is),* key.] One of a pair of sticks or blocks of wood, held in the hands and clicked together to the rhythm of music.

cla·ver, klä′vėr, klä′vėr, *v.i.* [Origin uncertain.] *Sc.* to talk idly; gossip.—**cla·ver,** *n. Sc.* idle talk.

clav·i·chord, klav′i·kard″, *n.* [M.L. *clavi-chordium,* < L. *clavis,* key, and *chorda,* string.] An early stringed musical instrument with a keyboard, whose tones were produced by the action of metal pins: now superseded by the pianoforte.

clav·i·cle, klav′i·kl, *n.* [L. *clavicula,* dim. of *clavis,* key.] *Anat., zool.* a bone of the pectoral arch; in man, either of two slender bones each articulating with the sternum and a scapula and forming the anterior part of a shoulder; the collar-bone.—**cla·vic·u·lar,** kla·vik′yu·lėr, *a.*

cla·vier, kla·vēr′, klav′ē·ėr, klä′vē·ėr, *n.* [Fr. *clavier,* keyboard, also G. *klavier,* keyboard instrument (< Fr.), < L. *clavis,* key.] The keyboard of a musical instrument. Any musical instrument with a keyboard, as a harpsichord, clavichord, or pianoforte.

claw, kla, *n.* [O.E. *clawu, clá,* a claw = D. *klaauw,* Icel. *klō,* Dan. and Sw. *klo,* G. *klaue,* a claw; allied to *cleave,* to adhere.] The sharp hooked nail of a mammal, bird, or other animal; loosely, the whole foot of an animal with hooked nails; a hooked extremity belonging to any animal member or appendage; the pincer at the end of certain limbs of lobsters, scorpions, and other arthropods; anything shaped like the claw of an animal, as the curved forked end of a hammer, used for drawing nails; that part of a jewelry setting that secures the stone; that end of a derrick hoist that has a pronged grasp.

claw, kla, *v.t., v.i.* To tear, scratch, pull, dig, or seize with or as with claws or nails.

claw ham·mer, *n.* A hammer furnished with two curved claws at one end of the head, between which nails may be caught for pulling.

claw hatch·et, *n.* A hatchet with a sharp chopping blade on one edge, and a cleft or claw at the back for pulling nails from the material into which they have been driven.

clay, klā, *n.* [O.E. *clæg* = D. and G. *klei.*] A natural earthy material, plastic when wet, resulting from the decomposition of certain rocks, consisting essentially of a hydrated silicate of aluminum, and used chiefly for making bricks or pottery; loosely, earth or mud; earth considered as the material from which the human body was orig. formed, Gen. ii. 7; Job, xxxiii. 6; hence, the human body; flesh as opposed to spirit; *fig.* anything which is easily shaped or influenced.—*v.t.* To treat with clay; cover or daub with clay.—**clay·ey,** *a.* Consisting of, resembling, or containing clay; covered or daubed with clay.

clay·bank, klā′bangk″, *n.* A dun-yellowish color; a horse of this color.

clay·more, klā′mōr″, klā′mạr″, n. [Gael. *claidheammor—claidheam*, a sword, and *mor*, great.] Formerly the large two-handed sword of the Scottish Highlanders; now a basket-hilted, double-edged broadsword.

clay pig·eon, n. *Skeet, trapshooting*, a saucer of baked clay or other material to be thrown into the air by a trap as a target. *Slang*, a person who is in a vulnerable position with respect to attack by others.

clean, klēn, a. [O.E. *clǣne*, clean, clear, = D. and G. *klein*, small.] Free from foreign or extraneous matter; unadulterated; pure; free from dirt or filth; unsoiled or unstained hence, free from any form of defilement; morally pure; innocent; upright; honorable, *Bib.* free from or not causing ceremonial defilement. Sometimes, free from dirty habits, as an animal; cleanly; free from defect or blemish; neatly made or proportioned; shapely, or trim; clever or dexterous, as action; free from encumbrances or obstructions; as, a *clean* harbor; without irregularity or unevenness; as, a *clean* cut; complete or perfect; as, a *clean* sweep; regarding an atomic or hydrogen bomb, having little or no fallout. *Slang*, not involved with police; having no concealed weapons; being without money.

clean, klēn, v.t. To make clean; with *off*, to remove in the process of cleaning.—v.i. To perform or to undergo cleaning.

clean, klēn, adv. In a clean manner; cleanly; wholly, completely, or quite.

clean-cut, klēn′kut′, n. Clear-cut; distinctly outlined or defined; well-cut; shapely; of a well-defined or well-constituted character or personality, as a person.

clean·er, klē′nèr, n. One who cleans, esp. one whose business is cleaning; as, a dry *cleaner*; the operator or owner of a dry-cleaning plant; an apparatus that cleans; as, a vacuum *cleaner*; a preparation for cleaning, as a detergent. *Pl.* a plant for dry cleaning.

clean-hand·ed, klēn′han′did, a. Having clean hands; *fig.* free from moral taint or suspicion.

clean-limbed, klēn′limd″, a. Having well-shaped limbs; shapely; well-proportioned.

clean·li·ness, klen′lē·nis, n. The condition or habit of keeping clean.

clean·ly, klen′lē, a.—*cleanlier, cleanliest*. Free from dirt, filth, or any foul matter neat; carefully avoiding filth.—adv. klēn′lē. In a clean manner; neatly; without filth; adroitly; dexterously.

clean out, v.t. *Slang*, to empty, as a store, of popular times; to deprive of resources. To empty for the purpose of cleaning or rearranging.

clean room, n. *Engin.* a room in which the air is kept aseptically clean for manufacturing such specialized items as precision parts.

cleanse, klenz, v.t.—*cleansed, cleansing*. [O.E. *clǣnsian < clǣne* clean.] To make clean; to free from filth, or whatever is unseemly, noxious, or offensive; to purify. —**cleans·er**, klen′zèr, n.

clean·up, klēn′up″, n. An act or instance of cleaning; a special undertaking; a reform, as the eradication of crime and corruption; the periodical disposal or tidying up of debris or litter; the material thus collected. *Slang*, a large profit or return on a bet or an investment; a killing. *Milit.* the liquidation of the remnants of an enemy or an area.

clean up, v.i. *Slang*, to realize a large profit in a short time.

clear, klēr, a. [O.Fr. *cler* (Fr. *clair*), < L. *clarus*, clear, bright.] Bright or shining; free from darkness, obscurity, or cloudiness; transparent or pellucid; of a pure, even color, as the complexion; easily seen, heard, or understood; distinct; evident; plain; free from confusion, uncertainty, or

doubt, as a person; perceiving or discerning distinctly; convinced or certain; serene or untroubled; free from guilt or blame; innocent; free from obstructions or obstacles; open; as, a *clear* space; unentangled or disengaged; free; quit or rid of; without obligation or liability; free from debt; without deduction or diminution; as, a *clear* thousand; hence, without limitation or qualification; as, the *clear* contrary; absolute; sheer.

clear, klēr, v.t. To make clear; free from darkness, cloudiness, muddiness, indistinctness, confusion, uncertainty, obstruction, contents, entanglement, obligation, or liability; free from imputation or guilt; prove or declare to be innocent; pass without entanglement or collision; as, to *clear* a rock at sea; leap over without touching; get past or over; free, as a ship or cargo, from legal detention at a port by satisfying the customs and other required conditions; gain; as, *clear* a profit; pass, as checks, through a clearing house; remove so as to leave something clear, used with *away*.—v.i. To become clear; with *away*, pass away or disappear, as clouds or mist; exchange checks and bills, and settle balances, as in a clearing house; specif. of a ship, to comply with the customs and other conditions legally imposed upon leaving or entering a port; leave port after having complied with such conditions.

clear, klēr, adv. In a clear manner; clearly; distinctly; entirely or quite. Also **clear·ly**.

clear, klēr, n. A clear or unobstructed space. —**clear·ness**, n. The quality of being clear.

clear·ance, klēr′ans, n. The act of clearing; a clear space; a clearing; *mech.* an intervening space, as between machine parts, for free play; *naut.* the clearing of a ship at a port, or the official certificate or papers, 'clearance papers,' indicating this; *banking*, the exchange of checks and drafts between members of a clearing house; sale of merchandise reduced in price; as, in a *clearance* sale; *government* and *milit.* permission to use or have access to classified material.

clear-cut, klēr′kut′, a. Cut or formed with clearly defined outlines; distinctly defined.

clear·head·ed, klēr′hed′id, a. Having a clear head or understanding; having acute discernment or keen intelligence.

clear·ing, klēr′ing, n. The act of one who clears; *banking*, the act of exchanging drafts on each other and settling the differences; among *railroads*, the act of distributing the proceeds of the through traffic passing over several lines; a place or tract of land cleared of wood or cultivation.

clear·ing, klēr′ing, n. *Stock market*, the act of transferring cash and securities between buyers and sellers.

clearing house, n. An institution through which the claims of banks against one another are settled: at the Stock Exchange and the Board of Trade, similar clearing houses exist for the facilitation of trading in stocks, grain, or other commodities.

clear sail·ing, n. *Colloq.* the prospect of accomplishing a certain goal without interference, as: They'll have *clear sailing* on the rest of the work.

clear-sight·ed, klēr′sī′tid, a. Seeing with clearness; having acuteness of mental discernment; discerning; perspicacious.—**clear·sight·ed·ness**, n.

clear-starch, klēr′stärch″, v.t. To stiffen with clear or colorless starch.

clear·wing, klēr′wing″, n. A moth with wings for the most part destitute of scales and transparent; esp. any of those constituting the family *Aegeriidae*, many species of which are, in the larval stage, injurious to fruit-trees and other plants, or any of certain sphinx moths.

cleat, klēt, n. [Allied to G. *klate, klatte*, a claw.] A piece of wood or iron used in a ship to fasten ropes upon; a piece of iron, leather, or rubber worn on a shoe to provide traction; *carp.* a piece of wood nailed on transversely to a piece of joinery for the purpose of securing it in its proper position, or for strengthening.

cleat, klēt, v.t. To strengthen with a cleat or cleats; to injure with a cleat.

cleav·a·ble, klē′va·bl, a. Capable of being divided or split.

cleav·age, klē′vij, n. The act of cleaving or splitting; the manner in which rocks or mineral substances regularly split according to their natural joints, or regular structure; *biol.* early divisions of fertilized eggs into smaller cells; *chem.* splitting of molecules or compounds into simpler molecules or compounds. Space between a woman's breasts, esp. as visible with a low neckline. A difference in opinions or interests between opposing groups.

cleave, klēv, v.t.—past *cleft, cleaved, clove*, pp. *cleft, cleaved*, or *cloven*, ppr. *cleaving*. [O.E. *clēofan* = G. *klieben < Gr. glyphein, carve*.] To part by or as by a cutting blow, esp. along a natural line of division, as the grain of wood; split; rend apart; rive; to penetrate or pass through; as to *cleave* the water; to make by or as by cutting; as, to *cleave* a path through the wilderness; to separate or sever; to divide into groups having opposing views.—v.i. To part or split. To penetrate or pass, used with *through*. To adhere; to be attached physically, or by affection or other tie, used with *to*.

cleav·er, klē′vèr, n. One who or that which cleaves; a butcher's instrument for cutting carcasses into joints or pieces. A ridge of rock extending from an expanse of snow or ice, as from a glacier.

cleav·ers, klē′vèrz, n. [Appar. < *cleave*.] A plant, *Galium aparine*, in the family *Rubiaceae*, with short hooked bristles by which it adheres to the fur of animals or to clothing; any of certain related species.

cleek, klēk, n. [Cf. *clutch*.] *Sc.* an iron hook, as for suspending a pot over a fire; *golf*, a club having a wooden head with a long, narrow face.

clef, klef, n. [Fr. *clef*, L. *clavis*, a key.] A character in music, placed at the beginning of a staff, to determine the degree of elevation to be given to the notes belonging to it as a whole.

cleft, kleft, n. [past and pp. of *cleave*, to divide.] A space or opening made by splitting; a crack; a crevice.

cleft, kleft, a. Partially split; divided halfway; having deep fissures; in a plant leaf, split almost to the midrib.

cleft pal·ate, n. A congenital malformation in which more or less of the palate is wanting, so as to leave a longitudinal gap in the upper jaw, often an accompaniment of harelip.

cleis·tog·a·my, **clis·tog·a·my**, klī·stog′-a·mē, n. [Gr. *kleistos*, closed, and *lamos*, marriage.] *Bot.* the characteristic of producing both fully developed flowers, plus small, inconspicuous, self-pollinating flowers as in the pansy and some violets.— **cleis·to·gam·ic**, **clis·to·gam·ic**, a.— **cleis·tog·a·mous**, **clis·tog·a·mous**, a.

clem·a·tis, klem′a·tis, n. [Gr. *klēmatis*.] The generic name of woody climbing plants of the crowfoot family having white or purple blossoms.

clem·en·cy, klem′en·sē, n. [L. *clementia*, < *clemens, clementis*, merciful.] Mildness of temper as shown by a superior to an inferior; disposition to spare or forgive; mercy; leniency; softness or mildness of the elements.

clem·ent, klem′ent, a. Mild in temper and

disposition; gentle; lenient; merciful; kind; tender, compassionate.—**clem·ent·ly**, *a.* With mildness of temperature; mercifully.

clench, klench, *v.t.* [M.E. *clenchen*; akin to D. *klinken*, clench, rivet.] To clinch, as a nail or screw bent and flattened; close, as the hands or teeth, tightly; grasp firmly, or grip; *naut.* to fasten with a clinch.

clench, klench, *n.* The act of clenching; the end of a nail or screw bent and flattened in clinching; tight hold; grip.—**clench·er**, *n.*

clep·sy·dra, klep′si·dra, *n.* pl. **clep·sy·dras**, **clep·sy·drae**. [Gr. *klepsydra*, < *kleiptein*, to steal, to hide, and *hydōr*, water.] A name common to devices of various kinds for measuring time by the regulated discharge of water; a water clock.

clep·to·ma·ni·a, klep″to·mā′ne·a, klep″-to·mān′ya, *n.* Compulsive stealing. Also *kleptomania*.

clere·sto·ry, **clear·sto·ry**, klēr′stōr″ē, klēr′star″ē, *n.* pl. **clere·sto·ries**, **clear·sto·ries**. *Arch.* an outside wall of a building, rising above an adjoining roof and having a series of windows which admit daylight to the interior; the upper part of the nave, transepts, and choir of a church, perforated by a series of windows above the aisle-roofs or triforium and forming the chief source of light for the building. Any similar construction, as that for ventilating a railroad car.

cler·gy, klėr′jē, *n.* pl. **cler·gies**. [O.Fr. *clergie*, < L. *clericus*, Gr. *klērikos*, clerical, < *klēros*, a lot, an allotment, the clergy.] The body of men set apart and consecrated, by due ordination, to the service of God in the Christian church; the body of ecclesiastics, in distinction from the laity.

cler·gy·man, klėr′jē·man, *n.* pl. **cler·gy·men**. The minister of a Christian church; one who is a member of the clergy.

cler·ic, kler′ik, *a.* [L.L. *clericus*, < Gr. *klērikos*, < *kleros*, clergy, orig. lot, allotment.] Pertaining to the clergy; clerical.—*n.* A member of the clergy.

cler·i·cal, kler′i·kal, *a.* Of, pertaining to, or characteristic of the clergy or a clergyman; upholding the power or influence of the clergy, esp. in politics; as, a *clerical* party. Pertaining to a clerk or office worker; as, a *clerical* error.—*n.* A cleric.

cler·i·cal col·lar, *n.* A stiff, slender white collar which stands upright and is fastened at the back of the neck and worn by certain members of the clergy.

cler·i·cal·ism, kler′i·ka·liz″um, *n.* Clerical principles; clerical power or influence, esp. in politics; support of such power or influence.—**cler·i·cal·ist**, *n.*

cler·i·hew, kler′i·hū″, *n.* A light verse form, usually two couplets in length, rhyming *aabb* and usually dealing with a person whose name constitutes the first rhyme.

cler·i·sy, kler′i·sē, *n.* [M.L. *clericia*, < L.L. *clericus*.] Learned men as a class; intelligentsia.

clerk, klėrk, *Brit.* klärk, *n.* [O.E. *clerc*, *cleric* and O.Fr. Fr. *clerc*, < L.L. *clericus*. CLERIC.] A person who performs general duties in an office or who keeps records and accounts; a salesperson; minor official who keeps records and performs routine assignments for a court or legislature; a cleric.—*v.i.* To act or serve as a clerk.—**clerk·ly**, *a.* Of or pertaining to a clerk or clerks.

clerk reg·u·lar, *n.* A member of a religious order bound by vows of religion and living in community, but engaged in active teaching or preaching outside the community.

clerk·ship, klėrk′ship, *Brit.* klärk′ship, *n.* The position or business of a clerk; a medical student's tour of duty in a hospital clinic.

clev·er, klev′ėr, *a.* [Connected with O.E. *cliver*, a claw, and with *cleave*, to adhere.] Intelligent; quick-witted; physically dexterous; ingenious.—**clev·er·ly**, *adv.*—**clev·er·ness**, *n.*

clev·is, klev′is, *n.* pl. **clev·is·es**. A piece of metal, usually U-shaped, with a pin or bolt passing through holds at the two ends, used for attaching or suspending parts.

clew, clue, klö, *n.* A ball of thread; *naut.* a corner or loop of a sail; *pl.* hammock cords; usu. *clue*, a guide in the solution of a mystery.—*v.t.* To coil or roll into a ball; *naut.* to haul or raise up or down, as a sail.

cli·ché, klē·shā′, *n.* [Fr., < *clicher*, to stereotype, < older *cliquer*, to fasten, make firm, < root of *clinch*, *clench* (omitting the nasal).] A hackneyed word, phrase, or idea; *print.* a stereotype or electrotype plate.

click, klik, *v.i.* [An imitative word expressing a slighter sound than *clack*; comp. *clack*, *cluck*, *clink*, *clank*; D. *klikken*, Fr. *cliquer*, to click.] To make a small sharp sound, or a succession of small sharp sounds, as by a gentle striking; to tick.—*v.t.* To move with a clicking sound.

click, klik, *v.i. Slang*, In the entertainment field, to have a very favorable reception by audiences; to agree, fit, or get along well together, as: The members *click* so well, they are bound to be successful.

click, klik, *n.* A slight, sharp sound, as of the cocking of a pistol; any of a class of sounds in South African languages, produced by withdrawing the tongue by a sucking action from a part of the mouth with which it has been in contact; some clicking mechanism, as a detent or a pawl.

cli·ent, klī′ent, *n.* [L. *cliens* (*client-*), for *cluens*, prop. ppr. of *cluere*, hear. LOUD.] Anyone under the patronage or protection of another; a dependent; a vassal; a follower; one who resorts to another for professional or business services; a customer. —**cli·en·tage**, klī′en·tij, *n.*—**cli·en·tal**, klī·en′tl, klī′en′tl″, *a.*

cli·en·tele, klī″en·tel′, *n.* [L. *clientela*.] A body of clients or dependents; one's clients collectively.

cliff, klif, *n.* [O.E. *clif*, a rock, a cliff = D. *klif*, Icel. *klif*, a cliff; akin also Dan. *klippe*, Sw. *klippa*, G. *klippe*, a crag.] A precipice; the steep and rugged face of a rocky mass; a steep rock; a headland.

cliff dwell·er, *n.* A member of one of the aboriginal tribes in the southwestern U.S. who built their dwellings in natural recesses in cliffs; *slang*, an individual who resides in large urban apartment building.—**cliff dwell·ing**, *n.*

cliff-hang·er, klif′hang′ėr, *n.* A drama characterized by sustained suspense; *sports*, a contest in which the outcome remains uncertain to the last moments.—**cliff-hang·ing**, *a.* Pertaining to the suspenseful nature of a cliff-hanger.

cli·mac·ter·ic, klī·mak′tėr·ik, klī″mak·-tėr′ik, *n.* [L. *climactericus*, < Gr. *klimaktērikos*, < *klimaktēr*, step of a ladder, < *klimax*.] A critical period in life; a year, usually one ending a period or an odd multiple of seven years, supposed to be marked by important changes in health, constitution, etc.; as, the grand *climacteric*, the sixty-third year; hence, any critical period; *physiol.* the menopause; also a corresponding period in the male.—**cli·mac·ter·i·cal**, *a.*

cli·mac·tic, klī·mak′tik, *a.* Pertaining to a climax.

cli·mate, klī′mit, *n.* [L. *clima*, Gr. *klima*, *klimatos*, a slope, a zone of the earth, a clime, < *klinō*, to bend, referring to the inclination of the earth from the equator to the pole.] The condition of a region in relation to the various phenomena of the atmosphere, as temperature, wind, moisture and miasmata, esp. as they affect the life of animals or men; a tendency suggestive of the mood and temper of a social or political group; the social and political conditions prevailing at a certain time in a specified area.—**cli·mat·i·cal·ly**, *adv.*—**cli·mat·ic**, **cli·mat·i·cal**, **cli·mat·al**, *a.* Pertaining to a climate or climates; limited by a climate.

cli·ma·tol·o·gy, klī″ma·tol′o·jē, *n.* The science of climates; an investigation of the causes on which the climate of a place depends.—**cli·ma·to·lo·gist**, klī″ma·tol′o·jist, *n.*—**cli·ma·to·log·i·cal**, **cli·ma·to·log·ic**, *a.*—**cli·ma·to·log·i·cal·ly**, *adv.*

cli·max, klī′maks, *n.* [L. < Gr. *klimax*, a ladder, < *klinō*, to slope.] A figure of speech or rhetorical device in which the language rises step by step in dignity, importance, and force; in a play or novel, the highest point of suspense, conflict or tension when the plot takes a major turn; the highest point of anything; the culmination; acme; an orgasm.

cli·max, klī′maks, *v.i.* To reach the highest point of anything; to reach orgasm.—*v.t.* To bring to a point of culmination.

climb, klīm, *v.i.* [O.E. *climban* = D. and G. *klimmen*.] To mount or ascend with difficulty; to rise slowly by continued effort; to achieve social eminence or higher professional position; *bot.* to ascend by twining or by means of tendrils or adhesive fibers, as a vine. To slope upward.— **climb down**, to descend.—*v.t.* To ascend, go up, or get to the top of.—**climb·a·ble**, *a.*

climb, klīm, *n.* A climbing; an ascent by climbing; a place to be climbed.

climb·er, klī′mėr, *n.* One who or that which climbs; a device to assist in climbing, as spiked shoes. *Bot.* a plant that rises by attaching itself to some support. *Ornith.* one of an order of climbing birds, including the parrots and woodpeckers. *Colloq.* one who aggressively seeks a higher social position.

climb·ing fish, *n.* A small East Indian fish, *Anabas scandens*, which is able to live for a considerable time out of water and to travel for some distance on land, and is reputed to climb trees. Also **climb·ing perch**.

climb·ing i·ron, *n.* An iron frame with spiked claws, strapped to one's boots as a help in climbing trees, poles, or ice-covered mountains.

clime, klīm, *n. Poet.* a tract or region of the earth; climate.

clinch, klinch; *v.t.* [Later form of *clench*.] To secure, as a driven nail, by beating down the point; to fasten together thus; rivet; to settle a matter as by a finishing stroke; fix or confirm decisively.—*v.i. Sports*, to grapple, as in fighting or boxing.

clinch, klinch, *n. Slang*, a close embrace.— *v.t. Slang*, to hold tight in an embrace.

clinch·er, klin′chėr, *n.* A person or thing that clinches; *colloq.* something decisive; a conclusive factor in an issue; a telling argument in a debate.

cling, kling, *v.i.*—**clung**, **clinging**. [O.E. *clingan*, to adhere, to dry up or wither; Dan. *klynge*, to grow in clusters; *klynge*, a heap, a cluster.] To adhere closely; to remain attached; to hold fast, esp. by winding round or embracing.—**cling·ing·ly**, *adv.*—**cling·er**, *n.* One who or that which clings.

cling·stone, kling′stōn″, *a.* Having a stone to which the pulp adheres closely, as certain peaches.—*n.* A clingstone or cling peach.

clin·ic, klin′ik, *n.* [Gr. *klinikos*, < *klinē*, a bed, < *klinō*, to recline.] A medical institution in which a group of physicians jointly examine and treat patients; the examination and treatment of patients in the presence of medical students; a place for the examination and treatment of nonresident patients, as in a hospital.

clin·i·cal, klin′i·kal, *a.* Pertaining to a clinic; based on examination or diagnosis in a clinic; dealing with the study of patients as opposed to laboratory experiment; objective.—**clin·i·cal·ly,** adv.

clin·i·cal psy·chol·o·gy, n. That branch of psychology which deals with the scientific, analytical examination and treatment of neurotic states and other abnormalities of human behavior.

clin·i·cal ther·mom·e·ter, n. A calibrated instrument used in medical practice for determining body temperature.

cli·ni·cian, kli·nish'an, n. A physician who studies diseases at the bedside, or is skilled in clinical methods.

clink, klingk, v.i. [An imitative word, akin to *click* and *clank*; compare D. *klinken,* to tinkle; Dan. *klinge,* to jingle; Icel. *klingja,* G. *klingen,* to ring, to chink.] To ring or jingle; to give out a small sharp sound or a succession of such sounds, as by striking small metallic bodies together.—v.t. To cause to produce a small, sharp, ringing sound.

clink, klingk, n. A sharp ringing sound made by the collision of small metallic bodies.

clink, klingk, n. [< the *Clink,* a prison in Southwark, London.] *Slang,* a prison, jail, or lockup.

clink·er, kling'ker, n. [D. *klinker,* kind of brick, < *klinken* = E. *clink,* v.] A kind of hard Dutch brick used for paving; a partially vitrified mass of brick; a mass of incombustible matter fused together, as in the burning of coal; slag; *geol.* volcanic material; the scale of oxide formed on iron during forging.

clink·er, kling'ker, n. *Slang,* a blunder; a flop; *Brit.* an excellent product.

clink·er-built, kling'ker-bilt", a. Having the outside planks or metal plates overlapping one another; pertaining to a ship's hull constructed of overlapping planks. Also **clinch·er-built,** klin'cher-bilt". Cf. *carvel-built.*

cli·nom·e·ter, kli·nom'i·ter, kli·nom'i·ter, n. An instrument for measuring inclination, as the dip of strata or the heeling of a ship.—**cli·no·met·ric, cli·no·met·ri·cal,** a. Pertaining to or determined by a clinometer; pertaining to oblique crystalline forms, or to solids which have oblique angles between the axes.—**cli·nom·e·try,** n.

clin·quant, kling'kant, a. [Fr., ppr. of obs. *clinquer,* clink, tinkle, glitter.] Glittering, as with tinsel; tinseled; decked with garish finery.—n. Imitation gold leaf; tinsel.

Cli·o, kli'ō, n. Gr. Mythol. the Muse who was supposed to preside over history; *astron.* the name of an asteroid; *zool.* a genus of mollusks.

clip, klip, v.t.—*clipped, clipping.* [Cf. Icel. *klippa,* clip.] To cut, or cut off or out, as with shears; trim by cutting; to cut or trim the hair or fleece of; shear; to pare the edge, as of a coin, fraudulently; to cut short; curtail, esp. to omit, as syllables of words, in pronouncing; *slang,* to cheat or overcharge; *football,* to block, as an opposing player, by hitting his legs illegally from behind.—v.i. To cut; to move swiftly.

clip, klip, n. An act of clipping; anything clipped off, esp. the wool shorn at a single shearing of sheep; *colloq.* a smart blow or stroke, as with the hand; *colloq.* a rapid gait or motion.

clip, klip, v.t. [O.E. *clyppan,* embrace.] To encompass; to hold in a tight grip; to fasten together.

clip, klip, n. A device for gripping and holding tightly; a metal clasp; a jewelry piece which may be clipped on a dress for decoration; a flange on the upper surface of a horseshoe.

clip art·ist, n. *Slang,* one who makes a profession of swindling or robbing.

clip·board, klip'bōrd", klip'bárd", n. A small-sized writing board, fitted with a clip or other device to hold sheets of paper.

clip joint, n. *Slang,* a place of entertainment notorious for swindling or overcharging.

clip·per, klip'er, n. An instrument used for cutting, esp. hair or lawn grass; *naut.* a sailing vessel built and rigged for speed.

clip·ping, klip'ing, n. The act of one who or that which clips; a piece clipped off or out, as from a newspaper.—a. That clips; as, *clipping* shears.—**clip·ping·ly,** adv.

clip·sheet, klip'shēt", n. *Journalism,* a sheet of paper printed only on one side so that its contents can be conveniently clipped and mounted for reproduction.

clique, klēk, klik, n. [Fr. < O.Fr. *cliquer,* make a sharp sound.] An exclusive set of persons; a coterie.—v.i. To form, or associate in, a clique.—**cliqu·ey, cliqu·y, cliqu·ish,** a.—**cliqu·ish·ness,** n.

clit·o·ris, klit'er·is, klī'ter·is, n. [N.L. < Gr. *kleitoris,* < *kleiein,* shut.] *Anat.* a small erectile organ of female mammals, located at the anterior part of the vulva, and homologous to the penis of the male.—**clit·o·ral, clit·or·ic,** a.

clo·a·ca, klō·ā'ka, n. pl. **clo·a·cae,** klō·ā'sē. [L., a common sewer.] A sewer; privy; *zool.* a cavity in birds, reptiles, many fish, and lower mammalia, into which both the rectum and the urinogenital ducts open, causing ejection of both waste and reproductive matter through the single wide opening.—**clo·a·cal,** a.

cloak, klōk, n. [O. and Provinc. Fr. *cloque,* L.L. *cloca, clocca,* a bell, a kind of horseman's cape of a bell shape; same word as *clock.*] A loose outer garment worn over other clothes; a thing which conceals; a disguise.

cloak, klōk, v.t. To cover with a cloak; to disguise.

cloak-and-dag·ger, klōk'an·dag'er, a. *Colloq.* an extravagant reference to the adventurous aspects of international espionage and intrigue.

cloak-and-sword, klōk'an·sard', a. Pertaining to the romantic literature of the adventures of legendary heroes who wore capes and carried swords; of or relating to any exaggerated account of gallant adventure.

clob·ber, klob'er, v.t. *Slang,* to beat up; to defeat overwhelmingly.—n. *Brit.* and *Australian slang,* clothing.

cloche, klōsh, kläsh, n. [Fr., lit. bell.] A woman's hat, close-fitted to the face, with a deep crown and narrow brim; a bell-glass under which plants are grown.

clock, klok, n. [Originally a bell. O.E. *clucga,* Icel. *klukka,* Dan. *klokke,* Sw. *klocka,* D. *klok,* G. *glocke,* a bell or clock; Ir. and Gael. *clog,* a bell or clock.] Any of several devices, other than the watch, that measure time and indicate the hours, minutes, and often seconds by the movement of hands over a dial; the signal-producing device in a synchronous computer; a vertical design embroidered on the side or sides of men's socks or textured stockings; *astron.* (cap.) the constellation *Horologium.*—v.t. To time or test, as with a stopwatch.

clock·wise, klok'wīz", adv., a. In the direction of rotation of the hands of a clock; pertaining to circular movement from the horizontal left to the horizontal right.

clock·work, klok'wurk", n. The machinery of a clock; a complex mechanism of wheels producing regularity of movement similar to that of a clock; precision.

clod, klod, n. [A slightly modified form of *clot*; akin Dan. *klode,* a globe or ball, *klods,* a block or lump.] A lump or mass in general; a lump of earth, soil, and grass, or clay; a dull, gross, stupid person; a numskull; a clodhopper.—**clod·dish,** klod'ish, a. Clownish; boorish; doltish; uncouth; ungainly.—**clod·dy,** klod'ē, a. Consisting of clods; abounding with clods; earthy; gross in sentiments or thoughts.

clod·hop·per, klod'hop"er, n. A country bumpkin; a hayseed; a clumsy boor; a clod; *pl.* big heavy shoes.—**clod·hop·ping,** klod'hop"ing, a. Uncouth; clownish; rude.

clog, klog, klåg, n. [Akin Sc. *clag,* a clog, an impediment, *clag,* to clog, as with something viscous or sticky, < O.E. *clæg,* clay. CLAY.] An encumbrance that hinders motion or renders it difficult, as a piece of wood or a weight fastened to an animal's leg; hindrance; encumbrance; impediment; a sort of shoe with a wooden sole; *Brit. slang,* a short, thick piece of wood.

clog, klog, klåg, v.t.—*clogged, clogging.* To impede the movements of by a weight, or by something that sticks or adheres; to encumber, restrain, or hamper; to choke up; to obstruct so as to hinder passage through; to throw obstacles in the way of; to hinder; to overfill; to trammel.—v.i. To become loaded or encumbered with extraneous matter; to dance a clog dance.

clog dance, n. A dance in which the feet, shod with clogs, perform a noisy accompaniment to the music.

cloi·son, kloi'zon, n. One of the fine metal dividing strips used in cloisonné enamels to keep the color areas separate.

cloi·son·né, kloi"zo'nā, Fr. klwä·zą·nā', a. [Fr., < *cloison,* partition, < L. *claudere,* shut, close.] Partitioned: applied to enamel in which thin metal bands, fixed on edge to a ground, outline the design and form partitions between the colors.—n.

clois·ter, kloi'ster, n. [O.Fr. *cloistre,* Fr. *cloître*; < L. *claustrum,* a bolt, enclosed place, *claudo, clausum,* to shut.] An arched way or covered walk running round the walls of certain portions of monastic and collegiate buildings; a place of religious retirement; a monastery; a convent; any arcade or colonnade round an open court; a piazza.

clois·ter, kloi'ster, v.t. To confine in a cloister or convent; to shut up in retirement from the world; to furnish with a cloister or cloisters; immure.

clois·tral, kloi'stral, a. Of or pertaining to a cloister; secluded; solitary; limited in outlook as if isolated from the world.

clone, klōn, n. [Gr. *klon,* twig, slip, < *klan,* break.] A group of cultivated plants consisting of individuals derived from a single original seedling or stock, the propagation having been by the use of vegetative parts such as buds, grafts, tubers, or other asexual methods of reproduction.—**clon·al,** klōn'al, a. Of, pertaining to, occurring in, or as a clone.

clon·ic, klon'ik, klō'nik, a. [< Gr. *klonos,* a shaking.] *Pathol.* convulsive, with alternate relaxation.—**clon·ic spasm,** a spasm in which the muscles or muscular fibers rapidly contract and relax alternately, as in epilepsy: used in contradistinction to *tonic spasm.*—**clo·nus,** klō'nus, n.

clop, kläp, v.i.—*clopped, clopping.* To produce a sharp, hollow sound, as if by a horse's hoof or a wooden shoe striking pavement.—n. The sound made by clopping.

clos·a·ble, close·a·ble, klōz'a·bl, a. That may be closed.

close, klōz, v.t.—*closed, closing.* [Fr. *cloo,* pp. of *clore,* to shut up; < L. *claude, clausum,* to shut; seen also in *concluds, exclude, include, seclude, cloister,* etc.] To bring together the parts of; to shut, as a door, window, book, eyes, or hands; make fast; to end, finish, conclude, complete; to fill or stop up; to consolidate: often followed by *up.*—v.i. To come together; to unite; to end, terminate, or come to a period; to shut or become closed. To engage in close encounter or to grapple, followed by *with*; to come to an agreement, followed by *with.*

close, klōz, n. An arriving at a conclusion; the conclusion or end of a period in time;

the final passage, as in a novel or play; *mus.* a cadence or point of rest in a piece.

close, klōs, *n.* [Fr. *clos,* an enclosed place.] *Brit.* an enclosed place, esp. the precinct of a cathedral or abbey; *Brit. dial.* a courtyard or the narrow entry passage leading to it; a dead-end road or alley.

close, klōs, *a.—closer, closest.* [O.Fr. Fr. *clos,* pp. of *clore,* < L. *claudere,* shut, E. *close.*] Closed; shut in or enclosed; without opening, or with all openings covered or closed; confined or narrow; as, *close* quarters; lacking fresh or freely circulating air; as, a *close* room; heavy or oppressive, as the air; narrowly confined, as a prisoner; strictly guarded; secluded or retired; hidden or secret; practicing secrecy, as a person; reserved or reticent; parsimonious, stingy, or niggardly; scarce, as money; not open to public or general admission or competition; as, a *close* corporation; under prohibition as to hunting or fishing, as a season; having the parts near together; as, a *close* texture; compact or condensed; near, or near together, in space, time, or relation; in immediate proximity, as, *close* contact; intimate or confidential; as, *close* friendship; fitting tightly, as a cap; not deviating from the subject under consideration; as, to pay *close* attention; strict, searching, or minute; as, *close* investigation; not deviating from a model or original; as, a *close* translation, a *close* copy; nearly even or equal, as a contest; *phonetics,* uttered with a relatively contracted opening of the oral cavity.— **close reef,** *naut.* the last ordinary reef in a sail, producing the greatest reduction in size.

close, klōs, *adv.* Tightly, so as to leave no opening; in strict confinement; in contact, or very near in space or time.— **close·ly,** klōs′lē, *adv.* In a close manner; so as to be close; compactly; nearly; intimately; intently; rigidly; narrowly; strictly; with strict adherence to an original.— **close·ness,** klōs′nes, *n.* The state or quality of being close, in the various senses of the word.

close cor·po·ra·tion, *n.* Closed corporation.

closed, klōzd, *a.* Forming a barrier; as, a *closed* gate; finished or brought to a conclusion; as, a *closed* issue; restricted to a few; as, the stockholders of a *closed* corporation; strictly excluding foreign influences; as, a *closed* policy; being or forming an independent entity; as, a *closed* committee; limited as to season of the year for hunting or fishing; as, a *closed* season. *Phon.* of a syllable that ends in a consonant or cluster of consonants. *Math.* having the property of producing only elements of the same set when mathematical elements of a certain set are operated upon.

closed chain, *n. Chem.* one of the organic compounds, such as benzene, whose carbon atoms are linked directly, or by other atoms, in a cyclic formation.

closed cir·cuit, *n. Elect.* an unbroken circuit permitting a continuous current flow.

closed-cir·cuit tel·e·vi·sion, *n.* A television system wherein the cameras, receivers, and all controls are linked by cables without open circuits; a method of telecasting by wire to certain viewing sets, as in theaters or clubs for watching special events.

closed cor·por·a·tion, *n.* An incorporated enterprise whose stock ownership is restricted to a few individuals. Also *close corporation.*

closed-end, klōzd′end″, *a.* Issued to the fully authorized amount; as, a *closed-end* mortgage; having a limited capitalization of shares of stock that can be liquidated only in the open market; as, a *closed-end* investment trust.

closed shop, *n.* A place of business in which, by contract between the employer and the labor union, only union members can work.

close·fist·ed, klōs′fis′tid, *a.* Miserly; niggardly; penurious.

close for·ma·tion, *n. Aeron.* a flight formation in which the airplanes fly at a minimum distance from one another, usually for protection against fighter attack.

close-grained, klōs′grānd′, *a.* Having a compact, fine-grained texture, as wood.

close har·mo·ny, *n. Mus.* a simultaneous combination of tones in which the supporting notes stay near the melody, lying within an octave or less range.

close-hauled, klōs′hạld′, *a. Naut.* sails set in order to sail as nearly against the wind as possible.

close-mouthed, klōs′mouthd′, klōs′moutht′, *a.* Reticent; uncommunicative.

close-out, klōz′out″, *n.* A clearance sale of merchandise in a retail store.

close-reefed, klōs′rēfd′, klōz′rēfd′, *a. Naut.* of a sail, having the last reef taken in; of a vessel, having the sail or sails so reefed.

close shave, *n. Slang.* A narrow escape; a rescue from imminent danger.

clos·et, kloz′it, *n.* [O.Fr. *closet,* dim. of *clos,* E. *close, n.*] A private room, esp. one of comparatively small size, as for retirement, counsel, or devotions; a small room, enclosed recess, or cabinet for storage of items such as clothing, provisions, and utensils; a water closet or toilet.

clos·et, kloz′it, *v.t.—closeted, closeting.* To shut up in a private place for a confidential interview or for intensive work, often used in the passive or reflexively; as, to be *closeted* with the trustees, *to closet* oneself in the laboratory.

clos·et dra·ma, *n.* A play to be read rather than acted.

close-up, klōs′up″, *n. Photog.* a photograph taken near the subject; *Motion pictures, TV,* a detailed or enlarged picture of a person or activity achieved by bringing the camera close to the subject; also **close-shot.**

clo·sure, klō′zhẽr, *n.* The act of closing; an end or conclusion; that which closes or shuts; cloture. *Math.* the characteristic of being mathematically closed.

clo·sure, klō′zhẽr, *v.t., v.i.—closured, closuring.* To cloture.

clot, klot, *n.* [Older form of *clod,* and formerly used in same sense; O.E. *clot,* a mass; D. *kloot,* a ball or globe; Sw. *klot,* a sphere; *klots,* a block; G. *kloss,* a clod, a lump, *klotz,* a block; akin *cloud.*] A coagulated mass of soft or fluid matter, as of blood or cream.

clot, klot, *v.i.—clotted, clotting.* To coagulate, as soft or fluid matter, into a thick, inspissated mass.—*v.t.* To cause to coagulate; to make or form into clots.—**clot·ty,—** *clottier, clottiest. a.* Full of clots; resembling a clot; coagulated.

cloth, klạth, kloth, *n. pl.* **cloths.** [O.E. *cláth* = D. *cleed,* Icel, *klæthi,* Dan. and Sw. *klæde,* G. *kleid,* cloth.] Any fabric of wool, hair, cotton, flax, hemp, or man-made filaments, formed by weaving; a tablecloth; *naut.* canvas used to make or reinforce a sail.—**the cloth,** *n.* A professional dress, specifically that of a clergyman.

clothe, klōTH, *v.t.—clothed* or *clad, clothing.* To cover with garments; to dress; to furnish or supply with clothes or raiment; *fig.* to cover or surround as if by clothing; to cloak.

clothes, klōz, klōTHz, *n. pl.* [A plural of *cloth,* though it cannot now be said to have a singular.] Garments worn by human beings; dress; apparel; vesture; the covering of a bed; bedclothes.

clothes·horse, klōz′hạrs″, klōTHz′hạrs″, *n.* A frame to hang clothes on; a person who dresses in the latest styles and is excessively

interested in clothes and fashions; a fashion model.

clothes·line, klōz′līn, klōTHz′līn″, *n.* A strong line of rope, plastic cord, or wire on which clothes are hung to dry.

clothes·pin, klōz′pin″, klōTHz′pin″, *n.* A spring clamp, or forked piece of plastic or wood, used to fasten articles on a line to dry.

clothes tree, *n.* An upright stand on which to hang clothes.

cloth·ier, klōTH′yẽr, klōTH′ē·ẽr, *n.* A manufacturer or retailer of cloth or of clothes; a tailor.

cloth·ing, klō′THing, *n.* Garments collectively; clothes; raiment; apparel.

clo·ture, klō′chẽr, *n.* [Fr.] *Parliamentary procedure,* termination of a debate usually by calling for a vote. Also *closure—v.t. clotured, cloturing.*

cloud, kloud, *n.* [Prob. < O.E. *clūd,* mass of rock, hill.] A visible collection of particles of water or ice suspended in the air, usually at a considerable elevation above the earth's surface; any similar mass, as of smoke or flying dust; a dim or obscure area in something otherwise clear or transparent; an ill-defined patch or spot differing in color from the surrounding surface; a throng or multitude; anything that obscures, darkens, or threatens, as with gloom or trouble.

cloud, kloud, *v.t.* To overspread or cover with or as with a cloud or clouds; overshadow; obscure or darken; to make indistinct; render gloomy; place under a cloud, as of suspicion or disgrace; to variegate with ill-defined patches of another color.—*v.i.* To grow cloudy; become clouded; to reveal by facial expression one's trouble, distress, or anxiety.

cloud·ber·ry, kloud′ber″ē, kloud′be·rē, *n. pl.* **cloud·ber·ries.** The orange-yellow edible fruit of the plant, *Rubus chamæmorus,* a small raspberry of the northern hemisphere; the plant. Also **baked-ap·ple ber·ry.**

cloud·burst, kloud′bụrst″, *n.* A sudden, violent downpour of rain.

cloud cham·ber, *n. Phys.* a device for observing or photographing the path of electrically charged particles, based on the principle that supersaturated vapor condenses more readily on charged particles than on neutral molecules. Also **Wil·son cloud cham·ber; fog cham·ber.**

cloud cov·er, *n.* Partial or complete cover of the sky by clouds; also **cloud·age.** *Aeron.* the protection from being seen afforded by flying into or behind a cloud.

cloud deck, *n. Aeron.* the upper surface of a cloud.

cloud·i·ly, kloud′i·lē, *adv.* In a cloudy manner; darkly; obscurely.—**cloud·i·ness,** kloud′ē·nes, *n.* The state of being cloudy.

cloud seed·ing, *n.* The technique of sowing clouds from an aircraft with an inoculant, such as dry ice particles or silver iodide crystals, so as to induce or increase precipitation.

cloud ver·ti·go, *n. Aeron.* a vertigo or dizziness sometimes suffered by fliers as a result of losing orientation when going through clouds.

cloud·y, kloud′ē, *a.—cloudier, cloudiest.* Of the nature of a cloud; resembling or pertaining to clouds; overcast with clouds; as, a *cloudy* sky; not clear or transparent; having cloudlike markings; obscure or indistinct; darkened by gloom or trouble; under suspicion or disgrace; as, a *cloudy* reputation.

clough, kluf, klou, *n.* [M.E.; origin uncertain.] *Brit.* A narrow valley; a ravine; a glen.

clout, klout, *n.* [O.E. *clút,* a clout, a patch; Dan. *klud,* Sw. *klut,* a clout; also W. *clwt,* Ir. and Gael. *clud,* a clout.] *Archery,* the mark fixed in the center of a target, or the shot that hits it; *colloq.* a hard blow, struck usually with the fist; *baseball*, a long hard-hit ball; *archaic*, a patch or rag.

clout, klout, *n. Slang*, influence or pressure, usu. unwelcome, based on the power to collect a debt, enforce some other obligation, or withhold a benefit.

clout, klout, *v.t. Colloq.* To strike forcefully, esp. with the hand. To stud or fasten with nails; *archaic*, to patch.

clove, klōv, *n.* [Sp. *clavo*, a clove, a nail, < L. *clavus*, a nail, from its resemblance to a nail in shape.] The dried flower bud of a tropical evergreen tree, *Eugenia aromatica*, of the myrtle family, used whole or ground as a very pungent, aromatic spice; the tree yielding cloves.

clove, klōv, *n.* [O.E. *clufe*, a bulb.] One of the small bulbs formed in the axils of the scales of a mother bulb, as in garlic.

clove, klōv, *n. Brit.* a denomination of weight, as for wool and cheese, usually about eight pounds.

clo·ven, klō′ven, *a.* Divided; parted; cleft; split.

clo·ven foot, *n.* A foot or hoof, as in sheep or oxen, divided into two parts; the symbol of Satan, evil, temptation, or devilish character.—**clo·ven-foot·ed**, *a.*

clove pink, *n.* A pink, *Dianthus caryophyllus*, with a spicy scent like that of cloves; a carnation.

clo·ver, klō′vėr, *n.* [O.E. *clæfre* = D. *klaver*, L.G. *klever*, Dan. *klover*, Sw. *klofver*, perhaps < root of *cleave*, from its trifid leaves.] Any leguminous herb of the genus *Trifolium*, bearing three-lobed leaves and roundish heads or oblong spikes of small flowers, several species being widely cultivated for fodder.—**to be in clo·ver**, *colloq.* to be in most enjoyable circumstances; to live luxuriously or in abundance.

clo·ver·leaf, klō′vėr·lēf″, *n.* A road plan laid out in the form of a four-leaf clover, designed to route traffic at different circular levels to prevent merging traffic from crossing major intersections.

clown, kloun, *n.* [Icel. *klunni*, a clumsy, boorish fellow; Fris. *klonne*, a bumpkin; allied to Sw. *klunn*, a block.] A jester; joker; buffoon; a performer in a circus or play usually in ridiculous dress and make-up. An awkward country fellow; a man of coarse manners; a person without refinement; a boor; a lout; a churl.—*v.i.* To act in jesting or grotesque manner, as a clown.

clown·ish, kloun′ish, *a.* Of or pertaining to clowns; rude; coarse; awkward; ungainly. —**clown·ish·ly**, *adv.* In a clownish manner. —**clown·ish·ness**, *n.* Boorishness; ridiculousness.

cloy, kloi, *v.t.* [O.Fr. *cloyer*, to stop up, equivalent to *clouer*, *cloer*, originally to fasten with a nail, O.Fr. *clo*, Fr. *clou*, < L. *clavus*, a nail.] To gratify to excess so as to cause loathing; to surfeit.—*v.i.* To cause surfeit.—**cloy·ing·ly**, *adv.*

club, klub, *n.* [A Scandinavian word; Icel. *klubba*, *klumba*, Sw. *klubba*, Dan. *klub*, a club.] A stick or piece of wood with one end thicker and heavier than the other, capable of being used as a weapon; *golf*, a staff with a crooked and heavy head for driving the ball. A playing card with a figure resembling a 3-leaf clover; *pl.* the suit so marked. A select number of persons in the habit of meeting for the promotion of some common object such as athletics, literature, science, politics. A clubhouse; a nightclub; a group of persons who participate in a plan wherein they agree to make regular payments or purchases in order to secure some benefits; as, a book *club*, an investment *club*.

club, klub, *v.i.*—**clubbed**, **clubbing**. To form a club or combination for a common purpose or to combine to raise a sum of money, often followed by *together*.—*v.t.* To beat with a club; to use as a club by brandishing with the small end; to contribute for a common fund or purpose.

club, klub, *a.* Pertaining to a club; made up of a combination of foods offered at a fixed price on the menu; as, a *club* luncheon.

club·by, klub′ē, *a.* Characteristic of a club; intimately associated.

club car, *n.* A railroad passenger car containing easy chairs, card tables, beverage bar, or buffet; a lounge car.

club chair, *n.* A comfortable upholstered chair with heavy sides and a slightly low back.

club·foot, klub′fụt″, *n. pl.* **club·feet.**— A short misshapen foot of congenital origin.— **club·foot·ed**, *a.* Having a clubfoot.

club·house, klub′hous″, *n.* A house or building occupied by a club; an athletic team's locker room.

club sand·wich, *n.* A triple-decker sandwich, usually combining white meat of fowl, bacon or ham, lettuce, tomato, and dressing.

club steak, *n.* A steak usually cut from the rib end of the short loin.

club·wom·an, klub′wụm″an, *n. pl.* **club·-wom·en.** A woman actively involved in club activities, esp. charitable and civic enterprises.

cluck, kluk, *v.t.* [Imit.: cf. G. *glucken*, Dan. *klukke*, Sw. *klucka*, also O.E. *cloccian*, cluck.] To utter the cry or call of a hen brooding or with young chicks; to make a similar sound.—*v.i.* To call by clucking.

cluck, kluk, *n.* A sound uttered by a hen; a clucking sound; *slang*, a stupid person.

clue, clew, klö, *n.* [O.E. *cliwe*, *cliwen*, a ball of thread = D. *kiuwen*, a clue; akin to L. *globus*, *glomus*, a mass.] A ball of thread; information that contributes to the solution of a problem, crime, or mystery, or is a guide through a complicated procedure.

clum·ber, klum′bėr, *n.* [From *Clumber*, estate of the Duke of Newcastle in Nottinghamshire, England.] One of a breed of spaniels with short legs and long, heavy body, valued as retrievers. Also **clum·ber span·iel.**

clump, klump, *n.* [Same as D. *klomp*, Dan. Sw. and G. *klump*, a lump, a clod.] A shapeless mass; a lump; a cluster of trees or shrubs; a dull, heavy noise; a clumsy, slow moving gait; *bacteriology, immunology*, an aggregation of particles such as red blood cells or bacteria which have undergone agglutination.—**clump·y**, klump′ē, *a.*

clump, klump, *v.t.* To gather into or form a clump; mass; *bacteriology, immunology*, to cause formation of clumps through agglutination.—*v.i.* To walk in a clumsy, lumbering manner; *bacteriology, immunology*, to form or be formed into a clump through agglutination.

clum·sy, klum′zē, *a.*—**clumsier**, **clumsiest.** [M.E. *clumsen*, *clomsen*, to benumb or stupefy; allied to Sw. *klummsen*, benumbed, Icel. *klumsa*, lockjaw, D. *kleumen*, to be benumbed; the root being same as in *clump*, etc.] Awkward; ungainly; without dexterity or grace; badly constructed; awkwardly done or said; tactless; unskillfully performed.—**clum·si·ly**, *adv.*—**clum·si·ness**, *n.*

Clu·ny lace, klö′nē, *n.* [From *Cluny*, town in east-central France.] Formerly, a kind of lace having the pattern darned on a square-meshed net ground; now, usually, a lace of the guipure class, often made of heavy linen thread.

clu·pe·id, klö′pē·id, *n.* [N.L. *Clupeidæ*, pl., < *Clupea*, the herring genus, L. *clupea*, kind of small river-fish.] Any of the *Clupeidæ*, a family of chiefly marine fishes, including the herrings, shad, sardines, and menhaden.—*a.* Pertaining to the clupeids; belonging to the *Clupeidæ*.—**clu·pe·oid**, *a.* Herring-like; of the herring family.—*n.* A clupeoid fish.

clus·ter, klus′tėr, *n.* [< M.E. < O.E. *cluster*; same root as Sw. and Dan. *klase*, Icel. *klasi*, a cluster.] A number of things, as fruits, growing naturally together; a bunch; a number of individuals of any kind collected or gathered into a body; an assemblage; a group; a swarm; a crowd; *milit.* a medal award attached to a ribbon, representing a class of recognitions; as, the oak-leaf *cluster*; *phon.* the occurrence of two or more consonants in succession pronounced in a single utterance.

clus·ter, klus′tėr, *v.i.* To grow or be assembled in clusters or groups.—*v.t.* To collect into a cluster or group; to produce in a cluster or clusters.

clus·tered, klus′tėrd, *a. Arch.* pertaining to several shafts grouped closely around a central pier; as, a *clustered* column.

clutch, kluch, *v.t.* [O.E. *clucche*, *cloche*, < *cloche*, a claw, a softened form of older *cloke*, a claw, Sc. *cluik*, *cluke*, a claw; allied to *claw*.] To seize, clasp, or grip with the hand; to hold tightly.—*v.i.* To seek to seize and hold; to use the clutch of a car or other vehicle.

clutch, kluch, *n.* A grasping or gripping with the fingers; a paw, talon or grasping hand; *usu. pl.* merciless power or mastery; as, fall into his *clutches*. A device for grasping and holding; *mach.* a contrivance for connecting shafts with each other or with wheels, so that they may be disengaged at will; the lever or control that operates this contrivance; *slang*, a crucial situation; an emergency; *sports*, a critical moment in play, as: *baseball*, He was a good hitter in a *clutch*.— *a.* Of a purse without a handle, small enough to grasp easily.

clutch, kluch, *n.* [A form of *cluck*, cry of a brooding hen.] The eggs laid and hatched by a bird at one time; a brood of chickens.

clut·ter, klut′ėr, *n.* [A modification of *clatter*.] Confused noise; bustle; confusion; litter.

clut·ter, klut′ėr, *v.t.* To put in a clutter; to crowd together in disorder.—*v.i.* To make a bustle or disturbance.

clut·ter, klut′ėr, *n. Electronics*, atmospheric noise; extraneous signals, echoes, or reflections on a radarscope or radio receiver which interfere with the reception of the desired signal. Also, *grass, snow, interference.*

Clydes·dale, klīdz′dāl″, *n.* One of a breed of draft horses combining activity, strength, and endurance, orig. raised in the valley of the upper Clyde (Clydesdale), Lanarkshire, Scotland.

clyp·e·ate, klip′ē·āt″, *a.* [L. *clypeus*, a shield.] *Bot.* shaped like a round buckler; shield-shaped; scutate. Also **clyp·e·i·-form**, klip′ē·i·form.

clys·ter, klis′tėr, *n.* [Gr. *klystēr*, < *klyzō*, to wash or cleanse.] *Med.* a liquid substance injected into the lower intestines to purge or cleanse them, or to relieve from costiveness; an enema.

cne·mis, nē′mis, *n. pl.* **cnem·i·des.** [N.L., < Gr. *cnēmis*, greave, legging, < *cnēmē*, lower leg.] *Anat.* The leg from knee to ankle; the shin-bone or tibia.—**cne·-mi·al**, nē′mi·al, *a.*

C-note, sē′nōt″, *n. Slang*, a one hundred-dollar bill.

co·ac·er·vate, kō·as″ėr·vāt′, *n. Chem.* a liquid colloidal suspension that is partially coagulated into droplets and is in a reversible state, but may be an intermediate stage in the coagulation of the suspension.— **co·ac·er·va·tion**, kō·as″ėr·vā′shan, *n. Chem.* the process of forming a coacervate.

coach, kōch, *n.* [Fr. *coche*, < Hung. *kocsi*; named < a village in Hungary.] A large, enclosed, four-wheeled carriage, often a public passenger vehicle; a class of airline travel less luxurious and less costly than first class; a railroad passenger-car, esp. one of the ordinary kind, as distinguished from a parlor-car or a sleeping-car; a bus that conveys public passengers; a private tutor who prepares a candidate for an examination; one who instructs others in preparation for an athletic contest; a member of a baseball club stationed near first or third base to advise the players of his team while they run the bases; one who instructs a performer; as, a drama *coach*, a voice *coach*.

coach, kōch, *v.t.* To give instruction or advice to, in the capacity of a coach.—*v.i.* To act as a coach; study with or be instructed by a coach.

coach dog, *n.* One of a breed of dogs trained to accompany a vehicle, resembling the pointer in form and stature, and of a white color profusely marked with small black or liver-colored spots. Also *Dalmatian*.

coach·man, kōch′man, *n.* pl. **coach·men.** A man employed to drive a coach or carriage; a certain kind of artificial fly for angling.—**coach·man·ship,** *n.* The work of a coachman; skill in driving a coach.

co·ac·tion, kō·ak′shan, *n.* Action in concert; *ecology*, the interplay existing between member organisms of plant and animal communities.—**co·act,** *v.i.*—**co·-ac·tive,** *a.*

co·ac·tive, kō·ak′tiv, *a.* [< L. *cōgere* (pp. *cōactus*), to drive together, force.] Forcing or compelling; compulsory.

co·ad·ju·tor, kō·aj′u·tẽr, kō″a·jō′tẽr, *n.* [L. *coadjutor*—prefix *co*, *ad*, to, and *juvo*, *jutum*, to help.] One who aids another; an assistant; a fellow helper; an associate; a fellow worker; a colleague; *theol.*, a bishop who is appointed to aid a diocesan bishop, and, generally, be his successor. Also **bish·op co·ad·ju·tor.**—**co·ad·ju·tress, co·ad·ju·trix,** kō·aj′u·tris, kō·aj′u·triks, *n.* A female assistant or fellow helper.

co·ad·u·nate, kō·aj′u·nit, kō·aj′u·nāt″, *a.* [L. *coadunatus.*] *Biol.* united or joined together, esp. during the growing process, as leaves united or grown together at the base.—**co·ad·u·na·tion,** *n.*

co·ag·u·la·bil·i·ty, kō·ag′ū·la·bil″i·tē, *n.* The capacity of being coagulated.—**co·ag·u·la·ble,** kō·ag′ū·la·bl, *a.* Capable of becoming coagulated.

co·ag·u·lant, kō·ag′ū·lant, *n.* That which produces coagulation. Also **co·ag·u·la·tor,** ko·ag′ū·lā·tor, *n.*

co·ag·u·lase, kō·ag′ū·lās, *n.* Any of several antibody-producing enzymes causing coagulation of blood.

co·ag·u·late, kō·ag′ū·lāt″, *v.t.*, *v.i.*—*coagulated*, *coagulating*. [L. *coagulo*, *coagulatum*, < *coagulum*, rennet.] To change from a fluid into a substance of glutinous consistency; to curdle, congeal, or clot.—**co·ag·u·la·tion,** *n.*

co·ag·u·lum, kō·ag′ū·lum, *n.* pl. **co·ag·u·la.** A coagulated mass, as curd; *med.* a blood clot or clump.

coak, kōk, *n.* [Origin uncertain.] *Carp.* a projection from the end of a piece of wood fitting into a hole in another piece at their joint, or a cylinder or pin of hard wood or the like fitted into both pieces; a dowel. —*v.t.* To unite, as the ends of two pieces of wood, by means of a coak or coaks.

coal, kōl, *n.* [O.E. *col* = D. *kool* = G. *kohle* = Icel. *kol*.] A black or dark-brown combustible mineral substance consisting of carbonized vegetable matter found in beds in the earth and mined for use as a fuel; as, hard *coal* or anthracite, soft or bituminous *coal*, and brown *coal* or lignite; a piece of this substance; a glowing hot fragment; as a live *coal* or ember.—**to haul** or **rake o·ver the coals,** *colloq.* to heap severe criticism upon.

coal, kōl, *v.t.* To burn to coal or charcoal; to provide with coal.—*v.i.* To take in coal for fuel, as a vessel.

coal·er, kō′lẽr, *n.* One who provides coal; something used to haul or transport coal, as a railroad or ship.

co·a·lesce, kō′a·les′, *v.i.*—*coalesced*, *coalescing.* [L. *coalesco*—prefix *co*, and *alesco*, to grow up, < *alo*, to nourish.] To unite by growth into one body; to fuse; to grow together physically; combine; blend; to join or unite into one body, party, society, or the like.—*v.t.* To cause to unite into one.—**co·a·les·cence,** *n.* The act of coalescing or uniting; the state of being united or combined.—**co·a·les·cent,** *a.* Growing together; uniting.

coal field, *n.* An area containing coal deposits.

coal·fish, kōl′fish″, *n.* pl. **coal·fish, coal·-fishes.** A species of cod, growing to the length of two feet or more, found on the northern coasts of Europe, and so named from the color of its back; a sablefish.

coal gas, *n.* The gas formed by burning coal; a gas used for illuminating and heating, produced by distilling bituminous coal.

co·a·li·tion, kō″a·lish′an, *n.* Union into one body or mass; voluntary union of individual persons, parties, or states for a common object or cause; an alliance; a league.—**co·a·li·tion·ist,** *n.* One who favors or joins a coalition.

coal meas·ures, *n.* pl. *Geol.* coal-bearing strata; specif. a portion of the Carboniferous system, characterized by coal deposits.

coal mine, *n.* A mine or pit from which coal is obtained.—**coal min·er,** *n.*—**coal min·ing,** *n.*

coal oil, *n.* *Dial.* an oil obtained by distilling coal, formerly used for illuminating purposes; kerosene.

Coal·sack, kōl′sak, *n.* *Astron.* any of several dark areas in the Milky Way, esp. one located near the Northern Cross in the constellation Cygnus, and another near the Southern Cross and the constellation Crux.

coal tar, *n.* A thick, black, viscid liquid which is formed during the distillation of bituminous coal, as in the manufacture of illuminating gas, and which upon further distillation yields various important products, as benzene, anthracene, and phenol, from which are derived a large number of dyes and synthetic compounds, and a final residuum, coal-tar pitch.

coam·ing, kō′ming, *n.* *Naut.* a raised border around a hatchway or other opening in a deck, designed to prevent water from running below; one of the pieces, esp. of the fore-and-aft pieces, of such a border. A similar border on the roof of a building.

co·apt, kō·apt′, *v.t.* [L.L. *coaptatus*, pp. of *coaptare*, < L. *co-*, with, and *aptare*, fit, < *aptus*.] To fit together, as in the setting of broken bones.—**co·ap·ta·tion,** kō″ap·tā′shan, *n.*

co·arc·tate, kō·ärk′tāt, kō·ärk′tit, *a.* [L. *coarctatus*, pp. of *coarctare*, *coartare*, < *co-*, with, and *artare*, press together.] Pressed together; compressed; contracted; *entom.* of a pupa, enclosed in an oval corneous case, and having no external indication of the organs.—**co·arc·ta·tion,** *n.*

coarse, kōrs, kạrs, *a.* [COURSE.] Of ordinary or inferior quality; common; base; lacking in fineness of texture or structure, or in elegance of form; rough; loose; crude; rude; ribald; vulgar; gross; indelicate in taste, language or manners; unpolished; unrefined, as in metals; harsh, grating in tone or color.—**coars·en,** kor′sen, kạr′sen, *v.t.* To render coarse or vulgar; to roughen.— *v.i.* To become coarse.—**coarse·ly,** kōrs′lē, *adv.* In a coarse manner.

coast, kōst, *n.* [O.Fr. *coste* (Fr. *côte*) < L. *costa*, rib, side.] The side, edge, or margin of the land next to the sea; the seashore, or the region adjoining it. (*Cap.*) in the U.S.,

the region bordering on the Pacific Ocean. The boundary or border of a maritime country; a snowy or icy hillside or incline down which one may slide on a sled.

coast, kōst, *v.i.* To slide on a sled down a snowy or icy hillside or incline; descend a hill, as on a bicycle, without using pedals or propelling power; to move or advance without added effort or power.—*v.t.* To sail along the shoreline of; to cause to move without power.

coast·al cur·rent, *n.* A current, usually parallel to the shoreline, with a speed of flow that is comparatively steady.

coast·al plain, *n.* *Geol.* a plain bordering on an ocean or other large body of water.

coast·er, kō′stẽr, *n.* One who or that which coasts; a vessel engaged in coastwise trade; one who lives near a coast; one who coasts on a sled or a bicycle; a sled used in coasting; an amusement railway with dips and curves, on which cars run by gravity; formerly, a tray, sometimes on wheels, for holding a decanter to be passed around a dining table; a small mat, dish, or tray placed under an object to protect a surface from moisture or scratching.

coast·er brake, *n.* A form of brake in bicycles which are fitted with a freewheel, operated by back pressure on the pedals: so called because a person may coast with such a bicycle when the pedals are stationary.

Coast Guard, *n.* That branch of the U.S. military service which in wartime under the Navy Dept. is responsible for guarding coasts, and in peacetime under the Transportation Dept. is detailed to ice patrol, lifesaving, and enforcement of customs, navigation, and immigration laws.

coast·line, kōst′līn″, *n.* The shoreline; the land and water along the shoreline.

coast·ward, coast·wards, kōst′wẽrd, kōst′wẽrdz, *adv.* Toward the coast.

coast·wise, kōst′wīz″, *adv.*, *a.* Along the coast.

coat, kōt, *n.* [O.Fr. *cote*, Fr. *cotte*, a coat < L.L. *cota*, a coat, < O.G. *cotte*, a coarse mantle, G. *kutte*, a cowl: allied to *cot*.] A warm outer garment covering at least the upper part of the body; a layer of one substance covering another; a coating; the external covering as fur, hair, or wool of an animal.

coat, kōt, *v.t.* To cover with a coat; to spread over with a coating or layer of any substance.

co·a·ti, kō·ä′tē, *n.* pl. **co·a·tis,** kō·ä′tēz. [Brazilian.] Either of two tropical American animals constituting the genus *Nasua*, related to the racoon, but having an elongated body, a long tail, and an attenuated, flexible snout. Also **co·a·ti·mon·di, co·a·ti·mun·di,** kō·ä′tē·mun′dē.

coat·ing, kō′ting, *n.* Any substance spread over for cover or protection; a thin external layer, as of paint or plastic; cloth for coats.

coat of arms, *n.* A representation of the armorial insignia depicted on a coat worn by knights over their armor; an escutcheon or shield of arms.

coat of mail, *n.* Defensive armor worn on the upper part of the body, consisting of a network of iron or steel rings, laid over each other like the scales of a fish, and fastened to a strong linen or leather jacket.

coat·tails, on the, *prep. phr.* In the path of; in the wake of; usually suggesting an achievement made easier by following another person's efforts, as: He won the election *on the coattails* of his celebrated father.

co·au·thor, kō·ạ′thẽr, kō·ạ″thẽr, *n.* One who writes a book or article with one or more other authors.—*v.t.* To write, as an article or book, with someone else.

coax, kōks, *v.t.* [< O.E. *cokes*, a fool; to *coax* one being thus to make a *cokes*, or fool, of him.] To influence or persuade by gentle urging, flattery, or fondling; to wheedle; to maneuver an object by adroit handling, as: The furniture movers *coaxed* the piano through the door.—**coax·er,** kōk'sẽr, *n.* One who coaxes; a wheedler.—**coax·ing·ly,** kōk'sing·lē, *adv.*

co·ax·i·al, kō·ak'sē·al, *a.* Having a common axis; placed or mounted concentrically on the same shaft.—**co·ax·i·al·ly,** *adv.*

co·ax·i·al ca·ble, *n.* An insulated cable, consisting of an insulated conductor tube surrounding a core of conducting material, used for the transmission of multiple telephone, telegraph, and television signals.

cob, kob, *n.* [Probably, in some meanings, < W. *cob,* a top, a tuft.] A corncob, the central kernel-bearing part of an ear of corn. *Brit. dial.* any rounded heap or small mass; a leader or top man. A coin, specif. a piece of eight or old Spanish peso; a male swan; a short-legged, stocky horse, esp. one with an exaggeratedly high gait; a mixture of clay and straw used in building.

cob, cobb, kob, *n.* [= East Fries. *kobbe.*] *Brit. dial.* a gull, esp. the great black-backed gull, *Larus marinus.*

co·balt, kō'bạlt, *n.* [G. *kobalt,* prob. = *kobold,* goblin.] *Chem.* sym. Co, at. no. 27; a silver-white, magnetic metallic element that is tough, lustrous, and ductile, found in and with various ores such as iron and nickel: usage includes preparation of alloys and compounds, the silicates of which yield blue coloring for ceramics, inks, and paints. See Periodic Table of Elements.

co·balt blue, *n.* A blue to green pigment compounded essentially of cobalt oxide and alumina; a deep blue color.

co·bal·tic, kō·bạl'tik, *a. Chem.* Of or pertaining to compounds in which cobalt has a valence of three.

co·bal·tite, kō·bạl'tīt, kō'bạl·tīt″, *n.* A silver-white mineral, cobalt sulfarsenide, CoAsS; sometimes called **co·balt·ine.**

co·bal·tous, kō·bạl'tus, *a. Chem.* Of or pertaining to compounds in which cobalt has a valence of two.

co·balt 60, *n.* A heavy radioactive isotope of cobalt, having a mass number of 60, and used as a source of gamma rays, chiefly in radiotherapy.

cob·ble, kob'l, *v.t.*—*cobbled, cobbling.* [O.Fr. *cobler,* to join or knit together, < L. *copulare,* to couple.] To make or repair, as shoes; to put together or mend coarsely or clumsily.—**cob·bler,** *n.*

cob·ble, kob'l, *n.* [< *cob,* a lump.] A naturally rounded rock fragment, formerly used for paving. Also *cobblestone.*—*v.t.*—*cobbled, cobbling.* To pave with cobblestones.—**cob·bles,** *n. pl. Chiefly Brit.* lumps of coal resembling cobbles. Also *cob coal.*

cob·ble·stone, kob'l·stōn″, *n.* A cobble.

cob coal, *n.* Coal in large round pieces; any piece of such coal. Also *cobbles.*

co·bi·a, kō'bē·a, *n.* A large fish, *Rachycentron canadus,* found in the waters off Japan, the East Indies, and in temperate and tropical seas off the eastern coast of the Americas.

cob·nut, kob'nut, *n.* The nut of certain cultivated varieties of hazel; a tree bearing such nuts, as *Corylus avellana.*

COBOL, Cobol, kō'bōl, kō'bạl, *n.* [< *common business oriented language.*] *Computer,* a computer language, using common English words, that is particularly suited to processing large files of data.

co·bra, kō'bra, *n.* Any of several venomous hooded snakes, genus *Naja,* of Asia and Africa, esp. the spectacled cobra, *N. naja,* of India; the skin as used for leather, esp. for shoes and belts.

cob·web, kob'web″, *n.* [O.E. *coppe,* a spider, seen in *attor-coppe,* a spider.] The network

spun by a spider to catch its prey; any single thread formed by a spider; the thread or web which an insect larva spins; anything resembling a cobweb either in texture, as something flimsy or finespun, or intent, as an entangling, intricate plot; *pl.* anything muddled, confused, or disorganized; as, *cobwebs* in her thinking.—**cob·webbed,** *a.*—**cob·web·by,** *a.*

co·ca, kō'ka, *n.* [Sp. < Peruvian.] A shrub, *Erythroxylum coca,* native in the Andes and cultivated elsewhere, or its dried leaves, which are chewed for their stimulant properties and which yield cocaine and other alkaloids.

co·caine, kō·kān', kō'kān, kō'ka·ēn″, *n.* [< *coca.*] A bitter crystalline alkaloid, $C_{17}H_{21}NO_4$, obtained from coca leaves, used in medicine as a local anesthetic and as a narcotic.

co·cain·ism, kō·kā'niz·um, kō'kā·niz″um, *n. Pathol.* Addiction to the habitual use of cocaine; the general breakdown due to excessive or habitual use of cocaine.

co·cain·ize, kō·kā'nīz, kō'ka·nīz″, *v.t.*—*cocainized, cocainizing.* To treat with or affect by cocaine.

coc·cid, kok'sid, *n.* Any insect of the large family *Coccoidea,* as scale insects and mealybugs.

coc·cid·i·oi·do·my·co·sis, kok·sid″ē·oi″dō·mī·kō'sis, *n. Pathol.* a fever and pulmonary disease or sometimes a skin infection in the form of lesions, occurring in man and some animals, and caused by inhaling the spores of the fungus *Coccidiodes immitis.*

coc·cid·i·o·sis, kok·sid″ē·ō'sis, *n. Vet. pathol.* a disease occurring in domestic and wild animals, rarely in humans, in which the intestines are infested with coccidia.

coc·cid·i·um, kok·sid'ē·um, *n. pl.* **coc·cid·ia,** kok·sid'ē·a. Any individual organism of an order of protozoans which are usually intestinal parasites in vertebrates.

coc·coid, kok'oid, *a.* Resembling or pertaining to a coccus; berrylike; spherical, as certain microorganisms.—*n.* A coccoid microorganism.

coc·cus, kok'us, *n. pl.* **coc·ci,** kok'sī. [N.L. < Gr. *kokkos,* grain, seed.] *Bact.* a globular or spherical bacterium, as in staphylo*coccus,* micro*coccus. Bot.* one of the carpels in the flower of a schizocarp plant. *Zool.* any of the homopterous insects of the genus *Coccus,* as the cochineal insects.

coc·cyx, kok'siks, *n. pl.* **coc·cy·ges,** kok·sī'jēz, **coc·cyx·es,** kok'·sik·sēz. [N.L., < Gr. *kokkux,* coccyx, orig. cuckoo.] *Anat.* a small triangular bone forming the lower extremity of the spinal column in man, consisting of four ankylosed rudimentary vertebrae; a corresponding part in certain other animals.—**coc·cyg·e·al,** kok·sij'ē·al, *a.*

Co·chin Chi·na, kō'chin chī'na, *n., a.* A term applied to a large variety of the domestic fowl which was imported from Cochin China, now South Vietnam.

coch·i·neal, koch″i·nēl', koch'i·nēl″, *n.* [F. *cochenille,* < Sp. *cochinilla,* < L. *coccinus,* scarlet, < *coccum,* < Gr. *coccos,* grain, seed, kermes.] A red dyestuff consisting of the dried bodies of the females of a scale-insect, *Coccus cacti,* which lives on various cactuses, as the nopal, of Mexico, Central America, and other warm regions; the insect itself.

coch·le·a, kok'lē·a, *n.* [L., a snail or snail's shell.] A bony structure in the internal ear, so called from resembling a snail shell; a spiral staircase; a tower containing a spiral staircase.—**coch·le·ate, coch·le·at·ed,** kok'lē·it, kok'lē·āt″, *a.* Spiral.

cock, kok, *n.* [O.E. *coc* = O.Fr. *coc,* Fr. *coq,* = M.L. *coccus;* prob. ult. imit.] The male

of the domestic fowl; the male of any of various birds, esp. of the gallinaceous kind; a figure or representation of a cock; one of the national emblems of France: from a word play on the Latin *gallus,* a cock, and *Gallus,* a Gaul; a weather vane in the shape of a cock; a weathercock; a leader or ruling spirit, often one who makes a vainglorious show of leadership or victory; as, *cock* of the walk; a device for permitting or arresting the flow of a liquid or gas from a receptacle or through a pipe; a faucet, tap, or valve; in a firearm, that part of the lock which by its fall or action causes the discharge; the hammer; the position into which the cock or hammer of a firearm is brought by being drawn partly or completely back, preparatory to firing; the gnomon of a sundial. *Sports,* the mark aimed at in the game of curling; *slang,* a cock-and-bull story.

cock, kok, *v.t.* To turn, set up, or tilt to one side, often in an assertive or jaunty manner; as, to *cock* one's hat to one side of the head, to *cock* one's head; to prepare to discharge, as a firearm.

cock, kok, *n.* [Dan. *kok,* a heap, a pile; Icel. *kökkr,* a lump.] A small conical pile of hay, so shaped for shedding rain.

cock·ade, ko·kād', *n.* [F. *cocarde,* < *coq,* cock.] A knot of ribbon, a rosette, or the like, worn on the hat as a badge or a part of a livery.—**cock·ad·ed,** ko·kā'ded, *a.*

cock-a-hoop, kok″a·hŏp', kok″a·hup', kok'·a·hŏp″, *a. Brit.* elated; joyous; triumphal.

Cock·aigne, Cock·ayne, ko·kān′, *n.* [O.Fr. *cokaigne;* origin uncertain.] An imaginary land of luxury and idleness.

cock-a-leek·ie, kok″a·lē'kē, *n.* A thick chicken and leek soup of Scottish origin.

cock·a·lo·rum, kok″a·lōr'um, *n.* [A humorous formation simulating Latin.] A person who assumes a pretentious manner; a self-important person; *colloq.* boastful talk.

cock-and-bull sto·ry, *n.* An improbable story given out as true.

cock·a·tiel, cock·a·teel, kok″a·tēl′, *n.* [D. *kaketielje;* cf. *cockatoo.*] A small, long-tailed Australian parrot, *Calopsitta novæ-hollandiæ,* common as a pet.

cock·a·too, kok'a·tö″, *n. pl.* **cock·a·toos.** [Malay *kakatua.*] Any of the crested parrots constituting the genus *Cacatua* or subfamily *Cacatuinæ,* of the East Indies or Australia.

cock·a·trice, kok'a·tris, *n.* [O.Fr. *cocatris,* < a M.L. form < L. *calcare,* tread, used to render Gr. *ichneumon,* "tracker," E. *ichneumon.* In later use associated with the cock.] A mythical serpent with deadly glance, reputed to be hatched by a serpent from a cock's egg, and commonly represented with the head, legs, and wings of a cock and the body and tail of a serpent; in the Bible, a venomous serpent.

cock·boat, kok'bōt″, *n.* A small boat, esp. one used as a tender. Also **cock·le·boat,** *cockleshell.*

cock·cha·fer, kok'chā″fẽr, *n.* A large scarabæid beetle, *Melolontha vulgaris,* of Europe, in both the larval and perfect forms destructive to forest vegetation; any of various allied beetles.

cock·crow, kok'krō″, *n.* The time at which cocks crow; early morning. Also **cock·crow·ing,** kok'krō″ing.

cocked hat, *n.* Any of various styles of hat having the brim turned up on two opposite sides or triangularly on three sides; a hat pointed before and behind, and in lateral view a triangular form, worn as part of certain naval, military, and other official costumes.

cock·er·el, kok'er·el, kok'rel, *n.* [Dim. of *cock.*] A young domestic cock.

cock·er span·iel, *n.* One of a breed of small spaniels trained for use in hunting or kept as pets.

---

cock·eye, kok′ī, *n.* An eye that squints, or is affected with strabismus.

cock·eyed, kok′īd, *a.* Having a squinting eye. *Slang*, absurdly wrong; foolishly twisted to one side; intoxicated.

cock·fight, kok′fīt, *n.* A fight between gamecocks which have been fitted with steel spurs.—**cock·fight·ing**, *n.*

cock·horse, kok′hȧrs″, *n.* A child's rocking horse.

cock·i·ly, kok′i·lē, *adv. Colloq.* in a cocky manner; smartly; pertly.—**cock·i·ness**, *n.*

cock·le, kok′el, *n.* [O.Fr. Fr. *coquille*, < L. *conchylium*, < Gr. *konchylion*, < *kogche*, mussel or cockle, E. *conch*.] Any of the bivalve mollusks, with somewhat heart-shaped, radially ribbed valves, which constitute the genus *Cardium*, esp. *C. edule*, the common edible species of Europe; any of various allied or similar mollusks; a cockle-shell; a small shallow or light boat; a small crisp confection of sugar and flour, bearing a motto; a wrinkle or pucker; *pl.* deep emotions; as, the *cockles* of the heart.

cock·le, kok′el, *n.* [O.E. *coccel*, tares; comp. Gael. *cogal*, Fr. *coquiole*, cockle.] A plant that grows among corn; the corn cockle; a weed such as rye grass, or darnel.

cock·le, kok′el, *v.i.*—*cockled, cockling.* To contract into wrinkles; pucker; of the sea, to rise into short, irregular waves.—*v.t.*

cock·le·bur, kok′el·bȯr, *n.* Any plant of the genus *Xanthium*, comprising coarse weeds with spiny burs; the burdock, *Arctium lappa*.

cock·le·shell, kok′el·shel″, *n.* The shell of the cockle, or one of its valves; a small, light boat.

cock·loft, kok′lȧft, kok′lȯft″, *n.* [Lit. a loft for cocks to roost in.] A small loft in the top of a house; a small garret.

cock·ney, kok′nē, *n. pl.* **cock·neys.** [M.E. *cokeney*, appar. "cock's egg," an imperfect egg (M.E. *ey*, egg).] (*Often cap.*) a native of the East End of London. The dialect of that district.—*a.* Of or pertaining to cockneys or their dialect.—**cock·ney·dom**, *n.* The region of cockneys; cockneys collectively.—**cock·ney·ish**, *a.* Cockney-like.—**cock·ney·ism**, *n.* Cockney quality or usage; a cockney peculiarity, as of speech.

cock·pit, kok′pit″, *n.* In some airplanes, an enclosed space containing a seat for a pilot or passenger; a pit or enclosed place for cockfights; a place where a contest is fought, or which has been the scene of many contests or battles; *naut.* a depression in the deck of a boat, esp. in yachts, the pit abaft the cabin occupied by the helmsman.

cock·roach, kok′rōch″, *n.* [Sp. *cucaracha*, a wood louse, a cockroach.] Any of various usu. nocturnal insects of the family *Blattidae*, very troublesome in houses, where they may multiply to a great extent, infesting kitchens and pantries.

cocks·comb, koks′kōm″, *n.* The comb or caruncle of a cock; the cap of a professional fool, resembling a cock's comb; a garden plant, *Celosia cristata*, with flowers, commonly crimson or purple, in a dense spike somewhat resembling the comb or crest of a cock. A fop; also *coxcomb*.

cock·shy, kok′shī″, *n. pl.* **cock·shies.** *Brit.* The act of throwing an object at a target, orig. a cock; the object thrown at; hence, an object of attack; a booth or the like where objects are thrown at targets, as for a prize.

cock·spur, kok′spȯr″, *n.* A spur of a cock; any of several plants with spur-like thorns or branches, esp. *Cratægus crus-galli*, a North American species of hawthorn.

cock·sure, kok′shȯr″, *a.* [Appar. < *cock*.] Perfectly sure or certain; over-confident.—**cock·sure·ly**, *adv.*—**cock·sure·ness**, *n.*

cock·tail, kok′tāl″, *n.* Any of various drinks, containing such alcoholic beverages as gin, whiskey, or brandy mixed with other liquors or juices; an appetizer, usually consisting of sea food, fruits, or juices, served as a first course of a meal.—*a.* Pertaining to a cocktail; designed for semi-formal attire.

cock·tail, kok′tāl″, *n.* A horse with a docked tail; a horse which is not thoroughbred.

cock·y, kok′ē, *a.*—*cockier, cockiest. Colloq.* arrogantly smart; pertly self-assertive; conceited.

co·co, kō′kō, *n. pl.* **co·cos.** [Pg. *coco*, < *coco*, a bugbear, a distorted mask, from the monkeylike face at the base of the nut.] The coconut palm.

co·coa, kō′kō, *n.* [Corruption of *cacao*.] The roasted, husked, and ground seeds of the cacao, *Theobroma cacao*, from which much of the fat has been removed; a hot beverage made from this powder.

co·coa but·ter, *n.* A fatty substance pressed from the seeds of the cacao, used in making soaps and cosmetics.

co·co·bo·lo, kō″kō·bō′lō, *n.* [Sp.] Any of several dark-colored hard woods of the West Indies and Central America, used in cabinet making. Also **co·co·bo·la.**

co·con·scious, kō·kon′shus, *a. Psychol.* pertaining to a mental process apart from the stream of consciousness, but influencing the latter, often in the form of unintended utterances or in hallucinations.—*n.* The process itself; also **co·con·scious·ness.**

co·co·nut, co·coa·nut, kō′ko·nut, *n.* The nut of the coconut palm, large, hard-shelled, with a white edible meat, and containing a milky liquid.

co·co·nut palm, *n.* A tall, slender tropical tree, *Cocos nucifera*, with an edible fruit.

co·coon, ko·kōn′, *n.* [Fr. *cocon*, < *coque*, a shell, < L. *concha*, shellfish.] The silky tissue or envelope which the larvae of many insects spin as a covering for themselves while they are in the chrysalis state; a similar soft case for eggs of spiders and earthworms; a protective airtight seal, usually of polyvinyl chloride, sprayed on guns and large machinery of ships during extended storage periods.

co·cotte, kō·kot′, ko·kot′, *Fr.* kȧ·kȧt′, *n. pl.* **co·cottes**, kō·kots′, ko·kots′, *Fr.* kȧ·kȧt′. A prostitute.

coc·o·zel·le, kok″o·zel′ē, *n.* A variety of squash, dark green with yellowish stripes, similar to zucchini in appearance.

cod, kod, *n. pl.* **cod, cods.** [D. *kodde*, a club, from its large club-shaped head.] A large food fish, *Gadus callarias*, usually weighing between 10 and 35 pounds found in the colder regions of the North Atlantic Ocean; also **cod·fish.** Any fish of the family *Gadidae*, including a fish of the Pacific Ocean that is very similar to the Atlantic cod; any one of several fishes similar to cod, as the ling.

C.O.D., c.o.d., abbr. for collect on delivery; payment at the time delivery is made to the purchaser; *Brit.* cash on delivery.

co·da, kō′dȧ, *n.* [It., < L. *cauda*, a tail.] *Mus.* a section at the end of a movement, usually distinct from the previous parts of the movement, that is added to obtain a fuller, more forceful ending.

cod·dle, kod′el, *v.t.*—*coddled, coddling.* [Origin uncertain: cf. *caudle*.] To nurse or care for tenderly or indulgently; to pamper; to cook slowly and gently; as, to *coddle* an egg.

code, kōd, *n.* [Fr. < L. *codex.* CODEX.] Any systematic collection or digest of the existing laws of a country; as, the Civil *Code* of France; any system or collection of rules and regulations; a system of signals for communication by telegraph, heliograph, or other device; a system of arbitrarily chosen words, used for brevity or secrecy; a cipher; numbers, letters or combinations of both used to represent or identify a thing, as in a storage system; *computer*, a set of symbols having a special set of rules for their use and which represent information in a form that can be used by a computer.

code, kōd, *v.t.*—*coded, coding.* To arrange in a code; enter in a code; to translate into a code or cipher; *computer*, to translate into a code that can be transmitted to and processed by a computer.

co·dec·li·na·tion, kō″dek·li·nā′shan, *n. Astron.* the complementary angle of the declination of a celestial point.

code con·ver·sion, *n. Computer*, the conversion of data from one code to another.

co·de·fend·ant, kō″di·fen′dant, *n.* A joint defendant; one of two or more defendants to a single legal action, criminal or civil.

co·deine, kō′dēn, *n.* [Gr. *codeia*, head, poppy-head.] A white, crystalline, slightly bitter alkaloid, $C_{18}H_{21}NO_3$, obtained from opium, used in medicine as an analgesic, sedative, and hypnotic.

co·det·ta, kō·det′a, *It.* kȧ·det′tä, *n.* [It.] *Mus.* a short coda.

co·dex, kō′deks, *n. pl.* **co·di·ces**, kō′di·sēz″. A manuscript volume of ancient origin, as a Greek or Latin classic, or the Scriptures; *obs.* a body of laws.

codg·er, koj′ėr, *n.* [Probably a form of *cadger*.] *Slang*, a curious old fellow; a character; *Brit.* a mean, miserly man.

cod·i·cil, kod′i·sil, *n.* [L. *codicillus*, dim. of *codex*.] A supplement to a will, containing an explanation, modification, or revocation of something contained in the will.—**cod·i·cil·la·ry**, kod″i·sil′a·rē, *a.*

cod·i·fi·ca·tion, kod″i·fi·kā′shan, kō″di·fi·kā′shan, *n.* The act, process, or result of codifying.

cod·i·fy, kod′i·fī″, kō′di·fī″, *v.t.*—*codified, codifying.* To reduce to a code or digest, as laws.

cod·ling, kod′ling, *n.* A young cod. *Brit.* an elongated cooking apple. An unripe apple.

cod·ling moth, *n.* A small moth, the larva of which feeds on tree-borne fruit.

cod-liv·er oil, *n.* A pale yellow oil extracted from cod livers, and from fish livers of related species, used chiefly in medicine as a source of vitamins A and D.

co·ed, kō′ed′, kō′ed″, *n.* A female student in a coeducational institution, as a college or university.

co·ed, co·ed, kō′ed′, kō′ed″, *a.* Pertaining to coeducation or to a coed; for or including both sexes; as, a *co-ed* college.

co·ed·u·ca·tion, kō″ej·u·kā′shan, *n.* Education of persons of both sexes in the same classes of an institution.—**co·ed·u·ca·tion·al**, *a.*—**co·ed·u·ca·tion·al·ly**, *adv.*

co·ef·fi·cient, kō″e·fish′ent, *a.* Cooperating.—*n.* That which unites in action with something else to produce an effect; *math.* a factor of an algebraic term that multiplies the other terms, as, in the term $3x$, 3 and x are *coefficients* of each other; in the term $4xy$, x is the *coefficient* of $4y$, 4 is the *coefficient* of xy, and y is the *coefficient* of $4x$; *phys.* a parameter; a numerical quantity, constant for a given substance under given circumstances, that is combined with the variable factors to calculate the kind and amount of change occurring in a substance or body.

coe·la·canth, sē′la·kanth, *n.* A fish thought to be extinct until one species, *Latimeria chalumnae*, was found in 1938.

coe·len·ter·ate, si·len′te·rāt″, si·len′te·rit, *n.* An animal of the phylum *Coelenterata*, consisting of invertebrates that are radially symmetrical, as hydras, jellyfish, corals.

coe·len·ter·on, si·len′te·ron, *n. pl.* **coe·len·ter·a**, si·len′te·ra. The saclike internal cavity of a coelenterate.

coe·li·ac, sē′lē·ak″, *a.* Celiac.

coe·lom, sē′lom, *n.* [Gr. *koilōma*, a cavity.] *Zool.* in most many-celled animals, the main body cavity, lined by epithelium, that contains the intestines and some other organs.

coe·lo·stat, sē′lo·stat″, n. [L. cœlum, cælum, sky, and Gr. statos, standing.] Astron. an instrument in which a reflected image of the sky is made to appear stationary by means of a mirror which revolves slowly by clockwork.

coe·no·bite, sē′no·bīt″, sen′o·bīt″, n. Cenobite.

co·en·zyme, kō·en′zīm, n. Biol. an organic compound that works as a catalyst in conjunction with an enzyme or enzyme system.

co·e·qual, kō·ē′kwal, a. Equal with another person or thing; of the same rank, dignity, or power.—n. One who is equal to another.—**co·e·qual·i·ty,** kō″ē·kwol′i·tē, n. The state of being coequal.—**co·e·qual·ly,** kō·ē′kwal·lē, adv.

co·erce, kō·ûrs′, v.t.—coerced, coercing. [L. coerceo—prefix co-, and arcere, to shut up, confine.] To restrain by force, particularly by moral force, as by law or authority; to repress; to compel to compliance; to constrain.—**co·er·ci·ble,** kō·ûr′si·bl, a. Capable of being coerced.—**co·er·cion,** kō·ûr′shon, n. The art of coercing; restraint; compulsion; constraint.—**co·er·cive,** kō·ûr′siv, a. Capable of coercing; restrictive; able to force into compliance.—**co·er·cive·ness,** n.—**co·er·cive·ly,** kō·ûr′siv·lē, adv. By constraint or coercion.

co·e·ta·ne·ous, kō″i·tā′nē·us, a. [L. coætaneus—prefix co-, and ætas, age.] Of the same age with another; beginning to exist at the same time; coeval.—**co·e·ta·ne·ous·ly,** adv. Of or from the same age or beginning.

co·e·ter·nal, kō″i·tûr′nal, a. Equally eternal with another.—**co·e·ter·nal·ly,** adv. With coeternity, or equal eternity.—**co·e·ter·ni·ty,** n. Existence from eternity equal with another eternal being; equal eternity.

co·e·val, kō·ē′val, a. [L. coævus—con-, and ævum, age.] Of the same age; having lived for an equal period; existing at the same time, or of equal antiquity or duration.—n. One who is a contemporary; one who lives at the same time.

co·ex·ec·u·tor, kō″ig·zek′ū·tėr, n. A joint executor, as of a will.—**co·ex·ec·u·trix,** kō″ig·zek′ū·triks, n. pl. **co·ex·ec·u·tri·ces.** A female coexecutor.

co·ex·ist, kō″ig·zist′, v.i. To exist at the same time with another.—**co·ex·ist·ence,** n. Existence at the same time with another; the peaceful existence with one another, of two or more nations or societies which differ in ideas.—**co·ex·ist·ent,** a. Existing at the same time with another.

co·ex·ten·sive, kō″ik·sten′siv, a. Equally extensive; having equal scope or extent.—**co·ex·ten·sive·ly,** adv.

cof·fee, ka′fē, kof′ē, n. [< It. caffè < Turk. kahve < •Ar. qahwah.] A beverage prepared from the roasted and ground or crushed seeds, called coffee beans, of certain plants or trees of the genus Coffea, grown in the uplands of tropical regions; these seeds, or a tree or shrub yielding such seeds; a cup of coffee; as, two coffees without cream; a social function at which coffee is served, as: The Homecoming schedule included several coffees for alumni. A color, medium- to dark-brown, resembling the beverage coffee with cream.

cof·fee·house, ka′fē·hous″, kof′ē·hous″, n. A restaurant which specializes in different kinds of coffee and light refreshments, and sometimes features entertainment; a similar eating place of seventeenth-century England which was used for informal meetings and discussions.

cof·fee klatch, cof·fee klatsch, n. A small social gathering, esp. of women, for informal conversation while drinking coffee.

cof·fee·pot, ka′fē·pot″, kof′ē·pot″, n. An appliance used for making or serving coffee.

cof·fee shop, n. A small restaurant, frequently in a hotel, which serves snacks and light meals.

cof·fee ta·ble, n. A low table most commonly placed before a living room sofa, for serving coffee or holding ash trays, beverage glasses, etc. Also **cock·tail ta·ble.**

cof·fee tree, n. Any tree, as Coffea arabica, which yields coffee beans; a tall North American tree, Gymnocladus dioica, known as Kentucky coffee tree, whose seeds have been used as a substitute for coffee; the cascara buckthorn.

cof·fer, ka′fėr, kof′ėr, n. [O.Fr. cofre (Fr. coffre), chest, < L. cophinus, basket.] A box or chest, esp. a safe for valuables; an ornamental sunken panel in a ceiling, vault, or soffit; any of various boxlike enclosures, as a caisson or cofferdam. Pl. a treasury; funds or pecuniary resources.—v.t. To deposit or lay up in a coffer or chest; to ornament with coffers or sunken panels.

cof·fer·dam, ka′fėr·dam″, kof′ėr·dam″, n. A water-tight enclosure, as one constructed of piles and clay and used, after pumping the water out, when laying foundations of bridges, repairing ships, or doing other work below the surface of the water.

cof·fin, ka′fin, kof′in, n. [O.Fr. cofin, a chest, L. cophinus, a basket.] The chest or box in which a dead human body is buried or interred in a vault; the hard substance forming a horse's hoof.—v.t. To put or enclose in a coffin.

cof·fin, ka′fin, kof′in, n. Atomic technology slang, the heavy lead box containing radioactive materials for transport.

cof·fin bone, n. A small bone enclosed in the hoof of a horse.

cof·fin cor·ner, n. Football, the area between the ten-yard line and the goal line of a football field, toward which punts are often directed, in the hope that the ball will roll out of bounds near the opponent's goal line.

cof·fle, kof′el, n. [Ar. qāfilah, caravan.] A train of men or beasts, esp. of slaves, fastened together.

cog, kog, kȧg, n. [M.E. cogge = Sw. kugge.] A tooth or projection, usually one of a series, on a wheel, for transmitting motion to or receiving motion from a corresponding tooth or part on another wheel with which it engages; a cogwheel; an unimportant person or part in a large organization.

cog, kog, kȧg, n. Carpentry, a projecting member on a beam which fits into a slot in another beam.—v.t., v.i.—cogged, cogging. To connect by a cog.

co·gent, kō′jent, a. [L. cogens, cogentis, forcing, compelling, < cogo—con-, together, and ago, to lead or drive.] Having the power to convince, compel, or persuade by means of a clear, forcible presentation of facts, ideas, and arguments; incisive; pertinent; relevant; convincing.—**co·gen·cy,** n. The quality or state of being cogent.—**co·gent·ly,** adv. In a cogent manner.

cog·i·ta·ble, koj′i·ta·bl, a. Capable of being conceived; thinkable.

cog·i·tate, koj′i·tāt″, v.i.—cogitated, cogitating. [L. cogito, cogitatum—co- for con-, together, and agito, to shake, to agitate.] To think deeply; to meditate; to ponder. —v.t. to think about; to devise.—**cog·i·ta·tion,** koj·i·tā′shan, n. The act of cogitating or thinking; thought; meditation; contemplation.

cog·i·ta·tive, koj′i·tā″tiv, a. Having the power of cogitating; meditative; given to thought; thoughtful.—**cog·i·ta·tive·ly,** adv. In a cogitative or thinking manner.

cog·nac, kōn′yak, kon′yak, Fr. ka·nyak′, n. [Fr.] A kind of French brandy, so called from the town of the same name, where large quantities are made.

cog·nate, kog·nāt, a. [L. cognatus—prefix co- for con-, with, and gnatus, old form of natus, born.] Allied by blood; kindred by birth; connected by the mother's side. Related in origin generally; proceeding from the same stock or root; of the same family, as words, roots, languages; allied in nature; having affinity of any kind; as, cognate sounds.

cog·nate, kog·nāt, n. One connected with another by ties of birth; a relation connected by the mother's side; anything related to another by origin or nature.

cog·na·tion, kog·nā′shan, n. [L. cognatio.] Relationship by blood or by descent from the same original.

cog·ni·tion, kog·nish′on, n. [L. cognitio(n-), < cognoscere, come to know, recognize, acknowledge, < co-, with, and gnoscere, noscere, know.] The act or fact of coming to know or of knowing; perception; cognizance; knowledge.—**cog·ni·tive,** kog′ni·tiv, a.

cog·ni·za·ble, kog′ni·za·bl, kon′i·za·bl, kog·nī′za·bl, a. Capable of falling under notice or observation; capable of being known, perceived, or apprehended; capable of falling under judicial notice.—**cog·ni·za·bly,** adv. In a cognizable manner.

cog·ni·zance, kog′ni·zans, kon′i·zans, n. [O.Fr. cognoissance, connoissance.] Knowledge or notice; perception; observation. Law, judicial or authoritative notice or knowledge; the right to try and to determine causes. Her. a crest; a badge; a badge worn by a retainer or soldier to indicate the person or party to which he belonged.

cog·ni·zant, kog′ni·zant, kon′i·zant, a. Acquainted with followed by of; having obtained knowledge of; competent to take legal or judicial notice.

cog·nize, kog·nīz′, v.t.—cognized, cognizing. To recognize as an object of thought; to perceive; to become conscious of.

cog·no·men, kog·nō′men, n. pl. **cog·no·mens, cog·nom·i·na,** kog·nom′i·na. [L. cognomen—prefix co for con-, and nomen, formerly gnomen, a name.] Strictly, the last of the three names by which a Roman of good family was known, indicating the family to which he belonged; hence a surname or distinguishing name in general.— **cog·nom·i·nal,** a.

co·gno·scen·ti, kon″ya·shen′tē, kog″no·shen′tē, n. pl., sing. **co·gno·scen·te.** Persons who have or claim to have special knowledge and appreciation of a particular field, esp. in fashion, literature, or the fine arts; connoisseurs.

cog·nos·ci·ble, kog·nos′i·bl, a. [< L. cognosco, COGNITION.] Capable of being known; subject to judicial investigation.— **cog·nos·ci·bil·i·ty,** n.

cog·no·vit, kog·nō′vit, n. [L., "he has acknowledged."] Law, an acknowledgment or confession by a defendant that the plaintiff's cause, or a part of it, is just, wherefore the defendant, to save expense, suffers judgment to be entered without trial.

cog rail·way, n. A railroad constructed on a steep incline with cogs or teeth on the rail which mesh with a cogwheel on the locomotive to provide traction.

Cogs·well chair, n. An armchair with sloping back and open sides, generally with legs of the cabriole type. Also **Cox·well chair.**

cog·wheel, kog′hwēl″, kog′wēl″, n. A wheel with teeth; a gear wheel.

co·hab·it, kō·hab′it, v.i. [L. cohabito, < co-, with, and habito, to dwell.] To dwell or live together as husband and wife: often applied to persons not legally married, and suggesting sexual intercourse; obs. to reside together.—**co·hab·i·ta·tion,** n.

co·heir, kō·âr′, n. A joint heir; one who succeeds to a share of an inheritance divided among two or more.—**co·heir·ess**, kō·âr'is, n. A joint heiress.

co·here, kō·hēr', v.i.—cohered, cohering. [L. cohæro—cə for con, and hæro, to stick together.] To stick or cleave together; to be united; to keep in close contact as parts of the same mass; to agree or be logically consistent, as parts of a discourse or argument.

co·her·ence, kō·hēr'ens, n. A cleaving together; due agreement, as of ideas; consistency. Also **co·her·en·cy**, kō·hēr'en·sē.

co·her·ent, kō·hēr'ent, a. Sticking together; tending to remain united; having an agreement or harmony of parts, as of a pattern. Logical; consistent; as, a coherent argument or discourse, a coherent speaker. —**co·her·ent·ly**, adv. In a coherent manner.

co·he·sion, kō·hē'zhan, n. [Fr. cohésion.] The act or state of cohering, uniting, or sticking together. Physics, the force which unites the molecules of a body and prevents decomposition; bot. the union of like parts, such as petals.

co·he·sive, kō·hē'siv, a. Cohering; sticking together.—**co·he·sive·ly**, adv.—**co·he·sive·ness**, n. The quality of, or tendency to, unite by cohesion.

co·hort, kō'hərt, n. [L. cohors, cohortis.] In Roman armies, the tenth part of a legion, a body of about 500 or 600 men; a band or body of warriors in general; a group; as, a cohort of enthusiastic followers; a companion.

co·hosh, kō'hosh, kō·hosh', n. [N. Amer. Ind.] Any of several medicinal North American plants, as Cimicifuga racemosa or black cohosh, and Caulophyllum thalictroides or blue cohosh.

coif, koif, n. [Fr. coiffe, L.L. cofia, cufia, < M.H.G. kuffe, kupfe, a kind of cap.] Any of various types of close-fitting hoodlike caps, worn by both sexes from about 1200 A.D., esp. such a cap still worn under a veil by some orders of nuns; a white close-fitting cap formerly worn by barristers and sergeants at law in England; the office of sergeant at law; her. a protective cap of padded cloth, leather, or metal worn under a helmet or a hood of mail.—v.t. To cover or dress with or as with a coif; to dress, as hair.

coif·feur, kwä·fOER', n. [Fr., < coiffer. COIFFURE.] A hairdresser.

coif·fure, kwä·fyur', Fr. kwä·fYR', n. [Fr., < coiffer, furnish with a coif or headcovering, dress the hair of, < coiffe, E. coif.] A head covering or headdress; a style of hair arrangement.—v.t.—coiffured, coiffuring. To arrange or dress, as the hair.

coil, koil, v.t. [O.Fr. coillir, cueillir, < L. colligere, to collect.] To gather, as a rope or chain, into a series of rings one above another; to twist or wind spirally.—v.i. To form rings or spirals; to wind; to follow a circular course.

coil, koil, n. A ring or series of rings or spirals into which a rope, chain, or other pliant body is wound; a pipe wound in spiral form or connected pipes arranged in a series, as in a radiator; elect. wire, esp. wire turned into a spiral, used as a conductor or inductor.

coin, koin, n. [Fr. coin, a wedge, the die with which money is stamped, a coin, a corner < L. cuneus, a wedge.] A piece of metal, as gold, silver, copper, or an alloy, converted into money by impressing some stamp on it; such pieces collectively; money; arch. an exterior angle or corner of a building; a quoin.

coin, koin, v.t. To make into money by stamping; to mint; to make, fabricate, or invent; as, to coin an expression.

coin·age, koi'nij, n. The act or process of coining money; coin; money coined; the

act of inventing, forming, or producing; what is fabricated or invented, as a word.

co·in·cide, kō"in·sīd', v.i.—coincided, coinciding. [M.L. coincidere, < L. co-, with, and incidere, fall on. INCIDENT.] To occupy the same place in space, the same point or period in time, or the same relative position; to correspond exactly, as in nature or character; to agree or concur, as in opinion.

co·in·ci·dence, kō·in'si·dens, n. The condition or fact of being coincident; an instance of agreement in circumstances, character, opinion, or sentiment; exact correspondence, esp. a striking occurrence of two or more events at one time, apparently by mere chance.

co·in·ci·dent, kō·in'si·dent, a. Occupying the same place or position; happening at the same time; corresponding, or of a similar nature; in exact agreement.

co·in·ci·den·tal, kō·in"si·den'tal, a. Involving coincidence; happening or existing simultaneously.—**co·in·ci·den·tal·ly**, adv.—**co·in·ci·dent·ly**, adv.

co·in·her·it·ance, kō"in·her'i·tans, n. Joint inheritance.—**co·in·her·it·or**, kō"in·her'i·tėr, n. A joint heir; a coheir.

co·in·stan·ta·ne·ous, kō"in·stan·tā'nē·us, a. Happening at the same instant.—**co·in·stan·ta·ne·ous·ly**, adv.

co·in·sur·ance, kō"in·shur'ans, n. Insurance jointly with another or others, esp. a form of fire insurance in which a person taking out insurance on property for less than its full value is regarded as a joint insurer and becomes jointly responsible for losses; concurrent acceptance of risk for one piece of property by two underwriters.

co·in·sure, kō"in·shur', v.t., v.i.—coinsured, coinsuring. To insure jointly with another or others; esp. to insure on a basis of coinsurance.

coir, koir, n. A species of yarn manufactured from the husk of coconuts, and formed into cordage, sailcloth, matting.

co·i·tion, kō·ish'an, n. [L. coitio—con, and eo, itum, to go.] A coming together; copulation.

co·i·tus, kō'i·tus, n. Sexual intercourse.—**co·i·tal**, a.

coke, kōk, n. Slang, cocaine. (Cap.) a soft drink: Coca-Cola. (Trademark.)

coke, kōk, n. [Origin uncertain.] A fuel with a high carbon content obtained by the destructive distillation of coal and used esp. in the production of metals; the residues resulting from similar treatment of other carbonaceous materials, as petroleum.

coke, kōk, v.t., v.i.—coked, coking. To convert into coke.

col, kol, Fr. kal, n. pl. **cols**. [Fr., < L. collum, neck.] Geol. a gap or saddle-shaped depression in a ridge or between two peaks of a mountain chain, usually forming a pass; the point at which the divide comes in a steeply sloping valley. Meteor. the relatively narrow column of low pressure occurring between two anticyclones.

co·la, kō'la, n. Plural of colon.

co·la, kō'la, n. Any of several carbonated soft drinks made from various sweeteners, aromatic materials, and acids, and from the extracts of kola nut seeds and coca plant leaves.

col·an·der, kul'an·dėr, kol'an·dėr, n. [< L. colans, colantis, ppr. of colo, to strain, < colum, a colander.] A vessel with a bottom perforated with little holes, used for straining liquids; a strainer.

co·lat·i·tude, kō·lat'i·tōd", kō·lat'i·tūd", n. [Abbrev. of complement and latitude.] The complement of the latitude, or the difference between a certain latitude and that of 90 degrees.

col·can·non, kol·kan'on, kạl·kan·on, n. An Irish dish made of cabbage and potatoes boiled and mashed together and seasoned.

col·chi·cine, kol'chi·sēn", kol'chi·sin", kol'ki·sēn", kol'ki·sin", n. A very poisonous, nearly odorless yellow alkaloid, $C_{22}H_{25}NO_6$, present in crystal or amorphous powder form and derived from the plant Colchicum autumnale, commonly called meadow saffron. Med. the compound colchicine tannate used to alleviate the symptoms of gout; biol. a synthetic used to induce chromosome polyploidy in plants, important in the development of new horticultural and agricultural varieties.

col·chi·cum, kol'chi·kum, kol'ki·kum, n. [L., a plant with a poisonous root < Colchis, the native country of Medea, the famous sorceress.] A genus of liliaceous plants, Colchicum, the most familiar species being the meadow saffron, a plant with a solid bulblike rootstock and purple, crocus-like flowers, found in various parts of Europe.

col·co·thar, kol'ko·thar, n. [Probably of Ar. origin.] The brownish-red peroxide of iron, used for polishing glass and as a pigment.

cold, kōld, a. [O.E. cald, ceald, = D. koud = G. kalt = Icel. kaldr = Goth. kalds, cold; all orig. pp. < a Teut. verb-stem (cf. O.E. calan, be cold) akin to L. gelidus, icy cold.] Producing or feeling, esp. in a high degree, the peculiar sensation resulting when heat is withdrawn from the body; chilly; frigid; having a temperature sensibly lower than the normal temperature of the body; having a relatively low temperature; having no warmth, or having lost warmth. Fig. deficient in passion, emotion, enthusiasm, or ardor; apathetic; indifferent; imperturbable; void of sensual desire; chaste; not affectionate, cordial, or friendly; unresponsive; failing to excite feeling or interest; depressing or dispiriting; faint or weak, as a scent; of coloring, inclining to blue or gray, rather than red or yellow.

cold, kōld, n. The relative absence of heat; a condition of low temperature; the sensation produced by loss of heat from the body; chill. A viral infection of the upper respiratory passages, popularly believed to be caused by exposure to cold, characterized by catarrh, hoarseness, and coughing; also **com·mon cold**.

cold-blood·ed, kōld'blud'id, a. Having cold blood; noting or pertaining to animals, as fishes and reptiles, whose blood temperature ranges from the freezing point upward, in accordance with the temperature of the surrounding medium; fig. lacking in emotion; unimpassioned; unsympathetic; cruel.—**cold-blood·ed·ly**, adv.—**cold-blood·ed·ness**, n.

cold chis·el, n. A strong chisel of tempered steel for cutting cold metal.

cold cream, n. A heavy, oily, cosmetic cream used for cleansing and lubricating the skin.

cold cuts, n. pl. Various sliced cold meats and cheeses.

cold deck, cold-deck, n. Slang, a deck of playing cards which have been secretly marked or stacked and exchanged for the deck in use, for fraudulent purposes.—v.t.

cold feet, n. Colloq. loss of courage or confidence for carrying out some undertaking proposed or begun.

cold frame, n. A glass-topped frame placed over a bed of seedlings or plants to protect them against cold.

cold front, n. The zone between two masses of air in which the cooler mass is in process of replacing the warmer.

cold·ness, kōld'nes, n. The state or quality of being cold; frigidity; sexual indifference.

cold rub·ber, n. Chem. a synthetic rubber of great durability, made at relatively low temperature and used mainly for tire retreads.

cold shoul·der, *n. Colloq.* an open show of coldness, indifference, or neglect in one's treatment of another; as, to give the *cold shoulder.*—**cold-shoul·der**, *v.t.*

cold sore, *n.* A vesicular eruption about the mouth often accompanying a cold or a febrile condition.

cold sweat, *n.* A chill characterized by perspiration, often induced by a state of nervousness.

cold war, *n.* The intense political, economic, and psychological contest for national advantage which does not reach the point of actual military operations.

cold wave, *n.* A considerable fall in temperature which occurs rapidly and affects a wide area.

cole, kōl, *n.* [< L. *colis, caulis,* a cabbage-stalk, a cabbage.] The rape plant, and others of the genus *Brassica;* colewort.

co·lec·to·my, ko·lek'to·mē, *n. pl.* **co·lec·to·mies.** *Surg.* complete or partial removal of the large intestine or colon.

cole·man·ite, kōl'ma·nīt", *n.* [From W. T. *Coleman,* of San Francisco.] A mineral consisting of a hydrous borate of calcium, $Ca_2B_6O_{11}\cdot5H_2O$, occurring in California in colorless to white monoclinic crystals with a brilliant luster, and utilized in the manufacture of borax.

co·le·op·ter, kō"lē·op'tėr, *n. Aeron.* an aircraft that lands and takes off vertically, having an annular wing. Also **fly·ing bar·rel.**

co·le·op·ter·ous, kō"lē·op'tėr·us, *a.* [< N.L. *coleoptera,* < Gk. *koleos,* sheath, *pteron,* wing.] *Entom.* belonging to a large order of insects, *Coleoptera,* including beetles, characterized by horny front wings encasing membranous hind wings.

cole·slaw, kōl'slȧ", *n.* A salad made of raw, sliced cabbage leaves.

co·le·us, kō'lē·us, *n. pl.* **co·le·us·es,** L. **co·le·i.** [N.L. (so called < the union of the filaments about the style), < Gr. *koleos,* sheath.] Any plant of the menthaceous genus *Coleus,* native to tropical Asia and Africa, species of which are cultivated for their showy colored foliage.

cole·wort, kōl'wurt", *n.* Any plant of the genus *Brassica,* which includes the cabbage, which does not form compact heads, as kale or rape.

col·ic, kol'ik, *n.* [L. *colicus,* Gr. *kōlikos,* < *kōlon,* the colon.] A painful spasm of the intestines, esp. of the colon, sometimes accompanied by fever or inflammation.—**col·ick·y**, kol'i·kē, *a.*

col·ic, kol'ik, *a.* Pertaining to the colon.

col·ic·root, kol'ik·rōt", kol'ik·rụt", *n.* Either of two North American liliaceous herbs, *Aletris farinosa* and *A. aurea,* having a root which is reputed to relieve colic; any of certain other plants reputed to cure colic.

col·ic·weed, kol'ik·wēd", *n.* Plants of the genus *Corydalis;* Dutchman's-breeches.

col·in, kol'in, *n.* [Fr.] The Virginian quail or American partridge; the bobwhite.

Col·i·se·um, kol'i·sē'um, *n.* Colosseum.

co·li·tis, ko·lī'tis, kō·lī'tis, *n.* [N.L.] *Pathol.* inflammation of the colon.

col·lab·o·rate, ko·lab'o·rāt", *v.i.*—**collaborated, collaborating.** [L.L. *collaboratus,* pp. of *collaborare,* < L. *com-,* with, and *laborare,* E. *labor, v.*] To work together with others, esp. on a literary or artistic endeavor; to cooperate with the enemy of one's country.—**col·lab·o·ra·tion,** *n.*—**col·lab·o·ra·tor,** *n.*

col·lab·o·ra·tion·ism, ko·lab"o·rā'shan·iz·um, *n.* The practice of collaboration with an enemy.—**col·lab·o·ra·tion·ist,** *n.*

col·lage, ko·läzh', kō·läzh', *Fr.* kạ·läzh', *n.* [Fr. glueing, pasting, < *coller,* to paste.] An art form in which diverse materials such as bits of newspapers, magazines, drawings, etc., are arranged and mounted to form a pleasing arrangement.

col·la·gen, kol'a·jen, *n.* The protein which makes up the major portion of the white fiber in connective tissues of vertebrates, particularly in the skin, bones, and tendons, yielding glue and gelatin when boiled.

col·lapse, ko·laps', *v.i.*—**collapsed, collapsing.** [L. *collabor, collapsus*—*col* for *con,* and *labor, lapsus,* to slide or fall (whence *lapse*).] To break down, disintegrate; to fall in or cave in suddenly; to come to nothing; to break down physically.—*v.t.* To cause to collapse.—**col·lap·si·ble,** *a.*

col·lapse, ko·laps', *n.* A falling in or together, as of the sides of a hollow vessel; a more or less sudden failure of the vital powers; a sudden and complete failure of any kind; a breakdown.

col·lar, kol'ėr, *n.* [L. *collare,* Fr. *collier,* a collar, < L. *collum,* the neck.] That part of a shirt or coat which is usually folded over and worn around the neck; an object worn around the neck, such as a chain worn by knights; part of the harness of a draft animal; an identifying or restraining band around an animal's neck.

col·lar, kol'ėr, *v.t.* To seize by the collar; to put a collar on.

col·lar·bone, kol'ėr·bōn", *n.* The clavicle.

col·lard, kol'ard, *n.* [Corruption of *colewort.*] A smooth-leaved variety of kale, cultivated chiefly in southern U.S. for use as a vegetable.

col·late, ko·lāt', ko·lāt', kol'āt, *v.t.*—**collated, collating.** [L. *confero, collatum,* to bring together, compare, bestow—*col* for *con,* and *fero, latum,* to carry.] To bring together and compare; to examine critically, as books or data, noting points of agreement and disagreement; to gather and arrange in order, or to check and correct the order of, as the sheets of a book for binding; *data processing,* to check and merge, as cards, from two or more comparably ordered sets into one or more similarly ordered new sets.—*v.i. Eccles.* to confer or bestow a benefice on a cleric.

col·lat·er·al, ko·lat'ėr·al, *a.* [L.L. *collateralis*—*col* for *con,* and L. *lateralis,* < *latus,* a side.] At the side; side by side; parallel; acting indirectly; acting through side channels; accompanying but subordinate; auxiliary; subsidiary. Descending from the same ancestor, but not in direct line, as distinguished from *lineal.* Guaranteed by property pledged as security.

col·lat·er·al, ko·lat'ėr·al, *n.* Property pledged as a guarantee of payment for an obligation or loan. A collateral relative.

col·la·tion, ko·lā'shan, ko·lā'shan, kō·lā'shan, *n.* The act of collating; a comparison, esp. the comparison of manuscripts or editions of books; the presentation of a clergyman to a benefice by a bishop who has the benefice in his own gift, or by neglect of the patron has acquired the patron's rights; the reading of passages in Scripture in monasteries, followed by a discussion and light repast; a light lunch or supper allowed on a day of fasting; any light meal.

col·league, kol'ēg, *n.* [L. *collega,* a colleague—*col* for *con,* and stem of *lego, legatum,* to send on a mission.] A partner or associate in the same office, employment, or commission, civil or ecclesiastical.—**col·league·ship,** *n.* The state of being a colleague in office or special work.

col·lect, kol'ekt, *n.* A short comprehensive prayer; a form of prayer adapted to a particular day or occasion.

col·lect, ko·lekt', *v.t.* [L. *colligo, collectum*—*col* for *con,* and *lego,* to gather.] To gather into one body or place; to assemble or bring together; to take or regain possession of; to receive or to obtain payment of.—*v.i.* To gather; to assemble; to accumulate; to run together.—**col·lect one·self,** to recover from surprise or a disconcerted state.—**col·lect·i·ble, col·lect·a·ble,** *a.*—**col·lect·a·bil·i·ty, col·lect·i·bil·ity,** *n.*

col·lect, ko·lekt', *a., adv.* Due for payment by the recipient on delivery; as, a *collect* telegram.

col·lec·ta·ne·a, kol"ek·tā'nē·a, *n. pl.* [L., things collected.] A selection of passages from various authors, usually made for the purpose of instruction; a miscellany.

col·lect·ed, ko·lek'tid, *a.* Gathered together; not disconcerted; cool; firm; prepared; self-possessed.—**col·lect·ed·ly,** *adv.* —**col·lect·ed·ness,** *n.*

col·lec·tion, ko·lek'shan, *n.* The act or practice of collecting or of gathering; that which is collected or gathered together, as stamps, paintings, and other objects of interest; that which is collected for a charitable, religious, or other purpose; the gathering of voluntary contributions from the congregation at a church service; the jurisdiction of a collector; a collectorship.

col·lec·tive, ko·lek'tiv, *a.* [L. *collectivus.*] Formed by collection; forming a collection or aggregate; aggregate; combined; pertaining to a group of individuals taken together; *bot.* of a fruit, formed by the coalescence of the pistils of several flowers, as the mulberry or the pineapple; *gram.* of nouns, expressing under the singular form a plurality of individual objects or persons, as *herd, jury, clergy,* which as subjects may take their verbs in either the singular or the plural, according to whether they are used to express more prominently the idea of unity or of plurality; in accordance with the tenets of collectivism.—**col·lec·tive·ly,** *adv.*

col·lec·tive, ko·lek'tiv, *n.* A collective body; an aggregate; *gram.* a collective noun, as *people, mob, audience.*

col·lec·tive bar·gain·ing, *n.* The practice or principle of bargaining as with reference to wages, hours of work, and other benefits, by employees collectively with their employers, or by representatives of bodies of employees with employers or their representatives.

col·lec·tive farm, *n.* A farm jointly operated by a community or group under state control, esp. in a communist country; a collective.

col·lec·tive se·cu·ri·ty, *n.* The principle or arrangement whereby a group of nations agrees to defend the security of individual members of the group by joint action against external aggression.

col·lec·tiv·ism, ko·lek'ti·viz"um, *n.* The socialistic doctrine that the land and means of production and distribution should belong to the people collectively.—**col·lec·tiv·ist,** *n.*—**col·lec·tiv·is·tic,** *a.*

col·lec·tiv·i·ty, kol"ek·tiv'i·tē, *n.* Collective character; a collective whole; the people collectively; collectivism.

col·lec·ti·vize, ko·lek'ti·vīz", *v.t.*—**collectivized, collectivizing.** To make collective; gather into one; combine; to place under the collective control of a people; to organize, as an industry, along collectivistic lines.—**col·lec·ti·vi·za·tion,** *n.*

col·lec·tor, ko·lek'tėr, *n.* One who collects; esp. one who collects objects of interest; an officer appointed to collect and receive customs, duties, or taxes, within a certain district.—**col·lec·tor·ship,** *n.* The office or jurisdiction of a collector.

col·leen, kol'ēn, ko·lēn', *n.* [Ir. *cailin.*] *Ir.* a girl.

col·lege, kol'ij, *n.* [L. *collegium,* a society, guild, or fraternity, < *collegia,* a colleague.] An institution of higher learning leading to the bachelor's degree; a subdivision of a university; as, the *college* of engineering;

a school for specialized instruction; as, a business *college*; the physical plant of a college; a society of men invested with certain powers and rights, performing certain duties or engaged in some common pursuit; as, the *College* of Surgeons.

col·le·gi·al, ko·lē′jē·al, ko·lē′jal, *a.* Pertaining to a college; collegiate.

col·le·gian, ko·lē′jan, ko·lē′jē·an, *n.* A member of a college; a college student.

col·le·giate, ko·lē′jit, ko·lē′jē·it, *a.* Of or pertaining to a college or college students; as, *collegiate* studies, *collegiate* styles; constituted after the manner of a college.

col·le·giate church, *n.* A church that has no cathedral, but does have a college of canons, or a dean, as Westminster Abbey; in the U.S., a church in an association of churches; a consolidation of previously separate churches under a common pastor or pastors.

col·le·gi·um, ko·lē′jē·um, *n.* pl. **col·le·gi·a**, ko·lē′jē·a. An inner circle of an organization with authority divided almost equally among its members, esp. such a group in the political organization of Soviet Russia.

col·let, kol′it, *n.* [Fr. *collet*, dim. of *col* < L. *collum*, neck.] *Mech.* a collar or enclosing band. The enclosing rim within which a jewel is set.—*v.t.*—*colleted, colleting.* To set in a collet.

col·lide, ko·līd′, *v.i.*—*collided, colliding.* [L. *collido*—*col* for *con*, and *lædo*, to strike.] To strike or dash against each other; to meet in shock; to meet in opposition or antagonism.

col·lie, kol′ē, *n.* [Origin doubtful.] A breed of dog with a coat of long hair, esp. common in Scotland, and much esteemed as a sheep dog, also popular as a family pet.

col·lier, kol′yẽr, [< *coal.*] *Chiefly Brit.* a coal miner. A ship used to transport coal; a crewman on such a ship.

col·lier·y, kol′ya·rē, *n.* pl. **col·lier·ies.** *Chiefly Brit.* a coal mine together with its buildings and machinery.

col·li·gate, kol′i·gāt″, *v.t.*—*colligated, colligating.* [L. *colligo*—*col* for *con*, and *ligo*, to bind.] To bind or fasten together; to connect by observing a certain relationship or similarity; as, to *colligate* phenomena.—**col·li·ga·tion**, *n.* The act of colligating; *logic*, that process by which many isolated facts are brought together under one general conception, observation, or principle.

col·li·mate, kol′i·māt, *v.t.*—*collimated, collimating.* [< a false reading of L. *collineatus* (taken as *collimatus*), pp. of *collineare*, < *com-*, with, and *lineare*, reduce to a straight line.] To bring into line; make parallel; adjust accurately the line of sight, as of a telescope or transit.—**col·li·ma·tion**, *n.*

col·li·ma·tor, kol′i·mā″tẽr, *n.* A fixed telescope for use in collimating other instruments; a device to transmit parallel rays of light, as the receiving telescope of a spectroscope; a device which confines a stream of particles into a beam where the paths of the particles are nearly parallel.

col·lin·e·ar, ko·lin′ē·ar, *a.* Lying in the same straight line.—**col·lin·e·ar·i·ty**, ko·lin′ē·ar′i·tē, *n.*—**col·lin·e·ar·ly**, *adv.*

col·lins, kol′inz, *n.* A tall iced drink with lime or lemon juice, sugar, and carbonated water added to a base of gin, vodka, or other liquors.

col·li·sion, ko·lizh′on, *n.* [L. *collisio.*] The act of striking or dashing together; the violent meeting and mutual striking of two or more moving bodies, or of a moving body with a stationary one; opposition; antagonism; interference.

col·li·sion course, *n.* The course of a rapidly moving object which, if unaltered, will cause it to collide: said of a missile or vehicle; a course of policy or activity which is rapidly approaching serious difficulty.

col·lo·cate, kol′o·kāt″, *v.t.*—*collocated, collocating.* [L. *colloco*—*col* for *con*, together, and *loco*, to place, *locus*, a place.] To set or place with, or in relation to; to station; to place in the proper order; as, to *collocate* past actions; to arrange, as words, in sentence form.—**col·lo·ca·tion**, kol″o·kā′shan, *n.*

col·lo·di·on, ko·lō′dē·on, *n.* [Gr. *kolla*, glue, and *eidos* resemblance.] A substance prepared by dissolving guncotton in ether, or in a mixture of ether and alcohol: used as a substitute for adhesive plaster in the case of slight wounds, and in the processing of photographic film and plates.

col·logue, ko·lōg′, *v.i.*—*collogued, colloguing.* *Colloq.* to plot together; to conspire in secret.

col·loid, kol′oid, *n. Chem.* A liquid mixture or gas with very fine suspended particles of liquid or solid that will not pass through a semi-permeable membrane, and having a high ratio of surface area to volume that results in an extremely slow rate of sedimentation or settling out: the suspended particles are too small to be visible under an ordinary light microscope, but can be studied through their reflected light and by the electron microscope. *Med.* a gelatinous or homogenous substance found normally in the thyroid and in some diseased tissues.

col·lop, kol′op, *n.* [M.E. *colope, colloppe*; origin uncertain.] *Brit. dial.* a small slice of bacon, or other meat; a small slice or piece of anything; a fold or roll of flesh on the body.

col·lo·qui·al, ko·lō′kwē·al, *a.* Peculiar to the language of conversation; pertaining to conversation.—**col·lo·qui·al·ly**, *adv.*

col·lo·qui·al·ism, ko·lō′kwē·a·liz″um, *n.* A word or phrase peculiar to the language of common conversation.

col·lo·qui·um, ko·lō′kwē·um, *n.* pl. **col·lo·qui·ums, col·lo·qui·a**, ko·lō′kwē·a. A group conference or informal seminar.

col·lo·quy, kol′o·kwē, *n.* pl. **col·lo·quies.** [L. *colloquium*—*col-*. together, and *loquor*, to speak.] A conversation or dialog; a conference. The governing body in certain Protestant churches.—**col·lo·quist**, *n.*

col·lo·type, kol′o·tīp, *n.* [Gr. *kolla*, glue, and *-type* < L. *typus* < Gr. *typos*, impression, < Gr. *typpein*, strike.] A photomechanical process of printing in ink from a gelatin plate; the plate itself or a print made from it.

col·lude, ko·lōd′, *v.i.*—*colluded, colluding.* [L. *colludere* (pp. *collusus*), < *com-*, with, and *ludere*, play.] To act jointly through a secret understanding; conspire in a fraud.—**col·lud·er**, *n.*

col·lu·sion, ko·lō′zhan, *n.* [L. *collusio*(n-), < *colludere*, E. *collude*.] Secret agreement for a deceitful or fraudulent purpose, esp. between persons appearing or pretending to be adversaries or competitors.—**col·lu·sive**, *a.* Involving collusion; fraudulently prearranged.—**col·lu·sive·ly**, *adv.*—**col·lu·sive·ness**, *n.*

col·lu·vi·um, ko·lō′vē·um, *n.* pl. **col·lu·vi·a, col·lu·vi·ums**, ko·lō′vē·a. Loose deposits of soil and disintegrated rock brought chiefly by gravity to the foot of a slope or cliff.—**col·lu·vi·al**, *a.*

col·ly, kol′ē, *v.t.*—*collied, collying.* [Akin to *coal.*] *Brit. dial.* To blacken as with coal dust; begrime.—*n. Brit. dial.* Coal dust; grime.

col·lyr·i·um, ko·lēr′ē·um, *n.* pl. **col·lyr·i·a, col·lyr·i·ums**, ko·lēr′ē·a. [L.] A lotion for the eye; eyewash.

col·o·cynth, kol′o·sinth, *n.* [Gr. *kolokynthis*, a gourd or pumpkin.] A Mediterranean plant, *Citrullus colocynthis*, of the gourd family; the fruit; a purgative derived from the fruit.

co·logne, ko·lōn′, *n.* [For *Cologne water*

(made at Cologne, Germany, since 1709).] A scented toilet water.

Co·lom·bi·an, ko·lum′bē·an, *Sp.* ka·-lam′byän, *a.* Characteristic of the kind of people, crafts, and customs that prevail in Colombia, a republic in northwest S. America.—*n.* An inhabitant of Colombia.

co·lon, kō′lon, *n.* pl. **co·lons, co·la**, kō′la. [L., < Gr. *kolon*, food, colon.] *Anat.* that portion of the large intestine which extends from the cecum to the rectum.

co·lon, kō′lon, *n.* pl. **co·lons.** [L., < Gr. *kōlon*, limb, member, clause.] A point of punctuation (:) intermediate in force between the semicolon and the period, marking off the main portion of a sentence from what follows, such as an explanation, quotation, or list, and following the salutation of a business letter: a colon also separates hours from minutes in time expressions and numbers from other numbers in mathematical proportions. *Anc. pros.* one of the members or sections of a rhythmical period, consisting of a sequence of from two to six feet united under a principal ictus or beat; pl. **co·la.**

co·lon, kō′lon, *n.* A colonial plantation owner or farmer, particularly one in Algeria.

colo·nel, kur′nel, *n.* [Formerly also *coronel*, which is an old French form and has given the modern pronunciation; Fr. *colonel*, O.Fr. *colonnel*, < It. *colonello*, a colonel, a little column, dim. of *colonna*, L. *columna*, a column; the name was originally given to the leading company in a regiment.] A commissioned officer ranking in most armies above a lieutenant colonel and below a brigadier general, and traditionally the chief commander of a regiment of troops.—**colo·nel·cy, colo·nel·ship**, *n.* The office, rank, or commission of a colonel.

Colo·nel Blimp, *n.* [From the character of that name created by David Low, British cartoonist.] An elderly government official or army officer noted for pomposity and short-sightedness or hostility toward modern procedures; in a broad sense, a pompous, elderly reactionary.

co·lo·ni·al, ko·lō′nē·al, *a.* Of or pertaining to a colony or colonies; esp. pertaining to the thirteen British colonies which became the United States of America, or to their period; pertaining to the architecture and furniture of the British colonies in America during the 17th and 18th centuries, or to imitations of this craftsmanship.—*n.* An inhabitant of a colony.—**co·lo·ni·al·ly**, *adv.*

co·lo·ni·al·ism, ko·lō′nē·a·liz″um, *n.* The colonial system; the policy advocating this system.

col·o·nist, kol′o·nist, *n.* An inhabitant of or settler in a colony; a member of a colonizing expedition.

col·o·ni·za·tion, kol″o·ni·zā′shan, *n.* The act of colonizing or state of being colonized.—**col·o·ni·za·tion·ist**, *n.* An advocate of colonization.

col·o·nize, kol′o·nīz″, *v.t.*—*colonized, colonizing.* To plant or establish a colony in; to send a colony to; to establish a colony of.—*v.i.* To move and settle a colony.—**col·o·niz·er**, *n.*

col·on·nade, kol″o·nād′, *n.* [It. *colonnata*, < *colonna*, a column.] *Arch.* any series or range of columns placed at regular intervals from each other, and usually giving support to a roof structure; trees planted in a row on both sides of a road or driveway.

col·o·ny, kol′o·nē, *n.* pl. **col·o·nies.** [L. *colonia*, < *colo, cultum*, to till (hence *cultivate, culture*).] A body of people transplanted from their mother country to a remote province or country, and remaining subject to or connected with the jurisdiction of the parent state; the country planted or colonized; any group of individuals with common or similar language, interests, or occupations, living in close association; as, a *colony* of Poles, an artist *colony*; the section inhabited by such a group; a number of animals or plants living or growing together; circumscribed aggregation of bacteria, produced by a single cell, and usually growing together in or on solid matter.

col·o·phon, kol′*o*·fon″, kol′*o*·fon, *n*. [L.L. < Gr. *kolophōn*, summit, finishing touch.] An inscription commonly used in former times to terminate a manuscript or book, and often giving the subject, author, or printer, and the date and place of production; in modern use, an inscription or printer's device at the end of a book; a publisher's device as used on a title page.

col·o·pho·ny, kol′*o*·fō″nē, ko·lof′*o*·nē, *n*. [L. *Colophonia* (*resina*), (resin) of Colophon (Ionian city in Asia Minor).] Common rosin, the hard amorphous substance derived from the oleoresin of the pine.

col·or, *Brit*. **col·our**, kul′ẽr, *n*. [L. *color, color*.] The visual property of an object apart from its form, dependent upon a response to light, including the attributes of hue, brightness, and saturation; any hue or tint as distinguished from white, black, or gray; that which is used for coloring, as a pigment, paint, or dye; the healthy ruddiness of a complexion; the natural hue of the skin, esp. complexion; a blush; the skin pigmentation of a Negro or other non-Caucasian; a false show; pretext; guise; plausibility; vivid and lifelike quality, as in literary imagery; *art*, the overall impression produced by hues in a painting; *art*, *liter*. a true-to-life effect created by specific treatment of the idiosyncrasies of a particular locale or time; as, local *color*; *mus*., *phon*. timbre; *law*, a prima facie or apparent authority or right; *mining*, a speck of gold settling in a miner's pan as a result of washing gold-containing gravel.—**col·ors**, *n. pl*. A flag, ensign, or standard borne in an army or fleet; a color used for identification, as of a badge or uniform; one's personal beliefs; general character or nature; as, to show one's true *colors*; *U.S. Navy*, a salute to the national flag when it is hoisted at sunrise or lowered at sunset.—**call to the col·ors**, to summon for military service.—**change col·or**, to turn red, as from selfconsciousness; to turn white, as from fright.—**lose col·or**, to become pale.—**serve with the col·lors**, to serve in the armed forces.

col·or, *Brit*. **col·our**, kul′ẽr, *v.t*. To impart color to; to dye; to tinge; to paint; to stain. *Fig*. to clothe with an appearance different from the real; to make plausible; to give a distinctive character to; influence.—*v.i*. To blush; to take on or become different in color.—**col·or·er**, *n*.

col·or·a·ble, *Brit*. **col·our·a·ble**, kul′ẽr·*a*·bl, *a*. Capable of being colored; specious or plausible; pretended; deceptive.—**col·or·a·bly**, *adv*.

Col·o·ra·do bee·tle, *n*. The potato beetle.

col·or·ant, kul′ẽr·ant, *n*. [Fr. *colorant*, prop. ppr.] A coloring matter; dye; pigment.

col·or·a·tion, *Brit*. **col·our·a·tion**, kul″*o*·rā′shan, *n*. Coloring; the state of being colored; the tints of an object.

col·o·ra·tu·ra, kul′ẽr·*a*·tụr′*a*, kul″ẽr·*a*·tyụr′*a*, *n*. [= G. *coloratur*, < *coloratura*, < L.L. *coloratura*, coloring, < L. *colorare*, E. *color*, *v*.] Runs, trills, and other florid decorations in vocal music; ornamented musical style or performance; a soprano capable of this style.—*a*. Also **col·or·a·ture**, kul′ẽr·*a*·chụr′.

col·or·bear·er, *Brit*. **col·our·bear·er**, kul′ẽr·bâr″ẽr, *n*. One who carries the colors or standard, as of a military body.

col·or-blind, *Brit*. **col·our-blind**, kul′ẽr-

blīnd″, *a*. Incapable of accurately distinguishing colors; having an imperfect perception of colors.—**col·or blind·ness**, *n*. Total or partial incapability of distinguishing colors, arising from some defect in the eye, though otherwise vision may be perfect.

col·or·breed, kul′ẽr·brēd″, *v.t*.—*colorbred, colorbreeding*. To develop desired colors by selective breeding.

col·or·cast, kul′ẽr·kast″, *n*. A broadcast of a television program in color.—*v.t*., *v.i*.—*colorcast, colorcasting*.

col·ored, *Brit*. **col·oured**, kul′ẽrd, *a*. Having color; of or pertaining to nonwhite people in general; pertaining to people of African descent. *Fig*. slanted; prejudiced; as, a point of view *colored* by circumstances; *bot*. of some color other than green, as a leaf.

col·or·fast, kul′ẽr·fast″, kul′ẽr·fäst″, *a*. Keeping its original shade of color without fading in the sunlight, or running in the wash; as, a *colorfast* fabric.—**col·or·fast·ness**, *n*.

col·or·ful, *Brit*. **col·our·ful**, kul′ẽr·fụl, *a*. Abounding in color; *fig*. richly picturesque; as, a *colorful* historical period; presenting or suggesting vivid or striking scenes; as, a *colorful* narrative.—**col·or·ful·ly**, *adv*.—**col·or·ful·ness**, *n*.

col·or guard, *Brit*. **col·our guard**, *n*. A guard having charge of the colors, the flag, as of a regiment.

col·or·if·ic, kul″*o*·rif′ik, *a*. Having the quality of tingeing; able to give color or tint to other bodies; pertaining to color.

col·or·im·e·ter, kul″*o*·rim′i·tẽr, *n*. An instrument for measuring the depth of color in a liquid by comparison with a standard liquid of the same tint.

col·or·ing, *Brit*. **col·our·ing**, kul′ẽr·ing, *n*. The act or art of applying colors; color applied; something used to impart color, as a dye; appearance with regard to color, as of a complexion; distinctive quality or tendency; a specious appearance; show.

col·or·ist, *Brit*. **col·our·ist**, kul′ẽr·ist, *n*. One who colors; a painter whose works emphasize the use of colors.

col·or·less, *Brit*. **col·our·less**, kul′ẽr·lis, *a*. Destitute of color; pale and wan; washed-out; wanting in spirit or character; vapid; uninteresting.

col·or phase, *n*. A genetically-caused deviation from the standard color of the coat or covering of an animal; an animal showing such a deviation; a pelage color that differs according to age or season.

col·or ser·geant, *Brit*. **col·our ser·geant**, *n*. A sergeant who has charge of batallion or regimental colors.

co·los·sal, ko·los′al, *a*. Like a colossus; greatly exceeding the standard size; very large; huge; gigantic.

Col·os·se·um, Col·i·se·um, kol″*o*·sē′um, *n*. [M.L. *Colosseum* also *Coliseum*, prop. neut. of L. *colosseus*, colossal, < *colossus*.] The greatest ancient amphitheater in Rome begun by the emperor Vespasian and finished 80 A.D. by Titus; (*l.c.*) a name applied to various other amphitheaters and large theaters and halls.

co·los·sus, ko·los′us, *n*. pl. **co·los·si, co·los·sus·es**, ko·los′ī. [Gr. *kolossos*, a colossal statue.] A statue of a gigantic size or of size much greater than the natural, such as the statue of Apollo which formerly stood at the entrance to the port of ancient Rhodes; any object of gigantic size.

co·los·to·my, ko·los′to·mē, *n*. *Surg*. a procedure resulting in the formation of an artificial anus by making an incision from the colon through the wall of the abdomen; the opening which results from this operation; the act of bringing together two separate parts of the intestine.

co·los·trum, ko·los′trum, *n*. [L.] The first milk secreted in the breasts after childbirth, containing a large amount of protein and immunizing factors for the newborn.

col·por·teur, kol′pôr″tẽr, kol′par″tẽr, *Fr*. kạl·par·tOER′, *n*. [Fr.—*col*. < L. *collum*, the neck, and *porteur*, a carrier, < L. *porto*, to carry.] A book peddler; one who travels from place to place distributing Bibles and other religious material.—**col·por·tage**, kol′pôr″tij, *n*. A colporteur's work.

colt, kōlt, *n*. [O.E. *colt*, a young ass, a young camel; akin. Sw. *kult*, a young boar, a stout boy.] A young male horse; a young donkey or mule; young person or novice.

col·ter, coul·ter, kōl′tẽr, *n*. [L. *culter*, a knife, a coulter.] A sharp iron blade or wheel inserted into the beam of a plow for the purpose of cutting the ground and facilitating the separation of the furrow slice by the plowshare.

colt·ish, kōl′tish, *a*. Of or like a colt; frisky; gay; playful; not easily restrained.

colts·foot, kōlts′fụt″, *n*. pl. **colts·foots**. A perennial composite Old World herb, *Tussilago farfara*, with yellow flowers, so called from the shape of its large, rounded leaves which were once used in medicine.

col·u·brid, kol′u·brid, kōl′ụ·brid, *n*. Any of a family, *Colubridae*, of worldwide, nonpoisonous snakes, including about two-thirds of all living snakes.

col·u·brine, kol′ū·brīn″, kol′ū·brin, kol′ụ·brīn″, kol′ụ·brin, *a*. [L. *colubrinus*, < *coluber*, a serpent.] Of or like a snake; belonging or pertaining to the family *Colubridae*, of snakes, esp. to the subfamily *Colubrinae*.

co·lu·go, ko·lö′gō, *n*. pl. **co·lu·gos**. [E. Ind.] The flying lemur.

col·um·bar·i·um, kol″um·bâr′ē·um, *n*. pl. **col·um·bar·i·a**, kol″um·bâr′ē·a. [L. *columba*, pigeon.] A sepulchre or similar construction with recesses for urns containing the ashes of the dead; one of these recesses. A dovecote; also **col·um·bar·y**.

Co·lum·bi·a, ko·lum′bē·a, *n*. [From Christopher *Columbus*, discoverer of America.] *Poetic*, the United States, esp. as a feminine personification.—**Co·lum·bi·an**, *a*. Pertaining to the United States, to America, or to Christopher Columbus.

co·lum·bic, ko·lum′bik, *a*. *Chem*. of or pertaining to columbium; niobic.

col·um·bine, kol′um·bīn″, kol′um·bin, *a*. [L. *columbinus*, < *columba*, a pigeon.] Like or pertaining to a pigeon or dove; of a dove color.

col·um·bine, kol′um·bīn″, *n*. [L. *columbina*.] A plant of the crowfoot family, genus *Aquilegia*, with showy variously-colored flowers, so called because the curved petals and wing-like sepals resemble a flock of pigeons, as *A. caerula*, state flower of Colorado.

co·lum·bite, ko·lum′bīt, *n*. A black crystalline mineral consisting of a compound of iron and columbium, containing often manganese and tantalum.

co·lum·bi·um, ko·lum′bē·um, *n*. [N.L., from *Columbia*, the United States.] *Chem*. the former name for niobium: Sym. Cb.

col·umn, kol′um, *n*. [L. *columna*, akin to *columen, culmen*, top (see *culminate*), *celsus*, high, *excellere*, raise, rise, E. *excel*, also to E. *hill*.] *Arch*. a long, slender upright shaft or pillar, esp. a decorative or supporting member, typically consisting of a cylindrical shaft with a base and capital; any column-like object, mass, or formation; as, a *column* of figures, the spinal *column*; one of the two or more vertical rows of lines of type or printed matter on a page, separated by a rule or blank space; a special department of a newspaper or magazine, furnished regularly by a particular writer or editor, and usu. focusing on a certain topic, as politics, art, or advice to the lovelorn; *milit.* a formation of troops narrow laterally and extended from front to rear; a line of ships following one after another; *bot.* a columnlike body formed by the union of stamens and style in an orchid.—**col·umned,** *a.*

co·lum·nar, ko·lum′nėr, *a.* [L.L. *columnaris.*] Of, pertaining to, or of the nature of a column or columns; columnlike.

col·um·ni·a·tion, ko·lum″nē·ā′shan, *n.* The use or arrangement of columns in a structure.

col·umn·ist, kol′um·nist, kol′u·mist, *n.* The editor or writer of a special column in a newspaper.

co·lure, ko·lụr′, kō·lụr′, kō′lụr, *n.* [Gr. *kolouros,* docktailed (with *grammē,* a line, understood)—*kolos,* stunted, and *oura,* a tail, because a part is always beneath the horizon.] *Astron.* either of the two great circles of the celestial sphere which intersect each other at right angles in the poles of the world, one of them passing through the solstitial and the other through the equinoctial points of the ecliptic, the points where they intercept the ecliptic being called cardinal points.

co·ma, kō′ma, *n. pl.* **co·mas.** [N.L., < Gr. *cōma,* < *ceīsthai,* lie.] A state of prolonged unconsciousness, usually due to disease or injury, from which it is difficult or impossible to rouse a person; stupor.

co·ma, kō′ma, *n. pl.* **co·mae,** co′mē. [L., < Gr. *comē,* hair.] *Bot.* a tuft of silky hairs at the end of a seed; *astron.* the nebulous envelope surrounding the nucleus of a comet; *optics,* the blurred appearance or hazy border surrounding an object viewed through a lens which is not free from spherical aberration.—**co·mal,** *a.*

Co·ma Ber·e·ni·ces, kō′ma ber″e·nī′sēz, *n.* A northern constellation. Also **Ber·e·ni·ce's Hair.**

Co·man·che, kō·man′che, ko·man′che, *n. pl.* **Co·man·ches, Co·man·che.** A North American plains Indian of Shoshonean origin now living in Oklahoma; the language of the Comanche.

Co·man·che·an, kō·man′chē·an, ko·man′chē·an, *a.* [From *Comanche,* town and county in north-central Texas.] *Geol.* noting or pertaining to a geological period or a system of rocks in North America equivalent to the earlier portion of the Cretaceous period or system.—*n.* The Comanchean period or system.

co·mate, kō′māt, *a.* [L. *comatus,* < *coma,* hair, E. *coma.*] *Bot.* hairy; tufted.

co·mate, kō·māt′, *n.* A mate or companion.

com·a·tose, kom′a·tōs′, kō′ma·tōs″, *a.* Pertaining to coma; drowsy; lethargic.

comb, kōm, *n.* [O.E. *camb* = D. *kam* = G. *kamm.*] A toothed instrument of bone, metal, plastic, or rubber, for arranging, cleansing, or adjusting the hair, or for keeping it in place; a curry-comb; a card for dressing wool; any comblike instrument, object, or formation; the fleshy growth on the head of the domestic fowl.

comb, kōm, *v.t.* To dress, as the hair, with or as with a comb; card, as wool; to search thoroughly.—*v.i.* To roll over or break at the crest, as a wave.

com·bat, kom·bat′, kom′bat, kum′bat, *v.t.* —*combated, combating, combatted, combatting.* [Fr. *combattre,* < L. *com-,* with, and *battere,* for *batteuere,* beat.] To fight or contend against; oppose.—*v.i.* To fight; to do battle.

com·bat, kom′bat, kum′bat, *n.* Fighting between organized forces, as the military, or between individuals; a battle or skirmish in war; a struggle; a conflict.

com·bat·ant, kom·bat′ant, kom′ba·tant, kum·bat′ant, kum′ba·tant, *a.* Combating; fighting; disposed to combat or contend.

Her. rampant as as if in combat, as two lions facing each other.—*n.* One who takes part in combat, fighting, or in any conflict.

com·bat fa·tigue, *n.* A psychoneurotic disorder caused by intense stresses of exhaustion and anxiety occurring under wartime combat conditions. Also **bat·tle fa·tigue.**

com·bat jac·ket, *n.* The waist-length jacket formerly worn as part of a service uniform. Also **bat·tle jac·ket, Eis·en·how·er jac·ket.**

com·bat zone, *n.* The battle area of military operations stretching from the front lines of fighting to the boundary of the communications zones.

combe, comb, kōm, kōm, *n.* [O.E. *cumb.*] *Brit.* a narrow valley or deep hollow, esp. one enclosed on all but one side. Also **coomb,** kōm.

comb·er, kō′mėr, *n.* A machine or machine operator that combs cotton or wool for weaving; a long, curling wave.

com·bin·a·ble, kom·bī′na·bl, *a.* That may be combined; admitting of combination. —**com·bin·a·bil·i·ty,** *n.*

com·bi·na·tion, kom″bi·nā′shan, *n.* [L.L. *combinatio(n-).*] The act of combining, or the resulting state; a number of things combined, or something formed by combining; an alliance of persons or parties; the set or series of numbers or letters used in setting the mechanism of a certain type of lock used on safes, called a combination lock, or the parts of the mechanism operated by this; a suit of underwear in one piece; chemical union; *math.* the arrangement of a number of individuals into various groups, each group containing a given number of the individuals; as, *a, b,* and *c* into *ab, ac,* and *bc;* one of the groups formed.—**com·bi·na·tion·al,** *a.*

com·bi·na·tive, kom′bi·nā″tiv, kom·bī′na·tiv, *a.* Tending to combine; uniting; resulting from combination. Also **com·bi·na·to·ry,** kom·bī′na·tōr″e, kom·bī′na·tar″ē.

com·bine, kom·bīn′, *v.t.*—*combined, combining.* [L.L. *combinare,* < L. *com-,* with, and *bini,* two at a time.] To bring or join into a close union or whole; unite; associate; to cause to coalesce, as in one body or substance; to possess or exhibit in union; as, a plan which *combines* the best features of several other plans.—*v.i.* To come together, as into one body; unite; coalesce; specif. to enter into chemical union; often, to unite for a common purpose or end; join forces; league together; form a combination.

com·bine, kom′bīn, kom·bīn′, *n.* Group of persons or associations leagued together in a joint undertaking; a harvesting machine which cuts and threshes grain while traveling across a field.

com·bine, kom′·bīn, *v.t.*—*combined, combining.* To harvest with a machine that performs all threshing operations as it moves across the fields.

comb·ings, kō′mings, *n. pl.* Hairs removed with a comb.

comb·ing wool, *n.* A quality of wool, consisting of long staples and strong fibers, which is esp. suitable for worsted fabrics.

com·bin·ing form, *n.* A word element used for combining with other words or word elements, as 'Anglo-,' in 'Anglophile.'

com·bin·ing weight, *n. Chem.* equivalent weight.

com·bo, kom′bō, *n. pl.* **com·bos.** A group of three or four musicians who play jazz or music for dancing.

com·bust, kom·bust′, *a.* [L. *combustus,* pp. of *comburere,* burn up (see *urere,* burn).]

Astrol. so near the sun as to be obscured by it, as a planet.

com·bus·ti·bil·i·ty, kom·bus′ti·bil′i·tē, *n.* The state or quality of being combustible. Also **com·bus·ti·ble·ness,** kom·bus′ti·bl·nes.

com·bus·ti·ble, kom·bus′ti·bl, *a.* [Fr. *combustible,* < L. *comburo, combustum,* to consume—*comb,* for *cum* or *con,* and *uro,* to burn; same root as Gr. *auein,* to kindle; Skt. *ush,* to burn.] Capable of catching fire and burning; flammable. *Fig.* fiery or irascible; hot tempered.—*n.* A substance that can readily catch fire and burn.

com·bus·tion, kom·bus′chan, kom·bush′chan, *n.* [L.L. *combustio(n-),* < L. *comburere* (pp. *combustus).*] The act or process of burning; the action of fire on inflammable material; violent excitement; tumult. *Chem.* rapid oxidation with heat and, usually, light; chemical combination attended by energy radiation in the form of heat and light; slow oxidation not accompanied by high temperature and light.—**com·bus·tive,** *a.* Pertaining to or characterized by combustion.

com·bus·tor, kom·bus′tėr, *n. Avi.* the term applied to the unit formed by the combustion chamber, flame holder, igniter, and injection system in a ramjet engine that initiates and sustains combustion; *aerospace,* combustion chamber.

come, kum, *v.i.*—*past* **came,** pp. **come,** ppr. **coming.** [O.E. *cuman* = G. *kommen.*] To move toward the speaker or toward something. To happen; to approach or arrive in succession; as, when we *come* to the second chapter; to be of similar quality or type, as: This *comes* closest to what I want. To arrive at through a changed condition, as: The water *came* to a boil. To appear as a result of, as: This *comes* of carelessness. To move toward or progress in the sense of achievement; as, to *come* up the hard way; to extend or reach, as: The dress *comes* to her knees. To become, seem to become, turn out to be, get to a given place; as, to *come* loose or untied, to *come* true, to *come* to life; to occur to the mind, as: The name *came* to him in a flash. To occur or befall, as: No good will *come* of this. To emanate, be derived, or originate, as: He *comes* from England. To enter a specified state or condition, as, to *come* into use; to be classified or part of; as, to *come* under my jurisdiction; to be obtainable; as, to *come* in two colors; to germinate, as grain; *slang,* to reach an orgasm; *colloq.* to assume a role; as, to *come* as the haughty queen.—*impv.* To call attention or remonstrate, as: *Come,* that will do!—**come a·part at the seams,** *slang,* to lose one's self-possession; to panic.— **come at,** to master or attain.—**come by,** to come into possession of, as: He *comes by* his blue eyes honestly. *Colloq.* visit or drop in. —**come in·to,** to gain possession of, as: She will *come into* a fortune.—**come through,** to survive an ordeal; *slang,* to give money or other aid, as: They usually *come through* with a gift. *Slang,* to perform as hoped, as: We know you'll *come through.* —**come to pass,** to occur: preceded by *it.*

come a·bout, *v.i.* To come to pass; occur. *Naut.* to change the course of a sailing vessel by tacking; to turn.

come a·cross, *v.t.* To meet or find by chance.—*v.i.* To be comprehensible or capable of being interpreted accurately, as: The message of this ad does not *come across.* *Slang,* to do or give what was promised or is requested; as, to *come across* with a loan.

come a·long, *v.i.* To improve or show progress, as: The patient is *coming along* nicely. To arrive, as: The next bus *comes along* later.—*Impv.* to urge another person to hurry.

come a·round, *v.i.* Come round.

come·back, kum′bak″, *n. Slang.* A successful attempt to regain one's lost skill or public acceptance; a recovery of strength or health; a terse retort or clever response to what has been said.

come back, *v.i.* To return to health or to a former position or success; to return to a person's memory, as: Your name *comes back* to me now. To reply wittily or tartly.

co·me·di·an, ko·mē′dē·an, *n.* An actor or player in comedy; a writer of comedy; a professional entertainer who amuses an audience by means of jokes and various antics of comic behavior; any amusing or comical person.—**co·me·di·enne**, ko·mē″dē·en′, *n.* A female comedian.

co·me·dic, ko·mē′dik, ko·med′ik, *a.* Of or pertaining to comedy.

com·e·do, kom′i·dō″, *n.* pl. **com·e·dos**, **com·e·do·nes**, kom″i·dō′nēz. [L. glutton < *comedere.* COMESTIBLE.] A hardened plug of sebum in a skin duct; a blackhead.

come·down, kum′doun″, *n. Colloq.* an unexpected or humiliating descent from dignity, importance, or prosperity.

come down, *v.i.* To be humbled; to lose rank or position; to be transmitted through generations; to contract an illness, usually with *with.*

com·e·dy, kom′i·dē, *n.* pl. **com·e·dies.** [Gr. *comedie* (Fr. *comedie*), < L. *comoedia,* < Gr. *cōmōdia,* < *cōmos,* revel and *aeidein,* sing.] A dramatic composition of light and humorous character, typically with a happy or cheerful ending; that branch of the drama which concerns itself with this form of composition; the comic element of drama, of literature generally, or of life; any literary composition dealing with a theme suitable for comedy, or employing the methods of comedy; any comic or humorous incident or series of incidents.

com·e·dy of man·ners, *n. Liter.* a genre of comic satire dealing with customs, esp. of fashionable society.

come-hith·er, kum″hiTH′ẽr, ko·miTH′ẽr, *a.* Alluring, subtly beckoning, or inviting; as, a *come-hither* look.

come in, *v.t.* To enter; to become fashionable; to be brought into use; to be among winners in a competition; as, to *come in* fourth; to receive, used with *for*; as, to *come in for* criticism; *impv.* to respond to a signal, used in communications, as: *Come* in, New York. To yield or come to maturity, as of a crop or oil well.

come·li·ness, kum′lē·nes, *n.* The quality of being attractive in appearance.

come·ly, kum′lē, *a.* [M.E. *cumli,* < O.E. *cymlic,* comely, < *cyme,* suitable, < *cuman,* to *come.*] Handsome; graceful; pleasing in appearance.

come off, *v.i.* To happen or take place; to be successful, as: The play *came off* well. To arrive at the end of or achieve, as: He *came off* with first place.

come-on, kum′on″, kum′ạn″, *n. Slang.* anything intended to lure another, frequently in the sense of victimizing him.

come on, *v.i.* To show progress; to thrive; to appear or start, as of a theatrical act or of natural phenomena, as: The storm *came on* suddenly. To encounter unexpectedly; as, to *come on* or *upon* a former pupil; *colloq. impv.* to hurry another person; *colloq. impv.* to try to persuade, as in saying please; *slang,* to make one's personality felt, to make an impression; as, to *come on* strong.

come out, *v.i.* To appear after being obscured or kept secret; to become available; to state one's views; as, to *come out* for the opposition; to speak or reveal, used with *with*; as, to *come out with* a strange tale; to make a formal debut into society; to terminate or turn out, as: He *came out* second in the competition.

come-out·er, kum·ou′tẽr, *n.* A reformer; one who leaves an established order, as a political or religious body, and wishes to change or replace it.

come o·ver, *v.i.* To change one's mind or position, as in adopting the opposition's point of view; to make an informal or impromptu visit.—*v.t.* To have an effect on; as: A strange feeling *came over* her.

com·er, kum′ẽr, *n.* One who comes, as: All *comers* are welcome. *Colloq.* one who shows promise of future achievement or distinction.

come round, *v.i.* To regain consciousness, recover; to gradually see and embrace another's views; to recover from hurt or angry feelings, as: He is angry now, but he will *come round.* To call upon or visit informally; *naut.* to tack or come about. Also *come around.*

co·mes·ti·ble, ko·mes′ti·bl, *a.* [O.Fr. Fr. *comestible,* < L.L. *comestibilis,* < L. *comedere* (pp. *comestus*), eat up, < *com-,* altogether, and *edere,* eat.] Edible; eatable. —*n.* pl. **co·mes·ti·bles.** *Usu. pl.* something edible; articles of food.

com·et, kom′it, *n.* [L. *cometa,* < Gr. *kometēs,* long-haired, a comet, < *komé,* hair; from the appearance of its tail.] One of the celestial bodies, orbiting the sun in eccentric paths ranging from slightly elliptical through parabolic, with periods of revolution ranging from a few years through millions of years, each of which is composed of a small dense nucleus surrounded by a large tenuous envelope of gases and dust, called the coma, that extends into a long tail.—**com·et·ar·y,** kom′i·ter″ē, **co·met·ic,** ko·met′ik, *a.*

come to, *v.i.* To amount to, as: My bill *came to* six dollars. To regain consciousness; *naut.* to anchor or sail a boat closer to the wind.

com·et seek·er, *n.* A telescope of wide range, used in searching for comets. Also **com·et find·er.**

come up, *v.i.* To be spoken of or arise; as, a matter that did not *come up* in the conversation; to appear before an authoritative body; as, a case that *comes up* in court; to equate or compare, as: His new novel does not *come up* to his earlier ones. To suggest or supply what is wanted or lost, used with *with*; as, to *come up with* an idea, to *come up with* the missing jewels. *Brit.* to enroll in a university.

come·up·pance, kum″up′ans, *n. Colloq.* a deserved punishment or reprimand, as: He is flouting the rules now, but he'll get his *comeuppance* soon.

com·fit, kum′fit, kom′fit, *n.* [Fr. *confit,* pp. of *confire,* to preserve, to make into a sweetmeat, < *conficere.*] A dry sweetmeat; any kind of fruit or root preserved with sugar and dried.

com·fort, kum′fẽrt, *v.t.* [O.E. *confort,* < O.Fr. *conforter,* to comfort, < L.L. *confortare,* to strengthen—*con,* intens., and L. *fortis,* brave.] To raise from depression; to soothe when in grief or trouble; to bring solace or consolation to; to console, to cheer; to hearten; to solace; to enliven.

com·fort, kum′fẽrt, *n.* [O.Fr. *confort.*] Relief in affliction; consolation; solace; the feeling of relief or consolation; a person or thing that affords consolation; a cause or matter of relief or satisfaction; a state of ease, with freedom from pain and anxiety, and satisfaction of bodily wants; that which promotes such a state. *U.S.* a comforter; a bedcover.—**com·fort·less,** kum′fẽrt·les, *a.* Without comfort; without affording or being attended by any comfort.

com·fort·a·ble, kumf′ta·bl, kum′fẽr·ta-·bl, *a.* Being in comfort or in a state of ease or moderate enjoyment; giving comfort; affording help, ease, or consolation.—**com·fort·a·ble·ness,** *n.* The state of being comfortable.—**com·fort·a·bly,** *adv.* In a comfortable manner; in a manner to give comfort or consolation.

com·fort·er, kum′fẽr·tẽr, *n.* One who or that which comforts; (*cap.*) the Holy Spirit; (*l.c.*) a woolen scarf for wrapping round the neck in cold weather; *U.S.* a light, warm bedcover.

com·fort sta·tion, *n.* A small building with toilet facilities for use by the public, such as in a park or at a beach.

com·fy, kum′fē, *a.*—*comfier, comfiest. Colloq.* comfortable.

com·ic, kom′ik, *a.* [L. *comicus,* < Gr. *cōmikos,* < *cōmos,* revel.] Of, pertaining to, or of the nature of comedy, as distinct from *tragedy*; acting in or composing comedy; humorous; funny; laughable.

com·ic, kom′ik, *n.* A comic actor or performer; a comic paper or periodical.

com·i·cal, kom′i·kal, *a.* Pertaining to or of the nature of comedy; resembling comedy; exciting mirth; droll; funny; strange, queer, or odd.—**com·i·cal·i·ty,** *n.* pl. **com·i·cal·i·ties.** Comical quality; something comical.—**com·i·cal·ly,** *adv.*—**com·i·cal·ness,** *n.*

com·ic re·lief, *n.* A comic element inserted into a serious work, to relieve its tension and to broaden its scope by contrasting the humorous with the tragic.

com·ic strip, *n.* A series of narrative cartoons appearing in sequence, usually in a newspaper.

com·ing, kum′ing, *n.* Approach; arrival; advent.—**com·ing,** *a.* That comes; approaching; on the way to note or distinction.

co·mi·ti·a, ko·mish′ē·a, *n.* pl. **co·mi·ti·a.** [L.] A legislative assembly or meeting among the ancient Romans.—**co·mi·tial,** ko·mish′al, *a.* Pertaining to the comitia.

com·i·ty, kom′i·tē, *n.* pl. **com·i·ties.** [L. *comitas,* < *comis,* mild, affable.] Mildness and suavity of manner; courtesy; civility; good breeding; *international law,* courtesy between nations, as the respect which one nation shows for the laws of another. See *comity of nations.*

com·i·ty of na·tions, *n.* That courtesy by which the laws and institutions of one country are recognized and to some extent given effect by the government of another within its territory.

com·ma, kom′a, *n.* pl. **com·mas,** in pros. **com·ma·ta**, kom′ạ·tạ. [L., < Gr. *comma,* short clause, < *coptein,* strike, cut.] A mark of punctuation (,) used to indicate the smallest interruptions in continuity of thought or grammatical construction within a sentence. *Anc. pros.* a fragment or smaller section of a colon; the part of a dactylic hexameter ending or beginning with the caesura. Any pause or interval.

com·ma ba·cil·lus, *n.* A bacterial microorganism, *Vibrio comma,* the cause of Asiatic cholera, often occurring in the form of a slightly curved rod: formerly supposed to be a bacillus but later found to be a spirillum.

com·ma fault, *n. Gram.* the misuse of a comma to separate main clauses not connected by a coordinating conjunction. Also **com·ma blun·der.**

com·mand, ko·mand′, ko·mänd′, *v.t.* [O.Fr. *comander* (Fr. *commander*), < M.L. *commandare,* < L. *com-,* with, and *mandare,* commit, enjoin.] To order or direct with authority; to have or exercise power or authority over; to have subject to one's bidding or disposal; to exact or secure deservedly, as: He *commands* the respect of his pupils. To dominate or overlook by reason of location; as, a hill *commanding* the sea; to have charge of a military or naval unit.—*v.i.* To issue orders; to have or exercise power or authority; to be commander; to occupy a dominating position; to look down on or over a region.

com·mand, ko·mand′, ko·mänd′, *n.* The act of commanding or ordering; an authoritative order; possession of controlling authority; a position or post in which one has the right to command; a body of troops, a district, or any division of authority under a commander; the power of dominating or viewing a region by reason of location, and the extent or degree of this view, as: The bluff overlooks the valley with a wide *command.* Mastery; as, good *command* of the language; ability to control; as, to be in *command* of one's emotions; an electric impulse which starts a mechanism, as a control in a spacecraft; *computer*, a control signal or an instruction in computer language.

com·mand, ko·mand′, ko·mänd′, *a.* Done in answer to a command; as, a *command* performance for a royal audience.

com·man·dant, kom″an·dant′, kom″an·dänt′, *n.* [Fr., orig. ppr. of *commander*, E. *command.*] The commanding or chief officer, irrespective of rank, of a place or military body; as, the *commandant* of a navy yard, with the rank of captain.

com·man·deer, kom″an·dēr′, *v.t.* [D. *commandeeren*, < F. *commander*, E. *command.*] To order or force into active military service; to seize, as private property, for military or other public use; to seize arbitrarily.

com·mand·er, kom″an·dēr′, *n.* One authorized to command; a leader or chief officer, esp. of a military organization; *U.S. Navy*, an officer below a captain and above a lieutenant-commander; the chief officer of certain divisions in police or fire departments; the officer who presides at meetings of certain societies, esp. secret orders or veterans' groups; a member of a high division in a modern, honorary order of knighthood.—**com·mand·er·ship**, *n.*

com·mand·er in chief, *n.* pl. **com·mand·ers in chief.** One who has supreme command of the armed forces of a nation, as: The president is the *commander in chief* of the U.S. armed forces. The officer in charge of a major armed force, frequently encompassing more than one service or forces from more than one country.

com·mand·er·y, ko·man′de·rē, ko·män′de·rē, *n.* pl. **com·mand·er·ies.** [Fr. *manderie.*] A local branch or lodge of certain secret orders; a district of a commander, esp. of certain medieval orders of knights; the rank of a commander.

com·mand·ing of·fi·cer, *n.* The commissioned officer in charge, usually below the rank of brigadier general, who is in command of an organization or base.

com·mand·ment, ko·mand′ment, ko·mänd′ment, *n.* [O.Fr. Fr. *commandement.*] The act, fact, or power of commanding; a command or mandate; a divine command; any one of the *Ten Commandments* delivered to Moses on Mount Sinai (Ex. xx. 2–17).

com·man·do, ko·man′dō, *n.* pl. **com·man·dos**, **com·man·does.** [D., < Pg. *commando*, < *commandar*, *v.*, = E. *command.*] A military task force specially trained to conduct surprise raids inside enemy territory; a member of such a force. —*a.* Of or relating to a raid or any troops, as guerrilla fighters or saboteurs, employing the shock tactics of commando units.—*v.t.* To remark upon.

com·mand pi·lot, *n.* The highest aeronautical rating in the U.S. Air Force granted to an active senior pilot.

com·mem·o·rate, ko·mem′o·rāt″, *v.t.*— *commemorated*, *commemorating.* [L. *commemoratus*, pp. of *commemorare*, < *com-*, with, and *memorare*, bring to remembrance,

< *memor*, mindful: see *memory.*] To call to remembrance; make honorable mention of; to honor the memory of by some solemnity or celebration; to serve as a memento of.—

com·mem·o·ra·ble, ko·mem′o·ra·bl, *a.*

com·mem·o·ra·tion, ko·mem″o·rā′shan, *n.* [L. *commemoratio(n-).*] The act of commemorating; a service or celebration in memory of some person or event; a memorial.

com·mem·o·ra·tive, ko·mem′o·rā″tiv, ko·mem′ér·a·tiv, *a.* Serving to commemorate.—**com·mem·o·ra·to·ry**, ko·mem′ér·a·tōr″ē, ko·mem′ér·a·tar″ē, *a.*

com·mence, ko·mens′, *v.i.*—*commenced*, *commencing.* [Fr. *commencer*, < a (hypothetical) L.L. *cominitiare*—L. prefix *com-*, and *initiare*, to begin. INITIATE.] To begin; to take rise or origin; to have first existence; to begin to be, as in a new state or character. —*v.t.* To begin; to enter upon; to perform the first act of.

com·mence·ment, ko·mens′ment, *n.* The act of commencing; rise; origin; the ceremony of graduation at which diplomas are granted, and in higher institutions of learning, degrees are conferred, in recognition of the completion of academic courses.

com·mend, ko·mend′, *v.t.* [L. *commendo*, to commit, to commend—*com-*, and *mando*, to commit to; the same word as *command* with a different signification.] To commit, deliver, entrust, or give in charge (N.T.); to represent as worthy of confidence, notice, regard, or kindness; to recommend; with reflexive pronoun, to call for notice or attention as: This subject *commends* itself to our attention. To mention with approbation; to mention by way of keeping in memory.—*v.i.* To approve; to praise.—

com·mend·a·ble, *a.* Capable or worthy of being commended or praised; praiseworthy; laudable.—**com·mend·a·bly**, *adv.* In a praiseworthy manner.

com·men·da·tion, kom′en·dā′shan, *n.* [L. *commendatio.*] The act of commending; praise; favorable representation in words. —**com·mend·a·to·ry**, ko·men′da·tōr″ē, *a.* Serving to commend; presenting to favorable notice or reception; expressing praise; laudatory.

com·men·sal, ko·men′sal, *n.* [L. *com*, with, and *mensa*, table.] A habitual mealtime companion; *biol.* a commensal plant or animal. —*a.* Pertaining to eating at the same table; *biol.* pertaining to organisms which live on or in one another without being parasitic. —**com·men·sal·ism**, ko·men′sal·iz·um, *n.* The state of being commensal.

com·men·su·ra·ble, ko·men′sér·a·bl, ko·men′shèr·a·bl, *a.* [L.L. *commensurabilis*, < *commensurare.*] Having a common measure or divisor; suitable in measure; proportionate.—**com·men·su·ra·bil·i·ty**, *n.*—**com·men·su·ra·ble·ness**, *n.*—**com·men·su·ra·bly**, *adv.*

com·men·su·rate, ko·men′sér·it, ko·men′shèr·it, *a.* Reducible to a common measure; of equal size or duration; corresponding in amount, degree, or magnitude; adequate; commensurable.—**com·men·su·rate·ly**, *adv.*—**com·men·su·ra·tion**, *n.*

com·ment, kom′ent, *v.i.* [L. *commentor*, < *commentus*, pp. of *comminiscor*, to reflect on < *com-*, with, together with, and stem *min*, seen in *memini*, to remember, and in E. *mind.*] To make remarks or observations; to write notes criticizing, illustrating, or explaining a literary passage or work; to make annotations.—*v.t.* To remark upon.

com·ment, kom′ent, *n.* An expression of opinion, an observation, or a criticism; a remark; a note intended to illustrate, criticize, or explain a literary passage; annotation; exposition.

com·men·tar·y, kom′en·ter″ē, *n.* pl. **com·men·tar·ies.** A series or collection of

comments or annotations; a treatise or essay that serves for explanation; a memoir or historical narrative; as, the *Commentaries* of Caesar; anything meant to explain or illustrate; a comment.—**com·men·tar·i·al**, *a.*

com·men·ta·tor, kom′en·tā″tèr, *n.* A person who gives or writes a commentary; an annotator; one who reports and analyzes news, weather, or athletic contests on radio or television.—**com·men·tate**, *v.t.*, *v.i.*— *commentated*, *commentating.*

com·merce, kom′érs, *n.* [Fr. *commerce*, < L. *commercium*, *com-*, with, and *merx* (*merc-*), goods, wares, merchandise.] Interchange of goods or commodities, esp. on a large scale between different countries, as "foreign *commerce*" or between different parts of the same country, as "internal *commerce*"; business intercourse; social intercourse; sexual intercourse.

com·mer·cial, ko·mur′shal, *n.* An announcement made over radio or television concerning the product or service of an advertiser.

com·mer·cial, ko·mur′shal, *a.* Pertaining to commerce or trade; dealing with or depending on commerce; carrying on commerce; produced for mass consumption, with profit as a primary aim, and often of inferior quality.—**com·mer·cial·ly**, *adv.*

com·mer·cial bank, *n.* A bank that includes among its services checking accounts and short-term loans to business.

com·mer·cial·ism, ko·mur′sha·liz″um, *n.* The doctrine and methods of commerce or commercial men; overemphasis on profits. —**com·mer·cial·ist**, *n.*—**com·mer·cial·is·tic**, *a.*

com·mer·cial·ize, ko·mur′sha·līz″, *v.t.*— *commercialized*, *commercializing.* To render commercial in character, methods, or spirit; to make available for sale; to seek commercial profit from.—**com·mer·cial·i·za·tion**, *n.*

com·mer·cial pa·per, *n.* Negotiable paper such as promissory notes or drafts, given in the due course of business.

com·mer·cial trav·e·ler, *n.* A traveling agent, as for a wholesale business house, who solicits orders for goods; a traveling salesman.

com·mie, kom′ē, *n. Slang*, (*often cap.*), a communist.

com·mi·na·tion, kom″i·nā′shan, *n.* [L. *comminatio(n-).*] A threatening; a threat of punishment or vengeance; a denunciation. —**com·mi·na·tor**, *n.*—**com·min·a·to·ry**, ko·min′a·tōr″ē, kom′in·a·tōr″ē, *a.*

com·min·gle, ko·ming′gel, *v.t.*, *v.i.*—*commingled*, *commingling.* To mix together; to mingle in one mass; to blend.

com·mi·nute, kom′i·nöt″, kom′i·nūt″, *v.t.* —*comminuted*, *comminuting.* [L. *comminuo*, *comminutum*, to make small—*com-*, with, and *minuo*, to lessen; root *min*, as in *minor*, less.] To make small or fine; to reduce to minute particles or to a fine powder; to pulverize. —*a.* Reduced into small parts or particles.

com·mi·nu·tion, kom′i·nö″shan, kom′i·nū″shan, *n.* The act of comminuting or reducing to a fine powder or to small particles; pulverization.

com·mis·er·ate, ko·miz′e·rāt″, *v.t.*—*commiserated*, *commiserating.* To feel sorrow, pain, or regret for, through sympathy; to compassionate; to pity.—**com·mis·er·a·tive**, *a.* Compassionate.—**com·mis·er·a·tive·ly**, *adv.*

com·mis·er·a·tion, ko·miz″e·rā′shan, *n.* The act of commiserating: a sympathetic suffering of pain or sorrow for the afflictions or distresses of another; pity; compassion.

com·mis·sar, kom′i·sär″, kom′i·sär′, *n.* [Fr. *commissaire*, M.L. *commissarius*, one to whom something is entrusted.] A Communist party official in charge of teaching party doctrine; formerly, the head of a government department in the Soviet Union.

com·mis·sar·i·at, kom″i·sâr′ē·at, n. The department of an army which supplies equipment and provisions for the troops; the body of officers in that department; the office or duties of a commissary; the district over which the jurisdiction of a commissary extends. Any of the departments of government within the Union of Soviet Socialist Republics until 1946, and now called the ministry.

com·mis·sar·y, kom′i·ser″ē, n. pl. **com·mis·sar·ies**. One to whom is committed some charge, duty, or office by a superior authority; a store for equipment, provisions, or food operated for military, lumber camp, mining personnel, etc.; a dining room for motion picture and television personnel; food supplies in general.

com·mis·sion, ko·mish′on, n. [O.Fr. Fr. commission, < L. commissio(n-), < committere.] The act of committing or giving in charge; authoritative charge or direction; authority committed, as for particular actions or functions; the position or rank of an officer in the army or navy; an instrument or warrant granting authority to act in a given capacity or conferring a particular rank; a body of persons authoritatively charged with particular functions; the condition of being placed under special authoritative charge; in naval use, the condition of a ship assigned to the charge of an officer for active service; hence, the condition of anything in active service or use; as, to be in or out of commission; a task or matter committed to one's charge; authority to act as agent for another or others in commercial transactions; a sum or percentage allowed to the agent for his services; the committing or perpetrating of a crime, error, or the like.

com·mis·sion, ko·mish′on, v.t. To give a commission to; authorize; delegate; send on a mission; to put in commission, as a warship; to give a commission or order for.

com·mis·sion·aire, ko·mish″o·nâr′, n. [Fr. commissionnaire.] In European cities, a person whose business it is to execute miscellaneous small commissions for the public; a messenger or porter.

com·mis·sioned, ko·mish′ond, a. Furnished with a commission; as, commissioned officers, army and navy officers holding rank by commission, including in the U.S. second lieutenants, ensigns, and all those above them.

com·mis·sion·er, ko·mish′o·nėr, n. One who commissions; a person who has a commission or warrant from proper authority to perform some office or execute some business; an officer having charge of some department of the public service; sports, the administrative official of professional leagues.

com·mis·sion mer·chant, n. A merchant engaged in buying or selling goods for others on commission.

com·mis·sion plan, n. The system of municipal government in which each department of the executive and legislative branches is administered by an elected city commissioner.

com·mis·sure, kom′i·shur″, n. [L. commissura, < committere.] A joint, seam, or suture; specif. bot. the joint or face by which one carpel coheres to another; anat., zool. a connecting band of nerve-tissue.—**com·mis·su·ral**, ko·mish′ėr·al, a.

com·mit, ko·mit′, v.t.—committed, committing. [L. committere (pp. commissus), bring together, join, entrust, do, < com-, with, and mittere, send.] To give in trust or charge; consign for safe-keeping; consign for preservation; as, to commit to writing, to commit to memory; to consign to custody, as

to a mental institution or prison; to refer, as to a committee, for consideration; to do; to perpetrate, as a crime, error, or folly; to bind by pledge or assurance.

com·mit·ment, ko·mit′ment, n. The act of committing, or the state of being committed; consignment, as to a hospital or prison; a warrant committing a person to prison; perpetration or commission, as of a crime; the act of committing, pledging, obligating, or engaging oneself, as to take on financial responsibilities.

com·mit·tal, ko·mit′al, n. Commitment.

com·mit·tee, ko·mit′ē, n. A person or a group of persons appointed to investigate, report, or act in special cases; a group of its members selected by a legislative body to act on certain legislative matters.

com·mit·tee·man, ko·mit′ē·man, ko·mit′ē·man″, n. A member of a committee; the party leader of a municipal precinct or ward.—**com·mit·tee·wo·man**, n.

com·mit·tee of the whole, n. A committee of a legislative body consisting of all the members present, sitting in a deliberative rather than a legislative character, for informal consultation and preliminary consideration of matters awaiting legislative action.

com·mix, ko·miks′, v.t., v.i. [L.]To mix or mingle; to blend.

com·mix·ture, ko·miks′chur, n. The act of mixing; the state of being mingled; the mass formed by mixing; a compound.

com·mode, ko·mōd′, n. [Fr. commode, < L. commodus, fit, convenient, useful, < com-, with, and modus, measure, E. mode.] A low cabinet or chest of drawers; a stand or cupboard for a washbasin; a stand or stool containing a chamber pot; a toilet. A large, high headdress worn by women about 1700.

com·mo·di·ous, ko·mō′dē·us, a. [L.L. commodiosus, < L. commodus, useful.] Roomy and convenient; spacious and suitable; serviceable.—**com·mo·di·ous·ly**, adv.—**com·mo·di·ous·ness**, n.

com·mod·i·ty, ko·mod′i·tē, n. pl. **com·mod·i·ties**. [O.Fr. commodite, Fr. commodité, < L. commoditas, < commodus.] Something that is of use or is valuable; an article of trade or commerce.

com·mod·i·ty ex·change, n. An organized trading center where commodities such as butter, sugar, coffee, or grains are bought and sold.

com·mo·dore, kom′o·dōr″, kom′o·dar″, n. [< Sp. commendador, a commander, or < Pg. capitao mor, superior captain.] A commissioned officer in the U.S. Navy, ranking under a rear admiral, who commands a detachment of ships in the absence of an admiral; the senior captain when three or more ships of war are cruising in company; the senior captain of a line of merchant vessels; the president or chief officer of a yachting club.

com·mon, kom′on, a. [O.Fr. comun (Fr. commun), < L. communis, appar. < com-, with, and -munis, bound, as in immunis, not bound, exempt.] Of or pertaining to a community at large, in the sense of public; as, common language; belonging to or equally shared by two or more individuals; as, common property; joint or united; as, a common front against the enemy. Occurring regularly or frequently in the sense of familiar or ordinary; as, a common headache; widespread or general; as, common knowledge; simple and rudimentary in nature; as, common courtesy, vulgar or unprincipled, as: Her clothes were tasteless and common. Second rate or inferior in quality; as: The cabinets were made of the most common wood. Lacking in rank, status, or distinction; as, a common foot soldier. Gram. of a word which refers to any of a

general group or class; as, a common noun; of a word, designated as being of common gender, in which masculine or feminine gender is not indicated, as child, person, individual; not belonging to an inflectional paradigm, in which a noun does not change its word form whether used as a subject or object. Math. belonging equally to two or more quantities.—**com·mon·ly**, adv.—**com·mon·ness**, n.

com·mon, kom′on, n. A tract of land possessed or used in common, esp. by all the members of a community; law, the right to take a profit from the land or waters of another, as by pasturing cattle, or catching fish; eccles. a religious service suitable for any of various festivals, or, specifically, the ordinary of the mass.—**in com·mon**, in joint possession, use, action, or relation.

com·mon·age, kom′o·nij, n. The use of anything in common, esp. a pasture; the right to such use; the state of being held in common; that which is so held, as land; the commonalty.

com·mon·al·ty, kom′o·nal·tē, n. pl. **com·mon·al·ties**. [O.Fr. communalté (Fr. communauté), < O.Fr. Fr. comunal.] The common people as distinguished from the nobility or those in authority; an incorporated body or its membership; the general body or mass, as of mankind. Also **com·mon·al·i·ty**, kom″o·nal′i·tē.

com·mon car·ri·er, n. An individual or a corporation whose business is the transportation of goods or passengers, as a railroad or a bus company.

com·mon de·nom·i·na·tor, n. Math. in a set of fractions, a number that is a multiple of all the divisors in the set; a characteristic, trait, or theme shared by or common to a group.

com·mon di·vi·sor, n. Math. a number or expression that divides two or more numbers or expressions without leaving a remainder.

com·mon·er, kom′o·nėr, n. One of the common people; a member of the commonalty; at Oxford University, a student who pays for his own board and other expenses, and is not supported by any foundation; one who has a joint right in common land.

com·mon frac·tion, n. Math. an arithmetic relationship expressed by a numerator and denominator separated by either a diagonal line, as 3/4, or by a horizontal line, as $\frac{3}{4}$.

com·mon law, n. The English system of law, as distinct from the civil or Roman law and the canon or ecclesiastical law; the unwritten law, esp. of England, based on usage and custom, as distinct from statute law; law of general application throughout a political entity, distinguished from law of specialized application, such as admiralty.

com·mon-law mar·riage, n. A marriage established by mutual agreement and cohabitation of a man and a woman, but not solemnized by a civil or religious ceremony.

com·mon log·a·rithm, n. A logarithm with the base 10.

com·mon mar·ket, n. A customs union; a partnership of nations established for economic purposes whereby tariff restrictions among the members are eliminated and common tariff restrictions toward other trading nations are adopted; (cap.) that association formed in 1958 by Belgium, France, Italy, Luxembourg, the Netherlands, and West Germany which is officially known as the European Economic Community.

com·mon meas·ure, n. Mus. in the U.S., four quarter notes to the bar; same as 4/4 or common time; poet. a strictly rhymed stanza of four iambic lines.

a- fat, fāte, fär, fâre, fall;   **e-** met, mē, mēre, hėr;   **i-** pin, pine;   **o-** not, nōte, mōve;   **u-** tub, cūbe, bull;   **oi-** oil;   **ou-** pound.

com·mon mul·ti·ple, *n. Math.* a number which is a multiple of each of two or more numbers, quantities, or expressions.

com·mon·place, kom′on·plās″, *n.* A common or customary subject of remark; a stock remark; a trite saying; a platitude; something taken for granted.

com·mon·place, kom′on·plās″, *a.* Not novel or striking; trite; common or ordinary.—**com·mon·place·ness,** *n.*

com·mon room, *n.* A lounge or other room, esp. in schools, which serves a variety of social purposes.

com·mons, kom′onz, *n. pl.* The lower house of the British Parliament or of the Canadian Parliament; (*cap.*) the representatives of this body; (*l.c.*) *Brit.* food provided at a common table, as in colleges; hence, a dining hall.

com·mon sense, *n.* Sound practical judgment; the natural intelligence or understanding of mankind in general. —**com·mon-sense,** **com·mon·sense,** *a.*—**com·mon·sen·si·ble,** **com·mon·sen·si·cal,** *a.*

com·mon stock, *n.* Securities which represent an ownership interest in a corporation, the holders of which securities receive dividends, when paid, only after the obligations of floating debt, bond interest, and preferred stock are met.

com·mon time, *n.* Musical time or rhythm with four beats to a measure. Also *common measure.*

com·mon touch, *n.* The personal quality of appeal to the common people.

com·mon trust fund, *n.* A joining or combination of two or more trust funds to secure greater efficiency in handling and diversity in investment risks.

com·mon·weal, kom′on·wēl″, *n.* The welfare of the public. Also **com·mon weal.**

com·mon·wealth, kom′on·welth″, *n.* The body politic or people of a nation, state, or other political unit; a nation or state with a representative form of government in which supreme authority is vested in the people; a republic; *Eng. history,* (*cap.*) the English state from the death of Charles I in 1649 to the Restoration in 1660; (*cap.*) a group of sovereign states and their dependencies linked by common objectives and formally associated by compact; as, the British *Commonwealth;* (*cap.*) an association of former colonies, esp. colonies which were part of the British Commonwealth; as, the *Commonwealth* of Australia; (*cap.*) loosely, any state of the United States; the official designation of Kentucky, Massachusetts, Pennsylvania, and Virginia, four states of the United States; (*cap.*) the official designation of Puerto Rico, a polity which is locally autonomous but united on a voluntary basis with the United States.

com·mon year, *n.* A calendar year of 365 days; a year which does not contain the intercalary day allotted to leap year.

com·mo·tion, ko·mō′shan, *n.* [L. *commotio,* < *commoveo, commotum.*] Agitation; tumult of people; disturbance; perturbation; disorder of mind; excitement; political or social unrest.

com·move, ko·mōv′, *v.t.*—*commoved, commoving.* [O.Fr., Fr. *commouvoir,* < L. *commovere,* < *com-,* altogether, and *movere,* E. *move.*] To move violently; agitate; excite.

com·mu·nal, ko·mūn′al, kom′ū·nal, *a.* [Fr. *communal,* < M.L. *communalis,* < *communa,* E. *commune.*] Pertaining to a commune or a community; characterized by common sharing and use of property by group members in a community.

com·mu·nal·ism, ko·mūn′a·liz″um, kom′ū·na·liz″um, *n.* A theory or system of government according to which each commune is virtually an independent state, and

the nation merely a federation of such states. —**com·mu·nal·is·tic,** *a.* Referring to the beliefs, principles, or practices of communal living and ownership.

com·mu·nal·i·ty, kom″ū·nal′it·ē, *n.* Group solidarity; communal character or state; similar opinions and feelings in a group.

Com·mu·nard, kom′ū·närd″, *n.* [Fr.] A member or supporter of the Paris Commune of 1871.

com·mune, ko·mūn′, *v.i.*—*communed, communing.* [Fr. *communier;* L. *communico,* to communicate, < *communis,* common. COMMON.] To converse; to talk together familiarly; to impart sentiments mutually; to interchange ideas or feelings; to partake of the Eucharist.

com·mune, kom′ūn, *n.* [Fr. Commune, < M.L. *communia,* < L. *communis.*] A community; the smallest administrative division, in many European countries, governed by a mayor and assisted by a municipal council; a small rural community organized as a collective unit; a unit of government holding to revolutionary or communist principles.

com·mu·ni·ca·ble, ko·mū′ni·ka·bl, *a.* [M.L. *communicabilis.*] Capable of being communicated or imparted; as, a *communicable* disease; communicative; ready to converse or to impart information.—**com·mu·ni·ca·bil·i·ty,** **com·mu·ni·ca·ble·ness,** *n.*—**com·mu·ni·ca·bly,** *adv.*

com·mu·ni·cant, ko·mū′ni·kant, *a.* Communicating; esp. partaking of the Eucharist; being a communicant.—*n.* One who communicates; an informant; one who partakes, or is entitled to partake, of the Eucharist; a member of a church.

com·mu·ni·cate, ko·mū′ni·kāt″, *v.t.*—*communicated, communicating.* [L. *communicatus,* pp. of *communicare,* < *communis.* COMMON.] To give to another; impart; transmit, as a disease; to impart knowledge of; make known; to administer the Eucharist to.—*v.i.* To have interchange of thoughts; hold communication; of rooms or buildings, to join or be joined, as: The campus buildings *communicate* by means of a central court.

com·mu·ni·ca·tion, ko·mū″ni·kā′shan, *n.* [L. *communicatio(n-).*] The act or fact of communicating; transmission; the imparting or interchange of thoughts, opinions, or information by speech, writing, or signs; that which is communicated or imparted; a document or message imparting views or information; passage, opportunity of passage, or a means of passage, between places.

com·mu·ni·ca·tion in·tel·li·gence, *n. Milit.* Intelligence developed from analyzing enemy communications; the organization that gathers and develops such information.

com·mu·ni·ca·tions, ko·mū″ni·kā′shanz, *n. pl. but sing. in constr.* A system of facilities used for communicating messages or orders; an organization that develops, operates, and maintains services for communication, as in industry or the military; *milit.* a system of routes or facilities for transporting persons and goods. The technology or industry of transmitting messages by means of a system of electrical or electronic facilities; see *telecommunications.* The combined study of effective communication in all forms, including speech and writing, and graphic and dramatic arts.

com·mu·ni·ca·tions sat·el·lite, *n. Aerospace,* an artificial earth-orbiting satellite designed to relay electronic communications, as radio, telephone, and television, between distant parts of the world.

com·mu·ni·ca·tive, ko·mū′ni·kā″tiv, ko·mū′ni·ka·tiv, *a.* Inclined to communicate

or impart; disposed to impart or disclose information or opinions; talkative; of or pertaining to communication.—**com·mu·ni·ca·tive·ly,** *adv.*

com·mun·ion, ko·mūn′yan, *n.* [L. *munio(n-),* < *communis.*] The act of sharing, or holding in common, or the state of things so held; participation; community; association or fellowship; mutual intercourse; a spiritual interchange of ideas or feelings, usu. between man and nature or the supernatural; often, religious fellowship or intercourse; ecclesiastical union; a body of persons having one common religious faith; a religious denomination. (*Often cap.*) participation in the sacrament of the Lord's Supper; the act of consuming the elements of the Eucharist; the celebration of the Lord's Supper; the Eucharist.—**com·mun·ion·ist,** *n.*

com·mu·ni·qué, ko·mū″ni·kā′, ko·mū′·ni·kā″, *n.* [Fr.] An official communication, as from the government to the press or the public.

com·mun·ism, kom′ū·niz″um, *n.* [= Fr. *communisme,* < L. *communis* (or Fr. *commun*): COMMON.] A theory or system of social organization based on the holding of property in common, actual ownership being ascribed to the community as a whole or to the state; an economic theory or system by which the state controls the means of production and the distribution and consumption of industrial products, the first modern example being in the Soviet Union; communalism; (*cap.*) standardized concept based on works of Karl Marx and Friedrich Engels.

com·mun·ist, kom′ū·nist, [= Fr. *communiste.*] *n.* An advocate of communism; a member of the Communist party; (*usu. cap.*) a Communard.—*a.*—**com·mu·nis·tic,** *a.*—**com·mu·nis·ti·cal·ly,** *adv.*

com·mu·ni·ta·ri·an, ko·mū″ni·târ′ē·an, *n.* A member of a communistic community; an advocate of such communities.—*a.*

com·mu·ni·ty, ko·mū′ni·tē, *n. pl.* **com·mu·ni·ties.** [L. *communitas,* < *communis:* see *commom.*] The state of being held in common; common possession, enjoyment, liability, etc.; common character; agreement; identity; social intercourse; association; life in association with others; the social state; a number of individuals associated together by the fact of residence in the same locality, or of subjection to the same laws and regulations; a number of persons having common ties or interests and living in the same locality; hence, any body or group living together, esp. a monastic body; a communistic society; the body of people of a place; the public.

com·mu·ni·ty cen·ter, *n.* A place provided by a residential community for its members to gather for recreational, social, or educational activities.

com·mu·ni·ty chest, *n.* A fund accumulated through voluntary contributions by members of a community for the support of local charity; (*cap.*) an organized fundraising campaign for several charities.

com·mu·ni·ty prop·er·ty, *n.* Any property jointly owned by husband and wife.

com·mu·nize, kom′ū·nīz″, *v.t.*—*munized, communizing.* [L. *communis.* COMMON.] To transfer individual ownership of (property) to community ownership; to impose communistic systems and rule on (a country or its people).

com·mut·a·ble, ko·mū′ta·bl, *a.* [L. *commutabilis.*] Capable of being commuted; exchangeable.—**com·mut·a·bil·i·ty,** **com·mut·a·ble·ness,** *n.*

com·mu·tate, kom′ū·tāt″, *v.t.*—*commutated, commutating.* [Back-formation from *commutator.*] *Elect.* to reverse the direction of an electric current) by a commutator; to use a commutator to convert (alternating current) into direct current or vice versa.

com·mu·ta·tion, kom″ū·tā′shan, n. [L. *commutatio(n-).*] The act or process of commuting; exchange; substitution; the substitution of one kind of payment for another; the changing of a penalty or prison sentence for another less severe; repeated travel between home and work.

com·mu·ta·tion tick·et, n. A transportation ticket issued at a reduced rate, as by a bus or a railroad company, entitling the holder to be carried over a given route a certain number of times or during a certain period.

com·mu·ta·tive, ko·mū′ta·tiv, kom′u·tā″tiv, a. [M.L. *commutativus.*] Of or pertaining to exchange, substitution, or interchange; pertaining to mutual dealings; *math.* combining quantities in a calculation where the result does not depend on the order in which the quantities are combined; as, the *commutative* law of multiplication.—**com·mu·ta·tive·ly,** adv.

com·mu·ta·tor, kom′ū·tā″tėr, n. [N.L., < L. *commutare,* E. *commute.*] *Elect.* A device for reversing the direction of a current, or for changing direct current into alternating current or vice versa; in a dynamo or motor, a segmented revolving part through which current is conveyed to the brushes.

com·mute, ko·mūt′, v.t.—*commuted, commuting.* [L. *commutare* (pp. *commutatus*), < *com-,* with, and *mutare,* change.] To exchange for another or something else; give and take reciprocally; interchange; change (one kind of payment) into or for another as by substitution; change (an obligation or penalty) for one less burdensome or severe; *elect.* to alter or direct (a current) by a commutator.—*v.i.* To make substitution; compensate; serve as a substitute; make a collective payment, esp. of a reduced amount, as an equivalent for a number of payments; use a commutation-ticket; travel daily from the suburbs to the city to work; *math.* to arrive at the same result regardless of the order in which an operation is performed on two or more quantities.

com·mut·er, ko·mū′tėr, n. One who travels to and from a location regularly, as to the city from the suburbs for work.

co·mose, kō′mōs, a. [L. *coma,* hair.] Hairy; comate; tufted.

com·pact, kom′pakt, n. [L. *compactum,* a compact, < *compaciscor, compactus,* to make an agreement—*com,* together, and *paciscor,* to fix, settle, covenant.] An agreement; a contract, covenant, bargain, or settlement between parties.

com·pact, kom′pakt, n. A small case, usu. carried in a woman's purse, containing a mirror and holding face powder and sometimes rouge; an economically-operated small model of a standard-sized automobile.

com·pact, kom′pakt′, a. [L. *compactus,* pp. of *compingo, compactum,* to join or unite.] Closely and firmly united, as the parts or particles of solid bodies; having the parts or particles close; solid; dense; not diffuse; not verbose; concise; composed.

com·pact, kom′pakt′, v.t. To thrust, drive, or press closely together; to join firmly; to consolidate; to make close; to unite or connect firmly, as in a system.

com·pact·i·ble, kom·pakt′i·bl, a. Having the qualities, as looseness of soil, for being compacted.

com·pac·tion, kom·pak′shan, kom·pak′-shan, n. The process of compacting or being compacted; *geol.* decrease in amount of soil bulk due to weight of upper deposits, evaporation, or other causes.

com·pan·ion, kom·pan′yon, n. [Akin D. *kampanje,* poop deck.] *Naut.* a covering

or hood over the top of a companionway; a companionway.

com·pan·ion, kom·pan′yon, n. [O.Fr. *compaignon,* Fr. *compagnon.*] One who accompanies another; a mate; a comrade; an associate; a member of the lowest rank in an order of knighthood; a person employed to afford company or assistance to another; a mate or match for a thing.

com·pan·ion, kom·pan′yon, v.t. To be a companion to; to accompany.

com·pan·ion·a·ble, kom·pan′yo·na·bl, a. Fit for good fellowship; qualified to be agreeable in company; sociable.—**com·-pan·ion·a·ble·ness,** n.—**com·pan·ion·a·bly,** adv.

com·pan·ion·ate, kom·pan′yo·nit, a. Of or like companions.

com·pan·ion·ate mar·riage, n. A form of marriage allowing divorce by mutual consent of a couple who have agreed to remain childless, and holding neither person legally responsible for or to the other.

com·pan·ion·ship, kom·pan′yon·ship″, n. The state or relation of a companion; the presence of a companion; association as companions; fellowship; a body of companions.

com·pan·ion·way, kom·pan′yon·wā″, n. *Naut.* The space or shaft occupied by the steps leading down from the deck to a cabin; the steps leading from one deck to another.

com·pa·ny, kum′pa·nē, n. pl. **com·pa·nies.** [O.Fr. *compaignie* (Fr. *compagnie*), < *compain.*] Companionship; fellowship; association; a number of individuals assembled or associated together; a party; a band; a companion or companions; an assemblage of persons for social purposes; a guest or guests; society collectively, esp. a number of persons united or incorporated for joint action; a medieval trade guild, or a corporation historically representing such a guild; as, the *Company* of Stationers of the City of London; an association for carrying on a commercial enterprise; the member or members of a firm not specifically named in the firm's title; *milit.* a subdivision of an infantry regiment or battalion, commanded by a captain; *naut.* a ship's crew, including the officers.—**keep com·pa·ny,** to go out exclusively with one member of the opposite sex; to associate with or be friendly with.—**part com·pa·ny,** to discontinue friendship or an association.

com·pa·ny un·ion, n. A labor union consisting of the employees of only one company, and not affiliated with a national union.

com·pa·ra·ble, kom′par·a·bl, a. [L. *comparabilis.*] Capable of being compared; having enough characteristics in common suitable for comparison.—**com·pa·ra·bil·it·y, com·pa·ra·ble·ness,** n.—**com·pa·ra·bly,** adv.

com·par·a·tive, kom·par′a·tiv, a. [L. *comparativus.*] Estimated by comparison; not positive or absolute; involving comparison as a method of study, esp. the comparison of different things belonging to the same science or study; as, *comparative* anatomy; having the power of comparing different things; as, the *comparative* faculty. *Gram.* expressing a greater degree; expressing more than the positive but less than the superlative: applied to forms of adjectives and adverbs.

com·par·a·tive, kom·par′a·tiv, n. *Gram.* the comparative degree, or that form of an adjective or adverb expressing it; as, *prettier* and *more beautiful* are the *comparatives* of *pretty* and *beautiful.*

com·par·a·tive lin·guis·tics, n. The scientific study of the historical development of language, with emphasis upon

languages and dialects that have a common origin.

com·par·a·tive re·li·gion, n. A comparative study and classification of the origin and growth of the interrelations and influences of the various religious systems.

com·pa·ra·tor, kom′pa·rā″tėr, n. [L., a comparer.] Any of various instruments for making comparisons, as of lengths or distances, or tints of color; one who detects and compares deviations from a standard measure.

com·pare, kom·pâr′, v.t.—*compared, comparing.* [L. *comparare,* < *compar,* equal, like, < *com-,* with, and *par,* equal.] To examine and note the similarities and differences of (two or more things, ideas, or people); to ascertain the resemblance or difference of, the agreement or disagreement; *gram.* to modify (an adjective or adverb) by inflection of the positive, comparative, or superlative degrees so as to express different degrees of the quality or manner denoted by the simple form.—*v.i.* To bear comparison; to contrast one thing with another.

com·pare, kom·pâr′, n. Comparison, as: His craftsmanship is beyond *compare.*—**com·par·er,** n.

com·par·i·son, kom·par′i·son, n. [O.Fr. Fr. *comparaison,* < L. *comparatio(n-),* < *comparare,* E. *compare.*] The act of examining in order to discover how one thing compares to another, esp. with an eye to their like or unlike characteristics; a comparative estimate or statement; capability of being compared or likened; *gram.* the modification of an adjective or adverb to express degrees of quality, quantity, or intensity.

com·par·i·son sheet, n. A detailed record of time studies made up to assist in determining basic fundamental data.

com·part, kom·pärt′, v.t. [L.L. *compartiri,* divide, share, < L. *com-,* with, and *partire,* divide.] To divide into parts or distinct spaces.

com·part·ment, kom·pärt′ment, n. [Fr. *compartiment,* L.L. *compartimentum,* < L. *comparitor,* to divide, share, < *pars, partis,* a part.] A division or separate part of a general design, as a building, railroad car, picture, or plan.—*v.t.* To mark or partition into compartments.—**com·part·men·tal,** a. Of, pertaining to, or divided into compartments.—**com·part·ment·ed,** a. Marked or partitioned into compartments.

com·part·men·tal·ize, kom·pärt·men′ta·līz, kom″pärt·men′ta·līz″, v.t.—*compartmentalized, compartmentalizing.* To divide into separate or distinct compartments.

com·pass, kum′pas, n. [O.Fr. Fr. *compas,* appar. < M.L. *compassus,* circle, compasses, < L. *com-,* with, and *passus,* step, pace.] An instrument for determining directions, consisting essentially of a freely pivoting magnetized needle or bar which points to the magnetic north. *Sometimes pl.,* an instrument for describing or drawing circles, etc., and measuring distances, consisting generally of two movable legs hinged at one end; also **pair of com·pass·es.** The enclosing line or limit of any area; measurement round, as: The dog was confined within the *compass* of the fence. Space within limits; area, extent, range, or scope, as of time, space, interest, concern, or knowledge, due or proper limits; moderate bounds, as: His enthusiasm knew no *compass. Music,* the total range of tones of a voice or musical instrument.

com·pass, kum′pas, v.t. [O.Fr. Fr. *compasser.*] To go, or move around; make the circuit of; to surround; enclose; encircle, to grasp, as with the mind; comprehend; to attain or achieve; accomplish; obtain, as: He was unable to *compass* his ambitions. To contrive or scheme.

com·pass, kum′pas, *a.* Curved; forming an arc; as, a *compass* window, or a roof with *compass* rafters.

com·pass card, *n.* A circular card attached to the pivot of a mariner's compass, on which the 32 points indicating direction, and usually the 360° of a circle, are marked.

com·pas·sion, kom·pash′on, *n.* [O.Fr. Fr. *compassion,* < L.L. *compassio(n-),* < *compati,* suffer with, < L. *com-,* with, and *pati,* suffer.] A sympathetic emotion created by the misfortunes of another, accompanied by a desire to help; pity; mercy.

com·pas·sion·ate, kom·pash′a·nit, *a.* Having or showing compassion; pitying; merciful; charitable.—**com·pas·sion·ate·ly,** *adv.*—**com·pas·sion·ate·ness,** *n.*

com·pas·sion·ate, kom·pash′a·nāt″, *v.t.* —*compassionated, compassionating.* To feel compassion for; take pity on.

com·pass plant, *n.* Any of various plants whose leaf edges or branches tend to point north and south; esp. *Silphium laciniatum,* a composite plant of the American prairies.

com·pass rose, *n.* A circle marked by 32 points or 360 degrees numbered clockwise from true or magnetic north, and printed on a chart to measure the angle from the compass needle to a heading for navigation or plotting purposes; a similar design, often ornamental, used on maps to indicate points of the compass.

com·pa·thy, kom′pa·thē, *n.* Feelings shared with another or others, such as grief or joy.

com·pat·i·bil·i·ty, kom·pat″i·bil′i·tē, *n.* The quality of being compatible; consistency; suitability. Also **com·pat·i·ble·ness,** kom·pat′i·bl·nis.

com·pat·i·ble, kom·pat′i·bl, *a.* [Fr. *compatible,* L.L. *compatibilis*—L. *com,* together, and *patior,* to suffer.] Capable of existing together in harmony; congenial; agreeable; congruous; *television,* capable of receiving color broadcasts in black and white on TV sets without special adaptation; *chem.* referring to the formation of a mixture that is not changed or separated by chemical interaction.—**com·pat·i·bly,** *adv.* In a compatible manner; fitly; suitably.

com·pa·tri·ot, kom·pā′trē·ot, *Brit.* kom·pa′trē·ot, *n.* [Fr. *compatriote,* < L.L. *compatriota,* < L. *com-,* with, and L.L. *patriota,* countryman.] A fellow countryman or fellow countrywoman.—**com·pa·tri·ot·ic,** *a.*—**com·pa·tri·ot·ism,** *n.*

com·peer, kom·pēr′, kom′pēr, *n.* An equal; a companion; an associate; a mate.

com·pel, kom·pel′, *v.t.*—*compelled, compelling.* [L. *compello, compulsum,* to drive together—*com,* and *pello,* to drive; hence *compulsion, compulsory.*] To drive or urge with force; to constrain; to oblige or necessitate; to subject; to cause to submit; to take by force or violence.—**com·pel·la·ble,** *a.*—**com·pel·ler,** *n.*—**com·pel·ling·ly,** *adv.*

com·pel·la·tion, kom″pe·lā′shan, *n.* [L. *compellatio(n-),* < *compellare,* address.] The act or the mode of addressing a person; form of address or designation; an appellation.

com·pend, kom′pend, *n.* Compendium.

com·pen·di·ous, kom·pen′dē·us, *a.* [L. *compendiosus.*] Containing the substance of a comprehensive subject in abbreviated form; succinct; concise.—**com·pen·di·ous·ly,** *adv.*—**com·pen·di·ous·ness,** *n.*

com·pen·di·um, kom·pen′dēum, *n. pl.* **com·pen·di·ums, com·pen·di·a.** [L. *compendium,* a shortening.] A brief treatment or summary of a larger work or body of knowledge; an abridgment; a listing in the sense of inventory.

com·pen·sa·ble, kom·pen′sa·bl, *a.* [Fr.]

Entitled or entitling to compensation; that can be compensated.

com·pen·sate, kom′pen·sāt, *v.t.*—*compensated, compensating.* [L. *compensatus,* pp. of *compensare,* < *com-,* with, and *pensare,* freq. of *pendere,* weight.] To counterbalance or offset; make up for; to make up for something; to recompense; *mech.* to counterbalance (a force or the like); adjust or construct so as to offset or counterbalance variations or produce equilibrium. —*v.i.* Provide or be an equivalent; make up; make amends.—**com·pen·sa·tive,** *a.*—**com·pen·sa·tor,** *n.* Any of various mechanical devices for effecting compensation.—**com·pen·sa·to·ry,** kom·pen′sa·tor″ē, kom·pen′sa·tẹr″ē, *a.*

com·pen·sa·tion, kom″pen·sā′shan, *n.* The act of compensating; that which is given or serves as an equivalent for services, debt, want, loss, or suffering; amends; indemnity; recompense; that which supplies the place of something else or makes good a deficiency.—**Com·pen·sa·tion Act for Work·men,** any of a number of state laws providing for the compensation of a workman by his employer in case of accident.

com·pete, kom·pēt′, *v.i.*—*competed, competing.* [L. *competere* (pp. *competitus*), contend for, earlier come together, agree, be fit, < *com-,* with, and *petere,* fall on, aim at, seek.] To contend with another for some prize or advantage, as in athletics or business; engage in a contest; vie.

com·pe·tence, kom′pi·tens, *n.* State of being competent; adequacy; sufficiency; property or means of subsistence sufficient to furnish the necessaries and conveniences of life. Also **com·pe·ten·cy.**

com·pe·tent, kom′pi·tent, *a.* [Fr. *compétent,* < *competer,* to be sufficient; L. *competo,* to be suitable.] Answering all requirements; suitable; fit; adequate; having legal capacity or power; rightfully or lawfully belonging.—**com·pe·tent·ly,** *adv.*

com·pe·ti·tion, kom″pi·tish′an, *n.* [L.L. *competitio.*] The act of competing; mutual contest or striving for the same object; rivalry; a trial of skill proposed as a test of superiority or comparative fitness.—**com·pet·i·tive,** kom·pet′i·tiv, *a.* Relating to competition; as, *competitive* prices.

com·pet·i·tor, kom·pet′i·tẹr, *n.* One who competes; a rival for sales of the same or similar merchandise.—**com·pe·ti·tory,** *a.* In competition or rivalry.

com·pi·la·tion, kom″pi·lā′shan, *n.* The act of compiling or collecting from written or printed documents or books; that which is compiled, such as a book or treatise drawn up by compiling.

com·pile, kom·pīl′, *v.t.*—*compiled, compiling.* [L. *compilo,* to pillage.] To put (various materials) into a volume; to draw together; to translate (a code) into machine language for use by a computer. —**com·pil·er,** kom·pī′lẹr, *n.* One who compiles.

com·pla·cence, kom·plā′sens, *n.* A feeling of quiet pleasure based on self-satisfaction.

com·pla·cen·cy, kom·plā′sen·sē, *n. pl.* **com·pla·cen·cies.** Complacence, usu. coupled with lack of awareness of existing or potential problems.

com·pla·cent, kom·plā′sent, *a.* [L.L. *complacens* (-*ent*-), ppr. of *complacere,* take pleasure, L. please at the same time, be pleasing. < L. *com-,* with, and *placere,* please.] Pleased with oneself or one's own merits or advantages; self-satisfied; complaisant.—**com·pla·cent·ly,** *adv.*

com·plain, kom·plān′, *v.i.* [Fr. *complaindre,* < L.L.] To utter expressions of grief, pain, uneasiness, censure, or resentment; to lament; to murmur; to bewail; to make a formal accusation against a person; to make a charge, followed by *of.*—

com·plain·a·ble, *a.*—**com·plain·er,** *n.* —**com·plain·ing·ly,** *adv.*

com·plain·ant, kom·plā′nant, *n.* One who complains or makes a complaint; a complainer; *law,* one who prosecutes by complaint, or commences a legal process against an alleged offender; a plaintiff.

com·plaint, kom·plānt′, *n.* [Fr. *complainte.*] Expression of grief, regret, pain, censure, or resentment; lamentation; murmuring; a finding fault; the cause or subject of complaint or murmuring; a malady; an ailment; a disease: usually applied to disorders not serious; a charge; a representation of injuries suffered; accusation; *law,* the first allegation made by a plaintiff in a civil court.

com·plai·sance, kom·plā′sans, kom·plā′zans, kom′pla·zans″, *n.* [Fr. *complaisance,* < *complaisant,* ppr. of *complaire,* to please = L. *complacere.* COMPLACENT.] A pleasing deportment; affability; civility; courtesy; desire to please; disposition to oblige.

com·plai·sant, kom·plā′sant, kom·plā′zant, kom′pla·zant″, *a.* [Fr. ppr. of *complaire,* please, humor, < L. *complacere,* take pleasure.] Disposed to please; obliging; agreeable; gracious; compliant.—**com·plai·sant·ly,** *adv.*—**com·plai·sant·ness,** *n.*

com·plect·ed, kom·plek′tid, *a.* Colloq. complexioned; as, dark-*complected.*

com·ple·ment, kom′ple·ment, *n.* [L. *complementum,* that which fills up, later fulfillment, accomplishment, < *complere,* fill up, complete. Cf. *compliment.*] That which completes or makes perfect, specif. a word or words used to complete a grammatical construction; full quantity or amount; complete allowance, specif. the full number of officers and crew required to man a ship; the quantity or amount which when added completes a whole; either of two parts or things needed to complete each other; *geom.* the angular amount needed to bring a given arc or angle to 90°. The interval which when added to a given interval completes a musical octave.—kom′ple·ment″, *v.t.* To complete; form a complement to.

com·ple·men·tal, kom″ple·men′tal, *a.* Forming a complement; completing; complementary.

com·ple·men·ta·ry, kom·ple·men′ta·rē, kom·ple·men′trē, *a.* Completing; supplying a deficiency; complemental.

com·ple·men·ta·ry an·gle, *n.* An angle in relation to another given angle where the combination produces an angle of 90 degrees.

com·ple·men·ta·ry col·ors, *n. pl.* Primary or secondary colors in the spectrum which, when combined, make another color.

com·ple·men·ta·tion, kom″ple·men·tā′shan, *n.* The principle in linguistics governing the relation of members of linguistic units that have no environment in common; as, *t* in *tone* and *t* in *stone,* the former being aspirated and the latter unaspirated. Also **com·ple·men·ta·ry dis·tri·bu·tion.**

com·ple·ment fix·a·tion, *n.* In immunological experimentation, a process which involves the addition of complement to a substance produced by the union of an antigen and its antibody.

com·plete, kom·plēt′, *a.* [L. *completus,* pp. of *completo, completum,* to fill up.] Having no deficiency; wanting no part or element; perfect; thorough; consummate in every respect; finished; ended; concluded.— **com·plet·a·ble,** *a.*—**com·plete·ly,** *adv.* —**com·plete·ness,** *n.*—**com·ple·tive,** *a.* —**com·ple·tive·ly,** *adv.*

com·plete, kom·plēt′, *v.t.*—*completed, completing.* To make complete; to finish; to end; to perfect; to fulfill, to accomplish; to realize.

com·plete fer·ti·liz·er, *n.* A fertilizer consisting of phosphoric acid, potash, and nitrogen in prescribed proportions.

com·ple·tion, kom·plē'shan, *n.* Act of completing, finishing, or perfecting; state of being complete or completed; perfect state; fulfillment; accomplishment.

com·plex, kom·pleks', kom'pleks, *a.* [L. *complexus,* pp. of *complecti,* entwine, embrace, < *com-,* with, and *plectere,* plait.] Composed of interconnected parts; compound; composite; esp. characterized by an involved combination of parts; complicated; intricate.—**com·plex sen·tence,** *n. Gram.* a sentence containing one or more dependent clauses in addition to the principal clause.

com·plex, kom'pleks, *n.* [L. *complexus,* n., < *complecti.*] A structural whole comprising interconnected parts; as, a school *complex,* an industrial *complex;* a complicated assemblage of particulars. *Psychoanalysis,* a group of ideas or mental processes which for some reason has been inhibited or restrained, or has not been assimilated by or brought into harmony with the main body of the mental processes, and which is regarded as the causative agent in the production of certain abnormal mental states; an emotional experience which has been repressed because of its painful or disagreeable content. *Colloq.* a fixed idea; an obsessive or predominating notion.

com·plex frac·tion, *n.* A fraction in which either the numerator or denominator or both contain a fraction or a mixed number.

com·plex·ion, kom·plek'shan, *n.* [L. *complexio, complexionis,* a combination, in L.L. physical constitution, < *ccmplector, complexus.*] The temperament, habitude, or natural disposition of the body or mind; physical character or nature; the color or hue of the skin, particularly of the face; the general appearance of anything.—**com·plex·ioned,** *a.* Having a complexion of this or that kind; having a certain hue, esp. of the skin.

com·plex·i·ty, kom·plek'si·tē, *n. pl.* **com·plex·i·ties.** The state or quality of being complex; intricacy; something complex.—**com·plex·ly,** *adv.*—**com·plex·ness,** *n.*

com·pli·ance, kom·plī'ans, *n.* The act of complying with a demand or an order; an acquiescence or yielding; a disposition to yield to others.

com·pli·an·cy, kom·plī'an·sē, *n. pl.* **com·pliancies.** Compliance.

com·pli·ant, kom·plī'ant, *a.* Complying; yielding; obliging.—**com·pli·ant·ly,** *adv.*

com·pli·ca·cy, kom'pli·ka·sē, *n. pl.* **com·pli·ca·cies.** The state of being complex or intricate.

com·pli·cate, kom'pli·kāt', *v.t.*—*complicated, complicating.* [L. *complicatus,* pp. of *complicare,* < *com-,* with, and *plicare,* fold.] To fold or twine together; combine intricately with; render complex, intricate, or involved.—*v.i.* To become intricate.

com·pli·cate, kom'pli·kit, *a.* Composed of various parts intimately united; complex; involved; intricate; *bot.* folded together lengthwise.

com·pli·cat·ed, kom'pli·kā"tid, *a.* Composed of intricately connected parts; involved; difficult to comprehend.—**com·pli·cat·ed·ly,** *adv.*—**com·pli·cat·ed·ness,** *n.*

com·pli·ca·tion, kom"pli·kā'shan, *n.* The act of complicating or state of being complicated; entanglement; complexity; something complicated; an aggregate of things involved, mixed up, or mutually united; that which complicates or causes complication; *med.* a secondary illness which may develop during a primary disease.—**com·pli·ca·tive,** kom'pli·kā"tiv, *a.*

com·plic·i·ty, kom·plis'i·tē, *n. pl.* **com·**plic·i·ties. The state of being an accomplice; partnership in crime.

com·pli·er, kom·plī'ér, *n.* [COMPLY.] One who complies.

com·pli·ment, kom'pli·ment, *n.* [Fr. *compliment,* It. *complimento,* < *complire,* to fill up, to satisfy, L. *compleo, complere,* to complete: same word as *complement,* which formerly was used in this sense.] An act or expression of civility, respect, or regard; delicate flattery; expression of commendation or admiration; praise.—**com·pli·ments,** *n.* Good wishes.

com·pli·ment, kom'pli·ment", *v.t.* To pay a compliment to; to flatter or gratify by expressions of approbation, esteem, or respect, or by acts implying respect and approbation.—**com·pli·ment·a·ble,** *a.*—**com·pli·ment·er,** *n.*—**com·pli·ment·ing·ly,** *adv.*

com·pli·men·ta·ry, kom"pli·men'ta·rē, kom"pli·men'trē, *a.* Full of or using compliments; intended to express or convey a compliment or compliments; expressive of civility, regard or praise.—**com·pli·men·ta·ri·ly,** *adv.*

com·pline, kom'plin, *n.* [< Fr. *complie,* < L. *completae (horae),* "complete hours": so-called because this service completes the religious exercises of the day.] *Eccles.* The last of the seven canonical hours in the Roman Catholic breviary; the last prayer at night, to be recited after sunset. Also **com·plin.**

com·ply, kom·plī', *v.t.*—*complied, complying.* [Appar. < It. *complire,* fulfill, complete, < L. *complere,* complete.] To fulfill; execute.—*v.i.* To be complaisant or accommodating; to act in accordance with wishes, requests, commands, requirements, or conditions; acquiesce; yield; conform.

com·po, kom'pō, *n. pl.* **com·pos.** Shortened form of *composition,* esp. as the name of various composite substances in industrial use.

com·po·nent, kom·pō'nent, *n.* [L. *compono,* construct.] A constituent. *Phys.* the effective part of a force or velocity in a given direction; one of any number of vectors which are added together to form a vector sum.

com·po·nent, kom·pō'nent, *a.* Composing; constituting; entering into as a part.

com·port, kom'pōrt, kom'part, *n.* [Appar. a corruption of *compote.*] A dish, usually having a supporting stem, for holding compotes and fruit; a compote.

com·port, kom·pōrt', kom·part', *v.t.* [Fr. *comporter,* bear, behave, < L. *comportare,* carry together, < *com-,* with, and *portare,* carry.] To bear or conduct (oneself); behave.—*v.i.* To agree or accord with; suit.

com·port·ment, kom·pōrt'ment, kom·part'ment, *n.* Behavior; demeanor; deportment.

com·pose, kom·pōz', *v.t.*—*composed, composing.* [< Fr. *composer,* to compose, < prefix *com,* and *poser,* to place, L. *pausare* (see POSE), but early identified with L. *compono, compositum,* to compound, < *com-,* and *pono,* to place; so also *dispose, expose.*] To form by uniting two or more things; to form, frame, or fashion; to form by being combined or united; to constitute; to make; to write, as an author; to become the author of, as a book, a piece of music; to calm; to quiet; to appease; to settle; to adjust, as differences, etc.; to place in proper form; to dispose; *fine arts,* to arrange the leading features of; *printing,* to set in proper order for printing, as type in a composing stick.—*v.i.* To practice literary, musical, or artistic composition.

com·posed, kom·pōzd', *a.* Free from disturbance or agitation; calm; sedate; quiet; tranquil.—**com·pos·ed·ly,** *adv.*

com·pos·er, kom·pō'zèr, *n.* One who or that which composes; one who writes an original work; most commonly, one who composes musical pieces.

com·pos·ing stick, *n. Print.* a compositor's hand-held tray, in which type is set.

com·pos·ite, kom·poz'it, *a.* [L. *compositus,* pp. of *componere,* put together, compound, compose, < *com-,* with, and *ponere,* place, put: cf. *compose.*] Made up of various parts or elements; compound; *(cap.), arch.* noting or pertaining to a classical (Roman) order in which the capital contains features of other orders; *(l.c.), bot.* belonging to *Compositæ,* the largest vegetable family of plants, including the daisy, dandelion, and aster, in which the florets are borne in a close head resembling a single flower.

com·pos·ite, kom·poz'it, *n.* Something composite; a compound; *bot.* a composite plant.—**com·pos·ite·ly,** *adv.*—**com·pos·ite·ness,** *n.*

com·pos·ite num·ber, *n. Math.* a number exactly divisible by some number other than itself.

com·pos·ite school, *n. Canada,* a secondary school which gives courses in commerical, industrial, and academic subjects.

com·po·si·tion, kom"po·zish'on, *n.* [O.Fr. Fr. *composition,* < L. *compositio(n-),* < *componere.* COMPOSITE.] The act of combining parts to form a whole; the manner in which such parts are combined; the resulting state or product; make-up or constitution; a compound or composite substance; *gram.* the creation of compound words like *campfire.* The act or the manner of composing prose or verse or a musical or artistic work; the resulting production or work; a short essay written as a school exercise; the setting up of type for printing. A settlement by mutual agreement; an agreement or compromise, esp. one by which a creditor accepts partial payment from a debtor; a sum of money so paid.—**com·pos·i·tive,** kom·poz'i·tiv, *a.*

com·po·si·tion of forc·es, *n. Mech.* the union or combination of two or more forces acting in the same or in different directions into a single equivalent force, called the resultant.

com·pos·i·tor, kom·poz'i·tèr, *n.* [L., a composer, arranger, < *componere.* COMPOSITE.] *Printing,* one who sets type; a typesetter.

com·pos men·tis, kōm'pōs men'tis, *a. Brit.* kom'pos men'tis. [L., having control of one's mind.] Of sound mind.

com·post, kom'pōst, *n.* [O.Fr. *compost,* < L. *compositus.* COMPOSITE.] A composition or compound; esp. a mixture of various substances, as dung or dead leaves, for fertilizing land.—*v.t.* To treat with or make into compost.

com·po·sure, kom·pō'zhèr, *n.* The state of being composed; a settled state of mind; sedateness; calmness; tranquillity.

com·po·ta·tion, kom"po·tā'shan, *n.* [L. *compotatio*—*com,* with, and *potatio,* < *poto,* to drink.] The act of drinking alcoholic beverages or tippling together.—**com·po·ta·tor,** kom' po·tā"tèr, *n.* One who drinks with another.

com·pote, kom'pōt, *Fr.* kạn·pōt', *n.* [Fr.] Fruit, generally such stone fruit as peaches, apricots, or cherries, stewed or preserved in syrup and served as dessert; a decorative dish, often footed, sometimes covered.

com·pound, kom·pound', *v.t.* [M.E. *compounen,* < O.Fr. *compondre* < L. *componere.* COMPOSITE.] To put together into a whole; combine; to make or form by combining parts or elements; construct; to make up or constitute; to aggravate or heighten by adding something new; as: His desolation was *compounded* by her indifference. To settle or adjust by agreement, esp. for a reduced amount, as a debt; to agree, for a consideration, not to prosecute a crime; *elect.* to wind (a dynamo or a motor) so that part of the field-magnet coils are in series with the armature circuit and part are shunted from it so the machine can regulate itself.—*v.i.* To make a bargain; come to terms; compromise; settle a debt by compromise.

com·pound, kom′pound, kom·pound′, *a.* Composed of two or more parts, elements, or ingredients; involving two or more actions or functions; composite.

com·pound, kom′pound, *n.* Something formed by compounding or combining parts, elements, or ingredients; *chem.* a distinct substance which is designated by a definite formula when produced by combining two or more different elements in fixed proportion by weight.

com·pound, kom′pound, *n.* [Cf. Malay *kampong,* enclosure.] A large area enclosed by a wall or fence; in the Orient, such an enclosure containing homes and commercial buildings of Europeans; in Africa, such an area for native laborers; *milit.* any enclosure, but esp. one for prisoners of war.

com·pound air·craft, *n.* A helicopter equipped with fixed wings and propeller or jet engines.

com·pound-com·plex, kom′pound·kom′-pleks, *a. Gram.* pertaining to a sentence in which there are two or more independent clauses and one or more dependent clauses.

com·pound frac·ture, *n.* A fracture in which a bone is broken and the fracture exposed by laceration of the tissues.

com·pound in·ter·est, *n.* That interest computed from the principal plus its accrued interest.

com·pound leaf, *n.* A leaf composed of a number of leaflets on a common stalk. It may be either digitately or pinnately compound, and the leaflets themselves may be compound.

com·pound mi·cro·scope, *n.* An optical instrument for magnifying objects, consisting of two lenses of different focal lengths mounted on the same viewer.

com·pound num·ber, *n.* A quantity expressed in more than one denomination or unit, as the length 1 foot 6 inches.

com·pound sen·tence, *n.* A sentence consisting of two or more independent clauses, usu. connected by one or more conjunctions.

com·pound word, *n.* A word made up of two or more words which retain their separate form and signification.

com·pra·dor, kom″pra·dạr′, *n.* [Pg., a buyer, purveyor.] In many countries, a native agent or factotum, as of a foreign business house. Also **com·pra·dore.**

com·pre·hend, kom″pri·hend′, *v.t.* [L. *comprehendo*—*com-,* together, *præ,* before, *hendere,* to catch.] To take into the mind; to grasp by the understanding; to possess or have in idea; to understand; to take in or include within a certain scope; to include by implication or signification; to embrace; to comprise.

com·pre·hen·si·bil·i·ty, kom″pri·hen′-si·bil′i·tē, *n.* The quality of being comprehensible; the capability of being understood.

com·pre·hen·si·ble, kom″pri·hen′si·bl, *a.* [L. *comprehensibilis.*] Capable of being comprehended; capable of being understood; conceivable by the mind; intelligible. Also **com·pre·hend·i·ble.** *a.*—**com·pre·-hen·si·ble·ness,** *n.*—**com·pre·hen·si·bly,** *adv.*

com·pre·hen·sion, kom″pri·hen′shan, *n.* [L. *comprehensio.*] The act of comprehending, including, or embracing; a comprising; inclusion; capacity of the mind to understand; power of the understanding to receive and contain ideas; capacity of knowing.

com·pre·hen·sive, kom″pri·hen′siv, *a.* Having the quality of comprehending or embracing a great number or a wide extent; of extensive application; wide in scope; having the power to comprehend or understand.—**com·pre·hen·sive·ly,** *adv.*—**com·pre·hen·sive·ness,** *n.*

com·press, kom·pres′, *v.t.* [L. *compressus,* pp. of *comprimere,* < *com-,* together, and *premere,* press.] To press together; force into a smaller space; to form into a solid mass; condense.—**com·press·i·ble,** *a.*—**com·press·i·bil·i·ty,** *n.*

com·press, kom·pres, *n. Med.* a soft pad, usually of cloth, used as a means of applying pressure, moisture, cold, heat, or medication. An apparatus or establishment for compressing cotton bales.

com·pressed, kom·prest′, *a.* Pressed into a smaller area; condensed; squeezed together; *bot.* flattened laterally or along the length; *zool.* narrow from side to side, and therefore of greater height than width.

com·pressed air, *n.* Air which has been mechanically compressed, and which, on account of its expansive force, is used to operate such mechanisms as drills.

com·pres·sion, kom·presh′on, *n.* The act of compressing or the state of being compressed; also **com·pres·sure.** The process of reducing the volume of the working substance in an internal-combustion engine while increasing its pressure.—**com·-pres·sion·al,** *a.*

com·pres·sion cham·ber, *n. Aeron.* a strongly built chamber in which air pressure can be increased to two or more atmospheres for testing the functional processes of personnel and equipment.

com·pres·sive, kom·pres′iv, *a.* Having power to compress; tending to compress.—**com·pres·sive·ly,** *adv.*

com·pres·sor, kom·pres′ẽr, *n.* [L.] One who or that which compresses; *anat.* a muscle that compresses some part of the body; *surg.* an instrument for compressing a part of the body. A machine that reduces the volume of gases and increases their pressure so they can be used in refrigeration or for driving an engine.

com·prise, kom·prīz′, *v.t.*—*comprised, comprising.* [Fr. *compris,* part. of *comprendre,* L. *comprehendo,* to comprehend. COMPREHEND.] To contain; to include; to consist of; be made up of, as: The United States *comprises* various states. To form; to make up, as: Twenty-six characters *comprise* our alphabet.

com·pro·mise, kom′pro·mīz″, *n.* [O.Fr. Fr. *compromis* < L. *compromissum,* prop. pp. neut. of *compromittere.*] An agreement to abide by the decision of an arbiter; arbitration; a settlement of differences by mutual concessions; an adjustment of conflicting claims or principles by the sacrifice or surrender of a part of each; anything resulting from compromise; something intermediate between different things; a compromising or endangering, as of reputation.

com·pro·mise, kom′pro·mīz″, *v.t.*—*compromised, compromising.* To settle by a compromise; to bring to terms; to render liable to suspicion by lax conduct; endanger, as to reputation; involve unfavorably; commit.—*v.i.* To make a compromise.—**com·pro·mis·er,** *n.*—**com·pro·mis·ing·ly,** *adv.*

comp·trol·ler, kon·trō′lẽr, *n.* A controller; an officer who examines expenditures and checks finances of a company.—**comp·-trol·ler·ship,** *n.* The office of comptroller.

com·pul·sion, kom·pul′shan, *n.* [L. *compulsio, compulsionis,* constraint, compulsion, < *compello, compulsum,* to compel.] The act of compelling or the state of being compelled; a strong, irresistible impulse to carry out an act.

com·pul·sive, kom·pul′siv, *a.* Exercising compulsion; compulsory; dictated by irresistible psychological urges.—**com·pul·-sive·ly,** *adv.* By or under compulsion.

com·pul·so·ry, kom·pul′so·rē, *a.* Exercising compulsion; compelling; constraining; enforced; due to compulsion; mandatory; as a *compulsory* contribution.—**com·pul·so·ri·ly,** *adv.*

com·punc·tion, kom·pungk′shan, *n.* [L. *compunctio,* to sting.] A questioning of the rightness of one's actions; a qualm; an uneasiness of mind or conscience; regret for wrongdoing or for causing pain or unhappiness; guilt; remorse.—**com·-punc·tious,** kom·pungk′shus, *a.*

com·pur·ga·tion, kom″pẽr·gā′shan, *n.* [L.L. *compurgatio(n-),* < L. *compurgare,* purify completely, < *com-,* altogether, and *purgare,* purge.] Formerly, in common law, the legal clearing of one accused, by the oaths of persons testifying to his innocence or veracity; in general, a vindication of one accused.—**com·pur·ga·tor,** kom′pẽr·gā″tẽr, *n.*—**com·pur·ga·to·ry,** kom·pụr′ga·tōr″ē, kom·pụr′ga·tạr″ē, *a.*

com·put·a·ble, kom·pūt′a·bl, *a.* Capable of being computed, numbered, or reckoned.—**com·put·a·bil·i·ty,** *n.*

com·pu·ta·tion, kom″pū·tā′shan, *n.* [L. *computatio.*] The act or process of computing, reckoning, or estimating; calculation; the result of a computation.—**com·pu·ta·tion·al,** *a.*—**com·pu·ta·tive,** *a.*—**com·pu·ta·tive·ly,** *adv.*

com·pute, kom·pūt′, *v.t.*—*computed, computing.* [L. *computo,* to calculate—*com,* together, and *puto,* to reckon, esteem, whence also *dispute, impute.* To *count* is really the same as this word.] To determine by calculation; to count; to reckon; to calculate; to estimate.—*v.i.* To reckon by means of a computer or data processing machine.—*n.* Computation, reckoning.

com·put·er, kom·pū′tẽr, *n.* An electronic contrivance which solves problems and does complicated calculations by processing data according to prescribed, programmed instructions and then produces and/or retains the outcome of these processes; one who computes; a reckoner; a calculator.

com·put·er·i·za·tion, kom·pū″te·rī·zā′-shan, *n.* The operation or procedure of computerizing.

com·put·er·ize, kom·pū′te·rīz″, *v.t.*—*computerized, computerizing.* To execute, regulate, or store with a computer; to furnish with computers.

com·put·er lan·guage, *n.* Letters, numbers, and arithmetical symbols combined to form a symbolic language which can be fed into a computer.

com·put·er pro·gram, *n.* A system or design for finding the solution to a problem on a computer: a set of ordered instructions for a computer.

com·put·er u·til·i·ty, *n.* A service which provides computational ability to several clients; a "time-shared" computer system.

com·rade, kom′rad, *Brit.* kom′rid, kum′rid, *n.* [O.E. *camarade, camerade,* < Sp. *camarada,* Fr. *camarade,* one who occupies the same chamber, < L. *camera,* a chamber.] A close friend or intimate associate; a companion in work, interests, or activities; a fellow soldier or other fighting man; (*cap.*) a Communist party member or person holding strong leftist political views.—**com·rade·ship,** *n.* The state or feeling of being a comrade; companionship.

Com·sat, kom′sat″, *n.* The short form of *communications satellite;* a man-made device designed to revolve in a closed path or orbit around the earth, relaying or reflecting electromagnetic signals used for communicative purposes.

---

ch- chain, G. na*ch*t; **th-** THen, thin; **w-** wig, hw as sound in whig; **z-** zh as in azure, zeal. *Italicized vowel* indicates schwa sound.

Com·ti·an, kom'tē·an, a. Of or pertaining to the French philosopher Auguste Comte, 1798–1857, or his system of philosophy. See *positivism*.—**Comt·ism**, n. The philosophical system founded by Auguste Comte; positivism.—**Comt·ist**, n.

con, kon, v.t.—*conned, conning*. [A form of *can*.] To peruse carefully and attentively; to study over; to learn; *naut.* to direct the steering of, as a ship.

con, kon, adv. [Abbrev. < L. *contra*, against.] Against, in the phrase *pro and con*, for and against.—n. A statement, argument, or consideration supporting the negative side of a question; as, to discuss the *pros* and *cons*.

con, kon, v.t.—*conned, conning. Slang.* To deceive or swindle; to trick; to persuade through deception.—a.

co·na·tion, kō·nā'shan, n. [L. *conatio(n)-*, < *conari* (pp. *conatus*), endeavor, try.] *Psychol.* one of the three modes, together with cognition and affection, of mental function; a conscious effort to carry out seemingly volitional acts.

co·na·tive, kon'a·tiv, kō'na·tiv, a. [L. *conatus*, pp.] *Psychol.* pertaining to or of the nature of conation as distinguished from feeling and cognition; *gram.* expressing endeavor or effort; as, a *conative* verb.

co·na·tus, kō·nā'tus, n. pl. **co·na·tus**. [L. < *conari*.] An effort or striving; *biol.* a natural force or tendency simulating a human effort; *philos.* a term used by Spinoza for the striving of all living things toward self-affirmation and self-preservation.

con bri·o, kon brē'ō, adv. *Mus.* energetically, with vigor: used as a direction to the performer.

con·cat·e·nate, kon·kat'e·nāt', v.t.—*concatenated, concatenating.* [L. *concateno, concatenatum*, to link together.] To link together; to unite in a successive series or chain, as things depending on each other.—a. Linked together.—**con·cat·e·na·tion**, kon·kat'e·nā'shan, n.

con·cave, kon·kāv', a. [L. *concavus*—*con-*, and *cavis*, hollow.] Hollow and curved or rounded, as the inner surface of a spherical body; incurved—v.t.—*concaved, concaving.* To make concave.—**con·cave·ly**, adv. —**con·cave·ness**, n.

con·cave, kon'kāv, n. A concave surface, line, or segment; an arch or vault; a cavity.

con·cav·i·ty, kon·kav'i·tē, n. pl. **con·cav·i·ties**. A concave surface, or the space contained in it; hollowness.

con·cav·o-con·cave, kon·kā'vō·kon·kāv', a. Concave or hollow on both surfaces, as a lens.

con·ca·vo-con·vex, kon·kā'vō·kon·veks', a. Concave on one side and convex on the other; pertaining to a lens in which the concave face has a greater degree of curvature than the convex face, the lens being thinnest in the middle.

con·ceal, kon·sēl', v.t. [< L. *concelo*.] To hide; to withdraw from observation; to cover or keep from sight; to keep close or secret; to refrain from disclosing; to withhold from utterance or declaration.—**con·ceal·a·ble**, a.—**con·ceal·ment**, n. The act of concealing, hiding, or keeping secret; the state of being hid or concealed; privacy; shelter from observation; cover from sight.

con·cede, kon·sēd', v.t.—*conceded, conceding.* [L. *concedo, concessum*, to yield, grant.] To admit as true, just, or proper; to grant; to let pass undisputed; to grant as a privilege; to yield up; to allow; to acknowledge, as an opponent's victory, before an official decision has been made.—v.i. To make concession; to grant a request or petition; to yield.—**con·ced·er**, n.

con·ceit, kon·sēt', n. [M.E. *conceyte*; related to *conceive* as *deceit* to *deceive*.] An exaggerated opinion of one's own worth or importance; that which is conceived in the mind; a thought; an idea; favorable opinion; esteem; imagination or fancy; a fancy or whim; an ingenious or witty thought or expression; a fanciful metaphor, esp. of strained or far-fetched nature; the use of such metaphors as a literary characteristic.

con·ceit·ed, kon·sē'tid, a. Having an exaggerated opinion of oneself, or of one's qualities or abilities, vain.—**con·ceit·ed·ly**, adv.—**con·ceit·ed·ness**, n.

con·ceiv·a·ble, kon·sē'va·bl, a. Capable of being conceived, thought, imagined, or understood. — **con·ceiv·a·bil·i·ty**, con·ceiv·a·ble·ness, n.—**con·ceiv·a·bly**, a.

con·ceive, kon·sēv', v.t.—*conceived, conceiving.* [O.Fr. *conceveir* (Fr. *concevoir*), < L. *concipere* (pp. *conceptus*), < *con-*, with, and *capere*, take.] To become pregnant with; to form in the mind; form a notion or idea of; imagine; to form, as a notion, opinion, or purpose; to experience or entertain, as a feeling; to express, as in words. —v.i. To become pregnant; to form an idea of; think.—**con·ceiv·er**, n.

con·cen·ter, kon·sen'tẽr, v.i. To converge or meet in a common center; to combine or be united in one object.—v.t. To draw or direct to a common center; to concentrate.

con·cen·trate, kon'sen·trāt', v.t.—*concentrated, concentrating.* [Fr. *concentrer*- L. *con-*, together, and *centrum*, a center.] To bring to a common center or point of union; to cause to come together to one spot or point; to bring to bear on one point; to direct toward one object, as all one's attention; in chemical manipulations, to intensify by removing nonessential matter; to reduce to a state of great strength and purity.—v.i. To approach or meet in a common point or center.—**con·cen·tra·tive**, a.—**con·cen·tra·tor**, n.

con·cen·trate, kon'sen·trāt', n. A concentrated form of something; a product of concentration.

con·cen·tra·tion, kon"sen·trā'shan, n. The act of concentrating; concentrated state; exclusive attention to one object; close mental application; something concentrated.

con·cen·tra·tion camp, n. Barracks with stockade, patrolled by the military, used for the detention and punishment of people politically, economically, or racially adverse to the policies of the government, esp. in Europe during World War II.

con·cen·tric, kon·sen'trik, a. [M.L. *concentricus*, < L. *con-*, with, and *centrum*, center.] Having a common center, as circles or spheres; specif. *mineral.* occurring in or having parallel layers arranged about a common center. Also **con·cen·tri·cal**.—**con·cen·tri·cal·ly**, adv.—**con·cen·tric·i·ty**, kon"sen·tris'i·tē, n.

con·cept, kon'sept, n. [L. *conceptus*, a conceiving, a thought, < *concipere*.] That which is conceived in the mind; a general notion or idea; a conception.

con·cep·ta·cle, kon·sep'ta·kl, n. [L. *conceptaculum*, < *concipere*.] *Biol.* in certain algae and fungi, an external organ or cavity enclosing reproductive bodies.

con·cep·tion, kon·sep'shon, n. [O.Fr. Fr. *conception*, < L. *conceptio(n)-*, < *concipere*.] The act of conceiving, or the state of being conceived; the inception of pregnancy; the inception of life; beginning; that which is conceived; the embryo or fetus; the act or power of forming notions, ideas, or concepts; a notion or idea; a concept; a design or plan. —**con·cep·tion·al**, a.—**con·cep·tive**, a.

con·cep·tu·al, kon·sep'chō·al, a. [L. *conceptus*, a thought.] Pertaining to concepts or their formation.

con·cep·tu·al·ism, kon·sep'chō·a·liz"um, n. The philosophical doctrine, midway between nominalism and realism, that universals have existence, in that they exist in the mind; the doctrine that general and abstract terms, as *horse, red*, can be fully represented in thought.—**con·cep·tu·al·ist**, n.—**con·cep·tu·al·is·tic**, a.—**con·cep·tu·al·ly**, adv.

con·cep·tu·al·ize, kon·sep'chō·a·līz", v.t. —*conceptualized, conceptualizing.* To form into a concept.—v.i. To think in concepts.—**con·cep·tu·al·i·za·tion**, n.

con·cern, kon·sẽrn', v.t. [M.L. *concernere*, relate to, L.L. mix.] To relate to; be connected with; be of interest or importance to; affect; to interest, engage, or involve: used reflectively or in the passive, often with *with* or *in*; as, to *concern* oneself *with* a matter, to be *concerned in* a transaction; to disquiet or trouble, now used in the passive, as: He was *concerned* about my health.

con·cern, kon·sẽrn', n. Relation; important relation or bearing; interest; participation; solicitude or anxiety; a matter or affair; a matter that engages one's attention, interest, or care; a commercial or manufacturing firm or establishment.

con·cerned, kon·sẽrnd', a. Interested; troubled or anxious.—**con·cern·ed·ly**, adv.

con·cern·ing, kon·sẽr'ning, prep. [Orig. ppr.] Relating to; regarding; about.

con·cern·ment, kon·sẽrn'ment, n. Relation or bearing; interest; anxiety or solicitude; a concern in which one is involved.

con·cert, kon·sẽrt', v.t. [Fr. *concerter*, < It. *concertare*: cf. L. *concertare*, contend, also *conserere* (pp. *consertus*), join together.] To contrive or arrange by agreement; plan; devise; *mus.* to arrange in parts for several voices or instruments.—v.i. To plan or act together.

con·cert, kon'sẽrt, kon'sert, n. [Fr. *concert*, < It. *concerto*, < *concertare*.] Agreement of two or more in a design or plan; combined action; accord or harmony; a musical performance in which several singers or players, or both, participate.—**con·cert·mas·ter**, n. The first violinist of an orchestra, who is usually also the assistant conductor.

con·cert·ed, kon·sẽr'tid, a. Contrived or arranged by agreement; planned or devised together; done in concert; *mus.* arranged in parts for several voices or instruments.

con·cer·ti·na, kon"sẽr·tē'na, n. [< *concert*, n.] A small, portable bellowslike musical instrument, commonly with polygonal ends, similar in principle to the accordion but with a more limited range.—**con·cer·ti·nist**, n.

con·cer·ti·no, kon"cher·tē'nō, It. kan"·cher·tē'na, n. pl. **con·cer·ti·ni**, kon"cher·tē'nē. [It., dim. of *concerto*.] *Mus.* A short concerto; in a concerto grosso, the group of solo instruments.

con·cer·to, kon·cher'tō, It. kan·cher'ta, n. pl. **con·cer·tos**, It. **con·cer·ti**, kan·cher'tē. [It.] A musical composition, usu. in a symphonic form, for one principal instrument, with accompaniments for a full orchestra.

con·cer·to gros·so, kon·cher'tō grō'sō, It. kan·cher'tō gras'sa, n. pl. **con·cer·ti gros·si**, kon·cher'tē grō'sē. A musical arrangement which alternates full orchestration with instrumental solos.

con·cert pitch, n. *Mus.* a pitch slightly higher than the ordinary pitch, used in tuning instruments for concert use.

con·ces·sion, kon·sesh'an, n. [L. *concessio(n)-*, < *concedere*. CONCEDE.] The act of conceding or yielding, as a right or privilege, or as a point or fact in an argument; that which is conceded; esp. something conceded by a government or a controlling authority, as a grant of land; a right, privilege, or franchise granted by a controlling authority to an individual, organization, or corporation to perform some special service or to conduct special sales activities within the limits of a larger enterprise, such as to vend cigarettes at a ball game, or to operate a beauty salon in a department store.

con·ces·sion·aire, kon·sesh″o·nâr′, n. [Fr.] One to whom a concession has been granted, as by a government or a business. Also **con·ces·sion·er.**

con·ces·sive, kon·ses′iv, a. [L.L. *concessivus.*] Tending or serving to concede; *gram.* expressing concession, as the conjunction *through.—n. Gram.* a concessive word, clause, or sentence.—**con·ces·sive·ly,** adv.

conch, kongk, konch, n. pl. **conchs, con·ches,** kongks, kon′chiz. [L. *concha,* < Gr. *cogchē,* mussel or cockle.] A shellfish, or its shell; any of several marine gastropods esp. *Strombus gigas;* the spiral shell of a gastropod, often used as a trumpet; *arch.* the concave interior surface of a dome.

con·chif·er·ous, kong·kif′er·us, a. Shell-bearing; *zool.* belonging or pertaining to the *Conchifera,* a group or class of mollusks including the oyster and clam.

con·chol·o·gy, kong·kol′o·jē, n. That department of zoology dealing with the nature, formation, and classification of the shells of mollusks.—**con·chol·o·gist,** n.

con·cierge, kon′sē·ârzh′, Fr. ka̱n·syerzh′, n. [Fr.; origin uncertain.] In France, one who has charge of the entrance of a building; a janitor or doorkeeper.

con·cil·i·ar, kon·sil′ē·êr, a. [< L. *concilium,* a council.] Pertaining to, relating to, or put forth by a council.

con·cil·i·ate, kon·sil′ē·āt″, v.t.—concili-ated, conciliating. [L. *conciliatus,* pp. of *conciliare,* bring together, < *concilium,* assembly, union.] To overcome, as distrust or hostility, by soothing or pacifying means; placate; win over; to win or gain, as regard or favor; to render accordant or compatible; reconcile.—**con·cil·i·at·ing·ly,** adv.

con·cin·ni·ty, kon·sin′i·tē, n. pl. **con·cin·ni·ties.** [L. *concinnitas,* < *concinnus,* well put together.] Harmonious adaptation of parts; fine adjustment of words and clauses in discourse or writing; elegance of structure or style; an example of rhetorical elegance.

con·cise, kon·sīs′, a. [L. *concisus,* pp. of *concidere,* cut off.] Expressing much in few words; brief and comprehensive; lacking superfluity and elaboration; succinct; terse. —**con·cise·ly,** adv.—**con·cise·ness,** n.

con·ci·sion, kon·sizh′on, n. [L. *concisio(n-),* < *concidere,* cut up or off.] Concise quality; brevity; terseness.

con·clave, kon′klāv, kong′klāv, n. [L. *conclave,* a private room, a closet—*con-,* together, and *clavis,* a key.] The private assembly or meeting of the cardinals for the election of a pope; the body of cardinals; a meeting of individuals with special power or influence; a secret assembly.

con·clude, kon·klōd′, v.t.—concluded, concluding. [L. *concludo—con,* and *claudo,* to shut; whence also *clause, close.*] To shut up or enclose (*N.T.*); to include or comprehend; to infer or arrive at by reasoning; to deduce, as from premises; to judge; to end, finish, bring to a conclusion; to settle or arrange finally; as, to *conclude* an agreement or a peace.—*v.i.* To infer; to form a final judgment; to come to a decision; to resolve; to determine, generally followed by an infinitive or a clause; to end; to make a finish.—**con·clud·er,** n.

con·clu·sion, kon·klō′zhan, n. [L. *con-clusio(n-).*] The end or close; the final part; the last main division of a discourse, containing a summing up of the points; a result, issue, or outcome; a deduction or inference; a proposition concluded or inferred from premises; final decision;

final settlement or arrangement, as of a treaty; *law,* an estoppel; *gram.* the con-cluding clause of a conditional sentence.

con·clu·sive, kon·klō′siv, a. Serving to settle or decide a question; decisive; convincing.—**con·clu·sive·ly,** adv.—**con·clu·sive·ness,** n.

con·coct, kon·kokt′, kon·kokt′, v.t. [L.] To form and prepare in the mind; to devise; to plot; to plot, as a scheme; to mix by combining different ingredients, as in cooking.—**con·coc·tion,** n. [L. *concoctio.*] The act of mixing ingredients or concocting; the thing concocted.—**con·coc·tive,** a.

con·com·i·tance, kon·kom′i·tans, n. The state of being together; connection with another thing. Also **con·com·i·tan·cy,** kon·kom′i·tan·sē.

con·com·i·tant, kon·kom′i·tant, kon·kom′i·tant, a. [L. *com,* together, and *comitor,* to accompany, < *comes,* a com-panion.] Accompanying; concurrent; attending; of things or circumstances.—*n.* A thing that accompanies another; an accompaniment; an accessory.—**con·com·i·tant·ly,** adv.

con·cord, kon′kard, kong′kard, n. [O.Fr. Fr. *concorde,* < L. *concordia,* < *concors,* of the same mind, < *con-,* with, and *cor* (*cord-*), heart.] Agreement between persons; concurrence in opinions or sentiments; unanimity; accord; hence, peace; some-times, a compact or treaty; agreement between things; harmony; *mus.* a har-monious combination of tones sounded together; *gram.* agreement of words gram-matically connected, as in gender, number, case, or person.

con·cord·ance, kon·kar′dans, kon·kar′dans, n. The state of being concordant; agreement; harmony; an alphabetical index of the principal words of a book, as of the Bible, with a reference to the passage in which each occurs and usually some part of the context; an alphabetical index of subjects or topics.

con·cord·ant, kon·kar′dant, kon·kar′dant, a. Agreeing; harmonious; correspondent; consistent.—**con·cord·ant·ly,** adv.

con·cor·dat, kon·kar′dat, n. [Fr. < M.L. *concordatum,* prop. pp. neut. of L. *con-cordare,* agree, E. *concord, v.*] An agreement; a compact; esp. an agreement between the Pope and a secular government regarding the regulation of ecclesiastical matters.

con·course, kon′kōrs, kon′ka̱rs, kong′kōrs, kong′ka̱rs, n. [Fr. *concours,* < L. *concursus,* < *concurro,* to run together—*con-,* and *curro,* to run.] A moving, flowing, or running together; confluence; a meeting or coming together of people; the people assembled; a crowd; a street, road or other broad thoroughfare; grounds used for racing or other athletic sports; an open space where people congregate, as in a railroad terminal.

con·cres·cence, kon·kres′ens, n. [L. *con-crescentia,* < *concrescere,* grow together, harden.] A growing together, as of parts or cells; coalescence.—**con·cres·cent,** a.

con·crete, kon′krēt, kon·krēt′, a. [L. *concretus,* pp. of *concrescere,* grow together, harden, < *con-,* with, and *crescere,* grow.] Formed by coalescence of separate particles into a mass; united in a coagulated, con-densed, or solid state; made of concrete; of an idea, term, or name, representing or applied to an actual substance or thing, as opposed to an abstract quality; hence, in general, constituting an actual thing or instance; particular, as opposed to general; pertaining to or concerned with realities or actual instances rather than abstractions; *math.* noting a number which relates to a particular object or thing.—**con·crete·ly,** adv.—**con·crete·ness,** n.

con·crete, kon′krēt, kon·krēt′, n. A mass formed by coalescence or concretion of

particles of matter; an artificial stonelike material used for foundations, made by mixing cement, sand, and broken stones with water, and allowing the mixture to harden; this material strengthened by a system of embedded iron or steel bars, netting, or the like, used for building; as, "reinforced *concrete*"; any of various other artificial building or paving materials, as those containing tar; a concrete idea or term; a concrete object or thing.

con·crete, kon·krēt′, v.t.—concreted, con-creting. To form into a mass by coalescence of particles; render solid; unite or combine, as qualities or attributes; to make concrete, as an idea.—kon·krēt′, kon′krēt, v.i. To coalesce into a mass; become solid; harden.

con·crete, kon·krēt′, kon·krēt′, v.t.—con-creted, concreting. To treat or lay with concrete.—*v.i.* To use or apply concrete.

con·cre·tion, kon·krē′shan, n. [L. *con-cretio(n-).*] The act or process of con-creting; the state of being concreted; coalescence; congelation; a solid mass formed by or as by coalescence or cohesion; *pathol.* a tophus or other hard inorganic mass found in the body; *geol.* a more or less rounded mass of mineral matter occurring in sandstone or clay, usually calcareous or siliceous and often composed of concentric layers deposited about a fossil, grain of sand, or other nucleus.—**con·cre·tion·al,** a.—**con·cre·tion·ar·y,** a.—**con·cre·tive,** a.—**con·cre·tive·ly,** adv.

con·cu·bi·nage, kon·kū′bi·nij, n. The state of being a concubine; cohabitation without benefit of religious or legal sanction. —**con·cu·bi·nar·y,** kon·kū′bi·ner″ē, a.

con·cu·bine, kong′kū·bīn″, kon′kū·bīn″, n. [L. *concubina,* < *concumbo,* lie together.] A woman who cohabits with a man without being legally married to him; a mistress; a secondary wife among certain polygamous peoples.

con·cu·pis·cence, kon·kū′pi·sens, n. [L. *concupiscentia,* < *concupisco,* to lust after.] Lust; ardent sexual longing; physical desire. —**con·cu·pis·cent,** kon·kū′pi·sent, a. Im-moderately desirous; lustful.—**con·cu·pis·ci·ble,** a.

con·cur, kon·kêr′, v.i.—concurred, con-curring. [L. *concurro,* to run together—*con-,* and *curro,* to run.] To agree, be in harmony; as, to *concur* with a person in an opinion; to combine; to unite in con-tributing to a common object; to coincide or take place simultaneously.

con·cur·rence, kon·kêr′ans, kon·kur′ans, n. The act of concurring; a simultaneous happening in time and place; cooperation or combination of agents, circumstances, or events; accordance in opinion; agreement.

con·cur·rent, kon·kêr′ant, kon·kur′ant, a. Concurring; tending to or meeting at the same point; occurring or existing together or side by side; having equal authority or jurisdiction; coordinate; acting in con-junction; cooperating or contributing to the same matter; accordant or agreeing.— *n.* One who or that which concurs.—**con·cur·rent·ly,** adv.—**con·cur·rent·ness,** n.

con·cur·rent res·o·lu·tion, n. In a legislative assembly, a resolution adopted by both branches, but unlike a joint resolution in the respect that it does not require the signature of the chief executive.

con·cuss, kon·kus′, v.t. [L. *concussus,* pp. of *concutere.*] To shake or shock; to injure (the brain) by concussion.

con·cus·sion, kon·kush′on, n. [L. *con-cussio(n-).*] The act of shaking or shocking, as by a blow; shock occasioned by the impact of a collision; injury to the brain or spine, from a blow or fall.—**con·cus·sive,** a.

con·demn, kon·dem′, v.t. [L. *condemnare,* < *con-,* altogether, and *damnare,* E. *damn.*]

To pronounce adverse judgment on; express strong disapproval of; censure; to afford occasion for convicting, as: His very looks *condemn* him. To pronounce to be guilty; sentence to punishment; doom; to adjudge to be unfit for use or service, as a ship; pronounce to be forfeited, as a prize of war; *law*, declare subject to use for a public purpose, under the right of eminent domain.—**con·dem·na·ble,** kon·dem′na·bl, *a.* [L.L. *condemnabilis.*] Deserving to be condemned.—**con·demn·er,** kon·dem′ẽr, *n.*

con·dem·na·tion, kon″dem·nā′shan,kon″-dem·nā′shan, *n.* [L. *condemnatio(n-).*] The act of condemning; the state of being condemned; cause for condemning.—**con·-dem·na·to·ry,** kon·dem′na·tōr″ē, *a.*

con·dem·na·tion pro·ceed·ings, *n. pl.* *Law,* the litigation required for seizure of property for public use.

con·den·sa·ble, con·den·si·ble, kon·-den′sa·bl, *a.* Capable of being condensed.

con·den·sate, kon·den′sāt, *n.* Something produced by condensation, as water from steam.

con·den·sa·tion, kon″den·sā′shan, kon″-den·sā′shan, *n.* [L. *condensatio.*] The act of condensing or making more compact; consolidation; the act of reducing a gas or vapor to a liquid or solid form; the reduction of a literary work to a more concise form; the product of such reduction; as, the *condensation* of a novel.—**con·den·sa·-tion·al,** *a.*

con·den·sa·tion trail, *n.* A visible trail of condensed water vapor or ice crystals left behind an aircraft in motion through the air. Also *contrail,* **va·por path, va·por scarf,** *vapor trail.*

con·dense, kon·dens′, *v.t.—condensed, condensing.* [L. *condenso—con-,* and *denso,* to make dense.] To make more dense or compact; to reduce the volume of; to consolidate; to compress or abridge; as, to *condense* a magazine article; to reduce, as a gas or vapor, to the condition of a solid or liquid.—*v.i.* To become more compact, as the particles of a body; to change from the vaporous to the liquid state.

con·densed, kon·denst′, *a.* Made dense or close in texture or composition; compressed; compact; *print.* denoting type that is narrow in relation to its height.

con·densed milk, *n.* Sweetened milk reduced by evaporation to a thick consistency.

con·dens·er, kon·den′sẽr, *n.* One who or that which condenses; an apparatus for condensing vapor to a liquid or solid form. *Elect.* a device for accumulating and holding a charge of electricity; a capacitor. *Opt.* a combination of lenses that concentrates and focuses light rays.

con·de·scend, kon″di·send′, *v.i.* [Fr. *condescendre*—L. *con-,* with, and *descendo.*] To descend voluntarily for a time to the level of an inferior; to stoop; to lower oneself intentionally; to assume or behave in a patronizing manner.—**con·de·scend·ing,** kon″di·sen′ding, *a.* Marked or characterized by condescension; stooping to the level of one's inferiors.—**con·de·scend·ing·ly,** *adv.*

con·de·scen·sion, kon″di·sen′shan, *n.* The act of condescending; the act of voluntary stooping to an equality with inferiors; a patronizing attitude on the part of a superior.—**con·de·scend·ence,** *n.*

con·dign, kon·dīn′, *a.* [L. *condignus,* well worthy—*con-,* and *dignus,* worthy.] Well deserved; merited; suitable: now always applied to punishment or something equivalent.—**con·dign·ly,** *adv.*

con·dig·ni·ty, kon·dig′ni·tē, *n. Philos.* a quality of merit which implies an equation of service rendered and its recompense.

con·di·ment, kon′di·ment, *n.* [L. *condimentum,* < *condio,* to season, pickle.] Something used to season food; a sauce, spice, or relish.

con·dis·ci·ple, kon″di·sī′pl, *n.* A student associate; a fellow learner; a schoolmate.

con·di·tion, kon·dish′on, *n.* [O.Fr. *condicion* (Fr. *condition*), < L. *condicio(n-),* erron. *conditio(n-),* agreement, stipulation, circumstances.] Something demanded as an essential part of an agreement; a stipulation; a circumstance indispensable to some result; a prerequisite; that on which something else is contingent; a requirement imposed on a college student who fails to reach a prescribed standard in a study; the study or subject to which the requirement is attached; a restricting, limiting, or modifying circumstance; situation with respect to circumstances; state of health; social position; quality or character; a characteristic; *logic,* the antecedent expressing the condition of a hypothetical proposition; *gram.* the protasis of a conditional sentence.

con·di·tion, kon·dish′on, *v.t.* [O.Fr. *condicioner* (Fr. *conditionner*).] To subject to something as a condition; make conditional on; to form or be a condition of; determine, limit, or restrict, as a condition; to make, as something, a condition; stipulate; to impose a condition on (a student); to subject to particular conditions or circumstances; to test, as a commodity, to ascertain its condition; to put in fit or proper state.—*v.i.* To make conditions.—**con·di·tion·er,** *n.* One who or that which conditions; *milling,* a machine for drying damp or musty grains.

con·di·tion·al, kon·dish′a·nal, *a.* Provisional; subject to or contingent upon conditions; *logic,* implying an hypothesis; *gram.* involving or expressing a condition.—**con·di·tion·al·i·ty,** *n.*—**con·di·tion·al·-ly,** *adv.*

con·di·tion·al sale, *n.* A type of sale in which the goods are delivered to the buyer but the title to them is retained by the seller until such time as the purchase price is paid in full.

con·di·tioned, kon·dish′ond, *a.* Being in a certain condition; circumstanced; having a nature or disposition as specified; *psychol.* trained to a certain response.

con·di·tioned re·flex, *n. Psychol.* a learned, automatic response to a particular stimulus induced by training. Also *conditioned response.*

con·di·tioned re·sponse, *n. Psychol.* conditioned reflex.

con·dole, kon·dōl′, *v.i.—condoled, condoling.* [L.L. *condoleo—con-,* with, and L. *doleo,* to grieve, whence *doleful, dolor.*] To express pain or grief at the distress or misfortunes of another; to express sympathy to one in grief or misfortune, followed by *with.*—**con·do·la·to·ry,** *a.*

con·do·lence, kon·dō′lens, *n.* The act of condoling; expression of sympathy with another's grief.—**con·do·ler,** *n.*

con·dom, kon′dom, kon′dom, *n.* A thin sheath, often of rubber, worn over the penis during coitus for the purpose of preventing conception and venereal infection.

con·do·min·i·um, kon″do·min′ē·um, *n.* pl. **con·do·min·i·ums.** [L. *con,* and *dominium,* rule.] Joint rule or control; a residential building consisting of multiple units, each under individual ownership, but subject to certain joint agreements and regulations; one residential unit in such a building; *internat. law,* joint dominion over a territory by two or more states.

con·do·na·tion, kon″dō·nā′shan, *n.* [L. *condonatio.*] The act of condoning or pardoning a wrong act; the implied forgiving or pardon of an offense by overlooking it.

con·done, kon·dōn′, *v.t.—condoned, condoning.* [L. *condonare,* to pardon.] To

pardon; to overlook (an offense); *law,* to forgive, or to act so as to imply forgiveness of (a violation of the marriage vow).

con·dor, kon′dor, *n.* [Sp. < Peruvian *cuntur.*] A large American vulture, *Vultur gryphus,* also inhabiting the higher regions of the Andes, having the head and upper part of the neck bare, with blackish plumage varied round the neck and wings with white. A former gold coin of Ecuador and Chile, bearing the figure of a condor.

con·dot·tie·re, kạn″do·tyâr′ā, *It.* kạn″-dạt·tye′Rĕ, *n. pl.* **con·dot·tie·ri,** kạn″do-·tyâr′ē, *It.* kạn″dạt·tye′Rĕ. [It. ult. < L. *conducere,* lead together, also hire.] A professional military captain or leader of mercenaries, in the service of princes or states at war, esp. in Italy in the 14th and 15th centuries; a professional soldier.

con·duce, kon·dōs′, kon·dūs′, *v.i.—conduced, conducing.* [L. *conduco,* to conduce—*con-,* and *duco,* to lead; *conduct* is from the same verb.] To combine with other things in bringing about or tending to bring about a result; to contribute to a result, usually followed by *to.*—**con·duc·i·ble,** *a.* [L. *conducibilis.*]—**con·duc·i·ble·ness,** *n.*

con·du·cive, kon·dō′siv, kon·dū′siv, *a.* Having the quality of conducing, promoting, or furthering; tending to advance or bring about; followed by *to.*—**con·du·cive·ness,** kon·dū′siv·nes, *n.*

con·duct, kon·dukt′, *v.t.* [L. *conductus,* pp. of *conducere.*] To lead or guide; escort; to direct in action or course; manage; carry on; to direct as leader; as, to *conduct* an orchestra; to behave, as oneself; to serve as a channel or medium for; *phys.* to serve as a medium for transmitting heat or electricity.—*v.i.* To lead; to act as conductor; *phys.* to transmit heat or electricity.—**con·duct·i·-bil·i·ty,** *n.*—**con·duct·i·ble,** *a.*

con·duct, kon′dukt, *n.* [M.L. *conductus, n.,* < L. *conducere.*] Personal behavior or deportment; the act of conducting; guidance; escort; direction or management; execution.

con·duct·ance, kon·duk′tans, *n. Elect.* power of a conductor to transmit a current.

con·duc·tion, kon·duk′shan, *n.* [L. *conductio(n-).*] A conducting, as of water through a pipe; *phys.* transmission through a conductor, as the conveyance of heat through a body by the raising of the temperature of its particles but without the visible transfer of matter, or the conveyance of electricity through a body without any sensible transfer of its particles; *physiol.* transmission of an impulse along nerve fibers.

con·duc·tiv·i·ty, kon″duk·tiv′i·tē, *n.* pl. **con·duc·tiv·i·ties.** Power of conducting heat, electricity, or sound.—**con·duc·tive,** kon·duk′tiv, *a.*

con·duc·tor, kon·duk′tẽr, *n.* [L.] One who conducts; a leader; a guide; a director or manager; the director of an orchestra or chorus, who indicates to the performers the rhythm and expression of the music as by motions of a baton; the official in charge of a railroad train, or other public vehicle; a substance capable of transmitting heat, electricity, or sound; a lightning rod.—**con·duc·to·ri·al,** *a.*—**con·duc·tor·ship,** *n.*—**con·duc·tress,** *n.*

con·duit, kon′dwit, kon′dō·it, kon′dū·it, kon′dit, *n.* [Fr. *conduit,* pp. of *conduire,* L. *conducere, conductum,* to conduct.] A pipe, tube, or other channel for the conveyance of fluids; a tube or pipe for protecting electric wires or cables.

con·du·pli·cate, kon·dō′pli·kit, kon·dū′-pli·kit, *a.* Doubled or folded over or together; *bot.* applied to leaves in the bud when they are folded down the middle, so that the halves of the lamina are applied

a- fat fāte fär fâre, fall; **e-** met, mē, mẽre hẽr; **i-** pin, pīne; **o-** not, nōte, mŏve; **u-** tub, cūbe, bull; **oi-** oil; **ou-** pound.

together by their faces.—**con·du·pli·ca·-tion,** *n.*

con·dyle, kon′dīl, kon′del, *n.* [L. *condylus,* Gr. *kondylos,* a knuckle, a joint.] *Anat.* a protuberance on the end of a bone serving to form an articulation with another bone.—**con·dy·lar, con·dy·loid,** kon′di·loid″, *a.*

cone, kōn, *n.* [L. *conus,* < Gr. *conos.*] A geometrical solid generated by the revolution of a right-angled triangle upon one of its legs as an axis, 'right circular cone'; a similar solid with an axis oblique to the base, 'oblique circular cone'; a similar solid having an ellipse or the like for a base; a surface generated by a moving straight line, one point of which is fixed, which constantly touches a fixed curve; a solid figure rising from a circular base and regularly tapering to a point; anything cone-shaped, as a volcanic peak. *Bot.* the more or less conical multiple fruit of the pine or fir; a strobile.

cone, kōn, *v.t.*—*coned, coning.* To shape like a cone or the segment of a cone.—*v.i.* To bear cones.

cone·flow·er, kōn′flou″er, *n.* Any plant of the genus *Rudbeckia,* having flowers with a cone-shaped disk, as *R. hirta,* the yellow daisy; any of various allied plants as *Brauneria purpurea,* the purple cone-flower.

con·el·rad, kon′el·rad″, *n.* [< *con*(trol) (*of*) *el*(ectromagnetic) *rad*(iation).] An emergency radio broadcasting system whereby official Civil Defense information and instructions may be broadcast to the public during enemy attack or any emergency situation, involving the continued operation of certain AM stations on special frequencies of 640 or 1240 kilocycles, the signals being so arranged as to deny navigational aid to enemy bombers.

cone·nose, kōn′nōz″, *n.* A large blood-sucking insect, *Triatoma sanguisuga,* a species of assassin bug infesting houses in the southern and western U.S.

Con·es·to·ga wag·on, kon′i·stō′ga wag′on, kon″i·stō′ga wag′on, *n.* A large, broad-wheeled, covered wagon used during the western migration of American pioneers. So named from Conestoga, Pennsylvania.

co·ney, kō′nē, kun′ē, *n.* A rabbit found in Europe; rabbit fur; a rabbit coat dyed and clipped to look like seal; a grouper fish found in tropical Atlantic waters. Also **co·ny,** kō′nē, kun′e, pl. **co·nies.**

con·fab, kon′fab, *n. Colloq.* Discussion; conversation.—*v.i.*—*confabbed, confabbing. Colloq.* To discuss or converse; to chat.

con·fab·u·late, kon·fab′ū·lāt″, *v.i.*—*confabulated, confabulating.* To chat; converse informally; *psychol.* to engage in fantasy to replace memory loss.—**con·fab·u·la·tion,** kon·fab″ū·lā′shan, *n.*—**con·fab·u·la·tor,** *n.*

con·fect, kon·fekt′, *v.t.* [L. *confectus,* pp. of *conficere,* < *con-,* together, and *facere,* make.] To make up, compound, or prepare from ingredients or materials; to make into a preserve; to construct, form, or make; to mix, as ingredients.—*n.* A preserved, candied, or other sweet confection.

con·fec·tion, kon·fek′shan, *n.* [O.Fr. Fr. *confection,* < L. *confectio*(n-), < *conficere.*] The process of compounding, preparing, or making; a medicinal preparation made with the aid of sugar, honey, or syrup; a sweet preparation, liquid or dry, of fruit, as candy or a preserve; a candy or bonbon; a ready-made garment, as an elaborate and elegant article of feminine dress.

con·fec·tion·a·ry, kon·fek′sha·ner″ē, *a.* Of the nature of a confection; pertaining to confections or their making.—*n.* pl. **con·fec·tion·a·ries.** Confectionery; candy.

con·fec·tion·er, kon·fek′sha·nẽr, *n.* One who makes or sells candies, bonbons, and sometimes ice cream and cakes.

con·fec·tion·er·y, kon·fek′sha·ner″ē, *n.* pl. **con·fec·tion·er·ies.** Confections or sweetmeats collectively; the work or business of a confectioner; a confectioner's shop.

con·fed·er·a·cy, kon·fed′ẽr·a·sē, kon·-fed′ra·sē, *n.* pl. **con·fed·er·a·cies.** A union of persons or parties; a league or alliance of persons, parties, or states for the purpose of acting on mutual goals; a combination of persons for unlawful purposes; a conspiracy.—**The Con·fed·er·a·cy,** *n. U.S. hist.* the southern states which seceded from the Union in 1860-1861.

con·fed·er·ate, kon·fed′e·rāt″, *v.t., v.i.*—*confederated, confederating.* [L.L. *confœdreatus,* pp. of *confœderare,* < L. *con-, with,* and *fœderare,* E. *federate.*] To unite in a league or alliance, or a conspiracy.

con·fed·er·ate, kon·fed′ẽr·it, kon·fed′rit, *a.* Confederated; united in a league or alliance, or a conspiracy; (*cap.*) *U.S. hist.* pertaining to the southern States which seceded from the Union in 1860-61 and formed a separate government.

con·fed·er·ate, kon·fed′ẽr·it, kon·fed′rit, *n.* One united with others in a confederacy; an ally; an accomplice; (*cap.*) an adherent of the Confederate States of America.

Con·fed·er·ate Me·mo·ri·al Day, *n. U.S.* in the south, the day which commemorates the Confederate forces of the Civil War, the date varying in different areas: April 26 in Alabama, Florida, Georgia, Mississippi; May 10 in North Carolina, South Carolina; May 30 in Virginia; and June 3 in Kentucky, Louisiana, Tennessee.

con·fed·er·ate rose, *n.* A shrub, *Hibiscus mutabilis,* native to China, having large flowers which deepen in color soon after opening and having a large fruit. Also **cot·ton rose, Con·fed·er·ate rose.**

con·fed·er·a·tion, kon·fed″e·rā′shan, *n.* [L.L. *confaederatio*(n-).] The act of confederating, or the state of being confederated; a league or alliance; a body of confederates, esp. of states more or less permanently united for common purposes; *Canada,* the federation of 1867 of Ontario, Quebec, Nova Scotia and New Brunswick.—**the Con·fed·er·a·tion,** the ten provinces comprising Canada.—**con·fed·er·a·tive,** kon·fed′e·rā″tiv, kon·fed′ẽr·a·tiv, *a.* Pertaining to a confederation.

con·fer, kon·fer′, *v.t.*—*conferred, conferring.* [L. *confero,* to bring together, compare, bestow.] To give or bestow: with *on* or *upon* before the recipient. *Confer* differs from *bestow* in that it always implies a certain amount of condescension or superiority on the part of the giver.—*v.i.* To consult together on some special subject; to compare opinions; formerly often simply to discourse or talk, but now to converse on some serious or important subject.—**con·fer·ee,** *n.* One on whom something is conferred.—**con·fer·ment,** *n.*—**con·fer·ra·ble,** *a.*—**con·fer·ral,** *n.*—**con·fer·rer,** *n.*

con·fer·ence, kon′fẽr·ens, kon′frens, *n.* [Fr. *conférence.*] The act of conferring or consulting together; a meeting for consultation, discussion, or instruction between individuals or groups; a meeting of the representatives of different foreign countries; a meeting of representatives of two legislative bodies; *eccles.* a meeting of the clergy, clergy and layman, or of an association of churches. An association of athletic teams.—**con·fer·en·tial,** kon″fe·ren′shal, *a.*

con·fess, kon·fes′, *v.t.* [Fr. *confesser,* < L. *confiteor, confessum.*] To admit or acknowledge, as a crime, a fault, a debt, or something that is against one's interest or reputation; to own to; to disclose. *Rom. Cath. Ch.* to disclose (sins) to a priest in private with a view to absolution; to hear or

receive the confession of: said of the priest. To declare belief in; to grant, concede, admit.—*v.i.* To make confession or avowal; to disclose faults; to make known one's sins to a priest.

con·fess·ed·ly, kon·fes′id·lē, *adv.* By general confession or admission; admittedly.

con·fes·sion, kon·fesh′on, *n.* The act of confessing; the act of making an avowal; that which is confessed. *Rom. Cath. Ch.* a disclosing of sins or faults to a priest; the unburdening of the conscience to a confessor.—**con·fes·sion of faith,** *n.* A statement which comprises the articles of faith that a person or a church accepts as true.

con·fes·sion·al, kon·fesh′o·nal, *n.* [Fr. *confessional,* L.L. *confessionale.*] A compartment or cell in which a priest sits to hear confessions.—*a.* Of or pertaining to a confession.

con·fes·sor, kon·fes′ẽr, *n.* One who confesses; one who acknowledges a crime or fault; a priest who hears confession and has the power to grant absolution; one who makes a profession of his faith and adheres to it in the face of persecution.

con·fet·ti, kon·fet′ē, *It.* kan·fet′tē, *n.* pl. but sing. in constr. [It., < L. *confectus:* CONFECT.] Narrow streamers or bits of colored paper thrown at weddings, parties, and carnivals; a confection; a bonbon.

con·fi·dant, kon″fi·dant′, kon″fi·dänt′, kon′fi·dant″, kon′fi·dänt″, *n.* [O.Fr.] A person entrusted with the confidence of another; one to whom secrets are confided; a confidential friend.—**con·fi·dante,** *n.* A female confidant.

con·fide, kon·fīd′, *v.i.*—*confided, confiding.* [L. *confidere,* < *con-,* altogether, and *fidere,* trust.] To have full trust or faith; to show trust by imparting secrets.—*v.t.* To entrust; commit to the charge, knowledge, or good faith of; tell in assurance of secrecy.

con·fi·dence, kon′fi·dens, *n.* [L. *confidentia.*] Full belief in the trustworthiness or reliability of a person or thing; presumption; self-reliance, assurance, or aplomb; boldness; the confiding of private matters; a confidential communication; confidential relationship.

con·fi·dence game, *n.* A kind of swindle in which the swindler gains the confidence of his victim in order to fleece him at cards, betting, or appropriation of funds intended for investment. Also *Brit.* **con·fi·dence trick.**—**con·fi·dence man,** *n.* One who swindles by a confidence game.

con·fi·dent, kon′fi·dent, *a.* Full of confidence; certain; relying on oneself; full of assurance; bold, sometimes overbold; cocksure; presumptuous.—**con·fi·dent·ly,** *adv.*

con·fi·den·tial, kon″fi·den′shal, *a.* Intended to be treated as private, or kept in confidence; spoken or written in confidence; secret; enjoying the confidence of another; entrusted with secrets or with private affairs.—**con·fi·den·tial·ly,** *adv.*

con·fid·ing, kon·fī′ding, *a.* Trusting; reposing confidence; trustful.—**con·fid·ing·ly,** *adv.*—**con·fid·ing·ness,** *n.*

con·fig·u·ra·tion, kon·fig″ū·rā′shan, *n.* [L.L. *configuratio*(n-), < L. *configurare.*] The relative disposition of the parts or elements of a thing; external form, as resulting from this; conformation. *Astron.* relative position or aspect of the planets or other heavenly bodies; a group of stars. *Psychol.* a gestalt; *chem., phys.* space relationship of atoms in a molecule, or of electrons and nucleons in an atom.

con·fig·ure, kon·fig′ūr, *v.t.*—*configured, configuring.* [L. *configurare,* pp. *configuratus.*] To make or arrange in a certain form; to cause to conform; to shape.

con·fine, kon′fīn, *n.* [L. *confinis,* bordering, adjoining, *confine,* a border—*con,* and *finis,* end, border, limit. FINE.] *Usu. pl.* Border; boundary; frontier; limit, as: His remarks went beyond the *confines* of good taste.

con·fine, kon·fīn′, *v.t.*—*confined, confining.* [Fr. *confiner.*] To limit or restrain; enclose within bounds or restrict; to shut away or imprison.—**con·fin·er,** *n.*

con·fined, kon·fīnd′, *a.* Restricted to quarters; being in childbirth.

con·fine·ment, kon·fīn′ment, *n.* The act of confining; the state of being confined; restriction; imprisonment; lying-in for childbirth.

con·firm, kon·fėrm′, *v.t.* [L. *confirmo*—*con-,* and *firmo,* to make firm, < *firmus,* firm.] To make firm or more firm; to strengthen; to settle or establish; to make certain; to put past doubt; to assure; to verify; to sanction; to ratify; to strengthen in resolution, purpose, or opinion; to administer the rite of confirmation to.—**con·firm·a·ble,** *a.*

con·fir·ma·tion, kon″fėr·mā′shan, *n.* The act of establishing; establishment; corroboration; the act of rendering valid; that which confirms; the ceremony of laying on hands by a bishop in the admission of baptized persons to the full enjoyment of Christian privileges, a rite of the Roman, Greek, and English churches; a ceremony which confirms Jewish adolescents in their traditional heritage. Convincing testimony. **con·fir·ma·tive,** *a.*

con·fir·ma·to·ry, kon·fėr′ma·tōr″ē, kon·fėr′ma·tǎr″ē, *a.* Serving to confirm; giving additional strength, force, or stability, or additional assurance or evidence.

con·firmed, kon·fėrmd′, *a.* Fixed; settled; settled in certain habits or state of health; as, a *confirmed* drunkard or invalid; having received the rite of confirmation.—**con·firm·ed·ly,** kon·fur′mid·lē, *adv.*—**con·firm·ed·ness,** *n.*

con·fis·ca·ble, kon·fis′ka·bl, kon·fī′ska·bl, *a.* Capable of being confiscated; liable to forfeiture.

con·fis·cate, kon′fis·skāt″, kon·fis′kāt, *v.t.*—*confiscated, confiscating.* [L. *confiscatus,* pp. of *confiscare,* < *con-,* with, and *fiscus,* basket, chest, treasury.] To seize as forfeited to the public treasury; appropriate, by way of penalty, to public use; to seize by or as if by authority; to appropriate summarily.

con·fis·cate, kon′fis·skāt″, kon·fis′kāt, *a.* Seized; forfeited; appropriated by the government; deprived of possessions by confiscation.—**con·fis·ca·tion,** *n.* [L. *confiscatio(n-).*] The act of confiscating, or the state of being confiscated.—**con·fis·ca·tor,** *n.*—**con·fis·ca·to·ry,** kon·fis′ka·tǎr″ē, *a.* Characterized by or effecting confiscation.

Con·fit·e·or, kon·fit′ē·ėr, *n.* [L., "I confess."] *Rom. Cath. Ch.* a form of prayer beginning with "Confiteor," in which general confession of sins is made.

con·fi·ture, kon′fi·chụr′, *n.* [Fr. < L. *confectura,* < *conficere.*] A confection; a preserve, as of fruit.

con·fla·grant, kon·flā′grant, *a.* [L. *conflagrans (-ant-),* ppr. of *conflagrare.*] Burning or blazing.

con·fla·gra·tion, kon″fla·grā′shan, *n.* [L. *conflagratio*—*con-,* with, and *flagro,* to burn, whence *flagrant.*] A great fire, or the burning of any great mass of combustibles.

con·fla·tion, kon·flā′shan, *n.* [L.L. *conflatio(n-)* < L.L. *conflatus,* pp. of *conflare,* blow together, fuse, < *con-,* with, and *flare,* blow.] The act or result of merging various elements; specif. the formation of a text by a combination of two readings; a composite reading or text.—**con·flate,** kon·flāt′, *a.*

con·flict, kon′flikt, *n.* [L. *conflictus,* a conflict, < *confligo*—*con-,* together, and *fligo,* to strike, to dash.] A fight, struggle, or combat; a controversy or quarrel; active

opposition; contention; strife or incompatibility, as, a *conflict* in luncheon dates.

con·flict, kon·flikt′, *v.i.* To meet in opposition or hostility; to contend; to strive or struggle; to be in opposition; to be contrary; to be incompatible or at variance. —**con·flict·ing, con·flic·tive,** *a.* Being in opposition; contrary; contradictory; incompatible.—**con·flic·tion,** *n.*

con·flict of in·ter·est, *n.* The situation in which the private financial interests of a public officeholder stand to benefit by the influence from this position; the interference of one personal interest with another.

con·flu·ence, kon′flö·ens, *n.* [L. *confluentia,* < *confluo*—*con-,* and *fluo,* to flow.] A flowing together; the meeting or junction of two or more streams of water; the body of water so joined; the place of meeting; a crowd; a concourse.

con·flu·ent, kon′flö·ent, *a.* [L. *confluens.*] Flowing together; meeting in their course, as two streams; meeting; running together; *bot.* united at some part.—*n.* A tributary stream.

con·flux, kon′fluks, *n.* A flowing together; a meeting or joining; a crowd; a multitude. Also *confluence.*

con·fo·cal, kon·fō′kal, *a. Math.* having the same focus or foci.

con·form, kon·fǎrm′, *v.t.* [L. *conformo*—*con-,* and *forma,* form.] To make of the same form or character; to make like; as, to *conform* anything to a model; to bring into harmony or correspondence; to adapt; to submit: often *refl.*—*v.i.* To act in conformity or compliance; to comply with the usages of the Church of England.—**con·form·er, con·form·ist,** *n.*—**con·form·ism,** *n.*

con·form·a·ble, kon·fǎr′ma·bl, *a.* Corresponding in form, character, manners, or opinions; submissive, compliant, or acquiescent; *geol.* (strata or groups of strata) lying in parallel planes having the same dip.— **con·form·a·bil·i·ty,** *n.* The state or quality of being conformable.—**con·form·a·bly,** *adv.* In conformity.

con·form·ance, kon·fǎr′mans, *n.* Conformity.

con·for·ma·tion, kon″fǎr·mā′shan, *n.* The act or process of conforming, as in adaptation or adjustment; a symmetrical arrangement of parts; agreement or correspondence with a plan or model; structure, shape, or contours, esp. of an animal, as: The horse had a jumper's *conformation.*

con·form·i·ty, kon·fǎr′mi·tē, *n. pl.* **con·form·i·ties.** Correspondence in form or manner; agreement; congruity; likeness; harmony; accordance; (*often cap.*) compliance with the usages or principles of the Church of England.

con·found, kon·found′, kon·found′, *v.t.* [Fr. *confondre,* < L. *confundo*—*con-,* together, and *fundo, fusum,* to pour out, whence *fuse, confuse, refuse,* etc.] To confuse; bewilder; to mistake (one) for another; to contradict; to increase the confusion of; to perplex with terror, surprise, or astonishment; to astound; to mingle confusedly together.—**con·found·er,** *n.*

con·found·ed, kon·foun′ded, *a. Colloq.* bothersome; annoying; damned: used as a euphemism; as, a *confounded* lie.—**con·found·ed·ly,** *adv.*

con·fra·ter·ni·ty, kon″fra·tėr′ni·tē, *n. pl.* **con·fra·ter·ni·ties.** [M.L. *confraternitas,* < *confrater.*] A brotherhood; a society or body of men united for some purpose or in some profession; esp. a brotherhood devoted to some particular religious or charitable service.

con·frere, kon′frâr, *n.* [Fr., < M.L. *confrater,* < L. *con-,* with, and *frater,* brother.] A fellow member of a fraternity or profession; a colleague.

con·front, kon·frunt′, *v.t.* [Fr. *confronter*— L. *con-,* together, and *frons, frontis,* the countenance or front.] To stand facing; to face; to stand or be in front of, providing resistance, as an obstacle; to meet in hostility; to oppose; to set face to face; to bring together for purposes of comparison or examination.—**con·fron·ta·tion, con·front·ment,** kon″frun·tā′shon, *n.* The act of confronting.—**con·front·er,** *n.*

Con·fu·cian, kon·fū′shan, *a.* Of or pertaining to Confucius, Chinese philosopher, or to his doctrines or followers.—*n.* A follower of Confucius.

Con·fu·cian·ism, kon·fū′sha·niz″um, *n.* The moral doctrines of Confucius, advocating filial piety, justice, and fidelity.— **Con·fu·cian·ist,** kon·fū′shan·ist, *n.*

con·fuse, kon·fūz′, *v.t.*—*confused, confusing.* [L. *confusus,* < *confundo,* CONFOUND.] To mix up without order or clearness; to throw together indiscriminately; to derange; disorder, jumble; to confound; to perplex or bewilder; to embarrass; to disconcert.— **con·fus·ed·ly,** kon·fū′zid·lē, *adv.*—**con·fus·ed·ness,** *n.*

con·fu·sion, kon·fū′zhan, *n.* [L. *confusio.*] A state in which things are confused; an indiscriminate mingling; disorder; tumultuous condition; perturbation of mind; embarrassment; distraction; disconcertment.

con·fu·ta·tion, kon″fū·tā′shan, *n.* The act of confuting, disproving, or proving to be false or invalid.—**con·fu·ta·tive,** kon·fū′ta·tiv, *a.* Designed to confute.

con·fute, kon·fūt′, *v.t.*—*confuted, confuting.* [L. *confuto,* to cool down by cold water, to confute—*con-,* together, and *futis,* a pitcher, < root of *fundo,* to pour.] To prove, as an argument or statement, to be false, defective or invalid; to disprove; to overthrow; to convict of error by argument or proof.— **con·fut·er,** *n.*

con·ga, kong′ga, *n. pl.* **con·gas.** [Sp.] A Cuban dance, characteristically performed by a group who form a single winding line and follow a leader; the music for this dance.—*v.i.* **congaed, congaing.**

con·gé, kon′zhā, kon·jā, *Fr.* kạN·zhā′, *n. pl.* **con·gés.** [Fr.] Leave to depart; dismissal; *arch.* a type of concave molding. Also **con·gee.**

con·geal, kon·jēl′, *v.t.* [L. *congelare*—*con-,* together, and *gelare,* to freeze, < *gelu,* cold, whence also *gelid, jelly.*] To change from a fluid to a solid state by cold or a loss of heat; to freeze; to coagulate; to check the flow of.—*v.i.* To pass from a fluid to a solid state by cold; to coagulate.—**con·geal·a·ble,** *a.*—**con·geal·ment,** *n.* Congelation.

con·ge·la·tion, kon″je·lā′shan, *n.* [L. *congelatio.*] The act or process of congealing; the state of being congealed; that which is congealed or solidified.

con·ge·ner, kon′je·nėr, *n.* [L.—*con-,* together, and *genus, generis,* a kind or race.] One of the same kind or class; a plant or animal belonging to the same genus as another.—**con·ge·ner·ic,** kon″je·ner′ik, *a.* Being of the same kind, nature, or class; belonging to the same genus. Also **con·gen·er·ous,** kon·jen′ėr·us.

con·gen·ial, kon·jēn′yal, *a.* [L. *con-,* with, and *genius,* spirit, E. *genius.*] Compatible in spirit, feeling, and temper; sympathetic; agreeable or pleasing; existing together sociably and harmoniously.—**con·ge·ni·al·i·ty, con·gen·ial·ness,** kon·jē″nē·al′i·tē, *n.*—**con·gen·ial·ly,** *adv.*

con·gen·i·tal, kon·jen′i·tal, *a.* [L. *congenitus*—*con-,* and *genitus,* born, root *gen,* to produce.] Existing in an individual from birth; as, a *congenital* deformity; relating to existing characteristics dating from birth which are not hereditary.

con·ger, kong′gėr, *n.* [L. *conger, congrus,* < Gr. *goggros.*] A large marine eel,

Conger conger, sometimes growing to the length of 10 feet, used for food along the coasts of Europe; any of certain other eels or eellike fishes of the family *Congridae*. Also **con·ger eel**.

con·ge·ries, kon·jēr'ēz, *n. sing. or pl. in constr.* [L., < *congero*, to amass—*con-*, and *gero*, to bear.] A collection of several particles or bodies in one mass or aggregate; an aggregate; a heap.

con·gest, kon·jest', *v.t.* [L. *congestus*, pp. of *congerere*, bring together < *con-*, with, and *gerere*, bear.] To heap together; to collect in undue quantity; to fill to excess; overcrowd; *pathol.* to cause an unnatural accumulation of blood in the vessels of, as an organ or part.—*v.i.* To gather or collect together in undue quantity; to become congested.—**con·ges·tion**, *n.* [L. *congestio(n-)*.] A heaping together; an overcrowded condition; *pathol.* an inflammation or excess of fluid in an organ or part.—**con·ges·tive**, *a.* Pertaining to or characterized by congestion.

con·glo·bate, kon·glō'bāt, kong'glō·bāt", *a.* [L. *conglobatus*—*con-*, and *globus*, a ball.] Formed or gathered into a ball or small spherical body; combined into one mass.—*v.t.*—*conglobated, conglobating.* To collect or form into a ball; to combine into a round mass.—*v.i.* To assume a round or globular form.—Also **con·globe**.

con·glo·ba·tion, kon"glō·bā'shan, kong'-glō·bā'shan, *n.* The act of forming or gathering into a ball; a round body.

con·glom·er·ate, kon·glom'e·rāt", *v.t.*—*conglomerated, conglomerating.* [L. *conglomeratus*, pp. of *conglomerare*, < *con-*, with, and *glomerare*, form into a ball, < *glomus*, ball.] To gather into a ball or rounded mass; bring together into a cohering mass; form into a whole, without regard to homogeneity or congruity of the parts.—*v.i.* To collect or cluster together.

con·glom·er·ate, kon·glom'ér·it, *n.* Anything composed of heterogeneous materials or elements; *geol.* a rock consisting of rounded and water-worn pebbles, embedded in a finer cementing material; consolidated gravel.

con·glom·er·ate, kon·glom'ér·it, *a.* Gathered into a rounded mass; consisting of parts so gathered; clustered; *bot.* densely clustered; *geol.* made up of heterogeneous material cemented together loosely.—**con·glom·er·at·ic**, kon·glom"e·rat'ik, *a.*

con·glom·er·a·tion, kon·glom"e·rā'shan, *n.* [L.L. *conglomeratio(n-)*.] The act of conglomerating, or the state of being conglomerated; that which is conglomerated; a cohering mass; a cluster; a heterogeneous combination.

con·glu·ti·nate, kon·glöt'i·nāt", *v.t.*—*conglutinated, conglutinating.* [L. *conglutino*—*con-*, and *glutino*, < *gluten*, glue.] To glue together; to unite by some glutinous or tenacious substance; to reunite; to cement.—*v.i.* To coalesce; to become united by the intervention of some glutinous substance.—*a.* Glued together; *bot.* united by some adhesive substance, but not organically united.—**con·glu·ti·na·tion**, *n.*

Con·go col·or, kong'gō kul'ér, *n.* [From the *Congo (Kongo)* in Africa.] *Chem.* one of a group of coaltar colors or dyes, red, violet, or yellow, possessing the property of dyeing cotton and other vegetable fibers without the presence of a mordant. Also **Con·go dye**.

Con·go·lese, kong"gō·lēz', kong"gō·lēs', *a.* Of or pertaining to the diversified languages and peoples comprising the Congo in central Africa.—*n. pl.* **Con·go·lese**. An inhabitant or native of the Congo; the official language spoken by the natives of the Congo.

con·go snake, *n.* A snakelike amphibian, *Amphiuma means*, of the southeastern U.S., having small forelimbs, each with several toes, and attaining a length of three feet. Also **Con·go eel**.

con·gou, kong'gö, *n.* [Chinese *kung-fu*, labor.] A kind of black tea from China.

con·grat·u·late, kon·grach'u·lāt", *v.t.*—*congratulated, congratulating.* [L. *congratulator*—*con-*, and *gratulor*, < *gratus*, grateful, pleasing. GRACE.] To express sympathetic pleasure on some piece of good fortune happening to, as another party; to compliment upon a happy event; to wish joy to; to felicitate.—**con·grat·u·lant**, kon·grach'u·-lant, *a.* Congratulating; expressing pleasure in another's good fortune.—**con·grat·u·-la·tor**, *n.* One who congratulates.—**con·grat·u·la·to·ry**, kon·grach'u·la·tōr"ē, kon·grach'u·la·tar"ē, *a.* Containing or expressing congratulation.

con·grat·u·la·tion, kon·grach"u·lā'shan, *n.* The act of congratulating; words used in congratulating; *usu. pl.* expressions to a person of pleasure in his good fortune.

con·gre·gate, kong'gre·gāt", *v.t.*—*congregated, congregating.* [L. *congregatus*, pp. of *congregare*, < *con-*, with, and *gregare*, collect into a flock, < *grex*, flock.] To bring together in a crowd, body, or mass; assemble; collect.—*v.i.* To flock together; gather; meet.—*a.* Congregated; assembled; collective.—**con·gre·ga·tive**, *a.* Tending to congregate.—**con·gre·ga·tive·ness**, *n.*—**con·gre·ga·tor**, *n.*

con·gre·ga·tion, kong"gre·gā'shan, *n.* [L. *congregatio(n-)*.] The act of congregating; a congregated body; an assemblage; a body of persons assembled for religious worship and instruction; a body of persons associated together for the purpose of holding religious services in common; in the Old Testament, the Israelites; in the New Testament, the Christian church or a particular assemblage of worshipers; in the Roman Catholic Church, a committee of cardinals or other ecclesiastics; a religious community or order with a common rule but not under solemn vows; an associated group of monasteries.

con·gre·ga·tion·al, kong"gre·gā'sha·nal, *a.* Pertaining to a congregation; recognizing the governing power of the congregation; (*cap.*) pertaining or adhering to a form of church government in which each congregation or church acts as an independent, self-governing body, while maintaining fellowship with other like congregations.—**con·gre·ga·tion·al·ly**, *adv.*

Con·gre·ga·tion·al Chris·tian, *a.* Pertaining to a denomination developed in the United States in 1931 by the union between the Congregational Church and the Christian Church.

con·gre·ga·tion·al·ism, kong"gre·gā'sha·na·liz"um, *n.* The principle of church government by individual congregations; (*cap.*) the system of government and doctrine of the Congregational churches.—**con·gre·ga·tion·al·ist**, *n.* One who holds to the congregational principle of church government; (*cap.*) a member of the Congregational denomination.

con·gress, kong'gris, *n.* [L. *congressus*, < *congredi*, come together, < *con-*, with, and *gradi*, walk, go, < *gradus*, step.] The act of coming together; an encounter; an interview; sexual intercourse; social intercourse; a formal meeting or assembly of representatives for the discussion, arrangement, or promotion of some matter of common interest; the national legislative body of a nation, esp. of a republic; (*cap.*) the national legislative body of the U.S., consisting of the Senate and the House of Representatives; this body as it exists for the two years during which the representatives hold their seats; as, the 69th *Congress*.—**con·gres·sion·al**, kon·gresh'o·nal, *a.* Of or pertaining to a congress; (*Cap.*) pertaining to the Congress of the U.S.—**con·gres·sion·al·ly**, *adv.*

con·gress boot, *n.* A high shoe with elastic sides, popularly worn by men in the late nineteenth and early twentieth centuries.

con·gres·sion·al dis·trict, *n. Govt.* one of the federal districts into which a state is divided, each electing its representative to the U.S. House of Representatives.

Con·gres·sion·al Med·al of Hon·or, *n.* Medal of Honor.

Con·gres·sion·al Rec·ord, *n.* The official record of Congressional proceedings, published on a daily basis while Congress is convened.

con·gress·man, kong'gris·man, *n. pl.* **con·gress·men**. (*Often cap.*) a member of the U.S. Congress, esp. of the House of Representatives.—**con·gress·wom·an**, kong'gris·wum"an, *n. pl.* **con·gress·wom·en**. (*Often cap.*) a female member of the U.S. Congress.

con·gru·ence, kong'grö·ens, *n.* [L. *congruentia*.] Suitableness of one thing to another; agreement; consistency; *math.* a statement that two figures or numbers are congruent. Also **con·gru·en·cy**, kong'grö·en·sē, pl. **con·gru·en·cies**.

con·gru·ent, kong'grö·ent, *a.* Conforming; agreeing; corresponding; *geom.* of figures, capable of being superimposed so that they coincide at all points; as, *congruent* circles; *math.* referring to numbers with the same remainders when divided by a given number.—**con·gru·ent·ly**, *adv.*

con·gru·i·ty, kon·grö'i·tē, kon·grö'i·tē, *n. pl.* **con·gru·i·ties**. The state or quality of being congruous; agreement between things; suitableness; consistency; *geom.* the condition of coinciding exactly when superimposed.

con·gru·ous, kong'grö·us, *a.* [L. *congruus*, < *congruere*.] Agreeing or harmonious in character; accordant; consonant; consistent; appropriate or fitting; having harmony of parts; *geom.* having congruity.—**con·gru·ous·ly**, *adv.*—**con·gru·ous·ness**, *n.*

con·ic, kon'ik, *a.* [Gr. *konikos*.] Having the form of, pertaining to, or resembling a cone.—*n. Geom.* a conic section.—**con·i·cal**, *a.* Conic; cone-shaped.—**con·i·cal·ly**, *adv.*—**con·i·cal·ness**, *n.*

con·ics, kon'iks, *n.* The branch of mathematics dealing with conic sections, the ellipse, the parabola, and the hyperbola.

con·ic sec·tion, *n. Math.* the locus of a point which moves in a curve so that its distance from a fixed point, called the focus, is in an unvarying ratio, called the eccentricity, to its distance from a fixed straight line, called the directrix: examples are an ellipse, or a hyperbola.

co·nid·i·um, kō·nid'ē·um, ko·nid'ē·um, *n. pl.* **co·nid·i·a**. kō·nid'ē·a, ko·nid'ē·a. [N.L., dim. < Gr. *konis*, dust.] In fungi, a propagative body or cell which is asexual in its origin and functions.—**co·nid·i·al**, **co·nid·i·an**, *a.*

co·ni·fer, kō'ni·fèr, kon'i·fèr, *n.* [L. *conifer*, cone-bearing, < *conus*, cone, and *ferre*, bear.] Any of a group of evergreen trees and shrubs, family *Coniferae*, including the pine, fir, spruce, and other cone-bearing trees.

co·ni·ine, kō'nē·ēn", kō'nē·in, kō'nēn, *n.* A highly poisonous volatile alkaloid, $C_8H_{17}N$, constituting the active principle of the poison hemlock. Also **co·nin**, **co·nine**.

co·ni·um, kō'nē·um, *n.* [L.L., < Gr. *coneion*, hemlock.] The poison hemlock, *Conium maculatum*; a preparation of this plant, used in medicine.

con·jec·tur·al, kon·jek'chér·al, *a.* Pertaining to, or of the nature of conjecture; involving conjecture; problematical; given to making conjectures.—**con·jec·tur·al·ly**, *adv.*

---

con·jec·ture, kon·jek'chẽr, *n.* [Fr. *conjecture,* L. *conjectura,* a conjecture, lit. a throwing or putting of things together.] A guess or inference based on the supposed possibility or probability of a fact, or on slight evidence; an opinion formed on insufficient or presumptive evidence.

con·jec·ture, kon·jek'chẽr, *v.t.—conjectured, conjecturing.* To conclude or suppose from grounds or evidence insufficient to ensure the reliability of the opinion; surmise; guess.—*v.i.* To form conjectures.

con·join, kon·join', *v.t.* [*Con* and *join;* Fr. *conjoindre.*] To join together or in one; to unite; to associate or connect.—*v.i.* To become united or joined.

con·joint, kon·joint', *a.* [O.Fr. Fr. *conjoint,* pp. of *conjoindre.*] Joined together; united; combined; associated; pertaining to or formed by two or more in combination; joint.—**con·joint·ly,** *adv.*

con·ju·gal, kon'ju·gal, *a.* [L. *conjugalis,* < *conjux, conjunx,* husband or wife, < *conjungere.*] Of, pertaining to, or of the nature of marriage; matrimonial; pertaining to the relation of husband and wife; connubial.— **con·ju·gal·i·ty,** *n.*—**con·ju·gal·ly,** *adv.*

con·ju·gant, kon'ju·gant, *n.* One of a pair of conjugating sex cells or organisms.

con·ju·gate, kon'ju·gāt", *v.t.—conjugated, conjugating.* [L. *conjugo, conjugatus,* to couple—*con-,* and *jugo,* to yoke.] *Gram.* to inflect (a verb) through some or all of its several voices, moods, tenses, numbers, and persons in a prescribed order.—*v.i. Biol.* to join in conjugation.

con·ju·gate, kon'ju·git, kon'ju·gāt", *n. Gram., rhet.* one of a group of words having a common derivation.

con·ju·gate, kon'ju·git, kon'ju·gāt, *a.* Joined together or operating as if joined, esp. in a pair; coupled; *gram.* having a common derivation and usually a kindred meaning; *bot.* having a pair of leaflets, as a pinnate leaf; *math.* so related, as two points or quantities, as to be interchangeable with regard to certain properties.—**con·ju·gate·ly,** *adv.*—**con·ju·gate·ness,** *n.*

con·ju·gat·ed pro·tein, *n.* A compound consisting of a protein combined with a nonprotein, as hemoglobin.

con·ju·ga·tion, kon'ju·gā'shan, *n.* A joining together; conjunction. *Gram.* the inflection of a verb in its different forms; a class of verbs conjugated in the same way; the presentation of inflectional verb forms in a prescribed arrangement. *Biol.* the union of two sex cells, or gametes; the temporary union of ciliated protozoans in which nuclear material is exchanged.— **con·ju·ga·tion·al,** *a.*—**con·ju·ga·tion·al·ly,** *adv.*—**con·ju·ga·tive,** *a.*

con·junct, kon·jungkt', kon'jungkt, *a.* [L. *conjunctus,* pp. of *conjungere.* CONJOIN.] Conjoined; associate; formed by conjunction.

con·junct, kon·jungkt', kon'jungkt, *n. Logic,* either of the two statements in a compound proposition.

con·junc·tion, kon·jungk'shan, *n.* [L. *conjunctio.*] Union; connection; association; *astron.* that position of a planet in which it is in a line with the earth or another planet and the sun; *gram.* any one of a group of words, such as *and, but, because,* serving to unite words, sentences, or clauses of a sentence, and indicating their relation to one another. —**con·junc·tion·al,** *a.*—**con·junc·tion·al·ly,** *adv.*

con·junc·ti·va, kon"jungk·tī'va, *n.* pl. **con·junc·ti·vas, con·junc·ti·vae.** *Anat.* the mucous membrane which lines the inner surface of the eyelids, and covers the anterior surface of the eyeball.—**con·junc·ti·val,** *a.*

con·junc·tive, kon·jungk'tiv, *a.* [L. *conjunctivus.*] Uniting; serving to connect. *Gram.* of or like a conjunction; uniting, as such conjunctive adverbs as *moreover, yet;* of a verb, subjunctive.—**con·junc·tive·ly,** *adv.*

con·junc·ti·vi·tis, kon·jungk"ti·vī'tis, *n.* [< *conjunctiva,* and Gr. *-itis,* inflammation.] Inflammation of the conjunctiva.

con·junc·ture, kon·jungk'chẽr, *n.* Combination of circumstances or affairs; esp. a critical time, proceeding from a union of circumstances; a crisis of affairs.

con·jur·a·tion, kon"ju·rā'shan, *n.* The act of binding by an oath; adjuration; an incantation; a spell.

con·jure, kon'jẽr, kon·jur', *Brit.* kun'jẽr, *v.t.—conjured, conjuring.* [L. *conjuro,* to swear together, to conspire.] To call on or summon by a sacred name or in a solemn manner; to adjure, kon·jur'. To affect or effect by magic or enchantment; to call up or bring into existence, usu. with *up,* kon'jẽr.—kon'jẽr, *v.i.* to practice the arts of a conjurer; to use magic.—**con·jur·er, con·jur·or,** *n.* A magician; one who practices legerdemain; a juggler.

conk out, *v.i. Slang.* To become unconscious; to break down, as a motor.

con man, *n. Slang.* A confidence man; a swindler.

con·nate, kon'āt, *a.* [L. *con-,* and *natus,* born.] Existing from birth; born or created together; congenial or related in nature; *biol.* congenitally joined or fused into one body.—**con·nate·ly,** *adv.*

con·nat·u·ral, ko·nach'ẽr·al, *a.* Connected by nature or belonging to by nature; inborn; having the same or an allied nature.— **con·nat·u·ral·ly,** *adv.*

con·nect, ko·nekt', *v.t.* [L. *connectere* (pp. *connexus, conectere,* < *con-,* with, and *nectere,* bind.] To bind or fasten together; join or unite; link, as two things together or one with another; to establish communication between; put in communication (with); to bring into association or relation; associate, as with something.—*v.i.* To become connected; join or unite; be in communication; of scheduled airplanes or railroad trains, to arrive at a time when passengers may proceed, without undue delay, on another, departing plane or train. —**con·nect·a·ble, con·nect·i·ble,** *a.*— **con·nec·tor, con·nect·er,** *n.*

con·nect·ed, ko·nek'tid, *a.* Bound or fastened together; joined in order or sequence, as words or ideas; associated.— **con·nect·ed·ly,** *adv.*—**con·nect·ed·ness,** *n.*

con·nec·ting rod, *n.* A rod or bar connecting movable parts, esp. one on a steam engine or gas engine, to transfer power or motion to a piston rod, etc.

con·nec·tion, *Brit.* **con·nex·ion,** ko·nek'shan, *n.* [L. *connexio(n-).*] The act of connecting, or the state of being connected; junction; union; union in due order or sequence of words or ideas; contextual relation; communication; association; relationship; sexual relation; anything that connects; a bond or tie; a connecting part; a person related to another or others, esp. by marriage or distant consanguinity; a body of persons connected, as by political or religious ties; a religious denomination; the meeting of means of conveyance for transfer of passengers without delay.

con·nec·tive, ko·nek'tiv, *n.* Anything that serves to connect; *gram.* a word used to connect words, phrases, clauses, and sentences, as a conjunction.—**con·nec·tive·ly,** *adv.*—**con·nec·tiv·i·ty,** *n.*

con·nec·tive, ko·nek'tiv, *a.* Having the power of connecting; tending to connect; connecting.

con·nec·tive tis·sue, *n.* A tissue which connects, supports, or surrounds other tissues or organs, and occurs in various forms throughout the body.

conn·ing tow·er, kon'ing tou'ẽr, *n.* [See *con.*] A low, circular armored structure on a war vessel, occupied by the commanding officer or the helmsman during an engagement; the observation tower on a submarine serving also as the entrance to the interior.

con·nip·tion, ko·nip'shan, *n.* [A made word.] *Colloq.* a fit of hysterics or hysterical excitement. Also **con·nip·tion fit.**

con·niv·ance, con·niv·ence, ko·nī'vans, *n.* [Earlier *connivence,* < L.L. *conniventia.*] The act of conniving; feigned ignorance or tacit encouragement of wrongdoing.

con·nive, kon·nīv', *v.i.—connived, conniving.* [L. *conniveo,* to wink, to connive at— *con-,* together, and *niveo,* to wink.] To overlook a fault or other act and allow it to pass unnoticed, usu. followed by *at;* to conspire; to be sympathetic toward something others are against, usu. followed by *at.*

con·niv·ent, ko·nī'vent, *a. Biol.* converging, as petals.

con·nois·seur, kon"o·sur', kon'o·sūr', *n.* [Fr. (now *connaisseur*), O.Fr. *conoissere,* < L. *cognoscere,* come to know.] One competent to pass critical judgments in an art, esp. one of the fine arts, or in matters of taste.— **con·nois·seur·ship,** *n.*

con·no·ta·tion, kon"o·tā'shan, *n.* Implication of a word or phrase in addition to its literal meaning; *logic,* the sum of the qualities thought essential to a term.— **con·no·ta·tive,** *a.*

con·note, ko·nōt', *v.t.—connoted, connoting.* [M.L. *connotare* (pp. *connotatus*), < L. *con-,* with, and *notare,* mark, E. *note, v.*] To denote secondarily; signify in addition to the primary meaning; imply; to involve as a condition or accompaniment.—**con·no·tive,** *a.* Connotative.—**con·no·tive·ly,** *adv.*

con·nu·bi·al, ko·nö'bē·al, ko·nū'bē·al, *a.* [L. *connubialis,* < *connubium,* marriage— *con-,* and *nubo,* to marry.] Pertaining to marriage; nuptial; belonging to the state of wedlock.—**con·nu·bi·al·i·ty,** *n.* The state of being connubial.—**con·nu·bi·al·ly,** *adv.* In a connubial manner; as man and wife.

co·noid, kō'noid, *a.* [Gr. *conoeidēs,* < *conos,* cone, and *eidos,* form.] Resembling or approaching a cone in shape; conoidal.—*n.* A geometrical solid formed by the revolution of a conic section about one of its axes; a geometrical surface generated by a straight line moving so as to touch a fixed straight line and a fixed curve, and continue parallel to a given plane; any object, as a bullet, approaching a cone in shape.— **co·noi·dal,** ko·noi'dal, *a.* Pertaining to or of the nature of a conoid; approaching a cone in shape.

con·quer, kong'kẽr, *v.t.* [O.Fr. *conquerre* (also *conquerir,* Fr. *conquérir*), < L. *conquærere, conquirere* (pp. *conquisitus*), < *con-,* altogether, and *quærere,* seek.] To acquire by force of arms; win in war; gain or obtain by effort; to overcome by force; subdue; vanquish; gain the victory over; surmount.—*v.i.* To make conquests; gain the victory.—**con·quer·a·ble,** *a.*—**con·quer·ing·ly,** *adv.*—**con·quer·or,** *n.*

con·quest, kon'kwest, kong'kwest, *n.* [O.Fr. *conqueste, conquest* (Fr. *conquête, conquêt*), < M.L. fem. and neut. forms < L. *conquirere* (pp. *conquisitus*). CONQUER.] The act of conquering; acquisition by force; captivation, as of favor or affections; vanquishment; that which is conquered or won.—**the Con·quest,** the conquering of England by William, Duke of Normandy, in 1066.

con·qui·an, kong'kē·an, *n.* [Sp. *con quién,* "with whom?"] A card game for two players, the object being to form sets of three or four cards of the same denomination or sequences of three or more cards of the same suit, as in rummy.

con·quis·ta·dor, kon·kwis′ta·dạr″, *Sp.* kạng·kēs″tä·THẠR′, *n.* pl. **con·quis·ta·dors,** Sp. **con·quis·ta·dor·es.** [Sp.] A conqueror: used esp. of the Spanish conquerors of Mexico and Peru in the 16th century.

con·san·guine, kon·sang′gwin, *a.* [L. *consanguineus,* < *con-,* with, and *sanguis,* blood.] Of the same blood; consanguineous. —*n.* One of the same blood as, or related by birth to, another.

con·san·guin·e·ous, kon″sang·gwin′ē·us, *a.* Of the same blood; related by birth; akin; pertaining to consanguinity; related as having had the same ancestor.—**con·san·-guin·e·ous·ly,** *adv.*

con·san·guin·i·ty, kon″sang·gwin′i·tē, *n.* The condition of being of the same blood; relationship by blood; kinship; *fig.* relationship or affinity.

con·science, kon′shens, *n.* [O.Fr. Fr. *conscience,* < L. *conscientia,* < *consciens* (*-ent-*), ppr. of *conscire,* be conscious of, < *con-,* with, and *scire,* know.] The guiding recognition of right and wrong as regards one's actions and motives; the faculty which decides upon the moral quality of one's actions and motives, enjoining one to conformity with the moral law; conscientiousness; *psychol.* a part of the superego.—**in all con·science,** in all reason and fairness; in truth; assuredly.

con·science clause, *n.* A clause or article inserted in an act or law, which relieves persons whose conscientious or religious scruples forbid their compliance with it.

con·science mon·ey, *n.* Money paid to relieve the conscience, as for obligations previously evaded.

con·sci·en·tious, kon″shē·en′shus, *a.* Influenced by conscience; governed by a strict regard to the dictates of conscience, or by the known or supposed rules of right and wrong; painstaking; careful.—**con·sci·en·-tious·ly,** *adv.*—**con·sci·en·tious·ness,** *n.*

con·sci·en·tious ob·jec·tor, *n.* One who objects, from conscientious scruples, to some course of action or procedure, esp. one who, when called upon in time of war to fight for his country, refuses to do so because of religious or moral principles.

con·scious, kon′shus, *a.* [L. *conscius,* < *con-,* with, and *scire,* know.] Inwardly sensible or aware of one's own existence, emotions, and thoughts, or of external objects and conditions; mentally alert; endowed with consciousness; aware of what one is doing; present to consciousness; known to oneself; sometimes, deliberate or intentional; directing one's thoughts and attention unduly toward oneself; self-conscious; betraying self-consciousness.—*n.* The upper level of mental life marked by awareness.—**con·scious·ly,** *adv.*

con·scious·ness, kon′shus·nis, *n.* The state of being conscious; inward sensibility of something; knowledge of one's own existence, sensations, cognitions; the thoughts and feelings, collectively, of an individual, or of an aggregate of people; as, the moral *consciousness* of a nation; activity of mental faculties; as, to regain *consciousness* after fainting.

con·scious·ness-ex·pand·ing, kon′shus·-nis·ik·spand′ing, *a.* Causing the mental state of perception or awareness to be greatly intensified, as: LSD is a *consciousness-expanding* drug.

con·script, kon′skript, *n.* [L. *conscriptus,* < *conscribo,* to enroll—*con-,* with, and *scribo,* to write.] A recruit obtained by conscription.—*a.* Enrolled; drafted.—kon·skript′, *v.t.* To draft; to enroll by compulsion for military service.

con·script fa·thers, *n.* pl. A title of the senators of Rome; any legislators.

con·scrip·tion, kon·skrip′shan, *n.* [L. *conscriptio.*] A compulsory enrollment of

males of a certain age for military or naval service; a draft; a compulsory payment exacted by a government during wartime.

con·se·crate, kon′se·krāt″, *v.t.*—*consecrated, consecrating.* [L. *consecro*—*con-,* with, and *sacro,* to consecrate, < *sacer,* sacred. SACRED.] To make or declare to be sacred with certain ceremonies or rites; to appropriate to sacred uses; to enroll among deities or saints; to canonize; to give episcopal rank to; to dedicate with solemnity; to render venerable; to make respected; to hallow.—**con·se·cra·tive,** *a.*—**con·se·-cra·tor,** *n.*—**con·se·cra·to·ry,** kon′se·-kra·tōr″ē, kon′se·kra·tạr″ē, *a.*

con·se·cra·tion, kon″se·krā′shan, *n.* The act or ceremony of consecrating or separating from a common to a sacred use; dedication of a person or thing to the service and worship of God, by certain rites or solemnities; dedication; the ceremony of elevating a priest to the dignity of a bishop; the giving of the bread and wine of the Eucharist their sacred character in the mass or communion service.

con·se·cu·tion, kon″se·kū′shan, *n.* [L. *consecutio(n-),* < *consequi,* follow after.] Succession; sequence; logical sequence.

con·sec·u·tive, kon·sek′ū·tiv, *a.* [Fr. *consécutif,* < L. *consequi.*] Following one another in uninterrupted intervals; uninterrupted in course or succession; successive; marked by logical sequence; *gram.* expressing consequence or result; as, a *consecutive* clause.—**con·sec·u·tive points,** *n. pl.* Math. two or more points infinitely close one to another on the same branch of a curve.—**con·sec·u·tive·ly,** *adv.*—**con·-sec·u·tive·ness,** *n.*

con·sen·su·al, kon·sen′shō·al, *a.* [L. *consensus.* CONSENSUS.] Formed or existing by consent; *physiol.* pertaining to involuntary movement accompanying voluntary movement, as the contraction of the iris when the eye is opened to receive the light; *psychol.* pertaining to reflex action initiated by a distinctly conscious sensation.—**con·sen·su·al·ly,** *adv.*

con·sen·sus, kon·sen′sus, *n.* [L. < *consentire.*] A general agreement or concord; majority of opinion.

con·sent, kon·sent′, *v.i.* [L. *consentio,* to agree—*con-,* with, and *sentio, sensum,* to feel, perceive, think; akin *sense, sentiment.*] To agree; to accord; to yield, as to persuasion; to comply; to acquiesce or accede.

con·sent, kon·sent′, *n.* Voluntary approval of what is done or proposed by another; permission; acquiescence; concurrence; compliance; accord of minds; agreement in opinion or sentiment.—**con·sent·er,** *n.*

con·sen·ta·ne·ous, kon″sen·tā′nē·us, *a.* [L. *consentaneus,* < *consentire.*] Agreeing or accordant; done by common consent; unanimous.—**con·sen·ta·ne·i·ty,** **con·-sen·ta·ne·ous·ness,** kon·sen″ta·nē′i·tē, *n.* **con·sen·ta·ne·ous·ly,** *adv.*

con·sen·tience, kon·sen′shens, *n.* [See *consentient.*] Agreement or accordance.

con·sen·tient, kon·sen′shent, *a.* [L. *consentiens* (*-ent-*), ppr. of *consentire.*] Agreeing or accordant; unanimous, as an opinion; acting in agreement or harmony.

con·se·quence, kon′se·kwens″, kon′se·-kwens, *n.* [L. *consequentia,* < *consequor.*] The effect, result, or outcome which follows any act, cause, principles, or series of actions; an event or effect produced by some preceding act or cause; inference; deduction; conclusion from premises; importance.—**in con·se·quence of,** as the effect of; by reason of; through.

con·se·quent, kon′se·kwent″, kon′se·-kwent, *a.* [L. *consequens* (*-ent-*), ppr. of *consequi,* follow after, < *con-,* with, and *sequi,* follow.] Following as an effect or result; resulting; following as a logical

conclusion; logically consistent.—**con·se·-quent·ly,** *adv.*

con·se·quent, kon′se·kwent″, kon′se·kwent, *n.* An effect or result; anything that follows upon something else; *logic,* a conclusion or inference; *math.* the second term of a ratio.

con·se·quen·tial, kon″se·kwen′shal, *a.* [L. *consequentia.*] Of the nature of a consequence; following as an effect or result, or as a logical conclusion or inference; consequent; resultant; logically consistent; of consequence or importance; self-important; pompous.—**con·se·quen·-ti·al·i·ty,** **con·se·quen·tial·ness,** *n.*— **con·se·quen·tial·ly,** *adv.*

con·serv·a·ble, kon·sẽr′va·bl, *a.* Capable of being conserved; preservable.

con·serv·an·cy, kon·sẽr′van·sē, *n.* pl. **con·serv·an·cies.** [For earlier *conservacy,* < M.L. *conservatia.*] Conservation, as of rivers or forests; *Brit.* a commission or court regulating fisheries and navigation.

con·ser·va·tion, kon″sẽr·vā′shan, *n.* [L. *conservatio(n-).*] The act of conserving; preservation and protection from loss, injury, or decay; official supervision of rivers, forests, and other natural resources; a district under such supervision.—**con·-ser·va·tion·al,** *a.*

con·ser·va·tion·ist, kon″sẽr·vā′sha·nist, *n.* One who advocates or promotes conservation, esp. of the natural resources of a country; one engaged in protecting game and fish, preserving forests, conserving food and fuel supply in the public interest.

con·ser·va·tion of en·er·gy, *n. Phys.* the principle that the total energy of a closed system is constant, regardless of the change in form of the energy.

con·ser·va·tion of mass, *n. Phys.* The principle that the total mass of any closed system is constant, regardless of its changes in form or reactions between the parts; the principle that matter cannot be destroyed or created.

con·serv·a·tism, kon·sẽr′va·tiz″um, *n.* [< *conservative.*] The disposition to preserve what is established; opposition to innovation or change; the principles and practices of political conservatives.—**con·-serv·a·tist,** *n.* A conservative.

con·serv·a·tive, kon·sẽr′va·tiv, *a.* Tending to preserve; preservative; inclined to keep up existing institutions and customs; opposed to radical changes or innovations; moderate, cautious. *Brit.,* (*cap.*) pertaining to the Conservatives or their party's principles.—**con·serv·a·tive·ly,** *adv.*— **con·serv·a·tive·ness,** *n.*

con·serv·a·tive, kon·sẽr′va·tiv, *n.* One whose principles, methods, and habits are moderate and cautious; one who avoids extremes; an advocate of political caution; *Brit.,* (*cap.*) a member of the Conservative party in Great Britain. A preservative.

con·ser·va·toire, kon·sẽr″va·twär′, kon·-sẽr′va·twär″, *Fr.* kạn·seR·vä·twär′, *n.* [Fr.] A conservatory, as of music or any of the other fine arts.

con·ser·va·tor, kon′sẽr·vā·tor, kon·sẽr′-va·tor, *n.* [L.] One who conserves or preserves; a protector; a guardian; a custodian; a person or institution designated to protect and direct another's interests. *Brit.* a person working for the conservancy commission; a conservation worker.

con·serv·a·to·ry, kon·sẽr′va·tōr″ē, kon·-sẽr′va·tạr″ē, *n.* pl. **con·serv·a·to·ries.** [M.L. *conservatorius* (as *n., conservatorium*).] A greenhouse, usually glass enclosed, for the displaying and growing of plants; a place for instruction in music and declamation; a school of music.—*a.* Serving or adapted to conserve; preservative.

con·serve, kon·sẽrv′, *v.t.*—*conserved, conserving.* [O.Fr. Fr. *conserver,* < L. *conservare* (pp. *conservatus*), < *con-,* with, and *servare*, keep.] To keep in a safe or sound state; preserve from loss, decay, waste, or injury; keep unimpaired; to preserve, as fruit, with sugar; *phys.* to maintain a constant balance of energy during a physical or chemical change.—**con·serv·er**, *n.*

con·serve, kon′sẽrv, kon·sẽrv′, *n.* [O.Fr. Fr. *conserve.*] That which is conserved; a confection; a preserve; a jam consisting of several fruits cooked together with sugar.

con·sid·er, kon·sid′ẽr, *v.t.* [L. *considero*, to view attentively, to consider: originally (like *contemplor*) an augurial term—*con-*, together, and *sidus, sideris*, a constellation.] To think on with care; to ponder; to study; to meditate on; to observe and examine; to respect; to take into view or account, or have regard to, in examination or in forming an estimate; to judge to be; as, to *consider* a man wise.—*v.i.* To think seriously, maturely, or carefully; to reflect.

con·sid·er·a·ble, kon·sid′ẽr·a·bl, *a.* [M.L. *considerabilis.*] Worthy of consideration; important; of distinction; being of an amount or extent worthy of attention; fairly large or great—*n. Colloq.* Much; a great deal.—**con·sid·er·a·bly**, *adv.*

con·sid·er·ate, kon·sid′ẽr·it, *a.* [L. *consideratus.*] Given to consideration or to sober reflection; circumspect; discreet; prudent; characterized by consideration or regard for another's circumstances and feelings.—**con·sid·er·ate·ly**, *adv.*—**con·sid·er·ate·ness**, *n.*

con·sid·er·a·tion, kon·sid″e·rā′shan, *n.* [L. *consideratio(n-).*] The act of considering; reflection, meditation, or deliberation; a thought or reflection; regard or account; something taken, or to be taken into account; a recompense for service rendered; a compensation; thoughtful or sympathetic regard or respect; thoughtfulness for others; estimation; esteem; importance or consequence. *Law*, that which a contracting party accepts as an equivalent for a service; the price of a promise.

con·sid·ered, kon·sid′erd, *a.* Arrived at by careful thought and evaluation; as, his *considered* opinion; looked upon with respect.

con·sid·er·ing, kon·sid′ẽr·ing, *prep.* [Orig. ppr.] Taking into account; in view of.—**con·sid·er·ing·ly**, *adv.*

con·sign, kon·sin′, *v.t.* [L. *consigno*, to seal or sign.] To give or hand over; to transfer or deliver over into the possession of another or into a different state; as, to *consign* a body to the grave; to deliver or transfer in charge or trust; to entrust, as goods, to a factor for sale; to commit for permanent preservation; as, to *consign* to writing.—**con·sig·na·tion**, kon″sig·nā′shan, *n.* The act of consigning.—**con·sign·er, con·sign·or**, *n.*

con·sign·ee, kon″si·nē′, kon″si·nē′, kon·si·nē′, *n.* The person to whom goods or other things are consigned.

con·sign·ment, kon·sin′ment, *n.* The act of consigning; the act of sending off goods to an agent for sale; goods sent or delivered to an agent for sale.

con·sist, kon·sist′, *v.i.* [L. *consisto*—*con-*, and *sisto*, to stand.] To be comprised or contained, followed by *in*; to be composed or to be made up, followed by *of*; to be compatible, consistent, or harmonious, followed by *with.*

con·sist·en·cy, kon·sis′ten·sē, *n. pl.* **con·sist·en·cies.** Coherence; firmness; solidity; degree of density or viscosity; agreement; congruity. Also **con·sist·ence.**

con·sist·ent, kon·sis′tent, *a.* Agreeing; compatible; not self-contradictory; uniform.—**con·sist·ent·ly**, *adv.*

con·sis·to·ry, kon·sis′to·rē, *n. pl.* **con·sis·tor·ies.** [L.L. *consistorium*, place of assembly, < L. *consistere.*] A council chamber; an assembly or council, esp. any of various ecclesiastical councils or tri-

bunals, as in certain Reformed churches; a court corresponding to a session in Presbyterian churches; in the Roman Catholic Church, a senate consisting of the whole body of the cardinals, usually presided over by the Pope, which deliberates upon the affairs of the church; the meeting of any such body; the place where it meets.—**con·sis·to·ri·al**, kon″si·stōr′ē·al, *a.*

con·so·ci·ate, kon·sō′shē·āt″, *v.t.*—*consociated, consociating.* [L. *consociatus*, pp. of *consociare*, < *con-*, with, and *sociare*, join.] To bring together.—*v.i.* To associate.

con·so·ci·ate, kon·sō′shē·it, kon·sō′shē·āt″, *a.* Associated; joined in a consociation.—*n.* One associated with another or others; an associate; partner; a companion.

con·so·ci·a·tion, kon·sō″sē·ā′shan, kon·sō″shē·ā′shan, *n.* [L. *consociatio(n-).*] Association of persons or things; fellowship; a confederation or union of churches, esp. Congregational churches.—**con·so·ci·a·tion·al**, *a.*—**con·so·ci·a·tion·ism**, *n.*

con·so·la·tion, kon″so·lā′shan, *n.* [L. *consolatio.*] The act of consoling; a comfort; solace; one who or that which offers consolation; *sports*, a game or contest between those persons or teams eliminated before the final competition.—**con·sol·a·to·ry**, kon·sol′a·tōr″ē, kon·sol′a·tar″ē, *a.* Tending to console or give comfort.

con·sole, kon·sōl′, *v.t.*—*consoled, consoling.* [L. *consolor*, to console.] To cheer, as a person, in distress or depression; to comfort; to soothe; to solace.—**con·sol·a·ble**, *a.*—**con·sol·er**, *n.*

con·sole, kon′sōl, *n.* [Fr. origin uncertain.] Any bracket or bracketlike support; a corbel; desklike structure containing the keyboards of an organ, esp. when separate from the body of the instrument; a cabinet, standing on the floor, which holds a radio, TV, or phonograph; the control unit of a computer or an electronic system.

con·sole ta·ble, *n.* A table supported by consoles or brackets fixed to a wall; a table, with curved console-like legs, which fits against a wall.

con·sol·i·date, kon·sol′i·dāt″, *v.t.*—*consolidated, consolidating.* [L. *consolido, consolidatum*—*con-*, and *solidus*, solid.] To make solid or compact; to harden or make dense and firm; to bring together into one close mass or body; to make firm or establish; *milit.* to regroup for strength after action.—*v.i.* To grow firm and hard; to unite and become solid.

con·sol·i·dat·ed school, *n.* A public school, esp. in rural areas, formed by combining schools from several districts.

con·sol·i·da·tion, kon·sol″i·dā′shan, *n.* [L.L. *consolidatio(n-).*] The act of consolidating, or the state of being consolidated; solidification; strengthening; unification; merger; combination; a consolidated whole; a merger of two or more corporations by dissolving old corporations and creating a single new one.—**con·sol·i·da·tor**, *n.*

con·som·mé, kon″so·mā′, *Fr.* kaN·sa·mā′, *n.* [Fr., prop. pp. of *consommer*, < L. *consummare.*] A strong, clear soup made by boiling meat long and slowly, until all the flavor and nutritive properties are extracted.

con·so·nance, kon′so·nans, *n.* The state of being consonant; correspondence of sounds; harmony of sounds; *fig.* accord or agreement; *mus.* a simultaneous combination of tones, as of a note and its fifth, that is agreeable to the ear. *Phys.* sympathetic vibration; resonance. Also **con·so·nan·cy.**

con·so·nant, kon′so·nant, *a.* [L. *consonans* (-*ant*-), ppr. of *consonare*, sound together, < *con-*, with, and *sonare*, sound.] Corresponding in sound, as words; harmonious, as sounds; in agreement; agreeable or accordant to; consistent with; consonantal; *mus.* constituting a consonance; *phys.*

characterized by or pertaining to consonance.—**con·so·nant·ly**, *adv.*

con·so·nant, kon′so·nant, *n.* One of the partly closed speech sounds which are combined with more open sounds, called *vowels*, to form syllables; an element of speech other than a vowel; a letter or character representing such a sound or element.

con·so·nan·tal, kon″so·nan′tal, *a.* Of, pertaining to, or of the nature of a consonant; marked by consonant sounds.—**con·so·nan·tal·ly**, *adv.*

con·so·nant shift, *n.* The consistent differences in consonant articulation in the history of any language or dialect.

con·sort, kon′sart, *n.* [L. *consors*—*con-*, and *sors*, a lot.] A partner; an intimate associate, particularly a wife or husband; *naut.* any vessel accompanying another.

con·sort, kon·sart′, *v.t.* To associate; sound in harmony.—*v.i.* To associate; have intercourse; to agree or harmonize.

con·sor·ti·um, kon·sar′shē·um, *n. pl.* **con·sor·ti·a**, kon·sar′shē·a. An association or union; a combination of financial institutions and capitalists for the purpose of carrying into effect some financial operation requiring large sources of capital; *Brit.* teams of companies as joint producers of atomic power plants.

con·spe·cif·ic, kon″spi·sif′ik, *a.* Of the same species.

con·spec·tus, kon·spek′tus, *n. pl.* **con·spec·tus·es.** [L., < *conspicere*, view, survey, < *con-*, together, and *specere*, look at.] A general summary; a digest; a résumé.

con·spic·u·ous, kon·spik′ū·us, *a.* [L. *conspicuus*, < *conspicere.*] Easy to be seen; clearly visible; catching the eye; readily attracting the attention; striking; noteworthy.—**con·spic·u·ous·ly**, *adv.*—**con·spic·u·ous·ness**, *n.*

con·spic·u·ous con·sump·tion, *n.* Ostentatious buying, use, and display for status rather than for the utilitarian value of the goods.

con·spir·a·cy, kon·spir′a·sē, *n. pl.* **con·spir·a·cies.** [L. *conspiratio*, < *conspiro.*] The secret plotting of two or more persons to do a wrongful act; a plot so devised; a group of conspirators.

con·spir·a·tor, kon·spir′a·tẽr, *n.* [M.L.] One who conspires; a joint plotter.

con·spir·a·tor·ial, kon·spir″a·tōr′ē·al, kon·spir″a·tar′ē·al, *a.* Of or relating to conspiracy or conspirators.

con·spire, kon·spir′, *v.i.*—*conspired, conspiring.* [O.Fr. Fr. *conspirer*, < L. *conspirare* (pp. *conspiratus*), < *con-*, with, and *spirare*, breathe.] To agree together, esp. secretly, to do something reprehensible or illegal; combine for an evil or unlawful purpose; plot; to act in combination; contribute jointly to a result.—*v.t.* To plot, as something evil or unlawful.—**con·spir·er**, *n.*—**con·spir·ing·ly**, *adv.*

con·sta·ble, kon′sta·bl, *Brit.* kun′sta·bl, *n.* [O.Fr. *conestable* (Fr. *connétable*), < L.L. *comes stabuli*, "count of the stable," master of the horse.] In medieval monarchies, the highest ranking official of the household, court, or army; the keeper or governor of a royal fortress or castle; a military officer; now esp. any of various officials who keep the peace and perform minor judicial duties; *Brit.* a policeman.—**con·sta·ble·ship**, *n.*

con·stab·u·lar·y, kon·stab′ū·ler″ē, *n. pl.* **con·stab·u·lar·ies.** A district under the jurisdiction of a constable; the body of constables of a district or locality; a body of officers of the peace organized on a military basis.—*a.*

con·stan·cy, kon′stan·sē, *n.* [L. *constantia.*] The quality of being unchanging or unwavering in thought, deed, or purpose; steadfastness; faithfulness.

con·stant, kon′stant, *a.* [O.Fr. Fr. *constant,*

---

a- fat, fāte, fär, fâre, fall;　**e-** met, mē, mẽre, hẽr;　**i-** pin, pīne;　**o-** not, nōte, möve;　**u-** tub, cūbe, bull;　**oi-** oil;　**ou-** pound.

< L. *constans* (*constant-*), ppr. of *constare*, stand together, stand firm, < *con-*, with, and *stare*, stand.] Standing firm in mind or purpose; invariable or unchanging; uniform; always present; continuing without pause.—**con·stant·ly**, *adv.*

con·stant, kon′stant, *n.* Something constant, invariable, or unchanging; *math.* a quantity assumed to be invariable throughout a given discussion; *phys.* a numerical quantity expressing a relation or value, as of a physical property of a substance, which remains unchanged under certain conditions.

con·stel·late, kon′ste·lāt″, *v.t.*—*constellated, constellating.* To cluster, as stars in a constellation.

con·stel·la·tion, kon″ste·lā′shan, *n.* [O.Fr. *constellacion* (Fr. *constellation*), < L.L. *constellatio(n-).*] Any of various groups of fixed stars to which definite names have been given, as Ursa Major, Ursa Minor, Bootes, Cancer, Orion; a division of the heavens occupied by such a group; the grouping of the stars as supposed to influence events, esp. at the time of a person's birth; *fig.* any brilliant assemblage.—**con·stel·la·to·ry**, kon·stel′a·tōr″ē, *a.*

con·ster·nate, kon′stẽr·nāt″, *v.t.*—*consternated, consternating.* To overwhelm with astonishment or confusion.

con·ster·na·tion, kon″stẽr·nā′shan, *n.* [L. *consternatio*, < *consterno.*] Dismayed astonishment; alarm that results in confusion; fear; paralyzing wonder.

con·sti·pate, kon′sti·pāt″, *v.t.*—*constipated, constipating.* [L. *constipatus*, pp. of *constipare*, < *con-*, together, and *stipare*, crowd, pack.] *Med.* To cause constipation in; to make costive.

con·sti·pa·tion, kon″sti·pā′shan, *n.* [L.L. *constipatio(n-).*] The state of being constipated; a condition of the bowels marked by irregular or difficult evacuation.

con·stit·u·en·cy, kon·stich′ō·en·sē, *n.* pl. **con·stit·u·en·cies.** A body of constituents; the body of voters, or, loosely, of residents, in a district represented by an elective officer; the district itself; any body of supporters or customers; a clientele. *Canada*, a riding or district represented by a member of Parliament or a member of the Legislative Assembly.

con·stit·u·ent, kon·stich′ō·ent, *a.* [L. *constituens* (*-ent-*), ppr. of *constituere.*] Constituting; empowered to appoint or elect a representative; as, a *constituent* body; having power to frame or alter a political constitution; as, a *constituent* assembly; serving to make up a thing; component; constituting.—**con·stit·u·ent·ly**, *adv.*

con·stit·u·ent, kon·stich′ō·ent, *n.* One who or that which establishes or determines; that which constitutes or composes, as a part, or an essential part; an essential ingredient; one who elects or assists in electing another as his representative in a deliberative or administrative assembly.

con·sti·tute, kon′sti·tōt″, kon′sti·tūt″, *v.t.* —*constituted, constituting.* [L. *constitutus*, pp. of *constituere*, < *con-*, together, and *statuere*, set up, set, establish.] To compose; form; to appoint to an office or function; make or create; as, to be *constituted* captain; to set up or establish; give legal form to; to make up or form of elements or material.

con·sti·tu·tion, kon″sti·tō′shan, kon″sti·tū′shan, *n.* [L. *constitutio(n-).*] The act of constituting, or the state of being constituted; establishment; formation; a decree, law, or regulation, as one made by a superior civil or ecclesiastical authority; hence, any established arrangement or custom; the way in which anything is constituted; make-up or composition; esp. the physical character of the body as to strength or health; character or condition

of mind; disposition; temperament; the system of fundamental principles according to which a nation, state, corporation, or the like is governed, or the document embodying these principles; as, the *Constitution* of the U.S.; any system of fundamental principles of action.

con·sti·tu·tion·al, kon″sti·tō′sha·nal, kon″sti·tū′sha·nal, *a.* Pertaining to the constitution or composition of a thing; essential; belonging to or inherent in a person's constitution of body or mind; affecting the bodily constitution; pertaining to, in accordance with, or subject to the constitution of a state.

con·sti·tu·tion·al, kon″sti·tō′sha·nal, kon″sti·tū′sha·nal, *n.* A walk or other exercise taken for the benefit of health.

con·sti·tu·tion·al·ism, kon″sti·tō′sha··na·liz″um, kon″sti·tū′sha·na·liz″um, *n.* The theory or principle of constitutional rule or authority; constitutional principles; adherence to a constitution.

con·sti·tu·tion·al·i·ty, kon″sti·tō′sha··nal′i·tē, kon″sti·tū′sha·nal′i·tē, *n.* The quality of being constitutional; accordance with the constitution of a state or nation.

con·sti·tu·tion·al·ly, kon″sti·tō′sha·na··lē, kon″sti·tū′sha·na·lē, *adv.* In a constitutional manner; in consistency with a national constitution or law; in accordance with the constitution of mind or body; in reference to the fundamental or essential makeup or structure.

con·sti·tu·tive, kon′sti·tō″tiv, kon′sti··tū″tiv, *a.* Forming, composing, enacting, or establishing; constituting; instituting. *Chem.* relating to the arrangement of atoms or molecules in a substance.—**con·sti·tu··tive·ly**, *adv.*

con·strain, kon·strān′, *v.t.* [O.Fr. *constreindre, constraindre* (Fr. *contraindre*), < L. *constringere* (pp. *constrictus*), draw together, constrict, constrain, < *con-*, together, and *stringere*, draw tight.] To force, compel, or oblige; bring about by compulsion; as, to *constrain* obedience; to confine forcibly, as by bonds; hence, to repress or restrain; *mech.* to prevent the occurrence of motion in (a body), except in a particular manner or direction.—**con··strain·a·ble**, *a.*—**con·strained**, *a.*—**con·strain·ed·ly**, *adv.*—**con·strain·er**, *n.*

con·straint, kon·strānt′, *n.* [O.Fr. *constrainte* (Fr. *constrainte*).] The act of constraining, or the condition of being constrained; compulsion; confinement or restriction; repression of natural feelings and impulses; unnatural restraint in manner; embarrassment; something that constrains.

con·strict, kon·strikt′, *v.t.* [L. *constrictus*, pp. of *constringere.*] To draw together as by an encircling pressure; compress; cramp; to cause to contract or shrink.—**con·stric··tive**, *a.*—**con·stric·tion**, *n.*

con·stric·tor, kon·strik′tẽr, *n.* [N.L.] One who or that which constricts; a serpent that crushes its prey in its coils; *anat.* a muscle that constricts or draws parts together.

con·struct, kon·strukt′, *v.t.* [L. *constructus*, pp. of *construere*, pile or put together, construct, < *con-*, together, and *struere*, pile up, build, make: cf. *construe.*] To form by putting together parts; build; frame; devise; *geom.* to draw, as a figure, so as to fulfill given conditions.—**con·struct·i·ble**, *a.*—**con·struc·tor, con·struc·ter**, *n.*

con·struct, kon′strukt, *n. Philos., psychol.* the result of intellectual perception and consideration of things and ideas received through the senses.

con·struc·tion, kon·struk′shan, *n.* [L. *constructio(n-)*, < *construere.*] The act or art of constructing; the way in which a thing is constructed; a building; the act or manner of constructing. *Gram.* the arrangement and

connection of words in a sentence according to established usages; syntactical connection. Explanation or interpretation, as of a law or a text, or of conduct.—**con·struc··tion·al**, *a.*—**con·struc·tion·al·ly**, *adv.*

con·struc·tion·ist, kon·struk′sha·nist, *n.* One who construes or interprets, esp. laws.

con·struc·tive, kon·struk′tiv, *a.* [M.L. *constructivus.*] Constructing, or tending to construct; of, pertaining to, or of the nature of construction; structural; deduced by construction or interpretation; inferential; virtual; intended to be helpful; as, *constructive* criticism.—**con·struc·tive·ly**, *adv.*— **con·struc·tive·ness**, *n.*

con·struc·tiv·ism, kon·struk′ti·viz″um, *n.* (*Often cap.*) the nonrepresentational style of art which uses modern industrial materials such as plastics and glass to organize planes and volume in an extremely formal expression.

con·struc·tor, con·struc·ter, kon·struk′tẽr, *n.* [M.L.] One who constructs; a builder; as, a naval *constructor*, one of a corps of naval officers charged with the construction and repair of warships.— **con·struc·tor·ship**, *n.*

con·strue, kon·strō′, *Brit.* kon′strō, *v.t.* —*construed, construing.* [L. *construere.*] To arrange or combine, as words, syntactically; to analyze the grammatical construction of, as a sentence; to translate, esp. orally; to show the meaning or intention of; interpret, as a law; put one's own interpretation on; to deduce by construction or interpretation; infer.—*v.i.* To admit of grammatical analysis or interpretation.—**con′stru·a··ble**, *a.*—**con·stru·er**, *n.*

con·sub·stan·tial, kon″sub·stan′shal, *a.* Of one and the same substance, essence, or nature.—**con·sub·stan·ti·al·i·ty**, kon″·sub·stan″shē·al′i·tē, *n.*—**con·sub·stan··tial·ly**, *adv.*

con·sub·stan·ti·a·tion, kon″sub·stan″·shē·ā′shan, *n.* [N.L. *consubstantiatio(n-).*] *Theol.* the substantial union of the body and blood of Christ with the eucharistic elements after consecration.

con·sue·tude, kon′swi·tōd″, kon′swi·tūd″, *n.* [L. *consuetudo* (*consuetudin-*), < *consuescere* (pp. *consuetus*), accustom, < *con-*, with, and *suescere*, become used, accustom: cf. *custom.*] Custom, esp. as having legal force; usage; familiarity; social intercourse.—**con·sue·tu·di·na·ry**, kon′swi·tōd′i·ner″ē, *a.* Customary.

con·sul, kon′sul, *n.* [L. prob. < *consulere*, deliberate.] Either of the two chief magistrates of the ancient Roman republic; one of the three supreme magistrates of the French republic from 1799 to 1804; an agent appointed by one country to reside in a foreign city or town and care for the commercial and other interests there of citizens of his own country.—**con·su·lar**, *a.* —**con·sul·ship**, *n.*

con·su·lar a·gent, *n.* An officer performing the duties of a consul at a place of minor commercial importance.

con·su·late, kon′su·lit, *n.* [L. *consulatus.*] The office or position of a consul; the premises officially occupied by a consul.

con·sul gen·er·al, *n.* pl. **con·suls gen·er··al.** A consular officer of the highest rank.

con·sult, kon·sult′, *v.i.* [L. *consulto*, intens. < *consulo*, to consult.] To seek the opinion or advice of another; to take counsel together; to deliberate in common.—*v.t.* To ask advice of; to seek the opinion of as a guide to one's own judgment; to have recourse to for information or instruction.

con·sult·ant, kon·sul′tant, *n.* One who consults; one who offers business, professional, or expert advice for a fee.

con·sul·ta·tion, kon″sul·tā′shan, *n.* The act of consulting; deliberation by two or more persons with a view to some decision; a meeting of physicians to consult concerning a patient's case.

con·sult·a·tive, kon·sul'ta·tiv, *a.* Of or pertaining to consultation; advisory. Also **con·sul·ta·to·ry, con·sul·tive.**

con·sum·a·ble, kon·söm'a·bl, *a.* Capable of being consumed.

con·sume, kon·söm', *v.t.*—*consumed, consuming.* [L. *consumere* (pp. *consumptus*), < *con-*, altogether, and *sumere*, take, use, spend.] To destroy, as by decomposition or burning; to destroy or expend by use; use up; waste; squander; to devour.—*v.i.* To be consumed; suffer destruction; waste away.

con·sum·ed·ly, kon·sö'mid·lē, *adv.* [*Consumed* formerly had sense of deuced, confounded.] *Brit.* Extremely; greatly; to excess.

con·sum·er, kon·sö'mèr, *n.* One who or that which consumes; *econ.* the buyer or user of commodities and services, as opposed to *producer.*

con·sum·er cred·it, *n.* Credit given to an individual by a store, bank, or finance company, through charge accounts, installment plans, or money loans to finance the purchase of consumer goods or defray personal expenses.

con·sum·er goods, *n. pl.* Goods, such as clothing and food, which are made for the consumer and are not intended to be used in further production.

con·sum·mate, kon'su·māt', *v.t.*—*consummated, consummating.* [L. *consummatus*, pp. of *consummare*, < *con-*, altogether, and *summa*, top, culmination, completion, E. *sum.*] To bring to completion; complete; perfect; fulfill; to complete (a marriage) by sexual intercourse.—**con·sum·ma·tion**, *n.*

con·sum·mate, kon·sum'it, kon'su·mit, *a.* Complete or perfect; supremely qualified; of the highest quality.—**con·sum·mate·ly**, *adv.*

con·sump·tion, kon·sump'shan, *n.* [L. *consumptio(n-)*, < *consumere.*] The act of consuming, or the state of being consumed; destruction; decay; destruction by use. *Pathol.* tuberculosis; progressive wasting of the body, esp. from tuberculosis of the lungs. *Econ.* the using up of commodities or services, as opposed to their *production.*

con·sump·tive, kon·sump'tiv, *a.* Tending to consume; destructive; wasteful; pertaining to consumption by use. *Pathol.* pertaining to or of the nature of tuberculosis; disposed to or affected with consumption.— *n.* One who suffers from tuberculosis.

con·tact, kon'takt, *n.* [L. *contactus*, < *contingo, contactum*, to touch—*con-*, and *tango* (root *tag*), to touch.] A state or condition of touching; touch; proximity or association; connection; a junction of two electrical conductors through which current flows; a carrier of contagion; one who provides access to an advantageous opportunity, as: His *contacts* led to sales.—*a.*

con·tact, kon'takt, *v.t.* To bring into contact; *colloq.* to get in touch with.—*v.i.* To be in contact.

con·tact lens, *n.* A small prescription lens to correct vision, which is applied directly to the surface of the cornea, and held in place by surface tension of the eye fluid.

con·tact print, *n.* *Photog.* a positive photographic print made by passing light through a negative which is held in direct contact with a photosensitive paper, plate, or film.

con·ta·gion, kon·tā'jon, *n.* [L. *contagio(n-)*, < *contingere*, touch. CONTINGENT.] The communication of disease by direct or indirect contact; a disease so communicated; the medium by which a contagious disease is transmitted; pestilential influence; hurtful contact or influence; moral corruption; the communication of

any influence, as enthusiasm, from one to another.

con·ta·gious, kon·tā'jus, *a.* [L.L. *contagiosus.*] Causing or involving contagion; noxious; communicable by contagion, as a disease. *Fig.* tending to spread from one to another; as, *contagious* laughter; communicable.—**con·ta·gious·ly**, *adv.*—**con·ta·gious·ness**, *n.*

con·ta·gi·um, kon·tā'jum, kon·tā'jē·um, *n. pl.* **con·ta·gi·a**, kon·tā'ja, kon·tā'jē·a. [L.] The medium by which a contagious disease is communicated, as a virus.

con·tain, kon·tān', *v.t.* [O.Fr. Fr. *contenir*, < L. *continere* (pp. *contentus*), hold together, hold, hold back.] To have within itself; hold within fixed limits; to be capable of holding; have capacity for; to be equal to, as: A quart *contains* two pints. To have as contents or constituent parts; comprise; include; to keep within proper bounds; restrain, as oneself or one's feelings or passions; to retain; *math.* to be divisible by, esp. without a remainder.—*v.i.* To restrain oneself or one's feelings.—**con·tain·a·ble**, *a.* That may be contained.

con·tain·er, kon·tā'nèr, *n.* That which contains; a vessel, receptacle, carton, case, or other containing or enclosing structure.

con·tain·er·i·za·tion, kon·tā"nèr·i·zā'shan, *n.* The procedure of shipment of goods in reusable containers, as in a truck trailer which may be transferred unopened to a ship or a railroad flatcar.—**con·tain·er·ize**, *v.t.*—*containerized, containerizing.* To package in uniform reusable containers preparatory to shipment.

con·tain·ment, kon·tān'ment, *n.* The policy, process, or result of containing, esp. as in preventing a hostile power from territorial or ideological expansion.

con·tam·i·nant, kon·tam'i·nant, *n.* Something which causes contamination, such as waste materials emptied into the source of water supply, or noxious fumes into the air.

con·tam·i·nate, kon·tam'i·nāt", *v.t.*—*contaminated, contaminating.* [L. *contaminatus*, pp. of *contaminare*, ult. < *con-*, with, and *tangere*, touch.] To render impure by contact or mixture; defile; pollute; taint; corrupt.—**con·tam·i·na·tive**, *a.*—**con·tam·i·na·tor**, *n.*

con·tam·i·na·tion, kon·tam"i·nā'shan, *n.* [L.L. *contaminatio(n-)*.] The act of contaminating, or the state of being contaminated; something that contaminates.

conte, kạNt, *n. pl.* **contes**, kạnt. [Fr. = E. *count*, *n.*] A tale or short story, esp. of extraordinary and usually imaginary events.

con·temn, kon·tem', *v.t.* [L. *contemno.*] To despise; to consider and treat as mean and despicable; to scorn; to reject with disdain.—**con·tem·nor**, kon·tem'èr, kon·tem'nèr, *n.*

con·tem·plate, kon'tem·plāt", kon·tem'-plāt, *v.t.*—*contemplated, contemplating.* [L. *contemplatus*, pp. of *contemplari*, < *con-*, with, and *templum*, open space for augurial observations, E. *temple.*] To look at or view with continued attention; observe thoughtfully; to consider thoroughly and deliberately.—*v.i.* To think studiously upon past events and future possibilities; meditate.

con·tem·pla·tion, kon"tem·plā'shan, *n.* [L. *contemplatio(n-)*.] The act of contemplating; thoughtful observation; attentive consideration; religious meditation; matter for reflection or meditation; prospect or expectation; as, to act in *contemplation* of probable changes; purpose or intention; as, projects in *contemplation.*

con·tem·pla·tive, kon·tem'pla·tiv, kon'-tem·plā"tiv, *n.* One given to contemplation. —*a.*—**con·tem·pla·tive·ly**, *adv.*—**con·tem·pla·tive·ness**, *n.*

con·tem·po·ra·ne·ous, kon·tem"po·rā'nē·us, *a.* [L. *contemporaneus.*] Living,

happening, or belonging within the same time period; contemporary.—**con·tem·po·ra·ne·ous·ly**, *adv.*—**con·tem·po·ra·ne·ous·ness**, *n.*

con·tem·po·rar·y, kon·tem'po·rer"ē, *a.* Existing or occurring at the same time; belonging to the same age or date.

con·tem·po·rar·y, kon·tem'po·rer"ē, *n. pl.* **con·tem·po·rar·ies.** One belonging to the same time or period with another or others; a person of the same age as another. —**con·tem·po·rar·i·ness**, *n.*

con·tempt, kon·tempt', *n.* [L. *contemptus*, < *contemnere*: see *contemn.*] The feelings or actions with which one regards anything considered mean, vile, or worthless; disdain; scorn; the state of being despised; dishonor; disgrace; *law*, disobedience to, or open disrespect for, the rules or orders of a court or legislature.

con·tempt·i·ble, kon·temp'ti·bl, *a.* [L. *contemptibilis.*] Worthy of contempt; deserving scorn or disdain; mean; vile.— **con·tempt·i·ble·ness**, *n.* The state of being contemptible.—**con·tempt·i·bly**, *adv.* In a contemptible manner; meanly; in a manner deserving of contempt.

con·temp·tu·ous, kon·temp'chö·us, *a.* Manifesting or expressing contempt or disdain; scornful.—**con·temp·tu·ous·ly**, *adv.*—**con·temp·tu·ous·ness**, *n.*

con·tend, kon·tend', *v.i.* [L.] To struggle in opposition; as, to *contend* with the enemy for control of the airstrip; to strive in rivalry; as, to *contend* for first prize; to assert or maintain rigorously, as: He *contended* he was innocent.—**con·tend·er**, *n.* One who contends; a combatant or rival.

con·tent, kon·tent', *a.* [O.Fr. Fr. *content*, < L. *contentus*, satisfied, pp. of *continere.*] Having the desires limited by what one has; satisfied, as with something specified; easy in mind; willing or resigned; assenting; wholly at ease.

con·tent, kon·tent', *v.t.* To make content; to quiet, so as to stop complaint or opposition; to appease; to make easy in any situation; to please or gratify.

con·tent, kon'tent, *rarely* kon·tent', *n.* [L.] *Usu. pl.* that which is contained, as in a cask or book. The substance or purport, as of a document; the sum of the attributes or notions composing a given conception; the substance or matter of cognition, etc.; power of containing; capacity; volume; area; extent; size.

con·tent, kon·tent', *n.* The state or feeling of being contented; contentment; *Brit.* in the British House of Lords, an affirmative vote or voter.

con·tent·ed, kon·ten'tid, *a.* Satisfied with what one has or with one's circumstances; easy in mind; not complaining, opposing, or demanding more.—**con·tent·ed·ly**, *adv.* —**con·tent·ed·ness**, *n.*

con·ten·tion, kon·ten'shan, *n.* [L. *contentio(n-)*, < *contendere*: see *contend.*] The act of contending; a struggling together in opposition; strife; a quarrel; a striving in rivalry; competition; a contest; strife in debate; a dispute; a controversy; a point contended for in controversy.

con·ten·tious, kon·ten'shus, *a.* [L. *contentiosus.*] Given to or causing contention; argumentative; as, a *contentious* person; characterized by or involving controversy; as, a *contentious* point or issue; *law*, pertaining to causes between contending parties.—**con·ten·tious·ly**, *adv.*—**con·ten·tious·ness**, *n.*

con·tent·ment, kon·tent'ment, *n.* [Fr. *contentement.*] The state or feeling of being contented; content; a resting or satisfaction of mind without disquiet or craving for something else; acquiescence in one's own circumstances. *Contentment* is passive, *satisfaction* is active. The former implies the absence of fretting or craving, the latter an active feeling of pleasure.

con·ter·mi·nous, kon·tėr′mi·nus, *a*. [L. *conterminus*.] Having a common boundary; bordering; contiguous; meeting at the ends; having the same boundaries or limits; coextensive. Also **con·ter·mi·nal**.—**con·ter·mi·nous·ly**, *adv*.—**con·ter·mi·nous·ness**, *n*.

con·test, kon·test′, *v.t*. [O.Fr. Fr. *contester*, < L. *contestari*, call to witness, bring a legal action, < *con-*, with, and *testari*, bear witness, < *testis*, a witness.] To call in question; argue against; dispute; to struggle or fight for, as in battle; contend for in rivalry.—*v.i*. To contend; compete. —**con·test·a·ble**, *a*.—**con·test·er**, *n*.

con·test, kon′test, *n*. A struggle for victory, or superiority; struggle in arms; dispute; debate; controversy; strife in argument. **con·test·ant**, *n*.

con·tes·ta·tion, kon″te·stā′shan, *n*. [L. *contestatio(n-)*.] The act of contesting.

con·text, kon′tekst, *n*. [L. *contextus*, connection, < *contexo*—con-, and *texo*, to weave.] The parts of a written or spoken communication which precede or follow a word, sentence, or passage, and affect its meaning; as, distortion by quoting out of *context*. The surrounding environment, circumstances, or facts which help give a total picture of something.

con·tex·ture, kon·teks′chėr, *n*. The act, process, or manner of interweaving several parts into one body; a structure so interwoven; fabric; the disposition and union of the constituent parts of a thing with respect to each other; constitution.

con·ti·gu·i·ty, kon″ti·gū′i·tē, *n*. pl. **con·ti·gu·i·ties**. The state of being contiguous; closeness of situation or place; a linking together, as of a series of objects.

con·tig·u·ous, kon·tig′ū·us, *a*. [L.] Situated so as to touch or almost touch; meeting or joining at the surface or border; close together; neighboring; bordering or adjoining.—**con·tig·u·ous·ly**, *adv*.—**con·tig·u·ous·ness**, *n*.

con·ti·nence, kon′ti·nens, *n*. [L. *continentia*, < *continens*.] Self-restraint, esp. in regard to sexual passion or indulgence. Also **con·ti·nen·cy**.—**con·ti·nent**, *a*.—**con·ti·nent·ly**, *adv*.

con·ti·nent, kon′ti·nent, *n*. [L. *continens* (-ent), holding together, continuous, also holding or containing, ppr. of *continere*. CONTAIN, also CONTINENT.] A continuous tract or extent, as of land; the mainland, as distinguished from islands or peninsulas; one of the seven main land masses of the globe: Europe, Asia, Africa, North America, South America, Australia, and Antarctica. —**the Con·ti·nent**, the mainland of Europe, as distinguished from the British Isles.

con·ti·nen·tal, kon″ti·nen′tal, *n*. (*Usually cap.*) an inhabitant of a continent, esp. of the mainland of Europe; (*cap*), *Amer. hist.* a soldier of the Continental army in the Revolutionary War; (*l.c.*) a piece of paper money issued by the Continental Congress that lost most of its value before the war's end; thus the phrase, *not worth a continental*.

con·ti·nen·tal, kon″ti·nen′tal, *a*. Of, pertaining to, or of the nature of a continen (*usually cap.*) of or pertaining to the mair land of Europe; (*cap.*), *Amer. hist.* of o: pertaining to the colonies during and immediately after the Revolutionary War; as, the *Continental* Congress.—**con·ti·nen·tal·ly**, *adv*.

con·ti·nen·tal code, *n*. The international Morse code, used in radiotelegraphy.

con·ti·nen·tal shelf, *n*. *Geog.* the submerged edge of a continent.

con·tin·gence, kon·tin′jens, *n*. A state of touching, or tangency; contingency.

con·tin·gen·cy, kon·tin′jen·sē, *n*. pl. **con·tin·gen·cies**. The state or character of being contingent; dependence on chance, or on the fulfillment of some condition; a contingent event; a possibility; a thing contingent or conditional on something uncertain; an adjunct.

con·tin·gent, kon·tin′jent, *a*. [L. *contingens* (-ent), ppr. of *contingere*, touch, border on, reach, befall, happen.] Happening by chance or without known cause; fortuitous; accidental; liable to happen or not; uncertain; possible; dependent for existence, occurrence, character, etc., on something not yet certain, often followed by *on* or *upon*; provisionally liable to exist, occur, or take effect; conditional; *logic*, such that truth or falsity cannot be logically established, but must be decided empirically for the specific instance.

con·tin·gent, kon·tin′jent, *n*. Something contingent; a contingency; the proportion that falls to one in a division, as a share to be contributed or furnished; a quota of troops furnished; hence, any one of the representative groups composing an assemblage; as, the New York *contingent* at a national convention.—**con·tin·gent·ly**, *adv*. —**con·tin·gent·ness**, *n*.

con·tin·gent fund, *n*. A sum of money put aside to provide for any unexpected expense or loss, as a lawsuit.

con·tin·u·al, kon·tin′ū·al, *a*. [Fr. *continuel*, L. *continuus*.] Proceeding without interruption or cessation; not intermittent; unceasing; of frequent recurrence; often repeated; incessant.—**con·tin·u·al·ly**, *adv*.

con·tin·u·ance, kon·tin′ū·ans, *n*. [O.Fr. *continuance*, < *continuer*, E. *continue*.] The act or fact of continuing; continuation; duration; a continuation or sequel; *law*, postponement, as of a trial or suit, to a future date.

con·tin·u·ant, kon·tin′ū·ant, *n*. *Phon.* a consonant, such as *f* or *v*, which may be prolonged in utterance, as distinguished from a 'stop,' as *p* or *b*, which involves a complete closing of the vocal organs.—*a*.

con·tin·u·a·tion, kon·tin″ū·ā′shan, *n*. [L. *continuatio*.] The act of continuing or prolonging; extension or carrying on to a further point; a prolongation.

con·tin·u·a·tive, kon·tin′ū·ā″tiv, kon·tin″ū·a·tiv, *a*. [L.L. *continuativus*.] Tending or serving to continue, or to cause continuation or prolongation; *gram.* expressing continuance of thought.—*n*. Something continuative; *gram.* a continuative word or expression.—**con·tin·u·a·tive·ly**, *adv*.— **con·tin·u·a·tive·ness**, *n*.

con·tin·u·a·tor, kon·tin′ū·ā″tėr, *n*. That which continues; one who carries forward anything that had been begun by another.

con·tin·ue, kon·tin′ū, *v.t.—continued, continuing*. [O.Fr. Fr. *continuer*, < L. *continuare* (pp. *continuatus*), < *continuus*.] To make continuous; to extend from one point to another in space; prolong; to cause to last or endure; maintain or retain, as in a position; go on with or persist, as in an action; to carry on from the point of suspension or interruption, as a narrative; to carry on by means of a successor or successors; to carry over, postpone, or adjourn, as a legal proceeding.—*v.i*. To go forward in any course or action; keep on; to go on after suspension or interruption; to last or endure; to remain in a place; abide; remain in a particular state or capacity.— **con·tin·u·er**, *n*.

con·tin·ued, kon·tin′ūd, *a*. Protracted or extended; proceeding without cessation; resuming after an interruption; unceasing.

con·tin·ued frac·tion, *n*. A fraction having a denominator which contains a fraction which in turn contains a fraction, and so on.

con·tin·u·ing, kon·tin′ū·ing, *a*. Enduring or lasting; characterized by uninterrupted flow or extension in time or space; continuous.

con·ti·nu·i·ty, kon″ti·nö′i·tē, kon″ti·nū′i·tē, *n*. pl. **con·ti·nu·i·ties**. The state or quality of being continuous; a continuous or connected whole; specif. a scenario or other dramatic script for the stage, movies, or television written in such a form as to give the action in detail.

con·tin·u·ous, kon·tin′ū·us, *a*. [L. *continuus*, < *continere*, hold together.] Holding together without break or interruption; uninterrupted in substance; having the parts in immediate connection; uninterrupted in time, sequence, existence, or action; without cessation. Also *continuing*.—**con·tin·u·ous·ly**, *adv*.—**con·tin·u·ous·ness**, *n*.

con·tin·u·um, kon·tin′ū·um, *n*. pl. **con·tin·u·a**, kon·tin′ū·a. That which is continuous and homogenous, of which no separate parts are evident; an ordered, uninterrupted extent, series, or whole; broadly, continuity. *Math.* a set of elements which may have a third element interpolated between any two; the set of all real numbers.

con·tort, kon·tȯrt′, *v.t*. [L. *contortus*, pp. of *contorquere*, < *con-*, together, and *torquere*, twist.] To twist, as the body; to bend out of shape; distort.—**con·tor·tion**, kon·tȧr′shan, *n*. The act of contorting, or the state of being contorted; a writhing, esp. spasmodically; distortion; a distorted form. —**con·tor·tive**, *a*.

con·tort·ed, kon·tȧr′tid, *a*. Twisted to an extreme degree; convoluted.

con·tor·tion·ist, kon·tȧr′sha·nist, *n*. One who practices contortion, esp. one who performs gymnastic feats involving contorted postures.

con·tour, kon′tụr, *n*. [Fr. *contour*—con-, and *tour*, a turn, revolution, turner's lathe, < L. *tornus*, Gr. *tornos*, a lathe; hence also Fr. *tourner*, E. *turn*.] The outline of a figure or body; the line that defines or bounds a solid body; the periphery considered as distinct from the object.

con·tour, kon′tụr, *v.t*. To make or form the contour or outline of; to mark with contour lines; to build in conformity to a contour.

con·tour, kon′tụr, *a*. *Agric.* referring to a method of plowing the land along its natural ridges in order to reduce erosion.

con·tour feath·er, *n*. Any of the feathers which form the surface plumage of a bird and determine the contour of the body.

con·tour fly·ing, *n*. Flying an airplane along the side of a mountain or ridge at a constant altitude.

con·tour line, *n*. *Surv.* a line carried along the surface of a region at a uniform height above sea level; the representation of such a line on a map.

con·tour map, *n*. A topographic map where irregularities of contour are shown by the relative spacing of lines known as contour intervals.

con·tour sheet, *n*. A fitted bed sheet, elasticized at the corners, to keep the sheet secure and free of wrinkles.

con·tra·band, kon′tra·band″, *n*. [It. *contrabbando* or Sp. *contrabando*, < L. *contra*, against, and M.L. *bandum*, *bannum*, proclamation, E. *ban*, *n*.] Illegal or prohibited traffic; smuggling; anything prohibited by law to be imported or exported; goods imported or exported contrary to law or proclamation; specif. goods which, by international law, subjects of neutral states cannot supply to one belligerent in time of war except at the risk of seizure and confiscation by the other; in the U.S., during the Civil War, a Negro slave who escaped to or was brought within the Union lines.—*a*. Prohibited by law, proclamation, or treaty to be imported or exported; *fig.* forbidden; unauthorized.—**con·tra·band·- age, con·tra·band·ism,** *n.*—**con·tra·- band·ist,** *n.*

con·tra·bass, kon'tra·bās", *n.* [It.] The member of a family of musical instruments with a range below bass; the double bass.

con·tra·bas·soon, kon'tra·ba·sön', kon'- tra·ba·sön', *n.* A bassoon pitched an octave lower than the ordinary bassoon: the deepest-toned and largest member of the oboe family. Also *double bassoon.*

con·tra·cep·tion, kon'tra·sep'shan, *n.* The prevention of conception or impregnation, by deliberate measures.—**con·tra·cep·tive,** kon'tra·sep'tiv, *a.* Tending or serving to prevent conception or impregnation; pertaining to contraception.—*n.* A contraceptive agent or device.

con·tract, kon·trakt', *v.t.* [Fr. *contracter,* L. *contraho, contractum,* to draw.] To draw together or into a smaller compass, either in length or breadth; to reduce in size or duration; condense; lessen; to betroth or affiance; to bring on, incur, acquire, as vicious habits or debts; *gram.* to shorten (a word) by combining or omitting a letter or syllable.—*v.i.* To be drawn together; to become shorter or narrower; to shrink; to bargain; to make a mutual agreement as between two or more persons. —**con·tract·ed,** *a.*—**con·tract·i·bil·i·ty,** **con·tract·i·ble·ness,** *n.*—**con·tract·i·ble,** *a.*

con·tract, kon'trakt, *n.* An oral, written, or implied agreement between two or more persons; a formal covenant of marriage; *law,* an enforceable pact.

con·tract bridge, *n.* A variety of bridge in which only the number of tricks named in the final bid, or contract, can count toward game, additional tricks being counted above the line

con·trac·tion, kon·trak'shan, *n.* [L. *contractio.*] The act of contracting, drawing together, or shrinking; the act of shortening, narrowing, or lessening dimensions by causing the parts to approach nearer to each other; the state of being contracted; the shortening of a word or words by the omission of one or more letters or syllables, as 'won't' for 'will not' or 'nat'l' for 'national.'—**con·trac·tive,** *a.* Tending to contract.

con·trac·tor, kon'trak·tẽr, kon·trak'tẽr, *n.* [L.L.] One who or that which contracts; one who contracts to furnish supplies or perform work at a certain price or rate; one who contracts to construct buildings; *anat.* a muscle that contracts or draws together some part of the body; *bridge,* the player who makes the final bid, or this player's partner.

con·trac·tu·al, kon·trak'chö·al, *a.* Of, pertaining to, or of the nature of a contract.

con·trac·ture, kon·trak'chẽr, kon·trak'- shẽr, *n.* [L. *contractura.*] *Med.* a permanent shortening of a muscle due to spasm, scar, or paralysis.

con·tra·dict, kon'tra·dikt', *v.t.* [L. *contradico, contradictum—contra,* and *dico,* to speak, whence *diction,* etc.] To assert not to be so, or to assert to be contrary to what has been asserted; to deny; to be directly contrary to.—**con·tra·dict·a·ble,** *a.* —**con·tra·dict·er,** *n.*—**con·tra·dic·tious,** *a.*

con·tra·dic·tion, kon'tra·dik'shan, *n.* [L. *contradictio(n-).*] The act of contradicting; assertion of the contrary or opposite; direct opposition or repugnance between things compared; inconsistency; absolute logical inconsistency; a self-contradictory statement or phrase.

con·tra·dic·to·ry, kon'tra·dik'to·rē, *a.* Contradicting; affirming the contrary; implying a denial of what has been

asserted; inconsistent with one another; directly opposite.—**con·tra·dic·to·ri·ly,** *adv.*—**con·tra·dic·to·ri·ness,** *n.*

con·tra·dic·to·ry, kon'tra·dik'to·rē, *n.* pl. **con·tra·dic·to·ries.** A proposition which denies or opposes another in all its terms.

con·tra·dis·tinc·tion, kon'tra·di·stingk'- shan, *n.* Distinction by opposite qualities or characteristics; as, drama in *contradistinction* to farce.—**con·tra·dis·tinc·tive,** *a.* Having the quality of, or characterized by, contradistinction; opposite in qualities.— **con·tra·dis·tinc·tive·ly,** *adv.*

con·tra·dis·tin·guish, kon'tra·di·sting'- gwish, *v.t.* To distinguish by contrasting opposite qualities; discriminate by direct contrast.

con·trail, kon'trāl, *n.* [*con(densation)* and *trail.*] The visible condensed moisture left in the sky by a plane, rocket, or missile. Also *condensation trail.*

con·tra·in·di·cate, kon'tra·in'di·kāt", *v.t.* —*contraindicated, contraindicating. Med.* of a symptom or condition, to give indication against the advisability of (a particular or usual remedy or treatment).—**con·tra·- in·di·cant,** *n.*—**con·tra·in·di·ca·tion,** *n.* —**con·tra·in·di·ca·tive,** *a.*

con·tral·to, kon·tral'tō, *n.* pl. **con·tral·tos,** It. **con·tral·ti,** kon·tral'tē. [It., < *contra,* against, counter to, and *alto,* alto.] *Mus.* the lowest female voice or voice-part, intermediate between soprano and tenor; a singer with a contralto voice.—*a.* Pertaining to the contralto or its range.

con·tra·po·si·tion, kon'tra·po·zish'on, *n.* [L.L. *contrapositio(n-),* < L. *contraponere,* place opposite.] A placing over against, or in contrast to; opposite position; antithesis. —*v.t.*

con·trap·tion, kon·trap'shan, *n.* [A made word.] *Colloq.* a contrivance; a device.

con·tra·pun·tal, kon'tra·pun'tal, *a. Mus.* pertaining to counterpoint.—**con·tra·pun·- tal·ly,** *adv.*—**con·tra·pun·tist,** *n.*

con·tra·ri·e·ty, kon'tra·rī'i·tē, *n.* pl. **con·tra·ri·e·ties.** [L. *contrarietas.*] The state or quality of being contrary; opposition in fact, essence, quality, or principle.

con·tra·ri·wise, kon'trer·ē·wiz", *adv.* In a contrary manner; on the contrary; in the opposite way; perversely.

con·tra·ry, kon'trer·ē, kon·trâr'ē, *a.* [L. *contrarius,* < *contra,* in opposition.] Opposite in nature or character; diametrically opposed; mutually opposed; being the opposite one of two; antagonistic or hostile; hence, perverse; opposite in direction or position; untoward or unfavorable; *bot.* at right angles.—**con·- tra·ri·ly,** *adv.*—**con·tra·ri·ness,** *n.*

con·tra·ry, kon'trer·ē, kon·trâr'ē, *n.* pl. **con·tra·ries.** That which is contrary or opposite; as, to prove the *contrary* of a statement; either of two contrary things, statements, or propositions; hostility; a denial.—**by con·tra·ries,** by way of opposition; contrary to expectation.—**on the con·tra·ry,** in extreme opposition to what has been stated.—**to the con·tra·ry,** to the opposite or different effect; in opposition to or reversal of something stated.

con·trast, kon·trast', *v.t.* [Fr. *contraster,* < It. *contrastare,* < M.L. *contrastare,* withstand, oppose, < L. *contra,* against, and *stare,* stand.] To set in opposition in order to show unlikeness; compare by observing differences; place in immediate relation in order to heighten an effect by emphasizing differences; to afford or form a contrast to; set off.—*v.i.* To exhibit unlikeness on comparison; form a contrast.—**con·trast·- a·ble,** *a.*—**con·trast·ing·ly,** *adv.*—**con·- tras·tive,** *a.* Affording a contrast.

con·trast, kon'trast, *n.* The act of contrasting; the state of being contrasted; a striking exhibition of unlikeness; some-

thing strikingly different. *Photog.* the difference between light and dark areas of a negative or print.

con·trast·y, kon·tras'tē, kon'tras·tē, *a. Photog.* displaying decided gradations between the light and dark portions of a photographic print.

con·tra·vene, kon'tra·vēn', *v.t.*—*contravened, contravening.* [L. *contravenio—contra,* against, and *venio,* to come, as in *convene.*] To come or be in conflict with; to obstruct in operation; to act so as to violate; to transgress.—**con·tra·ven·er,** *n.*

con·tra·ven·tion, kon'tra·ven'shan, *n.* The act of contravening, violating, or transgressing; violation; opposition.

con·tre·danse, con·tra·dance, kon'tri·- dans", kon'tri·däns", *Fr.* kan·tri·däns, *n.* [Fr., a corruption of E. *country-dance.*] A graceful dance, based on the country-dance, in which the partners stand opposite one another; a variation of the quadrille; a piece of music suitable for such a dance.

con·tre·temps, kon'tre·tän", *Fr.* kan·- tre·tän', *n.* pl. **con·tre·temps.** [Fr.] An unexpected and untoward incident; an embarrassing conjuncture; a hitch.

con·trib·ute, kon·trib'ūt', *v.t.*—*contributed, contributing.* [L. *contribuo—con-,* and *tribuo,* to grant, assign, or impart.] To give or grant in common with others; to give to a common fund or for a common purpose; to pay as a share; to submit for publication. —*v.i.* To give a part; to lend a portion of power, aid, or influence; to have a share in any act or effect, with *to.*—**con·trib·ut·- a·ble,** *a.*—**con·trib·u·tor,** *n.*

con·tri·bu·tion, kon'tri·bū'shan, *n.* [L.L. *contributio(n-).*] The act of contributing; something contributed; specif. an article contributed to a magazine; an impost or levy.—**con·trib·u·tive,** *a.* Tending to contribute; contributing.—**con·trib·u·- tive·ly,** *adv.*

con·trib·u·to·ry, kon·trib'ū·tōr"ē, kon·- trib'ū·tar"ē, *a.* Contributing; furnishing something toward a result; subject to contribution or levy; pertaining to or of the nature of contribution.—*n.* pl. **con·trib·- u·to·ries.** One who or that which contributes.—**con·trib·u·to·ry neg·li·gence,** *n. Law,* negligence on the part of a person injured which has contributed to bring about the injury.

con·trite, kon·trit', kon'trit, *a.* [L. *contritus,* pp. of *conterere,* grind, wear down, < *con-,* together, and *terere,* rub.] Broken in spirit by a sense of guilt; penitent; proceeding from contrition.—**con·trite·ly,** *adv.*—**con·- trite·ness,** *n.*

con·tri·tion, kon·trish'on, *n.* [L.L. *contritio(n-).*] The condition of being contrite; sincere penitence; *theol.* sorrow for and detestation of sin with a true purpose of amendment.

con·triv·ance, kon·trī'vans, *n.* The act of contriving, inventing, devising, or planning; the thing contrived; the faculty of contriving; an artifice; scheme; invention.

con·trive, kon·trīv', *v.t.*—*contrived, contriving.* [O.E. *contreven, controven,* < O.Fr. *controver* (Fr. *controuver*), < *con-,* with, and *trover,* find.] To plan with ingenuity; devise; invent; manage to do something. —*v.i.* To form schemes or designs; plan; to plot.—**con·triv·er,** kon·trī'vẽr, *n.*— **con·triv·a·ble,** *a.*

con·trived, kon·trivd', *a.* Affected; simulated; artificial.

con·trol, kon·trōl', *v.t.*—*controlled, controlling.* [O.Fr. *contreroller* (Fr. *contrôler*), < *contrerolle,* "counter-roll," < L. *contra,* against, and M.L. *rotulus,* E. *roll.*] To check or regulate; to exercise restraint or direction over; dominate; command; to hold in check; curb; to overpower.— **con·trol·la·bil·i·ty,** *n.*—**con·trol·la·ble,**

a.—**con·trol·la·bly,** *adv.*—**con·trol·ling,** *a.*

con·trol, kon·trōl', *n.* The act or power of controlling; regulation; domination or command; check or restraint; something that serves to control; a standard of comparison in scientific experimentation; a person who acts as a check; a controller. *Mach.* a regulating or controlling device or mechanism; *often pl.* a set of such devices.

con·trol ex·per·i·ment, *n.* An experiment or experimental device used to observe and evaluate the reliability and findings of another experiment.

con·trol·ler, kon·trō·lėr, *n.* [Fr. *contrôleur.*] One employed to check income and expenditures; a comptroller; one who regulates, directs, or restrains; a regulating mechanism.—**con·trol·ler·ship,** *n.*

con·trol·ling in·ter·est, *n.* A majority stock ownership in a corporation, held by an individual or group of individuals, which gives them control over policy.

con·trol roc·ket, *n. Aerospace,* a low-thrust, auxiliary rocket engine which has its exhaust nozzle pointed toward the direction of flight to adjust the heading, velocity, deceleration, and separation of stages of a long range ballistic missile. Also *retro-rocket;* **ver·nier en·gine.**

con·trol tow·er, *n.* A tower at an airfield with the necessary equipment and personnel to observe and direct air and ground traffic in the takeoff and landing areas.

con·tro·ver·sial, kon″tro·vėr′shal, *a.* Of, pertaining to, or of the nature of controversy; polemical; given to controversy; disputatious; subject to controversy; debatable.—**con·tro·ver·sial·ist,** *n.* One who engages or is skilled in controversy; a disputant.—**con·tro·ver·sial·ly,** *adv.*—**con·tro·ver·sial·ism,** *n.*

con·tro·ver·sy, kon′tro·vėr″sē, *n.* pl. **con·tro·ver·sies.** [L. *controversia,* < *controversus,* turned against, < *contro-* (= *contra-*), against, and *versus,* pp. of *vertere,* turn.] Dispute, debate, or contention; disputation concerning a matter of opinion.

con·tro·vert, kon′tro·vert″, kon″tro·vert′, *v.t.* To contend against in discussion; dispute; deny; oppose; to contend about in discussion; debate; discuss.—*v.i.* To engage in controversy.—**con·tro·vert·er,** *n.*—**con·tro·vert·i·ble,** *a.* That may be controverted.—**con·tro·vert·i·bly,** *adv.*

con·tu·ma·cious, kon″tụ·mā′shus, kon″tū·mā′shus, *a.* [Obs. Fr. *contumacieux,* < *contumace,* < L. *contumacia,* E. *contumacy.*] Exhibiting contumacy; stubbornly perverse or rebellious; wilfully and obstinately disobedient.—**con·tu·ma·cious·ly,** *adv.*—**con·tu·ma·cious·ness, con·tu·mac·i·ty,** kon″tụ·mas′i·tē, kon″tū·mas′i·tē, *n.*

con·tu·ma·cy, kon′tụ·ma·sē, kon′tū·ma·sē, *n.* pl. **con·tu·ma·cies.** [L. *contumacia,* < *contumax,* stubborn, contumacious.] Stubborn perverseness or rebelliousness; wilful and obstinate resistance or disobedience to authority; *law,* wilful disobedience to an order or summons of a court.

con·tu·me·li·ous, kon″tụ·mē′lē·us, kon″tū·mē′lē·us, *a.* [L. *contumeliosus.*] Indicating or expressive of contumely; contemptuous; insolent; rude and sarcastic; disposed to utter reproach or insult; insolent; proudly rude.—**con·tu·me·li·ous·ly,** *adv.*—**con·tu·me·li·ous·ness,** *n.*

con·tu·me·ly, kon′tụ·me·lē, kon′tū·me·lē, kon′tụ′me·lē, kon′tū′me·lē, kon′tum·lē, *n.* [L. *contumelia.*] Haughtiness and contempt in language or behavior; contemptuous or insulting language; haughty insolence.

con·tuse, kon·tōz′, kon·tūz′, *v.t.*—*contused, contusing.* [L. *contundo, contusum*—*con-,* and *tundo,* to beat, same root as Skt. *tud,* to

beat.] To wound or injure by bruising; to injure without breaking the flesh.

con·tu·sion, kon·tō′zhen, kon·tū′zhen, *n.* [L. *contusio.*] A severe bruise on the body; a hurt or injury as to the flesh or some part of the body without breaking of the skin, as by a blunt instrument or by a fall.

co·nun·drum, ko·nun′drum, *n.* [Origin obscure.] A whim or conceit; a pun; a riddle the answer to which involves a pun or play on words; anything that puzzles.

con·va·lesce, kon″va·les′, *v.i.*—*convalesced, convalescing.* To grow better after sickness; to recover health.

con·va·les·cence, kon″va·les′ens, *n.* [L. *convalesco,* to grow stronger—*con-,* and *valesco,* to get strength, *valeo,* to be strong.] The gradual recovery of health and strength after being ill; the state of a person renewing his vigor after sickness or weakness.—**con·va·les·cent,** kon″va·les′ent, *a.* Recovering health and strength after sickness or debility.—*n.* One who is recovering his health after sickness.

con·vect, kon·vekt′, *v.t.* To move, as a gas or fluid, by convection.—*v.i.* To circulate heat by convection.

con·vec·tion, kon·vek′shan, *n. Phys.* the movement of currents in a fluid or gas of uneven temperature due to the variation of its density and the resultant action of gravity; the circulation of heat thus effected. *Meteor.* vertical movement of air currents, esp. the upward flow of warm air.

con·vec·tor, kon·vek′tėr, *n.* Any device or fluid circulating heat by convection.

con·vene, kon·vēn′, *v.i.*—*convened, convening.* [L. *convenio.*] To come together; to meet; to meet in the same place; to assemble: rarely said of things.—*v.t.* To cause to assemble; to call together; to convoke; to summon judicially to meet or appear.—**con·ven·er,** kon·vē′nėr, *n.* One who convenes or meets with others; one who convenes or calls a meeting.

con·ven·ience, kon·vēn′yans, *n.* [L. *convenientia.*] The quality of being convenient; adaptiveness for easy use; a situation or a time convenient for one; as, to do a thing at one's *convenience;* a convenient appliance, utensil, or an easily prepared food. *Brit.* a water closet.

con·ven·ient, kon·vēn′yant, *a.* [L. *conveniens (-ent-),* ppr. of *convenire,* agree, accord, suit, be proper.] Agreeable to the needs or purpose; well suited with respect to facility ro ease in use; in satisfactory nearness.—**con·ven·ient·ly,** *adv.*

con·vent, con′vent, *n.* [L. *conventus,* meeting, assembly, company, M.L. *convent,* < L. *convenire:* see *convene.*] A community of persons devoted to religious life under a superior; a society of monks, friars, or nuns: in popular usage, only of nuns; the building or buildings occupied by such a society; a monastery or nunnery: in popular usage, a nunnery.

con·ven·ti·cle, kon·ven′ti·kl, *n.* [L. *conventiculum,* dim. of *conventus,* meeting.] A secret or unauthorized meeting, esp. for religious worship, as those held by Protestant dissenters from the Church of England during the period when they were prohibited by law; a place of meeting or assembly, esp. a nonconformist meeting place.—**con·ven·ti·cler,** *n.* An attendant or supporter of conventicles.—**con·ven·tic·u·lar,** kon″ven·tik′ya·lėr, *a.*

con·ven·tion, kon·ven′shan, *n.* [L. *conventio(n-),* meeting, agreement, < *convenire.*] A coming together; a meeting or assembly; esp. a formal assembly, as of representatives or delegates, for action on particular matters; the calling together of an assembly; an agreement, compact, or contract; specif. an international agreement, esp. one other than a treaty and dealing with a

specific matter, as postal service, copyright, or patents; general agreement or consent; accepted usage, esp. as a standard of procedure; sometimes, conventionalism; a rule, method, or practice established by general consent or accepted usage; *bridge,* a bid that conveys information to one's partner according to a prearranged understanding.

con·ven·tion·al, kon·ven′sha·nal, *a.* [L.L. *conventionalis.*] Of or pertaining to a convention or assembly, agreement, or compact; established by general consent or accepted usage; traditional, rather than spontaneous or original. *Fine arts,* in accordance with accepted models or traditions; stylized rather than in precise imitation of nature.—**con·ven·tion·al·ism,** *n.* Adherence or the tendency to adhere to that which is conventional; something conventional.—**con·ven·tion·al·ist,** *n.*—**con·ven·tion·al·i·ty,** kon·ven″sha·nal′i·tē, *n.* pl. **con·ven·tion·al·i·ties.** Conventional quality or character; adherence to convention; a conventional practice, principle, or form; *pl.* the conventional rules of propriety, with *the.*

con·ven·tion·al bomb, *n.* Any nonatomic bomb designed primarily for explosive effect as distinguished from a chemical bomb, incendiary bomb, or other special purpose bombs.

con·ven·tion·al·ize, kon·ven′sha·na·līz″, *v.t.*—*conventionalized, conventionalizing.* To render conventional; to bring under the influence of conventional rules; to render observant of the conventional rules of society.—**con·ven·tion·al·i·za·tion,** *n.*

con·ven·tion·eer, kon·ven″sha·nēr′, *n.* One who attends a convention.

con·ven·tu·al, kon·ven′chō·al, *n.* A member of a convent or monastery; (*cap.*) one of an order of Franciscan friars which in the 15th century was separated from the Observants, and which follows a mitigated rule.—*a.* Belonging to or characteristic of a convent.—**con·ven·tu·al·ly,** *adv.*

con·verge, kon·vėrj′, *v.i.*—*converged, converging.* [L.L. *convergere,* < L. *con-,* together, and *vergere,* incline, E. *verge.*] To tend to meet in a point or line; to focus; incline toward each other, as lines which are not parallel; *fig.* to tend to a common result or conclusion.—*v.t.* To cause to converge.—**con·verg·ing·ly,** *adv.*

con·ver·gence, kon·vėr′jens, *n.* The act or fact of converging; convergent state or quality.—**con·ver·gent,** *a.* Converging; formed by convergence, as of lines. Also **con·ver·gen·cy.**

con·vers·a·ble, kon·vėr′sa·bl, *a.* [Fr. *conversable,* < M.L. *conversabilis,* < L. *conversari.*] Agreeable; easy to talk with; able to or desirous of conversing.

con·ver·sant, kon·ver′sant, kon′vėr·sant, *a.* [O.Fr. *conversant,* < L. *conversans (-ant-)* ppr. of *conversari.*] Pertaining to familiarity in the sense of being knowledgeable or experienced, as: Reading kept him *conversant* with current issues. Having regular or frequent personal association.—**con·ver·sance, con·ver·san·cy,** *n.*

con·ver·sa·tion, kon″vėr·sā′shan, *n.* [Fr. *conversation,* L. *conversatio,* intercourse.] Informal oral communication; verbal exchange of ideas, sentiments or observations; the act, process, or instance of verbal exchange; association or intimate acquaintance; *law,* moral conduct or behavior; as, criminal *conversation* or adultery.—**con·ver·sa·tion·al,** kon·vėr·sā′shan·al, *a.*—**con·ver·sa·tion·al·ly,** *adv.*

con·ver·sa·tion·al·ist, kon″vėr·sā′sha·na·list, *n.* One who excels in and enjoys good conversation. Also **con·ver·sa·tion·ist.**

con·ver·sa·tion piece, *n.* An object, as of home decoration, so novel or unusual that it

con·verse, kon·vẽrs', v.i.—conversed, conversing. [Fr. converser; L. conversor, to associate with.] To exchange informal verbal communication; to talk, speak, or chat informally.—**con·verse,** kon'vẽrs, n. A conversation or discussion.—**con·vers·er,** n.

con·verse, kon·vẽrs', kon'vẽrs, a. [L. conversus, turned round, converto, conversum, to turn round.] Turned about or reversed in order, direction, or relationship; in opposition or contrariwise to an existing order.—**con·verse·ly,** adv.

con·verse, kon'vẽrs, n. A thing which is the opposite or contrary of another; esp. one form of words that corresponds to another form of words but with a significant pair of terms interchanged in place; as, 'warm in winter but cold in summer' is the converse of 'cold in winter but warm in summer'; logic, a proposition obtained by conversion.

con·ver·sion, kon·vẽr'zhan, kon·vẽr'shan, n. [L. conversio(n-), < convertere: see convert.] The act or state of converting; a physical transformation from one state or form to another; a change in character, form, or function; the diversion of a thing from its original, proper, or intended use; a spiritual change from sinfulness to righteousness; a change from one religion, political party, or allegiance to another; law, unauthorized appropriation of another's property; logic, the transposition of the terms of logical proposition; math. a change in a mathematical expression by clearing of fractions; football, the scoring of a point after touchdown; basketball, scoring on a free throw.

con·vert, kon·vẽrt', v.t. [L. convertere (pp. conversus), turn about, turn, change, < con-, altogether, and vertere, turn.] To effect a change in from one form, condition, or set of properties to another, in the sense of transmuting or transforming; to exchange for an equivalent; as, to convert francs into dollars; to alter from an original use; as, to convert a classroom into a laboratory; to appropriate wrongfully to one's own use; to cause a change in from one belief, view, or allegiance to another; to effect a change in from one religion to another; to change in character; chem. to cause (a substance) to undergo a chemical change; law, to assume unlawful rights of ownership; logic, to subject (a proposition) to logical conversion. —v.i. To become converted; sports, to complete the point after touchdown in football, or to score on a free throw in basketball.

con·vert, kon'vẽrt, n. One who is converted; one who experiences a change of creed, belief, religion, or allegiance in the sense of conversion.

con·vert·er, kon·vẽr'tẽr, n. One who or that which converts, specif. one who converts raw textile fabrics into the finished product by bleaching, dyeing, or glossing; metal. a vessel in which pig iron is converted into steel by the Bessemer process; elect. a device for changing the form of electrical energy, as from direct to alternating current; a radio device for changing one frequency to another; a device which adapts a television receiver to include additional channels, specif. UHF channels; physics, a reactor for converting fuels.

con·vert·i·ble, kon·vẽr'ti·bl, a. [L.L. convertibilis.] Capable of being converted; interchangeable or equivalent; transformable; having a top which may be lowered or removed, as of an automobile.—**con·vert·i·bil·i·ty, con·vert·i·ble·ness,** n.—**con·vert·i·bly,** adv.

con·vert·i·ble, kon·vẽr'ti·bl, n. Something capable of being converted or altered for another use, purpose, or function; an automobile having a folding top.

con·vert·i·ble bond, n. Finance, a bond which, at the discretion of the holder, may be exchanged for common stock of the company at a fixed price.

con·vert·i·ble life in·sur·ance, n. A limited type of life insurance, such as term or group insurance, which gives the insured the right to change the policy into an expanded or more permanent form without new evidence of insurability.

con·vert·i·ble stock, n. Preferred stock which may be exchanged for common stock upon exercise of the owner's option.

con·vert·i·plane, con·vert·a·plane, kon·vẽr'ti·plān, n. An aircraft that combines the landing and take-off characteristics of a rotary-wing helicopter with the high forward speed of a fixed-wing plane.

con·vex, kon' veks , kon·veks', a. [L. convexus, carried round, rounded.] Denoting a surface that is curved or rounded outward, as the exterior of a sphere or circle: opposite of concave.—kon'veks, n. A convex part.—**con·vex·ness,** n.—**con·vex·ly,** adv.

con·vex·i·ty, kon·vek'si·tē, n. pl. con·vex·i·ties. State of being convex; the exterior surface of a convex body.

con·vex·o-con·cave, kon·vek'sō·kon·kāv', a. Convex on one side and concave on the other, as a lens; specif. pertaining to a lens in which the convex face has a greater degree of curvature than the concave face, the lens being thickest in the middle.

con·vey, kon·vā', v.t. [O.Fr. conveier, convoyer, L.L. conviare, to convey, to convoy—L. con-, with, and via, a way.] To carry, bear, or transport; to transmit; hand over; to communicate by any medium, as words, appearance, or bodily attitude. Law, to transfer rights, real estate, or other property from one person to another.—**con·vey·a·ble,** kon·vā'a·bl, a.

con·vey·ance, kon·vā'ans, n. The act of conveying; the act of bearing, carrying, or transporting; transmission; transference; the means by which anything is conveyed, esp. a vehicle or carriage of some kind. Law, the transmitting or transferring of property from one person to another; the document by which property is transferred.

con·vey·an·cing, kon·vā'an·sing, n. Law, the examination of titles, and the drawing of deeds or leases for the conveyance of property from one person to another.—**con·vey·an·cer,** kon·vā'an·sẽr, n.

con·vey·er, con·vey·or, kon·vā'ẽr, n. Law, that which, or one who, conveys, as in a transfer of property; a mechanical contrivance for transporting material, as from one part of a building to another.

con·vict, kon·vikt', v.t. [L. convictus, pp. of convincere.] To prove or find guilty of an offense, esp. after trial before a legal tribunal; prove or declare guilty of wrong-doing or error; to impress with the sense of guilt.

con·vict, kon'vikt, n. One who has been convicted, as before a legal tribunal; a convicted person undergoing penal servitude.

con·vic·tion, kon·vik'shan, n. [L.L. convictio(n-), < L. convincere.] The act of convicting, as before a legal tribunal, or the fact or state of being convicted; the act of convincing, or bringing to a recognition of the truth of a thing, or the state of being convinced; settled persuasion; a fixed or firm belief.—**con·vic·tion·al,** a.

con·vince, kon·vins', v.t.—convinced, convincing. [L. convinco, convictum—con-, and vinco, to vanquish.] To persuade or satisfy by evidence; to bring to full belief or acquiescence by satisfactory proofs or

arguments; to compel to yield assent.—**con·vin·ci·ble,** a. Capable of conviction.

con·vinc·ing, kon·vins'ing, a. Having qualities that persuade one of the reality and credibility of something; believable. —**con·vinc·ing·ly,** adv.—**con·vinc·ing·ness,** n.

con·viv·i·al, kon·viv'ē·al, a. [L. conviva, a guest—con-, and vivo, victum, to live, whence victuals, vital, vivid.] Relating to a feast or entertainment; festal; social; jovial.—**con·viv·i·al·i·ty,** n. The good humor or mirth indulged in at an entertainment; a convivial spirit or disposition.—**con·viv·i·al·ly,** adv.

con·vo·ca·tion, kon'vo·kā'shan, n. [L. convocatio(n-).] The act of convoking, or the fact or state of being convoked; a number of persons met in answer to a summons; an assembly; a provincial synod or assembly of the clergy of the Church of England; an assembly of the clergy of the division of a diocese in the American Protestant Episcopal Church.—**con·vo·ca·tion·al,** a.

con·voke, kon·vōk', v.t.—convoked, convoking. [L. convoco, to convoke.] To call together; to summon to meet; to assemble by summons.—**con·vok·er,** n.

con·vo·lute, kon'vo·lōt', v.t.—convoluted, convoluting. [L. convolutus, pp. of convolvere.] To coil up; form into a twisted shape.

con·vo·lute, kon'vo·lōt', a. Rolled up together, or one part over another; bot. coiled up longitudinally, so that one margin is within the coil and the other without, as a leaf in the bud.—**con·vo·lut·ed,** a.—**con·vo·lute·ly,** adv.

con·vo·lu·tion, kon"vo·lō'shan, n. A rolling or coiling together; rolled up or coiled condition; a turn or winding of anything coiled; a whorl; a sinuosity, esp. one of the sinuous folds or ridges of the surface of the brain.—**con·vo·lu·tion·al, con·vo·lu·tion·ar·y,** a.

con·volve, kon·volv', v.t.—convolved, convolving. [L. convolvere (pp. convolutus), < con-, together, and volvere, roll.] To roll or wind together; coil; twist.—v.i. To form convolutions.—**con·volve·ment,** n.

con·vol·vu·lus, kon·vol'vū·lus, n. pl. **con·vol·vu·lus·es,** L. **con·vol·vu·li,** kon·vol'vū·li. [L., bindweed, < convolvere.] Any plant of the genus Convolvulus, which comprises erect, twining, or trailing herbs with trumpet-shaped flowers, certain of which are cultivated for ornament. Also morning glory.—**con·vol·vu·la·ceous,** a.

con·voy, kon'voi, kon·voi', v.t. [O.Fr. convoier (Fr. convoyer).] To accompany or escort, now usually for protection; as, a merchantman convoyed by a warship.

con·voy, kon'voi, n. [O.Fr. Fr. convoi.] The act of convoying; the protection afforded by an escort; an escort, esp. for protection, as an armed force or warship; a party, supply of stores, or ship convoyed.

con·vulse, kon·vuls', v.t.—convulsed, convulsing. [L. convulsus, pp. of convellere.] To shake violently; cause violent agitation or disturbance in; specif. to affect with successive violent and involuntary contractions of the muscles; affect with irregular spasms; to cause to laugh violently.

con·vul·sion, kon·vul'shan, n. [L. convulsio(n-).] A convulsing or being convulsed; violent agitation or disturbance; commotion. Often pl., pathol. a violent and involuntary spasmodic contraction of the muscles; an affliction marked by such contractions. A violent fit of laughter.—**con·vul·sion·ar·y,** kon·vul'sha·ner"ē, a.

con·vul·sive, kon·vul'siv, a. Tending to convulse; of the nature of or characterized by convulsion; affected with convulsion.—**con·vul·sive·ly,** adv.

coo, kö, v.i.—cooed, cooing. [Imit.] To utter the soft, murmuring sound characteristic of pigeons or doves, or a similar sound; to murmur or talk fondly or amorously.—*v.t.* To utter by cooing.—*n.* A cooing sound.—**coo·er,** *n.*—**coo·ing·ly,** *adv.*

cook, kụk, *n.* [O.E. *cōc,* < L. *coquus,* a cook, < *coquere,* cook.] One whose occupation is the preparation of food by heat or otherwise, for the table; one who cooks; a chef.

cook, kụk, *v.i.* To act as cook; prepare food by the action of heat; of food, to undergo cooking.—*v.t.* To prepare (food) by the action of heat, as by boiling, baking, or roasting; subject (anything) to the action of heat. *Colloq.* to concoct or invent falsely, often with *up;* alter surreptitiously or falsify. *Slang,* to ruin or spoil.

cook·book, kụk′bụk″, *n.* A book containing recipes and instructions for cooking. Also **cook book.**

cook·e·ry, kụk′e·rē, *n.* pl. **cook·er·ies.** The art or practice of cooking; a place for cooking.

cook·ie, cook·y, kụk′ē, *n.* pl. **cook·ies.** [D. *koekje,* dim. of *koek,* cake.] A small, flat, sweet cake.

cook·out, kụk′out″, *n.* A group-gathering at which a meal is cooked and eaten outdoors; a barbecue.

cool, kōl, *a.* [O.E. *cōl;* akin to E. *cold, chill.*] Moderately cold; neither warm nor very cold; imparting or permitting a sensation of moderate coldness; as, a *cool* dress; not excited by passion; calm; unmoved; deliberate; relaxed; deficient in ardor or enthusiasm; lacking in cordiality; as, a *cool* reception; calmly audacious or impudent; of a color, producing a cool impression; *colloq.* of a number or sum, without exaggeration or qualification; as, a *cool* thousand dollars; *slang,* attractive or excellent.—**cool·ish,** *a.*—**cool·ly,** *adv.*—**cool·ness,** *n.*

cool, kōl, *v.i.* [O.E. *cōlian.*] To become cool; to lose the heat of passion or emotion; become less ardent or cordial; become more moderate.—*v.t.* To make cool; impart a sensation of coolness to; to abate the ardor or intensity of; allay, as passion or emotion; moderate.

cool, kōl, *n.* That which is cool; the cool part, place, or time; as, the *cool* of the evening; coolness; composure.

cool·ant, kōl′ạnt, *n.* A substance, usually a fluid or a gas, used to dissipate heat in the operation of tools, machines, or motors.

cool·er, kōl′ẽr, *n.* That which cools or makes cool; a vessel or apparatus for cooling liquids; any of several iced alcoholic drinks. *Slang,* a jail; a jail cell for violent prisoners.

cool-head·ed, kōl′hed′id, *a.* Calm; free from excitement or passion; not easily excited.—**cool-head·ed·ness,** *n.*

coo·lie, coo·ly, kō′lē, *n.* pl. **coo·lies.** [E. Ind.] In old times among Europeans in India and China, an unskilled native laborer; such a laborer employed as cheap labor elsewhere.

cool·ing-off per·i·od, *n.* A period of time agreed upon by two disputing factions for moderating tensions and to permit negotiation; *labor relations,* an 80-day limit for labor negotiations set by the Taft-Hartley Act.

coon, kōn, *n. Colloq.* a racoon.

coop, kōp, kụp, *n.* [M.E. *cupe,* cf. O.E. *cȳpe,* basket, D. *kuip,* tub, G. *kufe,* coop, tub, vat, L. *cupa,* tub, cask.] A box or the like, as with bars or wires on one side or more, in which fowl are confined for fattening or transportation; an enclosure, cage, or pen for poultry; any narrow confining thing or place, as a room or cell; *slang,* a prison.

coop, kōp, kụp, *v.t.* To place in or as in a coop; confine narrowly: often with *up;* as, to remain *cooped up* in one place.

co-op, kō′op, kō·op′, *n.* A house, store, or business enterprise owned cooperatively; a cooperative society.

coop·er, kō′pẽr, kụp′ẽr, *n.* [M.E. *couper* = D. *kuiper* = G. *küfer.*] One who makes or repairs vessels formed of staves and hoops, as barrels, casks, and tubs.—*v.t.* To make or repair (casks and barrels).—*v.i.* To work as a cooper.

coop·er·age, kō′pẽr·ij, kụp′ẽr·ij, *n.* The work or business of a cooper, or the place where it is carried on; the price paid for coopers' work.

co·op·er·ate, kō·op′e·rāt″, *v.i.*—*cooperated, cooperating.* [L.L. *cooperatus,* pp. of *cooperari,* < L. *co-,* with, and *operari.*] To work or act together or jointly; unite in producing an effect; to practice economic cooperation.

co·op·er·a·tion, kō·op″e·rā′shạn, *n.* [L.L. *cooperatio(n-).*] The act or fact of cooperating; joint operation or action; the combination of persons for purposes of production, purchase, or distribution for their joint benefit; a state of organisms living in a colony, the mutual benefits of which are greater than the disadvantages of overcrowding.

co·op·er·a·tive, kō·op′e·rā″tiv, kō·op′-ẽr·a·tiv, *a.* Cooperating; of or pertaining to cooperation; pertaining to economic cooperation; as, a *cooperative* society or a *cooperative* store.—*n.* One who cooperates; specif. a member of a cooperative society or organization; a cooperative society; a business organization established for the purpose of providing its members with goods at a cost lower than that available to the general public.—**co·op·er·a·tive·ly,** *adv.*—**co·op·er·a·tor,** *n.*

co-opt, kō·opt′, *v.t.* [L. *cooptare.*] To elect into a body by the votes of the existing members; to deputize.—**co-op·ta·tion,** kō·op·tā′shạn, *n.*—**co-op·ta·tive,** kō·op′-ta·tiv, *a.*—**co-op·tion,** kō·op′shạn, *n.*

co·or·di·nate, kō·ạr′di·nit, kō·ạr′di·nāt″, *a.* [L.] Of the same order or degree; equal in rank or importance; involving coordination; *math.* pertaining to coordinates.—**co·or·di·nate·ly,** *adv.*—**co·or·di·nate·ness,** *n.*

co·or·di·nate, kō·ạr′di·nāt″, *v.t.*—*coordinated, coordinating.* To place or class in the same order, rank, or division; to place or arrange in due order or proper relative position; combine in harmonious relation or action.—*v.i.* To become coordinate; to assume proper order or relation; act in harmonious combination.—**co·or·di·na·tive,** *a.*—**co·or·di·na·tor,** *n.*

co·or·di·nate, kō·ạr′di·nit, kō·ạr′di·nāt, *n.* One who or that which is equal in rank or importance; an equal; *math.* a number, or one of a set of numbers, which locates a point in space in relation to a line, or a system of lines.

co·or·di·nate, kō·ạr′di·nit, kō·ạr′di·nāt″, *n.* Often *pl.* a line of clothing or furniture consisting of separate pieces, manufactured of the same or harmonious materials and designated to be worn or used together.

co·or·di·na·tion, kō·ạr″di·nā′shạn, *n.* The act of coordinating, or the state of being coordinated; a making or being coordinate; due ordering or proper relation; harmonious combination.

coot, kōt, *n.* [M.E. *coote, cote,* = D. *koet.*] Any of various widely distributed swimming and diving birds of the genus *Fulica,* as *F. americana* and the European *F. atra,* "bald coot." *Slang,* a stupid or foolish person, often with *old.*

coot·ie, kō′tē, *n.* [Army slang, prob. < World War I.] A louse.

cop, kop, *n.* [O.E. *cop,* copp, top, summit: cf. D. *kop,* G. *kopf,* head.] A conical mass of

thread as wound on a spindle in a spinning machine.

cop, kop, *v.t.*—*copped, copping.* [Origin uncertain.] *Slang,* to catch; lay hold of; to steal.—*n. Slang,* a policeman.

co·pa·cet·ic, co·pe·set·ic, kō″pa·set′ik, *a.* [Creole *coup esètique,* capable of being coped with successfully.] *Slang,* entirely satisfactory.

co·pai·ba, kō·pā′ba, kō·pī′ba, *n.* [Sp. and Pg. *copaiba;* from Brazilian name.] An oleoresin with aromatic odor and acrid taste, obtained from various tropical, chiefly South American, trees of the genus *Copaifera,* used formerly in medicine as a stimulant, expectorant, and diuretic, and now in varnishes and lacquers; the copaiba tree. Also **co·pai·va.**

co·pal, kō′pal, kō′pal, *n.* [Sp. *copal,* < Mex. *copalli,* resin.] A hard, lustrous resin yielded by various tropical trees, used chiefly in making varnishes.

co·par·ce·nar·y, kō·pär′se·nẽr″e, *n.* Joint heirship; copartnership; joint ownership. Also **co·par·ce·ny.**—**co·par·ce·ner,** *n.* A coheir or coheiress.

co·part·ner, kō·pärt′nẽr, kō′pärt″nẽr, *n.* A partner with others; one who is jointly concerned with one or more persons in carrying on a business; a sharer; a partaker. —**co·part·ner·ship,** *n.*

cope, kōp, *n.* [M.E. *cope, cape,* < M.L. *capa,* E. *cape.*] A cloak or cape, specif. a long mantle of silk or other material worn by ecclesiastics over the alb or surplice in processions and on other occasions; any cloaklike or canopylike covering; the vault of heaven or the sky; a coping.

cope, kōp, *v.t.*—*coped, coping.* To furnish with or as with a cope; to cover with or as with a coping.—*v.i.* To slope downward like a coping.

cope, kōp, *v.i.*—*coped, coping,* [O.Fr. *coper,* to strike (Fr. *couper,* to cut), < *colp, cop* (Fr. *coup*), a blow.] To strive or contend on equal terms or with equal strength, usu. followed by *with;* to deal with successfully.

cope, kōp, *v.t.* To join or form without mitering; to notch; to shape (a fitting) in conformity with the shape of another part.

Co·per·ni·can, kō·pẽr′ni·kan, ko·pẽr′-ni·kan, *a.* Of or pertaining to the astronomer Copernicus, 1473–1543, who promulgated the astronomical theory that the earth and the planets revolve in orbit around the sun.

cope·stone, kōp′stōn, *n.* The top stone of a building or the like; a stone used for or in a coping; *fig.* the crowning or finishing touch.

cop·i·er, kop′ē·ẽr, *n.* One who copies; a machine that makes copies.

co·pi·lot, kō′pī″lot, *n.* A pilot on certain aircraft who assists the first pilot in the performance of his duties.

cop·ing, kō′ping, *n.* The uppermost course of a wall or the like, usually made sloping so as to carry off water; a section of woodwork, the ends of which are cut to fit a molding.

cop·ing saw, *n.* A saw with a narrow blade stretched in a U-shape frame, and used to cut fancy patterns in wood.

co·pi·ous, kō′pē·us, *a.* [L. *copiosus,* < *copia,* plenty. COPY.] Having or yielding an abundant supply; exhibiting abundance or fullness, as of words; large in quantity or number; abundant; plentiful; unlimited.— **co·pi·ous·ly,** *adv.*—**co·pi·ous·ness,** *n.*

co·pol·y·mer, kō·pol′a·mẽr, *n. Chem.* a compound made by polymerizing two or more dissimilar monomers.

co·pol·y·mer·ize, kō·pol′a·me·rīz″, *v.t., v.i.*—*copolymerized, copolymerizing.* To subject to or undergo a change analogous to polymerization but with a union of unlike monomers.—**co·pol·y·mer·i·za·tion,** *n.*

cop·per, kop′er, *n.* [O.E. *coper, copor,* < L.L. *cuprum,* for L. *Cyrium,* "Cyprian metal," < Cyrus, the island of Cyprus in the eastern Mediterranean.] *Chem.* a malleable, ductile metallic element having a characteristic reddish-brown color, a good conductor of electricity, used for electric wiring, for alloys such as brass or bronze, and for electroplating. Sym. Cu, at. no. 29. See Periodic Table of Elements. A copper coin, as the English penny or the U.S. cent; a vessel made of copper, esp. a large boiler for cooking or laundry; a copper plate with an engraved or etched design, prepared for printing. *a.* Made of copper; pertaining to copper; copper-colored.—**cop·per·y,** *a.*

cop·per, kop′ér, *v.t.* To cover, coat, or sheathe with copper; in the game of faro, to indicate that the player wishes to bet against a certain card; hence, to bet against (a tip); to act in opposition to (a scheme).

cop·per·head, kop′ér·hed″, *n.* A venomous snake, *Agkistrodon contortrix,* of the U.S. having a copper-colored head, and reaching a length of about 3 feet; (often *cap.*) a Northern sympathizer with the South during the American Civil War.

cop·per·plate, kop′ér·plāt″, *n.* A plate of copper on which something is engraved or etched for printing; a print from such a plate; engraving or printing of this kind.—*a.* Engraved or etched on copper, or printed from a copperplate.

cop·per py·ri·tes, *n.* Chalcopyrite.

cop·per·smith, kop′ér·smith″, *n.* A worker in copper; one who manufactures copper utensils.

cop·pice, kop′is, *n.* [O.Fr. *copeiz, coupiez,* wood newly cut, < *couper, coper,* to cut < L.L. *colpus,* L. *colaphus,* Gr. *kolaphos,* a blow.] Copse.

cop·ra, kop′ra, *n.* [E. Ind.] The dried kernel or meat of the coconut, from which coconut oil is expressed.

cop·ro·lite, kop′ro·līt, *n.* A roundish, stony mass of petrified fecal matter of animals.

copse, kops, *n.* A wood of small trees; a growth of underwood or brush wood; a wood cut at certain times for fuel or other purposes.

Copt, kopt, *n.* [Cf. Ar. *Qibtī,* Copt, Gr. *Aigyptios,* Egyptian.] One of the natives of Egypt descended from the ancient Egyptians; an Egyptian Christian of the sect of the Monophysites.—**Cop·tic,** *a.* Of or pertaining to the Copts.—*n.* The language of the Copts, still used in the Coptic Church.

cop·ter, kop′tér, *n. Colloq.* helicopter.

cop·u·la, kop′ū·la, *n.* pl. **cop·u·las, cop·u·lae,** kop′ū·lē″. [L., a band, bond, < *co-,* together, and *apere,* fasten, join.] Something that connects or links together; *gram., logic,* that word or part of a proposition, esp. a form of the verb *be,* which expresses the relation between the subject and the predicate; *anat.* a connecting bone or cartilage.—**cop·u·lar,** *a.*

cop·u·late, kop′ū·lāt″, *v.i.*—copulated, copulating. To unite in sexual embrace.—**cop·u·la·tion,** kop′ū·lā′shan, *n.* [L. *copulatio.*] The act of copulating; coition.—**cop·u·la·to·ry,** *a.*

cop·u·la·tive, kop′ū·lā″tiv, kop′ū·la·tiv, *a.* [L.L. *copulativus.*] Serving to unite or couple; as, a *copulative* conjunction like *and, also, but, likewise, further, moreover, as well as;* involving connected words or clauses; as, a *copulative* sentence; of the nature of a copula; as, a *copulative* verb, such as *became* in "He *became* captain." Of or pertaining to copulation.—*n.* A copulative word; a copulative conjunction.—**cop·u·la·tive·ly,** *adv.*

cop·y, kop′ē, *n.* pl. **cop·ies.** [O.Fr. Fr. *copie,* < L. *copia,* plenty, abundance, facilities, M.L. a copy or transcript, < L.

co-, together, and *ops,* power, means, wealth.] A transcript, reproduction, or imitation of an original; one of the various examples or specimens of the same book, engraving, or the like; that which is to be transcribed, reproduced, or imitated; material written for a newspaper or an advertisement; written material to be set in type.

cop·y, kop′ē, *v.t.*—copied, copying. To make a copy of; transcribe; reproduce; to follow as a pattern or model; imitate; to produce as a copy of something else.—*v.i.* To make a copy or copies; make or do something in imitation of something else.

cop·y·book, kop′ē·buk″, *n.* A book for or containing copies, as of documents; a school book in which samples are written or printed for learners to imitate.

cop·y·boy, kop′ē·boi″, *n.* An errand boy employed in a newspaper office.

cop·y·cat, kop′ē·kat″, *n.* One who imitates the actions of another in an irksome way; one who lacks originality.

co·py desk, *n.* The desk in a newspaper office at which copy is edited.

cop·y·hold, kop′ē·hōld″, *n.* Formerly in England, a tenure of lands of a manor by transcript of the roll or record of the manorial court; an estate held by this tenure.

cop·y·hold·er, kop′ē·hōl″dér, *n.* One who or that which holds copy, esp. for a typesetter; a proofreader's assistant who reads the copy aloud, or follows it while the proof is read, for the detection of deviations from it in the proof.

cop·y·ist, kop′ē·ist, *n.* A copier; a transcriber of documents.

cop·y·read·er, kop′ē·rē″dér, *n.* One who edits copy for a newspaper or other publication and writes headlines.

cop·y·right, kop′ē·rīt″, *n.* The exclusive privilege which the law allows an author or his assignee of printing, reprinting, publishing, and selling his own original work; an author's exclusive right of property to his work for a certain time.—*a.* Relating to, or protected by the law of copyright.—*v.t.* To secure by copyright, as a book.

co·quet, kō·ket′, *v.i.*—coquetted, coquetting. [Fr. *coqueter.*] To trifle in love; flirt.

co·quet·ry, kō′ki·trē, kō·ke′trē, *n.* pl. **co·quet·ries.** [Fr. *coquetterie.*] The flirtatious behavior of a coquette.

co·quette, kō·ket′, *n.* [Fr., fem. of *coquet.*] A woman who endeavors to gain the admiration and affections of men for mere self-gratification; a flirt.—**co·quet·tish,** *a.*—**co·quet·tish·ly,** *adv.*

co·quil·la nut, ko·kēl′ya nut, ko·kē′ya nut, *n.* [Pg. *coquilho,* dim. of *coco,* coconut.] The elongated oval fruit or nut of a South American palm, *Attalea funifera,* having a very hard brown shell often used in turnery.

co·qui·na, kō·kē′na, *n.* [Sp., shell-fish, cockle.] A small clam of the genus *Donax* used for making chowder; a soft, whitish rock composed of fragments of marine shells.

cor·a·cle, kar′a·kl, kor′a·kl, *n.* [W. *corwgl.*] A small boat made by covering a wicker frame with leather, horsehide, etc., used in various parts of the British isles, originally by the ancient Britons.

cor·a·coid, kar′a·koid″, kor′a·koid″, *a.* Referring to a bone or bony process in various vertebrates, as birds and reptiles, extending between the shoulder blade and breastbone.—*n.* This process or bone.

cor·al, kar′al, kor′al, *n.* [O.Fr. *coral* (Fr. *corail*), < L.L. *corallum,* L. *corallium* < Gr. *korallion.*] The hard, calcareous, red, white, or black skeleton of any of various marine invertebrate animals; such skeletons collectively, as forming reefs or islands; an animal of this kind; something made of coral, as an ornament; the unimpregnated roe or eggs of the lobster, which when boiled assume the color of red coral; the

color, usu. a deep pink.—*a.* Composed of or containing coral; of or like coral.

cor·al bells, *n.* The alumroot plant cultivated in many varieties, native to southwestern U.S., bearing many small, red, bell-shaped flowers.

cor·al·ber·ry, kar′al·ber″ē, kor′al·ber″ē, *n.* pl. **cor·al·ber·ries.** A North American shrub, *Symphoricarpos symphoricarpos,* bearing clusters of coral-red berries in the axils of the leaves. Also **In·di·an cur·rant.**

cor·al·line, kar′a·lin, kar′a·līn″, kor′a·lin, kor′a·līn″, *n.* [L.L. *corallinus.*] Any alga or seaweed of the genus *Corallina* or related genera, having a red color and calcareous fronds; any of various corallike animals.—*a.* Of or like coral; coral-colored.

cor·al·lite, kar′a·līt″, kor′a·līt″, *n. Paleon.* a fossil coral; *zool.* the coral skeleton of an individual polyp.

cor·al·loid, kar′a·loid″, kor′a·loid″, *a.* Having the form or appearance of coral. Also **cor·al·loi·dal.**

cor·al reef, *n.* An extensive reef built by the gradual deposit of coral and other organic matter, part of which has become limestone.

cor·al snake, *n.* Any of various snakes of the venomous genus *Micrurus* of tropical New World areas, having brilliant bands of red, black, yellow, or white, esp. *M. fulvius* of southern U.S.

co·ran·to, ko·ran′tō, ko·rän′tō, kō·ran′tō, kō·rän′tō, *n.* pl. **co·ran·tos, co·ran·toes.** Courante.

cor·ban, kar′ban, *Heb.* kaR·bän′, *n.* [Heb. *corbân,* an offering, sacrifice.] Among the ancient Hebrews, a solemn consecration of anything to God, as of oneself, one's services, or possessions; an alms basket; a treasury of the church.

cor·beil, kar′bel, *Fr.* kaR·bā′, *n.* [Fr. *corbeille,* < L. *corbicula,* dim. of *corbis,* a basket.] *Arch.* a carved basket with sculptured flowers and fruits, esp. on a capital.

cor·bel, kar′bel, *n.* [L.L. *corbella,* a dim. < L. *corbis,* a basket.] *Arch.* a piece of stone, wood, or iron projecting from the vertical face of a wall to support a super-incumbent object.—*v.t.*—corbeled, corbeling, corbelled, corbelling. *Arch.* to support on a corbel or corbels; to provide with corbels.

cor·bel·ing, cor·bel·ling, kar′be·ling, *n. Arch.* the construction of corbels; work consisting of corbels; specif. an overlapping arrangement of stones, each course projecting beyond the one below.

cor·bie, cor·by, kar′bē, *n.* A raven; a crow.

cor·bie·step, kar′bē·step″, *n.* One of a series of steplike projections on the sloping sides of a gable, from the eaves to the apex of the roof. Also **cor·bel step, crow·step.**—**cor·bie ga·ble,** *n.* Gable with corbiesteps.

cor·bi·na, kar′bī′na, *n.* Any of several American marine and game fishes, esp. the bluish-gray, dark-spotted whiting, *Menticirrhus undulatus,* popular with surf casters along the California coast.

cord, kard, *n.* [O.Fr. Fr. *corde,* < L. *chorda,* cord, string.] A string or small rope composed of several strands twisted or woven together; something resembling a cord or rope; a cordlike rib on the surface of cloth; hence, a ribbed fabric, esp. corduroy; *pl.* corduroy breeches or trousers; *sing.* in *fig.* use, any influence which binds or restrains. A measure of cut wood orig. measured with a cord, equal to 128 cubic feet, or a pile 8 feet long, 4 feet high, and 4 feet broad; *anat.* a cord like structure; as, the spinal *cord* or the vocal *cords.*—*v.t.* To furnish with a cord; bind or fasten with cords; to pile or stack up, as wood, in cords.

cord·age, kar′dij, *n.* Cords or ropes collectively, esp. in a ship's rigging; quantity of wood measured in cords.

a- fat, fāte, fär, fâre, fall;   **e-** met, mē, mēre, hėr;   **i-** pin, pīne;   **o-** not, nōte, möve;   **u-** tub, cūbe, bull;   **oi-** oil;   **ou-** pound.

cor·date, kạr'dāt, *a.* [N.L. *cordatus,* < L. *cor* (*cord-*), heart.] Heart-shaped, as a shell; esp. of leaves, heart-shaped with the attachment at the notched end.—**cor·date·ly,** *adv.*

cord·ed, kạr'did, *a.* Furnished with, made of, or in the form of cords; ribbed, as a fabric; bound with cords; of wood, stacked up in cords.

Cor·de·lier, kạr″de·lēr', *n.* [Fr.] A Franciscan friar, so called from his girdle of knotted cord; *pl.* a certain Parisian political club at the time of the French Revolution, which met in an old convent of the Cordeliers or Franciscans.

cor·delle, kạr·del', *n.* [Fr. dim. of *corde,* E. *cord.*] A towline formerly used on river boats in Canada and U.S.—*v.t.*—**cordelled, cordelling.** To tow a boat with a cordelle.

cor·dial, kạr'jal, *Brit.* kạr'dē·al, *a.* [Fr. *cordial,* < L. *cor, cordis,* the heart; same root as E. *heart.*] Proceeding from the heart; courteous and gracious; warm; affectionate; refreshing; invigorating.—**cor·dial·i·ty, cor·dial·ness,** kạr·jal'i·tē, kạr″jē·al'i·tē, *Brit.* kạr·dē·al'i·tē. *n.*—**cor·dial·ly,** *adv.*

cor·dial, kạr'jal, *Brit.* kạr'dē·al, *n.* Something that strengthens, invigorates, or stimulates; an aromatic, sweetened alcoholic liquor; a liqueur; a medicinal drink.

cor·di·er·ite, kạr'dē·e·rīt″, *n. Mineral.* a silicate of aluminum, iron, and magnesium in shades of blue, violet, and pale yellow with vitreous luster.

cor·di·form, kạr'di·fạrm″, *a.* Heart-shaped.

cor·dil·le·ra, kạr'dil·yâr'a, kạr·dil'ėr·a, *n.* [Sp., < L. *chorda,* a string.] A ridge or chain of mountains; specifically, the mountain range of the Andes in South America.—**cor·dil·le·ran,** *a.*

cord·ing, kạr'ding, *n.* A heavy cord used for decorative or ornamental purposes, often interwoven with fabric or with metallic or contrasting thread.

cord·ite, kạr'dīt, *n.* A gunpowder, resembling brown cord, composed of nitroglycerin, guncotton, and mineral jelly.

cor·don, kạr'don, *n.* [Fr. *cordon,* < *corde,* E. *cord.*] A cord or braid worn for ornament or as a fastening; a ribbon worn, usually diagonally across the breast, as a badge of a knightly or honorary order; a line of sentinels, military posts, or the like, enclosing or guarding a particular place; a line beyond which passage is prohibited, as about an infected district. *Fort.* a projecting course of stones at the base of a parapet; the coping of an escarp. *Arch.* a stringcourse.

cor·don·bleu, *Fr.* kạr·dạN″ blœ', *n.* pl. **cor·dons bleus,** kạr·dạN″ blœ″. The blue-ribbon badge worn by knights under the Bourbon dynasty of France; one qualified to wear this badge; a person distinguished in his field, esp. a notable chef.

Cor·do·van, kạr'do·van, *a.* Of or pertaining to Cordova, Spain; (*l.c.*) designating a kind of leather made orig. at Cordova, at first of goatskin tanned and dressed, but later also of split horsehide; made of this leather.—*n.* A native or inhabitant of Cordova; (*l.c.*) cordovan leather.

cor·du·roy, kạr'du·roi″, kạr″du·roi', *n.* [Appar. < Fr. *corde du roi,* "king's cord" (not found, however, in Fr. as a name for the fabric).] A thick cotton stuff corded or ribbed on the surface; *pl.* trousers or breeches made of this; *sing.* a corduroy road.—*a.* Made of corduroy; resembling corduroy; specif. constructed of logs laid together transversely, as a road across swampy ground.

cor·du·roy, kạr'du·roi″, kạr″du·roi', *v.t.* To form, as a road, by laying logs together transversely; to make a corduroy road over.

cor·du·roy bridge, *n. Canada,* a bridge or road surfaced with logs laid crosswise.

cord·wood, kạrd'wụd″, *n.* Wood cut into lengths suitable for use as fuel and stacked in cords; logs cut into lengths of approximately four feet and stacked in cords; trees which, failing to meet the standard required for lumber, are suitable only for use as fuel.

core, kōr, kạr, *n.* [M.E. *core:* cf. L. *cor,* heart.] The central part of a fleshy fruit, containing the seeds; the central part of anything; the innermost or most essential part of anything; *foundry,* an inner mold placed within an outer mold to fill a space intended to be left hollow in a casting; *elect.* the piece of iron, bundle of iron wires, or the like, forming the central or inner portion of an electromagnet or induction-coil; *teleg.* the central conducting wires in a submarine or subterranean cable; *carp.* layer of wood which forms a base for veneers.

core, kōr, kạr, *v.t.*—**cored, coring.** To remove the core of fruit; to cut from the central part of something; *foundry,* to make or mold metal on a core.

core, kōr, kạr, *n. Brit.* a group of miners in one shift; the time spent underground by a shift of miners.

co·re·li·gion·ist, kō″ri·lij'o·nist, *n.* An adherent of the same religion as one's own.

co·re·op·sis, kōr″ē·op'sis, kạr″ē·op'sis, *n.* [N.L., < Gr. *coris,* bug, and *opsis,* appearance; so called from the form of the seed.] Any plant of the genus *Coreopsis,* including familiar garden herbs with yellow, brownish-red, or yellow and red flowers.

co·re·spond·ent, kō″ri·spon'dent, kōr″i-·spon'dent, kạr'i·spon″dent, kor'i·spon″dent, *n. Law,* a joint respondent, esp. in a divorce proceeding.

co·ri·a·ceous, kōr″ē·ā'shus, kạr″ē·ā'shus, kor″ē·ā'shus, *a.* [L. *coriaceus,* < *corium,* leather.] Consisting of leather or resembling leather; tough and leathery.

co·ri·an·der, kōr″ē·an'dėr, kạr″ē·an'dėr, kor″ē·an'dėr, *n.* [L. *coriandrum,* < Gr. *koriandron,* coriander.] An annual plant of the carrot family, the seeds of which are aromatic and flavorful and are used in certain liqueurs, and in cookery.

Co·rin·thi·an, ko·rin'thē·an, *a.* Pertaining to Corinth, a city of ancient Greece noted for its artistic adornment, luxury, and licentiousness; hence, ornate, as literary style; luxurious; licentious; amateur; *arch.* noting or pertaining to one of the three Greek orders, distinguished by a capital adorned with rows of acanthus leaves.—*n.* A native or inhabitant of Corinth; a gay, licentious, or shameless fellow; a man of fashion; a wealthy amateur sportsman, esp. an amateur yachtsman; *pl.* the two books of epistles of the New Testament addressed by St. Paul to the Corinthians.

Co·ri·o·lis force, kạr″ē·ō'lis fôrs, *n. Phys.* the deflective effect of the earth's rotation on any object in motion such as a projectile or aircraft, which diverts it to the right of velocity in the northern hemisphere, and to the left in the southern hemisphere.

co·ri·um, kōr'ē·um, kạr'ē·um, *n.* pl. **co·ri·a,** kōr'ē·ä, kạr'ē·ä. [L., skin, hide, leather.] *Anat.* The sensitive vascular layer of the skin beneath the epidermis; the derma; the corresponding layer of the mucous membrane.

cork, kạrk, *n.* [M.E. *cork* = D. *kurk* = *kork*; perhaps through Sp. < L. *cortex,* bark, or possibly L. *quercus,* oak.] The outer bark of a species of oak, *Quercus suber,* of Mediterranean countries, used for making stoppers for bottles, insulation or floats; the tree itself; something made of cork; a piece of cork, or of other material as rubber, used as a stopper for a bottle;

bot. an outer tissue of bark, produced by and exterior to the phellogen.—*v.t.* To provide or fit with cork or a cork; stop with or as with a cork, often with *up;* to blacken with burnt cork.

cork·age, kạr'kij, *n.* The corking or uncorking of bottles or a charge made for this; specif. a charge made by hotels for uncorking and serving bottles of wine or other liquor not purchased from the house.

cork·er, kạr'kėr, *n.* One who or that which corks. *Slang,* something that closes a discussion or settles a question; something striking or astonishing; something very good of its kind.

cork·ing, kạr'king, *a. Slang,* excellent or fine.

cork·screw, kạrk'skrö″, *n.* An instrument consisting of a metal screw or helix with a sharp point and a transverse handle, used to draw corks from bottles.—*a.* Resembling a corkscrew; helical or spiral.—*v.t.* To cause to advance in a spiral or zigzag course; to draw with or as with a corkscrew.—*v.i.* To move in a spiral course.

cork·wood, kạrk'wụd″, *n.* Cork; the light and porous wood of any of certain trees and shrubs, as the balsa, *Ochroma lagopus,* or, esp. in the U.S., a stout shrub or small tree, *Leitneria floridana,* with shining deciduous leaves; any of these trees or shrubs.

corm, kạrm, *n.* [N.L. *cormus,* < Gr. *cormos,* tree-trunk with boughs lopped off, < *ceirein,* cut short, shear.] *Bot.* a fleshy, bulblike, subterranean stem, producing leaves and buds on the upper surface and roots usually on the lower, and sometimes covered by a few membranous scales, as in the crocus. See *bulb, tuber.*

cor·mo·rant, kạr'mėr·ant, *n.* [O.Fr. *cormaran* (Fr. *cormoran*), < M.L. *corvus marinus,* sea-raven.] Any bird of the genus *Phalacrocorax,* comprising large, voracious waterbirds with a long neck, webbed feet, and a pouch under the beak in which they hold captured fish: used in eastern Asia to catch fish by banding the necks so they cannot swallow their catch; *colloq.* a greedy or rapacious person.—*a.* Gluttonous.

corn, kạrn, *n.* [O.E. *corn* = D. *koren* = G. *korn* = Icel. *korn* = Goth. *kaurn;* akin to L. *granum,* grain.] A small, hard seed or fruit, esp. of a cereal plant; collectively, the seeds of cereal plants, or the plants themselves, used for food, in Great Britain esp. of grain, in England esp. of wheat, and in Scotland esp. of oats; in the U.S., commonly restricted to maize or Indian corn.

corn, kạrn, *v.t.* To granulate, as gunpowder; to preserve and season with salt in grains; lay down in brine, as meat; to plant with corn; to feed with corn.—*v.i.* Of plants, to form corns or seeds.

corn, kạrn, *n.* [L. *cornu,* a horn.] A hard excrescence or induration of the skin on the toes or some other part of the feet, often painful, caused by the pressure of shoes.

cor·na·ceous, kạr·nā'shus, *a.* [L. *cornus,* cornel, < *cornu,* horn.] Belonging to the *Cornaceae,* a family of plants, mostly shrubs and trees, including the cornel or dogwood, and the tupelo.

corn bor·er, *n.* Any of a variety of moths of European origin, the larvae of which are destructive to corn by boring into the crown and stem.

corn bread, *n.* A kind of bread made of corn meal.

corn·cob, kạrn'kob″, *n.* The elongated woody receptacle in which the grains of an ear of maize are embedded; a tobacco pipe with a bowl made of this cob.

corn cock·le, *n.* An annual plant, *Agrostemma githago,* and of the pink family, bearing red flowers common as a weed among crops of grain and along roadsides.

corn col·or, *n.* A light, soft yellow.— **corn-col·ored,** *a.* Of the color of corn; of the color of light blonde hair.

corn·crib, kạrn′krib″, *n.* A ventilated structure used for the storage of unhusked or unshelled corn.

corn dodg·er, *n.* A kind of cake, popular in southern U.S., made of corn meal fried or baked hard.

cor·ne·a, kạr′nē·a, *n.* [N.L., fem. of L. *corneus,* horny.] *Anat.* the transparent anterior part of the external coat of the eye, covering the iris and the pupil.— **cor·ne·al,** *a.*

corn ear·worm, *n.* A moth of the cutworm variety, the larvae of which are destructive to corn, tomatoes, and cotton.

corned, kạrnd, *a.* Preserved or cured with salt; as, *corned* beef.

cor·nel·ian, kạr·nēl′yan, *n.* Carnelian.

cor·ne·ous, kạr′nē·us, *a.* Horny; hard.

cor·ner, kạr′nẽr, *n.* [O.Fr. *cornere, corniere,* < *corne,* horn, hornlike projection, < L. *cornu,* horn.] The meeting place of two converging lines or surfaces; as, the *corner* of a room; an angle; a projecting angle, esp. the place where two streets meet; sometimes, an end or margin; the space between two converging lines or surfaces near their intersection; any narrow, secluded, or secret place; any part, even the least or the most remote; a region or quarter; as, all the *corners* of the earth; a piece to protect the corner of anything; a monopoly of the available supply of a stock or commodity, for the purpose of raising the price.—*a.* Located at or on a corner; used or suitable for use on or in a corner.

cor·ner, kạr′nẽr, *v.t.* To furnish with corners; to place in or drive into a corner; to force into an awkward or difficult position, or one from which escape is impossible; to drive an auto around a sharp turn at high speed.—*v.i.* To meet in, or be situated on or at, a corner.—**cor·nered,** *a.* Having a corner or corners; as, four-*cornered;* forced into a difficult or undesirable position.—**cor·ner·er,** *n.*

cor·ner·stone, kạr′nẽr·stōn″, *n.* A stone which lies at the corner of two walls, and serves to unite them; specif. a stone built into a corner of the foundation of an important edifice as the actual or nominal starting point in building, usually laid with formal ceremonies, and often hollowed out and made the repository of documents; something of fundamental importance to a belief or an ideology.

cor·net, kạr′net′, *n.* [O.Fr. Fr. *cornet,* horn, also Fr. *cornette,* headdress, standard, cavalry cornet, < O.Fr. *corne,* < L. *cornu,* horn.] A brass wind instrument of the trumpet class, with valves and pistons; a little cone of paper twisted at the end, used for enclosing candy, etc.; the great white cap worn by certain congregations of nuns.—**cor·net·ist, cor·net·tist,** *n.* A player upon the cornet.

corn flour, *n.* Flour made from the grain of corn. Also *Brit.* cornstarch.

corn·flow·er, kạrn′flou′ẽr, *n.* Any of several plants growing in grainfields, as *Centaurea cyanus,* an asteraceous plant with blue, varying to white, flowers, growing wild in Europe and often cultivated in the U.S.—**corn·flow·er blue,** *n.* A deep blue color resembling the cornflower.

cor·nice, kạr′nis, *n.* [Fr. *cornice,* now *corniche,* < It. *cornice,* possibly < L. *cornix,* crow: cf. *corbel,* ult. < L. *corvus,* raven.] A horizontal molded projection which crowns or finishes a wall or building; specif. the uppermost member of an entablature, resting on the frieze; any of various other ornamental moldings or bands, as for concealing hooks or rods from which curtains are hung.

cor·niche, kạr′nish, kạr·nēsh′, *n.* A road which follows the edge of a cliff.

cor·nic·u·late, kạr·nik′ū·lāt″, kạr·nik′ū·lit, *a.* [L. *corniculatus,* < *corniculum,* dim. of *cornu,* horn.] Horned; having small horn-like processes.

Cor·nish, kạr′nish, *a.* Pertaining to Cornwall, in England; applied to a domestic English fowl bred for meat.—*n.* The ancient language of Cornwall, a dialect of the Celtic.

Corn·ish game hen, *n.* An English breed of chicken crossed with other breeds to produce a type of hen particularly desirable for roasting.

Corn Law, *n. Eng. hist.* one of a series of laws regulating the home and foreign grain-trade, repealed in 1846.

corn meal, *n.* Coarsely-ground meal made of corn; *Sc.* oatmeal.—**corn·meal,** *a.*

corn pone, *n.* Corn bread, esp. of a plain or simple kind popular in southern U.S.

corn pop·py, *n.* Corn rose.

corn rose, *n.* The common red poppy, *Papaver rhoeas;* the corn cockle. Also *corn poppy.*

corn snow, *n. Skiing,* snow in the form of pellets resulting from the melting and subsequent freezing of a layer of snow.

corn·starch, kạrn′stärch″, *n.* A starch, or a starchy flour made from corn, used for thickening puddings and gravies.

corn sug·ar, *n.* A sugar made from corn-starch; dextrose.

corn syr·up, *n.* A sweet syrup prepared from the grain of corn.

cor·nu, kạr′nū, kạr′nö, *n.* pl. **cor·nu·a,** kạr′nū·a, kạr′nö·a. [L.] A horn, or horn-like part or process.

cor·nu·co·pi·a, kạr′nu·kō′pē·a, *n.* [L.L., for L. *cornu copiæ,* "horn of plenty."] The fabulous horn of the goat Amalthea, which suckled Zeus, represented as overflowing with flowers and fruit, and symbolizing plenty; hence, an overflowing supply; a horn-shaped or conical receptacle or ornament.—**cor·nu·co·pi·ate,** kạr′nu·kō′pē·it, *a.* Having the shape of a cornucopia.

cor·nute, kạr·nöt′, kạr·nūt′, *a.* [L. *cornutus,* < *cornu,* horn.] Having horns; horn-shaped; *bot., zool.* furnished with a horn-like appendage or process. Also **cor·nut·ed.**

corn whis·key, *n.* A whiskey distilled, often illegally, from a mash of at least 80 percent corn grain.

corn·y, kạr′nē, *a.*—**cor·ni·er, corniest.** Of, pertaining to, or abounding in corn; *slang,* unpleasantly sentimental or unsophisticated, as certain literature or music. Pertaining to or having corns on the feet.

co·rol·la, kō·rol′a, *n.* [L. *corolla,* dim. of *corona,* a crown.] *Bot.* the part of a flower inside the calyx, surrounding the parts of fructification, and composed of one or more petals, generally to be distinguished from the calyx by the fineness of its texture and the gayness of its colors.—**co·rol·late, co·rol·lat·ed,** kō·rol′āt, kō·rol′lāt″, *a.*

cor·ol·lar·y, kạr′o·ler″ē, kor′o·ler″ē, *Brit.* ko·rol′a·rē, *n.* pl. **cor·ol·lar·ies.** [L.L. *corollarium,* corollary, L. gift, gratuity, orig. garland, < L. *corolla:* see *corolla.*] A mathematical proposition incidentally proved in proving another; hence, an immediate or easily drawn inference; a natural consequence or result.

co·ro·na, ko·rō′na, *n.* pl. **co·ro·nas, co·ro·nae,** ko·rō′nē. [L. garland, wreath, E. *crown.*] A crown or garland, esp. that bestowed upon the ancient Romans as a reward for distinguished services; a circular chandelier suspended from the roof or vaulting of a church; a white or colored circle of light seen round a luminous body, esp. the sun or moon; *meteor.* such a circle due to the diffraction produced by thin clouds or mist in the atmosphere; *astron.* a

luminous envelope outside of the sun's chromosphere, observable during eclipses and remarkable for its radiating streamers; *arch.* the part of a cornice supported by and projecting beyond the bed molding, and surmounted by the cymatium; *anat.* the upper portion or crown of a part, as of the head or a tooth; *bot.* a crownlike appendage, esp. one on the inner side of a corolla.

Co·ro·na Aus·tra·lis, ko·rō′na a·strā′lis, *n.* The southern constellation that touches the constellation Sagittarius on the south. Also **South·ern Crown.**

Co·ro·na Bo·re·al·is, ko·rō′na bôr″ē·al′is, ko·rō′na bạr′ē·al′is, ko·rō′na bôr″ē·ā′lis, ko·rō′na bạr′ē·ā′lis, *n.* The northern constellation that lies between Boötes and Hercules. Also **Northern Crown.**

cor·o·nach, kạr′o·nach, kor′o·nach, *n.* [Gael. and Ir.] *Sc. Ir.* a dirge.

cor·o·nal, ko·rōn′al, kạr′o·nal, kor′o·nal, *a.* [L. *coronalis,* < *corona.*] Pertaining to or resembling a crown or corona; *anat.* noting or pertaining to a suture extending across the skull between the frontal bone and the parietal bones.—kạr′o·nal, kor′o·nal, *n.* A crown or coronet; a garland; *anat.* the coronal suture.—**cor·o·nal·ly,** *adv.*

cor·o·nar·y, kạr′o·ner″ē, kor′o·ner″ē, *a.* Of or like a crown; pertaining to either or both of the two arteries of the heart.—*n.* A coronary artery; thrombosis.

cor·o·nar·y throm·bo·sis, *n.* Clotting of blood in one of the arteries of the heart.

cor·o·na·tion, kạr″o·nā′shan, kor″o·nā′shan, *n.* [O.Fr. *coronacion,* < L. *coronare,* to crown.] The act or ceremony of investing with a crown; the crowning of a sovereign; completion of a work.

cor·o·ner, kạr′o·nẽr, kor′o·nẽr, *n.* [A.Fr. *corouner,* "officer of the crown," < *coroune.*] An officer, as of a county or municipality, whose chief function in modern times is to investigate, by inquest before a jury, any death not clearly due to natural causes.—**cor·o·ner·ship,** *n.*

cor·o·net, kạr′o·nit, kạr′o·net″, kor′o·nit, kor′o·net″, kạr′o·net′, kor″o·net′, *n.* [O.Fr. *coronnette,* dim. of *corone.*] A small or inferior crown; specif. a crown representing a dignity inferior to that of the sovereign; a crownlike headdress or ornament for the head, as of gold or jewels; some crownlike part; the lowest part of the pastern of a horse, just above the hoof.—**cor·o·net·ed,** *a.* Adorned with or wearing a coronet.

co·ro·no·graph, ko·rō′no·graf″, ko·rō′no·gräf, *n.* A telescope fitted with devices to simulate an eclipse, used for observing and photographing the corona of the sun.

cor·po·ral, kạr′pẽr·al, kạr′pral, *a.* [L. *corporalis* (as *n.,* M.L. *corporale* < *corpus,* body).] Of or pertaining to the human body; bodily; physical; corporeal or material. *Zool.* pertaining to the body proper as distinguished from the head and limbs.—*n. Eccles.* a fine cloth on which the consecrated elements are placed during the celebration of the Eucharist.—**cor·po·ral·i·ty,** *n.* —**cor·po·ral·ly,** *adv.*

cor·po·ral, kạr′pẽr·al, kạr′pral, *n.* [Corrupted < Fr. *caporal,* It. *caporale,* < *capo,* L. *caput,* the head.] The noncommissioned officer of a company of soldiers next below a sergeant; on warships, a petty officer who attends to police matters; a noncommissioned officer of low rank in the Marine Corps.

cor·po·ral pun·ish·ment, *n.* Infliction of physical pain as punishment.

cor·po·rate, kạr′pẽr·it, kạr′prit, *v.t.*—**corporated, corporating.** [L. *corporatus,* pp. of *corporare,* < *corpus,* body.] To incorporate; unite in one body.—*a.* United in one body; pertaining to a united body, as of persons considered collectively as an individual; forming a corporation; of or pertaining to a corporation.—**cor·po·rate·ly**, *adv.*—**cor·po·ra·tive**, kȧr′po·rā″tiv, kȧr′pẽr·a·tiv, kȧr′pre·tiv, *a.*

cor·po·ra·tion, kȧr″po·rā′shan, *n.* [L.L. corporatio(n-).] A number of persons united or regarded as united in one body; specif. an artificial person, created by law, or under authority of law, from a group or succession of natural persons, and having a continuous existence irrespective of that of its members, and powers and liabilities distinct from those of its members.

cor·po·ra·tion, kȧr″po·rā′shan, *n. Slang,* the large and prominent abdomen of a stout man.

cor·po·rat·ism, kȧr′po·ra·tiz″um, kȧr′pra·tiz″um, *n.* The system of, the principles underlying, or the practices involved in the organization of legal corporations. Also **cor·po·rat·iv·ism**, kȧr′po·rā″ti·viz″um, kȧr′pẽr·a·ti·viz″um.

cor·po·ra·tive state, *n. Polit., philos.* a category of state in which the governmental economic and political authority is exercised through corporate bodies based on occupational or trade interests.

cor·po·re·al, kȧr·pōr′ē·al, kȧr·par′ē·al, *a.* [L. *corporeus,* < *corpus,* body.] Of the nature of the physical body; bodily; of the nature of matter; material; tangible; pertaining to material things.—**cor·po·re·al·i·ty**, cor·po·re·al·ness**, kȧr·pōr·ē·al′i·tē, *n.*—**cor·po·re·al·ly**, *adv.*

cor·po·re·i·ty, kȧr″po·rē′i·tē, *n.* [M.L. *corporeitas,* < L. *corporeus.*] Corporeal nature or quality; materiality.

cor·po·sant, kȧr′po·zant″, *n.* [Pg. *corpo santo,* "holy body."] A light, due to atmospheric electricity, sometimes seen on the mastheads or yard-arms of ships and on church-towers or tree-tops. Also **Saint El·mo's Fire, co·ro·na dis·charge.**

corps, kōr, kȧr, *n. pl.* **corps,** kōrz, *Fr.* kȧr. [Fr. CORPSE.] A body or number of persons associated or acting together. *Milit.* an organized military body consisting of officers and men or of officers alone; as, the U.S. Marine *Corps, Corps* of Engineers, or Signal *Corps;* a tactical unit with two or more divisions and other troops.

corps de bal·let, kȧr″ de ba·lā′, kȧr″ de bal′ā, *Fr.* kȧr de bä·lā′, *n.* The chorus of dancers in a ballet company who perform together and have no solo parts.

corpse, kȧrps, *n.* [O.Fr. Fr. *corps,* earlier *cors,* < L. *corpus,* body.] A dead body, usually of a human being.

corps·man, kōr′man, kȧr′man, *n. pl.* **corps·men.** An enlisted man in the U.S. Navy who assists the medical officer.

cor·pu·lent, kȧr′pū·lent, *a.* [L. *corpulentus,* < *corpus,* body.] Large or bulky of body; portly; stout; fat.—**cor·pu·lence, cor·pu·len·cy**, *n.*—**cor·pu·lent·ly**, *adv.*

cor·pus, kȧr′pus, *n. pl.* **cor·po·ra**, kȧr′pẽr·a. [L.] The body of a man or animal, especially a dead body; the essential part or substance of something; a body of works or complete collection of laws or writings, usually of one type; as, the *corpus* of Romantic poetry; *finance,* principal, as differentiated from interest or income; *anat.* the principal part of a bodily organ. A collection of recorded speech patterns made for the purpose of analyzing a dialect or language.

cor·pus cal·lo·sum, kȧr′pus ka·lō′sum, *n. pl.* **cor·po·ra cal·lo·sa**, kȧr′pẽr·a ka·lō′sa. *Anat.* the large band of nervous tissue joining the two cerebral hemispheres in the brain of man and other mammals.

cor·pus·cle, kȧr′pu·sel, kȧr′pus·el, *n.* [L. *corpusculum,* dim. of *corpus,* body.] A minute particle; a minute body forming a more or less distinct part of an organism; a minute or elementary particle of matter, as an electron, molecule, or atom; *physiol.* a cell, especially one having a distinct

function and form; as, red and white blood cells or *corpuscles.* Also **cor·pus·cule.**—**cor·pus·cu·lar**, kȧr·pus′kya·lẽr, *a.*—**cor·pus·cu·lat·ed**, kȧr·pus′kya·lā″tid, *a.*

cor·pus de·lic·ti, kȧr′pus di·lik′tī, *n. pl.* **co·po·ra de·lic·ti**. *Law,* the essential fact or element of a criminal case which proves that a crime was committed, as, in a murder case, proof that killing occurred; the substance on which a crime was committed, as the body of a victim, or the remains of a burned house.

cor·pus lu·te·um, kȧr′pus lö′tē·um, *n. pl.* **cor·po·ra lu·te·a**, kȧr′pẽr·a lö′tē·a. *Anat.* the yellowish endocrine tissue formed in the ovary of mammals by rupture of a Graafian follicle after ovulation which, during pregnancy, secretes the hormone progesterone; *pharm.* the hormonal substance comprised chiefly of progesterone, made from the corpus luteum of hogs or cows and used in the treatment of ovarian irregularities.

cor·rade, ko·rād′, kȧ·rād′, *v.t.*—**corraded, corrading.** [L. *corradere* (pp. corrasus), < *com-,* together, and *radere,* scrape.] To scrape or rub together; wear by scraping. *Geol.* of rock fragments carried by streams, to wear down by being rubbed together; to erode.—**cor·ra·sion**, ko·rā′zhan, *n.*—**cor·ra·sive**, kȧ·rā′siv, *a.*

cor·ral, ko·ral′, *n.* [Sp.] A pen or enclosure for horses and cattle; an enclosure formed of wagons during an encampment, for defense against attack.—**cor·ral**, *v.t.*—**corralled, corralling.** To confine in, or as in a corral; to seize or capture.

cor·rect, ko·rekt′, *v.t.* [L. *correctus,* pp. of *corrigere,* < *com-,* together, and *regere,* keep straight, direct.] To set right; remove the errors or faults of; rectify; to point out or mark the errors in; to admonish or rebuke in order to cause amendment; discipline; punish; to counteract the operation or effect of something hurtful; *math., physics,* to alter or adjust so as to bring into accordance with a standard or the like.—*a.* In accordance with an acknowledged or accepted standard; proper; conforming to fact or truth; free from error; accurate.—**cor·rect·a·ble, cor·rect·i·ble**, *a.*—**cor·rect·ing·ly**, *adv.*—**cor·rect·ness**, *n.*—**cor·rec·tor**, *n.*—**cor·rect·ive·ly**, *adv.*

cor·rec·tion, ko·rek′shan, *n.* [L. *correctio(n-).*] The act of correcting, or the state of being corrected; that which is substituted or proposed for what is wrong; an alteration.—**cor·rec·tion·al**, *a.*—**cor·rec·tion·al·ly**, *adv.*

cor·rect·i·tude, ko·rek′ti·töd″, ko·rek′ti·tūd″, *n.* Propriety of conduct and manners.

cor·rec·tive, ko·rek′tiv, *a.* Tending to correct; having the quality of correcting; remedial; as, *corrective* physical exercises.—*n.*—**cor·rec·tive·ly**, *adv.*

cor·re·late, kȧr′e·lāt″, kor′e·lāt″, *v.i.*—**correlated, correlating.** To have a mutual relation; stand in correlation.—*v.t.* To place in or bring into mutual relation or orderly connection.—*a.* Mutually related; correlated.—*n.* Either of two related things, esp. when one implies the other; to order one or a member of a series to correspond with one or a member of another series.

cor·re·la·tion, *Brit.* also **co·re·la·tion**, kȧr″e·lā′shan, kor″e·lā′shan, *Brit.* kō″ri·lā′shan, *n.* The act of correlating, or the state of being correlated; mutual relation of two or more things or parts; corresponding relationship between organisms in processes, qualities, and structure.

cor·rel·a·tive, ko·rel′a·tiv, *a.* Being in correlation; mutually related; so related that each implies or complements the other. —*n.* Either of two things, as two terms, which are correlative.—**cor·rel·a·tive·ly**,

adv.—**cor·rel·a·tive·ness, cor·rel·a·tiv·i·ty**, ko·rel′a·tiv′i·tē, *n.*

cor·re·spond, kȧr″i·spond′, kor″i·spond′, *v.i.* To be similar or analogous; be in agreement or conformity; agree with; to communicate by exchange of letters.—**cor·re·spond·ing**, *a.*—**cor·re·spond·ing·ly**, *adv.*

cor·re·spond·ence, kȧr″i·spon′dens, kor″i·spon′dens, *n.* The act or fact of corresponding; relation of similarity or analogy; agreement; conformity; intercourse; also **cor·re·spon·den·cy**. Communication by exchange of letters; letters that pass between correspondents; letters addressed to a newspaper, etc.

cor·re·spond·ence school, *n.* A school which mails instructional materials and tests to non-resident students who complete the work and send it back to the school for grading.

cor·re·spond·ent, kȧr″i·spon′dent, kor″i·spon′dent, *a.* Corresponding.—*n.* A thing that corresponds to something else; one who has regular business relations with another, esp. at a distance; one who communicates by letters; one who contributes to a newspaper, esp. one employed to report news regularly from a distant place.—**cor·re·spond·ent·ly**, *adv.*

cor·re·spon·sive, kȧr″i·spon′siv, kor″i·spon′siv, *a.* Responsive to one another.

cor·ri·da, kȧ·rē′dä, *n.* [Sp.] A bullfight.

cor·ri·dor, kȧr′i·dẽr, kȧr′i·dȧr″, kor′i·dẽr, kor′i·dȧr″, *n.* [Fr. *corridor,* < It. *corridore,* < *correre,* < L. *currere,* run.] A gallery or passage connecting parts of a building; a passage into which several apartments open; a narrow tract of land forming a passageway, as one belonging to an inland country and affording access to the sea.

Cor·rie·dale, kȧr′ē·dāl″, kor′ē·dāl″, *n.* A breed of sheep originally raised in New Zealand and valuable for market lambs and high quality wool.

cor·ri·gen·dum, kȧr″i·jen′dum, kor″i·jen′dum, *n. pl.* **cor·ri·gen·da**, kȧr″i·jen′dä, kor″i·jen′dä. [L. neut. gerundive of *corrigere.*] A printing or typographic error detected after publication and corrected separately on an added page.

cor·ri·gi·ble, kȧr′i·ji·bl, kor′i·ji·bl, *a.* [Fr., < L. *corrigo,* to correct.] Capable of being corrected, amended or reformed.—**cor·ri·gi·bil·i·ty**, *n.*—**cor·ri·gi·bly**, *adv.*

cor·ri·val, ko·rī′val, *n.* [L. *corrivalis.*] A rival; a competitor.—*a.* Being in rivalry or competition.

cor·rob·o·rant, ko·rob′ẽr·ant, *a.* Confirming; authenticating.

cor·rob·o·rate, ko·rob′o·rāt″, *v.t.*—**corroborated, corroborating.** [L. *corroboro, corroboratum—con-,* and *roboro,* to strengthen, < *robur,* strength.] To strengthen or give additional strength to; to confirm; to authenticate; to add assurance to; as, to corroborate testimony, news.—**cor·rob·o·ra·tion**, ko·rob″o·rā′shan, *n.*—**cor·rob·o·ra·tive**, *a.*—**cor·rob·o·ra·to·ry**, *a.*

cor·rode, ko·rōd′, *v.t.*—**corroded, corroding.** [L. *corrodo—cor-,* for *con-,* and *rodo,* to gnaw, whence also *rodent, erode.*] To eat away by degrees; to wear away or diminish by chemical action, as: Nitric acid corrodes copper. *Fig.* to gnaw or prey upon; to consume by slow degrees.—**cor·rod·i·ble**, *a.* That may be corroded.

cor·ro·sion, ko·rō′zhan, *n.* The action of corroding, eating, or wearing away by slow degrees, as the chemical effect of acids on metals.

cor·ro·sive, ko·rō′siv, *a.* Having the power to corrode or eat into a substance; fretting or irritating.—*n.* That which has the quality of eating or wearing gradually. —**cor·ro·sive·ly**, *adv.*—**cor·ro·sive·ness**, *n.*

cor·ro·sive sub·li·mate, *n. Chem.* bichloride of mercury, $HgCl_2$, an acrid, highly poisonous salt prepared by sublimation, and used as an antiseptic in medicine.

cor·ru·gate, kạr′u·gāt″, kor′u·gāt″, *v.t.*—*corrugated, corrugating.* [L. *corrugatus,* pp. of *corrugare,* < *com-,* altogether, and *rugare,* wrinkle, < *ruga,* a wrinkle.] To wrinkle; in general, to draw or bend into folds or alternate furrows and ridges.—*v.i.* To become corrugated.—*a.* Corrugated; wrinkled; furrowed.—**cor·ru·ga·tion,** *n.* The act of corrugating, or the state of being corrugated; a wrinkle, fold, furrow, or ridge.

cor·ru·gat·ed i·ron, *n.* Sheet iron or galvanized iron, strengthened by being bent into a series of parallel grooves and ridges, and often used for roofing.

cor·rupt, ko·rupt′, *v.t.* [L. *corruptus,* pp. of *corrumpere, com-,* altogether, and *rumpere,* break.] To change from a sound to a putrid or putrescent state; infect or taint; contaminate; to vitiate morally; pervert; deprave; to vitiate the integrity of; make venal; bribe; to debase language or a word. —*v.i.* To become corrupted or corrupt. —**cor·rupt·er, cor·rup·tor,** *n.*—**cor·rup·ti·ble,** *a.*—**cor·rup·ti·bil·i·ty, cor·rup·ti·ble·ness,** *n.*—**cor·rup·ti·bly,** *adv.*—**cor·rup·tive,** *a.*—**cor·rupt·ly,** *adv.* —**cor·rupt·ness,** *n.*

cor·rupt, ko·rupt′, *a.* Corrupted; putrid; infected or tainted; depraved or debased; dishonest or venal; influenced by bribery; vitiated by errors or alterations, as a text or a word.

cor·rup·tion, ko·rup′shan, *n.* [L. *corruptio(n-).*] The act of corrupting, or the state of being corrupt; putrefactive decomposition; putrid matter; moral perversion; depravity; perversion of integrity; corrupt or dishonest proceedings; bribery; perversion from a state of purity; debasement, as of a language; a debased form of a word.

cor·sage, kạr·säzh′, *n.* [O.Fr. Fr. *corsage,* < *cors.*] A bouquet to be worn by a woman; the body or waist of a woman's dress; a bodice.

cor·sair, kạr′sâr, *n.* [Fr. *corsaire,* < M.L. *cursarius,* < *cursus,* hostile excursion, booty, L. a running, E. *course.*] A privateer, esp. on the Barbary coast; a pirate; a vessel used by pirates.

cor·se·let, kạr″se·let′, kạrs′lit, *n.* [Fr., dim. of O.Fr. *cors,* L. *corpus,* the body.] A lightly boned or unboned corset worn by women, kạr″se·let′. A section of armor which covered the wearer's torso, kạrs′lit; also **cors·let,** kạrs′lit.

cor·set, kạr′sit, *n.* [O.Fr. Fr. *corset,* dim. of *cors.*] A shaped, close-fitting, sometimes reinforced undergarment extending above and below the waist line, worn chiefly by women to shape and support the body.— *v.t.*—**cor·set·ed,** *a.* Wearing a corset.— **cor·se·tiere,** kạr″se·tiẽr′, *n.* A woman who makes or sells corsets.

Cor·si·can, kạr′si·kan, *a.* Relating to the people and island of Corsica, a French domain located in the Mediterranean.—*n.*

cor·tege, *Fr.* cor·tège, kạr·tezh′, kạr·täzh′, *n.* [Fr. *cortège,* < It. *corteggio,* < *corte,* = E. *court.*] A train of attendants; a procession, esp. at a funeral.

cor·tex, kạr′teks, *n.* pl. **cor·ti·ces,** kạr′ti·sēz″. [L. *cortex, corticis,* bark; whence *cork.*] Bark, as of a tree; *anat.* the outermost section of an organ as of the brain or the adrenal glands.

cor·ti·cal, kạr′ti·kal, *a.* Belonging to, consisting of, or resembling the cortex; relating to the cerebral cortex.—**cor·ti·cate, cor·ti·cat·ed,** *a.*

cor·ti·cos·te·rone, kạrt″i·kos′te·rōn″, kạrt′i·kōs′te·rōn″, *n.* A steroid hormone, $C_{21}H_{30}O_4$, of the adrenal cortex.

cor·tin, kạr′tin, kạr′tin, *n.* A hormone secreted by the adrenal cortex.

cor·ti·sone, kạr′ti·sōn″, kạr′ti·zōn″, *n.* Steroid hormone of the adrenal cortex; *pharm.* generic name of an adrenal-steroid hormone which can be administered either orally or intramuscularly to cause remission, but not cure various collagen diseases.

co·run·dum, ko·run′dum, *n.* [Tamil *kuruntam,* < Skt. *kuruvinda,* ruby.] A mineral of the aluminum oxide group characterized by hardness and crystal forms, including such gemstones as the sapphire and the ruby, and other varieties used as abrasives.

cor·us·cate, kạr′u·skāt″, kor′u·skāt″, *v.i.*— *coruscated, coruscating.* [L. *curosco, coruscatum,* to flash.] To flash; to lighten; to gleam; to glitter.—**cor·us·ca·tion,** *n.* A sudden burst of light in the clouds or atmosphere; a flash of wit.—**co·rus·cant,** *a.*

cor·vée, kạr·vā′, *n.* [Fr. *corvée,* < M.L. *corrogata,* required work, < L. *corrogare.*] Formerly, labor, as on the repair of roads, exacted by a feudal lord; labor required by public authorities in place of taxes to maintain roads.

cor·vette, kạr·vet′, *n.* [Fr. *corvette,* < L. *corbita,* a ship of burden, < *corbis,* a basket.] Formerly, a flush-decked vessel without a quarter-deck, and having only one tier of guns in the sailing navies; a ship smaller than a destroyer bearing both anti-submarine and antiaircraft guns.

cor·vine, kạr′vin, kạr′vin, *a.* [L. *corvinus,* < *corvus,* raven.] Pertaining to or resembling a crow; belonging or pertaining to the *Corvidae,* a family of birds including the crows, ravens, and jays.

Cor·vus, kạr′vus, *n. Astron.* a small southern constellation between Virgo and Hydra.

cor·y·phae·us, kạr″i·fē′us, kor″i·fē′us, *n.* pl. **cor·y·phae·i,** kạr″i·fē′ī, kor″i·fē′ī. [L., < Gr. *coryphaios,* < *copyphē,* head.] The leader of the chorus in the ancient Greek drama; the leader of any chorus or group of singers.

cor·y·phée, kạr″i·fā′, kor″i·fā′, *Fr.* kạ·rē·-fā′, *n.* [Fr., < L. *coryphæus.* CORYPHAEUS.] A ballet dancer who takes a leading part as a member of a small ensemble; a chorus girl.

co·ry·za, ko·rī′za, *n.* [L.L., < Gr. *coryza.*] *Pathol.* Acute inflammation of the mucous membrane of the nasal cavities; cold in the head; a respiratory disease found in domestic animals.

cos, kos, kạs, *n.* Romaine.

Co·sa Nos·tra, kō′za nōs′tra, *n.* [It. lit. 'our thing.'] A secret society of criminal activity in the U.S., related to the Mafia in its Italian-Sicilian origin.

co·se·cant, kō·sē′kant, kō·sē′kant, *n.* [< *complement* and *secant.*] *Trig.* in a right-angle triangle, the cosecant of the base angle that is less than 90° is the number obtained after dividing the hypotenuse by the perpendicular: multiplied by the sine, it equals one.

co·seis·mal, kō·sīs′mal, kō·sīz′mal, *a.* Noting or pertaining to a line or curve connecting or comprising points on the earth's surface where an earthquake wave arrives simultaneously.—*n.* A coseismal line or the like.—**co·seis·mic,** *a.* Coseismal.

co·sig·na·to·ry, kō·sig′na·tōr″ē, kō·-sig′na·tar″ē, *n.* pl. **co·sig·na·to·ries.** One who is joint signer of a promissory note, a treaty, or other agreement.

co·sine, kō′sīn, *n.* [*Complement* and *sine.*] *Trig.* in a right-angle triangle, the cosine of the base angle that is less than 90° is the number obtained after dividing the base by the hypotenuse: multiplied by the secant, it equals one.

cos let·tuce, *n.* [< Cos (*Kos*), island off the coast of Asia Minor.] A kind of lettuce, including the romaine and other varieties, with erect oblong heads and crisp leaves.

cos·met·ic, koz·met′ik, *a.* [Gr. *kosmētikos,* < *kosmos,* order, beauty.] Beautifying; improving beauty, particularly the beauty of the complexion.—*n.* Any preparation that helps to beautify and improve the skin, esp. the facial complexion.

cos·mic, koz′mik, *a.* [Gr. *kosmikos.*] Of or pertaining to the cosmos; as, *cosmic* philosophy; characteristic of the cosmos; immeasurably extended in space or time; vast; forming a part of the material universe, esp. outside of the earth; orderly or harmonious.—**cos·mi·cal,** *a.* Cosmic; *astron.* occurring at sunrise, as the rising or setting of a star.—**cos·mi·cal·ly,** *adv.*

cos·mic dust, *n.* Matter in fine particles existing in or falling from space.

cos·mic noise, *n. Aerospace,* static caused by an extra-terrestrial phenomenon, as sunspots.

cos·mic ray, *n.* An electromagnetic ray of extremely high frequency and energy content that originates in outer space and bombards the atoms of the earth's atmosphere, producing mesons and penetrating barriers impervious to all other radiation.

cos·mog·o·ny, koz·mog′o·nē, *n.* pl. **cos·mog·o·nies.** [Gr. *kosmogonia—kosmos,* world, and root *gen,* to bring forth.] The origin or creation of the world or universe; creation; a doctrine of the formation of the universe.—**cos·mo·gon·ic, cos·mo·gon·i·cal,** koz″mo·gon′ik, *a.*—**cos·mog·o·nist,** *n.*

cos·mog·ra·phy, koz·mog′ra·fē, *n.* pl. **cos·mog·ra·phies.** [L.L. *cosmographia,* < Gr. *kosmographia.*] The science which describes and maps the heavens and the earth, embracing astronomy, geography, and sometimes geology; a description or representation of the universe in its main features.

Cos·mo·line, koz′mo·lēn″, *n.* Heavy grease used to protect weapons. (Trademark.)— *v.t.*—*cosmolined, cosmolining.* (*l.c.*) to coat weapons with heavy grease.

cos·mol·o·gy, koz·mol′o·jē, *n.* The general science or theory of the cosmos or material universe, its parts, elements, and laws.— **cos·mo·log·ic, cos·mo·log·i·cal,** koz″-mo·loj′ik, koz″mo·loj′i·kal, *a.*—**cos·mol·o·gist,** *n.*

cos·mop·o·lis, koz·mop′o·lis, *n.* A city inhabited by people from many lands.

cos·mo·pol·i·tan, koz″mo·pol′i·tan, *a.* Pertaining to or characteristic of a cosmopolite; belonging to all parts of the world; having no local or national attachments; *bot., zool.* widely distributed over the globe. —*n.* A cosmopolite.—**cos·mo·pol·i·tan·ism,** *n.* Cosmopolitan character.—**cos·mo·pol·i·tan·ize,** *v.t.*—*cosmopolitanized, cosmopolitanizing.* To render cosmopolitan.

cos·mop·o·lite, koz·mop′o·līt″, *n.* [Gr. *kosmopolitēs,* < *kosmos,* world, and *politēs,* citizen, < *polis,* city, state.] A citizen of the world, or one at home in all parts of the world; a person free from national or local attachments or prejudices; an animal or plant of world-wide distribution.—**cos·-mop·o·lit·ism,** *n.*

cos·mos, koz′mos, koz′mōs, *n.* pl. **cos·mos, cos·mos·es.** [Gr. *kosmos,* order, ornament, and hence the universe as an orderly and beautiful system.] The universe as an embodiment of order and harmony; a system of order and harmony; *bot.* a plant of the genus *Cosmos,* a full-blooming annual with showy flowers.

Cos·mos, koz′mōs, koz′mas, *n.* The general name given to each one of the numbered series of Soviet unmanned earth satellites, one of their tasks being to test equipment for manned space flights.

Cos·sack, kos′ak, kos′ak, *n.* [Turk. *quzzāq,* adventurer, freebooter.] One of a people of southern European Russia and adjoining parts of Asia, noted as horsemen or light cavalry; a privileged military class in Russia under the czars.

cos·set, kos′it, *n*. A pet lamb, or any other pet.—*v.t.* To pamper; coddle; fondle.

cost, kạst, kost, *n*. [O.Fr. *cost* (Fr. *coût*).] The price paid or charged for something; outlay or expenditure, as of time or labor; that which must be given to acquire, produce, accomplish, or maintain anything; a sacrifice, loss, or penalty endured, for a thing; *pl., law,* expenses in litigation or other legal transaction.

cost, kạst, kost, *v.i.*—*cost, costing.* [O.Fr. *coster* (Fr. *coûter*), < L. *constare*, stand together, cost.] To require an expenditure of money as stated; to require a expenditure of effort, time, or labor; entail a particular sacrifice, loss, or penalty; to estimate or determine the cost, as of production.—*v.t.* To require a price of; to cause to suffer a loss or penalty; to determine or estimate the cost of.

cos·ta, kos′ta, kạ′sta, *n*. pl. **cos·tae**, kos′tē, kạ′stē. [L., rib, side.] A rib or riblike part, as of a leaf or insect wing; a ridge.—**cos·tal**, **cos·tate**, *a*.

cost ac·count·ing, *n*. The classifying, recording, and analyzing in a systematic manner the cost of materials, labor, and overhead involved in a company's production or its rendering of a service.—**cost ac·count·ant**, *n*.

cos·tard, kos′tard, kạ′stard, *n*. [M.E., perhaps < O.Fr. *coste*, < L. *costa*, rib.] A large English apple used in cooking.

Cos·ta Ri·can, kos′ta rē′kan, kạ′sta rē′kan, kō′sta rē′kan, *Sp.* kạs′tä Rē′kän, *a*. Relating to the people and culture of Costa Rica, a republic in Central America, located between Panama and Nicaragua.—*n*. An inhabitant or native of Costa Rica.

cos·ter·mon·ger, kos′tẽr·mung″gẽr, kos′tẽr·mong″gẽr, kạ′stẽr·mung″gẽr, kạ′stẽr·mong″gẽr, *n*. [Earlier *costardmonger:* see *costard.*] *Brit.* a peddler of fruit, vegetables, and fish.

cos·tive, kos′tiv, kạ′stiv, *a*. [Contr. < It. *costipativo*, < L. *constipo*, to cram, to stuff.] Having the bowels bound; constipated.—**cos·tive·ly**, *adv*.—**cos·tive·ness**, *n*.

cost·ly, kạst′lē, kost′lē, *a*.—*costlier, costliest.* Costing much; of great price or value; sumptuous; occasioning great expense; lavish or extravagant; entailing great sacrifice; detrimental.—**cost·li·ness**, *n*.

cost·mar·y, kost′mâr″ē, kạst′mâr″ē, *n*. pl. **cost·mar·ies.** [M.E. *cost* (< L. *costum*, kind of aromatic plant) and *Mary.*] A perennial plant, *Chrysanthemum balsamita*, with fragrant leaves, used as a pot-herb, in salads, and for flavoring.

cost of liv·ing, *n*. The relationship of the average cost of consumer goods and services to the national level of individual or family incomes.

cost-of-liv·ing in·dex, kạst′ov·liv′ing in′deks, kost′ov·liv′ing in′deks, *n*. An index indicating the weighted average of prices of 296 commodities purchased by consumers, used esp. to adjust wages to compensate for changes in the purchasing power of money. Also **con·sum·er price in·dex.**

cost-plus, kạst′plus′, kost′plus′, *a*. The cost of production plus an additional fee or percentage as an agreed rate of profit; as, a *cost-plus* contract.

cos·trel, kos′trel, kạ′strel, *n*. [O.Fr. *costerel*, appar. orig. a flask hung at the side, < *coste*, < L. *costa*, rib, side.] An ancient bottle or vessel of leather, earthenware, or wood, often of flattened form and commonly having an ear or ears to suspend it by, as from the waist.

cos·tume, kos′tōm, kos′tūm, *n*. [Fr. *costume*, < It. *costume*, < L. *consuetudo*, custom.] The style of dress, including ornaments and hair styles, peculiar to a nation, class, or period; fashion of dress appropriate to a particular occasion or season; as, court *costume,* winter *costume*; dress or garb belonging to another period or place, as worn on the stage or at balls; a set of outer garments, esp. an ensemble or outfit worn by a woman.—ko·stōm′, ko·stūm′, *v.t.—costumed, costuming.* To furnish with a costume or dress; provide appropriate dress for.—**cos·tum·er**, ko·stō′mẽr, ko·stū′mẽr, *n*. One who makes or deals in costumes. Also *Fr.* **cos·tu·mier**, ko·stō′mē·ẽr, ko·stū′mē·er, *Fr.* kạs·tY·myä′.

co·sy, co·sey, kō′zē, *a*. Cozy.

cot, kot, *n*. [Anglo-Ind. < Hind *khāt*.] A light portable bed, as one of canvas or the like, stretched on a frame; a light bedstead; *Brit.* a small bed or crib for a child; *naut.* a swinging bed made of canvas.

cot, kot, *n*. [O.E. *cot*, neut. (also *cote*, fem.), = D., L.G., and Icel. *kot* = G. *koth*.] A small or humble dwelling; a cottage; a small erection for shelter or protection; a sheath or covering, as to protect a finger.

co·tan·gent, kō·tan′jent, kō′tan″jent, *n*. [N.L. *cotangens* (-*ent*-).] *Trig.* the tangent of the complement of a given angle or arc; the ratio between the side adjacent to an acute angle in a right-angle triangle and the side opposite the angle.—**co·tan·gen·tial**, kō″tan·jen′shal, *a*.

cote, kōt, *n*. [O.E. *cote:* see *cot.*] A shelter for small animals, such as sheep, pigs, or pigeons; *Brit. dial.* a cot or small house.

co·teau, kạ·tō′, kō·tō′, *Fr.* kạ·tō′, *n*. pl. **co·teaux**, kạ·tōz′, kō·tōz′, *Fr.* kạ·tō′. [Fr., dim. of *côte,* hillside, < L. *costa,* rib, side.] *Chiefly Canadian.* An upland; a broad, flat-topped ridge of moderate elevation.

co·te·rie, kō′te·rē, *n*. [Fr., < L.L. *coteria,* an association of villagers, *cota,* a cottage.] A set or circle of friends who are in the habit of meeting for social or literary intercourse; a clique.

co·ter·mi·nous, kō·tẽr′mi·nus, *a*. Conterminous.

co·thur·nus, kō·thụr′nus, *n*. pl. **co·thur·ni**, kō·thụr′nī. [L., < Gr. *cothornos.*] The buskin or high shoe of the Greeks and Romans, specif. the high, thick-soled shoe worn by ancient Greek and Roman tragic actors, often taken as symbolic of tragedy; an elevated style of enacting Greek and Roman tragedy. Also **co·thurn,** kō′thụrn, kō·thụrn′.

co·tid·al, kō·tīd′al, *a*. Pertaining to a coincidence of tides; noting a line connecting points where it is high tide at the same time.

co·til·lion, co·til·lon, kō·til′yan, ko·til′-yan, *Fr.* kạ·tē·yaN′, *n*. [Fr. *cotillon,* old dance for four or eight persons, cotillion, lit. 'petticoat,' dim. of O.Fr. *cote,* E. *coat.*] Any of various dances of the quadrille kind; in the U.S., a complex dance, or entertainment of dancing, consisting of picturesque or elaborate patterns; the music for this type of dancing; *U.S.* a formal dance at which debutantes are presented socially.

cot·ta, kot′a, kạ′ta, *n*. [M.L.] A short surplice, sleeveless or with short sleeves, worn esp. by church choristers.

cot·tage, kot′ij, *n*. [M.L. *cotagium,* < *cota,* cot, = E. *cote.*] A small dwelling of humble character; a small country residence or detached suburban house; one of several detached houses forming an institution, as a resort or a hospital; a temporary residence, as at a lake or resort.—**cot·tag·er**, *n*.

cot·tage cheese, *n*. A kind of soft white cheese made of skim-milk curds.

cot·tage pud·ding, *n*. A dessert consisting of cake with a topping of sweet sauce.

cot·ter, kot′ẽr, *n*. [Origin obscure.] A wedge, key, or the like, fitted or driven into an opening in order to secure something or hold parts together.

cot·ter, cot·tar, kot′ẽr, *n*. [M.L. *cotarius,* < *cota,* cot, = E. *cote.*] One occupying a cottage and land, by tenure of labor, esp. a Scottish or Irish peasant or farm laborer.

cot·ter pin, *n*. A half-round metal strip, bent double and used as a fastener by flaring the two ends in an open position in order to hold the pin in place.

cot·ton, kot′on, *n*. [O.Fr. Fr. *coton,* < Ar. *qutun.*] The soft white, downy hairs or fibers attached to the seeds of plants of the mallow-like tropical genus *Gossypium,* used in making thread or fabric; a plant yielding cotton, as *G. hirsutum,* "upland cotton" or *G. barbadense,* "sea-island cotton"; such plants collectively, as a cultivated crop; cloth or thread made of cotton; any soft, downy substance resembling cotton, growing on some other plant.—**cot·ton·y**, kot′o·nē, *a*. Of the nature of or resembling cotton; covered with a down or nap resembling cotton; woven or composed of cotton.

cot·ton, kot′on, *v.i. Colloq.* To fraternize; to agree or get on with.—**cot·ton to,** *slang,* to be attracted to a person or idea.

cot·ton can·dy, *n*. A candy made from whipped spun sugar, wound around a stick or in a cone-shaped paper container.

cot·ton gin, *n*. A machine for separating the fibers of cotton from the seeds, invented by Eli Whitney in the 18th century.

cot·ton grass, *n*. Any of the rushlike plants of the genus *Eriophorum,* found in swampy places and bearing spikes resembling tufts of cotton.

cot·ton·mouth, kot′on·mouth″, *n*. The water moccasin snake.

cot·ton·seed, kot′on·sēd″, *n*. pl. **cot·ton·seeds, cot·ton·seed.** The seed of the cotton plant, yielding an oil which is used as a substitute for olive oil and in cooking.

cot·ton stain·er, *n*. A type of insect that punctures and damages the developing seeds of cotton and stains the fibers with an indelible yellow or red juice.

cot·ton·tail, kot′on·tāl, *n*. The common North American rabbit, genus *Sylvilagus,* named for its fluffy white tail.

cot·ton·weed, kot′on·wēd″, *n*. Any of certain plants with stems and leaves covered with a soft, fine hair; the cudweed.

cot·ton·wood, kot′on·wụd″, *n*. Any of several American species of poplar, as *Populus deltoides,* with cottonlike tufts on the seeds.

cot·ton wool, *n*. Cotton in its raw state, as on the boll or gathered for use.

cot·y·le·don, kot″i·lēd′on, *n*. [Gr. *kotylēdōn,* < *kotylē,* a hollow.] *Bot.* The seed leaf; the first leaf or leaves of the embryo plant.—**cot·y·le·don·al, cot·y·le·don·ar·y**, *a*.

couch, kouch, *v.t.* [Fr. *coucher,* O.Fr. *clocher,* Pr. *colcar,* It. *colcare,* < L. *collocare,* to lay, to place.] To cause to lie down; to put down, as for sleep; to lower a weapon into attack position; to express in words, as: He *couched* his criticism in formal language.—*v.i.* To lie down, as on a bed or place of repose; to stoop; to bend the body or back; to wait in ambush.

couch, kouch, *n*. An upholstered piece of living room furniture seating at least two persons and long enough to lie down on; an animal's den; an otter's burrow.—**couch·ant**, kouch′ant, *a*. Lying down; squatting.

couch grass, *n*. Any of various grasses, esp. *Agropyron repens,* known chiefly as troublesome weeds, and characterized by creeping rootstocks which spread rapidly.

cou·gar, kō′gẽr, *n*. pl. **cou·gars, cou·gar.** [Native name modified.] A quadruped of the cat family, one of the most dangerous animals of the Americas. Also **cat·a·mount**, *mountain lion, panther, puma.*

cough, kạf, kof, *n.* [Imitative of the sound; D. *kuch,* a cough.] Expulsion of air from the lungs marked by sudden loud noise; an illness characterized by such a condition.— *v.i.* To expel air noisily from the lungs. —*v.t.* To expel from the lungs by coughing.—**cough up,** *slang,* to hand over money.

could, kụd. [O.E. *coude, cuthe,* pret. of *cunnan,* to be able.] The past form of can.

could·n't, kụd'ent. Contraction of could not.

cou·lée, kö'lē, *Fr.* kö·lā', *n.* [Fr. < *couler,* flow, slide, < L. *colare,* strain.] A stream of lava; *western U.S.* a deep ravine or gulch, usually dry, which has been worn by running water.

cou·lisse, kö·lēs', *n.* [Fr. < *couler:* see *coulée.*] A grooved piece of wood, or groove in which something slides; one of the side scenes of a stage in a theater.

cou·loir, köl·wär', *Fr.* kö·lwär', *n.* [Fr. < *couler.*] A steep gorge or gully on the side of a mountain.

cou·lomb, kö'lom, kö·lom', *Fr.* kö·lọN', *n.* [From C. A. *Coulomb* (1736–1806), French physicist.] The quantity of electricity transferred by a current of one ampere in one second.—**cou·lom·bic,** *a.*

coul·ter, köl'tẽr, *n.* Colter.

cou·ma·rin, kö'ma·rin, *n.* [Fr. *coumarine,* < *coumarou.*] A white crystalline substance with a vanillalike odor, obtained from the tonka bean and certain other plants, or prepared synthetically, and used for flavoring and perfume. Also **cu·ma·rin.**

cou·ma·rone, kö'ma·rōn", *n.* A colorless liquid compound, C_8H_6O, derived from coal tar naphtha and used to form coumarone resins for use in such things as printing inks, adhesives, and pipe oils.

coun·cil, koun'sil, *n.* [Fr. *concile,* < L. *concilium—con-,* together, and root *cal,* to summon; akin conciliate, reconcile. This word is often improperly confounded with *counsel.*] An assembly convened for consultation, deliberation, and advice; a group elected or appointed to act in an advisory, administrative, or legislative capacity; an executive body of persons who hold equal rank, power, and authority; a federation of organizations; the governing body of such a federation; a local chapter of a parent organization.—**coun·cil·lor, coun·cil·or,** koun'si·lẽr, koun·slẽr, *n.* A member of a council.—**coun·cil·man,** *n.* A member of a council.—**coun·cil·lor·ship,** *n.*

coun·sel, koun'sel, *n.* [Fr. *conseil,* < L. *consilium,* advice, from *consulo,* to consult, deliberate. Akin *consult.*] Advice; information or opinion given to aid the judgment or actions of another; consultation or deliberation about future actions; deliberate purpose; secret opinions or purposes; as, to keep one's counsel. *Law,* a lawyer engaged in a court trial or managing a case in court; a lawyer appointed as an advisor.

coun·sel, koun'sel, *v.t.*—*counseled, counseling, Brit. counselled, counselling.* To advise or give deliberate opinion; to exhort, warn, admonish, or instruct; to recommend.

coun·sel·ing, *Brit.* **coun·sel·ling,** koun'-se·ling, *n.* The act or process of giving professionally competent advice, as: She asked the Dean of Women for *counseling.* Specifically, the use of psychological methods in professional guidance of an individual.

coun·se·lor, *Brit.* **coun·sel·lor,** koun'se·-lẽr, *n.* Any person who gives counsel or advice; an adviser; one whose profession is to give legal advice and manage cases in court; a lawyer; *Brit.* a barrister. A supervisor at a summer camp for children. —**coun·se·lor·ship,** *Brit.* **coun·sel·lor·-ship,** *n.* The office or duties of a counselor.

count, kount, *n.* [O.Fr. *conte* (Fr. *comte*), < L. *comes (comit-),* companion, later a title of office or honor, < *com-,* with, and *ire,* go.] A rank and accompanying title in the order of nobility; in some European countries, a nobleman corresponding in rank to the English earl.

count, kount, *n.* [O.Fr. *conte,* (Fr. *compte, conte*), < L.L. *computus,* < L. *computare.*] The act of counting; enumeration; reckoning; calculation; the number representing the result of a process of counting; a tally; the total number; an accounting; regard, notice, or consideration; *law,* a distinct charge in an indictment; *boxing,* a referee's call of the seconds from one to ten after a fighter has been knocked down.

count, kount, *v.t.* [O.Fr. *conter* (Fr. *compter, conter*), < L. *computare.* COMPUTE.] To number; to enumerate by units or groups in their regular order of progression; to name, one by one; as, a succession of units or groups, to reach a total; to tally or reckon; to compute; to name (numerals) in order; to check by numbering in the sense of inventory; to consider or regard; to estimate or esteem.—*v.i.* To indicate numbers in order by groups; to enumerate the units in a group; to add or total; to be of value or significance; to take into consideration.— **count·a·ble,** *a.*

count·down, kount'doun", *n.* The count by seconds prior to the firing of a missile or space rocket, or the discharge of an explosive, with the precise moment of firing designated as zero.

coun·te·nance, koun'te·nans, *n.* [Fr. *contenance,* demeanor, way of acting or holding oneself, < *contenir,* to contain.] The whole form of the face; the features considered as a whole; the visage; the face; appearance or expression of the face. Permission; favor expressed toward a person; goodwill; support.

coun·te·nance, koun'te·nans, *v.t.*—*countenanced, countenancing.* To allow; to tolerate. To favor; to encourage; to aid, to support; to abet.—**coun·te·nanc·er,** *n.*

count·er, koun'tẽr, *n.* [O.Fr. *comptoer, comptoir* (Fr. *comptoir*), < M.L. *computatorium,* counting-house, counting-table, < L. *computare,* E. *count, compute.*] A table or board on which money is counted, business is transacted, or goods are laid for examination; in a restaurant, a flat serving area with seating facilities on one side; in a kitchen, a long working space which may also be used as an eating surface; anything used in keeping account, as in games, esp. a piece of metal, ivory, wood, or other material; an imitation coin or token.

count·er, koun'tẽr, *n.* One who counts; an apparatus for keeping count of revolutions or other movements of an object; a device for measuring radioactivity by the ionization of gas in a special tube; as, a Geiger counter.

coun·ter, koun'tẽr, *adv.* [O.Fr. Fr. *contre,* < L. *contra,* adv. and prep., in opposition, against.] In the opposite direction; in opposition; contrary.—*a.* Opposite; opposed; contrary; serving as a check; duplicate.—*v.t.* To go counter to; oppose; controvert; to meet or answer a move or blow by another in return.—*v.i.* To make an opposing move; to give a blow while receiving or parrying one, as in boxing.

coun·ter, koun'tẽr, *n.* That which is counter, opposite, or contrary to something else; that portion of the stern of a boat or vessel extending from the water line to the full outward swell; a piece of stiff leather forming the back of a shoe or boot around the heel; a circular parry in fencing; a blow delivered in receiving or parrying another blow, as in boxing; *mus.* any voice part set in contrast to a principal melody or part; as, the *counter*-tenor.

coun·ter·act, koun"tẽr·akt', *v.t.* To act in

opposition to; to hinder, defeat, or frustrate by contrary agency; to oppose, withstand, contravene, or resist.—**coun·ter·ac·tion,** *n.* Action in opposition; hindrance; resistance.—**coun·ter·ac·tive,** *a.* Tending to counteract.—**coun·ter·ac·tor,** *n.*

coun·ter·at·tack, koun'tẽr·a·tak", *n.* An attack designed to counteract another attack; a responsive attack.—koun"tẽr·a·-tak', *v.t., v.i.* To attack as an offsetting or responsive measure.

coun·ter·at·trac·tion, koun"tẽr·a·trak'-shan, *n.* Attraction of an opposite character; an attraction, counter or rival to another attraction.

coun·ter·bal·ance, koun"tẽr·bal'ans, *v.t.*—*counterbalanced, counterbalancing.* To serve as a balance to; to weigh against with an equal weight; to act against with equal power or effect.—*n.* Equal weight, power, or agency acting in opposition to anything; counterpoise.

coun·ter·bore, koun'tẽr·bõr", koun'tẽr·-bạr", koun"tẽr·bõr', koun'tẽr·bạr', *v.t.*— *counterbored, counterboring.* To bore out a cylindrical hole for a certain distance so as to form a flat-bottomed enlargement for receiving the head of a screw or the like; form a counterbore or counterbores in.—*n.* An enlargement of a hole made by counterboring; a tool for counterboring a hole.

coun·ter·brace, koun'tẽr·brās", *n. Engin.* a brace which transmits a strain in an opposite direction from a main brace.—*v.t.* *counterbraced, counterbracing.* To brace in opposite directions.

coun·ter·change, koun"tẽr·chānj', *v.t.*— *counterchanged, counterchanging.* To change to the opposite; cause to change places or qualities; to alternate; diversify.—*n.* Transposition; interchange; exchange.

coun·ter·charge, koun'tẽr·chärj", *v.t.*— *countercharged, countercharging.* To charge in return; make an accusation against (one's accuser).—*n.* An opposing accusation.

count·er check, *n.* A blank check obtained at a bank, made available for making a withdrawal from that bank or for use in making a deposit.

coun·ter·check, koun"tẽr·chek', *v.t.* To check by contrary action or some obstacle; to verify by a second check.—koun"tẽr·-chek", *n.* A restraining action; a check confirming a previous check.

coun·ter·claim, koun'tẽr·klām", *n.* A claim set up against another claim.—koun"-tẽr·klām", *v.i., v.t.* To set up (a counterclaim).—**coun·ter·claim·ant,** *n.*

coun·ter·clock·wise, koun"tẽr·klok'wīz", *adv., a.* In a direction opposite to that in which the hands of a clock rotate; from right to left.

coun·ter·es·pi·o·nage, koun"tẽr·es'pē·-o·näzh", koun"tẽr·es'pē·o·nij, *n.* The measures taken by a nation through its intelligence agency to detect and defeat enemy espionage.

coun·ter·feit, koun'tẽr·fit, *a.* [O.Fr., Fr. *contrefait,* pp. of *contrefaire,* < M.L. *contrafacere,* imitate, counterfeit.] Made to imitate, and pass for, something else; not genuine; spurious; forged.—*n.* An imitation designed to pass as an original; a forgery.

coun·ter·feit, koun'tẽr·fit, *v.t.* To imitate with intent to defraud; to make as a counterfeit; to forge; to make a pretense of; to simulate; to assume the appearance of.— *v.i.* To make counterfeits, as of money; to feign or dissemble.—**coun·ter·feit·er,** *n.*

coun·ter·foil, koun'tẽr·foil", *n.* A detachable stub, usually part of a check, money order, or other such instrument, retained by the issuer as a record of the transaction.

coun·ter·glow, koun'tẽr·glō", *n. Astron.* a patch of extremely faint luminosity seen in the heavens near the ecliptic at a point exactly opposite to the sun. Also *gegenschein.*

coun·ter·in·tel·li·gence, koun″tẽr·in-·tel′i·jens, *n.* The activity of an intelligence agent or agency in combating sabotage or other activity by enemy intelligence.

coun·ter·ir·ri·tant, koun″tẽr·ir′i·tant, *n. Med.* an agent for producing irritation in one part of the body to counteract irritation or relieve pain or inflammation elsewhere.

coun·ter·mand, koun″tẽr·mand′, koun″-tẽr·mänd′, *v.t.* [Fr. *contremander—contre,* and *mander,* L. *mando,* to command.] To revoke, as a former command; to order or direct in opposition to an order before given, thereby annulling it.—koun″tẽr·-mand″, koun′tẽr·mänd″, *n.*

coun·ter·march, koun″tẽr·märch′, *v.i.* To march in a contrary direction; march back.—*v.t.* To cause to march back.—koun′tẽr·märch″, *n.* A military evolution by which a body of marching men change direction without breaking formation; *fig.* a complete reversal of conduct or measures.

coun·ter·meas·ure, koun′tẽr·mezh″ẽr, *n.* An action intended as a retaliation against another measure.

coun·ter·mine, koun′tẽr·mīn″, *n. Milit.* a mine intended to intercept or destroy an enemy's mine. A counterplot.—koun″tẽr-·mīn′, *v.i.—countermined, countermining.* To make or place countermines.—*v.t.* To oppose or defeat by a countermine; to counterplot.

coun·ter·of·fen·sive, koun″tẽr·o·fen′siv, *n. Milit.* a major military action undertaken to combat an attacking enemy force.

coun·ter·pane, koun′tẽr·pān″, *n.* [< older *counterpoint,* O.Fr. *contrepoinct,* corruptly derived < L.L. *culcita puncta,* stitched quilt.] A bedcover; a coverlet for a bed; a quilt.

coun·ter·part, koun′tẽr·pärt″, *n.* A copy; duplicate; a thing which fits together, completes, or complements another; a person or thing which closely resembles another; one whose title, authority, or responsibility is the same as that of another person.

coun·ter·plot, koun′tẽr·plot″, koun″tẽr-·plot′, *v.t., v.i.—counterplotted, counter-plotting.* To oppose or frustrate (a plot) by another plot or stratagem.—koun′tẽr·plot″, *n.* A plot or artifice set afoot in order to oppose another; *liter.* a secondary plot used to enhance the main plot by contrast or variation.

coun·ter·point, koun′tẽr·point″, *n.* [O.Fr. Fr. *contrepoint,* < M.L. *contrapunctum,* < L. *contra,* against, and *punctus,* pp. of *pungere,* prick.] *Mus.* A melody or voice-part added to another as accompaniment; the art of adding one or more melodies to a given melody according to fixed rules; the art of polyphonic or concerted composition.

coun·ter·poise, koun′tẽr·poiz″, *n.* [O.Fr. *contrepois* (Fr. *contrepoids*).] A counter-balancing weight; any equal and opposing power or force; the state of being in equilibrium.—*v.t.—counterpoised, counter-poising.* To balance by an opposing weight; counteract by an opposing force; to bring into equilibrium; to weigh, as one thing against another.

coun·ter·pose, koun′tẽr·pōz″, *v.t.—coun-terposed, counterposing.* To place in an opposing position.

coun·ter·pro·pos·al, koun′tẽr·pro·pō′zal, *n.* A proposal which is offered for con-sideration as a substitute for another one.

coun·ter·punch, koun′tẽr·punch″, *n.* A blow which is given in quick retaliation, as in boxing.

coun·ter·rev·o·lu·tion, koun′tẽr·rev′o-lö′shan, *n.* A revolution opposed to a former one, and restoring or attempting to restore a former state.

coun·ter·shaft, koun′tẽr·shaft″, koun′tẽr·-shäft″, *n.* An intermediate shaft driven by a belt or gearing from a main shaft; a jackshaft.

coun·ter·sign, koun′tẽr·sīn″, *n.* A sign used in reply to another sign; a private signal, as a word, phrase, or number, which must be given to pass a sentry; a watchword; a sign or mark put on some-thing to authenticate or identify it; a signature added to another signature, as for authentication.

coun·ter·sign, koun′tẽr·sīn″, koun″tẽr-·sīn′, *v.t.* To sign opposite to or in addition to another signature; add one's signature to (something already signed by another) by way of authentication; to confirm; ratify.—**coun·ter·sig·na·ture,** *n.*

coun·ter·sink, koun′tẽr·singk″, koun″tẽr-·singk′, *v.t.—countersank* or *countersunk, countersinking.* To form a cavity in (timber or other materials) so as to receive the head of a bolt or screw and make it flush with the surface; to sink, as the head of a screw or bolt, below or even with the surface, by making a depression for it in the material.—*n.* A drill or brace bit for countersinking; the cavity made by countersinking.

coun·ter·spy, koun′tẽr·spī″, *n. pl.* **coun·ter·spies.** One who spies against the espio-nage activities of an enemy country.

coun·ter·vail, koun″tẽr·vāl′, *v.t.* [Fr. *contre-valoir.* AVAIL.] To act with equivalent force or effect against; to compensate for.

coun·ter·weigh, koun″tẽr·wā′, *v.t.* To weigh against; to counterbalance.—**coun·ter·weight,** koun′tẽr·wāt″, *n.* A weight in the opposite scale. Also *counterpoise.*

coun·ter·word, koun′tẽr·wụrd″, *n.* A word which, through common usage, has acquired a meaning less specific than its original meaning, as *grand, awful, swell.*

coun·tess, koun′tis, *n.* [O.Fr. *contesse* (Fr. *comtesse*), < M.L. *comitissa,* fem. of L. *comes.*] The wife or widow of a count in the nobility of continental Europe, or of an earl in the British peerage; a woman having the rank of a count or earl in her own right.

count·ing house, *n. Chiefly Brit.* a building or office appropriated to bookkeeping, as in a mercantile or manufacturing establish-ment.—**count·ing room,** *n.* A room used as a counting house.

count·less, kount′lis, *a.* Incapable of being counted; innumerable.

count noun, *n.* A noun which may be pluralized and is used with limiting adjec-tives such as numerals, or *many* or *few*; as opposed to a mass noun, such as *happiness* or *air,* which remains singular.

coun·tri·fy, kun′tri·fī″, *v.t.—countrified, countrifying.* To impart the characteristics of the country or of rural life; to make rustic.—**coun·tri·fied,** *a.*

coun·try, kun′trē, *n. pl.* **coun·tries.** [O.Fr. *contree* (Fr. *contrée*), < M.L. *contrata,* lit. "that which lies opposite or before one," < L. *contra,* against.] A tract of land of undefined extent, considered apart from geographical or political limits; a region; a district; land, with reference to character or features; the territory of a nation; a state distinct in name, race, and language; the land of one's birth or citizenship; rural districts, as opposed to cities or towns; the people of a district, state, or nation; the public; the body of voters; *law,* the public at large, as represented by a jury.—*a.* Of or pertaining to a country or one's own country; pertaining to the country, or rural districts; rural; rustic.

coun·try club, *n.* A club in the country or a suburban area, with a house, grounds, and facilities for such sports as golf, tennis, and swimming.

coun·try-dance, kun′trē·dans″, kun′trē-·däns″, *n.* [So named as being of rural origin.] A dance of rural, or native, English origin in which the partners face each other in two lines.

coun·try·man, kun′trē·man, *n. pl.* **coun·-**

try·men. A native or inhabitant of a particular region; a man of one's own country; a compatriot; a man who lives in the country; a rustic.

coun·try·seat, kun′trē·sēt″, *n. Brit.* a country estate, often used by its owner for only part of the year.

coun·try·side, kun′trē·sīd″, *n.* A particular section of a country; a rural area; the land adjacent to, but outside, the corporate limits of a city or town; its inhabitants.

coun·ty, koun′tē, *n. pl.* **coun·ties.** [L.L. *comitatus, < comes, comitis,* a count.] *U.S.* the largest geographic division for admini-strative purposes within a state. One of the main administrative, judicial, and political divisions of Great Britain and Ireland; one of the larger local administrative units, as in Canada; the people inhabiting a county.—*a.* Pertaining to a county.

coun·ty a·gent, *n.* An employee of both the federal and state governments, whose job is to go into rural areas and further farming, marketing, and home economics skills by means of talks, demonstrations, etc.

coun·ty seat, *n.* The town or city in which county government is centered.

coup, kö, *n. pl.* **coups,** köz, *Fr.* kö. [Fr. *coup,* O.Fr. *coup, colp,* < L. *colaphus,* < Gr. *colophos,* blow, < *colaptein,* strike.] A stroke or blow. A sudden, highly successful stroke or move; a quick-witted scheme or achievement.

coup d'é·tat, kö′dā·tä′, *Fr.* kö·dä·tä′, *n. pl.* **coups d'é·tat,** köz′dä·tä′, *Fr.* kö·dä·tä′. [Fr. 'stroke of state.'] A sudden and de-cisive measure in politics, esp. one effecting a change of government illegally or by force.

coupé, coupe, kö·pā′, köp, *n.* [Fr. *carosse coupé,* cut-off coach.] An enclosed four-wheeled carriage seating two inside and a driver outside; an enclosed two-door automobile.

cou·ple, kup′l, *n.* [O.Fr. *cople* (Fr. *couple*), < L. *copula,* band, bond.] A combination of two; a brace or pair; a man and a woman united by marriage or betrothal, or associ-ated as partners in a dance or the like; two of the same sort connected or considered together; *mech.* a pair of equal, paralleled forces acting in opposite directions and tending to produce rotation. *Colloq.* a small number; a few.—*a. Colloq.* two, used with a; as, a *couple* more streets.

cou·ple, kup′l, *v.t.—coupled, coupling.* [O.Fr. *copler* (Fr. *coupler*), < L. *copulare*: see *copulate.*] To fasten, link, or associate together in a pair or pairs; to join or connect; to unite in matrimony or sexual union; *elect.* to join or associate by means of a coupler.—*v.i.* To join in a pair; to copulate.

cou·pler, kup′lẽr, *n.* One who or that which couples or links together; a device in an organ for connecting keys, manuals, or a manual and pedals, so that they are played together when one is played. *Elect.* a device for transfering electrical energy from one circuit to another, as a transformer which joins parts of a radio apparatus together by means of induction; a pneumatic device for joining two railroad cars.

cou·plet, kup′lit, *n.* [Fr. dim. of *couple.*] Two successive lines of verse, esp. two that rhyme.

cou·pling, kup′ling, *n.* The act of bringing or joining together; sexual union; anything that couples; any of various mechanical devices for uniting or connecting parts or things; the part of the body of a four-footed animal which connects the hindpart to the forepart; a means for joining two electric circuits so that power or energy may be transferred from one to the other.

cou·pon, kö′pon, kū′pon, *n.* [Fr. < *couper,* to cut.] An interest certificate printed at the bottom of transferable bonds, and so called because it is cut off or detached and given up when a payment is made; generally, one of a series of tickets or forms which binds the issuer to make certain payments, perform some service, make certain concessions, or give value for certain amounts at different periods, on presentation of the ticket by the ticket holder.

cour·age, kur′ij, kur′ij, n. [Fr. *courage*, < L. *cor*, the heart, whence also *cordial*, etc.] That quality of mind which enables a person to encounter danger and difficulties with firmness, or without fear; bravery; intrepidity; valor; boldness; resolution.—**cou·ra·geous,** ko·rā′jus, a.—**cou·ra·geous·ly,** adv.—**cou·ra·geous·ness,** n.

cou·rante, ku·ränt′, Fr. kö·RäNT′, n. [Fr. *courante*, prop. fem. of *courant*, ppr.] An old-fashioned dance characterized by a running or gliding step; a piece of music for or suited to this dance; a movement in the classical suite, following the allemande.

cou·reur de bois, kö·RŒR de bwä′, n. pl. **cou·reurs de bois.** [Fr. "runner of woods."] One of a class of hunters and trappers of French blood or descent found in Canada and adjoining parts of North America.

cour·i·er, kur′ē·ėr, n. [Fr. *courrier*, < *courir*, < L. *curro*, to run.] A messenger, carrying urgent news or reports and generally traveling in haste; the conveyance used by this messenger, such as a special plane or automobile. *Brit.* one employed by travelers to make and take charge of their travel arrangements.

course, kōrs, kars, n. [O.Fr. *cours* (also *course,* fem.), < L. *cursus,* a running, course, < *currere,* run.] The path or route along which anything moves; a way or channel in which water flows; the ground or water on which a race is run or sailed; a racecourse; the direction in which anything moves or runs; the continuous passage of time; progress onward or through a succession of stages; customary manner of procedure; regular or natural order of events; a particular manner of proceeding; a number of things in regular sequence; a systematized or prescribed series, as of studies, lectures, medical treatments; a part of a meal served at one time; a continuous horizontal or inclined range of stones, bricks, or the like, in a wall or the face of a building; the pursuit of game with hounds; a race of dogs after a hare. *Naut.* the lowest square sail on any mast of a square-rigged ship; the point of the compass toward which a ship sails. *Pl.* the menses.—**of course,** in the common manner of proceeding; hence, naturally; as would be expected in the circumstances; obviously.

course, kōrs, kars, v.t.—**coursed, coursing.** To chase or pursue; to run through or over; to cause to run; to pursue or hunt, as game, with hounds, esp. by sight and not by scent; cause, as dogs, to pursue game. —v.i. To practice coursing; to run; move swiftly; to follow a course; direct one's course.—**cours·er,** n.

cours·ing, kōr′sing, kar′sing, n. The sport of pursuing hares, with hounds, when the game is started in sight of the hounds.

court, kōrt, kart, n. [O.Fr. *cort, court* (Fr. *cour*), < L. *cors, cortis,* contracted < *cohors, cohortis,* a yard, a *court*—*co*- for *con*-, and *hor,* a root seen in *hortus,* a garden, also in *garden, garth.*] An enclosed uncovered area, whether behind or in front of a house, or surrounded by buildings; a courtyard; an alley, lane, close, or narrow street; the place of residence of a king or sovereign prince; all the surroundings of a sovereign in his regal state; the collective body of persons who compose the retinue or council of a sovereign; a hall, chamber, or place where justice is administered; the persons

or judges assembled for hearing and deciding causes, as distinguished from the counsel or jury; any judicial body, civil, military, or ecclesiastical; the sitting of a judicial assembly; space prepared for playing such games as basketball, tennis, and squash racquets; a motel; attention directed to a person in power to gain favor; civility; flattery; address to gain favor; as, to pay *court* to a person.

court, kōrt, kart, v.t., v.i. To endeavor to gain the favor of or win over by attention and flattery; to seek the affections or love of; to woo; to solicit for marriage; to solicit; to seek; as, to *court* applause; to hold out inducements to; to invite.

court card, n. *Brit.* a face card: the king, queen, or jack of any deck of cards.

cour·te·ous, kėr′tē·us, a. Polite, considerate of others; having courtly manners.— **cour·te·ous·ly,** adv.—**cour·te·ous·ness,** n.

cour·te·san, cour·te·zan, kōr′ti·zan, kar′ti·zan, kėr′ti·zan, n. A prostitute, esp. one whose associates are wealthy, aristocratic, or of the nobility.

cour·te·sy, kėr′ti·sē, n. pl. **cour·te·sies.** Politeness of manners combined with kindness; polished manners or urbanity shown in behavior toward others; an act of civility or respect; a favor or indulgence, as contradistinguished from right.

court·house, kōrt′hous″, kart′hous″, n. A building in which established courts are held; *U.S. dial.* the county seat.

cour·ti·er, kōr′tē·ėr, kar′tē·ėr, n. One who attends or frequents the court of a sovereign; one who courts or flatters another to obtain favor.

court·ly, kōrt′lē, kart′lē, a.—**courtlier, courtliest.** Relating or pertaining to a king's court; refined and dignified; elegant; polite; courteous.—adv. In a courtly manner.— **court·li·ness,** n.

court·ly love, n. The amorous affairs of medieval ladies and their lovers conducted according to an idealized formula.

court-mar·tial, kōrt′mär″shal, kōrt′mär′-shal, kart′mär″shal, kart′mär′shal, n. pl. **courts-mar·tial.** A court consisting of military or naval officers, and sometimes enlisted personnel, for the trial of military or naval offenses; a trial by court-martial.— v.t.—**court-martialed, court-martialing,** *Brit.* **court-martialled, court-martialling.**

court of ap·peals, n. *Law,* an appellate court which ranks between the lower court of trials and the highest court, both in the U.S. federal system and in some state systems; *Brit.* high court in London from which appeals may be made only to the House of Lords.

court of claims, n. A court acting to determine the accuracy of bills rendered against a division of a government and to provide for their payment; a court meeting annually in Washington, D.C. to judge claims brought against the U.S. government.

Court of St. James, n. The royal court in London, England.

court plas·ter, n. A kind of coated silk adhesive plaster.

court·room, kōrt′rōm″, kōrt′rum″, kart′-rōm″, kart′rum″, n. A room housing a court of law, in which trials are held.

court·ship, kōrt′ship, kart′ship, n. The act of courting or soliciting favor; wooing; period of time during which such wooing takes place.

court ten·nis, n. The older form of tennis, played in an indoor court.

court·yard, kōrt′yärd″, kart′yärd″, n. A court or enclosure around a house or adjacent to it.

cous·in, kuz′in, n. [Fr. *cousin,* < L.L. *cosinus,* for L. *consobrinus,* a cousin—*con,* and *sobrinus,* akin to *soror,* a sister.] The son or daughter of an uncle or aunt; in a

wider and now less usual sense, one collaterally related more remotely than a brother or sister; a people or a nation with similar ancestors, language, or culture; a term of address used by a monarch to a nobleman; a close friend.—**cous·in·hood,** n. The state of being cousins; the individuals connected with a family regarded collectively.—**cous·in·ly,** a. Like or becoming a cousin.—**cous·in·ship,** n. The state of being cousins; cousinhood.— **cous·in·ger·man,** kuz′in·jėr′man, n. pl. **cous·ins·ger·man.** A first or full cousin.

couth, kōth, a. [Back formation < uncouth.] Having breeding, polish, or sophistication. *Brit.* friendly, kind, or pleasant.

cou·ture, kō·tūr′, Fr. kö·TYR′, n. The business of custom dressmaking, designing, and selling fashionable women's clothing; fashion designers and establishments collectively.

cou·tu·rier, kō·tūr′ē·ā″, kō·tūr′ē·ėr, kō·tūr′yä, Fr. kö·TY·RYä′, n. [Fr., < *couture,* sewing, L. *consuere,* sew together.] A dressmaker; a person who designs, makes, and sells fashionable women's clothes.—**cou·tu·ri·ère,** kō·tūr′ē·ėr, kō·tūr′ē·er″, Fr. kö·TY·RYer″, n. A female couturier.

cou·vade, kō·väd′, n. A custom among some primitive peoples in which the father, at the birth of a child, enacts various rituals associated with childbirth, such as being confined to bed and fasting.

co·va·lence, kō·vā′lens, n. *Chem.* the number of electron pairs shared by different atoms.—**co·va·lent,** a.

co·va·lent bond, n. *Chem.* the bond produced by the sharing of an electron pair by two atoms in a chemical process.

co·var·i·ant, kō·vâr′ē·ant, a. Varying according to a certain mathematical relationship with another coexisting factor.

cove, kōv, n. [O.E. *cofa,* chamber.] A hollow or recess in the side of a mountain; a sheltered nook; a small sheltered bay, inlet, or creek; a cave or cavern. *Arch.* a concavity; a concave molding or member.— v.t, v.i.—**coved, coving.** To form into or become a hollow or arch.

cove, kōv, n. [Origin obscure; first in rogues' slang.] *Brit. slang.* A man or boy; a fellow.

co·vel·lite, kō·vel′īt, kō′ve·līt″, n. [From N. *Covelli,* who in 1839 found it in lava from Vesuvius.] A native sulfide of copper, CuS, of an indigo blue color, occurring in masses.

cov·e·nant, kuv′e·nant, n. [O.Fr. *covenant, convenant,* orig. ppr. of *convenir,* < L. *convenire,* agree.] An agreement between two or more persons to do or refrain from doing some act; a compact; a contract; in Biblical usage, the agreement or engagement of God with man as set forth in the Old and the New Testament. *Law,* a formal agreement of legal validity; an incidental clause in such legal agreement.—**cov·e·nan·tee,** n. The one to whom a promise by covenant is made.—**cov·e·nan·ter, cov·e·nan·tor,** n. One who enters into a covenant.

cov·e·nant, kuv′e·nant, v.i. To enter into a covenant.—v.t. To agree to by covenant; stipulate.

Cov·ent Gar·den, kuv′ent gär′den, kov′-ent gär′den, n. A market district in London; a famous theater in London.

Cov·en·try, kuv′en·trē, kov′en·trē, n. [From *Coventry,* town in Warwickshire, England.] A place to which persons are said to be sent when excluded from social relations; the situation of one socially ostracized or deliberately ignored, because of objectionable conduct.

cov·er, kuv′ėr, v.t. [O.Fr. *covrir* (Fr. *couvrir*), < L. *cooperire,* < *co*-, altogether, and *operire,* cover.] To put something over or upon, as for protection or concealment; overlay or overspread; put a cover or covering on; clothe; invest; put one's hat on (one's head); to match or equal the amount of (money wagered by another gambler); to play a card of higher value than (one previously played); accept the conditions of (a bet); to serve as a covering for; extend over; occupy the surface of; of a male animal, to copulate with (the female); of a bird, to brood or sit on, as eggs or chicks; to shelter or protect; serve as a defense to; to hide from view; screen; to aim directly at, as with a pistol; to have within range, as a fortress does certain territory; to include, comprise, or provide for; to act as reporter or photographer of or at, as occurrences or performances, as for a newspaper; to pass or travel over; to suffice to defray or meet, as a charge or expense; offset (an outlay, loss or liability); *milit.* to be in line with by occupying a position directly before or behind, as: One soldier or one body of troops *covers* another.—*v.i.* To provide or serve as a covering; to act in place of someone who is absent; to protect a partner by playing a card of higher value than one previously played; to become covered; to put one's hat on.—**cov·er·er,** *n.*

cov·er, kuv′ẽr, *n.* That which covers, as the lid of a vessel, the binding of a book, the wrapper of a letter; protection, shelter, or concealment; a screen or cloak; woods or underbrush serving to shelter and conceal wild animals or game; a covert; funds to cover liability or secure against risk of loss; a set of utensils, plate, knife, fork, laid at table for one person.—**cov·ered,** *a.* Provided with a covering; having a cover; clothed with some growth; as, moss-*covered*; wearing one's hat.—**cov·er·less,** *a.*

cov·er·age, kuv′ẽr·ij, *n.* A covering, or provision for something by agreement or contract; that which is so covered. *Communications,* the sending and receiving areas of radio or television stations; the number of readers in an area served by a publication; the writing, publishing, or broadcasting of news. *Insurance,* protection against a specific risk or risks.

cov·er·all, kuv′ẽr·ạl″, *n.* A loose one-piece outer work garment worn to protect other clothing. Also **cov·er·alls.**

cov·er charge, *n.* A predetermined charge added to the bill at night clubs or restaurants to pay for entertainment.

cov·er crop, *n.* An agricultural product, as vetch, grown esp. during the winter to provide fertilization and prevent soil erosion, weed growth, and nutrient loss by leaching.

cov·ered smut, *n.* A disease of grains, characterized by a fungus covering of spore masses.

cov·ered wag·on, *n.* A large wagon with high curved hoops covered by a canvas top, used to transport pioneers westward during the 19th century.

cov·er·ing, kuv′ẽr·ing, *n.* Something placed over or around a thing to conceal, shield, or provide warmth; the act of one who covers.—*a.* That covers; concealing; explanatory; as, a *covering* message; shielding; as, a *covering* barrage of artillery fire.

cov·er·let, kuv′ẽr·lit, *n.* [M.E. *coverlite,* appar. < O.Fr. *covrir,* cover and *lit,* bed.] A bedspread; a counterpane; a covering.

cov·er point, *n.* Cricket, lacrosse, a player who supports the player called *point.*

co·versed, kō′vẽrst, *a.* Trig. in the phrase *coversed sine,* the versed sine of the complement of an angle or arc.

cov·ert, kuv′ẽrt, kō′vẽrt, *a.* [O.E. *covert* (Fr. *couvert*), pp., *covert, coverte* (Fr. *couvert, couverte*), *n.,* < *covrir,* cover: see *cover.*] Covered; sheltered; *fig.* concealed. Secret; disguised; *law,* under cover or

protection of a husband.—*n.* A covering or cover; shelter; concealment; disguise; a hiding place; a thicket giving shelter to wild animals or game; *pl. ornith.* the smaller and weaker feathers of a bird that cover the bases of the large feathers of the wing and tail.—**cov·ert·ly,** *adv.*—**cov·ert·ness,** *n.*

co·vert cloth, *n.* A twilled cloth woven with ply yarns of cotton, wool, or worsted, used for raincoats and overcoats.

cov·er·ture, kuv′ẽr·chẽr, *n.* [O.Fr. *coverture* (Fr. *couverture*).] A cover or covering; shelter; concealment; *law,* the status of a married woman considered as under the protection and authority of her husband.

cov·er-up, kuv′ẽr·up″, *n.* Whatever is done to conceal wrongdoing, esp. a distraction so that there will not be an investigation.—**cov·er up,** *v.i.* To conceal or minimize wrongdoing.

cov·et, kuv′it, *v.t.* [O.Fr. *coveitier* (Fr. *convoiter*), ult. < L. *cupere,* desire.] To wish for, esp. eagerly; to desire inordinately, or without due regard to the rights of others; desire wrongfully.—*v.i.* To have an inordinate or wrongful desire.—**cov·et·a·ble,** *a.*—**cov·et·er,** *n.*

cov·et·ous, kuv′i·tus, *a.* [O.Fr. *coveitos* (Fr. *convoiteux*).] Eagerly desirous, esp. inordinately desirous of possessions or wealth; grasping; avaricious; eager to possess that to which one has no right.—**cov·et·ous·ly,** *adv.*—**cov·et·ous·ness,** *n.*

cov·ey, kuv′ē, *n.* [O.Fr. *covee* (Fr. *couvée*), orig. pp. fem. of *cover* (Fr. *couver*), brood, incubate, < L. *cubare,* lie.] A brood or small flock of quail, partridges, or similar birds. *Fig.* a company; a group.

cow, kou, *n.* pl. **cows,** archaic, **kine,** kin. [O.E. *cū* = D. *koe* = G. *kuh* = Icel. *kȳr,* cow.] The female of a bovine animal, esp. of the domestic species *Bos taurus*; the female of various other large animals, as the elephant, whale, seal, or alligator.

cow, kou, *v.t.* [Dan. *kue,* Icel. *kúga,* to depress, subdue, keep under.] To daunt; dishearten; intimidate; overawe.

cow·age, cow·hage, kou′ij, *n.* [Hind. *kawanch.*] The short, brittle hairs of the pods of a leguminous plant, which easily penetrate the skin, and produce an intolerable itching; these hairs when administered in honey or molasses to expel parasitic worms; the pods of this plant. Also **cow·itch,** kou′ich.

cow·ard, kou′ard, *n.* [O.Fr. *coart* (Fr. *couard*), < *coue, coe,* < L. *cauda,* tail.] One who lacks courage to meet danger or difficulty; one who is basely timid; a craven.—*a.* Destitute of courage; cowardly.—**cow·ard·ly,** *a., adv.*—**cow·ard·li·ness,** *n.*

cow·ard·ice, kou′ẽr·dis, *n.* [O.Fr. *coardise* (Fr. *couardise*).] Want of courage; ignoble fear; pusillanimity.

cow·bane, kou′bān,″ *n.* Any of several parsleylike plants considered poisonous to cattle, as the water hemlock, *Cicuta virosa,* or an American swamp plant, *Oxypolis rigidior.*

cow·bell, kou′bel,″ *n.* A bell hung around the neck of a cow, to ring and thereby indicate her whereabouts.

cow·ber·ry, kou′ber″ē, kou′be·rē, *n.* pl. **cow·ber·ries.** The berry or fruit of any of various shrubs, as *Vaccinium vitis-idaea,* that grow in pastures; any of these shrubs.

cow·bird, kou′bụrd,″ *n.* Any of the American blackbirds constituting the genus *Molothrus,* esp. *M. ater,* of North America: so called because they accompany cattle. Also **cow black·bird.**

cow·boy, kou′boi,″ *n.* A man who looks after cattle on a large ranch or stock farm and does this work on horseback; a man who possesses the skills of a cowboy, esp. those associated with the rodeo; *slang,* an automobile driver who is reckless and

speedy; *U.S. history,* a member of a guerrilla band in the American Revolution accused of being pro-British.

cow·catch·er, kou′kach″ẽr, *n.* A frame fixed to the front of a locomotive, for clearing the track of obstructions; also *pilot.* *Slang,* in radio and television, a brief commercial of a subordinate product or service broadcast before the principal part of the program.

cow col·lege, *n. Slang,* a small agricultural college situated in a rural area.

cow·er, kou′ẽr, *v.i.* [Same word as Sc. *curr,* to squat; Icel. *kúra,* Dan. *kure,* Sw. *kura,* to doze, to rest; G. *kauren,* to cower.] To crouch in fear; to stoop or sink downward, as from terror.—**cow·er·ing·ly,** *adv.*

cow hand, *n.* An employee on a cattle ranch; a cowpoke or cowboy.

cow·herd, kou′hụrd, *n.* One whose occupation is the tending of cows.

cow·hide, kou′hīd,″ *n.* The hide or skin of a cow, made or to be made into leather; a strong whip made of such leather.—*v.t.* *cowhided, cowhiding.* To whip with a cowhide lash.

cowl, koul, *n.* [O.E. *cūle, cūgele,* < L.L. *cuculla,* L. *cucullus,* hood.] A hooded garment worn by monks; the hood of this garment; a hood-shaped covering for a chimney or ventilating shaft, to increase the draft.—*v.t.* To cover with a cowl.—**cowl·ed,** *a.*

cow·lick, kou′lik,″ *n.* A tuft of hair growing in a wayward direction and turned up, often over the forehead, so that it appears as if licked by a cow.

cowl·ing, kou′ling, *n.* A metal covering for an engine; *aeron.* the removable housing for an aircraft component, used for the purpose of protecting, streamlining, or regulating the flow of cooling air.

cowl·staff, koul′staf,″ koul′stäf,″ *n. Brit. colloq.* a staff or pole on which a vessel or weight is carried between two persons.

cow·man, kou′man, *n.* pl. **cow·men.** *Western U.S.* An owner of cattle; a rancher; a cowherd or cowboy.

co-work·er, kō·wẽr′kẽr, kō′wẽr″kẽr, *n.* One who works with another; a co-operator.

cow·pea, kou′pē,″ *n.* A beanlike annual plant, *Vigna sinensis,* extensively cultivated in the southern U.S. for forage or fertilizer, and having seeds used for food; the seed. Also *black-eyed pea.*

Cow·per's gland, kou′pẽrz gland,″ kö′pẽrz gland,″ *n. Anat.* one of two small glands on either side of the urethra and near the base of the prostate in the male, discharging a mucous substance into the urethra.

cow·poke, kou′pōk,″ *n. Western slang.* A cowhand; a cowboy.

cow po·ny, *n.* A small saddlehorse ridden in herding cattle.

cow·pox, kou′poks,″ *n.* A disease which appears on the teats of the cow in the form of vesicles or blisters; the fluid or virus contained therein is capable of immunizing man against smallpox.

cow·ry, cow·rie, kou′rē, *n.* pl. **cow·ries.** [Hind. *kaurī.*] The shell of any of the marine mollusks constituting the genus *Cypraea,* as that of *C. moneta,* used as money in certain parts of Asia and Africa; or that of *C. tigris,* a large, handsome shell often used as a home decoration; the animal itself, found in warm seas.

cow·slip, kou′slip, *n.* [O.E. *cu-slyppe, cu-sloppe,* the latter part of the name apparently meaning dung.] A perennial herb of the primrose family, growing in moist places in Britain; *U.S.* the marsh marigold.

cox·a, kok′sa, *n.* pl. **cox·ae,** kok′sē. [L., hip.] *Anat.* the joint of the hip; *zool.* the first or proximal segment or joint of the leg in insects and other arthropods.—**cox-**

al, *a.*—**cox·al·gi·a**, kok·sal'jē·*a*, kok·sal'ja, *n. Pathol.* pain in the hip.—**cox·al·gic**, *a.*

cox·comb, koks'kōm, *n.* [*Cock's comb.*] A vain showy fellow; a superficial pretender to knowledge or accomplishments; a fop; a dandy.—**cox·comb·i·cal**, koks·kom'i·kal, koks·kō·mi·kal, *a.*

cox·swain, kok'san, kok'swān", *n.* [Earlier *cockswain.*] The steersman of a boat; on a ship, one who has charge of a boat and its crew; *sports*, in a racing shell, the one who steers and calls the rhythm of the oarsmen's strokes.

coy, koi, *a.* [O.Fr. *coi, coy, coit,* < L. *quietus,* quiet.] Shrinking from familiarity; shy; modest; reserved; distant; backward; bashful.—**coy·ly**, *adv.* In a coy manner; with disinclination to familiarity.—**coy·ness**, *n.* The quality of being coy; bashfulness; shyness; reserve; modesty.

coy·o·te, ki·ō'tē, ki'ōt, *n.* [Sp. *coyote,* Mex. *coyotl.*] The American prairie wolf noted for its howling at night; in Amer. Indian folklore, the trickster of the Indian; *slang,* a contemptible person.

co·yo·til·lo, kō"yō·tēl'yō, ki"ō·tēl'yō, *Sp.* ka"ya·tē'ya, *n.* A Mexican plant of the buckthorn family, bearing poisonous fruit.

coy·pu, koi'pö, *n. pl.* **coy·pus, coy·pu.** The native name of a South American rodent, a large, beaverlike, semiaquatic mammal, valued for its soft brown fur called nutria.

coz, kuz, *n. Colloq.* cousin.

coz·en, kuz'en, *v.t.* [A form of *cousin;* Fr. *cousiner,* to sponge upon people under pretext of relationship, < *cousin,* a cousin.] To cheat; to defraud; to deceive; to beguile.—*v.i.* To cheat; to act deceitfully.—**coz·en·age**, *n.*—**coz·en·er**, *n.*

co·zy, kō'zē, *a.*—**cozier, coziest.** [Akin to Norse *koselig,* cosy, *kose sig,* to enjoy one's ease.] Well sheltered, snug; comfortable; social.—*n. pl.* **co·zies.** A kind of padded covering or cap put over a teapot to keep the tea warm. Also *cosey, cosy,* **co·zie, co·zey.**—**co·zi·ly**, *adv.*—**co·zi·ness**, *n.*

crab, krab, *n.* [O.E. *crabba* = D. *krab* = G. *krabbe* = Icel. *krabbi.*] A crustacean with a short, broad, more or less flattened body, the abdomen or so-called tail being small and folded under the thorax; any of various other crustaceans resembling the true crabs; any of various large mechanical contrivances for hoisting or drawing; *slang,* an ill-tempered or crabbed person; (*cap.*) the zodiacal constellation or sign Cancer.

crab, krab, *v.i.*—**crabbed, crabbing.** To catch crabs; to act like a crab in crawling backward or sideways.—*v.t. Slang,* to find fault with; to complain.—**crab·by, crab·bed**, krab'id, *a.* Ill-tempered; sour; peevish.—**crab·bed·ly**, *adv.*—**crab·bed·ness**, *n.*

crab ap·ple, *n.* A small, sour wild apple, cultivated for its fruit used in making jelly; any tree bearing crab apples.

crab cac·tus, *n.* A Brazilian cactus with leaflike stems and red flowers and fruit. Also **Christ·mas cac·tus.**

crab grass, *n.* An annual grass with decumbent leaves, often found as a weedy pest in lawns and other grassy areas.

crab louse, *n.* A small, blood-sucking, wingless insect parasitic on mammals. Also **bod·y louse.**

crab·stick, krab'stik", *n.* A walking stick or club made of the wood of the crab apple tree; *colloq.* an ill-tempered person.

crack, krak, *v.t.* [An imitative word; O.E. *cracian,* to crack; G. *krachen,* to crack; D. *krak,* a crack; Gael. *knac,* a crack, as of a whip, etc.] To rend, break, or burst; to break partially; to break without an entire severance of the parts; to throw out or utter with smartness; as, to *crack* a joke; to snap; to cause to make a sharp sudden noise like a whip. To break open, into, or

through, as a safe, a secret code, or a barrier.—*v.i.* To break with a sharp sound; to burst; to open in chinks; to be fractured without quite separating into different parts; to give out a loud or sharp sudden sound; to fail or give way, as or as if under strain.—**crack a book**, *slang,* to open a book, esp. a textbook, for studying.

crack, krak, *n.* A chink or fissure; a partial separation of the parts of a substance, with or without an opening; a burst of sound; a sharp or loud sound uttered suddenly; a violent report; injury or impairment to the intellect or to the character; flaw; blemish.

crack, krak, *a. Colloq.* having qualities to be proud of; first-rate; excellent; as, a *crack* regiment, a *crack* horse.

crack·down, krak'doun", *n.* The sudden and severe enforcement of existing regulations.—**crack down**, *v.i.*

crack·er, krak'ér, *n.* A thin, crisp biscuit; a small kind of firework filled with powder, which explodes with a sharp noise or with a series of sharp cracks; one who or that which cracks.

crack·ers, krak'érz, *n. Brit. slang,* crazy, insane.

crack·ing, krak'ing, *a.* Excellent; outstanding.—*adv. Slang,* to begin quickly, hurriedly; as, to get *cracking.*

crack·ing, krak'ing, *n.* The act of one who or that which cracks; specif. in the distillation of petroleum or the like, the process of breaking down certain hydrocarbons into simpler ones of lower boiling points, by means of excess heat or distillation under pressure, in order to give a greater yield of low-boiling fractions that could be obtained by simple distillation.

crack·le, krak'el, *v.i.*—**crackled, crackling.** [Dim. of crack.] To make slight, sudden, sharp noises, rapidly repeated, as the tiny explosive sounds of burning wood; to be vibrant or sparkling, as: Her conversation *crackles* with enthusiasm; to change by cracking or forming a web of tiny surface cracks, as: Paint, improperly applied, may *crackle.*—*v.t.* To crumple or break with a cracking noise; to cover with a network of minute cracks, as of crazed glass or pottery.—**crack·led**, *a.* Covered with a network of minute cracks, as ceramics or glass; covered with a crisp, browned, and wrinkled skin or rind, as roast pork.—**crack·ly**, *a.*—**cracklier, crackliest.** Having a tendency to crackle; easily crumbled or broken.

crack·le, krak'el, *n.* The act of crackling; a crackling noise; liveliness or sparkle; a network of fine cracks, as in the glaze of some kinds of porcelain; ceramics or other ware with such a glaze. Also called **crack·le·ware.**

crack·lings, krak'lings, *n. Southeast U.S.* a term applied to the crisp, browned residue of pork fat after it has been rendered.

crack·nel, krak'nel, *n.* A hard brittle cake or biscuit; *pl.* cracklings.

crack·pot, krak'pot", *n. Slang,* an eccentric person with impractical, or actually insane ideas.—*a. Slang,* eccentric; impractical; insane; as, a *crackpot* scheme.

crack-up, krak'up", *n.* A collision; an accident or crash resulting in damage to a vehicle; *colloq.* loss or breakdown of a person's health, especially mental and emotional. Collapse or failure, as of negotiations, alliances, or an understanding.

cra·dle, krād'el, *n.* [O.E. *cradol.*] A little bed or cot for an infant, usually one constructed to admit of a rocking or swinging motion; *fig.* the place where anything is nurtured during its early existence. Any of the various contrivances likened to a child's cradle, as the framework on which a ship rests during construction or repair; *mining,*

a kind of box on rockers used by miners for washing auriferous gravel or sand to separate the gold; *agric.* a frame of wood attached to a scythe, for laying grain evenly as it is cut. An engravers' tool for laying mezzotint grounds.—*v.t.,* *v.i.*—**cradled, cradling.**

cra·dle hill, *Canada,* a small mound possibly formed by the uprooting of a tree.

craft, kraft, kräft, *n.* [O.E. *craeft,* craft, cunning, force, a craft = G. Sw. Icel. and Dan. *kraft,* D. *kracht,* power, faculty; < root of which *cramp* is a nasalized form, akin to Skt. *grabh.* to grasp.] Dexterity in a particular manual occupation; cunning skill or artifice used to deceive; guile; an occupation or employment requiring skills; manual art; trade; the members of a trade collectively; a vessel, such as a ship or airplane; a group of ships or airplanes taken as a whole.

crafts·man, krafts'man, kräfts'man, *n. pl.* **crafts·men.** An artisan; an artificer; a mechanic; one skilled in a manual occupation.—**crafts·man·ship**, *n.*

craft un·ion, *n.* A labor union composed of working people of the same craft or occupation, as a meat-cutters union.

craft·y, kraf'tē, kräf'tē, *a.*—**craftier, craftiest.** Characterized by, having, or using craft; cunning; sly.—**craft·i·ly**, *adv.* In a crafty manner; cunningly; slyly; deceitfully.—**craft·i·ness**, *n.*

crag, krag, *n.* [Gael. *creag,* Ir. *craig,* W. *careg,* a rock, stone.] A steep, rugged rock; a rough broken rock, or point of a rock.—**crag·ged**, krag'id, *a.* Full of crags or broken rocks.—**crag·gy**, krag'ē, *a.*—**crag·gi·ness**, *n.* The state of being craggy.

crake, krāk, *n.* [Imitative of the bird's cry; comp. L. *crex,* Gr. *krex,* a landrail; Icel. *kraka,* to croak.] A grallatorial bird of various species belonging to the family of the rails.

cram, kram, *v.t.*—**crammed, cramming.** [O.E. *crammian,* to cram; Dan. *kramme,* to crush; Sw. *krama,* to press; akin cramp.] To fill, as an object, by force or compression, with more than it can conveniently hold; to force or stuff hastily or carelessly, frequently used with *down* or *into;* as, to *cram* all one's belongings *into* a small suitcase; to fill with an excess of food, esp. to force-feed, as poultry, in order to fatten for market; to eat greedily, hastily, or in a rough manner; to stuff, as knowledge, into the mind or to prepare, as oneself or another person, by filling the mind with information, as in hurried studying for an examination.—*v.i.* To eat greedily; to fill one's mind with information, as in hurried study for an examination.—**cram·mer**, *n.*

cram·bo, kram'bō, *n. pl.* **cram·boes.** [Origin doubtful.] A game in which one person gives a word or a line of verse to which another finds a rhyme; any poor or foolish rhyme.

cramp, kramp, *n.* [Cf. M.D. and M.L.G. *krampe,* O.H.G. *chramph,* hook.] A small metal bar with bent ends, for holding together timbers, masonry, etc.; a clamp; a portable frame or tool with a movable part which can be screwed up to hold things together; hence, anything that confines or restrains; a cramped state or part.—*v.t.* To fasten or hold with a cramp; to confine narrowly; to restrict; restrain; hamper.—*a.* Cramped; hard to decipher or understand; difficult; knotty.—**cramp one's style**, *slang,* to hinder or thwart the exercise of a person's full capabilities.

cramp, kramp, *n.* [O.Fr. Fr. *crampe* < Teut., and akin to E. *cramp.*] An involuntary, spasmodic, painful contraction of a muscle or muscles, as from a slight strain or a sudden chill; a sudden, violent abdominal pain; *pl.* continuing abdominal pain, as in painful menstruation.—*v.t.* To affect with or as with a cramp.

cramp·fish, kramp′fish″, *n.* pl. **cramp·fish, cramp·fish·es.** *Ichth.* the electric ray.

cram·pon, kram′pon, *n.* [Fr. *crampon.*] An apparatus used in raising heavy objects, as timber or stones for building, consisting of two hooked pieces of iron hinged together; an iron plate fitted with spikes, worn on the bottom of a shoe to facilitate climbing or walking on snow or ice. Also **cram·poon.**

cran·age, krā′nij, *n.* The use of a crane to move goods, esp. to load or unload a ship; the charge made for this.

cran·ber·ry, kran′ber″ē, kran′be·rē, *n.* pl. **cran·ber·ries.** [= G. *kranbeere, kranichbeere,* 'crane berry.' CRANE.] The red, acid fruit or berry of any plant of the genus *Vaccinium,* as *V. oxyoccus,* 'small cranberry' or 'European cranberry,' or *V. macrocarpus,* 'large cranberry' or 'American cranberry,' used in making sauce, jelly, etc.; the plant itself.—**cran·ber·ry tree,** *n.* A tree or shrub, *Viburnum opulus,* as the honeysuckle, bearing red berries and white cymose flowers. Also, *snowball, guelder rose.*

cran·ber·ry glass, *n.* A clear ruby-red glass.

cran·dall, kran′dal, *n.* [Prob. from *Crandall,* proper name.] A hammerlike tool for dressing soft stone.—*v.t.* To treat or dress with a crandall.

crane, krān, *n.* [O.E. *cran,* akin to G. *kranich.*] Any of a group of large wading birds, family *Gruidae,* with very long legs and neck; popularly, any of various similar birds, as the great blue heron, *Ardea herodias.* A device for moving heavy weights, having two motions, one a direct lift and the other a horizontal movement, and consisting in one of its simplest forms of an upright post turning on its vertical axis and bearing a projecting arm on which the hoisting tackle is fitted; any of various similar devices, as a horizontally swinging arm by a fireplace, used for suspending pots over the fire; *motion pictures, TV,* a boom for moving cameras; (*cap.*), *astron.* the southern constellation Grus.—*v.t., v.i.—craned, craning.* To stretch (the neck) as a crane does; to hoist, lower, or move by or as by a crane.

cra·ni·al in·dex, *n.* The ratio of the full breadth of the skull to its full length, multiplied by 100.

cra·ni·al nerve, *n.* One of the nerves that originate in the brain and come through openings in the skull.

cra·ni·ol·o·gy, krā″nē·ol′o·jē, *n.* The science that deals with the size, shape, and other characteristics of skulls.

cra·ni·om·e·try, krā″nē·om′i·trē, *n.* The science of the measurement of skulls.

cra·ni·um, krā′nē·um, *n.* pl. **cra·ni·ums, cra·ni·a,** krā′nē·a. [M.L., < Gr. *cranion.*] The skull of a vertebrate; that part of the skull which encloses the brain.— **cra·ni·al,** krā′nē·al, *a.*—**cra·ni·ate,** krā′nē·it, krā′nē·āt″, *a.*—**cra·ni·al·ly,** *adv.*

crank, krangk, *n.* [M.E. *cranke;* O.E. *cranc-staef,* weaver's implement; akin to E. *cringe, crinkle.*] *Mach.* a device for conveying motion, consisting in its simplest form of an arm or handle secured at right angles to a shaft, which receives or imparts the motion; *colloq.* a bad-tempered, irritable person. A person subject to eccentric or impracticable notions, often one overzealous or fanatical in advocating his beliefs; an eccentric notion or whim.—*v.t. Mach.* to turn with a crank or move or set in operation by means of a crank.

crank·case, krangk′kās″, *n.* In an internal-combustion engine, the case which encloses the crankshaft, connecting rods, and allied parts.

crank·pin, krangk′pin″, *n.* A pin or cylinder at the outer end of a crank, holding a connecting rod.

crank·shaft, krangk′shaft″, krangk′shäft″, *n.* A shaft receiving motion from, or imparting motion to a crank.

crank·y, krang′kē, *a.—crankier, crankiest.* Ill-tempered; cross; crotchety; liable to lurch or capsize.—**crank·i·ly,** *adv.—* **crank·i·ness,** *n.*

cran·ny, kran′ē, *n.* pl. **cran·nies.** [Fr. *cran,* a notch, < L. *crena,* a notch; comp. G. *krinne,* a rent.] A small narrow opening, fissure, crevice, or chink, as in a wall or other substance.—*v.i.* To become intersected with or penetrated by crannies or clefts.—**cran·nied,** *a.* Having chinks, fissures, or crannies.

crap, krap, *n.* Craps; a throw of 2, 3, or 12 on the dice in craps: a losing throw. *Slang,* nonsense; junk; misleading statements.— *v.i.* To lose the dice by throwing a 7 before making the point. Also **crap out.—crap·shoot·er,** krap′shoo″tėr, *n.* A player of craps.

crape, krāp, *v.t.—craped, craping.* Crepe.— *n.* Crepe.

crape myr·tle, *n.* A tall shrub native to China, having large showy flowers, now widely cultivated in western and southern U.S. as an ornamental shrub. Also, *crepe myrtle.*

crap·pie, krap′ē, *n.* [Origin obscure.] A small sunfish, *Pomoxys annularis,* of the central parts of the U.S.

craps, kraps, *n.* [Appar. < *crabs,* as used in the old game of 'hazard.'] A game of chance using two dice, in which a first throw of 7 or 11 wins, while a first throw of 2, 3, or 12 loses, and a first throw of any other number can win only if repeated in subsequent throws before a 7 appears.

crap·u·lous, krap′ū·lus, *a.* Drunk; ill as a result of intemperance; associated with drunkenness. Also **crap·u·lent.—crap·u·lence,** krap′ū·lens, *n.* [L. *crapulo,* intoxication.] Drunkenness; the sickness occasioned by intemperance.

crash, krash, *v.t.* [M.E.; imit.] To break in pieces violently and noisily; to shatter; to force or drive in, through, or out with violence and noise; *aeronautics,* to cause an aircraft to make a landing in an abnormal manner, usually damaging or wrecking the apparatus.—*v.i.* To break or fall to pieces with noise; to make a loud, clattering noise, as of something dashed to pieces; to move or go with a crash; to strike with a crash; *aeronautics,* to land in an abnormal manner. —*n.* A breaking or falling to pieces with loud noise; the shock of collision and breaking; *fig.* a sudden and violent falling to ruin; as, the stock market *crash* of 1929. A sudden, loud noise, as of something dashed to pieces; the sound of thunder or loud music; *aeronautics,* an act of crashing.

crash, krash, *n.* [Prob. < Russ.] A coarsely woven fabric, usually linen or cotton, used for towels, draperies or clothing.

crash, krash, *a.* Of or pertaining to hasty, intensive effort, reflecting a condition of emergency; as, a *crash* program to rebuild.

crash dive, *n.* A sudden dive made by a submarine, generally for the purpose of avoiding attack from plane or vessel.— **crash-dive,** krash′dīv″, krash′dīv′, *v.t., v.i.* —past *crash-dived* or *crash-dove,* pp. *crash-dived,* ppr. *crash-diving.*

crash hel·met, *n.* A sturdy helmet heavily padded, worn for protection by pilots, cyclists, and auto race drivers.

crash-land, krash′land′, *v.t., v.i. Avi.* to land (an airplane in an emergency) where normal procedures are impossible, causing damage to the craft.

crash pro·gram, *n.* An emergency program having priority over all others, set up in government, science, or other important areas; any intensive course or program.

cra·sis, krā′sis, *n.* pl. **cra·ses,** krā′sēz. [Gr. *krasis,* a mixing.] *Gram.* a figure by which two different letters are contracted into one long letter or into a diphthong. Also *synaeresis.*

crass, kras, *a.* [L. *crassus.*] Gross; thick; coarse; not thin, nor fine: applied to fluids and solids; dense; stupid; obtuse.—**cras·si·tude,** kras′i·tōd″, kras′i·tūd″, *n.* Grossness; coarseness; thickness.—**crass·ness,** *n.* Grossness.—**crass·ly,** *adv.*

crate, krāt, *n.* [L. *cratis,* wickerwork.] A basket or hamper of wickerwork, for the transportation of crockery; any openwork casing, as a box made of slats for packing and transporting commodities.—*v.t.— crated, crating.* To put or pack in a crate.

cra·ter, krā′tėr, *n.* [L. < Gr. *crater,* orig. bowl for mixing wine and water in, < *kerannynai,* mix.] A cup-shaped depression or cavity marking the orifice of a volcano; a bowl-shaped depression made by the impact of a meteorite; a bowllike opening at the mouth of a geyser; a hole, pit, or depression in the ground caused by an explosion; originally, a large bowl used by ancient Greeks and Romans; *elect.* a cavity formed in the positive carbon of an arc-lamp using continuous current.—**cra·ter·al,** *a.*—**cra·tered,** *a.* Having a crater.— **cra·ter·i·form,** krā′tėr·i·farm, kra·ter′i·farm, *a.* Having the form of a crater; bowl-shaped.

craunch, kränch, *v.t., v.i., n.* Crunch.

cra·vat, kra·vat′, *n.* [Fr. *Cravate,* a Croat, and hence a cravat, because it was adopted in the 17th century from the Croats who entered the French service.] A man's neckcloth or scarf; a necktie.

crave, krāv, *v.t.—craved, craving.* [O.E. *crafian,* to ask—Icel. *krefja,* Sw. *kräfva,* Dan. *kraeve,* to crave, to ask.] To ask for with earnestness; to beg for urgently; to entreat, implore, solicit; to call for, as a gratification; to long for; to require or demand, as a passion or appetite.—*v.i.* To beg, ask, beseech, or implore; to long or hanker eagerly, followed by *for.*—**crav·er,** *n.*—**crav·ing,** *n.* Vehement or earnest desire; a longing.—**crav·ing·ly,** *adv.*

cra·ven, krā′ven, *a.* [O.Fr. *cravanter,* to overthrow, < L.L. *crepantare,* < L. *crepare,* to break; akin to *crevice, crepitate.*] Cowardly; lacking courage.—*n.* A coward; one without moral strength.—**cra·ven·ly,** *adv.*

craw, krą, *n.* [Of same origin as Dan. *kro,* D. *kraag,* G. *kragen,* the throat, craw.] An enlargement of the gullet in front of the stomach of fowls; the stomach of an animal.

craw·fish, krą′fish″, *n.* Crayfish.—*v.i.* To back out or retreat from a position or undertaking.

crawl, krąl, *v.i.* [Of same origin as Sw. *kräla,* also *krafla,* Icel. *krafla,* Dan. *kravle,* G. *krabbeln,* to crawl.] To move slowly in a prone position by thrusting or drawing the body along the ground; to move slowly on the hands and knees; of plants or vines, to grow or spread by extending tendrils; to creep; to move or walk slowly, or timorously; to feel as if things were creeping on one's person; to behave meanly or despicably.—*n.* The act of crawling; slow creeping motion; a swimming stroke performed in a face down position from which the swimmer uses an alternate overarm stroke combined with a flutter kick while turning the head from side to side; *Brit.* going from one pub to another.—**crawl·ing·ly,** *adv.* In a crawling manner.

crawl, krąl, *n.* [= *kraal.*] An enclosure in shallow water on the seacoast, for containing fish or turtles.

crawl·er, krạ′lẽr, *n.* One who or that which crawls; a creeper; a reptile; a worm used as fish bait; a tread for a tractor; a garment for a baby.

crawl space, *n.* An open area in a building which provides for ventilation, maintenance, and storage, but is too low to allow a person to stand erect.

crawl·y, krạ′lē, *a.—crawlier, crawliest.* Having the sensation of contact with crawling things; creepy; giving a queasy feeling.

cray·fish, krā′fish, *n. pl.* **cray·fish·es, cray·fish.** Any of numerous fresh-water crustaceans of the genera *Cambarus* and *Astacus,* closely related to and resembling the lobsters but smaller. Also *crawfish.*

cray·on, krā′on, krā′on, *n.* [Fr. *crayon* < *craie,* L. *creta,* chalk.] A pencil of white or colored chalk or wax used in drawing on paper; a drawing made with crayons.—*v.t.* To draw or sketch with a crayon.

craze, krāz, *v.t.—crazed, crazing.* [M.E. *crasen,* break, akin to Fr. *écraser,* crush < Scand.] To make small cracks on the surface of, as on pottery; crackle; to impair in intellect; make insane.—*v.i.* To become minutely cracked, as the glaze on the surface of pottery; to become insane.

craze, krāz, *n.* A minute crack in the glaze of pottery; an insane condition; a mania; an unreasoning liking or fancy for some object of interest or popularity, esp. as current among the public generally; a rage; a fad.

cra·zy, krā′zē, *a.—crazier, craziest.* Deranged in mind; insane; unsound; eccentric; *slang,* very eager, or very infatuated, usu. followed by *about.*—**cra·zi·ly,** *adv.*—**cra·zi·ness,** *n.*

cra·zy bone, *n.* The elbow; the funny bone.

cra·zy quilt, *n.* A quilt made of patches of irregular shape combined with little or no regard to pattern.

cra·zy·weed, krā′zē·wēd″, *n.* The loco weed.

creak, krēk, *v.i.* [Imitative of a more acute and prolonged sound than *crack;* comp. Fr. *criquer,* to creak; W. *crecian,* to scream.] To make a sharp, harsh, grating sound or some continuance, as by the friction of hard substances.—*v.t.* To cause to make a harsh protracted noise.—*n.* A sharp, harsh, grating sound.—**creak·y,** krē′kē, *a.—creakier, creakiest.*

cream, krēm, *n.* [O.Fr. *cresme* (Fr. *crème*), < L.L. *chrisma.*] The fatty part of milk, which rises to the surface when the liquid is allowed to stand; something containing or resembling this substance, as a table delicacy; a confection; an emulsified cosmetic; *fig.* the best part of anything. A yellowish white color.—**cream·y,** *a.—creamier, creamiest.*—**cream·i·ly,** *adv.*—**cream·i·ness,** *n.*

cream, krēm, *v.t.* To coat with a cosmetic cream; *slang,* to beat decisively.

cream, krēm, *v.i.* To form cream; hence, to froth; to foam.—*v.t.* To allow (milk) to form cream; separate as cream; take the cream or best part of; add cream to (tea or coffee). *Cooking,* to work, as shortening and sugar, to a smooth, creamy mass; to prepare, as vegetables, with cream, milk, or a cream sauce.

cream cheese, *n.* Any of various soft, rich, unripened cheeses made of cream, or with an extra proportion of cream.

cream·er, krē′mẽr, *n.* A refrigerator in which milk is placed to facilitate the formation of cream; a vessel or apparatus for separating cream from milk; a small jug or pitcher for holding cream.

cream·er·y, krē′me·rē, *n. pl.* **cream·er·ies.** An establishment engaged in the production of butter and cheese; a place for the sale of milk and its products; formerly, a place where milk was set to form cream.

cream of tar·tar, *n.* Purified and crystallized

potassium bitartrate, $KHC_4H_4O_6$, which is used in baking powder, in medicine, and in treating metals.

crease, krēs, *n.* [Prob. related to O.Fr. *creast,* a line, ridge, or furrow.] A line or mark made by folding or doubling anything; hence, a similar mark, however produced; the name given to certain lines marking boundaries in various sports, esp. hockey; a wrinkle in the skin.

crease, krēs, *v.t.—creased, creasing.* To make a crease or mark in, as by folding or doubling; to wound superficially with a gunshot.—*v.i.* To become creased.—**creas·y,** krē′sē, *a.—creasier, creasiest.*

creas·er, krēs′ẽr, *n.* A tool or a sewing machine attachment for making creases on leather or cloth, as guides to see by; *bookbinding,* a tool for making the band impression distinct on the back or for making blind lines or creases on covers.

cre·ate, krē·āt′, *v.t.—created, creating.* [L. *creatus,* pp. of *creare,* bring into being.] To bring into being; cause to exist; produce; specif. to evolve from one's own thought or imagination; to be the first to represent, as a part or role; to make by investing with new character or functions; constitute; appoint; to be the cause or occasion of; give rise to.—*v.i.*

cre·a·tion, krē·ā′shan, *n.* The act of creating, producing, or causing to exist; especially, the act of bringing the world into existence; the act of investing with a new character; the act of making or inventing; the production of that which is original, innovative, or imaginative.—**cre·a·tion·al,** *a.* Pertaining to creation.

cre·a·tive, krē·ā′tiv, *a.* Having the power to create, or exerting the act of creating.—**cre·a·tive·ly,** *adv.*—**cre·a·tive·ness,** *n.*—**cre·a·tiv·i·ty,** krē″ā·tiv′i·tē, *n.*

cre·a·tive ev·o·lu·tion, *n. Philos.* the continuous formation of the universe as brought about by the life force.

cre·a·tor, krē·ā′tẽr, *n.* [L.] One who or that which creates, produces, causes, or constitutes; *(cap.)* the almighty Maker of all things.

crea·ture, krē′chẽr, *n.* [O.Fr. *creature* (Fr. *créature*), < L.L. *creatura,* < L. *creare.*] Anything created, animate or inanimate; an animate being; an animal, distinct from man; a human being or person; something produced by or springing from something else; a result or product; a person owing his rise and fortune to another, or subject to the will or influence of another.—**crea·ture·ly,** *a.* Of or pertaining to a creature or creatures. Also **crea·tur·al.**

crea·ture com·forts, *n. pl.* Those things, as food, clothing, and shelter, which minister to bodily comfort.

crèche, kresh, krãsh, *Fr.* kRĕsh, *n.* [Fr. *crèche,* manger.] *Brit.* an institution or establishment where, for a small payment, children are taken care of during the day. An asylum for foundlings; a representation of the manger and the Holy Family.

cre·dence, krēd′ens, *n.* [L.L. *credentia,* belief, < L. *credens, credentis,* pp. of *credo,* to believe. CREED.] Reliance on evidence derived from sources other than personal knowledge, as from the testimony of others; belief or credit. *Eccles.* the small table by the side of the altar or communion table, on which the bread and wine are placed before they are consecrated.—**cre·dent,** krēd′ent, *a.* Believing.

cre·den·dum, kri·den′dum, *n. pl.* **cre·den·da,** kri·den′da. [L.] A thing to be believed; an article of faith.

cre·den·tial, kri·den′shal, *n.* A title or claim to confidence or credit; *pl.* testimonials or documents giving a person belief, credit, or authority.—*a.* Giving a basis for confidence.

cre·den·za, kri·den′za, *n.* A buffet or sideboard often without legs.

cred·i·ble, kred′i·bl, *a.* [L. *credibilis.*] Capable of being believed; such as one may believe; worthy of credit, reliance, or confidence as to truth and correctness: applied to persons and things.—**cred·i·bil·i·ty, cred·i·ble·ness,** *n.*—**cred·i·bly,** *adv.* In a credible manner; so as to command belief; as, to be *credibly* informed.

cred·it, kred′it, *v.t.* [Fr. *crédit;* L. *creditum.*] To believe; to have faith in the truth of; to sell or lend on the basis of future payment; to trust; to enter upon the credit side of an account; to give credit for; to ascribe or attribute to a person or thing; to give educational credits to.—**cred·it·a·ble,** kred′it·a·bl, *a.* Deserving or bringing admiration, credit, honor, or reputation.—**cred·it·a·bil·i·ty,** kred′i·ta·bil′i·tē, *n.* The quality of being creditable.—**cred·it·a·bly,** kred′i·ta·blē, *adv.* Reputably; with credit; without disgrace.

cred·it, kred′it, *n.* Reliance on the truth or genuineness of something; belief; trust; approval or honor given for some quality or action; reputation or influence derived from the confidence or good opinion of others; trustworthiness; esteem; good name; a source of honor or good standing; reputation for commercial solvency or stability; the selling of goods or lending of money on the basis of future payment; the time extended for payment for goods or services sold on trust; a sum of money deposited in an account against which one may draw. *Bookkeeping,* an entry on the right-hand side of an account indicating a payment or other item lessening the claim against a debtor; any of the sums or the total entered on the right-hand side of an account. *Educ.* recorded acknowledgment of the work of a student in a particular course of study.

cred·it card, *n.* A small card establishing the right of its holder to credit on certain purchases, as meals, lodging, gasoline, or merchandise.

cred·it line, *n.* A line of copy accompanying a publication or show, giving the source of a published article or the contribution of a particular person; the maximum amount of credit that a customer is allowed by a store, bank, or the like.

cred·i·tor, kred′i·tẽr, *n.* One who gives goods or money on credit; one to whom money is due.

cred·it un·ion, *n.* A cooperative association in which members may keep money that accrues interest, and from which they may borrow at low interest rates.

cre·do, krē′dō, krā′dō, *n. pl.* **cre·dos.** [L., "I believe": the first word of the Apostles' and the Nicene Creed in Latin.] The Apostles' or the Nicene Creed; a musical setting of the creed, usually of the Nicene Creed; any creed or formula of belief.

cred·u·lous, krej′u·lus, *a.* [L. *credulus,* < *credo,* to believe.] Apt to believe without sufficient evidence; easily deceived; stemming from gullibility or credulity; as, a con man's *credulous* victim.—**cred·u·lous·ly,** kred′ū·lus·lē, *adv.*—**cred·u·lous·ness, cre·du·li·ty,** kre·dö′li·tē, kre·dū′li·tē, *n.*

Cree, krē, *n. pl.* **Crees, Cree.** A N. American Indian tribe formerly found in Manitoba, Saskatchewan, and Montana; an Algonquin language of the Cree Indians.

creed, krēd, *n.* [O.E. *crēda,* < L. *credo:* see *credo.*] An authoritative, formulated statement of the chief articles of Christian belief, as the Apostles', the Nicene, or the Athanasian Creed; in general, any formula of religious belief, as of a particular denomination; an accepted system of religious belief; any system of belief or of

---

a- fat, fāte, fär, fâre, fạll; **e-** met, mē, mēre, hẽr; **i-** pin, pīne; **o-** not, nōte, mȯve; **u-** tub, cūbe, bụll; **oi-** oil; **ou-** pound.

opinion.—**creed·al**, cre·dal, a.—**creed·**·less, a.

creek, krēk, krik, n. [M.E. creke, crike: cf. D. kreek, Fr. crique, creek, Icel. kriki, crack, nook.] A small stream, as a branch of a river; a rivulet. Brit. a small inlet or bay; a narrow or winding passage.

Creek, krēk, n. pl. **Creeks**, **Creek**. A powerful alliance of Muskogean Indians formerly occupying a large part of Alabama, Georgia, and northern Florida; a Muskogean language of the Creek Indian.

creel, krēl, n. [Perhaps through Fr. < L. craticula, dim. of cratis, wickerwork.] A wickerwork basket, esp. one used by anglers for holding fish; a wickerwork trap to catch fish or lobsters; a framework for holding bobbins in a spinning machine.

creep, krēp, v.i.—crept, creeping. [O.E. crēopan = D. kruipen = Icel. krjúpa.] To move with the body prone and near the ground, as a reptile; to move on hands and knees, as a child; to move slowly, imperceptibly, or stealthily; to slip, shift, or move gradually from one position to another; metals, to change shape as a result of stress or high temperature; bot. to spread or grow over a surface.—**creep·ing**, a. Referring to that which creeps; as, a creeping vine.—**creep·ing·ly**, adv.

creep, krēp, n. The act of creeping; an unpleasant sensation of horror; an enclosure that permits entry of young animals only; slang, an odd, loathsome, or obnoxious person.—**the creeps**, colloq. a feeling of repulsion or fear similar to that which produces goose flesh: generally used as the object of give.—**creep·y**, krē'pē, a. Producing a nervous, shivery, fearful sensation; cheap; inferior.—**creep·i·ness**, n.

creep·er, krē'pėr, n. One who or that which creeps; one of a breed of domestic fowls with short legs; any of various birds that creep about on trees or bushes; as, the black-and-white creeper; a plant which grows along the land by sending or shooting out stems; as, the Virginia creeper; a grappling device for dragging the bottom of a river; a spiked piece of iron worn on the heel of shoes to prevent slipping; pl. a loose one-piece garment, usually bifurcated, worn by infants.

creese, kris, krēs, n. [Malay krîs.] A short sword or heavy dagger with a wavy blade, used by the Malays. Also **crease**.

cre·mate, krē'māt, v.t.—cremated, cremating. [L. crematus, pp. of cremare, consume by fire.] To consume by fire; burn, esp. to reduce a corpse to ashes.—**cre·ma·tion**, kri·mā'shan, n. [L. crematio(n-).] The act or custom of cremating.—**cre·ma·tion·ist**, n. One who advocates cremation instead of burial of the bodies of the dead.

cre·ma·tor, krē'mā·tėr, n. [L.L.] One who cremates; a furnace for cremating dead bodies or other matter.—**cre·ma·to·ry**, a. Of or pertaining to cremation.—n. A furnace or an establishment for cremating dead bodies or other matter.—**cre·ma·to·ri·um**, krē"ma·tōr'ē·um, krē"ma·tạr'ē·um, krem"a·tōr'ē·um, krem"a·tạr'ē·um, n. pl. **cre·ma·to·ri·ums**, **cre·ma·to·ri·a**. [N.L.] A crematory.

crème, krem, krēm, krām, Fr. krem, n. [Fr.] Cream; a cream-like preparation or liquid; one of a class of liqueurs of thick, oily, or syrupy consistency.

crème de ca·ca·o, krem" de kō'kō, krem" de kä·kä'ō, Fr. krem de kä·kä·ō', n. A sweet liqueur flavored with chocolate and vanilla.

crème de la crème, krem' de lä krem', n. [Fr.] The finest; the very best part; literally, 'cream of the cream.'

crème de menthe, krem" de menth', krem" de mint', Fr. krem de mäNt', n. [Fr. "cream

---

of mint."] A green or white liqueur flavored with mint.

Cre·mo·na, kri·mō'na, It. kre·mạ'nä, n. A general name given to the violins made at Cremona in North Italy in the 17th and 18th centuries.

cren·el, kren'el, n. [O.Fr. crenel (Fr. créneau), dim. of cren (Fr. cran), notch.] One of the openings between the merlons of a castle battlement; a crenature.—v.t. creneled, crenelled, creneling, crenelling. To furnish with crenels or battlements; arch. to form with square indentations as a molding. Also **cren·e·late**, **cren·el·late**.—**cren·el·at·ed**, **cren·el·lat·ed**, a.

cren·u·late, kren'ū·lāt", kren'ū·lit, a. Having the edge cut into very small scallops, as a leaf or a shell. Also **cren·u·lat·ed**.—**cren·u·la·tion**, kren"ū·lā'shan, n.

cre·o·dont, krē'o·dont", n. [N.L. Creodonta, pl., < Gr. kreas, flesh, and odous(odont-), tooth.] Any of the Creodonta, a group of primitive carnivorous mammals, characterized by small brains, regarded as the ancestors of the modern carnivores.

Cre·ole, krē'ōl, n. [Fr. créole, < Sp. criollo.] Orig., in the West Indies and Spanish America, one born in the region but of European, usually Spanish, ancestry; similarly, in Louisiana and elsewhere, a person born in the region but of French ancestry; in general, a person born in a place but of foreign ancestry, as distinguished from the aborigines and half-breeds.—a. Of, belonging to, or characteristic of the Creoles; as, a Creole dialect, Creole French; (l.c.) bred or growing in a country, but of foreign origin, as, an animal or plant; cookery, pertaining to a sauce made of tomatoes and peppers, served with rice or meats.

cre·o·lized, krē'o·līzd", a. Pertaining to a language which is a blend of two languages.

cre·o·sol, krē'o·sōl", krē'o·sạl", krē'o·sol", n. [< creosote.] Chem. a colorless oily liquid with an agreeable odor and burning taste, resembling carbolic acid, obtained from wood tar and guaiacum resin.

cre·o·sote, krē'o·sōt", n. [Gr. kreas, flesh, and sozein, save.] An oily liquid with a burning taste and a penetrating odor, obtained by the distillation of wood tar, and used as a preservative and antiseptic.—v.t.—creosoted, creosoting. To treat with creosote.—**cre·o·sote bush**, n. An evergreen shrub, Covillea or Larrea mexicana, of northern Mexico and adjacent regions, bearing resinous foliage with a strong odor of creosote.

crêpe, krāp, Fr. krep, n. [Fr. crêpe, earlier crespe, < L. crispus, curled, crimped, E. crisp.] A thin, light fabric of silk, cotton, or other fiber, with a finely crinkled or ridged surface; esp. a black or white silk fabric of this kind, used for mourning veils, trimmings, etc.; a band or piece of this material, as for a token of mourning. Also **crape**.—**crepe**, v.t.—creped, creping. To cover, clothe, or drape with crepe; to frizzle or curl; to form into ringlets. Also **crape**.—**crêpe de Chine**, krāp" de shēn', n. [Fr. "crape of China."] A light, soft, thin silk fabric with minute irregularities of surface.

crepe myr·tle, **crêpe myr·tle**, n. Crape myrtle.

crepe pa·per, n. A decorative paper, wrinkled to resemble crepe fabric, and used as a fancy wrapping on packages and for other purposes of ornamentation.

crepe rub·ber, n. A synthetic rubber which has been given a crinkled surface, generally used for shoe soles; a crude rubber formed into crinkled sheets.

crêpe su·zette, krāp"sö·zet', Fr. krep"sy·zet', n. pl. crêpes su·zette. A pancake, rolled or folded, heated in an orange sauce flavored with liqueur and served flaming as a dessert.

---

crep·i·tate, krep'i·tāt", v.i.—crepitated, crepitating. [L. crepito, crepitatum, freq. < crepo, to tackle (whence crevice).] To burst with a small sharp abrupt sound rapidly repeated, as salt in fire or during calcination; to crackle; to snap.—**crep·i·tant**, krep'i·tant, a. Crackling.

cre·pus·cule, kri·pus'kūl, krep'u·skūl", n. [O.Fr. crepuscule (Fr. crépuscule), < L. crepusculum, twilight, < creper, dark, obscure.] Twilight; dusk.—**cre·pus·cu·lar**, kri·pus'kū·lėr, a. [L. crepusculum, twilight.] Pertaining to twilight; glimmering; flying or appearing in the twilight or evening, or before sunrise, as certain insects.

cres·cen·do, kri·shen'dō, kri·sen'dō, It. kre·shen'dạ, a. [It., gerund of crescere, < L. crescere.] Mus. gradually increasing in force or loudness: opposed to decrescendo or diminuendo.—n. pl. **cres·cen·dos**, It. **cres·cen·di**, kre·shen'dē. An increase in force or loudness; a crescendo passage.

cres·cent, kres'ent, n. [L. crescens (crescent-), ppr. of crescere, grow, increase; as n., through O.Fr. cressant (Fr. croissant).] The crescent moon; the convexo-concave figure of the moon in its first or last quarter; the Turkish or Islamic emblem; hence, the Turkish or Islamic power; any crescent-shaped object, as a croissant.—a. Increasing or growing, as the new moon or the moon during its first quarter; shaped like the moon during its first quarter.—**cres·cen·tic**, kre·sen'tik, a. Crescent-shaped.

cres·cive, kres'iv, a. Increasing or growing.—**cres·cive·ly**, adv.

cre·sol, krē'sōl, krē'sạl, krē'sol, n. [< creosote.] Chem. any one of three colorless, poisonous isomeric phenols, C_7H_8O, occurring in coal tar and wood tar, and mainly used as a disinfectant.

cress, kres, n. [O.E. caerse, cresse—D. kers, G. kresse, Sw. karse.] Any of various plants in general use as a salad; as, watercress, common in streams and having a pungent taste, or garden cress, a dwarf cultivated species.

cres·set, kres'it, n. [O.Fr. crusset, crasset; akin to E. cruse, G. kruse, a jar.] A lamp or firepan suspended on pivots and carried on a pole, or to a beacon light in a kind of iron basket; a large lamp used ornamentally in churches.

crest, krest, n. [O.Fr. creste (Fr. crête), < L. crista.] A tuft or other natural growth on the top of an animal's head, as the comb of a cock; anything resembling or suggesting such a tuft; her. a figure borne above the escutcheon in a coat of arms, sometimes used separately as a cognizance. The head or top of anything; the summit of a hill, etc.; fig. the highest or best of the kind; arch. the ornamental part which surmounts a roof-ridge, wall, etc. A ridge or ridgelike formation; the ridge of the neck of a horse, dog, etc., or the mane growing from this; the foamy top of a wave; archaic, courage.— v.t. To furnish with a crest: to serve as a crest for; crown or top; to reach, as the crest or summit of.—v.i. To form or rise into a crest, as a wave.—**crest·ed**, a. Having or bearing a crest.—**crest·ing**, n. Arch. an ornamental finish of stone, metal, or the like, surmounting a wall, roof-ridge, etc.—**crest·less**, a.

crest·fall·en, krest'fạ"len, a. Dejected; discouraged; sunk; bowed; dispirited.

cre·ta·ceous, kri·tā'shus, a. [L. cretaceus, < creta, chalk.] Composed of, having the qualities of, or abounding with chalk. (Cap.) geol. of or referring to the last period of the Mesozoic era, lasting from 70 to 135 million years ago, which saw the extinction of giant reptiles and development of early mammals; referring to this period's system of strata, containing immense chalk beds.—n. (Cap.), geol. the Cretaceous period.

Cre·tan, krēt′an, *a.* Of or pertaining to the Mediterranean island of Crete or its inhabitants.—*n.*

cre·tin, krēt′in, krē′tin, *n.* [Fr. (orig. Swiss) *crétin,* by some connected with *chrétien,* Christian.] A person afflicted with cretinism. —**cre·tin·ism,** krēt′e·niz″um, *n. Pathol.* a chronic disease, due to absence or deficiency of the normal thyroid secretion, characterized by physical deformity, stunted growth, idiocy, and in many cases, goiter.

cre·tonne, kri·ton′, krē′ton, *n.* [Fr.] A cotton cloth with various textures of surface printed with pictorial and other patterns, and used for curtains and for covering furniture.

cre·vasse, kre·vas′, *n.* [Fr. *crevasse.*] A fissure or rent: generally applied to a fissure across a glacier, and in the U.S. to a breach in the embankment of a river.—*v.t.* —*crevassed, crevassing.*

crev·ice, krev′is, *n.* [Fr. *crevasse,* < *crever,* L. *crepare,* to burst, to crack.] A crack; a cleft; a fissure; a cranny; a rent.

crew, krö, *n.* [O.Fr. *creue* (Fr. *crue*), increase, augmentation, orig. pp. fem. of *creistre* (Fr. *croître*), < L. *crescere,* grow, increase.] A body of persons engaged upon a particular work; as, a train *crew. Naut.* the company of men who man a ship or boat; the common sailors of a ship's company; a particular gang of a ship's company responsible for one job; as, gunnery *crew.* A gang or crowd, usu. a derogatory term.

crew cut, *n.* A haircut in which the hair is cropped close to the scalp.

crew·el, krö′el, *n.* [< D. *krul,* a curl.] A kind of fine worsted or thread of silk or wool, used in embroidery and fancy work; the embroidery made of this floss or yarn.— **crew·el·work,** krö′el·wurk, *n.*

crib, krib, *n.* [O.E. *crib* = D. *krib* = G. *krippe.*] A child's bed with high, usu. slatted sides; a manger in which animals are fed; a framework enclosure such as a stall or pen in which cattle are stabled; a small narrow room or any cramped habitation; a petty theft; *colloq.* a device, such as a list of correct answers, a translation, or other illicit aid, sometimes called a pony, employed by students for cheating; *cribbage,* a set of cards made up by equal contributions from each player's hand, and belonging to the dealer.—*v.t.*—*cribbed, cribbing.* To shut up or confine in a criblike enclosure; to provide with cribs, racks, or stalls; to line with timber or planking; *colloq.* to pilfer or steal, as a passage from an author. To translate by means of a crib. —*v.i.* To practice cribbing. *Colloq.* to pilfer or steal; of students, to use a translation or other illicit aid.—**crib·ber,** *n.*

crib·bage, krib′ij, *n.* A game of cards, for two, three, or four players, a characteristic feature of which is the crib, which is composed of the players' discards.

crib·bing, krib′ing, *n.* A self-injurious habit of horses in which they bite their manger while noisily drawing in their breath. Also **crib·bit·ing.**

crib·ri·form, krib′ri·fạrm″, *a.* [L. *cribrum,* sieve.] Having the form of a sieve; perforated with many small openings.

crick, krik, *n.* [Akin to *crook.*] A painful muscle spasm, esp. of the neck or back.— *v.t.*

crick·et, krik′it, *n.* [O.Fr. *criquet,* from its sharp creaking sound; comp. D. *kriek,* a cricket, *krieken,* to chirp.] An insect of the family *Gryllidae,* noted for the chirping or creaking sound produced by the male by rubbing the bases of its wing cases against each other.

crick·et, krik′it, *n.* [Fr. *criquet,* a kind of game.] A popular outdoor game, played esp. in England, by two sides of eleven each, with bats, ball, and wickets; honorable,

gentlemanly behavior.—*v.i.* To engage in the game of cricket.

cri·er, krī′er, *n.* One who cries; an official, as of a court or a town, who makes public announcements; one who cries goods for sale; a hawker.

crime, krim, *n.* [O.Fr. Fr. *crime,* < L. *crimen,* accusation, fault, offense, crime.] An act or omission, esp. one of a grave nature, punishable by law as forbidden by statute or injurious to the public welfare; hence, serious violation of human law; as, steeped in *crime;* more generally, any offense, esp. one of a grave character; hence, serious wrongdoing; sin.

Cri·me·an, krī·mē′an, krī·mē′an, *a.* Of or pertaining to the Crimea, a large peninsula extending into the Black Sea from the north; as, the *Crimean* War, a war allying Great Britain, France, Turkey, and Sardinia against Russia, carried on chiefly in the Crimea, from 1854 until 1856.

crim·i·nal, krim′i·nal, *a.* Guilty of a crime; felonious; partaking of the nature of a crime; involving a crime; pertaining to acts which violate public law; *law,* relating to crime: opposed to *civil.* Also **crim·i·nous.**—*n.* A person guilty of crime; a person indicted or charged with a public offense and found guilty; a culprit; a malefactor.—**crim·i·nal·i·ty,** krim″i·nal′-i·tē, *n.*—**crim·i·nal·ly,** *adv.*

crim·i·nal law, *n.* Any of the legal enactments dealing with crimes and their punishment.

crim·i·nate, krim′i·nāt″, *v.t.*—*criminated, criminating.* [L. *criminor, criminatus.*] To accuse or charge with a crime; to involve in a crime or the consequences of a crime.— **crim·i·na·tion,** *n.* The act of criminating; accusation; a charge.—**crim·i·na·tive, crim·i·na·to·ry,** krim′i·nā″tiv, krim′i·na·tōr″ē, krim′i·na·tạr″ē, *a.* Relating to accusation; accusing.

crim·i·nol·o·gy, krim″i·nol′o·jē, *n.* The scientific study of crime, penal treatment, and the behavior of convicts and criminals. **crim·i·nol·o·gist,** *n.*—**crim·i·no·log·i·cal,** *a.*—**crim·i·no·log·i·cal·ly,** *adv.*

crimp, krimp, *v.t.* [A lighter form of *cramp;* D. *krimpen,* Dan. *krympe,* G. *krimpen,* to shrink; akin *crumple.*] To curl or wave (the hair); to flute or make ridges on; to bend (the edges in metalworking); to bend into shape; to press (the ends of something) together; to check, arrest, or hinder; *cooking,* to gash (the flesh of a fish) with a knife, to give it greater hardness and make it more crisp.—*n.* Something that has been crimped; curled or waved hair; a machine used for crimping; the waviness of wool fibers; something that cramps or prevents; a ridge or crease formed in sheet metal for fastening purposes.—**crimp·y,** *a.* —*crimpier, crimpiest.*

crimp, krimp, *n.* A person who decoys or entraps others into military service or work aboard ship, by methods of swindling, deception, or forcible persuasion.—*v.t.*

crim·son, krim′zon, krim′son, *n.* [O.Fr. *cramoisin,* < L.L. *carmesinus,* < Ar. *kermez, qirmiz,* the kermes insect, which yields the dye; akin *carmine.*] Any color of the rather indefinite range of deep, vivid, purplish reds.—*a.* Of a deep red color.—*v.t.* To dye with crimson; to make red.—*v.i.* To become of a crimson color; to be tinged with red; to blush.

cringe, krinj, *v.i.*—*cringed, cringing.* [M.E. *crenge,* < O.E. *cringan, crincan,* yield, fall in battle, prob. orig. "bend, contract, shrink."] To shrink, bend, or crouch, from fear or servility; cower; fawn.—*n.* A cringing; a servile or fawning obeisance.—**cring·er,** *n.* —**cring·ing·ly,** *adv.*

crin·kle, kring′kl, *v.i., v.t.*—*crinkled, crinkling.* [= D. *krinkelen;* akin to E. *cringe* and

crank.] To fold or bend in the sense of crumple; to wrinkle or ripple; to make slight, sharp sounds; to rustle.—*n.* A turn or twist; a wrinkle; a ripple; a crinkling sound.—**crin·kly,** *a.*—*crinklier, crinkliest.*

crin·o·line, krin′o·lin, krin′o·lēn″, *n.* [Fr., < *crin,* < L. *crinis,* hair.] A kind of starched cotton fabric used for stiffening or distending garments; a petticoat of stiff material, formerly worn by women under a full skirt; hence, a hoop skirt.

cri·ol·lo, krē·ō′lō, *Sp.* krē·ạ′ya, *n.* A person of European, esp. Spanish, blood born in Spanish America; any breed of domestic animal developed in Latin America.

cri·o·sphinx, krī′o·sfingks″, *n. pl.* **cri·o·sphinx·es, cri·o·sphin·ges,** krī′o·sfin″jēz. [Gr. *krios,* a ram, and *sphinx,* sphinx.] A sphinx having the head of a ram.

crip·ple, krip′l, *n.* [O.E. *crypel*—G. *kruppel,* Icel. *kryppil,* a cripple, D. *kreupel,* lame; < stem of *creep.*] One who has lost or never enjoyed the use of his limbs; a partially disabled or lame person or animal.—*a.* Lame; inferior.—*v.t.*—*crippled, crippling.* To disable by injuring the limbs; to lame; to disable.

cri·sis, krī′sis, *n. pl.* **cri·ses,** krī′sēz. [L. *crisis,* Gr. *krisis,* < the root of *krinō,* to separate, to determine. CRIME.] The change of a disease which indicates recovery or death; the decisive state of things, or the point of time when an affair has reached its height, and must soon terminate or suffer a material change; turning point.

crisp, krisp, *a.* [O.E. *crisp, crips,* < L. *crispus,* curled, crisp.] Easily broken or crumbled; brittle; possessing a certain degree of firmness and freshness; fresh; brisk, effervescing or foaming; sparkling; curling in small stiff or firm curls.—*v.t.* To curl; to contract or form into ringlets; to wrinkle or curl into little undulations; to ripple.—*v.i.* To form little curls or undulations; to curl.—*n. Brit.* potato chip.—**crisp·ly,** *adv.* In a crisp manner.— **crisp·ness,** *n.* State of being crisp. Also **crisp·i·ness.**—**crisp·y,** *a.* Curled; formed into ringlets; brittle; dried so as to break short.

cris·pate, kris′pāt, *a.* [L. *crispatus,* pp. of *crispare,* curl, wave, < *crispus,* E. *crisp.*] Crisped, or curled. Also **cris·pat·ed.**— **cris·pa·tion,** kri·spā′shan, *n.* The act of crisping or curling, or the state of being crisped; a slight contraction; a minute undulation.

crisp·er, kris′per, *n.* One who or that which crisps or curls; an instrument for crisping cloth; the storage compartment of a refrigerator especially adapted for preserving the freshness of vegetables.

criss·cross, kris′krạs, kris′kros″, *n.* [For *christ-cross.*] A cross-shaped mark of one who cannot write; a crossing or intersection; a children's game, tick-tack-toe.—*a.* Crossed; crossing; marked by crossings.— *adv.* In a crisscross manner; crosswise.—*v.t., v.i.* To mark with or form crossing lines.

cris·tate, kris′tāt, *a.* [L. *cristatus,* < *crista,* a crest.] Crested; tufted. Also **cris·tat·ed,** kris′tā·tid.

cri·te·ri·on, krī·tēr′ē·on, *n. pl.* **cri·te·ri·a, cri·te·ri·ons,** krī·tēr′ē·ạ. [Gr. *kriterion,* < root of *krinō,* to judge.] A standard of judging; any established law, rule, principle, or fact by which a correct judgment may be formed.

crit·ic, krit′ik, *n.* [L. *criticus,* Gr. *kritikos,* < *kritēs,* a judge, < *krinō,* to judge.] A person skilled in judging the merit of anything by certain standards or criteria; a judge of merit or excellence in the fine arts; a writer whose chief function it is to pass judgment on matters of literature and art; a reviewer; one who judges with severity; one who censures or finds fault.

crit·i·cal, krit′i·kal, *a.* Relating to criticism; belonging to the art of a critic; passing judgment upon literary and artistic matters; inclined to make nice distinctions; exact; fastidious; inclined to find fault or to judge with severity; pertaining to the crisis or turning point of a disease; pertaining to any crisis; decisive; important, as regards consequences; momentous; attended with danger or risk; dangerous; hazardous.—**crit·i·cal·ly**, *adv.* In a critical manner; with nice discernment or scrutiny; at the exact time; in a critical situation, place, or condition.—**crit·i·cal·ness**, *n.*

crit·i·cal an·gle, *n. Opt.* the angle of incidence of a ray passing from one medium into a less refracting medium, when it emerges along the bounding surface.

crit·i·cal point, *n. Aeron.* a point in flight at which it is equally quick to proceed to the destination or to return to the point of departure.

crit·i·cal tem·per·a·ture, *n. Physics*, that temperature of a gas above which no pressure, however great, can liquefy it.

crit·i·cism, krit′i·siz″um, *n.* The art of judging with propriety the beauties and faults of a literary performance or of any production in the fine arts; the art of judging the merit of any performance; a critical judgment; a detailed critical examination of the history, origin, and the like of literary texts; a critique.

crit·i·cize, *Brit.* **crit·i·cise**, krit′i·siz″, *v.i.* —criticized, criticizing, *Brit.* criticised, criticising. To judge critically, estimating beauties and defects; to pick out faults; to utter censure.—*v.t.* To examine or judge critically; to pass judgment on with respect to merit or blame.—**crit·i·ciz·a·ble**, *a.*

cri·tique, kri·tēk′, *n.* [Fr.] A written estimate of the merits of a performance, especially of a literary or artistic performance; a criticism.

crit·ter, krit′ėr, *n. U.S. Dial.* Creature; domestic animal.

croak, krōk, *v.i.* [Purely imitative, like M.H.G. krochzen, G. krächzen, Fr. croasser, L. crocire, crocitare, Gr. krōzein, to croak.] To make a low, hoarse noise in the throat, as a frog, a raven, or crow; to speak with a low, hollow voice; to forebode evil; to complain; to grumble; *slang*, to die.—*v.t.* To utter in a low hollow voice; to murmur out; to announce or herald by croaking; *slang*, to kill.—*n.* The low, harsh sound uttered by a frog or a raven, or a like sound.—**croak·y**, krō′kē, *a.*—*croakier, croakiest.*

croak·er, krō′kėr, *n.* Someone or something which croaks; a fish that makes croaking or grunting noises; a habitual complainer or grumbler.

Cro·a·tian, krō·ā′shan, krō·ā′shē·an, *a.* Pertaining to Croatia, an area east of the Adriatic Sea, and its people and their Slavic dialect. Also **Cro·at**, krō′at.

cro·chet, krō·shā′, *Brit.* krō′shā, krō′shē, *n.* [Fr. crochet, O.Fr. crochet, croquet, hook, implement, dim. of croc, hook.] A kind of knitting done with a needle having at one end a small hook for drawing the thread or yarn into place; the work or fabric made.—*v.t., v.i.*—crocheted, crocheting. To knit by crochet.—**cro·chet·er**, *n.*

crock, krok, *n.* [O.E. crocca—D. kruik, Icel. krukka, Dan. krukke, G. krug, an earthen vessel, pitcher.] An earthen vessel; *Brit. dial.* a pot or pitcher. The soot or smut from pots and kettles.—*v.t. Brit. dial.* to injure or disable. To soil with smut.—*v.i. Brit. dial.* to become ill. Of cloth, to give off color or crock when rubbed.—**crock·er·y**, krok′e·rē, *n.* Earthenware; vessels formed of clay, glazed and baked.

crock·et, krok′it, *n.* [Akin to crochet or to crook.] An architectural ornament, usually in imitation of curved and bent foliage,

placed on the angles of the inclined sides of pinnacles, canopies, and gables.

croc·o·dile, krok′o·dīl″, *n.* [L. crocodilus, < Gr. krokodeilos.] Any of the large, thick-skinned, lizard-like reptiles which constitute the genus Crocodylus, order Crocodilia, inhabiting the waters of tropical Africa, Asia, Australia, and America, esp. C. niloticus of the Nile; in a wider sense, any animal of the order Crocodilia, including the alligators of America and the gavial of India; the skin of these reptiles tanned for use in luggage, shoes, handbags, and wallets; *fig.* one who sheds crocodile tears or makes a hypocritical show of sorrow.—**croc·o·dil·i·an**, krok″o·dil′ē·an, *a.* Of or pertaining to the crocodile; *specif.* pertaining to the crocodilians, order Crocodilia; hypocritical.—*n.*

croc·o·dile bird, *n.* An African plover, Pulvianus aegyptius, which often perches upon crocodiles and feeds on their insect parasites.

cro·cus, krō′kus, *n.* pl. **cro·cus·es.** [L. < Gr. krokos, crocus, saffron.] Any of the small bulbous plants constituting the iridaceous genus Crocus, much cultivated for their showy, solitary flowers, which commonly appear before the leaves in early spring, though some species, as C. sativus, the source of saffron, blossom in autumn; formerly, any of several metallic oxides resembling saffron; now, a polishing powder consisting of iron oxide.

croft, kraft, kroft, *n.* [O.E. CROFT.] *Brit.* A small piece of enclosed ground for tillage or pasture; a very small agricultural holding, as one worked by a Scottish crofter.—**croft·er**, *n. Brit.* One who cultivates a croft; one who rents and tills a croft in parts of Scotland.—**croft·ing**, *n.* The tenancy of crofts; the holding of a crofter.

crois·sant, *Fr.* kʀwä·säɴ′, *n.* A crescent-shaped roll of bread dough originated in France.

Croix de Guerre, kʀwäd·e·geʀ′, *n.* A military decoration awarded by France for distinguished gallantry in action.

Cro-Mag·non, krō·mag′non, krō·mag′non, krō·man′yon, *Fr.* kʀō·mä·naɴ′, *a.* [Cro-Magnon, a cave near Les Eyzies, France.] Pertaining to a group of tall, erect, prehistoric people who lived in southwestern Europe and used bone and stone implements.—*n.* One of this group.

crom·lech, krom′lek, *n.* [W. cromlech—crom, bent, concave, and llech, a flat stone.] An ancient structure consisting of two or more large unhewn stones fixed upright in the ground supporting a large flat stone in a horizontal position, probably a sepulchral monument; a dolmen.

crone, krōn, *n.* [Formerly crony, < D. karonje, a hussy, a slut, lit. a carrion. CARRION.] A contemptuous term for an old woman.

cro·ny, krō′nē, *n.* pl. **cro·nies.** An intimate companion; an associate; a familiar friend.

crook, kruk, *n.* [M.E.: cf. Icel. krōkr, crook, hook.] A bent or curved implement, piece, or appendage; a hook; the hooked part of anything; an instrument or implement having a bent or curved part, as a shepherd's staff or as the crozier of a bishop or abbot; the act of crooking or bending; a bending, turn, or curve; *colloq.* a dishonest person, esp. a sharper, swindler, or thief.—*v.t.* To cause to assume an angular or curved form; bend; curve; make a crook in; *colloq.* to cheat or steal.—*v.i.* To bend.

crook·ed, kruk′id, *a.* Bent; not straight; curved; deformed; not straightforward or honest; dishonest; fraudulent.—**crook·ed·ly** *adv.*—**crook·ed·ness**, *n.*

crook·ed knife, *n. Canada*, a knife with a hooked blade used esp. by Indians in making canoes and snowshoe frames.

Crookes tube, kruks tōb, *n.* [From

Sir W. Crookes (1832–1919), English scientist.] A form of vacuum tube used to demonstrate cathode ray properties.

crook·neck, kruk′nek″, *n.* A variety of squash with a long, recurved neck.

croon, krōn, *v.i.* [Cf. M.H.G. kronen, murmur, grumble, M.D. kronen, D. kreunen, groan.] To utter a low murmuring sound; sing softly and monotonously. Sc., North Eng. to bellow or roar.—*v.t.* To sing in a low murmuring tone.—*n.* The act or sound of crooning.

crop, krop, *n.* [O.E. crop, cropp, = D. krop = G. kropf: cf. croup and group. Some E. senses are from crop, v.] The cultivated produce of the ground, as grain or fruit, while growing or when gathered; the yield of such produce for a particular season; the yield of some other product in a season; a supply produced; the stock or handle of a whip; a short riding whip with a loop instead of a lash; an entire tanned hide of an animal; the act of cropping; a cutting off, as of the hair; a style of wearing the hair cut short, or a head of hair so cut; a mark produced by clipping the ears, as of an animal; *geol.* an outcrop of a vein or seam. A special pouchlike enlargement of the gullet of many birds, in which the food undergoes partial preparation for digestion, or a similar organ in other animals; the craw.

crop, krop, *v.t.*—cropped, cropping. To cut off or remove (the head or top) of a plant; to cut off the ends of a part of; cut short; clip (the ears or hair of); to cut closely (the margins of a book); to remove by or as by cutting; to cause to bear a crop or crops.—*v.i.* To bear or yield a crop or crops; to come to the surface of the ground, as a vein of ore, usually with *up* or *out*; *fig.* to appear incidentally or unexpectedly, usually with *up* or *out*.

crop-eared, krop′ērd″, *a.* Having the ears cropped for identification; as, a crop-eared horse. *Brit. hist.* having the hair cropped short, so that the ears are conspicuous; a punishment applied to English Puritans and Roundheads.

crop·per, krop′ėr, *n.* One who or that which crops; one who raises a crop, esp. on shares; a plant which furnishes a crop; a cloth-shearing machine.—**come a crop·per**, to fall heavily, as from a horse, or to undergo a disastrous failure or collapse.

cro·quet, krō·kā′, *Brit.* krō′kā, krō′kē, *n.* [Appar. a var. of Fr. crochet, hook, hooked implement: O.Fr. croquet.] A lawn game played by knocking wooden balls through a set of wickets by means of mallets; in this game, the act of driving away an opponent's ball by striking one's own when the two are in contact.—*v.t.*—croqueted, croqueting. To drive away (a ball) by a croquet.

cro·quette, krō·ket′, *n.* [Fr. < croquer, crunch.] A mixture of minced meat or fish, combined with rice, potato, or other material shaped into a cylindrical or conical form, coated with bread crumbs, and fried in deep fat.

cro·qui·gnole, krō′ki·nōl″, krō′kin·yōl″, *n.* A special hair fashion in which the hair is wound toward the head on curlers, forming a circular style.

cro·quis, kʀa·kē′, *E.* krō·kē′, *n.* pl. **cro·quis.** *Fr.* a rough sketch.

cro·sier, krō′zhėr, *n.* [Cf. O.Fr. crosser (M.L. crociarius), bearer of a crozier or pastoral staff, < croce (M.L. crocia), crozier.] The pastrol staff of a bishop or an abbot, hooked at one end like a shepherd's staff; *bot.* the circinate young frond of a fern. Also **cro·zier.**

cross, kras, kros, *n.* [Prov. cros, Fr. croix, < L. crux, crucis, a cross used as a gibbet, from same root as that of W. crog, a cross, crwg, a hook; Ir. crohaim, to hang; Gael. crocan, a hook.] An instrument on which malefactors were formerly put to death, consisting of two pieces of timber placed across each other, either in form of +, T, or ×, variously modified; (cap.) that on which Christ suffered. The symbol of the Christian religion; fig. the religion itself. An ornament in the form of a cross; a monument with a cross upon it to excite devotion, such as were formerly set in marketplaces; any figure, mark, or sign in the form of a cross, or formed by two lines crossing each other, such as the mark made instead of a signature by those who cannot write; anything that thwarts, obstructs, or perplexes; hindrance, vexation, misfortune, or opposition; a mixing of breeds; a hybrid.—a. Transverse; passing from side to side; falling athwart. Adverse; thwarting; untoward. Snappish; perverse; intractable; peevish; fretful; ill-humored; contrary. Contradictory; perplexing; made or produced by the opposite party; as, a cross question.

cross, krạs, kros, v.t. To draw or run (a line) across; cancel by marking crosses on or over; to make the sign of the cross upon; to pass from side to side of; to pass or move over; to thwart, obstruct, hinder, embarrass; to contradict; to counteract; to clash with; to be inconsistent with; to cause to interbreed; to mix the breed of.—v.i. To lie or be athwart; to move or pass across.—adv. Not parallel; crosswise.—**cross one's path,** to come upon unexpectedly.—**crossed check,** n. Brit. a check crossed with two lines, between which may be written the name of a banking firm or the words "and Co.", such marks being made as an additional security that the sum shall be paid to the proper party.—**cross·ing,** n. The act of one who crosses; an intersection; a place specially set apart or adapted for passing across, as on a street or line of rails. —**cross·ly,** adv. In a cross manner; athwart; transversely; unfortunately; peevishly; fretfully.

cross·bar, krạs′bär″, kros′bär″, n. A transverse bar, line, or stripe; a horizontal bar used for exercises in a gymnasium.

cross·bill, krạs′bil″, kros′bil″, n. One of several species of birds belonging to the finch family, the mandibles of whose bill curve opposite ways and cross each other above the points.

cross·bones, krạs′bōnz″, kros′bōnz″, n. pl. A symbol of death, consisting of two human thigh or arm bones placed crosswise, generally in conjunction with a skull; the design of the flag of pirate ships.

cross·bow, krạs′bō″, kros′bō″, n. A medieval weapon formed by placing a bow transversely on a stock from which stones or arrows were released.

cross·bred, krạs′bred″, kros′bred″, a. Applied to an animal produced from a male and female of different breeds.

cross·breed, krạs′brēd″, kros′brēd″, v.t., v.i. —n. A breed produced from parents of different breeds.—**cross·breed·ing,** n. The system of breeding animals, such as horses, cattle, dogs, and sheep, from individuals of two different strains or varieties.

cross bun, n. Brit. hot cross bun.

cross-check, krạs′chek″, kros′chek″, v.i. To check again, or against other authorities; hockey, to make an illegal move to counter an opponent.—v.t.

cross-coun·try, krạs′kun″trē, kros′kun″trē, a. Directed across fields or open country; not following the roads or the great highways.—krạs″kun′trē, kros″kun′trē, n. Any of the cross-country sports.

cross·cur·rent, krạs′kẻr″ent, krạs′kur″ent, kros′kẻr″ent, kros′kur″ent, n. A current of air or water moving across a main stream; a conflict of feeling or opinion.

cross·cut, krạs′kut″, kros′kut″, n. A cross section; a short cut; something that cuts

across; a cutting that crosses the lode in mining.—a. Made or used for the purpose of cutting across.—v.t.—crosscut, crosscutting. To cut across; to intersect.—**cross--cut saw,** n. A saw adapted for cutting timber across the grain.

crosse, krạs, kros, n. [Fr. crosse, O.Fr. croce, stick with curved end, crozier, akin to croc, hook.] A kind of long-handled racket used in the game of lacrosse.

cross·ex·am·ine, krạs′ig·zam′in, kros′ig--zam′in, v.t.—cross-examined, cross-examining. Law, to examine (a witness) anew, to test the validity of previous testimony.—**cross-ex·am·in·a·tion,** n. Law, the examination or interrogation of a witness called by one party by the opposing party or his counsel.

cross-eye, krạs′ī″, kros′ī″, n. Strabismus.

cross-fer·ti·li·za·tion, krạs′fẻr″ti·li·zā′shan, kros′fẻr″ti·li·zā′shan, n. Bot. the fertilization of the ovules of one plant by the pollen of another; the fecundation of a pistillate plant by a staminiferous one, by the agency of insects, or the action of wind and water. Biol. the fertilization of an organism by the fusion of male and female gametes from separate individuals of the same species.—cross-fer·ti·lize, v.t.—**cross-fer·ti·liz·a·ble, cross-fer·tile,** a.

cross-file, krạs′fil, kros′fil, v.i.—cross-filed, cross-filing. Politics, to file one's candidacy for more than one political party in a primary election.

cross fire, n. Milit. a term used to denote that the lines of fire from two or more positions cross one another; a sharp exchange of words.

cross-grained, krạs′grānd″, kros′grānd″, a. Having the grain or fibers transverse or irregular, as timber; perverse; intractable.

cross hair, n. A very fine strand of quartz fiber or other material, or a line ruled on glass, forming a cross with another strand or line, and employed in a telescope, microscope, or the like, to define a line of sight.

cross·hatch, krạs′hach″, kros′hach″, v.t. To hatch or shade with two series of parallel lines crossing each other.—n.—**cross--hatch·er,** n.—**cross-hatch·ing,** n.

cross·head, krạs′hed″, kros′hed″, n. Mach. a beam or rod stretching across the end of the piston of a reciprocating engine and moving between parallel guides; print. a heading stretching across a full column or between sections of text.

cross-link, krạs′lingk″, kros′lingk″, n. Chem. a connecting unit, analogous to the rung of a ladder, such as a chemically bonded atom or group of atoms, which links chains of atoms in a protein, plastic, or other complex molecule.—v.t. To couple by cross-links.—v.i. To make cross-links.

Cross of Lor·raine, n. A type of cross with two crossarms of different length, the upper shorter than the lower.

cross·patch, krạs′pach″, kros′pach″, n. Colloq. an ill-humored person.

cross·piece, krạs′pēs″, kros′pēs″, n. A piece of any material placed across something; a transverse piece.

cross·pol·li·na·tion, krạs′pol″i·nā′shan, kros′pol″i·nā′shan, n. Bot. cross-fertilization.—**cross-pol·li·nate,** v.t.

cross-pur·pose, n. A contrary purpose; a misunderstanding; an inconsistency.

cross-ques·tion, krạs′kwes′chan, kros′-kwes′chan, v.t. To cross-examine.

cross ref·er·ence, n. A reference from one part of a book, list, or card file to another where additional information on the subject is to be had.—**cross-re·fer,** krạs″ri·fur′, kros″ri·fur′, v.t., v.i.—cross-referred, cross-referring.

cross·road, krạs′rōd″, kros′rōd″, n. A road that crosses another. Pl. the place where one road intersects another; the

point at which a fateful decision must be made.

cross·ruff, krạs′ruf″, kros′ruf″, n. Bridge, whist, a series of successive tricks in which each of two partners trumps the other's lead.—v.t., v.i.

cross sec·tion, n. The cutting of any body at right angles to its length, often used to examine the area of the surface thus exposed; a sample showing all aspects.

cross-ster·ile, krạs′ster′il, kros′ster′il, a. Having the quality of being mutually incapable of reproducing when cross-fertilization is attempted, used in referring to two species, or individual organisms of plants.—**cross-ste·ril·i·ty,** n.

cross-stitch, krạs′stich″, kros′stich″, n. A kind of stitching employing pairs of diagonal stitches of the same length crossing each other in the middle at right angles.

cross street, n. A street crossing another street, or one running transversely to main streets.

cross talk, n. The mixed sounds heard in radio or telephone transmission due to interference from another electronic transmitter.

cross·tie, krạs′ti″, kros′ti″, n. A tie placed transversely to form a foundation or support, as under a railroad track.

cross·walk, krạs′wạk″, kros′wạk″, n. A specially marked pedestrian lane, as across a street or highway.

cross·wise, krạs′wiz″, kros′wiz″, a., adv. In the form of a cross; across. Also **cross·-ways.**

cross·word puz·zle, krạs′wurd″ puz′el, kros′wurd″ puz′el, n. A puzzle in which words corresponding to given meanings are to be supplied and fitted into a particular figure divided into spaces, the letters being arranged both horizontally and vertically.

crotch, kroch, n. [Same as CRUTCH.] A fork or forking; the parting of two branches; the part of the human body where the legs are joined; the part of a pair of trousers where the two legs meet.

crotch·et, kroch′it, n. [Fr. crochet, dim. < croc, a hook.] A peculiar turn of the mind; a whim or fancy; a perverse conceit; print. a bracket; surg. an instrument with a sharp hook. Any unusual or odd device; mus. a black-faced note with a stem.—**crotch·et·y,** kroch′i·tē, a. Full of crotchets; whimsical; grouchy; odd.—**crotch·et·i·ness,** n.

cro·ton, krōt′on, n. [N.L. < Gr. kroton, a tick, also a plant having tick-like seeds.] Any of the chiefly tropical plants constituting the genus Croton; among florists, any plant of the related genus Phyllaurea or Codiaeum, cultivated for the ornamental foliage.

crouch, krouch, v.i. [A softened form of crook, with modification of meaning.] To bend or stoop low with limbs hugging the body; to lie close to the ground, as an animal; to bend servilely, or cringe.—v.t. To bend, esp. in humility or fear.

croup, krōp, n. [Sc. croup, roup, hoarseness; allied to Goth. hropjan, to croak, to call; O.E. hreópan, to call.] An inflammation of the respiratory passages characterized by highly labored breathing and a hoarse, rasping cough.—**croup·y,** adj.—croupier, croupiest.

croup, krōp, n. [Fr. croupe, the rump, croup.] The highest part of the hind quarters or rump of a four-legged animal, esp. a horse; the area of an animal's rump behind the loin.

crou·pi·er, krō′pē·ẻr, krō′pē·ā″, Fr. krō··pyā′, n. [Fr. croupier, < croupe, the rump or hinder part.] An employee of a gambling establishment who supervises a gaming table, accepting bets and paying off wagers; one who, at a public dinner party, sits at the lower end of the table as assistant chairman.

crous·tade, krō·städ′, *n.* [Fr.] A thin, crisp shell, either fried or baked, which is served with a filling of meat, fish, or other foods.

crou·ton, krō′ton, krō·ton′, *n.* [Fr. *croûte*: see *crust*.] A small piece of fried or toasted bread used as a garnish for salads and soups.

crow, krō, *n.* [O.E. *crāwe* = D. *kraai* = G. *krähe*; < the Teut. verb represented by E. *crow*.] Any of the oscine birds constituting the genus *Corvus*, family *Corvidae*, with lustrous black plumage and a characteristic harsh cry or caw; any of various similar birds of other families; an iron bar with a slightly bent or beaked end, used as a lever; a crowbar; (*cap.*) *astron.* the southern constellation Corvus. (*Cap.*) a member of a tribe of Siouan Indians of eastern Montana; the language of this people.—**as the crow flies,** utilizing the most direct route, usually a straight line.

crow, krō, *n.* The cry of a rooster or cock; an exultant or exuberant human cry.—*v.i.* To make the shrill cry of a cock; to utter noises indicative of pleasure; to exult or gloat; to boast.

crow·bar, krō′bär″, *n.* A bar of iron or steel with a bent and sometimes forked end, used as a lever.

crow·boot, krō′bōt″, *n. Canada,* a boot usually made of muskrat fur with a moose-hide sole.

crowd, kroud, *n.* [O.E. *crūdan,* to press; O.D. *cruden,* to press, to push; L.G. *krūden,* to oppress.] A number of persons or things collected or closely pressed together; an audience; a number of persons congregated without order; a throng; the lower orders of people; the populace; the mob.

crowd, kroud, *v.i.* [O.E. *crūdan* = M.D. *kruyden* (D. *kruien*).] To press forward; advance by pushing; to congregate in numbers; throng; swarm.—*v.t.* To push or shove; press closely together; compress; force into a confined space; to fill full or to excess; fill by crowding or pressing into; to beset, encumber, or incommode, as with excess of numbers; *colloq.* to urge, press by solicitation, or annoy by urging.—**crowd sail,** *naut.* to set all the sail a ship can possibly stand.

crown, kroun, *n.* [A.Fr. *coroune,* O.Fr. *curune, corone* (Fr. *couronne*), < L. *corona,* garland, wreath, crown.] An ornamental fillet for the head, as the wreath or garland conferred by the ancients as a mark of victory or distinction; hence, honorary distinction or reward; specif. a decorative fillet or covering for the head, worn as a symbol of sovereignty; the power or dominion of a sovereign; (*cap.*) with *the,* the sovereign as head of the state, or the supreme governing power of a state under a monarchical government; (*l.c.*) an exalting or chief attribute. Any of various coins, orig. one bearing the representation of a crown or a crowned head; formerly a British silver coin of the value of 5 shillings; sometimes, a krone or a krona. Something having the form of a crown, as the corona of a flower; the top or highest part of anything, as of the head, a hat, a mountain; the head itself; the part of a cut gem above the girdle; that part of a tooth which appears beyond the gum; an artificial substitute, as of gold or porcelain, for the crown of a tooth; the grinding surface of a tooth; the leaves and living branches of a tree; the highest or most perfect state of anything; crown glass.—*a.* Of or pertaining to a crown or the Crown; of or pertaining to the sovereign or his authority.

crown, kroun, *v.t.* To place a crown or garland upon the head of; specif. to invest with a regal crown, or with regal dignity and power; to honor as with a crown; reward; invest with honor and dignity; to

surmount as with a crown; surmount as a crown does; to complete worthily, or bring to a successful or effective conclusion; *dentistry,* to cover the top of a tooth with a false crown; *colloq.* to hit on the head.

crown ant·ler, *n.* A topmost branch or antler of a stag's horn.

crown col·o·ny, *n.* A British colony over which the crown has some control of legislation and administration, as distinguished from one having a constitution and representative government.

crown·er, krou′nẽr, krō′nẽr, *n. Brit. dial.* coroner.

crown glass, *n.* A glass containing silicon, potassium or sodium, and calcium but no lead, blown and whirled into sheets, formerly used for windows; an alkali-lime silicate optical glass of low refraction.

crown land, *n.* [< G. *kronland.*] Land belonging to the crown, the revenue of which goes to the reigning sovereign.

crown lens, *n. Opt.* the convex, crown glass constituent of an achromatic lens.

crown prince, *n.* [< G. *kronprinz.*] The heir apparent of a monarch.—**crown prin·cess,** *n.* [< G. *kronprinzessin.*] The wife of a crown prince; a female heir apparent.

crow's-foot, krōz′fụt″, *n. pl.* **crow's-feet.** *Usu. pl.* a wrinkle at the outer corner of the eye. A caltrop, as for obstructing the passage of cavalry; *tailoring,* a three-pointed embroidered figure used as a finish, as at the end of a seam or opening.

crow's-nest, krōz′nest″, *n. Naut.* a box or shelter for the lookout man, secured near the top of a mast.

croze, krōz, *n.* [Origin uncertain.] The groove at the ends of the staves of a barrel or cask into which the edge of the head fits; a tool for cutting such a groove.

cro·zier, krō′zhẽr, *n.* Crosier.

cru·cial, krō′shal, *a.* [Fr. *crucial,* < L. *crux* (*cruc-*), E. *cross.*] Critical; decisive, as between two hypotheses; of the form of a cross; cross-shaped.—**cru·cial·ly,** *adv.*

cru·ci·ate, krō′shē·it, krō′shē·āt″, *a.* [N.L. *cruciatus,* < L. *crux* (*cruc-*), E. *cross.*] Of the form of a cross; cross-shaped.—**cru·ci·ate·ly,** *adv.*

cru·ci·ble, krō′si·bl, *n.* [M.L. *crucibulum,* night-lamp, melting-pot; origin uncertain.] A vessel of clay, porcelain, graphite, platinum, or the like, in which metals can be melted or heated; in a metallurgical furnace, the hollow part at the bottom, in which molten metal collects; a severe test.—**cru·ci·ble steel,** steel made in a crucible, esp. a high-grade steel prepared by melting together selected materials.

cru·ci·fer, krō′si·fẽr, *n.* [L.L. *crucifer,* < L. *crux* (*cruc-*), cross, and *ferre,* bear.] A cross-bearer, as in ecclesiastical processions; *bot.* a cruciferous plant.—**cru·cif·er·ous,** krō·sif′ẽr·us, *a.* Bearing a cross; *bot.* belonging or pertaining to the family *Cruciferae* or *Brassicaceae,* whose members bear flowers having a cross-like, four-petaled corolla.

cru·ci·fix, krō′si·fiks, *n.* [L. *crucifixus,* pp. of *crucifigere,* earlier *cruci figere,* "fix to a cross."] An image of Jesus Christ crucified on the cross; the cross as a symbol of Christianity.

cru·ci·fix·ion, krō′si·fik′shan, *n.* [L.L. *crucifixio(n-),* < L. *crucifigere.*] The act of crucifying; (*cap.*) the putting to death of Christ upon the cross. A picture or representation of this; severe persecution, pain, or suffering.

cru·ci·form, krō′si·fạrm, *a.* Cross-shaped.

cru·ci·fy, krō′si·fī″, *v.t.*—*crucified, crucifying.* [O.Fr. Fr. *crucifier,* L.L. *crucificare,* for L. *crucifigere.* CRUCIFIX.] To put to death by nailing or otherwise affixing to a cross; excruciate or torment; treat with grievous severity.—**cru·ci·fi·er,** *n.*

crude, krōd, *a.*—*cruder, crudest.* [L. *crudus,* raw, crude, rough. CRUEL.] Being in a raw or unprepared state, as manufacturing materials; underdeveloped or imperfect, as ideas or opinions; lacking finish or polish, as literary or artistic work; lacking in culture, refinement, tact, or the like, as persons or their behavior or speech.—**crude·ly,** *adv.*—**crude·ness,** *n.*—**cru·di·ty,** krō′di·tē, *n. pl.* **cru·di·ties.** The state or quality of being crude; anything crude.

crude oil, *n.* Petroleum in an unrefined state.

cru·el, krō′el, *a.* [Fr. *cruel,* < L. *crudelis,* cruel.] Disposed to give pain to others in body or mind; destitute of pity, compassion, or kindness: applied to persons; exhibiting or proceeding from cruelty; causing pain, grief, or distress; inhuman; tormenting, vexing.—**cru·el·ly,** *adv.*—**cru·el·ness,** *n.* —**cru·el·ty,** krō′el·tē, *n.* [O.Fr. *cruelté,* L. *crudelitas.*] The state or character of being cruel; savage or barbarous disposition; any cruel or unjust act.

cru·et, krō′it, *n.* [M.E. *cruette,* appar. dim. < O.Fr. *crue, cruie,* pitcher, pot, < Teut., and akin to Fr. *cruche,* pitcher, and E. *crock.*] A glass bottle, esp. one for holding vinegar or oil for the table.

cruise, krōz, *v.i.*—*cruised, cruising.* [D. *kruisen,* cross, cruise, < *kruis,* = E. *cross, n.*] To sail to and fro, or from place to place, as in search of hostile ships, or for pleasure; to move around without a special reason or destination but available for duty or service, as police cars, or taxis; to operate, as an airplane, at less than maximum speed.—*v.t.* To cruise over; *forestry,* to survey (wooded land) in order to estimate the amount and value of the timber.—*n.* An act of cruising; a voyage made by cruising.

cruis·er, krō′zẽr, *n.* One who or that which cruises, as a person or a ship; an armed vessel or warship of fair or superior speed, used to protect a nation's commerce, give battle to an enemy's ships, or perform other duties; one of a class of warships just below the armored cruiser class; a squad car used for police patrol.—**ar·mored cruis·er,** one of a class of warships below the battleship class, having less armor and armament and greater speed than a battleship.—**bat·tle cruis·er,** a fast armored warship of a class between battleships and armored cruisers.—**pro·tec·ted cruis·er,** a cruiser having an armored deck but no vertical side armor.

crul·ler, krul′ẽr, *n.* [Prob. of Dutch origin: cf. D. *krullen,* curl.] A light, sweet cake cut in circular form from a rolled dough and fried in deep fat. Also **krul·ler.**

crumb, krum, *n.* [O.E. *cruma* = D. *kruim* = G. *krume.*] A small particle of bread or cake that breaks or falls off; the soft inside part of bread; a small particle or portion of anything; *slang,* a useless or despicable person.—*v.t.* To break into crumbs or small fragments; *cookery,* to dress or prepare with breadcrumbs.

crum·ble, krum′bl, *v.t.*—*crumbled, crumbling.* [For earlier *crimble,* < O.E. *cruma,* E. *crumb.*] To break into crumbs; reduce to small fragments.—*v.i.* To fall into small particles; become disintegrated; all to decay.—*n. Dial.* a small or tiny crumb or fragment. Something crumbling or crumbled.—**crum·bly,** *a.*—*crumblier, crumbliest.* Likely to crumble.—**crum·bli·ness,** *n.*—**crum·blings,** *n. pl.*

crump, krump, krụmp, *v.t.* [Imit.] To crunch with the teeth.—*v.i.* To make a crunching sound, as in walking over snow, or as snow when trodden on; to make a loud, crashing sound, as a cannon or a bursting shell.—*n.* A crunching sound; *Brit.* a heavy blow. A loud, crashing sound, as of a bursting shell; a soldier's term for a large explosive shell.

crum·pet, krum′pit, n. [Origin uncertain.] *Chiefly Brit.* a kind of light, soft cake resembling a muffin, cooked on a griddle or the like, and often toasted for eating; *slang,* an attractive girl or woman.

crum·ple, krum′pel, v.t.—*crumpled, crumpling.* [M.E. (first in *crumpled,* pp.), freq. < O.E. *crump, crumb,* crooked.] To make crooked; bend together; contort; bend spirally; to crush into irregular creases or folds; rumple; to ripple.—v.i. To become crumpled; contract into folds or wrinkles; shrivel.—n. An irregular fold or wrinkle produced by crumpling.—**crum·pler,** n.—**crum·ply,** a. Full of crumples or wrinkles.

crunch, krunch, v.t. [Var. of *craunch.*] To crush with the teeth; chew with a crushing noise; to crush or grind noisily.—v.i. To chew with a crushing sound; to produce, or proceed with, a crushing noise.—n. The act or sound of crunching.—**crunch·y,** krun′chē, a.—*crunchier, crunchiest.*

cru·node, krö′nŏd, n. [Irreg. < *crux,* cross, and *nodus,* E. *node.*] *Geom.* a point at which a curve crosses itself.

crup·per, krup′ér, krŭp′ér, n. [O.Fr. *crupiere* (Fr. *croupière*), < *crupe*: see *croup.*] A leather strap attached to the back of the saddle of a harness, and passing in a loop under a horse's tail, for preventing the saddle from slipping forward; the rump or buttocks of a horse.

cru·ral, krŭr′al, a. [L. *cruralis,* < *crus,* leg.] Pertaining to the leg or the hind limb; of or pertaining to the leg proper, or crus.

crus, krus, krŏs, n. pl. **cru·ra,** krŭr′a. [L. leg.] *Anat.* & *zool.* that part of the leg or hind limb between the femur or thigh and the ankle or tarsus; the shank; any of various parts likened to a leg, as one of a pair of supporting parts.

cru·sade, krö·sād′, n. [Fr. *croisade* (also Sp. *cruzada*), < *croiser* (Sp. *cruzar*), mark with a cross, < L. *crux,* cross.] (Often *cap.*) any of the military expeditions undertaken by the Christians of Europe in the 11th, 12th, and 13th centuries for the recovery of the Holy Land from the Mohammedans. Any war carried on under papal sanction; in general, any aggressive movement for the defense or advancement of an idea or cause, or against a public evil.—v.i. —*crusaded, crusading.* To go on or engage in a crusade.—**cru·sad·er,** n. One who engages in a crusade; (*often cap.*) one of those who took part in the Crusades of the Middle Ages.

cruse, kröz, krŏs, n. [M.E. *cruse, cruce*: cf. Icel. *krūs,* pot, tankard, D. *kroes,* cup, pot.] An earthen pot or bottle, or any small vessel for liquids.

crush, krush, v.t. [Appar. < O.Fr. *croissir, crash, gnash, break,* crush, prob. < Teut.] To press and bruise, as between two hard bodies; squeeze or batter out of shape or normal condition; crumple, as by rough handling; to press or squeeze forcibly or violently; to put down, overpower, or subdue completely; overwhelm; to oppress grievously; to break into small fragments or particles, as ore or stone; to force out by pressing or squeezing.—v.i. To become crushed; to advance with crushing; press or crowd forcibly.—n. The act of crushing, or the state of being crushed, esp. the crowding together of persons or things, or the mass crowded together; a great crowd or a crowded social gathering; *colloq.* an intense infatuation, usu. short-lived.— **crush·er,** n. One who or that which crushes; a machine for crushing ore and stone.—**crush·ing,** a. Bruising; overwhelming.—**crush·ing·ly,** adv.

crust, krust, n. [O.Fr. *crouste* (Fr. *croûte*), < L. *crusta,* hard surface, rind, shell, crust.] The hard outer portion of a loaf of bread; the outside covering of a pie; any more or

less hard external covering or coating; a scab; the exterior portion of the earth, accessible to examination; the hard outer shell or covering of an animal or plant.—v.t. To cover with or as with a crust; encrust; to form a crust.—v.i. To form or contract a crust; to form into a crust.

crus·ta·cean, kru·stā′shan, a. [N.L. *Crustacea,* neut. pl. of *crustaceus,* E. *crustaceous.*] Belonging to the *Crustacea,* a class of chiefly aquatic arthropods, including the lobsters, shrimps, crabs, barnacles, and wood lice, commonly having the body covered with a hard shell or crust.—n. A crustacean animal.—**crus·ta·ce·ol·o·gy,** kru·stā′shē·ol′o·jē, n. The science or study of crustaceans.

crus·ta·ceous, kru·stā′shus, a. [N.L. *crustaceus,* < L. *crusta,* shell, E. *crust.*] Of the nature of or pertaining to a crust or shell; having a hard covering, as an animal; belonging to the *Crustacea;* crustacean.

crus·tal, krus′tal, a. Of or pertaining to a crust, as that of the earth.

crust·y, krus′tē, a.—*crustier, crustiest.* Of the nature of or resembling a crust; having a crust; surly or irascible in manner or speech.—**crust·i·ly,** adv.—**crust·i·ness,** n.

crutch, kruch, n. [O.E. *crycc* = D. *kruk* = G. *krücke*: cf. *crook.*] A staff or support to assist a lame or infirm person in walking, now usually with a crosspiece at one end to fit under the armpit; any of various devices resembling this in shape or use; a forked support or part; the crotch of the human body; the forked leg rest or pommel of a side saddle; that which is used as an expedient when needed resources are inadequate.—v.t. To support with or as with a crutch; prop or sustain.

crux, kruks, n. pl. **crux·es,** L. **cru·ces,** krö′sēz. [L., cross, torment, trouble.] A cross; a fundamental point; something that torments by its puzzling nature; a perplexing difficulty; (*cap.*) *astron.* the Southern Cross, a southern constellation having its four chief stars arranged in the form of a cross.—**crux an·sa·ta,** kruks′an·sā′ta, n. pl. **cru·ces an·sa·tae,** krö′sēz an·sā′tē. A cross in the form of *T* with a loop at the top.

cry, krī, v.i.—*cried, crying.* [O.Fr. Fr. *crier,* < L. *quiritare,* cry, shriek, lament.] To call loudly; shout; to utter inarticulate sounds, esp. of lamentation or grief; to shed tears; to give forth vocal sounds or characteristic calls, as animals; yelp, as hounds in the chase.—v.t. To utter or pronounce loudly; call out; to announce orally in public; sell by outcry; sometimes, to proclaim the marriage banns of.—**cry down,** to condemn by proclamation; to disparage; belittle.—**cry up,** to praise; extol.—**cry wolf,** to give a false alarm.—**cry·ing,** a. That cries; clamorous; wailing; weeping; demanding remedy, or notorious; as, a *crying* evil.—**cry·ing·ly,** adv.

cry, krī, n. pl. **cries,** krīz. [O.Fr. Fr. *cri.*] The act or sound of crying; any loud utterance or exclamation; a shout; a scream; a wail; an entreaty or appeal; an oral proclamation or announcement; a call of wares for sale, as by a street vender; public report; an opinion generally expressed; a battle cry; a political or party catchword; a fit of weeping; the vocal utterance or characteristic call of an animal; the yelping of hounds in the chase; hence, a pack of hounds.

cry·ba·by, krī′bā″bē, n. pl. **cry·ba·bies.** A person who cries or complains with little provocation.

cry·mo·ther·a·py, krī″mō·thèr′a·pē, n. [Gr. *krymos,* icy cold.] Cryotherapy.

cry·o·bi·ol·o·gy, krī″ō·bī·ol′o·jē, n. The study of the effects that very low temperatures have on biological systems.

cry off, v.i. *Brit.* to get out of an agreement or promise.

cry·o·gen, krī′ō·jen, n. A substance for producing low temperatures; a freezing mixture.—**cry·o·gen·ic,** krī′ō·jen′ik, a.— **cry·o·gen·ics,** n. pl., sing. in constr. That branch of physics dealing with very low temperatures, at which gases such as oxygen liquefy.

cry·o·gen·ic lake, n. *Geol.* a lake in an area of permanently frozen ground, the water being formed by local thawing.

cry·o·lite, krī′o·līt″, n. *Chem.* a fluoride of sodium and aluminum used as an electrolyte in the extraction of aluminum from its oxide. Also used in ceramics and as an insecticide.

cry·om·e·ter, krī·om′i·tėr, n. A thermometer for the measurement of low temperatures, frequently containing alcohol instead of mercury.

cry·o·phyte, krī′ō·fīt, n. *Bot.* a plant growing on ice and snow, usually an alga, but sometimes a moss, fungus, or bacterium: abundance of algae may cause the phenomenon of red snow.

cry·os·co·py, krī·os′ko·pē, n. pl. **cry·os·co·pies.** [*cryo* and *scopy.*] *Phys.* the determination of the freezing points of liquids, often performed to determine the constituents of the liquid, and the study of effects of changes in freezing point caused by addition of solutes to a solution.— **cry·o·scop·ic,** krī″o·skop′ik, a.—**cry·o·scope,** krī′a·skōp, n. *Phys.* an instrument for determining the freezing points of liquids.

cry·o·stat, krī′o·stat″, n. A thermostat for use in maintaining low temperatures.

cry·o·sur·ger·y, krī″o·sèr′jèr·ē, n. Surgery with special instruments using extreme cold to destroy or remove diseased tissue.

cry·o·ther·a·py, krī″ō·ther′a·pē, n. Treatment of disease by means of cold. Also *crymotherapy.*

crypt, kript, n. [L. *crypta,* < Gr. *krypte,* prop. fem. of *kryptos,* hidden, < *kryptein,* hide.] A subterranean chamber or vault, esp. one beneath the main floor of a church, used as a burial place. *Anat.* a follicle; a glandular cavity.—**crypt·al,** a.

crypt·a·nal·y·sis, krip″ta·nal′i·sis, n. The study and solution of secret, written codes or cyphers.

cryp·tic, krip′tik, a. [L.L. *crypticus,* < Gr. *kryptikos,* < *kryptein,* hide.] Hidden; secret; occult; indicating the use of code or cipher; *zool.* fitted for concealing. Also **cryp·ti·cal.**—**cryp·ti·cal·ly,** adv.

cryp·to, krip′tō″, n. pl. **cryp·tos.** One who is secretly a member of a party or group.

cryp·to·clas·tic, krip″to·klas′tik, a. *Geol.* composed of fragments too small to be seen by the unaided eye.

cryp·to·crys·tal·line, krip″tō·kris′ta·lin, krip″tō·kris′ta·līn″, a. Indistinctly crystalline; noting or pertaining to rocks whose crystals are so small as to be indistinguishable, even with the microscope.

cryp·to·gam, krip′to·gam″, n. [Fr. *cryptogame* = N.L. *cryptogamus,* cryptogamous, < Gr. *kryptos,* hidden, and *gamos,* marriage.] *Bot.* any of the *Cryptogamia,* an old primary division of plants comprising those without stamens and pistils, and therefore without flowers and seeds, as the ferns, mosses, and thallophytes; a plant without a true seed.—**cryp·to·gam·ic,** a. Of or pertaining to the cryptogams.—**cryp·tog·a·mous,** krip·tog′a·mus, a. Having the characters of the cryptogams.

cryp·to·gen·ic, krip″to·jen′ik, a. Being of obscure or unknown origin, as a disease.

cryp·to·gram, krip′to·gram″, n. A piece of writing in secret characters; something written in cipher.—**cryp·to·gram·mat·ic,** krip″to·gra·mat′ik, a.

cryp·to·graph, krip′to·graf″, krip′to·gräf″, n. A cryptogram; a system of secret writing;

a cipher; the form or method of writing employing secret characters.—*v.t.*—**cryp·tog·ra·phy**, krip·tog′ra·fē, *n.* The process or art of writing in secret characters, or in cipher; anything so written.—**cryp·to·graph·ic**, krip″to·graf′ik, *a.*—**cryp·tog·ra·pher**, krip·tog′ra·fêr, **cryp·tog·ra·phist**, *n.*

cryp·tol·o·gy, krip·tol′o·jē, *n.* Occult or enigmatical language; cryptography and cryptanalysis.

cryp·to·nym, krip′to·nim, *n.* A secret name.—**cryp·ton·y·mous**, krip·ton′i·mus, *a.* Having the name concealed; anonymous.

cryp·to·zo·ite, krip″to·zō′īt, *n.* A malarial parasite in that stage of its life cycle when it lives in tissue cells before proceeding to invade the blood cells.

crys·tal, kris′tal, *n.* [O.Fr. Fr. *cristal*, < L. *crystallum*, < Gr. *krystaggos*, ice, crystal, < *kryos*, icy cold, frost.] A clear, transparent mineral resembling ice, esp. the transparent or nearly transparent form of pure quartz; anything made of or resembling such a substance; glass of a high degree of brilliance; sometimes, cut glass; the glass cover over the face of a watch; *chem.*, *mineral.* a body having a specific internal structure and enclosed by symmetrically arranged plane surfaces, formed by the solidification of a substance, and consisting of a single element or a compound; *radio*, the piece of galena, carborundum, or the like forming the essential part of a crystal detector, or the detector itself.—*a.* Composed of crystal; resembling crystal; clear; transparent; *radio*, pertaining to or employing a crystal detector.—**crys·tal·lif·er·ous**, kris″ta·lif′êr·us, *a.* Bearing, containing, or yielding crystals. Also **crys·tal·lig·er·ous**, kris″ta·lij′êr·us.

crys·tal de·tec·tor, *n.* A device for rectifying the alternating currents in a radio receiving apparatus, consisting essentially of a crystal, as of galena or carborundum, which permits a current to pass freely in one direction only.

crys·tal gaz·ing, *n.* A steady staring at a crystal or glass ball or other clear object in order to arouse visual perceptions, as of distant happenings or the future; the act of making decisions or predicting the future without the necessary facts to reinforce these ideas.—**crys·tal gaz·er**, kris′tal gā″zêr, *n.*

crys·tal·line, kris′ta·lin, kris′ta·lin″, *a.* Consisting of crystal; relating or pertaining to crystals or crystallography; resembling crystal; pure; clear; transparent; pellucid.—**crys·tal·line lens**, *n. Anat.* the lens of the eye.

crys·tal·lite, kris′ta·līt″, *n.* A minute mineral body resulting from the crystallizing process and found in igneous rock.—**crys·tal·lit·ic**, kris″ta·lit′ik, *a.* Consisting of or containing crystallite.

crys·tal·lize, kris′ta·līz″, *v.t.*—*crystallized, crystallizing.* [= Fr. *crystalliser*.] To form into crystals; cause to assume crystalline form; *fig.* to give definite or concrete form to.—*v.i.* To form crystals; become crystalline in form; *fig.* to assume definite or concrete form.—**crys·tal·lized**, *a.* Formed into crystals; crystalline; candied, as ginger.—**crys·tal·liz·er**, *n.*—**crys·tal·liz·a·ble**, *a.* Capable of being crystallized.—**crys·tal·li·za·tion**, kris″ta·li·zā′shan, *n.* The act of crystallizing; the process of forming crystals; a crystallized body or formation.

crys·tal·log·ra·phy, kris″ta·log′ra·fē, *n.* The science of crystallization, teaching the principles of the process, and the forms and structure of crystals.—**crys·tal·log·ra·pher**, *n.*

crys·tal·loid, kris′ta·loid″, *a.* Resembling a crystal.—*n. Chem.* a substance, such as salt, which crystallizes, forms a true solution, and in solution form easily passes through

membranes. *Bot.* a minute, crystal-shaped mass of albuminoid matter found in the cells of certain seeds.—**crys·tal·loid·al**, *a.*

crys·tal vi·o·let, *n. Chem.* chloride used in diagnostic medicine as a stain and an acid-base indicator.

crys·tal vi·sion, *n.* Visual perception, as of distant happenings or the future, supposed to be aroused by crystal gazing; the image or images which seem to be perceived.

CST, C.S.T., *n.* Central Standard Time.

cte·noid, tē′noid, ten′oid, *a.* [Gr. *ktenoeides*.] *Zool.* comblike or pectinate, as the scales of certain fishes; having such scales.

cten·o·phore, ten′o·fōr″, ten′o·fạr″, tē′no·fōr″, tē′no·fạr″, *n.* [N.L. *Ctenophora*, pl.] Any of the free-swimming aquatic animals of the class *Ctenophora*, resembling jellyfishes.

cub, kub, *n.* [Origin obscure.] The young of certain animals, as the fox or bear; an awkward or uncouth youth; an inexperienced newspaper reporter.

cub, kub, *n.* Any of several closely similar types of small, light, single engine monoplanes with a closed cabin.

Cu·ban, kū′ban, *Sp.* kö′vän, *a.* Of or pertaining to Cuba, in the West Indies.—*n.* A native or inhabitant of Cuba.

Cu·ban heel, *n.* A broad, medium high heel, slightly curved, used on women's shoes.

cu·ba·ture, kū′ba·chêr, *n.* The determination of the cubic contents of a solid; cubic contents. Also **cub·age**.

cub·by, kub′ē, *n.* pl. **cub·bies**. A snug, confined place; a cubbyhole.—**cub·by·hole**, kub′ē·hōl″, *n.* A small enclosed space; a very small, snug room or place.

cube, kūb, *n.* [Fr. *cube*, < L. *cubus*, < Gr. *kubos*, die, cube.] *Geom.* a solid bounded by six equal squares, the angle between any two adjacent faces being a right angle; *math.* the third power of a quantity; as, the *cube* of 4 is 4 × 4 × 4, or 64.—*v.t.*—*cubed, cubing.* To measure the cubic contents of; to raise to the third power; find the cube of.—**cube root**, *n.* A quantity of which a given quantity is the cube; as, for the given quantity 64, 4 is the *cube root*.

cube, kūb, *n.* One of several tropical American plants used in manufacturing insecticides and fish poisons.

cu·beb, kū′beb, *n.* [Fr. *cubèbe*, < Ar. *kabābah*.] The spicy fruit or berry of an East Indian climbing shrub of the pepper family, *Piper cubeba*, dried in an unripe but fully grown state, formerly used medicinally in the treatment of urinary and bronchial disorders, and frequently smoked in cigarette form.

cu·bic, kū′bik, *a.* [L. *cubicus*, < Gr. *kubikos*.] Having the form of a cube; of three dimensions, solid, or pertaining to solid content; as, a *cubic* foot, the volume of a cube whose edges are each a foot long; *math.* being of the third power or degree; *crystal.* belonging or pertaining to the isometric system of crystallization.—**cu·bic meas·ure**, the measurement of volume in cubic units; a system of such units, esp. that in which 1,728 cubic inches = 1 cubic foot, 27 cubic feet = 1 cubic yard.—**cu·bi·cal**, *a.* Cubic.—**cu·bi·cal·ly**, *adv.*—**cu·bi·cal·ness**, *n.*

cu·bi·cle, kū′bi·kl, *n.* [L. *cubiculum*, < *cubare*, lie.] A bedchamber, esp. one of a number of small ones in a divided dormitory; any small space or compartment partitioned off; a carrel.

cu·bi·form, kū′bi·fạrm″, *a.* Having the form of a cube.

cub·ism, kū′biz·um, *n.* That revolutionary phase, developed in Paris in the early 20th century, of the modern art movement which concerned itself with expressing the idea of the whole structure of a given object by reducing the surfaces to geometric planes

and organizing them without regard to representational accuracy.

cu·bit, kū′bit, *n.* [L. *cubitum*, also *cubitus*, elbow, cubit.] An ancient linear unit based on the length of the forearm, usually from 17 to 21 inches.—**cu·bi·tal**, kū′bi·tal, *a.* [L. *cubitalis*.] Of or pertaining to the forearm; of the length of a cubit.—**cu·bi·tus**, kū′bi·tus, *n.* [L.] *Anat.* the forearm.

cu·boid, kū′boid, *a.* [Gr. *kuboeides*, cubelike.] Resembling a cube in form; *anat.* noting or pertaining to the outermost bone of the distal row of tarsal bones.—*n.* Something resembling a cube in form; *anat.* the cuboid bone; *math.* a rectangular parallelepiped.—**cu·boi·dal**, *a.*

cub scout, *n.* A member of that division of the Boy Scouts of America comprising boys 8 to 11 years of age.

cuck·ing stool, kuk′ing stōl″, *n.* [Cf. obs. *cuck*, void excrement.] A former instrument of punishment consisting of a chair in which an offender, as a dishonest tradesman, was strapped, to be jeered at and pelted by the crowd, or, sometimes, to be ducked.

cuck·old, kuk′old, *n.* [O.Fr. *cucuault*, < *cucu*, cuckoo; in allusion to the female cuckoo's laying eggs in the nests of other birds.] The husband of an unfaithful wife.—*v.t.* To make a cuckold of (a husband).—**cuck·old·ly**, *adv.*—**cuck·old·ry**, kuk′ol·drē, *n.*

cuck·oo, kö′kö, kụk′ö, *n.* pl. **cuck·oos**. [O.Fr. *cucu* (Fr. *cuocou*), cuckoo; imit. of the bird's call: cf. D. *koekoek*, L.G. *kukuk*, G. *kuckuk*, L. *cuculus*, Gr. *kokkux*, cuckoo.] Any bird of the genus *Cuculus*, esp. a common European migratory bird, *Cuculus canorus*, noted for its characteristic call, and for the female's habit of laying her eggs in the nests of other birds, for the young to be reared by foster parents; any other bird of the family *Cuculidae* of which *C. canorus* is a member; the call of the cuckoo, or an imitation of it; a fool or simpleton.—*v.i.*—*cuckooed, cuckooing.* To utter the call of the cuckoo, or an imitation of it.—*v.t.* To repeat monotonously.—*a. Slang.* Foolish; crazy.

cuck·oo clock, *n.* A clock which announces the hours by a sound like the call of the cuckoo.

cuck·oo·flow·er, kö′kö·flou″er, kụk′ö·flou″er, *n.* Any of various cress plants, as the lady's smock or the ragged robin.

cuck·oo·pint, kö′kö·pīnt″, kụk′ö·pīnt″, *n.* [Earlier *cuckoo-pintle*.] A common European species of arum, *Arum maculatum*. Also *wake-robin*.

cuck·oo·spit, kö′kö·spit″, kụk′ö·spit″, *n.* A frothy secretion found on plants, exuded as a protective covering by the young of certain insects as the froghoppers; an insect secreting this.

cu·cu·li·form, kū·kū′li·fạrm″, *a.* [L. *cucullus*, hood, and *-form.*] Pertaining to an order of birds, *Cuculiformes*, which includes road runners and cuckoos.

cu·cul·late, kū′ku·lāt″, kū·kul′āt, *a.* [L.L. *cucullatus*, hooded, < L. *cucullus*, hood.] Cowled; hooded; resembling a cowl or hood. Also **cu·cul·lat·ed**.—**cu·cu·late·ly**, *adv.*

cu·cum·ber, kū′kum·bêr, *n.* [O.Fr. *cocombre* (Fr. *concombre*), < L. *cucumis* (*cucumer-*).] A cucurbitaceous creeping plant, *Cucumis sativus*, occurring in many cultivated forms, yielding a long fleshy fruit which is commonly eaten green in a salad and when young used for pickling; the fruit of this plant; any of various allied or similar plants, or its fruit.—**cu·cum·ber tree**, *n.* Any of several American magnolias, esp. *Magnolia acuminata*; any of certain other trees, as the *Averrhoa bilimbi* of the East Indies.

cu·cu·mi·form, kū·kū′mi·fạrm″, *a.* [L.] Shaped like a cucumber; approximately cylindrical, with rounded or tapering ends.

---

cu·cur·bit, kū·kẽr'bit, *n*. [L. *cucurbita*, gourd.] A gourd; any cucurbitaceous plant; a roundish vessel formerly used as the lower part of a distilling apparatus.—**cu·cur·bi·ta·ceous**, kū·kẽr"bi·tā'shus, *a*. Belonging to the *Cucurbitaceae*, or gourd family of plants, which includes the pumpkin, squash, cucumber, muskmelon, watermelon, and colocynth.

cud, kud, *n*. [O.E. *cud*, the cud, what is chewed, < *ceowan*, to chew.] Food regurgitated from the first stomach of a ruminating animal into its mouth in order to be chewed again; a portion of tobacco held in the mouth and chewed; a quid.—**chew the cud**, *fig*. to ponder; to reflect; to ruminate.

cud·bear, kud'bâr", *n*. [From Dr. *Cuthbert* Gordon (18th century), who patented it.] A red or violet coloring matter obtained from various lichens, esp. *Lecanora tartarea*, used in coloring drugs and foods.

cud·dle, kud'l, *v.t.*—*cuddled, cuddling*. [Origin uncertain.] To draw or hold close in an affectionate manner; hug tenderly; fondle.—*v.i.* To lie close and snug; nestle; curl up in going to sleep.—*n*. An act of cuddling; a hug or embrace.—**cud·dle·some**, kud'l·som, *a*.—**cud·dly**, *a*.

cud·dy, kud'ē, *n*. pl. **cud·dies**. [Origin uncertain.] A small cabin on a ship or boat, esp. one under the poop; a small room; a cupboard.

cud·dy, kud'ē, kŭd'ē, *n*. pl. **cud·dies**. [Origin uncertain.] *Sc.*, *Brit. dial.* a donkey; *fig*. a stupid fellow.

cudg·el, kuj'el, *n*. [O.E. *cycgel*, perh. < *cog*, a short piece of wood.] A short, thick stick; a club.—*v.t.*—*cudgeled, cudgeling*, *Brit. cudgelled, cudgelling*. To beat with a cudgel or thick stick; to beat in general.—**cudg·el one's brains**, to try to understand or recall something; to ponder.

cud·weed, kud'wēd", *n*. Any of the woolly, lilylike herbs constituting the genus *Gnaphalium*; any of various plants of allied genera.

cue, kū, *n*. [Formerly *q*, *qu*, as if an abbreviation, possibly for L. *qualis*, of what kind, or *quando*, when.] Any sound, word, or action that serves as the signal for any other sound, word, or action in a theatrical production; a guiding hint or suggestion; the part one is to play at a particular juncture; the course of action one ought to pursue.—*v.t.*—*cued, cuing*.—**cue in**, to give information to someone.

cue, kū, *n*. [Fr. *queue*.] A queue of hair; a queue or file, as of persons awaiting their turn; a long, straight tapering rod tipped with a soft pad, used to strike the ball in billiards and pool.—*v.t.*—*cued, cuing*. To twist or braid into a queue, as hair; to strike a ball with a cue stick.—**cue ball**, *n*. *Billiards*, the ball struck by the cue as distinguished from the other balls on the table.

cues·ta, kwes'ta, *n*. A hill characterized by a gradual incline on one face and a steep incline on the other.

cuff, kuf, *n*. [M.E. *cuffe, coffe*, glove, mitten; origin uncertain.] A fold, band, or variously shaped piece serving as a trimming or finish for a sleeve at the wrist; a turned-up fold at the bottom of trouser legs; a separate or detachable band or piece of linen or other material worn about the wrist, inside or outside of the sleeve; a handcuff.—*v.t.* To make or put cuffs on; to put handcuffs on.—**off the cuff**, *slang*, speaking in an impromptu, or unrehearsed way; giving advice or information unofficially or informally.—**on the cuff**, *slang*. With the agreement to pay later; on a charge account, or on credit.

cuff, kuf, *n*. [Akin to Sw. *kuffa*, Hamburg dialect *kuffen*, to cuff.] A blow with the

fist; a stroke.—*v.t.* To strike with the fist, as a man; to buffet.

cui·rass, kwi·ras', *n*. [Fr. *cuirasse*, < *cuir*, L. *corium*, leather. The cuirass was originally made of leather.] A breastplate; a piece of defensive armor made of iron plate, covering the trunk of the body.—*v.t.* To equip with a cuirass.—**cui·ras·sier**, kwēr"a·sēr', *n*. A soldier wearing a cuirass or breastplate.

Cui·se·naire rod, kwiz"e·nâr' rod, *n*. Any one of a coordinated set of 10 differently colored groups of wooden rods, the width and depth of all rods remaining at 1 centimeter, each group differing only in length ranging from 1 centimeter to 10 centimeters, each group one centimeter longer than the preceding group: used in elementary schools for the visualization and understanding of basic mathematical concepts and processes.

cui·sine, kwi·zēn', *n*. [Fr., < L. *coquina*, art of cooking, a kitchen, < *coquo*, to cook.] A manner, quality, or style of cooking; cookery.

cuisse, kwis, *n*. [O.Fr. *cuissaux*, pl. of *cuissel*, < *cuisse*, thigh, < L. *coxa*, hip.] *Her*. a piece of armor to protect the thigh.

culch, kulch, *n*. Cultch.

cul-de-sac, kul'de·sak', kul'de·sak, kul'de·sak', kul' de·sak, *Fr.* kyd·e·säk', *n*. pl. **culs-de-sac**. [Fr. "bottom of sack."] A saclike cavity, tube, or the like, open only at one end, as the caecum; a street, lane, or other passage closed at one end; *milit*. the situation of a military force hemmed in on all sides except behind. Any situation in which movement or progress is blocked.

cu·let, kū'lit, *n*. [Dim. of Fr. *cul*, bottom: cf. Fr. *culasse*, culet.] The flat face forming the bottom of a gem; the part of medieval armor protecting the back of the body below the waist.

cu·lex, kū'leks, *n*. pl. **cu·li·ces**, kū'li·sēz". Any of a large group of mosquitoes that includes the common mosquito found in North America and Europe.

cu·lic·id, kū·lis'id, *n*. [N.L. *Culicidæ*, pl., < L. *culex*, gnat.] Any of the *Culicidae*, a family of two-winged insects including the mosquitoes.—*a*. Pertaining to the culicids; belonging to the *Culicidae*.

cu·li·nar·y, kū'li·ner"ē, kul'i·ner"ē, *a*. [L. *culinarius*, < *culina*, a kitchen.] Relating to the kitchen, or to the art of cooking.

cull, kul, *v.t.* [O.Fr. *cuillir, coillir* (Fr. *cueillir*), < L. *colligere*, E. *collect*.] To choose or select; pick; to collect or gather; pluck; to gather the choice things or parts from.—*n*. The act of culling; something picked out and put aside as inferior.

cul·len·der, kul'en·dẽr, *n*. Colander.

cul·let, kul'it, *n*. Broken glass for remelting.

cul·lis, kul'is, *n*. [Fr. *coulisse*, a groove, from *couler*, to run.] *Arch*. a gutter in a roof.

cul·ly, kul'ē, *n*. pl. **cul·lies**. [Origin uncertain.] A man or fellow; one who is easily imposed upon or cheated; a dupe; a gull.—*v.t.*—*cullied, cullying*. To cheat, deceive, or trick.

culm, kulm, *n*. [M.E. *culme*; perhaps akin to *coal*.] Coal dust or refuse coal; anthracite, esp. of inferior grade.

culm, kulm, *n*. [L. *culmus*, a stalk.] *Bot*. the jointed stem of grasses, which is herbaceous in most, but woody and treelike in the bamboo.—**cul·mif·er·ous**, kul·mif'ẽr·us, *a*. Bearing culms.

cul·mi·nant, kul'mi·nant, *a*. Culminating; at the peak.

cul·mi·nate, kul'mi·nāt", *v.i.*—*culminated, culminating*. To reach or cease at the highest point, as of rank, power, quality, or development; to finish or end; come to a concluding point; *astron*. to reach its highest altitude, as a celestial body.—*v.t.* To bring to a climax or conclusion.

cul·mi·na·tion, kul"mi·nā'shan, *n*. The process of culminating; that in which

something culminates; summit; acme; *astron*. the transit of a heavenly body over the meridian.

cu·lotte, kō·lot', kū·lot', *n*. [Fr., lit. breeches.] A woman's skirt or dress divided like trousers but cut full so as to appear to be a skirt. Also **cu·lottes**.

cul·pa·ble, kul'pa·bl, *a*. [L. *culpabilis*, < *culpa*, a fault.] Deserving censure; blamable, blameworthy; immoral: said of persons or their conduct.—**cul·pa·bil·i·ty**, **cul·pa·ble·ness**, kul"pa·bil'i·tē, *n*.—**cul·pa·bly**, *adv*.

cul·prit, kul'prit, *n*. [From an old legal formula abbreviated *cul. prit*, for A.Fr. *culpable* (or L. *culpabilis*), guilty, and *prit* or *prest* (O.Fr. *prest*), ready.] A person arraigned for an offense; hence, one guilty of an offense or fault; an offender.

cult, kult, *n*. [L. *cultus*, < *colere*, cultivate, till, worship.] A system of religious worship, esp. with reference to its rites and ceremonies; a sect adhering to a common ideology or doctrine or leader, esp. when such adherence or devotion is based on fanatical beliefs or dogma; an instance of fixed, almost religious veneration for a person or thing, esp. by a body of admirers.—**cul·tic**, **cult·ish**, **cul·tu·al**, kul'chō·al, *a*.

cultch, kulch, *n*. The spawn of the oyster; stones, shells, and other stuff used to form a bed for the spawn of the oysters. Also **culch**.—*v.t.* To make a bed with cultch for the spawn of the oysters. Also **culch**.

cul·ti·gen, kul'ti·jen, *n*. A cultivated plant of unknown ancestry.

cul·ti·var, kul'ti·vär", kul'ti·vẽr, *n*. A kind of organism that is produced and can sustain itself only under cultivation.

cul·ti·vate, kul'ti·vāt", *v.t.*—*cultivated, cultivating*. [M.L. *cultivatus*, pp. of *cultivare*, < *cultivus*, tilled, < L. *colere*.] To prepare for crop raising, as land; till; use a cultivator on; to promote or improve the growth of, as a plant, by labor and attention; produce by culture. To develop or improve by education or training; train; refine; to promote the growth or development of, as an art or science; to devote oneself to, as an art, pursuit, or practice; to seek, to promote or acquire, as an acquaintance, interest, or taste; seek the acquaintance or friendship of.—**cul·ti·va·tion**, *n*.—**cul·ti·va·ble**, **cul·ti·vat·a·ble**, *a*.

cul·ti·vat·ed, kul'ti·vā"tid, *a*. Prepared for or subjected to cultivation, as land; produced or improved by cultivation, as a plant. Improved by education or training; cultured; refined.

cul·ti·va·tor, kul'ti·vā"tẽr, *n*. One who or that which cultivates; an agricultural implement for loosening earth and destroying weeds drawn between rows of growing plants.

cul·trate, kul'trāt, *a*. [L. *cultratus*, knife-shaped, < *culter*, knife.] *Bot*. sharp-edged and pointed, as a leaf. Also **cul·trat·ed**, kul'trā·tid.

cul·tur·al, kul'chẽr·al, *a*. Of or pertaining to culture; educational; refined. Of, pertaining to, or produced by the cultivation of plants.—**cul·tur·al·ly**, *adv*.

cul·tur·al an·thro·pol·o·gy, *n*. The study of the origins, variability, development, and history of the cultures of human societies.

cul·tur·al lag, *n*. *Sociol.*, *anthropol.* a marked discrepancy between the degrees of development of various aspects of a culture, such as results when the nonmaterial features of a culture fail to develop apace with technology. Also **cul·ture lag**.

cul·ture, kul'chẽr, *n*. [L. *cultura*, < *colere*. CULT.] The acquired ability of an individual or a people to recognize and appreciate generally accepted esthetic and intellectual excellence; the esthetic and intellectual achievement of civilization; a particular state or stage of civilization, as in the case of a certain nation or period; as, Chinese *culture*. *Anthropol.*, *sociol.* the total of human behavior patterns and technology communicated from generation to generation. *Biol.*, *med.* the cultivation of microorganisms, as bacteria, for scientific study or medicinal use; the product or growth resulting from such cultivation. *Agric.* the action or practice of cultivating the soil; tillage; the raising of plants or animals, esp. with a view to their improvement.—*v.t. cultured*, *culturing*. To subject to culture; cultivate. *Biol.*, *med.* to develop, as bacteria, in an artificial medium; to introduce a culture into.—**cul·ture·less**, *a.*

cul·tured, kul′chẽrd, *a.* Cultivated; enlightened or refined; precipitated by or grown in an artificial medium.

cul·tured pearl, *n.* A pearl, the formation of which is artificially induced by the insertion of a piece of foreign matter into the fleshy part of selected oysters.

cul·tur·ist, kul′chẽr·ist, *n.* A cultivator; an advocate or devotee of culture.

cul·tus, kul′tus, *n.* pl. **cul·tus·es**, **cul·ti**, kul′tī. [L. CULT.] A cult.

cul·tus, kul′tus, *n.* [Chinook *cultus*, worthless.] Lingcod. Also **cul·tus cod**.

cul·ver, kul′vẽr, *n.* [O.E. *culfre*.] *Brit. dial.* a pigeon; a dove.

cul·ver·in, kul′vẽr·in, *n.* [O.Fr. Fr. *coulevrine*, < *couleuvre*, < L. *colubra*, serpent.] A form of musket used in the Middle Ages; a heavy cannon used in the 16th and 17th centuries.

cul·vert, kul′vẽrt, *n.* [Origin uncertain.] A drain, as under a road or sidewalk, for the passage of water; a sewer; a conduit.

cum, kum, kụm, *prep.* [L.] With; together with; including.—*a.* Including; as, magna *cum laude*, *cum dividend*.

cum·ber, kum′bẽr, *v.t.* [M.E. *cumbren*.] To overload, to overburden; to retard; to obstruct.—*n.* Hindrance; burdensomeness. —**cum·ber·some**, *a.*—**cum·ber·some·ly**, *adv.*—**cum·ber·some·ness**, *n.*—**cum·brance**, kum′brans, *n.* That which cumbers or encumbers; an encumbrance.—**cum·brous**, kum′brus, *a.* Serving to cumber or encumber.—**cum·brous·ly**, *adv.*—**cum·brous·ness**, *n.*

cum·in, kum′in, *n.* [L. *cuminum*, *cyminum*, < Gr. *cuminon*.] A small plant, *Cuminum cyminum*, of the parsley family, native to Egypt and Syria and long cultivated for its aromatic seedlike fruit used in cookery and medicine; the fruit or seeds of this plant.

cum lau·de, kụm lou′dä, kụm lou′de, kụm lou′dē, kụm lạ′dē, *a.*, *adv.* [L. lit. with praise.] With honor: used to designate an academic rank of graduates, above average, but lower than *magna cum laude* and *summa cum laude*.

cum·mer·bund, kum′·ẽr·bund″, *n.* [Hind. *kamarband*, "loin band."] A wide sash wrapped about the waist, esp. a horizontally pleated one worn with men's formal dress.

cum·quat, kum′kwot, *n.* Kumquat.

cum·shaw, kum′shạ, *n.* [Prob. < Chinese.] Among Chinese, a gift given with his purchase to a customer by a merchant; something given as a compliment or for good measure; a lagniappe; a gratuity or tip; *milit.* favors or goods, such as coffee, traded between two military units for other favors or goods, which could not be secured through official channels or could be secured only with great difficulty.

cu·mu·late, kū′mū·lāt″, *v.t.*—*cumulated*, *cumulating*. [L. *cumulatus*, pp. of *cumulare*, heap up, < *cumulus*, a heap.] To heap up; amass; accumulate.—kū′mū lit, kū′mū·lat″, *a.* Cumulated; heaped up.—**cu·mu·la··tion**, *n.*

cu·mu·la·tive, kū′mū·lā″tiv, kū′mū·la·tiv, *a.* Increasing by accumulation or successive additions; formed by or resulting from accumulation or the addition of successive parts or elements; increasing the amount or force of something else by forming an addition, or a number of successive additions, to it; pertaining to or characterized by accumulation.—**cu·mu·la·tive·ly**, *adv.* —**cu·mu·la·tive·ness**, *n.*—**cu·mu·la·tive div·i·dend**, *n.* A dividend which if not paid in full when due must be paid before dividends are paid on the common stock.—**cu··mu·la·tive pre·ferred stock**, *n.* Stock bearing cumulative dividends.—**cu·mu·la·tive sys·tem of vot·ing**, *n.* A system which gives each voter as many votes as there are persons to be elected to an office, allowing him to cast them all on one candidate or to distribute them.

cu·mu·lo·cir·rus, kū″mū·lō·sir′us, *n.* pl. **cu·mu·lo·cir·rus**. Cirrocumulus.

cu·mu·lo·nim·bus, kū″mū·lō·nim′bus, *n.* pl. **cu·mu·lo·nim·bus**. [CUMULUS and NIMBUS.] A cloud with a cumulus-like summit and a nimbus-like base, characteristic of thunderstorms; a thundercloud.

cu·mu·lo·stra·tus, kū″mū·lō·strā′tus, kū″mū·lō·strat′us, *n.* pl. **cu·mu·lo·stra··tus**. Stratocumulus.

cu·mu·lus, kū″mū·lus, *n.* pl. **cu·mu·li**, kū″mū·lī. [L., a heap.] A heap or pile; a cloud with domelike summit or made up of rounded heaps, seen in fair weather.— **cu·mu·lous**, kū′mū·lus, *a.*

cunc·ta·tion, kungk·tā′shan, *n.* [L. *cunctatio*(n-), < *cunctari*, delay.] Tardy action; delay.—**cunc·ta·to·ry**, kungk′ta·tōr″ē, kungk′ta·tạr″ē, *a.*—**cunc·ta·tor**, *n.*

cu·ne·ate, kū′nē·it, kū′nē·āt″, *a.* [L. *cuneatus*, pp. of *cuneare*, make wedge-shaped, < *cuneus*, wedge.] Wedge-shaped; of leaves, triangular, and tapering to a point at the base. Also **cu·ne·at·ed**.—**cu··ne·ate·ly**, *adv.*—**cu·ne·at·ic**, kū′nē·at′ik, *a.* Cuneiform; cuneate.—**cu·ne·al**, kū′nē·al, *a.*

cu·ne·i·form, kū·nē′i·fạrm″, kū′nē·i··fạrm″, *a.* [L. *cuneus*, wedge, and *-form*.] Having the form of a wedge; wedge-shaped, as the characters used in writing in ancient Persia and Assyria; noting or pertaining to this kind of writing; *anat.* noting or pertaining to any of various wedge-shaped bones, as the tarsus.—*n.* Cuneiform characters or writing; *anat.* a cuneiform bone.—**cu·ne·i·form·ist**, *n.* One versed in the subject of cuneiform writing.

cu·nic·u·lus, kū·nik′ū·lus, *n.* pl. **cu··nic·u·li**, kū·nik′ū·lī. [L., underground passage, burrow, orig. rabbit.] An underground passage, as a burrow or a drain.

cun·ner, kun′ẽr, *n.* [Origin obscure.] Either of two small edible fishes, *Crenilabrus melops*, of the British coasts, and *Tautogolabrus adspersus*, of the Atlantic coast of North America.

cun·ni·lin·gus, kun″i·ling′gus, *n.* Oral stimulation of the female genitalia. Also **cun·ni·linc·tus**, kun″i·lingk′tus.

cun·ning, kun′ing, *n.* [M.E., verbal noun of *cunnen*, < O.E. *cunnan*, know, be able.] Ability, skill, or expertise; skill employed in a crafty manner; skillful deceit; craftiness; guile.—*a.* Exhibiting ingenuity; artfully subtle or shrewd; crafty; sly; guileful; quaintly pleasing or attractive.—**cun·ning··ly**, *adv.*—**cun·ning·ness**, *n.*

cup, kup, *n.* [O.E. *cuppe*, < M.L. *cuppa*, *cupa*, cup, < L. *cupa*, tub, cask.] A small, open vessel, as of porcelain or metal, used esp. to drink from, made either with or without a handle; the chalice used in the Eucharist; the wine of the Eucharist; a loving cup; an ornamental cup or other vessel or article, as of precious metal, offered as a prize for a contest; the containing part of a goblet or the like; any cuplike utensil, organ, part, or cavity; a cupping glass; a cup with its contents; the quantity contained in a cup; any of various beverages, as a mixture of wine and various ingredients; as, claret *cup*; *fig.* something to be partaken of or endured, as suffering. *Pl.* the drinking of intoxicating liquors; a state of intoxication; (*cap.*), *astron.* the southern constellation, Crater.—*v.t.*—*cupped*, *cupping*. To take or place in or as in a cup; to use a cupping-glass on.—*v.i.* To become cup-shaped; to use a cupping glass.—**cup·ful**, *n.* pl. **cup·fuls** or **cups·ful**.—**cupped**, *a.* Cup-shaped.

cup·bear·er, kup′bâr″ẽr, *n.* An attendant who fills and serves cups of wine or other liquors to the guests.

cup·board, kub′ord, *n.* A closet with shelves for dishes; *Brit.* any small closet or cabinet.

cup·cake, kup′kāk″, *n.* A small cake for an individual serving, baked in a cup-shaped compartment of a pan.

cu·pel, kū′pel, kū·pel′, *n.* [Fr. *coupelle*, < M.L. *cupella*, dim. of *cupa*, *cuppa*, E. *cup*.] A small, cuplike porous vessel, usually made of bone ash, used in assaying, as for separating gold and silver from lead; a receptacle or furnace bottom in which silver is refined.—*v.t.*—*cupeled*, *cupeling*, *cupelled*, *cupelling*. To heat or refine in a cupel.—**cu·pel·la·tion**, *n.*

cup·hold·er, kup′hōl″dẽr, *n.* A competitor who has won and retained a specific championship in which a cup or similar trophy is awarded.

Cu·pid, kū′pid, *n.* [L. *Cupido*, lit. "desire, passion," < *cupere*, desire.] The Roman god of love, son of Venus, commonly represented as a winged boy with bow and arrows; (*l.c.*) a similar winged being, or a representation of one, esp. as symbolical of love.—**play cu·pid**, to be instrumental in arranging a love match.

cu·pid·i·ty, kū·pid′i·tē, *n.* [L. *cupiditas*, < *cupidus*, desirous, < *cupio*, to desire; akin *covet*.] An eager desire to possess something; inordinate or unlawful desire, esp. of wealth or power; avarice; covetousness.

Cu·pid's bow, *n.* The bow which is traditionally associated with the ancient Roman god of love; a line that resembles the curve of this bow, esp. as descriptive of the upper lip.

cu·po·la, kū′po·la, *n.* pl. **cu·po·las**. [It. dome, < L.L. *cupula*, dim. of L. *cupa*, tub, cask.] *Arch.* a vault or dome built on a circular or polygonal base and constituting a roof or ceiling; a comparable smaller structure atop a roof or dome, sometimes serving as a belfry, light tower, or lookout; any of various domelike structures; *metal.* a furnace in the shape of a vertical cylinder, used for melting iron.—**cu·po·lat·ed**, *a.* Having a cupola; shaped like a cupola.

cup·ping, kup′ing, *n.* The process of drawing blood from the body by the application of a cupping glass over a slight incision, or to the surface of the body without an incision, an early remedy, as for the relief of internal congestion.—**cup·per**, kup′ẽr, *n.* One who performs the operation of cupping.—**cup·ping glass**, *n.* A glass vessel in which a partial vacuum is created, as by heat, used in the process of cupping.

cup plant, *n.* A tall, yellow-flowered, native U.S. plant, *Silphium perfoliatum*, of the composite family, with large opposite leaves, the upper pairs being connate at their base and forming a cuplike cavity; rosinweed.

cu·pre·ous, kū′prē·us, kö′prē·us, *a.* *Chem.* consisting of or containing copper; copper-colored; similar to copper.

cu·pric, kū′prik, kö′prik, *a.* *Chem.* containing copper in its bivalent form; as, *cupric* oxide.

cu·prif·er·ous, kū·prif′ẽr·us, kö·prif′ẽr·us, *a. Chem.* yielding copper.

cu·prite, kū′prīt, kö′prīt, *n.* A reddish mineral, cuprous oxide, Cu_2O, an important copper ore occurring as crystals and granular masses.

cu·prous, kū′prus, kö′prus, *a. Chem.* containing copper in its univalent form; as, *cuprous* oxide.

cup shake, *n.* Wind shake.

cu·pule, kū′pūl, *n.* [N.L. *cupula,* dim. of M.L. *cupa, cuppa,* E. *cup.*] *Bot.* a cup-shaped involucre consisting of indurated, cohering bracts, as in the acorn; *zool.* a small cup-shaped sucker or similar organ or part.—**cu·pu·late,** kū′pū·lāt″, kū′pū·lit, *a.* Having or shaped like a cupule. Also **cu·pu·lar.**

cur, kụr, *n.* [Sw. *kurre,* D. *korre,* a dog, from root of Icel. *kurra,* to grumble or mutter.] A worthless dog; mongrel; a mean, contemptible person.

cur·a·ble, kūr′a·bl, *a.* [L.L. *curabilis.*] Able to be cured.—**cur·a·bil·i·ty, cur·a·ble·ness,** *n.*—**cur·a·bly,** *adv.*

cu·ra·çao, cu·ra·çoa, kūr″a·sō′, kūr″a·sō′a, *n.* A liqueur or cordial flavored with orange peel, cinnamon, and mace, so named from the island of Curaçao, where it was first made.

cu·ra·cy, kūr′a·sē, *n. pl.* **cu·ra·cies.** The office or position of a curate.

cu·ra·re, cu·ra·ri, kū·rär′ē, *n.* [Carib.] A blackish, resinlike substance from *Strychnos toxifera* and other tropical plants of the genus *Strychnos,* used by South American Indians for poisoning arrows, employed in physiological experiments for arresting the action of the motor nerves; a plant yielding it.—**cu·ra·rize,** kūr′a·rīz″, kū·rär′īz, *v.t.—curarized, curarizing.* To administer curare to, as in vivisection.—**cu·ra·ri·za·tion,** *n.*

cu·ras·sow, kūr′a·sō″, kū·ras′ō, *n.* [< the island of *Curaçao.*] Any of various large, arboreal, South and Central American birds of the family *Cracidae,* somewhat resembling the turkey and sometimes domesticated.

cu·rate, kūr′it, *n.* [M.L. *curatus,* < *cura,* cure of souls.] A clergyman employed as assistant or deputy of a rector or vicar.

cur·a·tive, kūr′a·tiv, *a.* Serving to cure or heal; pertaining to curing or remedial treatment; remedial.—*n.* A curative agent; a remedy.—**cur·a·tive·ly,** *adv.*—**cur·a·tive·ness,** *n.*

cu·ra·tor, kū·rā′tẽr, kūr′ā·tẽr, *n.* [L. < *curare* (pp. *curatus*), care for, have charge of.] The director of a museum or art gallery; an overseer. *Law,* a guardian, esp. of property, appointed by a court.—**cu·ra·to·ri·al,** kūr″a·tōr′ē·al, kūr″a·tạr′ē·al, *a.*—**cu·ra·tor·ship,** *n.*

curb, kụrb, *n.* [Fr. *courber,* to bend, < L. *curvare,* < *curvus,* curved.] Any thing that restrains or controls; a restraint; the part of a horse's halter used in restraining the animal; an enclosing framework or border. The border, as of stone, at the outer edge of a sidewalk; also *Brit.* **kerb.** A market for the sale of securities not dealt in on the stock exchange.—*v.t.* To put a curb on, as on a horse; to control as with a curb; restrain; check; to furnish with or protect by a curb or curbstone—**curb bit,** *n.* A horse's bit having a curb.—**curb·a·ble,** *a.*—**curb·ing,** *n.* The material, as stones, forming a curb; a curb or part of one.—**curb·less,** *a.* Without curb; unrestrained.—**curb·like,** *a.*

curb roof, *n.* A roof with two slopes to each face.

curb·stone, kụrb′stōn″, *n.* One of the stones, or a range of stones, forming a curb, as along the outer edge of a sidewalk.

cur·cu·li·o, kụr·kū′lē·ō″, *n. pl.* **cur·cu·li·os.** [L., weevil.] Any snout beetle or weevil, esp. one of various forms injurious to fruit.

cur·cu·ma, kụr′kū·ma, *n.* [N.L. < Ar. *kurkum,* saffron, turmeric.] Any plant of the genus *Curcuma,* of the East Indies, yielding turmeric and other tropical herbs of the ginger family.

curd, kụrd, *n.* [M.E. origin uncertain.] (*Often pl.*) a substance consisting of casein, obtained from milk by coagulation, used for making cheese or eaten as food. Any substance resembling this.—*v.t., v.i.* To turn into curd; coagulate; congeal.

cur·dle, kụr′dl, *v.i.—curdled, curdling.* To coagulate; to thicken or change into curd; to freeze; to congeal; to go bad; to spoil.—*v.t.* To change into curd; to coagulate; to congeal; to sour; to spoil.

cure, kūr, *v.t.—cured, curing.* [O.Fr. *curer* (Fr. *curer,* cleanse), < L. *curare* (pp *curatus*), care for, have charge of, treat medically, cure.] Restore to health; relieve or rid of something troublesome or detrimental, as a bad habit; to remove by remedial means, as a disease; remedy or eradicate, as an evil; to prepare, as meat or fish, for preservation, by salting or drying; to vulcanize.—*v.i.* To effect a cure; to become cured.—**cur·er,** *n.*

cure, kūr, *n.* [O.Fr. Fr. *cure,* < L. *cura,* care.] Spiritual charge or supervision of the people in a certain district, as a parish; the office or district of one exercising such care; a method or course of remedial treatment, as for disease; successful remedial treatment; restoration to health; a means of healing or curing; a remedy; the act or a method of curing meat or fish.—**cur·er,** *n.*

cu·ré, kū·rā′, Fr. ky·RĀ′, *n. pl.* **cu·rés,** kū·rāz′, kūr′āz, *Fr.* ky·RĀ′. [Fr. < M.L. *curatus.* CURATE.] In French use, a parish priest.

cure-all, kūr′ạl″, *n.* A cure for all ills; a panacea.

cu·rette, kū·ret′, *n.* [Fr. < *curer,* cleanse.] A scoop-shaped surgical instrument for removing or scraping away foreign matter and granulations from the walls of a body cavity, as the uterus.—*v.t.—curetted, curetting.* To scrape with a curette.—**cu·rette·ment,** *n.*—**cu·ret·tage,** *n.*

cur·few, kụr′fū, *n.* [O.Fr. *cuevrefu* (Fr. *couvre-feu*), "cover-fire."] A police or military order requiring withdrawal of persons from the streets or closing of businesses or places of assembly at a specified hour; the ringing of a bell at a fixed hour as a signal for covering or extinguishing fires, as practiced in medieval Europe; the giving of a signal, at a certain hour in the evening; the time of ringing, the bell itself, or its sound.

cu·ri·a, kūr′ē·a, *n. pl.* **cu·ri·ae,** kūr′ē·ē. [L. and M.L.] One of the political subdivisions of each of the three tribes of ancient Roman citizens; the building in which such a division or group met, as for worship or public deliberation; the senate house in ancient Rome; the senate of ancient Italian towns; a court of justice or administration. (*Often cap.*) the Papal court; the Pope and those about him in Rome engaged in the administration of the Roman Catholic Church.—**cu·ri·al,** *a.*

cu·ri·age, kūr′ē·ij, *n.* The strength of radioactivity as stated in curies.

cu·rie, kūr′ē, kū·rē′, *n.* [From Madame *Curie,* co-discoverer of radium.] *Chem.* the official international unit of radioactivity: 3.70 × 10^{10} disintegrations per second.

Cu·rie point, *n.* [From Pierre *Curie,* co-discoverer of radium.] *Phys.* the temperature at which a body, as iron, loses its permanent magnetization.

cu·ri·o, kūr′ē·ō″, *n. pl.* **cu·ri·os.** [Short for *curiosity.*] Any article, object of art, or piece of bric-à-brac, etc., valued as a curiosity.

cu·ri·o·sa, kūr′ē·ō′sa, *n. pl.* Books or pamphlets written on unusual or erotic subjects.

cu·ri·os·i·ty, kūr″ē·os′i·tē, *n. pl.* **cu·ri·os·i·ties.** [L. *curiositas.*] The state or feeling of being curious; a strong desire to see something novel or to discover something unknown; a desire to see what is new or unusual, or to gratify the mind with new discoveries; inquisitiveness; a curious or singular object.

cu·ri·ous, kūr′ē·us, *a.* [O.Fr. *curios* (Fr. *curieux*), < L. *curiosus,* careful, inquiring, inquisitive, < *cura.*] Desirous of learning or knowing; often inquisitive or prying; exciting attention or interest because of strangeness or novelty; odd; in booksellers' and collectors' catalogues, of books, indelicate, indecent, or obscene.—**cu·ri·ous·ly,** *adv.*—**cu·ri·ous·ness,** *n.*

cu·ri·um, kūr′ē·um, *n.* [From Pierre and Marie *Curie.*] *Chem.* a silvery, metallic, radioactive element formed as a by-product of atomic bombardment, sym. Cm, at. no. 96. See Periodic Table of Elements.

curl, kụrl, *v.t.* [M.E. *curlyd, crulled,* pp.; akin to D. *krullen,* G. *krollen,* Sw. *krulla,* curl.] To form into ringlets; to form into a spiral or curved shape; coil; make undulations in.—*v.i.* To form curls or ringlets, as the hair; to coil; become curved or undulated; *sports,* to play at curling.—*n.* A ringlet of hair; anything of a spiral or curved shape; a coil; a convolution; an undulation; any of various diseases of plants in which the leaves curl up; the act of curling, or the state of being curled.—**curl·er,** *n.* One who or that which curls; a player at curling.

cur·lew, kụr′lö, *n.* [O.Fr. Fr. *courlieu;* perhaps imit.] Any of the migratory shore birds, with a long, slender, curved bill, which constitute the genus *Numenius,* as *N. arquatus,* the common curlew of Europe, or *N. longirostris* the "long-billed curlew" of America; any of various similar birds.

curl·i·cue, kụr′li·kū″, *n.* A fancy curl or scroll-like twist. Also **curl·y·cue.**—*v.t., v.i. —curlicued, curlicuing.*

curl·ing, kụr′ling, *n. Sports,* a game played on the ice by two opposing teams of four members each, in which curling stones are slid toward a target called the tee.—**curl·ing stone,** *n.* A large ellipsoid stone, or sometimes an iron object, used in the game of curling, having one smooth and one rough side, and a curved handle.

curl·ing i·ron, *n.* A metal instrument, usu. tongs, that curls or waves the hair when the locks are twined around the heated rod. Also **curl·ing i·rons, curl·ing tongs.**

curl·pa·per, kụrl′pā″pẽr, *n.* A piece of paper with which a lock of hair is rolled up tightly, to remain until curled.

curl·y, kụr′lē, *a.—curlier, curliest.* Curling or tending to curl; having curls, as hair; having a wavy grain; as *curly* maple.—**curl·i·ness,** *n.*

cur·mudg·eon, kẽr·muj′on, *n.* [Word of uncertain origin.] A testy, cranky, snappish person, esp. an older man.—**cur·mudg·eon·ly,** *a.*

curn, kụrn, *n.* [= *corn.*] *Sc.* A grain; a small quantity or number.

curr, kụr, *v.i.* [Imit.] To make a low, murmuring sound, like the purring of a cat or cooing of a dove.

cur·rant, kụr′ant, kur′ant, *n.* [A.Fr. (*raisins de*) *Corauntz,* (raisins of) Corinth: so called as coming from Corinth in Greece.] A small seedless raisin, produced chiefly in California and the Levant, used in cooking, baking, and jellies; the small, edible, acid round fruit or berry of certain wild or cultivated shrubs of the genus *Ribes;* the shrub itself; any of various similar fruits or shrubs.—**cur·rant worm,** *n.* Any of several insect larvae destructive to currants.

cur·ren·cy, kụr′en·sē, kur′en·sē, *n. pl.* **cur·ren·cies.** Circulation, as of coin or paper money; that which is current as a medium of exchange; the money in actual use; general acceptance; prevalence; vogue.

cur·ren·cy ex·change, *n.* A type of business which specializes in, and charges a fee for, various simple monetary services, as cashing checks, issuing or cashing money orders.

cur·rent, kŭr′ent, kur′ent, *a.* [O.Fr. *curant* (Fr. *courant*), < L. *currens* (current-), ppr. of *currere*, run.] Prevalent, generally accepted, or in vogue; as, *current* styles; of the present time or closest to the present; as, the *current* issue of a magazine; circulating, or passing from one to another, as a coin; publicly reported or known; as *current* information.—*n.* A flowing or flow, as of a river; that which flows, as a stream; the portion of a body of water or air moving in a certain direction; any discernible course, trend, or general tendency, as of time or events; *elect.* a movement or flow of electricity; the rate or measure of this flow, usually expressed in amperes.— **cur·rent·ly,** *adv.*—**cur·rent·ness,** *n.*

cur·rent as·sets, *n. Finance*, the assets of a company which are reasonably expected to be realized in cash, or to be sold or consumed during the normal operating cycle.

cur·rent li·a·bil·i·ties, *n. Finance*, debts of a business or corporation, payable within one year.

cur·ri·cle, kĕr′i·kl, *n.* [L. *curriculum*, < *curro*, to run.] A chaise or carriage with two wheels, drawn by two horses abreast.

cur·ric·u·lum, ku·rik′ū·lum, *n.* pl. **cur·ric·u·lums, cur·ric·u·la,** ku·rik′ū·la. [L.] A specified fixed course of study in a university, college, or school; the total of all courses offered in the school.—**cur·ric·u·lar,** *a.*

cur·ric·u·lum vi·tae, ku·rik′ū·lum vī′tē, *Lat.* kŏr·Rik′ụ·lụm″ wē′tī, *n.* pl. **cur·ric·u·la vi·tae.** A résumé of one's career and qualifications usu. submitted when applying for a position.

cur·ri·er, kŭr′ē·er, kur′ē·er, *n.* [O.Fr. *corier*, < L. *coriarius*, tanner, currier, < *corium*, skin, hide, leather; now associated with *curry*.] One who dresses and colors leather after it is tanned; one who curries a horse.—**cur·ri·er·y,** *n.* pl. **cur·ri·er·ies.** The occupation or business of a currier, or the place where it is carried on.

cur·rish, kŭr′ish, *a.* Of or pertaining to a cur; curlike; snarling; quarrelsome; contemptible.—**cur·rish·ly,** *adv.*—**cur·rish·ness,** *n.*

cur·ry, cur·rie, kŭr′ē, kur′ē, *n.* pl. **cur·ries.** [E. Ind. (Dravidian).] An East Indian sauce or relish in many varieties, containing a mixture of turmeric and other spices, seeds, vegetables, and fruits, eaten with rice or combined with meat, fish, or other food; curry powder; a dish prepared with such a sauce or with curry powder.—*v.t.*—*curried, currying.* To prepare food with a curry sauce or with curry powder.—**cur·ried,** *a.*

cur·ry, kŭr′ē, kur′ē, *v.t.*—*curried, currying.* [Fr. *courroyer, corroyer*, originally to prepare, put right, or made ready in general.] To treat, as leather after it is tanned, by scraping, cleansing, beating, and coloring; to rub and clean (a horse) with a comb; *colloq.* to beat, drub, or thrash.—**cur·ry fa·vor,** to seek favor by officiousness, kindness, flattery, caresses, and the like.—

cur·ry·comb, *n.* An iron instrument or comb with very short teeth, for combing and cleaning horses.—*v.t.* To rub down or comb with a currycomb.

curse, kŭrs, *v.t.*—*cursed* or *curst, cursing.* [O.E. *cursian*, < *curs*, a curse—a word of doubtful connections.] To utter a wish of evil against; to execrate; to blast; to blight; to vex, harass, or torment with great calamities.—*v.i.* To utter imprecations; to

use blasphemous or profane language; to swear.—*n.* A malediction; the expression of a wish of evil to another; an imprecation; that which brings evil or severe affliction; torment; great vexation; condemnation or sentence of divine vengeance on sinners.— **curs·ed,** kŭr′sid, kŭrst, *a.* Being under a curse; execrable; hateful; detestable; abominable; wicked; vexatious; troublesome.— **curs·ed·ly,** *adv.*—**curs·ed·ness,** *n.*—**curst,** kŭrst, *a.* Cursed.

cur·sive, kĕr′siv, *a.* [M.L. *cursivus*, < L. *currere*, run.] Printed or written in a running or flowing hand, with the letters joined one to another.—*n.* A printed, cursive character used to imitate handwriting; a manuscript written in cursive characters.—**cur·sive·ly,** *adv.*

cur·so·ri·al, kŭr·sōr′ē·al, kŭr·sạr′ē·al, *a.* [L. *cursorius*, < *cursor*, runner.] *Zool.* fitted for running, as the limbs of an animal; having limbs adapted for running, as certain birds and insects.

cur·so·ry, kŭr′so·rē, *a.* [L. *cursorius*.] Rapidly done, often without noticing details; hasty; superficial.—**cur·so·ri·ly,** *adv.*—**cur·so·ri·ness,** *n.*

curt, kĕrt, *a.* [L. *curtus*, cut short, clipped, mutilated.] Short or shortened; brief or terse, as speech or style; abrupt or rudely short, as speech or manner.—**curt·ly,** *adv.* —**curt·ness,** *n.*

cur·tail, kĕr·tāl′, *v.t.* [O.Fr. *courtault,* M.Fr. *courteau,* < *court,* L. *curtus,* short.] To cut off the end of a part of; to make short; to shorten in any manner; to abridge; to diminish.—**cur·tail·ment,** *n.*

cur·tail step, kŭr′tāl step, *n.* [Origin uncertain.] The first or bottom step of a stair, when it is finished in a curved line at its outer ends.

cur·tain, kŭr′tan, kur′tin, *n.* [O.Fr. *curtine,* Fr. *courtine,* < L.L. *cortina,* curtain.] A movable hanging piece of material used to screen, conceal, or adorn; anything serving to shut off, cover, or conceal; as, a *curtain* of artillery fire; *theatr.* a hanging drapery separating the auditorium from the stage; the time at which the curtain is scheduled to rise signalling the start of a theatrical production; the fall or descent of the curtain at the conclusion of a scene or act of a play. *Fort.* the part of a wall or rampart connecting two bastions, towers, or the like; *arch.* a flat portion of a wall, connecting two towers, projecting structures, or the like.—*v.t.* To provide, shut off, conceal, or adorn with or as with a curtain or curtains.—**cur·tain lec·ture,** *n.* A scolding given privately, orig. behind the bed curtains at night, by a wife to her husband. —**cur·tain rais·er,** *n.* A short play acted before a principal play.

cur·tain call, *n.* The presentation of the cast of a theatrical or other production in response to the applause of the audience at the end of the performance.

cur·tate, kŭr′tāt, *a.* [L. *curtatus,* pp. of *curtare,* shorten, < *curtus,* cut short, clipped.] Shortened or reduced; abbreviated.

cur·ti·lage, kŭr′ti·lij, *n.* [O.Fr. *cortillage,* < *cortil,* < M.L. *cortile,* court, yard, < *cortis,* E. *court.*] *Law,* the area of land occupied by a dwelling and its yard and outbuildings, actually enclosed or considered as enclosed.

curt·sy, kŭrt′sē, *n.* pl. **curt·sies.** [= *courtesy.*] A bow made by women, consisting of a bending of the knees and a lowering of the body.—*v.i.*—*curtsied, curtsying.* To make a curtsy.

cu·rule, kūr′öl, *a.* [L. *curulis:* cf. *currulis, curulis,* pertaining to a chariot, < *currus,* chariot.] Noting a special form of chair or seat used by the highest magistrates of ancient Rome; privileged to sit in such a chair; of the highest rank.

cur·va·ceous, kŭr·vā′shus, *a. Colloq.* of a woman, having a shapely figure with pronounced curves.

cur·va·ture, kŭr′va·chẽr, *n.* [L. *curvatura.*] The act of curving; a curved condition; the degree of curving; a curve or bend.

curve, kŭrv, *n.* [L. *curvus,* bent, curved.] A continuously bending line without angles; any curved outline, form, thing, or part; a curving; a curved ruler used by draftsmen; *math.* a line no part of which is straight and whose coordinates are continuous functions of a single independent variable or parameter; *baseball,* a ball pitched with a spin causing it to veer.—*v.t., v.i.—curved, curving.* To bend in a curve; cause to take, or take the course of, a curve.—*a.* Curved.— **curv·ed·ness,** *n.*

cur·vet, kŭr′vit, *n.* [It. *corvetta,* < L. *curvus,* bent, curved.] A prancing leap of a horse in which the animal's forelegs are raised off the ground and then the hind legs spring in quick succession so that all four legs are in midair for an instant; *fig.* a prank or frolic.—kĕr·vet′, kŭr′vit, *v.i.*—*curvetted, curvetting, curveted, curveting.* To leap in a curvet, as a horse; to cause one's horse to do this; *fig.* to leap and frisk.—*v.t.* To cause to make a curvet.

cur·vi·lin·e·ar, kŭr′vi·lin′ē·er, *a.* [L. *curvus* and *linea,* a line.] Having the shape of a curved line; consisting of or bounded by curved lines. Also **cur·vi·lin·e·al,** kŭr″vi·lin′ē·al.—**cur·vi·lin·e·ar·i·ty,** kŭr″vi·lin″ē·ar′i·tē, *n.*—**cur·vi·lin·e·ar·ly,** *adv.*

cu·sec, kū′sek, *n.* A rate of one cubic foot per second.

cu·shaw, ka·shạ′, *n.* [N. Amer. Ind.] Any of various crookneck squashes, esp. varieties of *Cucurbita moschata.*

cush·ion, kŭsh′on, *n.* [O.Fr. *cussin, coissin* (Fr. *coussin*), < M.L. *coxinus,* < L. *coxa,* hip.] A baglike case filled with a soft material, used to support or ease the body in reclining, sitting, or kneeling; anything that resembles this in appearance, properties, or use; a pillow; the elastic raised rim of the top of a billiard table; something used to counteract the shock or jolt of moving machinery parts, as a kind of padding or a body of air or steam; a reserve fund to provide for unanticipated expenses; *Canada,* the surface of the rink on which ice hockey is played.—*v.t.* To place on or support by a cushion; to furnish with a cushion or cushions; to check motion, as of a piston, by a cushion of steam; to form something, as steam, into a cushion; to suppress quietly by ignoring; to soften or decrease the effect or impact of, as: Her criticism was *cushioned* by a soft smile.

Cush·it·ic, ku·shit′ik, *n.* [Named for Cush, an area of biblical times which was located near the Nile River.] A group of languages, part of a larger family of African-Asian languages, spoken in various East African sections, especially Ethiopia and Somaliland.—*a.* Referring to Cushitic.

cush·y, kŭsh′ē, *a.*—*cushier, cushiest.* [Cf. *cushion.*] *Slang,* comfortable or easy; as, a *cushy* job.—**cush·i·ly,** *adv.*

cusk, kusk, *n.* pl. **cusk, cusks.** [Origin unknown.] An edible marine fish similar to a cod and obtained along both coasts of the northern Atlantic; the American burbot.

cusp, kusp, *n.* [L. *cuspis* (cuspid-), point.] A point or pointed end; *astron.* a point of a crescent, esp. of the moon; *astrol.* the entrance of a house in the calculation of nativities; *geom.* a point where two branches of a curve meet, end, and are tangent; *arch.* a decorative figure formed by the intersection of two arcs or curved members; *anat. zool., bot.* a point, projection, or protuberance, as on the crown of a tooth.—

cusped, cus·pate, kus'pit, kus'pāt, **cus·- pat·ed,** *a.*

cus·pid, kus'pid, *n.* A cuspidate tooth; a canine tooth.—**cus·pi·dal,** kus'pi·dal, *a.* Pertaining to, or having a cusp; cuspidate. —**cus·pi·date,** kus'pi·dāt', *a.* Having a cusp or cusps; ending in a cusp or sharp point, as a canine tooth. Also **cus·pi·dat·- ed.—cus·pi·da·tion,** kus'pi·dā'shan, *n.* Decoration with cusps, as in architecture.

cus·pi·dor, kus'pi·dȯr", *n.* [Pg. < *cuspir*, to spit.] A spittoon.

cuss, kus, *n.* [Vulgar form of *curse.*] *Colloq.* A curse; a fellow.—*v.t., v.i. Colloq.* to curse; to criticize harshly.—**cuss·ed,** *a.* Cursed; mean.—**cuss·ed·ly,** *adv.*—**cuss·- ed·ness,** *n.* Tendency toward perversity; stubbornness.

cus·tard, kus'tẽrd, *n.* [Probably a corrup- tion of old *crustade,* a kind of stew served up in a raised *crust.*] A mixture of milk, eggs, and sweetening, which is baked, boiled, or frozen.

cus·tard ap·ple, *n.* [< the yellowish pulp.] The large, dark-brown, roundish fruit of a West Indian tree; any of several soft, pulpy edible fruits grown primarily in tropical America; any of the trees or shrubs of the family *Annonaceae* bearing such fruit; the North American papaw or its fruit.

cus·tard glass, *n.* An opaque glass which is creamy buff in color.

cus·to·di·an, ku·stō'dē·an, *n.* One who has the care or custody of anything; a guard- ian; a caretaker.—**cus·to·di·an·ship,** *n.*

cus·to·dy, kus'to·dē, *n. pl.* **cus·to·dies.** [L. *custodia,* < *custos, custodis,* a watchman, a keeper.] A keeping; a guarding; guardian- ship; care, in the sense of protection; the state of being held in keeping or under guard; imprisonment.—**cus·to·di·al,** ku·- stō'dē·al, *a.* Relating to custody or guard- ianship.

cus·tom, kus'tom, *n.* [O.Fr. *costume* (Fr. *coutume*), < L. *consuetudo* (*consuetudin-*), custom.] A habitual practice, either of an individual or a group; established usage; the usual way of acting in given circum- stances; convention; *law,* a long-established practice which has acquired the force of law. Habitual patronage of a business establishment; the customers of a business firm, collectively. A tax, tribute, or service due a feudal lord from his tenants; a toll or duty; *pl.* duties or tariffs imposed by law on imports or exports.—*a.* Made to order or esp. for an individual; as, *custom*-made shoes; dealing in things so made or doing work to order, as *custom* tailor.—**cus·tom·- a·ble,** *a.* Customary.

cus·tom·ar·y, kus'to·mer"ē, *a.* According to custom or established usage; usual; habitual; in common practice.—*n. pl.* **cus·tom·ar·ies.** A book containing the legal customs and rights of a locality.— **cus·tom·ar·i·ly,** *adv.*—**cus·tom·ar·i·- ness,** *n.*

cus·tom-built, kus'tom·bilt', *a.* Designed or made to meet an individual customer's specifications. Also *custom-made.*

cus·tom·er, kus'to·mẽr, *n.* One who trades regularly at a particular shop; a patron; a purchaser or buyer; *colloq.* a person with whom one has to deal, in the sense of fellow or chap; as, a queer *customer.*

cus·tom·er's man, *n. Stock market,* a registered representative of a member firm of the stock exchange, meeting the require- ments of the exchange as to background and knowledge of the securities business. Also **reg·is·tered rep·re·sent·a·tive.**

cus·tom house, *n.* A government office where customs or duties are collected and sailing clearances are obtained.

cus·tom·ize, kus'to·mīz, *v.t.*—*customized, customizing.* To design, construct, fit, or alter to an individual's specifications.

cus·tom-made, kus'tom·mād, *a.* Custom- built.

cut, kut, *v.t.*—*cut, cutting.* [Of Celtic origin; akin. W. *cwt,* a short piece, *cwtogi,* to curtail; Ir. *cut,* a short tail; *cutach,* bob- tailed.] To separate or divide, as the parts of, by an edged instrument, or as an edged instrument does; to make an incision in; to put an abrupt end to; to sever; to strike sharply, as with a whip; abridge or shorten, as by editing; *motion picture,* to stop shooting, as a sequence or scene; *radio, TV,* to stop taping or recording or broad- casting; *card playing,* to divide, as a pack of cards, at random into two or more parts; *sports,* to hit, as a ball, in a way as to make it change its course. To fell, as a tree; to mow or reap, as grass or hay; to sever and remove, as the nails or hair; to fashion by, or as by, cutting or carving; to hew out; to carve; to grow, as baby teeth out of gums; to wound the sensibilities of; to affect deeply; to inter- sect; to cross, as: One line *cuts* another. *Colloq.* to no longer have anything to do with; to quit; to shun the acquaintance of; to snub or shun; to absent oneself from; as, to *cut* a class.—*v.i.* To admit of being cut; to change direction sharply; *motion picture, TV,* to shift suddenly from one shot to another; *slang,* to run away or make off.

cut, kut, *n.* The act of cutting; a stroke or a blow, as with a knife or whip; an act or speech which wounds the feelings; an excision or omission of a part; a part excised or omitted; a piece of meat cut off; the quantity cut, as of lumber; a reduction in price; a passage or course straight across; as, a short *cut*; the manner or fashion in which anything is cut; style; manner; kind; the result of cutting, as an incision or wound; a passage or channel made by cutting or digging; *print.* an engraved block or plate used for printing, or an impression from it; *colloq.* a refusal to recognize an acquaintance; *colloq.* an absence when attendance is required. A cutting of the cards in card-playing; one of several pieces of straw or paper, used in drawing lots; as, to draw *cuts* for a thing; *colloq.* a share or percentage of a profit; *baseball,* a swing at a ball with a bat.—**a cut a·bove,** *colloq.* being somewhat better than.

cut, kut, *a.* That has been cut or incised; as, a *cut* diamond; watered or diluted; as, a *cut* whiskey; reduced; castrated.

cut-and-dried, kut"an·drīd', *a.* Fixed or settled in advance; lacking freshness or spon- taneity; in accordance with a set pattern.

cu·ta·ne·ous, kū·tā'nē·us, *a.* [L. *cutis,* skin.] Of, pertaining to, or affecting the cutis or skin.—**cu·ta·ne·ous·ly,** *adv.*

cut·a·way, kut'a·wā", *a.* Of a coat, having the skirt cut away from the waist in front in a curve or slope.—*n.* A cutaway coat; *motion picture, TV,* a sudden shift from one scene to another, showing a different but related action.

cut back, *v.t.* To make short by removing the end; to prune.—*v.i.* To go back while pre- senting a story, esp. in a movie, to show past events; *football,* to run suddenly in a differ- ent direction.—**cut·back,** kut'bak", *n.* A cut in production because of decline in demand; the cancellation of an order for war materiel.

cutch, kuch, *n.* Catechu.

cut down, *v.t.* To reduce, as something, in size, number, or quantity by removing un- necessary parts; to curtail; to destroy, knock down by force, or kill.—*v.i.* To reduce quantity or volume.—**cut·down,** kut'doun", *n.* Diminution; reduction.

cute, kūt, *a.*—*cuter, cutest.* [For *acute.*] *Colloq.* Quaintly pleasing or engagingly attractive; cunning; mentally acute; clever; shrewd.—**cute·ly,** *adv.*—**cute·ness,** *n.*

cut glass, *n.* Glass with patterns shaped or ornamented into its surface.—**cut-glass,** *a.*

cut-grass, kut'gras", kut'gräs", *n.* Any of various grasses with blades whose rough edges cut the flesh when drawn against it, esp. grasses of the genus *Leersia,* as *L. oryzoides.*

cu·ti·cle, kū'ti·kl, *n.* [L. *cuticula,* dim. of *cutis,* skin.] The epidermis; non-living skin which frames the nails of fingers and toes; any superficial integument, membrane, or the like; *bot.* a very thin transparent film covering the surface of plants and derived from the outer surfaces of the epidermal cells.—**cu·tic·u·lar,** kū·tik'ū·lẽr, *a.*

cut·ie, kū'tē, *n. Slang,* a clever person who tries to outsmart others; a cute person; *colloq. specif.* a cute, attractive girl.

cut in, *v.i.* To force oneself into a position belonging to others, or into a sequence or order, out of turn; to enter or join abruptly; to interrupt a talk or discussion; to inter- rupt a dancing couple to partner one of them.—**cut-in,** kut'in', *n.* Any thing cut in; act of cutting in; *colloq.* a share; as, *cut-in* on a fee; *motion picture,* an insertion, as of a close up, which interrupts the continuity of a scene; *radio and TV,* a commercial or station identification announcement in- serted into a broadcast.—*a.*

cu·tis, kū'tis, *n. pl.* **cu·tes, cu·tis·es,** kū'tēz. [L. skin.] The corium, or true skin, beneath the epidermis.—**cu·tis ve·ra,** kū'tis vēr'a, *n.* [L., "true skin."] The cutis.

cut·lass, kut'las, *n.* [Fr. *coutelas,* < O.Fr. *coutel,* knife < L. *cultellus.*] A short, heavy, slightly curved sword.

cut·ler·y, kut'le·rē, *n.* [Fr. *coutelier,* < L. *culter,* a knife.] The business of making, sharpening, repairing, or vending knives and other cutting instruments; such instru- ments collectively, esp. those for cutting and serving food.—**cut·ler,** kut'lẽr, *n.* One whose occupation is cutlery; a knife grinder.

cut·let, kut'lit, *n.* [Fr. *côtelette,* dim. of *côte,* < L. *costa,* rib.] A slice of meat for broiling or frying, orig. one, as of mutton, containing a rib, but now commonly one cut from the leg, esp. of veal or mutton; a kind of croquette in a flattened form, made of minced chicken, lobster, or the like.

cut off, *v.t.* To separate; shut out; dis- inherit; intercept; interrupt; bring to a sudden end.—**cut-off,** kut'ạf", kut'of", *n.* A cutting off, or something that cuts off; a shorter passage or way, as one across a bend; the arresting of the passage of steam or working fluid to the cylinder of an engine, or the mechanism effecting it.

cut-off point, *n. Aerospace,* a point on the trajectory of a ballistic missile or other air- borne object at which the fuel is exhausted or cut off.

cut out, *v.t.* To remove by cutting or carving; to shape or form by, or as by, cutting; to fashion; to replace, as an op- ponent; *naut.* to seize and carry off, as a vessel from a harbor.—*v.i. Colloq.* To cease; to leave hastily.—**cut·out,** kut'out", *n.* A cutting out; something that cuts out; a device for breaking an electric circuit or for eliminating part of it; a device in the exhaust pipe of an internal-combustion engine exhausting through a muffler, which when open permits the engine to exhaust directly into the air; something cut out from something else.

cut·o·ver, kut'ō"vẽr, *n.* The portion of a timbered area from which all trees have been cut.—*a.*

cut·purse, kut'pẽrs", *n.* A pickpocket; formerly, one who stole by cutting purses, a practice common when men wore purses at their waists.

cut-rate, kut'rāt", *a.* Sold or selling below the usual price.

cut·ter, kut'ẽr, *n.* One who or that which cuts; a medium-sized boat for rowing or sailing, or a launch, belonging to a ship of

war; a one-masted boat or vessel with a comparatively narrow and deep hull, rigged more or less like a sloop; a lightly armed government vessel or steamship, used to prevent smuggling and enforce the customs regulations; a small, light sleigh, usually for one horse.

cut·throat, kut'thrōt", n. A murderer; one who would probably cut throats.—a. Murderous; cruel; ruthless. Of, or pertaining to card games, such as three-handed poker, or cutthroat contract.

cut·throat trout, n. A spotted trout with a red streak under the lower jaw.

cut·ting, kut'ing, n. The act of one who or that which cuts; something cut off; a small shoot cut from a plant to start a new plant; a recording; *Brit.* a clipping from a newspaper. Something produced by cutting; an excavation made through rising ground, as in constructing a road.—a. Pertaining to, or dividing by or as by, a cut; piercing, as a wind; wounding the feelings severely, as a remark.—**cut·ting·ly**, adv.

cut·tle, kut'l, n. [O.E. *cudele*.] A cuttlefish. —**cut·tle·bone**, kut'l·bōn, n. The calcareous internal shell or plate of true cuttlefishes, used to make powder for polishing, and fed to canaries to supply the necessary lime in their diet.—**cut·tle·fish**, kut'l·fish, n. pl. **cut·tle·fish**, **cut·tle·fish·es**. Any of various cephalopods, esp. of the genus *Sepia*, having sucker-bearing arms and the power of ejecting a black inklike fluid when disturbed.

cut·up, kut'up", n. *Colloq.* one who clowns or plays pranks.

cut·wa·ter, kut'wạ"tẽr, kut'wot"er, n. The fore part of a ship's stem or prow, which cuts the water; the sharp edge of a pier of a bridge, which resists the action of water or ice.

cut·work, kut'wụrk", n. A kind of openwork embroidery in which material is cut out from within a stitched design.

cut·worm, kut'wụrm", n. Any of various caterpillars of certain nocturnal moths, which feed at night on the stems of plants, cutting them off at or near the ground.

cu·vette, kö·vet', kū·vet', n. *Chem.* a small tube or vessel, often transparent, used in an experimental laboratory. Also **cur·vette**.

C.W.A.C., CWAC. Abbreviation for Canadian Women's Army Corps.

cy·an·a·mide, sī·an'a·mid, sī·an'a·mīd", sī"a·nam'īd, sī"a·nam'id, n. *Chem.* a white crystalline compound prepared by the action of ammonia on cyanogen chloride.

cy·a·nate, sī'a·nāt", n. *Chem.* a salt of cyanic acid.

cy·an·ic, sī·an'ik, a. [Gr. *kyanos*, dark-blue; in part with reference to *cyanogen.*] Blue, applied esp. to a series of colors in flowers, including the blues and all colors which tend toward blue; pertaining to or containing cyanogen.

cy·a·nide, sī'a·nīd, sī'a·nid, n. *Chem.* a combination of cyanogen with an element or a radical; as, potassium *cyanide*, a powerful poison.—v.t.—*cyanided, cyaniding* To treat with cyanide, as an ore in the process of extracting gold.—**cy·a·nide pro·cess**, n. A method of extracting silver and gold from ores.

cy·a·nine, sī'a·nēn", sī'a·nin, n. Any of several groups of dyes used in photography that sensitize photographic film to a wider color range.

cy·a·no, sī'a·nō", a. *Chem.* containing or pertaining to the cyanogen group.

cy·a·no·co·bal·a·min, sī"a·nō·kō·bal'a·min, n. *Chem.* vitamin B$_{12}$.

cy·an·o·gen, sī·an'o·jen, n. [Fr. *cyanogène*, < Gr. *kyanos*, dark-blue, and *gen-*, bear, produce.] *Chem.* a univalent radical, CN, consisting of one atom of carbon and one of nitrogen, occurring in various compounds,

---

some of which are blue; a poisonous, flammable gas, C$_2$N$_2$.—**cy·a·no·ge·net·ic, cy·-a·no·gen·ic**, a.

cy·a·no·sis, sī"a·nō'sis, n. [N.L., < Gr. *kyanosis*, dark-blue color, < *kyanos.*] *Pathol.* blueness or lividness of the skin, as from imperfectly oxygenated blood.— **cy·a·not·ic**, a.—**cy·a·nosed**, a.

cy·ber·nate, sī"bẽr·nāt, v.t.—*cybernated, cybernating.* To equip, as a manufacturing process, with machines that regulate themselves to such an extent that little or no human control is needed.

cy·ber·net·ics, sī"bẽr·net'iks, n. pl. but sing. in constr. The study of control and communication systems in animals, men, and machines.—**cy·ber·net·ic**, sī"bẽr·-net'ik, a.

cy·borg, sī'bạrg, n. An organism with a physically implanted or physically connected electric or mechanical device, wherein the device corrects a physiological malfunction, maintains normal functions in a hostile environment, or enlarges the normal physical capacities of the body.

cy·cad, sī'kad, n. [N.L. *Cycas* (*Cycad-*), the typical genus, < Gr. *kukas*, erron. for *koikas*, acc. pl. of *koix*, kind of palm.] Any of the *Cycadaceae*, a family of tropical cone-bearing plants intermediate in appearance between the tree ferns and the palms, many having a thick, unbranched columnar trunk which bears a crown of large pinnate leaves.

cyc·la·men, sik'la·men, sik'la·men", n. [< Gr. *kyklos*, a circle, referring to the round-shaped rootstock.] A genus of low-growing herbaceous plants, with fleshy rootstocks and very handsome flowers.

cy·cle, sī'kl, n. [L.L. *cyclus*, < Gr. *kyklos*, ring, circle, wheel, round, revolution, cycle.] An orbit in the heavens; a round of years or a recurring period of time, esp. one in which certain events or phenomena repeat themselves in the same order and at the same intervals; hence, any long period of years; an age; any round of operations or events; a series which returns upon itself; any complete course or series; specif. one of the complete series of changes in the working fluid in the cylinder of an internal-combustion engine; a complete or double alternation of reversal of an alternating electric current; a series of poetic or prose narratives gathering round some mythical or heroic theme; as, the Arthurian *cycle*, the Charlemagne *cycle*; a bicycle, tricycle, or the like.—v.i.—*cycled, cycling.* To move or revolve in cycles; pass through cycles; to ride a bicycle, tricycle, or the like; travel by cycle.—**cy·cler**, n. One who cycles.

cy·cle, sī'kl, n. *Computer,* the smallest period of time in which a computer can finish an action; a series of operations in a computer, repeated as a single entity.

cy·clic, sī'klik, sik'lik, a. [Fr. *cyclique*, < L. *cyclicus*, < Gr. *kyklikos.*] Of or pertaining to a cycle or cycles; revolving or recurring in cycles; characterized by recurrence in cycles; *bot.* arranged in whorls, as the parts of a flower; of a flower, having the parts so arranged; *chem.* noting or pertaining to a compound whose structural formula contains a closed chain or ring of atoms. Also **cy·cli·cal.**—**cy·cli·cal·ly**, adv.

cy·cli·cal stocks, n. pl. *Stock market,* certain stocks, as of the textile and steel industries, that tend to follow the up-and-down trends of the total business community.

cy·cli·cal the·o·ry, n. A theory which sees fluctuations in business conditions as recurring in a predictable pattern according to specified periods of time.

cy·clist, sī'klist, n. One who rides a bicycle, tricycle, or motorcycle; a cycler.

cy·clo·graph, sī'klo·graf", sī'klo·gräf", sik'lo·graf", sik'lo·gräf", n. A device for

---

drawing curves or arcs; *photog.* a form of camera for obtaining a panoramic view of the periphery of an object, as a vase.

cy·cloid, sī'kloid, a. [Gr. *kykloeides*, < *kyklos*, circle, and *eidos*, form.] Resembling a circle; smooth and more or less circular in form, with concentric striations, as the scales of certain fishes; having such scales, as a fish; cyclothymic.—n. *Geom.* a curve generated by a point on the circumference of a circle when the circle is rolled along a straight line and kept always in the same plane; a cycloid fish.—**cy·cloi·dal**, a.—**cy·-cloi·dal·ly**, adv.

cy·clom·e·ter, sī·klom'i·tẽr, n. A device for recording the revolutions of a wheel and hence the distance traversed by a wheeled vehicle; an implement which measures circular arcs.

cy·clone, sī'klōn, n. [< Gr. *kyklos*, a circle.] A circular or rotary storm of immense, destructive force, revolving at enormous speed around a calm center, and at the same time advancing at a rate varying from 20 to 40 miles an hour, rotating in the Northern Hemisphere from right to left, and in the Southern Hemisphere from left to right.—**cy·clon·ic**, **cy·clo·nal**, a.— **cy·clon·i·cal·ly**, adv.

Cy·clo·pe·an, sī"klo·pē'an, a. Of or characteristic of the Cyclops, one of a race of mythological giants having a single eye in the middle of the forehead; (*sometimes l.c.*) gigantic; vast; (*usu. l.c.*) noting an early style of masonry employing massive, irregular stones.

cy·clo·pe·di·a, cy·clo·pae·di·a, sī"klo·-pē'dē·a, n. [N.L., < Gr. *kyklos*, circle, and *paideia*, education.] An encyclopedia.— **cy·clo·pe·dic, cy·clo·pae·dic**, a.—**cy·-clo·pe·dist, cy·clo·pae·dist**, n.

cy·clo·pro·pane, sī"klo·prō'pān, sik'lo·-prō'pān, n. A flammable gas, C$_3$H$_6$, used as an anesthetic.

cy·clo·ram·a, sī"klo·ram'a, sī"klo·rä'ma, n. [Gr. *kyklos*, circle, and *orama*, view.] A pictorial representation, as of a landscape or a battle, on the wall of a cylindrical room or hall, appearing in perspective to the spectators occupying a position in the center; a curved backdrop, as a screen or curtain, used as the background in a stage setting.—**cy·clo·ram·ic**, a.

cy·clo·stome, sī'klo·stōm", sik'lo·stōm", n. Any eellike aquatic vertebrate of the class *Cyclostomata* including the lampreys and hagfishes and characterized by pouchlike gills and a circular suctorial mouth without jaws.—a. Having a circular mouth; belonging or pertaining to the *Cyclostomata.*

cy·clo·thy·mi·a, sī"klo·thī'mē·a, sik"lo·-thī'mē·a, n. *Psychiatry,* a mild psychosis of the manic-depressive type, in which the personality alternates between depressive and elated states.—**cy·clo·thyme**, n. An individual afflicted with cyclothymia.— **cy·clo·thy·mic**, a.

cy·clo·tron, sī'klo·tron", sik'lo·tron", n. *Phys.* a device for imparting high speed and energy to charged particles as the cumulative effect of subjecting them repeatedly to an alternating electric field of relatively low voltage, through which they are guided in a spiral path by the use of magnets.

cyg·net, sig'nit, n. [Dim. of Fr. *cygne*, < L. *cygnus*, a swan.] A young swan.

Cyg·nus, sig'nus, n. *Astron.* a northern constellation in the Milky Way, the Swan, including the bright star Deneb.

cyl·in·der, sil'in·dẽr, n. [L. *cylindrus*, < Gr. *kylindros*, roller, cylinder, < *kylindein*, roll.] A geometrical solid generated by the revolution of a rectangle about one of its sides, constituting a figure enclosed by two parallel circular bases and a curved surface whose elements are perpendicular to the bases, called "right circular cylinder"; a

---

ch- chain, G. na*ch*t;   **th-** THen, thin;   **w-** wig, hw as sound in whig;   **z-** zh as in azure, zeal.   *Italicized vowel* indicates schwa sound.

similar solid in which the elements of the curved surface are oblique to the circular bases, called 'oblique circular cylinder'; any solid bounded by two parallel planes and a curved surface generated by a moving straight line which constantly touches a fixed curve and is always parallel to its original position; a curved surface generated in this manner; any cylinderlike object or part, whether solid or hollow; the rotating part of a revolver, which contains the chambers for the cartridges; the chamber in an engine in which the working fluid acts upon the piston; the cylindrical chamber of a pump, in which the piston moves the fluid; in certain printing presses, a rotating cylinder which produces the impression to be printed, or either of two cylinders which rotate against each other in opposite directions; *archaeol.* a cylindrical tablet of clay or stone with cuneiform inscriptions, worn as a seal or talisman by the Babylonians and related peoples.—*v.t.* To furnish with a cylinder or cylinders; to subject to the action of a cylinder or cylinders.

cy·lin·dric, si·lin′drik, *a.* [Gr. *kylindricos.*] Of, pertaining to, or of the form of a cylinder.—**cy·lin·dri·cal·ly**, *adv.*—**cyl·in··droid**, sil′in·droid″, *n.* A solid having the form of a cylinder with equal and parallel elliptical bases. Also **cy·lin·dri·cal**, si··lin′drik·al.

cy·ma, si′ma, *n.* pl. **cy·mas**, **cy·mae**, si′mē. [Gr. *kyma*, a wave, a sprout, < *kyō*, to swell.] *Arch.* a molding of a cornice, the profile of which is a double curve, concave joined to convex; an ogee molding. *Bot.* a cyme.

cy·ma·ti·um, si·mā′shē·um, *n.* pl. **cy·ma·ti·a**, si·mā′shē·a. [L., < Gr. *kymation*, dim. of *kyma*, E. *cyma.*] *Arch.* a cyma, esp. the capping or crowning molding of a cornice, placed above the corona.

cym·bal, sim′bal, *n.* [L. *cymbalum*, Gr. *kymbalon*, a cymbal, < *kymbos*, hollow.] A musical instrument, circular and hollow like a dish, made of brass or bronze, two of which are struck glancingly together, producing a sharp ringing sound.—**cym··bal·ist**, *n.* One who plays the cymbals.

cym·bid·ium, sim·bid′ē·um, *n.* Any variety of the genus *Cymbidium*, terrestrial orchid with boat-shaped flowers which range in color from pale cream to bronze, popularly used for corsages.

cyme, sim, *n.* [Gr. *kyma*, a wave, a sprout. CYMA.] *Bot.* an inflorescence of the definite or determinate class, in which the flowers are in racemes, corymbs, or umbels, the successive central flowers expanding first.—**cy·mose**, si′mōs, si·mōs′, *a.* Containing or pertaining to a cyme; in the form of a cyme.—**cy·mose·ly**, *adv.*

cy·mene, si′mēn, *n.* [L. *cyminum.*] *Chem.* a liquid hydrocarbon with a pleasant smell, occurring in the volatile oil of the common cumin, *Cuminum cyminum*, and used in the manufacture of resins and metal polishes and as a solvent.

cy·mo·gene, si′mo·jēn″, *n. Chem.* a mixture of very volatile inflammable hydrocarbons, principally butane, obtained at the beginning of the distillation of crude petroleum, and used for producing low temperatures by evaporation.

cyn·ic, sin′ik, *n.* [L. *cynicus*, < Gr. *kynikos*, doglike, churlish, Cynic, < *kyon* (*kyn-*) dog.] (*Cap.*), *philos.* one of a sect of ancient Greek philosophers who taught that pleasure is an evil if sought for its own sake, and made an ostentatious show of contempt for riches and enjoyment; (*l.c.*) a sneering faultfinder; one who disbelieves in the goodness of human motives, and who is given to displaying his disbelief by sneers and sarcasm.—*a.* (*Cap.*) Of or pertaining to Cynic philosophy or Cynic philosophers;

cynical.—**cyn·i·cism**, sin′i·siz″um, *n.* The practice of a cynic; a morose contempt of the pleasures and arts of life.

cyn·i·cal, sin′i·kal, *a.* (*Cap.*) Of, pertaining to, resembling, or suggestive of the Cynics or their doctrines; (*l.c.*) like or characteristic of a cynic.—**cyn·i·cal·ness**, *n.*—**cyn·i··cal·ly**, *adv.*

cy·no·sure, si′no·shŏr″, sin′o·shŏr″, *n.* [Gr. *kynosoura*, lit. dog's tail, the Little Bear—*kyŏn*, *cynos*, a dog, and *oura*, tail.] (*Cap.*) an old name of the constellation Ursa Minor or the Little Bear, which contains the polestar, and thus has long been noted by mariners and others; (*l.c.*) anything that strongly attracts attention; a center of attraction.

cy·pher, si′fẽr, *n.* Cipher.

cy pres, si′prā′, *n. Law*, the practice of carrying out the wishes of a testator as closely as possible when these wishes are impossible, impractical, or illegal to administer exactly as directed.—*adv.*

cy·press, si′pres, *n.* [O.Fr. *cipres* (Fr. *cyprès*), < L.L. *cypressus*, < Gr. *kyparissos.*] Any of the evergreen trees constituting the pine family, genus *Cupressus*, distinguished by dark-green, scalelike, overlapping leaves, a hard, durable wood, and symmetrical growth; any of various other pine trees allied to the true cypress of the southern U.S.; the wood of any such tree; any of various other plants in some way resembling the true cypress; the branches of the true cypress, used as an emblem of mourning.

cy·press vine, *n.* An annular garden plant, *Quamoclit pennata*, with finely parted leaves and scarlet or white tubular flowers.

Cyp·ri·an, sip′rē·an, *a.* Pertaining to Cyprus, esp. as the reputed birthplace of Aphrodite, and ancient home of her worshipers; lewd; licentious. Also **Cyp·ri·ote**.

cyp·ri·pe·di·um, sip″ri·pē′dē·um, *n.* [N.L.] Any plant of the genus *Cypripedium*, comprising orchids having large drooping flowers with a protruding saclike labellum; a lady's-slipper.

cyr·to·sis, sẽr·tō′sis, *n.* [N.L. < Gr. *kyrtosis*, < *kyrtos*, curved.] *Pathol.* an abnormal curvature of the spine and of the limbs.

cyr·to·style, sẽr′to·stil, *n.* [Gr. *kyrtos*, curved, and *stylos*, pillar, column.] *Arch.* a portico with columns arranged in a projecting curve.

cyst, sist, *n.* [N.L. *cystis*, < Gr. *kystis*, bladder, bag, pouch.] A bladder, sac, or vesicle; *pathol.* a closed bladderlike sac formed in animal tissues, containing fluid or semifluid morbid matter; *zool.* a capsule or resistant covering, esp. the sac developed by larval tapeworms which live in the tissues of certain animals; *bot.* a cell or cavity enclosing reproductive bodies.—**cys·tec··to·my**, sis·tek′tō·mē, *n.* pl. **cys·tec·to·mies**. *Surg.* excision of a cyst or bladder.—**cys·tic**, sis′tik, *a.* Pertaining to or having a cyst or cysts; encysted.

cys·tic fi·bro·sis, *n. Pathol.* a hereditary disease appearing in childhood, involving the pancreas and lungs.

cys·ti·tis, si·sti′tis, *n. Pathol.* inflammation of the bladder.

cys·to·cele, sis′to·sēl″, *n.* [Gr. *kelē*, a tumor.] *Pathol.* a hernia or rupture formed by the protrusion of the urinary bladder into the vagina.

cys·toid, sis′toid, *a.* Resembling a cyst, but having no membrane; bladderlike.—*n.* A cystoid structure.

cys·to·scope, sis′to·skōp″, *n. Med.* an instrument for examining the interior of the bladder.—**cys·to·scop·ic**, sis″to·skop′ik, *a.*

cy·to·ar·chi·tec·ture, si″tō·är′ki·tek″·chẽr, *n.* The cell structure of a bodily tissue or part.

cy·to·chem·is·try, si″to·kem′i·strē, *n.*

The science of the structure and chemistry of living cells.

cy·to·chromes, si′to·krōmz″, *n.* A class of iron-containing proteins found in cells of animals and plants dependent upon oxygen.

cy·to·gen·e·sis, si″to·jen′i·sis, *n.* [Gr.] *Biol.* the origin and development of cells in animal and vegetable structures. Also **cy·tog·e·ny**.—**cy·to·ge·net·ic**, **cy·to·gen·ic**, si″tō·je·net′ik, *a.*—**cy·to·ge·net··ics**, *n.*

cy·to·ki·ne·sis, si″tō·ki·nē′sis, si″tō·ki··nē′sis, *n.* Cytoplasmic changes during fertilization and cell division.

cy·tol·o·gy, si·tol′o·jē, *n.* The scientific study of the structure, functions, and life cycle of cells.—**cy·tol·o·gist**, *n.*—**cy·to··log·i·cal**, *a.*

cy·tol·y·sis, si·tol′i·sis, *n. Physiol.* the dissolution or degeneration of cells.

cy·to·plasm, si′to·plaz″um, *n. Biol.* the living substance or protoplasm of a cell exclusive of the nucleus.—**cy·to·plas·mic**, *a.*

cy·to·tax·on·o·my, sit″ō·tak·sän′ō·mē, *n.* Classification of plants and animals according to characteristics of the chromosomes.—**cy·to·tax·o·nom·ic**, *a.*

cy·to·trop·ic, si″to·trop′ik, *a. Biol.* drawn toward or having an attraction for cells, as various viruses; of or pertaining to propensity of cells to be drawn toward or to move away from each other, singly or in groups.—**cy·tot·ro·pism**, si·to′tro·piz″um, *n.* The tendency of cells to move.

czar, zär, *n.* [Russ. *tsar*, < L. *Cæsar*, Cæsar.] An emperor or king; (*cap.*) the former emperor of Russia; (*often cap.*) an autocratic master or leader. Also *tsar.*—**cza·ri·na**, zä·rē′na, *n.* A czar's wife; a Russian empress. Also **czar·it·za**, *tsarina.*

czar·das, chär′däsh, *n.* [Hung.] A Hungarian national dance in two movements, one slow and the other fast.

czar·dom, zär′dom, *n.* The power of a czar; land ruled by a czar. Also *tsardom.*

czar·e·vitch, zär′e·vich, *n.* [Russ. *tsarevich.*] A son of a czar; in earlier use, any son of the emperor of Russia; later, the eldest son. Also *tsarevitch.*—**cza·rev·na**, zä·rev′na, *n.* [Russ. *tsarevna.*] A daughter of a czar; in later use, in Russia, the wife of the czarevitch. Also *tsarevna.*

czar·ism, zär′iz·um, *n.* The rule of the czars in Russia; a dictatorship. Also *tsarism.*—**czar·ist**, zär′ist, *n.* A follower of the czar or of czarism. Also *tsarist.*

Czech·o·slo·va·kian, chek″o·slo·vä′kē··an, *a.* Of or pertaining to the inhabitants and languages of Czechoslovakia, the most western Slovak country. Also **Czech.**—*n.* A native of Czechoslovakia; the Czech and Slovak languages. Also **Czech.**

D

D, d, dē, *n.* In the English alphabet, the fourth letter and the third consonant, representing a dental sound; the Roman numeral for 500; *mus.* the second note of the natural scale, corresponding to the French and Italian *re.* A grade which denotes poor performance by a student.

'd. Contraction of verb auxiliaries *did, had, would,* and *should,* as: Where'd he go? I'd already gone. We'd like to go.

dab, dab, *v.t.*—**dabbed, dabbing.** [Allied to O.D. *dabben*, to dabble, probably also to *dub.*] To strike quickly but lightly with the hand or with some soft or moist substance; to apply lightly, as salve to a burn.—*n.* A gentle blow with the hand or some soft substance; a quick but light blow; a small lump or mass of anything soft or moist.

dab, dab, *n.* A name common to many species of the flatfish, but esp. to a kind of flounder found along the European and American coasts of the Atlantic Ocean.

dab·ber, dab′ẽr, *n.* One who or that which dabs; a cushionlike or cotton-tipped article used for applying liquids, or pastes.

dab·ble, dab′l, *v.t.*—*dabbled, dabbling.* [< *dab.*] To wet; to moisten; to spatter; to sprinkle.—*v.i.* To play in water, as with the hands; to splash in mud or water; to do or engage in anything in a superficial manner. —*dab·bler*, *n.* One who dabbles in water or mud; a superficial, casual participant; as, a *dabbler* in politics.

dab·chick, dab′chik″, *n.* [*Dab* equivalent, to *dip*, and *chick*, from its habit of dipping or diving below the water.] The little grebe, a small swimming and diving bird.

da ca·po, dä kä′pō, *It.* dä kä′pa, *a., adv.* [It., "from (the) head."] *Mus.* from the beginning: a direction to repeat.

dace, dās, *n. pl.* **dac·es**, or, esp. collectively, **dace**. [O.Fr. *dars*, dace, = *dart*, E. *dart.*] A small fresh-water fish, *Leuciscus leuciscus*, of Europe, with a stout body; any of several similar or related fishes of the U.S.

dachs·hund, daks′hụnd″, daks′und″, dash′-hụnd″, dash′und, *Ger.* däks′hụnt″, *n.* [G., < *dachs*, badger, and *hund*, dog.] One of a German breed of small hounds with a long body and very short legs.

da·coit, da·koit, da·koit′, *n.* In India, Pakistan, and Burma, one of a class of robbers who plunder in bands.—**da·coit·y**, *n.* pl. **da·coit·ies**. The system or an incident of robbing by bands of dacoits.

Da·cron, dā′kron, dā′kron, dak′ron, dak′-ron, *n.* A synthetic fiber characterized by resilience and resistance to wrinkling; the fabric woven of this fiber. (Trademark.)

dac·tyl, dak′til, dak′til, *n.* [Gr. *daktylos*, a finger, a dactyl, which, like a finger, consists of one long and two short members.] A poetical foot of three syllables, the first long and the others short, or the first accented, the others not; a finger or toe.— **dac·tyl·ic**, dak·til′ik, *a.* Pertaining to or consisting chiefly or wholly of dactyls.—*n.* A dactylic verse.

dac·ty·lol·o·gy, dak″ti·lol′o·jē, *n. pl.* **dac·ty·lol·o·gies**. The art of communicating ideas or thoughts by the fingers; the language of the deaf and dumb.

dad, dad, *n.* [Akin W. *tad*, Skt. *tata*, Hind. *dada*, Gypsy *dad*, *dada*, L. *tata*, Gr. *tata*, Lapp *dadda*—father.] *Colloq.* father. Also **dad·dy**, dad′ē, pl. **dad·dies**.

da·da, dä′dä, *n.* (*Often cap.*) A style in art and literature which flourished briefly after World War I, protesting against restraint, social convention, and logic.—**da·da·ism**, *n.*

dad·dy-long·legs, dad′ē·lạng′legz″, dad′-ē·lọng′legz″, *n. pl.* **dad·dy-long·legs**. Any of the arachnids constituting the order *Phalangidea*; a harvestman; *Brit.* any of the long-legged insects constituting the family *Tipulidae*, as a crane fly.

da·do, dā′dō, *n. pl.* **da·does**, **da·dos**. [It., die, cube, pedestal, = E. *die.*] The part of a pedestal between the base and the cornice or cap; a similar part in other structures, as at the bottom of an exterior wall; the lower part of an interior wall, often finished with fabric, wallpaper, or paint; *carp.* a rectangular groove made to receive a board.— *v.t.* Provide with a dado; cut a groove in.

dae·dal, dēd′al, *a.* [L. *Dædalus*, Gr. *Daidalos*, an ingenious artist.] Showing artistic skill; ingenious; mazy; intricate.

dae·mon, dē′mon, *n.* See *demon.*

daff, daf, *v.i.* [M.E. *daffe:* cf. *daft.*] *Sc., North. Eng.* to dally; make sport; play.

daf·fo·dil, daf′o·dil, *n.* [For M.E. *affodylle*, < L. *asphodelus.*] A species of plant, *Narcissus pseudonarcissus*, with single or double yellow nodding flowers, blooming in the spring; formerly, any plant of the genus *Narcissus.* Also **daf·fo·dil·ly**, **daf·-fo·down·dil·ly**, daf″o·doun″dil′ē.

daff·y, daf′ē, *a.*—*daffier, daffiest. Colloq.* silly; weak-minded.

daft, daft, däft, *a.* [= *deft.*] Simple or foolish; mad or crazy; *Sc.* madly gay.— **daft·ly**, *adv.*—**daft·ness**, *n.*

dag, dag, *n. Canadian.* A heavy, triangular blade with a double cutting edge, used as a weapon and tool by Indians.

dag·ger, dag′ẽr, *n.* [W. *dagr*, Ir. *daigear*, Armor. *dager*, *dag*, a dagger or poniard; Gael. *daga*, a dagger; Fr. *dague*, a dagger.] A weapon resembling a short sword, with a sharp-pointed blade, used for stabbing at close quarters; *print.* a mark of reference in the form of a dagger, †.—*v.t.* To stab with a dagger; *print.* to mark using a dagger.—**at dag·gers drawn**, on hostile terms; at war.—**look or speak dag·gers**, to look or speak fiercely, savagely.

da·go·ba, dä′go·ba, *n. pl.* **da·go·bas**. [Singhalese *dāgaba.*] In Buddhist countries, specif. in Ceylon, a dome-shaped monumental structure containing relics of Buddha or of some Buddhist saint; a stupa.

da·guerre·o·type, da·ger′o·tīp″, da·ger′ē·o·tīp″, *n.* [From L. J. M. *Daguerre* (1789–1851), French inventor.] An early photographic process in which the impression was made on a silver surface sensitized to the action of light by iodine, and then developed by mercury vapor; a picture made by this process.—*v.t. daguerreotyped, daguerreotyping.* To photograph by the daguerreotype process.—**da·guerre·o·typ·er**, **da·guerre·o·typ·ist**, *n.*—**da·-guerre·o·ty·py**, *n.* The daguerreotype process.

dah, dä, *n.* The dash used in the code of telegraphy or radio, represented by a tone interval approximately three times as long as the dot.

da·ha·be·ah, dä″ha·bē′a, *n.* [Egyptian name.] A boat used on the Nile for the conveyance of travelers, formerly having sails, but now motorized.

dahl·ia, dal′ya, däl′ya, *Brit.* dāl′ya, *n.* [N.L. from A. *Dahl*, Swedish botanist.] Any plant of the asterlike genus *Dahlia*, native to Mexico and Central America, widely cultivated for its showy, variously colored flowers.

da·hoon, da·hön′, *n.* [Origin uncertain.] An evergreen shrub or small tree, *Ilex cassine*, native to the southern U.S.

Dail Eir·eann, dạl ar′ạn; *Irish*, THạl âr′ạn, *n.* The lower house of parliament in Ireland.

dai·ly, dā′lē, *a.* [O.E. *dæglic.*] Of, pertaining to, occurring, or issued each successive day or, sometimes, each successive weekday.— *n. pl.* **dai·lies**. A newspaper published each weekday; anything appearing each day.— *adv.* Every day; day by day.—**dai·li·ness**, *n.*—**dai·ly dou·ble**, *n. Horse Racing*, a combination bet in which the better attempts to pick the winners in two specified races in the course of a day.

dai·mon, dī′mōn, *n.* [Gr. *daimōn*, deity, fate.] *Myth.* a demon or attendant spirit; a genius.

dai·myo, **dai·mio**, dī′mū, *n. pl.* **dai·myo**, **dai·myos**. [Japanese.] *Hist.* a feudal lord in Japan.

dain·ty, dān′tē, *a.*—*daintier, daintiest.* [< O.Fr. *daintie, dainté*, pleasantness, an agreeable thing.] Delicately beautiful; delicious, as food; overly particular in taste; fastidious.—**dain·ti·ly**, *adv.* In a dainty manner.—**dain·ti·ness**, *n.*

dain·ty, dān′tē, *n. pl.* **dain·ties**. A delicacy.

dai·qui·ri, dī′ki·rē, dak′i·rē, *n. pl.* **dai·qui·ris**. [Cuba.] A cocktail made of rum, lime juice, and sugar.

dair·y, dâr′ē, *n. pl.* **dair·ies**. [M.E. *deyerie*, < *deie*, *daie*, maid, dairymaid, < O.E. *dæge* (= Icel. *deigja*), lit. "kneader," "bread-maker," akin to *dāh*, E. *dough.*] A place, as a room or building, where milk and cream are kept and made into butter and cheese; a shop where milk, and butter are sold; the business of producing, processing, bottling, and distributing milk, and manufacturing butter and cheese; a dairy-farm.—**dair·y farm**, *n.* A farm devoted chiefly to the production of milk.—**dair·y far·mer**, *n.*—**dair·y farm·ing**, *n.*—**dair·-y·ing**, *n.* The business of a dairy.

dair·y cat·tle, *n. pl.* Cows that are raised for their milk.

dair·y·man, *n. pl.* **dair·y·men**. An owner, manager, or an employee of a dairy.—**dair·y·maid**, dâr′ē·mād″, *n.* A female who milks cows and works in a dairy.

da·is, dā′is, dī′is, dās, *n.* [O.Fr. *dais*, *deis*, a dining table, < L. *discus*, a dish, a quoit.] A raised platform in a hall for a throne, speaker's desk, or table for prominent persons.

dai·sy, dā′zē, *n. pl.* **dai·sies**. [O.E. *daeges-ēage*, "day's eye."] An often cultivated composite plant of the genus *Bellis* or *Chrysanthemum*, having flowers with a yellow disk and white or pink rays.

dak, dauk, dawk, dạk, däk, *n.* [Hind. *dāk.*] In the East Indies, transportation, as of letters or of travelers, by relays of men or horses; the post or mail; any arrangement for transportation or travel by relays.

Da·ko·ta, da·kō′ta, *n. pl.* **Da·ko·tas**. A tribe of Indians living on the plains of N. America; a member of this tribe; the language of this tribe which is related to Sioux.

dale, dāl, *n.* [O.E. *dael* = Icel. Sw. Goth., etc., *dal*, G. *thal*, a valley.] A low place between hills; a vale or valley.—**dales·man**, dālz′man, *n.* One living in a dale or valley, esp. in northern England.

dalles, dalz, *n. pl.* [Canadian Fr., < Fr. *dalle*, gutter, trough.] Rapids flowing over a flat rock bottom in a narrowed portion of a river. Also **dells**.

Dal·lis grass, *n.* A perennial grass introduced as pasture grass in southern U.S.

Dall sheep, **Dall's sheep**, dạl shēp, dạlz shēp, *n.* A wild sheep with curved horns, found in the mountains of the northwestern part of N. America.

dal·ly, dal′ē, *v.i.*—*dallied, dallying.* [Probably allied to G. *dalen, dallen, tallen*, to speak or act childishly, to trifle, to toy; or perhaps E. *doll.*] To amuse oneself with idle play; to play, esp. to trifle; to linger; to delay amorously.—**dal·li·ance**, dal′ē·ans, dal′yans, *n.* The act of dallying, trifling, deferring, or delaying.—**dal·li·er**, *n.*

Dal·ma·tian, dal·mā′shan, *a.* Of or pertaining to Dalmatia, an area on the Adriatic sea, or its inhabitants.—*n.* A native or inhabitant of Dalmatia. A large, short-haired, white dog marked with black or brown spots. Also **Dal·ma·tian dog**, **coach dog**.

dal·mat·ic, dal·mat′ik, *n.* [L.L. *dalmatica*, prop. fem. of L. *dalmaticus*, Dalmatian.] *Rom. Cath. Ch.* an ecclesiastical vestment worn over the alb by the deacon, as at the celebration of the Mass, and worn by bishops on certain occasions. A similar robe worn by English monarchs at coronation.

dal se·gno, däl sān′yō, *It.* däl se′nū, *adv. Mus.* directing the performer to go back to the sign that marks the beginning of the repeat.

dal·ton·ism, dạl′to·niz″um, *n.* [John *Dalton*, the chemist, who suffered from this defect, and was the first to call attention to it.] (*Sometimes cap.*) Color blindness, esp. the inability to differentiate between red and green.

dam, dam, *n.* [M.E. *dam* = D. *dam* = G. *damm* = Icel. *dammr.*] A barrier to obstruct the flow of a liquid, esp. one of earth or masonry, built across a stream; a body of water confined by a dam; any dam-like barrier, as one to keep out water or gas from a mine.—*v.t.*—*damned*, *damming*. To furnish with a dam; obstruct or confine with a dam; in general, to stop up or shut up.

dam, dam, *n.* [A form of *dame*.] A female parent: used now only of quadrupeds, unless in contempt.

dam·age, dam'ij, *n.* [O.Fr. *damage*; Fr. *dommage*, < L.L. *damnaticum*, < L. *damnum*, loss, injury.] Any hurt, injury, or harm to person, property, character, or reputation; *law*, *usu. pl.* the estimated money equivalent for detriment or injury sustained; *colloq.* charge or expense.—*v.t.* —*damaged*, *damaging*. To injure; to impair; to lessen the soundness, goodness, or value of.—*v.i.* To become injured or impaired in soundness or value.—**dam·age·a·ble**, *a.* —**dam·age·a·ble·ness**, **dam·ag·a·bil-·i·ty**, *n.*—**dam·ag·er**, *n.*—**dam·ag·ing**, *a.* Capable of injuring; causing injury.

dam·an, dam'an, *n.* [Ar.] A small, rabbit-like, ungulate mammal, *Procavia syriaca*, of Syria and Palestine, the cony (coney) of the Bible; any of various other animals of the same genus.

Dam·a·scene, dam'a·sēn″, dam″a·sēn′, *a.* [L. *Damascenus*.] Of or pertaining to the city of Damascus, in Syria; (*l.c.*) of or pertaining to the art of damascening or to damask.—*n.* An inhabitant of Damascus; (*l.c.*) work or patterns produced by damascening.

dam·a·scene, dam'a·sēn″, dam″a·sēn′, *v.t.*—*damascened*, *damascening*. To ornament or form designs, as on metal, by inlaying with gold or other precious metals, or by etching; to produce a wavy or variegated pattern, as on metal, like the one on the sword blades of Damascus. Also **dam·a·skeen**, dam'a·skēn″, dam″a·skēn′. —**dam·a·scen·ing**, *n.* The act or art of producing damascened metal or articles; the design, pattern, or wavy appearance on damascened metal. Also **dam·a·skeen-·ing**.

Da·mas·cus steel, da·mas'kus stēl′. [From *Damascus*, city in Syria, famous for metal-work and fabrics.] A kind of steel originally made in the East, chiefly at Damascus, and used for making sword blades, the surfaces of which exhibit a wavy or variegated pattern; a product of similar appearance, as that produced by welding iron and steel together, or by etching a wavy pattern on ordinary steel. Also **da·mas·cus**.

dam·ask, dam'ask, *a.* [M.E. *damaske*, < L. *damascus*, < Gr. *Damaskos*, Damascus.] Of, from, or named for the city of Damascus in Syria; as, *damask* silk or linen, *damask* rose; pink, as the damask rose.— *n.* Damascus steel, or the peculiar pattern or wavy appearance on its surface; a fabric of silk, linen, cotton, or wool, with a woven, often elaborate pattern; the pink color of the damask rose.—*v.t.* To damascene by inlaying; to weave or adorn with elaborate designs; to make of the pink color of the damask rose.

dam·ask rose, *n.* A color of deep pink or rose.

dame, dām, *n.* [O.Fr. Fr. *dame*, < L. *domina*, mistress, lady, fem. of *dominus*, master, lord.] *Archaic*, a woman of authority, as a female ruler, the mistress of a household, or the mistress of a school; an elderly matron; *slang*, a woman; *Brit.* (*cap.*) the legal title prefixed to the Christian name and surname of the wife of a knight or baronet; the distinctive title employed before the name of a woman upon whom a dignity corresponding to that of a knight has been conferred; as, *Dame* Nellie Melba.

dame's vi·o·let, *n.* A perennial garden plant, *Hesperis matronalis*, with spikes of fragrant white or purple flowers. Also **dame's rock·et**, **gar·den rock·et**.

dam·mar, dam'ér, *n.* [Malay *damar*, resin.] A fossilous resin from various coniferous trees of the genus *Dammara*, of India and the islands of the southwestern Pacific, which is much used for making colorless varnish; any of various similar resins from trees of other genera. Also **dam·ar**, **dam·mer**.

damn, dam, *v.t.* To condemn or censure; as, to *damn* a book; to bring condemnation upon, as: His actions *damned* him. To condemn to hell. To use the word *damn* when swearing or cursing.—*v.i.* To curse; to employ the word *damn.*—*n.* Uttering *damn* as a curse; the smallest, most worthless bit; as, not amount to a *damn.*—*adv.*, *adj.* Damned.—*interj.* An oath expressing anger or frustration.—**damn·ing**, *a.* That damns or condemns; occasioning condemnation.—**damn·ing·ly**, *adv.*

dam·na·ble dam'na·bl, *a.* [O.Fr. Fr., < L.L. *damnabilis.*] Worthy of condemnation; detestable, abominable, or outrageous.— **dam·na·ble·ness**, *n.*—**dam·na·bly**, *adv.*

dam·na·tion, dam·nā'shan, *n.* The act of damning or the state of being damned; a cause of being damned; *theol.* a sin deserving eternal punishment; an oath or curse.—*interj.* An oath or expression of anger or disappointment.

dam·na·to·ry, dam'na·tōr″ē, dam'-na·tạr″ē, *a.* [L. *damnatorius.*] Conveying or occasioning condemnation; damning.— **damned**, damd, *a.* Condemned, esp. to eternal punishment; accursed: often used profanely, or as an emphatic expletive or intensive.—*adv.* Slang, very; to an extreme degree; as, *damned* hard.

dam·ni·fy, dam'ni·fī″, *v.t.*—*damnified*, *damnifying*. Law, to cause damage or loss to.

damp, damp, *a.* [Same word as D. and Dan. *damp*, G. *dampf*, steam, vapor, fog, smoke.] Moderately wet; moist; humid. —*n.* Moist air; humidity; moisture; a noxious exhalation issuing from the earth, deleterious or fatal to animal life, such as exists in old disused wells, in mines, and coal pits.—*v.t.* To dampen; moisten; to stifle or suffocate; dull or deaden; check or retard the action, as of a vibrating string; to deaden the energy or ardor of; depress; discourage; *elect.* to cause, as the members of a group or series of consecutive oscillations or waves, to fall off in amplitude as the end of the group or series is approached.— *v.i. Hort.* to rot, with *off*; *elect.* to lessen progressively in amplitude.

damp·en, dam'pen, *v.t.*—To make damp; moisten; to dull or deaden; depress; damp. —*v.i.* To become damp; to become depressed.

damp·er, dam'pér, *n.* One who or that which damps; an iron plate sliding across a flue of a furnace to check or regulate the draft of air; a piece of mechanism in a pianoforte which, after the finger has left the key, checks a long-continued vibration of the strings; *elect.* a device which diminishes the oscillation of a suspended or freely moving mechanism.

damp·ing-off, dam'ping·af′, dam'ping·of′, *n.* The diseased condition of cuttings or seedlings due to certain fungi and evidenced by rotting and wilting.

dam·sel, dam'zel, *n.* [Fr. *demoiselle*, O.Fr. *damoisele*, *damisele*, < L:L. *dominicella*, dim. of L. *domina*, *domna*, a mistress.] A young woman; a maiden; a girl; *archaic*, a young maiden of noble birth. Also **dam·o·zel**, **dam·o·sel**.

dam·son, dam'zon, *n.* [M.E. *damascene*, "plum of Damascus," < L. *Damascenus*, E. *Damascene*.] The small dark-blue or purple plum, *Prunus insititia* or *Prunus domestica insititia*, introduced into Europe from Asia Minor; the tree bearing this fruit.

dam·son-cheese, *n.* A damson plum preserve with a consistency of soft cheese.

dance, dans, däns, *v.i.*—*danced*, *dancing*. [O.Fr. *dancer* (Fr. *danser*); prob. < Teut.] Move with the feet or body rhythmically and in a more or less set succession of movements, esp. to music; engage, or take part, in a dance; to leap, skip, as from excitement or emotion; move nimbly or quickly; to bob up and down.—*v.t.* To cause to dance; to perform, or take part in (a dance); to bring about or cause to be by dancing.—**dance at·ten·dance**, to attend assiduously or obsequiously, as on a person. —**dan·cer**, dan'sér, däns'ér, *n.*

dance, dans, däns, *n.* [O.Fr. *dance* (Fr *danse*).] A succession of more or less regularly ordered steps and movements of the body, usually performed to musical accompaniment; an act or round of dancing; any of the many regulated successions of steps which constitute particular forms of dancing; any recurring leaping, springing, or similar movement; a piece of music suited in rhythm to a particular form of dancing; a social gathering for dancing; a ball.

dan·de·li·on, dan'de·lī″on, *n.* [Fr. *dent de lion*, "lion's tooth" (with allusion to the toothed leaves).] A common composite plant, *Taraxacum officinale*, abundant as a weed, characterized by deeply toothed leaves and golden-yellow flowers; any other plant of the genus *Taraxacum*.

dan·der, dan'dér, *n.* [Origin obscure.] Anger or temper.

dan·dle, dan'dl, *v.t.*—*dandled*, *dandling*. [Allied to G. *tand*, prattle, frivolity, *tändeln*, to trifle, to dandle.] To shake or jolt on the knees or in one's arms, as an infant; to fondle, amuse, or treat as a child; to pet.—**dan·dler**, *n.*

dan·druff, dan'druf, *n.* [Origin unknown.] A scurf which form on the scalp and comes off in small scales or particles. Also **dan-·driff**.—**dan·druff·y**, *a.*

dan·dy, dan'dē, *n. pl.* **dan·dies**. [Perhaps a use of *Dandy*, var. of *Andy*, for *Andrew*, man's name.] A man conspicuous for careful elegance of dress and appearance; a fop; *slang*, something very fine or first-rate; *paper-making*, a dandy roller.—*a.*—*dandier*, *dandiest*. Foppish; affectedly neat or fine; *slang*, fine or first-rate.—**dan·dy·ish**, **dan·-di·a·cal**, *a.*—**dan·dy·ism**, *n.*—**dan·di·fy**, *v.t.*—*dandified*, *dandifying*.—**dan·di·ly**, **dan·di·a·cal·ly**, *adv.*

dan·dy roll·er, *n. Paper-making*, a roller for compacting the web of paper-pulp and impressing the watermark. Also **dan·dy roll**.

Dane, dān, *n.* [L.L. *Dani*, pl.] A native or inhabitant of Denmark; a person of Danish descent.—One of a breed of large, powerful, short-haired dogs, somewhat resembling the mastiff but slighter in build. Also **Great Dane**.

dane·geld, dān'geld″, *n.* [Celt, *geld* = O.E. *geld*, *gild*, a payment.] (*Often cap.*) An annual tax laid on the English nation in early times for maintaining forces to oppose the Danes, or to furnish tribute to procure peace, and later continued as a land tax. Also **dane·gelt**, dän'gelt″.

Dane·law, dān'lạ″, *n.* [For O.E. *Dena lagu*, Danes' law.] The Danish law anciently in force in the districts of northern and northeastern England which were occupied or held by the Danes; that part of England under this law. Also **Dane·lagh**, dän'lạ″.

dan·ger, dān'jèr, *n.* [Formerly control, power, Fr. *danger*, O.Fr. *dangier*, *dongier*, a feudal term for right to woods and waters, < L.L. *dominiarium*, < L. *dominus*, a lord; akin *dominion*, *dame*, *damsel*.] Exposure to destruction, ruin, injury, loss, pain, or other evil; peril; risk; hazard; jeopardy.

a- fat, fāte, fär, fâre, fạll; **e-** met, mē, mēre, hèr; **i-** pin, pīne; **o-** not, nōte, mŏve; **u-** tub, cūbe, bụll; **oi-** oil; **ou-** pound.

dan·ger·ous, dān'jêr·us, *a*. Attended with danger; perilous; hazardous; unsafe; full of risk; creating danger.—**dan·ger·ous·ly**, *adv*. In a dangerous manner or condition.—**dan·ger·ous·ness**, *n*.

dan·gle, dang'gl, *v.i*.—*dangled, dangling*. [Allied to Dan. *dingle*, Sw. and Icel. *dingla*, to swing.] To hang loose, shaking, or waving; to hang and swing; to hang about or be dependent on, with *about* or *after*; *gram*. to be in a sentence without the necessary syntactic relation to the remainder of the sentence.—*v.t*. To cause to dangle; to swing.—*n*.—**dan·gler**, *n*.—**dan·gling·ly**, *adv*.

Dan·ish, dā'nish, *a*. Belonging or pertaining to Denmark, the Danes, or their language. —*n*. The language of the Danes.

Dan·ish pas·try, *n*. A light pastry made from dough leavened with yeast, and often containing a filling, such as fruit, nuts, or cheese.

dank, dangk, *a*. [Nasalized form allied to *daggle* and Sw. *dagg*, dew.] Damp, esp. disagreeably damp; moist; humid.—**dank·ish**, *a*.—**dank·ly**, *adv*.—**dank·ness**, *n*.

dan·seuse, Fr. dän·sœz', *n*. pl. **dan·seuses**, Fr. dän·sœz'. [Fr., fem. of *danseur*, dancer, < *danser*, E. *dance*.] A professional female dancer, esp. a ballet dancer.

Dan·tesque, dan·tesk', *a*. In the style of the poet *Dante* (1265–1321), characterized by impressive elevation of style with deep solemnity or somberness of feeling. Also **Dan·te·an**, dan'tē·an, dan·tē'an.

daph·ne, daf'nē, *n*. [L., < Gr. *daphne*, laurel.] The laurel, *Laurus nobilis*; any plant of the genus *Daphne*, of Europe and Asia, comprising small shrubs of which some species, as *D. mezereum*, are cultivated for their fragrant flowers.

dap·per, dap'êr, *a*. [M.E. *dapyr*, neat: cf. D. *dapper*, G. *tapfer*, brave, stout, gallant.] Neat; trim; smartly dressed; small and active.—**dap·per·ly**, *adv*.—**dap·per·ness**, *n*.

dap·ple, dap'l, *n*. [Origin uncertain: cf. Icel. *depill*, spot, dot.] Spots or small blotches of coloring differing from their background coloring; the state or quality of being so marked; an animal with a mottled skin or coat.—*a*. Spotted.—*v.t., v.i*. —*dappled, dappling*. To mark or become marked with spots of color.—**dap·pled**, *a*. —**dap·ple-gray**, *a*. Gray with spots and patches of a darker shade.

darb, därb, *n*. *Slang*, something superb or splendid.

dar·bies, där'bēz, *n. pl. Brit. slang*, handcuffs.

dar·by, där'bē, *n. pl.* **dar·bies**. [From *Darby* or *Derby*, proper name.] A plasterer's tool for leveling a surface of plaster.

Dar·by and Joan, *n*. [Perhaps from an 18th century poem.] The typical "old married couple" contentedly leading a life of placid, uneventful domesticity.

dare, dâr, *v.i*.—past *dared* or archaic *durst*, pp. *dared*, ppr. *daring*. [O.E. *dear, durran*, 1st and 3d pers. sing. pres. ind. of *durran*, akin to O.H.G. *giturran*, Goth. *gadaursan*, dare, Gr. *thrasus*, bold, Skt. *dharsh-*, dare.] To have the necessary courage or boldness for something.—*v.t*. To have the necessary courage for; venture on; to venture to expose oneself to; meet defiantly; to defy or challenge, as someone, to do something challenging; seek to provoke to action, as by asserting another's lack of courage.—*n*. An act of daring or defying; a defiance; a challenge.—**dar·er**, *n*.

dare·dev·il, dâr'dev'il, *n*. One who fears nothing; one who is recklessly daring. —*a*. Recklessly brave.—**dare·dev·il·try, dare·dev·il·ry**, *n*.

dare say, dâr'sā', *v.t*. To think (something) as probable.—*v.i*. To agree; to suppose.

dar·ing, dâr'ing, *n*. Adventurous courage; boldness; intrepidity.—*a*.—**dar·ing·ly**, *adv*.—**dar·ing·ness**, *n*.

Dar·jee·ling, där·jē'ling, *n*. A variety of tea grown esp. in the area around Darjeeling, a mountainous district of West Bengal, India.

dark, därk, *a*. [O.E. *deorc*, dark: cf. O.H.G. *tarchannan*, conceal.] Devoid of or deficient in light; unilluminated; radiating or reflecting little light; dim, approaching black in hue; as, a *dark* brown; not fair; as, a *dark* complexion; devoid of moral or spiritual light; evil; wicked; iniquitous; characterized by or producing gloom; cheerless; dismal; sad; sullen; frowning; obscure to the understanding; difficult to interpret or explain; hidden or secret; silent or reticent; unable to see; mentally or spiritually blind; unenlightened; destitute of knowledge or culture.—*n*. Darkness; night; nightfall; a dark place; a dark color; obscurity; secrecy; ignorance.—**dark·en**, *v.i*. To become dark or darker; become obscure; grow clouded, as with gloom or anger; become blind.—*v.t*. To make dark or darker; deprive of light; shut out the light of; obscure; dim; cloud; render gloomy; sully; make blind; deprive of mental or spiritual light.—**dark·en·er**, *n*. —**dark·ish**, *a*. Somewhat dark.—**dark·ly**, *adv*.—**dark·ness**, *n*.—**Dark Con·ti·nent**, *n*. A term formerly applied to Africa, when it was little known.

dark ad·ap·ta·tion, *n*. The process by which the eye adjusts to a reduced amount of light.—**dark-a·dap·ted**, *a*.

Dark Ag·es, *n. pl*. The era in European history, extending from about A.D. 476 to the end of the tenth century, or in more general terms, to the Renaissance; the Middle Ages.

dark-field mi·cro·scope, därk'fēld" mī'kro·skōp". *n. Phys*. an ultramicroscope.

dark horse, *n*. A race horse whose capabilities are not known; any competitor about whom nothing certain is known or who unexpectedly comes to the front; one unexpectedly receiving a nomination, as at a political convention.

dark lan·tern, *n*. A hand lantern whose light can be obscured by an opaque slide or cover at the opening.

dar·kle, där'kl, *v.i*.—*darkled, darkling*. [< *darkling*, *adv*., taken as ppr.] To show indistinctly; to grow dark; to darken with anger or gloom.

dark·ling, därk'ling, *adv*. In the dark; at night.—*a*. Happening or done in darkness; dark.

dark·ling bee·tle, *n*. Any of the numerous brown or black hard-bodied, slow-moving beetles of the family *Tenebrionidae*, which feed on decayed plants, grain that is stored, and fungi.

dark·room, därk'rōm", därk'rụm", *n*. *Photog*. a room from which the actinic rays of light have been excluded, used for the manufacturing, handling, and developing of photographic materials sensitive to light.

dark·some, därk'sụm, *a*. *Poet*. Somber; gloomy; dark.—**dark·some·ness**, *n*.

dar·ling, där'ling, *n*. [O.E. *dēorling*, < *dēore*, E. *dear*.] A person very dear to another; one much beloved; a person or thing in great favor.—*a*. Very dear; dearly loved; favorite; full of charm.—**dar·ling·ly**, *adv*.—**dar·ling·ness**, *n*.

darn, därn, *v.t., v.i*. [Origin uncertain.] To mend with rows of stitches run from side by side, sometimes with crossing and interwoven rows to fill up a gap; sew with such stitches, as in embroidery.—*n*. An act of darning; a darned place in a garment.—**darn·er**, *n*.

darn, därn. A euphemistic var. of *damn*.

dar·nel, där'nel, *n*. [M.E. *darnel*: cf. Fr. dial. *darnelle*.] An annual grass, *Lolium temulentum*, found as a weed in grainfields; any grass of the genus *Lolium*.

darn·ing, där'ning, *n*. The act of one who darns; the result produced; articles darned, or to be darned.—**darn·ing nee·dle**, *n*. A long needle with a long eye, used in darning. A dragonfly; also *darn·er*.

dart, därt, *n*. [O.Fr. *dart* (Fr. *dard*); prob. < Teut.] A long, slender, pointed missile weapon thrown by the hand or otherwise; *pl. but sing. in constr.* a game in which such a missile is thrown at a target. Something resembling such a weapon, as the sting of an insect; a tapering seam made to adjust the fit of a garment; a sudden swift movement.—*v.t*. To throw or thrust suddenly and rapidly; shoot; emit; to pierce with or as with a dart.—*v.i*. To move swiftly, like a dart.

dart·er, där'têr, *n*. One who throws or shoots darts; one who or that which darts or moves swiftly; specif. any of the small fresh-water fishes of the perch family in America which dart quickly when disturbed; a snakebird.

Dar·win·i·an, där·win'ē·an, *a*. Of or pertaining to Charles *Darwin*, the celebrated naturalist, or to his doctrines.—*n*. A believer in Darwinism.—**Dar·win·ism**, där'win·iz"um, *n*. The doctrine, taught by Darwin, of the origin and modifications of the species on the basis of the survival of the fittest.—**Dar·win·ist**, *n*.

dash, dash, *v.t*. [M.E. *dasshen*; prob. < Scand.] To strike violently, esp. so as to break to pieces; as, to *dash* the glass in anger; to throw or thrust violently or suddenly; to splash violently; to throw something into so as to produce a mixture; qualify or adulterate by admixture; to ruin or frustrate, as hopes or plans; to depress or dispirit; confound or abash; to write or sketch hastily; mark with a dash; underline; *Brit*. to damn: a euphemism, as used in imprecations.—*v.i*. To strike with violence; to move with violence; as, to *dash* away from here; rush; smash.

dash, dash, *n*. A violent blow or stroke; *fig*. a check or discouragement; the throwing or splashing of liquid against a thing; the sound of the splashing; a small spot or patch, as of color; a small quantity of anything thrown into or mingled with something else; a touch or tinge; a hasty stroke, as of a pen; a line produced by or as by such a stroke; a horizontal line of varying length, used in writing and printing as a mark of punctuation, as to note an abrupt break or pause in a sentence, or to begin and to end a parenthetic clause, as an indication of omission of letters or words or of intermediate terms of a series, as a dividing line between distinct portions of matter, and for other purposes; a short line used in musical notation, as a vertical one placed over or under a note to indicate a staccato effect; an impetuous movement; a rush; a sudden onset; a sprint or short race; as, a hundred-yard *dash*; spirited action; vigor in action or style; an ostentatious display; as, to cut a *dash*; a dashboard.

dash·board, dash'bōrd", dash'bärd", *n*. A partition below the windshield of an automobile or airplane which serves as an instrument panel; a board or panel on the front of a horse-drawn vehicle to intercept mud, water, or snow.

da·sheen, da·shēn', *n*. [Appar. a corruption of Fr. *de Chine*, of China, whence the plant is supposed to have been derived.] A variety of the taro, *Caladium colocasia*, introduced into the southern U.S. from the West Indies, and cultivated for its edible corms and tubers, which are used like potatoes; a corm or a tuber of this plant.

dash·ing, dash'ing, *a.* Impetuous; spirited; showy; brilliant.

das·tard, das'tẻrd, *n.* [Icel. *daestr*, exhausted; akin to *daze*, the suffix being *-ard*.] A coward; a poltroon; one who furtively does base acts.—*a.* Cowardly; meanly; shrinking from danger.—**das·tard·li·ness,** *n.*—**das·tard·ly,** *a.*

das·y·ure, das'ē·ụr, *n.* [N.L. *Dasyurus*, < *dasys*, hairy, shaggy, thick, and *oura*, tail.] Any of the small carnivorous marsupials constituting the genus *Dasyurus*, native in Australia and Tasmania.—**das·y·u·rine,** das''i·ụr'in, das''i·ụr'in, *a.*

da·ta, dā'ta, dat'a, dä'ta, *pl.* of *datum*.

da·ta proc·ess·ing, *n.* The processing of information by computing machines which sort, classify, and perform computations on cards or tapes fed into them.

date, dāt, *n.* [O.Fr. *date* (Fr. *datte*), < L. *dactylus*, < Gr. *daktylos*.] The oblong, fleshy, one-seeded fruit of a species of palm, *Phoenix dactylifera*; the tree bearing this fruit. Also *date palm*.

date, dāt, *n.* [Fr., < L. *datum*, given, used in a Roman letter as "given" (at such a place and such a time).] The time when any event happened, when anything was transacted, or when anything is to be done; that addition to a writing which specifies the year, month, and day when it was given or executed; the period of time at or during which one has lived or anything has existed. *Colloq.* an appointment; a person of the opposite sex with whom one has an appointment for a social engagement.—*v.t.—dated, dating.* To write down the date on; to append the date to; to note or fix the time of; to denote clearly the age of; to mark with traits particular to a certain period; *colloq.* to make an appointment with a person of the opposite sex for a social engagement.—*v.i.* To reckon time; to begin at a certain date; as, to *date* from the 10th century; to have a certain date.—**date·less,** *a.* Having no date; undated; so old as to be beyond date; having no fixed limit; eternal.—**dat·a·ble, date·a·ble,** *a.*—**dat·er,** *n.*—**out of date,** obsolete; behind the times.—**up to date,** modern; in the latest style.—**pre·date,** to date prior to the time of issuance.—**post·date,** to date subsequent to the time of issuance.

date line, *n.* A theoretical line coinciding with the meridian of 180° from Greenwich, the regions on either side of which are counted as differing by one day in their calendar dates.—**date·line,** dāt'līn'', *n.* A line in a letter, newspaper article, or the like, giving the date and often the place of origin.—*v.t.—datelined, datelining.*

date palm, *n.* The species of palm, *Phoenix dactylifera*, which bears dates, having a stem usually from 60 to 80 feet in height, terminating in a crown of pinnate leaves.

da·tive, dā'tiv, *a.* [L. *dativus*, < *do*, to give.] *Gram.* in certain inflected languages, pertaining to the case of nouns and pronouns which have the function of an indirect object.—*n.* The dative case; a form or word in the dative case.

da·tum, dā'tụm, dat'ụm, dä'tụm, *n. pl.* **da·ta, da·tums,** dā'ta, dat'a, dä'ta. [L.] Some fact, proposition, quantity, or condition granted or known, esp. when it is to be used for further research or reasoning. *Surv., engin.* any base line used for measuring elevation; the starting point of a scale; *pl.* **da·tums.**

daub, dạb, *v.t.* [O.Fr. *dauber*, to plaster, < L. *dealbare*, to whitewash—*de*, intens., and *albus*, white.] To smear with soft adhesive matter, as with mud or slime; to plaster; to soil; to defile; to besmear; to paint coarsely; to lay or put on without taste.—*v.i.* To daub a thing; to paint coarsely.—*n.* A crude substance or material used to

daub walls; the act of daubing or anything daubed; a smear or smearing; a coarse painting.—**daub·er,** *n.*—**daub·y,** *a.*

daugh·ter, dạ'tẻr, *n.* [O.E. *dóhtor* = D. *dochter*, Dan. *dotter*, Icel. *dóttir*, G. *tochter*, Gr. *thygatẽr*, Pers. *doktarah*, Skt. *duhitri*, Lith. *dukté*,—daughter.] In relation to her real or adopted parents, a female child of any age; a female descendant; a female person having a spiritual relationship similar to the physical one of child to parent; as, a *daughter* of Israel; the female offspring of an animal or plant.—*a.*—**daugh·ter-in-law,** *n. pl.* **daugh·ters-in-law.** A son's wife.—**daugh·ter·ly,** *a.*

daunt, dạnt, dänt, *v.t.* [O.Fr. *danter*, Fr. *dompter*, to tame; < L. *domitare*, a freq. of *domo*, to tame, < root of *dominus*, a lord.] To intimidate; to dishearten; to check by fear.—**daunt·less,** *a.* Bold; not discouraged; fearless; intrepid; not timid.—**daunt·less·ly,** *adv.*—**daunt·less·ness,** *n.*

dau·phin, dạ'fin, *Fr.* dō·faN', *n. pl.* **dau·phins,** *Fr.* dō·faN'. [Fr. *dauphin*, the title originally of the lords of *Dauphiny*, and afterward attached to the French crown along with this province, < L. *delphinus*, a dolphin, the crest of the lords of Dauphiny.] (*Often cap.*) Prior to the revolution of 1830, the eldest son of the King of France.—**dau·phine,** dä'fên, *Fr.* dō·fên', *n. pl.* **dau·phines,** *Fr.* dō·fên'. (*Often cap.*) The wife of the dauphin.

dav·en·port, dav'en·pōrt'', dav'en·pạrt'', *n.* [From *Davenport*, proper name.] A kind of large sofa or divan, often one convertible into a bed.

dav·it, dav'it, dā'vit, *n.* [Origin unknown.] *Naut.* either of the two cranelike devices projecting over the side or stern of a vessel, and used for suspending or lowering and hoisting cargo, boats, or anchors by means of pulleys.

da·vy, dā'vē, *n.* [Named for its inventor; English chemist Sir Humphry *Davy*.] A miner's safety lamp with the flame enclosed by a wire screen. Also **Da·vy lamp.**

Da·vy Jones, dā'vē jōnz'. *n. Naut.* the spirit of the sea; the sailor's devil.—**Da·vy Jones's lock·er,** *n.* The ocean's bottom, esp. as the grave of all who perish at sea.

daw, dạ, *n.* [< *cry*.] A jackdaw.

daw·dle, dạd'l, *v.i.—dawdled, dawdling.* [Akin to *daddle*, and probably to *dowdy*, a slattern.] To waste time; to trifle; to saunter along.—*v.t.* To waste by trifling.—**daw·dler,** *n.*—**daw·dling·ly,** *adv.*

dawn, dạn, *v.i.* [O.E. *dagain*, to dawn or become day, < *daeg*, day.] To grow light; to begin to develop or appear; to begin to be realized or understood, as: The truth *dawns* upon me.—*n.* The first appearance of light in the morning; beginning; rise; first appearance; as, the *dawn* of civilization.

day, dā, *n.* [O.E. *daeg* = D. *dag* = G. *tag* = Icel. *dagr* = Sw. and Dan. *dag* = Goth. *dags,* day.] The interval of light between two successive nights; the time between sunrise and sunset; daylight; the portion of a day allotted to labor; as, an eight-hour *day*; a day as a point or unit of time, or on which something occurs; a day assigned to a particular purpose or observance; as, New Year's *Day*; a day of contest, or the combat or conflict of such a day; as, to win the *day*; a period of power or influence; as, a man who has had his *day*; *usu. pl.*, a particular time or period; as, in *days* of old; in the daytime, as: He prefers working *days.* Often *pl.*, a period of life or activity; as, to end one's *days* in peace.—**so·lar day,** *n. Astron.* the period during which the earth makes one revolution on its axis; the interval of time which elapses between two consecutive returns of the same terrestrial meridian to the sun.—**mean so·lar day,** *n.*

Astron. twenty-four hours or the average length of the solar day.—**civ·il day,** *n. Astron.* a period reckoned from midnight to midnight and equivalent in length to the mean solar day, as contrasted with a similar period reckoned from noon to noon known as the **as·tro·nom·i·cal day,** *n.*

day blind·ness, *n.* A defect of vision causing one to see less by day or in bright light than by night or in dim light. Also *hemeralopia.*

day·book, dā'bụk'', *n.* A book in which are recorded the debits and credits or accounts of the day; a diary.

day·break, dā'brāk'', *n.* The dawn or first appearance of light in the morning.

day coach, *n.* A railroad passenger car of the ordinary kind, as distinguished from a sleeping car, a parlor car, or a dining car.

day·dream, dā'drēm'', *n.* A reverie; a visionary fancy indulged in when awake.—*v.i.* To have reveries.—**day·dream·er,** *n.*

day·flow·er, dā'flou''ẻr, *n.* Any plant of the genus *Commelina*, of the spiderwort family, mostly bearing cymes of small blue flowers.

day la·bor·er, *Brit.* **day la·bour·er,** *n.* One who works by the day, as an unskilled laborer.

day let·ter, *n.* A telegram at a reduced rate or charge for a limited number of 50 words, sent either by day or night, but at a slower speed than regular service.

day·light, dā'līt'', *n.* The light of day; *fig.* openness or publicity; daytime; daybreak. —**day·light sav·ing time,** *n.* Time usually one hour later than standard time, to provide extra evening daylight.

day lil·y, *n.* Any plant of the liliaceous genus *Hemerocallis*, with yellow or orange flowers which commonly last only for a day; any plant of the liliaceous genus *Niobe* or *Funkia*, with white or blue flowers.

day·lin·er, *n.* An express train connecting two cities, or a daytime train connecting the suburbs and the city.

day nurs·er·y, *n.* A nursery for the care of small children during the day, esp. while the mothers are at work.

Day of A·tone·ment, *n.* A Jewish holiday occurring ten days after the Jewish New Year, a day of purification from sins of the past year through fasting and prayer. Also *Yom Kippur.*

day school, *n.* A school held in the daytime, as distinguished from night school; a school held on weekdays, as distinguished from Sunday school; a school at which board and lodging are not furnished for the pupils, as distinguished from boarding school.

days of grace, *n. pl.* Days, commonly three, allowed by law or custom for payment after a bill, note, or insurance premium falls due.

day·star, dā'stär'', *n.* The morning star; *poet.* the sun.

day·time, dā'tīm'', *n.* The time of daylight, between sunrise and sunset.

daze, dāz, *v.t.—dazed, dazing.* [M.E. *dasen*; < Scand.] To stun or stupefy, as by a blow, a shock, or strong drink; confuse or bewilder; dazzle.—*n.* The state of being dazed.—**daz·ed·ly,** dā'zid·lē, *adv.*

daz·zle, daz'l, *v.t.—dazzled, dazzling* [Freq. of *daze*.] To overpower or dim, as the vision, by intense light; to bewilder by brilliancy or display of any kind.—*v.i.* To be overpowered by light; to be overpoweringly bright; *fig.* to excite admiration by brilliancy.—*n.* The act or fact of dazzling; bewildering brightness.—**daz·zle·ment,** *n.* The act of dazzling, or the state of being dazzled; that which dazzles.—**daz·zler,** *n.* —**daz·zling·ly,** *adv.*

D-day, *n. Milit.* the day planned for an attack against the enemy, usually unannounced.—**D-Day,** *n.* June 6, 1944, the date on which the Allied forces of World War II invaded Western Europe.

---

a- fat, fāte, fär, fâre, fạll;   e- met, mē, mẽre, hẻr;   i- pin, pīne;   o- not, nōte, mŏve;   u- tub, cūbe, bụll;   oi- oil;   ou- pound.

DDT, *n.* [< (D)ichloro-(D)iphenyl-(T)richloroethane.] The powerful insecticide, $C_{14}H_9Cl_5$.

dea·con, dē′kon, *n.* [O.E. *dēacon, diacon*, < L.L. *diaconus*, < Gr. *diákonos*, servant, minister, deacon.] A lay church official or subordinate minister; a member of the clerical order below a priest in the Anglican, Greek Orthodox, or Roman Catholic churches.—**dea·con·ess**, dē′ko·nis, *n.* A female deacon; in certain Protestant churches, one of an order of women who care for the sick and poor.—**dea·con·ry**, *n.* pl. **dea·con·ries.** The office of a deacon; deacons collectively.—**dea·con-ship**, *n.*

de·ac·ti·vate, dē·ak′ti·vāt″, *v.t.*—*deactivated, deactivating.* To cause to become inactive; to render ineffective or inoperative; as, to *deactivate* a bomb; *milit.* to demobilize or dissolve a (military unit).—**de·ac·ti·va·tion**, dē·ak″ti·vā′shan, *n.*

dead, ded, *a.* [O.E. *deád* = D. *dood*, Dan. *dod*, Icel. *dauthr*, Goth. *dauths*, death, die.] Deprived or devoid of life; not alive; inanimate; lacking sensation; numb; resembling death; deep and sound; as, a *dead* sleep; not capable of an emotional or intellectual response; insensitive; unfeeling; not burning, extinguished; as, *dead* coals, a *dead* desire; unfruitful, barren, infertile; as, *dead* land; having ceased working or producing, no longer in operation; as, a *dead* battery; no longer considered relevant, interesting, or important; as, a *dead* issue; dreary, spiritless, unexciting; devoid of action or amusements; as, a *dead* party; not having the usual business or trade activity; not bouncy and resilient; as, a *dead* tennis ball; unvarying or unbroken; as, a *dead* level; commercially unproductive; not in use; as, *dead* capital; unreverberating, dull, heavy; as, a *dead* sound; tasteless, flat; as, *dead* beer; cut off from the rights of a citizen, as a prisoner for life; no longer spoken or in common use by a people, said of a language; no longer in effect, defunct; as, a *dead* law; having no gloss, warmth, or brightness; as, a *dead* white; in a state of spiritual death; perfectly still or motionless; as, *dead* waters; precise, exact; as, *dead* center; sure or unerring as death; as, a *dead* shot; sudden, sharp; as, a *dead* stop; complete, absolute; as, a *dead* silence; *colloq.* completely exhausted; tired out; doomed; *sports,* out of play; as, a *dead* ball; *elect.* not connected to a voltage source, and thus not conveying electricity; uncharged; *print.* not to be used, or already used, as copy or composed type.—*adv.* To the last degree; completely; as *dead* tired; abruptly and completely; as, to stop *dead.*—*n.* The time when there is a remarkable stillness and gloom; the culminating point, as the coldest part of winter or darkest part of night.—**the dead**, those who are dead; the deceased; the departed.

dead·beat, ded′bēt′, *a.* Beating without recoil, as the movement in a clock; free from oscillation, as the pointer of an electric meter.

dead·beat, ded′bēt″, *n. Slang.* One who avoids paying for what he gets; a debtor; a sponger; an idler.

dead cen·ter, *Brit.* **dead cen·tre**, *n.* Either of two positions of the crank in a reciprocating engine in which the connecting rod has no power to turn the crank, occurring when the crank and connecting rod are in the same straight line, at each end of a stroke. Also *dead point.*

dead·en, ded′en, *v.t.* To weaken in sensitivity, intensity, vitality, or animation; benumb; dull; to reduce the speed of; to reduce in brilliance or sound; make soundproof; deprive of life.—*v.i.* To become dead.—**dead·en·er**, *n.*—**dead·en-**

ing, *n.* A material used to soundproof a room; a material used to diminish gloss.

dead-end, ded′end′, *a.* Closed at one end; leading nowhere.—**dead end**, *n.* An end, as of a street or pipe, that has no opening; a cul-de-sac; an impasse.

dead·fall, ded′fạl″, *n.* A trap, esp. for large game, in which a weight falls upon and crushes the prey; a mass of fallen trees and underbrush.

dead hand, *n. Law.* The perpetual holding of land, esp. by a corporation or charitable trust; a mortmain.

dead heat, *n.* A race in which two or more competitors finish at the same time so that no one is the winner.

dead let·ter, *n.* An act, such as a law or ordinance, which has lost its force even though it has not been formally repealed or abolished; a letter which the post office is unable to deliver or to return to the sender.

dead·line, ded′lin″, *n.* A line or limit that must not be crossed; the latest possible time for doing something.

dead load, *n.* The constant weight which a structure, such as a bridge or building, is calculated to support, comprising the weight of the component parts and permanent accessories.

dead·lock, ded′lok″, *n.* A state of affairs in which action is for the time impossible, due to unwillingness of opposing forces to yield or compromise, as: Labor-management talks were at a *deadlock.*—*v.t.* To bring to a deadlock, as: One minor point *deadlocked* the talks.—*v.i.* To reach a deadlock.

dead·ly, ded′lē, *a.*—*deadlier, deadliest.* [O.E. *dēadlīc.*] Causing or likely to cause death; fatal; aiming to kill or destroy; as, *a deadly* foe; implacable; with great precision or effectiveness; as, *deadly* aim; enervating or undermining; as, the *deadly* effects of certain habits; resembling or suggestive of death; excessive; as, *deadly* haste; *colloq.* unbearably dull; as, a *deadly* conversation. —*adv.* In a manner resembling or suggesting death; as, *deadly* pale; excessively or completely; as, *deadly* silent.—**dead·li·ness**, *n.*

dead·ly sin, *n.* Any of seven sins: pride, lust, envy, anger, covetousness, gluttony, and sloth, considered by some to be the cause of spiritual death.

dead march, *n.* Solemn music for a funeral procession, esp. that played at a military funeral.

dead pan, *n. Slang,* a face completely without expression.—**dead·pan**, *a. Slang,* without facial expression; with pretended seriousness or detachment.—*adv.*—*v.i.*

dead point, *n.* Dead center.

dead reck·on·ing, *n.* The calculation without celestial observation of the position of a ship or airplane by studying the course followed, the distance covered, and the known or expected drift; the position so calculated.

dead space, *n.* Space which is not utilized; *physiol.* the part of the respiratory system through which air passes to reach the bronchioles and alveoli.

dead weight, *n.* The heavy, unrelieved weight of anything inert; a heavy or oppressive burden; the weight of a railroad car or other vehicle, as distinct from its load.

dead·wood, ded′wụd″, *n.* The dead limbs upon a tree; dead branches or trees; anything or anyone that is useless.

deaf, def, *a.* [O.E. *deáf* = D. *deof*, Dan. *dov*, Icel. *daufr*, G. *taub*—deaf; akin Sc. *daft*, stupid, Icel. *dofi*, torpor.] Lacking the sense of hearing, either wholly or in part; not willing to listen or hear; inattentive; unheeding.—**deaf·en**, *v.t.* To make deaf; to stun with loud noise; *arch.* to soundproof.—*v.i.* To bring on deafness or stun someone with loud noise.—**deaf·en·ing·ly**, *adv.*—

deaf·ly, *adv.*—**deaf-mute**, def′mūt, def·-mūt′, *n.* A person who is both deaf and dumb, esp. one whose dumbness dates from birth or early life.—**deaf·ness**, *n.*

deal, dēl, *n.* [O.E. *dæl* = D. *deel* = G. *teil* = Goth. *dails*, part, portion, share.] A quantity, amount, extent, or degree; as, a good *deal*, a great *deal*; the act of dealing or distributing; the distribution to the players of the cards used in a game; *colloq.* a business transaction; *colloq.* a bargain or arrangement for mutual advantage, as in commerce or politics, often a secret or underhand one; treatment; as, a bad *deal.* —*v.t.*—*dealt, dealing.* To distribute among a number of recipients, as the cards required in a game; apportion; to give to one as his share or portion; to administer or deliver; as, to *deal* a blow.—*v.i.* To distribute the cards required in a game; to treat; trade or do business; as, to *deal* with a firm, to *deal* in an article; occupy oneself or itself, with *in* or *with*; to take action with respect to a thing or person; conduct oneself toward persons in a specified way, as: We must *deal* justly with offenders.

deal, dēl, *n.* [M.L.G. *dele* = D. *deel* = G. *diele*, board, plank.] A board or plank, esp. of fir or pine, and usually more than 7 inches wide and 6 feet long, and less than 3 inches thick; such boards collectively; wood of fir or pine, such as deals are made from.—*a.*

de·a·late, dē′ā·lāt″, dē′ā·lit, *a. Entom.* wingless, as a result of friction or biting. Also **de·a·lat·ed**, dē′ā·lā″tid.—*n.* A dealate insect.—**de·a·la·tion**, *n.*

deal·er, dē′lẽr, *n.* One who conducts himself toward a person or persons in a specified way; as, a square *dealer*; a trader, esp. one who buys articles and sells them without altering their condition; a wholesale merchant; the player who distributes the cards in a game; *stock market,* an individual or firm that buys securities from or sells securities to a client.

deal·fish, dēl′fish″, *n.* pl. **deal·fish·es, deal·fish.** Any of the deep-sea fishes constituting the genus *Trachypterus*, characterized by a long, compressed, tapelike body.

deal·ing, dē′ling, *n.* The act of one who deals; action with respect to matters or persons; conduct toward others; *pl.* intercourse, as of friendship or business; trading.

de·am·i·nate, dē·am′i·nāt″, *v.t.*—*deaminated, deaminating. Chem.* to remove an amino group from a compound. Also **de·am·i·nize**, dē·am′i·niz″.—*deaminized, deaminizing.*

dean, dēn, *n.* [O.Fr. *dean, deien*, Mod.Fr. *doyen*, < L. *decanus*, one set over ten persons, < *decem*, ten.] An administrative officer of a college or university, under the president, supervising students in regard to discipline or their choice of courses, or heading the faculty of a division or college; head of the chapter of a collegiate church or cathedral; a priest charged by a bishop with supervising one district of a diocese; a senior member of any body; an acknowledged leader in a profession.—**dean·er·y**, *n.* pl. **dean·er·ies.** The office or jurisdiction of a dean; the official residence of a dean.—**dean·ship**, *n.*

dear, dēr, *a.* [O.E. *dēore* = D. *dier* = G. *teuer* = Icel. *dȳrn*.] Beloved or loved; regarded with esteem or affection; of great value or importance; precious; high-priced, costly, or expensive; heartfelt or earnest; as, one's *dearest* desire.—*n.* One who is dear; a beloved one; often used in direct address; as, my *dear.*—*adv.* Dearly; fondly; at great cost.—*interj.* An exclamation indicating surprise, distress, or other emotion.— **dear·ly**, *adv.*—**dear·ness**, *n.*

---

ch- chain, G. na*ch*t;   **th-** THen, thin;   **w-** wig, hw as sound in whig;   **z-** zh as in azure, zeal.   *Italicized vowel* indicates schwa sound.

dearth, dẽrth, *n.* [M.E. *derthe*, < *dere*, E. *dear*.] Scarcity or scanty supply of anything; want or lack; scarcity of food; famine.

dear·y, dear·ie, dẽr'ē, *n.* pl. **dear·ies.** *Colloq.* dear or darling.

death, deth, *n.* [O.E. *dēath* = D. *dood* = G. *tod* = Icel. *daudhr* = Goth. *dauthus*, death; akin to E. *dead* and *die*.] The act or fact of dying; the total and permanent cessation of all the vital functions of an animal or plant; the state of being dead; *fig.* loss or absence of spiritual life; loss or deprivation of civil life; extinction or destruction; bloodshed or murder; a cause or occasion of death; a pestilence; as, the black *death*; (*often cap.*) the annihilating power personified, usually as a skeleton.— **death·less,** *a.*—**death·ly,** *a., adv.*

death·bed, deth'bed″, *n.* The bed on which a person dies or is confined in his last illness; the last hours of life.

death ben·e·fit, *n.* Money payable to the beneficiary of the deceased under an insurance policy or pension plan.

death·blow, deth'blō″, *n.* A blow causing death; anything which extinguishes hope or ruins one's prospects.

death cam·ass, *n.* Any of several plants of the genus *Zigadenus*, found in the southern and western U.S. and Canada, which are poisonous to grazing livestock.

death cup, *n.* A common, extremely poisonous mushroom, *Amanita phalloides*, having a cuplike enlargement which receives the base of the stem; the enlargement itself.

death du·ty, *n. Brit.* inheritance tax.

death house, *n.* A building or part of a prison where persons condemned to death are held, awaiting execution.

death mask, *n.* A cast of a person's face taken just after death.

death rate, *n.* The ratio between the number of deaths and the total population of a specific place and time.

death rat·tle, *n.* A rattling sound made by a person immediately before dying, caused by air passing through mucus in the throat.

death's-head, deths'hed″, *n.* A human skull, esp. as a symbol of mortality.

death's-head moth, *n.* The large European hawk moth, *Acherontia atropos*, with markings on the back of the thorax resembling the figure of a skull.

death·trap, deth'trap″, *n.* A structure or situation involving imminent risk of death.

death war·rant, *n.* An official order for the execution of the sentence of death; a catastrophe that causes utter ruin; something that ends all hope.

death·watch, deth'woch″, deth'wạch″, *n.* A watch or vigil beside anyone dying or dead; a guard set over a condemned person before execution; newsmen awaiting an expected development in news.

death·watch, deth'woch″, deth'wạch″, *n.* Any small beetle of the family *Anobiidae*, which makes a sound like the ticking of a watch, a sound supposed to presage death. Also **death·watch bee·tle.**

de·ba·cle, dā·bä'kl, dä·bak'el, de·bä'kl, de·bak'el, *n.* [Fr., < *débâcler*, to break up— *de*, not, and *bâcler*, to bar, < L. *baculus*, a bar.] A calamitous breakdown, rout, or collapse, as of an enterprise; a sudden breaking up of ice in a river; *geol.* a sudden outbreak of water.

de·bar, di·bär', *v.t.*—**debarred, debarring.** To bar from a place or circumstance; to preclude; to hinder; to prohibit.—**de·bar·ment,** *n.* The act of debarring.

de·bark, di·bärk', *v.t., v.i.* [Fr. *débarquer*—*de*, and *barque*, a boat or bark.] To land from a ship or aircraft; to disembark.—**de·bar·ka·tion,** dē″bär·kā'shạn, *n.*

de·base, di·bās', *v.t.*—**debased, debasing.** To lower in quality, dignity, or character; to degrade; to abase; to lower the value,

as of a coin, by increasing the proportion of base metal.—**de·base·ment,** *n.* The act of debasing, or the state of being debased.— **de·bas·er,** *n.*—**de·bas·ing·ly,** *adv.*

de·bate, di·bāt', *v.i.*—**debated, debating.** [O.Fr. *debatre* (Fr. *débattre*), *batre*, beat, E. *bate*.] To engage in discussion, esp. in a legislative or other public assembly; to deliberate or consider.—*v.t.* To dispute about; discuss or argue, as a question, in a public assembly; to deliberate upon or consider. —*n.* Contention by argument; discussion; a discussion, esp. of public question in an assembly; deliberation or consideration.— **de·bat·a·ble,** di·bā'ta·bl, *a.* Capable of being debated; disputable by argument; open to question; in some doubt.—**de·bat·er,** *n.*—**de·bat·ing·ly,** *adv.*

de·bauch, di·bạch', *v.t.* [Fr. *débaucher*, O.Fr. *desbaucher*, < *des-* and *-baucher*, of uncertain origin and meaning.] To seduce from virtue or morality; to corrupt by sensuality or intemperance; in general, to corrupt or pervert; deprave.—*v.i.* To indulge in a debauch.—*n.* [Fr. *débauche*.] A period of excessive indulgence in sensual pleasures, esp. in drinking; the practice of such indulgence; debauchery.—**deb·au·chee,** deb″ạ·chē', deb'ạ·shē', *n.* [Fr. *débauché*, pp.] One addicted to excessive indulgence in sensual pleasures.—**de·bauch·er,** *n.*—**de·bauch·ment,** *n.*

de·bauch·er·y, di·bạ'che·rē, *n.* pl. **de·bauch·er·ies.** Excessive indulgence in sensual pleasures; intemperance.

de·ben·ture, di·ben'chẽr, *n.* [L. *debentur*, "there are owing."] A certificate of indebtedness; a certificate of drawback issued at a custom house; an instrument in which a corporation or company acknowledges indebtedness for a specified sum on which interest is due until the principal is paid; *Brit.* a security of a corporation issued in the form of stock, the certificates of which entitle the owner to an annuity.— **de·ben·tured,** *a.* Furnished with or secured by a debenture.

de·bil·i·tate, di·bil'i·tāt″, *v.t.*—**debilitated, debilitating.** [L. *debilito, debilitatum*, to weaken, < *debilis*, weak.] To weaken; to enfeeble.—**de·bil·i·ta·tion,** *n.* The act of weakening; the state of enfeeblement.

de·bil·i·ty, di·bil'i·tē, *n.* pl. **de·bil·i·ties.** [L. *debilitas*.] A state of general bodily weakness; feebleness.

deb·it, deb'it, *n.* [L. *debitum*, something owed, < *debeo*, to owe—*de*, from, and *habeo*, to have.] That which is entered in an account as a debt; a recorded item of debt; that part of an account in which is entered any article of goods furnished, or money paid to or on account of a person.—*v.t.* To charge with or as a debt; as, to *debit* a person *for* or *with* goods; to enter on the debtor side of a book.

deb·o·nair, deb″o·nâr', *a.* [Fr. *debonnaire* —*de*, from, *bon*, good, and *aire* (L. *area*), place, extraction.] Characterized by courtesy, affability, and charm; well-bred; winning; carefree. Also **deb·o·naire, deb·on·naire.**—**deb·o·nair·ly,** *adv.*—**deb·o·nair·ness,** *n.*

de·bouch, di·bōsh', di·bouch', *v.i.* [Fr. *déboucher*, < *dé-* and *bouche*, mouth, < L. *bucca*, cheek, mouth.] To march out from a narrow or confined place into open country, as a body of troops; in general, to issue or emerge.—*v.t.* To cause to emerge.

dé·bou·ché, dā·bō·shā', *n.* [Fr.] *Milit.* an opening or passage where troops may debouch; any place of exit; an outlet.— **de·bou·chure,** di·bō'shụr, di·bō·shụr', *n.* [Appar. a pseudo-French formation, on the analogy of (Fr.) *embouchure*.] A mouth or outlet, as of a river or a pass.—**de·bouch·ment,** di·bōsh'ment, di·bouch'ment, *n.* The act or fact of debouching.

dé·bride·ment, di·brēd'ment, dā·brēd'-ment, *n. Surg.* the removal of foreign matter or contaminated tissue from a wound to prevent the spread of infection.

de·brief, dē·brēf', *v.t.* To interrogate (military or government personnel) at the end of a mission or period of service to obtain useful data; to instruct (military or government personnel) not to reveal top secret or classified information.—**de·brief·ing,** *n.*

de·bris, de·brē', dā'brē, *Brit.* deb'rē, *n.* [Fr., < *dé*, L. *dis*, asunder, apart, and *briser*, to break.] Rubbish; fragments; ruins; *geol.* any accumulation of broken and detached matter, as that from the waste of rocks.

debt, det, *n.* [O.Fr. *debte* (now *dette*), L. *debita*, things due.] That which one person is bound to pay to or perform for another; an obligation; the state of owing something to another; as, to be in *debt*; *theol.* a trespass or sin.—**debt of hon·or,** a gambling debt.— **debt·or,** det'ẽr, *n.* [L. *debitor*.] A person who owes another; one indebted or in debt.

de·bunk, di·bungk', *v.t. Colloq.* to show the error in false or high-flown opinions, statements, or claims, as: Informed studies have *debunked* the legend of Paul Bunyan.— **de·bunk·er,** *n.*

de·but, dé·but, dā·bū', di·bū', dā'bū, deb'ū, *n.* [Fr., *débuter*, make the first stroke in a game, make one's first appearance, begin.] A first appearance in society or before the public; the start of a career or profession.—**deb·u·tant, déb·u·tant,** deb'-ū·tänt″, deb'ya·tänt″, *n.* One making a debut, as an actor or singer appearing for the first time before the public.—**deb·u·tante, déb·u·tante,** deb'ū·tänt″, deb'ū·tant″, *n.* A young woman making a debut, esp. into society.

de·cade, dek'ād, *n.* [L. *decas, decadis*, Gr. *dekas*, < *deka*, ten.] A period of ten years; a group or set consisting of ten.

dec·a·dence, dek'a·dens, di·kād'ens, *n.* [Fr. *décadence*, < M.L. *decadentia*, < L. *de*, from and *cadere*, fall.] A falling off or away from a state of excellence or prosperity; decline; decay; deteriorated condition. Also **dec·a·den·cy.**

dec·a·dent, dek'a·dent, di·kād'ent, *a.* [Fr. *décadent*, < *décadence*.] Falling off or deteriorating; being in a state of decline or decay; pertaining to or suggestive of the decadents.—*n.* One who is decadent; (*often cap.*) one of a group of French and English writers and artists toward the end of the 19th century whose work was characterized by great refinement or subtlety of style with a marked tendency toward the artificial and abnormal, and was thus held to exemplify a general decadence.—**dec·a·dent·ly,** *adv.*

dec·a·gon, dek'a·gon″, *n.* [Gr. *deka*, ten, and *gōnia*, a corner.] *Geom.* a closed plane figure having ten sides and ten angles.— **de·cag·o·nal,** de·kag'o·nal, *a.*

dec·a·gram, dek'a·gram″, *n.* [Fr. *déca-gramme*, Gr. *deka*, ten, and Fr. *gramme*.] See Metric System table.

dec·a·he·dron, dek″a·hē'dron, *n.* pl. **dec·a·he·drons, dec·a·he·dra,** dek″a·hē'dra. [Gr. *deka*, ten, and *hedra*, a seat, a base.] *Geom.* a solid figure having ten sides or faces.

de·cal, dē'kal, di·kal', dek'al, *n.* The process of transferring a design or picture from a specially prepared paper, which serves as a backing, to the surface of wood, glass, plaster, or other materials; the picture or design transferred or to be transferred in this manner. Also **de·cal·co·ma·ni·a,** di·kal″ko·mā'nē·a, di·kal'ko·mān'ya.

de·cal·ci·fy, dē·kal'si·fī″, *v.t.*—**decalcified, decalcifying.** To deprive, as a bone, of lime or calcareous matter.—**de·cal·ci·fi·ca·tion,** dē·kal″si·fi·kā'shạn, *n.*—**de·cal·ci·fi·er,** *n.*

de·ca·les·cence, dē″ka·les′ens, *n.* In the heating of iron, the sudden absorption of heat observed as it passes a certain temperature, and structural changes occur.—**de·ca·les·cent**, *a.*

dec·a·li·ter, *Brit.* **dec·a·li·tre**, dek′a·lē″tèr, *n.* See Metric System table.

Dec·a·logue, dek′a·lạg″, dek′a·lǒg″, *n.* [Gr. *deka*, ten, and *logos*, a word.] The Ten Commandments or precepts given by God to Moses at Mount Sinai. Also **dec·a·logue**, **Dec·a·log.**

dec·a·me·ter, *Brit.* **dec·a·me·tre**, dek′a·mē″tèr, *n.* See Metric System table.

de·cam·e·ter, de·kam′et·ėr, *n.* A line of poetry of ten feet.

de·camp, di·kamp′, *v.i.* [Fr. *décamper.*] To depart from a camp or camping ground; to break camp; to depart, esp. in a sudden and secret manner.—**de·camp·ment**, *n.*

dec·a·nal, dek′a·nal, di·kān′al, *a.* [L.L. *decanus.*] Of or pertaining to a clerical dean or deanery.

dec·ane, dek′ān, *n. Chem.* any one of several liquid hydrocarbons, $C_{10}H_{22}$, of the methane series, which occur in isomeric forms.

dec·a·no·ic ac·id, *n. Chem.* capric acid.

de·cant, di·kant′, *v.t.* [Fr. *décanter*, < M.L. *decanthare*, < L. *de*, from, and M.L. *canthus*, *cantus*, corner, side, E. *cant*.] To pour off gently, as liquor, without disturbing the sediment; to pour from one vessel into another.—**de·can·ta·tion**, dē″kan·tā′shan, *n.* The act or process of decanting.

de·cant·er, di·kan′tèr, *n.* A vessel used for decanting, or for receiving decanted liquors; a vessel, usually an ornamental bottle, from which wine, brandy, or other beverages are served.

de·cap·i·tate, di·kap′i·tāt″, *v.t.*—*decapitated, decapitating.* [M.L. *decapitatus*, pp. of *decapitare*.] To cut off the head of; kill by beheading.—**de·cap·i·ta·tion**, di·kap″i·tā′shan, *n.*—**de·cap·i·ta·tor**, *n.*

dec·a·pod, dek′a·pod″, *n.* [N.L. *Decapoda*, pl., < Gr. *deka*, ten, and *pous* (*pod*-), foot.] Any of the *Decapoda*, an order of ten-footed crustaceans, which includes the lobsters and crabs; an order of ten-armed cephalopods, which includes the cuttlefishes and squids.—*a.* Belonging to the *Decapoda*; having ten feet or legs.—**de·cap·o·dous**, de·kap′o·dus, *a.*

de·car·bon·ate, dē·kär′bo·nāt″, *v.t.*—*decarbonated, decarbonating.* To deprive of carbon dioxide or carbonic acid.—**de·car·bon·a·tion**, dē·kär″bo·nā′shan, *n.*

de·car·bon·ize, dē·kär′bo·nīz, *v.t.*—*decarbonized, decarbonizing.* To remove carbon from a substance or motor, as from an automobile engine.—**de·car·bon·i·za·tion**, dē·kär″bo·ni·zā′shan, *n.* Also *decarburize.*

de·car·bu·rize, dē·kär′ba·rīz″, dē·kär′bū·riz″, *v.t.*—*decarburized, decarburizing.* See *decarbonize.*

dec·are, dek′âr′, de·kâr′, *n.* See Metric System table.

dec·a·stere, dek′a·stèr″, *n.* See Metric System table.

dec·a·style, dek′a·stīl″, *a.* [Gr. *dekastylos.*] Having ten columns in front, as a temple or a portico. Also **dec·a·styl·ar.**

de·cath·lon, di·kath′lon, *n.* [Gr. *deka*, ten, and *athlon*, *athlos*, contest.] An athletic contest comprising ten different exercises or events, and won by the contestant having the highest total score.

de·cay, di·kā′, dē·kā′, *v.i.* [O.Fr. *decair* (also *dechaeir*, Fr. *dechoir*), < L. *de*, from, and *cadere*, fall.] To fall away from a state of excellence or prosperity; deteriorate; become impaired; decline; to fall into ruin; waste or wear away; specif. to become decomposed; rot.—*v.t.* To cause to decay.—*n.* The process of decaying, or the resulting state; a gradual falling into an inferior condition; progressive decline; impairment; loss of strength, health, or intellect; a wasting disease; a falling into ruin; a wasting or wearing away; dilapidation; decomposition or rotting; a cause of decaying or deterioration. *Phys.* see *radioactive decay.*—**de·cay·a·ble**, *a.* Liable to decay.—**de·cayed**, *a.* Having fallen away or declined from the former state of excellence or well-being; reduced in fortune; affected with physical decay, as buildings, teeth, or fruit.—**de·cay·less**, *a.* Not subject to decay.—**de·cayed·ness**, *n.*

de·cease, di·sēs′, *n.* [Fr. *décès*, < L. *decessus*, departure—*de*, and *cedo*, *cessum*, to go.] Departure from this life; death.—*v.i.* To depart from this life; to die.—**de·ceased**, di·sēst′, *a.* Departed from life; dead.—*n.* A dead person or persons.—**de·ce·dent**, di·sēd′ent, *n.* A deceased person.

de·ceit, (di·sēt′, *n.* [O.Fr. *deceite*, < L. *decepta*, pp. fem. of *decipere*.] The act or practice of deceiving; concealment or perversion of the truth for the purpose of misleading; deception; fraud; cheating; an act or device intended to deceive; a trick or stratagem; deceitfulness.—**de·ceit·ful**, *a.* Full of deceit; given to deceiving; misleading; fraudulent; deceptive.—**de·ceit·ful·ly**, *adv.*—**de·ceit·ful·ness**, *n.*

de·ceive, di·sēv′, *v.t.*—*deceived, deceiving.* [O.Fr. *deceveir* (Fr. *décevoir*), < L. *decipere* (pp. *deceptus*), catch, ensnare, deceive, < *de*, from, and *capere*, take.] To cause to believe what is false or disbelieve what is true; mislead; delude; to disappoint, with regard to hopes or expectations.—*v.i.* To practice deceit; act deceitfully.—**de·ceiv·er**, *n.*—**de·ceiv·ing·ly**, *adv.*—**de·ceiv·a·ble**, *a.*—**de·ceiv·a·bly**, *adv.*—**de·ceiv·a·ble·ness**, *n.*—**de·ceiv·a·bil·i·ty**, di·sē·va·bil′i·tē, *n.*

de·cel·er·ate, dē·sel′e·rāt, *v.t.*—*decelerated, decelerating.* [L.] To decrease the velocity of.—*v.i.* To decrease in velocity.—**de·cel·er·a·tion**, dē·sel″e·rā′shan, *n.* The act of decelerating; decrease in velocity.

de·cel·er·on, dē·sel′e·ron″, *n. Aeron.* an aileron that acts as a speed brake, used esp. on certain types of jet aircraft.

De·cem·ber, di·sem′bèr, *n.* [L. < *decem*, ten, this being the tenth month among the early Romans, who began the year in March.] The twelfth and last month of the year.

de·cen·cy, dē′sen·sē, *n.* pl. **de·cen·cies.** [L. *decentia.*] The state or quality of being decent; propriety in actions or discourse; decorum; modesty; something that is decent or becoming; *pl.* the standards of decent living and proper conduct.

de·cen·na·ry, di·sen′a·rē, *n.* pl. **de·cen·na·ries.** [L. *decennium*, a period of ten years—*decem*, ten, and *annus*, a year.] A period of ten years. Also **de·cen·ni·um.**—**de·cen·ni·al**, di·sen′ē·al, *a.*, *n.* Continuing for ten years; consisting of ten years; happening every ten years.—**de·cen·ni·al·ly**, *adv.*

de·cent, dē′sent, *a.* [L. *decens, decentis*, ppr. of *decet*, it becomes; akin *decorate*, *decorum*.] Having a character that gains general approval; suitable, as to words, behavior, dress, and ceremony; decorous; free from immodesty; passable; respectable.—**de·cent·ly**, *adv.* In a decent manner; passably; *colloq.* fairly.—**de·cent·ness**, *n.*

de·cen·tral·ize, dē·sen′tra·līz″, *v.t.* To distribute what has been centralized; to remove from direct connection with a central authority.—**de·cen·tral·i·za·tion**, dē·sen″tra·li·zā′shan, *n.* The act of distributing administrative powers or activities, as of a government or industry, over a wider area; dispersal of persons and industries from cities to outlying areas.

de·cep·tion, di·sep′shan, *n.* [L. *deceptio, deceptionis*, a deceiving.] The act of deceiving or misleading; the state of being deceived or misled; that which deceives; trick.—**de·cep·tive**, di·sep′tiv, *a.* Tending to deceive; having power to mislead.—**de·cep·tive·ly**, *adv.*—**de·cep·tive·ness**, *n.*

dec·i·are, des′ē·âr′, des′ē·är″, Fr. dā·sē·är′, *n.* See Metric System table.

dec·i·bel, des′i·bl″, *n. Phys.* a dimensionless measure of the ratio of two powers, equal to 10 times the logarithm to the base 10 of the ratio of two powers, P_1/P_2. The power P_2 may be a reference power, such as 1 milliwatt for electricity. Used in acoustics to express the intensity of a sound wave, equal to 20 times the common logarithm of the ratio of the pressure produced by the sound wave to a reference pressure of 0.0002 dyne per square centimeter. Used for expressing transmission gains, losses, and levels, and for measuring relative intensities of sounds. Sym. db.

de·cide, di·sīd′, *v.t.*—*decided, deciding.* [L. *decido—de*, and *caedo*, to cut, seen also in *concise, precise, excision*.] To determine or settle, finally or authoritatively; to conclude; to end; to bring to a decision.—*v.i.* To determine; to come to a conclusion; to pronounce a judgment.—**de·cid·a·ble**, *a.* Capable of being decided.—**de·cid·ed**, *a.* Resolute; determined; free from hesitation or wavering; unquestionable.—**de·cid·ed·ly**, *adv.*—**de·cid·ed·ness**, *n.*—**de·cid·er**, *n.*

de·cid·u·a, di·sij′ö·a, *n.* pl. **de·cid·u·as**, **de·cid·u·ae.** [N.L., prop. fem of L. *deciduus.*] *Physiol.* a membrane which arises from the alteration of the upper layer of the mucous membrane of the uterus, after the reception into the latter of the fertilized ovum, and which, in higher mammals, is cast off at parturition.—**de·cid·u·al**, *a.* Of or pertaining to the decidua.—**de·cid·u·ate**, *a.* Characterized by or having a decidua; as, a *deciduate* mammal; partly composed of a decidua; as, a *deciduate* placenta.

de·cid·u·ous, di·sij′ö·us, *a.* [L. *deciduus*, < *decidere*, fall off, < *de*, from, and *cadere*, fall.] Falling off or shed at a particular season or stage of growth, as leaves, horns, or teeth; shedding the leaves annually, as trees and shrubs; *fig.* not permanent; transitory.—**de·cid·u·ous·ly**, *adv.*—**de·cid·u·ous·ness**, *n.*

dec·i·gram, des′i·gram″, *n.* See Metric System table.

dec·ile, des′il, des′īl, *n.* One of the intervals of a frequency distribution wherein the total number of cases is divided into ten equal groups; any of these ten groups.—*a.*

dec·i·li·ter, des′i·lē″tèr, *n.* See Metric System table.

de·cil·lion, di·sil′yon, *n.* [L. *decem*, ten and E. (m)*illion.*] In Great Britain and Germany, the tenth power of a million, represented by 1 followed by 60 ciphers; in France and the U.S., a thousand nonillions, represented by 1 followed by 33 ciphers.—**de·cil·lionth**, *a.*, *n.*

dec·i·mal, des′i·mal, *a.* [L. *decimus*, tenth, < *decem*, ten.] Of or pertaining to tens; numbered or proceeding by tens; having a tenfold increase or decrease.—**dec·i·mal frac·tion**, *n.* A fraction with a denominator of 10, or a power of 10, expressed by a point or dot placed to the left of the numerator, as: $7/10 = .7$, $3/1000 = .003$. Also *decimal.*—**dec·i·mal sys·tem**, *n.* A system of weights, measures, and moneys based on multiples of ten; the metric system; *library science*, a classification for books, dividing all knowledge into ten classes, indicating the specific subject of each book by a number ranging from .001 to 999.—**dec·i·mal point**, *n.* The point or dot expressing the denominator.—**dec·i·mal·ize**, des′i·ma·līz″, *v.t.*—*decimal-*

---

ch- chain, G. na*ch*t; **th-** *TH*en, thin; **w-** wig, hw as sound in whig; **z-** zh as in azure, zeal. *Italicized vowel* indicates schwa sound.

ized, decimalizing. To reduce to a decimal system.

dec·i·mate, des′i·māt″, *v.t.*—*decimated, decimating.* [L.] To select by lot and punish with death every tenth man of; to destroy a great but indefinite number of; take a tenth from or of.—**dec·i·ma·tion,** des″i·mā′shan, *n.*—**dec·i·ma·tor,** *n.*

dec·i·me·ter, des′i·mē″tẽr, *n.* See Metric System table.

de·ci·pher, di·sī′fẽr, *v.t.* To explain (what is written in ciphers) by finding what each character or mark represents; decode; to discern the meaning of, as what is written in obscure or badly formed characters; to discover or explain the meaning of, as of something difficult to be understood.—**de·ci·pher·a·ble,** *a.*—**de·ci·pher·ment,** *n.*

de·ci·sion, di·sizh′an, *n.* [L. *decisio, decisionis.*] The act of deciding a question or issue; final judgment or opinion; determination or conclusion, as of a contest or event; a statement of a conclusion; unwavering firmness.

de·ci·sive, di·sī′siv, *a.* Final; conclusive; marked by prompt determination.—**de·ci·sive·ly,** *adv.*—**de·ci·sive·ness,** *n.*

dec·i·stere, des′i·stẽr″, *n.* See Metric System table.

deck, dek, *v.t.* [M.D. *decken* (D. *dekken*) = G. *decken,* cover; akin to E. *thatch.*] To clothe or attire in something ornamental; array; adorn; to cover or furnish with or as with a deck. [= D. *dek.*] A flooring extending from side to side of a ship or a part of a ship, forming a covering for the space below; any platform or part resembling this; a platform or flight deck on an airplane; a pack of playing cards; *slang,* a package of narcotics.—**decked,** *a.* Having a deck or decks; as, a three-*decked* ship.—**deck·er,** *n.* Something having a deck or decks; as, a three-*decker.*

deck chair, *n.* A reclining chair which folds, often used on ship decks, beaches, and lawns.

deck hand, *n.* A seaman who does menial tasks, esp. on a ship's deck.

deck·house, dek′hous″, *n.* pl. **deck·hous·es.** *Naut.* a cabin or other enclosure built on the upper deck of a ship.

deck·le, dek′l, *n.* [G. *deckel,* dim. of *decke,* cover.] *Papermaking.* Any contrivance to keep the paper pulp from spreading beyond desired limits, thus determining the size or the width of the sheet; a deckle edge. —**deck·le edge,** the rough edge of untrimmed paper, formed by the deckle; the ragged edge of handmade paper.—**deck·le-edged,** *a.*

de·claim, di·klām′, *v.i.* [L. *declamare* (pp. *declamatus*).] To speak aloud rhetorically; make a formal speech or oration; to inveigh against; to recite in public to exhibit elocutionary skill; to speak or write for oratorical effect, without sincerity or sound argument.—*v.t.* To utter aloud in a rhetorical manner; to recite as an exercise in elocution.—**de·claim·er,** *n.*

dec·la·ma·tion, dek″la·mā′shan, *n.* [L. *declamatio(n).*] The act or art of declaiming; that which is declaimed; an exercise in oratory or elocution; impassioned or bombastic oratory; speech or writing for oratorical effect; *mus.* the proper rhetorical enunciation of the words, esp. in recitatives and dramatic music.—**de·clam·a·to·ry,** di·klam′a·tōr″ē, di·klam′a·tar″ē, *a.* [L. *declamatorius.*] Pertaining to or characterized by declamation; merely rhetorical.

de·clar·ant, di·klâr′ant, *n.* [L. *declarans* (*-ant-*), ppr. of *declarare.*] One who makes a declaration; *law,* an alien who states his intention of becoming a U.S. citizen by signing his first papers.

dec·la·ra·tion, dek′la·rā′shan, *n.* [L. *declaratio(n), < declarare.*] The act of declaring; a positive, explicit, or formal statement; an announcement; an assertion; a proclamation; as, a *declaration* of war; that which is proclaimed, or the document embodying the proclamation; as, the *Declaration* of Independence; a statement of goods or wealth liable to duty or taxes; *law,* the formal statement in which a plaintiff presents his claim in an action; a complaint. A bid or contract in the game of bridge; in other card games, an announcement of points made.—**de·clar·a·tive,** de·clar·a·to·ry,** di·klar′a·tiv, di·klar′a·tōr″ē, di·klar′a·tar″ē, *a.* Serving to declare, make known, or explain; of the nature of a declaration or formal assertion.

de·clare, di·klâr′, *v.t.*—*declared, declaring.* [O.Fr. *declarer* (Fr. *déclarer*), < L. *declarare* (pp. *declaratus*), < *clarus,* E. *clear.*] To make clear or plain; to make known, esp. in explicit or formal terms; to proclaim; to announce officially; to state emphatically; to affirm; to manifest or reveal, as: His membership in the Masons *declares* his sympathies. To make a full statement of dutiable goods, taxable income, or wealth; in the game of bridge, to make a bid; in other games, to announce(points made.)—*v.i.* To make a declaration; to proclaim oneself.—**de·clar·a·ble,** *a.*—**de·clared,** *a.* Openly or formally made known; avowed. —**de·clar·ed·ly,** *adv.*—**de·clar·er,** *n.* One who declares; *bridge,* the one who plays the hand.

de·class, dē·klas′, dē·kläs′, *v.t.* [Fr.] To remove or degrade from one's class; cause to lose standing.

dé·clas·sé, dā″kla·sā′, dā″kla·sā′, *Fr.* dā·klä·sā′, *a.* [Fr., pp.] Declassed; belonging to or characteristic of a lower or low social order.—**dé·clas·sée,** *a.* Fem. of *déclassé.*

de·clas·si·fy, dē·klas′i·fī″, *v.t.*—*declassified, declassifying.* To remove security classification from, as secret information.

de·clen·sion, di·klen′shan, *n.* [Irreg. (prob. through Fr. *déclinaison*) < L. *declinatio(n).*] The act or fact of declining, or bending or sloping downward; a sinking down, as of the sun toward setting; deterioration; decline; sunken or fallen condition; deviation, as from a standard; *gram.* the formation of the cases of a noun, pronoun, or adjective by the addition of inflectional endings to the stem; the setting forth in order of the cases of such a word; a class of such words of a language, grouped according to their inflectional endings.—**de·clen·sion·al,** *a.*

dec·li·nate, dek′li·nāt″, dek′li·nit, *a.* [L. *declinatus,* pp. of *declinare.*] *Bot., zool.* bent or bending downward or aside.

dec·li·na·tion, dek″li·nā′shan, *n.* The act of moving, sloping, or bending down; deterioration; a deviation from a standard; the act of refusing; a refusal; *astron.* the distance of a heavenly body from the celestial equator, measured on a great circle passing through the pole and through the body; *phys.* the variation of the magnetic needle from the true meridian of a place.—**de·clin·a·to·ry,** di·klī′na·tōr″ē, di·klī′na·tar″ē, *a.* Of or pertaining to declination; characterized by declining; intimating refusal.—**dec·li·nom·e·ter,** *n.* An instrument for measuring declination.

de·clin·a·ture, di·klī′na·chẽr, *n.* The act of declining or refusing; a refusal.

de·cline, di·klīn′, *v.i.*—*declined, declining.* [L. *declino,* to bend down or aside.] To lean downward; to bend over; to sink to a lower level; to draw toward a close; to become impaired, as health; to courteously refuse. —*v.t.* To bend downward; to cause to bend; to refuse; *gram.* to inflect through case and number.—**de·clin·er,** *n.*

de·cline, di·klīn′, *n.* [O.Fr. *declin* (Fr. *déclin*).] A downward incline or slope; progress downward or toward a close; a gradual loss, as in value; deterioration; diminution, esp. gradual fall in price or value; a gradual decay of physical powers; an ending or last part.—**de·clin·a·ble,** *a.*

de·cliv·i·ty, di·kliv′i·tē, *n.* pl. **de·cliv·i·ties.** [L. *declivitas,* a declivity, < *declivis* sloping—*de,* and *clivus,* sloping; same root as in *decline.*] Slope or inclination downward; a slope or descent of the ground.—**de·cliv·i·tous, de·cli·vous,** di·kliv′i·tus, di·klī′vus, *a.* Sloping downward.

de·coct, di·kokt′, *v.t.* [L. *decoquo, decoctum,* to boil down—*de,* and *coquo,* to cook, to boil.] To extract the strength or flavor of by boiling.—**de·coc·tion,** di·kok′shan, *n.* [L. *decoctio(n-).*] The act of decocting; an extract obtained by decocting; a liquid in which a substance, usually animal or vegetable, has been boiled, and which thus contains the soluble constituents or principles of the substance.

de·code, dē·kōd′, *v.t.*—*decoded, decoding.* To translate, as a coded message, into the original language or form.

de·col·late, di·kol′āt, *v.t.*—*decollated, decollating.* [L. *decollo, decollatum.*] To behead.—**de·col·la·tion,** dē″ko·lā′shan, *n.*

dé·colle·tage, dā″kol·täzh′, dā″kol·e·täzh′, dek″o·le·täzh′, *Fr.* dā·kal·täzh′, *n.* The low-cut neckline of a dress or garment; a garment with such a neckline.

dé·colle·té, dā″kol·tā′, dā″kol·e·tā′, dek″-o·le·tā′, *Fr.* dā·kal·tā′, *a.* [Fr. < *de-* and *collet,* collar.] Having the neck and shoulders exposed, as when wearing a low-necked garment; of a garment, having a neckline that is low cut.

de·col·or·a·tion, dē·kul″ẽr·ā′shan, *n.* [L. *decoloratio, decolorationis,* discoloring—*de,* from, and *color,* color.] The removal of color; abstraction or loss of color.—**de·col·or·i·za·tion,** *n.* The process of depriving of color.—**de·col·or·ant,** dē·kul′ẽr·ant, *n.* A substance having properties that bleach or remove color.

de·com·pen·sa·tion, dē″kom·pen·sā′shan, *n. Med.* the inability of a diseased organ to compensate for its deficiency, esp. the loss of compensation in the functioning of the heart.—**de·com·pen·sate,** *v.i.*—*compensated, decompensating.*

de·com·pose, dē″·kom·pōz′, *v.t.*—*decomposed, decomposing.* [Fr. *decomposer*—*de,* from, and *composer,* to compose.] To separate into constituent parts or elementary particles; decay or rot.—*v.i.* To become resolved into constituent elements; decay, rot, or putrefy.—**de·com·po·si·tion,** *n.*

de·com·pound, dē″kom·pound′, *v.t.* To compound a second time or further; to decompose.—*a.* Composed of things which are themselves compound; as, a *decompound* leaf.—*n.* Something further compounded, or composed of parts which are themselves compound.

de·com·press, dē″kom·pres′, *v.t.* To release from pressure or compression, as in an air lock or decompression chamber. —*v.i.*

de·com·pres·sion, dē″kom·presh′an, *n.* The process of decreasing or removing air pressure from a chamber; an adjustment to normal atmospheric pressure undergone by a person after flying to high altitudes or coming out of a deep water dive; *surg.* the technique or operation used to reduce pressure upon an organ.

de·con·tam·i·nate, dē″kon·tam′i·nāt, *v.t.* —*decontaminated, decontaminating.* To purify; to free from harmful substances, as poisonous gas radioactivity.

de·con·trol, dē″kon·trōl′, *v.t.*—*decontrolled, decontrolling.* To bring out of a controlled state; release or remove from control; as, to *decontrol* industries subjected to governmental control.—*n.* The act of decontrolling, or the state of being decontrolled.

de·cor, dé·cor, dā´kạr´, di·kạr´, dā´kạr, *n.* [Fr., < *décorer,* decorate, < L. *decorare.*] Style of decoration, usually interior; as, Victorian *decor;* a decoration, esp. on the stage; scenic decoration or effect; theatrical scenery.

dec·o·rate, dek´o·rāt´, *v.t.—decorated, decorating.* [L. *decoratus,* pp. of *decorare,* < *decus,* ornament, akin to *decor,* what is becoming.] To furnish or deck with something becoming or ornamental; to furnish a home, office, or other interior in a particular style, as Early American; embellish; to confer distinction upon by the badge of an order or a medal of honor.—**dec·o·rat·ed,** *a.* Ornamented; adorned; embellished; *arch.* noting or pertaining to the Gothic style prevalent in England throughout the greater part of the 14th century, characterized by more or less elaborate decoration.

dec·o·ra·tion, dek´o·rā´shạn, *n.* [M.L. *decoratio(n-).*] The act of decorating; adornment; embellishment; that which decorates; an embellishment or ornament; a badge of an order or a medal conferred and worn as a mark of honor.

dec·o·ra·tive, dek´ẽr·a·tiv, dek´ra·tiv, dek´o·rā´tiv, *a.* Serving or tending to decorate; purely ornamental or serving only to decorate.—**dec·o·ra·tive·ly,** *adv.* —**dec·o·ra·tive·ness,** *n.*

dec·o·ra·tor, dek´o·rā´tẽr, *n.* One who decorates, esp. one who professionally decorates houses or buildings, particularly in their interior.—*a.* Pertaining to materials or practices generally preferred by decorators; as, *decorator* fabrics.

dec·o·rous, dek´ẽr·us, di·kōr´us, di·kạr´us, *a.* [L. *decorus,* becoming.] Suitable to the time, place, and occasion; becoming; seemly; proper; befitting, as of speech, behavior, or dress.—**dec·o·rous·ly,** *adv.* —**dec·o·rous·ness,** *n.*

de·cor·ti·cate, dē·kạr´ti·kāt´, *v.t.—decorticated, decorticating.* [L. *decortico, decorticatum—de,* not, and *cortex,* bark.] To strip off the bark of; to peel; to husk.—**de·cor·ti·ca·tion,** dē·kạr´ti·kā´shạn, *n.*

de·co·rum, di·kōr´um, di·kạr´um, *n.* [L., what is becoming.] Propriety of speech, appearance, or behavior; seemliness; decency.

de·coy, di·koi´, dē´koi, *n.* [D. *eende-kooi,* a duck-cage.] A place into which wild fowl are enticed and trapped, such as a pond; a fowl, or the likeness of one, employed to entice other fowl into a net or within range of shot; a thing or person intended to lead into a snare; a stratagem employed to mislead or lead into danger; an object used to deflect radar waves and to serve as deception for radar detectors.—di·koi´, *v.t.* To lead or lure by artifice into a snare; to entrap by any means which deceive; to allure, attract, or entice.

de·crease, di·krēs´, *v.i.—decreased, decreasing.* [O.Fr. *decreistre* < L. *decrescere* < *de,* down from, and *crescere,* grow.] To grow less; diminish gradually; lessen.—*v.t.* To make less; cause to diminish.—dē´krēs, di·krēs´, *n.* The process of growing less, or the resulting condition; gradual diminution; the amount by which a thing is lessened.— **de·creas·ing·ly,** *adv.*

de·cree, di·krē´, *n.* [O.Fr. *decre* (Fr. *décret*) < L. *decretum,* prop. pp. neut. of *decernere,* decide, decree.] An ordinance or edict promulgated by civil or other authority; an authoritative decision; *law,* a judicial decision; *theol.* one of the eternal purposes of God, by which events are foreordained.—*v.t.—decreed, decreeing.* To ordain or pronounce by decree; decide authoritatively.—*v.i.* To ordain or decide.— **de·cree·a·ble,** *a.* That may be decreed.

dec·re·ment, dek´re·ment, *n.* [L. *decrementum* < *decrescere.*] A gradual diminution or lessening; the amount lost by diminution; *math.* a decrease in a variable.

de·crep·it, di·krep´it, *a.* [L. *decrepitus,* broken down, worn out—*de,* from and *crepare,* to make a noise, hence originally noiseless.] Broken down or weakened by long use; wasted or worn by the infirmities of old age.—**de·crep·i·tude,** di·krep´i·tōd´, *n.* The state of being decrepit; weakened, as from the infirmities of age.—**de·crep·it·ly,** *adv.*—**de·crep·it·ness,** *n.*

de·crep·i·tate, di·krep´i·tāt´, *v.t.—decrepitated, decrepitating.* [L. *decrepo,* to break or burst, to crackle—*de* and *crepo.*] To roast or calcine in a strong heat, with a continual bursting or crackling of the substance.—*v.i.* To crackle when roasting.— **de·crep·i·ta·tion,** di·krep´´i·tā´shạn, *n.*

de·cre·scen·do, dē´´kri·shen´dō, dā´´kri·shen´dō, *a.* [It., gerund of *decrescere,* < L. *decrescere.* DECREASE.] *Mus.* gradually decreasing in force or loudness; diminuendo; opposed to *crescendo.*—*n.* pl. **de·cre·scen·dos.** *Mus.* a gradual decrease in force or loudness; a decrescendo passage.

de·cres·cent, di·kres´ent, *a.* [L. *decrescens* (-*ent-*), ppr. of *decrescere.*] Decreasing; waning, as the moon.

de·cre·tal, di·krēt´al, *a.* [L.L. *decretalis* (as *n.,* M.L. *decretale*), < L. *decretum.*] Pertaining to, of the nature of, or containing a decree or decrees.—*n.* A papal decree or epistle authoritatively determining some point of doctrine or ecclesiastical law; *pl.* (*cap.*) the body or collection of such decrees as a part of the canon law.—**de·cre·tal·ist, de·cre·tist,** *n.* One versed in the Decretals.

de·cre·tive, di·krē´tiv, *a.* Pertaining to or having the authority of a decree.

dec·re·to·ry, dek´ri·tōr´´ē, dek´ri·tạr´´ē, *a.* [L. *decretorius,* < *decernere,* decide, decree.] Pertaining to or of the nature of an authoritative decision or decree; definitive; decisive.

de·cry, di·krī´, *v.t.—decried, decrying.* [Fr. *décrier,* O.Fr. *descrier—des* (= L. *dis*), and *crier,* to cry.] To censure as faulty, mean, or worthless; to clamor against; to express open disapproval of; to lower in value officially, as a coin.—**de·cri·al,** di·krī´al, *n.* The act of decrying.—**de·cri·er,** *n.*

de·cum·bent, di·kum´bent, *a.* [L. *decumbens* < *decumbo,* to lie down—*de* and *cumbo,* for *cubo,* to lie.] Lying down; reclining; recumbent; *bot.* resting on the ground, as a shoot or stem, but with an ascending extremity.—**de·cum·bence, de·cum·ben·cy,** *n.*—**de·cum·bent·ly,** *adv.*

dec·u·ple, dek´ụ·pel, *a.* [L.L. *decuplus,* < L. *decem,* ten.] Tenfold; containing ten times as many.—*n.* A number ten times repeated.—*v.t.—decupled, decupling.* To increase ten times.

de·curved, dē·kụrvd´, *a.* Bent down or curved downward, as the bill of a bird.

de·cus·sate, di·kus´āt, dek´a·sāt´, *v.t., v.i. —decussated, decussating.* [L. *decusso,* to divide crosswise in the form of a cross, < *decussis,* the number 10, which the Romans represented by X.] To intersect so as to make acute angles; to intersect; to cross, as lines, rays of light, leaves, or nerves in the body.—di·kus´āt, di·kus´it, *a.* Crossed; intersected; *bot.* arranged in pairs alternately crossing each other at regular angles. —**de·cus·sate·ly,** di·kus´it·li, *adv.*—**de·cus·sa·tion,** dē´´ka·sā´shạn, dek´´a·sā´shạn, *n.* The act of crossing at right or at acute angles; the crossing of two lines, rays, or nerves, which meet in a point and then proceed and diverge.

de·dans, de·dän´, *n.* pl. **de·dans,** de·dän´. [Fr., interior, noun use of *dedans,* adv., within.] *Court tennis,* an open gallery for spectators, at the service end of the court; the spectators behind this opening at a match of court tennis.

ded·i·cate, ded´i·kāt´, *v.t.—dedicated, dedicating.* [L. *dedico—de,* and *dico, dicare,* to devote, dedicate.] To set apart and consecrate to a divine being, or to a sacred purpose; to appropriate to any person or purpose; *often refl.,* to give wholly or earnestly up to. To inscribe or address to a patron, friend, or public character; as, to *dedicate* a book.—*a.* Consecrated or devoted; appropriated.—**ded·i·ca·tor,** *n.*—**ded·i·ca·to·ry, ded·i·ca·tive, ded·i·ca·tion·al,** ded´i·ka·tōr´´ē, ded´i·ka·tạr´´ē, *a.* Serving to dedicate; serving as a dedication; of or pertaining to dedication.

ded·i·ca·tion, ded´´i·kā´shạn, *n.* The act of dedicating; consecration or devotion to a sacred use or cause; appropriation; an address prefixed to a book, and inscribed to a friend of the author, some public character, or other person, as a mark of love or esteem.

de·dif·fer·en·ti·a·tion, dē·dif´´e·ren´´shē·ā´shạn, *n. Biol.* a reverting of cells to a more primitive or general state, often prior to a more important change such as regeneration of a limb.

de·duce, di·dōs´, di·dūs´, *v.t.—deduced, deducing.* [L. *deducere* (pp. *deductus*), < *de,* from, and *ducere,* lead.] To derive, as a conclusion, from something known or assumed; infer; to draw or obtain from some source; to trace the course of.— **de·duc·i·ble,** *a.* That may be deduced.

de·duct, di·dukt´, *v.t.* To subtract or separate, in numbering, estimating, or calculating; to infer; to take away or detract.— **de·duct·i·ble,** *a.*—**de·duct·i·bil·i·ty,** *n.*

de·duc·tion, di·duk´shạn, *n.* [L. *deductio, deductionis.*] The act of subtracting; that which is deducted; abatement; the method of deducing from premises; conclusion derived from the given premises.—**de·duc·tive,** di·duk´tiv, *a.* Pertaining to deduction; deduced from premises.— **de·duc·tive·ly,** *adv.*

deed, dēd, *n.* [O.E. *daed,* a deed, < *dón,* to do = Icel. *dáð,* D. and Dan. *daad,* Goth. *deds,* G. *that,* a deed.] That which is done or performed; an act; an exploit; achievement; *law,* a writing containing some contract or agreement, esp. an instrument conveying real estate to a purchaser or donee.—*v.t.* To transfer by deed.—**deed·less,** *a.*—**in deed,** in fact, in reality; often united to form the single word *indeed.*

deem, dēm, *v.t.* [O.E. *déman,* to deem, to judge, < *dóm,* doom, judgment; Icel. *dœma,* Dan. *dømme,* Goth. (*ga*)*domjan,* to judge; < root of *do.*] To think, judge, believe, or have an opinion.—*v.i.* To think or suppose.

deep, dēp, *a.* [O.E. *deop* = D. *diep* = G. *tief* = Icel. *djúpr* = Goth. *diups,* deep.] Situated far down from the surface; having a specified dimension downward, inward, or backward; as, a tank eight feet *deep;* extending to or coming from a depth; as, a *deep* dive, a *deep* breath; difficult to understand; abstruse; lying below the surface; as, a speech of *deep* significance; not superficial; grave or serious; heartfelt; as, *deep* sorrow; absorbing; as, *deep* study; great in measure or degree; intense or extreme; as, *deep* sleep, *deep* color; low in pitch, as sound; having intellectual powers characterized by profound insight or learning; shrewd or artful; much involved; as, *deep* in debt; absorbed; as, *deep* in thought; *baseball,* in reference to a long hit or a defensive position, in the farthest part of the outfield; *football,* of a defensive back, positioned well back of the line of play in order to defend against forward passes.— *adv.* Profoundly; intensely; to or at a considerable or specified depth; far on in time.—**deep·ly**, *adv.* Far below the surface; profoundly; thoroughly; to a great degree; intensely; gravely; with low or deep tone; with artfulness; as, a *deeply* laid plot.—**deep·ness**, *n.*

deep, dēp, *n.* The sea or ocean; the deep part of an ocean or other body of water; any great depth in space or time; the part of greatest intensity; as the *deep* of winter; something profound or incomprehensible. *Naut.* one of the fathom points on a hand lead line, distinguished from the *marks* by being unmarked.

deep·en, dē'pen, *v.t.* To make deep or deeper; to intensify; to make more grave.—*v.i.* To become more deep, in all its senses.

deep-root·ed, dēp'rö'tid, dēp'rут'id, *a.* Deeply rooted; firmly implanted or established.

deep-sea, dēp'sē', *a.* Relating or belonging to the deeper parts of the ocean; as, *deep-sea* diver, *deep-sea* navigation.

deep-seat·ed, dēp'sē'tid, *a.* Situated far beneath the surface; deeply rooted or lodged; firmly implanted; as, a *deep-seated* sense of obligation.

deep space, *n.* Space beyond the solar system's limits.

deer, dēr, *n. pl.* deer; occasionally, esp. with reference to different species, deers. [O.E. *dēor* = D. *dier* = G. *tier* = Icel. *dȳr.*] Any ruminant animal of the family *Cervidae*, most of the males of which have solid deciduous horns or antlers; any of the smaller species of this family, as distinguished from the moose, elk, reindeer, or the like.

deer fly, *n.* Any of several varieties of blood-sucking winged insects, the female of which attacks deer, livestock, and man.

deer·hound, dēr'hound", *n.* A hound formerly used for hunting deer, esp. one of a Scottish breed allied to and resembling the greyhound but larger and having a shaggy coat.

deer mouse, *n.* A widely distributed white-footed mouse, *Peromyscus leucopus*, of North America.

deer·skin, dēr'skin", *n.* The hide of a deer; leather made from this; a garment made of such leather.—*a.*

de·es·ca·late, dē·es'ka·lāt, *v.t.*, *v.i.* To bring about a reduction in scope or extent; as, to *de-escalate* military plans in war.—**de·es·ca·la·tion**, dē·es'ka·lā'shan, *n.*

dee·wan, di·wän', *n.* A government official, in Moslem countries. Also **de·wan.**

de·face, di·fās', *v.t.*—defaced, defacing. To destroy or mar the face or surface of; to disfigure; to erase or obliterate.—**de·face·ment**, *n.* The act of defacing; injury to the surface or exterior; that which mars or disfigures.—**de·fac·er**, *n.*

de fac·to, dē·fak'tō, *a.*, *adv.* [L.] In fact; actually existing, whether lawfully or not.

de·fal·cate, di·fal'kāt, di·fạl'kāt, *v.t.*—defalcated, defalcating. [M.L. defalcatus, pp. of defalcare, < de, from, and M.L. falcare, cut with sickle, < L. falx, sickle.] *Archaic*, to cut off or deduct a part from; to curtail.—*v.i.* To embezzle; to misappropriate funds.—**de·fal·ca·tion**, *n.* A misappropriation of money held in trust, or a sum misappropriated; embezzlement; *archaic*, deduction or reduction.

def·a·ma·tion, def"a·mā'shan, dē"fa·mā'shan, *n.* The uttering or publishing of slanderous words with the purpose of injuring another's reputation; slander; calumny.—**de·fam·a·to·ry**, di·fam'a·tōr"ē, di·fam'a·tạr"ē, *n.* Containing defamation; slanderous.

de·fame, di·fām', *v.t.*—defamed, defaming. [L.L. *defamare*—de, not, and L. fama, fame.] To slander; to calumniate; to libel; to bring into disrepute.—**de·fam·er**, *n.*

de·fault, di·fạlt', *n.* [O.Fr. defaute (also

---

defaut, Fr. *défaut*), < *defaillir*, < *de*- and *faillir*, E. *fail*.] Failure to act; neglect; failure to meet financial obligations; *law*, failure to perform an act of obligation legally required, esp. to appear in court or to plead at a time assigned; want, lack, or absence; *sports*, failure to compete in or finish a scheduled contest.

de·fault, di·fạlt', *v.i.* To fail in fulfilling or satisfying an engagement, claim, contract, or agreement; *sports*, to fail to play or complete play in a scheduled match, or to lose the contest through such a failure.—*v.t.* To fail to act or pay; *sports*, to fail to play when scheduled, or to forfeit by failure to play; *law*, to give judgment against on account of failing to appear and answer.—**de·fault·er**, *n.*

de·fea·sance, di·fē'zans, *n.* [O.Fr. *defesance*, < *defaire*, *desfaire*, undo.] A rendering null and void; *law*, a condition on the performance of which a deed or other instrument is defeated or rendered void; a collateral deed or other writing embodying such a condition.—**de·fea·si·ble**, di·fē'zi·bl, *a.* That may be abrogated or annulled.

de·feat, di·fēt', *n.* [Fr. *défaite*, < *défaire*, to undo, O.Fr. *desfaire*—L. *dis*, and *facere*, to do.] An overthrow; loss of battle; check, rout, or destruction of an army by the victory of an enemy; a frustration by rendering null and void, or by prevention of success.—*v.t.* To overcome or vanquish; to overthrow; to frustrate; to prevent the success of; to disappoint; to render null and void.

de·feat·ism, di·fē'tiz·um, *n.* Expectation of or resignation to defeat.—**de·feat·ist**, *n.*

def·e·cate, def'e·kāt', *v.t.*—defecated, defecating. [L. defæco—de, and fæx, dregs.] To clear from dregs or impurities; to clarify or purify; to void, as excrement, from the bowels.—*v.i.* To become clear or pure by depositing impurities; to void excrement.—**def·e·ca·tion**, def"e·kā'shan, *n.*

de·fect, dē'fekt, di·fekt', *n.* [L. defectus, pp. of deficio, defectum, to fail—de, from, and facio, to make, to do.] A fault; an imperfection; that which is wanting to make a perfect whole; blemish; deformity.

de·fec·tion, di·fek'shan, *n.* [L. defectio, defectionis.] The act of abandoning a person or cause to which one is bound by allegiance or duty, or to which one has attached himself; a falling away; apostasy; backsliding.—**de·fect**, di·fekt', *v.i.* To abandon a cause, party, or person, esp. in order to follow another.—**de·fec·tor**, *n.*

de·fec·tive, di·fek'tiv, *a.* [L. defectivus, imperfect.] Wanting either in substance, quantity, or quality, or in anything necessary; imperfect; faulty; marked by a subnormal condition, either mental or physical; *gram.* wanting some of the usual forms of declension or conjugation; as, a *defective* noun or verb.—*n.* One who is physically or mentally deficient.—**de·fec·tive·ly**, *adv.*—**de·fec·tive·ness**, *n.*

de·fend, di·fend', *v.t.* To protect or support against any assault or attack; to protect by opposition or resistance; to vindicate, uphold, or maintain uninjured by force or by argument, as rights and privileges; *law*, to come forward as defendant in; as, to *defend* an action; to act as lawyer for.—*v.i.* To show opposition or resistance; *law*, to contest and try to defeat a claim or demand made against another.—**de·fend·er**, *n.*

de·fend·ant, di·fen'dant, *n.* *Law*, the person against whom a charge is made in a lawsuit.

de·fen·es·tra·tion, dē·fen"i·strā'shan, *n.* [L. *de*, < and *fenestra*, window.] The act of throwing out of a window.

de·fense, *Brit.* **de·fence**, di·fens', dē'fens, *n.* [O.Fr. defense (Fr. *défense*), < L.L. *defensa*, < L. *defendere*.] Resistance against

---

attack; protection; the practice or art of defending oneself against attack, as in fencing or boxing; something that defends, esp. a fortification; the defending or maintaining of a cause or the like by speech or argument; a speech or argument in vindication; *law*, the denial or pleading of the defendant in answer to the claim or charge against him; the proceedings adopted by a defendant, or his legal agents, for defending himself; a defendant and his legal agents collectively; *sports*, the protection of oneself or the goal against attack, as in hockey, football, and fencing; the team trying to thwart the attack of the team controlling the ball or puck.—**de·fense·less**, *Brit.* **de·fence·less**, *a.* Without defense; unprotected.—**de·fense·less·ly**, *Brit.* **de·fence·less·ly**, *adv.*—**de·fense·less·ness**, *Brit.* **de·fence·less·ness**, *n.*

de·fense mech·an·ism, *n. Physiol.* the reaction of an organism in self-protection against an invading microorganism; *psychol.* the unconscious process of excluding from the mind unacceptable or painful thoughts.

de·fen·si·ble, di·fen'si·bl, *a.* [L.L. *defensibilis*.] Capable of being defended against assault or injury; capable of being defended in argument; justifiable.—**de·fen·si·bil·i·ty**, **de·fen·si·ble·ness**, di·fen"si·bil'i·tē, *n.*—**de·fen·si·bly**, *adv.*

de·fen·sive, di·fen'siv, *a.* [Fr. *défensif*.] Serving to defend; proper for or suited to defense; carried on in resisting attack or aggression; of or relating to defense.—*n.* An attitude or position of defense or resistance to aggression or attack; as, to be on the *defensive.*—**de·fen·sive·ly**, *adv.* In a defensive manner; on the defensive; in defense.

de·fer, di·fur', *v.t.*—deferred, deferring. [O.Fr. *differre*, L. *differo*, to delay—*dis*, from, and *fero*, to carry.] To delay; to postpone; *milit.* officially to postpone induction into the armed forces.—*v.i.* To delay; to procrastinate.—**de·fer·ment**, *n.* The act of deferring; *milit.* official postponement of service in the armed forces.—**de·fer·rer**, *n.*—**de·ferred**, *a.*—**de·fer·ra·ble**, *n.*

de·fer, di·fur', *v.i.*—deferred, deferring. [L. *defero*, to carry down or away, hand over, refer—*de*, down, and *fero* to carry.] To yield to another's opinion; to submit or give way courteously or from respect; as, to *defer* to a friend's judgment.—*v.t.* To present for decision; to refer.—**de·fer·ence**, def'ẹr·ens, *n.* A yielding in opinion or judgment of another; respect; courteous consideration.—**def·er·en·tial**, def"e·ren'shal, *a.* Expressing deference; accustomed to defer.—**def·er·en·tial·ly**, *adv.*—**de·fer·rer**, *n.* One who defers in regard to opinion.

def·er·ent, def'ẹr·ent, *a.* Showing deference; *anat.* serving to convey away; as, a *deferent* duct.

de·fer·ves·cence, dē"fẹr·ves'ens, def"ẹr·ves'ens, *n. Med.* a lowering of fever.

de·fi·ance, di·fī'ans, *n.* [O.Fr. *defiance*, *deffiance*, < *defier*.] The act of defying; a challenge to meet in combat or contest; a daring or bold resistance to authority or to any opposing force; open disregard; as, in *defiance* of criticism.—**de·fi·ant**, *a.* Characterized by or showing defiance.—**de·fi·ant·ly**, *adv.*

de·fi·cien·cy, di·fish'en·sē, *n. pl.* **de·fi·cien·cies.** The state of being deficient; a failing; shortage; want, either total or partial; a defect; a deficit.

de·fi·cien·cy dis·ease, *n. Pathol.* a disease due to a dietary insufficiency, as of vitamins, minerals, or other essential elements.

de·fi·cient, di·fish'ent, *a.* [L. *deficiens* (-ent-), ppr. of *deficere*, be wanting.] Wanting some element or characteristic necessary to completeness, or having an

---

a- fat, fāte, fär, fâre, fạll;   **e-** met, mē, mēre, hẽr;   **i-** pin, pīne;   **o-** not, nōte, mõve;   **u-** tub, cūbe, bụll;   **oi-** oil;   **ou-** pound.

insufficient measure of it; falling short of a standard; defective; wanting or lacking. —**de·fi·cient·ly,** adv.

def·i·cit, def'i·sit, Brit. di·fis'it, n. [L., "there is wanting," 3d pers. sing. pres. ind. of deficere.] A falling short; the amount by which a sum of money falls short of the required amount. Finance, a state, at a given time in business, or in public revenues and spending, when liabilities exceed assets; the amount by which assets fall short of liabilities; loss in business; any deficiency.

def·i·cit fi·nan·cing, n. Finance, the raising of money by a government or public body to meet expenditures that exceed public revenues.

def·i·cit spend·ing, n. The practice of incurring expenses beyond income, esp. by a government.

de·fi·er, di·fi'er, n. One who defies.

def·i·lade, def"·i·lād', v.t.—defiladed, defilading. [Fr. défiler, defilade, orig. unthread, < de, (dis-) and -filer as in enfiler.] Fort. To arrange the plan and profile of a fortification so as to protect its lines from enfilading fire, or fire from nearby heights, and its interior from reverse fire.—n. Fort. the determination of the directions and heights of the lines of natural or artificial obstacles needed to defilade a fortification.

de·file, di·fil', v.t.—defiled, defiling. [L. prefix de, and O.E. fýlan (M.E. and Sc. file, to defile), < ful, foul.] To soil or sully; to tarnish, as a reputation; to make ceremonially unclean; to corrupt the chastity of; to violate.—**de·file·ment,** n. The act of defiling, or state of being defiled.—**de·fil·er,** n. One who or that which defiles.

de·file, di·fil', dē'fil, v.i.—defiled, defiling. [Fr. défiler—de, and file, a row or line, < L. filum, a thread.] To march off in a line, or file by file.—n. A narrow passage in which troops may march only in a file, or with a narrow front; a long pass, as between hills.

de·fine, di·fin', v.t.—defined, defining. [O.Fr. definer, for definir (Fr. définir), < L. definire (pp. definitus), limit, determine, explain, terminate, < de-, completely, and finire bound, limit, terminate, E. finish.] To state or set forth the meaning or significance, as of a word or phrase; to explain the nature or essential qualities of; to determine or fix the boundaries or extent of; make clear the outline or form of; fix or lay down definitely; specify distinctly; to be a distinguishing feature of; characterize.—**de·fine·ment,** n. The act of defining; description; definition.—**de·fin·er,** n.—**de·fin·a·ble,** a.—**de·fin·a·bil·i·ty,** n.—**de·fin·a·bly,** adv.

de·fin·i·en·dum, di·fin"ē·en'dum, n. pl. **de·fin·i·en·da,** di·fin"ē·en'da. The term to be defined, as in a dictionary entry; logic, the expression to be defined in terms of a previous expression.

de·fin·i·ens, di·fin'ē·enz, n. pl. **de·fin·i·en·tia,** di·fin"ē·en'cha, di·fin"ē·en'chē·a. A description or statement that defines something; that part of a statement which defines.

def·i·nite, def'i·nit, a. [L. definitus, pp. DEFINE.] Clearly defined or determined; not vague or general; fixed; precise; exact; having fixed limits; of persons, clear or specific in thought or statement; gram. specifying precisely or with limitation; as, the definite article; bot. of stamens, of a constant number not exceeding twenty; of an inflorescence, determinate.—**def·i·nite·ly,** adv.—**def·i·nite·ness,** n.

def·i·nite in·te·gral, n. Math. a number that is the difference between values of the indefinite integral of the independent variable at two designated values.

def·i·ni·tion, def"i·nish'an, n. [L. definitio, definitionis.] The act of defining; a brief and precise description of a thing by its properties; an explanation of the significance or meaning of a word or thing; the quality or power of making a thing sharp and clear; as, the definition of a telescope; the sharpness, resolution, and brilliance of an image, as a photograph; clarity, esp. of sound reproduction on a radio or TV set. —**def·i·ni·tion·al,** a.

de·fin·i·tive, di·fin'i·tiv, a. [L. definitivus, < definire.] Reliable and ostensibly exhaustive; as, a definitive report on Shakespeare; having the function of deciding or settling; determinative; conclusive; final; settled in a conclusive or final manner; serving to fix or specify definitely; precisely expressed; affording a solution or final answer; as, definitive treatment for illness; biol. having its final or complete form; as, a definitive organ.—**de·fin·i·tive·ly,** adv.—**de·fin·i·tive·ness,** n.

de·fin·i·tive host, n. Biol. an organism, infected by a parasite, in which the parasite attains sexual maturity and can reproduce itself.

def·i·nit·ize, def'i·ni·tīz", di·fin'i·tīz", v.t. —definitized, definitizing. To finalize in a clear form; make definite; to express with clarity and exactitude.

de·fin·i·tude, di·fin'i·töd", di·fin'i·tūd", n. The quality of being definite; precision.

def·la·grate, def'le·grāt", dē'fle·grāt", v.t. —deflagrated, deflagrating. [L. deflagro, deflagratum—de, intens., and flagro, to burn.] To set fire to; to cause to burn rapidly; to consume.—v.i. To burn rapidly, or with violent combustion.—**def·la·gra·tion,** n. —**def·la·gra·ble,** a.

de·flate, di·flāt', v.t.—deflated, deflating. To release the distending gas or air from; to lower (another's opinion of himself) or reduce (his hopes); finance, to reduce from an inflated level, as currency or prices.—v.i. To lose fullness through the escape of gas or air.—**de·fla·tion,** di·flā'shan, n. A deflating; finance, a reduction in the volume of currency outstanding; a reduction in the volume of purchasing power.—**de·fla·tion·ary,** di·flā'sha·ner"ē, a.

de·flect, di·flekt', v.i. [L. deflecto—de, from, and flecto, to turn or bend.] To turn away or aside; to deviate from a true course or right line; to swerve.—v.t. To cause to turn aside; to turn or bend from a straight line.—**de·flec·tive,** di·flek'tiv, a. —**de·flec·tor,** di·flek'tèr, n. An implement used for measuring the deviations in a compass caused by electrical currents and surrounding metal; that which deflects.

de·flec·tion, Brit. **de·flex·ion,** di·flek'shan, n. [L.L. deflexio(n)-.] The act of deflecting, or the state of being deflected; a turning from a true course or right line; a bending, esp. downward; deviation; amount of deviation; opt. the bending of rays of light from a straight line; the deviation or swing of the needle or indicator of a measuring instrument from the position regarded as zero.

de·flow·er, di·flou'er, v.t. [Fr. déflorer; L.L. defloro, < L. de, from, and flos, floris, a flower.] To deprive of virginity; to violate; ravish; to strip of flowers; to rob of beauty and freshness.—**def·lo·ra·tion,** def"lo·rā'shan, n. The act of deflowering or taking away a woman's virginity.

de·fo·li·ant, dē·fō'lē·ant, n. A preparation used for stripping leaves from plants.

de·fo·li·ate, dē·fō'lē·āt", v.t.—defoliated, defoliating. [M.L. defoliatus, pp. of defoliare, < L. de- and folium, leaf.] To strip or deprive prematurely of leaves.—v.i. To shed or lose leaves.—dē·fō'lē·it, dē·fō'lē·āt, a.—**de·fo·li·a·tion,** n.—**de·fo·li·a·tor,** n.

de·force, di·fōrs', di·fàrs', v.t.—deforced, deforcing. [O.Fr. deforcer, < de- and forcer, E. force.] Law, to withhold by force or violence, as from the rightful owner; to deprive forcibly or wrongfully of property. —**de·force·ment,** n.—**de·for·ciant,** di·fōr'shant, di·fàr'shant, n.

de·for·est, dē·fàr'ist, dē·for'est, v.t. To divest of forests or trees.—**de·for·est·a·tion,** n.—**de·for·es·ter,** n.

de·form, di·fàrm', v.t. [L. deformo—de, and forma, form.] To mar or injure the form of; to disfigure; to render ugly or unpleasing; to disfigure the moral beauty of; as, vices that deform character; to alter in form or transform.—v.i. To become deformed or disfigured.—**de·for·ma·tion,** dē"fàr·mā'shan, def"èr·mā'shan, n. The act of disfiguring or defacing; a disfigurement or defacement; a change in form, esp. one for the worse; an alteration in form or shape or the state of being so altered.—**de·formed,** di·fàrmd', a. Disfigured; distorted; misshapen; ugly.—**de·form·ed·ly,** di·for'mid·lē, adv.—**de·form·ed·ness,** n.

de·form·i·ty, di·fàr'mi·tē, n. pl. **de·form·i·ties.** [L. deformitas.] The state of being deformed; some deformed or misshapen part of the body; distortion; irregularity of shape or features; ugliness; anything that destroys beauty, grace, or propriety.

de·fraud, di·frad', v.t. [L. defraudare, < de-, and fraudare, cheat, < fraus, E. fraud.] To deprive of some right or property by fraud; cheat.—**de·frau·da·tion,** dē·frà·dā'shan, n.—**de·fraud·er,** n.

de·fray, di·frā', v.t. [Fr. defrayer—de, and frais, expense, < L.L. fractus or fractum, expense, compensation, < L. frango, fractum. to break.] To pay or arrange for payment of.—**de·fray·al,** de·fray·ment, n. —**de·fray·er,** n.—**de·fray·a·ble,** a.

de·frock, dē·frok', v.t. Eccles. To deprive, as a priest or minister, of the right to exercise the functions of his office.

de·frost, di·frast', di·frost', v.t. To remove frost or ice from; to thaw.—v.i. To thaw; to become free of ice.—**de·frost·er,** di·fra'stèr, di·fros'tèr, n.

deft, deft, a. [O.E. daeft, fit, convenient < (ge)dafam, to become, to befit; Goth gadaban, to befit.] Dexterous; clever; apt.— **deft·ly,** adv.—**deft·ness,** n.

de·funct, di·fungkt', a. [L. defunctus, pp. of defungi, discharge, finish, die, < de-completely, and fungi, perform.] Deceased; dead; extinct; no longer in use or in effect; as, a defunct law.—**the de·funct,** n. A dead person, esp. one recently deceased.— **de·funct·ness,** n.

de·fy, di·fi', v.t.—defied, defying. [Fr. défier, O.Fr. desfier, lit. to renounce faith or allegiance, < L. dis, apart, and fides, faith.] To provoke to combat or strife, by appealing to the courage of (another); dare; to challenge or resist boldly; to brave. —di·fi', dē'fi, n. A challenge.

de·gas, dē·gas', v.t.—degassed, degassing. To remove gas.—**de·gas·ser,** n.

de·gauss, dē·gous', v.t. To render nonmagnetic, as a steel hull of a ship, through the use of electrical coils that cancel the ship's magnetic field.

de·gen·er·ate, di·jen'e·rāt", v.i.—degenerated, degenerating. [L. degeneratus, pp. of degenerare, < degener, that departs from its race or kind, base, < de, from, and genus, race, kind.] To fall away from the normal state or condition; decline in physical, mental, or moral qualities; deteriorate.— di·jen'èr·it, n. One who has retrograded from a normal type or standard, as in morals or character; one exhibiting certain morbid physical and mental traits and tendencies, esp. from birth; one given to sexual perversion.—**de·gen·er·ate·ly,** adv.— **de·gen·er·ate·ness,** n.—**de·gen·er·a·cy,** n.

de·gen·er·ate, di·jen′ĕr·it, a. Fallen from a higher physical or moral condition; declined physically or morally from the normal standard of one's race, kind, or former self; characterized by or associated with degeneracy; base or mean; as, *degenerate* arts or times.

de·gen·er·a·tion, di·jen″e·rā′shan, n. The process of degenerating, or the state of being degenerate; deterioration; degradation; degeneracy. *Biol.* progressive deterioration or simplification; reversion to a less highly organized or a simpler type. *Pathol.* a process by which normal tissue becomes converted into or replaced by tissue of an inferior quality; as, fatty *degeneration*; the morbid condition produced by such a process.—**de·gen·er·a·tive**, di·jen′e·rā″tiv, di·jen′ĕr·a·tiv, a. Tending to degenerate; characterized by degeneration.

de·glu·ti·tion, dē″glụ·tish′an, n. [L. *deglutio, deglutitum*, to swallow.] The act of swallowing; the process by which animals swallow.

deg·ra·da·tion, deg″ra·dā′shan, n. The act of degrading; the state of being degraded; *geol.* a wearing down by erosion.

de·grade, dē·grād′, di·grād′, v.t.—*degraded, degrading*. [O.Fr. *degrader* (Fr. *dégrader*), < M.L. *degradare*, reduce in rank.] To reduce from a higher to a lower rank or degree; deprive of office, rank, degree, or title, esp. as a punishment; to lower in dignity or estimation; bring into contempt; to lower in quality or moral character; debase; deprave; to bring down in value or marketability; to reduce in amount, strength, or intensity; *biol.* to lower in the scale of classification; *chem.* to reduce in complexity, as a compound; *geol.* to wear down by erosion.—v.i. To become lower in grade, type, or character; deteriorate; degenerate.—**de·grad·ed**, a. Reduced or lowered in rank, estimation, character, or quality; vulgarized; debased; degenerate.—**de·grad·ing**, a.—**de·grad·ing·ly**, adv.

de·gree, di·grē′, n. A step or stage in a process, course of action, scale, or classificatory order; a stage in a scale of rank or dignity; relative rank or station in society; a stage in a scale of intensity or amount; relative extent, measure, or scope; the 360th part of the circumference of a circle, often indicated by the sign °, as 65°; one of the divisions or units of measure marked on a scale of a measuring instrument, as on a thermometer; *geog.* a line or point on the surface of the earth defined by its angular distance from 0° to 180° east or west of a standard meridian, or from 0° to 90° north or south of the equator; a legal measure of culpability or of the gravity of a crime; as, murder in the first *degree*; *educ.* an academic title awarded by institutions of learning upon completion of a course of study or as an honorary recognition of achievement; *gram.* one of the three forms, positive, comparative, or superlative, used in the comparison of an adjective or adverb. *Math.* the sum of the exponents of the unknown quantities or variables in an algebraic term, as a^3 and a^2b are both of the third degree; the exponent of the highest degree term in an equation or polynomial. *Genetics*, a certain step or distance in a line of genealogical descent, indicating the proximity of relationship. *Mus.* a space or line of the musical staff; a note, step, or tune of the scale.—**by de·grees**, in easy stages; gradually.—**to a de·gree**, to a great extent; to a small extent; somewhat.

de·gree-day, di·grē′dā″, n. A unit indicating that the mean outdoor temperature of any given day is one degree above or below a given standard temperature such as 65°F.;

as, a day with a mean outdoor temperature of 60° would have 5 *degree-days*.

de·gree of free·dom, n. The number of unrestricted, randomly sampled units entering into calculation of a statistic.

de·gres·sion, di·gresh′an, n. [L. *degredi* (pp. *degressus*), go down, < *de*, down from, and *gradi*, walk, go, < *gradus*, step, E. *grade*.] A going down; descent; the decrease in rate for sums below a certain amount, in degressive taxation.—**de·gres·sive**, di·gres′iv, a. Noting or pertaining to a form of taxation in which the rate is constant on sums of and above a certain fixed amount, but diminishes gradually on sums below it.

de·gum, dē·gum′, v.t.—*degummed, degumming*. To free from gum or similar substances.

de·gust, di·gust′, v.t. [L.] To taste.—**de·gus·ta·tion**, dē″gu·stā′shan, n.

de·hisce, di·his′, v.i.—*dehisced, dehiscing*. [L. *dehisco*, to gape—*de*, intens., and *hisco*, to gape.] *Bot.* to open, as the capsules or seed vessels of plants.—**de·his·cence**, di·his′ens, n. *Bot.* the splitting of an organ in accordance with its structure, as the opening of the parts of a capsule or the cells of anthers.—**de·his·cent**, di·his′ent, a. *Bot.* Opening; dehiscing.

de·horn, dē·hârn′, v.t. To deprive of horns, as cattle; prevent the growth of the horns of.—**de·horn·er**, n.

de·hu·man·ize, dē·hū′ma·nīz″, dē·ū′ma·-nīz″, v.t.—*dehumanized, dehumanizing*. To deprive of the character of humanity; to deprive of tenderness or softness of feeling; to bring about a loss of individuality.

de·hu·mid·i·fi·er, dē″hū·mid′i·fī″er, dē″ū·mid′i·fī″er, n. An appliance used to remove moisture from the air.

de·hu·mid·i·fy, dē″hū·mid′i·fī″, dē″ū·-mid′i·fī″, v.t.—*dehumidified, dehumidifying*. To remove moisture, as from the air within an enclosed space.—**de·hu·mid·i·fi·ca·tion**, n.

de·hy·drate, dē·hī′drāt, v.t.—*dehydrated, dehydrating*. To remove water from (a substance or mixture); to remove water from (food) by chemical process, as a means of preservation.—v.i. To lose water or moisture.—**de·hy·dra·tion**, n. The loss or removal of water.—**de·hy·dra·tor**, n.

de·hy·dro·gen·ate, dē·hī′dro·je·nāt″, dē·hi·droj′e·nāt″, v.t.—*dehydrogenated, dehydrogenating*. *Chem.* to remove hydrogen from (a substance).

de·hyp·no·tize, dē·hip′no·tīz″ v.t.—*dehypnotized, dehypnotizing*. To bring out of the hypnotic state, as: The psychoanalyst *dehypnotized* the patient.

de·ice, dē·īs′, v.t.—*deiced, deicing*. To remove from or keep free of ice.—**de·ic·er**, dē·ī′ser, n. A device or chemical substance for preventing the accumulation of ice on airplane surfaces, streets, or parts of a motor.

de·i·cide, dē′i·sīd″, n. [L.L. *deicida*, < L. *deus*, god, and *-cide*, < L. *-cida*, killer, or *-cidium*, a killing, < *caedere*, kill.] One who kills a god; the killing of a god.—**de·i·ci·dal**, a.

deic·tic, dīk′tik, a. [Gr. *deicticos*, serving to show, < *deicnunai*, show.] Demonstrating or proving directly.

de·i·fy, dē′i·fī″, v.t.—*deified, deifying*. [L. *deus*, a god, and *facio*, to make.] To make a god of; to exalt to the rank of a deity; to treat as an object of supreme regard; to make godlike; to elevate spiritually.—**de·if·ic**, dē·if′ik, a. Making divine.—**de·i·fi·ca·tion**, dē″i·fi·kā′shan, n.—**de·i·form**, dē·-i·fârm″, a. Of a godlike form.

deign, dān, v.i. [O.Fr. *deignier* (Fr. *daigner*), < L. *dignare, dignari*, deem worthy, < *dignus*, worthy.] To consider something fitting or in accordance with one's dignity;

condescend; vouchsafe.—v.t. To condescend to give or grant.

de·in·dus·tri·al·i·za·tion, dē·in·dus′-trē·a·li·zā″shan, n. Action taken to decrease or destroy industrial capacity, usually of a country defeated in war.

de·ism, dē′iz·um, n. [Fr. *déisme*, < L. *Deus*, God.] The doctrine or creed of a deist.—**de·ist**, dē′ist, n. [Fr. *déiste*.] One who believes in the existence of a God or supreme being but denies revealed religion, basing his belief on the light of nature and reason; one who believes in a God who created the universe but takes no part in its operations.—**de·is·tic**, **de·is·ti·cal**, dē·-is′tik, dē·is′ti·kal, a.—**de·is·ti·cal·ly**, adv.

de·i·ty, dē′i·tē, n. pl. **de·i·ties**. [O.Fr. *deite* (Fr. *déite*), < L.L. *deitas*, < L. *deus*, god; akin to L. *divus*, divine, *Jovis*, Jove, Gr. *Zeus* (gen. *Dios*), Zeus, Skt. *deva*, god, *dyāus*, heaven, and O.E. *Tīw*, the Teutonic god of war.] The estate or rank of a god; divine character or nature; godhood, esp. the character or nature of the Supreme Being; a god or goddess; a person or thing deified.—**the De·i·ty**, the Supreme Being; God.

dé·jà vu, dā·zhä vy′, n. [Fr. lit. *already seen*.] A hackneyed, overworked plot in film or narrative; *psychol.* the feeling of having experienced at some prior time something actually being experienced for the first time.

de·ject, di·jekt′, v.t. [L. *dejicio, dejectum—de*, down, and *jacio*, to throw.] To cast down; to depress the spirits of; to dispirit; discourage; dishearten.—**de·ject·ed**, di·jek′tid, a. Downcast; depressed; sad; sorrowful.—**de·ject·ed·ly**, adv.—**de·jec·ted·ness**, n.

de·jec·ta, di·jek′ta, n. pl. Excrements.

de·jec·tion, di·jek′shan, n. The state of being downcast; depression of mind; lowness of spirits; *physiol.* excrement.

de ju·re, dē jụr′ē, *Lat.* de ụ′ʀe. [L., "from right or law."] By right; according to law; a phrase sometimes used adjectively, as: A *de jure* ruler has a legal right to rule, whether actually exercising it or not. See *de facto*.

de·lam·i·nate, dē·lam′i·nāt″, v.i.—*delaminated, delaminating*. To split into laminae or thin layers.—**de·lam·i·na·tion**, dē·lam″i·nā′shan, n. A splitting apart into layers; *embryol.* the splitting of a primitive blastoderm into two layers of cells.

Del·a·ware, del′a·wâr″, n. An Algonquian language spoken by the Delaware Indians; one of the members of that tribe; *hort.* a sweet grape used in wine-making; the vine bearing this type of grape.

de·lay, di·lā′, v.t. [Fr. *délai*, It. *dilata*, delay, < L. *dilatus*.] To prolong the time of doing or proceeding with; to put off; to defer; to retard; to stop, detain, or hinder for a time.—v.i. To linger; to stop for a time.—n. A lingering; a putting off or deferring; procrastination.—**de·lay·er**, n.

de·le, dē′lē, n. [L., impv. of *delere*, do away with, E. *delete*.] A direction, usually represented by the symbol ϑ on a printer's proof, with express indication of the matter to be omitted.—v.t.—*deled, deleing*. To indicate for omission; delete; take out; omit.

de·lec·ta·ble, di·lek′ta·bl, a. [L. *delectabilis*, < *delectare*, to delight.] Delightful; highly pleasing; affording great joy or pleasure.—**de·lec·ta·ble·ness**, **de·lec·ta·bil·i·ty**, n.—**de·lec·ta·bly**, adv.—**de·lec·ta·tion**, dē″lek·tā′shan, n. Delight.

del·e·ga·cy, del′e·ga·sē, n. pl. **del·e·ga·cies**. The position or commission of a delegate; the sending or appointing of a delegate; a body of delegates.

del·e·gate, del′e·gāt″, v.t.—*delegated, delegating*. [L. *delegatus*, pp. of *delegare*, < *de*, from, and *legare*, send, depute.] To send or appoint as a deputy or representative; to assign or entrust (powers or functions) to another.—del′e·gāt″, del′e·git, n. One delegated to act for or represent another; a deputy; a representative, as in a convention or other assembly; the representative of a Territory in the House of Representatives of the U.S.; a member of the lower house in the Maryland, Virginia, and West Virginia legislatures.—del·e·ga·ble, a.

del·e·ga·tion, del″e·gā′shan, n. [L. delegatio(n-).] The act of delegating, or the fact of being delegated; a body of persons delegated to represent others, as in a convention or other assembly.

de·lete, di·lēt′, v.t.—deleted, deleting. [L. deleo, deletum, to blot out, to destroy.] To blot out; to erase; to strike or mark out, as with a pen or pencil.—de·le·tion, di·lē′shan, n. [L. deletio.] The act of deleting; an erasure; a passage deleted.

del·e·te·ri·ous, del″i·tēr′ē·us, a. [L.L. deleterius, < Gr. dēlētērios, noxious, < dēleomai, to injure.] Injurious; pernicious; harmful to health or well-being.

delft, delft, n. [For Delft ware.] A kind of earthenware with a white glaze that is decorated in colors, esp. blue, and originally made at Delft, in Holland; any pottery resembling this. Also delf, delft·ware.

de·lib·er·ate, di·lib′e·rāt″, v.t.—deliberated, deliberating. [L. deliberatus, pp. of deliberare, < de-, completely, and librare, balance, weigh.] To weigh in the mind; consider.—v.i. To think carefully or attentively; reflect about a decision or choice to be made; to consult or confer formally; hold formal discussion, as with reference to proposed measures.—de·lib·er·a·tor, n.

de·lib·er·ate, di·lib′ér·it, a. Carefully weighed or considered; studied; intentional; characterized by deliberation; careful or slow in deciding; leisurely in movement or action; slow; unhurried.—de·lib·er·ate·ly, adv.—de·lib·er·ate·ness, n.

de·lib·er·a·tion, di·lib″e·rā′shan, n. [L. deliberatio(n-).] The act of deliberating; careful consideration before decision; formal consultation or discussion, as in a legislative assembly; deliberate quality; leisureliness of movement or action; slowness.—de·lib·er·a·tive, a.—de·lib·er·a·tive·ly, adv.—de·lib·er·a·tive·ness, n.

del·i·ca·cy, del′i·ka·sē, n. pl. del·i·ca·cies. Exquisite quality or character; as, the delicacy of a jeweler's filigree work; something delightful or pleasing, esp. to the palate; fineness of texture or quality; softness; subtle quality; fineness of perception or feeling; sensitiveness; the quality of requiring or involving great care or tact; as, negotiations of great delicacy; exactness of action or operation; minute accuracy; fineness of feeling with regard to what is fitting, proper, or correct; consideration for the feelings of others; frailty, as of health; bodily weakness; liability to sickness.

del·i·cate, del′i·kit, a. [L. delicatus, delightful, luxurious, soft, tender, dainty, usually associated with L. deliciae, delight. DELICIOUS.] Fine in texture, quality, or construction; susceptible to sickness or bodily harm; weakly; easily damaged, or fragile; soft or faint, as color or light so fine or slight as to be scarcely perceptible; subtle; exquisite or refined in perception or feeling; distinguishing subtle differences; fine or exquisite in action or execution, as an instrument; requiring great care or tact; as, a delicate mission; regardful of what is becoming and proper; regardful of the feelings of others; dainty or choice, as food; excessively particular; fastidious.—del·i·cate·ly, adv.—del·i·cate·ness, n.

del·i·ca·tes·sen, del″i·ka·tes′en, n. [G., < Fr. délicatesse, delicacy, < délicat, < L. delicatus, E. delicate.] A store, or department of a store, which sells table delicacies such as cooked meats, smoked fish, sausages, cheese, salads, pickles, and canned goods that are either ready to be served or require little preparation; usu. construed as pl., the ready-to-eat foods that are sold in such a place, as: Delicatessen are served at the lodge.

de·li·cious, di·lish′us, a. [Fr. délicieux, < L. deliciæ, delight.] Highly pleasing to the sense of taste or smell; delightful.—de·li·cious·ly, adv.—de·li·cious·ness, n.

de·lict, di·likt′, n. [L. delictum, pp. neut. of delinquere, fail, commit a fault.] Law. A transgression; an offense; a misdemeanor.

de·light, di·līt′, v.t. [O.E. delite, < O.Fr. deliter, deleiter, < L. delecto, to delight, < delicio, to allure.] To provide great pleasure; to please highly.—v.i. To have or take great pleasure, usually followed by in.—n. A high degree of pleasure or satisfaction of mind; joy; rapture; that which gives great pleasure.—de·light·ed, di·lī′tid, a. Experiencing delight.—de·light·ed·ly, adv.

de·light·ful, di·līt′ful, a. Highly pleasing; charming.—de·light·ful·ly, adv.—de·light·ful·ness, n.

de·light·some, di·līt′som, a. Delightful; pleasurable.—de·light·some·ly, adv.—de·light·some·ness, n.

de·lim·it, di·lim′it, v.t. [Fr. délimiter, < L. delimitare (pp. delimitatus), < de, from, and limitare, E. limit.] To fix or mark the limits of, as a boundary; demarcate; define. Also de·lim·i·tate, di·lim′i·tāt″.—de·lim·i·ta·tion, n.—de·lim·i·ta·tive, a.

de·lin·e·ate, di·lin′ē·āt″, v.t.—delineated, delineating. [L. delineo, delineatum—de, down, and linea, a line.] To draw the lines which describe the form of; to sketch or design; to portray with accuracy; to depict, or describe verbally.—de·lin·e·a·tion, di·lin″ē·ā′shan, n. The act or process of delineating; representation or portrayal, whether pictorially or in words; sketch; description.—de·lin·e·a·tor, n.

de·lin·quent, di·ling′kwent, a. [L. delinquens (-ent-), ppr. of delinquere, fail, commit a fault, < de, from, and linquere, leave.] Failing in or neglectful of a duty or obligation; guilty of a misdeed or offense; of financial obligations, overdue or past due in payment.—n. One who is delinquent, esp. a juvenile delinquent.—de·lin·quent·ly, adv.—de·lin·quen·cy, di·ling′kwen·sē, n. pl. de·lin·quen·cies.

del·i·quesce, del″i·kwes′, v.i.—deliquesced, deliquescing. [L. deliquesco—de, and liquesco, to melt, < liqueo, to become liquid.] To melt gradually and become liquid by attracting and absorbing moisture from the air, as certain salts, acids, and alkalies; bot. to repeatedly subdivide into many branches.—de·li·ques·cence, del″i·kwes′ens, n. The process of deliquescing; the resulting liquid.—del·i·ques·cent, a.

de·lir·i·ous, di·lēr′ē·us, a. Pathol. characteristic of or pertaining to delirium. Fig. wildly enthusiastic.—de·lir·i·ous·ly, adv.—de·lir·i·ous·ness, n.

de·lir·i·um, di·lēr′ē·um, n. pl. de·lir·i·ums, de·lir·i·a, di·lēr′ē·a. [L. < delirare, be deranged, rave, lit. go out of the furrow, in plowing.] Pathol. more or less temporary disorder of the mental faculties, as in fevers and intoxication, characterized by restlessness, excitement, delusions, and hallucinations. Fig. a state of violent excitement or emotion; mad rapture or enthusiasm.—de·lir·i·um tre·mens, di·lēr′ē·um trē′menz. [N.L., "trembling delirium."] Pathol. a violent delirium due to excessive indulgence in alcoholic liquors.

del·i·tes·cent, del″i·tes′ent, a. [L. delitescens (-ent-), ppr. of delitescere, hide away.] Latent; concealed.—del·i·tes·cence, del″i·tes·cen·cy, n.

de·liv·er, di·liv′ér, v.t. [O.Fr. delivrer (Fr. délivrer), < M.L. deliberare, < L. de, from, and liberare, set free, < liber, free.] To carry and turn over to the intended recipients things such as letters or goods; to give into another's possession or keeping; to give forth or emit; to give forth in words, utter, or pronounce; as, to deliver a course of lectures, to deliver a verdict; to discharge, launch, or direct; to cast, throw, or project; to set free or liberate; to release or save, as from evil or trouble; to aid in the process of giving birth to, as offspring; to aid in the process of being born; of oneself, to disburden of thoughts or opinions.—v.i. To give birth; to make delivery; to pronounce an opinion or verdict.—de·liv·er·a·ble, a.—de·liv·er·er, n.

de·liv·er·ance, di·liv′ér·ans, n. The act of delivering or condition of being delivered, as from captivity, oppression, or danger; an opinion or decision communicated, esp. publicly; archaic, an utterance.

de·liv·er·y, di·liv′e·rē, n. pl. de·liv·er·ies. The act of delivering mail or goods; a surrender, as of prisoners; the utterance of words; oratorical style; the act or manner of giving or throwing, as of a ball; a rescuing or liberation from difficulty or unpleasantness; the state of being delivered of, or giving birth to a child; parturition; thing delivered; the goods transferred from seller to buyer; law, the act of giving into another's possession by legal process.

dell, del, n. [M.E. delle, akin to E. dale.] A deep natural hollow, often with wooded slopes; a small valley; a vale.

de·lo·cal·ize, dē·lō′ka·līz″, v.t.—delocalized, delocalizing. To remove from the proper or usual locality; free from local limitations or provincialities.—de·lo·cal·i·za·tion, n.

de·louse, dē·lous′, dē·louz′, v.t.—deloused, delousing. To free from parasitic lice.

Del·phic, del′fik, a. Pertaining to Delphi in ancient Greece, and to Apollo's oracle of that place; oracular; ambiguous. Also Del·phi·an, del′fē·an.

del·phi·nine, del′fi·nēn″, del′fi·nin, n. [N.L. Delphinium, < Gr. delphinion, larkspur.] Chem. a bitter, poisonous, crystalline alkaloid, $C_{33}H_{45}NO_9$, obtained from various species of larkspur, genus Delphinium, esp. D. staphisagria.

del·phin·i·um, del·fin′ē·um, n. pl. del·phin·i·ums, del·phin·i·a, del·fin′ē·a. [Gr. delphinion, larkspur.] A large genus of principally perennial plants, widely found in the northern temperate zone, that have palmate leaves and showy spikes of flowers, esp. the cultivated variety; larkspur.

Del·phi·nus, del·fī′nus, n. Astron. a small northern constellation, the Dolphin.

Del·sar·ti·an, del·sär′tē·an, a. Pertaining to a system of aesthetic gymnastics developed by François Delsarte, 1811-1871.

del·ta, del′ta, n. [L., < Gr. delta.] The fourth letter of the Greek alphabet; the fourth of any series, esp. in scientific classification; (cap.) a communications code word to designate the letter D. Anything triangular, like the Greek capital Δ; a triangular tract of alluvial land between diverging branches of the mouth of a river, often intersected by other branches; as, the delta of the Nile.—del·ta·ic, del·tā′ik, a. Of, pertaining to, or forming a river delta; having a delta. Also del·tic.

del·ta ray, n. An electron ejected by recoil when a rapidly moving particle, such as an alpha particle, passes through matter; sometimes applied to any secondary ionizing particles, not only electrons, ejected by recoil as a primary ionizing particle passes through matter.

del·toid, del'toid, n. [Gr. *deltoeides.*] A large triangular-shaped muscle covering the joint of the shoulder and serving to raise the arm laterally.—*a.* Triangular; shaped like the Greek capital delta, Δ.—**del·toi·dal,** *a.*

de·lude, di·lōd', *v.t.*—*deluded, deluding.* [L. *deludo*—*de,* and *ludo,* to play, *ludus,* sport, whence also *ludicrous, elude, illusion.*] To cause to entertain foolish or erroneous notions; to lead from truth or into error; to mislead; to beguile.—**de·lud·er,** *n.*—**de·lu·sive,** di·lō'siv, *a.* Tending to mislead the mind; deceptive; beguiling. Also **de·-lu·so·ry,** di·lō'so·rē.—**de·lu·sive·ly,** *adv.*—**de·lu·sive·ness,** *n.*

del·uge, del'ūj, *n.* [Fr. *déluge,* < L. *diluvium,* a flood, a deluge—*di* for *dis,* asunder, away, and *luo = lavo,* to wash; akin *lave, ablution.*] An inundation; a flood; anything resembling an inundation; anything that overwhelms, as a great calamity.—**the Del·uge,** *n.* The great flood covering the earth in the days of Noah.—*v.t.*—*deluged, deluging.* To overflow, as with water; to inundate; to drown; to overwhelm.

de·lu·sion, di·lō'zhan, *n.* The act of deluding; the state of being deluded or misled; false impression or belief; *psychiatry,* an abnormal phenomenon whereby a belief is held in the presence of evidence normally sufficient to destroy it.—**de·lu·sion·al,** *a.*

de·luxe, de luxe, de·lŭks', de·luks', *Fr.* de·lyks', *a.* [Fr.] Of superior quality or elegance.—*adv.* In an elegant manner.

delve, delv, *v.i.*—*delved, delving.* [O.E. *delfan* = D. *delven,* dig.] To carry on laborious research for information; *archaic,* to dig.—*v.t. Archaic,* to dig or excavate.—*n. Archaic,* a pit or cave.—**delv·er,** *n.*

de·mag·net·ize, dē·mag'ni·tīz', *v.t.*—*demagnetized, demagnetizing.* To deprive of magnetic polarity; to take away the magnetic properties from, as: The mechanic demagnetized the electromagnet.—**de·-mag·net·i·za·tion,** *n.*—**de·mag·net·iz·er,** *n.*

dem·a·gogue, dem·a·gog, dem'a·gag", dem'a·gog", *n.* [Gr. *demagogos = demos,* the people, and *agogos,* a leader.] A person who makes use of popular emotions and prejudices for personal power; in ancient times, a popular leader.—**dem·a·gogu·-er·y,** dem'a·ga"gu·rē, dem'a·gog"u·rē, *n.*—**dem·a·gog·ic, dem·a·gog·i·cal,** *a.*—**dem·a·gogu·ism, dem·a·gog·ism,** *n.*

de·mand, di·mand', di·mänd', *v.t.* [O.Fr. Fr. *demander,* < M.L. *demandare,* demand, L. give in charge, entrust, < L. *de,* from, and *mandare,* commit, enjoin.] To ask for with authority, or to claim as a right; to ask for peremptorily or urgently; to lay formal, legal claim; to summon, as to court; to call for or require as just, proper, or necessary; as, a task which *demands* patience; to ask authoritatively or peremptorily to be told; as, to *demand* a person's name.—*v.i.* To make a demand; to inquire or ask.—**de·-mand·a·ble,** *a.* Capable of being demanded.—**de·mand·ant,** *n.* One who demands. *Law,* the plaintiff in a real action; any plaintiff.—**de·mand·er,** *n.*

de·mand, di·mand', di·mänd', *n.* [O.Fr. Fr. *demande.*] The act of demanding; an authoritative or peremptory request or claim; as, a note payable on *demand;* a requisition; a legal claim; call or desire, as for a commodity; the state of being in request for purchase or use; as, an article in great *demand;* an urgent or pressing requirement; as, *demand* upon one's time or one's resources; an inquiry or question; that which is demanded; *econ.* the desire to purchase a commodity coupled with the power to purchase it, or the quantity of it demanded at a particular price.

de·mand de·pos·it, *n. Banking,* a deposit which may be withdrawn by the depositor at any time without prior notice.

de·mand·ing, di·man'ding, *a.* Exacting; requiring a high degree of precision or attention; claiming more than is normally necessary in a situation or in the performance of a task.

de·mand loan, *n.* Call loan.

de·mand note, *n.* A written promise to pay a sum of money upon request.

de·man·toid, di·man'toid, *n.* [G. *demant,* diamond.] A green andradite of brilliant luster that is used as a gem. Also **U·ra·li·-an em·er·ald.**

de·mar·ca·tion, dē"mär·kā'shan, *n.* [Fr. *démarcation*—*de,* down, and *marquer,* to mark.] The act or process of marking off, or of defining the limits or boundaries of anything; separation; distinction. Also **de·mar·ka·tion.**—**de·mar·cate,** di·mär'kāt, dē"mär·kāt", *v.t.*—*demarcated, demarcating.* To mark the limits or boundaries of. Also **de·mark.**

deme, dēm, *n.* [Gr. *demos.*] An administrative subdivision of ancient Attica and of modern Greece.

de·mean, di·mēn', *v.t.* [O.Fr. *demener* (Fr. *démener*), < *de*- and *mener,* bring, lead, L. *minare,* drive.] Of oneself, to conduct or behave in a specified manner.—**de·mean·or,** *Brit.* **de·mean·our,** *n.* Way of acting; conduct; behavior; bearing.

de·mean, di·mēn', *v.t.* To lower in dignity or standing; to debase or degrade; esp. of oneself, to lower or humiliate.

de·ment·ed, di·men'tid, *a.* [L. *demens, dementis,* out of one's mind—*de,* out of, and *mens,* the mind.] Mad; insane.

dé·men·ti, dā·män'tē, *Fr.* dā·mäN·tē', *n.* pl. **dé·men·tis.** [Fr., < *démentir,* give the lie to, contradict, < *dé*- and *mentir,* < L. *mentiri,* lie.] Official denial, as of a report, given by a government for diplomatic reasons.

de·men·tia, di·men'sha, di·men'shē·a, *n.* [L.] *Psychiatry,* any condition of deteriorated mentality, esp. a decline in the appropriateness of a person's emotional responses and in his intellectual powers.

de·men·tia prae·cox, di·men'sha prē'koks, di·men'shē·a prē'koks, *n.* Schizophrenia.

de·mer·it, dē·mer'it, *n.* [O.Fr. *demerite* (Fr. *démérite*) < L. *demeritum,* pp. neut. of *demerere,* deserve.] A censurable or punishable quality; a fault; lack of merit; in schools, a mark against a pupil for misconduct or deficiency, usually entailing a loss of privilege.

de·mesne, di·mān', di·mēn', *n.* [O.Fr. *demaine, domaine,* < L. *dominus,* a lord.] An estate in land; the land adjacent to a manorhouse or mansion kept in the proprietor's own hands, as distinguished from lands held by his tenants; territory.

dem·i·god, dem'ē·god", *n.* A personage whose qualities approach the divine; a figure in mythology more gifted than a mortal but not a god.

dem·i·john, dem'i·jon", *n.* [Fr. *dame-jeanne,* < Ar. *damagan* < *Damaghan,* a town in Khorassan once famous for its glassworks.] A glass vessel or bottle with a large body and small neck, enclosed in wickerwork.

de·mil·i·ta·rize, dē·mil'i·ta·rīz", *v.t.*—*demilitarized, demilitarizing.* To deprive of military character; free from militarism; remove the military organization from; place under civil instead of military control.—**de·mil·i·ta·ri·za·tion,** *n.*

dem·i·mon·daine, dem"ē·mon·dān', *Fr.* de·mē·maN·den', *n.* [Fr.] A woman of the demimonde.

dem·i·monde, dem'ē·mond", *Fr.* de·- **mē·maNd',** *n.* [Fr., "half-world"; a term introduced by A. Dumas the younger.] The world or class of women who have become socially declassed, or of doubtful reputation and standing, as intermediate between those of unquestioned respectability and the courtesan class.

dem·i·rep, dem'ē·rep", *n.* [Short for *demi-reputation.*] A woman of doubtful or compromised reputation.

de·mise, di·mīz', *n.* [Lit. a laying off or aside, < Fr. *démettre*—*de,* L. *dis,* aside, and *mettre,* to put, L. *mitto,* to send.] The death of a person; decease; termination of the operation or existence of a thing or institution; as, the *demise* of vaudeville. *Law,* a conveyance of an estate; the transfer of an estate because of a death. The transfer of sovereignty.—*v.t.*—*demised, demising. Law,* to transfer or convey, as an estate, for a specified period. To bequeath; to grant by will.—*v.i.* To pass by will or inheritance.—**de·mis·a·ble,** *a.*

dem·i·sem·i·qua·ver, dem"ē·sem'ē·-kwā"vèr, *n. Music,* a thirty-second note.

de·mis·sion, di·mish'an, *n.* [Fr. *démission,* < *démettre,* send or put away, < L. *de*- or *dis*- and *mittere,* send.] Relinquishment or resignation, esp. of an office; abdication.

de·mit, di·mit', *v.t.*—*demitted, demitting.* To resign or relinquish, as an office or position of dignity.—*v.i.* To resign.

dem·i·tasse, dem'i·tas", *Fr.* de·mē·täs', *n.* [Fr., "half-cup."] A small cup such as is used for serving black coffee after dinner; the contents of such a cup.

dem·i·urge, dem'ē·èrj", *n.* [Gr. *demiourgos,* worker for the people, artificer, maker, < *demios,* of the people (< *demos,* people, and *ergos,* working, worker.] *Philos.* The Platonic Craftsman who orders and arranges the physical world, bringing it, as far as possible, into conformity with the best and most rational pattern. In Gnosticism, the creator of positive evil, specif, of the material world.

dem·i·volt, dem'ē·võlt", *n.* In horseback riding, a half turn made by a horse with forelegs raised.

de·mob, dē·mob', *v.t.*—*demobbed, demobbing. Brit. colloq.* to demobilize or disband.—*n. Brit. colloq.* the act of demobilization; one who has been honorably discharged from the military service.

de·mo·bi·lize, dē·mō'bi·līz", *v.t.*—*demobilized, demobilizing. Milit.* of troops, to disarm and dismiss; to disband.—**de·mo·-bi·li·za·tion.**

de·moc·ra·cy, di·mok'ra·sē, *n.* pl. **de·-moc·ra·cies.** [Fr. *démocratie,* < Gr. *democratia,* < *demos,* people, and *cratein,* rule.] Government by the people; a form of government in which the supreme power is vested in the people and exercised by them or their elected agents; a state having such a form of government; in a restricted sense, a state in which the supreme power is vested in the people and exercised directly by them rather than by their elected representatives; a state of society characterized by nominal equality of rights and privileges; political or social equality; democratic spirit; the common people of a community as distinguished from any privileged class; the common people with respect to their political power; (*cap.*), *U.S. politics,* the principles of the Democratic party, or the members of the Democratic party collectively.

dem·o·crat, dem'o·krat", *n.* [Fr. *démocrate.*] An advocate of democracy; one who adheres to the principles of political or social equality for all; (*cap.*), *U.S. politics,* a member of the Democratic party.

dem·o·crat·ic, dem"o·krat'ik, *a.* [Gr. *democraticos.*] Pertaining to or of the nature of democracy; advocating or upholding democracy; catering to the tastes or serving the interests of the masses; pertaining to or characterized by the principle of political or social equality for all; (*cap.*), *U.S. politics*, of or pertaining to the Democratic party; *U.S. hist.* noting or pertaining to a party whose distinctive principles included a strict interpretation of the Constitution with respect to the powers delegated to the general government and those reserved by the individual states.—**dem·o·crat·i·cal·ly**, *adv.*

Dem·o·crat·ic-Re·pub·li·can par·ty, *n. U.S. hist.* a political party composed of merging groups who opposed the Federalist party.

de·moc·ra·tize, di·mok'ra·tīz", *v.t.—democratized, democratizing.* To render democratic; give democratic character to; remove class distinctions from; bring to a common level.—**de·moc·ra·ti·za·tion**, *n.*

de·mod·ed, dē·mō'did, *a.* [Fr. *démodé*, pp. of *démoder*, put out of fashion.] No longer in fashion.

de·mod·u·late, dē·moj'u·lāt", dē·mod'ū·lāt", *v.t.—demodulated, demodulating. Radio*, to detect or intercept a modulated signal.—**de·mod·u·la·tion**, *n.*

de·mog·ra·phy, di·mog'ra·fē, *n.* [Gr. *dēmos*, people, and *graphō*, to write.] The science of statistics on populations, such as records of births, deaths, marriages, and diseases.—**de·mog·ra·pher, de·mog·ra·phist**, *n.*—**de·mo·graph·ic, de·mo·graph·i·cal**, *a.* —**de·mo·graph·i·cal·ly**, *adv.*

dem·oi·selle, dem"wä·zel', *Fr.* de·mwä·zel', *n.* [Fr. DAMSEL.] A young lady; a damsel; the Numidian crane, *Anthropoides virgo*, of northern Africa, Asia, and Europe, having long white plumes behind the eyes; any of various slender-bodied dragonflies, family *Agridae*, which hold their wings vertically when at rest.

de·mol·ish, di·mol'ish, *v.t.* [Fr. *démolir, démolissant,* < L. *demolior—de,* down, and *molior,* to build, < *moles,* mass.] To throw or pull down; to raze; to destroy, as a structure or artificial construction; to ruin. —**de·mol·ish·er**, *n.*

dem·o·li·tion, dem"o·lish'an, dē"mo·lish'an, *n.* The act of demolishing; destruction; ruin; *pl.* highly explosive materials used particularly for destruction during war.

dem·o·li·tion bomb, *n.* A bomb that explodes after a short penetration, accomplishing damage and destruction by surface blast and underground explosion.

de·mon, dē'mon, *n.* [L. *dæmon,* spirit, evil spirit, < Gr. *daimon,* deity, tutelary divinity, genius; later, evil spirit.] An evil spirit; a devil; an atrociously wicked or cruel person; an evil passion or influence; a person of great energy. *Mythol.* a supernatural being classed between gods and men; also *daemon.*—**de·mo·ni·an**, *a.*— **de·mon·ic, de·mon·i·cal**, di·mon'ik, *a.*— **de·mon·i·cal·ly**, *adv.*—**de·mon·i·za·tion**, *n.*—**de·mon·ize**, *v.t.*

de·mon·e·tize, dē·mon'i·tīz", dē·mun'i·tīz", *v.t.—demonetized, demonetizing.* To deprive of standard value, as money; to withdraw from circulation.—**de·mon·e·ti·za·tion**, *n.*

de·mo·ni·ac, di·mō'nē·ak", dē"mo·nī'ak, *a.* [L.L. *dæmoniacus.*] Of, pertaining to, or of the nature of a demon or demons; inspired as if by a demon; demonic; characteristic of a demon or evil spirit; fiendish; possessed by an evil spirit, or pertaining to such possession; raging; frantic. Also **de·mo·ni·a·cal.**—*n.* One seemingly possessed by a demon or evil spirit; a lunatic.—**de·mo·ni·a·cal·ly**, dē"mo·nī'ik·lē, *adv.*

de·mon·ism, dē"mo·niz"um, *n.* Belief in demons; worship of demons; study of demons. See *demonology.*—**de·mon·ist**, *n.*

de·mon·ol·a·try, dē"mo·nol'a·trē, *n.* The worship of demons.—**de·mon·ol·a·ter**, *n.* —**de·mon·ol·a·trous**, *a.*—**de·mon·ol·a·trous·ly**, *adv.*

de·mon·ol·o·gy, dē"mo·nol'o·jē, *n.* The doctrine of demons; the study of demons or of beliefs about demons.—See *demonism.*—**de·mon·ol·o·gist**, *n.*—**de·mon·og·ra·phy**, dē"mo·nog'ra·fē, *n.* Descriptive demonology.—**de·mon·og·ra·pher**, *n.*

dem·on·strate, dem'on·strāt", *v.t.—demonstrated, demonstrating.* [L. *demonstro—de,* intens., and *monstro,* to show, < *monstrum,* a portent, a monster.] To point out with perfect clearness; to show clearly; to make evident; to exhibit; to exhibit the merits and operation of; to show or prove to be certain; to prove beyond the possibility of doubt.—*v.i.* To perform a demonstration or show; to instruct by using examples; to congregate, march, picket, or otherwise seek or force public attention and support to a cause; to show military force.—**de·mon·stra·ble**, di·mon'stra·bl, dem'on·stra·bl, *a.* Capable of being demonstrated, proved, or exhibited.—**de·mon·stra·bil·i·ty**, *n.*—**de·mon·stra·bly**, *adv.*

dem·on·stra·tion, dem"on·strā'shan, *n.* An exhibition of the merits and operation of a product; a manifestation; an outward show; the act of exhibiting proof beyond the possibility of doubt; a proof by logical or mathematical reasoning; a group action in public, such as marching or picketing, to attempt to attain a certain goal; as, a *demonstration* against unfair labor practices; *milit.* an operation, such as the massing of men at a certain point, performed for the purpose of deceiving the enemy.

de·mon·stra·tive, de·mon'stra·tiv, *a.* Serving to demonstrate; showing or proving by certain evidence; invincibly conclusive; characterized by or given to the strong exhibition of any feeling; outwardly expressive of feelings or emotions; *gram.* clearly indicating that to which it refers; as, a *demonstrative* adjective or a *demonstrative* pronoun.—*n. Gram.* a word that clearly indicates the object to which it refers, as *this* or *there.*—**de·mon·stra·tive·ly**, *adv.*— **de·mon·stra·tive·ness**, *n.*

dem·on·stra·tor, dem'on·strā"tėr, *n.* One who demonstrates or exhibits the merits or operation of something to the public, as a device or food product; an article or product used for purposes of demonstration, such as an automobile or radio; one who participates in group action, such as marching or picketing, to attempt to attain a certain goal.

de·mor·al·ize, di·mạr'a·līz", di·mor'a·līz", *v.t.—demoralized, demoralizing.* To weaken or destroy the moral influence of; to deprive of spirit, courage, discipline, or the like; reduce to a state of weakness or disorder; to corrupt or undermine the morals of; pervert morally.—**de·mor·al·i·za·tion**, *n.*—**de·mor·al·iz·er**, *n.*

de·mos, dē'mos, *n.* [Gr. *demos.*] The people or commons of an ancient Greek state; the populace; the mob; *sociol.* a human group regarded as a political unit.

de·mote, di·mōt', *v.t.—demoted, demoting.* To reduce to lower rank.—**de·mo·tion**, *n.*

de·mot·ic, di·mot'ik, *a.* Of or pertaining to the common people; popular; noting or pertaining to the ancient Egyptian handwriting of ordinary life, a simplified form of the hieratic character; pertaining to the spoken form of Modern Greek that is based on popular use.

de·mount, dē·mount', *v.t.* To remove from its mounting, setting, or place of support, as a gun or a vehicle tire; take apart.—**de·mount·a·ble**, *a.* That can be demounted; as,

a *demountable* wheel rim.—**de·mount·a·bil·i·ty**, *n.*

de·mul·cent, di·mul'sent, *a.* [L. *demulcens, demulcentis,* ppr. of *demulceo* to stroke down.] Softening; mollifying.—*n.* Any medicine which lessens the effects of irritation, as mucilaginous substances.

de·mur, di·mėr', *v.i.—demurred, demurring.* [Fr. *demeurer,* to delay, to stay, < L. *demorari—de,* and *mora,* delay.] To object, esp. because of scruples.—*n.* Exception taken; objection stated.—**de·mur·ral**, *n.*

de·mure, di·mūr', *a.—demurer, demurest.* [M.E. *demure,* appar. for *mure,* grave, discreet, < O.Fr. *meur,* < L. *maturus,* ripe.] Sedate; decorous; affectedly prim. —**de·mure·ly**, *adv.*—**de·mure·ness**, *n.*

de·mur·rage, di·mėr'ij, *n.* [O.Fr. *demourage,* < *demourer,* E. *demur.*] *Com.* The detention of a vessel by a freighter, as in loading or unloading, beyond the time agreed upon; similar detention of a freight train or truck; a charge for such detention.

de·mur·rer, di·mėr'ėr, *n.* One who demurs; *law,* a pleading which claims that the contentions submitted by the opposing party are insufficient in law to warrant his justification in bringing action. A demur.

de·my, di·mī', *n. pl.* **de·mies**. [Fr. *demi,* < L. *dimidius,* half, < *di-,* for *dis-,* apart and *medius,* middle.] A size of writing, measuring 16 × 21 inches. *Brit.* a size of writing paper 15½ × 20 inches and a size of printing paper 17¼ × 22½ inches; a foundation scholar at Magdalen College, Oxford, England, so called because originally he received half the allowance of a fellow.

den, den, *n.* [O.E. *denn.* a cave or lurking-place; akin *denu,* E. *dene,* a valley.] A cave or subterranean recess, used for concealment, shelter, protection, or security; a hiding place or lair of any wild, predatory animal; any squalid place of resort; a wooded hollow; a quiet retreat, as a room for reading; a group of cub scouts, part of the program of the Boy Scouts of America.— *v.i.—denned, denning.*

den·a·ry, den'a·rē, dē'na·rē, *a.* [L. *denarius,* < *deni,* ten at a time, < *decem,* ten.] Of or pertaining to the number ten; proceeding by tens; decimal.

de·na·tion·al·ize, dē·nash'a·na·līz", *v.t.* —*denationalized, denationalizing.* To deprive of national status, national attachments or characteristics; to remove from government ownership or control; as, the government's mandate to *denationalize* the steel industry.

de·nat·u·ral·ize, dē·nach'ėr·a·līz", *v.t.—denaturalized, denaturalizing.* To render unnatural; to alienate from nature; to deprive of naturalization or acquired citizenship in a foreign country.—**de·nat·u·ral·i·za·tion**, *n.*

de·na·ture, dē·nā'chėr, *v.t.—denatured, denaturing.* To change the nature of; to render unfit for human consumption, without impairing usefulness for other purposes, as alcohol; *biochem.* of a protein, to change from its original condition by chemical or physical means. Of fissionable material, to make unsuitable for use in an atomic weapon by adding nonfissionable material. Also **de·na·tur·ize.**—**de·na·tur·ant**, *n.* —**de·na·tur·a·tion, de·na·tur·i·za·tion**, *n.*

den·dri·form, den'dri·fạrm", *a.* [Gr. *dendron,* a tree.] Having the form or appearance of a tree.

den·drite, den'drīt, *n.* [Gr. *dendrites,* of a tree, < *dendron,* tree.] A branching figure or marking, resembling a tree or shrub in form, found on or in certain stones or minerals, and due to the presence of a foreign mineral; a stone or mineral so marked; any arborescent crystalline growth; any of the hairlike, branching processes

---

ch- chain, G. na*ch*;   **th-** THen, thin;   **w-** wig, hw as sound in whig;   **z-** zh as in azure, zeal.   *Italicized vowel* indicates schwa sound.

of neurons which carry impulses to nerve cell bodies.—**den·drit·ic**, den·drit′ik, *a.* Formed or marked like a dendrite; arborescent. Also **den·drit·i·cal.—den·drit··i·cal·ly**, *adv.*

den·dro·chro·nol·o·gy, den″drŏ·kro·nol′·o·jē, *n.* The study of growth rings on trees as a means of establishing dates.—**den·dro··chron·o·log·i·cal,** den″drŏ·kron″o·loj′i·kal, *a.*—**den·dro·chron·o·log·i·cal·ly,** *adv.*—**den·dro·chro·nol·o·gist,** *n.*

den·droid, den′droid, *a.* [Gr. *dendroeides.*] Treelike; arborescent. Also **den·droi·dal.**

den·drol·o·gy, den·drol′o·jē, *n.* That branch of botany dealing with shrubs and trees.—**den·drol·o·gist,** den·drol′o·jist, *n.*—**den·dro·log·ic,** den·drol·o·gous, den″·dro·loj′i·kal, *a.*—**den·dro·log·i·cal,** *a.*

dene, dean, dēn, *n.* [O.E. *denu,* valley, akin to *denn,* E. *den.*] *Brit.* A valley, particularly a deep, narrow, wooded valley or dell, esp. one through which a stream flows: frequently used in place names; a sandy area or sand hill near the sea.

Den·eb, den′eb, *n. Astron.* a star of the first order of brightness in the constellation Cygnus, the Swan.

den·e·ga·tion, den″e·gā′shan, *n.* [Fr. *dénégation,* < L. *denegare.* DENY.] Denial; contradiction.

de·ne·go·ti·ate, dē″ni·gō′shē·āt″, *v.t.*—*denegotiated, denegotiating.* Of agreements, esp. those of a political or economic nature, to negotiate termination of.

den·gue, deng′gā, deng′gē, *n.* [W. Ind. Sp.; of African origin.] *Pathol.* an infectious, eruptive, usually epidemic fever of warm climates, characterized esp. by severe pains in the joints and muscles; breakbone fever. Also **den·gue fe·ver.**

de·ni·a·ble, di·nī′a·bl, *a.* Capable of being denied.

de·ni·al, di·nī′al, *n.* The act of denying; contradiction of a statement; refusal to believe a doctrine; disbelief in the existence or reality of a thing; refusal to recognize or acknowledge; a disowning or disavowal; the refusal of a claim, request, or of a person making a request; restriction of one's own impulses.

de·nic·o·tin·ize, dē·nik′o·ti·nīz″, *v.t.*—*denicotinized, denicotinizing.* To remove nicotine or part of the nicotine, as from tobacco.

de·ni·er, di·nī′ĕr, *n.* One who denies.

de·nier, de·nēr′, den′yer, *Fr.* de·nyä′, *n.* [O.Fr. Fr. *denier,* < L. *denarius.*] Any of certain old French coins of little value, orig. of silver but later of copper, de·nēr′. A unit of weight designating the fineness of silk or synthetic filaments and yarns, equal to one yarn weighing one gram per 9000 meters: used esp. in grading women's hosiery, den′yer.

den·i·grate, den′i·grāt″, *v.t.*—*denigrated, denigrating.* To blacken; to defame.—**den·i·gra·tion,** *n.*—**den·i·gra·tor,** *n.*

den·im, den′im, *n.* [Fr. *serge de Nîmes,* serge of Nîmes, France.] A heavy, twilled cotton fabric used for overalls, sport clothes, and upholstery; *pl.* overalls, or similar apparel, made of this fabric.

de·ni·trate, dē·nī′trāt, *v.t.*—*denitrated, denitrating. Chem.* to remove oxides of nitrogen from, as a substance.—**de·ni·tra·tion,** *n.*

de·ni·tri·fy, dē·nī′tri·fī″, *v.t.*—*denitrified, denitrifying. Chem.* to remove nitrogen from, as compounds.—**de·ni·tri·fi·ca·tion,** *n.*—**de·ni·tri·fy·ing bac·te·ri·a,** *n. pl.* Soil bacteria that convert nitrogen compounds into free nitrogen which escapes into the air, contributing to soil depletion.

den·i·zen, den′i·zen, *n.* [O.Fr. *deinzein,* < *deinz, denz* (Fr. *dans*), within, in, < L. *de,* from, and *intus,* within.] An inhabitant or dweller in a particular place; a person who

frequents a place; anything adapted to a new place or condition, as a naturalized foreign word, or an animal or plant not indigenous to a place but successfully naturalized; *Brit.* an alien admitted to residence and certain rights of citizenship in a country.—*v.t.* Said of persons, to make a denizen of; to naturalize; *Brit.* to admit to residence and certain rights of citizenship.

de·nom·i·nate, di·nom′i·nāt″, *v.t.*—*denominated, denominating.* [L. *denomino—de,* intens., and *nomino,* to nominate.] To give a name or epithet to; to name, call, or designate.

de·nom·i·na·tion, di·nom″i·nā′shan, *n.* [L. *denominatio(n).*] The act of denominating; a name or designation, esp. one for a class of things; a collection or society of individuals called by the same name, esp. a religious sect; one of the grades or degrees in a series of designations of quantity, value, measure, or weight; as, money of small denomination.—**de·nom·i·na·tion·al,** *a.* Of or pertaining to a denomination, esp. a religious denomination; sectarian.—**de·nom·i·na·tion·al·ly,** *adv.*—**de·nom·i·na·tion·al·ism,** *n.* Denominational or sectarian spirit or policy; the tendency to divide into denominations or sects.

de·nom·i·na·tive, di·nom′i·nā″tiv, di·nom′i·na·tiv, *a.* [L.L. *denominativus.*] Conferring or constituting a distinctive denomination or name; appellative; *gram.* formed from a substantive or an adjective, as a denominative verb.—*n. Gram.* a denominative word, esp. a verb.

de·nom·i·na·tor, di·nom′i·nā″tĕr, *n.* [M.L.] *Math.* That term of a fraction, usually written under the line, which indicates its denomination, or shows the number of equal parts into which the unit is divided; a divisor.

de·no·ta·tion, dē″nŏ·tā′shan, *n.* [L. *denotatio(n-).*] The act or fact of denoting, marking out, or indicating; indication; something that denotes; a mark, sign, or symbol; a name or designation that specifies; that which a term denotes; signification or meaning, esp. the primary meaning of a word, as distinguished from its connotation.—**de·no·ta·tive,** *a.* Having the quality of denoting.—**de·no·ta·tive·ly,** *adv.*

de·note, di·nōt′, *v.t.*—*denoted, denoting.* [L. *denotare* (pp. *denotatus*).] To stand as a symbol for; to indicate or make known; to be a name or designation for; designate, esp. to designate merely, without implication or connotation.—**de·note·ment,** *n.*—**de·no·tive,** *a.*—**de·not·a·ble,** *a.*

de·noue·ment, dā″nŏ·män′, *n.* [Fr. also *dénoûment,* < *dénouer,* untie, < *dé-* and *nouer,* < L. *nodare,* knot, tie, < *nodus,* a knot.] The final disentangling of the intricacies of a plot, as of a drama or novel; the solution of a difficulty or mystery.

de·nounce, di·nouns′, *v.t.*—*denounced, denouncing.* [O.Fr. *denoncier* (Fr. *dénoncer*), < L. *denuntiare,* < *de-* and *nuntiare,* announce, declare, < *nuntius,* messenger.] To condemn openly; assail with censure; to make formal accusation against to the authorities; inform against; of treaties and similar documents, to give formal notice of the termination of.—**de·nounce·ment,** *n.*—**de·nounc·er,** *n.*

dense, dens, *a.*—*denser, densest.* [L. *densus,* thick, thickly set; akin to Gr. *dasus,* hairy, shaggy, thick.] Having the component parts closely compacted together; compact or closely set, as parts or objects; profound or intense, as ignorance; thick-headed, obtuse, or stupid, as persons; deep or dark, as color; *photog.* of a developed negative, relatively opaque, and yielding prints with strong contrasts of light and shade.—**dense·ly,** *adv.*—**dense·ness,** *n.*

den·si·fy, den′si·fī″, *v.t.*—*densified, densifying.* To permeate, as wood, with resin under heat and pressure in order to harden it.

den·sim·e·ter, den·sim′i·tĕr, *n.* An apparatus for ascertaining the relative density or specific gravity of a substance.—**den·si·met·ric,** den″si·me′trik, *a.*

den·si·tom·e·ter, den″si·tom′i·ter, *n.* A special type of densimeter for measuring optical density of a material such as a photographic negative.

den·si·ty, den′si·tē, *n. pl.* **den·si·ties.** [L. *densitas.*] The state or quality of being dense; compactness; closely set or crowded condition; specif. the mass or amount of matter per unit of bulk or volume; *elect.* the quantity of electricity per unit of area on a charged surface; *photog.* relative opacity of a developed negative.

dent, dent, *n.* [Var. of *dint.*] A hollow or depression in a surface, as from a blow.—*v.t.* To make a dent in or on.—*v.i.* To sink in, making a dent; to become indented.

dent, dent, *n.* [Fr. *dent,* < L. *dens* (*dent-*), tooth.] A tooth-like projection, as a tooth of a gearwheel or a comb.

den·tal, den′tal, *a.* [L. *dens* (*dent-*), tooth.] Of or pertaining to the teeth; of or pertaining to dentistry; *phon.* of speech sounds, formed by placing the tip of the tongue against or near the upper front teeth, as *d, t, n.*—*n. Phon.* a dental sound.—**den·tal·ize,** den′ta·līz″, *v.t.*—*dentalized, dentalizing. Phon.* to convert into a dental sound.—**den·tal·i·za·tion,** *n.*

den·tal floss, *n.* A soft thread coated with wax, used to clean between teeth.

den·tal hy·gien·ist, *n.* One who assists a dentist in the minor functions of dentistry, such as cleaning teeth and taking x-rays.

den·tal tech·ni·cian, *n.* A specialist who makes dental appliances.

den·tate, den′tāt, *a.* [L. *dentatus,* < *dens* (*dent-*), tooth.] Toothed; notched. *Biol.* having a toothed margin, or toothlike projections or processes; specif. of a leaf, having sharp marginal teeth directed outward. Also **den·tat·ed.—den·tate·ly,** *adv.*—**den·ta·tion,** *n.* Dentate state or form.

den·ti·cle, den′ti·kl, *n.* [L. *denticulus.*] A small tooth or projecting point.—**den·tic·u·late, den·tic·u·lat·ed,** den·tik′ū·lit, den·tik′ū·lāt, *a.* Having small teeth or pointed projections, as a leaf, calyx, or seed; finely dentate; *arch.* having dentils.—**den·tic·u·la·tion,** *n.* The state of being denticulate; a denticle or series of denticles.

den·ti·form, den′ti·farm″, *a.* Having the form of a tooth.

den·ti·frice, den′ti·fris, *n.* [L. *dens,* and *frico,* to rub.] A powder, paste, or liquid to be used in cleaning the teeth.

den·tig·er·ous, den·tij′e·rus, *a.* [L. *dens* (*dent-*), tooth.] Bearing or supplied with teethlike parts.

den·til, den′til, den′til, *n.* [Obs. Fr. *dentille,* dim. < L. *dens* (*dent-*), tooth.] *Arch.* one of a series of small rectangular blocks protruding like a row of teeth, as under a cornice.

den·ti·lin·gual, den″ti·ling′gwal, *a.* [L. *dens* (*dent-*), tooth, and *lingua,* tongue.] *Phon.* of speech sounds, uttered with the cooperation of the teeth and the tongue: said esp. of the sounds of *th* in *thin* and *this.*

den·tin, den′tin, den′tin, *n.* [L. *dens* (*dent-*), tooth.] *Anat.* the hard calcareous tissue beneath the enamel and the cement of a tooth, enclosing the pulp, and composing the greater part of the tooth. Also **den·tine,** den′tēn.—**den·tin·al,** *a.*

den·tist, den′tist, *n.* [Fr. *dentiste,* < *dent,* < L. *dens* (*dent-*), tooth.] A doctor who cares for and treats the teeth, gums, and oral cavity; Doctor of Dental Surgery. Abbr. D.D.S.

den·tist·ry, den'ti·strē, *n.* That profession which deals with the diagnosis, prevention, and treatment of oral malformations, and any disease affecting the teeth and their related structures.

den·ti·tion, den·tish'an, *n.* [L. *dentitio.*] The process of the cutting of teeth in infancy; that period during which the teeth develop; the tooth system, including number, kind, and arrangement of teeth, that is peculiar to man and other animals.

den·tu·lous, den'che·lus, *a.* Possessing teeth.

den·ture, den'chèr, *n.* False teeth; one or more artificial teeth used to replace natural teeth.

den·u·da·tion, den″ū·dā'shan, dē″nu·dā'shan, den″nū·dā'shan, *n.* [L.L. *denudatio(n-).*] The act of denuding; denuded or bare condition; *geol.* the laying bare of rock by erosive processes.—**de·nu·da·tive,** di·nū'da·tiv, di·nū'da·tiv, *a.*

de·nude, di·nōd', di·nūd', *v.t.*—denuded, denuding. [L. *denudo*—*de-,* and *nudus,* naked.] To make bare or naked; to strip; *geol.* to subject to an erosive process. Also **den·u·date,** den'ū·dāt″, di·nō'dāt″, di·nū'dāt.

de·nu·mer·a·ble, di·nō'mèr·a·bl, di·nū'mèr·a·bl, *a.* Pertaining to something which may be counted.

de·nun·ci·ate, di·nun'sē·āt″, di·nun'shē·āt″, *v.t., v.i.*—denunciated, denunciating. [L. *denuntiatus,* pp. of *denuntiare.*] To denounce; condemn openly.—**de·nun·ci·a·tion,** *n.* [L. *denuntiatio(n-).*] The act of denouncing; open and vehement condemnation; an invective; an accusing before a public prosecutor; formal notice of the termination of an international agreement, either in whole or part.—**de·nun·ci·a·tive, de·nun·ci·a·tory,** *a.*—**de·nun·ci·a·tor,** *n.*

de·ny, di·nī', *v.t.*—denied, denying. [O.Fr. *denier* (Fr. *denier*), < L. *denegare,* < *de-,* and *negare,* say no.] To assert the negative of, as a statement or an alleged fact; declare not to be true; to refuse to believe, as a doctrine; reject as false or erroneous; to refuse to believe in the existence or reality of; to refuse to recognize or acknowledge, as a person or thing; disown; disavow; repudiate; to refuse to grant, as a claim or request; to withhold the use or enjoyment of; to refuse access to one visited, as: He *denied* himself to callers.—**de·ny one·self,** to refrain from the gratification of one's desires; exercise self-denial.—**de·ny·ing·ly,** *adv.*

de·o·dar, dē'o·där″, *n.* [Hind. < Skt. *devadāru,* "wood of the gods."] A species of cedar, *Cedrus deodara,* a large tree valued for its durable wood, native to the Himalayas.

de·o·dor·ant, dē·ō'dèr·ant, *n.* An agent for destroying odors; a preparation for checking or masking body odors.

de·o·dor·ize, dē·ō'do·rīz″, *v.t.*—deodorized, deodorizing. To rid of odor or smell, esp. of fetid odor resulting from impurities.—**de·o·dor·iz·er,** dē·ō'dèr·ī″zèr, *n.*—**de·o·dor·i·za·tion,** *n.*

de·on·tol·o·gy, dē″on·tol'o·jē, *n.* [Gr. *deon,* that which is binding or needful, prop. ppr. neut. of *dein,* bind.] The study of duty or moral obligation; ethics.—**de·on·to·log·i·cal,** dē·on″to·loj'i·kal, *a.*—**de·on·tol·o·gist,** *n.*

de·ox·i·dize, dē·ok'si·dīz″, *v.t.*—deoxidized, deoxidizing. [Prefix *de-,* not, and *oxide,* or the first part of *oxygen.*] *Chem.* to deprive of oxygen, or reduce from the state of an oxide. Also **de·ox·i·date.**—**de·ox·i·di·za·tion,** *n.*—**de·ox·i·diz·er,** *n.*

de·ox·y·gen·ate, dē·ok'si·je·nāt″, *v.t.*—deoxygenated, deoxygenating. To remove oxygen from.—Also **de·ox·y·gen·ize.**

de·ox·y·ri·bo·nu·cle·ic ac·id, dē·ok″-si·rī'bō·nö·klē'ik as'id, dē·ok″si·rī'bō-nū·klē'ik as'id, dē·ok″si·rī″bō·nö·klē'ik as'id, dē·ok″si·rī″bō·nū·klē'ik as'id, *n.* See *DNA.*

de·part, di·pärt', *v.i.* [Fr. *départir*—*de-,* and *partir,* to separate.] To go or move away; to leave or desist, as from a practice; to forsake, abandon, deviate; to die; to decease.—*v.t.* To leave; to retire or go away from.

de·part·ed, di·pär'tid, *a.* Gone; dead.—**the de·part·ed,** *n.* The person who is dead, or, collectively, those who are dead.

de·part·ment, di·pärt'ment, *n.* [O.Fr. *departement* (Fr. *département*), < *departir.*] A distinct part of anything arranged in divisions; a division of a complex whole or organized system; a division of business or official duties or functions; one of the separate branches of a governmental organization; one of the large districts into which a country, as France, is divided for administrative purposes; any of the divisions of a school or college concentrating on a particular area of knowledge; any sphere of knowledge, interest, or responsibility; one of the sections of a retail store.—**de·part·men·tal,** di·pärt·men'tal, dē″pärt·men'tal, *a.*—**de·part·men·tal·ly,** *adv.*

de·part·men·tal·ize, di·pärt·men'ta·līz″, de″pärt·men'ta·līz″, *v.t.*—departmentalized, departmentalizing. To divide into its constituent parts, such as the various academic disciplines of a curriculum.—**de·part·men·tal·i·za·tion,** *n.*

de·part·ment store, *n.* A large retail establishment in which many different lines of merchandise are carried in separate departments under one general management.

de·par·ture, di·pär'chèr, *n.* [O.Fr. *departeure,* < *departir.*] The act of departing; a going away; a setting out or starting; divergence or deviation. *Navig.* the distance due east or west from a particular meridian; the bearing or position of a vessel, taken usually at the beginning of the voyage for the purpose of setting the course. The distance due east or west on a survey line.

de·paup·er·ate, di·pa'pèr·it, *a.* [M.L. *depauperatus,* pp. of *depauperare,* < L. *de-* and *pauperare,* make poor, < *pauper,* poor.] *Biol.* poorly developed in physical form.—**de·pau·per·a·tion,** *n.*

de·pend, di·pend', *v.i.* [L. *dependeo,* to hang down—*de-,* down, and *pendeo,* to hang.] To be related to anything in regard to existence, operation, or effects; to be contingent or conditioned, followed by *on* or *upon,* as: We *depend on* air for respiration. To rest with confidence; to trust, with *on* or *upon;* to hang down, followed by *from.*

de·pend·a·ble, di·pen'da·bl, *a.* Capable of being depended on; trustworthy.—**de·pend·a·bly,** *adv.*—**de·pend·a·bil·i·ty,** *n.* Reliability.

de·pend·ence, de·pend·ance, di·pen'dens, *n.* A state of being dependent; connection and support; mutual connection; interrelation; a state of relying on another for support or existence; a state of being subject to the operation of any other cause; reliance; confidence; trust.

de·pend·en·cy, de·pend·an·cy, di·pen'den·sē, *n.* pl. **de·pend·en·cies.** The state of being dependent; dependence; now generally, a territory remote from the state to which it belongs, but subject to its rule; an annex to a building.

de·pend·ent, de·pend·ant, di·pen'dent, di·pen'dant, *n.* One who is sustained by another, or who relies on another for support or favor; a retainer; a follower; a servant.—*a.* Hanging down; relying on something else for support; *gram.* not used in isolation; as, a *dependent* clause.

de·perm, dē·pųrm', *v.t. Naut.* of the steel hull of a ship, to demagnetize as a protection against magnetic mines. See *degauss.*

de·per·son·al·ize, dē·pėr'so·na·līz″, *v.t.*—depersonalized, depersonalizing. To deprive of personality or personal quality.—**de·per·son·al·i·za·tion,** *n.*

de·pict, di·pikt', *v.t.* [L. *depingo, depictum*—*de-,* and *pingo,* to paint.] To form a likeness of in colors; to paint; to portray; to represent in words; to describe.—**de·pic·tor, de·pict·er,** *n.*—**de·pic·tion,** *n.*

dep·i·late, dep'i·lāt″, *v.t.*—depilated, depilating. [L. *depilo, depilatum.*] To strip of hair.—**dep·i·la·tion,** *n.*

de·pil·a·to·ry, di·pil'a·tōr″ē, *n.* pl. **de·pil·a·to·ries.** A cosmetic employed to remove superfluous hairs from the human skin.—*a.* Having the quality or power to remove hair from the skin.

de·plane, dē·plān', *v.i.*—deplaned, deplaning. To leave an airplane.

de·plete, di·plēt', *v.t.*—depleted, depleting. [L. *depletus,* pp. of *deplere.*] To decrease the fullness of; reduce the stock or amount of; *med.* to empty or relieve as by bloodletting or purging.—**de·ple·tive, de·ple·to·ry,** di·plē'to·rē, *a.*

de·ple·tion, di·plē'shan, *n.* The state or act of being depleted; *geol.* the reduction of natural resources, such as forests, at a faster rate than replenishment.

de·plor·a·ble, di·plōr'a·bl, *a.* Lamentable; grievous; miserable; wretched; pitiable.—**de·plor·a·ble·ness, de·plor·a·bil·i·ty,** *n.*—**de·plor·a·bly,** *adv.*

de·plore, di·plōr', *v.t.*—deplored, deploring. [L. *deploro.*] To feel or express deep and poignant grief for; to lament; to mourn; to consider unfortunate.

de·ploy, di·ploi', *v.t.* [Fr. *deployer,* O.Fr. *desploier, despleier.*] *Milit.* To spread out, as troops, so as to form an extended front of small depth; to arrange in formation. Loosely, to redistribute appropriately or strategically.—*v.i.* To spread out with extended front.—*n. Milit.* a deploying.—**de·ploy·ment,** *n.*

de·plume, dē·plöm', *v.t.*—deplumed, depluming. [M.L. *deplumare.*] To deprive of plumage or feathers; pluck; to strip of honor, possessions, or wealth.—**de·plu·ma·tion,** *n.*

de·po·lar·ize, dē·pō'la·rīz″, *v.t.*—depolarized, depolarizing. To deprive of polarity or polarization; demagnetize.—**de·po·lar·i·za·tion,** dē·pō·la·ri·zā'shan, *n.*—**de·po·lar·iz·er,** *n.*

de·pone, di·pōn', *v.t., v.i.*—deponed, deponing. [L. *deponere* M.L. testify.] To testify under oath; depose.

de·po·nent, di·pō'nent, *a. Gram.* denoting a verb with a passive or middle voice form, but active in meaning.—*n.* A deponent verb. One who gives written testimony under oath.

de·pop·u·late, dē·pop'ū·lāt″, *v.t.*—depopulated, depopulating. [M.L. *depopulatus,* pp. of *depopulare.*] To deprive of inhabitants, wholly or in part, as by destruction or expulsion; reduce the population of.—**de·pop·u·la·tion,** *n.*—**de·pop·u·la·tor,** *n.*

de·port, di·pōrt', di·pąrt', *v.t.* [Fr. *déporter,* to banish; O.Fr. *se deporter,* to amuse oneself; L. *deporto,* to banish.] To eject from a country under compulsory edict; to carry away; to conduct or behave, followed by *oneself.*—**de·port·a·ble,** *a.*

de·por·ta·tion, dē″pōr·tā'shan, *n.* The lawful removal from a state or country of an alien whose presence is undesirable; the function of deporting.

de·por·tee, dē″pōr·tē', *n.* One deported, or under orders for deportation from a country.

de·port·ment, di·pōrt'ment, *n.* Manner of acting in relation to the duties of life; behavior; demeanor; carriage; conduct.

de·pos·al, di·pō′zal, *n.* The act of deposing from sovereignty or divesting of office.

de·pose, di·pōz′, *v.t.—deposed, deposing.* [Fr. *déposer.*] To remove from a throne or other high office; to divest of office; *law,* to testify, esp. in writing and under oath.— *v.i. Law,* to give testimony, esp. written testimony under oath.—**de·pos·a·ble**, *a.*—**de·pos·er**, *n.*

de·pos·it, di·poz′it, *v.t.* [L. *depositum,* something deposited, a deposit, < *depono, depositum.* DEPONE, POSITION.] To place or set down with care; of coins or tokens, to insert in a coin-operated machine; to lay down or precipitate by natural processes; to entrust for safekeeping or other purpose; to put down as a pledge or partial payment. —*v.i.* To be put down; precipitated; settled; inserted, as in a coin-operated machine; left with, as for safekeeping; given to, as for a security pledge.—*n.* That which is laid down; any matter laid down or precipitated by natural processes; the natural sediment in a bottle of wine; the coating of metal formed by electrolytic action; *geol., min.* mineral masses, as oil or coal, accumulated by water, wind, erosion, or other natural forces; anything entrusted to the care of another; a sum of money lodged in a bank; a pledge; a thing given as security or for part payment.—**de·pos·i·tor**, *n.* One who or that which deposits; one who deposits money in a bank.

de·pos·i·tar·y, di·poz′i·ter″ē, *n. pl.* **de·pos·i·tar·ies.** A person with whom anything is left or lodged in trust; a guardian, a depository.

dep·o·si·tion, dep″o·zish′an, dē″po·zish′an, *n.* [L. *depositio(n-), deponere.*] A deposing or removal from an office or position; the process of depositing; the thing deposited. *Law,* the giving of testimony under oath; the testimony so given; a statement under oath, taken down in writing, to be used in court in place of the oral testimony of the witness. *Eccles.* the interment of the mortal remains of a saint.

de·pos·i·to·ry, di·poz′i·tor″ē, di·poz′i·tar″ē, *n.* A place where anything is lodged for safekeeping; a person to whom a thing is entrusted for safekeeping.

de·pot, dē′pō, *milit. and Brit.* dep′ō, *n.* [Fr. *dépôt,* O.Fr. *depost,* < L. *depono, depositum,* to deposit.] A railroad station; a place of deposit; a depository; a building for receiving goods for storage or sale. *Milit.* the headquarters of a regiment; formerly, a station where recruits for different regiments were received and drilled.

dep·ra·va·tion, dep″ra·vā′shan, *n.* [L. *depravatio.*] The act of depraving or corrupting; the state of being depraved; corruption; deterioration.

de·prave, di·prāv′, *v.t.—depraved, depraving.* [L. *depravo,* to make crooked, to deprave.] To make bad or worse; to impair the good qualities of; to vitiate; to corrupt. —**de·prav·er**, *n.*

de·praved, di·prāvd′, *a.* Corrupted; perverted; immoral.

de·prav·i·ty, di·prav′i·tē, *n. pl.* **de·prav·i·ties.** The state of being depraved; an act or practice exhibiting corrupted morals.

dep·re·cate, dep′re·kāt″, *v.t.—deprecated, deprecating.* [L. *deprecor, deprecatus,* to pray against, to ward off by prayer.] To plead or argue earnestly against; to urge reasons against; to express strong disapproval of.— **dep·re·cat·ing·ly**, *adv.*—**dep·re·ca·to·ry**, **dep·re·ca·tive**, *a.*

dep·re·ca·tion, dep″re·kā′shan, *n.* The act of deprecating; entreaty; disapproval.

de·pre·ci·a·ble, di·prē′shē·a·bl, *a.* Susceptible to depreciation; capable of being decreased in value.

de·pre·ci·ate, di·prē′shē·āt″, *v.t.—depreciated, depreciating.* [L. *depretio,* to lower the price of.] To bring down the price or value of; to cause to be less valuable; to diminish the purchasing power of, as money; to represent as of little value or merit, or of less value than is commonly supposed; to lower in estimation, undervalue, decry, disparage or underrate.—*v.i.* To fall in value.—**de·pre·ci·a·tive**, **de·pre·ci·a·to·ry**, di·prē′shē·a·tōr″ē, *a.*—**de·pre·ci·at·ing·ly**, *adv.*—**de·pre·ci·a·tor**, *n.*

de·pre·ci·a·tion, di·prē″shē·ā′shan, *n.* The act of depreciating; reduction in value or worth; a lowering or undervaluing in estimation; the state of being undervalued; *accounting,* an allowance to account for decline in condition, deducted in computing the value of a business or property.

dep·re·date, dep′ri·dāt″, *v.t.—depredated, depredating.* [L. *depraedor,* to pillage.] To plunder; to pillage; to waste; to spoil.— **dep·re·da·tion**, *n.* The act of depredating; a robbing; a pillaging by men or animals; a laying waste.—**dep·re·da·tor**, *n.*—**dep·re·da·to·ry**, dep′ri·dā″to·rē, di·pred′a·tōr″ē, *a.*

de·press, di·pres′, *v.t.* [L. *deprimo, depressum,* to depress.] To press down; to let fall to a lower state or position; to lower; to render dull or languid; to deject or make sad; to humble, abase, bring into adversity; to lower in value.—**de·pres·sive**, *a.*

de·pres·sant, di·pres′ant, *a. Med.* Having the quality of depressing or lowering the vital activities; sedative.—*n.* A depressant substance or agent; a sedative.

de·pressed, di·prest′, *a.* Dejected; dispirited; discouraged; sad; humbled; languid; dull; suffering economic adversity, esp. unemployment and poverty. *Bot., zool.* flattened in shape; flattened as regards the under and upper surfaces.

de·pres·sion, di·presh′an, *n.* A hollow; the state or feeling of being depressed in spirits; a low state of strength; *econ.* a period of subnormal economic activity, marked by severely cut production, sinking profits and wages, a falling stock market, and much unemployment.—**de·pres·sion an·gle**, *n. Astron.* an angle in a vertical plane between the local horizontal and the descending line.

de·pres·so·mo·tor, di·pres″ō·mō′tėr, *a. Med.* causing a retardation of motor activity; as, *depressomotor* nerves.—*n.* A depressomotor agent, as bromine.

de·pres·sor, di·pres′er, *n.* [N.L.] One who or that which depresses. *Anat.* a muscle that draws down a part of the body; a nerve whose stimulation causes a decrease in bodily activity, as of blood pressure. *Med.* an instrument for pressing down a protruding part during surgery or an examination.

de·pres·su·rize, dē·presh′u·rīz″, *v.t.— depressurized, depressurizing.* To lessen pressure of.

dep·ri·va·tion, dep″ri·vā′shan, *n.* [M.L. *deprivatio(n-).*] The act of depriving, or the fact of being deprived; dispossession; expulsion from office; loss. Also **de·pri·val**, di·prī′val.—**de·priv·a·tive**, di·priv′a·tiv, *a.* Tending to deprive.

de·prive, di·prīv′, *v.t.—deprived, depriving.* [O.Fr. *depriver,* < M.L. *deprivare.*] To divest of something possessed or enjoyed; to expel from office; strip.—**de·priv·er**, *n.*—**de·priv·a·ble**, *a.*

depth, depth, *n.* [M.E. < *deep.*] The quality of being deep; measure or distance downward, inward, or backward; deepness, as of water; abstruseness, as of a subject; intellectual penetration, sagacity, or profundity, as of persons; gravity or seriousness; emotional profundity; as, *depth* of sorrow; intensity, as of silence or color; lowness of pitch; a deep part or place, as of the sea; an unfathomable space, or abyss; a deep or underlying region, as of feeling; the remotest or most extreme part, as of space; the inmost part; as, the *depth* of woods; the part of greatest intensity, as of night or winter.—**depth·less**, *a.* Without depth; shallow; superficial; of immeasurable depth; fathomless.

depth charge, *n.* A bomb which is dropped or thrown into the water from a ship or an airplane and explodes at a predetermined depth, used to destroy submarines and other underwater targets. Also **depth bomb.**

depth per·cep·tion, *n.* Visual skill in judging relationships of space between objects at varying distances and angles from the observer.

depth psy·chol·o·gy, *n. Psychol.* the field of psychology which emphasizes the importance of unconscious motivation.

dep·u·rate, dep′ū·rāt″, *v.t.—depurated, depurating.* [L.L. *depuro, depuratum,* to purify.] To free from impurities; to purify; to clarify.—**dep·u·ra·tion**, *n.*—**dep·u·ra·tor**, *n.*

dep·u·ta·tion, dep″ū·tā′shan, *n.* A special commission or authority to act as the substitute of another; the person or persons appointed to transact business for another.

de·pute, de·pūt′, *v.t.—deputed, deputing.* [Fr. *députer,* < L. *deputo,* to destine, allot.] To appoint, as a substitute or agent, to act for another; to appoint and send with a special commission or authority to act for the sender.

dep·u·tize, dep′ū·tīz″, *v.t.—deputized, deputizing.* [< *deputy.*] To appoint as deputy; depute.

dep·u·ty, dep′ū·tē, *n. pl.* **dep·u·ties.** [O.Fr. *depute* (Fr. *depute*), prop. pp. of *deputer,* E. *depute.*] A person appointed or authorized to act for another or others; a substitute; an authorized representative or agent; a person representing a constituency in any of certain legislative bodies; a person elected or appointed to assist a public official and to take over the position in case of vacancy.—*a.* Acting as deputy for another.—**dep·u·ty·ship**, *n.*

de·rac·in·ate, di·ras′i·nāt″, *v.t.—deracinated, deracinating.* [Fr. *deraciner.*] To pluck up by the roots; to alienate from one's native culture.—**de·rac·i·na·tion**, *n.*

de·rail, dē·rāl′, *v.i.* [Fr. *dérailler,* < *de-* and *rail,* rail.] Of a train, to run off the rails or track.—*v.t.* To cause to run off the rails.—*n.* A switch designed to divert a train or car from the track in an emergency. Also **de·rail·er.—de·rail·ment**, *n.*

de·range, di·rānj′, *v.t.—deranged, deranging.* [Fr. *déranger,* O.Fr. *desrengier.*] To disturb the arrangement or order of; throw into confusion; to disturb the proper condition, action, or functions of; to unsettle the reason of; make insane.—**de·ranged**, *a.* Disarranged; disordered; insane.—**de·range·ment**, *n.*

Der·by, dėr′bē, *Brit.* där′bē, *n. pl.* **Der·bies.** A celebrated horse race in England, originated in 1780 by the twelfth Earl of Derby, and run annually at Epsom, near London; any of several other annual horse races; as, the Kentucky Derby, held the first Saturday in May, in Louisville, Ky. (*l.c.*) a contest open to all; a stiff felt hat with rounded crown and narrow brim, worn chiefly by men.

der·e·lict, der′e·likt, *a.* [L. *derelictus,* pp. of *derelinquere,* forsake utterly.] Left or abandoned by the owner or guardian; as, a *derelict* ship; dilapidated; neglectful of duty; delinquent.—*n.* One guilty of neglect of duty; a vagrant; *naut.* a vessel abandoned at sea; *law,* land left dry by a change of the water line.

der·e·lic·tion, der″e·lik′shan, *n.* [L. *derelictio(n-),* < *derelinquere.*] The act of abandoning, or the state of being abandoned; a leaving dry of land by change of the water line; the land left dry; culpable abandonment or neglect, as of duty; delinquency.

de·ride, di·rīd′, *v.t.*—*derided, deriding.* [L. *derideo.*] To laugh at in contempt; to turn to ridicule or make sport of; to treat with scorn by laughter; to mock; to ridicule.—**de·rid·er,** *n.*—**de·rid·ing·ly,** *adv.*

de ri·gueur, de ri·gur′, *Fr.* de RĒ·gŒR′, *a.* [Fr. *compulsory.*] Required by rules of etiquette or fashion.

de·ri·sion, di·rizh′an, *n.* [L. *derisio.*] The act of deriding, or the state of being derided; contempt manifested by laughter; mockery; ridicule; scorn.

de·ri·sive, di·rī′siv, *a.* Expressing or characterized by derision; mocking; ridiculing.—**de·ri·sive·ly,** *adv.*—**de·ri·sive·ness,** *n.*—**de·ri·so·ry,** di·rī′so·rē, di·rī′zo·rē, *a.*

der·i·va·tion, der″i·vā′shan, *n.* [L. *derivatio(n-).*] The act of deriving, or the fact of being derived; a drawing or obtaining, as from a source; extraction; source or root; the formation of a word from a root, stem, or the like; the tracing of the origin of a word; a statement or theory of such origin or formation; something derived; a derivative.—**der·i·va·tion·al,** *a.*

de·riv·a·tive, di·riv′a·tiv, *a.* [L.L. *derivativus.*] Derived; drawn or having proceeded from a source or from something else; not original or primitive; secondary; pertaining to derivation.—*n.* Something derived or derivative; a word derived from another word or from a root, stem, or the like; *chem.* a substance or compound obtained from, or so constituted as to be regarded as derived from, another substance or compound.—**de·riv·a·tive·ly,** *adv.*

de·rive, di·rīv′, *v.t.*—*derived, deriving.* [L. *derivare.*] To draw or obtain from a source or origin; to take, as a word, from a particular source; form from a root, stem or the like; *chem.* to obtain, as one substance or compound, from another. To trace from a source or origin, as a custom or word; declare to come from a particular source; to obtain by reasoning; deduce.—*v.i.* To come from a source; originate.—**de·rived,** *a,* Drawn, obtained, or descended from a source.—**de·rived u·nit,** *n. Phys.* any of the units of area, velocity, etc., which are derived from fundamental units.—**de·riv·er,** *n.*—**de·riv·a·ble,** *a.*

der·ma, dur′ma, *n.* [N.L. < Gr. *derma, dermat-,* skin.] The corium, or true skin, beneath the epidermis; the skin in general. Also *dermis.*—**der·mal,** *a.* Of or pertaining to the derma or the skin; cutaneous.—**der·ma·ti·tis,** dur″ma·tī′tis, *n.* [N.L.] *Pathol.* inflammation of the derma.

der·mat·o·gen, der·mat′o·jen, dur′ma·to·jen, *n.* [Gr. *derma, dermatos,* skin, *gen,* to produce.] A cellular layer at the tip of a root or stem from which the epidermis is produced.

der·ma·toid, dur′ma·toid″, *a.* Resembling skin; skinlike.

der·ma·tol·o·gy, dur″ma·tol′o·jē, *n.* The science of the skin and its diseases.—**der·ma·to·log·i·cal,** *a.*—**der·ma·tol·o·gist,** *n.*

der·ma·to·phyte, dur′ma·to·fīt″, der·mat′o·fīt″, *n.* [Gr. *phyton,* a plant.] *Pathol.* a parasitic plant, infesting the skin and the hair and nails of men and animals, giving rise to various forms of skin disease, as ringworm.

der·ma·to·sis, dur″ma·tō′sis, *n.* pl. **der·ma·to·ses,** dur″ma·tō′sēz. [N.L. < Gr. *derma (dermat-),* skin.] *Pathol.* any disease of the skin.

der·mis, dur′mis, *n.* Derma.

der·moid, dur′moid, *a.* Skinlike; dermatoid; dermal.

der·o·gate, der′o·gāt″, *v.t.*—*derogated, derogating.* [L. *derogo, derogatum,* to repeal part of a law, to restrict, to modify.] To lessen the worth of; to disparage.—*v.i.* To detract; to have the effect of lowering or diminishing, as a reputation; to lessen by taking away a part, used with *from;* as, *ridicule derogates from* a person's dignity.

der·o·ga·tion, der″o·gā′shan, *n.* The act of derogating; a lessening of value or estimation; detraction; disparagement.

de·rog·a·to·ry, di·rog′a·tōr′ē, *a.* Having the effect of derogating or detracting from; disparaging; stating a low estimation of.—**de·rog·a·to·ri·ness,** *n.* The quality of being derogatory.—**de·rog·a·to·ri·ly,** di·rog″a·tōr′i·lē, di·rog″a·tōr″i·lē, *adv.* In a detracting manner.

der·rick, der′ik, *n.* [The name of a London hangman of the 17th century, applied first to the gallows, and hence to a contrivance resembling it.] An apparatus for hoisting heavy weights, usually consisting of a boom, supported by a central post, with a tackle rigged at the end; a tower-like framework built over an oil well or deep drilling hole to hold drilling hoisting equipment.

der·ri·ere, *Fr.* **der·ri·ère,** der″ē·âr′, *Fr.* de·RYER′, *n.* The buttocks; behind; rear; rump.

der·ring-do, der′ing·dö′, *n.* [Orig. a phrase in Chaucer's "Troilus and Cressida," M.E. *dorryng don,* "daring (to) do".] Daring deeds.

der·rin·ger, der′in·jèr, *n.* [After Henry Derringer, a 19th century American gunsmith.] A shortbarreled pistol of large caliber, now usually breech-loading.

der·ris, der′is, *n.* Any of the genus *Derris,* East Indian leguminous plants, including some containing rotenone, a source of an insecticide.

der·vish, dèr′vish, *n.* [Turkish *dervis,* Pers. *darvēsh,* poor, indigent, a dervish.] A member of a Muslim religious order of friars or monks whose devotional exercises are expressed in frenzied whirling and dancing, often accompanied by loud singing and shouting; someone or something which dances or whirls like a dervish.

de·sal·i·nate, dē·sal′i·nāt″, *v.t.*—*desalinated, desalinating.* Desalt.

de·salt, dē·salt′, *v.t.* To remove salt from, esp. from sea water, usually to freshen for consumption.—**de·salt·er,** *n.*

des·cant, dis·cant, des′kant, *n.* [O.Fr. *descant, deschant* (Fr. *déchant*), < M.L. *discantus,* < L. *dis-,* apart, and *canere,* sing.] *Mus.* a melody or counterpoint accompanying a simple musical theme and usually written above it; in part-music, the soprano; the art of singing or composing music in parts; a harmonized composition; an instrumental prelude consisting of variations on a theme; in general, a song or melody. A variation upon anything; comment on a subject, esp. an extended and varied comment; a disquisition or discourse.—des′kant, dis·kant′, *v.i. Mus.* to sing or play a melody in harmony with the chief melody; in general, to sing; to make comments on a subject; discourse at length and with variety.—**des·cant·er,** *n.*

de·scend, di·send′, *v.i.* [Fr. *descendre.*] To move from a higher to a lower place; to move, come, or go downward; to run or slope down; to invade or fall upon hostilely; to arrive in a multitude; to proceed from a source or origin; to be derived; to pass from one heir to another; to pass, as from general to particular considerations; to lower or degrade oneself; to stoop.—*v.t.* To walk, move, or pass downward upon or along; to pass from the top to the bottom of.—**de·**

scend·i·ble, di·sen′da·bl, *a.* Capable of being conveyed by inheritance. Also **de·scend·a·ble.**

de·scend·ant, di·sen′dant, *n.* An individual proceeding from an ancestor in any degree; anything derived from a prototype; an offspring.—**de·scend·ent, de·scend·ant,** di·sen′dent, *a.* Descending from a common ancestor or prototype.

de·scend·er, di·sen′dèr, *n. Print.* The part of a lower-case letter that goes below the body; a letter with a descender, as p, q, j, and y.

de·scent, di·sent′, *n.* [Fr. *descente.*] The act of descending or passing from a higher to a lower place; inclination downward; declivity; decline, as in station, virtue, quality, or the like; transmission by succession or inheritance; a proceeding from a progenitor; lineage; a generation; a single degree in the scale of genealogy.

de·scribe, di·skrīb′, *v.t.*—*described, describing.* [L. *describo,* to write down, to delineate.] To depict or portray orally or in writing; to present a mental image by means of words; to delineate or trace the form or figure of; as, to *describe* a geometric figure.—*v.i.* To use the power of describing.—**de·scrib·a·ble,** *a.*—**de·scrib·er,** *n.*

de·scrip·tion, di·skrip′shan, *n.* [L. *descriptio, descriptionis.*] The act of describing; delineation; an account of the properties or appearance of a thing, given so that another person may form a concept of it; the combination of qualities which constitute a class, species, or individual.

de·scrip·tive, di·skrip′tiv, *a.* Containing description; having the quality of representing.—**de·scrip·tive·ly,** *adv.*—**de·scrip·tive·ness,** *n.*

de·scrip·tive ge·om·e·try, *n.* An application of geometry in the projection of defined figures, which makes it possible for the mathematician to deduce their projective as well as their metrical properties; in general, geometry used and applied in terms of projections.

de·scrip·tive lin·guis·tics, *n.* The study of language which deals with the grammar and classification, without referring to origins.

de·scry, di·skrī′, *v.t.*—*descried, descrying.* [O.Fr. *descrier,* to decry, to make an outcry on discovering something.] To espy; to discover; to see or behold from a distance.

des·e·crate, des′e·krāt″, *v.t.*—*desecrated, desecrating.* [< L. *de-,* from, away, and *sacer,* sacred.] To divert from a sacred to a profane purpose or character; to render unhallowed; to profane.—**des·e·cra·tion,** *n.*

de·seg·re·gate, dē·seg′re·gāt″, *v.t.*—*desegregated, desegregating.* To abolish racial segregation in.—*v.i.*—**de·seg·re·ga·tion,** dē″seg′re·gā′shan, dē′seg″re·gā′shan, *n.*

de·sen·si·tize, dē·sen′si·tīz″,*v.t.*—*desensitized, desensitizing.* To make less sensitive; *physiol.* to remove the sensitivity or reactivity, as of an organ or tissue, to an outside stimulus, by means of desensitizing injections; *photog.* to make less sensitive to light.—**de·sen·si·ti·za·tion,** *n.*—**de·sen·si·tiz·er,** *n.*

des·ert, dez′èrt, *n.* [L. *desertus,* pp. of *desero, desertum,* to forsake—*de-,* away, and *sero, sertum,* to unite.] A wilderness; a vast sandy or rocky expanse, almost destitute of moisture and vegetation; a region devoid of something, as: That country is a spiritual *desert.*—*a.* Lying waste; uncultivated and uninhabited; pertaining to a wilderness.

de·sert, di·zèrt′, *v.t.* [Fr. *déserter* < M.L. *desertare,* freq. of L. *deserere,* abandon, forsake.] To abandon or forsake; depart from; esp. of military personnel, to leave in violation of duty.—*v.i.* To forsake one's duty; of military personnel, to leave the service without permission.—**de·sert·er,** *n.*

One who deserts, applied to military personnel who desert from service.

de·sert, di·zèrt′, *n*. [O.Fr. *deserte*, merit, < *deservir*, to deserve.] The quality of deserving either reward or punishment; reward or punishment merited; merit.— **de·serts**, *n. pl.* Deserved punishment or reward, as: He received his just *deserts*.

de·ser·tion, di·zèr′shan, *n*. [L.L. *desertio(n-)*, < L. *deserere*.] The act of deserting, esp. in violation of duty or obligation; abandonment; the state of being deserted; desolation; *law*, willful abandonment, esp. of one's wife or husband, in violation of legal or moral obligation.

de·serve, di·zèrv′, *v.t.*—*deserved, deserving*. [O.Fr. *deservir, desservir*, < L. *deservio*, to serve diligently—*de-*, intens., and *servio*, to serve.] To merit; to be worthy of, as reward or punishment, praise or censure, because of one's actions, qualities, or situation, whether good or evil.—*v.i.* To be deserving of, or to be entitled to a reward or punishment.—**de·served**, *a*. Merited; earned.—**de·serv·ed·ly**, di·zèr′vid·lē, *adv.*—**de·serv·er**, *n*.

de·serv·ing, di·zèr′ving, *a*. Worthy of reward or praise; meritorious.—**de·serv·ing·ly**, di·zèr′ving·lē, *adv*.

de·sex, dē·seks′, dē′seks, *v.t.* To spay or castrate.

de·sex·u·al·ize, dē·seksh′u·wa·līz″, dē·sek′sha·līz″, *v.t.*—*desexualized, desexualizing*. To divest of the sex or sexual power of; to remove the sexual quality from or any sexual connection with, esp. by diverting the interest or energy, as in sublimation.—**de·sex·u·al·i·za″tion**, *n*.

des·ha·bille, dez″a·bēl′, *n*. Dishabille.

des·ic·cant, des′i·kant, *a*. Drying.—*n*. A medicine or application that has drying qualities.

des·ic·cate, des′i·kāt″, *v.t.*—*desiccated, desiccating*. [L. *desicco*, to dry up—*de*, intens., and *sicco*, to dry, < *siccus*, dry.] To dry; to remove moisture from; to dehydrate, as food.—*v.i.* To become dry.—**des·ic·ca·tion**, *n*.—**des·ic·ca·tive**, *a*.

des·ic·ca·tor, des′i·kā″tér, *n*. One who or that which desiccates; an apparatus for drying fruit or milk; *chem.* an apparatus for absorbing the moisture present in a chemical substance.

de·sid·er·ate, di·sid′e·rāt″, *v.t.*—*desiderated, desiderating*. [L. *desidero, desideratum*, to long for, to feel the want of.] To feel the want of; to miss; to want; to desire.—**de·sid·er·a·tion**, *n*.

de·sid·er·a·tive, di·sid′e·rā″tiv, di·sid′ér·a·tiv, *a*. Having or implying desire; expressing or denoting desire.—*n*. A verb formed from another verb which expresses a desire to do the action implied in the original verb; as, in Latin, *edere*, to eat, *esurire*, to be hungry.

de·sid·er·a·tum, di·sid″e·rā′tum, *n. pl.* **de·sid·er·a·ta**, di·sid″e·rā′ta. [L.] That which is not possessed, but which is desirable; something much wanted.

de·sign, di·zīn′, *v.t.* [Fr. *désigner*, designate, indicate, also obs. *dessigner, desseigner* (It. *disegnare*), design, plan.] To prepare the preliminary sketch or the plans for; to draw the outline or figure of; to plan and fashion artistically or skillfully as for a model or pattern; to furnish or decorate with a design or designs. To form or conceive in the mind; contrive; plan; contemplate; to intend; as, a gesture *designed* to express contempt.—*v.i.* To make drawings, preliminary sketches or plans; to plan and fashion the form and structure of an object, decorative scheme, or work of art; to have intentions or purposes.

de·sign, di·zīn′, *n*. [= Fr. *dessein*, plan, purpose, *dessin*, drawing, sketch, pattern,

design.] An outline, sketch, or plan, as of a work of art, an edifice, or a machine to be executed or constructed; the combination of details or features, as of a picture, building or bridge; the pattern or device of artistic work; a thing artistically designed; a piece of artistic work; the art of designing; as, a school of *design*. Intention, purpose, or aim; a plan conceived in the mind; a project; a scheme; sometimes, a hostile plan, or evil, crafty, or selfish intention; the object of a plan or purpose; the end in view; the adaptation of means to a preconceived end; a contrivance.

des·ig·nate, dez′ig·nāt″, *v.t.*—*designated, designating*. [L. *designatus*, pp. of *designare*, mark out, indicate, appoint.] To mark or point out; indicate; show; specify; to name or entitle; to nominate or select, as for a duty or office; appoint; assign; set apart.—dez′ig·nit, dez′ig·nāt″, *a*. Designated, as to an office; nominated or appointed to an office, but not yet installed; as, an alderman-*designate*.—**des·ig·na·tive**, **des·ig·na·to·ry**, dez′ig·na·tōr″ē, dez″ig·nā′to·rē, *a*. Serving to designate.—**des·ig·na·tor**, *n*.—**des·ig·nee**, *n*.

des·ig·na·tion, dez″ig·nā′shan, *n*. The act of designating; a distinctive appellation; an assignment; appointment.

de·sign·er, di·zī′nér, *n*. One who designs; one who makes designs, as for works of art, machines, clothing; one who devises artistic or decorative patterns; a contriver; a schemer or intriguer.

de·sign·ing, di·zī′ning, *a*. Scheming; artful.—**de·sign·ing·ly**, *adv*.

des·i·nence, des′i·nens, *n*. [Fr. *désinence*, < L. *desinere*.] Termination or ending, as of a line of verse; *gram.* a termination, ending, or suffix of a word.

de·sir·a·ble, di·zīér′a·bl, *a*. Worthy of being desired; pleasing, excellent, or fine; alluring; advisable or advantageous.—*n*. One who or that which is desirable.—**de·sir·a·bil·i·ty**, **de·sir·a·ble·ness**, *n*.—**de·sir·a·bly**, *adv*.

de·sire, di·zīér′, *v.t.*—*desired, desiring*. [O.Fr. *desirer* (Fr. *désirer*), < L. *desiderare*; *desiderate*.] To wish or long for; crave; want; to express a wish to obtain; ask for, or request.—*v.i.* To have or feel a desire.—**de·sired**, *a*. Longed for or coveted; suitable or prescribed; as, the *desired* amount.—**de·sir·er**, *n*.

de·sire, di·zīér′, *n*. The fact or state of desiring; a longing or craving; a wish; sexual appetite; an expressed wish; a request; something or someone desired.—**de·sir·ous**, di·zīér′us, *a*. Having or characterized by desire; desiring.—**de·sir·ous·ly**, *adv*.—**de·sir·ous·ness**, *n*.

de·sist, di·zist′, di·sist′, *v.i.* [L. *desisto*.] To cease to act or proceed; to leave off; to discontinue or stop.—**de·sist·ance**, **de·sist·ence**, *n*.

desk, desk, *n*. [M.E. *deske* = It. *desco*, < M.L. *discus*, table, L. *discus*, disk, disc.] A table or similar piece of furniture, as in a school, office, or study, with a usu. level surface for reading, writing, or drawing, and often with drawers and compartments for papers, pens, books, and other supplies; a frame for supporting a book from which the service is read in a church; a pulpit; a department of an organization responsible for specified functions; as, the city *desk* of a newspaper; a stand or counter where certain dealings with the public are transacted; as, an information *desk*.—*a*.

desk·man, desk′man″, desk′man, *n*. *pl.* **desk·men**. *Journalism*, a newspaper staff member who works from his desk, writing and editing copy based on news telephoned in by reporters. A person, esp. with managerial functions, who works mainly at his desk.

des·mid, des′mid, *n*. [N.L. *Desmidium*, the typical genus, < Gr. *desmos*, band, chain.] *Bot.* any of the microscopic, unicellular fresh-water algae constituting the family *Desmidiaceae*.

des·moid, des′moid, *a*. [Gr. *desmos*, band, chain, ligament, also *desme*, bundle, < *dein*, bind.] *Anat.* resembling a ligament; ligamentous; *pathol.* resembling a bundle, as applied to certain fibrous tumors.

des·o·late, des′o·lāt″, *v.t.*—*desolated, desolating*. [L. *desolatus*, pp. of *desolare*, leave alone, forsake, < *de-*, and *solus*, alone.] To make unfit for habitation; lay waste; devastate; to deprive of inhabitants; depopulate; to render disconsolate; to forsake or abandon.

des·o·late, des′o·lit, *a*. Dreary or dismal; barren or waste; devastated; deprived of inhabitants or dwellings; deserted; lonely; forsaken; miserable or disconsolate.—**des·o·late·ly**, *adv*.—**des·o·late·ness**, *n*.

des·o·la·tion, des″o·la′shan, *n*. [L.L. *desolatio(n-)*.] The act of desolating, or the state of being desolated; dreariness; barrenness or ruin; depopulation; deprivation of companionship or comfort; loneliness; sadness.

des·ox·y·ri·bo·nu·cle·ic ac·id, des·ok′si·rī′bō·nō·klē′ik as′id, des·ok″si·rī′bō·nū·klē′ik as′id, des·ok′si·rī″bō·nō·klē′ik as′id, des·ok′si·rī″bō·nū·klē′ik as′id, *n*. Deoxyribonucleic acid. Also **DNA**.

de·spair, di·spâr′, *v.i.* [O.Fr. *desperer* (now *desesperer*), < L. *despero*—*de-*, away, and *spero*, to hope.] To give up all hope or expectation, followed by *of*; to lose all hope.—*n*. Hopelessness; desperation; that which causes despair, as: His thievery was her *despair*.—**de·spair·ing**, *a*. Indulging in despair; prone to despair; indicating despair.—**de·spair·ing·ly**, *adv*.

des·per·a·do, des″pe·rä′dō, des″pe·rā′dō, *n. pl.* **des·per·a·does**, **des·per·a·dos**. A fearless, reckless criminal or outlaw, esp. one in the early history of western U.S.

des·per·ate, des′pér·it, des′prit, *a*. [L. *desperatus*, pp. of *despero*, to despair.] Without hope; proceeding from despair; reduced to extremity and reckless of consequences; frantic. Irretrievable; past cure, or hopeless; as, a *desperate* disease, situation, or undertaking. Having a pressing demand or desire, as: They were *desperate* for food. Excessive; intense; as: He had a *desperate* desire to win.—**des·per·ate·ly**, *adv*.—**des·per·ate·ness**, *n*.

des·per·a·tion, des″pe·rā′shan, *n*. The state of being desperate; a giving up of hope leading to a disregard of safety or danger.

des·pi·ca·ble, des′pi·ka·bl, di·spik′a·bl, *a*. [L.L. *despicabilis*, < L. *despicor, despicatus*, to despise, < *despicio*.] Deserving of being despised; contemptible; base; mean; vile; worthless.—**des·pi·ca·ble·ness**, *n*.—**des·pi·ca·bly**, *adv*.

de·spise, di·spīz′, *v.t.*—*despised, despising*. [O.Fr. *despiz*, pp. of *despire*, to despise, < L. *despicere*, to despise—*de-*, down, and *specio*, to look.] To have the lowest opinion of; to contemn; to disdain; to scorn.—**de·spis·a·ble**, *a*.—**de·spis·er**, *n*.

de·spite, di·spīt′, *n*. [O.Fr. *despit*, M.Fr. *depit*, < L. *despectus*, a looking down upon, a despising, < *despicio*, to despise.] Extreme malice; contemptuous hate; an act of spite or contempt.

de·spite, di·spīt′, *prep*. In spite of; notwithstanding.

de·spite·ful, di·spīt′ful, *a*. Full of despite or spite; malicious.—**de·spite·ful·ly**, *adv*.—**de·spite·ful·ness**, *n*.

de·spoil, di·spoil′, *v.t.* [O.Fr. *despoiller*, L. *despolio*, to rob, plunder—*de-*, intens., and *spolio*, to spoil.] To take from by force; to rob; to strip of possessions.—**de·spoil·er**, *n*.—**de·spo·li·a·tion**, di·spō′lē·ā′shan, *n*.

The act of despoiling; a stripping; state of being despoiled. Also **de·spoil·ment.**

de·spond, di·spond′, des′pond, *v.i.* [L. *despondere*, promise, give up, lose (heart), < *de-*, from and *spondere*, promise.] To lose heart, courage, or hope; become depressed. —*n.* Despondency.—**de·spond·ing·ly,** *adv.*

de·spond·en·cy, di·spon′den·sē, *n.* Condition of being despondent; depression of spirits from loss of courage or hope; dejection. Also **de·spond·ence.**

de·spond·ent, di·spon′dent, *a.* Having a feeling of despondency; greatly discouraged, dispirited, or dejected.—**de·spond·ent·ly,** *adv.*

des·pot, des′pot, des′pot, *n.* [Gr. *despotēs*, master, lord.] An absolute ruler; an autocrat; a tyrant or oppressor; *hist.* a title given to Byzantine emperors, bishops of the Eastern Orthodox Church, and certain Italian leaders during the Renaissance.—**des·pot·ic,** di·spot′ik, *a.* Of, pertaining to, or of the nature of a despot or despotism; autocratic; arbitrary; tyrannical.—**des·pot·i·cal·ly,** *adv.*

des·pot·ism, des′po·tiz″um, *n.* The rule of a despot; the exercise of absolute authority; tyranny; an absolute or autocratic form of government; a country ruled by a despot.

des·qua·mate, des′kwa·māt″, *v.i.*—*desquamated, desquamating.* [L. *desquamatus*, pp. of *desquamare*, < *de-* and *squama*, scale.] To come off in scales, as the epidermis in certain diseases; scale or peel off.—**des·qua·ma·tion,** des″kwa·mā′shan, *n.*—**des·quam·a·tive,** *a.*

des·sert, di·zėrt′, *n.* [Fr. *dessert*, < *desservir*, to clear the table—*des-* (L. *dis-*), and *servir*, to serve.] A course of ice cream, pudding, pastry, or fruit served following a meal; any dish served following the main course.

des·sert·spoon, di·zėrt′spön″, *n.* A spoon intermediate in size between a tablespoon and teaspoon, used for eating desserts such as ice cream.

des·sert wine, *n.* A sweet wine served with the dessert course or between meals.

de·ster·i·lize, dē·ster′i·līz″, *v.t.*—*desterilized, desterilizing.* To take from an idle state and put it into use, as latent gold issued for currency.—*n.*—**de·ster·i·li·za·tion,** dē·ster″i·li·zā′shan, *n.*

des·ti·na·tion, des″ti·nā′shan, *n.* [L. *destinatio.*] The predetermined end of a journey or voyage; the place to which a thing is addressed; predetermined object, end, or design; the purpose for which anything is intended or appointed.

des·tine, des′tin, *v.t.*—*destined, destining.* [O.Fr. Fr. *destiner,* < L. *destinare* (pp. *destinatus*), make fast, establish, appoint.] To appoint or ordain beforehand, as by divine decree; to set aside for a particular use; design; intend.—**des·tined,** *a.* Foreordained or predetermined; designed or intended; bound for a certain destination.

des·ti·ny, des′ti·nē, *n.* pl. **des·ti·nies.** [O.Fr. *destinee* (Fr. *destiné*), < L. *destinata,* fem. of *destinatus,* pp. of *destinare,* establish, appoint.] That which is destined or predetermined to happen; the predetermined course of events; fate; one's lot or fortune; the power or agency which determines the course of events; (*cap.*) this power personified or represented as a goddess.—**the Des·ti·nies,** the Fates.

des·ti·tute, des′ti·töt″, des′ti·tūt″, *a.* [L.] Not having or possessing; wanting, followed by *of*; not possessing the necessities of life; in abject poverty; entirely without the means of subsistence.

des·ti·tu·tion, des″ti·tö′shan, des″ti·tū′shan, *n.* [L. *destitutio(n-),* < *destituere.* DESTITUTE.] Want of the means of subsistence; utter poverty; destitute condition; deprivation; want.

de·stroy, di·stroi′, *v.t.* [O.Fr. *destruire* (now *détruire*), < L. *destruo,* destroy.] To knock to pieces; to demolish; to ruin; to annihilate; to put an end to; to cause to cease; to kill or slay; to ravage; to spoil; to make ineffective or neutral.—*v.i.* To lead to destruction.

de·stroy·er, di·stroi′er, *n.* One who or that which destroys; a small, swift class of naval vessel, intended for the destruction of torpedo craft and for escort duty, which is armed with guns, torpedoes, and guided missiles.

de·stroy·er es·cort, *n.* A small naval vessel of the destroyer class used on the surface to detect submarines.

de·stroy·ing an·gel, *n.* Any of various poisonous mushrooms of the genus *Amanita.*

de·struct, di·strukt′, *a.* Having the propensity to destroy, as an apparatus in a missile, which will destroy it under certain circumstances.—*n.* The act or process of intentionally damaging an object.—*v.t.* To destroy.

de·struc·tion, di·struk′shan, *n.* [L. *destructio.*] The act of destroying; demolition; a pulling down; subversion; overthrow; ruin, by whatever means; extermination; death; murder; slaughter; the state of being destroyed.—**de·struct·i·ble,** di·struk′ti·bl, *a.*—**de·struct·i·bil·i·ty,** di·struk″ti·bil′·i·tē, *n.*

de·struc·tive, di·struk′tiv, *a.* Causing destruction; having a tendency to destroy; ruinous; deprecating, as: The instructor offered only *destructive* criticism.—**de·struc·tive·ly,** *adv.*—**de·struc·tive·ness,** *n.*—**de·struc·tiv·i·ty,** dē″struk·tiv′i·tē, *n.*

de·struc·tive dis·til·la·tion, *n. Chem.* the distillation of organic products at high temperatures, by which the elements are separated or evolved into new forms; a chemical process involving the decomposition of organic substances by heating and the collection of the gaseous or volatile products which evolve from this process, such as the collection of gas from decomposed coal.

de·struc·tor, di·struk′ter, *n. Brit.* a furnace for burning refuse; incinerator. *Aerospace,* a missile used to destroy flying objects.

des·ue·tude, des′wi·töd″, des′wi·tūd″, *n.* [L. *desuetudo—de-,* not, and *suesco,* to accustom oneself.] Disuse; something no longer practiced or customary.

de·sul·fu·rize, *Brit.* **de·sul·phu·rize,** dē·sul′fū·rīz″, dē·sul′fu·rīz″, *v.t.*—*desulfurized, desulfurizing.* To deprive of sulfur. Also **de·sul·fur·ate,** dē·sul′fū·rāt″, dē·sul′fu·rāt″.—**de·sul·fu·ri·za·tion, de·sul·fu·ra·tion,** *n.*

des·ul·to·ry, des′ul·tōr″ē, des′ul·tar″ē, *a.* [L. *desultorius,* pertaining to a *desultor,* or rider in the circus, < *desilio, desultum,* to leap down—*de-,* down, and *salio,* to leap.] Passing from one thing or subject to another without order or natural connection; rambling; unconnected; deviating from the main topic; as, a *desultory* comment.—**des·ul·to·ri·ly,** *adv.* In a desultory manner; without method; loosely.—**des·ul·to·ri·ness,** *n.*

de·tach, di·tach′, *v.t.* [Fr. *détacher,* O.Fr. *destachier.*] To unfasten and separate; disengage; disunite. *Milit.* to separate, as a number of troops from a main body, for a special purpose; send away on a special mission, as a regiment or ship.—**de·tach·a·ble,** *a.*—**de·tach·a·bil·i·ty,** di·tach″a·bil′i·tē, *n.*—**de·tach·er,** *n.*

de·tached, di·tacht′, *a.* Separated or disengaged; separate; unattached; standing apart; impartial; as, a *detached* opinion.

de·tach·ment, di·tach′ment, *n.* The act of detaching, or the condition of being detached; a state of aloofness, as from worldly affairs, or from the concerns of others; objectivity or impartiality; something detached, as a number of troops separated from a main body for special service.

de·tail, di·tāl′, *v.t.* [Fr. *détailler,* to cut in pieces—*de-,* and *tailler,* L.L. *taleare, taliare,* to cut, < L. *talea,* a cutting.] To relate, report, or narrate in particulars; to enumerate one by one the particulars of; *milit.* to appoint to a particular service; to decorate with a fine design.

de·tail, di·tāl′, dē′tāl, *n.* An item; a particular; the treatment of items or particulars; *art,* a minor part or element considered essential to the total effect. *Milit.* an individual or small body; a small detachment on special duty.—**in de·tail,** item by item; individually; part by part.

de·tailed, di·tāld′, dē′tāld, *a.* Characterized by many particulars; having details treated thoroughly; exact.

de·tail man, *n.* A representative of a manufacturer of drugs and other medical supplies who calls on physicians, pharmacists, and medical institutions to promote the sale of products.

de·tain, di·tān′, *v.t.* [Fr. *détenir,* L. *detineo,* to detain.] To keep or restrain from proceeding; to hinder; to hold in custody; *archaic,* to keep back or from; to withhold. —**de·tain·ment,** *n.*

de·tain·er, di·tā′nėr, *n.* [A.Fr. *detener,* inf., O.Fr. *detenir.*] *Law,* the detaining or keeping possession of what belongs to another; the detaining of a person in custody; a writ for the further detention of a person already in custody; detention.

de·tect, di·tekt′, *v.t.* [L. *detectus,* pp. of *detegere,* uncover, discover, < *de-* and *tegere,* cover.] To discover or catch in the performance of some act, as a criminal; to find out the action or character of; as, to *detect* a hypocrite; to bring to light; discover the presence, existence, or fact of; *radio,* to subject to the action of a detector. —**de·tect·a·ble, de·tect·i·ble,** *a.*

de·tec·ta·phone, di·tek′ta·fōn″, *n.* A sensitive device used to transmit telephone conversations, as of persons under suspicion, so that they may be heard in another room or place.

de·tec·tion, di·tek′shan, *n.* [L.L. *detectio(n-).*] The act of detecting, or the fact of being detected; discovery, as of an error or crime. *Radio,* demodulation.

de·tec·tive, di·tek′tiv, *n.* A member of the police force whose function is it secretly to obtain information and evidence, as of offenses against the law; a person employed unofficially by individuals for secret investigations and protection.—*a.* Serving to detect; having the function of detecting; pertaining to detection or detectives; as, a *detective* story.

de·tec·tor, di·tek′ter, *n.* [L.L.] One who or that which detects; any of various instruments or devices for indicating the presence or the state of a thing. *Radio,* a device for detecting electric oscillations or waves; specif. a device which rectifies the alternating currents in a radio receiver; as, a crystal *detector* of a vacuum-tube.

de·tent, di·tent′, *n.* [L. *detentus,* a keeping back.] A pin, stud, or lever which halts or releases for action a part of a clock, or other machine; a lock.

dé·tente, dā·tänt′, *Fr.* dā·täNt′, *n.* pl. **dé·tentes.** A thaw in tension, as between two countries; a lessening of hostility.

de·ten·tion, di·ten′shan, *n.* [L.L. *detentio(n-),* < *detinere.*] The act of detaining, or the state of being detained; forced stoppage; a keeping in custody; confinement; the withholding of what belongs to or is claimed by another.—*a.* Of, pertaining to, or used for the purpose of detention; as, a *detention* camp.

de·ter, di·tụr´, v.t.—deterred, deterring. [L. deterreo, to frighten from, to prevent—de, from, and terreo, to frighten.] To discourage and prevent from acting or proceeding, when there is a supposed or real difficulty or danger ahead.—**de·ter·ment**, n.—**de·ter·rent**, a. Intended or tending to deter; restraining.—n. Something that deters; known superiority in military strength, weaponry, or retaliatory capacity sufficient to restrain a potential aggressor.

de·terge, di·tụrj´, v.t.—deterged, deterging. [L. detergeo.] To cleanse; to wash or clear away unclean or offending matter from.

de·ter·gen·cy, di·tụr´jen·sē, n. The state or quality of being detergent; cleansing or purging power. Also **de·ter·gence**.

de·ter·gent, di·tụr´jent, a. Cleansing; purging.—n. Anything that has a strong cleansing power, as soap, a chemical substance, or a synthetic preparation having cleansing properties; an oil-soluble substance used in lubricating oil.

de·te·ri·o·rate, di·tēr´ē·o·rāt″, v.i.—deteriorated, deteriorating. [L. deterioro, deterioratum, < deterior, worse, < de, as exterior < ex, interior < in.] To grow worse or inferior in quality, value, or character; to be impaired in quality; to degenerate; to decompose.—v.t. To make worse; to reduce in quality.—**de·te·ri·o·ra·tion**, di·tēr″ē·o·rā´shan, n.—**de·te·ri·o·ra·tive**, a.

de·ter·mi·na·ble, di·tụr´mi·na·bl, a. Capable of being determined, ascertained, or decided; law, liable to be brought to a conclusion.—**de·ter·mi·na·ble·ness**, n.—**de·ter·mi·na·bly**, adv.—**de·ter·mi·na·cy**, n.

de·ter·mi·nant, di·tụr´mi·nant, n. That which determines or causes determination; math. a square algebraic array of quantities called elements, which symbolizes the sum of specified products of these elements.

de·ter·mi·nate, di·tụr´mi·nit, a. [L. determinatus.] Limited; fixed; definite; established; settled; positive; decisive, conclusive; fixed in purpose; resolute; bot. of cyme or inflorescence, restricted in further growth.—v.t.—determinated, determinating. To ascertain; to clearly establish the identity of.—**de·ter·mi·nate·ly**, adv.—**de·ter·mi·nate·ness**, n.

de·ter·mi·na·tion, di·tụr´mi·nā´shan, n. The act of deciding; firm resolution; settled purpose; the mental habit of settling upon some line of action with a fixed purpose to adhere to it; adherence to aims or purposes; resoluteness; the act of establishing or verifying a position, quality, or certain information after careful examination; law, a decision concluding a controversy; the fixing of the character, position, extent, or amount of anything; biol. the ascertaining of the classification of a plant or animal; logic, the definition of a concept according to its component parts; the addition of distinguishing factors to narrow the meaning of a concept; an inclination or proceeding toward a particular end or object.—**de·ter·mi·na·tive**, di·tēr´mi·nā″tiv, di·tēr´mi·na·tiv, a. Having power to determine or direct to a certain end; directing; limiting; bounding.—n. Something that serves to determine.—**de·ter·mi·na·tive·ly**, adv.—**de·ter·mi·na·tive·ness**, n.—**de·ter·mi·na·tor**, n.

de·ter·mine, di·tụr´min, v.t.—determined, determining. [L. determino.] To settle, fix, establish; to end or settle conclusively, as by the resolution of a doubtful or controverted point; to settle ultimately; to come to a fixed resolution and intention in respect of; to set bounds or limits to; to give a bent or direction to; to influence the choice of; to cause to come to a conclusion or resolution; to ascertain, as after investigation or reasoning; to cause or regulate;

chiefly law, to bring to an end; logic, to qualify by the addition of differentials.—v.i. To resolve; to decide; to settle on some line of conduct; chiefly law, to terminate.

de·ter·mined, di·tụr´mind, a. Having a firm or fixed purpose; manifesting firmness or resolution; resolute; decided.—**de·ter·mined·ly**, adv.—**de·ter·mined·ness**, n.

de·ter·min·er, di·tụr´mi·nẽr, n. One who or that which decides or determines; gram. a limiting adjective, modifying a noun, and typically placed before a descriptive adjective; as, an excellent idea; your handsome son.

de·ter·min·ism, di·tụr´mi·niz″um, n. Philos. the doctrine that all existences and happenings are the inevitable outcome of preceding conditions, and esp. that man's actions are not based on a free will, but are determined by inherited or environmental influences.—**de·ter·min·ist**, n., a.—**de·ter·min·is·tic**, di·tụr´mi·nis´tik, a.—**de·ter·min·is·ti·cally**, adv.

de·ter·rent, di·tụr´ent, a., n. See deter.—**de·ter·rence**, n.

de·ter·sive, di·tụr´siv, a. Having power to cleanse; cleansing.—n. That which has the power of cleansing; a detergent.

de·test, di·test´, v.t. [L. detestor, to invoke a deity in cursing, to detest—de-, intens., and testor, to call to witness, < testis, a witness.] To abhor; to abominate; to hate extremely.—**de·test·a·ble**, di·tes´ta·bl, a. Extremely hateful; abominable; very odious; deserving abhorrence.—**de·test·a·ble·ness**, **de·test·a·bil·i·ty**, di·tes″ta·bil´i·tē, n.—**de·test·a·bly**, adv.—**de·test·er**, n.

de·tes·ta·tion, dē´te·stā´shan, n. Extreme hatred; abhorrence; a person or thing loathed.

de·throne, dē·thrōn´, v.t.—dethroned, dethroning. To remove or drive from a throne; to depose.—**de·throne·ment**, n.—**de·thron·er**, n.

det·i·nue, det´i·nö″, det´i·nū″, n. [O.Fr. detenue, detention, orig. pp. fem. of detenir, E. detain.] Law, the unlawful detention of personal property, or a common-law action to recover the property so detained.

det·o·nate, det´o·nāt″, v.i.—detonated, detonating. [L. detonatus, pp. of detonare, thunder forth, < de-, from, and tonare, thunder.] To explode suddenly and violently.—v.t. To cause to explode.—**det·o·na·ble**, a. Tending to detonate; explosive. Also **det·o·nat·a·ble**.

det·o·na·tion, det″o·nā´shan, n. The act of detonating; an explosion.

det·o·na·tor, det´o·nā″tẽr, n. A device that explodes; a device, as a percussion cap, or an explosive, used for causing another substance to explode.

de·tour, dē´tụr, di·tụr´, n. [Fr.] The use of an alternate road when a more direct road is impassable; a roundabout or circuitous way; a deviation from a direct route or course of action.—v.i. To make a detour.—v.t. To cause to make a detour.

de·tox·i·cate, dē·tok´si·kāt″, v.t.—detoxicated, detoxicating. Detoxify.—**de·tox·i·ca·tion**, dē·tok″si·ka´shan, n.

de·tox·i·fy, dē·tok´si·fī″, v.t.—detoxified, detoxifying. To remove poisonous qualities or effects from.—**de·tox·i·fi·ca·tion**, dē·tok″si·fi·kā´shan, n.

de·tract, di·trakt´, v.t. [L. detracto.] To divert or distract.—v.i. To take away a part, lessen, as: Her gaudy clothes detract from her beauty.—**de·tract·ing·ly**, adv.—**de·trac·tor**, n. One who disparages.

de·trac·tion, di·trak´shan, n. [L. detractio.] The act of detracting; disparagement of, or injury to, the reputation of another; envious or malicious deprecation of a person, or denial of his merits.—**de·trac·tive**, a.—**de·trac·tive·ly**, adv.

de·train, dē·trān´, v.t. To cause to leave a train; as, to detrain troops.—v.i. To leave a railroad train.

de·trib·al·ize, dē·trī´ba·līz″, v.t.—detribalized, detribalizing. To cause a breakdown of tribal unity, allegiances, customs, and organization, generally through exposure to another culture.—**de·trib·al·i·za·tion**, dē·trī″ba·li·zā´shan, n.

det·ri·ment, de´tri·ment, n. [L. detrimentum, loss, damage, < deterere, rub away.] Loss, damage, or injury; that which causes loss, damage, or injury.—**det·ri·men·tal**, de″tra·men´tal, a. Causing damage or loss; injurious; prejudicial.—n. A damaging, harmful, or undesirable person or thing.—**det·ri·men·tal·ly**, adv.

de·tri·tion, di·trish´an, n. [L. deterere (pp. detritus).] The act of wearing away by rubbing.

de·tri·tus, di·trī´tus, n. [L. detritus, n., a rubbing away, < deterere (pp. detritus), rub away, < de-, from, and terere, rub.] Particles of rock or other material worn away from a mass, as by the action of water; any disintegrated material; debris; as, the layer of detritus on the bottom of the Atlantic ocean.—**de·tri·tal**, a.

de·trude, di·trōd´, v.t.—detruded, detruding. [L. detrudo—de-, down, and trudo, to thrust.] To thrust down or away; to push down.—**de·tru·sion**, di·trö´zhan, n. The act of thrusting or driving down.

de·trun·cate, di·trung´kāt, v.t.—detruncated, detruncating. [L. detrunco.] To cut off; to lop; to shorten by cutting off a piece.—**de·trun·ca·tion**, dē″trung·kā´shan, n.

deuce, dös, dūs, n. [O.Fr. deus (Fr. deux), < L. duos, acc. masc. of duo, two.] In card games or dice, two; a card, or the side of a die, having two spots; slang, two dollars; tennis, a stage of the score when each side has gained three points or the score 40 in a game, or five games in a set, and either side must gain two more points or games in succession to win.—a. Two.

deuce, dös, dūs, n. [M.E. deus, identical with E. deuce (the two at dice being the lowest and worst throw).] The devil: used in mild imprecations, as: Where the deuce did you find that hat?

deuc·ed, dö´sid, dū´sid, döst, dūst, a. Brit. colloq. devilish; excessive.—adv.—**deuc·ed·ly**, dö´sid·lē, dū´sid·lē, adv.

deuc·es wild, n. A variety of poker and other card games in which each deuce may be used to represent any other card named by the holder.

deu·ter·ag·o·nist, dö″te·rag´o·nist, dū″·te·rag´o·nist, n. [Gr. deuteragonistes, < deuteros, second, and agonistes, contender, actor, E. agonist.] In ancient Greek drama, the character of second importance after the protagonist: often the antagonist.

deu·ter·an·o·pi·a, dö″tẽr·a·nō´pē·a, dū″·tẽr·a·nō´pē·a, n. A type of color blindness in which a person cannot distinguish green and red.—**deu·ter·an·ope**, dö´tẽr·a·nōp″, dū″tẽr·a·nōp″, n. A person who has deuteranopia.

deu·te·ri·um, dö·tēr´ē·um, dū·tēr´ē·um, n. [N.L., < Gr. deuteros, second.] Phys., chem. a nonradioactive isotope of hydrogen that has twice the mass of ordinary hydrogen; the nucleus of an atom of deuterium, containing one neutron and one proton. Also **heav·y hy·dro·gen**.

deu·te·ri·um ox·ide, n. Chem. heavy water, D_2O.

deu·ter·o·ca·non·i·cal, dö´te·rō·ka··non´i·kal, dū″te·rō·ka·non´i·kal, dö″te·rō·ka·non´i·kal, dū″te·rō·ka·non´i·kal, a. Of or forming a second canon; the books of the Bible received by the Roman Catholic Church and regarded by it as canonical, commonly known as the Apocrypha.

deu·ter·og·a·my, dö″te·rog′a·mē, dū″-te·rog′a·mē, *n.* [Gr. *deuteros*, second, and *gamos*, marriage.] A second marriage after the death or divorce of the first husband or wife.—**deu·ter·og·a·mist,** *n.* One who marries a second time.

deu·ter·on, dö′te·ron″, dū′te·ron″, *n. Phys.* the nucleus of the deuterium atom; a nuclear particle with one positive charge, and a mass number 2.

deu·to·plasm, dö′to·plaz″um, dū′to·plaz″um, *n. Biol.* that portion of the yolk of ova which furnishes nourishment for the embryo.

deut·sche mark, doi′che märk, *n.* See Money table.

deut·zi·a, döt′sē·a, dūt′sē·a, doit′sē·a, *n.* [N.L.; from J. *Deutz*, Dutch patron of botanic sciences.] Any of the shrubs constituting the saxifragaceous genus *Deutzia*, bearing white or pink bell-shaped flowers, much cultivated for ornament.

de·va, dev, dā′va, däv, *n.* [Skt.] *Hindu mythol.* a god or divinity; one of an order of good spirits.

de·val·u·ate, dē·val′ū·āt″, *v.t.*—*devaluated, devaluating.* To reduce the value of; to fix a lower legal value on (currency).—**de·val·u·a·tion,** dē·val′ū·ā′shan, *n.*—**de·val·ue,** *v.t.*—*devalued, devaluing.*

De·va·na·ga·ri, dā″va·nä′ga·rē″, *n.* In India, an alphabet used for writing Sanskrit, Hindi, and some other languages. Also **Na·ga·ri,** nä′ga·rē.

dev·as·tate, dev′a·stāt″, *v.t.*—*devastated, devastating.* [L. *devasto, devastatum*, to lay waste—*de-*, intens., and *vasto*, to lay waste.] To lay waste; to ravage; to desolate; to get the better of; to conquer.—**dev·as·ta·tion,** dev″a·stā′shan, *n.* [L. *devastatio.*]—**dev·as·ta·tor,** *n.*—**dev·as·ta·tive,** *a.*

de·vel·op, di·vel′up, *v.t.* [Fr. *développer*, O.Fr. *desvoloper*—prefix *des-*, L. *dis-*, apart.] To gradually acquire, as a taste; to cause to evolve to a higher or more useful stage; to bring about growth or enlargement; to cause to become active; to unfold gradually; as, to *develop* an idea; to disclose or show all the ramifications of; *biol.* to make to pass through the process of natural evolution; *photog.* to bring out the latent image on a sensitized surface by the action of chemical agents; *mus.* to work out and expand, as a musical idea; *math.* in a series, to express in an extended form.—*v.i.* To advance from one stage to another by a process of natural or inherent evolution; to grow or expand by a natural process; to be evolved; to increase capabilities and become more mature; to be disclosed; to become manifest in all its parts.—**de·vel·op·a·ble,** *a.*

de·vel·op·er, di·vel′o·pêr, *n.* One who or that which develops; a chemical used to develop photographs; an individual who invests in and develops real estate by building homes.

de·vel·op·ment, di·vel′up·ment, *n.* The act or process of developing; unfolding; the unraveling of a plot; a gradual growth or advancement through progressive changes; the organic changes which take place in animal and vegetable bodies, from their embryo state until they arrive at maturity; *photog.* the process following exposure, by which the image on the plate is rendered visible; *mus.* the portion of a musical composition in which a theme is developed; a large group of similarly constructed homes or apartments, usu. built by the same builder.

de·vest, di·vest′, *v.t.* [Obs. Fr. *devestir* (Fr. *dévêtir*), O.Fr. *desvestir*, < L. *vestire*, clothe.] *Law*, to deprive of a right or title, or to take away(a right or title); divest.

de·vi·ance, dē′vē·ans, *n.* A condition, quality, or behavior which differs from an accepted standard. Also **de·vi·an·cy.**

de·vi·ate, dē′vē·āt″, *v.i.*—*deviated, deviating.* [L. *devio, deviatum*—*de-*, from, and *via*, way.] To turn aside or wander from the common or right way, course, or line; to diverge; to err; to swerve; to vary from a uniform state.—*v.t.* To cause to deviate.

de·vi·ate, dē′vē·it, *a.* Differing or departing from the prevailing behavior patterns of a given society. Also **de·vi·ant.**—*n.* Something or someone differing from a norm; a person differing, as in social attitudes or practices, from the standards of his group; an item in a statistical series which is markedly different from the norm. Also **de·vi·ant.**

de·vi·a·tion, dē″vē·ā′shan, *n.* A turning aside from the right way, course, or line; variation from a common or established rule or standard; *navig.* the deviation of a ship's compass from the true magnetic meridian, caused by the near presence of magnetism.

de·vice, di·vīs′, *n.* [O.Fr. *devise*, a device; Fr. *deviser*, to imagine, devise; < L. *divido, divisum*, to divide.] That which is formed by design or invented for a specific use; a scheme, contrivance, stratagem, project; something fancifully conceived, as an ornamental design; an emblematic design, such as a family or institutional crest; *usu. pl.* desire, will, or inclination, as: He would be an artist, if left to his own *devices.*

dev·il, dev′il, *n.* [O.E. *deófol*, < L. *diabolus*, Gr. *diabolos*, the accuser, < *diaballō*, to accuse.] An evil spirit or being; (*sometimes cap.*) the evil one, represented in Scripture as the traducer, tempter, and leader or ruler of hell. A very wicked person; a dashing, somewhat reckless, energetic person; an unfortunate, wretched person; as, poor *devil*; a printer's errand boy; a machine, as for cutting up rags and old cloth or preparing material for carding; anything very difficult or annoying.—**the dev·il,** an expletive expressing surprise, anger, or annoyance.—**dev·il·ish,** *a.* Having qualities of the devil; pertaining to the devil; diabolical; evil or mischievous; excessive.—**dev·il·ish, dev·il·ish·ly,** *adv.*—**dev·il·ish·ness,** *n.*—**dev·il·ment,** *n.* Trickery, roguishness; prank.—**dev·il·try,** *n.* pl. **dev·il·tries.** Extreme wickedness; reckless mischief; evil witchcraft. Also **dev·il·ry.**

dev·il, dev′il, *v.t.*—*deviled, deviling, Brit. devilled, devilling.* To season highly and chop fine, as in preparing food; *colloq.* to tease or pester; to cut up by an instrument called a devil.

dev·il·fish, dev′il·fish″, *n.* Any of various giant rays, genus *Manta* or *Mobula*, found in tropical seas; any large cephalopod, especially the octopus.

dev·il-may-care, dev′il·mā·kâr′, *a.* Unconcerned with consequences; reckless; happy-go-lucky; jaunty.

dev·il's ad·vo·cate, *n. R. Cath. Ch.* a person appointed to raise arguments against claims for beatification or canonization. One who defends a bad cause or argues an opposing position in order to stimulate argument.

dev·il's food cake, *n.* [Named for its stark color contrast to angel food cake.] A very rich chocolate cake.

dev·il's paint·brush, *n.* Any of several European hawkweeds found growing as weeds in the eastern U.S.

dev·il·wood, dev′il·wụd″, *n.* A small, hardwood tree, *Osmanthus americanus*, of the olive family, found in the southern U.S.

de·vi·ous, dē′vē·us, *a.* [L. *devius.*] Circuitous or indirect; rambling; erring or going astray; deceptive or tricky.—**de·vi·ous·ly,** *adv.*—**de·vi·ous·ness,** *n.*

de·vise, di·vīz′, *v.t.*—*devised, devising.* [Fr. *deviser*, to devise or invent, to dispose of; DEVICE.] To invent, contrive, or form in the mind; to plan; to scheme or plot; *law*, to

give or bequeath, as property, esp. real property, by will.—*v.i.* To lay a plan; to form a scheme.—**de·vis·a·ble,** *a.* Capable of being contrived or being bequeathed. **de·vis·al,** *n.* The act of bequeathing or of contriving.

de·vise, di·vīz′, *n. Law*, the act of bequeathing real property by will; a will or testament, or portion of such, disposing of real property; a share of an estate bequeathed.—**de·vi·see,** di·vī·zē′, dev′i·zē′, *n. Law*, the person to whom a devise is made.—**de·vi·sor,** di·vī′zêr, *n. Law*, one who devises property in a will.

de·vi·tal·ize, dē·vīt′a·līz″, *v.t.*—*devitalized, devitalizing.* To deprive of vitality; to weaken.—**de·vi·tal·i·za·tion,** dē·vī″ta·li·zā′shan, *n.*

de·vit·ri·fy, dē·vi′tri·fī″, *v.t.*—*devitrified, devitrifying.* To deprive of the character or transparent appearance of glass.—**de·vit·ri·fi·ca·tion,** dē·vi″tri·fi·kā′shan, *n.*

de·vo·cal·ize, dē·vō′ka·līz″, *v.t.*—*devocalized, devocalizing. Phon.* to deprive of vocal or sonant quality, as: The voiced *s* in the verb *close* is *devocalized* in the adverb *close*.—**de·vo·cal·i·za·tion,** dē·vō″ka·li·zā′shan, *n.*

de·void, di·void′, *a.* [Orig. pp. of obs. *devoid, v.,* < O.Fr. *desvuidier*, empty out.] Empty, void, or destitute, usually with *of.*

de·voir, de·vwär′, dev′wär, *Fr.* de·vwär′, *n.* [Fr. < L. *debere*, to owe, whence *debt.*] An act of civility or respect; duty; *pl.* respects or compliments paid as an obligation.

dev·o·lu·tion, dev″o·lö′shan, *n.* [M.L. *devolutio(n-)*, < L. *devolvere.* DEVOLVE.] The act or fact of devolving; passage onward from stage to stage; the transmitting or passing of property by inheritance or succession; the passing on to a successor of an unexercised right; the delegation of duty or responsibility to another; *biol.* degeneration, as opposed to *evolution.*

de·volve, di·volv′, *v.t.*—*devolved, devolving.* [L.] To transfer or delegate, as a duty or responsibility to another; to pass on; to hand down.—*v.i.*

Dev·on, dev′on, *n.* One of a noted breed of cattle, usually of a red color, originating in Devonshire, England.

De·vo·ni·an, de·vō′nē·an, *a.* Of or pertaining to Devonshire, England; *geol.* a term applied to the fourth period of the Paleozoic era, which preceded the Silurian period and was followed by the Mississippian period; pertaining to the rock strata of this period.—*n. Geol.* the Devonian system.

Dev·on·shire cream, *n. Brit.* a cream that has been clotted, or thickened, by cooking.

de·vote, di·vōt′, *v.t.*—*devoted, devoting.* [L. *devoveo, devotum*, to vow anything to a deity, to devote.] To give(one's complete attention)or to apply(one's time)zealously to some activity, pursuit, or cause; to dedicate by a solemn act; to consecrate.—**de·vote·ment,** *n.*

de·vot·ed, di·vō′tid, *a.* Feeling or displaying devotion; ardent or zealous; loyal, dedicated; devout.—**de·vot·ed·ly,** *adv.*—**de·vot·ed·ness,** *n.*

dev·o·tee, dev″o·tē′, *n.* One who is wholly devoted; one who is absorbed in religious duties and ceremonies; a fervent admirer.

de·vo·tion, di·vō′shan, *n.* [O.Fr. *devocion* (Fr. *dévotion*), < L. *devotio(n-)*, < *devovere.* DEVOTE.] The act of devoting, or the state of being devoted; dedication; consecration; zealousness in religious observance or worship; *usually pl.* an act of worship or prayer. Earnest attachment to a cause or person.—**de·vo·tion·al·ism,** *n.* The quality or state of one exhibiting marked religious devotion.—**de·vo·tion·al·ist,** *n.*

de·vo·tion·al, di·vō′sha·nal, *a.* Pertaining to or characterized by devotion; used in religious worship.—*n.* A worship service.—**de·vo·tion·al·ly**, *adv.*

de·vour, di·vour′, *v.t.* [O.Fr. *devorer* (Fr. *dévorer*), < L. *devorare*.] To eat up voraciously, ravenously, or greedily; to consume destructively, recklessly, or wantonly; to destroy or waste; to swallow up or engulf; to take in greedily with the senses or intellect; to absorb or engross wholly.—**de·vour·er**, *n.*—**de·vour·ing·ly**, *adv.*—**de·vour·ing·ness**, *n.*

de·vout, di·vout′, *a.* [Fr. *dévot*, devout; L. *devotus.* DEVOTE.] Displaying a solemn and reverential devotion to religion and religious exercises; expressing religious devotion or piety; warmly devoted; sincere.—**de·vout·ly**, *adv.* In a devout manner; piously; religiously; earnestly.—**de·vout·ness**, *n.*

dew, dö, dū, *n.* [O.E. *deáw*, D. *dauw*, Dan. *dug*, G. *thau*—dew.] The aqueous vapor or moisture which is deposited in small drops, especially during the night, from the atmosphere, on the surfaces of bodies when they have become colder than the surrounding atmosphere; something fresh as dew.—*v.t.* To wet with dew; to bedew.—**dew·drop**, *n.* A drop of dew.

Dew·ar flask, dō′ar flask, dō′ar fläsk, dū′ar fläsk, *n.* [After its inventor, Scottish scientist Sir James *Dewar*.] A double-walled vessel that keeps its contents at a near constant temperature by means of a vacuum created between its outer and inner walls and a silvered interior to prevent heat transfer; a prototype of the present-day thermos and originally developed to keep gases in a liquefied state. Also **Dew·ar ves·sel, Dew·ar**.

dew·ber·ry, dö′ber″ē, dō′be·rē, dū′ber″ē, dū′be·rē, *n. pl.* **dew·ber·ries**. The sweet, edible fruit of any of several species of trailing plants, genus *Rubus*, related to and resembling blackberries; the plant bearing such fruit.

dew·claw, dö′klǎ″, dū′klǎ″, *n.* A functionless inner claw or digit on the foot of some dogs, cats, and other mammals, not reaching the ground in walking; an analogous false hoof of deer, hogs, and the like.

Dew·ey dec·i·mal clas·si·fi·ca·tion, *n.* [Named for Melvil *Dewey*, U.S. librarian.] *Library science*, the system of classification of books and other printed matter in ten basic categories which are subdivided and labeled with a decimal system. Also **Dew·ey dec·i·mal sys·tem, dec·i·mal clas·si·fi·ca·tion**.

dew·fall, dō′fǎl″, dū′fǎl″, *n.* The formation or deposition of dew; the time when this begins in the evening.

dew·lap, dō′lap″, dū′lap″, *n.* The fold of skin that hangs from the throat of oxen or cows, or a similar appendage in other animals.—**dew·lapped**, *a.*

DEW line, *n.* [< (*D*)istant (*E*)arly (*W*)arning.] A line of radar stations at about the seventieth parallel of the N. American continent, designed for distant early warning of the approach of foreign aircraft.

dew point, *n.* The temperature at which the air becomes saturated with moisture; the temperature at which dew will form; an indicator of humidity. Also **dew-point tem·per·a·ture**.

dew worm, *n.* A long, thick earthworm used as bait; a night-crawler.

dew·y, dö′ē, dū′ē, *a.*—*dewier, dewiest*. Of or pertaining to dew; like dew; moist with, or as with, dew; falling gently, or refreshing, like dew; as, *dewy* sleep.—**dew·i·ly**, *adv.*—**dew·i·ness**, *n.*

dew·y-eyed, dō′ē·īd″, dū′ē·īd″, *a.* Showing youthful innocence and idealism; having a fresh and untouched appearance; naïve and trusting.

dex·ter, dek′stėr, *a.* [L. *dexter*, right, on the right, dexterous, favorable.] Pertaining to or situated on the right side; right; right-hand. *Her.* on the right of an escutcheon situated to the right of the bearer, and hence to the left of the spectator: opposed to *sinister*.

dex·ter·i·ty, dek·stėr′i·tē, *n.* [L. *dexteritas.*] The quality of being dexterous; manual adroitness or skill; adroitness in the use of the body generally; mental adroitness or skill; cleverness; right-handedness.

dex·ter·ous, dek′strus, dek′stėr·us, *a.* [L. *dexter.*] Having skill with the hands; adroit or skillful in bodily movements generally; deft; nimble; having mental adroitness or skill; clever; done with or exhibiting dexterity; right-handed, or using the right hand in preference to the left. Also **dex·trous**.—**dex·ter·ous·ly, dex·trous·ly**, *adv.*—**dex·ter·ous·ness, dex·trous·ness**, *n.*

dex·trad, dek′strad, *adv.* [L. *dexter*, right.] *Anat., zool.* to the right: opposed to *sinistrad*.

dex·tral, dek′stral, *a.* [L. *dexter*, right.] Of or pertaining to the right side; right; right-handed; of a spiral shell, having the whorl rising from left to right, as viewed from the outside.—**dex·tral·ly**, *adv.*

dex·tran, dek′stran, *n. Chem.* a white gum-like substance, produced by bacterial action and used as a blood plasma substitute.

dex·trin, dex·trine, dek′strin, dek′strēn, *n.* [L. *dexter*, right.] A group of water soluble gummy substances formed from starch by the action of heat or weak acids, used as an adhesive, a substitute for gum arabic, or for sizing paper and textiles.

dex·tro, dek′strō, *a. Chem.* dextrorotatory.

dex·tro·glu·cose, dek″strō·glö′kōs, *n. Chem.* dextrose.

dex·tro·gy·rate, dek″strō·jī′rit, dek″strō·jī′rāt, *a. Optics, crystal.* dextrorotatory.

dex·tro·ro·ta·tion, dek″strō·rō·tā′shan, *n. Optics, crystal.* a turning of the plane of polarization of light to the right.

dex·tro·ro·ta·to·ry, dek″strō·rō′ta·tōr″ē, dek″strō·rō′ta·tạr″ē, *a. Optics, crystal. chem.* turning or causing to turn toward the right or in a clockwise direction, as the plane of polarization of light in certain crystals and compounds. Also **dex·tro·ro·ta·tary**.

dex·trorse, dek′strạrs, dek·strạs′, *a.* [L. *dextrorsum*, toward the right side—*dexter*, right, and *vorsum*, for *versum*, turned.] *Bot.* turned toward the right; rising from left to right, as a spiral line, helix, or climbing plant. Also **dex·tror·sal**.

dex·trose, dek′strōs, *n. Chem.* the sugar found in blood and in many plants; corn sugar. Also *dextroglucose*.

dhar·ma, där′ma, dur′ma, *n.* [Skt. *dharma*.] *Hinduism, Buddhism*, law, or conformity to law, esp. religious law; religion; virtue; essential character; religious duty; rules of conduct as laid down in sacred writings.

dhar·na, dhur·na, där′na, dur′na, dėr′na, *n.* [Hind. *dharnā*.] The practice, in India, of sitting at a person's door without tasting food until he complies with some demand, as for payment of a debt, for a raise in wages, or the like; as, to sit *dharna*; something of the nature of a 'sit-in' practiced by some demonstrators in U.S. to get their grievances redressed.

dhow, dow, dou, *n.* An Arab vessel, generally lateen-rigged, employed in mercantile trading; in ancient days, used for carrying slaves from the east coast of Africa to the Persian Gulf and the Red Sea.

di·a·base, dī′a·bās″, *n. U.S.* a minor intrusive rock, esp. of labradorite and pyroxene; *Brit.* a dark-colored igneous rock consisting essentially of augite and feldspar.—**di·a·ba·sic**, dī″a·bā′sik, *a.*

di·a·be·tes, dī″a·bē′tis, dī″a·bē′tēz, *n.* [N.L. < Gr. *diabētēs, diabainein*, go through.] *Pathol.* any one of various abnormal urinary conditions, esp. diabetes mellitus.—**di·a·be·tes mel·li·tus**, dī″a·bē′tis me·lī′tus, dī″a·bē′tēz me·lī′tus, *n. Pathol.* a chronic disease characterized by excessive sugar in the blood and intermittent or continued presence of sugar in the urine, increased excretion of urine and accompanying thirst, and often by increased appetite plus weight loss, alleviated by regular injection of insulin.—**di·a·be·tes in·sip·i·dus**, dī″a·bē′tis in·sip′i·dus, dī″a·bē′tēz in·sip′i·dus, *n. Pathol.* a disease characterized by chronic excretion of large amounts of unconcentrated urine and extreme thirst, alleviated by a pituitary hormone extract.—**di·a·bet·ic**, dī″a·bet′ik, dī″a·bē′tik, *a.* Of, pertaining to, or affected with diabetes.—*n.* A person suffering from diabetes.

di·a·ble·rie, di·a·ble·ry, dē·ä′ble·rē, *Fr.* dyä·ble·rē′, *n. pl.* **di·a·ble·ries**. [Fr. *diablerie*, < *diable*, devil.] Devilry; mischief; wickedness; sorcery; witchcraft.

di·a·bol·ic, dī″a·bol′ik, *a.* [L. *diabolus*, the devil.] Devilish; pertaining to the devil; infernal; impious; atrocious.—**di·a·bol·i·cal**, *a.*—**di·a·bol·i·cal·ly**, *adv.*—**di·a·bol·i·cal·ness**, *n.*

di·ab·o·lism, dī·ab′o·liz″um, *n.* [Gr. *diabolos*, E. *devil.*] *Theol.* action aided by the devil; sorcery; witchcraft; action befitting the devil; deviltry; doctrine concerning devils; belief in or worship of devils. The character or condition of a devil.—**di·ab·o·list**, *n.*

di·ab·o·lize, dī·ab′o·liz″, *v.t.*—*diabolized, diabolus*, E. *devil.*] A game consisting of represent as diabolical; subject to diabolical influence.

di·ab·o·lo, dē·ab′o·lō″, *n.* [It., < L.L. *diabolus*, E. *devil.*] A game consisting of rotating, tossing, and catching a piece of wood shaped like a top, by means of a cord fastened at the ends of two sticks held in the hands; the piece of wood used in this sport.

di·a·chron·ic, dī″a·kron′ik, *a.* Dealing with the study of language changes over a period of time; historical.

di·a·cid, dī·as′id, *a. Chem.* capable of combining with two molecules of a monobasic acid; containing two replaceable hydrogen atoms.—*n.*

di·ac·o·nal, dī·ak′o·nal, *a.* [L. *diaconus*, Gr. *diakonos*, a deacon.] *Eccles.* pertaining to a deacon.—**di·ac·o·nate**, dī·ak′o·nit, dī·ak′o·nāt, *n.* The office of a deacon; a body of deacons.

di·a·crit·ic, dī″a·krit′ik, *a.* [Gr. *diakritkos, diakrinein*, separate one from another.] Serving to distinguish.—*n.* A modifying mark, point, or sign.—**di·a·crit·i·cal**, dī″a·krit′i·kal, *a.* Distinctive; capable of distinguishing or discerning.—**di·a·crit·i·cal mark, point**, or **sign**, *n.* A symbol added or put adjacent to a letter or character to distinguish it from another of similar form, to give it a particular phonetic value or to indicate stress, as a circumflex.—**di·a·crit·i·cal·ly**, *adv.*

di·a·dem, dī′a·dem″, *n.* [Gr. *diadēma*—*dia*, and *deō*, to bind.] A crown; a headband or fillet worn as a badge of royalty; royal power.—*v.t.* To adorn with or as with a diadem; to crown.

di·ad·ro·mous, dī·ad′ro·mus, *a. Ichth.* pertaining to fish that migrate between salt and fresh waters; *bot.* describing a leaf having fan-like venation.

di·aer·e·sis, dī·er′i·sis, *n. pl.* **di·aer·e·ses**. [Gr. *diairesis*, < *diairein*, to divide.] Separation of one syllable into two; a mark which signifies such a division, as the umlaut in naïve, chloë; usu. used to separate the pronunciation of two vowels. Also **di·er·e·sis**.—**di·ae·ret·ic**, dī″e·ret′ik, *a.*

di·a·ge·ot·ro·pism, dī″a·jē·o′tro·piz″um, *n. Bot.* the tendency of plants, or parts of plants such as the roots, to grow at a right angle to the direction of gravity. Also

di·a·ge·ot·ro·py.-di·a·ge·o·trop·ic, dī″·a·jē″o·trop′ik, *a.*

di·ag·nose, dī″ag·nōs″, dī′ag·nōz″, dī″ag·nōs′, dī″ag·nōz′, *v.t.—diagnosed, diagnosing. Med.* to ascertain the cause, as of an illness or disease, by studying symptoms. To determine the nature or cause, as of a malfunction, by means of scientific analysis; as, to *diagnose* the noise in a motor; to establish or verify, as the cause or nature of a problem.

di·ag·no·sis, dī″ag·nō′sis, *n.* pl. **di·ag··no·ses,** dī″ag·nō′sēz. [Gr. *diagnōsis—dia-*, through, and *gignōskō*, to know.] *Med.* identifying of diseases by their distinctive marks or symptoms; the conclusion reached; scientific determination of any kind.

di·ag·nos·tic, dī″ag·nos′tik, *a.* Distinguishing; characteristic; indicating the nature of a disease.—*n.* A sign or symptom by which a disease is known.—**di·ag·nos··tics,** *n.* pl. constr. as sing. That branch of medicine dealing with the diagnosis of diseases.—**di·ag·nos·ti·cal·ly,** *adv.*—**di··ag·nos·ti·cian,** dī″ag·no·stish′an, *n.*

di·ag·o·nal, dī·ag′o·nal, *a.* [Gr. *diagōnios*, from angle to angle.] *Math.* extending from one angle to the opposite, nonadjacent angle of a quadrilateral figure and dividing it into two triangles; lying in an oblique direction.—*n.* A straight line drawn between nonadjacent or opposite angles of a quadrilateral, or other polygon; something in a diagonal pattern; cloth woven in a diagonal pattern; a virgule.—**di·ag·o·nal·ly,** *adv.*

di·a·gram, dī′a·gram″, *n.* [Gr. *diagramma —dia*, and *grapho*, to write.] A figure or drawing made for the purpose of demonstrating the properties of any geometrical figure, as a triangle or a circle; a drawing that shows the structure or operation of an object or system.—**di·a·gram·mat·ic,** dī″·a·gra·mat′ik, *a.* Also **di·a·gram·mat·i·cal.**—**di·a·gram·mat·i·cal·ly,** *adv.*

di·a·gram, dī′a·gram″, *v.t.—diagramed, diagraming, Brit. diagrammed, diagramming.* To describe by means of a diagram; to represent by a diagram.

di·al, dī′al, dīl, *n.* [L.L. *dialis*, daily, < L. *dies*, a day.] The face of a watch, clock, or other timekeeper, such as a sundial; any usually circular plate or face with graduations on which a pointer moves to indicate a measurement, as in a gas meter or speedometer; a rotating disk for electrical connection and/or regulation of a device; as, the *dial* of a radio, a telephone *dial.*

di·al, dī′al, dīl, *v.t.—dialed, dialing, Brit. dialled, dialling.* To indicate with, or as with, a dial; to regulate or select by turning a dial; as, to *dial* the radio to a station, to *dial* a telephone number.

di·a·lect, dī′a·lekt″, *n.* [L. *dialectus,* < Gr. *dialektos,* discourse, language, dialect, < *dialegesthai*, converse, discuss, argue.] Manner of speaking; phraseology; idiom; a form of a language prevailing in a particular district, and marked by peculiarities of vocabulary or pronunciation; a special variety or branch of a language, or one of a number of languages regarded as a family; a form of language characteristic of a particular profession or trade.—**di·a·lec··tal,** dī″a·lek′tal, *a.*—**di·a·lec·tal·ly,** *adv.*

di·a·lec·tic, dī″a·lek′tik, *a.* [L. *dialecticus,* < Gr. *dialektikos* (as n., L. *dialectica,* < Gr. *dialektika,* < *dialegesthai*.] Of, pertaining to, or of the nature of logical argumentation; dialectal. Also **di·a·lec··ti·cal,** dī″a·lek′ti·kal.—*n.* The art or practice of logical discussion, as in a question-and-answer dialogue, employed to investigate the truth of a theory or opinion; logical argumentation; *often pl.* logic or a branch of logic; the Hegelian method of investigation, adopted by the dialectical materialists, based on the idea of

opposition between two contradictory but interacting forces (thesis and antithesis) and their continual reconciliation on a higher level (synthesis); that part of Kantian philosophy that admits the futility of trying to apply the perceptions of the mind to objects transcending experience.—**di·a·lec·ti·cian,** dī″a·lek·tish′an, *n.* One skilled in dialectics; a student specializing in dialectics.—**di·a·lec·ti·cism,** dī″a·lek′ti·siz″um, *n.* Dialectical speech or effect; dialectal phraseology.—**di·a·lec·ti·cal·ly,** *adv.*

di·a·lec·ti·cal ma·te·ri·al·ism, *n.* A philosophy founded by Karl Marx and Friedrich Engels, which forms the basis of Communist doctrine: it combines the materialistic idea of matter over mind with the Hegelian dialectic in which opposing forces are constantly being reunited at a higher level.

di·a·lec·tol·o·gy, dī″a·lek·tol′o·jē, *n.* The study of dialects; that branch of linguistics which encompasses dialects.—**di·a·lec··tol·o·gist,** *n.*—**di·a·lec·to·log·i·cal,** *a.*

di·a·log·ic, dī″a·loj′ik, *a.* [Gr. *dialogikos,* < *dialogos.*] Pertaining to or of the nature of dialogue; taking part in a dialogue. Also **di·a·log·i·cal.**—**di·a·log·i·cal·ly,** *adv.*

di·a·logue, dī′a·lag″, dī′a·log″, *n.* [Fr. *dialogue,* < Gr. *dialogos,* dialogue, < *dialegomai,* to dispute.] A conversation between two or more persons; a formal conversation in theatrical performances; a composition in which two or more persons are represented as conversing on some topic; a frank exchange of ideas or views on a specific issue in an effort to attain mutual understanding.—*v.i.—dialogued, dialoguing.* To participate in a dialogue.—*v.t.* To express in the form of a dialogue. Also **di·a·log.**—**di·a·log·uer, di·a·log·er,** *n.*—**di·al·o·gist,** dī·al′o·jist, *n.* A speaker in a dialogue; a writer of dialogues.—**di·a·lo·gis·tic,** dī″a·lō·jis′tik, *a.*—**di·a·lo·gis··ti·cal·ly,** *adv.*

di·al·y·sis, dī·al′i·sis, *n.* pl. **di·al·y·ses,** dī·al′i·sēz. [Gr. *dialysis,* a separation.] *Chem.* the act or process of separating the crystalloid elements of a body from the colloid by diffusion through a membrane.—**di·a·lyt·ic,** dī″a·lit′ik, *a.*—**di·a·lyze, Brit. di·a·lyse,** dī′a·līz″, *v.t.* To separate by a dialyzer.—**di·a·lyz·er, Brit. di·a·lys·er,** *n.* The parchment paper, or septum, stretched over a ring used in the operation of dialysis.

di·a·mag·net·ic, dī″a·mag·net′ik, *a.* Pertaining to a class of substances which, when freely suspended and exposed to a magnet, lies at right angles to the poles of the magnet; having a magnetic permeability less than that of a vacuum.—**di·a·mag·net·i··cal·ly,** *adv.*—**di·a·mag·net·ism,** dī″a··mag′ni·tiz″um, *n.* The characteristic phenomena of diamagnetic bodies.—**di·a··mog·net,** *n.* A diamagnetic substance.

di·am·e·ter, dī·am′i·tẽr, *n.* [Gr. *diametros.*] *Geom.* a straight line passing through the center of a circle or other curvilinear figure, terminated by the circumference, and dividing the figure into two equal parts; a straight line through the center of any figure or body; the measure transversely through a cylindrical body; thickness.—**di·a·met·ric, di·a·met·ri·cal, di·am·e·tral,** dī″a·me′trik, dī″a·me′tri·kal, dī·am′i·tral, *a.* Of or pertaining to a diameter; directly opposed.—**di·a·met··ri·cal·ly,** *adv.*

dia·mond, dī′mond, dī′a·mond, *n.* [Fr. *diamant,* corrupted from *adamant.*] A naturally crystallized, nearly pure carbon; a piece of this substance, important to industry because it is the hardest substance known, used in rock drills, tools for cutting glass, and as an abrasive powder; a

clear, flawless piece of this stone, valued as a precious gem of great refractive power, esp. after being cut and polished; an article of jewelry, esp. an engagement ring, furnished with such a gem; crystallized carbon produced by artificial means; a four-sided figure with the sides equal or nearly so, and having two obtuse and two acute angles, called also a lozenge; a red, lozenge-shaped mark on a playing card, or a card so marked; *print.* a type of small size, 4½ point; *baseball,* the infield or entire playing field; *pl.* but construed as *sing.* or *pl.* the suit of cards so marked.—*a.* Resembling a diamond; consisting of diamonds; set with a diamond or diamonds.—*v.t.* To ornament with, or as if, with diamonds.

dia·mond·back rat·tle·snake, *n.* Any of several poisonous rattlesnakes, characterized by a diamond-shaped pattern on the back.

dia·mond·back ter·ra·pin, *n.* Any of several edible turtles of the genus *Malaclemys,* common to the coastal waters of southeastern U.S., characterized by a diamond-shaped pattern on the back.

di·a·mon·dif·er·ous, dī″a·mon·dif′e·rus, *a.* Yielding diamonds; diamantiferous.

di·an·drous, dī·an′drus, *a.* [Gr. *di,* twice, and *anēr, andros,* a male.] *Bot.* having two stamens.

di·a·no·et·ic, dī″a·nō·et′ik, *a.* [Gr. *dianoetikos,* < *dia,* and *noeō,* to revolve in the mind.] Capable of thought; thinking; intellectual.—**di·a·no·et·i·cally,** *adv.*

di·an·thus, dī·an′thus, *n.* [N.L. < Gr. *diós,* of Zeus, and *anthos,* flower.] *Bot.* any plant of the genus *Dianthus,* as the carnation, pink, and sweet william.

di·a·pa·son, dī″a·pā′zon, dī″a·pā′son, *n.* [Gr. *diapasōn,* lit. through all (notes).] *Mus.* a bursting forth of harmony; the entire compass of a voice or an instrument; a pitchpipe or tuning fork; a standard of pitch; a name of either of two main stops in the organ, given because they extend through the scales of the instrument.—**di·a·pa·son·al,** *a.*

di·a·pause, dī″a·pąz″, *n. Zool.* a period of inactivity in insects and other arthropods during which growth stops; a period of sexual inactivity in annelids.

di·a·pe·de·sis, dī″a·pi·dē′sis, *n.* pl. **di·a··pe·de·ses,** dī″a·pi·dē′sēz. *Physiol.* the process by which the blood passes through the capillary walls into the tissues.

dia·per, dī′pẽr, dī′a·pẽr, *n.* [Fr. *diapré,* pp. of *diaper,* to variegate with colors; < L.L. *diasprus,* a kind of precious cloth, < It. *diaspro,* jasper.] A soft, absorbent cloth drawn up between the legs and fastened at the waist of infants too young to be toilet-trained; a fabric with an all-over pattern of figures; used orig. in the Middle Ages; the pattern itself.—*v.t.* To put a diaper on; to decorate with a diaperlike pattern.

di·aph·a·nous, dī·af′a·nus, *a.* Almost totally transparent, as filmy fabric; translucent; extremely delicate in form.—**di·aph·a·nous·ly,** *adv.*—**di·aph·a·ne·i··ty, di·aph·a·nous·ness,** dī·af″a·nē′i·tē, dī″a·fa·nē′i·tē, *n.*

di·a·phone, dī′a·fōn″, *n.* A low-pitched foghorn, the sound of which can be heard from afar. *Phon.* a phoneme occurring in one dialect which resembles a phoneme of another dialect of the same language, but differs phonetically; *ling.* the group of variants of a given phoneme, including all of the phonetically different sounds.

di·a·phragm, dī′a·fram″, *n.* [L.L. *diaphragma,* < Gr. *diaphragma,* < *diaphrassein,* to barricade < *dia-,* between, and *phrassein,* fence in.] A partition or septum; a plate with a circular hole, used in cameras and optical instruments to cut off marginal beams of light; a vibrating disk in a telephone or a phonograph; *anat.*

the partition separating the chest cavity from the abdominal cavity in mammals; *physical chem.* a semipermeable membrane; a porous plate separating two liquids; a device placed over the uterine cervix for contraception.—*v.t.* To furnish or act upon with a diaphragm; *photog.* to reduce the aperture, as of a lens or objective, by means of a diaphragm.—**di·a·phrag·mat·ic,** dī″a·frag·mat′ik, a.—**di·a·phrag·mat·i·cal·ly,** *adv.*

di·a·pos·i·tive, dī″a·poz′i·tiv, dī″a·poz′-tiv, *n.* A photographic transparent positive, as a lantern slide.

di·ar·chy, dy·ar·chy, dī·är′kē, *n.* pl. **di·ar·chies, dy·ar·chies.** [Gr.] Government in which the supreme power is vested in two persons.—**di·ar·chi·al,** dī·är′kē·al, *a.*

di·a·rist, dī′a·rist, *n.* One who keeps a diary.

di·ar·rhe·a, dī″a·rē′a, *n.* [Gr. *diarrhoia.*] *Pathol.* an ailment characterized by abnormally frequent and fluid evacuation of the intestines. Also **di·ar·rhoea.—di·ar·rhe·al, di·ar·rhe·ic, di·ar·rhet·ic,** dī″a·ret′ik, *a.* Also **di·ar·rhoe·al, di·ar·rhoe·ic, di·ar·rhoet·ic.**

di·ar·thro·sis, dī″är·thrō′sis, *n.* pl. **di·ar·thro·ses,** dī″är·thrō′sēz. [Gr.] *Anat.* a joint in which the bones revolve freely in every direction, as in the shoulder joint.—**di·ar·thro·di·al,** *a.*

di·a·ry, dī′a·rē, *n.* pl. **di·a·ries.** [L. *diarium,* < *dies,* day.] A daily record, esp. of the writer's own experiences or observations; a book for keeping such a record; a printed book for containing memoranda with reference to each day of the year.

Di·as·po·ra, dī·as′pėr·a, *n.* [Gr. *diaspora,* a scattering, < *diaspeirein,* scatter about.] The dispersion of Jews to areas outside Palestine since the 6th century B.C. Babylonian Exile; the areas so settled; the Jewish people, collectively, now living outside Israel. (*l.c.*) a dispersion, scattering, or decentralization, as of national or religious groups living outside their homeland but maintaining their cultural identity; the people of such a group.

di·a·spore, dī′a·spōr″, dī′a·spär″, *n.* [Gr. *diaspora,* a scattering (see *Diaspora*); < its action before the blowpipe.] The mineral hydroxide of aluminum, occurring in crystals, or more usually in layers or scaly masses.

di·a·stase, dī′a·stās″, *n.* [Gr. *diastasis,* separation.] An enzyme found in barley and oats after germination, so called because in solution it possesses the property of causing starch to convert first into dextrin and then into sugar.—**di·a·sta·sic, di·a·stat·ic,** dī″a·stat′ik, *a.*

di·as·ta·sis, dī·as′ta·sis, *n.* pl. **di·as·ta·ses,** dī·as′ta·sēz. *Med.* dislocation or separation of bones without fracture; pertaining to the heart, the rest period between the diastole and the systole.

di·as·to·le, dī·as′to·lē″, *n.* [L.L. < Gr. *diastole,* a putting asunder, dilatation, lengthening, < *diastellein,* put asunder.] *Physiol.* the normal rhythmical dilatation of the heart, esp. that of the ventricles; any of various other rhythmical dilatations; *anc. pros.* the lengthening of a syllable regularly short, esp. before a pause or at the ictus.—**di·as·tol·ic,** dī″a·stol′ik, *a.*

di·as·tro·phism, dī·as′tro·fiz″um, *n.* [Gr. *diastrophm,* < *diastrephein,* distort.] *Geol.* The action of the forces which caused the deformation of the earth's crust, producing continents and mountains; such a deformation.—**di·a·stroph·ic,** dī″a·strof′ik, *a.*

di·a·tes·sa·ron, dī″a·tes′a·ron″, *n.* [Gr. *dia tessarōn,* by four.] A harmony of the four gospels, *Matthew, Mark, Luke,* and *John,* arranged as a single narration.

di·a·ther·mic, dī″a·thėr′mik, *a.* [Gr.] Having the property of transmitting radiant heat; relating to diathermy. Also **di·a·ther·ma·nous,** dī″a·thėr′ma·nus.—**di·a·ther·mic sur·ger·y,** surgery performed by the use of a high-frequency electric arc to cut living tissue and thus eliminate excessive bleeding.

di·a·ther·my, dī′a·thėr″mē, *n.* The application of electric current to produce heat in tissues below the skin for therapeutic purposes. Also **di·a·ther·mi·a.**

di·ath·e·sis, dī·ath′i·sis, *n.* pl. **di·ath·e·ses,** dī·ath′i·sēz. *Pathol.* predisposition to certain diseases rather than to others; the tendency to a particular mental development.—**di·a·thet·ic,** dī″a·thet′ik, *a.*

di·a·tom, dī′a·tom, dī′a·tom, *n.* [N.L. *Diatoma,* a genus of diatoms, < L.Gr. *diatomos,* verbal adj. of Gr. *diatemnein,* cut through.] Any of numerous microscopic, unicellular, marine or fresh-water algae, characterized by siliceous cell walls or shells consisting of two valves, which form extensive fossil deposits in many localities. —**di·a·to·ma·ceous,** dī″a·to·mā′shus, *a.* Of or pertaining to diatoms; consisting of or containing diatoms or their fossil remains.— **di·a·to·ma·ceous earth,** *n.* See *diatomite.*

di·a·tom·ic, dī″a·tom′ik, *a.* *Chem.* having two atoms in the molecule; containing two replaceable atoms or groups.

di·at·o·mite, dī″a·to·mīt′, *n.* Deposited material consisting of siliceous diatom skeletons, when dry resembling chalk or dry clay, used for filtration, as a polishing agent, and a source of silica. Also *diatomaceous earth.*

di·a·ton·ic, dī″a·ton′ik, *a.* [Gr.] *Mus.* of the standard major or minor scales, those having eight tones to the octave, five whole tones and two semitones; applied to chords, intervals, and melodic progressions belonging to one of these scales.—**di·a·ton·i·cal·ly,** *adv.*

di·a·tribe, dī′a·trīb″, *n.* [Gr. *diatribē,* a discussion, amusement, passing of time.] An abusive, bitter harangue in which a person denounces, criticizes, or attacks something or someone.

di·az·o, dī·az′ō, dī·ā′zō, *a. Chem.* signifying that a compound contains a group of two nitrogen atoms, N_2, united with one hydrocarbon radical or with one hydrocarbon radical and another atom or group of atoms. Such compounds are used esp. in making dyes and pigments.—**di·az·o·tize,** dī·az′o·tīz, *v.t.*—*diazotized, diazotizing. Chem.* to treat so as to convert into a diazo compound.

di·az·o dye, *n.* A dye that is produced by chemical reaction of materials after they are absorbed by the fibers of a fabric; a developed dye.

dib, dib, *v.i.*—*dibbed, dibbing.* [Cf. *dab.*] To fish by letting the bait bob lightly on the water. Also *dibble.*

di·ba·sic, dī·bā′sik, *a.* [Gr. *di-,* two, and *basis,* base.] *Chem.* of acids, containing two hydrogen atoms that can be replaced by basic atoms or radicals; containing two univalent metallic or basic atoms.

dib·ble, dib′l, *n.* [< *dib,* a form of *dip.*] A pointed instrument used in gardening and agriculture to make holes for planting seeds or bulbs. Also **dib·ber,** dib′ėr.—*v.t.*— *dibbled, dibbling.* To plant with a dibble; dig with a dibble.—*v.i.* To dib.

di·bran·chi·ate, dī·brang′kē·it, dī·brang′-kē·āt″, *a.* [N.L. *Dibranchiata,* pl., < Gr. *di-,* two, and *branchia,* gills.] Belonging to the *Dibranchiata,* a subclass of cephalopods with two gills, including the squids and octopuses.—*n.* A dibranchiate cephalopod.

dibs, dibz, *n.* pl. *Slang,* small amounts of money.—**dibs on (some·thing),** *slang,* an expression used primarily by children to

declare a claim, as to a privilege or to the possession of an object.

di·cast, dī′kast, dik′ast, *n.* [Gr. *dikastēs,* < *dikazein,* judge, < *dikē,* right, justice.] In ancient Athens, one of 6,000 citizens chosen annually as eligible to try cases in the courts of law in a capacity that combined the functions of the modern judge and juryman.—**di·cas·te·ry,** dī·kas′te·rē, *n.* pl. **di·cas·te·ries.** [Gr. *dicasterion.*] One of the courts in which the dicasts sat; a body of dicasts.—**di·cas·tic,** *a.*

dice, dīs, *n. pl.* [Pl. of *die.*] Small cubes whose sides are marked with different numbers of spots from one to six, thrown from a box or the hand in games; the game played; any small cubes or square blocks. —**no dice,** *slang,* no; a refusal; in vain.

dice, dīs, *v.i.*—*diced, dicing.* To play at dice. —*v.t.* To cut into small pieces or cubes, as vegetables; to decorate with cubelike figures; to checker; to lose or win, as money, at dice.—**dic·er,** *n.*

di·cen·tra, dī·sen′tra, *n.* [N.L., < Gr. *di-,* two, and *centron,* sharp point, spur.] Any of the plants constituting the genus *Dicentra,* with racemes of drooping flowers having a two-spurred or heart-shaped corolla, as the Dutchman's-breeches or the bleeding heart.

di·chlam·y·de·ous, dī″kla·mid′ē·us, *a.* [Gr. *di-,* two, and *chlamys,* (*chlamyd-*), mantle.] *Bot.* having both a calyx and a corolla.

di·chlo·ride, dī·klōr′īd, dī·klar′īd, *n. Chem.* bichloride.

di·chog·a·mous, dī·kog′a·mus, *a.* [Gr. *dicha,* in two, and *gamos,* marriage.] *Bot.* having the stamens and pistils maturing at different times, thus preventing self-fertilization, as a monoclinous flower: opposed to *homogamous.* Also **di·cho·gam·ic,** dī″kō·gam′ik.—**di·chog·a·my,** *n.*

di·chot·o·mize, dī·kot′o·mīz″, *v.t.*—*dichotomized, dichotomizing.* To divide into parts; divide into pairs.—*v.i.* To separate into two parts; become dichotomous. —**di·chot·o·mist,** *n.*—**di·chot·o·mis·tic,** *a.*—**di·chot·o·mi·za·tion,** *n.*

di·chot·o·mous, dī·kot′o·mus, *a.* [Gr. *dichotomos,* cut in two, < *dicha,* in two, and *temnein,* cut.] Divided or dividing into two parts; characterized by or involving successive division or branching into two parts; pertaining to dichotomy.—**di·chot·o·mous·ly,** *adv.*

di·chot·o·my, dī·kot′o·mē, *n.* pl. **di·chot·o·mies.** [Gr. *dichotomia.*] Division into two parts or categories; dichotomous division; *logic,* classification by division, or by successive subdivision, into two mutually exclusive groups or sections; *bot.* a mode of branching by constant bifurcation; *astron.* the phase of the moon, or of an inferior planet, when half of its disk is visible.— **di·cho·tom·ic,** dī·ke·tom′ik, *a.*—**di·cho·tom·i·cal·ly,** *adv.*

di·chro·ic, dī·krō′ik, *a.* [Gr. *dichroos,* of two colors.] Having or exhibiting dichroism. Dichromatic. Also **di·chro·it·ic,** dī″krō·it′ik.

di·chro·ism, dī′krō·iz″um, *n. Crystal.* the property of a uniaxial crystal of exhibiting different colors in two different directions when viewed by transmitted light; *chem.* the property of certain solutions of exhibiting different colors in different degrees of concentration.

di·chro·ite, dī′krō·it″, *n. Mineral.* cordierite.

di·chro·mate, dī·krō′māt, *n. Chem.* a salt of the theoretical dichromic acid. Also *bichromate.*

di·chro·mat·ic, dī″krō·mat′ik, dī″kro·mat′ik, *a.* Having or showing two colors; dichromic; *zool.* displaying two color phases in a species, independently of sex or age; *ophthalm.* characterizing or exhibiting dichromatism. Also *dichroic, dichromic.*

---

a- fat, fāte, fär, fâre, fạll; **e-** met, mē, mēre, hėr; **i-** pin, pīne; **o-** not, nōte, mōve; **u-** tub, cūbe, bụll; **oi-** oil; **ou-** pound.

di·chro·ma·tism, dī·krō′ma·tiz″um, n. The quality or condition of being dichromatic; *ophthalm.* a form of colorblindness in which only two of the three primary colors are perceived.

di·chro·mic, dī·krō′mik, a. Dichromatic; as, *dichromic* vision; *chem.* of a compound, having two chromium atoms; *crystal.* dichroic.

di·chro·mic ac·id, n. *Chem.* a theoretical acid, $H_2Cr_2O_7$, known only through dichromates.

di·chro·scope, dī′kro·skōp″, n. [Gr. *di-chroa,* and *skopeo,* to see.] An instrument used for testing the dichroism of crystals. Also **di·chro·o·scope.—di·chro·scop·ic,** dī″kro·skop′ik, a.

dick, dik, n. [From *Dick,* for *Richard,* man's name.] *Brit.* a man or fellow; *slang,* a detective.

dick·cis·sel, dik·sis′el, n. [Imit. of its note.] The blackthroated bunting, *Spiza americana,* a bird of the eastern and central U.S.

dick·ens, dik′inz, n. [Probably a fanciful euphemism for *devil*; akin L.G. *duker, duks,* the deuce.] Devil or deuce, usu. preceded by *the* and used as a mild expletive as: Where *the* dickens is my hat?

dick·er, dik′ẽr, v.i. [Origin uncertain.] To bargain; to haggle.—v.t. To trade with haggling.—n. A bargain.

dick·ey, dick·y, dick·ie, dik′ē, n. pl. **dick·eys, dick·ies.** Any of various items of apparel worn by men or women to fill in a neckline or jacket opening and simulate a sweater, shirt, or blouse, esp. a man's shirt front worn with formal or clerical dress; a bib for a child; a male donkey; any donkey. *Chiefly Brit.* the driver's seat on the outside of a carriage, or a seat at the back of a carriage or of a two-seater automobile. A small bird, as a sparrow; also **dick·ey·bird, dick·y·bird.**

di·cli·nous, dī′kli·nus, dī·klī′nus, a. *Bot.* having the stamens in one flower and the pistils in another, on the same plant or on two separate plants.—**di·cli·nism, di·cli·ny,** n.

di·cot·y·le·don, dī·kot′a·lēd′on, dī″kot·a·lēd′on, n. *Bot.* any plant of the subclass *Dicotyledones,* the paramount and more numerous subclass of flowering plants, the seeds of which contain a pair of cotyledons or opposite seed leaves. Also **di·cot, di·cot·yl.—di·cot·y·le·don·ous,** a. Of or relating to the subclass *Dicotyledones*; having two cotyledons.

di·crot·ic, dī·krot′ik, a. [Gr. *dikrotos.*] *Physiol.* Having two arterial beats for one heartbeat, as certain pulses; pertaining to such a pulse.—**di·cro·tism,** dī′kro·tiz″um, n.

Dic·ta·phone, dik′ta·fōn″, n. (*Sometimes l.c.*) a dictating machine. (Trademark.)

dic·tate, dik′tāt, dik·tāt′, v.t.—dictated, dictating. [L. *dicto, dictatum,* a freq. of *dico, dictum,* to say.] To deliver or enounce with authority, as an order, command, or direction; to instruct to be said or written; to utter or read aloud for a person or a machine to record.—v.i. To say aloud, as in giving dictation; to give orders or act in an overbearing manner.—**dic·tate,** dik′tāt, n. An order delivered; a command; a rule, maxim, or precept; as, the *dictates* of reason.

dic·tat·ing ma·chine, n. A machine which records verbal dictation for later playback and transcription.

dic·ta·tion, dik·tā′shan, n. [L.L. *dictatio(n-).*] The act of dictating for reproduction in writing; the material which is dictated; the act of prescribing positively or authoritatively; dictatorial or imperious direction; something dictated or prescribed. *Mus.* performance of musical passages for a student to reproduce; the passages so performed.

dic·ta·tor, dik·tā′tẽr, dik·tā′tẽr, n. [L.] A person exercising absolute authority, esp. in government; a ruler who employs his absolute powers oppressively or tyrannically; one who authoritatively prescribes, as in the areas of fashion, conduct, usage; one who dictates; a chief magistrate appointed in ancient Rome in times of emergency.—**dic·ta·tor·ship,** n. A form of government characterized by absolute authority; a country having such a government; absolute authority; the office of a dictator.

dic·ta·to·ri·al, dik″ta·tōr′ē·al, dik″ta·tär′ē·al, a. [L. *dictatorius.*] Of or pertaining to a dictator; characteristic of a dictator; inclined to dictate or command; imperious; overbearing. Also **dic·ta·to·ry.—dic·ta·to·ri·al·ly,** adv.—**dic·ta·to·ri·al·ness,** n.

dic·ta·tor·ship of the pro·le·tar·i·at, n. Absolute rule by the propertyless working class, considered in Marxist theory to be a necessary stage in the establishment of a communistic social system.

dic·tion, dik′shan, n. [L. *dictio,* < *dico, dictum,* to speak.] A person's choice or selection of words in speaking or writing; one's manner of voicing sounds in speaking or singing; enunciation.

dic·tion·ar·y, dik′sha·ner″ē, n. pl. **dic·tion·ar·ies.** [L.L. *dictionarium.*] A book containing words of a language arranged in alphabetical order, with explanations of their meanings, pronunciations, etymologies, and other information; a lexicon; a word book; any work which communicates information on an entire subject or branch of a subject, under entries or heads arranged alphabetically.

Dic·to·graph, dik′to·graf″, dik′to·gräf″, n. [L. *dictum,* something said.] (*Sometimes l.c.*) a telephonic device with a highly sensitive transmitter obviating the necessity of a mouthpiece, used for secretly listening to or obtaining a record of conversations. (Trademark.)

dic·tum, dik′tum, n. pl. **dic·ta, dic·tums,** dik′ta. [L., something said, a saying, a command, prop. pp. neut. of *dicere,* say.] An authoritative utterance or pronouncement; a saying or maxim. *Law,* an expression of opinion by a judge on a legal point aside from the issues of the case under consideration; also *obiter dictum.*

did, did, v.t. Past tense of *do.*

di·dac·tic, dī·dak′tik, a. [Gr. *didaktikos,* < *didasko,* to teach.] Intended to instruct; containing doctrines, principles, rules, or moral precepts; tending to lecture or teach unnecessarily; pedantic. Also **di·dac·ti·cal,** dī·dak′ti·kal.—**di·dac·tics,** n. pl. but sing. in constr. The science or art of teaching.—**di·dac·ti·cal·ly,** adv.—**di·dac·ti·cism,** n.

di·dap·per, dī′dap″ẽr, *Brit.* did′a·pẽr, n. The dabchick or little grebe.

did·n't, did′ant. Contraction of did not.

di·do, dī′dō, n. pl. **di·does, di·dos.** [Origin uncertain.] *Usu. pl., colloq.* A prank; an antic; a disorderly performance.

di·dym·i·um, dī·dim′ē·um, di·dim′ē·um, n. [N.L., < Gr. *didymos,* twin.] *Chem.* a substance containing neodymium and praseodymium, formerly supposed to be an element, and called the 'twin brother of lanthanum.'

did·y·mous, did′i·mus, a. *Bot.* twin; produced in pairs.

di·dyn·a·mous, dī·din′a·mus, a. *Bot.* having two pairs of stamens, the pairs being of unequal length.

die, dī, v.i.—died, dying. [M.E. *dien, deien,* = Icel. *deyja* = O.H.G. *touwen,* die.] To suffer the total and permanent cessation of all the vital functions; cease to live. To cease to exist; come to an end, as: The project *died* due to a lack of funds. To be reduced in number by death; become extinct, with *off* or *out,* as: The cattle are *dying off.* The species *died out.* To pass gradually away or fade away; lose force, strength, or active qualities, often with *away, down,* or *out,* as: The fire *died out.* The excitement *died down.* To cease to function; stop, as: The motor *died.* To suffer pain or illness; as, *dying* with a toothache; to suffer mental anguish; as, *die* of embarrassment; to experience extreme excitement or hilarity; as, *dying* of laughter; *colloq.* to desire greatly, as: I'm *dying* for some water. *Poet.* to languish or faint, esp. with longing or passion; *theol.* to lose spiritual life; *theatr.* to fail; flop.—**die hard,** to struggle fiercely but futilely against death or defeat; to refuse to admit defeat; to be obstinate.—**nev·er say die,** never give up

die, dī, n. pl. **dice.** [M.E. *de,* < O.Fr. *de,* Fr. *dé,* = It. *dado* (DADO), < L. *datum,* pp. neut. of *dare,* give.] A small cube or block whose sides are marked with different numbers of spots. Any small cube or square block.—n. pl. **dies.** *Arch.* the cubical dado of a pedestal. *Mach.* any of various devices for cutting or shaping material, as an engraved stamp for impressing a design upon some softer material, as in coining money; one of a pair of stamps formed as counterparts, for impressing, shaping, or forming something; a hollow device of steel, often composed of several pieces to be fitted into a stock, for cutting threads, as on bolts or pipes; one of the separate pieces of such a device; a metal block with small perforations through which metal or plastic is forced; in a punching machine, a perforated block upon which the object to be punched is rested.—**the die is cast,** a decision has been made or an action taken, the consequences of which are irrevocable.—v.t.—died, dieing. To impress or shape with a die.

die·back, dī′bak″, n. *Bot.* a pathological condition in woody plants in which the branches die due to parasites, viruses, fungi, or conditions of environment.

di·e·cious, dī·ē′shus, a. Dioecious.

die down, v.i. To become quiet or calm; diminish; abate; *bot.* of the aboveground parts of certain plants, to wither away, usu. as part of a normal growth cycle.

die-hard, dī′härd″, n. One who resists to the last; one who resists change, esp. a political conservative.—a. Obstinate; stubbornly conservative. Also **die·hard.**

diel·drin, dēl′drin, n. *Chem.* a light tan, flaked solid, poisonous compound, $C_{12}H_8$-OCl_6, used as an insecticide.

di·e·lec·tric, dī″i·lek′trik, n. [Gr. *dia-,* through, and E. *electric.*] *Phys., elect.* a nonconducting or insulating material; a material which admits electrostatic and magnetic lines of force but resists passage of electric current.

di·en·ceph·a·lon, dī″en·sef′a·lon″, n. *Anat.* the posterior part of the prosencephalon, or forebrain.—**di·en·ce·phal·ic,** dī″en·se·fal′ik, a.

di·er·e·sis, dī·er′i·sis, n. pl. **di·er·e·ses,** dī·er′i·sēz″. Diaeresis.

die·sel, dē′zel, n. (*Sometimes cap.*) a wheeled vehicle that is driven by a diesel engine.—a. Of or pertaining to a vehicle or machine powered by a diesel engine; as, a *diesel* truck; pertaining to a diesel engine; as, *diesel* fuel.—**die·sel·ize,** v.t.—dieselized, dieselizing. To equip with a diesel engine.

die·sel en·gine. [Named for Dr. Rudolf *Diesel,* of Munich, the inventor.] (*Sometimes cap.*) a type of internal-combustion engine in which a heavy oil is sprayed into the cylinder after the air in it has been compressed to incandescence, causing the ignition of the oil, which undergoes a form of combustion slower than an explosion, and thus activates the piston.

---

ch- chain, G. na*ch*t;   **th-** *TH*en, thin;   **w-** wig, hw as sound in whig;   **z-** zh as in azure, zeal. *Italicized vowel* indicates schwa sound.

die·sink·er, dī′sing″kėr, *n.* An engraver of dies for coins, etc.—**die·sink·ing**, *n.*

di·e·sis, dī′i·sis, *n.* pl. **di·e·ses**, dī′i·sēz. *Typog.* the double dagger.

die·stock, dī′stok″, *n. Mach.* a stock for holding the dies used in cutting threads, as on pipes and screws. Also **die stock, die plate, screw stock.**

di·es·trous, dī·es′trus, *a. Zool.* pertaining to the sexually quiescent period in a female mammel between two periods of estrus. Also **di·es·tru·al**, dī·es′tru·wal.

di·et, dī′it, *n.* [O.Fr. *diète*, L.L. *dieta*, Gr. *diaita*, a way of living, diet.] A person's or an animal's regular food and drink; course of food and drink prescribed, as for health reasons, and limited in kind and quantity; whatever is provided or used habitually; as, a steady *diet* of television.—*v.t.* To furnish diet or meals for; to prescribe a particular diet for.—*v.i.* To eat according to rules prescribed, esp. in order to lose weight.—**di·et·er**, *n.*

di·et, dī′it, *n.* [Fr. *diete*, < L.L. *dieta*, the space of a day, < L. *dies*, a day, whence also *dial, diary*.] An assembly of dignitaries or delegates for legislative, ecclesiastical, or other purposes; session; (*often cap.*) the legislative or administrative assemblies of certain countries, as Japan, or formerly, of the Holy Roman Empire; as, the *Diet* of Worms.

di·e·tar·y, dī′i·ter″ē, *a.* Pertaining to diet or the rules of diet.—*n.* pl. **di·e·tar·ies.** An allowance of food for an individual or a group, regulated by certain factors, as availability, medical orders, or economic controls; as, the American *dietary*, prison *dietary; obs.* a system or course of diet.

di·e·tar·y law, *n. Judaism*, any of the laws prescribing which foods and food combinations may be eaten, plus various regulations pertaining to cooking and eating utensils and special treatment of foods before use.

di·e·tet·ic, dī′i·tet′ik, *a.* Pertaining to diet, or to the rules for regulating diet; prepared for special diets, as through use of sugar or salt substitutes; as, *dietetic* carbonated drinks. Also **di·e·tet·i·cal**, dī·i·tet′i·kal.—**di·e·tet·i·cal·ly**, *adv.*—**di·e·tet·ics**, dī″·i·tet′iks, *n. pl., sing. or pl. in constr.* The science of planning and regulating feeding according to nutritional principles.

di·e·ti·tian, di·e·ti·cian, dī′i·tish′an, *n.* One skilled in dietetics; one who arranges diets.

di·et kitch·en, *n.* A kitchen, as one in a hospital, for preparing and dispensing special diets.

dif·fer, dif′ėr, *v.i.* [L. *differo*—prefix *dif, dis-* and *fero*, to bear, to carry.] To be unlike, dissimilar, distinct, or various, in nature, condition, form, or qualities; to disagree; contend; be at variance. *Archaic*, to dispute; quarrel.

dif·fer·ence, dif′ėr·ens, dif′rens, *n.* [O.Fr. *difference* (Fr. *différence*), < L. *differentia*.] The state or relation of being different; dissimilarity; an instance of unlikeness or dissimilarity; a point in which things differ; a character which one thing has and an other has not; a distinguishing characteristic; distinction or discrimination; an important or decisive alteration in or effect on a state of affairs, used with *make* and an article or adjective or both; as, *makes a difference, makes no difference*; a disagreement in opinion; a dispute or quarrel; the degree in which one thing differs from another. *Math.* the amount by which one quantity is greater or less than another; the remainder in subtraction; *Logic*, that which causes a distinction; differentia; *Her.* an alteration to a coat of arms to distinguish it from another which would be otherwise identical.—*v.t.*— *differenced, differencing.* To cause or consti-

tute a difference in or between; make different; to perceive the difference in or between; discriminate; *her.* to add a distinguishing mark to.—**split the dif·fer·ence**, to share the remaining quantity equally; to meet halfway; compromise.

dif·fer·ent, dif′ėr·ent, dif′rent, *a.* Of various natures, forms, or qualities; unlike; dissimilar. Distinct; separate; not the same; various. Unusual; novel.—**dif·fer·ent·ly**, *adv.*—**dif·fer·ent·ness**, *n.*

dif·fer·en·ti·a, dif″e·ren′shē·a, *n.* pl. **dif·fer·en·ti·ae**, dif″e·ren′shē·ē. [L., difference.] The character or attribute by which one species is distinguished from all others of the same genus; the distinguishing attribute of any entity.

dif·fer·en·ti·a·ble, dif″e·ren′shē·a·bl, *a.* Capable of being differentiated.—**dif·fer·en·ti·a·bil·i·ty**, *n.*

dif·fer·en·tial, dif″e·ren′shal, *a.* [L. *dif·ferentia*, E. *difference*.] Of or pertaining to difference or diversity; exhibiting or depending upon a difference or distinction between things, individuals, or groups; as, a *differential* rate; constituting a difference; distinguishing; distinctive; pertaining to distinguishing characteristics in rate, quantity, or degree; *math.* pertaining to or involving differentials; as, a *differential* coefficient; *phys., mach.* pertaining to or involving the difference of two or more motions or forces.—*n.* The amount or degree of difference between comparable things; a differentiating characteristic. *Com.* a differential duty or rate; the difference involved in a differential rate. *Math.* an infinitesimal difference between consecutive values of a variable quantity; *elect.* a coil of wire in which the polar action produced is opposite to that of another coil; *mach.* a differential gear in the transmission system of an engine which allows for the difference in speed of two driving wheels.—**dif·fer·en·tial·ly**, *adv.* In a differential manner; with reference to a difference, as between quantities of forces; distinctively, or by way of difference.

dif·fer·en·tial cal·cu·lus, *n.* A branch of mathematics which investigates the relationship between the variables and the rate of change in functions.

dif·fer·en·tial e·qua·tion, *n. Math.* an equation that includes differentials or derivatives of functions.

dif·fer·en·tial gear, *n. Mach.* an epicyclic train of gears to link two shafts or axles in the same line, equally apportioning the driving force but letting one axle spin with greater speed than the other, esp. useful when a car turns curves.

dif·fer·en·ti·ate, dif″e·ren′shē·āt″, *v.t.*— *differentiated, differentiating.* [L. *differentia*, E. *difference*.] To mark off by differences; distinguish; alter or change; make different by modification, as a biological species; to perceive the difference in or between; *math.* to obtain the differential or the differential coefficient of.—*v.i.* To become unlike or dissimilar; change in character; to perceive or make a distinction; *biol.* of tissues or cells, to develop into more specialized structures.

dif·fer·en·ti·a·tion, dif″e·ren′shē·ā′shan, *n.* The act or process of differentiating, or the resulting state; *biol.* the modification of cells, tissues, and body parts as they develop into mature structure and function; *math.* the finding of a differential or a differential coefficient.—**dif·fer·en·ti·a·tor**, *n.*

dif·fi·cult, dif′i·kult″, dif′i·kụlt″, *a.* [Back formation < *difficulty.*] Hard to make, do, or perform; not easy; arduous; hard to contend with; hard to understand; hard to please; stubborn.—**dif·fi·cult·ly**, *adv.*

dif·fi·cul·ty, dif′i·kụl″tē, dif′i·kụl·tē, *n.*

pl. **dif·fi·cul·ties.** [Fr. *difficulté*; L. *difficultas*, < *difficilis*, difficult—*dis-*, priv., and *facilis*, easy to be made or done.] The state or quality of being difficult; that which is hard to be performed or surmounted; a perplexity; *usu. pl.* an embarrassing state of affairs, esp. financial. A trouble; a problem; an objection; a falling out; a controversy; a quarrel.

dif·fi·dence, dif′i·dens, *n.* [L. *diffidentia, diffidens*, ppr. of *diffido*, to distrust—*dis-*, not, and *fido*, to trust.] Lack of self-confidence; modest reserve.—**dif·fi·dent**, *a.* Characterized by diffidence.—**dif·fi·dent·ly**, *adv.*

dif·flu·ent, dif′lö·ent, *a.* [L. *diffluens* (-*ent*-), ppr. of *diffluere*, flow apart or away.] Tending to flow away; readily dissolving.—**dif·flu·ence**, *n.*

dif·fract, di·frakt′, *v.t.* [L. *diffringo, diffractum*—prefix *dif-, dis-*, and *frango*, to break.] To break; to bend from a straight line; to deflect.—**dif·frac·tion**, *n. Phys.* the deflection of waves into an interference pattern which occurs when light or other waves pass around an object in their path.—**dif·frac·tive**, *a.* Causing diffraction.

dif·frac·tion grat·ing, *n. Phys.* a narrow strip of polished glass or metal inscribed with many fine, equidistant, parallel lines, used for diffracting light in spectrum analysis.

dif·fuse, di·fūz′, *v.t.*—*diffused, diffusing.* [L. *diffundo, diffusum*—prefix, *dif-, dis-*, and *fundo, fusum*, to pour.] To pour out and allow or cause to flow or spread, as a fluid; to send out or give out in all directions; distribute; disseminate; spread, as light, information, or happiness; to spread by or subject to diffusion.—*v.i.* To spread; to be subjected to diffusion.—di·fūs′, *a.* Widely spread; lacking conciseness; wordy; verbose; *bot.* spreading widely, horizontally, and irregularly.—**dif·fuse·ly**, di·fūs′lē, *adv.*—**dif·fuse·ness**, *n.*—**dif·fuse·er**, di·fū′zėr, *n.* One who or that which diffuses; a material or a device used to lessen glare from a lighting fixture; *phys.* a device, usually within a machine such as a pump or compressor, for lowering the speed and increasing the pressure of a fluid by increasing the cross-sectional size of the tube or vessel through which it flows. Also **dif·fu·sor.**

dif·fus·i·ble, di·fū′zi·bl, *a.* Capable of being diffused.—**dif·fus·i·bil·i·ty, dif·fus·i·ble·ness**, *n.*

dif·fu·sion, di·fū′zhan, *n.* The act of diffusing or the condition of being diffused; wordiness in speech or writing; diffuseness; the breaking up and spreading of light rays, esp. when they are filtered through a translucent material; *phys.* the intermingling of molecules of different substances, or of the same substance at different concentrations, as a result of their random thermal motion; *anthropol., sociol.* the spreading of the characteristics of one culture to another.—**dif·fu·sion·al**, *a.*

dif·fu·sive, di·fū′siv, *a.* Having the quality of diffusing or becoming diffused; having a tendency to diffuse; diffuse as regards written or spoken expression.—**dif·fu·sive·ly**, *adv.*—**dif·fu·sive·ness**, *n.*

dig, dig, *v.t.*—*dug, digging.* [Probably connected with *dike* or *dyke, ditch*; O.E. *dic*, a dike or a ditch, *dician*, Dan. *dige*, to make a ditch.] To break up, turn, or remove, as with a spade or other sharp instrument; to excavate; to form in the ground by digging and removing the loose soil; as, to *dig* a basement; to raise from the earth by digging, as coal; to jab, thrust, or drive. *Slang*, to understand; to like; to pay attention to;—*v.i.* To work with a spade or other similar instrument; to work one's way or progress by or as by moving aside or removing material, often followed by *through*; to search through; *Brit. colloq.* to dwell as a renter or lodger.—**dig in**, to excavate trenches, esp. for defense in battle; to entrench oneself in a position, either physically or figuratively. To begin to apply oneself vigorously, as to one's work or to eating a meal; also **dig in·to.**—*n.* A sharp poke; an unkind remark. The site of an archaeological excavation; the excavation; *pl. Brit. colloq.* lodgings; also *diggings.*

dig·a·my, dig′*a*·mē, *n.* [L.L. *digamia*, < Gr. *digamos.*] Second marriage; the act of marrying again after a first marriage has been legally ended by divorce or by the death of one's first spouse.—**dig·a·mist**, *n.* —**dig·a·mous**, *adj.*

di·gas·tric, dī·gas′trik, *a.* [Gr. *di-*, double, and *gastēr*, belly.] *Anat.* of a muscle, having a double belly.—*n.* A double muscle that pulls the lower jaw downward and backward.

Dig·by chick·en, *n. Canadian*, a herring that has been smoke-cured.

di·gen·e·sis, dī·jen′i·sis, *n. Biol.* successive generation by two different processes, as sexual and asexual.—**di·ge·net·ic**, dī″je··net′ik, *a.*

di·gest, di·jest′, dī·jest′, *v.t.* [L. *digero*, *digestum*, to distribute, dispose, digest food —*di-* for *dis-*, asunder, and *gero*, *gestum*, to bear.] To convert, as food or drink, in the alimentary canal into a form absorbable by the body tissues; to arrange methodically in the mind; to think out; to order for being conveniently consulted or studied; classify; to summarize; to abridge; *chem.* to soften, decompose, or prepare, as with heat, moisture, or chemicals; *fig.* to bear with patience or with an effort; brook; put up with.—*v.i.* To undergo digestion, as food; to digest food or drink; *chem.* to be digested by means of heat, moisture, or chemicals.—dī′jest, *n.* A systematic compilation, as of literary or scientific material, frequently abridged or summarized; *law*, a compilation or synopsis, as of statutes or court decisions, systematically arranged.— **the Di·gest**, a collection of Roman laws, arranged under proper titles by order of the Emperor Justinian.—**di·gest·er**, *n.* One who digests; one who compiles a digest; that which assists the digestion of food; *chem.* a vessel in which substances may be digested.—**di·gest·i·ble**, *a.*—**di·gest·i··bil·i·ty, di·gest·i·ble·ness**, *n.*

di·ges·tion, di·jes′chan, di·jesh′chan, dī·· jes′chan, dī·jesh′chan, *n.* [L. *digestio.*] The process which food undergoes, primarily through the action of enzymes in the alimentary canal, whereby it is prepared for absorption into and nourishment of the body tissues; *chem.* a process whereby substances are treated, as with heat, moisture, or chemicals, to change their state or composition; the state resulting from either of these processes; the act, function, or operation of digesting; the ability to digest.—*n.* Any preparation or medicine which aids digestion.—**di·ges·tive**, di·jes′· tiv, dī·jes′tiv, *a.* Pertaining to digestion; having the power to promote digestion.— **di·ges·tive·ly**, *adv.*—**di·ges·tive·ness**, *n.*

dig·ger, dig′ėr, *n.* One who or that which digs; an implement or machine for digging. (*Cap.*) a member of any of several Indian tribes of western N. America that used roots as a major item of diet; also **Dig·ger In·di·an.**

dig·ger wasp, *n.* Any of a large group of solitary wasps of the family *Sphecidae*, most of which build their nests in burrows in the ground and provision them for their young with the bodies of spiders or insects which they have paralyzed by stinging.

dig·gings, dig′ingz, *n. pl. Sometimes constr. as sing.* An area of excavation, esp. a mining

area. Material removed from an excavation. —dig′inz, *Brit. colloq.* lodgings.

dig·it, dij′it, *n.* [L. *digitus*, a finger.] A finger or a toe; the breadth of a finger, or ¾ inch; *astron.* the twelfth part of the diameter of the sun or moon; *arith.* any positive integer under 10, including 0, so called from counting on the fingers.— **dig·it·al**, dij′i·tal, *a.* [L. *digitalis.*] Of or pertaining to digits; resembling a finger or fingers; also *digitate.*—*n.* A key of the organ, piano, or other keyboard instrument.

dig·it·al com·put·er, *n.* A computer in which information is represented in discrete units, using coded digits to indicate all the variables of a problem and providing solutions calculated mathematically, esp. in a binary system.

dig·i·tal·in, dij″i·tal′in, dij″i·tā′lin, *n.* A white, crystalline powder, $C_{36}H_{56}O_{14}$, a glucoside of digitalis used in medicine; any of several mixtures of glucosides extracted from digitalis.

dig·i·tal·is, dij″i·tal′is, dij″i·tā′lis, *n.* Any of several Eurasian herbs of the genus *Digitalis* of the figwort family, esp. *D. purpurea*, the common foxglove; the dried and powdered leaf of foxglove containing several important glucosides and serving as a powerful heart stimulant and a diuretic.— **dig·i·tal·ize**, dij′i·tal·iz″, dij·i·tal′īz, *v.t.* —*digitalized*, *digitalizing. Med.* to administer digitalis to in the treatment of heart disease.—**dig·i·tal·iz·a·tion**, *n. Med.* the process of administering digitalis in the course of treatment; the physiological effect induced by this.

dig·i·tate, dij′i·tāt″, *a. Bot.* having sections or parts, as leaflets, radiating like the fingers on a hand; *zool.* possessing digits or digitlike appendages. Also **dig·i·tat·ed.**— **dig·i·tate·ly**, *adv.*—**dig·i·ta·tion**, dij″i·· tā′shan, *n. Biol.* a division into fingerlike appendages or parts; any of such appendages or parts.

dig·i·ti·grade, dij′i·ti·grād″, *n.* [L. *digitus*, and *gradior*, to go.] An animal that walks on its toes, as the dog or cat.—*a.* Walking on the toes without any weight put on the sole of the foot.

dig·i·tox·in, dij″i·tok′sin, *n.* A bitter, odorless, white, highly poisonous leaflet or powder, $C_{41}H_{64}O_{13}$, the most active glucoside of digitalis, used as a heart stimulant; a cardiotonic mixture of digitalis glucosides, primarily digitoxin.

di·glot, dī′glot, *a.* [Gr. *diglottos*, < *di-*, two, and *glotta*, *glossa*, tongue.] Using or containing two languages; bilingual.—*n.* A bilingual book or edition.—**di·glot·tic**, dī″glot′ik, *a.*

dig·ni·fied, dig′ni·fīd″, *a.* Invested with dignity; marked with dignity or loftiness; noble; stately in deportment.—**dig·ni··fied·ly**, *adv.*

dig·ni·fy, dig′ni·fī″, *v.t.*—*dignified*, *dignifying.* [Fr. *dignifier*—L. *dignus*, worthy, and *facere*, to make.] To invest with honor or dignity; to elevate to a high office; to honor; to try to bestow undeserved dignity upon; to give a prestigious name or title to.

dig·ni·tary, dig′ni·ter″ē, *n. pl.* **dig·ni··tar·ies.** One who holds high rank or office, esp. in government.—**dig·ni·tar·i·al**, *a.*

dig·ni·ty, dig′ni·tē, *n. pl.* **dig·ni·ties.** [L. *dignitas.*] Formal or restrained deportment, demeanor, or speech; self-respect; majesty or stateliness; the state or quality of being worthy of respect, honor, or esteem; comparative importance, place, or excellence; rank; an elevated position, title, or rank.

di·graph, dī′graf, dī′gräf, *n.* [Gr.] A union of two vowels or of two consonants, representing a single sound of the voice, as *ea* in *head.*—**di·graph·ic**, dī″graf′ik, *a.*

di·gress, di·gres′, dī·gres′, *v.i.* [L. *digredior*,

digressus, to step apart.] To depart or wander from the main subject of a discourse, argument, or narration.

di·gres·sion, di·gresh′an, dī·gresh′an, *n.* [L. *digressio.*] The act of digressing; the part or passage of a discourse which deviates from the main subject.—**di·gres·sion·al**, *a.*

di·gres·sive, di·gres′iv, dī·gres′iv, *a.* Apt to digress; characterizing or characterized by digression.—**di·gres·sive·ly**, *adv.*— **di·gres·sive·ness**, *n.*

di·he·dral, dī·hē′dral, *a.* [Gr. *di*, two, and *hedra*, seat, base.] Having, or formed by, two plane faces; two sided; pertaining to or having a dihedral angle; *aeron.* pertaining to the upward or, rarely, downward slant of an aircraft wing or tailplane.—**di·he·dral an·gle**, *n. Geom.* the angle between two intersecting planes.

di·he·dral, dī·hē′dral, *n. Geom.* a figure formed by two intersecting planes; also *dihedral angle*, **di·he·dron.** *Aeron.* the upward (*positive*) or downward (*negative*) incline of an aircraft's wing or other supporting surface in relation to the horizontal; esp. the angle thus formed.

di·hy·brid, dī·hī′brid, *n. Biol.* the offspring or strain produced by parents which differ in two specific genetic factors.—*a.*

di·kast, dī′kast, dik′ast, *n.* Dicast.

dik-dik, dik′dik″, *n.* [A native East Afr. name.] Any of several small African antelopes, of the genera *Madoqua* and *Rhynchotragus*, which stand twelve to fourteen inches high.

dike, dīk, *n.* [O.E. *dic*, D. *dijk*, Dan. *dige*, a bank of earth, a ditch, the ditch being excavated and the bank formed by the same operation. *Ditch* is a softened form of this.] An embankment constructed to restrain flood waters; an artificially created waterway, as a ditch; a bank of debris that results from material being excavated; a raised causeway; a barrier or obstacle; *Brit.* a low wall of earth or stone to enclose land. *Geol.* a tabular mass of igneous rock which has intruded, while molten, into fissures of older rock beds. Also **dyke.**—*v.t.*—*diked*, *diking.* To surround with a dike; to secure by a bank; to drain by one or more dikes or ditches.

di·lac·er·ate, di·las′e·rāt″, dī·las′e·rāt″, *v.t.*—*dilacerated*, *dilacerating.* [L. *dilacero.*] To tear into pieces; to rend asunder. —**di·lac·er·a·tion**, *n.*

di·lap·i·date, di·lap′i·dāt″, *v.t.*—*dilapidated*, *dilapidating.* [L.] To cause to decay or fall into partial ruin through misuse or neglect.—*v.i.* To fall to partial ruin.— **di·lap·i·da·tion**, *n.*—**di·lap·i·da·tor**, *n.*

di·lap·i·dat·ed, di·lap′i·dā″tid, *a.* In a run-down condition; reduced to decay.

di·lat·an·cy, di·lāt′an·sē, dī·lāt′an·sē, *n.* The property of dilating. *Phys.* the property of granular masses of expanding in the volume they occupy when they change in shape, due to the increase of space between the particles; the property of some suspensions or colloids which increase in viscosity, and set to a solid, due to pressure, agitation, or expansion, as quicksand or wet sand.—**di·lat·ant**, di·lāt′ant, dī·lāt′ant, *a.* Dilating or expanding; pertaining to or characterized by dilatancy. —*n.* An agent or instrument that dilates something; a surgeon's dilator; a substance having the property of dilating or expanding; a substance having the property of dilatancy.

dil·a·ta·tion, dil″a·tā′shan, dī″la·tā′shan, *n.* The act of expanding, or dilating; the state of being expanded or distended; something which is dilated. *Med.* a pathological enlargement, as of an organ or passageway; an induced, temporary enlargement of an opening or passageway, as to aid examination; the establishment of or restoration to normal size of an abnormally small canal or orifice. Also **di·la·tion,** dī·lā′shan, di·lā′shan,

di·late, dī·lāt′, di·lāt′, *v.t.—dilated, dilating.* [L. *dilato,* to make wider.] To expand or swell out, esp. by filling; to distend; to enlarge in all directions.—*v.i.* To expand, swell, or extend in all directions; to discourse at length, usu. followed by *on* or *upon.*—**di·lat·a·bil·i·ty, di·lat·a·ble·ness,** *n.*—**di·lat·a·ble,** *a.*—**di·lat·a·bly,** *adv.*—**di·lat·ing·ly,** *adv.*

di·lat·ed, dī·lā′tid, di·lā′tid, *a.* Expanded from a side, or in all directions; broadened; also **di·lat·ate.—di·lat·ed·ly,** *adv.*—**di·lat·ed·ness,** *n.*

di·la·tive, dī·lā′tiv, di·lā′tiv, *a.* Tending or causing to dilate.

dil·a·tom·e·ter, dil″a·tom′i·tèr, *n. Phys.* a device used to measure the thermal expansion of substances.—**dil·a·to·met·ric,** *a.*

di·la·tor, di·lat·er, di·lā′tèr, di·lā′tèr, *n.* One who or that which dilates; *med.* an implement used to dilate an opening or canal of the body.

dil·a·to·ry, dil′a·tōr″ē, dil′a·tạr″ē, *a.* [Fr. *dilatoire,* L.L. *dilatorius,* < L. *differo, dilatum.*] Marked with or given to procrastination or delay; slow; tardy; making delay or resulting in delay.—**dil·a·to·ri·ly,** *adv.*—**dil·a·to·ri·ness,** *n.*

di·lem·ma, di·lem′a, *n.* [L.L., < Gr. *dilēmma.*] A situation requiring a choice between equally objectionable alternatives; an embarrassing situation; a problem that seems incapable of being resolved satisfactorily; *logic,* a form of argument in which two or more alternatives presented to an antagonist are equally conclusive against him.—**dil·em·mat·ic,** dil″e·mat′ik, *a.*

dil·et·tan·te, dil″i·tan′tē, dil″i·tän′tä, dil″i·tänt′, dil′i·tänt″, *n. pl.* **dil·et·tan·tes,** *It.* **dil·et·tan·ti,** dil″i·tän′tē, dil′i·tän′tē. [It., prop. ppr. of *dilettare,* < L. *delectare,* E. to *delight.*] One who pursues an art or science desultorily or merely for amusement; a dabbler; a lover or amateur of an art or science, esp. of a fine art.—*a.* Being a dilettante; of or pertaining to dilettantes.—**dil·et·tan·tish, dil·et·tan·te·ish,** *a.*—**dil·et·tant·ism, dil·et·tan·te·ism,** *n.*

dil·i·gence, dil′i·jens, *n.* [L. *diligentia,* carefulness, diligence, < *diligo,* to love earnestly.] Steady application; constant effort to accomplish what is undertaken; industry; care; perseverance.

dil·i·gence, dil′i·jens, *n.* [Fr.] A kind of four-wheeled public stagecoach in use, esp. in France, during the 18th century.

dil·i·gent, dil′i·jent, *a.* [L. *diligens, diligentis.*] Constant in effort to accomplish what is undertaken; attentive; industrious; done with painstaking care and perseverance.—**dil·i·gent·ly,** *adv.*

dill, dil, *n.* [M.E. *dile,* Sw. *dill,* G. *dill,* dill; possibly < its soothing qualities in *dilling* or *dulling* pain.] *Arethum graveolens,* of the parsley family, a plant indigenous to Europe, which bears seeds and yellow flowers both of which are aromatic and used primarily for flavoring; the foliage or seeds of this plant; a dill pickle.—**dill pick·le,** a dill-flavored, pickled cucumber.

dil·ly·dal·ly, dil′ē·dal″ē, dil·ē·dal′ē, *v.i.—dillydallied, dillydallying.* [A reduplication of *dally.*] To loiter; to delay; to trifle.

dil·u·ent, dil′ū·ent, *a.* [L. *diluens, diluentis.*] Having the effect of diluting.—*n.* That which dilutes.

di·lute, di·lōt′, dī·lōt′, *v.t.—diluted, diluting.* [L. *diluo, dilutus.*] To render liquid or more liquid, esp. by mixing with water; to weaken by an admixture.—*a.* Diluted, reduced in strength by intermixture.—**di·lut·er, di·lu·tor,** *n.*—**di·lute·ness,** *n.*

di·lu·tion, di·lō′shan, dī·lō′shan, *n.* The

act of diluting; the state of being diluted; that which is diluted.

di·lu·vi·al, di·lö′vē·al, *a.* [L. *diluvium,* a deluge, < *diluo.* DILUTE.] Pertaining to or resulting from a flood or deluge, esp. the flood in the Biblical story of Noah. Gen. vi–ix. *Geol.* formed by floods; made up of or pertaining to diluvium.

di·lu·vi·um, di·lö′vē·um, *n. pl.* **di·lu·vi·a,** di·lö′vē·a. [L., flood, < *diluere,* wash to pieces, wash away.] *Geol.* coarse, superficial deposits formerly attributed to a general deluge but now regarded as glacial drift. Also **di·lu·vi·on.**

dim, dim, *a.—dimmer, dimmest.* [O.E. *dim,* dark, obscure = O.Fris. *dim,* Icel. *dimmr,* dim.] Somewhat dark; not clearly seen, heard, understood, or remembered; obscure; faint; vague; not luminous; having the luster obscured; not seeing clearly; not likely to be successful, as: Prospects are *dim.* —*n.* The short-range beam of a headlight, as of an automobile.—*v.t.—dimmed, dimming.* To render dim or less clear; to decrease the brightness of, as headlights.— *v.i.* To become dim or dimmer.—**dim·ly,** *adv.*—**dim·ness,** *n.*—**take a dim view of,** to look upon pessimistically or disapprovingly.

dime, dīm, *n.* [Fr. *dime,* a tenth, a tithe, O.Fr. *disme,* < L. *decimus,* tenth, < *decem,* ten.] A silver coin of the United States and Canada equal to ten cents; the tenth of a dollar.

di·men·hy·dri·nate, dī″men·hī′dri·nāt″, *n. Pharm.* a synthetic, white, crystalline powder, $C_{17}H_{22}NO \cdot C_7H_6ClN_4O_2$, used to prevent or relieve nausea, esp. that caused by motion, and in the treatment of certain allergies.

dime nov·el, *n.* A cheap paperback novel characterized by sensationalism or melodrama: a term in use from 1850 to 1920.

di·men·sion, di·men′shan, *n.* [L. *dimensio(n-),* < *dimetiri,* measure off.] Magnitude measured in a particular direction, specif. length, breadth, thickness, or time. Usu. *pl.* measure, size, or magnitude; degree, scope, or range.—**di·men·sion·less,** *a.*—**di·men·sion·al,** *a.*—**di·men·sion·al·i·ty,** *n.*—**di·men·sion·al·ly,** *adv.*

dim·er·ous, dim′ėr·us, *a.* [Gr. *dimeres.*] Consisting of or divided into two parts; *bot.* of flowers, having two members in each whorl; *entom.* having two joints in each tarsus. Also **di·mer·ic.—dim·er·ism,** *n.*

dime store, *n.* A five-and-ten.

dim·e·ter, dim′i·tèr, *n.* [Gr. *dimetros.*] *Pros.* a line having two metrical feet.

di·min·ish, di·min′ish, *v.t.* [O.Fr. *demenuiser,* < L. *diminuo,* to lessen.] To cause to be or appear less or smaller by any means; to impair, degrade, or belittle. —*v.i.* To become, or appear, less or smaller; decrease.—**di·min·ish·a·ble,** *a.*—**di·min·ish·ment,** *n.*

di·min·ished, di·min′isht, *a.* Made smaller; lessened; *mus.* of an interval, smaller by a half step than the corresponding perfect or minor interval.

di·min·ish·ing re·turns, *n. pl. Econ.* The successively lower rate of output which is yielded when a single production factor continues to be increased beyond a certain optimum point while the other factors remain constant; any benefits which beyond a certain point do not increase proportionately to increased investment, as of time, money, or effort.

di·min·u·en·do, di·min″ū·en′do, *a., adv.* [It., gerund of *diminuire,* < M.L. *diminuere.* DIMINISH.] *Mus.* gradually diminishing in force or loudness; decrescendo, as opposed to *crescendo.*—*n. pl.* **di·min·u·en·dos.** *Mus.* a gradual decrease in force or loudness; such a passage.

dim·i·nu·tion, dim″i·nö′shan, dim″i·nū′-shan, *n.* [L. *diminutio(n-),* for *deminutio(n-),*

< *deminuere.* DIMINISH.] The act, fact, or process of diminishing; lessening; reduction; *law,* an omission in the record of a case sent up to a court of review; *mus.* repetition of a theme in notes with decreased time value.

di·min·u·tive, di·min′ū·tiv, *a.* [M.L. *diminutivus,* for L.L. *deminutivus.*] Characterized by diminution; small; little; tiny; *gram.* of certain affixes or words formed by their addition, signifying smallness, familiarity, endearment, or contempt, as: *Lambkin* is a *diminutive* word formed by adding the *diminutive* suffix—*kin* to the word *lamb.*—*n.* A diminutive specimen or form of anything; a small thing or person; *gram.* a diminutive word or affix.— **di·min·u·tive·ly,** *adv.*—**di·min·u·tive·ness,** *n.*

dim·is·so·ry, dim′i·sōr″ē, dim′i·sạr″ē, *a.* [L.L. *dimissorius.* DISMISS.] Sending away or granting leave to depart; as, a *dimissory* letter granting a clergyman leave to move to another diocese.—**dim·is·so·ri·al,** *n.* A dimissory letter.

dim·i·ty, dim′i·tē, *n. pl.* **dim·i·ties.** [It. *dimito,* L.L. *dimitum,* < Gr. *dimitos,* dimity.] A fine cotton fabric, usually white, often with a slightly raised check, stripe, or cord design woven of a heavier thread.

dim·mer, dim′ėr, *n.* One who or that which dims; a rheostatic device in a lighting system which makes possible gradual variation in the intensity of illumination. *Pl.* automobile parking lights; headlights switched to low beam.

di·mor·phism, di·mạr′fiz″um, *n.* [Gr. *di-,* double, and *morphē,* form.] *Bot.* the appearance of analogous organs of plants, as flowers or fruits, under two very dissimilar forms, either on the same plant or on separate plants of the species; *zool.* difference of form between animals of the same species; *crystal.* the property shown by some substances of crystallizing in two distinct forms.—**di·mor·phous, di·mor·phic,** *a.* Characterized by dimorphism.

dim·out, dim′out′, *n.* The process or the result of restricting the use of, or partially concealing, night lighting, as of a city or a ship, as a precaution against an air attack.

dim·ple, dim′pl, *n.* [Probably a diminutive form connected with *dip* or *deep*; akin G. *dümpel, tümpel,* a pool.] A small natural depression in the cheek or other part of the human body; a slight depression or indentation on any surface.—*v.i.—dimpled, dimpling.* To form or show dimples.—*v.t.* To mark with dimples.—**dim·ply,** *a.*

dim·wit, dim′wit, *n. Slang,* a stupid or obtuse person.—**dim·wit·ted,** *a.*—**dim·wit·ted·ly,** *adv.*

din, din, *n.* [O.E. *dyn, dyne,* noise, thunder; Icel. *dynr, din, dynia,* to resound; < same root as Skt. *dhvan,* to sound.] Noise; particularly loud, confused sound that is continued.—*v.t.—dinned, dinning.* To deafen with continued or confused sound.

di·nar, di·när′, *n.* [Ar. and Pers., < Gr. *dēnarion,* < L. *denarius.*] Any of certain Oriental coins, esp. gold coins of ancient Arab governments; monetary units in Iraq, Kuwait, Jordan, Tunisia, and Yugoslavia, of denominations varying from country to country.

dine, dīn, *v.i.—dined, dining.* [Fr. *dîner,* O.Fr. *disner,* L.L. *disnare.*] To eat the chief meal of the day; to take dinner; to have any meal.—**dine out,** to take dinner elsewhere than at one's own residence, esp. at a fine restaurant.—**din·ing room,** A room to dine in; a place for public dining.

din·er, dī′nėr, *n.* One who dines; a railroad dining car; a restaurant shaped like a railroad car.

di·nette, dī·net′, *n.* A small dining area off the kitchen.

---

a- fat, fāte, fär, fâre, fạll;   **e-** met, mē, mēre, hėr;   **i-** pin, pīne,   **o-** not, nōte, mŏve,   **u-** tub, cūbe, bụll;   **oi-** oil;   **ou-** pound.

ding, ding, v.i. [Imit.] To sound as a bell when struck; to ring, esp. continuously; to keep talking importunately.—adv., n. A word imitative of the sound of a stroke of a bell or the like.

ding-dong, ding'dang", ding'dong", n. The sound of bells, or any similar sound of repeated strokes.—v.i.—a.

din·ghy, ding'gē, n. pl. din·ghies. [Hindi.] An East Indian boat varying in size in different localities; a small boat used by a ship, esp. a tender for a sailboat, a rubber life raft. Also **din·gey, dingy, dinky.**

din·gle, ding'gl, n. [Apparently a form of O.E. dimble, a bell or dingle, and dimple.] A narrow dale or valley between hills; a small secluded and embowered valley.

din·gle·ber·ry, n. A woody bush of the southwestern U.S.; its globe-shaped, dark red, edible berry.

din·go, ding'go, n. pl. din·goes. A wolflike wild Australian dog with a reddish- or yellowish-brown coat.

din·gus, ding'us, n. pl. ding·us·es. Colloq. something whose name is forgotten or unknown.

din·gy, din'jē, a. dingier, dingiest. [Probably connected with dung.] Of a dirty white or dusky color; soiled; sullied; dusky.—ding'gē, n. pl. din·gies. Dinghy.—din·gi·ness, n.—din·gi·ly, adv.

din·ing car, n. A railroad car in which meals are served to passengers.

dink·ey, ding'kē, n. pl. dink·ies. [Amer.] A small locomotive used for hauling logs, shunting freight cars, and similar jobs; any small thing. Also **dinky.**

dink·y, ding'kē, a.—dinkier, dinkiest. [Sc. dink, neat.] Small; insignificant; Brit. colloq. neat; spruce; nattily attired.—n. pl. dink·ies. Dinghy.

din·ner, din'ẽr, n. The chief meal of the day; a formal meal in honor of a person or an event.

din·ner jack·et, n. A tuxedo jacket for semiformal evening wear.

din·o·flag·el·late, din"o·flaj'e·lāt", n. One of the plantlike flagellates of the order Dinoflagellata, which constitute an important part of the mass of various marine organisms.

di·no·saur, dī'no·sạr", n. [Gr. deinos, terrible, and sauros, a lizard.] Paleon. one of a group of terrestrial, fossil reptiles, some carnivorous, some herbivorous, the largest species weighing between 40 and 50 tons.—di·no·sau·ri·an, dī"no·sạr'ē·an, a., n. (Cap.)

di·no·there, dī'no·thēr", n. [Gr. deinos-, terrible, and thērion, wild beast.] Paleon. a gigantic, extinct, two-tusked mammal allied to the elephant, occurring in Asia and Europe during the later Tertiary period.

dint, dint, n. [O.E. dynt, a blow, O.E. and Sc. dunt, Icel. dyntr, a stroke.] Means; force; the mark made by a blow; a dent.—v.t. To make a dint in; to dent.—by dint of, by the power of; by means of.

di·o·cese, dī'o·sēs", dī'o·sis, n. [Gr. dioikēsis, administration, a province or jurisdiction—dia-, and oikēsis, residence, < oikeō, to dwell, oikos, a house.] The circuit or extent of a bishop's jurisdiction.—di·oc·e·san, dī·os'i·san, a. Pertaining to a diocese.—n. A bishop in charge of a diocese; the clergy of a diocese.

di·ode, dī'ōd, n. Electronics, a type of electron tube which has an anode and a cathode, used primarily as a rectifier.

di·oe·cious, dī·ē'shus, a. [Gr. di-, two, and oikos, house.] Biol. having the male and female organs in separate and distinct individuals; bot. of a plant species, having the androecium and the gynoecium in separate flowers on different plants. Also di·e·cious, di·oi·cous, dī·oi'kas.

Di·o·ny·si·a, dī"o·nish'ē·a, dī"o·nis'ē·a, n. pl. [L., < Gr. Dionysia.] Festivals in honor of Dionysus, the Greek god of wine and fertility, celebrated periodically in various parts of ancient Greece.—Di·o·nys·i·ac, a. [Gr. Dionysiakos.] Pertaining to the Dionysia or to Dionysus; Bacchic.—Di·o·ny·si·a·cal·ly, adv.

Di·o·ny·sian, dī"o·nish'an, dī"o·nis'ē·an, a. Pertaining to Dionysus, the Greek god of wine and fertility; of a reckless, sensual, or frenzied nature.

di·op·side, dī·op'sīd, dī·op'sid, n. [Fr. < Gr. di-, two, and opsis, appearance.] Mineral. a variety of pyroxene occurring in various colors, most commonly pale to medium green.

di·op·ter, Brit. **di·op·tre,** dī·op'tẽr, n. [Gr. diopter, a spy.] Opt. in lenses, the unit of refractive power, being that of the reciprocal of the focal length, expressed in meters. Abbr. D.

di·op·tom·e·ter, dī"op·tom'i·tẽr, n. An instrument which measures the eye's accommodation and refraction.—di·op·tom·e·try, n.

di·op·tric, dī·op'trik, a. [Gr. dioptrikos.] Of or pertaining to dioptrics; assisting vision by refracting light, as a lens; pertaining to the refraction of light, as by lenses.—di·op·tri·cal·ly, adv.—di·op·trics, n. pl. construed as sing. The branch of optics concerned with light refraction by lenses.

di·o·ram·a, dī"o·ram'a, dī"o·rä'ma, n. [Gr. dia-, through, and horama, a view.] A painted scene in three dimensions, viewed through an aperture; a spectacular picture or scene of any size, with or without translucent features; an exhibit, as presented in a museum, showing wild animals or human beings against a realistically painted scene of their habitat.—di·o·ram·ic, a.

di·o·rite, dī'o·rīt", n. [Fr. < Gr. diorizein, distinguish, < dia-, through, and crizein, bound.] An igneous rock commonly consisting essentially of feldspar and hornblende.—di·o·rit·ic, dī"o·rit'ik, a.

di·ox·ide, dī·ok'sīd, dī·ok'sid, n. Chem. an oxide consisting of two atoms of oxygen per molecule, as CO_2, carbon dioxide.

dip, dip, n. The act of dipping; a plunge into water, as for a brief swim; a lowering momentarily; a sinking down; a short downward plunge, as of an airplane; a quantity taken up by dipping, as a scoop of ice cream; a candle made by repeatedly dipping a wick into melted tallow; a liquid or sauce into which something is dipped; a slight or temporary decrease; a downward extension or inclination; the degree of such an extension; the angular amount by which the horizon lies below the level of the eye; a hollow or depression in the land; the angle which a freely poised magnetic needle makes with the plane of the horizon. Geol, and mining, the downward inclination of a stratum or vein; the angle between a stratum or similar geological feature and the horizontal plane; gymnastics, an exercise on the parallel bars in which a performer, standing on his hands, lowers his body until his chin is level with the bars and then elevates himself by straightening his arms; slang, a pickpocket.

dip, dip, v.t.—dipped, dipping. To plunge temporarily into a liquid, as to moisten, coat, or dye; to obtain or take up by bailing or ladling; to lower and raise again; as, to dip a flag in salute; to immerse, as animals, in a germicidal or antiseptic solution; to make, as a candle, by repeatedly dipping a wick into melted tallow.—v.i. To plunge into water or other liquid and emerge quickly; to plunge the hand or a dipper down into or below a surface, esp. to withdraw something; to sink or drop down

suddenly; to incline or slope downward; to decrease slightly and usu. temporarily, as: Prices dipped. To engage slightly in the study of a subject or the reading of a book.

di·phase, dī'fāz", a. Elect. having two phases. Also **di·pha·sic.**

di·phen·yl, dī·fen'al, dī·fēn'al, n. Biphenyl.

di·phen·yl·a·mine, dī·fen"il·a·mēn", dī·fen"il·am'in, n. Chem. an aromatic, crystalline, benzene derivative used chiefly in the preparation of various dyes and in stabilizing explosives.

di·phos·gene, dī·fos'jēn, n. A colorless liquid compound, $ClCOOCCl_3$, used as a poison gas in World War I and now used chiefly in organic synthesis.

diph·the·ri·a, dif·thēr'ē·a, dip·thēr'ē·a, n. [Gr. diphtera, a membrane.] An epidemic inflammatory disease of the air passages, and especially of the throat, characterized by the formation of a false membrane, now controlled by vaccine injections.—diph·the·rit·ic, dif"the·rit'ik, dip"the·rit'ik, a. Connected with, relating to, or formed by diphtheria. Also **diph·the·ri·al, diph·ther·ic.**

diph·thong, dif'thang, dif'thong, dip'-thang, dip'thong, n. [Gr. diphthongos—di-, twice, and phthongos, sound.] A continuous monosyllabic speech sound made by gliding from the articulatory position for one vowel toward that for another, as oy in toy.—diph·thong·i·za·tion, n.—diph·thong·ize, v.t.—diphthongized, diphthongizing.

diph·y·o·dont, dif'ē·o·dont", a. [Gr. diphues, double, and odous (odont) tooth.] Having two successive sets of teeth, as most mammals.

di·plex, dī'pleks, a. Pertaining to sending two signals over the same communications path in the same direction at the same time.

dip·lo·coc·cus, dip"lo·kok'us, n. pl. dip·lo·coc·ci, dip"lo·kok'sī. [Gr. diploos, double, and kokkos, a berry.] Bact. a form of parasitic bacteria occurring in pairs.—dip·lo·coc·cal, dip·lo·coc·cic, a.

dip·lo·e, dip'lō·ē", n. [N.L., < Gr. diploē, fold, doubling, < diploos, double.] Anat. the cancellate bony tissue between the hard inner and outer walls of the bones of the cranium.—dip·lo·ic, di·plō'ik, dip·lo·et·ic, dip"lō·et'ik, a.

dip·loid, dip'loid, a. Twofold; biol. having the two sets of chromosomes characteristic of a somatic cell.—n. Biol. a diploid cell or organism.

di·plo·ma, di·plō'ma, n. [Gr. diplōma, a paper folded double, a license, < diploō, to fold, diploos, double.] A document signed by competent authority, conferring some power, privilege, or honor, as that given to graduates of colleges and universities upon completion of graduation requirements; an official document.

di·plo·ma·cy, di·plō'ma·sē, n. The science or art of conducting negotiations between nations; the forms of international negotiations; dexterity or skill in managing negotiations of any kind.

dip·lo·mat, dip'lo·mat", n. A person representing his government in negotiations with other nations and international organizations; a person who is tactful in any situation.—dip·lo·mat·ic, dip"lo·mat'ik, a. Pertaining to the management of any negotiations; skillful in gaining one's ends by tact and cleverness.—dip·lo·mat·i·cal·ly, adv.—dip·lo·mat·ics, n. pl. construed as sing. Diplomacy; the science of deciphering old writings, to ascertain their authenticity.—dip·lo·mat·ist, di·plō'ma·tist, n. A person skilled in diplomacy; Brit. one employed by the Foreign Office as a diplomat.

dip nee·dle, *n.* A magnetic needle mounted so as to be capable of moving freely about its center of gravity in a vertical plane, and indicating by its dip the direction of the earth's magnetism. Also **dip·ping nee·dle.**

dip·no·an, dip'nō·an, *a.* [N.L. *Dipnoi,* pl., < Gr. *dipnoos,* having two breathing apertures.] *Ichth.* belonging or pertaining to the *Dipnoi,* a group of fishes having both gills and lungs.—*n.* A *dipnoan* fish.

di·pole, dī'pōl", *n. Phys.* a pair of opposite and equal electrical charges or magnetic poles of opposite signs separated by a short distance; a radio or television antenna having two equal horizontal rods extending in opposite directions from the connection to the lead-in wire. *Chem.* a molecule showing separation of positive and negative charges.—**di·po·lar,** dī·pō'lar, *a.*

dip·per, dip'ėr, *n.* One who or that which dips; any of various diving birds, esp. of the genus *Cinclus,* as *C. aquaticus,* the common European water ouzel; a vessel provided with a handle and used to dip liquids.—**Big Dip·per,** *astron.* the group of seven bright stars in Ursa Major resembling a dipper in outline.—**Lit·tle Dip·per,** *astron.* a similar group in Ursa Minor.

dip·sa·ca·ceous, dip"sa·kā'shus, *a.* [N.L. *Dipsacus,* the typical genus, < Gr. *dipsakos,* teasel.] Belonging to the *Dipsacaceae,* or teasel family of plants.

dip·so·ma·ni·a, dip"so·mā'nē·a, *n.* [N.L. < Gr. *dipsa,* thirst, and *mania,* E. *mania.*] *Pathol.* an irresistible, generally periodic, craving for intoxicating drink.—**dip·so·ma·ni·ac,** dip"so·mā'nē·ak", *n.*—**dip·so·ma·ni·a·cal,** dip"so·ma·nī'a·kal, *a.*

dip·stick, dip'stik", *n.* A wood or metal stick with markings to measure depth, used to indicate the amount of oil in the crankcase of an automobile or gasoline in a tank.

dip·ter·on, dip'te·ron", *n.* pl. **dip·ter·a,** dip'tėr·a. [Gr. *di-,* double, and *pteron,* wing.] Any of an order of insects, *Diptera,* characterized by one pair of membranous wings, including such insects as houseflies, mosquitoes, and gnats.—**dip·ter·an,** *a.,n.*—**dip·ter·ous,** dip'tėr·us, *a.*

dip·tych, dip'tik, *n.* [L.L. *diptycha,* pl., < Gr. *diptycha,* neut. pl. of *diptychos,* double-folded.] A hinged two-leaved tablet used by the ancient Greeks and Romans for writing on with the stylus; a pair of pictures or carvings on two panels hinged together, esp. used to decorate an altar.

dire, dīr, *a.*—*direr, direst.* [L. *dirus,* terrible.] Dreadful; horrible; in extreme circumstances; as, *dire* poverty; disastrous; as, a *dire* calamity.—**dire·ly,** dīr'lē, *adv.*—**dire·ness,** *n.*

di·rect, di·rekt', dī·rekt', *a.* [L. *dirigo, directum,* to set in a straight line, to direct—*di-* for *dis-* intens., and *rego, rectum,* to make straight. RIGHT, REGENT.] Characterized by a straight, uninterrupted route or method; the shortest, nearest, least complicated way; free of interruption or intervention in the sense of immediate; straightforward, candid, or clear; pertaining to a causal relationship, as: Inflation was a *direct* result of the government's fiscal policies. A lineal or unbroken line of descent; precise reproduction of another's words; as, a *direct* quote; absolute or exact; as, a *direct* copy. *Astron.* pertaining to celestial bodies appearing to move from west to east; moving in an orbital path the same as the earth's in its revolution around the sun. *Chem.* pertaining to dyes not requiring a mordant; *elec.* continuous, rather than alternating, current; *govt.* pertaining to efforts made by voters without an intervening agency, as a referendum; *math.* expressing a positive relationship in the terms of a proportion.

di·rect, di·rekt', dī·rekt', *v.t.* To guide or lead by instruction or information; to control, manage, or govern; to command; to address,(either verbal remarks or written communications); *fig.* to point the way; as, to *direct* her. To point out the way to a location; to project toward a specific place; as, to *direct* a broadside; *mus.* to conduct(a group).—*v.i.* To act as a guide; to give commands or orders.—*adv.* In a straight line or straightforward manner.—**di·rect·ly,** *adv.*—**di·rect·ness,** *n.* The state or quality of being direct.

di·rect ac·tion, *n.* An action, usually by a group, against an authority or a power such as an institution, where forceful means are employed to attain an end, as in the use of the boycott, picketing, or strikes.

di·rect cur·rent, *n. Elect.* a current flowing in one direction in a circuit. Abbr. *DC.*

di·rect·ed, di·rek'tid, dī·rek'tid, *a.* Characterized by direction; guided; controlled; prescribed; *math.* having an assigned direction or value, either positive or negative; as, a *directed* number.

di·rec·tion, di·rek'shan, dī·rek'shan, *n.* The course or line along which anything moves or is directed; the region toward which something is directed, as north; management; an order; the act of directing an orchestra or a theatrical production; a trend of thought or action; as, the *direction* of modern drama; the address on a letter. *Mus.* phrases or symbols on written music indicating how it is to be rendered.

di·rec·tion·al, di·rek'sha·nal, dī·rek'sha·nal, *a.* Pertaining to or indicating direction in space. *Radio,* adapted for indicating the direction of signals received; adapted for transmitting signals in a certain direction.

di·rec·tion find·er, *n. Radio,* a device on a receiver to detect the direction of incoming radio waves.

di·rec·tion in·di·ca·tor, *n.* An aircraft compass used to aid a pilot in flying a predetermined course by a comparison of two indicators giving the actual heading and the desired heading.

di·rec·tive, di·rek'tiv, dī·rek'tiv, *a.* Having the power of directing.—*n.* An authoritative instruction or direction; as, a *directive* to the employees from the foreman.

di·rect light·ing, *n.* A system of lighting in which the greatest part of the light from the source is cast on the illuminated area.

di·rect·ly, di·rekt'lē, dī·rekt'lē, *adv.* In a direct manner; in a straight line or course; immediately; instantly; soon; without delay; expressly; without circumlocution or ambiguity; following immediately in order. *Math.* in direct proportion.

di·rect ob·ject, *n. Gram.* the word, phrase, or clause upon which the verb acts or toward which it directs its action, as 'ball' in 'the boy threw the ball.'

di·rec·tor, di·rek'tėr, dī·rek'ter, *n.* One who or that which directs; one who superintends, governs, or manages; specifically, one of a body appointed to direct, control, or superintend the affairs of a company; a person who directs the action, staging, and music of a production for stage, film, TV, or radio.—**di·rec·to·rate,** di·rek'tėr·it, dī·rek'tėr·it, *n.* The office of a director; a body of directors.—**di·rec·to·ri·al,** *a.*—**di·rec·tor·ship,** *n.* The office of a director.

di·rec·to·ry, di·rek'to·rē, dī·rek'trē, dī·rek'to·rē, dī·rek'trē, *n.* A book containing an alphabetical list of the inhabitants of a city, or town, or of persons of a particular category; a board in the lobby of a public building listing names and room numbers of the occupants; board of directors; directorate; (*cap.*) during the French Revolution, a body established by the Convention in 1795, and composed of five members.—*a.*

di·rect pri·mary, *n.* A preliminary election in which members of a party select their candidates by a direct vote.

di·rec·tress, di·rek'tris, dī·rek'tris, *n.* A female who directs or manages a business or a production.

di·rec·trix, di·rek'triks, dī·rek'triks, *n.* pl. **di·rec·trix·es,** **di·rec·tri·ces,** *Geom.* a straight line which has a strictly proportionate frame of reference to a curve.

di·rect tax, *n.* An income, general, property, or poll tax paid directly by the taxpayer.

dirge, dėrj, *n.* [A contraction of L. *dirige* ("direct," imperative of *dirigere,* to direct), the first word in a psalm or hymn formerly sung at funerals.] A song or tune often heard at funerals and intended to express grief, sorrow, and mourning; a musical composition expressing sorrow.

dir·ham, dir·ham', *n.* See Money table.

dir·i·gi·ble, dir'i·ji·bl, di·rij'i·bl, *n.* A balloon or airship, driven by motors, whose course can be directed by means of steering or directing apparatus.—*a.* That may be directed, turned, or guided.

dirk, dėrk, *n.* [Origin doubtful.] A type of dagger.—*v.t.* To stab.

dirn·dl, dėrn'dl, *n.* A type of woman's dress with full skirt and close-fitting bodice, commonly of colorful and strikingly patterned material, derived from Tyrolean peasant use; the full skirt of this type.

dirt, dėrt, *n.* [Icel. *drit,* dirt, excrement, *drita,* Sc. *drite,* O.E. (ge) *dritan,* to go to stool.] Any foul or filthy substance, as excrement, mud, mire, dust; loose soil or earth; whatever, adhering to anything, renders it foul or unclean; obscenity in speech, writing, or pictures; mean or petty gossip. *Placer mining,* earth from which gold is separated; also *pay dirt.*

dirt·y, dėr'tē, *a.*—*dirtier, dirtiest.* Foul; nasty; filthy; not clean; impure; mean; tiresome; underhand; as, a *dirty* trick; lamentable; as, a *dirty* shame; not sportsmanlike; dull; as, a *dirty* color; sleety, rainy, or sloppy, as weather.—*v.t.*—*dirtied, dirtying.* To make dirty or filthy; to soil.—**dirt·i·ly,** *adv.*—**dirt·i·ness,** *n.*

dis·a·bil·i·ty, dis"a·bil'i·tē, *n.* pl. **dis·a·bil·i·ties.** The state or quality of being mentally or physically disabled or unable; weakness; impotence; incapacity; inability to hold a certain job because of a physical or mental handicap; want of legal qualifications.—**dis·a·ble·ment,** dis·ā'bl·ment, *n.*

dis·a·ble, dis·ā·bl, *v.t.*—*disabled, disabling.* To deprive of competent strength or power, physical or mental; to injure so as to no longer be fit for certain duties or services; to incapacitate, to cripple; to deprive of legal qualifications.—**dis·a·bled,** *a.* Injured; incapacitated.

dis·a·buse, dis"a·būz', *v.t.*—*disabused, disabusing.* [Fr. *désabuser,* to disabuse.] To free from mistaken or erroneous notions or beliefs; to set right.

di·sac·cha·ride, dī·sak'a·rīd", dī·sak'a·rid, *n.* Any of a class of sugars yielding two monosaccharide molecules upon hydrolysis.

dis·ac·cord, dis"a·kard', *n.* Lack of harmony; disagreement.—*v.i.* To disagree.

dis·ad·van·tage, dis"ad·van'tij, dis"ad·vän'tij, *n.* Absence or deprivation of advantage; that which prevents success or renders it difficult; any detriment to interest, fame, credit, profit, or other good.—*v.t.*—*disadvantaged, disadvantaging.* To deprive of advantage.

dis·ad·van·taged, dis"ad·van'tijd, dis"ad·vän'tijd, *n.* Those deprived of such advantages as good housing, medical care, and education.—*a.* Underprivileged.

dis·ad·van·ta·geous, dis·ad·van·ta'jus, dis"ad·van·tä'jus, *a.* Attended with disadvantage; unfavorable to success or prosperity; detrimental.—**dis·ad·van·ta-- geous·ly,** *adv.*—**dis·ad·van·ta·geous·ness,** *n.*

dis·af·fect, dis″a·fekt′, *v.t.* To alienate the affection of; to make less friendly or less faithful, as to a person, party, government, or cause; to make discontented or unfriendly.—**dis·af·fec·tion,** *n.* Alienation of affection, attachment, or good will; disloyalty, esp. toward a government or authority

dis·af·fil·i·ate, dis″a·fil′ē·āt″, *v.t.*—*disaffiliated, disaffiliating.* To separate or remove from an affiliation or association; as, to *disaffiliate* oneself from an organization.— *v.i.* To end an affiliation.—**dis·af·fil·i·a·tion,** dis″a·fil′ē·ā′shan, *n.*

dis·af·firm, dis″a·fėrm′, *v.t.* To deny; to contradict; *law*, to annul, as a judicial decision, by a contrary judgment of a superior tribunal.—**dis·af·fir·ma·tion,** dis″af·er·mā′shan, *n.*—**dis·af·fir·mance,** *n.*

dis·af·for·est, dis″a·far′ist, dis″a·for′ist, *v.t.* To strip of forests or trees; deforest. *Law*, to remove from legal classification as a forest. Also **dis·for·est.**

dis·a·gree, dis″a·grē′, *v.i.*—*disagreed, disagreeing.* To differ, as: The witnesses′ stories *disagree.* To be of an opposite or different opinion; to be unsuitable or to cause harm to, as to the stomach; to quarrel.—**dis·a·gree·ment,** dis″a·grē′ment, *n.* Want of agreement; difference, discrepancy, or lack of similarity; difference of opinion; a falling out; a quarrel; a discord.

dis·a·gree·a·ble, dis″a·grē′a·bl, *a.* The reverse of agreeable; unpleasant; offensive to the mind or to the senses; repugnant; obnoxious.—*n.*—**dis·a·gree·a·ble·ness,** *n.*—**dis·a·gree·a·bly,** *adv.*

dis·al·low, dis″a·lou′, *v.t.* [O.Fr. *desalouer.*] To refuse to allow; refuse to admit the truth or validity of, as of a statement or claim; reject.—**dis·al·low·ance,** *n.*—**dis·al·low·a·ble,** *a.*

dis·ap·pear, dis″a·pēr′, *v.i.* To vanish from sight; to go away or out of sight; to cease to be or exist; to gradually vanish from sight or cease to be seen—**dis·ap·pear·ance,** dis″a·pēr′ans, *n.* Act of disappearing; removal from sight.

dis·ap·point, dis″a·point′, *v.t.* [Fr. *désappointer,* originally to remove from an appointment or office.] To fall short of fulfilling the hopes or expectations of; to hinder the fulfillment of, as of hopes or expectations.

dis·ap·point·ment, dis″a·point′ment, *n.* Defeat or failure of expectation, hope, desire, or intention.—**dis·ap·point·ed,** dis″a·poin′tid, *a.* Frustrated; thwarted; downhearted.

dis·ap·pro·ba·tion, dis″ap·ro·bā′shan, *n.* Disapproval; censure, expressed or unexpressed.—**dis·ap·pro·ba·tive, dis·ap·pro·ba·to·ry,** *a.*

dis·ap·prove, dis″a·prööv′, *v.t.*—*disapproved, disapproving.* To regard as wrong or objectionable; to censure.—*v.i.* To express or feel disapproval, used with *of* before the object.—**dis·ap·prov·al,** dis″a·prö′val, *n.* Disapprobation.—**dis·ap·prov·ing·ly,** *adv.* With distaste.

dis·arm, dis·ärm′, *v.t.* To take the arms or weapons from, usually by force or authority; to reduce to peacetime proportions, as an army or navy; to deprive of means of attack, defense, or power to terrify; to render harmless; to turn suspicion or hostility into friendliness, as: His kindness *disarmed* us.—*v.i.* To lay down arms; to disband armed forces; to limit armaments and forces to peacetime proportions.

dis·ar·ma·ment, dis·är′ma·ment, *n.* The act of disarming; the reduction of a national armament to peacetime size.

dis·arm·ing, dis·är′ming, *a.* Tending to allay suspicion or animosity; pleasing; ingratiating.

dis·ar·range, dis″a·rānj′, *v.t.*—*disarranged, disarranging.* To put out of order; to unsettle or disturb the order or due arrangement of.—**dis·ar·range·ment,** *n.* Disorder.

dis·ar·ray, dis″a·rā′, *v.t.* To throw into disorder; to undress; to divest of clothes.—*n.* Disorder; confusion; disordered dress.

dis·ar·tic·u·late, dis″är·tik′ū·lāt′, *v.t.*—*disarticulated, disarticulating.* To take apart at the joints.—*v.i.* To come apart at the joints.—**dis·ar·tic·u·la·tion,** dis″är·tik″ū·lā′shan, *n.*

dis·as·sem·ble, dis″a·sem′bl, *v.t.* To take apart, as the component parts of a motor or structure.

dis·as·so·ci·ate, dis″a·sō′shē·āt″, dis″a·sō′sē·āt″, *v.t.*—*disassociated, disassociating.* To dissociate.

dis·as·ter, di·zas′tėr, di·zä′stėr, *n.* [Fr. *désastre*—dis-, and L. *astrum,* a star; a word of astrological origin.] Any unfortunate event, esp. a great misfortune causing widespread damage or suffering; calamity.—**dis·as·trous,** di·zas′trus, di·zä′strus, *a.* Occasioned or accompanied by disaster; calamitous.—**dis·as·trous·ly,** *adv.*

dis·a·vow, dis″a·vou′, *v.t.* To deny cognizance of or a responsibility for; to disown; to repudiate; to reject.—**dis·a·vow·al,** *n.* Denial; repudiation.

dis·band, dis·band′, *v.t.* To break up, as a band or body of men; to dismiss from military service; to disperse.—*v.i.* To break up and retire from military service.—**dis·band·ment,** *n.*

dis·bar, dis·bär′, *v.t.*—*disbarred, disbarring.* To expel from being a member of the bar or from the legal profession; to remove from the bar of a particular court.

dis·be·lief, dis″bi·lēf′, *n.* Denial of belief; skepticism.—**dis·be·lieve,** dis″bi·lēv′, *v.t.* —*disbelieved, disbelieving.* To hold not to be true or not to exist.—*v.i.* To deny the truth of any position.—**dis·be·liev·er,** *n.*

dis·burse, dis·bėrs′, *v.t.*—*disbursed, disbursing.* [O.Fr. *desborser*—prefix dis-, and L.L. *bursa,* a purse. PURSE.] To pay out as money; to expend; to spread out.—**dis·burse·ment,** dis·bėrs′ment, *n.* A sum paid out.—**dis·burs·er,** *n.*

disc, disk, *n., v.t.* See *disk.*

dis·calced, dis·kalst′, *a.* [L. *discalceatus.*] Unshod; barefooted, as certain religious congregations of men and women. Also **dis·cal·ce·ate,** dis·kal′sē·it, dis·kal′sē·āt″.

dis·cant, dis′kant, dis·kant′, *n., v.i.* See *descant.*

dis·card, di·skärd′, *v.t.* To reject; to cast aside as no longer usable; as, to *discard* old books; in a card game, to throw from one′s hand.—*v.i.* In a card game, to eliminate one or more cards from one′s hand.—dis′kärd, *n.* The act of discarding; that which is rejected or cast aside; in cards, one or more cards which are discarded.

dis·cern, di·sėrn′, di·zėrn′, *v.t.* [L. *discerno*—dis-, and *cerno,* to separate or distinguish, akin to Gr. *krino,* to judge (whence *critic*); Skt. *kri,* to separate.] To perceive or note as being different; to discriminate by the eye, some other sense, or the intellect.—*v.i.* To see or understand differences.—**dis·cern·er,** *n.* A clear-sighted observer; one who knows and judges.—**dis·cern·i·ble,** di·sėr′ni·bl, di·zėr′ni·bl, *a.* Distinguishable. Also **dis·cern·a·ble.** —**dis·cern·i·ble·ness, dis·cern·a·ble·ness,** *n.*—**dis·cern·i·bly, dis·cern·a·bly,** *adv.*

dis·cern·ing, di·sėr′ning, di·zėr′ning, *a.* Capable of discriminating.—**dis·cern·ing·ly,** *adv.*

dis·cern·ment, di·sėrn′ment, di·zėrn′ment, *n.* Acuteness of judgment; the power

to perceive differences between things or ideas, as well as their relationships.

dis·cerp·ti·ble, di·sėrp′ti·bl, di·zerp′ti·bl, *a.* Capable of being torn apart; divisible.

dis·charge, dis·chärj′, *v.t.*—*discharged, discharging.* [O.Fr. *deschargier* (Fr. *décharger*).] To relieve of a charge or load; to relieve or free of anything; to relieve oneself, as of an obligation or responsibility; to relieve or deprive, as of an office or employment; to dismiss from service. To clear of a charge or accusation; to set free from custody or legal restraint; to send away or to allow to go; to release from military service. To rid of a charge of electricity; to unload, as a cargo; to let go or shoot, as a missile; to pour forth, as water; to emit, as an oath; to pay a debt; to pay off, as a creditor; to fulfill, perform, or execute a duty or function; to rid, as a fabric of dye. *Law,* to set aside or annul, as an order of a court.— *v.i.* To discharge a burden or load; to throw off a burden; to deliver a charge or load; to emit contents; to come or pour forth.—**dis·charge·a·ble,** *a.*—**dis·char·ger,** *n.*

dis·charge, dis′chärj, dis·chärj′, *n.* The act of discharging a ship or a gun; a sending or coming forth, as of water from a pipe; ejection; emission; something discharged or emitted; the rate at which something is discharged or the quantity discharged; a relieving or being relieved of obligation or liability; the fulfilling of an obligation; the payment of a debt; the performance or execution, as of a duty; release or dismissal from office, employment, or military duty. *Law,* annulment, as of a court order; acquittal or exoneration; release from custody. A sending away or allowing to go; a certificate of release, as from obligation or liability; *elect.* the withdrawing or transference of an electric charge; the equalization of the difference of potential between two terminals.

dis·ci·flo·ral, dis″i·flōr′al, *a. Bot.* having flowers in which the receptacle is expanded into a conspicuous disk, as the sunflower.

dis·ci·ple, di·sī′pl, *n.* [O.Fr. Fr. *disciple,* < L. *discipulus,* < *discere,* learn.] A follower of a particular teacher; an adherent of the principles of some leader of thought, esp. one of the twelve personal followers of Jesus Christ; sometimes, any follower of Christ.—**dis·ci·ple·ship,** *n.*

Dis·ci·ples of Christ, *n.* A denomination of Christians, founded in the U.S. in the early part of the 19th century by Alexander Campbell, 1788–1866, which rejects all formulas or creeds, accepts the Bible alone as a sufficient and infallible rule of faith and practice, and administers baptism by immersion only.

dis·ci·plin·a·ble, dis′i·plin″a·bl, *a.* Subject to or meriting discipline or correction; capable of being disciplined or instructed.

dis·ci·pli·nar·i·an, dis″i·pli·nâr′ē·an, *n.* One who disciplines or advocates strict maintenance of discipline.—*a.* Disciplinary.

dis·ci·pli·nar·y, dis′i·pli·ner″ē, *a.* Of, pertaining to, or comprising discipline; intended to enforce or restore discipline.

dis·ci·pline, dis′i·plin, *n.* [O.Fr. Fr. *discipline,* < L. *disciplina,* < *discipulus,* E. *disciple.*] A state of order maintained by training and control; a particular system of regulations for conduct; instruction and exercise designed to train to proper conduct or action; systematic training under direction and control; drill; punishment inflicted by way of correction and training; the training effect of experience, adversity, etc.; a branch of instruction or learning. *Eccles.* the methods or rules employed in regulating the conduct of the members of a church; the system of government regulating the practices of a church as distinguished from its doctrine; religious mortification or penance; an instrument of punishment, esp. a scourge for religious penance.—*v.t. disciplined, disciplining.* To bring to a state of order and obedience by training and control; to subject to discipline or punishment; to correct; to chastise; to train by instruction and exercise; drill.—**dis·ci·plin·er,** *n.*—**dis·ci·plin·al,** *a.*

disc jock·ey, *n.* See *disk jockey.*

dis·claim, dis·klām′, *v.t.* To deny responsibility for or approval of; disown; disavow; to deny the validity or authority of; as, to *disclaim* an accusation; *law,* to deny or relinquish all claim to.—*v.i. Law,* to deny or relinquish a claim.—**dis·claim·er,** dis·klā′mer, *n.* A person who disclaims; an act of disclaiming; a means, such as a written statement, of disclaiming; *law,* a renunciation or giving up of a claim.

dis·cla·ma·tion, dis″kla·mā′shan, *n.* The act of disclaiming; renunciation; disavowal. —**dis·clam·a·to·ry,** dis·klam′a·tōr″ē, *a.*

dis·close, di·sklōz′, *v.t.*—*disclosed, disclosing.* To allow to be seen; to bring to light; to make known; reveal; tell.— **dis·clos·er,** *n.*—**dis·clo·sure,** di·sklō′zher, *n.* The act of making known or revealing what was secret; that which is disclosed or made known.

dis·cob·o·lus, di·skob′o·lus, *n. pl.* **dis·cob·o·li,** di·skob′o·lī′, di·skob′o·lē″. [L., < Gr. *diskobolos.*] A thrower of the discus in ancient Greece; (*cap.*) a famous statue by the Greek sculptor Myron, 5th century B.C.

dis·cog·ra·phy, di·skog′ra·fē, *n.* A systematic classification of phonograph records; the methods used in such classification. Also **dis·kog·ra·phy.**

dis·coid, dis′koid, *a.* [< Gr. *diskos,* disk, and *eidos,* form.] Having the form of a disk; flat and circular; *bot.* of a composite flower-head, consisting of a disk only. Also **dis·coi·dal,** dis·koi′dal.

dis·col·or, *Brit.* **dis·col·our,** dis·kul′er, *v.t.* To alter or mar the hue or color of.—*v.i.* To alter in color; fade.—**dis·col·or·a·tion,** *Brit.* **dis·col·our·a·tion,** dis·kul″o·rā′shan, *n.* Alteration of color; a discolored spot.

dis·com·bob·u·late, dis′kom·bob′ya·lāt′, *v.t.*—*discombobulated, discombobulating. Colloq.* To disconcert; perplex; upset.

dis·com·fit, dis·kum′fit, *v.t.* [O.Fr. *disconfire, disconfit* < L. *dis-,* and *conficere,* to achieve.] To rout, defeat, or scatter in flight; to disconcert, foil, or frustrate the plans of.—**dis·com·fi·ture,** dis·kum′fi·cher, *n.* Rout; defeat; frustration; disappointment; embarrassment.

dis·com·fort, dis·kum′fert, *n.* Annoyance, minor pain, or uneasiness.—*v.t.* To disturb the peace or happiness of; to make uneasy; to pain slightly.

dis·com·mend, dis″ko·mend′, *v.t.* To blame; to censure; to expose to censure or bad feeling.—**dis·com·mend·a·ble,** *a*

dis·com·mode, dis″ko·mōd′, *v.t.*—*discommoded, discommoding.* To inconvenience; to incommode.—**dis·com·mo·di·ous,** *a.*— **dis·com·mo·di·ous·ly,** *adv.*—**dis·com·mo·di·ous·ness,** *n.*

dis·com·pose, dis″kom·pōz′, *v.t.*—*discomposed, discomposing.* To disorder, disturb, or disarrange; to disturb the peace and quietness of; to agitate, ruffle, fret, or vex.— **dis·com·po·sure,** dis″kom·pō′zher, *n.* The state of being discomposed; agitation or perturbation of mind.

dis·con·cert, dis″kon·sert′, *v.t.* To throw into disorder or confusion; to undo, as a concerted scheme or plan; to baffle; to frustrate; to discompose or disturb the self-possession of; to confuse.—**dis·con·cert·ing,** *a.*—**dis·con·cert·ing·ly,** *adv.*—**dis·con·cert·ing·ness,** *n.*—**dis·con·cer·tion, dis·con·cert·ment.**

dis·con·cert·ed, dis″kon·sèr′tid, *a.* Disturbed; embarrassed; discomposed;

confused.—**dis·con·cert·ed·ly,** *adv.*— **dis·con·cert·ed·ness,** *n.*

dis·con·form·i·ty, dis·kon·far′mi·tē, *n. pl.* **dis·con·form·i·ties.** Nonconformity. *Geol.* a division of parallel rock strata usually indicated in relief through erosion of the different strata at different rates.

dis·con·nect, dis″ko·nekt′, *v.t.* To separate or sever the connection between; to disunite; to detach.—**dis·con·nec·tion,** *Brit.* **dis·con·nex·ion,** dis·kon·nek′shan, *n.* The act of disconnecting; separation; want of union.—**dis·con·nect·ed,** *a.*—**dis·con·nect·ed·ly,** *adv.*—**dis·con·nect·ed·ness,** *n.*

dis·con·so·late, dis·kon′so·lit, *a.* [L. *dis-,* and *consolatus,* pp. of *consolor,* to console, to be consoled.] Destitute of consolation; hopelessly dejected; miserable; marked by or causing sadness; gloomy.— **dis·con·so·late·ly,** *adv.*—**dis·con·so·la·tion,** dis·kon″so·lā′shan, **dis·con·so·late·ness,** *n.*

dis·con·tent, dis″kon·tent′, *n.* One who is discontented; a malcontent. Want of contentment; uneasiness of mind; dissatisfaction. Also **dis·con·tent·ment.**—*a.* Uneasy; dissatisfied.—*v.t.* To make dissatisfied.

dis·con·tent·ed, dis″kon·ten′tid, *a.* Not contented; dissatisfied; not pleased with one's circumstances.—**dis·con·tent·ed·ly,** *adv.*—**dis·con·tent·ed·ness,** *n.*

dis·con·tin·ue, dis″kon·tin′ū, *v.t.*—*discontinued, discontinuing.* To continue no longer; to cease from; to stop; to put an end to; *law,* to abandon or terminate some legal action.—*v.i.* To cease; to stop.—**dis·con·tin·u·ance,** dis″kon·tin′ū·ans, *n.* Any act of discontinuing; breaking off; interruption; *law,* the termination or interruption of any legal action on the part of the plaintiff by failure to proceed or by written notice.— **dis·con·tin·u·a·tion,** dis″kon·tin″ū·ā′shan, *n.* Cessation.

dis·con·ti·nu·i·ty, dis″kon·ti·nö′i·tē, dis″kon·ti·nū′i·tē, *n.* Want of continuity or uninterrupted connection; disunion of parts.

dis·co·phile, dis′ko·fīl″, *n.* An avid student and collector of phonograph records, usually limited to one or more types of music, such as opera. Also **dis·ko·phile.**

dis·cord, dis′kard, *n.* [Fr. *discorde,* L. *discordia,* disagreement, < *discors,* discordant—*dis-,* and *cor, cordis,* the heart.] Want of concord or agreement; opposition of opinions; disagreement; contention; strife; *mus.* a union of sounds disagreeable or grating to the ear; dissonance.—dis′kard′, *v.i.* To disagree; to be out of harmony or concord; to clash.

dis·cord·ance, dis·kar′dans, *n.* Disagreement; opposition; an inharmonious state; dissonance. Also **dis·cor·dan·cy,** dis·kar′dan·sē, *pl.* **dis·cor·dan·cies.**—**dis·cord·ant,** dis·kar′dant, *a.* Disagreeing; incongruous; being at variance; dissonant; harsh; jarring.—**dis·cord·ant·ly,** *adv.*

dis·co·theque, dis″kō·tek′, *n.* A small and informal nightclub, popularized in the U.S. in the 1960's, where the patrons dance to recorded music. Also **dis·co·thèque.**

dis·count, dis′kount, *n.* [O.Fr. *descompte.*] Any deduction from the customary price of goods; a deduction made in the amount due on a bill because of prompt payment of the bill. *Banking,* an interest deduction made in advance on a note; the act of discounting. *Fig.* an allowance made or a distortion, esp. a distortion of the truth.— **dis·count·a·ble.**—**dis·coun·ter,** *n.*

dis·count, dis′kount, *n.* The difference between the original price of a security and the price to which it may subsequently drop in the market; the amount below face or par value for which a security sells.

dis·count, dis′kount, dis·kount′, *v.t.* To lend or advance a sum of money, deducting

the interest from the principal; to deduct a portion of a bill because of prompt payment or payment in advance; to offer for sale at a lower than customary price; to estimate or take into account beforehand. *Fig.* to leave out of account or disregard; to make an allowance for, as: They *discounted* his statement because of his known predjudice.

dis·coun·te·nance, dis·koun′te·nans, *v.t.* —*discountenanced, discountenancing.* To put to shame; to abash; to discourage, check, or restrain.—*n.* Disapproval.

dis·count house, *n.* A retail store that sells consumer goods at below usual prices.

dis·count rate, *n.* The interest rate on loans charged to member banks by the Federal Reserve Bank; the rate of interest deducted on commercial paper.

dis·cour·age, di·skèr′ij, di·skur′ij, *v.t.*— *discouraged, discouraging.* To dishearten; to deprive of self-confidence; to attempt to repress or prevent by pointing out difficulties; to dissuade, usu. with *from.*—**dis·cour·age·ment,** *n.* The act of discouraging; the act of deterring or dissuading from an undertaking; that which discourages or dampens ardor or hope; the state of being discouraged.—**dis·cour·ag·ing,** *a.*—**dis·cour·ag·ing·ly,** *adv.*

dis·course, dis′kōrs, dis′kars, *n.* [Fr. *discours,* < L. *discursus,* a running about, a conversation, < *discurro,* to ramble—*dis-,* and *curro,* to run.] Verbal communication, as conversation or speech; a formal, systematic examination of a subject, either written or oral, as a dissertation.—*v.i. discoursed, discoursing.* To express ideas orally, as to converse or talk; to communicate, esp. in a formal manner, one's thoughts concerning a subject, used with *on* or *upon.*

dis·cour·te·ous, dis·kèr′tē·us, *a.* Wanting in courtesy; uncivil; rude.—**dis·cour·te·ous·ly,** *adv.*—**dis·cour·te·ous·ness,** *n.*— **dis·cour·te·sy,** dis·kèr′ti·sē, *n. pl.* **dis·cour·te·sies.** Want of courtesy; incivility; rudeness of manner; an act of disrespect.

dis·cov·er, di·skuv′er, *v.t.* [O.Fr. *descovrir.*] To disclose or reveal; to espy; to detect; to have the first sight of or obtain the first knowledge of.—**dis·cov·er·a·ble,** *a.* Capable of being discovered, brought to light, exposed, found out, or made known. —**dis·cov·er·er,** di·skuv′èr·er, *n.* One who discovers; one who first sees or espies; one who finds out or first comes to the knowledge of some thing.

dis·cov·er·y, di·skuv′e·rē, *n. pl.* **dis·cov·er·ies.** The act of discovering; a disclosing or bringing to light; that which is discovered; *law,* disclosure ordered by juridical authority, as of documents or facts.

dis·cred·it, dis·kred′it, *n.* Some degree of disgrace or reproach; disesteem; disrepute; want of belief, trust, or confidence; disbelief; something that injures reputation.— *v.t.* To give no credit to; to withhold belief, credit, or confidence in; to deprive of credit or good reputation; to bring into some degree of disgrace or disrepute; to give no credence to.—**dis·cred·it·a·ble,** dis·kred′i·ta·bl, *n.* Injurious to reputation; disgraceful; disreputable.—**dis·cred·it·a·bly,** *adv.*

dis·creet, di·skrēt′, *a.* [Fr. *discret,* < L. *discretus,* pp. of *discerno,* to discern.] Prudent in conduct; circumspect; cautious; heedful; guarded.—**dis·creet·ly,** *adv.*— **dis·creet·ness,** *n.*

dis·crep·an·cy, di·skrep′an·sē, *n. pl.* **dis·crep·an·cies.** [L. *discrepantia,* < *dis·crepo,* to give a different sound, to vary— *dis-,* and *crepo,* to creak.] A difference or inconsistency between facts, testimony, or theories; disagreement; divergence. Also **dis·crep·ance.**—**dis·crep·ant,** di·skrep′ant, *a.* Differing or diverging; disagreeing; dissimilar.—**dis·crep·ant·ly,** *adv.*

---

a- fat, fāte, fär, fâre, fall;   **e-** met, mē, mēre, hėr;   **i-** pin, pīne,   **o-** not, nōte, move;   **u-** tub, cūbe, bu̱ll;   **oi-** oil;   **ou-** pound.

dis·crete, di·skrēt′, *a.* [L. *discretus*, separated, set apart. DISCREET.] Separate or distinct from others; consisting of individual parts; disjunct.

dis·cre·tion, di·skresh′*a*n, *n.* [Fr. *discretion*, L. *discretio*.] The quality of being discreet; circumspection; judgment that is sound, prudent, tactful; the ability to make such judgment; individual freedom of decision or choice, as: The selection was left entirely to his *discretion.*—**dis·cre·tion·ar·y**, di·skresh′*o*·ner″ē, *a.* Left to a person's own discretion or judgment. Also **dis·cre·tion·al**.

dis·crim·i·nant, di·skrim′i·nant, *n. Math.* an expression that classifies or acts as a criterion of the behavior of another function or set of relations.

dis·crim·i·nate, di·skrim′i·nāt″, *v.t.*—*discriminated, discriminating.* [L. *discriminatus,* pp. of *discriminare,* < *discrimen,* a space between, distinction, difference, < *discernere,* separate, distinguish between, discern, < *dis-,* apart, and *cernere,* separate.] To make or constitute a distinction in or between; differentiate; to note or distinguish as different.—*v.i.* To make a distinction, as in favor of or against a person or thing, esp. to make a distinction between persons on the basis of race or religion rather than individual merit; distinguish accurately.—**dis·crim·i·na·ble**, *a.* Able to be distinguished.—**dis·crim·i·nate**, di·skrim′i·nit, *a.* Marked by discrimination; making subtle distinctions. —**dis·crim·i·nate·ly**, *adv.*

dis·crim·i·nat·ing, di·skrim′i·nā″ting, *a.* That discriminates; differentiating; distinctive; specif. differential, as a duty or a tariff; possessing the ability to make subtle distinctions.—**dis·crim·i·nat·ing·ly**, *adv.*

dis·crim·i·na·tion, di·skrim′i·nā′shan, *n.* [L.L. *discriminatio*(n-).] The act of discriminating or differentiating, or the resulting state; differentiation; the making of a difference in particular cases, as in favor of or against a person, particularly when influenced by race or creed rather than individual merit; the power of making subtle distinctions; discriminating judgment.

dis·crim·i·na·tive, di·skrim′i·nā″tiv, di·skrim′i·na′tiv, *a.* Discriminating, esp. of a duty or a tariff; producing distinctions; characteristic. Also **dis·crim·i·na·to·ry**, di·skrim′i·na·tōr″ē.—**dis·crim·i·na·tive·ly**, *adv.*

dis·crim·i·na·tor, di·skrim′i·nā″ter, *n.* Someone or something that discriminates; *elect.* a circuit that can be made to accept or reject different kinds of signals.

dis·crown, dis·kroun′, *v.t.* To depose; to dispossess of the crown.

dis·cur·sive, di·skėr′siv, *a.* [Fr. *discursif,* < L. *discursus.*] Passing rapidly from one subject to another; desultory; rambling; digressional; argumentative; marked by reasoning; rational.—**dis·cur·sive·ly**, *adv.* —**dis·cur·sive·ness**, *n.*

dis·cus, dis′kus, *n.* pl. **dis·cus·es.** [L., < Gr. *diskos,* discus, disk, dish, < *dicein,* throw.] A circular plate of stone or metal for throwing to a distance as a gymnastic exercise, as among the ancient Greeks and Romans; a competitive modern athletic event in which the discus is thrown.

dis·cuss, di·skus′, *v.t.* [L. *discussus,* pp. of *discutere,* lit. "strike asunder."] To treat as the subject of conversation or writing; to examine by argument or reason; to consider formally in verbal or written form; to debate; to talk over informally; *civil law,* to exhaust legal proceedings against, as the actual debtor or his property, before proceeding against a person secondarily liable for a debt.—**dis·cuss·er**, *n.*—**dis·cuss·i·ble**, **dis·cuss·a·ble**, *a.*

dis·cus·sant, di·skus′ant, *n.* One who takes part in a formal discussion, as in a symposium.

dis·cus·sion, di·skush′an, *n.* The act of discussing; examination by argument; a debate.

dis·dain, dis·dān′, *v.t.* [O.Fr. *desdaigner,* Fr. *dédaigner.*] To regard as worthless or unworthy; to scorn; to reject with contempt. —*n.* A feeling of contempt; an attitude of superiority; haughtiness; scorn.—**dis·dain·ful**, dis·dān′ful, *a.* Full of or expressing disdain; contemptuous; scornful; haughty.—**dis·dain·ful·ly**, *adv.*—**dis·dain·ful·ness**, *n.*

dis·ease, di·zēz′, *n.* [O.Fr. *desaise.*] An impairment of the functioning of a system of the human body, or an organ or part thereof; a similar disorder in animals or plants; the breakdown of a material under special conditions. —*v.t.*—*diseased, diseasing.* To make ill.—**dis·eased**, *a.* Affected with disease; unwholesome.

dis·em·bark, dis″em·bärk′, *v.t.* To remove from on board ship to land; to put on shore; to land.—*v.i.* To leave a ship and go on shore; to land.—**dis·em·bar·ka·tion**, **dis·em·bark·ment**, *n.*

dis·em·bod·y, dis″em·bod′ē, *v.t.*—*disembodied, disembodying.* To divest of the body, as a spirit or ghost; to set free from the flesh.—**dis·em·bod·i·ment**, *n.*

dis·em·bogue, dis″em·bōg′, *v.i.*—*disembogued, disemboguing.* To flow or pour forth, as from a channel; to discharge water, as streams and rivers flowing into larger bodies of water.—*v.t.* To pour out; to empty.—**dis·em·bogue·ment**, *n.* Discharge of waters by a stream.

dis·em·bow·el, dis″em·bou′el, *v.t.*—*disemboweled, disemboweling, Brit. disembowelled, disembowelling.* To deprive of the bowels or of parts analogous to the bowels; to eviscerate; to gut.—**dis·em·bow·el·ment**, *n.*

dis·en·chant, dis″en·chant′, dis″en·chänt′, *v.t.* To free from enchantment; to free from fascination or pleasing delusion; to disillusion.—**dis·en·chant·er**, *n.*—**dis·en·chant·ment**, *n.*

dis·en·cum·ber, dis″en·kum′bėr, *v.t.* To free from encumbrance, obstructions, or impediments.

dis·en·fran·chise, dis″en·fran′chīz, *v.t.*— *disenfranchised, disenfranchising.* To disfranchise; to deprive of the right to vote or some other right of citizenship.

dis·en·gage, dis″en·gāj′, *v.t.*—*disengaged, disengaging.* To set free from attachment; to extricate; *milit.* to withdraw from confrontation, as with enemy forces.—*v.i.* To extricate oneself; to become unattached. —**dis·en·gage·ment**, dis″en·gāj′ment, *n.* Freedom from obligation or engrossing occupation; the act of disengaging.

dis·en·tail, dis″en·tāl′, *v.t. Law,* to free from the rule of descent, said of an estate; to free from entailment.

dis·en·tan·gle, dis″en·tang′gl, *v.t.*—*disentangled, disentangling.* To free from entanglements; to unravel; to extricate from perplexity or complications; to disengage.—**dis·en·tan·gle·ment**, *n.*

dis·en·thrall, dis·en·thral, dis″en·thrạl′, *v.t.*—*disenthralled, disenthralling.* To liberate; to free from slavery or involuntary servitude.—**dis·en·thrall·ment, dis·en·thral·ment**, *n.*

dis·e·qui·lib·ri·um, dis·ē″kwi·lib′rē·um, dis″ē·kwi·lib′rē·um, *n.* A loss or lack of balance, esp. in economic affairs; instability.—**dis·e·quil·i·brate,** dis″i·kwil′-i·brāt″, dis·ē″kwi·lī′brāt, *v.t.* To put out of balance.—**dis·e·quil·i·bra·tion,** dis·ē″-kwi·li·brā′shan, dis″i·kwil′i·brā′shan, *n.*

dis·es·tab·lish, dis″e·stab′lish, *v.t.* To bring about the end of, as an establishment; of an established or state church, to deprive of exclusive government recognition or support.—**dis·es·tab·lish·ment**, *n.* The act of disestablishing; the act of withdrawing a church from its connection with the state.

dis·es·teem, dis″e·stēm′, *n.* Want of esteem; disfavor; low regard.—*v.t.* To regard as unworthy of esteem.

di·seur, dē·zụr′, *Fr.* dē·ZŒR′, *n.* pl. **di·seurs.** [Fr., one who says or tells.] A professional public entertainer who performs monologues and recitations.—**di·seuse,** *Fr.* dē·ZŒZ′, *n.* [Fr.] Fem of *diseur.*

dis·fa·vor, *Brit.* **dis·fa·vour,** dis·fā′vėr, *n.* The state of being unacceptable, disliked, or opposed; a lack of favor; disapproval; displeasure; an unkind act.—*v.t.* To withdraw or withhold favor, friendship, or support from.

dis·fig·ure, dis·fig′ūr, *v.t.*—*disfigured, disfiguring.* To spoil in appearance; to mar, impair, or make unsightly.—**dis·fig·ur·a·tion,** *n.* The act of disfiguring; that which disfigures, as a blemish. Also **dis·fig·ure·ment.**—**dis·fig·ur·er,** *n.*

dis·fran·chise, dis·fran′chīz, *v.t.*—*disfranchised, disfranchising.* To deprive of the rights and privileges of a free citizen; to deprive of any franchise, esp. of the right of voting.—**dis·fran·chise·ment,** dis·fran′-chiz·ment, *n.* The act of disfranchising; the state of being disfranchised.

dis·gorge, dis·gạrj′, *v.t.*—*disgorged, disgorging.* [O.Fr. *desgorger,* to vomit.] To eject or discharge from the stomach, throat, or mouth; to vomit; to force out or discharge violently, as: A volcano *disgorges* lava. To empty or pour out the contents of, as of the stomach.—*v.i.* To give up or eject something, esp. plunder or ill-gotten gains.

dis·grace, dis·grās′, *n.* A state of being out of favor; a state of dishonor, shame, or infamy; ignominy; that which causes shame or dishonor.—*v.t.*—*disgraced, disgracing.* To put out of favor; to bring shame or reproach on; to humiliate; to dishonor.— **dis·grace·ful,** *a.* Entailing disgrace; shameful; infamous; dishonorable.—**dis·grace·ful·ly,** *adv.*—**dis·grace·ful·ness,** *n.*

dis·grun·tle, dis·grun′tl, *v.t.*—*disgruntled, disgruntling.* To displease; to make discontented; to put in a bad mood.— **dis·grun·tled,** *a.*—**dis·grun·tle·ment,** *n.*

dis·guise, dis·gīz′, di′skīz′, *v.t.*—*disguised, disguising.* [O.Fr. *desguiser,* Fr. *déguiser.*] To alter the ordinary appearance of, making identification difficult or impossible; to hide or mask a true identity of; to conceal or obscure by false representation.—*n.* That which disguises; anything serving to conceal or mask identity, character or manner. —**dis·guis·a·ble,** *a.*—**dis·guis·er,** *n.*

dis·gust, dis·gust′, di·skust′, *n.* [O.Fr. *desgust,* Fr. *dégoût.*] Distaste; nausea; aversion excited by something offensive in the manners, conduct, language, or opinions of others; loathing; repugnance.—*v.t.* To cause to feel disgust; to excite aversion or nausea in; to offend the taste of.—**dis·gust·ed,** *a.* Experiencing disgust.—**dis·gust·ing,** *a.* Producing or causing disgust; nauseous; loathsome; nasty. Also **dis·gust·ful.**—**dis·gust·ing·ly,** *adv.*

dish, dish, *n.* [O.E. *disc,* a dish; like D. *disch,* G. *tisch,* a table, < L. *discus,* Gr. *diskos,* a quoit or disk.] A broad open vessel made of various materials, used esp. for serving food; loosely, any utensil employed in preparing, serving, or eating food; any particular kind of food; the quantity accommodated by a dish, or dishful; the concavity of certain wheels, as those of vehicles. *Slang,* a woman, usually an attractive one; something preferred or suited to one's skills.—*v.t.* To put into a dish; to make concave in the center, as a wheel. *Brit. slang*, to get the better of or cheat.—**dish it out,** *colloq.* to administer or dispense, esp. something non-material, as physical or verbal abuse, praise, or flattery. —**dish out,** *colloq.* to distribute or give out, as gossip, or esp. something material, as money or treats.

dish, dish, *n. Astron.* a parabolic reflector type of radio or radar antenna, used esp. for radio telescopes.

dis·ha·bille, dis″*a*·bēl′, *n.* [Fr.] A state of partial undress or of loose or negligent dress; *fig.* disorder or confusion, as: My mind is in a state of complete *dishabille.* Also **des·ha··bille,** dez″*a*·bēl′.

dis·har·mo·ni·ous, dis″här·mō′nē·us, *a.* Inharmonious; discordant. Also **dis·har··mon·ic,** dis″här·mon′ik.—**dis·har·mo·· nize,** dis·här′mo·nīz″, *v.t., v.i.*—*disharmonized, disharmonizing.* To make or be inharmonious.—**dis·har·mo·ny,** dis·här′· mo·nē, *n. pl.* **dis·har·mon·ies.** Discord; something discordant.

dish·cloth, dish′klôth″, dish′kloth″, *n.* A cloth used for washing dishes. Also *Brit.* **dish·clout,** dish′klout″.

dish·cloth gourd, *n.* Vegetable sponge.

dis·heart·en, dis·här′ton, *v.t.* To discourage; to deprive of courage; to depress the spirits of; to deject; to dispirit.— **dis·heart·en·ing,** *a.*

di·shev·el, di·shev′el, *v.t.*—*disheveled, disheveling, dishevelled, dishevelling.* [O.Fr. *descheveler,* Fr. *décheveler.*] To let hang in loose disorder; to rumple, tangle, muss, as hair or clothing; to cause untidiness in, as a person.—**di·shev·eled, di·shev·elled,** *a.* Disarranged; tousled; rumpled; having unkempt hair or an untidy appearance.—**di·shev·el·ment,** *n.*

dis·hon·est, dis·on′ist, *a.* Not honest; inclined or apt to deceive, cheat, pilfer, embezzle, or defraud; arising from or characterized by lack of honesty; fraudulent. —**dis·hon·est·ly,** *adv.*—**dis·hon·es·ty,** dis·on′i·stē, *n. pl.* **dis·hon·es·ties.**

dis·hon·or, *Brit.* **dis·hon·our,** dis·on′ẽr, *n.* Want of honor; disgrace; shame; anything that disgraces; nonpayment of a note or other commercial paper when due.—*v.t.* To disgrace; to bring shame on; to stain the character of; to violate the chastity of; to refuse or decline to accept or pay, as a bill of exchange.—**dis·hon·or·a·ble,** dis·on′ẽr··*a*·bl, *a.* Shameful; disgraceful; base; bringing shame; damaging the reputation; unprincipled; as, *dishonorable* behavior.— **dis·hon·or·a·ble·ness,** *n.*—**dis·hon·or·· a·bly,** *adv.*

dis·hon·or·a·ble dis·charge, *n. Milit.* the formal separation of a person from military service under dishonorable conditions.

dish·rag, dish′rag″, *n.* Any type of dishcloth.

dish·tow·el, dish′tou″el, *n.* An absorbent cloth for drying dishes.

dish·wash·er, dish′wosh″ẽr, dish′wȧ″shẽr, *n.* One who washes dishes; a machine used for washing dishes.

dish·wa·ter, dish′wȧ″tẽr, dish′wot″ẽr, *n.* Water in which dishes are washed.—**dull as dish·wa·ter,** *colloq.* Very boring; uninteresting.

dis·il·lu·sion, dis″i·lö′zhȧn, *v.t.* To disenchant; to free from illusion.—*n.* Disenchantment.—**dis·il·lu·sion·ment,** *n.*

dis·in·cline, dis″in·klīn′, *v.t.*—*disinclined, disinclining.* To make unwilling or reluctant. —**dis·in·cli·na·tion,** dis·in″klĭ·nā′shȧn, *n.*—**dis·in·clined,** *a.*

dis·in·fect, dis″in·fekt,′ *v.t.* To cleanse of infection by destroying or inhibiting the activity of disease-producing microorganisms.—**dis·in·fect·ant,** dis″in·fek′tȧnt, *n.* A chemical substance or other agent, such as ultraviolet light, used to disinfect inanimate objects.—**dis·in·fec·tion,** *n.*

dis·in·fla·tion, dis″in·flā′shȧn, *n. Econ.* the planned reversal of inflationary pressures by governmental action.

dis·in·gen·u·ous, dis″in·jen′ū·us, *a.* Not ingenuous; not open, frank, or candid; insincere; falsely attempting to appear ingenuous.—**dis·in·gen·u·ous·ly,** *adv.* —**dis·in·gen·u·ous·ness,** *n.*

dis·in·her·it, dis″in·her′it, *v.t.* To deprive of an inheritance, as by omission from a will; to dispossess of natural, hereditary, or customary rights or privileges.—**dis·in·· her·i·tance,** *n.*

dis·in·te·grate, dis·in′te·grāt″, *v.t.*—*disintegrated, disintegrating.* [L.] To separate the component particles of; to reduce in powder or fragments; to destroy the cohesion or unity of.—*v.i.* To break into component particles or parts. *Phys.* to sustain a change in nuclear composition.—**dis·in·· te·gra·tion,** dis·in″te·grā′shȧn, *n.* The act of separating the component particles of a substance; the gradual wearing down of rocks by atmospheric influence.—**dis·in·· te·gra·tive,** *a.*—**dis·in·te·gra·tor,** *n.*

dis·in·ter, dis″in·tẽr′, *v.t.*—*disinterred, disinterring.* To take out of a grave, as a dead body, or out of the earth; to bring from obscurity into view.—**dis·in·ter·ment,** *n.*

dis·in·ter·est, dis·in′tẽr·ist, dis·in′trist, *n.* Absence of interest; indifference. Freedom from self-interest.—*v.t.* To divest of interest or concern.—**dis·in·ter·es·ted,** *a.* Free from considerations of personal interest or advantage; not influenced by selfish motives.—**dis·in·ter·est·ed·ly,** *adv.*— **dis·in·ter·est·ed·ness,** *n.*

dis·join, dis·join′, *v.t.* To disunite or prevent the union of; separate; detach.—*v.i.* To be separated; to part.

dis·joint, dis·joint′, *v.t.* To separate at the joints; to put out of joint; to dislocate; to break the natural order and relationships of; to derange; to render incoherent.—*v.i.* To fall into pieces; to separate at the joints; to become dislocated.—**dis·joint·ed,** dis·· join′tid, *a.* Unconnected; incoherent; out of joint; separated at the joint.—**dis·joint·· ed·ness,** *n.*—**dis·joint·ly,** *adv.*

dis·junct, dis·jungkt′, *n. Logic,* any one of the alternatives in a disjunction.

dis·junct, dis·jungkt′, *a.* [L. *disjunctus,* pp. of *disjungere.*] Disjoined; separated; *entom.* having the head, thorax, and abdomen separated by deep constrictions; *mus.* pertaining to a progression of melody by intervals exceeding a second.

dis·junc·tion, dis·jungk′shȧn, *n.* [L. *disjunctio(n-), < disjungere.*] The act of disjoining, or the state of being disjoined; disunion; separation; *logic,* the relation between the terms of a disjunctive proposition; the proposition itself.

dis·junc·tive, dis·jungk′tiv, *a.* [L. *disjunctivus.*] Serving to disjoin; characterized by or involving disjunction. *Gram.* connecting words, phrases, and clauses disjoined in meaning, as the conjunctions *but* and *yet,* or *and nor*; alternative. *Logic,* alternative; as, a *disjunctive* proposition, one which asserts that one or the other of two things is true.—*n. Gram.* a disjunctive conjunction; *logic,* a disjunctive proposition. In general, a statement involving alternatives.—**dis·junc·tive·ly,** *adv.*

disk, disc, disk, *n.* [L. *discus,* discus, disk, dish.] Any thin, flat, circular plate or object; a phonograph record; an area which is or which appears to be round and flat, as the sun; *bot.,* *zool.* any of various roundish, flat structures or parts; in such flowers as the daisy, the central portion of the flower head, composed of tubular florets; *agric.* one of the concave circular cutters on a disk harrow.—*v.t.* To make a phonographic recording of; *agric.* to harrow.—**disk·like, disc·like,** *a.*

disk jock·ey, *n.* A person who conducts a radio program combining recorded music, commercial announcements, and informal comments. Also *disc jockey.*

disk wheel, *n.* A wheel without spokes, having a central steel disk which is mounted on the hub, used esp. on automobiles.

dis·like, dis·līk′, *n.* A feeling of aversion; distaste; antipathy; repugnance.—*v.t.*— *disliked, disliking.* To feel dislike toward; to regard with aversion.—**dis·lik·a·ble,** *a.*

dis·lo·cate, dis′lō·kāt″, *v.t.*—*dislocated, dislocating.* To move out of place; displace; *med.* to wrench out of proper position or joint, esp. a bone. To disrupt the established order of.—**dis·lo·ca·tion,** dis″lō′kā′shȧn, *n.* The act or result of dislocating; *geol.* the displacement of parts of rocks, or portions of strata, from the positions which they originally occupied.

dis·lodge, dis·loj′, *v.t.*—*dislodged, dislodging.* To remove or force from the fixed position or place occupied; to drive from any place of hiding or defense, or from a position seized.—*v.i.* To go from a lodging place.—**dis·lodg·ment, dis·lodge·ment,** *n.*

dis·loy·al, dis·loi′al, *a.* Not loyal or true to allegiance or obligation; faithless; false; perfidious; treacherous.—**dis·loy·al·ly,** *adv.*—**dis·loy·al·ty,** dis·loi′al·tē, *n. pl.* **dis·loy·al·ties.** The quality of being disloyal; want of fidelity; violation of allegiance; a disloyal deed.

dis·mal, diz′mal, *a.* [Origin uncertain. According to one derivation, < L. *dies malus,* an evil day; according to another, < O.Fr. *dismal,* L. *decimalis, decem,* ten, referring to the day of paying tithes.] Dark, gloomy, or cheerless; depressing; as, *dismal* weather; melancholy; sorrowful; depressed, as: I feel so *dismal.* Very bad; calamitous; as, a *dismal* failure; *obs.* unlucky.—*n. Southern U.S.* a swampy area; *pl., colloq.* doldrums; blues.

dis·man·tle, dis·man′tl, *v.t.*—*dismantled, dismantling.* [O.Fr. *desmanteler, desmanteller,* lit. to deprive of cloak or mantle.] To deprive of dress; to strip; to divest; more generally, to deprive or strip of furniture, equipment, fortifications, and the like; to disassemble; take apart.

dis·mast, dis·mast′, dis·mäst′, *v.t.* To deprive of a mast or masts; to break off and carry away the masts from.

dis·may, dis·mā′, *v.t.* [Same word as Sp. and Pg. *desmayar,* to fall into a swoon, but no doubt directly from the French.] To deprive entirely of courage or resolution; to discourage, with some feeling of dread or consternation; daunt; to disillusion or depress; to distress or alarm.—*n.* A complete giving way of boldness or spirit; loss of courage together with consternation; disillusionment; distress.—**dis·may·ing·· ly,** *adv.*

dis·mem·ber, dis·mem′bẽr,.*v.t.* To divide limb from limb; to separate the members of; to mutilate; to sever and distribute the parts of; to divide into separate territories; partition.—**dis·mem·ber·ment,** *n.*

dis·miss, dis·mis′, *v.t.* [< L. *dimitto, dimissum,* to dismiss.] To send away; to permit to depart; to discard; to remove from office, service, or employment; to disregard; *law,* to reject as unworthy of notice, or of being granted.—**dis·mis·sal,** dis·mis′al, *n.* The act of dismissing; the state of being dismissed; a notification of discharge. Also, *rare,* **dis·mis·sion.**

dis·mount, dis·mount′, *v.i.* To get off or alight, as from a horse.—*v.t.* To knock, throw, or pull from a mounted position; unhorse; to remove from a mounting or setting, as a tire from a rim; to disconnect component parts of, as of a mechanism.— *n.* The act or style of dismounting.

dis·o·be·di·ence, dis″o·bē′dē·ens, *n.* Neglect or refusal to obey; want of obedience.—**dis·o·be·di·ent**, dis″o·bē′di·ent, *a.* Neglecting or refusing to obey; rebellious; unruly.—**dis·o·be·di·ent·ly**, *adv.*

dis·o·bey, dis″o·bā′, *v.t., v.i.* To neglect or refuse to obey.—**dis·o·bey·er**, *n.*

dis·o·blige, dis″o·blīj′, *v.t.—disobliged, disobliging.* To act counter to the will or desires of; fail to oblige or do a friendly service; to offend; to impose upon; to inconvenience.—**dis·o·blig·ing**, *a.* Not obliging; not disposed to gratify the wishes of another; unaccommodating.—**dis·o·blig·ing·ly**, *adv.*

dis·or·der, dis·ar′dėr, *n.* Want of order or regular disposition; irregularity; unmethodical distribution; confusion; tumult; disturbance of the peace; disturbance or interruption of the normal, healthy functions of the body or mind; sickness; derangement. —*v.t.* To disrupt the order of; to derange; to throw into confusion; to disturb or interrupt the natural functions of; to produce sickness or indisposition in; to disturb the reason or judgment.

dis·or·dered, dis·ar′dėrd, *a.* Lacking order or methodical arrangement; confused; suffering disorder in physical or mental health.—**dis·or·dered·ly**, *adv.*—**dis·or·dered·ness**, *n.*

dis·or·der·ly, dis·ar′dėr·lē, *a.* Being without proper order; marked by disorder; confused; unmethodical; irregular; tumultuous; unruly; violating laws governing order and morality.—*adv.* In an unorderly manner.—**dis·or·der·li·ness**, *n.*

dis·or·der·ly con·duct, *n. Law*, a usually indefinite term signifying a petty offense against public peace, decorum, or morality.

dis·or·der·ly house, *n.* A house of prostitution or an illegal gambling establishment.

dis·or·gan·ize, dis·ar′ga·nīz″, *v.t.—disorganized, disorganizing.* To disturb or destroy the organic structure or orderly arrangement of; to throw into confusion or disorder. —**dis·or·gan·i·za·tion**, dis·ar″ga·ni·zā″shan, *n.* The act of disorganizing; the state of being disorganized.

dis·o·ri·ent, dis·ōr′ē·ent″, dis·ar′ē·ent″, *v.t.* To cause to lose one's bearings; to confuse. Also **dis·o·ri·en·tate**—*disorientated, disorientating.*—**dis·o·ri·en·ta·tion**, *n.* The state of being disoriented; *psychiatry*, temporary or permanent loss by an individual of his perception of space, time, or identity.

dis·own, dis·ōn′, *v.t.* To refuse to acknowledge as belonging to oneself; to deny; to repudiate.

dis·par·age, di·spar′ij, *v.t.—disparaged, disparaging.* [O.Fr. *desparagier*.] To bring reproach or discredit upon; lower the estimation of; to speak of slightingly; depreciate; belittle.—**dis·par·age·ment**, *n.* The act of disparaging; something that causes loss of dignity or reputation.—**dis·par·ag·ing·ly**, *adv.*

dis·pa·rate, dis′pėr·it, di·spar′it, *a.* [L. *disparatus*, pp. of *disparare*, separate.] Distinct in kind; essentially different; dissimilar; unlike.—**dis·pa·rate·ly**, *adv.*—**dis·pa·rate·ness**, *n.*

dis·par·i·ty, di·spar′i·tē, *n. pl.* **dis·par·i·ties.** [Fr. *disparité*, < L. *dispar*, unequal.] Inequality; difference in degree, age, rank, condition, or excellence; dissimilitude; unlikeness.

dis·pas·sion, dis·pash′an, *n.* Freedom from passion; the state or quality of being unexcitable or impartial. Also **dis·pas·sion·ate·ness.**

dis·pas·sion·ate, dis·pash′o·nit, *a.* Free from passion; calm; composed; unemotional, unbiased; impartial.—**dis·pas·sion·ate·ly**, *adv.*

dis·patch, **des·patch**, di·spach′, *v.t.* [O.Fr. *despecher*, Fr. *dépêcher*, to dispatch, to

expedite < L.L. *dispedico*—L. *dis-*, apart, and *pedica*, a snare, or < L.L. *dispactare*, < L. *dis-*, and *pango, pactum*, to fasten.] To send or send away, particularly on special business, often implying haste; to put to death; to kill; to perform or execute speedily; to finish.—*n.* The act of putting to death; prompt settlement; speedy and efficient performance; haste; a message sent or to be sent with haste, esp. an official communication sent by diplomatic or military courier; *journalism*, a news story transmitted by a reporter or a news service; an organization or a means for the fast and efficient sending of messages or goods.—

dis·patch·er, des·patch·er, *n.* One who dispatches, esp. one who routes or schedules planes, trains, buses, trucks, or taxicabs.

dis·pel, di·spel′, *v.t.—dispelled, dispelling.* [L. *dispello*.] To scatter by force; to disperse; to dissipate; to drive away, as clouds, doubts, or fears.

dis·pen·sa·ble, di·spen′sa·bl, *a.* Capable of being spared or dispensed with; not essential; capable of being dispensed or administered.—**dis·pen·sa·bil·i·ty**, **dis·pen·sa·ble·ness**, di·spen″sa·bil′i·tē, *n.*

dis·pen·sa·ry, di·spen′sa·rē, *n. pl.* **dis·pen·sa·ries.** A place in which medicines are dispensed; a charitable establishment where medicines and medical advice are given gratis or for a nominal amount to those who otherwise could not afford them.

dis·pen·sa·tion, dis″pen·sā′shan, *n.* The act of dispensing or dealing out; something which is dispensed; a specific plan or system of management or administration; *theol.* an ordering and management of worldly affairs by divine authority, specifically one of several moral and religious systems believed to be revelations of divine will; as, Mosaic *dispensation*, Christian *dispensation*. *Rom. Cath. Ch.* the granting of permission, or the document granting permission, to do what is forbidden by laws or canons, or to omit something which is commanded.—**dis·pen·sa·tion·al**, *a.*—**dis·pen·sa·to·ry**, di·spen′sa·tōr″ē, *n. pl.* **dis·pen·sa·to·ries.** A book containing formulas, preparation methods, and uses of medicines; a pharmacopoeia; a dispensary.

dis·pense, di·spens′, *v.t.—dispensed, dispensing.* [L. *dispenso*, to weigh out or pay, to manage, to act as steward.] To deal or divide out in parts or portions; to distribute; to administer; to apply, as laws to particular cases; *Rom. Cath. Ch.* to grant dispensation to; to relieve, excuse, or set free from an obligation. To make up and distribute, as medicines.—**dis·pense with**, to give up or do without; to do away with.—**dis·pens·er**, dis·pen′sėr, *n.* One who or that which dispenses or distributes; a holder, device, or machine which dispenses its contents in prescribed portions; as, a soap *dispenser*.

dis·perse, di·spėrs′, *v.t.—dispersed, dispersing.* [L. *dispersus*, pp. of *dispergere*.] To scatter; send or drive off in various directions; to distribute, diffuse, or disseminate; to dissipate or dispel; *chem., phys.* to subject to dispersion.—*v.i.* To separate or move apart in various directions; become dissipated or dispelled.—**dis·pers·ed·ly**, *adv.*—**dis·pers·er**, *n.*—**dis·pers·i·ble**, *a.*

dis·per·sion, di·spėr′zhan, di·spėr′shan, *n.* The act of dispersing or scattering; the state of being scattered or separated into remote parts; also **dis·per·sal**, di·spėr′sal. (*Cap.*) Diaspora. *Phys.* the separation of light waves, radiation, complex sound waves, etc., into components; as, the *dispersion* of white light into its various color components by means of a prism. *Chem.* a system of minute, discrete particles suspended in a solid, liquid, or gas, such as smog or homogenized milk. *Statistics*, the placing of values of a variable in certain

relationships around the average of a distribution.—**dis·per·sive**, *a.* Tending to scatter or dissipate.—**dis·per·sive·ly**, *adv.* —**dis·per·sive·ness**, *n.*

dis·per·soid, di·spėr′soid, *n. Chem.* a chemical formation which occurs when the finely divided particles of one substance are in a state of dispersed suspension in another substance.

dis·pir·it, di·spir′it, *v.t.* To depress the spirits of; to deprive of courage; to discourage; to dishearten; to deject.—**dis·pir·it·ed**, *a.* Discouraged; depressed; spiritless.—**dis·pir·it·ed·ly**, *adv.*—**dis·pir·it·ed·ness**, *n.*

dis·place, dis·plās′, *v.t.—displaced, displacing.* [Fr. *desplacer* (now *deplacer*).] To put out of place; dislodge; to remove from a position or office; to put something else in the place of; replace.—**dis·place·a·ble**, *a.* That may be displaced.—**dis·place·ment**, *n.* The act of displacing or the state of being displaced; dislocation or the amount of dislocation; the distance between the original position and the new position to which an object has moved; removal from an office; replacing of one thing by another; *phys.* the weight or the volume of water displaced by a floating body, as a ship, which is a weight equivalent to that of the floating body; *mach.* the volume of space displaced by a single movement of a piston; *psychoanal.* the process of shifting emotional fixation or attachment from one object or person to a usually less important object or person.—**dis·placed per·son**, one who, for military or political reasons, is unable or unwilling to return to his own country.

dis·play, di·splā′, *v.t.* [O.Fr. *desployer*, Fr. *déployer—des*, equal to L. *dis*, and *ployer*, same as *plier*, < L. *plicare*, to fold.] To set in view ostentatiously; to show; *print.* to give prominence in print, as by bold captions.—*n.* An unfolding; an exhibition of anything to the view; ostentatious show; exhibition; parade.

dis·play type, *n. Print.* type, of large size and boldness, used esp. in headlines to command the attention of readers.

dis·please, dis·plēz′, *v.t.—displeased, displeasing.* To offend somewhat; to dissatisfy; to annoy; to make angry, usually in a slight degree.—*v.i.* To produce displeasure.— **dis·pleas·ure**, dis·plezh′ėr, *n.* The feeling of one who is displeased; dissatisfaction; anger; vexation; annoyance.

dis·port, di·spōrt′, di·spart′, *v.t.* [O.Fr. *desport*, Fr. *déport*, properly diversion resorted to in order to divert the thoughts.] To conduct (oneself) in a gay, sportive manner.—*v.i.* To be amused or diverted.

dis·pos·a·ble, di·spō′za·bl, *a.* Subject to disposal; free to be used or employed as occasion may require.

dis·pos·a·ble per·son·al in·come, *n.* The amount of income available for spending in a given year, after deduction of personal taxes.

dis·pos·al, dis·pō′zal, *n.* The act of disposing; a setting or arranging; power of ordering, arranging, or distributing; management; power or right of bestowing; the act of selling or parting with; alienation.—**dis·pos·er**, di·spō′zėr, *n.*—**dis·pos·a·bil·i·ty**, dis·pos·a·ble·ness, *n.*

dis·pose, di·spōz′, *v.t.—disposed, disposing.* [Fr. *disposer*, to dispose, arrange.] To arrange, place about, or distribute; to set in order; to apply to a particular end or purpose; to set (the mind) in a particular frame; to incline to.—*v.i.* To regulate, determine, or settle.—**dis·pose of**, to part with; to alienate; to sell; to put into another's hand or power; to bestow; to do with, make use of, use, or employ, as oneself or one's time; to put away or get rid of.

dis·po·si·tion, dis″po·zish′an, *n.* [L. *dispositio,* arrangement.] The act of disposing or state of being disposed; manner in which things are arranged; natural fitness or tendency; temper or emotional constitution of the mind; inclination; propensity.

dis·pos·sess, dis″po·zes′, *v.t.* To put out of possession by legal action; to deprive of the occupancy or ownership of; to dislodge.

dis·proof, dis·pröf′, *n.* The act of disproving; proof to the contrary; confutation; refutation.

dis·pro·por·tion, dis″pro·pōr′shan, dis″pro·pär′shan, *n.* Want of proportion of one thing to another, or between the parts of a thing; want of symmetry; disparity; inequality.—*v.t.* To violate due proportion or symmetry in.—**dis·pro·por·tion·al, dis·pro·por·tion·ate,** *a.* Not having due proportion to something else; lacking proportion or symmetry of parts; unequal; inadequate.—**dis·pro·por·tion·ate·ness,** *n.* Unsuitableness in form, bulk, or value to something else.—**dis·pro·por·tion·ate·ly,** *adv.* With want of proportion of symmetry; unsuitably; inadequately; unequally. Also **dis·pro·por·tion·al·ly.**

dis·prove, dis·pröv′, *v.t.*—*disproved, disproving.* To prove to be false or erroneous; to confute; to refute.—**dis·prov·a·ble,** *a.*

dis·put·a·ble, di·spū′ta·bl, dis·pū′ta·bl, *a.* Capable of being disputed; liable to be called in question, controverted, or contested.—**dis·put·a·bil·i·ty,** *n.*—**dis·put·ant,** di·spūt′ant, *n.* One who disputes; one who argues in opposition to another.—*a.* Disputing; engaged in controversy.

dis·pu·ta·tion, dis″pū·tā′shan, *n.* [L. *disputatio.*] Verbal controversy; an academic exercise consisting of the defense of a thesis against opponents.—**dis·pu·ta·tious, dis·put·a·tive,** dis″pū·tā′shus, di·spū′ta·tiv, *a.* Fond of arguing; characterized by disputes.—**dis·pu·ta·tious·ly,** *adv.*—**dis·pu·ta·tious·ness,** *n.*

dis·pute, di·spūt′, *v.i.*—*disputed, disputing.* [L. *disputo,* to compute, to weigh, examine, investigate, discuss.] To debate; to quarrel.—*v.t.* To call in question; to contest; to make the subject of a disputation; to oppose.—*n.* Controversy in words; a quarrel.—**dis·put·er,** *n.* One who disputes or who is given to disputes.

dis·qual·i·fy, dis·kwol′i·fī″, *v.t.*—*disqualified, disqualifying.* To make unfit; to deprive of the qualities or properties necessary for any purpose, as: Weakness *disqualified* him for labor. To disbar from competition because of violation of the rules; to deprive of legal capacity, power, or right.—**dis·qual·i·fi·ca·tion,** dis·kwol″i·fī·kā′shan, *n.* Disability; legal incapacity; act of making ineligible; disbarment from competition because of violation of the rules.

dis·qui·et, dis·kwī′it, *n.* Uneasiness; anxiety.—*v.t.* To deprive of peace or tranquillity; to disturb or harass.—**dis·qui·et·ing,** *a.*—**dis·qui·et·ly,** *adv.*—**dis·qui·e·tude,** dis·kwī′i·töd″, dis·kwī′i·tūd, *n.* Want of tranquillity; uneasiness.

dis·qui·si·tion, dis″kwi·zish′on, *n.* [L. *disquisitio,* < *disquiro, disquisitum,* to investigate.] A formal inquiry into any subject, by discussion of the facts and circumstances bearing on it; a dissertation; an essay.

dis·re·gard, dis″ri·gärd′, *n.* Want of regard, notice, or attention; neglect; slight.—*v.t.* To take no notice of; to neglect to observe; to pay no heed to; as, to *disregard* instructions; to treat as unworthy of regard or notice.—**dis·re·gard·ful,** *a.* Neglectful; heedless.

dis·re·la·tion, dis″ri·lā′shan, *n.* Lack of a suitable connection; want of a proper relationship.

dis·re·mem·ber, dis″ri·mem′bėr, *v.t., v.i. Colloq.* Chiefly in southern U.S., to neglect to remember; to forget.

dis·re·pair, dis″ri·pâr′, *n.* A state of needing repair.

dis·rep·u·ta·ble, dis·rep′ū·ta·bl, *a.* Not reputable; of bad reputation; dishonorable; discreditable; low; mean.—**dis·re·pute, ta·ble·ness, dis·rep·u·ta·bil·i·ty,** *n.*—**dis·rep·u·ta·bly,** *adv.*—**dis·re·pute,** dis″ri·pūt′, *n.* Loss or want of reputation; discredit; dishonor.

dis·re·spect, dis″ri·spekt′, *n.* Lack of respect or reverence; incivility or rudeness; a discourtesy.—*v.t.* To treat rudely, irreverently, or without respect; to show disrespect.—**dis·re·spect·a·ble,** *a.* Not respectable; unworthy of respect.

dis·re·spect·ful, dis″ri·spekt′ful, *a.* Displaying a lack of respect; manifesting disrespect; irreverent; uncivil.—**dis·re·spect·ful·ly,** *adv.*—**dis·re·spect·ful·ness,** *n.*

dis·robe, dis·rōb′, *v.t., v.i.*—*disrobed, disrobing.* To divest of garments; to undress.

dis·rupt, dis·rupt′, *v.t.* [L. *disruptus,* pp. of *disrumpo (dirumpo),* to break or burst asunder.] To throw into disorder or upset; to impede or halt a normal continuity; to break apart.—**dis·rup·tion,** dis·rup′shan, *n.* [L. *disruptio.*] The act of disrupting or breaking up; a disrupted or disordered condition.—**dis·rup·tive,** dis·rup′tiv, *a.* Causing, or tending to cause, disruption; produced by or following on disruption.—**dis·rup·tive·ly,** *adv.*—**dis·rup·tive·ness,** *n.*—**dis·rupt·er,** *n.*

dis·sat·is·fac·tion, dis″sat·is·fak′shan, *n.* A feeling of discontent; a lack of satisfaction or gratification.—**dis·sat·is·fac·to·ry,** dis″sat·is·fak′to·rē, *a.* Causing dissatisfaction; giving discontent; displeasing.—**dis·sat·is·fy,** dis·sat′is·fī, *v.t.*—*dissatisfied, dissatisfying.* To fail to satisfy; to render discontented; to displease.

dis·sect, dis·sekt′, dī·sekt′, *v.t.* [L. *disseco, dissectum.*] To anatomize; to divide, separate, or cut apart, esp. an animal body or plant for scientific investigation and study; to examine minutely and critically, as: The editor *dissected* his manuscript.—**dis·sect·ed,** *a.*—**dis·sec·tion,** *n.* The act of dissecting or anatomizing; the state of being dissected.—**dis·sec·tor,** *n.* One who dissects; an anatomist.

dis·seize, *Brit.* **dis·seise,** dis·sēz′, *v.t.*—*disseized, disseizing, Brit. disseised, disseising.* [Prefix *dis,* neg., and *seize;* Fr. *dessaisir,* to dispossess.] *Law.* To dispossess wrongfully; to deprive of actual seizin or possession.—**dis·sei·zee,** *Brit.* **dis·sei·see,** dis″sē·zē′, dis·sē·zē′, *n.* One who is disseized.—**dis·sei·zor,** *Brit.* **dis·sei·sor,** *n.* One who dispossesses another.

dis·sem·blance, di·sem′blans, *n.* The act of dissembling; feigning; dissimulation. Lack of resemblance; dissimilarity.

dis·sem·ble, di·sem′bl, *v.t.*—*dissembled, dissembling.* [O.Fr. *dessembler* (Fr. *dissimuler*), < L. *dissimulo.*] To hide under an assumed manner; to conceal or disguise by a false outward show; to feign; as, to *dissemble* love, hate, or opinions.—*v.i.* To try to appear other than one's natural self; to put on an assumed manner or outward show; to conceal real facts, motives, intentions, or sentiments under some pretense.—**dis·sem·bler,** *n.* One who dissembles; one who conceals his real thoughts or feelings.

dis·sem·i·nate, di·sem′i·nāt″, *v.t.*—*disseminated, disseminating.* [L. *dissemino, disseminatum,* to scatter seed.] To spread or scatter, as seeds; to diffuse; to scatter widely as by sowing, esp. information, knowledge, or doctrines; to broadcast.—**dis·sem·i·na·tion,** *n.* The act of disseminating.—**dis·sem·i·na·tive,** *a.* Tending to disseminate or become disseminated.—**dis·sem·i·na·tor,** *n.*

dis·sem·i·nule, di·sem′i·nūl″, *n. Bot.* any one of the regenerative parts of a plant, as a bud, spore, or seed.

dis·sen·sion, di·sen′shan, *n.* [L. *dissensio.*] Disagreement in opinion, usually producing heated debates or angry words; strife; discord; a quarrel; breach of friendship and union.—**dis·sen·tious,** di·sen′shus, *a.*

dis·sent, di·sent′, *v.i.* [L. *dissentio,* to think otherwise, to dissent.] To disagree in opinion; to differ; to think in a different or contrary manner, used with *from; eccles.* to differ from an established church in regard to doctrines, rites, or government.—*n.* Difference of opinion; disagreement, esp. of a judge, from the majority opinion of his colleagues. Declaration of disagreement in opinion; *eccles.* separation from an established church.—**dis·sent·ing,** *a.* Disagreeing in opinion; having the character of dissent; belonging to or connected with a body of dissenters.—**dis·sent·er,** *n.* One who dissents; one who differs in opinion, or one who declares his disagreement; *eccles.* one who separates from the service and worship of any established church.

dis·sen·tient, di·sen′shint, *a.* Disagreeing with a majority opinion; declaring dissent; voting differently.—*n.* One who disagrees and declares his dissent.

Dis·sent·ing, di·sen′ting, *a. Brit.* pertaining to a Protestant not conforming to the Church of England.—**Dis·sent·er,** *n.*

dis·sep·i·ment, di·sep′i·ment, *n.* [L. *dissepimentum—dis-,* asunder, and *sepio,* to enclose, < *sepes,* a hedge.] A partition in certain hollow parts of animals and plants; one of the partitions in the ovary or fruits of some plants formed by the sides of cohering carpels.

dis·ser·tate, dis′ėr·tāt″, *v.i.*—*dissertated, dissertating.* [L. *dissertatus,* pp. of *dissertare,* freq. of *disserere.*] To treat of a subject in a discourse; compose a dissertation.—**dis·ser·ta·tion,** dis″ėr·tā′shan, *n.* [L. *dissertatio(n-).*] A formal discourse on a subject; a written thesis, esp. of a doctoral candidate; a disquisition.—**dis·ser·ta·tor,** *n.*

dis·serve, dis·sėrv′, *v.t.*—*disserved, disserving.* To do the reverse of a service to; to do an injury or ill turn to.—**dis·serv·ice,** dis·sėr′vis, *n.* An ill turn or injury.

dis·sev·er, di·sev′ėr, *v.t.* To part; to divide asunder; to separate; to disunite.—**dis·sev·er·ance, dis·sev·er·ment,** *n.*

dis·si·dent, dis′i·dent, *a.* [L. *dissidens, dissidentis,* ppr. of *dissideo,* to disagree.] Dissenting; disagreeing with an opinion or group.—*n.* One who dissents from others; a dissenter.—**dis·si·dence,** dis′i·dens, *n.* Disagreement; dissent; nonconformity.

dis·sil·i·ent, di·sil′ē·ent, *a.* [L. *dissilio,* to leap asunder.] Bursting and opening with force, as the dry pod or capsule of a plant.

dis·sim·i·lar, di·sim′i·lėr, *a.* Not similar or resembling; unlike; different.—**dis·sim·i·lar·i·ty,** di·sim″i·lar′i·tē, *n.*—**dis·sim·i·lar·ly,** *adv.*

dis·sim·i·late, di·sim′i·lāt″, *v.t., v.i.*—*dissimilated, dissimilating.* To make or become unlike.—**dis·sim·i·la·tion,** *n.* A making or becoming unlike; *biol.* catabolism; *phon.* change of one of two similar sounds which would otherwise occur near together in a word.—**dis·sim·i·la·tive, dis·sim·i·la·to·ry,** *a.*

dis·si·mil·i·tude, dis″si·mil′i·töd″, dis″si·mil′i·tūd″, *n.* [L. *dissimilitudo,* < *dissimilis,* unlike.] Unlikeness; difference; a point of difference.

dis·sim·u·late, di·sim′ū·lāt″, *v.t.*—*dissimulated, dissimulating.* [L. *dissimulatus,* pp. of *dissimulare,* disguise, conceal.] To disguise or conceal under a false semblance;

dissemble.—*v.i.* To use dissimulation; **dissemble.**—**dis·sim·u·la·tion,** *n.* [L. *dissimulatio(n-).*] The act of dissimulating; feigning; hypocrisy.—**dis·sim·u·la·tive,** *a.* —**dis·sim·u·la·tor,** *n.*

dis·si·pate, dis'i·pāt″, *v.t.*—*dissipated, dissipating.* [L. *dissipatus,* pp. of *dissipare,* scatter abroad, disperse, demolish, squander.] To scatter in various directions; disperse; dispel; to squander; waste.—*v.i.* To become scattered or dispersed; be dispelled; disintegrate; to indulge in extravagant, intemperate, or dissolute pleasures; practice dissipation.—**dis·si·pat·ed,** *a.* Indulging in or characterized by excessive devotion to pleasure; intemperate; dissolute.—**dis·si·pa·ted·ly,** *adv.*—**dis·si·pat·ed·ness,** *n.*—**dis·si·pa·tive,** *a.* —**dis·si·pa·tor,** *n.*

dis·si·pa·tion, dis″i·pā'shan, *n.* [L. *dissipatio(n-).*] The act of dissipating; the state of being dissipated; dispersion; a wasting by misuse; a diversion; undue or vicious indulgence in pleasure; intemperance; dissolute mode of living.

dis·so·cial, di·sō'shal, *a.* Disinclined to, or unsuitable for, society; not social; not reconcilable. Also **dis·so·ci·a·ble.**—**dis·so·ci·a·bil·i·ty,** *n.*

dis·so·ci·ate, di·sō'shē·āt″,*v.t.*—*dissociated, dissociating.* [L. *dissociatus,* pp. of *dissociare.*] To sever the association of; disunite; separate; *chem.* to subject to dissociation.— *v.i.* To withdraw from association; *chem.* to undergo dissociation.—**dis·so·ci·a·tive,** *a.*

dis·so·ci·a·tion, di·sō″sē·ā'shan, di·sō″- shē·ā'shan, *n.* The act of dissociating, or the state of being dissociated; disunion; *chem.* the change of a complex substance into two or more new substances, under circumstances which permit at least partial recombination to form the original substance, as the *dissociation* of water to form hydrogen and oxygen; the separation of the molecule of an electrolyte into its constituent ions; *psychol.* a process whereby a group of ideas and feelings function more or less independently of the rest of the personality, as when under hypnosis or in certain psychotic or neurotic disorders.

dis·sol·u·ble, di·sol'ū·bl, *a.* [L. *dissolubilis.*] Capable of being dissolved or melted; capable of disintegration.—**dis·sol·u·bil·i·ty,** *n.*

dis·so·lute, dis'o·lōt″, *a.* [L. *dissolutus,* pp. of *dissolvo.*] Loose in behavior and morals; debauched.—**dis·so·lute·ly,** *adv.*—**dis·so·lute·ness,** *n.* Dissipation.

dis·so·lu·tion, dis″o·lō'shan, *n.* [L. *dissolutio,* a breaking up, a loosening, < *dissolvo.*] The act of dissolving; liquefaction; a breaking up; dispersal; the termination of a bond or partnership; the breaking up or a terminating of the activity of an organization, business, or governing body; decomposition; death.

dis·solve, di·zolv', *v.t.*—*dissolved, dissolving.* [L. *dissolvo,* to break up, to separate.] To melt; to liquefy; to make into a solution; to disunite; break up; terminate, as a parliament; to break or make no longer binding, as an alliance; to solve, explain, or resolve, as a doubt; to make disappear; to move the emotions of; to destroy the power of or render ineffectual, as a spell; to destroy, disintegrate, or consume.—*v.i.* To melt; to liquefy; to be converted into solution; to slowly disappear; to be emotionally shaken; to be dismissed; to break up; to be decomposed; to waste away; to gradually disappear from or come into view in a motion picture or television fade-out.—*n.* A simultaneous fading out of one scene, on a motion picture or TV screen, while fading in another.—**dis·solv·er,** *n.*—**dis·solv·a·ble,** *a.*

dis·sol·vent, di·zol'vent, *a.* Having power to melt or dissolve other substances.—*n.* Anything that dissolves; a substance that has the power of converting a solid substance into a fluid, or of separating its parts so that they mix with a liquid; a solvent.

dis·so·nance, dis'o·nans, *n.* [Fr. *dissonance,* L. *dissonantia,* discordance.] Discord; a mixture or union of harsh, inharmonious sounds.—**dis·so·nant,** dis'o·nant, *a.* Discordant; harsh; jarring; inharmonious; unpleasant to the ear. Disagreeing; incongruous.—**dis·so·nant·ly,** *adv.*

dis·suade, di·swād', *v.t.*—*dissuaded, dissuading.* [L. *dissuadeo,* to advise against.] To attempt to draw or divert from a measure by reason; to divert by persuasion; to turn from a purpose by argument. Opposite of *persuade.*—**dis·suad·er,** *n.*

dis·sua·sion, di·swā'zhan, *n.* An act of dissuading.—**dis·sua·sive,** di·swā'siv, *a.* Tending to dissuade.—**dis·sua·sive·ly,** *adv.*—**dis·sua·sive·ness,** *n.*

dis·sym·met·ric, dis″si·me'trik, *a.* Not symmetric; having the same form but not superposable, as the right and left hands; reversely symmetric. Also **dis·sym·met·ri·cal.**—**dis·sym·me·try,** dis·sim'i·trē, *n.* Absence of symmetry; a dissymmetric, or reversely symmetric, form or character.

dis·taff, dis'taf, dis'täf, *n.* [O.E. *distæf.*] A staff with a cleft end, formerly used for holding the fibers from which thread was drawn in spinning by hand; an analogous part of a spinning-wheel, for holding flax to be spun; any work, traditionally that of women; with reference to the distaff as a woman's implement, the female sex; a female heir.—*a.* Pertaining to a woman; as, the *distaff* side of the family.

dis·tal, dis'tal, *a.* Applied to the end of a bone, limb, or organ in plants and animals farthest removed from the point of attachment; situated at the extremity; most distant from the center.

dis·tance, dis'tans, *n.* [Fr. *distance,* L. *distantia,* < *disto,* to stand apart.] An interval or space between two objects; the length of the shortest line between separated things, places, or locations; remoteness of place; the respectful avoidance of familiarity; reserve which one assumes from being offended, or from dislike; *mus.* the interval between two tones; *arts,* the area of a painting showing things as distant. *Horse racing,* in a heat race, a point 240 yards from the finish that a horse must reach before the winner finishes in order to qualify for the next heat.—*v.t.*—*distanced, distancing.* To place at a distance; to leave at a great distance; to outdo or excel greatly.

dis·tant, dis'tant, *a.* [L. *distans,* standing apart, ppr. of *disto.*] Separate or removed; remote in place, in time, or in a line of succession or descent; apart in kind or nature; slight; as, a *distant* resemblance; characterized by haughtiness or indifference; reserved; shy; pertaining to something going a great distance or coming from a great distance; as, a *distant* message.—**dis·tant·ly,** *adv.* Remotely; at a distance; with reserve.

dis·taste, dis·tāst', *n.* Dislike of food or drink; disinclination.—**dis·taste·ful,** *a.* Unpleasant to the taste or liking; disagreeable; slightly repulsive.—**dis·taste·ful·ly,** *adv.*—**dis·taste·ful·ness,** *n.*

dis·tem·per, dis·tem'pėr, *n.* Ill humor; one of several highly contagious diseases of animals, esp. one affecting young dogs; political unrest; riot.—*v.t.* To derange the bodily functions or mental state of.

dis·tem·per, dis·tem'pėr, *v.t.* [O.Fr. *destremper* (Fr. *détremper*), < M.L. *distemperare,* dilute, soak.] To paint in distemper. —*n.* A method of painting in which the colors are mixed with some binding medium, such as gum or glue, to obtain a mat surface and to effect rapid drying; the pigment, or the ground, so prepared; tempera; a painting done by this method.

dis·tem·per·oid, dis·tem'pėr·oid, *a.* Of or pertaining to a weakened canine distemper virus used for immunization against natural distemper.

dis·tend, di·stend', *v.t.* [L.] To stretch or swell out by force acting from within; to dilate; to expand; to swell; of the bladder or the lungs, to puff out.—*v.i.* To become inflated or distended; to swell.—**dis·ten·si·bil·i·ty,** *n.*—**dis·ten·si·ble,** *a.*—**dis·ten·sion, dis·ten·tion,** *n.*

dis·tich, dis'tik, *n.* [Gr. *distichon*—*di,* twice, and *stichos,* a row, a line, a verse.] A couplet; a couple of verses or poetic lines making complete sense.—**dis·ti·chal,** *a.*

dis·till, *Brit.* **dis·til,** di·stil', *v.t.*— *distilled, distilling.* [Fr. *distiller,* < L. *destillo,* to trickle down.] To subject to the process of distillation; to concentrate or purify by distillation; as, to *distill* alcohol from grain; to obtain or extract by distillation; to yield or give forth in drops.—*v.i.* To go through a process of distillation; to condense or fall in drops from a still after distillation; to drop; to trickle or fall in drops or a thin film of moisture.—**dis·till·a·ble,** *a.* Fit for distillation or capable of being distilled.—**dis·tilled,** *a.* Made by distillation.

dis·til·la·tion, dis″ti·lā'shan, *n.* The volatilization of a liquid by heating in a retort or still and condensing the resultant vapor by cooling; the purification or refinement of a substance, or the separation of different substances, by this process; a distillate; the essence of something; the act of distilling or the condition of being distilled.—**dis·til·late,** dis'ti·lit, dis'ti·lāt″, di·stil'it, *n.* The fluid which is the condensed end product of distillation; anything like a distillate, as the essence or concentration of something.

dis·till·er, di·stil'ėr, *n.* One who distills; one whose occupation is to distill alcoholic liquors; a device, as a still, for distilling.— **dis·till·er·y,** di·stil'e·rē, *n.* pl. **dis·till·er·ies.** The building and works where distilling, esp. of alcoholic liquors, is carried on.

dis·tinct, di·stingkt', *a.* [L. *distinctus,* pp. of *distinguo.*] Separated or distinguished by some feature; not the same in number or kind; different; well-defined; sharp and clear; obvious; plain; unmistakable; notable; as, a *distinct* honor.—**dis·tinct·ly,** *adv.* In a distinct manner; clearly; obviously; plainly; precisely.—**dis·tinct·ness,** *n.*

dis·tinc·tion, di·stingk'shan, *n.* [L. *distinctio.*] The act of separating or distinguishing; that which is distinguished as different; a contrast; a note or mark of difference; distinguishing quality; eminence or superiority; elevation or honorable estimation; that which confers or marks eminence or superiority; a title or honor of some kind.—**dis·tinc·tive,** di·stingk'tiv, *a.* Marking or indicating distinction or difference.—**dis·tinc·tive·ly,** *adv.*—**dis·tinc·tive·ness,** *n.*

dis·tin·gué, dis″tang·gā', di·stang·gā', Fr. dē·stan·gā', *a.* [Fr. (fem. *distinguée*).] Distinguished; having an air of distinction: said esp. of persons.

dis·tin·guish, di·sting'gwish, *v.t.* [L. *distinguo,* to mark off, to distinguish.] To mark or set apart as different or separate from others; to perceive or recognize the individuality of; to note as differing from something else by some mark or quality; to classify or divide by any mark or quality which constitutes difference; to separate from others by some mark of honor or preference; to make eminent or known.—*v.i.*

To make a distinction; to find or show the difference.—**dis·tin·guish·a·ble**, *a.* Capable of being distinguished or recognized; capable of being defined or classified; worthy of note or special regard.—**dis·tin·guish·a·ble·ness**, *n.*—**dis·tin·guish·a·bly**, *adv.*—**dis·tin·guish·ing**, *a.* Constituting difference or distinction from everything; peculiar; characteristic.

dis·tin·guished, di·sting'gwisht, *a.* Separated from others by superior or extraordinary qualities; eminent; extraordinary; transcendent; noted; famous; celebrated.

Dis·tin·guished Con·duct Med·al, *n.* A British military decoration awarded for gallantry in action. Abbr. *D.C.M.*

Dis·tin·guished Fly·ing Cross, *n.* A military decoration awarded for heroism or extraordinary achievement while participating in aerial flight. Abbr. *D.F.C.*

Dis·tin·guished Serv·ice Cross, *n.* A military decoration awarded to a member of the army for extraordinary heroism in operations against the enemy. Abbr. *D.S.C.*

Dis·tin·guished Serv·ice Med·al, *n.* A military decoration awarded persons for exceptionally meritorious service in a duty of great responsibility. Abbr. *D.S.M.*

Dis·tin·guished Serv·ice Or·der, *n.* A British decoration since 1866, awarded for distinguished service in war. Abbr. *D.S.O.*

dis·tort, di·start', *v.t.* [L. *distorqueo, distortum.*] To twist out of natural or regular shape; to force or put out of the true bent or direction; to change from the true meaning; to pervert; *electron.* of a signal, to reproduce inaccurately by changing the frequency of the output wave.—**dis·tort·ed,** *a.* Twisted out of natural or regular shape; shaped abnormally or awry; *electron.* pertaining to an inaccurately reproduced signal.—**dis·tor·tion,** *n.* The act of distorting; a twisting or writhing motion; an unnatural direction of parts from any cause, as a curved spine, a wry mouth, or squinting; a perversion of the true meaning of words; *electron.* an inaccurate reproduction of a signal, caused by a change in the frequency of the output wave; *optics,* a lack of proportion in an image resulting from an aberration of the lens.—**dis·tor·tion·al,** *a.*

dis·tract, di·strakt', *v.t.* [L. *distraho, distractum,* to pull asunder, to perplex.] To turn or draw from any object or point; to divert (the attention) toward various other objects; to perplex, confound, or harass with conflicting emotions; to render frantic; to provide a diversion.—**dis·tract·ing·ly,** *adv.*—**dis·tract·ed,** *a.* Disordered in intellect; perplexed; frantic.—**dis·tract·ed·ly,** *adv.*

dis·trac·tion, di·strak'shan, *n.* The act of distracting; the state of being distracted; that which distracts; confusion from multiplicity of objects crowding on the mind and calling the attention different ways; frenzy; extreme perturbation or agony of mind, as from pain or grief. Anything giving the mind a new and more pleasant occupation; a diversion.—**dis·trac·tive,** *a.*

dis·train, di·strān', *v.t.* [O.Fr. *destraindre,* < L. *distringere,* to draw apart, to exact a pledge.] *Law,* to seize, as goods or chattels, for debt.—*v.i. Law,* to levy a distress.—**dis·train·a·ble,** *a.*—**dis·train·er, dis·train·or,** *n.*—**dis·traint,** di·strānt', *n. Law,* a distress or act of distraining.

dis·trait, di·strā', *Fr.* dēs·tRe', *a.* [Fr.] Absent-minded; inattentive because of distracting preoccupation.

dis·traught, di·strạt', *a.* [Old pp. of *distract.*] Distracted; disturbed mentally.

dis·tress, di·stres', *n.* [O.Fr. *destresse, destrece,* oppression, < *destrecer,* to oppress, < a hypothetical L.L. *districtiare,* < L.

districtus, pp. of *distringo,* to draw apart, hinder, molest.] Extreme pain; anguish of body or mind; that which causes suffering; affliction; calamity; adversity; misery; a state of danger. *Law,* the act of distraining; the seizure of any personal chattel as a pledge for the payment of rent or debt, or the satisfaction of a claim.—*v.t.* To afflict with pain or anguish; to harass; to grieve; to make miserable.—**dis·tress·ful,** *a.* Inflicting or bringing distress; calamitous; proceeding from pain or anguish; indicating distress.—**dis·tress·ful·ly,** *adv.* In a distressful manner.—**dis·tress·ful·ness,** *n.*—**dis·tress·ing,** *a.* Very afflicting; affecting with severe pain.—**dis·tress·ing·ly,** *adv.*

dis·tress, di·stres', *a.* Of or pertaining to merchandise sold at a loss; involving distrained goods; as, a *distress* sale.

dis·trib·u·tar·y, di·strib'ū·ter"ē, *n.* pl. **dis·trib·u·tar·ies.** A branch of a river which flows from the main stream and does not join it again, as opposed to a *tributary,* which flows into the main stream.

dis·trib·ute, di·strib'ūt, *v.t.*—*distributed, distributing.* [L. *distribuo, distributum,* to divide, distribute.] To divide among two or more; to deal out; to give or bestow in parts or portions; to dispense; to deliver, as newspapers, to a prescribed destination; to divide, as into classes, orders, genera; *logic,* to use, as a term, in its fullest meaning; encompassing all members of the class referred to; *printing,* to separate, as type, and place the individual units in their proper storage compartments.—**dis·trib·ut·a·ble,** *a.* Capable of being distributed.—**dis·trib·u·tee,** di·strib"ū·tē', *n. Law,* a person entitled to share in the apportionment of an estate.—**dis·trib·u·tor,** *n.* One who or that which distributes or deals out; a person or company that markets a product for the manufacturer, especially a wholesaler with exclusive sales rights in a given area; a device in a combustion engine which distributes electrical current to the spark plugs in the right sequence for firing.

dis·tri·bu·tion, dis"tri·bū'shan, *n.* [L. *distributio.*] The act of distributing or dealing out; the act of separating into distinct parts or classes; that which is distributed; the arrangement, position, or frequency of something in an area; as, *distribution* of troops, or of stars in the galaxy; the geographical range of a species; the division of the personal property of an estate among heirs; the marketing of a product; *statistics,* see *frequency distribution.*—**dis·tri·bu·tion·al,** *a.*—**dis·trib·u·tive,** di·strib'ū·tiv, *a.* Pertaining to distribution; serving to distribute; expressing separation or division; *gram.* referring singly to the persons or things of a group, as: *Each* and *either* are *distributive* adjectives. *Logic,* distributed, as a term, throughout a proposition; *math.* pertaining to an operation which produces the same result when performed on the whole as when performed on each part with the results combined.—**dis·trib·u·tive·ly,** *adv.*—**dis·trib·u·tive·ness,** *n.*

dis·trict, dis'trikt, *n.* [Fr. *district,* < M.L. *districtus,* territory under jurisdiction, < *distringere,* constrain, coerce.] A division of territory, as of a country, state, or county, marked off for administrative, electoral, or other purposes; a region or locality; *Brit.* a city or county subdivision similar to a ward or precinct in the U.S.—*v.t.* To divide into districts.

dis·trict at·tor·ney, *n.* The prosecuting officer of a federal judicial district, or of a state, or any district thereof.

dis·trust, di·strust', *v.t.* To doubt or suspect the truth, fidelity, firmness, sincerity, reality, sufficiency, or goodness of;

to have no faith, reliance, or confidence in; to be suspicious of.—*n.* Doubt or suspicion; want of confidence, faith, or reliance.—**dis·trust·ful,** dis·trust'fụl, *a.* Apt to distrust; wanting confidence; suspicious; mistrustful; apprehensive; not confident.—**dis·trust·ful·ly,** *adv.*—**dis·trust·ful·ness,** *n.*

dis·turb, di·stĕrb', *v.t.* [L. *disturbo,* to throw into disorder—*dis-,* asunder, and *turbo,* to confuse, < *turba,* a crowd, tumult.] To excite from a state of rest or tranquillity; to stir; to move; to discompose; to agitate; to throw into confusion or disorder; to disquiet; to render uneasy; to ruffle; to move from any regular course, operation, or purpose; to make irregular; to interfere with; to interrupt.—**dis·turb·er,** *n.*

dis·turb·ance, di·stĕr'bans, *n.* The act of disturbing; that which disturbs; interruption of peace or quiet; interruption of settled state of things; violent change; derangement; perturbation; agitation; disorder of thoughts; confusion; agitation in the body politic; a disorder; a tumult.

dis·turbed, di·stĕrbd', *a.* Exhibiting symptoms which indicate a mental or emotional abnormality.

di·sul·fate, dī·sul'fāt, *n. Chem.* a salt of disulfuric acid; a bisulfate; a pyrosulfate.—**di·sul·fide,** dī·sul'fīd, *n. Chem.* an inorganic compound having two sulfur atoms joined with an element or radical.—**di·sul·fu·ric acid,** *Chem.* a crystalline acid, $H_2S_2O_7$, obtained when sulfur trioxide is dissolved in sulfuric acid; pyrosulfuric acid.

dis·un·ion, dis·ūn'yon, *n.* A state of not being united; separation; a breach of concord and its effect; dissension.—**dis·u·nite,** dis"ū·nīt', *v.t.*—*disunited, disuniting.* To separate; to disjoin; to part; to raise dissension between.—*v.i.* To fall asunder; to become separate.—**dis·u·ni·ty,** *n.* pl. **dis·u·ni·ties.** A lack of unity.

dis·un·ion·ist, *n.* An advocate of disunion; in U.S. politics during the Civil War period, an advocate of secession.

dis·use, dis·ūs', *n.* Cessation of use, practice, or exercise.—**dis·ūz',** *v.t. disused, disusing.* To cease to use; to omit or neglect to practice.

dis·u·til·i·ty, dis"ū·til'i·tē, *n.* The quality of causing inconvenience, fatigue, or harm; injuriousness.

di·syl·la·ble, dī'sil·a·bl, di·sil'a·bl, *n.* A word consisting of two syllables. Also **dis·syl·la·ble,** di·sil'a·bl, dis'sil"a·bl, dī'sil·a·bl.—**di·syl·lab·ic,** dī"si·lab'ik, dis"i·lab'ik, *a.* Having or pertaining to two syllables. Also **dis·syl·lab·ic,** dis"i·lab'ik, dis"si·lab'ik.

dit, dit, *n.* A click or quick tone used in radio or International Morse Code to designate a dot.

ditch, dich, *n.* [A softened form of *dike,* formerly applied to the embankment as well as to the ditch.] A trench made by digging in the earth, particularly for draining wet land, for guarding an enclosure, or for preventing an enemy from access; a long artificial channel dug to contain water.—*v.t.* To dig a ditch in; to drain by means of a ditch; to surround with a ditch; of a vehicle, to force or drive into the ditch; of a train, to derail; of land-based aircraft, to crash-land in water and abandon. *Slang,* to be absent without valid reason, esp. of a student from class.—*v.i.* To dig a ditch.—**ditch·er,** *n.*

ditch reed, *n.* A tall reed with broad flat leaves found in damp areas of N. America and used for weaving lattices, mats, and screens. Also **gi·ant reed.**

dith·er, diTH'ẽr, *n.* [Origin uncertain.] Trembling; quivering; a state of great agitation, excitement, or confusion.—*v.i.*

---

a- fat, fāte, fär, fâre, fạll; **e-** met, mē, mēre, hẽr; **i-** pin, pīne; **o-** not, nōte, mŏve; **u-** tub, cūbe, bụll; **oi-** oil; **ou-** pound.

To act hesitantly, irresolutely, or in a disturbed or excited manner.

dith·y·ramb, dith′*i*·ram″, dith′*i*·ramb″, *n.* [Gr. *dithyrambos.*] A hymn among the ancient Greeks composed in a wildly enthusiastic style; any poem of an impetuous and irregular character.—**dith·y·ram·bic,** dith″*i*·ram′bik, *a.* Pertaining to or resembling a dithyramb; wild; enthusiastic.

dit·to, dit′ō, *n. pl.* **dit·tos.** [It. *ditto* (now *detto*), said, aforesaid, < L. *dictus,* pp. of *dicere,* say.] The aforesaid; the same: a term used in accounts, lists, or the like to avoid repetition; also *ditto mark. Colloq.* a duplicate or copy.—*adv.* As already stated.—*v.t.*—*dittoed, dittoing.* To duplicate; copy.

dit·to·graph, dit′o·graf″, dit′o·gräf″, *n.* A letter or letters repeated by error in printing or copying.

dit·to mark, *n. Often pl.* two small marks (″) placed beneath a previously written item to indicate the repetition of that item.

dit·ty, dit′ē, *n. pl.* **dit·ties.** [O.Fr. *ditté,* story, poem, etc., < L. *dictatum,* pp. of *dictare,* to dictate.] A song; a little poem to be sung.

dit·ty bag, *n.* A bag used by sailors to hold sewing implements, etc.—**dit·ty box,** *n.* A small box used like a ditty bag.

di·u·ret·ic, dī″ū·ret′ik, *a.* [Gr. *diourētikos,* < *dia,* through, and *ouron,* urine.] Having the power to increase the amount of urine discharged.—*n.* A medicine that increases the secretion of urine.—**di·u·re·sis,** dī″ū·rē′sis, *n. Med.* an excessive flow of urine.

di·ur·nal, dī·ur′nal, *a.* [L. *diurnalis,* < *diurnus,* daily, < *dies,* a day.] Belonging to the period of daylight, as distinguished from the night; happening every day. *Bot.* pertaining to flowers that are open by day and closed at night.—**di·ur·nal·ly,** *adv.*

di·va, dē′vä, *n. pl.* **di·vas,** **di·ve,** dē′väs, dē′vä. [It. < L. *diva,* goddess.] A great woman singer, esp. of opera; a prima donna.

di·va·gate, dī′va·gāt″, *v.i.*—*divagated, divagating.* [L.L. *divagatus,* pp. of *divagari,* < L. *vagari,* wander, < *vagus,* wandering, E. *vague.*] To wander; stray. To digress.—**di·va·ga·tion,** *n.*

di·va·lent, dī·vā′lent, *a.* Bivalent.

di·van, di·van′, dī·vän′, dī′van, *n.* [Turk. *divān* = Ar. *diwān,* < Pers. *diwān.*] A long, cushioned seat, often without arms or a back; a sofa or couch; a kind of coffee house or smoking room; in Turkey and other Moslem countries, a council of state, council chamber, judgment hall, or bureau of state. A collection of Persian or Urdu poems by a single author; also *diwan.*

di·var·i·cate, di·var′*i*·kāt″, di·var′*i*·kāt″, *v.i.*—*divaricated, divaricating.* [L. *divaricatus,* pp. of *divaricare,* < *varicare,* straddle, < *varus,* bent.] To spread apart; branch; diverge; *bot., zool.* to branch at a wide angle.—**di·var·i·cate·ly,** *adv.*—**di·var·i·ca·tion,** *n.*

dive, dīv, *v.i.*—past *dived* or *dove,* pp. *dived,* ppr. *diving.* [O.E. *dyfan,* to dive = Icel. *dýfa,* to dip, to dive.] To plunge head-first into water; to submerge, as a submarine or skin diver; to plunge deeply; to penetrate suddenly into anything, as with the hand; to enter deeply into anything, as a hobby or discussion; to dart; *aeron.* of an airplane, to plunge downward at a greater angle than when gliding.—*v.t.* To precipitate a descent of (something); to plunge into or through something.—*n.* An act of diving; the submerging of a skin diver or submarine; a downward plunge of an airplane; a sudden dart; a sharp or sudden decline; *colloq.* a disreputable place for drinking and gambling; *slang,* a prearranged, faked knockout in a boxing match.—**div·er,** dī′vėr, *n.* One who or that which dives; one who works under water, usu. in special dress; any of various birds that habitually dive; *Brit.* a

loon.—**dive bomb·er,** *n.* An airplane that drops its bombs while in a steep dive.—**dive-bomb,** *v.t., v.i.* To attack with or as with a dive bomber.

di·verge, di·vėrj′, dī·vėrj′, *v.i.*—*diverged, diverging.* [L. *di-* for *dis-,* asunder, and *vergo,* to incline.] To tend or proceed from a common point in different directions; to deviate from a given course or line; to differ or vary.—*v.t.* To turn aside or turn away.—**di·ver·gence,** **di·ver·gen·cy,** di·vėr′jens, di·vėr′jens, dī·vėr′jen·sē, dī·vėr′jen·sē, *n.* The act of diverging; a receding from each other; a deviation; a going farther apart.—**di·ver·gent,** *a.* Diverging; separating or receding from each other, as lines from the same point.—**di·ver·gent·ly,** *adv.*

di·vers, dī′vėrz, *a.* [Fr. *divers,* < L. *diversus,* diverse, turned away.] Various.

di·verse, di·vurs′, dī·vurs′, dī′vurs, *a.* [L. *diversus.*] Different; unlike; of sundry types or forms.—**di·verse·ly,** dī·vurs′lē, *adv.*—**di·verse·ness,** *n.*—**di·ver·si·fi·ca·tion,** *n.* The act of diversifying; the state of being diversified.

di·ver·si·form, di·vur′si·farm″, dī·vur′si·farm″, *a.* Of various forms.

di·ver·si·fy, di·vur′si·fī″, dī·vur′si·fī″, *v.t.*—*diversified, diversifying.* [Fr. *diversifier* —L. *diversus,* and *facio,* to make.] To make diverse or various in form or qualities; to give variety or diversity to; *finance,* to buy (securities) in varied businesses or industries.—**di·ver·si·fied,** *a.*

di·ver·sion, di·vur′zhan, di·vur′shan, dī··vur′zhan, dī·vur′shan, *n.* The act of diverting or turning aside from any course; that which diverts the mind from care, business, or study; sport; play; pastime; *milit.* a feint or other movement made to mislead an enemy as to the real point of attack.—**di·ver·sion·ar·y,** *a.*—**di·ver·sion·al,** *a.*—**di·ver·sion·ist,** *n.*

di·ver·si·ty, di·vur′si·tē, dī·vur′si·tē, *n.* [L. *diversitas.*] The state of being diverse; difference; variety, as in interests or investments.

di·vert, di·vurt′, dī·vurt′, *v.t.* [L. *diverto, diversum,* to turn aside.] To turn off from any course; to turn aside; as, to *divert* a stream or traffic; to please; to entertain.—**di·vert·er,** *n.* One who or that which diverts.—**di·vert·ing,** *a.* Causing diversion; amusing.—**di·vert·ing·ly,** *adv.*

di·ver·tic·u·lum, dī″vėr·tik′ya·lum, *n. pl.* **di·ver·tic·u·la,** dī″vėr·tik′ya·la. *Anat.* a blind, tubular sac or process branching off from a canal or cavity.

di·ver·ti·men·to, di·vėr″te·men′tō, *It.* dē·ver″tē·men′ta, *n. pl.* **di·ver·ti·men·ti,** di·vėr″tē·men′tē. [It.] Any of various pieces of light instrumental chamber music in several movements, such as a fantasia.

di·ver·tisse·ment, di·vėr′tis·ment, *Fr.* dē·ver·tēs·mäN′, *n.* [Fr. < *divertir.*] A diversion or entertainment interlude, esp. a short ballet; a divertimento.

di·ver·tive, di·vėr′tiv, dī·vėr′tiv, *a.* Serving to divert; amusing.

di·vest, di·vest′, dī·vest′, *v.t.* [O.Fr. *devestir,* < L.*devestio,* to undress.] To strip; to deprive, used with *of;* to free.

di·vide, di·vīd′, *v.t.*—*divided, dividing.* [L. *divido,* to divide—*di-* for *dis-,* asunder, and *vid,* a root signifying to cut or separate, akin to Skt. *vyadh,* to penetrate.] To part or separate into pieces; to cut or otherwise separate into two or more parts; to cause to be separate; to classify; to keep apart, as by a partition or by an imaginary line or limit; to make partition of among a number; to disunite in opinion or interest; to set at variance.—*v.i.* To become separated; to part from a common interest or outlook; to fork, as a road; to do mathematical division; to vote by the division of a legislative house, as in the British Parliament, into two parts,

the "ayes" dividing from the "noes."—*n.* The watershed of a district or region.—**di·vid·a·ble,** di·vī′da·bl, *a.* Capable of being divided.—**di·vid·ed,** *a.* Parted, separated, or disunited; showing divisions; at variance in feeling.—**di·vid·er,** *n.* One who or that which divides; *pl.* an instrument for dividing lines; compasses.

div·i·dend, div′i·dend″, *n.* [L., lit. 'a thing to be divided.'] *Math.* a sum or a number to be divided. Something extra or beyond the expected; the proportion of profit or gain made by a corporation which is divided among the stockholders; the sum that falls to the share of each; *law,* the share of the fund realized from the effects of a bankrupt, and apportioned according to the amount of the debt due to each creditor. A refund in money allocated by an insurance company to policyholders.

div·i·dend yield, *n.* The current yearly stock dividend divided by the current market price per share of stock outstanding.

div·i·na·tion, div″i·nā′shan, *n.* [L. *divinatio.*] The act of foretelling future events, or discovering things secret or obscure, by supernatural means; unusual insight; intuitive perception.—**di·vin·a·to·ry,** di·vin′a·tōr″e, di·vin′a·tar″ē, *a.*

di·vine, di·vīn′, *a.* [L. *divinus,* divine, religious, divinely inspired, godlike, < *divus,* divine, a deity or divinity.] Pertaining to God, or to a heathen deity or false god; partaking of the nature of God; godlike; heavenly; sacred; holy; excellent in the highest degree; relating to divinity or theology. *Colloq.* very delightful; wonderful.—*n.* A minister of the gospel; a priest; a clergyman; a theologian.—*v.t.*—*divined, divining.* [L. *divino.*] To foretell; to predict; to prognosticate; to conjecture; to guess.—*v.i.* To use or practice divination; to prognosticate; to guess; to prophesy.—**di·vine·ly,** *adv.*—**di·vine·ness,** *n.*

Di·vine Lit·ur·gy, *n.* A prescribed form for eucharistic worship in the Eastern Orthodox Church.

di·vine right of kings, *n.* The belief that the king's right to rule is derived directly from God.

div·ing bell, *n.* An apparatus, originally bell-shaped, in which persons can descend into the water and remain for a length of time, compressed air being pumped into the bell by assistants on the surface.

di·vin·ing rod, *n.* A forked stick, usu. of hazel, which is believed useful for indicating the presence of water or metal deposits. Also **dows·ing rod.**

di·vin·i·ty, di·vin′i·tē, *n. pl.* **di·vin·i·ties.** [L. *divinitas.*] The state of being divine; divineness; deity; godhead; divine element; divine nature; a celestial being; awe-inspiring character or influence; sacredness; the science of divine things; theology. (*Cap.*) God; Deity.

div·i·nize, div′i·nīz″, *v.t.*—*divinized, divinizing.* [Fr. *diviniser,* < *divin.*] To make or consider divine; to deify.—**div·i·ni·za·tion,** *n.*

di·vis·i·ble, di·viz′i·bl, *a.* [L. *divisibilis,* < *divido.*] Capable of division; that may be separated or disunited; separable.—**di·vis·i·bil·i·ty,** *n.* The quality of being divisible.—**di·vis·i·bly,** *adv.*—**di·vis·i·ble·ness,** di·viz′i·bl·nes, *n.*

di·vi·sion, di·vizh′on, *n.* [L. *divisio.*] The act of dividing or separating into parts; the state of being divided; separation; something that separates or traces the boundaries of, as a partition or dividing line; a section of a country, company, or government, divided for administrative, political, or other reasons; a distributing or apportioning; a part separated from the whole, as a segment or section; discord; dissension; variance; the separation of members, as in a legislature, into two groups for ascertaining the vote; *biol.* a number of plants or animals forming a part of a larger group, class, or category; *hort.* plant propagation in which segments are separated from the parent and used to produce new plants; *arith.* the process of finding the quotient, or, how many times a number, the divisor, is contained in another, the dividend; *milit.* a self-contained administrative and tactical organization, smaller than a corps, larger than a brigade; *nav.* a tactical group of ships forming part of a squadron.— **di·vi·sion of labor**, specialization; division of work processes into separate, smaller functions.—**di·vi·sion·al**, *a.*

Di·vi·sion·ism, di·vizh′a·niz″um, *n.* (*Sometimes l.c.*) *fine arts*, the pointillistic theory and practice of applying small dots of pure color, to be blended by the observer's eye as the painting is viewed from a distance.

di·vi·sive, di·vī′siv, *a.* Serving or tending to divide; causing dissension or strife.— **di·vi·sive·ly**, *adv.*—**di·vi·sive·ness**, *n.*

di·vi·sor, di·vī′zẽr, *n. Arith.* the number by which the dividend is divided.

di·vorce, di·vōrs′, di·vạrs′, *n.* [O.Fr. Fr. *divorce* < L. *divortium* < *divortere, divertere,* separate.] A legal dissolution of the marriage relation; any formal separation of man and wife according to established custom; a complete separation of any kind; as, the *divorce* of church and state.—*v.t.*— *divorced, divorcing.* To separate by divorce; of one's marriage partner, to rid oneself of by divorce; to separate; cut off.—**di·vorce·- a·ble**, *a.*—**di·vor·cé**, di·vōr′sā, *n.* A divorced man.—**di·vor·cee, di·vor·cée,** di·vōr·sē′, di·vōr·sā′, di·vōr′sā, di·vōr′sē, *n.* A divorced woman.—**di·vorce·ment**, *n.* An act of divorcing; divorce.

div·ot, div′ot, *n.* [Origin obscure.] *Sc.* a piece of turf or sod, as for covering a cottage; *golf,* a piece of turf cut out with a club in making a stroke.

di·vulge, di·vulj′, *v.t.*—*divulged, divulging.* [L. *divulgo,* to spread among the people.] To tell or make known, as what was before private or secret; to reveal; to disclose; to let be known.—**di·vul·gence, di·vulge·- ment**, *n.*—**di·vulg·er**, *n.*

di·vul·sion, di·vul′shan, *n.* [L. *divulsio,* a tearing asunder, < *divello, divulsum,* to pluck or pull asunder.] The act of pulling or tearing apart; a rending asunder; violent separation; laceration.—**di·vul·sive**, di·- vul′siv, *a.* Tending or having power to pull asunder or rend.

di·wan, di·wän′, di·wạn′, *n.* Dewan. A collection of poems by a single author in Persia; also *divan.*

Dix·ie, dik′sē, *n.* The southern states of the U.S., esp. the states comprising the Confederacy during the Civil War; the most popular of the many songs of the same name, written in 1859 by D. D. Emmett. Also **Dix·ie Land, Dix·ie·land.**

Dix·ie·crat, dik′sē·krat″, *n.* [*Dixie* and (*demo*)*crat.*] A southern Democrat, esp. one who left the Democratic Party in 1948 to support a states rights party opposing civil rights.—**Dix·ie·crat·ic**, *a.*

Dix·ie·land, dik′sē·land″, *a.* Relating to a jazz style of New Orleans origin, usu. played by a small ensemble, and characterized by a strong two-beat or four-beat rhythm and solo or group improvisation.

di·zy·got·ic, dī″zī·got′ik, *a.* Describing fraternal twins.

diz·zy, diz′ē, *a.*—*dizzier, dizziest.* [O.E. *dysig,* foolish; akin to L.G. *dusig, dōsig,* Ò.D. *duyzigh,* Mod.D. *duizelig,* dizzy, Dan. *dosig,* drowsy.] Having a sensation of whirling with instability or proneness to fall; giddy; mentally confused or dazed; causing giddiness; as, a *dizzy* height; caused or characterized by giddiness; *colloq.*

silly.—*v.t.*—*dizzied, dizzying.* To make dizzy or giddy; to confuse.—**diz·zi·ly,** *adv.*—**diz·zi·ness**, *n.* State of being dizzy; vertigo.

D lay·er, *n.* A layer of the ionosphere which tends to form in the D region, usually containing some quantities of ionized gases.

DNA, *n. Biochem.* deoxyribonucleic acid, a compound found in chromosomes consisting of a long chain molecule comprising many repeated and varied combinations of four nucleotides, one of which is the sugar deoxyribose: subdivisions of the molecule are believed to be the genes.

do, dō, du̇, *v.t.*—pres. sing. *do, do* or archaic *doeth* or *doth*; pres. pl. *do*; past sing. *did, did* or archaic *didst, did*; past pl. *did*; pp. *done*; ppr. *doing.* [O.E. *don,* pret. *dyde,* D. *doen,* G. *thun,* do; related to L. *dere,* Gr. *tithanai,* Skt. *dha,* put.] To perform, as an act; to complete or accomplish, as: He *did* the work. To exert, as: I *did* my utmost. To be the cause of; as, to *do* good, to *do* harm; to give or render; as, to *do* justice; to deal with, in the manner appropriate to the act; as, to *do* dishes, to *do* one's hair; to cover or traverse; as, to *do* a hundred miles an hour; to suffice, as: It will *do* me for the present. To remain a period of time; as, to *do* a second term in office; to change the language of, as: They are *doing* Cervantes' novel in musical form.—*v.i.* To conduct oneself; as, to *do* badly; to fare, as: The patient is *doing* as well as expected. To suffice for the purpose, as: This will *do.* To take place, as: What's *doing* at the club? —*aux. v.* In interrogative, negative, or inverted construction, *do* is used for idiomatic word order and has no special meaning, as: *Do* you know where you are going? We *do* not wish to go there. *Do* expresses emphasis in such constructions as: I *do* work. *Do* is used in elliptical constructions, as: *Did* you go? I *did.*—**do ·way with**, to put an end to; as, to *do away with* unnecessary tasks.—**do by**, to treat, as: He *does* well *by* his children.—**do one proud**, to be a source of pride or credit, as: The child *did his mother proud.*—**do or die**, to make a very great effort.—**do out of**, to cheat or swindle, as: The peddler *did* him *out of* five dollars.—**do o·ver**, to repeat; to redecorate; as, to *do* the dining room *over.* —**do up**, to wrap up; to arrange, as the hair; to exhaust, as: The work *did* me *up.* —**do with·out**, to dispense with; as, to *do without* a car.—**have to do with**, to have a connection or an association with, as: What does that *have to do with* the problem?— **make do**, to get along despite inadequacy; as, to *make* old clothes *do.*—**do's and don'ts**, rules or regulations; as, the *do's and don'ts* of etiquette.

do, dō, *n.* pl. dos. *Mus.* the name given to the first of the syllables used in solmization; the first or key note of the diatonic scale.

do·a·ble, dö′a·bl, *a.* Capable of being done or executed.

dob·bin, dob′in, *n.* [Var. of *Robin,* for *Robert,* man's name.] A quiet, plodding horse for farm work or family use.

Do·ber·man pin·scher, dō′bẽr·man pin′shẽr, *n.* One of a breed of medium to large, short-haired dogs developed in Germany, usually having a brown, black, or bluish-gray coat with rust markings.

dob·son, dob′son, *n.* [Origin obscure.] A hellgrammite; the larva of any of various other insects of the same family, *Corydalidæ.*—**dob·son fly**, *n.* The adult insect, *Corydalus cornutus,* having membranous wings and, in the male, large hornlike mandibles.

do·cent, dō′sent, *Germ.* dō·tsent′, *n.* A university teacher; a guide in a museum or art gallery.

Do·ce·tism, dō·sēt′iz·um, dō′se·tiz″um, *n.* The belief of an early Christian sect that Jesus Christ had only a spiritual body and could not suffer physical pain.—**Do·ce·tic,** dō·sēt′ik, dō·set′ik, *a.* Pertaining to the belief of Docetism.

doch-an-dor·rach, doch′an·dôr′ach, *n. Sc., Ir.* stirrup cup; a drink at parting. Also **doch-an-dor·ris.**

doc·ile, dos′il, *Brit.* dō′sil, *a.* [L. *docilis,* < *doceo,* to teach.] Easily managed; teachable; easily instructed; ready to learn; tractable. —**doc·ile·ly**, *adv.*—**do·cil·i·ty**, do·sil′i·- tē, dō·sil′i·tē, *n.*

dock, dok, *n.* [O.E. *docce,* G. *docke.*] The common name of various species of perennial herbs, most of them troublesome weeds with stout root-stalks, erect stems, and broad leaves.

dock, dok, *n.* [M.E. *dok*: cf. Icel. *dockr.*] The solid or fleshy part of an animal's tail, as distinguished from the hair; the part of a tail left after cutting or clipping.—*v.t.* To cut short or cut off, as the end of a body part; as, to *dock* a dog's tail; to deprive of benefits, usually as a penalty; as, to *dock* a sum from an employee's pay.

dock, dok, *n.* An enclosure artificially formed on the side of a harbor or the bank of a river for reception of ships; a wharf; the waterway existing between two piers or wharves; such a waterway together with surrounding piers and wharves. A shipping or loading platform for any type of vehicle, such as trucks or freight trains. A repair shed or hangar for aircraft.—*v.t.* To bring, guide, or haul into dock.—*v.i.* To come into dock.

dock, dok, *n.* [D. *dok,* G. *docke,* Sw. *docka,* a dock, Flem. *docke,* a kind of cage; perhaps < L. *doga,* a kind of vessel, < Gr. *dochē,* receptacle, < *dechomai,* to receive.] The place, often enclosed, where a criminal stands or sits during a trial.

dock, dok, *v.t. Aerospace,* to join and couple together two or more orbiting objects in outer space.—**dock·ing**, *n.* A rendezvous and coupling of orbiting objects.

dock·age, dok′ij, *n.* The charge for the use of a dock; facilities for docking a vessel; the act of docking a ship; a deduction from, or curtailment of, wages; waste material in grains, easily removed by any of several separating processes.—**dock·er**, *n.* A worker at the wharves; a longshoreman; one who or which docks or cuts short. —**dock·yard**, dok′yärd, *n.* A yard or repository containing naval stores and facilities for building or repairing ships.— *Brit.* a navy yard.

dock·et, dok′it, *n.* An abridgement, abstract, or digest; a list of causes in court for trial, or of the names of the parties who have causes pending; any similar list; *chiefly Brit.* an official memorandum or entry of a proceedings in a legal cause, or a register of such entries. *Brit.* a writing on a letter or document, stating its contents; any statement of particulars attached to a package; a label; a ticket.—*v.t.*—*docketed, docketing.* To make an abstract or entry of in a docket; endorse with a memorandum, as of contents; mark with a ticket.

dock·hand, dok′hand″, *n.* A laborer on docks.

doc·tor, dok′tẽr, *n.* [L., < *doceo, doctum,* to teach.] A person duly licensed to practice medicine; a physician, dentist, or veterinarian; a learned man; one who has received the degree of this name from a university, being thus a *doctor* of divinity, laws, philosophy, etc.—*v.t.* To serve as physician to; to treat with remedies; to repair or patch up; to falsify; to drug or adulterate, as wine or food.—*v.i.* To practice medicine as a physician, dentist, or veterinarian; *dial.* to take or receive medicine or medical treatment.—**doc·tor·al**, *a.* Relating to the degree of a doctor, or the program of required study or research leading to the degree.—**doc·tor·ate**, dok′tẽr·it, *n.* The university degree of doctor.—**doc·tor·-ship**, *n.* The degree of a doctor; doctorate.

doc·tri·naire, dok″tri·nâr′, *n.* [Fr., < L. *doctrina*; name originally given to certain French politicians after the Restoration of 1815.] One who theorizes or advocates important changes in political or social matters without a sufficient regard to practical considerations; a political theorist. —*a.* Concerning or pertaining to a doctrinaire; dogmatic; theoretical rather than practical.

doc·trine, dok′trin, *n.* [O.Fr. Fr. *doctrine*, < L. *doctrina*, teaching, learning, < *doctor*.] That which is taught; teachings collectively; a body or system of teachings relating to a particular subject; a system of beliefs advocated; a particular principle taught or advocated; as, the Monroe *doctrine*; a tenet or dogma.—**doc·tri·nal**, dok′tri·nal, *Brit.* dok·trin′al, *a.* Pertaining to doctrine; containing a doctrine.—**doc·tri·nal·ly**, *adv.* In the form of doctrine or instruction; by way of teaching or positive direction.

doc·trine of de·scent, *n. Biol.* the theory that all the presently existing plants and animals are directly descended from previous plants and animals.

doc·u·ment, dok′ū·ment, *n.* [O.Fr. Fr. *document*, < L. *documentum*, lesson, example, M.L. official paper, < L. *docere*, teach.] A written or printed paper furnishing information or evidence; a legal or official paper.—*v.t.* To support by documentary evidence; to furnish with documents, evidence, or the like.—**doc·u·men·tal**, *a.*

doc·u·men·ta·ry, dok″ū·men′ta·rē, *a.* Pertaining to, consisting of, or derived from documents.—*n. pl.* **doc·u·men·ta·ries.** A dramatic or instructive presentation prepared for motion pictures or TV, and providing a complete record of a place, person, or subject of unusual interest or special significance.—**doc·u·men·ta·ri·ly**, *adv.*

doc·u·men·ta·tion, dok″ū·men·tā′shan, *n.* The use of documentary evidence; a furnishing with authentic documents.

dod·der, dod′ẽr, *n.* [Dan. *dodder*, Sw. *dodra*, G. *dotter*, of unknown derivation.] The name of certain leafless pink or white parasitic plants, the common English species of which are found on nettles, vetches, furze, or flax. Also **love vine.**—**dod·dered**, *a.* Overgrown with dodder; of trees, having the top branches blasted or withered.

dod·der, dod′ẽr, *v.i.* To tremble or shake, as from old age or lack of strength.—**dod·dered**, *a.* Feeble; senile; shaky, as from weakness. Also, **dod·der·ing, dod·-der·ly**—**dod·der·er**, *n.*

do·dec·a·gon, dō·dek′a·gon, *n.* [Gr. *dodekagonon.*] A polygon having twelve sides and twelve angles.—**do·de·cag·o·nal**, dō″de·-kag′o·nal, *a.*

do·dec·a·he·dron, dō·dek″a·hē′dran, dō″dek·a·hē′dran, *n. pl.* **do·dec·a·he·-drons,** do·dec·a·he·dra.** [Gr. *dodekaedron.* A solid figure having twelve faces.—**do·dec·a·he·dral**, *a.*

do·dec·a·phon·ic, dō·dek″a·fon′ik, *a.* Pertaining to the mechanical twelve-tone technique of musical composition.—**do·-dec·a·pho·nism**, *n.*—**do·dec·a·phon·ist**, *n.*—**do·dec·a·pho·ny**, *n.*

dodge, doj, *v.i.*—*dodged, dodging.* [Origin uncertain.] To move back and forth or to and fro; move aside or change position suddenly, as to avoid a blow or to get behind something; hence, to use evasive methods; prevaricate.—*v.t.* To elude by a sudden shift of position or by strategy;

hence, to deal indirectly or evasively with; trifle with; to follow stealthily; to move or drive about.—*n.* An act of dodging; a springing aside; a shifty trick; *colloq.* an ingenious expedient or contrivance.—**dodg·er**, *n.* One who dodges; a shifty person; a small handbill.—**dodg·er·y**, *n. pl.* **dodg·er·ies.** An act or instance of evading; trickery.—**dodg·y**, *a.*—*dodgier, dodgiest.*

do·do, dō′dō, *n. pl.* **do·dos, do·does.** [Pg. *doudo, doido,* foolish, silly.] A clumsy, flightless, extinct bird, *Didus ineptus,* related to the pigeons, but closer in size to the turkey, formerly found on the islands of Mauritius and Réunion; *colloq.* one who is slow-witted or hopelessly behind the times.

doe, dō, *n. pl.* **does, doe.** [O.E. *dá,* Dan. *daa.*] The female of the deer, goat, antelope, and rabbit, corresponding to the masculine *buck.* —**doe·skin**, *n.* The skin of a doe; a compact, short-napped cloth.

do·er, dö′ẽr, *n.* One who performs what is required, as opposed to a mere talker or theorizer.

doesn't, duz′ent. Contraction of does not.

doff, dof, daf, *v.t.* [Contr. for *do off,* like *don* for *do on.*] To take off, as clothing; to remove or lift up in greeting, as the hat; to discard or get rid of.

dog, dąg, dog, *n.* [O.E. *docga*; origin unknown.] A domesticated carnivorous quadruped of many varieties, the so-called *Canis familiaris*; any animal belonging to the same family, *Canidæ,* which includes the wolves, jackals, and foxes; the male of such an animal; any of various animals allied to or suggesting the dog; a prairie-dog; a dogfish; a despicable fellow; a fellow in general; as, a gay *dog*; (*cap.*) either of two constellations, Canis Major, "Great Dog," and Canis Minor, "Little Dog," situated near Orion. An andiron; any of various mechanical devices, as for gripping or holding something.—*v.t.*—*dogged, dogging.* To follow or track like a dog, esp. with hostile intent; to hound; to drive or chase with a dog or dogs; to fasten or grip with a mechanical dog.—*adv.* Completely or extremely, usu. used in combination; as, *dog-tired.*—**dog in the man·ger**, *n.* A person who, like the dog in the fable, churlishly keeps possession of something which is of no particular use to himself.—**to go to the dogs**, to go to ruin.

dog·bane, dąg′bān″, dog′bān″, *n.* A North American bitter plant of the *Apocynum* genus; wolfsbane.

dog·ber·ry, dąg′ber″ē, dog′ber″ē, dąg′be·-rē, dog′be·rē, *n. pl.* **dog·ber·ries.** The berry of several plants including the dog-wood, bearberry, and dogrose.

dog·cart, dąg′kärt″, dog′kärt″, *n.* A horse-drawn, two-wheeled carriage with the occupants sitting back to back on two transverse seats; a cart drawn by dogs.

dog·catch·er, dąg′kach″ẽr, dog′kach″ẽr, *n.* An official employed by a community or animal welfare organization to find and impound stray dogs and other homeless animals.

dog col·lar, *n.* A collar worn by dogs. *Slang,* a clergyman's collar; a necklace forming a high collar around a woman's neck.

dog days, *n. pl.* The days when Sirius, the Dog Star, rises and sets with the sun, extending from about July 3 to about August 11, a time of midsummer heat.

doge, dōj, *n.* [It.] The chief magistrate of the former republics of Venice, 697–1797, and Genoa, 1339–1797.

dog-ear, dąg′ẽr, dog′ẽr, *n.* The corner of a leaf in a book turned down.—*v.t.* To turn down in dog-ears.—**dog-eared**, *a.* Having the corners of pages turned down from careless handling; as, a *dog-eared* book.

dog-eat-dog, dąg′ẽt·dąg′, dog′ẽt·dog′, *a.* Characterized by ruthless competition.

dog·face, dąg′fās, dog′fās″, *n. Slang,* a soldier in the U.S. Army, esp. an infantryman.

dog fen·nel, *n.* An annual weed, *Eupatorium capillifolium*; mayweed.

dog·fight, dąg′fīt″, dog′fīt″, *n.* A fight between or as if between dogs; tenacious combat between fighter airplanes.

dog·fish, dąg′fish″, dog′fish″, *n. pl.* **dog·-fish, dog·fish·es.** A name given to several small sharks and other various fish, as the bowfin.

dog·ged, dą′gid, dog′id, *a.* Tenacious; obstinate.—**dog·ged·ly**, *adv.*—**dog·ged·ness**, *n.*

dog·ger·el, dą′gẽr·el, dog′ẽr·el, *a.* An epithet originally applied to a kind of loose, irregular measure in burlesque poetry; now, more generally, verses defective in rhythm and sense.—*n.* Doggerel verses.

dog·gish, dą′gish, dog′ish, *a.* Like a cur; snappish; surly; pretentiously stylish.—**dog·gish·ness**, *n.*

dog·gone, dąg′gąn″, dąg′gon′, dog′gąn″, dog′gon′, *v.t.*—*doggoned, doggoning.* [Appar. < the Scottish imprecation *dog on it!*] *Slang,* to damn.—*n. Slang,* a word used in vague malediction or as a substitute for profanity.—**dog·goned**, *a. Slang,* cursed; confounded.

dog·house, dąg′hous″, dog′hous″, *n.* A dog's shelter, usu. resembling a tiny house; *aerospace slang,* a protuberance or blister that houses an instrument or instruments on an otherwise smooth skin of a rocket.—**in the dog·house**, *slang,* in disfavor.

do·gie, dō′gē, *n.* An orphan calf in a western cattle herd.

dog·leg, dąg′leg, dog′leg″, *a.* Having a sharp angle like a dog's leg.—*n. Aerospace,* a directional turn made in a launch trajectory to achieve a more favorable orbit inclination; *golf,* a fairway that includes a sharp right or left turn.

dog·ma, dąg′ma, dog′ma, *n. pl.* **dog·mas, dog·ma·ta.** [Gr. *dogma,* that which seems true, an opinion, < *dokeō,* to seem.] A settled opinion or belief; a tenet, as of a religious faith; an opinion or doctrine received on authority, as opposed to one obtained from experience or demonstration.—**dog·mat·ic, dog·mat·i·cal**, dąg′mat′ik, dog·mat′ik, dąg·mat′i·kal, dog·mat′i·kal, *a.* Pertaining to a dogma or dogmas; having the character of a dogma; disposed to assert opinions with overbearing or arrogance; dictatorial; arrogant; authoritative; positive.—**dog·mat·i·cal·ly**, *adv.*—**dog·-mat·i·cal·ness**, *n.*

dog·mat·ics, dąg·mat′iks, dog·mat′iks, *n. pl. but sing. in constr.* Doctrinal theology; the essential doctrines of Christianity. Also **dog·mat·ic the·ol·o·gy.**—**dog·ma·tism**, dąg′ma·tiz″um, dog′ma·tiz″um, *n.* The quality of being dogmatic; arrogant assertion of opinion or belief; *philos.* a system of speculative reasoning based on certain a priori principles or self-evident truths, opposed to *skepticism.*—**dog·ma·tist**, dąg′ma·tist, dog′ma·tist *n.* One who is dogmatic; an upholder of dogmas; an arrogant advancer of principles or opinions.

dog·ma·tize, dąg′ma·tiz″, dog′ma·tiz″, *v.i.*—*dogmatized, dogmatizing.* To teach or assert opinions with bold and undue confidence; to assert principles arrogantly or authoritatively.—*v.t.* To state or deliver as dogma.—**dog·ma·tiz·er**, *n.*—**dog·ma·ti·za·tion**, *n.*

do-good·er, dö′gụd′ ẽr, *n.* One who works actively for social reform, often without a realistic grasp of the problems involved.

dog rose, *n.* The wild rose, *Rosa canina,* with pink flowers.

dog sled, *n.* A sled pulled by dogs. Also **dog sledge.** *Canadian,* **dog train.**

Dog Star, *n.* Either of the two stars Sirius, a star of the first magnitude, and Procyon, a bright star in Canus Minor.

dog tag, *n.* A disk fastened to a dog's collar giving the animal's identifying license number, which is registered and issued by local community authorities; one of the pair of identification tags worn by a member of the armed forces.

dog·tooth, dog'tŏth, *n.* A sharp-pointed human tooth situated between the incisors and the bicuspids; a canine tooth; an eyetooth.

dog·tooth vi·o·let, *n.* A plant of the genus *Erythronium*, esp. an early spring-flowering European bulbous herb, *E. denscanis*, which produces a solitary purple bloom; any of several related American woodland plants, as *E. Americanum*, yielding yellow flowers, or *E. albidum*, displaying white or pinkish-purple blossoms. Also **dog's tooth vi·o·let.**

dog·trot, dog'trot", *n.* A gentle trot like that of a dog.—*v.i.* To progress at an easy pace.

dog·watch, dog'woch", dog'wąch", *n. Naut.* one of the two watches of two hours each, between 4 and 6 p.m. and between 6 and 8 p.m.; a night shift; *journalism slang*, the period after a newspaper's regular editions have gone to press when a reduced staff remains on duty.

dog·wood, dog'wųd", *n.* Any of several trees or shrubs of the genus *Cornus*, some bearing small flowers having showy, white-to-pinkish, petallike bracts.

doi·ly, doi'lē, *n. pl.* **doi·lies.** [Said to be named from the first maker, an English draper.] A small, ornamental, cloth mat; a small place mat or decorative table runner.

do·ing, dŏ'ing, *n.* A performance; personal effort, as: To win will take some *doing*; action or cause; as, an accident not of his *doing*; *pl.* social activities; events; deeds.

do-it-your·self, dŏ'it·yẽr·self', *a.* Pertaining to supplies and materials manufactured and marketed esp. for the use of hobbyists or amateurs.—**do-it-your·self·er,** *n.*

dol·ce, dŏl'chā, *It.* dạl'che, *a.* [It., < L. *dulcis*, sweet.] *Mus.* sweet; soft.—*n.* Instruction to the performer to play the music sweetly and softly.

dol·drums, dŏl'drumz, dol'drumz, *n. pl. Naut.* the parts of the ocean near the equator that abound in calms, squalls, and light baffling winds; low spirits; a period of inactivity.

dole, dŏl, *n.* [O.Fr. *dole,* Fr. *deuil,* mourning, < L. *doleo,* to grieve.] *Archaic,* grief; sorrow.—**dole·ful,** *a.* Full of or causing grief; expressing grief; mournful; melancholy.—**dole·ful·ly,** *adv.*—**dole·ful·ness,** *n.*—**dole·some,** *a. Archaic,* doleful.

dole, dŏl, *n.* That which is dealt out or distributed; that which is given in charity; gratuity, esp. money distributed by the government to an unemployed person.—*v.t.* —*doled, doling.* To deal out; to distribute in small portions.

dol·er·ite, dol'e·rīt", *n.* [Fr. *dolérite,* < Gr. *doleros,* deceptive.] A coarse-grained variety of basalt; any of various other igneous rocks, as diabase; an igneous rock, similar to basalt, whose composition can be determined only when examined under a microscope.—**dol·er·it·ic,** dol'e·rit'ik, *a.*

dol·i·cho·ce·phal·ic, dol"i·kō·se·fal'ik, *a.* [Gr. *dolichos,* long, and *kephalé,* head.] Long-headed; having a breadth of skull small in proportion to the length from front to back: opposed to *brachycephalic.* Also **dol·i·cho·ceph·a·lous,** dol"i·kō·sef'a·lus. —**dol·i·cho·ceph·a·ly,** *n.*—**dol·i·cho·ceph·a·lism,** *n.*

dol·i·cho·cra·nic, dol"i·kō·krā'nik, *a.* Having a skull with a cranial index of less than 75; proportionately smaller in breadth than in length.

doll, dol, *n.* [< *Doll, Dolly,* for *Dorothy,* woman's name.] A toy representing a child or other human being; a child's toy baby;

a pretty but expressionless woman; *slang,* a man or woman who is considered attractive by the opposite sex;—**doll up,** *slang,* to dress elegantly or in a showy manner.— **doll·ish, doll·like,** *a.*—**doll·ish·ly,** *adv.*— **doll·ish·ness,** *n.*

dol·lar, dol'ẽr, *n.* [L.G. *daler* = D. *daalder,* < G. *thaler,* for *Joachimsthaler,* "coin of Joachimsthal," place of silver mines in Bohemia.] The monetary unit of the U.S.; the corresponding unit, coin, or note in Canada and several other countries or territories.

dol·lar di·plo·ma·cy, *n.* A foreign policy considered to have as its primary aim the promotion and protection of private investments abroad; a diplomacy which advocates use of financial resources to achieve objectives.

dol·lar sign, *n.* The character $ meaning dollar or dollars when placed before a number as, $5 (five dollars). Also **dol·lar mark.**

dol·lop, dol'op, *n.* [Origin obscure.] A lump; a small mass.

doll·y, dol'ē, *n. pl.* **doll·ies.** A child's name for a doll. A low platform on rollers or wheels, used for transporting heavy objects; a platform on wheels to hold a television or movie camera. A small railroad locomotive for specialized uses, as switching, in railroad yards or at construction sites. A piece of metal or wood placed on the head of a pile to absorb the blows while it is being driven; a tool for holding the head of a rivet while the other end is being headed; a wooden stick for stirring clothes being laundered in a washtub.—*v.t.*—*dollied, dollying.* To transport on or handle with a dolly.—*v.i.* To move a television or movie dolly to various positions to achieve different camera angles.

dol·man, dŏl'man, dol'man, *n.* [Fr. *dolman,* *doliman,* < Turk. *dolaman.*] A long outer robe worn by Turks; a woman's outer garment with dolman sleeves.

dol·man sleeve, *n.* A sleeve in a woman's outer garment, having a wide armhole and tapering to fit closely at the wrist.

dol·men, dŏl'men, dol'men, *n.* [Armor. *dolmen;* Gael. *tolmen—dol, tol,* a table, and *men,* a stone.] *Archaeol.* a rude ancient structure, probably of sepulchral origin, consisting of one large unhewn stone resting on two or more others placed erect; also applied to structures where several blocks are raised upon pillars to form a sort of gallery.

do·lo·mite, dŏ'lo·mīt", dŏl'o·mīt",*n.*[From D. G. de *Dolomieu* (1750–1801), French geologist.] A native carbonate of calcium and magnesium, called *dolomite marble* when in granular crystalline rock masses.— **do·lo·mit·ic,** dŏl'o·mit'ik, *a.*

do·lor, *Brit.* **do·lour,** dŏ'lẽr, *n.* [Fr. *douleur,* < L. *dolor, doloris,* grief, pain, < *doleo,* to grieve.] Grief; sorrow; lamentation.—**do·lor·ous,** dol'ẽr·us, dŏ'lẽr·us, *a.* Sorrowful; doleful; expressing pain or grief; woeful, as: The famine created a *dolorous* situation among the peasants.—**do·lor·ous·ly,** *adv.*—**do·lor·ous·ness,** *n.*

dol·phin, dol'fin, dạl'fin, *n.* [O.Fr. *daufin,* *delfin* (Fr. *dauphin*), < L. *delphinus,* < Gr. *delphis,* dolphin.] Any of various cetaceans of the family *Delphinidae,* some of which are commonly called porpoises, esp. *Delphinus delphis,* which has a long, sharp nose and abounds in the Mediterranean and the temperate Atlantic; either of two large pelagic fishes constituting the genus *Coryphaena,* esp. *C. hippurus,* remarkable for its changes of color when removed from the water; *naut.* a post or buoy to which to moor a vessel. *Astron.* the northern constellation Delphinus.—**dol·phin strik·er,** *naut.* a martingale spar under the end of a bowsprit.

dolt, dŏlt, *n.* [Probably connected with E. *dull,* O.E. *dol.* dull, stupid; *dwelan,* to err,

to be stupid.] A dull, stupid fellow; a blockhead.—**dolt·ish,** *a.* Dull in intellect. —**dolt·ish·ly,** *adv.*—**dolt·ish·ness,** *n.*

Dom, dom, *n.* [Pg. and Fr. *dom* = Sp. *don,* < L. *dominus,* master, lord.] A title prefixed to the name of certain Portuguese and Brazilian dignitaries; a title given to certain Roman Catholic ecclesiastics, esp. Benedictine and Carthusian monks.

do·main, dō·mān', *n.* [Fr. *domaine,*O. Fr. *domeine* (also *demeine*), orig. adj., < L. *dominicus,* belonging to a lord.] Absolute ownership of property; property so owned; possession or dominion; a territory under rule or influence; a realm; *fig.* a field of action, influence, or thought; as, the *domain* of commerce, of science, or of letters.—**do·ma·ni·al,** *a.*

dome, dōm, *n.* [L. *domus,* house; in part through Fr. *dôme,* < It. *duomo,* cathedral, cupola, dome.] A large hemispherical or approximately hemispherical roof; a cupola, esp. a large one; anything shaped like a cupola. *Crystal.* a form whose planes intersect the vertical axis, but are parallel to one of the lateral axes.—*v.t.*—*domed, doming.* To cover with or as with a dome; to shape like a dome.—*v.i.* To rise or swell as a dome.

domes·day, dōmz'dā', dōmz'dā", *n.* Old form of *doomsday.*—**Domes·day Book,** a record of a survey of the lands of England made by order of William the Conqueror about 1086, giving the ownership, extent, and value of the properties.

do·mes·tic, do·mes'tik, *a.* [L. *domesticus,* < *domus,* house.] Of or pertaining to the home, the household, or household affairs; devoted to home life or affairs; of or pertaining to one's own or a particular country as apart from other countries; belonging, existing, or produced within a country; as, *domestic* trade, *domestic* manufactures; not foreign; of an animal, living with man; tame.—*n.* A hired household servant; *pl.* home manufactures or goods.— **do·mes·ti·cal·ly,** *adv.*

do·mes·tic an·i·mal, *n.* Any of various animals, reclaimed from a wild state and adapted to live with man, such as the horse, cow, or dog.

do·mes·ti·cate, do·mes'ti·kāt", *v.t.*—*domesticated, domesticating.* [M.L. *domesticatus,* pp. of *domesticare,* < L. *domesticus.*] To convert to domestic uses; to tame, as an animal; to naturalize; to fit for life in a home.—**do·mes·ti·ca·ble,** *a.* Capable of being domesticated.—**do·mes·ti·ca·tion,** *n.*—**do·mes·ti·ca·tor,** *n.*

do·mes·tic fowl, *n.* Poultry, as a chicken, duck, turkey, or goose.

do·mes·tic·i·ty, dō"me·stis'i·tē, *n. pl.* **do·mes·tic·i·ties.** The state of being domestic; home life; home chores; *pl.* domestic affairs.—**do·mes·ti·cize,** *v.t.*— *domesticized, domesticizing.*

do·mes·tic sci·ence, *n.* Home economics.

dom·i·cal, dō'mi·kal, dom'i·kal, *a.* Domelike; having a dome or domes.—**dom·i·cal·ly,** *adv.*

dom·i·cile, dom'i·sīl", dom'i·sil, dō'mi·sīl", dō'mi·sil, *n.* [O.Fr. Fr. *domicile,* < L. *domicilium,* < *domus,* house.] A place of residence; an abode; a house or home; *law,* the place where one has his home or permanent residence, to which, if absent, he intends to return.—*v.t.*—*domiciled, domiciling.* To establish in a domicile.—*v.i.* To have one's domicile, with *at* or *in;* dwell. —**dom·i·cil·i·ar·y,** *a.*—**dom·i·cil·i·ate,** *v.t., v.i.*—*domiciliated, domiciliating.* To domicile.—**dom·i·cil·i·a·tion,** *n.*

dom·i·nance, dom·i·nan·cy, dom'i·nans, dom'i·nan·sē, *n.* Ascendency; rule; authority.

dom·i·nant, dom'i·nant, *a.* [L. *dominans,* ppr. of *dominor,* to rule, < *dominus,* lord, master.] Ruling; prevailing; governing; predominant; *genetics*, designating a genetic character or trait that overshadows the effect of recessive characters in an organism; *ecology*, one of those plants or animals that, by its presence, influences other living things in the area. *Mus.* pertaining to or based on the dominant; as, a *dominant* chord.—*n. Mus.* the fifth tone of the diatonic scale; *genetics*, a dominant trait or character.— **dom·i·nant·ly**, *adv.*

dom·i·nate, dom′i·nāt″, *v.t.*—*dominated, dominating*. To have power or sway over; to govern; to triumph over; to overlook from a greater height.—*v.i.* To predominate; to occupy a higher position.

dom·i·na·tion, dom″i·nā′shan, *n.* The exercise of power in ruling; dominion; government; arbitrary authority; tyranny. —**dom·i·na·tions**, *n. Theol.* the fourth rank or order in the angelic hierarchy.—**dom·i·na·tive**, dom′i·nā″tiv, dom′i·na·tiv, *a.* Presiding; governing; controlling.—**dom·i·na·tor**, *n.* One that dominates; a ruler or ruling power.

dom·i·neer, dom″i·nēr′, *v.i.* To rule arbitrarily or with insolence.—*v.t.* To govern harshly or overbearingly; to order or command insolently.—**dom·i·neer·ing**, *a.* Inclined to domineer; overbearing.—**dom·i·neer·ing·ly**, *adv.*—**dom·i·neer·ing·ness**, *n.*

do·min·i·cal, do·min′i·kal, *a.* [L.L. *dominicalis*, connected with Sunday, < L. *dominicus* (*dies dominica*, Sunday), pertaining to a lord or master, < *dominus*, lord.] Noting or marking the Lord's Day or Sunday; relating to Christ as Lord.—**do·min·i·cal let·ter**, one of the seven letters, A, B, C, D, E, F, G, used in almanacs to mark the Sundays throughout the year.

Do·min·i·can, do·min′i·kan, *a.* Of or pertaining to St. Dominic, 1170-1221, or the mendicant religious order founded by him; of or pertaining to the Dominican Republic in the West Indies.—*n.* A member of the order of St. Dominic; a black friar; a native or inhabitant of the Dominican Republic.

dom·i·nie, dom′i·nē, dō′mi·nē, *n.* [< L. *domine*; vocative case of *dominus*, a lord or master.] A minister of the Dutch Reformed Church; *dial.* a clergyman. *Sc.* a schoolmaster; a pedagogue.

do·min·ion, do·min′yan, *n.* [O.Fr. *minion*, < L. *dominium*, lordship, ownership, < *dominus*, master, lord.] The power or right of governing and controlling; sovereign authority; rule; control; lands or domains subject to sovereignty or control; a territory under its own form of government; as, the *Dominion* of Canada; a territory constituting a self-governing commonwealth and being one of a number of such territories united in a community of nations. *Pl. Theol.* dominations; *law*, dominium.

do·min·i·um, do·min′ē·am, *n. Law.* Ownership; exclusive right of possession or use. Cf. *condominium*.

dom·i·no, dom′i·nō″, *n. pl.* **dom·i·noes**. [Fr., a winter covering for the head worn by priests, < *dominus*, lord.] A masquerade dress, consisting of a loose cloak and usu. a half mask; the half mask itself; a person wearing a masquerade costume. A small, flat, rectangular block, used in a game, divided into two equal parts that are either blank or dotted as dice; *pl.* a game played with twenty-eight flat blocks, dotted, as on dice, with a certain number of points.

don, don, *n.* [Sp. *don* = Pg. *dom*, < L. *dominus*, master, lord.] (*Cap.*) a Spanish title prefixed to a man's Christian name. (*l.c.*) a Spanish lord or gentleman; a person

of great importance; in the English universities, a head, fellow, or tutor of a college.

don, don, *v.t.*—*donned, donning*. [To *do on*: opposed to *doff*.] To put on; to dress in; to assume.

do·ña, *Sp.* dạ′nyä, *n.* [< L. *domina*, fem. of *dominus*.] A title of respect prefixed to a woman's Christian name; a lady of quality. Also **do·na**, *Port.* dō′nä, **don·na**, *It.* dạn′nä.

do·nate, dō′nāt, dō·nāt′, *v.t.*—*donated, donating*. [< L. *donare*, to donate.] To make a gift of.—*v.i.* To contribute.

do·na·tion, dō·nā′shan, *n.* [L. *donatio*, an offering, < *dono*, to give; *donum*, a gift, < *do*, to give.] The act of giving or bestowing; that which is gratuitously given; a grant; a gift.

don·a·tive, don′a·tiv, dō′na·tiv, *a.* Of the nature of a donation; vested or vesting by donation, as a benefice.—*n.* A gift or donation.

do·na·tor, dō′nāt″ẽr, dō·nāt′ẽr, *n.* A donor.

done, dun, *a.* Executed; completed; finished; settled; cooked sufficiently; worn out.

do·nee, dō·nē′, *n.* The recipient of a gift or grant.

don·jon, dun′jon, don′jon, *n.* [Fr., < L.L. *domnio, domnionis*, for L. *dominio*, *dominium*.] The principal tower of a castle, commonly used as a prison or stronghold.

Don Juan, don wän′, don jō′an, *Sp.* dạn hwän′, *n.* A legendary Spanish nobleman of dissolute life; a libertine or rake.

don·key, dong′kē, dung′kē, *n. pl.* **don·keys**. [< a little *dun* animal.] An ass; a stupid or obstinate fellow.—**don·key en·gine**, *n.* A small steam engine used where no great power is required, and often to perform some subsidiary operation.

don·nish, don′ish, *a.* Resembling, or characteristic of, an English University don; formal; pedantic.—**don·nish·ly**, *adv.*—**don·nish·ness**, *n.*

don·ny·brook, don′ē·bruk″, *n.* [From *Donnybrook* Fair, until 1885 an annual event in Dublin, Ireland.] A wild fight; an uproarious brawl.

do·nor, dō′nẽr, *n.* [O.Fr. *doneor* (Fr. *donneur*), < L. *donator*, < *donare*.] One who gives or donates; *law*, one who gives property by gift or legacy, or who confers a power; *med.* a person or animal furnishing blood for transfusion, or biological tissue for transplant.—**do·nor·ship**, *n.*

do-noth·ing, dō′nuth″ing, *n.* One who does nothing; an idler.—*a.* Doing nothing; idle; indolent; characterized by an unwillingness to work toward a goal.

Don Quix·o·te, don″kē·hō′tē, don kwik′sat, *Sp.* don kē·hạ′te, *n.* [From *Don Quixote de la Mancha*, a novel by Cervantes.] One having lofty but impractical ideals.

don't, dōnt. Contraction of *do not*.—*n.* An instruction not to do something.

don·to·ped·a·lo·gy, don·tō·pi·dạl′ō·jē, *n.* [Lit. the practice of putting one's foot in one's mouth. Phrase coined by Prince Philip of England.] The tendency to make disconcerting blunders in speaking.

doo·dad, dō′dad, *n. Colloq.* any trifling ornament or bit of decorative finery; a gadget.

doo·dle, dōd′el, *n.* [Origin obscure.] *Colloq.* an aimless design or scribble.—*v.i., v.t.*—*doodled, doodling*. To sketch or scribble while the mind is preoccupied.

doom, dōm, *n.* [*dom* = O.E. O.Fris. *dom*, Goth. *doms*, Icel. *dómr*, the same word as the suffix *-dom* in *kingdom*, etc., and derived probably from verb *to do*.] A judgment or judicial sentence; passing of sentence; the final judgment; the state to which one is doomed or destined; fate; fortune, generally evil; adverse issue; ruin; destruction.—*v.t.* To condemn to any punishment; to consign by a decree or sentence; to pronounce sentence or judg-

ment on; to ordain as a penalty; to decree. —**crack of doom**, dissolution of nature.

dooms·day, dōmz′dā″, *n.* [O.E. *dōmes dæg*.] The day of the Last Judgment, at the end of the world; any day of sentence or condemnation; a day of final dissolution, as at the end of the world.—**Dooms·day Book**, *n.* The Domesday Book.

door, dōr, *n.* [O.E. *dór, dúru* = O.E. *dur, dor*, Icel. *dyr*, Goth. *daur*, G. *thür*, L. *fores*, Gr. *thura*, Ir. *dorus*, Skt. *dvâra*, door.] An opening or passage into a room, house, or building by which persons enter and leave; a solid barrier that covers the opening of a cabinet, room, or the like, usu. opening and closing by means of hinges or by sliding in a groove; a means of approach or access.—**next door to**, *fig.* near to; bordering on.—**out of doors**, out of the house; in the open air.—**in doors**, within the house; at home.—**door·way**, *n.* The entranceway into a room or house.

door·jamb, dōr′jam″, *n.* The vertical sides of a door frame which support the lintel.

door·knob, dōr′nob″, *n.* The knob or handle which releases the doorcatch, allowing the door to be opened.

door·mat, dōr′mat″, *n.* A small rug or pad placed near an entrance for cleaning dirt and mud from shoes before entering; *slang*, a person who submits to ill-treatment without protest.

door·nail, dōr′nāl″, *n.* The large-headed nail used in former times for reinforcing or ornamenting doors, and against which a knocker was struck.—**dead as a door·nail**, certainly dead.

door·sill, dōr′sil″, *n.* The sill or threshold of a doorway.

door·step, dōr′step″, *n.* A step at a door, raised above the level of the ground outside; one of a series of steps leading from the ground to a door.

dope, dōp, *n.* [D. *doop*, a dipping, sauce, < *doopen*, dip, baptize.] Any thick liquid or pasty preparation, as a sauce, lubricant, etc. *Slang*, the treaclelike preparation of opium used for smoking; any addictive drug; a stimulant, as one wrongfully given to a racehorse to induce greater speed; information or data, as on the previous performances of a racehorse; a calculation or forecast based on such information or data; a person under the influence of, or addicted to, the use of drugs; an unintelligent person. An absorbent material used to absorb and hold a liquid, as in the manufacture of dynamite.—*v.t.*—*doped, doping*. *Slang*. To affect with stupefying or stimulating drugs; to work or make out by calculation, inference, etc., as a problem, or plan.—*v.i. Slang*, to use stupefying or stimulating drugs.—**dope fiend**, *n. Slang*, a person addicted to the use of dope or drugs.

dope·ster, dōp′stẽr, *n.* A person who forecasts the results of a sports contest, an election, or other events, the outcome of which is uncertain.

dop·ey, dop·y, dō′pē, *a.*—*dopier, dopiest. Slang*, affected by or as by dope; dullwitted; slow.—**dop·i·ness**, *n.*

dop·ing, dō′ping, *n. Chem.* a trace impurity introduced into a pure crystal to obtain desired physical properties, esp. electrical: used esp. in laser crystals and semiconductors.—**dop·ing**, *n.*

dop·pel·gäng·er, dop′el·gang″ẽr, *n.* [G., 'double-goer.'] An apparitional double or counterpart of a living person.

Dop·pler ef·fect, *n.* [From C. *Doppler*, Austrian physicist.] The change in wave frequency when the source of waves moves toward or away from the observer, as the change in pitch of the whistle of an oncoming or receding train. Used in navigation and radar. Also **Dop·pler shift**.

---

ch- chain, G. na*cht*;   **th-** THen, thin;   **w-** wig, hw as sound in whig;   **z-** zh as in azure, zeal.   *Italicized vowel* indicates schwa sound.

Dor·cas so·ci·e·ty, dạr'kas, *n.* [From *Dorcas,* a Christian woman at Joppa who worked for the poor (Acts ix. 36).] A society of church women who provide clothing for the poor.

Dor·ic, dạr'ik, dōr'ik, *a.* Pertaining to the Dorians, a people of ancient Greece. Also **Do·ri·an,** dōr'ē·an.—*n.* The language of the Dorians, a dialect of ancient Greece.—**Dor·ic or·der,** *arch.* the oldest and simplest of the three orders of Grecian architecture, characterized by channeled columns having no base, flutings that are few, large, and not deep, and a capital of simple character. —**Do·ri·an mode,** *mus.* a mode utilizing the tones represented by the white keys on a piano and ranging from D to D on an ascending scale. Also **Dor·ic mode.**

dor·king, dạr'king, *n.* (*Often cap.*) a species of domestic fowl, distinguished by having five claws on each foot, so named because bred largely at *Dorking* in Surrey, England.

dor·mant, dạr'mant, *a.* [O.Fr. Fr. *dormant,* ppr. of *dormir,* < L. *dormire,* sleep, be inactive.] Sleeping; lying asleep or as if asleep; inactive as in sleep; torpid; in a state of rest or inactivity; quiescent; inoperative; in abeyance; accomplished or applied during dormancy; *her.* of an animal, lying down with its head on its forepaws, as if asleep.—**dor·man·cy,** dạr'man·sē, *n.*

dor·mer, dạr'mẽr, *n.* [O.Fr. *dormeor,* < L. *dormitorium.*] A dormer window.—**dor·mered,** *a.* Having dormer windows.— **dor·mer win·dow,** *n.* A vertical window in a projection built out from a sloping roof; the whole projecting structure.

dor·mie, dor·my, dạr'mē, *a.* [Origin obscure.] *Golf,* of a player or side, being as many holes ahead in a match as there remain holes to be played.

dor·mi·ent, dạr'mē·ent, *a.* [L. *dormiens* (*dormient-*), ppr. of *dormire,* sleep.] Sleeping; dormant.

dor·mi·to·ry, dạr'mi·tōr"ē, dạr'mi·tạr"ē, *n. pl.* **dor·mi·to·ries.** [L. *dormitorium.*] A sleeping room, esp. a large room containing a number of beds; a residence hall, as at a college, with rooms for sleeping. Also **dorm.**

dor·mouse, dạr'mous", *n. pl.* **dor·mice.** [M.E. *dormowse;* perhaps in part < O.Fr. *dormir,* sleep, in allusion to its hibernation.] Any of the small old-world rodents which constitute the family *Gliridae,* resembling small squirrels in appearance and habits.

dor·nick, dạr'nik, *n.* A stone of small size, or a chunk of rock; a thick damask linen cloth used as a carpet.

dorp, dạrp, *n.* [D. = E. *thorp.*] A village; a hamlet.

dor·sad, dạr'sad, *adv.* [L. *dorsum,* back.] *Anat.* toward the back: opposed to *ventrad.*

dor·sal, dạr'sal, *a.* [M.L. *dorsalis,* < L. *dorsum,* back.] *Anat., zool.* of, pertaining to, or on the back of the body; as, the *dorsal* fin of a fish. *Bot.* situated away from or directed away from the axis.—**dor·sal·ly,** *adv.*

Dor·set Horn, *n.* An English breed of sheep with thick wool of medium length, named after the county of Dorset, England.

dor·si·ven·tral, dạr"si·ven'tral, *a. Bot.* having differences in structure between upper and lower sides of a leaf, as in most foliage leaves; *zool.* dorsoventral.—**dor·si·ven·tral·ly,** *adv.*—**dor·si·ven·tral·i·ty,** *n. pl.* **dor·si·ven·tral·i·ties.**

dor·so·lat·er·al, dạr"sō·lat'ẽr·al, *a. Anat., zool.* of or pertaining to the back and sides.

dor·so·ven·tral, dạr"sō·ven'tral, *a. Zool.* extending from the dorsal to the ventral side of the body; *bot.* dorsiventral.— **dor·so·ven·tral·ly,** *adv.*

dor·sum, dạr'sum, *n. pl.* **dor·sa.** [L.] *Anat.* the back, as of the body; the back or outer surface of an organ or part of the body.

do·ry, dōr'ē, *n. pl.* **do·ries.** [Origin uncertain.] A small boat; esp. a boat with a narrow, flat bottom and high, flaring sides, usually propelled by oars, and used for fishing.

do·ry, dōr'ē, *n. pl.* **do·ries.** [Fr. *dorée,* lit. gilded.] Any of several food fish, *Zeus faber,* as the wall-eyed pike or perch of North America, and the John Dory of Europe. Also **do·ree.**

dos·age, dō'sij, *n.* The administration of medicine in doses; the amount of medicine to be administered; the operation of dosing wine.

dose, dōs, *n.* [Fr. *dose,* < M.L. *dosis,* < Gr. *dosis,* a giving, gift, portion, dose, < *didonai,* give.] A quantity of medicine prescribed to be taken at one time; a definite quantity of anything analogous to medicine; a portion or allotment of something nauseous or disagreeable; a quantity of sugar or other material added to wine to give it a particular characteristic; the amount of radiation absorbed by a given material; *slang,* a case of venereal disease.—*v.t.*—**dosed, dosing.** To administer or apportion in doses; to give doses to; of wine, to add a dose to.— *v.i.* To take a dose.

do·si·do, dō'sē·dō', *Fr.* **dos·à·dos,** *n. Square dance,* a figure in which two dancers pass by, circling each other back to back; a vehicle in which the occupants sit back to back; any structure or piece of furniture with a back to back seating arrangement.

do·sim·e·ter, dō·sim'e·tẽr, *n.* An apparatus for measuring minute doses of radiation or x-rays.—**do·sim·e·try,** dō·sim'i·trē, *n.* The measurement of doses of medicine; the process of measuring doses of radiation.— **do·si·met·ric,** dō·si·me'trik, *a.*

doss, dos, *n.* [Origin uncertain.] *Brit. slang,* a bed, esp. one in a cheap lodging house; sleep.—*v.i.* To sleep in an improvised bed.

dos·sal, dos'al, *n.* [L.L. *dorsale,* < L. *dorsum,* back.] An ornamental cloth hung at the back of an altar, a throne, or a seat Also **dos·sel.**

dos·si·er, dos'ē·ā", dos'ē·ẽr, *Fr.* dạ·syā', *n.* [Fr., < *dos,* back.] A collection of documents or papers containing detailed information about a person or subject.

dot, dot, *n.* [O.E. *dott,* a spot or speck (whence Sc. *dottle,* a small lump): akin L.G. *dutte,* a plug, a stopper; D. *dot,* a small bundle.] A small point or spot made with a pen or other pointed instrument; a speck, used in marking a writing; a precise point; *teleg.* a sound signal, shorter than a dash, representing a letter or part of a letter in the language of a telecommunication code, as in the Morse Code of telegraphy; *mus.* a point marked after a note or rest to indicate a measure of time value: when marked over or under a note, it indicates that the note is to be played staccato.—*v.t.*—**dotted, dotting.** To mark with dots; to mark or diversify with small detached objects, as clumps of trees.—*v.i.* to make dots or spots.—**dot·ter,** *n.*—**dot·ty,** *a. Slang,* eccentric; crazy.

dot, dot, *n.* [Fr. < L. *dos* (*dot-*), dowry, endowment.] The portion brought by the wife to the husband upon marriage, the income of which is in his control; a dowry. —**do·tal,** dōt'al, *a.*

dot·age, dō'tij, *n.* Feebleness or imbecility, particularly in old age; childishness of old age; senility; extravagant fondness; foolish affection.—**dot·ard,** dō'tẽrd, *n.* One whose intellect is impaired by age; a senile.

dote, dōt, *v.i.*—**doted, doting.** [The same word as O.D. *doten,* to dote; akin to D. *dut,* a nap, *dutten,* to take a nap; Icel. *dotta,* to nod with sleep.] To love to excess or extravagance; as, to *dote* on a person; to have the intellect impaired by age, so that the mind wanders or wavers; to be in a

state of senile silliness. Also **doat.**—**dot·er,** *n.*—**dot·ing·ly,** dō'ting·lē, *adv.*

dot·ted swiss, *n.* A thin cotton fabric with ornamental raised dots or other patterns. Also **Swiss mus·lin.**

dot·ter·el, dot·trel, dot'ẽr·el, do'trel, *n.* [From the bird's supposed stupidity.] A species of plover, breeding in the highest latitudes of Asia and Europe, and migrating to the shores of the Mediterranean.

Dou·ay Ver·sion, dö'ā vụr'zhan, dō'ā vụr'shan, *n.* English translation of the Vulgate Bible, the authorized version for the Roman Catholic Church, written at Rheims and Douai and completed in 1610. Also **Dou·ay Bi·ble, Dou·ay Rheims Bi·ble.**

dou·ble, dub'l, *a.* [O.Fr. *duble, double* (Fr. *double*), < L. *duplus,* < Gr. *diploos,* double.] Twofold in form, size, amount, or extent; composed of two like parts or members; paired; twice as great, heavy, or strong; of extra size or weight; *bot.* of flowers, having the number of petals largely increased; *mus.* of musical instruments, designed to produce simultaneously a tone an octave lower than another. *Fig.* twofold in character, meaning, or conduct; ambiguous; deceitful; hypocritical; insincere. *Chem.* of the nature of a double salt.—**doub·le·ness,** *n.*

dou·ble, dub'l, *n.* Something double; a twofold size, amount, or measure; twice as much; a fold; a sharp backward bend, as of a road; a sudden turn back on a course; a duplicate or counterpart; a wraith; *astron.* a double star; *milit.* a double-quick pace; *pl.* a tennis game or match in which two players are engaged on each side. *Motion pictures,* a stand-in or stunt artist who substitutes for a star. *Theatr.* an actor who performs two roles in one play. *Baseball,* a two-base hit. *Bowling,* two strikes in succession. *Bridge,* the doubling of an opponent's bid.—*adv.* Twofold; doubly.

dou·ble, dub'l, *v.t.*—**doubled, doubling.** To increase by an equal amount; to make double or twice as great in number, size, or value; multiply by two; to couple; to duplicate; to bend or fold with one part upon another, usu. with *over, up,* or *back;* clench, as the fist; to sail around, as a projecting area of land; as, to *double* Cape Horn; *mus.* of a note, to add the upper or lower octave to.—*v.i.* To become double or twice as great; to turn back on a course; to bend or fold; to use trickery; to share quarters with another, with *up;* to march at a double-quick pace; to serve or perform in two capacities.—**dou·bler,** *n.*

dou·ble bass, *n.* The largest and deepest-toned musical instrument of the viol kind.

dou·ble bas·soon, *n.* Contrabassoon.

dou·ble boil·er, *n.* A cooking utensil consisting of two pots, one smaller and fitting in the top of another, the lower pot being used for boiling water which cooks or heats food in the upper pot.

dou·ble-breast·ed, dub'l·bres'tid, *a.* Applied to a coat or vest with an overlapping front, having a double row of buttons and a single row of buttonholes.

dou·ble coun·ter·point, *n. Mus.* a two-part or invertible counterpoint in which the two voices can exchange positions.

dou·ble cross, *n.* A betrayal of a person, esp. a colleague or associate; an act of treachery or perfidy; *genetics,* a cross between first-generation hybrids in which four separate inbred lines are thus involved. —**dou·ble-cross,** *v.t.* To betray or deceive by underhanded dealing.

dou·ble dag·ger, *n. Typog.* a mark ‡ used to indicate a reference such as a footnote. Also *diesis.*

dou·ble-deal·ing, dub'l·dē'ling, *n.* Duplicity; the profession of one thing and the practice of another.—*a*. Given to duplicity; deceitful.—**dou·ble-deal·er**, *n*.

dou·ble-deck·er, dub′l-dek′ẽr, *n*. A bus with a lower and upper floor of seats; a ship with two decks above the waterline; a sandwich with two layers of filling in three slices of bread; a double-layered cake; an ice-cream cone with two scoops of ice cream.

dou·ble en·ten·dre, dub′l än·tän′dre, dub′l än·tänd′re, *Fr.* dö·blän·tän′dRe, *n*. pl. **dou·ble en·ten·dres**. [Fr.] A double meaning; a word or expression with two meanings, one often indelicate.

dou·ble en·try, *n*. A mode of bookkeeping in which two entries are made of every transaction, one to the debit side of one account, and the other to the credit side of another account, in order that the one may balance the other.

dou·ble-faced, dub′l·fāst″, *a*. Deceitful; hypocritical; showing two sides or faces.

dou·ble-head·er, dub′l·hed′ẽr, *n. Sports*, two games played in immediate succession on the same day, for which spectators are charged one admission only.

dou·ble im·age, *n. TV*, two images partially overlapping in a television receiver, caused by reception of the picture signal by both direct and reflected paths, the latter arriving slightly later on the screen; also **ghost**.

dou·ble in·dem·ni·ty, *n*. A clause in a life or accident insurance policy which grants double payment of the policy's face value if death results from accident.

dou·ble jeop·ard·y, *n*. The unlawful procedure of subjecting a person to a trial on two separate occasions for the same offense.

dou·ble-joint·ed, dub′l·join′tid, *a*. Having joints that allow unusual freedom of motion.

dou·ble neg·a·tive, *n*. A construction in syntax in which two negative words or expressions are used within the same clause, intended to give a single negation: an incorrect usage in English but correct in many foreign languages.

dou·ble play, *n. Baseball*, a defensive play by which two base runners are put out in one play of the ball.

dou·ble-reed, dub′l·rēd′, *a. Mus.* pertaining to wind instruments having two reeds fastened together, as the bassoon and the oboe.

dou·ble re·frac·tion, *n. Opt.* the bending of light through a crystal resulting in the formation of two rays.

dou·ble salt, *n. Chem.* a complex compound containing two salts.

dou·ble stand·ard, *n*. A set of principles or a code that discriminates between two groups, esp. the moral standard which applies more stringent rules to women than to men.

doub·let, dub′lit, *n*. [O.Fr. Fr. *doublet*, < *double*, E. *double*, *a*.] A close-fitting outer body-garment, with or without sleeves, formerly worn by men; one of, or a pair of like things; a duplicate; a couple; one of two words in the same language representing the same original, as the English *benison* and *benediction*; an unintentional repetition in printed matter; *pl*. two dice on each of which the same number of spots turns up at a throw. Something formed by a union of two like things, as a counterfeit gem made of two pieces of crystal with a layer of color between them.

dou·ble take, *n*. A delayed second look or reaction evincing surprise to what at first appeared unsurprising.

dou·ble time, *n*. Double-quick time or step; *milit.* a rate of marching in which 180 paces, each of three feet, are taken per minute. A rate of pay twice that of the regular wage scale.—**dou·ble-time**, *v.i.*—*double-timed*, *double-timing*.

dou·bloon, du·blön′, *n*. [Fr. *doublon*, Sp. *doblon*.] An old gold coin of Spain and the Spanish American colonies.

dou·bly, dub′lē, *adv*. In a double manner or degree; in two ways.

doubt, dout, *v.i.* [O.Fr. *doubter*, < L. *dubitare*, to doubt, < same stem as *dubius*, doubtful, < *duo*, two. Akin *dubious*, *dual*, etc.] To waver or fluctuate in opinion; to be uncertain respecting the truth or fact; to be undetermined.—*v.t.* To question or hold questionable; to withhold assent from; to hesitate to believe; to suspect.

doubt, dout, *n*. A fluctuation of mind respecting the truth or correctness of a statement or opinion, or the propriety of an action; uncertainty; suspicion.—**doubt·a·ble**, *a*. Liable to be doubted.—**doubt·er**, *n*.—**doubt·ing·ly**, *adv*.

doubt·ful, dout′ful, *a*. Entertaining doubt; not settled in opinion; undetermined; wavering; dubious; ambiguous; not clear in its meaning; not obvious, clear, or certain; questionable; not without suspicion; not confident; not without fear.—**doubt·ful·ly**, *adv*.—**doubt·ful·ness**, *n*.

doubt·less, dout′lis, *adv.*, *a*. Without doubt or question; unquestionably.—**doubt·less·ly**, *adv*. Unquestionably.

douche, dösh, *n*. [Fr., < It. *doccia*, conduit, showerbath, ult. < L. *ducere*, lead.] A jet or current of water or the like applied to a particular part or cavity of the body for hygienic or medicinal purposes; the application of such a jet; an instrument for administering it.—*v.t.*—*douched*, *douching*. To apply a douche to; douse.

dough, dō, *n*. [O.E. *dág*, *dáh* = D. *deeg*, Icel. and Dan. *deig*, Goth. *daigs*, G. *teig*, dough; akin Goth. *deigan*, to mold, to form.] A pasty mixture; a mass composed of flour or meal moistened and kneaded but not baked. *Slang*, money.

dough·boy, dō′boi″, *n*. During World War I, the nickname for an infantryman in the U.S. army; *chiefly Brit.* a yeast dough dumpling.

dough·nut, dō′nut″, *n*. A small roundish cake, usually with a hole in the center, usu. deep-fat fried.

dough·ty, dou′tē, *a*.—*doughtier*, *doughtiest*. [O.E. *dohtig*, *dyhtig*, < *dugan* (Sc. *dow*), to be able; Dan. *dygtig*, G. *tuchtig*, able, fit. Do, *v.i.*] Brave; valiant.—**dough·ti·ly**, *adv*.—**dough·ti·ness**, *n*.

Doug·las spruce, **fir**, or **pine**, *n*. [From David *Douglas* (1798–1834), Scottish botanist and traveler.] A coniferous tree, *Pseudotsuga taxifolia*, of western N. America, often over 200 feet high, and yielding a strong, durable timber.

Dou·kho·bors, **Du·kho·bors**, dö′kō·barz″, *n. pl.* [Russ. *Dukhobortsy*, "spirit wrestlers," contenders against the Holy Spirit.] A Russian Christian religious sect of peasants, dating from the 18th century, a large body of whom migrated to Canada in 1899, who reject civil and religious authority and believe in obeying the inner voice.

dour, dụr, dour, dou′ẽr, *a*. [L. *durus*, hard.] Sullen; gloomy; stern.—**dour·ly**, *adv*.—**dour·ness**, *n*.

douse, dous, *v.t.*—*doused*, *dousing*. [Origin doubtful; akin Sw. *dunsa*, to plump; D. *doesen*, to strike.] To plunge into water; to immerse; to splash water or any liquid on; to dip; *naut*. to strike or lower in haste, as sails; to slacken suddenly; *colloq*. to put out or extinguish.—*v.i.* To fall or be plunged suddenly into water.—*n*. A drenching.

DOVAP, dō′vap, *n*. An acronym for Doppler, velocity, and position; same as Doppler radar, a radar tracking system for determining the velocity and position of airborne vehicles by the change in frequency with which energy reaches a receiver when the receiver and energy source are in motion relative to each other.

dove, duv, *n*. [M.E. *duve* = D. *duif* = G. *taube* = Icel. *dūfa* = Goth. *dūbō*, dove; prob. from the Teut. verb stem represented by E. *dive*.] Any bird of the pigeon family, *Columbidæ*; a symbolic messenger of peace, usu. depicted carrying an olive branch; (*cap.*) the Holy Ghost (Luke iii. 22).

dove·cote, duv′kōt″, *n*. A structure, usually at a height above the ground, for the roosting and breeding of domestic pigeons. Also **dove-cot**.

dove·kie, duv′kē, *n*. [Dim. of *dove*.] A small arctic auk, *Plautus alle*; *Brit.* the black guillemot.

dove·tail, duv′tāl″, *n. Carp.* a tenon or tongue resembling a dove's tail spread or a reversed wedge; the mortise or cavity into which such a tenon fits; a joint or fastening formed by one or more such tenons and mortises.—*v.t.*, *v.i.* To join or fit together by means of a dovetail or dovetails; *fig.* to join or fit together compactly or harmoniously.

dow·a·ger, dou′a·jẽr, *n*. [< a form *dowage*, < Fr. *douer*, to endow.] A widow who has property or a title inherited from her deceased husband; an addition to a widow's title, to distinguish her from the wife of the present bearer of her husband's title; as, the *dowager* empress; an elderly woman of dignified bearing.

dow·dy, dou′dē, *a*.—*dowdier*, *dowdiest*. [Akin to O.E. *dowde*, *dowd*, dull, sluggish; E. *dawdle*, L.G. *dödeln*, to be slow; provinc. E. *daw*, a sluggard.] Shabby, not stylish; frumpy.—*n*. A poorly-dressed woman; a dowdy woman.—**dow·dy·ish**, *a*.—**dow·di·ly**, *adv*.—**dow·di·ness**, *n*.

dow·el, dou′el, *n*. [Fr. *douille*, a groove or socket; L.L. *ductile*, a gutter, < L. *duco*, to lead.] A wooden or iron pin or tenon used to join together edgewise two pieces of any substance; a piece of wood driven into a wall to receive nails of baseboards.—*v.t.*—*doweled*, *doweling*, *dowelled*, *dowelling*. To fasten by means of dowels, as two boards together by pins inserted in the edges.—**dow·el pin**, *n*. A pin inserted in the edges of boards to fasten them together.

dow·er, dou′ẽr, *n*. [Fr. *douaire*, < L.L. *dotarium*, < L. *doto*, *datum*, to endow, < *dos*, *dotis*, a dower, whence also *dotal*, *dowager*.] That with which one is endowed; *law*, that part of the real estate, of which her husband died possessed, which is allowed the widow for as long as she lives.—*v.t.* To furnish with dower or a portion; to endow.

dow·itch·er, dou′ich·ẽr, *n*. [Prob. N. Amer. Ind.] *Ornith.* a shore bird, *Limnodromus griseus*, related to snipes and sandpipers, having a snipelike bill which it jabs perpendicularly into the mud flats.

Dow-Jones av·er·ages, *n. pl. U.S. stock market*, a report issued daily to guide investors, showing the relative price of stocks for 30 leading industrials, 20 leading railroads and 15 leading public utilities, based on a formula developed by Charles H. Dow and Edward D. Jones, American economists. (Trademark.)

down, doun, *adv*. [Late O.E. *dūne*, for *adūne* (E. *adown*), earlier *of dūne*, "from (the) hill."] From higher to lower; in a descending direction or order, as from the top, head, or beginning; into or in a lower position or condition; to or at a low point, degree, rate, or pitch; below the horizon; as, the sun going *down*; in a prostrate, depressed, or degraded condition; in due place, position, form, or state; as, to settle *down* to work, to pay cash *down*, to jot *down* an address; *golf*, behind an opponent a specified number of holes, opposed to *up*. Sometimes, by ellipsis of a verb, used as if an imperative, as: Down, Towser! Down with you! Down with tyranny!—*prep*. In a descending direction on, over, or along.—*a*.

Downward; going or directed downward; downcast; dejected.—*n.* A downward movement; a descent; *fig.* a reverse; *football*, the declaring of the ball as down or out of play, or the play immediately preceding this.— *v.t.* To put or throw down; subdue.—*v.i.* To go down; fall.

down, doun, *n.* [Same word as Icel. *dún*, Dan. *duun*, G. *daune*, down.] The fine soft plumage of birds under the outer feathers, esp. on the breasts of waterfowl; the soft hair of the human face when beginning to appear; the pubescence of plants, a fine hairy substance; any fine feathery or hairy substance of vegetable growth.—*v.t.* To cover, stuff, or line with down.

down, doun, *n.* [O.E. *dún*, a hill; L.G. *dünen*, Fris. *dunen*, D. *duin*, a dune; O.H.G. *dún*, *dûna*, promontory, Sw. dial. *dun*, a hill; also W., Ir., and Gael. *dun*, a hill, hillock.] *Archaic*, a dune or sand hill near the sea; *pl.* an open, undulating, grassy tract; (*cap.*) any sheep of the breeds originating in the downs of southern England.

down·beat, doun'bēt", *n. Mus.* any first beat of a measure; the downward stroke of the conductor's baton indicating the principally accented note of the measure.

down·bow, doun'bō", *n. Mus.* a stroke used in playing a stringed instrument in which the direction of the movement of the bow over the strings is downward or toward the player.

down·cast, doun'kăst", doun'kast", *a.* Cast downward; directed to the ground; as, *downcast* eyes; in low spirits; dejected.

down·fall, doun'fạl", *n.* A sudden descent or fall from a position of power, honor, wealth, fame, or the like; ruin; destruction; the thing causing a downfall; a fall, esp. one that is heavy or sudden, of rain or snow.—**down·fall·en**, *a.*

down·grade, doun'grād", *n.* A gradually descending slope, as of a road; a decrease, as of income, status, or moral strength.— *v.t.*—*downgraded, downgrading.* To reduce the quality or status of; to attack, as a person's reputation or social position.—*a., adv.*

down·haul, doun'hạl", *n. Naut.* a rope for hauling down a sail.

down·heart·ed, doun'här'tid, *a.* Sad; low in spirits.—**down·heart·ed·ly**, *adv.*— **down·heart·ed·ness**, *n.*

down·hill, doun'hil", *n.* A slope; a skiing race.—doun'hil', *adv.* Downward; down a hill; of or toward a reduced state of health or economic position.—*a.* Sloping or going downward.

down·pour, doun'pōr", *n.* An especially heavy, usually sudden, rain.

down·range, doun'rānj", *a.* Of or relating to the airspace extending away from the launching site on a given rocket test range. —doun'rānj', *adv.*

down·right, doun'rīt", *adv.* In plain terms; completely; thoroughly.—*a.* Directly to the point; to the utmost degree; as, a *downright* falsehood.—**down·right·ly**, *adv.* —**down·right·ness**, *n.*

down·stage, doun'stāj, *n. Theatr.* the front of a stage, immediately behind the footlights.—*a., adv.*

down·stairs, doun'stârz', *n. pl. but sing. in constr.* The lower floor or floors of a building.—*adv.* Down the stairs; to or on a lower floor.—*a.* Pertaining to or situated on a lower floor.

down·stream, doun'strēm', *adv.* In the direction of the current of a river or stream.

down·swing, doun'swing", *n. Golf,* a downward swing, opposed to backswing. *Com.* a tendency downward in business activity.

down·throw, doun'thrō", *n.* A throwing down or being thrown down; an overthrow; *geol.* a downward displacement of rock on one side of a fault.

down·time, doun'tīm", *n.* An interval, during regular working hours, when a factory, a department, or an employee is not productive because of an unexpected situation, such as a breakdown of a machine or a failure of electric current.

down-to-earth, doun' tö ụrth', *a.* Realistic, practical.

down·town, doun'toun', *n.* The main part or business section of a city or town.— *a.* Pertaining to, or located in, the business district.—*adv.*

down·trend, doun'trend', *n.* A tendency toward a downward movement, esp. in business affairs.

down·trod·den, doun'trod"en, *a.* Tyrannized over; oppressed. Trampled. Also **down·trod.**

down·turn, doun'tẽrn", *n.* A downward trend, esp. a decline in business. Also *downtrend.*

down·ward, doun'wẽrd, *adv.* From a higher place to a lower; in a descending course; in a course or direction from a spring or source; in a course of descent from an ancestor. Also **down·wards**, **down·ward·ly.**—*a.* Moving or extending from a higher to a lower place; as, a *downward* course; descending from a head, origin, or source; tending to a lower condition or state.—**down·ward·ness**, *n.*

down·wind, doun'wind', *a., adv. Naut.* in the same direction the wind is blowing; with the wind blowing from behind; on the lee side or leeward.

down·y, dou'nē, *a.*—*downier, downiest.* Covered with down or nap; covered with pubescence or soft hairs, as a plant; made of down; soft, calm, soothing.—**down·i·ness**, *n.*

down·y mil·dew, *n.* Any fungus of the family *Peronosporaceae* causing the white downy mass on the underside of leaves on a host plant; the plant disease produced by the downy mildew.

dow·ry, dou'rē, *n. pl.* **dow·ries.** The money, goods, or estate which a woman brings to her husband in marriage; a natural talent. Also **dow·er·y**, *dower.*

dowse, douz, *v.i.*—*dowsed, dowsing.* To use a divining rod to locate underground water or mineral deposits.—**dows·ing rod**, *n.* A divining rod.

dox·ol·o·gy, dok·sol'o·jē, *n.* [Gr. *doxologia*, a praising—*doxa*, praise, glory, and *legō*, to speak.] A short hymn or words of praise ascribing glory to God, and used in worship. —**dox·o·log·i·cal**, dok·so·loj'i·kal, *a.*

doy·en, doi·en', doi'en, Fr. dwA·yan', *n.* [Fr.] A dean; the senior member of a body, class, or profession.—**doy·enne**, doi·en', Fr. dwA·yen', *n.* Fem. of *doyen.*

doy·ley, doi'lē, *n.* See *doily.*

doze, dōz, *v.i.*—*dozed, dozing.* [Akin to Dan. *dôse*, to doze—*dôs*, drowsiness; G. *dôseln*, *doseln*, to doze; Provinc. G. *dosen*, to slumber; allied to *dizzy* and *daze*.] To sleep lightly; to be dull or half asleep.—*v.t.* To pass or spend in drowsiness; to make dull; to stupefy.—*n.* A light sleep; a slumber.—**doz·er**, dō'zẽr, *n.*—**doz·y**, dō'zē, *a.*—*dozier, doziest.* Drowsy; inclined to sleep.—**doz·i·ly**, *adv.*—**doz·i·ness**, *n.*

doz·en, duz'en, *n. pl.* **doz·ens**; after a numeral **doz·en**. [O.Fr. Fr. *douzaine*, < *douze*, < L. *duodecim*, twelve.] A group of twelve units or things.—*a.* Twelve.— **doz·enth**, *a.* Twelfth.

doz·er, dō'zẽr, *n. Colloq.* a bulldozer or tractor-driven machine used in land clearance.

D.P., *n.* Displaced person; one who is exiled from his homeland because of war or tyrannical rule. Also **DP.**—*a., adv. Pharm.* in prescriptions, with a proper direction.

drab, drab, *n.* [Fr. *drap*, L.L. *drappus*,

cloth, < a Teut. root seen in E. *trappings*.] A thick woolen cloth of a dun or dull-brown color; a dull brownish-yellow color. —*a.*—*drabber, drabbest.* Being of a dull color; like the cloth so called; cheerless.— **drab·ly**, *adv.*—**drab·ness**, *n.*

drab, drab, *n.* [A Celtic word; Ir. *drabhog*, a slut, dregs, < *drab*, a spot, a stain; Gael. *drabach*, dirty, slovenly; *drabag*, a drab; akin to *draff*.] A strumpet; a slattern.—*v.i.* —*drabbed, drabbing.* To associate with prostitutes or slatterns.

drab·ble, drab'l, *v.i.*—*drabbled, drabbling.* [M.E. *drabelen* = L.G. *drabbeln*.] To become wet and dirty as by trailing over wet ground; draggle.—*v.t.* To draggle; make wet and dirty.—**drab·bler**, *n. Naut.* a piece of canvas laced to the bottom of the bonnet of a sail, to increase its depth.

dra·cae·na, dra·sē'na, *n.* Any ornamental tropical plant belonging to the lily family of the genera *Dracaena* or *Cordyline*, bare branches of which end in sword-shaped leaves.

drachm, dram, *n. Brit.* dram. Drachma.

drach·ma, drak'ma, *n. pl.* **drach·mas**, **drach·mae**, drak'mē. [L. < Gr. *drachmē*, a drachm, < *drassomais*, to grasp with the hand.] An ancient Greek silver coin; a monetary unit of modern Greece; an ancient Greek unit of weight; one of several modern weights, esp. a dram.

dra·co·ni·an, drā·kō'nē·an, *a.* [From *Draco* an Athenian lawmaker.] Harsh; rigorous.

draft, *chiefly Brit. also* **draught**, draft, dräft, *n.* [M.E. *draght*, later *draught, draft*, < O.E. *dragan*.] The act of pulling or drawing loads; a pull or haul; a team of animals for pulling a load; the drawing in of a fish net; a take of fish; the act of inhaling; that which is inhaled; the drawing of a liquid from its receptacle, as of ale from a cask; drinking, or a drink or potion; a current of air in an enclosed space, as in a room; a device for regulating a current of air, as in a fireplace; the taking of supplies, forces, or money from a given source; the selecting of persons for compulsory military service; a drain or heavy demand made on anything; a written order drawn by one person on another for the payment of money; the depth of water a vessel draws with a certain load; the act of drawing or delineating; a drawing, sketch, or design, as a construction plan; a first or preliminary form of any writing, subject to revision and copying; *sports*, a method of apportioning promising new players among professional teams; *metal.* the slight taper given to a pattern in order that it may be drawn from the sand without injury to the mold; *masonry*, a line or border chiseled at the edge of a stone, to serve as a guide in leveling the surfaces.—*a.* Suited for pulling heavy loads; as, a *draft* horse; being a tentative sketch, design, or outline; drawn from a cask; as, *draft* beer.—*v.t.* To draw or pull; take by draft, as for military service; draw the outlines or plan of, or sketch; draw up in written form; as, *draft* a reply.—**on draft**, of beer, ready to be drawn from a cask, rather than from a sealed can or bottle.— **draft·er**, *Brit.* **draught·er**, *n.*

draft dodg·er, *n.* One who evades or tries to evade compulsory service in the armed forces.

draft·ee, draf·tē', dräf·tē', *n.* One who is drafted, as for military service.

draft horse, *n.* A horse for drawing heavy loads.

drafts·man, drafts'man, dräfts'man, *n. pl.* **drafts·men.** One who draws, sketches, plans, or designs; one employed in making mechanical drawings, as of machines and structures. One who draws up documents. Also **draughts·man.—drafts·man·ship**, *n.*

a- fat, fāte, fär, fâre, fạll; **e-** met, mē, mēre, hér; **i-** pin, pīne; **o-** not, nōte, mōve; **u-** tub, cūbe, bụll; **oi-** oil; **ou-** pound.

draft·y, *Brit.* **draught·y**, draf'tē, dräf'tē, *a.*—*draftier, draftiest, draughtier, draughtiest.* Characterized by or allowing air currents to enter; as, a *drafty* room.—**draft·i·ly**, *Brit.* **draught·i·ly**, *adv.*—**draft·i·ness**, *Brit.* **draught·i·ness**, *n.*

drag, drag, *v.t.*—*dragged, dragging.* [M.E. *draggen*: cf. Icel. *draga*, also O.E. *dragan*, E. *draw.*] To draw with force, effort, or difficulty; pull heavily or slowly along; haul; trail; to search with a drag, grapnel, or the like; to break land with a drag or harrow; *fig.* to bring in, as an irrelevant matter. To protract or pass tediously, often with *out* or *on.*—*v.i.* To be drawn or hauled along; trail on the ground; to move heavily or with effort; to use a drag or grapnel; dredge; proceed or pass with tedious slowness.—**drag·ging·ly**, *adv.*—**drag one's feet.** *Slang*, to intentionally work or perform in a laggardly manner; to dawdle.

drag, drag, *n.* Something used by or for dragging, as a dragnet or a dredge; a grapnel, net, or other apparatus dragged through water in searching, as for dead bodies; a heavy harrow; a stout sledge or sled; a four-horse coach with seats inside and on top; a device for checking the rotation of the wheels of a vehicle; a kind of floating anchor used to keep a ship's head to the wind or to check drifting; *fig.* anything that retards progress. The act of dragging; slow, laborious movement or procedure; retardation; the scent or trail of a fox or other hunted animal; something, such as aniseed, dragged over the ground to leave an artificial scent; a hunt with such a scent; *aeron.* the total force of the air acting parallel and opposite to an aircraft direction of flight. A draw or puff on a cigarette. *Slang*, a boring thing or person; transvestite clothing; *slang*, a man's date, as: Come to the party stag or *drag.* *Slang*, a street; as, the main *drag.*—**drag race**, *n.* A short race between two or more cars to see which one accelerates fastest.

dra·gée, dra·zhā', *n.* [Fr.] A sweetmeat in the form of a chocolate- or sugar-coated nut; a ball-shaped candy, usually silver in color, used as a decoration for cakes; a sugar-coated medicine.

drag·ger, drag'ėr, *n.* Someone or something that drags; a boat that operates a dragnet.

drag·gle, drag'el, *v.t.*—*draggled, draggling.* [Dim. < *drag*, or a form of *drabble.*] To wet and make dirty by dragging on damp ground or mud, or on wet grass; to drabble. —*v.i.* To be drawn on the ground; to become wet or dirty by being drawn on the mud or wet grass; to straggle.

drag·gle·tail, drag'el·tāl", *n.* A slut; an untidy person; one wearing wet, dirty clothes.

drag·hound, drag'hound", *n.* A hound trained to follow a drag or artificial scent.

drag hunt, *n.* A hunt in which dogs and horsemen follow an artificial scent.

drag link, *n. Mach.* a link used to connect the cranks of two parallel shafts.

drag·net, drag'net", *n.* A net drawn along the bottom of water or along the ground to catch something; any system for catching a person, esp. a fugitive criminal.

drag·o·man, drag'o·man, *n. pl.* **drag·o·mans, drag·o·men.** [Sp. *dragoman*, < Ar. *tarjumān*, an interpreter, < *tarjama*, to interpret.] An interpreter and travelers' guide or agent in Near Eastern countries; an interpreter attached to an embassy or a consulate.

drag·on, drag'on, *n.* [Fr. *dragon*, < L. *draco*, Gr. *drakōn* < root *drak* or *derk*, as in *derkomai*, to see; Skt. *darc*, to see; so called from its fiery eyes.] A mythical, monstrous animal resembling a winged crocodile, with fiery eyes, crested head, enormous

claws, and often spouting fire. A small Asian lizard, having an expansion of skin on each side, which forms a wing, serving to sustain the animal when it leaps from branch to branch; a fierce, violent person, male or female; a spiteful, watchful woman; a short carbine, carried by the original dragoons.—**drag·on·ish**, *a.*

drag·on·et, drag"o·net', drag'o·nit, *n.* A little dragon; any small, brightly colored marine fish of the genus *Callionymus*, found in shallow tropical and temperate waters.

drag·on·fly, drag'on·flī", *n. pl.* **drag·on·flies.** Any of the large, harmless insects constituting the order *Odonata* that feed on mosquitoes, gnats, and flies, and are characterized by a long, slender body, large head, enormous eyes, and two pairs of large, reticulate, membranous wings.

drag·on li·zard, *n.* A monitor lizard, *Varanus komodoensis*, of Komodo and adjacent Indonesian islands, the largest of all known lizards, attaining a length of 10 to 11 feet. Also *Komodo dragon* or *lizard*, *giant lizard.*

drag·on's blood, *n.* Any of several water-insoluble, deep-red resins used as a pigment; specif. the resin obtained from the fruit of the Malayan rattan palm, *Daemonorops*, used for coloring varnish and in photoengraving.—**drag·on tree**, *n.* An evergreen tree of the Canary Islands, one of the plants that produce dragon's blood.

dra·goon, dra·gōn', *n.* [< Fr. *dragon*, the carbine carried by the original dragoons raised by Marshal Brissac in 1660, on the muzzle of which, from the old fable that the dragon spouts fire, the head of the monster was worked.] Originally a soldier serving both on foot and horseback, and armed with a short musket; in more recent times, a heavily armed cavalryman; currently, a member of a military unit formerly composed of such cavalrymen, esp. in the British army.—*v.t.* To subjugate by harsh use of troops; to harass; to persecute; to compel by violent measures.

drain, drān, *v.t.* [O.E. *drēahnian*, strain; prob. akin to E. *dry.*] To draw off gradually, as a liquid; to remove by degrees, as through conduits or by filtration; to draw off or take away completely; to withdraw liquid gradually from; to make empty or dry by drawing off liquid; to deprive of possessions or resources by gradual withdrawal; to exhaust.—*v.i.* To flow off gradually; to become empty or dry by the gradual flowing off of moisture.—**drain·er**, *n.*

drain, drān, *n.* The act of draining or drawing off; a gradual or continuous outflow, expenditure, or depletion; that which causes such outflow; that by which anything is drained, as a pipe or conduit.—**drain·a·ble**, *a.*

drain·age, drā'nij, *n.* The act or process of draining; a system of drains, artificial or natural; that which is drained off; sewage; *surg.* a slow draining off of fluids, as from wounds.

drain·pipe, drān'pīp", *n.* A pipe used for draining; a wastepipe or sewer.

drake, drāk, *n.* [M.E. *drake* = L.G. *drake.*] The male of any bird of the duck family.

drake, drāk, *n.* [O.E. *draca*, < L. *draco.*] Formerly, a small, brass cannon. Any of various ephemerids or mayflies used as bait by anglers; also **drake fly.**

dram, dram, *n.* [Contr. < *drachma.*] *Apothecaries' weight*, a weight equal to one eighth of an ounce, or 60 grains; *avoirdupois weight*, the sixteenth part of an ounce; a small drink of alcoholic liquor; any small amount.—**dram·shop**, dram'shop", *n.* Formerly, a barroom.

dra·ma, drä'ma, dram'a, *n.* [L.L. *drama*, < Gr. *drama* (*dramat-*), < *dran*, do.] A

composition in prose or verse presenting in dialogue a story of life or character, esp. one intended to be acted on the stage; a play; the branch of literature having such compositions as its subject; dramatic art or representation; any series of events having dramatic interest and leading up to a climax.

Dram·a·mine, dram'a·mēn", *n.* A remedy for motion sickness, dimenhydrinate. (Trademark.)

dra·mat·ic, dra·mat'ik, *a.* Of or pertaining to the drama; appropriate to or in the form of a drama; theatrical; characterized by the force and effect appropriate to the drama.— **dra·mat·i·cal·ly**, *adv.*

dra·mat·ics, dra·mat'iks, *n. pl.* Amateur theatrical productions; excessive emotional behavior; *sing. or pl. in constr.* the art of producing or acting plays.

dram·a·tis per·so·nae, dram'a·tis pėr·sō'nē, drä'ma·tis pėr·sō'nī, *n. pl.* [L.] The characters in a play; *sing. in constr.* the list of characters in a play.

dram·a·tist, dram'a·tist, drä'ma·tist, *n.* The author of a dramatic composition; a playwright.

dram·a·ti·za·tion, dram"a·ti·zā'shan, drä"ma·ti·zā'shan, *n.* The act of dramatizing; construction or representation in dramatic form; a dramatized version.

dram·a·tize, dram'a·tīz", drä'ma·tīz", *v.t.* —*dramatized, dramatizing.* To compose in the form of a drama; to adapt to the form of a play.—*v.i.* To be acceptable for dramatization; to speak, write, or conduct oneself in an exaggerated manner.

dram·a·tur·gy, dram'a·tėr"jē, drä'ma·tėr"jē, *n.* [Gr. *dramatourgia*, dramatic composition—*drama*, and *ergon*, work.] The technique and art of composing dramas and presenting them on the stage.—**dram·a·tur·gic**, dram·a·tur·gi·cal, *a.*—**dram·a·tur·gi·cal·ly**, *adv.*—**dram·a·tur·gist**, *n.*

dram·mock, dram'ok, *n.* [Gael. *dramag*, foul mixture.] *Sc. and North. Eng.* meal mixed with water, without being cooked. Also **drum·mock, dram·mach.**

drape, drāp, *v.t.*—*draped, draping.* [O.Fr. Fr. *draper*, < *drap*, < M.L. *drappus*, cloth.] To cover or hang with cloth or some fabric in graceful folds; adorn with drapery; to adjust, as hangings or clothing, in graceful folds.—*v.i.* To fall, hang, or become arranged in folds.—*n.* A curtain or drapery for covering windows; the manner in which cloth hangs.

drap·er, drā'pėr, *n.* [O.Fr. Fr. *drapier.*] *Brit.* A maker of cloth; a dealer in cloths; a retail merchant who sells clothing and dry goods.

dra·per·y, drā'pe·rē, *n. pl.* **dra·per·ies.** [O.Fr. Fr. *draperie.*] Fabric coverings, hangings, or clothing disposed in loose, graceful folds, or with a view to decorative effect; hangings or draped clothing, as represented in sculpture or painting; the draping or disposing of fabrics in graceful folds. *Brit.* the business of a draper; dry goods.

dras·tic, dras'tik, *a.* [Gr. *drastikos*, < *dran*, to do, to act.] Acting with strength or violence; severe; as, *drastic* punishment.— **dras·ti·cal·ly**, *adv.*

draught, draft, dräft, *n.* Older form of *draft*, still prevalent in British use; as, a *draught* of fish, a ship's *draught*, a *draught* of ale or beer.—*v.t.* See *draft.*—**draught·y**, draf'tē, dräf'tē, *a.* See *drafty.*

draughts, drafts, dräfts, *n. pl.*, *sing. or pl. in constr.* [Orig. pl., with reference to the moves.] *Brit.* the game of checkers.— **draughts·man**, drafts'man, dräfts'man, *n. pl.* **draughts·men.** A piece at draughts; a checker. A draftsman.—**draught·board**, draft'bōrd", draft'bard", dräft'bōrd", dräft'bard", *n.* A checkerboard. Also **draughts·board.**

---

ch- chain, G. na*ch*t;   **th-** THen, thin;   **w-** wig, hw as sound in whig;   **z-** zh as in azure, zeal.   *Italicized vowel* indicates schwa sound.

Dra·vid·i·an, dra·vid′ē·an, _a._ Of or pertaining to a race or body of peoples mostly of southern India and Ceylon; of or pertaining to the group or family of languages spoken by them, including Tamil, Telugu, Kanarese, and Malayalam. —_n._ A member of the Dravidian race; the Dravidian family of languages, also **Dra··vid·i·an lan·guages.**

draw, drą, _v.t._—past _drew_, pp. _drawn_, ppr. _drawing._ [O.E. _dragan_ = Icel. _draga_, draw, = Goth. _-dragan_ = D. _dragen_ = G. _tragen_, carry, bear.] To cause to move in a particular direction as by a pulling force; to pull, haul, or drag; to lead or take along. To obtain or remove, as from a receptacle or source; as, to _draw_ water; to extract; as, to _draw_ a cork; to extract by infusion or distillation; as, to _draw_ tea. To bring toward in the sense of enticing; to attract, as: Honey _draws_ flies. To take in as by sucking or inhaling; as, to _draw_ a breath of air; to deduce or infer; as, to _draw_ a conclusion; to derive or acquire from a source, as: The composer _drew_ his melodies from folk songs. To drain; as, to _draw_ a pond. To eviscerate; as, to _draw_ a chicken. To sketch in lines or words; to delineate or depict; as, to _draw_ images with poetry; to create graphically in lines; as, to _draw_ a picture; to mark, lay out, or trace. To close or shut; as, to _draw_ the blinds; to fill up; as, to _draw_ a bath. To select or acquire by chance, as: He _drew_ the winning ticket. To make or manufacture by stretching or hammering, as wire or dies; to wrinkle or shrink by contraction. To accumulate or gain; as, to _draw_ interest. To formulate; to specify in legal form; as, to _draw_ one's will. To leave, as a contest, undecided; to tie. _Archery_, to bend, as a bow. _Naut._ of a vessel, to need (a certain amount of water) to float.

draw, drą, _v.i._ To exert a pulling, moving, or attracting force; to move, go, or pass gradually, as: The night _draws_ near. To take out a sword, pistol, or similar instrument for action, as: The bandit _drew_ first. To come out of a mold, as in casting; to produce or have a draft of air, as a pipe or flue; to effect drainage. To leave a contest undecided; to settle in water, as a boat. To levy or call for money or supplies; to make demands, esp. a formal written demand, as for money due or on deposit. To shrink or contract; to wrinkle or pucker up. To use or practice the art of tracing or delineating figures; to practice drawing. _Med._ to cause blood or pus to concentrate at one point. _Archery_, to pull back a bowstring.

draw, drą, _n._ The act, process, or result of drawing; that which is drawn, as the movable part of a drawbridge; a lot or chance picked at random; a tie or undecided contest; a land basin into or through which water drains; something which attracts attention or patronage; a card dealt to replace a discard in poker; the dry channel left by a stream; _archery_, the force to pull a bow fully, or the distance from the string to the back of the drawn bow.

draw·back, drą′bak″, _n._ That which detracts from profit or pleasure; a discouragement or hindrance; a disadvantage; an objectionable feature. A certain amount of duties or customs dues paid back or remitted.

draw·bar, drą′bär″, _n._ An iron rod with an eye at each end for use in coupling railroad cars; a bar in a fence, which can be removed to allow passage; a back beam at the rear of a tractor to which implements are hitched.

draw·bore, drą′bōr″, drą′bȯr″, _n. Carp._ a hole pierced through a tenon so that when a mortise or drawbore pin is driven in, the mortised and tenoned parts are drawn snugly together.

draw·bridge, drą′brij″, _n._ A bridge which may be drawn up, let down, or drawn aside to allow or hinder navigation of ships, boats, barges, etc.

draw·ee, drą·ē′, _n._ The person on whom an order or bill of exchange is drawn.

draw·er, drȧr, drą′ėr, _n._ One who draws, in the sense of a draftsman; one who draws an order, draft, or bill of exchange. A sliding storage compartment in a piece of furniture that may be pulled out and pushed back; _pl._ an undergarment for the lower part of the body; underpants, drȧr.

draw·ing, drą′ing, _n._ The act of a person or thing that draws; that which is drawn; representation by lines; delineation of form without reference to color; a sketch, plan, or design. Something determined by drawing lots; a lottery; the time of selection for a lottery or raffle.

draw·ing card, _n._ A speaker, entertainer, or performance attracting large audiences; anything which serves to attract patrons, customers, or the like.

draw·ing room, _n._ [Formerly _withdrawing room_, a room to which the company withdrew from the dining room.] _U.S._ a private room in a railway passenger car; a room in a house for receiving company.

drawl, drąl, _v.t._ [A dim. form < _draw_ or _drag_.] To utter or pronounce in a slow manner by prolongation of the vowels.—_v.i._ To speak with slow utterance.—_n._ A drawling manner of speech.—**drawl·er,** _n._—**drawl·ing·ly,** _adv._

drawn, drąn, _a._ Haggard; taut or tense; undecided, as a contest in which neither side has won; disemboweled, as a fowl; melted and made into a sauce, as butter.—**drawn work,** a needlework design formed by the pulling out of rows of threads.

draw out, _v.t._ To persuade to speak freely; to make longer; to take more time for; to remove, as money, from a place of deposit.

draw·plate, drą′plāt″, _n._ A plate of hard steel, pierced with conical holes, for reducing and elongating wire by drawing it through the holes.

draw pok·er, _n._ A game of poker in which players are dealt five cards and, after betting, are entitled to replace up to three cards.

draw·string, drą′string″, _n._ A cord inserted around the opening of a bag, garment, or curtain, serving to close the opening when the cord is pulled. Also **draw string.**

draw up, _v.t._ To arrange into position, as troops; to stand erect; to bring to a stop; to draft in legal form.

dray, drā, _n._ [M.E. _draye_; akin to E. _draw._] A low, strong cart without fixed sides, for carrying heavy loads; a sledge or sled.—_v.t._ To convey on a dray.—**dray·age,** drā′ij, _n._ Carriage by dray, or a charge made for it.—**dray·horse,** _n._—**dray·man,** drā′man, _n. pl._ **dray·men.**

dread, dred, _v.t._ [M.E. _dreden_, prob. for _adreden,_ < O.E. _ondrǣdan_ = O.H.G. _intrātan,_ fear.] To fear greatly; regard with awe; to anticipate with terror or apprehension.—_v.i._ To be in great fear.—_n._ Great fear; terror or apprehension as to something future.—_a._ Dreaded; dreadful.

dread·ful, dred′ful, _a._ Full of dread or fear; inspiring dread or fear; terrible; extremely bad, unpleasant, or ugly; awe-inspiring or great.—_n. Brit._ a cheap, lurid story, as of crime or adventure; a periodical given to highly sensational matter.—**dread·ful·ly,** _adv._—**dread·ful·ness,** _n._

dread·nought, dred′nąt″, _n._ A battleship with a main battery composed exclusively of guns of 10″ caliber or greater. A heavy cloth; a garment of this cloth.

dream, drēm, _n._ [M.E. _dreem_ = D. _droom_ = G. _traum_ = Icel. _draumr_, dream.] A succession of images or ideas present in the mind during sleep; the sleeping state in which this occurs; an involuntary vision occurring to one awake; a visionary fancy voluntarily indulged in while awake; a reverie; an aim or hope; sometimes, a wild or vain fancy; an object seen in a dream; something of beauty or charm associated with dreams rather than with reality.—**dream·ful,** _a._—**dream·ful·ly,** _adv._—**dream·ful·ness,** _n._—**dream·less,** _a._—**dream·less·ly,** _adv._—**dream·less·ness,** _n._

dream, drēm, _v.i._—_dreamed_ or _dreamt_ (dremt), _dreaming._ To have a dream or dreams; be conscious of images and thoughts during sleep; to indulge in daydreams or reveries; give way to visionary thought or speculation; to think or conceive of something in a very remote way.—_v.t._ To have a dream about; see or imagine in sleep or in a vision; to imagine, as if in a dream; to fancy; suppose vaguely or indefinitely; pass or spend time in dreaming, often followed by _away._

dream·er, drēm′ėr, _n._ One who dreams; one who indulges in daydreams or in visionary thought or speculation.

dream·land, drēm′land″, _n._ The land or region seen in dreams; the land of imagination or fancy; the region of reverie.

drear·y, drēr′ē, _a._—_drearier, dreariest._ [O.E. _drēorig_, bloody, sad, sorrowful, _drēor_, blood, < _drēosan_ (Goth. _driusan_), to fall, with common conversion of _s_ into _r_; akin to G. _traurig_, sad, _trauern_, to mourn.] Dismal; gloomy; causing gloom or sadness; sorrowful or sad; oppressively monotonous. —**drear,** drēr, _a. Liter._ dismal.—**drear·i·ly,** _adv._ Gloomily; dismally.—**drear·i·ness,** _n._

dredge, drej, _n._ [Akin to _drag._] A contrivance for gathering objects or material from the bed of a river, lake, or harbor, by dragging along the bottom; a dredging machine.—_v.t._—_dredged, dredging._ To gather and bring up with a dredge, as oysters; to clear out or deepen with a dredge, as a channel.—_v.i._ To use a dredge.—**dredg·er,** _n._ One who uses a dredge; a boat used in dredging; a dredging machine.

dredge, drej, _v.t._—_dredged, dredging._ [O.Fr. _dragie_ (Fr. _dragée_), < L. _tragemata_, pl. < Gr. _tragēmata_, pl., sweetmeats, dessert, < _tragein, trogein_, nibble, eat (fruit, dessert, etc.).] _Cooking_, to sprinkle with some powdered preparation or substance, esp. flour. To sprinkle a powdered substance over.—**dredg·er,** drej′ėr, _n._ A container with a perforated top for sprinkling flour.

dreg, dreg, _n. Usu. pl._ the sediment of liquors; lees; grounds; any waste or worthless residue; refuse; _sing._ a small remnant; any small quantity; a drop.—**dreg·gy,** _a._

D region, _n._ The lowest region of the ionosphere, existing between about 25 and 40 miles above the earth's surface.

drench, drench, _v.t._ [O.E. _drencan, drencean,_ to give to drink, to drench, < _drincan,_ to drink.] To wet thoroughly; to soak; to saturate; to purge (an animal) violently with medicine.—_n._ A large drink or draft; a dose of liquid medicine for a beast, as a horse.—**drench·er,** _n._

dress, dres, _v.t._ [O.Fr. Fr. _dresser,_ erect, arrange, dress, ult. < L. _directus,_ straight, direct.] To put clothes upon; to furnish with clothes; to trim, adorn, embellish; to clean, as a fowl, for the table or market; to make straight; bring into line, as troops; to prepare by special processes, as skins, fabrics, timber, stone; to cultivate, as land; of hair, to comb out and fix; to apply bandages or medications to.—_v.i._ To come into line, as troops; to clothe or attire oneself; to put on or wear formal or elegant attire, often with _up._

dress, dres, *n.* Clothing; apparel; attire; the outer garment of girls and women consisting of skirt and blouse in one piece; a frock; formal clothes; outer covering, as the plumage of birds; a certain aspect or appearance; guise.—*a.* Pertaining to or used for dresses; appropriate for formal affairs; specifying formal attire.

dres·sage, dre·säzh′, *Fr.* dre·säzh′, *n.* The procedure of training a horse to perform highly-skilled maneuvers in obedience to a rider's almost imperceptible cues; the carrying out by a horse of such maneuvers.

dress cir·cle, *n.* A circular or curving division of seats in a theater or concert hall, usually the first gallery, orig. set apart for spectators in evening dress.

dress down, *v.t.* To reprimand strongly.—**dress·ing down,** *n.*

dress·er, dres′ẽr, *n.* [O.Fr. *dreçor* (Fr. *dressoir*), < *dresser*, E. *dress.*] A bureau or chest of drawers for clothing, often with a mirror; a cupboard for dishes and cooking utensils.

dress·er, dres′ẽr, *n.* One who helps another dress, as a valet; one who assists actors in making costume changes; one who dresses wounds; one who dresses in a distinctive manner; as, a fancy *dresser*; any of several tools used to dress stone or other materials.

dress·ing, dres′ing, *n.* The act of one who or that which dresses; that with which something is dressed, as bandages for a wound or manure for fertilization; a mixture, as of bread and seasonings, for stuffing fowl; a sauce added to a dish; as, salad *dressing.*

dress·ing gown, *n.* A loose gown or robe worn at home while attending to one's appearance or lounging.

dress·ing room, *n.* A room used while dressing; a room backstage in a theater where costumes and makeup are changed; a room in a store where clothes may be tried on before being bought.

dress·ing sta·tion, *n. Milit.* a first-aid center for those wounded in battle.

dress·ing ta·ble, *n.* A vanity or small table, usu. furnished with a mirror and several drawers, in front of which a woman sits while putting on makeup or doing her hair.

dress·mak·er, dres′māk″ẽr, *n.* A person whose occupation is making or altering women's clothing to order.—*a.* Of women's clothing, having softly rounded lines and delicate detail, as opposed to being severely tailored.—**dress·mak·ing,** *n.*

dress pa·rade, *n.* A ceremonial parade of the military in dress uniforms.

dress re·hears·al, *n.* A play rehearsal, complete with costumes, makeup, scenery, props, and lighting, simulating and preceding the first public performance.

dress shirt, *n.* A man's shirt, esp. one with a starched or pleated front and French cuffs, for semiformal or formal evening wear.

dress suit, *n.* A man's formal evening suit.

dress u·ni·form, *n.* A military uniform worn for ceremonies or formal social occasions.

dress·y, dres′ē, *a.*—*dressier, dressiest. Colloq.* Elaborate or rather formal in attire; chic; smartly elegant; showy in dress.—**dress·i·ly,** *adv.* **dress·i·ness,** *n.*

drib, drib, *v.i.*—*dribbed, dribbing.* [Var. of *drip.*] To drip; dribble.—*n.* A drop; a trifling quantity; a driblet.—**dribs and drabs,** small quantities.

drib·ble, drib′l, *v.i.*—*dribbled, dribbling.* [Freq. of *drib,* in part confused with *drivel.*] To fall or flow in drops or small quantities; trickle; to drivel or slaver.—*v.t.* To let fall in drops; give out in small portions; *sports,* to move along by a rapid succession of short kicks, bounces, or pushes.—*n.* A

dropping or dripping; a small trickling stream; a small quantity of liquid; a drop; a small quantity of anything; *sports,* the act of dribbling.—**drib·bler,** *n.*

drib·let, drib′lit, *n.* One of a number of small pieces or parts; a small sum doled out as one of a series. Also **drib·blet.**

dried-up, drīd′up′, *a.* Lacking moisture; wrinkled with age.

dri·er, dry·er, drī′ẽr, *n.* One who or that which dries; a mechanical contrivance or apparatus for removing moisture; any substance added to paints and varnishes to make them dry quickly.

drift, drift, *n.* [M.E. *drift,* < O.E. *drifan,* E. *drive.*] The act of moving or driving something along by, or as by, a current of air, water, or similar force; something heaped or piled into masses by currents of air or water, as snow or sand; material driven or carried from one place to another in masses, as snow or detritus. The course along which something is directed. Tenor or meaning; as, the *drift* of the President's speech; a direction in which something moves; a tendency; as: The *drift* toward war was evident. *Phys., geog.* a broad, shallow, usually slow-moving ocean current; *naut.* the rate at which a current of water moves; the direction of a current of water. *Aeron.* the deviation of aircraft from a set course due to winds. *Mach.* a round, tapering piece of steel used to enlarge holes in metal or to bring holes into line. *Min.* a horizontal passage in a mine. *Milit.* a tool used to clean an ordnance piece. *Electronics,* a temporary deviation in operating characteristics of a circuit, tube, or similar part.

drift, drift, *v.i.* To be driven or carried along by currents of water or air; to be piled in heaps, as snow or sand; to be covered by such a drift. To move smoothly and effortlessly; to move along the path of least resistance; *fig.* to be carried along by force of circumstances; to move along without specific direction, guidance, or control. To vary or veer from a set course; to vary from such a course aimlessly.—*v.t.* To form into piles, heaps, or drifts by currents of air, water, or similar forces; to carry along, as in a current. To enlarge or shape, as a hole, with a steel drift. *Min.* to excavate horizontally; *ranching,* to drive slowly, as livestock.—**drif·ter,** *n.*—**drift·ing·ly,** *adv.*—**drift·less,** *a.*

drift·age, drif′tij, *n.* The act or process of drifting, esp. through action of wind or water; deviation from a set course caused by drifting; something that drifts or that which is carried along or deposited by air or water currents. *Navig.* the amount of drift away from a set course.

drift·wood, drift′wụd″, *n.* Wood floating on, or cast ashore by, the water; something that drifts aimlessly.

drift·y, drif′tē, *a.* Of the nature of, or characterized by, drifts; forming or full of drifts.

drill, dril, *v.t.* [D. *drillen,* turn around, bore, train; cf. M.L.G. *drillen,* roll, turn.] To pierce or bore with a drill, as a hole; to pierce or bore a hole in; to instruct and exercise in military tactics and the use of arms; to discipline; to teach by repetition; to shift or shunt, as cars or engines.—*v.i.* To bore holes with, or as with, a drill; to go through exercises in military or other training.—**drill·a·ble,** *a.*—**drill·er,** *n.*

drill, dril, *n.* [D. *dril.*] A tool or machine for drilling or boring holes in metal, stone, or other hard substances; a gastropod, *Urosalpinx cinerea,* destructive to oysters; the act or method of training in military tactics and the use of arms; an exercise in such training; any strict, methodical training, instruction, or exercise.

drill, dril, *n.* A small furrow made in the soil, in which to sow seeds; a ridge on top of which such a furrow is made; a row of seeds or plants thus sown; a machine for sowing seeds in rows, now usually having contrivances for making furrows and for covering the seeds when sown.—*v.t.* To sow or raise in drills, as seed or crops; to plant in drills, as the ground.

drill·ing, dril′ing, *n.* The act of a person or thing that drills; material removed by a drill in operation.

drill·ing, dril′ing, *n.* [G. *drillich,* < L. *trilix (trilic-),* having three threads.] A stout twilled cotton or linen fabric used for linings, pockets, overalls, or summer clothing. Also **drill.**

drill·mas·ter, dril′mas″tẽr, dril′mä″stẽr, *n.* One who gives practical instruction in military tactics and the use of arms; one who trains in fundamentals, esp. where mechanical drills are needed; *educ.* the instructor's aide, esp. in language teaching, who serves as the speaker supplying the model utterances to be imitated by the learner.

drill press, *n.* A machine fitted with one or more drills for boring holes in metal.

dri·ly, drī′lē, *adv.* See dryly.

drink, dringk, *v.i.*—past *drank* (formerly *drunk*), pp. *drunk* (formerly *drank* or *drunken*), ppr. *drinking.* [O.E. *drincan* = D. *drinken* = G. *trinken* = Icel. *drekka* = Goth. *drigkan,* drink.] To swallow water or other liquid; imbibe; partake of anything as if to satisfy thirst; specif. to imbibe alcoholic liquors, esp. habitually or to excess; tipple.—**to drink to,** to salute in drinking; drink in honor of; drink with wishes for the furtherance of.—*v.t.* To swallow; imbibe; to take in in any manner, as moisture; absorb; to take in through the senses with eagerness and pleasure; gaze upon or listen to attentively or rapturously; to swallow the contents of; to drink in honor of, or with wishes for the success, furtherance, or accomplishment of; as, to *drink* a toast to.

drink, dringk, *n.* [O.E. *drinc, drinca.*] Any liquid which is swallowed, as to quench thirst or for nourishment; a beverage; specif. alcoholic liquor; excessive indulgence in alcoholic liquor; a draft or a serving of liquid; a large body of water, as: He fell into the *drink.*—**drink·a·ble,** *a.*

drink·er, dringk′ẽr, *n.* One who drinks; esp. one who drinks alcoholic liquors habitually or to excess.

drip, drip, *v.i.*—*dripped, dripping.* [O.E. *drypan,* to drip, to drop = Dan. *dryppe,* Icel. *drjúpa,* D. *druipen,* G. *triefen.*] To fall in drops; to have any liquid falling in drops.—*v.t.* To let fall in drops.

drip, drip, *n.* A falling in drops; that which trickles; liquid that falls or trickles in particles; as, the *drip* or *drippings* of fat from cooking meat; the sound made by falling drops. *Arch.* a large flat part of the cornice projecting to throw off water; any device for shedding rainwater. *Med.* a device for administering fluid slowly and continuously, esp. into a vein; the material so injected. *Slang,* a dull, unattractive, inept person.

drip-dry, drip′drī′, drip′drī″, *v.i.*—*drip-dried, drip-drying.* Of a fabric article, to dry wrinkle-free, or nearly so, when hung up dripping wet.—*v.t.* To hang up while dripping wet and allow to dry hanging, as an article of clothing.—**drip′drī″,** *a.*

drip·ping, drip′ing, *n. Usu. pl.* the fat which falls from meat in roasting; anything that drips.—*a.* Very wet.

drip·py, drip′ē, *a.* Dripping; rainy; drizzly.

drip·stone, drip′stōn″, *n. Arch.* a projecting molding or cornice used to throw off the rain. *Geol.* calcium carbonate, $CaCO_3$, as it appears in stalactites and stalagmites.

drive, drīv, *v.t.*—pret. *drove* (archaic *drave*), pp. *driven,* ppr. *driving.* [O.E. *drifan* = D. *drijven* = G. *treiben* = Icel. *drifa* = Goth. *dreiban,* drive.] To send along, away, off, in, out, or back by compulsion; force along; cause and guide the movement, as of an animal or vehicle; convey in a vehicle; to keep going, as machinery; propel; impel, constrain, or urge; compel, overwork, or overtask; to carry through vigorously, as business or a bargain; *min.* to excavate horizontally; *sports,* to hit or propel, as a puck or ball; *golf,* to hit from a tee with a golf club; *baseball,* to cause (a base runner) to advance or score by a base hit or sacrifice fly.—*v.i.* To go along before an impelling force; rush or dash violently; strike or aim; proceed or work vigorously; act as driver; go or travel in a driven vehicle; to hit a golf ball from a tee.

drive, drīv, *n.* The act of driving; a moving along of game, cattle, or floating logs, in a particular direction; the animals or logs that are driven; a propelling or forcible stroke; a vigorous onset or onward course; a strong military offensive; a united effort to accomplish some purpose, as to raise money for a government loan or for some philanthropic object; vigorous pressure or effort in business; a trip in a driven vehicle; a road for driving; a driving mechanism of a motorcar; a driveway; *min.* a drift, or horizontal excavation or tunnel. *Psychol.* a strong, motivating urge that stimulates a response; an instinctive need. *Sports,* a golf shot from a tee; the flight of a ball or puck hit with much force.

drive-in, *n.* A theater, restaurant, bank, or other business that caters to customers who remain in their automobiles while being served.—*a.*

driv·el, driv′el, *v.i.*—driveled, driveling, *Brit.* drivelled, drivelling. [O.E. *dreflian.*] To let saliva flow from the mouth; slaver; to talk childishly or idiotically; utter silly nonsense.—*v.t.* To utter childishly or idiotically; to waste childishly.—*n.* Saliva flowing from the mouth; slaver; childish or idiotic nonsense; silly talk; twaddle.—**driv·el·er,** *Brit.* **driv·el·ler,** *n.*

driv·er, drī′vẽr, *n.* One who or that which drives; one who drives an animal, animals, or a vehicle, as a cowboy or chauffeur; *mach.* a part that transmits force or motion; *golf,* a wooden-headed club with a long shaft, used for making long shots from the tee; *Brit.* a locomotive engineer.—**driv·er·less,** *a.*

driv·er's li·cense, *n.* A legal permit to drive a motorized vehicle on a public way.

driv·er's seat, *n.* The position or seat from which a vehicle is operated; *colloq.* the position of power in an organized group, a governing body, or a dispute.

drive shaft, *n.* A shaft that transmits power to the mechanical parts of machines.

drive·way, driv′wā″, *n.* A road, esp. a private drive, leading from a public road to a building or other structure or enclosure; any roadway used for driving on.

driv·ing, drī′ving, *a.* Having great force; communicating power.

driz·zle, driz′el, *v.i.*—drizzled, drizzling. [A dim. < O.E. *drysnian,* Goth. *driusan,* to fall; like Prov. G. *drieseln,* to drizzle.] To rain in small drops; to fall from the clouds in very fine particles.—*v.t.* To shed in small drops or particles.—*n.* A small or fine rain.—**driz·zly,** driz′lē, *a.* Shedding fine rain.

drogue, drōg, *n.* A sea anchor made from a bucket or canvas bag; a device, shaped like a funnel, used by airplanes in flight for refueling purposes; a device shaped like a cylinder, towed by an airplane, and used

as a decelerating influence, also used to decelerate an astronaut's capsule.

droit, droit, *Fr.* drwä, *n.* pl. **droits,** *Fr.* drwä. [O.Fr. Fr. *droit,* < M.L. *directum,* right, prop. neut. of L. *directus,* straight, direct.] A legal right or claim; that to which one has a legal right or claim; a due; a perquisite; custom duties.

droi·tu·ral, droi′chẽr·al, *a.* [Fr. *droiture,* < M.L. *directura,* right, L. a making straight, < L. *dirigere.*] *Law,* relating to the right of property, as distinguished from the right of possession.

droll, drōl, *a.* [Same word as Fr. *drôle,* D. *drol,* G. *droll,* a thick, short person, a droll; Gael. *droll,* a slow, awkward person; perhaps from Icel. and Sw. *troll,* a kind of imp or hobgoblin.] Comical; humorously odd; amusing.—*n.* One whose occupation or practice is to amuse by odd tricks; a jester; a buffoon; something exhibited for mirth or sport.

droll·er·y, drō′le·rē, *n.* pl. **droll·er·ies.** The quality of being droll; something done to cause mirth; sportive tricks; buffoonery; fun; a comical way of acting or talking; humor.

drom·e·dar·y, drom′e·der″ē, drum′e·der″ē, *n.* pl. **drom·e·dar·ies.** [L. *dromedarius,* a dromedary, < Gr. *dromas, dromados,* running, < stem of *dramein,* to run.] A species of camel, *Camelus dromedarius,* with one hump, found in Arabia and northern Africa.

drone, drōn, *n.* [O.E. *drān,* the dronebee; L.G. and Dan. *drone,* Sw. *dron, drönje,* G. *drohne,* from the sound it makes; akin *humblebee,* G. *hummel,* and the verb *hum.*] The male honeybee, having no sting and collecting no honey; an idler; a parasite; one who earns nothing and does no work; a humming or low sound; the instrument of humming; a monotonous or long-winded speaker; a remote-control device on a pilotless boat or airplane.

drone, drōn, *v.i.*—droned, droning. [Dan. *dröne,* Sw. *dröna,* to drone; akin Goth. *drunjus,* a sound.] To make a low, heavy, dull sound; to hum; to snore; to talk in a dull monotonous tone; to live in idleness.—*v.t.* To read or speak in a dull, monotonous, droning manner, often with *on.*—**dron·er,** *n.*—**dron·ing·ly,** *adv.*

drool, drōl, *v.i.* [Contraction of *drivel.*] To slaver; to water at the mouth.—*v.t.*—*n.* Senseless talk; drivel.

droop, drōp, *v.i.* [A form of *drip, drop.*] To sink or hang down; to bend downward, as from weakness or exhaustion; to languish from grief or other cause; to fail or sink; to decline; to be dispirited.—*v.t.* To let sink or hang down.—*n.* The act of drooping or of falling or hanging down; a drooping position or state.—**droop·ing·ly,** *adv.* —**droop·y,** *a.*—droopier, droopiest. Lacking spirit; dejected; sagging.

drop, drop, *n.* [O.E. *dropa* = O.S. *dropo* = O.H.G. *troffo* (G. *tropfen*) = Icel. *dropi.*] A small quantity of liquid which falls or is produced in a more or less spherical mass; a liquid globule; the quantity of liquid contained in such a mass; a very small quantity of liquid; a minute quantity of anything; *usu. pl.* liquid medicine given in drops. Something like or likened to a drop, as a pendant or a lozenge; the act of dropping, as men or supplies by parachute; a fall or descent; the distance or depth to which anything drops; a steep slope; the newborn young of animals, as the litter of a cat; a fallen fruit; that which drops or is used for dropping; as, a *drop* curtain; a trap door in the scaffold of a gallows, on which the criminal about to be executed is placed; a heavy weight or hammer that falls between guides; a drop press; a slit or depository for dropping

mail; *baseball,* a ball so delivered by the pitcher that it shoots suddenly downward as it approaches the batter; *milit.* men or supplies parachuted from an airplane.—**to get,** or **have, the drop on one,** to get, or have, the chance to shoot before an antagonist can use his weapon.

drop, drop, *v.i.*—dropped, dropping. [O.E. *dropian,* secondary form of *drēopan* = O.S. *driopan* = O.H.G. *triofan* (G. *triefen*) = Icel. *drjūpa,* drip, drop.] To fall in globules or small portions, as a liquid; to discharge moisture in globules; drip; to fall vertically or sink to the ground; have an abrupt descent; fall wounded, dead, or unconscious; to squat or crouch, as a dog at the sight of game; to quit or withdraw; as, to *drop* from a contest; to come to an end; cease; lapse; disappear; to fall lower in condition or degree; to pass without effort into some condition; as, to *drop* asleep; to move down gently, as with the tide or a light wind; to come or enter casually or unexpectedly, used with *in* or *into.*—*v.t.* To let fall in globules or small portions; distill; shed, as tears; to let fall or cause to fall like a drop; allow to sink or cause to sink to a lower position; of animals, give birth to; to utter or express casually or incidentally, as a hint; send, as a note, in a casual or offhand manner; *slang,* lose or part with, as money. Bring to the ground by a blow or shot; set down, as from a ship or vehicle; omit, as a letter or syllable, in pronouncing or writing; let droop or cast down, as the eyes; to lower in pitch or loudness, as the voice; to cease to keep up or have to do with; have done with; dismiss; to give up, as an idea; to leave; to decrease, as in value; to parachute or airdrop, as men or supplies, to the ground.

drop ceil·ing, *n.* A false ceiling below the original, usually constructed in the process of remodeling to improve heating, lighting, acoustics, or the general appearance of a room.

drop cur·tain, *n.* A curtain lowered, as between the acts of a play, to shut off the stage from the view of the audience.

drop-forge, drop′fôrj″, drop′färj″, *v.t.*—drop-forged, drop-forging. To forge by the impact of a falling mass or weight, the hot piece of metal usually being placed between dies and subjected to the blow of a drop-hammer or the like.—**drop for·ging,** *n.* A forging caused by the impact of a dropped weight; an object so forged.

drop goal, *n. Brit.* a goal made by a drop kick in rugby.

drop ham·mer, *n.* A machine for embossing or forging, consisting of a weight raised vertically and allowed to drop suddenly on metal resting on an anvil. Also *drop press.*

drop kick, *n. Football,* a kick given a football as it hits the ground after being dropped, to direct it toward the opponent's goal posts.—**drop-kick,** *v.t.* To kick the football in making a drop kick; to score three points with a successful drop kick.— *v.i.* To make a drop kick.—**drop-kick·er,** *n.*

drop leaf, *n.* One of two extensions used to enlarge a table hinged to the ends or sides of a table-top in such a way that it may be lowered to a hanging position when not needed.—**drop-leaf,** *a.*

drop·light, drop′līt″, *n.* A suspended electric light that can be raised or lowered by its cord.

drop off, *v.i.* To fall asleep; to die. Of a surface level, to fall away sharply; to decrease or decline, as: The birth rate *dropped off* last year.—*v.t.* To deliver; as, to *drop off* a package; to deposit.—**drop-off,** drop′af″, drop′of″, *n.* An abrupt declivity; a decline or decrease.

drop·out, drop'out", *n.* A withdrawal; one who withdraws, as from membership; one who withdraws before completion of a course of instruction; a person who discontinues his formal education prior to graduation, as from high school or college.

drop·page, drop'ij, *n.* That portion of a fruit crop that falls to the ground before it is ready for picking.

drop·per, drop'ẽr, *n.* One who or that which drops; a tube of glass or similar material with a flexible rubber bulb at one end and a small orifice at the other, for drawing a liquid and expelling it in drops.

drop press, *n.* A drop hammer; a punch press.

drop ship·ment, *n.* A shipment of merchandise delivered directly to retailers by the manufacturer or other suppliers but billed through the wholesaler or distributor.

drop sonde, drop'sond", *n. Meteor.* a radiosonde fitted with a parachute in order to be dropped from an aircraft for measurement of atmospheric conditions as it descends.

drop·sy, drop'sē, *n.* [Formerly *hydropsy*, < Gr. *hydrōps*, dropsy, < *hydōr*, water.] *Med.* an abnormal collection of serous fluid in any cavity of the body, or in the cellular tissue; edema.—**drop·si·cal**, drop'si·kal, *a.* —**drop·sied**, *a.*—**drop·si·cal·ly**, *adv.*—**drop·si·cal·ness**, *n.*

dros·ky, dros'kē, *n.* pl. **dros·kies.** [Russ. *drozhki.*] A kind of light four-wheeled carriage used chiefly in Russia, having a long bench on which the passengers sit sideways or astride. Also **drosh·ky**, drosh'kē, pl. **drosh·kies.**

dro·soph·i·la, drō·sof'i·la, dro·sof'i·la, *n.* [N.L. < Gr. *drosos*, dew and *philos*, loving.] A genus of flies, esp. *Drosophila melanogaster*, widely used in genetic experiments.

dross, drȧs, dros, *n.* [O.E. *dros, drosn*, < *dreósan*, to fall; D. *droes*, Icel. *tros*, rubbish; Sc. *drush*, dregs; Dan. *drysse*, to fall.] The refuse or impurities on the surface of melted metal; waste matter.—**dros·sy**, drȧ'sē, dros'ē, *a.*—**drossier, drossiest.** Like dross; worthless.

drought, drout, *n.* [Contr. < O.E. *drugath, drugoth*, < *drige, dryge*, dry; like D. *droogte*, < *droog*, dry.] Dry weather; want of rain; a long period of dry weather that affects crops; thirst; scarcity; lack. Also **drouth**, drouth.—**drought·y**, drou'tē, *a.* —*droughtier, droughtiest.* Arid; thirsty.

drove, drōv, *n.* [O.E. *dráf*, < *drifan*, to drive.] A number of animals, as oxen, sheep, or swine, driven in a body; a crowd of people in motion; a flock; a chisel used in stonework.

dro·ver, drō'vẽr, *n.* One who drives cattle or sheep to market, or from one locality to another; a cattle merchant.

drown, droun, *v.t.* [< O.E. *druncnian*, to sink in water, to be drunk, < *druncen*, pp. of *drincan*, to drink; Dan. *drukne*, to drown.] To deprive of life by immersion in water or other fluid; to overflow, overwhelm, or inundate; to put an end to, as if by drowning; to overpower.—*v.i.* To be suffocated in water or other fluid.

drowse, drouz, *v.i.*—*drowsed, drowsing.* [O.E. *driusan*, sink, become inactive or sluggish.] To be listless, sleepy, or half asleep.—*v.t.* To make drowsy or sleepy; to pass or spend in drowsing; as, to *drowse* away the afternoon.—*n.* A condition of drowsing or of being half asleep.

drows·y, drou'zē, *a.*—*drowsier, drowsiest.* Inclined to sleep; half asleep; marked by or resulting from sleepiness; dull or sluggish. —**drows·i·ly**, *adv.*—**drows·i·ness**, *n.*

drub, drub, *v.t.*—*drubbed, drubbing.* [Prov. E. *drab*; akin to Icel. and Sw. *drabba*, to beat; G. *treffen*, to hit.] To beat with a stick or other object; to thrash; to cudgel; to defeat in a particularly decisive or humiliating way.—*n.* A blow with a stick or cudgel.—**drub·ber**, *n.*—**drub·bing**, *n.* A cudgeling; a sound beating; a decisive defeat.

drudge, druj, *v.i.*—*drudged, drudging.* [Softened form of M.E. *druggen, drug*, to work laboriously; origin doubtful.] To work hard; to labor in menial work; to labor with fatigue.—*n.* One who labors hard in servile employment; a slave.—**drudg·er·y**, druj'e·rē, *n. pl.* **drudg·er·ies.** Ignoble toil; hard work in servile occupations.—**drudg·ing·ly**, *adv.*

drug, drug, *n.* [O.Fr. Fr. *drogue*, origin uncertain.] Formerly, any ingredient used in chemistry, pharmacy, dyeing, or the like; now, any medicinal substance for internal or external use; often, a habit-forming medicinal substance; a narcotic; a commodity that is overabundant, or in excess of demand in the market.—*v.t.*—*drugged, drugging.* To mix, as food or drink, with a drug, esp. a narcotic or poisonous drug; to administer medicinal drugs to; to stupefy or poison with a drug; to administer anything nauseous to; to surfeit.

drug·get, drug'it, *n.* [Fr. *droguet*, dim. of *drogue*, drug, trash.] A cloth of wool and other fibers used as a floor covering.

drug·gist, drug'ist, *n.* A pharmacist; the operator or owner of a drugstore.

drug·store, drug'stōr", drug'star", *n.* A place of retail business where prescriptions are filled, and drugs and miscellaneous merchandise are sold.

dru·id, drö'id, *n.* [Fr. *druide*, < L. *druidæ, druides*, pl.; < Celtic.] (*Often cap.*) one of an order of priests or ministers of religion among the ancient Celts of Gaul, Britain, and Ireland.—**dru·id·ess**, *n.* A female druid.—**dru·id·ic, dru·id·i·cal**, *a.* Of or pertaining to the druids.—**dru·id·ism**, drö'i·diz"um, *n.* The religion or rites of the druids.

drum, drum, *n.* [= D. *trom* = L.G. *trumme* = Dan. *tromme* = Sw. *trumma*, drum.] A musical instrument of the percussive class, consisting of a hollow body covered at one or both ends with a tightly stretched membrane, or head, which is struck with a stick, a pair of sticks, or the hand; the sound produced by this instrument, or any noise suggestive of it. Something resembling a drum in shape or structure or in the noise it produces, as the tympanum or middle ear; a cylindrical part of a machine; a cylindrical box or receptacle; a natural organ by which an animal produces a loud or bass sound. A drumfish or any of several fish of the family *Sciaenidae* that makes a drumming noise.

drum, drum, *v.i.*—*drummed, drumming.* To beat or play on a drum; beat on anything rhythmically; to make a sound like that of a drum; to resound. To create interest or solicit trade or customers.—*v.t.* To beat rhythmically; to perform by drumming; to call or summon by or as by beating a drum. To solicit or obtain, as trade or customers: usu. with *up*. To expel or dismiss in disgrace: usu. with *out*. To drive or force by persistent repetition.

drum·fish, drum'fish", *n.* Any of various fishes of the North American Atlantic coast, producing a drumming sound, esp. in the breeding season.

drum·lin, drum'lin. [Celtic name.] *Geol.* an elongated mound of glacial material. Also **drum.**

drum ma·jor, *n.* The chief or first drummer of a regiment; the marching leader of a band or drum corps.—**drum ma·jor·ette**, *n.* A female drum major.

drum·mer, drum'ẽr, *n.* One who beats a drum; a commercial traveler.

drum·stick, drum'stik", *n.* A stick for beating a drum; the lower joint of the leg of a dressed fowl.

drunk, drungk, *a.* Intoxicated with strong drink; having one's mental and physical faculties impaired by excessive drinking; overwhelmed or dominated by some feeling or emotion, as if by alcohol; of or pertaining to intoxication.—*n.* A bout or spell of drinking to intoxication; a fit of drunkenness; a drunken person.

drunk·ard, drung'kẽrd, *n.* One who is frequently intoxicated; an inebriate.

drunk·en, drung'ken, *a.* Intoxicated; drunk; given to drunkenness; pertaining to or proceeding from intoxication; unsteady; lurching.—**drunk·en·ly**, *adv.*—**drunk·en·ness**, *n.*

drunk·om·e·ter, drung·kom'i·tẽr, *n.* An instrument used to measure the alcoholic content in the bloodstream by testing the breath.

dru·pa·ceous, drö·pā'shus, *a. Bot.* drupelike; pertaining to or producing drupes.

drupe, drōp, *n.* [N.L. *drupa*, drupe, L. *drupa, druppa*, = Gr. *druppa*, overripe olive.] A fruit, as the peach, cherry, or plum, consisting of an outer skin, *epicarp*, a pulpy and succulent layer, *mesocarp*, and a hard or woody inner shell or stone, *endocarp*, which usually encloses a single seed.— **drupe·let**, *n.* A little drupe, as one of the individual pericarps composing the blackberry.

druse, drōz, *n.* [G. *druse*, < Czech. *druza.*] A surface or crust composed of small projecting crystals; a rock cavity lined with such crystals.

dry, drī, *a.*—*drier, driest.* [O.E. *dryge*, akin to D. *droog*, L.G. *drog*, and G. *trocken*, dry.] Free from moisture; not wet or damp; lacking rain or humidity, as a climate or season; characterized by absence, deficiency, or failure of natural or ordinary moisture; not under water; as, *dry* land; depleted or devoid of water or other liquid; as, a *dry* well; not yielding milk; as, a *dry* cow; free from or unaccompanied by tears; as, *dry* eyes; drained away or evaporated; as, a *dry* stream; desiring drink, thirsty; causing thirst; eaten or served without butter or the like; as, *dry* toast; of bakery goods, stale; of cooked food, not juicy enough to be tasty; free from sweetness; as, a *dry* wine; of a cocktail, mixed with dry vermouth; mixed with comparatively little dry vermouth; as, a *dry* martini; characterized by or favoring prohibition of the manufacture and sale of alcoholic liquors for use as beverages; of or pertaining to nonliquid substances or commodities; as, *dry* measure; not producing hoped-for results; unfruitful; stated in a straight-faced, brisk, pithy manner; as, *dry* humor; unemotional, indifferent, or cold; dull or uninteresting; as, a *dry* topic; plain, unadorned, or straightforward; as, a list of *dry* facts; *art*, having sharply defined outlines or lacking warmth and gradation in color.—**dry·ly**, *adv.*—**dry·ness**, *n.*

dry, drī, *v.t.*—*dried, drying.* [O.E. *drȳgan.*] To make dry; free from moisture or liquid; desiccate.—*v.i.* To become dry; lose moisture.—**dry up**, to become totally dry; to cease to be productive; to cease to be, as: Communication between the couple dried up. *Slang*, to discontinue talking.

dry, drī, *n. pl* **drys.** *Colloq.* a prohibitionist. Any dry place, esp. dry land.

dry·ad, drī'ad, drī'ad, *n. pl.* **dry·ads, dry·a·des**, drī'a·dēz". [Gr. *dryas, dryados*, < *drys*, an oak, a tree.] (*Often cap.*) *myth.* a nymph of the woods, or a deity supposed to preside over woods.

dry bat·ter·y, *n. Elect.* a dry cell, or a voltaic battery consisting of a number of dry cells.

dry cell, *n. Elect.* a voltaic cell whose liquid constituents have been made more or less solid by means of absorbent material.

dry-clean, drī′klēn, *v.t.* To clean (textiles) with solvents other than water, as carbon tetrachloride.—**dry clean·er,** *n.* A solvent used to dry-clean fabrics; a person engaged in dry cleaning as a business.—**dry clean··ing,** *n.*

dry dock, *n.* A basinlike structure from which the water can be removed after the entrance of a ship, used during cleaning, construction, or repairs.—**dry-dock,** *v.t.* To put in a dry dock.

dryer, drī′ẽr, *n.* See *drier.*

dry farm·ing, *n.* A method of farming practiced in regions of slight or insufficient rainfall, depending largely upon tillage methods which make the soil receptive to moisture and prevent evaporation.—**dry farm·er,** *n.*—**dry-farm,** *v.i., v.t.*

dry fly, *n.* An artificial fly made to float on the water, used in fishing.

dry goods, *n. pl.* Textile fabrics and related articles of trade, as distinguished from groceries, hardware, and other goods.

dry hole, *n. Geol.* any well drilled for oil or gas that does not produce the quantity to be profitable commercially.

Dry Ice, *n.* Solidified carbon dioxide, usually in the shape of blocks, used as a refrigerant because it reverts directly to a gas without liquefying. (Trademark.)

dry·ing, drī′ing, *a.* Producing dryness; having the quality of rapidly becoming dry and hard upon exposure to air.

dry·ing oil, *n.* An oily, organic liquid such as linseed, tung or soybean oil, or a mixture of a natural oil with a synthetic resin which, when spread thinly and exposed to the air, hardens to a tough, elastic film: used in paint and varnish.

dry kiln, *n.* A heated oven or chamber for controlled drying or seasoning of lumber.

dry meas·ure, *n.* System of units of capacity used to measure dry commodities. *U.S.* two pints make one quart, eight quarts make one peck, four pecks make one bushel of 2150.42 cubic inches; *Brit.* two pints make one quart, four quarts make one gallon, two gallons make one peck, four pecks make one bushel of 2219.36 cubic inches, and eight bushels make one quarter.

dry·o·pith·e·cine, drī″ō·pith′e·sīn″, *n.* A member of a subfamily of Old World apes regarded as the possible ancestors of man and present-day anthropoids.—*a.*

dry plate, *n. Photog.* a glass plate in a camera, coated with a sensitized silver halide emulsion, upon which an image can be produced by exposure to a lighted object and subsequent development of the plate.

dry·point, drī′point″, *n. Engraving,* a technique utilizing only a sharp-pointed needle to cut fine lines on copper; a print made by this process.

dry rot, *n.* A decay of seasoned timber causing it to become brittle and to crumble to a dry powder, due to various fungi; any of various diseases of vegetables or plants due to fungi; any concealed or unsuspected inward decay.—**dry-rot,** *v.t., v.i.*

dry run, *n.* A military practice exercise without the use of live ammunition. Any trial run or rehearsal.

dry·salt·er, drī′sạl″tẽr, *n. Brit.* One who deals in those chemicals and their extracts that make up various drugs, dyes, and gums; *colloq.* a dealer in salted and dried meats, pickles, sauces, and other foods.—**dry·salt·er·y,** *n. pl.* **dry·salt·er·ies.** *Brit.* the store or business of a drysalter.

dry-shod, drī′shod″, *a.* Having dry feet or shoes.

dry wash, *n.* Clean, dry, unironed laundry.

d.t.'s, *n. pl. construed as sing.* Abbreviation for delirium tremens.

du·ad, dō′ad, dū′ad, *n.* [= *dyad.*] A group of two; a pair.

du·al, dō′al, dū′al, *a.* [L. *dualis,* < *duo,* two; akin *duel, double, doubt, dubious.*] Of or indicating two; consisting of two parts; twofold; double; having two different natures; *gram.* referring to a word form that denotes two.—*n. Gram.* the dual number in a language or a word form with such a number.—**du·al·i·ty,** dō·al′i·tē, dū·al′i·tē, *n.* A dual state or quality.—**du·al·ly,** *adv.*

du·al car·riage·way, *n. Brit.* a highway divided by a grassy strip or a fence separating streams of traffic moving in opposite directions.

du·al·ism, dō′a·liz″um, dū′a·liz″um, *n.* A twofold division; *philos.* any system holding that all phenomena in the universe can be explained in terms of two fundamental and exclusive principles, such as mind and matter, being and nonbeing. *Theol.* the doctrine that there are two distinct eternal principles, one good and the other evil; the belief that man embodies two irreducible elements such as body and soul.—**du·al·ist,** *n.* A believer in dualism.—**du·al·is·tic,** *a.*—**du·al·is·ti·cal·ly,** *adv.*—**du·al·ize,** *v.t.*

du·al-pur·pose, *a.* Serving or meant to serve two functions; bred for two reasons, as cattle reared for their milk and meat.

dub, dub, *v.t.*—*dubbed, dubbing.* [M.E. *dubben;* < O.Fr. (cf. O.Fr. *aduber,* later *adouber,* dub knight, equip, dress, adjust), but ult. origin uncertain.] To strike lightly with a sword in the ceremony of conferring knighthood; to make or designate as a knight; to invest with any dignity or title; to style, name, or call by a descriptive nick-name; *Brit.* to dress, trim, or crop, as certain fowl; to smooth by cutting or rub-bing, as wood or leather; to execute (a golf shot) poorly; to botch or do poorly.—*v.i.* To make a thrusting or poking movement.

dub, dub, *n. Slang,* one who is awkward or unskillful.

dub, dub, *v.t.*—*dubbed, dubbing.* [< *double.*] To equip, as a film, with a new sound track; used with *in,* to add (music, dialogue, or other sounds) to a film or radio, or television tape recording; to transfer (recorded material) to a new record or tape.—*n.* Any sounds added to a sound track.—**dub·ber,** *n.*

dub, dub, *n. Sc.* a puddle or pool.

dub·bin, dub′in, *n.* A preparation used in dressing leather. Also *dubbing.*

dub·bing, dub′ing, *n.* The conferring of knighthood; the materials used for the body of an angler's fly; dubbin.

du·bi·e·ty, dō·bī′i·tē, dū·bī′i·tē, *n. pl.* **du·bi·e·ties.** [L. *dubietas.*] Doubtfulness; a feeling of doubt. Also **du·bi·os·i·ty,** dō″-bē·os′i·tē, dū″bē·os′i·tē.

du·bi·ous, dō′bē·us, dū′bē·us, *a.* [L. *dubius,* moving alternately in two opposite directions, < root of *duo,* two.] Doubtful; occasioning or involving doubt; of question-able ethics or taste; as, a *dubious* business arrangement, a *dubious* remark; of uncertain event or issue; wavering or fluctuating in opinion.—**du·bi·ous·ly,** *adv.* —**du·bi·ous·ness,** *n.*

du·bi·ta·ble, dō′bi·ta·bl, dū′bi·ta·bl, *a.* [L. *dubito,* to waver in opinion.] Liable to be doubted; doubtful; uncertain.—**du·bi··ta·bly,** *adv.*—**du·bi·ta·tion,** dō″bi·tā′shan, dū″bi·tā′shan, *n.* The act of doubting or hesitating; doubt.

du·cal, dō′kal, dū′kal, *a.* [L. *ducalis,* pertaining to a leader, < *dux, ducis,* a leader.] Pertaining to a duke.—**du·cal·ly,** dō′ka·lē, dū′ka·lē, *adv.* After the manner of a duke; *her.* with a coronet of a duke.

du·cat, duk′at, *n.* [Fr. *ducat,* It. *ducato,* < L.L. *ducatus,* a duchy (the particular duchy originating the name being uncertain), < L. *dux.*] A gold coin formerly common to several European states; *slang,* a ticket to a theater or sports performance.

du·ce, dō′chā, It. dō′che, *n. pl.* **du·ces,** It. **du·ci,** dō′chäs, It. dō′chē. Leader, esp. a dictator.—**il Du·ce,** *n.* Title applied to Benito Mussolini, premier of Italy and leader of Italian fascism, 1922–43.

duch·ess, duch′is, *n.* [Fr. *duchesse,* < *duc,* duke.] The wife or widow of a duke; a woman who has the sovereignty of a duchy.

duch·y, duch′ē, *n. pl.* **duch·ies.** [Fr. *duché.*] The territory controlled or governed by a duke or duchess; a dukedom.

duck, duk, *n.* Any of numerous species of waterfowl of the family *Anatidae* that have a small, more or less depressed body, a short neck, broad, flat bill, short legs, a waddling gait, and a marked difference in the plumage of the sexes; the flesh of the bird used as food; any female duck; *slang,* any person; *Brit. colloq.* a term of endearment.

duck, duk, *v.t.* [Akin to D. *duiken,* to bend the head, duck, dive, Dan. *dukke,* to dive, G. *tauchen,* to dip, to dive.] To plunge under water for a brief period of time; to bow; to stoop or nod in order to escape a blow; to evade a responsibility.—*v.i.* To plunge or dip into water briefly; to drop the head suddenly; to bow; to evade a dis-agreeable task.—*n.* An example of ducking. —**duck·er,** duk′ẽr, *n.*

duck, duk, *n.* [Same word as D. *doek,* Sw. *duk,* G. *tuch,* cloth.] A type of coarse, tightly-woven cloth resembling canvas; *pl.* slacks made of duck.

duck, duk, *n. Milit.* a truck which can be used on land and in water.

duck·bill, duk′bil″, *n.* A small aquatic monotreme, *Ornithorhynchus anatinus,* of Australia and Tasmania, having webbed feet and a beak like that of a duck. Also **duck-billed plat·y·pus,** *platypus.*

duck·board, duk′bōrd″, duk′bạrd″, *n.* A board or a section or structure of boarding laid as a floor or track over wet or muddy ground.

duck call, *n.* A gadget or device for imitating duck calls.

duck·ing stool, *n.* A stool or chair in which offenders were formerly tied and then plunged into water.

duck·ling, duk′ling, *n.* A young duck.

duck·pins, duk′pinz″, *n. pl. but sing. in constr.* A type of bowling game using a smaller ball and pins shorter and thicker than regulation tenpins.

ducks and drakes, *n.* The game of skipping shells or flat stones across the surface of still water. Also **duck and drake.**—**play ducks and drakes with,** to use carelessly or to spend foolishly. Also **make ducks and drakes of.**

duck soup, *n. Slang,* a goal that is easily attained or accomplished, as: Learning a new card trick is *duck soup* to that expert.

duck·weed, duk′wēd″, *n.* Any member of the family *Lemnaceæ,* esp. of the genus *Lemma,* comprising small aquatic plants which float free on still water.

duck·y, duk′ē, *a.*—*duckier, duckiest. Slang,* delightful; highly pleasing; darling.—*n. Brit. slang,* sweetheart, pet: a term of affection or familiarity.

duct, dukt, *n.* [L. *ductus,* leading, conduct, conduit, < *ducere,* lead.] Any pipe, tube, canal, or conduit by which fluid or other substances are conducted or conveyed; *anat.* a tube, canal, or vessel conveying a bodily fluid, esp. a glandular secretion; *elect.* a tubular channel or pipe for con-ductors such as telephone or telegraph cables and electric power lines; *bot.* an extended tube or cavity produced by a series of elongated plant cells whose end walls have disintegrated.—*v.t.* To transport by means of a duct.—**duct·less,** *a.*

duc·tile, duk'til, duk'til, *a.* [L. *ductilis,* < *ducere,* lead.] Capable of being hammered out thin, as certain metals; malleable; capable of being drawn out into wire or threads, as gold; capable of being molded or shaped; plastic; *fig.* susceptible of being led or drawn; compliant; tractable; capable of being directed through channels, as water.—**duc·tile·ly,** *adv.*—**duc·til·i·ty,** *n.*

duc·tule, duk'tōl, duk'tūl, *n.* A duct of small size.

dud, dud, *n. Milit. slang,* a shell or bomb that fails to explode; *slang,* a person, thing, or undertaking that fails.—*a.* Inoperative; useless.

dude, dōd, dūd, *n.* A man whose appearance shows excessive care and delicacy; a dandy; a fop; *colloq.* a city-bred person, esp. an Easterner who spends a vacation on a ranch.

du·deen, dö·dēn', *n. Irish,* a short clay tobacco pipe.

dude ranch, *n.* A ranch operated for, or accommodating tourists, where they may board and enjoy ranch life.

dudg·eon, duj'on, *n.* [Origin unknown.] Anger; resentment; malice; ill will; discord.

duds, dudz, *n. pl.* [M.E. *dudde;* origin unknown.] *Colloq.* Clothes; one's belongings in general.

due, dö, dū, *a.* [O.Fr. *deu* (Fr. *dû*), pp. of *deveir* Fr. < L. *debere,* owe.] Owed or payable as an obligation or debt, esp. payable at once because the required date has been reached; owed or owing because of a moral or natural right; that ought to be given or rendered; rightful, proper, or fitting; as, a *due* reward; adequate or sufficient; as, *due* cause for dismissal; under engagement as to time; expected or scheduled to be ready, arrive, or be present; as, *due* home at midnight.—*n.* That which is due or owed; *pl.* a charge or fee paid at regular intervals, as for the privilege of membership in a club.—*adv.* Directly or straight; as, *due* east.—**due bill,** *n.* A brief written acknowledgment of indebtedness, not payable to order or transferrable by mere endorsement.—**due date,** *n.* The maturity date of a bond, bill, or note; the specific date when a debt becomes payable.—**due to,** *prep.* Attributable, as to a cause.

du·el, dö'el, dū'el, *n.* [Fr. *duel* = It. *duello,* < M.L. *duellum* a combat between two (< L. *duo,* two), orig. an early form of L. *bellum,* war.] A prearranged combat between two persons, fought with deadly weapons according to an accepted code of procedure, esp. to settle a private quarrel; any contest between two persons or parties.—*v.i.*—*dueled,dueling,Brit. duelled, duelling.* To fight a duel.—**du·el·ist,** *Brit.* **du·el·list,** *n.* One who fights duels. Also **du·el·er,** *Brit.* **du·el·ler.**

du·el·lo, dö·el'ō, dū·el'ō, *It.* dö·el'lạ, *n. pl.* **du·el·los,** *It.* **du·el·li,** *It.* dö·el'lē. [It.] The practice or art of dueling; the code of rules regulating dueling.

du·en·na, dö·en'a, dū·en'a, *n.* [Sp. *duenna, dueña,* a form of *doña,* fem. of *don,* < L. *domina,* a mistress.] In Spanish and Portuguese families, an older woman appointed to serve as chaperon to the young ladies; a governess.

due pro·cess of law, *n.* A course of legal proceedings in accordance with established rules and principles for enforcing and protecting individual rights. Also **due pro·cess.**

du·et, dö·et', dū·et', *n.* [It. *duetto,* < *duo,*

two.] A musical composition for two voices or two instruments.

duff, duf, *n.* [Var. of *dough.*] A flour pudding boiled or steamed, usu. containing raisins, currants, and spices. Decaying vegetable matter covering forest ground.

duff, duf, *v.t.* [Appar. < *duffer* (recorded earlier).] *Slang,* to manipulate so as to make it pass for something new or different; misrepresent; fake. *Brit.* to misjudge one's swing in golf so that the club hits the ground behind the ball.

duf·fel, duf·fle, duf'el, duf'l, *n.* [From *Duffel,* a Belgian manufacturing town.] A kind of coarse woolen cloth having a thick nap; supplies and equipment for camping.

duf·fel bag, *n.* A large canvas bag, cylindrical in shape when packed, used by campers, hunters, and members of the armed forces for carrying personal items.

duf·fel coat, duf·fle coat, *n.* A knee-length coat, usually hooded, made of coarse wool.

duff·er, duf'ėr, *n.* A stupid, ineffectual, or clumsy person; a person who is inept at a particular sport or game; a dull, irresolute old man; something useless or inferior; a peddler of cheap, flashy articles.

dug, dug, *n.* [Akin to Sw. *dägga,* Dan. *dægge,* to suckle; < root seen in Skt. *duh,* to milk.] The pap or nipple of a female mammal.

du·gong, dö'gong, *n.* [Malayan.] A herbivorous mammal of the Indian Ocean and Red Sea, related to the manatee or sea cow, and having flipperlike forelimbs and a rounded, paddlelike tail.

dug·out, dug'out', *n.* A boat made by hollowing out a large log; an underground shelter for troops in trenches; a shelter at the side of a baseball field containing the players' bench.

dui·ker, dī'kėr, *n. pl.* **dui·ker, dui·kers.** [D., diver, diver buck.] Any of the small African antelopes constituting *Cephalophus* and related genera, so-called from their habit of plunging through and under bushes instead of leaping over them. Also **dui·ker·bok.**

duke, dök, dūk, *n.* [Fr. *duc,* < L. *dux, ducis,* a leader, < *duco,* to lead (seen also in duct, ducat, conduct, produce, educate, etc.); cog. O.E. *toga,* a leader, E. *tug* and *tow.*] A nobleman of the highest rank after a prince; the ruler of a duchy; *slang, pl.* fists or hands.—**duke·dom,** *n.* The office or rank of a duke; a duchy.

dul·cet, dul'sit, *a.* [O.Fr. *dolcet,* L. *dulcis,* sweet.] Sweet to the ear; melodious; harmonious; agreeable to the mind or feelings.—*n.* An organ stop producing a tone similar to that of the dulciana but pitched an octave higher.—**dul·cet·ly,** *adv.* —**dul·cet·ness,** *n.*

dul·ci·an·a, dul''sē·an'a, dul''sē·ä'na, *n.* [N.L. < L. *dulcis,* sweet.] An organ stop having metal pipes, and giving thin, incisive, somewhat stringlike tones.

dul·ci·fy, dul'si·fī'', *v.t.*—*dulcified, dulcifying.* [L.L. *dulcificare,* < L. *dulcis,* sweet, and *facere,* make.] To sweeten; render more agreeable; mollify; appease.—**dul·ci·fi·ca·tion,** dul''si·fi·kā'shạn, *n.*

dul·ci·mer, dul'si·mėr, *n.* [Sp. *dulcemele,* It. *dolcimelo,* < L. *dulcis,* sweet.] A musical instrument of trapezoidal form, whose wire strings are struck with hammers held in each hand; an instrument similar to the guitar whose strings are plucked.

dul·cin·e·a, dul''sin'ē·a, dul''si·nē'a, *n.* [< *Dulcinea* (< Sp. *dulce* < L. *dulcis,* sweet), name given by Don Quixote, in Cervantes's romance, to his peasant ladylove.] A ladylove; a mistress; a sweetheart.

dull, dul, *a.* [M.E. *dul, dull,* akin to O.E. *dol,* foolish, stupid, D. *dol,* G. *toll,* mad.] Deficient in understanding or intelligence;

obtuse; stupid; lacking keenness of perception in the senses or feelings; insensible; unfeeling; not intense or acute; as, a *dull* pain; slow in motion or action; not brisk; sluggish, as trade; drowsy or heavy; listless or spiritless; causing ennui or depression; tedious; uninteresting; not sharp, as a knife; blunt, as a point; not bright, intense, or clear, as color, light, or sound; lusterless; dim; muffled.—*v.i.* To make or become dull.—**dull·ish,** *a.*—**dull·ness, dul·ness,** *n.*—**dul·ly,** *adv.*—**dull·ard,** dul'ard, *n.* A person who is stupid.

dulse, duls, *n.* [Gael. *duilliasg,* Ir. *duileasg,* dulse.] An edible, reddish-brown or purple seaweed.

du·ly, dö'lē, dū'lē, *adv.* In a due manner; properly or fittingly; in due season; punctually; adequately or sufficiently.

du·ma, dö'ma, *Russ.* dö'mä, *n.* A representative assembly or council in Russia; (*cap.*) the Russian parliament created in 1905 by Czar Nicholas II, and overthrown by the Bolshevist revolution in 1917.

dumb, dum, *a.* [O.E. *dumb* = Goth. *dumbs,* Dan. *dum,* G. *dumm,* dumb, stupid; allied to *dim,* and perhaps Goth. *daubs,* deaf.] *Colloq.* slow-witted. Mute; without the power of speech; silent; unaccompanied by speech; mimed; as, *dumb* show. *Naut.* without means of propulsion—*v.t.* To silence; deaden.—**dumb·ly,** *adv.*—**dumb·ness,** *n.*

dumb·bell, dum'bel'', *n. Usu. pl.* a weight used for exercising, consisting of two iron or wooden balls with a short bar between them for grasping; *slang,* a stupid person.

dumb show, *n.* A part of dramatic representation performed pantomimically; gestures without words; pantomime.—**dumb-show,** *a.*

dumb·struck, dum'struk'', *a.* Temporarily without speech, because of astonishment or confusion.

dumb·wait·er, dum'wā''tėr, *n.* A small elevator, consisting of a framework with shelves, pulled up and down in a shaft to convey food, small articles, or garbage from floor to floor in a building; a server or other portable stand.

dum·dum, dum'dum'', *n.* [*Dum-Dum,* India.] A soft-nosed bullet which expands on striking.

dum·found, dum·found', dum'found'', *v.t.* To strike dumb with amazement; to astound. Also **dumb·found, dum·found·er, dumb·found·er.**

dum·my, dum'ē, *n. pl.* **dum·mies.** *Slang,* The exposed hand in bridge which is played by the declarer along with his own hand; the player whose hand is exposed; a copy or sham object doing service for a real one; a figure on which merchants display clothing; a person secretly acting as an agent for another; material prepared for the printer; one who is unable to speak; one who is usually silent; one who is stupid.—*a.* Sham; fictitious; counterfeit; artificial; seeming to act for oneself while really acting for another.—*v.t.*—*dummied, dummying.* To prepare material contemplated for printing, often used with *up.*

dump, dump, *v.t.* [M.E. *dumpen, v.t.* and *v.i.,* plunge down: cf. Norw. *dumpa,* Dan. *dumpe,* fall suddenly, Sw. *dumpa,* dip, *dimpa,* tumble, fall.] To throw down in a mass; fling down or drop heavily; to empty out by tilting or overturning; to get rid of suddenly and irresponsibly; *com.* to put on the market, as goods, in large quantities and at a low price; esp. to do this in a foreign country at a price below that charged in the home country or below the cost of production.—*v.i.* To fall suddenly; to throw away garbage.—*n.* A mass of material, as rubbish, dumped or thrown down, or a place where it is deposited; a collection of military supplies, deposited at some point, as near a battlefront, to be distributed for use; the act of dumping; *slang*, a dilapidated place.—**dump·er**, *n.*

dump·ling, dump′ling, *n.* A rounded mass of boiled or steamed dough, often served with stewed meat; a kind of pudding consisting of a wrapping of dough enclosing an apple or other fruit, and boiled or baked; *colloq.* a short and stout person or animal.

dumps, dumps, *n. pl.* [Perhaps akin to *damp.*] *Colloq.* a dull, gloomy state of mind. —**dump·ish**, *a.*—**dump·ish·ly**, *adv.*— **dump·ish·ness**, *n.*

dump truck, *n.* A truck with a special kind of body that can be tilted back to unload the contents through a rear opening.

dump·y, dum′pē, *a.*—**dumpier, dumpiest.** Short and thick.—**dump·i·ly**, *adv.*— **dump·i·ness**, *n.*

dump·y lev·el, *n.* A spirit level used in surveying, mounted under a short telescope that is fixed to a table and capable only of rotary movement in a horizontal plane.

dun, dun, *v.t.*—**dunned, dunning.** [A form of *din.*] To call on for payment repeatedly; to urge importunately.—*n.* One who duns; an urgent demand for payment.

dun, dun, *a.* [O.E. *dunn*, perhaps < W. *dwn*, Gael. *donn*, dun.] Of a grayish brown or dull brown color; marked by dullness and gloom.—*n.* A dull, greyish brown color; a dun-colored horse with a black tail and mane; an immature mayfly; an artificial fly imitating this insect, used in fishing.— **dun·ness**, *n.*

Dun·can Phyfe, dung′kan fīf′, *a.* Of, pertaining to, or constituting furniture designed by, or made in the style of, the American cabinetmaker, Duncan Phyfe, 1768–1854.

dunce, duns, *n.* [From *Duns Scotus*, the leader of the Schoolmen of the 14th century, opposed to the revival of classical learning; hence this name was given to his followers in contempt by their opponents.] An ignoramus; a person too stupid to learn; a dullard.

dun·der·head, dun′dėr·hed″, *n.* [Akin Dan. *dummerhoved*, a dunderhead, lit. stupid-head, < *dum*, stupid.] A dunce. Also **dun·der·pate**, dun′dėr·pāt″.—**dun·- der·head·ed**, *a.*

dun·drea·ries, dun″dri′ar·ēz, *n. pl.* Long side whiskers worn without a beard.

dune, dūn, *n.* [O.E. *dūn*, down.] A hill or ridge of sand formed by wind, and most often found near lakes and oceans or in deserts.

dung, dung, *n.* [O.E. *dung*, G. *dung*. Sw. *dynga*, manure pile.] The excrement of animals.—*v.t.* To manure with dung.— **dung·y**, *a.*

dun·ga·ree, dun″ga·rē′, *n.* [Anglo-Indian, low, common, vulgar.] A coarse, durable cotton, generally blue, used for work clothes, overalls, or pants. *Pl.* such clothing made of this cotton twill; blue jeans.

dung bee·tle, *n.* Any of various scarabaeid beetles that feed upon or breed in dung.

dun·geon, dun′jon, *n.* [Fr. *dongeon, donjon.*] A strong, close prison or cell, generally underground; donjon.

dung·hill, dung′hil″, *n.* A heap of dung; the place where dung is kept collected; a repugnant or vile place, thing, or situation.

du·nite, dō′nīt, dun′īt, *n.* [From *Dun* Mountain, in New Zealand.] An igneous rock of the peridotite group, having granitic structure, composed chiefly of olivine, ranging from yellow to dark green in color, and found in North Carolina, Georgia, and New Zealand.

dunk, dungk, *v.t.* [Amer. < L.G. *dunken*, to dip.] To dip into a liquid before eating; to

dip or temporarily submerge into a liquid.— *v.i.* To dip or submerge a person, thing, or oneself in water or other liquid.—**dunk·er**, *n.*

Dunk·er, dung′kėr, *n.* A member of a Christian sect founded in Germany and reorganized in the U.S., characterized by the practice of threefold immersion in baptism.—Also **Dun·kard, Tun·ker**, dung′kėrd, tung′kėr.

dun·lin, dun′lin, *n. pl.* **dun·lins, dun·lin.** A red-backed sandpiper, *Erolia alpina*, about eight inches long: found widely in the Northern Hemisphere.

dun·nage, dun′ij, *n.* Temporary blocks or braces installed to protect freight in the hold of a ship, in a railroad car, or in a truck; padding used in a shipping container; baggage.—*v.t.*—*dunnaged, dunnaging.* To stow or secure with pieces of wood; to pack with dunnage.

du·o, dō′ō, dū′ō, *n. pl.* **du·os.** [It. < L. *duo*, two.] A pair; *mus.* a duet.

du·o·de·cil·lion, dō″ō·di·sil′yan, dū″ō·- di·sil′yan, *n. pl.* **du·o·de·cil·lions.** A cardinal number indicated by 1 followed by 39 zeros in the American and French numbering systems, and by 1 followed by 72 zeros in the British and German systems.

du·o·dec·i·mal, dō″o·des′i·mal, dū″o·- des′i·mal, *a.* [L. *duodecim*, twelve.] Proceeding in computation by twelves; of or referring to 12 or twelfths. Also *duodenary.* —*n.* One part of 12 equal parts; a number in a numbering system with base 12.

du·o·dec·i·mo, dō″o·des′i·mō, dū″o·- des′i·mō, *n. pl.* **du·o·dec·i·mos.** A book in which a sheet is folded into 12 leaves or 24 pages; the size of a book consisting of sheets so folded: usu. indicated as 12mo. Also *twelvemo.*—*a.* Having or consisting of 12 leaves to a sheet.

du·o·den·a·ry, dō″o·den′a·rē, dō″o·- dē′no·rē, dū″o·den′a·rē, dū″o·dē′no·rē, *a.* [L. *duodenarius.*] Duodecimal.

du·o·de·num, dū″o·dē′num, dū·od′e·num, *n. pl.* **du·o·de·na, du·o·de·nas.** [< L. *duodeni*, twelve each, so called because its length is about twelve fingers' breadth.] The first portion of the small intestine, extending from the stomach to the jejunum. —**du·o·de·nal**, dū″o·dēn′al, dū″od′e·nal, *a.* Connected with or relating to the duodenum.

du·o·logue, dō′o·lag″, dō′o·log″, dū′o·- lag″, dū′o·log″, *n.* [L. *duo*, two, *-logue*, < *dialogue.*] A dialogue or conversation between two persons; a dramatic performance limited to two actors.

du·op·o·ly, dō·op′o·lē, dū·op′o·lē, *n. pl.* **du·op·o·lies.** A marketing situation which exists when there are only two sellers. See *monopoly.*

du·op·so·ny, dū·op′so·nē, *n. pl.* **du·op·- so·nies.** A marketing situation which exists when there are only two buyers.

dup, dup, *v.t.*—**dupped, dupping.** [For *do up.*] *Archaic*, to raise the latch of; to open.

dupe, dōp, dūp, *n.* [Fr. *dupe*, a name sometimes given to the hoopoe, and hence, from the bird being regarded as stupid, applied to a stupid person.] A person who is easily cheated, or one easily led astray by his credulity.—*v.t.*—*duped, duping.* [Fr. *duper.*] To make a dupe of; to trick; to deceive.— **dup·a·ble**, *a.*—**dup·a·bil·i·ty**, *n.*—**dup·- er**, *n.*—**dup·er·y**, dū′pe·rē, *n.* The art of duping or an instance of it; the condition of one who is duped.

dupe, dōp, dūp, *a., n., v.t.*—*duped, duping. Slang*, duplicate.

du·ple, dō′pl, dū′pl, *a.* [L. *duplus*, DOUBLE.] Having two members or parts; double; twofold, as: A *duple* ratio is one like 2 to 1 or 8 to 4. *Mus.* characterized by two or a multiple of two beats to the measure; as, *duple* meter.

du·plex, dō′pleks, dū′pleks, *a.* [L.] Double; twofold; *mach.* having two working parts that operate at the same time or in an identical manner; of a system allowing simultaneous telecommunications in opposite directions over one channel.—*n.* Anything that is double or twofold. An apartment of rooms on two floors; also **du·plex a·part·ment.**—**du·plex·i·ty**, *n.*

du·pli·cate, dō′pli·kāt, dū′pli·kāt, *v.t.*— *duplicated, duplicating.* [L. *duplicatus*, pp. of *duplicare*, double, < *duplex.*] To double; make two-fold; to copy exactly; to reproduce in every detail.—dō′pli·kit, dū′pli·kit, *a.* Double; consisting of or existing in two corresponding parts of examples; exactly like or corresponding to something else.— **du·pli·cate bridge**, *n.* A form of bridge in which identical hands are pre-dealt to sets of players in order to compare scores.

du·pli·cate, dō′pli·kit, dū′pli·kit, *n.* One of two things exactly alike; a copy exactly like an original; in general, anything corresponding in all respects to something else; a counterpart or double.—**in du·pli·- cate**, in two copies, exactly alike.

du·pli·ca·tion, dō″pli·kā′shan, dūp″li·kā′- shan, *n.* [L. *duplicatio(n-).*] The act of duplicating, or the state of being duplicated; a duplicate.—**du·pli·ca·tive**, *a.*

du·pli·ca·tor, dō′pli·kā″tėr, dū′pli·kā″tėr, *n.* One who or that which duplicates, esp. a machine for producing copies.

du·plic·i·ty, dō·plis′i·tē, dū·plis′i·tē, *n.* [O.Fr. *duplicite* (Fr. *duplicité*), < L.L. *duplicitas*, doubleness, < L. *duplex.*] The fact or practice of speaking or acting in two ways in relation to the same matter with intent to deceive; double-dealing; the state or quality of being twofold or double; *law*, the pleading of two or more distinct matters in one plea.

du·ra·ble, dur′a·bl, *a.* [O.Fr. Fr. *durable*, < L. *durabilis*, < *durare*, last.] Lasting or enduring; holding out well against wear or any destructive change.—**du·ra·bil·- i·ty, du·ra·ble·ness**, *n.*—**du·ra·bly**, *adv.*

du·ra·ble goods, *n. pl.* Merchandise that can be used over a long period of time, as machinery, automobiles, and appliances. Also **hard goods.**

Du·ral·u·min, du·ral′ū·min, dyu̇·ral″ū·- min, *n.* [G., from *Düren*, town in Rhenish Prussia where it was first made, and *alumin*, aluminum.] A strong, light alloy of aluminum, copper, manganese, magnesium, and small amounts of iron and silicon, used mainly in aircraft construction. (Trademark.)

du·ra ma·ter, dur′a mā′tėr, *n.* [M.L. "hard mother."] *Anat.* the tough, fibrous membrane forming the outermost of the three coverings of the brain and spinal cord.

du·ra·men, du·rā′min, dū·rā′min, *n.* [L. *duramen*, hardness, < *durus*, hard.] The central wood or heartwood of an exogenous tree.

dur·ance, dur′ans, *n.* [Apparently shortened from *endurance*, from the hardships of imprisonment.] Imprisonment; custody.

du·ra·tion, du·rā′shan, *n.* [L.L. *duratio*, < *durare*, to last.] Continuance in time; the time during which anything lasts.

dur·bar, dur′bär, *n.* [Hind. and Pers. *darbâr*—Pers. *dâr*, door, and *bâr*, court, audience, assembly.] *Ind.* An audience room in the palaces of the native princes; state levee or audience held by the governor-general, or by a native prince, before India became a republic; an official reception; royal court or assembly.

du·ress, du·res′, dyu̇·res′, dur′is, dyur′is, *n.* [O.Fr. *duresse*, hardship, constraint, < L. *duritia*, harshness, hardness, < *durus*, hard.] Coercion; imprisonment; restraint of liberty; *law*, restraint or coercion which renders void a contract or legal act.

Dur·ham, dẽr'am, *n.* One of a breed of short-horned cattle originating in the county of Durham, England.

du·ri·an, dụr'ē·an, *n.* [Malay *durian*, < *dūrī*, thorn.] The edible fruit of a tree of the East Indies, *Durio zibethinus*, with a hard, prickly rind, tasty flesh, and very offensive odor.

dur·ing, dụr'ing, dẽr'ing, *prep.* [< L. phrase *vita durante*, while life lasts.] Throughout the course or existence of; at a point in.

dur·mast, dẽr'mast", dẽr'mäst", *n.* A European oak, *Quercus sessiliflora* or *Q. petraea*, with a heavy, elastic wood, highly valued for use in making furniture or constructing buildings.

du·ro, dụr'ō, *Sp.* dō'Rạ, *n.* pl. **du·ros.** The silver dollar or peso of Spain and some countries of Spanish America.

du·roc, dẽr'ok, *n.* (*Often cap.*) any of a breed of red American hogs noted for their hardiness.

du·rom·e·ter, dụ·rom'e·tẽr, *n.* An instrument used for measuring hardness, consisting of a small drill or indenter point working under pressure.

dur·ra, dụr'a, *n.* [Ar.] A species of grain sorghum much cultivated in Africa, Asia, the south of Europe, and warm, dry regions of the U.S. Also **In·di·an mil·let, Guin·ea corn.**

du·rum wheat, dẽr'um hwēt, dyẽr'um hwēt, dẽr'um wēt, dyẽr'um wēt, *n.* A variety of wheat that yields a flour used for the production of spaghetti, macaroni, and related foods.

dusk, dusk, *a.* [M.E. *deosc, dosc:* cf. O.E. *dox*, dark.] Dark; tending to darkness; dusky.—*n.* The darker stage of twilight; moderate darkness; shade; gloom.—*v.i.* To become dusk; grow dark; present a dusky appearance.—*v.t.* To make dusky; darken; dim.—**dusk·y**, *a.*—*duskier, duskiest.* Somewhat dark; dark-colored, esp. having dark-colored skin; deficient in light; dim; gloomy.—**dusk·i·ly**, *adv.*—**dusk·i·ness**, *n.*

dust, dust, *n.* [O.E. *dūst* = M.L.G. = *dust* = Icel. *dust*, dust: cf. G. *dunst*, vapor.] Earth or other matter in fine, dry particles, so small and light as to be easily raised and carried by the wind; any finely powdered substance; a cloud of finely powdered earth or other matter in the air, as that raised by the trampling of persons or animals; *fig.* confusion or turmoil; surface of the earth; the ground, esp. as a burial place; that to which anything, as the human body, is reduced by disintegration or decay; low or mean condition; *Brit.* dust, ashes, and other refuse from a house. Gold dust.—**dust·less**, *a.*—**dust·like**, *a.*

dust, dust, *v.t., v.i.* To free from dust; wipe the dust from; to sprinkle with dust or powder; strew or sprinkle as dust.

dust bowl, *n.* An area subject to violent and frequent dust storms, esp. an area in S. central U.S., formerly plagued by such storms.—**dust bowl·er**, *n.*

dust dev·il, *n.* A small whirlwind, filled with sand and dust, commonly seen in hot, dry regions. Also **dust whirl.**

dust·er, dus'tẽr, *n.* One who or that which dusts; an apparatus for sprinkling a dust or powder on something; anything, as a cloth or a machine, for removing dust; a long, light overgarment to protect the clothing from dust; a woman's short, light-weight dressing gown. A trial wellhole which fails to reach water, or an unproductive boring for oil or gas. Also **dry hole.**

dust·ing, dus'ting, *n.* Process of removing dust; a sprinkling of a dry substance; *slang*, a defeat by a beating.

dust jack·et, *n.* A removable paper cover for a book, used to protect the binding. Also **book jack·et.**

dust·man, dust'man", dust'man, *n.* pl. **dust·men.** *Brit.* One employed to remove garbage or other waste. The sandman.

dust·pan, dust'pan", *n.* A utensil into which dust is swept for the purpose of removal.

dust storm, *n.* A wind storm which raises dense masses of dust into the air, occurring during a drought in areas of arable land, as distinguished from a sandstorm which occurs in desert regions.

dust·y, dus'tē, *a.*—*dustier, dustiest.* Filled or covered with dust; clouded with or as with dust; of the nature of dust; powdery.—**dust·i·ly**, *adv.*—**dust·i·ness**, *n.*

Dutch, duch, *n.* [G. *deutsch*, German, Germanic, pertaining to the Germanic or Teutonic race; O.H.G. *diutisc*, < *diot*, O.E *theod*, Goth. *thiuda*, people.] *Pl.* originally, the Germanic race or the German peoples generally, now only the people of the Netherlands and their immediate descendants. The language of these people; *U.S., pl.* the Pennsylvania Dutch.—*a.* Pertaining to the Netherlands, its people, or their languages. *U.S.* of or relating to the Pennsylvania Dutch; *slang*, disfavor.

dutch, duch, *adv.* (*Often cap.*) with each person paying his own expenses.

Dutch clo·ver, *n.* White clover, a valuable pasture plant.

Dutch cour·age, *n.* False courage motivated by intoxicants.

Dutch door, *n.* A door divided horizontally, allowing the upper half to be opened while the lower remains shut, or vice versa.

Dutch elm dis·ease, *n.* *Plant pathol.* a disease of elms caused by a fungus, *Ceratostomella ulmi*, which is transmitted by bark beetles, and which causes defoliation, decay, and death of the elm.

Dutch·man, duch'man, *n.* pl. **Dutch·men.** A native of the Netherlands; *building*, a wedge or other contrivance used to hide or counteract a structural fault; *theatr.* a narrow strip of canvas that conceals the crack between two scenery flats.

Dutch·man's-breech·es, *n. pl., sing. or pl. in constr.* [So named for the shape of the flowers.] A wild spring-flowering herb, *Dicentra cucullaria*, with creamy white double-spurred blossoms.

Dutch ov·en, *n.* A cast iron pot or any heavily constructed kettle with a close-fitting cover; a metal utensil, that opens in front, used for roasting close to an open fire or on top of a stove; a brick oven in which the walls are preheated for cooking.

Dutch treat, *n.* A meal or entertainment for which each person pays his own expenses.

Dutch un·cle, *n.* *Colloq.* a person who bluntly and sternly criticizes or admonishes someone else.

du·te·ous, dō'tē·us, dū'tē·us, *a.* Dutiful; obedient.—**du·te·ous·ly**, *adv.*—**du·te·ous·ness**, *n.*

du·ti·a·ble, dō'tē·a·bl, dū'tē·a·bl, *a.* Subject to the imposition of duty or customs.

du·ti·ful, dō'ti·ful, dū'ti·ful, *a.* Performing the duties or obligations required by law, justice, or propriety; obedient; submissive to superiors; respectful; reverential; required by duty; expressive of respect or a sense of duty; as, *dutiful* care.—**du·ti·ful·ly**, *adv.*—**du·ti·ful·ness**, *n.*

du·ty, dō'tē, dū'tē, *n.* pl. **du·ties.** [< due.] That which a person is bound by any natural, moral, or legal obligation to do or perform; the obligation to do something; an act of obedience or respect, esp. respectful conduct toward one's parents or elders; any task one is asked to perform; an action or task required by any business, office, or service; active military service; a tax, esp. an import tax.

du·um·vir, dō·um'vẽr, dū·um'vẽr, *n.* pl. **du·um·virs, du·um·vi·ri**, dū·um'vi·rē.

[L., for *duovir*, usually pl. *duoviri*, < *duo*, two, and *viri*, pl. of *vir*, man.] *Rom. hist.* one of two officers or magistrates united in the same public office; either of two persons jointly holding power.

du·um·vi·rate, dō·um'vẽr·it, dū·um'vẽr·it, *n.* [L. *duumviratus*.] A union of two men in the same office, as in ancient Rome; an association of two persons in any office; the office or government of such persons.

du·ve·tyn, dō'vi·tēn", *n.* A soft, flexible, closely woven fabric of wool, cotton, silk, or synthetic fibers, with a thick, fine, velvety nap. Also **du·ve·tine, du·ve·tyne.**

dwarf, dwạrf, *n.* [O.E. *dweorg* = D. *dwerg* = G. *zwerg* = Icel. *dvergr*.] A human being much smaller than the ordinary stature or size; a pygmy; an animal or plant much below the ordinary size of its kind or species; a mythical being, usually small and ugly, credited with magical powers.—*a.* Of unusually small stature or size; dwarfish; diminutive.

dwarf, dwạrf, *v.t.* To render dwarf or dwarfish; hinder from growing to the natural size; prevent the due intellectual or moral development of; to render insignificant in extent or character; to cause to appear or seem small, as by comparison.—*v.i.* To become dwarfed or smaller.—**dwarf·ish**, *a.*—**dwarf·ish·ly**, *adv.*—**dwarf·ish·ness**, *n.*

dwell, dwel, *v.i.*—*dwelt* or sometimes *dwelled, dwelling.* [M.E. *dwellen*, delay, tarry, abide, earlier tr., O.E. *dwellan*, *dwelian*, lead astray, hinder, delay, = Icel. *dvelja*, delay, intr. tarry, wait.] To abide as a permanent resident; to reside; to live; to continue for a time; linger or pause in thought or action; to place emphasis upon a point in a discourse.

dwell·ing, dwel'ing, *n.* A place of residence or abode; a house.

dwin·dle, dwin'dl, *v.i.*—*dwindled, dwindling.* [Freq. < O.Fr. and Sc. *dwine*; O.E. *dwinan*, to pine, waste away = D. *dwijnen*, Icel. *dvina*, Dan. *tvine*, to pine.] To diminish gradually; to become small and insignificant; to shrink; to waste away; to degenerate.—*v.t.* To cause to diminish gradually; to make smaller.

DX, abbr. indicating distance in radio transmissions, as between distant stations. Also **D.X.**

dy·ad, dī'ad, *n.* [L.L. *dyas* (dyad-), < Gr. *dyas* (dyad-), < *duo*, two.] A group of two; a couple; *chem.* an element, atom, or radical having a valence of two; *biol.* a secondary morphological unit, consisting of an aggregate of monads.—**dy·ad·ic**, dī·ad'ik, *a.*

dy·ar·chy, dī'är·kē, *n.* pl. **dy·ar·chies.** [Gr. *duo*, two, *archē*, rule.] See *diarchy*.

dyb·buk, dib·buk, dib'uk, *Heb.* dē·bōk', *n.* pl. **dyb·buks, dib·buks, dyb·bu·kim, dib·bu·kim**, di·bụk'im, *Heb.* dē"bō·kēm'. A demon or the spirit of a dead person that, according to medieval Jewish belief, enters a living person and controls his actions until exorcised by religious means.

dye, dī, *n.* [O.E. *dēag, dēah*.] Color or hue, esp. as produced by dyeing; a coloring material or matter; a liquid containing coloring matter for imparting a particular hue to cloth, paper, or hair.

dye, dī, *v.t.*—*dyed, dyeing.* [O.E. *dēagian*.] To give a new and often permanent color to, esp. by treating or impregnating with dye; to impart, as color, by means of a dye.—*v.i.* To impart color by treating with dye; to become colored when treated with a dye.—**dy·er**, *n.*—**dy·a·ble**, *a.*

dyed-in-the-wool, dīd'n·the·wụl', *a.* *Colloq.* confirmed; complete and unqualified; as, a *dyed-in-the-wool* conservative.

---

ch- chain, G. na*ch*t;   **th-** THen, thin;   **w-** wig, hw as sound in whig;   **z-** zh as in azure, zeal.   *Italicized vowel* indicates schwa sound.

dy·er's-weed, dī'erz·wēd″, *n.* Any of various plants yielding dyes, as the weld, *Reseda luteola,* the dyeweed, *Genista tinctoria,* or the woad, *Isatis tinctoria.*

dye-stuff, dī'stuf″, *n.* Coloring matter used in dyeing.

dye-weed, dī'wēd″, *n.* A fabaceous shrub, *Genista tinctoria,* a native of the Old World, bearing yellow flowers and yielding a yellow dye; woadwaxen. Also **dy·er's-broom.**

dye-wood, dī'wụd″, *n.* Any wood yielding a coloring matter used for dyeing.

dy·ing, dī'ing, *a.* Ceasing to exist; nearing death; given, uttered, or manifested just before death; as, *dying* words; pertaining to or associated with death; as, *dying* hour; drawing to a close; fading away.—*n.* The act or process of ceasing to exist.

dyke, dīk, *n., v.t.* See *dike.*

dy·nam·e·ter, dī·nam'i·tėr, *n. Opt.* an instrument for determining the magnifying power of a telescope.

dy·nam·ic, dī·nam'ik, *a.* [Gr. *dynamikos,* powerful, efficacious, < *dynamis,* power, < *dynasthai,* be able.] Of or pertaining to force not in equilibrium, or to force in any state; pertaining to dynamics; pertaining to or characterized by energy or effective action; active; energetic, forceful, or effective; *med.* functional, not organic, as a disease.—*n.* Dynamics; motive force.—**dy·nam·i·cal,** *a.*—**dy·nam·i·cal·ly,** *adv.*

dy·nam·ics, dī·nam'iks, *n. Phys.* the study of the description and the causes of the motion of systems of particles under the influence of forces: opposed to *kinematics* and *statics.*

dy·na·mism, dī'na·miz″um, *n.* [Gr. *dynamis,* power: DYNAMIC.] Any of various doctrines or philosophical systems which seek to explain the phenomena of nature by the action of some force; great energy or vitality.

dy·na·mite, dī'na·mīt″, *n.* An explosive consisting of nitroglycerin in an absorbent substance.—*v.t.* To shatter with dynamite. —**dy·na·mit·ic,** dī·*na*·mit'ik, *a.*—**dy·na·mit·er,** *n.* One who uses dynamite, esp. for purposes of revolution.

dy·na·mo, dī'na·mō″, *n.* Dynamoelectric machine; a machine for converting energy from a mechanical into an electrical form by the use of electromagnets; a generator; *slang,* an energetic person.

dy·na·mo·e·lec·tric, dī″na·mō·i·lek'trik, *a.* Pertaining to the conversion of mechanical energy into electric energy, or vice versa. Also **dy·na·mo·e·lec·tri·cal.**

dy·na·mom·e·ter, dī″no·mom'i·tėr, *n.* An instrument for measuring force or power, esp. that of machines or the strength of materials.—**dy·na·mo·met·ric, dy·na·mo·met·ri·cal,** *a.* Of or pertaining to the measurement of force.

dy·na·mo·tor, dī'na·mō″tėr, *n.* A combined electrical motor and generator, used for changing electric current from one type to another or for changing voltages, esp. in portable radio equipment.

dy·nast, dī'nast, dī'nast, *Brit.* din'ast, *n.* [L. *dynastes,* < Gr. *dynastes,* < *dynasthai,* be able, have power.] A ruler or potentate, esp. a hereditary ruler.

dy·nas·ty, dī'na·stē, *Brit.* din'a·stē, *n. pl.* **dy·nas·ties.** [Gr. *dynasteia,* sovereignty, < *dynastēs,* a lord or chief, < *dynamai,* to be strong, *dynamis,* power.] A succession of rulers of the same line or family, who govern a particular country; the period during which they rule.—**dy·nas·tic, dy·nas·ti·cal,** *a.*—**dy·nas·ti·cal·ly,** *adv.*

dyne, dīn, *n.* [Gr. *dynamis,* power, DYNAMIC.] *Phys.* the unit of force in the centimeter-gram-second system, being that force which, acting on a mass of one gram, gives it an acceleration of one centimeter per second per second. Abbr. *dyn.*

Dy·nel, dī·nel', *n.* A strong, fast-drying, noncombustible synthetic fiber used in textiles and wigmaking; fabric or yarn made of this synthetic fiber. (Trademark.)

dy·node, dī'nōd, *n. Electronics,* an electrode whose function is to produce secondary emission of electrons for amplification of the electric current in an electron tube. Also *electron multiplier.*

dys·bar·ism, dis'bä·riz″um, *n.* A bodily condition, the symptoms of which include headaches, bends, and mental disturbances, resulting from the existence of a pressure differential between the surrounding air pressure and the pressure of dissolved and free gases within the body tissues, fluids, and cavities.

dys·cra·sia, dis·krā'zha, dis·krā'zē·a, *n.* [M.L. < Gr. *dyskrasia,* < *dyskratos,* badly tempered.] *Pathol.* a generally faulty or disordered condition of the body.—**dys·cras·ic,** dis·kraz'ik, dis·kras'ik, *a.*

dys·en·ter·y, dis'en·ter″ē, *n.* [L. *dysenteria,* < Gr. *dysenteria,* < *dys-,* ill, and *enteron,* intestine.] *Pathol.* an infectious disease characterized by inflammation and ulceration of the lower portion of the bowels, with diarrhea that soon becomes mucous and hemorrhagic; *colloq.* diarrhea.—**dys·en·ter·ic,** *a.*

dys·func·tion, dis·fungk'shan, *n. Med.* abnormal or impaired functioning, as of an organ.—**dys·func·tion·al,** *a.*

dys·gen·ics, dis·jen'iks, *n. pl. but sing. in constr.* The scientific study of factors that cause degeneration in the type of offspring produced.

dys·lo·gis·tic, dis″lo·jis'tik, *a.* [Formed on the model of *eulogistic, dys* signifying ill, and the word having therefore the opposite signification of *eulogistic.*] Conveying censure, disapproval, or opprobrium; uncomplimentary.—**dys·lo·gis·ti·cal·ly,** *adv.*

dys·pep·sia, dis·pep'sha, dis·pep'sē·a, *n.* [L. < Gr. *dyspepsia,* < *dyspeptos,* hard to digest, < *dys-,* hard, and *peptein,* cook, digest.] Impaired digestion; indigestion.— **dys·pep·tic,** *a.* Pertaining to, subject to, or suffering from dyspepsia; morbidly gloomy; peevish or cross.—*n.* A person subject to or suffering from dyspepsia.—**dys·pep·ti·cal·ly,** *adv.*

dys·pha·gia, dis·fā'ja, dis·fā'jē·a, *n.* [Gr. *dys,* ill, and *phagō,* to eat.] *Pathol.* difficulty in swallowing.—**dys·phag·ic,** dis·faj'ik, *a.*

dys·pho·ri·a, dis·fōr'ē·a, dis·fạr'ē·a, *n.* A general feeling of anxiety, depression, and restlessness.—**dys·phor·ic,** dis·fạr'ik, dis·for'ik, *a.*

dys·pla·si·a, dis·plā'zha, dis·plā'zhē·a, dis·plā'zē·a, *n.* Abnormal development or growth, as of cells, organs, or tissues; abnormality in anatomic structure due to such growth.—**dys·plas·tic,** dis·plas'tik, *a.*

dys·pro·si·um, dis·prō'sē·um, dis·prō'-shē·um, *n.* [N.L.] *Chem.* a metallic rare-earth element which forms highly magnetic compounds, used in nuclear reactions as a neutron absorber; in compound form used primarily as a high purity semiconductor. Sym. Dy, at. no. 66.

dys·tel·e·ol·o·gy, dis″tel·ē·ol'o·jē, dis″-tē·lē·ol'o·jē, *n. Philos.* the doctrine of purposelessness in nature, as opposed to design.—**dys·tel·e·o·log·i·cal,** dis″tel·ē·o·loj'i·kal, dis″tē·lē·o·loj'i·kal, *a.*—**dys·tel·e·ol·o·gist,** *n.*

dys·tro·phy, dis'tro·fē, *n.* [N.L. *dystrophia,* < Gr. *dys-,* ill, and *trephein,* nourish.] *Med.* faulty nutrition or abnormal development; *pathol.* any of several neuromuscular ailments marked by degeneration or weakness of muscle. Also **dys·tro·phi·a,** di·strō'fē·a.—**dys·troph·ic,** dis·trof'ik, *a.*

dys·u·ri·a, dis·ūr'ē·a, *n.* [Gr. *dysouria.*] *Pathol.* difficulty or pain in discharging urine.—**dys·u·ric,** *a.*

E

E, e, ē, *n.* The second vowel and the fifth letter of the English alphabet, occurring more frequently than any other letter of the alphabet; the graphic representation of this letter; any spoken sound represented by this letter; anything shaped like the letter E. *U.S.* a school grade of fifth rank indicating failure or sometimes a conditional pass; a school grade equated with excellent or outstanding achievement. (*Cap.*) *mus.* the third tone in the natural scale of C; the written musical note representing this tone. (*l.c.*) *math.* the base of the system of natural logarithms.

each, ēch, *a.* [O.E. *ǣlc,* < *ā,* ever, and *gelīc,* like.] Every one of any number separately considered or treated; every one of two or more considered individually, as: *Each* child carried his lunch to school.—*pron.* Each one; all of a group or aggregate considered one by one, as: *Each* struggled manfully with the job.—*adv.* To, for, or from each; apiece, as: They received one apple *each.*

each oth·er, *pron.* Each the other, as: They struck *each other.* Used also as a compound reciprocal pronoun in oblique cases, as: They struck at *each other.*

ea·ger, ē'gėr, *a.* [O.E. *egre,* O.Fr. *eigre,* Mod.Fr. *aigre,* eager, sharp, biting, < L. *acer, acris,* sharp.] Characterized by enthusiastic, keen, ardent, or impatient feelings, interests, or desires; marked by great earnestness or diligence.—**ea·ger·ly,** ē'gėr·lē, *adv.*—**ea·ger·ness,** ē'gėr·nes, *n.*

ea·ger bea·ver, *n. Slang,* an overly zealous or diligent individual, particularly one who seems to seek special favor by his zealous performance.

ea·gle, ē'gl, *n.* [Fr. *aigle,* < L. *aquila, fem.,* an eagle.] A common name for many large, very strong birds of prey of the family *Accipitridae,* characterized by a hooked beak, sharp talons, and great powers of flight and vision; a representation of such a bird, often used as an emblem; any seal or standard having such a figure, as the military standard of ancient Rome and the seal or standard of the U.S.; *milit.* insignia of rank worn by a colonel or naval captain. A former gold coin of the U.S. worth ten dollars; a reading desk or lectern in the form of an eagle with expanded wings; *golf,* a score of two under par on any but a par-three hole. (*Cap.*) *astron.* the constellation Aquila.—**eag·let,** ē'glit, *n.* A young eagle.

ea·gle eye, *n.* Unusually keen visual power; the ability to watch or observe carefully, esp. details, as: He read the contract with an *eagle eye.* One who possesses an eagle eye.—**ea·gle-eyed,** *a.*

ea·gre, ē'gėr, ā'gėr, *n.* [O.E. *eágor, égor,* Icel. *ǽgir,* the sea.] A tidal wave moving up a river or estuary at spring tide; a bore. Also **ea·ger.**

ear, ēr, *n.* [O.E. *eare* = D. *oor,* Icel. *eyra,* Dan. *ore,* G. *ohr,* L. *auris,* G. *ous.*] The organ of hearing which, in man and higher animals, is composed of the external ear, a cartilaginous funnel for collecting the sound waves and directing them inward, the middle ear, called typanum or drum, and the internal ear or labyrinth; the external ear alone; the sense of hearing; the power to distinguish sounds, esp. acute perception of the differences of musical tone and pitch; a favorable hearing; attention; heed; a part of any inanimate object resembling an ear; a projecting part from the side of anything, as the handle of a pitcher.—**eared,** ērd, *a.* Having ears or ear-like protrusions.—**be all ears,** to give one's full attention.—**bend**

one's ear, *slang,* to talk constantly to a person, often boring him.—**fall on deaf ears,** to go unheeded or be ignored.—**in one ear and out the oth·er,** heard but put out of mind.—**pin one's ears back,** *slang,* to defeat someone thoroughly; to beat someone soundly.—**up to the ears,** deeply involved; almost fully immersed.

ear, ēr, *n.* [O.E. *ear,* D. *aar,* G. *ähre,* an ear.] A spike or head of corn or other grain; that part of cereal plants which contains the flowers and seeds.—*v.i.* To form ears, as corn.—**eared,** ērd, *a.*

ear·ache, ēr'āk", *n.* Pain in the ear.

ear·drop, ēr'drop", *n.* A pendent earring.

ear·drum, ēr'drum", *n.* The tympanic membrane which separates the middle ear from the external ear.

ear·ful, ēr'ful, *n.* pl. **ear·fuls.** A large quantity of oral news or gossip, esp. when unsolicited; a harsh verbal rebuke.

earl, url, *n.* [O.E. *eorl,* Icel., Dan., and Sw. *jarl,* an earl.] *Brit.* a nobleman, the third in rank, being directly below a marquis, and above a viscount.—**earl·dom,** url'dom, *n.* The rank of an earl.

ear·lap, ēr'lap", *n.* The lobe of the ear; the whole external ear; one of the flaps attached to a cap, for covering the ears in cold weather.

earl mar·shal, *n.* An officer of state in Great Britain who serves as the head of the College of Arms, as a marshal of state processions, and, on ceremonial occasions, as a royal attendant.

ear lobe, *n.* The soft, pendent part of the human ear or the ear of certain fowls.

ear·ly, ur'lē, *adv.*—**earlier, earliest.** [O.E. *ærlīce,* < *ær.* ERE.] In or during the first part of some division of time, or of some course or series; far back in time; anciently; before the usual or appointed time.—*a.* Of, pertaining to, or occurring near the beginning of some division of time, or of some course or series; belonging to a period far back in time; ancient; occurring before the usual or appointed time; occurring in the near future.—**ear·li·ness,** *n.*

ear·ly bird, *n. Colloq.* a person who arises early; a person who arrives before others.—**Ear·ly Bird,** *n.* A communications satellite used to transmit microwave signals between North America and Europe.

ear·mark, ēr'märk", *n.* A mark on the ear for distinguishing ownership of sheep, pigs, or cattle; any mark for distinction or identification.—*v.t.* To distinguish by putting an earmark on; to set apart, as funds, for a specific purpose.

ear·muff, ēr'muf", *n. often pl.* one of a pair of adjustable coverings for protecting the ears in cold weather.

earn, urn, *v.t.* [O.E. *earnian,* earn, akin to O.H.G. *arnon,* reap, G. *ernte,* harvest.] To gain by labor or service rendered; to gain as a due return or profit; to get as one's desert or due; to bring about or procure as deserved; to merit as compensation; deserve.

ear·nest, ur'nist, *a.* [O.E. *eorneste.*] Serious in intention, purpose, or effort; sincerely zealous; characterized by or evincing depth and sincerity of feeling; of serious importance, or demanding serious attention.—*n.* [O.E. *eornost* = D. and G. *ernst.*] Seriousness, as of intention or purpose.—**in ear·nest,** seriously; having, or with, a serious purpose.—**ear·nest·ly,** *adv.*—**ear·nest·ness,** *n.*

ear·nest, ur'nist, *n.* [< W. *ernes,* earnest or pledge, < *ern,* a pledge.] Something paid, delivered, or done beforehand, as a pledge and security for the whole, or as a token of more to come; anything which gives assurance, promise, or indication of what is to follow; token.—**ear·nest mon·ey,** *law,* money paid as earnest to bind a bargain or ratify and prove a sale.

earn·ings, ur'ningz, *n. pl.* That which is earned; what is gained or deserved by labor, services, or performance; wages; reward; recompense; profit.

ear·phone, ēr'fōn", *n.* A device, worn over or in the ear, in which electrical energy is converted into sound waves.

ear·ring, ēr'ring", ēr'ing, *n.* An ornament worn on or hanging from the lobe of the ear.

ear shell, *n.* Abalone.

ear·shot, ēr'shot", *n.* The distance within which a sound can be heard; hearing distance.

ear·split·ting, ēr'split"ing, *a.* Extremely loud; distressingly shrill; deafening.

earth, urth, *n.* [O.E. *eorthe* = D. *aarde* = G. *erde* = Icel. *jördh* = Goth. *airtha,* earth.] (*Often cap.*) the planet which is third in order from the sun, with an equatorial diameter of 7,926 miles, a polar diameter of 7,900 miles, a mass of approximately six sextillion tons, and a mean density of about 5.6 times that of water. The human inhabitants of the globe, as: The plague of war swept the *earth.* This planet as the habitat of man, often in contrast to heaven and hell; the realm of temporal affairs as opposed to spiritual matters. Broadly, the surface of this planet; the fragmental material constituting the surface of this planet, esp. cultivable soil or dirt, as contrasted with rock or sand; the dry land of this planet, as opposed to sea or air; the ground. The lair of any burrowing animal. *Chem.* any of several metallic oxides difficult to reduce, such as alumina. *Elect.* the ground that forms part of an electric current.—*v.t.* To drive into hiding, as an animal; to heap up or mound with soil for protection, as: He *earthed* his rose bushes for the winter.—*v.i.* To hide in the ground; to burrow.—**on earth,** among many possibilities: used as an intensive, as: Where *on earth* did you find that dress ?

earth·born, urth'bòrn", *a.* Born on the earth; originating from the earth or earthly life; mortal; human.

earth·bound, urth'bound", *a.* Firmly fixed in or to the earth; attached or restricted to the land or surface of the earth; directed toward the earth; as, an *earthbound* parachutist; possessing only earthly or material interests; unimaginative.

earth·en, ur'than, *a.* Made of earth; composed of baked clay; earthly or worldly.—**earth·en·ware,** *n.* Pottery made of hardened or baked, coarse clay fired at low heat.

earth·light, urth'līt", *n.* Earthshine.

earth·ling, urth'ling, *n.* An inhabitant of the earth; a mortal; one devoted to worldly affairs; a worldling.

earth·ly, urth'lē, *a.*—**earthlier, earthliest.** Pertaining to the earth or this world; worldly; also, among the things of this earth; possible; conceivable; as, of no *earthly* use.—**earth·li·ness,** *n.*

earth·quake, urth'kwāk", *n.* A trembling or undulation of a part of the earth's crust, due to the faulting of underlying rock, volcanic activity, or other disturbances.

earth sci·ence, *n.* Any science dealing with the earth or any part or aspect of it, as geology, geography, oceanography, or seismology.

earth·shak·ing, urth'shā"king, *a.* Affecting fundamental principles or issues; of key importance; consequential.

earth·shine, urth'shīn", *n. Astron.* reflected light from the earth which faintly illuminates the parts of the moon not lighted by the sun's rays, as during the moon's crescent phase. Also *earthlight.*

earth·star, urth'stär", *n.* A fungus of the genus *Geaster,* with an outer covering which splits into the form of a star.

earth·ward, urth'wėrd, *adv.* Toward the earth. Also **earth·wards.**—*a.* Headed or moving toward the earth.

earth·work, urth'wurk", *n. Milit.* a fortification constructed of earth; the operations involved in excavating and embanking earth, as for construction projects.

earth·worm, urth'wurm", *n.* Any of the segmented worms found in the earth, esp. one of the very widespread family *Lumbricidae,* which is often used as bait by anglers, and which by its burrowing movements loosens and aerates the soil. Also *angleworm.*

earth·y, ur'thē, *a.*—**earthier, earthiest.** Composed of earth or soil; like earth or having some of its properties; crude, gross, or unrefined; as, an *earthy* tale; unaffected, natural or down-to-earth.—**earth·i·ness,** *n.*

ear trum·pet, *n.* An instrument formerly used to aid hearing, usu. in the shape of a cone or funnel which was held to the ear to collect and direct sound waves.

ear·wax, ēr'waks", *n.* A yellowish waxlike secretion from certain glands in the external auditory canal, acting as a lubricant, and arresting the entrance of dust. Also *cerumen.*

ear·wig, ēr'wig", *n.* [O.E. *ēarwicga,* 'ear insect.'] Any of numerous beetlelike insects constituting the family *Forficulidae,* having a long narrow body and a pair of pincers at the posterior end of the abdomen, and incorrectly believed to creep into and injure the human ear.—*v.t.*—*earwigged, earwigging.* To assail with covert representations or insinuations; work upon by covert statements.

ease, ēz, *n.* [Fr. *aise,* ease; O.Fr. *eise, ayse, aize,* ease; Pr. *aise,* It. *agio,* O.It. *asio,* ease; all words of very doubtful origin.] Freedom from labor, physical pain, disturbance, excitement, or annoyance; freedom from concern, anxiety, solicitude, or anything that troubles the mind; tranquillity; repose; freedom from constraint, formality, stiffness, harshness, or unnatural arrangement; unaffectedness; freedom from financial need.—**at ease,** *milit.* of soldiers standing or marching, free to assume a relaxed stance, but required to keep in place and remain silent.

ease, ēz, *v.t.*—*eased, easing.* To free from pain, suffering, anxiety, care, or any disquiet or annoyance; to relieve; to give rest to; to mitigate; to alleviate; to assuage; to allay; to abate or remove in part; to move with care; as, to *ease* an auto into a small parking space; to render less difficult; to facilitate; to release from pressure or restraint by moving gently.—*v.i.* To diminish pressure or tension; to become less painful; to move or be moved with care.

ease·ful, ēz'ful, *a.* Giving ease; restful.—**ease·ful·ly,** *adv.*

ea·sel, ē'zel, *n.* [D. *ezel* = G. *esel,* easel, lit. 'ass': akin to E. *ass.*] A frame in the form of a tripod, for supporting an artist's canvas, a blackboard, or the like; any similar frame used to display objects such as china plates or paintings.

ease·ment, ēz'ment, *n.* Convenience; accommodation; that which gives ease or relief; *law,* a privilege without profit which one proprietor has, entitling him to some specific, limited use in the estate of another.

eas·i·ly, ē'zi·lē, ēz'lē, *adv.* In an easy manner; without any difficulty; beyond question.—**eas·i·ness,** ē'zi·nes, *n.* The state or quality of being easy.

east, ēst, *n.* [O.E. *ēast* = D. *oost,* G. *ost,* Icel. *aust;* connected with L. *aurora* (anc. *ausosa*), Lith. *auszra,* the red of the morning. Skt. *ushas,* the dawn, < a root *us,* to burn, as in L. *urere,* to burn.] One of the four cardinal points of the compass; the point in the heavens where the sun is seen to rise at the equinox, or the corresponding point on the earth; the point of the horizon lying on the right hand when one's face is turned toward the north pole; (*cap.*) areas lying east of a definite or implied point; the region or countries which lie east of Europe; the Orient; the eastern region of the U.S. *Eccles.* the space near the high altar at the extreme end of the Church.—*a.* Toward or in the direction of the rising sun; coming from the east; opposite from west.—*adv.* In an easterly direction; eastward; in the east.

east·bound, ēst'bound", *a.* Directed or travelling eastward.

east by north, *n. Navig.* a point on the compass indicating a direction north of east by one point.

east by south, *n. Navig.* a point on the compass indicating a direction south of east by one point.

East·er, ē'stèr, *n.* [O.E. *ēastre*, pl. *ēastron* (= O.H.G. *ōstarūn*, G. *Ostern*, pl.), from the name (Northumbrian *Eostre*) of a Teutonic goddess of spring, orig. of dawn; akin to E. *east.*] An annual Christian festival in commemoration of the resurrection of Jesus Christ, observed on the first Sunday after the full moon that occurs on or next after March 21. Also **East·er Sun·day.**— **East·er egg**, an egg ornamented by dyeing, or an ornamental imitation of an egg, or a confection in the form of an egg, used at Easter as a gift or decoration.—**East·er lil·y**, one of the several kinds of white lilies that blossom in early spring.—**East·er Mon·day**, the day after Easter.

east·er·ly, ē'stèr·lē, *a.* Coming from the east, esp. pertaining to the wind; moving or directed eastward; situated or looking toward the east.—*adv.* On the east; in the direction of east; from the east.—*n. pl.* **east·er·lies.** A wind coming from the east.

east·ern, ē'stèrn, *a.* [O.E. *easterne.*] Lying toward or situated in the east; directed or proceeding toward the east; coming from the east, as a wind; (*often cap.*) of or pertaining to the east; as, the *Eastern* Church or an *Eastern* Congressman; (*usu. cap.*) oriental.—*n.* One living in an eastern region or country; (*cap.*) a member of the Eastern Church.—**East·ern·er**, *n.* A person of or from the eastern U.S.—**east·ern·most**, *a.* Farthest east.

East·ern Hem·i·sphere, *n.* The half of the earth east of the Atlantic Ocean, comprising the land masses of Africa, Asia, Australia, and Europe.

East·ern Or·tho·dox Church, *n.* The faith, practice, membership, and government of the Christian churches that are in communion with the ecumenical patriarch of Constantinople, including the autocephalous Greek and Russian Orthodox Churches.

East·ern Stand·ard Time, *n.* (*Sometimes l.c.*) see *Standard Time.* Abbr. EST, e.s.t., E.S.T.

East·er·tide, ē'stèr·tīd", *n.* The Easter season; in various churches, the time extending from Easter Sunday to Ascension Day, to Whitsunday, or to Trinity Sunday.

East In·di·an, *a.* Of or pertaining to the East Indies, a vague collective name for India, Indonesia and other countries in S.E. Asia, and the Malay Archipelago.—*n.* A native or inhabitant of the East Indies.

east·ing, ē'sting, *n. Navig.* the distance east made good or gained on any course to the eastward; easterly direction.

East·lake, ēst'lāk", *a.* Designating or pertaining to a style of design in late 19th century English and U.S. furniture, characterized by sturdy rectangular lines and named after Charles L. *Eastlake*, English art critic and painter.

east·ward, ēst'wèrd, *adv.* Toward the east. Also **east·wards.**—*a.* Going, tending,

facing, or located toward the east.—*n.* The direction facing the east; the eastern part or point.

eas·y, ē'zē, *a.*—*easier, easiest.* [O.Fr. *aisie* (Fr. *aisé*), pp. of *aisier*, E. *ease*, v.] Having or characterized by ease; free from pain or discomfort; comfortable; free from anxiety or care; tranquil; free from want; conducive to ease or comfort; not difficult; requiring no great effort or labor; obtained with little effort; not burdensome or oppressive; not difficult to influence; compliant; readily imposed upon; not harsh or strict; lenient; indulgent; free from formality, constraint, or embarrassment; smooth or flowing; moderate; gentle; fitting loosely; not difficult to obtain.—**on eas·y street**, in a situation of financial ease or independence; in a wealthy and luxurious state.—*adv.* In an easy manner; comfortably.

eas·y·go·ing, ē'zē·gō'ing, *a.* Taking matters in an easy way; characterized by comfortable unconcern; calm, relaxed.—**eas·y·go·ing·ness**, *n.*

eas·y mark, *n. Slang*, one who can easily be victimized, cheated, or fooled.

eas·y mon·ey, *n.* Money which can be obtained at low interest rates or with little effort; money obtained by fraud.

eat, ēt, *v.t.*—past *ate*, āt, *Brit.* et; pp. *eaten*; ppr. *eating.* [O.E. *etan* = D. *eten* = G. *essen* = Icel. *eta* = Goth. *itan*, eat; akin to L. *edere*, Gr. *edein*, Skt, *ad-*, eat.] To take into the mouth and swallow for nourishment; to masticate and swallow (food); to devour, as food; to consume by or as by devouring; ravage or devastate; wear or waste away; corrode; pierce or gnaw into.—*v.i.* To consume food; take a meal; to make a way, as by gnawing or corrosion.—**eats**, *n. pl. Slang*, food; a meal.—**be eat·ing some·one**, to trouble a person, as: His worried frown indicated that something was *eating* him.—**eat crow**, to do something extremely disagreeable and humiliating, under compulsion.—**eat hum·ble pie**, to apologize.—**eat one's words**, to be forced to retract one's statements.—**eat·er**, *n.*

eat·a·ble, ē'ta·bl, *a.* Fit to eat; edible.—*n. Usu. pl.* articles of food.

eat·ing, ē'ting, *n.* The act of one who or that which eats; the consuming of food; food with reference to the quality perceived when eaten, as: This fish is delicious *eating.*—*a.* Fit to eat, esp. when raw.

eau de Co·logne, ō"de ko·lōn', *n. pl.* **eaux de Co·logne.** [Fr., < L. *aqua*, water.] A perfumed toilet water originally manufactured at Cologne, Germany.

eau de vie, ō" de vē', *Fr.* ōde vē', *n. pl.* **eaux de vie.** [Fr., lit. water of life.] Brandy, esp. a coarser variety.

eaves, ēvz, *n. pl.* [O.E. *efes* = M.L.G. *ovese* = O.H.G. *obasa* = Icel. *ups*, eaves; prob. akin to E. *over.*] The overhanging lower edge of a roof.

eaves·drop, ēvz'drop", *v.i.*—*eavesdropped, eavesdropping.* To listen clandestinely to a private conversation.—*v.t.* To listen clandestinely.—**eaves·drop·per**, *n.*

ebb, eb, *n.* [O.E. *ebbe, ebba*; D. *eb, ebbe*, G. and Dan. *ebbe*, Sw. *ebb*; allied to E. *even*, G. *aben*, to fall off, to sink.] The return of tidewater toward the sea; a decline; decay.—*v.i.* To flow back, as the water of a tide; to recede; to decay; to decline.

ebb tide, *n.* The flowing back of tidewater; the receding tide.

eb·on·ite, eb'o·nīt", *n.* Vulcanite, esp. when black.

eb·on·ize, eb'o·nīz, *v.t.*—*ebonized, ebonizing.* To color black, by staining or finishing, in imitation of ebony.

eb·on·y, eb'o·nē, *n. pl.* **eb·on·ies.** [L. *ebenus*, Gr. *ebenos.*] A hard, black, heavy wood from tropical trees of the genus *Diospyros*, capable of taking on a fine

polish, and used extensively for fine furniture and cabinetwork; the tree yielding such wood; any similar wood or tree yielding a similar wood; a deep, rich, black color.—*a.* Consisting of ebony; black like ebony; dark. Also **eb·on**, eb'on.

e·brac·te·ate, ē·brak'tē·āt", *a.* [L. *e*, not, and *bractea*, a thin plate.] *Bot.* without bracts.

e·bul·lience, i·bul'yens, *n.* A boiling over; overflow; a bursting forth of feelings or thoughts; exhilaration. Also **e·bul·lien·cy**, pl. **e·bul·lien·cies.**

e·bul·lient, i·bul'yent, *a.* Boiling over; extremely enthusiastic, excited, or demonstrative.

eb·ul·li·tion, eb"u·lish'an, *n.* [L. *ebullitio*, < *ebullio—e, ex*, out, up, and *bullio*, to boil, < *bulla*, a bubble.] The phenomenon or act of boiling; effervescence; a sudden outward display of feeling, as of anger.

e·car·i·nate, ē·kar'i·nāt, *a. Biol.* lacking a carina or keel; as, an *ecarinate* flower.

ec·cen·tric, *Brit. also* **ex·cen·tric**, ik·sen'-trik, ek·sen'trik, *a.* [L. *eccentricus—ex*, from, and *centrum*, center.] Deviating from the usual practice; odd. *Math.* not having the same center though situated one within the other; not concentric, usu. in reference to two circles. *Mach.* having the axis away from the center; *astron.* deviating from the circular, as an ellipse.—*n.* An eccentric person; a mechanical contrivance for converting circular into reciprocating rectilinear motion, as a disk placed off center on a revolving shaft.—**ec·cen·tri·cal·ly**, *adv.*

ec·cen·tric·i·ty, ek"sen·tris'i·tē, *n.* pl. **ec·cen·tric·i·ties.** Behavior that deviates from the usual; oddity; whimsicality; *math.* the constant ratio of the distance of any point on a conic section from a fixed point to its distance from a fixed line.

ec·cle·si·as·tic, i·klē"zē·as'tik, *a.* [Gr. *ekklēsiastikos*, < *ekklēsia*, an assembly, the church, < *ekkaleō*, to call forth or convoke —*ek*, and *kaleo*, to call.] Pertaining or relating to the church or the clergy. Also **ec·cle·si·as·ti·cal.**—*n.* A clergyman. —**ec·cle·si·as·ti·cal·ly**, *adv.*

ec·cle·si·as·ti·cism, i·klē"zē·as'ti·siz"-um, *n.* Strong adherence to the principles of the church, or to ecclesiastical observances.

ec·cle·si·ol·o·gy, i·klē"zē·ol"a·jē, *n.* [Gr. *ekklēsia*, the church, and *logos*, discourse.] The science and theory of church building and decoration; the study of basic church doctrine.

ec·cri·nol·o·gy, ek"ri·nol'o·jē, *n. Anat., physiol.* the study of secretions and secretory glands.

ec·dys·i·ast, ek·diz'ē·ast", *n.* [Coined by H. L. Mencken.] A woman who does a striptease.

ec·dy·sis, ek'di·sis, *n.* pl. **ec·dy·ses.** [Gr., < *ekdyō*, to strip off—*ek*, out of, and *dyō*, to enter.] The act of shedding or casting an outer coat or integument, as in the case of serpents, crustaceans, or certain insects.

e·ce·sis, i·sē'sis, *n. Ecology*, the establishment of an animal or plant in a new environment.—**e·ce·sic**, *a.*

ech·e·lon, esh'e·lon", *n.* [Fr. *échelon*, < *échelle*, ladder, < L. *scala*, E. *scale.*] A degree of rank or authority, as: Financially, he is in the upper *echelon*. A formation of troops in which groups are disposed in parallel lines, each to the right or left of the one in front, so that the whole presents the appearance of steps; one of the groups of a command so disposed; a similar disposition of the ships of a fleet.—*v.t., v.i.* To form in echelon.

e·chid·na, i·kid'na, *n.* pl. **e·chid·nas, e·chid·nae.** [N.L. < Gr. *echidna* adder, viper.] *Zool.* a spiny, coarse-haired, insectivorous animal of the genus *Tachyglossus*,

---

a- fat, fāte, fär, fâre, fâll; **e-** met, mē, mère, hèr; **i-** pin, pīne; **o-** not, nōte, möve; **u-** tub, cūbe, bull; **oi-** oil; **ou-** pound.

belonging to the most primitive order of mammals, the *Monotremes*, and found in Australia, Tasmania, and New Guinea, related to the platypus with which it provides an evolutionary link from the reptiles to birds. Also *spiny anteater*.

ech·i·nate, ek´i·nāt″, ek´i·nit, *a*. [L. *echinatus*, < *echinus*.] Spiny; bristly. Also **ech·i·nat·ed**.

e·chi·no·derm, i·kī´no·dẽrm″, ek´i·no·-dẽrm″, *n*. [Gr. *echinos*, sea urchin, and *dermos*, skin.] Any marine animal of the phylum *Echinodermata*, such as the sea urchin or starfish, having radial appendages, symmetrical body structure, and a spiny calcareous exoskeleton.—**e·chi·no·der·-ma·tous**, i·kī″no·dẽr´ma·tus, ek´i·no·dẽr´ma·tus, *a*.

e·chi·noid, i·kī´noid, ek´i·noid″, *a*. Resembling an echinus or sea urchin.—*n*. A sea urchin.

e·chi·nu·late, i·kin´ū·lat, i·kīn´ū·lat, i·kin´ū·lāt″, i·kīn´ū·lāt″, *a*. Possessing prickles or short spines.

e·chi·nus, i·kī´nus, *n. pl.* **e·chi·ni**, i·kī´nī. The generic name for the sea urchin. *Arch.* a rounded molding below the abacas at the top of a Doric column; the corresponding segment of a column of another order.

ech·o, ek´ō, *n. pl.* **ech·oes**. [L. *echo*, < Gr. *echo*, sound, echo.] A repetition of sound, produced by the reflection of sound waves; the sound so produced; any repetition or close imitation of the ideas or opinions of another; one who imitates another; one who assents obsequiously to another's opinions; a sympathetic response, as to sentiments expressed; anything suggestive of an echo, as a response to a partner's signal in card playing. *Mus.* a very soft repetition of a phrase; a part of a large organ for the production of echo-like effects; also **ech·o·or·gan**; a single stop so used; also **ech·o·stop**. (*Cap.*) the personification of echo; *class. myth.* a mountain nymph who pined away for love of the beautiful youth Narcissus until only her voice remained.—**ech·o·less**, *a*.

ech·o, ek´ō, *v.i.*—echoed, echoing. To be repeated by or as by an echo; to emit an echo; resound with an echo.—*v.t.* To repeat by or as by an echo; to repeat or imitate the words or sentiments of.—**ech·o·er**, *n*.

Ech·o, ek´ō. *n*. A communications code word that designates the letter E.

e·cho·ic, e·kō´ik, *a*. Echolike; imitative of some sound; onomatopoetic.—**ech·o·-ism**, ek´ō·iz″um, *n*. The formation or use of echoic words; onomatopoeia.

ech·o·la·li·a, ek″ō·lā´lē·a, *n*. An infant's normal imitation of sounds made by others; *psychiatry*, uncontrollable repetition of another person's words.

ech·o·lo·ca·tion, ek″ō·lō·kā´shan, *n. Elect.* a method by which the location or distance of an object is determined by the reflection of sound waves off the object.

ech·o sound·er, *n*. A sonar device used to determine the depth of a body of water or of an object under water. Also *sonic depth finder*.

é·clair, ā·klâr´, i·klâr´, ā´klâr, *Fr.* ā·kleR´, *n*. An oblong pastry puff, filled with custard, whipped cream, or ice cream, and usually iced with chocolate.

ec·lamp·si·a, i·klamp´sē·a, *n*. [N.L., < Gr. *eklampein*, shine forth, < *ek*, out of, and *lampein*, shine.] *Pathol.* a form of toxemia, marked by convulsions of a recurrent nature, and happening during pregnancy or childbirth.—**ec·lamp·tic**, *a*.

é·clat, ā·klä´, *n*. [Fr., a splinter, noise, brightness, magnificence, < *éclater*, to split, to shiver, to glitter; < O.H.G. *skleizan*, G. *schleissen*, *schlitzen*, to split; E.

slit, slice, slate.] Brilliancy of success; renown; a burst, as of applause; acclamation.

ec·lec·tic, i·klek´tik, *a*. [Gr. *eklektikos*—*ek*, and *lego*, to choose.] Choosing what seems best from the doctrines, works, or styles of others; composed of such selections.—*n*. One who follows an eclectic method.—**ec·lec·ti·cal·ly**, *adv*.—**ec·lec·ti·cism**, *n*. The doctrine or practice of an eclectic approach or method.

e·clipse, i·klips´, *n*. [O.Fr. *eclipse* (Fr. *éclipse*), < L. *eclipsis*, < Gr. *ekleipsis*, < *ekleipein*, leave out, leave off, be eclipsed, < *ek*, out of, and *leipein*, leave.] The interception or obscuration of the light of the sun, moon, or other heavenly body, by the intervention of another heavenly body either between it and the eye or between it and the source of its illumination; any obscuration of light; any obscuration or overshadowing; loss of brilliance or splendor.—*v.t.*—eclipsed, eclipsing. To cause to suffer eclipse; to cast a shadow upon; obscure; deprive of luster; to render dim by comparison; surpass.

e·clip·tic, i·klip´tik, *a*. [L. *ecliptious*, < Gr. *ekleiptikos*, < *ekleipein*. ECLIPSE.] *Astron.* Pertaining to an eclipse; pertaining to the ecliptic.—*n. Astron.* the great circle formed by the intersection of the plane of the earth's orbit with the celestial sphere; the apparent annual path of the sun in the heavens; an analogous great circle on a terrestrial globe.

e·clo·sion, i·klō´zhan, *n. Entom.* the hatching from its egg of a larva; the coming forth of an adult insect from the pupal case.

e·col·o·gy, i·kol´o·jē, *n*. [Gr. *oikos*, a dwelling, and *logos*, a discourse.] The branch of biology that studies the relationships between organisms and their total environment, both animate and inanimate; also *bionomics*. The branch of sociology concerned with human populations, their environment, spatial distribution, and resulting cultural patterns.—**ec·o·log·i·cal**, ek″o·loj´i·kal, ē″ko·loj´i·kal, *a*.—**ec·o·log·i·cal·ly**, *adv*.—**e·col·o·gist**, *n*.

e·con·o·met·rics, i·kon″o·me´triks, *n. pl. but sing. in constr.* The use of statistical techniques in analyzing economic data and problems.

e·co·nom·ic, ē″ko·nom´ik, ek″o·nom´ik, *a*. [L. *œconomicus*, < Gr. *oikonomikos*, < *oikonomia*. ECONOMY.] Of or relating to the production, distribution, and consumption of goods and income; pertaining to an economy or system of industrial or commercial organization or operation; pertaining to the material welfare of a community, nation, or individual; of or pertaining to the science of economics; pertaining to the means of living or to the arts by which human needs and comforts are supplied; as, *economic* botany; utilitarian. Thrifty or frugal; also *economical*.

e·co·nom·i·cal, ē″ko·nom´i·kal, ek″o·-nom´i·kal, *a*. Characterized by economy or thrifty management; avoiding waste or extravagance; economic.—**e·co·nom·i·cal·ly**, *adv*.

e·co·nom·ics, ē″ko·nom´iks, ek″o·nom´iks, *n. pl. but sing. in constr.* The science treating of the production, distribution, and consumption of wealth, or the material welfare of mankind; political economy; economic questions, affairs, or aspects.

e·con·o·mist, i·kon´o·mist, *n*. One versed in the science of economics.

e·con·o·mize, i·kon´o·mīz″, *v.t.*—economized, economizing. To manage economically; use sparingly; use to the best advantage.—*v.i.* To practice economy in expenditure; avoid waste or extravagance.—**e·con·mi·za·tion**, *n*.—**e·con·o·miz·er**, *n*.

e·con·o·my, i·kon´o·mē, *n. pl.* **e·con·o·-mies**. [L. *œconomia*, < Gr. *oikonomia*, < *oikos*, house, and *nemein*, deal out, manage.] Thrifty management; frugality in the expenditure or consumption of money or materials; a saving; the management of the resources of a country, with regard to its productivity; as, the national *economy*; the disposition or regulation of the parts or functions of any complex whole; a judicious or sparing use of anything.

ec·o·spe·cies, ek´ō·spē″shēz, ek´ō·spē″sēz, ē″kō·spē″shēz, ē″kō·spē″sēz, *n. Ecol.* a species, approximately comparable to the taxonomic species, whose members are particularly adapted to their environment and reproduce among themselves without loss of fertility.—**ec·o·spe·cif·ic**, *a*.

ec·o·sphere, ek´ō·sfēr″, ē″kō·sfēr″, *n*. Any area in which life can exist; specif. that part of the atmosphere, extending to 13,000 feet above sea level, in which normal breathing is possible.

ec·o·sys·tem, ek´ō·sis″tem, ē´kō·sis″tem, *n*. The basic ecological unit, made up of a community of organisms interacting with their inanimate environment.

ec·o·tone, ek´o·tōn″, ē´ko·tōn″, *n*. A transition zone between neighboring plant communities, as grassland and forest, in which organisms of both compete for dominance.

ec·ru, ek´rö, ā´krö, *a*. [Fr. raw, unbleached.] Pale yellowish brown or beige in color, as raw silk or unbleached linen.—*n*. Ecru color.

ec·sta·sy, ek´sta·sē, *n. pl.* **ec·sta·sies**. [O.Fr. *extasie* (Fr. *extase*), < L.L. *ecstasis*, < Gr. *ekstasis*, < *existanai*, put out of place or out of the normal mental state, < *ex*, out of, and *instanai*, set up, stand.] A state of intense, overpowering emotion; a state of exultation or mental rapture induced by beauty, music, or artistic creations; rapturous delight; a transport of any emotion; as, an *ecstasy* of fear; mental transport or rapture from the contemplation of divine things; the frenzy of poetic inspiration.—**ec·stat·ic**, ek·stat´ik *a*. [Gr. *ekstatikos*.] Of, pertaining to, or characterized by ecstasy; subject to or in a state of ecstasy; rapturous.—*n*. One subject to fits of ecstasy; *pl*. raptures.—**ec·stat·i·cal·ly**, *adv*.

ec·to·blast, ek´to blast″, *n. Embryol.* ectoderm.—**ec·to·blas·tic**, *a*.

ec·to·derm, ek´to·dẽrm″, *n. Embryol.* the outer primary layer of cells in the embryo of any metazoan animal: opposed to *endoderm*.—**ec·to·der·mal**, **ec·to·der·mic**, *a*.

ec·tog·e·nous, ek·toj´e·nus, *a*. Capable of developing outside of the host, as certain pathogenic bacteria. Also **ec·to·gen·ic**, ek″tō·jen´ik.

ec·to·mere, ek´to·mēr″, *n. Zool.* any of the cells, formed from the fertilized egg, which eventually make up the ectoderm.—**ec·to·mer·ic**, *a*.

ec·to·morph, ek´to·mạrf″, *n*. A type of body structure, characterized by linearity and leanness, developed by the relative dominance of tissues derived from the ectoderm, the outermost of the three cell layers of the embryo; a person having this type of body structure.—**ec·to·mor·phic**, *a*. Of, pertaining to, or characteristic of ectomorphs.—**ec·to·morph·y**, *n*.

ec·to·par·a·site, ek″tō·par´a·sit″, *n*. An external parasite: opposed to *endoparasite*.—**ec·to·par·a·sit·ic**, ek″tō·par″a·sit´ik, *a*.

ec·to·plasm, ek´to·plaz″um, *n. Biol.* the outer portion of the cytoplasm in a cell. *Spiritualism*, a supposed emanation from the body of a medium while in a trance; that of which a materialized spirit or the like is held to be composed, or to which spiritualistic phenomena are attributed.—**ec·to·plas·mic, ec·to·plas·mat·ic,** *a.*

ec·u·men·i·cal, ek″ū·men′i·kal, *Brit.* ē″kū·men′i·kal, *a.* [L. *œcumenicus,* Gr. *oikoumene,* the habitable earth, < *oikos,* a habitation.] General; universal; of or representing the whole Christian Church or the whole Catholic Church; fostering world-wide Christian unity. Also **ec·u·men·ic,** ek″ū·men′ik, *Brit.* ē″kū·men′ik.—**ec·u·me·nic·i·ty,** ek″ū·me·nis′i·tē, ek″-ū·me·nis′i·tē, *n.* United Christianity. —**Ec·u·men·i·cal Coun·cil,** *n. R. Cath. Ch.* an assembly, called by the Pope, of cardinals and bishops whose decrees are ratified by the Pope.

ec·u·men·i·cal pa·tri·arch, *n.* The patriarch of Constantinople, the highest official of the Greek Orthodox Church.

ec·u·me·nism, ek′ū·me·niz″um, *n.* A movement which promotes unity among Christians and encourages a mutually cooperative relationship between Christian and non-Christian faiths. Also **ec·u·men·i·cal·ism, ec·u·men·i·cism.—ec·u·me·nist,** *n.*

ec·ze·ma, ek′se·ma, eg′ze·ma, ig·zē′ma, *n.* [N.L., < Gr. *ekxema,* < *ekxein,* boil out.] *Pathol.* an inflammatory disease of the skin attended with itching and the exudation of serous matter.—**ec·zem·a·tous,** *a.*

e·da·cious, i·dā′shus, *a.* [L. *edax,* < *edo,* to eat.] Eating; given to eating; voracious.—**e·dac·i·ty,** i·das′i·tē, *n.* [L. *edacitas.*] Ravenousness; voracity; gluttony.

E·dam, ē′dam, ē′däm, *D.* ä·däm′, *n.* [From the village of Edam, near Amsterdam, Netherlands.] A pressed, fine-flavored, yellow Dutch cheese made in flattened balls, and coated with red paraffin. Also **E·dam cheese.**

e·daph·ic, i·daf′ik, *a.* Pertaining to the soil and soil factors; affected by soil rather than climate.—**e·daph·i·cal·ly,** *adv.*

Ed·dic, ed′ik, *a.* Of, pertaining to, or like the *Edda,* either of two collections of Icelandic myths and poetry dating from the 12th and 13th centuries. Also **Ed·da·ic,** e·dā′ik.

ed·dy, ed′ē, *n. pl.* **ed·dies.** [< Icel. *itha,* an eddy.] A current of air or water turning round in a direction contrary to the main stream, esp. a current moving circularly; a small whirlpool; any substance moving in a similar manner.—*v.i.*—**eddied, eddying.** To move circularly, or in eddies.—*v.t.* To cause to move in an eddy.

e·del·weiss, ād′el·vīs″, ād′el·wīs″, *n.* [G. *edel,* noble, *weiss,* white.] A composite herb of the genus *Leontopodium,* growing in the Alps and having white, woolly foliage in flowerlike clusters.

e·de·ma, i·dē′ma, *n. pl.* **e·de·ma·ta,** i·dē′-ma·ta. [N.L., < Gr. *oidema,* < *oidein,* swell.] *Pathol.* a swelling due to excessive accumulation of fluid in a serous cavity or connective tissue. Also **oe·de·ma.—e·dem·a·tous, e·dem·a·tose,** *a.*

E·den, ēd′en, *n.* [Heb. *ēden,* delight, pleasure, a place of pleasure.] The garden in which Adam and Eve first lived; a paradise.—**E·den·ic,** ē·den′ik, *a.*

e·den·tate, ē·den′tāt, *a.* [L. *edentatus,* pp. of *edentare,* deprive of teeth, < *e,* out of, and *dens (dent-),* tooth.] Toothless; belonging or pertaining to the *Edentata,* an order of mammals, including the sloths, armadillos, and South American anteaters, in which the incisors and canines, or all the teeth, are lacking.—*n.* An edentate mammal.

e·den·tu·lous, ē·den′chu·lus, i·den′chu·-lus, *a.* Without teeth.

edge, ej, *n.* [O.E. *ecg.* = D. *egge* = G. *ecke* = Icel. *egg,* edge; akin to L. *acies,* edge, point, Gr. *akis,* point. Skt. *acri,* edge, corner.] The thin, sharp side of the blade of a cutting instrument or weapon; the sharpness proper to a blade; cutting or wounding quality; sharpness or keenness of language, argument, appetite, desire; fitness for action or operation; something resembling a cutting edge, as the crest of a ridge; the line in which two surfaces of a solid object meet; one of the narrow surfaces of a thin, flat object; as, a book with gilt *edges*; a border or margin; the brink or verge, as of a precipice; *slang,* intoxication from drinking.—**on edge,** eager or impatient; in a state of acute and uncomfortable sensibility; as, nerves *on edge,* to set the teeth *on edge.*—**have the edge on,** to have the advantage.

edge, ej, *v.t.*—**edged, edging.** To put an edge on; sharpen; to provide with an edge or border; to move edgeways; move or force gradually or by imperceptible degrees.—*v.i.* To move edgeways; advance gradually or by imperceptible degrees.—**edged,** *a.* Having an edge; sharp.

edge tool, *n.* A tool having a sharp cutting edge.

edge·wise, ej′wīz″, *adv.* With the edge directed forward; in the direction of the edge; sideways. Also **edge·ways.**

edg·ing, ej′ing, *n.* The act of one that edges; something that serves for an edge or border; trimming for edges.

edg·y, ej′ē, *a.*—**edgier, edgiest.** Sharp-edged; sharply defined; irritable or nervous.—**edg·i·ly,** *adv.*—**edg·i·ness,** *n.*

edh, ети, *n.* See *eth.*

ed·i·ble, ed′i·bl, *a.* [L.L. *edibilis,* < L. *edo,* to eat.] Fit to be eaten as food; eatable; esculent.—*n.* Anything that may be eaten for food; an article of food; a comestible.—**ed·i·bil·i·ty, ed·i·ble·ness,** *n.*

e·dict, ē′dikt, *n.* [L. *edictum,* < *edico,* utter or proclaim—*e,* out, and *dico,* to speak.] An order issued by a ruler as a law requiring obedience; an authoritative proclamation of command or prohibition; a decree.—**e·dic·tal,** ē·dik′tal, *a.* Pertaining to an edict.—**e·dic·tal·ly,** *adv.*

ed·i·fice, ed′i·fis, *n.* [L. *aedificium,* a building.] A building, esp. a structure impressive in size and appearance.—**ed·i·fi·cial,** ed″i·fish′al, *a.* Pertaining to an edifice or structure; structural.

ed·i·fy, ed′i·fī″, *v.t.*—**edified, edifying.** [Fr. *édifier,* < L. *aedificare,* to build, erect, construct—*aedes,* a house and *facio,* to make.] To instruct and improve in knowledge generally, and particularly in moral and religious knowledge.—**ed·i·fi·er,** *n.*—**ed·i·fy·ing,** *a.* Adapted to edify; having the effect of instructing and improving.—**ed·i·fi·ca·tion,** ed′i·fi·kā′shan, *n.* The act of edifying; improvement and progress of the mind in knowledge, in morals, or in faith and holiness.

ed·it, ed′it, *v.t.* [Partly < L. *editus,* pp. of *edere,* give forth, < *e,* out of, and *dare,* give; partly < E. *editor.*] To prepare or revise(literary matter)for publication, as an editor does; to supervise or direct the publication of(a newspaper, magazine, or other printed matter); to act as editor of; to adapt (film), as for television or motion pictures, by rearranging, cutting, and splicing.

e·di·tion, i·dish′an, *n.* [L. *editio(n-).*] The form in which a literary work is published; as, Milman's *edition* of Gibbon, a one-volume *edition* of Shakespeare; the whole number of copies of a book or newspaper, printed from one set of types and issued at one time; esp. one of a number of printings of the same book, issued at different times, and differing from one another by alterations or additions; a form of anything, printed or not, for public presentation; as, the newest *edition* of a play.

ed·i·tor, ed′i·tẽr, *n.* [L.] One who edits or prepares literary matter, or a particular edition of a literary work, for publication; the supervising director of a newspaper or other periodical, or of a special department of one.—**ed·i·tor·ship,** *n.* The office or function of an editor; editorial direction.

ed·i·to·ri·al, ed″i·tōr′ē·al, *a.* Written by an editor, as a note or an article; having reference to the artistic and literary divisions of a publishing firm rather than to the business divisions.—*n.* An article, as in a newspaper, written by the editor or under his direction, and setting forth the position or opinion of the publication upon some subject; a statement of opinion broadcast by a radio or television station.—**ed·i·to·ri·al·ly,** *adv.*—**ed·i·to·ri·al·ist,** *n.*

ed·i·to·ri·al·ize, ed″i·tōr′ē·a·līz″, *v.i.*—**editorialized, editorializing.** To set forth one's position or opinion on some subject in, or as if in, an editorial; to express personal opinion when reporting facts, as in a radio or television newscast.

ed·u·cate, ej′u·kāt″, ed′ū·kāt″, *v.t.*—**educated, educating.** [L. *educo, educatum,* < *educo, eductum,* to lead forth, to bring up a child—*e,* out, and *duco,* to lead.] To advance the mental, aesthetic, physical, or moral development of, esp. by teaching or schooling; to send to school; to qualify by instruction for the business and duties of life; to teach; to instruct; to train; to rear.—*v.i.* To instruct or train a person or a group of persons.—**ed·u·ca·ble, ed·u·cat·a·ble,** *a.*—**ed·u·cat·ed,** *a.*

ed·u·ca·tion, ej″u·kā′shan, ed″ū·kā′shan, *n.* The process of educating, teaching, or training; a part of or a stage in this training; the learning or development which results from this process of teaching or training; the process of imparting or acquiring skills for a particular trade or profession; a kind of schooling; instruction and discipline in general; erudition; the academic discipline dealing with teaching and learning methods in the schools.—**ed·u·ca·tion·al,** *a.*—**ed·u·ca·tion·al·ly,** *adv.*

ed·u·ca·tion·al psy·chol·o·gy, *n.* The branch of psychology which investigates educational problems through psychological methods and concepts.

ed·u·ca·tive, ej′u·kā″tiv, ed′ū·kā″tiv, *a.* Tending to or having the power to educate.

ed·u·ca·tor, ej′u·kā″tẽr, ed′ū·kā″tẽr, *n.* One who or that which educates; a person directly involved in planning or directing the learning process.—**ed·u·ca·tion·ist,** ej″u·kā′sha·nist, ed″ū·kā′sha·nist, *n.* One well versed in educational theory and method; a professional educator. Also **ed·u·ca·tion·al·ist,** ej″u·kā′sha·nal·ist, ed″-ū·kā′sha·nal·ist.

e·duce, i·dös′, i·dūs′, *v.t.*—**educed, educing.** [L.] To bring or draw out; to extract; to deduce.—**e·duc·i·ble,** *a.* Capable of being educed.—**e·duc·tion,** i·duk′shan, *n.* The act of educing, drawing out, or bringing into view; anything educed.—**e·duc·tor,** *n.*

e·dul·co·rate, i·dul′ko·rāt″, *v.t.*—**edulcorated, edulcorating.** [= Fr. *édulcorer,* < L. *e,* out of, and L.L. *dulcorare,* sweeten, < *dulcor,* sweetness.] *Chem.* to free from acids, salts, or impurities by washing.—**e·dul·co·ra·tion,** *n.*

Ed·ward·i·an, ed·wạr′dē·an, ed·wär′dē-an, *a.* Pertaining to the characteristics and time of Edward VII of England; opulent; ornate.—*n.* A person suggestive of the Edwardian era.

eel, ēl, *n. pl.* **eels, eel.** [O.E. *ael* = Dan., D., and G. *aal,* Icel. *all;* not connected with Gr. *echis,* Skt. *ahi,* a serpent; L. *anguilla,* an eel.] A fish characterized by its slimy serpent-like elongated body, the absence of ventral fins, and the continuity of the dorsal and anal fins around the extremity of the tail.—**eel-like,** *a.*—**eel·y,** *a.*

eel·grass, ēl'gras″, ēl'gräs″, n. An underwater plant, *Zostera marina*, having long narrow leaves.

eel·pout, ēl'pout″, n. [O.E. *aele-puta*.] The name of two different species of fish, the viviparous blenny and the burbot.

eel·worm, ēl'wẽrm″, n. A worm of the family *Anguillulidae*, esp. any plant-parasitic roundworm.

e'en, ēn. Contraction of even.

e'er, âr. Contraction of ever.

ee·rie, ēr'ē, a.—eerier, eeriest. [O.E. *earh*, timid.] Frightening; disquieting because of weirdness or gloominess; suggesting supernatural influence or potential danger; strange. Also **ee·ry**.—**ee·ri·ly**, adv.—**ee·ri·ness**, n.

ef·fa·ble, ef'a·bl, a. [L. *effabilis*, < *effari*, utter.] Utterable; expressible.

ef·face, i·fās', v.t.—effaced, effacing. [Fr. *effacer*, O.Fr. *esfacier*.] To rub out or obliterate; to wipe out; to render inconspicuous; as, to be self-*effacing*.—**ef·face·a·ble**, a.—**ef·fac·er**, n.—**ef·face·ment**, n.

ef·fect, i·fekt', n. [O.Fr. *effect* (Fr. *effet*), < L. *effectus*, < *efficere* (pp. *effectus*), bring about, effect.] That which is produced by some agency or cause; a result; a consequence; power to produce results; force; validity; the result intended; purport or intent; tenor or significance; the state of being operative; operation or execution; accomplishment or fulfillment; the result upon the mind of what is apprehended by the faculties; a mental impression produced, as by a painting or speech; a combination, as of form, color, light, and shade, producing a particular mental impression. *Pl.* goods; movables; personal estate; property.—v.t. To bring about; accomplish; fulfill; produce or make.—**for ef·fect**, for the mere impression on the mind of others; as, to talk *for effect*.—**in ef·fect**, in result or consequences, as: The two methods are the same *in effect*. In fact or reality, as: It is no other *in effect* than what it seems. In operation, as a law.—**ef·fect·er**, n.—**ef·fect·i·ble**, a. Capable of being effected.

ef·fec·tive, i·fek'tiv, a. [L. *effectivus*, < *efficere*, bring about, accomplish.] Serving to effect the purpose; producing the intended or expected result; capable of producing effect; adapted for a desired end; in force or operation; actual; fit for action or duty, as soldiers or sailors; producing a striking impression, as a performance or picture; striking; picturesque.—n. One, esp. a soldier, fit for duty or active service; the effective total of a military force.—**ef·fec·tive·ly**, adv.—**ef·fec·tive·ness**, n.

ef·fec·tor, i·fek'tẽr, n. *Physiol.* a motor nerve which transforms nerve impulses into physical action.

ef·fec·tu·al, i·fek'chŏ·al, a. [O.Fr. *effectuel*, < M.L. *effectualis*, < L. *effectus*, E. *effect*.] Producing, or capable of producing, an intended effect; adequately answering its purpose; valid or binding, as an agreement or document.—**ef·fec·tu·al·i·ty**, n. pl. **ef·fec·tu·al·i·ties**.—**ef·fec·tu·al·ly**, adv.—**ef·fec·tu·al·ness**, n.

ef·fec·tu·ate, i·fek'chŏ·āt″, v.t.—effectuated, effectuating. [Fr. *effectuer*.] To bring to pass; to achieve; to accomplish; to fulfill.—**ef·fec·tu·a·tion**, n.

ef·fem·i·nate, i·fem'i·nit, a. [L. *effeminatus*, < *effeminor*, to grow or make womanish; < *ex*, out, and *femina*, woman.] Having qualities unsuitable to a man; womanish; soft, delicate, or comfort-loving to an unmanly degree.—i·fem'i·nāt″, v.t. *effeminated, effeminating.* To make womanish or effeminate.—v.i. To grow womanish or weak.—**ef·fem·i·na·cy**, i·fem'i·na·sē, n. pl. **ef·fem·i·na·cies**. The state or character of being effeminate.—**ef·fem·i·nate·ly**, adv.—**ef·fem·i·nate·ness**, n.

ef·fen·di, i·fen'dē, n. pl. **ef·fen·dis**. [Turk.] A title of respect originating in Turkey; now used in addressing educated men or members of the aristocracy in eastern Mediterranean countries.

ef·fer·ent, ef'ẽr·ent, a. [L. *efferens* (-ent-), ppr. of *efferre*, bring out, raise, exalt, < *ex*, out of, and *ferre*, bear.] *Physiol.* conveying outward from a central organ or point: opposed to *afferent*; specif., conveying impulses from a nerve center to an effector.—**ef·fer·ent·ly**, adv.—**ef·fer·ence**, n.

ef·fer·vesce, ef'ẽr·ves', v.i.—effervesced, effervescing. [L. *effervesco*—*ef*, ex, out of, and *fervesco*, to begin boiling, < *ferveo*, to be hot.] To bubble, hiss, and froth, as when the gaseous part escapes from a liquid; to show signs of excitement.—**ef·fer·ves·cence**, n. The bubbling, frothing, or sparkling of a fluid which takes place when some part of the mass flies off in a gaseous form; strong manifestation of feeling.—**ef·fer·ves·cent**, ef'ẽr·ves'ent, a. Effervescing.—**ef·fer·ves·cent·ly**, adv.

ef·fete, i·fēt', a. [L. *effetus*, < *ex*, out of, and *fetus*, breeding, having brought forth.] Lacking vitality; exhausted; incapable of bearing young.—**ef·fete·ly**, adv.—**ef·fete·ness**, n.

ef·fi·ca·cious, ef″i·kā'shus, a. [L. *efficax*, efficacious, *efficio*. EFFECT.] Effectual; producing the effect intended or desired.—**ef·fi·ca·cious·ly**, adv.—**ef·fi·ca·cious·ness**, n.

ef·fi·ca·cy, ef'i·ka·sē, n. pl. **ef·fi·ca·cies**. [L. *efficacia*, efficacy.] Power to produce effects; effectiveness. Also **ef·fi·ca·ci·ty**, ef″i·kas'i·tē.

ef·fi·cien·cy, i·fish'en·sē, n. pl. **ef·fi·cien·cies**. [L. *efficientia*.] Competence for one's duties; power of producing intended effect in relation to cost in time, money, and energy; the ratio of resulting useful work to the energy expended.

ef·fi·cien·cy en·gi·neer, n. A person who analyzes the component parts of a job, procedure, or business operation with the purpose of achieving the desired results with a minimum expenditure of cost, time, and effort. Also **ef·fi·cien·cy ex·pert**.

ef·fi·cient, i·fish'ent, a. Acting or functioning competently; able to be used with satisfaction and economy; competent; causing desired effects.—**ef·fi·cient·ly**, adv.

ef·fi·gy, ef'i·jē, n. pl. **ef·fi·gies**. [L. *effigies*, < *effingere*, form, fashion, < *ex*, out of, and *fingere*, form, mold.] A representation or image of something, esp. a sculptured likeness of a person; a stuffed figure representing an obnoxious person.

ef·flo·resce, ef″lo·res', v.i.—effloresced, efflorescing. [L. *effloresco*—*ef* for *ex*, and *floresco*, < *floreo*, to blossom, < *flos*, a flower.] To burst into bloom, as a flower. *Chem.* to change over, upon exposure to air, to a whitish, mealy, or crystalline powder, from a gradual decomposition; to become covered with a whitish powdery crust.

ef·flo·res·cence, ef″lo·res'ens, n. The act or process of flowering; the time of flowering; fullness of development. *Chem.* the formation of a whitish substance on the surface of certain bodies, as salts; the powder or crust thus formed; *pathol.* a redness or eruption on the skin.—**ef·flo·res·cent**, ef″lo·res'ent, a. Flowering. *Chem.* encrusted or covered with efflorescence; liable to effloresce.

ef·flu·ence, ef'lö·ens, n. [Fr. *effluence*, < L. *effluo*, to flow out—*e*, ex, and *fluo*, to flow.] The act of flowing out; that which flows out or issues.—**ef·flu·ent**, ef'lö·ent, a. Flowing out; emanating; emitted.—n. The act or process of flowing out; a stream that flows out of another stream or out of a lake.

ef·flu·vi·um, i·flö'vē·um, n. pl. **ef·flu·vi·a**, **ef·flu·vi·ums**, i·flö'vē·a. Something flowing out in a subtle or invisible form; emanation, esp. a noxious or disagreeable exhalation.—**ef·flu·vi·al**, a.

ef·flux, ef'luks, n. [L. *effluere* (pp. *effluxus*).] Outward flow, as of water; that which flows out; an effluence.—**ef·flux·ion**, n. A flowing out.

ef·fort, ef'ẽrt, n. [Fr. *effort*—L. *ef* for *ex*, out, and *fortis*, strong.] An exertion of strength or power, whether physical or mental; strenuous exertion to accomplish an object; something produced by conscious mental or physical exertion; endeavor; *Brit.* an organized fund-raising drive in a community.—**ef·fort·less**, a. Making no effort.—**ef·fort·less·ly**, adv.—**ef·fort·less·ness**, n.

ef·fron·ter·y, i·frun'te·rē, n. pl. **ef·fron·ter·ies**. [Fr. *effronterie*, < L. *effrons*, *effrontis*, barefaced.] Audacious impudence or boldness; shamelessness; an example of such bold behavior.

ef·fulge, i·fulj', v.i.—effulged, effulging. [L. *effulgeo*—*ef* for *ex*, out, and *fulgeo*, to shine.] To shine with splendor.—**ef·ful·gence**, n. Great luster or brightness; splendor.—**ef·ful·gent**, a.—**ef·ful·gent·ly**, adv.

ef·fuse, i·fūz', v.t.—effused, effusing. [L. *effundo*, *effusum*, to pour out—*ef* for *ex*, out, and *fundo*, *fusum*, to pour.] To pour out, as a fluid; to flow.—v.i. To emanate; to flow out.—i·fūs', a. Spilling out; *bot.* spread out in a loose arrangement. Noting shells with lips that are separated by a gap or groove.

ef·fu·sion, i·fū'zhan, n. The act of pouring out; that which is poured out; a free and unrestrained expression of feeling. *Pathol.* the escape of any fluid out of the vessel containing it into a cavity of the body; the escaping fluid itself.

ef·fu·sive, i·fū'siv, a. Showing overflowing kindness or cordiality; without reserve.—**ef·fu·sive·ly**, adv.—**ef·fu·sive·ness**, n.

eft, eft, n. [O.E. *efete*.] Formerly, any small lizard or lizardlike animal; now, usually, a newt in its terrestrial stage of development.

e·gad, i·gad', ē'gad', interj. [Probably a euphemistic corruption of 'by God.'] An exclamation expressing exultation or surprise.

e·gads but·ton, n. *Slang*, in rocketry, the switch used to destroy in flight a missile which is malfunctioning. Also **chick·en switch**.

e·gal·i·tar·i·an, i·gal″i·târ'ē·an, a. Pertaining to the belief that all men are equal.—n. One who believes in the equality of all mankind.—**e·gal·i·tar·i·an·ism**, n.

e·gest, ē·jest', v.t. [L. *egestus*, pp. of *egerere*, < *e*, out of, and *gerere*, bear.] To discharge from the body; void; excrete.—**e·ges·ta**, ē·jes'ta, n. pl. [L.] Matter egested from the body; excrement.—**e·ges·tion**, ē·jes'chan, ē·jesh'chan, n. [L. *egestio(n-)*.] The process of egesting; the voiding of the refuse of digestion.—**e·ges·tive**, a.

egg, eg, n. [Icel. *egg* = O.E. *æg* = D. and G. *ei*: cf. L. *ovum*, Gr. *ōon*, egg.] The roundish reproductive body in a shell or membrane, produced by the female of animals, and consisting of the ovum or female reproductive cell together with its appendages; the body of this sort produced by birds, esp. by the domestic hen; anything resembling a hen's egg; *biol.* the ovum or female reproductive cell. *Slang*, a person; an aerial bomb. *Brit.* an immature person.—**lay an egg**, *theater*, to have an unsuccessful performance. To fail in any endeavor.

egg, eg, v.t. [O.E. *ecgian*, *eggian*, to incite, to sharpen; Icel. *eggja*, to egg.] To incite, urge, or provoke, usu. followed by *on*. To pelt with eggs.

egg and dart, *n.* An egg-shaped ornament alternating with a dartlike ornament, carved in relief on moldings. Also **egg and tongue, egg and an·chor.**

egg·beat·er, eg'bē″tėr, *n.* A portable hand or electric tool for beating eggs, and whipping cream and batters. Also *Brit.* **eggwhisk.**

egg·head, eg'hed″, *n.* Colloq. an intellectual.

egg·nog, eg'nog″, *n.* A drink of eggs beaten up with sugar, milk, nutmeg, and sometimes alcoholic liquor.

egg·plant, eg'plant″, eg'plänt″, *n.* A plant, *Solanum melongena,* with purplish egg-shaped fruit which is served as a vegetable.

egg·shell, eg'shel″, *n.* The shell or calcareous covering of an egg; a pale yellow color.—*a.* Fragile and thin; as, *eggshell* porcelain; having a slight gloss; as, *eggshell* finish; colored pale yellow.

egg·whisk, eg'hwisk″, eg'wisk″, *n. Brit.* eggbeater.

e·gis, ē'jis, *n.* Aegis.

eg·lan·tine, eg'lan·tīn″, eg'lan·tēn″, *n.* [Fr. *églantine,* O.Fr. *aiglent,* < a form of *aculentus,* prickly, < L. *aculeus,* a spine, a prickle, *acus,* a needle.] An old and poetical name for the sweetbrier or wild rose.

e·go, ē'gō, eg'ō, *n.* pl. **e·gos.** [L. *ego,* I.] The "I" or self as distinguished from the selves of others; *philos.* the individual's mental states and sensual experiences, as known through direct introspection; *psychoanal.* that part of the psyche that is conscious, experiencing, and reacting to the outside world, and thus acting as mediator between the id's unconscious primitive impulses and society's expectations. Egotism; vanity; self-esteem; self-concept.

e·go·cen·tric, ē″gō·sen′trik, eg′ō·sen′trik, *a.* Having or regarding self as the center of all things, esp. in relation to the world; involved with one's own concerns and relatively unaware of others' concerns; self-centered.—*n.* An egocentric person.—**e·go·cen·tric·i·ty,** *n.*—**e·go·cen·trism,** *n.*

e·go i·de·al, *n. Psychoanal.* a desired and actively sought standard of personal excellence, derived from the total of positive identifications with parents or other esteemed persons.

e·go·ism, ē′gō·iz″um, eg′ō·iz″um, *n.* [Fr. *égoïsme,* < L. *ego,* I.] The habit of valuing everything only in reference to one's personal interest; pure selfishness; self-conceit; egotism: opposed to *altruism*; *ethics,* the view that the motivating force and ultimate end of an individual's actions should be his own welfare only; *metaph.* the doctrine that nothing certainly exists but the ego or mind of the individual.

e·go·ist, ē′gō·ist, eg′ō·ist, *n.* [Fr. *égoïste.*] A self-centered or selfish person; an egotist; a conceited individual.—**e·go·is·tic, e·go·is·ti·cal,** *a.* Characterized by or proceeding from egoism or selfishness; egotistic; concerned with oneself and one's own gratifications.—**e·go·is·ti·cal·ly,** *adv.*

e·go·ma·ni·a, ē″gō·mā′nē·a, eg′ō·mān′ya, eg′ō·mā′nē·a, eg′ō·mān′ya, *n.* [EGO.] Egotism developed to an abnormal degree.

e·go·tism, ē′gō·tiz″um, eg′ō·tiz″um, *n.* The practice of too frequently using the word *I*; hence, a practice of speaking or writing too much about oneself; an objectionable amount of pride; a passionate and exaggerated love of self, leading one to refer all things to oneself, and to judge everything by its relation to one's interests or importance.—**e·go·tist,** ē′gō·tist, eg′ō·tist, *n.*—**e·go·tis·tic, e·go·tis·ti·cal,** ē″gō·tis′tik, eg″ō·tis′tik, *a.*—**e·go·tis·ti·cal·ly,** *adv.*

e·gre·gious, i·grē′jus, i·grē′jē·us, *a.* [L. *egregius,* lit. out of the common flock.] Extraordinary or remarkable in a bad sense or for undesirable characteristics; flagrant; as, an *egregious* blunder; *archaic,* remark-able or distinguished.—**e·gre·gious·ly,** *adv.* —**e·gre·gious·ness,** *n.*

e·gress, ē′gres, *n.* [L. *egressus,* < *egredior*—*e,* and *gradior,* to step.] The act of going or issuing out; the right to depart; a way or a means of departing; an exit; *astron.* the passing of a heavenly body from eclipse, occultation, or transit.—*i·gres′, v.i.* To go out; to issue forth; to emerge.—**e·gres·sion,** i·gresh′an, *n.* [L. *egressio.*] Egress; emergence.

e·gret, ē′grit, eg′rit, *n.* [Fr. *aigrette,* a dim. from an old form *aigre,* < O.H.G. *heigro,* a heron, Sw. *hager,* Icel. *hegri,* a heron. *Heron* has the same origin.] Any of those species of herons which have long, white, flowing plumes during their breeding period. A plume of an egret; also *aigrette.*

E·gyp·tian, i·jip′shan, *a.* Of or pertaining to Egypt or its people; as, *Egyptian* architecture.—*n.* A native or inhabitant of Egypt; the extinct Afro-Asiatic language of the ancient Egyptians.—**E·gyp·tian·ize,** i·jip′sha·nīz, *v.t.*—*Egyptianized, Egyptianizing.* To make Egyptian in appearance or customs.—*v.i.* To become, or become like, an Egyptian.

E·gyp·tian cot·ton, *n.* A strong, silky, long-staple cotton cultivated mainly in Egypt.

E·gyp·tol·o·gy, ē″jip·tol′o·jē, *n.* The science or study of Egyptian antiquities.—**E·gyp·tol·o·gist,** *n.* One well acquainted with the antiquities of Egypt, esp. the hieroglyphic inscriptions and documents.

eh, ā, e, *interj.* An utterance expressing surprise or doubt, or requesting information or confirmation: often corresponds to 'What did you say?' or 'Don't you agree?'

ei·der, ī′dėr, *n.* [Icel. *ædhr* (*ædhar-dun,* eiderdown).] Any of several large sea ducks of the genus *Somateria* and allied genera of the northern hemisphere; also **ei·der duck.** The choice down from the female eider duck; also *eiderdown.*

ei·der·down, ī′dėr·doun″, *n.* Down or soft feathers from the breast of the female eider; a comforter stuffed with eiderdown.

ei·det·ic, ī·det′ik, *a.* Of, referring to, or composed of visual images that can be reproduced from memory with almost photographic accuracy.—**ei·det·i·cal·ly,** *adv.*

ei·do·lon, ī·dō′lon, *n.* pl. **ei·do·la, ei·do·lons,** ī·dō′la, ī·dō′lonz. [IDOL.] An unreal or spectral form; a phantom.

eight, āt, *a.* [O.E. *eahta* = D. and G. *acht* = Icel. *atta* = Goth. *ahtau,* eight; akin to L. *octo,* Gr. *oktō,* Skt. *ashta,* eight.] One more than seven in number.—*n.* A cardinal number between seven and nine, or a symbol representing it; a set of eight persons, as the crew of a racing boat; a playing card with eight spots.

eight·ball, āt′bạl″, *n. Pool,* a black ball marked with the number eight.—**be·hind the eight ball,** in an extremely disadvantageous position or perplexing situation.

eight·een, ā′tēn′, *n.* A cardinal number, eight plus ten; the symbol representing this sum; a set of 18 persons or things.—**eight·eenth,** ā′tēnth′, *a.* Next in order after the seventeenth; being one of eighteen equal units or parts.—*n.* Eighteenth unit or part, esp. of one; the eighteenth in a series.

eight·een·mo, ā′tēn′mō, *n.* [< *eighteen* and -*mo,* in L. *decimo,* tenth.] The size of a book in which a sheet is cut into eighteen leaves.

eight·fold, āt′fōld″, *a.* Eight times the number or quantity; made up of eight parts.—*adv.*

eighth, ātth, *a.* Next in order after the seventh; being one of eight equal units or parts.—*n.* Eighth unit or part, esp. of one; the eighth in a series; *mus.* an octave.

eighth note, *n. Mus.* a musical note having one eighth the time value of a whole note. Also *Brit.* quaver.

eight·y, ā′tē, *n.* pl. **eight·ies.** A cardinal number, eight times ten; fourscore; a symbol for this number; a set of 80 persons or things.—*a.* Adding up to 80 in number.—**eight·i·eth,** ā′tē·ith, *a., n.*

Ein·stein·i·an, in·stī′nē·an, *a.* Of or pertaining to Albert *Einstein,* theoretical physicist, or his theories, esp. that of relativity.

ein·stein·i·um, in·stī′nē·um, *n.* [From Albert *Einstein.*] A synthetic, radioactive, metallic element. Sym. Es, at. no. 99.

eis·tedd·fod, ā·steTH′vod, ī·steTH′vod, *n.* [W.] A meeting of bards and minstrels in Wales; a periodical Welsh festival for the recitation of poems and performances on the harp.—**eis·tedd·fod·ic,** *a.*

ei·ther, ē′THėr, ī′THėr, *a., pron.* [O.E. *aegther;* contracted from *aeghwæther,* compounded of *a* = *aye,* the augment *ge,* and *hwæther.*] One or the other; one of two things; each of two; the one and the other.—*conj.* A disjunctive conjunction always used as correlative to and preceding *or;* as, *either* the one *or* the other.—*adv.* Too; also; likewise.

e·jac·u·late, i·jak′ū·lāt″, *v.t.*—*ejaculated, ejaculating.* [L. *ejacular, ejaculatus*—*e-,* out, and *jaculum,* a dart, < *jacio,* to throw.] To exclaim; to utter suddenly and briefly; to eject swiftly from a living body, esp. to eject at orgasm.—*v.i.* To eject semen.—i·jak′ū·lit, *n.* The semen ejected in an ejaculation.—**e·jac·u·la·tion,** i·jak″ū·lā′shan, *n.* The uttering of a short sudden exclamation; the exclamation uttered; the sudden discharge of semen by the male reproductive organs.—**e·jac·u·la·to·ry,** i·jak′ū·la·tōr″ē, i·jak′ū·la·tär″ē, *a.*

e·ject, i·jekt′, *v.t.* [L. *ejicio, ejectum*—*e-,* and *jacio,* to throw.] To throw out; to cast out; to drive away; to expel; to dismiss from office; to turn out.—**e·ject·a·ble,** *a.*—**e·jec·tion,** i·jek′shan, *n.* [L. *ejectio.*] The act of ejecting; dismissal; dispossession; expulsion; rejection.—**e·jec·tive,** *a.*

e·jec·ta, i·jek′ta, *n. pl.* Material ejected, as from a volcano in eruption.

e·jec·tion cap·sule, *n.* A detachable pressurized cockpit on certain aircraft which, in an emergency, may be ejected as a unit and parachuted to the ground.

e·jec·tion seat, *n.* An emergency escape seat designed to catapult a flyer from an airplane with sufficient force to clear the airplane completely.

e·ject·ment, i·jekt′ment, *n.* A casting out; a dispossession; *law,* action to repossess and recover ownership of real property and costs and damages.

e·jec·tor, i·jek′tėr, *n.* Someone or something that ejects; the mechanism in a gun that throws out the empty cartridge after firing; a pump used for removing gas or fluid.

eke, ēk, *v.t.*—*eked, eking.* [O.E. *ēcan,* to increase, to eke, Icel. *auka,* Goth. *aukan,* L. *augeo* (whence *augment*), Gr. *auxanō,* to increase.] *Archaic,* to add to; to enlarge by addition.—*adv.* [O.E. *ēāc,* D. *ook,* Sw. *och,* Dan. *og,* G. *auch,* and.] *Archaic,* also; likewise; in addition.

eke out, *v.t.* To provide for or remove, as some insufficiency, by an expedient, as: He *eked* out his knowledge of new math from his child's first textbook. To make, as a living, only by hard labor; to extend, as one's resources, by economical use.

el, el, *n.* (*Often cap.*) elevated train.

e·lab·o·rate, i·lab′o·rāt″, *v.t.*—*elaborated, elaborating.* [L. *elaboro, elaboratum*—*e-,* out, and *laboro,* to labor, < *labor,* labor.] To work out or complete with great detail; to work out fully or perfectly; to produce with labor.—*v.i.* To give more detailed treatment.—i·lab′ėr·it, *a.* Wrought with labor; executed with exactness; highly finished; marked by great detail or complexity.—**e·lab·o·rate·ly**, *adv.*—**e·lab·o·rate·ness**, *n.*—**e·lab·o·ra·tion**, *n.* The act of elaborating; careful or laborious finish bestowed; anything that is elaborated.—**e·lab·o·ra·tive**, *a.*—**e·lab·o·ra·tor**, *n.*

é·lan, ā·län′, *Fr.* ā·läN′, *n.* [Fr.] Dash; impetuous ardor.

e·land, ē′land, *n.* pl. **e·lands, e·land.** [D. *eland,* an elk.] Either of two large African antelopes, genus *Taurotragus,* with short spiral horns.

el·a·pid, el′a·pid, *n.* Any of the family of extremely poisonous snakes, genus *Elapidae,* which includes the cobras, corals, and poisonous snakes found in the warmer areas of both hemispheres.—*a.*

e·lapse, i·laps′, *v.i.*—*elapsed, elapsing.* [L. *elabor, elapsus,* to slip away—*e,* out, and *labor, lapsus,* to glide.] To slip or glide away; to pass away silently: said of time.

e·las·mo·branch, i·las′mo·brangk″, i·laz′mo·brangk″, *n.* [N.L. *Elasmobranchii,* pl., < Gr. *elasmos,* metal plate, and *bragchia,* gills.] Any of the *Elasmobranchii,* a group of fishes with plate-like gills and having cartilaginous rather than bony skeletons, including the sharks and rays.—*a.*

e·las·tic, i·las′tik, *a.* [Fr. *élastique,* L.L. *elasticus,* < Gr. *elastos,* beaten out, extensible, < *elaunō,* to drive, to beat out.] Of solids, capable of spontaneously recovering original shape, size, and form after being altered by some force such as stretching, bending, or pressure; of gases, capable of indefinite expansion. Capable of easy adjustment to circumstances; adaptable; flexible. Capable of readily recovering from depression or exhaustion; buoyant. Capable of springing back or rebounding; bouncy.—**e·las·ti·cal·ly,** *adv.*

e·las·tic, i·las′tik, *n.* A flexible or stretchable fabric endowed with elasticity by the interweaving of rubber threads; something made from such fabric; cords, strings, or bands made of rubber.

e·las·tic·i·ty, i·la·stis′i·tē, ē″la·stis′i·tē, *n.* The quality or state of being elastic; adaptability; resilience; flexibility; buoyancy; *phys.* the capability of a body to recover its original size and shape after it has been altered.

e·las·ti·cize, i·las′ti·sīz″, *v.t.*—*elasticized, elasticizing.* To make or render elastic, as by equipping with elastic bands, as: She *elasticized* the sleeves of the sweater she knitted.—**e·las·ti·cized,** *a.* Marked by or possessing the nature of elasticity, as: He wore *elasticized* hose for medical reasons.

e·las·tin, i·las′tin, *n. Biochem.* the protein or albuminoid which constitutes the basic substance of elastic tissue, as found in tendons and cartilage.

e·las·to·mer, i·las′ta·mėr, *n. Chem.* any elastic substance having physical qualities resembling natural rubber.—**e·las·to·mer·ic,** i·las″to·mer′ik, *a.*

e·late, i·lāt′, *v.t.*—*elated, elating.* [L. *elatus,* pp. of *efferre,* bring out, raise, exalt.] To put in high spirits; to make proud; to make happy.—*a. Liter.* marked by raised spirits; elated.—**e·lat·ed,** i·lā′tid, *a.* Exultant; joyful.—**e·lat·ed·ly,** *adv.*—**e·lat·ed·ness,** *n.*

el·a·ter, el′a·tėr, *n.* [Gr. *elatēr,* a driver.] *Bot.* an elastic spiral filament found in certain plants, as liverworts, which assists in the dispersion of spores; *entom.* any of various small beetles of the family *Elateridae,* esp. the click beetle.

e·lat·er·ite, i·lat′e·rīt″, *n.* A brownish, rubberlike natural mineral resin.

e·la·tion, i·lā′shan, *n.* State of joy or exaltation; a feeling of great pride and happiness.

E lay·er, *n.* A radio reflective layer of the ionosphere occurring from 55 to 85 miles above the earth, and lying immediately below the F layer. Also **Heav·i·side lay·er.**

el·bow, el′bō, *n.* [O.E. *elnboga* = G. *elbogen,* orig. 'arm bow.'] The outer part of the bend or joint of the arm; the angle at this joint when bent; the portion of a sleeve that covers this joint; something bent like the elbow, as a sharp turn in a road or river, or a piece of pipe bent at an angle; the upper end joint in the anterior limb of a quadruped.—*v.t.* To push with, or as with, the elbow; jostle; to make, as one's way, by so pushing.—*v.i.* To elbow one's way.

el·bow grease, *n. Colloq.* energetic labor, esp. physical, as: Digging a ditch requires *elbow grease.*

el·bow·room, el′bō·rŏm″, el′bō·rṳm″, *n.* Room to extend the elbows; ample room; free scope.

eld, eld, *n.* [O.E. *ældu, yldu,* < *ald, eald,* E. *old.*] *Archaic.* Age; old age; an old person.

el·der, el′dėr, *n.* [O.E. *ellern, ellen;* the *d* has been inserted in later times; D. *elloorn,* the elder.] Any tree or shrub of the honeysuckle family, genus *Sambucus,* with white flowers and purple berrylike drupes.

eld·er, el′dėr, *a.* [O.E. *yldra, eldra,* the compar. degree of *eald,* old.] Having lived a longer time; of greater age; prior in origin; senior in rank; pertaining to earlier times.

eld·er, el′dėr, *n.* [O.E. *ealdor,* an ancestor, a chief, a prince.] One who is older than another or others; an ancestor; a person of great influence in a tribal community; a lay official in Presbyterian churches; a Mormon priest.—**eld·er·ship,** *n.* The office of an elder.

el·der·ber·ry, el′dėr·ber″ē, el′dėr·be·rē, *n.* pl. **el·der·ber·ries.** The fruit of the elder, used in making jelly, pie, and wine.

el·der·ly, el′dėr·lē, *a.* Somewhat old; advanced beyond middle age; pertaining to one advanced in age.—**eld·er·li·ness,** *n.*

eld·er states·man, *n.* A highly respected senior member of a group or organization, usu. functioning as a consultant or advisor, esp. in governmental affairs.

eld·est, el′dist, *a.* [O.E. *eldesta,* superl. of *eald, ald,* old.] Oldest; most advanced in age.

eld·est hand, *n.* The card player to whom the first card is dealt; the player to the left of the dealer. Also **eld·er hand.**

El Do·ra·do, el″ do·rä′dō, el″ do·rä′dō, *Sp.* el dạ·RÄ′ᴛʜạ, *n.* [Sp. the golden—*el,* the, and *dorado,* gilt.] A legendary treasure country or city believed to exist in South America or other territory explored by the Spanish conquerors; any region rich in gold or treasure of any kind.

el·dritch, el′drich, *a.* [Origin uncertain.] Weird; uncanny; unearthly. Also **el·drich, el·ritch.**

El·e·at·ic, el″ē·at′ik, *a.* Of or pertaining to *Elea,* an ancient Greek town, or to a philosophical school that originated there. —*n.* An adherent of the Eleatic philosophy, founded by Parmenides and developed by Zeno.—**El·e·at·i·cism,** *n.*

el·e·cam·pane, el″e·kam·pān′, *n.* [L. *inula,* elecampane, and M.L. *campana,* prob. 'of the fields,' < L. *campus,* field.] A plant, *Inula helenium,* with large yellow flowers and aromatic leaves and root.

e·lect, i·lekt′, *v.t.* [L. *eligo, electum—e-,* out, and *lego, lectum,* to pick, choose.] To select for an office by vote or designation; to pick out or select; to choose; to determine in favor of, as: He *elected* to go.—*v.i.* To make a choice.—*a.* Chosen or elected; chosen but not inaugurated, consecrated, or invested with office; as, a bishop-*elect. Theol.* chosen for eternal life; predestinated in the divine counsels.—*n.* pl. **e·lect.** One or

several chosen or set apart; *theol.* those esp. favored by God.

e·lec·tion, i·lek′shan, *n.* [L. *electio.*] The act of electing; the act of choosing a person to fill an office or employment by vote; power to choose or select; choice; liberty to choose or act; as: It is at his *election* to accept or refuse. *Theol.* predetermination by God for heaven.

e·lec·tion·eer, i·lek″sha·nēr′, *v.i.* To work or exert oneself in any way to obtain the election of a candidate or party.— **e·lec·tion·eer·er,** *n.*

e·lec·tive, i·lek′tiv, *a.* Chosen by election; dependent on choice; bestowed or passing by election; pertaining to or consisting in choice or right of choosing; exerting the power of choice; optional; *chem.* having a tendency to mix with certain substances and not others.—*n.* In education, an optional course of study, as opposed to a *required* course.—**e·lec·tive·ly,** *adv.*— **e·lec·tive·ness,** *n.*

e·lec·tor, i·lek′tėr, *n.* One who elects or has the right of electing; a person who has the right of voting for any functionary; specif. one of the persons elected, by vote of the people, to the electoral college, designed to elect the President and Vice-President of the U.S.; (*usu. cap.*) *hist.* one of the German princes with power to elect the Holy Roman Emperor.—**e·lec·tor·al,** i·lek′tėr·al, *a.* Pertaining to election or electors; consisting of electors.

e·lec·tor·ate, i·lek′tėr·it, *n.* A body of electors; the dignity or territory of an Elector of the Holy Roman Emperor.

E·lec·tra com·plex, i·lek′tra kom′pleks, *n.* [From *Electra,* who, in Gr. legend, persuaded her brother to kill their mother to avenge their father's murder.] *Psychoanal.* the unresolved, usu. unconscious, libidinal feelings of a daughter toward her father, accompanied by jealousy of her mother.

e·lec·tress, i·lek′tris, *n.* A woman elector; (*usu. cap.*) the wife or widow of an Elector of the Holy Roman Empire.

e·lec·tric, i·lek′trik, *a.* [N.L. *electricus,* < L. *electrum,* < Gr. *elektron,* amber (as a substance that develops electricity under friction).] Pertaining to, consisting of, containing electric charge or electric current; producing, conveying, operated, or produced by electricity; *fig.* stirring, exhilarating.—**e·lec·tri·cal,** i·lek′tri·kal, *a.*—**e·lec·tri·cal·ly,** *adv.*—**e·lec·tri·cal·ness,** *n.*

e·lec·tric, i·lek′trik, *n.* A vehicle that operates by electricity, such as a streetcar, automobile, or railroad locomotive.

e·lec·tri·cal tran·scrip·tion, *n.* An electric record used esp. for later broadcasting; a radio rebroadcast from such a record.

e·lec·tric chair, *n.* A chair used in prisons for executions by electrocution; the penalty or sentence of death by electrocution.

e·lec·tric charge, *n. Phys.* the presence of an uncancelled, excess of either positive particles (protons), or negative particles (electrons), in a substance.

e·lec·tric eel, *n.* A fish, *Electrophorus electricus,* of eellike form, having the power of giving off strong electric discharges, which serve as a means of offense and defense. It is found in the fresh waters of northern S. America, and sometimes attains a length of over 6 feet.

e·lec·tric eye, *n.* A photoelectric cell; an electric device in which the electric current is controlled by variations in light intensity.

e·lec·tric field, *n. Phys.* a quantitative description of the attraction or repulsion of one electric charge by another; at any one point, it is the ratio of the force exerted on a positive test charge, placed at that point, to the magnitude of the charge.

---

ch- chain, G. na*ch*t;   **th-** *TH*en, *th*in;   **w-** *w*ig, *hw* as sound in *wh*ig;   **z-** *zh* as in a*z*ure, *z*eal.   *Italicized vowel* indicates schwa sound.

e·lec·tri·cian, i·lek·trish′an, ē″lek·trish′-an, n. One who makes, repairs, installs, or operates electric devices or equipment.

e·lec·tric·i·ty, i·lek·tris′i·tē, ē″lek·tris′i·tē, n. Phys., chem. a natural phenomenon known only by its effects, as electric charge, electric current, electric field, electromagnetism; the science that concerns itself with this phenomenon; the measurable existence or flow of subatomic particles more or less freed from their association from any particular molecule or atom. Infectious excitement; keen anticipation.

e·lec·tric ray, n. A fish of the ray family Torpedinidae, capable of emitting electric discharges.

e·lec·tri·fy, i·lek′tri·fī″, v.t.—electrified, electrifying. To equip with electricity; to equip for operation by electricity; to charge with electricity; to affect by electricity. Fig. to give a sudden shock; to thrill.—e·lec·tri·fi·ca·tion, n.—e·lec·tri·fi·er, n.

e·lec·tro·a·nal·y·sis, i·lek″trō·a·nal′i·sis, n. Chemical analysis by electrolysis. —e·lec·tro·an·a·lyt·ic, e·lec·tro·an·a·lyt·i·cal, a.

e·lec·tro·car·di·o·gram, i·lek″trō·kär′dē·o·gram″, n. The record produced by an electrocardiograph. Also cardiogram, EKG, E.K.G., ECG, E.C.G.

e·lec·tro·car·di·o·graph, i·lek″trō·kär′dē·o·graf″, i·lek″trō·kär′dē·o·gräf″, n. An electric instrument used in medical diagnosis to detect and record the heartbeat.—e·lec·tro·car·di·o·graph·ic, a.—e·lec·tro·car·di·o·graph·i·cal·ly, adv.—e·lec·tro·car·di·og·ra·phy, i·lek″trō·kär″dē·og′ra·fē, n.

e·lec·tro·chem·is·try, i·lek″trō·kem′i·strē, n. The branch of chemistry that studies electrically produced chemical changes and production of electricity by chemical change.—e·lec·tro·chem·i·cal, a.—e·lec·tro·chem·i·cal·ly, adv.

e·lec·tro·cute, i·lek′tro·kūt″, v.t.—electrocuted, electrocuting. To execute or kill by means of an electric current or shock.—e·lec·tro·cu·tion, n.

e·lec·trode, i·lek′trōd, n. One of the conductors or terminals, either the cathode or anode, by which an electric current enters or leaves an electrolytic cell, vacuum tube, or the like.

e·lec·tro·de·pos·it, i·lek″trō·di·poz′it, v.t. Chem. to deposit by electrolysis.—n. Chem. a deposit as of metal, produced by electrolysis.—e·lec·tro·dep·o·si·tion, n.

e·lec·tro·dy·nam·ics, i·lek″trō·dī·nam′iks, n. pl. but sing. in constr. Phys. the study of the interactions of moving electric charges.—e·lec·tro·dy·nam·ic, e·lec·tro·dy·nam·i·cal, i·lek″trō·dī·nam′ik, a.

e·lec·tro·dy·na·mom·e·ter, i·lek″trō·dī″na·mom′i·tėr, n. An instrument for measuring electric currents by electrodynamic action.

e·lec·tro·en·ceph·a·lo·graph, i·lek″trō·en·sef′a·lo·graf″, i·lek″trō·en·sef′a·lo·gräf″, n. A device for recording the spontaneous electrical activity of the brain by means of leads attached to the scalp. Also encephalograph.—e·lec·tro·en·ceph·a·lo·gram, i·lek″trō·en·sef′a·lo·gram″, n. A tracing made by an electroencephalograph.—e·lec·tro·en·ceph·a·log·ra·pher, n.—e·lec·tro·en·ceph·a·lo·graph·ic, a.—e·lec·tro·en·ceph·a·log·ra·phy, i·lek″trō·en·sef″a·log′ra·fē, n.

e·lec·tro·form, i·lek′tro·farm″, v.t. To make or form, as an object, by electrodeposition of metal on a mold.—e·lec·tro·form·ing, n. The act or process of making an object by electroplating a removable mold.

e·lec·tro·graph, i·lek′tro·graf″, i·lek′tro·gräf″, n. A device for the electrical transmission of pictures; a picture produced by an electrograph; a device for electrolytically etching metal plates to be used in printing.—e·lec·trog·ra·phy, i·lek·trog′ra·fē, ē″lek·trog′ra·fē, n.—e·lec·tro·graph·ic, a.

e·lec·tro·jet, i·lek′tro·jet″, n. A layer of ions in the upper atmosphere of the earth, found in areas of auroral phenomena.

e·lec·tro·ki·net·ic, i·lek″trō·ki·net′ik, i·lek″trō·kī·net′ik, a. Phys. of or pertaining to the effects of electricity in motion.—e·lec·tro·ki·net·ics, n. pl. but sing. in constr. Phys. the study of electrokinetic effects.

e·lec·trol·y·sis, i·lek·trol′i·sis, ē″lek·trol′i·sis, n. Chem., phys. the decomposition of a chemical compound by an electric current; the destruction of tumors or hair roots by an electric current.—e·lec·tro·lyze, i·lek′tro·līz″, v.t.—electrolyzed, electrolyzing. To decompose by electrolysis.—e·lec·tro·ly·za·tion, n.—e·lec·tro·lyz·er, n.

e·lec·tro·lyte, i·lek′tro·līt″, n. Chem., phys. a substance whose solutions are capable of conducting electric current, esp. a compound that decomposes by electrolysis. Also e·lec·tro·lyt·ic con·duc·tor.

e·lec·tro·lyt·ic, i·lek″tro·lit′ik, a. Pertaining to electrolysis or to an electrolyte. Also e·lec·tro·lyt·i·cal, i·lek″tro·lit′i·kal.

e·lec·tro·mag·net, i·lek″trō·mag′nit, n. A magnet consisting of a core, usu. of soft iron, magnetized by an electric current passing through a wire coiled around the core.

e·lec·tro·mag·net·ic spec·trum, n. The complete range of wavelengths and frequencies of electromagnetic radiation from gamma rays to the longest radio waves and including light waves.

e·lec·tro·mag·net·ic wave, n. Phys. A wave whose characteristics are variations of electric and magnetic fields, such as a radio wave or a light wave.

e·lec·tro·mag·net·ism, i·lek″trō·mag′ni·tiz″um, n. The study of the relation between electric currents and magnetism; magnetism caused by electric current.—e·lec·tro·mag·net·ic, a. Pertaining to electromagnetism or an electromagnet.—e·lec·tro·mag·net·i·cal·ly, adv.

e·lec·tro·met·al·lur·gy, i·lek″trō·met′a·lur″jē, i·lek″trō·me·tal′ėr·jē, n. The use of electricity for producing heat or for electrolysis in the processing of metals.

e·lec·trom·e·ter, i·lek·trom′i·tėr, ē″lek·trom′i·tėr, n. An instrument for measuring electric potential or differences of electric potential between two conductors.

e·lec·tro·mo·tive, i·lek″tro·mō′tiv, a. Pertaining to, causing, or tending to cause an electric current.

e·lec·tro·mo·tive force, n. Elect. the amount of energy supplied by a source of electricity, such as a dry cell, usu. measured in volts.

e·lec·tron, i·lek′tron, n. Elect. an elementary particle of negative charge found outside the nucleus of an atom.

e·lec·tro·neg·a·tive, i·lek″trō·neg′a·tiv, a. Elect. having a charge of negative electricity. Chem. referring to the degree of an atom's tendency to attract and hold valence electrons.—e·lec·tro·neg·a·tiv·i·ty, n.

e·lec·tron gun, n. Phys. an electrode together with the apparatus for controlling the size and shape of the beam of electrons emitted from the electrode.

e·lec·tron·i·cist, i·lek·tron′i·sist, ē″lek·tron′i·sist, n. One who composes electronic music.

e·lec·tron·ics, i·lek·tron′iks, ē″lek·tron′iks, n. pl. but sing. in constr. The branch of physics that studies the behavior and applies the effects of the flow of electrons in vacuum tubes, gases, and semiconductors. —e·lec·tron·ic, a. Relating to or using devices operating by principles of electronics.—e·lec·tron·i·cal·ly, adv.

e·lec·tron lens, n. Phys. an electromagnetic or electrostatic device used to reflect and focus electron beams in an electron microscope, in a manner analogous to optical lenses focusing beams of light.

e·lec·tron mi·cro·scope, n. Phys. an instrument which utilizes the short wavelength of an electron beam, rather than light waves, to obtain magnification and resolution of minute structures for which a light microscope is inadequate. It contains an electron gun whose beam is refracted and focused onto a specimen by an electron lens system; the image is magnified and projected onto a fluorescent screen or stage. —e·lec·tron mi·cros·co·py, n.

e·lec·tron mul·ti·pli·er, n. Elect. a dynode.

e·lec·tro·nog·ra·phy, i·lek″tro·nog′ra·fē, n. A printing process in which the ink is transferred electrostatically.—e·lec·tron·o·gra·phic, a.

e·lec·tron op·tics, n. pl. but sing. in constr. Phys. the study of electron diffraction phenomena, which are in direct analogy to the effect of lenses on light, and the use of electron beams to determine microstructure of many substances.

e·lec·tron tube, n. Any of numerous devices consisting of a sealed glass tube containing a vacuum or a gas at low pressure, in which controlled conduction of electrons occurs. Also vacuum tube.

e·lec·tron volt, n. Phys. the kinetic energy acquired by an electron or particle of similar charge when falling through a potential difference of one volt.

e·lec·tro·pho·re·sis, i·lek″trō·fo·rē′sis, n. Physical chem. the movement of particles suspended in a fluid under the influence of an electric field.

e·lec·troph·o·rus, i·lek·trof′ėr·us, ē″lek·trof′ėr·us, n. pl. e·lec·troph·o·ri, i·lek·trof′o·rī″, ē″lek·trof′o·rī. [N.L.] A simple instrument for generating static electricity by means of induction.

e·lec·tro·plate, i·lek′tro·plāt″, v.t.—electroplated, electroplating. To plate or give a coating of silver or other metal by means of electrolytic deposition.—n. Articles coated by the process of electroplating.

e·lec·tro·pos·i·tive, i·lek″tro·poz′i·tiv, a. Physical chem. containing positive electricity; tending to pass to the negative pole in electrolysis; basic, as an element or radical. —n. An electropositive body.

e·lec·tro·scope, i·lek′tro·skōp″, n. An instrument for detecting the presence of small charges or voltages of electricity.

e·lec·tro·shock, i·lek′tro·shok″, n. Psychiatry, treatment of a mental disorder by electric shock administered to the brain.

e·lec·tro·stat·ic gen·er·a·tor, n. Phys. a generator producing high-voltage, static electric charges. Also Van de Graaff generator.

e·lec·tro·stat·ics, i·lek″trō·stat′iks, n. pl. but sing. in constr. Phys. the branch of electromagnetism that studies and works with the effects of stationary electric charges. —e·lec·tro·stat·ic, a.—e·lec·tro·stat·i·cal·ly, adv.

e·lec·tro·stat·ic u·nit, n. Elect. any of several units in a system based on the force with which a static charge repels an equal static charge at a distance of one centimeter in a vacuum. Abbr. esu, ESU.

e·lec·tro·sur·ger·y, i·lek″trō·sėr′je·rē, n. Use of electricity in surgery.—e·lec·tro·sur·gi·cal, a.—e·lec·tro·sur·gi·cal·ly, adv.

e·lec·tro·ther·a·py, i·lek″trō·ther′a·pē, n. The treatment of disease by the use of brief, non-convulsive electric shocks.

e·lec·tro·ther·mal, i·lek″trō·thėr′mal, a. Pertaining to heat produced by electricity; relating to the combination of electricity and heat.—e·lec·tro·ther·mic, a.

e·lec·trot·o·nus, i·lek·trot′o·nus, ē″lek·-trot′o·nus, *n.* [N.L. < *electro-*, form of Gr. *electron*, amber, used to represent E. *electric*, and Gr. *tonos*, tension.] The altered state of a nerve during the passage of an electric current through it.—**e·lec·tro·ton·ic,** i·lek″tro·ton′ik, *a.*

e·lec·tro·type, i·lek′tro·tīp″, *n.* The process of producing copies of types, woodcuts, medals, and the like by means of the electric deposition of copper upon a mold taken from the original; a copy thus produced.—*v.t.*—*electrotyped, electrotyping.* To make an electrotype of.—**e·lec·tro·typ·er,** *n.*

e·lec·tro·va·lence, i·lek″trō·vā′lens, *n. Chem.* a digit indicating the number of charges transferred in an atom resulting in the formation of ions; the number of negative or positive charges gained by an atom in the gain or loss of electrons. Also **e·lec·tro·va·len·cy,** i·lek″trō·vā′len·sē.—**e·lec·tro·va·lent,** *a.*

e·lec·trum, i·lek′trum, *n.* [L. < Gr. *elektron.*] A pale yellow alloy of gold and silver.

e·lec·tu·ar·y, i·lek′chŏo·er″ē, *n. Veter. med.* a medicinal paste usu. composed of a powder mixed with honey or syrup.

el·ee·mos·y·nar·y, el″e·mos′i·ner″ē, el″e·moz′i·ner″ē, el″ē·mos′i·ner″ē, el″ē·moz′i·ner″ē, *a.* [L.L. *eleemosynarius,* < Gr. *eleémosynē,* alms, < *eleeō,* to pity, *eleos,* compassion.] Relating to charity; supported by or dependent on charity.

el·e·gance, el′e·gans, *n.* Elegant quality; something elegant; an elegant characteristic; a refinement. Also **el·e·gan·cy.**

el·e·gant, el′e·gant, *a.* [O.Fr. *elegant* (Fr. *elegant*), < L. *elegans* (-ant-), fastidious, nice, fine, elegant, connected with *eligere,* pick out, choose.] Tastefully fine or luxurious in dress, manners, appointments; gracefully refined, as in tastes, habits, or literary style; nice, choice, or excellent in quality or kind, as a contrivance, preparation, or process; characterized by a graceful distinction in form or appearance; in general, choice, fine, or pleasingly superior. —**el·e·gant·ly,** *adv.*

el·e·gi·ac, el″e·jī′ak, el″e·jī′ak, i·lē′jē·ak″, *a.* Pertaining to the elegiac couplet, which has a first line of six dactyls and a second line of either five or six dactyls in which the unaccented parts of the third and sixth feet have been dropped; comprising or pertaining to elegy; expressing sorrow or lamentation.—*n.*

e·le·git, i·lē′jit, *n. Law,* a writ of execution by which any or all of a debtor's property is held by his creditor until the debt is paid.

el·e·gy, el′i·jē, *n.* pl. **el·e·gies.** [L. *elegia,* < Gr. *elegeia,* < *elegos,* a lament.] A mournful or plaintive poem, or a funeral song; a poem or a song expressive of sorrow and lamentation; a dirge; *class. poetry,* any poem written in elegiac verse.—**el·e·gist,** el′i·jist, *n.* A writer of elegies.—**el·e·gize,** el′i·jīz″, *v.i.*—*elegized, elegizing.* To write or compose elegies.—*v.t.* To celebrate or lament in an elegy.

el·e·ment, el′e·ment, *n.* [O.Fr. *element* < L. *elementum,* a first principle, rudiment.] A component or constituent part of a whole; one of the substances, usu. earth, water, air, or fire, formerly considered as constituting the material universe; the natural habitat or environment of an animal or person, as: He's in his *element* now. *Pl.* weather conditions, esp. severe; as, exposed to the *elements*; the basic principles of an art or science; the bread and wine used in the Eucharist. *Chem.* one of a class of substances that consist solely of atoms of the same atomic number. *Math.* a member of a class or set; any unit of the data necessary for calculation. *Geom.* any one of the points,

lines, planes, or other geometric forms which compose a figure; *elect.* an integral unit within an electrical instrument having terminals for direct connection with some other unit.

el·e·men·tal, el″e·men′tal, *a.* Of, or relating to a fundamental constituent; simple; uncompounded; pertaining to rudiments or first principles; basic; of or pertaining to the four elements or any one of them; pertaining to the great forces of nature; referring to the chemical elements.

el·e·men·ta·ry, el″e·men′ta·rē, el″e·men′-trē, *a.* Containing or relating to first principles or rudiments; referring to an elementary school; simple or uncompounded; having the characteristics of an element or principal substance; primary; of or referring to the great forces of nature or the four elements; elemental; *chem.* referring to one or more of the elements.—**el·e·men·ta·ri·ly,** *adv.*—**el·e·men·ta·ri·ness,** *n.*

el·e·men·ta·ry par·ti·cle, *n. Phys.* Fundamental particle.

el·e·men·ta·ry school, *n.* A school covering the first 6 to 8 years of instruction in fundamentals, as reading, to children 6 to 12 or 14 years old.

el·e·mi, el′e·mē, *n.* The resinous exudation from various trees, used in the manufacture of perfumes, ointments, and varnish. Also *gum elemi.*

e·len·chus, i·leng′kus, *n.* pl. **e·len·chi,** i·leng′kī, i·leng′kē. [L. < Gr. *elegchos,* < *elegchein,* cross-examine, refute.] A logical refutation; an argument which refutes another argument by proving the contrary of its conclusion; a false refutation; a sophistical argument.—**e·lenc·tic,** *a.*

el·e·phant, el′e·fant, *n.* [L. *elephantus,* also *elephas* (*elephant-*), < Gr. *elephas* (*elephant*), elephant, ivory.] Any of large hoofed mammals with the nose drawn into a long, prehensile proboscis or trunk and lower incisor teeth that form tusks of ivory, comprising two existing species: *Elephas maximus,* of Asia with comparatively small ears, and *Loxodonta africana,* of Africa with large flapping ears.

el·e·phan·ti·a·sis, el″e·fan·tī′a·sis, el″e·-fan·tī′a·sis, *n.* [< Gr. *elephas,* E. *elephant.*] *Pathol.* a chronic disease, due to lymphatic obstruction by filarial worms, characterized by enormous enlargement of the parts affected and hardening and fissuring of the skin, which becomes like an elephant's hide.

el·e·phan·tine, el″e·fan′tin, el″e·fan′tīn, el″e·fan′tēn, *a.* Pertaining to the elephant; resembling an elephant; huge; immense.

el·e·phant shrew, *n.* Any of the small, leaping, mouselike insectivorous animals of the family *Macroscelididæ* of Africa, which have a long snout suggesting the proboscis of an elephant.

el·e·vate, el′e·vāt″, *v.t.*—*elevated, elevating.* [L. *elevo, elevatum,* to lift up—*e-,* out, up, and *levo,* to raise, < *levis,* light in weight.] To raise; to raise from a low or deep place to′a higher place; to raise to a higher state or station; to improve, refine, or dignify; to augment or swell; to make louder.

el·e·vat·ed, el′e·vā″tid, *a.* Raised; exalted; dignified; elated; excited.

el·e·vat·ed rail·road, *n.* A railway with tracks on an elevated structure, as above surface or ground traffic.

el·e·va·tion, el″e·vā′shan, *n.* [L. *eleva-tio(n-).*] The height to which anything is elevated; the angle at which anything is raised above a horizontal direction; altitude above ground level; an elevated place; an eminence; loftiness; grandeur or dignity; nobleness; the act of elevating or the state of being elevated; *arch.* a drawing or design which represents an object or structure as being projected geometrically on a vertical plane, esp. one showing the exterior as seen from

the front or the side; *surv.* a particular height above a given level.—**the El·e·va·tion,** *R. Cath. Ch.* the lifting up of the host and chalice in the service of the mass.

el·e·va·tor, el′e·vā″tèr, *n.* One who or that which elevates, raises, lifts, or exalts; a mechanical contrivance for raising passengers or goods from a lower place to a higher one; a hoist; a granary provided with devices for lifting grain; an airfoil on the tail of an airplane for producing up and down motion.

el·ev·en, i·lev′en, *n.* [O.E. *endleofan, endlufon,* = D. *elf* = G. *eilf* = Icel. *ellifu* = Goth. *ainlif,* eleven; < the Teut. stem represented by E. *one,* with a termination occurring also in E. *twelve.*] The cardinal number between 10 and 12; a symbol, like 11 or xi, representing it; a set of 11 persons or things.—*a.*

e·lev·enth, i·lev′enth, *a.* Next after the tenth; pertaining to one of eleven equal parts.—*n.* The eleventh member of a series; an eleventh part.—**the e·lev·enth hour,** *fig.* the last possible hour for doing something, an allusion to the parable of the laborers in the vineyard from Matt. xx.1–16.

el·e·von, el′e·von″, *n. Aeron.* A control surface which combines the functions of an elevator and an aileron.

elf, elf, *n.* pl. **elves,** elvz. [O.E. *aelf* = Icel. *álfr,* elf, = G. *alp,* nightmare, incubus.] A small imaginary being with magical powers, usu. thought to be in human form; a sprite; a fairy; a mischievous person; a dwarf or a small child.—**elf·in,** el′fin, *a.* Pertaining to elves; elflike.—*n.* An elf.— **elf·ish,** el′fish, *a.* Elflike; elfin; mischievous. Also **elv·ish.**—**elf·ish·ly,** *adv.*—**elf·ish·ness,** *n.*

e·lic·it, i·lis′it, *v.t.* [L. *elicio, elicitum*—*e-,* out, and *lacere,* to allure; akin *delicate, delight.*] To bring or draw out; to bring to light by reasoning or discussion; as, to *elicit* the truth; to educe; to evoke, as: The speech *elicited* much controversy.—**e·lic·i·ta·tion,** *n.*—**e·lic·i·tor,** *n.*

e·lide, i·līd′, *v.t.*—*elided, eliding.* [L. *elido*—*e-,* out, and *lædo,* to strike.] To omit or slur over in pronunciation, as a vowel, consonant, or syllable; to suppress, abridge, or leave out.—**e·lid·i·ble,** *a.*

el·i·gi·ble, el′i·ji·bl, *a.* [Fr. *éligible,* < L. *eligo*—*e-,* out, and *lego,* to choose.] Fit to be chosen for some purpose or duty; worthy of choice; desirable; legally qualified to be chosen.—*n.* A person who is eligible.— **el·i·gi·bil·i·ty,** el″i·ji·bil′i·tē, *n.* The state or condition of being eligible; capability of being chosen.—**el·i·gi·bly,** *adv.*

e·lim·i·nate, i·lim′i·nāt″, *v.t.*—*eliminated, eliminating.* [L. *elimino, eliminatum*—*e-,* out, and *limen,* threshold.] To take out or separate as being neither necessary nor an element of value; to set aside as unimportant or not to be considered; of an organism, to discharge wastes; *math.* to cause to disappear from an equation.—**e·lim·i·na·tion,** i·lim″i·nā′shan, *n.* The act of eliminating; *math.* the solution of a set of equations by successive removal of variables.—**e·lim·i·na·tive,** *a.*—**e·lim·i·na·tor,** *n.*

e·li·sion, i·lizh′an, *n.* The act of eliding; the cutting off or suppression of a vowel or syllable in pronunciation or verse.

e·lite, i·lēt′, ā·lēt′, *n.* [Fr. lit. elected or select.] Those who are choice or select; the best; a kind of typewriter type having twelve characters to the linear inch.—*a.*

e·lit·ism, i·lē′tiz·um, ā·lē′tiz·um, *n.* The practice of rule by the elite class; the belief that this practice should prevail; a pride in belonging to an elite class.—**e·lit·ist,** *n.*

e·lix·ir, i·lik′sèr, *n.* [M.L. *elixir,* < Ar. *al-iksir,* philosophers' stone, prob. < Gr. *xerion,* a drying powder for wounds, < *xeros,* dry.] *Phar.* an aromatic, sweetened

---

ch- chain, G. na*ch*t; **th-** THen, thin; **w-** wig, hw as sound in whig; **z-** zh as in azure, zeal. *Italicized vowel* indicates schwa sound.

alcoholic liquid containing medicinal agents, or for use as a vehicle for such agents; an alchemic preparation previously thought to be capable of changing base metals into gold, or for prolonging life; the quintessence or absolute embodiment of anything; a sovereign remedy.

E·liz·a·beth·an, i·liz′a·bē′than, i·liz′a-·beth′an, a. Pertaining to Queen Elizabeth I of England (1533–1603) or her period; as, *Elizabethan* poetry; of or relating to the architectural style of the times of Elizabeth and James I, when the debased Gothic and Italian were combined, characterized by large windows, tall and highly decorated chimneys, and much ornament.—*n.* Any Englishman, but esp. one notable in the arts or literature, who lived during the reign of Elizabeth I.

elk, elk, *n.* pl. **elks, elk.** [Icel. *elgr,* O.H.G. *elaho,* Sw. *elg;* akin to L. *alces,* an elk.] In Europe and Asia, the largest member of the deer family, genus *Alces,* similar to the moose; in America, the wapiti, a member of the deer family, next in size to the moose; a leather used esp. for sport shoes, originally elkskin but now generally calfskin or cowhide. (*Cap.*) a member of the *Benevolent and Protective Order of Elks,* a fraternal organization.

elk·hound, elk′hound″, *n.* One of a breed of dogs having a short, compact body and gray coat, originally raised in Norway for hunting game. Also **Nor·we·gian elk·-hound.**

ell, el, *n.* [O.E. *eln;* D. *ell, elle,* G. *elle,* O.H.G. *elna,* Sw. *aln,* Icel. *alin,* Goth. *aleina;* akin to L. *ulna,* Gr. *ōlenē,* the forearm, and hence, a measure of length.] Any of various measures of length once used for cloth.

ell, el, *n.* Something shaped like an L; an extension to a building, at right angles to one end. Also **el.**

el·lipse, i·lips′, *n.* [Gr. *elleipsis,* an omission or defect, < *elleipo,* to leave out—*el,* out, and *leipō,* to leave.] *Geom.* An oval figure produced when any cone is cut by a plane which passes through it, not parallel to or cutting the base; a closed plane curve such that the sum of the distances of one of the points on the curve from two fixed points, called foci, is constant.

el·lip·sis, i·lip′sis, *n.* pl. **el·lip·ses,** i·lip′-sēz. *Gram.* the omission from any syntactical construction of one or more words or elements which the hearer or reader may easily supply, as: He ordered red wine not white (white *wine* understood.) *Print.* the marks or mark (— or ∗∗∗ or . . .) denoting the omission or suppression of letters or words.

el·lip·soid, i·lip′soid, *n. Geom.* a solid figure, all plane sections of which are ellipses or circles.—*a.*—**el·lip·soi·dal,** i·-lip·soid′al, el″ip·soid′al, *a.*

el·lip·ti·cal, i·lip′ti·kal, *a.* Pertaining to an ellipse; having the form of an ellipse; pertaining to ellipsis. Also **el·lip·tic,** i·lip′tik.—**el·lip·ti·cal·ly,** *adv.*—**el·lip·-ti·ci·ty,** i·lip·tis′i·tē, el″ip·tis′i·tē, *n.*

elm, elm, *n.* [O.E. *elm,* D. *olm,* Icel. *álmr,* Dan. *ælm, alm;* akin to L. *ulmus,* Bohem. *gilm* (pron. *yilm*), elm.] A valuable timber and shade tree of the genus *Ulmus* found in North America and Europe.

elm·blight, elm′blīt, *n. Plant pathol.* Dutch elm disease.

el·o·cu·tion, el″o·kū′shan, *n.* [L. *elocutio,* < *eloquor, elocutus,* to speak out—*e-,* out, and *loquor,* to speak.] The art of speaking effectively in public; the manner in which a speech is delivered.—**el·o·cu·tion·ar·y,** el″o·kū′sha·ner″ē, *a.*—**el·o·cu·tion·ist,** *n.*

E·lo·him, el″ō·hēm′, e·lō′him, *liturgical use* el″ō·kēm′, *n.* A Hebrew name for God used in the Old Testament in passages originat-

ing in the later periods of biblical history.—**E·lo·his·tic,** e″lō·his′tik, *a.* Pertaining to certain passages in the Old Testament, esp. in the Pentateuch, in which the Almighty is always spoken of as *Elohim.*

e·loign, i·loin′, *v.t.* [Fr. *éloigner,* O.Fr. *esloignier,* < L. *ex-* out of, and *longe,* long, far.] To remove to a distance. Also **e·loin.**—**e·loign·ment,** *n. Law,* the removal of a person or goods from legal jurisdiction.

e·lon·gate, i·lạng′gāt, i·long′gāt, ē′lạng-·gāt″, ē′long·gāt″, *v.t.*—**elongated, elongating.** [L.L. *elongatus,* pp. of *elongare,* remove, prolong, < L. *e-* out of, and *longe,* long, far, *longus,* long.] To draw out to greater length; lengthen; extend.—*v.i.* To increase in length.—*a.* Outstretched; protracted; elongated.—**e·lon·ga·tion,** *n.* The act of elongating or the state of being elongated; that which is elongated; an elongated part; an extension; *astron.* the angular distance of a planet from the sun, or of a satellite from its primary.—**e·lon·gat·ed,** *a.*

e·lope, i·lōp′, *v.i.*—**eloped, eloping.** [< D. *loopen,* the same word as G. *laufen,* Goth. *hlaupan,* to run, to leap, E. *leap,* with prefix *e-* out, away.] To run away to be married, usu. without parental knowledge or consent; to run away with a lover.—**e·lope·ment,** *n.*—**e·lop·er,** *n.*

el·o·quence, el′o·kwens, *n.* The action, practice, or art of using language with fluency, power, and aptness; eloquent language or discourse.

el·o·quent, el′o·kwent, *a.* Having the power of expressing strong emotions vividly and appropriately, as an orator; impellingly expressive, as a great work of art or music; characterized by eloquence, as a speech.—**el·lo·quent·ly,** *adv.*

else, els, *a.* [O.E. *elles,* else, otherwise; akin to O.H.G. *eli, ali,* Goth. *alis;* L. *alius,* Gr. *allos,* another.] Other; in addition; as, nothing or nobody *else,* nowhere *else,* who *else.*—*adv.* Otherwise; if the fact were different, as: He was ill, or *else* he would have come.

else·where, els′hwâr″, els′wâr″, *adv.* In, at, or to another place.

e·lu·ci·date, i·lū′si·dāt″, *v.t.*—**elucidated, elucidating.** [L.L. *elucido, elucidatum*—L. *e-,* out, and *lucidus,* bright.] To make clear or manifest; to explain; to remove obscurity from and render intelligible.—**e·lu·ci·da·tion,** *n.*—**e·lu·ci·da·tive,** *a.*—**e·lu·ci·da·tor,** *n.*

e·lude, i·lūd′, *v.t.*—**eluded, eluding.** [L.] To escape the comprehension of, as: Your meaning *eludes* me. To evade or avoid by stratagem, deceit, or dexterity; as, to *elude* pursuers.

e·lu·sion, i·lū′zhan, *n.* An escape by artifice or deception; an evasion.

e·lu·sive, i·lū′siv, *a.* Tending to elude a clear understanding or expression; evasive. Also **e·lu·so·ry,** i·lū′so·rē.—**e·lu·sive·ly,** *adv.*—**e·lu·sive·ness,** *n.*

e·lute, ē·lūt′, i·lūt′, *v.t.*—**eluted, eluting.** *Chem.* To wash out, as an adsorbed material, using a solvent.—**e·lu·tion,** *n.*

e·lu·tri·ate, i·lū′trē·āt″, *v.t.*—**elutriated, elutriating.** [L. *elutrio, elutriatum,* < *eluo, elutum,* to wash off—*e-,* off, and *luo,* to wash.] To purify, remove, or separate by washing and straining, or decanting.—**e·lu·tri·a·tion,** *n.*—**e·lu·tri·a·tor,** *n.*

e·lu·vi·a·tion, i·lū″vē·ā′shan, *n.* The movement of suspended particles within the soil, caused by an excess of rainfall over evaporation.—**e·lu·vi·ate,** i·lū′vē·āt″, *v.i.* —*eluviated, eluviating.* To go through the process of eluviation.

e·lu·vi·um, i·lū′vē·um, *n.* pl. **e·lu·vi·a,** i·lū′vē·a. [N.L., < L. *eluere,* wash out or away, < *e-,* out of, and *luere,* wash.] *Geol.* a deposit of soil, dust, or other debris that is produced by the decomposition and

weathering of rock and is found where this process takes place; rock debris drifted and laid down by wind action.—**e·lu·vi·al,** i·lū′vē·al, i·lū′vyal, *a.*

el·ver, el′vêr, *n.* An immature eel.

elv·ish, el′vish, *a.* Pertaining to elves or fairies; mischievous, as if done by elves; elfish.

E·ly·si·um, i·lizh′ē·um, i·lē′zhē·um, i·liz′ē·um, i·lē′zē·um, i·lizh′um, *n.* [L., < Gr. *ēlysion (pedion),* the Elysian fields.] *Mythol.* a place assigned to good souls after death; any exquisitely happy place; paradise.—**E·ly·si·an,** i·lizh′an, i·lē′zhan, *a.*

el·y·tron, el′i·tron″, *n.* pl. **el·y·tra,** el′i·tra. [Gr., a cover, sheath, < *elyō,* to roll around.] The wing sheath or coriaceous membrane which forms the forewing in certain insects, as beetles, serving to cover and protect the posterior wing.—**el·y·troid,** el′i·troid″, *a.* Like an elytron.

em, em, *n. Print.* the square of any size of type used as the unit of measurement for printed matter; orig. the portion of a line occupied by the letter *m.*

e·ma·ci·ate, i·mā′shē·āt″, *v.i.*—**emaciated, emaciating.** [L. *emacio, emaciatum*—*e-,* intens., and *macies,* leanness.] To lose flesh gradually; to become lean from loss of appetite or other cause.—*v.t.* To cause to lose flesh gradually; to reduce to leanness.—**e·ma·ci·at·ed,** *a.* Thin; wasted.—**e·ma·-ci·a·tion,** i·mā″shē·ā′shan, i·mā″sē·ā′shan, *n.* The act of making or becoming lean or thin in flesh; the state of being reduced to leanness.

em·a·nate, em′a·nāt″, *v.i.*—**emanated, emanating.** [L. *emano, emanatum*—*e-,* out, and *mano,* to flow.] To flow forth; to proceed from something as the source, fountain, or origin.—*v.t.* To give forth; to discharge.

em·a·na·tion, em″a·nā′shan, *n.* The act of emanating; that which emanates, issues, flows, or proceeds from any source, substance, or body.—**em·a·na·tion·al,** *a.* —**em·a·na·tive,** em′a·nā″tiv, *a.*

e·man·ci·pate, i·man′si·pāt″, *v.t.*—**emancipated, emancipating.** [L. *emancipo, emancipatum*—*e-,* out, *manus,* the hand, and *capio,* to take.] To restore from bondage to freedom; to free from bondage, restriction, or restraint of any kind; to liberate from subjection, controlling power, or influence. —**e·man·ci·pa·tion,** i·man″si·pā′shan, *n.* The act of emancipating; deliverance from bondage or controlling influence; liberation. —**e·man·ci·pa·tion·ist,** *n.* One who supports emancipation.—**e·man·ci·pa·tor,** i·man′si·pā″tèr, *n.* One who emancipates.

e·mar·gi·nate, i·mär′ji·nāt, *a.* [L. *emarginatus*—*e-,* not, and *margo, marginis,* border, margin.] Having a notched margin; *bot.* having a shallow notch at the apex, as a leaf. Also **e·mar·gi·nat·ed,** i·mär′ji·-nā″tid.

e·mas·cu·late, i·mas′kū·lāt″, *v.t.*—**emasculated, emasculating.** [L. *e-,* not, and *masculus,* dim. of *mas,* a male.] To castrate; to deprive of masculine vigor; to render effeminate; of written or spoken language, to impoverish or deprive of potent qualities by excision.—i·mas′kū·lit, i·mas′kū·lāt″, *a.* Effeminate.—**e·mas·cu·la·tion,** *n.*— **e·mas·cu·la·tor,** *n.*—**e·mas·cu·la·to·ry,** i·mas′kū·la·tōr″ē, i·mas′kū·la·tạr″ē, *a.*

em·balm, em·bäm′, *v.t.* [Prefix *em,* and *balm,* balsam.] Of a dead body, to protect from decay by treating with drugs and chemicals; to preserve from loss or decay. —**em·balm·er,** *n.*—**em·balm·ment,** *n.*

em·bank, em·bangk′, *v.t.* [Prefix *em,* and *bank.*] To enclose with a bank; to defend by banks, mounds, or dikes.—**em·bank·ment,** em·bangk′ment, *n.* The act of surrounding or defending with a bank; a mound or bank raised to hold back water or to carry railroads and roadways.

em·bar·go, em·bär′gō, *n.* pl. **em·bar·-goes.** [Sp. *embargo,* an embargo, embarrassment, lit. what serves as a bar—prefix *em* for *in,* and L.L. *barra,* a bar; akin *embarrass.*] A restraint or prohibition imposed by a government on merchant vessels to prevent their entering or leaving its ports; an order issued by a government regulatory agency restricting, prohibiting, or regulating the transportation of freight; any legal restriction on commerce; a restraint or hindrance imposed on anything.—*v.t.—embargoed, embargoing.* To put an embargo on.

em·bark, em·bärk′, *v.t.* [Fr. *embarquer,* < *em-* (< L. *im-,* in) and *barque,* E. *bark.*] To put or receive on board a ship; of a person, to involve in an enterprise; of money, to venture or invest in an enterprise.—*v.i.* To board a ship, as for a voyage; to engage in an enterprise or a business.—**em·bar·ka·-tion, em·bar·ca·tion, em·bark·ment,** *n.*

em·bar·rass, em·bar′as, *v.t.* [Fr. *embarrasser,* < Sp. *embarazar* or It. *imbarazzare,* < L. *im-,* in, and M.L. *barra,* E. *bar.*] To cause to feel self-conscious; to confuse, disconcert, or abash; to render difficult or intricate, as a question or problem; complicate; to put obstacles or difficulties in the way of; impede; hamper; to beset with financial difficulties.—*v.i.* To feel self-conscious.—**em·bar·rassed·ly,** em·bar′ast·lē, em·bar′a·sid·lē, *adv.*—**em·bar·rass·ing·ly,** *adv.*

em·bar·rass·ment, em·bar′as·ment, *n.* The state of being embarrassed; abashment; confusion of mind; anything which embarrasses; an exorbitant amount.

em·bas·sa·dor, em·bas′a·dėr, *n.* An ambassador.

em·bas·sy, em′ba·sē, *n.* pl. **em·bas·sies.** The mission or function of an ambassador; a body of persons entrusted with ambassadorial functions; an ambassador together with his staff; a legation; the official office and residence of an ambassador.

em·bat·tle, em·bat′l, *v.t.—embattled, embattling.* To arrange in order of battle; to array for battle; to furnish with battlements.—**em·bat·tle·ment,** *n.*

em·bay, em·bā′, *v.t.* To enclose in a bay or inlet; to landlock.—**em·bay·ment,** em·bā′ment, *n.* Any bay or similar-appearing terrestial formation; that action by which bay formation takes place.

em·bed, em·bed′, *v.t.—embedded, embedding.* To fix or enclose in a surrounding mass; to lay in or as in a bed.—**em·bed·ment,** *n.*

em·bel·lish, em·bel′ish, *v.t.* [Fr. *embellir*—prefix *em-,* and *belle,* L. *bellus,* pretty, beautiful.] To adorn; to beautify with decorative devices; to decorate; to heighten the attractiveness, as of a story, by adding imaginary statements.—**em·bel·lish·ment,** *n.* The act of embellishing or state of being embelished; adornment; ornament; decoration; the addition of fabricated statements to a recital of facts.

em·ber, em′bėr, *n.* [O.E. *æmyrian,* cinders; Dan. *emmer,* Icel. *eimyrja,* embers.] A small live coal or glowing piece of wood; *pl.* the smoldering remains of a fire.

Em·ber days, *n. pl.* [O.E. *ymbrine, ymbrene,* the circle or course of the year, < *ymb* or *emb,* round, and *rinnan,* to run.] Days for fasting and penitence, occurring quarterly each year on the Wednesdays, Fridays, and Saturdays after the first Sunday in Lent, Whitsunday, September 14th, and December 13th, as celebrated in the Rom. Cath. Ch. and other Western churches.

em·bez·zle, em·bez′l, *v.t.—embezzled, embezzling.* [O.Fr. *embeasiler,* to filch, *besler,* to deceive; origin doubtful.] To appropriate fraudulently to one's own use that which is entrusted to one's care.—**em·bez·zle·ment,** *n.*—**em·bez·zler,** *n.*

em·bit·ter, em·bit′ėr, *v.t.* To make bitter or more bitter; to create feelings of hostility or bitterness.—**em·bit·ter·ment,** *n.*

em·blaze, em·blāz′, *v.t.—emblazed, emblazing.* To kindle; to light up or make bright, as by a blaze.—**em·blaz·er,** *n.*

em·bla·zon, em·blā′zon, *v.t.* To depict, as an armorial ensign on a shield; to decorate in bright colors; to celebrate; proclaim sensationally.—**em·bla·zon·er,** *n.*—**em·blaz·on·ment,** em·blā′zon·ment, *n.*—**em·bla·zon·ry,** em·blā′zon·rē, *n.*

em·blem, em′blem, *n.* [L. *emblema,* inlaid work, ornamentation, < Gr. *emblēma,* an insertion, *emballein,* throw in.] An object, or a representation of it, symbolizing something, as a quality, state, or class of persons; a symbol; a sign, design, or figure used symbolically as the distinctive badge of something, as of a person, family, or nation; an allegorical drawing or picture with explanatory writing; a fable or allegory capable of being expressed pictorially.—*v.t.* To represent by an emblem.—**em·blem·at·ic,** em″ble·mat′ik, *a.* Pertaining to, of the nature of, or serving as an emblem; symbolic; typical. Also **em·blem·at·i·cal.**—**em·blem·at·i·cal·ly,** *adv.*—**em·blem·a·tist,** em·blem′a·tist, *n.* A designer, maker, or user of emblems.—**em·blem·a·tize,** em·blem′a·tīz″, *v.t.—emblematized, emblematizing.* To serve as an emblem of; represent by an emblem; symbolize.

em·ble·ments, em′ble·ments, *n. pl.* [O.Fr. *emblaement,* < *emblaer* (Fr. *emblaver*), < M.L. *imbladare,* sow with grain.] *Law,* the products of annual cultivation of the land which lawfully belong to the tenant.

em·bod·y, em·bod′ē, *v.t.—embodied, embodying.* To lodge in or invest with a body; to incarnate; to provide with a concrete form; to render obvious to the senses or mental perception; as, to *embody* thought in words; to form or collect into a body or united mass; to collect into a whole.—**em·bod·i·ment,** em·bod′ē·ment, *n.* The act of embodying or investing with a body; the state of being embodied; bodily or material representation; the act of collecting or forming into a body or united whole.—**em·bod·i·er,** *n.*

em·bold·en, em·bōl′den, *v.t.* To give boldness or courage to; to encourage.

em·bo·lec·to·my, em″bo·lek′to·mē, *n. pl.* **em·bo·lec·to·mies.** *Surg.* removal of an embolus.

em·bol·ic, em·bol′ik, *a. Embryol.* of or pertaining to an emboly; *pathol.* pertaining to an embolus or to embolism.

em·bo·lism, em′bo·liz″um, *n.* An intercalation; the time intercalated. *Med.* blockage of a blood vessel by an embolus; broadly, an embolus.

em·bo·lus, em′bo·lus, *n.* pl. **em·bo·li,** em′bo·lī. [Gr. *embolos,* wedge or plug.] *Med.* an abnormal particle circulating in the bloodstream, as an air bubble or blood clot.

em·bo·ly, em′bo·lē, *n.* pl. **em·bo·lies.** *Embryol.* the intrusion or growth of one part into another, as in the invagination of the blastula wall by gastrula formation.

em·bos·om, em·buz′om, em·bŏ′zom, *v.t.* To enclose; to take into or hold in the bosom; to cherish.

em·boss, em·bås′, em·bos′, *v.t. Metalworking,* to fashion relief or raised work on; to represent in relief, as a surface design.—**em·boss·er,** em·bå′sėr, em·bos′ėr, *n.*—**em·boss·ment,** *n.*

em·bou·chure, äm″bu·shur′,äm′bu·shur″, *Fr.* aN·bö·shyR′, *n.* [Fr., < prefix *em,* and *bouche,* mouth.] A mouth of a river. *Mus.* the part of a wind instrument to which the mouth is applied; the shaping of the lips to this mouthpiece.

em·bowed, em·bōd′, *a.* Bent outward, as an archery bow; vaulted or arched.

em·bow·el, em·bou′el, em·boul′, *v.t.—emboweled, emboweling, embowelled, embowelling.* To disembowel.

em·bow·er, em·bou′ėr, *v.i.* To lodge or rest in a bower.—*v.t.* To shelter, as with foliage.

em·brace, em·brās′, *v.t.—embraced, embracing.* [Fr. *embrasser,* to embrace—*em-,* in, and *bras,* the arm.] To take or clasp in the arms, or to press to the bosom as an expression of affection; to hug. To accept, receive, or avail oneself of; as, to *embrace* an idea or opportunity. To adopt, to make one's own, as: He *embraced* the Moslem faith. To enclose, encompass, or contain, as: A redwood fence *embraced* the rose gardens. To take in or include, as: His painting *embraced* most of the newer art techniques.—*v.i.* To participate in an embrace.—*n.* The act of embracing.—**em·brace·ment,** *n.*—**em·brac·er,** *n.*—**em·brace·a·ble,** *a.*

em·brac·er·y, em·brā′sa·rē, *n. Law,* an attempt to influence a jury, by promises, persuasions, entreaties, money, or the like.—**em·brace·or,** em·brā′sėr, *n. Law,* one who practices embracery.

em·branch·ment, em·branch′ment, em·bränch′ment, *n.* A branching or ramification; a branch.

em·bran·gle, em·brang′gl, *v.t.—embrangled, embrangling.* To confuse; entangle; embroil. Also **im·bran·gle.—em·bran·gle·ment,** *n.*

em·bra·sure, em·brā′zhėr, *n.* [Fr.] *Fort.* an opening in a wall or parapet through which cannons may be pointed and fired; *arch.* the enlargement of the opening of a door or window on the inside of the wall. *Dentistry,* a space between adjacent teeth.

em·brit·tle, em·brit′l, *v.t.—embrittled, embrittling.* To make brittle.—*v.i.* To become brittle.—**em·brit·tle·ment,** *n.*

em·bro·cate, em′brō·kāt″, *v.t.—embrocated, embrocating.* [M.L. *embrocatus,* pp. of *embrocare,* < L.L. *embrocha,* < Gr. *embrochē,* lotion.] To moisten and rub with a liniment or lotion.—**em·bro·ca·tion,** *n.* The act of embrocating a bruised or diseased part of the body; the liquid used for this; a liniment or lotion.

em·broi·der, em·broi′dėr, *v.t.* To adorn, as a fabric, or make, as a design, with ornamental needlework; to embellish, as a tale, with imaginary details.—*v.i.* To do embroidery.—**em·broi·der·y,** em·broi′de·rē, em·broi′drē, *n.* pl. **em·broi·der·ies.** The art of working with needle and thread to form raised, decorative designs on fabric; embroidered designs or an object decorated with such designs; an embellishment of a story with fictitious detail.—**em·broi·der·er,** *n.*

em·broil, em·broil′, *v.t.* [Prefix *em-,* and *broil,* a noisy quarrel.] To mix up or entangle in a quarrel or disturbance; to intermix confusedly; to involve in contention or trouble.—**em·broil·ment,** *n.*

em·brown, em·broun′, *v.t.* To make brown.—*v.i.* To become brown.

em·brue, em·brö′, *v.t.—embrued, embruing.* Imbrue.

em·bry·o, em′brē·ō″, *n.* pl. **em·bry·os.** A multicellular organism in the process of development from the fertilized or parthenogenetically activated ovum until birth or metamorphosis; a young plant within the seed, before the beginning of its rapid growth and referred to as the "germ" of a seed; in mammals, the early stage of development in the womb; in man, the stage until the end of the second month after conception. Something in an as yet undeveloped state; as, the *embryo* of an idea.—**em·bry·on·ic, em·bry·on·al,** *a.* Of or pertaining to an embryo; in the beginning stage; rudimentary.—**em·bry·on·i·cal·ly, em·bry·on·al·ly**, *adv.*—**em·bry·on·at·ed**, *a.* Having an embryo.

em·bry·og·e·ny, em″brē·oj′e·nē, *n.* [Gr. *embryon*, and root *gen*, to produce.] The formation and development of embryos; the study of such formation and development. Also **em·bry·o·gen·e·sis**, em″brē·ō·jen′i·sis.—**em·bry·o·gen·ic, em·bry·o·ge·net·ic**, em″brē·ō·jen′ik, em″brē·ō·je·net′ik, *a.*

em·bry·ol·o·gy, em″brē·ol′o·jē, *n.* [Gr. *embryon*, and *logos*, discourse.] The study of the development of embryos; the development process itself.—**em·bry·o·log·ic, em·bry·o·log·i·cal**, em″brē·o·loj′ik, em″brē·o·loj′i·kal, *a.*—**em·bry·o·log·i·cal·ly**, *adv.*—**em·bry·ol·o·gist**, *n.*

em·bry·on·ic disk, *n. Biol.* the blastodisc or blastoderm; the homologous disk of cells of the blastocyst from which the embryo of a placental mammal develops.

em·bry·on·ic lay·er, *n. Biol.* the germ layer.

em·bry·on·ic mem·brane, *n. Zool.* an extra embryonic structure in vertebrates, mainly nutritive and protective, which lies outside the embryo proper but is derived from the zygote; the yolk sac.

em·bry·o·phyte, em″brē·o·fīt″, *n. Bot.* any plant that produces an embryo and has vascular tissue, thus excluding thallophytes.

em·bry·o sac, *n.* [Gr. *embryon*, an embryo.] *Bot.* a multi-nucleate oval cell in the ovule of seed-bearing plants in which fertilization of egg and development of embryo occur.

em·bry·o·tic, em″brē·ot′ik, *a.* In the beginning stage; rudimentary.

em·cee, em′sē′, *v.i.—emceed, emceeing.* [< the abbr. *M.C.*, master of ceremonies.] To function as the master of ceremonies.—*v.t.* To act as the master of ceremonies for.—*n.* The master of ceremonies.

e·meer, e·mēr′, *n.* Emir.

e·mend, i·mend′, *v.t.* [L. *emendare*.] To free from faults or errors; correct; now, usu., to amend, as a text, by removing errors.—**e·mend·a·ble**, *a.*

e·men·date, ē′men·dāt″, i·men′dāt, *v.t.—emendated, emendating.* [L. *emendatus*, pp. of *emenare*.] To emend, as a text.—**e·men·da·tion**, ē″men·dā′shan, em″en·dā′shan, *n.* The act of emending, or the fact of being emended; a correction, as in a text.—**e·men·da·tor**, *n.*—**e·men·da·to·ry**, *a.*—**e·mend·er**, *n.*

em·er·ald, em′ẽr·ald, em′rald, *n.* [O.Fr. *esmeralde* (Fr. *émeraude*), < L. *smaragdus*, < Gr. *smaragdos*, a green precious stone.] A green transparent variety of beryl used as a gemstone; *Brit. print.* a 6½ point type of a size between nonpareil and minion.—*a.* Of a clear deep green color.—**Em·er·ald Isle**, *n.* Ireland, so called from its verdure.

e·merge, i·mẽrj′, *v.i.—emerged, emerging.* [L. *emergo, emersum.*] To rise out of or come forth from a fluid or other surrounding substance; to come into notice; to arise from a state of obscurity; to come into existence through evolution; to develop from an inferior condition.

e·mer·gence, i·mẽr′jens, *n.* The act or occasion of emerging; *biol.* an outgrowth on the surface of a plant.

e·mer·gen·cy, i·mẽr′jen·sē, *n.* pl. **e·mer·gen·cies.** A sudden, usu. unexpected, occasion or combination of events calling for immediate action.

e·mer·gent, i·mẽr′jent, *a.* Emerging; rising into view or notice; unexpected; coming suddenly; calling for immediate action; urgent; pressing.—*n.* Something coming into existence; an aquatic plant with vegetative growth mostly above the water.

e·mer·gent ev·o·lu·tion, *n. Philos., biol.* the theory that at certain critical stages in evolution, sudden new characteristics appear which make possible a new level of development.

e·mer·i·tus, i·mer′i·tus, *a.* [L. *emeritus*, having served out his time.] Retired from the performance of public duty because of age, length of service, or infirmity, but retaining the honorary title of the position; as, a professor *emeritus*.—*n.* pl. **e·mer·i·ti**, i·mer′i·tī″, i·mer′i·tē″.

e·mersed, i·mẽrst′, *a. Bot.* standing out of or rising above the surrounding water, as the leaves or stem of an aquatic plant.

e·mer·sion, i·mẽr′shan, *n.* The reappearance of a heavenly body after an eclipse or occultation.

em·er·y, em′e·rē, em′rē, *n.* [Fr. *émeri*, O.Fr. *esmeril*, < It. *smiriglio*, < Gr. *smyris, smiris, smēris*, < *smaō*, to rub.] A mineral substance consisting of a hard, grayish-black variety of corundum, used for grinding and polishing metals, hard stones, and glass.—**em·er·y board**, a strip, usu. cardboard, coated with powdered emery, used in manicuring.—**em·er·y cloth**, an emery-coated polishing cloth for metals.

e·met·ic, e·met′ik, *a.* [L. *emeticus*, < Gr. *emeticos*, < *emein*.] Inducing vomiting, as a medicinal substance.—*n.* An emetic medicine or agent.—**e·met·i·cal·ly**, *adv.*

em·e·tine, em′i·tēn″, em′i·tin, *n.* An alkaloid with emetic and other medicinal properties, used chiefly in the treatment of amoebic dysentery.

e·meu, ē′mū, *n.* Emu.

em·i·grant, em′i·grant, *n.* One who emigrates, as from one country to another, esp. one who emigrates from his native country.—*a.*

em·i·grate, em′i·grāt″, *v.i.—emigrated, emigrating.* [L. *emigro, emigratum*, to migrate, to emigrate.] To quit one country, state, or region and settle in another; to remove from one country or state to another induce to emigrate.—**em·i·gra·tion**, em″i·grā′shan, *n.* The act of emigrating; departure of inhabitants from one country or state to another for the purpose of residence; a body of emigrants.

é·mi·gré, em′i·grā″, Fr. ā·mē·grā″, *n.* pl. **é·mi·grés**, em′i·grāz″, Fr. ā·mē·grā′. [Fr. pp. of *émigrer*, < L. *emigrare*.] In French use, an emigrant, esp. one of the royalists who became refugees from France during the revolution that began in 1789; one who goes into voluntary exile because of political conditions in his native land.

em·i·nence, em′i·nens, *n.* [Fr. *éminence*, < L. *eminentia*, < *eminens, eminentis*, < *emineo—e-*, out, and *mineo*, to project, to jut.] A station of distinction due to office, rank, or personal achievements; a person of outstanding attainments; something prominent; a title for a cardinal; a hill. Also **em·i·nen·cy.**

em·i·nent, em′i·nent, *a.* High in office, rank, or public esteem; lofty; conspicuous.—**em·i·nent·ly**, *adv.*

em·i·nent do·main, *n.* The dominion of a government over all the property within the state, by which it can appropriate private property for public use, compensation being given to the owner.

e·mir, e·mēr′, *n.* An Arabian chieftain or prince; a title of honor of the descendants of Mohammed; the title of certain Turkish officials. Also *emeer*.—**e·mir·ate**, *n.* The office of an emir. Also **e·meer·ate.**

em·is·sar·y, em′i·ser″ē, *n.* pl. **em·is·sar·ies.** [L. *emissarius*, < *emitto, emissum*, to send out.] A person sent on a mission; an intelligence operative; a secret agent or spy.

e·mis·sion, i·mish′an, *n.* [L. *emissio.*] The act or a case of emitting; that which is emitted; an issuing, as of dollar bills; release of fluid, such as semen, from the body. *Electronics*, the movement of electrons from the cathode or heated filament of a tube.—**e·mis·sive**, *a.*

e·mit, i·mit′, *v.t.—emitted, emitting.* [L.] To throw or give out, as light, heat, steam; to send forth; to put forth and circulate, as currency; to voice; to utter, as a sound.—**e·mit·ter**, *n.*

em·men·a·gogue, e·men′a·gag″, e·men′a·gog″, e·mē′na·gag″, e·mē′na·gog″, *n.* [Gr. *emmena*, the menses—*em-*, in, *mēn, mēnos*, month, and *agō*, to lead.] A medicine taken to promote the menstrual discharge.

em·me·tro·pi·a, em″i·trō′pē·a, *n.* [N.L. < Gr. *emmetros*, in measure.] The normal refractive condition of the eye, in which the rays of light are accurately focused on the retina and there is perfect vision.—**em·me·trop·ic**, em″·i·trop′ik, *a.*

e·mol·lient, i·mol′yent, *a.* [L. *emolliens, emollientis*, pp. of *emollio*.] Softening; making supple; relaxing; soothing to the skin.—*n.* A medicine which softens and relaxes living tissues that are inflamed.

e·mol·u·ment, i·mol′ū·ment, *n.* [L. *emolumentum*, a working out.] The profit arising from office or employment; compensation for services; remuneration.

e·mote, i·mōt′, *v.i.—emoted, emoting.* To show emotion; to behave with exaggerated emotion or expression, as in acting.—**e·mot·er**, *n.*

e·mo·tion, i·mō′shan, *n.* [L. *emovere* (pp. *emotus*), move out, stir up.] An affective state of consciousness in which joy, sorrow, fear, hate, or the like is experienced: distinguished from the cognitive and volitional states of consciousness; any of the feelings of joy, sorrow, fear, hate, love, or the like; any agitated or intense state of mind, usu. with concurrent physiological changes; an occurrence of this; that which brings about any intense state of feeling.—**e·mo·tion·al**, i·mō′sha·nal, *a.* Pertaining to or characterized by emotion; attended by or producing emotion; appealing to emotions.—**e·mo·tion·al·ly**, *adv.*—**e·mo·tion·less**, *a.*

e·mo·tion·al·ist, i·mō′sha·na·list, *n.* One who appeals to the emotions unduly; one who bases theories of conduct on the emotions; one easily affected by emotion.—**e·mo·tion·al·is·tic**, *a.*—**e·mo·tion·al·ism**, i·mō′sha·na·liz″um, *n.* The character of being emotional; tendency to emotional excitement; undue emotion.

e·mo·tion·al·i·ty, i·mō″sha·nal′i·tē, *n.* Emotional state or quality.

e·mo·tion·al·ize, i·mō″sha·na·līz″, *v.t.—emotionalized, emotionalizing.* To render emotional; treat as a matter of emotion.

e·mo·tive, i·mō′tiv, *a.* Having to do with emotions; indicating or producing emotion.—**e·mo·tive·ly**, *adv.*—**e·mo·tiv·i·ty**, e·mo·tive·ness, ē″mō·tiv′i·tē, *n.*

em·pale, em·pāl′, *v.t.—empaled, empaling.* Impale.

em·pan·el, em·pan′el, *v.t.—empaneled, empanelled, empaneling, empanelling.* Impanel.

em·pa·thize, em′pa·thīz″, *v.i.—empathized, empathizing.* To feel or regard with empathy.

em·pa·thy, em′pa·thē, *n.* [Gr. *en-*, in, and *pathein*, suffer, feel: formed as an equivalent of G. *einfühlung*, lit. 'in-feeling.'] *Psychol.* mental entrance into the feeling or spirit of another person or thing; appreciative perception or understanding.—**em·pa·thet·ic, em·path·ic**, em·path′ik, *a.*

em·pen·nage, äm″pe·näzh′, Fr. äN·pe·näzh′, *n.* [Fr., < *empenner*, feather (an arrow), < *em-* (< L. *in*, in) and *penne*, < L. *penna*, feather.] The assembly at the rear end of an aircraft comprised of the horizontal and vertical stabilizers and their associated control surfaces. Also **tail as·sem·bly.**

em·per·or, em'pẽr·ẽr, *n.* [Fr. *empereur,* < L. *imperator,* < *impero, imperatum,* to command.] The sovereign or supreme monarch of an empire; a title of dignity superior to that of king.

em·per·y, em'pe·rē, *n. pl.* **em·per·ies.** Empire; unrestricted dominion.

em·pha·sis, em'fa·sis, *n. pl.* **em·pha·ses,** em'fa·sēz. [L. *emphasis,* < Gr. *emphasis,* significance, < *emphainein,* exhibit, indicate.] Stress laid upon, or importance or significance attached to, anything; special and significant stress of voice laid on particular words or syllables; intensity or force of expression or action; prominence, as of outline.

em·pha·size, *Brit.* also **em·pha·sise,** em'fa·sīz″, *v.t.*—*emphasized, emphasizing.* To give emphasis to; lay stress upon; stress.

em·phat·ic, em·fat'ik, *a.* Uttered with emphasis; characterized by direct and forceful speech or action; forcible; expressive; striking; boldly marked or outlined.— **em·phat·i·cal·ly,** *adv.*

em·phy·se·ma, em″fi·sē'ma, em'fi·zē'ma, *n.* [Gr. *emphysēma,* < *emphysaō,* to inflate.] *Pathol.* distention or puffiness caused by the presence of air in body tissues or organs; esp. a disease of the lungs characterized by a thinning of the lung tissues and a loss of their elasticity.—**em·phy·se·ma·tous,** em″fi·sem'a·tus, em″fi·sē'ma·tus, em″fi·zem'a·tus, em″fi·zē'ma·tus, *a.*

em·pire, em'pīr, *n.* [Fr. *empire,* < L. *imperium.*] The territory, countries, or peoples under the dominion of an emperor or other powerful sovereign; the territory or government of an emperor: usu. an area of greater extent than a kingdom; supreme power in governing; supreme dominion; sovereignty; imperial power; anything resembling an empire in power and scope, as a powerful and influential enterprise under the exclusive control of a single individual, family, or set of associates.

Em·pire, em'pī·er, om·pēr', *a.* Characteristic of or relating to a particular style in clothing, architecture, ornamentation, and furnishings developed during the Empire period in early 19th-century France; of a gown, having the high waistline and décolleté bodice of this period.

em·pir·ic, em·pir'ik, *n.* [L. *empiricus,* < Gr. *empeirikos,* experienced.] One who relies only on experience and observation. A quack.

em·pir·i·cal, em·pir'i·kal, *a.* Pertaining to experiments or experience; depending upon experience or observation alone, without due regard to science and theory.— **em·pir·i·cal·ly,** *adv.*

em·pir·i·cal for·mu·la, *n. Chem.* a formula which shows the relative number of atoms that combine to form a compound and does not necessarily show the total number of atoms in a molecule of the compound.

em·pir·i·cism, em·pir'i·siz″um, *n.* The quality or method of being empirical; *philos.* the belief that knowledge is derived from experiment or experience. Quackery. —**em·pir·i·cist,** *n.*

em·place, em·plās', *v.t.*—*emplaced, emplacing.* [Fr. *emplacer,* < *em-* (< L. *in,* in) and *place.*] To put in place or position.— **em·place·ment,** *n.* A putting in place or position; location; *fort.* the space or platform for a gun or battery and its accessories.

em·plane, em·plān', *v.t., v.i.*—*emplaned, emplaning.* Enplane.

em·ploy, em·ploi', *v.t.* [Fr. *employer,* < L. *implicare,* to infold, involve, engage.] To engage in one's service; to keep busy or at work; to make use of; to apply or devote to an object; to occupy.—*n.* A state of being engaged for wages; employment.—**em·ploy·a·ble,** *a.*—**em·ploy·a·bil·i·ty,** *n.*

em·ploy·ee, em·ploy·e, em·ploi'ē, em″ploi·ē', *n.* [The English form of the French *employé.*] One who works for an employer for salary or wages.

em·ploy·er, em·ploi'ẽr, *n.* One that employs.

em·ploy·ment, em·ploi'ment, *n.* The act of employing or using; the state of being employed; occupation; business; that which one undertakes to occupy his time.

em·poi·son, em·poi'zon, *v.t.* To embitter; to destroy all pleasure in; to pervert.— **em·poi·son·ment,** *n.*

em·po·ri·um, em·pŏr'ē·um, em·par'ē·um, *n. pl.* **em·po·ri·ums, em·po·ri·a.** [L., < Gr. *emporion,* < *emporos,* traveler, merchant.] A town or city of important commerce, esp. a principal center of trade; a place of business, esp. a department store carrying a wide variety of merchandise.

em·pow·er, em·pou'ẽr, *v.t.* To authorize; to warrant; to license.—**em·pow·er·ment,** *n.*

em·press, em'pris, *n.* The consort or spouse of an emperor; a woman who rules an empire.

emp·ty, emp'tē, *a.* [O.E. *aemti, aemtig, ēmtig,* vacant, free, idle; *aeⁿtian,* to be at leisure, to be vacant, < *aemta, ēmta,* quiet, leisure.] Containing nothing; void of contents or appropriate contents; not occupied; not inhabited; *math.* of a set, having no members. Destitute of force, effect, or sincerity; as, *empty* remarks, *empty* promises; destitute of sense, knowledge, or judgment; vacuous; feeling hunger; unproductive.—*n.* Any type of container that is empty.—*v.t.*—*emptied, emptying.* To remove the contents from; to discharge.—*v.i.* To become empty.— **emp·ti·ness,** *n.*—**emp·ti·ly,** *adv.*

emp·ty-hand·ed, emp'tē·han'did, *a.* Having or carrying nothing in the hands; without gain or acquisition.

emp·ty-head·ed, emp'tē·hed'id, *a.* Without thought; flighty.

em·pur·ple, em·pẽr'pl, *v.t.*—*empurpled, empurpling.* To tinge or color with purple.

em·py·e·ma, em″pē·ē'ma, em″pī·ē'ma, *n.* [Gr. *empyēma,* < *em-,* in, and *pyon,* pus.] *Med.* a collection of pus in some cavity of the body, esp. in the cavity of the chest. Also **py·o·thor·ax.**—**em·py·e·mic,** *a.*

em·pyr·e·al, em·pir'ē·al, em″pi·rē'al, em″pi·rē'al, *a.* [L.L. *empyræus,* < Gr. *empyros,* prepared by fire, fiery, scorched.] Formed of pure fire or light; refined beyond aerial substance; pertaining to the highest and purest region of heaven, according to ancient cosmology. Also *empyrean.*

em·py·re·an, em'pi·rē'an, em″pi·rē'an, em·pir'ē·an, *n.* The highest heaven, where the pure element of fire was supposed by the ancients to exist; the firmament.—*a.*

e·mu, ē'mū, *n.* An Australian bird about five feet high, flightless, three-toed, and closely related to the cassowary. Also *emeu.*

em·u·late, em'ū·lāt″, *v.t.*—*emulated, emulating.* [L.] To strive to equal or excel in qualities or actions; copy; to vie with; to come forward as a rival of.—**em·u·la·tor,** *n.*

em·u·la·tion, em″ū·lā'shan, *n.* The act of emulating; desire or ambition to equal or excel others.—**em·u·la·tive,** em'ū·lā·tiv, *a.*—**em·u·la·tive·ly,** *adv.*

em·u·lous, em'ū·lus, *a.* Desirous or eager to imitate, equal, or excel another; arising from the desire to emulate.—**em·u·lous·ly,** *adv.*—**em·u·lous·ness,** *n.*

e·mul·si·fy, i·mul'si·fī″, *v.t.*—*emulsified, emulsifying.* To make or form into an emulsion.—**e·mul·si·ble,** *a.*—**e·mul·si·fi·ca·tion,** *n.*—**e·mul·si·fi·er,** *n.*

e·mul·sion, i·mul'shan, *n.* [< L. *emulgeo, emulsum,* to milk out.] Any milklike substance or preparation; *chem.* a mixture of two immiscible liquids which are kept in suspension, one within the other, such as butterfat in milk; *photog.* a coating on photographic films, plates, or paper, sensitive to rays of light.—**e·mul·sive,** *a.*

e·mul·soid, i·mul'soid, *n. Chem.* a liquid mixed in another liquid and forming a colloidal system; an emulsion.—**e·mul·soi·dal,** i·mul·soid'al, ē″mul·soid·al'a, *a.*

en, en, *n. Print.* half of the width of an em.

en·a·ble, en·ā'bl, *v.t.*—*enabled, enabling.* To make able; to supply with physical, moral, or legal power; to furnish with sufficient means, ability, or authority; to make easy or possible.—**en·a·bling,** *a.* Granting special or unusual power or sanction; as, an *enabling* act or statute.

en·act, en·akt', *v.t.* To make, as a bill, into an act or established law; to act or perform; to act the part of or represent on the stage. —**en·ac·tive,** *a.* Having power to enact; establish as a law.—**en·ac·tor,** *n.*

en·act·a·ble, *a.*—**en·ac·tor,** *n.*

en·act·ment, *n.* The act of enacting or the state of being enacted; a law enacted; a decree; an act.—

e·nam·el, i·nam'el, *n.* [Prefix *en-,* and old *amel, ammel, amile,* enamel, < O.Fr. *esmail,* Mod.Fr. *émail,* enamel, < G. *schmelzen,* to smelt.] A substance resembling glass, but differing from it by a greater degree of fusibility or opacity, used as an ornamental or protective coating for various metal, glass, or pottery articles; a smooth, glossy surface of various colors, resembling enamel; any of the glossy paints or varnishes; enamelware; artistic work done in enamel; *dentistry,* the smooth hard substance which covers the crown of a tooth, overlying the dentine.—*v.t.*—*enameled, enamelled, enameling, enamelling.* To lay enamel on; to paint in enamel; to form a glossy surface like enamel upon; to variegate or adorn with different glossy colors.—*v.i.* To practice the use of enamel or the art of enameling.—**e·nam·el·er, e·nam·el·ler,** *n.* —**e·nam·el·ist, e·nam·el·list,** *n.*—**e·nam·el·ware,** *n.* Enameled articles, esp. cooking utensils.

en·am·or, *Brit.* **en·am·our,** en·am'ẽr, *v.t.* [O.Fr. *enamourer* < L. *amor,* love.] To inflame with love; charm; captivate: usu. in the past participle, followed by *of* or *with.* —**en·am·ored·ness,** *Brit.* **en·am·oured·ness,** *n.*

en·an·ti·o·morph, i·nan'tē·o·marf″, *n. Chem., crystal.* either of a pair of chemically identical crystals or chemical compounds whose molecular configurations are mirror images of each other and which have no planes of symmetry.—**en·an·ti·o·mor·phic,** *a.*—**en·an·ti·o·mor·phism,** *n.*— **en·an·ti·o·mor·phous,** *a.*

en·ar·thro·sis, en″ar·thrō'sis, *n.* [Gr.] *Anat.* a ball-and-socket joint.

en·cae·ni·a, en·sēn'ya, en·sē'nē·a, *n. pl., sing* or *pl. in constr.* [L., < Gr. *enkainia.*] Festive ceremonies commemorating the founding of a city or the consecration of a church; (*cap.*) ceremonies held at Oxford University, England, in honor of founders and benefactors.

en·cage, en·kāj', *v.i.*—*encaged, encaging.* To shut up or confine in or as in a cage.

en·camp, en·kamp', *v.i.* To take up position in a camp; to make a camp.—*v.t.* To form into or place in a camp.—**en·camp·ment,** en·kamp'ment, *n.* The act or an instance of encamping; a campsite or the accommodations or persons occupying it.

en·cap·su·late, en·kap'su·lāt″, *v.t.*—*encapsulated, encapsulating.* [L.] To enclose in or as in a capsule.—*v.i.* To become enclosed in or as in a capsule. Also **en·cap·**

sule.—en·cap·su·la·tion, n.—en·cap·su·lat·ed, a.

en·case, en·kās′, v.t.—encased, encasing. To confine or package in or as in a case. Also incase.

en·case·ment, en·kās′ment, n. The state of being encased; the act of encasing.

en·caus·tic, en·ka′stik, a. [L. encausticus, < Gr. enkanstikos, < enkaiein, burn in.] Noting, pertaining to, or produced by a process of painting with wax colors fixed with heat, or any process by which colors are burned in.—n. The art, process, or practice of encaustic painting; material produced by an encaustic process.—en·caus·ti·cal·ly, adv.

en·ceinte, en·sānt′, Fr. än·saNt′, a. [Fr.] Pregnant; with child.

en·ceinte, en·sānt′, Fr. än·saNt′, n. [Fr.] A wall or enclosure, as of a fortified place; the place thus enclosed.

en·ce·phal·ic, en″se·fal′ik, a. Belonging or relating to the brain or to other structures within the cranial cavity.

en·ceph·a·li·tis, en·sef″a·lī′tis, n. Pathol. inflammation of the brain.—en·ceph·a·lit·ic, en·sef″a·lit′ik, a.

en·ceph·a·lo·gram, en·sef′a·lo·gram″, n. Med. an X-ray photograph of the brain. Also encephalograph.—en·ceph·a·log·ra·phy, n. The technique or act of taking X-ray photographs of the brain, usu. after replacing the cerebrospinal fluid with oxygen or another gas.

en·ceph·a·lo·graph, en·sef′a·lo·graf, en·sef′a·lo·gräf, n. An encephalogram; an electroencephalograph.

en·ceph·a·lo·my·e·li·tis, en·sef″a·lō·mī·e·lī′tis, n. Pathol. inflammation of the brain and spinal cord.

en·ceph·a·lon, en·sef′a·lon″, n. pl. en·ceph·a·la, en·sef′a·la. [Gr. enkephalos, within the head.] The brain.

en·chain, en·chān′, v.t. To fasten with or as if with chains; to hold fast; restrain.—en·chain·ment, n.

en·chant, en·chant′, en·chänt′, v.t. [Fr. enchanter, to sing, < L.] To subdue or influence by charms or spells; bewitch; to fascinate; to delight in a high degree; to charm, captivate, or enrapture; to endow with a magical quality.—en·chant·er, en·chan′tèr, en·chän′tèr, n. One who enchants; a sorcerer or magician; one who charms or delights.—en·chant·ress, en·chan′tris, en·chän′tris, n. A female enchanter; sorceress; a captivating woman.

en·chant·ing, en·chan′ting, en·chän′ting, a. Charming; delightful; bewitching.—en·chant·ing·ly, adv.

en·chant·ment, en·chant′ment, en·chänt′ment, n. The act, art, or action of enchanting; the state of being enchanted; that which enchants.

en·chase, en·chās′, v.t.—enchased, enchasing. [Fr. enchâsser, < L. capsa, a chest, a case, < capio, to take or receive.] To put in an ornamental setting, as a gem; to adorn with embossed work, inlay, or engraving.

en·chi·la·da, en″chi·lä′da, en″chi·lad′a, n. In Mexican cuisine, a spicy meat or cheese mixture rolled up in a tortilla, with a chili-seasoned sauce poured over it.

en·chi·rid·i·on, en″ki·rid′ē·an, en″ki·rid′ē·an, n. pl. en·chi·rid·i·ons, en·chi·rid·i·a. [L.L., < Gr. encheiridion, < en-, in, and cheir, hand.] A handbook; a manual.

en·cho·ri·al, en·kōr′ē·al, en·kạr′ē·al, n. Belonging to or used in a country: used esp. of demotic writing; native; indigenous.

en·ci·pher, en·sī′fèr, v.t. To put, as a letter, into cipher.

en·cir·cle, en·sèr′kl, v.t.—encircled, encircling. To form a circle about; enclose; surround; encompass; to move circularly around.—en·cir·cle·ment, n.

en·clasp, en·klasp′, en·kläsp′, v.t. To clasp; to embrace. Also in·clasp.

en·clave, en′klāv, Fr. äN·kläv′, n. [Fr. en-, in, and L. clavis, a key.] An outlying part of a country or a small autonomous territory entirely or nearly surrounded by the territory of another power; an area primarily populated by a minority group.

en·clit·ic, en·klit′ik, a. [Gr. enklitikos, inclined, < enklinō, to incline.] Gram. pertaining to a word connected to a preceding word and so closely related that it loses its independent accent, as men in laymen.—n. Gram. an enclitic word.

en·close, en·klōz′, v.t.—enclosed, enclosing. To shut in, or confine on all sides; to surround; to put in an envelope with a letter or in a package; to contain; include. Also inclose.—en·clo·sure, en·klō′zhèr, n. The act of enclosing; the state of being enclosed; that which is enclosed, as a space enclosed or fenced, or something enclosed along with a letter. Also inclosure.

en·code, en·kōd′, v.t.—encoded, encoding. To convert, as a message, into code.

en·co·mi·um, en·kō′mē·um, n. pl. en·co·mi·ums, en·co·mi·a. [Gr enkōmion, a laudatory ode—en, in, and kōmos, a revel, a procession in honor.] A eulogy; a formal statement in praise of something or someone.—en·co·mi·ast, en·kō′mē·ast″, n. [Gr. enkōmiastēs.] One who authors or delivers an encomium; a eulogist.—en·co·mi·as·tic, a. Bestowing praise; laudatory. Also, en·com·mi·as·ti·cal.

en·com·pass, en·kum′pas, v.t. To form a circle about; encircle; enclose; surround; to envelop; to include.—en·com·pass·ment, n.

en·core, äng′kōr, äng′kạr, än′kōr, än′kạr, interj. [Fr. still, yet, further, besides, = It. ancora; origin uncertain.] Again; once more. —n. A demand by an audience, usu. expressed through applause, for a repetition, as of a song, or for an additional number or piece; that which is performed in response to such a demand.—v.t.—encored, encoring. To call for a repetition of; to call for an encore from.

en·coun·ter, en·koun′tèr, n. [Fr. encontre—en-, and contre, L. contra, against.] A sudden, casual, or accidental meeting; a hostile meeting; conflict; a minor battle. —v.t. To meet face to face; to meet suddenly or unexpectedly; to meet in opposition; to engage with in battle; to be confronted with or contend against, as opposition, problems, or adversities.—v.i. To meet each other unexpectedly; to meet, esp. in hostile fashion.

en·cour·age, en·kèr′ij, en·kur′ij, v.t.—encouraged, encouraging. [Fr. encourager—en-, and courage.] To inspire with courage, confidence, or hope; embolden; to stimulate or help; to support or countenance.—en·cour·age·ment, n. The act of encouraging; the state of being encouraged; that which encourages; incitement; incentive.—en·cour·ag·ing, a. Inspiring with courage or hope for success.—en·cour·ag·ing·ly, adv.

en·crim·son, en·krim′zon, v.t. To make crimson; redden.

en·croach, en·krōch′, v.i. [Prefix en, and Fr. crocher, to hook on, < croc, a hook.] To trespass or intrude on the rights or possessions of another by gradual advances; to make gradual inroads; to assail gradually and stealthily.—en·croach·er, n.—en·croach·ment, n. The act of encroaching.

en·crust, en·krust′, v.t. To cover with a crust.—en·crus·ta·tion, en″kru·stā′shan, n. Incrustation.

en·cum·ber, en·kum′bèr, v.t. [O.Fr., Fr. encombrer, < M.L. incombrare, < L. in-, in, and M.L. combrus, obstruction, obstacle.] To impede or hamper; retard; to burden

with obligations or debt; to load or fill with what is obstructive or superfluous; to render difficult; complicate. Also incumber. —en·cum·brance, en·kum′brans, n. That which encumbers; a burden; a hindrance; something useless or superfluous; an annoyance or trouble; a dependent person, esp. a child; law, a burden or claim on property, as a mortgage.—en·cum·branc·er, n. Law, one who holds an encumbrance.

en·cyc·li·cal, en·sik′li·kal, en·sī′kli·kal, a. [Gr. enkyklikos—en-, in, and kyklos, a circle.] Of a letter, sent to many persons or places; intended for wide, general circulation. Also en·cyc·lic.—n. Rom. Cath. Ch. an encyclical letter, a letter sent by the Pope to all bishops of the church.

en·cy·clo·pe·di·a, en·sī″klo·pē′dē·a, n. [Gr. enkyklopaideia.] A work in which various branches of knowledge are discussed separately, and usu. in alphabetical order; a dictionary of things, not words. Also en·cy·clo·pae·di·a.—en·cy·clo·pe·dic, en·cy·clo·pe·di·cal, en·sī″klo·pē′dik, en·sī″klo·pē′di·kal, a. Pertaining to an encyclopedia; such as is embraced in an encyclopedia; universal as regards knowledge and information.—en·cy·clo·pe·di·cal·ly, adv.

en·cy·clo·pe·dism, en·sī″klo·pē′diz·um, n. The possession of a wide range of information; extensive learning. Also en·cy·clo·pae·dism.

en·cy·clo·pe·dist, en·sī″klo·pē′dist, n. The compiler of an encyclopedia, or one who assists in such compilation. Also en·cy·clo·pae·dist.

en·cyst, en·sist′, v.t., v.i. [Gr.] To enclose or become enclosed in a cyst, sac, or vesicle.—en·cyst·ment, en·cys·ta·tion, n.

end, end, n. [O.E. ende = Icel. endi, Dan. and G. ende, Goth. andeis, the end; Skt. anta, end, death.] The extreme point of a line, or of anything that has more length than width; as, the end of the street; the termination, conclusion, or last part of a portion of time, of an action, of a state of things, or of a quantity of materials; as, end of the year, generosity without end; the close of life; death; consequence; issue; result; the ultimate point or thing at which one aims or directs his views; purpose; scope; aim; remnant or fragment; a portion or share of something; extreme limit of something; bounds; slang, the limit of one's patience. Football, either of the two linemen at each side of a scrimmage line; the position played by these linemen.—on end, resting on one end; upright; continuously; uninterruptedly.—make both ends meet, to live within one's income.—at loose ends, without work; lack of recreation.—at wit's end, puzzled, confused.—go off the deep end, to go to extremes; lose control of one's emotions.

end, end, v.t. To put an end to or be the end of; to finish; to close, conclude, terminate; to destroy; to put to death. Brit. dial. to stack wheat, hay, or grain in a barn.—v.i. To come to an end; to terminate; to die; to close; to conclude; to cease.—end·er, n. One who or that which ends or finishes.

en·dam·age, en·dam′ij, v.t.—endamaged, endamaging. To bring loss or damage to; to damage; to harm; to injure.—en·dam·age·ment, n.

en·da·moe·ba, en″da·mē′ba, n. pl. en·da·moe·bae, en·da·moe·bas, en″da·mē′bē. Parasitic amoebas which cause amoebic dysentery in man. Also en·da·me·ba.—en·da·moe·bic, en·da·me·bic, a.

en·dan·ger, en·dān′jèr, v.t. To put in danger; to bring into peril; to expose to loss or injury.—en·dan·ger·ment, n.

en·darch, en′därk, *a. Bot.* xylem or wood whose development is toward the center of the stem.

end brain, end′brān′, *n.* The telencephalon, a subdivision of the forebrain.

end bulb, *n.* Tactile corpuscle, or the end of a nerve enclosed by a bulbous enlargement of the surrounding sheath of connective tissue.

en·dear, en·dēr′, *v.t.* To make beloved; to bind by ties of affection and love.— **en·dear·ment**, en·dēr′ment, *n.* The act of endearing; the state of being beloved; *usu. pl.* action or words showing affection.

en·deav·or, *Brit.* **en·deav·our**, en·dev′ėr, *n.* [Fr. *en-*, in, and *devoir*, duty, < L. *debere*, to owe, to be under obligation (whence debt).] A serious effort; a strenuous attempt.—*v.i.* To labor or exert oneself; to try; to attempt.—*v.t.* To try to effect.— **en·deav·or·er**, *Brit.* **en·deav·our·er**, *n.*

en·dem·ic, en·dem′ik, *a.* [Fr. *endémique*, < Gr. *endēmios—en-*, in, among, and *demos*, people.] Of a disease, peculiar to a people, locality, or region. Also **en·dem·i·cal**, en·dem′i·kal.—*n.* A disease to which inhabitants of a particular region are subject.—**en·dem·i·cal·ly**, *adv.*—**en·de·mic·i·ty**, en·de·mism, en″de·mis′i·tē, en′de·miz′um, *n.*

en·der·mic, en·dėr′mik, *a.* [Gr. *en*, in, and *derma*, skin.] Acting on or through the skin, as a medicine.—**en·der·mi·cal·ly**, *adv.*

end·ing, en′ding, *n.* The act of putting or coming to an end; termination; conclusion; the close of life; the last part; the final syllable or letter of a word.

en·dive, en′dīv, än′dēv, *Fr.* än·dēv′, *n.* A plant, *Cichorium endivia*, having thin curled leaves, widely cultivated in the U.S. for use in salads. Also *escarole*.

end·less, end′lis, *a.* Having no end or conclusion; interminable; incessant; continual; forming a closed loop.—**end·less·ly**, *adv.*—**end·less·ness**, *n.*

end man, *n.* A man at one end of a row or line; a man at either end of the line of performers of a minstrel troupe, who plays on the bones or the tambourine and carries on humorous dialogue with the interlocutor.

end·most, end′mōst″, *a.* Farthest; most remote; as, the *endmost* tip of the peninsula.

en·do·bi·ot·ic, en″dō·bī″ot′ik, en″dō·bē·ot′ik, *a.* Living within the tissues of a plant or animal.

en·do·blast, en′dō·blast″, *n. Biol.* endoderm; hypoblast.—**en·do·blas·tic**, *a.*

en·do·car·di·um, en″dō·kär′dē·um, *n. pl.* **en·do·car·di·a.** [Gr. *endon*, within, and *kardia*, the heart.] *Anat.* a colorless transparent membrane which lines the interior of the heart.—**en·do·car·di·al**, en″dō·kär′dē·al, *a.* Relating to the endocardium; located in the interior of the heart.— **en·do·car·di·tis**, en″dō·kär·dī′tis, *n.* Inflammation of the internal parts of the heart.

en·do·carp, en′dō·kärp″, *n.* [Gr. *endon*, within, *karpos*, fruit.] *Bot.* the inner layer of the pericarp or fruit wall.—**en·do·car·pal**, **en·do·car·pic**, *a.*

en·do·cra·ni·um, en″dō·krā′nē·um, *n. pl.* **en·do·cra·ni·a.** *Anat.* the tough fibrous membrane covering the brain, known as the dura mater; inner surface of the cranium.

en·do·crine, en′dō·krin, en′dō·krīn″, en″dō·krēn″, *a.* [Gr. *endon*, within, and *krinein*, separate.] *Anat., physiol.* designating any of the various glands, as the thyroid, suprarenal, or pituitary glands, which produce and release certain important internal secretions directly to the blood or lymph; of, or pertaining to, these glands; as, *endocrine* function, *endocrine* disorders. See *ductless gland.*—*n.* An endocrine gland or its internal secretion.

en·do·cri·nol·o·gy, en″dō·kri·nol′o·jē, en″dō·krī·nol′o·jē, *n.* The science that deals with the endocrine glands and their relation to bodily changes and disease.— **en·do·crin·o·log·ic**, **en·do·crin·o·log·i·cal**, en″dō·krin′o·loj′ik, *a.*—**en·do·cri·nol·o·gist**, *n.*

en·do·derm, en′dō·dėrm″, *n.* [Gr. *endon*, within, and *derma*, skin.] The innermost of three germ layers of an embryo from which is derived the epithelium of the digestive and respiratory tracts. Also *entoderm.*— **en·do·der·mal**, **en·do·der·mic**, *a.*

en·do·der·mis, en″dō·dėr′mis, *n. Bot.* a layer of cells just inside the cortex and most conspicuous in roots.

en·do·don·tia, en″dō·don′sha, en″dō·don′shē·a, *n.* The branch of dentistry specializing in diseases of the tooth's pulp. Also **en·do·don·tics**, en″dō·don′tiks.— **en·do·don·tic**, *a.*—**en·do·don·tist**, en″dō·don′tist, *n.*

en·do·en·zyme, en″dō·en′zīm, *n. Biochem.* an enzyme that operates inside the cell.

en·dog·a·my, en·dog′a·mē, *n.* [Gr. *endon*, within, *gamos*, marriage.] The custom of marrying within the tribe: opposite of *exogamy*; sexual reproduction between persons who are closely related.—**en·dog·a·mous**, **en·do·gam·ic**, *a.*

en·do·gen, en′dō·jen″, en′dō·jen, *n.* [Gr. *endon*, within, root *gen*, to produce.] *Bot.* any plant, as the monocotyledons, whose stems were once thought to develop from the inside.—**en·dog·e·nous**, en·doj′e·nus, *a.* Pertaining to endogens; *biol.* growing, developing, or originating from within; *physiol., biochem.* of or pertaining to the anabolism of the nitrogenous parts of cells and tissues.—**en·dog·e·nous·ly**, *adv.*

en·dog·e·ny, en·doj′e·nē, *n. Biol.* growth from a deep-seated layer; development from within. Also **en·do·gen·e·sis.**

en·do·lymph, en′dō·limf″, *n.* [Gr. *endon*, within, E. *lymph*.] *Anat.* a limpid fluid in the labyrinth of the ear.—**en·do·lym·phat·ic**, en″dō·lim·fat′ik, *a.*

en·do·morph, en′dō·märf″, *n. Mineral.* a mineral enclosed within another mineral. *Psychol.* a type of body structure characterized by soft roundness, massive digestive viscera, and comparatively weak muscle and bone structure, developed by the dominance of tissues derived from the endoderm, the innermost of the three cell layers of the embryo; a person having this type of body structure.—**en·do·mor·phic**, *a.* Of, pertaining to, or characteristic of endomorphs. —**en·do·mor·phy**, *n.*

en·do·mor·phism, en″dō·mär′fiz·um, en″dō·mär′fiz·um, *n. Geol.* the alteration produced in an intrusive rock by reaction with the rock surrounding it.

en·do·par·a·site, en″dō·par′a·sīt″, *n.* [Gr. *endon*, within, and E. *parasite*.] A parasite living within the internal organs of animals.

en·do·phyte, en′dō·fīt″, *n. Bot.* a plant which lives, usu. parasitically, within another plant.—**en·do·phyt·ic**, en″dō·fit′ik, *a.*

en·do·plasm, en′dō·plaz″um, en′dō·plaz″um, *n.* [Gr. *endon*, within, and *plasma*. PLASMA.] The inner, partially fluid part of the cytoplasm of a cell.—**en·do·plas·mic**, *a.*

end or·gan, *n. Physiol.* any specialized structure which forms the peripheral terminus of a path of nervous conduction.

en·dorse, en·dars′, *v.t.*—*endorsed, endorsing.* [Prefix *en-*, and L. *dorsum*, a back.] To write on the back of, as one's name as payee, on the back of a check, to obtain the cash or credit represented on the face of the document; to assign by writing one's name on the back; to assign or transfer by

endorsement; to sanction, ratify, or approve; to acknowledge the receipt, as of a sum specified, by one's signature.—**en·dor·see**, **en·dor·ser**, *n.*

en·dorse·ment, en·dars′ment, *n.* The act of endorsing; the signature of the holder of a note or bill of exchange written on its back; ratification, sanction, or approval. A provision added to an insurance contract whereby the scope of its coverage is restricted or enlarged.

en·do·scope, en′dō·skōp″, *n. Med.* an instrument designed to give a view of some internal part, or hollow organ, of the body, such as the womb.—**en·dos·co·py**, *n.*— **en·do·scop·ic**, en″dō·skop′ik, *a.*

en·do·skel·e·ton, en″dō·skel′i·ton, *n. Zool.* the internal skeleton or framework of the body of an animal: opposed to *exoskeleton.* —**en·do·skel·e·tal**, *a.*

en·dos·mo·sis, en″dos·mō′sis, en″doz·mō′sis, *n.* Osmosis from without inward; in the phenomena of osmosis, the action or flow of fluid from a solution of lesser osmotic pressure to one of greater: opposed to *exosmosis.* Also **en·dos·mos**, en′dos·mōs″, en′doz·mōs.—**en·dos·mot·ic**, en″dos·mot′ik, en″doz·mot′ik, *a.*—**en·dos·mot·i·cal·ly**, *adv.*

en·do·sperm, en′dō·spėrm″, *n.* [Gr. *endon*, within, *sperma*, seed.] *Bot.* the albuminous tissue which surrounds the embryo in many seeds, and contains the supply of food for the germinating embryo.— **en·do·sper·mic**, **en·do·sper·mous**, *a.*

en·do·spore, en′dō·spōr″, en′dō·spar″, *n. Bact.* a spore formed within a cell.— **en·do·spor·ic**, *a.*—**en·do·spo·ri·um**, en″dō·spōr′ē·um, en″dō·spar′ē·um, *n. pl.* **en·do·spo·ri·a**, en″dō·spō·por′ous, en″dos′pėr·us, en″dō·spōr′us, en″dō·spar′us, *a.*

en·dos·te·a, en·dos′tē·um, *n. pl.* **en·dos·te·a** [Gr. *endon*, within, *osteon*, bone.] *Anat.* the lining membrane of the narrow cavity of a bone.—**en·dos·te·al**, *a.*— **en·dos·te·al·ly**, *adv.*

en·do·the·ci·um, en″dō·thē·shē′um, en″dō·thē′sē·um, *n. pl.* **en·do·the·ci·a.** [Gr. *endon*, within, *thēkē*, a cell.] *Bot.* the fibrous cellular tissue lining an anther, that aids in the dehiscence of the sporangum releasing pollen.

en·do·the·li·um, en″dō·thē′lē·um, *n. pl.* **en·do·the·li·a.** [Gr. *endon*, without, *thēlē*, a nipple.] A delicate membrane lining the heart, blood vessels, and body cavities.— **en·do·the·li·al**, en·do·the·li·oid, *a.*

en·do·ther·mic, en″dō·thėr′mik, *n.* [Gr. *endon*, within, *thermos*, heat.] Of a chemical reaction, involving absorption of heat, or of the compound so formed.—**en·do·ther·mal**, *a.*

en·do·tox·in, en″dō·tok′sin, *n.* The poison liberated at the death and disintegration of a microorganism, such as *Eberthella typhi*, the typhoid fever agent.

en·dow, en·dou′, *v.t.* [< L. *dos, dotis*, a dowry, < root seen in L. *do*, Gr. *didōmi* to give.] To furnish with a permanent fund or provision for support; to furnish with any gift, quality, or faculty.—**en·dow·ment**, *n.* Revenue or property permanently appropriated to any person or place; that which is given or bestowed on the person or mind; natural capacity.

end pa·per, *n.* A sheet of paper, one half of which is pasted inside the cover of a book, the other half of which forms the fly leaf.

end plate, *n.* One of the main end timbers of a mine shaft; *physiol.* the ending of a motor nerve, usu. embedded in muscle fiber.

end run, *n. Football*, a running play where the ball carrier tries to run wide around his own left or right flank.

end-stopped, end′stopt′, *a. Pros.* of or denoting a line of verse in which the end of a syntactic unit, as a clause or phrase, coincides with the end of the line.

end ta·ble, *n.* A small table placed at the end of a couch or next to a chair.

en·due, en·dö′, en·dū′, *v.t.—endued, enduing.* [L. *induo,* to put on.] To invest or endow with special qualities; to take on or assume; to don or clothe. Also **in·due.**

en·dur·ance, en·dur′ans, en·dēr′ans, *n.* Permanence; a continuing or bearing up under pain or distress without yielding; fortitude.

en·dure, en·dur′, en·dēr′, *v.t.—endured, enduring.* [Fr. *endurer,* < L. *durare,* to last.] To last; to abide; to suffer or sustain without yielding; to bear with patience or without opposition; to bear; to undergo, suffer, or experience; as, to *endure* great moral pressure.—*v.i.* To last; to sustain or support without breaking or yielding; to bear with patience; to merit lasting recognition, as: The works of Shakespeare have *endured* for centuries.—**en·dur·a·ble,** *a.*—**en·dur·a·bly,** *adv.*

en·dur·ing, en·dur′ing, en·dēr′ing, *a.* Permanent; lasting.—**en·dur·ing·ly,** *adv.* —**en·dur·ing·ness,** *n.*

end·ways, end′wāz″, *adv.* On or at the end; with the end forward or upward; in the direction of the length. Also **end-wise,** end′wiz″.

en·e·ma, en′e·ma, *n.* [Gr. *enema,* < *enienai,* to send in < *hiēni,* to send.] The injection of fluid into the rectum for cleansing, diagnosis, etc.; the liquid injected.

en·e·my, en′e·mē, *n.* pl. **en·e·mies.** [Fr. *ennemi,* < L. *inimicus—in-,* neg., and *amicus,* a friend.] One hostile to another; a foe; an adversary; a hostile military force; that which is harmful.

en·er·get·ic, en″ēr·jet′ik, *a.* [Gr. *energētikos.*] Acting with or exhibiting energy; operating with force, vigor, and effect; vigorous. Also **en·er·get·i·cal.—en·er·get·i·cal·ly,** *adv.*

en·er·get·ics, en″ēr·jet′iks, *n. pl. but sing. in constr. Phys.* the study of energy.

en·er·gize, en′ēr·jīz″, *v.i.—energized, energizing.* To act with energy or force; to act in producing an effect.—*v.t.* To give strength or force to; to give active vigor to. —**en·er·gi·zer,** *n.*

en·er·gy, en′ēr·jē, *n.* pl. **en·er·gies.** [Gr. *energeia.*] Inherent power; the power of operating, whether exerted or not; power vigorously exerted; strength of expression; *phys.* the actual or potential ability to do work.

en·er·gy lev·el, *n. Phys.* one of a series of stable states of matter, marked by a distinct level of constant energy, and distinguishable from others in the series by that level of energy. Also **en·er·gy state.**

en·er·vate, en′ēr·vāt″, *v.t.—enervated, enervating.* [L. *enervo, enervatum—e-,* out, away, and *nervus,* a nerve.] To deprive of nerve, force, or strength; to weaken.— i·nēr′vit, *a.* Without strength or force; weakened; debilitated. Also **en·er·vat·ed,** en′ēr·vā·tid.—**en·er·va·tion,** *n.*

en·fee·ble, en·fē′bl, *v.t.—enfeebled, enfeebling.* To weaken; to debilitate.— **en·fee·ble·ment,** *n.*

en·feoff, en·fef′, en·fēf′, *v.t.* [Prefix *en-,* and L.L. *feoffo,* to confer a fief or feud. FIEF.] *Law,* to give a fief or fee to.—**en·feoff·ment,** *n. Law,* the act of enfeoffing; the instrument or deed by which one is enfeoffed.

en·fet·ter, en·fet′ēr, *v.t.* To bind with, or as with, fetters.

en·fi·lade, en′fi·lād″, en″fi·lād′, *n.* [Fr. *en-* and *file,* a row, a rank, < *fil,* a thread, L. *filum.*] *Milit.* a position of troops subjecting them to fire from the flanks along the length of the line; the fire thus directed; *arch.* an arrangement of doors, arches, or columns in parallel and opposite rows to provide an effect of endless vista.—*v.t.—enfiladed, enfilading. Milit.* to fire in the flank of a troop; to be in position to deliver such fire; *arch.* to form an enfilade.

en·flame, en·flām′, *v.t., v.i.—enflamed, enflaming.* Inflame.

en·fleu·rage, *Fr.* äN·flœ·Räzh′, *n.* [Fr. < *enfleurer,* impregnate with the perfume of flowers, < *en-* and *fleur,* flower.] A process of extracting perfumes by exposing inodorous oils or fats to the exhalations from the flowers: used when the flower oils are too delicate or fugitive to undergo distillation.

en·fold, en·fōld′, *v.t.* To swathe or wrap up, as with a garment; to clasp in the arms; to form into folds.

en·force, en·fōrs′, en·fars′, *v.t.—enforced, enforcing.* [Prefix *en,* and *force;* Fr. *enforcir.*] To put into execution or force compliance with, as of laws; to add strength or emphasis to, as of opinions or contentions; to compel or impose upon by force.—**en·force·a·bil·i·ty,** *n.*—**en·force·a·ble,** *a.*—**en·force·ment,** *n.*—**en·forc·er,** *n.*

en·fran·chise, en·fran′chiz, *v.t.—enfranchised, enfranchising.* [O.Fr. *enfranchir (enfranchiss-),* < *en-* and *franc,* free, E. *frank.*] To set free; to liberate, as from slavery; release from obligation; to grant a franchise to; admit to citizenship, esp. to the right of voting; *fig.* to naturalize, as foreign words. Also *affranchise, franchise.*— **en·fran·chise·ment,** en·fran′chiz·ment, *n.* —**en·fran·chis·er,** *n.*

en·gage, en·gāj′, *v.t.—engaged, engaging.* [Fr. *engager—en-,* and *gager,* < *gage,* a pledge.] To hire or employ; to bind by a pledge or contract; to betroth; to attract; to occupy the attention of; to do battle with; *milit.* to attack; *mech.* to cause to interlock or mesh, as gears; to touch or interlock, as weapons in fencing.—*v.i.* To promise or pledge oneself; to undertake or occupy oneself; *milit.* to begin combat. *Mech.* to mesh; to be in gear.

en·gaged, en·gājd′, *a.* Occupied; employed; enlisted; affianced; committed; *milit.* in combat with; *mech.* meshed or in gear; *arch.* of a column, actually or seemingly attached in some measure to the main structure.

en·gage·ment, en·gāj′ment, *n.* Act of engaging; act or state of betrothal; appointment; agreement or contract; occupation; period of employment; *milit.* conflict between warring factions; *mech.* act or state of meshing.

en·gag·ing, en·gā′jing, *a.* Winning; attractive; tending to draw the attention or the affections; pleasing.—**en·gag·ing·ly,** *adv.*

en·gar·land, en·gär′land, *v.t.* To encircle with a garland.

en·gen·der, en·jen′dēr, *v.t.* [Fr. *engendrer,* < L. *ingenero—in-,* and *genero,* to beget, < *genus, generis,* birth, descent.] To beget; to produce; to cause to exist; to cause, excite, stir up.—*v.i.* To be caused or produced.

en·gine, en′jin, *n.* A machine for applying thermal energy to produce force and motion; as, the internal combustion motor of an automobile or the diesel *engine* of a truck, train, or ship; a locomotive; any instrument by which an effect is produced, esp. one of destruction or ingenuity; as, an *engine* of war, a fire *engine;* any mechanical device.

en·gi·neer, en″ji·nēr′, *n.* One who devises, designs, or builds according to the practices of engineering; one who operates a machine or locomotive; a person who skillfully manages a project. *U.S. Army,* a member of the Corps of Engineers engaged in constructing forts, bridges, roads, etc.; *orig.* one who managed military machines.—*v.t.* To perform the duties of an engineer; to direct, superintend, or maneuver by contrivance.

en·gi·neer·ing, en″ji·nēr′ing, *n.* The art of executing a practical application of scientific knowledge; the professional knowledge and work of an engineer; the profession of constructing and using mechanical devices; the management of an intricate enterprise.

en·gine·ry, en′jin·rē, *n. pl.* **en·gine·ries.** Machines in general; *milit.* artillery or other instruments of war; a skillful contrivance.

en·gird, en·gērd′, *v.t.—engirt* or *engirded, engirding.* To encompass. Also **en·gir·dle,** en·gēr′dl.

en·gla·cial, en·glā′shal, *a. Geol.* frozen within a glacier; believed to have been ice-locked in a glacier in former times.— **en·gla·cial·ly,** *adv.*

Eng·lish, ing′glish, ing′lish, *a.* [O.E. *englisc,* < *Engle,* Angle, the Angles.] Of, pertaining to, or characteristic of England or its inhabitants; of or pertaining to the English language.—*n.* The English language, spoken in the U.S., England, and areas now or previously controlled by Great Britain; *pl. in constr.* the English people. A particular style of the English language as used in a given time or area or by an individual; as, Canadian *English,* Chaucerian *English;* a school subject or course in English composition and literature; an English translation, as of a foreign word; an understandable version of anything obscure or very technical; *print.* a type size, 14-point, between pica and Columbian; *(sometimes l.c.)* a spinning motion imparted to a ball by striking it off-center, as in billiards, or by the manner of releasing it, as in bowling.—*v.t.* To translate into English; to anglicize, as a foreign word into English.—**Eng·lish·ism,** ing′gli·shiz″um, ing′li·shiz″um, *n.* An idiomatic expression characteristic of the English; also *Briticism.* An affinity for whatever is English.— **Eng·lish·ry,** ing′glish·rē, ing′lish·rē, *n.* A population of English birth or descent; specif. the English residing in Ireland; the fact of being English.

Eng·lish horn, *n.* A woodwind instrument somewhat larger than the oboe and having a pitch a fifth lower.

Eng·lish·man, ing′glish·man, ing′lish··man, *n. pl.* **Eng·lish·men.** A native or naturalized citizen of England. Also **Eng·land·er.**

Eng·lish muf·fin, *n.* A round, flat muffin made of bread dough, usually halved and toasted for serving.

Eng·lish set·ter, *n.* Any of a breed of medium-sized, long-haired bird dogs with a flat, silky coat of white with red or black markings, and having fine fur on the tail and legs.

Eng·lish son·net, *n.* A poem in iambic pentameter composed of three quatrains plus a concluding couplet, with the rhyme scheme *abab cdcd efef gg.* Also *Shakespearean sonnet.*

Eng·lish spring·er span·iel, *n.* A medium-sized spaniel, used for hunting, having a silky coat that is usu. black and white.

Eng·lish toy span·iel, *n.* A British-bred small spaniel characterized by a small, upturned nose and a rounded head.

Eng·lish wal·nut, *n.* The walnut tree, *Juglans regia,* having hard, richly-grained wood and bearing a widely-used edible nut; the nut of this tree.

Eng·lish·wom·an, ing′glish·wum″an, ing′lish·wum″an, *n. pl.* **Eng·lish·wom·en.** A woman born in England; a woman who is a naturalized citizen of England.

a- fat, fāte, fär, fâre, fall; **e-** met, mē, mēre, hèr; **i-** pin, pīne; **o-** not, nōte, möve; **u-** tub, cūbe, bull; **oi-** oil; **ou-** pound.

en·glut, en·glut', v.t.—*englutted, englutting.* [O.Fr. *englotir* (Fr. *engloutir*), < M.L. *inglutire,* < L. *in-,* in, and *glutire,* swallow.] To swallow or gulp down.

en·gorge, en·gārj', v.t.—*engorged, engorging.* [Fr. *engorger,* < *en-,* and *gorge,* E. gorge.] To swallow greedily; to glut or gorge; *pathol.* to congest with blood.—**en·gorge·ment,** *n.* The act of engorging, or the state of being engorged; *pathol.* congestion with blood.

en·graft, en·graft', en·gräft', v.t. *Bot.* to graft, as a scion, to another type of plant for propagation; to insert; to attach; to set firmly. Also **in·graft.**

en·grail, en·grāl', v.t. [Fr. *engrêler,* to engrail, < *grêle, gresle,* hail.] To decorate or indent the edge of with concave curves or notches; *minting,* to pattern the edge of, as a coin, with raised dots.—**en·grailed,** en·grāld', a. Her. indented on the edge with small concave curves.

en·grain, en·grān', v.t. Ingrain.

en·gram, en·gramme, en'gram, n. [Gr. *en-,* upon, and *granna,* mark.] *Biol.* an ineradicable mark left by a stimulus in the protoplasm of a tissue; *psychol.* a lasting, subconscious memory of a psychical experience.—**en·gram·mic,** a.

en·grave, en·grāv', v.t.—*engraved, engraving.* To cut, as figures, letters, or devices, into a hard substance, like stone, metal, or wood; as, to *engrave* the wedding date on a ring; to picture or represent by incisions, as on stone, metal, or wood, for printing purposes; to print from such a surface; to impress deeply; fix in the mind or memory.—**en·grav·er,** *n.*

en·grav·ing, en·grā'ving, n. The art of cutting designs or writing into any hard substance; specif. the art of forming designs on the surface of metal plates or blocks of wood for the purpose of taking off impressions or prints of these designs; a design so engraved; an engraved plate or block; an impression or print taken from an engraved surface.

en·gross, en·grōs', v.t. [O.Fr. *engrossier,* make big or bigger, A.Fr. *engrosser,* write large, also O.Fr. *en gros,* in large quantities, by wholesale; all < L. *in-,* in, and L.L. *grossus,* thick, E. gross.] To occupy wholly, as the mind or attention; absorb; to write or copy in a large, legible hand or in a formal manner for preservation, as a public document or record; to acquire the whole of in order to control the market; monopolize.—**en·grossed,** a. Wholly absorbed; preoccupied.—**en·gross·ing,** a. Fully occupying the mind or attention; absorbing.—**en·gross·ing·ly,** adv.—**en·gross·er,** n.—**en·gross·ment,** n. The act of engrossing; the state of being completely engaged; absorption; an engrossed work, as a document.

en·gulf, en·gulf', v.t. To swallow up in, or as in, a gulf or whirlpool; to overwhelm; to immerse.—**en·gulf·ment,** n.

en·hance, en·hans', en·häns', v.t.—*enhanced, enhancing.* [Pr. *enanser,* to advance, enhance, < *enant, enans,* forward.] To heighten; intensify; make greater; increase, as price, value, beauty, or pleasure.—**en·hance·ment,** n.

en·har·mon·ic, en"här·mon'ik, a. [L.L. *enharmonicus,* < Gr. *enarmonikos,* < *en-,* in, and *armonia,* E. harmony.] *Mus.* noting or pertaining to a style of music, or a scale or instrument, employing intervals smaller than a semitone; esp. pertaining to a use of notes which differ in name and in position on the staff, as G♯ and A♭, but which refer to identical tones or keys on fixed-note instruments like the piano.—**en·har·mon·i·cal·ly,** adv.

en·heart·en, en·här'ten, v.t. To give renewed hope or fortitude to; to produce inspiration in.

e·nig·ma, e·nig'ma, n. [L. *aenigma,* < Gr. *ainigma,* < *ainissesthai,* speak darkly, < *ainos,* tale, fable.] Anything or anyone puzzling or inexplicable; a saying, question, pictorial representation, or the like, containing a hidden meaning to be discovered; a riddle.—**en·ig·mat·ic, en·ig·mat·i·cal,** en"ig·mat'ik, ē"nig·mat'i·kal, a. [L.L. *aenigmaticus.*] Perplexing; mysterious.—**en·ig·mat·i·cal·ly,** adv.

en·isle, en·īl', v.t.—*enisled, enisling.* To make an island of; place on an island; isolate.

en·jamb·ment, en·jam'ment, en·jamb'-ment, Fr. äN·zhänb·män', n. [Fr. *enjambement—en-,* in, *jambe,* leg.] *Pros.* the running on of a verse from one line or couplet to another without a hesitation at the end of the line.

en·join, en·join', v.t. [Fr. *enjoindre,* < L. *injungo.*] To admonish, instruct, or command with authority.—**en·join·er,** n.—**en·join·ment,** n.

en·joy, en·joi', v.t. [O.Fr. *enjoier,* to receive with joy.] To feel or perceive with pleasure; to have, possess, and use with satisfaction.—**en·joy·a·ble,** a. Capable of being enjoyed or of yielding enjoyment.—**en·joy·a·ble·ness,** n.—**en·joy·a·bly,** adv.—**en·joy·ment,** n. Satisfaction or pleasure in the possession or occupancy of anything; that which causes joy or gratification; delight.

en·kin·dle, en·kin'dl, v.t.—*enkindled, enkindling.* To kindle; to set on fire; to inflame; to excite; to rouse into action.—v.i. To take fire; to be inflamed; to be roused into action.

en·lace, en·lās', v.t.—*enlaced, enlacing.* To fasten or encircle with, or as with, a lace or cord; to encircle; to interweave or entwine.—**en·lace·ment,** n.

en·large, en·lärj', v.t.—*enlarged, enlarging.* To make larger; to extend; to expand; to make more comprehensive.—v.i. To grow larger; to speak or write with greater detail.—**en·large·a·ble,** a.—**en·larg·er,** n. An optical instrument used to project images larger than the negative upon photographic printing material.

en·large·ment, en·lärj'ment, n. The act of enlarging or state of being enlarged; an addition; expansion of intellectual powers; a detailed discourse. *Photog.* a photograph which has been printed larger than the size of the original negative.

en·light·en, en·lit'en, v.t. To illuminate; to give intellectual light to; to impart knowledge; to instruct.

en·light·en·ment, en·lit'en·ment, n. Act of enlightening; state of being enlightened. —**the En·light·en·ment,** a philosophical and cultural movement of the 17th and 18th centuries, characterized by a questioning of established beliefs, an emphasis on the free use of reason, the development of scientific empiricism, and a predominant concern for the dignity and welfare of mankind.

en·list, en·list', v.t. To enroll for service in the military; to employ in advancing some interest.—v.i. To enroll in the armed services voluntarily; to enter heartily into a cause.—**en·list·ment,** n. The act of enlisting; the raising of soldiers by enlisting.—**en·list·ed,** a.

en·list·ed man, n. A man in the U.S. armed forces who ranks below a commissioned officer or warrant officer.

en·liv·en, en·li'ven, v.t. To give life, action, or motion to; to make vigorous or active; to give spirit or vivacity to; to make sprightly, gay, or cheerful.—**en·liv·en·er,** n.

en masse, än mas', en mas', Fr. äN mas', adv. [Fr.] As a whole; all together; in a body.

en·mesh, en·mesh', v.t. To catch in; to entangle. Also **im·mesh, in·mesh.**

en·mi·ty, en'mi·tē, n. pl. **en·mi·ties.** [Fr. *inimitié,* O.Fr. *enemistie,* corresponding to a L. form *inimicitas,* < *inimicus,* unfriendly.] Hostility; ill will.

en·ne·ad, en'ē·ad", n. [Gr. *ennea,* nine, *ad* as in *monad, triad, myriad.*] A collection of nine.

en·ne·a·gon, en'ē·a·gon", n. [Gr. *ennea,* nine, and *gōnia,* angle.] A closed plane figure having nine angles and nine sides; a nonagon.

en·ne·a·he·dron, en"ē·a·hē'dron, n. pl. **en·ne·a·he·dra.** [Gr. *ennea,* nine, and *edna,* seat, base.] A solid figure having nine faces.—**en·ne·a·he·dral,** a.

en·no·ble, en·nō'bl, v.t.—*ennobled, ennobling.* [Fr. *ennoblier.*] To make noble; to raise to nobility; to dignify; to elevate in degree, qualities, or excellence.—**en·no·ble·ment,** n.—**en·no·bler,** n.

en·nui, än·wē', än'wē, Fr. äN·nwē', n. [Fr. O.Fr. *anui,* annoy, like Old Venetian *inodio,* < L. *in odio,* in hate, in disgust.] A feeling of weariness arising from lack of occupation or lack of interest in present scenes and surrounding objects; listlessness; boredom; tedium.

e·nol·o·gy, ē·nol'o·jē, n. A science that deals with wine and the making of wine. Also *oenology.*

e·nor·mi·ty, i·nār'mi·tē, n. pl. **e·nor·mi·ties.** [L. *enormitas.*] The state or quality of being enormous, immoderate, or excessive; a very grave offense against order, right, or decency; an atrocious crime; an atrocity.

e·nor·mous, i·nār'mus, a. [L. *enormis.*] Great beyond or exceeding the common measure; excessively large; excessively wicked; atrocious.—**e·nor·mous·ly,** adv.—**e·nor·mous·ness,** n.

e·nough, i·nuf', a. [O.E. *genōg, genōh,* = D. *genoeg* = G. *genug* = Icel. *gnōgr* = Goth. *ganōhs,* enough.] Adequate for the want or need; sufficient for the purpose or to satisfy desire.—n. An adequate quantity or number; as much as is needed or desired; a sufficiency.—adv. In a quantity or degree that answers a purpose or satisfies a need or desire; sufficiently; fully or quite, as: He is ready *enough* to accept the offer. Tolerably or passably.

e·nounce, i·nouns', v.t.—*enounced, enouncing.* [Fr. *énoncer,* L. *enuncio.*] To declare; to enunciate; to state, as a proposition or argument.

e·now, i·nou', i·nō', a. adv. An old form of *enough.*

en·phy·tot·ic, en"fī·tot'ik, a. *Bot.* of or denoting a regional plant disease which occurs regularly but not severely.—n.

en·plane, en·plān', v.t., v.i.—*enplaned, enplaning.* To go aboard an airplane.

en prise, än"prēz', Fr. äN prēz', a. Of a chess piece, liable to capture.

en·quire, en·kwīr', v.t., v.i.—*enquired, enquiring.* Inquire.—**en·quir·er,** n. Inquirer. —**en·quir·y,** n. Inquiry.

en·rage, en·rāj', v.t.—*enraged, enraging.* To make furious; to exasperate.

en·rap·ture, en·rap'chèr, v.t.—*enraptured, enrapturing.* To transport with rapture; to delight beyond measure.—**en·rapt,** a.

en·reg·is·ter, en·rej'i·stèr, v.t. [Fr. *enregistrer,* < *en-* and *registre,* E. register.] To register; record.

en·rich, en·rich', v.t. To supply with abundant wealth or property; to supply with an abundance of anything desirable; to increase the nutritive value of, as foodstuffs, by adding vitamins and minerals; to improve by fertilizing, as soil; to supply with anything ornamental; to adorn.—**en·rich·ment,** n.—**en·rich·er,** n.

en·robe, en·rōb', v.t.—*enrobed, enrobing.* To clothe with attire; to attire.

en·roll, en·rōl', v.t.—enrolled, enrolling. To write in a roll or register; to insert or enter the name of in a list or catalogue; to record; to insert in records; to wrap.—v.i. To register oneself or cause oneself to be registered.—**en·roll·ment**, **en·rol·ment**, n. The act of enrolling or registering; the number registered, as for a particular course or school.

en·root, en·rōt', en·rŭt', v.t. To fix by the root; fig. to fix fast; implant deeply.

en route, än rōt', en rōt', Fr. äN Rōt', adv. [Fr.] On the way; along the way.

en·san·guine, en·sang'gwin, v.t.—ensanguined, ensanguining. [Prefix en-, and L. sanguis, sanguinis, blood.] To stain or cover with blood; to crimson.

en·sconce, en·skons', v.t.—ensconced, sconcing. To cover or shelter; to settle comfortably.

en·scroll, en·skrōl', v.t. To write or record on a scroll; inscroll.

en·sem·ble, än·säm'bl, än·sämb'bl, Fr. äN·säN'ble, n. [Fr. < L. insimul, at the same time.] All the parts of anything taken together so that each part is considered only in relation to the whole; the general effect of a whole work of art, as a picture, piece of music, or drama; the complete outfit of a person, esp. when all the parts blend or harmonize; combined performance of a full group of singers, players, or the like; the full group thus performing; the appearance at one time of the entire cast of a production.

en·sheathe, en·shēтн', v.t.—ensheathed, ensheathing. To wrap in, or as in, a sheath. Also **en·sheath, in·sheathe, in·sheath**.

en·shrine, en·shrīn', v.t.—enshrined, enshrining. To enclose in, or as in, a shrine; to preserve with care; to cherish.

en·shroud, en·shroud', v.i. To cover with, or as with, a shroud; to envelop with anything which conceals.

en·si·form, en'si·fŏrm", a. [L. ensiformis, ensis, sword, and forma, form.] Having the shape of a sword; sword-shaped: said of leaves of plants, or of a cartilage at the lower part of the human sternum or breastbone.

en·sign, en'sīn, en'sin, n. [Fr. enseigne, a sign, an ensign, < L. insigne, a sign, a badge—in-, and signum, a mark, a sign.] A flag, banner, or standard distinguishing office, rank, or nationality, esp. of an army or ship, en'sīn. Milit. the lowest commissioned officer in the United States Navy, ranking below a lieutenant, junior grade; formerly a commissioned officer of lowest rank in a British regiment of infantry, the one who carried the standard, en'sīn.—**en·sign·cy, en·sign·ship**, n. The rank, office, or commission of an ensign.

en·si·lage, en'si·lij, n. [Fr. ensilage, < Sp. ensilar, to store grain in an underground receptacle, < en-, in, and silo, < L. sirus, a pit.] A mode of storing green fodder in pits or silos, the substance stored being tightly pressed and undergoing a slight fermentation; the substance thus treated.—v.t.—ensilaged, ensilaging. To ensile.

en·sile, en·sil', en'sil, v.t.—ensiled, ensiling. To store by the process of ensilage.

en·sky, en·skī', v.t.—enskied or enskyed, enskying. To place in the sky; fig. to place in an exalted position.

en·slave, en·slāv', v.t.—enslaved, enslaving. To make a slave of; to master or overpower, as: LSD has enslaved him.—**en·slave·ment**, n.—**en·slav·er**, n.

en·snare, en·snâr', v.t.—ensnared, ensnaring. To capture in a snare; to trap; to involve by a trick. Also **in·snare**.—**en·snare·ment**, n.—**en·snar·er**, n.—**en·snar·ing·ly**, adv.

en·snarl, en·snär'l, v.t. To tangle in a snarl.

en·soul, en·sōl', v.t. To endow with a soul. Also **in·soul**.

en·sphere, en·sfēr', v.t.—ensphered, ensphering. To enclose in or make into a sphere.

en·sue, en·sō', v.i.—ensued, ensuing. [Prefix en-, and sue; O.Fr. ensuir, < L. insequor, to follow upon.] To follow as a consequence; to follow in a train of events or course of time; to succeed; to come after.—**en·su·ing**, a.—**en·su·ing·ly**, adv.

en suite, äN swēt', adv., a. [Fr.] In a series; in succession.

en·sure, en·shur', v.t.—ensured, ensuring. To make sure or secure; to make certain; to turn out, arise, or follow; to make safe.—**en·sur·er**, n.

en·swathe, en·swoтн', en·swäтн', v.t.—enswathed, enswathing. To swathe; to wrap up. Also **in·swathe**.—**en·swathe·ment**, n.

en·tab·la·ture, en·tab'la·chėr, n. [O.Fr. entablature—en-, and table; L. tabula, a board, plank.] Arch. the superstructure which lies horizontally upon the columns and consists of three principal divisions: the architrave, the frieze, and the cornice. Any similar part.

en·ta·ble·ment, en·tā'bl·ment, n. Arch. a platform which supports a statue or other upright structure above the dado of a pedestal.

en·tail, en·tāl', v.t. To limit an inheritance to a specified line of heirs, so that a landed estate cannot be alienated or bequeathed; to confer as if by entail; to cause to descend to a fixed series of possessors; to impose a burden upon someone; to bring on or involve; as, a loss entailing no regret.—n. The act of entailing, or the state of being entailed; the rule of descent settled for an estate; that which is entailed, as an estate; any predetermined order of succession, as to an office.—**en·tail·er**, n.—**en·tail·ment**, n.

en·tan·gle, en·tang'gl, v.t.—entangled, entangling. To tangle so as not to be easily separated; to make confused or disordered; to involve in anything complicated; to involve in difficulties, embarrassments, or contradictions; to hamper.—**en·tan·gle·ment**, n. The act of entangling or state of being entangled; a complication.—**en·tan·gler**, n.

en·tel·e·chy, en·tel'e·kē, n. pl. **en·tel·e·chies**. [L. entelechia, < Gr. entelecheia, < enteleiechein, be in fulfilment or completion.] Philos. a realization or actuality as opposed to a potentiality.

en·tente, än·tänt', Fr. äN·täNt', n. [Fr.] A mutual understanding between two or more nations to follow a common course of action; a coalition of nations or parties to such a mutual understanding.

en·ter, en'tėr, v.t. [Fr. entrer, < L. intrare, to enter, < intro, into the inside—in-, in, and root seen in trans, across, and in Skt. tri, to pass.] To come or go into in any manner whatever; to pierce; to penetrate; to insert or place; to begin or commence upon, as a new period or stage in the progress of life, a new profession, etc.; to engage or become involved in; to join; to become a member of; to set down in a book or other record; to enroll; to inscribe; of a ship, to report at the custom house on arrival in port. Law, to go in or upon and take possession, as of lands; to place in regular form before a court.—v.i. To come in; to go or pass in; to embark or enlist in an affair, business, or profession; to become a member; to begin to talk of or examine a subject; as, to enter the discussion; to be enrolled in a school; to join a competition; as, to enter late in the race.—**to en·ter in·to**, to get into the inside or interior of; to penetrate; to engage in; as, to enter into business; to deal with or treat

by way of discussion, argument, and the like; to be an ingredient in; to form a constituent part in.—**en·ter·a·ble**, a.

en·ter·al, en'tėr·al, a. Having reference to the enteron or alimentary canal.—**en·ter·al·ly**, adv.

en·ter·ec·to·my, en"te·rek'tō·mē, n. [Gr. enteron, intestine, and ec, out of, and tomia, E. -tomy.] Surg. removal of a portion of the intestine.

en·ter·ic, en·ter'ik, a. [Gr. enterikos, < enteron, intestine.] Belonging or relating to the intestines; as, enteric or typhoid fever.

en·ter·i·tis, en"te·rī'tis, n. Pathol. inflammation of the intestines, esp. the small intestine.

en·ter·o·coc·cus, en"te·rō·kok'us, n. pl. **en·ter·o·coc·ci**, en"te·rō·kok'sī, en"te·rō·kok'sē. A streptococcus usu. found in the intestine.—**en·ter·o·coc·cal**, a.

en·ter·o·co·li·tis, en"te·rō·kō·lī'tis, en"te·rō·ko·lī'tis, n. Pathol. inflammation of the small and large intestines.

en·ter·o·hep·a·ti·tis, en"te·rō·hep"a·tī'tis, n. Veter. med. an infectious, often fatal, disease affecting the intestines and liver of various wild birds, turkeys, and chickens.

en·ter·on, en'te·ron", n. pl. **en·ter·a**. [N.L. < Gr. enteron.] Anat., zool. the alimentary canal; specif. the digestive tract of the fetus or embryo.

en·ter·os·to·my, en"te·ros'tō·mē, n. pl. **en·ter·os·to·mies**. Surg. an incision into the intestine through the abdominal wall, to allow for drainage or feeding.

en·ter·prise, en'tėr·priz", n. [Fr. entreprendre < L. prehendo, prendo.] That which is undertaken or attempted; a project attempted; particularly a bold, arduous, or hazardous undertaking; an active and enterprising spirit; readiness to engage in undertakings of difficulty, risk, or danger; a firm or business.—**en·ter·pris·er**, en'tėr·prī'zėr, n. One who engages in an enterprise or business.—**en·ter·pris·ing**, en'tėr·prī'zing, a. Having a disposition for or tendency to engage in enterprises; ready to start and carry on untried schemes.—**en·ter·pris·ing·ly**, adv.

en·ter·tain, en'tėr·tān', v.t. [Fr. entretenir, to maintain—entre = L. inter, between, and tenir = L. tenere, to hold.] To treat with hospitality; to amuse; to take into consideration.—v.i. To provide diversions, amusements, or entertainment for; to receive company.—**en·ter·tain·er**, n.

en·ter·tain·ment, en"tėr·tān'ment, n. The act of entertaining; the receiving and accommodating of guests; something that serves for amusement, as a dramatic performance.—**en·ter·tain·ing**, a. Affording entertainment; amusing; diverting.—**en·ter·tain·ing·ly**, adv.

en·thal·py, en'thal·pē, en·thal'pē, n. pl. **en·thal·pies**. Phys. a measurement of heat change in a thermodynamic system; heat flow into a closed system when pressure is constant: expressed by the equation $H = U + pV$ where H is the enthalpy, U is the internal energy of the system, p the pressure and V the volume.

en·thrall, en·thral', en·thral', v.t.—enthralled, enthralling. To enslave; to charm or to captivate. Also **in·thral, in·thrall**.—**en·thrall·ment, en·thral·ment**, n.

en·throne, en·thrōn', v.t.—enthroned, enthroning. To place on a throne; to invest with sovereign authority; to exalt to an elevated place or seat; to induct or install, as a bishop, into the powers and privileges of a vacant see. Also **in·throne**.—**en·throne·ment**, n. The act of enthroning or state of being enthroned. Also **en·thron·i·za·tion**.

en·thuse, en·thōz', v.i., v.t.—enthused, enthusing. Colloq. To arouse enthusiasm; to exhibit enthusiasm.

en·thu·si·asm, en·thŏ′zē·az″um, n. [Gr. *enthousiasmos*, < *enthousiazō*, to infuse a divine spirit, < *enthous*, *entheos*, inspired, divine.] A keen and active interest; ardent zeal in pursuit of an object; any pursuit where such zeal or keen interest is displayed.

en·thu·si·ast, en·thŏ′zē·ast″, n. [Gr. *enthousiastēs*.] One full of enthusiasm for something; a person of ardent zeal.

en·thu·si·as·tic, en·thŏ′zē·as′tik, a. Filled with or characterized by enthusiasm; prone to enthusiasm; ardent; devoted.—**en·thu·si·as·ti·cal·ly**, adv.

en·thy·meme, en′thi·mēm″, n. Logic, a syllogism, with one implied premise.

en·tice, en·tīs′, v.t.—*enticed*, *enticing*. [O.Fr. *enticer*, *entiser* = Mod.Fr. *attiser*, < *tison*, L. *titio*, a firebrand.] To draw on by exciting hope or desire; to allure or attract.—**en·tice·ment**, n. The act of inducing, esp. to evil; the state of being induced; allurement; attraction.—**en·tic·er**, n.—**en·tic·ing**, a.—**en·tic·ing·ly**, adv.

en·tire, en·tīer′, a. [O.Fr. Fr. *entier*, < L. *integer*, untouched, whole.] Whole; complete; having all the parts or elements; full or thorough; as, *entire* freedom of choice; not broken, mutilated, or decayed; intact; not gelded; unimpaired or undiminished; being wholly of one piece; undivided; continuous; having an unbroken outline; without notches or indentations, as leaves or shells. —n. Brit. a kind of malt liquor; porter.— **en·tire·ly**, adv. Wholly or fully; completely or unreservedly; solely or exclusively; heartily or sincerely.—**en·tire·ness**, n.—**en·tire·ty**, n. pl. **en·tire·ties**. [O.Fr. < *entierete*, < L. *integritas*.] The state of being entire; completeness; that which is entire; the whole.

en·ti·tle, en·tī′tl, v.t.—*entitled*, *entitling*. [O.Fr. *entituler*.] To furnish with a title, right, or claim; to give a name or title to; to designate.—**en·ti·tle·ment**, n.

en·ti·ty, en′ti·tē, n. pl. **en·ti·ties**. [L.L. *entitas*, < *ens*, *entis*, a thing.] A being or species of being; an existing thing; being or existence; essence.

en·to·blast, en′tō·blast″, n. [Gr. *entos*, within, and *blastos*, bud.] Biol. the endoderm. Also *endoblast*.—**en·to·blas·tic, en·do·blas·tic**, en″tō·blas′tik, a.

en·to·derm, en′to·dêrm″, n. Endoderm. —**en·to·der·mal, en·to·der·mic**, a.

en·tomb, en·tōmb′, v.t. To deposit in a tomb; to bury; to inter. Also **in·tomb**.— **en·tomb·ment**, n.

en·to·mol·o·gy, en″to·mol′o·jē, n. pl. **en·to·mol·o·gies**. [Gr. *entomon*, an insect, < *entomos*, cut in—*en-*, in, and *temno*, to cut; < the thorax being almost divided from the abdomen.] That branch of zoology which deals with the structure, habits, and classification of insects.—**en·to·mo·log·ic, en·to·mo·log·i·cal**, en″to·mo·loj′i·kal, a. —**en·to·mo·log·i·cal·ly**, adv.—**en·to·mol·o·gist**, n.

en·to·moph·a·gous, en″to·mof′a·gus, a. Feeding on insects; insectivorous.

en·to·moph·i·lous, en″to·mof′i·lus, a. Of or relating to a plant whose fertilization is effected by insects.—**en·to·moph·i·ly**, n.

en·to·mos·tra·can, en″to·mos′tra·kan, a. [N.L. *Entomostraca*, pl., < Gr. *entomos*, cut in pieces, and *ostracon*, shell.] Belonging to the *Entomostraca*, a subclass of crustaceans which have a moderately simple organization, including the cirripeds.—n. An entomostracan crustacean.—**en·to·mos·tra·cous**, a.

en·tou·rage, än″tu·räzh′, Fr. äN·tö·räzh′, n. [Fr. *entour*, around.] The retinue of a person; associates; the surrounding environment.

en·to·zo·on, en″to·zō′on, n. pl. **en·to·zo·a**, en″to·zō′a. [N.L.] An internal parasite,

as an intestinal worm.—**en·to·zo·an**, a., n. —**en·to·zo·ic**, a. Living as a parasite inside another animal.

en·tr'acte, än·trakt′, Fr. äN·träkt′, n. [Fr.] The interval between the acts of a drama; a short musical entertainment performed during such interval.

en·trails, en′trālz, en′tralz, n. pl. [Fr. *entrailles*; < L.L. *intralia*, < L. *inter*, within.] The internal parts of animal bodies; the bowels; the viscera; the guts; the insides of anything.

en·train, en·trān′, v.t. To put aboard a train.—v.i. To board a train.—**en·train·er**, n.

en·train·ment, en·trān′ment, n. Phys. a process in which droplets of fluid or gas molecules adjacent to a moving stream are carried along by the stream, which process is especially pertinent to a jet; chem. the entrapment of air bubbles in concrete to improve its properties; the process of carrying off liquid droplets during distillation.

en·trance, en′trans, n. [< *enter*.] The act of entering into a place; the power or liberty of entering; admission. The doorway or passage by which a place may be entered; also **en·trance·way**. An actor's first appearance on stage; the act of taking possession, as of an office.

en·trance, en·trans′, en·träns′, v.t.— *entranced*, *entrancing*. To fill with delight or wonder; to enrapture; to throw into a trance.—**en·trance·ment**, n.—**en·tranc·ing**, a.—**en·tranc·ing·ly**, adv.

en·trant, en′trant, n. One who enters; one who begins a new course of life; one becoming a member for the first time of any association or body; one taking part in a contest.

en·trap, en·trap′, v.t.—*entrapped*, *entrapping*. To catch as in a trap; to ensnare; to bring by artifice into a difficult or compromising position.—**en·trap·ment**, n.

en·treat, en·trēt′, v.t. [O.Fr. *entraiter*, to treat of.] To ask earnestly; to beseech; to plead for; to solicit pressingly.—**en·treat·ing·ly**, adv.—**en·treat·ment**, n.—**en·treat·y**, en·trē′tē, n. Urgent plea; earnest petition; supplication.

en·tre·chat, Fr. äN·tRe·shä′, n. [Fr.] Ballet, a leap during which the feet are struck together a number of times.

en·trée, än′trā, n. [Fr.] Entry; freedom of access; a way of obtaining access; Brit. a dish served before the main course or between courses at dinner; U.S. a dish served as the main course.

en·tre·mets, än′tre·mā″, Fr. äN·tRe·me′, n. pl. **en·tre·mets**, än′tre·māz″, Fr. äN·tRe·me′. [Fr. *entre*, between, and *mets*, a dish.] A side dish or minor dish served at the table.

en·trench, en·trench′, v.t. To dig or cut a trench or trenches around; to fortify with a ditch and parapet; to lodge within, or as within, an entrenchment; to place in a strong position.—v.i. To invade; to encroach, with *on* or *upon*.—**en·trench·ment**, n. The act of entrenching; fort. a work consisting of a ditch and a parapet constructed for a defense against an enemy. Any protection.

en·tre·pôt, än′tre·pō″, Fr. äN·tRe·pō′, n. [Fr. < L. *inter*, between, and *positum*, placed.] A warehouse for the depositing of goods; a center for the distribution or repackaging of merchandise.

en·tre·pre·neur, än″tre·pre·nêr′, än″tre·pre·nŷr′, Fr. äN·tRe·pRe·nœr′, n. [Fr. *entreprendre*, to undertake.] The person who organizes, manages, and assumes the risks of a business; a successful businessman.— **en·tre·pre·neur·i·al**, a.—**en·tre·pre·neur·ship**, n.

en·tre·sol, en′têr·sol″, än′tre·sol″, Fr.

äN·tRe·sal′,′ n. [Fr.] Arch. a low story between two others of greater height, esp. when the lower story is the ground floor; a mezzanine.

en·tro·py, en′tro·pē, n. [Gr. *en-*, in, *tropē*—transformation.] Phys. a measure of the degree to which the energy in a closed thermodynamic system or process has ceased to be available energy. In a reversible process, the entropy remains the same; in natural irreversible processes, the entropy increases, as: In the universe as a whole, the *entropy* is said to be increasing. The degree of uniformity in anything; sameness.

en·trust, en·trust′, v.t. To trust or confide to the care of; to commit with confidence; as, to *entrust* a thing *to* a person, or a person *with* a thing; consign; commit; confide.— **en·trust·ment**, n.

en·try, en′trē, n. pl. **en·tries**. [Fr. *entrée*.] The act of entering; entrance; entranceway; one placed in a contest; the act of recording in a book; any single item entered or set down; the giving of an account of a ship's cargo or exhibition of her papers in order to obtain permission to land goods; *law*, the act of taking possession of lands or tenements.

en·twine, en·twīn′, v.t.—*entwined*, *entwining*. To twine; to twist around or together.—v.i. To become twisted or twined. Also **in·twine**.

en·twist, en·twist′, v.t. To twist together or about. Also **in·twist**.

e·nu·cle·ate, i·nö′klē·āt″, i·nū′klē·āt″, v.t.—*enucleated*, *enucleating*. [L. *enucleatus*, pp. of *enucleare*, < *e-*, out of, and *nucleus*, kernel, E. *nucleus*.] To remove, as a kernel, tumor, or eyeball, from its enveloping cover; biol. to deprive of the nucleus.— i·nö′klē·it, i·nö′klē·āt″, i·nū′klē·it, i·nū′klē·āt″, a. Having no nucleus.—**e·nu·cle·a·tion**, n.—**e·nu·cle·a·tor**, n.

e·nu·mer·ate, i·nö′me·rāt″, i·nū′me·rāt″, v.t.—*enumerated*, *enumerating*. [L. *enumero*, *enumeratum*—*e-*, out, and *numerus*, number.] To mention one by one; to number; to count; to recount.—**e·nu·mer·a·ble**, a.— **e·nu·mer·a·tion**, n. The act of enumerating; a list.—**e·nu·mer·a·tive**, a. Counting; reckoning up.—**e·nu·mer·a·tor**, n.

e·nun·ci·ate, i·nun′sē·āt″, i·nun′shē·āt″, v.t.—*enunciated*, *enunciating*. [L. *enuntiatus*, pp. of *enuntiare*. ENOUNCE.] To utter or pronounce, esp. in a particular manner; to announce or proclaim; to state or declare definitely, as a theory.—v.i. To utter or pronounce words in a particular manner.— **e·nun·ci·a·ble**, a.—**e·nun·ci·a·tion**, n. [L. *enuntiatio(n-)*.] The act or the manner of enunciating; announcement; statement; utterance or pronunciation.—**e·nun·ci·a·tive, e·nun·ci·a·to·ry**, a. Serving to enunciate; declaratory; pertaining to vocal utterance.—**e·nun·ci·a·tor**, n.

en·ure, en·ūr′, v.i., v.t.—*enured*, *enuring*. Inure.

en·u·re·sis, en″ū·rē′sis, n. [Gr.] Pathol. incontinence or involuntary discharge of urine.—**en·u·ret·ic**, en″ū·ret′ik, a., n.

en·vel·op, en·vel′up, v.t.—*enveloped*, *enveloping*. [Fr. *envelopper*, It. *invillupare*, to envelop.] To cover, as by wrapping or folding; to enwrap or wrap up; to surround entirely; to cover on all sides; to form a covering about; to outflank or turn (the enemy's line) so that it is partially surrounded.—**en·vel·op·ment**, n. The act of enveloping; that which envelops.

en·ve·lope, en′ve·lōp″, än′ve·lōp″, n. An enclosing paper cover, usu. sealable, as for a letter; what is wrapped around or envelops something; a wrapper; biol. an integument; the membrane covering an organ; electron. the metal or glass casing that covers a vacuum tube; geom. a surface or curve to which another surface or curve is tangent in accordance with a definite system of variation or movement; *bot.* the calyx or corolla surrounding the stamens and pistils; *aeron.* the outer covering of a balloon or airship distended by means of enclosed gas. Also **en·vel·op.**

en·ven·om, en·ven'om, *v.t.* To taint or impregnate with venom or poison; to imbue with bitterness or malice.

en·vi·a·ble, en'vē·a·bl, *a.* Exciting or capable of exciting envy; highly desirable. —**en·vi·a·bly,** *adv.*—**en·vi·a·ble·ness,** *n.*

en·vi·ous, en'vē·us, *a.* [Fr. *envieux.*] Feeling or harboring envy; tinctured with envy; excited or directed by envy.— **en·vi·ous·ly,** *adv.*—**en·vi·ous·ness,** *n.*

en·vi·ron, en·vī'ron, en·vī'ĕrn, *v.t.* [Fr. *environner—en-,* and O.Fr. *vironner,* to veer, to environ, < *virer,* to veer.] To surround, encompass, or encircle; to hem in; to envelop.

en·vi·ron·ment, en·vī'ron·ment, en·vī'ĕrn·ment, *n.* All the physical, social, and cultural factors and conditions influencing the existence or development of an organism or assemblage of organisms; the act of surrounding; the state of being surrounded; that which surrounds; surroundings.— **en·vi·ron·men·tal,** *a.*—**en·vi·ron·men·tal·ly,** *adv.*

en·vi·rons, en·vī'ronz, en·vī'ornz, en'vĕr·onz, en'vi·ornz, *n. pl.* Areas surrounding a city or other specific place; the vicinity.

en·vis·age, en·viz'ij, *v.t.*—*envisaged, envisaging.* [Fr. *envisager—en-,* in, and *visage,* face.] To contemplate; to form a mental picture of.

en·vi·sion, en·vizh'an, *v.t.* To picture in one's mind, esp. a future happening.

en·voy, en'voi, än'voi, *n.* [Fr. *envoyer,* to send, < L. *via,* a way.] One dispatched upon an errand or mission; a messenger; a diplomatic agent ranking below an ambassador; a person delegated to negotiate a treaty or transact other business with a foreign ruler or government; a diplomatic agent sent on a special mission.

en·voy, en'voi, *n.* The concluding lines to a poem or prose piece, often serving as a dedication; a brief, final stanza of a ballade. Also **en·voi.**

en·vy, en'vē, *n. pl.* **en·vies.** [Fr. *envie,* < L. *invidia,* envy, < *invidus,* envious.] Discontent or jealousy excited by the sight of another's superiority or success; a feeling that makes a person begrudge another his good fortune; resentment; malice; object of envy.—*v.t.*—*envied, envying.* [Fr. *envier.*] To feel envy toward or on account of; to regard with jealousy and longing; to desire earnestly.—**en·vi·er,** *n.*—**en·vy·ing·ly,** *a.*

en·wind, en·wind', *v.i.*—*enwound, enwinding.* To enfold or coil about. Also **in·wind.**

en·womb, en·wŏm', *v.t.* To enclose in or as in a womb.

en·wrap, en·rap', *v.t.*—*enwrapped, enwrapping.* To envelop; to occupy completely, as: He was *enwrapped* in thought.

en·wreathe, en·rēTH', *v.t.*—*enwreathed, enwreathing.* To encircle, as with a wreathe. Also **in·wreathe.**

en·zo·ot·ic, en"zō·ot'ik, *a.* [Gr. *en-,* among, and *zōon,* an animal.] Limited to the animals of a district: said of diseases.—*n.* A disease affecting the animals of a district.

en·zyme, en'zim, *n.* [Gr.] *Biochem.* a very large class of protein substances that are produced by living cells and are essential to life by acting as catalysts in the metabolism of the organism.—**en·zy·mat·ic,** en·zy··mic,** en"zī·mat'ik, en"zi·mat'ik, en·zī'mik, en·zī'mik, *a.*—**en·zy·mat·i·cal·ly,** **en·zy·mi·cal·ly,** *adv.*

en·zy·mol·o·gy, en"zī·mol'o·jē, en"zi·mol'o·jē, *n.* A branch of science that deals with the nature and activity of enzymes.— **en·zy·mol·o·gist,** *n.*

E·o·cene, ē'o·sēn", *a.* [Gr. *ēōs,* the dawn, and *kainos,* recent.] *Geol.* of or pertaining to an epoch of the early Tertiary period of the Cenozoic era which began approximately 55 million years ago and lasted about 20 million years, during which time modern mammals developed.—*n.* The Eocene epoch.

e·o·hip·pus, ē"ō·hip'us, *n.* A small, primitive horse from the Eocene epoch of the western U.S. and Europe with four-toed forefeet and three-toed hindfeet.

e·o·li·an, ē·ō'lē·an, *a. Geol.* pertaining to sand or other deposits arranged or transported by the wind, or to the erosive action of the wind; (*cap.*) Aeolian.

e·o·lith, ē'o·lith, *n.* [Gr. *ēōs,* dawn, and *lithos,* stone.] A chipped flint, the oldest known type of prehistoric stone implement. —**e·o·lith·ic,** ē"o·lith'ik, *a. Archeol.* of or pertaining to the early part of the Stone Age, characterized by the use of eoliths.

e·on, ae·on, ē'on, ē'on, *n.* [Gr. *aiōn,* age, duration, eternity.] A long, indefinite space of time; an age; a division of geologic time, usu. of more than one era.

e·o·sin, ē'o·sin, *n.* [Gr. *ēōs,* dawn.] *Chem.* a red crystalline powder, $C_{20}H_8Br_4O_5$, used primarily to dye fabrics a rose red color, and to stain specimens for microscopic examination; any of several similar dyes. Also **e·o·sine,** ē'o·sin, ē'·o·sēn".

e·o·sin·o·phil, ē"o·sin'o·fil, *n. Biol.* a microorganism, cell, or substance readily stained by eosin. Also **e·o·sin·o·phile,** ē"o·sin'o·fīl".—**e·o·sin·o·phil·ic,** *a.*

e·pact, ē'pakt, *n.* [Gr. *epaktos,* brought in or on—*epi,* on, and *agō,* to lead.] *Astron.* the number of days, usually about eleven, by which the solar year exceeds the lunar year; the age in days of the moon on Jan. 1 of any year, used in calculating the date of Easter.

ep·ar·chy, ep'är·kē, *n. pl.* **ep·ar·chies.** [Gr. *eparchia.*] In ancient Greece, a province; in modern Greece, one of the administrative subdivisions of a province; *Gr. Orthodox Church,* a diocese or archdiocese.

ep·au·let, ep'e·let", ep'e·lit, ep"e·let', *n.* [Fr. *épaulette.*] A shoulder piece; an ornamental decoration worn on the shoulder, especially by military and naval officers. Also **ep·au·lette.**

é·pée, ā·pā', *n.* [Fr.] *Fencing,* a blunt-tipped sword having a tapered three-sided blade without a cutting edge; the art of fencing with this weapon.—**é·pée·ist,** *n.*

ep·ei·rog·e·ny, ep"i·roj'e·nē, *n. Geol.* great heaving and settling movements of the earth's crust resulting in vertical displacement or tilting of the strata over large portions of a continent or ocean basin. Also **e·pei·ro·gen·e·sis,** **ep·i·rog·e·ny,** i·pī"rō·jen'i·sis.—**e·pei·ro·gen·ic,** i·pī"rō·jen'ik, *a.*

ep·en·ceph·a·lon, ep"en·sef'a·lon", *n. pl.* **ep·en·ceph·a·lons, ep·en·ceph·a·la.** [Gr. *epi,* on, and *enkephalon,* the brain.] *Anat.* the rhombencephalon or hindbrain; the metencephalon.—**ep·en·ce·phal·ic,** ep"en·se·fal'ik, *a.*

ep·en·the·sis, e·pen'thi·sis, *n. pl.* **ep·en·the·ses,** e·pen'thi·sēz". [Gr. *epi,* on, en, in, and *tithēmi,* to put.] *Gram.* the development of a letter or sound in the middle of a word. —**ep·en·thet·ic,** ep"en·thet'ik, *a.*

é·pergne, i·pĕrn', ā·pârn', *n.* [Apparently < Fr. *épargne,* thrift, economy.] A centerpiece, often elaborately ornamented, consisting of several dishes grouped vertically or radially about an upright center support and used to hold pastry, fruit, or the like.

ep·ex·e·ge·sis, ep·ek"si·jē'sis, *n. pl.* **ep·ex·e·ge·ses,** ep·ek"si·jē'sēz. [Gr. *epexēgēsis, epexegeisthai,* explain in addition, < *epi,* on, to, and *exegeisthai.* EXEGESIS.] *Rhet.* the addition of a word or words to explain a

preceding word or sentence; the word or words so added.—**ep·ex·e·get·ic, ep·ex··e·get·i·cal,** ep"ek"si·jet'ik, *a.*—**ep·ex·e··get·i·cal·ly,** *adv.*

e·phebe, i·fēb', ef'ēb, *n.* In ancient Greece, a youth just entering manhood or attaining citizenship.—**e·phe·bic,** *a.*

e·phed·rine, i·fed'rin, ef'i·drēn", ef'i·drin, *n.* [N.L. *Ephedra,* a genus of plants, < L., the plant horsetail, < Gr. *ephedra, epi,* on, and *edra,* seat, and *ine.*] *Chem.* a crystalline alkaloid, $C_{10}H_{15}NO$, found in species of *Ephedra* or synthesized, used medicinally in the treatment of colds, asthma, and hay-fever. Also **e·phed·rin.**

e·phem·er·a, i·fem'ĕr·a, *n. pl.* **e·phem·er·as, e·phem·er·ae,** i·fem'e·rē". Something existing or lasting a very short time; an ephemerid or mayfly.

e·phem·er·al, i·fem'ĕr·al, *a.* [Gr. *ephemeros,* lasting but a day, short-lived—*epi,* and *hēmera,* a day.] Short-lived; fleeting; continuing or existing one day only. —*n.* Anything fleeting or short-lived, as certain flowers.—**e·phem·er·al·i·ty,** *n. pl.* **e·phem·er·al·i·ties.** The condition or quality of being ephemeral; also **e·phem·er·al·ness.**—**e·phem·er·al·ly,** *adv.*

e·phem·er·id, i·fem'ĕr·id, *n.* [N.L.] Any of the mayflies, short-lived insects of the order *Ephemeroptera.*

e·phem·er·is, i·fem'ĕr·is, *n. pl.* **e·phem·er·i·des,** ef"e·mer'i·dēz". [Gr., a diary.] *Astron.* a table indicating the positions of the heavenly bodies from day to day or at regular intervals throughout the year; an astronomical almanac.

e·phem·er·on, i·fem'e·ron", i·fem'ĕr·on, *n. pl.* **e·phem·er·a, e·phem·er·ons.** Anything ephemeral.—**e·phem·er·ous,** *a.*

ep·i·blast, ep'i·blast", *n. Embryol.* the ectoderm.—**ep·i·blas·tic,** *a.*

e·pib·o·ly, i·pib'o·lē, *n. pl.* **e·pib·o·lies.** *Embryol.* the surrounding of a group of cells by another more rapidly dividing group.—**ep·i·bol·ic,** ep"i·bol'ik, *a.*

ep·ic, ep'ik, *a.* [L. *epicus,* < Gr. *epikos,* < *epos,* a word, a song.] Of, pertaining to, or resembling an epic; heroic; majestic; imposingly great; of extraordinary scope. size, or extent. Also **ep·i·cal.**—*n.* An extended narrative poem in elevated style, typically centered upon a hero, and describing extraordinary achievements and events; any work of art whose subject or scale resembles an epic; events or achievements worthy of epic treatment.

ep·i·ca·lyx, ep"i·kā'liks, ep"i·kal'iks, *n. pl.* **ep·i·ca·lyx·es, ep·i·ca·ly·ces,** ep"i·kā'li·sēz, ep"i·kal'i·sēz. *Bot.* a ring of bracts or leaves which resemble a calyx and surround the base of the true calyx.

ep·i·car·di·um, ep"i·kär'dē·um, *n. pl.* **ep·i·car·di·a.** [N.L., < Gr. *epi,* on, and *cardia,* heart.] *Anat.* the inner serous layer of the pericardium, lying directly upon the heart.—**ep·i·car·di·al, ep·i·car·di·ac,** *a.*

ep·i·carp, ep'i·kärp", *n.* [Gr. *epi,* on, and *karpos,* fruit.] *Bot.* the outermost layer of the pericarp of a fruit.

ep·i·cene, ep'i·sēn, *a.* [L. *epicœnus,* < Gr. *epicoinos,* < *epi,* on, and *koinos,* common.] Of or having the characteristics of both sexes; weak; non-masculine; *gram.* of nouns, having but one form of gender to denote both sexes.—*n.* One who is epicene. —**ep·i·cen·ism,** *n.*

ep·i·cen·ter, *Brit.* **ep·i·cen·tre,** ep'i·sen"tĕr, *n.* [Gr. *epicentros.*] That part of the earth's exterior immediately above the source of an earthquake. Also *Brit.* **ep·i·cen·trum.**

ep·i·cot·yl, ep"i·kot'il, ep"i·kot'il, *n.* [Gr. *epi,* above, and *cotyl(edon).*] *Bot.* in seedlings, that part of the stem immediately above the cotyledons.—**ep·i·cot·y·le·don·ar·y,** ep"i·kot"i·lē'don·er"ē, *a.*

ep·i·crit·ic, ep″*i*·krit′ik, *a. Physiol.* relating to cutaneous sensitivity to very small variations in heat, cold, or pain stimuli.

ep·i·cure, ep′*i*·kūr″, *n.* [After *Epicurus,* a Greek philosopher who taught that pleasure and pain are the chief good and chief evil.] A person of refined and discriminating taste, esp. a connoisseur of good food and wines; *archaic,* one devoted to sensual enjoyments.—**e·pi·cu·re·an**, ep″*i*·kū·rē′an, ep″*i*·kūr′ē·an, *a.* Luxurious; given or pertaining to sensual pleasures or luxury. (*Cap.*) pertaining to Epicurus or his teachings.—*n.* A man devoted to sensual pleasures or luxuries; an epicure. (*Cap.*) a follower of Epicurus.—**Ep·i·cu·re·an·ism**, *n.* The principles or philosophical doctrines of Epicurus; attachment to sensual enjoyments and luxurious habits.—**ep·i·cur·ism**, *n.* The practices of an epicure.

ep·i·cy·cle, ep′*i*·sī″kal, *n.* [L.L. *epicyclus,* < Gr. *epicyclos,* < *epi,* on, and *cyclos,* circle.] *Ptolemaic astron.* a small circle, the center of which moves around in the circumference of a larger circle; a circle which rolls, exteriorly or interiorly, around the circumference of another circle.—**ep·i·cy·clic**, ep″*i*·sī′klik, *a.*—**ep·i·cy·clic train**, *mach.* any train of gears, the axes of the wheels of which revolve around a common center.—**ep·i·cy·cloid**, ep″*i*·sī′kloid, *n. Geom.* a curve generated by the motion of a point on the circumference of a circle which rolls upon the convex side of a fixed circle.—**ep·i·cy·cloi·dal**, *a.*

ep·i·dem·ic, ep″*i*·dem′ik, *a.* [Gr. *epi,* upon, and *demos,* people.] Common to or affecting a whole people, or a great number in a community at the same time; as a contagious disease; widely prevalent. Also **ep·i·dem·i·cal.**—*n.* An occurrence of an epidemic disease; an outbreak of anything which spreads or increases rapidly; as, an *epidemic* of shootings.—**ep·i·dem·i·cal·ly**, *adv.*—**ep·i·de·mic·i·ty**, ep″*i*·de·mis′*i*·tē, *n.*

ep·i·de·mi·ol·o·gy, ep″*i*·dē″mē·ol′o·jē, *n.* The science concerned with the study and control of epidemic diseases.—**ep·i·de·mi·o·log·i·cal**, **ep·i·de·mi·o·log·ic**, ep″*i*·dē″mē·o·loj′*i*·kal, ep″*i*·dē″mē·o·loj′ik, *a.*—**ep·i·de·mi·o·log·i·cal·ly**, *adv.*—**ep·i·de·mi·ol·o·gist**, *n.*

ep·i·der·mis, ep″*i*·dėr′mis, *n.* [L.L., < Gr. *epidermis,* < *epi,* on, and *derma,* skin.] *Anat.* the outer, non-vascular, non-sensitive layer of the skin, covering the true skin or cutis; *zool.* any of various outer integuments or coverings, as the chitinous covering of the shells of many mollusks; *embryol.* the ectoderm; *bot.* the surface layer of cells of leaves and other soft plant parts.—**ep·i·der·mal**, **ep·i·der·mic**, *a.*—**ep·i·der·mi·cal·ly**, *adv.*—**ep·i·der·moid**, **e·pi·der·moi·dal**, *a.*

ep·i·di·a·scope, ep″*i*·dī′a·skōp″, *n.* A device which projects images of opaque objects or images printed on transparent material: used in optics.

ep·i·did·y·mis, ep″*i*·did′*i*·mis, *n.* pl. **ep·i·di·dym·i·des**, ep″*i*·di·dim′*i*·dēz″. [N.L., < Gr. *epididymis,* < *epi,* on, and *didymos,* testicles.] *Anat.* an elongated oblong body, chiefly convoluted tubes, resting upon and alongside the testicle.—**ep·i·did·y·mal**, *a.*

ep·i·dote, ep′*i*·dōt″, *n.* [Fr., < Gr. *epi,* and *didonai,* to give.] A group of silicate minerals of a green color occurring in metamorphic rock.—**ep·i·dot·ic**, ep″*i*·dot′ik, *a.*

ep·i·fo·cal, ep″*i*·fō′kal, *a.* Directly above the focus, or true center of disturbance, of an earthquake.

ep·i·gas·tric, ep″*i*·gas′trik, *a.* [Gr. *epi,* and *gastēr,* belly.] Pertaining to or lying upon the upper and anterior part of the

abdomen.—**ep·i·gas·tri·um**, ep″*i*·gas′trē·um, *n.* pl. **ep·i·gas·tri·a**, ep″*i*·gas′trē·a. The upper part of the abdomen.

ep·i·gene, ep′*i*·jēn″, *a.* [Gr. *epi,* upon, and root *gen,* to produce.] *Geol.* formed or originating on the surface of the earth.

ep·i·gen·e·sis, ep″*i*·jen′*i*·sis, *n.* [Gr. *epi* and *genesis,* generation.] *Biol.* the theory that an organism develops through differentiation of its initially structureless entity: opposed to *preformation; geol.* a change in the structure of a rock caused by external forces.—**ep·i·ge·net·ic**, ep″*i*·je·net′ik, *a.* Pertaining to or produced by epigenesis.—**ep·i·gen·ic**, ep″*i*·jen′ik, *a.* Relating to deposition or structure after formation of the enclosing rock.

e·pig·e·nous, *i*·pij′e·nus, *a.* Growing upon the surface, as on a leaf or other part of a plant.

ep·i·ge·ous, ep″*i*·jē′us, *a.* [Gr. *epigeios, epigaios,* < *epi,* on, and *ge,* earth.] *Bot.* growing on or close to the ground; of cotyledons, borne above ground in germination. Also **ep·i·ge·al.**

ep·i·glot·tis, ep″*i*·glot′is, *n.* pl. **ep·i·glot·tises**, ep″*i*·glot·ti·des, ep″*i*·glot′*i*·dēz. [Gr. *epiglōttis*—*epi,* on, and *glōttis.*] *Anat.* a thin cartilaginous plate behind the tongue, which covers the glottis like a lid during the act of swallowing and thus prevents food or drink from entering the larynx.—**ep·i·glot·tal**, **ep·i·glot·tic**, **ep·i·glot·tid·e·an**, ep″*i*·glo·tid′ē·an, *a.*

ep·i·gon, ep′*i*·gon″, *n. Bot.* the bag enclosing the spore case of the young liverwort.

ep·i·gone, ep′*i*·gōn″, *n.* A mediocre imitator of a writer, painter, or other creative person. Also **ep·i·gon**, ep′*i*·gon″.

ep·i·gram, ep′*i*·gram″, *n.* [Gr. *epigramma,* an inscription—*epi,* upon, and *gramma,* a writing, < *graphō,* to write.] A brief, witty, pointed, often antithetical saying; a short poem, usu. satirical, the last line of which often contains an unexpected change of thought or biting comment.—**ep·i·gram·mat·ic**, **ep·i·gram·mat·i·cal**, ep″*i*·gra·mat′ik, *a.*—**ep·i·gram·mat·i·cal·ly**, *adv.*—**ep·i·gram·ma·tist**, ep″*i*·gram′a·tist, *n.*—**ep·i·gram·ma·tize**, ep″*i*·gram′a·tīz″, *v.t.*—*epigrammatized, epigrammatizing.* To represent or express by or in epigrams.—*v.i.* To make an epigram.

ep·i·graph, ep′*i*·graf″, ep′*i*·gräf″, *n.* [Gr. *epigraphē*—*epi,* and *graphō,* to write.] An inscription on a building, tomb, or monument. A quotation or motto, at the beginning of a book, or at its divisions, which gives the theme.

e·pig·ra·phy, *i*·pig′ra·fē, *n.* The study, deciphering, and interpretation of inscriptions; epigraphs collectively.—**e·pig·ra·phist**, **e·pig·ra·pher**, *n.*

ep·i·lep·sy, ep′*i*·lep″sē, *n.* [Gr. *epilepsia*—*epi,* upon, and *lambanō, lēpsomai,* to take, to seize.] *Pathol.* a chronic nervous disease characterized by brief convulsive seizures and loss of consciousness.—**ep·i·lep·tic**, ep″*i*·lep′tik, *a.* Pertaining to, or affected with, epilepsy.—*n.* One affected with epilepsy.—**ep·i·lep·ti·form**, **ep·i·lep·toid**, ep″*i*·lep′ti·fąrm″, ep″*i*·lep′toid, *a. Pathol.* similar to epilepsy.

ep·i·logue, **ep·i·log**, ep′*i*·ląg″, ep′*i*·log″, *n.* [L. *epilogus,* < Gr. *epilogos,* conclusion—*epi,* and *legō,* to speak.] A section following a piece of literature that terminates or amplifies the preceding expression; a speech or short poem addressed to the spectators by one of the actors, after the conclusion of a drama.—**e·pil·o·gist**, *i*·pil′o·jist, *n.*

ep·i·mor·pho·sis, ep″*i*·mąr′fo·sis, ep″*i*·mąr·fō′sis, *n. Zool.* a type of regeneration, esp. in invertebrate animals, which involves cell proliferation and subsequent differentiation.

epi·my·si·um, ep″*i*·miz′ē·um, *n. Anat.* the sheath of a muscle formed by connective tissue.

ep·i·nas·ty, ep′*i*·nas″tē, *n.* [Gr. *epi,* on, and *nastos,* pressed close, compact, < *nassien,* press close.] *Bot.* increased growth along the upper surface of an organ or part, causing the part to bend downward, as the opening of a bud: a condition occurring when certain chemicals, as weed-killers, are applied.—**ep·i·nas·tic**, *a.*

ep·i·neph·rine, **ep·i·neph·rin**, ep″*i*·nef′rin, ep″*i*·nef′rēn, *n. Biochem.* an adrenal gland hormone that raises blood pressure, having among its many medicinal uses that of heart stimulant and of muscle relaxant in asthma.

ep·i·neu·ri·um, ep″*i*·nur″ē·um, ep″*i*·nėr′ē·um, *n.* pl. **ep·i·neu·ri·a**. [N.L., < Gr. *epi,* on, and *neuron,* nerve.] *Anat.* the dense sheath of connective tissue which surrounds the trunk of a nerve.—**ep·i·neu·ri·al**, *a.*

E·piph·a·ny, *i*·pif′a·nē, *n.* pl. **E·piph·a·nies**. [Gr. *epiphaneia,* appearance, < *epiphainō,* to appear—*epi,* upon, and *phainō,* to show.] *Eccles.* a Christian festival held on January sixth commemorating the manifestation of Jesus Christ to the Magi; (*l.c.*) a manifestation, esp. of a divinity.

ep·i·phe·nom·e·nal·ism, ep″ē·fe·nom′*i*·na·liz″um, *n.* A doctrine concerned with the relationship between body and mind which states that consciousness or mental activity is but a by-product of neural or body processes and has no effect upon them.

ep·i·phe·nom·e·non, ep″ē·fe·nom′e·non″, ep″ē·fe·nom′e·non′, *n.* pl. **ep·i·phe·nom·e·na**. A secondary phenomenon that accompanies another but is incapable in itself of producing results; *pathol.* a secondary or additional symptom or complication arising during the course of a malady.—**ep·i·phe·nom·e·nal**, *a.*—**ep·i·phe·nom·e·nal·ly**, *adv.*

e·piph·o·ra, *i*·pif′ėr·a, *n. Pathol.* excessive flow of tears due to a disorder of the lacrimal glands; *rhet.* a method of giving emphasis by echoing the last word of successive sentences, clauses, or verses.

e·piph·y·sis, *i*·pif′*i*·sis, *n.* pl. **e·piph·y·ses**, *i*·pif′*i*·sēz. [N.L., < Gr. *epiphysis,* < *epiphyesthai,* grown on.] *Anat.* a part or process of a bone which is separated from the main body of the bone by a layer of cartilage, and which finally becomes united with the bone through further ossification; the pineal body of the brain.—**ep·i·phys·i·al**, **ep·i·phys·e·al**, ep″*i*·fiz′ē·al, *i*·pif″*i*·sē′al, *i*·pif″*i*·zē′al, *a.*

ep·i·phyte, ep′*i*·fīt″, *n.* [Gr. *epi,* on, and *phyton,* plant.] *Bot.* any of various plants, as certain mosses, lichens, and orchids, growing upon another plant for mechanical support, but not parasitic; an air plant or aerophyte.—**ep·i·phyt·ic**, ep″*i*·fit′ik, *a.*—**ep·i·phyt·i·cal·ly**, *adv.*

ep·i·phy·tot·ic, ep″*i*·fī·tot′ik, *a. Bot.* of or pertaining to a plant disease which attacks many plants in a widespread area.—*n.* An epidemic of such a disease.

ep·i·rog·e·ny, ep″*i*·roj′e·nē, *n.* See *epeirogeny.*

e·pis·co·pa·cy, *i*·pis′ko·pa·sē, *n.* pl. **e·pis·co·pa·cies**. Government of the church by bishops; that form of church government in which there are three distinct orders of ministers, namely bishops, priests or presbyters, and deacons; the order of bishops; the office or incumbency of a bishop.

e·pis·co·pal, *i*·pis′ko·pal, *a.* [L.L. *episcopalis,* < *episcopus,* bishop.] Pertaining to a bishop; based on or recognizing a governing order of bishops; (*cap.*) used in the titles of various churches, and esp. to designate the Anglican Church or some branch of it; as,

the Protestant *Episcopal* Church in the U.S.
—e·pis·co·pal·ly, *adv.*

e·pis·co·pa·lian, i·pis″ko·pāl′yan, i·pis″ko·pā′lē·an, *a.* Pertaining or adhering to the episcopal form of church government; (*cap.*) pertaining to the Episcopal Church of the Anglican communion.—*n.* An adherent of the episcopal system; (*cap.*) a member of the Episcopal Church.—e·pis·co·pa·lian·ism, *n.*

e·pis·co·pal·ism, i·pis′ko·pa·liz″um, *n.* The theory of church polity according to which the supreme ecclesiastical authority is vested in the episcopal order as a whole, and not in any individual except by delegation.

e·pis·co·pate, i·pis′ko·pit, i·pis′ko·pāt″, *n.* A bishopric; the office and dignity of a bishop; the collective body of bishops.

ep·i·sode, ep′i·sōd″, ep′i·zōd″, *n.* [Gr. *epeisodion*, a parenthetic addition, neut. of *episodios*, coming in besides, < *epi*, and *eisodos*, entrance] An incident in the course of a series of events, as in a person's life or experience; an incident or digression in a piece of writing or an oral account. *Motion Pictures, Radio, TV,* one of the parts of a serial. *Mus.* a digressive passage.—ep·i·sod·ic, ep′i·sod·i·cal, ep″i·sod′ik, ep″i·zod′ik, *a.*—ep·i·sod·i·cal·ly, *adv.*

e·pis·ta·sis, i·pis′ta·sis, *n. pl.* e·pis·ta·ses, i·pis′ta·sēz″. *Genetics,* the suppressive action one gene exercises over the effect of another not allelomorphic to it.

ep·i·stax·is, ep″i·stak′sis, *n.* [Gr. *epi*, upon, and *staxis*, a dropping.] *Pathol.* bleeding from the nose.

ep·i·ste·mic, ep″i·stē′mik, ep″i·stem′ik, *a.* Of or relating to knowledge or the obtaining of it.—ep·i·ste·mi·cal·ly, *adv.*

e·pis·te·mol·o·gy, i·pis″te·mol′o·jē, *n.* [Gr. *episteme*, knowledge (< *epistasthai*, know).] The theory or study of the origin, nature, methods, and limits of knowledge.—e·pis·te·mo·log·i·cal, i·pis″te·mo·loj′i·kal, *a.*—e·pis·te·mol·o·gist, *n.*

ep·i·ster·num, ep″i·stèr′num, *n. pl.* ep·i·ster·na. [Gr. *epi*, upon, and *sternon*, the breastbone.] *Entomol.* a lateral portion of a segment of an arthropod; *anat.* the uppermost of the three parts of the sternum.

e·pis·tle, i·pis′l, *n.* [O.Fr. *epistle* (Fr. *épître*), < L. *epistola* < Gr. *epistolē*, message, letter, < *epistellein*, send to, < *epi*, on, to, and *stellein*, send.] A letter, esp. a formal or morally instructive letter; a literary piece, usu. in verse, written in the form of a letter. (*Cap.*) one of the apostolic letters of the New Testament; (*often cap.*) an extract, usu. from one of the Epistles of the New Testament, forming part of the Eucharistic service in certain churches.—e·pis·to·lar·y, i·pis′to·ler″ē, *a.* [L. *epistolaris*.] Of, pertaining to, or appropriate for correspondence; contained in, or carried on by, letters.

e·pis·to·ler, i·pis′to·lèr, *n.* [Fr. *épistolier*.] (*Often cap.*) one who reads the epistle in the Eucharistic service. A writer of epistles. Also e·pis·tler.

ep·i·style, ep′i·stīl″, *n.* [L. *epistylium*, < Gr. *epistylion*, < *epi*, on, and *stylos*, pillar, column.] *Arch.* an architrave.

ep·i·taph, ep′i·taf″, ep′i·täf″, *n.* [Gr. *epi*, upon, and *taphos* or *taphē*, a tomb.] An inscription on a tomb or monument in honor or memory of the dead; a brief composition, often poetic, written to praise someone deceased.—*v.t.*—ep·i·taph·ic, ep″i·taf′ik, *a.*—ep·i·taph·ist, *n.*

e·pit·a·sis, i·pit′a·sis, *n.* [N.L. < Gr. *epitasis*, < *epiteinein*, intensify, < *epi*, on, and *teinein*, stretch.] In the ancient drama, that part of a play in which the action is developed, following the protasis and leading up to the catastrophe.

ep·i·the·li·o·ma, ep″i·thē″lē·ō′ma, *n. pl.* ep·i·the·li·o·mas, ep·i·the·li·o·ma·ta, ep″i·thē″lē·ō′ma·ta. [N.L. < *epithelium*.] *Pathol.* a malignant growth or cancer consisting chiefly of epithelial cells.—ep·i·the·li·om·a·tous, ep″i·thē″lē·om′a·tus, *a.*

ep·i·the·li·um, ep″i·thē′lē·um, *n. pl.* ep·i·the·li·ums, ep·i·the·li·a, ep″i·thē′lē·a. [N.L. < Gr. *epi*, on, and *thēlē*, nipple.] *Biol.* any tissue which covers an external or internal surface, or lines a cavity or the like, and which performs protective, secreting, or other functions, as the epidermis or the lining of blood vessels.—ep·i·the·li·al, *a.*—ep·i·the·li·oid, *a.*

ep·i·thet, ep′i·thet″, *n.* [Gr. *epitheton*, a name added, < *epi*, upon, and *tithēmi*, to place.] A descriptive word or phrase expressing some real or implied quality of a person or thing, often used to designate the person or thing in place of the name, as 'Charles the Great' for Charlemagne; an invective or term of abuse.—ep·i·thet·ic, ep·i·thet·i·cal, *a.*

e·pit·o·me, i·pit′o·mē, *n.* [Gr. *epitomē*, < *epi*, upon, and *tomē*, a cutting, < *temnō*, to cut.] A summary or abstract of a book or other writing; a compendium; abridgement; *fig.* a person or thing that typifies the whole; as: She was the *epitome* of gentleness.—e·pit·o·mize, i·pit′o·mīz″, *v.t.*—*epitomized, epitomizing.* To make a summary of; to abstract; to typify.

ep·i·zo·ic, ep″i·zō′ik, *a.* Living on the outer surface of an animal.—ep·i·zo·ism, *n.*—ep·i·zo·ite, *n.*

ep·i·zo·on, ep″i·zō′on, ep″i·zō′on, *n. pl.* ep·i·zo·a, ep″i·zō′a. [Gr. *epi*, upon, and *zōon*, animal.] A parasitic animal which lives on the body of other animals.

ep·i·zo·ot·ic, ep″i·zō·ot′ik, *a.* [Gr. *epi*, upon, and *zōon*, animal.] Pertaining to any disease that is prevalent among many animals of the same kind at the same time.—*n.* An epizootic disease.—ep·i·zo·ot·i·cal·ly, *adv.*

ep·och, ep′ok, *Brit.* ē′pok, *n.* [M.L. *epocha*, < Gr. *epochē*, pause, < *epechein*, hold on, check, < *epi*, on, and *echein*, have, hold.] A particular period of time as marked by distinctive character, events, or the like; a point of time from which succeeding years are numbered, as at the beginning of a system of chronology; the beginning of any distinctive period in the history of anything; a point of time distinguished by a particular event or state of affairs. *Astron.* an arbitrarily fixed instant of time or date, usu. the beginning of a century or half century, used as a reference in giving the elements or the life of a planetary orbit; the longitude of a planet as seen from the sun at such an instant or date. *Geol.* an interval of geologic time, less than a period.—ep·och·al, *a.* Of or pertaining to an epoch or epochs; of the nature of an epoch.—ep·och·mak·ing, *a.* Opening a new era, as in human history, thought, or knowledge; as, an *epoch-making* discovery.

ep·ode, ep′ōd, *n.* [Gr. *epōdē*—*epi*, upon, and *ōdē*, a song, an ode.] *Pros.* the third or last part of an ode, an ancient Greek ode being divided into strophe, antistrophe, and *epode;* a type of lyric poem in which a long verse is followed by a shorter one.

ep·o·nym, ep′o·nim, *n.* [Gr. *epi*, upon, and *onyma*, a name.] A real or imaginary person for whom something is named; one whose name is the popular designation for something.—ep·o·nym·ic, ep·on·y·mous, *a.* Giving one's name to a place, institution, syndrome, or disease.—ep·on·y·my, e·pon′i·mē, *n.* The development of proper names from eponyms or the supposition of a real or fictitious eponym for a proper name.

ep·o·pee, ep′o·pē″, ep″o·pē′, *n.* [Fr. *épopée*, Gr. *epopoiia*—*epos*, a word, an epic

poem, and *poieō*, to make.] An epic poem; the subject of an epic poem; an epic. Also ep·o·poe·ia, ep″o·pē′a.

ep·os, ep′os, *n.* [Gr.] A long narrative poem or a group of such poems on an epic theme; a series of events suitable for epic treatment. Also *epic.*

ep·ox·y, e·pok′sē, *n. pl.* ep·ox·ies. *Chem.* see *epoxy resin.*—*a.* Of or referring to a compound containing an oxygen atom united with two carbon atoms that are already joined in some other way.

ep·ox·y res·in, *n. Chem.* any one of a group of resins containing at least one epoxy compound, useful for its characteristics of toughness, adhesiveness, corrosion and chemical resistance, and good dielectric properties; in finished products used principally for surface coatings, adhesives, and electrical insulation. Also *epoxy.*

ep·si·lon, ep′si·lon″, ep′si·lon, *Brit.* ep·sī′lon, *n.* The fifth letter of the Greek alphabet, E, ε. *Math.* a small positive number used to show that a given series or quantity of numbers is zero or close to zero.

Ep·som salt, ep′som salt, *n. Usu. pl.* hydrated magnesium sulfate: used in the leather industry, in dyeing and finishing textiles, and in medicine as a cathartic.

eq·ua·ble, ek′wa·bl, ē′kwa·bl, *a.* [L. *æquabilis, æquo,* to make equal, < *æquus,* equal.] Characterized by uniformity or evenness; fair; uniform in action; steady; even.—eq·ua·bil·i·ty, eq·ua·ble·ness, *n.*—eq·ua·bly, *adv.*

e·qual, ē′kwal, *a.* [L. *æqualis,* < *æquus,* level, even.] Alike, as in quantity, degree, value, or size; of the same rank, ability, or merit; as great as another, followed by *to* or *with,* as: The velocity of sound is not *equal* to that of light. Having adequate power, ability, or means, as: He was not *equal* to the task. Evenly proportioned or balanced; as, an *equal* mixture, an *equal* contest; uniform in operation or effect; as, *equal* laws; even or regular, as motion; level; as, an *equal* plain.—*n.* One who or that which is equal.—*v.t.*—*equaled, equaling, equalled, equalling.* To be or become equal to; to match; to make or do something equal to.—e·qual·ly, *adv.* In an equal manner or measure; to an equal extent or degree; in uniform manner or degree.—e·qual·ness, *n.*

e·qual·i·tar·i·an, i·kwol″i·târ′ē·an, *a.* Pertaining or adhering to the doctrine of equality among men.—*n.* One who adheres to the doctrine of equality among men.—e·qual·i·tar·i·an·ism, *n.*

e·qual·i·ty, i·kwol′i·tē, *n. pl.* e·qual·i·ties. [L. *æqualitas.*] The state of being equal; likeness in size, number, quantity, value, qualities, or degree.

e·qual·ize, ē′kwa·līz″, *v.t.*—*equalized, equalizing.* To make equal; to render uniform.—e·qual·i·za·tion, *n.*

e·qual·iz·er, ē′kwa·lī″zèr, *n.* One who or that which equalizes; *mech.* any of various devices or appliances for equalizing strains or pressures between parts of a mechanism; *elect.* a device used for equalizing voltage of current from two or more generators; *slang,* a weapon, esp. a pistol or other firearm.

e·qual tem·per·a·ment, *n.* The tuning of a keyboard instrument in which the pitch of tones varying less than a semitone, as G♯ and A♭, are treated enharmonically.

e·qua·nim·i·ty, ē″kwa·nim′i·tē, ek″wa·nim′i·tē, *n.* [L. *æquanimitas,* < *æquanimis,* having an even mind, < *æquus* and *animus,* mind.] Evenness of mind or temper; calmness; composure; self-possession.—e·quan·i·mous, i·kwan′i·mus, *a.* Of an even temper; not easily elated or depressed.

e·quate, i·kwāt′, *v.t.*—*equated, equating.* [L. *æquatus,* pp. of *æquare,* < *æquus.*]

equation 332 **equivocation**

To state the equality of or between; to put in the form of an equation; to make equal; to reduce to an average; to make such correction or allowance in, as will reduce to a common standard of comparison; to regard, treat, or represent as equivalent.

e·qua·tion, i·kwā′zhan, *n.* [L. *æquatio(n-).*] The act of making equal; equalization; equally balanced state; equilibrium; reduction to a mean or a normal value; *math.* an expression of, or a proposition asserting, the equality of two quantities, usu. employing the sign = between them; *chem.* a symbolic representation of a reaction.—**e·qua·tion of time,** the difference between mean solar time and apparent solar time.—**e·qua·tion·al,** *a.* Pertaining to or involving equations.—**e·qua·tion·al·ly,** *adv.*

e·qua·tor, i·kwā′tèr, *n.* [L.L. *æquator,* < L. *æquo, æquatum,* to make equal.] That great circle of the earth whose plane is perpendicular to the earth's axis, thus dividing the earth into the northern and southern hemispheres; a circle dividing the surface of any celestial body or any surface into two parts, usu. equal and symmetrical.

e·qua·to·ri·al, ē″kwa·tŏr′ē·al, ē″kwa·tăr′ē·al, ek″wa·tŏr′ē·al, ek″wa·tăr′ē·al, *a.* Of, pertaining to, or near an equator, esp. the equator of the earth; of, or similar to, the regions of the earth's equator.—*n.* A telescope having two axes of motion, one parallel to the earth's axis, and the other at right angles to it.—**e·qua·to·ri·al·ly,** *adv.*

eq·uer·ry, ek′we·rē, *n.* pl. **eq·uer·ries.** An officer attendant upon nobles or princes, and who takes care of their horses; *Brit.* a certain officer of the royal household.

e·ques·tri·an, i·kwes′trē·an, *a.* [L. *equestris,* < *eques,* horseman, < *equus,* horse; akin Gr. *hippos,* Skt. *açva,* horse; Gr. *ōkys,* swift.] Pertaining to horses or horsemanship; representing a person on horseback; pertaining to the class or rank of knights in ancient Rome.—*n.* A rider on horseback.—**e·ques·tri·enne,** i·kwes′tri·en, *n.* [Spurious French form.] A female rider.

e·qui·an·gu·lar, ē″kwē·ang′gū·lèr, ē″kwē·ang′gya·lèr, *a. Geom.* consisting of or having all the angles equal.

e·qui·ca·lor·ic, ē″kwi·ka·lŏr′ik, ē″kwi·ka·lär′ik, *a.* Marked by the ability to yield equal amounts of energy in the body.

e·qui·dis·tance, ē″kwi·dis′tans, *n.* Equal distance.—**e·qui·dis·tant,** ē″kwi·dis′tant, *a.* Being at an equal distance from some point or place.—**e·qui·dis·tant·ly,** *adv.*

e·qui·lat·er·al, ē″kwi·lat′èr·al, *a.* [L. *æquus,* equal, and *latus, lateris,* a side.] Having all the sides equal.—*n.* A geometric form with all sides equal; a side equal to all others.

e·quil·i·brant, i·kwil′i·brant, *n. Phys.* a system of forces, or a single force, that counterbalances to produce equilibrium.

e·qui·li·brate, i·kwil′i·brāt″, ē″kwi·li′brāt, *v.t.*—**equilibrated, equilibrating.** [L. *æquus,* equal, and *libro,* to poise, < *libra,* a balance.] To balance equally; to keep in equilibrium.—*v.i.* To balance.—**e·qui·li·bra·tion,** ē″kwi·li·brā′shan, i·kwil″i·brā′shan, *n.* Equipoise; the state of being equally balanced.—**e·qui·li·bra·tor,** ē″kwi·li′brā·tèr, i·kwil′i·brā″tèr, *n.*—**e·qui·li·bra·tory,** *a.*

e·quil·i·brist, i·kwil′i·brist, *n.* One who balances equally; one who keeps his balance in unnatural positions and perilous movements, as a tightrope walker.—**e·quil·i·bris·tic,** *a.*

e·qui·lib·ri·um, ē″kwi·lib′rē·um, *n.* pl. **e·qui·lib·ri·ums, e·qui·lib·ri·a.** [L. *æquilibrium,* < *æquus,* equal, and *libra,* balance.] Equal balance between opposing forces; a state of rest due to the action of counteracting forces; mental balance; *chem.* the state of a chemical system when no further change occurs in it. Equal balance between any powers or influences; equality of effect; due or just relationship.

e·qui·mo·lal, ē″kwi·mō′lal, *a.* Having an equal number of moles or gram molecules; having equal molal concentration. Also **e·qui·mo·lar.**

e·quine, ē′kwin, *a.* [L. *equinus,* < *equus,* a horse. EQUESTRIAN.] Pertaining to or resembling a horse.—*n.* A horse.

e·qui·noc·tial, ē″kwi·nok′shal, *a.* Of or relating to the equinoxes; equality of day and night; occurring or manifested at or near the time of an equinox; pertaining to the regions of the equinoctial line or the equator; *bot.* opening consistently at a specific time, as a flower.—*n.* The celestial equator; a severe storm.—**e·qui·noc·tial points,** the two points where the equator and the ecliptic intersect.

e·qui·noc·tial cir·cle, *n.* The celestial or heavenly equator. Also **e·qui·noc·tial line.**

e·qui·noc·tial storm, *n.* Line storm.

e·qui·nox, ē″kwi·noks′, ek′wi·noks″, *n.* [L. *æquinoctium,* < *æquus,* equal, and *nox,* night.] The time when the sun crosses the equator and day and night are of equal length all over the world; as, the vernal *equinox* on about March 21, the autumnal *equinox* on about September 23; one of two equinoctial points.

e·quip, i·kwip′, *v.t.*—**equipped, equipping.** [Fr. *equiper,* O.Fr. *esquiper,* to fit out a ship, < the Teut. stem *skip,* to provide, arrange, as in Icel. *skipa,* to arrange; akin E. *ship, shape.*] To provide with everything necessary for an expedition, voyage, or undertaking; to fit out for sea, as a ship; to dress; to prepare, as oneself, for some particular duty or service.—**e·quip·per,** *n.*

eq·ui·page, ek′wi·pij, *n.* [Fr. *equipage.*] A carriage with a horse or horses; materials with which a person or thing is equipped; equipment; the furniture and supplies of an armed ship. *Archaic,* a body of retainers; a set of household articles; a collection of personal belongings.

e·quip·ment, i·kwip′ment, *n.* Articles used in equipping; the act of equipping or fitting out; the knowledge and skill enabling one to perform a task; furnishings; as, office *equipment.*

e·qui·poise, ē″kwi·poiz′, ek′wi·poiz″, *n.* [L. *æquus,* equal, and E. *poise.*] Equality of weight or force; due balance; equilibrium.

e·qui·pol·lence, ē″kwi·pol′ens, *n.* [Fr. *equipollence*—L. *æquus,* equal, and *polleo,* to be able.] Equality of power or force; *logic,* an equivalence between two or more propositions. Also **e·qui·pol·len·cy.**

e·qui·pol·lent, ē″kwi·pol′ent, *a.* Having equal power, force, or signification; equivalent; *logic,* able to be deduced from two propositions or statements.—*n.* An equivalent.

e·qui·pon·der·ate, ē″kwi·pon′de·rāt″, *v.i.*—**equiponderated, equiponderating.** [L. *æquus,* equal, and *pondero,* to weigh, < *pondus, ponderis,* weight.] To be equal in weight; to weigh as much as another thing.—*v.t.* To counterbalance.—**e·qui·pon·der·ance,** ē″kwi·pon′dèr·ans, *n.* Equality of weight; equipoise. Also **e·qui·pon·der·ancy.**—**e·qui·pon·der·ant,** *a.* Being of the same weight.

e·qui·po·tent, ē″kwi·pōt′ent, *a.* [L. *æquus,* equal, and *potens,* E. *potent.*] Equal in power, ability, or capacity.

e·qui·po·ten·tial, ē″kwi·po·ten′shal, *a. Phys.* having uniform potential at all points.

eq·ui·se·tum, ek′wi·sē·tum, *n.* pl. **eq·ui·se·tums, eq·ui·se·ta.** [L. *equus,* a horse, and *seta,* a bristle.] Any plant of the genus *Equisetum,* related to the ferns and including the horsetails. Also *scouring rush.*—**e·qui·se·ta·ceous,** *a.*

eq·ui·ta·ble, ek′wi·ta·bl, *a.* [Fr. *équitable,* < L. *æquitas,* equity, < *æquus,* equal.] Possessing or exhibiting equity; equal in regard to the rights of persons; just; fair; impartial; *law,* pertaining to a court of equity.—**eq·ui·ta·ble·ness,** *n.*—**eq·ui·ta·bly,** *adv.*

eq·ui·tant, ek′wi·tant, *a.* [L. *equitans (-ant-),* ppr. of *equitare,* ride.] *Bot.* straddling or overlapping, as leaves whose bases overlap the leaves above or within them.

eq·ui·ta·tion, ek″wi·tā′shan, *n.* The act or art of riding on horseback; horsemanship.

eq·ui·ty, ek′wi·tē, *n.* pl. **eq·ui·ties.** [O.Fr. *equite* (Fr. *equité*) < L. *æquitas,* < *æquus,* equal, just.] The quality of being fair or impartial; fairness; impartiality; that which is fair and just; justice or right. *Law,* a system of jurisprudence that includes a body of legal rules and doctrines determining what is equitable and fair, which supplements and remedies the defects of common and statute law; any system of jurisprudence incorporating such a body of supplementary and remedial rules and doctrines; an equitable right or claim. *Stock market,* the ownership interest of a share of common stock in a corporation; the difference in the market value of a security and the amount still owed the broker on its purchase when bought on margin. The value of a property in excess of all liens and claims against it.

e·qui·ty cap·i·tal, *n. Finance,* that part of capital resulting from the sale of stock.

e·quiv·a·lence, i·kwiv′a·lens, ē″kwi·vā′lens, *n.* The state or fact of being equivalent; equality in value, force, or significance; also **e·quiv·a·len·cy.** *Chem.* the quality of having equal valence. *Logic, math.* the relationship existing between two statements in which they are either both true or both false; the relationship existing between two propositions in which each logically implies the other, and to deny one while affirming the other would produce a contradiction.

e·quiv·a·lent, i·kwiv′a·lent, ē″qwi·vā′lent, *a.* [L.L. *æquivalens (-ent-),* ppr. of *æquivalere,* have equal power, < L. *æquus,* equal, and *valere,* be strong, be worth.] Equal in value, measure, force, effect, or significance; corresponding in position or function; *geom.* having the same extent, as a triangle and a square of equal area; *math.* capable of a one-to-one correspondence, as two sets; *chem.* endowed with an equal capacity to combine or react chemically.—*n.* That which is equivalent; something equal, tantamount, or corresponding to something.—**e·quiv·a·lent·ly,** *adv.*

e·quiv·a·lent weight, *n. Chem.* the weight of an element that will combine with, or can replace, one atomic weight of hydrogen or one-half atomic weight of oxygen.

e·quiv·o·cal, i·kwiv′o·kal, *a.* [L. *æquus,* equal, and *vox, vocis,* voice.] Being of doubtful signification; capable of being understood in different senses; ambiguous; susceptible to double meaning; uncertain; dubious; unsatisfactory; suspicious; capable of being ascribed to different motives; doubtful; questionable.—**e·quiv·o·cal·i·ty, e·quiv·o·ca·cy,** *n.*—**e·quiv·o·cal·ly,** *adv.*—**e·quiv·o·cal·ness,** *n.*

e·quiv·o·cate, i·kwiv′o·kāt″, *v.i.*—**equivocated, equivocating.** To use ambiguous expressions with a view to mislead; to quibble.—**e·quiv·o·ca·tor,** *n.*

e·quiv·o·ca·tion, i·kwiv″o·kā′shan, *n.* The act of equivocating; the use of words or expressions that are susceptible to double meanings, with a view to mislead; prevarication; quibbling; an ambiguous statement.

eq·ui·voque, eq·ui·voke, ek'wi·vōk″, ē′-kwi·vōk″, n. [Fr. *équivoque.*] An ambiguous term or expression; a pun; double meaning.

e·ra, ēr′a, ē′ra, n. [L.L. *æra,* number or epoch by which reckoning is made, prob. the same word as L. *æra,* counters, pl. of *æs,* copper, bronze.] A period of time marked by distinctive character or events; a point of time from which succeeding years are numbered; the beginning of a system of chronology that is computed from a given date; a period in which years are numbered and dates are determined from a point in the past; a distinctive date, event, or character forming the beginning of an age or period.

e·ra·di·ate, i·rā′dē·āt″, v.t., v.i.—*eradiated, eradiating.* To radiate.

e·rad·i·cate, i·rad′i·kāt, v.t.—*eradicated, eradicating.* [L. *eradico, eradicatum*—*e-,* out, and *radix, radicis,* a root.] To destroy thoroughly; to eliminate by erasing or by chemical means; to extirpate; to pull up by the roots.—**e·rad·i·ca·ble,** i·rad′i·ka·bl, a.—**e·rad·i·cant,** i·rad′i·kant″, a., n.—**e·rad·i·ca·tion,** i·rad″i·kā′shan, n.—**e·rad·i·ca·tive,** a.—**e·rad·i·ca·tor,** n.

e·rase, i·rās′, v.t.—*erased, erasing.* [L. *erado, erasum*—*e-,* out, and *rado, rasum,* to scrape, to scratch.] To rub or scrape out, as letters or characters written, engraved, or painted; to efface; to obliterate; to eliminate, as recorded material, from magnetic tape or wire; *slang,* to do away with by killing.—v.i. To become erased easily; remove marks from.—**e·ras·a·ble,** a.—**e·ras·a·bil·i·ty,** i·rās″a·bil′i·tē, n.

e·ras·er, i·rā′sêr, n. One who or something which erases; an implement, as a piece of rubber or cloth, used to erase writing or other marks.

E·ras·tian·ism, i·ras′cha·niz″um, i·ras′tē·a·niz″um, n. [Named for Thomas *Erastus,* sixteenth-century German-Swiss theologian.] The doctrine that the church should be subordinate to the state in ecclesiastical and other matters.—**E·ras·tian,** i·ras′chan, i·ras′tē·an, a. Pertaining to Erastianism.—n.

e·ras·ure, i·rā′shêr, n. The act of erasing or scratching out; obliteration; the impression left on a surface after erasing.

er·bi·um, êr·bē′um, n. [From *Ytterby,* in Sweden.] *Chem.* a metallic element of the rare-earth series, used in certain alloys and lasers. Sym. Er, at. no. 68. See Periodic Table of Elements.

ere, âr, conj., prep. [O.E. *aer* = D. *eer,* Icel. *ár,* Goth. *air,* before, sooner, earlier.] *Poet.* before, in respect to time; sooner than.

e·rect, i·rekt′, v.t. [L. *erectus,* pp. of *erigere,* set upright, raise up, build, < *e-,* out of, and *regere,* direct.] To raise and set in an upright or perpendicular position; to build or construct, as a building; to set up or establish, as an institution, to found; to form into; as, to *erect* territory into a state; *geom.* to draw or construct, as a line or figure, upon a given base; *opt.* to change, as an inverted image, to a normal position; *physiol.* to cause, as a body part, to become stiffly upright. To cause to come into being; as, to *erect* a social barrier.—a. Upright in position or posture; as, to stand or sit *erect;* raised or directed upward; as, a dog with ears *erect; bot.* vertical.—**e·rect·a·ble,** a.—**e·rect·er,** e·rec·tive, a. Tending to erect.—**e·rect·ly,** adv.—**e·rect·ness,** n.

e·rec·tile, i·rik′til, i·rik′til, a. [Fr. *érectile.*] Capable of being erected or set upright; *anat.* susceptible of being distended with blood and becoming rigid, as tissue.—**e·rec·til·i·ty,** i·rek·til′i·tē, ē″rek·til′i·tē, n.

e·rec·tion, i·rek′shan, n. [L. *erectio(n-).*] The act of erecting; the state of being erected; something constructed, as a

building or other structure; *physiol.* a distended and rigid state of an organ or part which contains erectile tissue, esp. of the penis or the clitoris.

e·rec·tor, i·rek′têr, n. One who or that which erects; *anat.* a muscle that raises or erects another body part.

E re·gion, n. That part of the ionosphere 40 to 90 miles above the earth's surface, containing the daytime E layer and the sporadic E layer.

ere·long, âr·lạng′, âr·long′, adv. Archaic, before long; soon.

er·e·mite, er′e·mīt″, n. [L. *eremita;* Late Gr. *eremites,* < Gr. *eremeos,* alone, desert.] A hermit, esp. for religious reasons; a religious recluse; one who lives in a wilderness.—**er·e·mit·ic, er·e·mit·i·cal,** er″e·mit′ik, a. Relating to, having the character of, or like an eremite.—**er·e·mit·ism,** n.

ere·now, âr·nou′, adv. Archaic, before this time.

e·rep·sin, i·rep′sin, n. *Biochem.* a proteolytic mixture containing peptidases and found in intestinal secretions.

er·e·thism, er′e·thiz″um, n. [Gr. *erethismos,* irritation, < *erethizō,* to stir.] *Physiol.* an abnormal excitement or irritability in any organ or tissue.—**er·e·this·mic, er·e·this·tic, er·e·thit·ic, e·re·thic,** e·reth′ik, e·reth′ik, a.

ere·while, âr·hwīl′, âr·wīl′, adv. Archaic, a while before.

erg, urg, n. [Gr. *ergon,* work.] *Phys.* the unit of work in the centimeter-gram-second system, being the amount of work done by a steady force of one dyne moving through a distance of one centimeter in the direction of the force.

er·go, ur′gō, er′gō, adv., conj. [L.] Therefore.

er·go·cal·cif·er·ol, ur″gō·kal·sif′e·rōl″, ur″gō·kal·sif′e·rạl″, ur″gō·kal·sif′e·rol″, n. Calciferol.

er·go·graph, ur′go·graf″, ur′go·gräf″, n. A device for measuring and recording muscular work completed.—**er·go·graph·ic,** a.

er·gom·e·ter, êr″gom′et·êr, n. *Phys.* a device for measuring the work done by a set of muscles.

er·go·no·vine, ur″go·nō′vēn, ur″go·nō′vin, n. *Pharm.* a crystalline alkaloid made from ergot, used esp. to prevent hemorrhage after childbirth or abortion.

er·gos·ter·ol, ur″gos′te·rōl″, ur·gos′te·rạl″, ur″gos′te·rol″, n. *Biochem.* a sterol obtained from ergot or yeast which, when treated with ultraviolet radiation, is converted to vitamin D and used to prevent or cure rickets.

er·got, ur′got, ur′got, n. [Fr. *ergot,* < O.Fr. *argot,* cock's spur.] *Plant pathol.* A fungus, *Claviceps purpurea,* whose growth affects and eventually replaces the grain of cereal, esp. rye, with a hard, dark-colored body; one of the bodies so produced; a source of alkaloids used in medical practice.—**er·got·ic,** ur″got′ik, a.—**er·got·ized.** Containing or infected with ergot.

er·got·a·mine, ur·got′a·mēn″, ur·got′a·min, n. An alkaloid extracted from ergot, used chiefly in treating migraine and stimulating labor contractions.

er·got·ism, ur′go·tiz″um, n. *Plant pathol.* a diseased condition of rye due to the growth of the fungus, *Claviceps purpurea; pathol.* a disease resulting from the consumption of foods prepared from rye and other cereals affected with this fungus.

er·i·ca·ceous, er″i·kā′shus, a. [N.L. *Erica,* the heath genus, < Gr. *ereiē,* heath.] Belonging to the *Ericaceæ,* or heath family of plants, which includes the heath, arbutus, azalea, rhododendron, and American laurel.

er·i·coid, er′i·koid″, a. Similar to a heath.

E·rie, ēr′ē, n. pl. E·rie, E·ries. A member of an American Indian tribe that once lived

on the southern shore of Lake Erie; the language spoken by the Erie people.

Er·in, er′in, ēr′in, âr′in, n. [Uncertain origin.] *Poet.* Ireland.

er·i·na·ceous, er″i·nā′shus, a. Of or similar to a hedgehog.

er·is·tic, e·ris′tik, a. [Gr. *eristikos,* contentious, < *eris,* strife.] Pertaining to disputation or controversy; controversial; captious. Also **er·is·ti·cal.**—n. One who enters into controversy; the art of disputation.

Er·len·mey·er flask, ur′len·mī″êr flask, er′len·mī′êr fläsk, ur′len·mī′ur fläsk, er′len·mī″êr fläsk, n. A conical laboratory flask with a broad, flat base and narrow neck.

er·mine, ur′min, n. pl. er·mine, er·mines. [O.Fr. *ermine,* Mod.Fr. *hermine,* < the Teut.] A small mammal of the weasel family, *Mustela erminea,* found in Europe, with a white winter coat and black tail; any of other similar weasels which have a white winter fur; the white fur itself, often with the black tail fur interspersed for contrast; the dignity of a king, judge, or other dignitary, whose robe is trimmed with ermine.—**er·mined,** a. Clothed with ermine.

erne, ern, urn, n. [O.E. *earn* = Dan. and Sw. *ærn,* an eagle, allied to G. *aar,* an eagle, and to Skt. *ara,* swift, < *ri,* to go.] A sea eagle, esp. the white-tailed sea eagle.

e·rode, i·rōd′, v.t.—*eroded, eroding.* [L. *erodere* (pp. *erosus*), < *e-,* out of, and *rodere,* gnaw.] To eat out or away; to destroy by slow consumption; to form, as a channel, by eating or wearing away; to slowly wear away, as the earth's surface, by the action of wind or water.—v.i. To become eroded.

e·rod·ent, i·rōd′ent, a. Eroding; erosive.

e·rog·e·nous, i·roj′e·nus, a. [< Gr. *erōs,* love, and *-genous.*] Inducing sexual desire; sexually excitable; as, the body's *erogenous* zones.

e·rose, i·rōs′, a. [L. *erosus,* pp. of *erodere,* < *e-,* out of, and *rodere,* gnaw.] Uneven, as if gnawed away; *bot.* having the margin irregularly incised, as a leaf.

e·ro·sion, i·rō′zhan, n. [L. *erosio.*] The act or operation of eating or wearing away; *geol.* the wearing away of soil or rock by the influence of water, ice, winds, and other forces of nature.

e·ro·sive, i·rō′siv, a. Having the property of eating away, corroding, or wearing away; causing erosion.—**e·ro·sive·ness, e·ro·siv·i·ty,** n.

e·rot·ic, i·rot′ik, a. [Gr. *erotikos,* < *erōs, erōtos,* love.] Pertaining to or prompted by sexual love; increasing sexual desire; moved by sexual desire. Also **e·rot·i·cal.**—n. An amorous composition or poem; an erotic person.—**e·rot·i·cal·ly,** adv.

e·rot·i·ca, i·rot′i·ka, n. pl. Items of literature or art having a sexual theme.

e·rot·i·cism, i·rot′i·siz″um, n. A sexual quality; use of sexually stimulating themes in art, literature, and drama; a condition of sexual excitement; an unusually insistent sexual desire.

e·ro·to·gen·ic, i·rō″to·jen′ik, i·rot″o·jen′-ik, a. Erogenous.

err, ur, er, v.i. [L. *erro, erratum,* to wander, to err; allied to G. *irren,* to wander, to go astray.] To wander; to go astray, esp. in thought; to be wrong; to deviate from the path of duty; to fail morally; to transgress; to blunder; *archaic,* to stray.

er·ran·cy, ur′an·sē, n. pl. er·ran·cies. The fact or state of erring.

er·rand, er′and, n. [O.E. *ærende* = O.H.G. *arunti* = Icel. *eyrendi,* errand, message.] A trip to convey a message or execute a commission; a journey for a specific purpose; the purpose of any short trip or journey; a commission; a service or favor done for another; as, to do his mother's *errands.*

er·rant, er′ant, *a.* [O.Fr. Fr. *errant,* prop. ppr. of O.Fr. *errer,* journey, travel (< M.L. *iterare,* < L. *iter,* way, journey).] Journeying or traveling, as a medieval knight in quest of adventure; wandering or straying; deviating from the regular or proper course.—**er·rant·ly,** *adv.*

er·rant·ry, er′an·trē, *n.* pl. **er·rant·ries.** An errant condition or deed; behavior suggestive of a knight-errant.

er·rat·ic, i·rat′ik, *a.* [L. *erraticus,* < *errare,* wander, E. *err.*] Wandering; not fixed; as, an *erratic* star; having no certain course; deviating from the proper or usual course in conduct or opinion; eccentric; queer. *Med.* irregular; changeable; moving from point to point, as rheumatic pains. *Geol.* of or pertaining to a boulder, or something similar, transported from its original site to an unusual location, as by glacial action.—*n.* A wanderer; an erratic or eccentric person; *geol.* an erratic boulder or block.—**er·rat·i·cal·ly,** *adv.*—**er·rat·i·cism,** *n.*

er·ra·tum, i·rā′tum, i·rä′tum, *n.* pl. **er·ra·ta.** [L. *erratum,* a blunder.] An error or mistake in writing or printing; *pl.* a list of mistakes in writing or printing.

err·ing, ur′ing, er′ing, *a.* Wandering; going astray; in error; wrong; sinning.—**err·ing·ly,** *adv.*

er·ro·ne·ous, e·rō′nē·us, e·rŏ′nē·us, *a.* [L. *erroneus.*] Characterized by or containing error; wrong; mistaken; false; inaccurate.—**er·ro·ne·ous·ly,** *adv.*—**er·ro·ne·ous·ness,** *n.*

er·ror, er′or, *n.* [O.Fr. *error* (Fr. *erreur*), < L. *error,* < *errare,* wander, E, *err.*] A deviation from accuracy or correctness; a mistake, as in action or procedure; an inaccuracy, as in speaking or writing; the belief of what is not true; a false belief; departure from moral right; wrong-doing; a moral offense; *math.* the difference between the observed or approximately determined value and the true value of a quantity; *baseball,* a faulty defensive play other than a wild pitch or a passed ball, which allows a runner to safely reach base, or to advance one or more bases. *Christian Science,* false illusions about reality.—**er·ror·less,** *a.*

er·satz, er′zäts, er′sats, *a.* [G.] Acting as a substitute; serving as an artificial or synthetic, and often inferior, replacement.—*n.*

Erse, ẽrs, *a.* [A variation of *Irish.*] Pertaining to the Gaelic-speaking people in Ireland and Scotland or to their language.—*n.* The Scottish-Gaelic or Irish-Gaelic language.

erst, ẽrst, *adv.* [O.E. *ǣrest,* superl. of *ǣr.* ERE.] *Archaic,* a while ago; formerly.

erst·while, ẽrst′hwīl″, ẽrst′wīl″, *a.* Former. —*adv. Archaic,* a while before; formerly.

er·u·bes·cence, er″u·bes′ens, *n.* [L. *erubesco,* to become red—*e-,* and *ruber,* red (whence *rubric.*)] The act of turning red; redness of the skin or surface of anything; blushing.—**er·u·bes·cent,** *a.* Red or reddish; blushing.

e·ruct, i·rukt′, *v.t.,v.i.* [L. *eructo, eructatum* —*e-,* out, and *ructo,* to belch.] To eject, as wind from the stomach; to belch; to emit violently, as matter from a volcano. Also **e·ruc·tate.**—**e·ruc·ta·tion,** i·ruk·tā′shan, *n.* [L. *eructatio.*] The act of belching wind from the stomach; a belch.

er·u·dite, er′ū·dīt″, er′u̇·dīt″, *a.* [L. *eruditus,* < *erudio,* to polish, to instruct— *e-,* out, and *rudis,* rough, rude.] Learned; scholarly.—**er·u·dite·ly,** *adv.*—**er·u·dite·ness,** *n.*

er·u·di·tion, er″ū·dish′an, er″u̇·dish′an, *n.* Knowledge gained chiefly from books and study; scholarship.

e·rum·pent, i·rum′pent, *a.* [L. *erumpens* (*-ent*), ppr. of *erumpere.* ERUPT.] Bursting forth; *bot.* prominent, as if bursting through the epidermis.

e·rupt, i·rupt′, *v.i.* [L. *eruptus,* ppr. of *erumpere,* < *e-,* out of, and *rumpere,* break.] To burst forth, as volcanic matter; to eject matter, as a volcanic geyser; to burst forth in a sudden or violent manner; to break out in a rash or blemish; of teeth, to break through the skin of the gums.—*v.t.* To cause to burst forth; to eject, as volcanic matter; to force through the gums, as teeth; to break out.

e·rup·tion, i·rup′shan, *n.* [L. *eruptio(n-).*] A bursting forth; an issuing forth suddenly and violently; an outburst; an outbreak; that which bursts forth. *Geol.* the ejection of molten rock, as from a volcano; the ejection of water, as from a geyser. *Pathol.* the breaking out of a rash; a rash or exanthema.

e·rup·tive, i·rup′tiv, *a.* Bursting forth, or tending to burst forth; pertaining to or of the nature of an eruption; *geol.* of rocks, formed by the eruption of molten material; *pathol.* causing an eruption or rash.—*n. Geol.* an eruptive rock.—**e·rup·tive·ly,** *adv.*—**e·rup·tive·ness,** *n.*

e·ryn·go, i·ring′gō, *n.* pl. **e·ryn·goes,** **e·ryn·gos.** [L. *eryngion,* < Gr. *ēryggion,* dim. of *ēryggos,* eryngo.] Any plant of the genus *Eryngium,* consisting of coarse herbs with toothed or spiny leaves, esp. the seaholly, an ornamental grown for its misty blue flowerheads. Also **e·rin·go.**

er·y·sip·e·las, er″i·sip′e·las, ēr″i·sip′e·las, *n.* [Gr. *erythros,* red, and *pella,* skin.] An infectious skin disease characterized by fever and inflammation, affecting subcutaneous tissue, caused by a specific streptococcus.—**er·y·si·pel·a·tous,** er″i·si·pel′a·tus, ēr″i·si·pel′a·tus, *a.*

er·y·the·ma, er″i·thē′ma, *n.* [N.L. < Gr. *erythēma, erythainein,* redden, < *erythros,* red.] *Pathol.* abnormal redness of the skin due to local congestion, as in inflammation. —**er·y·the·mat·ic,** **er·y·them·a·tous,** er″i·thi·mat′ik, er″i·them′a·tus, *a.*

e·ryth·rism, i·rith′riz·um, *n.* [Gr. *erythros,* red.] Abnormal or excessive redness, as of plumage or hair.—**er·y·thris·mal,** er″i·thriz′mal, *a.*

e·ryth·ro·blast, i·rith′rō·blast″, *n. Anat.* one of the nucleated cells found in bone marrow from which the red blood cells are formed.

e·ryth·ro·cyte, i·rith′rō·sīt″, *n.* [Gr. *erythro,* red, and *cyte,* hollow, vessel.] The red blood cell, containing hemoglobin, and carrying oxygen to the cells and tissues and carbon dioxide to the respiratory organs.—**e·ryth·ro·cyt·ic,** **e·ryth·roid,** i·rith″rō·sit′ik, *a.*

e·ryth·ro·cy·tom·e·ter, i·rith″rō·sī·tom′i·tẽr, *n.* An instrument for counting red blood cells.

e·ryth·ro·my·cin, i·rith″rō·mī′sin, *n.* An antibiotic used in treating amoebic and other diseases, and produced by the actinomycete, *Streptomyces erythraeus.*

e·ryth·ro·poi·e·sis, i·rith″rō·poi·ē′sis, *n.* The production of red blood corpuscles.—**e·ryth·ro·poi·et·ic,** i·rith″rō·poi·et′ik, *a.*

es·ca·drille, es″ka·dril′, *Fr.* es·kä·drē′ye, *n.* [Fr. dim. of *escadre,* squadron, < It. *squadra.*] A squadron or divisional unit of the European air forces, esp. in France, usu. containing six planes.

es·ca·lade, es″ka·lād′, *n.* [Fr. through Sp. or It. < M.L. *scalare,* climb by ladder, < L. *scala,* flight of steps, ladder, E. *scale.*] A scaling or mounting by means of ladders, esp. in an assault upon a fortified place.—*v.t.—escaladed, escalading.* To mount, pass, or enter by means of ladders. —**es·ca·lad·er,** *n.*

es·ca·late, es′ka·lāt″, *v.t.—escalated, escalating.* [< *escalade.*] To gradually increase in scope or intensity; as, to *escalate* a war; to raise or go up on, or as if on, a moving

stairway.—**es·ca·la·tion,** es″ka·lā′shan, *n.*

es·ca·la·tor, es′ka·lā″tẽr, *n.* [L. *e-,* out of, from, and *scala,* flight of steps.] A moving staircase that either ascends or descends continuously by means of an endless belt, used to carry passengers, as from one floor to another in a department store.

es·ca·la·tor clause, *n.* A provision in a contract stating that the wages of labor union members may be raised or lowered, so as to conform with the rise or fall of living costs.

es·cal·lop, e·skol′op, e·skal′op, *n., v.t.* See *scallop.*

es·ca·pade, es″ka·pād′, es″ka·pād′, *n.* [Fr. < It. *scappata* < *scappare.* ESCAPE.] An adventurous action contrary to usual or accepted behavior; a deviation from confining rules; an impulsive action performed without regard for consequences; an escape from confinement.

es·cape, e·skāp′, *v.i.—escaped, escaping.* [O.Fr. *escaper, eschaper* (Fr. *échapper*), = It. *scappare,* appar. orig. 'slip out of one's cloak,' < L. *ex-,* out of, and M.L. *cappa,* cloak, E. *cape.*] To slip or get away, as from confinement or restraint; to avoid capture, punishment, or any threatened evil; to issue from a confining enclosure, as a fluid; to fade or slip away, as from the memory; *bot.* to grow wild, as a plant just introduced.—*v.t.* To get away from; as, to *escape* prison; slip out inadvertently, as a remark; to elude, as a threatened danger; to fail to be noticed or recollected by.—**es·cap·er,** *n.*—**es·cap·a·ble,** *a.*

es·cape, e·skāp′, *n.* The act or instance of escaping, or the fact of having escaped; a slipping or getting away from confinement or restraint; a respite from reality; leakage, as of water or gas; a means of escaping; as, a fire *escape; bot.* a plant once under cultivation, now growing wild.—*a.* Affording a respite from reality; as, an *escape* novel; allowing a means of evading obligation; as, an *escape* clause.

es·ca·pee, es·skāp′ē, *n.* One who has escaped, esp. from imprisonment.

es·cape hatch, *n.* An emergency exit, usu. on an aircraft or submarine.

es·cape mech·an·ism, *n. Psychol.* involuntary or unconscious measures used by an individual to avoid anxieties, unpleasant realities, or responsibilities.

es·cape·ment, e·skāp′ment, *n.* The device in a timepiece which controls and maintains the constant rate of the wheels; the spacing mechanism of a typewriter which controls and regulates the horizontal motion of the carriage. *Archaic,* the act of escaping; a way of escape; an outlet.

es·cape rock·et, *n. Aerospace,* a small rocket engine attached to the end of an escape tower of a space capsule, and used to provide additional thrust for separation of the capsule from the booster in an emergency.

es·cape tow·er, *n. Aerospace,* a trestle tower on top of a space capsule which connects the capsule to the escape rocket during lift-off, protecting the capsule from the heat of the escape rocket.

es·cape ve·loc·i·ty, *n. Phys.* the minimum speed which a body must acquire in order to escape the gravitational field of a planet or celestial body.

es·cap·ist, e·skā′pist, *n.* One who seeks escape from unpleasant reality in daydreams and fancies.—*a.*—**es·cap·ism,** *n.*

es·ca·role, es″ka·rōl′, *n.* [Fr. < It. *scariola.*] A broad-leaved endive, used for salads.

es·carp, e·skärp′, *n.* [Fr. *escarpe,* < It. *scarpa.*] *Fort.* the inner slope or wall of the ditch surrounding a rampart; any similar steep slope.—*v.t.* To make into an escarp; give a steep slope to; furnish with escarps.—

---

ch- chain, G. na*ch*t;   **th-** THen, thin;   **w-** wig, hw as sound in whig;   **z-** zh as in azure, zeal.   *Italicized vowel* indicates schwa sound.

es·carp·ment, *n.* Ground cut into the form of an escarp or steep slope; the precipitous face of a ridge of land, extent of rock, or the like; a cliff.

es·char, es'kär, es'kėr, *n.* [Gr. *eschara,* a fireplace, a scab.] A crust or scab on the skin caused by burns or caustic applications.—**es·cha·rot·ic,** es″ka·rot'ik, *a.* Caustic; having the power of searing or destroying the flesh.—*n.* An application which sears or destroys flesh.

es·char, es'kär, es'kėr, *n.* Esker.

es·cha·tol·o·gy, es'ka·tol'o·jē, *n.* [Gr. *eschatos,* last, and *logos,* discourse.] *Theol.* the doctrine of the last or final things, as death, judgment, and the destination of the soul.—**es·cha·to·log·i·cal,** es″ka·to·loj′i·kal, *a.*—**es·cha·to·log·i·cal·ly,** *adv.*—**es·cha·tol·o·gist,** *n.*

es·cheat, es·chēt', *n.* [O.Fr. *eschete,* < *escheir, escheoir,* Mod.Fr. *echoir,* < L. *excadēre*—*ex-,* and *cadēre,* to fall.] The reverting of any land or tenements to the state or sovereign due to lack of qualified heirs; the property which falls to the state in this way; the right to such land.—*v.i.* To become an escheat.—*v.t.* To cause to be an escheat; to forfeit.—**es·cheat·a·ble,** *a.*—**es·cheat·age,** es·chē′tij, *n.* The right of succeeding to an escheat.

es·chew, es·chō', *v.t.* [O.Fr. *eschever,* Fr. *eschiver,* to avoid, to shun, < O.G. *skiuhan,* G. *scheuen,* to avoid; akin to E. *shy.*] To shun; to avoid.—**es·chew·al,** *n.*—**es·chew·er,** *n.*

es·cort, es'kart, *n.* [Fr. *escorte,* < It. *scorta,* < *scorgere,* guide, < L. *ex-,* out of, and *corrigere,* set right, E. *correct.*] A male who accompanies a woman on a social engagement; a body of persons, or a single person, accompanying another or others for protection, guidance, or chivalry; specif. an armed guard, as armed vessels accompanying merchant ships; protection, safeguard, or guidance on a journey.—e·skart', *v.t.* To attend or accompany as an escort.

es·cri·toire, es″kri·twär', *n.* [O.Fr. *escritoire,* < L. *scriptorium,* connected with writing, *scribo, scriptum,* to write.] A desk or chest of drawers with a compartment for writing materials; a writing desk.

es·crow, es'krō, e·skrō', *n.* [A.Fr. *escrowe,* O.Fr. *escroe,* piece· of parchment, scroll (Fr. *écrou,* entry in a jail register); < Teut., and akin to E. *shred.*] *Law,* a written document fully executed by the parties, but deposited with a third person, by whom it is held until the fulfillment of some condition, at which time it is delivered to the grantee.—*v.t.*

es·cu·lent, es'kū·lent, *a.* [L. *esculentus,* < *esca,* food, < *edo,* to eat.] Capable of or fit for being used as food; edible.—*n.*

es·cutch·eon, e·skuch'on, *n.* [O.Fr. *escuchon* (Fr. *écusson*), < *escu,* < L. *scutum,* shield.] The shield, or shield-shaped surface, on which armorial bearings are depicted; a hatchment; something resembling an escutcheon or a shield, as the panel on a ship's stern bearing her name; the protective metal plate around a keyhole or light switch.—**es·cutch·eoned,** *a.*

es·ker, es·kar, es'kėr, *n.* [Ir. *eiscir.*] *Geol.* a long, linear ridge of sand and gravel formed by a flowing stream in or under a stagnant glacier. Also *eschar.*

Es·ki·mo, es'ki·mō″, *n.* pl. **Es·ki·mos, Es·ki·mo.** [Algonquian name for the people, meaning eaters of raw flesh: by themselves called *Innuit.*] A people, characterized by short or medium stature, stout build, light-brown complexion, and a broad, flat face, inhabiting the arctic coasts of America from Greenland to Alaska and a small part of the adjacent Asiatic coast; the language of this region excluding southern Alaska. Also *Esquimau.*—*a.* Of or pertaining to their language. Also **Es·ki·mo·an, Es·qui·mau·an.**

Es·ki·mo dog, *n.* One of a breed of strong dogs used by the Eskimos for pulling sleds and hunting.

e·soph·a·gus,oe·soph·a·gus, i·sof'a·gus, ē·sof'a·gus, *n.* pl. **e·soph·a·gi, oe·soph·a·gi,** i·sof'a·jī″, ē·sof'a·jī″. [N.L. *œsophagus,* < Gr. *oisophagos,* perhaps < *oisein,* fut. used with *pherein,* bear, and *phagein,* eat.] The muscular tube in man and higher animals extending from the pharynx to the stomach and through which food passes; the gullet.—**e·soph·a·ge·al, oe·soph·a·ge·al,** i·sof″a·jē′al, ē″so·faj′ē·al, *a.*

es·o·ter·ic, es'o·ter'ik, *a.* [Gr. *esotericos,* < *esōterō,* compar. of *esō,* within, *ēs, eis,* into.] Understood only by those few with pertinent interest or knowledge; belonging or pertaining to an inner or select circle, as of disciples; communicated to or understood by the initiated only, as a doctrine; private or secret; profound or recondite.— *n.* An esoteric doctrine; one initiated or believing in esoteric doctrines.—**es·o·ter·i·cal,** *a.* Esoteric.—**es·o·ter·i·cal·ly,** *adv.* **es·o·ter·i·cism, es·o·te·rism,** es'o·te·riz″um, *n.*

es·o·ter·i·ca, es″o·ter′i·ka, *n. pl.* Matters understood only by those who have special knowledge or interest; obscure items.

es·pa·drille, es″pa·dril″, *n.* [Fr.] A sandal with a sole made of rope, held on by a thong laced through the canvas upper and tied around the ankle.

es·pal·ier, e·spal'yėr, *n.* [Fr. < It. *spalliera,* lit. 'shoulder support,' < *spalla,* shoulder, < L. *spatula,* broad piece.] A trellis or framework on which fruit trees or shrubs are trained to grow in flattened form; a tree or plant thus trained.—*v.t.* To train on or furnish with an espalier.

es·par·to, e·spar'tō, *n.* [Sp., < L. *spartum,* Gr. *sparton, spartos.*] Any of two or three species of grass, esp. *Stipa tenacissima,* found in southern Spain and North Africa, and extensively exported for use in the manufacture of such items as paper, matting, and baskets. Also **es·par·to grass.**

es·pe·cial, e·spesh'al, *a.* [O.Fr. *especial,* Fr. *spécial,* L. *specialis,* of particular sort or kind, special, < *species,* kind.] Of a distinct sort or kind; special; particular; marked; peculiar.—**es·pe·cial·ly,** *adv.*—**es·pe·cial·ness,** *n.*

Es·pe·ran·to, es″pe·rän'tō, es″pe·ran′tō, *n.* [From *Esperanto,* pseudonym of L. L. Zamenhof (1859–1917), Russian physician, who in 1887 proposed this language.] An artificial language designed as an international medium, based on words and forms common to the principal European languages.—**Es·pe·ran·tism,** *n.*—**Es·pe·ran·tist,** *n.*

es·pi·al, e·spi′al, *n.* The act of spying; observation; discovery.

es·pi·o·nage, es″pē·o·näzh″, es'pē·o·nij, es″pē·o·näzh′, *n.* The practice of spying; the use of spies by one government for securing confidential information from another.

es·pla·nade, es″pla·nād′, es″pla·näd′, *n.* [Fr. < the old verb *esplaner,* to make level, < L. *explanare*—*ex-,* and *planus,* plain, level.] Any open level space, esp. one for public walks or drives, as near the seaside.

es·pouse, e·spouz', *v.t.*—*espoused, espousing.* [O.Fr. *espouser* (Fr. *épouser*) < L. *sponsare,* to betroth, to espouse, freq. of *spondeo, sponsum,* to pledge oneself.] To embrace or to adopt, as a cause or quarrel; to give or take in marriage; to promise, engage, or bestow in marriage by contract or pledge; to betroth; to marry; to wed.— **es·pous·al,** e·spou'zal, *n.* [O.Fr. *espousaille,* L. *sponsalia,* espousals, pl. n. of *sponsalis,* relating to betrothal.] The act of espousing or betrothing; marriage; the adopting or taking up of a cause.—**es·pous·er,** *n.*

es·pres·so, e·spres′ō, *n.* [It.] Strong coffee brewed by steam pressure forced through finely ground or powdered coffee beans.

es·prit, e·sprē', *n.* [Fr. < L. *spiritus,* E. *spirit.*] Spirit; intelligence; wit.

es·prit de corps, e·sprē′ de kar', *n.* [Fr. 'spirit of body.'] A sense of union, common interests and responsibilities, as developed among a body of associated persons.

es·py, e·spi′, *v.t.*—*espied, espying.* [O.Fr. *espier,* It. *spiare;* same word as *spy.*] To see at a distance; to descry; to discover, as something concealed.

Es·qui·mau, es'ku·mō″, *n.* pl. **Es·qui·maux,** es'ku·mō″, es'ku·mōz″. [Fr.] Eskimo.

es·quire, e·skwīer', es'kwīer, *n.* [O.Fr. *esquier* (Fr. *ecuyer*), < L.L. *scutarius,* shieldbearer, < L. *scutum,* shield.] (*Cap.*) a title of respect or courtesy placed in abbreviated form after the surname, usu. in a written address: applied esp. to lawyers; *Brit.* a title applied to a commoner who is thought to have reached the social level of a gentleman. Abbr. *Esq.* Any of various officials in the service of a king or nobleman; a man belonging to the order of English gentry ranking next below a knight; a gentleman who attends or escorts a lady in public.—*v.t.*—*esquired, esquiring.* To raise to the rank of esquire; to address as "Esquire"; to escort as an esquire.

es·say, es'ā, e·sā', *n.* [Fr. *essayer.*] An effort made for the performance of anything; a trial, attempt, or endeavor; a test or experiment, es'ā, e·sā'. A short, literary composition, intended to prove some particular point or illustrate or interpret a particular subject, es'ā.—es'ā, e·sā', *v.t.* To exert, as one's power or faculties, on; to attempt; to try, as an experiment.— **es·say·er,** es'ā·ėr, e·sā'ėr, *n.* One who essays; one who writes essays; an essayist. —**es·say·ist,** es'ā·ist, *n.* A writer of an essay or essays.

es·sence, es'·ens, *n.* [Fr. < L. *essentia,* < *esse,* to be; akin *entity.*] That which constitutes the particular nature of a thing; intrinsic value; the necessary and significant nature of a particular entity, as man as a rational animal. The individual properties of any plant or drug extracted, refined, or distilled into a condensed form; an extract; a perfume.

Es·sene, es'ēn, e·sēn', *n.* [L. *Esseni,* pl., < Gr. *Essēnos.*] One of a brotherhood or monastic order of Jews in ancient Palestine, first appearing in the 2nd century B.C., characterized by asceticism, celibacy, and the strict observance of the non-Levitical portion of the Mosaic law.—**Es·se·ni·an,** e·sē′nē·an, *a.*—**Es·se·nism,** *n.*

es·sen·tial, e·sen'shal, *a.* [M.L. *essentialis.*] Pertaining to, constituting, or entering into the essence or nature of a thing; important; fundamental; inherent; basic; absolutely necessary; indispensable; containing an essence of a plant or drug; *med.* idiopathic.— *n.* Something belonging to the essence or nature of a thing; something indispensable; basic; necessary; a chief point.—**es·sen·ti·al·i·ty,** e·sen″shē·al'i·tē, *n.*—**es·sen·tial·ly,** *adv.*—**es·sen·tial·ness,** *n.*

es·sen·tial a·mi·no ac·id, *n.* *Biochem.* an amino acid which cannot be synthesized by the body and is required for growth and survival.

es·sen·tial·ism, e·sen'sha·liz″um, *n.* *Educ.* a doctrine or theory that there are definite traditional standards, concepts, and procedures which are indispensable to a society, and which all students must be systematically schooled in, despite differing aptitudes.

es·sen·tial oil, *n.* Any of a class of oils obtained from plants, possessing the characteristic odor of the plant, and volatilizing completely when heated: used chiefly in making perfumes and flavors.

es·so·nite, es′o·nīt″, *n.* A yellow to brown gem, softer than a true hyacinth; a variety of grossularite.

EST, E.S.T., e.s.t. *n.* Abbr. for Eastern Standard Time.

es·tab·lish, e·stab′lish, *v.t.* [O.Fr. *establir* (Fr. *établir*), < L. *stabilio*, to make firm, to establish, < *sta*, root of *sto*, to stand.] To make firm or stable; to install or settle on a permanent basis; to prove or verify; as, to *establish* the facts; to institute and ratify; to enact or decree authoritatively and for permanence; as, to *establish* law and order; to ordain; to originate and secure permanently; as, to *establish* a custom; to found permanently; as, to *establish* a business; to set up, as a state or national institution; as, to *establish* a church.— **es·tab·lish·er,** *n.*

es·tab·lished church, *n.* A church recognized by law as the official church of a nation. Also *state church.*

es·tab·lish·ment, e·stab′lish·ment, *n.* That which has been established; the act of establishing; the state of being established; the power structure of an established order of society; a public or private institution; a place of business or residence and everything connected with it; a permanent civil or military organization; the state church; confirmation.—**the Es·tab·lish·ment,** those members of a society or particular field who form the power structure of that group.

es·tan·cia, e·stän′sē·a, *Sp.* es·tän′syä, *n.* pl. **es·tan·cias.** [Sp. < M.L. *stantia*, < L. *stare*, stand.] In Spanish America, a landed estate; a stock farm.

es·tate, e·stāt′, *n.* [O.Fr. *estat* (Fr. *etat*), < L. *status.*] Landed property, esp. a large amount of property with a manor house on it. *Law*, property or possessions; the amount of one's holdings in land and other property; property left at a person's death. *Brit.* a housing project; a major social group having political power; social status or rank.—*v.t.*—**estated, estating.** *Archaic*, to establish in or as in an estate.

es·tate wag·on, *n. Brit.* station wagon.

es·teem, e·stēm′, *v.t.* [Fr. *estimer*, L. *aestimare, estimatum*, < same root as Skr. *esha*, a wish, G. *heischen*, to desire. Akin *aim.*] To have a high regard for; to respect; to admire; to regard as having a certain value; as, to *esteem* his opinions valuable. —*n.* Favorable opinion; high regard.

es·ter, es′tėr, *n.* [G. *essigäther*, ethyl acetate < *essig*, vinegar, and *äther*, ether.] *Chem.* one of a class of organic compounds corresponding to inorganic salts; a compound formed by the reaction of an alcohol with an acid and the elimination of water.— **es·ter·i·fy,** e·ster′i·fī″, *v.t., v.i.*—**esterified,** *esterifying.*—**es·ter·i·fi·ca·tion,** *n.*

es·ter·ase, es′te·rās″, *n. Biochem.* an enzyme which hastens the hydrolysis or decomposition of esters into an acid and an alcohol.

es·the·sia, es·thē′zha, es·thē′zhē·a, es·-thē′zē·a, *n.* [Gr. *aisthēsis*, perception, sensibility.] Capacity for experiencing sensations; sensibility; feeling. Also **aes·the·sia.**—**es·the·sis,** es·thē′sis, *n.* Elementary sensation; feeling. Also **aes·the·sis.**

es·the·si·om·e·ter, es·thē″zē·om′i·tėr, *n.* [Gr. *aisthesis*, perception, sensation.] *Med.* an instrument for determining the degree of tactile sensibility.

es·thet·ic, es·thet′ik, *a.* Aesthetic.—**es·-thete,** *n.* Aesthete.

Es·tho·ni·an, es·stō′nē·an, es·thō′nē·an, *a., n.* See *Estonian.*

es·ti·ma·ble, es′ti·ma·bl, *a.* Capable of being estimated or valued; worthy of esteem or respect; deserving of good opinion or high regard.—**es·ti·ma·ble·-ness,** *n.*—**es·ti·ma·bly,** *adv.*

es·ti·mate, es′ti·māt″, *v.t.*—**estimated, estimating.** [L. *aestimatus*, pp. of *aestimare*, judge the value of, rate.] To form an approximate judgment or opinion regarding such items as the value, amount, size, or weight of; calculate approximately; to form an opinion of; judge.—*v.i.* To submit approximate figures, as of the cost of work to be done.—es′ti·mit, es′ti·māt, *n.* An approximate judgment or calculation, as of the value or amount of something; an approximate statement of the charge for certain work to be done; a judgment or opinion, as of the qualities of a person or thing; estimation or judgment.—**es·ti·ma·tive,** es′ti·mā″tiv, *a.* Pertaining to or capable of estimating.—**es·ti·ma·tor,** *n.*

es·ti·ma·tion, es″ti·mā′shan, *n.* [L.] Judgment or opinion; the act of estimating or appraising; estimate; valuation in respect of excellence or merit; esteem; repute; approximate calculation.

es·ti·val, es′ti·val, e·stī′val, *a.* Aestival.

es·ti·vate, es′ti·vāt″, *v.i.*—**estivated, estivating.** Aestivate. **es·ti·va·tion,** es″ti·vā′shan, *n.*

es·toile, e·stoil′, e·twäl′, *n.* [O.Fr. *estoile* (Fr. *étoile*), < L. *stella*, star.] *Her.* a star-shaped figure, commonly having six points and wavy rays.

Es·to·ni·an, e·stō′nē·an, *a.* Of or pertaining to Estonia, formerly an independent republic, now a part of the Soviet Union; of or relating to the Finno-Ugric language spoken by the inhabitants of Estonia. —A member of the people who inhabit Estonia, Livonia, or certain other regions of Russia; the language of the inhabitants. Also *Esthonian.*

es·top, e·stop′, *v.t.*—**estopped, estopping.** [O.Fr. *estoper* (Fr. *étouper*), stop up, < L. *stuppa*, tow.] *Law*, to hinder or prevent by estoppel.

es·top·pel, e·stop′el, *n.* [O.Fr. *estoupail,* stopple, stopper.] *Law*, a bar or impediment preventing one from asserting a fact or claim, arising from a previous action, or a failure to act, by which one has admitted, implied, or established the contrary.

es·to·vers, e·stō′vėrz, *n. pl.* [O.Fr. *estover,* noun use of *estovoir,* be necessary.] *Law*, necessaries allowed by law, as wood and timber to a tenant or alimony to a wife.

es·trade, e·sträd′, *n.* [Fr. road, highway, later raised platform through Pr. or It. < L.L. *strata,* paved way.] A raised platform; a dais.

es·tra·di·ol, es″tra·dī′ōl, es″tra·dī′al, es″tra·di·ol, *n.* A hormone used to treat estrogen deficiency and some menopausal and postmenopausal symptoms. Also **oes·tra·di·ol.**

es·trange, e·stranj′, *v.t.*—**estranged, estranging.** [O.Fr. *estrangier* (Fr. *étranger*), < L. *extraneare,* < *extraneus,* that is without, foreign.] To turn away in feeling or affection; to alienate the affections of; to cause to be strange or as a stranger; to remove to, or keep at, a distance; to divert from the original use or possessor.— **es·trange·ment,** *n.*—**es·tran·ger,** *n.*

es·tray, e·strā′, *n.* [O.Fr. *estraier.*] *Law*, a domestic animal, as a horse or a sheep, found wandering or without an owner. Anything strayed away.—*v.i.* To stray.

es·treat, e·strēt′, *n.* [O.Fr. *estraite,* < L. *extraho, extractum,* to draw out.] *Law*, an exact copy of an original record or writing, as of one under which a fine is levied.—*v.t. Law*, to levy, as fines under an *estreat;* to make an *estreat* of, as of a fine levied.

es·tri·ol, es′trē·ōl″, es′trē·al″, es′trē·ol″, *n. Biochem.* an estrogenic substance found in the urine of pregnant women. A pharmaceutical preparation from this substance. Also **oes·tri·ol.**

es·tro·gen, es′tro·jen, *n.* [L. *estrus,* frenzy, and *gen,* producer.] *Biochem.* a female hormone which induces estrus, causes sexual receptivity, and promotes the development of secondary sex characteristics in the female. Also **oes·tro·gen.**—**es·tro·gen·ic,** oes·tro·gen·ic, *a.*

es·trone, es′trōn, *n. Biochem.* a female sex hormone, used in treating estrogen deficiency and some menopausal and postmenopausal symptoms. Also **es·trin, oes·trin, oes·trone.**

es·trous, es′trus, *a.* Of or pertaining to the estrus. Also **oes·trous.**

es·trous cy·cle, *n. Zool.* the complete cycle of reproductive changes in female mammals, running from the start of one period of estrus to the start of the next.

es·trus, es′trus, *n. Zool.* the point of highest sexual excitability in the female, during which conception is possible; the period of heat. Also **es·trum, oes·trus.**—**es·tru·al,** es′trō·al, *a.*

es·tu·ar·y, es′chō·er″ē, *n.* pl. **es·tu·ar·ies.** [L. *aestuarium,* < *aestuo,* to boil or foam, *aestus,* heat, tide.] The wide mouth of a river where the tide meets the currents; a firth.—**es·tu·a·rine,** es′chō·a·rīn″, es′chō·ėr·in, *a.* Of or pertaining to an estuary; formed in an estuary.

e·su·ri·ent, i·sur′ē·ent, *a.* [L. *esuriens* (-*ent*-), ppr. of *esurire,* desire to eat, < *edere,* eat.] Hungry; greedy.—**e·su·ri·ence, e·su·ri·en·cy,** *n.*—**e·su·ri·ent·ly,** *adv.*

e·ta, ā′ta, ē′ta, *n.* [Gr. *eta;* akin to Heb. *hēth.*] The seventh letter of the Greek alphabet, the symbols for which are H, η; the sound represented by this letter.

é·ta·gère, ā·tä·zheR′, *n.* [Fr., < *étage,* story, = E. *stage.*] An ornamental cabinet of open shelves suitable for bric-à-brac.

et·a·mine, et′a·mēn″, *n.* [Fr. *étamine,* O.Fr. *estamine,* < L. *stamen,* warp, thread.] A lightweight fabric of wool, cotton, or silk, with an open, canvaslike weave.

é·tape, ā·tap′, *Fr.* ā·täp′, *n.* [Fr.; akin to E. *staple.*] A place at which troops halt for the night; the distance marched by them during the day. *Archaic,* an allowance of provisions for troops on the march.

et·cet·er·a, et·set′ėr·a, et·se′tra, *n.* pl. **et·cet·er·as.** [L.] A number of other things or persons unspecified; *pl.* extras or additional items.—**et cet·er·a,** and others; and the rest; and so forth. Abbr. *etc.*

etch, ech, *v.t.* [D. *etsen,* < G. *ätzen,* corrode, etch; akin to E. *eat.*] To cut, bite, or corrode with an acid; engrave by the corrosive action of an acid so as to form a design or picture in furrows which when charged with ink will give an impression on paper; to produce or copy by this method, as on copper; to draw clearly, as a person's likeness; to impress firmly on the mind.— *v.i.* To practice etching.—*n.* A chemical used for etching.—**etch·er,** *n.*

etch·ing, ech′ing, *n.* The process or art of one who etches; a process for forming a design or drawing on a metal plate from which an ink impression on paper can be taken; the design or picture produced.

e·ter·nal, i·tėr′nal, *a.* [Fr. *éternel;* L. *aeternus, aeviternus,* < *aevum,* an age, and a suffix -*ternus.*] Having no beginning or end of existence; everlasting; endless; continued without interruption; ceaseless; perpetual.—**the E·ter·nal,** *n.* An appellation for God.—**e·ter·nal·ly,** *adv.*—**e·ter·nal·i·ty,** e·tėr·nal′i·tē, **e·ter·nal·ness,** i″tėr·nal′i·tē, *n.*

e·terne, i·tėrn′, *a.* [O.Fr. *eterne,* < L. *aeternus,* for *aeviternus,* < *aevum,* eternity, age, akin to Gr. *aiōn*, E. *æon*.] *Archaic*, eternal or everlasting.

e·ter·ni·ty, i·tẽr´ni·tē, *n*. pl. **e·ter·ni·-ties**. The condition or quality of being eternal; being without beginning or end; endless past time or endless future time; the state or condition which begins at death; immortality.

e·ter·nize, i·tẽr´nīz, *v.t.*—*eternized, eternizing*. [Fr. *éterniser*.] To make eternal or endless; to perpetuate; to make forever famous; to immortalize.—**e·ter·ni·za·tion**, i·tẽr´ni·zā´shan, *n*.

e·te·sian, i·tē´zhan, *a*. [L. *etesius*, < Gr. *etēsios*, annual, < *etos*, a year.] (*Often cap*.) recurring every year: applied to the periodical winds in the Mediterranean.

eth, eTH, *n*. The Anglo-Saxon letter ð, capital form Ð, equivalent to the English *th*; in modern phonetic systems, a symbol representing the sound of *th* in *then*. Also *edh*.

eth·ane, eth´ān, *n*. [< *ether*.] *Chem*. an odorless, colorless, flammable gas derived from natural gas, used in organic synthesis and as a refrigerant or fuel.

eth·a·nol, eth´a·nōl″, eth´a·nạl″, eth´a·-nol″, *n*. *Chem*. ethyl alcohol.

eth·ene, eth´ēn, *n*. *Chem*. ethylene.

e·ther, ē´thẽr, *n*. [L. *aether*, < Gr. *aithēr*, upper air, sky, akin to *aithein*, kindle, light up, Skt. *idh*-, kindle.] *Chem*. a highly volatile and inflammable colorless liquid, $(C_2H_5)_2O$, used mainly as an anesthetic and a solvent, the most common forms of which are diethyl ether and ethyl ether. The medium formerly believed to fill the upper regions of space; the clear sky; the heavens; the upper regions of space.

e·the·re·al, i·thẽr´ē·al, *a*. Delicate and airy; as, an *ethereal* beauty; heavenly; celestial; pertaining to the atmosphere in space, as opposed to the earth. *Chem*. containing or relating to ether. Also **e·ther·ic**.—**e·the·re·al·i·ty**, i·thẽr´ē·al´i·tē, *n*.—**e·the·re·al·ly**, *adv*.—**e·the·re·al·ness**, *n*.

e·the·re·al·ize, i·thẽr´ē·a·līz″, *v.t.*—*etherealized, etherealizing*. To render spiritlike or ethereal. Also **e·the·ri·al·ize**.—**e·the·re·al·i·za·tion**, i·thẽr´ē·al·i·zā´shan, *n*.

e·ther·i·fy, i·thẽr´i·fī″, ē´thẽr·i·fī″, *v.t.*—*etherified, etherifying*. To convert into ether.—**e·ther·i·fi·ca·tion**, i·thẽr´i·fi·cā´shan, *n*.

e·ther·ize, ē´thẽ·rīz″, *v.t.*—*etherized, etherizing*. To subject to the influence of ether.—**e·ther·i·za·tion**, *n*.

eth·ic, eth´ik, *a*. [L. *ethicus*, < Gr. *ēthicos*, < *ēthos*, custom, disposition, character.] Pertaining to morals; ethical.—*n*. A system or philosophy of conduct and principles practiced by a person or group; as, the Christian *Ethic*, the personal *ethic*; ethics.—**eth·i·cal**, eth´i·kal, *a*. Pertaining to morals or the principles of morality; pertaining to right and wrong in conduct; in accordance with the rules for right conduct or practice; pertaining to drugs that have been proven by clinical trial and are available to the public only through a physician's prescription.—**eth·i·cal·ly**, *adv*.—**eth·i·cal·ness**, *n*.—**eth·i·cize**, eth´i·sīz″, *v.t.*—*ethicized, ethicizing*. To make ethical; regard or treat as ethical.

eth·ics, eth´iks, *n. pl. but sing. in constr*. The principles of morality, or the field of study of morals or right conduct.—*n. pl., sing. or pl. in constr*. A particular ethical system; the rules of conduct recognized in respect to a particular class of human actions; as, medical *ethics*; moral principles, as of an individual.

E·thi·o·pi·an, ē″thē·ō´pē·an, *a*. [L. *Aethiops*, < Gr. *Aithiops*.] Pertaining to Ethiopia, a region of Africa south of Egypt; *zoogeog*. belonging to Africa south

of the tropic of Cancer.—*n*. A native of Ethiopia.

E·thi·op·ic, ē″thē·op´ik, ē″thē·ō´pik, *a*. Relating to Ethiopia; of or pertaining to the Semitic language of ancient Ethiopia.—*n*. The literary and ecclesiastical language of ancient Ethiopia.

eth·moid, eth´moid, *a*. [Gr. *ēthmoeidēs*, < *ēthmos*, strainer, sieve, and *eidos*, form.] *Anat*. noting or pertaining to a bone of the skull situated at the root of the nose, and containing numerous perforations for the filaments of the olfactory nerve. Also **eth·moi·dal**.—*n*. The ethmoid bone.

eth·narch, eth´närk, *n*. [Gr. *ethnarchēs*, < *ethnos*, race, nation, and *archein*, lead, rule.] The sovereign of a nation or a province.—**eth·nar·chy**, *n. pl*. **eth·nar·chies**. [Gr. *ethnarchia*.] The government or jurisdiction of an ethnarch.

eth·nic, eth´nik, *a*. [L.L. *ethnicus*, < Gr. *ethnicos*, national, gentile, heathen, *ethnos*, race, nation.] Of, pertaining to, or peculiar to a people, esp. to those groups sharing a common language or set of customs or traits; pertaining to such peoples, their origin, characteristics, and classification; pertaining to nations not Jewish or Christian; coming from or belonging to the distinctive, cultural, or aesthetic traditions of a particular country or people; as, *ethnic* music. Also **eth·ni·cal**.—**eth·ni·cal·ly**, *adv*.

eth·no·cen·tric, eth″nō·sen´trik, *a*. *Sociol*. pertaining to the belief that one's own culture is superior to that of other ethnic groups; pertaining to the tendency to compare foreign cultures unfavorably with one's own.—**eth·no·cen·tric·al·ly**, *adv*.—**eth·no·cen·tric·i·ty**, eth″nō·sen·tris´i·tē, *n*.—**eth·no·cen·trism**, *n*.

eth·nog·e·ny, eth·noj´e·nē, *n*. A branch of ethnology which studies the origin of races and ethnic groups.—**eth·no·gen·ic**, eth″-nō·jen´ik, *a*.—**eth·nog·e·nist**, *n*.

eth·nog·ra·phy, eth·nog´ra·fē, *n*. A branch of anthropology that deals with the scientific description and classification of various cultures.—**eth·nog·ra·pher**, *n*.—**eth·no·graph·ic**, **eth·no·graph·i·cal**, eth″no·graf´ik, *a*.—**eth·no·graph·i·cal·ly**, *adv*.

eth·nol·o·gy, eth·nol´o·jē, *n*. A branch of anthropology that deals with the various groups of mankind, their origin, distinctive characteristics, customs, and distribution.

e·thol·o·gy, ē·thol´o·jē, ē·thol´o·jē, *n*. [Gr. *ethos* or *ēthos*, manners, morals, and *logos*, discourse.] The science of ethics or human character formation; the study of animal behavior.—**eth·o·log·i·cal**, eth″o·-loj´i·kal, *a*.

e·thos, ē´thos, eth´os, *n*. [Gr. *ēthos*.] The characteristic spirit, as of a people; character or disposition; *liter*. the moral factor which influences a man's actions.

eth·yl, eth´il, *n*. [*Ether*, and Gr. *hyle*, matter.] *Chem*. a univalent hydrocarbon radical. (*Cap*.) tetraethyl lead, or motor fuel to which it has been added as an anti-knock compound. (Trademark.)—**e·thyl·ic**, e·thil´ik, *a*.

eth·yl ac·e·tate, *n*. *Chem*. a colorless, flammable, fragrant liquid, used as a paint or lacquer solvent, and in perfumes and organic syntheses.

eth·yl al·co·hol, *n*. *Chem*. grain alcohol; a colorless, limpid, volatile liquid, used as a solvent, an intermediate in organic synthesis, or in beverages.

eth·yl·ate, eth´i·lāt″, *v.t.*—*ethylated, ethylating*. *Chem*. to introduce one or more ethyl radicals into a compound.—**eth·yl·a·tion**, *n*.

eth·yl cel·lu·lose, *n*. *Chem*. an ethyl ether of cellulose; a white, granular, thermoplastic solid which can be made with slightly varying chemical composition and

properties: used as an adhesive, a protective coating, or a toughening agent for plastics.

eth·yl·ene, eth´i·lēn″, *n*. *Chem*. a sweet-smelling, colorless gas derived from petroleum and natural gas, used in the manufacture of plastics and certain types of rubber, in the coloration of fruits, and in increasing the rate of seedling and plant growth; a plant hormone.

eth·yl·ene gly·col, *n*. *Chem*. ethylene alcohol, CH_2OHCH_2OH, the simplest of the glycol group, a clear, colorless, syrupy liquid with a sweet taste: used in automobile radiator antifreeze and brake fluid, and in organic synthesis and the manufacture of plastics.

eth·yl e·ther, *n*. See *ether*.

e·ti·o·late, ē´tē·o·lāt″, *v.t., v.i.*—*etiolated, etiolating*. [Fr. *étioler*, blanch: cf. *éteule*, stubble, < L. *stipula*, stalk, straw.] To make or become white through loss of normal color, as from lack of sunlight; blanch.—**e·ti·o·la·tion**, ē″tē·ō·lā´shan, *n*.

e·ti·ol·o·gy, ē″tē·ol´o·jē, *n*. The study of causation in the fields of pathology, biology, philosophy, and physics.—**e·ti·o·lo·gist**, *n*.—**e·ti·o·log·i·cal**, ē″tē·o·loj´i·kal, *a*.—**e·ti·o·log·i·cal·ly**, *adv*.

et·i·quette, et´i·kit, et´i·ket″, *n*. [Fr. *étiquette*, O.Fr. *estiquette*, label, ticket, billet, < *estiquier*, fix, stick; < Teut., and akin to E. *stick*.] Conventional requirements as to social behavior; proprieties of conduct as established in any class or community or for any occasion; prescribed or accepted code of usage in matters of ceremony, as at a court, in official or other formal observances, or in polite society generally.

E·ton jack·et, ēt´on jak´it, *n*. A boy's short jacket reaching only to the waistline, as those worn by students at Eton College, England; a similar short jacket worn by women.—**E·ton col·lar**, a large stiff collar worn over an Eton jacket.

E·trus·can, i·trus´kan, *a*. Relating to Etruria, an ancient country in west central Italy; of or relating to the language or art of Etruria.—*n*. A native of ancient Etruria. Also **E·tru·ri·an**, i·trụr´ē·an.

é·tude, ā´tōd, ā´tūd, ā·tōd´, ā·tūd´, *Fr.* ā·tyd´, *n*. [Fr.] *Mus*. a composition intended mainly for the practice of some point of technique; a study.

e·tui, ā·twē´, et´wē, *n*. [Fr.] A pocket case for small articles, such as needles and pins or toilet articles. Also **e·twee**.

et·y·mol·o·gize, et″i·mol´o·jīz″, *v.i.*—*etymologized, etymologizing*. To search into the origin of words.—*v.t*. To trace the etymology of; to give the etymology of.

et·y·mol·o·gy, et″i·mol´o·jē, *n. pl*. **et·y·mol·o·gies**. [L. *etymologia*, < Gr. *etymologia*, < *etymon* (ETYMON) and *legein*, speak.] Explanation of the origin and linguistic changes of a particular word; the derivation of a word; the branch of philology concerned with the origin and history of words.—**et·y·mo·log·ic**, **et·y·mo·log·i·cal**, et″i·mo·loj´ik, *a*.—**et·y·mo·log·i·cal·ly**, *adv*.—**et·y·mol·o·gist**, *n*.

et·y·mon, et´i·mon″, *n. pl*. **et·y·mons**, **et·y·ma**, et´i·ma. [L. *etymon*, < Gr. *etymon*, the original sense, form, or element of a word, prop. neut. of *etymos*, true, real.] A primary word or root from which derivatives are formed; the primitive form of a word.

eu·caine, ū·kān´, *n*. A white, odorless, crystalline powder, $C_{15}H_{21}NO_2$, used as a local anesthetic.

eu·ca·lyp·tol, ū″ka·lip´tōl, ū″ka·lip´tạl, ū″ka·lip´tol, *n*. Cineole. Also **eu·ca·lyp·tole**.

eu·ca·lyp·tus, ū″ka·lip´tus, *n. pl*. **eu·ca·lyp·ti**, eu·ca·lyp·tus·es. [N.L. < Gr. *eu-*,

a- fat, fāte, fär, fâre, fạll; e- met, mē, mēre, hẽr; i- pin, pīne; o- not, nōte, mōve; u- tub, cūbe, bụll; oi- oil; ou- pound.

well, and *calyptos*, covered, < *calyptein*, cover (with allusion to the cap covering the buds).] Any member of the genus *Eucalyptus*, including many tall, aromatic, evergreen trees, native to Australia and extensively cultivated in California, Florida, and the Mediterranean, which yield a valuable timber, and bear leaves containing an oil used in medicine. Also **eu·ca·lypt.**

Eu·cha·rist, ū′ka·rist, *n.* [Gr. *eucharistia*, thanksgiving, the Lord's Supper; *eucharistos*, grateful.] The Christian sacrament of the Lord's Supper; the Holy Communion; the consecrated elements of bread and wine; (*l.c.*) thanksgiving.— **Eu·cha·ris·tic, Eu·cha·ris·ti·cal,** *a.*

eu·chre, ū′kėr, *n.* [Origin uncertain.] A game of cards played by two, three, or four persons, usu. with the 32 highest cards in the pack; an instance of euchring or being euchred.—*v.t.*—*euchred, euchring.* To get the better of in a hand at euchre, by the opponent's failure to win three tricks after having made the trump; *colloq.* to outwit or get the better of, as by scheming.

eu·chro·ma·tin, ū·krō′ma·tin, *n. Genetics,* chromosome material containing the genetically active portion of chromatin.— **eu·chro·mat·ic,** *a.*

eu·chro·mo·some, ū·krō′mo·sōm″, *n. Genetics,* any chromosome which is not a sex chromosome. Also *autosome.*

eu·clase, ū′klās, *n.* [Gr. *eu*, and *klaō*, to break.] A mineral, beryllium aluminum silicate, pale green, blue, or yellow in color and very brittle.

Eu·clid·e·an, Eu·clid·i·an, ū·klid′ē·an, *a.* [From the Greek geometrician *Euclid*, of about 280 B.C.] Of or pertaining to Euclid, his geometry, or the geometry based on his or similar postulates.

eu·de·mon·ism, eu·dae·mon·ism, ū·dē′mo·niz″um, *n.* [Gr. *eudaimōn*, happy.] *Ethics,* a doctrine which holds that human happiness is a moral obligation achieved from right action by reason.—**eu·de·mon·ist,** *n.*—**eu·de·mon·ic,** ū″di·mon′ik, *a.*

eu·di·om·e·ter, ū″dē·om′i·tėr, *n.* [Gr. *eudios*, fine, clear, as weather.] A device used in the analysis and volumetric measurement of gases.—**eu·di·o·met·ric, eu·di·o·met·ri·cal,** ū″dē·o·me′trik, *a.*—**eu·di·om·e·try,** ū″dē·om′i·trē, *n.* The measurement and analysis of gases with the eudiometer.

eu·gen·ic, ū·jen′ik, *a.* [Gr. *eu*-, well, and *gen*, bear, produce.] Pertaining to or bringing about improvement in the type of offspring produced.—**eu·gen·i·cist,** *n.* One versed in eugenics; an advocate of eugenic measures. Also **eu·ge·nist,** ū′je·nist.

eu·gen·ics, ū·jen′iks, *n. pl. but sing. in constr.* The science of improving the qualities of the human species; the science of bringing about an improved type of offspring of the human species.

eu·ge·nol, ū′je·nōl″, ū′je·nal″, ū′je·nol″, *n.* [N.L. *Eugenia*, genus of tropical plants.] *Chem.* a colorless, aromatic, oily compound, $C_{10}H_{12}O_2$, contained in clove oil and used chiefly in perfumes and as a flavoring agent.

eu·gle·na, ū·glē′na, *n.* Any of various microscopic green protozoa with a single flagellum and a red eyespot, which have both animal and plant traits and are used in biological research.—**eu·gle·noid,** *a.*

eu·gle·noid move·ment, *n.* The wriggling movement characteristic of euglena and various other protozoa, achieved by contraction of one body part and dilation of another.

eu·he·mer·ism, ū·hē′me·riz″um, ū·hem′e·riz″um, *n.* [From *Euhemerus,* 4th century B.C. Greek writer.] The method or system of interpretation which holds that myths are based upon traditional accounts of actual history.—**eu·he·mer·ist,** *n.*—**eu·he·mer·is·tic,** *a.*—**eu·he·mer·is·ti·cal·ly,** *adv.*—**eu·he·mer·ize,** *v.t.*—*euhemerized, euhemerizing.*

eu·la·chon, ū′la·kon″, *n. pl.* **eu·la·chon, eu·la·chons.** The candlefish, one of the smelt family, found on the north Pacific coast. Also *Canadian,* **oo·li·chan.**

eu·la·mel·li·branch, ū″la·mel′i·brank, *n.* Any bivalve mollusk, as the oyster, clam, and fresh-water mussel, belonging to the *Eulamellibranchia* order.

eu·lo·gi·um, ū·lō′jē·um, *n. pl.* **eu·lo·gi·a, eu·lo·gi·ums.** Any eulogy.

eu·lo·gize, ū′lo·jīz″, *v.t.*—*eulogized, eulogizing.* To speak or write in commendation of another; to extol in speech or writing; to praise.—**eu·lo·gi·za·tion,** *n.*—**eu·lo·giz·er,** *n.*—**eu·lo·gist,** *n.*

eu·lo·gy, ū′lo·jē, *n. pl.* **eu·lo·gies.** [Gr. *eulogia*—*eu*-, well, and *logos,* speech, < *lego,* to speak.] Praise; a speech or writing in commendation of a living or dead person citing his valuable qualities or services.— **eu·lo·gis·tic,** *a.*—**eu·lo·gis·ti·cal·ly,** *adv.*

eu·nuch, ū′nuk, *n.* [L. *eunuchus,* < Gr. *eunouchos,* chamber attendant, < *eune,* bed, and *echein,* have, hold, keep.] A castrated male employed in a harem or as a court chamberlain; a male deprived of the testes.

eu·on·y·mus, ū·on′i·mus, *n.* Any of several shrubs, vines, or small trees of the genus *Euonymous,* usu. found in northern temperate areas. Also **e·von·y·mus.**

eu·pa·to·ri·um, ū″pa·tōr′ē·um, ū″pa·tar′ē·um, *n.* [N.L. < Gr. *eupatorion;* named from Mithridates *Eupator,* king of Pontus 120?–63 B.C.] Any plant of the genus *Eupatorium,* as the thoroughwort or joe-pye weed.

eu·pat·rid, ū·pa′trid, ū′pa·trid, *n. pl.* **eu·pat·ri·dae,** ū·pa′tri·dē. [Gr. *eupatrides,* < *eu*-, good, and *patēr,* father.] One of the hereditary aristocrats of ancient Athens and other states of Greece, who were exclusively vested with the powers of making and administering the law; an aristocrat or patrician.

eu·pep·sia, ū·pep′sha, ū·pep′sē·a, *n.* [Gr. *eupepsia*—*eu*-, and *pepsis,* digestion, < *peptō,* to digest.] Good digestion. Also **eu·pep·sy.** —**eu·pep·tic,** ū·pep′tik, *a.* Having good digestion; cheerful.

eu·phe·mism, ū′fe·miz″um, *n.* [Gr. *euphēmismos*—*eu*-, well, and *phemi,* to speak.] The substitution of an agreeable or inoffensive word or phrase for one which may be indelicate or unpleasant; the term so substituted.—**eu·phe·mist,** *n.*—**eu·phe·mis·tic, eu·phe·mis·ti·cal,** *a.*—**eu·phe·mis·ti·cal·ly,** *adv.*

eu·phe·mize, ū′fe·mīz″, *v.t.*—*euphemized, euphemizing.* To express by means of a euphemism.—**eu·phe·miz·er,** *n.*

eu·pho·ni·ous, ū·fō′nē·us, *a.* Agreeable to the ear; characterized by euphony.— **eu·pho·ni·ous·ly,** *adv.*—**eu·pho·ni·ous·ness,** *n.*

eu·pho·ni·um, ū·fō′nē·um, *n.* A musical instrument resembling the baritone tuba, but having a higher range and mellower tone.

eu·pho·nize, ū′fo·nīz″, *v.t.*—*euphonized, euphonizing.* To make euphonious.

eu·pho·ny, ū′fo·nē, *n.* [L.L. *euphonia,* < Gr. *phonia,* < *euphonos,* well-sounding, < *eu*- and *phone,* sound, voice.] Agreeableness of sound; pleasing effect to the ear, as of uttered speech. *Phon.* a tendency to modify pronunciation and alter the form of words to achieve greater ease in speaking.— **eu·phon·ic, eu·phon·i·cal,** ū·fon′ik, *a.* Of, pertaining to, or characterized by euphony.—**eu·phon·i·cal·ly,** *adv.*

eu·phor·bi·a, ū·far′bē·a, *n.* [N.L. for L. *euphorbea,* an African plant; named from *Euphorbus,* a Greek physician.] Any plant of the genus *Euphorbia,* consisting mostly of herbs and shrubs with an acrid milky juice having medicinal or poisonous properties; a spurge.—**eu·phor·bi·a·ceous,** ū·far″bē·ā′shus, *a.* Belonging to the *Euphorbiaceae,* or spurge family of plants, which includes the spurges, the rubber tree, castor oil, and cassava plants.

eu·pho·ri·a, ū·fōr′ē·a, ū·far′ē·a, *n.* [Gr. *eu*-, well, *phoreo,* I possess.] A feeling of well-being not always justified by physical health; a mood of elation.

eu·pho·tic, ū·fō′tik, *a. Biol.* pertaining to or constituting that portion of a body of water which has sufficient light to allow photosynthesis.

eu·phu·ism, ū′fū·iz″um, *n.* An ornate style of writing marked by the frequent use of alliteration, antitheses, and mythological similes, in imitation of the writings of the Elizabethan, John Lyly, and his character, *Euphues;* any ornate style of writing or speaking; an instance of such style or language.—**eu·phu·ist,** *n.*—**eu·phu·is·tic,** *a.*—**eu·phu·is·ti·cal·ly,** *adv.*

eu·plas·tic, ū·plas′tik, *a.* [Gr. *euplastos,* easy to mold, < *eu*-, and *plassein,* form, mold.] *Physiol.* capable of being transformed into organized tissue.

eup·ne·a, eup·noe·a, ūp·nē′a, *n.* [Gr. *eu*-, well, *pneō,* I breathe.] Easy, natural breathing.

Eur·a·sian, ū·rā′zhan, ū·rā′shan, *a.* Of or pertaining to Europe and Asia taken together; of mixed European and Asiatic descent.—*n.* A person of mixed European and Asiatic descent.

Eur·at·om, ū·rat′om, *n.* [From *Eur(opean) Atom(ic) (Energy) (Community)*.] An organization, created March 25, 1957, of Belgium, France, Italy, Luxembourg, the Netherlands, and West Germany, which seeks to cooperate in developing and exploiting nuclear energy for peaceful uses.

eu·re·ka, ū·rē′ka, *interj.* [Gr. *(h)eurēka,* I have found, perf. ind. act. of *(h)euriskō,* to find.] The exclamation of Archimedes, when, after long study, he discovered a method of detecting the amount of alloy in King Hiero's crown; an expression of triumph at a discovery or supposed discovery; motto of the state of California.

eu·rhyth·mics, eu·ryth·mics, ū·riTH′miks, *n. pl., sing. or pl. in constr.* [Gr. *eurythmos,* in good rhythm.] The art of gracefully responsive motions of the body inspired through physical sensibility to music; musical interpretation through body movement.—**eu·rhyth·mic, eu·ryth·mic,** *a.*

eu·rhyth·my, eu·ryth·my, ū·riTH′mē, *n.* Rhythmical movement or order; harmonious proportion.

eu·ri·pus, ū·rī′pus, *n. pl.* **eu·ri·pi,** ū·rī′pī. [L. < Gr. *euripos,* < *eu*- and *ripe,* impetus, rush.] A strait where the tide flows with violent and dangerous fluctuation; (*cap.*) the strait between the islands Euboea and Boeotia in Greece.

Eu·ro·pe·an, ūr″o·pē′an, *a.* Of or pertaining to Europe, its inhabitants, or its culture.—*n.* A native or inhabitant of Europe; a person of European descent.— **Eu·ro·pe·an·ism,** *n.* European characteristics, ideas, methods, sympathies; a European trait or practice.—**Eu·ro·pe·an·ize,** *v.t.*—*Europeanized, Europeanizing.* To cause to become European, as in ideas, manners, or characteristics.—**Eu·ro·pe·an·i·za·tion,** *n.*

Eu·ro·pe·an plan, *n.* A hotel policy of charging a fixed rate for room and service, meals being extra.

eu·ro·pi·um, ū·rō′pē·um, *n. Chem.* the most reactive element of the rare-earth series, used in oxide form as a neutron absorber in nuclear reactions and in color television tubes to obtain truer reds and more brightness. Sym. Eu, at. no. 63.

eu·ry·ha·line, ūr″*i*·hā′lin, ūr″*i*·hā′lin, ūr″*i*·hal′in, ūr″*i*·hal′ĭn, *a. Ecol.* able to exist in waters having great variations in salinity.

eu·ry·therm, ūr′*i*·thèrm″, *n.* An organism having the ability to adjust physically to widely varying degrees of heat and cold.—**eu·ry·ther·mal, eu·ry·ther·mic, eu·ry·ther·mous,** *a.*

eu·ry·top·ic, ūr″*i*·top′ik, *a.* Of an organism, having an exceptional ability to adjust to variations in environmental conditions.

Eu·sta·chian tube, ū·stā′shan tōb, ū·stā′shan tūb′, ū·stā′kē·an tōb, ū·stā′kē·an tūb′, *n.* [Named after Bartolommeo *Eustachio*, an Italian anatomist.] The tube between the middle ear, or tympanum, and the pharynx. Also **au·di·to·ry ca·nal.**

eu·sta·cy, ū′sta·sē, *n. pl.* **eu·sta·cies.** *Geol.* a worldwide alteration in the level of the sea, usu. due to repositioning of continental glaciers.—**eu·stat·ic**, ū·stat′ik, *a.*

eu·tec·tic, ū·tek′tik, *a.* [Gr. *eutēktos*, easily melted, < *eu-* and *tēkein*, melt.] Of greatest fusibility: said of an alloy or solid solution with a melting point usu. lower than that of any other alloy or mixture composed of the same ingredients; of or pertaining to such an alloy or solution, or to its attributes. —*n.*—**eu·tec·toid**, ū·tek′toid, *a., n.*

eu·tha·na·sia, ū″tha·nā′zha, ū″tha·nā′zhē·a, ū″tha·nā′zē·a, *n.* [Gr. *eu-*, well, and *thanatos*, death.] A painless putting to death of persons having an incurable disease; an easy death. Also **mer·cy kill·ing.**

eu·then·ics, ū·then′iks, *n. pl. but sing. in constr.* [Gr. *euthēnia*, plenty, prosperity, well-being.] The science of improving the physical and intellectual capacities of man by control and improvement of living conditions.

eu·the·ri·an, ū·thēr′ē·an, *a.* Of or referring to a large group, *Eutheria*, composed of the placental mammals.—*n.*

eu·tro·phy, ū′tro·fē, *n.* [Gr. *eutrophia*, < *eu-* and *trephein*, nourish.] *Med.* healthful, normal nutrition. *Ecol.* the condition of a lake rich in nutrient plant and animal life and sometimes causing pollution and decay. —**eu·troph·ic**, ū·trof′ik, *a.*

eux·e·nite, ūk′se·nīt″, *n.* [Gr. *euxeuos*, hospitable.] A rare mineral of metallic, brownish cast, composed of such valuable elements as calcium, cerium, columbium, germanium, titanium, uranium, and yttrium.

e·vac·u·ant, i·vak′ū·ant, *a.* Evacuating; *med.* promoting evacuation, esp. from the bowels; diuretic.—*n. Med.* an evacuant medicine or agent.

e·vac·u·ate, i·vak′ū·āt″, *v.t.—evacuated, evacuating.* [L. *evacuatus*, pp. of *evacuare*, < *e-*, out of, and *vacuus*, empty, E. *vacuous.*] To make empty, or expel the contents of; as, to *evacuate* the stomach by an emetic; to deprive of something essential; to leave empty; to vacate; to withdraw from or quit, as an occupied town or fort; to discharge or eject, as through the excretory passages, esp. from the bowels; to remove from a place, as troops, wounded soldiers, or inhabitants.—*v.i.* To leave or withdraw from a place, as in an emergency.— **e·vac·u·a·tive**, *a.—***e·vac·u·a·tor**, *n.—* **e·vac·u·a·tor·y**, *a.*

e·vac·u·a·tion, i·vak″ū·ā′shan, *n.* [L.L. *evacuatio*(*n-*).] The act or process of evacuating, or the condition of being evacuated; a making empty of contents; expulsion, as of contents; discharge, as of waste matter through the excretory passages, esp. from the bowels; that which is

evacuated or discharged; *milit.* the withdrawal or removal of troops, wounded soldiers, or equipment, as from a battle area.

e·vac·u·ee, i·vak′ū·ē″, i·vak″ū·ē′, *n.* One who is removed, for safety or protection, from a disaster area or an area threatened by danger.

e·vade, i·vād′, *v.t.—evaded, evading.* [L. *evado—e-*, and *vado*, to go, as in *invade, pervade;* akin to E. *wade.*] To avoid, escape from, or elude in any way, as by dexterity, artifice, sophistry, address, or ingenuity; to elude doing; to shun replying directly, as to a question; to escape the grasp or comprehension of; to baffle or foil.—*v.i.* To escape; to avoid a question.—**e·vad·a·ble, e·vad·i·ble**, *a.* Capable of being evaded.— **e·vad·er**, *n.—***e·vad·ing·ly**, *adv.*

e·vag·i·nate, i·vaj′i·nāt″, *v.t.—evaginated, evaginating.* [L. *evaginatus*, pp. of *evaginare*, < *e-*, out of, and *vagina*, sheath.] To turn inside out or cause to protrude by eversion, as a tubular organ.—**e·vag·i·na·tion**, *n.*

e·val·u·ate, i·val′ū·āt″, *v.t.—evaluated, evaluating.* [Fr. *évaluer*, O.Fr. *esvaluer*, < *es-* (< L. *ex*, out of) and *value*, E. *value.*] To ascertain the value of; to appraise carefully; *math.* to ascertain the numerical value of.—**e·val·u·a·ble**, i·val′ū·a·bl, *a.* —**e·val·u·a·tion**, *n.—***e·val·u·a·tive**, *a.—* **e·val·u·a·tor**, *n.*

ev·a·nesce, ev″a·nes′, ev′a·nes″, *v.i.— evanesced, evanescing.* [L. *evanesco—e-*, and *vanesco*, to vanish, < *vanus*, vain, empty.] To vanish; to disappear slowly; to be dissipated, as vapor.

ev·a·nes·cent, ev″a·nes′ent, *a.* Vanishing; fleeting; passing away; liable to disappear or end; almost imperceptible.—**ev·a·nes·cent·ly**, *adv.—***ev·a·nes·cence**, *n.*

e·van·gel, i·van′jel, *n.* [L. *evangelium*, the gospel; Gr. *euangelion*, good tidings, the gospel—*eu*, well, good, and *angellō*, to announce.] The gospel; (*usu. cap.*) one of the gospels or four New Testament books under the names of Matthew, Mark, Luke, and John. Good tidings or news. An evangelist.

e·van·gel·i·cal, ē″van·jel′i·kal, ev″an·jel′i·kal, *a.* [L.L. *evangelicus*, < Gr. *euangelikos.*] Of or pertaining to the gospel or the four Gospels; pertaining to the Protestant churches which hold to the doctrines of Christ's teachings, salvation by faith and personal conversion, and the superiority of preaching over ritual; spiritually minded; zealous for practical Christian living; seeking the conversion of sinners; evangelistic.—*n.* An adherent of evangelical doctrines; a member of an evangelical church or party. Also **e·van·gel·ic.—e·van·gel·i·cal·ism**, *n.* Evangelical doctrines or principles; adherence to them, or to an evangelical church or party. Also **e·van·gel·i·cism.—e·van·gel·i·cal·ly**, *adv.—***e·van·gel·i·cal·ness**, *n.*

e·van·ge·lism, i·van′je·liz″um, *n.* The fervent, zealous preaching or promulgation of the gospel; the work of an evangelist; evangelicalism; zeal.—**e·van·ge·lis·tic**, *a.* —**e·van·ge·lis·ti·cal·ly**, *adv.*

e·van·ge·list, i·van′je·list, *n.* [L.L. *evangelista*, < Gr. *euangelistēs*, < *euangelizesthai*, E. *evangelize.*] (*Often cap.*) any of the gospel writers, Matthew, Mark, Luke, or John. A preacher of the gospel, as one who brings it to a heathen nation; an occasional or itinerant preacher; a revivalist; a patriarch in the Mormon Church.

e·van·ge·lize, i·van′je·liz, *v.t.—evangelized, evangelizing.* To instruct in the gospel; to preach the gospel to and convert.—*v.i.* —To preach the gospel.—**e·van·ge·li·za·tion**, *n.—***e·van·ge·liz·er**, *n.*

e·van·ish, i·van′ish, *v.i. Poet.* to vanish; to disappear.—**e·van·ish·ment**, *n.*

e·vap·o·rate, i·vap′o·rāt″, *v.i.—evaporated, evaporating.* [L. *evaporo, evaporatum—e-*, out, and *vapor*, vapor.] To be changed to vapor; to pass off in vapor; to disappear; to produce moisture.—*v.t.* To convert or resolve, as into vapor; to cause to evaporate; to take out of, as the moisture or vapor from fruit; to cause to disappear.—**e·vap·o·ra·ble**, i·vap′ér·a·bl, *a.* Capable of being converted into vapor or of being dissipated by evaporation.

e·vap·o·rat·ed milk, *n.* Unsweetened, concentrated milk reduced by evaporation to one half or less of its bulk and packaged in cans.

e·vap·o·ra·tion, i·vap″o·ra′shan, *n.* The act or process of evaporating; the conversion of a liquid by heat into vapor or steam. —**e·vap·o·ra·tive**, i·vap′o·rā″tiv, i·vap′er·a·tiv, *a.—***e·vap·o·ra·tive·ly**, *adv.—* **e·vap·o·ra·tor**, *n.*

e·vap·o·rim·e·ter, i·vap″o·rim′i·tèr, *n.* An instrument for ascertaining the quantity of a fluid evaporated in a given time; an atmometer. Also **e·vap·o·rom·e·ter, e·vap·o·ra·tion gauge.**

e·vap·o·tran·spi·ra·tion, i·vap″ō·tran″spi·rā′shan, *n.* The process by which the earth's surface or soil loses moisture by evaporation of water and by transpiration from plants; the volume of water lost in this process.

e·va·sion, i·vā′zhan, *n.* [L.L. *evasio* (*n-*), < L. *evadere.*] The act of evading, avoiding, shirking, or escaping; the means used to evade, avoid, or shirk; a subterfuge; an excuse; an equivocation; the avoiding of an argument, accusation, or interrogation.

e·va·sive, i·vā′siv, *a.* Tending to avoid or shirk; characterized by evasion; equivocating.—**e·va·sive·ly**, *adv.—***e·va·sive·ness**, *n.*

eve, ēv, *n.* [Short for *even, evening.*] The day or the latter part of the day before a church festival or other event; the period just preceding some event; as, on the *eve* of a revolution; the evening.

e·vec·tion, i·vek′shan, *n.* [L. *evectio*(*n-*), < *evehere*, carry forth or up,—*e-*, out of, and *vehere*, carry.] *Astron.* a periodical variance of the moon's orbit caused by the attraction of the sun.—**e·vec·tion·al**, *a.*

e·ven, ē′ven, *a.* [O.E. *efen* = D. *even* = G. *eben* = Icel. *jafn* = Goth. *ibns*, even.] Level or flat, as ground; free from inequalities or smooth, as a surface; free from variations or fluctuations, as motion; uniform in character, as color; equable or unruffled, as temperament; equitable, impartial, or fair, as actions; on the same level, as *even* with the ground; in the same plane or line; parallel, as a course; accordant or exactly adjusted, as one thing with another; in a state of equilibrium, as a balance; leaving no balance of debt on either side, as accounts; equal in measure or quantity; of a number, exactly divisible by two: opposed to *odd;* denoted by such a number, as the *even* pages of a book; exactly expressible in integers without fractional parts, as an *even* mile or an *even* hundred. —**e·ven·ly**, *adv.—***e·ven·ness**, *n.*

e·ven, ē′ven, *adv.* In an even manner; evenly; just; as, *even* now; fully or quite; as, *even* to death; still; yet; indeed; used as an intensive to stress something unexpected or to emphasize the comparative degree. *Archaic*, exactly or precisely; as: It was *even* so.

e·ven, ē′ven, *v.t.* To make even; to level; to smooth; to place in an even state as to claim or obligation, as accounts; to balance, often followed by *up.—v.i.* To become even.

e·ven, ē′ven, *n.* [O.E. *aefen, éfen.*] *Archaic*, evening.

e·ven·fall, ē′ven·fal″, *n.* The beginning of evening; early evening; twilight.

e·ven-hand·ed, ē′ven·han′did, a. Impartial; equitable; just.

eve·ning, ēv′ning, n. [O.E. ǣfnung, verbal noun (like morning), < ǣfen, efen, evening; cog.G. ābend, Sw. afton, Icel. aftan, Dan. aften, evening. Akin to O.E. æf, of, off; G. ab, of, L. ab, Skt. apa, from.] The close of the day and the beginning of darkness or night; the time from sunset until darkness; the latter part of the afternoon and the earlier part of the night; a period of ending or dwindling, as the latter part of life, strength, or glory; a night's entertainment or activity.—a.

eve·ning dress, n. Formal clothes worn for social occasions in the evening.

eve·ning prayer, n. (Often cap.) Evensong; vespers; a prayer service held in the evening in the Anglican Church.

eve·ning prim·rose, n. Any of several plants of the family Onagraceae, esp. Oenothera biennis, whose fragrant yellow flowers open at dusk.

eve·nings, ēv′ningz, adv. In or during the evening on a regular basis or habitually, as: She sang in the choir evenings.

eve·ning star, n. A bright planet, such as Venus, visible in the western sky at or soon after sunset; any planet, visible to the naked eye, seen anywhere in the sky from sunset to midnight. A bulbous plant, Cooperia drummondii, found in the southwestern U.S., with fragrant, white, star-shaped, night-blooming flowers.

e·ven-mind·ed, ē′ven·min′did, a. Not easily ruffled, disturbed, or prejudiced; calm; equable.—e·ven-mind′ed·ness, n.

e·ven·song, ē′ven·sang′, ē′ven·song″, n. The evening prayer service in the Anglican Church; vespers in the Roman Catholic Church.

e·vent, i·vent′, n. [L. eventus, evenire, come out, happen, turn out, < e-, out of, and venire, come.] Anything that happens or is regarded as happening; the fact of happening; as, resources available in the event of war; an occurrence, esp. one of some importance; the outcome, issue, or result of anything; sports, each of the items in a program of various contests.—at all e·vents, in an·y e·vent, whatever happens; in any case.—in the e·vent, if.

e·vent·ful, i·vent′ful, a. Full of events or incidents, esp. of a striking character; as, an eventful period; having important issues or results; momentous.—e·vent·ful·ly, adv.—e·vent′ful·ness, n.

e·ven·tide, ē′ven·tīd″, n. [O.E. ǣfentīd.] Poet. evening.

e·ven·tu·al, i·ven′chö·al, a. Coming later or happening as a consequence or final result; consequential; final; ultimate.—e·ven·tu·al·ly, adv. In the event; in the final result or issue.

e·ven·tu·al·i·ty, i·ven″chö·al′i·tē, n. pl. e·ven·tu·al·i·ties. That which may happen; a contingent result.

e·ven·tu·ate, i·ven′chö·āt″, v.i.—eventuated, eventuating. To result, as a consequence; to happen; to come to pass.

ev·er, ev′ėr, adv. [O.E. ǣfre, always; allied to Goth. aiws, time, aiw, ever; Icel. ǣfi, an age, the space of life; L. ǣvum, Gr. aiōn, Skt. âyus, an age. Akin aye, every.] At any time past or future; at all times; always; eternally; constantly; incessantly; continually; in any degree.

ev·er·glade, ev′ėr·glād″, n. A tract of low, swampy land more or less covered with tall grass.—the Ev·er·glades, an extensive marshy region in southern Florida.

ev·er·green, ev′ėr·grēn″, a. Always green; of trees or shrubs, having green leaves throughout the year; fresh and vigorous at all times.—n. An evergreen plant with needle-shaped leaves, esp. pine, spruce, or fir; pl. evergreen branches used for decoration, as at Christmas.

ev·er·last·ing, ev″ėr·las′ting, ev″ėr·lä′sting, a. Lasting forever; eternal; perpetual; continuing indefinitely; incessant; tiresome.—n. Eternity; (cap.) God. Bot. any of various flowers which retain their shape and color when dried, esp. certain species of the asteraceous genus, Helichrysum.—ev·er·last·ing·ly, adv.—ev·er·last·ing·ness, n.

ev·er·more, ev″ėr·mōr′, ev″ėr·mȯr′, adv. Always; eternally; continually; from this time forward.

e·vert, i·vėrt′, v.t. [L. everto, eversum—e-, and verto, to turn.] To turn outward or inside out.—e·ver·sion, i·vėr′zhan, i·vėr′shan, n.—e·ver·si·ble, i·vėr′si·bl, a.

e·ver·tor, i·vėr′tėr, n. A muscle that causes an outward rotation of a part.

eve·ry, ev′rē, a. [O.E. everich, everilk, < O.E. ǣfre, ever, and ǣlc, each.] Each individual of the whole number without exception; each of a number singly or one by one; all conceivable, total.—eve·ry·bod·y, ev′rē·bod″ē, pron. Every person.—eve·ry·one, ev′rē·wun″, ev′rē·wun, pron. Every person; everybody.—eve·ry·where, ev′rē·hwâr″, ev′rē·wâr″, adv. In every place.

eve·ry·day, ev′rē·dā″, a. Of or pertaining to every day; daily; of or for ordinary days as contrasted with Sundays or gala days; as, everyday clothes; such as is met with every day; ordinary; commonplace.

eve·ry·thing, ev′rē·thing″, pron. Every object or particular of an aggregate or total; all; something extremely important, as: This news means everything to us.

e·vict, i·vikt′, v.t. [L. evictus, pp. of evincere, overcome completely, recover (property) by judicial decision, prove, < e-, out, and vincere, conquer.] To expel by force; to expel (a tenant) from property by a legal process or by virtue of a superior title; to recover (property) by such means.—e·vic·tion, n.—e·vic·tor, n.

ev·i·dence, ev′i·dens, n. [Fr. évidence, < L. evidentia—e-, and video, visum, to see.] That which makes evident or provides a sign or indication of something; that which shows or establishes the truth or falsity of something; proof; testimony; law, that which is legally submitted to a competent tribunal as a means of ascertaining the truth of anything under investigation.—state's ev·i·dence, evidence for the prosecution given by an accomplice in a crime.—in ev·i·dence, easily seen or noticed; conspicuous.—v.t.—evidenced, evidencing. To prove; to support by testifying; to show or indicate.—ev·i·den·tial, ev″i·den′shal, a. Affording evidence; pertaining to or based on evidence.—ev·i·den·tial·ly, adv.

ev·i·dent, ev′i·dent, a. [L. evidens.] Easily seen or understood; clear to the mind or vision; manifest; obvious; plain.—ev·i·dent·ly, ev′i·dent·lē, ev′i·dent″lē, ev″i·dent′lē, adv.

e·vil, ē′vil, a. [O.E. yfel = D. euvel = G. übel = Goth. ubils, evil.] Morally wrong; immoral; sinful; wicked; causing injury, mischief, trouble, or pain; bad; harmful; repulsive; characterized or accompanied by misfortune or suffering; unfortunate; disastrous; due to bad character or conduct.—adv. In an evil manner; badly; ill.—e·vil·ly, adv.—e·vil·ness, n.

e·vil, ē′vil, n. That which is evil; evil quality, intention, or conduct; harm; misfortune; sin; something evil; anything causing injury or harm.—e·vil·do·er, n.—e·vil·do·ing, n.

e·vil eye, n. The power, superstitiously attributed to certain persons, to inflict bad luck or injury by a look.

e·vil-mind·ed, ē′vil·mīn′did, a. Having evil dispositions or intentions; disposed to mischief or sin; inclined to an indecent interpretation of things done or said.—e·vil-mind·ed·ly, adv.—e·vil-mind·ed·ness, n.

e·vince, i·vins′, v.t.—evinced, evincing. [L. evinco, to vanquish, to prove or show.] To show; to prove; to manifest; to make evident; to display as something belonging to one's own nature or character; as, to evince fear.—e·vin·ci·ble, a.

e·vis·cer·ate, i·vis′e·rāt″, v.t.—eviscerated, eviscerating. [L. evisceratus, pp. of eviscerare, < e-, out of, and viscera, entrails.] To remove the viscera from; disembowel; fig. to deprive of vital or essential parts.—e·vis·cer·a·tion, i·vis″e·rā′shan, n.

ev·i·ta·ble, ev′i·ta·bl, a. [L. evitabilis, < evitare.] Avoidable.

ev·o·ca·tion, ev″o·kā′shan, n. [L. evocatio(n-).] The act of evoking; a calling forth esp. of a spirit or a mental image; law, formerly the summoning or removal of a case from a lower court to a higher one; embryol. induction of a particular development process in an embryo by an evocator which diffuses from neighboring tissues.

e·voc·a·tive, i·vok′a·tiv, i·vō′ka·tiv, a. Tending to evoke; as, an evocative literary passage. Also e·voc·a·to·ry.—e·voc·a·tive·ly, adv.—e·voc·a·tive·ness, n.

ev·o·ca·tor, ev′o·kā″tėr, n. One who evokes, esp. one who calls up spirits; a chemical which induces evocation in an embryo.

e·voke, i·vōk′, v.t.—evoked, evoking. [L. evocare (pp. evocatus), < e-, out of, and vocare, call.] To call up, produce, or elicit, as a response, a memory, or a feeling; to invoke or call forth, as a supernatural spirit; to produce artistically or imaginatively, as in creating vivid mental pictures by skillful description.—ev·o·ca·ble, ev′o·ka·bl, a.

ev·o·lute, ev′o·lōt″, n. [L. evolutus, pp. of evolvere. EVOLVE.] Geom. a curve which is the locus of the center of curvature of another curve, called the involute, or the envelope of the normals to the latter; the curve from which an involute is formed by the unwrapping of a flexible and inextensible string. See involute.

ev·o·lu·tion, ev″o·lö′shan, Brit. also ē′vo·lö′shan, n. [L. evolutio(n-), < evolvere.] Development; any process of formation or growth; continuous progress from unorganized simplicity to organized complexity; something evolved; a product; a movement, or one of a series of movements, of troops or ships, as for disposition in order of battle or in line on parade; any similar movement. Chem. an evolving or giving off of gas or heat; math. the formation of an involute; the extraction of roots from powers; biol. development from a rudimentary to a more complex state; in modern use, the fact or doctrine of the descent of all living things from a few simple forms of life, or from a single form.—ev·o·lu·tion·al, ev·o·lu·tion·ar·y, a.—ev·o·lu·tion·ism, n.—ev·o·lu·tion·ist, n.

e·volve, i·volv′, v.t.—evolved, evolving. [L. evolvere (pp. evolutus), roll out, unroll, unfold, < e-, out, and volvere, roll.] To develop by degrees; as, to evolve a plan; to develop, as by a process of growth to a more highly organized condition; to give off or emit, as odors or vapors.—v.i. To come forth gradually into being; develop; evolution.—e·volv·a·ble, a.—e·volve·ment, n.—e·volv·er, n.

e·vul·sion, i·vul′shan, n. [L. evulsio(n-), < evellere, pluck out, < e-, out, and vellere, pluck.] The act of plucking or pulling out; forcible extraction.

ev·zone, ev′zōn, n. A Greek soldier of an elite infantry unit whose uniform is distinguished by a skirt of heavy white cotton.

ewe, ū, dial. yō, n. [O.E. ēowu; allied to Fris. ei, O.H.G. avi, ou, Icel. â, L. ovis, Gr. oïs,

Skt. *avi*, a sheep.] A female sheep, goat, or related animal.

ewe-neck, ū′nek, *n.* A neck like that of a ewe, hollowed rather than arched convexly: considered a defect in horses and dogs.—**ewe-necked,** *a.*

ew·er, ū′ér, *n.* [< O.Fr. *ewe,* Mod.Fr. *eau,* water, < L. *aqua,* water.] A large pitcher, with a wide spout and a handle, used for pouring water.

ex, eks, *prep.* [L. *ex,* also *e-, prep.,* out of, from, beyond.] *Com.* free of charges until the time of removal out of; as, *ex* elevator, *ex* ship; *finance,* without, not including, or without the right to have; as, *ex* coupon, *ex* dividend, *ex* interest.

ex·ac·er·bate, ig·zas′ér·bāt″, ik·sas′ér·bāt″, *v.t.*—exacerbated, exacerbating. [L. *exacerbo, exacerbatum—ex-,* intens., and *acerbus,* harsh, sharp, sour.] To increase the violence, intensity, or bitterness of, as a disease or unfriendly feelings; to irritate, exasperate, or embitter.—**ex·ac·er·ba·tion,** *n.*

ex·act, ig·zakt′, *v.t.* [L. *exactus,* pp. of *exigere,* drive out, force out, require, complete, measure by a standard, < *ex-,* out, and *agere,* drive, do, act.] To force or compel the payment, yielding, or performance of; to extort; to call for, demand, or require.—**ex·act·a·ble,** *a.*—**ex·ac·tor, ex·act·er,** *n.*

ex·act, ig·zakt′, *a.* Strictly accurate or correct; precise; conforming perfectly to the requirements or conditions of the case; admitting of no deviation, as laws or discipline; strict or rigorous.—**ex·act·ness,** *n.*

ex·act·ing, ig·zak′ting, *a.* Severe, or unduly severe, in demands or requirements, as a person; requiring close application or attention, as a task.—**ex·act·ing·ly,** *adv.*—**ex·act·ing·ness,** *n.*

ex·ac·tion, ig·zak′shan, *n.* The act of exacting; extortion; that which is exacted; fees, rewards, or contributions levied with severity or injustice.

ex·act·i·tude, ig·zak′ti·tŏd″, ig·zak′ti·tūd″, *n.* [Fr.] The quality of being exact; exactness.

ex·act·ly, *adv.* In an exact manner; just or precisely, as: Do *exactly* as you please. Quite right; that's so.

ex·ag·ger·ate, ig·zaj′e·rāt″, *v.t.*—exaggerated, exaggerating. (L. *exaggeratus,* pp. of *exaggerare,* < *ex-,* out, and *aggerare,* heap up, < *agger,* heap, mound.] To magnify beyond truth or reason; overstate; represent disproportionately; to increase or enlarge abnormally.—*v.i.* To employ exaggeration, as in speech or writing.—**ex·ag·ger·at·ed,** *a.* Unduly magnified; abnormally increased or enlarged.—**ex·ag·ger·at·ed·ly,** *adv.*—**ex·ag·ger·at·ing·ly,** *adv.*—**ex·ag·ger·a·tor,** *n.*

ex·ag·ger·a·tion, ig·zaj″e·rā′shan, *n.* [L. *exaggeratio(n-).*] The act of exaggerating, or the state of being exaggerated; an overstatement or magnification; an exaggerated form of something.—**ex·ag·ger·a·tive,** ig·zaj″e·rā′tiv, ig·zaj′ér·a·tiv, *a.* Also **ex·ag·ger·a·to·ry.**

ex·alt, ig·zalt′, *v.t.* [L. *exaltare,* < *ex-,* out, and *altus,* high.] To raise up or elevate in rank, honor, power, character, or quality; to dignify; glorify; ennoble; to stimulate, as the imagination; to attribute exaltation to; praise; extol; raise in degree; intensify; heighten.—**ex·al·ter,** *n.*

ex·al·ta·tion, eg″zal·tā′shan, *n.* [L.L. *exaltatio(n-).*] The act of exalting or the state of being exalted; elevation, as in rank, power, or character; elation of mind or feeling, sometimes abnormal in character; abnormal intensification of the action of an organ; *astrol.* the most influential position of a planet in the zodiac.

ex·alt·ed, ig·zal′tid, *a.* Elevated, as in rank

or character; dignified; lofty; noble; rapturously excited.—**ex·alt·ed·ly,** *adv.*—**ex·alt·ed·ness,** *n.*

ex·am, ig·zam′, *n. Colloq.* examination.

ex·am·i·na·tion, ig·zam″i·nā′shan, *n.* The act of examining or state of being examined; a careful search, inquiry, or inspection; a process for testing qualifications, knowledge, progress, or skills of students or candidates; a particular test, as an essay on the subject being tested; *law,* formal inquiry into facts by testimony or interrogation; a medical inspection for health.—**ex·am·i·na·to·ri·al,** ig·zam″i·na·tōr′ē·al, ig·zam″i·na·tàr′ē·al, *a.*

ex·am·ine, ig·zam′in, *v.t.*—examined, examining. [L. *examino, examinatum,* < *examen, examinis,* for *exagmen,* < *ex-,* out, and *ago,* to bring, to do.] To inspect or observe carefully; to question, as a witness or an accused person; to inquire into the qualifications, capabilities, knowledge, or progress of; to inspect medically; to test.—**ex·am·in·a·ble,** *a.*—**ex·am·in·er,** *n.*

ex·am·i·nant, *n.* One who examines or inspects.—**ex·am·i·nee,** *n.* One who undergoes an examination.

ex·am·ple, ig·zam′pl, ig·zäm′pl, *n.* [L. *exemplum,* < *eximo,* to take out or away—*ex-,* out, and *emo, emptum,* to take, to purchase.] A sample or specimen that typifies the aggregate; a model; one who or that which is proposed or is proper for imitation; a former instance to be followed or avoided; such an instance held out as a caution or warning to others; a particular case illustrating a general rule or position.—*v.t. exampled, exampling.* To present or serve as an example of; exemplify.

ex·an·i·mate, ig·zan′i·mit, ig·zan′i·māt″, *a.* [L. *exanimatus,* pp. of *exanimare,* deprive of breath, life, or spirit, < *ex-* priv. and *anima,* air, breath, life.] Inanimate or lifeless; lifeless in appearance; spiritless; disheartened.—**ex·an·i·ma·tion,** *n.*

ex·an·the·ma, eg″zan·thē′ma, *n.* pl. **ex·an·the·ma·ta,** ex·an·the·mas, eg″zan·them′a·ta, eg″zan·thē′ma·ta, [L.L. < Gr. *exanthema, exanthein,* blossom out, break out, < *ex-,* out, and *anthein,* blossom, < *anthos,* a flower.] *Pathol.* an eruption or rash on the skin; an eruptive disease, esp. one attended with fever, as smallpox or measles. Also **ex·an·them,** eg·zan′them, ig·zan′them.—**ex·an·the·mat·ic, ex·an·them·a·tous,** *a.*

ex·arch, ek′särk, *n.* [L.L. *exarchus,* < Gr. *archos,* < *ex-,* out, and *archein,* lead, rule.] The ruler of a province in the Byzantine Empire; *Eastern Ch.* a bishop ranking below a patriarch and above a metropolitan, now a patriarch's deputy.—*a. Bot.* having the first-formed wood or xylem tissue appearing near the periphery of the stem.—**ex·ar·chate,** ek′sär·kāt″, ek·sär′kät, *n.* [M.L. *exarchatus.*] The office, jurisdiction, or province of an exarch.

ex·as·per·ate, ig·zas′pe·rāt″, *v.t.*—exasperated, exasperating. [L. *exaspero, exasperatum,* to irritate.] To irritate extremely; to enrage; to anger; to excite or inflame.—*a.*—**ex·as·per·a·tion,** ig·zas″pe·rā′shan, *n.*

ex·ca·vate, eks′ka·vāt″, *v.t.*—excavated, excavating. [L. *excavatus,* pp. of *excavare,* < *ex-,* out, and *cavare,* make hollow, < *cavus,* hollow.] To make hollow by removing the inner part; make a hole or cavity in, as by digging; to make a hole or tunnel in, by removing material; to expose or lay bare by digging; unearth.—**ex·ca·va·tion,** *n.* [L. *excavatio(n-).*] The act of excavating; a hole or cavity made by excavating.—**ex·ca·va·tor,** *n.* One who or that which excavates; a machine used in excavating.

ex·ceed, ik·sēd′, *v.t.* [L. *excedo—ex-,* out, and *cedo,* to go.] To pass or go beyond; to proceed beyond the given or supposed

limit, measure, or quantity of; to surpass; to excel.—*v.i.* To excel over others.

ex·ceed·ing, ik·sē′ding, *a.* Great in extent, quantity, degree, or duration; exceptional.—**ex·ceed·ing·ly,** *adv.* Extremely; very much.

ex·cel, ik·sel′, *v.t.*—excelled, excelling. [L. *excello—ex-,* and root seen in Gr. *kellō,* to impel, L. *celsus,* raised high.] To surpass in good qualities or laudable deeds; to outdo in comparison; to transcend.—*v.i.* To be eminent or distinguished; to surpass others.

ex·cel·lence, ek′se·lens, *n.* The state of excelling in anything; superiority; any valuable quality; anything meritorious. (*Usu. cap.*) excellency, a title of honor given to persons of high rank.

ex·cel·len·cy, ek′sē·len·sē, *n.* pl. **ex·cel·len·cies.** (*Usu. cap.*) a title of honor given to governors, ambassadors, ministers, and the like; the person bearing such a title.

ex·cel·lent, ek′se·lent, *a.* Extremely good; choice.—**ex·cel·lent·ly,** *adv.*

ex·cel·si·or, ik·sel′sē·ér, ek·sel′sē·ér, *a.* [L. compar. of *excelsus,* high, prop. pp. of *excellere.*] (*Cap.*) upward: used as the motto of the State of New York.—*n.* A kind of fine wood shavings, used for stuffing or packing; a 3-point printing type, smaller than brilliant.

ex·cept, ik·sept′, *v.t.* [Fr. *excepter,* L. *excipio, exceptum—ex-,* out, and *capio,* to take.] To take or leave out of any number specified; to exclude.—*v.i.* To object; to take exception, usu. followed by *to.*—*prep.* With exception of; excepting.—*conj.* Excepting; unless.

ex·cept·ing, ik·sep′ting, *prep.* With exception of; excluding; unless; except.

ex·cep·tion, ik·sep′shan, *n.* The act of excepting or excluding; exclusion; one who or that which is excepted or excluded; an objection; that which is or may be offered in opposition to a rule, proposition, statement, or allegation; *law,* a written or oral objection. Offense; slight anger or resentment; as, to take *exception* at a severe remark, to take *exception* to what was said.—**ex·cep·tion·a·ble,** *a.* Liable to exception or objection; objectionable.

ex·cep·tion·al, ik·sep′sha·nal, *a.* Out of the ordinary; relating to or forming an exception; unusual; remarkable; superior; *educ.* of a child, intellectually superior or handicapped either physically or mentally and therefore requiring special training.

ex·cep·tive, ik·sep′tiv, *a.* Including an exception; making exception.

ex·cerpt, ik·sèrpt′, *v.t.* [L. *excerpo, excerptum—ex-,* out, and *carpo,* to pick.] To pick out or extract from a book or other literary composition, esp. for purposes of quotation; to cull; to select; to cite.—ek′sèrpt, *n.* An extract from a book or writing of any kind.—**ex·cerp·ter, ex·cerp·tor,** *n.*—**ex·cerpt·i·ble,** *a.*—**ex·cerp·tion,** *n.*

ex·cess, ik·ses′, ek′ses, *n.* [O.Fr. *exces* (Fr. *excès*), < L. *excessus,* < *excedere.*] A going beyond ordinary or proper limits; exuberance or superabundance; superfluity; an extreme or excessive amount or degree; the fact of exceeding something else in amount or degree; preponderance; the amount or degree by which one thing exceeds another; intemperance.—ek′ses, ik·ses′, *a.* Being more than or above what is necessary, usual, or specified.—**ex·cess pro·fits tax,** an additional tax on business profits which are in excess of the average profits for a number of base years, or of a fixed percentage of capitalization.

ex·ces·sive, ik·ses′iv, *a.* Exceeding the usual or proper limit or degree; characterized by excess; immoderate; extravagant; unreasonable.—**ex·ces·sive·ly,** *adv.*—**ex·ces·sive·ness,** *n.*

ex·change, iks·chānj′, *n.* [O.Fr. *eschange* (Fr. *échange*).] The act of exchanging; a parting with a thing in return for some equivalent; the giving up or resigning of something for something else; as, the *exchange* of a crown for a cloister; the replacing of one thing by another; a return; as, to receive gold in *exchange* for silver; the act of giving and receiving reciprocally; as, an *exchange* of blows or gifts. A place for exchanging commodities, items, or services; a place where merchants, brokers, or bankers meet to transact business; a central office or station; as, a telephone *exchange*. *Finance*, a system for settling accounts in different locations without actual transfer of money through use of documents, called bills of *exchange*, which represent money values; a transfer of credits which discharges obligations in different locations; the percentage charged for exchanging money or financial instruments; the mutual transfer of equivalent sums of money, as in the currencies of two different countries.

ex·change, iks·chānj′, *v.t.—exchanged, exchanging.* [O.Fr. *eschangier* (Fr. *échanger*), < M.L. *excambiare,* < L. *ex-,* out and M.L. *cambiare,* E. *change.*] To part with for some equivalent; to give up (something) for something else; to replace by another or something else, as: Please *exchange* this purchase for me. To give and receive, as things, reciprocally; to give to and receive from each other, as things of the same kind; as, to *exchange* blows or gifts; to interchange.—*v.i.* To make an exchange; to pass or be taken in exchange or as an equivalent.—**ex·change·-a·ble,** *a.*—**ex·change·a·bil·i·ty,** *n.*—**ex·chan·ger,** *n.*—**ex·change stu·dent,** a student attending school in a foreign country in exchange for a student sent from that country to his.

ex·chang·ee, iks·chän·jē′, iks·chän′jē, eks″-chän·jē′, *n.* A person who participates in an exchange program.

ex·change rate, *n.* The value of the currency of one country in relation to the value of the currency of another country; the ratio or percentage at which two currencies are traded; the difference in value between two or more currencies or in the value of the same currency at two or more places. Also **rate of ex·change.**′

ex·cheq·uer, eks′chek·ẽr, iks·chek′ẽr, *n.* [O.Fr. *eschequier,* Fr. *echiquier,* a chessboard. The term was applied to a court of finance because the court at first held meetings around a table covered with a checkered cloth; accounts were taken by means of counters on the checks.] The treasury of a nation or organization; *Brit. (often cap.)* the revenue department of the British government; an office in medieval England responsible for the management of the royal revenue.

ex·cide, ik·sīd′, *v.t.—excided, exciding.* [L. *excidere* (pp. *excisus*), < *ex-,* out of, and *caedere,* cut.] To cut out; excise.

ex·cip·i·ent, ik·sip′ē·ent, *n.* [L. *excipiens* (*-ent-*), ppr. of *excipere,* take out.] *Pharm.* a more or less inert substance, as sugar or jelly, used as the medium or vehicle for the administration of an active medicine.

ex·cise, ek′sīz, ek′sīs, ik·sīz′, *n.* [Prob. < M.D. *excijs,* < O.Fr. *acceis,* a tax, ult. < L. *ad-,* to, and *censere,* tax.] An inland tax or duty on certain commodities, as spirits or tobacco, levied on their manufacture, sale, or consumption within the country; also **ex·cise tax.** A tax levied for a license to carry on certain trades or to pursue certain sports; *Brit.* that branch of the civil service charged with the collection of excise duties.—ik·sīz′, *v.t.—excised, excising.* To impose an excise on.—**ex·cis·a·ble,** *a.* Subject to excise duty.

ex·cise, ik·sīz′, *v.t.—excised, excising.* [< L. *excido, excisum—ex-,* out, and *caedo,* to cut.] To cut out or off; to remove by cutting, as in surgery; to delete or expunge.—**ex·ci·sion,** ek·sizh′ən, ik·sizh′ən, *n.* The act of cutting out; *surg.* resection; *eccles.* excommunication.—**ex·cis·a·ble,** ek·sī′za·bl, *a.*

ex·cise·man, ek′sīz·man, *n.* pl. **ex·cise·-men.** *Brit.* an officer who collects excise taxes and enforces excise laws.

ex·cit·a·ble, ik·sī′ta·bl, *a.* Capable of being excited; easily excited or stirred up; *physiol.* able to react to stimulus or to be aroused to activity by a stimulus.—**ex·cit·a·bil·i·ty, ex·cit·a·ble·ness,** ik·sī″ta·bil′i·tē, *n.*—**ex·cit·a·bly,** *adv.*

ex·cit·ant, ik·sīt′ənt, ek′si·tənt, *a.* [L. *excitans* (*-ant-*), ppr.] Exciting or tending to excite; stimulating.—*n.* Something that excites; a stimulant.

ex·ci·ta·tion, ek″sī·tā′shən, *n.* The act of exciting; condition of being excited; *biol.* the activating of an individual, organ, or tissue, as by electrical stimulation, and the condition resulting.

ex·cit·a·tive, ik·sī′ta·tiv, *a.* Having power to excite; tending to excite. Also **ex·cit·a·-to·ry,** ik·sī′ta·tōr″ē, ik·sī′ta·tȧr″ē.

ex·cite, ik·sīt′, *v.t.—excited, exciting.* [Fr. *exciter,* < L. *excito—ex-,* and *cito,* intens. of *cieo* or *cio,* to excite, call; akin to Gr. *kiō,* to go, *kineō,* to move.] To call into action; to animate; to rouse, provoke, or stir up the feelings of; to cause to act, as that which is dormant, sluggish, or inactive; *physiol.* to produce a reaction in or increase the activity of, as of a nerve or muscle; *phys.* to raise, as an atom, to a state of higher energy above the ground state; *elect.* to develop electrical or magnetic activity in.

ex·cit·ed, ik·sī′tid, *a.* Emotionally aroused; stimulated; agitated; revealing intense feelings.—**ex·cit·ed·ly,** *adv.*—**ex·cit·ed·-ness,** *n.*—**ex·cit·ed state,** *n. Phys.* an energy level of a system, as an atom or molecule, which is higher than the ground state, or lowest level.

ex·cite·ment, ik·sīt′mənt, *n.* The act of exciting; the state of being excited; agitation; that which excites or arouses; that which moves, stirs, or induces action.

ex·cit·er, ik·sī′tẽr, *n.* One who or that which excites. *Elect.* a generator supplying an electric field used to drive a larger direct current generator; a device that supplies the carrier frequency voltage, as in an FM system, the unit including the frequency generating, modulating, and multiplying circuits of the transmitter.

ex·cit·ing, ik·sī′ting, *a.* Calling or rousing into action; producing excitement; thrilling.—**ex·cit·ing·ly,** *adv.*

ex·ci·tor, ik·sī′tẽr, ik·sī′tȧr, *n. Physiol.* a nerve whose stimulation produces greater action in the part supplied.

ex·claim, ik·sklām′, *v.i.* [L. *exclamo—ex-,* and *clamo,* to call.] To cry out or say suddenly and emotionally.—*v.t.* To utter with strong emotion; vociferate.

ex·cla·ma·tion, ek″sklȧ·mā′shən, *n.* The act of exclaiming or making an outcry; ardent expression of discontent or protest; vehement vociferation; an emphatic or passionate utterance, usu. spontaneous; an interjection.

ex·cla·ma·tion point, *n.* A mark or sign (!) in written or printed matter, used with an interjection or exclamation to indicate forcefulness, strong emotion, or surprise. Also **ex·cla·ma·tion mark.**

ex·clam·a·to·ry, ik·sklam′a·tōr″ē, ik·-sklam′a·tȧr″ē, *a.* Expressing exclamation; pertaining to or characterized by exclamation.—**ex·clam·a·to·ri·ly,** *adv.*

ex·clave, eks′klāv, *n.* [L. *ex-,* out of, and L. *clavis,* key, as in *enclave.*] A section of a country set apart from the rest by surrounding alien territory.

ex·clo·sure, ik·sklō′zhẽr, *n.* An area closed off, as by fences, to keep out intruders.

ex·clude, ik·sklōd′, *v.t.—excluded, excluding.* [L. *excludere* (pp. *exclusus*,), *ex-,* out of, and *cludere, claudere,* shut, close.] To shut or keep out; prevent entry of; to prohibit from inclusion; deny consideration; to expel or eject.—**ex·clud·a·bil·i·ty,** *n.*—**ex·clud·a·ble, ex·clud·i·ble,** *a.*—**ex·clud·er,** *n.* **ex·clu·so·ry,** ik·sklō′sa·rē, *a.*

ex·clu·sion, ik·sklō′zhən, *n.* [L. *exclusio(n-).*] The act of excluding or the state of being excluded; expulsion; that which is excluded or expelled.—**ex·clu·sion·ism,** ik·sklō′zha·niz″um, *n.* The principle, policy, or practice of exclusion, as from rights or privileges.—**ex·clu·si·ble, ex·-clu·sion·ar·y,** *a.*—**ex·clu·sion·ist,** *n.*

ex·clu·sion prin·ci·ple, *n. Phys.* the law that, in any given atom or molecule, no two electrons, protons, or neutrons will occupy the same energy level.

ex·clu·sive, ik·sklō′siv, *a.* Having the power or effect of excluding; owned, used, or controlled by one person or group; as, *exclusive* rights to publish a novel; shutting out others from association; snobbish; permitting or catering to a select clientele; complete, undivided; as, *exclusive* attention to one's work; incompatible; as, mutually *exclusive* ideas; sole or only; as, the *exclusive* means of transportation.—*n. Journ.* a news story or report released to or obtained by a news organization having the privilege of first usage. An exclusive right or privilege, as a franchise to sell goods in a given territory.—**ex·clu·sive of,** not including or taking into consideration.—**ex·clu·sive·ly,** *adv.*—**ex·clu·sive·ness, ex·clu·siv·i·ty,** eks″klō·siv′i·tē, *n.*

ex·cog·i·tate, eks·koj′i·tāt″, *v.t.—excogitated, excogitating.* [L. *excogitatus,* pp. of *excogitare,* < *ex-,* out, and *cogitare,* think, E. *cogitate.*] To think out; contrive; devise.—**ex·cog·i·ta·tion,** *n.*—**ex·cog·i·ta·tive, ex·cog·i·ta·ble,** *a.*—**ex·cog·i·ta·tor,** *n.*

ex·com·mu·ni·cate, eks″ko·mū′ni·kāt″, *v.t.—excommunicated, excommunicating.* [L. *ex-,* out, and *communico, communicatum,* to communicate, < *communis,* common.] To expel or eject from the communion of the church and deprive of spiritual advantages by ecclesiastical censure; to expel from any association and deprive of the privileges of membership.—eks″ko·mū′ni·kit, eks″ko·-mū′ni·kāt″, *n.* One who is excommunicated; one cut off from any privilege. Also **ex·com·mu·ni·cant.**—eks″ko·mū′ni·kit, eks″ko·mū′ni·kāt″, *a.* Deprived of communion with the church.—**ex·com·mu·ni·ca·ble,** *a.* Liable or deserving to be excommunicated; punishable by excommunication.—**ex·com·mu·ni·ca·tor,** *n.*

ex·com·mu·ni·ca·tion, eks″ko·mū′ni·kā′shən, *n.* The act of excommunicating or the state of being excommunicated; expulsion from the communion of a church and deprivation of its rights, privileges, and advantages.—**ex·com·mu·ni·ca·tive,** *a.* Serving to expel from communion with the church.—**ex·com·mu·ni·ca·to·ry,** *a.* Relating to or causing excommunication.

ex·co·ri·ate, ik·skōr′ē·āt″, ik·skȧr′ē·āt, *v.t.—excoriated, excoriating.* [L.L. *ex·corio—*L. *ex-,* and *corium,* skin, hide.] To break or wear off the cuticle of; to abrade a part of the skin so as to reach the flesh; to denounce scathingly.—**ex·co·ri·a·tion,** *n.* The act of excoriating; abrasion; a verbal whipping.

ex·cre·ment, ek′skre·ment, *n.* [L. *ex·crementum,* < *excerno, excretum,* to sift out—*ex-,* out, and *cerno,* to separate.] Refuse matter discharged from the body after digestion.—**ex·cre·men·tal, ex·cre·men·-ti·tious,** ek″skre·men′tal, ek″skre·men·-tish′us, *a.*

ex·cres·cence, ik·skres′ens, *n.* [L. *ex-crescentia,* < *excrescens.*] Abnormal growth or increase; an outgrowth; a natural outgrowth, esp. an abnormal or unsightly outgrowth on an animal or plant; any disfiguring addition.

ex·cres·cent, ik·skres′ent, *a.* [L. *excrescens* (*-ent-*), ppr. of *excrescere,* grow out, < *ex-,* out of, and *crescere,* grow.] Growing out from something else, esp. growing abnor-mally out of something else; superfluous; *phon.* arising as a mere euphonic addition, as the sound of *t* in *against.*

ex·cre·ta, ik·skrē′ta, *n. pl.* [L. neut. pl. of *excretus.*] Excreted matter; the excretions of the body, as sweat or urine.—**ex·cre·tal,** *a.*

ex·crete, ik·skrēt′, *v.t.*—*excreted, excreting.* [L. *excretus,* pp. of *excernere,* sift out, dis-charge, < *ex-,* out of, and *cernere,* separate, sift.] To separate and eliminate from an organic body; separate and expel from the blood or tissues, as waste or harmful matters.—**ex·cre·tion, ex·cres·cen·cy,** ik·skres′en·sē, *n.* The act of excreting; the substance excreted, as sweat, urine, or certain plant juices.—**ex·cre·tive,** *a.* Serv-ing to excrete.—**ex·cre·to·ry,** *a.* Pertaining to or concerned in excretion; having the function of excreting.

ex·cru·ci·ate, ik·skrö′shē·āt″, *v.t.*—*ex-cruciated, excruciating.* [L. *excrucio, ex-cruciatum—ex-,* and *crucio,* to torment, < *crux,* a cross.] To cause extreme pain to; to torture; to cause extreme mental agony to.

ex·cru·ci·at·ing, ik·skrö′shē·ā″ting, *a.* Extremely painful; intensely distressing; torturing; agonizing.—**ex·cru·ci·at·ing·-ly,** *adv.*—**ex·cru·ci·a·tion,** *n.*

ex·cul·pate, ek′skul·pāt″,ik·skul′pāt,*v.t.*—*exculpated, exculpating.* [L.L. *exculpo, ex-culpatum*—L. *ex-,* and *culpo, culpatum,* to blame, < *culpa,* a fault.] To clear from a charge or imputation of fault or guilt.—**ex·cul·pa·tion,** *n.* Exoneration; the act of relieving from blame.—**ex·cul·pa·to·ry,** *a.* Containing evidence to clear from blame.

ex·cur·rent, ik·skur′ent,ik·skur′ent, *a.* [L. *excurrens* (*-ent-*), ppr. of *excurrere.*] Flowing outward; *zool.* having a current that flows outward: used esp. to describe the channels in sponges. *Bot.* having the axis prolonged so as to form an undivided main stem or trunk, as the stem of the spruce; projecting beyond the apex, as the midrib in certain leaves.

ex·cur·sion, ik·skur′zhan, ik·skur′shan, *n.* [L. *excursio*(*n-*), < *excurrere.*] A trip made for a particular reason and with the inten-tion of returning soon; a trip made at specially reduced fares; a group taking such a trip; divergence or digression; *phys.* the departure of a body from its mean position or proper course; *mech.* the range of stroke of any moving part.—*v.i.* To make an excursion.—*a.* Pertaining to or intended for use on excursions.—**ex·cur·sion·al, ex·cur·sion·ar·y,** *a.*—**ex·cur·sion·ist,** *n.*

ex·cur·sive, ik·skur′siv, *a.* Of speech or thought, rambling; wandering.—**ex·cur·sive·ly,** *adv.*—**ex·cur·sive·ness,** *n.*

ex·cur·sus, ek·skur′sus, *n. pl.* **ex·cur·sus·es, ex·cur·sus.** [L.] A dissertation appended to a book, discussing some im-portant point or topic more fully than could be done in the body of the work.

ex·cus·a·to·ry, ik·skū′za·tōr″ē, ik·skū′-za·tar″ē, *a.* Making excuse; containing excuse or apology; apological.

ex·cuse, ik·skūz′, *v.t.*—*excused, excusing.* [O.Fr. Fr. *excuser,* < L. *excusare,* < *ex-,* out of, and *causa,* cause, judicial proceeding.] To offer an apology for; seek to remove the

blame from; to serve as an apology or justification for; pardon or forgive; to seek or obtain exemption or release for; to re-lease from an obligation or duty; dispense with.—**ex·cus·a·ble,** *a.*—**ex·cus·a·bly,** *adv.*—**ex·cus·er,** *n.*

ex·cuse, ik·skūs′, *n.* The act of excusing; a reason or an expression of regret for failure to perform adequately; an explanation for an absence.—**ex·cuse·less,** *a.*—**ex·cus·er,** *n.*—**ex·cus·ing·ly,** *adv.*

ex·e·at, ek′sē·at″, *n.* Authorization given by a bishop for a priest to absent himself from his diocese; *Brit.* official authorization enabling a student to leave his university for a period of time.

ex·ec., ig·zek′, *n.* Executive officer; an executive; an executor.

ex·e·cra·ble, ek′si·kra·bl, *a.* Hateful; detestable; abominable; extremely bad.—**ex·e·cra·ble·ness,** *n.*—**ex·e·cra·bly,** *adv.*

ex·e·crate, ek′si·krāt″, *v.t.*—*execrated, exe-crating.* [Fr. *exécrer,* < L. *execror—ex-,* and *sacer,* consecrated or dedicated to a deity, accursed.] To denounce as evil or detest-able; to invoke a curse upon or to curse; to detest utterly; to abhor; to abominate.—**ex·e·cra·tive,** *a.*—**ex·e·cra·tor,** *n.*

ex·e·cra·tion, ek″si·krā′shan, *n.* The act of execrating; a curse pronounced; impreca-tion of evil; utter detestation; the object execrated.

ex·e·cute, ek′se·kūt″, *v.t.*—*executed, execut-ing.* [O.Fr. *executer* (Fr. *exécuter*), L. *executus,* pp. of *exequi,* for *exsequi,* < *ex-,* out, and *sequi,* follow.] To carry through to the end; to inflict capital punishment on, esp. in accordance with legal sentence; to perform or do skillfully; to put into effect; to administer, transact, or carry through in the manner prescribed by law; to produce by following a plan or design.—**ex·e·cut·a·ble,** *a.*—**ex·e·cut·er,** *n.*

ex·e·cu·tion, ek″se·kū′shan, *n.* [O.Fr. *execucion* (Fr. *exécution*), < L. *executio*(*n-*).] The act or process of executing; the state or fact of being executed; mode or style of performance; technical skill, as in music; the infliction of capital punishment, or, formerly, of any legal punishment; effective action or use, esp. of weapons; destructive work or effect; *law,* a judicial writ directing the enforcement of a judgment or court decree.—**ex·e·cu·tion·er,** *n.* An official who inflicts capital punishment in pursuance of a legal warrant; one who executes.

ex·ec·u·tive, ig·zek′ū·tiv, ig·zek′yu·tiv, *a.* [Fr. *exécutif.*] Pertaining to or suited for executing or carrying into effect; charged with or pertaining to execution of laws or administration of affairs; made for or used by an executive or executives.—*n.* The executive branch of a government; the person or persons in whom the supreme executive power of a government is vested; any person or body charged with administra-tive work; a person skilled in such work.—**ex·ec·u·tive·ly,** *adv.*

ex·ec·u·tive a·gree·ment, *n.* An agree-ment between the U.S. and another nation, made by the President without senatorial approval, and pertaining to matters not warranting a formal treaty.

ex·ec·u·tive coun·cil, *n.* A council charged with supreme executive authority; a council that acts as advisory aide to a government head.

Ex·ec·u·tive Man·sion, *n.* (*Also l.c.*) *U.S.* the White House, in Washington, D.C., offi-cial residence of the President; the official residence of a governor of one of the states.

ex·ec·u·tive of·fic·er, *n. Milit.* the assist-ant to a commanding officer; the naval or military officer who is second in command.

ex·ec·u·tive or·der, *n.* (*Often cap.*) a command having the power of law, issued by the President or other head of state.

ex·ec·u·tive ses·sion, *n.* A legislative session, usu. not open to the public.

ex·ec·u·tor, ig·zek′yu·tėr, ig·zek′ū·tėr, *n.* [O.Fr. *executor* (Fr. *exécuteur*), < L. *executor,* < *exequi,* < *ex-,* out, and *sequi,* follow.] One who executes, carries out, per-forms, or fulfills; *law,* a person appointed by a testator to carry out the provisions of his will.—**ex·ec·u·to·ri·al,** ig·zek″yu·tōr′-ē·al, ig·zek″yu·tar′ē·al, ig·zek″ū·tōr′ē·al, ig·zek″ū·tar′ē·al, *a.*—**ex·ec·u·tor·ship,** *n.* The office of an executor.

ex·ec·u·to·ry, ig·zek′ū·tor″ē, ig·zek′ū·-tar″ē, *a.* Executive; operative; *law,* per-taining to what is yet to be executed or performed.

ex·e·ge·sis, ek″si·jē′sis, *n. pl.* **ex·e·ge·ses,** ek″si·jē′sēz. [N.L. < Gr. *exēgēsis,* < *exēgeisthai,* explain, < *ex-,* out of, and *hēgeisthai,* lead.] Critical explanation or interpretation, esp. of Scripture.—**ex·e·get·ic, ex·e·get·i·cal,** ek″si·jet′ik, *a.* [Gr. *exegetikos.*]—**ex·e·get·i·cal·ly,** *adv.*

ex·e·gete, ek′si·jēt″, *n.* One skilled in exegesis. Also **ex·e·get·ist.**

ex·e·get·ics, ek″si·jet′iks, *n. pl. but sing. in constr.* The science which lays down the principles and art of scriptural inter-pretation.

ex·em·plar, ig·zem′plėr, ig·zem′plär, *n.* [L. *exemplum,* < *eximo,* to take away—*ex-,* out, and *emo,* to take.] A model, original, or pattern to be copied or imitated; a person who serves as a model; an example that is typical; a specimen or copy, as of a book.

ex·em·pla·ry, ig·zem′pla·rē, ′eg′zem·-plėr″ē, *a.* [L.L. *exemplaris,* < L. *exemplum.*] Serving as a model, pattern, illustration, or specimen; worthy of imitation; commend-able; such as may serve for a warning; as, an *exemplary* punishment; illustrative; typical.—**ex·em·pla·ri·ly,** *adv.*—**ex·em·pla·ri·ness,** *n.*

ex·em·pli·fy, ig·zem′pli·fī″, *v.t.*—*exem-plified, exemplifying.* [L.L. *exemplifico,* to exemplify—L. *exemplum,* an example, and *facio,* to make.] To show or illustrate by example; to serve as an example or instance of; *law,* to make, under seal, an attested copy or transcript.—**ex·em·pli·fi·a·ble,** *a.*—**ex·em·pli·fi·ca·tion,** *n.* The act of exemplifying; a showing or illustrating by example; that which exemplifies.

ex·em·plum, ig·zem′plum, *n. pl.* **ex·em·-pla,** ig·zem′pla. An anecdote or story narrated to support a contention or illus-trate a moral; an example.

ex·empt, ig·zempt′, *v.t.* [Fr. *exempter;* L. *eximo, exemptum,* to take out, to remove—*ex-,* out, and *emo,* to buy, to take.] To free or permit to be free from any burden, promise, or duty, to which others are subject; to grant immunity to.—*a.* Not liable; not in-cluded; freed; free.—*n.*—**ex·emp·tion,** *n.* The act of exempting; the state of being exempt; immunity; *U.S.* one who or that which constitutes a deduction on an income-tax form.

ex·en·ter·ate, ek·sen′te·rāt″,*v.t.*—*exenter-ated, exenterating.* [L. *exenteratus,* pp. of *exenterare,* < Gr. *ex-,* out of, and *enteron,* intestine.] To surgically excise the contents of a body cavity, as of the pelvis; to eviscerate.—*a.*—**ex·en·ter·a·tion,** *n.*

ex·e·quy, ek′se·kwē, *n. pl.* **ex·e·quies.** [L. *exequaie,* pl. < *exequi, exsequi,* follow out.] A funeral rite or ceremony; *pl.* a funeral procession.

ex·er·cise, ek′sėr·sīz″, *n.* [O.Fr. Fr. *ex-ercise,* < L. *exercitium,* < *exercere,* drive on, keep active or busy, < *ex-,* out, and *arcēre,* keep.] Bodily or mental exertion for the sake of training or improvement; a putting into action, use, operation, or effect; the act or state of being in use or operation; something done or performed as a means of practice or training; something done as an exhibition or test of proficiency; a performance, procedure, or ceremony; as, graduation *exercises*.

ex·er·cise, ek'sėr·sīz", *v.t.*—exercised, exercising. To put through exercises, or forms of practice or exertion, designed to train, develop, or keep in condition; to put into action, practice, or use, as: He *exercised* his rights. To exert or bring to bear; as, to *exercise* influence; to drill; as, to *exercise* troops; to occupy the attention of; to perturb or worry.—*v.i.* To go through exercises; to take bodily exercise.—**ex·er·cis·er**, *n.*—**ex·er·cis·a·ble**, *a.*

ex·er·ci·ta·tion, ig·zėr"si·tā'shan, *n.* [L. *exercitatio(n-)*, < *exercitare*, exercise diligently, practice, freq. of *exercere*.] *Archaic.* Exercise or exertion, as of faculties or powers; practice or training; an exercise or performance; an exercise or display of skill, esp. a disquisition or discourse.

ex·ergue, ig·zėrg', ek'sėrg, *n.* [Fr. < Gr. *ex-*, out and *ergon*, work.] *Numis.* The small space below the main device on a coin or medal; anything inscribed in this space.—**ex·ergu·al**, ig·zėr'gal, *a.*

ex·ert, ig·zėrt', *v.t.* [L. *exerto, exserto,* to stretch out, to thrust forth, freq. < *exsero, exsertum,* to thrust out or forth—*ex-*, out, and *sero*, to join.] To put forth or exercise, as strength, force, or ability; to put in action with vigor; to strive to bring into active operation; as the mind or the bodily powers. *Refl.* to use efforts; to put forth one's powers.—**ex·er·tion**, *n.* The act of exerting; a putting forth of power; an effort; a striving or struggling; endeavor; trial.

ex·e·unt, ek'sē·unt, *v.i.* Go out: a stage direction referring to two or more of the actors.

ex·fo·li·ate, eks·fō'lē·āt", *v.i.*—exfoliated, exfoliating. [L. *exfolio, exfoliatum,* to strip of leaves—*ex-*, and *folium,* a leaf.] To separate and come off in scales; to split into scales; to grow or spread by, or as if by, producing leaves.—*v.t.* To free from scales, splinters, or laminae; to free from scales in removing the surface of; to grow or spread by, or as if by, producing leaves.—**ex·fo·li·a·tion**, *n.*—**ex·fo·li·a·tive**, eks·fō'lē·ā"tiv, eks·fō'lē·a·tiv, *a.*

ex·ha·la·tion, eks"ha·lā'shan, eg"za·lā'shan, *n.* [L. *exhalatio.*] The act or process of exhaling; that which is exhaled or emitted; vapor; emanation; effluvium.

ex·hale, eks·hāl', ig·zāl', *v.i.*—exhaled, exhaling. [L. *exhalo—ex-*, out, and *halo*, to breathe.] To breathe out; to eject breath or vapor; to rise or pass off as vapor.—*v.t.* To expel from or let out of the lungs; to emit or give off, as vapor, sound, or an odor.—**ex·hal·ant**, eks·hā'lant, ig·zā'lant, *a.* Having the quality of exhaling or emitting.—*n.* A duct with the function of exhaling.

ex·haust, ig·zȧst', *v.t.* [L. *exhaustus,* pp. of *exhaurire,* < *ex-*, out of, and *haurire,* draw, drain.] To draw out or drain off; to use up or consume completely; to expend wholly; to empty by drawing out the contents; to create a vacuum in; to deprive of ingredients by use of solvents, as a drug; to deprive wholly of useful or essential properties, as soil; to drain of possessions or resources, as a person or country; to wear out or fatigue greatly, as a person; to draw out all that is essential, as in a subject; to treat or study thoroughly.—*v.i.* To pass out or escape, as spent steam from a cylinder; to discharge contents; as, an engine which *exhausts* directly into the air.—**ex·haust·er**, *n.* —**ex·haust·i·bil·i·ty**, *n.*—**ex·haust·i·ble**, *a.*

ex·haust, ig·zȧst', *n. Engin.* the act or process of exhausting, as the drawing off of air from a vessel; the escape of the spent steam or working fluid from the cylinder of an engine after completing its work; an exhausting apparatus, as a pump for removing air from a building; a passage through which exhausted material, as spent steam, escapes; exhausted material, as spent steam.

ex·haust·ed, ig·zȧs'tid, *a.* Completely consumed, spent, or drained; greatly fatigued.—**ex·haust·ed·ly**, *adv.*—**ex·haust·less**, ig·zȧst'lis, *a.* Untiring; inexhaustible; marked by an inability to be exhausted.—**ex·haust·less·ly**, *adv.*—**ex·haust·less·ness**, *n.*

ex·haus·tion, ig·zȧs'chan, ig·zȧsh'chan, *n.* The act or process of exhausting, or the state of being exhausted; extreme weakness or fatigue.—**ex·haust·ing**, *a.* Marked by a tiring or fatiguing manner or quality.

ex·haus·tive, ig·zȧs'tiv, *a.* Serving to explore or test all elements of a subject; comprehensive; thorough; tending to exhaust or drain, as of resources or strength.—**ex·haus·tive·ly**, *adv.*—**ex·haus·tive·ness**, *n.*

ex·hib·it, ig·zib'it, *v.t.* [L. *exhibitus,* pp. of *exhibere* < *ex-*, out, and *habere,* have, hold.] To offer or expose to view; present for inspection; to place on display, as in a competition or show; to manifest or reveal by outward signs; as, to *exhibit* anger; *law,* to submit, as a document, in a court, or to present officially for consideration, as a petition or charge; *med.* to administer, as a remedy.—*v.i.* To make or give an exhibition; present something to public view.—**ex·hib·it·a·ble**, *a.*—**ex·hib·i·tor, ex·hib·i·ter**, *n.*—**ex·hib·i·to·ry**, *a.*

ex·hib·it, ig·zib'it, *n.* An exhibiting or exhibition; that which is exhibited; an object or a collection of objects shown in an exhibition or fair; *law,* a document or other object exhibited in court and referred to and identified as evidence.

ex·hi·bi·tion, ek"si·bish'an, *n.* [L. *exhibitio(n-)*.] An exhibiting, showing, or presenting to view; a show; a public display, as of works of art, manufactured products, or athletic feats; *Canada,* a large fair or exposition; *Brit.* a grant given to a college student, usu. as a result of a competitive examination.

ex·hi·bi·tion·er, ek"si·bish'a·nėr, *n. Brit.* a student who receives an exhibition, or allowance, at a college or university.

ex·hi·bi·tion·ism, ek"si·bish'a·niz"um, *n.* An exaggerated propensity for showing off one's talents or traits or for attracting attention to oneself; *psychiatry,* a form of sexual perversion marked by a usu. compulsive display of the sex organs.—**ex·hi·bi·tion·ist**, *n.*—**ex·hi·bi·tion·is·tic**, *a.*

ex·hib·i·tive, ig·zib'i·tiv, *a.* Serving for exhibition; tending to exhibit, usu. with *of.*

ex·hil·a·rate, ig·zil'a·rāt", *v.t.*—exhilarated, exhilarating. [L. *exhilaro—ex-*, and *hilaro,* to make merry, < *hilaris,* merry, jovial.] To make cheerful or merry; to stimulate.—**ex·hil·a·rant**, ig·zil'ėr·ant, *a.* Exhilarating.—*n.* That which exhilarates.—**ex·hil·a·rat·ing**, *a.* Stimulating.—**ex·hil·a·ra·tive, ex·hil·a·ra·to·ry**, *a.*

ex·hil·a·ra·tion, ig·zil"a·rā'shan, *n.* The act of exhilarating; the feeling of cheerfulness.

ex·hort, ig·zȧrt', *v.t.* [L. *exhortor—ex-*, and *hortor,* to encourage, to advise.] To appeal to and encourage by earnest admonition; to advise or caution.—*v.i.* To use constructive criticism to encourage and incite.—**ex·hor·ta·tive, ex·hor·ta·to·ry, ex·hor·ta·tiv**, ig·zȧr'ta·tōr"ē, ig·zȧr'ta·tȯr"ē, *a.* —**ex·hort·er**, *n.*—**ex·hort·ing·ly**, *adv.*

ex·hor·ta·tion, eg"zȧr·tā'shan, ek"sȧr·tā'shan, *n.* The act or practice of exhorting; language intended to incite and encourage; a persuasive discourse; an admonition.

ex·hume, ig·zōm', ig·zūm', eks·hūm', *v.t.* —exhumed, exhuming. [Fr. *exhumer,* to dig out of the ground—L. *ex-*, out, and *humus,* earth, ground (akin *humble*).] To dig up after having been buried; to disinter; to revive, as something obscure or neglected; reestablish.—**ex·hu·ma·tion**, eks"hū·mā'shan, *n.*—**ex·hum·er**, *n.*

ex·i·gen·cy, ek'si·jen·sē, *n.* pl. **ex·i·gen·cies.** [Fr. *exigence,* < L. *exigo,* to drive out or forth, to demand, to exact.] A state of being urgent; a situation which demands immediate attention and prompt solution; an emergency; *usu. pl.* intrinsic requirements or circumstantial necessities. Also **ex·i·gence.**

ex·i·gent, ek'si·jent, *a.* Urgent; demanding prompt attention or immediate action; requiring a great deal; demanding. Also **ex·i·geant.**—**ex·i·gent·ly**, *adv.*

ex·i·gi·ble, ek'si·ji·bl, *a.* That may be exacted; demandable; requirable.

ex·ig·u·ous, ig·zig'ū·us, ik·sig'ū·us, *a.* [L. *exiguus,* scanty.] Small; slender; inadequate in number or amount.—**ex·i·gu·i·ty, ex·ig·u·ous·ness**, ek"si·gū'i·tē, *n.* Smallness; slenderness.—**ex·ig·u·ous·ly**, *adv.*

ex·ile, eg'zīl, ek'sīl, *n.* [Fr. *exil,* banishment, *exile,* an exiled person, < L. *exsilium,* banishment, *exsul,* a banished person—*ex-*, out, and root of *salio,* to leap; Skt. *sar,* to go.] Removal or separation from one's native country, either voluntary or forced by authority; a person expelled from his country or one who chooses to reside in another.—*v.t.*—exiled, exiling. To banish; to cause to be an exile.—**ex·il·a·ble**, *a.*—**ex·il·er**, *n.*—**ex·il·ic**, eg·zil'ik, ek·sil'ik, *a.*

ex·im·i·ous, eg·zim'ē·us, *a.* [L. *eximius,* < *eximere,* take out.] *Archaic.* Distinguished; eminent; excellent.

ex·ist, ig·zist', *v.i.* [Fr. *exister,* < L. *existo—ex-*, and *sisto,* to stand, as in *assist, consist.*] To have actual being or reality; to be; to live; to continue to have life; to occur in certain places or under specific conditions.

ex·ist·ence, ig·zis'tens, *n.* The state of existing; the condition of being; the form of being which consists in interaction with other things; state of being actual; the condition of objectivity; life; living; an entity.—**ex·ist·ent**, ig·zis'tent, *a.* Having being; having existence.—*n.* One who or that which exists.

ex·is·ten·tial, eg"zi·sten'shal, ek"si·sten'shal, *a.* Relating to, of, or pertaining to existence; of the doctrine of existentialism. —**ex·is·ten·tial·ly**, *adv.*

ex·is·ten·tial·ism, eg"zi·sten'sha·liz"um, ek"si·sten'sha·liz"um, *n.* The term for various philosophical doctrines based on the concept that the individual is entirely free, and must therefore accept commitment and full responsibility for his acts and decisions in an uncertain and purposeless world.— **ex·is·ten·tial·ist**, *n., a.*

ex·is·ten·tial quan·ti·fi·er, *n. Philos.* a term in formal logic expressing that a given formula with a free variable *x* holds for one or more but not all values of *x* usu. within a certain range. Also **ex·is·ten·tial op·er·a·tor.** See *Universal quantifier.*

ex·it, eg'zit, ek'sit, *n.* [L., he goes out < *exeo,* to go out—*ex-*, out, and *eo,* to go.] A passage out of; the departure of a player from the stage when he has performed his part; any departure; the act of quitting the stage of action; death.—*v.i.* To leave.

ex li·bris, eks lī'bris, eks lē'bris, *n.* pl. **ex li·bris.** [L. 'from the books.'] From the library of, a phrase inscribed in or on a book before the owner's name; a bookplate.

Ex·moor, eks'mụr", *n.* A moorish area in Devonshire County in S.W. England; a breed of Devonshire horned sheep used

---

ch- chain, G. na*ch*t; **th-** THen, thin; **w-** wig, hw as sound in whig; **z-** zh as in azure, zeal. *Italicized vowel* indicates schwa sound.

for mutton; a breed of ponies native to the Exmoor area.

ex·o·bi·ol·o·gy, ek″sō·bī·ol′o·jē, n. Aerospace. That field of biology which deals with the effects of environments outside the earth on living organisms; a search for life forms evolved and existing outside the earth.

ex·o·carp, ek′sō kärp″, n. [Gr. exo-, outside, karpos, fruit.] Bot. epicarp.

ex·o·crine, ek′sō·krin, ek′sō·krīn″, ek′so·krĕn″, a. Secreting externally through a duct: used esp. in referring to certain glands.

ex·o·der·mis, ek″sō·dèr′mis, n. Bot. a temporary layer of cortical cells performing a protective function in some roots lacking secondary thickening, as orchids.

ex·o·don·tia, ek″so·don′sha, ek″so·don′shē·a, n. The branch of dentistry which deals with tooth extraction. Also **ex·o·don·tics**.

ex·o·dus, ek′so·dus, n. [Gr. exodos—ex-, and hodos, way.] Departure from a place, esp. by a large number of people; mass migration. (Cap.) the migration from Egypt by Moses and the Israelites.

ex·o·en·zyme, ek″sō·en′zīm, n. Biochem. an enzyme which performs its function outside the cell which produces it.

ex·o·er·gic, ek″sō·èr′jik, a. Of or pertaining to a reaction accompanied by a release of energy.

ex of·fi·ci·o, eks o·fish′ē·ō″, adv., a. [L. 'from office.'] By virtue of official position; as, ex officio authority.

ex·og·a·my, ek·sog′a·mē, n. Marriage outside the tribe; sexual reproduction by organisms of no relation.—**ex·og·a·mous**, ek·sog′a·mus, a.

ex·o·gen, ek′so·jen, n. [Fr. exogène.] Bot. any plant of the obsolete class Exogenæ, including the dicotyledons, whose stems grow by successive concentric layers on the outside.—**ex·og·e·nous**, ek·soj′e·nus, a. Growing by additions on the outside. Bot. belonging to the exogens; of plants, as the dicotyledons, having stems which grow by the addition of an annual layer of wood to the outside beneath the constantly widening bark; pertaining to plants having such stems.—**ex·og·e·nous·ly**, adv.

ex·on·er·ate, ig·zon′e·rāt″, v.t.—exonerated, exonerating. [L. exonero, exoneratum—ex-, not, and onus, oneris, a load.] To relieve or clear of a charge or of blame; to discharge of responsibility, obligation, duty, or liability.—**ex·on·er·a·tion**, n.—**ex·on·er·a·tive**, a.

ex·oph·thal·mos, ek″sof·thal′mos, ek″sof·thal′mos, n. [N.L., < Gr. exophthalmos, with prominent eyes, < ex-, out, and ophthalmos, eye.] Pathol. protrusion of the eyeball from the eye socket, usu. caused by excessive activity of the thyroid gland. Also **ex·oph·thal·mus**, **ex·oph·thal·mia**, ek″sof·thal′mus, ek″sof·thal′mē·a.—**ex·oph·thal·mic**, a.

ex·o·ra·ble, ek′so·ra·bl, a. [L. exorabilis, < ex-, and oro, to pray.] Capable of being moved or persuaded by entreaty.

ex·or·bi·tance, ig·zor′bi·tans, n. [L.L. exorbitantia, < exorbito, to go out of the track—L. ex-, out, and orbita, a rut made by a wheel, < orbis, a circle.] A going beyond rule or ordinary limits; excess; extravagance; as, exorbitance of demands, of prices. Also **ex·or·bi·tan·cy**, pl. **ex·or·bi·tan·cies**.

ex·or·bi·tant, ig·zar′bi·tant, a. Going beyond the established limits of right or propriety; excessive; extravagant; enormous.—**ex·or·bi·tant·ly**, adv.

ex·or·cise, **ex·or·cize**, ek′sar·sīz″, v.t.—exorcised, exorcising. [Fr. exorciser, < Gr. exorkizo—ex-, intens., and horkizo, to bind by oath < horkos, an oath.] To expel or cast out, as an evil spirit, by conjurations,

prayers, and ceremonies; to purify of unclean spirits by adjurations and ceremonies; to deliver from the influence or presence of malignant spirits or demons.—**ex·or·cis·er**, **ex·or·cist**, ek′sar·sist, n.

ex·or·cism, ek″sar·siz″um, n. The act of exorcising; the prayer or charm used to expel evil spirits.—**ex·or·cis·tic**, a.

ex·or·di·um, ig·zar′dē·um, ik·sar′dē·um, n. [L. < exordior, to begin a web, to lay the warp—ex-, and ordior, to begin a web, to begin.] The beginning of anything; specif. the introductory part of a discourse.—**ex·or·di·al**, a.

ex·o·skel·e·ton, ek″sō·skel′i·ton, n. Zool. an external protective covering or integument, esp. when hard, as the shell of crustaceans, the carapace of turtles, and the scales and plates of fishes: opposed to endoskeleton.—**ex·o·skel·e·tal**, a.

ex·os·mo·sis, ek″sos·mō′sis, ek″soz·mō′sis, n. Osmosis from within outward; in osmosis, the action or flow of fluid passing from a region of greater concentration to a region of lesser concentration: opposed to endosmosis. Also **ex·os·mose**, ek″sos·mōs′, ek″soz·mōs.—**ex·os·mot·ic**, ek″sos·mot′ik, ek″soz·mot′ik, a.

ex·o·sphere, ek′sō·sfēr″, n. [Gr. exō-, outside and sphaira, sphere.] The outermost layer of the atmosphere, extending about 200 to 400 miles from the earth's surface.

ex·o·spore, ek′so·spōr″, ek′so·spar″, n. Bot. the outer layer of a spore.—**ex·o·spor·al**, **ex·o·spor·ous**, ek″so·spōr′al, ek″so·spar′al, ek·sos′pèr·al, a.

ex·os·to·sis, ek″so·stō′sis, ek″so·stō′sis, n. pl. **ex·os·to·ses**, ek″so·stō′sēz, ek″so·stō′sēz. [Gr. ex-, and osteon, a bone.] Pathol. any abnormal protuberance or enlargement of a bone or tooth.

ex·o·ter·ic, ek″so·ter′ik, a. [L. exotericus, < Gr. exōterikos, < exōterō, compar. of exō-, outside.] Pertaining to the outside; external; not belonging or pertaining to the inner or select circle: opposed to esoteric; suitable for the general public; commonplace; simple.—**ex·o·ter·ics**, **ex·o·ter·i·ca**, ek″so·ter′i·ka, n. pl. Exoteric doctrines, discourses, or works.—**ex·o·ter·i·cal·ly**, adv.

ex·o·ther·mic, ek″sō·ther′mik, a. [Gr. exō-, outside, thermos, heat.] Chem. formed with or involving evolution of heat: opposed to endothermic. Also **ex·o·ther·mal**.

ex·o·tic, ig·zot′ik, a. [L. exoticus, < Gr. exōtikos, < exō-, outside, < ex, ek, out of.] Of foreign origin or character; not native; introduced from abroad, but not fully naturalized or acclimatized; strikingly beautiful and unusual in appearance; as, an exotic woman; mysterious; different; strange; pertaining to stripteasing; as, an exotic dancer.—n. Anything exotic, as a plant.—**ex·ot·i·cal·ly**, adv.—**ex·ot·ic·ness**, n.

ex·ot·i·cism, ig·zot′i·siz″um, n. Tendency to adopt what is exotic; exotic quality or character; anything exotic, as a foreign word or idiom.—**ex·ot·i·cist**, n.

ex·o·tox·in, ek″sō·tok′sin, n. Biochem. a soluble toxin formed within and secreted by a microorganism which is not itself toxic.

ex·pand, ik·spand′, v.t. [L. expandere (pp. expansus), < ex-, out, and pandere, spread, extend.] To spread out or unfold; spread out to view or display, as: A peacock expands his feathers. To express in fuller form or greater detail; to develop, as a statement; to increase in extent, size, or volume. Dilate; distend; enlarge; make broader in scope, or more comprehensive.—v.i. To spread out; unfold; develop; to express in fuller form, usu. followed by on or upon; to increase, as in extent or bulk; become dilated or enlarged; increase in scope.—**ex·pand·ed**, a. Spread out;

extended; increased in area, bulk, or volume.—**ex·pand·a·ble**, a.—**ex·pand·a·bil·i·ty**, n.—**ex·pand·ing·ly**, adv.—**ex·pand·ed type**, print. a kind of type somewhat wider than is usual for its height.

ex·pand·er, ik·span′dèr, n. That which expands; med. one of the colloidal substances used as a substitute for plasma to expand the volume of blood.

ex·panse, ik·spans′, n. [L. expansum, neut. of expansus, pp. of expandere. EXPAND.] That which is expanded; an uninterrupted space or area, esp. one of considerable extent; a wide extent of anything; expansion or extension.

ex·pan·si·ble, ik·span′si·bl, a. Capable of being expanded, extended, dilated, or diffused.—**ex·pan·si·bil·i·ty**, n.

ex·pan·sile, ik·span′sil, ik·span′sīl, a. Capable of expanding or of being dilated; of or pertaining to expansion.

ex·pan·sion, ik·span′shan, n. [L.L. expansio(n-).] The act of expanding or the state of being expanded; spreading out; increase in size or volume; dilatation; distension; enlargement; the amount or degree of expanding; anything spread out; an expanse; an expanded, dilated, or enlarged portion or form of a thing; math. the development at length of an expression indicated in a contracted form; mach. increase of volume of the working medium in the operation of an engine, as of steam in the cylinder.—**ex·pan·sion·ism**, n. A national policy of expansion, as of territory or currency.—**ex·pan·sion·ist**, n.—**ex·pan·sion·ary**, **ex·pan·sion·al**, a.

ex·pan·sive, ik·span′siv, a. Tending to cause expansion; as, the expansive force of heat; tending to expand or capable of expanding; pertaining to or characterized by expansion; fig. effusive, as persons, feelings, or utterances; expanding over a large area; extensive; having a wide range; comprehensive; psychiatry, characterized by delusions of self-grandeur.—**ex·pan·sive·ly**, adv.—**ex·pan·sive·ness**, **ex·pan·siv·i·ty**, ek″span·siv′i·tē, n.

ex par·te, eks pär′tē, a. [L.] One-sided; partial; law, made or done by or on behalf of one party in a suit.

ex·pa·ti·ate, ik·spā′shē·āt″, v.i.—expatiated, expatiating. [L. exspatior, exspatiatus—ex-, and spatior, to walk about, < spatium, space.] To rove or wander without prescribed limits; to enlarge in discourse or writing; to be copious in argument or discussion.—**ex·pa·ti·a·tion**, n.—**ex·pa·ti·a·tor**, n.

ex·pa·tri·ate, eks·pā′trē·āt″, v.t.—expatriated, expatriating. [M.L. expatriatus, pp. of expatriare, < L. ex-, out of, and patria, fatherland.] To banish, as a person, from his native country; to withdraw, as oneself, from residence in one's native country.—v.i. To withdraw from citizenship in one country to become a citizen of another.—a. Expatriated.—n. An expatriated person.—**ex·pa·tri·a·tion**, n.

ex·pect, ik·spekt′, v.t. [L. expectare, for exspectare, < ex-, out, and spectare, look at or to.] To await or look forward to; to anticipate the occurrence or birth of; to regard as likely to occur; to suppose or surmise; to consider probable, due, or right.—v.i. To be pregnant; to wait.—**ex·pect·a·ble**, a.—**ex·pect·a·bly**, adv.—**ex·pect·er**, n.—**ex·pect·ing·ly**, adv.

ex·pect·an·cy, ik·spek′tan·sē, n. pl. **ex·pect·an·cies**. The act or state of expecting, or the state of being expected; an object of expectation.

ex·pect·ant, ik·spek′tant, a. Expecting or anticipating; having expectations; pregnant.—n. One who waits in expectation.—**ex·pect·ant·ly**, adv.

ex·pec·ta·tion, ek″spek·tā′shan, *n.* [L. *expectatio(n-)*.] The act or state of expecting, or the state of being expected; anticipation; expectant mental attitude; something expected; the degree of probability of the occurrence or receiving of something.—**ex·pec·ta·tion of life,** the duration of life which may be expected as shown by mortality tables.—**ex·pect·a·tive,** ik·spek′ta·tiv, *a.* Of or pertaining to expectation; characterized by expectation.

ex·pect·ed val·ue, *n. Statistics,* the weighted sum or average of the probability distribution of random variables, which may be finite or in an infinite sequence of numbers. Also **ex·pec·ta·tion val·ue, mean val·ue.**

ex·pec·to·rant, ik·spek′to·rant, *a.* Having the quality of promoting discharges from the mucous membrane of the lungs or trachea.—*n.* A drug which promotes such discharges.

ex·pec·to·rate, ik·spek′to·rāt, *v.t.*—*expectorated, expectorating.* [L. *expectoro, expectoratum*—*ex-,* and *pectus, pectoris,* the breast (whence *pectoral*).] To eject from the trachea or lungs; to discharge, as phlegm or other matter, by coughing, hawking, and spitting.—*v.i.* To eject matter by coughing and spitting; to spit.—**ex·pec·to·ra·tion,** *n.* The act of expectorating; the matter expectorated.

ex·pe·di·en·cy, ik·spē′dē·en·sē, *n.* pl. **ex·pe·di·en·cies.** [L. *expediens,* pp. of *expedio,* to set free.] Propriety under the particular circumstances of a case; advisability in view of the desired end; the seeking of immediate or selfish gain or advantage at the expense of genuine principle. Also **ex·pe·di·ence.**—**ex·pe·di·en·tial,** ik·-spē″dē·en′shal, *a.*

ex·pe·di·ent, ik·spē′dē·ent, *a.* Tending to achieve desired results by the most direct, sometimes ruthless, method; proper under the circumstances; conducive to selfish ends; acting for expedience.—*n.* Means employed to accomplish an end; means devised or employed in an exigency; device; contrivance.—**ex·pe·di·ent·ly,** *adv.*

ex·pe·dite, ek′spi·dīt″, *v.t.*—*expedited, expediting.* [L. *expeditus,* pp. of *expedire,* extricate, help forward, send off or dispatch, orig. 'free the feet of,' < *ex-,* out of, and *pes (ped-),* foot.] To facilitate the motion or progress of; hasten; to accomplish promptly, as a piece of business; to dispatch; to issue, as a document.

ex·pe·dit·er, ex·pe·di·tor, ek′spi·dī″tèr, *n.* One who expedites, esp. one, as in a government or business organization, whose job is to make sure that materials are promptly delivered when needed.

ex·pe·di·tion, ek″spi·dish′an, *n.* [L. *expeditio(n-).*] An excursion, journey, or voyage made for some specific purpose, as of war or exploration; the body of persons or ships engaged in such an excursion; promptness in action.—**ex·pe·di·tion·ar·y,** *a.* Pertaining to or composing an expedition; as, an *expeditionary* force.

ex·pe·di·tious, ek″spi·dish′us, *a.* Performed with or characterized by efficiency and celerity; quick; hasty; speedy.—**ex·pe·di·tious·ly,** *adv.*—**ex·pe·di·tious·ness,** *n.*

ex·pel, ik·spel′, *v.t.*—*expelled, expelling.* [L. *expellere* (pp. *expulsus*), < *ex-,* out of, and *pellere,* drive.] To drive or force out or away; discharge or eject; as, to *expel* air from the lungs; compel to depart from a place; as, to *expel* a traitor or an invader from a country; to cut off from membership or relations; as, to *expel* a student from a college.—**ex·pel·la·ble,** *a.*—**ex·pel·lant, ex·pel·lent,** *a.* Expelling; serving to expel. —*n.* An expellant medicine.—**ex·pel·ler,** *n.* —**ex·pel·lee,** *n.*

ex·pend, ik·spend′, *v.t.* [L. *expendere* (pp. *expensus*), weigh out, pay out, < *ex-,* out, and *pendere,* weigh.] To pay out; disburse; spend; to consume by use; use up, as time or energy.—**ex·pend·a·bil·i·ty,** ik·spend″a·bil′i·tē, *n.*—**ex·pend·er,** *n.*

ex·pend·a·ble, ik·spen′da·bl, *a.* Able to be disposed of without irreparable loss; conveniently replaced. *Milit.* able to be sacrificed, as men, supplies, or equipment, toward achievement of a military objective.

ex·pend·i·ture, ik·spen′di·chèr, *n.* The act of expending; disbursement; consumption; that which is expended; expense.

ex·pense, ik·spens′, *n.* [M.L. *expensa,* prop. fem. of L. *expensus,* pp. EXPEND.] Cost or charge; that which is expended; an outlay, esp. of money; a cause or occasion of expenditure. *Pl.* charges incurred by a person in the execution of his duties; money paid to a person to reimburse him for such charges.—**at the ex·pense of,** with the sacrifice or loss of; as, quantity *at the expense of* quality.

ex·pense ac·count, *n.* An account of expenses incurred by the employee which are to be refunded by the employer.

ex·pen·sive, ik·spen′siv, *a.* Entailing great expense; costly.—**ex·pen·sive·ly,** *adv.*—**ex·pen·sive·ness,** *n.*

ex·pe·ri·ence, ik·spēr′ē·ens, *n.* [O.Fr. *experience* (Fr. *expérience*), < L. *experientia,* < *experiens (-ent-),* ppr. of *experiri* (pp. *expertus*), try, undergo—*ex-,* out, and *per-,* occurring also in *peritus,* experienced, skilled.] The process or fact of personally observing, encountering, or undergoing something; as, to have had *experience* in teaching; a particular instance of personally encountering or undergoing something; as, to have a strange *experience*; the observing, encountering, or undergoing of things generally as they occur in the course of time; as, the range of human *experience*; knowledge or practical wisdom gained from what one has observed, encountered, or undergone; as, men of ripe *experience.*

ex·pe·ri·ence, ik·spēr′ē·ens, *v.t.*—*experienced, experiencing.* To have experience of; meet with; undergo; feel; to learn by experience.—**ex·pe·ri·ence re·li·gion,** to become converted to religion.—**ex·pe·ri·enced,** *a.* Taught by or having experience; wise or skillful through experience in a particular sphere of activity; endured.

ex·pe·ri·en·tial, ik·spēr″ē·en′shal, *a.* Pertaining to or derived from experience.—**ex·pe·ri·en·tial·ly,** *adv.*

ex·per·i·ment, ik·sper′i·ment, *n.* [O.Fr. *experiment,* < L. *experimentum,* < *experiri,* try.] A test or trial; a tentative procedure; a controlled project to establish a hypothesis, illustrate a known law or effect, or discover one which is unknown; the conducting of such projects.—ek·sper′i·ment″, *v.i.* To test; to make experiments.—**ex·per·i·men·ta·tion,** ik·sper″i·men·tā′shan, *n.* The act or practice of experimenting.—**ex·per·i·ment·er,** *n.*

ex·per·i·men·tal, ik·sper″i·men′tal, *a.* Pertaining to, derived from, or founded on experiment; of the nature of an experiment; tentative; based on or derived from experience; empirical.—**ex·per·i·men·tal·ly,** *adv.*—**ex·per·i·men·tal·ism,** *n.*—**ex·per·i·men·tal·ist,** *n.* One who experiments.

ex·per·i·ment sta·tion, *n.* An establishment in which experiments in a particular line of research or activity are systematically carried on.

ex·pert, ik·spurt′, ek′spurt, *a.* [L. *experius,* having made trial, experienced, *experior,* to try.] Experienced; taught by use or practice; skillful; dexterous; adroit; having a facility of operation or performance from

practice.—ek′spurt, *n.* A skillful or practiced person; an authority in a particular field; a scientific or professional witness who gives evidence on matters connected with his profession.—ek′spurt, *v.t., v.i.*—**ex·pert·ly,** *adv.*—**ex·pert·ness,** *n.*

ex·per·tise, ek″spèr·tēz′, *n.* An interpretation or opinion from an expert; specialized knowledge.—**ex·pert·ize,** *Brit.* **ex·per·tise,** ek′sper·tīz″, *v.t., v.i.*—*expertized, expertizing, Brit. expertised, expertising.* To offer an opinion based on thorough study.—**ex·pert·ism,** *n.* Detailed knowledge or experience in a particular field.

ex·pi·ate, ek′spē·āt″, *v.t.*—*expiated, expiating.* [L. *expio, expiatum,* to make satisfaction—*ex-,* out, and *pio,* to appease, to propitiate, < *pius,* pious.] To atone for; to make redress or reparation for.—**ex·pi·a·ble,** ek′spē·a·bl, *a.*—**ex·pi·a·tor,** *n.*—**ex·pi·a·tion,** *n.*—**ex·pi·a·to·ry,** *a.* Having the power to make atonement or expiation.

ex·pi·ra·tion, ek″spi·rā′shan, *n.* [L. *exspiratio.*] The act of breathing out; emission of breath; exhalation; close, end, conclusion, or termination; expiry.—**ex·pir·a·to·ry,** ik·spīer′a·tōr″ē, ik·spīer′a·tạr″ē, *a.* Pertaining to the expiration of breath.

ex·pire, ik·spīer′, *v.t.*—*expired, expiring.* [L. *exspiro*—*ex-,* out, and *spiro,* to breathe.] To breathe out; to expel from the lungs in the process of respiration: opposed to *inspire;* to exhale.—*v.i.* To emit breath; to die; to come to an end, as an agreed period of time.—**ex·pir·y,** *n.* pl. **ex·pir·ies.** Expiration of breath; termination.

ex·plain, ik·splān′, *v.t.* [L. *explano*—*ex-,* and *plano,* to make plain, *planus,* level, plain.] To make plain or understandable; to clear of obscurity; to make clear or evident; to expound; to give or show the meaning or reason for.—*v.i.* To give explanations.—**ex·plain·a·ble,** *a.*—**ex·plain·er,** *n.*

ex·pla·na·tion, ek″spla·nā′shan, *n.* [L. *explanatio.*] The act of explaining; a making clear or understandable; an exposition; the clearing up of a misunderstanding; interpretation.—**ex·plan·a·to·ry,** ik·splan′a·tōr″ē, ik·splan′a·tạr″ē, *a.* Serving to explain; containing explanation. Also **ex·plan·a·tive.**—**ex·plan·a·to·ri·ly,** **ex·plan·a·tive·ly,** *adv.*

ex·plant, eks·plant′, eks·plänt′, *v.t.* To transfer, as live fragments of plant or animal tissue, to a nutrient material.—*n.* A fragment of living tissue kept alive for study.—**ex·plan·ta·tion,** *n.*

ex·ple·tive, ek′sple·tiv, *a.* [Fr. *explétif,* < L. *expleo, expletum,* to fill full—*ex-,* intens., and *pleo,* to fill.] Superfluous; possessing many expletives, as a sentence. Also **ex·ple·to·ry,** ek′sple·tōr″ē, ek′sple·tạr″ē.—*n.* An additional word, syllable, or phrase used to fill a vacancy but not to alter the meaning of a sentence; an obscene or profane word or phrase; a needless interjection.

ex·pli·ca·ble, ek′spli·ka·bl, ik·splik′a·bl, *a.* Capable of being explained.

ex·pli·cate, ek′spli·kāt″, *v.t.*—*explicated, explicating.* [L. *explico, explicatum,* to unfold—*ex-,* not, and *plico,* to fold.] To interpret clearly and simply the meaning or sense of; to explain; to logically develop the implications of.—**ex·pli·ca·tion,** ek″spli·kā′shan, *n.*—**ex·pli·ca·tive,** ek′spli·ca·tō·ry, ek′spli·kā″tiv, ik·splik′a·tiv, ek′spli·ka·tōr″ē, ek′spli·ka·tạr″ē, *a.* Serving to unfold or explain.—**ex·pli·ca·tor,** *n.*

ex·plic·it, ik·splis′it, *a.* [L. *explicitus,* disentangled, < *explico, explicitum,* to unfold, to disentangle.] Precise and distinct in expression; leaving nothing to be implied; unequivocal; thoroughly formulated or developed; unreserved; outspoken.—**ex·plic·it·ly,** *adv.*—**ex·plic·it·ness,** *n.*

ex·plode, ik·splōd′, *v.i.*—*exploded, exploding.* L. *explodere* (pp. *explosus*) < *ex-,* out of, from, and *plodere, plaudere,* clap.] To expand with force and noise because of rapid chemical change or decomposition, as gunpowder or nitroglycerin; to burst, fly into pieces, or break up violently with a loud report, as a boiler from excessive pressure of steam; to burst forth violently or noisily with emotion; as, *explode* with laughter.—*v.t.* To cause to break apart or blow up noisily; to detonate; to discredit, disprove, or cause to be rejected, as a belief. —**ex·plod·er,** *n.*—**ex·plo·si·ble,** *a.* Capable of being exploded.—**ex·plo·si·bil·i·ty,** ik·splō″zi·bil′i·tē, ik·splō″si·bil′i·tē, *n.* **ex·plod·ed,** ik·splō′did, *a.* Depicted, as in a photograph or drawing, so as to show the parts of a system or mechanism separately, while retaining their actual relationship to each other; as, an *exploded* view of an engine.

ex·plod·ent, ik·splŏd′ent, *n.* An explosive. **ex·ploit,** ek′sploit, ik·sploit′, *n.* [O.Fr. *esploit* (Fr. *exploit*), < L. *explicitum,* neut. of *explicitus,* pp. of *explicare,* unfold, display.] A deed that is striking or notable; a feat or heroic act.—ik·sploit′, *v.t.* [O.Fr. *exploitier* (Fr. *exploiter*).] To utilize for profit; to use selfishly for one's own ends; to promote.—**ex·ploit·a·ble,** *a.*—**ex·ploit·a·tive, ex·ploit·a·to·ry, ex·ploit·ive,** *a.*—**ex·ploit·er,** *n.*

ex·ploi·ta·tion, ek″sploi·tā′shan, *n.* The act or process of exploiting; utilization for profit, as of natural resources; selfish utilization; use of public relations and publicity to promote an enterprise or person.

ex·plo·ra·tion, ek″splō·rā′shan, *n.* The act of engaging in close examination; scrutiny; travel for purposes of discovery; a search into unknown areas. *Med.* examination of a wound or organ.—**ex·plor·a·tive, ex·plor·a·to·ry,** ik·splôr′a·tiv″, ik·splar′a·tiv″, ik·splôr′a·tōr″ē, ik·splar′a·tar″ē, *a.*

ex·plore, ik·splôr′, ik·splar′, *v.t.*—*explored, exploring.* [L. *exploro,* to cry aloud, to explore—*ex-,* out, and *ploro,* to bewail.] To travel or range over with the intent of making discovery, esp. geographical discovery; to investigate; to scrutinize; *med.* to examine closely, as in probing an organ.— *v.i.* To engage in systematic investigation.— **ex·plor·a·ble,** *a.*—**ex·plor·ing·ly,** *adv.*

ex·plor·er, ik·splôr′ẽr, ik·splar′ẽr, *n.* One who explores, esp. one who journeys into unknown areas in search of knowledge; a person who travels for the purpose of research in anthropology, geography, or other fields. A boy who is affiliated with the program of the Boy Scouts of America devoted to exploring. *Surg., dentistry,* an instrument used to examine or probe. *(Cap.)* one of a series of satellites produced by the government of the U.S.; as, *Explorer* I, designed for orbiting about the earth, launched in 1958.

ex·plo·sion, ik·splō′zhan, *n.* [L. *explosio(n-),* < *explodere.* EXPLODE.] The act of exploding; a violent, noisy expansion or bursting, as of gunpowder or a boiler; the noise itself; a violent outburst of emotion, as of laughter or anger; a sudden, widespread outcropping or increase; as, population *explosion; phon.* abrupt release of the breath in certain pronunciations of stop consonants, *p, b, t, d.*

ex·plo·sive, ik·splō′siv, *a.* [L. *explodere* (pp. *explosus*), E. *explode.*] Tending or serving to explode; pertaining to or of the nature of an explosion; *phon.* involving a slight explosion of the breath in certain pronunciations of the consonants, *p, b, t, d.* —*n.* An explosive agent or substance, as gunpowder; *phon.* an explosive consonant.— **ex·plo·sive·ly,** *adv.*—**ex·plo·sive·ness,** *n.* **ex·po·nent,** ik·spō′nent, ek′spō·nent, *n.* [L. *exponens, exponentis,* ppr. of *expono,* to

expose or set forth—*ex-,* out, and *pono,* to place.] One who expounds or explains anything; an interpreter; one who stands as a symbol, representative, or proponent of something; *math.* a number or symbol placed above and at the right of a quantity to denote the power to which the quantity should be raised, as a^2 denotes *a* raised to the second power.—**ex·po·nen·tial,** ek″spō·nen′shal, *a.* Of or pertaining to an exponent or exponents.—**ex·po·nen·tial·ly,** *adv.*

ex·port, ik·spōrt′, ik·spart′, ek′spōrt, ek′spart, *v.t.* [Fr. *exporter,* < L. *exporto—ex-,* out, and *porto,* to bear, to carry.] To send, as goods, for sale or consumption in foreign countries.—ek′spōrt, ek′spart, *n.* The act of exporting; exportation; the gross quantity of goods exported; a commodity that is exported.—ek′spōrt, ek′spart, *a.* Of or relating to exportation or to goods which can be exported.—**ex·port·a·ble,** *a.* Capable of being exported.—**ex·port·er,** *n.*

ex·por·ta·tion, ek″spōr·tā′shan, ek″spar·tā′shan, *n.* The act of exporting; the conveying or sending abroad of commodities, usu. for commerce.

ex·pose, ik·spōz′, *v.t.*—*exposed, exposing.* [Fr. *exposer*—prefix *ex-,* and *poser,* to set, to place.] To leave unprotected; to place in danger; to abandon; to uncover; to disclose or reveal, as a crime; to display; to exhibit as an object of worship; to lay open to examination; to hold up to censure by disclosing the faults of. *Photog., phys.* to subject to light or other radiant energy.—**ex·pos·er,** *n.*

ex·po·sé, ik″spō·zā′, *n.* [Fr.] Exposure; revelation of something concealed or discreditable.

ex·posed, ik·spōzd′, *a.* Put in danger; unprotected; open to the wind or cold; unsheltered; vulnerable; *photog.* pertaining to film or plates that have been subjected to light or other radiant energy.

ex·po·si·tion, ek″spo·zish′an, *n.* [Fr. *exposition,* L. *expositio.*] A laying open; a setting out to public view; explanation; interpretation; a laying open of the sense or meaning of; an exhibition or show; the first part of a sonata; the opening section of a fugue.—**ex·po·si·tion·al,** *a.*

ex·pos·i·tor, ik·spoz′i·tẽr, *n.* One who expounds or explains; an interpreter.— **ex·pos·i·to·ry, ex·pos·i·tive,** ik·spoz′i·tōr″e, ik·spoz′i·tar″ē, *a.* Serving to explain; tending to illustrate.

ex post fac·to, eks′ pōst″fak′tō, *a.* [For L.L. *ex postfacto,* 'from what is done afterward.'] Formulated after the fact; adding to or in some way altering previous requisites, thereby changing a previously determined situation.—*adv.* After the fact.—**ex post fac·to law,** a law made after an offense but operative with respect to it.

ex·pos·tu·late, ik·spos′cha·lāt″, *v.i.*—*expostulated, expostulating.* [L. *expostulo, expostulatum,* to demand vehemently, to find fault—*ex-,* and *postulo,* to demand, < *posco,* to ask urgently, to beg.] To reason earnestly with a person on some impropriety of his conduct; to remonstrate.—**ex·pos·tu·la·tion,** *n.* The act of expostulating; earnest protest; an address containing expostulatory statements.—**ex·pos·tu·la·tor,** *n.*—**ex·pos·tu·la·to·ry, ex·pos·tu·la·tive,** *a.*

ex·po·sure, ik·spō′zhẽr, *n.* The act of exposing or the state of being exposed; an act of abandoning without shelter or protection; disclosure of something private or secret; a laying open or subjecting to the action or influence of something; presentation to open and public view; position with regard to access of sunlight and wind; something exposed to view; *photog.* the act of exposing light-sensitive photographic

film; a section of film or plate for a single picture; the time required for light rays to produce the desired picture.

ex·po·sure me·ter, *n. Photog.* a device for measuring light intensity and indicating the correct shutter speeds and stops for photographic exposure.

ex·pound, ik·spound′, *v.t.* [O.Fr. *expondere,* < L. *exponere,* to set forth, to explain—*ex-,* out, and *pono,* to place.] To explain; to argue the defense of; to clear of obscurity; to interpret.—**ex·pound·er,** *n.*

ex·press, ik·spres′, *v.t.* [O.Fr. *expresser,* L. *exprimo, expressum—ex-,* out, and *premo,* to press.] To declare by words; to make known, esp. one's own opinions or ideas; to communicate or represent, as by a symbol or formula; to intimate, indicate, or denote; to press or squeeze out; to send or convey by an especially fast system; to emit, as if forced by pressure.—**ex·press·er,** *n.*—**ex·press·i·ble, ex·press·a·ble,** *a.*

ex·press, ik·spres′, *a.* Given in direct terms; clearly stated; explicit; precise; plain; designed or intended for a precise and definite purpose; special or specific; as, an *express* reason; pertaining to a particularly direct or fast means of transportation or delivery, as a train or highway. —*n.* Any regular provision made for the transmission of freight that is faster but more expensive than ordinary service; any vehicle or other conveyance sent on a special mission; a train which travels at a high rate of speed; that which is sent by express; a concern engaged in the business of express transportation or transmission. *Brit.* a messenger sent with haste on a particular errand or occasion; the dispatch sent through such a messenger.—*adv.* By way of express, as: Ship the goods *express.*

ex·press·age, ik·spres′ij, *n.* The transporting of parcels by express; the charge for such transporting.

ex·pres·sion, ik·spresh′an, *n.* [L. *expressio(n-).*] The act of expressing or setting forth in words; the manner or form in which a thing is put into words; a particular word, phrase, or form of words; wording; phrasing; the act of manifesting or revealing; indication of feeling, thought, or attitude, as shown on the face, in the voice, or in artistic execution; a look or intonation expressing feeling or personal reaction; the quality or ability of expressing emotion; the act of expressing or representing, as by symbols; a mathematical symbol or combination of symbols indicating a value or relation, as an algebraic quantity; the action of expressing or pressing out, as juice from a fruit.—**ex·pres·sion·less,** *a.*—**ex·pres·sion·less·ly,** *adv.*

ex·pres·sion·ism, ik·spresh′a·niz″um, *n.* [= Gr. *expressionismus.*] A movement in the arts emphasizing the free expression of the artist's subjective, emotional responses to objects and events, rather than their objective representation, and characterized by distortion or exaggeration of natural forms and intensification of color for purposes of expression.—**ex·pres·sion·ist,** *n.*—**ex·pres·sion·is·tic,** *a.*—**ex·pres·sion·is·ti·cal·ly,** *adv.*

ex·pres·sive, ik·spres′iv, *a.* Serving to express, utter, or represent; full of expression; vividly representing the meaning or feeling intended to be conveyed; significant. —**ex·pres·sive·ly,** *adv.*—**ex·pres·sive·ness,** *n.*

ex·press·ly, ik·spres′lē, *adv.* In an express manner; of set purpose; in direct terms; plainly.—**ex·press·ness,** *n.*

ex·press·man, ik·spres′man, *n.* pl. **ex·press·men.** One engaged in the express business.

ex·press ri·fle, *n.* A sporting rifle taking a large charge of powder and a light bullet, adapted for killing large game at short range.

ex·press·way, ik·spres'wā″, n. A highway, usu. with divided lanes and limited access, used for high-speed traffic.

ex·pro·pri·ate, eks·prō′prē·āt″, v.t.—expropriated, expropriating. [M.L. expropriatus, pp. of expropriare, < L. ex- priv. and proprius, one's own, E. proper.] To take or transfer, as real estate, from the owner, esp. to take for public use by the right of eminent domain; to dispossess of ownership.—**ex·pro·pri·a·tor**, n.—**ex·pro·pri·a·tion**, eks·prō″prē·ā′shan, n.

ex·pul·sion, ik·spul′shan, n. [L. expulsio, a driving out, < expello, to expel.] The act of driving out or expelling; the state of being expelled.—**ex·pul·sive**, ik·spul′siv, a. Having the power to expel.

ex·punc·tion, ik·spungk′shan, n. The act of erasing or expunging.

ex·punge, ik·spunj′, v.t.—expunged, expunging. [L. expungo, to prick out, to cross or blot out—ex-, out, and pungo, to prick.] To blot out; to obliterate; to annihilate.—**ex·pung·er**, n.

ex·pur·gate, ek′spėr·gāt″, ik·spur′gāt, v.t.—expurgated, expurgating. [L. expurgo, expurgatum—ex-, and purgo, to purge.] To purify or revise by removing objectionable or obscene material; as, to expurgate a novel; to delete or omit, as anything obscene, offensive, or erroneous, as: They expurgated several scenes from the film.—**ex·pur·ga·tion**, n.—**ex·pur·ga·tor**, n.—**ex·pur·ga·tory**, a. Cleansing; purifying; serving to expurgate.—**ex·pur·ga·to·ri·al**, a.

ex·qui·site, ek′skwi·zit, ik·skwiz′it, a. [L. exquisitus, pp. of exquirere, seek out, < ex-, out, and quaerere, seek.] Of exceptionally choice quality, as food, wines, laces, or fabrics; of rare excellence of production or execution, as works of art; of peculiar refinement or elegance, as taste, manners, or persons; of uncommon beauty or charm, or rare and appealing excellence, as a face, a flower, coloring, music, or poetry; extraordinarily fine or admirable, or consummate, as skill, nicety, care, gentleness, purity; intense, acute, or keen, as pleasure or pain; keenly or delicately sensitive or responsive to impressions; as, an exquisite ear for music. n.—A person, esp. a man, who is overly fastidious in dress; a dandy; a coxcomb.—**ex·qui·site·ly**, adv.—**ex·qui·site·ness**, n.

ex·san·gui·nate, eks·sang′gwa·nāt″, v.t.—exsanguinated, exsanguinating. [L. exsanguinatus, rendered bloodless, < ex- priv. and sanguis (sanguin-) blood.] To render bloodless; to drain the blood from.

ex·san·guine, eks·sang′gwin, a. Anemic.

ex·scind, ek·sind′, v.t. [L. exscindo, to cut out.] To cut out or off.

ex·sect, ek·sekt′, v.t. [L. exseco, to cut out.] To cut out or away.—**ex·sec·tion**, n.

ex·sert, eks·sėrt′, v.t. [L. exsertus, pp. of exsero, put forth.] To thrust out.—**ex·ser·tile**, eks·sėr′til, eks·sėr′til, a.—**ex·ser·tion**, n.

ex·sert·ed, eks·sėr′tid, a. Biol. Standing out; projected, as a stamen, beyond an encompassing part.

ex·sic·cate, ek′si·kāt″, v.t., v.i.—exsiccated, exsiccating. [L. exsicco, exsiccatum, to dry up—ex-, intens., and sicco, to dry.] To dry; to dehydrate.—**ex·sic·ca·tion**, n.—**ex·sic·ca·tor**, n.—**ex·sic·ca·tive**, a.

ex·stip·u·late, eks·stip′ū·lit, eks·stip′ū·lāt″, a. Bot. having no stipules. Also e·stip·u·late, ē·stip′ū·lit, ē·stip′ū·lāt″.

ex·tant, ek′stant, ik·stant′, a. [L. extans, exstans, extantis, exstantis, ppr. of exsto, to stand out—ex-, out, and sto, to stand.] Still existing; in being; not destroyed or lost.

ex·tem·po·ral, ik·stem′pėr·al, a. [L.

extemporalis, < ex tempore.] Archaic, extemporaneous; extempore.—**ex·tem·po·ral·ly**, adv.

ex·tem·po·ra·ne·ous, ik·stem″po·rā′nē·us, a. [L. extemporaneus—ex-, not, and tempus, temporis, time.] Performed, uttered, or made at the time, without previous thought or study; impromptu; off-hand; carefully thought out but delivered with reference to few or no notes, as a speech; accustomed to or capable of speaking or performing extemporaneously; made to meet an immediate need; improvised. Also Also **ex·tem·po·rar·y**, ik·stem′po·rer″ē.—**ex·tem·po·ra·ne·ous·ly**, **ex·tem·po·rar·i·ly**, ik·stem″po·râr′i·lē, adv.—**ex·tem·po·ra·ne·ous·ness**, n.

ex·tem·pore, ik·stem′po·rē, adv. [L. phrase ex tempore, same meaning.] Without previous thought or preparation; with reference to few notes or none.—a.

ex·tem·po·rize, ik·stem′po·rīz″, v.i.—extemporized, extemporizing. To speak without previous thought, study, or preparation; to discourse without notes or written composition.—v.t. To make or devise without forethought; provide for the occasion; prepare in great haste with the means within one's reach; as, to extemporize a speech.—**ex·tem·po·riz·er**, n.—**ex·tem·po·ri·za·tion**, ik·stem″po·ri·zā′shan, n.

ex·tend, ik·stend′, v.t. [L. extendere (pp. extentus, also extensus) stretch out, extend—ex-, out, and tendere, stretch, E. tend.] To stretch out in distance, space, or time; to pull out to the full length; to exert to the fullest; to straighten or hold out, as a hand or finger; to spread out in area; to enlarge in quantity by adulteration; to widen the scope of, as one's influence; to make more comprehensive, as the meaning of a word; to hold forth as an offer or grant; offer; grant; give; finance, to prolong the duration of, as a loan, beyond a previously specified limit; bookkeeping, to multiply the unit price by the number of units, placing the result in the proper column; law, to make seizure or levy upon by writ of extent; Brit. to assess or value.—v.i. To be or become extended or stretched out; to reach toward a particular point; to increase in length, area, or scope.—**ex·tend·i·ble**, a.—**ex·tend·i·bil·i·ty**, n.

ex·tend·ed, ik·sten′did, a. Stretched out; pulled out; straightened; continued or prolonged; widespread or extensive; having spatial magnitude; printing, of type, much wider than is usual for its height.—**ex·tend·ed·ly**, adv.—**ex·tend·ed·ness**, n.

ex·tend·er, ik·sten′dėr, n. That which is added to a product to increase the quantity; an adulterant.

ex·ten·si·bil·i·ty, ik·sten″si·bil′i·tē, n. The quality of being extensible.—**ex·ten·si·ble**, ik·sten′si·bl, a. Capable of being extended.

ex·ten·sile, ik·sten′sil, ik·sten′sīl, a. Anat., zool. extensible.

ex·ten·sion, ik·sten′shan, n. The act of extending; the state of being extended; the thing extended; that by which an object is extended; the range or degree to which a thing may be extended; an added portion; com. a written engagement on the part of a creditor, allowing a debtor further time to pay. An additional telephone, esp. one operating on the same line as another; phys. that property of a body by which it occupies a portion of space; anat. the act of straightening a limb; surg. the act of pulling an injured limb to restore it to its natural position; logic, the range of a term or concept as is indicated by the number of objects which it denotes or includes.—**ex·ten·sion·al**, a.—**ex·ten·sion·al·i·ty**, n.—**ex·ten·sion·al·ly**, adv.

ex·ten·si·ty, ik·sten′si·tē, n. [L. extensus

pp.] The quality of having extension; psychol. that element of sensation from which the perception of space or size is developed.

ex·ten·sive, ik·sten′siv, a. [L.L. extensivus.] Of great extent; wide; broad; great; comprehensive; noting or pertaining to a system involving operations carried on by methods not calculated to result in any high degree of effectiveness, as the cultivation of large areas of land, where land is cheap, with a minimum of labor and expense: opposed to intensive.—**ex·ten·sive·ly**, adv.—**ex·ten·sive·ness**, n.

ex·ten·som·e·ter, ek″sten·som′i·tėr, n. [L. extensus, pp.] An apparatus for measuring minute degrees of expansion, contraction, or deformation.

ex·ten·sor, ik·sten′sėr, ik·sten′sọr, n. Anat. a muscle which serves to extend or straighten any part of the body, as an arm or a finger: opposed to flexor.

ex·tent, ik·stent′, n. [O.Fr. estente, estendre, < L. extendere.] The space or degree to which a thing extends; length, area, amount, or scope; an extended space; a particular length, area, or volume; something having extension; U.S. law, a writ or levy by which a creditor has his debtor's lands valued and transferred to himself, for a term of years or absolutely. Brit. law, a writ to recover debts of record due to the crown, under which land may be seized; a seizure made under such a writ.

ex·ten·u·ate, ik·sten′ū·āt″, v.t.—extenuated, extenuating. [L. extenuo, extenuatum, to make thin or small, to lessen.] To weaken the import or force of; to mitigate; to underestimate; to attach little importance to.—**ex·ten·u·at·ing**, a.—**ex·ten·u·a·tion**, n. The act of extenuating; mitigation; that which serves to extenuate, as an excuse.—**ex·ten·u·a·tor**, n.—**ex·ten·u·a·to·ry**, ik·sten′ū·a·tōr″ē, ik·sten′ū·a·tạr″ē, a.

ex·te·ri·or, ik·stēr′ē·ėr, a. [L. compar. of exter or exterus, on the outside, outward.] External; outer; outward; situated or happening beyond the limits of; proper for use on the outside.—n. The outer surface; the outside; the external features.—**ex·te·ri·or·ly**, adv.

ex·te·ri·or an·gle, n. Geom. Any of the four angles formed outside two parallel lines cut by a third straight line; an angle outside a polygon between any of its sides and an extended adjacent side.

ex·te·ri·or·ize, ik·stēr′ē·o·rīz″, v.t.—exteriorized, exteriorizing. To externalize; to bring out or expose, as an internal organ from the body for surgery.—**ex·te·ri·or·i·za·tion**, ik·stē″rē·o·riz·ā′shan, n.

ex·ter·mi·nate, ik·stėr′mi·nāt″, v.t.—exterminated, exterminating. [L. extermino, exterminatum, to remove—ex-, and termino, to terminate, < terminus, a limit.] To destroy utterly; to extirpate; to root out; to eradicate.—**ex·ter·mi·na·tion**, n.—**ex·ter·mi·na·tor**, n.—**ex·ter·mi·na·tive**, **ex·ter·mi·na·to·ry**, a.

ex·tern, ek′stėrn, ik·stėrn′, a. [Fr. externe, < L. externus, < exter, outer, outward.] Archaic, outward or external.—n. A person connected with an institution but not residing in it, as a pupil in a boarding school or a member of the medical staff of a hospital. Also **ex·terne**.

ex·ter·nal, ik·stėr′nal, a. [L. externus, < exter, outer.] Of or pertaining to the outside or outer part; exterior; belonging to or coming from without; extrinsic; pertaining to the outward or visible appearance or show; as, external acts of worship; pertaining to that which is foreign, esp. foreign countries; applied or to be applied to the outside of the body; as, external medicines; metaph. belonging to the world of things

existing outside of the perceiving mind.—
n. The outside; that which is external; *pl.*
external or outward features or circumstances.—**ex·ter·nal·ly,** *adv.*

ex·ter·nal-com·bus·tion en·gine, ik·-
stur'nal kom·bus'chan en'jin, *n.* An engine
which receives its heat from fuel ignition
outside the engine cylinder.

ex·ter·nal·ism, ik·stėr'na·liz″um, *n.*
Attention or devotion to externals; undue
regard to externals.—**ex·ter·nal·ist,** *n.*—
ex·ter·nal·i·ty, ek″stėr·nal'i·tē, *n.* pl.
ex·ter·nal·i·ties. The state or quality of
being external; undue regard to externals;
something external; an outward feature or
circumstance.—**ex·ter·nal·ize,** *v.t.*—*exter-
nalized, externalizing.* To make external; to
find causation outside of the self.—**ex·-
ter·nal·i·za·tion,** ik·stur'nal·i·zā'shan, *n.*

ex·ter·o·cep·tive, ek″stėr·o·sep'tiv, *a.*
Physiol. of, relating to, or activated by
external stimuli; of or relating to the extero-
ceptors or the sensory responses recorded
through them.

ex·ter·o·cep·tor, ek″stėr·o·sep'tėr, *n.*
Physiol. a sensory receptor that responds to
stimuli from outside the organism.

ex·tinct, ik·stingkt′, *a.* [L. *extinctus,* pp. of
extinguo, exstinguo.] No longer in existence;
as, an *extinct* race; having ceased; no longer
in use; as, an *extinct* custom; having died
out; lapsed; as, an *extinct* title; extinguished;
quenched.—**ex·tinc·tive,** *a.*

ex·tinc·tion, ik·stingk'shan, *n.* The act of
extinguishing; the state of being extinguished; annihilation; a coming to an end;
a dying out, as of a species.

ex·tine, ek'stēn, ek'stīn, *n.* [L. *extimus,*
outermost, superl. of *exter,* outer.] *Bot.* the
outer coat of a pollen grain. Also **ex·ine,**
ek'sēn, ek'sin.

ex·tin·guish, ik·sting'gwish, *v.t.* [L. *ex-
tinguere* (pp. *extinctus*), for *exstinguere,* <
ex-, out, and *stinguere,* quench, orig.
prick.] To put out, as fire; to put out the
flame of, as of something burning; to
quench, as hopes or passions; to obscure
or eclipse, as by superior brilliancy; to
put an end to or wipe out of existence;
suppress; abolish; annihilate; to render
void, as a right or claim; to discharge, as
a debt, by payment.—**ex·tin·guish·a·ble,**
a.—**ex·tin·guish·er,** *n.* One who or that
which extinguishes; a conical cap for putting over a lighted candle to extinguish it;
any of various portable apparatus for
extinguishing fire.—**ex·tin·guish·ment,** *n.*

ex·tir·pate, ek'stėr·pāt″, ik·stėr'pāt, *v.t.*—
extirpated, extirpating. [L. *extirpo, exstirpo,
exstirpatum—ex-,* out, and *stirps,* the trunk
of a tree.] To pull or pluck up by the roots;
to root out; to eradicate; to destroy totally;
to exterminate.—**ex·tir·pa·tion,** *n.*—**ex·-
tir·pa·tor,** *n.*—**ex·tir·pa·tive,** *a.*

ex·tol, ik·stōl′, ik·stol′, *v.t.*—*extolled, ex-
tolling.* [L. *extollo,* to raise up—*ex-,* out, up,
and *tollo,* to raise; < same root as in *tolero,*
to endure, to tolerate.] To praise; to laud;
to applaud; to eulogize; to magnify; to
glorify. Also **ex·toll.**—**ex·tol·ler,** *n.*—
ex·tol·ling·ly, *adv.*—**ex·tol·ment, ex·-
toll·ment,** *n.*

ex·tort, ik·start′, *v.t.* [L. *extorqueo, ex-
tortum—ex-,* and *torqueo,* to twist.] To obtain
from a person by force or compulsion;
wrest or wring by physical force, torture, or
authority.—**ex·tor·ter,** *n.*—**ex·tor·tive,**
a.

ex·tor·tion, ik·star'shan, *n.* The act of
extorting; the act or practice of extorting
money from people by any undue exercise
of power; illegal compulsion to pay
money; that which is extorted.—**ex·tor·-
tion·ar·y,** ik·star'sha·ner″ē, *a. Archaic,*
extortionate.—**ex·tor·tion·ate,** ik·star'-
sha·nit, *a.* Practicing or characterized by
extortion; oppressive in exacting money.—

ex·tor·tion·ate·ly, *adv.*—**ex·tor·tion·er,**
ex·tor·tion·ist, *n.*

ex·tra, ek'stra, *a.* [Prob. orig. short for
extraordinary, < L. *extra-,* repr. *extra,*
adv. and prep., outside (of), without, <
exter, outer, outward.] Beyond or more than
what is usual, expected, or necessary;
additional; larger or better than what is
usual.—*n.* Something additional; a special
edition of a newspaper, in addition to the
regular editions; an auxiliary worker hired
during a busy season; an auxiliary actor
hired for a bit part, as in a mob scene; an
additional cost; something of superior
quality; *cricket,* a score or run not made
from the bat.—*adv.* In excess of the usual
or specified amount; beyond the ordinary
degree; unusually; uncommonly.

ex·tra-base hit, ek'stra bās'hit, *n. Baseball,*
a hit which advances the player more than
one base.

ex·tra·cel·lu·lar, ek″stra·sel'ū·lėr, *a.
Biol.* outside of a cell or cells.—**ex·tra·-
cel·lu·lar·ly,** *adv.*

ex·tract, ik·strakt′, *v.t.* [L. *extractus,* pp.
of *extrahere,* < *ex-,* out of, and *trahere,*
draw.] To draw or pull out by force; to
derive from a source; to formulate or
deduce; to obtain by force from someone
unwilling; to withdraw from a substance
by a chemical or mechanical operation; to
take or copy out, as a passage from a book;
to make excerpts, as from a book; *math.* to
determine, as the root of a number.—ek′-
strakt, *n.* [N.L. *extractum,* prop. neut. of L.
extractus, pp.] Something extracted; a
passage selected from a book or the like;
a concentrated preparation of a substance;
as, almond *extract.*—**ex·tract·a·ble, ex·-
tract·i·ble,** *a.*—**ex·tract·a·bil·i·ty, ex·-
tract·i·bil·i·ty,** *n.*

ex·trac·tion, ik·strak'shan, *n.* [L. *extractio.*]
The act of extracting or drawing out; the
state of being extracted; descent; lineage;
math. the operation of finding the root of a
given number or quantity. Something
extracted.

ex·trac·tive, ik·strak'tiv, *a.* Capable of
being extracted; tending or serving to extract; extracting; of or like an extract.—
n. That which may be or has been extracted.

ex·trac·tor, ik·strak'tėr, *n.* One who or
that which extracts; the mechanism in a
firearm or cannon which pulls an empty
shell casing out of the chamber for ejection;
med., dentistry, a forceps or other instrument
used in extracting or pulling.

ex·tra·cur·ric·u·lar, ek″stra·ka·rik'ū·-
lėr, *a.* Outside the scope of the curriculum,
esp. pertaining to school-approved and
affiliated student activities other than
academic studies, as choral groups, sports,
or school publications; relating to activities
outside one's established routine.

ex·tra·dite, ek'stra·dīt″, *v.t.*—*extradited,
extraditing.* To deliver or give up, as a
criminal, to the jurisdiction of another
authority; to obtain the deliverance or
extradition of.—**ex·tra·dit·a·ble,** *a.*

ex·tra·di·tion, ek″stra·dish'an, *n.* [L.
ex-, and *traditio,* a giving up, surrender, <
trado, traditum, to give up.] Delivery of a
criminal or fugitive from justice by one
country, state, or other authority to another,
on sufficient grounds shown.

ex·tra·dos, ek'stra·dos″, ek'stra·dōs″, ek·-
strā'dos, ek·strā'dōs, *n.* pl. **ex·tra·dos, ex·-
tra·dos·es.** [Fr. < L. *extra,* outside of, and
Fr. *dos,* < L. *dorsum,* back.] *Arch.* the
exterior curve or surface of an arch or
vault.

ex·tra·ga·lac·tic, ek″stra·ga·lak'tik, *a.*
Outside the Milky Way galaxy.

ex·tra·ju·di·cial, ek″stra·jö·dish'al, *a.*
Out of the ordinary course of legal procedure; beyond jurisdiction; not legally
justified.—**ex·tra·ju·di·cial·ly,** *adv.*

ex·tra·le·gal, ek″stra·lē'gal, *a.* Outside
the purview of the law; not within the scope
or extent of legal authority; outside the
protection of the law; of action, taken in any
other manner than provided by legal
authority.—**ex·tra·le·gal·ly,** *adv.* In a
manner outside the sphere of law.

ex·tra·mar·i·tal, ek″stra·mar'i·tal, *a.*
Pertaining to sexual relations other than
with one's husband or wife.

ex·tra·mun·dane, ek″stra·mun'dān, ek″-
stra·mun·dān′, *a.* Beyond the limit of the
material world.

ex·tra·mu·ral, ek″stra·mūr'al, *a.* [L.
extra, beyond, and *murus,* a wall.] Concerned with contests between athletic
teams or special groups from more than
one school or university; pertaining to
something beyond the walls or boundaries
of an organized community.—**ex·tra·-
mu·ral·ly,** *adv.*

ex·tra·ne·ous, ik·strā'ne·us, *a.* [L. *extraneus,* < *extra,* without, beyond; akin
strange.] Not belonging to a thing; superfluous; alien; outside of.—**ex·tra·ne·ous·-
ly,** *adv.*—**ex·tra·ne·ous·ness,** *n.*

ex·tra·nu·cle·ar, ek″stra·nö'klē·ėr, ek″-
stra·nū'klē·ėr, *a.* Within a living cell, but
outside the nucleus.

ex·traor·di·nar·y, ik·strar'di·ner″ē, ek″-
stra·ar'di·ner″ē, *a.* [L. *extraordinarius—
extra,* and *ordo, ordinis,* order.] Beyond an
ordinary, common, usual, or customary
order, method, or course; exceeding a
common degree or measure; exceptional;
remarkable; wonderful; special; particular;
sent for a special purpose or on a particular
occasion; as, an ambassador *extraordinary.*—
ex·traor·di·nar·i·ly, ik·strar″di·nâr'i·-
lē, ek″stra·ar″di·nâr'i·lē, *adv.* In an
extraordinary manner; in an uncommon
degree; remarkably; exceedingly; eminently.—**ex·traor·di·nar·i·ness,** *n.*

ex·tra point, *n. Football,* a point scored
after a touchdown by kicking the ball
between the goal posts; *pl.* two points
scored immediately after a touchdown by
running or passing the ball over the goal
line in one play.

ex·trap·o·late, ik·strap'o·lāt″, ek'stra·-
po·lāt″, *v.t., v.i.*—*extrapolated, extra-
polating. Math.* to approximate the values
of a variable beyond the range for which
values have been calculated. To project
data or experience, by inferences, into an
unknown area and thus achieve a conjectural
knowledge of the unknown, as: To write
credible science fiction an author must
extrapolate.—**ex·trap·o·la·tion,** *n.*—**ex·-
trap·o·la·tive,** *a.*—**ex·trap·o·la·tor,** *n.*

ex·tra·sen·so·ry, ek″stra·sen'so·rē, *a.*
Outside of the normal range of the senses.

ex·tra·sys·to·le, ek″stra·sis'to·lē, *n.
Pathol.* an abnormal contraction of the heart
causing a brief interruption of the normal
heartbeat.—**ex·tra·sys·tol·ic,** ek″stra·-
sis·tol'ik, *a.*

ex·tra·ter·res·tri·al, ek″stra·te·res′-
trē·al, *a.* Originating or existing outside
the limits of the earth.

ex·tra·ter·ri·to·ri·al, ek′stra·ter″i·tōr′-
ē·al, ek′stra·ter″i·tar'ē·al, *a.* Beyond
territorial jurisdiction; beyond the jurisdiction of the country in which one resides.
Also **ex·ter·ri·to·ri·al,** ek′stra·ter″i·tōr′ē·al,
eks″ter·i·tar'ē·al.—**ex·tra·ter·ri·to·ri·-
al·i·ty,** *n.* Exemption from a country's
laws, such as diplomatic immunity; jurisdiction by a foreign country over its
citizens in another country. Also **ex·ter·-
ri·to·ri·al·i·ty.**

ex·tra·u·ter·ine, ek″stra·ū′tėr·in, ek″-
stra·ū′te·rīn″, *a.* Situated or taking place
outside the uterus; as, an *extrauterine*
pregnancy.

ex·trav·a·gance, ik·strav'a·gans, *n.* [Fr.
extravagance—L. *extra,* beyond, and *vagans,*

ppr. of *vago, vagor,* to wander.] Unrestrained or fantastic excess, as of actions or opinions; an extravagant action or notion; excessive expenditure or outlay, as of money; an instance of wastefulness or prodigality. Also **ex·trav·a·gan·cy,** pl. **ex·trav·a·gan·cies.**

ex·trav·a·gant, ik·strav′a·gant, *a.* Spending more money than necessary; wasteful; exorbitantly priced; exceeding reason or necessity; lacking restraint; excessively elaborate or lavish.—**ex·trav·a·gant·ly,** *adv.*

ex·trav·a·gan·za, ik·strav″a·gan′za, *n.* An elaborate musical or dramatic production, noted for its free style and structure; a spectacular show or event.

ex·trav·a·gate, ik·strav′a·gāt″, *v.i.—extravagated, extravagating.* [M.L. *extravagatus,* pp. of *extravagari,* wander beyond, < L. *extra,* outside of, and *vagari,* wander.] *Archaic.* To wander or stray; to go beyond the bounds of propriety or reason.

ex·trav·a·sate, ik·strav′a·sāt″ *v.t.—extravasated, extravasating.* [L. *extra,* beyond, and *vas,* a vessel.] *Pathol.* to force or let out of the proper vessels, as blood; *geol.* to erupt or pour forth, as lava.—*v.i.* To ooze or pour forth by effusion or infiltration into the surroundings.—**ex·trav·a·sa·tion,** *n.* The act of extravasating; the state of being forced or let out of the ducts of the body that contain it; effusion.

ex·tra·vas·cu·lar, ek″stra·vas′kū·lêr, *a.* Being outside of the blood vessels or vascular system.

ex·tra·ve·hic·u·lar, ek″stra·vē·hik′ū·lar, *a.* Of or pertaining to that which is exterior or beyond the enclosure of an orbiting spacecraft; outside a vehicle traveling through outer space.—**ex·tra·ve·hic·u·lar ac·tiv·i·ty,** *n.*

ex·treme, ik·strēm′, *a.* [O.Fr. *extreme* (Fr. *extrême*), < L. *extremus,* superl. of *exter,* outer, outward.] Utmost or exceedingly great in degree; of a character farthest removed from the ordinary or average; going to greatly exaggerated lengths; located at the farthest limit or point from a center; farthest, utmost, or very far in any direction; exceeding the bounds of moderation; last or final.—*n.* The utmost or highest degree; one of two things as remote or different from each other as possible; an excessive length beyond the ordinary or average; as, to go to *extremes. Math.* the first or last term of a proportion or series. *Logic,* the subject or predicate of a syllogism's conclusion; either of two terms divided in the premises and joined in the conclusion.—**ex·treme·ly,** ik·strēm′lē, *adv.* In an extreme degree; exceedingly.—**ex·treme·ness,** *n.*

ex·treme·ly high fre·quen·cy, *n.* A radio frequency broadcast between 30,000 and 300,000 megacycles per second.

ex·treme unc·tion, *n. Rom. Cath. Ch.* a sacrament involving the anointing of a sick person with oil when on the point of death. Also **A·noint·ing of the Sick.**

ex·trem·ism, ik·strē′miz·um, *n.* Tendency or disposition to go to extremes, esp. in politics.—**ex·trem·ist,** *n.* One who goes to extremes; a supporter of extreme doctrines or practices, esp. in politics.—*a.* Belonging or pertaining to extremists; radical.

ex·trem·i·ty, ik·strem′i·tē, *n.* pl. **ex·trem·i·ties.** [O.Fr. *extremite* (Fr. *extrémité*), < L. *extremitas,* < *extremus.*] The extreme or terminal point, limit, or part of something; the ultimate in need or distress; moment of danger or approaching death; intense degree of pain or other feeling; the utmost or any extreme degree; an extreme measure; forced act or decision; *usu. pl.* the end part of a limb, or the limb itself, esp. the human hand or foot.

ex·tre·mum, ik·strē′mum, *n.* pl. **ex·tre·**

---

ma, ik·strē′ma. *Math.* the minimum or maximum value of a function.

ex·tri·ca·ble, ek′stri·ka·bl, ik·strik′a·bl, *a.* Capable of being extricated.

ex·tri·cate, ek′stri·kāt″, *v.t.—extricated, extricating.* [L. *extrico, extricatum—ex-,* and *tricae,* trifles, perplexity.] To free or remove from a difficulty; to disengage; to disentangle.—**ex·tri·ca·tion,** *n.*

ex·trin·sic, ik·strin′sik, *a.* [L. *extrinsecus,* from without—*exter,* outward, and *secus,* by, along with.] Not innate or inherent; extraneous or unessential; acquired or developed; originating from without; *anat.* esp. of a muscle, having its origin outside the part where it occurs or which it affects. Also **ex·trin·si·cal.—ex·trin·si·cal·ly,** *adv.*

ex·trorse, ek·strars′, *a.* [Fr. *extrorse,* < L. *extra,* on the outside, and *verto, versum,* to turn.] *Bot.* directed outward, or turned away from the axis.—**ex·trorse·ly,** *adv.*

ex·tro·ver·sion, ek″strō·vêr′zhan, ek″strō·vêr·shan, ek′strō·vêr″zhan, ek′strō·vêr″shan, ek″strō·vêr′zhan, ek′strō·vêr″shan, ek″stro·vêr″zhan, ek′stro·vêr″shan, *n. Psychol.* the act or characteristic of directing one's interest primarily toward what is outside the self; the state of being extroverted: opposed to *introversion;* also **ex·tra·ver·sion.** *Pathol.* a congenital turning inside-out, as of an organ.—**ex·tro·ver·sive, ex·tra·ver·sive,** *a.*—**ex·tro·ver·sive·ly, ex·tra·ver·sive·ly,** *adv.*

ex·tro·vert, ek′strō·vêrt″, ek′stra·vêrt″, *n. Psychol.* one whose interest and attention is directed primarily toward what is outside the self; one who relates to the external or objective; loosely, one who is outgoing, active, expressive, and gregarious: opposed to *introvert.—v.t.* To direct, as one's interest, toward external things.—*a.* Characterized by extroversion. Also **ex·tra·vert.** —**ex·tro·ver·ted, ex·tra·ver·ted,** *a.*

ex·trude, ik·strōd′, *v.t.—extruded, extruding.* [L. *extrudere* (pp. *extrusus*), < *ex-,* out of, and *trudere,* thrust.] To thrust out; force or press out; to expel; to form, as metal or plastic, by forcing through a die.— *v.i.* To protrude.—**ex·tru·sion,** ik·strō′zhan, *n.* The act of extruding, or the fact of being extruded; expulsion; protrusion.

ex·tru·sive, ik·strō′siv, *a.* Tending to extrude; pertaining to extrusion; *geol.* of rocks, having been forced out in a molten or plastic condition at the surface of the earth.

ex·u·ber·ance, ig·zō′bêr·ans, *n.* [Fr. *exubérance,* < L. *exuberantia—ex-,* intens., and *ubero,* to be fruitful, < *uber,* rich, fruitful.] The state or quality of being exuberant; an expression of this in speech or action. Also **ex·u·ber·an·cy.**

ex·u·ber·ant, ig·zō′bêr·ant, *a.* [L. *exuberans, exuberantis,* ppr. of *exubero.*] Full of joyful enthusiasm; high-spirited; unrestrained; overflowing; characterized by abundance, richness, or luxuriance; prolific.—**ex·u·ber·ant·ly,** *adv.*

ex·u·ber·ate, ig·zō′be·rāt″, *v.i.—exuberated, exuberating.* To be exuberant.

ex·ude, ig·zōd′, ik·sōd′, *v.i.—exuded, exuding.* [L. *exsudo,* to discharge by sweating—*ex-,* and *sudo,* to sweat.] To ooze; to seep out gradually, as sweat through the pores.— *v.t.* To discharge in such a manner; to give off diffusely; as, to *exude* an odor; *fig.* to express with one's entire·being; as, to *exude* hostility.—**ex·u·da·tion,** ek″sū′dā″shan, ek″su·dā·shan, eg″zu·dā·shan, *n.* The act or process of exuding. An exuded substance; also **ex·u·date.**

ex·ult, ig·zult′, *v.i.* [L. *exulto, exsulto,* to leap or jump about—*ex-,* and *salio, saltum,* to leap.] To be extremely elated; to rejoice in triumph.—**ex·ult·ing·ly,** *adv.*—**ex·ult·ant,** ig·zul′tant, *a.* Jubilant; rejoicing triumphantly.—**ex·ult·ant·ly,** *adv.*—**ex·ul·ta·tion,** eg″zul·tā′shan, ek″sul·tā′shan,

---

n. The act of exalting; great gladness. Also **ex·ult·ance, ex·ult·an·cy.**

ex·ur·ban·ite, eks·ųr′ba·nit″, *n.* A former city dweller who has moved to a semi-rural area beyond the suburbs, but who usu. continues to work in the city and retains his urban life style.—**ex·urb,** ek′sêrb, eg′zêrb, *n.* A community or region beyond a city's suburbs inhabited primarily by exurbanites.—**ex·ur·bi·a,** eks·ér′bē·a, *n.* Exurbs generally or collectively.

ex·u·vi·ae, ig·zō′vē·ē″, ik·sō′vē·ē″, *n. pl.* [L. < *exuo,* to put off, to strip.] Cast skins, shells, or coverings of animals.—**ex·u·vi·al,** *a.*—**ex·u·vi·ate,** ig·zō′vē·āt″, ik·sō′vē·āt″, *v.t., v.i.—exuviated, exuviating.* To shed or cast off, as the skins of snakes.—**ex·u·vi·a·tion,** *n.*

ey·as, i′as, *n.* [M.E. *neias,* < O.Fr. Fr. *niais,* being a nestling, < L. *nidus,* nest.] A nestling; *falconry,* a young hawk taken from the nest for training.

eye, ī, *n.* [M.E. *ye, eighe,* O.E. *ēage,* Dan. *öie,* D. *oog,* Icel. *auga,* G. *auge,* Goth. *ouga;* cog. L. *oculus,* Skt. *akshi—eye;* from a root meaning sharp.] An organ of sight, which, in man and other vertebrates, is normally one of a pair of globular bodies each consisting of a cornea, iris, pupil, lens, retina, and various muscles, nerves, and blood vessels, and set in an orbit or socket in the skull; the visible portion of the organ; the external area within or near the socket, including such supportive and protective structures as the eyelids; the iris in reference to its color; as, blue *eyes;* sight; delicate or accurate ocular perception; as, an eagle *eye;* power of seeing together with intellectual perception, discrimination, or appreciation; as, a discerning *eye;* a look or glance, as: Run your *eye* over these figures. View; regard; keen interest in; as, an *eye* to one's future, an *eye* for the girls; careful watch; surveillance; *often pl.* opinion or judgment. Anything resembling or suggesting an eye in shape, general appearance, or function, as the bud or shoot of a plant tuber, the hole in a needle, the circular catch of a hook-and-eye, a spot on the tail feathers of a peacock, a photoelectric cell, or a camera lens. The center of an object or of an activity; *meteor.* an area of relative calm in the center of a tropical cyclone; *slang,* a detective.—**an eye for an eye,** revenge equivalent to injury.—**catch some·one's eye,** attract someone's visual attention.— **eye of the wind,** *naut.* the direction opposite that of the wind.—**in a pig's eye,** *slang,* by no means; never.—**see eye to eye,** concur; agree.—**eyed,** *a.*—**eye·less,** *a.*—**eye·like,** *a.*

eye, ī, *v.t.—eyed, eying* or *eyeing.* To fix the eyes upon; to view; to observe or watch narrowly; to make an eyelike opening into something.—**eye·a·ble,** *a.*

eye·ball, ī′bạl″, *n.* The ball or globe of the eye.

eye bank, *n.* A place where corneas removed from newly-dead persons are stored until needed for transplantation to restore the sight of those with corneal defects.

eye·bolt, ī′bōlt″, *n.* A bolt with a loop or eyelike opening at one end for receiving a hook or rope.

eye·brow, ī′brou″, *n.* The arch or ridge forming the upper part of the orbit of the eye, or the fringe of hair growing upon it.

eye catch·er, *n.* Something which attracts the eye.—**eye·catch·ing,** *a.*

eye·cup, ī′kup″, *n.* A device for applying lotions to the eye, consisting of a cup or glass with a rim shaped to fit snugly about the orbit of the eye.

eye di·a·lect, *n.* The use of phonetic misspellings to represent dialectical pronunciations or the speech of uneducated persons, as '*dunno*' for *don't know.*

---

ch- chain, G. na*ch*t; **th-** THen, thin; **w-** wig, hw as sound in whig; **z-** zh as in azure, zeal. *Italicized vowel* indicates schwa sound.

eye·drop·per, ī′drop″ẽr, n. A dropper for administering eye drops.

eye·ful, ī′fụl″, n. pl. **eye·fuls.** A complete or satiating view of something; a visually attractive being, esp. a beautiful woman; a quantity of foreign matter in the eyes.

eye·glass, ī′glas″, ī′gläs, n. A single lens worn to assist vision, as a monocle; an eyepiece; an eyecup.—**eye·glass·es,** n. pl. A device for correcting defective vision or for protecting the eyes, consisting of two lenses set in a frame which holds them in place; also *glasses, spectacles.*

eye·hole, ī′hōl″, n. The socket or orbit of the eye; a hole to look through, as in a mask or a curtain; a circular opening, as for the insertion of a pin, hook, or rope.

eye·lash, ī′lash″, n. One of the hairs that edge the eyelid; the entire fringe of these hairs.

eye·let, ī′lit, n. A small hole to receive a lace or small rope or cord, or for ornamental purposes; a metal ring to line such a hole; an eyehole, as in a mask; a small opening or peephole in a wall.—*v.t.*—*eyeleted, eyeleting, eyeletted, eyeletting.*

eye·lid, ī′lid″, n. That portion of movable skin that serves as a cover for the eyeball.

eye·o·pen·er, ī′ō″pe·nẽr, n. A startling realization or experience; *slang,* an early morning drink of liquor.—**eye·open·ing,** a.

eye·piece, ī′pēs″, n. In an optical instrument, the lens or combination of lenses to which the eye is applied.

eye rhyme, n. A rhyme in appearance but not in sound, as *gone, lone,* often the result of changes in pronunciation.

eye·shot, ī′shot″, n. Range of vision; view.

eye·sight, ī′sīt″, n. The ability to see; vision; the extent of vision; view.

eye·sore, ī′sōr″, ī′sạr″, n. Something offensive to look at.

eye·spot, ī′spot″, n. A rudimentary light-sensitive organ occurring in many invertebrates; an eyelike spot, as on the tail of a peacock.

eye·stalk, ī′stạk″, n. *Zool.* the stalk or peduncle upon which the eye is borne in lobsters, shrimps, and certain other crustaceans.

eye·strain, ī′strān″, n. Discomfort or fatigue of the eyes due to their excessive or incorrect use or to uncorrected visual defects.

eye·tooth, ī′tōth″, n. pl. **eye·teeth.** An upper canine tooth.

eye·wash, ī′wosh″, ī′wạsh″, n. A lotion to cleanse or treat the eye; *slang,* flattery or nonsense.

eye·wink, ī′wingk″, n. A wink of the eye.

eye·wit·ness, ī′wit″nis, ī′wit′nis, n. One who sees an act or occurrence and can give a report of it.—ī′wit″nis, v.t. To witness; to behold.—a. Of or by an eyewitness.

ey·ra, âr′a, ī′ra, n. [S. Amer.] A jaguarundi.

eyre, âr, n. [O.Fr. *erre, eirre,* a journey, < L. *iter, itineris,* a journey.] *Archaic,* a journey or circuit, esp. of a court; *law,* a medieval court held in different English counties by itinerant justices.

ey·rie, ey·ry, âr′ē, ēr′ē, n. pl. **ey·ries.** Aerie.

F

F, f, ef, n. The sixth letter of the English alphabet, a consonant; the graphic representation of this letter; any sound represented by this letter; a device that reproduces this letter; anything in the shape of an F. (*Cap.*) the grade or rate in school most often indicating failure; one receiving such a

grade. *Mus.* the fourth note of the diatonic scale; the written musical note representing this tone.

fa, fä, n. *Mus.* the syllable for the fourth note of the diatonic scale.

fa·ba·ceous, fa·bā′shus, a. [L. *fabaceus,* < *faba,* bean.] Belonging to the *Fabaceae,* or bean family of plants; leguminous.

Fa·bi·an, fā′bē·an, a. [From Quintus *Fabius* Maximus, a Roman general who sought to wear out the enemy, Hannibal.] Characteristic or suggestive of using harassing tactics without risking a decisive battle. Designating or pertaining to a socialistic society, founded in London about 1884, advocating a moderate socialism to be spread gradually without attempts at revolutionary action.—n. A member of or sympathizer with the Fabian Society.—**Fa·bi·an·ism,** n.

fa·ble, fā′bl, n. [O.Fr. Fr. *fable,* < L. *fabula,* < *fari,* speak, say.] A story or tale, esp. a short story, often with animals or inanimate objects as speakers or actors, devised to convey a moral; a legend or myth; fiction or fabrication.—*v.i.*—*fabled, fabling.* To invent or tell a fable; fabricate.—*v.t.* To relate as if actually so.—**fa·bled,** a. Related or celebrated in fables; legendary; fictitious.—**fa·bler,** n.

fab·li·au, fab′lē·ō″, Fr. fá·blē·ō′, n. pl. **fab·li·aux,** fab′lē·ōz″, Fr. fá·blē·ō′. [Fr.] A kind of metrical tale, comic and ribald, common in French literature of the 12th and 13th centuries.

fab·ric, fab′rik, n. [O.Fr. Fr. *fabrique,* < L. *fabrica,* workshop, art, product of art, structure, < *faber,* artisan.] A woven, felted, or knitted cloth; texture or quality, esp. of textiles; mode of construction, structure, or framework; *petrog.* the pattern formed by crystal grains in a rock.

fab·ri·cant, fab′ri·kant, n. [Fr.] A manufacturer or builder.

fab·ri·cate, fab′ri·kāt″, v.t.—*fabricated, fabricating.* [L. *fabrico, fabricatum.*] To manufacture, build, make, or construct; to form into a whole by connecting the parts; to assemble; to form by art and labor; to invent or make up; to forge or devise falsely.—**fab·ri·ca·tion,** fab″ri·kā′shan, n. The act or process of fabricating; that which is fabricated; a falsehood.—**fab·ri·ca·tive,** a.—**fab·ri·ca·tor,** n.

Fab·ri·koid, fab′ri·koid″, n. A waterproof, leatherlike material made of cloth coated with pyroxlin. (Trademark.)

fab·u·list, fab′ya·list, fab′ū·list, n. A person who tells fables; one who prevaricates.

fab·u·lous, fab′ya·lus, fab′ū·lus, a. Incredible; remarkably good; wonderful or marvelous; having the nature of a fable; fictitious; invented; not real; mythical.—**fab·u·lous·ly,** adv.—**fab·u·lous·ness,** n.

fa·cade, fa·çade, fa·säd′, fä·säd′, n. pl. **fa·cades,** fa·sädz′, fa·sädz′, Fr. fä·säd′. [Fr. < It. *faciata,* a facade, < *faccia,* L. *facies,* the face.] Face or front view, esp. of a building; artificial or false appearance.

face, fās, n. [O.Fr. Fr. *face,* < L. *facies,* form, appearance, face.] The front part of the head, including in humans the forehead, chin, cheeks, eyes, nose, and mouth; the visage; an expression of the countenance; as, an unhappy *face;* a grimace or other expressive facial distortion; self-respect; favorable repute; audacious assurance or effrontery; appearance, show, or semblance; any surface; the front, functional, or most important surface; as, a clock *face;* the working or striking side, as of a tool; the finished side, as of fabric or leather; of a document, the manifest sense or express terms; the amount specified in a bill or note, exclusive of interest; as, *face* value.

Print. all type of one particular style; the surface, as of a plate or type, that imprints. *Geom.* any of the plane surfaces bounding a solid figure; *mining,* the front or end of a drift or excavation, where the material is being mined or was last mined; *fort.* either of the two outer sides which form the salient angle of a bastion; *milit.* any side of a battalion or the like, esp. when formed in a square.—**face to face,** in one another's actual company; confronting each other, followed by *with.*—**in the face of,** despite; notwithstanding.—**on the face of it,** according to appearances; manifestly.—**fly in the face of,** to act in open disregard of.—**lose face,** to undergo shame, disrepute, or loss of dignity.—**save face,** to retain one's self-respect or good reputation.—**show one's face,** to appear, esp. briefly.—**one's face,** in one's immediate presence.

face, fās, v.t.—*faced, facing.* To have or turn the face toward; look toward; to be situated opposite to, as: The hotels *face* Central Park. To come face to face with; to confront bodily, bravely, or impudently; to oppose with defiance; to confront without evasion; as, to *face* the facts; to smooth or flatten the surface of, as stone, *sewing,* to line, as a garment; *milit.* to cause, as an assembled troop, to turn in a certain direction on command. To overlay with a different material.—*v.i.* To have or turn the face in a given direction.

face brick, n. A brick of pleasing color and finish used for facing a wall or the exterior of a house.

face card, n. A jack, queen, or king in a deck of playing cards.

face-hard·en, fās′här″den, v.t. To harden the surface, as of steel or other metal, by chilling or casehardening.

face lift·ing, n. Plastic surgery for eliminating signs of aging on the face by raising sagging tissues and removing wrinkles.

face·plate, fās′plāt″, n. A perforated disk, affixed to the live spindle of a lathe, which holds the material being worked on.

fac·et, fas′it, n. [Fr. *facette,* dim. of *face.*] A small flat portion of a surface, esp. on a gem or crystal; *fig.* an aspect of a subject being discussed; *anat.* a flat smooth surface of a bone; *arch.* one of the fillets between the flutes of a column; *zool.* one of the corneal surfaces of a compound eye.—*v.t. faceted, faceting, facetted, facetting.* To cut facets on.—**fac·et·ed, fac·et·ted,** a. Having facets.

fa·ce·ti·ae, fa·sē′shē·ē″, n. pl. [L. < *facetus,* merry, elegant, < root of *facio,* to make.] Witty or humorous remarks or writings; jests; witticisms; coarsely humorous books or tales.

fa·ce·tious, fa·sē′shus, a. Flippant; jesting; without serious intent; witty; full of playful humor.—**fa·ce·tious·ly,** adv.—**fa·ce·tious·ness,** n.

fa·cial, fā′shal, a. Of or pertaining to the face; for the face.—n. A facial massage or beauty treatment.—**fa·cial·ly,** adv.

fa·ci·es, fā′shē·ēz″, ụ. pl. **fa·ci·es.** The general appearance of anything; *geol.* appearance or nature of one stratified part of a rock body as distinguished from other parts by composition; *med.* facial appearance indicative of a disease.

fac·ile, fas′il, *Brit.* fas′īl, a. [O.Fr. Fr. *facile,* < L. *facilis,* easy to do, easy, < *facere,* do, make.] Easily done, performed, or used; easy or unconstrained, as manners or persons; moving, acting, working, or proceeding with ease; superficial; skillful; affable or agreeable; easily persuaded or influenced.—**fac·ile·ly,** adv.—**fac·ile·ness,** n.

fa·cil·i·tate, fa·sil′i·tāt″, v.t.—*facilitated, facilitating.* [Fr. *faciliter,* < L. *facilitas,* easiness.] To make easy or less difficult.—

fa·cil·i·ta·tion, fa·sil″i·tā′shan, *n.* The act of facilitating; aid; *physiol.* increase of the response of nerve impulses along a particular pathway resulting from earlier or simultaneous stimulation.

fa·cil·i·ty, fa·sil′i·tē, *n. pl.* **fa·cil·i·ties.** [Fr. *facilité,* < L. *facilitas.*] The quality of being easily performed or guided; ease in performance; readiness proceeding from skill or use; dexterity; freedom from difficulty; the means by which the accomplishment of anything is rendered easier; *often pl.* something built and activated to serve a particular purpose; as, the school's luncheon *facilities.*

fac·ing, fā′sing, *n.* A covering in front for ornament, protection, defense, or other purposes; an ornamental or strengthening lining at the edge of a garment; *milit.* the movement of soldiers turning in response to a command; *pl.* the distinctive trimmings on a regimental coat or jacket.

fac·sim·i·le, fak·sim′i·lē, *n.* [L. *fac,* impv. of *facere,* do, make, and *simile,* neut. of *similis,* like.] An exact copy or likeness. *Communications,* a process by which written messages or pictures are electronically transferred, by means of radio, telegraph, or telephone, for instant reproduction at a distant place; also **fac·sim·i·le trans·mis·sion,** fax, faks. Such a reproduced message or picture; also **fax.**—*v.t.*—*facsimiled, facsimileing.* To reproduce or make a facsimile of. *Communications,* to send(a message or picture)by the process of facsimile; also **fax.**

fact, fakt, *n.* [L. *factum,* a thing done, prop. neut. of *factus,* pp. of *facere,* do, make.] Something that has really happened or is actually the case, as distinguished from something merely believed to be so; the quality of being real and actual; a truth known by actual observation or authentic testimony; *often pl., law,* something which is alleged to be; as, *facts* given but not trustworthy.

fac·tion, fak′shan, *n.* [L. *factio,* < *facio, factum,* to do.] A group within a larger organization, combined or acting in unison, usu. in opposition to the main group, party, or government; partisan discord or dissension.—**fac·tion·al,** fak′sha·nal, *a.*—**fac·tion·al·ly,** *adv.*—**fac·tion·al·ism,** *n.* Loyalty to a faction; a state of self-interest or factional conflict.

fac·tious, fak′shus, *a.* Given to faction; prone to dissent; pertaining to or proceeding from faction.—**fac·tious·ly,** *adv.*—**fac·tious·ness,** *n.*

fac·ti·tious, fak·tish′us, *a.* [L. *facticius,* < *facere,* do, make.] Contrived rather than spontaneous or natural; made, manufactured, or artificial; conforming to a conventional standard.—**fac·ti·tious·ly,** *adv.*—**fac·ti·tious·ness,** *n.*

fac·ti·tive, fak′ti·tiv, *a.* Causative; tending to make or cause. *Gram.* of transitive verbs, expressing an action that produces a new condition in the object, which is accomplished by the verb's taking an objective complement in addition to a direct object, as: They *elected* him *president.*

fac·tor, fak′tėr, *n.* [L. doer, maker, < *facere,* do, make.] A contributing element in bringing about any given result; *math.* one of two or more numbers, algebraic expressions, or the like, which when multiplied together produce a given product; *law,* in some states, a person accused as a garnishee. *Com.* a commission merchant; an agent entrusted with the possession and sale of goods on behalf of a client. *Biol.* a gene or similar unit responsible for hereditary characteristics.—*v.t. Math.* to resolve into factors; *Com.* to act as agent or factor for in commercial transactions.—**fac·tor·a·ble,** *a.*—**fac·to-**

ri·al, fak·tōr′ē·al, fak·tàr′ē·al, *a., n.*—**fac·tor·ship,** *n.*—**fac·tor·age,** *n.* The action or business of a factor; the allowance or commission paid to a factor.

fac·tor·ize, fak′to·rīz″, *v.t.*—*factorized, factorizing. Law,* to garnishee; *math.* resolve into factors.—**fac·tor·i·za·tion,** *n.*

fac·to·ry, fak′to·rē, *n. pl.* **fac·to·ries.** A building or collection of buildings used for the manufacture of goods; a trading establishment maintained in a foreign country by resident factors and merchants; *colloq.* an institution failing to encourage individual creativity, producing only uniformity.

fac·to·tum, fak·tō′tum, *n.* [L. *facio,* to do, and *totum,* the whole.] One hired to perform a variety of tasks.

fac·tu·al, fak′chō·al, *a.* Pertaining to facts; of the nature of fact; dealing only in fact.—**fac·tu·al·i·ty,** **fac·tu·al·ness,** fak″chō·al′i·tē, *n.*—**fac·tu·al·ly,** *adv.*

fac·tu·al·ism, fak′chō·a·liz″um, *n.* A reliance on factual evidence; a responsibility to fact; a theory which places great emphasis on fact.—**fac·tu·al·ist,** *n.*—**fac·tu·al·is·tic,** *a.*

fac·ture, fak′chėr, *n.* [L. *factura,* < *facere,* do, make.] The act, process, or manner of making; construction; the thing made.

fac·u·la, fak′ū·la, fak′ya·la, *n. pl.* **fac·u·lae,** fak′ū·lē″, fak′ya·lē″. [L. *facula,* a little torch, dim. of *fax,* a torch.] *Astron.* a bright patch sometimes seen on the sun's surface, most clearly visible near the edge.

fac·ul·ta·tive, fak′ul·tā″tiv, *a.* Conferring a privilege or permission, or the power of doing or not doing something; left to one's option or choice; optional; that may or may not take place; that may or may not assume a specified character; *biol.* organisms capable of either a parasitic or a nonparasitic life.—**fac·ul·ta·tive·ly,** *adv.*

fac·ul·ty, fak′ul·tē, *n. pl.* **fac·ul·ties.** [Fr. *faculté,* L. *facultas,* < *facio,* to do, to make.] A natural or acquired ability; extraordinary talent or skill; as, a *faculty* for painting; any mental or bodily power. *Educ.* the teaching staff of any institution of learning; one of the departments of a university; as, the *faculty* of Arts and Sciences. The individuals constituting one of the learned professions.

fad, fad, *n.* A passing fashion or mode of behavior pursued for a time with undue zeal.—**fad·dish,** fad′ish, *a.* Pertaining or given to fads.—**fad·dism,** *n.* Compulsive adherence to fads.—**fad·dist,** *n.* One who is inclined to adopt fads.

fade, fād, *v.i.*—*faded, fading.* [O.Fr. *fader,* < *fade,* prob. < L. *vapidus,* E. *vapid.*] To lose brightness or vividness, as color; to lose freshness and vigor; wither; fail gradually in strength or health; in general, to fail or disappear gradually; to die gradually.—*v.t.* To cause to fade.—**fade in,** *radio, TV, motion pictures, recording,* to introduce, as a sound or an image, gradually and with increasing intensity.—**fade-in,** *n.* An image or sound so introduced.—**fade out,** *radio, TV, motion pictures, recording,* to cause to fade or disappear, as a sound or an image.—**fade·a·way,** *n.* The act or instance of fading away.—**fade·less,** *a.* Not fading.—**fade·less·ly,** *adv.*

fa·er·ie, fa·er·y, fā′e·rē, fâr′ē, *n. pl.* **fa·er·ies.** The domain or land of the fairies; *archaic,* a fairy.—*a.* Like a fairy.

fag, fag, *v.t.*—*fagged, fagging.* [Prob. < verb *flag.*] To exhaust, usu. with *out.*—*v.i.* To become weary through work.—*n. Slang,* a man who is a homosexual. *Brit.* laborious toil; in some schools, a boy who performs menial services for another who outranks him in class standings.

fa·ga·ceous, fa·gā′shus, *a.* Pertaining to the beech family of shrubs and trees.

fag end, *n.* The unfinished or coarse end of a piece of cloth or web; the untwisted end portion of a rope; a remnant; the last, and usu. undesirable, part of anything.

fag·ot, fag·got, fag′ot, *n.* [O.Fr. Fr. *fagot;* origin uncertain.] A bundle of wood, sticks, or twigs used for fuel or in building fortifications; a bundle of iron or steel pieces to be rolled or hammered; *fig.* a collection; as, a *fagot* of selections.—*v.t.* To bind or make into a fagot; to ornament with fagoting.

fag·ot·ing, fag·got·ing, fag′o·ting, *n.* A kind of decorative drawn work in which threads of a fabric are pulled out in a horizontal line and the remaining cross threads are bundled in the middle in an hourglass design; a type of openwork embroidery in which crisscross stitches are made across an open seam.

fahl·band, fäl′band″, G. fäl′bänt″, *n.* [G. 'fallow band.'] *Mining,* a belt or zone of rock impregnated with metallic sulfides.

Fahr·en·heit, far′en·hīt″, G. fär′en·hīt″, *a.* [After Gabriel Daniel *Fahrenheit,* who first employed quicksilver in thermometers about 1720.] Of or pertaining to a thermometer with a scale, determined at normal atmospheric pressure, on which the boiling point of water is 212° above zero of the scale, the freezing point is 32° above zero of the scale, and zero is approximately the temperature produced by mixing snow and common salt in equal quantities by weight.

fa·ience, fa·ïence, fī·äns′, fä·äns′, Fr. fä·yäns′, *n.* [Fr.] A fine pottery or earthenware glazed and painted in various designs, named from *Faenza* in Italy.

fail, fāl, *v.i.* [Fr. *faillir,* to fail, < L. *fallere,* to deceive.] To become deficient; to be inadequate; to cease to be abundant; to fall short; to decay, decline, sink, or be diminished; to become weaker; to become extinct; to be entirely wanting; to stop functioning; to be unsuccessful in receiving a passing mark in; to be guilty of omission or neglect; to become insolvent or bankrupt.—*v.t.* To neglect, omit, or leave undone; to disappoint; to desert; to not have at hand when required; to not promote or grade, as a student, as ineligible for promotion.—*n.* Failure; deficiency; want.—**with·out fail,** without doubt; certainly.

fail·ing, fā′ling, *n.* An imperfection; a weakness in character or disposition; a foible; a fault; the act or state of a person or thing that fails.—*prep.* Lacking, without, or in default of.—**fail·ing·ly,** *adv.* In a failing manner; as, a *failingly* dim ray of sunlight.

faille, fil, fāl, Fr. fä′ye, *n.* [Fr.] A slightly lustrous, closely woven fabric characterized by indistinct, flat ribbing.

fail·safe, fāl′sāf″, *a. Electronics,* pertaining to a safety warning feature or system which reacts automatically to a possible source of failure, either functional or operational; *milit.* pertaining to an automatic response system that halts continuation of an air mission beyond a certain standard operating point without direct orders from a designated authority.

fail·ure, fāl′yėr, fāl′ūr, *n.* The act or instance of failing; the state of having failed to attain an objective; want of success; one who is unsuccessful; a deficiency, insufficiency, or total cessation of supply; nonperformance or omission of a duty or obligation; deterioration, esp. a waning of physical powers; a state of insolvency or bankruptcy.

fai·né·ant, fā′nē·ant, Fr. fe·nā·äN′, *n. pl.* **fai·né·ants,** fā′nē·ants, Fr. fe·nā·äN′. [Fr. *faire,* do, *néant,* nothing.] An idler; a do-nothing.—*a.*

faint, fānt, *v.i.* [O.Fr. *faint,* sluggish, negligent, pp. of *feindre,* L. *fingere,* to feign.] To become temporarily unconscious;

to swoon. *Archaic*, to lose spirit or courage; to become gradually indistinct.—*n.* A momentary loss of consciousness; a swoon. —*a.* On the verge of losing consciousness; indistinct or lacking brightness and vividness; feeble; weak.—**faint·ly**, *adv.*—**faint·ness**, *n.*

faint·heart·ed, fānt′här′tid, *a.* Cowardly; timorous; having lost courage.—**faint·heart·ed·ly**, *adv.*—**faint·heart·ed·ness**, *n.*

fair, fâr, *a.* Pleasing to the eye; pretty; light in hue; blond or light-complected; unblemished in appearance, quality, or character; without rage or turmoil; clear, bright, or sunny, as the mood of a person or the sky; clear; discernible, or legible, as handwriting; gentle, civil, or courteous, as one's manner; honest, open, frank, impartial, or unbiased; just; objective or dispassionate; legitimate, justifiable, or acceptable, as a course of action; good, select, or promising, as a choice; ample, reasonable, or adequate, as quantity or amount; mediocre; *naut.* assisting as utilizable, as wind or tide.—*adv.* Fairly. —**fair·ly**, *adv.* In an impartial manner; moderately; completely; suitable; legitimately; clearly.—**fair·ness**, *n.*

fair, fâr, *n.* A competitive exhibition of livestock and various products, often combined with entertainment, and held annually in various states; a public exhibit of the culture and particular achievements of different countries by the representatives of those countries; the exhibition and sale of products, usu. for the benefit of a charity.

fair ball, *n. Baseball*, any batted ball that lands and stays between the first and third base lines in the infield, or first lands but need not remain within the foul lines in the outfield, or remains within the foul lines while it passes beyond the outfield for a home run.

fair catch, *n. Football*, the catch of a kicked ball by a player who signals that he will not attempt a runback and therefore may not be tackled or hindered in any way.

fair·ground, fâr′ground″, *n. Usu. pl.* A place set aside for fairs, carnivals, and exhibitions.

fair·ish, fâr′ish, *a.* Reasonably good; as, *fairish* health; moderately large; fairly light in color.—**fair·ish·ly**, *adv.*

fair-mind·ed, fâr′mīn′did, *a.* Reasonable and unbiased; free from prejudice.—**fair-mind·ed·ness**, *n.*

fair-trade agree·ment, fâr′trād′ a·grē′ment, *n.* An arrangement, illegal in some states, in which a retailer agrees not to sell a manufacturer's product for less than a specified price.—**fair trade**, *v.t.* To distribute or sell, as a commodity, subject to a fair-trade agreement.—*a.*—**fair-trader**, *n.*

fair·way, fâr′wā″, *n. Golf*, the part of the course, between the tee and the green, where the grass is cut short; a path that is unobstructed; *naut.* a navigable waterway.

fair-weath·er, fâr′weŦH″ẽr, *a.* Intended for use or carried on in fair weather only; undependable in time of adversity; as, *fair-weather* friends.

fair·y, fâr′ē, *n. pl.* **fair·ies**. [O.Fr. *faerie*, Fr. *féerie*, the power of a fairy, enchantment; < O.Fr. *fae*, Fr. *fée*, It. *fata*, a fairy, lit. a fate, < L. *fatum*, fate.] An imaginary being or spirit having a small, graceful human form and superhuman attributes; an elf or fay.—*a.* Pertaining to or in some manner connected with fairies; coming from fairies; resembling a fairy. Also **fair·y·like**.—**fair·y·land**, *n.* The imaginary land or abode of fairies.

fair·y ring, *n.* A ring of mushrooms formed in a pasture or a lawn by the mycelia of a fungus, popularly supposed to be caused by fairies in their dances.

fair·y tale, *n.* A tale of magical creatures and their adventures, usu. told for the amusement of children; an unbelievable, imaginative statement or story; a lie. Also **fair·y sto·ry**.

faith, fāth, *n.* [O.Fr. *feid*, *fei* (Fr. *foi*), < L. *fides*, faith, < *fidere*, trust.] Confidence or trust in a person or thing; loyalty; fidelity to a person, promise, or commitment; belief not substantiated by proof; spiritual acceptance of truth or realities not certified by reason; belief in God; belief in the doctrines or teachings of a religion.—**in faith**, in truth; indeed.

faith·ful, fāth′ful, *a.* Strict in the performance of duty; unswervingly devoted; loyal to one's promises; trustworthy; adhering to fact or true to an original; as, a *faithful* copy.—*n. pl.* **faith·ful**, **faith·fuls**. The loyal adherents of any party or group; with *the*, believing members of the Christian church or of the Mohammedan faith.

faith·less, fāth′lis, *a.* Not adhering to vows or duty; not trustworthy; perfidious; without religious faith or belief.—**faith·less·ly**, *adv.*—**faith·less·ness**, *n.*

fake, fāk, *v.t.*—**faked**, **faking**. [E. dial., to patch, alter.] To prepare or change in order to impart a false character to; to simulate; *slang*, to act by improvising.—*v.i.* To pretend something.—*n.* A counterfeit or imitation offered as genuine; a fraud; one who fakes.—*a.*—**fak·er**, *n.*

fa·kir, fa·kēr′, fā′kẽr, *n.* [Ar. *faqīr*, poor.] A Muslim religious mendicant or ascetic; a Hindu devotee or ascetic of India.

Fa·lan·gist, fa·lan′jist, *n.* A member of the official fascist political party in Spain following the civil war of 1936–1939.

fal·cate, fal′kāt, *a.* [L. *falcatus*, < *falx* (*falc-*), sickle.] Curved like a sickle; hooked; *bot.* of fruits, shaped like a sickle. Also **fal·cat·ed**.

fal·chion, fal′chon, fal′shon, *n.* [O.Fr. *fauchon*, < M.L. *falcio(n-)*, < L. *falx*, (*falc-*), sickle.] A broad, short sword used in medieval times, having a convex edge curving sharply to the point.

fal·con, fal′kon, fal′kon, fạ′kon, *n.* [O.Fr. Fr. *faucon*, < L.L. *falco(n-)*, falcon (named from its hooked talons), < L. *falx* (*falc-*), sickle.] Any of various diurnal birds of prey of the family *Falconidae*, esp. of the genus *Falco*, having long pointed wings and a hooked bill; formerly any of various hawks trained to hunt other birds and game. An obsolete kind of cannon.

fal·con·er, fal′ko·nẽr, fal′ko·nẽr, fạ′kon·ẽr, *n.* [O.Fr. Fr. *fauconnier*.] One who hunts with falcons; one who breeds and trains hawks for hunting.

fal·co·net, fal′ko·net″, fal′ko·net″, fạ′ko·net″, *n.* A small falcon, esp. any of various Asiatic species.

fal·con·ry, fal′kon·rē, fal′kon·rē, fạ′kon·rē, *n.* [Fr. *fauconnerie*.] The sport of hawking; the training of falcons.

fal·de·ral, fal′de·ral″, *n.* Folderol.

fall, fạl, *v.i.*—past **fell**, pp. **fallen**, ppr. **falling**. [O.E. *feallan* = D. *vallen* = G. *fallen* = Icel. *falla*, fall.] To descend by the power of gravity from a higher to a lower place or position through loss or lack of support; to drop or come down suddenly from a standing or erect position; to lose high position, dignity, or character; to come as if by descending, as stillness, night, or silence; to become detached and drop off, as leaves; to issue forth; as, to let *fall* a remark; to hang down, or extend downward, as: Her hair *fell* to her shoulders. To sink to a lower level, as waves; to decline, as in strength; to ebb, as the tide; to slope, as land; to lose animation, as: Her face *fell*. To be cast down, as the eyes; to be

reduced, as the temperature; to become lowered, as the voice; to decrease, as in number, value, volume, degree, or quality; to come down in fragments or ruins; collapse; to succumb to attack, as a fortified place; to be overthrown, as a government; to do wrong or sin, esp. to give up one's chastity; to drop down wounded or dead, esp. to be slain; to be directed, as light or sight, on something; to come within the jurisdiction, scope, or limitation of something; to have a proper place, as: The accent *falls* on the first syllable. To come, as an inheritance, assignment, or duty, as: The jobs *fall* to him. To come by chance into a particular position; as, to *fall* among thieves; to enter into a particular emotional, mental, or physical state; as, to *fall* in love, to *fall* ill. To apply oneself or set about actively or heartily; as, to *fall* to work. To come to pass; occur; happen, as: Independence Day *falls* on Thursday this year.— *v.t.* To chop down or fell, as a tree.—**fall a·way**, to withdraw support or allegiance; to apostatize; to decline, decay, or perish; to become lean or emaciated.—**fall back**, to recede; to retreat; to give way.—**fall be·hind**, to drop back; to fail to pay on time.—**fall down**, to fail; to disappoint.— **fall for**, to be deceived by; to fall in love with.—**fall in**, to sink inward; to take one's proper place in line, as a soldier.—**fall in with**, to come together; to meet; to agree; to conform to.—**fall off**, to drop off; to separate or withdraw; to decrease in number, amount, or intensity; to diminish. —**fall on, fall up·on**, to assault; to discover by chance; to become the duty or responsibility of; to have or know; experience; as, to *fall on* hard times.—**fall out**, to drop out of one's place in line, as a soldier; to disagree or quarrel; to occur or happen.—**fall short**, to fail to reach a mark aimed at; to be or prove insufficient.—**fall through**, to come to naught; to fail.—**fall to**, to set to work; apply oneself; to begin to eat.

fall, fạl, *n.* The act of falling or dropping from a higher to a lower place or position; the descent of rain or snow; the quantity that descends; autumn, the season of the year when the leaves fall from trees; a sinking to a lower level; subsidence, as of waves; decline or decay; *usu. pl.* a cataract or waterfall; as, Niagara *Falls*. Downward direction or trend; the distance through which anything falls; a decrease, as in price or value; a falling from an erect position, as to the ground; a method of being thrown on one's back by an opponent in wrestling; a bout at wrestling; as, to try a *fall*; a felling of trees, or the timber cut down at one time; the surrender or capture, as of a city; a succumbing to temptation, or lapse into sin; a proper place; as, the *fall* of an accent on a syllable; a falling or hanging covering or piece of material, as of lace; a loosely hanging veil; a woman's long hair piece; *mech.* the part of the rope of a tackle to which the power is applied in hoisting; *pl.* the apparatus used in lowering or hoisting a ship's boat.—*a.* Of or pertaining to autumn.

fal·la·cious, fa·lā′shus, *a.* [L. *fallaciosus*.] Deceptive, misleading, or false; delusive; containing a fallacy; logically unsound.— **fal·la·cious·ly**, *adv.*—**fal·la·cious·ness**, *n.*

fal·la·cy, fal′a·sē, *n. pl.* **fal·la·cies**. [L. *fallacia*, < *fallax*, deceptive, < *fallere*, deceive.] Something deceptive, misleading, or false, esp. a misleading or unsound argument; the quality of being deceptive or erroneous; *logic*, any of various types of faults in arguments or syllogisms that render then logically unsound.

fall·en, fạ′len, *a.* Having dropped; prostrate; degraded; of a woman, no longer chaste; overthrown; slain.

---

a- fat, fāte, fär, fâre, fạll;   **e-** met, mē, mẽre, hẽr;   **i-** pin, pīne;   **o-** not, nōte, mŏve;   **u-** tub, cūbe, bụll;   **oi-** oil;   **ou-** pound.

fall guy, *n. Slang.* One who is made to take the blame for the base actions of another; scapegoat.

fal·li·ble, fal′i·bl, *a.* [L.L. *fallibilis,* < L. *fallo,* to deceive.] Liable to err or fail; capable of being mistaken or deceived; liable to be inaccurate or misleading.—**fal·li·bil·i·ty,** *n.*—**fal·li·bly,** *adv.*

fall·ing-out, fȧ′ling·out′, *n. pl.* **fall·ings-out, fall·ing-outs.** A quarrel or alienation of persons once on friendly terms or closely associated with one another.

fall·ing star, *n.* A meteor; a shooting star.

Fal·lo·pi·an tube, fȧ·lō′pē·an, *n.* [From Gabriello *Fallopio* (1523–62), an Italian anatomist.] (*Sometimes l.c.*) either of a pair of slender tubes which convey the ova from the ovaries to the cavity of the uterus.

fall·out, fȧl′out″, *n. Phys.* dust, soot, and other material blown into the atmosphere by a nuclear explosion, and usu. rendered radioactive by it; the descent of such particles. A by-product of any sort.

fal·low, fal′ō, *n.* [M.E. *falewen,* appar. < O.E. *fealh,* a harrow.] Land that has lain unseeded after plowing and harrowing; the state of being fallow; an interval during which land is left fallow.—*a.* Of land, plowed and left unseeded for a season or more; uncultivated or neglected.—*v.t.* To plow and harrow, as land, without seeding.—**fal·low·ness,** *n.*

fal·low, fal′ō, *a.* [O.E. *fealu* = D. *vaal* = G. *fahl, falb,* fallow, = Icel. *fölr,* pale.] Of a pale yellowish or brownish color.

fal·low deer, *n.* A European deer, *Dama dama,* with a yellowish coat.

false, fȧls, *a.*—**falser, falsest.** [L. *falsus,* feigned, spurious, deceptive, false, pp. of *fallere,* deceive.] Contrary to what is true or correct; erroneous, mistaken, untrue, or incorrect; uttering or declaring what is untrue; deceitful, treacherous, or faithless; deceptive; as, *false* appearances; not genuine; counterfeit or artificial; employed to deceive or mislead; *mus.* inaccurate in pitch; as, a *false* note; *biol.* having a deceptive resemblance to something that properly bears the name; as, the *false* Solomon's-seal; substituted for or supplementing, esp. temporarily.—*adv.* In a false manner; incorrectly or wrongly; treacherously or faithlessly.—**false·ly,** *adv.*—**false·ness,** *n.*

false·hood, fȧls′hud, *n.* An untrue statement; a lie; the act of lying or prevaricating; something that is untrue; want of truth or veracity.

false ho·ri·zon, *n.* A line marking the apparent meeting of ground and sky, used in instruments which measure altitude.

false rib, *n.* A rib which is not directly attached to the sternum.

fal·set·to, fȧl·set′ō, *n. pl.* **fal·set·tos.** [It. < L. *falsus,* false.] An artificially high tone; an unnaturally high voice, esp. in a man; a singer, esp. a man, who uses the tones above the natural compass of the voice.—*a.*—*adv.*

fals·ie, fȧl′sē, *n.* Usu. *pl.* a cup of rubber or fabric, placed inside a brassiere, making the breast appear larger or more shapely.

fal·si·fy, fȧl′si·fī″, *v.t.*—**falsified, falsifying.** [Fr. *falsifier,* < L. *falsus,* and *facio,* to make.] To make false, as by alteration or addition, esp. for the purpose of deception or fraud; to represent falsely; to disprove or confute.—*v.i.* To lie.—**fal·si·fi·ca·tion,** fȧl′si·fi·kā′shan, *n.* The act of falsifying; a counterfeiting.—**fal·si·fi·er,** *n.*

fal·si·ty, fȧl′si·tē, *n. pl.* **fal·si·ties.** That which is false; a lie; the quality of being false, deceitful, or insincere.

Fal·staff·i·an, fȧl′staf′ē·an, *a.* Pertaining to, characteristic of, or resembling the fictional Sir John Falstaff, a fat, jovial soldier known for his bawdy wit, swaggering manner, and cowardice, in Shakespeare's *Henry IV* and *The Merry Wives of Windsor.*

falt·boat, fält′bōt″, *n.* [G. *faltboot,* folding boat.] A light collapsible boat having a wooden, canvas-covered frame.

fal·ter, fȧl′tėr, *v.i.* [M.E. *falteren;* origin uncertain.] To become unsteady or hesitant in movement; to stagger, stumble, or totter; to speak hesitatingly or brokenly; stammer; to hesitate or waver in action or purpose; to begin to give way or lose one's resolution, courage, or powers.—*v.t.* To utter hesitatingly or brokenly.—*n.* An act of faltering; an unsteadiness of gait, voice, action, or sound.—**fal·ter·er,** *n.*—**fal·ter·ing·ly,** *adv.*

fame, fām, *n.* [Fr. *fame,* < L. *fama,* fame, renown, < *fari,* to speak.] Widespread renown or recognition; opinion of a person or thing held by the public; reputation.—*v.t.* To make famous; to have renown.—**famed,** fāmd, *a.* Much talked of; renowned; celebrated; acclaimed.

fa·mil·ial, fȧ·mil′yal, fȧ·mil′ē·al, *a.* Pertaining to or characteristic of a family; connected with or common to the family; as, a *familial* trait.

fa·mil·iar, fȧ·mil′yėr, *a.* [L. *familiaris,* < *familia,* a household, the servants of a family, < *famulus,* a servant.] Well-known; of everyday occurrence or use; well-acquainted; closely intimate; well-versed, as in a subject or study; exhibiting the manner of an intimate friend; informal; affable; characterized by ease or absence of stiffness; pertaining to a family.—*n.* An intimate; a close companion; a member of the household of a high ecclesiastical official; a person who frequents a place.—**fa·mil·iar·ly,** *adv.*

fa·mil·i·ar·i·ty, fȧ·mil″ē·ar′i·tē, *n. pl.* **fa·mil·i·ar·i·ties.** The state of being familiar; thorough acquaintance or knowledge of a person or subject; intimacy. *Pl.* actions characterized by too much license; liberties.

fa·mil·iar·ize, fȧ·mil′ya·rīz″, *v.t.*—**familiarized, familiarizing.** To make familiar or intimate; to accustom; to make intimately acquainted; to render conversant or fully acquainted by practice or customary use.—**fa·mil·iar·i·za·tion,** *n.* Act or process of making or becoming familiar.

fa·mil·iar spir·it, *n.* A spirit or demon supposed to be constantly at the command of some person; the spirit of a deceased person summoned by a medium to advise or predict.

fam·i·ly, fam′i·lē, fam′lē, *n. pl.* **fam·i·lies.** [L. *familia,* a household, the slaves or servants of a house, < *famulus,* a servant, a slave, < Oscan *famel,* a servant, < *faama,* Skr. *dhāman,* a house.] The unit consisting of parents and their children; the children, as distinguished from the *parents;* persons related by blood or marriage; those who are descendants of a common progenitor; a clan; noble or distinguished lineage; as, a man of *family;* the group of persons who live in one household and under one head; a group of people or things with a common or related characteristic, function, or origin; as, office *family,* woodwind *family;* a taxonomic classification of plants or animals which is above a genus and below an order; *math.* a set of surfaces or curves whose equations are related, differing only in their parameters. A class of languages sharing certain characteristics and seeming to have had a common origin; as, the Indo-European *family.*—*a.* Of or pertaining to a family.

fam·i·ly cir·cle, *n.* The section in an opera house or theater where inexpensive seats are located, usu. an upper balcony.

fam·i·ly man, *n.* A man who has a wife and a child or children; a man who is attentive to his family, and devoted to family life and domestic routine.

fam·i·ly name, *n.* A surname; the last name of an individual, shared by the members of his immediate family.

fam·i·ly tree, *n.* A chart or diagram outlining the lineage of a family from the earliest known ancestor, and showing all family members and their relationships. Also **ge·ne·a·log·i·cal tree.**

fam·ine, fam′in, *n.* [Fr. *famine,* < L. *fames,* hunger.] Widespread scarcity of food; a general shortage of anything; dearth; starvation.

fam·ish, fam′ish, *v.t., v.i.* [O.Fr. *famis,* starving, < L. *fames.*] To cause to suffer from hunger or thirst.—**fam·ish·ment,** *n.*—**fam·ished,** *a.* Suffering from extreme hunger.

fa·mous, fā′mus, *a.* [L. *famosus,* Fr. *fameux.*] Widely known; celebrated; renowned.—**fa·mous·ly,** *adv.* Ably; excellently; successfully.

fan, fan, *n.* [O.E. *fann,* < L. *vannus,* fan for winnowing grain.] A device for producing a cooling current of air; a hand implement for producing such currents, often made of parts which can be folded and which when spread out take the form of a sector of a circle; anything resembling or spread out like a fan, as the tail of a bird; any of various electric devices consisting of a series of radiating blades revolving to produce an air current; a device for winnowing grain.—**fan·like,** *a.*—**fan·ner,** *n.*

fan, fan, *v.t.*—**fanned, fanning.** To move or agitate, as air, with a fan; to cause air to blow upon, as from a fan; to stir to activity with or as with a fan; to blow upon, as if driven by a fan; to spread out like a fan; *agric.* to winnow.—*v.i.* To move or spread as a fan does; *baseball,* to strike out.

fan, fan, *n. Slang.* An enthusiast or devotee of any sport or amusement; an admirer, esp. of an actor or other public figure.

fa·nat·ic, fȧ·nat′ik, *n.* [L. *fanaticus,* inspired, enthusiastic, < *fanum,* a place dedicated to some deity, a temple.] Zealot; an extremist: often applied to followers of a religion or a political party.—*a.* Wildly enthusiastic; marked by extreme, uncritical zeal. Also **fa·nat·i·cal,** fȧ·nat′i·kal,—**fa·nat·i·cal·ly,** *adv.*—**fa·nat·i·cize,** *Brit.* also **fa·nat·i·cise,** fȧ·nat′i·sīz″, *v.t.*—*fanaticized, fanaticizing, Brit.* also *fanaticised, fanaticising.* To make fanatic.

fa·nat·i·cism, fȧ·nat′i·siz″um, *n.* Excessive zeal or unreasoning fervor, esp. religious or political; behavior marked by such zeal or fervor.

fan·ci·er, fan′sē·ėr, *n.* One having a specialized interest, esp. one who is engaged in breeding, for improvement, a particular variety of animal or plant; an enthusiast.

fan·ci·ful, fan′si·ful, *a.* Guided by fancy rather than by reason and experience; capricious; unreal; appealing to whimsy.—**fan·ci·ful·ly,** *adv.*—**fan·ci·ful·ness,** *n.*

fan·cy, fan′sē, *n. pl.* **fan·cies.** [Contr. of fantasy.] Imagination, esp. of a capricious or illusory type; specif. the faculty of creating decorative, light, and playful imagery, as in poetry or art; a mental image or conception; an idea or opinion with little foundation; a caprice or whim; capricious or arbitrary preference, inclination, or fondness; as, to take a *fancy* to; judgment, as in fashion or art; breeding of animals or plants to develop points of beauty or excellence; followers or enthusiasts of a particular class of things, as birds or dogs, or of a particular amusement.

fan·cy, fan′sē, *a.*—**fancier, fanciest.** Adapted to please the fancy or taste; not plain; ornamental; elegant; select or extra fine; as, *fancy* fruits; involving superior skills;

as, *fancy* footwork, *fancy* diving; bred, as an animal or plant, to develop special points of beauty or excellence; vari-colored, as a flower; unrealistic, extravagant, or excessive; as, *fancy* prices; based on ideas of the fancy or imagination; depending on the exercise of imagination or caprice; whimsical; irregular.—**fan·cy dress,** a masquerade costume.—**fan·cy dress ball,** a ball at which fancy dress is worn.—**fan·ci·ly,** *adv.* Elaborately; with imagination.—**fan·ci·ness,** *n.*

fan·cy, fan′sē, *v.t.—fancied, fancying.* To form a fancy or conception of; picture to oneself; imagine; to believe without being sure or certain; to take a liking to; like.

fan·cy-free, fan′sē-frē′, *a.* Free to daydream; not romantically involved.

fan·cy·work, fan′sē-wurk″, *n.* Ornamental needlework.

fan·dan·go, fan·dang′gō, *n. pl.* **fan·dan·gos.** [Sp. < W. Ind.] A lively Spanish or Spanish-American dance performed by a man and woman playing castanets; music for such a dance or its rhythm.

fan·fare, fan′fâr, *n.* [Fr.] A flourish of trumpets; a short cheerful tune for hunting horns; an orchestral passage for brass instruments. Ostentatious show; boast or bravado; *colloq.* publicity, advertising.

fan·fa·ron, fan′fa·ron″, *n.* [Fr. < Sp.] A swaggerer; an empty boaster.—**fan·fa·ron·ade,** fan″fa·ro·nād, *n.* Bluster.

fang, fang, *n.* [M.E. *fangen,* < O.E. *fōn* (pret. *fēng,* pp. *fangen*) = O.H.G. and Goth. *fāhan.*] A long, pointed tooth of an animal; one of the long, hollow, or grooved teeth of a poisonous snake by which venom is injected; a canine tooth; one of the two anterior appendages of a spider; the root of a tooth, or one of its prongs.—**fanged,** fangd, *a.* Having fangs.

fan·jet, fan′jet″, *n.* A jet engine in which additional thrust is obtained by a ducted fan in the front end which draws in extra air to be compressed and expelled; an aircraft powered by one or more such engines.

fan·light, fan′līt″, *n.* A transom window, usu. semicircular, above a door or larger window.

fan palm, *n.* Any palm with fan-shaped leaves, as the talipot.

fan·tail, fan′tāl″, *n.* A tail, end, or part shaped like a fan; one of a breed of domestic pigeons with a fan-shaped tail; a fish of the perch family; a fan-shaped part of a structure, as an arch; the rounded overhang on the stern of some ships.—**fantailed,** *a.* Having a fan-shaped tail.

fan-tan, fan′tan″, *n.* [Chinese.] A Chinese gambling game in which a pile of coins or counters is placed under a bowl, and bets are made on what the remainder will be after their sum has been divided by four; a card game in which the cards are played in sequence, the winner being the player who first gets rid of his cards.

fan·ta·si·a, fan·tā′zha, fan·tā′zhē·a, fan″ta·zē′a, *n.* [It. < L. *phantasia.*] A musical composition in fanciful or irregular, rather than strict form; a potpourri of well-known airs arranged with interludes and florid embellishments; a play or poem in which the author creates the illusion of a fantasy.

fan·ta·sied, fan′ta·sēd, fan′ta·zēd, *a.* Present solely in the imagination.

fan·tasm, fan′taz·um, *n.* Phantasm.

fan·tast, fan′tast, *n.* A fanciful person; a visionary; a person of fantastic ideas or mannerisms. Also **phan·tast.**

fan·tas·tic, fan·tas′tik, *a.* [Fr. *fantastique,* < Gr. *phantastikos,* present to the eye or mind < *phantazien,* to make visible.] Existing in imagination only; whimsical; capricious; formed as if by unrestrained

fancy; odd in appearance; highly irregular; grotesque; of incredible dimension; exaggerated; extravagant; exorbitant; not based on reality; illusory; irrational. Also **fan·tas·ti·cal,** fan·tas′ti·kal.—**fan·tas·ti·cal·ly,** *adv.*—**fan·tas·ti·cal·ness,** *n.*—**fan·tas·ti·cal·i·ty,** *n.*

fan·ta·sy, phan·ta·sy, fan′ta·sē, fan′ta·zē, *n. pl.* **fan·ta·sies, phan·ta·sies.** A creation of the imagination, esp. when unrestrained; a freely envisioned thought or invention; a whimsical notion; a caprice; a mental image, esp. when grotesque or odd; a hallucination; a supposition based on no solid foundation; *mus.* a fantasia. *Psychol.* the usu. pleasant process of subjectively solving complex problems by imagining them in concrete symbols and images; the images themselves.

fan·toc·ci·ni, fan″to·chē′nē, *n. pl.* [It.] Puppets worked by concealed wires or strings; a puppet show using fantoccini; marionettes.

fan·tom, fan′tom, *n.* Phantom.

fan trac·er·y, *n. Arch.* tracery which spreads over the surface of a vault, like the folds of a fan.

fan win·dow, *n. Arch.* a fan-shaped window whose sash is formed with radial bars, used often as a fanlight.

fan·wort, fan′wurt″, *n.* A plant, *Cabomba caroliniana,* of the water-lily family, found in ponds or shallow swamps and used in fish aquaria.

far, fär, *adv.—farther, farthest, further, furthest.* [O.E. *feorr* = D. *ver* = O.H.G. *fer* = Icel. *fjarri* = Goth. *fairra,* far; akin to Gr. *pera,* beyond, further, Skt. *paras,* beyond, far.] At or to a great distance; remote in space or time; to an advanced stage or degree; greatly or very much; as, *far* better; by a great interval; widely; as, *far* reaching; at or to a definite distance, point of progress, or degree, preceded by *as, so, how.*—**by far,** by a great extent; very much.—**far and a·way,** by far; unquestionably.—**in so far, so far as,** to such an extent.—*a.* Distant or remote in space or time; extending to a great distance; as, a *far* look ahead; more distant of the two; as, the *far* side.—**a far cry from,** removed from; very different from.

far·ad, far′ad, far′ad, *n.* [From Michael Faraday (1791–1867), English physicist.] The unit of electrical capacity; the capacity of a condenser which has a difference of potential of one volt when charged with one coulomb.—**far·a·day,** far′a·dē, far′a·dā″, *n. Elect.* a unit used in electrolysis, being a quantity of electricity equal to about 96,500 coulombs.—**fa·rad·ic,** fa·rad′ik, *a.* Applied to induced currents of electricity, as the secondary currents of induction coils, or to phenomena connected with them.—**fa·ra·dism,** far′a·dizm″, *n.* Induced electricity; its application for therapeutic purposes.—**far·a·dize,** far′a·dīz″, *v.t.—faradized, faradizing. Med.* to stimulate or treat, as a muscle, with induced electric currents.—**far·a·di·za·tion,** *n.*—**far·a·diz·er,** *n.*

far·an·dole, far′an·dōl″, Fr. fä·RÄN′dal′, *n.* [Fr. < Pr. *farandolo.*] A lively dance, of Provençal origin, in which all the dancers join hands and execute various figures.

far·a·way, fär′a·wā″, *a.* Situated at a great distance; as, *faraway* places; dreamy; as, a *faraway* look in the eyes.

farce, färs, *n.* [Fr. *farce,* It. *farsa,* < L. *farcio,* to stuff, from being stuffed or crammed with humor.] A play of a broadly comic character which depends for its humor upon low comic devices such as slapstick and extravagant situations; humor of this kind; ridiculous pretense; mere show. *Cooking,* stuffing; forcemeat.—*v.t.—farced, farcing.* [Fr. *farcir,* < L. *farcio,* to

stuff.] To introduce witty material into a speech, play, or literary composition.—**far·ci·cal,** fär′si·kal, *a.* Belonging to a farce; of the character of a farce; ludicrous.—**far·ci·cal·i·ty,** *n.*—**far·ci·cal·ly,** *adv.*

far·ci, far·cie, fär·sē′, *a.* [Fr. pp. of *farcir,* E. *farce.*] *Cooking,* stuffed.

far·cy, fär′sē, *n. Vet. pathol.* a disease of horses and cattle which affects the lymphatic glands and skin; a contagious form of glanders.

fare, fâr, *v.i.—fared, faring.* [O.E. *faran,* to go = Icel. Sw. *fara,* Dan. *fare,* D. *varen,* G. *fahren,* to go, same root as L. *per,* through, *porta,* gate, Gr. *poros,* passage, *peirō,* to pierce.] To be in a certain condition, as: We *fare* well. To eat or drink.—*n.* The price paid or charged for conveyance or transport; a passenger who pays for public conveyance; food; that which is offered for public use or enjoyment.—**far·er,** *n.*

fare-thee-well, fâr′THē·wel″, *n. Colloq.* completion; extreme; the utmost degree, as: The roast was cooked to a *fare-thee-well.*

fare·well, fâr′wel′, *interj.* An expression of leave-taking; good-by.—*n.* Good-by; an act of departure.—*a.* Final; of or pertaining to the act or occasion of parting; as, a *farewell* dinner.

far-fetched, fär′fecht′, *a.* Unbelievable; improbable; exaggerated; strained.

far-flung, fär′flung′, *a.* Distant; scattered; extending over a wide range of space or time.

far·i·na, fa·rē′na, *n.* [L. *farina,* flour < *far,* a sort of grain.] A fine, granular preparation of flour or meal, cooked as a cereal or used as a rich thickener in puddings, soups, etc.—**far·i·na·ceous,** far″i·nā′shus, *a.* Containing or yielding farina or flour; mealy. Also **far·i·nose,** far′i·nōs.

far·kle·ber·ry, fär′kl·ber″ē, fär′kl·be·rē, *n. pl.* **far·kle·ber·ries.** A small tree, *Batodendron arboreum,* of southeastern U.S., having small, black berries attractive to birds.

farm, färm, *n.* [O.Fr. Fr. *ferme,* < M.L. *firma,* < L. *firmare,* make firm, < *firmus,* E. *firm.*] A tract of land devoted to the production of crops, livestock, or poultry; a tract of water set aside for cultivating aquatic life; as, an oyster *farm*; *baseball,* a minor-league team operated by a major-league team to train players or keep them in reserve; *hist.* the system of awarding authority to collect public revenues from a district, formerly granted to a citizen upon payment of a fixed sum or a percentage.—*v.t.* To cultivate, as land; to let or lease, as taxes, for a fixed sum or percentage; to let or lease the labor or services of someone for hire.—*v.i.* To cultivate the soil; operate a farm.—**farm out,** to send out, as work, from the main organization to be taken care of by persons on the outside; to contract for the maintenance of, as of orphans; *baseball,* to situate, as a player, with a farm team.—**farm·ing,** *n.* The act or vocation of one who farms; agriculture.

farm·er, fär′mer, *n.* One who raises crops or animals; one who operates a farm; one who undertakes some service, as the charge and maintenance of orphans, at a fixed price.—**farm hand,** one who works on a farm, esp. for pay.

farm·house, färm′hous″, *n.* A residence on a farm.—**farm·stead,** färm′sted″, *n.* A farm with its buildings; a homestead.—**farm·yard,** färm′yärd″, *n.* An area surrounded by or connected with farm buildings.

farm·land, färm′land″, *n.* Land adapted to or under cultivation.

far·o, fâr′ō, *n.* [Said to be from *Pharaoh* having formerly been depicted on one of the cards.] A card game in which the players bet on the cards drawn from a box which contains the dealer's or banker's pack.

Far·o·ese, fâr″ō·ēz′, fâr″ō·ēs′, a. Pertaining to the Faeroe Islands, the inhabitants, or the Germanic language they speak.—n. pl. **Far·o·ese.**

far-off, fär′af′, fär′of′, a. Distant or faraway; remote in space or time.

far-point, fär′point″, n. Ophthalm. the most distant point at which an object is distinctly visible to the fully relaxed eye.

far·ra·go, fa·rä′gō, fa·rā′gō, n. pl. **far·ra·goes.** [L. < far, meal.] A mixture composed of various elements confusedly put together; a medley.—**far·rag·i·nous,** fa·raj′i·nus, a. Formed of various materials; mixed.

far-reach·ing, fär′rē′ching, a. Having wide influence and great effect.—**far-reach·ing·ly,** adv.—**far-reach·ing·ness,** n.

far·ri·er, far′ē·ėr, n. [O.Fr. ferrier, < ferrer, to shoe a horse, < L. ferrum, iron.] Brit. a shoer of horses; a veterinarian, esp. one who cares for horses.—**far·ri·er·y,** far′ē·e·rē, n. The art of shoeing horses; the place where a farrier works.

far·row, far′ō, n. [O.E. fearh, akin to D. varken, G. ferkel, L. porcus, a pig.] A litter of pigs.—v.t. To give birth to (young): said of swine.—v.i. To produce a litter of pigs.

far·row, far′ō, a. [Origin uncertain.] Pertaining to a cow which does not produce offspring in a certain breeding season.

far-see·ing, fär′sē′ing, a. Showing foresight; able to see things clearly at great distances.

far-sight·ed, fär′sī′tid, fär′sī″tid, a. Seeing more clearly at a distance than close at hand; seeing to a great distance; calculating carefully the distant results of present conduct; showing good judgment.—**far-sight·ed·ly,** adv.—**far-sight·ed·ness,** n.

far·ther, fär′THėr, a. [Not the original compar. of far, which was far-er (ferrer), but assimilated to further.] More remote; more distant than something else; tending to a greater distance; additional.—adv. At or to a greater distance or degree; at or to a more advanced stage; moreover.—**far·ther·most,** a. Being at the farthest distance; most remote.—**far·thest,** fär′THist, a. Superl. of far. At the greatest distance either in time or place.—adv. At or to the greatest distance, degree, or most advanced stage.

far·thing, fär′THing, n. [O.E. fēorthung, the fourth part of a thing, < fēortha, fourth.] Formerly, a small, copper, British coin equal to a fourth of a penny; a trifle.

far·thin·gale, fär′THing·gāl″, n. [O.Fr. vertugalle, vertugade, < Sp. verdugo, a rod or shoot of a tree, hence a hoop.] A hoop petticoat worn by women in the 16th and 17th centuries; the circles of hoops used to extend the petticoat.

fas·ces, fas′ēz, n. pl., sing. or pl. in constr. [L.] A bundle of rods, with an ax bound with them, formerly borne before the superior Roman magistrates as a badge of their power over life and limb; the symbol of the Fascist party in Italy.

fas·ci·a, fash′ē·a, n. pl. **fas·ci·ae, fas·ci·as,** fash′ē·ē″. [L., band.] A band or fillet; arch. a long, flat member or band, esp. a horizontal division of an architrave; biol. a distinctly marked band of color. Anat. a band or sheath of connective tissue investing, supporting or binding together internal organs or parts of the body; tissue of this kind; surg. a bandage.—**fas·ci·al,** a.—**fas·ci·ate, fas·ci·at·ed,** fash′ē·āt″, a. [L. fasciatus, pp. of fasciare, envelop with bands, < fascia.] Marked with a band or bands; bound with a band, fillet, or bandage. Bot. compressed into a band or bundle; grown together, as stems.—**fas·ci·ate·ly,** adv.—**fas·ci·a·tion,** n. Fasciated condition; a binding up or bandaging. Bot. the process of becoming fasciated, or the resulting state; a malformation in plants.

fas·ci·cle, fas′i·kl, n. [L. fasciculus, dim. of fascis, bundle.] A small bundle; a single part of a printed work issued in installments; bot. a close cluster, as of flowers or leaves; anat. a small cluster of nerve fibers within the central nervous system.—**fas·ci·cled,** **fas·cic·u·lar,** fa·sik′ū·lėr, a. Pertaining to or forming a fascicle; fasciculate.—**fas·cic·u·lar·ly,** adv.—**fas·cic·u·late, fas·cic·u·lat·ed,** fa·sik′ū·lit, fa·sik′ū·lāt″, a. Arranged in a fascicle or fascicles.—**fas·cic·u·late·ly,** adv.—**fas·cic·u·la·tion,** n.—**fas·ci·cule,** n. [Fr., < L. fasciculus.] A fascicle, esp. of a book.—**fas·cic·u·lus,** n. pl. **fas·cic·u·li.** [L.] A fascicle, as of nerve fibers or muscle fibers; a fascicle of a book.

fas·ci·nate, fas′i·nāt″, v.t.—fascinated, fascinating. [Fr. fasciner, L. fascino, fascinatum, to fascinate, bewitch.] To bewitch; to enchant; to attract by some powerful or irresistible influence; to captivate; to arouse the interest of; to mesmerize, as by terror or awe.—v.i. To exercise a bewitching or captivating power.—**fas·ci·nat·ing,** fas′i·nā″ting, a. Bewitching; enchanting; charming; captivating.—**fas·ci·nat·ing·ly,** adv.—**fas·ci·na·tion,** n. The act of fascinating, bewitching, or enchanting; enchantment; a charm.—**fas·ci·na·tor,** n. One who fascinates; formerly, a woman's head scarf of lace or crochet.

fas·cism, fash′iz·um, n. (Sometimes cap.) an autocratic system of government, headed by an absolute dictator, and characterized by strict social and economic regimentation, aggressive nationalistic policies often accompanied by racism, and forcible suppression of all criticism or opposition; the political philosophy, methods, or principles of fascism. (Cap.) a fascist movement, esp. that headed by Benito Mussolini from 1922–43 in Italy.—**fas·cist,** fash′ist, n. A person who believes in or is sympathetic to fascism; (often cap.) a member of a fascist party.—a. Of or pertaining to fascism. Also **fa·scis·tic,** fa·shis′tik.—**fa·scis·ti·cal·ly,** adv.

fash·ion, fash′an, n. [O.Fr. fachon, facion, < L. factio, a making, < facio, to make. FACT.] The make or form of anything; mode or way; the current vogue in dress, style, procedure, manners, living, or the arts.—v.t. To form; to give shape to.

fash·ion·a·ble, fash′a·na·bl, a. Conforming to the current fashion or established mode; of or pertaining to the world of fashion.—n. A person of fashion.—**fash·ion·a·ble·ness,** n.—**fash·ion·a·bly,** adv.—**fash·ion plate,** a picture of a clothing style; an outstandingly fashionable person who consistently dresses in the latest style.

fast, fast, fäst, a. [O.E. faest, fest, fast, firm = D. vast, Icel. fastr. Dan. fast, G. fest, firm, solid. Hence fast, quick, and verb to fast.] Swift; rapid. Firmly fixed; closed; steadfast; faithful; firm in adherence; not changeable; lasting. Dissipated; of questionable morals; devoted to pleasure. Of a timepiece, ahead of the true time.—**fast·ness,** n. [O.E. faestnes, firmness, a fortification.] The state of being firm or secure; strength; security; a fortress; swiftness.

fast, fast, fäst, adv. In a fast or quick manner; swiftly; rapidly; with quick steps or progression; of a timepiece, ahead of the true time; wastefully; with dissipation. Tightly; as, to stick fast; deeply, as: He was fast asleep.

fast, fast, fäst, v.i. [O.E. faestan, to fast; probably < faest, firm, steadfast, the meaning being to be steadfast in abstaining = D. vasten, Dan. faste, Icel. and Sw. fasta, G. fasten, Goth. fastan, to fast.] To abstain from food beyond the usual time; to go hungry; to abstain from food, or particular kinds of food, voluntarily, especially for religious reasons or to lose

weight.—n. Abstinence from food; a withholding from the usual quantity of nourishment; voluntary abstinence from food; the time of fasting.

fas·ten, fas′en, fä′sen, v.t. [O.E. faestnian, to secure.] To fix firmly; to make fast; to secure; to fix, as the attention, intently on; to unite closely; to attach; to impute.—v.i. To fix oneself or itself; to become attached.—**fas·ten·er,** n. One who or that which fastens.—**fas·ten·ing,** n. Anything that fastens, binds, or attaches.

fas·tid·i·ous, fa·stid′ē·us, a. [L. fastidiosus, < fastidium, loathing, fastidiousness, < fastus, haughtiness.] Hard to please; squeamish; delicate to a fault; overnice.—**fas·tid·i·ous·ly,** adv.—**fas·tid·i·ous·ness,** n.

fas·tig·i·ate, fa·stij′ē·it, fa·stij′ē·āt″, a. [L. fastigiatus, pointed, < fastigium, a top or peak.] Peaked or pointed at the top; bot. tapering up to a point, as the branches of an evergreen tree. Also **fas·tig·i·at·ed.**—**fas·tig·i·at·ed·ly,** adv.

fas·tig·i·um, fa·stij′ē·um, n. pl. **fas·tig·i·ums, fas·tig·i·a.** Med. the period of highest fever or greatest infection during the course of an illness.

fat, fat, a.—fatter, fattest. [O.E. foet = D. vet, Dan. fed, Icel. feitr, G. fett, fat.] Fleshy; plump; obese; corpulent; oily; greasy. Producing a large income; rich; fertile; nourishing.—v.t.—fatted, fatting. To make fat; to fatten.—v.i. To grow fat.—**fat·head,** n. Slang, a stupid person.—**fat·ling,** n. Any young animal fattened for slaughter, as a lamb, kid, or the like.—**fat·ly,** adv.—**fat·ness,** n.

fat, fat, n. A soft solid organic compound composed of carbon, hydrogen, and oxygen; a solid glycerol ester of higher fatty acids; the tissues of animals, and sometimes plants, that contain principally an oily or greasy substance; corpulence; the best or richest part of a thing.

fa·tal, fāt′al, a. [L. fatalis, < fatum, fate.] Deadly; mortal; destructive; calamitous; disastrous; determining or critically important; as, that fatal moment which led him to leave his country.—**fa·tal·ly,** fāt′a·lē, adv.

fa·tal·ism, fāt′a·liz″um, n. The doctrine that all things are predetermined or subject to fate.—**fa·tal·ist,** n.—**fa·tal·is·tic,** a.—**fa·tal·is·ti·cal·ly,** adv.

fa·tal·i·ty, fā·tal′i·tē, fa·tal′i·tē, n. pl. **fa·tal·i·ties.** [L. fatalitas.] A fixed unalterable course of things; a calamitous accident; a violent death.

fat·back, fat′bak″, n. A strip of fat from the back portion of a side of pork, cured by salting. Any of several fish, as the mullet and bluefish.

fate, fāt, n. [L. fatum, a prophetic declaration, oracle, pp. neut. of fari, speak.] The agency by which events are inevitably predetermined; destiny; that which is ordained to happen; one's appointed lot; death, destruction, or ruin. (Cap.), class. mythol. the goddess of fate; pl. the three goddesses, Clotho, Lachesis, and Atropos.—v.t.—fated, fating. To predetermine, as by the decree of fate; destine.—**fat·ed,** a. Having a particular fate or destiny; subject to, guided by, or predetermined by fate; doomed to destruction.—**fate·ful,** a. Involving momentous consequences; important; prophetic; ominous; fatal, deadly, or disastrous.—**fate·ful·ly,** adv.—**fate·ful·ness,** n.

fa·ther, fä′THėr, n. [O.E. faeder = D. vader, Icel. fathir, Dan. and Sw. fader, Goth. fadar, G. vater, L. pater, Gr. patēr, Pers. padar, Skt. pitri, father; perhaps from a root pa, to feed.] A man who begets a child; a male parent; a male ancestor; esp. the founder of a family or race; one who

---

exercises paternal care over another; a guardian or protector; a respectful means of address to an old man; a priest; (*usu. cap.*) the name of the first person in the Holy Trinity. An originator; as, the *father* of the automobile; a prototype or early form; *Brit.* the eldest member of a society or profession.—**fa·ther·hood,** fä′THẽr·-hụd″, *n.* The state of being a father; the character or authority of a father.—**fa·ther·less,** *a.* Without a living father; without a known father.—**fa·ther·like,** *a., adv.*—**fa·ther·li·ness,** *n.*—**fa·ther·ly,** *a., adv.*

fa·ther, fä′THẽr, *v.t.* To beget as a father; to profess or acknowledge oneself to be the author of; to act as a father toward; to accept responsibility for.

Fa·ther Christ·mas, *n. Brit.* Santa Claus.

fa·ther im·age, *n.* A man embodying the idealized concept of a father; father figure.

fa·ther-in-law, *n. pl.* **fa·thers-in-law.** The father of one's husband or wife.

fa·ther·land, fä′THẽr·land, *n.* [A literal translation of the G. *Vaterland.*] One's native country; the country of one's fathers or ancestors.

Fa·ther's Day, *n.* The third Sunday in June, set aside in the U.S. for honoring fathers.

fath·om, faTH′om, *n. pl.* **fath·oms, fath·-om.** [O.E. *fæthm,* the bosom, the space of both arms extended; Icel. *fathmr,* D. *vadem,* Sw. *famn,* G. *faden,* from a root meaning to stretch.] A measure of length containing six feet, used chiefly for measuring water depths.—*v.t.* To try the depth of; to sound; to penetrate or comprehend.—**fath·om·a·ble,** *a.*—**fath·om·less,** *a.*—**fath·om·less·ly,** *adv.*—**fath·om·less·ness,** *n.*

Fa·thom·e·ter, fa·THOM′i·tẽr, *n.* An instrument for measuring depths under water by means of the principles of sonar. (Trademark.) Also *sonic depth finder.*

fa·tid·ic, fā·tid′ik, fa·tid′ik, *a.* [L. *fatidicus,* < *fatum,* fate, and *dicere,* say.] Prophesying; prophetic. Also **fa·tid·i·cal.**

fa·tigue, fa·tēg′, *n.* [Fr. *fatiguer,* < L. *fatigo,* to weary.] Weariness from bodily labor or mental exertion; lassitude or exhaustion of strength; the cause of weariness; labor undergone; toil; the labors of a non-military type done by military men, as distinct from the use of arms; fatigue duty; *pl.* the rugged and durable clothes worn while on fatigue duty; *metal.* the tendency of a metal or material to weaken or break down under continued stress; *physiol.* a temporary loss or diminution in a bodily organ on account of continued stress.—*v.t.—fatigued, fatiguing.* To weary with labor or any bodily or mental exertion; to harass with toil; to exhaust the strength by severe or long-continued exertion.—*v.i.* To tire or wear out.—**fat·i·ga·ble,** fat′a·ga·bl, *a.*—Easily tired; fatigued.—**fat·i·ga·bil·i·ty,** *n.*

fats·hed·era, fat·sed′e·ra, fats·hed′e·ra, *n. Bot.* an ornamental plant of the aralia family, a hybrid between *Hedera helix* and *Aralia elata,* having lobed glossy leaves shaped like an open palm.

fat-sol·u·ble, fat′sol″ū·bl, fat′sol″ya·bl, *a. Chem.* pertaining to a substance soluble in fat or oil.

fat·ten, fat′en, *v.t.* To make fat; to feed for slaughter; to enrich; to make fertile; to increase in value.—*v.i.* To grow fat; to become plump or fleshy.—**fat·ten·er,** *n.*

fat·ty, fat′ē, *a.—fattier, fattiest.* Having the nature or qualities of fat; oily; greasy; composed of or containing much fat.—**fat·ti·ness,** *n.*—**fat·tish,** *a.*

fat·ty ac·id, *n. Chem.* any one of a group of saturated or unsaturated aliphatic acids such as stearic, palmitic, or oleic acid, that

---

are commonly found in natural fats and oils, and used mainly in soaps, detergents, lubricants, rubber products, and cosmetics.

fa·tu·i·ty, fa·tö′i·tē, fa·tū′i·tē, *n. pl.* **fa·tu·i·ties.** [L. *fatuitas,* < *fatuus,* silly.] A stupid or foolish act or remark; smug stupidity; foolishness.—**fat·u·ous,** fach′-ö·us, fach′ū·us, *a.* [L. *fatuus.*] Idiotically silly; foolish.—**fat·u·ous·ly,** *adv.*—**fat·u·ous·ness,** *n.*

fau·cet, fạ′sit, *n.* [Fr. *fausset,* < L. *falsus,* false.] A device with an adjustable valve which controls the flow of liquid from a pipe or container; tap.

faugh, fạ, *interj.* Exclamation of contempt, abhorrence, or disgust.

fault, fạlt, *n.* [O.Fr. Fr. *faute,* < L. *fallere,* deceive, disappoint, E. *fail.*] A defect or imperfection; a flaw; a failing; an error or mistake; a misdeed or transgression; delinquency; culpability; cause for blame; *geol., min.* a break in the continuity of a body of rock or of a vein, with dislocation along a plane of fracture; *elect.* an accidental defect in an electric circuit, as a new path opened to the current; *tennis,* a failure to serve the ball legitimately within the prescribed area of the court. *Hunting,* a break in the line of scent; a losing of the scent.—*v.t.* To find fault with, blame, or censure; *geol.* to cause a fault in.—*v.i.* To commit a fault; *geol.* to undergo a fault.—**at fault,** open to censure; blamable.—**find fault,** to seek out defects and make them known; to criticize.—**to a fault,** to such an extent as to constitute a fault; excessively.

fault·find·er, fạlt′fïn′dẽr, *n.* One who finds fault; one who complains or objects; a device for locating defects, as in an electric circuit.—**fault·find·ing,** fạlt′fïn′-ding, *n., a.*

fault·less, fạlt′lis, *a.* Without fault or flaw; perfect.—**fault·less·ly,** *adv.*—**fault·less·-ness,** *n.*

fault·y, fạl′tē, *a.—faultier, faultiest.* Containing faults or defects; having, or marked by, imperfections or failings; culpable or blamable; of the nature of a fault. Also **fault·ful.**—**fault·i·ly,** *adv.*—**fault·i·ness,** *n.*

faun, fạn, *n.* [L. *faunus,* a deity of the woods and fields.] *Rom. mythol.* one of a kind of demigods or rural deities, half-human, with pointed ears or horns, sometimes with the feet of a goat, and differing little from satyrs.

fau·na, fạ′na, *n. pl.* **fau·nas, fau·nae,** fạ′nē. [A Roman goddess of fields, cattle, etc.] A collective term for the animals or animal life peculiar to a region, epoch, or environment, corresponding to the word *flora* in respect to plants; a treatise on certain fauna.—**fau·nal,** *a.*—**fau·nal·ly,** *adv.*

fauv·ism, fō′viz·um, *n.* [< Fr. *les fauves,* the wild beasts.] (*Often ·cap.*) a movement chiefly in French art of the early 20th century, characterized by distorted flat patterns and violent colors: a movement more individualistic than collective, including such representative artists as Matisse, Vlaminck, and Rouault.—**fauv·ist,** *n.*

faux pas, fō pä′, *n. pl.* **faux pas,** fō päz′, Fr. fō pä′. [< Fr. lit. *false step.*] Social blunder; a breach of etiquette.

fa·vo·ni·an, fa·vō′nē·an, *a.* [L. *favonius,* the west wind.] Pertaining to the west wind; presenting favorable conditions.

fa·vor, *Brit.* **fa·vour,** fā′vẽr, *n.* [O.Fr. *favor* (Fr. *faveur*), < L. *favor,* < *favere,* be favorable.] Something done or granted out of good will; a kind act; good will or kind regard; as, to win *favor* in the sight of a superior; the state of being approved or held in high regard; as, in *favor* or out of *favor;* something bestowed as a token of good will or kind regard; a gift; partial or

---

biased kindness; leniency.—**in fa·vor of,** in support of; on the side of; to the advantage of.

fa·vor, *Brit.* **fa·vour,** fā′vẽr, *v.t.* [O.Fr. *favorer,* < M.L. *favorare,* < L. *favor.*] To regard with favor; have a liking or preference for; to show favor to; encourage; to deal with gently, spare, or ease; as, to *favor* a lame leg; to treat with partiality; lend support or confirmation to; to resemble, as: The baby *favored* his father.—**fa·vor·ing·ly,** *adv.*

fa·vor·a·ble, *Brit.* **fa·vour·a·ble,** fā′-vẽr·a·bl, *a.* [O.Fr. Fr. *favorable,* < L. *favorabilis,* in favor, winning favor, pleasing.] Advantageous; furnishing aid, advantage, or convenience; as, a *favorable* position; approving or commendatory; winning favor; pleasing.—**fa·vor·a·ble·-ness,** *n.*—**fa·vor·a·bly,** *adv.*

fa·vored, *Brit.* **fa·voured,** fā′vẽrd, *a.* Regarded or treated with favor; enjoying special favors or advantages; having a particular appearance; as, ill-*favored.*—**fa·vored·ly,** *adv.*—**fa·vored·ness,** *n.*

fa·vor·ite, *Brit.* **fa·vour·ite,** fā′vẽr·it, *n.* A person or thing regarded with special favor, preference, or affection; one unduly favored; the competitor most likely to win.—*a.* Regarded with particular affection or preference.—**fa·vor·ite son,** a candidate nominated at a national political convention by his own state's delegates.—**fa·vor·it·-ism,** fā′vẽr·i·tiz″um, *n.* Preferential treatment of one person or group over others having equal claims.

fa·vus, fā′vus, *n. pl.* **fa·vus·es.** [L. a honeycomb.] *Pathol.* a fungus-borne disease, *Trichophyton schonleinii,* attacking the scalp of humans or the skin of fowls and mammals, and characterized by yellowish dry incrustations resembling a honeycomb.

fawn, fạn, *n.* [Fr. *faon,* < a form *fetonus,* < L. *fetus,* progeny.] A young deer; a buck or doe of the first year; a light grayish brown color.—*a.* Of a light grayish brown color.—*v.i.* Of a deer, to bring forth a fawn.

fawn, fạn, *v.i.* [O.E. *fægnian,* Icel. *fagna,* to rejoice, flatter.] To seek favor by servile behavior or flattery; to toady; to show servile fondness, as a dog.

fawn lil·y, *n. Bot.* an herb of the genus *Erythronium,* having single nodding flowers, and leaves with brown or white spots. Also, *dog tooth violet.*

fay, fā, *n.* [Fr. *fée,* L.L. *fata,* a fairy.] A fairy; an elf.—*a.*

faze, fāz, *v.t.—fazed, fazing. Colloq.* To disturb; discomfit; daunt, as: Criticism does not *faze* him.

F clef, *n. Mus.* the clef that places F below middle C on the fourth line of the staff. Also *bass clef.*

fe·al·ty, fē′al·tē, *n. pl.* **fe·al·ties.** [O.Fr. *fealté, feauté,* fealty, < L. *fidelitas,* faithfulness, fidelity.] Faithfulness and loyalty of a feudal tenant or vassal to his lord; hence, faithfulness; fidelity.

fear, fẽr, *n.* [O.E. *faer,* fear, peril; Icel. *far,* harm, mischief; O.H.G. *fára,* danger, fright; Mod.G. *gefahr,* danger; < root of E. *fare,* to travel.] A painful emotion caused by an expectation of evil or of impending danger; anxiety; solicitude; awe and reverence for God; dread.—*v.t.* To feel fear or a painful apprehension of; to be afraid of; to suspect; to have a reverential awe of.—*v.i.* To be afraid.

fear·ful, fẽr′ful, *a.* Afraid; apprehensive; timorous; arising from lack of courage; producing fear. Terrible; dreadful; awful; extreme; as, a *fearful* headache.—**fear·ful·-ly,** *adv.*—**fear·ful·ness,** *n.*

fear·less, fẽr′lis, *a.* Bold; courageous; intrepid; undaunted.—**fear·less·ly,** *adv.*—**fear·less·ness,** *n.*

---

a- fat, fāte, fär, fâre, fạll; **e-** met, mē, mēre, hẽr; **i-** pin, pīne; **o-** not, nōte, möve; **u-** tub, cūbe, bụll; **oi-** oil; **ou-** pound.

fear·some, fēr′sum, *a.* Alarming; frightening.—**fear·some·ly,** *adv.*—**fear·some·ness,** *n.*

fea·sance, fē′zans, *n.* [A.Fr. *fesance,* O.Fr. Fr. *faisance,* < *faire,* do.] *Law,* performance, as of a condition, obligation, or duty.

fea·si·ble, fē′zi·bl, *a.* [Fr. *faisible,* < *faire, faisant,* to do or make, L. *facere,* to do, to make.] Capable of being accomplished; practicable; likely.—**fea·si·bil·i·ty, fea·si·ble·ness,** fē″ze·bil′i·tē, fē′zi·bl·nis, *n.*—**fea·si·bly,** *adv.*

feast, fēst, *n.* [O.Fr. *feste,* Fr. *fête,* < L. *festum,* a holiday, a feast, < *festus,* solemn, festive.] A sumptuous dinner or entertainment for a number of guests; a banquet; a delicious meal; *fig.* something particularly gratifying to the senses or the mind. A religious festival in commemoration of some great event, or in honor of some distinguished being.—*v.i.* To eat a meal of rich or sumptuous foods; to view with delight.—*v.t.* To entertain with a banquet; to gratify luxuriously.—**feast·er,** *n.*

feat, fēt, *n.* [Fr. *fait,* < L. *factum,* a deed, < *facio, factum,* to do.] An act, exploit, or accomplishment, esp. one marked by extraordinary strength, skill, or courage.

feath·er, feTH′ėr, *n.* [O.E. *fether* = D. *veder* = G. *feder* = Icel. *fjodhr,* feather; akin to L. *penna,* feather, Gr. *pteron,* Skt. *pattra,* feather, wing.] One of the epidermal structures covering the body of a bird and consisting of a hard, tubelike quill attached to the body and tapering into a thin stemlike portion, bearing a series of slender barbs which unite to form a flat structure on each side of the quill; condition, as of health or spirits; kindred; as, birds of a *feather;* something resembling a feather, as a tuft or fringe of hair; *rowing,* the act of feathering an oar.—**a feath·er in one's cap,** a mark of distinction; an honor. —**feath·ered,** *a.* Clothed, covered, or provided with or as with feathers; winged; swift.—**feath·er·less,** *a.* Without feathers. —**feath·er·y,** *a.* Consisting of feathers; resembling a feather or feathers, as in appearance or lightness; flimsy or unsubstantial; covered with feathers.

feath·er, feTH′ėr, *v.t.* To clothe or cover with or as with feathers; provide with feathers; *aeron.* to turn, as a propeller's blades, in the direction of flight in order to reduce propeller rotation; *rowing,* to turn, as an oar, to a nearly horizontal position as it returns for the next stroke.—*v.i.* To grow feathers; to be feathery in appearance; move like feathers; to feather an oar or airplane propeller.—**feath·er one's nest,** *slang.* To obtain money for oneself, either ethically or unethically; to make provisions for oneself, regardless of others' welfare.

feath·er bed·ding, feTH′ėr·bed″ing, *n. Slang,* an employment practice whereby employers are required to hire unnecessary workers to meet union standards which arbitrarily limit the activity or production of each worker.—**feath·er·bed,** feTH′ėr·bed, *v.i., v.t.*—**featherbedded, featherbedding.**—*a.*

feath·er·brain, feTH′ėr·brān″, *n.* A foolish person. Also **feath·er·head.**—**feath·er·brained,** *a.*

feath·er·edge, feTH′ėr·ej″, *n.* An edge as thin as a feather; the thinner edge of a wedge-shaped board; a tool used in plastering to give a smooth finish at corners and edges; in silver work, a pattern of fine oblique lines along the edge.—**feath·er·edged,** *a.*

feath·er·stitch, feTH′ėr·stich″, *n.* An embroidery stitch producing work in which a succession of small filaments or branches extend alternately on each side of a central stem.—*v.t.* To ornament by featherstitch.

feath·er·weight, feTH′ėr·wāt″, *n.* A boxer weighing between 118 and 126 pounds; a wrestler weighing between 123 and 134 pounds; the lightest weight that may be carried by a horse in a handicap; a frivolous or insignificant person or thing.—*a.* Of or pertaining to a featherweight; insignificant.

fea·ture, fē′chėr, *n.* [O.Fr. *faiture,* < L. *factura,* making, formation, < *facere,* do, make.] Any part of the face; a characteristic part of anything; something offered as a special attraction; a principal movie on a program; a special magazine or newspaper article; *pl.* the face or countenance.—*v.t. featured, featuring.* To resemble in features; depict; outline; to make a feature of, or give prominence to.—**fea·tured,** *a.* Given prominence to.—**fea·ture·less,** *a.* Uninteresting.

feb·ri·fuge, feb′ri·fūj″, *a.* Serving to dispel or reduce fever. Also **feb·ri·fug·al,** fi·brif′yu·gal, feb″ri·fū′gal.—*n.* A febrifuge medicine or agent; a cooling drink.

fe·brile, fē′bril, feb′ril, *Brit.* fē′brīl, *a.* [L. *febrilis.*] Feverish.

Feb·ru·ar·y, feb′rö·er″ē, feb′ū·er″ē, *n. pl.* **Feb·ru·ar·ies.** [L. *februarius,* < *februa,* purification, because the Roman feast of purification was held on the 15th.] The second month in the year, consisting ordinarily of 28 days, but of 29 in leap years.

fe·ces, fae·ces, fē′sēz, *n. pl.* [L. *fæces,* pl. of *fæx,* dregs.] Excrement. Dregs; sediment.— **fe·cal, fae·cal,** fē′kal, *a.*

feck·less, fek′lis, *a.* [Sc. for *effectless.*] Weak; impotent; listless; indolent. Irresponsible.

fe·cund, fē′kund, fē′kund, fek′und, fek′und, *a.* [L. *fecundus,* fruitful.] Fruitful; prolific; abundantly productive in children or vegetation; marked by especial productivity or inventiveness in intellectual matters.— **fe·cun·di·ty,** fi·kun′di·tē, *n.*

fe·cun·date, fē′kun·dāt″, fek′un·dāt″, *v.t.* —*fecundated, fecundating.* To make fruitful or prolific; *biol.* to impregnate.—**fe·cun·da·tion,** *n.*

fed·er·al, fed′ėr·al, *a.* [Fr. *federal,* < L. *fœdus* (*fœder*-), compact, league, akin to *fides,* faith.] Of or pertaining to a formal agreement among nations or states which acknowledge central jurisdiction over common affairs; pertaining to a union of states under a central government distinct from the governments of the individual states; as, the *federal* government of the U.S.; favoring a strong central government in such a union. (*Cap.*), *U.S. Hist.* pertaining to the Federalist party; relating to or sympathetic with the Federal government or the Union armies during the Civil War. —*n.* An advocate of federation or federalism; (*cap.*), *U.S. Hist.* in the Civil War, an adherent of the Union government; a soldier in the Federal army.—**fed·er·al·ism,** *n.* The federal principle of government; the principles of the Federalist party.—**fed·er·al·ist,** *n.* An advocate of federalism; (*cap.*), *U.S. Hist.* a member or supporter of the Federalist party.—*a.*— **fed·er·al·ize,** fed′ėr·a·līz″, *v.t.*—*federalized, federalizing.* To unite in a federal union; bring under the control of a federal union or government.—**fed·er·al·i·za·tion,** *n.*—**fed·er·al·ly,** *adv.*

Fed·er·al Re·serve Bank, *n.* See *Federal Reserve System.*

Fed·er·al Re·serve Board, *n.* See *Federal Reserve System.*

Fed·er·al Re·serve Dis·trict, *n.* See *Federal Reserve System.*

Fed·er·al Re·serve Sys·tem, *n.* A federal banking system, controlled by a central board of governors, the *Federal Reserve Board,* and established to facilitate the flow of money, regulate credit, and concentrate the national banking resources in a system of 12 *Federal Reserve Banks,* each serving as a source of discount and reserve and as a supervisory agent for the affiliated banks in its *Federal Reserve District.*

Fed·er·al Trade Com·mis·sion, *n.* A five-member board appointed by the President of the U.S. to prevent illegal acts leading to unfair competition in interstate trade. Abbr. *FTC, F.T.C.*

fed·er·ate, fed′e·rāt″, *v.t., v.i.*—*federated, federating.* [L. *fœderatus,* pp. of *fœderare,* < *fœdus,* compact, league.] To unite in a league or federation; to organize on a federal basis.—**fed′ėr·it,** *a.* Federated; allied.—**fed·er·a·tion,** fed″e·rā′shan, *n.* The act of federating or uniting in a league; the formation of a political unity, with a central government, out of a number of separate states, each of which retains control of its own internal affairs; a league or confederacy; a federated body formed by a number of states or societies.— **fed·er·a·tive,** *a.* Pertaining to or of the nature of a federation; inclined to federate. —**fed·er·a·tive·ly,** *adv.*

fe·do·ra, fi·dōr′a, fi·dar′a, *n.* [Said to take its name from *Fédora,* drama by V. Sardou.] A man's felt hat with a curled brim, worn with the crown creased lengthwise.

fed up, *a. Slang.* Having had more than enough of something; surfeited; annoyed; weary.

fee, fē, *n.* [A.Fr. *fee,* O.Fr. *fé* (Fr. *fief*), = M.L. *feudum, feodum;* appar. < Teut.] A remuneration for professional service, as of a physician; a charge fixed by law for the services of a public officer or for licenses, registrations, permits; a sum paid for a privilege; as, an admission *fee;* a gratuity or tip; *feud.* land owned by a feudal lord and granted to a tenant or vassal in exchange for personal services; *law,* currently, an estate of inheritance in land.—**fee sim·ple,** *pl.* **fees sim·ple.** A fee without limitation to any particular class of heirs.—**fee tail,** *pl.* **fees tail.** A fee limited to a particular class of heirs.—**in fee,** in undisputed possession or ownership.

fee, fē, *v.t.*—*feed, feeing.* To give a fee to; tip.

fee·ble, fē′bl, *a.*—*feebler, feeblest.* [O.Fr. *feble, feible* (Fr. *faible*), < L. *flebilis,* lamentable, < *flere,* weep.] Physically weak; weak intellectually or morally; lacking in force or effectiveness; lacking in volume, brightness, or distinctness.— **fee·ble·mind·ed,** fē′bl·mīn′did, *a.* Deficient in mentality.—**fee·ble·mind·ed·ness,** *n.*—**fee·ble·ness,** *n.*—**fee·bly,** *adv.*— **fee·blish,** *a.*

feed, fēd, *v.t.*—*fed, feeding.* [O.E. *fēdan,* < *fōda,* E. *food.*] To give food to; supply with nourishment; to yield or serve as food for; to furnish for consumption; to minister to or gratify; to provide with the requisite materials for maintenance or operation, as a machine; *theatr.* to furnish with lines or cues, as an entertainer.—*v.i.* To take food or eat, esp. used of livestock; to be nourished or gratified as if by food; to pass successively into a machine for the purpose of being processed or utilized.—*n.* Food, esp. for domestic animals; provender; fodder; an allowance of such food; the act of feeding; *colloq.* a meal, esp. an elaborate one; the act or process of feeding a furnace or other machine. The material, or the amount of it, so fed or supplied; a feeding mechanism.—**feed·er,** *n.* One who or that which supplies food or feeds something; something that ministers to the maintenance of something else, as a tributary stream or branch railroad; a person or device that feeds a machine; one who or that which takes food or nourishment; a livestock animal which is fattened for marketing.—**feed·stuff,** fēd′stuf″, *n.* A nutritive substance used as food for livestock.

feed·back, fēd′bak″, *n.* The return of a portion of the output of any energy-converting device or system to the input of the same system; *electron.* a system by which some of the energy from the output of a communications circuit is returned to the input circuit, either to increase or reduce the power or to regulate the quality of the signal; *psychol.* in an organism, a sensory or perceptual report of the result of any behavior which may reinforce or modify subsequent behavior; *computer,* the return of a portion of the output data to the input of the system for the purpose of self-correction or control.

feel, fēl, *v.t.*—*felt, feeling.* [O.E. *fēlan,* D. *voelen,* G. *fühlen,* to feel.] To perceive by the touch; to have sensation excited by contact with the body or limbs; to have a sense of; to be affected by; to be conscious, as of pain, pleasure, or disgrace; to experience; to suffer; to examine by touching; to be convinced of, or believe in; to think.—*v.i.* To have perception by touch, or by contact with the body; to have the sensibility or the passions moved or excited; to produce an impression on the nerves of sensation, as: Iron *feels* cold. To perceive oneself to be; as, to *feel* well; to know certainly or without misgiving; to have pity or compassion; as: I *feel* for the slum-dwellers.—*n.* The act of feeling; intuitive knowledge; sensation or impression on being touched; sense of touch; sensation of feeling something.—**feel·er,** fē′lèr, *n.* One who feels; an organ of touch in insects and others of the lower animals, as antennae or palpi; any device for the purpose of ascertaining the designs, opinions, or sentiments of others.

feel·ing, fē′ling, *a.* Possessing great sensibility; expressive of great sensibility; easily affected or moved; as, a *feeling* heart.—*n.* The sense of touch by which we perceive external objects which come in contact with the body; the sensation conveyed by the sense of touch; the act or power of feeling; physical sensation other than that due to sight, hearing, taste, or smell; as, a *feeling* of warmth, pain, or drowsiness; mental sensation or emotion; mental state or disposition; consciousness; impression; opinion; conviction; tenderness of heart; fine sensibility; *art,* the quality of exciting or expressing emotion; *pl.* sensitiveness; collective susceptibilities.—**feel·ing·ly,** *adv.*—**feel·ing·ness,** *n.*

feign, fān, *v.t.* [O.Fr. Fr. *feindre* (ppr. *feignant*), < L. *fingere,* pp. *fictus* (stem *fig-*), touch, form, mold, conceive, devise, feign; akin to Gr. *thigganein,* touch, Skt. *dih-,* stroke, smear, and E. *dough.*] To put on an appearance of or pretend; as, to *feign* sickness; to simulate; to sham; to invent fictitiously or deceptively, as a story or an excuse; to fable; to imitate deceptively, or counterfeit; as, to *feign* another's voice.—*v.i.* To make believe; pretend.—**feigned,** *a.*—**feign·ed·ly,** fā′nid·lē, *adv.*—**feign·ing·ly,** *adv.*—**feign·er,** *n.*

feint, fānt, *n.* [Fr. *feinte,* < *feindre,* E. *feign.*] A movement made with the object of deceiving; a pretense; a mock attack made on an adversary aimed at diverting his attention from the real point of attack; a feigned or assumed appearance.—*v.i.* To make a feint.

feist, fīst, *n. Dial.* A small dog; a cur. Also **fice, fist.**

feist·y, fī′stē, *a.*—*feistier, feistiest.* Excited; agitated; petulant; quarrelsome.

feld·spar, feld′spär″, or fel′spär″, *n.* [G. *feldspath,* 'field spar.'] Any of a group of crystalline minerals, all silicates of aluminum with potassium, sodium, calcium, or barium. Also **feld·spath.—feld·spath·ic, feld·spath·ose,** *a.* Of, pertaining to, or

containing feldspar.—**feld·spath·oid,** feld′-spa·thoid″, fel′spa·thoid″, *n.* Any of a group of minerals related to the feldspars.

fe·lic·i·tate, fi·lis′i·tāt″, *v.t.*—*felicitated, felicitating.* [Fr. *féliciter;* L.L. *felicito,* L. *felix, felicis,* happy.] To congratulate; to express joy or pleasure to another at his good fortune.—**fe·lic·i·ta·tion,** fi·lis″i-tā′shan, *n.* An expression of congratulation.—**fe·lic·i·ta·tor,** *n.*

fe·lic·i·tous, fi·lis′i·tus, *a.* Extremely appropriate, suitable, or well expressed; of a person, having a special ability for apt expression.—**fe·lic·i·tous·ly,** *adv.*—**fe·lic·i·tous·ness,** *n.*

fe·lic·i·ty, fi·lis′i·tē, *n. pl.* **fe·lic·i·ties.** [L. *felicitas,* < *felix,* happy.] The state of being happy; extreme enjoyment; source of happiness; skillfulness.—**fe·li·cif·ic,** fē″li·sif′ik, *a.* Promoting happiness.

fe·lid, fē′lid, *n.* A cat of the family *Felidae.*—*a.*

fe·line, fē′lin, *a.* [L. *felinus,* < *felis,* a cat.] Belonging to the cat family; like a cat; stealthy.—*n.*—**fe·line·ly,** *adv.*—**fe·lin·i·ty,** fi·lin′i·tē, *n.*

fell, fel, *v.t.* [O.E. *fellan,* < *feallan,* to fall; causative form of *fall.*] To cause to fall; to bring to the ground, either by cutting or by striking; to hew down; to knock down; *sewing,* to finish a seam by folding one raw edge over the other and then stitching along the folded edge.—**fell·a·ble,** *a.*—**fell·er,** fel′er, *n.* One who hews or knocks down; a sewing machine attachment for felling a seam.

fell, fel, *n.* [O.E. *fell* = Icel. < *fell,* G. *fell,* D. *vel,* Goth. *fill,* skin. Cogn. L. *pellis,* skin.] A skin or hide of an animal; fleece; a membrane beneath the skin; a seam sewed down level with the cloth; *Brit.* a moor or upland pasture.—**fell·mon·ger,** fel′mung″gèr, fel′mong″gèr, *n.* One who deals in or works on fells or hides.

fell, fel, *a.* [O.E. *fell,* D. *fel,* O.Fr. *fel, felle,* sharp, fierce, cruel, a word perhaps of Celtic origin.] Cruel; barbarous; inhuman; fierce; deadly.—**fell·ness,** *n.* Cruelty; ruthlessness.—**fell·ly,** fel′lē, *adv.*

fel·lah, fel′a, *n. pl.* **fel·lahs,** Ar. **fel·la·hin, fel·la·heen,** fel″a·hēn. [Ar.] A peasant or laborer in Egypt, Syria, and other Arabic-speaking countries.

fel·la·ti·o, fe·lā′shē·ō″, fe·lā′shē·ō″, *n.* Stimulation of the penis by oral means. Also **fel·la·tion,** fe·lā′shan, fe·lā′shan.

fel·low, fel′ō, *n.* [Icel. *fēlagi,* a partner, a sharer in goods, < *fēlag,* a community of goods (lit. a *fee-laying*), < *fē,* money, and *lag,* partnership, a laying.] A man or boy; companion; associate; an equal in rank, character or qualification; a peer; one of a pair, or of two things used together and suited to each other; a graduate student given a grant for further study; a person belonging to one of several learned societies.—*a.*

fel·low-man, fel′ō·man′, *n. pl.* **fel·low-men.** Another human being; a comrade. Also **fel·low·man.**

fel·low serv·ant, *n.* A person employed along with another or several others by a common employer.—**fel·low serv·ant rule,** *law,* the ruling that relieves an employer from any liability for injury to an employee caused by the carelessness or negligence of a fellow employee.

fel·low·ship, fel′ō·ship″, *n.* The condition or relation of being a fellow; community of interest; companionship; mutual intercourse; communion; friendliness; a body of fellows; a company; a guild or corporation; the position or emoluments of a fellow of a university; a foundation for the maintenance of such a fellow.

fel·low trav·el·er, *n.* A sympathizer of a group, organization, or party, but not a

participant by membership, usu. used to describe one who associates himself with the programs of the Communist party.—**fel·low-trav·el·ing,** *a*

fel·ly, fel′ē, *n. pl.* **fel·lies.** [O.E. *felg, felge* = Dan. *fælge,* D. *velg,* G. *felge,* a felly.] One of the curved pieces of wood which, joined together, form the circular rim of a wheel; the circular rim of a wheel. Also **fel·loe,** fel′ō.

fel·on, fel′on, *n.* [Fr. *félon,* a traitor, < L.L. *felo,* a felon.] A person who has committed a felony.—*a. Archaic,* traitorous; disloyal.—**fel·on·ry,** fel′on·rē, *n.* Felons collectively; the criminal inhabitants of a penal colony.

fel·on, fel′on, *n.* [M.E. *feloun,* appar. < M.L. *fello(n-),* an inflammatory swelling, perhaps < L. *fel,* gall, poison.] *Pathol.* an acute and painful inflammation of the deeper tissues of a finger or toe, usu. near the nail.

fel·o·ny, fel′o·nē, *n. pl.* **fel·o·nies.** [O.Fr. *felonie* (Fr. *félonie*).] *Law,* any crime of a more serious nature than a misdemeanor which, esp. in the U.S., is punishable by imprisonment for more than one year. *Early Eng. law,* any crime which occasioned the forfeiture of lands or goods.—**fe·lo·ni·ous,** fe·lō′nē·us, *a.* Of, involving, or pertaining to a felony. *Archaic,* villainous; traitorous.—**fe·lo·ni·ous·ly,** *adv.*—**fe·lo·ni·ous·ness,** *n.*

fel·site, fel′sīt, *n.* [< *fels(par)*.] A dense igneous rock or rock constituent consisting of minute crystals of feldspar and quartz.—**fel·sit·ic,** fel·sit′ik, *a.*

felt, felt, *n.* [O.E. *felt* = D. *vilt,* G. *filz,* felt; allied to Gr. *pilos,* wool wrought into felt, and to L. *pileus,* a felt hat or cap.] An unwoven cloth that is made by matting wool, hair, or fur into a compact substance by pressure, moisture, or heat; an article made of such material; anything resembling felt, as a mat made of asbestos fibers and used in building and insulating.—*v.t.* To make into felt; to cover with felt.—*v.i.* To become matted, as felt.—**felt·ing,** fel′ting, *n.* The process by which felt is made; the materials of which felt is made, or the felt itself.

fe·luc·ca, fe·luk′a, *n.* [It. *felucca, feluca,* < Ar. *felûkah,* < *fulk,* a ship.] A long, narrow vessel, once common in the Mediterranean, having lateen sails, and capable of being propelled by oars.

fe·male, fē′māl, *n.* [Fr. *femelle,* L. *femella,* a young girl, < *femina,* a woman.] An animal of the sex which conceives and gives birth to young; a girl or woman; *bot.* that portion of a flower called the pistil which receives the pollen or male element.

fe·male, fē′māl, *a.* Belonging to the sex which gives birth to young or produces eggs; pertaining to or characteristic of this sex; feminine. *Bot.* pertaining to any reproductive structure containing the egg which requires fertilization; pistillate. *Mech.* designating a part into which a corresponding part fits.

fem·i·ne·i·ty, fem″i·nē′i·tē, *n.* [L. *femineus,* feminine, < *femina,* woman.] Feminine nature; womanliness.

fem·i·nine, fem′i·nin, *a.* Pertaining to a woman or to the female sex; having the qualities commonly attributed to a woman; gentle; womanly; lacking in manly characteristics; effeminate; *gram.* denoting the gender of words which signify females, or the termination of such words; *pros.* denoting a rhyme of two or three syllables, the first of which is accented.—*n. Gram.* in declension, the feminine gender or a word of the feminine gender.—**fem·i·nin·i·ty,** fem″i·nin′i·tē, *n.* Quality of being feminine; womanly characteristics; effeminacy; women collectively. Also **fe·min·i·ty.**—**fem·i·nine·ly,** *adv.*—**fem·i·nine·ness,** *n.*

fem·i·nism, fem'i·niz"um, n. [L. *femina,* woman.] The doctrine advocating that social and political rights of women be equal to those possessed by men; (*sometimes cap.*) a movement to acquire such rights; *med.* in a male, the presence of feminine characteristics.—**fem·i·nist,** n.—**fem·i·nis·tic,** a.

fem·i·nize, fem'i·niz", v.t.—*feminized, feminizing.* [L. *femina,* woman.] To make feminine or womanish.—v.i. To acquire a feminine or effeminate character.—**fem·i·ni·za·tion,** fem'i·ni·zā'shan, n.

femme fa·tale, fem" fa·tal', fem" fa·täl', *Fr.* fäm fä·täl'; n. pl. **femmes fa·tales,** fem" fa·talz', fem"fa·tälz', *Fr.* fäm fä·täl'. [Fr. lit. 'fatal woman'.] A seductive or irresistible woman, esp. one who entices men into dangerous situations.

fe·mur, fē'mẽr, n. pl. **fe·murs, fem·o·ra,** fem'ẽr·a. [L. thigh.] *Anat.* a bone in the leg, extending from the hip to the knee; the thighbone. *Entom.* the third segment of an insect's leg, beginning at the base.—**fem·o·ral,** fem'ẽr·al, a.

fen, fen, n. [O.E. *fenn* = D. *veen* = G. *fenn* = Icel. *fen,* fen, = Goth. *fani,* mud.] Low land covered wholly or partially with water; boggy land; a marsh.—**fen·ny,** fen'ē, a.

fen, fen, n. Yuan. See Money table.

fence, fens, n. [Abbr. < *defence.*] A barrier forming a boundary to or enclosing some area, usu. constructed of railings, posts, boards, or wire; the art of fencing; a skill in argument and repartee. *Slang,* a purchase or receiver of stolen goods; a place dealing in stolen merchandise—**on the fence,** *colloq.* in a neutral or uncommitted position.—**fence·less,** a.—**fence·less·ness,** n.

fence, fens, v.t.—*fenced, fencing.* To enclose with a fence; to secure by an enclosure; to guard.—v.i. To practice fencing; to parry arguments; to equivocate.—**fenc·er,** n.

fencing, fen'sing, n. The art or sport of using a sword or foil in attack or defense; material used in making fences; that which encloses an area; fences.

fend, fend, v.t. [For *defend.*] To ward off or avert, usu. followed by *off*; as, to *fend off* blows.—v.i. To make defense; to offer resistance; to parry. *Colloq.* to manage without assistance; to provide, as a livelihood, used with *for.*

fen·der, fen'dẽr, n. One who or that which fends; that part of a vehicle covering each wheel, designed to prevent splashing; a projection at the front of a locomotive or street car for pushing aside obstructions; a metal screen or guard before a fireplace that holds back falling coals; *naut.* a cushion of rope, timber, or the like on a vessel which reduces shock and prevents chafing under impact.

fe·nes·tra, fi·nes'tra, n. pl. **fe·nes·trae,** fi·nes'trē. [L. *fenestra,* a window.] *Anat.* a natural perforation, esp. one in the bone between the tympanum and the inner ear; *entom.* a small transparent spot sometimes found in wings of butterflies and other insects; *arch.* a window or opening suggestive of a window.—**fe·nes·tral,** a.—**fe·nes·trate, fe·nes·trat·ed,** fi·nes'trāt, fi·nes'trā·tid, a. Having windows, openings or transparent areas.

fen·es·tra·tion, fen"i·strā'shan, n. *Arch.* the design and placement of the windows and other exterior openings in a building; *surg.* an operation to form an opening in the bone between the middle and inner ear.

Fe·ni·an, fē'nē·an, fēn'yan, n. [Ir. *Fiann, Fēinne,* legendary band of Irish warriors.] A member of an Irish revolutionary organization, founded in New York in 1858, dedicated to liberating Ireland from British rule.—a.—**Fe·ni·an·ism,** n.

fen·nel, fen'el, n. [O.E. *fenol, finol,* < L. *faeniculum,* fennel, dim. of *faenum,* hay.] An herb, *Foeniculum vulgare,* of the parsley family, having yellow flowers, and bearing aromatic seeds which are used in cooking and medicine; the seeds of this plant; any of various similar plants, as *Ferula communis,* 'giant fennel,' a tall, ornamental herb native of Mediterranean regions.

fen·nel·flow·er, fen'el·flou'ẽr, n. Any of the annual herbs of the genus *Nigella,*whose seeds are used in the East as a condiment and medicine.

fen·u·greek, fen'yu·grēk", fen'ū·grēk", n. [O.E. *fenogrecum,* < L. *fenum Graecum,* 'Greek hay.'] An herb, *Trigonella foenum-graecum,* indigenous to western Asia but extensively cultivated elsewhere for its mucilaginous seeds, which are used for food, seasoning, and in veterinary medicine.

fe·rae na·tu·rae, fē'rē na·tūr'ē, fē'rē na·tūr'ē, a. [L.] *Law,* of animals, wild or untamed: opposed to *domitae naturae.*

fe·ral, fēr'al, fer'al, a. [L. *fera,* wild beast, prop. fem. of *ferus,* wild.] Wild, or existing in a state of nature, as animals or sometimes plants; having reverted to the wild state, as from domestication; pertaining to or characteristic of wild animals; savage; brutal. Also **fe·rine,** fēr'in, fēr'in.—**fer·i·ty,** fer'i·tē, n. [L. *feritas,* < *ferus,* wild.] Wild, untamed, or uncultivated state; savagery; ferocity.

fe·ral, fēr'al, fer'al, a. [L. *feralis,* pertaining to the dead, < *ferre,* bear (with reference to funeral processions).] Pertaining to the dead; funereal; deadly; fatal.

fer-de-lance, fer"de·lans', fer"de·läns', n. [Fr. lit. 'iron (head) of lance.'] A large venomous snake of tropical America.

fer·e·to·ry, fer'i·tōr"ē, fer'i·tar"ē, n. pl. **fer·e·to·ries.** [M.E. *feretre,* < O.Fr. *fiertre,* < L. *feretrum,* < Gr. *pheretron,* < *pherein,* bear.] A shrine, usually portable, designed to hold the relics of saints; a reliquary.

fe·ri·a, fēr'ē·a, n. pl. **fe·ri·ae, fe·ri·as,** fēr'ē·ē". A holiday; *eccles.* any holiday not set forth by the church as a feast day.—**fe·ri·al,** a.

fer·ma·ta, fer·mä'ta, *It.* feR·mä'tä, n. pl. **fer·ma·tas,** *It.* **fer·ma·te,** feR·mä'te. [It.] *Mus.* the holding of a rest, chord, or note beyond the indicated time, at the performer's discretion. Sym. ⌢.

fer·ment, fẽr·ment', v.t. [L. *fermentare* (pp. *fermentatus*), < *fermentum.*] To act upon as a ferment; cause to undergo a change similar to that by which grape sugar is converted into ethyl alcohol in the presence of yeast. *Fig.* to agitate; excite; inflame; foment.—v.i. To be fermented; undergo fermentation; *fig.* seethe with agitation or excitement.—**fer·ment·a·ble,** a.

fer·ment, fẽr'ment, n. [L. *fermentum,* < *fervere,* boil.] Any of various agents or substances, as yeast, enzymes, or certain bacteria, capable of producing chemical changes, as effervescence or decomposition, in other substances. *Fig.* agitation; excitement; tumult.

fer·men·ta·tion, fẽr"men·tā'shan, n. The act or process of fermenting; a change brought about by a ferment; *fig.* agitation or excitement.—**fer·men·ta·tive,** fẽr'men'ta·tiv, a. Tending to produce or undergo fermentation; pertaining to fermentation.

fer·mi·on, fẽr'mē·on", n. [Named after Enrico *Fermi,* a 20th century physicist.] *Phys.* In quantum statistics, atomic and sub-atomic particles classified according to their energy levels; particles classified according to Fermi-Dirac statistics in which no more than one of a group of identical particles may occupy the same energy level.

fer·mi·um, fẽr'mē·um, n. [After Enrico *Fermi,* 20th century physicist.] A radioactive element produced by nuclear bombardment and other nuclear reactions.

Sym. Fm, at no. 100. See Periodic Table of Elements.

fern, fẽrn, n. [O.E. *fearn* = G. *farn, farren,* D. *varen,* fern; allied to Skt. *parna,* a wing or feather.] *Bot.* a seedless, flowerless plant of the class *Filicinae,* having large leaves, called fronds, which are usually compound and which bear, on their under surface or edge, sporangia containing minute spores.—**fern·er·y,** fẽr'ne·rē, n. pl. **fern·er·ies.** A place where ferns are artificially grown; a bed, garden, or display of ferns.—**fern·y,** a.—*fernier, ferniest.*

fe·ro·cious, fe·rō'shus, a. [Fr. *féroce*; L. *ferox, ferocis,* fierce, allied to *ferus,* wild.] Fierce; savage; cruel; brutal; *colloq.* intense or very great.—**fe·ro·cious·ly,** adv.—**fe·ro·cious·ness,** n.—**fe·ro·ci·ty,** fe·ros'i·tē, n.

fer·ret, fer'it, n. [Fr. *furet,* It. *furetto,* a ferret, < L. *fur,* a thief.] A domesticated, European polecat of the genus *Putorius,* bred to hunt rabbits and kill rats; *U.S.* the polecat or black-footed ferret, *Putorius nigripes*; any diligent searcher, as a detective or investigator.—v.t. To hunt, as rabbits, with ferrets; to drive out of a lurking place; to search out; as, to *ferret* out the facts.—**fer·ret·er,** n.

fer·ret, fer'it, n. [Older *foret,* < It. *fioretti,* floss silk, < L. *flos, floris,* flower.] A narrow tape of cotton, silk, or other fiber. Also **fer·ret·ing.**

fer·ri·age, fer'ē·ij, n. The act of conveying by ferry; the price charged for ferrying.

fer·ric, fer'ik, a. [L. *ferrum,* iron.] *Chem.* of or containing iron, esp. iron with a valance of three.—**fer·ric ox·ide,** *chem.* a dark-red iron oxide, Fe_2O_3, appearing in nature as hematite and rust, or derived through synthesis, and used mainly as a pigment and for polishing metals.

fer·rif·er·ous, fe·rif'ẽr·us, a. [L. *ferrum,* and *fero,* to produce.] Producing or yielding iron.

Fer·ris wheel, fer'is wēl, n. [From G.W.G. *Ferris,* the inventor.] An amusement ride consisting of a large upright wheel rotating about a fixed axis, and having passenger cars suspended around its rim.

fer·rite, fer'it, n. *Metal.* the pure metallic content of steel and iron; the main constituent of steel. *Chem.* any one of several types of multiple oxides containing ferric oxide and another oxide, each of which has different magnetic properties: used in rectifiers, semiconductors, dielectrics, computer memory tapes, and other electronic devices.

fer·ro·al·loy, fer"ō·al'oi, fer"a·loi", n. Any of several alloys of iron used with other material in the production of steel.

fer·ro·con·crete, fer"ō·kon'krēt, fer"ō·kon·krēt', n. A building material consisting of concrete in which steel rods are embedded; reinforced concrete.

fer·ro·e·lec·tric, fer"ō·i·lek'trik, n. *Phys., electron., chem.* a crystal, such as Rochelle salt, analogous to a ferromagnetic material, that spontaneously develops electric polarization and is capable of reversal of polarization, which makes it useful for detecting vibrations.—a. Pertaining to this crystal.

fer·ro·mag·net·ic, fer"ō·mag·net'ik, a. *Phys.* of or pertaining to a magnetic material, esp. a strong permanent magnet.

fer·ro·type, fer'o·tip", n. *Photog.* a print given a glossy surface by being pressed on a smooth metal plate when wet.—v.t.—*ferrotyped, ferrotyping.* To make(such a print)

fer·rous, fer'us, a. [L. *ferrum,* iron.] Pertaining to, obtained from, or containing iron, esp. bivalent iron.

fer·rous ox·ide, n. The monoxide of iron, FeO, which is soluble in acid but not in water. Also **i·ron mon·ox·ide.**

fer·rous sul·fate, *n. Chem., pharm.* a salt, FeSo₄·7H₂O, in the form of green crystals, which is a by-product of the pickling of steel, used in treating industrial waste and in medicine. Also **cop·per·as, green cop·-per·as, green vit·ri·ol.**

fer·ru·gi·nous, fe·rŏ̄'ji·nus, *a.* [L. *ferrugineus,* rusty, < *ferrugo, ferruginis,* iron rust, < *ferrum,* iron.] Containing iron; colored like iron rust.

fer·rule, fer'ul, fer'ŏl, *n.* [Fr. *virole,* < M.L. *virola,* < *viriæ,* bracelets.] A metal ring or cap put around the end of a post or tool handle, for strength or protection; a short tube put over a pipe joint for a tight fitting. —*v.t.*—*ferruled, ferruling.* To furnish with a ferrule.

fer·ry, fer'ē, *v.t.*—*ferried, ferrying.* [O.E. *ferian,* akin to *faren,* E. *fare.*] To carry, as passengers, vehicles, or goods, across a river or other narrow body of water by boat; to deliver, as an airplane, boat, or other craft, under its own power.—*v.i.* To travel by ferry.—*n.* pl. **fer·ries.** A place where ferry service is provided; the legal right to operate a ferry or ferry line and to charge a toll; a ferryboat.—**fer·ry·boat,** *n.* —**fer·ry·man,** *n.*

fer·tile, fur'til, *Brit.* fur'tīl, *a.* [Fr. *fertile,* < L. *fertilis,* < *fero,* to bear, to produce; same root as E. *bear.*] Producing or able to produce crops in abundance; able to produce offspring; prolific; productive, creative, or inventive; as, a *fertile* imagination. *Biol.* fertilized; capable of growth. *Bot.* capable of producing fruit; able to fertilize or be fertilized.—**fer·tile·ly,** *adv.*— **fer·tile·ness,** *n.*

fer·til·i·ty, fer·til'i·tē, *n.* [L. *fertilitas.*] The state of being fertile; the ability to produce offspring.

fer·ti·li·za·tion, fur″ti·li·zā'shan, *n.* The act or process of making fertile or productive; the application of a fertilizer; *biol.* the union of a sperm cell and an ovum.— **fer·ti·li·za·tion·al,** *a.*

fer·ti·lize, fur'ti·līz″, *v.t.*—*fertilized, fertilizing.* To make fertile; to make fruitful or productive; to enrich.—**fer·ti·liz·a·ble,** *a.*

fer·ti·liz·er, fur'ti·lī″zer, *n.* One who or that which fertilizes; any substance, such as manure or a chemical compound, used to enrich the soil.

fer·u·la, fer'u̇·la, fer'ū·la, *n.* pl. **fer·u·las, fer·u·lae,** fer'u̇·lē″, fer'ū·lē″. [L.] A genus of plants, *Ferula,* members of which yield asafetida, galbanum, and other strongly scented gum resins, and have many valuable medicinal properties.

fer·ule, fer'ul, fer'u̇l, *n.* [L. *ferula,* a twig, a cane, a switch, < *ferio,* to strike.] A flat piece of wood, a cane, or rod, used to punish children by striking them on the palm of the hand; classroom discipline.— *v.t.*—*feruled, feruling.* To punish with a ferule.

fer·vent, fur'vent, *a.* [L. *fervens, ferventis,* ppr. of *ferveo,* to boil, to ferment; akin *ferment.*] Ardent; earnest; animated; glowing with religious feeling; zealous; intensely warm.—**fer·vent·ly,** *adv.*—**fer·ven·cy,** fur'ven·sē, *n.* The state of being fervent; ardor; zeal.

fer·vid, fur'vid, *a.* [L. *fervidus,* < *ferveo.*] Impassioned; zealous; very hot; burning. —**fer·vid·ly,** *adv.*—**fer·vid·ness,** *n.*

fer·vor, fur'ver, *n.* [L. *fervor,* heat.] Intense feeling; passion; zeal; heat.

fes·cue, fes'kū, *n.* [O.E. *festue,* < O.Fr. *festu,* Fr. *fetu,* a straw; L. *festuca,* a shoot or twig.] Any grass of the genus *Festuca,* some of which are cultivated for meadows and lawns. Also **fes·cue grass.**

fest, fest, *n., combining form.* [G.: see *feast.*] A festival or festivity, much used in various humorous or slang formations; as, talk*fest,* gab*fest.*

fes·tal, fes'tal, *a.* [L. *festum,* a feast.] Pertaining or relating to a feast; festive.— **fes·tal·ly,** *adv.*

fes·ter, fes'ter, *v.i.* [O.Fr. *festrir,* to fester.] To suppurate; to form pus; to putrefy; to rankle, as a feeling of pique or resentment. —*n.* Act of festering or rankling.

fes·ti·val, fes'ti·val, *n.* [L. *festivus.*] A time of religious or other celebration; an occasion for rejoicing; a program of cultural events.—*a.* Pertaining to a feast or holiday.

Fes·ti·val of Lights, *n.* The Jewish holiday Hanukkah. See *Hanukkah.*

fes·tive, fes'tiv, *a.* [L. *festivus.*] Pertaining to or appropriate for a feast; joyous; gay.— **fes·tive·ly,** *adv.*—**fes·tive·ness,** *n.*

fes·tiv·i·ty, fe·stiv'i·tē, *n.* pl. **fes·tiv·i·ties.** [L. *festivitas.*] A joyous time or celebration; the condition or quality of being festive; social joy or gaiety; *pl.* the activities or events of a festive occasion.

fes·toon, fe·stŏn', *n.* [Fr. *feston,* lit. a festal garland; It. *festone,* < L. *festum,* a feast.] A swag, chain, or garland of flowers or foliage suspended so as to form hanging loops or curves; a fabric so draped; *arch.* a sculptured, painted, or molded reproduction of a festoon. Also **fes·toon·er·y,** pl. **fes·toon·er·ies.**—*v.t.* To adorn with festoons; to make into festoons; to connect by festoons.

fe·tal, foe·tal, fēt'al, *a. Embryol.* of, pertaining to, or having the character of a fetus.

fe·ta·tion, foe·ta·tion, fē·tā'shan, *n.* [L. *fetare,* bring forth, breed.] *Embryol.* the development of a fetus; pregnancy.

fetch, fech, *v.t.* [O.E. *feccan,* prob. var. of *fetian,* E. *fet.*] To go and bring back; to cause to come or succeed in bringing; to sell for or bring, as a price; *colloq.* to attract or captivate; to deal or strike, as a blow or stroke; *naut.* to reach or arrive at.— *v.i.* To go and bring things; *naut.* to move, go, or take a course; as, to *fetch* to windward. —*n.* The act of fetching; a bringing in from a distance, or the distance of fetching or reaching; the distance traveled by ocean waves; a trick or deceit.—**fetch·er,** *n.*— **fetch·ing,** *a. Colloq.* charming; captivating. —**fetch·ing·ly,** *adv.*

fetch, fech, *n.* [Origin obscure.] The apparition of a living person; a wraith.

fete, fête, fāt, *Fr.* fet, *n.* pl. **fetes,** fāts, *Fr.* fet. [Fr. < L. *festum,* a feast.] A feast; a holiday; a religious festival day; a large lavish party or entertainment.—*v.t.*— *feted, feting, fêted, fêting.* To entertain with a feast; to honor with a fete.

fet·e·ri·ta, fet″e·rē'ta, *n.* [Prob. native African.] A grain sorghum cultivated in the U.S. for grain and forage.

fe·ti·cide, foe·ti·cide, fē'ti·sīd″, *n.* [L. *fetus,* and *cædo,* to kill.] The destruction of a fetus.—**fe·ti·ci·dal,** *a.*

fet·id, fet'id, fē'tid, *a.* [L. *fætidus,* < *fæteo,* to stink.] Having an offensive smell.— **fet·id·ly,** *adv.*—**fet·id·ness,** *n.*

fet·ish, fet·ich, fet'ish, fē'tish, *n.* [Fr. *fétiche,* Pg. *feitiço,* sorcery, witchcraft, < L. *factitius,* artificial, < *facio,* to make.] Any object regarded as having mysterious powers; anything one irrationally or unquestioningly pursues or devotes oneself to. *Psychiatry,* any object or part of the body, not of the generative system, which arouses sexual interest.

fet·ish·ism, fet'i·shiz″um, fē'ti·shiz″um, *n.* Belief in or practice of assigning mysterious powers to an inanimate object; irrational or unquestioning pursuit of or devotion to anything. *Psychiatry,* belief in the potency of an object, esp. one associated with a beloved person, to stimulate sexual desire. —**fet·ish·ist,** *n.*—**fet·ish·is·tic,** *a.*

fet·lock, fet'lok″, *n.* [M.E. *fetelak, fitlok,* =

G. dial. *fissloch.*] A part of a horse's leg situated behind the joint between the cannon bone and the great pastern bone, bearing a tuft of hair; the tuft of hair itself. The joint at this point; also **fet·lock joint.** Also **fet·ter·lock.**

fe·tor, foe·tor, fē'ter, *n.* [L. *fœtor.*] Any strong offensive smell; stench.

fet·ter, fet'er, *n.* [O.E. *feter, fetor,* a fetter; O.G. *fezzera,* G. *fessel,* Icel. *fjöturr.* Probably connected with *foot.*] A chain or shackle by which a person or animal is confined by the foot. *Usu. pl.* Anything that confines or restrains from motion or expression; a restraint.—*v.t.* To put fetters on; to bind; to confine; to restrain.

fet·tle, fet'l, *v.t.*—*fettled, fettling.* [M.E. *fettlen,* put in order, arrange; perhaps orig. 'gird up,' < O.E. *fetel,* belt.] *Foundry,* to remove sand from, as a casting; *metal.* to line or repair, as the hearth of a furnace.—*n.* A state or condition; as, in fine *fettle;* sand or another agent used in fettling a furnace. —**fet·tling,** *n.* The material with which the hearth of a puddling furnace is lined.

fe·tus, foe·tus, fē'tus, *n.* pl. **fe·tus·es, foe·tus·es.** [L. < a root *fe,* implying fruitfulness, productiveness, as in *fecund.*] The young of an animal in the later stages of development but still confined to the womb or egg; an unborn human from after the third month of pregnancy until birth.

feud, fūd, *n.* [M.E. *fede,* < O.Fr. *fede, feide, faide,* feud; < Teut. (cf. G. *fehde*), and akin to E. *foe.*] A state of bitter and continuous mutual hostility, esp. such a state existing between two families or clans and marked by frequent armed conflicts; a quarrel or contention.—*v.i.* To quarrel, fight, or seek revenge.—**feud·ist,** *n.*

feu·dal, fūd'al, *a.* Of or pertaining to a system of political organization in medieval Europe in which land was granted by a lord to a vassal in exchange for military service; of, pertaining to, or of the nature of land held under this system.—**feud·ist,** *n.* A writer or authority on feudal law of the 9th to 15th centuries.

feu·dal·ism, fūd'a·liz″um, *n.* The medieval feudal system and its characteristics; the system of holding lands in fee, usu. in return for military services.—**feu·dal·ist,** fūd'a·list, *n.* A supporter of the feudal system.—**feu·dal·is·tic,** *a.*—**feu·dal·i·ty,** fū·dal'i·tē, *n.* The state or quality of being feudal.

feu·dal·i·za·tion, fūd″a·li·zā'shan, *n.* The act of feudalizing.—**feu·dal·ize,** fūd'a·līz″, *v.t.*—*feudalized, feudalizing.* To reduce to a feudal tenure; to conform to feudalism.

feu·da·to·ry, fū'da·tŏr″ē, fū'da·tar″ē, *a.* Under the sovereignty of another state; owing feudal loyalty.—*n.* pl. **feu·da·to·-ries.** A vassal holding his lands by feudal tenure; the land held; fief.

feuil·le·ton, foi'i·ton, *Fr.* fœy·e·taṇ', *n.* pl. **feuil·le·tons,** *Fr.* fœy·e·taṇ'. [Fr. < *feuillet,* dim. of *feuille,* leaf.] Part of a European newspaper or magazine devoted to light literature, criticism, or serialized fiction; any item printed in the feuilleton.— **feuil·le·ton·ist,** *n.* A writer of feuilletons.

fe·ver, fē'ver, *n.* [O.E. *fefer,* < L. *febris,* a fever; or < O.Fr. *fevre,* Mod.Fr. *fièvre,* of same origin.] An abnormal increase in body temperature; any disease having high temperature as a principal symptom; agitation or excitement by anything that strongly affects the passions; contagious zeal.—*v.t.* To put in a fever.—**fe·ver·ish,** *a.* Having fever, esp. a slight degree of fever; of, indicating, or pertaining to fever; tending to cause fever; infested with fever, as a country; excited, heated, uneasy, as though from fever.—**fe·ver·ish·ly,** *adv.*— **fe·ver·ish·ness,** *n.*

fe·ver blis·ter, *n.* An eruption around the mouth which may accompany a cold or fever. Also **fe·ver sore**, *cold sore*.

fe·ver·few, fē'vėr·fū″, *n.* [O.E. *feferfuge*, < L.L. *febrifugia*, < L. *febris*, fever, and *fugare*, put to flight.] A perennial European plant, *Chrysanthemum parthenium*, bearing small white flowers and formerly used as a medicine to reduce fever.

fe·ver·ous, fē'vėr·us, *a.* Feverish.—**fe·ver·ous·ly**, *adv.*

fe·ver·wort, fē'vėr·wu̧rt″, *n.* An herb, *Triostemum perfoliatum*, in the honeysuckle family, with emetic and purgative uses. Also **horse gen·tian**.

few, fū, *a.* [O.E. *fēawe*, pl., = O.H.G. *fōhe* = Goth. *fawai*; akin to L. *paucus*, Gr. *paupos*, little, pl. few.] Being of small number; not many; as, a book with *few* merits.—*n. sing. but pl. in constr.* A small number; a small amount; a minority, as: Many were asked to audition, but *few* were chosen.—*pron., pl. in constr.* A small number of individuals or things.—**the few**, a small number of persons or things separated or distinguished from a larger number; the minority; as, a measure which benefits *the few* at the expense of the many.

few·er, fū'ėr, *a.* Pertaining to a smaller number; of a smaller number.—*pron., pl. in constr.* A smaller number.

few·ness, fū'nis, *n.* The state of being few in number or small in quantity; scarcity.

fey, fā, *a.* [O.E. *fǣge*, Icel. *feigr*, near to death.] Under a spell; of the nature of fairies or sprites; elfin; enchanted. *Sc.* mentally disturbed by a feeling of impending death or calamity.

fez, fez, *n. pl.* **fez·zes**. [From the city of *Fez*, in Morocco.] A brimless felt cap, usu. red with a black tassle, shaped like a truncated cone, and worn by males in eastern Mediterranean countries.

fi·a·cre, fē·ä'kėr, fē·äk'ėr, *Fr.* fyä'kʀe, *n. pl.* **fi·a·cres**, *Fr.* fyä'kʀe. [Fr., from the Hotel St. *Fiacre*, where in 1640 the inventor of these carriages established an office for their hire.] A hackney coach or similar vehicle for hire.

fi·an·cé, fē″än·sā', fē·än′sā, *Fr.* fyäṅ·sā′, *n. pl.* **fi·an·cés**, *Fr.* fyäṅ·sā′. [Fr. pp. of *fiancer*, betroth.] A man pledged to be married.—**fi·an·cée**, fē″än·sā′, fē·än′sā, *Fr.* fyäṅ·sā′, *n. fem. pl.* **fi·an·cées**, *Fr.* fyäṅ·sā′.

fi·as·co, fē·as′kō, *n. pl.* **fi·as·cos**, **fi·as·coes**. [It. *fiasco*, a flask or bottle, a cry in Italy when a singer fails to please.] A complete and humiliating failure.

fi·at, fī'at, fī′at, *n.* [L. let it be done, < *fio*, to be done.] A decree or dictatorial order by a person or group having complete authority; sanction by a person in authority.—**fi·at mon·ey**, paper currency issued by a government as legal tender, which is not convertible into coin.

fib, fib, *n.* [Probably an abbr. and corruption of *fable*.] A falsehood, esp. one that is not malicious.—*v.i.*—*fibbed*, *fibbing*.—**fib·ber**, **fib·ster**, *n.*

fi·ber, *Brit.* **fi·bre**, fī'bėr, *n.* [Fr. *fibre*, < L. *fibra*, filament.] A slender filament; a fine threadlike part of a substance, as of wool, jute, or asbestos; *zool.* one of the threadlike elements composing the tissue of muscles and nerves. *Bot.* a slender threadlike root of a plant; filaments collectively; matter composed of filaments, esp. matter from the bast tissue or other parts of plants used for industrial purposes. *Fig.* material, stuff, or character; as, men of strong *fiber*.—**fi·bered**, *a.* Having fibers.

fi·ber·board, fī'bėr·bôrd″, fī′bėr·bärd″, *n.* A construction material of wood or other plant fiber compressed into large sheets.

fi·ber·glass, fī'bėr·glas″, fī′bėr·gläs″, *n.* Fine and flexible filaments of glass which

can be spun into textiles or matted for insulation; spun glass.

fi·bril, fī'bril, fib′ril, *n.* [N.L. *fibrilla*, dim. of L. *fibra*, E. *fiber*.] A small or very fine fiber or filament; *bot.* one of the hairs on the young roots of some plants. Also **fi·bril·la**, pl. **fi·bril·lae**, fī·bril′ē.

fi·bril·lar, fī'bri·lėr, fib′ri·lėr, *a.* Of, pertaining to, or composed of fibers or fibrils. Also **fi·bril·lar·y**.

fi·bril·la·tion, fī″bri·lā′shan, fib″ri·lā′shan, *n.* The process or act of the formation of fibrils. *Pathol.* the twitching of certain muscle fibers without coordination or control; erratic and irregular contractions of heart muscle fibers resulting in abnormally rapid heartbeats.

fi·bril·li·form, fī·bril′i·fa̧rm″, fi·bril′i·fa̧rm″, *a.* Of the form of a fibril or fibrils.—**fi·bril·lose**, fī'bri·lōs″, fib′ri·lōs″, *a.* Like or furnished with fibrils.

fi·brin, fī'brin, *n.* A fibrous, elastic, insoluble protein, formed by the interaction of fibrinogen with the enzyme thrombin, that promotes clotting to prevent blood loss.—**fi·brin·ous**, *a.*

fi·brin·o·gen, fī·brin′o·jen, *n.* A globulin in the blood that is a soluble protein and assists in producing fibrin for the clotting of blood.—**fi·brin·o·gen·ic**, **fi·bri·nog·e·nous**, fī″bri·nō·jen′ik, fī″bri·noj′e·nus, *a.* Producing fibrin.

fi·broid, fī'broid, *a. Pathol.* resembling or formed of fibrous tissue.—*n.* A fibroid tumor.

fi·bro·ma, fī·brō′ma, *n. pl.* **fi·bro·ma·ta**, **fi·bro·mas**, fī·brō′ma·ta. *Pathol.* a benign tumor or growth of fibrous matter.—**fi·brom·a·tous**, fī·brom′a·tus, *a.*

fi·brous, fī'brus, *a.* [N.L. *fibrosus*, < L. *fibra*, E. *fiber*.] Containing, consisting of, or resembling fibers.

fi·bro·vas·cu·lar, fī″brō·vas′kū·lėr, *a. Bot.* composed of a fibrous conductive tissue which conveys fluid from one part to another; as, *fibrovascular* bundles.

fib·u·la, fib′ū·la, *n. pl.* **fib·u·las**, **fib·u·lae**, fib′ū·las, fib′ū·lē. [L. a clasp, a brace, a pin.] *Anat.* the outer and lesser bone of the lower leg; *archaeol.* a clasp used by early Greeks and Romans, similar to a safety pin.—**fib·u·lar**, *a.*

fich·u, fish′ö, *Fr.* fē·shy′, *n. pl.* **fich·us**, fish′öz, *Fr.* fē·shy′. [Fr., origin uncertain.] A kind of kerchief of muslin, lace, or the like, generally triangular in shape, worn about the neck by women, with the ends drawn together or crossed on the breast.

fick·le, fik′l, *a.* [O.E. *ficol*, inconstant; akin to G. *ficken*, to move quickly to and fro.] Wavering; inconstant, esp. in affections; unstable; of a changeable mind; irresolute; not firm in opinion or purpose; capricious.—**fick·le·ness**, *n.*

fic·tile, fik′til, *Brit.* fik′til, *a.* [L. *fictilis*, < *fingo*, *fictum*, to form.] Molded or capable of being molded; made of soft clay or earthenware; pliable.

fic·tion, fik′shan, *n.* [L. *fictio*, a shaping, fashioning, < *fingo*, *fictum*, to fashion.] A creation of the imagination, esp. a fanciful story; a falsehood; a prose narrative of imagined events in the form of a novel, novella, or short story; the act of inventing or imagining. *Law*, an assumption that something false may be accepted as true.—**fic·tion·al**, *a.*—**fic·tion·al·ly**, *adv.*

fic·tion·al·i·za·tion, fik′sha·na·li″zā·shan, *n.* The act, procedure, or product of narrating an actual or historical event in fictional form. Also **fic·tion·i·za·tion**.—**fic·tion·al·ize**, **fic·tion·ize**, *fictionalized*, *fictionalizing*, *fictionized*, *fictionizing*, *v.t.*

fic·tion·eer, fik″sha·nēr′, *n.* An author who produces inferior fiction in quantity.

fic·tion·ist, fik′sha·nist, *n.* A writer of fiction; a writer of novels or short stories.

fic·ti·tious, fik·tish′us, *a.* [L. *fictitius*.] Feigned; not genuine; untrue. Of or pertaining to fiction; dealing with imaginary characters and events.—**fic·ti·tious·ly**, *adv.*—**fic·ti·tious·ness**, *n.*

fic·tive, fik′tiv, *a.* Feigned; fictional; imaginary; able to create imaginatively.—**fic·tive·ly**, *adv.*

fid·dle, fid′l, *n.* [O.E. *fithele* = L.G. *fidel*, Dan. *fiddel*, Icel. *fithla*, D. *vedel*; perh. borrowed < L.L. *vidula*, a viol.] *Colloq.* a stringed musical instrument in the viol family.—*v.i.*—*fiddled*, *fiddling*. To play on a fiddle or violin.—*v.t.* To play, as a tune, on a fiddle or violin.—**fid·dler**, *n.*

fid·dle, fid′l, *v.i.*—*fiddled*, *fiddling*. To waste time aimlessly; to putter; to make nervous or fidgety movements with the fingers or hands; to interfere or meddle.—**fid·dle a·way**, to waste, as time or energy.—**fid·dler**, *n.*

fid·dle, fid′l, *n. Naut.* a device, as a frame or ledge, used aboard ships, esp. in rough weather, to prevent dishes and other utensils from sliding off a table.

fid·dle·back, fid′l·bak″, *a.* Resembling the outline or back of a fiddle.—**fid·dle·back chair**, *n.*

fid·dle-fad·dle, fid′l·fad″l, *a. Colloq.* trifling; making a bustle about nothing.—*v.i.*—*fiddle-faddled*, *fiddle-faddling*. To trifle; to fuss over a trifle.—*n.* A triviality; nonsense.—**fid·dle-fad·dler**, *n.*

fid·dler crab, *n.* A small-sized crab, of the genus *Uca*, the male having an enlarged claw which it moves in a way resembling fiddling.

fid·dle·stick, fid′l·stik″, *n.* A violin bow; something inconsequential.—**fid·dle·sticks**, *interj. Trivia;* nonsense.

fid·dling, fid′ling, *a. Colloq.* trifling; trivial; insignificant.

fi·de·ism, fēd′ā·iz″um, *n.* A tenet that certain premises, as of religion and philosophy, need no rational explanation but should be accepted on faith.—**fi·de·ist**, *n.*

fi·del·i·ty, fi·del′i·tē, fī·del′i·tē, *n. pl.* **fi·del·i·ties**. [L. *fidelitas*, < *fidelis*, faithful, < *fides*, trust, faith, *fido*, to trust.] Marital faithfulness; careful and exact observance of duty; loyalty; exactness in reproduction; adherence to fact or truth; *electron.* the quality or degree of accuracy in sound reproduction, as of a radio.

fidg·et, fij′it, *v.i.* [Dim. of provincial *fidge*, *fike*, *fyke*, to be restless; akin to Icel. *fika*, to hasten; G. *ficken*, O.Sw. *fika*, to move quickly to and fro.] To make restless, twitchy movements; to have the jitters.—*v.t.* To cause to become restless or agitated.—*n. Usu. pl.* irregular, uneasy movements due to nervousness or restlessness. A nervous, jumpy person.—**fidg·et·y**, *a.* Given to fidgeting; restless; uneasy; needlessly and nervously fussy.

fi·du·cial, fi·dū′shal, fī·dū′shal, *a.* [L.L. *fiducialis*, < L. *fiducia*, trust, trustiness, < *fido*, to trust.] Based on trust or belief; *phys.* regarded as a standard of comparison or point of reference, as in measuring; fiduciary.—**fi·du·cial·ly**, *adv.*

fi·du·ci·ar·y, fi·dū′shē·er″ē, fī·dū′shē·er″ē, *a.* [L. *fiduciarius*, held in trust.] Of or indicating a trustee or his office; held in trust; accepted only because the public has faith in its value, as fiat money.—*n. pl.* **fi·du·ci·ar·ies**. One who holds a thing in trust for another; a trustee.

fie, fī, *interj.* [Interjectional expression corresponding to Sc. *feigh*, Fr. *fi*, G. *pfui*, *fi*, Dan. *fy*.] An exclamation denoting contempt, dislike, or disbelief, now usu. used humorously.

fief, fēf, *n.* [Fr. *fief*, < O.H.G. *fihu*, property, lit. cattle.] An estate held on feudal tenure.

field, fēld, *n.* [O.E. *feld,* a field = D. *veld* Dan. *felt,* G. *feld*; allied to *fold,* an enclosure, *fell,* a hill; Dan. *falle,* greensward; Sc. *fale, feal,* a turf.] A piece of land suitable for tillage or pasture; the open countryside; cleared land; cultivated ground; a distinct division of a farm; an area having a particular natural resource; as, oil *field*; an area set aside for a particular activity; as, playing *field,* air*field*; the ground where a battle is fought; the battle or action; the area where military operations are carried out; any large unbroken stretch of something; as, *field* of ice; a sphere of interest or knowledge; as, the *field* of chemistry; an area of operations that is away from the office or headquarters; as, to service customers in the *field*; the ground or blank space on which figures or designs are drawn, as on medals, coins, or flags; the surface of a heraldic shield or escutcheon. *Athletics,* all those entered in an event or contest; the area where such an event takes place; a particular section of this area; those players, esp. in football, who are in action; *horse racing,* the name applied to a group of several horses in a race, a wager on the group winning if any one of the horses finishes first; *baseball, cricket,* the team not at bat. *Phys.* the space within which a given force operates; as, magnetic *field*; *opt.* that area which can be seen through a lens, as of a telescope or other optical instrument.

field, fēld, *v.t.* To respond to satisfactorily, as to a difficult question. *Baseball,* of a defensive player, to catch or handle, as a batted ball.—*v.i.* To make a successful defensive play in baseball or cricket.

field, fēld, *a.* Of, related to, grown in, or inhabiting the fields; as, *field* flowers, *field* mice; used in the field; as, *field* boots, played in the field; as, *field* events in a track and field meet.

field ar·til·ler·y, *n.* Mobile artillery which accompanies troops in the field.—**Field Ar·til·ler·y,** a branch of the U.S. Army from 1907 to 1950.

field corn, *n.* Corn grown as feed for livestock.

field day, *n.* A day of outdoor sports and competition; an outdoor social gathering or picnic; a day for military field exercises; any occasion or 'time of unrestricted activity, excitement, or success.

field·er, fēl'dėr, *n. Baseball, cricket.* One who fields the ball; a defensive player positioned in the field.—**field·er's choice,** *baseball,* an attempt by a fielder to put out a player already on base rather than the batter, even though the play to first base could put out the batter.

field e·vent, *n.* An event at an athletic meet not performed on the running track, as the high jump, pole vault, or javelin throw.

field glass, *n.* A binocular telescope for outdoor use. Also **field glass·es.**

field goal, *n. Football,* a three-point goal scored from scrimmage by kicking the ball between an opponent's goal posts; *basketball,* a two-point goal scored while the ball is in play.

field grade, *n.* The U.S. army ranks including colonel, lieutenant colonel, and major.—**field of·fic·er,** a military officer of field grade.

field gun, *n.* A small, rapid-firing cannon mounted on wheels, used for support in the field; a fieldpiece.

field house, *n.* A building connected with an athletic field and providing locker rooms, storage space, showers, and other facilities; a building which encloses an area used for various indoor sports.

field mag·net, *n.* A magnet for producing a magnetic field, esp. in a dynamo or electric motor.

field mar·shal, *n.* An officer of the highest rank in many armies, such as the British and Canadian.

field mouse, *n.* One of several species of small rodent animals that live in open fields.

field of force, *n. Phys.* a space or region around the origin of a force, as an electric charge or magnetic attraction, in which the force is effective.

field of hon·or, *n.* The area where a duel takes place; any battlefield.

field·piece, fēld'pēs″, *n. Milit.* a gun or mounted cannon used in field battles. Also *field gun.*

field the·o·ry, *n. Phys.* a detailed, mathematically described theory of the movement, distribution, and effect of one or more fields of force.

field tri·al, *n.* A competitive trial of hunting dogs in actual performance in the field.

field wind·ing, *n. Elect.* the conducting coils wound on poles and connected in series producing the field magnet which regulates the current in a generator or electric motor.

field·work, fēld'wurk″, *n.* Investigation, exploration, or research performed outdoors by geologists, archaeologists, engineers, or surveyors. *Milit.* a temporary fortification constructed by field troops.

fiend, fēnd, *n.* [O.E. *feōnd, fynd,* a fiend, an enemy, < *feon,* to hate. Akin D. *vijand,* Icel. *fjandi,* Goth. *fjands,* G. *feind.*] An infernal being; an evil spirit; a demon; hence a diabolically cruel or malicious person. *Colloq.* an annoying or mischievous person; as, a *fiendish* child; one with an exaggerated interest in a subject, as in sports; one who overindulges, as in food; an addict.—**fiend·ish,** *a.*—**fiend·ish·ly,** *adv.*—**fiend·ish·ness,** *n.*

fierce, fērs, *a.* [O.Fr. *fiers, fiers,* < L. *ferus,* wild, rude, cruel, whence *fera,* a wild beast; akin *feral* and *ferocious.*] Savage; ferocious; easily enraged; furiously active, intense, or eager; vehement in anger or cruelty; violently aggressive or hostile in temperament or nature.—**fierce·ly,** *adv.*—**fierce·ness,** *n.*

fier·y, fīr′ē, fī′e·rē, *a.*—**fierier, fieriest.** Consisting of, attended or characterized by, or containing fire; characteristic of, suggestive of, or resembling fire; intensely hot; flashing or glowing, as the eye; intensely ardent, impetuous, or passionate; flammable; inflamed, as a tumor or sore; causing a burning sensation, as liquors or condiments. —**fier·i·ly,** *adv.*—**fier·i·ness,** *n.*

fi·es·ta, fē·es′ta, *Sp.* fyes′tä, *n. pl.* **fi·es·tas,** fē·es′taz, *Sp.* fyes′täs. [Sp.] A public or religious holiday in Spain or Latin America; a festive day or celebration; a feast.

fife, fīf, *n.* [Fr. *fifre,* a fife, < G. *pfeife,* = E. *pipe,* a word of onomatopoetic origin.] A small, high-pitched flute used mainly for military marches.—*v.i.* To play on a fife.— **fif·er,** *n.*

fif·teen, fif′tēn, *a.* [O.E. *fiftyne.*] One more than 14 in number; five more than 10.—*n.* The cardinal number between 14 and 16; a symbol representing it; a set of 15 persons or things.

fif·teenth, fif′tēnth, *a.* Following the fourteenth; being the ordinal of 15; being one of 15 equal parts into which anything is divided.—*n.* One of 15 equal parts; that which follows the fourteenth in a series.

fifth, fifth, *a.* Following the fourth; being the ordinal of five; being one of five equal parts into which anything is divided.—*n.* One of five equal parts; that which follows the fourth in a series. *Mus.* an interval consisting of five diatonic degrees. A fifth of a gallon, esp. of spirituous liquor.

fifth col·umn, *n.* Citizens residing in a country who are in sympathy with its enemies, and who are serving their interests or are ready to assist them in case they attack the country.—**fifth col·umn·ism,** *n.*— **fifth col·umn·ist,** *n.*

fif·ti·eth, fif′tē·ith, *a.* Following the forty-ninth; being the ordinal of 50; being one of 50 equal parts into which anything is divided.—*n.* One of 50 equal parts; that which follows the forty-ninth in a series.

fif·ty, fif′tē, *a.* [O.E. *fiftig.*] One more than 49 in number; five times 10; 40 plus 10.— *n. pl.* **fif·ties.** The cardinal number between 49 and 51; a symbol representing it; a set of 50 persons or things.—**fif·ty-fif·ty,** *a., adv. Colloq.* being shared equally, as profits, expenses, or payments; as, to go *fifty-fifty* on the luncheon check.

fig, fig, *n.* [Fr. *figue,* akin D. *vijg,* G. *feige,* < L. *ficus,* fig.] Any of the tropical trees or shrubs of the genus *Ficus* of the mulberry family, esp. the common fig tree, *F. carica,* cultivated for its edible fruit; a small pear-shaped fruit, a syconium, consisting of a hollow receptacle containing many ripe carpels which, erroneously called the seed, are embedded in the pulp. *Slang,* a contemptibly small amount, as: I do not care a *fig* for him.

fight, fīt, *v.i.*—**fought, fighting.** [O.E. *feohtan* = G. *fechten,* D. *vechten,* Dan. *fegte,* Icel. *flkta,* to fight.] To contend for victory in battle or in single combat; to contend in arms or otherwise; to strive or struggle; to resist or oppose.—*v.t.* To carry on or wage, as a battle; to contend with; to defend against; to oppose or resolve by striving or contending; to win or gain by struggle; as, to *fight* one's way; to manage or maneuver in a fight; as, to *fight* one's ship.—*n.* A contest; a battle; an engagement; verbal contention or argument; any struggle for victory; an inclination for fighting.—**fight·er,** fī′tėr, *n.* One who or that which fights; a combatant; *milit.* an aircraft equipped with weapons for the interception and destruction of enemy airplanes in the air.—**fight it out,** to struggle until a decisive result is attained.—**fight shy of,** to avoid, as from a feeling of dislike, fear, or mistrust.

fig leaf, *n.* The leaf of a fig tree, esp. in allusion to the first covering of Adam and Eve. Gen. iii. 7. *Fig.* anything designed to conceal what is shameful or indecorous.

fig·ment, fig′ment, *n.* [L. *figmentum,* < *fingo,* to feign.] An invention; a fiction; something feigned or imagined.

fig·ur·a·tion, fig″ū·rā′shan, fig″ya·ra′-shan, *n.* [L. *figuratio(n)-,* < *figurare,* E. *figure, v.*] The act of shaping into a particular figure; the resulting figure or shape; the act of representing figuratively; a figurative representation; the act of marking or adorning with figures or designs; *mus.* ornamentation by the use of passing tones or embellishments.

fig·ur·a·tive, fig′ūr·a·tiv, *a.* [L.L. *figur-ativus,* < L. *figurare,* E. *figure, v.*] Of the nature of or involving a figure of speech, esp. a metaphor; metaphorical, not literal; as, a *figurative* expression; abounding in figures of speech; as, *figurative* language; representing by means of a figure, emblem, or likeness, as in a drawing or sculpture; emblematic.—**fig·ur·a·tive·ly,** *adv.*—**fig·ur·a·ive·ness,** *n.*

fig·ure, fig′ūr, *Brit.* fig′ėr, *n.* [Fr. *figure,* < L. *figura,* figure, shape, < *fig,* root of *fingo,* to fashion.] The form of anything as expressed by the outline or contour; shape; the human shape or form; a pictorial representation of the human body or an object; appearance or impression made by a person; as, to cut a poor *figure*; an emblem or symbol; a number symbol; value or

figure 364 **fill out**

amount stated in numbers; mathematical calculations; a pattern or design; movements in a dance or skating; *mus.* a short related group of notes or chords that can grow into a composition or theme; *logic*, the form of a syllogism with respect to the relative position of the middle term; *geom.* an assembly of geometric elements placed in a particular form or shape; *opt.* the exact curve needed on the surface of an optical element, as the mirror of a reflecting telescope.—**cut a fig·ure**, to appear to advantage or disadvantage.—**fig·ure·less**, *a.*

fig·ure, fig′yėr, fig′ūr, *Brit.* fig′ėr, *v.t.*—*figured*, *figuring.* To compute or calculate numerically; to make a figure or likeness of; to cover or adorn with figures or ornamental designs; to imagine or picture mentally; to represent by a figure of speech. *Colloq.* to think about; consider; believe. *Mus.* to decorate with passing notes or other embellishments; to write figures over or under (the bass notes) to indicate accompanying chords.—*v.i.* To be a prominent personage; to compute; to make a figure.—**fig·ure out**, to solve.—**fig·ur·er**, *n.*

fig·ured, fig′yėrd, fig′ūrd, *a.* Formed or shaped; represented by a pictorial or sculptured figure; adorned with a pattern or design; figurative, as language; *mus.* having the accompanying chords indicated.

fig·ure eight, *n.* An aerial maneuver which traces the numeral eight; a skating pattern; a knot resembling the figure eight.

fig·ure·head, fig′ūr·hed″, *n.* A person who is nominally the head of a society, company, or group, but has no real authority or responsibility. *Naut.* an ornamental or carved figure, as a statue or bust, placed over the cutwater of a ship.

fig·ure of speech, *n.* A mode of expression, as a simile, metaphor, or hyperbole, where words are employed in a nonliteral or unusual sense for special effects, such as lending vividness or heightening beauty of style.

fig·ure skat·ing, *n.* A type of skating in which the skater traces or outlines prescribed figures or patterns.

fig·ur·ine, fig′yu·rēn′, fig′ū·rēn′, *n.* [Fr.] A small ornamental figure of china, pottery, or metalwork; a statuette.

fig·wort, fig′wụrt″, *n. Bot.* the common name for *Scrophulariaceae*, a large family of primarily herbaceous plants, many of which have two-lipped flowers arranged on spikes or racemes, including the foxglove and snapdragon; any plant of the genus *Scrophularia.*

fil·a·ment, fil′a·ment, *n.* [Fr. *filament*, < L. *filum*, thread.] A very fine thread or threadlike structure; a fiber or fibril; in an incandescent lamp, the threadlike, nearly infusible conductor which is placed in the bulb and heated to incandescence by the passage of electric current; *electron.* the direct or indirect heater of the cathode of an electron tube; *bot.* the stalklike portion of a stamen, supporting the anther.—**fil·-a·ment·ed**, *a.*—**fil·a·men·ta·ry, fil·a·-men·tous**, *a.*

fi·lar, fī′lėr, *a.* [L. *filum*, thread.] Of or pertaining to a thread; *opt.* having threads across the field of vision.

fil·a·ture, fil′a·chėr, *n.* [Fr. *filature*, < M.L. *filare*, spin, < L. *filum*, thread.] The act of forming into threads; the reeling of silk from cocoons; a reel for drawing off silk from cocoons; an establishment for reeling silk.

fil·bert, fil′bėrt, *n.* A tree or shrub of a species of hazel, esp. *Corylus avellana* of Europe; the thick-shelled edible nut of the hazel tree which matures about August 22nd, St. Philbert's day.

filch, filch, *v.t.* [For *filk*, < O.E. *fele*, Icel. *fela*, to steal, like *talk* and *tell*, *stalk* (verb)

and *steal*.] To steal, esp. something of little value; to pilfer; to purloin.—**filch·er**, *n.*

file, fīl, *n.* [O.E. *feol* = D. *vijl*, Dan. *viil*, G. *feile*, O.H.G. *vihila*, a file.] A tool, usu. of hardened steel, having sharp ridges across its surface, for cutting, abrading, and smoothing metal, wood, and other materials. —*v.t.*—*filed*, *filing.* To rub smooth, reduce, or cut with a file or as with a file.

file, fīl, *n.* [Fr. *fil*, thread, string, and *file*, file, row, < L. *filum*, thread.] A container, such as a cabinet or a folder, in which papers are arranged or classified for convenient reference; a collection of papers or records systematically arranged; a line of persons or things arranged one behind another, as distinguished from rank; a line of men standing or marching one behind the other in a military formation; one of the vertical rows of squares on a chessboard running directly from player to player.—**on file**, on or in a file for convenient reference.—*v.t.*—*filed*, *filing.* To place in a file; to arrange, as papers or records, methodically for preservation or reference; to send, as copy or a news story, to a newspaper.—*v.i.* To march or move in file; to register as a candidate.

file·fish, fīl′fish, *n. pl.* **file·fish, file·fish·es.** Any of various salt-water fishes of the family *Monacanthidae*, with spiny or granular skin, as the triggerfish.

fi·let, fi·lā′, fil′ā, *Fr.* fē·le′, *n.* [Fr. *filet*, net, netting, for *filé*, < *fil*, thread, string.] A lace or net with a square mesh. *Cooking*, a boneless piece of lean meat or fish, sometimes rolled and tied for roasting; also *fillet.*—*v.t.* To slice, as meat or fish, into filets; also *fillet.*

fi·let mi·gnon, fi·lā′ min·yon′, fi·lā′ min′yon, *Fr.* fē·le mē·nyạN′, *n. pl.* **fi·lets mi·gnons.** A small, boneless, and lean steak, cut from the tenderloin of beef.

fil·i·al, fil′ē·al, *a.* [Fr. *filial*, < L.L. *filialis*, < L. *filius*, a son, *filia*, a daughter.] Pertaining to or assuming the relation of a son or daughter; befitting a child in relation to his parents. *Genetics*, of or designating a generation successive to the parental.— **fil·i·al·ly**, *adv.*—**fil·i·al·ness**, *n.*

fil·i·ate, fil′ē·āt″, *v.t.*—*filiated*, *filiating.* [L. *filius*, son, *filia*, daughter.] *Law*, to establish judicially the paternity of, as an illegitimate child.—**fil·i·a·tion**, *n.* The fact of being the child of a certain parent, esp. the filial relationship of a son to his father; derivation; the relation of one thing to another from which it is derived; derivation or the formation of branches, esp. of a language or a culture; an offshoot; *law*, judicial determination of paternity.

fil·i·bus·ter, fil′i·bus″tėr, *n.* [Fr. *filibustier*, < *fribustier*, D. *vrijbuiter*, G. *freibeuter*, E. *freebooter*.] An effort by a minority group of legislators to defeat or delay legislation by obstructionist tactics, esp. by long speeches. A lawless adventurer, as a soldier of fortune; freebooter; buccaneer.—*v.i.* To defeat or delay legislation by obstructionist tactics. To act as a lawless adventurer or buccaneer.—*v.t.* To block, as legislation, by obstructionist tactics.

fil·i·form, fi′li·fạrm″, fī′li·fạrm″, *a.* [L. *filum*, thread.] Threadlike; filamentous.

fil·i·gree, fil′i·grē″, *n.* [Corruption of *filgrane* < Fr. *filgrane*, < It. *filigrana*, < L. *filum*, thread, and *granum*, grain.] Ornamental work of fine intertwisted wire, esp. jewelers' work of gold or silver in a delicate, lacy design; intricate ornamental openwork; anything very delicate or fanciful.—*a.* Composed of or resembling filigree.—*v.t.*—*filigreed*, *filigreeing.* To adorn with or form into filigree.—Also **fil·a·gree, fil·la·gree.**

fil·ings, fī′lingz, *n. pl.* Particles, esp. metal, removed by a file.

Fil·i·pi·no, fil″i·pē′nō, *n. pl.* **Fil·i·pi·nos.** [Sp.] A native or resident of the Philippine Islands.—*a.* Relating to or characteristic of the Philippines or their inhabitants.

fill, fil, *v.t.* [O.E. *fyllan* = D. *vullen* = G. *fullen* = Icel. *fylla* = Goth. *fulljan*, fill; from the Teut. adj. represented by E. *full.*] To make full, as of contents; put as much as can be held into; as, to *fill* a cup; supply to the fullest or the utmost; as, to *fill* the heart with joy; complete by inserting written matter or decorative work in, as blank spaces, usu. with *in*, *out*, or *up*; to close or repair, as a hole, crack, or cavity; as, to *fill* a tooth; furnish with an occupant or incumbent, as a vacancy or post; to occupy to the full capacity; to pervade; to hold or perform the duties of, as an office or position; satisfy, as food does; meet satisfactorily, as requirements; execute, as a business order; make up or compound, as a medical prescription; distend, as the wind does a sail; raise the level of, as an area of ground, with earth and rocks.—*v.i.* To become full; as, eyes *filling* with tears; become distended, as sails with wind; to fill a cup or other receptacle.—**fill the bill**, *colloq.* to satisfy the requirements of the case.—**fill one's shoes**, *colloq.* to assume another's position and responsibilities.

fill, fil, *n.* [O.E. *fyllo.*] A full supply or desired amount; as, one's *fill* of food or sleep; a quantity sufficient to fill something; as, a *fill* of tobacco for a pipe; a single filling or charge; a mass of earth and stones used to level an area of ground.

fill·er, fil′ėr, *n.* One who or that which fills; a thing or quantity of a material used to fill something or to augment contents; a liquid or paste used to stop up cracks or pores, as in preparing a surface for painting; a brief item of copy used to fill a vacant space in a newspaper or magazine.

fil·let, fil′it, *n.* [O.Fr. Fr. *filet*, dim. of *fil*, thread, string, < L. *filum*, thread.] A narrow band of ribbon worn around the head as a decoration; any narrow strip of material, as wood or metal. *Arch.* a narrow, often flat, molding between two larger moldings; the flat surface between two flutes of a column. *Anat.* a band of fibers; lemniscus. A line impressed on the cover of a book as a decoration; a tool for impressing such lines.—*v.t.* To bind or adorn with or as with a fillet.

fil·let, fi·let, fi·lā′, fil′ā, *n.* [< Fr. *fil*, thread, string.] *Cooking*, a boneless piece of meat, esp. beef tenderloin, or of fish; a piece of meat boned, rolled, and tied for roasting.—*v.t. Cooking*, to cut or prepare as a fillet; to cut fillets from.

fill-in, fil′in″, *n.* A person or thing serving as a replacement, supplement, or insertion; a brief, usually oral review of essential information.

fill·ing, fil′ing, *n.* The act of one who or that which fills; a making or becoming full; that which is put in to fill something; as, a gold *filling* in a tooth, a custard *filling* for a pie; the weft threads which interlace the warp in a woven fabric.

fill·ing sta·tion, *n.* Gas station.

fil·lip, fil′ip, *v.t.* To flick smartly with the finger by first curling the finger tightly against the thumb, then quickly straightening the finger; to form, as the fingers, into a fillip; to arouse or urge into action.—*n.* The fillip movement; a tap or strike made with a fillip; something which sharply rouses or stimulates.

fil·lis·ter, fil′i·stėr, *n.* [Origin unknown.] A plane for cutting rabbets or grooves; a rabbet or groove, as one on a window sash to hold the glass and putty.

fill out, *v.i.* To round out or become fuller, as the face or figure.

---

ch- chain, G. na*ch*t; **th-** THen, thin; **w-** wig, hw as sound in whig; **z-** zh as in azure, zeal. *Italicized vowel* indicates schwa sound.

fill up, *v.t.* To fill completely, as a receptacle or hole; to take up or occupy fully, as: These duties *fill up* the day.—*v.i.* To become filled to capacity.

fil·ly, fil′ē, *n.* pl. **fil·lies.** [A dim. form of *foal* = Icel. *fylja,* a filly, < *foli,* a foal.] A young female horse; *colloq.* a young girl.

film, film, *n.* [O.E. *filmen,* a skin; allied to *fell,* a skin.] A thin skin or membrane; a thin coating or overlay; a delicate network of fine threads, as gossamer or cobweb; a haze or blur. *Photog.* transparent, flexible material in strips or sheets of cellulose acetate, covered with an emulsion which is sensitive to light, used in taking photographs or making motion pictures. A motion picture; the cellulose acetate strips or rolls of reproductions projected on a screen; highly developed film containing an area carrying synchronized recorded sound; *pl.* the movie industry in general or motion pictures collectively. *Pathol.* an abnormal growth on the cornea.—*v.t.* To coat or cover with or as with a film; to produce a motion picture from; as, to *film* a documentary.—*v.i.* To become covered by a film; to be suitable for filming; to be occupied in the making of a motion picture. —**film·y,** *a.*—*filmier, filmiest.*—**film·i·ly,** *adv.*—**film·i·ness,** *n.*

film·dom, film′dom, *n.* The world of motion pictures; the movie industry; its personnel.

film·strip, film′strip″, *n.* A series of individual still pictures on a length of film, to be projected on a screen, sometimes having captions but without sound and usually needing narration: often used as a teaching aid.

fi·lose, fī′lōs, *a.* [L. *filum,* thread.] Thread-like; ending in a threadlike process.

fil·ter, fil′tẽr, *n.* [Fr. *filtre* = It. *filtro,* < M.L. *filtrum, feltrum,* felt (used as a filter); < the Teut. source of E. *felt.*] Any contrivance or porous substance, as felt, paper, charcoal, or sand, through which liquid or gas is passed to remove impurities or other matter; any device containing a filtering substance; *phys.* an apparatus which controls sound waves, light waves, or electrical currents by checking or lessening certain waves or frequencies without greatly affecting others; *photog.* a colored, translucent screen, usu. of glass, for a camera lens, used to control the intensity and type of light waves admitted.—*v.t.* To pass, as air, through a filter in order to strain or purify; to remove by the action of a filter; to act as a filter for.—*v.i.* To pass through or as through a filter, as: Water *filtered* through the roof.—**fil·ter·a·ble, fil·tra·ble,** *a.*—**fil·ter·a·bil·i·ty,** *n.*

fil·ter bed, *n.* A sand or gravel bed, as in a tank or reservoir, which filters water or sewage.

fil·ter tip, *n.* A cigar or cigarette end piece containing a substance which filters impurities out of the smoke; a cigar or cigarette which has such a tip.—**fil·ter-tipped,** *a.*

filth, filth, *n.* [O.E. *fylth,* < *fūl,* E. *foul.*] Foul matter; offensive or disgusting dirt; moral impurity or corruption; vulgar language; obscenity.

filth·y, fil′thē, *a.*—*filthier, filthiest.* Characterized by or of the nature of filth; disgustingly dirty; vile or obscene; highly offensive.—**filth·i·ly,** *adv.*—**filth·i·ness,** *n.*

fil·trate, fil′trāt, *v.t.*—*filtrated, filtrating.* [L.L. *filtro, filtratum.*] To filter.—*n.* The liquid which has been passed through a filter.—**fil·tra·tion,** fil·trā′shan, *n.*

fim·bri·a, fim′brē·*a, n.* pl. **fim·bri·ae,** fim′brē·ē″. [L.L., border, fringe.] *Biol.* a fringe or fringed border, as at the opening of tubes, esp. at the entrance of the Fallopian tubes.—**fim·bri·ate,** fim′brē·it,

fim′brē·āt″, *a.* Having a fringe; as, *fimbriate* petals. Also **fim·bri·at·ed,** fim′brē·ā″tid. —**fim·bri·a·tion,** *n.*

fin, fin, *n.* [O.E. *finn* = D. *vin* = L.G. *finne,* fin.] A membranous winglike or paddlelike organ attached to any of various parts of the body of fishes and certain other aquatic animals, used for propulsion, steering, or balancing; any part, as of a mechanism, resembling a fin; one of a pair of rubber, paddlelike attachments for the feet, used by swimmers, esp. skin divers, for added propulsion; *aeron.* an airfoil or vane attached longitudinally, as to an aircraft or rocket, to provide a stabilizing effect; *naut.* an attachment to the underwater part of a boat or submarine to aid stability. One of the protruding ridges of an engine cylinder or a radiator. *Slang,* a five-dollar bill; the arm or hand.—*v.t.*—*finned, finning.* To remove the fins from.—*v.i.* Of fish or aquatic mammals, to move the fins, esp. so violently as to extend them above the water.—**fin·less,** *a.*—**fin·like,** *a.*—**finned,** *a.* Having fins.

fi·na·gle, fe·na·gle, fi·nā′gl, *v.t.*—*finagled, finagling, fenagled, fenagling.* To acquire through chicanery or intrigue; to practice chicanery or intrigue on; to wangle.—*v.i.* To use intrigue, dishonesty, or deceit to achieve one's ends.—**fi·na·gler,** *n.*

fi·nal, fīn′al, *a.* [O.Fr. Fr. *final,* < L.L. *finalis,* < L. *finis,* end, E. *fine.*] Pertaining to or coming at the end; last in place, order or time; the ultimate; as, the *final* goal of all things; conclusive or decisive; relating to or constituting the end or purpose; as, a *final* cause.—*n.* Something final. *Usu. pl.* the last and decisive game or match in an athletic tournament; the last examination in a school course.

fi·na·le, fi·nal′ē, fi·nä′lē, *n.* [It. < L.L. *finalis,* E. *final.*] The final or concluding part, esp. if impressive or climactic, of an act of an opera, or of a musical composition; the concluding part of any performance or of any series.

fi·nal·ist, fīn′a·list, *n.* One who is entitled to take part in a final, decisive trial or round to determine the winner of a contest.

fi·nal·i·ty, fi·nal′i·tē, *n.* pl. **fi·nal·i·ties.** [L.L. *finalitas.*] The state or fact of being final, concluded, or irrevocable; the quality of or the manner suggesting conclusiveness or decisiveness; something that is final, as an act or utterance; a fundamental fact or belief.

fi·na·lize, fīn′a·liz″, *v.t.*—*finalized, finalizing.* To complete or make final; to arrange in final form; to sum up and set forth, as the details of a plan or proposal.

fi·nal·ly, fīn′a·lē, *adv.* At the final point or moment; in the end; in a final manner; conclusively or decisively.

fi·nance, fi·nans′, fī′nans, *n.* [Fr. < L.L. *financia,* a money payment, < *finare,* to pay a fine, < L. *finis.*] The management of pecuniary affairs, esp. in the fields of government, corporations, banking, and investment; the system of public revenue and expenditure; *pl.* income or resources of corporations, governments, or individuals.— *v.t.*—*financed, financing.* To supply with finances or money; provide capital for.—*v.i.* To conduct financial operations; manage finances.—**fi·nan·cing,** *n.* Raising or providing funds.—**fi·nan·cial,** fi·nan′shal, *a.* Of or pertaining to finance or money matters.—**fi·nan·cial·ly,** *adv.*

fin·an·cier, fin″an·sēr′, fī″·nan·sēr′, *Brit.* fi·nan′sē·er, *n.* [Fr.] One occupied with or skilled in financial affairs or operations.

fin·back, fin′bak″, *n.* Any whalebone whale of the genus *Balaenoptera,* having a prominent dorsal fin, as *B. physalus,* found on the Atlantic and Pacific coasts of the U.S. Also **fin·back whale.**

finch, finch, *n.* [O.E. *finc* = D. *vink* = G. *fink,* finch.] Any of the numerous small singing birds of the family *Fringillidae,* characterized by stout cone-shaped bills adapted for seed-eating, and including the buntings, sparrows, crossbills, goldfinches, grosbeaks, and linnets; any of various related birds.

find, find, *v.t.*—*found, finding.* [O.E. *findan* = D. *vinden* = G. *finden* = Icel. *finna* = Goth. *finthan,* find.] To come upon or encounter by chance; meet with; to discover, as: An astronomer *finds* a new star. To discover, learn, attain, or obtain by search or effort; as, to *find* the meaning of a word in a dictionary, to *find* time or money for a thing; to ascertain by study or calculation; as, to *find* the sum of several numbers; recover, as something lost; to meet with in experience or come to have; as, to *find* favor with the public; to discover or perceive upon examination or consideration; as, to *find* no harm in a proceeding; arrive at, as a destination, as: The arrow *found* its target. Gain or regain the use of; as, to *find* one's tongue; to provide or furnish; as, to *find* food and lodging for servants. *Law,* to determine after judicial inquiry; as, to *find* a person guilty; to agree upon and deliver, as a verdict.—*v.i. Law,* to determine an issue after judicial inquiry; render a verdict, as: The jury *found* for the plaintiff.—**find fault,** to discover or make known some defect or flaw; find cause for blame or complaint; express dissatisfaction. —**find one·self,** to come to a realization and acceptance of one's own capabilities and limitations and to conduct one's life accordingly.—**find out,** to discover or learn by search or inquiry; to detect, as an offense or fraud; to ascertain or discover the true character or identity of, as a person.

find, find, *n.* An act of finding; a discovery, esp. of something valuable; something that has been found.

find·er, fīn′dẽr, *n.* One who or that which finds; *astron.* a small telescope attached to a larger one for the purpose of finding an object more readily. *Photog.* a camera attachment or part which indicates how much subject area will be included in the finished picture; also **view·find·er.**

find·er's fee, *n. Business,* a commission or fee paid to one who introduces a customer, arranges financing, or independently performs similar negotiations or services on behalf of a commercial firm.

find·ing, fīn′ding, *n.* The act of one who or that which finds; discovery; something found or ascertained; *law,* a decision or verdict after judicial inquiry; *pl.* tools or materials used by artisans; as, shoemakers' or jewelers' *findings.*

fine, fin, *a.*—*finer, finest.* [O.Fr. Fr. *fin* = M.L. *finus,* appar. (as if meaning "brought to the final point," as of excellence) < L. *finire,* finish. FINISH.] Of the highest quality; of very high grade or quality; free from imperfections or impurities; choice, excellent, or admirable; as, a *fine* sermon; consisting of minute particles; as, *fine* sand, meal, or shot; very thin or slender; as, *fine* thread; keen or sharp, as a tool; delicate in texture; as, *fine* cloth; delicately fashioned; highly skilled or accomplished; as, a *fine* musician; trained to the proper degree, as an athlete; characterized by or affecting refinement or elegance; as, a *fine* lady; polished or refined; as, *fine* manners; affectedly ornate or elegant; as, *fine* language or writing; delicate or subtle, as a distinction; showy or smart, as dress; smartly dressed; good-looking or handsome; *metal.* having a high or a specified proportion of pure metal; as, gold 18 carats *fine.*— *adv. Colloq.* excellently; very well; finely.

Naut. as close to the wind as one can get.—*v.t.*—*fined, fining.* To make fine; purify, clarify, or refine; make small, thin, or slender.—*v.i.* To become fine; become pure, or clarify; become thin; dwindle.—**fine·ly,** *adv.*

fine, fīn, *n. Law,* a pecuniary payment exacted as punishment for an offense; any compensation coercively required of someone. *Eng. law,* a transfer of property by court decree in questions of possession, based on a quasi-legal hearing.—*v.t.*—*fined, fining.* To require monetary reparation on.—**in fine,** in short; finally.

fi·ne, fē′nā, *n.* [It.] *Mus.* end: a designation which marks the close of a repeated section or the close of a composition having several movements.

fine, fēn, *n.* [Fr.] A drink of brandy, usu. a commonplace bar brandy.

fine art, *n. pl.* **fine arts.** *Usu. pl.* art concerned with expressive and aesthetic beauty within the particular work itself, as painting, drawing, sculpture, architecture.

fine·ness, fīn′nis, *n.* The state or quality of being fine; the proportion of pure gold or silver in an alloy, often expressed as the number of parts in 1,000.

fin·er·y, fī′nė·rē, *n. pl.* **fin·er·ies.** Elaborate or showy adornment; fine clothes, jewels, or other ornamentation.

fines, fīnz, *n. pl.* A ground or powdered substance, as ore; a collection of minute particles of different sizes.

fines herbes, fēn′erbz′, fēn′urbz′, *Fr.* fēn zeRb′, *n. pl.* [Fr. fine herbs.] A combination of several finely-chopped herbs, as parsley, tarragon, chives, and chervil, used for seasoning in cooking.

fine·spun, fīn′spun′, *a.* Drawn to a fine thread; overrefined or subtle.

fi·nesse, fi·nes′, *n.* [O.Fr. Fr. *fin,* = M.L. *finus,* < L. *finire,* finish.] Delicacy of execution; subtlety of discrimination; artful management, as of a difficult situation requiring diplomatic handling; strategy; craft; an artifice; stratagem. In bridge and other card games, an attempt to win a trick with a lower card when a higher card not in sequence with it is held, in the hope that the holder of the intervening card has already played; certain similar plays in chess and other games.—*v.i.*—*finessed, finessing.* To make a finesse at cards.—*v.t.* To bring about or accomplish by finesse; in card games, to play as a finesse.

fin·ger, fing′gėr, *n.* [O.E. *finger* = D. *vinger* = G. *finger* = Icel. *fingr* = Goth. *figgrs,* finger.] Any of the terminal members of the hand other than the thumb; the part of a glove made to fit the finger; something resembling a finger in shape, intent, or use; the width of a finger, or ¾ inch; the length of a finger, or 4½ inches; any of various projecting parts of machines.

fin·ger, fing′gėr, *v.t.* To touch with the fingers; handle; toy or meddle with; to touch in such a way as to spoil; to pilfer. *Mus.* to play, as an instrument, with the fingers; to perform or mark, as a passage of music, with certain fingering.—*v.i.* To touch or handle something with the fingers; *mus.* to use the fingers in playing.

fin·ger board, *n. Mus.* the board at the neck of a stringed instrument, where fingers act on the strings; a keyboard.

fin·ger bowl, *n.* A bowl at a dining table to hold water for rinsing the fingers after eating.

fin·gered, fing′gėrd, *a.* Having fingers; having a particular number or kind of fingers; as, slippery-*fingered; biol.* digitate; *mus.* marked to indicate which fingers should be used to play the notes.

fin·ger·ing, fing′gėr·ing, *n.* The act of touching lightly or handling. *Mus.* the action of the fingers in playing on an instrument; the marking of the notes of a piece of music to guide the fingers in playing.

fin·ger·ling, fing′gėr·ling, *n.* A young fish, esp. a very small salmon or trout; something very small.

fin·ger·nail, fing′gėr·nāl″, *n.* The hard protective growth at the end of each of the fingers of the hand.

fin·ger paint·ing, *n. Art.* The technique of applying paint with the fingers on wet paper; a painting made by such a process.—**fin·ger-paint,** *v.i., v.t.*

fin·ger·print, fing′gėr·print″, *n.* An impression of the markings of the last joint of the thumb or a finger; this impression in ink, taken for purposes of identification.—*v.t.* To take the fingerprints of.

fin·ger·tip, fing′gėr·tip″, *n.* The tip of the finger.—**at one's fin·ger·tips,** readily available; at hand.

fin·i·al, fin′ē·al, fī′nē·al, *n.* [< L. *finio,* to finish. FINAL.] *Arch.* the ornamental termination of a pinnacle, canopy, gable, or the like. A terminal ornament or cap, as on a piece of furniture; the ornamental screw securing a lampshade.

fin·i·cal, fin′i·kal, *a.* [< *fine.*] Finicky, esp. affectedly fastidious.—**fin·i·cal·ly,** *adv.*—**fin·i·cal·ness, fin·i·cal·i·ty,** *n.*

fin·ick·y, fin′i·kē, *a.* Unduly particular; fussy. Also *finical.*—**fin·ick·ing.**—**fin·ick·i·ness,** *n.*

fin·is, fin′is, fē·nē′, fī′nis, *n. pl.* **fin·is·es.** [L.] End; conclusion.

fin·ish, fin′ish, *v.t.* [Fr. *finir,* ppr. *finissant* < L. *finio, finitum,* to finish, < *finis,* end.] To bring to an end; to arrive at the end of; to use up; to perfect; to polish to a high degree; *colloq.* to defeat or dispose of.—*v.i.* To complete a task; to come to an end of a work, project, or program; terminate.—*n.* The end or concluding stage of anything; perfection, as of detail, style, manner; that which completes, perfects, or polishes; a last coat, as of paint or varnish, applied to a surface.—**fin·ished,** *a.* Completed; polished to the highest degree; defeated.—**fin·ish·er,** *n.*

fin·ish·ing school, *n.* A private school which instructs young women in the social graces.

fi·nite, fī′nīt, *a.* [L. *finitus,* pp. of *finire.* FINISH.] Having bounds or limits; not too great or too small to be measured; not infinite or infinitesimal; subject to limitations or conditions, as of space, time, circumstances, or the laws of nature; *gram.* of verbs, limited by person, number, and tense, as distinguished from infinitives and participles. *Math.* of a line, having a termination; of a number or quantity, having limits and able to be determined by counting or measuring.—*n.* That which is finite, or finite things collectively, usu. preceded by *the.*—**fi·nite·ly,** *adv.*—**fi·nite·ness, fin·i·tude,** fin′i·tŏd″, fin′i·tūd″, *n.*

fink, fingk, *n. Slang.* A strikebreaker; a detective or policeman; an informant; a contemptible or undesirable person.—*v.i. Slang.* To inform, esp. to the police; to act as a strikebreaker.

Finn, fin, *n.* A native or inhabitant of Finland; one who speaks Finnish as a native language.

fin·nan had·die, fin′an had′ē, *n.* Smoked haddock. Also **fin·nan had·dock.**

Finn·ish, fin′ish, *a.* Belonging or pertaining to, or characteristic of Finland, the Finns, or their language.—*n.* A language of the Finno-Ugric subfamily which is the chief language of Finland, also spoken in parts of Sweden and Norway and in the Karelian region of the Soviet Union. Also **Finn·ic,** fin′ik.

Fin·no-U·gric, fin″ō·ŏ′grik, fin″ō·ū′grik, *a.* Of or pertaining to any of various peoples of eastern Europe and western parts of Siberia, esp. the Finns, Lapps, Estonians, and Hungarians; of or relating to the languages spoken by these peoples.—*n.* One of two subfamilies of the Uralic language family including Finnish, Lapp, Estonian, and Hungarian. Also **Fin·no-U·gri·an.**

fin·ny, fin′ē, *a.*—*finnier, finniest.* Having fins; of the nature of a fin; of, pertaining to, or containing fish.

fiord, fyôrd, fyârd, *Norw.* fyōR, fyuR, *n.* Fjord.

fip·ple flute, *n.* A flutelike instrument, as a recorder, with a slitted wooden plug at its mouthpiece.

fir, fėr, *n.* [O.E. *furh* = Icel. Sw. *fura,* Dan. *fyr, fyrre,* G. *föhre. Fir* represents an ancient word, which appears in L. as *quercus,* an oak, and probably meant originally, tree in general.] Any of several species of coniferous trees, genus *Abies,* of the pine family; the wood of a fir tree.

fire, fīėr, *n.* [O.E. *fyr* = Icel. *fyri,* Dan. and Sw. *fyr,* G. *feuer,* fire; cog. Gr. *pyr,* fire; allied to Skt. *pu,* to purify, as fire is the great purifying element.] Rapid combustion in which a substance ignites and burns, producing heat, light, and flame; fuel in combustion; burning which causes destruction, as of a house or town; conflagration; a firelike flash or spark; the discharge of a number of firearms; a rapid succession, as of questions; ardor of passion; liveliness of imagination; heat; fever; severe verbal criticism; harsh ordeal or trial.—*v.t.*—*fired, firing.* To set on fire; kindle; to add fuel to; to heat, as for baking or drying; to inflame or irritate; to animate; to cause to explode; to discharge, as a gun or shot; to throw or hurl; *colloq.* to discharge from a job.—*v.i.* To take fire; to be irritated or inflamed; to explode or shoot; to discharge artillery or firearms.—**on fire,** ignited; burning; eager; ardent.—**fire a·way,** to begin; to continue with vigor, esp. in interrogation.—**fire up,** to become irritated or angry.—**fir·er,** *n.*

fire·arm, fīėr′ärm,″ *n.* A weapon whose charge is expelled by the explosion of gunpowder, usu. a small weapon, as a rifle or revolver.

fire·ball, fīėr′bal″, *n.* A meteor having the appearance of a globular mass of light; lightning shaped like a ball; the center of a nuclear explosion; an old type of grenade; *slang,* a vigorous or energetic person.

fire blight, *n.* A highly destructive bacterial disease affecting some fruit trees, esp. apple and pear, in which the foliage appears burnt.

fire·boat, fīėr′bōt″, *n.* A boat equipped with water-pumping apparatus for extinguishing fires.

fire·brand, fīėr′brand″, *n.* A piece of burning wood; an incendiary; one who stirs up dissension or creates strife.

fire·break, fīėr′brāk″, *n.* A strip of land which has been cleared to prevent the spread of a forest or brush fire.

fire·brick, fīėr′brik″, *n.* A brick made of fire clay, capable of withstanding great heat, as of industrial furnaces.

fire·bug, fīėr′bug″, *n. Slang.* An arsonist; a pyromaniac.

fire clay, *n.* A type of clay capable of sustaining intense heat and used in making firebricks, gas retorts, crucibles, etc.

fire con·trol, *n. Milit.* the technically controlled delivery of gunfire or missiles on a target; the control of fires.

fire·crack·er, fīėr′krak″ėr, *n.* A firework consisting of a paper cylinder enclosing an explosive and a fuse which can be ignited.

fire-cure, fīėr′kur″, *v.t.*—*firecured, firecuring.* To preserve or cure, as meat or fish, by means of an open fire and smoke.—**fire-cured,** *a.*

---

ch- chain, G. na*ch*t;   **th-** THen, thin;   **w-** wig, hw as sound in whig;   **z-** zh as in azure, zeal.   *Italicized vowel* indicates schwa sound.

fire·damp, fīer′damp″, *n.* A highly combustible gas, predominately methane, formed in coal mines; the explosive mixture formed by methane gas and air.

fire de·part·ment, *n.* The department of public service assigned to the prevention and extinguishing of fires; the personnel of this department. Also *Brit.* **fire bri·gade.**

fire·drake, fīer′drāk″, *n.* [M.E. *fyrdrake,* < O.E. *fyrdraca.*] A mythical fire-breathing dragon.

fire drill, *n.* A practice drill for a company of firemen, or other similar group, to accustom them to their duties in case of fire; a drill for pupils in a school, or other individuals, to train them in the manner of exit to be followed in case of fire.

fire-eat·er, fīer′ē″tér, *n.* A magician who pretends to eat fire; a belligerent or quarrelsome person.

fire en·gine, *n.* A truck equipped to pump pressurized jets of water or fire-fighting chemicals to extinguish fires.

fire es·cape, *n.* Any device which enables the occupants of a building to escape during a fire, as a steel stairway affixed to the exterior of the building. *Brit.* a wheeled extension ladder.

fire ex·tin·guish·er, *n.* A portable device which is used to extinguish fires by ejecting chemicals or water in spray form.

fire·fly, fīer′flī″, *n.* *pl.* **fire·flies.** Any winged insect which gives off light, esp. members of the family *Lampyridae;* a lightning bug.

fire·guard, fīer′gärd″, *n.* A metal framework placed in front of a fireplace as protection; an outdoor area cleared of all flammable matter to prevent fire from spreading; a person employed to put out fires; a person employed to watch for the outbreak of fires.

fire·house, fīer′hous″, *n.* Fire station.

fire i·rons, *n. pl.* Tools or equipment for a fireplace, as poker, tongs, shovel, and andirons.

fire·light, fīer′līt″, *n.* The light from an open fire, as in a hearth or campfire.

fire·lock, fīer′lok″, *n.* A gunlock in which sparks from a flint ignite the priming; a gun with such a lock; a flintlock musket.

fire·man, fīer′man, *n. pl.* **fire·men.** A man employed to fight fires; a man who tends fires in a furnace or steam engine, as a stoker; *U.S. Navy,* an enlisted man whose duty it is to operate and care for a ship's machinery; *Brit.* a mine inspector.

fire o·pal, *n.* A semiprecious, usu. red, stone; girasol.

fire pink, *n.* A plant of the genus *Silene,* having a sticky calyx and stem and bearing crimson flowers; a catchfly.

fire·place, fīer′plās″, *n.* The lower part of a chimney which opens into a room and in which fuel is burned; a hearth; an outdoor construction of stone or brick built for open fires.

fire·plug, fīer′plug″, *n.* A hydrant which provides a water supply for extinguishing fires.

fire pow·er, *n. Milit.* the volume of projectiles that can be delivered on a specific target in a given period of time by a weapon or military unit, or by a tank or battleship. Also **fire·pow·er.**

fire·proof, fīer′prōf″, *a.* Proof against fire; almost totally resistant to fire; incombustible.—*v.t.* To make fireproof.—**fire·proofed,** *a.*

fire sale, *n.* A sale in which goods are offered at reduced prices because of damage by fire, smoke, or water.

fire screen, *n.* A screen, usu. of metal, placed before a hearth, esp. used to prevent damage caused by flying sparks.

fire·side, fīer′sīd″, *n.* The side of the fireplace; the hearth; home.—*a.* Informal or

friendly, as: President F. D. Roosevelt broadcast his *fireside* chats on radio.

fire sta·tion, *n.* A building which houses firemen and fire-fighting equipment; a firehouse.

fire·stone, fīer′stōn″, *n.* Any kind of stone which resists the action of fire; a flint used to strike fire.

fire storm, *n.* A severe air disturbance caused by a large fire, in which hot air rising over the fire causes strong winds of cooler air to rush in, speeding the spread of the fire.

fire tow·er, *n.* A tower from which forest rangers or wardens can watch for and report fires.

fire·trap, fīer′trap″, *n.* A building which could easily catch on fire and threaten its occupants.

fire wall, *n.* A fireproof wall built to keep a fire from spreading beyond a specified area; *aeron.* a fireproof bulkhead behind an aircraft engine designed to retard or prevent the spreading of a fire.

fire·ward·en, fīer′wạr″den, *n.* An officer responsible for preventing or extinguishing fires, as in a woodland or community.

fire·wa·ter, fīer′wạ″tér, fīer′wot″er, *n. Slang,* strong liquor: a term first used by American Indians.

fire·weed, fīer′wēd″, *n.* Any of numerous plants, of the genus *Epilobium,* as the willow herb, that grows abundantly on burned or cleared land.

fire·wood, fīer′wụd″, *n.* Wood for fuel, esp. logs cut in short lengths.

fire·works, fīer′wụrks″, *n. pl.* Firecrackers or other combustible or explosive devices for producing brilliant displays of light or loud noise, as on the Fourth of July; a pyrotechnic display; an explosive show of temper, esp. involving two people.

fir·ing, fīer′ing, *n.* The art of one who fires; the act or process of vitrifying, baking, or setting on fire; the discharge of firearms; material for burning; fuel.

fir·ing line, *n. Milit.* The place from which troops fire upon a target or enemy; the troops stationed at the line; the point of decisive action in an activity.

fir·ing pin, *n.* A pin that strikes the primer or detonator of a firearm, igniting the charge of the ammunition.

fir·ing range, *n.* An area equipped with targets for gunnery practice; the range or distance from a target at which a weapon can be fired effectively.

fir·ing squad, *n.* A military squad assigned to carry out an execution by shooting; a similar squad assigned to fire a salvo at the burial of a person receiving military honors.

fir·kin, fụr′kin, fér′kin, *n.* [M.E. *ferdekyn,* appar. a dim. < D. *vierde,* fourth.] *Brit.* a measure of capacity, usu. one quarter of a barrel; a small wooden vessel for butter or lard.

firm, fụrm, *n.* [It. and Sp. *firma,* signature, < L. *firmare,* confirm, E. *firm, v.*] A partnership of two or more persons for carrying on a business; a commercial concern; the name or style under which associated persons do business.

firm, fụrm, *v.t.* [O.Fr. *fermer,* make firm, fix (Fr. close), < L. *firmare,* make firm, confirm, < *firmus.*] To make firm in consistency or texture, as: Massage *firms* the skin. To tighten or fix securely in place; to confirm, bolster, or make definite, often followed by *up;* as, *firm up* an offer.—*v.i.* To become firm.

firm, fụrm, *a.* [O.Fr. Fr. *ferme,* < L. *firmus,* firm, stable, steadfast, strong.] Having a compact consistency; as, *firm* jelly; comparatively solid, stiff, or unyielding under pressure; securely held in place, fast, or immovable; as, a candle *firm* in its socket; fixed, settled, or unalterable, as a

belief or decree; steady, or not shaking; as, a *firm* hand; not fluctuating or falling, as prices or the market; not subject to change; as, a *firm* offer; steadfast or unwavering; showing resoluteness or determination.—**firm·ly,** *adv.*—**firm·ness,** *n.*

fir·ma·ment, fụr′ma·ment, fér′ma·ment, *n.* [L. *firmamentum,* < *firmo, firmatum,* to make firm.] The arch of heaven, or the sky and the celestial bodies.—**fir·ma·men·tal,** fụr″ma·men′tal, fér″ma·men′tal, *a.*

firn, firn, *n.* Névé.

first, fụrst, *a.* [O.E. *fyrst* = O.H.G. *furist* (G. *fürst,* prince) = Icel. *fyrstr,* foremost, first; a superl. form akin to E. *fore.*] Being before all others in time, order, rank, or importance; the ordinal of one; *mus.* highest or principal among several like voices or instruments; as, *first* violin in an orchestra.—*adv.* Before all others or anything else in time, order, rank, or importance; in the first place; before some other thing, event, or action; in preference to something else; sooner; for the first time.

first, fụrst, *n.* That which is before all others in time, order, rank, or importance; the beginning; the first part; the first member of a series; the highest place in competition; in an automobile, low gear; *Brit.* a place in the first or highest group in an examination for honors; *mus.* the highest or foremost among like instruments or voices.

first aid, *n.* Emergency aid or treatment given to the victim of an accident or sudden illness before regular medical services can be obtained.

first base, *n. Baseball,* the base that is to be reached first by a base runner; the position of the player defending the area around that base.—**get to first base,** *slang,* to achieve the first step toward a goal, usu. used in the negative.

first-born, fụrst′bạrn″, *a.* Of a child, first brought forth; eldest.—*n.* The child born first to a given parent or parents.

first cause, *n. Philos.* the basic source of all causality, which does not owe its existence to any other causative factor; prime mover in a chain of causality; (*cap.*) God, the self-created *First Cause* of all creation.

first class, *n.* The first, best, or highest rank, level, or grade of something; the finest class of passenger accommodations, as on an airplane, train, or steamship; a category of U.S. mail including letters, post cards, and sealed matter which may not be inspected; *Brit.* the group of individuals earning highest recognition in a university honors course.—**first-class,** *a., adv.*

first·hand, first-hand, fụrst′hand″, *a., adv.* Obtained from the first source or point of origin; direct.

first la·dy, *n.* (*Often cap.*) the wife of the U.S. president or a state governor; the wife of the chief executive of any country. An outstanding woman in an art, profession, or sport.

first lieu·ten·ant, *n. Milit.* a commissioned officer ranking below a captain and above a second lieutenant in the army, air force, and marine corps of most countries.

first·ling, fụrst′ling, *n.* The first of its kind to be produced or to appear; the first product or result, esp. the first offspring of an animal.

first·ly, fụrst′lē, *adv.* In the first place; first.

first mort·gage, *n.* A lien on real or personal property ranking above other liens.

first-night·er, fụrst′nī′tér, *n.* One who makes a practice of attending the theater or opera on the nights of the first public performances.

first of·fen·der, *n.* A person legally convicted for the first time of an offense against the law.

first pa·pers, *n. pl.* The initial step in the process of naturalization when an alien files his first application declaring his intention to become a citizen of the U.S.A.

first per·son, *n. Gram.* the linguistic forms of pronouns and verbs, used by the speaker or writer of a statement while referring to himself in that statement, as, *I, we, am;* a style of speech or writing characterized by a general use of linguistic forms of the first person.

first-rate, fŭrst′rāt′, *a.* Of the first rate or class; excellent; very good.—*adv.* Excellently; very well.—**first-rat·er,** *n.*

first read·ing, *n.* The formal stage of a Bill after its introduction in the U.S. House of Representatives, including a reading of the title of the Bill and the scheduling of it for the second reading.

first ser·geant, *n.* A senior officer of non-commissioned rank in the Army or Navy, in charge of the personnel management or administration of a company or other military unit.

first-string, fŭrst′string′, *a.* In the category of the most important or most highly esteemed; first-rate; regular, as against substitute or temporarily placed; as, the *first-string* quarterback in a football game.

first wa·ter, *n.* The purest luster or highest quality, applied principally to precious stones, as diamonds and pearls; *fig.* the first or highest quality or degree.

firth, fŭrth, *n.* [< Icel. *fjorth,* Dan. *fiord,* N. *fjord,* a firth.] *Chiefly Sc.* an estuary or narrow bay; as, *Firth* of Forth in Scotland. Also *frith.*

fis·cal, fis′kal, *a.* [L. *fiscus,* the state treasury.] Of or pertaining to financial affairs; pertaining to the public treasury or public revenues.—*n.* A revenue stamp; in the Philippines and some European countries, a public official, as a prosecutor.—**fis·cal·ly,** *adv.*—**fis·cal year,** a twelve-month period for which a complete financial accounting is made. Compare *calendar year.*

fish, fish, *n. pl.* **fish, fish·es.** [O.E. *fisc* = D. *visch* = G. *fisch* = Icel. *fiskr* = Goth. *fisks,* fish; akin to L. *piscis,* fish.] Popularly, one of the various aquatic animals including true fish, shellfish, starfish. *Zool.* a cold-blooded, completely aquatic vertebrate, having an elongated body, often covered with scales and with fins and gills, including the classes *Cyclostomata, Chondrichthyes,* and *Osteichthyes;* fish used as food. A strip of wood or iron used to strengthen a mast; *astron.* one of the signs of the zodiac, the constellation, Pisces; *slang,* an unexperienced, gullible person; an odd person; as, a queer *fish.*—**fish·like,** *a.*

fish, fish, *v.i.* [O.E. *fiscian.*] To catch or attempt to catch fish; to search for something; to attempt to catch onto something, esp. something underwater, using a hook, a dredge, or other specialized equipment; to seek to obtain something indirectly or by artifice; as, to *fish* for compliments.—*v.t.* To catch or attempt to catch, as fish or the like; to try to catch fish in, as a stream; to draw as by fishing, often followed by *up* or *out,* as: She *fished* her shoes *out* from under the bed. *Naut.* to reinforce or strengthen, as a mast or joint, by a narrow strip of wood or metal called a fish; to raise the flukes of (an anchor) to secure it to the deck or the side of a vessel.—**fish·a·ble,** *a.*—**go fish·ing,** *fig.* To scatter or extend widely one's search for information, evidence, political support, etc.; to withdraw from active participation.

fish-and-chips, fish″an·chips′, *n. pl.* Fried fish and French fried potatoes, a popular dish in the United Kingdom.

fish cake, *n.* A small ball of shredded fish, as codfish, mixed with mashed potato, seasoned, and fried. Also **fish ball.**

fish·er, fish′ẽr, *n.* [O.E. *fiscere.*] One who fishes; a fisherman; a North American mammal, *Martes pennanti,* related to the marten and the weasel; the dark brown pelt of this animal.

fish·er·man, fish′ẽr·man, *n. pl.* **fish·er·men.** One engaged in fishing, for profit or pleasure; a boat employed in fishing.

fish·er·y, fish′e·rē, *n. pl.* **fish·er·ies.** The occupation or industry of catching fish, shellfish, or other products of the sea or streams; a place where such an industry is regularly carried on; a fishing establishment; *law,* the right of fishing in certain waters.

fish·hook, fish′hụk″, *n.* A hook, usu. barbed, used for catching fish.

fish·ing, fish′ing, *n.* The art or practice of catching fish as an occupation or for sport and recreation.—*a.* Used or employed in fishery or by fishermen.

fish meal, *n.* A fertilizer and food for animals made from finely ground dried fish.

fish·mong·er, fish′mung″ẽr, fish′mong′ẽr, *n. Brit.* a dealer in fish.

fish stick, *n.* A commercially frozen, breaded and fried, oblong-shaped piece of fish.

fish sto·ry, *n. Colloq.* an extravagant or incredible story or tale.

fish·tail, fish′tāl″, *a.* Suggesting a fish's tail in shape or motion.—*n.* A transition piece of a turbojet engine.—*v.i. Aeron.* to swing the tail of an airplane from side to side, esp. in order to lose speed before touchdown; *colloq.* to swing an automobile or to skid, esp. with the weight of the car on the rear wheels.

fish·wife, fish′wīf″, *n. pl.* **fish·wives.** A woman who sells fish; a loud, vulgar, abusive woman.

fish·y, fish′ē, *a.*—*fishier, fishiest.* Pertaining to fishes; having the taste or odor of fish. *Colloq.* dubious; questionable; undependable.

fis·sile, fis′il, *a.* [L. *fissilis,* < *findere,* cleave, split.] Capable of being split or divided; cleavable; capable of nuclear fission.—**fis·sil·i·ty,** fi·sil′i·tē, *n.*

fis·sion, fish′an, *n.* [L. *fissio(n-),* < *findere* (pp. *fissus*), cleave, split.] The act of cleaving or splitting into parts; *biol.* the division of a cell or organism into new cells or organisms as a process of reproduction. *Phys.* the splitting of a nucleus of a heavy atom into nuclei of lighter atoms and the resultant release of energy. Also **nu·cle·ar fis·sion.**—**fis·sion·a·ble,** *a.*—**fis·sion·a·bil·i·ty,** fish″an·a·bil′i·tē, *n.*

fis·sion bomb, *n.* Atomic bomb.

fis·sip·a·rous, fi·sip′ẽr·us, *a.* Reproducing by fission or spontaneous division; tending to divide or separate into parts or factions, as an organization or party.—**fis·sip·a·rous·ly,** *adv.*—**fis·sip·a·rous·ness,** *n.*

fis·si·ped, fis′i·ped″, *a.* Having separated toes. Also **fis·sip·e·dal, fis·si·pe·di·al.** fi·sip′e·dal, fis′i·ped″al, fis″i·pē″dē·al.—*n.*

fis·sure, fish′ẽr, *n.* [Fr. < L. *fissura,* < *findo,* to split.] A cleft; a crack; a narrow opening caused by the breaking or separating of parts. *Anat.* any cleft or groove in an organ, as in the brain.—*v.t., v.i.*—*fissured, fissuring.* To cleave or make a fissure in; to crack or fracture.

fist, fist, *n.* [O.E. *fȳst* = D. *vuist* = G. *faust,* fist.] The hand closed tightly, with the fingers doubled into the palm; a grasp or hold; *print.* the index sign. *Colloq.* the hand; a person's handwriting.—*v.t.* To grasp in the fist; to clench, as the hand, into a fist; to strike with the fist.

fist·ic, fis′tik, *a.* Of or pertaining to boxing; of or pertaining to the fists; pugilistic.

fist·i·cuff, fis′ti·kuf″, *n.* A cuff or blow with the fists; *pl.* combat with the fists.—*v.t., v.i.* To strike or fight with the fists.—**fist·i·cuff·er,** *n.*

fis·tu·la, fis′chụ·la, *n. pl.* **fis·tu·las, fis·tu·lae,** fis′chụ·lē. [L. pipe, tube, reed, ulcer.] *Pathol.* an abnormal duct or passage caused by injury or disease, as one leading from an abscess to the body surface or from one cavity or hollow organ to another. *Vet. pathol.* any of various suppurative inflammations, as in the withers of a horse; also **fis·tu·lous with·ers.**—**fis·tu·lar, fis·tu·lous,** *a.* Tubelike; containing tubes or tubelike parts; *pathol.* pertaining to a fistula.

fit, fit, *n.* [O.E. *fitt,* fight, struggle.] An attack or manifestation of a disease characterized by loss of consciousness or by convulsions; an uncontrollable attack of any physical disturbance; as, a *fit* of coughing; an intensive but brief surge or occurrence of something; as, a *fit* of enthusiasm or activity; an uncontrolled expression of emotion.—**by fits and starts,** at irregular intervals; intermittently.—**throw a fit,** *slang,* to become enraged or violently angry.

fit, fit, *a.*—*fitter, fittest.* [M.E. *fyt;* origin uncertain: cf. *feat.*] Well adapted or suited, as for a purpose or occasion; as, *fit* to be eaten; worthy or deserving; as, not *fit* to be repeated; proper, becoming, or right as a course of action; as, to do as one sees *fit;* suitable by reason of qualifications, as for a position, office, or function; in a suitable condition, prepared, or ready; as, crops *fit* for gathering; in good physical condition; as, feeling *fit.*—**fit·ly,** *adv.*—**fit·ness,** *n.*—**fit to be tied,** *colloq.* deeply irked or angered.

fit, fit, *v.t.*—*fitted* or *fit, fitting.* To suit or be proper, becoming, or suitable for; to be of the right size or shape for, as: The keys *fit* the lock. To alter or adjust to a purpose; to adjust to a prescribed size or shape; as, to *fit* the dress to the figure; to put into exact place; as, to *fit* the clothes into one drawer; to render qualified or competent; to prepare, as: High schools *fit* students for college. To supply; as, to *fit* the door with a handle; to furnish or equip, often with *out;* as, to *fit out* a person for a hunting trip.—*v.i.* To be of the right size or shape for a particular person or thing as: The dress *fits.* To belong, go with, or be in agreement with, often followed by *in, into,* or *with,* as: You *fit into* our group easily.—*n.* The condition of fitting or being fitted, suited, or adapted; the manner in which a thing fits; as, a loose, tight, or perfect *fit;* something, esp. clothing, that fits well, as: This coat is a good *fit.*

fit, fit, *n. Archaic,* a division of a song, poem, or story.

fitch, fich, *n.* [O.D. *vitsche,* O.Fr. *fissau,* a polecat; akin *foist.*] The polecat of Europe, *Mustela putorius;* the fur of the polecat. Also **fitch·et, fitch·ew,** fich′it, fich′ō.

fit·ful, fit′fụl, *a.* Occurring in starts and stops; characterized by irregular, intermittent movement.—**fit·ful·ly,** *adv.*—**fit·ful·ness,** *n.*

fit·ment, fit′ment, *n.* Equipment; *usu. pl.* fittings or fixtures.

fit·ter, fit′ẽr, *n.* One who or that which fits; one who fits or alters garments; one who puts together the parts of machinery; a person who installs fittings or fixtures; one who outfits or supplies.

fit·ting, fit′ing, *n.* The act of one who or that which fits; the act of trying on clothes for the purpose of alteration; a standardized fixture or part; *pl.* furnishings or fixtures.—*a.* Fit or appropriate; suitable; proper.—**fit·ting·ly,** *adv.*—**fit·ting·ness,** *n.*

five, fiv, *a.* [O.E. *fíf* = Goth. *fimf,* Icel. *fimm,* Sw. and Dan. *fem,* D. *viif,* G. *fünf,*

Lith. *penki*, W. *pump*, Gael. *coig*, L. *quinque*, Gr. *pempe, pente*, Skt. *panchan*— five.] One more than four in number.—*n.* The cardinal number between four and six; a symbol representing this number; a set of five persons or things.—**five-fold**, *a.* Consisting of five parts; five times repeated; in fives.

five-and-ten, fīv′an·ten′, *n.* Originally, a store selling merchandise marked at 5 or 10 cents; a store selling mainly inexpensive items. Also **five-and-dime, five-and-ten-cent-store**, *dime store.*

five·fin·ger, fīv′fing″gėr, *n. Bot.* a species of the genus *Potentilla*, having leaves consisting of five leaflets; cinquefoil. *Zool.* a five-rayed starfish.

fiv·er, fī′vėr, *n. Slang*, a five-dollar bill; *Brit.* a five-pound note.

five-star, fīv′stär′, *a.* Having five stars indicating top military rank; as, a *five-star* general; of the best quality or merit.

fix, fiks, *v.t.* [L. *fixus*, pp. of *figere*, fix, fasten, drive in, pierce.] To make fast, firm, or stable; to place or attach permanently; to implant firmly, as principles; to settle definitely; to determine; to direct, as the eyes, steadily or unwaveringly; to look at with a steady gaze; to set or make rigid; to make permanent or stable; to repair; to put in order or good condition; to adjust or arrange; to provide or supply; to prepare, as a meal. *Slang*, to bribe, as a jury or athlete; to secure favorable action; to castrate or spay, as a pet; to beat up or cause to fail; to get even with. *Chem.* to make stable or more permanent by decreasing or destroying volatility; *photog.* to make permanent by chemical treatment, as a photographic negative.—*v.i.* To become fixed; to become firmly attached or implanted; to become stable or permanent; to assume a rigid or solid form; to become steadily directed, as the eyes or the attention; *dial.* to intend or plan.—**fix on** or **up·on**, to decide upon.—**fix·a·ble**, *a.*

fix, fiks, *n. Colloq.* a position from which it is difficult to escape; a predicament. The position of an aircraft or a ship as determined by bearings taken on two or more known points, by observations, or by radio. *Slang*, an act of determining the outcome of a sporting event or of obtaining immunity from the law by bribery or collusion; an injection of a narcotic, esp. heroin; the narcotic or quantity injected.

fix·ate, fik′sāt, *v.t.*—*fixated, fixating.* [Appar. a back-formation from *fixation*.] To fix; render stable or fixed; *psychoanalysis*, to concentrate, as the libido, on an infantile stage of emotional development or form of gratification.—*v.i.* To become fixed. *Psychoanalysis*, to develop a fixation; to suffer abatement at a particular stage of sexual or emotional development.

fix·a·tion, fik·sā′shan, *n.* [M.E. < M.L. *fixatio(n-)*, < *fixare*, freq. of L. *figere*. FIX.] The act of fixing or the state of being fixed; *chem.* reduction from a volatile or fluid to a stable or solid form. Popularly, an unhealthy obsession or compelling preoccupation. *Psychoanalysis*, an attaching or arresting of emotional and psychosexual development at an early or infantile stage, often due to a childhood trauma.

fix·a·tive, fik′sa·tiv, *a.* Serving to fix; making fixed or permanent.—*n.* A fixative substance; a varnish sprayed on drawings, esp. those done in crayon or chalk, to fix the colors and prevent blurring; a substance that impedes evaporation, used esp. in the manufacture of perfume; a hardening or preserving solution used to prepare material for microscopic study.

fixed, fikst, *a.* Made firm or permanent; firmly implanted; set or intent upon something; steadily directed; definitely or

permanently placed; stationary; definite, not fluctuating or varying; occurring on the same date each year; put in order; *colloq.* arranged privately or dishonestly; *chem.* non-volatile or not easily volatilized; as, a *fixed* oil.—**fix·ed·ly**, fik′sid·lē, *adv.*—**fix·ed·ness**, *n.*

fixed as·set, *n. Usu. pl.* an item of value of a relatively permanent nature, used to operate a business, but not intended to be converted to cash, as land, buildings, and equipment.

fixed charge, *n.* An expense that does not fluctuate and cannot be avoided, such as taxes or rent.

fixed star, *n.* A star so distant that it seemingly retains the same position with respect to the stars around it.

fix·er, fik′sėr, *n.* One who uses his influence or pays bribes to help himself or others gain special privileges, political favors, or immunity from the law.

fix·ing, fik′sing, *n.* The act of one who or that which fixes; *pl., colloq.* appropriate trimmings or accompaniments.

fix·i·ty, fik′si·tē, *n. pl.* **fix·i·ties.** [= Fr. *fixité*.] The state or quality of being fixed; stability; permanence; something fixed or stable.

fix·ture, fiks′chėr, *n.* [L.L. *fixura*.] Something securely fixed in position; a part of equipment permanently attached to a dwelling, automobile, or machine; as, a gas *fixture*; a person or thing long established in the same place or position. *Brit.* a fixed or appointed time for a sporting event; the event itself. *Law*, a personal chattel annexed to real property and legally regarded as a part of it.

fizz, fiz, *v.i.* [Imit.] To make a hissing or sputtering sound; to show exhilaration.—*n.* A hissing sound; effervescence. *Colloq.* spirit or verve; an effervescent drink; a mixed drink of lemon juice, sugar, soda, and liquor; as, gin *fizz.*

fiz·zle, fiz′l, *v.i.*—*fizzled, fizzling.* [Imit.: cf. *fizz* and *fissle.*] To make a hissing or sputtering sound esp. one that dies out weakly; *colloq.* to fail ignominiously after a more or less brilliant start.—*n.* A hissing or sputtering sound. *Colloq.* a fiasco; a failure.

fizz·y, fiz′ē, *a.*—*fizzier, fizziest.* Effervescent; bubbly.

fjeld, fyeld, *Norw.* fyel, *n.* [Norw.] A high, almost barren Scandinavian plateau.

fjord, fiord, fyōrd, fyard, *Norw.* fyŭr, fyör, *n.* [Dan. *fiord*; Icel. *fjörthr.* FIRTH.] A long, narrow sea inlet bordered by steep cliffs, as is common on the coast of Norway.

flab·ber·gast, flab′ėr·gast, *v.t.* [Origin obscure.]. To overcome with surprise and bewilderment; astound.

flab·by, flab′ē, *a.*—*flabbier, flabbiest.* [For earlier *flappy*, < *flap*.] Hanging loosely or limply, as flesh or muscles; flaccid; lacking firmness, force, or resilience, as character, principles, or utterances; feeble.—**flab·bi·ly**, *adv.*—**flab·bi·ness**, *n.*

fla·bel·late, fla·bel′it, fla·bel′āt, *a. Biol.* fan-shaped. Also **fla·bel·li·form.**

fla·bel·lum, fla·bel′um, *n. pl.* **fla·bel·la**, fla·bel′a. [L. fan, < *flare*, blow.] A fan, esp. one used in religious ceremonies; a fan-shaped structure.

flac·cid, flak′sid, *a.* [L. *flaccidus*, < *flaccus*, flabby.] Soft and limp; flabby; not firm; lacking vigor.—**flac·cid·ly**, *adv.*—**flac·cid·ness**, *n.*

flac·on, flak′on, *Fr.* flä·kạn′, *n.* [Fr.] A small bottle or flask with a stopper.

flag, flag, *v.i.*—*flagged, flagging.* [Appar. a later form of M.E. *flacken*, flap, flutter; = Icel. *flaka*, flap, hang loose.] To decline in vigor, energy, interest, or activity, as: The conversation *flags*. To hang loosely or limply, as sails; become limp; droop, as plants.

flag, flag, *n.* [= D. *vlag* = Dan. *flag* = Sw. *flagg* = G. *flagge*; appar. recorded first in

Eng.: cf. *flag*.] A piece of cloth, commonly bunting, of varying size, shape, design, and color, usually attached at one edge to a staff or cord, and used as an ensign, standard, symbol, or signal; as, the *flag* of a nation; something resembling a flag; the tail of a deer or of a setter dog; *mus.* a line or hook, attached to the end of the stem of a note, which indicates the note's value.—*v.t.* —*flagged, flagging.* To place a flag or flags over or on; decorate with flags; to signal or warn, as a person or motor vehicle, with or as with a flag; to decoy, as game, by waving a flag or the like to arouse curiosity.—**flag down**, to signal to stop, as a train, with or as with a flag.

flag, flag, *n.* [M.E. *flagge*; origin uncertain.] Any of various plants with long, sword-shaped leaves; as, the sweet *flag* or purple iris; the long, slender leaf of such a plant.—**flag·gy**, *a.*—*flaggier, flaggiest.* Profuse with or resembling flag plants.

flag, flag, *n.* [M.E. *flagge*, a turf: cf. Icel. *flag*, spot where a turf has been cut out, *flaga*, flag, or slab of stone.] A flat slab of stone used for paving; a flagstone. *Pl.* an area, as a walk, paved with flagstones; also *flagging.*—*v.t.*—*flagged, flagging.* To pave with flags.—**flag·gy**, *a.*—*flaggier, flaggiest.* Pertaining to flags or flagstone; having a structure like flagstone; laminate.

flag·el·lant, flaj′e·lant, fla·jel′ant, *n.* One who whips, esp. one who whips himself or is whipped by another for religious discipline or erotic excitement; *(often cap.)* a member of a fanatical religious sect of medieval Europe which practiced whipping in public.—*a.*—**flag·el·lant·ism**, *n.*

flag·el·late, flaj′e·lāt″, *v.t.*—*flagellated, flagellating.* [L. *flagello, flagellatum*, to beat or whip, < *flagellum*, a whip, scourge, dim. of *flagrum*, a whip, a scourge; akin *flail*.] To whip; to scourge.—**flag·el·la·tion**, *n.* A flogging, esp. for religious discipline or abnormal sexual gratification.

flag·el·late, flaj′e·lit, flaj′e·lāt″, *a.* [FLAGELLUM.] Having flagella; having the shape of a flagellum; of or caused by flagellates. Also **flag·el·lat·ed.**—*n.* A protozoan or alga with flagella.—**flag·el·la·tion**, *n.* The development or arrangement of flagella.

fla·gel·li·form, fla·jel′i·fạrm″, *a.* [L. *flagelliformis*.] Long, narrow, and flexible, like the lash of a whip.

fla·gel·lum, fla·jel′um, *n. pl.* **fla·gel·la**, fla·jel′a. [L. a whip, scourge, dim. of *flagrum*, a whip.] *Biol.* a long, lashlike appendage serving as an organ of locomotion in certain reproductive bodies, bacteria, and protozoa; a sensory organ in some arachnids.—**fla·gel·lar**, *a.*

flag·eo·let, flaj″o·let′, flaj″o·lā′, *n.* [Fr. dim. of O.Fr. *flageol, flajol*, flute.] A flute-like wind instrument, having a tubular mouthpiece, six or more holes, and sometimes keys; a fipple flute.

flag·ging, flag′ing, *a.* Weakening; declining; drooping. Also **flag·gy**—*flaggier, flaggiest.*—**flag·ging·ly**, *adv.*

flag·ging, flag′ing, *n.* Flagstones collectively; a pavement of flagstones. Also **flags.**

fla·gi·tious, fla·jish′us, *a.* [L. *flagitiosus*, > *flagitium*, a shameful act, < *flagito*, to demand or urge hotly or violently, < root *flag*, whence *flagro*, to burn, (as in *flagrant*).] Shamefully vicious; infamous.—**fla·gi·tious·ly**, *adv.*—**fla·gi·tious·ness**, *n.*

flag·man, flag′man, *n. pl.* **flag·men.** One who signals with or as with a flag, as at a railroad crossing.

flag of·fi·cer, *n.* A naval officer, having a rank above captain, who may display a flag denoting his rank; admiral.

flag of truce, *n. Milit.* a white flag carried as an indication of desire to parley with the enemy.

a- fat, fāte, fär, fâre, fall; **e-** met, mē, mēre, hėr; **i-** pin, pīne; **o-** not, nōte, mōve; **u-** tub, cūbe, bụll; **oi-** oil; **ou-** pound.

flag·on, flag′on, n. [O.Fr. Fr. *flacon* < M.L. *flasco(n-)*. FLASK.] A large bottle for wines or liquors; a vessel, esp. with a handle, spout, and lid, used for holding and carrying liquids, as at a table.

flag·pole, flag′pōl″, n. The pole or staff on which a flag is displayed. Also *flagstaff*.

flag rank, n. Any naval rank above captain.

fla·grant, flā′grant, a. [L. *flagrans, flagrantis*, ppr. of *flagro*, to burn.] Repugnantly glaring; heinous; notorious or scandalous. *Archaic*, burning, blazing, or glowing.— **fla·grant·ly**, adv.—**fla·gran·cy**, **fla·grance**, n.

flag·ship, flag′ship″, n. The ship which bears the flag officer or the commander and displays his flag.

flag·staff, flag′staf″, flag′stäf″, n. pl. **flag·staffs**, **flag·staves**, flag′stāvz″. A flagpole.

flag·stone, flag′stōn″, n. A flat slab of stone for paving; pl. a walk paved with such slabs. Flag; rock, such as limestone or shale, which can be split into such slabs.

flag·wav·ing, flag′wā″ving, n. An overly sentimental show of devotion to a country or a cause.

flail, flāl, n. [M.E. *fleil*, *flayel*, in part through O.Fr. *flaiel* (Fr. *fléau*), < L.L. *flagellum*, flail, L. whip, scourge. FLAGELLUM.] An instrument for threshing grain by hand, consisting of a staff or handle and a freely swinging stick or bar; formerly, a weapon resembling this.—v.t. To strike with or as with a flail; to thresh.

flair, flâr, n. [Fr. < *flairer*, smell, scent, < L. *fragare*. FRAGRANT.] Natural skill; innate talent; knack.

flak, flack, flak, n. [< G. *(fl)ieger*, aircraft + *(a)bwehr*, defense + *(k)anone*, gun.] Antiaircraft fire.

flake, flāk, n. [M.E. *flake*: cf. Icel. *floki*, felt; hair, wool, and E. *flock*, also *flaw* and *flay*.] A small, loosely cohering piece or mass, as of falling snow; a small detached bit of burning matter; a scale or a small, flat, exfoliated piece; a thin piece split off from the surface of anything; a stratum or layer; a loose sheet of ice; chip.—v.i.—*flaked*, *flaking*. To fall in flakes, as snow; fall like flakes of snow; to peel off or separate in flakes.—v.t. To cover with or as with flakes of snow; fleck; to form into flakes; to remove in flakes; to break flakes or chips from.—**flak·er**, n.

flake, flāk, n. [M.E. *flake*, *fleke*: cf. Icel. *flaki*, *fleki*, hurdle, wickerwork shield, = D. *vlaak*, hurdle.] A frame for drying fish.

flake white, n. Pure white lead in the form of flakes or scales, used as a pigment. Also **lead white**.

flak·y, flā′kē, a.—*flakier*, *flakiest*. Consisting of flakes; lying or cleaving off in flakes or layers; flakelike.—**flak·i·ly**, adv. **flak·i·ness**, n.

flam, flam, n. [Prob. imit.] A drumbeat made by striking the drum with the two sticks almost at the same instant, with the accent on the second sound.

flam, flam, n. [Origin uncertain.] A fabrication; an absurdity; a trick.—v.t.—*flammed*, *flamming*. To delude; cheat.

flam·bé, fläm·bā′, Fr. fläN·bā′, a. [Fr.] *Cooking*, served flaming in brandy or other liquor; *ceramics*, having iridescent, usu. red or blue streaks due to irregular glazing or firing.

flam·beau, flam′bō, n. pl. **flam·beaux**, **flam·beaus**, flam′bōz. [Fr. < *flambe*, a blaze, for *flamble*, < L. *flammula*, dim. of *flamma*, a flame.] A flaming torch; a torch; a large embellished candlestick.

flam·boy·ant, flam·boi′ant, a. [Fr., ppr. of *flamboyer*, to flame, flare, < O.Fr. *flambe*. FLAME.] Showily striking; dashing; florid or ornate; of wavy form, as the outline of a flame; *arch*. pertaining to the ornate Gothic style prevalent during the 15th and 16th centuries, characterized by wavy, flamelike tracery in the windows.— **flam·boy·ance**, **flam·boy·an·cy**, n.— **flam·boy·ant·ly**, adv.

flame, flām, n. [Fr. *flamme*, < L. *flamma*, a flame, for *flagma*, < the root *flag*, whence *flagro*, to burn, to blaze, as in *flagrant*, *conflagration*; root also in Gr. *phlegō*, to burn.] Burning vapor or gas rising from a fire in bright, hot gleams; a single tongue of light from a fire; a state of brilliant, animated combustion; anything suggesting a flame, as in brilliance or color; burning passion; ardor; *slang*, a sweetheart.—v.i.— *flamed*, *flaming*. To send out a flame or blaze; to shine with flamelike brilliance; glow; to act in a violent passion.—v.t. To subject to fire or flame.—**flam·ing**, a. Blazing; resembling a flame in heat or brilliance; ardent; passionate.—**flam·ing·ly**, adv.—**flam·er**, n.

flame cul·ti·va·tor, n. A flamethrower used for the destruction of small weeds.

fla·men·co, flä·meng′kō, n. pl. **fla·men·cos**. A style of dancing with clapping, stamping, and other vigorous movements, developed by the Spanish gypsies; a song or music in this style.

flame-out, **flame·out**, flām′out″, n. The sudden extinction of the flame-burning fuel of a jet engine.

flame·proof, flām′prōf″, a. Resistant to flames; slow to ignite.

flame·throw·er, flām′thrō″ėr, n. [Cf. G. *flammenwerfer*.] A weapon which shoots a stream of flaming liquid.

flame-tree, flām′trē″, n. An Australian ornamental tree, *Brachychiton acerifolium*, having bright scarlet flowers.

fla·min·go, fla·ming′gō, n. pl. **fla·min·gos**, **fla·min·goes**. [Pg. *flamingo* = Sp. *flamenco*, < L. *flamma*, E. *flame*.] Any of the wading birds of the genus *Phoenicopterus*, with very long neck and legs, webbed feet, a bent bill, and pinkish to scarlet plumage.

flam·ma·ble, flam′a·bl, a. Combustible; readily ignited or easily kindled; inflammable.—n. A combustible substance.— **flam·ma·bil·i·ty**, flam″a·bil′i·tē, n. The capacity or ability to support combustion.

flange, flanj, n. [Cf. *flank*.] A projecting rim, collar, or ridge, on a pipe, beam, wheel, or the like, intended to add strength, to facilitate the attachment of another part, or to guide the part along a stationary track.—v.i.—*flanged*, *flanging*. To project like, or take the form of, a flange.—v.t. To furnish with a flange.—**flang·er**, n.

flank, flangk, n. [Fr. *flanc*, Sp. and Pg. *flanco*, It. *fianco*, the flank; of Germanic origin ultimately, same as O.H.G. *hlanca*, side, loin, flank; akin G. *gelenk*, joint.] The fleshy part of the side of an animal or man, between the ribs and the hip; a cut of meat or flesh from this part; the side of anything, as of a building; *milit*. the extreme right or left side of an army, or the outer ships of a fleet; *fort*. the right or left side of a fortification; the side of the projecting part of a bastion; *mach*. the part of a gear tooth between the root and the pitch circle.—v.t. To stand or be at the side of; to place, as troops, so as to command or attack the side of; to pass around or turn the flank of.—v.i. To hold a position at the side.—**flank·er**, flang′kėr, n. One who or that which flanks; *milit*. a fortified position at either side for protection or attack; *football*, an offensive player who takes a position on the line to the right of the right end, or left of the left end.

flan·nel, flan′el, n. [Origin uncertain.] A warm, soft, woolen fabric with a slight nap; a soft, strong fabric made of cotton and wool or other similar blends. *Pl*. outer garments made of the woolen fabric, as trousers for boating or tennis; woolen undergarments.—v t.—*flanneled*, *flanneling*, *Brit. flannelled*, *flannelling*. To cover or clothe with flannel; to rub with flannel.— **flan·nel·ly**, a.—**flan·nel·ette**, **flan·nel·et**, n. A light cotton flannel having a nap on one side.

flap, flap, v.t.—*flapped*, *flapping*. To move, as wings, up and down; to cause to swing or sway loosely, esp. with noise; *colloq.* to toss, fold, or shut roughly or noisily; to strike with something broad and flexible.— v.i. To swing or sway loosely, as in the wind; to flutter; to move up and down; to strike a blow with something broad and flexible.

flap, flap, n. Anything broad and flexible that hangs loose or is attached by one movable end or side; the motion of anything broad and loose, or a stroke with it; the noise produced by something that flaps; a broad flat piece of any material. *Surg.* a portion of tissue partially separated from the base tissue; a portion of skin or flesh used in skin grafting. *Aeron.* a control surface of a plane used to increase the lift or drag of the airplane, or to aid in recovery from a dive; any rudder attached to a rocket, acting either in the air or within the jet stream. *Slang*, a state of confusion or haste. —**flap·py**, a.—*flappier*, *flappiest*.

flap·doo·dle, flap′dōd″el, n. *Slang*, nonsense.

flap·jack, flap′jak″, n. A griddlecake.

flap·per, flap′ėr, n. One who or that which flaps; a young wild bird that is first learning to fly. *Colloq.* a term popular in the 1920's denoting a young woman who flouted conventional restraints in her conduct and dress.

flare, flâr, v.i.—*flared*, *flaring*. [Origin unknown.] To blaze with a sudden burst of flame; to stream out, as the hair in a wind; to burn with an unsteady flame, as: A torch *flares* in the wind. *Fig.* to start or burst in sudden, fierce activity or passion, usu. with *up* or *out*, as: Persecutions *flare* up anew. To shine or glow; to spread gradually outward in form toward the edge or rim.—v.t. To spread out; to display conspicuously; to cause to burn with a swaying flame; to signal by flares of light; to light up with flame; to cause to spread gradually outward.

flare, flâr, n. The act or the effect of flaring; an unsteady or swaying flame or light, as of torches in the wind; a sudden blaze or burst of flame; a blaze of fire or light used to signal, illuminate, or guide; a combustible for burning used to produce such a blaze; a sudden burst, as of zeal or temper; glaring brightness or show; glare; a gradual spreading outward in form; as, a skirt with a slight *flare*; the part thus spread outward, as the end of a trumpet. *Photog.* a spot of light cast by the lens of a camera on the plate, resulting from reflection; light from reflection scattered by a lens.—**flar·ing**, a. Flaming; glaringly bright or showy; spreading outward in form.—**flar·ing·ly**, adv.

flare·back, flâr′bak″, n. A blast of flame which may issue from the breech of a large gun or cannon when it is opened after firing; *fig.* an outburst of something recurring suddenly; as, a *flareback* of winter.

flare-up, flâr′up″, n. A sudden bursting or flaring into flame or light; *fig.* an abrupt outburst of anger; a sudden intensification, as of violence; a sudden outbreak, as of disease.

flash, flash, n. A sudden, transitory outburst of flame or light; a sudden blaze instantly disappearing; a gleam; an instant; a sudden brief outburst or display, as of joy or wit; ostentatious display; a lock or dam used to cause an extra volume or rush of water, as for floating a boat over shoals; the sudden flow of water so produced. *Journ.* a brief initial report giving a hurried summary of an important news story, pending fuller details.—**flash in the pan,** *fig.* a sudden showy or pretentious outburst or effort, without any enduring result; one who makes such an effort.

flash, flash, *a.* Of short duration; showy; vulgarly ostentatious; counterfeit; gaudy; pertaining to the world or jargon of organized crime.

flash, flash, *v.i.* [M.E. *flaschen,* prob. imit.] To break forth into sudden flame or light, esp. intermittently; to burst suddenly into view or perception; to shine or gleam; to move quickly; to break into sudden action or speech; to act or speak angrily. *Archaic,* to make a sudden display.—*v.t.* To emit or send forth, as fire or light, in sudden flashes; to cause to flash, as powder by ignition or a sword by waving; to express or communicate by or as by a flash or flashes; to convey by instantaneous communication, as by telegraph; to form swiftly into vapor, as liquid; *colloq.* to make a sudden or ostentatious display of. *Glassmaking,* to coat with a film of colored, white, or opalescent glass. *Arch.* to protect with flashing.

flash·back, flash′bak″, *n.* A literary or cinematic technique which interjects previous action, thoughts, or events into the existing action without regard for chronology.

flash·board, flash′bōrd″, flash′bård″, *n. Engin.* a board, or one of a series of boards, as on a milldam, used to increase the depth of the water.

flash bulb, *n.* A flash lamp used to illuminate briefly any subject that is being photographed.

flash card, *n.* A card having words, numbers, or pictures, meant to elicit a quick response, used by students or teachers to drill arithmetic, spelling, reading, or foreign languages.

flash flood, *n.* A sudden, destructive flood caused by heavy rainfall in the immediate area.

flash gun, *n.* A device used in photography that ignites a flash bulb and operates a camera shutter at the same time.

flash·ing, flash′ing, *n.* The act of one who or that which flashes; pieces of sheet metal used to cover and protect certain joints and angles, as where a roof comes in contact with a wall or chimney; the producing of an artificial flash or flood of water; the act of flushing, as a sewer; *glassmaking,* the process or method by which glass is flashed.—*a.* Emitting flashes.—**flash·ing·ly,** *adv.*

flash lamp, *n. Photog.* a device producing a momentary light sufficiently bright for taking photographs. Also **flash·lamp.**

flash·light, flash′līt″, *n.* A flash of light or a light that flashes; a device for giving flashes of light for signaling, as in a lighthouse; a brilliant light synchronized with photographic equipment; a photograph made by such a light; a hand-held electric light powered by batteries.

flash·o·ver, flash′ō″vėr, *n.* A disruptive electrical discharge through or around the surface of a liquid or solid insulator.

flash point, *n. Chem.* the lowest temperature at which a combustible liquid gives off vapor in sufficient quantity to ignite momentarily upon application of a flame.

flash·tube, flash′tōb, flash′tūb″, *n. Photog.* a gas-filled glass bulb which, when electronically ignited, illuminates the subject with a momentary flash of brilliant light; flashbulb. *Electron.* an electronic tube, filled with gas, used to provide a flash of brilliant light for a stroboscope.

flash·y, flash′ē, *a.*—*flashier, flashiest.* Sparkling or brilliant, esp. in a superficial way or for the moment; showy; gaudy.—**flash·i·ly,** *adv.*—**flash·i·ness,** *n.*

flask, flask, fläsk, *n.* [O.E. *flasc, flasca, flaxa,* Dan. *flaske,* Sw. *flasca;* ultimate origin doubtful.] A type of bottle; a narrow-necked globular glass vessel, as used in a laboratory; a small flattened container, as of metal, usu. for carrying liquor on the person; a vessel for carrying gunpowder on the person; a container for molding sand in a foundry.—**flask·et,** flas′kit, flä′skit, *n.* A small flask.

flat, flat, *a.* [Not in O.E. = Icel. *flatr,* Sw. *flat,* Dan. *flad,* G. *flach,* flat; akin Gr. *platys,* Skt. *pritus,* broad.] Horizontal and level; even, without elevations or depressions; lying level with the ground; prostrate; lying with one surface completely against something; having a level appearance; shallow; as, a *flat* dish. Positive or absolute; as, a *flat* denial; without interest; dull; lifeless; tasteless or stale; having lost its carbonation; as, *flat* beer; deflated; as, a *flat* tire. Having no shine or gloss; fixed; without variation; having no depth; monotonous; commercially inactive; exact; as, one minute *flat. Mus.* below the natural or true pitch; not sharp or natural; *gram.* derived without change in form; *slang,* without money, broke.—*adv.* In a flat manner; precisely; completely, totally; *mus.* below the proper pitch; *finance,* without interest. Also **flat·ly.**—**flat·ness,** *n.*

flat, flat, *n.* Something flat; the flat part or side of anything; a plain; a level area of land; *colloq.* a deflated tire; *mus.* a mark (♭) placed before a note or in a space of the staff which indicates that all notes on the same degree or their octaves are lowered a semitone; the note thus lowered; *theatr.* a part of stage scenery consisting of canvas stretched across a wooden frame. A suite of rooms on one floor of a building used as a residence; a floor or story of an apartment building; a rough shallow box in which plants are started. *Usu. pl.* a woman's shoe with a low heel or no heel; a low or partially submerged area of land; a shoal or marsh.

flat, flat, *v.t.*—*flatted, flatting.* To make flat; *mus.* to lower, as a pitch, usu. by one semitone.—*v.i.* To become flat; to play or sing off key.

flat·boat, flat′bōt″, *n.* A large flat-bottomed boat used in shallow water, esp. on rivers. Also **flat·bot·tom,** flat′bot′om.

flat·car, flat′kär″, *n. U.S.* A railroad freight car having a platform with no enclosing sides or roof; platform car.

flat·fish, flat′fish″, *n. pl.* **flat·fish, flat·fish·es.** Any of a group of fish, including the halibut, flounder, and sole, having a greatly compressed body, swimming on one side, and having both eyes on the upper side in the adult.

flat·foot, flat′fụt″, flat′fụt′, *n. pl.* **flat·feet.** *Pathol.* a condition in which the arch of the foot is flattened so that the entire sole rests upon the ground; a human foot so formed. *Slang,* a policeman; *pl.* **flat·foots.**

flat-foot·ed, flat′fụt′id, *a.* Having flat feet; *colloq.* taking or showing an uncompromising stand in a matter; firm and explicit.—*adv.* In a determined or uncompromising manner. Also **flat-foot·ed·ly.—flat-foot·ed·ness,** *n.*

flat-hat, flat′hat″, *v.i.*—*flat-hatted, flat-hatting. Slang,* to fly a plane recklessly; to fly dangerously low.—**flat-hat·ter,** *n.*

Flat·head, flat′hed″, *n.* One of a small tribe of American Indians of northwestern Montana; a Chinook Indian.

flat·i·ron, flat′ī″ėrn, *n.* An iron having a flat face and used for pressing clothes.

flat sil·ver, *n.* Silver tableware; flatware.

flat·ten, flat′en, *v.t.* To make flat or level; to make prostrate.—*v.i.* To grow or become flat.—**flat·ten out,** to become level or stabilized; *aeron.* to maneuver an airplane

into a horizontal flight position.—**flat·ten·er,** *n.*

flat·ter, flat′ėr, *v.t.* [Fr. *flatter,* Pr. *flatar,* to pat, stroke, caress, flatter; perhaps < Icel. *flatr,* E. *flat;* compare also Icel. *flathra,* to fawn or flatter, *flathr,* flattery.] To gratify by excessive praise or insincere compliments, esp. for personal interests or motives; to gratify by favorable representation; to show advantageously; to beguile or encourage with false hopes.—*v.i.* To practice flattery.—**flat·ter·er,** *n.*—**flat·ter·ing·ly,** *adv.*

flat·ter, flat′ėr, *n.* One who or that which makes something flat, esp. a blacksmith's hammer with a broad face.

flat·ter·y, flat′e·rē, *n. pl.* **flat·ter·ies.** [Fr. *flatterie.*] The act of flattering; extravagant, usu. insincere praise.

flat·top, flat′top″, *n. U.S. Navy colloq.* an aircraft carrier.

flat·u·lent, flach′u·lent, *a.* [L.L. *flatulentus,* < L. *flatus,* a blowing, < *flo, flatum,* to blow.] Affected with or caused by gases generated in the alimentary canal; generating or apt to generate gas in the stomach; boastful; pretentious.—**flat·u·lence, flat·u·len·cy,** *n.*—**flat·u·lent·ly,** *adv.*

fla·tus, flā′tus, *n.* [L. a blowing, < *flare,* blow.] *Pathol.* an accumulation of gas in the stomach, intestines, or other body cavity.

flat·ware, flat′wâr″, *n.* Any eating utensil plated with or composed of silver; also *flat silver.* Tableware that is more or less flat, as a plate.

flat·wise, flat′wīz″, *adv.* With the flat side, instead of the edge, foremost or in contact. Also **flat·ways.**

flat·work, flat′wurk″, *n.* Any article, such as a sheet or tablecloth, which can be ironed in a mangle rather than by hand.

flat·worm, flat′wurm″, *n. Biol.* any platyhelminth, a worm having a soft, usu. flattened body.

flaunt, flạnt, *v.i.* [Connected with prov. G. *flander,* a rag or tatter, *flandern,* to flutter, G. *flattern,* to flirt, to flutter.] To make an ostentatious display; to move or act ostentatiously; to wave conspicuously; to be glaring or gaudy.—*v.t.* To display or parade ostentatiously, impudently, or offensively.—*n.* The act of flaunting.—**flaunt·er,** *n.*

flaunt·y, flạn′tē, *a.*—*flauntier, flauntiest.* Ostentatious; vulgarly or offensively showy; gaudy. Also **flaunt·ing.—flaunt·i·ly, flaunt·ing·ly,** *adv.*—**flaunt·i·ness,** *n.*

flau·tist, flạ′tist, flou′tist, *n.* [It. *flauto,* a flute.] A flutist.

fla·vin, flā′vin, *n. Chem.* a yellow dye of vegetable origin, and a constituent of flavoproteins.

fla·vine, flā′vin, flā′vēn, *n. Chem.* acriflavine hydrochloride, used as an antiseptic; flavin.

fla·vo·pro·tein, flā″vō·prō′tēn, flā″vō·prō′tē·in, *n. Biochem.* a flavin enzyme, consisting of a protein linked to coenzymes containing riboflavin, and taking part in tissue respiration as a catalyst of hydrogen removal.

fla·vor, *Brit.* **fla·vour,** flā′vėr, *n.* [O.Fr. *flauor, flaveure, flaur, flair,* an odor; all used also in reference to taste.] Taste; the quality of any substance which affects the taste; something providing flavor; flavoring; a characteristic quality of something; *archaic,* odor or fragrance.—*v.t.* To give flavor or some quality of taste to.— **fla·vored,** *Brit.* **fla·voured,** *a.*—**fla·vor·less,** *Brit.* **fla·vour·less,** *a.*

fla·vor·ful, flā′vėr·ful, *a.* Full of flavor; pleasant tasting. Also **fla·vor·ous, fla·vor·some,** *Brit.* **fla·vour·some.—fla·vor·ful·ly,** *adv.*

fla·vor·ing, *Brit.* **fla·vour·ing,** flā′vėr·ing, *n.* Any substance used for imparting flavor; seasoning.

---

a- fat, fāte, fär, fâre, fạll;   **e-** met, mē, mēre, hėr;   **i-** pin, pīne;   **o-** not, nōte, mōve;   **u-** tub, cūbe, bụll;   **oi-** oil;   **ou-** pound.

flaw, flạ, n. [O.E. *flōh,* that which has flown off, a fragment; Goth. *flagga,* a fragment; Sw. *flaga,* a flaw, *flaga sig,* to scale off, akin to *flake* and *flag;* akin. also W. *fflaw,* a splinter, *ffla,* a parting from.] Any imperfection; a defect; a fault; a crack or fissure; a defect in a legal document that may make it invalid.—*v.t.* To make or produce a flaw in.—*v.i.* To become defective.—**flaw·less,** *a.*—**flaw·less·ly,** *adv.*—**flaw·less·ness,** *n.*

flaw, flạ, n. [= D. *vlaag* = L.G. and Dan. *flage.*] A brief, sudden gust of wind; a short period of stormy weather.

flax, flaks, n. [O.E. *fleax* = D. *vlas* = G. *flachs,* flax.] Any plant of the genus *Linum,* esp. *L. usitatissimum,* a slender, erect, annual plant with blue flowers cultivated for its fiber; the fiber of this plant used in the manufacture of linen thread and fabrics.—**flax·en,** *a.* Made of flax; of the pale yellowish color of dressed flax.—**flax·y,** *a.*

flax·seed, flaks'sēd", n. The seed of the flax, used in making linseed oil and medicinal soothing agents. Also *linseed.*

flay, flā, *v.t.* [O.E. *flēan,* to flay; O.D. *vlaegen, vlaen,* to flay; akin *flake, flaw.*] To skin; to strip off the skin or outer layer of, esp. by whipping; to criticize ruthlessly; to cheat of money or goods by fraud; fleece.

F layer, n. *Meteor.* the area of the ionosphere formed in the F region between 85 and 220 miles above earth, consisting of the F_1 layer, appearing constantly, and the F_2 layer, appearing only during the day and having a lower electron density.

flea, flē, n. [O.E. *fleá,* < *fleôn, fleôgan,* to fly; D. *vloo,* Icel. *flō,* Sc. *flech,* G. *floh,* a flea.] Any of many small, wingless, bloodsucking insects of the order *Siphonaptera,* parasitic on warm-blooded animals, and able to leap relatively great distances.—**a flea in one's ear,** *slang.* A biting or upsetting reproach or rebuff; a hint.

flea·bane, flē'bān", n. A popular name for composite plants of the genus *Erigeron,* so called because of their supposed power of destroying or driving away fleas.

flea bee·tle, n. Any of several small leaping beetles that feed on and infest plants.

flea·bite, flē'bīt", n. The bite of a flea; the red spot on the skin produced by such a bite; a trifling wound or pain; *slang,* a slight inconvenience.

flea-bit·ten, flē'bit"en, a. Bitten or covered by fleas; *slang,* decrepit or run-down. Of horses, colored white and streaked or spotted with reddish-brown.

fleam, flēm, n. [D. *vlijm,* Fr. *flamme,* O.H.G. *fliedimā,* < L.L. *flevotomum, flebotomum,* < Gr. *phlebs, phlebos,* a vein, and *tomos,* a cutting.] *Surg.* A sharp instrument for opening veins; a lancet.

flea mar·ket, n. An outdoor market, esp. in Europe, where inexpensive and/or secondhand items are for sale.

flèche, flāsh, Fr. flesh, n. pl. **flè·ches,** flā'shiz, Fr. flesh. [Fr.] A narrow spire at the intersection of the nave and transepts of a church; *milit.* a projecting part of a fortification with two of its three walls forming an angle pointing forward.

fleck, flek, n. [Icel. *flekkr,* D. *vlek,* G. *fleck,* a spot; allied to *flick.*] A spot; a dapple; a little bit.—*v.t.* To spot; to streak.

flec·tion, Brit. **flex·ion,** flek'shan, n. [L. *flectio.*] The act of bending a limb of the body; the bending of a limb by exercising the flexor muscle; a curved or bowed part. —**flec·tion·al, flex·ion·al,** *a.*

fledge, flej, *v.i.*—*fledged, fledging.* [M.E. *flegge;* akin to E. *fly.*] Of a young bird, to acquire the feathers necessary for flight.—*v.t.* To bring up, as a young bird, until able to fly; to furnish with or as with feathers; to feather, as an arrow.—**fledg·y,** *a.*—*fledgier, fledgiest.* Feathered; feathery.

fledg·ling, Brit. **fledge·ling,** flej'ling, n. A young bird just fledged; *fig.* an inexperienced person.

flee, flē, *v.i.*—*fled, fleeing.* [O.E. *flēon* = G. *fliechen* Icel. *flȳja* = Goth. *thliuhan,* flee; long confused with the unrelated word *fly.*] To run away, as from danger or pursuers; take flight; depart or withdraw hastily; to move swiftly, fly, or speed, as a missile. —*v.t.* To run away from, as a place or person; to avoid by flight.

fleece, flēs, n. [O.E. *flēos* = D. *vlies* = G. *fliess.*] The coat of wool that covers a sheep or some similar animal; the wool shorn from a sheep at one time; something resembling a fleece of wool in quality, texture, or appearance; a soft, deep-piled fabric used in clothing, esp. as coat linings; the pile of this fabric.—*v.t.*—*fleeced, fleecing.* To cut or clip the fleece from; to strip of money or belongings; victimize; swindle; to cover or fleck with fleecelike masses, as: The fluff of the cottonwood trees *fleeced* the landscape.—**fleece·a·ble,** *a.*—**fleeced,** *a.* Having a fleece or soft nap.—

fleec·y, flē'sē, *a.*—*fleecier, fleeciest.* Covered with, made of, or similar to wool or fleece. Fluffy or soft.—**fleec·i·ly,** *adv.*—**fleec·i·ness,** *n.*

fleer, flēr, *v.i.* [M.E. *fleryen;* prob. < Scand.] To grimace, sneer, or laugh coarsely or mockingly; jeer.—*v.t.* To deride; laugh at mockingly.—*n.* A fleering look; a jeer or gibe.—**fleer·ing·ly,** *adv.*

fleet, flēt, a. [Icel. *fljotr,* O.E. *flēotan,* quick; allied to *flit* and *float.*] Swift of pace; nimble; light and quick in motion.—*v.i.* To fly or move swiftly; to hasten; *naut.* to alter one's position.—*v.t.* To skim over the surface of; to pass or cause to pass rapidly, as time; *naut.* to alter the position of.— **fleet·ly,** *adv.*

fleet, flēt, n. [O.E. *flēot,* ship, craft, < *flēotan,* float.] A unit of armed vessels; a number of warships under the command of a single officer or government; any group of ships or boats sailing in company, employed in the same service, or otherwise associated; a group of vehicles owned or operated as a unit, as airplanes, trucks, or cars.

fleet ad·mi·ral, n. The highest commissioned rank in the U.S. Navy, corresponding to General of the Army; a person holding this rank.

fleet·ing, flē'ting, a. Passing rapidly; transitory; as, *fleeting* moments.—**fleet·ing·ly,** *adv.*—**fleet·ing·ness,** *n.*

Fleet Street, n. The center of the newspaper world in London, England; *fig.* the British press.

Flem·ing, flem'ing, n. A native of Flanders, a group of adjacent provinces of western Belgium, northern France, and southwestern Netherlands; a speaker of Flemish.

Flem·ish, flem'ish, a. [M.D. *Vlaemisch.*] Of or pertaining to Flanders, its people, or their language.—*n.* The people of Flanders; the Flemings; the language of the Flemings, a form of Low German closely related to Dutch.

flense, flens, *v.t.*—*flensed, flensing.* [Dan. *flense;* D. *vlensen.*] To strip the blubber or skin from, as a whale or a seal.

flesh, flesh, n. [O.E. *flǣsc* = D. *vleesch* = G. *fleisch,* flesh, = Icel. *flesk,* pork.] The soft substance of an animal body, consisting of muscle and fat; such substance of animals considered as food, usu. excluding fish and sometimes fowl; meat; the body; man's physical or animal nature as distinguished from his moral or spiritual nature; mankind; living creatures in general; kindred or family; the soft, pulpy portion of a fruit or vegetable; the surface of an animal body, esp. with respect to its color.

flesh, flesh, *v.t.* To feed, as a hound or hawk, with flesh in order to make it more

eager for the chase; to incite and accustom to battle or bloodshed by an initial experience; to inflame the ardor or passions of by a taste of indulgence; to clothe or cover with flesh; to remove, as adhering flesh, from hides; to plunge, as a weapon, into the flesh; to make fleshy.—**flesh out,** to give substance to; to round out.

flesh col·or, n. A cream color with a pink tinge, supposed to resemble a white person's skin.—**flesh-col·ored,** *a.*

flesh·er, flesh'ėr, n. One who removes flesh from hides; a tool for fleshing hides.

flesh fly, n. Any of various flies of the family *Sarcophaga,* as the blowfly, whose eggs are deposited in living flesh.

flesh·ings, flesh'ingz, n. pl. Flesh-colored tights; bits of flesh scraped from hides.

flesh·ly, flesh'lē, a.—*fleshlier, fleshliest.* [O.E. *flǣsclīc.*] Of or pertaining to the flesh or body; bodily, corporeal, or physical; carnal, sensual, or lustful; as, *fleshly* appetites; worldly rather than spiritual; *obs.* fleshy.—**flesh·li·ness,** *n.*

flesh·pot, flesh'pot", n. A pot or vessel containing flesh or meat; a place catering to indulgences and pleasure, as an especially lavish night club; *pl.* the material comforts and sensual pleasures of high living.

flesh·y, flesh'ē, a.—*fleshier, fleshiest.* Having much flesh; plump; fat; of, pertaining to, or consisting of flesh; of fleshlike substance; pulpy and firm, as a fruit.—**flesh·i·ness,** *n.*

fletch, flech, *v.t.* [Prob. < *fletcher.*] To provide or equip with a feather, as an arrow.

fletch·er, flech'ėr, n. [O.Fr. *flechier,* < *fleche* (Fr. *flèche*), arrow.] One who makes or deals in arrows, or bows and arrows.

Fletch·er·ism, flech'e·riz"um, n. [From Horace *Fletcher* (1849–1919), a U.S. nutritionist.] The practice of chewing food until it is reduced to a liquefied mass, advocated as a health measure by Horace Fletcher and other nutritionists.—**Fletch·er·ize,** *v.t., v.i.*—*Fletcherized, Fletcherizing.* To masticate food thoroughly.

fleur-de-lis, fleur-de-lys, flụr"de·lē', flụr"de·lēs', Fr. flœr·de·lēs', n. pl. **fleurs-de-lis.** [Fr. *fleur de lis,* "flower of lily."] A heraldic device somewhat resembling three petals or floral segments, as of an iris, assembled in a cluster by an encircling band near the base, esp. used as the distinctive bearing of the royal family of France; the iris flower or plant.

fleu·ry, flụr'ē, flōr'ē, a. [Fr. *fleuré,* O.Fr. *floré,* < O.Fr. *flor* (Fr. *fleur*), E. *flower.*] *Her.* Decorated with fleurs-de-lis; of a cross, having each arm, or the upper part of one arm, ending in a fleur-de-lis. Also **flo·ry,** flär'ē.

flews, flōz, n. pl. [Origin unknown.] The large pendulous parts of the upper lip of certain dogs, as bloodhounds.—**flewed,** *a.*

flex, fleks, *v.t.* [< L. *flecto, flexum,* to bend.] To bend without breaking; to curve; to contract, as a muscle.—*v.i.* To form into folds; to clasp.—*n.* The act of flexing; *Brit.* an electric cord; *math.* an inflection point.— **flexed,** *a.*

flex·i·ble, flek'si·bl, a. [L. *flexibilis,* < *flecto, flexum.*] Capable of being bent; easily bent or pliant; yielding to persuasion or argument; capable of being adapted or modified. Also **flex·ile,** flek'sil.—**flex·i·bil·i·ty, flex·i·ble·ness,** *n.*—**flex·i·bly,** *adv.*

flex·ion, flek'shan, n. Flection.

flex·or, flek'sėr, n. [N.L.] *Anat.* a muscle which serves to flex or bend a joint of the body.

flex·u·ous, flek'shō·us, a. [L. *flexuosus.*] Winding or bending; having turns; wavering. Also **flex·u·ose,** flek'shō·ōs".—**flex·u·os·i·ty, flex·u·ous·ness, flex·u·ose·ness,** *n.*—**flex·u·ous·ly, flex·u·ose·ly,** *adv.*

flex·ure, flek′shẽr, *n.* [L. *flexura.*] The act of flexing or bending; the state of being flexed or bent; a fold; a bent part or thing. —**flex·ur·al,** *a.*

flib·ber·ti·gib·bet, flib′ẽr·tē·jib″it, *n.* [Appar. a made word.] A chattering or flighty person, usu. a woman.

flic, flēk, flik, *n.* [Fr.] *Colloq.* a Parisian policeman.

flick, flik, *n.* [Appar. imit.] A sudden light blow or stroke, as with a whip or a finger; the sound thus made; a sharp, quick movement; as, a *flick* of the wrist; something thrown off with a jerk; as, a *flick* of a spray. *Slang,* a motion picture.—*v.t.* To strike lightly with a whip or finger; to remove with such a stroke; to move with a sudden stroke or jerk.—*v.i.* To move with a jerk or jerks; to flutter.

flick·er, flik′ẽr, *v.i.* [O.E. *flicorian*; prob. imit.] To burn, shine, or emit light unsteadily; to move in a wavering manner; to quiver or vibrate; to flutter; to appear partially or momentarily, as a shadow.— *v.t.* To make flicker.—*n.* An act of flickering; a wavering or flashing movement or light; a momentary occurrence, as: He was gone in a *flicker. Often pl., slang,* a motion picture.—**flick·er·ing·ly,** *adv.*— **flick·er·y,** *a.*

flick·er, flik′ẽr, *n.* [Prob. imit. of the bird's note.] *Ornith.* a brown-backed woodpecker, *Colaptes auratus,* identified by its white rump, and native to eastern N. America.

flick·er·tail, flik′ẽr·tāl, *n.* A gopher or ground squirrel, *Citellus richardsoni,* common in the northwestern U.S. and Canada.

fli·er, fly·er, flī′ẽr, *n.* [Cf. *fly, v.i.*] Something that flies, as an insect; an aviator; one who or that which moves with great speed; a part of a machine having a rapid motion. *Colloq.* a flying jump or leap; a financial venture outside of one's ordinary business. A single one of a straight flight of steps, orig. a small handbill, now an advertisement of a special sale or event, distributed either as a handbill or a mailed insert or leaflet.

flight, flīt, *n.* [O.E. *flyht,* < *flēogan,* E. *fly.*] The act, manner, or power of flying; a trip in or by an airplane, as: He left on the morning *flight.* The distance covered or the course pursued by a flying object; a number of beings or things flying or passing through the air together; as, a *flight* of doves or swallows; swift movement in general, as of a missile; *fig.* a soaring above or transcending of ordinary bounds; as, a *flight* of fancy; a series of steps or stairs between two adjacent landings; a series, as of steps, ascending without change or direction. *U.S. Air Force,* a tactical unit of four or more aircraft. *Archery,* a light arrow for long-distance shooting; a contest with such arrows.—*v.i.* Of wildfowl, to fly together in a flock.—**flight·less,** *a.*

flight, flīt, *n.* [M.E. *fliht,* < O.E. *flēon,* E. *flee.*] The act of fleeing; hasty or precipitate departure.

flight con·trol, *n. Aeron.* the control of aircraft in flight, esp. control exercised by means of radio communication and electronic devices; (*often cap.*) an agency or activity providing such control. *Often pl.* the complete system of levers, cables, and control devices used for control of the movement of an aircraft.

flight deck, *n. U.S. Navy,* the upper deck of an aircraft carrier that serves as a runway from which planes land and take off. *Aeron.* in most planes, the front compartment used for the operation of the aircraft in flight.

flight en·gi·neer, *n.* A crew member of an airplane responsible for the mechanical performance of the aircraft in flight.

flight feath·er, *n. Ornith.* one of the large, stiff feathers of a bird's wing, essential for flight.

flight lieu·ten·ant, *n.* A commissioned rank in the Royal Air Force and Royal Canadian Air Force which corresponds to that of Captain in the U.S. Air Force; a person holding this rank.

flight path, *n. Aeron.* The path followed or made by an airborne aircraft, projectile, guided missile, or the like; the course of the center of gravity made by an aircraft in flight.

flight sur·geon, *n.* (*Often cap.*), *aeron.* a medical officer trained and qualified to tend to the medical needs of an aircraft crew.

flight·y, flī′tē, *a.*—*flightier, flightiest.* Moved by sudden and irrational whims; given to flights of fancy; fickle; capricious; slightly delirious or light-headed; mildly crazy.— **flight·i·ly,** *adv.*—**flight·i·ness,** *n.*

flim·flam, flim′flam″, *n.* [Origin uncertain: cf. *flam.*] *Colloq.* a trick or deception; trickery; mere nonsense.—*v.t.*—*flimflammed, flimflamming.* To trick; delude; cheat. —**flim·flam·mer,** *n.*

flim·sy, flim′zē, *a.*—*flimsier, flimsiest* [Perhaps connected with *film.*] Lacking in strength or solidity; unsubstantial; unconvincing; frail; trivial.—**flim·si·ly,** *adv.* —**flim·si·ness,** *n.*

flim·sy, flim′ze, *n. pl.* **flim·sies.** A lightweight typewriter paper used for carbon copies; a copy on this paper.

flinch, flinch, *v.i.* [Perhaps corrupted < *flench,* or < O.E. *flecche,* Fr. *flechir,* L. *flectere,* to bend.] To draw back from pain or danger; to wince. *Croquet,* to allow one's foot to slip off the ball when hitting the opponent's ball away.—*n.* The act of flinching.—**flinch·er,** *n.*—**flinch·ing·ly,** *adv.*

flin·ders, flin′dẽrz, *n. pl.* Fragments; splinters.

fling, fling, *n.* An act of flinging; a period of irresponsible fun or indulgence; a severe or contemptuous remark. A lively Scottish dance characterized by flinging movements of the legs and arms; also *Highland Fling.*

fling, fling, *v.t.*—*flung, flinging.* [Cf. Icel. *flengja,* whip, mod. ride furiously, Sw. *flanga,* fly, race, tear, romp.] To throw, cast off, or hurl, esp. with force or violence; to throw or move with impatience or disdain, as: He *flung* himself angrily from the room. To put suddenly or violently; as, to *fling* someone into prison; to discard; to send forth suddenly or rapidly; to throw to the ground; to energetically involve, as oneself, in a project.—*v.i.* To move with haste or violence; rush or dash; to speak angrily or abusively, usu. followed by *out;* to throw the body around.—**fling·er,** *n.*

flint, flint, *n.* [O.E. *flint* = M.L.G. *vlins* = O.H.G. *flins* = Dan. *flint.*] A hard siliceous, fine-grained rock, usu. a mixture of quartz and chalcedony; a piece of this used with a piece of steel to strike a spark or start a fire; something very hard and obdurate.

flint corn, *n.* A variety of Indian corn, *Zea mays indurata,* the kernels of which have a thick, hard, horny wall.

flint glass, *n.* A brilliant, lustrous glass containing lead oxide and used chiefly for optical lenses.

flint·lock, flint′lok″, *n.* A gunlock, characteristic of the small arms of the 17th and 18th centuries, in which a piece of flint strikes against steel and produces sparks which ignite the priming; a firearm with such a lock.

flint·y, flin′tē, *a.*—*flintier, flintiest.* Consisting or composed of flint; very hard; unmerciful; unyielding.—**flint·i·ly,** *adv.*— **flint·i·ness,** *n.*

flip, flip, *v.t.*—*flipped, flipping.* [A form of *flap.*] To propel or toss into the air, as a coin, with a sudden or snapping movement, esp. to cause to turn over; to flick; to turn over, as cards, esp. with a rapid motion or jerk.—*v.i.* To make a snapping or flicking movement; to strike at something quickly or sharply; to move suddenly or jerkily; *slang,* to react enthusiastically or violently.— *n.* An instance or act of flipping; a smart blow or flick; a somersault executed in the air; any of a number of sweetened mixed drinks.

flip, flip, *a.*—*flipper, flippest. Slang.* Impertinent; impudent; flippant.

FLIP, flip, *n.* [(*FL*)oating (*I*)nstrument (*P*)latform.] An ocean-going research vessel which can be towed into place horizontally and then flipped into vertical position to float bow-up like a buoy.

flip-flop, flip′flop″, *n.* The noise or movement of something swaying or flapping loosely; a quick change of direction or opinion; an advertising display having pages joined on top and turned in sequence; *gymnastics,* a backward flip in which the hands must touch the floor before the body returns to an upright position.—*v.i.*— *flip-flopped, flip-flopping.* To perform a backward flip; to flap; to move back and forth.—*adv.*

flip·pant, flip′ant, *a.* [Formed < *flip, flap,* akin Icel. *fleipa,* tattle, *fleipinn,* pert, petulant.] Frivolous; showing undue levity; lacking in seriousness; disrespectful.— **flip·pan·cy, flip·pant·ness,** *n.*—**flip·pant·ly,** *adv.*

flip·per, flip′ẽr, *n.* [< flip.] A broad, flat limb, as of a seal or whale, adapted for swimming. *Usu. pl.* a type of rubber shoe, greatly expanded at the toe, and worn for some forms of swimming; also *fins. Slang,* the hand.

flip side, *n. Slang,* the less popular side of a phonograph record.

flirt, flẽrt, *v.i.* To play at love; to engage in coquetry; to toy with an idea; to dart or move with short, quick movements; to expose oneself carelessly.—*v.t.* To throw or move with a jerk; to fling suddenly; to make coquettish motions with, as a fan.— *n.* Also **flirt·er.**—**flir·ta·tion,** *n.* A brief, trifling, amorous adventure.—**flir·ta·tious, flirt·y,**—**flir·ta·tious·ly,** *adv.*—**flir·ta·tious·ness,** *n.*

flit, flit, *v.i.*—*flitted, flitting.* [Dan. *flytte,* Sw. *flytta,* to remove; akin to *flee, fleet, flutter.*] To fly or dart; to move quickly and lightly, as: The hummingbird *flitted* from flower to flower. To flutter; to pass rapidly, as: The time *flitted* away. *Archaic,* to move.—*n.* A quick movement.—**flit·ter,** *n.*

flitch, flich, *n.* [O.E. *flicce* = M.L.G. *vlicke* = Icel. *flikki,* flitch.] A salted and cured cut of meat from the side of a hog; as, a *flitch* of bacon; a steak cut from a halibut. *Carp.* a slab cut lengthwise from the trunk of a tree; one of several planks fastened together to form a compound beam.—*v.t.* To divide into flitches.

flit·ter, flit′ẽr, *v.i., v.t.* Flutter.

fliv·ver, fliv′ẽr, *n.* [Origin obscure.] A small, inexpensive, and usu. old automobile. A failure or bungle.

float, flōt, *v.i.* [O.E. *flotian,* < *flēotan,* float.] To rest or move gently on the surface of a liquid; to be buoyant; to rest or move in a liquid; to drift; to rest or move on the air; to hover; to move gracefully or effortlessly; to move or hover before the eyes or in the mind; to pass from one to another, as: News of their divorce is *floating* around town. To move about in an irresponsible manner, as: He *floated* from job to job. To be unattached or uninvolved; to be launched, as a company or scheme; *com.* to be in circulation, as an acceptance; to be awaiting maturity.—*v.t.* To cause to float; to make smooth or level, as the surface of wet plaster; to launch, as a company or scheme; to get into operation; to put on the market, as a stock or bond; to cover with water; irrigate.—**float·a·ble**, *a.* Capable of floating or being floated on.—**float·a·bil·i·ty**, *n.*

float, flōt, *n.* [O.E. *flot*, a floating, *flota*, a ship, fleet.] Something that floats on a liquid surface or buoys up something on a liquid surface; a raft; a life preserver; a piece of cork that buoys up a baited line in the water and shows by its movement when a fish bites; an inflated sac that supports a plant or animal in the water; a hollow ball which, through its buoyancy, automatically regulates the level of a liquid in a tank or cistern. A platform on wheels carrying an elaborate tableau or other display as a part of a parade or procession; any of various tools for smoothing or leveling, as a plasterer's trowel; *aeron.* a boatlike underpart enabling an amphibious airplane to stay afloat in water; the value of uncollected checks in a stage of transfer from one bank to another; a milk shake or carbonated beverage with a scoop of ice cream floating in it; *usu. pl.* the footlights of a theater.

float·age, flō′tij, *n.* Flotage.

float·a·tion, flō·tā′shan, *n.* Flotation.

float·er, flō′tėr, *n.* One who or that which floats; one who continually changes his residence or employment; an independent voter; one who fraudulently votes in different places in the same election. *Insurance,* a policy of limited duration which insures household or personal property, esp. when that property is being transported.

float·ing, flō′ting, *a.* Buoyed upon water or liquid; having little or no attachment; not fixed or settled in a definite state; *pathol.* out of normal position; as, a *floating* kidney. *Finance,* in circulation or used and not permanently invested, as capital; not funded, as a debt. *Mach.* suspended to reduce vibration.—**float·ing·ly**, *adv.*

float·ing dock, *n.* A floating dry dock which can be lowered to enable a ship to enter and then can be raised to keep the ship above water.

float·ing is·land, *n.* A mass of earth and vegetation resembling an island, floating on a body of water; a custard dessert topped with meringue or whipped cream.

float·ing rib, *n.* One rib of the lowest pairs of ribs, not attached to the breastbone or other ribs.

float·plane, flōt′plān″, *n. Aeron.* an airplane equipped with buoyant landing gear, consisting of one or more floats in place of wheels.

floc, flok, *n.* A flaky mass of fine particles, as in a chemical precipitate. A soft fluffy tuft of cotton or wool, esp. used for stuffing mattresses or seats; also **flock**.—*v.i.* —**flocced, floccing.** To gather into a tuftlike mass.—*v.t.* To cause to accumulate into or form flocs.

floc·cose, flok′ōs, *a.* [L. *floccosus.*] *Bot.* Composed of or bearing tufts of woolly, or long, soft hairs; flocculent.

floc·cu·late, flok′ū·lāt″, flok′ya·lāt″, *v.i.*—*flocculated, flocculating.* [N.L. *flocculus.*] To form clusters or masses of loosely united particles, esp. in a chemical precipitate.—*v.t.* To cause to form masses or clusters of particles.—*n.* An aggregate of particles; a flocule.—*a. Entom.* having small tufts of hairs on the body.—**floc·cu·la·tion**, *n.*

floc·cule, flok′ūl, *n.* [N.L. *flocculus.*] Something resembling a small flock or tuft of wool; a small mass of soft, fluffy matter, esp. in a liquid.

floc·cu·lent, flok′ū·lent, *a.* Composed of a mass of loosely joined particles; similar to a

tuft of wool; covered by or having soft hair; *biol.* covered with a soft woolly or waxy secretion.—**floc·cu·lence**, *n.*

floc·cu·lus, flok′ū·lus, *n. pl.* **floc·cu·li.** [N.L. dim. of L. *floccus*, flock of wool.] Anything resembling a flock or tuft of wool; a floccule; flake; particle; *astron.* a cloudy area of brightness or darkness appearing on the sun; *anat.* a lobe of the cerebellum.

flock, flok, *n.* [O.E. *floc, flocc*, a flock, a company of men = Dan. *flok,* Sw. *flock,* Icel. *flokkr,* flock.] A group of animals of the same kind, esp. sheep or birds, that are assembled, fed, or herded together; a large group of people; any group under the supervision of a leader; a Christian congregation in relation to its pastor.—*v.i.* To gather in flocks or crowds.

flock, flok, *n.* [M.E. *flokke,* appar. < O.Fr. Fr. *floc,* < L. *floccus,* flock of wool: cf. M.D. and M.L.G. *vlocke,* O.H.G. *floccho,* flock, flake, Icel. *floki,* felt, hair, wool, and E. *flake.*] A lock or tuft of wool, hair, or cotton; wool or cotton waste used for stuffing mattresses and cushions; finely powdered wool or cloth applied as a decorative finish on wallpaper, display signs, etc., and as a protective coating on metal.—*v.t.* To stuff or cover with flock.

floe, flō, *n.* [Dan. *flage,* Sw. *flaga,* a floe; akin to *flake.*] A large mass of ice floating on the ocean; a floating section of a mass of ice. Also *ice floe.*

flog, flog, flog, *v.t.*—*flogged, flogging.* [Allied to Prov. E. *flack,* to beat; *flacket,* to flap about; perhaps also to *flap* or *flag.*] To beat or whip; to chastise with repeated blows; to criticize severely; to compel into action; *Brit.* to sell vigorously.—**flog·ger**, flog′ėr, *n.*—**flog·ging**, *n.* The act of beating or whipping; a beating.

flood, flud, *n.* [O.E. *flōd,* a flood = Fris., Dan. and Sw. *flod,* Icel. *flod,* D. *vloed;* < the root of *flow.*] A great flow of water; a body of water rising and overflowing the land; the flowing in of the tide; a flow or stream of anything fluid; a great outpouring; an overflowing; superabundance.—*v.t.* To overflow; to inundate; to supply excessively.—**flood·er**, *n.*

flood·gate, flud′gāt″, *n.* A gate in a canal or a river that is either opened or shut in order to control the flow and the depth of the water; anything used to restrain or control an outflow.

flood·light, flud′līt″, *n.* A lamp that projects a bright, broad beam of light, usu. used with a reflector.—*v.t.*—*floodlighted* or *floodlit, floodlighting.* To illuminate by floodlight.

flood plain, *n.* Level land along the course of a stream or river that is prone to flooding; a plain formed from soil deposited by floods.

flood tide, *n.* The rising or incoming tide; an apex; an enormous amount.

flood·wa·ter, flud′wạ″tėr, *n.* The water resulting from a flood.

floor, flōr, *n.* [O.E. *flōr,* a floor = D. *vloer,* a floor; G. *flur,* a field, a floor; W. *llawr,* the ground, a floor.] The part of a building or room upon which one walks; one level of a building containing rooms or apartments; a story; the horizontal parts of a building which divide that building into stories; a flat surface or bottom; as, the ocean *floor*; the level, supporting surface or platform of something constructed; a level area or platform with a special purpose; as, a dance *floor*; the minimum price paid or charged; the part of a legislative hall, auditorium, meeting house, or the like from which the members speak, as distinguished from the gallery; the right to speak in parliamentary procedure; as: Mr. Jones has the *floor.* *Stock market,* the trading room of a stock and commodity

exchange where securities are bought and sold.—*v.t.* To furnish with a floor; to strike or knock down level with the floor; to push to the floor, as an automobile accelerator, maximum speed; *colloq.* to confuse, as: The problem *floored* him.

floor·age, flōr′ij, *n.* The total area of a floor; the total floor space in a building.—**floor·ing**, flōr′ing, *n.* A floor; materials for floors.

floor·board, flōr′bōrd″, *n.* Any of the boards in a floor; the floor of an automobile.

floor lamp, *n.* A lamp whose base rests on the floor.

floor lead·er, *n.* A legislator who manages the activities of his party on the floor of the U.S. Senate or House of Representatives; a similar leader in a state legislature.

floor show, *n.* Singing, dancing, or other entertainment presented at a night club.

floor·walk·er, flōr′wạ″kėr, flạr′wạ″kėr, *n.* One who supervises sales personnel and directs customers in a retail store. Also *Brit.* **shop·walk·er.**

floo·zy, **floo·zie**, flō′zē, *n. pl.* **floo·zies.** *Slang.* A woman of loose morals; a prostitute. Also **floo·sy.**

flop, flop, *v.i.*—*flopped, flopping.* [Var of *flap.*] To fall or plump down suddenly, esp. with noise; drop or turn with a sudden bump or thud; to change suddenly, as from one side or party to another, often with *over; colloq.* yield, break down suddenly, or fail; to flap, as in the wind.—*v.t.* To drop or throw with a sudden bump or thud; to flap clumsily and heavily, as wings; to reverse or transpose, as the right and left sides in a photograph by inverting the negative.—*n.* The act or sound of flopping; a thud; *colloq.* a failure.—**flop·per**, *n.*

flop·house, flop′hous″, *n. Colloq.* a cheap rundown rooming house or hotel, usu. in the poor, disreputable part of a city.

flop·o·ver, flop′ō″vėr, *n.* Defective television reception characterized by a picture which continually crosses the screen vertically.

flop·py, flop′ē, *a.*—*floppier, floppiest.* Tending to flop.—**flop·pi·ly**, *adv.*—**flop·pi·ness**, *n.*

flo·ra, flōr′a, *n. pl.* **flo·ras**, **flo·rae.** [L. < *flos, floris,* a flower.] Plants, esp. those, indigenous to any district, region, or period; a systematic listing of any such plants; (*cap.*) the Roman goddess of flowers; the given name of a girl.—**flo·ral**, flōr′al, flạr′al, *a.*—**flo·ral·ly**, *adv.*

flo·ral en·vel·ope, *n. Bot.* the floral leaves of a flower collectively, as petals or sepals or both; a perianth.

Flor·en·tine, flạr′en·tēn″, flạr′en·tīn″, flor′en·tēn″, flor′en·tīn″, *a.* Of or pertaining to Florence, Italy.—*n.* A native of Florence.

flo·res·cence, flō·res′ens, flo·res′ens, *n.* [N.L. *florescentia,* < L. *florescens,* ppr. of *florescere,* begin to flower, < *florere.*] *Bot.* the act, state, or period of flowering. A flourishing period of prosperity.—**flo·res·cent**, *a.*

flo·ret, flōr′it, flạr′it, *n. Bot.* a small flower; a single small flower in the compact cluster forming the head of a composite plant.

flo·ri·at·ed, flōr′ē·ā″tid, flạr′ē·ā″tid, *a.* Decorated with floral ornament; having the shape of a flower.—**flo·ri·a·tion**, *n.*

flo·ri·bun·da, flōr″i·bun′da, *n. Bot.* any of various hybrid roses bearing open clusters of large flowers.

flo·ri·cul·ture, flōr′i·kul″chėr, *n.* [L. *flos, floris,* and *cultura.*] The cultivation of flowers or flowering plants.—**flo·ri·cul·tur·al**, *a.*—**flo·ri·cul·tur·al·ly**, *adv.*—**flo·ri·cul·tur·ist**, *n.*

flor·id, flōr′id, flạr′id, *a.* [L. *floridus,* < *flos, floris,* a flower.] Having a flowery, overly ornate style; showy; ruddy; flushed

with red; as, a *florid* complexion.—
flo·rid·i·ty, *n.*—**flor·id·ly**, *adv.*—**flor·**
id·ness, *n.*

Flor·i·da moss, *n.* Spanish moss.

flo·rif·er·ous, flō·rif′ĕr·us, *a.* Producing
flowers.—**flo·rif·er·ous·ly**, *adv.*—**flo·rif·**
er·ous·ness, *n.*

flo·ri·le·gi·um, flōr″i·lē′jē·um, flōr″i·
lē′jē·um, *n. pl.* **flo·ri·le·gi·a.** [N.L. < L.
florilegus, flower-culling, < *flos, flor-,*
flower, and *legere*, gather, choose.] A
selection of writings; an anthology.

flor·in, flor′in, *n.* A coin of Great Britain,
one-tenth £, or 2 shillings. The guilder of
the Netherlands. Also **gul·den, gild·er.**

flo·rist, flōr′ist, flor′ist, *n.* [L. *flos (flor-),*
flower.] One who cultivates flowers and
ornamental plants for sale; a dealer in
flowers and ornamental plants, including
artificial ones.—**flo·rist·ry**, *n.*

flo·ris·tics, flō·ris′tiks, flo·ris′tiks, *n. pl.,*
sing. or pl. in constr. A branch of the science
of phytogeography dealing with the distribution of plants upon the earth.—**flo·ris·**
tic, *a.* Pertaining to floristics, a flora, or
flowers.—**flo·ris·ti·cal·ly**, *adv.*

floss, flạs, flos, *n.* [It. *floscio, flosso*, soft,
flaccid, < L. *fluxus*, flowing, loose.] Silk or
silklike fiber in untwisted filaments;
untwisted silk or other strands used in
embroidery; the cottony fiber yielded by
the silk-cotton tree; any silky filamentous
matter, as cornsilk; any similar soft thread,
as that used to clean between the teeth. Also
floss silk.—**floss·y**, *a.*—*flossier, flossiest.* Of
or like floss; soft or silky; downy; *slang*,
showy or ostentatiously stylish.

flo·tage, floa·tage, flō′tij, *n.* The act or
state of floating; buoyancy; anything that
floats; flotsam; the portion of a ship's hull
above the water line.

flo·ta·tion, floa·ta·tion, flō·tā′shan, *n.*
The act or state of floating; the floating or
launching of a commercial venture or a
loan. *Metal.* a process for separating particles
of a powdered metal ore, based on their relative tendency to float or sink in a particular
fluid; any similar process based on relative
floating capacities.

flo·til·la, flō·til′a, *n.* [Sp. dim. of *flota*, a
fleet.] A little fleet; a fleet of small vessels;
a U.S. navy unit consisting of two or more
squadrons.

flot·sam, flot′sam, *n.* [< float.] *Maritime*
law, ship's cargo or wreckage found
floating on and recovered from a body of
water. *Fig.* hoboes; vagrants; wandering
refugees.—**flot·sam and jet·sam**, ship's
cargo or wreckage found floating or on
shore; miscellaneous, worthless, unimportant odds and ends; vagrants; drifters.

flounce, flouns, *v.i.*—*flounced, flouncing.*
[Cf. Sw. dial. *flunsa*, plunge.] To throw the
body about, as in floundering or struggling;
to go with an indignant or angry fling of the
body; to move in a self-conscious, exaggerated way.—*n.* A flouncing movement; a
sudden fling of the body in indignation or
anger.—**flounc·y**, *a.*—*flouncier, flounciest.*

flounce, flouns, *n.* [Originally *frounce*, < Fr.
froncis, a plait, < *froncer, fronser,* to
wrinkle, < L. *frons, frontis*, the front or
forehead.] A gathered or pleated strip of
fabric sewed horizontally around a dress or
skirt, with the lower edge loose.—*v.t.*
flounced, flouncing. To decorate with a
flounce or flounces.—**flounc·ing**, *n.* Fabric
used for flounces.—**flounc·y**, *a.*—*flouncier,*
flounciest.

floun·der, floun′dĕr, *n. pl.* **floun·der,**
floun·ders. [Gr. *flunder*, Sw. *flundra*, Dan.
flynder, flounder.] An edible flatfish.

floun·der, floun′dĕr, *v.i.* [D. *flodderen*, to
flap like a loose garment.] To slip or
stumble; to struggle to maintain or regain
balance, as in deep snow or mud; to be
clumsy or confused.—*n.*

flour, flour, flou′er, *n.* [Fr. *fleur*, a flower,
fleur de farine, flour, lit. 'flour of meal,' the
finest part of the meal.] The finely ground
meal of grain; the finer part of meal
separated by sifting; the fine powder of any
substance.—*v.t.* To convert into flour.—*v.i.*
To separate into tiny particles.—**flour·y**, *a.*
Consisting of or resembling flour; covered
with flour.

flour·ish, flur′ish, flur′ish, *v.i.* [O.Fr.
florir (floriss-) (Fr. *fleurir*) < L. *florere,*
flower, bloom, flourish, < *flos (flor-)*, akin
E. *flower*.] To be vigorous or in good
health; to thrive; to be at the height of
success or development; to be in its or one's
prime; to grow luxuriantly or thrive in
growth; to make strokes or flourishes with a
brandished weapon or the like; to add
embellishments to handwriting; to make an
ostentatious display. *Mus.* to play a showy
passage; to play in a showy manner; to
sound a fanfare.—*v.t.* To brandish or wave
about; to flaunt or display ostentatiously;
to adorn with decorative work or designs.—
flour·ish·er, *n.*—**flour·ish·ing**, *a.* Vigorous in growth; thriving; prosperous.—
flour·ish·ing·ly, *adv.*

flour·ish, flur′ish, flur′ish, *n.* A brandishing
or waving, as of a sword; an ostentatious
display; a decoration or embellishment,
esp. one of sweeping curves in writing.
Rhet. elaborate language; an expression
used merely for effect. *Mus.* an elaborate
passage or addition used only for display; a
fanfare.

flout, flout, *v.t.* [D. *fluiten, fluyten*, to play
on the flute, to whistle, to jeer, < *fluit*, a
flute.] To mock or insult; to treat with
contempt or disrespect; to jeer at; to defy.—
v.i. To behave with contempt, often with *at.*
—*n.* A mock; an insult.—**flout·er**, *n.*

flow, flō, *v.i.* [O.E. *flōwan* = D. *vloeien* =
Icel. *floa*; akin to E. *flood*, and perhaps to
fleet and *float.*] To move along in a stream,
as a liquid; to circulate, as the blood; to
proceed continuously and smoothly as a
stream of people or a line of verse; to fall
or hang loosely at full length, as hair; to
stream or well forth; to gush out; to issue or
proceed from a source; to discharge a
stream, as of blood; to rise and advance, as
the tide, opposed to *ebb*; to overflow or
abound with something.—*v.t.* To cause or
permit to flow; to cover with water or other
liquid; to flood.

flow, flō, *n.* The act of flowing; movement
in or as in a stream; any continuous
movement, as of thought, speech, or trade;
an outpouring or discharge of something, as
blood; the rise of the tide, opposed to *ebb*;
an overflowing; that which flows, as a
stream; the rate of flowing; the volume of
fluid that flows through a passage in a unit
of time; a small coastal channel; a wetland;
mach. advancing distortion of a metal part
under constant use at high temperature;
phys. the transfer of energy.

flow·age, flō′ij, *n.* An overflowing; a
flooded condition; floodwater.

flow chart, *n.* A detailed graphic representation, employing symbols, which illustrates the nature and sequencing of an
operation on a step-by-step basis: a chart
used in systems analysis and computer
technology.

flow chart sym·bol, *n.* A series of unique
graphic symbols representing persons,
places, actions, functions, and equipment
utilized in a flow chart: a symbol used
in systems analysis and computer technology.

flow·er, flou′ĕr, *n.* [O.Fr. *flor, flour* (Fr.
fleur), < L. *flos (flor-)*, flower.] *Bot.* the
blossom or bloom of a plant; the part of a
seed plant comprising the reproductive
organs and their surrounding covers, if any,
esp. when such covers, or envelopes, are

more or less conspicuous in form and color;
a single complex structure consisting of
pistil, stamens, corolla, and calyx; a plant
considered with reference to its blossom or
cultivated for its floral beauty; the state of
efflorescence or bloom; as, plants in *flower.*
An ornament representing a flower; an
ornament or figure of speech; the best or
finest member or part of a number, body,
or whole; as, the *flower* of the family; the
finest or choicest product of anything, as,
the *flower* of his genius; the best or finest
example of some quality; the finest or most
flourishing state or period, as of life or
beauty; the prime; *pl. chem.* a substance in
the form of a fine powder, esp. as obtained
by sublimation; as, *flowers* of sulfur.—
flow·ered, *a.*—**flow·er·less**, *a.*—**flow·er·**
like, *a.*

flow·er, flou′ĕr, *v.i.* To produce flowers,
as a plant; to blossom; to bloom; to come
into full development; to flourish.—*v.t.* To
cover or decorate with flowers or floral
designs.

flow·er·age, flou′ĕr·ij, *n.* The process,
time, or state of flowering; flowers collectively; an abundance of flowers; floral
ornament or decoration.

flow·er·et, flou′ĕr·it, *n.* A small flower;
a floret; a segment of a head of cauliflower.

flow·er girl, *n.* A young girl who carries and
sometimes scatters flowers in a wedding
procession; *Brit.* a woman or girl who sells
flowers in the street.

flow·er head, *n. Bot.* a compact, head-
shaped cluster of tiny flowers or florets all
combined into and enclosed by an involucre,
as in the daisy.

flow·er·pot, flou′ĕr·pot″, *n.* A pot or
container in which plants are grown.

flow·er·y, flou′e·rē, *a.* Full of flowers;
having floral designs; richly embellished
with ornate language; like a flower, as a
fragrance.—**flow·er·i·ly**, *adv.*—**flow·er·**
i·ness, *n.*

flow·ing, flō′ing, *a.* Moving in or as in a
stream; proceeding smoothly or with ease,
as language; smoothly and gracefully
continuous throughout the length, as lines
or curves; falling or hanging loosely at
full length, as hair; abounding, or having
in plentiful supply.—**flow·ing·ly**, *adv.*—
flow·ing·ness, *n.*

flown, flōn, *a.* Coated or decorated with
colors blending or flowing together, as
porcelain or ceramic ware.

flow·stone, flō′stōn″, *n. Geol.* a form of
limestone found where mineral matter has
been deposited by water flowing over rocks.

flu, flō, *n.* See *influenza.*

flub, flub, *v.t.*—*flubbed, flubbing.* To make a
mess of; to botch.—*v.i.* To act in a blundering manner.—*n.*

flub·dub, flub′dub″, *n.* [Prob. a made word.]
Colloq. pretentious nonsense or show;
claptrap. Also **flub·dub·ber·y**, *pl.* **flub·**
dub·ber·ies.

fluc·tu·ant, fluk′chō·ant, *a.* Unstable in
behavior; in a state of constant change;
fluctuating; moving like a wave. *Med.* of a
boil or abscess, having a compressible semiliquid center requiring lancing.

fluc·tu·ate, fluk′chō·āt,″ *v.i.*—*fluctuated,*
fluctuating. [L. *fluctuo, fluctuatum*, < *fluctus,*
a wave, < *fluo*, to flow.] To shift irregularly;
to move backward and forward, as in
waves; to be wavering or unsteady; to vary
markedly and without regularity or conformity; to oscillate; to vacillate; to have
relatively frequent and continuous but
undeterminate variations.—*v.t.* To cause
to undulate erratically.

fluc·tu·a·tion, fluk″chō·ā′shan, *n.* Continuing, usu. irregular movement or change;
a wavering; unsteadiness; a motion like
that of waves; a moving in this and that
direction; a rising and falling.

flue, flö, _n._ [Origin obscure.] The smoke passage in a chimney; any duct or passage for air, gases, or the like; in steam boilers, a pipe or tube through which hot gases are conveyed to heat surrounding water.

flu·ent, flö′ent, _a._ [L. _fluens, fluentis_, ppr. of _fluo, fluxum_, to flow; akin Gr. _phlyō_, to bubble over.] Flowing; having words at one's command and uttering them with facility and smoothness; voluble.—**flu·ent·ly**, _adv._—**flu·en·cy**, _n._

flue pipe, _n._ An organ pipe in which the air enters directly, without striking a reed, and produces a tone by flowing over an opening in the side.—**flue stop**, an organ stop that affects a number of flue pipes.

fluff, fluf, _n._ Light, downy particles, as of cotton; a downy mass; _colloq._ a mistake, esp. in speaking lines in a play or in broadcasting. Something light and trivial—**fluff·y**, _a._—_fluffier, fluffiest._—**fluff·i·ness**, _n._

fluff, fluf, _v.t._ To shake or pat, as a pillow, until light and fluffy, usu. with _up._—_v.i._ To become soft, light, and fluffy.

flu·id, flö′id, _a._ [L. _fluidus_, < _fluo_, to flow.] Capable of flowing; liquid; gaseous; opposite of _solid._ Not fixed or rigid; as, a _fluid_ position on a question.—_n._ A liquid or gas that flows freely; a substance whose particles on the slightest pressure move and change their relative position without separation.—**flu·id·i·ty**, _n._—**flu·id·ly**, _adv._—**flu·id·ness**, _n._

flu·id drive, _n._ A mechanical, usually automatic, system of power transmission in automobiles, in which a rotor, operating in an oil-filled sealed casing, forces another rotor to rotate in response to the driving force transmitted through the action of the oil, thus permitting a smooth drive of the engine in any of the gears.

flu·id·ex·tract, _n. Pharm._ a preparation of a vegetable drug in alcohol, so formulated that the strength of one cubic centimeter of the solution equals a gram of the dry drug.

flu·id me·chan·ics, _n. pl., sing. or pl. in constr._ An applied science which deals with the properties and principles of liquids and gases.

flu·id ounce, _n._ A measuring unit of liquid capacity equal to one-sixteenth pint in the U.S. and one-twentieth pint in Gr. Brit. Abbr. _fl. oz._

flu·i·dram, flö′i·dram″, _n._ A measuring unit of liquid capacity equal to one-eighth part of a fluid ounce. Also **flu·id dram, flu·id drachm.** See Measures and Weights table.

fluke, flök, _n._ [O.E. _flóc._] A flatfish or flounder; any of several trematode flatworms, parasitic in man, sheep, and snails; one of the lobes of a whale's tail.

fluke, flök, _n._ [Origin uncertain.] The part of an anchor, a flat triangular piece at the end of each arm, which catches in the ground; a barb, or the barbed head, of a harpoon, arrow, or the like.

fluke, flök, _n._ An accidental advantage or stroke of luck; lucky chance; an accidentally successful stroke, as in golf or billiards.—_v.t._—_fluked, fluking._ To hit, make, or gain by luck.—**fluk·y**, _a._—_flukier, flukiest._ Obtained by chance; uncertain, as a wind.

flume, flöm, _n._ [O.Fr. _flum_, < L. _flumen_, stream, river, < _fluere_, flow.] A deep, narrow passage containing a mountain torrent; an artificial channel or trough for conducting water, as one in which logs are transported.—_v.t._—_flumed, fluming._ To transport, as lumber, in a flume; to divert, as a river, by a flume.

flum·mer·y, flum′e·rē, _n._ pl. **flum·mer·ies.** [W. _llymru._] Oatmeal or flour boiled with water until thick; a sweet dessert, esp. a molded cold pudding, usu. served with a fruit sauce. _Fig._ an empty compliment; nonsensical talk; humbug.

flunk, flungk, _v.i._ [Origin uncertain.] _Colloq._ To fail, as a student in a course or examination; to give up; back out.—_v.t._ To fail in, as a course; to cause to fail, or give a failing grade to.—_n._ A flunking; a failure.—**flunk out**, to be dismissed or to dismiss from an educational institution because of failure to meet the academic requirements.—**flunk·er**, _n._

flun·ky, flun·key, flung′kē, _n._ pl. **flun·kies, flun·keys.** [L.G. _flunkern_, to flaunt; D. _flonkeren, flinkeren_, to glitter; or < _flank_, one who keeps at his master's flank.] A male servant in livery; a servile person.

flu·or, flö′ər, flö′ér, _n._ [So called from its use as a flux, < L. _fluor_, a flowing. < _fluere_, flow.] _Mineral._

flu·o·resce, flö″o·res′, flu·res′, flō·res′, _v.i._—_fluoresced, fluorescing._ [Back formation < _fluorescence._] To exhibit fluorescence.

flu·o·res·ce·in, flu·o·res·ce·ine, flö″o·res′ē·in, flu·res′ē·in, flō·res′ē·in, _n. Chem._ an orange-red crystalline powder, $C_{20}H_{12}O_5$, which in dilute alkaline solution gives off intense greenish-yellow fluorescence by reflected light and is reddish-orange by transmitted light: used for dyeing water in sea rescue operations, as a tracer to locate well impurities, and for wool and silk dyeing.

flu·o·res·cence, flö″o·res′ens, flu·res′ens, flō·res′ens, _n. Chem., phys._ the emission of electromagnetic radiation, esp. in the form of visible light, by certain substances called phosphors, as the result of absorption of other radiations such as an electric discharge or an ultraviolet light.

flu·o·res·cent lamp, _n._ A lamp which contains a fluorescent bulb in the shape of a tube; a tube whose inside walls are coated with a fluorescent substance and which is filled with argon and mercury vapor, so that, when an electric current is passed through the mercury-argon mixture, ultraviolet light is produced, absorbed by the phosphor, and re-emitted as visible light.

fluor·i·da·tion, flur″i·dā′shan, flōr″i·dā′shan, _n._ The addition of a fluoride to drinking water to prevent tooth decay.—**fluor·i·date**, _v.t._—_fluoridated, fluoridating._ To add a fluoride to.

flu·o·ride, flö′o·rīd″, flur′īd, flō′rīd, _n. Chem._ a compound of fluorine with another element or a radical.

fluor·i·nate, flur′i·nāt″, flōr′i·nāt″, _v.t._—_fluorinated, fluorinating. Chem._ to cause to combine or to treat with fluorine.—**fluor·i·na·tion**, _n._

flu·o·rine, flö′o·rēn″, flö′o·rin, flur′ēn, flur′in, flōr′ēn, flōr′in, _n._ [< _fluor._] _Chem._ an extremely reactive non-metallic element, a light-yellow corrosive gas, found naturally in combination in minerals such as cryolite. Sym. F, at. no. 9.

flu·o·rite, flö′o·rīt″, flur′īt, flōr′īt, _n. Mineral._ naturally occurring calcium fluoride, a transparent or translucent variously colored mineral, used as a flux in steel furnaces and in smelting, and as the principal source of fluorine. Also _fluorspar, fluor._

flu·o·ro·car·bon, flö″o·rō·kär′bon, flur″ō·kär′bon, flōr″ō·kär′bon, _n. Chem._ any of a number of extremely inert compounds of carbon and fluorine, some uses of which are as aerosol propellants, lubricants, refrigerants, solvents, and fire extinguishing agents.

flu·o·rom·e·ter, flö″o·rom′i·tėr, flu·rom′i·tèr, flō·rom′i·tèr, _n._ A device used to measure fluorescence. Also **flu·o·rim·e·ter.**—**flu·o·ro·met·ric**, flö″ér·o·me′trik, flur″o·me′trik, flōr″o·me′trik, _a._—**flu·o·rom·e·try**, _n._

fluor·o·scope, flur′o·skōp″, flōr′o·skōp″, flö′ér·o·skōp″, _n._ An instrument which permits the direct observation on a fluorescent screen of the shadows produced by x-rays or other radiation passing through an opaque object.—**fluor·o·scop·ic**, flur′o·skop′ik, _a._ Pertaining to the fluoroscope or to fluoroscopy.—**fluor·os·cop·i·cal·ly**, _adv._—**fluor·os·co·pist**, flu·ros′ko·pist, _n._—**fluor·os·co·py**, _n._ Examination by means of a fluoroscope.

flu·or·spar, flö′ər·spär″, flö′ér·spär″, _n._ Fluorite.

flur·ry, flur′ē, _n._ pl. **flur·ries.** [Of doubtful origin; akin Sw. _flurig_, disordered, _flur_, disordered hair.] A short-lived snowfall; a sudden gust of wind; sudden agitation, commotion, or bustle; _stock market_, a brief increase in trading activity.—_v.t._—_flurried, flurrying._ To agitate, confuse, or alarm; fluster.—**flur·ried**, _a._—**flur·ried·ly**, _adv._

flush, flush, _v.t._ [Origin uncertain.] To flood with water, esp. for cleansing purposes; wash out, as a sewer or toilet, by means of a sudden gush of liquid; to redden; cause to blush; to animate or elate.—_v.i._ To flow with a rush; flow and spread suddenly; to become suffused with color; redden; blush.—_n._ A rushing or overspreading flow, as of water; a blush; a rosy glow; freshness or vigor; a rush of emotion; elation.

flush, flush, _a._ Even or level, as with a surface; aligned; in one plane; as, the _flush_ deck of a ship; abutting; as close together as possible; well supplied, esp. with money; affluent; prosperous; abundant or plentiful, as money; suffused with a reddish color; blushing; full of vigor; lusty; full to overflowing.—_v.t._ To make flush or even.—_adv._ Squarely; evenly.—**flush·ness**, _n._

flush, flush, _v.t._ [M.E. _flusshen_, appar. imit.: cf. _flash._] To cause, as birds, to leave protective cover.—_v.i._ To fly out or start up suddenly, as birds when disturbed.

flush, flush, _n._ [Fr. (obs.) _flus_, for _flux_, flow, flush (cf. 'run of cards'), < L. _fluxus_, E. _flux._] In poker and certain other card games, a hand or set of cards all of the same suit.

flus·ter, flus′tėr, _v.t._ [Icel. _flauster_, fluster, _flaustra_, to be in a fluster; N. _flosa_, passion.] To agitate; to confuse; to befuddle with drink.—_v.i._ To become agitated or confused; to behave in a nervous, excited manner.—_n._ Agitation; confusion.

flute, flöt, _n._ [O.Fr. _fleute, flehute, flaute, flahute_; origin unknown.] A musical woodwind instrument consisting of a hollow cylindrical tube with a series of fingerholes or keys for producing tone variations, of two types: the recorder, blown through a mouthpiece at the upper end, and the transverse, blown across the edge of a hole in the side near the upper end; in an organ, a pipe or stop that produces a flutelike sound; _furniture, arch._ a furrow or groove as ornamentation on a column. A similar rounded groove or pleat, as in a ruffle, a design on glassware, or the edge of a pie crust.—_v.i._—_fluted, fluting._ To play on a flute; to produce or utter flutelike sounds.—_v.t._ To utter in flutelike tones; to form flutes, grooves, or furrows in.—**flut·ed**, _a._ Uttered in flutelike tones; having flutes or grooves; furrowed.—**flut·er**, _n._—**flut·ing**, _n._—**flut·ist**, _n._—**flute·like**, **flut·y**, _a._—_flutier, flutiest._

flut·ter, flut′ėr, _v.i._ [O.E. _floterian_, to fluctuate, < _flot_, the sea; allied to _float_, and to L.G. _fluttern_, G. _flattern_, to flutter.] To wave or flap in the wind; of birds, to move or flap the wings rapidly without flying or in short, erratic flights; to move with quick vibrations or undulations, as: Her eyelids _flutter._ To move about with quick, erratic motions; to be agitated or upset; to beat irregularly, as the heart.—_v.t._ To cause to flutter; to agitate or throw into confusion. —*n.* Quick and irregular motion; vibration; agitation or confusion; excited commotion, as: Her entrance caused a *flutter. Electron.* sound distortion caused by irregular frequency transmission.—**flut·ter·er,** *n.*—**flut·ter·ing·ly,** *adv.*—**flut·ter·y,** *a.*

flut·ter kick, *n.* An alternating kicking motion in swimming, the knees remaining rigid as in the crawl.

flu·vi·al, flō′vē·al, *a.* [L. *fluvialis, fluviaticus, fluviatilis,* < *fluvius,* a river, < *fluo,* to flow.] Of or pertaining to a river or rivers; produced by river action; growing or living in rivers. Also **flu·vi·a·tile,** flō′vē·a·til, flō′vē·a·til″.

flu·vi·o·ma·rine, flō″vē·ō·ma·rēn′, *a. Geol.* formed or deposited in estuaries in which both the action of the sea and the river are involved.

flux, fluks, *n.* [Fr. < L. *fluxus,* < *fluo,* to flow.] The state of flowing; constant change or movement; a flow or discharge; the inward flow of the tide; an evacuation of fluid matter from the body, esp. an abnormal discharge from the bowels; *metal.* the substance used to promote the fusion of metals or minerals; *phys.* the rate of flow at which a fluid, particles, or energy move across a given area.—*v.t., v.i.* To cause to flow; to make fluid; to fuse by melting; to flow.

flux gate, *n. Phys.* a device in a gyroscopic compass which detects the horizontal component of the earth's magnetic field and accordingly adjusts and maintains an aircraft's proper compass heading.

flux·ion, fluk′shan, *n.* A flux or flowing; perpetual change.—**flux·ion·al, flux·ion·ar·y,** *a.*

fly, flī, *n.* pl. **flies.** [Partly < O.E. *fleóge,* the insect, < *fleógan,* to fly, like G. *fliege,* < *fliegen.*] Any of numerous insects with one pair of transparent wings, of the order *Diptera,* esp. the common housefly, *Musca domestica;* any of various other winged insects, as the firefly. A hook dressed to resemble a fly or other insect, used by anglers.—**fly in the oint·ment,** anything, esp. a small thing, that takes away from the pleasure or usefulness of something else.

fly, flī, *n.* pl. **flies.** A flap of cloth covering a zipper or other fastener in a garment closing, esp. in a pair of men's trousers; a flap making up the door of a tent; a piece of canvas making up a second, outer roof on some tents. The act of flying; flight. *Brit.* a light carriage or hackney coach. The width of an extended flag from its staff to farthest edge; the flag's farthest edge. *Theatr.* an area over a theater stage, as for overhead lights and machinery for moving sets. *Baseball,* a ball batted high into the air and caught inside the foul lines. A flyleaf; a flywheel.

fly, flī, *v.i.*—past **flew,** pp. **flown,** ppr. **flying.** [O.E. *fleógan,* G. *fliegen,* Icel. *fljuga,* Dan. *flyve,* to fly.] To move through the air on wings; to move through the air by force of wind or other propulsion; to journey through the air in an aircraft; to run or pass with swiftness, as time; to move swiftly; to run away,; to flee or escape; to burst in pieces; to flutter or wave, as a flag; to be spent rapidly, said of money; to hunt or attack while flying, as a hawk; *baseball,* to bat a fly ball.—*v.t.* To operate, as an aircraft; to travel over in an aircraft; as, to *fly* the Atlantic; to transport or carry by aircraft.—**to fly at,** to rush at; to attack suddenly and forcefully.—**to fly in the face of,** to act in open defiance of or direct opposition to.—**to let fly,** to discharge, throw, or utter with violence.—**to fly off,** to leave in a hurry.—**to fly in·to,** to have a sudden, uncontrolled outburst, as of rage.—**fly·a·ble,** *a.*—**fly·a·bil·i·ty,** *n.*

fly, flī, *a.*—*flier, fliest. Brit. slang.* Mentally alert; sharp; nimble-witted; quick and agile in movement.

fly ag·a·ric, *n.* A deadly poisonous mushroom, *Amanita muscaria.*

fly·a·way, flī′a·wā″, *a.* Fluttering; streaming; flighty; frivolous. *Aeron.* of or pertaining to supplies and equipment of a military unit designed to be transported in the unit's own aircraft.

fly·blow, flī′blō″, *n.* The eggs or young larvae of a blowfly or flesh fly, deposited on food.—*v.t.*—past *flyblew,* pp. *flyblown,* ppr. *flyblowing.* To deposit eggs or larvae, on, as meat.—**fly·blown,** *a.* Tainted.

fly·boy, flī′boi″, *n. Slang.* A pilot of the U.S. Air Force; any member of that group.

fly·by, flī′bī, *n.* pl. **fly·bys.** A low flight over or past a given point by an airplane or space vehicle.

fly-by-night, flī′bī·nīt″, *n.* An unreliable person or business, esp. in matters of financial responsibility and payment of debts.—*a.* Not responsible or trustworthy, esp. in financial or business matters; not lasting; ephemeral; transitory.

fly cast·ing, *n. Angling,* the act or technique of casting with artificial flies, using a rod longer, lighter, and more flexible than a bait-casting rod.

fly·catch·er, flī′kach″ẽr, *n. Ornith.* any of the singing, perching birds of the family *Tyranmdae,* which feed on insects seized in flight.

fly·er, flī′ẽr, *n.* Flier.

fly gal·ler·y, *n. Theatr.* a narrow, elevated platform near the side of the stage proper from which lines are manipulated to control flying scenery. Also **fly floor.**

fly·ing, flī′ing, *a.* Capable of or suited for flight; moving through the air; moving rapidly; passing quickly or fleeting; as, *flying* moments; waving or floating freely in the air, as flags; trained for swift action or mobility; as, a *flying* squad of policemen; having or appearing to have wings.—*n.* The act of passing or traveling through the air; flight; the piloting of an aircraft.

fly·ing boat, *n. Aeron.* a kind of seaplane having a boatlike hull or fuselage, allowing the craft to float, take off, and land on water.

fly·ing bridge, *n. Naut.* the highest bridge or raised platform on a ship, where navigational instruments and controls are located.

fly·ing but·tress, *n. Arch.* a segment of an arch projecting diagonally downwards and joining a vaulted wall to another buttress, acting as a counterpoise.

fly·ing col·ors, *n. pl.* Complete success or excellence, as: He passed the test with *flying colors.*

Fly·ing Dutch·man, *n.* A legendary Dutch spectral or phantom ship supposedly seen off the Cape of Good Hope, believed to foretell foul weather or danger; the legendary captain of this ship; an opera by Richard Wagner.

fly·ing field, *n.* An area, on a smaller scale than an airport, with runways and facilities for servicing aircraft.

fly·ing fish, *n.* One of the fishes of the family *Exocoetidae,* found in tropical waters, and able to glide a short distance in the air by means of their large, winglike pectoral fins.

Fly·ing For·tress, *n.* A large, heavily-armed U.S. bomber, the piston-engined B-17, widely used in World War II.

fly·ing fox, *n.* Any fruit bat of the family *Pteropodidae,* with a foxlike head, esp. *Pteropus edulis,* of the Old World tropics.

fly·ing gur·nard, *n.* One of several varieties of marine fish whose colorful, large fins enable it to leap above the water and give the appearance of flying.

fly·ing jib, *n. Naut.* a sail extended outside of the jib on the extended jib boom.

fly·ing le·mur, *n.* A nocturnal mammal of the order *Dermoptera,* allied to primates, whose limbs are connected by wide, lateral folds of skin which aid it in making gliding leaps: found in tropical Asia, the East Indies, and the Philippines.

fly·ing ma·chine, *n.* A powered aircraft, esp. an early type of airplane.

fly·ing sau·cer, *n.* Any of various unidentified, disk-shaped, airborne objects reported in the mid-20th century and popularly regarded as secret missiles, ocular illusions, natural phenomena, or vehicles from outer space.

fly·ing squir·rel, *n.* A squirrel of the genus *Glaucomys,* having folds of skin extending between the fore and hind legs which enable it to make gliding leaps.

fly·leaf, flī′lēf″, *n.* pl. **fly·leaves.** A blank page at the beginning or end of a book or pamphlet.

fly·o·ver, flī′ō″vẽr, *n.* The act of flying over a given point on or above the earth by one or more aircraft. *Brit.* an overpass, as on a highway.

fly·pa·per, flī′pā″pẽr, *n.* A porous paper coated with a sticky substance or poison which kills flies.

fly·past, flī′past″, flī′päst″, *n.* Flyby.

fly·speck, flī′spek″, *n.* A speck or mark from the excrement of a fly; a minute spot; *fig.* something insignificant.—*v.t.* To mark with specks.

fly·trap, flī′trap″, *n.* A trap to catch or kill flies.

fly·way, flī′wā″, *n.* A generalized, natural air route regularly taken by migrating birds, such as the Mississippi *flyway.*

fly·weight, flī′wāt″, *n.* A boxer not weighing more than 112 lbs.

fly·wheel, flī′hwēl″, flī′wēl″, *n.* A heavy wheel or disk revolving on a shaft, used to ensure uniform motion in all working parts of a machine.

FM, F.M. Frequency modulation.

f-num·ber, *n. Photog.* a number established by dividing the focal length of a lens by its effective diameter, the smaller the number, the wider the opening, and the shorter exposure necessary. Also **fo·cal ra·tio.**

foal, fōl, *n.* [O.E. *fola* = O.H.G. *folo* = Icel. *foli* = Goth. *fula,* foal; akin to L. *pullus,* Gr. *polos,* young animal, foal.] A young horse, donkey, or related animal; a colt or filly.—*v.t., v.i.* To bring forth or give birth to, as a foal.

foam, fōm, *n.* [O.E. *fām* = G. *feim,* and dial. *faum,* foam; allied to L. *spuma,* foam, < *spuo,* to spit.] The mass of minute bubbles formed on the surface of liquids by fermentation or agitation; froth produced as a result of salivating or sweating; a substance used to extinguish fires, esp. in burning liquids, by smothering the flames with minute, heat resistant bubbles.—*v.i.* To gather foam; to froth; to become or be angry.—*v.t.* To cause to foam.—**foam·i·ly,** *adv.*—**foam·i·ness,** *n.*—**foam·y,** fō′mē, *a.* Covered with foam; frothy.

foam rub·ber, *n.* A spongy rubber, formed by latex which is whipped prior to vulcanization, and used for pillows and mattresses.

fob, fob, *n.* A short chain or ribbon, usu. decorative, attached to a watch and worn hanging from the pocket in which the watch is carried.

f.o.b. [(*f*)ree (*o*)n (*b*)oard.] *Com.* an abbreviation confirming an agreement that shipping charges on goods purchased and placed aboard a common carrier will be borne by the seller. Also **F.O.B.**

fo·cal, fō′kal, *a.* Of or pertaining to a focus; as, the *focal* distance or length of a lens. *Med.* confined to a localized area of the body.—**fo·cal·ize**, fō′ka·līz″, v.t.—focalized, focalizing. To focus.—v.i. To become focused.—**fo·cal·i·za·tion**, fō″ka·li·zā′shan, n.—**fo·cal·ly**, adv.

fo·cal in·fec·tion, n. Pathol. an infection in a specific, localized area which may enter the bloodstream and spread to other parts of the body.

fo·cal length, n. Opt. the distance from the optical center of a lens or mirror to the point where light rays converge. Also **fo·cal dis·tance**.

fo'c's'le, fo'c'sle, fōk′sel, n. Forecastle.

fo·cus, fō′kus, n. pl. **fo·cus·es, fo·ci**, fō′sī. [L., fireplace.] A point at which rays of light, heat, or the like, meet after being reflected or refracted; a point from which diverging rays appear to proceed, or a point at which converging rays would meet if they could be prolonged in the same direction. Opt. the position of an object, or the adjustment of an optical device, necessary to produce a clear image; as, in focus, out of focus; the clear and sharply defined condition of an image resulting from such position or adjustment; the focal point or the focal length of a lens. A central point, as of attraction, attention, or activity; geom. one of the points from which the distances to any point of a given curve are in a linear relation. The place where an earthquake starts; pathol. that part of the body where a disease develops or is localized.

fo·cus, fō′kus, v.t.—focused, focusing, focussed, focussing. To bring into focus, as an image; to concentrate; to adjust to a focus, as a camera lens or the eye.—v.i. To be focused; to be adjusted to a clear image. —**fo·cus·er**, n.

fod·der, fod′ēr, n. [O.E. fódder, fóder, < fóda, food = Icel. fóthr, L.G. foder, D. voeder, G. futter, fodder.] Food for cattle and other livestock, usu. corn, consisting of entire plants including stalks, leaves, and grain.—v.t. To feed with fodder.

foe, fō, n. [O.E. fá, fáh, an enemy, < same stem as fiend.] An enemy; one who entertains personal enmity; an enemy in war; a hostile or opposing army; an adversary.

foehn, föhn, fān, Ger. fœin. n. [G.] A dry, warm wind which blows down into the valleys of a mountain, esp. in the Alps.

foe·tal, fēt′al, a. Fetal.

foet·id, fet′id, a. Fetid.

foe·tus, fē′tus, n. Fetus.

fog, fog, fag, n. [Cf. Dan. fog, spray, shower, drift, Icel. fok, spray, drift (of snow, sand, ashes, etc.), fjūk, snowstorm, fjūka, be driven by the wind, as spray, snow, etc.] Condensed water vapor in the atmosphere near the earth's surface, often interfering with visibility; any darkened state of the atmosphere or the substance which causes it; photog. a blur on a negative or picture resulting from exposure to light other than that producing the image; chem. a mixture of liquid particles dispersed in gas.—v.t.—fogged, fogging. To envelop with or as with fog; to confuse; photog. to affect by fog.—v.i. To become enveloped or obscured with or as with fog.

fog, fog, fag, n. [W. ffwg, dry grass.] A second growth of grass after mowing; long grass that remains on land through the winter.

fog bank, n. A stratum or mass of fog as seen from a distance.—**fog·dog**, fog′dag″, fog′dog″, fag′dag″, fag′dog″, n. A bright spot sometimes seen in a fog bank.

fog·bound, fog′bound″, fag′bound″, a. Surrounded by fog; incapable of navigation due to heavy fog; as, a fogbound ship.

fog·bow, fog′bō″, fag′bō″, n. A whitish or yellow-colored bow, arc, or circle sometimes seen in fog; a rainbow created by fog droplets.

fog·gy, fog′ē, fag′ē, a.—foggier, foggiest. Filled

or abounding with fog; misty; dim; dull; bewildered. Photog. pertaining to a photographic print or plate which has been clouded during the process of developing. —**fog·gi·ly**, adv.—**fog·gi·ness**, n.

fog·horn, fog′harn″, fag′harn″, n. A loud horn for warning vessels of their proximity to the coast or to another ship during a fog; a loud, resonant voice.

fo·gy, fo·gey, fō′gē, n. pl. **fog·ies, fo·geys**. Colloq. an old-fashioned or extremely conservative person, usu. preceded by old. —**fo·gy·ism, fo·gey·ism**, n.—**fo·gy·ish, fo·gey·ish**, a.

foi·ble, foi′bl, n. [O.Fr. weak.] A trivial or minor fault; the weaker part of a sword blade, lying between the middle and the point.

foie gras, fwä·grä′, Fr. fwä·grä′, n. Liver from force-fed geese or ducks used as a table delicacy, and in paste form called pâté de foie gras.

foil, foil, n. [O.Fr. foil (also fem. foille, Fr. feuille), < L. folium, leaf; akin to Gr. phullon.] Metal hammered or rolled into a very thin sheet; as, gold foil or tin foil; the metallic backing applied to glass to form a mirror; a thin layer of metal placed under a gem to improve its color or brilliancy; a person or thing that serves to set off another distinctly or to advantage by contrast; arch. an arc or a rounded space between cusps, as in the tracery of a window or in other ornamentation. See airfoil, hydrofoil.—v.t. To cover or back with foil; to set off by contrast.—foiled, a. Arch. adorned with foils.

foil, foil, v.t. [O.Fr. Fr. fouler, trample, full (cloth).] To prevent from being successful; to frustrate or thwart, as efforts or attempts; hunting, to spoil, as a scent, by trampling so as to baffle pursuers.—n. Archaic, a defeat or check.—foil·er, n.

foil, foil, n. [Appar. < foil.] A blunt sword with a button at the point, for use in fencing; pl. the art or exercise of fencing with such swords.

foils·man, foilz′man, n. pl. **foils·men**. One who is expert at fencing with foils.

foin, foin, v.i. [M.E. foynen, appar. < O.Fr. foine (Fr. fouine), fish-spear, < L. fuscina, trident.] To thrust with a weapon; lunge.—n. Archaic, a thrust with a weapon.

foi·son, foi′zon, n. [O.Fr. Fr. foison, < L. fusio(n-), a pouring out, E. fusion.] Archaic, abundance, esp. an abundant harvest.

foist, foist, v.t. [D. vuist, fist; orig. perh. to insert by clever movements of the fist.] To pass off or impose, as an unworthy person or thing, upon another by deception or fraud, followed by on or upon; to insert surreptitiously or without warrant, followed by in or into.

fol·a·cin, fol′a·sin, n. Chem. folic acid.

fold, fōld, v.t. [O.E. fealdan = O.H.G. faldan = Icel. falda = Goth. falthan, fold.] To double or bend, as cloth or paper, over upon itself; to shut or bring into a compact form by bending and laying parts together, often with up; as, to fold up a map; to bring together or intertwine, as the arms or hands; to clasp or embrace; as, to fold her in his arms; to enclose, wrap, or envelop in something; to bend or wind, often with about or around; as, to fold one's arms about another's neck; of a bird, to bring, as wings, close to the body; cooking, to add to other ingredients by gently turning one part over another, usu. with in; as, to fold in the flour.—v.i. To become folded; colloq. to collapse or fail, esp. financially, sometimes with up.

fold, fōld, n. A folded part, form, or layer of something; as, a fold of cloth; a pleat; a flexure; a crease or line made by folding; a bend or waviness, as a hollow, in the terrain; geol. a bend or curvature in strati-

fied rock, as an anticline, syncline, or monocline; anat. a folded or doubled part of a membrane or other usu. flat structure; as, a vocal fold. A coil, as of the body of a serpent; an act of folding or doubling over.

fold, fōld, n. [O.E. fald = Dan. fold, Sw. falla, a fold, a pen.] A pen or enclosure for sheep or similar animals; a flock of sheep; a church or its congregation; any group having common goals, values, and beliefs.—v.t. To confine in a fold.

fold·a·way, fōld′a·wā″, a. Capable of being folded and put out of the way.

fold·boat, fōld′bōt″, n. A faltboat.

fold·er, fōld′ēr, n. One who or that which folds; a folded printed sheet, as a circular or a timetable; a protective covering, as of folded cardboard, for loose papers, reports, or the like.

fol·de·rol, fol′de·rol″, n. [Orig. meaningless syllables used in songs.] Nonsense; foolish talk or ideas; a trifle. Also falderal.

fold·ing door, n. A door made of hinged sections folded together when opened.

fold·ing mon·ey, n. Colloq. paper currency.

fo·li·a·ceous, fō″lē·ā′shus, a. [L. foliaceus, < folium, a leaf, akin to Gr. phyllon, a leaf.] Having or bearing leaves: said of sepals and bracts that resemble true leaves; consisting of leaves or thin laminae.

fo·li·age, fō′lē·ij, n. [Fr. feuillage, < feuille, L. folium.] Leaves collectively; the leaves of a plant; leaves or leafy growths represented in sculpture or architecture.

fo·li·age leaf, n. A typical green leaf, contrasted with a modified leaf such as a scale, bract, or tendril.

fo·li·ar, fō′lē·ēr, a. [L. folium, leaf.] Of or pertaining to a leaf.

fo·li·ate, fō′lē·āt″, v.t.—foliated, foliating. [M.L. foliatus, pp. of foliare, put forth leaves, < L. folium, leaf.] To shape like a leaf; to beat or roll, as gold, into thin sheets or foil; to separate into thin sheets; to spread over with a thin metallic backing, as glass; to number the folios or leaves of, as a book; arch. to decorate with foils or foliage.—v.i. To put forth leaves; to split into thin leaflike layers or laminae.—fō′lē·it, fō′lē·āt″, a. [L. foliatus, < folium.] Having or covered with leaves; leaflike. —**fo·li·at·ed**, fō′lē·ā″tid, a. Shaped like a leaf; consisting of thin leaflike layers or laminae. Arch. ornamented with foils or with representations of foliage; also foliate.

fo·li·a·tion, fō″lē·ā′shan, n. The act of foliating or bursting into leaf; the state of being in leaf; leaves or foliage; formation of metal into thin sheets; the application of foil to glass; the consecutive numbering of the folios or leaves of a book; geol. the structure of certain rocks resulting from the splitting of various minerals into leaflike layers; arch. ornamentation with foils or representations of foliage.

fo·lic ac·id, n. Chem. a member of the vitamin B complex, found in green plants, fresh fruits, liver, and yeast, used for treatment of nutritional anemia. Also folacin.— **fo·lic**, fō′lik, a. Chem. pertaining to folic acid.

fo·lie à deux, fo·lē′ a dö′, Fr. fạ·lē ä dœ′, n. Psychiatry, the simultaneous occurrence of the same abnormal mental condition in two closely associated persons.

fo·lic·o·lous, fō″lē·ik′o·lus, a. Growing on or parasitic upon leaves, as certain liverworts or fungi.

fo·li·o, fō′lē·ō″, n. pl. **fo·li·os**. [L., abl. of folium, leaf.] A sheet of paper folded once to make two leaves or four pages to each sheet; a volume printed on such sheets, having pages of the largest size; the size of such a volume; one of a collection of leaves, as of a manuscript or book, numbered consecutively on the front side only; the number of a page; a portfolio; *bookkeeping*, facing pages of an account book which have the same serial number; *law*, a certain number of words, in the U.S. generally 100, taken as a unit for estimating the length of a document.—*a.* Pertaining to or having the form of a folio.—*v.t.*—*folioed, folioing.* To number consecutively the leaves or pages of.

fo·li·o·late, fō'lē'o·lāt″, *a. Bot.* pertaining to or consisting of leaflets: often compounded; as, bi*foliolate.*

fo·li·ose, fō'lē·ōs″, *a. Bot.* Leafy; having leaflike appendages, as in lichens and liverworts. Also **fo·li·ous**, fō'lē·us.

fo·li·um, fō'lē·um, *n.* pl. **fo·li·a**, fō'lē·a. [L. leaf.] A lamella; *geol.*, *usu. pl.* thin leaflike strata or laminae frequently found in metamorphic rocks.

folk, fōk, *n. pl.* [O.E. *folc*, folk, a people or nation = L.G., Fris., Dan., and Sw. *folk*; Icel. *folk*; D. and G. *volk*; probably connected with E. *flock*; Lith. *pulkas*, multitude, crowd; but further connections doubtful.] People in general; a separate class of people; people as the preservers of culture, esp. the large proportion of the members of a society which represents its composite customs, traditions, and mores. Also **folks.**—*a.* Originating among or representative of the common people; as, *folk* music; having unknown origin and characterized by traditional forms; as, *folk* legend.—**folks**, *n. pl. Colloq.* the members of one's own family, esp. one's parents.—**folk·ish, folk·like**, *a.*

folk dance, *n.* A dance originated among and transmitted through the common people; a piece of music for such a dance.

folk·et·y·mol·o·gy, *n.* [G. *volksetymologie.*] The modification, through extended popular usage, of an unfamiliar word to give it an apparent correlation with a familiar or better understood word, often as a result of misconception of the word's source and derivation; as, *asparagus* to *sparrowgrass.*

folk·lore, fōk'lōr″, fōk'lar″, *n.* The traditional beliefs, customs, legends, and songs of a people that are handed down orally from generation to generation; the study of these traditions.—**folk·lor·ist**, *n.*—**folk·lor·ic, folk·lor·is·tic**, *a.*

folk·moot, fōk'mōt″, *n.* [O.E. *folcmot*, 'folk meeting.'] Formerly, in England, a general assembly of the people of a shire or town. Also **folk·mote**, fōk'mōt″.

folk mu·sic, *n.* Music, usually of simple character and anonymous origin, handed down orally among the common people and representative of their traditions, beliefs, and attitudes.

folk song, *n.* A song originating among and transmitted orally by the common people of a nation or area, often occurring in a number of versions and usually characterized by simple melody, narrative style, and verse repetition; a popular song written in imitation of this type by a known author.

folk·sy, fōk'sē, *a.*—*folksier, folksiest.* Sociable; informal; unpretentious; as, a *folksy* character.—**folk·si·ly**, *adv.*—**folk·si·ness**, *n.*

folk tale, *n.* A traditional tale or legend originating among a particular people, handed down, esp. by word of mouth, and sometimes in written form.—Also **folk sto·ry.**

folk·ways, fōk'wāz″, *n. pl.* Popular or traditional habits, customs, and standards of conduct informally established and perpetuated within a society. See *mores.*

fol·li·cle, fol'i·kl, *n.* [L. *folliculus*, dim. of *follis*, bellows, bag.] *Anat.* a small cavity, sac, or gland; *bot.* a dry, one-celled fruit, as of the milkweed, that grows from a single carpel and splits only along one seam.—**fol·lic·u·lar**, fo·lik'ū·lėr, fo·lik'ya·lėr, *a.* Pertaining to, consisting of, or like a follicle; provided with follicles; *pathol.* affecting or originating in a follicle.—**fol·lic·u·late, fol·lic·u·lat·ed**, *a.* Provided with or consisting of a follicle.

fol·li·cle-stim·u·lat·ing hor·mone, *n. Biochem.* a pituitary hormone that stimulates production of Graafian follicles in the female and spermatozoa in the male. Also **FSH.**

fol·lic·u·lin, fo·lik'ū·lin, fo·lik'ya·lin, *n. Biochem.* a female hormone produced by the ovarian follicles. Also *estrone.*

fol·low, fol'ō, *v.t.* [O.E. *folgian, fylgan,* = D. *volgen* = G. *folgen* = Icel. *fylgja,* follow; perhaps akin to E. *full.*] To go or come after; move behind in the same direction; to come after in natural sequence or order of time; succeed; come after as a result or consequence; result from; to accept the authority of or adhere to, as a leader; to comply with or obey, as advice; to imitate, as fashion; to move forward along, as a path; to endeavor to attain, as an ideal; to go in pursuit of; to engage in as a pursuit; as, to *follow* a profession; to watch the progress or course of; to attend to and comprehend, as an argument.—*v.i.* To go or come after a person or thing in motion; to come after something else in natural sequence or order of time; to result as an effect; occur as a consequence.—*n.* The act of following; *billiards*, a stroke which causes the cue ball to roll on after the object ball struck by it.—**fol·low suit**, *card playing*, to play a card of the same suit as that first played; *fig.* to follow the example of another.—**fol·low·a·ble**, *a.*

fol·low·er, fol'ō·ėr, *n.* One who or that which follows; one who follows another's beliefs or teachings, as a disciple or adherent; an imitator; an attendant, retainer, or servant; *Brit. colloq.* a male admirer or suitor of a young woman, esp. a maidservant; *mach.* a part of a machine that receives motion from, or follows the motion of, another part.

fol·low·ing, fol'ō·ing, *n.* A body of followers, attendants, or adherents.—*a.* That follows, esp. that comes after, or next in order or time; succeeding; that is now to follow; now to be mentioned, described, or related.

fol·low out, *v.t.* To follow or carry to a conclusion; to execute, as orders.

fol·low through, *v.i.* To extend or carry through a stroke or motion to its full extent, as in golf or tennis; to pursue an activity or plan, esp. to completion.—**fol·low-through**, *n.* The full completion of a stroke, as in golf or tennis; the part of such a stroke which follows impact with the ball; any act of carrying to completion.

fol·low up, *v.t.* To pursue closely; pursue to a conclusion; prosecute with energy, as something already begun; increase the effect of by further action.—**fol·low-up**, *n.* The act of following up; a letter or circular sent to a person to enhance the effect of a previous one, as in advertising; *journalism*, a news story giving additional or supplementary information on a previously published story.—*a.* Following an earlier action, procedure, or letter.

fol·ly, fol'ē, *n. pl.* **fol·lies**. [O.Fr. Fr. *folie*, < *fol.* FOOL.] The state or quality of being foolish; lack of understanding or good judgment; a foolish action, practice, or idea; an absurdity; a costly and foolish undertaking, esp. a pretentious building often left unfinished due to lack of funds. *Pl.* a musical revue or stage show.

Fol·som cul·ture, *n. Anthropol.* a 10,000- to 25,000-year-old hunter culture whose members inhabited a large part of North America east of the Rocky Mountains, discovered in 1926 when stone blades called 'Folsom points' were uncovered near Folsom, New Mexico.—**Fol·som man**, an individual of the Folsom culture.

fo·ment, fō·ment', *v.t.* [Fr. *fomenter*, L. *fomento*, < *fomentum*, for *fovimentum*, a warm application, < *foveo*, to warm, to cherish.] To foster; to promote or encourage; to instigate; as, to *foment* quarrels; to bathe with warm liquids.—**fo·men·ta·tion**, fō″men·tā'shan, *n.* Encouragement, esp. toward a destructive purpose; the applying of warm liquids to relieve pain; that which is applied, as a lotion or poultice.—**fo·ment·er**, *n.*

fond, fond, *a.* [O.E. *fonne*, to be foolish, fond, stupid; *fon*, a fool; akin to Icel. *fana*, to play the fool; Sw. *fane*, fatuous. The word is properly a past participle, whence the final *d*.] Having affection for, usu. followed by *of*; loving or tender; as, a *fond* glance; excessively affectionate; doting; cherished highly or unreasonably; as: He had *fond* hopes of becoming a millionaire.

fon·dant, fon'dant, *Fr.* faṇ dän', *n.* [Fr. prop. ppr. of *fondre*, melt.] Thick, creamy sugar paste, the basis of many candies; the candy made of such paste.

fon·dle, fon'dl, *v.t.*—*fondled, fondling.* To caress; to touch lovingly.—*v.i.* To exhibit affection by caressing.—**fon·dler**, *n.*

fond·ly, fond'lē, *adv.* Lovingly or affectionately.—**fond·ness**, fond'nis, *n.* Tender affection; strong preference.

fon·due, fon·dö', fon'dö, *Fr.* faṇ·dy', *n.* [Fr. prop. fem. of *fondu*, pp. of *fondre.*] A dish composed of melted cheese, usu. with white wine.

font, *Brit.* **fount**, font, fount, *n.* [Fr. *fonte* < *fondre*, melt, cast. FOUND.] A complete assortment of type of one style and size.

font, font, *n.* [O.E. *font* < M.L. *fons*, baptismal font, < L. spring, fountain.] A receptacle, usu. of stone, for the water used in baptism; a receptacle for holy water; the reservoir for oil in a lamp; *fig.* a source or origin.—**fon·tal**, fon'tal, *a.* Pertaining to or issuing from a font; *fig.* pertaining to or being the source of something.

fon·ta·nel, fon·ta·nelle, fon″ta·nel', *n.* [Fr. *fontanelle*, < *fontaine*, E. *fountain.*] *Anat.* one of the spaces, covered with a membranous structure, between certain bones of the fetal or young skull.

food, föd, *n.* [O.E. *fōda*, food; akin to O.H.G. *fuotan*, Icel. *faedha*, Goth. *fōdjan*, feed. FEED, FODDER, FOSTER.] A nourishing substance taken into and absorbed by an organism to sustain life and enable growth and repair of tissues; more or less solid nutriment, as opposed to drink; a particular kind of nutriment; as, a breakfast *food*; something for consumption or use; as, *food* for thought.—**food·less**, *a.*

food chain, *n.* A sequence of plants and animals in which the smallest one provides nourishment for a larger one, which in turn is consumed by a still larger one.

food poi·son·ing, *n.* An acute gastrointestinal ailment caused by food chemically contaminated by insecticides or by bacterial toxins.

food·stuff, föd'stuf″, *n.* A substance or material suitable for food.

foo·fa·raw, fö'fa·ra″, *n.* A fuss over something small or unimportant; gaudy finery.

fool, föl, *n.* [O.Fr. *fol* (Fr. *fol, fou*), n. and *a.*, < L. *follis*, bellows, bag, or ball inflated with air.] One who lacks judgment or sense; a silly or stupid person; one who is made to appear ridiculous or stupid, as: He made a *fool* of me. A dupe; a professional jester or buffoon formerly kept by a person of rank to provide amusing entertainment. *Slang*, an enthusiast; an ardent fan. *Brit.* a dessert made of stewed fruit which is crushed and mixed with cream.—*a.* Foolish; silly.

fool, föl, *v.i.* To act like a fool; jest or play.—*v.t.* To trick or deceive; to spend foolishly, as time or money, usu. with *away.*—**fool a·round,** to waste time.

fool·er·y, fö′le·rē, *n.* pl. **fool·er·ies.** Foolish action or conduct; an act of folly; a foolish action, performance, or thing.

fool·har·dy, föl′här″dē, *a.* [O.Fr. *fol hardi.*] Recklessly bold; foolishly adventurous; rash.—**fool·har·di·ly,** *adv.*—**fool·har·di·ness,** *n.*

fool·ish, fö′lish, *a.* Lacking good sense; silly; resulting from a lack of sense; unwise; as, a *foolish* decision—**fool·ish·ly,** *adv.*—**fool·ish·ness,** *n.*

fool·proof, föl′proof″, *a.* Infallible; involving no risk or chance or error; as, a *foolproof* plan.

fools·cap, fölz′kap″, *n.* [< the watermark used on the paper consisting of a fool's cap.] A legal ruled pad of paper with an approximate one-inch blank space at the top; *Brit.* the size of a sheet of writing or printing paper, usu. 13½ by 17 inches.

fool's cap, *n.* A cap or hood, usually with bells, formerly worn by jesters; also **fools·cap.** A conical paper cap formerly worn by troublesome or slow students as punishment; also **dunce cap.**

fool's er·rand, *n.* An absurd or useless errand or undertaking.

fool's gold, *n.* Iron or copper pyrites, which are sometimes mistaken for gold.

fool's par·a·dise, *n.* A state of illusory happiness; enjoyment based on false beliefs or hopes.

foot, fụt, *n.* pl. **feet.** [O.E. *fōt* = D. *voet* = G. *fuss* = Icel. *fotr* = Goth. *fotus,* foot; akin to L. *pes* (*ped-*), Gr. *pod-*, and Skt. *pad,* foot.] The terminal part of the vertebrate leg, on which the body stands and moves; in invertebrates, any part similar to a foot in position or function; any part or thing resembling a foot in form, use, or position, as the lower terminating part of a leg of a piece of furniture; a unit of measurement which in English-speaking countries is equal to 12 inches or 30.48 centimeters; walking or running motion; step; pace; the part of anything opposite the top or head; as, the *foot* of a mountain; the bottom or base, as of a page or ladder; that part of a bed or grave where the feet are placed; that part of a stocking or boot that covers the foot; the last of a series; *naut.* the lower edge of a sail; *pros.* the major unit of poetic meter consisting of a group of stressed and unstressed syllables. Soldiers who march or fight on foot; infantry as distinguished from cavalry.—**on foot,** on one's own feet; walking, as: He came *on foot.*

foot, fụt, *v.i.* To walk or dance, often followed by *it;* to move.—*v.t.* To set foot on; walk or dance on; to add, as a column of figures, and place the sum at the foot, often with *up; colloq.* to assume responsibility for, or settle, as a bill. To make or attach a foot to; as, to *foot* a stocking.

foot·age, fụt′ij, *n.* Length or extent in feet; as the *footage* of a film; a scene or scenes on a particular subject in a motion-picture; as, newsreel *footage; mining,* payment by the running foot of work done, or the amount so paid.

foot-and-mouth dis·ease, *n.* A highly contagious, febrile disease of cattle and other hooved animals marked by blisters in the mouth, and around the hooves, teats, and udder. Also **aph·thous fe·ver, hoof-and-mouth dis·ease.**

foot·ball, fụt′bạl, *n.* An outdoor game, amateur or professional, played by opposing teams of eleven men each, on a field 100 yards long with a goal at each end, points

being scored by getting the ball over the goal line or kicking it between the goalposts. An ellipsoidal ball used in this game, inflated and leather-covered, which may be carried, thrown, or kicked; also *pigskin. Brit.* rugby, played with an identical ball; soccer. *Canada,* a game similar to U.S. football, but played with teams of twelve men each. *Fig.* a controversial or difficult problem which is left unsolved by one responsible party and delegated to another for action.

foot·board, fụt′börd″, *n.* A board or small platform on which to support the foot or feet; an upright piece across the foot of a bedstead; a treadle.

foot·bridge, fụt′brij″, *n.* A bridge for pedestrians.

foot·can·dle, fụt″kan′dl, *n. Opt.* A unit of illumination equivalent to that produced by a standard candle at the distance of one foot; one lumen per square foot.

foot·ed, fụt′id, *a.* Provided with a foot or feet; having a certain number of feet: often used in combination; as, multi-*footed.*

foot·er, fụt′ẽr, *n.* One who goes on foot; a pedestrian; an indicated number of feet in height, length, or breadth; as, a six-*footer.*

foot·fall, fụt′fạl″, *n.* A footstep; the sound made by a footstep.

foot fault, *n. Tennis,* a fault called against a player for serving the ball without keeping both feet behind the base line.—*v.i.*

foot·gear, fụt′gẽr″, *n.* Articles used to cover the feet, as shoes or boots.

foot·hill, fụt′hil″, *n.* A low hill at the foot of a mountain or at the edge of a mountainous area.

foot·hold, fụt′hōld″, *n.* A place where one may tread or rest securely; firm standing; footing; stable position.

foot·ing, fụt′ing, *n.* A firm or secure position for the feet; foothold; a secure position or basis; as, a business on a sound *footing;* social, economic, or professional standing in relation to others, as: He was on an equal *footing* with his colleagues. The addition of a column of figures or the resulting sum; *building trades,* a foundation, as for a wall.

foot·lights, fụt′līts, *n. pl. Theatr.* a row of lights at the front of a stage, almost at the level of the performers' feet, used to illuminate the stage action. The stage or theater as a profession.

foot·lock·er, fụt′lok″ẽr, *n.* A small, stationary chest or trunk placed at the foot of a bed for storage of personal belongings, first used by soldiers.

foot·loose, fụt′lös″, *a.* Free to go about at will; not confined by ties or responsibilities. —**foot·loose and fan·cy free,** carefree, unattached.

foot·man, fụt′man, *n.* pl. **foot·men.** A liveried carriage attendant; a house servant.

foot·note, fụt′nōt″, *n.* A note of reference or explanation at the bottom of a page which documents or supplements the text; a statement, action, or event that is subordinate to a larger or more significant one.—*v.t.*—*footnoted, footnoting.* To supply with footnotes.

foot·pace, fụt′pās″, *n.* A walking pace; a raised portion of a floor; a stairway landing.

foot·pad, fụt′pad″, *n.* A robber who goes on foot and robs other pedestrians.

foot·path, fụt′päth″, *n.* A narrow path for pedestrians only. *Brit.* a sidewalk in town; a path in the country. Also **foot·way.**

foot-pound, fụt′pound′, *n. Phys.* a unit of work or energy; the work done by a force equal to one pound when it acts through a distance of one foot in the direction of the force. Abbr. *ft-lb, fp, f.p.*

foot-pound·al, fụt′poun′dal, *n. Phys.* The absolute unit of work in the foot-pound-second system of measurement; the work done by a one poundal force when it acts through a distance of one foot in the direction of the force.

foot-pound-sec·ond, fụt′pound′sek′ond, *n. Phys.* of or pertaining to the system of units of measurement in which the basic units of length, mass, and time are the foot, pound, and second. Abbr. *fps, f.p.s.*

foot·print, fụt′print″, *n.* The mark or impression left by a foot, as in sand or soft earth; an imprint of the sole of the foot made for identification purposes.

foot·rest, fụt′rest″, *n.* A support on which to rest the feet.

foot rot, *n. Veter. pathol.* an inflammatory infection of the feet of sheep or cattle, causing lameness; *bot.* a disease in plants that rots the stem near the ground.

foot sol·dier, *n.* An infantryman.

foot·sore, fụt′sör″, fụt′sạr, *a.* Having the feet sore or tender, as from much walking.

foot·stalk, fụt′stạk″, *n. Zool.* a stalk or a supportive structure resembling a stalk; *bot.* a stem or stalk; also *pedicel, peduncle.*

foot·step, fụt′step″, *n.* The act of taking a step; the distance traversed by one step; the sound of a step; a footprint; a stair.

foot·stool, fụt′stöl″, *n.* A low stool upon which to rest the foot or feet.

foot-ton, fụt′tun′, *n. Phys.* a unit of work equivalent to the energy expended in raising a ton of 2,240 pounds a distance of one foot.

foot·wall, fụt′wạl″, *n. Geol.* the top layer of the rock strata beneath a fault plane; *mining,* the top layer of rock strata lying beneath a bed of ore, a vein, or a lode.

foot·wear, fụt′wâr″, *n.* Protective covering for the feet, as boots, shoes, or slippers.

foot·work, fụt′wụrk″, *n.* Management or control of the feet, as in dancing or boxing; moving from place to place on foot, esp. for purposes of investigation or research.

fop, fop, *n.* [D. *foppen,* to banter, to make a fool of, *fopper,* a wag.] A vain man who is unduly concerned with his dress, appearance, and manners.—**fop·pish,** fop′ish, *a.* Like or suited to a fop; affected in dress or manners.—**fop·pish·ly,** *adv.*—**fop·pish·ness,** *n.*

fop·per·y, fop′e·rē, *n.* pl. **fop·per·ies.** The characteristics of a fop; something which is typical of or used by a fop.

for, fạr, *unstressed,* fẽr, *prep.* [O.E. *for,* also *fore,* before, for.] In the interest of or on behalf of; as, to act *for* a client; in place of, or instead of; as, a substitute *for* butter; in consideration of, or in return for; as, three *for* a dollar; in exchange for or as an offset to; as, blow *for* blow; in favor of, or on the side of; as, to stand *for* honest government; in honor of; as, to give a dinner *for* a person; with the object or purpose of; as, to go *for* a walk; conducive to; as, *for* the advantage of everybody; in order to obtain; as, a suit *for* damages; in order to save; as, to flee *for* one's life; with inclination or sensitivity toward; as, an eye *for* beauty; in proportion to; as, tiny *for* her age; with the purpose of reaching; as, to start *for* London; intended to belong to, suit the purposes or needs of, or be used in connection with; as, a picture book *for* children; in assignment or attribution to; as, an engagement *for* this evening; appropriate or adapted to; as, a subject *for* speculation; such as to allow of; as, too many *for* separate mention; such as results in; as, his reason *for* going; with regard or respect to; as, so much *for* that; as affecting the interests or circumstances of; as, bad *for* one's health; in the character of, or as being; as, to know a thing *for* a fact; by reason of, or because of; as, to shout *for* joy; in spite of; as, to love someone, *for* all that; during the continuance of; as, *for* a long time; to the extent or amount of; as, to walk *for* a mile; used to introduce an infinitive phrase equivalent to a noun clause such as *that he should*, as: It is time *for* him to leave home.—*conj.* Because; seeing that; since.

for·age, făr′ij, for′ij, *n.* [O.Fr. *forrage* (Fr. *fourrage*), < *forre, fuerre,* fodder; < Teut., and akin to E. *fodder.*] Food for horses and cattle; fodder; provender; the seeking or obtaining of such food; the act of searching for provisions of any kind; a raid.—*v.t.* *foraged, foraging.* To collect forage from; strip of supplies; plunder; to obtain by foraging; to supply with forage.—*v.i.* To wander in search of supplies; to hunt or search about; rummage; to make a raid.—**for·age cap,** a small, low, fatigue cap formerly worn by soldiers.—**for·ag·er,** *n.*

fo·ra·men, fō·rā′men, fo·rā′men, *n.* pl. **fo·ram·i·na,** fō·ram′i·na, fa·ram′i·na, fō·ram′i·na. [L., < *foro,* to bore.] A small natural opening or perforation in parts of animals, such as an opening by which nerves or blood vessels obtain a passage through bones.—**fo·ram·i·nal, fo·ram·i·nous,** fo·ram′i·nal, *a.*—**fo·ram·i·nate,** fō·ram′i·nit, *a.* Perforated; full of holes.

for·a·men mag·num, *n.* The occipital bone opening and passageway of the spinal cord that unites with the medulla oblongata.

for·as·much, făr′az·much′, fĕr·az·much′, *conj.* In view of the fact that; seeing that; since: followed by *as.*

for·ay, făr′ā, for′ā, *v.t., v.i.* [A form of *forage.*] To ravage; to pillage; to forage.—*n.* A predatory excursion; a raid.—**for·ay·er,** făr′ā·ĕr, for′ā·ĕr, *n.* A marauder.

forb, fărb, *n.* An herb, other than a grass, such as a legume, that is eaten by livestock.

for·bear, făr·bâr′, *v.t.*—past *forbore,* pp. *forborne,* ppr. *forbearing.* [O.E. *forberan.*] To refrain or desist from; to keep back; withhold; *archaic,* to endure.—*v.i.* To refrain; to be patient; to practice self-control when aroused or provoked.—**for·bear·er,** *n.*—**for·bear·ing·ly,** *adv.*

for·bear, făr·bâr″, *n.* Forebear.

for·bear·ance, făr·bâr′ans, *n.* The act of forbearing; a refraining from something; forbearing conduct or quality; patience; leniency; an abstaining from the enforcement of a right, as from collecting an overdue debt.

for·bid, fĕr·bid′, făr·bid′, *v.t.*—past *forbade, forbad;* pp. *forbidden,* ppr. *forbidding.* [O.E. *forbēodan.*] To command against an action; prohibit; to bid or command not to do; to hinder or prevent; render impossible; to exclude or bar from use.—**for·bid·dance,** *n.* The act of forbidding or the state of being forbidden.

for·bid·den, fĕr·bid′en, făr·bid′en, *a.* Prohibited; not permitted.

For·bid·den Cit·y, *n.* Formerly a walled section of Peking which contained the palace of the Chinese emperors and other royal buildings; Lhasa, capital city of the Chinese province of Tibet.

for·bid·den fruit, *n. Bib.* fruit of the tree of the knowledge of good and evil, of which Adam and Eve partook despite God's prohibition; any unlawful pleasure or immoral indulgence.

for·bid·ding, fĕr·bid′ing, făr·bid′ing, *a.* Grim or disagreeable; threatening; keeping one back from a nearer approach; repellent; causing aversion or dislike.—**for·bid·ding·ly,** *adv.*—**for·bid·ding·ness,** *n.*

for·bode, fōr·bōd′, *v.t., v.i.* Forebode.

force, fōrs, fărs, *n.* [O.Fr. Fr. *force,* < M.L. *fortia,* < L. *fortis,* strong.] Strength or power, esp. active power; impetus; physical strength or power. exerted upon an object; physical coercion; violence; *law,* unlawful

violence to persons or things. The power of overcoming resistance; power to influence or control; mental or moral strength; any body of persons combined for joint action; as, a police *force,* an office *force;* often *pl.* a body of armed men; as, the armed *forces.* Might, as of a ruler or realm; strength for war; any influence or agency analogous to physical force; as, a social *force;* binding power, as of an agreement; operation; as, a law now in *force. Phys.* an influence which produces or tends to produce motion or change of motion; the intensity of such an influence.—**force·less,** *a.*

force, fōrs, fărs, *v.t.*—*forced, forcing.* [O.Fr. Fr. *forcer,* < *force.*] To compel or oblige; to bring about or effect by force; to bring about of necessity; to put or impose forcibly, followed by *on* or *upon;* as, to *force* one's opinions *upon* another; to drive or propel against resistance; to make one's way by force; to overcome the resistance of; compel by force; to ravish or violate, as a woman; to obtain or draw forth by or as by force; extort; to take or enter by force; as, to *force* a stronghold; to break open, as a door or lock; to cause, as plants or fruit, to grow or mature by artificial means; to press, urge, or exert to violent effort or to the utmost; to use force upon. *Baseball,* to put out, as a runner, by compelling him to advance from one base to another in order to free a base for another runner; to allow, as a run, to be scored by walking the batter when there is already a runner on each base. *Cards,* to compel, as a player, to trump by leading a suit of which he has no cards; to compel to play so as to make known the strength of a hand held; to compel a player to play, as a particular card.—*v.i.* To make one's way by force.—**force·a·ble,** *a.*—**forc·er,** *n.*

forced, fōrst, fărst, *a.* Subjected to force; enforced or compulsory; as, *forced* labor; strained, unnatural, or affected; as, a *forced* smile.—**for·ced·ly,** fōr′sid·lē, făr′sid·lē, *adv.*

forced land·ing, *n. Avi.* a landing, either on land or water, made when it is impossible for the aircraft to remain airborne as a result of mechanical failure, combat damage, or the like.

force feed, *n.* A system of lubrication supplying oil under pressure, esp. to an internal-combustion engine.

force-feed, fōrs′fēd′, fărs′fēd′, *v.t.*—*forcefed, force-feeding.* To induce to eat by employing force, fear, or cajolery; to force acceptance, as of an idea.

force·ful, fōrs′ful, fărs′ful, *a.* Full of force; powerful; vigorous; effective; acting or driven with force.—**force·ful·ly,** *adv.*—**force·ful·ness,** *n.*

force ma·jeure, *Fr.* fărs mä·zhŒr′, *n.* pl. **forces ma·jeures.** [Fr.] *Law,* an unpredictable occurrence which may be judged sufficient cause to void a contract.

force·meat, fōrs′mēt″, fărs′mēt″, *n. Cookery,* meat or fish chopped fine and seasoned, either served alone or used a stuffing. Also *farce.*

for·ceps, făr′seps, for′seps, *n.* pl. **for·ceps, for·ci·pes,** făr′se·pēz″. [L.] An instrument, as pincers or tongs, for seizing and holding objects, as in surgical operations.

force pump, *n.* A pump which delivers liquid by means of pressure or force directly applied, so as to eject it forcibly to a great elevation, in contrast to a lift pump.

for·ci·ble, fōr′si·bl, făr′si·bl, *a.* Having force; exercising force; powerful; marked by force or violence; effective.—**for·ci·ble·ness,** *n.*—**for·ci·bil·i·ty,** *n.*—**for·ci·bly,** *adv.*

ford, fōrd, fărd, *n.* [O.E. *ford,* connected with *faran,* to go, to fare; akin G. *furt,* a ford, *fahren,* to go; allied to Gr. *poros,* a passage.]

A place in a river or other body of water where it is shallow enough to be passed by wading.—*v.t.* To pass or cross, as a stream, by wading.—**ford·a·ble,** *a.*

for·do, fore·do, făr·dō′, *v.t.*—past *fordid,* pp. *fordone,* ppr. *fordoing; foredid, foredone, foredoing.* To exhaust, overpower, or overcome, as by toil.

fore, fōr, făr, *a.* [< *fore-,* prefixal use of *fore, adv.,* in noun compounds: cf. *forepart.*] Situated at or toward the front, as compared with something else; first in place, time, order, or rank; forward; earlier.—*n.* The forepart of anything; the front; *naut.* the foremast.—**to the fore,** to or at the front; to or in a conspicuous place or position.

fore, fōr, făr, *prep., conj.* [O.E. *fore* = D. *voor* = G. *vor* = Goth. *faura,* before, for; akin to L. *præ,* before, *pro,* Gr. *pro,* before, for, Skt. *pra,* before.] *Archaic or dial.* before. Also **'fore.**—*interj. Golf,* a cry of warning to persons who may be in the path of one's hit ball.—*adv. Naut.* at or toward the bow.

fore-and-aft, fōr′and·aft′, făr′and·aft, fōr′-and·äft′, făr′and·äft, *a. Naut.* situated along or running parallel to the length of a ship; lengthwise.

fore·arm, fōr′ärm″, făr′ärm″, *n.* That part of the arm which is between the elbow and the wrist.

fore·arm, fōr′ärm′, făr′ärm′, *v.t.* To arm or prepare for attack or resistance before the time of need.

fore·bear, for·bear, fōr′bâr″, făr′bâr″, *n.* [Orig. Sc.] *Usu. pl.* Ancestors; forefathers.

fore·bode, for·bode, fōr·bōd′, făr·bōd′, *v.t.*—*foreboded, foreboding.* To bode beforehand; foretell; presage; to be prescient of; to feel a secret sense of, as of a calamity about to happen.—*v.i.* To make predictions.—**fore·bod·er,** *n.*

fore·bod·ing, fōr·bō′ding, făr·bō′ding, *n.* A prediction or omen; a portent; an inner sense of a coming event, esp. of a calamity.—*a.* Indicative of a coming event, esp. of a misfortune.—**fore·bod·ing·ly,** *adv.*—**fore·bod·ing·ness,** *n.*

fore·brain, fōr′brān″, făr′brān″, *n. Anat.* The anterior of the three major divisions of the embryonic vertebrate brain; the diencephalon and telencephalon, the segments of the adult vertebrate brain which develop from this tissue. Also **pros·en·ceph·a·lon.**

fore·cast, fōr′kast″, făr′kast″, fōr′käst″, făr′käst″, *v.t.*—*forecast* or *forecasted, forecasting.* To form an opinion beforehand; predict; to make a prediction, as of the weather; to serve as a forecast of; foreshadow; to contrive, or plan beforehand; prearrange.—*v.i.* To conjecture beforehand; make a forecast; to plan or arrange beforehand.—*n.* prediction, esp. as to the weather; a conjecture as to something in the future; a foreshadowing of something else to come; the act, practice, or faculty of forecasting.—**fore·cast·er,** *n.*

fore·cas·tle, fōk′sal, fōr′kas″al, fōr′kä″sal, făr′kas″al, făr′käs″al, *n. Naut.* A short raised deck in the forepart of a ship, in front of the foremast; the forward section of a vessel where the sailors' quarters are located; a structure above deck, in the bow of the ship, used to shelter supplies and machinery. Also **fo′c's′le, fo′c′sle.**

fore·close, fōr·klōz′, făr·klōz′, *v.t.*—*foreclosed, foreclosing.* [O.Fr. *forclos,* pp. of *forclore,* exclude, < *for-* (< L. *foris*), outside, and *clore,* L. *claudere,* shut.] *Law,* to deprive of the right to redeem mortgaged property; to take away the right to redeem, as a mortgage or pledge; exclude or bar; to hinder or prevent, as from doing something; to establish an exclusive claim to; to close, settle, or answer beforehand;

as, to *foreclose* objections.—*v.i.* To foreclose a mortgage.—**fore·clos·a·ble,** *a.*—**fore·clo·sure,** fōr·klō′zhèr, *n.* The act of foreclosing, esp. of foreclosing a mortgage.

fore·deck, fōr′dek″, fạr′dek″, *n. Naut.* the forepart of a ship's upper or main deck.

fore·do, fōr·dō′, fạr·dō′, *v.t.* Fordo.

fore·doom, fōr·dōm′, fạr·dōm′, *v.t.* To doom beforehand.—fōr′dōm″, fạr′dōm″, *n.* A predestination of condemnation or misfortune.

fore·fa·ther, fōr′fä″THèr, fạr′fä″THèr, *n.* An ancestor.

fore·fend, fōr·fend′, fạr·fend′, *v.t.* Forfend.

fore·fin·ger, fōr′fing″gèr, fạr′fing″ẽr, *n.* The finger next to the thumb. Also *index finger.*

fore·foot, fōr′fụt″, fạr′fụt″, *n.* pl. **fore·feet.** One of the anterior feet of a quadruped or multiped.

fore·front, fōr′frunt, fạr′frunt, *n.* The foremost or most eminent part, place, or position.

fore·gath·er, fōr·gaTH′ér, fạr·gaTH′ér, *v.i.* Forgather.

fore·go, fōr·gō′, fạr·gō′, *v.t.* Forgo.

fore·go, fōr·gō′, fạr·gō′, *v.t.,* *v.i.*—past *forewent,* pp. *foregone,* ppr. *foregoing.* To go before; to precede.—**fore·go·er,** *n.* One who goes before another; an ancestor; a progenitor.—**fore·go·ing,** *a.* Preceding; going before, in time or place; antecedent. —**fore·gone,** fōr·gon′, fōr′gon″, *a.* Past; preceding; predetermined.

fore·gone con·clu·sion, *n.* An obvious, inevitable result; a conclusion determined before consideration of evidence.

fore·ground, fōr′ground″, fạr′ground″, *n.* The part of a scene or picture which is, or is represented as being, nearest to the observer; the forefront.

fore·hand, fōr′hand″, fạr′hand″, *a.* A stroke in tennis and other racquet or paddle sports made with the palm turned in the direction in which the hand is moving; being in front or ahead; foremost or leading; done beforehand; given or made in advance, as a payment.—*n.* A forehand stroke; the part of a horse which is in front of the rider; *archaic,* the advantage; upper hand.—*adv.* With a forehand stroke.—**fore·hand·ed,** *a.* Forehand, as a stroke in tennis; providing for the future or the unexpected; prudent; thrifty; well-to-do.—**fore·hand·ed·ly,** *adv.* —**fore·hand·ed·ness,** *n.*

fore·head, fạr′id, for′id, fạr′hed″, for′hed″, *n.* [O.E. *forhēafod.*] The part of the face above the eyes; the brow.

for·eign, fạr′in, for′in, *a.* [Fr. *forain* < L.L. *foranus,* < L. *foras,* out of doors.] Belonging or relating to another country; located outside of one's own country; not of the country in which one resides; relating to dealings with other countries; carried on with another country or countries; as, *foreign* trade; alien; not one's own; not belonging or connected; not to the purpose, usu. with *to* or *from.*—**for·eign·er,** *n.* A person born in or belonging to a foreign country; an alien.—**for·eign·ism,** *n.* A foreign idiom or custom.—**for·eign·ness,** *n.*

for·eign af·fairs, *n.* *pl.* Diplomatic, commercial, or any other matters relating to activities between one nation and another; international activities.

for·eign bill, *n.* A bill of exchange authorizing a payment to a creditor in a foreign country.

for·eign ex·change, *n.* The transferring of funds to settle accounts with firms or residents in a foreign country.

for·eign min·is·ter, *n.* A cabinet minister in charge of foreign affairs; the equivalent of U.S. Secretary of State or Brit. Foreign Secretary.

for·eign serv·ice, *n.* (*Often cap.*) that branch of the U.S. State Department whose diplomatic and consular personnel represent the U.S. abroad.

fore·judge, fōr·juj′, fạr·juj′, *v.t.*—*forejudged, forejudging.* To judge beforehand or before hearing the facts and examining the evidence; to prejudge.—**fore·judg·er,** *n.*

fore·judge, fōr·juj′, fạr·juj′, *v.t.*—*forejudged, forejudging.* To forjudge.

fore·know, fōr·nō′, fạr·nō′, *v.t.*—past *foreknew,* pp. *foreknown,* ppr. *foreknowing.* To have previous knowledge of; to know beforehand.—**fore·know·a·ble,** *a.*—**fore·know·er,** *n.*—**fore·know·ing·ly,** *adv.*

fore·knowl·edge, fōr′nol″ij, fạr′nol″ij, fōr··nol′ij, fạr·nol′ij, *n.* Knowledge of a thing or event before it takes place; prescience.

fore·leg, fōr′leg″, fạr′leg″, *n.* One of the front or anterior legs, as of an animal or chair.

fore·lock, fōr′lok″, fạr′lok″, *n.* A lock or tuft of hair growing from the forepart of the head, esp. on horses.

fore·man, fōr′man, fạr′man, *n.* pl. **fore·men.** A man who supervises others, as in a work crew; the chairman of a jury who acts as its spokesman.—**fore·man·ship,** *n.*

fore·mast, fōr′mast″, fōr′mäst″, fạr′mast″, fạr′mäst″, *n. Naut.* the mast nearest the bow of a ship.

fore·most, fōr′mōst″, fạr′mōst″, fōr′most, fạr′most, *a.* [< O.E. *formest.*] First in place, rank, order, or time.—*adv.* In the first place.

fore·name, fōr′nām″, fạr′nām″, *n.* A name that precedes the family name or surname; the first name.—**fore·named,** *a.* Named or mentioned before in the same statement or writing; aforesaid.

fore·noon, fōr′nōn″, fạr′nōn″, *n.* The part of the day that comes before noon; the period from late morning to midday.— fōr′nōn″, *a.*

fo·ren·sic, fo·ren′sik, *a.* [L. *forensis,* < *forum,* forum.] Pertaining to, connected with, or used in courts of law or public discussion and debate; adapted or suited to argumentation; argumentative.—*n.* A spoken or written exercise in argumentation, as in a college.—**fo·ren·sics,** *n.* *pl.,* *sing.* or *pl.* *in constr.* The art or theory of debate and argumentation.—**fo·ren·si·cal·i·ty,** fo·ren″si·kal′i·tē, *n.*

fo·ren·sic med·i·cine, *n.* Medical knowledge as applied to issues involved in civil and criminal law, esp. in the proceedings in a court of law. Also *medical jurisprudence, le·gal med·i·cine.*

fore·or·dain, fōr″ạr·dān′, fạr″ạr·dān′, *v.t.* To ordain or appoint beforehand; to preordain; to predestine.—**fore·or·di·na·tion,** fōr″ạr·di·nā′shan, fạr″ạr·di·nā′shan, *n.* Predetermination; predestination.

fore·part, fōr′pärt″, fạr′pärt″, *n.* The most advanced part, or the first in time or place; the anterior part; the beginning.

fore·quar·ter, fōr′kwạr″tèr, fạr′kwar″tèr, *n.* One of the two halves of the front portion of the body of an animal, as of lamb or beef.

fore·run, fōr·run′, fạr·run′, *v.t.*—past *foreran,* pp. *forerun,* ppr. *forerunning.* To run before or to precede; to be a prediction or omen of; to be a herald of.—**fore·run·ner,** *n.* A person sent ahead to give notice of the approach of others; a harbinger; a sign or omen of something to follow; an ancestor; an antecedent.

fore·said, fōr′sed″, fạr′sed″, *a.* Spoken of or mentioned before; aforesaid.

fore·sail, fōr′sāl, fạr′sāl, *n. Naut.* a sail carried on the foreyard of a square-rigged vessel; the principal fore-and-aft sail set on the foremast of a schooner.

fore·see, fōr·sē′, fạr·sē′, *v.t.*—past *foresaw,* pp. *foreseen,* ppr. *foreseeing.* To see beforehand; to have prescience of; to foreknow—*v.i.* To exercise foresight.—**fore··**

see·a·ble, *a.*—**fore·see·a·bil·i·ty,** *n.*— **fore·se·er,** *n.*

fore·shad·ow, fōr·shad′ō, fạr·shad′ō, *v.t.* To give evidence of beforehand; to prefigure; to adumbrate.—*n.*—**fore·shad·ow·er,** *n.*

fore·shore, fōr′shōr″, fạr′shōr″, *n.* The strip of land along the edge of a body of water; the sloping part of an ocean, sea, or other shore between high and low water marks; a beach.

fore·short·en, fōr·shạr′ten, fạr·shạr′ten, *v.t. Art,* to represent a line, part, or object which lies in a plane not parallel to the surface of the canvas, as less than its true length in order to give the proper impression of distance to the eye. To abridge; to make compact.

fore·show, fōr·shō′, fạr·shō′, *v.t.*—past *foreshowed,* pp. *foreshown,* ppr. *foreshowing.* To show, represent, or exhibit beforehand; to prognosticate; to foretell.

fore·side, fōr′sīd″, fạr′sīd″, *n.* The front or upper side; land stretching along the sea.

fore·sight, fōr′sīt″, fạr′sīt″, *n.* Provident care for the future; insight; the act or power of foreseeing; prescience; foreknowledge. The sight on the muzzle of a gun.—**fore·sight·ed,** *a.* Having foresight; prescient; provident.—**fore·sight·ed·ly,** *adv.*—**fore·sight·ed·ness,** *n.*

fore·skin, fōr′skin″, fạr′skin″, *n. Anat.* the fold of skin which covers the glans of the penis; the prepuce.

fore·speak, fōr·spēk′, fạr·spēk′, *v.t.*—past *forespoke,* pp. *forespoken,* ppr. *forespeaking.* To foretell or predict; to proclaim, indicate, claim, or arrange in advance.

for·est, fạr′ist, for′ist, *n.* [O.Fr. *forest,* Mod. Fr. *forêt,* < L.L. *foresta,* a forest, < L. *foris, foras,* out of doors, abroad.] A large tract of land covered with trees; a tract of woodland and open uncultivated ground; a cluster. *Brit. law,* a district devoted to hunting, usu. a royal domain.—*a.* Of or pertaining to a forest; sylvan; rustic.—*v.t.* To convert into a forest.—**for·est·al,** *a.,* **fo·res·tial,** fo·res′chal, *a.*—**for·est·a·tion,** fạr″i·stā′shan, for″i·stā′shan, *n.* The act or process of planting a forest.

fore·stall, fōr·stạl′, fạr·stạl′, *v.t.* [M.E. *forstallen,* < O.E. *foresteall,* a standing before, intercepting, waylaying.] To prevent, hinder, or thwart by action in advance; to take measures concerning or to deal with in advance; as, to *forestall* the actions of others; to deal with, meet, or realize in advance of the natural or proper time; anticipate; to get ahead of in action; *business,* to buy in advance, as goods, in order to sell later at a higher price.

for·es·ter, fạr′i·stèr, for′i·ster, *n.* A person skilled in forestry, particularly one appointed to inspect and care for forests or trees. Any animal which lives in a forest; any of various moths of the family *Agaristidae*; a large, gray kangaroo, *Macropus canguru.*

for·est·ry, fạr′i·strē, for′i·strē, *n.* The science of developing and cultivating forests.

fore·taste, fōr′tāst″, fạr′tāst″, *n.* Anticipation; enjoyment in advance.—fōr·tāst′, fạr·tāst′, *v.t.* To have a foretaste of; to taste beforehand.

fore·tell, fōr·tel′, fạr·tel′, *v.t.*—*foretold, foretelling.* To tell of in advance; to predict; to prophesy; to foreshow.—*v.i.* To utter a prediction or a prophecy.—**fore·tell·er,** *n.*

fore·thought, fōr′thạt″, fạr′thạt″, *n.* A thinking beforehand; provident care; foresight. —*a.*—**fore·thought·ful,** *a.*—**fore·thought·ful·ly,** *adv.*—**fore·thought·ful·ness,** *n.*

fore·to·ken, fōr·tō′ken, fạr·tō′ken, *n.* [O.E. *foretācn.*] A premonitory token or sign.—*v.t.* To foreshadow; betoken beforehand.

---

fore·top, fōr′top″, fạr′top″, *n. Naut.* a platform at the head of a foremast.

for·ev·er, fạr·ev′ẽr, fẽr·ev′ẽr, *adv.* Eternally; continually.—**for·ev·er·more**, *adv.* For always; forever.—**for·ev·er·ness**, *n.* Endless or infinite time; eternity.

fore·warn, fōr·wạrn′, fạr·wạrn′, *v.t.* To warn beforehand; to give previous notice to.—**fore·warn·ing·ly**, *adv.*

fore·wom·an, fōr′wụm″an, fạr′wụm″an, *n.* pl. **fore·wom·en.** A woman who supervises others. Also **fore·la·dy,** pl. **fore·la·dies.**

fore·word, fōr′wụrd″, fōr′wẽrd, fạr′wụrd″, fạr′wẽrd, *n.* A preface; an introduction to a book or other printed matter.

fore·yard, fōr′yärd, fạr′yärd, *n. Naut.* the lower yard on the foremast.

for·feit, fạr′fit, *v.t.* [Fr. *forfait,* a crime, misdeed, < *forfaire,* to transgress, L.L. *foris facere,* to offend, L. *foris,* out of doors, beyond (seen also in *foreclose, forest*), and *facere,* to do.] To lose the right to, by some fault, crime, or neglect; to become, by misdeed, liable to be deprived of, as of an estate or one's life.—*n.* The act of forfeiting; that which is forfeited; a fine; a penalty; *pl.* a game in which an object or objects must be given up when certain rules are not met.—*a.* Forfeited or subject to be forfeited; liable to penal seizure.—**for·feit·a·ble**, *a.* Liable to be forfeited; subject to forfeiture.—**for·feit·er**, *n.*

for·fei·ture, fạr′fi·chẽr, *n.* The act of forfeiting; the losing, as of some right, privilege, estate, or honor, because of an offense, crime, breach of condition, or other act; that which is forfeited.

for·gath·er, fore·gath·er, fạr·gaTH′ẽr, *v.i.* [Akin to O.Fris. *forgathera,* to assemble.] To meet; to convene; to come or meet together accidentally.

forge, fōrj, fạrj, *n.* An apparatus in which metal is heated and softened before shaping; a workshop where metal is heated in such an apparatus; a furnace or industrial plant where metal is melted and refined.—*v.t.* *forged, forging.* To heat in a forge and form or shape; to form or make in any way; to invent, devise, or produce in order to deceive; to imitate fraudulently, as a signature or work of art.—*v.i.* To commit forgery; to work at a forge; to heat metal.—**forge·a·ble**, *a.*—**forg·er**, *n.*

forge, fōrj, fạrj, *v.i.*—*forged, forging.*—To move forward, esp. slowly or with difficulty, usu. with *ahead.*

for·ger·y, fōr′je·rẽ, fạr′je·rẽ, *n.* pl. **for·ger·ies.** The production of an imitation which is claimed to be genuine, as a coin or work of art; something produced by forgery; the act of fabricating or producing falsely. *Law,* the act of producing or altering fraudulently any writing which affects the legal rights of another; a forged signature.

for·get, fẽr·get′, *v.t.*—past *forgot,* pp. *forgotten, forgot,* ppr. *forgetting.* [O.E. *forgitan, forgietan.*] To lose remembrance of; to cease or fail to remember; be unable to recall; to omit or neglect unintentionally; to omit to take, or leave behind inadvertently; to omit to mention, or leave unnoticed; to omit to think of, or take note of; to neglect willfully; to overlook, disregard, or slight.—*v.i.* To cease or omit to think of something; to fail to remember at the proper time.—**for·get one·self,** to be unselfish; to speak or act without dignity or self control.—**for·get·ta·ble**, *a.*—**for·get·ter**, *n.*

for·get·ful, fẽr·get′fụl, *a.* Apt to forget; heedless or neglectful.—**for·get·ful·ly**, *adv.*—**for·get·ful·ness**, *n.*

for·get-me-not, fẽr·get′mē·not″, *n.* A small plant of the borage family, *Myosotis scorpioides,* bearing bright blue flowers, with yellow centers, and popularly regarded as the emblem of constancy and friendship.

forg·ing, fōr′jing, *n.* A piece of forged metalwork.

for·give, fẽr·giv′, *v.t.*—past *forgave,* pp. *forgiven,* ppr. *forgiving.* [O.E. *forgifan—for,* intens. and *gifan,* to give.] To cease to feel resentment against; to give up a claim on account of; to grant remission of an offense, debt, fine, or penalty; to pardon; to free from the consequences of an injurious act or crime.—*v.i.* To grant pardon to an offender.—**for·giv·a·ble**, *a.* Capable of being forgiven; pardonable.—**for·give·ness**, *n.* The act of forgiving; disposition or willingness to forgive.—**for·giv·er**, *n.*

for·giv·ing, fẽr·giv′ing, *a.* Disposed to forgive; inclined to overlook offenses; compassionate.—**for·giv·ing·ness**, *n.*

for·go, fạr·gō′, *v.t.*—past *forwent,* pp. *forgone,* ppr. *forgoing.* [Also spelled less correctly *forego;* < prefix *for,* intens., or with sense of away, and *go;* O.E. *forgān,* to forgo, pass over, neglect.] To voluntarily avoid enjoying or possessing; to give up, renounce, resign.—**for·go·er**, *n.*

for·judge, fore·judge, fạr·juj′, *v.t.*—*forjudged, forjudging, forejudged, forejudging. Law,* to evict or dispossess by a judgment of the court; to eject from court, as an attorney, for a legal violation.—**for·judg·ment**, *n.*

fork, fạrk, *n.* [O.E. *forca,* < L. *furca,* a fork.] A tool having a handle and two or more prongs or tines for holding, lifting, or piercing, as any of various agricultural implements; any pronged instrument for handling food at the table or in cooking; a tuning fork. A dividing into branches; the point at which a river or road splits into branches; any one of these branches.—*v.t.* To make fork-shaped; to pierce, raise, pitch, or dig with a fork. *Slang,* to yield, give, or hand, used with *over;* to pay or dispense, used with *out. Chess,* to attack two men simultaneously.—*v.i.* To form a fork; to divide into branches.—**forked**, fạrkt, fạr′kid, *a.* Having a fork or bifurcation; zigzag, as lightning.—**fork·ed·ly**, *adv.*—**fork·er**, *n.*—**fork·like**, *a.*—**fork·y**, *a.*—*forkier, forkiest.* Forked, as a beard.

fork·lift, fạrk′lift″, *n.* A machine consisting of two steel arms with fingers for securing and lifting heavy loads. Also **fork·lift truck.**

for·lorn, fạr·lạrn′, *a.* [M.E. *foreloren* < O.E. *forloren,* lose, utterly destroy.] Abandoned; bereft; unhappy; miserable; wretched, as in feeling, condition, or appearance.—**for·lorn·ly**, *adv.*—**for·lorn·ness**, *n.*

for·lorn hope, *n.* [D. *verloren hoop,* 'lost troop.'] A faint expectation of success; a vain hope; a dangerous or hopeless mission.

form, fạrm, *n.* [O.Fr. Fr. *forme,* < L. *forma,* form, shape.] External shape or appearance considered apart from color or material; a particular shape; a body, esp. that of a human being; a structural condition, character, or mode exhibited by a thing; as, water in the *form* of ice, a mild *form* of the disease; *gram.* a particular character as to spelling and inflection, exhibited by a word, as: The possessive *form* of *he* is *his.* Due or proper shape; good order; the manner or style of arranging and coordinating parts for a pleasing or effective result, as in literary composition; a prescribed or customary method of doing something; a set order of words, as for a religious ritual or a legal document; a document with blank spaces to be filled in with particulars; a specimen document to be used as a guide in preparing others for like cases; as, a *form* for a lease; a formality or ceremony, often with the implication of absence of real meaning; procedure according to a set order; conformity to the usages of society, often in deprecation, as: It is bad

form to do so. A manner or method of doing something, as: He runs fast but his *form* is bad. A condition, esp. a good condition with reference to fitness for performing, as, an athlete in good *form;* the lair of a hare; an image or likeness of a shape; as, the dressmaker's *form;* something that gives or determines shape, as molds for a concrete foundation; *philos.* that element which determines the mode in which a thing is, or is perceived. *Brit.* a rank or class of pupils in a school; a bench or long seat. *Print.* an assemblage of type set in a case to print from; *crystal.* the combination of all the like faces possible on a crystal of given symmetry.

form, fạrm, *v.t.* To give form or shape to; give a particular form to, or fashion in a particular manner; to mold by discipline or instruction; as, to *form* boys into men; to place in order, arrange, or organize; to construct, make, or produce; to frame in the mind; as, to *form* opinions; to develop; as, to *form* habits or friendships; to serve to make up or compose; serve for, or constitute, as: They *form* into committees. *Milit.* to draw up into lines or formations.—*v.i.* To take or assume form; be formed or produced; assume a particular form or arrangement.—**form·a·ble**, *a.* Capable of being formed.—**form·er**, *n.*

for·mal, fạr′mạl, *a.* Of or pertaining to the form, shape, structural condition, or mode of being of a thing, esp. as distinguished from the matter; being in accordance with prescribed or customary forms; as, a *formal* siege; made or done in accordance with forms ensuring validity; as, a *formal* authorization; being in accordance with conventional requirements; rigorously methodical; excessively regular or symmetrical; as, a *formal* garden; marked by form or ceremony; as, a *formal* occasion; observant of form, as persons; ceremonious, sometimes excessively so; punctilious or precise to affectation; being a matter of form only; perfunctory; referring to the use of language by educated speakers and writers, esp. that speech which excludes slang and colloquial terminology and that writing which contains no abbreviations nor elliptical constructions; *philos.* pertaining to form. —*n.* A social occasion requiring evening dress; something formal in style or character, as an evening gown.—**for·mal·ly**, *adv.*—**for·mal·ness**, *n.*

form·al·de·hyde, fạr·mal′de·hīd, fẽr·mal′de·hīd, *n. Chem.* a colorless, water-soluble, poisonous gas with a pungent odor: used, usu. in solution, in the manufacture of synthetic resins and other organic compounds, and as a preservative and disinfectant. Also *methanal.*

for·ma·lin, fạr′ma·lin, *n. Chem.* a 37% aqueous solution of formaldehyde. Also **for·mol.**

for·mal·ism, fạr′ma·liz″um, *n.* Strict adherence to or observance of prescribed or customary forms, as in religion or art. *Ethics,* a concept which holds that right and wrong are known by direct intuition and that an act is right or wrong irrespective of its consequences.

for·mal·i·ty, fạr·mal′i·tē, *n.* pl. **for·mal·i·ties.** The condition or quality of being formal; accordance with prescribed, customary, or due forms; conventionality; excessive regularity or stiffness; marked or excessive ceremoniousness; an established order or mode of proceeding; as, the *formalities* of judicial process; something done merely for form's sake; a requirement of custom or etiquette.

for·mal·ize, fạr′ma·liz″, *v.t.*—*formalized, formalizing.* To give a definite shape or form to; to make formal, esp. for the purpose of gaining official approval or authorized acceptance.—*v.i.* To be formal; act with formality.—**for·mal·i·za·tion,** *n.* —**for·mal·iz·er,** *n.*

for·mal log·ic, *n.* A division of logic dealing with deductive reasoning and with operations in which the form of the proposition is more important than the content.

for·mant, far′mant, *n. Acoustics, phon.* a significant acoustic element of a speech sound; specif. one of several energy bands typically appearing on a sound spectrogram or frequency profile of a particular phoneme.

for·mat, far′mat, *n.* The layout and physical appearance of a book, newspaper, or magazine including shape, size, type, and overall design; the general arrangement of a television or radio program; any general plan. *Computer,* the organization of input data on punch cards, magnetic tape, or other devices for transferral to internal storage.

for·mate, far′māt, *n. Chem.* a salt or ester of formic acid.

for·ma·tion, far·mā′shan, *n.* [L. *formatio(n-).*] The act or process of forming, or the state of being formed; the manner in which a thing is formed; disposition of parts; formal structure or arrangement; something formed; *milit.* a particular disposition of troops, as in columns or squares. *Geol.* strata formed during some subdivision of geological time; a body of sedimentary rock of practically the same kind throughout; a mass or deposit of rock or mineral of a particular composition or origin.

form·a·tive, far′ma·tiv, *a.* [O.Fr. Fr. *formatif.*] Giving form or shape; forming; shaping; fashioning; molding; pertaining to formation or development; as, the *formative* period of a nation; *gram.* serving to form words; as, a *formative* termination. *Biol.* concerned with the formation of an embryo, organ, or the like; capable of developing new cells or tissue by cell division; as, *formative* tissue.—*n. Gram.* an element of a word, as a prefix or a suffix, added to the base of a word to give it new grammatical form.—**form·a·tive·ly,** *adv.* —**form·a·tive·ness,** *n.*

form class, *n. Gram.* a linguistic class of words or forms with at least one grammatical characteristic in common, as the formation of the plural by adding -es, or the order of words in a sentence, as the position of a subject or direct object.

for·mer, far′mèr, *a.* [A compar. < O.E. *forma,* first. FOREMOST.] Before or preceding another in time; ancient; long past; preceding; earlier, as between two things mentioned together; first mentioned; having previously been.—**for·mer·ly,** *adv.* In time past, either in time immediately preceding or at an indefinite distance; previously.

form·fit·ting, farm′fit″ing, *a. Fashion,* fitting snugly or closely to the figure or body.

form ge·nus, *n. Zool.* a neutral taxonomic classification for organisms whose structural relationships to other classes are unclear.

for·mic, far′mik, *a.* [L. *formica,* ant.] *Zool.* relating to ants; *chem.* pertaining to or obtained from formic acid.

For·mi·ca, far·mī′ka, *n.* A laminated thermosetting plastic, resistant to heat and chemicals, used for furniture, counters, table tops, wall panels, etc. (Trademark.)

for·mic ac·id, *n. Chem.* a colorless, caustic, fuming liquid, HCOOH, found naturally in ants and produced synthetically, used principally in tanning and dyeing, in fumigants and insecticides, and as a solvent.

for·mi·car·y, far′mi·ker″ē, *n.* pl. **for·mi·car·ies.** A nest of ants; an anthill.

for·mi·da·ble, far′mi·da·bl, *a.* [L. *formidabilis,* < *formido,* fear.] Exciting fear or awe, due to strength or size; so strong or difficult as to discourage approach, encounter, or undertaking; arousing admiration or awe on account of greatness or grandeur; powerful; as, a *formidable* contestant; superior.—**for·mi·da·ble·ness, for·mi·da·bil·i·ty,** far″mi·da·bil′i·tē, *n.*

form·less, farm′lis, *a.* Not having any regular or definite shape.—**form·less·ly,** *adv.*—**form·less·ness,** *n.*

For·mo·san, far·mō′san, *a.* Relating to Formosa or Taiwan.—*n.* A resident of the island of Formosa or Taiwan; the language of the aborigines of that island in the China Sea.

for·mu·la, far′mū·la, *n.* pl. **for·mu·las, for·mu·lae,** far′mū·lē. [L. *formula,* dim. of *forma,* a form.] A prescribed form or method; a prescribed form of words or symbols in which something is stated; *med.* a prescription. *Eccles.* a written confession of faith; a formal enunciation of doctrines. *Math.* a rule, concept, or principle expressed in algebraic symbols; *chem.* an expression by means of symbols and letters of the constituents of a compound. A recipe or prescription; a preparation made according to such a recipe or prescription, esp. a liquid preparation, usually of milk or a milk substitute plus sugar and water, used to feed an infant.—**for·mu·la·ic,** *a.* Constituting a formula or formulas; in accordance with a formula.—**for·mu·la·i·cal·ly,** *adv.*

for·mu·lar·ize, far′mū·la·rīz, *v.t.*—*formularized, formularizing.* To reduce to a formula; to formulate.—**for·mu·lar·i·za·tion,** far″mū·ler·i·zā′shon, *n.*—**for·mu·lar·iz·er,** *n.*

for·mu·lar·y, far′mū·ler″ē, *n.* pl. **for·mu·lar·ies.** A book containing standard and prescribed formulas; a book of precedents; *relig.* a book describing rituals; *pharm.* a book listing pharmaceuticals and medical formulas.—*a.* Pertaining to a formula or formulas; prescribed; ritual.

for·mu·late, far′mū·lāt″, *v.t.*—*formulated, formulating.* To reduce to or express in a formula; to put into a precise and comprehensive statement; to invent or develop, as a new kind of perfume.—**for·mu·la·tion,** *n.*—**for·mu·la·ble,** *a.*—**for·mu·la·tor,** *n.*

for·mu·lism, far′mū·liz″um, *n.* Adherence to or systematic use of formulas; a system of formulas.—**for·mu·list,** *n.* One who adheres to or favors the use of formulas.—**for·mu·lis·tic,** *a.*

for·mu·lize, far′mū·līz, *v.t.*—*formulized, formulizing.* To formulate.—**for·mu·li·za·tion,** *n.*—**for·mu·li·zer,** *n.*

for·myl, far′mil, *n. Chem.* the radical O=CH— of formic acid.

for·ni·cate, far′ni·kāt″, *v.i.*—*fornicated, fornicating.* [L. *fornicor, fornicatus,* < *fornix,* a vault, a brothel, brothels in Rome being generally in vaults or cellars.] To commit fornication.

for·ni·cate, far′ni·kit, far′ni·kāt″, *a.* [L. *fornicatus,* < *fornix,* arch, vault.] Arched; vaulted. Also **for·ni·cat·ed.**

for·ni·ca·tion, far″ni·kā′shan, *n.* [L. *fornicatio.*] Sexual intercourse, with mutual consent, between two persons not married to each other. *Bib.* adultery; incest.—**for·ni·ca·tor,** *n.*—**for·ni·ca·tress,** *n.*—**for·ni·ca·to·ry,** far′ni·ka·tor″ē, *a.*

for·nix, far′niks, *n.* pl. **for·ni·ces,** far′ni·sēz. [L., arch, vault.] *Anat.* any of various arched or vaulted structures, as an arching fibrous formation in the brain.—**for·ni·cal,** *a.*

for·sake, far·sāk′, *v.t.*—past *forsook,* pp. *forsaken,* ppr. *forsaking.* [O.E. *forsacan,* to oppose, to renounce; prefix *for-,* and *sacan,* to contend; Dan. *forsage,* D. *versaken,* to deny. SAKE.] To quit or leave entirely; to desert; to abandon; to depart or withdraw from; to renounce; to reject.—**for·sak·en,** *a.*—**for·sak·en·ly,** *adv.*—**for·sak·en·ness,** *n.*

for·sooth, far·sōth′, *adv.* [M.E. *for* and *soth,* that is, for or in truth. O.E. *forsōth.*] *Archaic.* In truth; certainly; very well: now mainly used ironically or humorously.

for·swear, fore·swear, far·swâr′, *v.t.*—past *forswore,* pp. *forsworn,* ppr. *forswearing; foreswore, foresworn, foreswearing.* [Prefix *for* with negative sense.] To reject or renounce upon oath; to renounce earnestly or with protestations; *refl.* to swear falsely; to perjure (oneself).—*v.i.* To swear falsely; to commit perjury.—**for·swear·er, fore·swear·er,** *n.* One who forswears; one who is perjured.—**for·sworn, fore·sworn,** far·swōrn′, *a.* Perjured.

for·syth·i·a, far·sith′ē·a, far·sī′thē·a, fèr·sith′ē·a, fèr·sī′thē·a, *n.* [N.L. from W. Forsyth (1737-1804), British horticulturist.] A popular ornamental shrub of the genus *Forsythia,* of the olive family, cultivated for its showy yellow flowers which appear in early spring before the leaves.

fort, fôrt, *n.* [Fr. *fort,* noun use of *fort,* adj., < L. *fortis,* strong.] A strong or fortified place; a fortress; an armed place surrounded by defensive works and occupied by troops; a fortification.—*v.t.* To fortify.

for·ta·lice, far′ta·lis, *n.* [O.Fr. *fortalice, fortelesse,* < M.L. *fortalitia, fortalitium,* < L. *fortis,* strong.] A small fort; an outwork.

forte, fôrt, *n.* [< Fr. *fort,* strong part, the final *e* being an English insertion.] A particular talent or faculty of a person; a strong point; chief excellence; the strong portion of the blade of a sword, between the middle and the hilt.

for·te, far′tā, It. far′tā, *adv.* [It.] *Mus.* Loudly; forcefully: used as a direction to conductors and performers.—*a.* Loud; forceful.—*n.* A forte tone or passage.

forth, fôrth, *adv.* [O.E. *forth,* < *fore,* before; G. *fort,* on, further; D. *voord,* forward.] Onward or forward in time, place, or order; as, from that time *forth;* out, as from a state of concealment; from an interior; out into view; as, come *forth,* put *forth.*

forth·com·ing, fôrth′kum′ing, *a.* Soon to appear, arrive, or occur; available. Also *upcoming.*—*n.* A coming forth.

forth·right, fôrth′rīt″, *a.* Straightforward; direct; outspoken; frank.—fôrth″rīt′, fôrth′rīt″, *adv.* Directly forward; in a direct manner. Also **forth·right·ly.**—**forth·right·ness,** *n.*

forth·with, fôrth″with′, fôrth′wiTH′, *adv.* Immediately; without delay; directly.

for·ti·eth, far′tē·ith, *a.* Following the thirty-ninth; being the ordinal of 40; being one of 40 equal parts into which anything is divided.—*n.* One of 40 equal parts; that which follows the thirty-ninth in a series.

for·ti·fi·ca·tion, far″ti·fa·kā′·shan, *n.* The act of fortifying; something which fortifies; the art or science of erecting a military place of defense; *pl.* the works constructed for the purpose of strengthening a position. A fortified place; a fort.

for·ti·fy, far′ti·fī″, *v.t.*—*fortified, fortifying.* [Fr. *fortifier,* < L.L. *fortifico*—L. *fortis,* strong, and *facio,* to make.] To add strength to; to surround with fortification or armaments as a defense against attack; to give physical strength to; to furnish with means of resisting; to reinforce; strengthen morally or mentally; to encourage; to confirm; to strengthen or enrich by adding ingredients; to increase the alcoholic content of, as wine or liqueurs.—*v.i.* To construct' fortifications.—**for·ti·fi·a·ble,** fạr'·ti·fī"a·bl, *a.* **for·ti·fi·er,** *n.*

for·tis, fạr'tis, *a. Phon.* articulated with comparatively great muscular tension and explosive expiration.—*n.* pl. **for·tes,** fạr'tēz. A consonant so produced, as *f, k, p, s, t, ch, sh, th.*

for·tis·si·mo, fạr·tis'i·mō", *It.* fạr·tēs'·sē·mạ", *a.* [It., superl. of *forte.*] *Mus.* very loud.—*adv.* Very loudly.

for·ti·tude, fạr'ti·tōd", fạr'ti·tūd", *n.* [L. *fortitudo,* < *fortis,* strong.] The strength of mind which enables a person to encounter danger or to bear pain with coolness and courage; passive courage; resolute endurance.

for·ti·tu·di·nous, fạr"ti·tōd'i·nus, fạr"ti··tūd'i·nus, *a.* Having quiet courage and strength; marked by fortitude and endurance.

fort·night, fạrt'nīt", fạrt'nit, *n.* [Contr. < *fourteen nights,* time being formerly reckoned by nights.] The space of fourteen days; two weeks.—**fort·night·ly,** fạrt'nīt"lē, *adv.* Once a fortnight; every fortnight.—*a.* Occurring or appearing once a fortnight.—*n.* pl. **fort·night·lies.** A publication appearing every two weeks.

FORTRAN, fạr'tran, *n.* [(*FOR*)mula (*TRAN*)slation.] *Computer,* any of several alphanumeric coding systems for programming specific procedures, used esp. in solving scientific problems.

for·tress, fạr'tris, *n.* [Fr. *forteresse,* O.Fr. *fortelesse.*] A fortified place, esp. one of considerable extent and complication; a stronghold; place of security.—*v.t.* To fortify.

for·tu·i·tism, fạr·tō'i·tiz"um, fạr·tū'i·tiz"um, *n. Philos.* the doctrine or belief that adaptations in nature are produced by the haphazard, unplanned operations of natural causes.—**for·tu·i·tist,** *n.*

for·tu·i·tous, fạr·tō'i·tus, fạr·tū'i·tus, *a.* [L. *fortuitus,* < *fors, fortis,* chance.] Accidental; happening by chance; lucky.—**for·tu·i·tous·ly,** *adv.*—**for·tu·i·tous·ness,** *n.*

for·tu·i·ty, fạr·tō'i·tē, fạr·tū'i·tē, *n.* pl. **for·tu·i·ties.** The state or quality of being fortuitous; a chance happening; an accident.

for·tu·nate, fạr'chu·nit, *a.* [L. *fortunatus,* pp. of *fortunare,* E. *fortune.*] Having good fortune; receiving good from uncertain or unexpected sources; lucky; bringing or presaging good fortune; resulting favorably; auspicious.—**for·tu·nate·ly,** *adv.*—**for·tu·nate·ness,** *n.*

for·tune, fạr'chan, *n.* [L. *fortuna,* a lengthened form from stem of *fors, fortis,* chance, luck, < *fero,* to bring (as in *fertile*).] Great wealth or riches; one's total estate or amount of possessions; chance or luck, good or bad; *sometimes pl.* the good or ill that happens or may happen; as, the *fortunes* of war, the *fortunes* of success; (*often cap.*) the personified or deified power regarded as determining what may occur; fate or destiny; prosperity or good luck.

for·tune hunt·er, *n.* A man who seeks to attain wealth by marrying a rich woman.

for·tune·tell·er, fạr'chan·tel"ẽr, *n.* One who purports to predict the future and to tell people their fortune in life.—**for·tune··tell·ing,** *n., a.*

for·ty, fạr'tē, *n.* pl. **for·ties.** [O.E. *fēowertig*—*fēower,* four, and *tig,* ten.] One more than 39 in number; four times ten. The cardinal number between 39 and 41; a symbol representing it; a set of 40 persons or things; *pl.* the numbers between 40 and 49 inclusive; the years in the fourth decade of a lifetime or century—*a.*

for·ty-five, fạr'tē·fīv', *n.* The cardinal number between 44 and 46; a symbol

representing it; one more than 44 in number; 40 plus 5; a set of 45 persons or things. A .45 caliber pistol; a phonograph record meant to be played at 45 revolutions per minute.—*a.*

for·ty-nin·er, fạr"tē·nī'nẽr, *n.* A person who migrated to California when gold was discovered there in 1849.

for·ty winks, *n. pl., sing.* or *pl. in constr. Colloq.* a brief nap.

fo·rum, fōr'um, *n.* pl. **fo·rums,** L. **fo·ra,** fōr'a. [L.] The marketplace or public place of an ancient Roman city, the center of judicial and other public business, and a place of assembly for the people; *often fig.* a court or tribunal; as, the *forum* of conscience, the *forum* of public opinion; an assembly for the discussion of questions of public interest.

for·ward, fạr'wẽrd, *adv.* [O.E. *forweard,* < *for, fore,* before, and -*weard.*] Toward or at a place, point, or time in advance; onward; ahead; to the front; into view or consideration, or forth; as, to bring *forward* new evidence. Also **for·wards.**—*a.* Situated in the front or forepart; lying in advance; directed toward a point in advance; moving ahead; onward; well advanced, often beyond one's years; precocious; ready, prompt, or eager; presumptuous, pert, or bold; radical or extreme; of or pertaining to the future; as, *forward* buying.—*n. Sports,* a player stationed in advance of others on his team.—*v.t.* To send forward; transmit, as a letter, esp. to a new destination; to advance or help onward; promote or hasten, as an action or process.—**for·ward·ly,** *adv.*—**for·ward·ness,** *n.*

for·ward·er, fạr'wẽr·dẽr, *n.* A person who or that which forwards; specif. an individual, agent, or firm employed by a shipper to receive goods and to transmit them to a carrier for reshipment. Also **for·ward··ing·a·gent.**

for·ward·ing, fạr'wẽr·ding, *n.* The act of one who or that which forwards, esp. the service performed by a forwarder of goods; *bookbinding,* the preparation of a book for final covering.

for·ward pass, *n. Football,* an offensive play in which the ball is thrown from behind the line of scrimmage to a receiver positioned in the direction of the opponent's goal.

for·zan·do, fạrt·sän'dō, *It.* fạr·tsän'dạ, *a., adv.* [It.] Sforzando.

fosse, foss, fos, fạs, *n.* [Fr. *fosse* < L. *fossa,* a ditch.] *Fort.* a ditch or moat, usu. full of water, outside the walls of a fortified place.

fos·sette, fo·set', fạ·set', *n.* [Fr. *fossette,* dim. of *fosse.*] A dimple; *biol.* a little depression, as in a shell; *pathol.* a deep corneal ulcer of small circumference.

fos·sil, fos'il, *n.* [L. *fossilis,* < *fodere,* dig.] Any remains, impression, or trace of an animal or plant of a former geological age, found in the earth's crust or strata; *colloq.* an antiquated person or thing.—*a.* Of the nature of a fossil; dug out of the earth, or obtained by digging; as, *fossil* fuel; belonging to a past epoch or discarded system; antiquated.—**fos·sil·if·er·ous,** fos"i·lif'ẽr·us, *a.* Bearing or containing fossils, as rocks or strata.

fos·sil·ize, fos'i·līz",*v.t.*—*fossilized, fossilizing. Fig.* to change as if into mere lifeless remains or traces of the past; render rigidly antiquated, as persons or ideas.—*v.i.* To become fossilized, literally or figuratively.—**fos·sil·i·za·tion,** fos"i·li·za'shan, *n.*

fos·so·ri·al, fo·sōr'ē·al, fo·sạr'ē·al, *a.* [L. *fossor,* a digger, < *fodio, fossum,* to dig.] *Zool.* adapted for digging, as the feet or other parts of certain animals; pertaining to animals who burrow to find shelter or food.

fos·ter, fạs'tẽr, fos'tẽr, *v.t.*—*fostered, foster-*

ing. [O.E. *fostrian,* to nourish, *foster,* nourishment, *foda,* food.] To promote the growth of; encourage; sustain and promote; to bring up; nurture; to cherish.—**fos·ter·er,** *n.*

fos·ter child, *n.* A child supported financially or cared for by a person or persons not its natural parents; a child under the control of the community or state who is placed with foster parents. Also **fos·ter·ling.**

fos·ter par·ent, *n.* A person who supports financially, or cares for, a child not his own; a person engaged by a state or social agency to care for a child not his own.

Fou·cault pen·du·lum, fö·kō'pen'ju·lum, fö·kō' pen'du·lum, fö·kō' pen'dū·lum, *n.* [From Jean Bernard Léon *Foucault,* 1819–68, Fr. physicist.] *Astron., phys.* a pendulum, suspended by a wire about 200 feet in length, whose plane of swing deviates slowly with the earth's movement, thus demonstrating the earth's rotation.

fou·droy·ant, fö·droi'ant, *Fr.* fö·dRwä··yän', *a.* [Fr. ppr. of *foudroyer,* strike with lightning, < *foudre,* < L. *fulgur,* lightning.] Striking as with lightning; sudden and overwhelming in effect; stunning; dazzling; *pathol.* occurring suddenly in severe form, as a symptom or disease.

foul, foul, *a.* [O.E. *fūl,* foul = Icel. *full,* Dan. *fuul,* D. *vuil,* G. *faul,* Goth. *fuls,* putrid, corrupt; same root as L. *puteo,* to stink, Skt. *puy,* to be putrid.] Noxious or offensive to the senses; covered or clogged with extraneous matter which is injurious or offensive; filthy, or unclean; polluted; stormy or tempestuous; as, *foul* weather; obscene, profane, or abusive; as, *foul* language; morally offensive or repugnant; detestable or vile; as, *foul* deeds; dishonorable; unfair or unlawful; marred with errors or changes, as a manuscript; *sports,* denoting or pertaining to an act committed contrary to the rules of the game; *baseball,* of or denoting a ball hit outside one of the foul lines; *naut.* entangled, or involving danger of collision.—**foul, foul·ly,** *adv.* In a foul or unfair manner.

foul, foul, *n.* A colliding or entangling; an act contrary to the rules of a game or sport; *baseball,* a foul ball.—*v.t.* To make dirty; to defile; to soil; to obstruct or choke; to have a collision with; to cause to entangle or snare; to dishonor or degrade; to commit a foul or an unfair act against; *baseball,* to hit into foul territory, often followed by *away* or *off.*—*v.i.* To become foul or dirty; *sports,* to commit a foul; *baseball,* to hit a ball foul; *naut.* to come into collision; to become entangled or clogged.—**fall foul of, fall a·foul of, run foul of,** to run against or collide with, as ships; to clash or have a conflict with; to attack.—**foul up,** *slang,* to wreck; spoil; to bring about confusion or disorder; to blunder.

fou·lard, fö·lärd', fo·lärd', *n.* [Fr., origin unknown.] A soft, lightweight silk, rayon, or cotton cloth, plain or with a printed pattern, used for scarves, neckties, and other articles of clothing.

foul ball, *n. Baseball,* a batted ball that lands or is played outside the field of play as bounded by the foul lines. Also *foul.*

fouled-up, fould'up", *a. Slang,* in a state of confusion or disorder.—**foul-up,** *n. Slang.* A blunder; a muddle; a confused condition.

foul line, *n. Baseball,* one of the two lines extending from home plate past first and third base and continuing to the boundary of the field; *bowling,* a line across the alley which limits the area of fair delivery of the ball. *Basketball,* one of two fixed lines on the court from which free throw shots are made; also **free throw line.**

foul·mouthed, foul'mouтнd', foul'moutht', *a.* Using vile or obscene language; given to profane or abusive speech.

---

foul·ness, foul′nis, *n.* The quality or state of being foul or filthy; something which is foul; evilness.

foul play, *n.* A violent or treacherous act, often murder; an unfair act or infringement of the rules in a game or sport.

foul tip, *n. Baseball,* a pitched ball that lightly touches the bat and is thereby deflected behind the foul line.

found, found, *v.t.* [O.Fr. Fr. *fonder,* < L. *fundare,* lay the bottom of, found, < *fundus,* bottom.] To set up or establish on a firm basis or for enduring existence; as, to *found* a city; to lay the lowest part of, as a building, on a firm base or ground; to base or ground, usu. with *on* or *upon*; as, a story *founded on* fact.—*v.i.* To be founded or based, with *on* or *upon*.

found, found, *v.t.* [Fr. *fondre,* to melt, to cast, < L. *fundo, fusum,* to pour out.] To melt, as iron, and pour into a mold; to form by melting a metal and pouring it into a mold; to cast.

foun·da·tion, foun·dā′shan, *n.* [O.Fr. Fr. *fondation,* < L. *fundatio(n-).*] The act of founding or establishing; that on which something is founded; the natural or prepared ground or base on which some structure rests; the lowest division of a building or wall, usu. of masonry and partly or wholly below the surface of the ground; the basis or ground of anything; as, a report that has no *foundation* in fact; a donation or endowment for the support of an institution, as a hospital or research organization; an endowed institution. A foundation garment.—**foun·da·tion·al,** *a.*

foun·da·tion gar·ment, *n.* A woman's undergarment, as a corset, girdle, or brassiere, worn to firm or support the contours of the figure. Also *foundation.*

found·er, foun′dèr, *n.* One who founds or establishes, as a college, business, or social movement.

found·er, foun′dèr, *v.i.* [O.Fr. *fondrer,* < L. *fundus,* bottom.] To fill with water and sink, as a ship; to fall in or sink down, as buildings or ground; to stumble, break down, or go lame, as a horse; to fail utterly, as: His plans *foundered* at the start.—*v.t.* To cause to sink, as a ship; to cause, as a horse, to break down or go lame.—*n.* Lameness in the foot of a horse.

found·er, foun′dèr, *n.* One who casts metals in various forms.

found·ling, found′ling, *n.* [Dim. formed < *found,* as *darling* < *dear.*] A child found after being abandoned by its parents.

found·ry, foun′drē, *n. pl.* **found·ries.** [Fr. *fonderie.*] The art of casting metals; an establishment for casting metals; the class of cast metal objects; castings.

found·ry proof, *n. Print.* a proof submitted for final checking before printing plates are cast.

fount, fount, *n.* [L. *fons, fontis.*] A spring of water; a fountain; an origin; a source.

fount, fount, *n. Brit. print.* type font.

foun·tain, foun′tan, *n.* [O.Fr. Fr. *fontaine,* < L.L. *fontana,* prop. fem. of L. *fontanus,* of or from a spring, < *fons,* E. *fount.*] A spring or source of water; the source or head of a stream; the source or origin of anything; a jet or stream of water, made by mechanical means to spout or rise from an opening or structure, as to provide water for use, to cool the air, or to serve as an ornament; a structure for discharging such a jet or a number of jets, often elaborate with basins, sculptures, etc.; a structure, as in a public place, for furnishing a constant supply of fresh water for drinking; a soda fountain; a reservoir for a liquid to be supplied gradually or continuously, as for ink in a printing press.—**foun·tained,** *a.*—**foun·tain·less,** *a.*

foun·tain·head, foun′tan·hed″, *n.* A fountain or spring from which a stream flows; a primary source.

foun·tain pen, *n.* A pen with a reservoir which supplies ink continuously.

four, fōr, far, *a.* [O.E. *fēower* = Fris. *fiower,* Icel. *fjórir,* Dan. *fire,* G. and D. *vier,* Goth. *fidwor,* L. *quatuor,* Gr. *tettares,* Russ. *cetvero,* W. *pedwar,* Ir. *ceathair,* Skt. *chatvâr.*] One more than three in number; twice two.—*n.* The cardinal number between three and five; a symbol representing it; a set of four persons or things.

four·chette, fur·shet′, *n.* [Fr., dim. of *fourche,* < L. *furca,* E. *fork.*] A forked strip of material forming the sides of two adjacent fingers of a glove; *ornith.* the wishbone of a bird; *zool.* the frog of an animal's foot; *anat.* a small fold of membrane forming the posterior margin of the vulva.

four-cy·cle, fōr′sī″kl, far′sī″kl, *a.* Pertaining to a type of internal-combustion engine having a cycle of operations in which air or fuel is drawn into the cylinder, compressed, consumed, and exhausted in four successive piston strokes.—*n.* Also **four-stroke cy·cle.**

four-di·men·sion·al, fōr′di·men′sha·nal, *a.* Having or relating to four dimensions; *math.* having elements which need four coordinates to define them completely.

Four·drin·i·er, fur·drin′ē·èr, *n.* [Named after H. and S. *Fourdrinier,* E. papermakers of the 19th century.] A machine first constructed in 1803 and used to manufacture paper in a continuous strip or web. Also **Four·drin·i·er ma·chine.**

four flush, *n. Poker.* Four cards of a possible flush, which, with one card of a different suit, make up a hand; an imperfect flush of no value.—**four-flush,** *v.i.* To bet on an imperfect poker hand; *slang,* to bluff.—**four·flush·er,** *n. Slang.* One who bluffs; a cheat.

four·fold, fōr′fōld″, *a.* Consisting of four parts or units; quadruple.—*adv.*

four-foot·ed, fōr′fut′id, *a.* Having four feet; quadruped.

four-hand·ed, fōr′han′did, *a.* Involving four hands or players, as a game of cards; intended for four hands, as a piece of music for the piano; having four feet adapted for use as hands, as in monkeys; quadrumanous. Also **four-hand.**

Four Horse·men, *n. pl.* The riders of the four horses, described in the apocalyptic vision in Rev. 6: 2–8, which represent the four plagues of humankind: war, famine, pestilence, and death.

Four Hun·dred, *n.* The upper social stratum of a city or community, used with *the.* Also **400.**

Fou·ri·er·ism, fur′ē·e·riz″um, *n.* The system of social reform propounded by the French socialist F. M. Charles *Fourier,* 1772–1837, according to which society was to be organized into associations or communities called phalanxes, each large enough to be economically and socially self-sufficient.—**Fou·ri·er·ist, fou·ri·er·ite,** fur′ē·e·rīt″, *n.*

four-in-hand, fōr′in·hand″, *n.* A vehicle drawn by four horses and guided by one driver; a four-horse team. A necktie tied with a slipknot at the collar, with the ends hanging in front.

four-o'clock, fōr′o·klok″, *n.* A common garden plant, *Mirabilis jalapa,* having fragrant red, white, yellow, or variegated flowers which open late in the afternoon; any plant of the same genus.

four-post·er, fōr′pō′stèr, *n.* A bed having four tall posts at its corners, orig. for the support of a curtain or canopy.

four·ra·gère, fur′a·zhâr″, *Fr.* fö·Râ′-zheR′, *n.* [Fr., said to have originated in the *corde à fourrage,* 'cord for forage,' carried by mounted men for binding and transporting forage.] *Milit.* an ornament of cord worn on the shoulder, esp. such a cord awarded as an honorary decoration, as to the members of a regiment or other unit which has received a requisite number of citations.

four·score, fōr′skōr′, *a.* Four times twenty; eighty.

four·some, fōr′som, *n.* A game, esp. of golf, between two pairs of partners; the players in such a game; any group numbering four. —*a.* Pertaining to or composed of four persons or objects.

four·square, fōr′skwâr′, *a.* Having its four sides and angles equal; square; solid; firm; direct; blunt.—*adv.* Bluntly; frankly.—*n.* A square.

four·teen, fōr′tēn′, *a.* [O.E. *fēowertīene.*] One more than 13 in number; four and ten; twice seven.—*n.* The cardinal number between 13 and 15; a symbol representing it; a set of 14 persons or things.

four·teen·er, fōr′tē′nèr, *n.* A poetic line comprised of 14 syllables, esp. one of seven iambic feet.

four·teenth, fōr′tēnth″, *a.* Following the thirteenth; being the ordinal of 14; being one of 14 equal parts into which anything is divided.—*n.* One of 14 equal parts; that which follows the thirteenth in a series.

fourth, fōrth, *a.* [O.E. *fēowertha.*] Following the third; being the ordinal of four; being one of four equal parts into which anything is divided.—*n.* That which follows the third in a series; one of four equal parts; *mus.* the interval of notes which encompasses four tones in the diatonic scale, beginning the count with the first tone.—*adv.*—**the Fourth,** July 4th, Independence Day in the U.S.

fourth di·men·sion, *n. Phys.* in the space-time continuum of the theory of relativity, the dimension or coordinate that locates an event or point in time.

fourth es·tate, *n.* (*Often cap.*) the press: so called because of its modern equivalence in political power and influence to the three medieval European estates, the nobility, the clergy, and the commons.

fowl, foul, *n. pl.* **fowls, fowl.** [O.E. *fugel* = D. and G. *vogel* = Icel. *fugl* = Goth. *fugls,* fowl, bird; possibly akin to E. *fly.*] The domestic or barnyard cock or hen; any of various other wild gallinaceous or similar birds, as the turkey or duck; in market and household use, a full-grown domestic fowl for food purposes, as distinguished from a chicken or young fowl; the flesh or meat of a fowl; a bird of any kind.—*v.i.* To hunt or take wildfowl.—**fowl·er,** fou′lèr, *n.*

fowl·ing piece, *n.* A light shotgun for shooting wildfowl or other small game.

fox, foks, *n. pl.* **fox·es, fox.** [O.E. *fox* = D. *vos* = G. *fuchs,* fox.] Any of a group of wild carnivorous mammals of the dog family, esp. those constituting the genus *Vulpes,* smaller than wolves, having a pointed muzzle, erect ears, and a long, bushy tail, and proverbially noted for alertness and cunning; the fur of the fox; *fig.* a cunning or crafty person; (*cap.*) a member of an Indian tribe formerly inhabiting Wisconsin; *naut.* small cordage made by hand by twisting rope yarns together.—*v.t.* To outwit or deceive; to repair, as a shoe, by fitting with a new upper.—*v.i.* To act cunningly or craftily.

foxed, fokst, *a.* Stained or discolored by age or decay, as a book or paper.

fox·fire, foks′fīèr″, *n.* The phosphorescent light emitted by decaying timber infested with certain fungal growths; a fungus which causes decaying timber to emit such light.

fox·glove, foks′gluv″, *n.* Any flowering plant of the genus *Digitalis,* of the figwort family, esp. *D. purpurea,* used in medicine as the drug digitalin.

fox grape, *n.* A northern U.S. species of grape, *Vitis labrusca,* bearing purple-black fruit with a musky, sour flavor, from which various cultivated varieties, as the Concord grape, have been developed.

fox·hole, foks′hōl″, *n.* A small pit dug in a battle area for individual shelter from enemy fire.

fox·hound, foks′hound″, *n.* One of various breeds of fleet, keen-scented hounds trained to hunt foxes.

fox·ing, fok′sing, *n.* The pieces or piece of leather or other material with which the upper front portion of a shoe is covered or repaired.

fox squir·rel, *n.* Any of several North American arboreal squirrels varying in color and remarkable for its large size.

fox·tail, foks′tāl″, *n.* The tail of a fox; *bot.* any of various weedy grasses of the genus *Setarig,* with soft brushlike spikes of flowers.—**fox·tail mil·let,** *n.* An annual grass, *Setaria italica,* of numerous varieties, grown chiefly for hay; also **I·tal·ian mil·let.**

fox ter·ri·er, *n.* A small, smooth-haired or wire-haired terrier, formerly used to dig out foxes.

fox trot, foks′trot″, *n.* A social dance, in duple or quadruple time, characterized by various combinations of short, quick steps; a pace of a horse, consisting of a series of short steps that slacken from a trot to a walk.—**fox-trot,** *v.i.*—*fox-trotted, fox-trot-ting.*

Fox·trot, foks′trot″, *n.* A communications code word to designate the letter F.

fox·y, fok′sē, *a.*—*foxier, foxiest.* Cunning or crafty; of the color of the common red fox, a yellowish or reddish brown; discolored or foxed; of wine, having the musky flavor characteristic of certain American grapes, as the fox grape.—**fox·i·ly,** *adv.*—**fox·i·ness,** *n.*

foy, foi, *n.* [M.D. *foye,* prob. < O.Fr. *voie,* < L. *via,* way.] *Sc.* A feast or gift given by or to a person about to start on a journey; a feast held on some special occasion, as at the end of the harvest.

foy·er, foi′ẽr, foi′ā, *Fr.* fwä·yä′, *n.* [Fr. < L.L. *focarium,* a hearth, < L. *focus.*] A lobby or anteroom in a public building, as a theater; an entrance hall or vestibule in a private home or apartment.

fra·cas, frā′kas, *Brit.* frak′ä, *n. pl.* **fra·cas·es,** *Brit.* **frac·as.** [Fr. < *fracasser,* to crash; It. *fracassare,* to break.] An uproar; a noisy quarrel; a brawl.

frac·tion, frak′shan, *n.* [O.Fr. Fr. *fraction,* < L.L. *fractio(n-),* < L. *frangere,* break.] *Math.* a part of a unit; one or more of a number of equal parts into which a unit is divided; an arithmetical representation of such a part or parts, as ¾, in which the denominator 4 indicates the number of equal parts into which the whole is divided and the numerator 3 indicates how many of such equal parts are considered; a number which indicates the quotient or expresses the ratio between two quantities in the form x/y such that x is any real number and y is any real number not equal to zero; an analogous ratio of algebraic quantities. A part, as distinct from the whole of anything; a very small portion; a piece broken off; fragment or bit; the act of breaking, as of the bread in the Eucharist.—*v.t.* To divide into fractions; to fractionate.

frac·tion·al, frak′sha·nal, *a.* Of or pertaining to a fraction or fractions; constituting a fraction; small, inconsiderable, or insignificant; *chem.* of or denoting a process, as crystallization or distillation, by which a mixture is separated into its component ingredients according to their differing chemical or physical properties. Also **frac·tion·ar·y.**—**frac·tion·al·ly,** *adv.*

frac·tion·al cur·ren·cy, *n.* Coins or paper money of a smaller denomination than the primary monetary unit.

frac·tion·ate, frak′sha·nāt″, *v.t.*—*fractionated, fractionating.* To separate or divide into parts or components. *Chem.* to separate, as a mixture, into its ingredients or into portions having different properties, as by distillation or crystallization; to obtain by such a process.—**frac·tion·a·tion,** *n.*

frac·tious, frak′shus, *a.* [< Prov. E. *fratch,* to quarrel or chide.] Apt to quarrel; cross; irritable; peevish; unruly.—**frac·tious·ly,** *adv.*—**frac·tious·ness,** *n.*

frac·ture, frak′chẽr, *n.* [Fr. *fracture,* < L. *fractura,* < *frangere,* break.] The act of breaking, or the state of being broken; *med.* the breaking of a bone or cartilage and the resulting condition. A break, breach, or split; the characteristic appearance, specif. the texture, of a broken surface, as of a mineral.—*v.t.*—*fractured, fracturing.* To break or crack; to break up or separate into pieces.—*v.i.* To undergo fracture; break.

frag·ile, fraj′il, *Brit.* fraj′īl, *a.* [L. *fragilis,* < *frango,* to break.] Brittle; easily broken; delicate; frail; flimsy.—**frag·ile·ly,** *adv.*—**frag·ile·ness, fra·gil·i·ty,** fra·jil′i·tē, *n.*

frag·ment, frag′ment, *n.* [Fr. *fragment,* < L. *fragmentum, frangere,* break.] A part broken off; a detached portion of anything, esp. a portion that is incomplete or imperfect in character; an odd piece, bit, or scrap; a part of an unfinished whole; as, a *fragment* of a poem.—*v.t., v.i.* To break or separate into pieces or fragments. Also *fragmentate, fragmentize.*

frag·men·tal, frag·men′tal, *a.* Fragmentary; *geol.* noting or pertaining to rock or rocks made up of fragments or particles of older rocks; also *clastic.*—**frag·men·tal·ly,** *adv.*

frag·men·tary, frag′men·ter″ē, *a.* Composed of fragments; incomplete; broken; disconnected. Also *fragmental.*—**frag·men·tar·i·ly,** *adv.*—**frag·men·tar·i·ness,** *n.*

frag·men·tate, frag′men·tāt″, *v.t., v.i.*—*fragmentated, fragmentating.* To fragment.

frag·men·ta·tion, frag″men·tā′shan, *n.* A breaking up into fragments or parts. *Milit.* the rapid, forceful scattering of the fragments of an exploding shell, bomb, or grenade; the fragments so scattered.

frag·ment·ed, *a.* Reduced to fragments; lacking cohesion or unity.

frag·ment·ize, frag′men·tīz, *v.t., v.i.*—*fragmentized, fragmentizing.* To fragment.

fra·grance, frā′grans, *n.* The quality of being fragrant; sweetness of smell; pleasing scent; perfume. Also, *archaic,* **fra·gran·cy,** *pl.* **fra·gran·cies.**

fra·grant, frā′grant, *a.* [L. *fragrans (fragrant-),* ppr. of *fragrare,* emit an odor, smell sweet.] Emitting a pleasing odor; sweet-smelling; sweet-scented.—**fra·grant·ly,** *adv.*

frail, frāl, *n.* [O.Fr. *frael,* M.E. *frayel.*] A basket made of rushes, in which dried fruit is occasionally shipped; a unit of weight measure for raisins, usu. about 75 lb.

frail, frāl, *a.* [Fr. *frele,* O.Fr. *fraile,* L. *fragilis,* fragile.] Lacking physical strength and robust health; weak; delicate; fragile; not durable; susceptible to temptation.—**frail·ly,** *adv.*—**frail·ness,** *n.*

frail·ty, frāl′tē, *n. pl.* **frail·ties.** The condition or quality of being frail; liableness to be tempted; a fault proceeding from weakness of character; a foible.

fraise, frāz, *n.* [Fr., same word as *frieze* (on a building).] *Fort.* an ancient defense consisting of pointed stakes driven into the ramparts in a horizontal or inclined position.

frame, frām, *n.* A structure for admitting or enclosing something; as, a door *frame*; an enclosing border or case, as for a picture; something composed of parts fitted and joined together, forming a supporting structure or skeleton, as of a building or boat; a framework; a system, order, or way something is constructed; as, *frame* of government; the body, esp. the human body, with reference to its bone structure or build; a temporary state; as, in a good *frame* of mind; a machine or device which functions by means of or is built on a framework; as, a weaving *frame*; a unit of programmed instruction, esp. one requiring the student's answer; one exposure on a strip of movie film; *usu. pl.* the structure holding the lenses of eyeglasses; *slang,* a frame-up; *baseball slang,* an inning. *Bowling,* a turn to bowl, each player having ten turns in a game; the square on a scoring sheet in which the score for each turn is recorded. *Pool,* the triangular form used to set up the balls for a game; the balls so set up; the period of play required to pocket them.—*a.* Of a house, having the framework and exterior made of wood.—**frame·less,** *a.*

frame, frām, *v.t.*—*framed, framing.* [O.E. *framian,* avail, profit, < *fram,* adv., forward, forth, also prep.] To provide with or put into a frame, as a picture; to surround, as with a frame; to fashion or shape; to adapt to a particular purpose; as, to *frame* a message to be understood by all; to form or construct the frame of, by fitting and·uniting parts; to devise, compose, or make a draft of, as a plan or a law; to conceive or imagine, as ideas; to utter or express, as: *Frame* it in your own words. *Slang,* to contrive or devise fraudulently or falsely, as a charge against someone; to incriminate unjustly; to prearrange the result of, as a race or contest.—**fram·er,** *n.*

frame of ref·er·ence, *n. pl.* **frames of ref·er·ence.** A set of facts, ideas, or values which orient, provide special meaning, or serve as the framework for evaluating or understanding something.

frame-up, frām′up″, *n. Slang,* an act or plot devised to produce fraudulent or unjust results, such as the conviction of an innocent person or the predetermination of the outcome of a contest.

frame·work, frām′wurk″, *n.* A frame or structure composed of parts fitted together, esp. one designed to support or enclose something; as, the *framework* of a house; a basic system or structure around which something is built; as, the *framework* of his philosophy; frames collectively; work done in, on, or with a frame, as embroidery.

fram·ing, frā′ming, *n.* The act, process, or manner of constructing or contriving anything; the act of providing with a frame; a frame or a system of frames; framework.

franc, frangk, *Fr.* frän, *n.* The monetary unit of France and several other countries. See Moneys of the World table.

fran·chise, fran′chiz, *n.* [O.Fr. Fr. *franchise,* < *franc,* free, E. *frank.*] The right to vote; a privilege of a public nature conferred on an individual or a body of individuals by a governmental grant, as the right to be a corporation or to provide a public service or utility; the permission to sell a product, often within a specified territory, granted to a retailer by the manufacturer; *archaic,* a legal immunity or exemption from a particular burden or exaction.—*v.t.*—*franchised, franchising.* To invest with a franchise; to enfranchise.—**fran·chise·ment,** *n.*—**fran·chis·ee,** *n.*

Fran·cis·can, fran·sis′kan, *n.* A member of the mendicant religious order founded by St. Francis of Assisi about 1210.—*a.* Relating to St. Francis of Assisi or the Franciscans.

fran·ci·um, fran′sē·um, *n. Chem.* a radioactive element of the alkali-metal series

a- fat, fāte, fär, fâre, fall; e- met, mē, mēre, hẽr; i- pin, pīne; o- not, nōte, mōve; u- tub, cūbe, bull; oi- oil; ou- pound.

which is a disintegration product of actinium. Sym. Fr, at. no. 87.

fran·co·lin, frang′ko·lin, *n.* [Fr. *francolin,* < It. *francolino.*] *Ornith.* a gallinaceous bird of the genus *Francolinus,* partridgelike in appearance and native to the Mediterranean regions.

Fran·co·phile, frang′ko·fīl″, *a.* Having a strong admiration for France or French culture.—*n.* Also **Fran·co·phil,** frang′ko·fil.

fran·gi·ble, fran′ji·bl, *a.* [< L. *frango,* to break.] Breakable; brittle.—**fran·gi·bil·i·ty,** fran″ji·bil′i·tē, **fran·gi·ble·ness,** *n.*

fran·gi·pane, fran′ji·pān″, *n.* Frangipani.

fran·gi·pan·i, fran″ji·pan′ē, fran″ji·pä′nē, *n.* pl. **fran·gi·pan·is, fran·gi·pan·i.** [Said to be named after the inventor.] A perfume prepared from, or imitating the odor of, the flower of the red jasmine, *Plumeria rubra,* of tropical America; the tree or shrub itself, or another of the same genus; a type of pastry having a sweet, cream and almond filing. Also *frangipane.*

frank, frangk, *a.* [O.Fr. *franc,* < M.L. *francus,* free, < L.L. *Francus,* Frank.] Open or unrestrained, esp. in speech; candid; outspoken; free from concealment or hypocrisy; sincere; undisguised or plainly evident; as, a *frank* statement.—**frank·ly,** *adv.*—**frank·ness,** *n.*

frank, frangk, *n.* A signature or mark affixed to a letter or package to ensure its transmission free of charge; the letter or package that is being sent in such a way; the privilege of sending articles in such a way.—*v.t.* To mark a letter or package for transmission by public conveyance free of charge by virtue of official privilege; to send free of charge; to secure exemption for; to enable to pass freely, as: He was *franked* through customs.—**frank·er,** *n.* One who affixes the mark for free passage.

Frank·en·stein, frangk′ken·stīn″, *n.* [From the titular hero of Mary W. Shelley's story "Frankenstein," a young student who creates a destructive being, in human form, that he cannot control.] One who creates a monster or a destructive agency that he cannot control or that brings about his own ruin; often, the monster or destructive agency itself.

frank·furt·er, frangk′fèr·tèr, *n.* [G., after the city *Frankfurt* on the Main.] A small linked sausage composed of beef or pork that is smoked, seasoned, cooked, and put in casings. Also **frank·fort·er, frank·fort, frank·furt,** *hot dog.*

frank·in·cense, frang′kin·sens″, *n.* An aromatic gum-resin from various Asiatic and African trees of the genus *Boswellia,* used chiefly for burning as incense. Also *olibanum.*

Frank·ish, frang′kish, *a.* Of or relating to the culture or language of the Franks, an ancient Germanic people dwelling in the Rhine region.—*n.* Old Franconian: the West Germanic language of the Franks.

frank·lin·ite, frangk′li·nīt″, *n.* An oxide of manganese, iron, and zinc, faintly magnetic and black in color, found in Franklin, New Jersey; a zinc ore.

Frank·lin stove, *n.* A free-standing, cast-iron heating stove, invented by Benjamin Franklin, which is similar in appearance to a fireplace.

fran·tic, fran′tik, *a.* [O.Fr. *frenetique,* < L. *phreneticus,* < Gr. *phrenitis,* mental disorder, frenzy, < *phren,* the mind.] Overcome by uncontrollable feelings of fear, anxiety, grief, pain, or anger; frenzied.—**fran·ti·cal·ly, fran·tic·ly,** *adv.*—**fran·tic·ness,** *n.*

frap·pé, fra·pā′, *Fr.* frä·pā′, [Fr. pp. of *frapper* to strike, to chill.] *a.* Artificially chilled, as with ice; iced; frozen.—*n.* An iced or frozen refreshment.

frat, frat, *n. Slang,* a college or school fraternity.

fra·ter, frā′tèr, *n.* [L., brother; akin to E. *brother.*] A brother, as in a fraternity or a religious order; a comrade.

fra·ter·nal, fra·tụr′nal, *a.* [Fr. *fraternel;* L. *fraternus,* < *frater,* brother.] Brotherly; pertaining to a brother or brothers; belonging to a society of men or a confraternity.—**fra·ter·nal·ism,** *n.*—**fra·ter·nal·ly,** *adv.*

fra·ter·nal twin, *n.* One of a pair of twins each originating from separately fertilized ova, consequently having different hereditary features and not necessarily being identical or of the same sex.

fra·ter·ni·ty, fra·tụr′ni·tē, *n.* pl. **fra·ter·ni·ties.** [Fr. *fraternité;* L. *fraternitas.*] The state or relationship of a brother; a body or class of men associated for their common interest, business, or pleasure. *U.S.* a social or honorary society of male or female college students, designed as a brotherhood with a title in the form of Greek letters. *Brit.* a group of people gathered for a common purpose.

frat·er·nize, frat′er·nīz″, *v.i.*—*fraternized fraternizing.* To associate in a brotherly way; to have or hold close sympathies or intimate understandings with the enemy or inhabitants of a vanquished land, esp. when such behavior is contrary to military orders. —**frat·er·niz·er,** *n.*—**frat·er·ni·za·tion,** *n.*

frat·ri·cide, fra′tri·sīd″, frā′tri·sīd″, *n.* [L. *fratricidium,* the crime, *fratricida,* the criminal—*frater,* and *caedo,* to kill.] One who murders or kills a brother or sister; the murdering of a brother or sister.—**frat·ri·cid·al,** *a.* Pertaining to or involving fratricide.

frau, frou, *n.* pl. **fraus,** G. **frauen.** [G.] A woman; a married woman; a wife; (*cap.*) a German title equivalent to Mrs.

fraud, frạd, *n.* [O.Fr. *fraude,* < L. *fraus,* cheating, deceit.] Deceit or trickery deliberately practiced in order to gain some advantage dishonestly; an instance of such deceit; deception or artifice of any kind; anything contrived or intended to deceive; as: The letter is a *fraud.* A person who makes deceitful pretenses; a humbug; an imposter.—**fraud·ful,** *a.*—**fraud·ful·ly,** *adv.*

fraud·u·lent, frạ′ju·lent, *a.* Proceeding from or founded on the use of fraud; as, a *fraudulent* contract; given to using fraud. —**fraud·u·lent·ly,** *adv.*—**fraud·u·lence, fraud·u·len·cy,** *n.* pl. **fraud·u·len·cies.** —**fraud·u·lent·ness,** *n.*

fraught, frạt, *a.* [A participial form < old verb *fraught,* to load, a form of freight.] Filled, laden, charged, or abounding, usu. followed by *with;* as, a scheme *fraught with* mischief; *archaic,* freighted.

fräu·lein, froi′lin, frạ′lin, frou′lin, *n.* pl. **fräu·leins,** G. **fräu·lein.** [G. dim. of *frau.*] A young lady; an unmarried woman; (*cap.*) a German title equivalent to Miss.

Fraun·ho·fer lines, froun′hō″fèr linz″, *n. pl.* [From Joseph von *Fraunhofer,* a German optician and physicist.] The dark lines of the solar spectrum.

frax·i·nel·la, frak″si·nel′a, *n.* [N.L., dim. L. *fraxinus,* ash-tree.] *Bot.* gas-plant.

fray, frā, *v.t.* [Fr. *frayer,* < L. *fricare,* rub.] To cause weakening by rubbing, as threads or fibers; to wear by use, as material; to cause to ravel or tear, esp. at the ends, due to friction or constant contact. To irritate, as: Certain noises *fray* my nerves.—*v.i.* To become separated or pulled apart.—*n.* A worn or raveled section of material.

fray, frā, *n.* A quarrel or violent turmoil; a conflict; a brawl.

fra·zil, frā′zil, fraz′il, fra·zēl′, fra·zil′, *n.* Ice flakes which occur in rapids and rough waters and form ice banks near the shore.

fraz·zle, fraz′el, *v.i., v.t.*—*frazzled, frazzling.* [Var. of *fazel,* perhaps by association with *fray.*] To wear to threads; to tire out.— *n.* Condition of being wearied; a shred; a fragment.—**fraz·zled,** *a. Colloq.* worn out.

freak, frēk, *n.* [Origin uncertain: cf. O.E. *frician,* dance.] An unpredictable action or happening; an abnormal or unusual object; a person or animal exhibited as an example of a deviation from the normal. *Numis.* an imperfect coin accidentally put into circulation. *Philately,* a stamp unlike others of the same printing.—*a.*

freak, frēk, *v.t.* To streak or fleck, as with color; variegate.—*n.* A fleck of color.

freak·ish, frē′kish, *a.* Whimsical; capricious; grotesque.—**freak·ish·ly,** *adv.*—**freak·ish·ness,** *n.*

freak·y, frē′kē, *a.*—*freakier, freakiest.* Freakish.—**freak·i·ly,** *adv.*—**freak·i·ness,** *n.*

freck·le, frek′l, *n.* [O.E. *freckens, frekens* freckles (akin to *freak,* to variegate); Icel. *freknur,* Dan. *fregner,* freckles; akin G. *fleck,* a spot.] A brownish spot on the skin, particularly on the face, neck, and hands, often caused by exposure to the sun; any small spot or discoloration.—*v.t., v.i.*— *freckled, freckling.* To mark or become marked with freckles.—**freck·led,** *a.*— **freck·ly,** *a.*—*frecklier, freckliest.*

free, frē, *a.*—*freer, freest.* [O.E. *fri, freó* > Icel. *fri,* Dan. and Sw. *fri,* D. *vrij,* G. *frei,* Goth. *freis,* free; allied to *friend,* Goth. *frijon,* to love; Skt. *pri,* to love; perhaps also to L. *privus,* one's own, *privatus,* private.] Not being under physical or moral restraint; exempt from subjection to the will of others; not in confinement; not under an arbitrary or despotic government; capable of being used, enjoyed, or taken advantage of without charge; not obstructed; not bound by adherence to a form or rule; as, *free* verse; going beyond due limits in speaking or acting; voluntary; profuse; gratuitous; exempt; not encumbered, followed by *from* or *of;* invested with certain immunities or privileges. *Chem.* not chemically combined with any other body.—**free and eas·y,** unconstrained; regardless of conventionalities; casual.—**free·ly,** *adv.*

free, frē, *v.t.* To make free; to rescue or release from slavery, confinement, or the like; to exempt, as from some oppressive condition or duty; to disengage.—*adv.* In a free manner; without charge; gratuitously. —**to make free with,** to interfere with; to take liberties with; to help oneself to.

free a·gent, *n.* An athlete, entertainer, or other employee who, being released from a contract, may personally negotiate the terms of his future employment; one who is not responsible to any authority for his actions.

free a·long·side ship, free a·long·side ves·sel, *adv., a.* Delivered to the dock at which a ship is to be loaded without charge or liability to the buyer. Abbr. *f.a.s., F.A.S.*

free·boot·er, frē′bö″tèr, *n.* [D. *vrijbuiter,* G. *freibeuter.*] A buccaneer or pirate; a plunderer; a pillager.—**free·boot,** *v.i.*

free·born, frē′bạrn″, *a.* Born free; not in vassalage or servitude; inheriting liberty; pertaining to or befitting the freeborn.

free·dom, frē′dom, *n.* The state of being free; exemption from slavery, servitude, confinement, or constraint; liberty; independence; political liberty; frankness; openness; outspokenness; unrestrictedness; permission; liberality; particular privileges; as, the *freedom* of a city; ease or facility of doing, enjoying, or using something at will. Improper familiarity.

free·dom of the seas, *n.* The doctrine that merchant ships have the right to sail on all waters, except territorial, in both peace and war.

---

free en·ter·prise, *n.* A doctrine or type of economy under which private business is allowed to operate with minimum governmental control; capitalist economy.

free fall, *n.* The unguided descent of a body through the air; that portion of a parachute jump occurring before the parachute opens; the hypothetical state of unrestrained movement in a gravitational field.

free-float·ing, frē'flō'ting, *a.* Of or pertaining to unrestrained movement; lacking commitment as to doctrine; denoting absence of a specific cause.

free-for-all, frē'fèr·ạl', *n.* A competition, fight, or debate open to all, without any rules or regulations; a brawl or fight that is out of control.

free-form, frē'fạrm", *a. Art,* having an irregular outline or form; unrestrained by any set pattern; unconventional in concept, style, or presentation.

free gold, *n.* U.S. Treasury holdings of gold or gold certificates over and above the legal reserve; *min.* gold in a pure state.

free·hand, frē'hand", *a., adv.* Done or drawn by hand without assistance by any guiding or measuring instruments; as, a *freehand* sketch.

free hand, *n.* Freedom to act or decide on one's own initiative.

free-hand·ed, frē'han'did, *a.* Openhanded; liberal.—**free-hand·ed·ness,** *n.*—**free-hand·ed·ly,** *adv.*

free·hold, frē'hōld", *n. Law.* An estate in real property, held in fee simple, fee tail, or for life; the tenure by which such an estate is held.—*a.*—**free·hold·er,** *n.*

free-lance, frē'lans, frē'läns, *a.* Independent of or; pertaining to the manner of working of a writer, artist, or actor not under contract or employed by another.—*v.t.*—**free lance,** *n.* One who free-lances.

free love, *n.* The doctrine or practice of free choice in sexual relations, without restraint of legal marriage or of any continuing obligations.

free·ma·son, frē'mā'son, frē'mā'son, *n.* One of a class of skilled stoneworkers of the Middle Ages; a member of a society composed of such workers, with honorary members known as 'accepted masons' who were not connected with the building trades; (*cap.*) now, a member of a widely distributed secret order, Free and Accepted Masons, developed from societies of this kind, having for its object mutual assistance and the promotion of brotherly love among its members.—**free·ma·son·ic,** frē'ma·son'ik, *a.*—**free·ma·son·ry,** frē'mā"son·rē, *n.* Secret or tacit brotherhood; instinctive sympathy; (*cap.*) the principles, practices, and institutions of Freemasons.

free on board, *adv., a. Com.* without charge to the buyer for the placing of merchandise on board a common carrier at a designated point. Abbr. *f.o.b., F.O.B.*

free port, *n.* A port or part of a port where ships may be unloaded and goods deposited without payment of customs; a port open under equal terms to all vessels.

free rad·i·cal, *n. Chem.* an atom or combination of atoms which contains one or more unpaired electrons and is highly reactive and short-lived.

free·si·a, frē'zhē·a, frē'zē·a, frē'zha, *n.* [N.L.; from Fr. H. T. Freese (1795-1876), German botanist.] *Bot.* any plant of the genus *Freesia,* in the iris family, native to South Africa, and cultivated for its fragrant white, yellow, or rose-purple, tubular flowers.

free sil·ver, *n.* The free coinage of silver, usu. at a fixed ratio with gold.

free soil, frē'soil', *n.* U.S. territory already free of slavery before the Civil War.—**free-soil,** *a.*

free-spo·ken, frē'spō'ken, *a.* Accustomed to speaking without reserve; outspoken.—**free-spo·ken·ness,** *n.*

free-stand·ing, frē'stan'ding, *a.* Free of any apparent architectural support; balanced independently and of itself.

free·stone, frē'stōn", *n.* Any stone, esp. limestone or sandstone, which can be easily quarried and worked; a fruit having a stone from which the pulp is easily separated, as certain varieties of peaches.—*a.*

free·think·er, frē'thing'kèr, *n.* A person who forms his opinions without regard for authority or tradition, esp. in matters of religion.—**free·think·ing,** *n., a.*

free throw, *n. Basketball,* an unobstructed shot at the basket, worth one point if successful, and given a player who has been illegally interfered with by an opponent.

free trade, *n.* International trade without governmental regulation or custom duties; such trade where tariffs are used only as needed for revenue.—**free-trade,** *a.*—**free-trad·er,** *n.* An advocate of free trade. Also **free trad·er.**

free verse, *n. Pros.* verse which lacks a regular metrical pattern and which depends upon the natural rhythms of the spoken language.

free·way, frē'wā", *n.* A multiple-lane expressway which bypasses populated areas, and moves traffic without interruption by use of cloverleaves or interchanges.

free·wheel, frē'hwēl', frē'wēl', *n.* That form of rear wheel on a bicycle which has a clutchlike device for freeing or releasing it from the driving mechanism, as when the pedals are stopped in coasting; an automotive transmission system which allows the propeller or drive shaft to run freely when its speed is higher than that of the engine shaft.—*v.i.* To live unconcernedly, irresponsibly; to move along, or coast, with the wheels disengaged.

free will, *n.* The power of directing one's own actions without physical or divine forces; voluntariness; spontaneity; the doctrine that human actions reflect choice.

free·will, frē'hwil', frē'wil', *a.* Voluntary; freely given or done.

free world, *n.* Collectively, those countries outside the Communist orbit.

freeze, frēz, *v.i.*—past *froze,* pp. *frozen,* ppr. *freezing.* [O.E. *frysan, frēosan* = D. *vriezen,* Icel. *frjosa,* Dan. *fryse,* G. *frieren;* same root as L. *pruina,* hoarfrost.] To be congealed by cold; to be changed from a liquid to a solid state by the abstraction of heat; to be hardened into ice; to be of that degree of cold at which water freezes; to become chilled in body with cold; to become filled with ice, as pipes; to become rigid or fixed through fear; to adhere by the formation of ice; to become cold or unfriendly in manner; to be injured or killed by cold.—*v.t.* To congeal or cause to freeze; to harden into ice; to give the sensation of cold and shivering; to clog or block by ice, as a pipe; to make adhere or to fasten by ice; to harden or stiffen by freezing; to make rigid or motionless through fear or shock; to injure or kill by frost or cold; to quick-freeze; to make insensitive or anesthetize by cold; to act toward in a cold, unfriendly manner; to fix or set wages, rents, or prices at a specific level; to prohibit the liquidation, collection, or use of assets, loans, or funds by law.—*n.* The act of freezing; a weather condition of intense cold.—**freez·a·ble,** *a.*

freeze-dry, frēz'drī, *v.t.*—**freeze-dried,** *freeze-drying. Chem.* to dry, as frozen foods, vaccines, and blood plasma in a high vacuum for preservation at room temperature.—**freeze-dry·ing,** *n.*

freez·er, frē'zèr, *n.* One who or that which freezes; a cabinet, room, or refrigerator

maintained at sub-zero temperatures, for freezing and keeping perishable foods; a device for making ice cream.

freez·ing point, *n. Phys.* the temperature at which a liquid freezes; as, 0° centigrade or 32° Fahrenheit for water.

free zone, *n.* That part of a port or city where goods may be received and stored duty free.

F re·gion, *n.* The highest of the ionospheric regions, in which the F layers develop.

freight, frāt, *n.* [Akin *fraught:* cf. M.D. and M.L.G. *vrecht,* for *vracht,* also the related O.Fr. *fret.*] *U.S., Canada,* transportation of goods by water, air, or land, esp. by means of common carriers, as opposed to *express; Brit.* transportation of goods by water; the price paid for such transportation; *U.S., Canada,* the cargo, or any part of the cargo or lading carried for pay by water, air, or land; *Brit.* cargo carried by water. *U.S., Canada,* a train of cars for transporting goods or merchandise; also **freight train.**—*v.t.* To transport, as freight; send by freight; to load with goods for transportation; in general, to load; burden.

freight·age, frā'tij, *n.* The transportation of goods, or the price paid for this; freight, cargo, or lading.

freight·er, frā'tèr, *n.* A vessel engaged chiefly in the transportation of goods; a person whose occupation is to receive and forward freight; a person for whom freight is transported; one who loads freight.

frem·i·tus, frem'i·tus, *n.* pl. **frem·i·tus.** [L. < *fremere,* to murmur, to growl.] *Med.* palpable vibration, as of the walls of the chest.

French, french, *a.* [O.Fr. *franchois, françois,* Mod.Fr. *francais,* < *France,* which received its name from the *Franks.*] Of, pertaining to, or characteristic of France, its inhabitants, or its culture.—*n.* The Romance language of France and portions of Belgium and Switzerland and of certain other countries, primarily those colonized by France after the 16th century; collectively, the French people.—**French·man,** *n.* A native or naturalized citizen of France.—**French·wom·an,** *n.*

french, french, *v.t.* (*Sometimes cap.*) cooking, to prepare in the French manner; esp. to slice (string beans) lengthwise into thin strips before cooking.

French Can·a·da, *n.* The Canadian province of Quebec.—**French Ca·na·di·an,** *n.* A descendant of French settlers in Canada.—**French-Ca·na·di·an,** *a.*

French chalk, *n.* A variety of talc or soapstone resembling chalk, generally used by tailors for making lines on cloth.

French chop, *n.* A chop, usually of lamb's rib, with the meat scraped from the end of the bone.

French cuff, *n.* A cuff at the end of a sleeve of a shirt, formed by doubling over a band of the material and fastening with a link or a button.

French doors, *n. pl.* A pair of doors with full-length glass panels, hinged at the sides opposite to each other in a frame, and opening in the middle.

French dress·ing, *n. Cooking,* a popular U.S. salad dressing made of oil, vinegar, and various spices and seasonings.

French fried, *a.* (*Often l.c.*) fried in deep fat, esp. potato strips.—**French fries,** *n. pl.* (*Often l.c.*) deep-fried strips of potatoes; also *Brit. chips.*

French heel, *n.* A gracefully curved, high heel on women's shoes.—**French-heeled,** *a.*

French horn, *n.* A musical wind instrument of brass having several curves, and gradually widening from the mouthpiece to a flaring bell at the other end.

---

a- fat, fāte, fär, fâre, fạll;   **e-** met, mē, mēre, hèr;   **i-** pin, pīne;   **o-** not, nōte, mōve;   **u-** tub, cūbe, bụll;   **oi-** oil;   **ou-** pound.

French·i·fy, fren'chi·fī", v.t.—*Frenchified*, *Frenchifying*. To make appear French; to imbue with French tastes or manners.— v.i.—**French·i·fi·ca·tion**, fren"chi·fi·kā'-shan, n.

French leave, n. [After the 18th century French practice of leaving a party without informing the host.] A departure without proper notice or permission; a secret or hurried departure, as: The bookkeeper took *French leave* before the auditors arrived.

French pas·try, n. A variety of fancily decorated, often filled sweet pastries.

French tel·e·phone, n. A telephone with receiver and transmitter on the same handle.

French toast, n. Bread dipped in a batter of milk and eggs and fried, usually served with sugar or syrup.

French win·dow, n. A casement window with sashes opening in the middle.

fre·net·ic,phre·net·ic,fre·net'ik,a.[FREN-ZY.] Frenzied; frantic. Also **fre·net·i·cal**, **phre·net·i·cal.—fre·net·i·cal·ly**, adv.

fre·num, frae·num, frē'num, n. pl. **fre·nums, fre·na**, frē'na. [L. *frenum*, also *frænum*, bridle, curb, bit.] *Anat.* a ligament or fold of membrane which checks or restrains the motion of a part, as the one which binds down the under side of the tongue.

fren·zy, fren'zē, n. pl. **fren·zies**. [O.Fr. *frenesie* (Fr. *frenesie*), < L. *phrenesis*, Gr. *phrenitis*.] Violent mental agitation resembling temporary madness; wild excitement or enthusiasm; delirium.—v.t.—*frenzied*, *frenzying*. To affect with or drive to frenzy; render frantic.—**fren·zied**, a.—**fren·zied·-ly**, adv.

Fre·on, frē'on, n. *Chem.* any one of a group of fluorinated hydrocarbons used as refrigerants and aerosol propellants. (Trademark.)

fre·quen·cy, frē'kwen·sē, n. pl. **fre·quen·-cies**. The state or fact of being frequent; frequent occurrence or rate of recurrence; also **fre·quence**. *Phys.* the number of regularly recurring events of any given kind in a given unit of time; the number of cycles or complete alterations per second of an alternating electric current or of other waves. *Math.* the number of occurrences of a specific value or characteristic in relation to the number of possible occurrences.

fre·quen·cy dis·tri·bu·tion, n. *Statistics*, an arrangement of data, often a graphic representation, which subclassifies the possible values of a variable into categories or intervals.

fre·quen·cy mod·u·la·tion, n. *Electron.* a type of modulation of transmitted radio waves in which the frequency, rather than the amplitude, of the carrier wave is varied in accordance with a signal; specif. a broadcasting system using this type of modulation. Abbr. *FM, F.M.*

fre·quent, frē'kwent, a. [Fr. *frequent*, < L. *frequens, frequentis*, common, usual, full, crowded; same root as *farcio*, to cram (whence *farce*).] Happening or appearing often; occurring at short intervals; habitual or recurrent, as guests.—fri·kwent', frē'-kwent, v.t. [L. *frequento*; Fr. *frequenter*.] To visit often; to resort to, often or habitually. —**fre·quen·ta·tion**, frē"kwen·tā'shan, n. The act or custom of frequenting.—**fre·-quent·er**, n.—**fre·quent·ly**, adv. Often; at short intervals; repeatedly; commonly.— **fre·quent·ness**, n.

fre·quen·ta·tive, fri·kwen'ta·tiv, a. *Gram.* denoting or relating to a verb or verb form which expresses the frequent repetition of an action.—n. A verb, usually formed with the suffix -le or -er, which expresses the frequent occurrence or repetition of the action of the simple verb, as *dabble, chatter*.

fres·co, fres'kō, n. pl. **fres·coes, fres·cos**.

[It. *fresco*, fresh.] A method of painting on a plastered wall or ceiling, called *true fresco* when done before the plaster is dry, or *dry fresco* when done on dry plaster; a picture or design so painted.—v.t.— *frescoed, frescoing*. To paint in fresco.— **fres·co·er**, n.—**fres·co·ing**, n. The process of painting in fresco; frescoed decoration.

fresh, fresh, a. [O.E. *fersc*, whence *fresh* by a common metathesis = D. *versch*, Icel. *ferskr, friskr*, Dan. *fersk, frisk*, G. *frisch*; hence It. Sp. and Pg. *fresco*, Fr. *frais, fraiche*, fresh.] Of water, not salt; pure; not stale; full of health and strength; vigorous; bright; vivid; unimpaired by time; recently grown or obtained; not smoked, frozen or preserved; in good condition; not faded or worn; not exhausted with labor or exertion; youthful; healthy; inexperienced; untrained; newly arrived; original; additional; not previously known; *meteorol.* of a wind, moderately brisk. *Colloq.* impertinent; discourteous. *Brit. colloq.* slightly drunk. —n. A freshet; a spring of fresh water; the fresh or early part or time.—adv. Just recently.—**fresh·ly**, adv.—**fresh·ness**, n.

fresh·en, fresh'en, v.t. To make fresh; refresh, revive, or renew; to remove saltiness from.—v.i. To become or grow fresh; to become stronger or brisker, as wind; to make oneself clean or invigorated, usu. followed by *up*.—**fresh·en·er**, n.

fresh·et, fresh'it, n. A small stream of fresh water; a flood or overflowing, as of a river, due to heavy rains or melted snow.

fresh·man, fresh'man, n. pl. **fresh·men**. A first-year student in a high school or university; a novice.—a.

fresh-wa·ter, fresh'wạ"tèr, a. Of or pertaining to water that is fresh, or not salt; living in fresh water, or pertaining to fish or other animals doing this; accustomed to fresh water only, and not to the sea; of little experience or raw, as soldiers. Of slight attainments or minor standing; as, a *fresh-water* college.

fret, fret, v.i.—*fretted, fretting*. [O.E. *fretan* = D. *vretan* = G. *fressen* = Goth. *fraitan*, eat up, devour; from elements represented by E. *for-* and *eat*.] To become vexed or angry; to worry; to utter peevish expressions; to become eaten, worn, or corroded; to gnaw; cause corrosion; make a way by gnawing or corroding; to move in agitation or commotion, as water.—v.t. To irritate; tease; make angry; to gnaw; eat into; rub or wear away; fray; to form or make, as a hole, by wearing away; to agitate or disturb, as the surface of the sea or other body of water.—n. A state of irritation; vexation or anger; a gnawing or wearing away; erosion; corrosion; a worn or eroded place.

fret, fret, n. [O.Fr. *freter*, to interlace; *frettes*, a grating; perhaps < L. *ferrum*, iron. Akin also O.E. *fraetwe*, ornaments.] A kind of ornament formed of bands or fillets variously combined, but most frequently arranged in interlocking rectangular motifs.—v.t.—*fretted, fretting*. To ornament or furnish with frets.

fret, fret, n. [Origin uncertain.] *Mus.* any of the ridges set across the finger board of certain stringed instruments to serve as fixed points against which the strings may be pressed by the fingers to regulate the pitch of notes.—v.t.—*fretted, fretting*. To provide with frets.

fret·ful, fret'ful, a. Inclined to fret; irritable or peevish.—**fret·ful·ly**, adv.— **fret·ful·ness**, n.

fret saw, n. A small saw for cutting fretwork.

fret·work, fret'wèrk", n. Ornamental work, usu. openwork, consisting of a series or combination of frets.

Freud·i·an, froid'ē·an, a. Of or pertaining

to the Austrian physician, psychoanalyst, and psychopathologist Sigmund *Freud* (1856–1939), or his close associates and doctrines, esp. respecting the causes and treatment of neurotic and psychopathic states, and the interpretation of dreams.— n. An adherent of the doctrines of Freud.— **Freud·i·an·ism**, n.

fri·a·ble, frī'a·bl, a. [L. *friabilis*, < *frio, friatum*, to crumble down.] Easily crumbled or pulverized: often applied to rock or soil. **fri·a·bil·i·ty, fri·a·ble·ness**, frī"a·bil'i·-tē, n.

fri·ar, frī'ér, n. [< M.E. *frere*, Fr. *frère*, O.Fr. *freire*, a brother, < L. *frater, fratris*, a brother.] A man belonging to one of the Roman Catholic religious orders or brotherhoods, esp. the mendicant ones.

fri·ar's lan·tern, n. An ignis fatuus.

fri·ar·y, frī'a·rē, n. pl. **fri·ar·ies**. A monastery of friars; a brotherhood of friars.

frib·ble, frib'l, a. [Perhaps corrupted < Fr. *frivole*, frivolous.] Frivolous; trifling; silly.—n. A trifler; anything frivolous.—v.i. —*fribbled, fribbling*. To trifle.—v.t. To trifle away.—**frib·bler**, n.—**frib·bling**, a.

fric·an·deau, fric·an·do, frik'an·dō", frik"an·dō', n. pl. **fric·an·deaus, fric·an·-deaux, fric·an·does**. [Fr.] Veal or other meat larded, stewed, and served with a sauce.

fric·as·see, frik"a·sē', n. [Fr. *fricassée*, < *fricasser*, cook as a fricassee.] Meat, as chicken or veal, cut up, stewed, and served in a sauce made of its own juices.—v.t.— *fricasseed, fricasseeing*. To prepare as a fricassee.

fric·a·tive, frik'a·tiv, a. *Phon.* of consonants, characterized by the friction of the breath issuing through a narrow opening of the vocal passages, as *f, v, th, TH, s, z, sh, zh*, and *h*.—n.

fric·tion, frik'shan, n. [Fr. *friction*, < L. *frictio(n-)*, < *fricare*, rub.] The rubbing of the surface of one body against that of another; *mech., phys.* the resistance to the relative motion, as sliding or rolling, of surfaces of bodies in contact. Clashing or conflict, as of temperaments or opinions.— **fric·tion·al**, a. Of, pertaining to, or of the nature of friction; moved, worked, or produced by friction.—**fric·tion·al·ly**, adv. —**fric·tion·less**, a.

fric·tion clutch, n. *Mech.* a kind of loose coupling which connects two parts or systems of parts so that rotating motion is transferred from one to another by friction between them.

fric·tion drive, n. *Mech.* a system of power transmission which transmits motion between the driving and the driven machinery by surface friction, and which affords a wide variety of speed ratios.

fric·tion tape, n. *Elect.* a cloth tape, both insulating and adhesive, used esp. to cover and protect electrical conductors.

Fri·day, frī'dā, frī'dē, n. [O.E. *Frīgedæg*, G. *Freytag*, the day sacred to *Frigga*, or *Freya*, the Teutonic goddess.] The sixth day of the week; the day following Thursday.

fridge, frij, n. *Chiefly Brit. and Canadian*, *colloq.* refrigerator.

friend, frend, n. [O.E. *frēond* = *vriend* = G. *freund* = Icel. *frændi* = Goth. *frijonds*, all orig. ppr. of a verb (O.E. *freon*, love, free) < the source of E. *free*.] One attached to another by affection or regard; an intimate; an acquaintance; a member of the same nation or political group; (*cap.*) a member of the Society of Friends, the Christian sect called Quakers; a patron.—**friend at court, friend in court**, a friend who is in a position to further one's interests with others.—**friend·less**, a.— **friend·less·ness**, n.

friend·ly, frend'lē, a.—*friendlier, friendliest*. [O.E. *frēondlic*.] Characteristic of a friend;

like a friend; favorably disposed; inclined to approve, help, or support; not hostile.— *adv.* In a friendly manner; like a friend.— **friend·li·ly,** *adv.*—**friend·li·ness,** *n.*

friend·ship, frend'ship, *n.* A relationship of mutual regard; a feeling of liking and esteem.

fri·er, frī'ẽr, *n.* Fryer.

Frie·sian, frē'zhan, *a.* Frisian.

frieze, frēz, *n.* [Fr. *frise* = It. *fregio,* Sp. *friso,* probably < Ar. *ifriz,* a ledge or a wall.] *Arch.* that part of the entablature of a column which is between the architrave and cornice, usu. sculptured with figures or other ornaments.

frieze, frēz, *n.* [Fr. *frise,* probably from *Friesland,* once the principal seat of its manufacture.] A coarse woolen cloth having a shaggy nap on one side.

frig·ate, frig'it, *n.* [Fr. *frégate,* < It. *fregata.*] Orig. a swift, oared, war vessel; later, a sailing ship used in naval warfare. Presently, a destroyer-type ship in the U.S. Navy, larger than a destroyer and smaller than a cruiser, with a difference of about 1500 tons displacement; *Brit.* a naval vessel which is the same size as, or smaller than, a destroyer.

fri·gate bird, *n.* A long-winged, scissorlike tailed, black bird, *Fregata magnificens,* of warmer seas, with great soaring ability. Also **man-o'-war bird.**

fright, frīt, *n.* [O.E. *frytu, fyrhto,* fear; Dan. *frygt,* G. *furcht,* D. *vrucht,* fear. *Fear* is probably akin in origin.] Sudden and violent fear; terror; *colloq.* a person or object of a shocking, disagreeable, or ridiculous appearance.—*v.t.* To frighten; to alarm.

fright·en, frīt'en, *v.t.* To strike with fright; to terrify; to scare; to alarm suddenly; to drive away by scaring.—*v.i.* To become terrified.—**fright·en·ing·ly,** *adv.*

fright·ful, frīt'ful, *a.* Causing fright; terrible; dreadful; horrible or shocking. *Colloq.* awful or dreadful; as, a *frightful* time; extreme; as, a *frightful* fool.— **fright·ful·ly,** frīt'ful·lē, *adv.*—**fright·ful·ness,** *n.*

frig·id, frij'id, *a.* [L. *frigidus,* < *frigēre,* be cold, < *frigus,* cold, coldness.] Very cold in temperature; devoid of warmth of feeling; cold or indifferent; stiff or formal; abnormally unresponsive or indifferent to sexual intercourse; indifferent; without sympathy, passion, or sensitivity.—**frig·id·ly,** *adv.*— **fri·gid·i·ty, frig·id·ness,** *n.*

Frig·id·aire, frij'i·dâr', *n.* An electric refrigerator. (Trademark.)

frig·o·rif·ic, frig'o·rif'ik, *a.* [L. *frigorificus* —*frigus, frigoris,* cold, and *facio,* to make.] Causing cold; freezing.

fri·jol, frē'hōl, *Sp.* frē·hạl', *n.* pl. **fri·jo·les,** frē'hōlz, *Sp.* frē·hō'lēz, *Sp.* frē·hạ'les. [Sp. *frijol.*] A cultivated bean of the genus *Phaseolus,* much used for food in Mexico. Also **fri·jo·le,** frē·hō'lē.

frill, fril, *n.* [Origin uncertain.] A strip of cloth or lace, gathered or pleated at one edge and loose at the other, used as trimming on clothing; a strip of paper similarly cut, used to trim a portion of meat, as a chop, containing a bone; a ruff or fringe of hair or feathers about the neck of dogs or birds; an affectation of manner or style; an extravagance or nonessential.—*v.t.* To trim with a frill or form into a frill.—*v.i. Photog.* to become wrinkled at the edge as in a film or the gelatin coating of a plate.— **frill·ing,** *n.* Frilled trimming; frills.— **fril·ly,** *a.*

fringe, frinj, *n.* [Fr. *frange,* fringe, It. *frangia* < L. *fimbria,* fringe; akin to *fibra,* a fiber.] A decorative border of threads or strands, suspended loosely from a raveled edge or separate band, used on clothing or home furnishings; anything resembling a fringe or border; as, a *fringe* of long eye-

lashes; something marginal or supplementary in relationship to a prime process or consideration; a group apart from the mainstream of public opinion, usu. manifesting an extreme view; *opt.* one of the resultant light or dark bands caused by the diffraction or interference of light.—*v.t. fringed, fringing.* To adorn or border with, or as with, a fringe; to be or serve as a fringe or border for.—**fring·y,** *a.*

fringe ar·e·a, *n.* A region which has poor, weak, or distorted reception from a given broadcasting station; anything on the outer edge of the mainstream, as of popular opinion; as, a *fringe area* of discussion.

fringe ben·e·fit, *n.* Any benefit, such as paid holidays, insurance, or pensions, given an employee in addition to salary or wages; *fig.* any incidental benefit.

fringe tree, *n.* A shrub or small tree, *Chionanthus virginica,* belonging to the olive family, found in the southern U.S., bearing panicles of white flowers with long, narrow petals.

frip·per·y, frip'e·rē, *n.* pl. **frip·per·ies.** [Fr. *friperie,* O.Fr. *freperie,* < *frepe,* rag.] Finery in dress, esp. when tawdry or showy; an article of this kind; gaudy ornamentation; trifling articles. *Fig.* empty display; ostentation.—*a.*

Fri·sian, frizh'an, *a.* Of or pertaining to Friesland, a province of the Netherlands, its inhabitants, or their language.—*n.* One of the people of Friesland; the Germanic language spoken in Friesland; *Brit.* Holstein.

frisk, frisk, *v.i.* [O.Fr. Fr. *frisque;* origin uncertain.] To dance, leap, skip, or gambol, as in frolic.—*v.t.* To search for stolen property, concealed weapons, or other articles by feeling a person's clothing and pockets.—*n.* A leap, skip, or caper; a frolic; the act of searching or frisking.— **frisk·er,** *n.*—**frisk·ing·ly,** *adv.*

fris·ket, fris'kit, *n.* [Fr. *frisquette.*] *Print.* a sheet with parts cut out, or a frame for holding such a sheet, placed over a form so that only certain parts may be printed.

frisky, fris'kē, *a.*—**friskier, friskiest.** Lively; frolicsome; playful.—**frisk·i·ly,** *adv.;* **frisk·i·ness,** *n.*

frit, frit, *n.* [Fr. *fritte,* < It. *fritta,* < L. *frigere,* roast, E. *fry.*] *Glassmaking,* a calcined, partly fused material ready for complete fusion to form glass; *ceram.* partially fused material used as a basis for glazes; the composition from which artificial soft-paste porcelain is made.—*v.t. fritted, fritting.* To make into frit; fuse partially.

frith, frith, *n.* Firth.

frit·il·lar·i·a, frit″i·lâr'ē·a, *n.* [N.L., < L. *fritillus,* dice box.] Any plant of the liliaceous genus *Fritillaria,* comprising bulbous herbs with drooping, bell-shaped flowers.—**frit·il·lar·y,** frit′i·ler″ē, *n.* pl. **frit·il·lar·ies.** *Bot.* a fritillaria; *zool.* any of several brownish, spotted butterflies of the genera *Speyeria, Argynnis,* and allied genera.

frit·ter, frit'ẽr, *v.t.* [Fr. *friture,* lit. a frying, < L. *frigo, frictum,* to fry.] To waste or expend little by little; as, to *fritter* away life; to spend frivolously or on trifles. To cut or break into small pieces or fragments. —*v.i.* To become detached; to break; to lessen, shrink, or dwindle.—*n.* A fragment or shred.—**frit·ter·er,** *n.*

frit·ter, frit'ẽr, *n.* Batter shaped into a small cake and fried in deep fat or sautéed, sometimes with a filling of fruit or meat; as, an apple *fritter* or a corn *fritter.*

friv·ol, friv'ol, *v.i.*—**frivoled, frivoling,** *Brit.* **frivolled, frivolling.** [< *frivolous.*] To behave frivolously; trifle.—*v.t.* To spend frivolously, usu. with *away.*—**friv·ol·er,** *Brit.* **friv·ol·ler,** *n.*

fri·vol·i·ty, fri·vol'i·tē, *n.* pl. **fri·vol·i·ties.** The quality of being frivolous or trifling; the act, habit, or thing that is trifling.

friv·o·lous, friv'o·lus, *a.* [L. *frivolus,* frivolous, silly, trifling; same root as *frico,* to rub.] Of little weight, worth, or importance; trifling; characterized by unbecoming levity; silly.—**friv·o·lous·ly,** *adv.* —**friv·o·lous·ness,** *n.*

frizz, friz, *v.t.* [Fr. *friser,* O.Fr. *frizer,* to curl, *frise,* frieze cloth.] To curl tightly; to form into small, very tight or kinky curls.— *v.i.* To become frizzed.—*n.* That which is frizzed or curled, as hair; a curl. Also **friz.**

frizz, friz, *v.i., v.t.* [Imit.] To fry and make a sizzling or sputtering noise.

friz·zle, friz'l, *v.t., v.i.*—**frizzled, frizzling.** [Dim. < *frizz.*] To curl tightly or kink, as hair; to frizz.—*n.*

friz·zle, friz'l, *v.i., v.t.*—**frizzled, frizzling.** [< *frizz,* to sizzle.] To make a sizzling or sputtering noise, as in frying; frizz.—*v.t.* To fry or cook with a sizzling noise; to fry and make crisp or curled.—*n.* A tight or crisp curl.

friz·zly, friz'lē, *a.*—**frizzlier, frizzliest.** Frizzed, as hair; very curly; kinky. Also **friz·zy.**—**friz·zi·ly,** *adv.*—**friz·zi·ness,** *n.*

fro, frō, *adv.* [O.E. or Icel. *frá,* from; abbr. form of *from.*] From; away; back or backward; as, to and *fro.*—*prep. Sc.* from.

frock, frok, *n.* [O.Fr. Fr. *froc;* origin uncertain.] A woman's dress; a coarse outer garment with large sleeves worn by monks; the priestly or clerical office; a loose outer garment worn by peasants and workmen; a smock.—*v.t.* To provide with or clothe in a frock; to invest with priestly or clerical office.

frock coat, *n.* A fitted, double-breasted coat, having a knee-length skirt, worn by men.

froe, frō, *n.* Frow.

frog, frog, frạg, *n.* [O.E. *frogga,* akin to D. *vorsch,* G. *frosch,* Icel. *froskr,* frog.] Any of various tailless amphibians of the order *Salientia,* of the web-footed, aquatic genus *Rana,* having strong hind legs enabling them to leap; a slight hoarseness due to mucus on the vocal cords; a triangular horny substance in the sole of the hoof of a horse or other hoofed animal; a device in the rail of a railroad for connecting one track with another crossing or branching from it; an ornamental fastening for a coat or other garment; a small frame of wire, glass, pottery, or plastic, set in a vase for use as a flower holder.—*v.i.*—**frogged, frogging.** To catch or search for frogs.

frog·eye, frog'ī″, frạg'ī″, *n.* Any of several fungus diseases affecting the leaves of tobacco, soybeans, apples and other plants, producing small white spots in concentric rings.—**frog-eyed,** *a.* Affected with frogeye.

frog·hop·per, frog'hop″ẽr, frạg'hop″ẽr, *n.* A small leaping insect, the larvae of which are found on plants enclosed in a frothy liquid known as cuckoo-spit. Also *spittle bug.*

frog lil·y, *n.* The yellow pond lily.

frog·man, frog'man″, frạg'man, *n.* pl. **frog·men.** A person especially trained and equipped to swim under water, usu. for purposes of exploration and demolition.

frog spit, *n.* Any of several filamentous fresh-water algae forming floating masses. Also **frog spit·tle.**

frol·ic, frol'ik, *n.* [< D. *vroolijk,* < *vro* = O.Fris. *fro,* Dan. *fro,* glad, and *lijk* = E. *like;* G. *fröhlich,* < *froh,* joyful, and *lich,* like.] A wild or merry prank; a flight of levity or gaiety and mirth; a scene of gaiety and mirth; a merrymaking.—*v.i.*—**frolicked, frolicking.** To play merry pranks; to behave in ways of levity, mirth, and gaiety; to play in a light-hearted or lively manner; to romp.—**frol·ic·some**, frol′ic·som, *a.* Full of gaiety and mirth; sportive.—**frol·ic·some·ly**, *adv.*—**frol·ic·some·ness**, *n.*

from, frum, from, *unstressed* from, *prep.* [O.E. *fram*, prep., *from*, as adv. forward, forth; = O.H.G. and Goth. *fram*, prep. and adv., = Icel. *frā*, prep. (cf. *fro*), *fram*, adv.; ult. akin to E. *fore*.] A particle or function word specifying a starting point, source, or origin; as, a train running west *from* New York, to count *from* 1 to 10; a particle expressing removal or separation in space, time, or order; as, away *from* home; a particle expressing discrimination or distinction; as, to tell one tree *from* another; a particle indicating cause, reason, or instrumentality; as, to suffer *from* measles.

frond, frond, *n.* [L. *frons, frondis*, a leaf.] *Bot.* a large leaf, esp. that of a palm tree; a fern leaf; a leaflike extension of a plant, as a seaweed, which is not distinctly differentiated into stem and leaf.—**frond·ed**, *a.*

fron·des·cence, fron·des′ens, *n. Bot.* the process or period of coming into leaf; foliage.—**fron·des·cent**, *a.*

fron·dose, fron′dōs, *a.* [L. *frondosus*, < *frons.*] *Bot.* frondlike; having fronds.

front, frunt, *n.* [O.Fr. Fr. *front*, < L. *frons* (*front-*), forehead, front.] The foremost part or surface of anything; the part or side of anything which is directed forward; any side or face of a building, esp. that which has the main entrance; frontage. *Milit.* the foremost line or part of an army; a line of battle; place where active operations are carried on. A movement or coalition, usu. political, to achieve a common goal; an eminent person serving as a nominal official of a group or company to give it prestige; bearing or demeanor in confronting any situation; as, a calm *front*. *Colloq.* an outward appearance of wealth or position assumed to impress others; any person or business which masks or disguises illegal activity. *Meteorol.* a line which separates dissimilar masses of air.—*a.* Of or pertaining to the front; situated in or at the front.—*v.t.* To have the front toward; face; to meet face to face; confront, esp. in hostility or defiance; oppose; supply with a front; to serve as a front to.—*v.i.* To face or turn in some specified direction; serve as a mask or disguise for an illegal activity. —*adv.*

front·age, frun′tij, *n.* The front of a building or lot; the lineal extent of this front; the direction something faces; exposure; land abutting a body of water or a street; land between a building and the street.

fron·tal, frun′tal, *n.* [O.Fr. *frontel*, < M.L. *frontale*, < L. *frons*, E. *front*.] *Arch.* the façade of a building; *eccles.* a movable cover or hanging for the front of an altar.

fron·tal, frun′tal, *a.* [N.L. *frontalis*, < L. *frons*, E. *front*.] Pertaining to, in, or at the front; *anat.* noting or pertaining to the forehead or the bone or pair of bones forming the forehead.—**fron·tal·ly**, *adv.*

fron·tal bone, *n.* A membrane bone in the skull, one of a pair forming the forehead.

fron·tal lobe, *n.* The anterior or upper division of the cerebral hemisphere.

front-end load, *n. Investing*, all or a major part of the total load, or sales charge, which is deducted from early payments under a contractual plan for the long-range purchase of investment shares.

fron·tier, frun·tēr′, *n.* [O.Fr. *frontiere* (Fr. *frontière*), < M.L. *frontaria*, < L. *frons*, E. *front*.] The part of a country that faces or borders another country; that part of a country which forms the border of its settled or inhabited regions; a new or untapped area of knowledge or achievement.—*a.* Of or pertaining to a frontier;

situated on the frontier.—**fron·tiers·man**, frun·tērz′man, *n.* pl. **fron·tiers·men**. A man who lives on the frontier; a pioneer.

fron·tis·piece, frun′tis·pēs″, fron′tis·pēs″, *n.* [An altered form, simulating *piece*, of *frontispice*, < Fr. *frontispice*, < M.L. *frontispicium*, < L. *frons*, front, and *specere*, look at.] An illustration facing the title page of a book; formerly, the title page. *Arch.* the front of a building; a highly decorated façade; a pediment over a door, window, or gate.

front·let, frunt′lit, *n.* [O.Fr. *frontelet*, dim. of *frontel*, E. *frontal*.] An ornament worn on the forehead; the forehead of an animal; *ornith.* the forehead when marked by different color or texture of the plumage; *Judaism*, the phylactery placed on the forehead.

front mat·ter, *n.* The introductory matter which prefaces the main text of a book.

front of·fice, *n.* The executive staff of a firm or organization.

fron·to·gen·e·sis, frun″to·jen′i·sis, *n. Meteor.* the development of a front that causes clouds and precipitation and is formed by the fusion and interaction of two different masses or currents of air.

fron·tol·y·sis, frun·tol′i·sis, *n. Meteor.* the dissolution of a front between masses of air.

front·ward, frunt′wèrd, *adv.* Toward the front. Also **front·wards**.

frosh, frosh, *n.* pl. **frosh**. *Colloq.* a freshman in college; *Brit. dial.* a frog.

frost, frạst, frost, *n.* [O.E. *frost, forst*, = D. *vorst* = G. and Icel. *frost*, frost.] A state of the temperature which occasions the freezing of water; a covering of minute ice needles, as formed from the atmosphere at night, and appearing on the ground and exposed objects when these have cooled by radiation below the freezing point; frozen vapor; coldness of manner or temperament. *Slang*, a failure, esp. a play or social occasion; a coolness between persons.—*v.t.* To cover with frost; to give a frostlike surface to, as glass; to ice, as a cake; to damage, as plants, by frost.—*v.i.* To freeze; to become like frost.

frost·bite, frạst′bīt″, frost′bīt″, *n.* Damage to tissues in any part of the body, such as the nose and ears, occasioned by exposure to severe cold, resulting in inflammation and sometimes gangrene.—*v.t.*—*past frostbit*, pp. *frostbitten*, ppr. *frostbiting*. To damage by frost or severe cold.

frost·ed, frạ′stid, fros′tid, *a.* Covered with frost; having a frostlike surface; iced, as cake; quick-frozen, as applied to foods; prepared with ice cream; as, a *frosted* milk shake.

frost heave, *n.* Upward movement of soil or pavement when presence of ice crystals in the soil forces expansion.

frost·ing, frạ′sting, fros′ting, *n.* An edible, sweetened mixture used to cover cakes and other pastries; icing; a lusterless finish, as on metal or glass; a decorative material made from fine particles of glass.

frost·y, frạ′stē, fros′tē, *a.*—*frostier, frostiest.* Attended with or producing frost; freezing; very cold; lacking warmth of feeling; chilling; consisting of or covered with frost; resembling frost; white or gray, as the hair; pertaining to or characteristic of old age.—**frost·i·ly**, *adv.*—**frost·i·ness**, *n.*

froth, frạth, froth, *n.* [M.E. *frothe*: cf. Icel. *frodha*, froth, also O.E. *āfrēothan*, form froth.] An aggregation of bubbles, as on a liquid, from agitation or fermentation; foam; a foam of saliva issuing from the mouth, caused by certain diseases or exhaustion; something unsubstantial, light, or trivial.—*v.t.* To cause to foam; to emit like froth; to cover with froth.—*v.i.* To give off froth; to foam.

froth·y, frạ′thē, froth′ē, *a.*—*frothier, frothiest.* Of, like, or having froth; foamy; unsubstantial, light, trifling.—**froth·i·ly**, *adv.*—**froth·i·ness**, *n.*

frou-frou, frö′frö″, *n.* A rustling sound, as of taffeta or silk in women's apparel; elaborate ornamentation, esp. that on women's clothing.

frow, froe, frō, *Brit.* frou, *n.* A wedge-shaped tool with a handle at a right angle to the blade, used for splitting shingles; a steel wedge for splitting logs. *Brit.* an untidy woman.

fro·ward, frō′wèrd, frō′èrd, *a.* [< *fro* = from, and *-ward*, denoting direction; O.E. *fromweard*, turned away, about to depart.] Not willing to comply with what is right or reasonable; perverse; ungovernable; refractory; disobedient; peevish.—**fro·ward·ly**, *adv.*—**fro·ward·ness**, *n.*

frown, froun, *v.i.* [Fr. *frogner*, in *se refrogner*, to knit the brow, to frown; of doubtful origin.] To express displeasure, severity, sternness, or disapproval by contracting the brow; to scowl.—*v.t.* To show or express by scowling; to express disapproval by a grimace.—*n.* A contraction or wrinkling of the brow; a severe or stern look; a scowl.—**frown·ing·ly**, *adv.*

frowz·y, **frows·y**, frou′zē, *a.*—*frowzier, frowziest.* [Akin Prov. E. *froust*, a musty smell, also Prov. E. *frow*, a slattern, < D. *vrow*, G. *frau*, a woman.] Slovenly; not clean or neat in appearance. Having a stale, musty odor.

fro·zen, frō′zen, *a.* Preserved by quick freezing; as, *frozen* foods; congealed by cold; covered with ice, as a stream; obstructed by the formation of ice, as pipes; injured or killed by frost or cold; frigid, or very cold; chilly or cold in manner; as, a *frozen* stare; *fig.* rendered impossible of liquidation, as by business conditions; as, *frozen* assets, *frozen* loans.—**fro·zen·ly**, *adv.*—**fro·zen·ness**, *n.*

fruc·ti·fi·ca·tion, fruk″ti·fi·kā′shan, frụk″ti·fi·kā′shan, *n.* The act of fructifying; the fruiting of a plant. The fruit of a plant. The organs of fruiting.

fruc·ti·fy, fruk′ti·fī″, frụk′ti·fī″, *v.t.*—*fructified, fructifying.* To make fruitful; to render productive; to fertilize.—*v.i.* To bear or produce fruit.—**fruc·tif·er·ous**, fruc·tif′er·us, *a.* Fruit-bearing.

fruc·tose, fruk′tōs, frụk′tōs, *n.* [L. *fructus*, fruit.] *Chem.* a natural sugar, $C_6H_{12}O_6$, found in honey and many fruits, used in foods, medicines, and preservatives. Also *fruit sugar, levulose.*

fruc·tu·ous, fruk′chö·us, *a.* [O.Fr. *fructuous* (Fr. *fructueux*), < L. *fructuosus*, < *fructus*, E. *fruit*.] Fruitful; productive.

fru·gal, frö′gal, *a.* [L. *frugalis*, < *frugi*, lit. fit for food, hence worthy, temperate.] Economical in regard to expenditure; thrifty; sparing; not lavish; saving.—**fru·gal·i·ty**, frö·gal′i·tē, *n.* pl. **fru·gal·i·ties.** Thrift; prudent and sparing use of anything.—**fru·gal·ly**, *adv.*—**fru·gal·ness**, *n.*

fru·giv·o·rous, frö·jiv′er·us, *a.* [L. *frux, frugis*, and *voro*, to eat.] Feeding on fruits, as birds and other animals.

fruit, fröt, *n.* [O.Fr. Fr. *fruit*, < L. *fructus*, enjoyment, proceeds, fruit, < *frui*, enjoy.] *Often pl.* any product of vegetable growth useful to men or animals; as, *fruits* of the earth. *Bot.* the matured ovary of a plant with its contents and accessory parts; the pulpy edible substance covering the seeds of various flowering plants and trees; the spores and accessory organs of a cryptogam. Anything produced or occurring; product; result; profit; *slang*, a male homosexual.—*v.i., v.t.* To bear or bring to bear fruit.

fruit·age, frö′tij, *n.* The bearing of fruit; a quantity or yield of fruit or fruits, considered collectively; product or result, as of one's efforts.

fruit cake, *n.* A rich cake and traditional Christmas food containing nuts, raisins, currants, other dried or candied fruits, and spices.

fruit·er, frōt'ẽr, *n.* A ship employed in transporting fruit; a fruit grower or dealer.

fruit·er·er, frōt'ẽr·ẽr, *n. Brit.* A dealer in fruit; a fruit seller.

fruit fly, *n.* Any of several small flies of the family *Trypetidae*, whose larvae attack or feed on fruit or rotting vegetables; a fly of the genus *Drosophila* used in genetic research.

fruit·ful, frōt'ful, *a.* Bearing fruit abundantly; very fertile or productive; productive of results; as, a *fruitful* journey; profitable.—**fruit·ful·ly,** *adv.*—**fruit·ful·ness,** *n.*

fru·i·tion, frō·ish'an, *n.* [O.Fr. *fruition,* < L.L. *fruitio(n-),* < L. *frui,* enjoy.] Attainment of a goal; accomplishment; enjoyment, as of something realized; *hort.* condition of bearing fruit.

fruit·less, frōt'lis, *a.* Destitute or not bearing fruit; barren; without any production, advantage, or good effect; worthless.—**fruit·less·ly,** *adv.*—**fruit·less·ness,** *n.*

fruit sug·ar, *n.* Fructose.

fruit·y, frōt'ē, *a.*—*fruitier, fruitiest.* Resembling fruit; having the taste or flavor of fruit; of a wine, having a full-bodied fruit flavor; *fig.* cloyingly sweet or syrupy. *Slang,* mentally disturbed, odd, or eccentric; homosexual.

fru·men·ta·ceous, frō'men·tā'shus, *a.* [L. *frumentaceus,* < *frumentum,* grain; same root as *fructus,* fruit.] Having the character of or resembling wheat or other cereal grain.

fru·men·ty, frō'men·tē, *n.* [L. *frumentum,* grain.] *Brit.* a dish made of hulled wheat boiled in milk, sweetened, and seasoned. Also *furmenty,* **fur·me·ty, fro·men·ty.**

frump, frump, *n.* [Connected with *frampold,* or with Provinc. E. *frumple,* D. *frommelen,* to wrinkle or crumple.] A dowdy or cross-tempered, old-fashioned female.—**frump·ish, frump·y,** *a.*—*frumpier, frumpiest.*

frus·trate, frus'trāt, *v.t.*—*frustrated, frustrating.* [L. *frustratus,* pp. of *frustrari, frustrare,* < *frustra,* in vain.] To disappoint or thwart; to cause to have no effect; defeat; baffle; nullify.

frus·tra·tion, frus·trā'shan, *n.* Something that disappoints or thwarts; the state of being thwarted.

frus·tum, frus'tum, *n.* pl. **frus·tums, frus·ta,** frus'ta. [L., piece, bit.] *Geom.* the part of a solid, as a cone or pyramid, left after a top portion is cut off by a plane parallel to the base; the part of a solid between two cutting planes. *Arch.* a truncated column.

fru·tes·cent, frō·tes'ent, *a.* [L. *frutex, fruticis,* a shrub.] *Bot.* having the appearance or nature of a shrub.—**fru·tes·cence,** *n.*—**fru·ti·cose,** frō'ti·kōs″, *a.* Pertaining to shrubs; shrubby.

fry, frī, *v.t.*—*fried, frying.* [Fr. *frire,* to fry, < L. *frigo,* to fry, roast, or parch.] To cook in a pan over a fire using fat.—*v.i.* To be cooked in this way.—*n.* A social occasion on which fried food is served; as, a fish *fry;* a dish of anything fried.

fry, frī, *n.* [M.E. *fry,* akin Icel. *frjō, frae,* Goth. *fraiw,* seed.] The young of fishes or of some other animals, as frogs; adult fish of lesser size; a category of people, esp. children; as, small *fry.*

fryer, frier, frī'ẽr, *n.* A young chicken, suitable for frying; a cooking vessel intended for frying foods.

f-stop, ef'stop″, *n. Photog.* the setting for a camera lens opening as indicated by an f-number.

F₂ lay·er, *n.* See *F layer.*

fuch·sia, fū'sha, *n.* A house and garden plant, *Fuchsia hybrida,* in the evening-primrose family, with showy, colorful, drooping flowers; also **la·dy's-ear·drop.** Any plant of the genus *Fuchsia.* A vivid purplish-red color.

fuch·sin, fuk'sin, *n.* A coal-tar derivative dyestuff and bacterial dye, occurring as a greenish solid which forms deep-red or purple solutions; magenta. Also **fuch·sine,** fuk'sēn.

fu·coid, fū'koid, *a.* Resembling or allied to seaweeds of the genus *Fucus.*—*n.* A fucoid seaweed.

fu·cus, fū'kus, *n.* pl. **fu·cus·es, fu·ci,** fū'sī. [L., rock lichen.] *Bot.* any plant of the genus *Fucus* of olive-brown seaweed or algae with branching fronds and air bladders; rockweed.

fud·dle, fud'l, *v.t.*—*fuddled, fuddling.* [From a form *fuzzle,* akin to L.G. *fusslig,* G. *fusselig,* drunk.] To make foolish or stupid by drink; to make tipsy.—*v.i.* To tipple.—*n.* A confused or muddled state.

fud·dy-dud·dy, fud'ē·dud″ē, fud'ē·dud'ē, *n.* pl. **fud·dy-dud·dies.** *Colloq.* A stuffy or old-fashioned person; one who is fussy or excessively worried about trifles.

fudge, fuj, *v.i.*—*fudged, fudging.* [Origin uncertain.] To cheat or behave dishonestly; to fail to fulfill a promise or obligation; to welsh, often with *on.*—*v.t.* To dodge, evade, or fail to cope with, as an issue or responsibility; to make up, fake, or invent, as a false story.

fudge, fuj, *n.* A soft candy composed of sugar, butter, milk, and chocolate or other flavors. A made-up story; nonsense; a short section of typeset material, as a piece of late news, inserted in a newspaper.

Fu·e·gi·an, fū·ē'jē·an, fwä'jē·an, *a.* Of or pertaining to Tierra del Fuego, an area at the southern tip of South America, or to its inhabitants or culture.—*n.* An inhabitant of Tierra del Fuego; an Indian native to Tierra del Fuego.

fu·el, fū'el, *n.* [O.Fr. *fouaille,* < M.L. *focalia,* pl. of *focale,* fuel, < L. *focus,* hearth, fireplace.] Combustible matter used to maintain fire, as coal, wood, or oil; material which provides nourishment; a means of sustaining or increasing strong feeling.—*v.t.*—*fueled, fueling, Brit. fuelled, fuelling.* To supply with fuel.—*v.i.* To get or replenish fuel.

fu·el cell, *n. Chem., aerospace,* a device which converts chemical energy directly into electrical energy without needing recharging as does a storage battery: used, esp. in space vehicles; a fuel tank, esp. one of a number of fuel tanks as in an airplane's wing; a compartment within a fuel tank.

fu·el in·jec·tion, *n.* The forced spraying of fuel or fuel and air under pressure into the combustion chamber of an engine.—*a.* Of or pertaining to an engine that operates by using fuel injection.—**fu·el in·jec·tor,** *n.* A pump used for fuel injection.

fu·el oil, *n.* An oil used for fuel, esp. one used as a substitute for coal, as crude petroleum.

fug, fug, *n. Brit.* A stuffy atmosphere in a crowded place; stale air.

fu·ga·cious, fū·gā'shus, *a.* [L. *fugax* (*fugac-*) < *fugere,* flee.] Fleeting; transitory. *Bot.* of leaves or petals, falling or fading early.—**fu·ga·cious·ly,** *adv.*—**fu·ga·cious·ness, fu·gac·i·ty,** fū·gas'i·tē, *n.*

fu·gal, fū'gal, *a. Mus.* pertaining to or in the style of a fugue.—**fu·gal·ly,** *adv.*

fu·gi·tive, fū'ji·tiv, *a.* [O.Fr. Fr. *fugitif,* < L. *fugitivus,* < *fugere* = Gr. *pheugein,* flee.] Fleeing, or tending to flee; having taken flight, or run away; as, a *fugitive* slave; wandering; vagabond; fleeting or transitory; quickly fading, as colors; readily escaping, as odors; ephemeral.

occasional.—*n.* A runaway; a refugee.—**fu·gi·tive·ly,** *adv.*—**fu·gi·tive·ness,** *n.*

fugue, fūg, *n.* [Fr. *fugue,* < It. *fuga,* < L. *fuga,* flight, swift course, akin to *fugere,* flee.] *Mus.* a musical composition having two or more themes treated contrapuntally. *Psychol.* a long period of amnesia.—**fu·guist,** *n.* A composer or performer of fugues.

Füh·rer, Fueh·rer, fū'rẽr, G. fУ'RẼR, *n.* [G.] Leader.—**der Füh·rer,** the title used by Adolph Hitler, Nazi dictator of Germany from 1933 to 1945.

ful·crum, ful'krum, ful'krum, *n.* pl. **ful·cra, ful·crums.** [L., the post or foot of a couch, < *fulcio,* to support.] A prop or support; *mech.* that by which a lever is sustained or the point about which a lever turns in lifting a body; *usu. pl., zool.* any of several parts in an animal that support or perform as a hinge.—*v.t.* To provide with a fulcrum; to construct into a fulcrum.

ful·fill, ful·fil, ful·fil', *v.t.*—*fulfilled, fulfilling.* [A compound of *full* and *fill;* O.E. *fullfyllan.*] To accomplish or carry into effect, as a prophecy or promise; to perform; to meet or satisfy, as requirements; to complete.—*v. refl.* To realize one's full potentialities.—**ful·fill·er,** *n.*—**ful·fill·ment, ful·fil·ment,** *n.* An act of fulfilling; condition of being fulfilled.

ful·gent, ful'jent, *a.* [L. *fulgens, fulgentis,* < *fulgeo,* to shine.] Shining; dazzling; exquisitely bright.—**ful·gent·ly,** *adv.*

ful·gu·rant, ful'gūr·ant, *a.* Flashing like lightning. Also **ful·gu·rous.**

ful·gu·ra·tion, ful″gū·rā'shan, *n.* [L. *fulguratio,* < *fulgur,* lightning.] The flashing of or as of lightning; *med.* destruction, esp. of abnormal growths, by electricity.—**ful·gu·rate,** *v.i., v.t.*—*fulgurated, fulgurating.*

ful·gu·rite, ful'gū·rīt″, *n.* [L. *fulgur,* lightning.] An indentation formed in sand or rock by lightning; rocky matter fused by lightning.

fu·lig·i·nous, fū·lij'i·nus, *a.* [L. *fuliginosus* < *fuligo,* soot.] Sooty; smoky; having a dusky color.—**fu·lig·i·nous·ly,** *adv.*

full, ful, *a.* [O.E. *full, ful.*] Containing all that can be held; filled; as, a *full* cup, *full* sails; containing a plentiful amount or number; of the maximum size, amount, extent, or volume; as, a *full* mile, *full* growth; complete or entire; copious; ample in detail; satisfied, as with food; occupied with the thought or subject; filled or rounded out, as in form; wide, ample, or having ample folds, as garments or draperies; having ample volume and depth of sound; of dress, suited for formal or ceremonial wear.—**full·ness,** *n.* The state or quality of being full or filled.

full, ful, *adv.* Exactly, directly, or straight; as: He looked him *full* in the face. To the utmost extent or degree, esp. in compound words; as, *full*-blown; *often poet.* very or quite; as, *full* well, *full* sad.

full, ful, *n.* Complete measure; utmost extent; highest state or degree; as, fed to the *full,* the *full* of the moon.

full, ful, *v.t. Sewing,* to make full by gathering, tucking, or pleating.—*v.i.* Of the moon, to become completely illuminated.

full, ful, *v.t.* [O.Fr. Fr. *fouler,* < M.L. *fullare,* full (cloth), < L. *fullo(n-),* a fuller.] To cleanse and thicken, as cloth, by special moistening and heating processes in manufacture.—*v.i.* Of cloth, to become compacted or felted.

full·back, ful'bak″, *n. Football,* a backfield player with both offensive and defensive duties, usu. standing farthest behind the line of scrimmage, the position played by a fullback. In rugby, football, and field hockey, a chiefly defensive player stationed near his own goal.

full blood, *n.* Pure extraction; as, an Indian of *full blood*; whole blood or relationship through both parents; as, brothers of *full blood*; a thoroughbred animal.

full-blood·ed, fụl'blud'id, *a.* Of pure blood or extraction; thoroughbred; *fig.* vigorous; lusty.—**full-blood·ed·ness,** *n.*

full-blown, fụl'blōn', *a.* Fully expanded, as a blossom; mature; completely developed; as, a *full-blown* beauty.

full-bod·ied, fụl'bod'ēd, *a.* Satisfying in strength and flavor, as a beverage; vigorous or significant, as writing.

full dress, *n.* Attire which etiquette requires to be worn on formal or ceremonial occasions.—**full-dress,** *a.*

ful·ler's earth, *n.* A variety of clay and fine siliceous material, used in absorbing grease from fabric, in fulling and cleansing cloth, and as a dusting powder.

full-faced, fụl'fāst', *a.* Having a plump or round face; facing squarely toward the spectator.

full-fash·ioned, fụl'fash'ạnd, *a.* Made by a knitting process to conform to the contour of a part of the body, as hosiery.

full-fledged, fụl'flejd', *a.* Completely developed; matured; of full status or rank.

full house, *n. Poker,* a hand of playing cards containing three of a kind and a pair. Also **full hand.**

full-length, fụl'lengkth', fụl'length', *a.* Of usual, standard, or original length; unabridged; showing or suited to the full length of the human form, as a mirror.

full moon, *n.* The moon with its whole disk illuminated; the time when the moon is in this position.

full-scale, fụl'skāl', *a.* Equal in size or proportion to the original, as a model; complete; using all available resources; as, a *full-scale* revolt.

full stop, *n.* A full grammatical pause, as at the end of a sentence; a period.

full tilt, *adv.* At top speed or full potential.

full time, *n.* The length of time considered to constitute a complete work period, as: *A 40-hour week is considered to be full time.*—**full-time,** *a.* Working the full schedule of hours: opposed to *part-time.*

ful·ly, fụl'ē, *adv.* In a full manner; to the full extent; completely; entirely.

ful·mar, fụl'mẹr, *n.* [Perhaps < Icel. *fūll,* foul (with allusion to odor), and *mār,* gull.] A northern oceanic bird of the petrel family, esp. *Fulmarus glacialis.*

ful·mi·nant, ful'mi·nant, *a.* [L. *fulminans, fulminantis.*] Violent, sudden, intense; of a disease, showing rapid development or progression.

ful·mi·nate, ful'mi·nāt, *v.i.*—**fulminated, fulminating.** [L. *fulminatus,* pp. of *fulminare,* < *fulmen* (*fulmin-*) lightning, thunderbolt, < *fulgere,* flash, shine.] To explode with a loud noise; detonate; to issue denunciations or invectives.—*v.t.* To cause to explode; to denounce vehemently.—*n. Chem.* an unstable, explosive salt of fulminic acid.— **ful·mi·na·tion,** ful'mi·nā'shan, *n.*—**ful·mi·na·tor,** *n.*—**ful·mi·na·to·ry,** *a.*

ful·mi·nat·ing, ful'mi·nā'ting, *a.* Exploding; detonating; *pathol.* rapid and severe.— **ful·mi·nat·ing pow·der,** a powder that detonates.

ful·min·ic ac·id, ful·min'ik as'id, *n.* [< L. *fulmen.*] *Chem.* an unstable, explosive acid, HONC, known principally in the form of its salts, which are used as detonators.

ful·some, fụl'sọm, ful'sọm, *a.* Offensive, as from excess of praise or insincerity of motive; nauseous; disgusting.—**ful·some·ly,** *adv.*—**ful·some·ness,** *n.*

ful·vous, ful'vụs, *a.* [L. *fulvus,* yellow.] Yellow; tawny; of a tawny yellow color.

fu·mar·ic ac·id, fū·mar'ik as'id, *n. Chem.* a crystalline acid, $C_4H_4O_4$, derived from certain plants, fermentation of molasses,

and made synthetically, and used mainly in the manufacture of polyester and other resins.

fu·ma·role, fū'ma·rōl″, *n.* [It. *fumarola,* < L. *fumus,* smoke.] A hole from which smoke or gases issue in a volcanic locality.— **fu·ma·rol·ic,** fū″ma·rol'ik, *a.*

fum·ble, fum'bl, *v.i.*—**fumbled, fumbling.** [< D. *fommelen,* L.G. *fummeln,* to fumble, Sw. *fumla,* to handle feebly.] To feel or grope about; to search for or attempt something awkwardly; *sports,* to drop the ball or fail to handle it properly.—*v.t.* To make, deal with, or manipulate clumsily or ineffectively; *sports,* to drop or fall from one's grasp, as a ball.—*n.* An act or instance of fumbling.—**fum·bler,** *n.*

fume, fūm, *n.* [O.Fr. *fum,* < L. *fumus,* smoke, steam, fume.] Often *pl.* smoke, gas, or any smokelike or gaseous exhalation, esp. when odorous, stifling, or otherwise offensive; an angry or irritable mood.—*v.i.* —**fumed, fuming.** To emit fumes; to rise or pass off as fumes; to show irritation or anger.—*v.t.* To treat with fumes; to send forth, as fumes.—**fumed,** *a.* Darkened or colored by exposure to ammonia fumes, as oak and other woods.—**fum·ing·ly,** *adv.*— **fum·y,** *a.*

fu·mi·gant, fū'mi·gant, *n.* Any chemical compound or vapor used to fumigate.

fu·mi·gate, fū'mi·gāt″, *v.t.*—**fumigated, fumigating.** [L. *fumigo, fumigatum.*] To expose to fumes or vapors, esp. for disinfection or for destruction of vermin.— **fu·mi·ga·tion,** *n.*—**fu·mi·ga·tor,** *n.*— **fu·mi·ga·to·ry,** fū'mi·ga·tōr″ē, *a.*

fu·mi·to·ry, fū'mi·tōr″ē, *n. pl.* **fu·mi·to·ries.** [O.Fr. Fr. *fumeterre,* < M.L. *fumus terrae,* 'smoke of the earth.'] A climbing weed of the genus *Fumaria,* a source of several alkaloids of medicinal value.

fun, fun, *n.* [Prob. < M.E. *fonnen,* be foolish.] That which is diverting, amusing, or mirthful; recreation or play; playfulness or jollity.—*v.i.*—**funned, funning.** *Colloq.* to make fun; joke.—*a. Colloq.* entertaining or amusing.

fu·nam·bu·list, fū·nam'bū·list, *n.* [L. *funambulus,* a rope walker < *funis,* rope, and *ambulo, ambulatum,* to walk.] A performer in a circus or other show who does a balancing act on a slack, elevated wire or cable; a rope walker or rope dancer.

func·tion, fungk'shan, *n.* [Fr. *fonction,* L. *functio,* < L. *fungor, functus,* to perform, to execute.] The normal or proper activity of a person, institution, or thing; the specific duties of a person, esp. in a professional or an official capacity, as: *The function of a judge is to administer justice.* A formal or elaborate social occasion; *math.* the association of a particular quantity from one set with each quantity from another set, such that no change can be made in the former without producing a corresponding change in the latter; *gram.* the role of a linguistic form in a grammatical construction.—*v.i.* To perform usual or specified activity; to serve in a particular capacity.—**func·tion·less,** *a.*

func·tion·al, fungk'sha·nal, *a.* Of or pertaining to a function or functions; serving or having a particular use; capable of performing its function; designed for or suited to a utilitarian purpose; *med.,* *psychol.* affecting only the functions and not the structure of an organ.—**func·tion·al·ly,** *adv.*

func·tion·al dis·ease, *n. Pathol.* a disease in which there is a pathological change in the function of an organ, but no structural alteration in the tissues involved: opposed to *organic disease.*

func·tion·al·ism, fungk'sha·na·liz″um, *n. Arch.* a philosophy or principle of design

which holds that the utilitarian purpose of an object should influence or control its form, construction, and material composition; *psychol.* the point of view that considers mental phenomena as useful activities or processes in terms of need, effect, or achievement.—**func·tion·al·ist,** *n.,* *a.*—**func·tion·al·ist·ic,** fungk″sha·na·lis'tik, *a.*

func·tion·al shift, *n. Ling.* the assuming of one or more additional grammatical functions by a word without any change in its form.

func·tion·ar·y, fungk'sha·ner″ē, *n. pl.* **func·tion·ar·ies.** One who holds an office or trust; an official who has special duties.

func·tion word, *n.* A word, as a preposition, article, or conjunction, which serves a primarily grammatical function, indicating the relationship to other words with which it is used.

fund, fund, *n.* [Fr. *fond,* bottom, foundation, *fonds,* land, capital, stock, fund, < L. *fundus,* bottom, piece of land, estate.] A store or stock of something, esp. a stock of money. *Pl.* money in hand; pecuniary resources; the national debt, esp. in Great Britain, used with *the.*—*v.t.* To provide a fund to pay the interest or principal of, as a debt; to convert, as current debts, into a long-term debt represented by bonds; to provide funds for; to finance; to put into a fund; to invest.

fun·da·ment, fun'da·ment, *n.* [O.Fr. Fr. *fondement,* < L. *fundamentum,* < *fundare.*] The buttocks; the anus. *Geog.* the physical features of a particular region.

fun·da·men·tal, fun″da·men'tal, *a.* Of, pertaining to, or being the basis, root, or foundation of something; essential; elementary; primary.—*n.* A primary principle, rule, or law; something essential; *phys.* the lowest of the component frequencies of a periodic wave. *Mus.* the lowest frequency or pitch of a tone in a harmonic series; also **first har·mon·ic.**—**fun·da·men·tal·ly,** *adv.*

fun·da·men·tal·ism, fun″da·men'ta·liz″um, *n.* A belief that the Bible is to be accepted literally as an inerrant and infallible spiritual and historical document. (*Often cap.*) an early 20th century U.S. Protestant movement stressing this belief; any similar belief or movement.—**fun·da·men·tal·ist,** *n.,* *a.*—**fun·da·men·tal·is·tic,** fun″da·ment″al·is'tik, *a.*

fun·da·men·tal par·ti·cle, *n. Phys.* any subatomic particle, as a proton, neutron, electron, neutrino, or muon, found within or surrounding the nucleus of an atom, some of which are short-lived particles released from atoms under nuclear bombardment. Also **el·e·men·ta·ry par·ti·cle.**

fun·da·men·tal u·nit, *n. Phys.* one of the units, esp. of mass, length, or time, taken as a basis for a system of units.

fun·dus, fun'dus, *n. pl.* **fun·di,** fun'dī. [L.] *Anat.* the bottom of a hollow organ, or the part opposite to or remote from an aperture.—**fun·dic,** *a.*

fu·ner·al, fū'nẹr·al, *n.* [Fr. *funérailles,* < L. *funis, funeris,* a burial.] The ceremony or procession immediately prior to burying or cremating a dead person; obsequies.—*a.*

fu·ner·al di·rec·tor, *n.* An undertaker; one who manages funerals.

fu·ne·ral home, *n.* An establishment where a dead person is prepared for a funeral and where relatives and friends may view the body. Also **fu·ne·ral par·lor.**

fu·ner·ar·y, fū'ne·rer″ē, *a.* [L.L. *funerarius,* < L. *funus* (*funer-*), funeral.] Of or pertaining to a funeral or burial; as, a *funerary* urn.

fu·ne·re·al, fū·nēr'ē·al, *a.* [L. *funereus.*] Pertaining to a funeral; gloomy; mournful. —**fu·ne·re·al·ly,** *adv.*

fun·gal, fung´gal, *a.* Pertaining to or of the nature of a fungus; fungous.—*n.* A fungus.

fun·gi·ble, fun´ji·bl, *a.* [M.L. *fungibilis,* < L. *fungi,* perform, discharge.] *Law,* of such a nature that one item or part may be replaced by another of the same type; interchangeable; permitting substitution.—*n.* A fungible thing, as coins or grain.—**fun·gi·bil·i·ty,** fun´ji·bil´i·tē, *n.*

fun·gi·cide, fun´ji·sīd´, *n.* A chemical agent which eradicates fungi; a chemical which prevents future fungoid growths.—**fun·gi·cid·al,** *a.*—**fun·gi·cid·al·ly,** *adv.*

fun·gi·form, fun´ji·fạrm´, *a.* Having the form of a fungus, esp. a mushroom.

fun·go, fung´gō, *n. pl.* **fun·goes.** *Baseball.* The practice method whereby a coach or player hits the ball to the outfield by tossing the ball in the air and batting it as it falls; a ball hit in this manner.

fun·goid, fung´goid, *a.* Resembling a fungus; of the nature of a fungus; *pathol.* characterized by spongy growths resembling fungi.—*n.*

fun·gous, fung´gus, *a.* [L. *fungosus,* < *fungus,* fungus.] Pertaining to, resembling, or caused by fungi; *fig.* springing up or spreading rapidly but not enduring.

fun·gus, fung´gus, *n. pl.* **fun·gi, fun·gus·es,** fun´jī. [L. mushroom, fungus.] Any of the *Fungi,* a group of parasitic and saprophytic plants including mushrooms, molds, mildews, and smuts, characterized by absence of flowers, leaves, and chlorophyll. *Pathol.* a spongy growth.—*a.* Fungous.

fun house, *n.* A building constructed in an amusement area containing special equipment, as noisemakers or eerie lighting effects, to surprise or amuse patrons.

fu·nic·u·lar, fū·nik´ū·lêr, *a.* Of or related to a rope or cord; dependent upon the tension of a rope, cable, or cord; of or like a funiculus.—*n.* Funicular railway.

fu·nic·u·lar rail·way, *n.* A cable railway used for ascending and descending a mountain, with the cable simultaneously pulling up one car and lowering another. Also *funicular.*

fu·nic·u·lus, fū·nik´ū·lus, *n. pl.* **fu·nic·u·li,** fū·nik´ū·lī´. *Bot.* the stalk of an ovule. *Anat.* a part of the body resembling a cord, as the umbilical cord, spermatic cord, and small bundles of nerve fibers.

funk, fungk, *n. Chiefly Brit.* A coward; a state of extreme fright or dejection.—*v.t. Chiefly Brit.* To fear; to avoid doing or facing.—*v.i. Chiefly Brit.* To draw back because of fear.—**funk·y,** *a.*

fun·ki·a, fung´kē·a, füng´kē·a, *n.* A prominent-veined, basal-leafed ornamental plant of the genus *Hosta,* in the lily family, grown for both its foliage and its scapes of white to lavender, drooping flowers. Also *plantain lily.*

funk·y, fung´kē, *a.*—*funkier, funkiest. Slang,* foul-smelling; offensive. *Jazz,* marked by an earthy quality, with a basis in the blues.

fun·nel, fun´el, *n.* [Provinc. Fr. *enfouil,* a funnel, < L. *infundibulum,* a funnel—*in-,* into, and *fundo, fusum,* to pour.] A utensil, usu. a hollow cone with a slim tube or pipe extending from its narrowest point: used for conveying liquids or other free-moving substances downward, as into a narrow-necked bottle; anything in the shape of a funnel; any flue, chimney, or shaft providing ventilation or allowing the escape of smoke, esp. the smokestacks of steamships.

fun·nel, fun´el, *v.i.*—*funneled, funneling, Brit. funnelled, funnelling.* To be shaped like a funnel; to move through or as if through a funnel.—*v.t.* To shape like a funnel, as the hands; to cause to move through a funnel; to channel or direct through a passage or to a central point; as, to *funnel* requests through headquarters.

fun·nel cloud, *n.* A funnel-shaped cloud hanging from the heavy storm clouds of a tornado. See *tornado.*

fun·nel·form, fun´el·fạrm´, *a.* Having the shape of a funnel. *Bot.* of a corolla, funnel-shaped, as a morning glory. Also *infundibuliform.*

fun·nies, fun´ēz, *n. pl. Colloq.* cartoon or comic strips; that part of a newspaper or other publication containing comic strips.

fun·ny, fun´ē, *a.*—*funnier, funniest.* Affording fun; amusing; comical; intending to provoke amusement. *Colloq.* underhanded; involving deceit, or arousing suspicion.—*n. pl.* **fun·nies.** *Colloq.* an amusing remark or anecdote; a joke.—**fun·ni·ly,** *adv.*—**fun·ni·ness,** *n.*

fun·ny bone, *n.* The part of the elbow where the ulnar nerve passes by the internal condyle of the humerus, which when struck causes a peculiar, tingling sensation in the arm and hand; the crazy bone; a sense of humor.

fur, fụr, *n.* [Appar. < *fur, v.:* cf. O.Fr. *forreure,* fur lining or trimming, Fr. *fourrure,* fur.] The skin of certain animals, as the sable, ermine, and beaver, covered with a fine, soft, thick, hairy coating; the hairy coating on such a skin; such skins as a material for lining or trimming, or for entire garments; an article of apparel made of or with this material; any coating resembling or suggesting fur.—*a.*

fur, fụr, *v.t.*—*furred, furring.* To line, face, or trim with fur, as a garment; clothe with fur. To coat with deposited matter, as the tongue or the inside of a boiler. *Building,* to apply furring strips to.

fur·be·low, fụr´be·lō´, *n.* [Fr. dial. *falbala.*] A trimming, as a flounce or ruffle, on a woman's gown; any elaborate, showy, frequently superfluous trimming.—*v.t.* To ornament with or as with furbelows.

fur·bish, fụr´bish, *v.t.* [Fr. *fourbir,* < O.H.G. *furben,* to clean, to furbish, G. *fürben,* to sweep.] To rub or scour to brightness; to polish; to renovate: sometimes with *up.*—**fur·bish·er,** *n.*

fur·cate, fụr´kāt, *v.i.*—*furcated, furcating.* [L. *furca,* fork.] To form a fork; divide into branches.—fụr´kāt, fụr´kit, *a.* Forked.—**fur·ca·tion,** fêr·kā´shan, *n.*

fur·cu·la, fụr´kū·la, *n. pl.* **fur·cu·lae,** fụr´kū·lē´. [L., dim. of *furca.*] A forked part, esp. the bone formed by the union of the collarbones in many birds; the wishbone. Also **fur·cu·lum,** *pl.* **fur·cu·la.**

fur·fu·ra·ceous, fụr˝fū·rā´shus, *a.* [L. *furfuraceus.*] Scurfy; scaly or flaky, as with dandruff. Like bran.

fur·fur·al, fụr´fa·ral˝, fūr´fa·ral˝, *n.* [L. *furfur,* bran and E. *al(dehyde).*] *Chem.* an oily, colorless liquid with a penetrating odor, derived from oat or rice hulls and corncobs: used mainly as an organic solvent and in the manufacture of synthetic resins.

fu·ri·ous, fụr´ē·us, *a.* [O.Fr. Fr. *furieux,* < L. *furiosus,* < *furia,* E. *fury.*] Full of fury, violent anger, or rage; fiercely vehement; intensely violent, as wind or storms; of unrestrained energy or speed; as, a *furious* pace.—**fu·ri·ous·ly,** *adv.*—**fu·ri·ous·ness,** *n.*

furl, fụrl, *v.t.* [Contr. < *furdle,* for *fardle, fardel,* to make up in bundles.] To wrap or roll, as a flag or a sail, close to something, as a mast or pole, and fasten.—*v.i.* To become furled.—*n.* Something which is furled; the act or process of furling.

fur·long, fụr´lạng, fụr´long, *n.* [O.E. *furlang*—*furh,* a furrow, and *lang,* long.] A measure of length, equal to one-eighth of a mile, 40 rods, or 220 yards.

fur·lough, fụr´lō, *n.* [Dan. *forlov,* D. *verlof,* G. *verlaub,* leave, furlough, lit. leave off or away—*fur* being equivalent to *for-* in *forbear,* and *lough,* akin to *leave, lief.*] Leave or permission given, esp. to a soldier, to be absent from service for a certain time; the period of time granted.—*v.t.* To furnish with a furlough; to lay off, as workers.

fur·men·ty, fụr´men·tē, *n.* Frumenty. Also **fur·me·ty, fur·mi·ty,** fụr´mi·tē.

fur·nace, fụr´nis, *n.* [O.Fr. *fornais, fornaise* (Fr. *fournaise*), < L. *fornax* (*fornac-*), < *fornus, furnus,* oven.] A structure or apparatus in which to generate heat, as for melting ores, baking pottery, or heating houses; *fig.* any place of extreme heat.

fur·nish, fụr´nish, *v.t.* [O.Fr. *furnir* (*furniss-*) (Fr. *fournir*), accomplish, complete, supply, furnish; from Teut.] To provide or supply with something necessary, useful, or desired; to equip, as a house or room, with necessary appliances, as furniture.—**fur·nish·er,** *n.*

fur·nish·ing, fụr´ni·shing, *n.* That with which anything is furnished. *Pl.* fittings, appliances, or articles of furniture for a house or room; accessories of men's apparel.

fur·ni·ture, fụr´ni·chêr, *n.* [Fr. *fourniture,* < *fournir,* furnish.] Fitting, apparatus, or necessary accessories for something; the movable articles, as tables, chairs, desks, required for use or ornament in a house or office; *print.* pieces of wood or metal, less than type high, set in and about pages of type to fill them out and hold the type in place.

fu·ror, *Brit.* **fu·rore,** fūr´ạr, *n.* [L., < *furere,* rage, rave.] A general outburst of enthusiasm or excitement; a commotion; a prevailing mania for or against something. Fury; rage.

furred, fụrd, *a.* Made or lined with fur; wearing fur; covered with fur, as animals; coated with morbid matter, as the tongue.

fur·ri·er, fụr´ē·êr, *n.* A dealer in or dresser of furs and fur garments; one who makes fur garments or cleans and repairs them.

fur·ri·er·y, fụr´ē·e·rē, *n. pl.* **fur·ri·er·ies.** The trade or craft of a furrier.

fur·ring, fụr´ing, *n.* The act of lining or trimming clothing with fur; the fur used; a coating of matter on something, as on the tongue. *Building,* the nailing on of thin strips, as of wood or metal, to furnish a level surface for lathing or plastering or to provide air spaces; the strips used.

fur·row, fụr´ō, fur´ō, *n.* [O.E. *furh* = O.H.G. *furich,* G. *furche,* furrow; cogn. with L. *porca,* a ridge between furrows.] A trench in the earth made by a plow; a groove; a wrinkle in the face.—*v.t.* To make furrows in; to mark with or as with wrinkles.—*v.i.* To become furrowed.

fur·ry, fụr´ē, *a.*—*furrier, furriest.* Of or like fur; covered with fur; dressed in fur; coated with morbid matter, as the tongue.

fur·ther, fụr´ᴛʜêr, *adv.* [O.E. *furthor,* compar. of *fore,* before.] At or to a more advanced point in time or space; to a greater extent; farther; in addition; moreover.—*a.* [O.E. *furthra.*] Additional; more; more distant or remote; farther.

fur·ther, fụr´ᴛʜêr, *v.t.* [O.E. *fyrthrian.*] To help forward, as a work, undertaking, or cause; promote; advance.—**fur·ther·ance,** *n.* Promotion; advancement.—**fur·ther·er,** *n.*

fur·ther·more, fụr´ᴛʜêr·mōr˝, *adv.* Moreover; besides; in addition.

fur·ther·most, fụr´ᴛʜêr·mōst˝, *a.* Most distant or remote.

fur·thest, fụr´ᴛʜist, *a., adv.* Farthest.

fur·tive, fụr´tiv, *a.* [L. *furtivus,* < *furtum,* theft, < *fur,* thief.] Taken or done stealthily or in a manner to escape observation; as, a *furtive* glance; surreptitious; sly.—**fur·tive·ly,** *adv.*—**fur·tive·ness,** *n.*

fu·run·cle, fụr´ung·kl, *n.* [L. *furunculus,* a petty thief, a boil, dim. of *fur,* thief.] A boil or inflammatory sore.—**fu·run·cu·lar,** fu·run·cu·lous,** fụ·rung´kū·lêr, *a.*

fu·run·cu·lo·sis, fụ·rung″kū·lō′sis, *n.* [N.L.] *Pathol.* the condition marked by the tendency toward, or presence of, furuncles.

fu·ry, fūr′ē, *n. pl.* **fu·ries.** [O.Fr. Fr. *furie*, < L. *furia*, < *furere*, rage, rave.] Violent or unrestrained anger; rage; frenzy; intense vehemence or violence, as of storms or waves; unrestrained energy or speed; as, to work with *fury*; (*cap.*) one of the avenging female spirits of classical mythology. (*l.c.*) any avenging spirit; a fierce and violent person, esp. a woman.

furze, fụrz, *n.* [O.E. *fyrs.*] A plant of the leguminous genus *Ulex*, esp. *U. europaeus*, a low-growing, spiny shrub with yellow flowers. Also *Brit.* **gorse**, *whin.*—**furz·y**, *a.*

fus·cous, fus′kus, *a.* [L. *fuscus*, dark-colored.] Brownish or brownish-gray in color; dusky.

fuse, fūz, *n.* [A shortened form of *fusil*, a musket.] *Elect.* a safety device in an electric circuit, containing a strip of metal which melts when the current becomes excessive, thus breaking the circuit. A tube, cable, or wick filled with combustible matter, used to ignite an explosive charge. *Milit.* any mechanism or electronic device used to discharge a shell, missile, or the like; also *fuze.*—*v.t.*—**fused, fusing.** To furnish, as a bomb, with a fuse; also **fuze.**

fuse, fūz, *v.t.*—**fused, fusing.** [L. *fundo, fusum*, to pour out, to melt, to cast; hence *found* (to cast).] To blend or unite by or as by melting together; to melt or liquefy.—*v.i.* To melt by heat; to become intermingled and blended.

fused quartz, *n.* A type of silica glass made from pure quartz.

fu·see, fū·zē′, *n.* [Fr. *fusée*, < M.L. *fusata*, spindleful, orig. pp. fem. of *fusare*, work with a spindle; < L. *fusus*, spindle.] A match with a large head which ignites by friction and is not easily extinguished; the fuse of an explosive device; a signal light or flare used on railroads. *Horol.* a spirally grooved conical pulley and chain used in old-fashioned watches or clocks, for counteracting the diminishing power of the uncoiling spring.

fu·se·lage, fū′se·lij, fū″se·läzh′, fū′ze·lij, fū″ze·läzh′, *n.* [Fr., < *fuselé*, spindle-shaped, < *fuseau*, < L. *fusus*, spindle.] The main structure or central section of an airplane, which contains the crew, passengers, and cargo; body or hull.

fu·sel oil, *n.* [G. *fusel*, inferior liquor or spirits.] An acrid, oily, poisonous liquid consisting chiefly of amyl alcohol, often obtained as a by-product in the distillation of alcoholic liquors.

fu·si·ble, fū′zi·bl, *a.* Capable of being fused or melted.—**fu·si·bil·i·ty**, fū″zi·bil′i·tē, *n.* The quality or extent of being fusible.

fu·si·ble met·al, *n.* An alloy, as one of lead, tin, and bismuth, compounded to melt at a relatively low temperature, often used to make safety devices. Also **fu·si·ble al·loy.**

fu·si·form, fū′zi·fârm″, *a.* [L. *fusus*, spindle.] Spindle-shaped; rounded and tapering from the middle toward each end.

fu·sil, fu·sile, fū′zil, fū′sil, fū′sīl, *a.* [Fr. *fusile*, L. *fusilis.*] Made by melting. *Archaic*, capable of being melted; fusible; molten.

fu·sil, fū′zil, fū′sil, *n.* [Fr. *fusil*, orig. the part of the lock that struck fire, L.L. *focile*, < L. *focus*, a fire (whence also, *fuel*).] A light musket formerly used.

fu·sil·ier, fū″zi·lēr′, *n.* [Fr.] Orig. a soldier armed with a fusil; a soldier of certain British regiments.

fu·sil·lade, fū′si·läd″, fū′si·läd, fū′zi·läd, fū″zi·läd, *n.* [Fr., < *fusiller*, shoot, < *fusil.*] A simultaneous or continuous discharge of firearms; *fig.* a general discharge or outpouring of anything.—*v.t.*—**fusiladed, fusilading.** To attack or shoot by a fusillade.

fu·sion, fū′zhan, *n.* [L. *fusio(n-)*, < *fundere.*] The act of fusing; the state of being fused; a melting by heat; the uniting of various elements into a whole as if by melting together; something formed by fusing. *Polit.* the coalition of parties or factions; the group resulting from such coalition. *Phys.* the combining of the nuclei of atoms under intense heat to release nuclear energy; also **nu·cle·ar fu·sion:** compare *fission.*—**fu·sion·ism**, *n. Polit.* the policy or practice of fusion.

fu·sion·ist, *n. Polit.* one who advocates or supports a coalition of parties or factions.—*a.*

fu·sion bomb, *n.* A bomb that releases explosive energy through the fusing or uniting of the atomic nuclei of certain isotopes to form heavier nuclei under the influence of intense heat, esp. a *hydrogen bomb.*

fuss, fus, *n.* [Origin uncertain.] An excessive display of anxious activity, esp. over trifles; needless bustle; a disturbance or commotion.—*v.i.* To give excess attention to, usu. with *over*; make much ado about trifles or small details; to fidget or worry.—*v.t.* To bother with trifles.—**fuss·er**, *n.*

fuss·budg·et, fus′buj″it, *n. Colloq.* a fussy person; one overly concerned with trifles.

fuss·y, fus′ē, *a.*—**fussier, fussiest.** Excessively anxious or particular about trifles or petty details; fretful or complaining; elaborately made or trimmed, as clothing.—**fuss·i·ly**, *adv.*—**fuss·i·ness**, *n.*

fus·tian, fus′chan, *n.* [O.Fr. *fustaine*, Fr. *futaine*, It. *fustagno* from *Fostat*, the name of a suburb of Cairo, whence this fabric was first brought.] Originally, a coarse fabric of cotton and linen; now, a stout twilled fabric of cotton with a pile, as corduroy; an inflated style of speaking or writing; bombast.—*a.* Made of fustian; bombastic.

fus·tic, fus′tik, *n.* [Fr. and Sp. *fustoc*, < Ar. *fustuq*, akin to Gr. *pistakē*, pistachio tree; < Pers.] The wood of a large tropical tree, *Chlorophora tinctoria*, a member of the mulberry family, yielding a yellow dye; the tree itself, or the dye; any of several other dyewoods.

fus·ti·gate, fus′ti·gāt″, *v.t.*—**fustigated, fustigating** [L. *fustigo*, < *fustis*, a stick.] To beat with a cudgel; to beat; to criticize sharply.—**fus·ti·ga·tion**, *n.*

fus·ty, fus′tē, *a.*—**fustier, fustiest.** [O.Fr. *fusté*, tasting or smelling of the cask, *fust*, a cask, < L. *fustis*, a stick.] Moldy; musty; ill-smelling. Outmoded; fogyish; clinging to conservative ideas.—**fus·ti·ly**, *adv.*—**fus·ti·ness**, *n.*

fu·thark, fö′thark, *n.* [So-called from the first six letters, equivalent to *f, u, th, o, r, c.*] The runic alphabet. Also **fu·thorc, fu·thork.**

fu·tile, fūt′il, fū′til, *Brit.* fū′tīl, *a.* [Fr. *futile*, < L. *futilis*, leaky, vain, worthless, < *fundo, fusum*, to pour.] Serving no useful end; of no effect; vain, fruitless, or unsuccessful; worthless; trivial.—**fu·tile·ly**, *adv.*—**fu·tile·ness**, *n.*

fu·til·i·tar·i·an, fū·til″i·târ′ē·an, *a.* [Formed on the type of *utilitarian.*] Devoted to the belief that all human aims and hopes are futile; pessimistic.—*n.* One who adheres to this concept.—**fu·til·i·tar·i·an·ism**, *n.*

fu·til·i·ty, fū·til′i·tē, *n. pl.* **fu·til·i·ties.** The quality of being futile, or producing no valuable effect; uselessness; unimportance; that which is futile, as an effort, act, or occurrence.

fu·ture, fū′chẽr, *a.* [Fr. *futur*, < L. *futurus*, soon to be.] Of or connected with time to come; any time that is to be or come after the present. *Gram.* of a verb tense, expressing action or being in the time to come.—*n.* Time to come; what will exist or happen in the time to come; a state or condition yet to come, usu. a better or more prosperous time; as, to have a *future* in business. *Gram.* the future tense; a verb in the future tense.

fu·ture·less, fū′chẽr·lis, *a.* Having no prospect of future betterment.

fu·ture per·fect, *a. Gram.* pertaining to a verb tense indicating an action or state to be completed by a given future time: expressed in English by *will have* or *shall have*, followed by a past participle.—*n.*

fu·tures, fū′chẽrz, *n. pl.* Commodities or stocks purchased or sold on the basis of delivery at a future date.

fu·tur·ism, fū′cha·riz″um, *n.* A movement in the fine arts that originated prior to World War I, rejecting traditional forms of expression in order to portray the dynamic movement, speed, violence, and power of a mechanized era.—**fu·tur·ist**, *n.*—**fu·tur·is·tic**, fū″cha·ris′tik, *a.* Of the future or of futurism.—**fu·tur·is·tic·al·ly**, *adv.*

fu·tu·ri·ty, fū·tụr′i·tē, fū·tẽr′i·tē, fū·chụr′i·tē, *n. pl.* **fu·tu·ri·ties.** Future time; a future quality, state, or condition; future generations, collectively; a future or possible event; a futurity race.

fu·tu·ri·ty race, *n.* A horse race in which the horses, usu. two-year-olds, are entered far in advance of the race, sometimes at birth or earlier; any race for which competitors are selected long before the scheduled date.

fuze, fūz, *n.* See **fuse.**

fuzee, fū·zē′, *n.* Fusee.

fuzz, fuz, *n.* [Origin uncertain.] Loose, light, fibrous or fluffy matter; a coating of such matter. *Slang*, a policeman or other law officer; policemen collectively.—*v.i.* To form, or take on, fuzz; become fuzzy.—*v.t.* To cover with fuzz; make fuzzy; make unclear or confused, sometimes with *up.*

fuzz·y, fuz′ē, *a.*—**fuzzier, fuzziest.** Covered with fuzz; of the nature of or resembling fuzz; indistinct; hazy.—**fuzz·i·ly**, *adv.*—**fuzz·i·ness**, *n.*

fyce, fīs, *n.* Feist.

fyke, fīk, *n.* [D. *fuik.*] A bag-shaped net for catching fish.

fyl·fot, fil′fot, *n.* A swastika.

G

G, g, jē, *n.* The seventh letter of the English alphabet, with two sounds, a hard or guttural, as in *good*; a soft (= j), as in *gem*; the graphic representation of this letter; any spoken sound represented by this letter; anything shaped like the letter G. (*Cap.*) *mus.* the fifth tone and dominant of the scale of C major; also *sol.*

G, g (*Cap.*), *elect.* conductance; abbr. for *gauss. Psychol.* the general factor or root of intelligence. (*l.c.*), *phys.* gravity; the acceleration, due to gravity, with which any body falls freely to the earth in vacuo, its value being about 32 feet per second per second.—**g, g.**, *metrics*, a gram or grams.

gab, gab, *v.i.*—**gabbed, gabbing.** [Icel. *gabb*, mockery, *gabba*, to mock; akin D. *gabberen*, to joke, to chatter; Fr. *gaber*, to deceive; E. *gabble, gape.*] *Colloq.* to talk glibly; to prate; to talk idly.—*n. Colloq.* idle talk; chatter.—**gab·ber**, *n.*

gab, gab, *n.* [Origin obscure.] *Mech.* a hook, esp. on the rod transmitting the motion of an eccentric.

gab·ar·dine, gab′ẽr·dēn″, gab″ẽr·dēn′, *n.* A closely woven fabric with fine diagonal ribs on the face, and made of a cotton, rayon, or woolen cloth; a garment made of gabardine. Also **gab·er·dine.**

gab·ble, gab'l, *v.i.*—*gabbled, gabbling.* [Freq. < *gab*; akin to *gobble.*] To talk noisily and rapidly, or without meaning; to prate; to utter rapid inarticulate sounds.—*v.t.* to utter quickly and incoherently.—*n.* Loud or rapid talk without meaning; inarticulate sounds uttered rapidly, as by fowls.—**gab·bler,** *n.*

gab·bro, gab'rō, *n.* [It.] *Geol.* any one of a particular class of granular igneous rocks.—**gab·bro·ic, gab·bro·it·ic,** ga·brō'ik, gab·rō·it'ik, *a.*—**gab·broid,** gab'roid, *a.*

gab·by, gab'ē, *a.*—*gabbier, gabbiest. Colloq.* full of gab; loquacious.

gab·fest, gab'fest″, *n. Colloq.* an informal gathering at which people engage in prolonged, general talk.

ga·ble, gā'bl, *n.* [O.Fr. *gable,* O.H.G. *gabala,* G. *gabel,* fork.] *Arch.* that portion of a building encompassed or enclosed by the sloping ends, usu. triangular, of a ridged roof; a similar expanse of a gambrel roof; any architectural structure or ornament resembling a gable.—*v.t.*—*gabled, gabling.* To build with a gable or gables.—*v.i.* To be in the form of a gable or to end in a gable.—**ga·bled,** gā'beld, *a.*

ga·ble roof, *n. Arch.* a ridged roof terminating at both ends in a gable.

ga·blet, gā'blit, *n. Arch.* a small gable or gablelike ornament.

ga·ble win·dow, *n. Arch.* a window in or under a gable; a window having its upper part shaped like a gable.

ga·boon, ga·bön', ga·bōn', *n.* An African tree, *Aucoumea klaineana,* or its reddish-brown wood which is used mainly in furniture. Also **ga·boon ma·hog·a·ny,** *okoume.*

ga·by, gā'bē, *n. pl.* **ga·bies.** [Akin to *gape, gab.*] *Brit. Colloq.* A foolish person; a dunce.

gad, gad, *n.* [Icel. *gaddr,* Sw. *gadd,* Goth. *gazds,* a goad, a spike, a sting; akin to *goad;* cf. also Ir. *gada,* a bar or ingot of metal.] A spike or style; a sharp cattle goad; a wedge or ingot of steel or iron; a pointed wedgelike tool used by miners.—*v.t.*—*gadded, gadding.* Prick or dig with a gad; use a gad upon.

gad, gad, *v.i.*—*gadded, gadding.* [Probably from the restless running about of animals stung by the *gadfly.*] To rove or ramble idly or without any fixed purpose, usu. with *about;* to act or move without restraint.—*n.* The act of gadding.—**gad·der,** *n.*—**gad·ding·ly,** *adv.*

gad, Gad, gad, *n., interj. Colloq.* a form of God, often used as a mild oath.

gad·a·bout, gad'a·bout″, *n.* One who wanders aimlessly or socializes out of restless idleness; one who gads.—*a.* Fond of frivolous social activity.

gad·fly, gad'flī″, *n.* p. **gad·flies.** Any large fly of the family *Tebanidae,* as the horsefly that annoys or stings domestic animals; *fig.* a bothersome person who constantly annoys or irritates others.

gad·get, gaj'it, *n.* A small contrivance or device, unnamed or undefined; any novel device, interesting object, or trifle.

Ga·dhel·ic, ga·del'ik, *n., a.* Goidelic.

ga·doid, gā'doid, *a.* [N.L. *gadus,* cod, < Gr. *gádos,* kind of fish.] Resembling a cod; belonging to the *Gadidae,* a family of soft-finned fishes including the cod, haddock, hake, and pollack.—*n.* A gadoid fish.

gad·o·lin·ite, gad'o·lin·it″, *n.* [From J. *Gadolin,* 1760–1852, Finnish chemist.] A silicate mineral which is a source of several rare-earth elements including gadolinium.

gad·o·lin·i·um, gad″o·lin'ē·um, *n. Chem.* a metallic element of the rare-earth series which is highly magnetic esp. at low temperatures. Sym. Gd, at. no. 64. See Periodic Table of Elements.

ga·droon, ga·drön', *n.* [Fr. *godron,* O.Fr. *goderon;* origin unknown.] A band of ornamental grooving or reeding, often oval, used to embellish silver objects; *arch.* a molding characterized by convex carvings or indentations. Also **go·droon,** gō·drön'.—**ga·drooned,** *a.*—**ga·droon·age,** *n.*—**ga·droon·ing,** *n.*

gad·wall, gad'wal″, *n.* A large, edible, wild duck, *Anas strepera,* which is grayish-brown and inhabits temperate, fresh-water regions of N. America.

Gael·ic, gā'lik, *n.* [Gael. *Gaidhealach,* Gaelic, < *Gaidheal,* a Gael.] One of two Celtic languages, Irish Gaelic and Scottish Gaelic, in current use in Ireland and in the Highlands of Scotland.—*a.* Of or pertaining to the Gaels, esp. the Scottish Highlanders; of or belonging to the Goidelic subdivision of the Celtic language.—**Gael,** gāl, *n.* A Gaelic-speaking Celt of Ireland or Scotland, esp. a Scottish Highlander.

gaff, gaf, *n.* [O.Fr. Fr. *gaffe,* boat hook.] A strong hook with a handle used for landing large fish; a barbed fish spear; a metal spur for a gamecock. *Naut.* the spar extending the upper edge of a fore-and-aft sail; the spar used to hoist a ship's colors. A butcher's hook; a telephone lineman's climbing hook; a fraud; a gimmick. *Slang,* an ordeal or abuse; something difficult to endure; as, to stand the *gaff. Brit. slang,* a cheap place of entertainment.—*v.t.* To hook or land with a gaff; *slang,* swindle. *Brit. slang,* to gamble, esp. for petty stakes, as tossing coins.—**blow the gaff,** *Brit. slang.* To betray a secret; reveal a plot; inform on others.

gaffe, gaf, *n.* An impropriety; a faux pas.

gaf·fer, gaf'ér, *n.* [Contr. < *grandfather* or *good father.*] An old rustic, usu. said contemptuously or humorously. *Brit.* the foreman of workmen; an overseer. A master craftsman in glassblowing.

gaff top·sail, *n. Naut.* a light sail set above a gaff.

gag, gag, *v.t.*—*gagged, gagging.* [Prob. imit. of the sound made in choking.] To stop up, as the mouth, with something so as to prevent speech or sound; to silence by force or authority, as in suppressing free speech or in limiting debate; to hold open, as the jaws with an instrument, in a surgical operation; to cause to vomit; to choke or prevent passage through. *Slang,* to introduce, as amusing lines, into a stage play, sometimes with *up.*—*v.i.* To heave with nausea; to choke; *slang,* to joke or quip.

gag, gag, *n.* Something put into the mouth to prevent speech or sound; a surgical device for keeping the jaws open; limitation of speech, as in a legislative debate; something which suppresses or limits free speech. *Slang,* a joke, line, or story intended to produce laughter, as in a comedian's routine; a hoax or trick, as a practical joke.—**gag·man,** *n.* One who writes gags.

ga·ga, gä'gä, *a. Slang.* Doting; foolish.

gage, gāj, *n.* [Fr. *gage,* < L.L. *gadium, vadium,* < Goth. *wadi,* pledge, G. *wette,* a bet; or < L. *vas, vadis,* a surety, a pledge.] Something given as a security to ensure the fulfillment of some act; a pledge; something thrown down as a token of challenge to combat.

gage, gāj, *n., v.t.* Gauge.

gage, gāj, *n.* One of several varieties of plum, *Prunus domestica,* including greengage and golden gage.

gag·gle, gag'l, *v.i.*—*gaggled, gaggling.* [Imit.] To utter the cry of a goose; cackle.—*n.* A flock of geese; any group or cluster.

gag rule, *n.* A rule or law restricting or preventing discussion or expression of opinion, as in a deliberative body. Also **gag law.**

gahn·ite, gä'nīt, *n.* [From J. G. *Gahn* (1745–1818), Swedish chemist.] A dark-colored mineral, $ZnAl_2O_4$, containing aluminum and zinc.

gai·e·ty, gay·e·ty, gā'i·tē, *n. pl.* **gai·e·ties, gay·e·ties.** [Fr. *gaieté, gaîté.*] The state of being gay or cheerful; gay spirits; cheerful liveliness; merrymaking or festivity; showiness; finery.

gail·lar·di·a, gā·lär'dē·a, *n.* [N.L.; from M. *Gaillard* de Marentonneau.] Any plant of the genus *Gaillardia,* in the composite family, native to N. America, several species of which are cultivated for their showy flowers with yellow, red, purple, or variegated rays. Also *blanket-flower.*

gai·ly, gay·ly, gā'lē, *adv.* In a gay manner; cheerfully or merrily; brightly or showily.

gain, gān, *v.t.* [O.Fr. *gaignier, waignier* (Fr. *gagner*), gain, < O.H.G. verb meaning "to pasture, hunt for food," < O.H.G. *weida* (G. *weide*), pasture, hunting, = O.E. *wath,* Icel. *veidhr,* hunting.] To obtain or earn as a profit or advantage, esp. by effort; succeed in getting; win, as in competition; to attain or reach, as a destination; to win over or persuade to one's friendship or purposes, often followed by *over;* to make or acquire an increase of; as, to *gain* five pounds.—*v.i.* To profit; benefit; to improve; make progress.—**gain on** or **up·on,** to encroach gradually on; to advance nearer to, as a person or thing pursued.—**gain·a·ble,** *a.* That may be gained.

gain, gān, *n.* [O.Fr. Fr. *gain.*] Profit or advantage. *Pl.* sums constituting profit. An increase or advance; a gaining or winning; *electron.* an increase in transmission signal power, as in an amplifier, usu. measured in decibels.

gain, gān, *n.* [Origin uncertain.] *Carp.* a groove or notch, as in a piece of lumber, designed to receive a projection of the same size and shape. Also *mortise.*

gain·er, gā'nér, *n.* One who or that which gains. *Diving,* a standing or running front dive in which the diver executes a backward somersault in midair. Also **full gain·er.** See *half gainer.*

gain·ful, gān'ful, *a.* Producing profit or advantage; lucrative.—**gain·ful·ly,** *adv.*—**gain·ful·ness,** *n.*

gain·less, gān'lis, *a.* Unprofitable; futile.—**gain·less·ness,** *n.*

gain·say, gān'sā″, *v.t.*—*gainsaid, gainsaying.* [O.E. *gegn-,* against (as in *again*), and E. *say.*] To contradict; to deny; to dispute.—*n.* Contradiction.—**gain·say·er,** *n.*

'gainst, genst, *Brit.* gänst. Contraction of against.

gait, gāt, *n.* [Akin Icel. *gata,* a way.] Walk; a manner of walking or stepping; carriage; any one of the paces of a horse, as the walk, canter, or trot.—*v.t.* To train, as a horse, in various gaits.—**gait·ed,** *a.* Having a particular gait: used in compounds; as, slow-*gaited.*

gait·er, gā'tér, *n.* [Fr. *guetre;* origin unknown.] A covering of cloth or leather for the ankle, instep, and sometimes also the lower leg, worn over a shoe; a cloth or leather shoe with elastic insertions at the sides; a cloth overshoe.

gal, gal, *n. Slang.* A girl; a girl friend.

gal, gal, *n. Phys.* a unit of measurement equiv. to 1000 milligals or one centimeter per second per second, used specif. in measuring acceleration, esp. of gravity.

ga·la, gā'la, gal'a, *Brit.* gä'la, *a.* [Fr., show, pomp; It. *gala,* finery; of Teut. origin; akin *gallant.*] Festive; suitable for a celebration.—*n.* An occasion of public festivity.

ga·lac·tic, ga·lak'tic, *a.* [Gr. *galaktikos,* < *gala* (*galakt*), milk, akin to L. *lac* (*lact*-), milk.] *Astron.* pertaining to the Galaxy or the Milky Way. *Med.* pertaining to milk; increasing the flow of milk.

ga·lac·tose, ga·lak'tōs, *n.* [Gr. *gala, galaktos,* milk.] A sweet substance, $C_6H_{12}O_6$, derived from milk sugar or lactose.

galah, ga·lä′, *n.* A cockatoo, *Kakatoë roseicapilla,* native to Australia and destructive to wheat crops.

gal·an·tine, gal′an·tēn″, gal″an·tēn′, *n.* [O.Fr. Fr. *galantine,* earlier *galatine;* origin uncertain.] Veal, chicken, or other meat boned, stuffed, boiled, and served cold with its own jelly.

Ga·la·tian, ga·lā′shan, *a.* Of or pertaining to Galatia, an ancient inland division of Asia Minor, or its inhabitants.—*n.* A native or inhabitant of Galatia; *pl.* the book of the New Testament addressed to the early Christian church in Galatia.

gal·a·vant, gal′a·vant″, *v.i.* Gallivant.

ga·lax, gā′laks, *n.* [N.L. < Gr. *gala, galaktos,* milk.] An evergreen herb of the southeastern U.S., *Galax aphylla,* whose leaves are used in quantity by florists.

gal·ax·y, gal′ak·sē, *n. pl.* **gal·ax·ies.** [Fr. *galaxie,* < Gr. *galaxias,* < *gala, galaktos,* milk.] Any one of the systems of stars held together gravitationally and separated from other systems by immense regions of space, as the Milky Way; an assemblage of splendid persons or things.

gal·ba·num, gal′ba·num, *n.* [L.; prob. < Heb.] A gum resin with a peculiar odor, obtained from certain Asiatic plants of the genus *Ferula* and used in medicines and incense.

gale, gāl, *n.* [Origin uncertain.] *Meteor.* a strong wind, specif. one between 32 and 63 miles per hour. *Fig.* a noisy fit or outburst, as of laughter.

gale, gāl, *n.* [Prob. a contr. of *gavel.*] *Brit.* a periodical payment of rent.

ga·le·na, ga·lē′na, *n.* [L., lead ore.] A mineral, lead sulfide, PbS, the principal ore of lead, characterized by a lead-gray color, a metallic luster, and perfect cubic cleavage. Also **ga·le·nite,** ga·lē′nīt.

Gal·i·le·an, gal″i·lē′an, *a.* Of, pertaining to, or invented by Galileo, the Italian physicist and astronomer.

gal·i·ma·ti·as, gal″i·mā′shē·as, gal″i·mat′ē·as, *n.* [Fr., origin doubtful.] Confused talk; nonsense.

gal·i·ot, gal·li·ot, gal′ē·ot, *n.* [Fr. *galiote,* dim. of *galie,* a galley.] A small galley or brigantine, moved by sails and oars; a two-masted Dutch cargo vessel.

gal·i·pot, gal·li·pot, gal′i·pot, *n.* [Fr. *galipot;* origin unknown.] A kind of turpentine exuded from the stem of certain species of pine.

gall, gal, *n.* [O.E. *gealla* = D. *gal* = G. *galle* = Icel. *gall;* akin to L. *fel,* Gr. *cholē,* gall, bile.] Something very bitter or severe; bitterness of spirit; rancor; bile, esp. that of an animal; impudence or effrontery.

gall, gal, *n.* [O.E. *gealla,* perhaps = *gealla,* E. *gall.*] A sore on the skin, esp. of a horse, due to rubbing; an excoriation; something irritating or vexing; a state of irritation or exasperation.—*v.t.* To make sore by rubbing; chafe; to fret and wear away by friction; annoy; harass; vex, as: The umpire's decision *galled* the player.—*v.i.* To become chafed.

gall, gal, *n.* [O.Fr. Fr. *galle,* < *galla.*] An abnormal vegetable growth or tumor on plants caused by certain parasites, insects, bacteria, fungi, viruses, injuries, or chemicals.

gal·lant, gal′ant, ga·lant′, ga·länt′, *a.* Brave, high-spirited, or chivalrous; as, a *gallant* soldier; polite and attentive to women; courtly; flamboyantly amorous; splendid or fine; stately; as, a *gallant* vessel; gay or showy, as in dress.—*n.* A gay, dashing man; a man of dauntless spirit; a man particularly attentive to women; a suitor or lover.—*v.t.* To court, as a woman; to escort.—*v.i.* To be a suitor or lover.

gal·lant·ry, gal′an·trē, *n. pl.* **gal·lant·ries.** [Fr. *galanterie.*] Dashing courage; heroic

bravery; gallant or courtly attention to women; a polite or chivalrous action or speech; gay or fine appearance.

gall blad·der, *n. Anat.* a small membranous sac, shaped like a pear, which receives and stores bile from the liver.

gal·le·on, gal′ē·on, gal′yon, *n.* [Sp. *galeon,* It. *galeone,* augmentatives from L.L. *galea,* a galley.] A large sailing ship formerly used by the Spaniards in war and commerce.

gal·ler·y, gal′e·rē, gal′rē, *n. pl.* **gal·ler·ies.** [O.Fr. Fr. *galerie,* < M.L. *galeria;* origin unknown.] A long covered walk or place for strolling; as, an aquarium *gallery;* a corridor with some specific importance, as its decoration or architectural design; a porchlike area, narrow passage, or large room used for public displays and sales, as of art and antiques; a raised platform or passageway along the outside or inside of a wall, as found in Spanish architecture; a platform or balcony which projects from an interior wall and contains seats for an audience, as in an opera or movie theater; the uppermost part of such a platform usu. having the most inexpensive seats; the occupants who sit upon this platform in theater; the general public, esp. when thought to be unrefined and undiscriminating in taste; spectators of a sport, as of bowling or tennis; *min.* an underground passage; *naut.* a platform extending from the stern of ancient sailing vessels.—**play to the gal·ler·y,** to seek favor and praise from the general public.—**gal·ler·ied,** *a.*

gal·le·ta, ga·yet′a, gī·et′a, *n.* [Sp.] A perennial grass of the *Hilaria* family, grown in southwestern U.S. and Mexico to make hay for cattle feeding.

gal·ley, gal′ē, *n. pl.* **gal·leys.** [O.Fr. *galie* (Fr. *galée*), < M.L. *galea,* < M.Gr. *galea;* origin unknown.] An early form of seagoing vessel propelled by oars and sometimes by sails; a large rowboat; the kitchen of a ship. *Print.* a long, narrow tray, usu. metal, to hold type which has been set; a galley proof.

gal·ley proof, *n. Print.* a proof taken from type on a galley to permit corrections before the page is printed.

gal·ley slave, *n.* A person condemned to work at the oar on a galley. *Fig.* a drudge; one who is overworked.

gall·fly, gal′flī, *n. pl.* **gall·flies.** An insect that causes galls on plants by depositing its eggs in the plant tissue.

Gal·lic, gal′ik, ga′lik, *a.* [L. *Gallicus,* < *Gallus,* a Gaul.] Of or pertaining to Gauls or Gaul; French.

gal·lic ac·id, *n. Chem.* a colorless or slightly yellow crystalline acid, $C_7H_6O_5 \cdot H_2O$, found in plant galls and used in photography as a developer, in dyeing, and in inks.

gal·li·cism, gal′i·siz″um, *n.* (*Often cap.*) a French idiom used in another language; a custom or mode of speech peculiar to the French.

gal·li·cize, gal′i·sīz″, *v.t.*—*gallicized, gallicizing.* (*Often cap.*) to make or become French in thought, custom, or language.

gall·ic·o·lous, ga·lik′o·lus, *a.* Causing galls; existing in galls.

gal·li·mau·fry, gal′i·mạ·frē, *n. pl.* **gal·li·mau·fries.** [Fr. *galimafrée,* a ragout; of uncertain origin.] A hodgepodge; a jumbled mixture or medley.

gal·li·na·ceous, gal″i·nā′shus, *a.* [L. *gallinaceus,* < L. *gallina,* hen.] Belonging or pertaining to the order *Galliformes,* which includes common poultry, pheasants, grouse, and partridges.—**gal·li·na·cean,** gal″i·nā′shan, *n.* A gallinaceous bird.

gall·ing, gạl′ing, *a.* Vexing; harassing; annoying.—**gall·ing·ly,** *adv.*

gal·li·nip·per, gal′i·nip″ėr, *n.* [Origin obscure.] A large mosquito, esp. the American *Psorophora ciliata.*

gal·li·ot, gal′ē·ot, *n.* Galiot.

gal·li·pot, gal′i·pot″, *n.* Galipot.

gal·li·um, gal′ē·um, *n.* [< *Gallia,* the Latin name for France.] A rare, silvery-white, metallic element which has a low melting point and a high boiling point. Sym. Ga, at. no. 31, at. wt. 69.72.

gal·li·vant, gal′i·vant″, *v.i.* [Probably a corrupt form of *gallant.*] To gad or run about; to flirt. Also *galavant.*

gall nut, *n.* A gall often found on oak trees, and resembling a nut. Also **gall-ap·ple.**

gal·lon, gal′on, *n.* [O.Fr. *galon, jalon;* Fr. *jale,* a jar, a bowl; origin unknown.] See Measures and Weights table.

gal·lon·age, gal′o·nij, *n.* Amount or capacity in gallons.

gal·loon, ga·lön′, *n.* [Fr. and Sp. *galon;* It. *galone,* < *gala,* show.] A kind of narrow ribbon or braid trimming made of cotton, silk, silver, or gold threads.—**gal·looned,** *a.*

gal·lop, gal′op, *v.i.* [O.Fr. *galoper, waloper,* Fr. *galoper;* Teut. *wallop.*] To move or run by leaps, as a horse; to ride at a gallop, or at full speed; *fig.* to go fast.—*v.t.* To cause to gallop, as a horse or other animal; to drive or convey at a gallop.—*n.* The fastest of the quadruped gaits, in which all four feet are off the ground simultaneously once during each stride; a run or ride at this gait; a rapid rate of going.—**gal·lop·er,** *n.*

gal·lo·pade, gal·o·pade, gal″o·pād′, *n.* [Fr. *galopade.*] The galop, a dance; the music for that dance.—*v.i.*—*galopaded, galopading.*

Gal·lo·phile, gal′o·fīl″, *n.* Francophile.

Gal·lo·way, gal′o·wā″, *n.* One of a breed of hornless cattle peculiar to Galloway, Scotland; one of a breed of small, strong horses first raised there.

gal·lows, gal′ōz, gal′oz, *n. pl.* **gal·lows·es, gal·lows.** [O.E. *galga, gealga* = D. *galg* = G. *galgen* = Icel. *galgi,* gallows, = Goth. *galga,* cross.] A wooden frame, consisting of a crossbeam on two uprights, on which condemned persons are executed by hanging; any similar structure.—*a.* Fit for the gallows.

gal·lows bird, *n. Colloq.* a person who deserves to be hanged.

gall·stone, gal′stōn″, *n. Pathol.* a stony particle or small stonelike mass formed in the gall bladder or biliary passages.

gal·lus, gal′us, *n. pl.* **gal·lus·es.** *Usu. pl., dial.* trouser suspenders.—**gal·lused,** *a.*

gall wasp, *n.* Any of the various insects belonging to the order *Hymenoptera* and the family *Cynipidae,* whose larvae form galls on plants; a gallfly.

Ga·lois the·o·ry, gal·wä thē′o·rē, *n.* [From Evariste *Galois,* Fr. mathematician, 1811–1832.] *Math.* that aspect of mathematics which deals with applying the theory of groups to the solution of polynomial equations.

ga·loot, gal·loot, ga·löt′, *n.* [Origin obscure.] *Slang,* an uncouth or clumsy fellow.

gal·op, gal′op, *n.* [Fr.] A lively, waltzlike dance in 2/4 time; the music for this dance. Also *gallopade.*

ga·lore, ga·lōr′, ga·lạr′, *adv.* [Ir. and Gael. *go leòr,* enough—*go,* to, and *leòr,* enough.] In profusion or abundance.

ga·losh, ga·loshe, ga·losh′, *n.* [Fr. *galoche,* < Gr. *kalopodion,* a wooden shoe.] *Usu. pl.* an overshoe worn to protect the regular shoe and foot during inclement weather.

ga·lumph, ga·lumf′, *v.i.* [Coined by Lewis Carroll in *Through the Looking-Glass.*] To gallop or prance; to go as in triumph; to bump along clumsily and pompously

gal·van·ic, gal·van′ik, *a. Elect.* of, pertaining to, or produced by galvanism, esp. by chemically produced electric current; voltaic. Affecting or affected as if by galvanism; shocking or stimulating.—

gal·van·ic bat·ter·y, voltaic battery.—**gal·van·i·cal·ly**, *adv.*

gal·van·ic cou·ple, *n.* Voltaic couple.

gal·va·nism, gal′va·niz″um, *n.* [From L. *Galvani* (1737–1798), Italian physician, discoverer of galvanism.] Current electricity, esp. as produced by chemical action; *med.* the application of voltaic or battery current to the body for therapeutic purposes.

gal·va·ni·za·tion, gal″va·ni·zā′shan, *n.* The act of galvanizing; the state of being galvanized.

gal·va·nize, gal′va·nīz″, *v.t.*—*galvanized, galvanizing.* To subject to galvanism; stimulate by or as by electric current; to coat, as iron, with zinc.—**gal·va·niz·er**, *n.*

gal·va·nom·e·ter, gal″va·nom′i·tēr, *n.* *Phys.* an instrument for detecting the existence and determining the strength and direction of an electric current.—**gal·va·no·met·ric**, gal″va·nō·me′trik, *a.*—**gal·va·nom·e·try**, *n.*

gal·va·no·scope, gal′va·nō·skōp″, gal·van′o·skōp″, *n.* Galvanometer.

gal·yak, gal′yak, *n.* A flat, sleek fur from the pelt of an unborn kid, lamb, or similar hoofed mammal.

gam·bier, gam·bir, gam′bēr, *n.* [Malay *gambīr.*] *Bot.* an astringent extract obtained from the leaves and young shoots of a tropical Asiatic vine, *Uncaria gambir,* used in medicine, dyeing, and tanning.

gam·bit, gam′bit, *n.* [Fr. < It. *gambetto,* a tripping up of one's legs, *gamba,* the leg.] *Chess,* the sacrifice of a pawn early in the game, for the purpose of taking up an attacking position. Any action, trick, or strategy intended to gain an initial advantage.

gam·ble, gam′bl, *v.i.*—*gambled, gambling.* [Prob. < a var. of M.E. *gamenen,* < O.E. *gamenian,* play, < *gamen,* E. *game.*] To play at any game of chance for stakes; to stake or risk money or anything of value on something involving chance or unknown contingencies; to take a risk.—*v.t.* To stake, bet, or wager; to squander by betting, usu. followed by *away.*—*n.* A venture in or as in gambling; any matter or thing involving risk or uncertainty.—**gam·bler**, *n.*

gam·boge, gam·bōj′, gam·bōzh′, *n.* [From *Camboja, Cambodia,* in Asia.] The gum resin or sap yielded by several species of trees, genus *Garcinia,* and used as a purgative in medicine and as a yellow pigment.

gam·bol, gam′bol, *v.i.*—*gamboled, gamboling, chiefly Brit. gambolled, gambolling.* [O.E. *gambolde, gambaude,* < Fr. *gambade, gambol, gambiller,* to wag the leg or kick, O.Fr. *gambe,* It. *gamba,* the leg, Fr. *jambe.*] To dance and skip playfully about; to leap; to frolic.—*n.* A frolic; a playful skip or leap.

gam·brel, gam′brel, *n.* [O.Fr. *gamberel,* butcher's *gambrel;* origin uncertain.] A bent piece of wood or iron used by butchers to hang a carcass on; the hock of an animal, esp. a horse.

gam·brel roof, *n.* A roof whose sides have two slopes, the lower one being the steeper,—**gam·brel-roofed**, *a.*

gam·bu·sia, gam·bū′zha, gam·bū′zhē·a, gam·bū′zē·a, *n. Ichth.* any of various surface-feeding fishes, genus *Gambusia,* which are stocked in fresh waters to eliminate mosquito larvae.

game, gām, *n.* [O.E. *gamen* = O.H.G. and Icel. *gaman,* amusement, sport.] An amusement or pastime; a diversion in the form of chance, skill, endurance, or a combination of these, pursued according to certain rules; as, card *games,* a *game* of football; the equipment employed in playing any of certain games; as, a store selling toys and *games;* a particular contest in the process of play, or a specific portion of play within the contest; as, to see a baseball *game,* to win

four *games* in a set of tennis; the state of a contest, indicated by the score, at a particular time, as: The *game* was two to one at the bottom of the ninth inning. The number of points necessary to win such a contest; a particular manner or quality of play, as: He plays a strong and consistent *game* of golf. *Fig.* a proceeding executed in the manner or spirit of a game; as, to play a waiting *game;* the use of skill and endurance, similar to that employed in a game, applied to a more general endeavor; as, the *game* of diplomacy; *colloq.* a pursuit, esp. a profession or line of business, characterized by chance or risk similar to that of a game, as: He made a fortune in the insurance *game.* A person's plan of action; a trick or dodge; wild animals, including birds and fish, which are hunted or taken for sport or profit; the flesh of wild animals used for food; *fig.* any object of pursuit or attack, as: The wealthy widow was so lonely that she was fair *game* for aspiring and selfish bachelors.—*a.*—*gamer, gamest.* Of or pertaining to animals hunted or taken as game; having the fighting or courageous spirit of a gamecock; plucky; *colloq.* having determination, spirit, or will, as: Having already failed three times, she was still *game* to try again.

game, gām, *a.* [Origin uncertain.] *Colloq.* lame, as a leg.

game, gām, *v.i.*—*gamed, gaming.* To play, sport, or jest; to play games, esp. games of chance for stakes; gamble.—*v.t. Archaic,* to squander in gambling; as, to *game* away a fortune.

game bird, *n.* A bird hunted for sport or profit, as pheasant or quail.

game·cock, gām′kok″, *n.* A male fowl used for cockfighting.

game fish, *n.* A food fish whose capture affords sport to the angler.

game fowl, *n.* A domestic fowl of a breed used for fighting.

game·keep·er, gām′kē″pēr, *n.* A person employed to look after the wild animals living on a game preserve, and to prevent illegal hunting, fishing, or other poaching.

gam·e·lan, gam′e·lan″, gam′e·lan *n.* A southeast Asian orchestra composed of string, wind, and percussion instruments; an instrument similar to a xylophone used in such an orchestra.

game law, *n.* A law to protect birds, fishes, and other wild animals by restricting the seasons and methods of capture.

game·ly, gām′lē, *adv. Colloq.* in a game or courageous manner.

game·ness, gām′nis, *n.* The quality of being game; courage; pluck.

games·man·ship, gāmz′man·ship″, *n.* The practice of using questionable but not illegal methods in order to win in a game.

game·some, gām′som, *a.* Sportive; playful; frolicsome.—**game·some·ly**, *adv.*—**game·some·ness**, *n.*

game·ster, gām′ster, *n.* A person addicted to gaming; a gambler; one skilled in games.

gam·e·tan·gi·um, gam″i·tan′jē·um, *n.* pl. **gam·e·tan·gi·a**, gam″i·tan′jē·a. [N.L. < Gr. *gametē,* wife, *gametēs,* husband, and *aggeion,* vessel.] *Bot.* an organ or body producing gametes.

gam·ete, gam′ēt, ga·mēt′, *n.* [Gr. *gametē,* wife, *gametēs,* husband, < *gamein,* marry, < *gamos,* marriage.] *Biol.* either of the two reproductive germ cells which unite to form a new organism.—**ga·met·ic**, ga·met′ik, *a.*—**gam·e·tal**, *a.*

game the·o·ry, *n.* A mathematical plan or theory applied in games, business situations, and military problems to determine how to achieve the most accurate results between at least two strategies. Also **the·o·ry of games.**

ga·me·to·cyte, ga·mē′tō·sīt″, *n. Biol.* a gamete-producing cell.

gam·e·to·gen·e·sis, gam″i·tō·jen′i·sis, *n. Biol.* the creation of gametes.—**gam·e·to·gen·ic, gam·e·tog·e·nous**, gam″i·toj′e·nus, *a.*

ga·me·to·phore, ga·mē′to·fōr″, ga·mē′to·far″, *n. Bot.* a part or structure producing gametes.

ga·me·to·phyte, ga·mē′to·fīt″, *n. Bot.* the sexual form of a plant in the alternation of generations, as opposed to *sporophyte.*

gam·ic, gam′ik, *a.* [Gr. *gamicos,* of or for marriage, < *gamos,* marriage.] *Biol.* sexual.

gam·in, gam′in, Fr. gä·man′, *n.* [Fr.; origin uncertain.] A street urchin; a neglected boy.—**gam·ine**, gam′ēn, gam′in, ga·mēn, Fr. gä·mēn, *n.* [Fr. fem. of *gamin.*] Tomboy; a saucy girl.

gam·ing, gā′ming, *n.* The act or practice of one who games; gambling.

gam·ma, gam′ä, *n.* The third letter of the Greek alphabet; third place or position in any scientific classification; *photog.* the amount of contrast in a developed photograph; *phys.* a magnetic intensity unit.—*a.*

gam·ma glob·u·lin, *n. Biochem.* a protein separated from blood and containing antibodies: used in inoculation against measles, poliomyelitis, and infectious hepatitis.

gam·ma i·ron, *n.* Austenite.

gam·ma na·sal, *n.* The Greek letter *gamma,* pronounced nasally, as in both ancient and modern Greek.

gam·ma rays, *n. Phys.* penetrating rays emitted from radioactive material and reducing the energy of the cell nucleus: used in radiotherapy.

gam·mer, gam′er, *n.* [Contr. of *good-mother* or *grandmother.*] An old wife or woman: the counterpart of *gaffer.*

gam·mon, gam′on, *n.* [Appar. < M.E. and O.E. *gamen,* E. *game.*] In backgammon, a double victory in which the winner discards all his counters before his opponent discards any.—*v.t.* To win a gammon over.

gam·mon, gam′on, *n.* [O.Fr. *gambon,* It. *gambone,* a big leg, a gammon, < *gamba,* a leg.] Smoked ham or the lower part from a side of bacon.

gam·o·gen·e·sis, gam″o·jen′i·sis, *n. Biol.* sexual reproduction.—**gam·o·ge·net·ic**, gam″ō·je·net′ik, *a.*—**gam·o·ge·net·i·cal·ly**, *adv.*

gamp, gamp, *n.* [From Sairey *Gamp* in Dickens' *Martin Chuzzlewit.*] *Brit. colloq.* a clumsy umbrella.

gam·ut, gam′ut, *n.* [M.L. *gamma ut,* < *gamma,* used to represent the first or lowest tone (G) in the medieval scale, and *ut,* later *do.*] The whole series of recognized musical notes; the whole range or series of anything.

gam·y, gā′mē, *a.*—*gamier, gamiest.* Having the flavor of game, esp. game that has been kept uncooked until almost tainted; strong-smelling; game or plucky, used chiefly of animals; scandalous, suggestive, or spicy; having a bad reputation.—**gam·i·ly**, *adv.*—**gam·i·ness**, *n.*

gan·der, gan′der, *n.* [O.E. *gandra,* for *ganra,* < the root *gan* seen in G. *gans,* a goose, *gänserich,* a gander.] The male of the goose.

gan·der, gan′der, *n. Slang,* a look or glance, usu. with *take.*

Gan·dhi·an, gän′dē·an, gan′dē·an, *a.* Of or relating to the doctrine of Mahatma Gandhi, Indian spiritual and nationalist leader, who advocated passive resistance as a means of opposing British colonial rule.

gan·dy dan·cer, gan′dē dan′sėr, *n. Slang,* a laborer who lays or repairs railroad tracks.

ga·nef, go·nef, gä′nef, *n.* [< Yiddish < Heb. *gannābh.*] *Slang,* petty thief; rogue; an unscrupulous person.

---

a- fat, fāte, fär, fâre, fall;   **e-** met, mē, mēre, hėr;   **i-** pin, pīne;   **o-** not, nōte, mōve;   **u-** tub, cūbe, bull;   **oi-** oil;   **ou-** pound.

gang, gang, *n.* [O.E. *gangan* = O.H.G. *gangan* = Goth. *gaggan*, go: cf. *go.*] A group; a number of young people closely associated socially; a set of persons working together in a squad or shift; as, a road *gang*; a company of persons working together for antisocial purposes; as, a *gang* of hoodlums; a number of similar tools, machines, or the like; as, a *gang* of saws.—*v.t.* To arrange or form into a gang; to attack, usu. followed by *up on*; as: The schoolboys *ganged up on* their classmate.—*v.i.* To arrange or behave as a gang.

gang·er, gang′ẽr, *n. Brit.* the foreman of a gang of workmen.

gang hook, *n.* Several fishing hooks joined together at the shanks to form a single unit.

gang·land, gang′land″, gang′land, *n.* The organized criminal elements of society; the underworld.

gan·gling, gang′gling, *a.* Awkwardly tall and slender, as a person; lank and loosely built.

gan·gli·on, gang′glē·an, *n.* pl. **gan·gli·a,** gang′glē·a, **gan·gli·ons,** gang′glē·a. [L.L., kind of swelling, < Gr. *ganglion,* tumor under the skin, on or near a tendon.] *Pathol.* an encysted tumor or enlargement in connection with the sheath of a tendon; *anat.* any aggregation of nerve cells or mass of gray matter forming a nerve center external to the central or cerebrospinal nervous system; *fig.* a center of force or activity.— **gan·gli·on·at·ed,** gang·gli·ate, gang·gli·at·ed, *a.*—**gan·gli·on·ic,** gang″glē·on′ik, *a.*

gan·gly, gang′glē, *a.*—*ganglier, gangliest.* Gangling; spindly.

gang·plank, gang′plangk″, *n.* A plank or long narrow structure used as a temporary bridge to permit access to or egress from a ship.

gang plow, *n.* A plow with several shares, or several plows in a common frame.

gan·grene, gang′grēn, gang·grēn′, *n.* [L. *gangraena,* < Gr. *gangraina,* < *graein,* gnaw.] *Pathol.* The dying of tissue, as from interruption of circulation; mortification.— *v.t., v.i.*—*gangrened, gangrening.* To affect or become affected with gangrene.— **gan·gre·nous,** gang′gre·nus, *a.*

gang·ster, gang′stẽr, *n.* One of a gang or syndicate of criminals; a mobster; a racketeer.

gangue, gang, *n.* [Fr. < G. *gang,* mineral vein, lode.] *Min.* the stony or earthy minerals occurring with the metallic ore in a vein or deposit.

gang up, *v.i. Colloq.* to group together in opposition.

gang·way, gang′wā, *n.* A passageway. *Naut.* any of various passageways on a ship; an opening in the rail or bulwarks of a ship for passing into or out of that ship; a gangplank. *Min.* a main passage or level. *Brit.* an aisle, as in a restaurant or theater; an aisle in the House of Commons separating the opposition party from the Government party. A temporary means of access formed by planks.—*interj.* Clear for passage, move out of the way.

gan·is·ter, gan′i·stẽr, *n.* [Origin unknown.] A hard siliceous rock occurring in some English coal seams, or an artificial mixture resembling it, used as a refractory material in the lining of furnaces.

gan·net, gan′it, *n.* [O.E. *ganot,* akin to D. *gent,* gander, and O.E. *gandra,* E. *gander.*] *Ornith.* any of the large, web-footed swimming birds of the genus *Sula,* as the solan, *S. bassana,* of the Atlantic coasts of Europe and America, or the booby, *S. leucogastra,* of the southern U.S. coast.

gan·oid, gan′oid, *a.* [Gr. *ganos,* brightness, and *eidos,* form, appearance.] Of fish-scales, having a smooth, shiny, enameled surface; belonging or pertaining to the *Ganoidei,* a

group of fishes many of which have such scales, including sturgeon.—*n.* A ganoid fish.

gant·let, gant′lit, gänt′lit, *n.* [< Sw. *gatlopp,* < *gata,* a street, a line of soldiers, and *lopp,* a course, akin to E. *leap,* D. *loopen,* to run.] A former military punishment. See *gauntlet.*

gant·let, gant′lit, *n.* The convergence of two railroad tracks to allow trains on either track to run through a tunnel or other narrow way.—*v.t.* To bring together, as two railroad tracks.

gan·try, gan′trē, *n.* pl. **gan·tries.** [Cf. O.Fr. *gantier,* var. of *chantier,* < L. *cantherius,* a supporting framework.] *Rail.* a framework used in displaying signals. A spanning framework or platform, as a bridgelike portion of certain cranes; *aerospace,* a movable scaffold used in the servicing and launching of rockets. A frame for supporting a barrel or cask. Also **gaun·try,** pl. **gaun·tries.**

gaol, jāl, *n. Brit.* jail.—**gaol·er,** *n. Brit.* jailer.

gap, gap, *n.* [M.E. *gap, gappe,* from Scand.: cf. Icel. *gap,* empty space, connected with *gapa,* gape. GAPE.] A break or opening; a breach; a vacant space or interval; a hiatus; a wide divergence; a blank or deficiency in something; a deep, sloping ravine or cleft cutting a mountain ridge; an opening between high rocks.—*v.t.*—*gapped, gapping.* To make a gap, opening, or breach in.

gape, gāp, gap, *v.i.*—*gaped, gaping.* [M.E. *gapen,* prob. from Scand.: cf. Icel. *gapa,* Sw. *gapa,* Dan. *gabe,* also D. *gapen,* G. *gaffen,* gape.] To stare with open mouth, as in wonder; to open the mouth wide, esp. as the result of weariness, attention, or astonishment; to open like a mouth; to yawn.—**gap·er,** *n.*—**gap·ing·ly,** *adv.*

gape, gāp, gap, *n.* The act of gaping; a yawn; a stare, as with open mouth; a breach or rent; *pl. but sing. in constr., veter. pathol.* a disease of poultry and other birds, attended with frequent gaping, due to infestation of the trachea and bronchi with a gape worm. —**the gapes,** a fit of yawning, as: Boredom gave him *the gapes.*

gape worm, *n.* A nematode worm, *Syngamus trachealis,* which causes the gapes in birds.

gapped scale, *n. Mus.* a scale which omits some notes from a complete series.

gar, gär, *n.* pl. **gar, gars.** [O.E. *gar,* spear.] Any of various N. Amer. fishes with a long, sharp snout or beak, esp. those of the family *Belonidae,* and of the ganoid family *Lepisosteidae.* Also *garfish.*

ga·rage, ga·razh′, ga·räj′, *n.* [Fr.] A place for sheltering or repairing motor vehicles.— *v.t.*—*garaged, garaging.* To store or place in a garage.

Gar·and ri·fle, gar′and ri′fl, ga·rand′rifl, *n.* [From John C. *Garand,* American inventor.] A semiautomatic, .30-inch caliber rifle, used by the U.S. Army in World War II and the Korean War. Also **M-1.**

garb, gärb, *n.* [Fr. *garbe* (now *galbe*), < It. *garbo,* grace; from Teut.] Fashion or mode of dress, esp. when particularly distinctive or characteristic; as, priestly *garb*; clothing. *Fig.* outward semblance or form.—*v.t.* To dress in a particular garb or manner.

gar·bage, gär′bij, *n.* [O.E. *garbash,* probably < *garble,* to sift; being thus what is sifted out, refuse.] Refuse; table waste; any worthless, offensive, or inferior matter; worthless goods. *Aerospace,* miscellaneous objects in orbit, esp. material broken away from a launch vehicle or satellite.

gar·ble, gär′bl, *v.t.*—*garbled, garbling.* [It. *garbellare,* < Ar. *gharbala,* sift.] To make unfair or misleading selections from, as from a text or speech; to mutilate so as to misrepresent; distort or jumble. *Archaic,* to free from dirt; sift or cleanse.—*n.* The process or act of garbling; something garbled.—**gar·bler,** *n.*

gar·den, gär′den, *n.* [O.Fr. *gardin, jardin* (Fr. *jardin*); < Teut. cf. G. *garten*; akin to E. *yard* and *garth.*] A plot of ground, usu. enclosed, devoted to the cultivation of useful or ornamental plants, vegetables, herbs, fruits, or flowers; a piece of ground or other space, commonly with ornamental plants and trees, used as a place of public resort; a highly cultivated region of luxuriant vegetation; a fertile and delightful spot.—*v.i.* To cultivate or tend a garden.— *v.t.* To cultivate, as a garden.—*a.* Pertaining to or produced in a garden; ordinary, common; hardy.—**gar·den·er,** gärd′nẽr, *n.*

gar·den cress, *n.* An herb, *Lepidium sativum,* used in cooking, esp. in salads. Also *peppergrass.*

gar·den he·li·o·trope, *n.* A common large perennial herb with small, fragrant, white or rose-colored flowers, *Valeriana officinalis,* used for ornamentation and as the source of the drug valerian.

gar·de·nia, gär·dē′nya, gär·dē′nē·a, *n.* [N.L. from Dr. Alexander *Garden,* 1730– 1791.] Any of the evergreen trees and shrubs of the genus *Gardenia,* native to the warmer parts of the Eastern Hemisphere, several species of which are cultivated for their fragrant, waxlike, white or yellow flowers.

gar·den·ing, gärd′ning, *n.* The cultivating of a garden; the work or art of a gardener.

gar·den-va·ri·e·ty, *a.* Ordinary; common.

gar·fish, gär′fish″, *n.* Gar.

gar·gan·tu·an, gär·gan′chŏ·an, *a.* [From the giant and king with the incredible capacity for food, *Gargantua,* hero of Rabelais' 16th century satiric novel of the same name.] Gigantic; enormous; prodigious.

gar·get, gär′git, *n.* [Cf. O.Fr. *gargate,* throat.] *Veter. pathol.* an inflamed condition of the head or throat of cattle and swine; inflammation of the udder in cows and ewes.

gar·gle, gär′gl, *v.i.*—*gargled, gargling.* [Fr. *gargouiller,* to gargle; L. *gurgulio,* the gullet; Gr. *gargarizō,* to rinse the mouth; G. *gurgel,* the throat, *gurgeln,* to gargle.] To wash or rinse the mouth or throat with a liquid preparation kept in motion by air expelled from the lungs; to make a sound like that of gargling.—*v.t.* To wash or rinse, as the mouth or throat, by gargling; to utter with a sound like that of gargling.—*n.* Any liquid preparation for washing the mouth and throat.

gar·goyle, gär′goil, *n.* [Fr. *gargouille,* spout.] *Arch.* a projecting spout for conducting rainwater from the gutters of a building, generally carved into a grotesque figure from whose mouth the water gushes; any grotesquely formed figure or ornament. —**gar·goyled,** *a.*

gar·ish, gär′ish, gar′ish, *a.* [< O.E. *gare,* to stare, probably a form of *gaze* with change from *z*-sound to *r.*] Gaudy; showy; overbright; dazzling.—**gar·ish·ly,** *adv.*— **gar·ish·ness,** *n.*

gar·land, gär′land, *n.* [O.E. *girlond, gerlond,* < Fr. *guirlande,* a garland, < O.H.G. *wiera,* a coronet, through *wierelen,* to plait.] A wreath or rope made of leaves, twigs, flowers, or the like, worn as decoration or as a sign of honor or victory; anything similar in appearance. A collection of printed literary pieces; an anthology.— *v.t.* To deck with a garland or garlands.

gar·lic, gär′lik, *n.* [O.E. *gärlēac,* < *gär,* spear, and *lēac,* leek.] A plant of the lily family, *Allium sativum,* with a strong-scented, pungent bulb used in cooking and medicine; any of various species of the same genus; the bulb or a clove of any such plant.—**gar·lick·y,** *a.*

gar·lic salt, *n.* A condiment made of salt mixed with ground dried garlic.

---

ch- chain, G. na*ch*t;   **th-** THen, thin;   **w-** wig, hw as sound in whig;   **z-** zh as in azure, zeal.   *Italicized vowel* indicates schwa sound.

gar·ment, gär′ment, _n._ [Fr. _garnement;_ O.Fr. _garniment,_ < _garnir,_ to garnish, to deck.] Any article of clothing; outside covering.—_v.t._ To clothe.

gar·ner, gär′nèr, _n._ [O.Fr. _gernier, garnier, granier_ (Fr. _grenier_), < L. _granarium._] A storehouse for grain; a granary; _fig._ a store of anything.—_v.t._ To store in a garner. _Fig._ to collect or deposit; to acquire.

gar·net, gär′nit, _n._ [O.Fr. Fr. _grenat,_ appar. (by reason of the red color) < L. _granatum,_ pomegranate, prop. neut. of _granatus,_ having grains or seeds, < _granum,_ E. _grain._] A hard, vitreous silicate mineral occurring in a number of varieties, all having the same general formula but differing in composition, and used as a gem or an abrasive; the common deep red transparent variety; the deep red color of this gem.

gar·net, gär′nit, _n. Naut._ a tackle fixed to a stay, and used to hoist cargo.

gar·net pa·per, _n._ A paper coated with crushed garnet, and used as an abrasive.

gar·ni·er·ite, gär′nē·é·rit″, _n._ [From Jules _Garnier,_ French geologist.] _Mineral._ a hydrous silicate of nickel and magnesium: an important ore of nickel.

gar·nish, gär′nish, _v.t._ [O.Fr. _garnir_ (_garniss-_), _warnir,_ fortify, equip, prepare, warn, Fr. _garnir,_ furnish, garnish; < Teut.: cf. _warn._] To adorn or decorate; to embellish or ornament; as, to _garnish_ a dish with parsley; to equip or furnish; to fit out. _Law,_ to serve with a legal warning or garnishment; to garnishee.—**gar·nish·a·ble,** _a._—**gar·nish·er,** _n._ One who garnishes or decorates; _law,_ one who serves with a garnishment.

gar·nish, gär′nish, _n._ Adornment or decoration; an ornament or embellishment; something added to a dish for flavor or decoration. _Slang,_ an unauthorized payment extorted from a new workman by his cohorts or boss; formerly, one paid in English jails by a new prisoner.

gar·nish·ee, gär″ni·shē′, _n. Law,_ a person served with a garnishment.—_v.t.—garnisheed, garnisheeing. Law,_ to make someone a garnishee; to attach, as money or property, by garnishment.

gar·nish·ment, gär′nish·ment, _n._ Adornment; decoration; an ornament or embellishment; act of garnishing; _law,_ a summons to appear in litigation already pending between others, or a warning served on a person to hold, subject to the court's direction, money or property in his possession belonging to the defendant.

gar·ni·ture, gär′ni·chèr, _n._ [Fr. _garniture,_ < _garnir,_ furnish, garnish.] Anything that garnishes, furnishes, or decorates; appurtenances or outfit; adornment or embellishment.

gar·pike, gär′pīk″, _n._ A gar.

gar·ret, gar′it, _n._ [O.Fr. _garite,_ a place of refuge or outlook, < _garer,_ to beware, < O.H.G. _werjan,_ Goth. _varjan,_ to defend. Akin _ward, guard, wary, warn._] That part of a house which is on the uppermost floor, immediately under the roof; a loft.

gar·ri·son, gar′i·son, _n._ [O.Fr. _garnison,_ < _garnir,_ to garnish.] A body of troops stationed in a fort or fortified place; a fort, military post, or fortified town furnished with troops.—_v.t._ To place a garrison in; to secure or defend by troops.

Gar·ri·son fin·ish, _n._ A surprise finish in a race where the winner comes from behind.

gar·ron, gar′on, _n._ [Ir. and Gael. _gearran._] A small, hardy horse bred in Ireland and Scotland; any similar horse.

gar·rot, gar′ot, _n._ [Fr. _garrot._] The golden-eye.

gar·rote, ga·rōt′, ga·rot′, _n._ [Sp. _garrote,_ orig. a stick (formerly used in drawing the cord tight in strangling), = Fr. _garrot,_ cudgel, stick for tightening the cord about a pack.] A Spanish mode of capital punishment by strangulation with an iron collar, or by injuring the spinal column at the base of the brain; the instrument used; strangulation or throttling, esp. for the purpose of robbery.—_v.t.—garroted, garroting.—**gar·rot·er,** n._

gar·ru·lous, gar′a·lus, gar′ū·lus, _a._ [L. _garrulus,_ < _garrio,_ to prate, to chatter; allied to Gr. _gēryō, garyō,_ to cry; Ir. _gairim,_ to bawl.] Excessively verbose; loquacious; characterized by diffuse or rambling speech.—**gar·ru·lous·ly,** _adv._—**gar·ru·lous·ness, gar·ru·li·ty,** ga·rō′li·tē, _n._

gar·ter, gär′tèr, _n._ [O.Fr. _gartier, jartier,_ < _garet_ (Fr. _jarret_), the bend of the knee; prob. from Celtic.] An elastic band worn around the leg or a supporter on an undergarment that holds up a stocking or sock; a band to hold up a sleeve. (_cap._), _Brit._ the blue velvet badge of the Order of the Garter; membership in the same; the order itself. —_v.t._

gar·ter snake, _n._ Any of the various harmless snakes of the genus _Thamnophis,_ having a brownish or greenish body and three longitudinal stripes, and commonly found in North and Central America.

garth, gärth, _n._ [Icel. _gardhr_ = O.E. _geard,_ E. _yard._] An open courtyard enclosed by a cloister.

gas, gas, _n._ pl. **gas·es.** [Coined by J. B. van Helmont (1577–1644), Flemish chemist; suggested by Gr. _chaos,_ chaos.] _Phys., chem._ a state of matter in which the molecules are free to move in any direction, expand to fill a container in which they are held, and tend to expand indefinitely when not confined. Any substance in the form of a gas or any mixture of gases except air; a substance in the form of a gas burned for illuminating or heating; a mistlike assemblage of fine particles suspended in the air, used to anesthetize or to asphyxiate, poison, or stupefy an enemy; the highly combustible mixture of air and firedamp found in coal mines; the exhalations which are a by-product of improperly digested food in the alimentary canal. _Colloq._ the accelerator pedal of a gasoline powered vehicle; gasoline. _Slang,_ empty or longwinded talk; one who or that which is quite novel, exciting, or satisfying; something or someone that makes a strong impact.—_v.t.— gassed, gassing._ To affect, overcome, or asphyxiate with gas or fumes; to supply, treat, or impregnate with gas; to singe with a gas flame to remove superfluous fibers. _Slang,_ to amuse successfully; to affect strongly.—_v.i._ To give off gas, as a storage battery; _slang,_ to indulge in empty talk.

gas at·tack, _n._ A military attack in which asphyxiating or poisonous gases are employed against the enemy, as by spraying from the air or by bombarding with gas shells.

gas·bag, gas′bag″, _n._ A bag for holding gas. _Slang,_ an empty, voluble talker; a windbag.

gas cham·ber, _n._ A chamber where a convicted prisoner is executed by the use of poisonous gas.

Gas·con, gas′kon, _n._ [Fr. akin; to _Basque._] A native of Gascony in France; (_l.c._) a boaster, a braggart.—_a._ Pertaining to Gascony or its inhabitants; (_l.c._) bragging, boastful.

gas·con·ade, gas″ko·nād′, _n._ [Fr.] A boast; bravado; bragging.—_v.i.—gasconaded, gasconading._—**gas·con·ad·er,** _n._

gas en·gine, _n._ An internal-combustion engine powered by a gas and air mixture.

gas·e·ous, gas′ē·us, gash′us, _a._ Of the nature of gas; pertaining to gas; in the form of gas; not solid. _Colloq._ wanting substance; indefinite.—**gas·e·ous·ness,** _n._

gas fit·ter, _n._ One who installs apparatus for the use of gas.—**gas fit·ting,** _n._ The work of a gas fitter; _pl._ the equipment for the use of gas for illuminating and heating purposes.

gash, gash, _n._ [Perhaps < O.Fr. _garser,_ to scarify, to pierce with a lancet; L.L. _garsa,_ scarification.] A deep and long cut or incision, esp. in flesh.—_v.t., v.i._

gas·hold·er, gas′hōl″dèr, _n._ A large container for storing natural or manufactured gas.

gas·i·fy, gas′i·fī″, _v.t.—gasified, gasifying._ To convert into gas.—_v.i._ To become gas.—**gas·i·fi·a·ble,** _a._—**gas·i·fi·ca·tion,** gas″i·fi·kā′shun, _n._—**gas·i·fi·er,** _n._

gas·ket, gas′kit, _n._ [Origin uncertain.] _Naut._ one of several lines used to bind a furled sail to a yard; _mech._ a ring of plaited hemp, tow, rubber, or metal used to make a joint watertight.

gas·kin, gas′kin, _n._ In quadrupeds, that part of the hind leg between the stifle and the hock.

gas·light, gas′līt″, _n._ Light made by the combustion of illuminating gas; a gas jet.

gas·lit, gas′lit″, _a._ Lighted by the combustion of illuminating gas; marked by extensive use of gaslight.

gas log, _n._ A gas burner, used in a fireplace, resembling a piece or several pieces of firewood.

gas mask, _n._ A masklike device which chemically filters the air, worn as protection against noxious gases used in warfare or incidental to certain industrial occupations.

gas·o·gene, gas′o·jēn″, _n._ [Fr. _gazogène,_ < _gaz,_ gas, and _-gène._] An apparatus for manufacturing aerated liquid.

gas·o·line, gas·o·lene, gas″o·lēn′, gas′o·lēn″, _n._ [< _gas_ and L. _oleum,_ oil.] A volatile flammable liquid, consisting of a mixture of hydrocarbons, obtained in the distillation of petroleum, and used chiefly as a solvent and as fuel for internal-combustion engines. Also _Brit. petrol._—**gas·o·line en·gine** or **mo·tor,** an internal-combustion engine using gasoline for fuel.

gas·om·e·ter, gas·om′i·tèr, _Brit._ gas·o′mē·tèr, _n._ An instrument or apparatus intended to measure or hold gases, gas·om′i·tèr. _Brit._ a reservoir of gas for piping into homes and factories, gas·o′mē·tèr.

gasp, gasp, gäsp, _v.i._ [M.E. _gaspen,_ < Scand. cf. Icel. _geispa,_ Sw. _gaspa,_ yawn.] To catch the breath, or labor for breath, with open mouth; to respire convulsively; to pant, as for air.—_v.t._ To breathe or utter with gasps.—_n._ A short, convulsive effort to breathe; a short, convulsive utterance or breath.—**gasp·ing·ly,** _adv._

gas·per, gas′pèr, gä′spèr, _n. Brit. slang,_ a cheap cigarette.

gas-plant, gas′plant″, gas′plänt″, _n. Bot._ a perennial herbaceous plant, _Dictamnus albus,_ of the rue family, having flowers that give off a flammable vapor in hot weather. Also _fraxinella._

gas·ser, gas′èr, _n._ One who or that which gasses; a well or boring yielding natural gas. _Slang,_ any thing or person that is remarkable in a good or bad sense.

gas shell, _n. Milit._ an explosive shell containing a poisonous gas.

gas sta·tion, _n._ A place where motor vehicles are serviced and gasoline, oil, etc., are sold. Also _filling station, service station._

gas·sy, gas′ē, _a.—gassier, gassiest._ Full of or containing gas; having a resemblance to gas. _Slang,_ full of empty talk; flatulent.—**gas·si·ness,** _n._

gas·tight, gas′tīt″, _a._ Made to prevent the entry or escape of gas.

gas·tral, ga·stral′, _a._ Pertaining to the stomach or digestive tract.

gas·tral·gi·a, ga·stral′jē·a, ga·stral′ja, _n._ [Gr. _gastèr, gastros,_ and _algos,_ pain.] Pain in the stomach, esp. neuralgic pain.

---

a- fat, fāte, fär, fâre, fạll;   **e-** met, mē, mēre, hèr;   **i-** pin, pīne;   **o-** not, nōte, mõve;   **u-** tub, cūbe, bụll;   **oi-** oil;   **ou-** pound.

gas·trec·to·my, ga·strek′to·mē, *n.* pl. **gas·trec·to·mies.** [Gr. *gastēr* (*gastr-*), belly, stomach, and *ek*, out of, and *-tomia*, E. *-tomy*.] *Surg.* the excision of the stomach or a portion of it.

gas·tric, gas′trik, *a.* [< Gr. *gastēr, gastros,* the belly or stomach.] Of or pertaining to the stomach.

gas·tric juice, *n. Biochem.* an acidic digestive fluid containing enzymes and hydrochloric acid, secreted by glands in the mucous membrane of the stomach.

gas·tric ul·cer, *n.* An open sore on the mucous membrane of the stomach, usu. caused by excessively acidic gastric juice.

gas·trin, gas′trin, *n. Biochem.* a hormone inducing secretion of gastric juices.

gas·tri·tis, ga·strī′tis, *n. Pathol.* chronic inflammation of the stomach, esp. of the mucous membrane.

gas·tro·in·tes·ti·nal, gas″trō·in·tes′ti·nal, *a.* Relating to or affecting the stomach and intestines.

gas·trol·o·gy, ga·strol′o·jē, *n.* [Gr. *gastrologia*.] The science of the structure, functions, and diseases of the stomach.—**gas·trol·o·gist,** *n.*

gas·tro·nome, gas′tro·nōm,″ *n.* A gourmet; an epicure. Also **gas·tron·o·mer, gas·tron·o·mist,** ga·stron′o·mėr.

gas·tron·o·my, ga·stron′o·mē, *n.* [Gr. *gastēr,* stomach, and *nomos,* a law.] The art of good eating; epicurism; culinary methods or customs.—**gas·tro·nom·ic,** gas″tro·nom′ik, *a.*—**gas·tro·nom·i·cal,** gas″tro·nom′ik, *a.*—**gas·tro·nom·i·cal·ly,** *adv.*

gas·tro·pod, gas′tro·pod,″ *n.* [N.L. *Gastropoda,* pl., < Gr. *gastēr,* belly, and *pous* (*pod-*), foot.] Any of the *Gastropoda,* a class of mollusks including the snails, whelks, and slugs, the members of which usually have a univalve shell and a disklike foot on the ventral surface of the body by means of which they move about.—*a.* Pertaining to the gastropods; belonging to the *Gastropoda.*—**gas·trop·o·dous,** ga·strop′o·dus, *a.*

gas·tro·scope, gas′tro·skōp,″ *n.* An instrument for inspecting the interior of the stomach.—**gas·tro·scop·ic,** gas″tro·skop′·ik, *a.*—**gas·tros·co·py,** ga·stros′ko·pē *n.*

gas·trot·o·my, ga·strot′o·mē, *n.* pl. **gas·trot·o·mies.** *Surg.* the operation of cutting into the abdomen or the stomach.

gas·tro·vas·cu·lar, gas″trō·vas′kū·lėr, *a. Zool.* serving for digestive and circulatory purposes; as, the *gastrovascular* body cavity of certain animals.

gas·tru·la, gas′tru̯·la, *n.* pl. **gas·tru·las, gas·tru·lae,** gas′tru̯·lē.″[N.L., dim. < Gr. *gastēr* (*gastr*), belly, stomach.] *Embryol.* an embryo of a metazoan, developed from the blastula, consisting of a cuplike body formed by two layers of cells.

gas·tru·la·tion, gas″tru̯·lā′shan, *n. Embryol.* the formation of a gastrula; any process, as invagination, by which a blastula or other form of embryo is converted into a gastrula.—**gas·tru·late,** *v.i.*—*gastrulating, gastrulating.*

gas tur·bine, *n.* A turbine engine activated by a stream of hot gases under pressure.

gas·works, gas′wu̯rks,″ *n. pl., but sing. in constr.* An establishment where illuminating and heating gas is manufactured.

gat, gat, *n.* [= *gate.*] A passage or channel between banks or cliffs, as along a coast.

gat, gat, *n.* [Abbr. of *Gatling gun.*] *Slang,* a gun, pistol, or revolver.

gate, gāt, *n.* [O.E. *geat,* gate, = D. and L.G. *gat* = Icel. *gat,* hole, opening.] A movable structure used to open or close any passageway; any passageway into and out of an enclosure, esp. one closed by a movable barrier; a structure built about such an opening and containing the barrier; a contrivance for regulating the passage of water or steam, as a valve; any natural means

of access or entrance, as a pass in a mountain range; anything providing access; as, the *gate* to wealth; a sash or frame for saws. The number of persons who pay an admission fee at an entrance; the total amount of money received from them. *Elect.* a signal which permits for a time the passage of other signals through a circuit. *Foundry,* a channel or opening in a mold, as the opening through which metal is poured; the waste metal cast in it.—*v.t.*—*gated, gating. Brit.* to punish by keeping within school boundaries, as a college student.

gate, gāt, *n.* [< Scand. Cf. Icel. *gata,* way, path, road, Sw. *gata,* Dan. *gade,* also G. *gasse,* Goth. *gatwo,* street.] *Sc., provinc. Eng.* a way, path, road, or street, as retained locally in street names; as, Canon*gate* in Edinburgh, Scotland, and Mickle*gate* in York, England.

gate·crash·er, gāt′krash,″ėr, *n. Colloq.* one who attends without an invitation or gains admission without paying.—**gate·crash·ing,** *n.*

gate·fold, gāt′fōld,″ *n.* An insert in a book or periodical that is larger than the other pages and is therefore folded.

gate·house, gāt′hous,″ *n.* A house at or over a gate, used as quarters by the gatekeeper of an estate, or by guards of a prison or fortified place; a structure at the gate of a dam or reservoir, with apparatus for regulating the flow of water.

gate·keep·er, gāt′kē″pėr, *n.* The person who has charge of a gate, esp. one who supervises the flow of traffic through it.

gate-leg ta·ble, gāt′leg″ tā′bl, *n.* A table with folding leaves or flaps, each flap supported when in use by legs that swing out from the frame and that may be pushed back to lower the flap.

gate·man, gāt′man,″ *n.* pl. **gate·men.** Gate-keeper.

gate·post, gāt′pōst,″ *n.* The post on which a gate swings, or the one against which it closes.

gate·way, gāt′wā,″ *n.* An entrance which is or may be closed with a gate; a structure which frames such an entrance; a means of entry, as: The Republic of the Philippines is the *gateway* to Asia.

gath·er, gaᴛʜ′ėr, *v.t.* [O.E. *gaderian, gadrian,* < *gador, geador,* together; cf. D. *gadern,* to gather, *te gader,* L.G. *to gader,* together.] To bring together; to collect; to assemble; to congregate; to harvest; to pluck; to accumulate; to amass; to draw together; to bring together in folds or plaits, as a garment; to pucker; to acquire or gain, with or without effort; as, to *gather* strength; to deduce by inference; to conclude; to attract; as, flowers *gathering* bees; to wrap about or enfold; as, to *gather* the coat around oneself.—*v.i.* To collect; to become assembled; to congregate; to take origin and grow; to come to a head, as a boil; to become folded or creased, as cloth.—**gath·er one·self to·geth·er,** to collect all one's powers for a strong effort.—**be gath·ered to one's fa·thers,** to die.—**gath·er·er,** *n.*

gath·er, gaᴛʜ′ėr, *n.* A plait or fold in cloth held in position by a thread drawn through it; a pucker; the act or instance of drawing together, collecting, or assembling.

gath·er·ing, gaᴛʜ′ėr·ing, *n.* The act of collecting or assembling; that which is gathered; a crowd; an assembly; the collection of food from the wilderness or from farm sources, as eggs from the nest; a fold or series of folds in a cloth; an abscess.

Gat·ling gun, gat′ling gun, *n.* [From R. J. *Gatling* (1818–1903), American inventor.] An early machine gun consisting of a revolving cluster of barrels around a central axis, each barrel being loaded and fired automatically during every revolution of the cluster.

GATT, gat, *n.* [(*G*)eneral (*A*)greement on (*T*)ariffs and (*T*)rade.] The General Agreement on Tariffs and Trade, an organization of 23 countries, including the U.S., established in 1947 to improve international trade by reductions in tariffs and by the elimination of unnecessary trade barriers.

gauche, gōsh, *a.* [Fr. < Teut.] Awkward; tactless; clumsy.—**gauche·ness, gau·che·rie,** gō″she·rē′, *Fr.* gōsh·e·rē′, *n.* Awkwardness; tactlessness; an awkward movement or act; a faux pas.

gau·cho, gou′chō, *Sp.* gou′cḥa, *n.* A cowboy of the S. American pampas, usu. of mixed Spanish and Indian blood.

gaud, gąd, *n.* [L. *gaudium,* joy, gladness; in later times something showy; akin *joy, jewel.*] A showy ornament or piece of finery.—**gaud·er·y,** gą′de·rē, *n.* pl. **gaud·er·ies.** Ostentatious finery or ornamentation.

gaud·y, gą′dē, *a.*—*gaudier, gaudiest.* Garish; tawdry; tastelessly or glaringly showy.—**gaud·i·ly,** *adv.*—**gaud·i·ness,** *n.*

gauf·fer, gą′fėr, gof′ėr, *n., v.t.* Goffer.

gauge, gage, gāj, *n.* A standard of measure, dimension, or capacity; a means of estimating or testing; criterion; any of various tools used for measuring or marking, as in the building trades or bookbinding; *rail.* the distance between the two rails of a railroad, the standard being 4 feet 8½ inches. A measure of the caliber of a shotgun; the standard of fineness of a stocking or other knitted fabric measured in the number of loops per 1½ inch; a device for checking the diameter of knitting needles for size and for measuring the number of rows or stitches per inch. *Naut.* the location of a ship in relation to another ship or the wind.

gauge, gage, gāj, *v.t.*—*gauged, gauging, gaged, gaging.* [O.Fr. *gauger,* perhaps of the same origin as *gallon,* and signifying to find the number of measures in a vessel.] To measure or to ascertain the contents or capacity of; to measure in respect to capability, power, or character; to appraise; to estimate; to make correspond to a standard. *Building,* to mix, as plaster, or to shape, as stones.—**gauge·a·ble, gage·a·ble,** *a.*—**gauge·a·bly, gage·a·bly,** *adv.*

gaug·er, gā′jėr, *n.* One who or the instrument which gauges; a customs official who measures and inspects dutiable goods; an inspector of machine-made work in a factory.

Gaul·ish, gą′lish, *a.* Pertaining to Gaul, the ancient Roman province of Gallia, its inhabitants, or their Celtic language.—*n.* That Celtic language, now extinct.

Gaull·ism, gō′liz·um, ga′liz·um, *n.* A conservative political movement arising in France after World War II under the leadership of Charles de Gaulle; the principles and practices of adherents to the movement.—**Gaull·ist,** *n.*

gaul·the·ri·a, gąl·thēr′ē·a, *n.* [N.L. from Dr. J. F. *Gaultier,* 1708–56, Canadian physician.] Any of the more than 100 species of evergreen shrubs of the genus *Gaultheria,* in the heath family, as *G. procumbens,* the American wintergreen.

gaunt, gąnt, *a.* [Cf. Norw. *gand,* a slender stick, a thin man.] Emaciated by age, hunger, or illness; haggard; of places and things, desolate.—**gaunt·ly,** *adv.*—**gaunt·ness,** *n.*

gaunt·let, gąnt′lit, gänt′lit, *n.* [Fr. *gantelet,* dim. < *gant,* a glove, < the Teut.; D. *want,* Dan. *vante,* Icel. *vöttr* (for *vantr*), a glove.] A glove with fingers covered with small plates, formerly worn as armor; a glove which covers both the hand and wrist; any type of protective glove, as used in industry.—**take up the gaunt·let,** to accept the challenge.—**throw down the gaunt·let,** to challenge.—**gaunt·let·ed,** *a.*

gaunt·let, gạnt′lit, gänt′lit, *n.* A method of punishment whereby two lines of men bearing weapons strike, whip, or beat the victim who must run between the lines; also *gantlet*. An attack coming from several sides; an extremely trying experience of any kind.—**run the gaunt·let,** to undergo this punishment; *fig.* to go through severe criticism, controversy, or ill-treatment.

gaur, gour, gou′ér, *n. pl.* **gaurs, gaur.** [Hind.] A wild ox of massive proportions, *Bibos frontalis gaurus,* found in southeastern Asia and Malaysia.

gauss, gous, *n.* [From the German mathematician, Karl Friedrich *Gauss,* 1777–1855.] *Phys.* the unit of magnetic induction or magnetic flux density in the electromagnetic system of measurement, equiv. to one maxwell per square centimeter.

gauze, gạz, *n.* [Fr. *gaze,* Sp. *gasa,* from the town *Gaza,* from which it was first brought.] A thin transparent fabric in an open mesh-like weave; any woven material resembling this; as, wire *gauze;* a loosely woven cotton bandage applied to wounds. A slight cloud, haze, or mist.—**gauz·y,** gạ′zē, *a.*—*gauzier, gauziest.* Like or made of gauze; thin as gauze.—**gauz·i·ness,** *n.*

ga·vage, ga·väzh′, *Fr.* gä·väzh′, *n.* [Fr., < *gaver,* to gorge with food.] Forced feeding, as of poultry or human beings, by means of a flexible stomach tube and a force pump.

gav·el, gav′el, *n.* [Origin uncertain.] A small mallet used by a presiding officer to signal for attention or order; a hammer used in masonry.—*v.t.*—*gaveled, gaveling, gavelled, gavelling.* Of a presiding officer, to use a gavel to demand silence or order.

gav·el, gav′el, *n.* [O.E. *gafol,* tribute, tax.] Rent or tribute paid in England in ancient and medieval times.

gav·el·kind, gav′el·kind″, *n.* [M.E. *gavelkynde, gavelikind,* < O.E. *gafol,* E. *gavel,* and *gecynd,* E. *kind.*] *Brit. law,* a land tenure, chiefly in Kent, England, by which estates were divided equally among the sons or other heirs; this custom of division in general; the land thus held.

gav·e·lock, gav′e·lok″, *n. Brit. dial.* an iron lever or crowbar.

ga·vi·al, gā′vē·al, *n.* [Hind. *ghariyāl.*] A large crocodile, *Gavialis gangeticus,* with elongated jaws, found in the Ganges and other certain rivers of India.

ga·votte, ga·vot′, *n.* [Fr., from *Gavot,* a native of the Pays de *Gap* in the Hautes Alpes, where the dance originated.] A lively old French dance in 4/4 time; music similar to the gavotte, sometimes included in a classical suite.—*v.i.*

gawk, gạk, *n.* [Origin uncertain.] An awkward, oafish person; a fool or simpleton.—*v.i.* To stare idly or stupidly; to gape.

gawk·ish, gạ′kish, *a.* Stupid, dull, awkward.—**gawk·ish·ly,** *adv.*—**gawk·ish·ness,** *n.*

gawk·y, gạ′kē, *a.*—*gawkier, gawkiest.* Awkward, clumsy, or ungraceful.—*n. pl.* **gawk·ies.** A clumsy person.—**gawk·i·ly,** *adv.*—**gawk·i·ness,** *n.*

gay, gā, *a.* [O.Fr. Fr. *gai;* < Teut.] In or showing a joyous, merry mood; cheerfully lively; given to or abounding in social or other pleasures; as, a *gay* social event. Given over to frivolous pleasure; dissipated; licentious. Bright or brilliantly colored; showily adorned. *Slang,* homosexual.—**gay·ness,** *n.*

ga·yal, ga·yäl′, *n.* [Hindi *gayāl.*] A domesticated ox, *Bos frontalis,* with slender horns and white legs, common in parts of India and thought to be a domesticated descendant of the gaur.

gay·e·ty, gā′i·tē, *n.* Gaiety.

gay·ly, gā′lē, *adv.* Gaily.

ga·za·bo, ga·zā′bō, *n. Slang,* a fellow.

gaze, gạz, *v.i.*—*gazed, gazing.* [Sw. *gasa,* to gaze; allied to E. *agast,* Goth. *usgaisjan,* to terrify.] To look steadily, intently, and earnestly; to look with eagerness or curiosity.—*n.* A fixed look.—**gaz·er,** *n.*

ga·ze·bo, ga·zē′bō, ga·zā′bō, *n. pl.* **ga·ze·bos, ga·ze·boes.** [Origin uncertain; now associated with *gaze.*] A structure commanding an extensive view, as a turret, belvedere, balcony, projecting window, or summerhouse.

gaze·hound, gạz′hound″, *n.* A dog that pursues by sight rather than by scent.

ga·zelle, ga·zel′, *n. pl.* **ga·zelles, ga·zelle.** [Fr. *gazelle,* < Ar. *ghazāl.*] Any of various small Asian and African antelopes of the genus *Gazella* and allied genera, noted for graceful movements and lustrous eyes.

ga·zette, ga·zet′, *n.* [Fr. < It. *gazzetta,* gazette, orig. a Venetian coin (as the price of the gazette), dim. < L. *gaza,* treasure.] A newspaper, now chiefly in names of newspapers; an official government journal or announcement, esp. in Great Britain, containing public notices and lists of government appointments and promotions.—*v.t.*—*gazetted, gazetting. Brit.* to announce or publish in a gazette.

gaz·et·teer, gaz″i·tēr′, *n.* [Fr. *gazettier,* now *gazetier.*] A geographical dictionary. *Archaic,* a journalist, esp. one appointed and paid by the government.

gaz·o·gene, gaz′o·jēn″, *n.* Gasogene.

gaz·pa·cho, gaz·pä′chō, *Sp.* gäth·pä′chō, gäs·pä′chō, *n.* A thick Spanish vegetable soup served cold.

G clef, *n. Mus.* the treble clef.

ge·an·ti·cline, jē·an′ti·klin″, *n.* [Gr. *gē,* earth, and E. *anticlinal.*] *Geol.* an upward fold encompassing a large part of the earth's surface. Also **ge·an·ti·cli·nal.**—**ge·an·ti·cli·nal,** *a.*

gear, gēr, *n.* [M.E. *gere,* prob. < Scand.: cf. Icel. *gervi, görvi,* gear, apparel, akin to O.E. *gearwe,* pl., clothes, ornaments, armor, *gearu,* ready.] *Mach.* a mechanism for transmitting or changing motion by interaction of parts, as by toothed wheels; an assembly of parts which serves a specific purpose in a machine; a toothed wheel which engages or meshes with another wheel or part; the meshing itself; the connection of a machine part with a motor or shaft; a particular connection governing speed and direction variations; as, reverse *gear. Naut.* the ropes, blocks, and other rigging of a particular sail or spar. Apparel or attire; movable property or goods; as, camping *gear;* apparatus or equipment; as, fishing *gear;* a harness, esp. for horses.

gear, gēr, *v.t. Mach.* to provide with gearing; connect by gearing; to put into gear. To provide with gear or equipment; harness; to adjust or regulate according to certain conditions; as, to *gear* instruction to student ability.—*v.i. Mach.* to fit exactly, as one part of gearing into another; come into or be in gear.

gear·box, gear box, gēr′boks″, *n.* A case or enclosure for the protection of gears; a motor vehicle transmission.

gear·ing, gēr′ing, *n. Mach.* collectively, the parts of a machine by which motion is transmitted or changed, esp. a train of toothed wheels; the act or operation of providing with gears.

gear·shift, gēr′shift″, *n. Mach.* a device by which transmission gears, as in an automobile, are engaged and disengaged.

gear·wheel, gear wheel, gēr′hwēl″, gēr′wēl″, *n.* A wheel having teeth or cogs which engage with the teeth of another wheel or part to transmit or receive motion; also **cog·wheel.**

geck·o, gek′ō, *n. pl.* **geck·os, geck·oes.** [Malay *gēkoq.*] A small, harmless lizard of the family *Gekkonidæ,* common in warm countries, having toes with adhesive disks.

gee, jē, *interj.* A word of command to horses, or other work animals, directing them to turn to the right; a similar command urging more speed, followed by *up.*—*v.i.*—*geed, geeing.* To turn to the right; to move faster, usu. followed by *up.*

gee, jē, *interj.* [Euphemism for *Jesus.*] A mild expression of wonder, astonishment, or enthusiasm. Also **gee whiz.**—*v.i.*—*geed, geeing. Colloq.* to agree; to go well together.

gee·gaw, gē′gạ″, *n.* Gewgaw.

geest, gēst, *n.* [L.G., dry or sandy soil.] *Geol.* old deposits produced by flowing water; coarse drift; gravel.

gee·zer, gē′zér, *n. Slang,* an odd character, usu. in friendly deprecation.

ge·fil·te fish, gefil′te fish, *n.* [< Yiddish, G., stuffed fish.] *Cookery,* a Jewish dish eaten as an appetizer or main dish, made of cooked and chilled ground fresh-water fish such as carp, pike, whitefish, or a combination of these, mixed with seasonings, crumbs, onion, and eggs. Also **ge·ful·te fish, ge·füll·te fish.**

ge·gen·schein, gā′gen·shin″, *n.* [G., counterglow.] *Astron.* a faint, round or elongated patch of light sometimes seen in the sky at night at a point directly opposite the sun. Also **counterglow.**

Ge·hen·na, gi·hen′a, *n.* [L.L., < Gr. *Geena,* < Heb. *Gē-Hinnōm,* valley of Hinnom.] *Bib.* the valley of Hinnom, near Jerusalem, regarded as a place of abomination; hell; in general, a place of extreme discomfort or suffering.

Gei·ger count·er, gī′gér koun′tér, *n.* [From Hans *Geiger,* German physicist.] *Phys.* an instrument for detecting and measuring radioactivity, consisting of a thin-walled, gas-filled metallic tube in which a needlelike electrode detects the passage of ionizing particles. Also **Gei·ger-Mül·ler count·er.**

gei·sha, gā′sha, gē′sha, *n. pl.* **gei·sha, gei·shas.** A Japanese girl trained to entertain men with dance, song, and conversation.

gel, jel, *n.* [< *gelatin.*] A jellylike, colloidal suspension, semisolid in consistency, as gelatin, glue, or agar-agar.—*v.i.*—*gelled, gelling.* To form a jellylike substance.

ge·län·de·sprung, ge·len′de·sprung″, *G.* ge·len′de·shprung″, *n. Skiing,* a maneuver in which a skier crouches low and thrusts himself into a jump with the aid of his poles, usu. to surmount an obstacle. Also **ge·län·de jump.**

gel·a·tin, jel′a·tin, *n.* [Fr. *gelatine,* It. and Sp. *gelatina,* < L. *gelo,* to congeal.] A glutinous protein obtained from various animal tissues, used in making various stiff, jellylike food products, and in photography, bacteriology, medicine, and other technical fields. Also **gel·a·tine,** jel′a·tēn.

ge·lat·i·nize, je·lat′i·nīz″, jel·a·ti·nīz″, *v.t.*—*gelatinized, gelatinizing.* To change into a jelly or cause to become gelatinous; to coat, as photographic paper, with gelatin.—*v.i.* To become a jelly or gelatinous. Also **ge·lat·i·nate.**—**ge·lat·i·ni·za·tion,** *n.*

ge·lat·i·nous, je·lat′i·nus, *a.* Of, pertaining to, or consisting of gelatin; resembling gelatin.—**ge·lat·i·nous·ly,** *adv.*—**ge·lat·i·nous·ness,** *n.*

ge·la·tion, je·lā′shan, je·lā′shan, *n.* [L. *gelatio(n-),* < *gelare,* freeze, congeal.] Solidification by cold; freezing.

geld, geld, *n.* [O.E. *geld, gield, gild,* payment, tribute, gild = D. and G. *geld,* money, = Icel. *gjald,* payment, = Goth. *gild,* tribute; < the Teut. verb represented by E. *yield.*] *Eng. hist.* a payment; a tax, esp. the tax paid to the crown by landholders under the Anglo-Saxon and Norman kings.

geld, geld, *v.t.*—*gelded* or *gelt, gelding.* [< Icel. *gelda,* Dan. *gilde,* G. *gelten,* to geld.] To castrate; to spay; *fig.* to weaken the force of.

geld·ing, gel′ding, n. A castrated animal, esp. a male horse.

gel·id, jel′id, a. [L. *gelidus,* < *gelo,* to freeze, seen also in *gelatin, congeal, jelly,* the root being that of *cool.*] Very cold; icy. —**ge·lid·i·ty,** je·lid′i·tē, n.—**gel′id·ly,** adv.

gel·ig·nite, jel′ig·nīt″, n. [< *gelatin* and L. *ignis,* fire.] A powerful explosive containing nitroglycerin, soluble guncotton, powdered wood, and potassium or sodium nitrate.

gel·se·mi·um, jel·sē′mē·um, n. pl. **gel·se·mi·ums, gel·se·mi·a.** [N.L. < It. *gelsomino,* jasmine.] A twining shrub of the genus *Gelsemium,* esp. the yellow jasmine, *G. sempervirens,* with fragrant yellow flowers; *pharm.* the root of the yellow jasmine, or the tincture from it, used as a drug.

gem, jem, n. [O.Fr. Fr. *gemme,* < L. *gemma,* bud, gem.] A precious or semiprecious stone, esp. when cut and polished for ornament; a jewel. *Fig.* something likened to a gem because of its beauty, perfection, or worth; something greatly prized; a highly esteemed person. *Cookery,* a kind of muffin; *Brit. print.* a 4-point printing type. —v.t.—**gemmed, gemming.** To adorn with or as with gems.

gem·i·nate, jem′i·nāt, v.i., v.t.—**geminated, geminating.** [L. *geminatus,* pp. of *geminare,* to double, < *geminus,* twin.] To become or cause to become doubled or paired.— jem′i·nit, jem′i·nāt″, a. Combined in a pair or pairs; coupled; binate.—**gem·i·nate·ly,** adv.—**gem·i·na·tion,** jem″i·nā′shun, n. A doubling; duplication; repetition, as the immediate repetition of a word or phrase for rhetorical effect, or the doubling of a consonant sound.

Gem·i·ni, jem′i·nī″, jem′i·nē, jim′i·nī″, jim′i·nē, n. pl. but sing. in constr. [L. twin brothers, Castor and Pollux.] *Astron.* a constellation including the bright twin stars, Castor and Pollux; *astrol.* third sign of the zodiac; *aerospace,* a U.S. manned spacecraft capable of rendezvous in orbit.

gem·ma, jem′a, n. pl. **gem·mae,** jem′ē. [L., bud, gem.] *Bot.* budlike protuberances, as of certain plants of the phylum *Bryophyta,* the mosses and liverworts, that can separate from the parent plant to grow independently; *zool.* a bud or protuberance which develops into a new organism, as in some coelenterates.—**gem·ma·ceous,** je·mā′shus, a.—**gem·mate,** jem′āt, v.i.— **gemmated, gemmating.** To put forth buds; increase by budding.—**gem·ma·tion,** n.

gem·mip·a·rous, je·mip′er·us, a. [L. *pario,* to produce.] Producing buds or gemmae; reproducing by buds, as the hydra.

gem·mule, jem′ūl, n. [L. *gemmula,* dim. of *gemma,* bud.] *Biol.* a small bud or gemma; a germinal mass of spores, as of sponges; one of the hypothetical units conceived by Darwin in the theory of pangenesis as the bearers of hereditary attributes.—**gem·mu·lif·er·ous,** a.

gem·ol·o·gy, gem·mol·o·gy, je·mol′o·jē, n. Scientific study of gems.—**gem·o·log·i·cal,** jem″o·loj′i·kal, a.—**gem·ol·o·gist,** n.

gems·bok, gemz′bok, n. pl. **gems·boks, gems·bok.** [S. Afr. D., 'chamois buck.'] A large antelope, *Oryx gazella,* of southern Africa, having long straight horns and a long tufted tail. Also **gems·buck.**

gem·stone, jem′stōn, n. A precious stone which can be refined by cutting and polishing for use in jewelry.

gen·darme, zhän′därm, Fr. zhän·därm′, n. [Fr. < the pl. *gens d'armes,* men at arms.] One of the armed police of France and some other European countries; *slang,* any policeman.

gen·dar·me·rie, gen·dar·me·ry, zhän·där′me·rē, Fr. zhäN·där·me·Rē′, n. [Fr.] A body of gendarmes.

gen·der, jen′dèr, n. [O.Fr. *gendre* (Fr. *genre),* < L. *genus (gener-),* race, kind, sort, gender.] *Gram.* any of the classes into which words, esp. nouns, pronouns, and their modifiers, are distinguished with reference to actual or ascribed sex or lack of it or to other characteristics, as being animate or inanimate; as, masculine, feminine, or neuter *gender;* membership in such a class; an ending or form denoting this membership. *Colloq.* sex, male or female, usu. humorous.

gene, jēn, n. [Gr. *gen-,* bear, produce.] *Biol.* the element or unit of a chromosome which carries and transfers an inherited characteristic from parent to offspring, and determines the development of some particular character or trait in the offspring.

ge·ne·a·log·i·cal, jē″nē·a·loj′i·kal, a. Pertaining to genealogy; exhibiting or tracing genealogies.—**ge·ne·a·log·i·cal tree,** a diagram showing the lineage of a family in the form of a tree. Also *family tree.*— **ge·ne·a·log·i·cal·ly,** adv.

ge·ne·al·o·gy, jē″nē·ol′o·jē, jē″nē·al′o·jē, n. pl. **ge·ne·al·o·gies.** [L. and Gr. *genealogia*—Gr. *genea,* family (root *gen,* to beget), and *logos,* discourse.] An account or record which traces the ancestry of a certain individual or family; descent from an ancestor; lineage; pedigree; the study of pedigrees or family history.—**ge·ne·al·o·gist,** n.

gene mu·ta·tion, n. *Biol.* a significant alteration in an organism due to a chemical rearrangement within the molecules of a gene.

gen·er·a·ble, jen′èr·a·bl, a. [L. *generabilis.*] Capable of being generated or produced.

gen·er·al, jen′èr·al, a. [O.Fr. *general* (Fr. *général),* < L. *generalis,* < *genus,* race or kind.] Pertaining to, affecting, including, or participated in by all members of a class or group; pertaining to the whole of something; common to many or most, though not universal; as, a *general* practice; prevalent; usual; not specialized and not limited to a precise application or area; as, the practice of *general* medicine; considered with reference to main elements or features rather than details or exceptions; as, a *general* knowledge of a subject; not specific or special; as, *general* instructions; indefinite or vague; having extended command, or superior or chief rank.— **gen·er·al·ly,** adv.—**gen·er·al·ness,** n.

gen·er·al, jen′èr·al, n. *Milit.* any general officer; a U.S. Army or Air Force officer ranking below General of the Army or Air Force and above lieutenant-general; the highest-ranking U.S. Marine Corps officer. *Eccles.* the chief of a religious order. The main or overall fact, statement, principle, or notion.—**gen·er·al·cy,** n. The office, rank, or tenure of a general.—**in gen·er·al,** with respect to the whole class referred to; commonly; usually; considering the whole and disregarding details.

Gen·er·al As·sem·bly, n. The main body of the United Nations, having representation for each member nation; the legislature in some states; the legislative body of some religious denominations, as the United Presbyterian Church.

Gen·er·al Court, n. Formerly, a Colonial assembly combining legislative and judicial functions; now, the state legislatures in New Hampshire and Massachusetts.

gen·er·al de·liv·er·y, n. A post office department in charge of mail that is held until called for by the addressee.

gen·er·al e·lec·tion, n. A national or state election in which all the eligible voters may participate; an election held to choose from the candidates nominated in preliminary elections.

gen·er·al·is·si·mo, jen″èr·a·lis′i·mō″, n. pl. **gen·er·al·is·si·mos.** [It.] The chief commander of several armies joining forces in a campaign; the supreme commanding officer of all armed forces in certain countries.

gen·er·al·ist, jen′èr·a·list, n. One who is knowledgeable in several different fields: opposed to *specialist.*

gen·er·al·i·ty, jen″e·ral′i·tē, n. pl. **gen·er·al·i·ties.** [L.L. *generalitas.*] Something that is general; a statement or principle that is undetailed, unspecific, or vague; the main body, greater part, or majority; the state or quality of being general.

gen·er·al·i·za·tion, jen″èr·a·li·zā′shan, n. The act or process of generalizing; a broad or general concept, statement, or principle derived from generalizing.

gen·er·al·ize, jen′èr·a·līz″, v.t.—**generalized, generalizing.** To make general; to bring into general use; to give a broad rather than a specific character or application to; to avoid making specific or detailed; to induce or formulate, as a general rule or conclusion, from particular facts or instances.—v i. To infer a general principle; to deal or indulge in generalities; *pathol.* to spread, as a disease or condition throughout the system.—**gen·er·al·iz·er,** n.

gen·er·al·ized, jen′èr·a·līzd″, a. Made general; *biol.* of an organism, not requiring a special environment for its existence.

gen·er·al of·fic·er, n. *Milit.* an officer, as a brigadier general, major general, or lieutenant general, ranking above a colonel.

gen·er·al or·der, n. *Milit.* Any order issued from a headquarters, and setting permanent policy for a command; any of the various permanent orders pertaining to the guard duties of a sentry.

gen·er·al part·ner, n. *Law,* a partner with unlimited liability for his company's debts.

gen·er·al prac·ti·tion·er, n. *Med.* a physician who does not confine his practice to a special field of medicine.

gen·er·al-pur·pose, jen′èr·al·pur′pos, a. Useful in several ways; fit for more than one purpose; as, a *general-purpose* encyclopedia.

gen·er·al se·man·tics, n. pl., sing. or pl. in constr. The field of study dealing with signs and symbols and all their meanings, connotations, and ambiguities in relation to human behavior.

gen·er·al·ship, jen′èr·al·ship″, n. The office of a general; military skill of a high commanding officer; wise management or judicious tactics.

gen·er·al staff, n. *Milit.* a group of military leaders, acting over and above the interests of any one service to determine military strategy and policy for a nation; the staff of officers assigned to aid the commanding officer of a division or larger unit in planning and management.

gen·er·al store, n. A retail store, selling merchandise of many kinds, usu. serving a rural region.

gen·er·ate, jen′e·rāt″, v.t.—**generated, generating.** [L. *genero, generatum,* to beget.] To procreate; to cause to be; to bring into existence; to produce, as heat or electricity; to be the stimulus for; as, laws which *generate* goodwill; *geom.* to create, as a line, figure, or plane, by a moving point, line, or figure.—**gen·er·a·tive,** a.—**gen·er·a·tive·ly,** adv.

gen·er·a·tion, jen″e·rā′shan, n. A single geneological succession in natural descent; the average period of time between one succession of children and the next, calculated at 30 years; people who are contemporary, or born and living at approximately the same time; such a group of people having approximately the same age, status, ideas, or problems; the act of generating; *geom.* the creation of a plane, figure, or line by the motion of another line, figure, or point.

gen·er·a·tive cell, *n.* A male or female reproductive cell; a gamete.

gen·er·a·tor, jen′e·rā″tẽr, *n.* [L.] One who generates; something that generates or produces; an apparatus for producing a gas or vapor; a machine by which mechanical energy is converted into electrical energy; a dynamo.

gen·er·a·trix, jen″e·rā′triks, *n. pl.* **gen·-er·a·tri·ces,** jen″ẽr·a·trī′sēz. [L.] *Geom.* a point, line, or figure whose motion gives rise to a line, surface, figure, or solid.

ge·ner·ic, je·ner′ik, *a.* [= Fr. *générique*, < L. *genus* (*gener*-), race, kind.] Pertaining to or characteristic of a genus, kind, or class, esp. a zoological or botanical genus; applicable or referring to all of the individuals forming a group, kind, or class; not registered as a trademark; as, a *generic* name of a drug, distinguished from its trade name. Also **ge·ner·i·cal.—ge·ner·-i·cal·ly,** *adv.*

gen·er·ous, jen′ẽr·us, *a.* [L. *generosus*, of honorable birth, generous, < *genus*, *generis*, birth, extraction, family.] Free and unselfish in giving; munificent; large, ample, or bountiful, as of size or proportions; noble in spirit; magnanimous; of wine, having a rich, full flavor.—**gen·-er·ous·ly,** *adv.*—**gen·er·os·i·ty,** jen″e·ros′i·tē, *n. pl.* **gen·er·os·i·ties.—gen·er·-ous·ness,** *n.*

gen·e·sis, jen′i·sis, *n. pl.* **gen·e·ses.** [Gr. *genesis*, < root *gen*, to beget.] The act of producing or giving origin; creation; origination; beginning; (*cap.*) the first book of the Old Testament.—**ge·nes·ic,** ji·nes′ik, ji·nē′sik, *a.*

gen·et, jen′it, ji′net′, *n.* [O.Fr. *genete* (Fr. *genette*), < Sp. *gineta*; from Ar. *jarnait.*] Any of the small carnivorous quadrupeds constituting the genus *Genetta*, allied to the civet cats.

gen·et, jen′it, *n.* Jennet.

ge·net·ic, je·net′ik, *a.* [< Gr. *genetēs*, a begetter, or *genesis*, generation.] Pertaining to the science of genetics; pertaining to genes; genic; pertaining to the origins or development of something. Also **ge·net·i·cal.—ge·net·i·cal·ly,** *adv.*

ge·net·ics, je·net′iks, *n. pl. but sing. in constr.* The science of the hereditary and evolutionary similarities and differences of related organisms, as produced by the interaction of the genes; the inherited features and characteristics of an organism or group or type of organisms.—**ge·net·i·cist,** je·net′i·sist, *n.* A specialist in the science of genetics.

ge·ne·va, je·nē′va, *n.* [< L. *juniperus*, juniper; *gin* is a contraction of this.] An alcoholic liquor made in the Netherlands.

Ge·ne·va bands, *n. pl.* [From *Geneva*, city in Switzerland.] Two bands or pendant strips of white cloth, worn at the collar as part of clerical dress.

Ge·ne·va Con·ven·tion, *n.* An international agreement dealing with the humane treatment of prisoners of war, wounded and dead combatants, and of civilian war victims, first signed at Geneva, Switzerland in 1864.

Ge·ne·va cross, *n.* A red Greek cross on a white ground, displayed to distinguish ambulances, hospitals, and persons serving the Red Cross society. Also *red cross.*

Ge·ne·va gown, *n.* A loose, full-sleeved black gown often worn by Protestant clergymen, so named from its use by the Swiss Calvinist clergy.

Ge·ne·van, je·nē′van, *a.* Pertaining to Geneva, Switzerland; of or relating to Calvinist doctrine.—*n.* An inhabitant of Geneva; a Calvinist.

gen·ial, jēn′yal, jē′nē·al, *a.* [L. *genialis*, < *genius*, social disposition, genius.] Characterized by kindly warmth of disposition; cordial; sympathetically cheerful; comfortably warm or mild, as a climate; contributing to life and comfort; as, the *genial* sun; marked by or pertaining to genius.—**ge·ni·al·i·ty,** jē′nē·al′i·tē, **gen·ial·ness,** *n.*—**gen·ial·ly,** *adv.*

ge·ni·al, je·nī′al, *a.* [Gr. *geneion*, chin, < *genus*, jaw.] *Anat.* of or pertaining to the chin.

gen·ic, jen′ik, *a. Biol.* of, pertaining to, or resulting from a gene or genes.—**gen·i·cal·ly,** *adv.*

ge·nic·u·late, je·nik′ū·lit, je·nik′ū·lāt″, *a.* [L. *geniculatus*, < *geniculum*, dim. of *genu*, knee.] Having kneelike joints; bent at an angle like the knee. Also **ge·nic·u·lat·ed.—ge·nic·u·late·ly,** *adv.*—**ge·nic·u·la·tion,** je·nik″ū·lā′shan, *n.*

ge·nie, jē′nē, *n. pl.* **ge·nies, ge·ni·i,** jē′nē·ī. [Fr. *génie*, < L. *genius*.] Any demon or spirit, specif. of Islamic mythology. Also *jinn.*

gen·i·pap, jen′i·pap,″ *n.* [From native name.] The edible fruit of a tropical American tree, *Genipa americana*, about the size of an orange and having a winelike flavor; the tree.

gen·i·tal, jen′i·tal, *a.* [L. *genitalis*, < *gignere* (pp. *genitus*), beget, bear.] Pertaining to procreation, or to the sexual organs.

gen·i·ta·li·a, jen″i·tā′lē·a, jen″i·tāl′ya, *n. pl.* [L.] The genitals.—**gen·i·tal·ic,** *a.*

gen·i·tals, jen′i·talz, *n. pl.* The organs of the system of reproduction, esp. the external organs.

gen·i·tive, jen′i·tiv, *a.* [L. *genitivus*, *genetivus*, lit. 'pertaining to generation,' < Gr. *genikos*, generic, < *genos*, race, kind.] *Gram.* pertaining to or indicating origin, source, possession, or the like: applied to a case in declension in Latin and other languages, similar to the possessive in English.—*n.* The genitive case, or a word in that case.—**gen·i·ti·val,** jen″i·tī′val, *a.*

gen·i·tor, jen′i·tẽr, *n.* [L., < *gignere* (pp. *genitus*), beget, bear.] A male parent; a father; a progenitor.

gen·i·to·u·ri·nar·y, jen″i·tō·yur′i·ner″ē, *a. Anat., physiol.* noting or pertaining to the genital and urinary organs.

gen·i·ture, jen′i·chẽr, *n. Astrol.* nativity.

gen·ius, jēn′yus, *n. pl.* **gen·ius·es.** [L., tutelary spirit, taste, inclination, talent, genius, orig. a male generative or creative principle, < *gen-* (as in *gignere*, pp. *genitus*, beget, bear) = Gr. *gen-* (as in *gignesthai*, *genesthai*, be born) = Skt. *jan-*, beget, bear, produce.] An unusual natural intellectual capacity as indicated in original and creative activity; a person who has unusual ability and very high intelligence, esp. one possessing an I.Q. of 140 or above; a natural aptitude for some specific thing; as, to have a *genius* for finance, for cooking, or for making friends; a person who has such an aptitude; a person who distinctively influences for good or evil the conduct, behavior, or destiny of another or others; the distinctive character, spirit, or associations, as of a nation, period, language, or institution. The attending or controlling spirit of a place or institution; in ancient belief, either of two mutually opposed spirits, one good and the other evil, supposed to attend a person throughout his life; pl. **gen·i·i,** jē′nē·ī.

gen·o·cide, jen′o·sīd,″ *n.* [Gr. *genos*, race, and -*cide*.] Deliberate mass murder of a race, people, or minority group.—**gen·-o·ci·dal,** *a.*

Gen·o·ese, jen″ō·ēz′, jen″ō·ēs′, *a.* Of or relating to Genoa, a port city in northwest Italy, or its inhabitants.—*n.* One who lives in or is a native of Genoa.

ge·nome, jē′nōm, *n. Biol.* either of the two sets of chromosomes in a zygote. Also **ge·nom,** jē′nom.

gen·o·type, jen′o·tīp″, *n. Biol.* the sum of the inherited characteristics in an individual; a group or class of organisms with the identical genetic composition; a type species.

gen·re, zhän′re, *Fr.* zhäN′Rɛ, *n.* [Fr. GENDER.] Kind; sort; style; a specific category of artistic or literary accomplishment distinguished by form, technique, and subject matter, as: Heroic characters and a lofty, grandiose style characterize the epic *genre*. *Fine arts,* a painting which portrays scenes of ordinary life; generally, this style of painting.—*a. Fine arts,* of or relating to genre.

gen·ro, gen′rō′, *n. pl.* (*Often cap.*) Japanese elder statesmen.

gens, jenz, *n. pl.* **gen·tes,** jen′tēz. [L., clan, race, people, < *gen*-, beget, produce.] A group of families in ancient Rome claiming descent from a common ancestor and united by a common name and common religious rites; *anthropol.* a tribe or clan, esp. one tracing descent through the male line; a well-defined group of allied organisms.

gent, jent, *n. Slang,* gentleman.

gen·teel, jen·tēl′, *a.* [Fr. *gentil*, < L. *gentilis*, belonging to the same family or nation, not foreign.] Well-bred; refined; free from anything low or vulgar; polished or polite; often, affecting or feigning politeness or delicacy.—**gen·teel·ly,** *adv.*—**gen·teel·-ness,** *n.*

gen·tian, jen′shan, *n.* [L. *gentiana*; said to be named from *Gentius*, an Illyrian king.] Any plant of the large genus *Gentiana*, comprising herbs most often having blue flowers, less often yellow, white, or red, esp. *G. crinita* of eastern North America, the 'fringed gentian,' or *G. lutea,* a yellow-flowered European species; any of various plants resembling the gentian; the root of *G. lutea* or a preparation of it used as a tonic or aid to digestion.

gen·tian vi·o·let, *n. Chem.* a dye used as a biological stain, as an acid-base indicator, and medicinally as a fungicide and bactericide.

gen·tile, jen′tīl, *a.* [L. *gentilis*, belonging to a clan, race, or people, national, L.L. foreign, pagan, heathen, < L. *gens*, clan, race, people. GENS.] (*Often cap.*) Of or pertaining to any people not Jewish, esp. Christians; heathen or pagan; among Mormons, not Mormon. Of or pertaining to a gens, tribe, or nation; *gram.* pertaining to nouns or adjectives expressing race, nationality, or local extraction.—*n.* (*Often cap.*) A person not a Jew, esp. a Christian; among Christians, one neither a Jew nor a Christian; a pagan or heathen; among Mormons, a non-Mormon.

gen·ti·lesse, jen′ti·les″, *n. Archaic,* courtesy; gentle and polite conduct.

gen·til·i·ty, jen·til′i·tē, *n. pl.* **gen·til·i·-ties.** [O.Fr. *gentilite*, gentilism, heathenism, also (with sense from *gentil*) gentle birth, < L. *gentilitas,* clan relationship, L.L. paganism, heathenism, < L. *gentilis.*] Superior refinement or elegance, whether possessed or affected; the condition of being wellborn; people of gentle birth; gentry.

gen·tis·ic ac·id, jen·tis′ik as′id, jen·tiz′ik as′id, *n. Pharm.* a crystalline compound, $(HO)_2C_6H_3COOH$, used primarily as an analgesic and diaphoretic.

gen·tle, jen′tl, *a.*—**gentler, gentlest.** [O.Fr. *gentil,* of good family, noble, excellent (Fr. *gentil,* nice, graceful, pretty), < L. *gentilis.*] Kindly, or amiable, esp. in disposition or manner; mild or moderate; not severe, violent, or loud; as, a *gentle* wind, a *gentle* sound; gradual, as a slope; tame or easily managed, as an animal; of, or characteristic of, good birth or family; wellborn; refined; honorable; courteous or generous; as, *gentle* reader; *archaic*, noble or chivalrous; as, a *gentle* knight.—*n. Archaic*, a person of gentle birth or good family.—*v.t. gentled, gentling.* To make mild or calm; soften; to tame, as a horse.—**gen·tle·ness,** *n.*—**gen·tly,** *adv.*

gen·tle breeze, *n. Meteor*, according to the Beaufort scale, a wind having a velocity of 8 to 12 miles per hour.

gen·tle·folk, jen'tl·fōk″, *n. pl.* Persons of good family and breeding. Also **gen·tle·folks.**

gen·tle·man, jen'tl·man, *n. pl.* **gen·tle·men.** [*Gentle*, that is, wellborn, and *man*; Fr. *gentilhomme.*] A man of good family or good social position; a man of good breeding, politeness, and courtesy; a man whose independent income raises him above a menial occupation or manual labor. *Often pl.* a polite or formal appellation by which men are addressed. A valet; as, a gentleman's *gentleman; Brit.* historically any man above the rank of yeoman, esp. a man without a title who bears a coat of arms.—**gen·tle·man·li·ness,** *n.*—**gen·tle·man·ly,** *a.*

gen·tle·man-at-arms, jen'tl·man·at·ärmz′, *n. pl.* **gen·tle·men-at-arms.** One of forty gentlemen who attend the British sovereign at various ceremonies. Also **gen·tle·man-pen·sion·er.**

gen·tle·men's a·gree·ment, *n.* An agreement which rests solely on the honor of the persons involved, being unenforceable by legal means; an unwritten understanding between persons or groups to exclude certain religious, racial, or nationality groups. Also **gen·tle·man's a·gree·ment.**

gen·tle sex, *n.* The female sex; women.

gen·tle·wom·an, jen'tl·wum″an, *n. pl.* **gen·tle·wom·en.** A woman of good family or good breeding; a woman who serves as personal attendant to a lady of high rank.

Gen·too, jen'tö, *n.* [Anglo-Ind. < Pg. *gentio*, gentile, pagan, applied to the Hindus as contrasted with the Mohammedans, < L. *gentilis.*] *Archaic.* An adherent of the Hindu religion, esp. a Telugu, a member of a Dravidian group in southern India; the language of the Telugus.—*a.*

gen·try, jen'trē, *n.* [M.E.; appar. a var. of *gentrice.*] Wellborn and well-bred people; in England, the class next below the nobility; persons of any particular group: used in humorous or ironic sense.

gen·u·flect, jen'ū·flekt″, *v.i.* [M.L. *genuflectere*, < L. *genu*, knee, and *flectere*, bend.] To bend the knee or knees as in worship; to express servile obedience by kneeling.—**gen·u·flec·tion,** *Brit.* **gen·u·flex·ion,** *n.*—**gen·u·flec·tor,** *n.*

gen·u·ine, jen'ū·in, *a.* [L. *genuinus*, native, natural, authentic, genuine, < *gen-*, beget, produce.] Proceeding from the reputed source or author, as a painting; authentic; not spurious; being truly such, rather than counterfeit or pretended; properly so called; sincere or free from pretense or affectation, as a person; belonging to or proceeding from the original stock, race, or breed; as, a *genuine* Arabian horse.—**gen·u·ine·ly,** *adv.*—**gen·u·ine·ness,** *n.*

ge·nus, jē'nus, *n. pl.* **gen·e·ra, ge·nus·es,** jen'ėr·a. [L. *genus, generis*, a kind, class = Gr. *genos*, race, family; < root *gen*, Skt. *jan*, to beget, the same as in E. *kin, kind.*] A kind, class, or sort; *logic*, a class of a greater extent than a species; *biol.* a category or class of animals and plants marked by certain common characteristics, usu. comprising several species, and forming a subdivision of a family.

ge·o·cen·tric, jē″ō·sen'trik, *a.* [Gr. *gē*, earth, and *kentron*, center.] *Astron.* measured or seen from the earth's center; having

reference to the earth for its center; seen from the earth or evaluated with earthly life as the basis. Also **ge·o·cen·tri·cal.**—**ge·o·cen·tri·cal·ly,** *adv.*

ge·o·chem·is·try, jē″ō·kem'i·strē, *n.* [Gr. *gē*, earth, and E. *chemistry.*] The science dealing with the chemical changes in, and the composition of, the earth's crust.—**ge·o·chem·i·cal,** *a.*—**ge·o·chem·ist,** *n.*

ge·o·chro·nol·o·gy, jē″ō·kro·nol'o·jē, *n.* The earth's chronology as determined by the study of geological data.—**ge·o·chro·nol·o·gist,** *n.*—**ge·o·chron·o·log·ic, ge·o·chron·o·log·i·cal,** jē″ō·kron″o·loj'ik, *a.*

ge·ode, jē'ōd, *n.* [L. *geodes,* < Gr. *geōdēs*, earthlike, < *gē*, earth, and *eidos*, form.] A hollow concretionary or nodular stone frequently lined with crystals; the cavity of this stone; any formation resembling this stone.—**ge·o·dal, ge·od·ic,** jē·ōd'al, jē·od'ik, *a.*

ge·o·des·ic, jē·ō·des'ik, *a.* Of or pertaining to geodesy; pertaining to the extension of theorems of plane geometry to figures drawn on curved surfaces.

ge·o·des·ic dome, *n. Arch.* a hemispherical structure of icosahedral facets, developed in the U.S. by R. Buckminster Fuller.

ge·o·des·ic line, *n.* The shortest line between two fixed points on a sphere or on any curved or otherwise mathematically defined surface. Also *geodesic.*

ge·od·e·sy, jē·od'i·sē, *n.* [Gr. *geodaisia,* < *gē*, earth, and *daiein*, divide.] That branch of applied mathematics which determines the shape and area of large tracts of land, the exact position of geographical points, and the curvature, shape, and dimensions of the earth. Also *geodetics.*—**ge·o·des·ic, ge·o·det·ic,** *a.*—**ge·od·e·sist,** *n.*

ge·o·det·ics, jē″o·det'iks, *n. pl. but sing. in constr.* Geodesy.

ge·o·dy·nam·ics, jē″ō·dī·nam'iks, *n. pl. but sing. in constr.* The science dealing with the natural forces and processes, volcanic or seismic, of the earth's interior and crust.—**ge·o·dy·nam·ic, ge·o·dy·nam·i·cal,** *a.*—**ge·o·dy·nam·i·cist,** *n.*

ge·og·no·sy, jē·og'no·sē, *n.* [Fr. *géognosie,* < Gr. *gē*, earth, and *gnōsis*, knowledge.] That branch of geology which is concerned with the constituent parts of the earth, its envelope of air and water, its crust, and its interior.—**ge·og·nos·tic, ge·og·nos·ti·cal,** jē″og·nos'tik, *a.*—**ge·og·nos·ti·cal·ly,** *adv.*

ge·og·ra·phy, jē·og'ra·fē, *n. pl.* **ge·og·ra·phies.** [Gr. *geōgraphia—gē*, the earth, and *graphē*, description.] The science which treats of the surface of the earth, dealing esp. with such aspects as topography, climate, the ocean, and plant and animal life, and with the political and social characteristics of the various peoples and nations who inhabit the earth; the topographical aspects of the earth or a particular area on the earth; as, the *geography* of South America; a book on the subject of geography.—**ge·o·gra·pher,** jē·og'ra·fėr, *n.* One who is versed in or compiles a treatise on geography.—**ge·o·graph·ic, ge·o·graph·i·cal,** jē″o·graf'ik, *a.*—**ge·o·graph·i·cal·ly,** *adv.*

ge·oid, jē'oid, *n.* [Gr. *geoidēs*, earthlike.] An imaginary surface which coincides with the mean sea level over the ocean and its extension under the continents; the geometric figure formed by this surface.—**ge·oi·dal,** jē·oi'dal, *a.*

ge·ol·o·gize, jē·ol'o·jīz″, *v.i.*—*geologized, geologizing.* To study geology; to make geological investigations.

ge·ol·o·gy, jē·ol'o·jē, *n. pl.* **ge·ol·o·gies.** [N.L. *geologia,* < Gr. *gē*, earth, and *-logia, legein*, speak.] The science that deals with

the physical history and structure of the earth and the physical changes which it has undergone or is still undergoing, esp. as recorded in rocks or rock formations; the geologic features or structure of a given region of the earth or of a celestial body; a treatise on geology.—**ge·o·log·ic, ge·o·log·i·cal,** jē·o·läj'i·kal, *a.*—**ge·o·log·i·cal·ly,** *adv.*—**ge·ol·o·gist,** *n.* (*See Table on next page.*)

ge·o·mag·net·ic, jē″ō·mag·net'ik, *a.* Of or pertaining to the earth's magnetism.—**ge·o·mag·ne·tism,** *n.*—**ge·o·mag·ne·tist,** jē″ō·mag'ne·tist, *n.*

ge·o·man·cy, jē'o·man″sē, *n.* [O.Fr. *geomancie* [Fr. *géomancie*), < M.L. *geomantia* Gr. *gē*, earth, and *manteia*, divination.] Divination determined by the figure created from a handful of earth thrown down at random, or by figures or lines formed by connecting a number of dots jotted down at random.—**ge·o·man·cer,** *n.*—**ge·o·man·tic,** *a.*

ge·om·e·ter, jē·om'i·tėr, *n.* [L. *geometra, geometres,* < Gr. *geometrēs*, land measurer, geometer, < *gē*, earth, and *metron*, measure.] Geometrician; a geometrid moth or its larva.

ge·o·met·ric, jē″o·me'trik, *a.* [Gr. *geometrikos.*] Pertaining to geometry; according to the rules or principles of geometry; done or determined by geometry; characterized by or forming straight lines, triangles, circles, or similar regular forms; as, a *geometric* design.—**ge·o·met·ri·cal,** *a.*—**ge·o·met·ri·cal·ly,** *adv.*

ge·om·e·tri·cian, jē·om″i·trish'an, jē″o·mi·trish'an, *n.* One skilled in geometry.

ge·o·met·ric mean, *n. Math.* the *n*th root of the product of *n* number of positive terms, as: The *geometric mean* of 5 and 45 is the square root of 5×45 ($\sqrt{225}$) or 15.

ge·o·met·ric pro·gres·sion, *n. Math.* a sequence in which the terms increase or decrease by a common ratio, as 2, 4, 8, 16. Also **ge·o·met·ric se·ries.**

ge·om·e·trid, jē·om'i·trid, *n.* Any of the *Geometridae*, a large family of usu. small, delicate, slender-bodied moths with broad wings, whose larvae are commonly called measuringworms or inchworms.—*a.*

ge·om·e·trize, jē·om'i·trīz″, *v.i.*—*geometrized, geometrizing.* To work by geometric methods.—*v.t.* To form geometrically.

ge·om·e·try, jē·om'i·trē, *n. pl.* **ge·om·e·tries.** [Gr. *geōmetria, gē*, the earth, and *metron*, measure—the term being originally equivalent to land measuring or surveying.] That branch of mathematics which treats of the properties, relationships, and measurement of points, lines, angles, surfaces, and solids; any system of geometry which has specific assumptions under which it operates; as, analytic *geometry*; a book or other writing on the subject of geometry.

ge·o·mor·phic, jē″o·mạr'fik, *a.* Of or pertaining to the surface features or form of the earth; having a form similar to that of the earth.

ge·o·mor·phol·o·gy, jē″o·mạr·fol'o·jē, *n.* The science which treats of the origin, development, and characteristics of the surface features of the earth.—**ge·o·mor·pho·log·ic, ge·o·mor·pho·log·i·cal,** jē″o·mär″pha·loj'i·kal, *a.*—**ge·o·mor·phol·o·gist,** *n.*

ge·oph·a·gy, jē·of'a·jē, *n.* [Gr. *gē*, the earth, and *phagō*, to eat.] The practice of eating earthy substances such as chalk or clay. Also **ge·o·pha·gi·a, ge·oph·a·gism,** jē″o·fā'ja, jē″o·fā'jē·a, jē·of'a·jiz″um.—**ge·oph·a·gist,** *n.*

ge·o·phys·ics, jē″ō·fiz'iks, *n. pl. but sing. in constr.* The physics or science of the earth, dealing with the relations between the earth's features and the agencies that produce them, including meteorology,

TABLE OF GEOLOGIC TIME

ERA	PERIOD		NORTH AMERICAN GEOLOGY	BIOLOGICAL FEATURES	TIME IN YEARS
CENOZOIC	Quaternary	(Epoch) Recent Pleistocene	Upwarp of Appalachian system, causing erosive sculpturing of new mountain profile; Rocky Mountains peneplained, then renewed in Cascadian uplift; geosyncline begun in Gulf of Mexico; formation of Basin and Range province, Columbia plateau, Sierra Nevada, California basin, and Coast Ranges	Diversification of mammals and birds; appearance of modern species and man	70,000,000 to Present
CENOZOIC	Tertiary	Pliocene Miocene Oligocene Eocene Paleocene			
MESOZOIC	Cretaceous		Renewed flooding of margins and center of continent, followed by reemergence in present outline; growth, lift, and volcanism of Mesocordilleran geanticline; Rocky Mountain geosyncline later buckled and upthrust in Laramide revolution, forming Rocky Mountain system; Appalachian system thickened and peneplained; Atlantic coast depressed	Large reptiles abruptly dying at end of period; appearance of marsupials and insectivores; deciduous trees in profusion: grass appearing; ammonites and belemnites dying, leaving essentially modern marine invertebrates	135,000,000 to 70,000,000
MESOZOIC	Jurassic		Erosion of Appalachians; arctic flooding of Rocky Mountain geosyncline, later drained by rising, volcanic Mesocordilleran geanticline (Nevadan disturbance); Pacific Coast submerged and volcanic	Age of dinosaurs, flying and marine reptiles; first birds appearing; diversification of small mammals; conifer forests; expansion of modern-appearing marine invertebrates	180,000,000 to 135,000,000
MESOZOIC	Triassic		Erosion and block faulting in new Appalachians; Cordilleran region reorganized into Mesocordilleran geanticline and Rocky Mountain geosyncline; Pacific Coast geosyncline formed	Reptiles becoming dominant; appearance of marine reptiles and dinosaurs; ammonites flourishing; small mammals late in period	225,000,000 to 180,000,000
PALEOZOIC	Permian		Profound, permanent alteration of ancient continent; major uplift, continuing from previous period; Appalachian geosyncline altered to anticlinorium (third generation of Appalachian Mountains); dead-sea evaporites formed in midcontinent; Trans-Pecos Permian basin; new Ouachita disturbance; Cordilleran region submerged; volcanism in north and west; arid climate	Sharp decline of swamp plants, giant insects, and amphibians; reptiles diverse; mammal-like reptiles appearing; ammonites flourishing; many other cephalopods declining; brachiopods declining; trilobites dying out	270,000,000 to 225,000,000
PALEOZOIC	Carboniferous — Pennsylvanian		Ouachita revolution; uplift of Arbuckle mountain system north of Llanoria; emergence of continent at close of period; tropical climate	Giant amphibians and primitive insects and spiders abundant in spore-bearing tree forests; primitive reptiles present at end of period; land snails appearing	330,000,000 to 270,000,000
PALEOZOIC	Carboniferous — Mississippian		Appalachia and Llanoria rising; continued limestone formation in Cordilleran geosyncline from Devonian submergence	Land life diverse; insects appearing; decline of corals; echinoderms and bryozoans expanding	350,000,000 to 330,000,000
PALEOZOIC	Devonian		Early sinking and submergence of Appalachia geosyncline, with heavy sedimentation spreading westward; submergence of Arctic region, spreading southward in Cordilleran geosyncline; Acadian disturbance in Appalachia (second generation of Appalachian Mountains) with volcanism	Decline of trilobites, expansion of brachiopods and corals; appearance of ammonites, amphibians, and primitive trees; sharks and land plants abundant	410,000,000 to 350,000,000
PALEOZOIC	Silurian		Flat continent; Appalachia gradually peneplained; sediments deposited in growing ocean embayments, which later withdrew, leaving a dead sea in northeastern U.S.	Continued dominance of invertebrates; corals and crinoids expanding; terrestrial life at end of period, with small plants and scorpions	440,000,000 to 410,000,000
PALEOZOIC	Ordovician		Greatest submergence, with brief periods of quiet emergence; uplift of Appalachia with geosyncline filling; Taconic disturbance (first generation of Appalachian Mountains)	Appearance of first primitive fish and of corals, crinoids, bryozoans, and clams; dominance of trilobites and cephalopods	500,000,000 to 440,000,000
PALEOZOIC	Cambrian		Appalachian and Cordilleran geosynclines formed between ancient borderlands (Appalachia and Cascadia) and central continental region; Ouachita geosyncline formed between borderland of Llanoria and continent; seas draining away at end of period, leaving low, flat relief	Abundance of fossil-forming life; trilobites and brachiopods common; first mollusks (gastropods); cephalopods at close of period	600,000,000 to 500,000,000
	Precambrian		Formation of Canadian shield; great igneous activity and diastrophism, alternating with quiet periods of sedimentation; glacial conditions in Upper Precambrian	Earliest evidence of life; soft-bodied animals and primitive plants in the ocean; jellyfish, worms, sponges, and algae	Formation of Crust to 600,000,000

oceanography, seismology, volcanology, magnetism, and other related fields.—
ge·o·phys·i·cal, *a.*—**ge·o·phys·i·cist,** *n.*
ge·o·phyte, jē′o·fīt″, *n. Bot.* a perennial plant, the overwintering or surviving buds of which lie underground.
ge·o·pol·i·tics, jē″ō·pol′i·tiks, *n. pl., sing. or pl. in constr.* The study of the influence or application of economic and geographical factors upon the politics of a state; a national policy formulated by the interrelation of geography and politics; a Nazi doctrine of expansionism which combined geographical, historical, racial, economic, and political factors to justify the extension of Germany's borders.—**ge·o·pol·i·tic, ge·o·po·lit·i·cal,** jē″ō·po·lit′i·kal, *a.*—**ge·o·po·lit·i·cal·ly,** *adv.*
ge·o·pon·ic, jē″o·pon′ik, *a.* [Gr. *gē*, the earth, and *ponos*, labor.] Pertaining to agriculture; bucolic; pastoral.—**ge·o·pon·ics,** *n. pl. but sing. in constr.* The art or science of farming.
geor·gette, jar·jet′, *n.* [For *Georgette crêpe*, so called from Mme. *Georgette*, Fr. modiste.] A fine transparent variety of silk crepe.
Geor·gian, jar′jan, *a.* Belonging or relating to the reigns of the first four Georges, kings of Great Britain from 1714 to 1830; the style or character of these periods; belonging or relating to George V of England, or his reign from 1910 to 1936; of or relating to Georgia in the U.S. or in the U.S.S.R.—*n.* A native of Georgia in the U.S., or of Georgia in the U.S.S.R.
geor·gic, jar′jik, *a.* Relating to husbandry.—*n.* A poem on an agricultural topic.
ge·o·strat·e·gy, jē″ō·strat′i·jē, *n.* That division of geopolitics which is concerned with strategy; a group of factors, esp. geographical, political, and strategic, which are characteristic of a specific area.—**ge·o·stra·te·gic,** jē″ō·stra·tē′jik, *a.*—**ge·o·strat·e·gist,** *n.*
ge·o·stroph·ic, jē″ō·strō′fik, *a.* Of or referring to a deflective force caused by the earth's rotation.
ge·o·syn·cline, jē″ō·sin′klīn, *n. Geol.* a synclinal fold which embraces a notable part of the earth's surface. Also *geosynclinal.*—**ge·o·syn·cli·nal,** jē″ō·sin·klīn′al, *a.*
ge·o·tax·is, jē″ō·tak′sis, *n. Biol.* movement of an organism in response to the directional stimulus of gravity.—**ge·o·tac·tic,** *a.*—**ge·o·tac·ti·cal·ly,** *adv.*
ge·o·tec·ton·ic, jē″ō·tek·ton′ik, *a.* Pertaining to the structure of the earth's crust or to the arrangement and form of the materials composing it.
ge·o·ther·mal, jē″ō·thur′mal, *a.* Of or pertaining to the internal heat of the earth. Also **ge·o·ther·mic.**
ge·ot·ro·pism, jē·o′tro·piz″um, *n.* [Gr. *gē*, earth, and *tropos*, a turning.] *Biol.* disposition or tendency to turn or incline gravitationally toward the earth, or in the case of negative *geotropism*, to turn away from the earth.—**ge·o·trop·ic,** jē″ō·trop′ik, *a.*
ge·ra·ni·a·ceous, ji·rā″nē·ā′shus, *a. Bot.* belonging to the geranium family, as the wild flowers of the genus *Geranium* and the cultivated house plant, *Pelargonium hortorum*, having five-petalled flowers and lobed, strongly-scented leaves.
ge·ra·ni·ol, je·rā′nē·al″, je·rā′nē·ōl″, *n.* An unsaturated alcohol, $C_{10}H_{17}OH$, primarily used in soaps and perfumes because of its fragrance.
ge·ra·ni·um, ji·rā′nē·um, *n.* [L., < Gr. *geranion*, crane's-bill, < *geranos*, crane.] Any of the plants of the genus *Geranium*, most of which have pink or purple flowers; a plant of the allied genus *Pelargonium*, of which many species are cultivated for their

showy flowers or their fragrant leaves; a deep, vivid red.
ge·rar·di·a, je·rär′dē·a, *n. Bot.* an herb of the genus *Gerardia*, belonging to the figwort family, and bearing purple, pink, or yellow flowers with distended bases.
ge·ra·tol·o·gy, jer″a·tol′o·jē, *n.* [Gr. *gēras* (*gērat*-), old age.] The study that treats of the decline of life, esp. of those animals threatened with extinction.
ger·bil, jur′bil, *n.* [Fr. *gerbille*, < *gerbo*, the Arabic name.] A small burrowing rodent related to the mouse, usu. found in the sandy parts of Africa and Asia, and popularized as a house pet in the U.S.
ge·rent, jēr′ent, *n.* [L. *gerens* (*gerent*-), ppr. of *gerere*, bear, conduct, manage.] A manager; a ruler.
ger·fal·con, jur′fal″kon, jur′fa″kon, *n.* Gyrfalcon.
ger·i·at·rics, jer″ē·a′triks, *n. pl. but sing. in constr.* The area of medicine which deals with the diseases of old age and the problems and care of aging persons.—**ger·i·at·ric,** *a.*—**ger·i·a·tri·cian, ger·i·at·rist,** jer″ē·a·trish′an, *n.*
germ, jurm, *n.* [Fr. *germe*, < L. *germen*, sprout.] A disease-producing microorganism; a seed; a bud; the earliest rudiment of a living organism; an embryo in its early stages; something that serves as source or seed; as, the *germ* of hate.
ger·man, jur′man, *a.* [O.Fr. Fr. *germain*, < L. *germanus*, german.] Having the same mother and father, or the same grandparents; born of a parental sibling, as a first cousin: used only in combination, as brother-*german*, cousin-*german*.
Ger·man, jur′man, *a.* Pertaining to Germany, its people, or their language.—*n.* One born in Germany or living there; a person of German ancestry; the Indo-European language spoken in Germany, Switzerland, and Austria. (*l.c.*) a social dance similar to a cotillion; a dance party where this dance is done.
ger·man·der, jer·man′dẽr, *n.* [M.L. *germandra*, by corruption < Gr. *khamaidrus*, < *khamai*, on the ground, and *drus*, tree, oak.] Any of the herbs or shrubs constituting the menthaceous genus *Teucrium*, as *T. chamaedrys*, a purple-flowered European species, and *T. canadense*, an American species; a species of speedwell.
ger·mane, jer·mān′, *a.* Significantly related; appropriate; relevant; pertinent.
Ger·man·ic, jer·man′ik, *a.* [L. *Germanicus*.] Of or pertaining to the Germans; German; pertaining to the Teutonic peoples, or to their group of languages; Teutonic.—*n.* A main division of the Indo-European language group, including German, Dutch, English, Flemish, Frisian, Afrikaans, Swedish, Danish, and Norwegian; the linguistic ancestor of these languages.
Ger·man·ism, jur′ma·niz″um, *n.* Characteristic German quality; German modes of thought, action, and the like; attachment to or affectation of what is German; a typical feature of the German language brought into another language.
Ger·man·ist, jur′ma·nist, *n.* One who specializes in the study of German literature, language, and culture.
ger·ma·ni·um, jer·mā′nē·um, *n.* A rare grayish-white metallic element, used in transistors, diodes, infrared optical equipment, and as an ingredient of glass lenses for cameras and microscopes. Sym. Ge, at. no. 32, at. wt. 72.59.
Ger·man mea·sles, *n. pl., sing. or pl. in constr. Med.* an infectious virus disease, less severe than measles, with such symptoms as fever, rash, and sore throat, and potentially damaging to an unborn child if the mother contracts the disease early in her pregnancy. Also *rubella.*

Ger·man shep·herd, *n.* Any of a breed of shepherd dogs marked by intelligence, and often used for police work and as guides for the blind.
Ger·man sil·ver, *n.* A usu. white alloy of copper, zinc, and nickel, used for making drawing instruments and utensils. Also *nickel silver.*
germ cell, *n. Biol.* A cell capable of sexual reproduction; sperm or egg cell.
ger·mi·cide, jur′mi·sīd″, *n.* [E. *germ*, L. *caedo*, I kill.] A substance that destroys germs.—**ger·mi·cid·al,** jur″mi·sīd′al, *a.*
ger·mi·nal, jur′mi·nal, *a.* [N.L. *germinalis*, < L. *germen*. GERM.] Pertaining to or of the nature of a germ or germ cell. *Fig.* in the earliest stage of development; embryonic.
ger·mi·nal disc, *n. Embryol.* A blastodisc; the part of a fertilized egg containing the first visible traces of the embryo proper.
ger·mi·nal ves·i·cle, *n. Embryol.* The nucleus of an ovum before the polar bodies are formed.
ger·mi·nant, jur′mi·nant, *a.* [L. *germinans, germinantis*.] Sprouting; beginning to grow; gradually developing; with the capacity to develop.
ger·mi·nate, jur′mi·nāt″, *v.i.*—germinated, germinating. [L. *germino, germinatum*, to bud, < *germen*.] To begin to develop; to start to grow. *Bot.* to begin to vegetate, as a plant or its seed; to sprout.—*v.t.* To cause to sprout or bud.—**ger·mi·na·tion,** jur″mi·nā′shun, *n.* The act of germinating; the first act of growth by an embryo plant.—**ger·mi·na·tive,** *a.*
germ lay·er, *n. Biol.* any one of the three embryonic cell layers: ectoderm, endoderm, mesoderm.
germ plasm, *n. Biol.* that part of the protoplasm of a cell containing the chromosomes and genes by which hereditary characteristics are transmitted. Also **id·i·o·plasm.**
germ war·fare, *n.* Biological warfare.
ger·on·toc·ra·cy, jer″on·tok′ra·sē, *n. pl.* **ger·on·toc·ra·cies.** [Gr. *gerōn, gerontos*, an old man, and *kratos*, power.] Government conducted by elders; that group of old men making up a governing body.
ger·on·tol·o·gy, jer″on·tol′o·jē, *n.* [Gr. *gerōn*, old man, and *-logy*.] The scientific study of the phenomenon of aging and its problems.—**ger·on·tol·o·gist,** *n.*
ger·ry·man·der, jer′i·man″dẽr, *n.* [From Elbridge *Gerry*, the governor of Massachusetts in 1812 when a district in the state was so formed, and (*sala*)*mander*, with allusion to the shape of the district.] *U.S. politics*, an arbitrary arrangement of the election districts of a state or county made to give one party an unfair advantage in elections.—*v.t.* To subject to a gerrymander, as a state; *fig.* to manipulate unfairly.—**ger·ry·man·der·er,** *n.*
ger·und, jer′und, *n.* [L.L. *gerundium*, < L. *gerere*, bear, conduct, carry on.] *Gram.* In Latin, a form of the verb used as a noun in the oblique cases of the singular; in English, the analogous *-ing* form of a verb used as a noun but retaining certain verbal functions such as being able to take an object or adverbial modifier, as: *Teaching* French is interesting.—**ge·run·di·al,** *a.*
ge·run·dive, je·run′div, *a.* [L.L. *gerundivus*.] *Gram.* resembling a gerund.—*n.* A Latin verbal adjective, of the nature of a future passive participle, with a stem form similar to the gerund, and expressing necessity or fitness; as, *legendus*, 'to be read,' in *liber legendus*, 'a book to be read,' or 'a book that should be read'; an analogous verbal adjective in other languages.—**ger·un·di·val,** jer″un·di′val, *a.*—**ge·run·dive·ly,** *adv.*
ges·so, jes′ō, *n.* [It. < L. *gypsum*. GYPSUM.] A preparation of plaster of Paris and glue used in sculpture, or as a surface for paint-

ing and gilding; a prepared surface made of such a preparation.

gest, geste, jest, *n. Archaic.* A tale, usu. in verse, of adventure or romance; an exploit.

ge·stalt, ge·shtält′, *n.* pl. **ge·stalts, ge··stal·ten,** ge·shtäl′ten. *Psychol.* a configuration, form, or pattern that, as a unified whole or functional unit, has properties which cannot be derived by summation of the separate parts.

Ge·stalt psy·chol·o·gy, *n.* The theory or school of psychology which explains a mental or physiological process as a unified and unanalyzable response to a total situation, and not as a summation of separate responses to the separate stimuli or components of a situation.

Ge·sta·po, ge·stä′pō, *G.* ge·shtä′pō, *n.* The German secret police organized under Hitler during the Nazi regime and known for its brutality.

ges·tate, jes′tät, *v.t.*—**gestated, gestating.** [L. *gestatus,* pp. of *gestare,* carry, freq. of *gerere,* bear.] To carry in the womb during pregnancy; *fig.* to form and gradually mature, as a project, in the mind.—**ges··ta·tion,** je·stä′shan, *n.*

ges·tic, jes′tik, *a.* Pertaining to gestures or motions of the body, esp. in dancing. Also **ges·ti·cal.**

ges·tic·u·late, je·stik′ū·lät″, *v.i.*—**gesticulated, gesticulating.** [L. *gesticulatus,* pp. of *gesticulari* < *gesticulus,* a gesticulation, dim. of *gestus,* bearing, gesture, E. *gest.*] To make or use gestures, esp. in an animated or excited manner.—*v.t.* To express by gestures.—**ges·tic·u·la·tion,** *n.*—**ges·tic··u·la·tive, ges·tic·u·la·to·ry,** *a.*—**ges··tic·u·la·tor,** *n.*

ges·ture, jes′chėr, *n.* [L.L. *gestura,* mode of acting, < L. *gestus,* posture, motion, < *gero, gestum,* to bear, to carry.] A motion or action intended to express an idea or feeling, or to enforce an argument or opinion; movement of the body or limbs; an action done as a token; as, a *gesture* of peace.—*v.t.* —*gestured, gesturing.* To express by gesture. —*v.i.* To make gestures.—**ges·tur·er,** *n.*

ge·sund·heit, ge·zụn′hīt, *interj.* [G., health.] An exclamation wishing good health, esp. to someone who just sneezed.

get, get, *v.t.*—past *got* or archaic *gat,* pp. *got* or *gotten,* ppr. *getting.* [M.E. *geten,* < Scan.: cf. Icel. *geta* = O.E. *-gitan, -gietan* = O.H.G. *-gezzan* (G. *-gessen* in *vergessen,* forget) = Goth. *-gitan,* akin to L. *-hendere* in *prehendere,* seize, take, and to Gr. *chandanein,* hold, contain.] To come into possession of or obtain by effort or contrivance; earn, gain, or win; as, to *get* an award for scholarship; attain or achieve, as reputation; learn, or commit to memory, as lessons in school; ascertain by calculation or experiment; obtain by entreaty or insistence, as permission or a confession; to receive, as a gift; acquire or come to have, as: They *get* skill through practice. Catch or contract, as an illness; receive or suffer, as an injury; receive as punishment, as a thrashing; to seek out and obtain, as a piece of information; succeed in finding, as a thing or person; capture; *colloq.* to corner, as in an argument; to influence or achieve power over; as, to *get* someone to eat; bring into a particular position, situation, or condition; as, to *get* a fire under control; prepare, as a meal; cause, as a person or thing, to be as specified; as, to *get* one's hair cut; to beget, now usu. of animals; to cause an emotional reaction in; as, fear *getting* to a person; *colloq.* to grasp the meaning of; as, to *get* the point of a lecture; *slang,* to perplex or nettle; *colloq.* to kill or to seek vengeance upon. The past participle *got* is used colloquially after *have* suggesting obligation or possession, as: I *have got* a cold; I *have got* to go.—*v.i.* To succeed in

coming, going, or arriving somewhere, usu. followed by *away, in, to, over,* or *through;* as, to *get* home, to *get through* an ordeal; to bring oneself into a particular situation or condition; as, to *get* into a rage, to *get* involved; attain or manage, followed by an infinitive; as, to *get to see* him; *colloq.* to leave at once; as, to *get* out of the house (also *slang,* git; as, git along); *colloq.* to initiate action, followed by a present participle; as, to *get going.*—**get a·cross,** *colloq.* to make a point or be understood.—**get a·long,** to make progress; proceed; advance; to fare in a specified manner; manage; take care of one's needs; to maintain harmonious relations, or agree, as with a person; to move on in years; grow older. Also *get on.*—**get a·round,** to travel extensively; to have many social contacts; to become widely known by going from one to another, as news. To circumvent or outwit; to cajole. Also *get round.*—**get at,** to reach; determine or ascertain; as, to *get* at the heart of the matter; approach in meaning; intend; to undertake or set oneself to; as, to *get* at one's chores; to sway or bribe; as, to *get* at the person in charge.—**get by,** to slip past without notice; to manage to exist or survive despite difficulties; to evade criticism or penalty.—**get e·ven with,** *colloq.* to be revenged.—**get off,** *colloq.* to escape penalty; to leave from; as, to *get off* the train.— **get on,** to get along; to board or mount, as a train or horse.—**get o·ver,** *colloq.* to recover, as from a condition.

get, get, *n.* Offspring; total progeny of an animal, esp. a stallion; *sports,* the return of a difficult shot, as in tennis.

get·a·way, get′a·wā″, *n.* An escape; the start, as of a race.—**get a·way,** *v.i.* To escape; to start, as in a race.—**get a·way with,** *colloq.* to manage to avoid; avoid the consequences of one's behavior.

Geth·sem·a·ne, geth·sem′a·nē, *n.* The garden near Jerusalem where Jesus was betrayed; an occasion or place of suffering.

get·ta·ble, get·a·ble, get′a·bl, *a.* Able to be got or procured; obtainable; available; accessible.

get·ter, get′ėr, *n.* Any person or thing that gets; *electron.* a substance, as barium or any other electropositive metal used to absorb residual gas in a vacuum tube or incandescent lamp; *Canadian,* poisoned bait for exterminating animal pests and vermin.

get-to·geth·er, get′to·geTH″ėr, *n.* A party or meeting, usu. small and informal.

get·up, get-up, get′up″, *n. Colloq.* Style, choice, or arrangement of clothing; one's outfit or costume; general style, appearance, or structure of something, esp. of a book or periodical. Enthusiasm; also **get-up-and-go.**

get up, *v.t.* To prepare, arrange, or organize; work up, as an emotion or feeling; acquire a knowledge of, as a subject; to dress or array, as the person, esp. in costume or unusual or elaborate fashion; produce in a specified manner or style with respect to appearance or externals, as a book.—*v.i.* To arise; rise from bed; raise oneself to a sitting or standing posture; to ascend or mount.

ge·um, jē′um, *n.* A plant of the genus *Geum,* in the rose family, having pinnate leaves, yellow, red, or white flowers, and tiny fruits with persistent spine-like styles. Also *avens.*

gew·gaw, gū′ga, gō′ga, *n.* [Formerly *gugawe, gygawe,* for old *givegove,* a reduplicated form < *give.*] A showy trifle; a pretty thing of little worth; a toy; a bauble.—*a.* Showy, but worthless.—**gew·gawed,** *a.*

gey·ser, gī′zėr, gī′sėr, *n.* [Icel. *geysir,* lit. the gusher, < *geysa,* to gush; allied to E. *gush.*] The name given to springs or natural fountains of hot water and steam characterized by periodic eruptions; the water rising

up in a column. *Brit.* a coiled, gas apparatus for rapid heating of water for the bath, ge′zėr.—**gey·ser·al, gey·ser·ic,** *a.*

gey·ser·ite, gī′ze·rīt″, gī′se·rīt″, *n.* A variety of opaline silica deposited around the orifices of geysers and hot springs.

ghar·ry, gar′ē, *n.* pl. **ghar·ries.** [Anglo-Ind. < Hind. *gārī.*] In India, Pakistan, and Egypt, a cart, carriage, or other wheeled vehicle, esp. a horse-drawn vehicle. Also **ghar·ri.**

ghast, gast, gäst, *a. Archaic,* ghastly.

ghast·ly, gast′lē, gäst′lē, *a.*—**ghastlier, ghastliest.** [M.E. *gastly,* < O.E. *gaestan,* terrify, E. *gast.* GHOST.] Frightful or dreadful; horrible; as, a *ghastly* crime; shocking; as, a *ghastly* mistake; suggestive of the color of a dead person or a ghost; as, a *ghastly* pallor.—*adv.*—**ghast·li·ness,** *n.*

ghat, ghaut, gät, *n.* [Hindi.] In India, a place along a river bank, usu. with a platform and stairs descending to the river, used for landing, washing, sun worship, and social gatherings.

gha·zal, ga·zal, ga·zal′, *n.* [Pers. and Ar. *ghazal.*] A lyric poem, in Urdu, Persian, or Arabic, in which the first two lines rhyme, with a corresponding rhyme in the second line of each succeeding couplet.

ghee, ghi, gē, *n.* [Hind. *ghī.*] In India and Pakistan, a kind of butter made from the milk of cows and buffaloes and clarified by boiling.

gher·kin, gụr′kin, *n.* [D. *agurkje;* < Slavic.] The small, spiny cucumber of the vine *Cucumis anguria,* of the West Indies and southern U.S., used for pickles; the plant yielding this cucumber; any small, immature fruit of a common variety of cucumber, when used for pickling.

ghet·to, get′ō, *n.* pl. **ghet·tos, ghet·toes.** [It.] A city area populated largely by people of a minority group, usu. due to financial or social restrictions imposed by the majority group; formerly, in countries of Europe, a section of a city in which Jews were required to live.

Ghib·el·line, gib′e·lin, gib′e·lēn, *n.* [It. *Ghibellino,* < G. *Waiblingen,* name of an estate belonging to the imperial family.] A member of the imperial and aristocratic party of medieval Italy which favored the German emperors and opposed the papal party known as Guelphs.

ghost, gōst, *n.* [O.E. *gāst* = D. *geest* = G. *geist,* spirit; prob. akin to E. *gast* and *ghastly.*] The soul or spirit of a dead person; a disembodied spirit, esp. one imagined to haunt the living; a specter or apparition; a mere shadow or semblance; as, the *ghost* of a smile; a distant possibility; as, a *ghost* of a chance; a spiritual being; *TV,* a duplicate image, usu. faint and slightly displaced from the main image, due to wave reflection; *opt.* a bright spot or secondary image, as from a defect in lenses. —*v.t.* Ghostwrite; to appear to or haunt.— *v.i.* Ghostwrite; to go about silently, like a ghost.—**give up the ghost,** to die.

ghost dance, *n.* A ritual dance, as that done by certain N. Amer. Indian tribes in the late 19th century, supposed to establish communication with the deceased.

ghost·ly, gōst′lē, *a.*—**ghostlier, ghostliest.** [O.E. *gāstlīc.*] Resembling, or pertaining to a ghost; suggestive of ghosts; spectral.— *adv.*—**ghost·li·ness,** *n.*

ghost town, *n.* A formerly flourishing town, now permanently abandoned.

ghost word, *n.* A word created by error or misunderstanding, never becoming an established part of the language.

ghost writ·er, *n.* A person who writes material that is to be spoken or published as the work of another. Also **ghost-writ·er.** —**ghost·write,** *v.t., v.i.*—past *ghostwrote,* pp. *ghostwritten,* ppr. *ghostwriting.*

ghoul, gōl, n. [Ar. *ghūl*.] An evil demon of Oriental stories, supposed to rob graves and feed on corpses; anyone who robs graves or the unburied dead; one who revels in what is revolting.—**ghoul·ish**, a. —**ghoul·ish·ly**, adv.—**ghoul·ish·ness**, n.

GI, jē′ī′, a. [Orig. < (*g*)alvanized (*i*)ron; later < (*g*)overnment (*i*)ssue.] *Milit.* of, suited to, or characteristic of an enlisted man of the U.S. armed forces; issued by a U.S. Army supply department; adhering or conforming to military regulations.— n. pl. **GI's** or **GIs**. A serviceman or ex-serviceman of the U.S. armed forces, esp. an enlisted man.—*v.t.*—**GI′d**, **GI′ing**. To clean, as barracks, for military inspection.— adv. In a manner conforming to military regulations. Also **G.I.**

gi·ant, jī′ant, n. [O.Fr. *geant*, *jaiant* (Fr. *géant*), < L. *gigas* (*gigant*-), < Gr. *gigas*, (*gigant*-).] An imaginary being of human form but superhuman size and strength; a person or thing of unusually great size; *fig.* one who towers above others or is eminent in endowments, achievements, or importance; as, an intellectual *giant*; *Gr. mythol.* one of a race of beings of more than human size and strength who were subdued by the Olympian gods.—a. Giantlike; of extraordinary size or strength; *fig.* great or eminent above others.—**gi·ant·ess**, jī′an-tis, n. A female giant.

gi·ant·ism, jī′an·tiz″um, n. The state of being gigantic in size. *Pathol.* abnormally great development in size or stature.

gi·ant pow·der, n. A form of dynamite composed of nitroglycerin and kieselguhr.

gi·ant star, n. *Astron.* a star, as Capella or Aldebaran, of great luminosity and mass, with a diameter much greater than the sun's.

gib, gib, n. [Origin obscure.] *Mech.* a thin piece of metal or wood, usu. wedge-shaped, fitted in to adjust a bearing or to hold parts together or in place.—*v.t.*— *gibbed*, *gibbing*. To secure with a gib or gibs.

gib·ber, jib′ėr, gib′ėr, v.i. [Akin to *jabber* and *gabble*, perhaps also to *gibe*.] To speak rapidly and inarticulately; to gabble or jabber; chatter.—n. Inarticulate talk.

gib·be·rel·lic ac·id, jib″e·rel′ik as′id, n. *Biochem.* a crystalline acid, $C_{18}H_{21}O_4$-COOH, derived from gibberellin and used to stimulate plant growth.

gib·ber·el·lin, jib″e·rel′in, n. *Chem.* a plant growth regulator produced by a fungus.

gib·ber·ish, jib′ėr·ish, gib′ėr·ish, n. Rapid and inarticulate talk; unintelligible language; speech or writing using obscure or excessively technical expressions.

gib·bet, jib′it, n. [Fr. *gibet*, O.Fr. *gibbet*; cf. O.Fr. *gibet*, a large stick.] A gallows with a crossbeam projecting from the top, on which notorious criminals were hanged and publically displayed.—*v.t.* To hang on a gibbet or gallows; to execute by so hanging; to hold up to ridicule or scorn.

gib·bon, gib′on, n. Any of various tailless apes of the genus *Hylobates*, of the East Indies and southern Asia, that are small, slender, and long-armed.

gib·bous, gib′us, a. Protuberant; convex; humpbacked. *Astron.* of a heavenly body, so illuminated as to be convex on both margins, as the moon when more than half full but less than full.—**gib·bous·ly**, adv. —**gib·bous·ness**, gib·bos·i·ty, gi·bos′i·tē, n.

gibe, jibe, jīb, v.i.—*gibed*, *gibing*. To utter derisive, sarcastic words; to flout; to jeer.— *v.t.* To taunt; to mock; to deride or sneer at.—n.—**gib·er**, n.—**gib·ing·ly**, adv.

gib·let, jib′lit, n. [O.Fr. *gibelet*, dish of game.] *Usu. pl.* the heart, liver, gizzard, or some other edible part of a fowl, often separated in cooking.

Gi·bral·tar, ji·brȧl′tėr, n. [From *Gibraltar*, the British fortress on the Mediterranean

coast of Spain.] An impregnable stronghold.

Gib·son, gib′son, n. [From the surname *Gibson*.] A martini cocktail made with gin and vermouth, and a small onion as garnish.

gid, gid, n. [< *giddy*.] *Veter. pathol.* a kind of staggers in sheep, caused by infestation of the brain with a larval tapeworm. Also *sturdy*.

gid·dy, gid′ē, a.—*giddier*, *giddiest*. [O.E. *gydig*, insane, < *god*, a god, a heathen deity.] *Pathol.* having a sensation of whirling or reeling about; affected with vertigo; dizzy. Inducing dizziness; inconstant; changeable; flighty; having the head turned; frivolous.—*v.t.*—*giddied*, *giddying*. —**gid·di·ness**, gid′i·nes, n.—**gid·di·ly**, adv.

Gid·e·ons In·ter·na·tion·al, n. A world-wide interdenominational organization of laymen, founded in 1899, which distributes copies of the Bible to motel and hotel rooms.

gift, gift, n. [O.E. *gift*, < *giefan*, to give.] That which is given or bestowed without charge; a present; a donation. The act, right, or power of giving. A natural quality or endowment; a talent.—**gift·ed**, a. Endowed with natural ability or talent.

gig, gig, n. [Origin obscure; perhaps imit.] A light, two-wheeled, one-horse carriage; *naut.* a ship's boat for either rowing or sailing; a long rowboat used chiefly for racing; *jazz*, a temporary professional engagement. *Milit.* a punishment or demerit.—*v.i.*—*gigged*, *gigging*. To ride in a gig.—*v.t. Milit.* To give out a gig; to punish by giving out a gig.

gig, gig, n. [< *fizgig*.] A fish spear; a device commonly with a cluster of four barbless hooks, for dragging through a school of fish in order to hook them through the body. A machine that raises the nap on cloth.— *v.t.*—*gigged*, *gigging*. To spear with a gig. To lift the nap on, as on cloth, with a gig.—*v.i.* To take fish with a gig.

gi·gan·tesque, jī″gan·tesk′, a. Befitting a giant.

gi·gan·tic, jī·gan′tik, a. [L. *giganticus*, < *gigas*, a giant.] Of the size or proportions of a giant; colossal; huge. Also **gi·gan·-te·an**.—**gi·gan·ti·cal·ly**, adv.

gi·gan·tism, jī′gan·tiz″um, n. *Pathol.* excessive growth of the body or parts of the body, most often caused by a malfunction of the pituitary gland; giantism.

gig·gle, gig′l, v.i.—*giggled*, *giggling*. [Imit.] To laugh in a silly or undignified way, as from nervousness or foolishness; to titter. —n.—**gig·gler**, n.—**gig·gle·some**, a.— **gig·gly**, a.—*gigglier*, *giggliest*.

gig·o·lo, jig′o·lō″, zhig′o·lō″, n. pl. **gig·o·los**. [Fr.] A man employed to be a woman's escort or dancing partner; a man who is financially supported by a woman not his wife.

gig·ot, jig′ot, n. [Fr., < O.Fr. *gigue*, the thigh, a fiddle, < O.G. *gige*, G. *geige*, a violin, from its shape.] A leg of mutton; a leg-of-mutton sleeve.

gigue, zhēg, n. [Fr.] A jig or other lively dance, often the concluding movement in a classical suite. Also **gi·ga**.

Gi·la mon·ster, hē′la mon′ster, n. [From the *Gila* River, in Arizona.] A large, venomous lizard, *Heloderma suspectum*, of the southwestern U S., having the skin studded with yellow or orange and black tubercles resembling nail heads.

gil·bert, gil′bėrt, n. [From the English physicist, William *Gilbert*, 1540–1603.] The centimeter-gram-second (cgs) unit of magnetomotive force.

gild, gild, v.t.—*gilded* or *gilt*, *gilding*. [O.E. *gyldan*, < *gold*.] To overlay with gold, either in leaf or powder; to give a golden hue to; to brighten; *fig.* to give a falsely attractive appearance to.—**gild the lil·y**, to

add ornamentation unnecessarily to an already beautiful object.—**gild·ed**, a.— **gild·er**, n.—**gild·ing**, n. The art of a gilder; a thin coating of gold leaf; *fig.* a superficially attractive appearance.

gild, gild, n. Guild.

gild·er, gil′dėr, n. A guilder.

gill, gil, n. [Dan. *giaelle*, Sw. *gäl*, *fisk-gel*, a fish gill; cf. Gael. *gial*, a jaw, a gill.] The respiratory organ of fishes and other animals which obtain oxygen from water; *bot.* the radiating plates on the underside of a mushroom. *Pl.* the flaps of flesh that hang below the beak of a fowl; *colloq.* the flesh under or about a person's chin; as, green around the *gills*.—*v.t.* To catch, as fish, in a gill net by the gills.

gill, ghyll, gil, n. [Icel. *gil*, a ravine.] *Brit. dial.* A ravine; a brook.

gill, jil, n. [O.Fr. *gelle*, a wine measure; akin to *gallon*.] A liquid measure of capacity equal to one-fourth pint. Abbr. *gi.*

gill net, n. A curtainlike net, suspended vertically in the water, with meshes of such size as to catch fish by the gills.

gill slit, n. *Zool.* one of the slitlike openings in the pharynx walls of fishes, through which water is ejected. An embryological opening into the pharynx of mammals, birds, and reptiles.

gil·ly flow·er, gil·li·flow·er, jil′ē·flou″ėr, n. [Corruption of M.E. *gilofre*, < O.Fr. *gilofre*, *girofle* (Fr. *girofle*), clove, < L. *caryophyllum*, < Gr. *karyophyllon*.] Any of various clove-scented flower plants as the wallflower, *Cheiranthus cheiri*, or the common stock, *Matthiola incana*.

Gil·son·ite, gil′so·nīt,′ n. [From S. H. *Gilson*, of Salt Lake City, Utah.] Uintaite. (Trademark.)

gilt, gilt, a. Gilded; golden in color.—n. The gold or other material applied in gilding; gilding.

gilt, gilt, n. A young female hog.

gilt-edged, gilt′ejd′, a. Having the edges gilded, as paper; of the highest order or quality, as securities. Also **gilt-edge**.

gilt·head, gilt′hed″, n. Any of various marine fishes with golden spots or streaks on the head, including the *Sparus auratus*, a percoid food fish found in the Mediterranean.

gim·bals, jim′balz, n. pl. but sing. in constr. [Formerly *gemmal*, *gimmal-ring*, < Fr. *gemelle*, < L. *gemellus*, twin, paired, double, < *geminus*, twin.] *Sometimes sing.* a contrivance consisting of two movable hoops supported on horizontal pivots that allows an object, as a mariner's compass, to suspend or incline freely and thus remain constantly level despite the position of its support. Also **gim·bal ring**.

gim·crack, jim′krak″, n. [Origin uncertain.] A showy, useless trifle; a trivial knicknack; any worthless article or object.—a.— **gim·crack·er·y**, jim′krak″e·rē, n.

gim·let, gim′lit, n. [O.Fr. *guimbelet* (Fr. *gibelet*); < Teut., and akin to E. *wimble*.] A small tool for boring holes, consisting of a steel shaft with a pointed screw at one end and a transverse handle at the other; a cocktail composed of lime juice, sugar, and either gin or vodka.—*v.t.*—*gimleted*, *gimleting*, *gimletted*, *gimletting*. To pierce with or as with a gimlet; to turn round like a gimlet.—a. Piercing.

gim·mick, gim′ik, n. [Origin uncertain.] A crafty or fraudulent device, as one for controlling gambling apparatus; a trick or stratagem; an ingenious expedient or new contrivance; a contrivance, the name of which is unknown or forgotten.

gimp, gimp, n. [Origin uncertain.] A flat trimming of cloth sometimes stiffened with wire, used on garments, furniture, curtains; a coarse glazed thread used to outline designs in lacemaking.

---

ch- chain, G. na*ch*t; **th-** THen, thin; **w-** wig, hw as sound in whig; **z-** zh as in azure, zeal. *Italicized vowel* indicates schwa sound.

gimp, gimp, *n. Slang.* A person who limps; a hobbling gait.—*v.i. Slang,* to limp, hobble.—**gimp·y,** *a.*—**gimpier, gimpiest.**

gin, jin, *n.* [< *engine.*] A machine for separating cotton from its seeds; as, a cotton *gin;* an apparatus for hoisting; a trap or snare for game.—*v.t.*—**ginned, ginning.** To clear, as cotton, of seeds with a gin; to catch or snare in a gin, as game.

gin, jin, *n.* [Abbr. of *geneva.*] A distilled alcoholic liquor made from a mash of rye or other grain and juniper berries; any similarly flavored liquor made from redistilled spirits with aromatics added.

gin, jin, *n. Cards,* gin rummy.—*v.t.*—**ginned, ginning.** To win, as a hand in gin rummy, by having all one's cards in sets.

gin·ger, jin′jẽr, *n.* [O.Fr. *gingibre* (Fr. *gingembre*), < L. *zingiber,* Gr. *zingiberis,* ginger; of Eastern origin.] The pungent, spicy rhizome of any of the reedlike plants of the genus *Zingiber,* used in cooking and medicine; any of these plants, native in the East Indies, but now cultivated in most tropical countries; a light sandy or tawny color. *Colloq.* spiciness or piquancy; spirit or animation.—*v.t.* To treat or flavor with ginger; *colloq.* to impart spiciness or piquancy to; to make spirited or lively.—*a.* Spiced with ginger.

gin·ger ale, *n.* A non-alcoholic, effervescing drink similar to ginger beer, but containing less ginger extract.

gin·ger beer, *n.* A non-alcoholic effervescing drink flavored with ginger.

gin·ger·bread, jin′jẽr·bred, *n.* A plain cake flavored with ginger, and usu. sweetened with molasses; a kind of cookie so flavored, often made in fanciful shapes, and sometimes gilded or frosted; showy ornamentation.—*a.* Showy; gaudy; tawdry.

gin·ger·bread tree, *n.* A tree, *Parinarium macrophyllum,* of western Africa, bearing the gingerbread plum, a large, mealy fruit.

gin·ger·ly, jin′jẽr·lē, *adv.* [Cf. O.Fr. *gensor, gentior,* pretty, orig. compar. of *gent.*] With extreme care or caution; cautiously; warily.—*a.* Cautious or wary.—**gin·ger·li·ness,** *n.*

gin·ger·snap, jin′jẽr·snap″, *n.* A thin, brittle cookie spiced with ginger and molasses.

gin·ger·y, jin′je·rē, *a.* Gingerlike; hot; pungent; spicy; tawny in color.

ging·ham, ging′am, *n.* [Malay *ginggang,* lit. 'striped.'] A cotton fabric woven of dyed yarns, usu. in striped, checked, or plaid patterns.

gin·gi·li, jin′ji·lē, *n.* pl. **gin·gi·lis.** [Hind. *jinjalī,* < Ar. *juljulān.*] The sesame plant or its oil.

gin·gi·val, jin·jī′val, jin′ji·val, *a.* Referring to the gums; *phon.* alveolar.

gin·gi·vi·tis, jin″ji·vī′tis, *n. Pathol.* inflammation of the gum tissues.

gink, gingk, *n.* [Origin obscure.] *Slang.* A person; a fellow, esp. an odd elderly man, often unpleasant and unkempt.

gink·go, gingk′gō, jingk′gō, *n.* pl. **gink·goes.** [Jap. *gingko.*] A large, ornamental, deciduous tree with fan-shaped leaves, *Ginkgo biloba,* native to China, and yielding an edible fruit or nut. Also **ging·ko, maid·en·hair tree.**

gin mill, *n. Slang,* a saloon or bar.

gin rum·my, *n. Cards,* a variation of the card game rummy in which either of the two players may lay down his hand, ending a game, when his unmatched cards total ten or less, or may win a bonus by matching all his cards before melding. Also **gin.**

gin·seng, jin′seng, *n.* [< Chinese.] Either of two plants, *Panax ginseng* of China and Korea, and *P. quinquefolius* of North America, yielding an aromatic root which is extensively used in medicine by the

Chinese; the root itself or a preparation made from it.

gip, jip, *n., v.t.*—**gipped, gipping.** Gyp.

Gip·sy, gip·sy, jip′sē, *n.* pl. **gip·sies.** Gypsy.

gi·raffe, ji·raf′, *Brit.* ji·räf′, *n.* [Fr. *giraffe,* now *girafe,* < Ar. *zarāfah.*] A long-necked, spotted ruminant, *Giraffa camelopardalis,* of Africa, the tallest of existing quadrupeds. (*Cap.*) *astron.* the northern constellation Camelopardalis.

gir·an·dole, jir′an·dōl″, *n.* A radiating and revolving firework; an ornamented candelabra, occasionally with a mirror behind it for light enhancement; a pendent jewel surrounded by smaller jewels or pendants, as an earring; a rotating water jet. Also **gi·ran·do·la,** ji·ran′do·la.

gir·a·sol, jir′a·sôl″, jir′a·sol″, *n.* [Fr. < It. *girasole*—*girare,* to turn, L. *gyrus,* a turn, and L. *sol,* the sun.] A variety of opal showing a reddish color when turned toward the light; Jerusalem artichoke. Also **gir·a·sole.**

gird, gurd, *v.t.*—**girded** or **girt, girding.** [O.E. *gyrdan* = D. *gorden* = G. *gürten* = Icel. *gyrdha,* gird; prob. akin to E. *yard.*] To bind or encircle, as a person's waist, with a belt or girdle; to equip, as with a sword, at the belt; to put on, as armor. *Fig.* to equip oneself for action; to invest or imbue, as with some quality or power. To surround; confine; hem in.

gird·er, gur′dẽr, *n.* A main horizontal supporting member in a floor or other structural work, as a beam of wood, steel, or reinforced concrete, esp. one bearing the ends of joists.

gir·dle, gur′dl, *n.* [O.E. *gyrdel,* < *gyrdan,* to gird; Sw. *gördel,* G. *gürtel.*] That which girds or encloses; an undergarment for the area of the body below the waist, worn by women and sometimes by men to give support and to improve the lines of the figure; a sash or belt; *anat.* the pelvic or pectoral arch. An encirclement of a tree made by removing the bark and cambium. The outer edge of a cut gem, which is held by the setting.

gir·dle, gur′dl, *v.t.*—**girdled, girdling.** To encompass with a belt; to circle. To cut a band, as around a tree or branch, through the bark and cambium.

gir·dler, gurd′lẽr, *n.* One who or that which girdles; a girdle maker; any insect, esp. a beetle, *Oncideres cingulata,* that bores a circular groove through the bark of twigs and stems. Also **twig gir·dler.**

girl, gurl, *n.* [M.E. *gurle, girle,* child; origin obscure.] A child or young person of the female sex; a young unmarried woman. *Colloq.* a woman; a female servant; a sweetheart.—**girl·hood,** *n.*

girl Fri·day, *n.* A female secretary or an executive assistant who is charged with a variety of duties in a business office.

girl friend, *n.* A girl a man regards with particular affection; a sweetheart; a female friend.

girl guide, *n.* A member of an organization of girls in Britain or Canada, the Girl Guides, similar to the Girl Scouts.

girl·ie, girl·y, gur′lē, *a.* Displaying sparsely clad or nude girls; as, a *girlie* magazine.

girl·ish, gur′lish, *a.* Like or pertaining to a girl; befitting a girl.—**girl·ish·ly,** *adv.*—**girl·ish·ness,** *n.*

girl scout, *n.* A member of an organization of girls, Girl Scouts, founded in the U.S. in 1912 by Juliette Low, and aiming to promote in its members good health, good citizenship, knowledge of homemaking, and good character.

Gi·ron·dist, ji·ron′dist, *n.* [Fr.] Member of the moderate Republican party formed in the French Legislative Assembly of 1791, and consisting of the Deputies for the Gironde district and their adherents.

girth, gurth, *n.* [M.E. *girth, gerth,* < Scand.: cf. Icel. *gjördh,* girdle, girth; akin to E. *gird.*] A band or girdle; specif. a band passed under the belly of a horse or other pack animal to secure a saddle or pack on its back; the measure around anything; circumference; compass.—*v.t.* to girdle; encircle; to equip, bind, or fasten with a girth.—*v.i.* To measure a specified amount in girth.

gist, jist, *n.* [O.Fr. *gist* (Fr. *gît*), 3d pers. sing. pres. ind. of *gesir* (Fr. *gésir*), lie, rest, < L. *jacēre,* to lie.] The ground on which a legal action rests; the substance or core of a matter; as, to give one the *gist* of an argument in a few words; the essential part.

git·tern, git′ẽrn, *n.* [O.D. *ghiterne,* L. < *cithara,* Gr. *kithari,* a kind of lyre.] An instrument of the guitar kind strung with wire; a cittern.

give, giv, *v.t.*—**gave, given, giving.** [O.E. *gifan* = Dan. *give,* Icel. *gefa,* D. *geven,* G. *geben,* Goth. *giban,* to give; probably causative from same root as L. *habeo,* to have (whence *habit,* etc.) = to make to have.] To place physically into or within another's grasp; to present as a gift; to donate; to offer; to exchange or trade; to lend; to permit; as, to *give* permission to; to perform; to sacrifice; as, to *give* one's life; to administer; as, to *give* first aid; to endow with a quality; as, to *give* form to a piece of clay; to be the material cause of, as: Food *gives* nourishment. To commit or relinquish; as to *give* oneself totally to one's job; to provide or yield; to impart, transmit, or convey; as, to *give* someone a cold, or to *give* my regards; to offer as entertainment; as, to *give* a party; *slang,* to be concerned about to a stated degree; as, to *give* a darn. To present as a toast; to assign or hand out; to ascribe; to pledge or promise; as, to *give* one's word; to accept or assume, usu. used in the passive voice, as: *Given* the present situation, the answer is clear.—*v.i.* To make gifts; to donate; to yield, as to pressure; to recede; to afford entrance or view.—**give ground,** to yield; to retreat before force. —**give way,** to retreat, to breakdown; to collapse under stress.—**giv·er,** *n.*

give, giv, *n.* The ability or tendency to yield under pressure; resilience; flexibility.

give-and-take, *n.* The process of making mutual concessions; compromise; a friendly exchange of point of view.

give a·way, *v.t.* To give as a present; to hand over, as the bride to the bridegroom, at a wedding; to betray; to divulge, as a secret.

give·a·way, giv′a·wā″, *n.* An accidental disclosure or betrayal; something given free of charge, esp. to promote business or publicity; in television or radio, a program where prizes are given to participants.

give in, *v.i.* To yield; to confess oneself defeated.

giv·en, giv′n, *a.* Bestowed; conferred; admitted; stated; disposed; as, *given* to arguing; assumed, as a fact.

giv·en name, *n.* First name, as distinguished from the surname; Christian name.

give off, *v.t.* To emit; to send forth, as an odor.

give out, *v.i.* To break down; become exhausted, as a supply.—*v.t.* To make known; to distribute.

give up, *v.t.* To surrender; hand over; to abandon all hope; to devote oneself fully to.—*v.i.* To abandon, as a plan, an activity, or a contest.

giz·zard, giz′ẽrd, *n.* [Fr. *gésier,* < L. *gigeria,* pl., entrails of poultry.] The portion of the stomach of birds in which food is digested after leaving the proventriculus; *colloq.* the innards collectively.

gla·bel·la, gla·bel'a, n. pl. **gla·bel·lae.** [N.L., prop. fem. of *glabellus*, smooth.] *Anat.* the flat area of the face between the eyebrows.

gla·brous, glā'brus, a. [L. *glaber*, smooth.] *Biol.* Smooth; having a surface devoid of hair or pubescence.

gla·cé, gla·sā', a. [Fr., pp. of *glacer*, < L. *glaciare*, freeze, < *glacies*, ice.] Frozen; frosted or iced, as cake; candied, as fruit or nuts; finished with a gloss, as kid or silk. —*v.t.*—*glacéed, glacéing.* To coat with icing.

gla·cial, glā'shal, a. [L. *glacialis*, < *glacies*, ice.] Abounding in, consisting of, or cold as ice; characterized by the presence of ice in extensive masses or glaciers; as, the *glacial* epoch or period; a geological epoch, the Pleistocene, during which much of the Northern Hemisphere was covered by great ice sheets; due to or associated with the action of ice or glaciers; bitterly cold; coldly unresponsive; as, a *glacial* manner. *Chem.* having or tending to assume an icelike form, as certain acids.—**gla·cial·ist**, n. A specialist in glacial geology; one who explains geological phenomena by the action of ice—**gla·cial·ly**, adv.

gla·ci·ate, glā'shē·āt", glā'sē·āt", v.i.—*glaciated, glaciating.* To be converted into ice.—*v.t.* To convert into or cover with ice; to act upon by glaciers.—**gla·ci·a·tion**, n. The process or result of glacial action.

gla·cier, glā'shẽr, n. [Fr. < *glace*, ice.] A vast accumulation of ice formed from snow, slowly descending from mountains, as valley *glaciers*, or spreading outward from centers, as continental *glaciers*.

gla·cier the·o·ry, n. *Geol.* the theory attributing important geological changes, as the erosion of valleys, to the action of glaciers during the Ice Age.

gla·ci·ol·o·gy, glā'shē·ol'o·jē, glā"sē·ol'o·jē, n. Any branch of the science of geology dealing with the formation, geographical distribution, movement, or effects of glaciers; the glacial characteristics of a particular country or area.—**gla·ci·ol·o·gist**, n.

gla·cis, glā'sis, glas'is, n. pl. **gla·cis**, **gla·cis·es.** [Fr. orig. 'icy or slippery place,' < *glacer*, freeze, make icy.] A gentle slope; a sloping embankment defending a fortification.

glad, glad, a.—*gladder, gladdest.* [O.E. *glæd* = Icel. *gladhr*, bright, glad, = D. *glad* and G. *glatt*, smooth; akin to L. *glaber*, smooth, hairless.] Cheerful, joyous, or merry; joyful or happy for a special reason; delighted or pleased, with *of, at*, or an inf. or clause; as, *glad* of one's success, *glad* at the news, *glad* to go, *glad* that one has come; characterized by or showing cheerfulness, joy, or pleasure; as, *glad* feelings, looks, smiles, or utterances; attended with or causing joy or pleasure; as, a *glad* occasion, *glad* tidings.—**glad·ly**, adv.—**glad·ness**, n.

glad, glad, n. *Colloq.* a gladiolus.

glad·den, glad'n, v.t. To make glad; to cheer.—*v.i.*

glade, glād, n. [Lit. a light or bright place, a glad place; Icel. *glathr*, bright, glad.] An open area in a wood or forest.

glad hand, n. *Colloq.* a hearty, enthusiastic greeting, often insincere or overly effusive. —**glad-hand**, v.t., v.i.—**glad-hand·er**, n.

glad·i·a·tor, glad'ē·ā"tẽr, n. [L., < *gladius*, a sword.] In the arenas of ancient Rome, a paid combatant, slave, or captive who, armed, fought to the death another person or an animal for the entertainment of the people; a combatant in general; a disputant. —**glad·i·a·to·ri·al**, a.

glad·i·o·lus, glad"ē·ō'lus, n. pl. **glad·i·o·li**, **glad·i·o·lus**, **glad·i·o·lus·es**, glad"ē·ō'li. [L., dim of *gladius*, sword.] Any

plant of the iris family, genus *Gladiolus*, native esp. to South Africa, with erect, swordlike leaves and spikes of brightly-colored flowers. Also **glad·i·o·la.**

glad·i·o·lus, glad"ē·ō'lus, n. pl. **glad·i·o·li**, glad"ē·ō'li. [L., dim. of *gladius*, sword.] *Anat.* the central part of the sternum.

glad·some, glad'som, a. Glad; cheerful or joyous; causing joy.—**glad·some·ly**, adv. —**glad·some·ness**, n.

Glad·stone, glad'stŏn, glad'ston, n. [From W. E. *Gladstone*, 1809–1898, British statesman.] A four-wheeled pleasure carriage with a calash top, two inside seats, and seats for driver and footman. A light traveling bag, opening flat into compartments; also **Glad·stone bag.**

glair, glâr, n. [Fr. *glaire*, < L. *clarus*, clear, the glair of an egg being the clear portion.] The white of an egg used as varnish to preserve paintings, and as a size in gilding; any similar viscous substance. Also **glaire.** —*v.t.* To varnish or smear with glair.— **glair·y**, a.—*glairier, glairiest.* Like glair, or possessing its qualities; covered with glair.

glam·or·ize, **glam·our·ize**, glam'o·rīz", v.t.—*glamorized, glamorizing, glamourized, glamourizing.* To make glamorous, romanticize.—**glam·or·i·za·tion**, **glam·our·i·za·tion**, glam"o·ri·zā'shun, n.— **glam·or·iz·er**, **glam·our·iz·er**, n.

glam·or·ous, **glam·our·ous**, glam'ẽr·us, a. Full of glamor, romantic attraction and excitement, or alluring charm.— **glam·or·ous·ly**, **glam·our·ous·ly**, adv. —**glam·or·ous·ness**, **glam·our·ous·ness**, n.

glam·our, **glam·or**, glam'ẽr, n. [Orig. Sc., corruption of *grammar*.] Excitement and allure; as, the *glamour* of being a film star; fascinating, bewitching, and often illusory charm.

glance, glans, gläns, v.i.—*glanced, glancing.* [M.E. *glaunche, glench*: cf. the earlier *glent*.] To look quickly or briefly; as, to *glance* at or over something; to allude to obliquely or in passing, often by way of censure or satire; to glide off in an oblique direction from an object struck, as a weapon or missile; to dart off or aside; to gleam or flash.—*v.t.* To shoot or hit obliquely. *Archaic*, to direct, as the eye in a glance or brief look; to cast or reflect, as a gleam.

glance, glans, gläns, n. A quick or brief look; a glancing off, as of an object after striking; a stroke in cricket in which the ball is allowed to glance off the bat; an allusion or reference, as in passing; a gleam or flash, as of light.

glance, glans, gläns, n. [G. *glanz*, lit. 'brightness,' 'luster.'] *Mining, mineral.* any of various ores having a luster which indicates their metallic nature.—**glance coal**, any hard, lustrous coal, esp. anthracite.

gland, gland, n. [Fr. *glande*, O.Fr. *glandre*, < L *glandula*, gland, dim. of *glans (gland-)*, acorn.] *Anat.* an organ by which certain constituents are separated from the blood for use in the body or for ejection from it, or by which certain changes are produced in the blood or lymph; any of various organs or structures likened to true glands; as, a lymph *gland*; *bot.* a secreting organ or structure, esp. one on or near a surface.

gland, gland, n. [Origin uncertain.] *Mach.* the cover or adjustable member of a stuffing box, by which the packing is compressed; any of various devices for clamping parts together.

glan·ders, glan'dẽrz, n. pl. but sing. in constr. *Veter. pathol.* a dangerous and contagious disease, chiefly of horses but capable of being transmitted to man, characterized by glandular swelling, nasal

discharge, and lesions of the lungs.— **glan·dered, glan·der·ous**, a.

glan·du·lar, glan'ju·lẽr, a. Consisting of a gland or glands; pertaining to glands. Also **glan·du·lous.**

glans, glanz, n. pl. **glan·des**, glan'dēz. [L., lit. 'acorn.'] *Anat.* the head of the penis, *glans penis*, or of the clitoris, *glans clitoridis.*

glare, glâr, v.i.—*glared, glaring.* [M.E. *glaren* = M.L.G. *glaren*.] To shine with a strong, dazzling light; to be intensely bright in color; to be too ornately or brilliantly ornamented; *fig.* to be obtrusively conspicuous. To glower; to look with a fierce or piercing stare.—*v.t.* To express, as hostility, by a frown or glower.—*n.* A strong, dazzling light; dazzling brilliance of light; shine; showy or dazzling appearance. A fierce or angry look.—**glar·y**, a.— *glarier, glariest.*—**glar·i·ness**, n.

glare, glâr, n. A bright, smooth surface, as of ice.—*a.* Bright and smooth, as ice; glassy. —**glar·y**, a.—*glarier, glariest.*

glar·ing, glâr'ing, a. Emitting or reflecting harshly dazzling or bright light; unpleasantly conspicuous; plainly obvious; flagrant; vulgarly showy; looking with anger or fierceness; staring.—**glar·ing·ly**, adv.—**glar·ing·ness**, n.

glass, glas, gläs, n. [O.E. *glaes*; L.G., D.G., Sw. and Icel. *glas*: Icel. also *gler*; akin to *glisten, glance, glare*.] A hard, brittle, transparent, artificial substance formed by the fusion of siliceous matter such as fine sand, with some alkali; something made of glass; a mirror; a glass vessel filled with running sand for measuring time; a drinking vessel without a handle; the quantity which such a vessel holds; glassware; an optical instrument, such as a lens, spyglass, or telescope; a barometer or thermometer; *pl.* a pair of eyeglasses, spectacles.—*a.* Made of glass; fitted with glass parts; pertaining to glass.—*v.t.* To put in a container of glass; to cover with glass; to equip with glass panes; to scan with an optical instrument; *liter.* to reflect or mirror.

glass block, n. *Construction*, one of the translucent blocks of glass, hollow or solid, usu. with any of several kinds of patterns on the outer surface, used for glazing an open side of a building or for partitioning between rooms. Also **glass brick.**

glass blow·ing, n. An ancient and still practiced art of producing fine glassware and glass ornaments by blowing through a long pipe which holds a blob of molten glass at its end.—**glass blow·er**, n.

glass·ful, glas'ful, gläs'ful, n. pl. **glass·fuls.** As much as a drinking glass will hold.

glass·ine, gla·sēn', n. A glossy, translucent paper resistant to air, water, or oil.

glass·mak·er, glas'mā"kẽr, gläs'mā"kẽr, n. One engaged in making glass or glassware. —**glass·mak·ing**, n.

glass snake, n. A North American snakelike lizard, genus *Ophisaurus*, so called from the brittleness of its tail.

glass·ware, glas'wâr", gläs'wâr", n. Articles made of glass.

glass wool, n. A fluffy, finely-spun glass product widely used for insulating material, filters, and the like.

glass·work, glas'wụrk", gläs'wụrk", n. The manufacture of glass and glassware; the fitting of glass; glazing; articles of glass collectively; glassware; ornamentation made of glass.

glass·works, glas'wụrks", gläs'wụrks", n. pl. usu. sing. in constr. A factory where glass is produced.

glass·wort, glas'wụrt", gläs'wụrt", n. Any of several herbaceous, succulent, leafless plants of the genus *Salicornia*, in the goosefoot family, native in salt water marshes and alkaline regions, whose ashes were once used as a source of soda for making glass. *Salsola kali*, the Russian thistle, a weed.

glass·y, glas′ē, glä′sē, *a.*—**glassier**, **glassiest**. Resembling glass, as in transparency or smoothness; fixed, unintelligent, or expressionless; as, a *glassy* stare; of the nature of glass; vitreous.—*n. pl.* **glass·ies**. A marble used for shooting other marbles.—**glass·i·ly**, *adv.*—**glass·i·ness**, *n.*

Glau·ber's salt, glou′bėrz salt, *n.* [From J. R. *Glauber*, German chemist.] A colorless, crystalline, sodium sulfate, $Na_2SO_4 \cdot 10H_2O$, used mainly in medicine as a cathartic, and in textile dyeing. Also **Glau·ber salt**, **Glau·ber's salts**.

glau·co·ma, glạ·kō′ma, glou·kō′ma, *n.* [Gr. *glaukōma*, < *glaukos*, sea-green.] A disease of the eye characterized by increased intraocular pressure and progressive loss of vision.—**glau·co·ma·tous**, glạ·kō′ma·tus, glạ·kom′a·tus, glou·kō′ma·tus, glou·kom′a·tus, *a.*

glau·cous, glạ′kus, *a.* [L. *glaucus*, < Gr. *glaukos*, bluish-green or sea-green.] Of a sea-green color; light green or bluish green in color; *bot.* covered with a fine bluish or whitish powder or bloom, as a fruit.—**glau·cous·ly**, *adv.*

glaze, glāz, *v.t.*—**glazed**, **glazing**. [M.E. *glasen*, < *glas*, glass.] To furnish or fit with glass, as a window; to produce a vitreous or glossy surface on, as pottery, by coating the ware with the proper materials and then firing in a kiln or by other methods; in general, to cover with a smooth and lustrous coating; give a glassy surface to, as by polishing; *painting*, to cover, as a painted surface, with a thin layer of transparent color.—*v.i.* To become glazed or glassy.—*n.* The vitreous or glossy surface or coating, as on glazed pottery and other ceramics, or the substance or material used to produce such a surface; any smooth, glossy surface or coating or a substance for producing it; a glassy coating of ice; *painting*, a thin layer of transparent color spread over a painted surface. *Cookery*, stock cooked down to a thin paste, for applying to the surface of meats; a substance, as sugar syrup, used to cover or coat a food.—**glaz·er**, *n.* One who or that which glazes.—**glaz·i·ness**, *n.*

gla·zier, glā′zhėr, *n.* [M.E. *glasier*, < *glas*, E. *glass*.] One who fits windows and picture frames with glass.—**gla·zier·y**, glā′zhe·rē, *n.* Glaziers' work.

glaz·ing, glā′zing, *n.* The act of furnishing or fitting with glass; the business of a glazier; glass set, or to be set, in frames; the act of applying a glaze; the glaze applied; the glassy surface or appearance of anything glazed.

gleam, glēm, *n.* [O.E. *glǣm*, a glittering; compare O.E. *glimo*, splendor, Sw. *glimma*, to flash; allied to *glimmer*, *glow*, *glance*.] A beam or flash of light; a ray; a subdued brightness or glow; a small stream of reflected light; a trace; as, a *gleam* of hope. —*v.i.* To shine or radiate softly; to glimmer; to appear briefly and clearly in, or as in, a flash of light.—**gleam·y**, *a.*—**gleamier**, **gleamiest**.

glean, glēn, *v.t.* [Fr. *glener*, < L.L. *glenare*, < W. *glain*, *glan*, clean; cf. O.E. *gilm*, a handful.] To gather, as scattered grain, from a reaped cornfield. *Fig.* to collect slowly and arduously, as data; to pick up here and there; to discover, as news.—*v.i.* To pick up anything slowly or by degrees. —**glean·a·ble**, *a.*—**glean·er**, *n.*

glean·ings, glē′nings, *n. pl.* Things gathered or acquired little by little, or in slow stages.

glebe, glēb, *n.* [Fr. *glèbe*, < L. *gleba*, a clod or lump of earth.] The land belonging to a parish church or ecclesiastical benefice.

glede, glēd, *n.* [O.E. *glida*, the kite, lit.

glider, from its gliding flight.] A bird of prey, the European kite. Also **gled**.

glee, glē, *n.* [O.E. *glēo*, *gliw*, *glig*, music, sport; Icel. *glȳ*, laughter.] Joy; merriment; mirth; gaiety; an unaccompanied musical composition consisting of two or more contrasted movements.—**glee·ful**, *a.* Full of glee; merry; gay, joyous. Also *archaic*, **glee·some**, *a.*

glee club, *n.* A group organized for singing songs.

gleed, glēd, *n. Brit. dial.* a glowing coal.

gleet, glēt, *n.* [O.Fr. *glette*, slime, phlegm; Sc. *glet*, *glit*, phlegm.] A transparent mucuous discharge from the urethra, an effect of gonorrhea; a thin fluid running from a sore.

glen, glen, *n.* [Ir. and Gael. *gleann*, W. *glynn*, a glen.] A secluded narrow valley; a dale; a depression or space between hills.

glen·gar·ry, glen·gar′ē, *n. pl.* **glen·gar·ries**. [From *Glengarry*, valley in Inverness, Scotland.] A Scottish cap with straight sides diminishing in height toward the back, a hollow or crease along the top, and sometimes short ribbon streamers at the back.

gli·a·din, glī′a·din, glī′a·din, *n. Chem.* any prolamin; any simple vegetable protein or globulin found in gluten, the protein of wheat and rye: used in the synthesis of spinal anesthetics and other drug preparations.

glib, glib, *a.*—**glibber**, **glibbest**. [Cf. D. *glibberig*, smooth, slippery; *glibberen*, < L.G. *glippen*, to slide; akin to *glide*.] Fluent; unctuous; having superficial, smooth words always ready; with more ease than sincerity in speech; smooth; slippery.—**glib·ly**, *adv.*—**glib·ness**, *n.*

glide, glīd, *v.i.*—**glided**, **gliding**. [O.E. *glīdan* = D. *glijden* = G. *gleiten*, glide: cf. *glede*.] To move smoothly along, without effort or difficulty, as a skater; to go quietly, stealthily, or unperceived; slip; steal; to pass quietly or imperceptibly, often with *by*, as time or life. *Aeron.* to move in the air, esp. at an easy angle downward, guided by air currents, gravity, or momentum already acquired.—*v.t.* To cause to glide. —*n.* The act of gliding; a gliding movement, as in dancing; *mus.* a slur; *phon.* a brief sound produced in passing from one definite speech sound to another.—**glide path**, **glide slope**, the path taken by an aircraft as it descends to the earth; a directed descent pattern.—**glid·er**, glī′dėr, *n.* One who or that which glides; *aeron.* an aircraft, usu. with no engine, controlled by use of air currents; a moving seat which glides, as opposed to swinging or rocking. —**glid·ing·ly**, *adv.*

glim·mer, glim′ėr, *v.i.* [Freq. of *gleam* = Dan. *glimre*, to glitter; < *glimme*, to gleam; cf. G. *glimmer*, a faint light; *glimmen*, to shine.] To shine faintly; to give a feeble light; to flicker; to appear indistinctly or dimly.—*n.* A faint and unsteady light; a shimmer; a twinkle; a vague perception; an inkling. Also **glim.**—**glim·mer·ing**, *n.* A glimmer; a glimpse.—*a.* Shining feebly; flickering.

glimpse, glimps, *n.* [Formerly *glimse*, from the stem of *gleam*, *glimmer*, etc., the *p* being inserted as in *empty*. Cf. Swiss *glumsen*, to glow; D. *glimpen*, *glinsen*, to sparkle.] A quick, passing view or look; a brief appearance; a slight suggestion or inkling.—*v.t.*—**glimpsed**, **glimpsing**. To get a quick view of.—*v.i.* To look fleetingly or glance, usu. followed by *at*.

glint, glint, *n.* [Of kindred origin with *glimpse*, *glimmer*, *glance*, etc.; cf. Dan. *glimt*, a gleam, *glimte*, to flash.] A flash; gleam; sheen or luster; a faint appearance or suggestion.—*v.i.* To gleam, sparkle, or flash; to dash or dart.—*v.t.* To cause to flash; to reflect.

glis·sade, gli·säd′, gli·sād′, *n.* [Fr. *glissade*; < *glisser*, to glide or slide.] A sliding or gliding down a slope or snowbank without skis. A gliding movement in ballet.—*v.i.*— **glis·sad·er**, *n.*

glis·san·do, gli·sän′dō, *n. pl.* **glis·san·di**, gli·sän′dē. [It. < Fr. *glissant*, ppr. of *glisser*, slide.] *Mus.* A quick, continuous sliding up or down the scale, as on a piano, harp, or trombone; a passage performed in this way.—*a.* Performed with a gliding effect.

glis·ten, glis′en, *v.i.* [O.E. *glisnian*, akin to G. *gleissen*, Icel. *glyssa*, O.G. *glizan*, to shine; same root as *glitter*, *gleam*, etc.] To shine or glow with a luster, as if wet; to sparkle with reflected light.—*n.* Glitter; sparkle.

glit·ter, glit′ėr, *v.i.* [Freq. from stem *glit*, seen in O.E. *glitnian*, to glitter = Sw. *glittra*, Icel. *glitra* (< *glita*, to shine), G. *glitzern*, to shine; akin to *gleam*, *glance*, etc.] To shine with a broken and scattered light; to gleam, sparkle, or glisten; to be showy or brilliant.—*n.* Bright sparkling light; brilliance; luster; splendor; sparkling ornamentation.—**glit·ter·y**, *a.*—**glit·ter·ing·ly**, *adv.*

gloam·ing, glō′ming, *n.* [O.E. *glōmung*, twilight, < *glom*, E. *gloom*.] The twilight; dusk.

gloat, glōt, *v.i.* [Allied to Sw. *glutta*, *glotta*, to look at with prying eyes; G. *glotzen*, to stare.] To contemplate with evil satisfaction; to gaze with admiration, eagerness, or desire.—*n.* The act of gloating; a sensation or reaction of selfish satisfaction.—**gloat·er**, *n.*—**gloat·ing·ly**, *adv.*

glob, glob, *n.* A drop of semi-liquid substance; a rounded lump or mass.

glob·al, glō′bal, *a.* Spherical; globe-shaped; pertaining to the earth; world-wide.—**glob·al·ly**, *adv.*

glo·bate, glō′bāt, *a.* [L. *globatus*.] Shaped like a globe; spherical. Also **glo·bat·ed**, **glo·boid**, **glo·bose**.

globe, glōb, *n.* [L. *globus*, a ball; Fr. *globe*, Sp. and It. *globo*.] The earth, usu. preceded by *the*; a sphere on whose surface is drawn a map or representation of the earth or of the heavens; a spherical solid body; a ball; any of several things somewhat spherical in shape, as a goldfish bowl.

globe·fish, glōb′fish″, *n. pl.* **globe·fish**, **globe·fish·es**. Any of several fishes, esp. those of the family *Tetraodontidae*, remarkable for being able to inflate themselves into a globular form. Also *blowfish*, *puffer*.

globe·flow·er, glōb′flou″ėr, *n. Trollius europaeus*, a European plant with a globular yellow flower; the related American plant.

globe·trot·ter, *n.* One who travels widely over the world.—**globe·trot·ting**, *n.*, *a.*

glo·bin, glō′bin, *n.* [L. *globus*, E. *globe*.] *Biochem.* a protein formed in the decomposition of hemoglobin.

glob·u·lar, glob′ū·lėr, *a.* Spherical; composed of globules; world-wide.—**glob·u·lar·i·ty**, *n.*—**glob·u·lar·ly**, *adv.*

glob·ule, glob′ūl, *n.* [L. *globulus*.] A small particle of matter of a spherical form.

glob·u·lin, glob′ū·lin, *n. Biochem.* any of several simple proteins which are insoluble in water, soluble in dilute solutions of salt, and coagulated by heat; as, gamma *globulin*.

glo·chid·i·ate, glō·kid′ē·it, glō·kid′ē·āt″, *a.* [Gr. *glōchis*, point of an arrow.] *Biol.* Barbed at the tip, as a hair or bristle; bearing barbs.

glock·en·spiel, glok′en·spēl″, glok′en·shpēl′, *n.* [G. < *glocke*, bell, and *spiel*, play.] A musical instrument consisting of a series of metal bars, mounted in a frame or support, and struck with hammers.

glom·er·ate, glom′ėr·it, *a.* Congregated; gathered into a round mass or dense cluster.—**glom·er·a·tion**, glom″e·rā′shan, *n.* The act of glomerating; conglomeration; an aggregate.

glom·er·ule, glom′e·röl″, *n.* [N.L. *glomerulus*, dim. of L. *glomus*, ball (of yarn, thread, etc.).] A compact cluster, as of capillary blood vessels; *bot.* a cyme condensed into a headlike cluster.—**glo·mer·u·lar**, glo·mer′ū·lėr, *a.*

gloom, glöm, *n.* [O.E. *glóm*, gloom, twilight, *glómung*, gloaming.] Obscurity; partial darkness; thick shade; dusk; heaviness, dejection, anger, sullenness; a depressing state of affairs; a dismal prospect.—*v.i.* To appear dimly; to look gloomy, sad, or dismal; to frown.—*v.t.* To make gloomy; to fill with gloom or sadness.—**gloom·ful**, *a.*—**gloom·ful·ly**, *adv.*—**gloom·less**, *a.*

gloom·y, glö′mē, *a.*—**gloomier, gloomiest.** Involved in gloom; imperfectly illuminated; dusky or dark; wearing the aspect of sorrow; dejected; doleful.—**gloom·i·ly**, *adv.*—**gloom·i·ness**, *n.*

glo·ri·fy, glör′i·fī″, *v.t.*—*glorified, glorifying.* [Fr. *glorifier*, < L. *gloria*, glory, and *facio*, to make.] To give or ascribe glory to; to praise; to magnify and honor; to extol; to make glorious; to exalt.—**glo·ri·fi·ca·tion**, glör″i·fi·kā′shan, *n.* The act of glorifying or the state of being glorified.—**glo·ri·fied**, *a.*—**glo·ri·fi·er**, *n.*

glo·ri·ole, glör′ē·öl, *n.* [Fr. < L. *gloriola*.] Aureole; a halo, as in ancient paintings, surrounding the heads of saints.

glo·ri·ous, glör′ē·us, glär′ē·us, *a.* [Fr. *glorieux*, L. *gloriosus*, < *gloria*.] Of exalted excellence and splendor; splendid; noble; illustrious or renowned; celebrated; magnificent or wonderful.—**glo·ri·ous·ly**, *adv.* —**glo·ri·ous·ness**, *n.*

glo·ry, glör′ē, *n. pl.* **glo·ries.** [L. *gloria*, fame, glory; allied to Gr. *kleos*, fame, *kleō*, to celebrate, *klyō*, to hear.] Praise, honor, or distinction accorded by common consent; something assuring fame or praise; thanksgiving expressed in adoration; renown, magnificence, resplendence; a state of greatness or happiness; the blessings of heaven; summit of wordly achievement; aureole; corona.—*v.i. gloried, glorying.* To exult with joy; to rejoice; to be boastful; to take pride in.

gloss, glos, *n.* [Akin to Icel. *glossi*, flame, brightness, *glys*, finery, whence *glysligr*, showy or specious; Sw. *glössa*, to glow; G. *glotzen*, to shine, to glance.] Brightness or luster, esp. from a smooth surface; polish; sheen; as, the *gloss* of silk; a false appearance or representation.—*v.t.* To give gloss or superficial luster to; to make smooth and shining; to give a false appearance to.

gloss, glos, *n.* [L. *glossa*, an obsolete or foreign word that requires explanation, < Gr. *glossa*, the tongue.] An explanation, as a marginal note or interlineation, of the meaning of some word in a text; a remark or comment intended to illustrate some point of difficulty; an interpretation; glossary; annotation.—*v.t.* To render clear by comments; to annotate; to illustrate; to give or render a false interpretation of, usu. with *over*.—*v.i.* Make glosses.

glos·sal, glos′al, *a.* Concerning the tongue.

glos·sa·ry, glos′a·rē, *n. pl.* **glos·sa·ries.** [L.L. *glossarium*.] A dictionary or vocabulary of the technical, dialectical, or obscure words of a specific field or work.—**glos·sar·i·al**, glo·sâr′ē·al, *a.* Connected with or relating to a glossary.—**glos·sa·rist**, *n.* One who compiles a glossary.

gloss·y, glos′ē, *a.*—**glossier, glossiest.** Having a gloss; having a smooth, shining surface; lustrous; specious; seemingly plausible.— **gloss·i·ly**, *adv.*—**gloss·i·ness**, *n.*

glost, glost, *n.* A ceramic glaze used on clay pottery; glazed ware.

glot·tal stop, *n. Phon.* a speech sound, plosive in character, as the sound of *tt* in the word *throttle*.

glot·tis, glot′is, *n. pl.* **glot·tis·es**, **glot·ti·des**, glot′i·dēz″. [Gr. *glōttis*, *glotta*, *glossa*, the tongue.] *Anat.* the opening at the upper part of the windpipe, and between the vocal chords, which, by its dilatation and contraction, contributes to the modulation of the voice.—**glot·tal**, glot′al, *a.* Relating to the glottis.

glove, gluv, *n.* [O.E. *glōf* = Icel. *glōfi*.] A covering for the hand, having a separate sheath for each finger and the thumb; a boxing glove.—*v.t.*—*gloved, gloving.* To cover with or as with a glove; provide with gloves; to serve as a glove for.—**han·dle with kid gloves**, to deal with considerately and tactfully.—**hand in glove**, in close association with; conspiratorial.—**glov·er**, *n.* One who makes or sells gloves.—**glove·less**, *a.*—**glove·like**, *a.*

glove com·part·ment, *n.* A recessed area in an automobile dashboard for retaining small articles.

glow, glō, *v.i.* [O.E. *glōwan* = D. *gloeien* = G. *glühen* = Icel. *glōa*, glow.] To emit bright light and heat without flame; to be incandescent; to shine like something intensely heated; to be lustrously red or brilliant; to be excessively hot; to feel an intense sensation of heat; to burn or be animated with emotion or passion; as, to *glow* with excitement.—*n.* The state of glowing; light such as is emitted by a body heated to luminosity; incandescence; brightness of color; vivid redness; a state of bodily heat; warmth of emotion or passion.—**glow·er**, *n.*

glow·er, glou′ėr, *v.i.* [Origin uncertain: cf. M.E. *gloren*, stare, glare.] To look angrily, with sullen dislike or discontent; scowl.— *n.* A glowering look.—**glow·er·ing·ly**, *adv.*

glow·ing, glō′ing, *a.* Incandescent; brilliantly luminous; rich and warm in coloring; exhibiting the glow of health or excitement; complimentary or favorable; ardent or impassioned.—**glow·ing·ly**, *adv.*

glow lamp, *n.* The vacuum tube in which electrons ionize a gas, emitting an observable glow.

glow·worm, glō′wụrm″, *n.* Any of various luminous insects or insect larvae; a European beetle, *Lampyris noctiluca*, the wingless female of which emits a greenish light from the end of the abdomen.

glox·in·i·a, glok·sin′ē·a, *n.* [N.L. from B.P. *Gloxin*, German botanist.] Any of the tropical American tuberous plants of the genus *Sinningia*, with large bell-shaped flowers in red, white, blue, or purple.

gloze, glōz, *v.t.*—*glozed, glozing.* [O.E. *glose*, a gloss or interpretation.] To justify or minimize, as a crime or error; palliate, usu. with *over*; extenuate.

glu·co·pro·tein, glö″kō·prō′tēn, glö″kō·prō′tē·in, *n.* Glycoprotein.

glu·cose, glö′kōs, *n.* [Fr. *glucose*, perhaps < Gr. *gleucos*, must, sweet new wine, < *glucus*, sweet.] *Chem.* a sugar, $C_6H_{12}O_6$, found in three forms, most commonly as dextrose which occurs in many fruits, animal tissues, and fluids, and is formed by the hydrolysis of carbohydrates; corn syrup, a mixture of dextrose, maltose, and dextrine used in bakeries and for candy-making.

glu·co·side, glö′kō·sīd″, *n.* Glycoside.— **glu·co·sid·ic**, glö″kō·sīd′ik, *a.*—**glu·co·sid·i·cal·ly**, *adv.*

glue, glö, *n.* [O.Fr. *glu*, < L.L. *glutis*, L. *gluten*, *glutinis*, glue; cf. W. *glyd*, viscous matter.] A strong adhesive consisting of impure gelatin, and used for uniting pieces of wood or other materials; any of various other binding preparations.—*v.t.*—*glued,*

gluing. To join or cover with glue or other viscous substance; to hold together, as if by glue; to fix; to rivet.—**glue·y**, *a.*— *gluier, gluiest.*—**glu·er**, *n.*

glum, glum, *a.*—*glummer, glummest.* [Akin to *gloom* and Sc. *gloum*, a frown.] Frowning; sullen.—**glum·ly**, *adv.*—**glum·ness**, *n.*

glu·ma·ceous, glö·mā′shus, *a. Bot.* Glumelike; consisting of or having glumes.

glume, glöm, *n.* [L. *gluma*, hull or husk (of grain), < *glubere*, peel.] *Bot.* one of the characteristic bracts of the inflorescence of grasses.—**glu·mif·er·ous**, glö·mif′er·us, *a.*

glut, glut, *v.t.*—*glutted, glutting.* [M.E. *glouten*, *glotten*: cf. O.Fr. *glout*, *glot*, gluttonous, greedy, *glouton*, glutton, *gloutir*, swallow.] To feed or fill to satiety; sate; to indulge to the utmost; to feed or fill to excess; to surfeit or cloy; to choke up, as a channel; to overstock, as a market.—*v.i.* To eat to satiety.—*n.* The act of glutting, or the state of being glutted; a full supply; a surfeit or excessive supply; *com.* a supply of goods in excess of the demand.

glu·tam·ic ac·id, glö·tam′ik as′id, *n. Biochem.* an amino acid that occurs in all complete proteins, used in the form of monosodium glutamate as a salt substitute and flavor intensifier.

glu·ten, glöt′en, *n.* [L. *gluten*, glue, akin to L.L. *glus*.] The tough, viscid nitrogenous substance which remains when the flour of wheat or other grain is washed with water to remove the starch; the protein in flour and bread.—**glu·ten bread**, bread made from gluten flour.—**glu·ten flour**, wheat flour from which a part of the starch has been removed, thus increasing the proportion of gluten.

glu·ti·nous, glö′ti·nus, *a.* [L. *glutinosus*, < *gluten*, glue.] Of the nature of glue; gluey; viscid; sticky.—**glu·ti·nos·i·ty**, glu·ti·nous·ness, glöt″i·nos′i·tē, *n.*—**glu·ti·nous·ly**, *adv.*

glut·ton, glut′n, *n.* [Fr. *glouton*, < L. *gluto*, *glutto*, a glutton, < *glutio*, to swallow.] One who indulges to excess in eating; a gormandizer; one who has an extraordinary capacity for something; as, a *glutton* for punishment. A wolverine of Northern Europe and Asia yielding a valuable fur.

glut·ton·ous, glut′n·us, *a.* Given to excessive eating; greedy.—**glut·ton·ous·ly**, *adv.*—**glut·ton·y**, *n.* Excess in eating or drinking.

gly·cer·ic, gli·ser′ik, glis′ėr·ik, *a.* Pertaining to, or derived from glycerin; as, *glyceric* acid, an acid obtained by the oxidation of glycerin.

glyc·er·ide, glis′e·rīd″, glis′ėr·id, *n. Chem.* any one of a group of esters of glycerol plus fatty acids, used mainly as plasticizers.— **glyc·er·id·ic**, glis″e·rid′ik, *a.*

glyc·er·in, glis′ėr·in, *n.* [Fr. *glycérine*, < Gr. *glyceros*, sweet.] *Chem.* glycerol. Also **glyc·er·ine**, glis′ėr·in, glis′e·rēn″, glis″e·rēn.—**glyc·er·in·ate**, glis′ėr·i·nāt″, *v.t.*— *glycerinated, glycerinating.* To mix or treat with glycerin.—**glyc·er·i·na·tion**, *n.*

glyc·er·ol, glis′e·röl″, glis′e·rol″, *n. Chem.* an odorless, colorless, syrupy, sweet-tasting liquid compound, $C_3H_5(OH)_3$, of the alcohol class, obtained by saponification of fats and oils: used in manufacturing alkyd resins and cellophane, and as a solvent and plasticizer; in very pure, nitrated form it is known as dynamite. Also *glycerin.*

glyc·er·yl, glis′ėr·il, *n. Chem.* the trivalent radical, C_3H_5, in glycerin and the glycerides.

gly·cine, glī′sēn, glī·sēn″, *n. Chem.* the simple amino acid, NH_2CH_2COOH, colorless, sweet, and crystalline: used chiefly in biochemical research, medicine, and organic synthesis.

gly·co·gen, glī′ko·jen, n. [Gr. glycys, sweet.] Chem. a white, amorphous, tasteless storage form of carbohydrate found mainly in the liver and muscles.

gly·co·gen·e·sis, glī″ko·jen′i·sis, n. Biochem. the transformation of glucose or other sugars in the body into glycogen.

gly·col, glī′kŏl, glī′kạl, glī′kol, n. [(Glyc)erin and alcoh(ol).] Chem. ethylene glycol; any of a group of alcohols of a similar type.— **gly·col·ic**, **gly·col·lic**, glī·kol′ik, a.

gly·col·ic ac·id, n. Chem. a crystalline, colorless compound, CH₂OHCOOH, obtained by oxidation of glycol, used in leather and textile dyeing. Also hydroxyacetic acid.

gly·col·y·sis, glī·kol′i·sis, n. pl. **gly·col·y·ses**. Biochem. the breakdown of carbohydrates by enzymes in a living organism.— **gly·co·lyt·ic**, glī″ko·lit′ik, a.— **gly·co·lyt·i·cal·ly**, adv.

gly·co·pro·tein, glī″kŏ·prō′tēn, glī″kŏ·prō′tē·in, n. Biochem. any of a group of conjugated proteins containing a protein plus a carbohydrate, as mucin. Also glucoprotein.

gly·co·side, glī′ko·sīd″, n. Chem. any of a group of organic compounds found abundantly in plants, which hydrolyze into sugars and other organic substances.— **gly·co·sid·ic**, glī″ko·sid′ik, a.

glyph, glif, n. [Gr. glyphē, carving, < glyphō, to carve.] Arch. an ornamental cavity or channel, esp. a vertical one in a Doric frieze. Sculp. a figure either sculptured or incised. Archaeol. A pictorial symbol; a hieroglyph.

gly·phog·ra·phy, glī·fog′ra·fē, n. [Gr. glyphē, carving.] An electrotype process by which a plate with a raised surface suitable for printing is made from an engraved plate.— **glyph·o·graph**, glif′o·graf″, glif′o·gräf″, n.— **gly·phog·ra·pher**, n.— **glyph·o·graph·ic**, glif″o·graf′ik, a.

glyp·tic, glip′tik, a. [Gr. glyptikos, < glyphein, carve.] Of or pertaining to carving or engraving on precious gems, or similar stones.—n. The art of carving or engraving, esp. on precious gems or related stones. Also **glyp·tics**, **glyp·tog·ra·phy**, glip·tog′ra·fē.

glyp·to·dont, glip′to·dont″, n. [N.L. < Gr. glyptos, and odoys, odont, tooth.] Paleon. an extinct armadillolike mammal of the genus Glyptodon, of the Pleistocene epoch.—a.

G-man, jē′man″, n. pl. **G-men**. A nickname for a special agent of the Federal Bureau of Investigation, a division of the U.S. Department of Justice.

gnarl, närl, n. [Back formation from gnarled.] A protuberance on the outside of a tree; a knot.—v.t. To twist or make twisted.— **gnarled**, närld, a. Knotty; cross-grained; bent; rugged.— **gnarl·y**, när′lē, a.—gnarlier, gnarliest.

gnash, nash, v.t. [Var. of earliest gnast: cf. Icel. gnastan, a gnashing.] To strike or grind together, as the teeth, esp. in rage or pain; to strike or grind the teeth upon; bite with grinding teeth.—v.i. To strike or grind teeth together.—n.— **gnash·ing·ly**, adv.

gnat, nat, n. [O.E. gnæt.] Any of various small dipterous insects, as the black fly of northern U.S. and Canada; any of certain small biting insects; a midge.

gnat·catch·er, nat′kach″ẽr, n. Any of various small, American, insectivorous birds of the genus Polioptila.

gnath·ic, nath′ik, a. [Gr. gnathos, jaw.] Pertaining to the jaw or jaws. Also **gnath·al**.

gnaw, nạ, v.t.—past gnawed, pp. gnawed, gnawn, ppr. gnawing. [O.E. gnagan = G. nagen = Icel. gnaga, gnaw.] To wear away or remove by persistent biting; to corrode; to bite persistently; to fret or torment by repeated annoyance.—v.i. To bite persistently; to cause corrosion; to produce an effect, as of corrosion; to produce pain or worry.— **gnaw·er**, n.

gnaw·ing, nạ′ing, n. The act of one who or that which gnaws; often pl. persistent pain; as, the gnawing of hunger.— **gnaw·ing·ly**, adv.

gneiss, nīs, n. [G.] A metamorphic rock similar to granite, but having a foliated arrangement of the constituent elements, esp. of the mica; any of a group of hard crystalline rocks containing feldspar.— **gneiss·ic**, **gneiss·ose**, a. Pertaining to, of the nature of, or resembling gneiss.— **gneiss·oid**, nī′soid, a. Resembling gneiss, as in structure.

gnome, nōm, n. [Gr. gnome, < gnōmē, intelligence.] An imaginary dwarfed and misshapen human being, supposedly inhabiting the subterranean parts of the earth, and guarding mines, esp. those of precious metals; a kind of goblin; an elemental spirit; any small misshapen person.

gnome, nōm, nō′mē, n. [Gr. gnōmē, a maxim.] A short statement of a proverbial truth; a maxim; a saw; an aphorism.— **gno·mic**, **gno·mi·cal**, a.

gno·mon, nō′mon, n. [L. < Gr. gnōmōn, one who knows, a judge, an indicator, < gignōskein, know.] An object which serves to indicate the hour of the day by casting its shadow upon a marked surface, esp. the vertical triangular plate of a sundial, geom. the part of a parallelogram which remains after a similar and smaller parallelogram has been taken away from one of its corners.— **gno·mon·ic**, **gno·mon·i·cal**, nō·mon′ik, a.

gno·sis, nō′sis, n. [N.L. < Gr. gnōsis, < gignōskein, know.] Knowledge; esp. a special knowledge of spiritual things; in relation to the ancient Gnostics, such knowledge as is divinely revealed or is attained through faith.

gnos·tic, nos′tik, a. [Gr. gnōstikos, < gignōskein, know.] Pertaining to knowledge; possessing knowledge, esp. esoteric knowledge of spiritual things; (cap.) pertaining to or characteristic of the Gnostics.—n. (Cap.) a member of any of certain sects among the early Christians who claimed to have superior knowledge of spiritual things, and who explained the world as created by power or agencies arising as emanations from the Godhead.— **Gnos·ti·cism**, n. The doctrines of the Gnostics.

gnu, nö, nū, n. pl. **gnu**, **gnus**. [Kafir nqu.] Any of several large African antelopes constituting the genus Connochaetes, with an oxlike head, curved horns, and a long, flowing tail. Also wildebeest.

go, gō, v.i.—past went, pp. gone, ppr. going. [O.E. gān = D. gaan = M.L.G. gān = O.H.G. gān, gēn, G. gehen, go.] To move, pass along, travel, proceed, or progress; to proceed toward a particular place; take a specified direction; as, to go due west; to move or pass away or out; depart; to continue, or be habitually, in a particular circumstance; as, to go in rags; to proceed according to; as, to go by the rules; to keep or be in motion, act, or function satisfactorily; act or operate with sound, as a bell or gun; to maintain an action; to pass or elapse, as time; to circulate, pass, or be valid; to be admissible or satisfactory; as, anything goes; to be known; as, to go under an alias; to have a general course, tendency, or character; compare; as, a good price as prices go; to harmonize or be compatible; as, colors that go well together; to turn out or result; as: How did the match go? To prove successful; to begin or come into action; as: Here goes! To pass, as by sale; to be given up or dispensed with; to be lost, come to an end, be consumed; to fail, lose strength, wear away or out; to die; to give way, as under pressure; to resort or have recourse; as, to go to court over a dispute; to carry an action to or beyond a given point; as, to go as high as ten dollars; to be capable of fitting in or around, or of being divided or contained; as, a book that will go into one's pocket, or a quantity which goes into twelve three times. To belong, as in a place, as: This book goes on the top shelf. To pass, be awarded, or transferred to a particular recipient, as: First prize goes to a dark horse. To be applied or appropriated, as: All the money goes for medicine. To contribute to a result; as, the items which go to make up a total; to conduce or tend, as: That just goes to show you. To reach or extend, in one direction or from one point to another; open into or lead to, as: Does that door go to the kitchen? To pass into a particular condition; as, to go to ruin; become; as, to go mad; to happen or occur, followed by on, as: What goes on here? To put oneself to; as to go to great lengths. Colloq. to have authority, as: What he says goes. To be worded, as a phrase, or composed, as a tune, in a certain way, as: How does that song go? To start or depart, used imperatively as an order or signal, as at the start of a race. To proceed on impulse, with determination, or quickly, used to intensify the verb which follows, as: He goes and spoils the plans. To be about to, intending, or destined to do something, used in the progressive followed by an infinitive, as: It is going to rain.—v.t. To go or proceed on, along, or through; as, going my way; to go to the extent of, or venture as far as. Colloq. To endure or tolerate; to risk, wager, or offer; as, to go five dollars on a race; to have a desire for; find enjoyable; to take over the responsibility for or function of; as, to go bail for someone. To yield, total, or measure; as of produce or crops, to go five pounds apiece.— **go a·bout**, to change the course of a vessel by wearing or tacking; to busy oneself with.— **go af·ter**, to try for; pursue; hunt for.— **go at**, to assail; to attack; to set about vigorously.— **go for**, to be taken or valued as; to attempt to obtain; to attack or assail; to prefer; to have an affinity for or be attracted by.— **go in for**, to make one's particular interest or amusement; as, to go in for stamp collecting.— **go off**, explode or burst, as fireworks; to happen or occur. —**go out**, to become outmoded or obsolete; to cease to work or operate, as a light; to take part in social activity; to date; to participate in a strike; to feel compassion, as: My heart goes out to her. To be a contender; as, to go out for the team.— **go o·ver**, to look over; to reexamine; to study again; to rehearse; to switch opinion or allegiance; to prove successful.— **go un·der**, to be submerged or overwhelmed; to succumb; to be ruined, as an enterprise.— **go up**, to rise or ascend; to advance or increase, as costs or values.— **go with**, to accompany; associate with; to socialize with or date; to harmonize with, as colors or styles.— **to go**, unexpired, remaining; as, 15 minutes to go; to be taken out and consumed elsewhere, as restaurant food.

go, gō, n. pl. **goes**. The act of going; as, the come and go of the seasons. Colloq. energy, spirit, or animation, as: That horse has lots of go. Colloq. a proceeding, turn of affairs, or state of things; a turn, chance, or attempt at something; something that proves successful; as, to make a go of a venture; a compact, or something fully agreed upon, as: It's a go. Colloq. the fashion, style, or rage.—a. Ready, esp. of rockets ready for launch, as: All systems are go.— **on the go**, *colloq.* constantly going; busy.—**no go**, *colloq.* of no use; futile.

go, gō, *n.* A Japanese game played by two players with black and white stones on a board marked in squares. Also **I-go**.

goad, gōd, *n.* [O.E. *gād*, a point of a weapon, a goad.] A pointed instrument, sometimes electrified, used to urge animals forward; anything that stimulates.—*v.t.* To drive with a goad; to incite, spur, or prod.

go-a·head, gō′a·hed″, *a.* Signifying permission to advance; moving ahead; making progress; forward-looking or enterprising; as, a *go-ahead* merchant.—*n.* Permission or notice to advance, as: The contractor received the *go-ahead* to begin building.

goal, gōl, *n.* [Fr. *gaule*, a pole, a word of Germanic origin, < Goth. *walus*, Fris. *walu*, Icel. *völr*, staff, rod.] The point set as the end of a race; an end toward which one directs his exertions; an aim or objective; in various games, the area, space, or object into which the players attempt to place the ball or puck; the act of scoring points in this way; the score which is made in this way.—*v.i.*

goal·keep·er, gōl′kē″pér, *n. Sports*, a player whose function is to guard the goal. Also **goal·ie**.

Go·a pow·der, gō′a pou′dér, *n.* [From *Goa*, a district in India.] A bitter powder extracted from a Brazilian tree and used for medicinal purposes.

goat, gōt, *n.* [O.E. *gāt* = D. *geit* = G. *geiss* = Icel. *geit* = Goth. *gaits*, goat; akin to L. *haedus*, kid.] Any animal of the genus *Capra*, family *Bovidae*, comprising various agile, hollow-horned ruminants closely related to the sheep, found native in rocky and mountainous regions of the Old World, and including domesticated forms common throughout the world; any of various allied animals, as *Oreamnos montanus*, Rocky Mountain goat, a ruminant of western North America; *fig.* a lustful man; *slang*, one who serves as a scapegoat, or suffers in the place of others. (*Cap.*) the zodiacal constellation or sign Capricorn.—**get one's goat**, *slang*, to disgust, anger, or annoy a person.—**goat·ish**, **goat·like**, *a.*

goat an·te·lope, *n.* Any of several mammals of the family *Rupicaprinae*, including the chamois, goral, and Rocky Mountain goat, which are related to the goats and have some characteristics of antelopes.

goat·ee, gō·tē′, *n.* A man's small, neat beard that is trimmed to a point and has no side whiskers.—**goat·eed**, *a.*

goat·fish, gōt′fish″, *n.* pl. **goat·fish**, **goat·fish·es**. Any of certain usu. red or gold-colored mullets of the family *Mullidae*, characterized by barbels under the jaw.

goat·herd, gōt′hûrd″, *n.* One whose occupation is to tend goats.

goats·beard, gōts′bērd″, *n.* A plant of the genus *Tragopogon*, as *T. porrifolius*, in the composite family, the vegetable salsify, also called vegetable oyster or oyster plant; an herb, *Aruncus sylvester*, in the rose family, with panicles of white flowers.

goat·skin, gōt′skin″, *n.* The skin or hide of a goat, or leather made from it.

goat·suck·er, gōt′suk″ér, *n.* Any of the wide-mouthed, chiefly nocturnal or crepuscular birds of the family *Caprimulgidae*, as the American whippoorwill and nighthawk, which feed on insects while in flight: once thought to suck the milk of goats.

gob, gob, *n. Colloq.* a sailor of the U.S. navy; a mass or lump. Pl., *colloq.* a great amount; a large quantity; as, *gobs* of whipped cream.

gob·ble, gob′l, *v.t.*—*gobbled*, *gobbling.* [A freq. < Fr. *gober*, to swallow.] To swallow in large pieces; to swallow hastily; *slang*, to grasp or seize eagerly, often followed by *up.* —*v.i.* To eat hurriedly; to make a noise in the throat, as by a male turkey.—*n.* A noise made in the throat, as that of a male turkey. —**gob·bler**, gob′lér, *n.* A male turkey.

gob·ble·dy·gook, **gob·ble·de·gook**, gob′l·dē·guk″, *n. Slang.* Pretentious, redundant, and obscure speech or writing; jargon.

Gob·e·lin, gob′e·lin, *Fr.* gȧ·blaɴ′, *n.* [From the *Gobelin* establishment in Paris where tapestry is made, orig. belonging to a family of dyers of that name.] A rich tapestry with ornate scenic or floral designs, originated in the 15th century; an imitation fabric made by machine.—*a.*— **Gob·e·lin stitch**, a vertical or slanting grounding stitch used in canvas work or needlepoint.

go-be·tween, gō′bi·twēn″, *n.* One who serves as a broker or agent between persons or groups of people; a mediator; an intermediary.

gob·let, gob′lit, *n.* [Fr. *gobelet*, dim. of O.Fr. *gobel*, a drinking glass, < L.L. *gobellus*, < L. *cupa*, a tub, a cask.] A drinking glass having a stem and a base; *archaic*, a kind of cup or drinking vessel without handles, sometimes having a cover.

gob·lin, gob′lin, *n.* [Fr. *gobelin*, L. *gobelinus*, Gr. *kobalos*, a kind of malignant being.] An evil or mischievous sprite, usu. thought to be extremely ugly.

go·bo, gō′bō, *n.* pl. **go·bos**, **go·boes**. *Movies, TV*, a dark screen used to create shadows and to shield the camera lens from direct light; an acoustic device to shield a microphone from unwanted sound.

go·by, gō′bē″, *n.* pl. **go·by**, **go·bies**. [L. *gobius*, *cobius*, < Gr. *kōbios*, kind of fish.] Any member of the *Gobiidae*, a family of small marine and fresh-water fishes, often having the ventral fins united to form a suctorial disk by which it clings to rocks.

go·cart, gō′kärt″, *n.* A simple framework device with casters or small wheels, designed to teach a small child to walk; a chairlike carriage or stroller for a small child; a handcart. A small, gasoline-powered racing vehicle consisting of a frame on small wheels, used for racing or recreational purposes; also **go·kart.**

God, god, *n.* [O.E. *god* = D. *god*, Icel. *goth*, *guth*, Dan. and Sw. *gud*, Goth. *guth*, G. *gott*; God; root unknown; not connected with *good.*] *Monotheism.* Creator and ruler of the universe; eternal, infinite Spirit; the Supreme Being, almighty and omniscient, worshipped by men; *O.T.* Jehovah.

god, god, *n.* A person, spirit, or object, worshipped and adored, to whom supernatural powers are attributed; a deity in mythology; an idol; a person possessing supreme authority; a person, as an athlete or other notable, who is publicly admired to a degree approaching worship; a person or thing valued above all.—*v.t.*—*godded*, *godding.* To make an idol of; deify.

god·child, god′chīld″, *n.* pl. **god·chil·dren.** A child for whom one has been sponsor at a baptism or at a corresponding ceremony of another faith.—**god·daugh·ter**, *n.*—**god·son**, *n.*

god·dess, god′is, *n.* A female deity; a woman who is adored; a very beautiful young lady.

go-dev·il, gō′dev′il, *n. Rail.* a small, open car propelled on the tracks either by hand or by gasoline. A sled used to transport tree trunks, ore, or rocks; an apparatus that is forced through a pipeline to remove obstructions; an explosive dropped into a well, esp. an oil well.

god·fa·ther, god′fä″тHér, *n.* A man who sponsors at baptism a child not his own progeny.

God-fear·ing, god′fēr″ing, *a.* Having a reverential fear of God; (*sometimes l.c.*) pious, devout.

god·for·sak·en, god′fér·sā″ken, god″fér·sā′ken, *a.* (*Sometimes cap.*) Forlorn, desolate, very remote; as, a *godforsaken* place; wretched or miserable; arousing pity.

god·head, god′hed″, *n.* [*God*, and suffix -*head*, same as -*hood.*] Godship; deity; divinity; divine nature or essence.—**The God·head**, the Deity; God; the Supreme Being.

god·hood, god′hud″, *n.* Divinity; divine character.

god·less, god′lis, *a.* Having or acknowledging no god; impious; ungodly; irreligious; wicked.—**god·less·ly**, *a.*—**god·less·ness**, *n.*

god·like, god′līk″, *a.* Resembling a god or God; divine; of superior excellence.— **god·like·ness**, *n.*

god·ling, god′ling, *n.* A minor or petty deity; a god whose influence is mainly local.

god·ly, god′lē, *a.*—*godlier, godliest.* Pious; revering God and His laws; devout; righteous.—*adv.* Piously; righteously.— **god·li·ly**, *adv.*—**god·li·ness**, *n.*

god·moth·er, god′muтH·ér, *n.* A female sponsor of a child at baptism.

go·down, go·doun′, *n.* In India and other Oriental countries, a warehouse or any other place for general storage.

god·par·ent, god′pâr″ent, god′par″ent, *n.* A sponsor of a child at its baptism.

go·droon, gō·drön′, *n.* Gadroon.

God's a·cre, *n.* [= G. *Gottesacker*, 'God's field.'] A churchyard; a burial ground.

god·send, god′send″, *n.* An unexpected acquisition or piece of good fortune, almost as if sent by God.

God·speed, god′spēd′, *n.* [A contraction of "I wish that *God* may *speed* you."] Success; a prosperous journey, usu. expressed as a wish; as, to bid a person *Godspeed.*

god·wit, god′wit, *n.* [Origin uncertain.] Any bird of the genus *Limosa*, which comprises wading birds related to snipes, and characterized by a long bill with a slight upward curve.

go·er, gō′ér, *n.* One who is a regular or frequent attender: usu. used by combining with another noun; as, *moviegoer.*

goe·thite, **gö·thite**, gō′thīt, gœ′tīt, *n.* A mineral iron hydroxide, FeO(OH), appearing as the commonest component of rust in the form of reddish-brown crystals or often in dark brown masses.

gof·fer, gof′ér, *n.* An ornamental fluted or ruffled border of lace or other fabric on women's apparel.—*v.t.* To frill or crimp as with a heated iron. Also **gauf·fer.**

go-get·ter, gō″get′ér, *n. Colloq.* An enterprising, enthusiastic individual; one who is ambitious and aggressive.

gog·gle, gog′l, *n.* [M.E. *gogelen*; perhaps < Celtic.] A stare; a wide-eyed look.—*v.i.* —*goggled, goggling.* To stare, esp. wide-eyed or with bulging protuberant eyeballs; of the eyes, to bulge and stare.—*v.t.* To cause to roll, as the eyes.—**gog·gle-eyed**, gog′līd″, *a.*

gog·gles, gog′lz, *n. pl.* Protective spectacles with special lenses, rims, or esp. side shields.

Goi·del·ic, goi·del′ik, *a.* Of the Gaels or their language.—*n.* The division of the Celtic languages including Irish Gaelic, Scottish Gaelic, and Manx: differentiated from Brythonic. Also **Gadhelic.**

go·ing, gō′ing, *n.* The act of moving, esp. of moving away; departure; the condition of the ground or the surface of a road, path, racetrack, or the like in reference to its suitability for walking, driving, or racing; the act of progressing toward a goal in any activity.—*a.* That goes; that moves or functions; functioning or operating successfully; as, a *going* business; standard, prevailing, or available; as, the *going* rate of exchange; existing.—**go·ings on**, **go-**

ings-on, *colloq.* activities; conduct, esp. such as evokes criticism.

goi·ter, goi·tre, goi′tẽr, *n.* [Fr. *goître,* < L. *guttur,* the throat.] A morbid enlargement of the thyroid gland, forming a protuberance on the side or front part of the neck.—**goi·trous,** goi′trus, *a.* Pertaining to goiter; affected with goiter.

gold, gōld, *n.* A metallic element of deep yellow color, noted for its malleability, ductility, and invulnerability to rust: used, when alloyed, for coins, jewelry, dentures, and filaments for threads and fabrics. Sym. Au, at. no. 79, at. wt. 196.967. A coin made of this metallic element; money, riches, wealth; that which is valuable or highly prized; a bright yellow color, like that of the metal.—*a.* Made of or consisting of gold; giving or producing gold; colored like gold; secured by the gold standard.

gold·beat·er, gōld′bē″tẽr, *n.* One whose occupation is to beat gold into thin leaves for gilding.—**gold·beat·ing,** *n.*

gold·brick, gōld′brik, *n.* A spurious imitation of gold in brick form. *Slang,* a person, esp. a soldier, who shirks his duties or avoids difficult assignments; also **gold·-brick·er.—gold-brick,** *v.t.* To defraud; to cheat.—*v.i.* To loaf; to be lax in the performance of one's duties.

gold·en, gōl′den, *a.* Made or consisting of gold; containing gold; of the color of gold; yellow; bright or shining, like gold; resembling gold in value; most excellent; exceedingly favorable, as an opportunity; flourishing or joyous, as a time or period; denoting the 50th in a series of events, esp. a 50th anniversary.—**gold·en·ly,** *adv.*—**gold·en·ness,** *n.*

gold·en calf, *n. Bib.* the golden idol devised by Aaron. Ex. xxxii. *Fig.* wealth as the object of undue reverence.

gold·en·eye, gōl′den·ī″, *n.* pl. **gold·en·eyes, gold·en·eye.** A diving duck, *Glaucionetta clangula,* having yellow eyes and, in the male, striking black and white markings.

gold·en glow, *n. Bot.* a tall cultivated variety of the coneflower, *Rudbeckia laciniata hortensia,* having large yellow double flowers and three to five parted leaves.

gold·en mean, *n.* The wise middle way between extremes.

gold·en re·triev·er, *n.* A hunting dog having a thick, golden-brown coat.

gold·en·rod, gōl′den·rod″, *n.* Any plant of the genus *Solidago,* most species of which bear numerous small yellow flowers, usu. arranged in panicles.

gold·en rule, *n.* An apothegm, stated variously, admonishing one to behave toward others as one wishes them to behave toward oneself, one version being that of Jesus Christ in his Sermon on the Mount: "Whatsoever ye would that men should do to you, do ye even so unto them." Matt. vii. 12.

gold·en sec·tion, *n. Esthetics,* the ratio between two line segments or the two dimensions of a plane geometric figure, esp. a rectangle, such that the smaller is to the greater as the greater is to the sum of both the smaller and greater.

gold-filled, gōld′fild, *a.* Composed of a base metal that has a gold overlay.

gold·finch, gōld′finch″, *n.* A European songbird, *Carduelis carduelis,* having wings marked with yellow; any of certain small American finches, esp. *Spinus tristis,* the male of which has yellow body plumage in summer.

gold·fish, gōld′fish″, *n.* pl. **gold·fish, gold·fish·es.** A small fish, *Carassius auratus,* of the carp family, originally native to China, and prized for aquariums and fishbowls because of its coloring, usu. yellow to orange.

gold foil, *n.* Gold in thin, pliable sheets less thin than gold leaf, used extensively in grounding designs in enameling and cloisonné.

gold leaf, *n.* Gold hammered into extremely thin sheets used primarily for gilding.

gold mine, *n.* A mine yielding gold; *fig.* a source of great wealth.

gold-of-pleas·ure, gōld′ov·plezh′ẽr, *n.* An annual herb, *Camelia sativa,* bearing a profusion of small yellow flowers.

gold·smith, gōld′smith″, *n.* A craftsman who makes, or a dealer who sells, jewelry or other objects fashioned from gold.

gold stand·ard, *n.* A monetary system in which the value of a national currency is based on gold of prescribed fineness and weight.

gold stick, *n.* In England, a gilded rod carried on state occasions by certain members of the royal household; the bearer thereof.

gold·stone, gōld′stōn″, *n.* Aventurine.

go·lem, gō′lem, gō′lem, *n.* [Heb., embryo, something unformed or incomplete.] In Jewish legend, a figure constructed to represent a human being, and endowed with life by human agency; *fig.* an automaton.

Golf, golf, galf, *Brit.* gof, *n.* A communications code word to designate the letter G.

golf, golf, galf, *Brit.* also gof, *n.* [D. *kolf,* a club to drive balls with; Dan. *kolbe,* a club.] A game played with clubs and a small white ball, generally over a large course with strategic obstacles, the object being to drive the ball, with as few strokes as possible, into nine or eighteen holes placed considerable distances apart.—*v.i.*—**golf cart,** a small, motor-driven or hand-drawn, wheeled vehicle used to transport a golfer or his equipment.—**golf course,** the ground or course on which golf is played; also **golf links.—golf club,** *n.*—**golf·er,** *n.*

Gol·go·tha, gol′go·tha, *n.* [Heb.] Place of the crucifixion of Jesus Christ; Calvary. Matt. xxvii. 33. (*l.c.*) scene of sacrifice; burial place.

gol·ly, gol′ē, *interj.* An expression of surprise or admiration.

gom·pho·sis, gom·fō′sis, *n.* pl. **gom·pho·ses,** gom·fō′sēz. [Gr., < *gomphos,* a nail.] *Anat.* an immovable peg and socket articulation, as the root of a tooth in the jaw socket.

go·nad, gō′nad, *n.* [N.L. *gonas,* < Gr. *gonē,* generation, seed.] *Anat.* a male or female reproductive gland that produces gametes, sperm, or ovum; a testis or ovary.

Gond, gōnd, *n.* A member of a group of aboriginal people belonging to the Dravidian stock, in the Madhya Pradesh state of central India.—**Gon·di,** gon′dē, *n.* A Dravidian dialect spoken by the Gonds.

gon·do·la, gon′do·la, *n.* [It. *gondola,* dim. of *gonda,* boat; origin uncertain.] A long, narrow boat with a high peak at each end and often a small cabin near the middle, used on the Venetian canals, and usu. propelled at the stern by a single oar or pole; a kind of lighter or barge; a railway freight car with low sides and no top.—**gon·do·lier,** *n.* A man who rows or poles a gondola.

gone, gan, gon, *a.* Departed; finished or consumed; over or past; as, *gone* ages; passed away or dead; lost, undone, or hopeless; as, a *gone* case; weak and faint; as, a *gone* feeling; pregnant. *Colloq.* exceptionally brilliant or outstanding; infatuated or enamoured, usu. followed by *on* or *upon.*—**far gone,** much advanced or deeply involved; almost exhausted; almost dead.—**gone·ness,** *n.* Faintness; exhaustion.—**gon·er,** ga′nẽr, gon′ẽr, *n. Colloq.* a person or thing that is dead, lost, or past recovery.

gon·fa·lon, gon′fa·lon, *n.* [It. *gonfalone* = Fr. *gonfalon, gonfanon,* O.Fr. *gonfanon, gunfanun,* < O.H.G. *gundfano,* 'war banner.'] A banner suspended from a crossbar, often having several streamers; the form of standard used esp. by the medieval Italian republics.—**gon·fa·lon·ier,** *n.* The bearer of a gonfalon; the chief magistrate or other official in a medieval Italian republic.

gong, gang, gong, *n.* [Malay]. A metallic disk which produces a sonorous sound when struck with a stick having a padded head; a saucer-shaped bell sounded by a hammer.

Gon·go·rism, gon′go·riz″um, gang′go·riz″um, *n.* [From Luis de *Gongora* y Argote, Sp. poet, 1561–1627.] An elaborate and embellished literary style marked by coined words, strained imagery, and other affected devices.—**gon·go·ris·tic,** gon″go·ris′tik, *a.*

go·ni·om·e·ter, gō′nē·om′i·tẽr, *n.* [Gr. *gōnia,* angle, and *metron,* measure.] An instrument for measuring solid angles, esp. those formed by the faces of mineral crystals.—**go·ni·o·met·ric, go·ni·o·met·ri·cal,** gō′nē·o·me′trik, *a.*—**go·ni·om·e·try,** *n.* The science of measuring solid angles.

gon·o·coc·cus, gon″o·kok′us, *n.* pl. **gon·o·coc·ci,** gon″o·kok′sī. [N.L. < Gr. *gonos,* offspring, seed, and N.L. *coccus.*] The bacterium that causes gonorrhea.—**gon·o·coc·cal,** *a.*

gon·o·gen·e·sis, gon″o·jen′e·sis, *n. Biol.* the process of maturation of the germ cells.

gon·oph, gon′of, *n.* Ganef.

gon·o·phore, gon′o·fōr″, *n.* [Gr. *gonos,* offspring, seed.] *Bot.* a prolongation of the axis of a flower, bearing the stamens and pistil above the perianth; *zool.* one of the generative buds or receptacles of the reproductive elements in hydrozoans.—**gon·o·phor·ic, gon·o·noph·o·rous,** gon″o·for′ik, gō·nof′ẽr·us, *a.*

gon·or·rhe·a, gon·or·rhoe·a, gon″o·rē′a, *n.* [Gr. *gonorrhoia—gonos,* semen, and *rheō,* to flow.] A contagious, inflammatory ailment of the male urethra or the female vagina, caused by the gonococcus and accompanied by secretions of mucus and pus.—**gon·or·rhe·al, gon·or·rhoe·al,** *a.*

goo, gō, *n. Slang.* Sticky matter; excessive sentimentality.—**goo·ey,** gō′ē, *a.—gooier, gooiest.*

goo·ber, gō′bẽr, *n.* [Angolan, *nguba.*] A peanut. Also **goo·ber pea.**

good, gud, *n.* That which is good; that which is righteous or virtuous; as, to be a power for *good* in the world; excellence or merit; as, to discern the *good* in a book; kindness or good deeds; as, to do *good;* advantage, desire, or benefit; as, to work for the common *good;* use, worth, or service, as: That broken hammer is of little *good. Pl.* property or possessions, usu. portable or movable; as, household *goods;* articles of trade, wares, or merchandise; as, to stock *goods* or to sell *goods;* cloth or fabric; as, curtain *goods. Slang,* that which has been offered, expected, or promised; as, to furnish the *goods;* that which is honest or genuine; as, the real *goods;* specific articles of proof or evidence, as: The thief had the *goods* with him.—*interj.* That is *good:* an elliptical expression of commendation or satisfaction.—**for good,** finally and permanently; forever; as, to leave a place *for good.*—**to make good,** to perform; to fulfill; to verify or establish, as an accusation; to make up a deficit; to make up for a defect; to maintain or carry out successfully.—**to the good,** on the side of profit or advantage, as: He came out five dollars *to the good* in that transaction.

good, gud, *a.—better, best.* [O.E. *gōd* = D. *goed* = G. *gut* = Icel. *godhr* = Goth. *goths,* good; perhaps orig. meaning 'fitting, suitable,' and akin to E. *gather*.] Of favorable quality or character; as, *good* weather, *good* shoes, *good* news; virtuous or morally excellent; as, *good* works; satisfactory or excellent in degree or kind; as, *good* food, a *good* book; responsible or trustworthy; as, a *good* face; physically beautiful or attractive; as, a *good* appearance; right or proper, as: Do what seems *good* to you. Appropriate or fitting for a particular purpose; as, *good* day for a swim; useful, advantageous, or profitable, as an idea or a trade; genuine or legally valid, as money or a title; endurable, used with *for*; as, *good for* a lifetime; real or true, as: He made *good* his threats. Reliable or economically safe; as, a *good* check; sound or valid; as, *good* judgment; guaranteed to give or pay, used with *for*; as, *good for* a loan; assured to cause a particular result, used with *for*; as, *good for* a joke; fertile or productive, as land; wholesome, as meat or fruit; sound or unimpaired, as eyes; agreeable or pleasant; as, a *good* time; amusing or jovial, as a joke; generous or kind; as, a *good* deed; sufficient or ample in quantity; as, *good* measure; full; as, a *good* day's journey; fairly great; as, a *good* deal of time; faithful or conforming; as, a *good* Catholic; competent or skillful; as, a *good* doctor; clever or adroit; as, *good* at sports; well-behaved, as a child; well-regarded or honorable; as, a *good* reputation; pertaining to a noble or respectable class; as, a *good* family; honorable or excellent, used formerly as an epithet of respect; as, my *good* sir; holy; as, *Good* Friday; intimate; as, a *good* friend.—**as good as**, practically or in effect; as, *as good as* finished.—**good and**, *colloq.* completely or entirely; as, *good and* hot.—**good·ish**, *a. Colloq.* Rather or fairly good; as, *goodish* cookies; rather large or considerable; as, *goodish* size.

good, gụd, *adv. Substandard colloq.* adequately, well, as: The machine runs *good*.

Good Book, *n.* (*Sometimes l.c.*) the Bible.

good-by, good-bye, gụd′bī′, *a., interj., n.* pl. **good-bys, good-byes**. [Corruption of *God be with you*.] Farewell.

good fel·low, *n.* One who is good natured, pleasant, and companionable.—**good-fel·low·ship**, *n.* Friendly convivial companionship; comradery.

good-for-nothing, gụd′fẽr·nŭth′ing, *a.* Worthless.—*n.* A worthless person.

Good Fri·day, *n.* Friday before Easter, a holy day of the Christian church, observed as commemorative of Christ's crucifixion.

good-heart·ed, gụd′här′tid, *a.* Considerate; charitable; kind.—**good-heart·ed·ly**, *adv.* —**good-heart·ed·ness**, *n.*

good hu·mor, *n.* A cheerful temper or state of mind.—**good-hu·mored**, *a.*—**good-hu·mored·ly**, *adv.*—**good-hu·mored·ness**, *n.*

good-look·ing, gụd′lụk′ing, *a.* Of pleasing appearance; attractive; handsome.

good·ly, gụd′lē, *a.*—**goodlier, goodliest**. Being pleasing in appearance; of a fine quality; large or considerable; as, a *goodly* share.

good na·ture, *n.* Natural mildness and kindness of disposition.—**good-na·tured**, gụd′nā′chẽrd, *a.* Having good nature; naturally mild in temperament.—**good-na·tured·ly**, *adv.*—**good-na·tured·ness**, *n.*

good-neigh·bor, gụd′nā′bẽr, *a.* Distinguished by or embracing the principle of mutual assistance and amicable political relations between countries; as, the *good-neighbor* policy among nations of the Americas.

good·ness, gụd′nis, *n.* The state or quality of being good; virtue or integrity; kindness; the best part of a thing, its essence; a euphemism for God; as, thank *goodness*.

good-tem·pered, gụd′tem′pẽrd, *a.* Having an agreeable disposition; not easily irritated or annoyed.—**good-tem·pered·ly**, *adv.*—**good-tem·pered·ness**, *n.*

good will, *n.* Friendly disposition; benevolence; favor; cheerful acquiescence; readiness or zeal; *com.* the intangible value of a business, due to custom, reputation, or projected earning power, as distinct from the tangible value of its stock or property. Also **good·will**.

good·y, gụd′e, *n.* pl. **good·ies**. *Usu. pl., colloq.* something good to eat or otherwise pleasing.—*interj.* Good: an expression of delight used esp. by children.

good·y-good·y, gụd′ē-gụd′ē, *n.* pl. **good·y-good·ies**. *Colloq.* a prissily or affectedly good or pious person.—*a.* Also **good·y**.

goof, gōf, *n. Slang.* A silly or stupid person; a dope; a mistake or error, esp. when the result of poor judgment or carelessness.—*v.i. Slang.* To make an error; blunder; to waste time, often with *off* or *around*.—*v.t. Slang.* To make a mess of; bungle, as: He *goofed* his chance to be promoted.—**goof-off**, *n. Slang,* an individual who constantly wastes time, neglects his job, or shrinks from responsibility.—*v.t.*

goof·y, gō′fē, *a.*—**goofier, goofiest**. *Slang.* Foolish; silly; stupid.—**goof·i·ly**, *adv.*—**goof·i·ness**, *n.*

gook, gụk, gōk, *n. Slang.* Dirt; any sticky or viscous substance.

goon, gōn, *n. Slang.* A stupid, silly, or unattractive person; a hoodlum, esp. one employed to intimidate opponents in a labor dispute.

goos·an·der, gō·san′dẽr, *n.* [Lit. goose-duck, < *goose*, and Icel. *andar*, genit. of *ōnd*, O.E. *ened*, a duck.] The merganser, a swimming bird of the Northern Hemisphere.

goose, gōs, *n.* pl. **geese**. [O.E. *gōs* (pl. *gēs*) = D. and G. *gans* = Icel. *gās*, goose; akin to L. *anser*, Gr. *chen*, Skt. *hansa*, goose.] Any of numerous wild or domesticated, web-footed birds of the family *Anserinæ*, esp. of the genus *Branta* and allied genera, mostly larger and with a longer neck than the ducks; the female of this bird, as distinguished from the male or gander; the flesh of the goose. A silly or foolish person; a simpleton.—**goos·ey**, *a.*—**goosier, goosiest**. Foolish.

goose·ber·ry, gōs′ber″ē, gōs′be·rē, gōz′ber″ē, gōz′be·rē, *n.* pl. **goose·ber·ries**. The small, edible, acid, globular fruit or berry of certain shrubs of the genus *Ribes*, esp. *R. grossularia*; the shrub itself.

goose egg, *n. Slang,* in athletic and other contests, a zero, indicating a miss or a failure to score.

goose flesh, *n.* A rough condition of the skin, resembling that of a plucked goose, induced by cold or fear. Also **goose bumps, goose pim·ples, goose skin**.

goose·foot, gōs′fụt″, *n.* pl. **goose·foots**. *Bot.* a family of plants, *Chenopodiaceae*, usu. with mealy leaves and inconspicuous flowers, with some species grown for their colorful foliage, others as vegetables including beet and spinach. A common weed, *Chenopodium album*, with leaves shaped like a goose's foot; also *lamb's-quarter*.

goose·neck, gōs′nek″, *n.* Something curved like the neck of a goose, as a drainpipe or a kind of movable stand for an electric lamp. —**goose-necked**, *a.*

goose step, *n.* A military exercise in which the body is balanced on one foot, without advancing, while the other foot is swung forward and back; a marching step in which the legs are swung high with straight, stiff knees.—**goose-step**, *v.i.* —*goose-stepped, goose-stepping.*

GOP, G.O.P. Abbr. for Grand Old Party: the Republican Party.

go·pher, gō′fẽr, *n.* [Fr. *gaufre*, honeycomb, in allusion to the burrow.] Any of various burrowing rodents of the family *Geomyidae*, common in the prairie regions of N. America; any of a large number of ground squirrels of the genus *Citellus*. A burrowing land tortoise, *Gopherus polyphemus*, of the southern U.S.

go·pher snake, *n.* A nonpoisonous snake, found in southern and western North America, that preys on small rodents. Also *Indigo snake, bullsnake*.

go·ral, gōr′al, *n.* See *goat antelope*.

Gor·di·an knot, gạr′dē·an not, *n.* [From the Greek legend about a knot tied by King *Gordius* of Phrygia, that, according to the oracle, would be untied by the future ruler of Asia: Alexander the Great cut the knot with his sword.] An intricate problem.—**cut the gor·di·an knot**, to solve an intricate problem boldly and quickly.

Gor·don set·ter, *n.* A breed of long-haired, black and tan bird dogs developed in Scotland about 1820, and named for the fourth Duke of Gordon.

gore, gōr, *n.* [O.E. *gor*, gore, filth, Icel. and Dan. *gor*, Sw. *gorr*.] Blood that is shed; clotted blood.

gore, gōr, *n.* [O.E. *gāra*, a point or corner of land, < *gār*, a spear; like Icel. *geiri*, a triangular piece, < *geirr*, a spear.] A tapering piece of cloth used as a panel in a skirt or sail to provide extra width; a gusset. A triangular piece of land.—*v.t.* To insert, as a gore.

gore, gōr, *v.t.*—**gored, goring**. Of a bull, elephant, etc., to pierce with a horn or tusk.

gorge, gạrj, *n.* [O.Fr. Fr. *gorge*, throat; origin uncertain.] A narrow ravine, esp. one through which a stream runs; a gluttonous meal; a choking or obstructing mass; as, an ice *gorge* in a river; anger or disgust; as, an insult that makes one's *gorge* rise; *fort.* the rear entrance or part of a bastion or outwork.—*v.t.*—**gorged, gorging**. To stuff with food: used reflexively or passively; satiate; to swallow greedily.—*v.i.* To eat greedily.

gor·geous, gạr′jus, *a.* [O.Fr. *gorgias*; origin uncertain.] Splendid in dress, appearance, or coloring; beautiful; magnificent. *Colloq.* Very pleasant; enjoyable; as, a *gorgeous* evening at the opera.—**gor·geous·ly**, *adv.*—**gor·geous·ness**, *n.*

gor·get, gạr′jit, *n.* [O.Fr. *gorgete*, dim. of *gorge*, throat.] A piece of armor for the throat; a covering for the neck and breast, as a wimple, formerly worn by women; a crescent-shaped badge formerly worn by military officers on a chain around the neck; a distinctively colored or textured patch on the throat of a bird or other animals.

Gor·gon·zo·la cheese, gạr″gon·zō′la chēz, *n.* [From *Gorgonzola*, town in northern Italy.] A strongly flavored, hard-pressed variety of white Italian cheese veined with mold.

go·ril·la, gō·ril′a, *n.* [N.L. < Gr. *gorilla*; of African origin.] A large and powerful anthropoid ape, *Gorilla gorilla*, of western equatorial Africa. *Slang.* A contemptuous term for an ugly, brutish person.

gor·mand, gạr′mand, *n.* Gourmand.

gorse, gạrs, *n.* [O.E. *gorst*.] *Chiefly Brit.* furze or whin.—**gors·y**, *a.*—**gorsier, gorsiest**.

gor·y, gōr′ē, *a.*—**gorier, goriest**. Bloody; bloodcurdling; extremely unpleasant; as, the *gory* details of his trial.

gosh, gosh, *Interj.* [Euphemism for *God*.] A mild oath; an expression of surprise or admiration.

gos·hawk, gos′hạk″, *n.* [O.E. *gōshafoc*, goose-hawk—so called from being flown at geese.] A kind of large, short-winged hawk, of the genus *Accipiter*, once frequently used in falconry.

gos·ling, goz'ling, *n.* [M.E.; dim. of *goose.*] A young goose; a foolish, inexperienced person.

gos·pel, gos'pel, *n.* [O.E. *gōdspel*, appar. orig. *gōd spel*, 'good tidings.'] The body of doctrine taught by Christ and the apostles; Christian revelation; glad tidings, esp. concerning salvation and the kingdom of God as announced to the world by Christ; the story of Christ's life and teachings, esp. as contained in the first four books of the New Testament; (*usu. cap.*) one of these books; (*often cap.*) an extract from one of these four Gospels or books, forming part of the Eucharistic service in certain churches. Something infallibly true or implicitly believed, as: His word is taken for *gospel* by the neighborhood children. A doctrine regarded as of prime importance.—*a.* Pertaining to the gospel; accordant with the gospel; evangelical.—**gos·pel mu·sic,** a highly rhythmic, religious music heard in Negro churches in the U.S.

gos·pel·er, gos·pel·ler, gos'pe·lėr, *n. Eccles.* one who reads or sings the gospel in the Eucharistic service. One who claims for his sect the exclusive possession of the true gospel: term used derisively.

gos·port, gos'pōrt", gos'part", *n. Aeron.* a flexible tube used for oral communication between two people in an airplane, esp. between an instructor and student.

gos·sa·mer, gos'a·mėr, *n.* [M.E. *gossomer, gosesomer,* appar. orig. 'goose summer' for a mild, late autumn period when geese are in season, and hence for the filmy matter seen in the air at that time.] A fine, filmy, cobwebby substance seen on grass and bushes or floating in the air in calm weather, esp. in autumn; any thin, light fabric or other delicate substance.—*a.* Of or like gossamer; thin; light; filmy.—**gos·sa·mer·y,** *a.*

gos·san, gos'an, goz'an, *n.* [Cornish.] *Geol.* decomposed rock of a reddish or ferruginous color, which often forms a large part of the outcrop of an iron-bearing vein. Also **i·ron hat.**

gos·sip, gos'ip, *n.* [O.E. *godsibb* < *god,* God, and *sibb,* relation.] Idle talk, rumors, or scandal; light, familiar talk or writing. A person, esp. a woman, given to idle talk or the spreading of reports about others; also **gos·sip·per.** *Archaic,* a godparent; a friend.—*v.t.*—*gossiped, gossiping, gossipped, gossipping.* To repeat as gossip.—*v.i.* To talk idly, esp. about other people; to go about tattling.—**gos·sip·ing·ly,** *adv.*—**gos·sip·ry,** *n. Archaic,* gossips or gossip, collectively.—**gos·sip·y,** *a.*

gos·sip·mon·ger, gos'ip·mung"gėr, gos'ip·mong"gėr, *n.* One particularly inclined to gossip.

Goth, goth, *n.* [L. *Gothi,* Goths.] One of an ancient Teutonic race of people who overran and conquered most of the Roman Empire in the 3rd to 5th centuries; a barbarian; a rude ignorant person.

Goth·ic, goth'ik, *a.* Pertaining to the Goths; pertaining to the Middle Ages; rude, barbarous; denoting a style of architecture utilizing the pointed arch, buttress, and ribbed vaulting current in western Europe from 1200 to 1500 A.D.; referring to a literary style in which a bleak and dismal setting, weird and often violent happenings, and a feeling of doom and decay are characteristic.—*n.* The language of the Goths; art and architecture in the Gothic style.

Goth·i·cism, goth'i·siz"um, *n.* Conformity to or enthusiasm for the Gothic style or principles of architecture, art, or literature; the style or principles themselves. (*l.c.*) Inelegance; barbarousness.

Goth·i·cize, goth'i·siz", *v.t.*—*Gothicized, Gothicizing.* To make Gothic, as in style.

gouache, gwäsh, gö·äsh', *Fr.* gwäsh, *n.* pl. **gouach·es,** *Fr.* gwäsh. [Fr. < It. *guazzo.*] A watercolor technique or painting in which opaque pigments mixed with gum have been used.

Gou·da, gou'da, gö'da, D. chou'dä, *n.* [From *Gouda,* a town in the Netherlands.] A mild yellow cheese, semisoft, with a red protective coating.

gouge, gouj, *n.* [O.Fr. Fr. *gouge,* M.L. *gubia, gulbia;* prob. < Celtic.] A chisel whose blade is shaped like a scoop, with a concave-convex cross section; the act of gouging; a groove or hole caused by gouging; *fig.* a swindle.—*v.t.*—*gouged, gouging.* To work upon with or as with a gouge, as in making grooves or holes; make with or as with a gouge, as a channel; to dig or force out with or as with a gouge; *fig.* to cheat or swindle.—**goug·er,** *n.*

gou·lash, gö'läsh, gö'lash, *n.* [Hung. *gulyas hus,* 'herdsman's meat.'] A stew of beef, veal, and vegetables, with paprika or other seasoning.

gourd, gōrd, gärd, gŭrd, *n.* [Fr. *gourde,* O.Fr. *gouorde, gougorde,* < L. *cucurbita,* a gourd.] The fruit of the family *Cucurbitaceae,* as melon, pumpkin, and the like; a pepo; the dried shell of this fruit, used for decoration or as a bottle.

gour·mand, gŭr'mand, *Fr.* gör·mäN', *n.* pl. **gour·mands,** *Fr.* gör·mäN'. [Fr. of Celtic origin; cf. W. *gormant,* that which tends to overfill; *gormodia, excess,* < *gor* excess.] An epicure; a gourmet; one who is informed about and enjoys good eating; *obs.* a glutton. Also *gormand.*—**gour·man·dism,** *n.*

gour·met, gŭr'mā, *Fr.* gör·me', *n.* pl. **gour·mets,** *Fr.* gör·me'. [Fr. < O.Fr. *gromet,* groom.] A connoisseur of food and drink; an epicure.

gout, gout, *n.* [Fr. *goutte,* L. *gutta,* a drop, from the old medical theory that diseases were due to the deposition of drops of morbid humor in the body.] *Pathol.* a disease caused by defective metabolism and characterized by inflamed joints, esp. in the big toe, and excessive uric acid in the bloodstream; a drop or clot, as of blood.

gout·y, gou'tē, *a.*—*goutier, goutiest.* Of or like gout; causing gout; resulting from gout; marked by gout.—**gout·i·ly,** *adv.*—**gout·i·ness,** *n.*

gov·ern, guv'ėrn, *v.t.* [Fr. *gouverner,* < L. *gubernare,* to govern, a form of Gr. *kybernan,* to govern.] To direct, control, or regulate by authority; to guide or influence; to restrain, check, keep under control; to steer or regulate the course of; *gram.* to necessitate the use of, as of a particular case; *mach.* to control, as engine speed, with a regulating mechanism.—*v.i.* To exercise authority; to administer the laws; to maintain control.—**gov·ern·a·ble,** *a.*—**gov·ern·ance,** guv'ėr·nans, *n.*

gov·ern·ess, guv'ėr·nis, *n.* [For earlier *governeress,* < O.Fr. *gouverneresse,* fem. of *gouverneur, governeor,* E. *governor.*] A female teacher hired to instruct and train children in a private household; *archaic,* a woman governor or ruler.

gov·ern·ment, guv'ėrn·ment, guv'ėr·ment, *n.* The exercise of political authority, direction, and restraint over the actions of the inhabitants of communities, societies, or states; the administration of public affairs; the governing organization or body of a nation, state, or community; the administration or executive power; the mode or system according to which the legislative, executive, and judicial powers are vested and exercised; as, a republican form of *government;* a province or division of territory ruled by a governor; regulation, control, or restraint. *Gram.* the influence

of the inflectional form of one word over the form or position of another word within a sentence.—**gov·ern·men·tal,** guv"ėrn·men'tal, *a.*—**gov·ern·men·tal·ly,** *adv.*

gov·er·nor, guv'ėr·nėr, *n.* One who governs; the supreme executive magistrate of a state of the U.S.; *Brit.* the official title of the representative of the British Crown serving in a colony or dependency of Great Britain; also *governor general. Brit. colloq.* a term of respect for an employer or one's father. A contrivance in mills and machinery for maintaining a uniform velocity with a varying resistance; a contrivance in a steam engine which automatically regulates admission of steam to the cylinder.—**gov·er·nor·ship,** *n.*

gov·er·nor gen·er·al, *n.* pl. **gov·er·nors gen·er·al.** A governor who has under him subordinate or deputy governors. *Brit.* governor or viceroy; also **gov·er·nor-gen·er·al.**—**gov·er·nor-gen·er·al·ship,** *n.*

gown, goun, *n.* [O.Fr. *goune,* L.L. *gunna,* furred robe, fur.] A woman's dress, esp. her formal attire; a dressing gown or a nightgown; the official robe worn by members of certain professions, as divinity, medicine, law, or by magistrates, university professors, or students; collectively, the students and faculty of a university, as distinguished from the people of the town; as, town and *gown.*—*v.t.* To put a gown on; to clothe or dress in a gown.—*v.i.* To put on a gown; to wear a gown or robe.—**gowns·man,** gounz'man, *n.* pl. **gowns·men.** One whose professional habit is a gown.

Graaf·i·an fol·li·cle, grä'fē·an fol'i·kl, *n.* [Named after Regnier de *Graaf,* 1641–73, a Dutch physician and anatomist.] One of the small sacs or vesicles in which an ovum develops in a mammalian ovary.

grab, grab, *v.t.*—*grabbed, grabbing.* [= M.L.G. *grabben* = Sw. *grabba;* perhaps akin to E. *grasp.*] To seize suddenly and eagerly; snatch; to take possession of in an unscrupulous manner; as, to *grab* land; to capture or arrest a person.—*v.i.* To make a grab or snatch.—*n.* The act of grabbing; a sudden, eager grasp or snatch; seizure or acquisition by violent or unscrupulous means; that which is grabbed; one who or that which grabs; a mechanical device for gripping objects.—**grab, grab·ba·ble,** *a.* Able to be grabbed.—**grab bag,** a bag or receptacle from which a person may draw, usu. after paying a small sum, and without examining any of the various articles within.—**grab·ber,** *n.*

grab, grab, *n.* [Ar. *ghurāb.*] An oriental vessel with triangular sails and usu. two masts.

grab·ble, grab'l, *v.i.*—*grabbled, grabbling.* [Freq. of *grab:* cf. D. *grabbelen.*] To feel or search with the hands; grope; to sprawl or scramble.

grab·by, grab'ē, *a.*—*grabbier, grabbiest.* Avaricious or greedy.

gra·ben, grä'ben, *n. Geol.* an elongated depression of the earth's surface caused by two or more faults.

grab off, *v.t.* To appropriate with haste or by force; as, to *grab off* territory.

grab rope, *n. Naut.* any of certain lines or ropes on a ship for taking hold of if necessary, as one for a boatman in another vessel to hold on to when coming alongside. Also **grab line.**

grace, grās, *n.* [Fr. < L. *gratia,* favor, < *gratus,* pleasant (seen also in *grateful, gratitude, agree, ingrate,* etc.); < a root seen in Gr. *chairō,* to rejoice, Gael. *gradh,* love, and E. *yearn.*] Elegance or dignity of form, movement, or expression; beauty, charm, or any pleasing attribute; favor, good will, or kindness; a sense of decency or propriety; a special dispensation or privilege; mercy or pardon; a temporary reprieve. *Law*, a period of time following the due date of a debt during which the debtor is allowed to make payment without penalty; also *days of grace*. *Theol.* the unmerited love and favor of God; divine influence renewing and morally strengthening man; a state of reconciliation with God. A short prayer before or after meals giving thanks or asking a blessing; *mus.* a grace note or notes; (*usu. cap.*) a title used in addressing a duke, duchess, or bishop, usu. preceded by *your, her,* or *his.*—**in the good** or **bad grace·es of,** in the favor or disfavor of.—**with good grace,** willingly or graciously.—**with bad grace,** reluctantly or ungraciously.

grace, grās, *v.t.*—*graced, gracing.* To lend or add grace to; to adorn; to dignify or honor; *mus.* to embellish with grace notes.

grace cup, *n.* A cup used to drink a final toast after grace has been said; the toast itself.

grace·ful, grās′ful, *a.* Marked by or displaying grace or elegance in form, action, or expression.—**grace·ful·ly,** *adv.*—**grace·ful·ness,** *n.*

grace·less, grās′lis, *a.* Void of grace or pleasing qualities; possessing no sense of propriety; unregenerate.—**grace·less·ly,** *adv.*—**grace·less·ness,** *n.*

grace note, *n. Mus.* a note added by way of ornament and written in smaller notation.

grace pe·ri·od, *n. Insurance,* a period of time, usu. 31 days, after the actual due date of a premium during which a policyholder may make payment of the premium before the policy lapses.

grac·ile, gras′il, *a.* [L. *gracilis*, slender.] Slender.—**grac·il·i·ty,** grac·ile·ness, gra·sil′i·tē, gra·sil′i·tē, *n.* Slenderness.

gra·ci·o·so, grä′shē·ō′sō, grä″sē·ō′sō, *Sp.* grä·thyō′sō, gRä·thyō′syō, *n. pl.* **gra·ci·o·sos.** The clownlike character in a Spanish comedy.

gra·cious, grā′shus, *a.* [Fr. *gracieux,* L. *gratiosus.*] Characterized by kindness, courtesy, or benevolence; tasteful or refined; polite in a condescending manner; merciful, used esp. of royalty.—**gra·cious·ly,** *adv.*—**gra·cious·ness,** *n.*

grack·le, grak′l, *n.* [L. *graculus,* a jackdaw, imitative of the cry.] Any of a number of long-tailed birds of N. America of the family *Icteridæ,* as the purple grackle, *Quiscalus quiscula;* any of various birds of the Old World which belong to the starling family, *Sturnidae.*

gra·date, grā′dāt, *v.i.*—*gradated, gradating.* [Back-formation from *gradation.*] To pass by insensible degrees, as one color into another.—*v.t.* To cause to gradate; to arrange in steps or grades.

gra·da·tion, grā·dā′shan, *n.* [L. *gradatio.*] An orderly arrangement or placing, according to relative rank, degree, size, or quality; a succession or change by gradual steps or degrees; the act of grading; the state of being graded; a degree or relative position in any order or series; the gradual blending of one tint into another; *ling.* ablaut.—**gra·da·tion·al,** *a.* Of, pertaining, or according to gradation.—**gra·da·tion·al·ly,** *adv.*

grade, grād, *n.* [Fr. *grade,* < L. *gradus,* a step, < *gradior, gressus,* to go, seen also in *congress, degrade, degree, egress, ingredient, progress, retrograde,* etc.] A degree in any series, rank, or order; relative position or standing, as in quality or seniority; one of the sections of a school system, as divided into the pupils' years of work; the group of pupils in one of these sections; a mark rating a pupil's work; a class comprising things of the same quality; the rate of ascent or descent, as of a sloping road; the part of a road which slopes; elevation or ground level; an animal with only one

parent of pure breed.—*v.t.*—*graded, grading.* To arrange in order according to size, quality, rank, or degree of advancement; to reduce, as a railway line, to such levels or degrees of inclination as may make it suitable for use; to improve the breed of, by crossing an animal of low grade with a pure-bred; to determine the grade of.—*v.i.* Blend; to form or be a grade or series.

grade cross·ing, *n.* A crossing of railroad tracks or highways, or of a railroad track and a highway, on the same level.

grad·er, grā′dèr, *n.* One who or that which grades; a pupil of a school grade; as, a *fifth grader;* a machine used for grading.

grade school, *n.* An elementary school in which the pupils are grouped into separate grades, usu. from the first grade to the eighth grade or from the first grade up to junior high school.

grade sep·a·ra·tion, *n.* Division of the grades of a railroad or highway crossing, as by an overpass or underpass, to avoid traffic jams or accidents.

gra·di·ent, grā′dē·ent, *n.* [L. *gradiens, gradientis,* ppr. of *gradior.*] Degree of slope or inclination, as of the ground; the rate of ascent or descent; a slope, incline, or grade. *Phys.* the rate of change, both in magnitude and direction, of a variable quantity such as temperature or pressure; a curve or diagram illustrating the degree of change in such a case.—*a.* Rising or descending by regular degrees of inclination; suited for walking, as the paws, feet, or claws of certain animals.

gra·din, grā′din, *Fr.* grä·daN′, *n. pl.* **gra·dins,** grā′dinz, Fr. grä·daN′. [Fr. < It. *gradino,* dim. of *grado,* < L. *gradus,* step, E. *grade.*] One of a series of tiered steps or seats; *eccles.* a shelf behind and above an altar. Also **gra·dine,** gra·dēn′.

grad·u·al, graj′ụ·al, *a.* [M.L. *gradualis* (as n., *graduale*), < L. *gradus,* step, E. *grade.*] Proceeding, changing, or moving by degrees or little by little; having a moderate inclination, as a slope.—*n. Eccles.* A response sung between the Epistle and the Gospel in the Eucharistic service; a book containing the words and music of the choral parts of the service.—**grad·u·al·ly,** *adv.*—**grad·u·al·ness,** *n.*

grad·u·al·ism, graj′ụ·a·liz″um, *n.* The practice or principle of attaining a goal gradually or by degrees.

grad·u·ate, graj′ō·āt′′, *v.t.*—*graduated, graduating.* [M.L. *graduatus,* pp. of *graduare,* admit to an academic degree, < L. *gradus,* step, E. *grade.*] To confer a degree or diploma upon at the close of a course of study, as in a university, college, or school; to divide into or mark with degrees, as the scale of a thermometer; to arrange in grades or gradations.—*v.i.* To receive a degree or diploma on completing a course of study; to change gradually.—*graj′ō·it,* graj′ō·āt, *a.* Of or pertaining to study beyond the bachelor's degree; as, a *graduate* school.—*graj′ō·it, graj′ō·āt, n.* One who has received an academic degree or diploma on completing a course of study; a graduated vessel for measuring, as a beaker.—**grad·u·a·ted,** *a.* Marked so as to indicate degrees or quantities; arranged in grades or gradations.—**grad·u·a·tor,** *n.*

grad·u·a·tion, graj′ō·ā′shan, *n.* [M.L. *graduatio(n-).*] The act of graduating or the state of being graduated; the ceremony of conferring degrees or diplomas, as at a college or school; a mark or marks, as on an instrument or a vessel, for indicating degree or quantity; these marks or divisions collectively.

gra·dus, grā′dus, *n. pl.* **gra·dus·es.** [Short for L. *gradus ad Parnassum,* 'steps to

Parnassus.'] A dictionary to aid in writing Latin or Greek verses; musical exercises of graduated difficulty.

graf·fi·to, gra·fē′tō, *n. pl.* **graf·fi·ti,** gra·fē′tē. [It. ult. < Gr. *graphein,* mark, draw, write.] *Archaeol.* an ancient drawing or writing scratched on a wall or other surface; *pl., sing.* or *pl. in constr.* inscriptions or drawings scrawled on walls, sidewalks, or the like.

graft, graft, gräft, *n.* [Earlier *graff,* < O.Fr. *grafe, greife* (Fr. *greffe*), orig. stylus, pencil, < L. *graphium, < Gr. graphium,* stylus, < *graphein,* write.] *Hort.* A shoot or part of a plant (the scion) inserted in a groove, slit, or the like in another plant or tree (the stock), so as to become nourished by and united with it; the plant or tree, the united stock and scion, resulting from such an operation; the place where the scion is inserted. A portion of living tissue transplanted by surgery from one body or part of a body to another.—*v.t.* To insert, as a scion of one plant, into another plant; to breed, as a fruit or plant, by grafting; to transplant by surgical grafting; *fig.* to attach or fix; as, to *graft* middle-class values onto the lower class.—*v.i.* To insert a graft or grafts; to become grafted.

graft, graft, gräft, *n.* [Cf. prov. Eng. or slang *graft,* work a job or trade, perhaps orig. 'digging': cf. *grave.*] The acquisition of gain or advantage by dishonest, unfair, or illegal means, esp. through the abuse of one's position or influence in politics or business; the gain or advantage acquired.—*v.i.* To practice graft.—*v.t.* To obtain by graft.—**graft·er,** *n.*

graft·age, graf′tij, gräf′tij, *n. Hort.* the technique and practice of grafting.

gra·ham flour, grā′am flour, *n.* Wheat flour made from the whole kernel; wholewheat flour.

Grail, grāl, *n.* [O.Fr. *graal, greal,* L.L. *gradalis, gradale;* perhaps < *cratella,* dim. of L. *crater,* Gr. *kratēr,* a cup.] The Holy Grail.

grain, grān, *n.* [Fr. *grain,* < L. *granum,* a grain, seed, kernel. Of same origin are *granite, grange, garner,* etc.] A single seed or fruit of a food plant, esp. of the cereal grasses; the gathered seeds or fruits of these plants in general, as wheat, rye, oats, and corn; the plants themselves; any small, hard particle, as of sand, sugar, or salt; a minute particle; a small amount; as, not a *grain* of sense; the smallest unit in certain U.S. and British systems of weight; the pattern or direction of the fibers or particles in wood, leather, or stone; the texture resulting from the arrangement of the fibers or particles; the side of leather from which the hairs have been eliminated; one's natural temperament.—**grain·less,** *a.*

grain, grān, *v.t.* To form into grains; to paint so as to give the appearance of grains or fibers; to take hairs off, as from skins; to finish the grain of, as of leather.—*v.i.* To form grains or to assume a granular form as the result of crystallization.—**grain·er,** *n.*

grain al·co·hol, *n.* An ethyl alcohol distilled from grains.

grain·field, grān′fēld″, *n.* An area of land where grain is grown.

grain rust, *n.* A rust which attacks the stems of wheat and other cereal grasses.

grains, granz, *n. pl. but sing. in constr.* [Same word as Dan. *green,* a branch, a prong; Icel. *grein,* a branch; akin *groin.*] A kind of harpoon with four or more barbed points used in fishing.

grain sor·ghum, *n.* Any of several kinds of sorghum, grown, esp. for grain or fodder.

grain·y, grā′nē, *a.*—*grainier, grainiest.* Grainlike or granular; full of grains or

grain; resembling the grain of wood.—
grain·i·ness, *n*.

gral·la·to·ri·al, gral″a·tōr′ē·al, gral″a·-
tạr′ē·al, *a*. [L. *grallator*, one who goes on
stilts, < *gralla*, stilts.] Belonging or
pertaining to the wading birds, as the
storks, cranes, and herons, which are
remarkable for their long legs.

gram, gram, *n*. [Pg. *grão*, < L. *granum*,
E. *grain*.] In the East Indies, the chick-pea,
Cicer arietinum, used as a food for both
man and cattle; any of various other plants,
as *Phaseolus aureus*, green gram, a bean
cultivated in India as a food crop.

gram, gramme, gram, *n*. [Fr. *gramme*, <
L.L. *gramma*, < Gr. *gramma*, a small
weight, orig. something drawn or written,
a character or letter, < *graphein*, write.]
See Metric System table.

gra·ma, grä′ma, *n*. [Sp. *grama*, grass.]
Any of various pasture grasses of the
western and southwestern U.S., esp. those
of the genus *Bouteloua*, as *B. gracilis*, blue
grama, the most common species. Also
gra·ma grass.

gram·a·ry, gram·a·rye, gram′a·rē, *n*.
[M.E. *grammarie, gramarye*: cf. O.Fr.
gramaire, grammar, also magic.] Occult
learning or magic.

gram at·om, *n*. *Chem*. the quantity of an
element whose weight in grams is numerically equal to that element's atomic
weight.

gra·mer·cy, gra·mu̇r′sē, *interj*. [O.Fr.
grand merci.] *Archaic*. Many thanks; an
exclamation of surprise or sudden feeling.

gram·i·ci·din, gram″i·sĭd′in, *n*. [*gram*
(-*positive*) and L. *cædere*, kill, and -*in*.]
Pharm. a powerful germicide.

gra·min·e·ous, gra·min′ē·us, *a*. [L.
gramineus, < *gramen, graminis*, grass.]
Like or pertaining to grass or the grass
family.

gram·i·niv·o·rous, gram″i·niv′ėr·us, *a*.
[L. *gramen* (*gramin-*), grass, and *vorare*,
devour.] Subsisting on grains or similar
food; pertaining to jaws and teeth suited for
feeding on seeds and grasses, as those of
particular rodents.

gram·mar, gram′ėr, *n*. [O.Fr. *gramaire*
(Fr. *grammaire*), < L. *grammatica*, < Gr.
grammatikē, grammar, prop. fem. of
grammatikos.] The study or science of the
usages of a language; the forms and syntax
of its words; the principles of correct
usage; a treatise on this subject; speech or
writing in accordance with established
grammatical usage, as: That sentence is
bad *grammar*. Grammatical forms and
usages collectively; as, a language having
little *grammar*; the elements of any science,
art, or subject; as, the *grammar* of painting;
a book presenting them; as, a *grammar* of
ornament.—**gram·mar·i·an**, gra·mâr′ē·-
an, *n*. One who specializes in the study
and proper use of grammar.

gram·mar school, *n*. Elementary school;
a graded public school intermediate
between a primary school and a high
school; *Brit*. a secondary school in which
the curriculum corresponds generally to
that of U.S. high schools; formerly, a school
for the teaching of Latin.

gram·mat·i·cal, gra·mat′i·kal, *a*. Of or
pertaining to /grammar; as, a *grammatical*
error; in accordance with the rules of
grammar, as; That sentence is not *grammatical*.—**gram·mat·i·cal·ly**, *adv*.—**gram·-
mat·i·cal·ness**, *n*.—**gram·mat·i·cal·i·ty**,
gra·mat″i·kal′i·tē, *n*.

gram·mat·i·cal mean·ing, *n*. The meaning of a word which is conveyed by
inflectional endings and syntax rather than
by semantic content.

gram mol·e·cule, *n*. *Chem*. that quantity
of a substance whose weight in grams is
numerically equal to that substance's

molecular weight. Also **gram·mo·lec·u·lar
weight**.—**gram·mo·lec·u·lar**, gram″mo·-
lek′ū·lẽr, *a*. Of or denoting a gram molecule.—**gram-mo·lar**, gram″mō′lẽr, *a*.

Gram-neg·a·tive, gram′neg′a·tiv, *a*. *Bact*.
denoting an inability, usu. of bacteria,
to hold the violet dye which is used
for classification purposes in Gram's
method.

gram·o·phone, gram′o·fōn″, *n*. *Brit*.
phonograph.

Gram-pos·i·tive, gram′poz′i·tiv, *a*. *Bact*.
denoting the ability of an organism to hold
the violet dye used in Gram's method of
typing bacteria.

gram·pus, gram′pus, *n*. [For M.E. *grapeys,
graspeys*, < O.Fr. *graspeis, craspois*, < M.L.
crassus piscis, 'fat fish.'] A large, marine
mammal of the dolphin family; any of
various related marine mammals, as the
killer whale.

Gram's meth·od, *n*. [From H. C. J. *Gram*,
Danish physician.] *Bact*. a method in
which an organism is stained, treated with
solution, and classified according to its
ability to retain the stain.

gram-var·i·a·ble, gram′vâr′ē·a·bl, *a*.
Characterized by irregular or inconsistent
stain retention according to Gram's
method.

gra·na·ry, grā′na·rē, gran′a·rē, *n*. pl.
gran·a·ries. [L. *granarium*, < *granum*.]
A storehouse for grain which has been
threshed; a region where grain is produced
in abundance.

grand, grand, *a*. [Fr. *grand*, < L. *grandis*,
great, grand, seen also in *aggrandize*.]
Vast in scope or size; great; illustrious;
high in power or dignity; noble; splendid;
principal or chief; as, a *grand* juror; pretentious; arrogant; comprehensive.—*n*.
Slang, a thousand dollars.—**grand·ly**, *adv*.
—**grand·ness**, *n*.

grand·aunt, grand′ant″, grand′änt″, *n*.
Great-aunt.

grand·ba·by, gran′bā′bē, *n*. A baby
grandchild.

grand·child, gran′chĭld″, *n*. A son's or
daughter's child.

grand·daugh·ter, gran′da̸″tėr, *n*. A daughter of a son or of a daughter.

grand duch·ess, *n*. The wife or widow of a
grand duke; a woman who governs a
grand duchy in her own right; a daughter of
a Russian czar or of a czar's son.

grand duch·y, *n*. A territory ruled by a
grand duke or grand duchess.

grand duke, *n*. The title of a sovereign of
certain European states; a Russian czar's
son or grandson.

gran·dee, gran·dē′, *n*. [Sp. *grande*, great,
grand.] A Spanish or Portuguese nobleman
of high rank; any man of high rank or social
position.

gran·deur, gran′jer, gran′ju̇r, *n*. [Fr.
grandeur, < *grand*.] The state or quality of
being grand; imposing or awesome greatness; majesty; magnificence; exalted rank,
dignity, or importance.

grand·fa·ther, gran′fä″THẽr, grand′fä″THẽr,
n. A father's or mother's father; ancestor,
forebear.

grand·fa·ther clause, *n*. *U.S. hist*. a
constitutional clause adopted to disenfran-
chise Negroes in some southern states by
exempting only those men who had voted
before 1867, or their lineal descendants,
from the high literacy and property qualifications required of new voters: declared
unconstitutional in 1915.

grand·fa·ther clock, *n*. A pendulum
clock encased in a tall cabinet which stands
directly on the floor. Also **grand·fa·ther's
clock**.

gran·dil·o·quence, gran·dil′o·kwens, *n*.
[L. *grandiloquens—grandis*, and *loquor*,
to speak.] Bombastic or lofty discourse;

high-sounding words.—**gran·dil·o·quent**,
gran·dil′o·kwent, *a*.

gran·di·ose, gran′dē·ōs″, *a*. [Fr.] Impressive because of inherent grandeur; imposing; aiming at or affecting grandeur;
grandiloquent; bombastic; pompous.—
gran·di·ose·ly, *adv*.—**gran·di·ose·ness**,
n.—**gran·di·os·i·ty**, gran″dē·os′i·tē, *n*.
pl. **gran·di·os·i·ties**.

gran·di·o·so, gran″dē·ō′sō, *a*. [It.] *Mus*.
grand or stately.—*adv*.

grand ju·ry, *n*. A specially impaneled jury
numbering 12 to 24 people whose duty it
is to hear accusations against offenders,
examine evidence of the state, and if just
cause exists, to find a bill of indictment.

grand lar·ce·ny, *n*. *Law*, theft of goods
valued above a specific amount.

grand mal, gran′mal′, *n*. *Pathol*. a severe
variety of epilepsy marked by convulsions,
stupor, and unconsciousness.

grand·moth·er, gran′muTH″ẽr, grand′-
muTH″ẽr, gram′muTH″ẽr, *n*. A father's or
mother's mother; a female forebear.

grand·neph·ew, gran′nef″ū, gran′nev″ū,
grand′nef″ū, grand′nev″ū, *n*. A grandson
of a brother or of a sister.

grand·niece, gran′nēs″, grand′nēs″, *n*. A
granddaughter of a brother or of a sister.

grand op·er·a, *n*. Opera similar in plot
and characterization to serious drama, but
having the text completely set to music.

grand·par·ent, gran′pâr″ent, gran′par″ent,
grand′pâr″ent, grand′par″ent, *n*. A parent
of a parent.

grand pi·an·o, *n*. A piano with strings
stretched horizontally in a harp-shaped
body.

Grand Prix, grän·prē′, *n*. pl. **Grand
Prixes, Grand Prix, Grands Prix**, grän·-
prēz′. Any of several major automobile
road races held in various countries.

grand slam, *n*. The winning of all the tricks
in one hand, as in bridge; *baseball*, a home
run hit with runners on all bases.

grand·son, gran′sun″, grand′sun″, *n*. A
son of a son or of a daughter.

grand·stand, gran′stand″, grand′stand″, *n*.
An elevated series of seats arranged one
row above another at a racecourse or
sports stadium, usu. with a roof; the spectators occupying these seats.—*v.i*. To
perform in a showy manner in order to
impress the spectators.

grand tour, *n*. Any extended tour; formerly,
an educational tour of continental Europe
for the sons of British aristocracy.

grand·un·cle, grand′ung″kl, *n*. The uncle
of one's father or mother; great-uncle.

grand vi·zier, *n*. The chief minister of the
former Turkish Empire and various
Moslem countries.

grange, grānj, *n*. [Fr. *grange*, a barn < L.L.
granea, granica, a barn < L. *granum*,
grain. GRAIN.] A farm, with its dwellings,
stables, barns, and other buildings; the
farm buildings of a feudal manor or religious
institution used for storage of grain; *Brit*.
a country residence and its outlying farm
buildings, esp. those of a gentleman
farmer. (*Cap*.) one of the local lodges of
the farmers' organization called 'The
Patrons of Husbandry'; the organization
itself.—**grang·er**, *n*. A farmer; (*often cap*) a
Grange member.—**grang·er·ism**, grān′-
je·riz″um, *n*. The laws and policies of the
Grangers.

grang·er·ize, grān′je·rīz″, *v.t*.—*granger-
ized, grangerizing*. [From J. *Granger*,
whose *Biographical History of England*
(1769) was arranged for such illustration.]
To illustrate, as a book, with additional
prints or engravings taken from other
books; to mutilate by cutting out photographs and illustrations.—**grang·er·i·za·-
tion**, grān″jẽr·i·zā′shun, *n*.—**grang·er·-
iz·er**, *n*.—**grang·er·ism**, *n*.

gran·ite, gran′it, n. [Fr. granit, < It. granito, lit. grained stone, < L. granum, a grain.] An unstratified igneous rock, one of the most abundant in the earth's crust, composed generally of grains or crystals of quartz, feldspar, and mica, united without regular arrangement; anything noted for its firm, enduring qualities.—**gra·nit·ic**, gra·nit′ik, a.

gran·ite pa·per, n. A varicolored fibrous paper resembling granite.

gran·ite·ware, gran′it·wâr″, n. Articles made of iron coated with vitreous enamel; pottery noted for its granitelike qualities.

gran·it·oid, gran′i·toid, a. Resembling granite.

gra·niv·o·rous, gra·niv′ĕr·us, a. [L. granum, grain, seed, and vorare, devour.] Feeding on grain or seeds.

gran·ny, gran·nie, gran′ē, n. pl. **gran·nies**. [Dim. of grandam, or of grandmother.] Colloq. a grandmother; an old woman. Southern U.S. a nurse or midwife; colloq. one exhibiting the fussiness of an old woman.

gran·ny knot, n. An incorrectly tied square knot which slips and jams easily.

gran·o·lith, gran′o·lith, n. Crushed granite mixed with cement and used for pavements.—**gran·o·lith·ic**, gran″o·lith′ik, a.

gran·o·phyre, gran′o·fīĕr″, n. [G. granophyr, < granit, granite, and porphyr, porphyry.] Any of a class of porphyritic igneous rocks in which the ground mass is a mixture of quartz and feldspar crystals.—**gran·o·phy·ric**, gran″o·fir′ik, a.

grant, grant, gränt, v.t. [O.Fr. graanter, creanter, promise, assure, authorize, grant, confirm, approve, < L. credens (credent)-ppr. of credere, trust, believe.] To give or accord; as, to grant permission; to bestow or confer, as a right, esp. by a formal act; to agree or accede to, as a request; to admit or concede, as for the sake of argument; transfer or convey, as property, esp. by deed or writing.—n. The act of granting; that which is granted, as a privilege or right, a sum of money, or a tract of land; law, a transfer or conveyance of property by deed or writing; a portion of land in Maine, New Hampshire, or Vermont, formerly granted by the state to a person or institution.—**grant·a·ble**, a.—**grant·er, grant·or**, n.

gran·tee, gran·tē′, grän·tē′, n. Law, one to whom a grant is made.

grant-in-aid, grant′in·ād′, n. pl. **grants-in-aid**. Financial aid or subsidy given by a central government to a state or local government for a construction project or other public program; such a grant of public or private funds given to an institution or individual for research or other educational projects.

gran·u·lar, gran′ū·lĕr, a. [< L. granum, grain.] Consisting of or resembling granules or grains.—**gran·u·lar·i·ty**, gran″ū·lar′i·tē, n.—**gran·u·lar·ly**, adv.

gran·u·late, gran′ū·lāt″, v.t.—granulated, granulating. [Fr. granular.] To form into grains or small masses; to raise in granules; to make rough on the surface.—v.i. To collect or be formed into grains; to become granular.—**gran·u·la·tive**, gran′ū·lā″tiv, gran′ū·la·tiv, a.—**gran·u·la·tor, gran·u·la·ter**, n.

gran·u·la·tion, gran″ū·lā′shan, n. The act or condition of granulating; the process of reducing into small grains; pathol. a process by which minute granular projections form on sores when healing; the granular projections themselves; astron. tiny short-lived specks on the photosphere of the sun which cause a mottled appearance.

gran·u·la·tion tis·sue, n. Med. tissue formed in the process of healing, which is made up of minute projections of flesh, and causes a granular appearance.

gran·ule, gran′ūl, n. [Fr., dim. < L. granum, a grain.] A little grain; a small particle; a pellet.

gran·u·lite, gran′ū·līt, n. A metamorphic rock consisting of uniform granules, usu. feldspar and quartz, and having distinct bands.—**gran·u·lit·ic**, gran″ū·lit′ik, a.

gran·u·lo·cyte, gran′ū·lō·sīt″, n. A white blood cell whose cytoplasm contains granules.—**gran·u·lo·cyt·ic**, gran″ū·lō·sit′ik, a.

gran·u·lo·ma, gran″ū·lō′ma, n. pl. **gran·u·lo·mas**, gran·u·lo·ma·ta, gran″ū·lō′ma·ta. A mass or growth of granulation tissue occurring during the process of infection.—**gran·u·lom·a·tous**, gran″ū·lom′a·tus, a.

gran·u·lose, gran′ū·lōs″, a. Granular; textured with granules.

grape, grāp, n. [O.Fr. grape, crape (Fr. grappe), cluster of fruit or flowers, orig. hook; < Teut. (cf. krapf, hook), and akin to E. cramp.] The edible, pulpy, smooth-skinned berry or fruit which grows in clusters on vines of the genus Vitis, and from which wine is made; any vine bearing this fruit; a dark purple color; grapeshot.—**grap·ey, gra·py**, a.—grapier, grapiest.

grape·fruit, grāp′frōt″, n. An edible, large, round, pale yellow fruit with an acid, flavorful pulp; the tree, Citrus paradisi. Also pomelo.

grape hy·a·cinth, n. Any plant of the genus Muscari, as M. botryoides, a species whose globular blue flowers resemble minute grapes.

grape·shot, grāp′shot″, n. Archaic, a cluster of small cast-iron balls used as a charge for a cannon.

grape sug·ar, n. Dextrose.

grape·vine, grāp′vīn″, n. A vine that bears grapes. An unauthenticated or baseless report; an informal method of communicating information from person to person.

graph, graf, gräf, n. [Gr. graphe, drawing, delineation, writing, < graphein, mark, draw, write.] A diagrammatic representation of a system of connections or relations between at least two things by a number of spots, lines, or bars; a pattern of lines which connect points; math. a curve or pattern representing an equation or function.—v.t. Math. To draw or plot, as a curve, from its equation or function; to draw, as a curve, representing an equation or function.

graph, graf, gräf, n. A letter of an alphabet as it might appear in any one of its forms, as C, c; a symbol for a sound or idea.

graph·eme, graf′ēm, n. The smallest written unit of an alphabet, a single letter; the aggregate of all written units or letters and letter combinations used to represent one phoneme, as the t in top, the tt in hitting, and the ed in packed.

graph·ic, graf′ik, a. [L. graphicus, < Gr. graphikos, pertaining to drawing, painting, or writing, < graphē.] Accurately or vividly described; lifelike; clearly delineated; pertaining to the use of diagrams, graphs, mathematical curves, or the like; of or pertaining to writing; as, graphic symbols; presenting an appearance like writing or printing; inscribed or written; geol. noting, pertaining to, or possessing that external texture of a rock characterized by seemingly written symbols produced by crystallization of certain elements; math. pertaining to the determination of values, the solving of problems, etc., by direct measurement on diagrams instead of by ordinary calculations; of or pertaining to the graphic arts. Also **graph·i·cal**.—**graph·i·cal·ly, graph·ic·ly**, adv.—**graph·ic·ness**, n.

graph·ic, graf′ik, n. A pictorial creation of graphic art; a chart, diagram, or map used in illustrated lectures and demonstrations; pl. the graphic arts.

graph·ic arts, n. pl. The visual arts in which representation, printing, ornamentation, or writing are produced on flat surfaces, as in painting or drawing; two-dimensional reproduction of those arts involved in the copying of original designs, as engraving, lithography, or etching.

graph·ics, graf′iks, n. pl. but sing. in constr. The science or art of drawing as used with mathematics and engineering; the science of calculating by means of diagrams.

graph·ite, graf′it, n. [G. graphit, < Gr. graphein, mark, draw, write.] Soft native carbon, having an iron-gray color and metallic luster, used in lead pencils, crucibles, and as a lubricant.—**gra·phit·ic**, gra·fit′ik, a.

graph·i·tize, graf′i·tīz″, v.t.—graphitized, graphitizing. To convert into graphite, as part of the carbon in steel; to cover with graphite, as the surface of an object.—**graph·i·ti·za·tion**, graf″ĭt″a·zā′shun, n.

graph·ol·o·gy, gra·fol′o·jē, n. [Gr. graphe, writing.] The study of handwriting, esp. for analysis of the writer's character.—**graph·ol·o·gist**, n.

Graph·o·phone, graf′o·fōn″, n. [Gr. graphein, write, and phone, sound.] (Sometimes cap.) A brand of phonographic machine; an early sound-reproducing machine employing a wax record. (Trademark.)

graph pa·per, n. A type of paper with printed ruled lines, usu. horizontal and vertical, forming a grid pattern on which graphs and curves are plotted.

grap·nel, grap′nel, n. [Dim. < Fr. grapin, a grapnel; of same origin as grape.] An instrument having several hooks or clamps for seizing and holding objects; a small anchor with four or five flukes or claws, used to hold boats or small vessels; a grappling iron. Also **grape·line, grap·lin, grap·line**.

grap·pa, gräp′pä, n. An Italian brandy processed from a wine press′ residue.

grap·ple, grap′l, n. [Appar. a dim. form < O.Fr. grape, hook; in later senses, < grapple, v.] A grapnel; a hooked device used to fasten and hold one ship to another; the act of grappling; a grip or close hold, as in wrestling; hand-to-hand combat.—v.t.—grappled, grappling. To seize, hold, or fasten with or as with a grapple; to seize and hold firmly in a struggle; engage in a struggle or a close encounter with.—v.i. To use a grapple; to hold or make fast to something as with a grapple; to seize another, or each other, in a firm grip, as in wrestling; to clinch; to contend or struggle, usu. followed by with, often fig.; as, to grapple with a difficult assignment.—**grap·pler**, n.

grap·pling, grap′ling, n. That by which anything, esp. a ship, is seized and held; a grapnel.

grap·pling i·ron, n. Grapnel. Also **grap·pling hook**.

grasp, grasp, gräsp, v.t. [M.E. graspen, grapsen; prob. akin to O.E. grāpian, E. grope.] To seize and hold by or as by clasping with the fingers; seize upon; hold firmly; to lay hold of with the mind; comprehend.—v.i. To make the motion of seizing; clutch something firmly or eagerly. —n. A grasping or gripping; a grip of the hand or of the arms; embrace; power of seizing and holding; hold, possession, or mastery, as, to wrest power from the grasp of a usurper; mental hold or ability to understand, as, a subject beyond one's grasp; broad or thorough comprehension.—**grasp·a·ble**, a.—**grasp·er**, n.

grasp·ing, gras′ping, gräs′ping, a. That seizes; fig. avaricious or greedy, as: He is a *grasping* individual.—**grasp·ing·ly**, *adv.*—**grasp·ing·ness**, *n.*

grass, gras, gräs, *n.* [O.E. *graes, gaers,* = D., G., Icel., and Goth. *gras,* grass; from the Teut. root whence E. *grow* and *green.*] Herbage, esp. the plants on which grazing animals pasture; any plant of the family *Gramineae* characterized by jointed stems, sheathing leaves, and flower spikelets; pasture land, as, half of the farm is *grass.* the grass-covered ground; lawn. Vertical lines on a radarscope which resemble lawn grass.—*v.t.* To feed with growing grass; to cover with grass or turf; to seed with grass; to lay on the grass, as for the purpose of bleaching.—*v.i.* To produce grass; to become covered with grass; to feed on growing grass; to graze.—**grass·y**, *a.*—*grassier, grassiest.*

grass cloth, *n.* A fabric woven from the fibers of the ramie or other tough-fibered grass.

grass green, *n.* The yellowish-green color of grass.

grass·hop·per, gras'hop″ĕr, gräs'hop″ĕr, *n.* A leaping insect of the order *Orthoptera,* commonly living in grass. *Colloq.* a type of light airplane.

grass·land, gras'land″, gräs'land″, *n.* Meadow land; permanent pasture; land which consists predominantly of grasses.

grass roots, *n. pl., sing. or pl. in constr.* An area comprising the small towns and rural sections of the U.S.; a hypothetical segment of the U.S. population residing outside the largest cities, and considered representative of the strongest, most admirable qualities of the national character; the basis or foundation of something. Also **grass-roots.**—**grass-roots,** *a.*

grass tree, *n.* Any member of the Australian lilylike genus *Xanthorrhoea,* comprising plants with a stout, woody stem, a tuft of long, grasslike leaves, and a dense flower spike.

grass wid·ow, *n.* [< *grass* and *widow;* the original force of *grass* being uncertain.] A woman who is separated or who lives apart from her husband, by reason of divorce or otherwise.—**grass wid·ow·er,** *n.* Masc. of grass widow.

grate, grāt, *n.* [M.L. *grata,* < L. *cratis,* wickerwork, hurdle.] A framework of parallel or crossed bars used as a partition, guard, or screen; a frame of metal bars for holding fuel in a fireplace or a furnace; a fireplace. *Min.* a screen for sifting ore.—*v.t.*—*grated, grating.* To fit with a grate.

grate, grāt, *v.t.*—*grated, grating.* [O.Fr. *grater* (Fr. *gratter*); < Teut. (cf. G. *kratzen,* to scratch).] To grind into particles by rubbing against a rough surface; to pulverize; to gnash, as the teeth; to scrape with a harsh, jarring noise; to irritate.—*v.i.* To scrape or rub noisily; to have an irritating effect, as: The sounds of squeaking chalk *grate* on my nerves.—**grat·er,** *n.*

grate·ful, *a.* [Obs. *grate,* pleasing, also thankful < L. *gratus.*] Appreciative of kindness shown or benefits received; thankful; expressive of gratitude; as, a *grateful* glance; pleasing, agreeable or welcome; as, *grateful* news; refreshing.—**grate·ful·ly,** *adv.*—**grate·ful·ness,** *n.*

grat·i·cule, grat'i·kūl″, *n.* [Fr., < M.L. *graticula,* for L. *craticula,* gridiron.] A design or plan divided into squares to facilitate copying, as in map making. *Opt.* a reticle.

grat·i·fi·ca·tion, grat″i·fi·kā'shan, *n.* [L. *gratificatio.*] The act of gratifying or pleasing; the state of being gratified; that which affords pleasure, enjoyment, or satisfaction.

grat·i·fy, grat'i·fī″, *v.t.*—*gratified, gratifying.* [Fr. *gratifier,* L. *gratificor—gratus,* pleasant, agreeable, and *facio,* to make.]

To give pleasure to; to satisfy desires, needs, or appetites; to indulge or humor.—**grat·i·fi·er,** *n.*—**gra·ti·fy·ing,** *a.* Capable of pleasing, satisfying, or producing gratification.

grat·in, grat'in, *Fr.* grä·taN′, *n.* [Fr. < *gratter,* scrape.] Au gratin.—**grat·in·ate,** *v.t.*—*gratinated, gratinating.* [= Fr.*gratiner*]. To prepare or cook au gratin.

grat·ing, grā'ting, *n.* A grate, or framework of parallel or crossed bars; a lattice, of metal or wood, used to close, cover, or partition off an opening. *Phys.* a series of fine parallel lines ruled very close together on a glass or polished metal surface, used to produce spectra by diffraction; also **dif·frac·tion grat·ing.**

grat·ing, grā'ting, *a.* Harsh or jarring, as sound; irritating or unpleasant in effect. —**grat·ing·ly,** *adv.*

gra·tis, grat'is, grā'tis, *adv.* [L. < *gratia,* favor.] For nothing; freely; without charge.—*a.* Given or done free of charge.

grat·i·tude, grat'i·tōd″, grat'i·tūd″, *n.* [L.L. *gratitudo.*] A warm and friendly appreciation of a kindness or a favor received; thankfulness; gratefulness.

gra·tu·i·tous, gra·tö'i·tus, gra·tū'i·tus, *a.* [L. *gratuitus,* < *gratus,* pleasing, agreeable.] Given without charge or recompense; free; not required, called for, or warranted by the circumstances; unjustified; as, a *gratuitous* assumption.—**gra·tu·i·tous·ly,** *adv.*—**gra·tu·i·tous·ness,** *n.*

gra·tu·i·tous con·tract, *n. Law,* a contract which benefits one party only and provides no recompense to the other. Also **con·tract of be·nef·i·cence.**

gra·tu·i·ty, gra·tö'i·tē, gra·tū'i·tē, *n.* pl. **gra·tu·i·ties.** A free gift; a donation; a tip; anything given without obligation or claim. *Brit.* a bonus for war veterans, or for military personnel on retirement or discharge.

grau·pel, grou'pel, *n.* [G. small hailstone.] *Meteor.* granules or pellets of soft hail or sleet. Also **snow pel·lets.**

gra·va·men, gra·vā'men, *n.* pl. **gra·vam·i·na,** gra·vam'i·na. [L. < *gravo,* to weigh down, < *gravis,* heavy.] *Law,* that part of an accusation which weighs most heavily against the accused; a grievance.

grave, grāv, *v.t.*—past *graved,* pp. *graven* or *graved,* ppr. *graving.* [O.E. *grafan,* to dig, to grave or carve = D. *graven,* Dan. *grave,* Icel. *grafa,* G. *graben,* to dig, to engrave; cogn. Ir. *grafaim,* to engrave, to scrape; Gr. *graphō,* to grave, to write.] To carve or cut; to engrave; to impress deeply, as on the mind.—**grav·er,** *n.* One who carves or engraves; an engraving tool; a burin.

grave, grāv, *n.* [O.E. *graef,* a grave, a trench, from stem of *grafan,* to dig or grave = Dan. *graf,* Icel. *gröf,* D. *graf,* G. *grab,* Russ. *grob,* a grave.] An excavation in the earth in which a dead body is buried; any place of interment; a tomb.

grave, grāv, *a.*—*graver, gravest.* [Fr. *grave,* < L. *gravis,* heavy (whence also *grief, aggravate, gravid, gravitate*); allied to Gr. *barys,* heavy, *baros,* weight (in *barometer*); Skt. *guru,* heavy.] Solemn; serious; important; momentous; critical or threatening; somber or drab, as color; *mus.* low in pitch.—**grave·ly,** *adv.*—**grave·ness,** *n.*

grave, grāv, gräv, *n.* An accent mark (ˋ) used in French to indicate a special pronunciation for certain vowels; in specific languages, used to indicate stress on certain syllables.

gra·ve, grä'vā, *It.* grä've, *a., adv. Mus.* slowly, with solemnity.

grav·el, grav'el, *n.* [Fr. *gravele,* < O.Fr. *grave,* sand or gravel, < the Celtic; Armor. *grouan,* sand; W. *grou,* pebbles, coarse gravel.] Small stones and pebbles loosely mixed; small stones and sand combined;

pathol. small crystals or calculi in the kidneys or bladder; the disease occasioned by such concretions.

grav·el, grav'el, *a.* Rasping or grating, as the sound of a voice.

grav·el, grav'el, *v.t.*—*graveled, graveling, Brit. gravelled, gravelling.* To cover with gravel; to puzzle; *colloq.* to annoy or provoke.

grav·el-blind, grav'el·blind″, *a.* Having very weak or poor vision: more blind than *sand-blind,* less blind than *stone-blind.*

grav·el·ly, grav'e·lē, *a.* Abounding in, consisting of, or resembling gravel; harsh or grating; as, *gravelly* speech.

grav·en, grā'ven, *a.* Of or denoting that which is deeply impressed or fixed; sculptured or carved; as, a *graven* image.

grave·stone, grāv'stōn″, *n.* A stone placed at a grave as a monument or marker.

grave·yard, grāv'yärd″, *n.* A place of burial or interment of the dead; a cemetery.

grave·yard shift, *n. Slang,* a work period beginning at or after midnight.

gra·vim·e·ter, gra·vim'i·tĕr, *n.* [L. *gravis,* heavy.] An instrument for determining specific gravities.—**grav·i·met·ric, grav·i·met·ri·cal,** grav″i·me'trik, grav″i·me'trik·al, *a.* Denoting measurement by weight.—**grav·i·met·ri·cal·ly,** *adv.*—**gra·vim·e·try,** gra·vim'i·trē, *n.* The measurement of weight or density; the determination of specific gravities.

grav·id, grav'id, *a.* [L. *gravidus,* < *gravis,* heavy.] Pregnant.—**gra·vid·i·ty,** gra·vid'i·tē, **grav·id·ness,** *n.*—**grav·id·ly,** *adv.*

grav·i·tate, grav'i·tāt″, *v.i.*—*gravitated, gravitating.* [Fr. *graviter,* < L. *gravitas,* < *gravis,* heavy.] To be affected by gravitation; to move under the influence of gravitation; to sink downward; *fig.* to have a tendency toward some attracting influence.—*v.t.* To move by gravitation.—**grav·i·ta·ter,** *n.*

grav·i·ta·tion, grav″i·tā'shan, *n.* The act or process of gravitating; *phys.* the force by which all masses or bodies are mutually attracted to each other. An attraction or tendency toward an object.—**grav·i·ta·tion·al,** *a.*—**grav·i·ta·tion·al·ly,** *adv.*—**grav·i·ta·tive,** grav'i·tā″tiv, *a.*

grav·i·ty, grav'i·tē, *n.* pl. **grav·i·ties.** Solemnity of deportment, character, or demeanor; seriousness; weightiness; enormity; as, the *gravity* of an offense. *Phys.* the force which causes bodies to tend toward a center of attraction, esp. toward the center of the earth; also *gravitation.* See *center of gravity, specific gravity.*—*a.* Of or pertaining to seriousness, solemnity, or weightiness.

gra·vure, gra·vur′, grä·vur′, *n.* [Fr. *engraving,* < *graver,* engrave; < Teut.] Intaglio printing from a plate made by a photomechanical process; a plate for intaglio printing made by photomechanical or other methods; a print made from such a plate. Also *photogravure, rotogravure.*

gra·vy, grā've, *n.* pl. **gra·vies.** [M.E. *gravey, grave;* origin obscure.] The fat and juices that drip from meat in cooking; these juices made into a sauce for meat and vegetables. *Slang,* money or gain easily or illegally obtained.—**gra·vy boat,** *n.* A small boat-shaped dish or vessel for serving gravy or sauce.

gray, grey, grā, *a.* [O.E. *graeg* = D. *grauw* = Icel. *grar,* gray.] Of a color between white and black, having little or no positive hue; ash-colored; lead-colored; not bright; as, a *gray* day; dismal or gloomy; as, a *gray* existence; dull, as in mood or outlook; dressed or habited in gray; as, a *gray* friar; gray-haired; old or ancient; pertaining to old age; mature, as experience; indeterminate.—*n.* Any neutral color consisting of a black and white mixture; something of this color, as cloth.—

a- fat, fāte, fär, fâre, fạll;   **e-** met, mē, mēre, hėr;   **i-** pin, pīne;   **o-** not, nōte, mŏve;   **u-** tub, cūbe, bụll;   **oi-** oil;   **ou-** pound.

v.t. To make *gray.*—**v.i.** To become *gray.*—**gray·ish, grey·ish,** *a.* Somewhat gray.—**gray·ly, grey·ly,** *adv.*—**gray·ness, grey·-ness,** *n.*

gray·beard, grey·beard, grā'bērd", *n.* An old man; one having maturity and long experience.

gray·fish, grey·fish, grā'fish", *n.* pl. **gray·fish·es, gray·fish, grey·fish·es, grey·fish.** The common dogfish, *Squalus acanthias.*

gray·hound, grā'hound", *n.* Greyhound.

gray·lag, grey·lag, grā'lag", *n.* [Perhaps named from its lagging behind other species in migrating.] The common gray wild goose, *Anser cinereus* or *A. anser* of Europe.

gray·ling, grā'ling, *n.* Any of the fresh-water fishes constituting the genus *Thymallus,* related to the trout, but having a longer and higher pectoral fin; any of the grayish or brownish butterflies belonging to the *Satyridae* family.

gray mat·ter, *n. Anat.* nerve tissue, as of the spinal cord and brain, made up of both nerve cells and nerve fibers, brownish gray in color. *Colloq.* brains; intelligence.

gray·wacke, grā'wak", grā'wak"e, *n.* [G. *grauwacke*—*grau,* gray, and *wacke,* a kind of rock.] A dark gray sandstone in which grains or fragments of various minerals or rocks, as feldspar and quartz, are embedded in a hard matrix.

graze, grāz, *v.i.*—*grazed, grazing.* [O.E. *grasian,* < *græs,* E. *grass*] To feed on growing herbage, as cattle; to pasture.—*v.t.* To put to feed on pasturage, as live-stock; to put to pasture.—*n.* A grazing or feeding on grass.—**graz·er,** *n.* An animal that grazes.

graze, grāz, *v.t.*—*grazed, grazing.* [Origin obscure.] To touch or rub lightly in passing; to abrade, scrape, or scratch lightly in passing.—*v.i.* To touch or rub something lightly, or so as to produce slight abrasion, in passing.—*n.* A grazing, touching, or rubbing lightly in passing; a slight abrasion or scratch.

gra·zier, grā'zhėr, *n.* One who raises cattle for the market.

graz·ing, grā'zing, *n.* Pasture land; a pasture.

grease, grēs, *n.* [O.Fr. *graisse, craisse* (Fr. *graisse*), < L. *crassus,* fat.] The melted or rendered fat of animals, esp. in a soft state; fatty or oily matter in general; a thick lubricant. Shorn wool which has not been cleansed of oily matter; also **grease wool.** *Veter. med.* an inflammation of a horse's skin in the fetlock region; also **grease-heel.** —**in the grease,** the state of wool or fur before being cleaned.

grease, grēs, grēz, *v.t.*—*greased, greasing.* To smear or anoint with grease; to soil with grease; to lubricate with grease; *fig.* to cause to run easily; to facilitate.—**grease the palm,** to bribe.—**greas·er,** *n.*

grease mon·key, *n. Slang,* an automobile or airplane mechanic.

grease paint, *n.* A heavy, oily variety of theatrical make-up used by performers.

grease·wood, grēs'wud", *n.* A shrub, *Sarcobatus vermiculatus,* of the alkaline regions of the western U.S., containing a small amount of oil and used for fuel; any of various similar shrubs.

greas·y, grē'sē, grē'zē, *a.*—*greasier, greasiest.* Composed of or containing grease; oily; smeared or soiled with grease; greaselike in appearance; *fig.* slippery or unsavory.—**greas·i·ly,** *adv.*—**greas·i·ness,** *n.*

great, grāt, *a.* [O.E. *great* = D. *groot* = *gross,* great.] Unusually or comparatively large in size or dimensions; as, a *great* fire; big; large; pregnant; as, *great* with child; large in number, numerous; unusual

or considerable in degree; of long duration; loud; as, a *great* cry; beyond what is ordinary, as in extent, scope, character; of much consequence; important; as, *great* issues at stake; chief or principal; as, the *great* seal; notable or remarkable; distinguished, illustrious, or famous; of high rank, official position, or social standing; of outstanding abilities or achievements; as, a *great* poet; of unusual excellence or merit; admirable or fine; of noble or superior character. *Genealogy,* being one generation more remote or removed from a relationship specified, used in compounds; as, *great*-grandfather, *great-great*-grandfather. *Colloq.* first-rate, fine, amusing; as, a *great* time; in an extreme degree; as, *great* friends; skillful or expert at; as, *great* at mathematics; much addicted to something, with *on*; as, to be *great on* finding fault; much in use or favor, as: Humor was a *great* word with physiologists.—**great·ly,** *adv.*—**great·ness,** *n.*

great, grāt, *n.* Collectively, those who have achieved outstanding success, as: Abraham Lincoln takes a rightful place among the *great. Usu. pl.* one who has attained distinction or renown; as, one of opera's *greats.*

great ape, *n.* Any of the four modern anthropoid apes: the gorilla, chimpanzee, gibbon, and orangutan.

great-aunt, grāt'ant", grāt'änt", *n.* A grandaunt.

Great Bear, *n.* A constellation in the northern sky, containing the Big Dipper. Also *Ursa Major.*

great cir·cle, *n.* A circle on the surface of a sphere, the plane of which passes through the center of the sphere.

great·coat, grāt'kōt", *n. Brit.* an overcoat.

Great Dane, *n.* A very large and powerful short-haired dog.

Great Di·vide, *n.* The Rocky Mountains: N. America's continental divide. *Fig.* A crisis; an important or crucial decision; dying or death.

great-heart·ed, grāt'här"tid, *a.* Having or showing a brave, noble, or generous heart; magnanimous. Also **great·heart·ed.** —**great-heart·ed·ness, great·heart·ed·-ness,** *n.*

great-neph·ew, grāt'nef"ū, grāt'nev"ū, *n.* A grandnephew.

great-niece, grāt'nēs", *n.* A grandniece.

great pow·er, *n.* A nation of the first rank in economic, military, and political strength.

Great Rus·sian, *n.* A Russian living in the northern or central part of the U.S.S.R.; the Slavic language of the northern and central part of the U.S.S.R.—*a.*

great seal, *n.* (*Often cap.*) an official seal, used by a government, corporation, or head of state, to stamp and thus authenticate important documents.

great-un·cle, grāt'ung"kl, *n.* A granduncle.

great year, *n. Astron.* a period during which a cycle of the precession of the equinoxes is completed, or about 26,000 years. Also *Platonic year.*

grebe, grēb, *n.* [Fr. *grèbe,* < Armor. *krib,* W. *crib,* a comb, a crest, one variety having a crest.] An aquatic bird of the family *Colymbidae,* having toes separate, but broadly fringed by a membrane, and legs set so far back that on land it assumes the upright position of the penguin.

Gre·cian, grē'shan, *a.* [L. *Graecia,* Greece, < *Graecus,* Greek.] Of or pertaining to Greece or its inhabitants; Greek.—*n.* A Greek; one versed in the Greek language or literature.

Gre·cism, grē'siz"um, *n.* [L. *Graecus,* Greek.] An idiom or peculiarity of the Greek language; the spirit of Greek thought, art, or culture; adoption or imitation of these. Also **Grae·cism.**

Gre·cize, grē'sīz, *v.t.*—*Grecized, Grecizing.* To impart Greek characteristics to; to translate into Greek.—*v.i.* To conform to what is Greek; to adopt Greek speech, idioms, or customs.

gree, grē, *v.t., v.i.*—*greed, greeing.* [For *agree.*] *Brit. dial.* to bring or come into accord; harmonize; agree.

greed, grēd, *n.* [Back-formation < *greedy.*] Inordinate or rapacious longing, esp. for wealth; desire for possessing or having more than one needs, esp. money or property; avarice.

greed·y, grē'dē, *a.*—*greedier, greediest.* [O.E. *graedig,* akin to *graedum,* with greed, Icel. *grādhr,* hunger, greed, Goth. *grēdus,* hunger.] Excessively eager for gain or wealth; desirous to have more than needed; avaricious; covetous; having an inordinate desire for food or drink; ravenous; voracious. In general, having eager desire; as, *greedy* for praise.—**greed·i·ly,** *adv.*—**greed·i·ness,** *n.*

Greek, grēk, *n.* [O.E. *Grēcas,* also *Crēcas,* pl. < L. *Graecus,* < Gr. *Graikos,* a Greek.] A native or inhabitant of ancient or modern Greece; a member of the Greek race; a member of the Greek Church; the language of the people of Greece, divided for convenience into ancient or classical Greek, Late Greek, Middle Greek, and Modern or New Greek, esp. that of the classical period. *Colloq.* anything unintelligible, as speech or statements, as: The letter, being in French, was *Greek* to him. The Greek alphabet, with the Roman (or English) equivalents, is here given:

Form		Equivalent	Name
A	α	a	alpha
B	β	b	beta
Γ	γ	g	gamma
Δ	δ	d	delta
E	ε	e (short)	epsilon
Z	ζ	z	zeta
H	η	e (long)	eta
Θ	θ, ϑ	th	theta
I	ι	i	iota
K	κ	k, c	kappa
Λ	λ	l	lambda
M	μ	m	mu
N	ν	n	nu
Ξ	ξ	x	xi
O	ο	o (short)	omicron
Π	π	p	pi
P	ρ	r	rho
Σ	σ, s	s	sigma
T	τ	t	tau
Υ	υ	u, y	upsilon
Φ	φ	ph	phi
X	χ	kh, ch	chi
Ψ	ψ	ps	psi
Ω	ω	o (long)	omega

—*a.* Of or pertaining to Greece, the Greeks, or their language; pertaining to the Greek Church.

Greek Cath·o·lic, *n.* Member of an Eastern Orthodox Church; one belonging to the Greek Orthodox Church.

Greek cross, *n.* A cross consisting of an upright crossed in the middle by a horizontal piece of the same length.

Greek fire, *n.* Any of various incendiary compositions consisting of substances such as pitch, asphalt, inflammable oils or sulphur, used by the Greeks and others in warfare during medieval times.

Greek Or·tho·dox, *a.* Of or pertaining to the Orthodox Church of Greece.

green, grēn, *a.* [O.E. *grēne* = D. *groen* = G. *grün* = Icel. *grœnn, grœnn,* green.] Of the color of growing herbage and foliage: in the spectrum, intermediate between yellow and blue; covered with a growth of herbage or foliage; as, *green* fields; characterized by the presence of verdure; as, a *green* Christmas; mild or temperate; as, a *green* winter; having a pale or sickly color, as from fear, jealousy, or illness; full of life and vigor; as, *green* old age; vigorous; undecayed; not fully developed or perfected in growth or condition; unripe or immature; unseasoned, as timber; not dried or cured; not fired, as bricks or pottery; immature in age or judgment; untrained; inexperienced; simple or gullible; fresh, recent, or new; as, a *green* wound.—**green·ly**, *adv.*

green, grēn, *n.* A green color; a green dye or pigment; any of various things of green color; green material or clothing; grassy land; a piece of grassy ground constituting a town or village common; in golf, a putting green. *Pl.* fresh leaves or branches of trees or shrubs, used for decoration; the leaves and stems of plants, as lettuce or spinach, used for food.—*v.i.*, *v.t.* To become or make green.

green al·ga, *n.* An alga of the *Chlorophyceae* family in which the cells bearing chlorophyll predominate.

green·back, grēn'bak", *n.* Any piece of U.S. paper money, the back of which is printed in green.

green bean, *n.* A string bean.

green·belt, grēn'belt", grēn'belt', *n.* An area of parkways, lawns, or wooded land surrounding a planned community. A judo belt bestowed on junior students who have achieved the first rank above a beginner.

Green Be·rets, *n. pl. Milit.* a specially trained task force in the U.S. Army, qualified to undertake unusually hazardous missions, and identified by their green berets.

green·bri·er, grēn'brī'ẽr, *n.* A climbing plant of the lily family, esp. *Smilax rotundifolia*, having greenish flowers, a thorny stem, and thick leaves.

green corn, *n.* Tender, edible ears of sweet corn.

green drag·on, *n. Bot.* a flowering herb, *Arisaema dracontium*, related to the jack-in-the-pulpit.

green·er·y, grē'ne·rē, *n. pl.* **green·er·ies.** Green foliage or vegetation; verdure; a place where green plants are raised or kept.

green-eyed, grēn'īd", *a.* Having green-colored eyes; jealous.

green finch, grēn'finch", *n.* A common European finch, *Chloris chloris*, olive-green with conspicuous yellow on wings and tail.

green·gage, grēn'gāj", *n.* [From Sir William *Gage*, who introduced this plum into England.] A species of plum having a green or yellow-green skin and a juicy greenish pulp.

green·gro·cer, grēn'grō"sẽr, *n. Brit.* a retailer of vegetables and fruit.—**green·gro·cer·y**, grēn'grō"se·rē, *n. pl.* **green·gro·cer·ies.**

green·horn, grēn'harn", *n.* [In allusion to the immature horns of a young animal.] A raw, inexperienced person. *U.S.* esp. during the 19th and early 20th centuries, a recent unassimilated immigrant.

green·house, grēn'hous", *n. pl.* **green·houses.** A heated glass building for growing young plants, and for commercially growing out of season plants and flowers.

green·ing, grē'ning, *n.* A variety of apple the ripe skin of which is green.

green·ish, grē'nish, *a.* Somewhat green; having a green tinge.—**green·ish·ness**, *n.*

green light, *n.* A signal of clearance or freedom to proceed, esp. a traffic signal light; *colloq.* permission.

green ma·nure, *n. Agric.* A field of green plants, plowed under while growing to decompose and thereby increase the soil's productiveness; manure which has not begun to decompose.

green mold, *n.* Blue mold.

green·ness, grēn'nis, *n.* The quality of being green; the quality of being immature; naiveté.

green·ock·ite, grē'no·kīt", *n.* [From Lord *Greenock*, 1783-1859.] A rare mineral consisting of cadmium sulfide, appearing in crystal form or as an earthy crust.

green on·ion, *n.* A scallion; a flavorful shallot which is used in salads or cooking.

green·room, grēn'rōm", grēn'rum", *n. Theater*, a room near the stage in a theater, in which actors and actresses relax while not performing.

green·sand, grēn'sand", *n.* A variety of sandstone containing green grains of glauconite which impart to it a greenish hue.

green·sick·ness, grēn'sik"nis, *n. Pathol.* an anemic condition occurring in young women and girls, characterized by a yellow-greenish skin pallor; chlorosis.—**green·sick**, *a.*

green snake, *n.* A nonvenomous, slender green snake of N. America, of the family *Colubridae*, feeding mainly on insects.

green soap, *n.* A soap, beneficial in the treatment of skin diseases, which has vegetable oils and potassium hydroxide as principal ingredients.

green·stone, grēn'stōn", *n.* Any of various dark-greenish igneous rocks taking their color from the chlorite they contain; nephrite.

green·sward, grēn'swạrd", *n.* Turf green with grass.—**green·sward·ed**, *a.*

green thumb, *n.* Superior ability to cultivate plants, esp. garden flowers.

green tur·tle, *n.* A large green-shelled sea turtle, *Chelonia mydas*, abundant in warm tropical waters, whose eggs and flesh are prized as food.

green veg·e·ta·bles, *n. pl.* Leafy plants, shoots, and legume fruits, esp. their green edible parts, such as cabbage, asparagus, green peas and their pods.

Green·wich Time, grin'ij tĩm, grin'ich tĩm", grẽn'ij tĩm", grẽn'ich tĩm", *n.* The mean standard time, determined from the prime meridian time at Greenwich, England, serving as the basis for calculating standard time elsewhere in the world. Also **Green·wich Mean Time**, **Green·wich Civ·il Time.**

greet, grēt, *v.t.* [O.E. *grētan*, to salute, hail, bid farewell = G. *grüssen*, D. *groeten*, to greet; compare Prov. E. and Sc. *greet*, Goth. *gretan*, Icel. *gráta*, to weep.] To address with expressions of kind wishes; to meet; to salute; to hail.—**greet·er**, *n.* —**greet·ing**, grē'ting, *n.* Salutation at meeting; compliment shown by one absent.

greg·a·rine, greg'a·rĩn", greg'ẽr·in, *n.* [N.L. *Gregarina*, the typical genus, < L. *gregarius*, E. *gregarious.*] One of the *Gregarinida*, a group of protozoans which are parasitic in insects and crustaceans.—*a.*

gre·gar·i·ous, gri·gâr'ē·us, *a.* [Lat. *gregarius*, < *grex, gregis*, a flock or herd; seen also in *aggregate, congregate, egregious.*] Sociable; cooperative; participating in groups; pertaining to a herd or flock; crowding; clustering; *bot.* growing in clusters.—**gre·gar·i·ous·ly**, *adv.*—**gre·gar·i·ous·ness**, *n.*

Gre·go·ri·an, gri·gōr'ē·an, gri·gar'ē·an, *a.* Relating to popes named Gregory or to those associated with them, esp. Pope Gregory I or Pope Gregory XIII.

Gre·go·ri·an cal·en·dar, *n.* The calendar now in general use introduced by Pope Gregory XIII in 1582 to provide corrections in the Julian Calendar.

Gre·go·ri·an chant, *n.* A plain song used in Roman Catholic and some other church services: its use was influenced by liturgical reforms which Pope Gregory I introduced.

greige, grā, grāzh, *n.* Woven fabric in the unfinished, unbleached, or undyed state before it is processed. Also **gray goods.**—*a.*

grei·sen, grī'zen, *n.* [G.] A crystalline rock composed chiefly of quartz and mica, common in the tin mines of Saxony.

grem·lin, grem'lin, *n.* Any unexplainable, disruptive influence; a fictitious ill-tempered elf or sprite, orig. blamed by aviation pilots in World War II for mechanical difficulties.

gre·nade, gri·nād', *n.* [Fr. *grenade* = Sp. *granada*, pomegranate, grenade, < L. *granatus*, having grains or seeds (*granatum*, pomegranate), < *granum*, E. grain.] A small explosive shell thrown by hand or discharged from a rifle; a glass missile containing chemicals, as for fire extinguishing.

gren·a·dier, gren"a·dẽr', *n.* [< *grenade.*] A member of a special regiment, as the *Grenadier* Guards of the British army; originally a soldier trained to use hand grenades. Any of the deep-sea fishes belonging to the family *Macruridae*, distinguished by their pointed tails and long bodies; also **rat·tail.**—**gren·a·dier·i·al**, *a.*

gren·a·dine, gren"a·dēn', gren'a·dēn", *n.* A thin, open-textured fabric, plain or patterned, woven in various fibers, as nylon, silk, cotton, or wool. A sweet red syrup obtained from pomegranates, used in mixed drinks.

Gresh·am's law, gresh'amz lạ, *n.* [From Sir T. *Gresham* (1519-1579), English financier.] *Econ.* the tendency of the inferior of two forms of currency in circulation together to circulate more freely than the superior, owing to the hoarding of the latter.

gres·so·ri·al, gre·sōr'ē·al, gre·sạr'ē·al, *a.* [N.L. *gressorius*, < L. *gradi*, walk, go.] *Zool.* adapted for walking, as the feet of some birds. Also **gres·so·ri·ous.**

grey, grā, *n.*, *a.*, *v.i.*, *v.t.* Gray.

grey fri·ar, *n.* (*Often cap.*) a friar of the Franciscan order.

grey·hound, grā'hound", *n.* [O.E. *grīghund* = Icel. *greyhundr*, greyhound (Icel. *grey*, dog); not connected with *gray.*] One of a breed of tall, slender dogs notable for keen sight and for fleetness; a swift ship, esp. an ocean liner. Also **grayhound.**

grey·lag, grā'lag", *n.* Graylag.

grib·ble, grib'l, *n.* [Origin obscure.] A small marine crustacean, *Limnoria terebrans*, destructive to submerged timber; any of certain related species.

grid, grid, *n.* [Back-formation < *gridiron.*] A grating; a gridiron; *elect.* a ridged or perforated lead plate used in a storage battery; *electron.* one of the interior elements of a vacuum tube; *surv.* base lines intersecting at right angles.

grid·dle, grid'l, *n.* [O.Fr. *gredil*, var. of *greil*, gridiron.] A flat, often heavy rimless frying pan used in cooking all types of hotcakes; any heated, flat area used for cooking.—*v.t.*—**griddled, griddling.**

grid·dle·cake, grid'l·kāk", *n.* A thin cake of batter cooked on a griddle; a pancake; a flapjack.

grid·i·ron, grid'ī"ẽrn, *n.* [M.E. *gredirne*, earlier *gredire*, appar. an altered form of *gredil*, E. *griddle.*] *Football*, the field of play; *cookery*, a utensil having parallel bars on which food may be broiled; any network or framework resembling this; *theater*, a structure above the stage of a theater, from which the drop scenes are manipulated.—*v.t.* To mark with parallel bars or lines like those of a gridiron.

grid leak, *n. Electron.* a high-resistance device which permits excessive charges on the grid to leak off or escape.

grief, grēf, *n.* [Fr. *grief*, grievance, what oppresses, < L. *gravis*, heavy.] Emotional pain or distress from an extreme cause, as affliction or bereavement; deep sorrow or sadness; the cause of such sadness.—**to come to grief**, to come to a bad end; to fail.—**grief-strick·en**, *a.* Afflicted with or overcome by grief.

griev·ance, grē'vans, *n.* An act or condition considered to be a justifiable reason for complaint, as substandard working conditions or unfair regulations; a cause, of grief, as a wrong or slight, real or imagined; a complaint.—**griev·ant**, *n.* A person filing a grievance for decision by an appointed authority, as an arbitrator.

grieve, grēv, *v.t.—grieved, grieving.* [O.Fr. *griever.*] To cause to feel grief; to make sorrowful.—*v.i.* To feel grief; to sorrow; to mourn.—**griev·er**, *n.*—**griev·ing·ly**, *adv.*

griev·ous, grē'vus, *a.* Causing grief or sorrow; serious; grave; severe; full of grief; expressing great grief or affliction. —**griev·ous·ly**, *adv.*—**griev·ous·ness**, *n.*

grif·fin, grif'in, *n.* [Fr. *griffon*, It. *grifone*, < L. *gryps, gryphus*, griffin, Gr. *gryps*, a griffon, < *grypos*, hook-beaked.] *Class. mythol.* a winged creature with the forepart of an eagle and the body of a lion. Also *griffon, gryphon.*

grif·fon, grif'on, *n.* [Fr. *griffon*, griffin.] One of a breed of coarse-haired hunting dogs; a small, wiry-haired pet dog of Belgian origin, resembling a Scotch terrier; a griffin.

grift, grift, *n. Slang,* any of various methods of gaining money by dishonest schemes, petty swindling, confidence games, or cheating.—*v.t.*—**grift·er**, *n.*

grig, grig, *n.* [Connected with *cricket*; in second sense with Sw. *kråka*, to creep.] *Dial.* A cricket; a grasshopper; a small eel; a merry or lively person.

gri·gri, grē'grē, *n.* Gris-gris.

grill, gril, *v.t.* [< Fr. *griller*, to broil, < *gril*, a gridiron, *grille*, a grate; O.Fr. *graille*, < L.L. *graticula*, corrupted < L. *craticula*, a small gridiron, dim. of *cratis*, a hurdle.] To broil on a gridiron or similar appliance; to mark with a pattern resembling a grill; *colloq.* to interrogate relentlessly.—*n.* A grate for broiling food over heat; a gridiron; grilled food; a grillroom.—**grill·-work**, *n.*

gril·lage, gril'ij, *n.* [Fr. < *grille*, a grate, a railing.] *Constr.* a heavy framework of beams used to sustain foundations on soft soil.

grille, grill, gril, *n.* [Fr.] A metal lattice or grating; a piece 'of ornamental ironwork; grillwork.

grill·room, gril'rōm", gril'rum", *n.* A restaurant that specializes in grilled food.

grim, grim, *a.—grimmer, grimmest.* [O.E. *grim*, fierce, ferocious; akin to *grama*, fury; Icel. *grimmr*, savage, angry, *gramr*, wrath; Dan. *grim*, ugly; D. *gram*, angry, *grimmen*, to growl; Gr. *grimm*, furious, *grimmen*, to rage; compare W. *grem*, a snarl, *gremiaw*, to snarl.] Of a forbidding or fear-inspiring aspect; fierce; stern; sullen; sour; surly.— **grim·ly**, *adv.*—**grim·ness**, *n.*

grim·ace, grim'as, gri·mās', *n.* [Fr. a wry face, < the Teutonic; cf. to D. *grimmen*, to snarl, to make faces.] A facial distortion expressing scorn, pain, disgust, affectation, disapproval, or other emotion; a smirk; a wry face.—*v.i.—grimaced, grimacing.* To make grimaces.

gri·mal·kin, gri·mal'kin, *n.* [For *gray-malkin*—*gray*, and *malkin*, that is *Molkin*, dim. < *Mary*; cf. *Tomcat.*] An old cat, esp. a female cat; a disagreeable old woman.

grime, grim, *n.* [Same as Dan. *grime*, a spot or streak, *grim*, soot, lampblack.] Dirt; foul matter; soot; dirt deeply ingrained.—*v.t.—grimed, griming.* To sully or soil deeply; to dirty.

Grimm's Law, *n.* [From Jakob L. K. Grimm in 'Deutsche Grammatik,' 1822.] *Linguistics*, a statement concerning the development of consonants from Proto-Indo-European into German.

grim·y, gri'mē, *a.—grimier, grimiest.* Full of grime; foul; dirty.—**grim·i·ly**, *adv.*—**grim·i·ness**, *n.*

grin, grin, *v.i.—grinned, grinning.* [O.E. *grennian*, grin: cf. G. *greinen* and *grinsen*, grin.] To smile broadly, or with a wide distention of the mouth; to draw back the lips so as to show the teeth, as a snarling dog or a person in pain.—*v.t.* To express or produce by grinning.—*n.* The act of grinning; a broad smile.—**grin·ner**, *n.*

grind, grind, *v.t.—ground, grinding.* [O.E. *grindan*, grind: cf. L. *frendere*, gnash the teeth, grind to pieces.] To reduce to fine particles, as by pounding or crushing; to pulverize; to wear smooth, or sharpen by friction; as, to *grind* a lens; to rub harshly or gratingly; rub or grate together; as, to *grind* one's teeth; to operate by turning a crank, as a coffee-mill; to oppress or torment; to teach in a dull manner; study or learn by close application.—*v.i.* To perform the act or operation of grinding something; to become ground; to rub harshly; grate. *Slang,* to work or study laboriously; to gyrate one's hips.—*n.* The act of grinding; a grinding sound; tiresome work; *slang,* an overly diligent student.

grind·er, grin'dėr, *n.* A person who sharpens tools or finishes rough materials; equipment for grinding. A molar tooth; *pl., slang,* the teeth.

grind·stone, grind'stōn", *n.* A revolving stone used for grinding or sharpening tools.—**keep one's nose to the grind·stone**, *colloq.* to work diligently and without unnecessary interruptions.

grin·go, gring'gō, *n.* pl. **grin·gos.** A foreigner in Spain or Spanish America, esp. an Englishman or an American: frequently derogatory.

grip, grip, *n.* [O.E. *gripe* = G. *griff*, grasp, hold, = Icel. *gripr*, possession.] The act of grasping; a seizing and holding fast; the strength of one's hand; a special mode of clasping hands, as among members of a secret society; grasp, hold, or control; as, to lose one's *grip* on a situation; mental or intellectual hold; as, to have a *grip* of a subject; something which seizes and holds, as a clutching device on a cable car; a handle or hilt; a small valise; grippe; *theatr.* stagehand.—*v.t.—gripped or gript, gripping.* To grasp or seize firmly; hold fast; *fig.* to take hold on (the mind); hold the interest or attention of; to attach by a grip or clutch.—*v.i.* To take firm hold; hold fast, as an anchor; to take hold on the mind; as, a story that *grips* the imagination. —**come to grips with**, grapple; firmly deal with; cope.

gripe, grip, *v.t.—griped, griping.* [O.E. *grīpan* = D. *grijpen* = G. *greifen* = Icel. *grīpa* = Goth. *greipan*, gripe, seize.] *Colloq.* to irritate, annoy. To produce pain in the bowels of, as if by constriction; to distress or oppress. *Archaic,* to seize and hold firmly; grip.—*v.i. Colloq.* To naggingly express dissatisfaction or resentment; grumble; complain. To suffer pain in the bowels.—*n. Colloq.* a complaint. *Usu. pl.* an intermittent spasmodic pain in the bowels. *Archaic,* grasp, hold, or control; that which grips or clutches.—**grip·er**, *n.*

grippe, grip, grip, *n.* [Fr.] *Pathol.* influenza. —**gripp·al, grippe·like**, *a.*

grip·sack, grip'sak", *n. Colloq.* a traveler's handbag or valise.

gri·saille, gri·zī', gri·zāl', *Fr.* grē·zä'ye, *n.* [Fr. < *gris*, gray.] A method of decorative painting in monochrome in various shades of gray, making objects appear to be in relief; a painting in this style.

gris·e·ous, gris'ē·us, griz'ē·us, *a.* [M.L. *griseus* = Fr. *gris*; < Teut.] Gray, esp. pearl-gray, often mottled.

gri·sette, gri·zet', *n.* [Fr. Orig. a gray woolen fabric, much used for dresses by women of the working classes, < *gris*, gray.] A young woman of the working class in France.

gris-gris, gree·gree, gri·gri, grē'grē, *n.* pl. **gris-gris, gree·grees, gri·gris.** An African charm, amulet, or incantation used as a protection or means of harming enemies.

gris·ly, griz'lē, *a.—grislier, grisliest.* [O.E. *grislic*, < *grisan* or *āgrīsan*, to dread, to fear greatly; allied to G. *grässlich*, horrible, *grausen*, horror; *grieseln*, to shudder.] Frightful; horrible; grim.—**gris·li·ness**, *n.*

grist, grist, *n.* [O.E. *grist*, a grinding, < *grindan*, to grind.] Grain ground or to be ground in a mill.—**grist for one's mill**, anything that can be turned to one's advantage or profit.

gris·tle, gris'l, *n.* [O.E. *gristle*, gristle; akin to *grist*, being named from the grinding or crunching it requires.] Cartilage.—**gris·tly**, gris'lē, *a.—gristlier, gristliest.* Consisting of or like gristle; cartilaginous.—**gris·tli·ness**, *n.*

grit, grit, *n.* [O.E. *grēot* = O.H.G. *grioz*, G. *griess*, grit, = Icel. *grjōt*, stones, rubble.] Fine, hard particles such as dust, grains of sand, or impurities in food; a coarse-grained siliceous rock, as sandstone; the structure of stone with regard to fineness or coarseness; *fig.* firmness of character; indomitable spirit; pluck.—*v.t.—gritted, gritting.* To grate or grind, as the teeth.—*v.i.* To produce a grating sound; grate.

grits, grits, *n. pl., sing. or pl. in constr.* [O.E. *grytta, gryttan*, grits or groats.] Hominy; coarsely ground grain often used as protein supplement. Also *hominy grits.*

grit·ty, grit'ē, *a.—grittier, grittiest.* Consisting of, containing, or resembling grit; sandy; containing fine, stony, or hard particles. *Colloq.* resolute; courageous; plucky.—**grit·ti·ly**, *adv.*—**grit·ti·ness**, *n.*

griv·et, griv'it, *n.* [Fr.]. A small green-gray Ethiopian monkey, *Cercopithecus aethiops.*

griz·zle, griz'l, *a.* [O.Fr. *grisel*, < O.Fr. and Fr. *gris*, gray; < Teut. (cf. G. *greis*, gray, hoary).] Gray.—*n.* The color gray; gray hair.—*v.t., v.i.—grizzled, grizzling.* To make or become gray.

griz·zle, griz'l, *v.i.* [Origin obscure.] *Brit.* to fret or sulk; whine.—*n. Brit.* a peevish mood.

griz·zled, griz'eld, *a.* Gray; having gray streaks.—**griz·zly**, griz'lē, *a.—grizzlier, grizzliest.* Grayish; as, the *grizzly* bear.

griz·zly bear, *n.* A large, savage bear, *Ursus horribilis*, grayish or brownish in color, found in western N. America.

groan, grōn, *v.i.* [O.E. *grānian*; perhaps akin to E. *grin*.] To utter a deep inarticulate sound expressive of grief, pain, or disapproval; moan; to make a deep sound resembling a groan; resound harshly; to suffer profoundly, usu. followed by *beneath* or *under*; be overburdened.—*v.t.* To utter or express with groans.—*n.* A groaning utterance or sound.—**groan·er**, *n.*—**groan·ing·ly**, *adv.*

groat, grōt, *n.* [D. *groot*, G. *grot*, that is, *great*, a great piece or coin.] An old English coin equal to fourpence; any of several European coins of small value; *fig.* anything of little worth.

groats, grōts, *n. pl., sing or pl. in constr.* [O.E. *grotan*, groats; akin *grits, grout.*] Oats, wheat, or other grain with the husks removed and the kernels broken into coarse fragments.

gro·cer, grō'sėr, *n.* [O.Fr. *grossier*, one who sells by wholesale, from *gros*, great.] A retail merchant selling food and household items.

ch- chain, G. na*ch*t; **th-** THen, thin; **w-** wig, hw as sound in whig; **z-** zh as in azure, zeal. *Italicized vowel* indicates schwa sound.

gro·cer·y, grō'se·rē, n. pl. **gro·cer·ies.** A retail store dealing in food and household items; pl. the goods sold by such stores.

Groe·nen·dael, grō'nen·däl", grō'nen·-däl', grä'nen·däl', gren'en·däl", n. A black-coated Belgian sheep dog, first raised in Groenendael, Belgium.

grog, grog, n. [From 'Old *Grog*,' a nick-name given British Admiral E. Vernon, 1684-1757, who diluted his sailors' rum.] A general term for strong drink; an alcoholic beverage, usu. rum diluted with water. A crushed ceramic material.—**grog·ger·y,** grog'e·rē, n. pl. **grog·ger·ies.** *Slang,* a barroom; tavern; also **grog·shop.**

grog·gy, grog'ē, a.—**groggier, groggiest.** In a state of exhaustion from lack of sleep; dizzy from illness or blows; *archaic,* drunken.—**grog·gi·ly,** adv.—**grog·gi·ness,** n.

grog·ram, grog'ram, n. [Fr. *grosgrain,* coarse grain, of a coarse texture.] A coarse fabric made of silk and mohair or silk and wool; a strong, coarse silk.

groin, groin, n. [Earlier *gryne,* M.E. *grynde*: cf. O.E. *grynde,* abyss, akin to *grund,* bottom, E. *ground.*] *Anat.* the fold or hollow on either side of the body where the thigh joins the abdomen; *arch.* the curved, projecting edge formed by the intersection of two vaults.

groin, groin, v.t. *Arch.* to form or build with groins.—**groin·ing,** n. *Arch.* Groined vaulting; the construction of such vaulting.

grom·met, grom'it, n. [Armor. *grom,* a curb.] *Mech.* an eyelet, ring, or washer used to reinforce an opening or to cushion or insulate that which passes through the opening; *naut.* a ring of rope, with or without a metal eye, used for securing sails, oars, or the like. Also *grummet.*

grom·well, grom'wel, n. [O.Fr. *gromil* (Fr. *grémil*); origin uncertain.] Any plant of the genus *Lithospermum,* comprising hairy herbs with white, yellow, or blue flowers and smooth, stony nutlets.

groom, grōm, grụm, n. [O.E. *grom,* boy; cf. O.D. *grom,* Icel. *gromr,* a youth. *Guma* (Goth. *guma,* O.H.G.) *homo* is the Teutonic word equivalent to L. *homo,* a man. Hence *bridegroom;* a man or boy who has charge of horses or the stable; one of several officers in the English royal household.—v.t. To make clean and neat; to curry or care for, as a horse; to train, condition, or otherwise prepare for a specific purpose, as for a job, position, or office.

grooms·man, grōmz'man, grụmz'man, n. pl. **grooms·men.** One who acts as attendant to a bridegroom at his marriage; the best man.

groove, grōv, n. [< D. *groeve, groef,* a furrow, a ditch, a channel = G. *grube,* a pit, hole, grave.] A furrow or long hollow, such as is cut by a tool; a narrow channel; *fig.* the fixed routine of one's life.—v.t. *grooved, grooving.* To cut a groove or channel in; to furrow.—**groov·er,** n.

groov·y, grōv'ē, a.—**groovier, grooviest.** Tending to be in a constant or fixed way of behaving or living; unchangeable; without divergence. *Slang,* exciting or stimulating; charming; as, a *groovy* performance.

grope, grōp, v.i.—*groped, groping.* [O.E. *grāpian.*] To search blindly; to feel one's way; to search perplexedly.—v.t. To search out by feeling one's way, as: They *grope* their way toward the exit.

gros·beak, grōs'bēk", n. Any of a group of finches distinguished by the thickness and strength of the conical bill.

gros·grain, grō'grān", n. [Fr. *gros grain,* 'large grain': cf. *grogram.*] A closely woven silk or rayon fabric with heavy transverse threads but little luster, often used for ribbons.

gross, grōs, a. [Fr. *gros,* big, thick, coarse; L.L. *grossus,* thick, crass; of doubtful origin.] Of or constituting a total without or prior to deductions, opposed to *net;* as, *gross* income; glaring or flagrant; as, a *gross* mistake, *gross* injustice; inelicate or obscene; coarse or unrefined; impercep-tive; great or enormous; obese; dense; visible to the naked eye.—v.t. To earn, as a total sum or profit, without or prior to deductions.—n. A totality prior to deduc-tions; *archaic,* chief part or bulk.—n. pl. **gross, gross·es.** Twelve dozen; 144 units. Abbr. *gr., gro.*—**gross·ly,** adv.—**gross·-ness,** n.

gross in·come, n. An individual's or business' total earnings and gains from all sources, including wages or salary, profits, gains resulting from the sale or disposition of property, interest, and dividends, prior to deductions. See *net income.*

gross na·tion·al prod·uct, n. *Econ.* the value in money of the total production of goods and services in a nation during a specified period of time, usually one year. Abbr. *GNP, G.N.P.* See *national income, net national product.*

gross prof·it, n. *Accounting,* the total receipts of a business, less the initial cost of goods sold, prior to deduction of operat-ing expenses and taxes. See *net profit.*

gros·su·lar·ite, gros'ū·la·rīt", n. A red, brown, yellow, green, or white garnet; hessonite.

grot, grot, n. *Poet.* a grotto.

gro·tesque, grō·tesk', n. [Fr. < *grotte,* a grotto, from the style of the paintings found in the ancient crypts and grottoes.] Any object that is fantastic, bizarre, ludicrous, ugly, or grotesque. *Art,* ornamental work consisting typically of medallions, sphinxes, or foliage combined with fanciful human or animal figures, forming a distorted or incongruous design.—a. Ridiculous or unnatural in design, appearance, or nature; atypical; bizarre.—**gro·tesque·ly,** adv.—**gro·tesque·ness,** n.

gro·tes·quer·y, gro·tes·quer·ie, grō·-tes'ke·rē, n. pl. **gro·tes·quer·ies.** A grotesque representation; a group of absurdly represented characters; something grotesque; the state of being grotesque.

grot·to, grot'ō, n. pl. **grot·toes, grot·tos.** [Fr. *grotte,* It. *grotta,* < L. *crypta,* Gr. *kryptē,* a cave, a vault, < *kryptō,* to con-ceal.] A cave, natural recess, or cavity in the earth; an artificially constructed cavern.

grouch, grouch, v.i. [Cf. *grudge.*] *Colloq.* To be sulky or morose; show discontent.—n. *Colloq.* A sulky or morose mood; a morose, irritable person.—**grouch·y,** grou'-chē, a.—**grouchier, grouchiest.**—**grouch·i·-ly,** adv.—**grouch·i·ness,** n.

ground, ground, n. [O.E. *grund,* ground; probably < *grindan,* to grind; G., Dan., and Sw. *grund,* D. *grond,* Icel. *grunnr,* Goth. *grundus,* ground; probably the original meaning was fine dust.] The surface of the earth; the soil; the bottom of a lake, ocean, or other body of water; land; estate; *sometimes pl.* land designated for a particular use; as, hunting *ground; pl.* the land around a building, constituting part of the total property. *Sometimes pl.* that on which anything may rest, rise, or originate; basis; foundation; support, as for a belief or argument; a cause or motivation for action. Topic for discussion; subject; *elect.* a general term for the connection of an electrical conductor to the earth; *paint.* the first layer of color on which the others are wrought; a foil or background that sets off anything. *Etching,* a composition spread over the surface of the plate to prevent the acid from eating into the plate. *Pl.* sediment at the bottom of a liquid; dregs; lees.—

v.t. To lay or set on the ground; to cause, as a ship, to run aground; to settle or establish, as on a foundation or basis; to fix or settle firmly; to found; to base; to provide a background, as for a painting; to thoroughly instruct in elements or principles; to cause, as an airplane or pilot, to be restricted to the ground; *elect.* to connect, as an electrical conductor, to a ground.—v.i. To run aground; *baseball,* to hit a ball on the ground. To strike the ground and remain fixed, as: The ship *grounded* in two fathoms of water.—**break ground,** to penetrate the soil for the first time; to take the first step in any undertaking.—**gain ground,** to advance; to obtain an advantage; to become more generally accepted or known.—**give ground,** to recede; to yield advantage.—**lose ground,** to withdraw from the position taken; to lose advantage; to decline in popularity or effect.—**stand one's ground,** to stand firm; to refuse to yield.

ground cher·ry, n. Any of the plants of the genus *Physalis* which have round berries enclosed in a ribbed husk, including *P. alkekengi,* the Chinese lantern plant.

ground con·nec·tion, n. *Elect.* A connec-tion of a conductor with the earth; a ground; a grounding connection.

ground cov·er, n. The low-growing plants and shrubs in a forest; a small, low plant, such as ivy, used as a ground covering in place of grass.

ground crew, n. Ground technicians responsible for the mechanical maintenance and servicing of aircraft.

ground ef·fect ma·chine, n. A vehicle which hovers immediately above land or water on a supporting cushion of air produced by downwardly thrusting fans, usu. achieving horizontal movement by means of a separate system of propulsion; a Hovercraft.

ground·er, groun'dẽr, n. *Baseball, soccer, cricket,* a ball batted, kicked, or thrown along the ground.

ground floor, n. The floor of a house on a level, or nearly so, with the exterior ground.—**in on the ground floor,** availing oneself of an exceptional opportunity as an early investor.

ground glass, n. Glass, the surface of which has been rendered lusterless and trans-lucent by treatment with an abrasive for optical or architectural purposes; glass which has been converted to a gritty or powdered form for use as an abrasive or polishing agent.

ground hog, n. A woodchuck.—**Ground-hog Day,** February 2nd, on which by tradition the ground hog emerges from hibernation and, if the day is sunny and he is frightened back into hibernation by his shadow, six more weeks of winter are forecast.

ground i·vy, n. A trailing plant, *Nepeta hederacea,* of the mint family, with rounded leaves and lavender flowers. Also **gill-o·-ver-the-ground.**

ground·less, ground'lis, a. Without sound cause; irrational; baseless; false.—**ground·-less·ly,** adv.—**ground·less·ness,** n.

ground·ling, ground'ling, n. A plant or animal that grows or remains close to the ground; a fish that swims close to the bottom; a person with poor taste, esp. in cultural areas; one who sits in a lower-priced seat at a theater or stadium; orig. a spectator who stood in a pit of the theater.

ground loop, n. A sharp turning of an airplane, caused by losing control or by trying to avoid an obstacle, during a landing or take-off run or while taxiing.

ground·mass, ground'mas", n. *Geol.* the crystalline, granular, or glassy base or matrix of a porphyry, in which the more prominent crystals are embedded.

ground·nut, ground'nut″, *n.* The peanut, earth nut, or goober, *Arachis hypogaea;* any of the edible fruits formed underground by such plants.

ground pine, *n.* A European bugle, or mint-like herb, *Ajuga chamaepitys,* having a resinous odor; a club moss, *Lycopodium obscurum,* or some allied species.

ground plan, *n.* A plan showing any floor of a building; any initial or basic plan.

ground plate, *n.* A bedplate under railroad ties; *elect.* a metal plate sunk in the ground to form the connection from a circuit to the earth. The lowest horizontal beam in a frame or building; also **ground·- sel, ground·sill.**

ground rent, *n.* Rent paid for the right to use another man's land, including the right to build on it.

ground school, *n.* A school in which a student undergoing instruction for an aeronautical rating receives training in the theoretical aspects of flying and in related subjects.—*a.*

ground·sel, ground'sel, *n.* [O.E. *grundeswelge,* earlier *gundeswelge,* appar. < *gund,* matter, pus, and *swelgan,* swallow (from its use in medicine).] A plant of the genus *Senecio,* of the composite family, bearing mostly yellow, tightly-clustered flowers.

ground squir·rel, *n.* Any of several animals allied to the true squirrels, as the chipmunks, gophers and other spermophiles, usu. having cheek pouches and living in holes.

ground state, *n. Phys.* the lowest possible energy level of a particle or system of particles. Also **ground lev·el.**

ground swell, *n.* A deep swell or rolling of the sea, occasioned along the shore by a distant storm or gale.

ground wa·ter, *n.* The source of fresh water beneath the earth's surface, as that supplying wells and springs, made available by the seepage of surface water.

ground wave, *n.* A radio wave that travels along or near the earth's surface.

ground·work, ground'wurk″, *n.* The work which forms the foundation of anything; a basis.

ground ze·ro, *n.* That point on the earth's surface, land or sea, vertically below or above the point of detonation of an atomic or hydrogen bomb. Also **hy·po·cen·ter.**

group, gröp, *n.* [Fr. *groupe,* < It. *gruppo, groppo,* knot, mass, heap, group; Teut. and akin to *crop.*] Any assemblage of persons or things; a cluster or aggregation; a number of persons or things ranged or considered together as being related in a scientific, natural, or other way; a number of persons, as in a community, united by common ties or interests, as of race, class, or occupation; *art,* an assemblage of figures arranged together, as in painting or sculpture; *geol.* a division in the classification of stratified deposits of a given geological era; *chem.* a number of atoms in a molecule connected or arranged together in some particular manner; a radical; *biol.* a number of animals or plants, classified together due to certain common traits or characteristics. *U.S. Air Force,* a unit immediately subordinate to a wing; *U.S. Army,* a unit comprising two or more battalions.—*v.t.* To arrange in or form into a group or groups; classify.—*v.i.* To form a group; be part of a group.—**group·- age,** *n.* Grouping; arrangement in a group or groups.

group dy·nam·ics, *n.* pl., *sing.* or pl. in *constr.* Sociological study of forces interacting within a human group; such interacting forces.

group·er, grö′pẽr, *n. pl.* **group·er, group·- ers.** [Pg. *garupa,* appar. < some S. Amer. name.] Any of numerous fishes of the genera *Epinephelus* and *Mycteroperca,* most of which are warm-water sea bass; as, the red grouper, an important food fish of the southern Atlantic coast of the U.S.

group·ing, grö′ping, *n.* Placing or manner of being placed in a group or groups; relative arrangement of persons, things, or parts as viewed or considered together in a group or groups.

group in·sur·ance, *n.* A single life, health, or accident insurance plan covering all the employees or members of an establishment, organization, office, or institution; an insurance plan available to or covering all the members of a group under a single contract, usu. without consideration of the age and physical condition of the persons insured or to be insured.

group ther·a·py, *n. Psychiatry,* a system of treatment for mentally ill or socially maladjusted persons, under which they share and try to solve their personal problems through group discussions.

grouse, grous, *n.* The common name of a number of ground-scratching game birds with mottled plumage, of the family *Tetraonidae,* more specif. applied to the red grouse, *Lagopus scoticus,* the black grouse, *Lyurus tetrix,* and the capercaillie, *Tetro urogallus,* all of Europe; also the spruce grouse, *Canachites canadensis,* and the ruffed grouse, *Bonasa umbellus,* of N. America.

grouse, grous, *v.i.*—**groused, grousing.** To grumble; complain.—*n.* Complaint.— **grous·er,** *n.*

grout, grout, *n.* [O.E. *grūt,* barley or wheat meal; Icel. *grautr,* porridge, akin to *groats, grits.*] A thin mortar used for pouring into the joints of masonry; a plaster for finishing a surface, as of a wall; coarse meal; a kind of heavy ale; *usu. pl.* lees, grounds, or dregs.—*v.t.* To fill or coat with grout.—**grout·er,** *n.*

grove, grōv, *n.* [O.E. *grāf,* a grove, < *grafan,* to dig, a grove being orig. an alley cut out in a wood; akin *grave.*] A cluster of trees, esp. when without underbrush; an assemblage of growing fruit or nut trees; a small wood.—**groved,** *a.*—**grove·less,** *a.*

grov·el, gruv′l, grov′l, *v.i.*—**groveled, groveling,** *Brit.* **grovelled, grovelling.** [From *groveling, adv.,* taken as present participle.] To lie or move with the face downward and the body prostrate, esp. as in abject humility or fear; *fig.* to humble oneself or act in an abject manner, as in fear or servility; continue, esp. willingly or contentedly, in an abject condition; take pleasure in mean or base things.—**grov·el·er,** *Brit.* **grov·el·ler,** *n.*—**grov·el·ing·ly,** *Brit.* **grov·el·ling·ly,** *adv.*

grow, grō, *v.i.*—past *grew,* pp. *grown,* ppr. *growing.* [O.E. *grōwan* = D. *groeien* = O.H.G. *gruoan* = Icel. *groa,* grow: cf. *grass* and *green.*] To undergo the process of development, esp. toward maturity; to survive, maintain life, or exist, as: The plant can *grow* under severe conditions. Be produced by natural processes, as leaves or fruit; arise or issue as from a germ, stock, or originating source, as: Love *grows* out of friendship. To increase by natural development; to increase gradually, or become greater; as, a fear, flood, or sum *grows,* heat or emotion *grows;* increase in influence or effect; as, a habit that *grows* on one; to become gradually attached or united; as, to *grow* fast to a thing; to become by degrees; come to be; as, to *grow* old or rich.—*v.t.* To cause to grow; cultivate, produce, or raise; to allow to grow; as, to *grow* a beard; to cover with a growth, used in the passive; as, a field *grown* with corn.—**grow up,** to spring up;

arise; to increase in growth; advance toward maturity; increase maturity.— **grow·a·ble,** *a.* Capable of being grown, as plants.—**grow·er,** *n.*—**grow·ing·ly,** *adv.*

grow·ing pains, *n.* pl. Dull, indefinite pains in the limbs during childhood and adolescence, commonly associated with the process of growing; emotional stresses of the preadult period; problems common to a new business or venture.

growl, groul, *v.i.* [Prob. imit.: cf. D. *grollen,* grumble.] To utter a deep guttural sound of anger or hostility, as a dog or a bear does; to rumble; to murmur or complain angrily; grumble.—*v.t.* To express by growling or grumbling.—*n.* The act or sound of growling; a rumbling; a grumbling or complaining.

growl·er, grou′lẽr, *n.* One who or that which growls; *Canada, naut.* an iceberg of a size large enough to be a danger to ships; *elect.* a device used for detecting short circuits by producing a growling sound if a short circuit is present; *slang,* a pitcher, pail, or other container brought by a customer for draft beer.

grown, grōn, *a.* Advanced in growth; arrived at full growth or maturity; as, a *grown* man; adult.

grown·up, grōn′up″, *n.* A fully grown person; an adult.

grown-up, grōn′up″, *a.* Suitable or appropriate to an adult; having reached physical or mental maturity.—**grown-up·ness,** *n.*

growth, grōth, *n.* The act, process, or manner of growing; development; gradual increase; production; condition or size attained, esp. at maturity; as, to come to the full *growth;* something that has grown, sprung up, or developed by or as by a natural process; as, a *growth* of weeds, the *growth* of a legend. *Pathol.* an abnormal tissue development, as a tumor.—**growth·less,** *a.* Deficient in growth.

growth stock, *n.* The common stock of a company which has a potential of future increase in business and profits.

GR-S, *n.* [(G)overnment (R)ubber and (S)tyrene.] Buna S, a synthetic rubber made at relatively low temperature, about 41°F., used esp. in the tread of tires.

grub, grub, *v.t.*—**grubbed, grubbing.** [M.E. *grubben,* dig: cf. G. *grübeln,* grub, rake, rack the brains.] To dig; to clear of roots; dig up, as trees, by the roots; uproot; extract, as by digging; *slang,* to provide with food.—*v.i.* To dig; to search, as by digging; to rummage; to lead a laborious or groveling life; drudge; *slang,* to take or eat food.—*n.* The larva of an insect, esp. of a beetle; a worm; a dull, plodding person; a drudge; *slang,* food or victuals.

grub·ber, grub′ẽr, *n.* One who grubs; a digger; a laborious worker; an implement for breaking up ground.

grub·by, grub′ē, *a.*—**grubbier, grubbiest.** Dirty; slovenly; infested with or affected by grubs or larvae.

grub·stake, grub′stāk″, *n.* Food, equipment, or money given to a prospector in return for a share of what he may find.—*v.t.* To provide with a grubstake.

Grub Street, *n.* A street in London, now Milton Street, reputedly once a gathering place of needy or second-rate writers; needy writers, collectively; *fig.* any poor or carelessly written literary work.—**Grub·- street, grub·street,** grub′strēt″, *a.*

grudge, gruj, *v.t.*—**grudged, grudging.** [Formerly *grucche, grutche, groche,* < O.Fr. *groucher, grouchier, groucer,* to grumble; of doubtful origin.] To permit or grant with reluctance; to begrudge.—*v.i.* To be envious; to feel ill will.—*n.* Reluctance felt in giving; ill will from envy or sense of injury.—**grudg·er,** *n.*—**grudg·- ing·ly,** *adv.* With reluctance.

gru·el, grö′el, *n.* [O.Fr. *gruel* (Fr. *gruau*), meal; from Teut. and akin to E. *grits, groats,* and *grout.*] A light, usu. thin, liquid food or cereal made by boiling meal, esp. oatmeal, in water or milk; any similar substance.

gru·el·ing, gru·el·ling, grö′e·ling, grö′-ling, *a.* Causing strain; severely testing one's strength or endurance, as in athletics or long-distance running.—*n.* A trying or exhausting procedure or experience.

grue·some, grö′som, *a.* [D. *gruwen,* Dan. *grue,* G. *grauen,* to shudder.] Horrible or frightening.—**grue·some·ly,** *adv.*—**grue·some·ness,** *n.*

gruff, gruf, *a.* [Same word as D. *grof,* Dan. *grov,* G. *grob,* coarse, blunt, rude.] Surly or stern in manner; harsh or blunt in speech. —**gruff·ish,** *a.*—**gruff·ly,** *adv.*—**gruff·ness,** *n.*

grum·ble, grum′bl, *v.i.*—*grumbled, grumbling.* [Perhaps same as D. *grommelen, grommen,* Fr. *grommeler,* to grumble; akin to O.E. *grimman,* to murmur, to rage; E. *grim.*] To express discontent or complaint; to murmur with discontent; to utter in a low voice; to rumble; to growl.—*v.t.* To express or utter by grumbling or in complaint.—*n.* A complaint; a discontented murmur; an utterance of complaint.— **grum·bler,** *n.*—**grum·bling·ly,** *adv.*

grum·met, grum′it, *n.* Grommet.

grump·y, grum′pē, *a.*—*grumpier, grumpiest.* [Connected with *grum, grumble.*] Surly; irritable; gruff. Also **grump·ish.**—**grump·i·ly,** *adv.*—**grump·i·ness,** *n.*—**grump,** *n.* An irritable, surly person.

grun·ion, grun′yan, *n.* A small edible fish, *Leuresthes tenuis,* of the silverside family, common off the coast of California, and known for spawning in underwater sand at high tide.

grunt, grunt, *v.i.* [O.E. *grunnettan,* freq. of *grunian,* grunt; cf. G. *grunzen* and L. *grunnire,* grunt.] To utter the deep guttural sound of a hog; to utter a similar sound; to grumble, as in discontent.—*v.t.* To express with a grunt.—*n.* A deep guttural sound, as that uttered by a hog; any similar utterance; any of various marine fish which emit a grunting sound when taken from the water.—**grunt·er,** *n.*—**grunt·ing·ly,** *adv.*

Gru·yère cheese, grö·yâr′ chēz, gri·yâr′ chēz, *Fr.* gRy·yeR′, *n.* [From *Gruyère,* district in Switzerland.] A firm pale-yellow variety of cheese usu. containing very few small holes.

gryph·on, grif′on, *n.* Griffin.

G-string, jē′string″, *n.* A narrow loincloth, esp. one worn as part of a stripteaser's or female entertainer's costume.

G-suit, jē′sōt″, *n.* An aviator's garment which exerts pressure on the abdomen and lower parts of the body to slow down or prohibit the blood's pooling below the heart during headward acceleration. Also **an·ti-G-suit.**

gua·cha·ro, gwä′cha·rō, *n.* pl. **gua·cha·ros.** [Sp.; prob. from native name.] A nocturnal, fruit-eating, South American bird, *Steatornis caripensis,* related to the goatsuckers, and valued for the edible oil yielded by the fat of its young. Also *oilbird.*

gua·co, gwä′kō, *n.* pl. **gua·cos.** [Sp.; from native name.] A climbing asteraceous plant, *Mikania guaco,* of tropical America, its medicinal leaves, or a substance obtained from them, used as an antidote for snakebites; a tropical American plant, *Aristolochia maxima,* also used for snakebites.

guai·a·col, gwī′a·kōl″, gwī′a·kal″, gwī′a·kol″, *n. Chem.* A colorless liquid, $CH_3·OC_6H_4OH$, resembling creosote, usu. obtained by distillation from guaiacum resin: used medicinally as an anesthetic and expectorant.

guai·a·cum, gwī′a·kum, *n.* [Native name.] A S. American tree of the genus *Guaiacum*; the resin obtained from it, used for medicinal purposes, and in the making of varnish; also **guai·ac,** gwī′ak″.—**guai·a·cic,** guī′a·-kik, *a.*

gua·na·co, gwä·nä′kō, *n.* pl. **gua·na·cos.** [Sp.; < Peruvian *huanacu.*] A wild ruminant mammal of S. America, *Lama guanicæ,* closely allied to the llama and alpaca and related to the camel.

gua·no, gwä′nō, *n.* pl. **gua·nos.** [Sp. < Peruvian *huanu,* dung.] A natural manure composed chiefly of the excrement of sea birds; any similar substance.

guar·an·tee, gar″an·tē′, *n.* [Appar. for *guaranty:* cf. Sp. *garante,* one who warrants.] A warrant, pledge, or formal assurance that stated specifications or obligations will be met, often given for genuineness, quality, or durability; that which is given as security; a guaranty; a guarantor; that person to whom a guaranty is given; something serving as security or collateral to indicate or assure a specified outcome.—*v.t.*—*guaranteed, guaranteeing.* To be or become a guaranty for; to make oneself answerable for, in behalf of one primarily responsible; to undertake to secure to another, as rights or possessions; engage to uphold or maintain; engage to protect or indemnify; engage, as to do something; to serve as a warrant or guaranty for.

guar·an·tor, gar′an·tar″, gar′an·tėr, *n.* One who or that which pledges or guarantees; one who gives or makes a guaranty.

guar·an·ty, gar′an·tē″, *n.* pl. **guar·an·ties.** [Fr. *garantie,* O.Fr. *guarantie,* < *guarant, warant,* warrant; < Teut.] The act of warranting or providing security; a warranty, pledge, or promise given by way of security; a formal or written assurance by which one person or party undertakes to be responsible for the carrying out of an obligation, or the condition or treatment of merchandise; something that serves as a warrant or security; one who warrants, or gives a formal assurance of being responsible for something.—*v.t.*—*guarantied, guarantying.* To guarantee.

guard, gärd, *v.t.* [O.Fr. *guarder, garder, warder* (Fr. *garder*), guard; < Teut.] To keep safe from harm or attack; protect or defend; to watch over in order to protect; attend or escort; to keep under close watch, as prisoners in order to prevent escape or outbreaks; to keep in check; as, to *guard* one's tongue; to provide with some safeguard or protective appliance. *Sports,* to hinder the actions of, as an opponent; to protect, as a goal.—*v.i.* To give protection; to keep watch; to take precautions, used with *against;* as, to *guard against* errors.

guard, gärd, *n.* [O.Fr. *guarde, garde,* (Fr. *garde*), < *guarder:* cf. *ward, n.*] Protection or defense; a posture of defense, as in fencing or boxing; the weapon or arms in such a posture; protective watch; vigilant care or heed; restraining watch, as over a prisoner or person under restraint; cautious restraint; a sentry; a member of a guarding force; *football,* a player situated on the line of scrimmage, who runs interference for the ball carrier and protects the passer from the onrushing defensive linemen. *Basketball,* on offense, the player who brings the ball upcourt and designates the plays; on defense, one who defends against the action of the offensive guard. *Brit.* the conductor of a railroad train; *(Cap.), pl.* certain household troops in the British army. A body of men charged with guarding a person or place from attack; a man or men who act as escort or watch over prisoners; a device intended or

serving to guard or protect.—**off one's guard,** unprepared; unwary.—**on one's guard,** in a position of readiness; watchful or vigilant; cautious; wary. Also **on guard.**

guard·ed, gär′did, *a.* Protected; defended. Cautious; circumspect; as, *guarded* behavior; framed or uttered with prudence.— **guard·ed·ly,** *adv.*—**guard·ed·ness,** *n.*

guard hair, *n.* Coarse, long outer hair which protects the soft underfur of certain animals.

guard·house, gärd′hous″, *n.* A house for the accommodation of guards; a building where military prisoners are confined.

guard·i·an, gär′dē·an, *n.* [Fr. *gardien.*] One who guards; one who has charge or custody of any person or thing; the head of a Franciscan monastery; *law,* one who is invested by law with care of the person and/or the estate of a minor or a person judged unable to administer his own affairs. —*a.* Protecting.—**guard·i·an·ship,** *n.*

guards·man, gärdz′man, *n.* pl. **guards·men.** A man who acts as a guard; a member of a guard; a member of the National Guard.

Guar·ne·ri·us, gwär·när′ē·us, *n.* pl. **Guar·ne·ri·us·es.** [From Giuseppe *Guarneri,* an Italian violin maker, 1683–1745.] A violin fashioned by Giuseppe Guarneri or one of his family.

Gua·te·ma·lan, gwä″te·mä′lan, *a.* Relating to a person, place, or thing associated with Guatemala, a republic in northern Central America, or its capital, Guatemala City.—*n.* A resident of Guatemala or Guatemala City.

gua·va, gwä′va, *n.* [Sp. < Carib. *guayabo,* the tree, *guayaba,* the fruit.] Any of various trees or shrubs of the genus *Psidium,* esp. P. *guajava,* of tropical or subtropical America, with a fruit used for making jelly or preserves; the fruit.

gua·yu·le, gwä·ū′lē, *Sp.* gwä·ū′le, *n.* [Sp.] A much-branched shrub, *Parthenium argentatum,* which is native to Texas and northern Mexico and is a source of rubber; the rubber produced by this plant.

gu·ber·na·to·ri·al, gö″bėr·na·tōr′ē·al, gö″bėr·na·tar′ē·al, gū″bėr·na·tōr′ē·al, gū″bėr·na·tar′ē·al, *a.* [L. *gubernator,* a governor. GOVERN.] Pertaining to a governor.

guck, guk, guk, *n. Slang,* something oozy, slimy, or repugnant.

gudg·eon, guj′on, *n.* [O.Fr. Fr. *goujon,* < L. *gobio,* var. of *gobius,* E. *goby.*] A small European fresh-water fish, *Gobio gobio,* of the carp family, easily caught, and much used for bait; any of several related fishes, as the minnow and burbot. *Fig.* a person who is easily duped; a bait or allurement.— *v.t.* To dupe; cheat.

gudg·eon, guj′on, *n.* [O.Fr. Fr. *goujon,* pin, gudgeon.] A metal pin or the like attached to the end of a wooden shaft to act as a journal; a pivot; a journal; a socket or eye for a pivot; a metallic pin for securing blocks or slabs of stone.

gudg·eon pin, *n. Brit.* wrist pin.

guel·der-rose, gel′dėr·rōz″, *n.* [From *Guelders,* or *Gelderland,* province of the Netherlands.] A variety of the European cranberry bush, *Viburnum opulus,* having large clusters of white flowers; snowball.

gue·non, ge·naN′, ge·non′, *n.* [Fr.; origin unknown.] Any of the agile, long-tailed African monkeys constituting the genus *Cercopithecus,* as the grivet and the green monkey.

guer·don, gur′don, *n.* [O.Fr. *guerdon,* It. *guiderdone,* < L.L. *widerdonum,* corrupted from O.G. *widarlōn* (O.E. *witherlēan*), a recompense, through the influence of the L. *donum,* a gift—from *widar* (G. *wider*), against, and *lōn,* reward (= E. *loan*).]

A reward; requital; recompense.—*v.t.* To give a guerdon to; to reward.

guern·sey, gŭrn'zē, *n.* pl. **guern·seys.** (*Cap.*) a breed of dairy cattle, native to the Isle of Guernsey, in the English Channel. A close-fitting woolen knitted shirt.—*a.*

guer·ril·la, gue·ril·la, ge·ril'la, *n.* [Sp. *guerrilla*, dim. of *guerra*, Fr. *guerre*, war, < O.H.G. *werra*, war.] One of a band of independent soldiers who prey on the enemy by harassment, surprise attack, and short, sharp engagements, often behind the lines.—*a.* Pertaining to guerrillas or their tactics.

guess, ges, *v.t.* [O.E. *gesse* = L.G. and D. *gissen*, Dan. *gisse*, Icel. *giska, gizka*, to guess, lit. 'to try to *get*'.] To deduce, infer, or surmise (factual information) with little or no real evidence or by chance; to deduce correctly; as, to *guess* an answer. *Colloq.* to think or believe.—*v.i.* To conjecture.— *n.* A conjecture; an estimate; an opinion reached by guessing.—**guess·er**, *n.*— **guess·work**, ges'wŭrk", *n.* Mere conjecture; an assumption.

guess·ti·mate, ges'ti·māt', *v.t.*—**guestimated, guestimating.** *Slang,* to evaluate without sufficient information.—ges'ti·mit, ges'ti·māt", *n.*

guest, gest, *n.* [O.E. *gæst, giest* = D. and G. *gast* = Icel. *gestr* = Goth. *gasts*, orig. 'stranger'; akin to L. *hostis*, stranger, enemy, and *hospes*, host, guest, stranger.] One who is afforded hospitality or entertainment in another's home or business establishment as a friend, visitor, patron, client, or customer either gratuitously or with payment for accommodations; one who replaces a regularly performing artist; *zool.* an organism which shares the food and dwelling of another organism.—*a.*

guff, guf, *n.* [Origin obscure.] *Slang.* Empty talk; humbug; nonsense.

guf·faw, gu·fa', gu·fạ', *n.* [Imitative.] A loud or sudden burst of laughter.—*v.i.* To burst into a loud or sudden laugh.

gug·gle, gug'l, *v.i.*—**guggled, guggling.** [Imitative, suggested by *gurgle*.] To make a sound like that of a liquid passing through a narrow aperture; to gurgle.—*n.* A sound of this kind; a gurgle.

guid·ance, gīd'ans, *n.* The act or service of counseling or supervising; the service provided by a vocational director or counselor; a program of an educational institution which provides testing, evaluation, and therapy services. A mechanism, system, or built-in device which guides the operation of a machine; the process of determining the flight path of a missile.

guide, *v.t.*—**guided, guiding.** [Fr. *guider*, It. *guidare*, Sp. *guiar*—of Teut. origin, and akin to G. *weisen*, to show, to lead, Goth. *witan*, to watch over; O.E. *witan*, to know, to *wit*, with change of *w* to *gu* as in *guile, guard.*] To lead or direct in a way; to conduct in a course or path; to direct; to regulate; to influence in conduct or actions; to give direction to; to instruct and direct; to superintend.—*v.i.* To function as a guide.—*n.* [Fr. *guide*, It. *guida*, Sp. *guia*.] A person who guides; a leader or conductor; one who conducts travelers or tourists in particular localities; one who or that which directs another in his conduct or course of life; a director; a regulator; a guidebook; a thumb index or projecting tab inserted in a reference work to facilitate its use; any of various contrivances intended to direct or maintain a fixed course or motion; a member of a marching unit who regulates the formations and establishes the alignment of the unit.—**guid·a·ble**, *a.* —**guide·less**, *a.*—**guid·er**, *n.*

guide·book, gīd'buk", *n.* A book for giving travelers or tourists information about the places they intend to visit.

guid·ed mis·sile, *n.* A rocket or other missile whose course is determined by self-contained instruments or radio signals.

guide·post, gīd'pōst", *n.* A post to which a signboard is attached for directing travelers.

gui·don, gī'don, *n.* [F. *guidon*, < It. *guidone*; akin to E. *guide*.] A small flag or streamer carried as a guide by troops, used for marking or signaling; the officer carrying it.

guild, gild, *n.* [O.E. *gild*, a payment, hence a society where payment was made for its protection and support, < *gildan*, to pay; D. *gild*, a guild.] In medieval times, an organization of merchants or artisans; an association of men having similar interests or engaged in the same business, often formed for mutual aid; *ecol.* a group of plants having specialized life patterns which make them in some degree parasitic or dependent upon other plants.—**guild·ship**, *n.*

guild·hall, gild·hall, gild'hạl", *n.* A town hall; a hall for meetings of a guild or corporation.

guild so·cial·ism, *n.* Control of state-owned industries by associations or guilds of workers, esp. the form of this theory developed in Britain in the early 20th century.

guile, gīl, *n.* [Fr. form of E. *wile*; O.Fr. *guile, guile*, < a Germanic form, with regular change of G. *w* into Romance *gu*, as in *guide*.] Craft; cunning; artifice; duplicity; deceit.—**guile·ful**, gīl'ful, *a.* Crafty; wily; intended to deceive.— **guile·ful·ly**, *adv.*—**guile·ful·ness**, *n.*— **guile·less**, gīl'lis, *a.* Free from guile; sincere.—**guile·less·ly**, *adv.*—**guile·less·ness**, *n.*

guil·le·mot, gil'e·mot", *n.* [Fr. *guillemot*, appar. dim. of *Guillaume*, William.] Any of various birds of the auk family constituting the genus *Cepphus*, native to the northern Atlantic coasts and characterized by a relatively narrow bill.

guil·loche, gi·lōsh', *n.* [Fr. *guillochis*; origin uncertain.] An architectural ornament composed of curved lines or strands interlacing or otherwise combined in a pattern.

guil·lo·tine, gil'o·tēn", gē'o·tēn", *n.* [From Dr. J. I. *Guillotin*, who introduced in the French Convention the motion for its use.] An instrument for beheading persons by means of a weighted blade which, when released, slides down between two upright posts; an instrument of similar design for cutting paper or metal; *Brit.* a method of shortening discussion of legislative business in Parliament by establishing a time limit.— gil'o·tēn', *v.t.*—**guillotined, guillotining.**

guilt, gilt, *n.* [O.E. *gylt*, a crime, < *gildan, gyldan*, to pay, to requite.] The fact of having performed a wrong act, esp. a violation of a law or a moral or ethical code; culpability; conduct or behavior encompassing such offenses; a feeling of shame or remorse due to personal responsibility, real or imagined, for an offense.— **guilt·less**, *a.* Free of guilt; innocent; without experience or knowledge, used with *of.*—**guilt·less·ly**, *adv.*

guilt·y, gil'tē, *a.*—**guiltier, guiltiest.** Having committed a crime or a moral wrong; judged responsible for an offense; culpable, often followed by *of*; as, *guilty of* a misdemeanor; pertaining to guilt; indicating guilt; as, a *guilty* look.—**guilt·i·ly**, *adv.*— **guilt·i·ness**, *n.*

guimpe, gimp, gamp, *n.* [Fr. *guimpe*, O.Fr. *guimple*, wimple; < Teut., and akin to E. *wimple.*] A vestlike piece of lace or similar material, worn at the neckline of a low-cut dress.

guin·ea, gin'ē, *n. Brit.* formerly a gold coin, now a money unit equivalent to 21 shillings.

guin·ea fowl, gin'ē foul, *n.* An African gallinaceous bird, *Numida meleagris*, related to the peacocks and pheasants, which usu. has dark gray plumage with small white spots, now raised throughout the world for food; any of a group of birds of which this species is the type.—**guin·ea hen**, *n.* The female of the guinea fowl.

guin·ea pig, gin'ē pig, *n.* A short-eared, short-tailed rodent of the genus *Cavia*, usu. white, black, and tawny, much used in biological experiments; any subject of experimentation.

guin·ea worm, gin'ē wŭrm, *n.* A parasitic nematode worm, *Dracunculus medinensis*, which causes illness in man and animals, found on the Guinea coast and other warm regions of Africa and Asia.

gui·pure, gi·pur', Fr. gē·pyr', *n.* [Fr., < *guiper*, cover or whip with silk, etc.; < Teut.] Any of various heavy laces in which the pattern is connected by bars or coarse stitches rather than worked on a net or mesh ground.

guise, gīz, *n.* [Fr. *guise*, the equivalent of E. *wise*, mode, fashion, O.H.G. *wīsa*, G. *weise*, with common change from *w* to *gu-* in words borrowed into Fr. from the German; compare *guile, wile.*] Outward appearance; dress; garb; assumed or deceptive appearance; pretense. *Archaic,* behavior; mode.

gui·tar, gi·tär', *n.* [Fr. *guitare*, < Sp. *guitarra*, < L. *cithara*.] A musical instrument with a long, fretted neck and a violin-like body, played by plucking the strings, usu. six in number, with the fingers or a pick.—**gui·tar·ist**, *n.*

gu·lar, gū'lẽr, gö'lẽr, *a.* [L. *gula*, throat.] Of, pertaining to, or situated on the throat.

gulch, gulch, *n.* [Allied to Sw. *gölka*, to swallow, D. *gulzig*, greedy.] A deep ravine caused by the action of water; the dry bed of a stream; a gully.

gulf, gulf, *n.* [O.Fr. Fr. *golfe*, < It. *golfo*, < L.Gr. *kolphos*, Gr. *kolpos*, bosom, hollow, gulf.] A portion of an ocean or sea extending into the land; as, the *Gulf* of Mexico; a deep hollow; a chasm or abyss; any wide separation, as in social, educational, or economic level; something that engulfs or swallows up; a whirlpool.—*v.t.* To consume; to swallow like a gulf or as in a gulf; engulf.—**gulf·y**, *a.*—*gulfier, gulfiest.*

Gulf States, *n. pl.* The states of Alabama, Florida, Mississippi, Louisiana, and Texas, all of which border on the Gulf of Mexico.

Gulf Stream, *n.* A warm ocean current that flows north from the Gulf of Mexico along the eastern U.S. coast.

gulf·weed, gulf'wēd", *n.* A coarse olive-brown seaweed, *Sargassum bacciferum*, found in tropical American waters, characterized by numerous berrylike air vessels.

gull, gul, *v.t.* [In Old and Prov. Eng., a young, unfledged bird, lit. 'a yellow bird,' from the yellowness of young birds, < O.E. *gul*, yellow.] To make a fool of; to mislead by deception; to trick.—*n.* One who is easily cheated.

gull, gul, *n.* [W. *gwylan*, Armor. *gwelan*, Corn. *gullan*, a gull.] Any of more than 40 species of swimming birds of the family *Larinæ*, having large wings, slender legs, and webbed feet.

Gul·lah, gul'a, *n.* Any one of a Negro people dwelling on the Sea Islands and along the coastal regions of South Carolina, Georgia, and northeastern Florida; the English dialect of these people.

gul·let, gul'it, *n.* [Fr. *goulet*, < L. *gula*, the throat.] The passage by which food and liquid are taken into the stomach; the esophagus; the throat or something resembling it; a gully or narrow valley.

gul·li·ble, gul'i·bl, *a.* Easily gulled or cheated; credulous.—**gul·li·bil·i·ty**, gul'i·bil'i·tē, *n.*—**gul·li·bly**, *adv.*

gul·ly, gul′ē, n. pl. **gul·lies.** [Fr. *goulet*, a gullet, a channel for water. GULLET.] A channel or valley worn in the earth by a current of water; a ravine; a ditch; a gutter; Sc., Brit. dial. a large knife.—v.t. gullied, gullying. To wear into a gully or channel.

gu·los·i·ty, gū·los′i·tē, n. Greediness; extreme appetite.

gulp, gulp, v.t. [A form of *gulf*, to swallow; same as D. *golpen*, to swallow greedily; Dan. *gulpe*, to disgorge.] To swallow eagerly, hastily, or in large mouthfuls, often followed by *down*; to hold back or suppress as if by swallowing.—v.i. To gasp, as when swallowing; to gasp, as in suppressing a sob.—n. The act of taking a large swallow; the amount taken.—**gulp·er**, n.

gum, gum, n. [O.E. *gōma*, Icel. *gómr*, G. *Gaumen*, palate, gum.] The fleshy tissue which covers the necks of the teeth and the parts of the jaws in which the teeth are set.—v.t. To chew, esp. without teeth; to shape by grinding, as a saw's teeth.—**gum·boil**, gum′boil″, n. A boil or small abscess on the gum.

gum, gum, n. [Fr. *gomme*, < L. *gummi*, Gr. *kommi*, gum.] A water-soluble, sticky substance which exudes from certain plants and trees and thickens or hardens when exposed to air; any of various similar substances secreted by plants, as resin; a gum tree; mucilage; glue; the adhesive on a postage stamp; chewing gum.—v.t.— gummed, gumming. To smear or stiffen with gum; to stick together with gum or a gumlike substance.—v.i. To exude or form gum; to become sticky or clogged with gummy material.—**gum up**, colloq. to spoil, bungle, or ruin.

gum am·mo·ni·ac, n. A gum resin from a Persian perennial herb, *Dorema ammoniacum*, used in medicine, porcelain cements, and some perfumes. Also *ammoniac*.

gum ar·a·bic, n. The gum of various species of acacia, which tends to harden in the air: used in medicine, inks, adhesives, and in certain foods as a thickener.

gum·bo, gum′bō, n. pl. **gum·bos.** The okra plant, or its edible pods; a soup, thickened with these pods, and often made with other vegetables, meat, chicken, or seafood; a kind of silty, fine soil found in southern and western U.S. which becomes very sticky when wet. (Often cap.) a patois spoken by some Negroes and Creoles in Louisiana.—a.

gum·drop, gum′drop″, n. A candy of gum arabic, gelatin, or the like, with sugar and flavoring.

gum e·las·tic, n. Rubber.

gum el·e·mi, n. Elemi.

gum·mite, gum′īt, n. An ore of gummy appearance, containing oxides of uranium, thorium, and lead.

gum·mo·sis, gu·mō′sis, n. [N.L., < L. *gummi*, E. *gum*.] Bot. an abnormal condition of plants, marked by the discharge of gum.

gum·my, gum′ē, a.—gummier, gummiest. Consisting of gum; of the nature of gum; exuding gum or covered with gum or other viscous matter; sticky. Also **gum·mous.**— **gum·mi·ness**, n.

gump·tion, gump′shan, n. [Orig. Sc.; origin obscure.] Colloq. Courage; pluckiness; personal initiative; shrewd, practical sense.

gum res·in, n. Any of various natural mixtures of gum and resin, obtained from certain plants.—**gum-res·i·nous**, a.

gum·shoe, gum′shō″, n. A shoe made of gum elastic or India rubber; a rubber overshoe; slang, a detective.—v.i.—gumshoed, gumshoeing. Slang, to walk softly or stealthily.

gum tree, n. Any tree that exudes gum, as the eucalyptus, the sour gum, or the sweet gum.

gun, gun, n. [M.E. *gunne*, *gonne*, perhaps < a Scand. feminine proper name (cf. Icel. *Gunna*, woman's name).] A metallic tube, with its stock or carriage and attachments, from which heavy missiles are thrown by the force of an explosive charge; milit. a piece of ordnance, esp. a long cannon or an automatic weapon. Any portable firearm, as a rifle; any similar device for projecting something; as, a cement *gun*; the discharge of a gun, as in a salute or signal. Slang, a professional gunman or killer; a throttle.—v.i.—gunned, gunning. To shoot with a gun; hunt with a gun.—v.t. To wound or kill with a gun, often followed by *down*; slang, to increase the supply of gasoline to, as an engine.

gun·boat, gun′bōt″, n. A small, armed vessel of light draft, used for visiting minor ports and patrolling rivers.

gun car·riage, n. The support or structure on which a gun is mounted or moved and on which it is fired.

gun·cot·ton, gun′kot″on, n. An explosive, high-nitrogen form of cellulose nitrate produced by treating cotton with a mixture of nitric and sulfuric acids and used to make smokeless powder.

gun dog, n. A dog, as a pointer or retriever, which is trained to aid sportsmen in hunting game with guns.

gun·fight, gun′fīt″, n. A fight utilizing guns, esp. a fight between two persons.— **gun·fight·er**, n.

gun·fire, gun′fīer″, n. The firing of a gun or guns; milit. the use of large or small firearms in war, as differentiated from other tactics or weapons.

gun·flint, gun′flint″, n. A piece of shaped flint, fixed in the hammer of a flintlock to fire the charge.

gunk, gungk, n. Colloq. Obnoxious material; sticky, greasy, or messy material sometimes having an offensive odor.

gun·lock, gun′lok″, n. The mechanism of a gun by which the hammer is controlled and the charge exploded.

gun·man, gun′man, n. pl. **gun·men.** A man armed with a gun, esp. one who uses his skill with a revolver unlawfully for hire; one who is an expert in the use of a gun.

gun met·al, n. Any of various alloys or metallic substances with a dark-gray or blackish color or finish, used for chains, belt buckles, and the like; a dark-gray color with a slightly bluish cast; a bronze formerly employed as a material for cannon. —**gun-met·al**, a.

gun moll, n. Slang. A girl friend or female accomplice of a gangster; female criminal.

gun·nel, gun′l, n. [Origin unknown.] Any of certain fishes of the blenny family, esp. *Pholis gunnellus*, found in the northern Atlantic.

gun·ner, gun′ēr, n. One who works a gun or cannon; U.S. Navy, Marine Corps, a warrant officer connected with or in charge of ordnance; a person who uses a gun for hunting; Brit., milit. an artilleryman.

gun·ner·y, gun′e·rē, n. The art of firing or managing guns; the science of artillery; collectively, guns.

gun·ner·y ser·geant, n. A noncommissioned U.S. Marine Corps officer ranking above a master sergeant and below a first sergeant.

gun·ny, gun′ē, n. pl. **gun·nies.** [Hindi.] A strong coarse cloth manufactured of jute and used for making bags and sacks; burlap.—**gun·ny-bag, gun·ny·sack**, n.

gun·pow·der, gun′pou″dēr, n. An explosive mixture of potassium nitrate, sulfur, and charcoal, for use in fireworks, blasting, and sometimes in certain guns.

gun room, n. In a British warship, orig. an apartment occupied by the gunner and his mates, now quarters for the junior officers.

gun·run·ner, gun′run″ēr, n. One who deals illegally in guns and ammunition, as in smuggling them into another country.— **gun·run·ning**, n.

gun·shot, gun′shot″, n. The projectile fired from a gun; the shooting of a firearm; the distance to which shot can be thrown so as to be effective.—a. Made by the shot of a gun; as, *gunshot* wounds.

gun-shy, gun′shī″, a. Frightened by guns or esp. the sound of gunfire; excessively fearful, wary, or distrustful.

gun·sling·er, gun′sling″ēr, n. Slang. One who fights with a gun; a gunman.

gun·smith, gun′smith″, n. One whose occupation is the making or repairing of small firearms.

gun·stock, gun′stok″, n. The wooden support or handle in which the barrel of a gun is fixed.

Gun·ter's chain, gun′tērz chān, n. [Named for Edmund *Gunter*, 1581–1626, English mathematician.] A surveyor's chain, 66 feet in length.

gun·wale, gun·nel, gun′l, n. [< *gun* and *wale*; so called because formerly guns were set upon it.] Naut. the upper edge of a ship's or boat's side.

gup·py, gup′ē, n. pl. **gup·pies.** A small, colorful tropical fish, *Lebistes reticulatus*, often prized and kept as an aquarium fish.

gurge, gurj, n. [L. *gurges*, a whirlpool.] Archaic, a whirlpool.

gur·gi·ta·tion, gur″ji·tā′shan, n. [L.L. *gurgitare* (pp. *gurgitatus*), engulf, flood, < L. *gurges*, whirlpool, gulf.] Surging rise and fall; ebullient motion, as of water.

gur·gle, gur′gl, v.i.—gurgled, gurgling. [Prob. imitative or connected with *gorge*; akin G. *gurgeln*, It. *gorgogliare*, to gurgle.] To run or flow in an irregular, noisy current, as water from a bottle; to flow with a murmuring sound.—v.t. To utter in a gurgling manner.—n. The sound made by a liquid flowing through a narrow opening.

Gur·kha, Ghur·ka, gur′ka, n. pl. **Gur·khas, Gur·kha.** A native of Nepal who belongs to a Rajput tribe famous for soldierly qualities; a member of a Gurkha regiment in the Indian army.

gur·nard, gur′nērd, n. [O.Fr. *gornart*, prob. lit. 'grunter' (from the sound made by the fish when taken out of the water), = Gr. *grognard*, grumbler, < *grogner*, grunt.] Any marine fish of the family *Triglidae*, having a spiny head and three pairs of free pectoral rays; any of various similar fishes.

gu·ru, gö′rö, gu·rö′, n. [Hind, *gurū*, < Skt. *guru*, teacher, orig. adj., heavy, weighty, worthy of honor.] In India, esp. among the Hindus, a religious teacher or spiritual guide.

gush, gush, v.i. [Icel. *gjosa*, to gush, *gusa*, a gush, to gush; a Scand. word, allied to O.E. *geōtan*, Goth. *giutan*, G. *giessen*, to pour; E. *gut*, *gust* (of wind), *geyser*.] To rush forth, as a fluid from confinement; to flow suddenly or copiously; to be extravagantly and effusively sentimental.—v.t. To emit suddenly, copiously, or with violence.—n. A sudden and violent issue of a fluid; an emission of liquid in a large quantity and with force; an outpour; an effusive display of sentiment.—**gush·er**, n. One who or that which gushes; an oil well that yields oil without being pumped; a person who is demonstratively sentimental.—**gush·ing**, a. —**gush·ing·ly**, adv.

gush·y, gush′ē, a.—gushier, gushiest. Characterized by very effusive talk or behavior; extremely sentimental; excessively enthusiastic.—**gush·i·ly**, adv.—**gush·i·ness**, n.

gus·set, gus′it, n. [Fr. *gousset*, a gusset, < *gousse*, a husk or shell.] A usu. triangular piece of cloth inserted in a garment or the like to strengthen or enlarge some part; something resembling such a piece of cloth in shape or function, as a plate uniting members of a steel framework.—*v.t.* To insert or apply, as a gusset.

gust, gust, *n.* [Icel. *gustr*, a blast of wind; allied to E. *gush*.] A violent blast of wind; a sudden rushing of fire, water, sound, or the like; a burst of passion.—*v.i.* To blow in gusts.—**gust·i·ly**, *adv.*—**gust·i·ness**, *n.* —**gust·y**, gus'tē, *a.*—*gustier, gustiest.* Subject to gusts; tempestuous.

gus·ta·to·ry, gus'ta·tō″rē, *a.* [L. *gustus*, a tasting, taste.] Of or pertaining to tasting. Also **gus·ta·tive.**

gus·to, gus'tō, *n.* [It.] Keen relish or zest; exuberance; enthusiasm; overabundant physical energy; personal taste or fancy.

gut, gut, *n.* [O.E. *gut, gutt,* gut, *guttas,* entrails; compare Prov. E. *gut,* a water channel, a drain; O.E. *gote,* a drain; from stem of O.E. *gēotan,* Goth. *giutan,* to pour out.] The intestinal canal from the stomach to the anus; an intestine; animal intestine used for making the strings of musical instruments, tennis rackets, and the like; a kind of silk used for making snells for fishhooks; a channel or passage; *pl.* the entrails or bowels. *Pl., slang,* pluck or courage; grit. —*v.t.* *gutted, gutting.* To remove or take out, as the entrails of; to eviscerate; to plunder the contents of; to destroy the inside of.

gut·less, gut'lis, *n.* Without courage; without confidence to act; without stamina or determination.

gut·ta, gut'a, *n.* pl. **gut·tae**, gut'ē. [L.] A drop or something droplike; *arch.* one of a series of pendent ornaments, usu. in the shape of a cone's frustrum, attached to the undersides of the mutules of a Doric entablature.

gut·ta-per·cha, gut'a·pur'cha, *n.* [Malay *gĕtah,* gum, balsam, and *pĕrcha,* kind of tree producing the substance.] The coagulated, milky juice of various Malaysian trees, esp. *Palaquium gutta,* used as for electrical insulation and in dentistry.

gut·tate, gut'āt, *a. Bot.* spotted, as if discolored by drops or having droplike spots; droplike. Also **gut·tat·ed.**—**gut·ta·tion**, gu·tā'shan, *n.* The exudation of water from plants.

gut·ter, gut'ér, *n.* [O.Fr. *goutiere* (Fr. *gouttière,* < *goute* (Fr. *goutte*), L. *gutta,* a drop.] A channel at the side or in the middle of a road or street for carrying off surface water; a channel at the eaves or on the roof of a building for drainage of rain water; any channel, trough, groove, or the like, esp. one for carrying off fluid; a furrow or channel made by running water; *bowling,* a channel or groove on each side of a bowling alley; *print.* the white space formed by the inner margins of facing pages in a book or magazine. *Fig.* the state of living in abject poverty; abode of the lowest class of people.—*v.t.* To form or cut in, as a channel or groove; to furnish with a gutter; *bowling,* to cause to roll into a gutter, as a bowling ball.—*v.i.* To form gutters, as water does; to flow in streams; to become channeled and lose molten wax, as a burning candle does.

gut·ter·snipe, gut'ér·snīp″, *n.* A person, esp. a child of the lowest economic or social class, usu. an inhabitant of an urban slum; a gamin.

gut·tur·al, gut'ér·al, *a.* [N.L. *gutturalis,* < L. *guttur,* throat.] Of or pertaining to the throat; harsh, rasping, or throaty, as certain vocal sounds.—*n.* A guttural sound; a velar.—**gut·tur·al·ly**, *adv.*— **gut·tur·al·ness, gut·tur·al·ism, gut·tur·al·i·ty**, gut″ér·al′i·tē, *n.*

gut·tur·al·ize, gut'ér·a·līz″, *v.t., v.i.*— *gutturalized, gutturalizing.* To utter in a

guttural manner; to velarize.—**gut·tur·al·i·za·tion**, gut″ér·al·i·zā'shan, *n.*

gut·ty, gut'ē, *a.*—*guttier, guttiest.* Courageous; challenging; extremely vital; very bold, as realistic details.

guv, guv, *n. Brit. slang.* A term used for one's father, or a superior; a shortened form of governor.

guy, gī, *n.* [O.Fr. *guis, guie,* a guide, < *guier,* guide.] A rope or appliance used to guide and steady something being hoisted or lowered, or to steady or secure anything liable to shift its position.—*v.t.* To guide, steady, or secure with a guy.

guy, gī, *n.* [From *Guy Fawkes.*] *Colloq.* a boy or man; a fellow. (*Usu. cap.*), *Brit.* a grotesque effigy of Guy Fawkes formerly carried about and burned in England on Nov. 5, Guy Fawkes Day; *Brit. slang,* a person of grotesque appearance.—*v.t. Colloq.* To jeer at or make fun of; ridicule.

guz·zle, guz'l, *v.i., v.t.*—*guzzled, guzzling.* [O.Fr. *goziller,* to gulp down; connected with Fr. *gosier,* the throat.] To drink greedily or excessively.—**guz·zler**, *n.*

gym, jim, *n. Colloq.* shortened form of gymnasiun or gymnastics.

gym·kha·na, jim·kä'na, *n.* [Appar. (*gym*)*nastics* and Hind. *khāna,* house.] *Brit.* A building or grounds for athletic events; a series of sports contests, as at a meet.

gym·na·si·ast, jim·nä'zē·ast″, *n.* [G.] A gymnast.

gym·na·si·um, jim·nä'zē·um, *n.* pl. **gym·na·si·ums, gym·na·si·a**, jim·nä'zē·a, jim·nä'zha. [L. < Gr. *gymnasion,* < *gymnazein,* train, exercise, < *gymnos,* naked, stripped, lightly clad.] A place or building for athletic exercises or contests; a school for gymnastics.

gym·na·si·um, jim·nä'zē·um, *G.* gim·nä'zē·u̇m″, **gym·nä'zē·u̇m″**, *n.* In continental Europe, a secondary school preparatory to the universities.

gym·nast, jim'nast, *n.* One who practices or teaches gymnastic exercises.

gym·nas·tic, jim·nas'tik, *a.* [L. *gymnasticus;* Gr. *gymnastikos.*] Pertaining to athletic exercises. Also **gym·nas·ti·cal.**— **gym·nas·ti·cal·ly**, *adv.*

gym·nas·tics, jim·nas'tiks, *n. pl.* Athletic exercises, esp. those performed on gymnasium apparatus; *sing. in constr.* the art of performing certain athletic exercises.

gym·no·sperm, jim'no·spurm, *n. Bot.* a class of seed plants, *Gymnospermae,* whose seeds are borne exposed and not in an ovary, as in the cone-bearing trees.

gym·no·spore, jim'no·spōr″, jim'no·spar″, *n. Bot.* a spore without a protective covering.

gyn·ae·ce·um, jin″a·sē'um, gī″na·sē'um, jī″na·sē'um, *n.* [L. < Gr. *gynaikeion,* prop. neut. of *gynaikeios,* of or for women, < *gyne,* woman.] Among the ancient Greeks, the part of a dwelling reserved for feminine use.

gy·nan·dro·morph, jī·nan'dro·marf″, gī·nan'dro·marf″, jī·nan'dro·marf″, *n. Biol.* a person having physical features characteristic of both sexes.

gy·nan·drous, ji·nan'drus, gī·nan'drus, jī·nan'drus, *a.* [Gr. *gynandros,* of doubtful sex, < *gynē,* woman, and *anēr* (*andr*), man.] *Bot.* having the pistils and stamens united in a column, as in orchids; evidencing gynandry.

gy·nan·dry, ji·nan'drē, gī·nan'drē, jī·nan'drē, *n.* Hermaphroditism; intersexuality; that condition in a plant or animal where both male and female reproductive organs exist. Also **gy·nar·chy**, jin'ér·kē, gī'nér·kē, jī'nér·kē.

gyn·e·coc·ra·cy, jin″e·kok'ra·sē, gī″ne·kok'ra·sē, jī″ne·kok'ra·sē, *n.* pl. **gyn·e·coc·ra·cies.** Political or governmental rule by women. Also **gy·nar·chy**, jin'ér·kē, gī'nér·kē, jī'nér·kē.

gyn·e·coid, jin'e·koid″, gī'ne·koid″, jī'ne·koid″, *a.* Womanlike; feminine.

gy·ne·col·o·gist,   **gy·nae·col·o·gist**, gī″ne·kol'o·jist, jin″e·kol'o·jist, jī″ne·kol'o·jist, *n. Med.* one who specializes in the field of gynecology.

gy·ne·col·o·gy,   **gy·nae·col·o·gy**, gī″ne·kol'o·jē, jin″e·kol'o·jē, jī″ne·kol'o·jē, *n.* [Gr. *gynē*(*gynaic-*), woman.] *Med.* that aspect of medical science which deals with the functions and diseases peculiar to women, esp. of the organs of reproduction. —**gyn·e·co·log·ic, gyn·e·co·log·i·cal**, jin″e·ko·loj'ik, gī″ne·ko·loj'ik, jī″ne·ko·loj'ik, *a.*

gy·noe·ci·um, ji·nē'sē·um, gī·nē'sē·um, jī·nē'sē·um, *n.* pl. **gy·noe·ci·a**. [N.L., orig. *gynaeceum,* but now regarded as < Gr. *gynē,* woman, and *oicos,* house.] *Bot.* the pistil, or the pistils collectively, of a flower.

gyp, jip, *n.* [Perhaps for *gypsy, gipsy.*] *Slang.* A swindle; a cheat; a swindler. *Brit.* a college servant in England.—*v.t.*— *gypped, gypping.* To swindle or cheat.— **gyp·per**, *n.*

gyp·soph·i·la, jip·sof'i·la, *n.* One of several varieties of annual or perennial herbs, usu. found in chalky soil, marked by profuse branching and fragrant, clustered flowers. Also *baby's-breath.*

gyp·sum, jip'sum, *n.* [L. < Gr. *gypsos,* chalk, gypsum.] A mineral, a hydrous sulfate of calcium, $CaSO_4 \cdot 2H_2O$, occurring in both crystalline and massive forms: used to make plaster of Paris, ornamental material, and fertilizer.—**gyp·se·ous**, *a.*

gyp·sy, jip'sē, *n.* pl. **gyp·sies**. [Corruption of *Egyptian.*] A person who leads a vagrant life; a wanderer; a hobo; a crafty woman. (*Cap.*) one of a nomadic, tawny-skinned, black-haired race of Hindu origin, now found universally; the language of these people; Romany.—*v.i.*—*gypsied, gypsying.* To live or roam as a Gypsy.—*a.* Camplike; picnic style; foot-loose. Also *Gipsy, gipsy.*—**gyp·sy·dom, gip·sy·dom, gyp·sy·hood, gyp·sy·ism**, *n.*

gyp·sy moth, *n.* A moth, *Porthetria dispar,* the larvae of which defoliate trees.

gy·rate, jī'rāt, jī·rāt', *v.i.*—*gyrated, gyrating.* [L. *gyratus,* pp. of *gyrare,* turn, wheel around, < *gyrus.*] To move in a circle or spiral; revolve round a fixed point or on an axis; rotate; whirl.— jī'rāt, *a. Bot.* circinate; *zool.* having convolutions.—**gy·ra·tor**, *n.*—**gy·ra·to·ry**, jī'ra·tōr″ē, *a.*

gy·ra·tion, jī·rā'shan, *n.* The act of gyrating; circular or spiral motion; revolution; rotation; whirling; a wheeling or rotating movement, as in dancing.

gyre, jīer, *n.* [L. *gyrus,* < Gr. *gyros,* ring, circle.] A circle; *poet.* a circular, spiral, or wheeling motion.

gy·rene, jī'rēn, jī·rēn', *n. Slang,* a U.S. Marine.

gyr·fal·con,   **ger·fal·con**, jur'fal″kon, jur'fa″kon, *n.* [L.L. *gyrofalco,* < *gyrus,* a circle, so called from its flight.] Any of a number of large, bold falcons of the arctic regions.

gy·ro, jī'rō, *n.* pl. **gy·ros.** Gyroscope; gyrocompass.

gy·ro·com·pass, jī'rō·kum″pas, *n.* A compass used in navigation which employs a continuously driven gyroscope so mounted that its axis maintains its position with reference to the true north.

gy·ro ho·ri·zon, *n. Aeron.* a flight instrument containing a gyroscope which shows any deviation of the plane from a flight position parallel to the horizon. Also *artificial horizon.*

gy·ro·plane, jī'ro·plān″, *n.* An aircraft, such as a helicopter or autogiro, having windmill-like wings that rotate about an approximately vertical axis.

---

ch- chain, G. na*ch*t;   **th-** THen, thin;   **w-** wig, hw as sound in whig;   **z-** zh as in azure, zeal.   *Italicized vowel* indicates schwa sound.

gy·ro·scope, jī′rọ·skōp″, n. [Fr. *gyroscope*.] An apparatus consisting of a heavy, swiftly rotating wheel, so mounted that its axis can turn freely in certain or all directions, and which is capable of maintaining the same absolute direction in space in spite of movements of the mountings or surrounding parts: used to maintain equilibrium and determine direction.—**gy·ro·scop·ic**, jī″rọ·skop′ik, a.—**gy·ro·scop·i·cal·ly**, adv.

gy·ro·sta·bi·liz·er, jī′rọ·stā′bi·li″zẽr, n. A device consisting essentially of a rotating gyroscope, used to stabilize a seagoing ship by counteracting its rolling motion. Also **gy·ro·scop·ic sta·bi·liz·er**.

gy·ro·stat, jī′rọ·stat″, n. A modification of the gyroscope, consisting of a rotating wheel pivoted within a rigid case, used for illustrating the dynamics of rotating bodies.—**gy·ro·stat·ic**, jī″rọ·stat′ik, a. Pertaining to the gyrostat or to gyrostatics.—**gy·ro·stat·i·cal·ly**, adv.—**gy·ro·stat·ics**, n. pl. but sing. in constr. Mech. the science which deals with the laws of rotating solids.

gy·rus, jī′rus, n. pl. **gy·ri**, jī′rī. [Gr. *gyros*, a circle.] Anat. a ridge or raised convolution, as on the surface of the brain.

gyve, jīv, n. [W. *gevyn*, Ir. *geibion*, < *geibhim*, to get, to hold; < L. *capio*, to take.] Usu. pl. A shackle, esp. for the legs; a fetter.—v.t.—*gyved, gyving*. To shackle; to chain.

H

H, h, āch, n. pl. **H's, Hs, h's, hs, aitch·es**, ā′chiz. The eighth letter of the English alphabet; the eighth in a series; the graphic representation of this letter, or anything resembling it; the spoken, aspirate sound represented by the letter *H*, often silent in such words of French origin as *hour, Heloise herb, heir*. (*Cap.*), chem. the symbol for hydrogen; slang, heroin.

ha, hä, interj. An exclamation denoting surprise, wonder, joy, or other sudden emotion. Also **hah**.

ha·ba·ne·ra, hä″ba·när′a, hä″ba·nyär′a, n. A slow Cuban dance; the music, in duple meter, for this dance.

ha·be·as cor·pus, hā′bē·as kạr′pus, n. [L. 'have thou the body.'] Law, a writ, the function of which is to release a person from unlawful detention, esp. to bring the accused before a court or judge to decide the legality of his detention. Also **ha·be·as cor·pus ad sub·ji·ci·en·dum**.

hab·er·dash·er, hab′ẽr·dash″ẽr, n. [Lit. a seller of *hapertas*, < O.Fr. *hapertas*, a kind of cloth.] The proprietor of a store which deals in men's furnishings; Brit. a dealer in notions and related goods.—**hab·er·dash·er·y**, pl. **hab·er·dash·er·ies**. n.

hab·er·geon, hab′ẽr·jen, n. [Fr. *haubergeon*, < *hauberc*, a hauberk.] A short coat of mail or armor consisting of a jacket without sleeves. Also **hauberk**.

ha·bil·i·ment, ha·bil′i·ment, n. [O.Fr. Fr. *habillement*, < *habiller*, to dress, < *habile*, fit.] Usu. pl. dress; attire; garb; accoutrements; equipment.

ha·bil·i·tate, ha·bil′i·tāt″, v.t.—*habilitated, habilitating*. [M.L. *habilitatus*, pp. of *habilitare*, < L. *habilus*.] Western U.S. to furnish, as a mine, with money or equipment.—**ha·bil·i·ta·tion**, ha·bil″i·tā′shan, n.

hab·it, hab′it, n. [O.Fr. *habit*, < L. *habitus*, condition, appearance, dress, < *habere*, have.] A disposition or involuntary tendency to act constantly in a certain manner, usu. acquired by frequent repetition; an addiction or usage; as, the *habit* of smoking, *habit*

of fault finding; a customary condition, constitution, or characteristic trait; biol. a characteristic form of an animal or plant; a costume indicating rank, membership in a religious order, or a special activity, as a riding *habit* or a nun's *habit*.—v.t. To dress; to clothe; to array.

hab·it·a·ble, hab′i·ta·bel, a. [O.Fr. Fr. *habitable*, < L. *habitabilis*.] Capable of being inhabited; suitable for a habitation.—**hab·it·a·bil·i·ty**, **hab·it·a·ble·ness**, hab″it·a·bil′i·tē, n.—**hab·it·a·bly**, adv.

ha·bi·tant, hab′i·tant, Fr. ä·bē·tän′, n. pl. **ha·bi·tants**, hab′i·tants, Fr. ä·bē·tän′. [O.Fr. Fr. *habitant*, < L. *habitans (-ant-)*, ppr. of *habitare*.] An inhabitant or resident of a place; in Canada or Louisiana, a farmer of French descent.

hab·i·tat, hab′i·tat″, n. [L. *habitat*, 'it dwells.'] The natural abode or locality of a plant or animal; a place where someone or something is usu. found.

hab·i·ta·tion, hab″i·tā′shan, n. [L. *habitatio*.] A residence or dwelling; a house or other place in which man or any animal dwells; act of inhabiting.

hab·it-for·ming, hab′it·fạr″ming, a. Tending to induce uncontrollable, habitual repetiton; addictive.

ha·bit·u·al, ha·bich′ọ·al, a. [Fr. *habituel*.] Formed or acquired by habit, frequent use, or custom; constantly practiced; customary; regular; as a matter of course.—**ha·bit·u·al·ly**, adv.—**ha·bit·u·al·ness**, n.

ha·bit·u·ate, ha·bich′ọ·āt″, v.t.—*habituated, habituating*. [L. *habituo, habituatum*.] To accustom; to make familiar by frequent use or practice; to familiarize.—**ha·bit·u·a·tion**, ha·bich″ọ·ā′shan, n.

hab·i·tude, hab′i·tōd″, hab′i·tūd″, n. [Fr. *habitude*, < L. *habitudo*.] Customary manner or mode of living, feeling, or acting.

ha·bit·u·é, ha·bich′ọ·ā″, ha·bich″ọ·ā′, Fr. ä·bē·twä′, n. pl. **ha·bit·u·és**, ha·bich′ọ·āz″, ha·bich″ọ·āz′, Fr. ä·bē·twä′. A frequenter of any place or type of place; as, a *habitué* of pool halls and bars.

ha·chure, ha·shụr′, hash′ụr, n. [Fr., < *hacher*, E. *hatch*.] In drawing or engraving, a line used in shading or the like, esp. one of the short lines representing the slopes of mountains, etc. on maps.—ha·shụr′, v.t. *hachured, hachuring*. To mark or shade with, or indicate by, hachures.

ha·ci·en·da, hä″sē·en′da, Sp. ä·syen′dä, n. pl. **ha·ci·en·das**. [Sp. landed property, estate, domestic work, < L. *facienda*, things to be done, neut. pl. gerundive of *facere*, do, make.] In Spanish-American countries, a landed estate, large farm, stock-raising ranch, or country house; a ranch building.

hack, hak, v.t. [O.E. = *haccian* (recorded in the compound *tohaccian*, hack to pieces) = D. *hakken* = G. *hacken*, hack.] To make irregular cuts in or upon, as with heavy blows; to roughen; to break up, as the surface of the ground; to cut, reap, or uproot; to kick the shins of intentionally, as in soccer.—v.i. To make rough cuts or notches; deal cutting blows; to kick an opponent's shins intentionally, as in soccer; to emit short, frequently repeated coughs.—n. A tool or instrument, as an ax, hoe, or pick for hacking or cutting; a cut, gash, or notch; a cutting blow; a short, broken cough.—**hack·er**, n.

hack, hak, n. [Short for *hackney*.] A horse kept for common hire or adapted for general work; sometimes, an old or worn-out horse; a coach or carriage kept for hire; a hackney; colloq. a taxicab. A person who hires himself out for general work, esp. general literary work. A frame or rack to hold fodder for cattle, or for drying fish or cheese.—a. Of a hired sort; much in use; hackneyed or trite.—v.t. To let out for hire;

put to indiscriminate use; to render trite or stale by frequent use.—v.i. To ride on the road, or to ride at an ordinary pace.

hack·a·more, hak′a·mōr″, n. [Sp. *jaquima*.] A bitless bridle used esp. to train or break horses, specif. that mechanism which causes parts of the bridle to apply pressure to the nose and top of the head when the reins are tightened.

hack·ber·ry, hak′ber″ē, n. pl. **hack·ber·ries**. [< Prov. E. *hagberry*.] The sweet fruit of the elmlike tree, genus *Celtis*; the tree itself or its wood. Also *hagberry, hedgeberry, sugarberry*.

hack·ie, hak′ē, n. Slang, a cabdriver.

hack·le, hak′l, n. A comb for dressing flax or hemp; one of the long, slender feathers on the neck or saddle of certain birds much used in making artificial flies for anglers; the neck plumage of the domestic cock; a kind of artificial fly for anglers; usu. pl. the hairs or ruff on the back of a dog's neck.—v.t.—*hackled, hackling*. To comb, as flax or hemp, with a hackle; to equip with a hackle. To cut roughly; to mangle.—**hack·ler**, n.—**hack·ly**, a. Rough or jagged as if hacked.

hack·ma·tack, hak′ma·tak″, n. Bot. a common name for the American larch, *Larix laricina*, a species of tree in the pine family. Also *tamarack*.

hack·ney, hak′nē, n. pl. **hack·neys**. [O.Fr. *haquenee*, a horse, Sp. *hacanea*, a nag; probably from O.D. *heckeneye, hakkenei*, a hackney; lit. perhaps a hacked or docktailed nag.] A trotting horse used for riding or to pull a light vehicle. (*Cap.*) a special English breed characterized by unusually high-stepping gait. A hired carriage.—a.—v.t. To overuse, wear out, or make trite. See *hack*.—**hack·neyed**, a. Discussed endlessly; overworked, trite, commonplace.—**hack·ney coach**, a coach kept for hire.

hack·saw, hak′sạ″, n. A hand saw used for cutting metal, consisting of a narrow, fine-toothed blade anchored in a metal frame.

hack·work, hak′wụrk″, n. Routine work, esp. writing or art, done for hire in accordance with a specified formula, offering little or no creative opportunity.

had·dock, had′ok, n. pl. **had·dock, had·docks**. [M.E. *haddok*; origin unknown.] A food fish, *Melanogrammus aeglefinus*, of the N. Atlantic, allied to but smaller than the cod.

hade, hād, v.i.—*haded, hading*. Geol. to incline from a vertical position.—n. Geol. the inclination of a vein or a rock fault plane from a vertical position.

Ha·des, hā′dēz, n. [Gr. *Haidēs*.] Class. mythol. the subterranean world of departed spirits; the lord of the lower world, Pluto. The abode or state of the dead, in the Revised Version of the New Testament; (l.c.) hell.—**Ha·de·an**, hā·dē′an, hā′dē·an, a.

hadj, haj, n. Hajj.

had·n't, had′nt. Contraction of had not.

hae·ma·tox·y·lin, hē″ma·tok′si·lin, hem″a·tok′si·lin, n. Hematoxylin.

hae·ma·tox·y·lon, hē″ma·tok′si·lon″, hem″a·tok′si·lon″, n. A small, thorny, tropical American tree, *Haematoxylon campechianum*, in the legume family, with corrugated, clustered trunks; the heartwood of this tree from which the dye, hematoxylin, is obtained. Also *logwood*.

haf·ni·um, haf′nē·um, häf′nē·um, n. Chem. a metallic element found in zirconium ores. Sym. Hf, at. no. 72, at. wt. 178.49.

haft, haft, häft, n. [O.E. *hæft*, a haft = D. and G. *heft*, a handle; Icel. *hepti* (= *hefti*), a haft, < the stem of *have* or *heave*.] A handle of an implement or weapon.—v.t. To furnish with a handle or hilt; to set in a haft.

haf·ta·rah, häf·tạr′a, Heb. häf·tä·Rä′, n. pl. **haf·ta·roth, haf·ta·rahs**, häf·tạr′ōt, Heb. häf·tä·Rät′. A passage from the Book of

Prophets which is read or chanted during a Jewish synagogue service, often by a Bar Mitzvah celebrant, after reading the Parashah on the Sabbath and other holy days.

hag, hag, häg, *n.* [Shortened < O.E. *haegtesse;* akin to G. *hexe,* D. *heks,* a witch; probably < O.E. *haga,* a hedge, G. *hag,* a wood (the meaning being woman of the woods).] An ugly old woman; a witch; a sorceress.—**hag·born,** *a.* Born of or produced by a witch.

hag, hag, *n.* [Cf. Icel. *högg,* a stroke, hewing, gap, ravine.] *Brit. dial.* Wild, broken ground; a firm spot in a bog; a soft spot in boggy land; a cutting, as of wood.

hag·ber·ry, hag'ber″ē, *n.* pl. **hag·ber·ries.** Hackberry.

hag·don, hag'don, *n.* Any one of the shearwaters, a group of N. Atlantic seabirds having long, narrow wings.

hag·fish, hag'fish″, *n.* pl. **hag·fish, hag·fish·es.** Any of several eellike marine cyclostomes of the order *Hyperotreta,* having a circular suctorial mouth and horny teeth which tear into and devour other fish.

Hag·ga·dah, hä·gä′da, *Heb.* hä·gä·dä′, hä·ga·da′, *n.* pl. **Hag·ga·dahs, Hag·ga·doth,** ha·gä′dōs, ha·gä′dōt, *Heb.* hä·gä·dạt′, hä·gä·dōs′. [*Heb. haggādāh,* 'narrative,' < *higgid,* tell.] *Judaism.* A book containing the Seder service observed during Passover; the non-legal portion of rabbinical literature, esp. the free exposition or illustration, chiefly homiletical, of the Scripture.

hag·gard, hag′ẽrd, *a.* [Fr. *hagard,* orig. a wild falcon, < G. *hag,* a wood. In secondary sense perh. for *hagged,* that is, *hag*-like.] Appearing wasted by want or suffering; having a worn and pale appearance; gaunt; tired; *falconry,* wild or untamed.—*n.* *Falconry,* an untrained hawk, captured as an adult.—**hag·gard·ly,** *adv.*

hag·gis, hag′is, *n.* [< *hag,* to chop, a form of *hack;* cf. Fr. *hachis,* a hash.] A Scottish dish, commonly boiled in a calf's or sheep's stomach, and made of the animal's heart and liver minced with suet, onions, oatmeal, and seasoning.

hag·gle, hag′l, *v.i.*—*haggled, haggling.* [Freq. of *hag,* for *hack,* to hack.] To bargain or deal with in a quibbling, petty way; to dispute over small points.—*v.t.* To cut into small pieces; to mangle.—*n.* The act or process of haggling.—**hag·gler,** *n.*

Hag·i·og·ra·pha, hag″ē·og′ra·fa, hā″jē·og′ra·fa, *n. pl., sing. or pl. in constr.* [L.L. < Gr. *agiographa, agios,* sacred, and *graphein,* write.] The books which form the third of the three ancient divisions of the Old Testament, comprising Psalms, Proverbs, Job, Song of Solomon, Ruth, Lamentations, Ecclesiastes, Esther, Daniel, Ezra, Nehemiah, and I and II Chronicles.—**hag·i·og·ra·pher, hag·i·og·ra·phist,** *n.* A writer of sacred books; one of the writers of the Hagiographa; a writer of lives of the saints; a hagiologist.—**hag·i·og·ra·phy,** *n.* pl. **hag·i·og·ra·phies.** Hagiology.—**hag·i·o·graph·ic, hag·i·o·graph·i·cal,** hag″ē·o·graf′ik, hā″jē·o·graf′ik, *a.*

hag·i·ol·a·try, hag″ē·ol′a·trē, hā″jē·ol′a·trē, *n.* The worship of saints.—**hag·i·ol·a·ter,** *n.*—**hag·i·ol·a·trous,** *a.*

hag·i·ol·o·gy, hag″ē·ol′o·jē, hā″jē·ol′o·jē, *n.* pl. **hag·i·ol·o·gies.** That branch of literature which deals with the lives and legends of the saints; the list or legends of the saints; a work on the lives and legends of the saints.—**hag·i·o·log·ic, hag·i·o·log·i·cal,** hag″ē·o·loj′ik, hā″jē·o·loj′ik, *a.*—**hag·i·ol·o·gist,** *n.*

hag·i·o·scope, hag′ē·o·skōp″, hā″jē·o·skōp, *n.* An opening in an inside wall or other barrier in a church, to afford a view of the chief altar to worshipers in the chapels or side aisles.—**hag·i·o·scop·ic,** hag″ē·o·skop′ik, hā″jē·o·skop′ik, *a.*

hag·rid·den, hag′rid″en, *a.* Tormented; sorely troubled.—**hag·ride,** hag′rīd, *v.t.* Torment or harass.

hah, hä, *interj.* Ha.

ha-ha, hä″hä′, hä′hä″, *n., interj.* [Imit.] The sound of laughter, expressing amusement, triumph, or derision. Also *haw-haw.*

ha-ha, hä″hä″, *n.* [Reduplicated form of *haw,* a hedge; Fr. *haha.*] A fence or hedge sunk in a ditch to avoid interference with the view from a garden.

Hah·ne·mann·i·an, hä″ne·man′ē·an, hä″ne·mä′nē·an, *a.* [From Samuel *Hahnemann,* German physician, 1755–1843.] Pertaining to Dr. Hahnemann's theories on homeopathic medicine.—**Hah·ne·mann·ism,** *n.* The theories of Dr. Hahnemann; original homeopathy.

haik, hīk, hāk, *n.* [Ar. *hayk* < *hāk,* to weave.] An oblong piece of cloth covering the head and body, used as an outer garment by the Arabs.

hai·ku, hī′kö, *n.* pl. **hai·ku.** [Jap.] A Japanese form of verse comprising respectively three unrhymed lines of five, seven, and five syllables; a poem in this form.

hail, hāl, *v.t.* [M.E. *hail, heyl,* prop. adj., hale, sound, well, < Icel. *heill,* hale, whole.] To salute or greet; to welcome; applaud or commend; to call out to, esp. in order to attract attention.—*v.i.* To call out in order to attract attention, as from a ship.—*n.* A salutation or greeting; the act of hailing; a shout or call to attract attention.—*interj.* A salutation; hello: an exclamation of approval or greeting.—**hail from,** to come from; to claim as one's place of birth or residence.—**with·in hail·ing dis·tance,** within sound of a loud shout.—**hail·er,** *n.*

hail, hāl, *n.* [O.E. *hagal, hagol* = G., D., Dan., and Sw. *hagel,* Icel. *hagl,* hail; root doubtful.] Small masses or pellets of ice or frozen vapor which fall during showers or storms; any showering suggestive of falling hail—*v.i.* To pour down hail; to fall in the manner of hail.—*v.t.* To shower or cast down like hail, as curses.

hail-fel·low, hāl′fel′ō, *a.* Cordial or jovial.—hāl′fel′ō, *n.* A genial person or hearty companion. Also **hail fel·low, hail-fel·low well met.**

Hail Ma·ry, *n.* Ave Maria.

hail·stone, hāl′stōn″, *n.* A single pellet of hail.

hail·storm, hāl′stạrm″, *n.* A storm having hail.

hair, hâr, *n.* One of the fine filaments which grow from the skin of animals and man; the mass of such fibers forming an extra thick covering on parts of the human body, as on the head; such fibers forming the outer protective coat of mammals; similar filamentous fibers covering the body of an insect; *bot.* such filaments on the epidermis of plants. A slight measure; a precise or minute degree; a fraction, as of time or space; as, missed by a *hair.*—*a.* Of or with hair; for hair; as, a *hair* spray.—**get in one's hair,** annoy or irritate someone.—**hair of the dog that bit one,** *slang,* an alcoholic drink taken as a hangover remedy.—**let one's hair down,** to relax; to lose one's inhibitions; to dismiss one's reserve and assume free and easy behavior.—**with·out turn·ing a hair,** remaining unperturbed; containing one's emotional reactions.—**hair·less,** *a.*

hair·breadth, hâr′bredth″, hâr′bretth″, *n.* The diameter or breadth of a hair; a minute distance.—*a.* Very narrow; as, a *hair-breadth* escape. Also **hair's-breadth, hairs·breadth.**

hair·brush, hâr′brush″, *n.* A brush for dressing and grooming hair.

hair·cloth, hâr′klạth″, hâr′kloth″, *n.* A cloth woven with either horse or camel hair, used

primarily in upholstery or in the stiffening of fabrics.

hair·cut, hâr′kut″, *n.* The act of trimming or cutting and shaping the hair; the style of the cut.

hair·do, hâr′dö″, *n.* pl. **hair·dos.** Coiffure; any arranged style for a woman's hair; hair so dressed.

hair·dress·er, hâr′dres″ẽr, *n.* One who styles women's hair. *Brit.* a barber.

haired, hârd, *a.* Having hair; characterized by a certain type of hair: used in combination; as, brown-*haired.*

hair·line, hâr′lin″, *n.* The beginning of the scalp or the hair above the brow on a human head; a very slender line, as a stroke made in writing or a stripe on a textile fabric; a fabric woven with very fine lines or stripes; *print.* a very thin line on a type face, as of the serif; a style of type consisting entirely of such lines.

hair·piece, hâr′pēs″, *n.* A switch of synthetic or human hair worn to complement a woman's hairdo by giving it extra fullness or length; postiche; toupee.

hair·pin, hâr′pin″, *n.* A doubled pin of metal or plastic used by women to hold hair in place.—*a.* Sharply curved or U-shaped, as a turn in a road.

hair-rais·ing, hâr′rā″zing, *a.* Frightening or terrifying; exciting.—**hair-rais·er,** *n.* A thriller; a melodrama; something which excites or terrorizes.

hair seal, *n.* Any of various earless seals of the subfamily *Phocinae,* with coarse hair and no soft underlying fur.

hair shirt, *n.* A shirt made of coarse animal hair and worn as a penance by religious ascetics.

hair space, *n.* *Print.* the thinnest metal space used to separate letters, words, or symbols.

hair·split·ter, hâr′split″ẽr, *n.* One who makes excessively fine distinctions.—**hair·split·ting,** *n., a.*

hair·spring, hâr′spring″, *n.* *Horol.* the fine, often spiral, spring which regulates the action of the balance wheel of a watch or timepiece.

hair·streak, hâr′strēk″, *n.* A butterfly of the *Lycaenidae* family, distinguished by thin stripes on its underwings.

hair stroke, *n.* A fine stroke or line in writing or printing.

hair trig·ger, *n.* A trigger of a firearm, so delicately adjusted that the slightest pressure will discharge the weapon.—**hair-trig·ger,** *a.* Responsive to the slightest stimulus; easily activated.

hair·y, hâr′ē, *a.*—*hairier, hairiest.* Covered with hair; having abundant hair; hirsute; of or similar to hair. *Slang,* undesirable, unpleasant, or difficult.—**hair·i·ness,** *n.*

Hai·tian, Hay·tian, hā′shan, hä′tē·an, *a.* Of or pertaining to Haiti, a republic in the West Indies, or its people.—*n.* A native or inhabitant of Haiti. The French dialect of Haiti; also **Hai·tian Cre·ole.**

hajj, hadj, haj, *n.* pl. **hajj·es, hadj·es.** [Ar. *hajj,* < *hajja,* set out, go on a pilgrimage.] A pilgrimage to Mecca, considered the duty of every Muslim.—**haj·ji, hadj·i,** haj′ē, *n.* pl. **haj·jis, hadj·is.** A Muslim who has performed his *hajj:* often used as a title.

hake, hāk, *n.* pl. **hake, hakes.** [M.E. *hake;* origin uncertain.] Any of the edible marine fishes constituting the genus *Merluccius,* related to and resembling the cod, as *M. bilinearis,* the silver *hake* of the New England coast; any of various related marine fishes, esp. of the genus *Urophycis,* as the white *hake.*

ha·kim, hä·kēm′, hä′kēm, *n.* [Ar. *hakīm.*] In Muslim countries, a physician, hä·kēm′; also **ha·keem.** A governor, judge, or ruling authority in Muslim countries, hä′kēm.

---

ch- chain, G. na*ch*t;   **th-** THen, thin;   **w-** wig, hw as sound in whig;   **z-** zh as in azure, zeal.   *Italicized vowel* indicates schwa sound.

Ha·la·kah, hä·lạ´кнạ, *Heb.* hä·lä·кнä´, hä·lạ·кʌạ´, *n. pl.* **Ha·la·kahs,** *Heb.* **Ha·la·koth,** hä·lạ·кнōs´, hä·lä·кнạt´. [Heb. *hălākāh,* 'rule to go by,' *hālak,* walk, go.] The body of traditional laws of the Jews, supplementing and interpreting the law of the Scripture, and comprising the legal aspects of the Talmud, as opposed to *Haggadah*; (*l.c.*) any of these laws. Also **Ha·la·chah.—ha·lak·ic,** ha·lak´ik, *a.—* **ha·la·kist,** hä´lạ·kist, ha·lä´kist, *n.* A writer or scholar of the Halakah.

hal·berd, hal´bẽrd, hạl´bẽrd, *n.* [Fr. *halle-barde,* < O.G. *helmparte, helmbarte,* a halberd—*helm,* a handle, a helm, and *parte, barte,* an ax.] A military weapon consisting of a combination of a spear and battle-ax with a handle about six feet long, used esp. in the 15th and 16th centuries. Also **hal·bert.—hal·berd·ier,** hal´bẽr·dẽr´, *n.*

hal·cy·on, hal´sē·on, *n.* [L. *halcyon,* < Gr. *halkyōn,* a kingfisher, said to be < *hals,* the sea, and *kyō,* to conceive.] A bird, allegedly the kingfisher, fabled to have the power of charming and calming the winds and waves during the winter solstice, when it hatched its young in a nest built on the sea; a kingfisher.—*a.* Pertaining to the halcyon; calm, quiet, and peaceful; flourishing and prosperous; carefree and happy.—**hal·cy·on days,** the seven days before and seven after the winter solstice; any days of peace and tranquillity.

hale, hāl, *v.t.—haled, haling.* [O.Fr. Fr. *haler,* hale, haul; < Teut.: cf. G. *holen,* fetch, haul.] To compel to comply; as, to *hale* before the magistrate.

hale, hāl, *a.—haler, halest.* [O.E. *hal* = Icel. *heill,* hale, whole.] Free from disease or bodily infirmity; robust; vigorous.—**hale·ness,** *n.*

half, haf, häf, *n. pl.* **halves,** havz, hävz. [O.E. *healf* = O.H.G. *halba,* Icel. *halfa,* Goth. *halba,* side, part.] One of the two equal, or approximately equal, parts into which anything is or may be divided; one part with an equal remainder; one of two parts or members associated together as a pair. *Sports,* one of two equal periods of play, as in football.—*a.* Being one of the two equal or approximately equal parts into which anything is or may be divided; being equal to only about half of full measure; as, *half* speed; partial or incomplete.—*adv.* To the extent or measure of half; as, a bucket *half*-full of water; in part, or partly; to some extent; to a great extent, preceded by *not;* as, *not half* bad.—**half·ness,** *n.*

half-and-half, haf´an·häf´, häf´an·häf´, *a.* Half one thing and half another; half the thing specified and half not.—*n.* Cream and milk mixed in equal parts; a mixture of two things in equal parts; *Brit.* a mixture of two malt liquors, esp. porter and ale.—*adv.* In two equal portions.

half·back, haf´bak´, häf´bak´, *n. Football.* One of two ball carriers in the offensive backfield, positioned behind the line and usu. on either side of the fullback; the position filled by such a player; any of the players behind the forward line in soccer or rugby.

half-baked, haf´bākt´, häf´bākt´, *a.* Insufficiently cooked, as food; incompletely planned; lacking mature judgment; *colloq.* half-witted.

half bind·ing, *n.* A style of binding books in which the back and corners are leather and the sides are paper or cloth; the binding itself.—**half-bound,** haf´bound´, häf´bound´, *a.*

half-bred, häf´bred´, häf´bred´, *a.* Referring to a person or animal having mixed blood strains; hybrid.

half-breed, haf´brēd´, häf´brēd´, *n.* One born of parents of different races, specif. applied to the offspring of an American Indian and a white person.—*a.*

half broth·er, *n.* A male offspring having one parent in common with another offspring.

half-caste, haf´kast´, häf´käst´, *n.* A person of mixed race, esp. one of mixed European and Hindu parentage.

half-cell, haf´sel´, häf´sel´, *n. Phys., chem.* an electrolytic cell in which ionization takes place between a single electrode and the electrolytic solution.

half cock, *n.* The position of the hammer of a firearm when raised halfway and held by the mechanism so that the trigger will not operate.—**half-cocked,** haf´kokt´, häf´kokt´, *a.* Of a firearm, with the hammer in the position of half cock.—**go off half-cocked,** *slang.* To act prematurely; take action without due preparation or forethought.

half gain·er, *n.* A standing or running front dive that ends, by means of a half backward somersault in the air, as a back dive.

half-heart·ed, haf´här´tid, häf´här´tid, *a.* Lacking eagerness or enthusiasm; indifferent.—**half-heart·ed·ly,** *adv.*—**half-heart·ed·ness,** *n.*

half-hour, haf´our´, haf´ou´ẽr, häf´our´, häf´ou´ẽr, *n.* The half of an hour; an interval of thirty minutes.—**half·hour·ly,** *a., adv.*

half-length, haf´lengkth´, haf´length´, häf´lengkth´, häf´length´, *n.* One of two equal parts in distance, height, or extent; that which shows half of the height of something, esp. a portrait.—*a.* Of or concerning one of two equal parts as measured in distance, height, or extent; concerning the viewing or fitting of half the body, as: The mirror shows only a *half-length* view.

half·life, haf´līf´, häf´līf´, *n. pl.* **half·lives.** *Phys.* the length of time in which one half of the radioactive atoms present in a substance will decay.

half-light, haf´līt´, häf´līt´, *n.* A partial light or one that is obscured, as at twilight or dawn.

half-mast, haf´mast´, häf´mäst´, *n.* A position halfway or less below the top of a mast, staff, or pole; as, a flag at *half-mast* in respect for the dead; half-staff; a signal of distress.—*v.t.* To hang at half-mast, as a flag.

half-moon, haf´mön´, häf´mön´, *n.* The moon at the quarters, when half its disk appears illuminated; a crescent-shaped object; the white base of a fingernail.— **half·moon,** *n.* An edible fish found off the coast of southern California.

half nel·son, *n. Wrestling,* a hold in which a wrestler standing behind his opponent places one arm under the corresponding arm of the opponent so that the hand grips the nape of the opponent's neck.

half note, *n. Mus.* a note equivalent to one half of a whole note. Also *minim.*

half pint, *n.* A dry or liquid measure equal to $\frac{1}{4}$ of a quart; *slang,* a very short person.

half sis·ter, *n.* A female offspring having one parent in common with another offspring.

half-slip, haf´slip´, häf´slip´, *n.* A slip without a bodice; a petticoat.

half sole, *n.* That part of the sole of a boot or shoe which extends from the shank or arch to the end of the toe.—**half-sole,** haf´sōl´, häf´sōl´, *v.t.—half-soled, half-soling.* To repair by putting on a new half sole.

half-staff, haf´staf´, häf´stäf´, *n.* Half-mast.

half step, *n. Milit.* in quick time, a 15-inch marching step; in double time, an 18-inch step; *mus.* a semitone.

half tide, *n.* The tide when halfway between the ebb and flood.

half-tim·bered, haf´tim´bẽrd, häf´tim´-bẽrd, *a. Arch.* having the frame and principal supports of timber, but with the spaces filled in with masonry or plaster.—**half-tim·ber·ing,** *n.*

half time, *n. Sports,* a rest period for players of football, basketball, or other games, after half the game has been played.—*a.*

half ti·tle, *n.* The title of a book, often shortened, appearing alone on a full page which precedes the title page or the first page of text, or used at the head of the first page of text.

half-tone, haf´tōn´, häf´tōn´, *n. Photog.* a tone intermediate between the extreme lights and shades of a picture; *photo-engraving,* a process in which gradation of tone, as in a photograph, is obtained by a system of minute dots between fine intersecting black lines produced by a screen placed in the camera a short distance in front of the sensitized plate; a metal plate made by this process, or a print from it.

half tone, *n. Mus.* a semitone.

half-track, haf´trak´, häf´trak´, *n. Milit.* a type of armored military vehicle propelled by caterpillar treads at the rear and conventional wheels at the front.—**half-tracked,** *a.*

half-truth, haf´trōth´, häf´trōth´, *n.* A partially true assertion usu. intended to be deceptive or evasive.

half vol·ley, *n.* A stroke, as in handball or tennis, when the ball is hit the instant it bounces from the playing area or ground.— **half-vol·ley,** haf´vol´ē, häf´vol´ē, *v.t., v.i. —half-volleyed, half-volleying.*

half·way, haf´wā´, häf´wā´, *adv.* Half over the way; as, to go *halfway* to Rome; to or at half the distance, as: The rope reaches only *halfway.* To half the full extent, as: The morning is *halfway* over.—*a.* Midway between two points; going to or covering only half the full extent, or partial; as, *halfway* measures.

half-wit, haf´wit´, häf´wit´, *n.* A feeble-minded person; one who lacks mental acuity.—**half-wit·ted,** *a.*—**half-wit·ted·ness,** *n.*

hal·i·but, hol·i·but, hal´i·but, hol´i·but, *n. pl.* **hal·i·but, hal·i·buts.** [M.E. *haly-butte,* appar. < *haly,* holy, and *butte,* kind of fish; perhaps so called for being eaten on holy days.] Either of the two largest species of flatfish, *Hippoglossus hippoglossus* of the N. Atlantic, or *Hippoglossus stenolepsis* of the N. Pacific, important food fish sometimes weighing several hundred pounds; any of various other similar flatfishes.

hal·ide, hal´īd, hä´līd, hä´lid, *n.* [Gr. *hals, als,* salt.] *Chem.* a binary compound formed by the direct union of a halogen with a more electropositive element or radical.—*a.* Of the nature of or pertaining to halide; haloid.

hal·i·dom, hal´i·dom, *n.* A holy place; a sanctuary.

hal·ite, hal´īt, hä´līt, *n.* [Gr. *hals (al-),* salt.] *Chem., mineral.* natural sodium chloride, NaCl; rock salt.

hal·i·to·sis, hal´i·tō´sis, *n.* Condition of having foul or offensive breath.

hall, hạl, *n.* [O.E. *heal, heall* = Icel. *holl,* hall, Sw. *hall,* D. *hal.* < root signifying to cover.] A large room, esp. one for public assembly including conventions, weddings, and entertainments; a room at the entrance of a house; an anteroom; a passageway connecting other areas in a house or public building; a manor house; the principal room in a medieval castle; a college or section of a college. *Brit.* a large room in which students dine in common; the students' dinner.

hal·le·lu·jah, hal´e·lö´yạ, *interj.* [Heb. *hallĕlūyāh,* 'praise ye Jehovah.'] Praise ye the Lord!—*n.* An exclamation of 'hallelujah!'; a song of praise to God. Also **hal·le·lu·iah.**

hall·mark, hạl´märk´, *n.* The official stamp of the Goldsmith's Hall in London, England, attesting that articles in gold and silver meet the legal standard; any mark certifying quality.—*v.t.* To mark with a hallmark.

hal·lo, hal·loo, ha·lō′, ha·lö′, *interj.* [Cf. G. *halloh!* and Fr. *halle,* an exclamation used to cheer on dogs; *haller,* to encourage dogs.] An exclamation to invite attention; a hunting cry to set a dog on the chase.—*n.* The shout "halloo."—*v.i.* To call "halloo"; to shout; to cry, as after dogs.—*v.t.* To shout to.

hal·low, hal′ō, *v.t.* [O.E. *hālgian,* to hallow, < *halig,* holy.] To consecrate; to honor as sacred.—**hal′lowed,** *a.*

Hal·low·een, hal″o·wēn′, hal″ō·ēn′, hol″o·wēn′, hol″ō·ēn′, *n.* [For *Allhallows even* (eve).] The evening of Oct. 31, the eve of Allhallows or All Saints′ Day, on which celebrants wear disguises and play pranks. Also **Hal′low·e′en.**

Hall·statt, Hall·stadt, hal′stat, häl′shtät, *a.* Noting or pertaining to a pre-Christian stage of culture in central Europe, characterized by the use of bronze, the introduction of iron, and artistic work in pottery and jewelry, as shown by relics found near Hallstatt, Austria. Also **Hall·statt·an, Hall·stat·ti·an, Hall·stad·tan,** hal·stat′an, häl·shtät′an, hal·stat′ē·an, häl·shtät′ē·an.

hal·lu·ci·nate, ha·lö′si·nāt″, *v.t.*—*hallucinated, hallucinating.* [L. *hallucinatus,* pp. of *hallucinari,* better *alucinari,* wander in the mind, dream: cf. Gr. *aluein,* wander in the mind.] To affect with hallucination.

hal·lu·ci·na·tion, ha·lö″si·nā′shan, *n.* [L. *hallucinatio(n-).*] *Psychol.* an apparent perception, as by sight or hearing, for which there is no real external cause, as distinguished from *illusion.* The imagined object of an hallucination; a false notion; a delusion.—**hal·lu·ci·na·to·ry,** ha·lö′si·na·tör″ē, *a.* —**hal·lu·ci·na·tion·al, hal·lu·ci·na·tive,** *a.*

hal·lu·cin·o·gen, ha·lö′si·no·jen″, hal″ū·sin′o·jen, *n.* A chemical substance or drug such as LSD or mescaline that causes hallucinations.—**hal·lu·ci·no·gen·ic,** ha·lö″si·nō·jen′ik, *a.*

hal·lu·ci·no·sis, ha·lö″si·nō′sis, *n. Psychiatry,* a disordered mental condition marked by hallucinations.

hal·lux, hal′uks, *n.* pl. **hal·lu·ces,** hal′ū·sēz. [N.L. for L. *allex,* great toe.] The innermost of the five digits normally present in the hind foot of air-breathing vertebrates; in man, the great toe; in birds, the inner toe or hind toe.

hall·way, hal′wā″, *n.* A corridor, entrance-hall, or passage, as in a building.

halm, häm, *n. Brit.* haulm.

ha·lo, hā′lō, *n.* pl. **ha·los, ha·loes.** [L. *halos,* < Gr. *halōs,* threshing-floor (on which the oxen trod out a circular path), disk, halo.] *Art,* a disk or circle of light represented about the head of a sacred person, as a saint or angel. An ideal glory investing an object viewed reverently or sentimentally, usu. denoting goodness or sanctity. *Meteor.* a circle of light seen around a luminous body, esp. the moon or the sun, due to the refraction produced by ice particles in the atmosphere; something resembling a halo, such as a nimbus or an aureola.—*v.t., v.i.—haloed, haloing.*

hal·o·gen, hal′o·jen, hā′lo·jen, *n.* [Gr. *hals* (*al-*), salt.] *Chem.* any of the elements astatine, chlorine, iodine, bromine, and fluorine, and sometimes the radical cyanogen, which forms a salt by direct union with a metal.—**ha·log·e·nous,** ha·loj′e·nus, *a.*

hal·o·gen·ate, hal′o·je·nāt″, hā′lo·je·nāt″, *v.t.—halogenated, halogenating. Chem.* to treat or combine with a halogen; to add a halogen to, esp. to an organic compound.—**hal·o·gen·a·tion,** *n.*

hal·oid, hal′oid, hā′loid, *a.* [Gr. *hals,* sea-salt, and *eidos,* resemblance.] *Chem.* resembling common salt in composition;

formed by the combination of a halogen and a metal.—*n.*

hal·o·mor·phic, hal″o·mar′fik, *a.* Influenced by the presence of an alkali or a neutral salt, or both; as, *halomorphic* soil.—*v.t.* **hal·o·mor·phism,** *n.*

hal·o·phile, hal′o·fīl″, *n.* [Gr. *hals* (*al-*), salt.] A plant or animal that thrives in salt marshes.—**ha·loph·i·lous,** ha·lof′i·lus, *a.*

hal·o·phyte, hal′o·fīt″, *n.* [Gr. *hals* (*al-*), salt.] A plant growing naturally in salt soil.—**hal·o·phyt·ic,** hal″o·fit′ik, *a.*

halt, halt, *a.* [O.E. *healt,* O.H.G. *halz* = Icel. *haltr* = Goth. *halts,* lame.] *Archaic,* lame; crippled; limping.—*v.i.* [O.E. *healtian.*] *Archaic,* to be lame; walk lamely; limp. To stand in doubt, waver, or hesitate; to proceed in a lame or faulty way, as reasoning, verse, rhyme, utterance.—*n. Archaic,* a halting movement or gait; a limp.—**halt·ing,** *a.*—**halt·ing·ly,** *adv.*

halt, halt, *n.* [G. *halt,* < *halten,* hold.] A stop; as, to call a *halt.*—*v.i.* To make a halt or temporary stop, as in marching or traveling.—*v.t.* To cause to halt; to restrain.

hal·ter, hal′ter, *n.* [O.E. *hælfter* = G. *halfter,* halter.] A rope or strap with a noose or headstall, for leading or tying horses or cattle; a rope with a noose for hanging lawbreakers; death by hanging. A woman′s sports top which fastens around the neck and leaves the back and arms exposed.—*v.t.* To put a halter on; to restrain, as by a halter; to catch with a noose; to hang, as a person.—*a.* Like or having a halter; as, a *halter* dress.

hal·ter·break, hal′ter·brāk″, *v.t.* To train, as a colt or other animal, to respond to a halter.

halve, hav, häv, *v.t.—halved, halving.* [M.E. *halven, halfen,* < *half.*] To divide into halves; share equally; give or take the half of; complete the half of. *Golf,* to play (a hole) in the same number of strokes.

hal·yard, hal·liard, hal′yerd, *n.* [*Hale* or *haul,* and *yard.*] *Naut.* a rope or tackle for hoisting and lowering sails, yards, or flags.

ham, ham, *n.* [O.E. *hamm* = D. *ham* = G. dial. *hamme,* ham.] The meat of a hog′s thigh used for food; the part of the leg behind the knee; *usu. pl.* the back of the thigh together with the buttocks. *Theatr.* an inferior performer who overacts. *Radio,* a licensed operator of an amateur radio station. *Sewing,* a cushion used for pressing the curved areas of garments.—*v.t.—hammed, hamming.* To perform with exaggerated gestures or speech.—*v.i.* To overplay a part.—*a.*—**ham·my,** *a.—hammier, hammiest.* Relating to the qualities of ham in taste, flavor, or appearance. Characteristic of one who is overdramatic in gesture and speech.

ham·a·dry·ad, ham″a·drī′ad, ham″a·drī′-ad, *n.* [Gr. *hamadryas,* < *hama,* together, and *drys,* a tree.] *Mythol.* a wood nymph, who lived and died with the tree to which she was attached. The king cobra, *Naja hannah.* A kind of baboon, *Papio hamadryas,* sacred to the ancient Egyptians.

ha·mal, ham·mal, ha·mäl′, ha·mal′, *n.* [Ar. *hammāl,* < *hamala,* carry.] An Oriental porter; in India and Pakistan, a male servant.

ham·burg·er, ham′bur″ger, *n.* Raw beef chopped or ground; a sandwich consisting of ground beef shaped into a patty, broiled, and placed between halves of a round bun.

hame, hām, *n.* [Same as D. *haam,* a hame.] One of two curved pieces in the harness of a draft horse, to which the traces are fastened.

Ham·il·to·ni·an, ham″il·tō′ne·an, *a.* [From Alexander *Hamilton,* Amer. political thinker and statesman, 1757–1804.] Of or pertaining to Hamilton or to the political ideas and philosophy of Hamilton, esp. his

emphasis on a strong central government, his advocacy of protective tariffs to safeguard the national economy, and his skepticism about the common man′s ability to understand political issues.—*n.* A supporter or believer in Hamilton′s doctrines.—**Ham·il·to·ni·an·ism,** *n.*

Ham·ite, ham′īt, *n. Bib.* a descendant of Ham, the second son of Noah. A member of any of various races, mainly Caucasian, of northern and eastern Africa, as the native Egyptians.—**Ham·it·ic,** ha·mit′ik, ha·mit′ik, *a.* Of or pertaining to Ham or the Hamites; noting or pertaining to the language of the Hamites.—*n.* A language subfamily from which Egyptian and other African languages are derived.

ham·let, ham′lit, *n.* [O.Fr. *hamelet,* dim. of *hamel* (Fr. *hameau*), hamlet; < Teut., and akin to E. *home.*] A small village; a cluster of houses in the country; *Brit.* a village without a church of its own, belonging to the parish of another village or town.

ham·mal, ha·mäl′, ha·mal′, *n.* Hamal.

ham·mer, ham′er, *n.* [O.E. *hamor* = D. *hamer* = G. *hammer* = Icel. *hamarr,* hammer.] A tool consisting of a solid head, usu. steel, set crosswise on a handle, used for beating metals or driving nails; a mallet or gavel, esp. one used by an auctioneer; any of various instruments or devices resembling a hammer in form, action, or use, as something which strikes a gong or doorbell; *mus.* one of the padded devices by which the strings of a piano are struck; *firearms,* that part of the lock which causes the discharge by its action; *sports,* a metal ball attached to a long, flexible handle, used in throwing contests; *anat.* the malleus; *fig.* an aggressive or destructive foe.—*v.t.* To beat or drive with a hammer; to form or build with a hammer. *Fig* to impress or teach by repetition; as, to *hammer* a rule into the students′ heads; to contrive or work out laboriously.—*v.i.* To strike blows with or as with a hammer, esp. repeatedly; *fig.* to make persistent or laborious attempts.—**ham·mer·er,** *n.*

ham·mer and sick·le, *n.* The Soviet Union′s emblem, consisting of a hammer crossing a sickle, which represents the worker and the peasant; any like emblem used by various communist parties.

ham·mer and tongs, *adv.* In a vigorous, loud, or rough manner.—*a.*

ham·mered, ham′erd, *a.* Indented with hammer marks, as the surface of some silver, brass, or other metal articles; made by hammering.

ham·mer·head, ham′er·hed″, *n.* Any of the voracious sharks constituting the family *Sphyrnidae,* characterized by a head expanded laterally so as to resemble a double-headed hammer, esp. *Sphyrna zygaena,* a widely distributed species. A brown African bird, *Scopus umbretta,* characterized by a head similar in shape to a claw hammer.

ham·mer·less, ham′er·lis, *a.* Having no hammer or no visible hammer: applied esp. to firearms which have the hammer or striking device concealed.

ham·mer lock, *n.* A hold in which a wrestler twists his opponent′s arm and forces it upward behind the back.

ham·mock, ham′ok, *n.* [Sp. *hamaca,* a word of West Indian origin.] A kind of hanging bed, consisting of a piece of canvas or netting, suspended from each end by cords and hooks.

ham·mock, ham′ok, *n.* [= *hummock.*] An elevated, thickly wooded tract of land within a marshy region, as the Florida Everglades. Also *hummock.*

ham·per, ham′per, *v.t.* [M.E. *hamperen,* = D. *haperen,* to stammer, falter, stick fast.] To impede in motion or progress; to encumber or restrain.—*n. Naut.* something that hampers or encumbers, but is still necessary equipment. *Fig.* anything which impedes.

ham·per, ham′pėr, *n.* [Contr. from *hanaper,* a container for goblets.] A kind of basket or wickerwork receptacle, used as a case for packing articles, for stowing picnic gear, or for storing laundry.

ham·ster, ham′stėr, *n.* [G.] A short-tailed, burrowing rodent, *Cricetus frumentarius* or *cricetus,* with large cheek pouches, inhabiting parts of Europe and Asia; any of various other rodents of the same genus and allied genera.

ham·string, ham′string″, *n.* In man, any of the tendons which bound the ham, or area behind the knee; in quadrupeds, the great tendon at the back of the hock.—*v.t. hamstrung* or *hamstringed, hamstringing.* To cut the hamstring or hamstrings of; to cripple, disable, or render powerless.

ham·u·lus, ham′ū·lus, *n.* pl. **ham·u·li,** ham′ū·lī″. [L., dim. of *hamus,* a hook.] *Biol.* a small hook or hooklike process.—**ham·u·lar, ham·u·late,** ham′ū·lāt″, *a.*

ham·za, häm′zä, *n.* The representation in English of the glottal stop in Arabic orthography, usu. an apostrophe.

hand, hand, *n.* [O.E. *hand* = D. and G. *hand* Icel. *hond* (*hand*-) = Goth. *handus,* hand.] The extremity of the arm, consisting of the palm, four fingers, and thumb; the corresponding part of the forelimb in any of the higher vertebrates; the terminal part of any limb when prehensile, as the hind foot of a monkey, claw of a crab, or talon of a hawk; agency or instrumentality; as, to die by one′s own *hand;* a part or share in something; as, to have a *hand* in a matter; side; as, on the right *hand;* a side of a subject or question; the hand as used in making a promise or taking an oath, and esp. as representing a woman promised, given, or won in marriage; a person who is engaged in performing a specific task; as, a book by several *hands;* a person employed in manual labor, as in a factory; member of a ship′s crew; a person with reference to action, ability, or skill; as, to be a poor *hand* at writing letters; a person considered a source, as of information or of supply; as, knowledge obtained at first *hand;* skill or knack at doing something, whether with the hands or otherwise; a turn or inning of play in certain games; a round or outburst of applause, as for an actor; style of handwriting; something resembling a hand in shape or function; a hand-shaped sign used in writing or printing to draw attention to something; the feel and finish of cloth or leather, esp. such qualities as smoothness, softness, warmth, and flexibility; a pointer or index on the dial of a clock or watch; a palmate root of ginger; a bundle of tobacco leaves tied together; one of the clusters forming a bunch of bananas; a lineal measure used in giving the height of horses, equal to four inches; *cards,* the cards dealt to or held by each player at one time; *pl.* possession or power, disposal or control; as, to put a matter into a person′s *hands.*—*a.* Made by, operated by, using, or belonging to the hand.—**at hand,** within reach; near by; near in time.—**at the hands of, at the hand of,** through the agency of someone or something.—**by hand,** done with the hands only, without mechanical help.—**from hand to mouth,** with attention to immediate wants only.—**hand o·ver fist,** *slang,* rapidly; in large quantities.—**hand to hand,** in close combat; at close quarters.—**in hand,** in immediate possession; as, cash *in hand;* in process; as, attending to the matter *in hand;* under control.—**off one′s hands,** out of one′s responsible charge or care.—**on hand,** in immediate possession; subject to disposal; before one for performance or atten-

tion, as a task, duty, or engagement; in attendance, or present.—**on one′s hands,** resting on one as a burden, responsibility, or task.—**out of hand,** no longer in process; over and done with; beyond control; at once; without delay.—**to hand,** within reach; at hand; into one′s immediate presence or possession.—**to have one′s hands full,** having all one can do.

hand, hand, *v.t.* To grasp, touch, manage, or work with the hands; to lead or conduct with the hand; as, to *hand* a child across the street; to deliver or pass with the hand or hands; to pass, transfer, or transmit, as: *Hand* me my hat.

hand and foot, *adv.* Entirely; fully; completely.

hand·bag, hand′bag″, *n.* A small purse for carrying in the hand, or a woman′s pocketbook, held in the hand or worn over the shoulder, for carrying small purchases, toilet articles, or money.

hand·ball, hand′bạl″, *n.* A game, with two or four players, played in an enclosed court in which a small rubber ball is batted with the hands against a wall; the ball used in this game.

hand·bill, hand′bil″, *n.* A printed paper or sheet to be circulated for the purpose of making some public announcement.

hand·book, hand′bụk″, *n.* A small book or treatise; a manual; an establishment where bets on horse races are accepted.

hand·breadth, hand′bredth″, hand′bretth″, *n.* The breadth of the hand; a unit of linear measure varying from 2½ to 4 inches; a palm. Also **hands·breadth, hand′s-breadth.**

hand·car, hand′kär″, *n. Rail.* a small car propelled by a hand mechanism or small motor to aid workmen in inspecting and repairing the tracks.

hand·clasp, hand′klasp″, hand′kläsp″, *n.* The clasping or shaking of hands by two persons to show greeting, congratulation, or the like; handshake.

hand·craft, hand′kraft″, hand′kräft″, *n.* Handicraft; craftsmanship.—hand′kraft′, hand′kräft′, *v.t.* To make or create by hand.—**hand·craft·ed,** *a.*

hand·cuff, hand′kuf″, *n.* [Modified < O.E. *handcops*—*hand,* the hand, *cops,* a fetter.] *Usu. pl.* a manacle or metal bracelet with lock, usu. in pairs chained together.—*v.t.* To put handcuffs on; to fetter.

hand down, *v.t.* To pass on in succession, as from father to son; to deliver to a lower court, as a decision.

hand·ed, hand′did, *a.* Having a hand possessed of a specified property: used esp. in compounds; as, right-*handed,* empty-*handed.*—**hand·ed·ness,** *n.* The tendency to utilize one hand more than the other.

hand·ful, hand′fụl″, *n.* pl. **hand·fuls.** As much as the hand will grasp or contain; a small quantity or number; as much as one can manage; *colloq.* a thing or person difficult to control.

hand gre·nade, *n.* A grenade or explosive shell which is thrown by hand and exploded by impact or by means of a fuse; a grenade or glass missile containing a chemical for extinguishing fire.

hand·gun, hand′gun″, *n.* Any small firearm that can be fired with a single-handed hold.

hand·i·cap, hand′dē·kap″, *n.* [Appar. orig. for *hand in cap.*] A race or other contest in which certain disadvantages or advantages of weight, distance, or time are placed upon competitors to equalize their chances of winning; the disadvantage or advantage itself; *fig.* any encumbrance or physical disadvantage.—*v.t.*—*handicapped, handicapping.* To assign or subject to, as competitors, a specific handicap; to penalize; *fig.* to serve as a handicap, as: Age *handicaps* him.—**hand·i·cap·per,** *n.* One who handicaps; one employed to determine the

amount of the handicaps in a contest; a newspaper employee whose selections of probable horse-racing winners are published as a betting guide.

hand·i·capped, hand′dē·kapt″, *a.* Physically or mentally disadvantaged; assigned a handicap, as a contestant.

hand·i·craft, hand′dē·kraft″, hand′dē·kräft″, *n.* [Equiv. to *hand-craft,* the *i* representing old prefix *ge,* as in *handiwork.*] The skill of one′s hands; work of an artisan, hobbyist, or tradesman, with or without special tools or equipment; a craft sometimes identified with a nation or region and oftentimes artistic; an object produced by handicraft.—**hand·i·craft·er,** *n.* One who engages in crafts as an occupation or hobby.—**hand·i·crafts·man,** *n.*

hand·i·ly, hand′di·lē, hand′di·lē, *adv.* In a handy manner; skillfully or dexterously; conveniently; easily or without difficulty; as, to pass a test *handily.*—**hand·i·ness,** *n.*

hand in glove, *adv.* Intimately involved.

hand in hand, *adv.* One hand enclosed in that of another; associating harmoniously; cooperatively; conjunctively; conjointly.

hand·i·work, hand′dē·wụrk″, *n.* [O.E. *handgeweorc,* < *hand,* the hand, and *geweorc* = *weorc,* work, with prefix *ge.*] Work done by the hands; an object that exhibits the hand skills of its maker; results influenced by or characteristic of a particular person or group.

hand·ker·chief, hang′kėr·chif, hang′kėr·chēf″, *n.* pl. **hand·ker·chiefs, hand·ker·chieves.** A hemmed square of cotton, linen, or silk carried for personal use or as a decorative accessory.

han·dle, han′dl, *n.* [O.E. *handle,* < *hand,* E. *hand.*] A part which is intended to be grasped by the hand; *fig.* that by which anything may be taken hold of; something that may be taken advantage of in effecting a purpose.—**fly off the han·dle,** to become disturbed esp. in an instant; to be angered suddenly and violently.—**han·dled,** *a.*

han·dle, han′dl, *v.t.*—*handled, handling.* [O.E. *handlian,* < *hand.*] To touch, feel, or use the hands on, as in picking up; to manage manually; manipulate; to manage, direct, or control; as, to *handle* troops in battle; wield, employ, or use; as, to *handle* one′s fists well in a fight; to deal with or treat, as a matter or subject, esp. to deal with or treat in a particular way; as, to *handle* a case or a person with discretion; to deal or trade in, as in goods.—*v.i.* To respond, perform, or behave in a specific way when handled or controlled, as: This boat *handles* well.—**han·dle·a·ble,** *a.*

han·dle·bar, han′dl·bär″, *n. Often pl.* a bar with a handle or handles, esp. the curved bar in front of the rider on a bicycle or motorcycle by which the vehicle is guided.

han·dle·bar mus·tache, *n.* A full, curving mustache.

han·dler, han′dlėr, *n.* One who handles; one who manually controls animals, esp. in exhibition or in hunting; *sports,* one who trains and advises a prizefighter.

han·dling, hand′ling, *n.* A touching; a use of the hand; a manner of treatment; a method of dealing with a subject, as in a book; action in commerce, including mechanical transportation, as of freight; training and discipline, as of a horse.

hand-me-down, hand′mē·doun″, han′mē·doun″, *n.* A used item of clothing passed from one person to another, esp. from an older to a younger sibling.—*a.*

hand-off, hand′af″, hand′of″, *n. Football,* the handing of the ball by one player, usu. the quarterback or an offensive back, to a nearby teammate.

hand·out, hand′out″, *n. Slang,* a portion of food or the like given to a beggar or other needy individual; anything given free of charge. *Journ.* a news item or prepared statement which is released for use by the press.

hand·o·ver, *v.t.* To give up control or give up possession of.

hand-pick, hand'pik', *v.t.* [Back formation from *hand-picked.*] To pick by hand; to select carefully; to choose for a specific purpose.

hand·rail, hand'rāl", *n.* A railing grasped by the hand for support, as along a balcony.

hand·saw, hand'sa̤", *n.* A saw which is designed for one-handed operation.

hands-down, handz'doun', *a.* Successful without effort; easy, as: It was a *hands-down* victory. Certain; without question.—*adv.*

hand·sel, hand'sel, *n.* [< *hand*, and stem *sell, sale*; Icel. *handsal* (< *hand*, and *sal*, sale), a bargain by shaking hands; Dan. *handsel*, hansel, earnest.] A gift given as a token of good luck or good will, esp. at New Year's or at the start of a new enterprise; the first use, specimen, or sale of something, considered a token of what is to come; a foretaste; a payment or first installment given as a pledge.—*v.t.*—*handseled, handseling, handselled, handselling.* To give a handsel to; to inaugurate; to experience or use for the first time. Also *hansel.*

hand·set, hand'set', *n.* A telephone unit combining a receiver and transmitter, mounted at either end of a handle.—*v.t.*—*handset, handsetting.* To assemble or set by hand, as type.—*a.* Printed from type which has been set by hand.

hand·shake, hand'shāk", *n.* The clasping of hands between two people in greeting, agreement, or farewell.

hand·some, han'som, *a.* [< *hand*, and term. *-some* = D. *handzaam*, tractable, serviceable, mild; G. *handsam*, convenient, favorable.] Possessing a form or appearance pleasing to the eye, and often impressive or manly; good-looking; ample, large, or generous; as, a *handsome* gift; gracious; as, *handsome* manners.—**hand·some·ly**, *adv.*—**hand·some·ness**, *n.*

hand·spike, hand'spīk", *n.* A bar used as a lever for raising weights.

hand·spring, hand'spring", *n. Gymnastics*, an acrobatic feat in which the body turns a complete circle in the air, touching ground with the hands first, then the feet.

hand·stand, hand'stand", *n.* The act of balancing the body upside down in a perpendicular position, on the palms of the hands.

hand-to-hand, hand'to·hand', *a.* At close range; in close touch, as fighting.—**hand to hand**, *adv.* At very close range.

hand-to-mouth, hand'to·mouth', *a.* Providing limited means of support; leading a financially insecure existence; having nothing to spare.

hand·weav·ing, hand'wē"ving, *n.* The craft or method of weaving a fabric on a handloom; the fabric woven on a handloom.

hand·wheel, hand'hwēl", hand'wēl", *n. Mech.* a wheel operated manually, which controls valves or other machine parts.

hand·work, hand'wu̥rk", *n.* Work done by the hands, as opposed to work done by machines.—**hand·worked**, *a.* Processed or made mainly by hand.

hand·wo·ven, hand'wō"ven, *a.* Hand-loomed; woven on a hand-controlled loom.

hand·writ·ing, hand'rī"ting, *n.* The style of writing peculiar to each person; calligraphy; writing done by hand.—**hand·write**, hand'rīt", *v.t.*—past *handwrote,* pp. *handwritten,* ppr. *handwriting.*

hand·y, han'dē, *a.*—*handier, handiest.* [Fr. *hand*; compare the D. and L.G. *handig*, handy.] Convenient; near or easily acces-

sible; easily maneuverable; skilled in using the hands.

hand·y·man, han'dē·man", *n.* pl. **hand·y·men.** One doing or hired to do odd jobs.

hang, hang, *v.t.*—*hung* or *hanged* (esp. for capital punishment and suicide), *hanging.* [In part O.E. *hōn* (pret. *heng*, pp. *hengen*), *v.t.* hang, suspend, execute by hanging on a cross or gibbet, in part the derived O.E. *hangian* (pret. *hangode*), *v.i.* hang, depend; akin D. *hangen*, G. *hangen*, Icel. *hanga*, *hengja*, and Goth. *hāhan*.] To fasten or attach, using only support from above; to suspend so as to allow free movement, as on a hinge; to suspend on a cross or gallows, esp. by the neck, as a method of capital punishment; to suspend thus as a means of suicide; to let droop or bend downward; as, to *hang* one's head in shame; to fasten in position, as the blade of a scythe; to attach, as paper, to walls; to furnish or decorate with something suspended or attached; as, to *hang* a room with pictures; to keep a jury from rendering a verdict by refusing to agree with the other jurors; *fine arts*, to display, as by attaching paintings to the walls in an exhibition; *slang*, cursed: used euphemistically for *damn*, as: I'll be *hanged* if I like that!

hang, hang, *v.i.* To be suspended; to dangle; to swing freely, as on a hinge; to die or be put to death by suspension from a cross or gallows; to bend forward or downward; to lean over; to rest, float, or hover in the air. To impend; to be imminent; to rest for support, followed by *on* or *upon*; to be dependent or contingent; to remain attentive, as to a person's words; to hold fast, cling, or adhere, often as an encumbrance, as: Remorse *hangs* heavy on my heart. To be burdensome, as dull hours; to remain in doubtful suspense, as: The trial *hangs* in the balance. To remain with motion or action suspended; to linger or loiter; to persist; to remain unsettled or unfinished; to fail to agree, as a jury; *fine arts*, to be on display, as in an exhibition.—**hang one on**, *slang*, to get very drunk.—**hang·a·ble**, *a.*

hang, hang, *n.* The action of hanging; the way in which a thing hangs; a slope or declivity; *colloq.* the precise manner or knack of using or doing something; as, to get the *hang* of a card trick; meaning or force; as, to get the *hang* of a sentence or a subject; concern, as: He doesn't give a *hang* about his test.

hang·ar, hang'ẽr, *n.* [Fr. *hangar*, a shed.] A shelter for housing or repairing airplanes.

hang a·round, *v.i. Colloq.* To loiter; to frequent a particular place or group.

hang back, *v.i.* To hesitate; to be reluctant to proceed.

hang·dog, hang'da̤g", hang'dog", *a.* Dejected or defeated; guilty or shifty in appearance.

hang·er, hang'ẽr, *n.* A shaped support or frame of wood, wire, or plastic for holding a garment when not in use; something by which a thing is hung, as a loop on a garment; one who hangs something; as, a paper-*hanger*; a kind of short sword; a hinged bracket on an automobile that holds the spring to the chassis; *Brit.* a small wooded section of sharply sloping land.

hang·er-on, hang'ẽr·on', hang'ẽr·a̤n', *n.* pl. **hang·ers-on.** A follower; a parasite; one who persistently frequents a person, group, or place, esp. with the hope of securing a personal advantage.

hang·ing, hang'ing, *n.* The action of one who or that which hangs; suspension; execution by suspending by the neck until dead; a slope; *usu. pl.* something that hangs or is hung, as drapery.—*a.* Dangling; suspended; fitted for an object which hangs; meriting, causing, or likely to inflict a

hanging; as, a *hanging* mob; overhanging; situated on a steep slope or at a height, as a garden; directed downward, as a look.

hang·ing in·den·tion, *n. Print.* a uniform indention of each line in a paragraph except the first.

hang·man, hang'man, *n.* pl. **hang·men.** One whose office is to hang persons condemned to death; a public executioner.

hang·nail, hang'nāl", *n.* [For *agnail.*] A small piece of skin, partly detached, at the base or side of a fingernail. Also *agnail.*

hang on, *v.i.* To continue; to persevere or persist; to cling to; to keep a telephone line open or connected.

hang·out, hang'out" *n. Colloq.* a place one visits frequently, as a clubroom or restaurant; living quarters.—**hang out**, *v.i.* To reside; to frequent, as a particular place.

hang·o·ver, hang'ō"vẽr, *n.* A situation or thing that remains from a former period; the physical discomfort suffered after over-indulgence in alcohol.

hang to·geth·er, *v.i.* To hold together; to be closely united; to be consistent or coherent, as: That alibi doesn't *hang together.*

hang up, *v.t.* To suspend, as on a hook or clothesline; to keep in or put into abeyance; to delay or hold back; to end, as a telephone dialogue.—*v.i.* To strand, as a ship on a reef; to break a telephone connection.—**hang-up**, hang'up, *n.* Delay; difficulty. *Slang*, obsession; problem.

hank, hangk, *n.* [M.E.: cf. Icel. *hǫnk*, hank, coil, skein.] A skein of thread or yarn; a definite length or weight of thread or yarn bought in bulk; a coil, knot, or loop, as of hair; *naut.* a fastener for a sail.

hank·er, hang'kẽr, *v.i.* [Allied to D. *hankeren*, to desire, to long for.] To long for; to persistently desire, followed by *after, for*, or an infinitive.—**hank·er·ing**, *n.* Yearning; craving; longing.—**hank·er·er**, *n.*

han·ky-pan·ky, hang'kē·pang'kē, *n.* [A made word: cf. *hocus-pocus.*] *Slang.* Trickery; underhanded dealing; questionable morals.

Han·o·ve·ri·an, han"ō·vẽr'ē·an, *a.* [From *Hanover*, a Prussian province; also the house of *Hanover*, sovereigns of Great Britain from 1714 to 1901.] Of or pertaining to the province of Hanover or to the former ruling house of Hanover.—*n.* A supporter of the house of Hanover.

Han·sa, han'sa, han'za, *n.* [G. *hanse, hansa*, league.] The Hanseatic League, a confederation of cities in W. Germany from the 13th to the 17th century, allied for mutual protection and commercial advantages; (*l.c.*) a medieval guild of merchants; a fee paid for membership in this guild. Also **Hanse.**—**Han·se·at·ic**, han"sē·at'ik, *a.*

Han·sard, han'sẽrd, *n. Brit., Canadian*, the official publication of the proceedings and debates of Parliament.

han·sel, han'sel, *n.* Handsel.—*v.t.*—*hanseled, hanseling, Brit. hanselled, hanselling.*

Han·sen's dis·ease, han'senz di·zēz", *n.* [From Armauer G. *Hansen*, Norwegian physician.] *Pathol.* leprosy.

han·som, han'som, *n.* [From J. A. *Hansom*, English patentee, 1803–82.] A low, covered, two-wheeled vehicle drawn by a horse, the driver being mounted on an elevated seat behind the cab. Also **han·som cab.**

hant, hant, *v.t., v.i., n. Dial.* haunt. Also **ha'nt.**

Ha·nuk·kah, hä'nu̇·ka, hä'nu̇·kä", hä'nu̇·kä", *Heb.* кнä·nö·kä', *n.* [Heb.] The Jewish Festival of Lights, lasting eight days, which commemorates the rededication of the Temple of Jerusalem after its defilement by the Syrians under King Antiochus. Also *Chanukah.*

hao·le, hou'lē, hou'lä, *n.* Among Hawaiians, one who is not a native Polynesian, esp. a white person.

hap, hap, *n.* [M.E. *hap,* < Scand.: cf. Icel. *happ,* hap, chance, good luck.] Chance or fortune; one's luck or lot; an occurrence, happening, or accident.—*v.i.*—*happed, happing.* [M.E. *happen.*] To happen.—**hap·less,** *a.* Luckless; unfortunate.—**hap·less·ly,** *adv.*—**hap·less·ness,** *n.*

hap·haz·ard, hap'haz"ĕrd, *n.* [< *hap* and *hazard.*] Chance or accident.—hap·haz'ĕrd, *a.* Accidental; aimless, determined by or dependent on mere chance; as, a haphazard performance.—*adv.*—**hap·haz·ard·ly,** *adv.*—**hap·haz·ard·ness,** *n.*

hap·log·ra·phy, hap·log'ra·fē, *n.* [Gr. *haploos,* single.] The unintentional omission of one or more repeated letters in writing or copying, as *rember* for *remember.*

hap·loid, hap'loid, *a.* Single; *biol.* possessing one set of chromosomes which are unpaired. Also **hap·loi·dic.**—*n. Biol.* a haploid cell or organism.—**hap·loi·dy,** *n.* The state of being a haploid.

hap·lol·o·gy, hap·lol'o·jē, *n.* [Gr. *haploos,* single.] *Gram.* the utterance of only one of two similar adjacent syllables or sounds, resulting in the contraction of a word, as in *idly* for *idlely.*

hap·lo·sis, hap·lō'sis, *n. Biol.* the development of the haploid number of chromosomes in the meiotic process.

hap·ly, hap'lē, *adv.* By luck or chance; by accident; perhaps.

hap·pen, hap'n, *v.i.* [M.E. *happenen,* < *happen,* E. *hap.*] To occur or take place; to come to pass by chance, without apparent reason or design; to befall; to chance; to have the fortune or lot, as: I *happened* to see him. To come upon by chance; as, to *happen* on a clue to a mystery; to be, come, or go by chance; as, to *happen* along.

hap·pen·ing, hap'e·ning, *n.* An event; an occurrence or gathering, usu. spontaneous; a spontaneous occurrence staged as a performance, and often involving interaction between the actors and audience.

hap·pen·stance, hap'en·stans", *n.* An occurrence caused by chance. Also **hap·pen·chance.**

hap·pi·ness, hap'ē·nis, *n.* The state or quality of being content; pleasure; felicity; aptness.

hap·py, hap'ē, *a.*—*happier, happiest.* [< *hap, n.*] Delighted, pleased, or glad; characterized by or indicative of pleasure or contentment; joyful; fortunate or lucky; felicitous; skillful or apt. Characterized by obsessive or impulsive behavior; crazy; quick to do or use something: used in combination; as, trigger-*happy.*—**hap·pi·ly,** *adv.*

hap·py-go-luck·y, hap'ē·gō·luk'ē, *a.* Trusting cheerfully to luck; carefree and lighthearted.—*adv. Archaic,* haphazardly.

Haps·burg, Habs·burg, haps'bŭrg, *Ger.* häps'bŭrкн, *a.* Pertaining to a prominent German family which provided rulers for Austria, Spain, Hungary, Bohemia, and the Holy Roman Empire from the 11th century to the 20th century.—*n.*

hap·ten, hap'ten, *n.* [G.] *Immunology,* a substance which reacts with an antibody only when they are together in a synthetic environment.

hap·tics, hap'tiks, *n. pl. but sing. in constr. Psychol.* the study of tactile sensations.—**hap·tic, hap·ti·cal,** *a.* Pertaining to tactile sensations.

ha·ra·ki·ri, här'a·kēr'ē, har'a·kēr'ē, har'ē·kēr'ē, *n.* [Jap. *hara,* belly, and *kiri,* cutting.] A traditional Japanese method of suicide, ceremonially performed by slashing the abdomen with a dagger; self-destruction or suicide. Also **ha·ri·ka·ri,** här'ē·kär'ē, har'ē·kar'ē.

ha·rangue, ha·rang', *n.* [Fr. *harangue,* < O.H.G. *hring,* ring, circle of people, arena, = E. *ring.*] A passionate, vehement, or loud speech or address, esp. to an assembly; a pompous, didactic, or scolding speech; a tirade.—*v.t.*—*harangued, haranguing.* To address in a harangue.—*v.i.* To deliver a harangue.—**ha·rangu·er,** *n.*

har·ass, har'as, ha·ras', *v.t.* [Fr. *harasser;* probably connected with Fr. *harier,* to harry, vex; *harer,* to set a dog on.] *Milit.* to annoy by repeated attacks or raids. To disturb or bother continually with worries, cares, or the like; to harry; to pester.

har·bin·ger, här'bin·jĕr, *n.* [O.E. *harbegier, harbergeour, harbesher,* one who provides harborage or lodging, a harbinger.] One who or that which precedes and foreshadows a future occurrence; omen; a forerunner or precursor; *archaic,* one who goes before to secure lodgings.—*v.t.* To act as a harbinger to; to presage.

har·bor, *Brit.* **har·bour,** här'bĕr, *n.* [M.E. *herbore, herboru, hereberge,* = Icel. *herbergi* = O.L.G. and O.H.G. *heriberga,* lit. 'army shelter'; from elements equivalent to O.E. *here,* army, and *beorgan,* protect.] A protected anchorage near a coast for ships, afforded by natural features of the coastline or by artificial construction; a similar area with facilities for ports or docks; a port; a place of shelter, haven, or refuge.—*v.t.* To give shelter or refuge to; to provide concealment for; to shelter; to maintain a habitat for, esp. an animal; to contain; to entertain within the mind, as thoughts and feelings.—*v.i.* To take shelter in a harbor.

har·bor·age, *Brit.* **har·bour·age,** här'bĕr·ij, *n.* Shelter for ships; harbor; a shelter or lodging.

har·bor mas·ter, *Brit.* **har·bour mas·ter,** *n.* An officer in charge of a harbor or port who enforces its regulations.

hard, härd, *a.* [O.E. *heard* = D. *hard* = G. *hart* = Icel. *hardhr* = Goth. *hardus,* hard; akin to Gr. *kratus,* strong, mighty.] Solid and firm to the touch; not easily penetrated, divided, or altered in shape; not soft; firmly formed or tight; as, a *hard* knot; difficult to do, accomplish, or perform; as, a *hard* task; carrying on with great exertion, energy, or persistence; as, a *hard* worker; difficult or troublesome with respect to a specified action; as, *hard* to please, *hard* of hearing; difficult to deal with, manage, control, or overcome; difficult to understand, explain, or solve; as, a *hard* subject; difficult to bear or endure; as, a *hard* life; severe or rigorous; as, a *hard* winter; rude or coarse; as, *hard* fare. Not easily impressed or moved, as persons; obdurate; unfeeling or pitiless; of a shrewd, practical nature; harsh or severe in dealing with others; as, a *hard* master; sometimes, niggardly, stingy; *colloq.* incorrigible or disreputable; as, a *hard* character. Based on actual facts; as, *hard* evidence; severe or rigorous in provisions; as, a *hard* bargain; searching; as, a *hard* look; harsh or unfriendly; as, *hard* feelings; vigorous or violent; as, a *hard* rain; harsh or unpleasant to the eye, ear, or esthetic sense; as, a *hard* face, *hard* outlines in a painting; *photog.* having great contrasts, or sharply defined shadows; of water, containing mineral salts which interfere with the action of soap; strong, spirituous, or intoxicating, as liquors; high and unyielding, as prices. *Econ.* in coin rather than paper currency; in coin, bills, or actual money as distinguished from other property; of currency, backed by financial stability and easily convertible into gold. *Phon.* having a guttural sound, as the *c* and *g* in *corn* and *get,* as distinguished from the soft *c* and *g* in *cite* and *gin;* of Slavic language consonants, not palatalized.—**hard up,** *slang,* urgently in need of something, usu. money.

hard, härd, *adv.* [O.E. *hearde.*] So as to be hard, solid, or firm; as, frozen *hard;* firmly or tightly; as, to hold *hard* by the wrist; with difficulty; as, breathing *hard;* harshly or severely; as, to treat or press *hard;* so as to involve severity or hardship; as, taxes bearing *hard* upon the poor; with great exertion, vigor, or violence; as, to work *hard;* earnestly, intently, or searchingly; as, to look *hard* at a thing or a person; being close or near, as in place, amount, or time; as, to follow *hard* after a person; *naut.* closely, fully, or to the extreme limit; as, *hard* alee. With bitter feelings, as: He took his humiliation *hard.*

hard-and-fast, härd'an·fast', härd'an·fäst', *a.* Firm and secure; strongly binding, strictly obligatory, or not to be set aside or violated; as, *hard-and-fast* rules.—**hard and fast,** *adv.* Firmly and securely; as, bound or held *hard and fast;* strictly or rigorously.

hard-bill, härd'bil", *n.* Any of various birds having a beak capable of cracking nuts or seeds.

hard-bit·ten, härd'bit'en, *a.* Hardened by conflict; tough; unyielding.

hard·board, härd'bōrd", härd'bärd", *n.* A board made of wood fibers that are compressed into sheets at a high temperature.

hard-boiled, härd'boild', *a.* Boiled until hard, as an egg. *Slang,* hardened by experience; not easily impressed or moved; unyielding or uncompromising; tough; as, a *hard-boiled* mayor; realistic; as, a *hard-boiled* approach to living.—**hard-boiled·ness,** *n.*

hard ci·der, *n.* Fermented cider.

hard clam, *n.* A thick-shelled clam; a quahog.

hard coal, *n.* Anthracite.

hard cop·y, *n. Computer,* readable communication, such as typewriting or printing, as distinguished from codes and special machine languages fed to a computer on perforated cards or tape, or on electromagnetic tape.

hard·core, härd'kōr', *a.* Aggressive; militant; unyielding; as, a *hard-core* criminal.

hard·en, här'den, *v.t.* To make hard or harder; made hardy, robust, or capable of endurance; make obdurate or unyielding; make unfeeling or pitiless.—*v.i.* To become hard or harder; become inured or toughened; become obdurate, unfeeling, or pitiless. Of prices or the market, to become higher or to stabilize.—**hard·ened,** *a.* Rendered hard; unfeeling; confirmed.—**hard·en·er,** *n.* A material blended with paints or varnishes to give durability to the finish; one who tempers tools used for cutting.—**hard·en·ing,** *n.* Any material used to harden other materials, esp. an alloy added to metal; the act or process of making hard.

hard goods, *n.* Merchandise designed to last a relatively long time, as machinery and appliances.

hard·hand·ed, härd'han'did, *a.* Having hands hardened by toil; ruling with a strong or cruel hand; severe.—**hard·hand·ed·ness,** *n.*

hard hat, *n.* A helmet, usu. metal but sometimes plastic, worn for protection.

hard-hat, härd'hat", *n. Slang,* a worker in the construction trades who wears a protective helmet.—*a.* Relating to the area or type of construction requiring the wearing of a protective helmet; as, the *hard-hat* industries.

hard·head, härd'hed", *n.* A shrewd, practical person; a stubborn person; a blockhead. Any of various fishes, as the gurnard *Trigla gurnardus,* and the menhaden.—**hard-head·ed, hard·head·ed,** *a.* Not easily moved or deceived; practical; shrewd; stubborn.—**hard-head·ed·ness, hard·head·ed·ness,** *n.*

hard-heart·ed, hard·heart·ed, härd'här'tid, *a.* Pitiless; unfeeling.—**hard-heart·ed·ly, hard·heart·ed·ly,** *adv.*—**hard-heart·ed·ness, hard·heart·ed·ness,** *n.*

har·di·hood, här′dē·hụd, *n.* Hardy spirit or character; boldness; daring; audacity; effrontery; temerity; robustness.

har·di·ment, här′dē·ment, *n.* [O.Fr. < *hardi,* E. *hardy.*] *Archaic,* boldness, daring, or hardihood.

har·di·ness, här′dē·nis, *n.* The quality or state of being hardy; robustness; capacity to endure; courage; boldness.

hard la·bor, *n.* Compulsory labor required of criminals as additional punishment to their imprisonment.

hard-line, härd′līn″, *a.* Holding fast to a rigid principle or course of action; favoring forceful action.

hard·ly, härd′lē, *adv.* Scarcely; barely; not quite; unlikely; severely; harshly.

hard ma·ple, *n.* Sugar maple.

hard·ness, härd′nis, *n.* The state or quality of being hard; impurity in water, caused by the presence of dissolved mineral salts, which reduces the cleansing power of soap. *Mineral.* the capacity of a mineral to scratch another or be scratched by another; see *Mohs scale.*

hard-of-hear·ing, härd′ov·hēr′ing, *a.* Of, concerning, or possessing an impaired sense of hearing.

hard pal·ate, *n.* See *palate.*

hard·pan, härd′pan″, *n.* A layer of firm detrital matter, as clay, underlying soft soil; hard unbroken ground. *Fig.* firm bottom or solid foundation; hard underlying reality; as, to get down to *hardpan.*

hard put, *a.* In a difficult situation; at a loss; not quite able.

hard rub·ber, *n.* Rubber that has been processed with a vulcanizing agent such as sulfur which unites its molecules into a comparatively inflexible product.

hards, härdz, *n. pl.* [< O.E. *heordan* (pl.), hards, tow; Icel. *hörr,* flax; same root as L. *caro,* to card, *carduus,* thistle, *coma,* hair; perhaps E. *hair.*] The refuse or coarse part of hemp or flax. Also **hurds.**

hard sauce, *n.* A mixture of butter and confectioners' sugar, with cream and extract flavoring added, which is well blended and then refrigerated before serving with a dessert such as steamed pudding.

hard·scrab·ble, härd′skrab″l, *a.* Of minimal return or yield for maximum effort.

hard sell, *n.* An aggressive sales technique using high pressure and direct appeal.

hard-set, härd′set′, *a.* Firmly or rigidly set; determined; obstinate; in a hard or difficult position; beset with difficulties; hard put to it, or finding it hard to do something.

hard-shell, härd′shel″, *a.* Having a hard shell, as a crab before molting; *fig.* rigid or uncompromising.

hard-shell clam, *n.* A quahog.

hard-shell crab, *n.* A crab that has not recently lost its shell, esp. the N. Amer. blue crab before molting.

hard·ship, härd′ship, *n.* A condition that is hard to bear; suffering; severe trial, oppression, or want; an instance of this; anything hard to bear.

hard·tack, härd′tak″, *n.* A type of hard biscuit made without salt, used chiefly as army rations or aboard ships. Also *ship biscuit, pilot biscuit.*

hard·top, härd′top″, *n.* An automobile model with the design of a convertible, but having a rigid roof of metal or of metal with a vinyl covering. A road or area treated with a tar mixture for durability.—*a.*

hard·ware, härd′wâr″, *n.* Metalware or articles, as tools, locks, hinges, cutlery, or utensils; physical equipment, as contrasted to ideas or design; *computer,* any mechanical, electrical, or electronic equipment, as distinguished from *software,* that includes the manuals, procedures, and specifications; *milit.* equipment or supplies made largely

of metal, from small fittings or tools to major items as aircraft and weapons.

hard wheat, *n.* A wheat with hard flinty kernels yielding a flour esp. adapted for making bread, macaroni, and the like.

hard·wood, härd′wụd″, *n.* The compact wood of such trees as hickory, oak, beech, ash, and cherry; any tree which yields such wood. *Forestry,* any broad-leafed tree, distinguished from a conifer or needle-leafed tree.—*a.* Consisting of hardwood.—**hard·wood·ed,** *a.* Pertaining to wood, esp. hardwood, that is difficult to work with or finish.

har·dy, här′dē, *a.*—*hardier, hardiest.* [Fr. *hardi,* bold, daring, properly the pp. of the old verb *hardir,* to make bold, < O.H.G. *hartjan,* < *hart* (E. *hard*), hard, bold.] Able to endure fatigue, hardship, and the like; bold, brave, or daring; intrepid; confident; full of assurance; rash; *bot.* of plants, capable of bearing exposure to cold weather.—**har·di·ly,** *adv.*

har·dy, här′dē, *n. pl.* **har·dies.** [Appar. < *hard.*] A chisel or fuller with a square shank for insertion into a square hole in a blacksmith's anvil.

hare, hâr, *n. pl.* **hares, hare.** [O.E. *hara* = D. *haas* = G. *hase* = Icel. *heri,* hare.] A small mammal of the genus *Lepus* in the family *Leporidae,* with long ears, a divided upper lip, a short tail, and lengthened hind legs adapted for leaping; any of various related animals; the common rabbit. (*Cap.*), *astron.* the southern constellation Lepus.—*v.i.* To run.

hare and hounds, *n.* An outdoor game in which certain players, the hares, leave a trail of paper called the scent, and are pursued by their opponents, the hounds, who try to catch the hares before they reach safety.

hare·bell, hâr′bel″, *n. Bot.* a species of the genus *Campanula,* in the bellflower family, having blue flowers shaped like bells.

hare·brained, hâr′brānd″, *a.* Giddy; heedless.

hare·lip, hâr′lip″, *n.* A congenital division or vertical fissure of the upper lip, sometimes extending to the palate; the deformed lip itself.

har·em, hâr′em, har′em, *n.* [Ar. *harīm,* anything prohibited, < *hharram,* to prohibit, the inmates of the harem being kept in strict seclusion.] The area reserved for women in a Muslim family; these women: wives, concubines, and servants; loosely, several females associated with any male. Also **ha·reem.**

har·i·cot, har′i·kō″, *n.* [Fr. a ragout; O.Fr. *harigoter,* to mince, *harigote,* a morsel.] A kind of ragout of meat and vegetables; the kidney bean or its pod or seed.

hark, härk, *v.i.* [Contr. < *hearken.*] *Usu. impv.* to listen; to hearken.—*interj.* Attention: a hunting cry used to stimulate or direct a pack of hounds. Also *harken, hearken.*

hark back, *v.i.* To revert to a previous situation; in hunting, to retrace a lost trail or scent.

har·ken, heark·en, här′ken, *v.i.* [O.E. *heorcnian, hyrcnian,* < *hyran,* to hear.] To listen; to pay attention; to give heed.—*v.t. Archaic,* to hear; to listen to.

harl, härl, *n. Brit.* a tangled mass or mixed quantity of some material.—*v.t.* To entangle or twist together; to confuse.

harl, härl, *n.* [Probably = *hardle,* < *hards.*] A filament, as of flax or hemp.

har·le·quin, här′le·kwin, här′le·kin, *n.* [Fr. *harlequin* (now *arlequin*), < It. *arlecchino*: cf. O.Fr. *Helequin, Hellekin, Herlequin,* name of a devil, or a troop of demons (*mesnie Helequin*), of medieval legend.] (*Cap.*) a comic pantomime character, usu. masked, dressed in parti-colored tights and bearing a wooden sword or magic wand; (*l.c.*) a buffoon; *ornith.* a bizarre appearing

duck, *Histrionicus histrionicus.*—*a.* Parti-colored; fantastically or strikingly variegated in color or ornamentation.—**har·le·quin·ade,** här′le·kwi·nād′, här′le·ki·nād′, *n.* A pantomime in which the Harlequin plays the principal part; buffoonery.—**har·le·quin·esque,** här′le·kwi·nesk′, här″le·ki·nesk′, *a.* In the style or manner of a harlequin.

har·lot, här′lot, *n.* [O.Fr. *harlot, herlot,* Pr. *arlot,* Sp. *arlote,* It. *arlotto,* a glutton, a lazy good-for-nothing, a word of uncertain origin; cf. W. *herlawd,* a stripling, *herlodes,* a damsel.] A woman who is promiscuous; a prostitute.—**har·lot·ry,** här′lo·trē, *n. pl.* **har·lo·tries.** The practice of prostitution; harlots as a group.

harm, härm, *n.* [O.E. *hearm,* harm, evil, grief = Dan., Sw., and G. *harm,* grief, offense; Icel. *harmr;* compare Skt. *çram,* to weary.] Physical or moral injury; hurt; damage.—*v.t.* To injure; to hurt; to damage.

har·mat·tan, här″ma·tan′, *n.* [W. Afr.] A dry, dusty land wind, occurring seasonally on the west coast of Africa.

harm·ful, härm′fụl, *a.* Inflicting harm; capable of causing hurt or damage; injurious.—**harm·ful·ly,** *adv.*—**harm·ful·ness,** *n.*

harm·less, härm′lis, *a.* Lacking ability or inclination to injure or harm; innocuous; inoffensive.—**harm·less·ly,** *adv.*—**harm·less·ness,** *n.*

har·mon·ic, här·mon′ik, *a.* [L. *harmonicus,* < Gr. *harmonikos, harmonia* < E. *harmony.*] Pertaining to or marked by harmony, agreement, or concord; concordant; consonant. *Mus.* musical; sounding together with pleasing effect; harmonious; pertaining to harmonics or overtones; referring to the arithmetical relationship between tonal vibrations; as, a *harmonic progression.*—*n. Mus.* the overtone of a fundamental; one of these tones produced as on a stringed instrument by lightly stopping a vibrating string. *Pl. but sing. in constr.* the doctrine or science of musical sounds.—**har·mon·i·cal,** *a.*—**har·mon·i·cal·ly,** *adv.*

har·mon·i·ca, här·mon′i·ka, *n.* [N.L. prop. fem. of L. *harmonicus,* E. *harmonic.*] Any of various musical instruments, esp. one having a set of small metallic reeds mounted in a case and played by the breath inhaling and exhaling; a mouth organ; any of the percussion instruments using graduated glass or metal bars for sounding elements.

har·mon·ic mo·tion, *n. Phys.* a simple periodic motion with a constant amplitude, such as the movement of a pendulum, or an oscillating motion that is a combination of such motions.

har·mon·i·con, här·mon′i·kon, *n.* [N.L. < Gr. *harmonikon,* neut. of *harmonikos,* E. *harmonic.*] Any of various musical instruments, as a harmonica or mouth organ.

har·mon·ic pro·gres·sion, *n. Math.* a number series, the terms of which have reciprocals forming an arithmetic progression.

har·mon·ics, här·mon′iks, *n. pl., sing. or pl. in constr.* That branch of acoustics which deals with musical sounds.

har·mo·ni·ous, här·mō′nē·us, *a.* [Fr. *harmonieux,* < *harmonie,* E. *harmony.*] Marked by agreement in feeling or action; as, a *harmonious* decision; forming a pleasingly consistent whole; exhibiting harmony; being in harmony; congruous; pleasing to the ear; tuneful.—**har·mo·ni·ous·ly,** *adv.*—**har·mo·ni·ous·ness,** *n.*

har·mo·nist, här′mo·nist, *n.* One skilled in musical harmony; a musician; a composer; one who makes a harmony, as by collating parallel texts in the Gospels.—**har·mo·nis·tic,** här″mo·nis′tik, *a.* Pertaining to a harmonist or harmony; pertaining to the collation and harmonizing of parallel passages, as of the Gospels.—**har·mo·nis·-ti·cal·ly,** *adv.*

har·mo·ni·um, här·mō′nē·um, *n.* [N.L. < L. *harmonia,* E. *harmony.*] A reed organ, in which air is forced outward through the reeds by foot-operated bellows.

har·mo·nize, här′mo·nīz″, *v.i.*—*harmonized, harmonizing.* [O.Fr. Fr. *harmoniser,* < *harmonie,* E. *harmony.*] To be in harmony, accord, or agreement; *mus.* to perform vocally or instrumentally in harmony.—*v.t.* To bring into harmony, accord, or agreement; *mus.* to set accompanying parts to, as to a melody. To demonstrate the harmony or agreement of.—**har·mo·niz·-er,** *n.*—**har·mo·ni·za·tion,** *n.*

har·mo·ny, här′mo·nē, *n.* pl. **har·mo·nies.** [L. and Gr. *harmonia,* < Gr. *harmos,* a suiting or fitting together, a joint, < *arō,* to fit, to adapt.] Accord in facts, views, or acts; sympathetic relationship; friendship; inner calm; a pleasing integration of components. *Mus.* the science of chords; coincident combination of musical tones. An arrangement of parallel literary passages or books, esp. the Gospels, intended to emphasize similarities.

har·mo·tome, här′mo·tōm″, *n.* A mineral belonging to the zeolite class, a hydrated silicate composed of aluminum, barium, and potassium.—**har·mo·tom·ic,** här″mo·-tom′ik, *a.*

har·ness, här′nis, *n.* [O.Fr. *harnas, herneis* (Fr. *harnais*); origin uncertain.] The working gear of a horse or other draft animal, except the ox; any similar combination of straps, bands, or the like; the routine of work, usu. preceded by *in*; as, to live and die *in harness*; the frame having the heddles and connected parts in a loom; the mechanism by which a large bell is suspended and rung.—*v.t.* To put a harness on; attach by a harness, as to a vehicle to be drawn; *fig.* to bring under conditions for working; as, to *harness* water power. *Archaic,* to array in armor.—**har·ness·er,** *n.*—**har·ness·like,** *a.*

har·ness horse, *n.* A horse trained to pull vehicles in harness, often for racing.

harp, härp, *n.* [O.E. *hearpe* = D. *harp,* Icel. *harpa,* Dan. *harpe,* G. *harfe,* a harp; perhaps same root as L. *carpo,* to pluck or twitch.] A musical instrument, played by both plucking and glissando techniques, consisting of graduated lengths of nylon or wire strings stretched within a triangular framework formed by a hollow sounding board, a post and crown, and a curved neck; any similar object or device.—*v.i.* To play on the harp; *colloq.* to dwell on a subject tiresomely and repeatedly, usu. followed by *on* or *upon.*—**harp·ist, harp·er,** *n.* A player on the harp.

har·poon, här·pōn′, *n.* [Fr. *harpon,* a harpoon, < *harper,* to clutch, < *harpe,* a claw, a hook, < Gr. *harpagē,* a hook, *harpazō,* to seize.] A spear or javelin, attached to a long cord, used to strike and kill whales and large fish.—*v.t.* To strike or capture with or as with a harpoon.—**har·poon·er,** *n.*

harp·si·chord, härp′si·kärd, *n.* [Obs. Fr. *harpechorde,* < It. *arpicordo,* < *arpa,* harp and *corda,* string, cord.] A keyboard instrument in general use from the 16th to the 18th century, and revived after 1900, in which the strings are plucked by leather or quill points connected with the keys.—**harp·si·chord·ist,** *n.*

har·py, här′pē, *n.* pl. **har·pies.** [Fr. *harpie,* < L. *harpyia,* Gr. *harpuia,* < root of *harpazō,* to seize.] A grasping, greedy person; an ill-tempered female. *Ornith.* a large and very powerful raptorial bird of Mexico and S. America, *Harpia harpyja*; also **har·py ea·gle.** (*Cap.*) *class. mythol.* any of several foul monsters having the face of a woman and the body of a bird.

har·que·bus, har·que·buse, har·que·-buss, här′kwe·bus, *n.* pl. **har·que·bus·es.** Arquebus.—**har·que·bus·ier,** *n.*

har·ri·dan, har′i·dan, *n.* [Akin Fr. *haridelle,* Prov. Fr. *hardele, harin,* a wornout horse, a jade.] A hag; an odious, shrewish old woman.

har·ri·er, har′ē·ėr, *n.* [< *hare.*] A small hound employed in hunting the hare; a cross-country runner.

har·ri·er, har′ē·ėr, *n.* [See *harry.*] One who or that which harries; any of the hawks of the genus *Circus,* family *Falconidae,* which prey on small animals.

har·row, har′ō, *n.* [Same word as Dan. *harve,* Sw. *harf,* a harrow; akin D. *hark,* G. *harke,* a rake.] An agricultural implement, consisting of a row of teeth, spikes, or upright disks protruding downward from a supporting frame, which is drawn across plowed soil to level it and crumble clods or to cover sown seed.—*v.t.* To draw a harrow over; to distress painfully; to torment; to harass.—*v.i.* To be prepared by harrowing, as a field.—**har·row·er,** *n.*

har·row·ing, har′ō·ing, *a.* Causing acute mental or emotional distress.—**har·row·ing·ly,** *adv.*

har·ry, har′ē, *v.t.*—*harried, harrying.* [O.E. *hergian,* to ravage, < *here* (genit. *herges*), an army; Icel. *herja,* to lay waste, to oppress; Dan. *hærge, hærje,* G. (*ver*)*heeren,* to ravage.] To pillage, plunder, or devastate; to harass; to torment or worry by recurrent attacks; to drive out or propel by harassment.—*v.i.* To make harassing raids.

harsh, härsh, *a.* [O.E. and Sc. *harsk,* harsh, acid; same as Dan. and O.Sw. *harsk,* rancid; G. *harsch,* harsh, rough; root doubtful; perhaps akin *hard.*] Grating or unpleasant to the senses, the mind, or the esthetic sense; crude; unrefined; acrid; rough; austere; severe; strident.—**harsh·en,** *v.i., v.t.*—**harsh·ly,** *adv.*—**harsh·ness,** *n.*

hart, härt, *n.* pl. **harts, hart.** [O.E. *heort* = L.G. and D. *hert,* Dan. *hiort,* Sw. *kjort,* Icel. *hjörtr,* G. *hirsch,* stag; lit. 'horned animal'; allied to Gr. *keras,* L. *cornu,* a horn.] A stag or male deer, esp. the red deer, *Cervus elaphus,* when he has passed his fifth year.

har·tal, här·täl′, *n.* *India,* a temporary cessation of commercial activity, esp. as a type of organized passive resistance.

har·te·beest, här′te·bēst″, härt′bēst″, *n.* pl. **har·te·beests, har·te·beest.** [S. Afr. D., 'hart beast.'] Any of various nearly extinct African antelopes, esp. *Alcelaphus caama,* having long, curving horns.

harts·horn, härts′hårn″, *n.* Antler of the hart, once used as an ammonia source. *Chem.* ammonium carbonate or sal volatile. Also *ammonium carbonate.*

har·um-scar·um, hâr′um·skâr′um, hâr′-um·skar′um, *a.* [Perhaps < O.E. *hare,* to frighten, or < *hare,* the animal, and *scare.*] Irresponsible, harebrained, or reckless.—*n.* A flighty, unsettled person.—*adv.* In a reckless or giddy manner.

ha·rus·pex, ha·rus′peks, har′u·speks″, *n.* pl. **ha·rus·pi·ces,** ha·rus′pi·sēz. [L. < *haru-* (Skt. *hira*), entrails, and *specere,* look at.] In ancient Rome, a minor priest who practiced divination from inspection of the entrails of animals killed in sacrifice. Also **a·rus·pex.**—**ha·rus·pi·cy, ha·rus·pi·ca·tion,** ha·rus′pi·sē, ha·rus″pi·kā′shan, *n.* Divination by or as by a haruspex.

har·vest, här′vist, *n.* [O.E. *hærfest* = O. Fris. *harvest,* G. *herbst,* D. *herfst,* Icel. *haust,* Sw. and Dan. *höst,* autumn, harvest.] The act or process of gathering any ripened crop; the time of such reaping and gathering; that which is reaped and gathered in; the product of any labor; gain; result; effect; consequence.—*v.t.* To reap or gather, as corn or fruit; to reap from, as fields; to gain or win by effort.—*v.i.* To

gather crops.—**har·vest·a·ble,** *a.* Ready for harvest.

har·ves·ter, här′vi·stėr, *n.* One who or that which harvests; a mower; a reaper; *zool.* a butterfly, *Feniseca tarquinius.*

har·vest fly, *n.* *Zool.* a N. American cicada, *Tibicen linnei,* reddish-brown in color and noted for the sharp trill it makes in late summer.

har·vest home, *n.* The bringing home of the harvest; the harvest feast; a festival observed in England at the end of harvest time; a song sung at this festival.

har·vest·man, här′vist·man, *n.* pl. **har·vest·men.** One who does harvesting; *zool.* any spider of the *Phalangida* order; also *daddy-longlegs.*

har·vest moon, *n.* The full moon at the time of harvest, or about the autumnal equinox.

has-been, haz′bin″, *n.* *Colloq.* One who has passed the period of his greatest effectiveness, achievement, or popularity; a thing no longer useful because of age or wear.

ha·sen·pfef·fer, hä′sen·fef″ėr, *n.* [G.] Stew made of rabbit that has been marinated in a sweet-sour sauce.

hash, hash, *n.* [Fr. *hacher,* E. to *hack.*] Cooked meat which has been chopped up and reheated with potatoes and other vegetables; a revision of old material; a jumble; a mess.—*v.t.* To chop into small pieces; to mince and mix; to talk over.—**hash over,** to discuss, consider, review.

hash·ish, hash·eesh, hash′ēsh, hash′ish, hä′shēsh, *n.* [Ar. *hashīsh.*] The flowering tops and leaves of the hemp *Canabis sativa,* which are drunk, chewed, or smoked for their narcotic and intoxicating effect; any of certain preparations made from this plant. See *cannabis.*

hash mark, *n.* *Milit. slang,* service stripe.

Ha·sid, hä′sid, *Heb.* кнä·sēd′, *n.* pl. **Ha·sid·im,** hä·sid′im, *Heb.* кнä″sē·dēm′. *Judaism,* one belonging to a sect founded in eastern Europe in the 18th century to stress the mystical elements of religion and encourage piety and optimism; one belonging to a sect founded in the 2nd century B.C. to oppose adoption of Hellenistic customs by the Jews. Also **Has·sid, Cha·sid.**—**Ha·sid·ic,** *a.*—**Has·i·dism,** *n.*

has·n't, haz′ant. Contraction of has not.

hasp, hasp, häsp, *n.* [O.E. *hæpse,* the hook of a hinge = Icel. *hespa,* G. *haspe, häspe,* a fastening; Dan. *haspe,* a hasp, a reel.] A clasp that passes over a staple, to be fastened by a padlock; a metal hook for fastening a door.—*v.t.*

has·sle, has′l, *n.* *Slang.* A disagreement or argument; a fight.

has·sock, has′ok, *n.* [Origin doubtful; cf. W. *hesg,* sedge, also Sw. *hwass,* rushes.] A footstool; a thick mat or cushion for kneeling. A thick clump of grass as found in a marsh; also *tussock.*

haste, hāst, *n.* [Same word as G., Sw., and Dan. *hast,* haste, whence O.Fr. *haste,* Fr. *hate,* haste; akin to *hate.*] Speed; swiftness; dispatch; expedition; rashness; quickness; precipitance; the state of being pressed by business; hurry; urgency.—*v.t., v.i. Chiefly poet.* To hasten; to hurry.—**make haste,** to hasten; to proceed rapidly.

has·ten, hā′sen, *v.i.* [< *haste.*] To move or act with haste; go or proceed with speed; hurry.—*v.t.* To cause to make haste; urge or impel to greater speed; accelerate, as a process; bring about more speedily, as an event.—**has·ten·er,** *n.*

hast·y, hā′stē, *a.*—*hastier, hastiest.* Moving or acting with haste; quick; speedy; precipitate; rash; inconsiderate; irritable; arousing or indicating impatience or anger; easily aroused to anger.—**hast·i·ly,** *adv.*—**hast·i·ness,** *n.*

---

a- fat, fāte, fär, fâre, fạll;　**e-** met, mē, mēre, hėr;　**i-** pin, pīne;　**o-** not, nōte, mōve;　**u-** tub, cūbe, bụll;　**oi-** oil;　**ou-** pound.

hast·y pud·ding, *n. U.S.* cornmeal mush; *Brit.* a pudding made of milk and flour boiled together quickly; oatmeal and water boiled together; porridge.

hat, hat, *n.* [O.E. *haet* = Dan. *hat*, Sw. *hett*, Icel. *hattr*, hat, < a root meaning to cover.] Any of various head coverings for both men and women, usu. with a crown, sides, and a continuous brim. *Rom. Cath. Ch.* the head covering of a cardinal; a cardinal's rank or office.—*v.t.*—*hatted, hatting.* To provide with a hat; bestow a hat upon.—**come with hat in hand,** to come humbly or respectfully.—**keep un·der one's hat,** to keep secret or confidential.—**pass the hat,** to collect money contributions, usu. at a meeting.—**take off one's hat to,** to recognize some superior quality or accomplishment in another.—**talk through one's hat,** to speak foolishly or irresponsibly.—**toss one's hat in the ring,** to enter a contest, esp. to become a candidate for political office.

hat·box, hat'boks", *n.* A case designed to hold one or more hats for storage or travel.

hatch, hach, *n.* [O.E. *haec*, gate, hatch: cf. D. and L.G. *hek*, fence, gate, Sw. *häck*, Dan. *hæk*, rack.] An opening in a ship's deck, a floor, or a roof; a hatchway; a cover for such an opening; a door, gate, or wicket with an opening over it; the lower half of a divided door; a floodgate. *Pl.* a ship's deck, as: The cargo was stored under *hatches*.

hatch, hach, *v.t.* [M.E. *hacchen*, akin to G. *hecken*, Sw. *häcka*, Dan. *hækka*, hatch.] To bring forth, as young, from the egg; to cause young to emerge from (the egg); to produce; devise; contrive secretly; as, to *hatch* a plot.—*v.i.* To be hatched.—*n.* The act of hatching; that which is hatched, as a brood.—**hatch·a·bil·i·ty,** *n.*—**hatch·a·ble,** *a.*—**hatch·er,** *n.*

hatch, hach, *v.t.* [Fr. *hacher*, to hack, to shade by lines.] To shade with parallel or crossed lines in drawing and engraving.—*n.* One of these fine lines or strokes.—**hatch·ing,** *n.* Shading made by parallel or crossed lines.

hatch·er·y, hach'e·rē, *n. pl.* **hatch·er·ies.** A place for hatching eggs, esp. fish or poultry eggs.

hatch·et, hach'it, *n.* [Fr. *hachette*, < *hacher*, to cut, < G. *hacken*, to cut.] A small ax with a short handle, used with one hand; a tomahawk.—**take up the hatch·et,** to make war.—**bur·y the hatch·et,** to make peace.

hatch·et face, *n.* A thin face having sharp, prominent features.—**hatch·et-faced,** *a.*

hatch·et man, *n. Colloq.* A hired murderer or henchman; one who enforces discipline for a superior; a writer or speaker who denounces others.

hatch·way, hach'wā", *n.* An opening covered by a hatch in a ship's deck for passage of cargo; a hatch; a similar opening in a floor or roof.

hate, hāt, *v.t.*—*hated, hating.* [O.E. *hate, hete*, hate, hatred, *hatian*, to hate; D. *haat*, Sw. *hat*, Icel. *hatr*, Goth. *hatis*, hate; Goth. *hatan*, Icel. and Sw. *hata*, D. *haten*, G. *hassen*, to hate.] To dislike greatly or intensely; to have a great aversion to; to loathe; to detest.—*v.i.* To experience dislike; to detest.—*n.* Great dislike or aversion; an object of extreme dislike or aversion.—**hat·er,** *n.*—**hate·a·ble, hat·a·ble,** *a.*

hate·ful, hāt'ful, *a.* Exciting animosity; odious; detestable. Feeling hatred; malevolent.—**hate·ful·ly,** *adv.*—**hate·ful·ness,** *n.*

ha·tred, hā'trid, *n.* Great dislike or aversion; detestation; active antipathy; animosity.

hat·ter, hat'ẽr, *n.* One who produces, sells, or refurbishes hats, usu. men's hats.

hau·berk, hạ'bụrk, *n.* [O.Fr. *hauberc*, < O.H.G. *halsberg* = hals, the throat, and *bergen*, to defend; O.E. *healsbeorg*, Icel.

---

hálsbjörg, a gorget. *Habergeon* is a diminutive.] A sleeveless, knee-length coat of mail, worn for protection in the Middle Ages.

haugh·ty, hạ'tē, *a.*—*haughtier, haughtiest.* [O.Fr. *hautain*, haughty, < *haut, haut,* < L. *altus,* high (whence *altitude, exalt*); *gh* was inserted through influence of *high*.] Proud; disdainful; contemptuous in manner; lofty; arrogant; supercilious.—**haugh·ti·ly,** *adv.*—**haugh·ti·ness,** *n.*

haul, hạl, *v.t.* [Same as D. *halen,* Icel. and Sw. *hala,* Dan. *hale,* to haul; G. *holen,* to fetch, to tow (whence Fr. *haler,* to haul); hence *halliard, halyard.*] To pull or draw with force; to transport, as in a truck or car; to drag; to tug; to compel, used with *up*; to change view or course of action.—*v.i.* To carry freight commercially; to tug. *Naut.* to change the direction in sailing; to sail nearer the wind.—*n.* A forceful pulling; that which is caught, taken, or received together; as, a good *haul* of lobsters; the distance something is carried.—**haul off,** to pull back the arm before striking a blow.—**long haul,** a rather long distance.—**haul·er,** *n.*

haul·age, hạ'lij, *n.* The act of hauling or drawing; the force expended in hauling; charges for hauling or towing.

haul·ier, hạl'yẽr, *n. Brit.* a commercial hauler or trucking company.

haulm, halm, hạm, *n.* [O.E. *healm* = D. and G. *halm* = Icel. *hālmr,* halm, straw: cf. L. *culmus,* stem, stalk, Gr. *kalamos,* reed.] *Chiefly Brit.* Stems or stalks collectively, as of grain, esp. as used for litter or thatching; a single stem or stalk.

haunch, hạnch, hänch, *n.* [Fr. *hanche,* the haunch, < Teut.; Fris. *hancke, hencke,* haunch; G. *hanke,* the haunch of a horse.] The hip; the fleshy hindquarter of a man or animal; flank; *food,* the upper leg and loin of beef, pork, or other meat animals. *Arch.* the middle part between the vertex or crown and the springing of an arch; the hance.—**haunched,** *a.*

haunt, hạnt, hänt, *v.t.* [Fr. *hanter,* to frequent, < Armor. *hent,* a way, *henti,* to frequent.] To frequent; to recur frequently to; to be much about; to appear spectrally to, as a ghost.—*v.i.* To be much about a place; to make frequent visits.—*n.* A place one frequents; a favorite resort; a common gathering place.—**haunt·er,** *n.*—**haunt·ing,** *a.* Lingering; often remembered; not easily forgotten; as, a *haunting* refrain.

Hau·sa, hou'sä, *n.* A people of the Sudan and Nigeria; their common language.

hau·sen, hạ'zn, G. hou'zen, *n.* [G. < O.H.G. *hūso.*] A large white sturgeon, *Acipenser huso,* of the Black Sea and Caspian Sea and their rivers, prized as a source of caviar. Also *beluga.*

haus·tel·lum, hạ·stel'um, *n. pl.* **haus·tel·la,** hạ·stel'a. [L. < *haurio, haustum,* to draw up.] *Biol.* the sucking organ of certain crustaceans and insects, otherwise called the proboscis or antlia.—**haus·tel·late,** hạ·stel'it, hạ'ste·lāt", *a.*

haut·boy, haut·bois, hō'boi, ō'boi, *n. pl.* **haut·boys, haut·bois.** [Fr. *hautbois*—*haut,* high, and *bois,* wood, from the high tone of the instrument.] An oboe; a wind instrument of wood, sounded through a double reed.

hau·teur, hō·tụr', Fr. ō·tœR', *n.* [Fr.] Pride; haughtiness; arrogance; a snobbish or spirited manner.

ha·üy·nite, ä·wē'nit, *n.* [From R. J. *Haüy,* 1743–1822, French mineralogist.] A silicate and sulfate mineral containing aluminum, calcium, and sodium, usu. having a bluish or greenish color, and found embedded in igneous rocks. Also **ha·üyne,** ä·wēn'.

have, hav, *v.t.*—*pres. sing. have,* or archaic *hast, has* or archaic

---

hath; *pres. pl. have*; *past sing. had, had* or archaic *hadst* or *haddest, had*; *past pl. had*; *subj. pres. have*; *subj. past had*; *pp. had*; *ppr. having.* [O.E. *habban,* < *hafian* (*fi* becoming regularly *bb* between vowels) = Dan. *have,* Icel. *hafa,* Goth. *habēn,* G. *haben,* to have; cogn. L. *capio,* to take (whence *capable,* etc.). *Behave, haft, haven* are connected.] To possess, as property or rights; to hold or control; to include or contain; to be in a particular relation to; as, to *have* a sister, to *have* an acquaintance; to accept, esp. as a partner in marriage; to possess as a characteristic or quality; as, to *have* blue eyes; to display or show; as, to *have* the audacity, to *have* compassion; to procure, receive, or obtain; as, to *have* it at all costs, to *have* news of; to be impelled or under necessity; as, to *have* to do the work; to experience or suffer from; to take part in or conduct; as, to *have* an argument; to maintain or hold in opinion; to bring about or cause to be; as, to *have* him arrested; to invite or extend hospitality to; as, to *have* overnight guests; to consume or partake of; as, to *have* dinner; to allow or tolerate; as, to *have* no argument; to bear or bring forth in childbirth; to place or hold in a particular position, often unfavorable; as, to *have* them cornered. *Slang,* to cheat; to bribe.—*aux. v.* Used with a past participle to form a present perfect, past perfect, or future perfect tense, as: I *have* come. She *had* gone. They will *have* finished.—**had bet·ter, had best,** should or ought to.—**have at,** to assail.—**have done,** to stop or complete.—**have had it,** *slang,* to have endured or tolerated all that is possible.—**have it in for,** *colloq.* to feel resentment or malice toward.—**have it out,** to pursue a discussion or conflict to a final decision.—**have to do with,** to be associated with.

have·lock, hav'lok, *n.* [From Sir H. *Havelock,* 1795–1857, British general.] A cap cover with a flap hanging over the neck, used for protection from the sun.

ha·ven, hā'ven, *n.* [O.E. *hæfen* = D. and L.G. *haven,* Icel. *höfn,* Dan. *havn,* G. *hafen*; connected with *have.*] A harbor or port; a bay, recess, or inlet which affords anchorage for ships; a shelter, asylum, or place of safety.—*v.t.* To shelter, as in a haven.

have-nots, hav'nots", *n. pl. Sometimes sing.* the underprivileged; persons or countries having few material possessions, as opposed to *haves.*—**haves,** havz, *n. pl. Sometimes sing.* a privileged country or group.

have·n't, hav'ent. Contraction of have not.

hav·er·sack, hav'ẽr·sak", *n.* [Fr. *havresac,* < D. *haverzak,* G. *hafersack,* a haversack, literally a sack for oats, < D. *haver,* G. *hafer,* Dan. *havre,* oats.] A strong cloth bag with a single strap, worn over the shoulder by soldiers, to carry provisions or supplies; any similar bag, esp. one carried on a hike or march.

hav·oc, hav'ok, *n.* [O.Fr. *havot,* pillage, plunder.] Devastation; wide and general destruction; disorder, confusion.—*v.t., v.i.*—*havocked, havocking.* To destroy; to lay waste.—**play hav·oc with,** to cause confusion in; to ruin.

haw, hạ, *n.* [O.E. *haga.*] The fruit of the hawthorn, *Crataegus oxyacantha,* or of other species of the same genus; any of various shrubs or small trees of this genus.

haw, hạ, *n.* The nictitating membrane in the eye of a dog, horse, and certain other animals.

haw, hạ, *interj.* A word of command to horses, usu. directing them to turn to the left, as opposed to *gee.*—*v.i., v.t.* To turn to the left.

haw, hạ, *v.i.* To falter in speaking; to stammer or hesitate in speech. See *hem.*—*n.* A meaningless utterance marking a hesitation in speech or a search for words.

---

ch- chain, G. na*ch*t;   **th-** *TH*en, thin;   **w-** wig, hw as sound in whig;   **z-** zh as in azure, zeal.   *Italicized vowel* indicates schwa sound.

Ha·wai·ian, ha·wī′an, ha·wä′yan, *a.* Of or pertaining to Hawaii or the Hawaiian Islands, the Hawaiian people, or their language.—*n.* An inhabitant of Hawaii; the Polynesian language of Hawaii.

Ha·wai·ian gui·tar, *n.* A guitar, having a long, fretted neck and six to eight strings, which is held horizontally and played by plucking with picks while moving a sliding bar across the strings for pitch.

haw-haw, ha′hạ″, *n., interj.* Ha-ha.

hawk, hạk, *n.* [O.E. *hafoc* = D. *havik*, G. *habicht*, Icel. *haukr*, a hawk.] Any of the daytime birds of prey of the family *Accipitrinae, Falconinae,* or *Buteoninae.* A swindler.—*v.i.* To hunt game with a hawk; to practice falconry; to fly or hunt in the manner of the hawk.—**hawk·er,** *n.*

hawk, hạk, *v.t.* [< D. *heukeren,* to retail, to huckster, *heuker,* a retailer; akin to G. *hōken, hōcken,* to retail, *höker, höcker,* a hawker, < *hocken, hucken,* to take upon the back, to squat. Compare *huckster.*] To sell, or try to sell, by crying in the streets or calling at people's doors.—*v.i.* To peddle merchandise from place to place.—**hawk·er,** *n.*

hawk, hạk, *v.t.* [Prob. imit.] To cough up, as phlegm.—*v.i.* To use a cough for clearing the throat.—*n.* An effort to force up phlegm by coughing; the sound made when clearing the throat of phlegm.

hawk·bill, hạk′bil″, *n.* Hawksbill.

hawk moth, *n. Entom.* any stout-bodied moth of the family *Sphingidae,* similar in manner of flying and feeding to a humming-bird, characterized by a long proboscis, and with forewings longer than hind wings. Also *sphingid, sphinx moth,* **hum·ming·bird moth.**

hawk's-beard, hạks′bērd″, *n. Bot.* any of several European herbs, genus *Crepis,* having yellow or orange flowers with hair-like tufts.

hawks·bill, hạks′bil″, *n.* A tropical sea turtle, having a mouth in the shape of a hawk's beak and a shell which provides the finest grade of commercial tortoise shell. Also *hawkbill,* **hawks·bill tur·tle.**

hawk·weed, hạk′wēd″, *n.* Any of the herbs with yellow, orange, or red flowers, constituting the genus *Hieracium;* any of various related plants.

haw·ser, hạ′zẽr, hạ′sẽr, *n.* [Formerly *halser.*] *Naut.* a large, heavy rope used in towing or securing a ship.

haw·thorn, hạ′thạrn″, *n.* Any of several species of thorny hardwooded ornamental shrubs of the rose family, genus *Crataegus,* native to the northern hemisphere, having white to red flowers and small, red pome fruits. *C. oxycantha,* the English hawthorn, widely planted in the U.S. Also **haw.**

hay, hā, *n.* [O.E. *hīeg* = D. *hooi* = G. *heu* = Icel. *hey* = Goth. *hawi,* hay; < the root of E. *hew.*] Grass cut and dried for use as fodder; grass mowed or ready for mowing.—*v.t.* To furnish with hay, as horses; to put under hay, as land; to convert into hay, as grass.—*v.i.* To cut and dry grass for use as fodder.—**not hay,** *slang,* not a little money.—**hit the hay,** *slang,* to go to bed.—**make hay while the sun shines,** to make the most of an opportunity at the proper time. —**hay·ing,** *n.* The process of making or storing hay.

hay, hā, *n.* [O.Fr. *haye,* kind of dance.] A kind of old country dance with winding movements.

hay·cock, hā′kok″, *n.* A conical pile of hay stacked outdoors; haystack.

hay fe·ver, *n. Pathol.* an allergy to the pollen of various plants, marked by sneezing, inflamed eyes, and other symptoms similar to a cold.

hay·fork, hā′fạrk″, *n.* A pronged fork for turning or lifting hay by hand; pitchfork; a mechanical fork for lifting hay.

hay·loft, hā′lạft″, hā′loft″, *n.* A loft in a stable or barn for the storage of hay; haymow.

hay·mak·er, hā′mā″kẽr, *n.* One who makes hay; one who spreads hay to dry after it is mowed; an apparatus for drying and curing hay. *Colloq.* a heavy-fisted swing; a knock-out blow.—**hay·mak·ing,** *n.*

hay·mow, hā′mou″, *n.* A mass of hay, esp. as stored in a barn; the place in a barn where hay is stored; hayloft.

hay·rack, hā′rak″, *n.* A rack for holding hay from which livestock is fed; a rack or framework mounted on a wagon, for use in carrying hay or straw; the wagon and rack together.

hay·seed, hā′sēd″, *n.* Grass seed, esp. that shaken out of hay; small bits of the chaff of hay. *Colloq.* a rustic; yokel.

hay·stack, hā′stak″, *n.* A hay pile, conical in shape and sometimes covered, built outdoors for drying and temporary preservation. *Brit.* **hay·rick.**

Hay·ti·an, hā′tē·an, *a.* Haitian.

hay·wire, hā′wiẽr″, *n.* Wire used to bind bales of hay.—*a.* [Said to refer orig. to the use of such wire for repairs about ranches, etc.] *Slang.* In disorder; broken down; out of control; wild or crazy; as, to go *haywire.*

haz·ard, haz′ẽrd, *n.* [O.Fr. *hasard, hasart* (Fr. *hasard);* prob. < Ar.] Exposure to danger or harm; a risk; peril; as, the *hazards* of war; chance; a chance; formerly, a game played with two dice like craps; *golf,* any of the various obstacles on the course.— *v.t.* [Fr. *hasarder.*] To take or run the risk of; to expose to danger; to stake; to venture or offer, as an opinion or conjecture. —**haz·ard·ous,** *a.* Full of risk; perilous; dependent on hazard or chance.—**haz·ard·ous·ly,** *adv.*—**haz·ard·ous·ness,** *n.*

haze, hāz, *n.* [Allied to O.E. *hasu,* dusky, dark; Icel. *hoss,* gray, dusky.] Mist, smoke, or a dusky vapor in the air; vagueness; mental fog.

haze, hāz, *v.t.*—*hazed, hazing.* [O.Fr. *haser,* to annoy.] To bully or humiliate, esp. school freshmen or newcomers; *naut.* to harass with overwork.—**haz·er,** *n.*

ha·zel, hā′zel, *n.* [O.E. *hæsel,* Icel. *hasl,* Dan. *hassel,* G. *hasel,* hazel.] *Bot.* any catkin-bearing shrub or small tree of the genus *Corylus,* native to N. America, Europe, and Asia, producing edible hazel-colored nuts, as *C. avellana,* the European filbert, and *C. americana,* the American hazelnut; the wood of this shrub; the nut fruit of this shrub. Also *hazelnut.* A light reddish-brown color.— *a.* Of a light reddish-brown color; as, *hazel* eyes; composed of hazel.—**ha·zel·ly,** *a.*

ha·zel·nut, hā′zel·nut″, *n.* The edible reddish-brown fruit of the hazel; the shrub bearing this fruit.

ha·zy, hā′zē, *a.*—*hazier, haziest.* Misty; mentally confused; vague.—**ha·zi·ly,** *adv.* —**ha·zi·ness,** *n.*

H-bomb, āch′bom″, *n.* Hydrogen bomb.

he, hē (*unstressed* ē), *pron.*—*sing nom.* he, *poss. his, obj.* him, *intens. and refl. himself;* *pl. nom. they, poss. their or theirs, obj. them.* [O.E. *hē* (gen. *his,* dat. *him,* acc. *hine*) = O.S. *he, hi,* = O.Fries. *hi,* he: cf. *her, it, hence, here,* and *hither.*] The nom. third pers. sing. masc. pron. representing the male being in question or last mentioned; the man or male; anyone, as: *He* who betrays his king must die.—*n. pl.* **hes.** A man or male animal, often used attributively; as, *he*-goat.

head, hed, *n.* [O.E. *heafod* = D. *hoofd* = G. *haupt* = Icel. *hofudh* = Goth. *haubith,* head.] The upper part of the human body, joined to the trunk by the neck; the corresponding part of an animal's body; the head considered as the seat of intellectual ability; mind or understanding; as, to have a good *head;* mental aptitude; as, to have a *head* for mathematics; presence of mind or self-control; as, to keep one's *head;* a person considered with reference to his mind, attributes, or position; as, wise *heads,* crowned *heads;* one to whom others are subordinate; a leader or chief; as, *head* of state; the chief or most important part; the position of greatest authority. A person or animal considered merely as one of a number or group; as, five dollars a *head;* collectively, a unit for enumerating or totaling; as, 10 *head* of cattle. That part of anything which is regarded as forming the top or upper end, or is opposite the foot, as the *head* of a cane, mast, staircase, or lake; anything resembling a head in form or position; as, the *head* of a pin; the end of something, as a bed or grave, toward which the head is placed; the top of a page or piece of writing or printing; something, as a title, at the top of a page, column, or section; a newspaper headline; froth or foam rising to the top of a liquid, as beer; either of two like ends, as of a barrel or drum, which is uppermost at any given time; the stretched membrane covering the end of a drum or similar percussion instrument; the obverse of a coin, bearing a head or other principal figure, as opposed to *tail;* the source of a river or stream. The foremost part or projecting end of anything; the front, as of a procession or military column; a projecting point of a coast, esp. when high, as a cape, headland, or promontory; the end or part of a machine, implement, or weapon, as a hammer, arrow, golf club, or lathe, which performs its main function, as striking or cutting; the maturing part of an abscess or boil; culmination or crisis; as, to bring matters to a *head;* the hair covering one's head; a topic or one of its chief divisions. A body of water kept at a height, as in a reservoir; the height of a body of fluid, used as a measure of its pressure; the pressure of a confined body, as of steam. *Bot.* a thick flower cluster attached directly to a common stem, as clover; the top part of a plant when compact or rounded, as the leaves of lettuce, leafstalks of celery, or flower buds of cauliflower. *Gram.* the word or words in an endocentric construction which have the same function as the construction itself; as, *flag* in *grand old flag.* *Naut.* the bow; the toilet aboard ship; *slang,* any bathroom.—**head o·ver heels,** in or as in an upside down position; to a great depth or entirely; as, *head over heels* in love; desperately.—**lose one's head,** to become uncontrollably excited; to lose one's restraint or self-discipline.—**not make head or tail of,** to fail to understand; to find incomprehensible.—**out of one's head,** demented, delirious, or crazy.—**o·ver one's head,** beyond one's comprehension; passing over or ignoring a superior; as to go *over* the supervisor's *head* with the problem.

head, hed, *v.t.* To lead or be at the head of; to outdo or surpass; to be the chief of; as, to *head* a committee; to put or stand at the top or beginning of, as of a page or list; to form or constitute the head or top of; to add or fit with a head; to direct the course of; as, to *head* one's boat for shore; to advance directly against the course of; as, to *head* into the wind; to get in front of so as to cause to turn back or aside, often used with *off;* to go round the head of, as of a stream; to shear or cut off the top branches of, as of a tree; to behead or decapitate; *soccer,* to strike, as a ball, with the head.—*v.i.* To move or be directed toward a point or in a specified direction; as, to *head* for the hills; to form or come to a head; to originate or rise, as a river.—*a.* Pertaining to the head; situated at the head, top, or front; as, the *head* division of a parade; coming from in front, as a wind; being in the position of leadership, command, or superiority; chief; principal.

head·ache, hed′āk″, *n.* A pain in the head. *Colloq.* a source of annoyance or worry; a vexatious situation or a baffling problem.—**head·ach·y**, hed′ā″kē, *a.*

head·band, hed′band″, *n.* A band worn around the head; a fillet; *print.* a band of decoration at the head of a chapter or at the top of a page in a book; an ornamental band, as of silk, attached at the ends of the inner back of a bound book.

head·board, hed′bōrd″, hed′bȧrd″, *n.* A vertical structure which forms or is placed at the head of anything, esp. a bed.

head·cheese, hed′chēz″, *n.* A preparation of parts of the head and feet of hogs or calves cut up, cooked, and seasoned, and formed into a jellied mass or loaf.

head cold, *n.* A variation of a common cold characterized by congestion of mucous membranes of the nasal passages and related tissues.

head·dress, hed′dres″, *n.* An ornamental head covering; a manner of dressing the hair; a coiffure.

head·ed, hed′id, *a.* Furnished with a head or heading; matured into a head, as a cabbage; having the kind of head specified: used in combination; as, clear-*headed*, long-*headed*.

head·er, hed′ér, *n.* A person or machine that removes the heads from something, as grain from stalks, or that puts heads on something, as nails; one who heads an organization; *building,* a brick or stone laid so that its end appears in the face of a wall; a timber or beam which fits between two long beams and supports the ends of short ones; *colloq.* a headfirst plunge or dive.

head·first, hed′fúrst′, *adv.* With the head in a forward position; rashly; with premature haste. Also **head·fore·most**.—*a.*

head gate, *n.* The upstream gate of a canal lock; a floodgate of a race, sluice, or the like.

head·gear, hed′gēr″, *n.* Any covering or protection for the head; the parts of a harness around an animal's head; *min.* a machine used for hoisting; *naut.* running rigging that controls headsails.

head·hunt·er, hed′hun″tèr, *n.* A member of a primitive tribe whose custom is to decapitate and preserve the heads of enemies; *slang,* a personnel recruiter; one who tries to deprive an opponent of influence or employment.—**head·hunt·ing**, *n., a.*—**head·hunt**, *v.i.*

head·ing, hed′ing, *n.* An object that acts as a front, beginning, or upper part of anything; the title of a chapter or page; a division of a discourse; *min.* a passage in a mine or tunnel used for ventilation or drainage; *aeron.* the horizontal direction in which the longitudinal axis of an aircraft is pointing.

head·land, hed′land, *n.* A point of land projecting out over the sea; a promontory; a strip of unplowed land alongside a fence or at the end of a plowed area.

head·less, hed′lis, *a.* Lacking a head; decapitated; lacking a leader; foolish or brainless.

head·light, hed′līt″, *n.* A brilliant light, with a reflector, on the front of a locomotive, automobile, or other vehicle.

head·line, hed′līn″, *n. Journ.* A title line over an article, often set in boldface type and briefly summarizing or suggesting content, as in a newspaper; the line at the top of a page, containing the title, pagination, or the like.—*v.t.*—*headlined, headlining.* To furnish with a headline; *theater,* to feature or to give top billing to.—**head·lin·er**, *n.* One to whom the headlines refer; the star performer in a theatrical production.

head·lock, hed′lok, *n. Wrestling,* a hold in which one contestant's head is held immobile by his opponent's encircling arm.

head·long, hed′lạng″, hed′lǒng″, *adv.* Head-first; rashly; unchecked by caution or fore-thought; precipitately; without delay.—*a.* Hasty, impetuous, or precipitate; with the head first.

head louse, *n.* One of a variety of the common louse, *Pediculus humanus capitis,* which lives chiefly on the human head and attaches its eggs to the hair.

head·man, hed′man, hed′man″, *n. pl.* **head·men.** [O.E. *hēafodman.*] A leader; a supervisor; a lesser leader of a primitive tribe.

head·mas·ter, hed′mas′tèr, hed′mä″stèr, *n. Brit.* the male principal of an elementary or secondary school; *U.S.* the male principal of a private school.

head·mis·tress, hed′mis′tris, *n. Brit.* the female principal of an elementary or secondary school; *U.S.* the female principal of a private school.

head·most, hed′mōst″, *Brit.* hed′most, *a.* Most advanced; first, foremost.

head·note, hed′nōt″, *n.* A written prefatory statement; such a statement preceding the report of a legal decision.

head-on, hed′on′, hed′ạn′, *a.* Meeting or coming together with the heads or fronts foremost, esp. pertaining to a collision between vehicles or persons, marked by direct confrontation or opposition.—*adv.* With the heads or fronts foremost, said of a collision.

head·phone, hed′fōn″, *n.* An earphone held in place by a band over the head.

head·piece, hed′pēs″, *n.* A helmet; the head, esp. as the seat of intellect; *print.* an embellishment at the top of a page.

head·pin, hed′pin″, *n.* The foremost bowling pin in a triangle of ten.

head·quar·ters, hed′kwȧr″tèrz, *n. pl.,* sing. or pl. in constr. The office of a commander of a military or political organization; a center of authority or order; the central office of a business.

head·race, hed′rās″, *n.* A channel for conveying water to a water wheel or similar device.

head·rest, hed′rest″, *n.* A device that supports the head.

head·room, hed′rōm″, hed′rụm″, *n.* Clear space in height to permit passage through a doorway or under an arch; headway.

head·set, hed′set″, *n.* A set of earphones.

head·ship, hed′ship″, *n.* The state or position of being a head or chief authority; supreme power.

head shrink·er, *n.* A primitive hunter who shrinks and preserves human heads as trophies; *slang,* psychiatrist.

head·spring, hed′spring″, *n.* The fountainhead or source of a stream; the source of anything. *Gymnastics,* a tumbling maneuver in which the head is used with the hands to help produce the needed spring.

head·stall, hed′stạl″, *n.* That section of a bridle which encircles an animal's head.

head start, *n.* A given or achieved advantage over others, as a handicap in a competitive event or race.

head·stock, hed′stok″, *n.* The frame supporting the moving parts of a machine; in a lathe, the assembly around the live spindle.

head·stone, hed′stōn″, *n.* The stone at the head of a grave; the chief stone or cornerstone of a foundation.

head·stream, hed′strēm″, *n.* A stream which is the origin of a river.

head·strong, hed′strạng″, hed′strǒng″, *a.* Restive, obstinate, or unmanageable; bent on pursuing one's own way.—**head·strong·ly**, *adv.*—**head·strong·ness**, *n.*

head tone, *n.* A vocal tone so produced as to bring the cavities of the nose and head into sympathetic vibration.

head·wait·er, hed′wā″tèr, *n.* One who supervises a public dining room, esp. the work of waiters and other employees serving food and drinks.

head·wa·ter, hed′wạ″tèr, hed′wot″ér, *n.* The part of a river near its source, or one of the streams that act as a source; *pl.* the tributaries at or near the source of a river.

head·way, hed′wā″, *n.* Motion forward or ahead; advance; progress or success in general; rate of progress; the interval between two trains or other vehicles traveling in the same direction over the same route; headroom.—**make head·way**, to move forward; to progress.

head·wind, hed′wind″, *n.* A wind directly opposed to a vehicle's course, esp. that of an airplane or ship.

head·work, hed′wúrk″, *n.* Mental or intellectual labor.—**head·work·er**, *n.*

head·y, hed′ē, *a.*—*headier, headiest.* Apt to affect the mental faculties; strongly intoxicating; as, a *heady* wine; exciting; as, *heady* news of his first promotion; rash or hasty; clever; headstrong.—**head·i·ly**, *adv.* In a rash, impetuous manner.—**head·i·ness**, *n.*

heal, hēl, *v.t.* [O.E. *haelan,* to heal, < *hāl,* whole, sound.] To make hale, sound, or whole; to cure of a disease or wound and restore to health; to reconcile, as a breach or difference; to purify or cleanse.—*v.i.* To grow sound; to return to a sound state, sometimes followed by *up* or *over.*—**heal·er**, *n.* One who heals, esp. by faith or other non-medical means.—**heal·a·ble**, *a.*

health, helth, *n.* [O.E. *haelth,* < *haelan,* to heal.] The sound condition of a living organism; physical or mental vigor; absence of ailments or defects; a wish offered for a person's well-being or happiness, as a toast.—**health·ful**, *a.* Full of health; free from disease; healthy; promoting health; wholesome.—**health·ful·ly**, *adv.*—**health·ful·ness**, *n.*

health·y, hel′thē, *a.*—*healthier, healthiest.* Enjoying or being in good health; hale or sound; indicative or pertaining to good health or a sound mentality; conducive to health; wholesome.—**health·i·ly**, *adv.*—**health·i·ness**, *n.*

heap, hēp, *n.* [O.E. *hēap,* heap, multitude, troop = D. *hoop* = M.L.G. *hōp* = O.H.G. *houf* (G. *haufe*).] A mass of things lying one on top of another; a pile. *Colloq.* quantity or number; a troop, multitude, or crowd. *Slang,* a dilapidated car; a jalopy.

heap, hēp, *v.t.* [O.E. *heapian.*] To gather, put, or cast in a heap, often followed by *up, on, together;* pile; *fig.* to accumulate or amass, often followed by *up;* as, to *heap up* riches; to cast or bestow in great quantity; as, to *heap* blessings upon a person; to load or supply abundantly; as to *heap* a person with benefits; to fill, as a vessel, to overflowing.—*v.i.* To become heaped or piled, as sand or snow; to rise in a heap or heaps.—**heap·er**, *n.*—**heap·y**, *a.*

hear, hēr, *v.t.*—*heard, hearing.* [O.E. *hýran, hēran,* to hear = O.Fris. *hera, hora,* Icel. *heyra,* D. *hooren,* G. *horen,* Goth. *hausjan.*] To perceive by the auditory sense; to learn or be made aware of by the ear; to listen, heed, attend, obey; to audit as one of a group of listeners; to give legal audience to.—*v.i.* To possess the faculty of perceiving and realizing sound; to acquire information; learn; to consider, usu. preceded by a negative and followed by *of,* as: He wouldn't *hear of* it. *Chiefly Brit.* to endorse a speaker, usu. impv., as: *Hear! Hear!*—**hear·er**, *n.*

hear·ing, hēr′ing, *n.* The act of perceiving sound; the faculty or sense by which sound is perceived; reach of sound; earshot; audience; an opportunity to be heard. *Law,* preliminary investigation of a case to determine its validity; a judicial investigation before a court.

---

hear·ing aid, *n.* A small, inconspicuous amplifying device, worn to correct or improve faulty hearing.

heark·en, här'ken, *v.i.*, *v.t.* Harken.

hear·say, hēr'sā", *n.* Rumor; common talk. —*a.*—**hear·say ev·i·dence,** *law,* evidence repeated at second hand, to which a witness cannot testify of his own direct personal knowledge, generally inadmissible in court.

hearse, hurs, *n.* [O.Fr. *herce,* (Fr. *herse*), harrow, frame for holding candles in church, < L. *hirpex, irpex,* large rake used as a harrow.] A funeral vehicle for transporting a dead person to the place of burial; a triangular framework for the 15 candles in use during the Rom. Cath. service of Tenebrae in Holy Week; a framework, often adorned with candles or epitaphs, which is placed over the coffin of a distinguished person.—**hearse·like,** *a.*

heart, härt, *n.* [O.E. *heorte* = D. *hart* = G. *herz* = Icel. *hjarta* = Goth. *hairtô,* heart; akin to L. *cor* (*cord-*), Gr. *kardia* and *kēr,* heart.] The hollow muscular organ of vertebrates which circulates blood throughout the body by means of rhythmic contractions and dilations; *fig.* the seat of emotion, affection, and passions: opposed to the head as the seat of intellect; the essence of personality; sensibility, sympathetic capacity, or empathy; moral nature or conscience; will or inclination; spirit, courage, or enthusiasm; a person; as, dear *heart;* memory; as, to learn by *heart;* the core or center part; the vital portion; breast or bosom; a figure or an object with rounded sides meeting in an obtuse point at the bottom and curving inward to a cusp at the top; a playing card of a suit marked with such figures in red. *Pl.* the suit of such cards; *sing. in constr.* a kind of card game in which the players try to avoid taking tricks containing hearts, or take all these tricks.—*v.t.* To fix in the heart.—**at heart,** intrinsically.—**break the heart of,** to disappoint greatly; to bring deep sorrow to. —**change of heart,** reversal of decision.— **eat one's heart out,** to grieve or suffer longing.—**from the heart, from the bot·tom of one's heart,** with sincerity.—**have one's heart in one's mouth,** to be very worried or frightened.—**lose heart,** become disheartened or discouraged.—**lose one's heart,** to fall in love.—**set one's heart on,** to have an intense desire for something.—**take to heart,** to take seriously.

heart·ache, härt'āk", *n.* Anguish of mind; grief.

heart at·tack, *n.* A sudden impairment in the heart's ability to function, often caused by an embolism or high blood pressure.

heart·beat, härt'bēt", *n.* The dual sound of the diastole and the systole which is made by the rhythmical contraction and dilation of the ventricles of the heart as blood is forced through its chambers.

heart block, *n.* An impairment of the ventricular beats of the heart.

heart·break, härt'brāk", *n.* Overwhelming sorrow or grief.—**heart·break·ing,** *a.*

heart·brok·en, härt'brō"ken, *a.* Deeply grieved; in despair.—**heart·brok·en·ly,** *adv.*—**heart·brok·en·ness,** *n.*

heart·burn, härt'burn", *n. Pathol.* Pyrosis; a burning sensation in the thorax and stomach, sometimes accompanied by a slight eructation of acid-tasting fluid. Also *cardialgia, water brash.*

heart·burn·ing, härt'bur"ning, *n.* Envious discontent; secret enmity or resentment.—*a.*

heart dis·ease, *n. Pathol.* an abnormality of the heart impairing its normal functioning.

heart·ed, här'tid, *a.* Having a particular kind of heart: used in combination; as, hard-hearted, faint-hearted.

heart·en, här'ten, *v.t.* To encourage; to instill confidence or courage in.

heart·felt, härt'felt", *a.* Deeply felt; earnest.

heart-free, härt'frē", *a.* Not amorously involved.

hearth, härth, *n.* [O.E. *heorth* = D. *haard* = G. *herd,* hearth.] The floor of a fireplace, usu. of brick or stone; the extension of this floor a short way into the room; any similar floor in a furnace or stove. *Fig.* the fireside; the home. Also *Brit.* **in·gle.** *Metal.* the bottom of a reverberatory furnace, or the lower part of a blast furnace; the fireplace of a forge.—**hearth·stone,** *n.* The stone forming the hearth.

heart·land, härt'land", härt'land", *n.* An area strategically or economically vital to the control of a country or region.

heart·less, härt'lis, *a.* Without sympathy or consideration; destitute of feeling or affection; cruel.—**heart·less·ly,** *adv.*—**heart·less·ness,** *n.*

heart mur·mur, *n. Pathol.* an abnormal heart sound, usu. audible with the aid of a stethoscope, and usu. indicating a structural or functional defect.

heart·rend·ing, härt'ren"ding, *a.* Grievous; overpowering with anguish; very distressing.—**heart·rend·ing·ly,** *adv.*

hearts·ease, härts'ēz, *n.* Emotional comfort; freedom from worry or care. *Bot.* a pansy or any similar flowering plant of the genus *Viola.* Also **heart's-ease.**

heart·sick, härt'sik", *a.* Sick at heart; pained in mind; deeply grieved or depressed. Also **heart·sore,** härt'sōr", härt'sor".— **heart·sick·ness,** *n.*

heart·strings, härt'stringz", *n. pl.* The strongest emotions or feelings, as: The tragedy pulled at her *heartstrings.*

heart·throb, härt'throb", *n.* A pulsating beat of the heart; an excessive emotional feeling; the object of one's ardent affection.

heart-to-heart, härt'to·härt', *a.* Candid; intimate.

heart·wood, härt'wŏd", *n. Bot.* the non-living and non-functioning center wood of a tree, usu. more compact and darker in color than the outer surrounding sapwood. Also *duramen.*

heart·y, här'tē, *a.*—**heartier, heartiest.** Proceeding from the heart; sincere; warm; cordial; zealous; sound and healthy; substantial or large to satisfaction; as, a *hearty* meal; requiring a large amount of food; as, a *hearty* appetite; loud and unrestrained; as, a *hearty* laugh.—*n.* A courageous fellow, esp. applied to a sailor; a friend.—**heart·i·ly,** *adv.*—**heart·i·ness,** *n.*

heat, hēt, *n.* [O.E. *haetu, haete,* < *hát,* hot; D. and L.G. *hitte,* Icel. *hiti,* Dan. *hede,* G. *hitze,* heat; Goth. *heito,* fever; root in Gr. *kaiō,* to burn.] A quality or condition of being hot; hotness or warmth; a degree of warmth; temperature; a single operation of increasing warmth or hotness; *phys.* the transfer of heat energy from one material to another by means of conduction, convection, or radiation; *metal.* one of several succeeding intensities of heat, as smelting. Abnormally high body temperature; a hot environment or climate; color or appearance of a material implying its temperature; depth of feeling; utmost ardor or violence; agitation or stress. *Zool.* period of sexual ardor in female animals; estrus. *Sports,* a single effort as in a race; a preliminary test to eliminate weaker contenders. *Slang,* increased enforcement of law; coercion.—*v.t.* To cause to feel or to make hot or warm; stimulate emotionally.—*v.i.* To be warm or hot; to become emotionally excited or aroused.—**heat·ed,** hē'tid, *a.* With heat; with intensity of feeling; animated.— **heat·er,** hē'tėr, *n.* One who or that which heats; an apparatus designed to produce heat, as for a room or building. *Slang,* pistol.—**heat·less,** *a.*

heat en·gine, *n.* A device that produces mechanical energy from heat, as an internal combustion engine.

heat ex·haus·tion, *n.* A physical condition caused by extended exposure to high temperature combined with exertion, and marked by faintness, nausea, and profuse sweating. Compare *heatstroke.* Also **heat pros·tra·tion.**

heath, hēth, *n. Brit.* a tract of open, uncultivated wasteland, often overgrown with heather and other shrubs; *bot.* a sturdy evergreen shrub of the *Ericaceae* family, as rhododendron and azalea.

hea·then, hē'THen, *n. pl.* **hea·thens, hea·then.** [O.E. *haethen* = D. *heiden* = G. *heide* = Icel. *heidhinn* = Goth. *haithnô;* commonly explained as meaning orig. 'heath dweller.'] A member of a people which does not acknowledge the Jewish, Christian, or Islamic God; a pagan or idolater; an irreligious or unenlightened person.—*a.* Pagan; pertaining to the heathen; irreligious or unenlightened.— **hea·then·dom, hea·then·ism,** *n.*—**hea·then·ish,** *a.*—**hea·then·ish·ly,** *adv.*

hea·then·ize, hē'THe·nīz", *v.t.*—**heathenized, heathenizing.** To make heathen or pagan.—*v.i.* To become heathen or pagan; to practice paganism.

heath·er, heTH'ėr, *n.* [Formerly *hadder;* cf. G. *heiter,* gay.] Common heath or *Calluna vulgaris,* a low shrub with clusters of rose colored flowers, very plentiful in Britain.— *a.* Also **heath·ered, heath·er·y.**

heath hen, *n. Brit.* female black grouse. An extinct N. American bird, *Tympanuchus cupido cupido,* similar to the prairie chicken.

heat light·ning, *n. Meteor.* flashes of light unaccompanied by thunder, seen near the horizon on summer evenings and thought to be reflections of distant lightning.

heat rash, *n.* Prickly heat.

heat·stroke, hēt'strōk", *n.* A state of collapse or prostration, usu. accompanied by high fever, brought on by exposure to heat, as of the sun or a furnace; sunstroke. Compare *heat exhaustion.*

heave, hēv, *v.t.*—**heaved** or **hove, heaving.** [O.E. *hebban* (past *hof, hefde,* pp. *hafen*) = D. *heffen* = G. *heben* = Icel. *hefja* = Goth. *hafjan,* heave, lift; akin to L. *capere,* take.] To raise or lift with effort or force; to hoist; to hurl or throw, as something heavy; to raise or force up or outward, causing a swelling motion, as the chest while panting; to utter with effort or pain, as a sigh or groan; *naut.* to haul, draw, or pull, as a cable; *geol.* to thrust, as a vein, out of place in a horizontal direction.—*v.i.* To rise as if thrust up; swell or bulge; rise and fall with a swelling motion, as the chest in hard breathing; to breathe with effort, or pant; to retch; to labor or strive to do something; *naut.* to haul or pull, as at a cable, or push, as at the bar of a capstan; to move a ship by such action: usu. followed by *about* or *ahead.*—*n.* The act of heaving; a lifting or upward movement; a rhythmical rise and fall, as of waves.—**heave ho!,** *naut.* a sailors' cry, usu. in unison, to urge greater effort in pulling or pushing.—**heave ho,** an act of expulsion, dismissal, or rejection, as: She gave her suitor the *heave ho.*—**heave in** or **in·to sight,** to rise into view as from below the horizon, as a ship at sea; in general, to come into view.—**heave to,** *naut.* to stop the headway, as of a vessel, esp. by bringing the head to the wind.—**heav·er,** *n.*

heav·en, hev'en, *n.* [O.E. *heofon,* heaven; < O.E. *hevan,* L.G. *heben,* Icel. *hifinn;* < root of *heave.*] *Theol.* the final place where the blessed go after death; the place where the blessed meet God; (*cap.*) an equivalent to God or Providence. Supreme felicity; bliss; a sublime or exalted condition; the blue expanse which surrounds the earth, and in which the sun, moon, and stars seem to be set. *Usu. pl.* The sky; the upper regions.—**heav·en·less,** *a.*

heav·en·ly, hev′en·lē, *a.* Celestial; beautiful; delightful; very happy; holy; divine; relating to the physical heavens, as: The stars are *heavenly* bodies.—*adv.*—**heav·en·li·ness,** *n.*

heav·en·ward, hev′en·wèrd, *adv., a.* Toward heaven.—**heav·en·wards,** *adv.*

heaves, hēvz, *n. pl. but sing. in constr.* [Pl. of *heave.*] *Veter. pathol.* a disease of horses, characterized by difficult breathing due to rupturing in the elastic network of the pulmonary system. Also *broken wind.*

heav·i·er-than-air, hev′ē·èr·тнan·âr′, *a. Aeron.* having a greater specific gravity than air: usu. pertaining to aircraft, as opposed to *lighter-than-air* balloons and dirigibles.

heav·i·ly, hev′i·lē, *adv.* With or as with a large weight, load, or burden; painfully or oppressively; with great force or intensity; severely; compactly or densely; clumsily or dully.

Heav·i·side lay·er, *n. Meteor.* a division of the ionosphere, usu. found at an altitude between 55 and 85 miles above the earth in the E-region, exhibiting free electron density and the reflection of low-frequency radio waves. Also *E layer, Kennelly-Heaviside layer.*

heav·y, hev′ē, *a.*—*heavier, heaviest.* [O.E. *hefig,* < *hefe,* weight, < *hebban,* E. *heave.*] Of great weight; hard to lift or carry; massive; of great amount; as, a *heavy* vote; of great force or intensity; as, a *heavy* sea, *heavy* sleep; being such in an unusual degree; as, a *heavy* drinker; of more than the usual, average, or specified weight; as, a *heavy* grade of paper; having much weight in proportion to bulk; grave or serious, as a fault or offense; harsh, severe, or burdensome, as penalties or taxes; grievous or distressing; oppressive; difficult or trying, as a task; depressed with trouble, sorrow, or care; as, a *heavy* heart; drooping with weariness, as the eyelids; weighted or laden; as, air *heavy* with moisture; broad, thick, or coarse; as, *heavy* features; ponderous, dull, or tedious; as, a *heavy* book; clumsy or sluggish; loud and deep, as sound; overcast or cloudy, as the sky; insufficiently raised or leavened, as bread; hard to digest; big with young; producing raw materials or machinery used in the manufacture of other goods; as, *heavy* industry; *phys.* of an isotope, having an atomic weight greater than normal; *theatr.* sober, serious, or somber, as a role. *Milit.* of or pertaining to guns of large caliber; as, *heavy* artillery; armed or equipped with powerful weapons.—*n. pl.* **heav·ies.** *Theatr.* a heavy part or character, or an actor who plays such parts; a villain. *Milit.* a gun of great weight or large caliber; *pl.* heavy cavalry.—*adv.*—**heav·i·ness,** *n.*

heav·y-du·ty, hev′ē·dō′tē, hev′ē·dū′tē, *a.* Constructed to withstand extremely hard usage or unusual stresses, as from heat, cold, friction, or pressure.

heav·y-foot·ed, hev′ē·fut′id, *a.* Awkward or ponderous in actions; *fig.* dull, slow, or unimaginative, as a musical composition; *slang,* tending to drive an automobile at high speed.

heav·y-hand·ed, hev′ē·han′did, *a.* Harsh, stern, demanding; clumsy or unskilled in manual tasks; having weary or weak hands. Also **hard-hand·ed.**—**heav·y-hand·ed·ly,** *adv.*—**heav·y-hand·ed·ness,** *n.*

heav·y-heart·ed, hev′ē·här′tid, *a.* Defeated; melancholy; mournful.—**heav·y-heart·ed·ly,** *adv.*—**heav·y-heart·ed·ness,** *n.*

heav·y hy·dro·gen, *n.* Deuterium.

heav·y-set, hev′ē·set′, *a.* Stocky; sturdy in

body build; compact; thickset; tending to be overweight.

heav·y spar, *n.* Barite.

heav·y wa·ter, *n.* A kind of water containing the hydrogen in its heavier isotopic form, deuterium, and used for scientific experiments.

heav·y·weight, hev′ē·wāt′, *n.* A boxer, wrestler, or other athlete of the heaviest class, usu. more than 175 pounds; a person considerably above average weight; *colloq.* anyone of superior intelligence, education, or skill.—*a.* Heavier or thicker than average, as paper stock.

heb·do·mad, heb′do·mad′, *n.* [L. *hebdomas (hebdomad-),* < Gr. *hebdomas (hepta-)* < *hepta,* seven.] The number seven; a group of seven, esp. a period of seven days; a week.—**heb·dom·a·dal,** heb·dom′a·dal, *a.* [L.L. *hebdomadalis.*] Weekly.—**heb·dom·a·dal·ly,** *adv.*—**heb·dom·a·dar·y,** heb·dom′a·der″ē, *a.*

he·be·phre·ni·a, hē″be·frē′nē·a, *n. Psychiatry,* a type of schizophrenia, occurring more often in the teen and preteen period of youth with disorders characterized by delusions, hallucinations, and childish, regressive behavior.—**he·be·phren·ic,** hē″be·fren′ik, *a.*

heb·e·tate, heb′i·tāt′, *v.t.*—*hebetated, hebetating.* [L. *hebeto, hebetatum,* < *hebes,* dull.] To dull; to blunt; to stupefy.—*v.i.* To become blunt or dull.—*a. Bot.* having a soft, blunt point.—**heb·e·ta·tion,** heb″i·tā′shan, *n.*—**heb·e·ta·tive,** *a.*

heb·e·tude, heb′i·töd″, heb′i·tūd″, *n.* [L. *hebetudo.*] Dullness; lethargy; stupidity.—**heb·e·tu·di·nous,** *a.*

He·bra·ism, hē′brā·iz″um, hē′brē·iz″um, *n.* A Hebrew usage or idiom; Hebrew character, spirit, thought, or practice.—**He·bra·ist,** *n.* One versed in the Hebrew language and learning; one imbued with the Hebraic spirit.—**He·bra·is·tic,** *a.*—**He·bra·ize,** *v.t.*—*Hebraized, Hebraizing.* To make more Hebraic; to conform to the Hebrew usage or type.—*v.i.* To utilize Hebrew expressions or practices.

He·brew, hē′brö, *n.* [O.Fr. *Hebreu* (Fr. *Hebreu*), < L. *Hebraeus,* < Gr. *Hebraios,* Hebrew; < Aramaic, and meaning lit. 'one from beyond.'] A member of that branch of the Semites descended from the line of Abraham; an Israelite; a Jew; the language of ancient and now modern Israel, which has been preserved in religious, literary, and scholarly use.—*a.*—**He·bra·ic,** hi·brā′ik, *a.*—**He·bra·i·cal·ly,** *adv.*

hec·a·tomb, hek′a·tōm″, hek′a·töm″, *n.* [Gr. *hekatombē—hekaton,* a hundred, and *bous,* an ox.] An ancient sacrifice of a hundred oxen; any great sacrifice of victims; a great number of persons or animals slaughtered.

heck, hek, *interj.* [Euphemism for *hell.*] *Slang,* an expression of disappointment or disgust.

heck·le, hek′l, *v.t.*—*heckled, heckling.* To harass by interrupting, as an entertainer or public speaker; badger.—**heck·ler,** *n.*

hec·tare, hek′târ, *n.* See Metric System table.

hec·tic, hek′tik, *a.* [Gr. *hektikos,* habitual, hectic, or consumptive, < *hexis,* habit of body, < *echō,* future, *hexō,* to have.] Pertaining to undue excitement, confusion, or turmoil; having a fluctuating fever characteristic of pulmonary tuberculosis.—**hec·ti·cal·ly,** *adv.*

hec·to·gram, hek′to·gram″, *n.* See Metric System table.

hec·to·graph, hek′to·graf″, hek′to·gräf″, *n.* An apparatus or process for reproducing written or drawn material by means of a thick sheet of gelatin and special ink.—*v.t.* —**hec·to·graph·ic,** hek″to·graf′ik, *a.*

hec·to·li·ter, hek′to·lē″tèr, *n.* See Metric System table.

hec·to·me·ter, hek′to·mē″tèr, *n.* See Metric System table.

hec·tor, hek′tèr, *n.* [From *Hector,* the son of Priam, a brave Trojan warrior.] A bully; a blustering, domineering fellow.—*v.t.* To treat with insolence; to bully.—*v.i.* To play the bully; to bluster.

he'd, hēd, *unstressed* ēd. Contraction of he had or he would.

hed·dle, hed′l, *n.* [By metathesis for *heald;* perhaps < O.E. *heald,* hold.] *Weaving,* one of the parallel threads or vertical cords with a center loop or eye which guides the warp threads.

hedge, hej, *n.* [O.E. *hecg,* a hedge, akin to *haga,* an enclosure; Icel. *hagi,* an enclosed field; D. *hegge,* a hedge.] A fence or barrier formed by bushes or small trees growing close together; any line of shrubbery closely planted; any barrier; a means of protection against a loss, as of a wager, through a counterbalancing action; a non-commital or guarded statement.—*v.t.*—*hedged, hedging.* To enclose; to obstruct; to hem in; to protect against a loss through a counterbalancing action.—*v.i.* To plant or care for a hedge; to avoid a direct statement.—**hedg·er,** *n.*

hedge·ber·ry, hej′ber′ē, *n. pl.* **hedge·ber·ries.** Hackberry.

hedge·hog, hej′hog″, hej′hag″, *n.* An Old World, insectivorous quadruped, of the *Erinaceus* genus, whose sides and back are covered with prickles or spines; the porcupine. *Milit.* a defensive construction or a portable obstacle against an advancing enemy; a defensive stronghold.

hedge·hop, hej′hop″, *v.i.*—*hedgehopped, hedgehopping.* To fly an airplane at a very low altitude, just skimming obstacles.

hedge·row, hej′rō″, *n.* A row of shrubs or trees forming a hedge.

hedge·spar·row, *n.* A small, sparrow-like, European bird, *Prunella modularis,* usu. found in hedges and copses. Also **dun·nock.**

he·don·ic, hē·don′ik, *a.* [Gr. *hēdomikos,* < *hēdonē,* pleasure.] Pertaining to or marked by pleasure; hedonistic; of or pertaining to hedonics or hedonism.—**he·don·ics,** *n. pl. but sing. in constr.* That branch of ethics which treats of pleasure; a branch of psychology concerned with the study of pleasant and unpleasant feelings.

he·don·ism, hēd′o·niz″um, *n.* The doctrine that the chief good and man's primary moral duty lie in the pursuit of pleasure; the psychological theory that man's actions are governed by a desire to experience pleasant feelings and avoid pain.—**he·don·ist,** *n.*—**he·do·nis·tic,** hē″do·nis′tik, *a.*

hee·bie-jee·bies, hē′bē·jē′bēz, *n. pl. Slang.* Condition of being nervous, keyed up, or edgy; the jitters.

heed, hēd, *v.t.* [O.E. *hēdan,* to heed; D. *hoeden,* to care for, *hoede,* care; G. *hüten,* to look after, < *hut,* protection; akin *hood.*] To listen to with care; to take notice of; to attend to.—*v.i.* To attend or give attention. —*n.* Care; attention; notice: often preceded by *give* or *take.*

heed·ful, hēd′ful, *a.* Attentive; cautious; mindful.—**heed·ful·ly,** *adv.*—**heed·ful·ness,** *n.*

heed·less, hēd′lis, *a.* Without heed; inattentive; careless.—**heed·less·ly,** *adv.*—**heed·less·ness,** *n.*

hee-haw, hē′ha″, *n.* [Imit.] The braying sound made by an ass; rude laughter; a guffaw.—*v.i.* To utter heehaws; bray; laugh rudely; guffaw.

heel, hēl, *v.i.* [Same as O.E. *heldan,* D. *hellen,* Dan. *helde,* Sw. *hälla,* to tilt.] *Naut.* to incline or cant over from a vertical position, as a ship.—*v.t.* To cause to lean or tilt.—*n.* The act of inclining.

heel, hēl, *n.* [O.E. *hel* = Icel. *haell,* D. *hiel,* the heel; radically akin to L. *calx,* the heel (seen in *inculcate*).] The hind part of the foot in man or of the hind foot of other vertebrates; that portion of the palm of the hand closest to the wrist; the hind part of a covering for the foot, as a shoe or stocking; the solid portion attached to the sole at the rear of a shoe or boot; something shaped like a human heel, or that occupies a corresponding position, as the crust of a loaf of bread; the latter or concluding part; as, the *heel* of a conference. *Naut.* the lower portion of a keel or mast; the inner portion of a boom. *Slang*, a loathsome individual; a scoundrel.—*v.t.* To add a heel to; to follow closely; to hit with the head of a golf club, as a golf ball; to supply with spurs, as a gamecock; to furnish with something, as money; to perform by the use of heels, as a dance.—*v.i.* To follow closely, at one's heels; to perform by using heels, as in dancing.—**at one's heels**, pursuing closely; close behind. Also **at heel.** —**down at the heels**, run-down, shabby, or impoverished.—**lay by the heels**, to imprison; to confine.—**show one's heels, take to one's heels**, to flee; to run away.

heel-and-toe, hēl'an·tō', *a.* Referring to a kind of pace, as in walking contests, in which the heel of the front foot touches the ground before the toes of the rear one leave it.

heeled, hēld, *a.* Having heels; as, high-*heeled. Slang*, armed or equipped with a gun; supplied with money; as, well-*heeled.*

heel·er, hē'lėr, *n.* One who heels shoes.—**ward heel·er**, *U.S.* a working aide for a political boss or machine.

heel·piece, hēl'pēs', *n.* A piece of material on the heel of a shoe or stocking.

heel·post, hēl'pōst', *n.* A post forming or fitted to the heel or end of something, as the post on which a gate or door is hinged.

heel·tap, hēl'tap', *n.* A small piece of leather or metal for the heel of a shoe; the dregs of liquor in a glass when the main portion has been drunk.

heft, heft, *n.* [< *heave*, to lift.] Weight; bulk. —*v.t.* To raise high; to measure the weight of by hoisting.—**heft·y**, hef'tē, *a.*—*heftier, heftiest.* Vigorous; strong; burly; heavy; large in bulk.

He·ge·li·an, hā·gā'lē·an, hi·jē'lē·an, *a.* [From G. *Hegel*, German philosopher, 1770-1831.] Characteristic of or pertaining to Hegel or his system of philosophy.—*n.* A follower of Hegel; an authority on his writing.—**He·ge·li·an·ism**, *n.* Hegel's system of philosophy, which equalizes the real and the rational and employs dialectic reasoning, the progression of thought through the successive stages of thesis, antithesis, and synthesis, to reach comprehension of the relationship between human consciousness and reality.

he·gem·o·ny, hi·jem'o·nē, hej'e·mō"nē, *n.* pl. **he·gem·o·nies.** [Gr. *hēgemonia*, < *hēgemōn*, guide, leader, < *hēgeomai*, to lead.] Leadership; predominance; preponderance of one state among several.—**heg·e·mon·ic**, hej'e·mon'ik, *a.*

he·gi·ra, hi·ji'ra, hej'ėr·a, *n.* [Ar. *hijrah*, departure, < *hajara*, to remove.] Any flight, usu. to escape danger. (*Cap.*) The flight of Mohammed from Mecca in 622 A.D.; the Moslem era. Also **he·ji·ra, He·ji·ra.**

heif·er, hef'ėr, *n.* [O.E. *heahfore*; origin doubtful.] A young cow which has not borne a calf.

heigh-ho, hi'hō', hā'hō', *interj.* An utterance of weariness or boredom; a cry of exultation.—**heigh**, *interj.* An exclamation used to call attention or give encouragement.

height, hīt, *n.* The state or condition of being tall or comparatively tall; the vertical distance from the lowest level to a given point; altitude or elevation; stature, as applied to living creatures. *Pl.* the highest

point, as: He reached the *heights* of his profession. *Often pl.* utmost degree in advancement, excellence or preeminence; a place of elevation; as, the *heights* overlooking the river.

height·en, hīt'en, *v.t.* To make or raise higher; to elevate; to increase; to augment; to intensify.—*v.i.* To become great or greater in amount, degree, or extent.—**height·en·er**, *n.*

height-to-pa·per, hīt'to·pā'pėr, *n. Print.* a standard applied to the height of printing type, in the U.S. usu. 0.9186 inch.

hei·nous, hā'nus, *a.* Of a completely abominable nature; utterly detestable; thoroughly evil.—**hei·nous·ly**, *adv.*—**hei·nous·ness**, *n.*

heir, âr, *n.* [O.Fr. *heir*, *eir* (Fr. *hoir*) < L. *heres*, heir.] An inheritor; one who inherits or is entitled to inherit; one who receives or is entitled to receive possession of property, a vested right, or liabilities on the death of the owner, either as his natural or as his legal successor; one who receives or is entitled to receive any gift, title, or endowment by inheritance or transmission; one to whom something falls, comes, or is due.—*v.t. Dial.* to inherit.—**heir·ess**, *n.* A female heir, esp. one inheriting or expected to inherit considerable wealth.—**heir·dom**, *n.* The position or rights of an heir; right of inheritance; inheritance. Also **heir·ship.**

heir ap·par·ent, *n.* pl. **heirs ap·par·ent.** An heir who is legally certain to inherit provided he survives the ancestor.

heir at law, *n.* pl. **heirs at law.** A person who after the death of an ancestor has legal right to the inheritance even though there has not been a will.

heir·loom, âr'lōm", *n.* [See *loom*, orig. tool or implement.] Any possession transmitted from generation to generation; *law*, a personal chattel that descends with an inheritance to the heir.

heir pre·sump·tive, *n.* pl. **heirs pre·sump·tive.** An heir whose expectation of inheritance may be nullified by the birth of a closer relative.

heist, hīst, *v.t. Slang.* To burglarize; to rob. —*n. Slang.* A robbery; a theft.

he·li·a·cal, hi·li'a·kal, *a.* [L. *heliacus*, < Gr. *helios*, the sun; akin L. *sol*, and W. *haul*, sun.] *Astron.* Emerging from the light of the sun or passing into it; rising or setting at approximately the same time as the sun. Also **he·li·ac**, hē'lē·ak".

he·li·an·thus, hē'lē·an'thus, *n.* [Gr. *helios*, the sun, and *anthos*, a flower.] A plant of the genus *Helianthus*, of herbaceous plants in the composite family, certain species of which are sunflowers.

hel·i·cal, hel'i·kal, *a.* Of, pertaining to, or shaped like a helix; spiral.—**hel·i·cal·ly**, *adv.*

hel·i·coid, hel'i·koid", hē'li·koid", *a.* [Gr. *helikoeides*, < *helix*, helix, and *eidos*, form.] Helixlike; coiled or curving as a spiral.—*n. Geom.* a warped surface generated by a straight line so moving as always to cut or touch a fixed helix.—**hel·i·coi·dal**, *a.*—**hel·i·coi·dal·ly**, *adv.*

hel·i·con, hel'i·kon", hel'i·kon, *n. Mus.* a large coiled bass tuba.

hel·i·cop·ter, hel'i·kop"tėr, hē'li·kop"tėr, *n. Aeron.* an aircraft sustained in the air by engine-propelled blades rotating on a vertical axis, capable of moving vertically as well as horizontally: in colloquial usage, *chopper, whirlybird*, or **egg·beat·er.** Also *gyroplane.*

he·li·o·cen·tric, hē'lē·ō·sen'trik, *a.* [Gr. *hēlios*, the sun, and *kentron*, center.] *Astron.* Relating to the sun as a center; appearing as if seen from the sun's center. Also **he·li·o·cen·tri·cal.**

he·li·o·gram, hē'lē·ō·gram", *n.* A heliographic message.

he·li·o·graph, hē'lē·ō·graf", hē'lē·ō·gräf", *n.* [Gr. *graphō*, to write.] A photoheliograph; a device which can be used for

signaling by reflecting light, esp. sunlight, into a movable mirror.—*v.t., v.i.* To communicate by reflecting the sun's rays.— **he·li·o·graph·ic**, *a.*—**he·li·og·ra·phy**, *n.*

he·li·ol·a·ter, hē'lē·ol'a·tėr, *n.* [Gr. *latrueō*, to worship.] A worshiper of the sun.— **he·li·ol·a·try**, *n.*

he·li·om·e·ter, hē'lē·om'i·tėr, *n. Astron.* an instrument used to determine the angular distance between two stars.— **he·li·o·met·ric**, **he·li·o·met·ri·cal**, hē"lē·o·me'trik, *a.*—**he·li·o·met·ri·cal·ly**, *adv.*—**he·li·om·e·try**, *n.*

he·li·o·scope, hē'lē·o·skōp", *n.* [Gr. *skopeō*, to view.] *Astron.* a telescope fitted with a device for viewing the sun without injury to the eyes.

he·li·o·stat, hē'lē·o·stat", *n.* [Gr. *statos*, fixed.] A contrivance consisting of a moving mirror which steadily reflects a sunbeam in one direction.—**he·li·o·stat·ic**, *a.*

he·li·o·tax·is, hē"lē·ō·tak'sis, *n.* The tendency of certain organisms to lean or turn toward or away from sunlight.—**he·li·o·tac·tic**, hē"lē·ō·tak'tik, *a.*

he·li·o·ther·a·py, hē"lē·ō·ther'a·pē, *n. Med.* treatment of disease by sunlight.

he·li·o·trope, hē'lē·ō·trōp", hēl'yo·trōp", *n.* [Fr. *heliotrope*, < L. *heliotropium*.] *Bot.* any herb or shrub of the genus *Heliotropium*, esp. *H. arborescens*, a garden plant with small, fragrant, purple flowers; a purple color, esp. when tinged with red; bloodstone, a form of quartz; *surv.* an instrument for reflecting the sun's rays to a distant point.

he·li·ot·ro·pism, hē"lē·o'tro·piz"um, *n. Bot.* the tendency of a plant or other organism to be influenced in its growth by the direction of sunlight falling on it: *positive heliotropism* is the tendency to grow toward light, *negative heliotropism*, away from light.—**he·li·o·trop·ic**, hē"lē·o·trop'ik, hē"lē·o·trō'pik, *a.*—**he·li·o·trop·i·cal·ly**, *adv.*

he·li·o·type, hē'lē·o·tīp", *n.* A photoengraving; collotype.—*v.t.*—**heliotyped**, *heliotyping.* To make a heliotype of.

hel·i·port, hel'i·pōrt", hel'i·part", *n.* [(*Heli*)copter and air(*port*).] A landing station for helicopters.

he·li·um, hē'lē·um, *n. Chem.* a gaseous, inert element usu. found in deposits of natural gas, nonflammable and lighter than air. Sym. He, at. no. 2, at. wt. 4.003. See Periodic Table of Elements.

he·lix, hē'liks, *n.* pl. **hel·i·ces**, **he·lix·es**, hel'i·sēz". [Gr. a winding, a spiral.] A spiral line, as of wire in a coil; something that is spiral; a circumvolution; *geom.* such a curve as is described by the thread of a screw; *arch.* a small volute or twist under the abacus of the Corinthian capital; *anat.* the whole circuit of the external ear.

hell, hel, *n.* [O.E. *hell* = D. *hel* = G. *holle* = Icel. *hel* = Goth. *halja*, hell; < root of O.E. *helan*, cover, hide.] *Theol.* the abode of evil and condemned spirits; the place or state of punishment of the wicked after death. Any state of torment or misery; as, a hell on earth; *slang*, an extreme condition; as, a *hell* of a mess.—*interj.* An expression of disgust or impatience.—**give some one hell**, *slang*, to rebuke severely.—**raise hell**, *slang.* To cause a commotion; to object vehemently.—**hell·ish**, *a.* Pertaining to hell; infernal; malignant; wicked; detestable.—**hell·ish·ly**, *adv.*—**hell·ish·ness**, *n.*

he'll, hēl, *unstressed* ēl, hil, il. Contraction of he will or he shall.

hell·bend·er, hel'ben"dėr, *n.* A large aquatic salamander, *Cryptobranchus alleganiensis*, common in the eastern U.S., esp. in the Ohio Valley.

hell-bent, hel'bent", *a. Slang.* Stubbornly determined; going ahead regardless of consequences.

hell·box, hel'boks", *n. Print.* a container which holds defective type discarded by a printer.

hell·broth, hel'brath", hel'broth", *n.* A witch's broth prepared for an evil purpose.

hell·cat, hel'kat", *n.* A furious vixen; a shrew; a hag or witch.

hel·le·bore, hel'e·bōr", *n.* [L. *helleborus, elleborus,* < Gr.] Any plant of the genus *Helleborus,* esp. *H. niger,* a European herb with showy flowers, popularly called the Christmas rose; any plant of the genus *Veratrum,* esp. *V. viride,* a coarse American herb; an insecticide or a cardiac medicine made from the root of the American herb.

Hel·len·ic, he·len'ik, he·lē'nik, *a.* [Gr. *hellenikos.*] Pertaining to the ancient Greeks, their language and culture; Grecian. —*n.* A language subfamily of the Indo-European group including both ancient and Modern Greek.—**Hel·len·ism**, hel'e·niz"- um, *n.* The character of the classical Greek civilization; the adoption of customs particular to the Greeks after the time of Alexander the Great; a Greek custom or idiom.—**Hel·len·ist**, hel'e·nist, *n.* One educated in the Greek language and culture. —**Hel·len·i·za·tion**, *n.* The adoption of Greek languages and customs.—**Hel·len·ize**, hel'e·nīz", *v.i.*

Hel·len·is·tic, hel"e·nis'tik, *a.* Of or pertaining to the period after Alexander the Great; pertaining to Hellenism or Hellenists. Also **Hel·len·is·ti·cal.**

hel·ler, hel'ėr, *n.* [Contraction of hellion, hell-raiser.] *Slang,* a troublemaker.

hell·gram·mite, hel'gra·mīt", *n.* Dobson; the aquatic larva of a large insect, *Corydalus cornutus,* used as bait by anglers.

hel·lion, hel'yon, *n. Colloq.* A mischievous person; an unruly troublemaker.

hel·lo, he·lō', he·lō', hel'ō, *interj.* [< *hallo, hollo.*] A greeting or an exclamation to attract attention, esp. used in answering the telephone; an exclamation of surprise.—*n.* pl. **hel·loes.** The call *hello,* as: I always get a friendly *hello* from him.—*v.i., v.t.* *helloed, helloing.* To call *hello.*

helm, helm, *n.* [O.E. *helma,* a helm; D. *helm,* a tiller; G. *helm,* a helve, a tiller; akin *helve.*] *Naut.* the instruments by which a ship is steered, consisting of a rudder, a tiller, and in large vessels a wheel; in a limited sense, the tiller or wheel. *Fig.* the place of direction, management, or control. —*v.t.* To steer; to guide.—**helm·less**, *a.*

hel·met, hel'mit, *n.* A defensive covering for the head, as that worn by participants in football, auto racing, and other dangerous sports; head armor composed of metal, leather, or plastic.—**hel·met·ed**, *a.*

hel·minth, hel'minth, *n.* [Gr. *helmins* (*helminth*), worm.] A worm; an intestinal worm, as the tapeworm and roundworm.— **hel·min·thic**, hel·min'thik, *a.* Pertaining to worms; expelling intestinal worms.— **hel·min·thol·o·gy**, hel"min·thol'o·jē, *n. Med.* the study and treatment of helminths, esp. of parasitic worms.—**hel·min·thi·a·sis**, hel"min·thī'a·sis, *n. Med.* an unhealthy condition of the body resulting from worms.

helms·man, helmz'man, *n.* pl. **helms·men.** The man at the helm or wheel who steers a ship.

help, help, *v.t.* [O.E. *helpan* = Goth. *hilpan,* D. *helpen,* Icel. *hjálpa,* Dan. *hjelpe,* G. *helfen,* to help— < same root as Skt. *kalp,* to be of service?] To provide assistance to; to contribute aid to; to cooperate with; to succor, to relieve; to remedy; to benefit; to promote; to be of use to; to facilitate; to avoid or prevent, usu. with *cannot,* as: You *can't help* but laugh. To serve; to furnish with; to appropriate for use; as, *help* myself to.—*v.i.* To be of use; to give aid or assistance, as: Every little bit *helps.*—*n.* Aid; assistance; remedy; succor; one who gives

assistance; a hired servant; collectively, a group of servants.—*interj.* A call for aid.— **help out,** to be of assistance.—**so help me,** a weak oath.

help·er, hel'pėr, *n.* One who helps, aids, or assists; an assistant, usu. unskilled.

help·ful, help'ful, *a.* Beneficial; useful; rendering aid.—**help·ful·ly**, *adv.*—**help·ful·ness**, *n.*

help·ing, hel'ping, *n.* An act of giving assistance; a single serving of food.— **help·ing hand,** assistance.

help·less, help'lis, *a.* Lacking help or strength; defenseless; weak; affording no help; perplexed or bewildered; as, a *helpless* expression.—**help·less·ly**, *adv.*—**help·less·ness**, *n.*

help·mate, help'māt", *n.* An assistant; a helper; a husband or wife. Also **help·meet.**

hel·ter-skel·ter, hel'tėr·skel'tėr, *adv.* [A term formed to express hustle; cf. G. *holter-polter,* D. *hulter de bulter,* Sw. *huller om buller.*] In confused haste; in a disordered way or manner.—*n.* Disorder; confusion; disarray; tumult.—*a.* Marked by confusion; hurried.

helve, helv, *n.* [O.E. *helfe,* O.H.G. *halbe, helbe;* same root as *helm* (of a ship), *hilt.*] The handle of an ax or hatchet.—*v.t.* *helved, helving.* To furnish with a helve, as an ax.

Hel·ve·tian, hel·vē'shan, *a.* Of or pertaining to Helvetia or to the Helvetii, the Celtic people of what is now Switzerland; Swiss. —*n.* One of the Helvetii; a Swiss.— **Hel·vet·ic**, hel·vet'ik, *a.* Helvetian.—*n.* A Swiss Protestant.

hem, hem, *n.* [O.E. *hem,* a hem; akin to Icel. *hemja,* Dan. *hemme,* O.Fris. *hemma,* D. and G. *hemmen,* to stop, check, restrain.] The border of a piece of cloth, made by doubling over the edge and sewing it down; any edge, border, margin.—*v.t.*—*hemmed, hemming.* To form a hem or border on; to border; to edge.—**hem in,** to enclose and confine.

hem, hem, *interj.* [Imit. and more correctly *hm.*] An exclamation, consisting of a sort of half-cough, expressing embarrassment or used to attract attention; ahem.—*v.i.* To make such a sound; to hesitate or stammer in speaking.—**hem and haw,** to speak vaguely, hesitantly; to avoid being explicit.

he·ma·cy·tom·e·ter, hē"ma·sī·tom'i·ter, hem"a·sī·tom'i·ter. *n.* Hemocytometer.

he·mal, haemal, hē'mal, *a.* [Cf. Gr. *haima,* blood.] Of or pertaining to the blood or blood vessels; noting, pertaining to, or situated on that side of the spinal column containing the heart and great blood vessels; hemic. Also **hem·a·tal**, hem'a·tl, hē'ma·tl.

he-man, hē'man", *n.* pl. **he-men.** A man notably muscular and tough.—*a.* Markedly virile.

hem·a·te·in, haem·a·te·in, hem"a·tē'in, hē"ma·tē'in, *n. Chem.* a reddish-brown crystalline substance, $C_{16}H_{12}O_6$, a product of hematoxylin by oxidation, useful as a stain in microscopic investigation.

he·mat·ic, hae·mat·ic, he·mat'ik, *a.* [Gr. *haimatikos,* < *haima,* blood.] Of or pertaining to blood; contained in blood; acting on the blood, as a medicine.—*n.* A hematic medicine.

hem·a·tin, haem·a·tin, hem'a·tin, hē'ma·tin, *n.* [Gr. *haima, haimat,* blood.] A reddish pigment containing iron, $C_{34}H_{32}N_4O_4FeOH$, produced in the decomposition of hemoglobin.

hem·a·tin·ic, haem·a·tin·ic, hem"a·tin'ik, hē"ma·tin'ik, *n.* A medicine, as a compound of iron, which tends to increase the amount of hematin or hemoglobin in the blood.

hem·a·tite, hem'a·tīt", hē'ma·tīt", *n.* [L. *haematites,* hamatite, < Gr. *haimatites,* blood-like, < *haima,* blood.] A native oxide of iron, Fe_2O_3, having a reddish color when

powdered; an important ore of iron.— **hem·a·tit·ic**, hem"a·tit'ik, hē"ma·tit'ik, *a.*

hem·a·to·crit, hem'a·tō·krit, hē'ma·tō·- krit, *n.* [Gr.] A centrifugal device for determining the percentage of red cells in a given amount of whole blood; the volume percentage of red blood cells in blood.

hem·a·tog·e·nous, haem·a·tog·e·nous, hem"a·toj'e·nus, hē"ma·toj'e·nus, *a.* Originating in the blood; blood-producing; spread by means of the bloodstream.

hem·a·tol·o·gy, haem·a·tol·o·gy, hem"a·tol'o·jē, hē"ma·tol'o·jē, *n.* That branch of medicine dealing with the blood and its diseases.—**hem·a·to·log·ic**, hem"a·to·loj'ik, hē"ma·to·loj'ik, *a.*—**hem·a·to·log·i·cal**, *a.*—**hem·a·tol·o·gist**, *n.*

hem·a·to·poi·e·sis, haem·a·to·poi·e·sis, hem"a·tō·poi·ē'sis, hē"ma·tō·poi·ē'- sis, *n.* [N.L. < Gr. *haimatopoiesis* (*poiein,* make).] The process of the formation of blood cells.—**hem·a·to·poi·et·ic, haem·a·to·poi·et·ic**, hem"a·tō·poi·et'ik, hē"ma·tō·poi·et'ik, *a.*

hem·a·to·sis, haem·a·to·sis, hem"a·tō'sis, hē"ma·tō'sis, *n. Physiol.* the change that takes place in venous blood as it converts into arterial blood by oxygenation in the lungs; the formation of the blood.

hem·a·tox·y·lin, haem·a·tox·y·lin, hē"ma·tok'si·lin, hem"a·tok'si·lin, *n.* [N.L. *Hæmatoxylon,* the logwood genus, < Gr. *haima* (*haimat-*), blood, and *xylon,* wood.] Colorless or pale yellow crystals, $C_{16}H_{14}O_6$·- $3H_2O$, obtained from logwood and used in the manufacture of stain and ink in textile and leather dyeing, and in microscopy.

hem·a·to·zo·on, haem·a·to·zo·on, hem"a·to·zō'on, hem"a·to·zō'on, hē"ma·to·zō'on, hē"ma·to·zō'on, *n.* pl. **hem·a·to·zo·a, haem·a·to·zo·a**, hem"a·to·zō'a, hē"ma·to·zō'a. [N.L. *hæmatozoon,* < Gr. *haima* (*haimat-*), blood, and *zoon,* animal.] An animal parasite living in the blood.— **hem·a·to·zo·ic**, *a.*

heme, hēm, *n. Biochem.* portion of the hemoglobin molecule which contains red pigmented iron, $C_{34}H_{32}N_4O_4Fe.$ Also *hematin.*

hem·er·a·lo·pi·a, hem"ėr·a·lō'pē·a, *n.* [N.L. < Gr. *hemeralops,* blind by day, < *hemera,* day, and *alaos, ōps,* eye.] *Pathol.* day blindness; a condition of the eyes in which distinct vision is possible only at night or in dim light.

hem·er·o·cal·lis, hem"er·o·kal'is, *n.* One of several species of the lily family with yellow, orange, or red flowers; (*cap.*) the genus of flowering plants comprising the day lilies.

he·mic, hae·mic, hē'mik, hem'ik, *a.* [Gr. *haima,* blood.] Of or pertaining to the blood.

hem·i·cel·lu·lose, hem"i·sel'ū·lōs", *n. Biochem.* a natural carbohydrate substance between sugar and cellulose in complexity, found mainly in the woody tissue of plants.

hem·i·cy·cle, hem'i·sī"kl, *n.* [Gr. *hēmi,* half, and *kyklos,* a circle.] A half circle; a semicircular building or area.—**hem·i·cy·clic**, hem"i·sī'klik, hem"i·sik'lik, *a.*

hem·i·dem·i·sem·i·qua·ver, hem"ē·dem"ē·sem'ē·kwā"vėr, *n. Mus.* a sixty-fourth note.

hem·i·he·dral, hem"i·hē'dral, *a.* [Gr.] Of a crystal, having only half the planes or faces required by the maximum symmetry. —**hem·i·he·dral·ly**, *adv.*

hem·i·hy·drate, hem"i·hī'drāt, *n. Chem.* a hydrate containing one half a molecule of water to one molecule of the compound from which it is formed.

hem·i·mor·phic, hem"i·mȯr'fik, *a.* [Gr.] Of a crystal, having the two ends of an axis unlike in their planes or modifications.— **hem·i·mor·phism**, *n.* The property of being hemimorphic.

hem·i·mor·phite, hem″i·mạr′fīt, n. Mineral. a hydrous zinc silicate, $Zn_2SiO_4 \cdot H_2O$, valuable as a zinc ore. Also *calamine*.

he·min, hae·min, hē′min, n. [Gr. *haima*, blood.] A reddish-brown crystalline compound, $C_{34}H_{32}N_4O_4FeCl$, derived by heating hemoglobin with sodium chloride and acetic acid, and used in tests to indicate the presence of blood. Also **Teich·mann's crys·tals.**

he·mip·ter·an, hi·mip′tẽr·an, n. Zool. a member of *Hemiptera*, a large insect order among which are the true bugs, plant lice, aphids, cicadas, and other related insects having mouths for sucking and piercing, often two sets of wings, and a life cycle that includes a partial metamorphosis. Also **he·mip·ter.—a.—he·mip·ter·ous,** a.

hem·i·sphere, hem′i·sfẽr″, n. [Gr. *hēmisphairion*.] One half of a sphere or globe; half of the terrestrial or of the celestial globe; a projection or map of either of these globes. Anat. either of the two convoluted parts, one on each side, which constitute a great part of the cerebrum.—**hem·i·spher·ic, hem·i·spher·i·cal,** hem″i·sfẽr′ik, a.—**hem·i·spher·oid,** hem″i·sfẽr′oid, n. The half of a spheroid.

hem·i·stich, hem′i·stik″, n. [L. *hemistichium*, < Gr. *hēmistichion*.] Pros. the exact or approximate half of a poetic verse or line, usu. divided by a caesura; an incomplete line or a line of less than the usual length.

hem·i·trope, hem′i·trōp″, a. [Fr. *hémitrope*, < Gr. *hēmi-*, half, and *-tropos*, turned, < *trepein*, turn.] Half-turned; *mineral.* specif. applied to a compound or twin crystal which has two similar parts or halves, one of which is turned halfway around upon the other. Also **hem·i·trop·ic,** hem″i·trop′ik.—n. A hemitrope crystal.

hem·line, hem′lin″, n. The finished lower edge of a garment or part of a garment.

hem·lock, hem′lok″, n. [O.E. *hemleác*, meadow death.] An evergreen coniferous tree in the pine family, of the genus *Tsuga*; the softwood of this tree. Any of various poisonous herbaceous plants; as, *Cicuta maculata*, water-*hemlock*, and *Conium maculatum*, poison-*hemlock*, both of the carrot family.

he·mo·cy·tom·e·ter, hē″mō·si·tom′i·tẽr, hem″ō·si·tom′i·tẽr, n. Med. an instrument used to count blood corpuscles. Also **he·ma·cy·tom·e·ter.**

he·mo·glo·bin, hae·mo·glo·bin, hē″mo·glō′bin, hem′o·glō″bin, hē″mo·glō′bin, hem″o·glō′bin, n. A red respiratory pigment occurring in the red corpuscles of the blood and composed of iron-containing protein matter which carries oxygen.—**he·mo·glo·bic, he·mo·glo·bin·ic, he·mo·glo·bin·ous,** a.

he·mo·phil·i·a, hae·mo·phil·i·a, hē″mo·fil′ē·a, hē″mo·fēl′ya, hem″o·fil′ē·a, hem″o·fēl′ya, n. Pathol. an inherited defect of males, transmitted through the mother, which leads to excessive bleeding due to deficiency of a coagulant factor in the blood. —**he·mo·phil·i·ac, hae·mo·phil·i·ac, he·mo·phile,** n. One having hemophilia. —**he·mo·phil·ic, hae·mo·phil·ic,** hē″mo·fil′ik, hem″o·fil′ik, a. Evidencing hemophilia. Also **hemophile.**

hem·or·rhage, Brit. **haem·or·rhage,** hem′ẽr·ij, hem′rij, n. A rapid and heavy flow of blood from a ruptured blood vessel.—v.i. —*hemorrhaged, hemorrhaging,* Brit. *haemorrhaged, haemorrhaging.*To bleed heavily. —**hem·or·rhag·ic,** Brit. **haem·or·rhag·ic,** hem″o·raj′ik, a.

hem·or·rhoid, haem·or·rhoid, hem′o·roid″, n. [L. < Gr.] Usu. pl., *pathol.* a swelling formed by the dilatation of a blood vessel at the anus. Also *piles.*— **hem·or·rhoi·dal, haem·or·rhoi·dal,** a.

he·mos·ta·sis, hae·mos·ta·sis, hi·mos′ta·sis, hē″mo·stā′sis, hem″o·stā′sis, n. The termination of bleeding; retardation of blood circulation; blood congestion, as in a localized part. Also **he·mo·sta·sia, hae·mo·sta·sia,** hē″mo·stā′zha, hē″mo·stā′zhē·a, hē″mo·stā′zē·a, hem″o·stā′zha, hem″o·stā′zhē·a, hem″o·stā′zē·a.

he·mo·stat, hē″mo·stat″, hem′o·stat″, n. An instrument or chemical used to check or arrest hemorrhaging. Also *hemostatic, haemostatic.*

he·mo·stat·ic, hae·mo·stat·ic, hē″mo··stat′ik, hem″o·stat′ik, n. Hemostat.—a. Causing bleeding to stop.

hemp, hemp, n. [O.E. *henep, hænep*, = D. *hennep* = G. *hanf* = Icel. *hampr*, hemp.] A tall annual herb, *Cannabis sativa*, native in Asia and cultivated in most temperate regions; the female plant, from which hashish and marijuana are produced; the tough fiber of the male plant, from which coarse fabrics and rope are made; any of various plants similar to or yielding hemp fibers; as, sisal *hemp*; *slang*, a hangman's rope.—**hemp·en,** a.

hemp net·tle, n. Bot. A bristly-haired mint, *Galeopsis tetrahit*, native to Eurasia and a common weed in the U.S.; any of various plants of the genus *Galeopsis*.

hem·stitch, hem′stich″, v.t. To embroider along a line from which threads have been drawn out, gathering the remaining threads so as to form decorative patterns.—n.

hen, hen, n. [O.E. *hen, henn* = D. *hen*, Icel. *haena*, G. *henne*, hen—the feminines corresponding to O.E. and Goth. *hana*, D. *haan*, G. *hahn*, Icel. *hani*, a cock, the root being same as in L. *cano*, to sing.] The female domestic barnyard fowl; the female of other gallinaceous birds, the lobster, and some fishes; *slang*, any woman, esp. a fussy older woman. Also *biddy*.

hen and chick·ens, n. pl. **hens and chick·ens.** The common houseleek, *Sempervivum tectorum*, a perennial succulent with overlapping leaves, which reproduces by offshoots which surround the parent plant.

hen·bane, hen′bān″, n. Bot. a poisonous viscid Eurasian herb, *Hyoscyamus niger*, of the nightshade family, which contains narcotic alkaloids and is in limited cultivation for sedative drugs. Also **hy·os·cy·a·mus,** hi·o·si′a·mus.

hence, hens, adv. [O.E. *hennes*, a genit. form < older *henne*; O.E. *heonan*, hence; G. *hin*, Goth. *hina*, hence; the pronominal element seen in *he* and *here*.] From this place; from this time; as, a week *hence*; as a consequence, inference, or deduction; therefore; thus; consequently.

hence·forth, hens′fōrth′, hens′fạrth′, hens′forth″, hens′fạrth″, adv. From this time forward. Also **hence·for·ward,** hens″fōr′wẽrd, hens′fạr·wẽrd, hens′for·wẽrd, hens′fạr′wẽrd.

hench·man, hench′man, n. pl. **hench·men.** [M.E. *henchemanne, henxtman,* prob. orig. meaning 'groom,' and appar. < O.E. *hengest*, stallion, horse, and *mann*, man.] A trusted attendant or follower; a close and obedient adherent, esp. one who carries out without demur or scruple the instructions of a leader, usu. for personal gain.— **hench·man·ship,** n.

hen·dec·a·gon, hen·dek′a·gon″, n. [Gr. *hendeka*, eleven, and *gōnia*, an angle.] Geom. a plane figure having eleven sides and as many angles.—**hen·de·cag·o·nal,** hen″de·kag′o·nal, a.

hen·dec·a·syl·la·ble, hen·dek′a·sil″a·bl, hen″dek·a·sil′a·bl, n. [Gr. *hendeka*, eleven, and *syllable*, a syllable.] A metrical line of eleven syllables.—**hen·dec·a·syl·lab·ic,** hen·dek″a·si·lab′ik, n., a.

hen·di·a·dys, hen·dī′a·dis, n. [N.L. < Gr. *hen dia dyoin*, 'one through two.'] Rhet.

a figure in which a single complex idea is expressed by two words connected by a copulative conjunction, as *deceit and thoughts*, meaning *deceitful thoughts*.

hen·e·quen, hen·e·quin, hen′e·kin, n. [Sp. *jeniquen*; from Carib. name.] Bot. a stemless plant, *Agave fourcroydes*, with basal rosettes of spiny erect leaves, native to Mexico; the hard wiry fiber from the leaves of this plant, used for making binder twine, lariats, and coarse fabrics.

hen·na, hen′a, n. [Ar. *hinnâ*.] Bot. a tropical plant, *Lawsonia inermis*; a dye made from the leaves of this plant and formerly used to tint hair red, now chiefly for dyeing fabrics and leather; the color of henna, a rich brownish red.—v.t. To color with henna dye or paste.

hen·ner·y, hen′e·rē, n. pl. **hen·ner·ies.** An enclosed place for hens or poultry.

hen·o·the·ism, hen′o·thē·iz″um, n. [Gr. *heis, henos*, one, and *theos*, god.] The worship of one deity as supreme while still recognizing other gods.

hen par·ty, n. Slang, a women's social gathering.

hen·peck, hen′pek″, v.t. To dominate, nag, or persistently annoy, as one's husband.

hen·ry, hen′rē, n. pl. **hen·ries, hen·rys.** [From Joseph Henry, Amer. physicist, 1797–1878.] Elect. the practical unit of inductance, equal to the inductance of a circuit in which an electromotive force of one volt is produced by an inducing current which varies at the rate of one ampere per second.

hep, hep, a. Slang, knowledgeable about the latest ideas, styles, or developments.—**hut, hup,** hep, *interj.* A word denoting the first beat when counting a marching rhythm.

hep·a·rin, hep′a·rin, n. Biochem. a complex blood anticoagulant found in various domestic animal tissues, esp. the liver.— **hep·a·rin·ize,** hep′ẽr·i·nīz″, v.t.—*heparinized, heparinizing.* To treat therapeutically with heparin in order to retard blood coagulation.

he·pat·ic, hi·pat′ik, a. [L. *hepaticus*, Gr. *hepatikos*, < *hēpar, hēpatos*, the liver.] Pertaining to the liver; *bot.* referring to the liverworts. Liver-colored.—n. A medication acting on the liver; *bot.* a liverwort.

he·pat·i·ca, hi·pat′i·ka, n. pl. **he·pat·i·cas, he·pat·i·cae,** hi·pat′i·sē. An early spring flower in the genus *Hepatica*, of the buttercup family, with light purple flowers and lobed basal leaves.

hep·a·ti·tis, hep″a·tī′tis, n. Pathol. inflammation of the liver.

hep·a·tize, hep′a·tīz″, v.t.—*hepatized, hepatizing.* [Akin Gr. *hēpatizein*, to like the liver, < *hēpar (hēpat-)*, liver.] Pathol. to convert, as spongy lung tissue, into liverlike tissue by congestion.—**hep·a·ti·za·tion,** n.

Hep·ple·white, hep′l·hwīt″, hep′l·wīt″, a. Pertaining to a style of English furniture characterized by slender, graceful lines, and designed by George Hepplewhite in the late 18th century.

hep·ta·chord, hep′ta·kạrd″, n. [Gr. *hepta*, seven, and *chorde*, chord.] Mus. A diatonic scale having seven notes; an instrument of ancient Greece with seven strings.

hep·tad, hep′tad, n. [L.L. *heptas (heptad-)*, < Gr. *heptás (heptad-)* < *heptá*, seven.] The number seven; a group of seven; *chem.* an element, atom, or radical having a valence of seven.

hep·ta·gon, hep′ta·gon″, n. [Gr. *hepta*, seven, and *gōnia*, an angle.] Geom. a plane figure having seven sides and seven angles. —**hep·tag·o·nal,** hep·tag′o·nal, a.

hep·ta·he·dron, hep″ta·hē′dron, n. pl. **hep·ta·he·drons, hep·ta·he·dra.** Geom. a solid figure having seven faces.—**hep·ta·he·dral, hep·ta·he·dri·cal,** a.

hep·tam·er·ous, hep·tam′ėr·us, *a.* [Gr. *hepta*, seven, and *meros*, a part.] Having seven parts; *bot.* consisting of seven parts to each whorl of a flower.

hep·tam·e·ter, hep·tam′i·tėr, *n.* [L.L. *heptametrum,* < Gr. *heptametron,* < *hepta*, seven, and *metron*, measure.] *Pros.* a verse consisting of seven metrical feet.—**hep·ta··met·ri·cal,** hep″ta·me′tri·kal, *a.*

hep·tane, hep′tān, *n.* [Gr. *hepta*, seven (with reference to the atoms of carbon).] *Chem.* any of several isomeric hydrocarbons of the methane series with the formula C_7H_{16}.

hep·tan·gu·lar, hep·tang′gū·lėr, *a.* Having seven angles.

hep·tar·chy, hep′tär·kē, *n. pl.* **hep·tar··chies.** [Gr. *hepta*, seven, and *arche*, rule.] A government by seven persons; a group of seven political units, as states or kingdoms, each ruled by its own leader; (*cap.*) the seven Anglo-Saxon kingdoms into which England was once divided.

her, hėr, *unstressed* ėr, *pron.* [O.E. *hire, heore,* genit. and dat. case of the pronoun, *heo,* she, the feminine of *he.* HE.] The objective case of *she,* as: I love *her.*—*pronominal a.* The possessive case of *she,* used as an attributive; as, *her* face.—**hers,** hėrz, *pron.* [< *her,* with *s* of the possessive case.] A possessive case of *she* used, instead of *her* and a noun, as subject, object, or predicate.—**her·self,** hėr·self′, *pron.* A reflexive or emphatic form of the third pers. sing. fem. pron., as: She improved *herself.* She *herself* is to blame. A denotation of a usual or customary state, as: She wasn't *herself* all evening.

her·ald, her′ald, *n.* [O.Fr. *herault, herald,* Fr. *heraut,* < O.H.G. *hariwalt* (G. *herold*), an officer of an army—*hari, heri,* an army (akin E. *harry*), and *waltan,* to rule (E. *wield*).] Formerly an officer or ambassador responsible for carrying messages between leaders, esp. in war; one who proclaims or announces; a bearer of messages; a forerunner. *Brit.* an official of tournaments; a tracer of genealogies; one who records and emblazons the arms of nobility and gentry. —*v.t.* To introduce or to give tidings of, as by a herald; to proclaim.—**he·ral·dic,** he·ral′dik, *a.*

her·ald·ry, her′al·drē, *n. pl.* **her·ald·ries.** The science of armorial bearings; the art of blazoning armorial bearings, of settling the right of persons to bear arms or to use certain bearings, of tracing and recording genealogies, of recording honors, and of deciding questions of precedence; the office or duty of a herald; a heraldic device, or a collection of such devices; a coat of arms; armorial bearings; heraldic symbolism; heraldic pomp or ceremony.

herb, ųrb, hųrb, *n.* [Fr. *herbe,* L. *herba,* herb, from a root meaning to eat or nourish, seen in Gr. *phorbē,* pasture, fodder.] Any plant with a soft or succulent stem which dies to the root every year; any similar plant, esp. used in medicines, scents, or seasonings.— **her·ba·ceous,** hųr·bā′shus, ųr·bā′shus, *a.* [L. *herbaceus.*] Pertaining to herbs; having the form or color of ordinary leaves.

her·bage, ųr′bij, hųr′bij, *n.* Herbs collectively; herbaceous vegetation; the succulent parts, as leaves and stems, of herbaceous plants; grass and other nonwoody growths.

her·bal, hųr′bal, ųr′bal, *n.* A book or discourse on plants or herbs; a herbarium.—*a.* Pertaining to herbs.

herb·al·ist, hųr′ba·list, ųr′ba·list, *n.* A person who collects plants; a dealer in medicinal plants. A healer who specializes in the curative properties of herbs; also *herb doctor.*

her·bar·i·um, hųr·bâr′ē·um, *n. pl.* **her··bar·i·ums, her·bar·i·a,** hųr·bâr′ē·a. A collection of dried plants systematically arranged; a contrivance for preserving dried specimens of plants.

herb doc·tor, *n.* One who prepares or prescribes herbs for their curative properties; a herbalist.

herb·i·cide, ųr′bi·sīd″, hųr′bi·sīd″, *n.* A chemical preparation or other agent for destroying or inhibiting growth of weeds, herbs, or other harmful vegetation.—**her··bi·cid·al,** *a.* Having a destructive effect on trees, herbs, and weeds.

her·biv·o·rous, hųr·biv′ėr·us, *a.* [L. *herba,* and *voro,* to eat.] Eating herbs; subsisting on plants, as: Cattle are *herbivorous.* —**her·biv·ore,** hųr′bi·vōr″, hųr′bi·vạr″, *n.* A herbivorous animal, esp. any member of that group of mammals, *Ungulata,* subsisting on plants.

herb·y, ųr′bē, hųr′bē, *a.*—**herbier, herbiest.** Abounding in herbs; grassy; pertaining to herbs; herblike.

her·cu·le·an, hėr″kū·lē′an, hėr·kū′lē·an, *a.* [From *Hercules,* a mythological hero noted for his strength.] Prodigious in strength, courage, vigor, or size; very difficult to perform; as, a *herculean* task; requiring the strength of an unusually powerful person; (*cap.*) of or pertaining to Hercules or his followers.

herd, hėrd, *n.* [O.E. *heord, herd* = Goth. *hairda,* D. *herde,* Dan. *hjord,* Icel. *hjörth,* G. *herde,* a herd, flock, drove, etc.] A group of animals, usu. of one kind, traveling, feeding, or kept together; flock; drove; derogatory term for the masses or common people; a group of people sharing a mutual bond; any large group; herder or keeper, used in combination; as, goat*herd,* swine*herd.*—*v.t., v.i.* To assemble in a group; to gather together; to care for; to drive.—**ride herd on,** to keep a watchful or protective eye on; to herd.— **herd·er,** *n.*

herds·man, hėrdz′man, *n. pl.* **herds·men.** A keeper or owner of a herd; one who tends or breeds livestock. Also *herder.* (*Cap.*), *astron.* Boötes, a constellation.

here, hēr, *adv.* [O.E. *hēr* = D. and G. *hier* = Icel. and Goth. *hēr,* from the pronominal stem represented by E. *he.*] In or at this particular place; towards this place, as: *Here* comes Mary. Now; at this point, as: We'll stop the lesson *here.* In this life, as: Man's days *here* are few. Used emphatically or indicatively, as: John *here* is a lawyer. *Here* is your pen.—*interj.* Present, as in answering a roll call. Used to call attention, to comfort, or rebuke, as: *Here,* quick! *Here,* don't worry. *Here,* now, less noise!— *n.* This place; this world; this life.—**here·· a·bout, here·a·bouts,** hēr′a·bout″, *adv.* About this place; in this neighborhood.— **here and there,** in several places; at intervals of space or time; to and fro.—**here·by,** hēr·bī′, hēr′bī″, *adv.* As a result of this; by this means.

here·af·ter, hēr·af′tėr, hēr·äf′tėr, *adv.* [O.E. *hēræfter.*] After this in order or time; in time to come; in the world to come.— hēr′af·tėr, *n.* Life after death; time to come; the future.

her·e·dit·a·ment, her″i·dit′a·ment, *n.* [L.L. *hereditamentum.*] *Law,* any property that may be inherited.

he·red·i·tar·y, he·red′i·ter″ē, *a.* [L. *hereditarius,* < *hereditas,* E. *heredity.*] Inherited; transmitted from predecessors; *biol.* descending from genetic inheritance, as opposed to acquired. *Law,* transmitted or transmissible in the line of descent by force of law; holding a title or position by inheritance; as, a *hereditary* peer.—**he·· red·i·tar·i·ly,** hi·red′i·târ′i·lē, hi·red′i·· ter″i·le, *adv.*—**he·red·i·tar·i·ness,** *n.*

he·red·i·ty, he·red′i·tē, *n. pl.* **he·red·i·· ties.** [L. *hereditas,* heirship, inheritance, < *heres,* E. *heir.*] Inheritance; tradition; *biol.*

the transmission of characteristics of parents to offspring through chromosomes which bear the genes; the tendency of an organism to manifest the qualities of its parentage; an individual's inherited traits and characteristics.

Her·e·ford, her′fėrd, her′e·fėrd, *n.* [From *Herefordshire,* England.] A breed of beef cattle usu. having a reddish body and a whitish face.

here·in, hēr·in′, *adv.* In this; in here; in this case; into here: usu. used at the beginning of the text of a legal contract or other document.

here·of, hēr·uv′, hēr·ov′, *adv.* Concerning this; of this; about this.

here·on, hēr·on′, hēr·an′, *adv.* On this; hereupon, as an occasion, writing, etc.

he·re·si·arch, he·rē′zē·ärk″, he·rē′sē·ärk″, her′e·zē·ärk″, her′e·sē·ärk″, *n.* [L.L. *hæresiarcha,* < Gr. *hairesiarchēs,* < *hairesis,* heresy, and *harchein,* lead, rule.] A leader in heresy; the chief of a heretical sect.

her·e·sy, her′i·sē, *n. pl.* **her·e·sies.** [O.Fr. *heresie* (Fr. *hérésie*), < L. *hæresis,* < Gr. *hairesis,* a taking, choice, principles, sect, heresy, < *hairein,* take.] A belief at variance with the accepted doctrine of a church; a belief opposed to authoritative opinion in any area of thought; the holding of such a conviction.

her·e·tic, her′i·tik, *n.* [O.Fr. *hereticque* (Fr. *hérétique*), < L.L. *haereticus* < Gr. *hairetikos,* able to choose, heretical, < *hairein,* take.] *Theol.* one who holds religious opinions contrary to the doctrines of his church. A dissenter from accepted beliefs or dogma of any kind.—**her′i·tik,** he·ret′ik, *a.* Also **he·ret·i·cal.**—**he·ret·i·cal·ly,** *adv.*

here·to, hēr·tö′, *adv.* To this, as to place, thing, document, or circumstance.

here·to·fore, hēr″to·fōr′, hēr″to·fạr′, *adv.* Previously; formerly; up to now.

here·un·der, hēr·un′dėr, *adv.* Under this; under authority of or in accordance with this.

here·un·to, hēr″un·tö′, *adv.* Hereto; to this: used esp. with a document; as, *here-unto* subscribed.

here·up·on, hēr″u·pon′, hēr″u·pạn′, *adv.* Upon this; following immediately after this, whether in time or consequence.

here·with, hēr·with′, hēr·wiTH′, *adv.* With this; along with this; by means of this; enclosed with this.

her·it·a·ble, her′i·ta·bl, *a.* [O.Fr. *héritable,* abbr. < L.L. *hereditábilis.*] Capable of being inherited; inheritable.—**her·it·a·· bil·i·ty,** *n.*—**her·it·a·bly,** *adv.*

her·it·age, her′i·tij, *n.* [O.Fr. *heritage,* < *heriter,* inherit, < L.L. *hereditare.*] That which comes to or belongs to one by reason of birth; as, the *heritage* of longevity; a legacy, as of culture or tradition; something allotted to or reserved for one; as, the *heritage* of a title; *law,* that which may be inherited through the legal process, as property or land.

her·i·tor, her′i·tėr, *n.* An inheritor. *Fem.* **her·e·trix, her·i·trix, her·i·tress,** her′i·· triks, her′i·tris.

herm, hėrm, *n.* [L. *Herma, Hermes,* < Gr. *Hermēs* (pl. *Hermai*).] *Gr. antiq.* a kind of monument or statue, common in ancient Athens, consisting of a head or bust, usu. that of the god Hermes, supported on a quadrangular pillar. Also *herma, hermes.*— **her·mae·an,** hėr·mē′an, *a.*

her·ma, hėr′ma, *n. pl.* **her·mae, her·mai,** hėr′mē, hėr′mī. Herm.

her·maph·ro·dite, hėr·maf′ro·dit″, *n.* [From *Hermaphroditos* of Greek mythology, son of *Hermes* and *Aphrodite,* who became united into one body with a nymph.] An animal or human being having the sexual characteristics of both male and female; *bot.* a flower that contains both the stamens and the pistils.—*a.* Including or being of both sexes; *fig.* combining diverse or opposing qualities.—**her·maph·ro·dit·ic,** her·maph·ro·dit·i·cal, hĕr·maf″ro·dit′ik, *a.*—**her·maph·ro·dit·i·cal·ly,** *adv.*—**her·maph·ro·dit·ism,** hur·maf′ro·di·tiz″um, *n.*

her·me·neu·tics, hur″me·nö′tiks, hur″me·nū′tiks, *n. pl. but sing. in constr.* [Gr. *hermēneutikos* < *hermēneus,* an interpreter, from *Hermēs,* Mercury.] The art or science of interpretation, esp. applied to the Scriptures.—**her·me·neu·tic,** her·me·neu·ti·cal, *a.*

her·mes, hĕr′mēz, *n. pl.* **her·mae, her·mai,** hĕr′mē, hĕr′mī. Herm.

her·met·ic, hur·met′ik, *a.* [Fr. *hermetique,* < the ancient *Hermes Trismegistus,* who was regarded as skilled in alchemy and occult science.] Airtight; pertaining to alchemy or occultism. Also **her·met·i·cal.**—**her·met·i·cal·ly,** *adv.*

her·mit, hĕr′mit, *n.* [O.Fr. *hermite, ermite* (Fr. *ermite*), < L.L. *eremita,* E. *eremite.*] A recluse; any person living in seclusion, esp. religious seclusion; *zool.* any of various animals of solitary habits; *cookery,* a spiced molasses cookie.

her·mit·age, hĕr′mi·tij, *n.* [O.Fr.] The habitation of a hermit; any secluded habitation. (*Cap.*) a French red wine produced in the region of Valence.

her·mit crab, *n. Zool.* any of numerous decapod crustaceans which protect their soft uncovered rear by occupying the cast-off shell of a univalve mollusk.

her·ni·a, hĕr′nē·a, *n. pl.* **her·ni·as, her·ni·ae,** hĕr′nē·ē″. [L.] *Pathol.* the projection of any internal organ or tissue through an abnormal aperture in the wall which encloses it, usu. in the abdominal area. Also *rupture.*—**her·ni·al,** *a.*—**her·ni·ate,** *v.i.*—*herniated, herniating.*—**her·ni·a·tion,** *n.*

he·ro, hĕr′ō, *n. pl.* **he·roes** [L. *heros,* < Gr. *hērōs.*] A man of distinguished valor, intrepidity, or fortitude; a central or prominent personage in any remarkable action or course of events; a man admired and venerated for his noble deeds or qualities; one invested with heroic qualities in the opinion of others; the principal male character in a poem, story, play, or the like, on whom the chief interest of the plot is centered. *Fem.* **he·ro·ine.** *Class. myth.* a man of superhuman strength, courage, or ability; an immortal being intermediate in nature between gods and men; a demigod. *U.S. colloq.* an oversize sandwich made with a long roll or with bread cut lengthwise.

he·ro·ic, hi·rō′ik, *a.* [L. *heroicus,* < Gr. *hērōikós.*] Pertaining to heroes, or men of distinguished valor; characteristic of or befitting a hero, as conduct; intrepid; brave; bold; of the nature of a hero; of or pertaining to the heroes of antiquity, as the *heroic* age; of a size larger than life but usu. less than colossal, as a statue; dealing with the deeds of heroes as, *heroic* poetry; used in heroic poetry as, *heroic* verse; resembling heroic poetry in language or style; magniloquent; grand; extravagant or bombastic; having or involving recourse to extreme measures as, *heroic* treatment; boldly experimental; daring. Also **he·ro·i·cal.**—*n.* Heroic verse; bombast.—**he·ro·i·cal·ly,** *adv.*—**he·ro·ic·ness, he·ro·i·cal·ness,** *n.*

he·ro·ic cou·plet, *n.* A verse form which consists of two lines which rhyme in iambic pentameter, often used in heroic poetry.

he·ro·ic stan·za, *n.* A four-line stanza or quatrain, consisting of two heroic couplets.

he·ro·ic verse, *n.* In classical poetry, the dactylic hexameter; in English, German, and Italian, the iambic pentameter; in French, the Alexandrine.

her·o·in, her′ō·in, *n.* [Appar. < *hero,* akin G. *heroin.*] *Pharm.* a morphine derivative,

$C_{21}H_{23}NO_5$, being white, odorless, and crystalline, and constituting a dangerously addictive narcotic.

her·o·ine, her′ō·in, *n.* Fem. of hero.

her·o·ism, her′ō·iz″um, *n.* [Fr. *héroïsme,* < *héros,* < L. *heros,* E. *hero.*] The qualities of a hero or heroine; heroic conduct; a heroic trait or action.

her·on, her′on, *n.* [O.Fr. *hairon* (Fr. *heron*); < Teut.] Any of the wading birds, family *Ardeidae,* having long bills, necks, and legs; as, the great white *heron,* the great blue *heron.* Also *Brit. dial.* **her·on·sew, her·on·shaw, her·on·shew.**—**her·on·ry,** *n. pl.* **her·on·ries.** A place where herons breed.

he·ro wor·ship, hĕr′ō·wur″ship, *n.* Veneration for great men; admiration, sometimes unwarranted, for an individual.—**he·ro·wor·ship,** *v.t.*—*hero-worshiped, hero-worshiping.* To have excessive admiration for; to express hero worship for; as, to *hero-worship* an athlete.—**he·ro·wor·ship·er,** *Brit.* **he·ro·wor·ship·per,** *n.*

her·pes, hĕr′pēz, *n.* [L. < Gr. *herpēs* (*herpet-*), *herpes,* < *herpein,* creep.] *Pathol.* any of certain inflammations of the skin or mucous membrane characterized by clusters of blisters, which often spread. Also **her·pes sim·plex.—her·pes zos·ter,** *n. Pathol.* a form of herpes characterized by blisters which sometimes form a girdle about the body; shingles.—**her·pet·ic,** hĕr·pet′ik, *a.*

her·pe·tol·o·gy, hĕr″pi·tol′o·jē, *n.* [Gr. *herpeton,* a reptile, < *herpō,* to creep, and *logos,* discourse.] *Zool.* that branch of study which has to do with reptiles and amphibians.—**her·pe·to·log·ic, her·pe·to·log·i·cal,** *a.*—**her·pe·to·log·i·cal·ly,** *adv.*—**her·pe·tol·o·gist,** *n.*

Herr, her, *n. pl.* **Her·ren,** her′en. [G.] In German use, gentleman or sir; as a title, equivalent to *Mister* (Mr.).

her·ring, her′ing, *n. pl.* **her·ring, her·rings.** [O.E. *hæring* = D. *haring* = G. *häring,* herring.] An important food fish, *Clupea harengus,* occurring abundantly in the N. Atlantic; any of closely related fishes or any fish of the family *Clupeidae:* often canned, pickled, or smoked and sold commercially.

her·ring·bone, her′ing·bōn″, *n.* A pattern made up of slanting parallel lines in rows, adjacent rows forming a V or inverted V and thus resembling the ribs of the herring, often used in textile weaves, embroidery, or masonry; *skiing,* a technique of climbing in which the skier points his skis outward in a V: the resultant tracks are in a herringbone pattern.—*a.* Resembling the spine of a herring.—*v.t.*—*herringboned, herringboning.* To put a herringbone design in or on.—*v.i.* To create a herringbone pattern; *skiing,* to ascend a slope using the herringbone technique.

her·ring gull, *n.* The most common gull in N. America, *Larus argentatus,* inhabiting both the seashore and inland waters.

hers, hĕrz, *pron.* See **her.**

her·self, hĕr·self′, *pron.* See **her.**

Hertz·i·an wave, heRts′sē·an wāv′, *n.* [From Heinrich R. *Hertz,* German physicist, 1857–1894.] *Phys.* an electromagnetic disturbance or radio wave, produced in the luminiferous ether and serving as a means of radio transmission.

he's, hēz, *unstressed* ēz. Contraction of he is or he has.

hes·i·tant, hez′i·tant, *a.* [L. *hæsitans, hæsitantis.*] Hesitating; wanting readiness of speech; lacking certainty.—**hes·i·tan·cy,** hez′i·tan·sē, *n. pl.* **hes·i·tan·cies.** The act of doubting; state of uncertainty. Also **hes·i·tance.**—**hes·i·tant·ly,** *adv.*

hes·i·tate, hez′i·tāt″, *v.i.*—*hesitated, hesitating.* [L. *hæsito, hæsitatum,* intens. < *hæreo, hæsum,* to stick, as in *adhere, cohere,*

inherent.] To stop or pause; to be reluctant in decision or action; to be doubtful as to fact, principle, or determination. To stammer; to stop in speaking.—**hes·i·tat·er, hes·i·ta·tor,** *n.*—**hes·i·tat·ing·ly,** *adv.*

hes·i·ta·tion, hez″i·tā′shan, *n.* [L. *hæsitatio, hæsitationis.*] The act of hesitating; a state of doubt or indecision; a pause or stammer in speech.—**hes·i·ta·tive,** hez′i·tā″tiv, *a.* Showing hesitation.—**hes·i·ta·tive·ly,** *adv.*

Hes·pe·ri·an, he·spēr′ē·an, *a.* [L. *hesperius,* western, < Gr. *hesperios* (= L. *vesper*), the evening. From the *Hesperides,* daughters of Atlas in Greek mythol. who guarded a garden of golden apples with the help of a dragon.] *Poet.* western; situated at the west. Of or pertaining to the Hesperides. —*n.* A Westerner; an Occidental.

hes·per·i·din, he·sper′i·din, *n. Chem.* hesperetin-rhamnoglucoside, $C_{28}H_{34}O_{15}$, a white glucoside powder derived from the peel of citrus fruits.

Hes·sian, hesh′an, *n.* [From *Hesse,* formerly a western principality of Germany.] A native of Hesse; a German-born soldier who fought as a mercenary for the British in the American Revolution; a mercenary; (*l.c.*) burlap.—*a.*

Hes·sian boots, *n. pl.* Knee-high military boots that have a dipped curve toward the calf with a pendant tassel in front, a 19th-century fashion copied from the Hessian troops.

Hes·sian fly, *n.* A small, two-winged insect, *Phytophaga destructor,* that is an egg-laying pest of winter wheat.

hess·ite, hes′it, *n.* [From G. H. *Hess,* Swiss chemist, 1802–1850.] Silver telluride, Ag_2Te, a rare, lead-gray, auriferous mineral.

hes·so·nite, hes′o·nīt″, *n.* Essonite.

he·tae·ra, hi·tēr′a, *n. pl.* **he·tae·rae, he·tae·ras,** hi′tēr·ē. [Gr.] A courtesan supported by a wealthy clientele. Also **he·tai·ra,** hi·tēr′a, *pl.* **he·tai·rai, he·tai·ras,** hi·tī′ri.—**he·tae·ric, he·tai·ric,** *a.*—**he·tae·rism, he·tai·rism,** *n.* Concubinage; in primitive societies, the system of communal marriages.

het·er·o·cer·cal, het″er·o·sur′kal, *a.* [Gr. *heteros,* other, different, *kerkos,* a tail.] *Zool.* having or pertaining to an asymmetrically divided tail or caudal fin in which the vertebral column continues into the upper, larger lobe, as in sharks and sturgeons.

het·er·o·chro·mat·ic, het″er·ō·krō·mat′ik, het″er·ō·kro·mat′ik, *a.* Relating to or containing various colors; composed of different frequencies or wavelengths; *genetics,* referring to heterochromatin.—**het·er·o·chro·ma·tism,** het″er·o·krō′ma·tiz″um, *n.*

het·er·o·chro·ma·tin, het″er·o·krō′ma·tin, *n. Genetics,* a component of chromatin, dense and easily stained, which evidences little genetic activity. Compare *euchromatin.*

het·er·o·clite, het′er·o·klīt″, *a.* [L.L. *heteroclitus,* < Gr. *heteroklitos,* < *heteros,* other, different, and *klinein,* incline, inflect.] *Gram.* irregular in declension or inflection, as a noun; *fig.* exceptional or anomalous. Also **het·er·o·clit·ic, het·er·o·clit·i·cal,** het″er·o·klit′ik.—*n. Gram.* a word irregular in declension or inflection; *fig.* a person or thing that deviates from the ordinary rule or form.

het·er·o·cy·clic, het″er·o·sī′klik, het″er·o·sik′lik, *a. Chem.* relating to or denoting an organic compound having a ring that contains one or more atoms other than carbon.

het·er·o·dox, het′er·o·doks″, *a.* [Gr. *heteros,* other, different, and *doxa,* opinion.] Contrary to established or generally accepted doctrines, standards, or opinions, esp. in theology; holding unorthodox

het·er·o·dox·y, n. pl. **het·er·-o·dox·ies.** Unorthodox state or quality; unorthodox belief or opinion.

het·er·o·dyne, het″ĕr·o·dīn″, a. [Gr. *heteros*, other, different, and *dynamis*, power.] *Radio*, pertaining to or denoting a method of altering the frequency of an incoming continuous wave signal by impressing upon it oscillations of a slightly different frequency, the interference resulting in fluctuations or beats with audio frequency.—*v.i.*—*heterodyned, heterodyning.* To produce a heterodyne effect.—*v.t.* To alter by the heterodyne method.

het·er·oe·cious, **het·er·e·cious,** het″e·rē′shus, a. [Gr. *heteros*, other, different, and *oikia*, house.] *Biol.* of a parasite, passing through different stages of growth on different hosts, as certain fungi.—**het·er·oe·cism,** het″e·rē′siz·um, n.

het·er·og·a·mous, het″e·rog′a·mus, a. [Gr. *heteros*, other, different, and *gamos*, marriage.] *Biol.* having unlike gametes, or reproducing by the union of such gametes, as opposed to *isogamous*; characterized by heterogenesis. *Bot.* having flowers or florets of two sexually different kinds, as opposed to *homogamous.*—**het·er·og·a·my,** n. The state of being heterogamous; heterogenesis.

het·er·o·ge·ne·ous, het″ĕr·o·jē′nē·us, het″ĕr·o·jēn′yas, a. [Gr. *heteros*, other, different, and *genos*, kind.] Differing in kind; having dissimilar or incongruous elements, as opposed to *homogeneous.*—**het·er·o·ge·ne·i·ty,** het″ĕr·ō·je·nē′i·tē, n.—**het·er·o·ge·ne·ous·ness,** het″ĕr·ō·je·nē′i·tē, n.—**het·er·o·ge·ne·ous·ly,** adv.

het·er·o·gen·e·sis, het″ĕr·o·jen′i·sis, n. *Biol.* Metagenesis; abiogenesis. See *alternation of generations.*—**het·er·o·ge·net·ic,** het″e·rō·je·net′ik, a.

het·er·og·e·nous, het″e·roj′e·nus, a. *Biol.* having a different source, usu. outside the organism.

het·er·og·o·nous, het″e·rog′o·nus, a. [Gr. *heteros*, other, different, and *gonos*, offspring, generation.] *Bot.* pertaining to two or more perfect flowers that differ as to the length of stamens and pistils and occur on different individuals of the same species; *biol.* pertaining to the alternation of two differing generations, one being dioecious, the other hermaphroditic; *zool.* alternation of a sexual generation with a parthenogenetic generation, as in female bees. Also **het·er·o·gon·ic,** het″ĕr·o·gon′ik.—**het·er·og·o·ny,** n.

het·er·og·ra·phy, het″e·rog′ra·fē, n. Spelling different from that in current use; spelling in which the same letter is used to represent different sounds in different words.—**het·er·o·graph·ic,** het″ĕr·o·graf′ik, a.

het·er·og·y·nous, het″e·roj′i·nus, a. [N.L. *heterogynus*, < Gr. *heteros*, other, different, and *gynē*, woman, female.] *Zool.* having females of two kinds, one sexual and the other abortive or neuter, as the ants.

het·er·ol·o·gous, het″e·rol′o·gus, a. [Gr. *heteros*, other, different, and *logos*, proportion, relation.] *Biol.* having a different relation; not corresponding; not homologous. *Pathol.* abnormal; consisting of tissue unlike the normal tissue of a part, as a tumor.

het·er·ol·o·gy, het″e·rol′o·jē, n. *Biol.* in similar bodily parts, a difference in important structures due to differences in origin. *Pathol.* an abnormality, deviating from the common type, as a tumor.

het·er·ol·y·sis, het″e·rol′i·sis, n. *Biochem.* the dissolution or destruction of cells in one species caused by the introduction of enzymes or lysins from another species.—**het·er·o·lyt·ic,** het″ĕr·o·lit′ik, a.

het·er·om·er·ous, het″e·rom′ĕr·us, a. [Gr. *heteros*, other, different, and *meros*, part.] *Bot.* having or consisting of parts which differ in quality, number of elements, or composition; as, a *heteromerous* flower.

het·er·o·mor·phic, het″ĕr·o·mar′fik, a. [Gr. *heteromorphos*, < *heteros*, other, different, and *morphē*, form.] *Biol.* of different or dissimilar form; deviating from normal structure or type. *Entom.* undergoing complete metamorphosis; *bot.* heterogonous.—**het·er·o·mor·phism, het·er·o·mor·phy,** n.

het·er·on·o·mous, het″e·ron′o·mus, a. [Gr. *heteros*, other, different, and *nomos*, law.] Subject to or involving different laws; subject to the law or will of another; *biol.* having different laws or modes of growth.

het·er·on·o·my, het″e·ron′o·mē, n. [Gr. *heteros*, different, *nomos*, law.] Subordination to the law or rule of another, as opposed to *autonomy.*

het·er·o·nym, het′ĕr·o·nim″, n. [Gr. *heteros*, other, *onyma*, name.] A word with the same spelling as another but a different pronunciation and meaning, as *tear*, to rip, and *tear*, a drop of fluid from the eye.—**het·er·on·y·mous,** het″e·ron′i·mus, a. Of, relating to, or like a heteronym; designated by different names, as two correlatives.

het·er·oph·o·ny, het″e·rof′o·nē, n. *Mus.* the simultaneous performance of a melody by two or more musicians, each adding individual variations to the orig. melodic line.—**het·er·o·phon·ic,** het″ĕr·o·fon′ik, a.

het·er·o·phyl·lous, het″ĕr·o·fil′us, a. *Bot.* having dissimilar leaves on the same stem or plant.—**het·er·o·phyl·ly,** n.

het·er·o·plas·ty, het′ĕr·o·plas″tē, n. *Surg.* an operation in which lesions are repaired with grafted tissue taken from another person or organism.

het·er·op·ter·ous, het″e·rop′tĕr·us, a. *Biol.* relating to an order, *Hemiptera*, or suborder, *Heteroptera*, in which the true bugs are included.

het·er·o·sex·u·al, het″ĕr·o·sek′shō·al, a. Of or pertaining to sexual orientation toward the opposite sex; *biol.* pertaining to different sexes.—n. One who is heterosexual.—**het·er·o·sex·u·al·i·ty,** het″ĕr·o·sek″shō·al′i·tē, n. Sexual attraction toward the opposite sex.

het·er·o·sis, het″e·rō′sis, n. *Biol.* an increased vigor or potential for growth as a result of cross-breeding of plants or animals. Also *hybrid vigor.*—**het·er·ot·ic,** het″e·rot′ik, a.

het·er·os·por·ous, het″e·ros′pĕr·us, het″ĕr·o·spōr′us, het″ĕr·o·spar′us, a. *Bot.* having more than one kind of spores, as distinguished from *homosporous.*—**het·er·os·po·ry,** het″e·ros′po·rē, n.

het·er·o·troph·ic, het″ĕr·o·trof′ik, a. *Biol.* using organic matter for a source of food, as all animals and non-green plants. Compare *autotrophic.*—**het·er·o·troph·i·cal·ly,** adv.

het·er·o·typ·ic, het″ĕr·o·tip′ik, a. *Biol.* pertaining to the primary stage of meiosis, the reduction division, marked by the splitting of chromosomes within a germ cell.

het·er·o·zy·go·sis, het″ĕr·ō·zī·gō′sis, n. *Biol.* the union of genetically unlike gametes which form a heterozygote.

het·er·o·zy·gote, het″ĕr·o·zī′gōt, het″ĕr·o·zig′ōt, n. *Genetics*, a hybrid animal or plant which does not breed true to type because it contains at least one pair of genes with different characteristics. Compare *homozygote.*—**het·er·o·zy·gous,** het″ĕr·o·zī′gus, a.

het·man, het′man, n. pl. **het·mans.** [Pol. < G. *hauptman*, head-man, chieftain.] A leader of the Cossacks. Also *ataman.*

het up, het′up′, a. *Dial.* distraught, excited.

heu·land·ite, hū′lan·dīt″, n. [From H. *Heuland*, a 19th-century English collector of minerals.] A mineral, one of the zeolites, consisting of hydrous calcium aluminosilicate, $CaAl_2Si_7O_{18} \cdot 6H_2O$.

heu·ris·tic, hū·ris′tik, a. [Gr. *heuriskein*, to find out.] Aiding or leading on toward discovery; following a teaching method that induces the student to make his own discoveries.—n. A heuristic technique or discussion.—**heu·ris·ti·cal·ly,** adv.

hew, hū, v.t.—past *hewed*, pp. *hewed* or *hewn*, ppr. *hewing.* [O.E. *hēawan* = D. *houwen* = G. *hauen.*] To strike forcibly with a cutting tool, as an ax or sword; to chop; to hack; to cut down or fell, as trees; to shape with cutting blows; to give rough form to.—v.i. To deal cutting blows; to adhere; to conform closely to a prescribed line of conduct.—**hew·er,** n.

hex, heks, v.t. To jinx; to bewitch; to put under an evil spell.—n. A jinx; a magic spell; a witch.—a. Hexagonal.—**hex·er,** n.

hex·a·chlo·ro·phene, hek″sa·klōr′o·fēn″, hek″sa·klạr′o·fēn, n. *Chem.* $(C_6HCl_3OH)_2$-CH_2, a bactericidal agent used in soaps, cosmetics, and deodorants.

hex·a·chord, hek′sa·kạrd″, n. *Mus.* a diatonic series of six tones, having a half step between the third and fourth tones and whole steps between the others.

hex·ad, hek′sad, n. [L.L. *hexas* (hexad-), Gr. *hexas* (hexad), < *hex*, six.] A group or series of six.—**hex·ad·ic,** a.

hex·a·gon, hek′sa·gon″, hek′sa·gon, n. [L. *hexagonum*, < Gr. *hexagōnos*, hexangular.] *Geom.* a plane figure having six angles and six sides.—**hex·ag·o·nal,** hek·sag′o·nal, a. Of, pertaining to, or having the form of a hexagon; having a hexagon as a base or cross section; as, a *hexagonal* pyramid; divided into hexagons, as a surface; *crystal.* noting or pertaining to a system of crystallization characterized by three equal lateral axes intersecting at angles of 60° and a vertical axis of different length at right angles to them.—**hex·ag·o·nal·ly,** adv.

hex·a·gram, hek′sa·gram″, n. A six-pointed starlike figure formed of two equilateral triangles placed concentrically with their sides parallel and on opposite sides of the center.

hex·a·he·dron, hek″sa·hē′dron, n. pl. **hex·a·he·drons, hex·a·he·dra,** hek″sa·hē′dra. [Gr. *hex*, six, and *hedra*, a base or seat.] A regular solid body having six sides.—**hex·a·he·dral,** a.

hex·a·hy·drate, hek″sa·hī′drāt, n. *Chem.* a compound which has six water molecules.—**hex·a·hy·drat·ed,** a.

hex·am·er·ous, hek·sam′ĕr·us, a. *Bot.* of flowers, having six members in each whorl; *zool.* having organs in six groups, radially arranged.

hex·am·e·ter, hek·sam′i·tĕr, n. [Gr. *hex*, six, and *metron*, measure.] *Pros.* a verse of six feet, the first four of which may be either dactyls or spondees, the fifth normally a dactyl, and the sixth usu. a spondee but sometimes a trochee.—a. Having six metrical feet.—**hex·a·met·ric, hex·a·met·ral,** hek″sa·met′rik, a.

hex·a·meth·yl·ene·tet·ra·mine, hek″sa·meth″i·lēn·tet′ra·mēn′, n. *Chem.* a crystalline powder, $C_6H_{12}N_4$, used in industry for making synthetic resins, and accelerating rubber vulcanization; *med.* an antiseptic and a diuretic. Also **hex·a·mine.**

hex·ane, hek′sān, n. [Gr. *hex*, six (with reference to the atoms of carbon).] *Chem.* any of five isomeric hydrocarbons, volatile and liquid in nature and usu. found in petroleum.

hex·an·gu·lar, hek·sang′gū·lĕr, a. [Gr. *hex*, six, and E. *angular.*] Having six angles.

hex·a·ni·trate, hek′sa·nī′trāt, n. *Chem.* a compound that contains nitrate groups of six.

Hex·a·pla, hek′sa·pla, n. pl. [Gr. *hexaplous*, sixfold.] A 3rd-century edition of the Old Testament in six versions arranged in six parallel columns; (*l.c.*) a similar edition of any text.—**hex·a·plar,** hek′sa·plar, a.

hex·a·pod, hek'sa·pod", n. [N.L. *Hexapoda* < Gr. *hexapous* (*-pod-*), six-footed, *hex*, six, and *pous* (*pod-*), foot.] One of the *Insecta*, formerly called *Hexapoda*, a class of arthropods having six feet, comprising the true insects.—*a.* Having six feet; belonging to the class *Insecta*.—**hex·ap·o·dous**, hek-sap'o·dus, *a.*

hex·o·san, hek'so·san", n. *Chem.* a hemicellulose which yields hexose sugar on hydrolysis.

hex·ose, hek'sōs, n. *Chem.* any of the simple sugars containing six atoms of carbon per molecule, as fructose or glucose.

hey, hā, *interj.* An exclamation, used to express joy or surprise and to call attention.

hey·day, hey·dey, hā'dā", n. [Equivalent to *highday*.] Period of optimum condition, vigor, or productivity; prime.

hi, hī, *interj.* [Cf. *hey* and *hoy*.] Hello; *Brit.* an exclamation used to attract attention.

hi·a·tus, hī·ā'tus, n. pl. **hi·a·tus·es, hi·a·tus.** [L. < *hiare*, to open or gape.] An interruption or break in continuity; an opening, gap, or lacuna; a vocal break or pause between two adjacent vowels in two successive syllables or words, as in *co-operate*; *anat.* any natural aperture, fissure, or cleft.

hi·ba·chi, hē·bä'chē, n. [Jap. 'fire bowl.'] A small cast-iron charcoal stove or brazier used for cooking and heating. Also **ha·ba·chi**, ha·bä'chē.

hi·ber·nac·u·lum, hī″bẽr·nak'ū·lum, n. pl. **hi·ber·nac·u·la**, hī″bẽr·nak'ū·la. [L. a winter residence, < *hibernus.*] *Biol.* a protective winter covering for a plant or animal part. Winter shelter for a dormant or hibernating animal; also **hi·ber·na·cle.**

hi·ber·nal, hī·bur'nal, *a.* [L. *hibernalis*, < *hibernus*, wintry, akin to *hiems*, winter; Gr. *chiōn*, Skr. *hima*, snow.] Belonging or relating to winter; wintry.

hi·ber·nate, hī'bẽr·nāt", *v.i.*—*hibernated, hibernating.* To pass the winter in a suspended, dormant, or torpid condition; to winter, as in a milder climate.—**hi·ber·na·tion**, n.—**hi·ber·na·tor**, n.

Hi·ber·ni·an, hī·bur'nē·an, *a.* [L. *Hibernia*, Ireland.] Pertaining to Ireland; Irish.—n. A native of Ireland.—**Hi·ber·ni·an·ism, Hi·ber·ni·cism**, hī·bur'ni·siz″um, n. An idiom or manner of speech peculiar to the Irish.

hi·bis·cus, hī·bis'kus, hi·bis'kus, n. pl. **hi·bis·cus·es.** [L. < Gr. *hibiskos*, mallow.] Any of the herbs, shrubs, or trees of the genus *Hibiscus*, in the mallow family, with large, showy, colored flowers, as in the cultivated shrub, rose-of-sharon.

hic, hik, *interj.* [Imit.] An exclamation which is, or resembles, the sound of a hiccup.—**hick**, *v.i.* To hiccup.

hic·cup, hik'up, hik'up, n. [Imit.] A quick, involuntary intake of breath suddenly checked by closure of the glottis, producing a characteristic sound; *usu. pl.* an attack of such spasms.—*v.i.*—*hiccuped, hiccuping; hiccupped, hiccupping.* To make the sound of a hiccup; to be affected with hiccups. Also **hic·cough.**

hick, hik, n. [From *Hick*, for *Richard*, man's name.] An unsophisticated yokel; a country bumpkin.—*a.* Pertaining to lack of sophistication or urbanity; as, a *hick* town.

hick·ey, hik'ē, n. pl. **hick·eys.** An expression for anything whose name is not known or remembered; thingamajig; also **doo·hick·ey, do-hick·ey.** *Elect.* a fitting used to install a fixture in an outlet box; a tool for manipulating or bending pipes and conduits; *slang*, a pimple, skin eruption, or a bruise.

hick·o·ry, hik'o·rē, hik'rē, n. pl. **hick·o·ries.** [N. Amer. Ind.] Any N. American tree of the genus *Carya*, some of which yield valuable hardwood and sweet, edible nuts;

the wood of such a tree; a switch or stick of this wood.

hi·dal·go, hi·dal'gō, *Sp.* ē·THäl'ga, n. pl. **hi·dal·gos**, hi·dal'gōz, *Sp.* ē·THäl'gas. [Sp., for *hijo de algo*, 'son of something.'] In Spain, a man of the lower nobility.

hid·den, hid'en, *a.* Concealed; secret; mysterious; obscure.—**hid·den·ness**, n.

hid·den·ite, hid'e·nīt", n. [From W. E. *Hidden*, mineralogist, 1853–1918.] A transparent green to yellow variety of spodumene, highly esteemed as a gem.

hide, hīd, *v.t.*—past *hid*, pp. *hidden* or *hid*, ppr. *hiding.* To conceal intentionally from sight; to prevent from being observed readily; to conceal from discovery; to secrete; to obstruct or block the view of; to conceal from knowledge or to maintain secrecy. *Bib.* to turn away, as the head, in displeasure, shame, or anger; to ignore.—*v.i.* To keep out of sight; to conceal oneself.—**hid·er**, n.

hide, hīd, n. The pelt of an animal either raw or tanned, esp. that of one of the larger animals; *slang*, the human skin.

hide, hīd, n. [O.E. *hīd.*] An Old English measure of land, usually 120 acres, considered adequate for supporting one family.

hide, hīd, *v.t.*—*hided, hiding.* To beat, whip, or thrash; to flog.—**hid·ing**, n.

hide-and-seek, hīd'an·sēk', n. A children's game in which the players who conceal themselves are sought by the player who is 'it.' Also **hide-and-go-seek**, hīd'an·gō·sēk'.

hide·a·way, hīd'a·wā", n. A place for escape or refuge; a retreat.—*a.* Hidden; as, a *hideaway* bed.

hide·bound, hīd'bound", *a.* Of an animal, having the hide or skin adhering closely to the back and ribs; of a tree, having the bark close or unyielding; *fig.* of a person, narrow-minded; rigidly fixed in opinion; ultraconservative.

hid·e·ous, hid'ē·us, *a.* [Fr. *hideux*, O.Fr. *hisdous*, rough, shaggy, hideous, < L. *hispidosus*, for *hispidus*, rough, shaggy.] Frightful or shocking to the senses; dreadful; shocking in a moral way; detestable; horrible.—**hid·e·ous·ly**, *adv.*—**hid·e·ous·ness**, n.

hide·out, hīd'out", n. A spot used for concealment, esp. as refuge from the authorities.—**hide out**, *v.i.* To go into concealment; to remain in hiding.

hi·dro·sis, hi·drō'sis, hī·drō'sis, n. [N.L., < Gr. *hidrosis*, < *hidroun*, sweat, perspire, < *hidros*, sweat.] *Pathol.* Perspiration, esp. excessive perspiration due to drugs, disease, or the like; any of certain diseases characterized by sweating.—**hi·drot·ic**, hi·drot'-ik, hī·drot'ik, *a.*

hie, hī, *v.i.*—*hied, hieing* or *hying.* [O.E. *hīgian*, strive: cf. D. *hijgen*, pant.] To hasten; speed; go in haste.—*v.t.* To hurry: used reflexively.

hi·e·mal, hī'e·mal, *a.* [L. *hiemalis*, < *hiems*, winter.] Of or relating to winter.

hi·er·arch, hī'e·rärk", hī'rärk, n. [Gr. *hieros*, sacred, and *archē*, rule.] One who rules or has authority in sacred things, as a bishop, high priest, or religious leader.

hi·er·ar·chy, hī'e·rär″kē, hī'rär·kē, n. pl. **hi·er·ar·chies.** A ranking of individuals, as a group of officials, according to their authority or function in a church or government; a logical arrangement of scientific or other items; the orders of angels.—**hi·er·ar·chal, hi·er·ar·chic, hi·er·ar·chi·cal**, *a.*—**hi·er·ar·chi·cal·ly**, *adv.*

hi·er·at·ic, hī″e·rat'ik, hī·rat'ik, *a.* [Gr. *hieratikos*, < *hieros*, holy.] Pertaining to priests; sacred; sacerdotal; of or relating to a mode of writing used by the ancient Egyptian priests, a development from the hieroglyphics; denoting or relating to certain styles of art fixed by religious

tradition. Also **hi·er·at·i·cal.**—**hi·er·at·i·cal·ly**, *adv.*

hi·er·oc·ra·cy, hī″e·rok'ra·sē, hī·rok'ra·sē, n. pl. **hi·er·oc·ra·cies.** [Gr. *hieros*, holy, and *kratos*, power.] Government by ecclesiastics.

hi·er·o·dule, hī'ẽr·o·dōl", hī'ẽr·o·dūl", hī'ro·dōl", hī'ro·dūl", n. [Gr. *hierodoulos*, < *hieros*, sacred, and *doulos*, slave.] *Gr. antiq.* a slave dwelling in a temple and dedicated to the service of a deity.—**hi·er·o·du·lic**, *a.*

hi·er·o·glyph·ic, hī″ẽr·o·glif'ik, hī″ro·glif'ik, *a.* [L.L. *hieroglyphicus*, < Gr. *hieroglyphikos*, < *hieros*, sacred, and *glyphein*, carve.] Pertaining to pictographic inscriptions in the form of symbolic characters used in ancient Egyptian records; having a hidden meaning; mysteriously symbolic; hard to decipher. Also **hi·er·o·glyph·i·cal.**—n. A picture or character representing a word or idea; a figure or device with a hidden meaning. *Pl.* the writing found on monuments and records of the ancient Egyptians; similar writings of other peoples; writing difficult to decipher. Also **hi·er·o·glyph.**—**hi·er·o·glyph·i·cal·ly**, *adv.*

hi·er·ol·o·gy, hī″e·rol'o·jē, hī·rol'o·jē, n. [Gr. *hieros*, sacred, and *logos*, discourse.] Sacred literature or learning.

hi·er·o·phant, hī'ẽr·o·fant", hī'ro·fant", hī·ẽr·o'fant", n. [Gr. *hierophantēs*—*hieros*, sacred, and *phaino*, to show.] A priest; one who expounds and interprets the rites and mysteries of religion; *specif.* the high priest of the ancient Eleusinian mysteries.

hi-fi, hī'fī", n. [(*hi*)gh (*fi*)delity.] Equipment used in reproducing sound with high fidelity.—*a.*

hig·gle, hig'l, *v.i.*—*higgled, higgling.* [A weaker form of *haggle*.] To bargain; to argue, often over petty, niggardly details; to haggle.—**hig·gler**, n. A peddler.

hig·gle·dy-pig·gle·dy, hig'l·dē·pig'l·dē, *adv.* Topsy-turvy; in confusion.—*a.* Jumbled; confused; chaotic.

high, hī, *a.* [O.E. *hēah* = D. *hoog* = G. *hoch* = Icel. *har* = Goth. *hauhs*, high.] Having a considerable or specified reach or extent upward; lofty; elevated; tall; situated far above the ground or some other base level; pertaining to highland or inland regions rather than those near sea level; extending to or from an elevation; as, a *high* dive. Exalted in rank or estimation; of a lofty or superior kind; as, *high* resolves; grave or serious; as, *high* treason; principal or main; as, the *high* altar of a church; rich or luxurious; as, *high* living; of great amount, degree, or force; as, a *high* price, *high* speed; expensive; denoted by a high number; as a *high* latitude; advanced to the utmost extent or culmination; as, *high* noon; fully advanced or come; as, *high* time to begin work; haughty or arrogant, as manner or expression; extreme in doctrine or opinion; elated or merry; as, *high* spirits; of meat, tending toward decomposition; of sounds, produced by relatively rapid vibrations; acute in pitch, as a note; shrill; *slang*, excited with drink.

high, hī, *adv.* At or to a high point, place, level, rank, amount, or degree; for high stakes; at or to a high pitch; richly or luxuriously; as, living *high*.—n. A position of height, as: The stocks reached a new *high*. A transmission gear in an automobile enabling rapid speed.—**high and low**, everywhere.—**on high**, at or to a height; above.

high·ball, hī'bạl", n. An iced alcoholic drink composed of liquor mixed with a carbonated beverage or water and served in a tall glass. *Rail.* a signal for a train to proceed; a signal for full speed.—*v.t.* To signal to, as a train's engineer, for a train to proceed.—*v.i. Slang*, of a train, to move at high or full speed.

high blood pres·sure, *n.* Abnormally high arterial blood pressure; hypertension.

high·born, hī′bȯrn″, *a.* Being of noble birth or ancestry.

high·boy, hī′boi″, *n.* A tall chest of drawers supported on legs.

high·bred, hī′bred″, *a.* Descended from superior bloodlines or stock; wellborn; highly refined; indicative of or marked by good breeding.

high·brow, hī′brou″, *n. Colloq.* an intellectual person or one with intellectual pretensions: sometimes used in a derogatory sense.—*a.* Also **high·browed.—high·-brow·ism,** *n.*

high·bush, hī′bush″, *a. Bot.* of or pertaining to certain tall upright shrubs bearing fruits; as, *highbush* blueberry, *Vaccinium corymbosum.*

high·chair, hī′chār″, *n.* A baby's chair with long legs and a removable food tray.

High Church, *a.* Placing great stress on church authority and jurisdiction, ritual and tradition, as well as holding a strict viewpoint on doctrine; pertaining to the High Church parties in the Church of England and in the Episcopal Church.— **High Church·man,** *n.*

high com·mand, *n.* Those in highest authority in a military, business, or other organization; the headquarters of a military operation.

high com·mis·sion·er, *n.* A representative of government stationed in another country, esp. within the British Commonwealth; the governing officer of a protectorate, territory, or the like; the head of an international commission.

high·er crit·i·cism, *n.* Study of the Bible concentrating on determination of dates of composition, historical credibility, authenticity, authorship, and purposes and intended meanings of the authors.

high·er-up, hī′ėr-up′, *n.* pl. **high·er-ups.** A person of superior rank, importance, or authority in any organization.

high ex·plo·sive, *n.* One of a class of extremely powerful, rapidly detonating explosives, esp. one based on nitroglycerine as TNT, frequently used as a bursting charge.

high·fa·lu·tin, hī″fa·lōt′in, *a. Colloq.* pompous or bombastic. Also **high·fa·lu·ting, hi·fa·lu·tin, hi·fa·lu·ting.**

high fash·ion, *n.* [< Fr. *haute couture.*] Style; sophistication; mode; *colloq.* the chief exponents of international dress designing.—*a.* Stylish; fashionable; avantgarde; pertaining to the designs of the most prestigious couturiers. Also **haute cou·ture,** ōt kö·tYR′.

high fi·del·i·ty, *n. Electron.* the reproduction of sound with minimal distortion of the original signals. Also **hi-fi.—***a.*

high·fli·er, high·fly·er, hī′flī′er, *n.* One who is extravagant or who tends to extremes in opinion, manner, or ambition.

high-flown, hī′flōn″, *a.* Extravagant or pompous in language or taste; pretentious.

high·fly·ing, hī′flī′ing, *a.* Extravagant in claims, expectations, or opinions; flying high.

high fre·quen·cy, *n.* An electromagnetic wave frequency between 3 and 30 megacycles per second, used in radio and television transmission.—*a.* Abbr. *hf, HF.*

high-grade, hī′grād′, *a.* Of excellent quality.

high-hand·ed, high·hand·ed, hī′han′did, *a.* Oppressive; domineering; arbitrary.— **high-hand·ed·ly,** *adv.***—high-hand·ed·-ness,** *n.*

high hat, *n.* Top hat.

high-hat, hī′hat′, *a. Colloq.* Condescending; arrogant; proud.—*v.t.***—high-hatted, high-**

hatting. To snub; to deal with in a patronizing manner.

High Hol·i·days, *n.* pl. *Judaism,* two important observances designated as special holy days: Rosh Hashanah and Yom Kippur.

high horse, *n.* An arrogant manner; a snobbish attitude.

high jump, *n. Track,* a jump for height, usually from a running start, over a crossbar placed between two vertical poles.

high·land, hī′land, *n.* An elevated or mountainous region.—*a.* Pertaining to or characteristic of a lofty, hilly region.— **high·land·er,** *n.* An inhabitant of a highland.

High·lands, hī′landz, *n.* pl. The lofty, elevated part of Scotland.—**High·land·er,** *n.* An inhabitant of the Highlands; member of a Highland military regiment.—**High·land fling,** a lively folk dance native to Scotland; also *fling.*

high-lev·el, hī′lev′el, *a.* Having high rank, status, or importance; originating or occurring at a high altitude.

high·light, hī′līt″, *n.* An interesting, important, or conspicuous point in an activity, scene, or the like; *art,* the area, plane, point, or edge on a represented form which reflects the most light.—*v.t.* To feature; focus one's attention on; *art,* to illuminate or give highlights to.

High Mass, *n. Eccles.* a liturgical function, essentially the same as a Low Mass, but enhanced by additional music, the singing of the liturgy, the use of incense, and assistance to the priest by a deacon and subdeacon.

high-mind·ed, hī′min′did, *a.* Characterized by lofty principles and feelings; honorable; magnanimous.—**high-mind·-ed·ly,** *adv.***—high-mind·ed·ness,** *n.*

high-muck-a-muck, hī′muk″a·muk′, hī′muk′a·muk″, *n. Slang,* a person of rank or influence who is pompously aware of his importance. Also **high-muck·e·ty-muck.**

high·ness, hī′nis, *n.* The state or quality of being high; (*cap.*) a form of address and title of honor for royalty or for others of high rank: used with *His, Her,* or *Your.*

high-oc·tane, hī′ok′tān, *a.* Of gasoline, having a high octane number, indicative of efficiency and good performance.

high-pres·sure, hī′presh′er, *a.* Having, exerting, or involving a pressure much greater than that of the atmosphere; of an engine, sustaining high steam pressure; *colloq.* intense, pressing, and insistent; as, a *high-pressure* salesman.—*v.t.***—high-pressured, high-pressuring.** To influence or persuade by aggressive and persistent tactics.

high priest, *n.* A chief priest; a person who wields or is capable of wielding power and influence in any sphere or domain, as in sports or the arts.

high-proof, hī′prööf′, *a.* Containing a high percentage of alcohol; as, *high-proof* spirits.

high re·lief, *n. Sculp.* relief in which half or more than half of the depth of the sculptured figure projects from the background. Also *alto-rilievo.*

high rise, *n.* A multistoried building, usu. an apartment building.—**high-rise,** *a.*

high·road, hī′rōd″, *n. Chiefly Brit.* a highway; *fig.* a reliable or easy course of action; as, the *highroad* to fortune.

high school, *n. U.S.* the secondary level of education following elementary school, and usu. including grades 9 or 10 through 12. Compare *junior high school* and *senior high school.*—**high-school,** *a.*

high seas, *n.* pl. The sea or ocean, lying outside the territorial jurisdiction of any nation and considered a common highway. —**high-sea,** *a.*

high-sound·ing, hī′soun′ding, *a.* Pretentious; pompous; ostentatious; with an impressive sound or implication.

high-spir·it·ed, hī′spir′i·tid, *a.* Having a courageous spirit; bold; energetic; elated.— **high-spir·it·ed·ly,** *adv.***—high-spir·it·-ed·ness,** *n.*

high-strung, hī′strung′, *a.* Having an unusually nervous, highly excitable temperament.

high·tail, hī′tāl′, *v.i. Colloq.* To leave or depart rapidly; to hurry or run away, usu. followed by *it.*

high tea, *n. Brit.* a meal, usu. with meat or fish, ordinarily served late in the afternoon or early in the evening.

high-ten·sion, hī′ten′shan, *a. Elect.* capable of carrying or operating under current of high voltage. Also **high volt·age, high po·ten·tial.**

high-test, hī′test′, *a.* Meeting difficult standards of quality; pertaining to gasoline having a relatively low boiling point.

high tide, *n.* The tide at its highest level; the time that the tide reaches this level; *fig.* peak or climax.

high-toned, hī′tōnd′, *a.* High-principled; dignified; characterized by dignity; as, a *high-toned* journal; affectedly or excessively stylish or superior.

high trea·son, *n.* Treason against the sovereign or state.

high wa·ter, *n.* Water at its highest level, as during a flood or at high tide.—**high-wa·ter mark,** the highest level that a body of water reaches; the mark indicating this level left by the receding waters; *fig.* any peak, climax, or high point.

high·way, hī′wā″, *n.* A public road, esp. a main route between two towns or cities; any principal route, whether on water or land; a direct course of action.

high·way·man, hī′wā″man, *n.* pl. **high·-way·men.** One, formerly on horseback, who waylays and robs on the highway.

high-wrought, hī′rȧt′, *a.* Wrought with exquisite art or skill; ornate; excited or agitated to a high degree.

hi·jack, high·jack, hī′jak″, *v.t., v.i.* [Said to have come from *hi, Jack!* as used by a robber in accosting an intended victim.] To rob in transit, as a person; to take by force, as something in transit; as, to *hijack* an aircraft.—**hi·jack·er,** *n.***—hi·jack·ing,** *n.*

hike, hīk, *v.i.—hiked, hiking.* To walk for exercise or pleasure, esp. a long distance. To rise out of place or position, as part of a garment, often with *up.—v.t. Colloq.* To move or raise with a sudden jerk, often with *up;* to increase sharply or unexpectedly, as prices, often with *up.—n.* A march or constitutional; a walk. *Colloq.* an increase or rise.—**hik·er,** *n.*

hi·lar·i·ous, hi·lâr′ē·us, hi·lar′ē·us, hī·-lâr′ē·us, hī·lar′ē·us, *a.* Exceedingly funny; laughter inducing.—**hi·lar·i·ous·ly,** *adv.* —**hi·lar·i·ous·ness,** *n.***—hi·lar·i·ty,** hi·-lar′i·tē, hi·lâr′i·tē, hī·lar′i·tē, hī·lâr′i·tē, *n.*

hill, hil, *n.* [O.E. *hyll* = M.D. *hille,* hill; akin to L. *collis,* hill, *culmen,* top, *columna,* column.] A conspicuous natural elevation of the earth's surface much smaller than a mountain; an artificial heap or pile; a little heap of earth packed at the roots of a young plant for support.—*v.t.* To form into a hill or a heap; to surround with hills, as plants. —**hill·er,** *n.* One who cultivates the soil to form hills of earth around plants; a tool for such work.—**hill·side,** *n.* The side or slope of a hill.—**hill·top,** *n.* The summit of a hill.—**hill·y,** *a.—hillier, hilliest.*

hill·bil·ly, hil′bil″ē, *n.* pl. **hill·bil·lies.** *Colloq.* a rustic or unsophisticated person originating or residing in a deprived backwoods area, usu. in or from the mountains of the southern U.S.—*a.*—

hill·bil·ly mu·sic, *U.S.* country-and-western music; the folk music of mountaineers or Westerners.

hill my·na, *n.* The myna of the genus *Gracula,* an Indian and Oriental bird, usu. black, which can be trained to imitate the human voice more distinctly than a parrot. Also **myna, mynah.**

hill·ock, hil′ok, *n.* [Dim. of *hill.*] A small hill, knoll, or mound.

hilt, hilt, *n.* [O.E. *hilt, hilte.*] The handle of a sword or dagger; the handle of any weapon or tool.—*v.t.* To furnish with a hilt.—**to the hilt,** absolutely or completely.

hi·lum, hī′lum, *n. pl.* **hi·la,** hī′la. [L. little thing, trifle.] *Bot.* the mark or scar on a seed produced by separation from its funiculus or placenta; the nucleus of a granule of starch; *anat.* the point at which vessels, ducts, or nerves enter or emerge from a bodily part. —**hi·lar,** hī′lẽr, *a.* Concerning or near a hilum.

him, him, *pron.* [In O.E. the dative of *he.*] The objective case of *he,* as: She likes *him.* Give it to *him.*—**him·self,** him·self′, im·self′, *pron.* A reflexive or emphatic form of *he,* as: He struck *himself.* He *himself* told me. A denotation of his usual or customary state, as: He is not *himself* at all.

hi·mat·i·on, hi·mat′ē·on̂, *n. pl.* **hi·mat·i·a,** hi·mat′ē·a. [Gr. *himation.*] *Gr. antiq.* a garment consisting of a rectangular piece of cloth thrown over the left shoulder and wrapped about the body.

Him·yar·ite, him′ya·rīt″, *n.* [Said to be named from an ancient king *Himyar.*] One of an ancient people of southern Arabia; a descendant of this ancient group.—**Him·yar·it·ic,** him″ya·rit′ik, *a.*

hin, hin, *n.* [Heb.] A Hebrew liquid measure containing about six quarts.

Hi·na·ya·na, hē″na·yä′na, *n.* A conservative school of Buddhism, believing in the nontheistic, contemplative life and in purification through one's own efforts.— **Hi·na·ya·nist,** *n.*—**Hi·na·ya·nis·tic,** *a.*

hind, hīnd, *n. pl.* **hinds, hind.** [O.E. *hind* = Icel. *hind,* hind: cf. D. and G. *hinde.*] The female of the deer, chiefly the red deer, esp. in and after the third year; any of various food fishes of the western Atlantic, as *Epinephelus maculosus,* the red hind.

hind, hīnd, *a.*—**hinder, hindmost** or **hindermost.** [O.E. *hind,* hind, *hindan,* behind; Goth. *hindana, hindar,* O.H.G. *hintar,* G. *hinten,* behind, *hinter,* hind; hence to *hinder.*] Pertaining to or situated at the part which follows or is behind; rear.

hind·brain, hīnd′brān″, *n. Anat.* the posterior of the vertebrate brain including, primarily, the pons, cerebellum, and medulla oblongata; rhombencephalon.

hin·der, hin′dẽr, *v.t.* [O.E. *hindrian,* to hinder, < *hinder,* compar. of hind.] To prevent from proceeding; to obstruct or impede; to check or retard; to thwart or stop; to interrupt.—*v.i.* To serve as an obstacle or impediment.—**hind·er·er,** *n.*

hind·er, hin′dẽr, *a.* In the rear; at the back.

hind·gut, hīnd′gut″, *n. Anat.* the posterior of the embryonic alimentary structure, from which the colon and rectum evolve.

Hin·di, hin′dē, *n.* [Hind. and Pers. *Hindī,* < Pers. *Hind,* India.] An Indo-Iranian vernacular language of northern India comprising various dialects; a form of Hindustani used as a literary language by Hindus.

hind·most, hīnd′mōst″, *Brit.* also hīnd′most, *a.* [O.E. *hindema,* hindmost; the *-most* is a corruption as in *foremost.*] Farthest behind; behind all others; last.

Hin·doo·ism, hin′dō·iz″um, *n.* Hinduism.

hind·quar·ter, hīnd′kwãr″tẽr, *n.* One of the posterior quarters when a half carcass of beef or lamb is sectioned; those parts of

an animal which are located to the rear of where the hind legs connect to the torso; *pl.* the rump.

hin·drance, hin′drans, *n.* The act of delaying, interrupting, or thwarting; the cause of such difficulty; impediment.

hind·sight, hīnd′sīt″, *n.* Rear sight of any firearm; perception, understanding, or judgment of an incident after it has happened.

Hin·du, Hin·doo, hin′dö, *n.* [Hind. and Pers. *Hindu,* < Pers. *Hind,* India.] Any adherent of Hinduism, a religion prevailing predominantly in India and Nepal; in general, any native of Hindustan, the primarily Hindu section of India.—*a.* Of or pertaining to the Hindus or Hinduism.

Hin·du·ism, hin′dö·iz″um, *n.* The religious and social system of the Hindus, a development of ancient Brahmanism with the accretion of Buddhistic and other elements, comprising a body of socio-religious practices, rites, beliefs, and doctrines, as of Karma, transmigration of soul, and veneration for the cow. Also *Hindooism.*

Hin·du·sta·ni, Hin·do·sta·ni, hin″du̇·stä′nē, hin″du̇·stan′ē, *n.* [Hind. and Pers. *Hindūstānī.*] One of the languages of Hindustan, orig. a dialect of Western Hindi spoken in and around Delhi, and later becoming current in other parts of India.— *a.* Of or pertaining to Hindustan, its people, or their language, esp. to the language called Hindustani.

hinge, hinj, *n.* [M.E. *heng, hing;* akin to E. *hang.*] The movable joint or device on which a door, gate, shutter, lid, or the like, turns or moves. A natural joint moving in only one plane, as the joint of the knee; also **hinge joint.** A central point, principle, or rule; a turning point or crisis; a type of gummed fastener used by stamp collectors to make postage stamps adhere in albums.— *v.t.*—**hinged, hinging.** To furnish with or attach by a hinge.—*v.i.* To hang or turn on, or as on, a hinge; to depend, usu. followed by *on.*

hin·ny, hin′ē, *n. pl.* **hin·nies.** [L. *hinnus.*] The offspring of a stallion and female donkey.

hint, hint, *n.* [Perhaps < O.E. *hente, hentan,* to seize; akin also Icel. *ymtr,* a muttering.] A suggestion; something insinuated rather than said; a clue; a small amount of something.—*v.t.* To suggest indirectly; to intimate.—*v.i.* To allude indirectly; to intimate: usu. followed by *at.*—**hint·er,** *n.*—**hint·ing·ly,** *adv.*

hin·ter·land, hin′tẽr·land″, *n.* [G. *hinter,* behind, back, and *land,* land.] Land lying behind a coastal district; country remote from urban centers; interior or back country.

hip, hip, *n.* [O.E. *hype* = Icel. *huppr,* Dan. *hofte,* Goth. *hups,* D. *heup,* G. *hufte;* akin to *heap,* perhaps to *hump.*] *Anat.* the side of the pelvis and upper region of the thigh with their fleshy covering parts; the haunch; the hip joint. *Arch.* the external angle at the junction of two sloping roofs or sides of a roof.—*v.t.*—**hipped, hipping.** To construct with a hip, as a roof.

hip, hip, *n.* [O.E. *heope.*] *Bot.* the ripe, fleshy fruit of the rose, esp. the wild rose.

hip, hip, *interj.* An exclamation used for a cheer, as: *Hip,* hip, hurrah!

hip, hip, *a. Slang.* Familiar with current trends and happenings; abreast of new ideas, styles, and fads; up-to-date; avant-garde; sophisticated; informed.

hip·bone, hip′bōn″, *n.* The innominate bone.

hip joint, *n.* The ball-and-socket joint between the hipbone and the femur.

hipped, hipt, *a.* Having hips; having hips of a particular kind, often in combination; as, wide-*hipped; arch.* constructed with a hip or hips, as a roof.

hipped, hipt, *a. Slang,* having a mental obsession; fanatically interested; as, *hipped* on modern art. *Brit. slang,* melancholy.

hip·pie, hip′ē, *n.* A young adult, usu. nonconformist in dress and behavior, and characterized esp. by pacifistic, anarchistic, anti-intellectual, or anti-establishment opinions or outlooks.

hip·po, hip′ō, *n. pl.* **hip·pos.** *Colloq.* hippopotamus.

hip·po·cam·pus, hip″o·kam′pus, *n. pl.* **hip·po·cam·pi,** hip″o·kam′pī. [L. < Gr. *hippokampos,* < *hippos,* horse, and *kampos,* sea monster.] *Class. myth.* a sea horse, a fish with two forefeet and a body ending in the tail of a dolphin; *zool.* a sea horse of the genus *Hippocampus;* *anat.* either of two ridges in each of the two large upper cavities in the interior of the brain.—**hip·po·cam·pal,** *a.*

hip·po·cras, hip′o·kras″, *n.* [Fr., lit. 'wine of *Hippocrates.*'] A medicinal cordial made of wine infused with spices.

Hip·po·crat·ic, hip″o·krat′ik, *a.* Pertaining to Hippocrates, a Greek physician, born 460 B.C.—**Hip·po·crat·ic oath,** a pledge embodying a code of ethics taken by those about to receive a degree in medicine.

hip·po·drome, hip′o·drōm″, *n.* [L. *hippodromos,* < Gr. *hippodromos,* < *hippos,* horse, and *dromos,* a running, course, race-course.] In ancient Greece and Rome, a course for horse races and chariot races; any arena or structure for equestrian and other displays, circuses, and the like.

hip·po·griff, hip·po·gryph, hip′o·grif″, *n.* [Fr. *hippogriffe,* < It. *ippogrifo,* < Gr. *hippos,* horse, and L. *gryphus,* griffin.] A mythological animal having the body and hind parts of a horse and the wings, claws, and head of a griffin.

hip·po·pot·a·mus, hip″o·pot′a·mus, *n. pl.* **hip·po·pot·a·mus·es, hip·po·pot·a·mi,** hip″o·pot′a·mī. [L. < Gr. *hippopotamos,* < *hippos,* horse and *potamos,* river.] A large herbivorous mammal, *Hippopotamus amphibius,* having a thick-skinned, hairless body, short legs, and large head and muzzle, found in and near the rivers and lakes of Africa, and able to remain under water for a considerable time.

hip roof, *n.* A type of roof with both sides and ends that slope.—**hip-roofed,** *a.*

hir·cine, hẽr′sīn, hẽr′sin, *a.* [L. *hircinus,* < *hircus,* a goat.] Pertaining to or resembling a goat; having a goatlike odor; lecherous.

hire, hīr, *v.t.* [O.E. *hȳr* = M.L.G. *hūre* = D. *huur* = G. *heuer,* hire.] To engage the services or labor of in exchange for payment; to obtain the temporary use of by paying; to grant the temporary use of or the services of for some compensation, often with *out.*—*v.i.* To engage oneself for a compensation, often with *out,* as: She *hired out* as a maid.—*n.* The price or compensation paid or contracted to be paid for the temporary use of something or for personal services or labor; the act of hiring or the fact of being hired.—**hir·er,** *n.*

hire·ling, hīr′ling, *n.* [O.E. *hȳrling.*] One serving for hire; a mercenary: used in contempt.—*a.* Serving or to be had for hire; venal; mercenary.

hire-pur·chase, hīr′pur′chas, *n. Brit.* buying on the installment plan. Also **hire-pur·chase sys·tem.**

hir·ing hall, *n.* A placement or employment office operated by a union for the benefit of its members.

hir·sute, hẽr′sōt, *a.* [L. *hirsutus,* shaggy.] Hairy; shaggy; of or relating to hair; *zool.* covered with long bristly hair; *bot.* having rather rough and coarse hairs.—**hir·sute·ness,** *n.*—**hir·su·tu·lous,** hẽr·sō′chu·lus, *a.* Slightly hirsute.

hi·run·dine, hi·run′din, hi·run′dīn, *a.* [L. *hirundo,* a swallow.] Swallowlike; pertaining to a swallow.

his, hiz, *pronominal a.* [In O.E. the genit. sing. of *hē,* he, and of *hit,* it.] The possessive case of the personal pronoun *he,* used as an attributive; as, *his* picture.—*pron.* Of or belonging to him: the possessive case of *he* used, instead of *his* and a noun, as subject, object, or predicate noun, as: *His* is the best, I read a book of *his.*

His·pan·ic, hi·span'ik, *a.* Spanish; pertaining to Latin America, Spain, and Portugal, their people, language, or culture. —**His·pan·i·cism,** *n.* A Spanish phrase or idiom.—**His·pan·i·cize,** *v.t.*—Hispanicized, Hispanicizing. To make Spanish, as in taste or style; to lead into Spanish influence.

his·pa·nism, his'pa·niz″um, *n.* (*Often cap.*) a Latin American movement directed toward promoting the Spanish language and culture.

his·pid, his'pid, *a.* [L. *hispidus,* rough, hairy.] *Biol.* Shaggy; bristly; covered with stiff bristles or spines.—**his·pid·i·ty,** his·pid'i·tē, *n.*—**his·pid·u·lous,** hi·spij'a·lus, *a. Biol.* having short bristly hairs.

hiss, his, *v.i.* [O.E. *hysian,* O.D. *hissen,* imit. of sound.] To make a sound like that of the letter *s,* as that of serpents or of water thrown on hot metal; to emit a similar sound in contempt or disapprobation.—*v.t.* To utter with a hissing sound; to condemn or express disapproval by hissing; to silence by uttering a hissing sound, often with *down* or *off.* —*n.* The sound made by propelling the breath between the tongue and upper teeth, as in pronouncing the letter *s,* especially as expressive of disapprobation; any similar sound.—**hiss·er,** *n.*

hist, hist, *interj.* A sibilant exclamation used to attract attention or command silence.

His·ta·drut, his·tä·drŏt′, *n.* [Heb.] The major trade union of Israel, established in 1920.

his·tam·i·nase, hi·stam'i·nās″, *n. Biochem.* an enzyme which deactivates a histamine, and therefore is used to treat certain allergies.

his·ta·mine, his'ta·mēn″, his'ta·min, *n.* [< (*hist*)*idine* and *amine.*] *Biochem.* an amine, found in the tissue of all plants and animals and released during allergic reactions, that dilates the capillaries, stimulates gastric secretion, and causes uterine contractions.—**his·ta·min·ic,** his″ta·min'ik, *a.*

his·to·gen·e·sis, his″to·jen'i·sis, *n. Biol.* the origin, development, and differentiation of tissues. Also **his·tog·e·ny,** his·toj'e·nē. —**his·to·ge·net·ic,** his″to·je·net'ik, *a.*— **his·to·ge·net·i·cal·ly,** *adv.*

his·to·gram, his'to·gram″, *n. Statistics,* a frequency distribution graph consisting of rectangles which correspond in width to class intervals and correspond in height to frequency values.

his·tol·o·gy, hi·stol'o·jē, *n. Biol.* the study of plant and animal tissues, esp. of their microscopic structures; the structure, esp. the microscopic structure, of a given tissue of an organism.—**his·to·log·ic,** his·to·· log′i·cal, his″to·loj′i·kal, *a.*—**his·to·log·· i·cal·ly,** *adv.*—**his·tol·o·gist,** *n.*

his·tol·y·sis, hi·stol'i·sis, *n. Biol.* the dissolution and breaking down of organic tissues.—**his·to·lyt·ic,** his″to·lit'ik, *a.*

his·tone, his'tōn, *n.* [Gr. *histos,* web, tissue.] *Biochem.* any of a class of protein substances, as globin, having marked basic properties and, on hydrolysis, yielding amino acids.

his·to·ri·an, hi·stōr'ē·an, hi·star'ē·an, *n.* A writer of history; an authority in history; one who compiles records or documents for a particular purpose; a chronicler.

his·tor·ic, hi·star'ik, hi·stor'ik, *a.* [L. *historicus,* < Gr. *historikos,* < *historia,* E. *history.*] Important or celebrated in history; memorable; historical.

his·tor·i·cal, hi·star'i·kal, hi·stor'i·kal, *a.* Of or pertaining to history; of the nature of or constituting history; following, or in accordance with history, esp. as opposed to legend or fiction; dealing with history; as, a *historical* work; using history as a basis; as, a *historical* novel; noted or celebrated in history; historic.—**his·tor·i·cal·ly,** *adv.* —**his·tor·i·cal·ness,** *n.*

his·tor·i·cal ma·te·ri·al·ism, *n.* The division of Marxist theory that deals with social history and causation. Compare *dialectical materialism.*

his·tor·i·cal pres·ent, *n. Gram.* the use of the present tense in an account of past actions.

his·tor·i·cal school, *n.* Any of several schools of thought which emphasize the importance of historical events and analysis in the study of law, economics, and related subjects.

his·to·ric·i·ty, his″to·ris'i·tē, *n.* Historical quality or authenticity based on fact.

his·to·ri·og·ra·pher, hi·stōr″ē·og′ra·fėr, hi·star″ē·og′ra·fėr, *n.* [L.L. *historiographus,* < Gr. *historiographos,* < *historia,* history, and *graphein,* write.] A historian, esp. an official historian, as of a public institution.—**his·to·ri·og·ra·phy,** *n.*— **his·to·ri·o·graph·ic, his·to·ri·o·graph·· i·cal,** *a.*—**his·to·ri·o·graph·i·cal·ly,** *adv.*

his·to·ry, his'to·rē, his'trē, *n. pl.* **his·to·· ries.** [L. *historia,* a history, < Gr. *historia,* a learning by inquiry, < *histor,* knowing, learned; same root as E. *wis, wit,* to know. *Story* is a short form of this.] That branch of knowledge which deals with events that have already taken place; the study or investigation of the past; a narrative or account, usu. chronological, of past events in the life of a nation, community, institution, or the like; the sum total of past happenings; anything that happened in the past; any past filled with unusual or memorable happenings; a drama dealing with past events; a story or tale.

his·tri·on·ic, his″trē·on'ik, *a.* [L. *histrionicus,* < *histrio,* an actor; same root as Skt. *has,* to laugh at.] Pertaining to actors or to acting; belonging to stage playing; theatrical; affected; melodramatic. Also **his·tri·· on·i·cal.**—**his·tri·on·i·cal·ly,** *adv.*

his·tri·on·ics, his″trē·on'iks, *n. pl., sing. or pl. in constr.* Dramatics or theatricals; affected behavior; an insincere display of emotion.

hit, hit, *v.t.*—hit, hitting. [O.E. *hyttan* = Icel. *hitta* = Sw. *hitta* = Dan. *hitte,* hit on, find.] To deal a blow to; to come against with an impact or collision; to reach with a missile, a weapon, a blow, or the like; as, to *hit* the mark; *baseball,* to strike, as a ball, with a bat; to drive or propel by a stroke; to reach or touch directly and effectively; as, to be *hit* by satire or innuendo; affect severely; as, to be badly *hit* in a financial panic; to succeed in representing, imitating, or producing exactly; as, to *hit* a likeness in a portrait; to conform to or suit exactly; as, to *hit* one's fancy. *Slang,* to attain or arrive at; as, to *hit* shore; to demand, as money, from; to be seen in; as, to *hit* the papers.—*v.i.* To deal a blow or blows; to strike with a missile or weapon; to come into collision, often with *against, on,* or *upon;* to come to light, with *upon* or *on;* as, to *hit on* a new way of doing something.—**hit it off,** to agree; get along with.—**hit or miss,** haphazard.

hit, hit, *n.* An impact, collision, or blow; any shot that reaches its objective; an effective remark or expression; a stroke of satire or censure, as: The letter contained severe *hits* at the administration. One who or that which is a noted success, as: His new album is a big *hit.* A stroke of good fortune; *backgammon,* a victory won by a player after his opponent has thrown off one or more men from the board; *baseball,* a base hit.

hit-and-run, hit'an·run', *a.* Designating or relating to the driver of an automobile who fails to stop or identify himself upon being involved in an accident; marked by quick action; as, a *hit-and-run* attack. *Baseball,* pertaining to a play in which the runner proceeds to the next base as the batter attempts to hit the ball.

hitch, hich, *v.t.* [Akin to Prov. E. *hick,* to hop or spring; G. dial. *hiksen,* to limp; Sc. *hotch,* to move by jerks, to hobble; Prov. E. *huck,* to shrug.] To fasten temporarily by a knot or hook; to harness or yoke, as a horse, to a vehicle, sometimes followed by *up;* to jerk or raise up; *slang,* to hitchhike; *colloq.* to marry.—*v.i.* To move jerkily or haltingly; to become entangled, caught, or hooked; to be linked or yoked; to hitchhike rides.—*n.* A sudden jerk, tug, or catch; a limp; an unexpected hindrance in plans; a device for attaching something temporarily; *naut.* a knot or noose in a rope for fastening it to an object. *Slang,* a period spent in military service; a ride or lift.—**hitch·er,** *n.*

hitch·hike, hich'hīk″, *v.i.*—hitchhiked, hitchhiking. To travel by signaling vehicles and obtaining free rides, often interspersed with stretches of walking.—*v.t.*—**hitch·· hik·er,** *n.*

hith·er, hiTH'ėr, *adv.* [O.E. *hider,* hither, Goth. *hidre,* Icel. *hethra,* hither.] To this place; here.—*a.* On this side or in this direction; nearer.—**hith·er and thith·er,** to this place and that; here and there.

hith·er·most, hiTH'ėr·mōst″, *a.* Closest to this place.

hith·er·to, hiTH'ėr·tō″, *adv.* To this time; until now. *Archaic,* to this place.

hith·er·ward, hiTH'ėr·wėrd, *adv.* Toward this place. Also **hith·er·wards.**

Hit·ler·ism, hit'ler·iz″um, *n.* The principles and practices of the Nazi party under Adolf Hitler.—**Hit·ler·ite,** hit'le·rīt″, *n.* One who adheres to Hitler's doctrines.—*a.* Referring to Hitler or Hitlerism.

Hit·tite, hit'īt, *n.* One of a powerful, civilized ancient people who flourished in Asia Minor and adjoining regions for about seven centuries before 1200 B.C. until subjugated by the Assyrians; a language of the Anatolian branch, used by the Hittites. —*a.* Referring to the Hittite people or their language.

hive, hīv, *n.* [O.E. *hȳf,* perhaps akin to Icel. *hūfr,* ship's hull, and L. *cupa,* tub, cask.] An artificial shelter for the habitation of a swarm of honeybees; a beehive; something resembling or suggesting this, as in structure, shape, or use; a place swarming with busy occupants; as, a *hive* of industry; the bees inhabiting a hive; a swarming or teeming multitude.—*v.t.*—hived, hiving. To gather into or cause to enter a hive, as bees; to shelter, as in a hive; to store up in a hive; to lay up for future use or enjoyment.—*v.i.* To enter a hive, as bees; to live together in the manner of bees; to dwell as in a hive.

hives, hīvz, *n. pl., sing. or pl. in constr.* [Perhaps akin to *heave.*] *Pathol.* a skin condition in which there is an eruption of itching wheals over the body; urticaria.

ho, hō, *interj.* An exclamation expressing surprise, exultation, or, when repeated, derisive laughter; a cry to attract attention.

hoar, hōr, *n.* [O.E. *hār,* hoary, grayhaired; Icel. *hārr,* hoar, *hœra,* gray hair, hoariness; cf. Sc. *haar,* a whitish mist.] Hoarfrost; an appearance of age or venerability.—*a. Archaic,* hoary.—**hoar·i·ness,** *n.*—**hoar·y,** *a.*—hoarier, hoariest. Gray or white as with age; of or pertaining to age or venerability; of a whitish or light gray color.

hoard, hōrd, *n.* [O.E. *hord* = O.E. and G. *hort,* Icel. *hood,* Goth. *huzd,* hoard, treasure; < root of *house*, and of L. *custos*, a guardian.] An accumulation of articles, money, or other valuables, preserved for future use, esp. when in quantities larger than ordinarily expected and in hidden stocks.—*v.t.* To collect and lay up in a hoard; to amass and preserve in secret.— *v.i.* To collect and form a hoard, as of money.—**hoard·er**, *n.*—**hoard·ing**, *n.* The act of accumulating, esp. secretly; *usu. pl.* that which is hoarded.

hoard·ing, hŏr′ding, *n.* [O.Fr. *horde*, a barrier.] *Brit.* A temporary enclosure around a building under construction or undergoing repairs; billboard.

hoar·frost, hŏr′frŏst″, hŏr′frŏst″, hȧr′frȯst″, hȧr′frŏst″, *n.* White frost; a coating of ice particles.

hoar·hound, hŏr′hound″, hȧr′hound″, *n.* Horehound.

hoarse, hŏrs, hȧrs, *a.* [O.E. *hās*, hoarse; husky = Icel. *hāss*, Dan. *haes*, D. *heesch*, G. *heiser*, hoarse: the *r* is intrusive.] Having a husky, harsh, rough, or grating voice, as when affected with a cold; sounding husky, harsh, or gruff.—**hoarse·ly**, *adv.*—**hoars·en**, *v.t.*, *v.i.* To make or to grow hoarse.— **hoarse·ness**, *n.*

ho·at·zin, hō·at′sin, wät′sin, *n.* A crested, olive-colored bird native to South America, genus *Opisthocomus*, noted for the claws which grow out of the wings of its young. Also **ho·ac·tzin**, hō·ak′tsin, wäk′tsin.

hoax, hŏks, *n.* [For *hocus*.] Something done for deception or mockery; a trick played upon another in sport or without malice; a practical joke.—*v.t.* To play a trick upon, for sport or for purposes of deception.—**hoax·er**, *n.*

hob, hob, *n.* [Origin obscure. Cf. *hub*.] A rounded peg or pin used as a target in certain games, as quoits; any of these games; a hobnail; a projection or shelf at the back or side of a fireplace; a tool or machine used for cutting gears and sprockets.

hob, hob, *n.* [From *Hob*, for *Robert*, or *Robin*, man's name.] A hobgoblin, elf, or sprite.—**to play hob, to raise hob**, *fig.* To cause mischief; create trouble or confusion.

hob, hob, *v.t.*—*hobbed, hobbing.* To provide with hobnails; *mach.* to cut with a hob.

Hobbes·i·an, hob′zē·an, *a.* Referring to the doctrines of Thomas Hobbes, an English philosopher, 1588–1679.—*n.* A follower of Thomas Hobbes or his doctrines.— **Hob·bism**, hob′iz·um, *n.*

hob·ble, hob′l, *v.i.*—*hobbled, hobbling.* [M.E. *hobelen* = D. *hobbelen*, toss, rock, stammer; a freq. form related to E. *hop*, and with sense in part affected by *hopple*.] To move unsteadily; wobble; to walk lamely; limp; *fig.* to proceed irregularly and haltingly, as in action or speech.—*v.t.* To cause to limp; to fasten together the legs of, as a horse or mule, so as to prevent free motion; to embarrass; impede; perplex.—*n.* The act or an act of hobbling; an uneven, halting gait; a limp; an awkward or difficult situation; a rope or strap used to hobble an animal; a fetter.

hob·ble·de·hoy, hob′l·dē·hoi″, *n.* An awkward, ungainly, adolescent boy.

hob·ble skirt, *n.* A woman's long narrow skirt so constricting below the knees that it interferes with normal walking.

hob·by, hob′ē, *n. pl.* **hob·bies.** An interesting activity carried on outside of a major occupation for mere pleasure or relaxation; avocation.

hob·by, hob′ē, *n. pl.* **hob·bies.** [Akin Fr. *hoberau*, dim. of O.Fr. *hobe*, a little bird of prey.] A small but strong-winged Old World falcon once used for hawking game.

hob·by-horse, hob′ē·hȧrs, *n.* A figure of a horse, or a stick with a horse's head, ridden

by children; a figure of a horse, supported about the waist of a performer in a morris dance or pantomime; a favorite occupation or frequent topic of interest.

hob·gob·lin, hob′gob″lin, *n.* [< *hob*, formerly a rustic, a clown, an elf; corruption of *Robin*, *Robert*.] A goblin; an elf; an imp; something causing dread or unreasonable fear.

hob·nail, hob′nāl″, *n.* [*hob*, a projection, and *nail*.] A nail with a thick strong head used for the soles of heavy boots and shoes; a decorative type of knob pattern on cloth materials or glassware.—**hob·nailed**, *a.* Set with hobnails; rough or rustic.

hob·nob, hob′nob″, *v.t.*—*hobnobbed, hobnobbing.* [Lit., 'have or not have, drink if it please you'—O.E. *habban*, to have, and *nabban*, for *ne habban*, not to have.] To associate amicably; to be on a familiar basis; to drink together sociably.

ho·bo, hō′bō, *n. pl.* **ho·boes, ho·bos.** A wanderer or vagrant, usually homeless and poor; a tramp; a migratory worker.— **ho·bo·ism**, *n.*

Hob·son's choice, *n.* [From Thomas *Hobson*, about 1544–1631, of England, who rented horses and insisted that each customer take the horse next to the stable door.] The choice of taking either the thing offered or nothing.

hock, hok, *n.* [M.E. *hoch, hogh, howh*, < O.E. *hōh*, heel.] The joint in the hind leg of the horse, ox, or similar animal corresponding to the ankle in man, but raised from the ground and thus appearing as if bent backward; the similar joint found in the same location in fowl.—*v.t.* To cripple or disable by cutting the tendons at the back of the knee; to hamstring.

hock, hok, *n.* Pawn; *slang*, prison.—*v.t. Slang*, to pawn.—**hock·er**, *n.*

hock, hok, *n.* [Shortened form of obs. *hockamore*, for *Hochheimer*.] *Chiefly Brit.* any white Rhine wine.

hock·ey, hok′ē, *n.* [< *hook*.] A game played on ice in which opposing teams, on skates, use long curved sticks to try to send a small disk, called a puck, into each other's goal; also **ice hock·ey.** A similar game played on a field with a ball rather than a puck; also **field hock·ey.**—**hock·ey stick,** a club curved at the lower end, used in the game of hockey to control the puck or ball.

ho·cus, hō′kus, *v.t.*—*hocused, hocusing, hocussed, hocussing.* [The *hocus* of *hocus-pocus*.] To cheat; to hoax or trick; to stupefy with drugs.

ho·cus-po·cus, hō′kus·pō′kus, *n.* [< juggler's jargon, simulating Latin.] A juggler's trick; sleight of hand; trickery or deception; a nonsense saying used to conjure or to cover up deception.—*v.t.*, *v.i.*—*hocus-pocused, hocus-pocusing, hocus-pocussed, hocus-pocussing.* To practice deception.

hod, hod, *n.* [North E. for *hold*.] A kind of trough or tray for carrying mortar and bricks to masons and bricklayers, fixed to the end of a pole, and carried on the shoulder.—**hod car·ri·er, hod·man,** one who carries bricks or mortar in a hod.

hodge·podge, hoj′poj″, *n.* [Corruption of *hotchpotch*.] A mixed mass; a jumble.

Hodg·kin's dis·ease, *n.* [From Dr. Thomas *Hodgkin*; 1798–1866, an English physician.] *Pathol.* a progressive disease marked by chronic inflammation and enlargement of the lymph nodes and other organs.

ho·dom·e·ter, hō·dom′i·tėr, *n.* Odometer.

hoe, hō, *n.* [O.Fr. Fr. *houe*; < Teut. (cf. G. *haue*), and akin to E. *hew*.] A long-handled farm or garden implement with a thin, flat blade usu. set transversely, and used for breaking up the surface of the ground or removing weeds; an implement used for mixing mortar, cement, or plastic.—*v.t.*

hoed, hoeing. To dig, scrape, weed, or cultivate with a hoe.—*v.i.* To work with a hoe.—**ho·er**, *n.*

hoe·cake, hō′kāk″, *n. Southern U.S.* a cake made with cornmeal, so called because orig. baked on a hoe.

hoe·down, hō′doun″, *n.* A dance featuring square and folk dances with hillbilly music; the music characteristic of such a dance.

hog, hag, hog, *n.* [M.E. *hog, hogge*; origin unknown.] A swine, esp. an adult domesticated swine raised for slaughter; a pig, boar, or other animal of the *Suidae* family; *fig.* a selfish, gluttonous, or filthy person.—*v.t.* —*hogged, hogging.* To arch, as the back, upward like that of a hog; to take more than one's share of; to cut, as a horse's mane, short.—*v.i.* To droop at both ends, as a ship.

ho·gan, hō′gan, hō′gan, *n.* [Navaho *qoghán*.] A Navaho Indian dwelling constructed of posts and sticks covered with earth.

hog·back, hag′bak″, hog′bak″, *n. Geol.* a sharply crested ridge of land formed by unequally eroded tilted layers of rock.

hog chol·er·a, *n. Veter. pathol.* a contagious, sometimes fatal disease affecting swine, caused by a filterable virus, and producing loss of appetite, emaciation, fever, and other symptoms.

hog·fish, hag′fish″, hog′fish″, *n. pl.* **hog·-fish, hog·fish·es.** Any of various fishes thought to resemble hogs in shape, as *Lachnolaimus maximus*, a crimson food fish; the pigfish, *Orthopristis chrysopterus*; the logperch, *Percina caprodes*.

hog·gish, hag′gish, hog′gish, *a.* Swinish; selfish; gluttonous; filthy.—**hog·gish·ly**, *adv.*—**hog·gish·ness**, *n.*

hog·nose, hag′nōz″, hog′nōz″, *n.* Any of the harmless American snakes constituting the genus *Heterodon*, notable for their hoglike snouts and their curious actions and contortions when disturbed. Also **hog·nose snake, hog·nosed snake.**

hog pea·nut, *n.* A twining plant, *Amphicarpa bracteata*, of the pea family, native to eastern U.S., bearing peanut-like fruits close to the ground or underground.

hogs·head, hagz′hed″, hogz′hed″, *n.* [Corrupted < D. *okshoofd*, Dan. *oxehoved*, the measure called a hogshead.] A large cask, esp. a cask containing from 63 to 140 gallons; a liquid measure of 63 gallons or 238.5 liters. Abbr. *hhd.*

hog·tie, hag′tī″, hog′tī″, *v.t.*—*hogtied, hogtying.* To tie together the four feet or both hands and feet of; render ineffective.

hog·wash, hag′wosh″, hag′wȧsh″, hog′-wosh″, hog′wȧsh″, *n.* Refuse or swill given to hogs. *Slang*, any worthless stuff; senseless, exaggerated talk or writing.

hoicks, hiks, hoiks, *interj.* [Origin unknown: cf. *yoicks*.] A cry used to incite hounds in hunting. Also **hoick.**—*v.t.*, *v.i.* To incite, as hounds, by the cry *hoicks.*

hoi·den, hoid′en, *n.*, *a.* Hoyden.

hoi pol·loi, hoi′ po·loi′. [Gr.] The many; the multitude: sometimes preceded erroneously by *the*, because *hoi* means 'the.'

hoist, hoist, *v.t.* To raise or lift, esp. by some mechanical appliance.—*n.* The act or an act of hoisting; a lift; an apparatus for hoisting; an elevator. *Brit.* a freight elevator. The vertical height of a sail or flag.—**hoist·er**, *n.*

hoi·ty-toi·ty, hoi′tē·toi′tē, *n.* [Cf. obs. or prov. *hoit*, indulge in riotous mirth.] Haughtiness; giddy behavior.—*a.* Assuming; haughty; giddy; flighty.

ho·kum, hō′kum, *n.* [< *hocus-pocus*.] Material introduced into a speech or drama to promote laughter or sentiment regardless of truth or falsity; nonsense; bunk.

Hol·arc·tic, hol·ärk′tik, hol·är′tik, hōl·-ärk′tik, hōl·är′tik, *a.* Pertaining to the

Palearctic and Nearctic, the two biogeographical regions of the Arctic.

hold, hōld, *v.t.*—*held, holding.* [O.E. *healdan* = Dan. *holde,* D. *houden,* Icel. *halda,* Goth. *haldan,* G. *halten,* to hold; hence *behold.*] To have or grasp in the hand; to bear, put, or keep in a certain position; as, to *hold* the hands up; to consider or regard, as: I *hold* him in honor. To contain or to have capacity to receive and contain; to retain within itself or to keep from running or flowing out; to keep or to be in possession of; to maintain, uphold, or preserve; set aside or reserve; to occupy, own, or keep; to have or to entertain; as, to *hold* enmity; to derive or deduce title to; as, to *hold* lands of the king; to stop, restrain, or withhold; to keep fixed, as to a certain line of action; to bind or oblige; as, to *hold* one to his promise; to keep in continuance or practice; to prosecute or pursue, as a course; to celebrate, solemnize, or carry out, as a meeting; to occupy or keep employed; to engage the attention of.—*v.i.* To take or keep a thing in one's grasp; to maintain an attachment; to continue firm; to adhere; to stand, be valid, or apply; as, the argument *holds* good; to stand one's ground; to refrain; to be dependent on for possessions; to derive right or title, with *of* or *from*; to stop, stay, or wait; remain faithful; remain in force or valid.—*impv.* To cease or give over.—**hold·a·ble,** *a.*—**hold back,** to check, withhold, retain.—**hold down,** to check, suppress.—**hold forth,** to speak in public; offer or extend.—**hold in,** to restrain, check, or repress.—**hold off,** to remain aloof; to keep from touching; to delay.—**hold on,** to continue, to maintain, to endure; to cling to; *Brit.* steady on!—**hold to·geth·er,** not to separate; remain united.—**hold wa·ter,** *fig.* to be logically sound or capable of standing investigation, as: This argument does not *hold water.*—**hold with,** to side or concur with; to support.

hold, hōld, *n.* The act of holding fast by a grasp of the hand or by some other physical means; as, to catch *hold;* something grasped for support; something to hold a thing by, as a handle; a nonphysical grasp,' control, controlling force, or dominating influence, as: The idea has a strong *hold* on the imagination. A receptacle for something; a holding or piece of property held; a prison or prison cell; *Brit.* a dwelling or habitation; *mus.* a fermata.

hold, hōld, *n.* [Var. of *hole.*] *Naut.* the interior of a ship below the deck, or below the lower deck, where the cargo is stowed. The baggage compartment of an airplane.

hold·er, hōl'dėr, *n.* One who or that which holds, esp. one who has the ownership, possession, or use of something; an occupant; a tenant; one in actual or constructive possession of a bill or note and legally entitled to receive payment thereon; something to hold a thing with; as, a pen*holder.*

hold·ing, hōl'ding, *n.* The act of one who or that which holds; tenure of land, esp. of a farm rented from another person; *often pl.* owned property of any kind, but esp. stocks and bonds. A business controlled by a holding company; *sports,* illegal interference with an opponent's actions.

hold·ing com·pa·ny, *n. Finance.* a company which owns sufficient stock in certain other companies to have effective control of them.

hold·out, hōld'out″, *n.* One who refuses to participate, as in a group or community program; *colloq.* a professional who delays signing a contract in the hope of obtaining some additional benefit.—**hold out,** *v.t.* To extend or stretch forth, as the hand; to propose or offer, as a business opportunity.

—*v.i.* To stand firm; to refuse to yield; to last or endure.

hold o·ver, *v.t.* To set aside or postpone for action or consideration at a future time.—*v.i.* To remain in office or in possession of land or the like after the expiration of a set time limit.—**hold·o·ver,** hōld'ō″vėr, *n. Colloq.* A person who remains in possession or in office beyond the regular term; something which remains behind from a former period; a lockup or cell for prisoners awaiting trial.

hold·up, hōld'up″, *n. Colloq.* a forcible stopping of a person or vehicle for the purpose of robbery; any proceeding likened to this, as an overcharge or extortion. A temporary halt in the progress of some activity.—**hold up,** *v.t.* To raise or keep in an erect position; to sustain or uphold; to show or exhibit; *colloq.* to halt and rob.—*v.i.* To endure; to remain undisturbed.

hole, hōl, *n.* [O.E. *hol,* hole, cave, den, orig. neut. of *hol,* = D. *hol* = G. *hohl* = Icel. *holr,* hollow; perhaps akin to O.E. *helan,* cover, hide.] A hollow place in a solid body or mass; a cavity; an excavation; an opening through anything; an aperture or perforation; an orifice; a gap or rent; a fault or flaw; the excavated habitation of an animal; a burrow; a small, dingy, or mean abode; a cell or dungeon; *colloq.* an embarrassing position or predicament; as, to find oneself in a *hole; sports,* a small cavity into which a marble, ball, or the like is to be played for a score in various games; a deep pond; a cove or small harbor.—*v.t.* —*holed, holing.* [O.E. *holian.*] To make a hole or holes in; make hollows or perforations in; sink, as a shaft; bore, as a tunnel; to putt or drive into a hole, as the ball in golf.—*v.i.* To make a hole or holes; to go into a hole; retire into a hole for the winter, as a hibernating animal, usu. with *up; golf,* to drive the ball into a hole, often with *out.* —**hole·y,** *a.*

hol·i·day, hol'i·dā″, *n.* A commemorative day of rest fixed by law or convention; a holy day; *pl., Brit.* a vacation or period of leave.—*a.* Pertaining to a joyous occasion or state of being.—*v.i. Brit.* to take a vacation, usu. with *at* or *in.*—**hol·i·day·er,** *n.* Vacationist.

ho·li·ly, hō'li·lē, *adv.* In a holy manner; piously or devoutly.

ho·li·ness, hō'lē·nis, *n.* The state or character of being holy; *(cap.)* with *His* or *Your,* a title of the Pope and formerly of other high ecclesiastical dignitaries.

ho·lism, hō'liz·um, *n. Philos.* the theory that a being has an identity other than and exceeding the total or sum of its parts.—**ho·list,** *n.*—**ho·lis·tic,** *a.*—**ho·lis·ti·cal·ly,** *adv.*

hol·land, hol'and, *n.* An unbleached, glazed or unglazed, linen or cotton textile used in the manufacture of upholstery, bookbindings, children's clothing, and, when heavily sized, window shades.

hol·lan·daise sauce, hol'an·dāz″ sạs, hol″an·dāz′ sạs, *n.* A lightly cooked sauce made with blended eggs, butter, vinegar or lemon juice, and seasonings to be served as a topping over such dishes as cooked broccoli, asparagus, and eggs Benedict.

Hol·lands, hol'andz, *n. pl. but sing. in constr.* A gin, first made in Holland, marked by the addition of juniper directly to the mash. Also **Hol·land gin.**

hol·ler, hol'ėr, *v.i. Colloq.* Complain loudly; cry out with surprise; shout to gain attention.—*v.t. Colloq.* To cry out, as: He *hollered* epithets after the runaway. To give verbal expression to, as an emotion. —*n. Colloq.* A loud wail or utterance of complaint or pain; a call to one out of normal hearing range; a loud cheer.

hol·lo, ho·lō', hol'ō, *interj.* A call to attract attention or express greeting; an exclamation of surprise, delight, or encouragement.

hol·low, hol'ō, *a.* [O.E. *holg, holh,* an empty space, < *hol,* a hole.] Containing an empty space within; having a vacant space within; not solid; concave; sunken; sounding as if reverberating from a cavity; deep or low; meaningless; not sincere or faithful; false; deceitful; hungry.—*n.* A depression or excavation below the general level or in the substance of anything; a cavity.—*v.t., v.i.* To make a hollow or cavity in, usu. with *out.*—**hol·low·ly,** *adv.*—**hol·low·ness,** *n.*

hol·low ware, *n.* Utensils or serving pieces made of glass, china, metal, and esp. silver; such pieces having some depth, as opposed to flatware.

hol·ly, hol'ē, *n. pl.* **hol·lies.** [M.E. *holi, holin,* < O.E. *holen, holegn,* holly; akin to D. and G. *hulst,* Fr. *houx,* holly.] Trees or shrubs of the genus *Ilex,* having handsome, glossy, spiny-toothed leaves and red berries; the foliage and berries, much used for Christmas decorations. See *ilex.*

hol·ly·hock, hol'ē·hok″, hol'ē·hạk″, *n.* [M.E. *holihoc,* < *holi,* holy, and *hoc,* mallow.] A tall, cultivated garden plant, *Althea rosea,* of the mallow family, a native of China, having coarse, wavy-edged leaves and spirelike spikes of showy, variously colored flowers.

Hol·ly·wood bed, *n.* A box spring and mattress on low legs or casters, without a footboard, and with or without a headboard.

holm, hōm, *n.* [O.E., L.G., G., and Dan. *holm,* a small island in a river; Sw. *holme,* Icel. *hólmr,* an island.] A river island; *Brit.* a low flat tract of rich land by the side of a river.

holm, hōm, *n.* [M.E. *holm,* for *holin,* holly.] *Brit.* the holly shrub or tree; the holm oak.

hol·mi·um, hōl'mē·um, *n. Chem.* a metallic element, one of the rare-earth series. Sym. Ho, at. no. 67, at. wt. 164.94.

hol·o·blas·tic, hol″o·blas′tik, hō″lo·blas′tik, *a. Biol.* pertaining to a fertilized ovum from which the embryo is formed by complete division or cleavage: opposed to *meroblastic.*—**ho·lo·blas·ti·cal·ly,** *adv.*

hol·o·caust, hol'o·kạst″, *n.* [L.L. *holocaustum,* < Gr. *holokauston,* neut. of *holokaustos,* burnt whole, < *holos,* whole, and *kaustos,* burnt, < *kaiein,* burn.] Vast or total destruction, usu. by fire; great loss of life and/or property by earthquake, flood, war, or otherwise. A sacrificial offering consumed by fire.—**hol·o·caus·tic,** *a.*

ho·lo·gram, hō'lo·gram, hol'o·gram, *n. Phys.* a three-dimensional image made by means of a laser beam.

hol·o·graph, hol'o·graf″, hol'o·gräf″, hō'lo·graf″, hō'lo·gräf″, *n.* A handwritten document, as a will, letter, or deed, which bears the signature of the author.—**hol·o·graph·ic, hol·o·graph·i·cal,** hol″o·graf'ik, *a.*

hol·o·he·dral, hol″o·hē′dral, hō″lo·hē′dral, *a. Crystal.* having the maximum planes or faces required for total symmetry.—**hol·o·he·drism,** *n.*—**hol·o·he·dron,** *n. pl.* **hol·o·he·drons, hol·o·he·dra.** A crystal or form with holohedral characteristics.

hol·o·phras·tic, hol″o·fras′tik, hō″lo·fras′tik, *a. Ling.* pertaining to or characterized by polysynthesism; expressing a whole phrase or sentence in a single word, as in the Eskimo language.

hol·o·phyt·ic, hol″o·fit′ik, hō″lo·fit′ik, *a. Bot.* autotrophic.

hol·o·type, hol'o·tīp″, hō'lo·tīp″, *n. Taxonomy,* a single animal or plant specimen selected by the discoverer for descriptive and taxonomical purposes to represent an entire species.—**hol·o·typ·ic,** hol″o·tip′ik, a.

hol·o·zo·ic, hol″o·zō′ik, hō″lo·zō′ik, a. Biol. assimilating solid organic food matter by ingestion, as most animals; heterotrophic.

Hol·stein, hōl′stīn, hōl′stēn, n. One of a breed of dairy cattle of large size, originating in North Holland and Friesland, having a white coat with jet black irregular patches. Also **Hol·stein-Frie·sian.**

hol·ster, hōl′stèr, n. [D. holster, a pistol case = O.E. hoolster, a cover.] A leather case for a pistol. usu. hung on a belt or saddle.

ho·ly, hō′lē, a.—holier, holiest. [O.E. hālig, holy, < hāl, whole; similarly D. and G. heilig, Icel. heilagr, Dan. hellig, holy; akin hale, heal, hallow, whole, etc., same root also in Gr. kalos, beautiful.] Consecrated to God; dedicated by religious authority; having qualities compelling worship and adoration; exalted by dedication to service of the church or of religion; saintly in character; awesome; of divine origin. —n. pl. ho·lies. A consecrated place.

Ho·ly Cit·y, n. A city held sacred by the adherents of a religion; heaven.

Ho·ly Com·mun·ion, n. The Eucharist; the act of receiving the consecrated element or elements of the Eucharist.

ho·ly day, n. A day appointed for religious observance, either as a feast or a fast.

Ho·ly Fa·ther, n. Rom. Cath. Ch. the Pope.

Ho·ly Ghost, n. The third person in the Trinity. Also Holy Spirit.

Ho·ly Grail, n. The chalice or cup used by Jesus Christ at the Last Supper; the goal of knightly pilgrimages; the object of any arduous quest. Also Grail.

Ho·ly Of·fice, n. The congregation of the Rom. Cath. Ch. concerned with the purity of dogma and the suppression of heresy. Also **Con·gre·ga·tion for the Doc·trine of the Faith.**

ho·ly of ho·lies, n. That portion of the Jewish tabernacle containing the Ark of the Covenant; any place of special sanctity.

ho·ly oil, n. Eccles. consecrated or sacramental oil, used in Greek, Latin, and Anglican rituals and sacraments; chrism.

ho·ly or·ders, n. Ordination; the clerical status of an ordained minister; the ranks of the Christian clergy.

Ho·ly Roll·er, n. A member of a religious sect whose services are noted for emotional religious expression; a humorous term for a religious fanatic.

Ho·ly Ro·man Em·pire, n. A loose confederation of western and central European states, ecclesiastically controlled by the Pope and existing as a political entity from 962 to 1806.

Ho·ly See, n. Rom. Cath. Ch. The See of Rome; the office or jurisdiction of the Pope; the papal court.

Ho·ly Spir·it, n. The third person in the Trinity. Also Holy Ghost.

ho·ly·stone, hō′lē·stōn″, n. A soft sandstone used by seamen for cleaning the decks of ships.—v.t.—holystoned, holystoning. To scrub with holystone.

Ho·ly Syn·od, n. The governing council of an Eastern Orthodox church.

Ho·ly Thurs·day, n. The Thursday preceding Easter; Maundy Thursday. Anglican Ch. Ascension Day.

ho·ly wa·ter, n. Eccles. water which has been blessed by a priest.

Ho·ly Week, n. The week preceding Easter.

Ho·ly Writ, n. Scriptures.

hom·age, hom′ij, om′ij, n. [O.Fr. homage (Fr. hommage), < M.L. hominaticum, homo (homin-), vassal, L. man.] Respect; an action showing respect. In feudal times, a vassal's formal acknowledgment of allegiance to his lord.—**hom·ag·er,** hom′a·jèr, om′a·jèr, n. One who owes or does homage; a vassal.

hom·bre, om′brä, om′brē, Sp. ạm′bRe, n. pl. **hom·bres,** om′bräz, om′brēz, Sp. ạm′bRes. [Sp. < L. homo, man.] Slang, a man.

hom·burg, hom′burg, n. A man's softcrowned felt hat, dented lengthwise, with an upturned brim.

home, hōm, n. [O.E. hām, home, dwelling = G. heim = Icel. heimr, abode, village = Goth. haims, village.] A dwelling or abode; a house or apartment that is the fixed residence of a person, a family, or a household; an accustomed or familiar neighborhood; one's native city, region, or country; the dwelling place of an animal; a region where something is native or common, as: Africa is the home of the ostrich. The habitat or seat; an institution for the care of the homeless, sick, infirm, or orphaned; in various games, the point which one tries to reach. Baseball, the plate at which the batter stands and toward which the pitcher delivers the ball; also **home plate.** Fig. heaven.—a. Of or connected with one's home; domestic; effective; to the point; being the headquarters; as, the home office.—adv. To or toward one's home or one's native country; to the point; to the mark aimed at; so as to produce an intended effect; as, to bring a lesson home to a person; effectively.—**at home,** in or about one's own familiar territory; conversant, familiar, or thoroughly acquainted; as, at home in a subject; at one's ease; as, to make oneself at home.—**home·less,** a. Lacking a home.—**home·less·ness,** n.

home, hōm, v.i.—homed, homing. To go or return home; to reside; to travel toward a target or airport, as a guided missile or plane.—v.t. To provide with a home; to send to a home; to direct toward a port, airport, or target, as a ship, plane, or missile, esp. by means of some automatic system of guidance.

home-and-home, hōm′and·hōm, a. Sports, pertaining to a series of games or contests scheduled by two teams, to take place in the city or in the sports facility of each opponent by turn.

home·bod·y, hōm′bod″ē, n. pl. **home·bod·ies.** A person whose main interest in life centers around the home; one who would rather remain at home.

home·bred, hōm′bred′, a. Originating at home; indigenous; lacking sophistication.

home·com·ing, hōm′kum″ing, n. A return to one's place of abode or home; a gathering of a group of people at an appointed time at a place which they once had frequented, as an annual celebration at high schools, colleges, and universities for returning alumni.

home e·co·nom·ics, n. The science of homemaking, including the study of nutrition, child care, clothing, budgeting, and the like. Also domestic science.

home front, n. The sector of civilian activity in a total war situation.

home·like, hōm′līk″, a. Having the characteristics of a home; warm, cozy, familiar.

home·ly, hōm′lē, a.—homelier, homeliest. Pertaining to home; unpretentious. Plain in appearance; unattractive.—**home·li·ness,** n.

home·made, hōm′mād′, a. Made at home; of domestic manufacture; of simple or crude design.

ho·me·op·a·thy, ho·moe·op·a·thy, hō″mē·op′a·thē, n. The system of treating disease by administering in minute quantities drugs which would, if given in larger doses to a healthy person, produce symptoms similar to those of the disease: opposed to allopathy.—**ho·me·o·path·ic,** a. **ho·me·o·path·i·cal·ly,** adv.—**ho·me·o·path, ho·me·op·a·thist,** n.

ho·me·o·sta·sis, hō″mē·o·stā′sis, n. Biol. the tendency of the physiological system of higher animals to maintain an environment of organic stability even when its natural function or condition has been disrupted. —**ho·me·o·stat·ic,** a.—**ho·me·o·stat·i·cal·ly,** adv.

ho·mer, hō′mèr, n. [Heb.] An ancient Hebrew unit of measure equiv. to about 100 gallons liquid measure or to about 11½ bushels dry measure.

hom·er, hō′mèr, n. Baseball, a home run.— v.i. Baseball, to hit a home run.

Ho·mer·ic, hō·mer′ik, a. Pertaining to the poet Homer; resembling Homer's verse or style; heroic.—**Ho·mer·i·cal·ly,** adv.

home rule, n. Government of a country, colony, city, or the like by the inhabitants themselves, esp. with regard to local matters.—**home rul·er,** one in favor of home rule.

home run, n. Baseball, a hit which, unaided by errors, allows the batter to circle the bases and return to home plate, scoring a run.

home·sick, hōm′sik″, a. Ill or depressed by a longing for home while absent from it.— **home·sick·ness,** n.

home·spun, hōm′spun″, a. Spun or made at home, as yarn or cloth; garments of such origin or character; plain or simple; unpolished or rude.—n. Cloth of a plain or simple weave made at home; cloth of similar appearance, commonly of loose texture, stout and durable.

home·stead, hōm′sted, hōm′stid, n. [O.E. hāmstede.] A home or dwelling, esp. a house with the ground and buildings immediately connected with it; law, a dwelling with its land and buildings, occupied by the owner as a home, and exempted by statute from seizure or forced sale for debt; land settled on under the Homestead Act.—v.i. To acquire or settle on a tract of land under the Homestead Act.—v.t. To settle on under the Homestead Act.—**Home·stead Act,** an act of Congress in 1862 allowing for the grant of a parcel of 160 acres of unappropriated public land in the West to a settler for development and eventual ownership.—**home·stead·er,** n.

home·stead law, n. Any law exempting home owners from seizure of property by creditors; also **home·stead ex·emp·tion law.** Any law granting or selling public land for settlement.

home·stretch, hōm′strech′, n. Horse racing, the section of a racecourse between the last curve and the finish; hence, the final phase of an activity or journey.

home·ward, hōm′wèrd, adv. Toward home; toward one's abode or native country. Also **home·wards.**—a. In the direction of home.

home·work, hōm′wurk″, n. Work to be done at home, esp. that assigned by a teacher to students.

home·y, hom·y, hō′mē, a.—homier, homiest. Informal, cozy, comfortable, as a home.—**home·y·ness, hom·i·ness,** n.

hom·i·ci·dal, hom″i·sīd′al, a. Pertaining to or involving homicide; as, a homicidal attack; inclined toward homicide; murderous.—**hom·i·ci·dal·ly,** adv.

hom·i·cide, hom′i·sīd″, n. [L. homicidium, the crime, homicida, the perpetrator— homo, man, and cœdo, to strike, to kill.] The killing of one human being by another, including acts of manslaughter, murder, accidental killing, and justifiable homicide; a person who kills another.

hom·i·let·ic, hom″i·let′ik, a. [Gr. homilētikos, < homilein, consort, converse, speak, < homilos, assembly.] Pertaining to preaching, sermons, or homilies; of or pertaining to homiletics. Also **hom·i·let·i·cal.**—**hom·i·let·i·cal·ly,** adv.—**hom·i·let·ics,** n. pl. but sing. in constr. The art of preaching; the branch of practical theology concerned with preparing and delivering sermons.

hom·i·ly, hom'i·lē, *n. pl.* **hom·i·lies.** [Gr. *homilia*, intercourse or conversation, instruction, a sermon, < *homilos*, a throng.] A religious discourse or sermon read or addressed to an audience; an admonitory discourse on moral or upright behavior.

hom·ing, hōm'ing, *a.* Coming home; in the direction of home or some specified point; as, a *homing* instinct.

hom·ing de·vice, *n. Aerospace*, any device used for homing aircraft; any device incorporated in a guided missile or the like to home it on target.

hom·ing pi·geon, *n.* A pigeon, frequently used for carrying messages, bred and trained to return home from great distances. Also **hom·er.**

hom·i·nid, hom'i·nid, *n. Anthropol.* any member of the family *Hominidae*, made up of modern man, his ancestors, and related extinct species. Also **ho·min·i·an, hom·o·nid.**—*a.*

hom·i·noid, hom'i·noid", *n. Zool.* any member of the superfamily *Hominoidea*, consisting of the great apes and man.—*a.* Pertaining to the superfamily *Hominoidea*; resembling man.

hom·i·ny, hom'i·nē, *n.* Corn hulled and sometimes coarsely ground, prepared for food by being boiled in water or milk.

hom·i·ny grits, *n. pl., sing. or pl. in constr.* Evenly-ground hominy, popular in southeastern U.S., and often used as a breakfast food.

Ho·mo, hō'mō, *n.* [L., man.] *Zool.* a genus of the order *Primates*, which includes all races of modern man, *Homo sapiens*, and various extinct species.

ho·mo·cer·cal, hō"mō·sur'kal, *a.* [Gr. *homos*, same, *kerkos*, tail.] *Ichthyol.* Having the lobes of the tail fin of equal size, as the cod or herring; denoting such a tail fin.

ho·mo·chro·mat·ic, hō"mō·krō·mat'ik, hō"mo·krō·mat'ik, hom"o·kro·mat'ik, *a.* Monochromatic; relating to or having one hue.

ho·moe·cious, hō·mē'shus, ho·mē'shus, *a. Biol.* of a parasite, spending its entire life on the same host.

ho·mo·e·rot·ic, hō"mō·i·rot'ik, *a.* Pertaining to erotic attraction to members of the same sex.—**ho·mo·e·rot·i·cism**, hō"mō·i·rot'i·siz"um, *n.*

ho·mog·a·mous, hō·mog'a·mus, *a.* [Gr. *homos*, same, and *gamos*, marriage.] *Bot.* Having flowers that are sexually alike; of a flower, having stamens and pistils maturing simultaneously, resulting in interbreeding. —**ho·mog·a·my**, *n.*

ho·mo·ge·ne·i·ty, hō"mo·je·nē'i·tē, hom"o·je·nē'i·tē, *n.* The state or quality of having like characteristics or uniformity of nature, composition, or structure.

ho·mo·ge·ne·ous, hō"mo·jē'nē·us, hō"mo·jēn'yus, hom"o·jē'nē·us, hom"o·jēn'yus, *a.* [M.L. *homogeneus*, < Gr. *homogenēs*, < *homos*, same, and *genos*, race, kind.] Of the same kind or nature; essentially alike; uniform in structure; similar; congruous; composed of parts all of the same kind; not heterogeneous. *Math.* of the same kind and commensurable; of the same degree or dimensions.—**ho·mo·ge·ne·ous func·tion**, *math.* a polynomial in two or more variables, all the terms being of the same degree.—**ho·mo·ge·ne·ous·ly**, *adv.*—**ho·mo·ge·ne·ous·ness**, *n.*

ho·mo·gen·e·sis, hō"mo·jen'i·sis, hom"o·jen'i·sis, *n. Biol.* the ordinary course of generation, in which the offspring is like the parents and runs through the same cycle of development.—**ho·mo·ge·net·ic**, hō"mo·je·net'ik, hom"o·je·net'ik, *a. Biol.* Pertaining to homogenesis; having a

common origin; derived from the same structure, however modified.

ho·mog·e·nize, ho·moj'e·nīz", hō·moj'e·nīz", *v.t.*—*homogenized, homogenizing.* To make homogeneous; to form by mixing and emulsifying; as, *homogenized* milk.— **ho·mog·e·ni·za·tion**, *n.*—**ho·mog·e·niz·er**, *n.*

ho·mog·e·nous, ho·moj'e·nus, hō·moj'e·nus, *a.* [Gr. *homogenēs.*] *Biol.* of organs or the like, corresponding in structure because of a common origin.—**ho·mog·e·ny**, *n.*

ho·mog·o·nous, ho·mog'o·nus, hō·mog'o·nus, *a.* [Gr. *homos*, same, and *gonos*, offspring, generation.] *Bot.* pertaining to a type of flower with equally long stamens and pistils: opposed to *heterogonous.*—**ho·mog·o·ny**, *n.*

ho·mo·graft, hō'mo·graft", hō"mo·gräft", hom'o·graft", hom'o·gräft", *n. Surg.* an organ or tissue removed from an individual and grafted to another of the same species: opposed to *heterograft.*

hom·o·graph, hom'o·graf", hom'o·gräf", *n.* A word which has exactly the same form as another, although it may have a different origin, meaning, or pronunciation as *wound*, an injury, and *wound*, coiled.—**hom·o·graph·ic**, hom"o·graf'ik, *a.*

Ho·mo hab·i·lis, hō"mō hab'i·lis, *n.* [Named in 1964 by Louis S. B. Leaky, Brit. anthropologist.] The earliest true man, a species of prehistoric man believed to have lived two billion years ago, and whose remains have been found in Tanzania, Africa.

ho·moi·o·ther·mal, hō·moi"o·thur'mal, *a. Zool.* Having or preserving a relatively constant body temperature independent of the surroundings; of or denoting a warm-blooded animal: opposed to *poikilothermal.* Also **ho·moi·o·ther·mic.**—**ho·moi·o·therm**, hō·moi'o·thurm", *n. Zool.* a homoiothermal organism.—**ho·moi·o·ther·my**, *n.*

Ho·moi·ou·si·an, hō"moi·ö'sē·an, hō"moi·ou'sē·an, *n. Theol.* an adherent of a 4th-century church party which asserted that the essence of the Son is similar to, but not the same as, that of the Father. —*a.*—**Ho·moi·ou·si·an·ism**, *n.*

ho·mol·o·gate, ho·mol'o·gāt", hō·mol'o·gāt", *v.t.*—*homologated, homologating.* [L.L. *homologo, homologatum*, < Gr. *homos*, same, and *logos*, discourse, *legō*, to speak.] To approve; to sanction; to ratify.—**ho·mol·o·ga·tion**, *n.*

ho·mol·o·gous, ho·mol'o·gus, hō·mol'o·gus, *a.* Related or similar in structure, nature, position, or value; *biol.* alike in origin and structure; *chem.* referring to a chemical series in which each successive compound has the same structure but differs slightly from the last by a regular increase in molecular weight; *med.* pertaining to a bacterium and its relationship to the serum derived from it.—**ho·mo·log·i·cal**, hō"mo·loj'i·kal, *a.*—**ho·mol·o·gize**, ho·mol'o·jīz", hō·mol'o·jīz", *v.i., v.t.* —**hom·o·logue**, hom'o·lag", hom'o·log", *n.*

ho·mol·o·gy, ho·mol'o·jē, hō·mol'o·jē, *n.* The state of being homologous; sameness of relation; correspondence, or an instance of correspondence; *biol.* homologous relation or correspondence.

ho·mol·o·sine pro·jec·tion, ho·mol'o·sin pro·jek'shan, ho·mol'o·sīn", hō·mol'o·sin, hō·mol'o·sīn", *n. Cartography*, an equal-area projection of the earth's surface with most distortion confined to ocean areas so that the continents can be shown with the least distortion possible.

ho·mo·mor·phic, hō"mo·mar'fik, hom"o·mar'fik, *a.* [Gr. *homos*, same, and *morphē*, shape.] *Biol.* having the same external appearance or form; *bot.* having perfect flowers of only one variety; *entom.* having a

similarity of form between the larval and adult stages.—**ho·mo·mor·phism, ho·mo·mor·phy**, *n.*—**ho·mo·mor·phous**, *a.*

hom·o·nym, hom'o·nim, *n.* A word spelled and pronounced like another, but differing in meaning, as *point*, a score, and *point*, to indicate; a word both homophonic and homographic with another; *biol.* a word selected to designate a certain genus or species, then rejected because it has already been used for a different genus or species. —**hom·o·nym·ic**, *a.*

ho·mon·y·mous, ho·mon'i·mus, hō·mon'i·mus, *a.* Having the same sound and spelling; homonymic. *Pathol.* denoting a type of double vision.—**ho·mon·y·my**, *n.*

Ho·mo·ou·si·an, hō"mō·ö'sē·an, hō"mō·ou'sē·an, *n. Theol.* a believer in an early Christian doctrine maintaining that the natures of the Son and God the Father are identical and consubstantial.—*a.*—**Ho·mo·ou·si·an·ism**, *n.*

hom·o·phone, hom'o·fōn", hō"mo·fōn" *n.* [Gr. *homos*, same, *phōnē*, sound.] A word of like sound with another but having different spelling, meaning, and derivation, as *right* and *write*; see *homonym.*—**ho·moph·o·nous**, ho·mof'o·nus, *a.*

hom·o·phon·ic, hom"o·fon'ik, hō"mo·fon'ik, *a.* [Gr. *homophōnia*, unison < *homophōnos.*] Alike in sound; *mus.* having one part or melody predominating.—**ho·moph·o·ny**, ho·mof'o·nē, *n.* The quality of being homophonic; homophonic music.

ho·mop·ter·ous, ho·mop'tĕr·us, hō·mop'tĕr·us, *a. Zool.* pertaining or relating to the *Homoptera* order of insects usu. having two pairs of wings and sucking mouth parts, as cicadas and aphids.—**ho·mop·ter·an**, *a., n.*

Ho·mo sa·pi·ens, hō'mō sā'pē·enz, *n.* The single surviving species of human evolutionary development, modern man, belonging to the genus *Homo* and the primate family *Hominidae.*

ho·mo·sex·u·al, hō"mo·sek'shö·al, hō"mō·sek'shö·al, *n.* One who is characterized by a sexual interest in a person of the same sex.—*a.*—**ho·mo·sex·u·al·i·ty**, hō"mo·sek"shö·al'i·tē, hō"mō·sek"shö·al'i·tē, *n.*

ho·mos·po·rous, ho·mos'pĕr·us, hō"mo·spōr'us, hō"mo·spar'us, *a. Bot.* having only one kind of spore, as distinguished from *heterosporous.*—**ho·mos·po·ry**, ho·mos'po·rē, hō·mos'po·rē, *n.*

ho·mo·tax·is, hō"mo·tak'sis, hom"o·tak'sis, *n.* [N.L. < Gr. *homos*, same, and *taxis*, arrangement.] Similarity of arrangement, as of geological strata which, though not necessarily contemporaneous, have the same relative position.—**ho·mo·tax·i·al, ho·mo·tax·ic**, *a.*—**ho·mo·tax·i·al·ly**, *adv.*

ho·mo·type, hō'mo·tīp", hom'o·tīp", *n. Biol.* That which has the same type of structure as something else; specif., any of two or more serially homologous parts or organs in an animal.—**ho·mo·typ·al, ho·mo·typ·ic**, hō"mo·tip'ik, hom"o·tip'ik, *a.*

ho·mo·zy·gote, hō"mo·zī'gōt, hō"mo·zig'ōt, hom"o·zī'gōt, hom"o·zig'ōt, *n. Genetics*, an animal or plant which breeds true to type, having inherited a pair of genes identical with respect to a characteristic.— **ho·mo·zy·gous**, *a.*

ho·mun·cu·lus, hō·mung'kū·lus, hō·mung'kya·lus, *n. pl.* **ho·mun·cu·li**, hō·mung'kū·li, hō·mung'kya·li. [L. dim. of *homo*, man.] Anciently, a belief in a miniature human body supposed to be found in the sperm and ovum; a little man; a dwarf; a human fetus.

hom·y, hō'mē, *a.*—*homier, homiest.* Homey.

Hon·du·ran, hon·dur'an, hon·dūr'an, *a.* Relating to Honduras, a republic in northeastern Central America.—*n.*

hone, hōn, n. [O.E. *hān,* Icel. *hein,* Sw. *hen,* a hone.] A stone used for sharpening instruments; a precision instrument for making and smoothing holes in metal parts. —*v.t.* To sharpen on a hone; *fig.* to smooth or finish as though with a sharpened edge; as, to *hone* a skill.

hone, hōn, *v.i.*—*honed, honing.* [Fr. *hogner,* O.Fr. *hoignier, vuingnier,* grumble, growl.] *Southern U.S.* To grumble or moan; to pine or yearn for.

hon·est, on'ist, *a.* [O.Fr. *honeste* (Fr. *honnête*), < L. *honestus,* honorable, respectable, worthy, virtuous, decent, < *honor, honos,* E. honor.] Without deceit or fraud; honorable in principles, intentions, and actions, as persons; not inclined to lie, cheat, or steal; showing uprightness, straightforwardness, or fairness; as, *honest* actions; gained by fair means; as, an *honest* penny; truthful or sincere, as persons, utterances, or feelings; frank, open, or without disguise; as, *honest* opposition; genuine or unadulterated, as commodities; respectable or reputable; estimable or worthy; as, these *honest* fellows.—**hon·-est·ly,** *adv.*—**hon·est·ness,** *n.*

hon·es·ty, on'i·stē, *n.* pl. **hon·es·ties.** [O.Fr. *honeste,* < L. *honestas.*] The quality or fact of being honest; uprightness, probity, or integrity; freedom from deceit or fraud; truthfulness, sincerity, or frankness. *Bot.* an herb of the mustard family, *Lunaria annua,* with purple flowers and semitransparent, satiny pods; also **sat·in-flow·er.**

hon·ey, hun'ē, *n.* pl. **hon·eys.** [O.E. *hunig* = D. and G. *honig* = Icel. *hunang* = Sw. *honung* = Dan. *honning,* honey.] A sweet, viscid fluid made by bees from the nectar collected from flowers, and stored in their nests or hives as food; any of various similar products produced by insects or in other ways; *fig.* sweetness, or something sweet, delicious, or delightful; as, the *honey* of His flattery; sweet one, a term of endearment.— *a.* Of or like honey; sweet; dear.—*v.t.*—*honeyed, honied, honeying.* To sweeten with or as with honey; to talk sweetly to; flatter. —*v.i.* To coax with flattery, usu. with *up.*—**hon·ey·ful, hon·ey·less, hon·ey·-like,** *a.*

hon·ey·bee, hun'ē·bē″, *n.* A bee that produces and stores honey, esp. *Apis mellifera.*

hon·ey·comb, hun'ē·kōm″, *n.* [O.E. *hunig-camb.*] A structure of wax containing rows of hexagonal cells formed by bees for the purpose of storing honey and their eggs; something resembling this; the reticulum of a ruminant.—*a.* Having the structure or appearance of a honeycomb; as, the *honeycomb* coral.—*v.t.* To pierce with many holes or cavities; as, a rock *honeycombed* with holes; *fig.* to penetrate in all parts; as, a city *honeycombed* with vice.

hon·ey·dew, hun'ē·dō″, hun'ē·dū″, *n.* A sweet saccharine substance exuded in dew-like drops in warm weather by the leaves of trees and other plants.

hon·ey·dew mel·on, *n.* A very sweet muskmelon with a white, smooth skin and delicate light-green pulp.

hon·ey eat·er, *n.* Any of numerous singing birds, belonging to the *Meliphagidae* family in Australia, capable of extracting nectar from flowers.

hon·ey guide, *n.* Any of numerous small birds belonging to the *Indicatoridæ* family found in Africa and Asia, noted particularly for directing human beings and animals to honeybee nests in order to obtain the honey and wax.

hon·ey lo·cust, *n.* A broad graceful N. Amer. tree, *Gleditsia triacanthos,* in the pea or legume family, usu. with large, conspicuous branched spines on trunk and branches and featherlike or lacy foliage, and bearing large pod fruits containing sweet pulp between the seeds.

hon·ey·moon, hun'ē·mön″, *n.* The first month, more or less, after marriage; a holiday spent by a newly married couple in traveling or visiting; the beginning period, generally harmonious, of any new position or venture.—*v.i.* To spend or have a honeymoon.—**hon·ey·moon·er,** *n.*

hon·ey·suck·le, hun'ē·suk″el, *n.* [O.E. *hunisūce,* privet, lit. 'honey-suck.'] Any of the upright or climbing shrubs belonging to the genus *Lonicera,* in the honeysuckle family, some of which are ornamental and cultivated for their fragrant, nectar-filled flowers; any of various other fragrant or ornamental plants.—**hon·ey·suck·led,** *a.*

hong, hong, *n.* [Chin.] In China, a succession of rooms or buildings forming a warehouse or factory; one of the foreign factories formerly maintained at Canton.

honk, hongk, hangk, *n.* [Imit.] The cry of a goose; any similar sound, as of an auto horn. —*v.t., v.i.*

honk·y-tonk, hong'kē·tongk″, hang'kē·-tangk″, *n.* [Origin uncertain.] *Slang.* A cheap, low-class bar or night club; the style of music played in such places, usu. on a piano with a distinctive tinny sound.—*a.*

hon·or, *Brit.* **hon·our,** on'ėr, *n.* [M.E. *onur, honour, honor,* < O.Fr. *onur, onor, honur, honor* (Fr. *honneur*), < L. *honor, honos,* honor, repute, official dignity, mark of honor, ornament.] High public esteem, credit, fame, or glory; as, a roll of *honor;* an exemplary sense of personal moral standards and conduct; as, a man of *honor;* high respect, as for worth or rank; such respect manifested; as, to be received with *honor;* a source or cause of credit or distinction; as, to be an *honor* to one's family; a special privilege or favor; chastity or purity in a woman; (*usu. cap.*) a deferential title, as for judges or mayors, preceded by *Your* or *His. Pl.* courtesies or civilities; as, to do the *honors* in serving as host; distinction or rank awarded for special proficiency in scholarship; as, to win university *honors;* a course of advanced study for very able students. *Bridge,* the ace, king, queen, jack, or ten of the trump suit or, in a no-trump hand, any of the four aces. *Golf,* the right to tee off first.—*v.t.* To hold in honor or high respect; to show respect to; treat with honor; to confer honor or distinction upon; to accept and pay when due, as a bill; to carry out or fulfill, as a promise.—**do hon·or to,** show honor or respect to; be a source of honor to.—**hon·or·er,** *n.*

hon·or·a·ble, *Brit.* **hon·our·a·ble,** on'ėr·a·bl, *a.* Worthy of being honored; illustrious or noble; motivated by principles of honor; conferring honor; consistent with honor or impeccable reputation; upright and laudable; regarded with esteem; accompanied with marks or testimonies of esteem. (*Cap.*) a title of distinction applied to certain members of noble families or persons in certain government positions; abbr. *Hon.*—**hon·or·a·ble·ness, hon·or·-a·bil·i·ty,** *n.*—**hon·or·a·bly,** *adv.*

hon·o·rar·i·um, ·on″o·râr′ē·um, *n.* pl. **hon·o·rar·i·ums, hon·o·rar·i·a,** on″o·râr′ē·a. [L.] A payment or reward given in recognition for services performed for which established practice or propriety discourages charging a fixed fee.

hon·or·ar·y, on′o·rer″ē, *a.* [L. *honorarius.*] Bestowed in honor; indicative of honor or distinction; intended merely to confer honor; as, an *honorary* degree; possessing a title or post without performing services or receiving benefit or reward; as, *honorary* secretary; trusting one's honor for payment or fulfillment, as of obligations or debts.— *n. Archaic,* an honorary degree or one who receives it; an honorary society.—**hon·or·-ar·i·ly,** *adv.*

hon·or·if·ic, on″o·rif′ik, *a.* [L. *honorificus.*] Granting or bestowing honor; expressing respect, as a title or grammatical form, in speaking about or addressing one of superior position. Also **hon·or·if·i·cal.**—*n.* Any title, word, phrase, or term of respect.— **hon·or·if·i·cal·ly,** *adv.*

hon·ors of war, *n. pl.* Certain courtesies or privileges that may be accorded a defeated military force.

hon·or sys·tem, *n.* A system of management, as in schools or penal institutions, whereby obedience to rules and the performance of duty generally are sought by making persons responsible for their own conduct, rather than by using special guards and penalties.

hooch, höch, *n.* [Short for *hoochinoo,* orig. the name (for *Hutsnuwu,* lit. 'grizzly bear fort') of an Indian tribe on Admiralty Island, Alaska, who made liquor.] *Slang,* alcoholic beverages, esp. when illicitly distilled or obtained.

hood, hụd, *n.* [O.E. *hōd* = D. *hoed,* G. *hut,* a hat; allied to D. *heed;* G. *hut,* D. *hoeden,* to protect; Skt. *chad,* to cover.] A soft covering of fabric for the head and neck; a cowl; anything that resembles a hood in form or in use, as the sepal or petal of some flowers or the crest distinguishing certain birds; an ornamental fold at the back of an academic gown or ecclesiastical robe; a covering for mechanical parts, as the *hood* over an automobile's engine; condition, state, or quality: used in combination; as *mother*hood, false*hood,* hardi*hood; falconry,* the cover for the hawk's head.—*v.t.*—**hood·like,** *a.*

hood, hụd, höd, *n. Slang,* hoodlum.

hood·ed, hụd′id, *a.* Having or covered with a hood; hood-shaped. *Zool.* having on the head a hoodlike formation, crest, arrangement of colors, or the like. *Bot.* hood-shaped, as certain petals, sepals, and leaves; also *cucullate.*—**hood·ed·ness,** *n.*

hood·lum, höd′lum, hụd′lum, *n.* A thug or gangster; a young rowdy; a destructive person.

hoo·doo, hö′dö, *n.* [Akin to voodoo.] Something which brings misfortune; a jinx. —*v.t.* To bring bad luck to.—**hoo·doo·ism,** *n.*

hood·wink, hụd′wingk″, *v.t.* To deceive; to take advantage of; to cheat.—**hood·wink·-er,** *n.*

hoo·ey, hö′ē, *n., interj. Slang,* nonsense.

hoof, hụf, höf, *n.* pl. **hoofs, hooves.** [O.E. *hōf* = D. *hoef* = G. *huf* = Icel. *hōfr,* hoof.] The horny covering protecting the ends of the digits or encasing the foot in certain animals; the foot of a hoofed animal, as the horse; *slang,* the human foot.—*v.i. Slang.* To travel on foot, usu. with *it;* to dance.—*v.t.* To kick, eject, trample.—**on the hoof,** alive; not butchered.

hoofed, hụft, höft, *a.* Having hoofs; ungulate.

hoof·er, hụf′ėr, hö′fėr, *n. Slang,* one who dances professionally.

hook, hụk, *n.* [O.E. *hōc,* hook, = D. *hoek,* hook, angle, corner, point of land.] A curved piece of metal or other firm material adapted to catch, hold, cut, or pull something, as a fishhook or sickle; something bent like a hook; *sports,* a mid-flight change in the direction of a ball hit, as in golf, or thrown, as in baseball and bowling; *boxing,* a short blow struck from the side.— **by hook or by crook,** by any means, fair or foul.—**hook and eye,** a fastening for garments.—**hook and lad·der truck,** a fire engine.—**on one's own hook,** on one's own account or responsibility; by one's own effort.—**off the hook,** released from a difficulty, responsibility, or obligation.

hook, hŭk, *v.t.* To fasten or catch hold of and lift or draw, as with a hook; *fig.* to secure by artifice. To use a hooked implement in making, as a rug; of a horned animal, to catch on, or attack with, the horns; to strike with a swinging stroke, as in various sports. *Slang,* to seize by stealth; pilfer; steal.—*v.i.* To curve or bend like a hook; to move with a sudden turn; to become attached or fastened by a hook.

hook·ah, hook·a, *n.* [Ar.] An Oriental tobacco pipe with a long pliable tube and water vase so constructed that the smoke is cooled as it passes through the water. Also *hubble-bubble, water pipe.*

hooked, hŭkt, *a.* Shaped like a hook; having one or more hooks; made using a hook; made by a process called hooking, as a rug; *slang,* addicted to the use of habit-forming drugs.—**hook·ed·ness,** *n.*

hook·er, hŭk′ẽr, *n. Slang.* A prostitute; a generous drink of liquor.

hook·up, hŭk′up″, *n. Electron.* a diagram of a radio or other apparatus, showing the arrangement and connection of the different elements; the apparatus. *Aeron.* the contact made by an aircraft in flight with the hose of a tanker aircraft for refueling purposes. *Colloq.* any alliance, cooperation, or relationship, as between persons, factions, or countries.

hook·worm, hŭk′wŭrm″, *n.* Any of certain bloodsucking nematode worms equipped with mouth hooks, which feed off of the lining of the intestine of men and animals, often causing a disease characterized by severe anemia.

hook·y, hŭk′ē, *n. Colloq.* An absence from school without justification; truancy: used mainly in the phrase *to play hooky.*

hoo·li·gan, hō′li·gan, *n.* [Irish surname.] A street ruffian or hoodlum.—*a.*—**hoo·li·gan·ism,** *n.*

hoop, hōp, hŭp, *n.* [Late O.E. *hōp* = O. Fries. *hōp* = D. *hoep,* hoop.] A circular band or ring of metal, wood, or other stiff material, used to hold together the staves of a cask, barrel, or the like; a large ring of metal, plastic, or wood for a ⌐child to use in play; a circular band of metal or plastic used to expand a woman's skirt; a hoop-like or ringlike structure; the band of a finger ring; an iron arch used in croquet; a wicket.—*v.t.* To bind or fasten with a hoop or hoops; to encircle.—**hoop·er,** *n.*—**hooped, hoop·like,** *a.*

hoop·la, hōp′lä, *n. Slang.* Lively and loud excitement; statements made for the purpose of confusing an issue.

hoop skirt, *n.* A bellshaped skirt made to stand out by a framework of light, flexible hoops.

hoo·ray, hu·rā′, *interj., v.i., n.* Hurrah.

hoose·gow, hoos·gow, hōs′gou, *n.* [Sp. *juzgado,* a court.] *Slang.* A place of confinement; a jail; a prison.

Hoo·sier, hō′zhẽr, *n.* A person from the state of Indiana, which is nicknamed the *Hoosier State.*

hoot, hōt, *v.i.* [M.E. *huten, hoten;* prob. imit.] To cry out or shout, esp. in disapproval or derision; of an owl, to utter its cry; to utter or make a similar sound.—*v.t.* To assail with cries or shouts of disapproval or derision; drive away by hooting, often used with *out, away,* or *off;* as, a speaker who was *hooted out* of the lecture hall; to express in hoots.—*n.* A cry or shout, esp. of disapproval or derision; the cry of an owl; any similar sound, as of a whistle, or horn; *colloq.* the least concern or smallest amount, as: He doesn't give a *hoot.*—**hoot·er,** *n.*—**hoot·ing·ly,** *adv.*

hoot·en·an·ny, hōt′e·nan″ē, *n. pl.* **hoot·en·an·nies.** A gathering, usu. informal, at which folk singers and musicians perform for entertainment or, esp. when the audience joins in, for group enjoyment; *slang,* a contrivance, so called when its proper name is not remembered, or cannot be readily recalled.

hop, hop, *v.i.*—**hopped, hopping.** [O.E. *hoppian* = Icel. and Sw. *hoppa* = Dan. *hoppe* = G. *hopfen;* cf. *hobble.*] To move by a short leap or succession of such leaps; to leap with a springy movement on one foot; to leap by lifting both or all feet, as a bird or frog; *colloq.* to make a short flight or trip.—*v.t.* To leap over; *colloq.* to climb aboard, as a train or bus.—*n.* An act of hopping, esp. a spring or leap on one foot. *Colloq.* a short trip in a plane; a kind of dance or a dance party.

hop, hop, *n.* [M.D. *hoppe* (D. *hop*) = L.G. *hoppe* = G. *hopfen,* the hop.] A twining plant, *Humulus lupulus,* in the mulberry family, with three- to five-lobed leaves; *pl.* the dried conelike fruits of the female plant used in brewing and medicine.—*v.t.*—**hopped, hopping.** To treat or flavor with hops.—**hop·bine,** hop′bīn″, *n.* The twining stem of the hop.

hope, hōp, *n.* [O.E. *hopa,* = D. *hoop,* Sw. *hopp,* Dan. *haab,* hope; G. *hoffen,* to hope; possibly akin to L. *cupio,* to desire.] The belief that one's desires may be attained; trust; someone or something in which confidence is placed; the thing hoped for or desired; that which gives hope.—*v.i.*—**hoped, hoping.** [O.E. *hopian.* D. *hopen,* to hope.] To have hope with the expectation of attainment; as, to *hope* for the best.—*v.t.* To trust; to desire with expectation; to long for or entertain hope for.—**hop·er,** *n.*

hope chest, *n.* A chest in which a young unmarried woman collects articles which may be of use to her when she is married.

hope·ful, hōp′ful, *a.* Full of hope; inspiring hope; promising.—*n.* A promising young person; one who aspires to something with hope.—**hope·ful·ly,** *adv.*—**hope·ful·ness,** *n.*

hope·less, hōp′lis, *a.* Despairing; affording no hope; desperate; incurable; impossible to correct, control, manage, or solve; incapable of reaching a goal.—**hope·less·ly,** *adv.*—**hope·less·ness,** *n.*

hop·head, hop′hed″, *n. Slang,* a person addicted to narcotic drugs, esp. to opium and its derivatives.

hop·lite, hop′līt, *n.* [Gr. *hoplitēs,* < *hoplon,* a weapon.] A soldier carrying heavy armor in the infantry of ancient Greece.

hop-o'-my-thumb, hop′o·mi·thum′, *n.* [Orig. *hop on* (or *upon*) *my thumb.*] A diminutive person.

hop·per, hop′ẽr, *n.* One who or that which hops; any insect adapted for leaping, such as a grasshopper or leafhopper; a large, funnel-shaped chamber for temporarily storing loose materials, such as grain or coal, which are later dispensed through the bottom.

hop·sack·ing, hop′sak″ing, *n.* A fabric of loose texture used for clothing; a loosely woven fabric of jute or hemp, used in making rough bags.

hop·scotch, hop′skoch″, *n.* A children's game in which the player, while hopping on one foot, moves a flat stone or the like according to a diagram traced on the ground.

hop·tree, hop′trē″, *n.* A N. American shrub or small tree, *Ptelea trifoliata,* with trifoliate leaves, clusters of small greenish-white flowers, and a flat, circular fruit surrounded by a wing: the fruit has been used as a substitute for hops. Also **wa·fer·ash.**

ho·ra, ho·rah, hōr′a, *n.* A Romanian and Israeli circle dance, or the music for such a dance.

ho·ral, hōr′al, *a.* [L.L. *horalis,* < L. *hora,* hour.] Pertaining to an hour or hours; hourly.

Ho·ra·tian, ho·rā′shan, hō·rā′shan, *a.* Relating to or resembling the works or style of the Latin poet Horace.

horde, hōrd, *n.* [Fr. *horde,* < Turk. and Pers. *ordû,* court, camp, horde.] A tribe, clan, or race of Asiatic or other nomads; a mob; a multitude; a gang; a pack, as of animals; a swarm, as of insects.—*v.i.*—**horded, hording.** To live in hordes; to huddle together.

hore·hound, hoar·hound, hōr′hound, *n.* [O.E. *hōrahūne—hōr,* hoar, and *hūne,* the generic name of these plants.] An aromatic medicinal herb, *Marrubium vulgare,* of the mint family, naturalized in the U.S., having white woolly leaves and clusters of small white flowers; any of various similar mint plants; a cough lozenge or candy flavored with an extract from this plant.

ho·ri·zon, ho·rī′zon, *n.* [O.Fr. *orizon* (Fr. *horizon*), < L. *horizon,* < Gr. *horizōn,* bounding circle, horizon, prop. ppr. of *horizein,* bound, < *horos,* boundary, limit.] The line or circle which forms the apparent boundary between earth and sky; *fig.* the limit or range of perception, knowledge, or the like. *Astron.* the plane which is tangent to the earth at the place of the observer, called *sensible horizon;* the great circle of the celestial sphere whose plane is parallel to the sensible horizon of a particular place, called *astronomical horizon, celestial horizon,* or *rational horizon. Geol.* a stratum or group of strata differing, as in fossils, from the deposits above or below.—**ar·ti·fi·cial ho·ri·zon,** a level reflector, as the surface of mercury in a dish, used in determining the altitudes of stars.—**ho·ri·zon·al,** *a.*

hor·i·zon·tal, hȧr″i·zon′tal, hor″i·zon′tal, *a.* [= Fr. *horizontal,* < L. *horizon,* E. *horizon.*] Of or pertaining to the horizon; situated on or occurring at the horizon; parallel to the plane of the horizon; level; at right angles to the vertical; neither vertical nor inclined; measured or contained in a plane parallel to the horizon; as, a *horizontal* distance; equal and nondiscriminatory; as, a *horizontal* levy.—*n.* A horizontal line, plane, or the like; horizontal position.—**hor·i·zon·tal·i·ty, hor·i·zon·tal·ness,** *n.*—**hor·i·zon·tal·ly,** *adv.*

hor·mone, hȧr′mōn, *n.* [Gr. *hormaō,* excite.] *Physiol.* a secretion of an endocrine gland, distributed in the blood stream or in bodily fluids to stimulate its specific functional effect in another part of the body. Such a substance produced synthetically.—**hor·mo·nal,** hȧr·mō′nal, *a.*—**hor·mo·noid,** *a.*

horn, hȧrn, *n.* [O.E. *horn,* a horn, a trumpet = Icel., Sw., Dan., and G. *horn,* D. *horen,* Goth. *haurn,* Armor. *corn,* L. *cornu,* Gr. *keras,* horn.] A hard projecting appendage growing on the heads of certain animals, as cattle, goats, and deer; the material of which such horns are composed; *mus.* a wind instrument, orig. made of horn, now of brass, esp. the French horn. Something similar to a horn, as in shape, position, or use; a powder flask; the antenna of an insect; an extremity of the crescent moon; the pommel of some saddles; a device for sounding a warning; *Bib.* a symbol of glory or power.—*v.t.* To butt or gore.—**horn·less,** *a.*—**horn·less·ness,** *n.*—**horn·like,** *a.*—**horn·y,** *a.*—**hornier, horniest.**

horn·beam, hȧrn′bēm″, *n.* A shrub or tree of the genus *Carpinus,* in the birch family, with striking, smooth, blue-gray bark and hard white wood, as *C. betulus,* or the American species *C. cariliniana.*

horn·bill, hȧrn′bil″, *n.* Any of the large African and Asian birds constituting the family *Bucerotidae,* characterized by a very large bill, often surmounted by a horny protuberance.

horn·blende, hạrn′blend, n. [G. horn, horn, and blende, < blenden, to dazzle, from its horny and glittering appearance.] A dark green or black lustrous mineral which is a common form of amphibole.—**horn·blen·dic,** hạrn·blen′dik, a.

horned, hạrnd, a. Having horns or projections resembling them. Cuckolded.—**horn·ed·ness,** hạr′nid·nis, n.

horned pout, n. Any of several fish with barbels on their heads, esp. *Ictalurus nebulosus;* bullhead; catfish. Also **horn pout.**

horned toad, n. Any of various small, harmless lizards of the genus *Phrynosoma* of western N. America, toadlike in appearance, with horny spines on the head. Also **horn toad, horned liz·ard.**

hor·net, hạr′nit, n. [O.E. hyrnet = M.L.G. hornte = O.H.G. hornaz, G. hornisse, hornet.] A large, strong, social wasp having an exceptionally severe sting, esp. *Vespa crabro,* 'European hornet,' or *V. maculata,* 'American' or 'white-faced hornet.'

horn in, v.i. Slang, to interrupt or thrust oneself in or into without invitation; as, to horn in with a remark.

hor·ni·to, hạr·nē″tō, Sp. ạr·nē′tạ, n. pl. **hor·ni·tos,** hạr·nē″tōz, Sp. ạr·nē′tạs. [Sp., dim. of horno, < L. furnus, oven.] Geol. a low oven-shaped mound, common in the volcanic regions of South America, usu. emitting hot smoke and vapors from its sides and summit.

horn-mad, hạrn′mad′, a. Angry enough to gore with the horns, as a bull or other horned animal; raging mad; furious.—**horn-mad·ness,** n.

horn of plen·ty, n. Cornucopia.

horn·pipe, hạrn′pīp″, n. Obs. a musical instrument similar to a clarinet. A lively dance, orig. of English sailors, or its music.

horn·stone, hạrn′stōn″, n. A variety of quartz resembling flint; chert.

horn·swog·gle, hạrn′swog″l, v.t.—**hornswoggled, hornswoggling.** Slang. To trick; hoax; dupe; cheat; deceive.

horn·tail, hạrn′tāl″, n. Any of various wasplike insects of the family *Siricidae,* so called from the female having a horn-shaped protuberance at the end of the abdomen.

horn·worm, hạrn′wụrm″, n. Any of various sphinx moth larvae, as the tobacco hornworm, characterized by a hornlike caudal projection.

hor·o·loge, hạr′o·lōj, hor′o·lōj″, n. [Fr. horologe, L. horologium, Gr. hōrologion—hōra, hour, and legō, to tell.] A mechanism for indicating the hours of the day, esp. an older timepiece, as the sundial; a timepiece of any kind.—**ho·rol·o·gy,** hạ·rol′o·jē, hō·rol′o·jē, n. The science of measuring time; the art of constructing machines for measuring time.—**ho·rol·o·ger, ho·rol·o·gist,** n.—**hor·o·log·ic, hor·o·log·i·cal,** hạr″o·loj′ik, hor″o·loj′ik, a.

hor·o·scope, hạr′o·skōp″, hor′o·skōp″, n. [Gr. hōroskopos—hōra, hour, and skopeō, to view.] A pattern or diagram of the heavens at a given time, used by astrologers to predict future events in the lives of persons, according to the position of the stars at the time of their birth.—**ho·ros·co·py,** hō·ros′ko·pē, hạ·ros′ko·pē, n. The predicting of future events by the disposition of the stars and planets.

hor·ren·dous, hạ·ren′dus, ho·ren′dus, a. [L. horrendus, gerundive of horrēre, bristle, shudder.] Dreadful; terrible; horrible.—**hor·ren·dous·ly,** adv.

hor·ri·ble, hạr′i·bl, hor′i·ble, a. [L. horribilis, < horreo, to bristle or stand on end, to be terrified.] Exciting or tending to excite horror; very disagreeable; dreadful; terrible; shocking; hideous; colloq. excessive. —**hor·ri·ble·ness,** n.—**hor·ri·bly,** adv.

hor·rid, hạr′id, hor′id, a. [L. horridus, < horreo, to bristle, to be terrified.] Exciting horror; dreadful; hideous; shocking; colloq. very offensive.—**hor·rid·ly,** adv.—**hor·rid·ness,** n.

hor·rif·ic, hạ·rif′ik, ho·rif′ik, a. [L. horrificus.] Causing horror.—**hor·rif·i·cal·ly,** adv.

hor·ri·fy, hạr′i·fī″, hor′i·fī″, v.t.—**horrified, horrifying.** [L. horror, and facio, to make.] To strike or impress with horror; to appall.—**hor·ri·fi·ca·tion,** hạr″i·fi·kā′shạn, n.—**hor·ri·fied,** a. Showing or accompanied by a feeling of horror.

hor·rip·i·la·tion, hạ·rip″i·lā′shạn, ho·rip″i·lā′shạn, n. [L. horreo, to bristle, and pilus, hair.] The bristling or standing on end of the hair as a result of fear or cold in such animals as dogs and cats; goose flesh.

hor·ror, hạr′ẽr, hor′ẽr, n. [L., < horreo.] A powerful feeling of fear, dread, abhorrence; that which excites horror. Pl., slang, the blues; delirium tremens.

hors d'oeu·vre, ạr dụrv′, Fr. ạR dŒ′vRe, n. pl. **hors d'oeu·vres, hors d'oeu·vre,** Fr. ạR dŒ′vRe. Usu. pl. an appetizer or relish.

horse, hạrs, n. pl. **hors·es, horse.** [O.E. hors = O.H.G. hros, G. ross, = Icel. hross, horse.] A large, solid-hoofed quadruped, *Equus caballus,* domesticated since prehistoric times, and employed as a beast of draft and burden and for carrying a rider; the mature male of this animal; a stallion or a gelding; any animal of the family *Equidae,* as the ass and zebra; a representation or figure of a horse; soldiers serving on horseback; as, a thousand horse; something on which a person rides, sits, or exercises, as if on a horse's back; a trestle; a man: used as a playful term. Slang, a crib, translation, or other illicit aid to study; heroin. Chess, colloq. a knight; min. a mass of rock enclosed within a lode or vein; gymnastics, a wooden block with four legs, covered with leather, and used in exercising and vaulting.

horse, hạrs, v.t.—**horsed, horsing.** To provide with a horse or horses; to set on horseback; to set or carry on a person's back; slang, to subject to teasing.—v.i. To mount a horse; to ride horseback; slang, to frolic, often with around.—a. Of or relating to a horse or horses; mounted on horseback; of unusual size; powered or drawn by horses.

horse·back, hạrs′bak″, n. The back of a horse; geol. a narrow elevation or ridge of earth or rock.—adv. On horseback.

horse·car, hạrs′kär″, n. U.S. a streetcar formerly drawn by a horse or horses. A vehicle equipped to transport horses.

horse chest·nut, n. Any of several trees of Asiatic origin, genus *Aesculus,* having large, palmate leaves, clusters of beautiful flowers, and often planted for ornament; the seed of this tree. See *buckeye.*

horse-cop·er, horse-coup·er, hạrs′kō″pẽr, n. Brit. a dealer in horses.

horse draw·ing, n. Canadian, a contest for draft horses to test their pulling power.

horse·flesh, hạrs′flesh″, n. The flesh of a horse; horses generally, esp. those used for driving, racing, or riding.

horse·fly, hạrs′flī″, n. pl. **horse·flies.** A large fly, genus *Tabanus,* that sucks the blood of horses, cattle, and other animals.

horse·hair, hạrs′hâr″, n. The hair of horses, particularly of the mane and tail; cloth or fabric produced from this hair.

horse·hide, hạrs′hīd″, n. The hide of a horse, or leather made from it; colloq. a baseball.

horse lat·i·tudes, n. pl. Meteor. either of two high pressure belts situated at about 30° N. or 30° S. latitude, between the region of westerly winds of higher latitudes and the region of the trade winds of the torrid zone, notorious for tedious calms.

horse·laugh, hạrs′laf″, hạrs′läf″, n. A loud, coarse, often scornful laugh.

horse·less car·riage, hạrs′lis kar′ij, n. Formerly, an automobile.

horse mack·er·el, n. Any of various large tuna, such as bluefin or dogtooth tuna; jack mackerel.

horse·man, hạrs′man, n. pl. **horse·men.** A man on horseback; a person skilled in horseback riding; one who raises, manages, tends, or trains horses. A soldier who served on horseback; cavalryman.—**horse·man·ship,** n.—**horse·wom·an,** n. pl. **horse·wom·en.**

horse·mint, hạrs′mint″, n. A wild mint, *Mentha longifolia,* orig. native to Europe but now found in parts of America; any of various other menthaceous plants, as *Monarda punctata,* an erect odorous herb.

horse net·tle, n. A prickly weed of the nightshade family, *Solanum carolinense.*

horse op·er·a, n. Slang, a motion picture or television play featuring the exploits and adventures of cowboys of the Wild West.

horse·play, hạrs′plā″, n. Rough or rowdy play or practical jokes; rude pranks.

horse·pow·er, hạrs′pou″ẽr, n. A unit for measuring power or rate of work, as of the engine of an automobile: equiv. to 550 foot-pounds per second. Abbr. hp, HP, h.p., H.P.

horse·pow·er-hour, hạrs′pou″ẽr·our″, hạrs′pou″ẽr·ou″ẽr, n. A unit of work or energy equal to the work performed by a piece of machinery operating at the rate of one horsepower for one hour.

horse·rad·ish, hạrs′rad″ish, n. A cultivated plant, *Armoracia lapathifolia,* of the mustard family, grown for its woody, aromatic roots; a condiment derived from its root.

horse sense, n. Colloq. practical good sense.

horse·shoe, hạrs′shō″, hạrsh′shö″, n. A metal plate, U-shaped to follow the outline of a horse's hoof to which it is attached for protection from rough surfaces; pl. a form of quoits played by tossing horseshoes over a peg.—v.t. To shoe, as a horse.—a. Resembling a horseshoe or its shape; as, a horseshoe arch.—**horse·sho·er,** n.

horse·shoe crab, n. A primitive arthropod of the genus *Limulus,* which has a carapace of horseshoe shape and is found along the Atlantic Coast. Also *king crab.*

horse·tail, hạrs′tāl″, n. A perennial herb of the genus *Equisetum,* related to ferns, which has hollow, jointed, grooved stems.

horse trade, n. A commercial, political, or other negotiation conducted with shrewdness and sharp bargaining.—**horse-trade,** hạrs′trād″, v.i.—**horse-traded, horse-trading.** To negotiate shrewdly; to haggle.—**horse trad·er,** n.

horse·weed, hạrs′wēd″, n. A N. American weed, *Erigeron canadensis,* of the composite family, with small linear leaves and many small heads of yellowish flowers, common in pastures, roadsides. See *bitterweed.*

horse·whip, hạrs′hwip″, hạrs′wip″, n. A kind of whip, usu. of leather, used to control horses.—v.t.—**horsewhipped, horsewhipping.** To lash or flagellate with or as with a horsewhip.—**horse·whip·per,** n.

hors·ey, hors·y, hạr′sē, a.—**horsier, horsiest.** Associated with the nature or quality of horses; engrossed with horses, as with their breeding or racing. Slang, appearing gross, crass, or clumsy.—**hors·i·ly,** adv.—**hors·i·ness,** n.

horst, hạrst, n. Geol. an elevated part of the earth's crust positioned between parallel faults.

hor·ta·tive, hạr′ta·tiv, a. [L. hortativus, < hortari, urge, exhort, < hori, urge.] Exhorting; urging.—**hor·ta·tive·ly,** adv.

hor·ta·to·ry, hạr′ta·tōr″ē, hạr′ta·tȧr″ē, a. [L.L. *hortatorius,* < L. *hortator.*] Of, pertaining to, or characterized by exhortation; exhorting; hortative.—**hor·ta·to·ri·ly,** adv.

hor·ti·cul·ture, hạr′ti·kul″chėr, n. [L. *hortus,* a garden (same root as *garden, yard*), and *cultura,* culture.] The cultivation of a garden; the science and art of cultivating flowers, herbs, shrubs, fruits, and garden vegetables.—**hor·ti·cul·tur·al,** hạr″ti·kul′chėr·al, a.—**hor·ti·cul·tur·al·ly,** adv.—**hor·ti·cul·tur·ist,** n.

hor·tus sic·cus, hạr′tus sik′us, n. [L., *lit.* 'a dry garden.'] A collection of specimens of plants carefully dried and preserved; herbarium.

ho·san·na, hō·zan′a, interj. [L.L. < Gr. *hōsanna,* < Heb. *hōshī‘āh-nnā,* save, pray!] An exclamation, used as an acclamation of praise to God or Christ.—n. pl. **ho·san·nas.** A joyful expression of praise or adoration.—v.t.—*hosannaed, hosannaing.* To praise or acclaim.

hose, hōz, n. pl. **hose.** [O.E. *hosa* = D. *hoos* = G. *hose* = Icel. *hosa,* hose.] *Pl.* an article of clothing for the foot and lower part of the leg; stockings; socks; formerly, a garment for the legs and waist, as tights or breeches, worn by men.—**ho·sier,** hō′zhėr, n. Brit. one who makes or deals in hose or stockings, or goods knitted or woven like hose.

hose, hōz, n. pl. **hos·es.** A flexible tube for conveying liquids to a desired point; as, a garden *hose;* Brit. a sheath, or sheathing part, as that enclosing the ear of grain. A socket, esp. one receiving the shaft or handle of a tool, golf club, or the like.—v.t.—*hosed, hosing.* To water, wash, or drench by means of a hose; *Canadian slang,* to defeat or deal with unscrupulously.

ho·sel, hō′zel, n. *Golf,* the cavity in the club head of an iron that encloses the shaft.

ho·sier·y, hō′zhe·rē, n. Socks or stockings of any kind. *Brit.* the business of a hosier.

hos·pice, hos′pis, n. [Fr. < L. *hospitium,* hospitality, a lodging, an inn.] A place of refuge for travelers, often operated by a religious order.

hos·pi·ta·ble, hos′pi·ta·bl, ho·spit′a·bl, a. [Obs. Fr. *hospitable,* < M.L. *hospitāre,* receive as a guest, < L. *hospes.*] Giving or affording a generous welcome and entertainment to guests or strangers; as, a *hospitable* host; inclined to, or characterized by, hospitality; as, a *hospitable* disposition; favorably receptive or open, usu. with *to;* as, a people *hospitable to* new ideas.—**hos·pi·ta·ble·ness,** n.—**hos·pi·ta·bly,** adv.

hos·pi·tal, hos′pi·tal, n. [O.Fr. *hospital* (Fr. *hôpital*), < M.L. *hospitale,* inn, hospice, prop. neut. of L. *hospitalis,* pertaining to guests, hospitable, < *hospes.*] An institution in which sick or injured persons are given medical, obstetric, psychiatric, or surgical treatment, or nursing care; a similar establishment for the care of animals; formerly, a charitable institution for the care and maintenance of the needy, infirm, aged, or orphaned.

hos·pi·tal·i·ty, hos″pi·tal′i·tē, n. pl. **hos·pi·tal·i·ties.** [L. *hospitalitas.*] The generous reception and gracious entertainment of strangers or guests; the disposition to extend friendly treatment to guests.

hos·pi·tal·i·za·tion, hos″pi·ta·li·zā′shan, n. The act, state, or duration of being hospitalized; *colloq.* insurance which provides payment of some or all of the subscriber's expenses incurred in the hospital.

hos·pi·tal·ize, hos′pi·ta·līz″, v.t.—*hospitalized, hospitalizing.* To place for care or treatment in a hospital.

hos·pi·tal ship, n. A vessel fitted up as a mobile hospital, as one accompanying a

fleet of warships or assigned to treat ailing or wounded soldiers.

host, hōst, n. [O.Fr. *hoste,* Fr. *hôte;* < L. *hospes, hospitis,* a host, for *hostipes,* < *hostis,* an enemy, a stranger.] One who receives and entertains another at his own house or elsewhere; a landlord of a hostel or an inn; an animal or plant organism upon which a parasite is dependent for its existence.—v.t.

host, hōst, n. [O.Fr. *hoste,* < L. *hostis,* a stranger, an enemy, in later usage an army.] A great number of things or persons; a multitude; armed forces.

host, hōst, n. [L. *hostia,* a sacrificial victim, < *hostire,* to strike.] (*Often cap.*) the altar bread or wafer in the Eucharist.

hos·tage, hos′tij, n. [O.Fr. *hostage.*] A person handed over or held as a pledge for the performance of certain conditions.

hos·tel, hos′tel, n. A lodging, supervised by adults, planned for the use of young hikers and bicyclists; also *youth hostel.* Brit. a student residence or dormitory; *archaic,* an inn.

hos·tel school, n. *Canadian,* a boarding school operated by the government for Indian and Eskimo children.

host·ess, hō′stis, n. [O.Fr. *hostesse* (Fr. *hôtesse*), fem. of *hoste,* E. *host.*] A female host; a woman who entertains a guest or guests; a woman employed by a restaurant, resort, airline, etc. to greet, seat, serve, and assist patrons.

hos·tile, hos′til, Brit. hos′tīl, a. [L. *hostilis,* < *hostis,* enemy.] Antagonistic; opposed in feeling, action, tendency, or character; of or pertaining to an enemy or actions characteristic of an enemy; unfriendly.—n. A hostile person; an enemy.—**hos·tile·ly,** adv.—**hos·til·i·ty,** ho·stil′i·tē, n. pl. **hos·til·i·ties.** [L.L. *hostilitas.*] Hostile state, feeling, or action; enmity; antagonism; a hostile act. *Pl.* acts of warfare; war.

hos·tler, hos′lėr, os′lėr, n. [O.Fr. *hostelier,* < *hostel,* Mod.Fr. *hôtel,* an inn, < L.L. *hospitale,* a hospital. HOTEL.] Formerly, the person who had the care of horses at an inn; one who services trucks, buses, or locomotives.

hot, hot, a.—*hotter, hottest.* [O.E. *hāt* = D. *heet* = G. *heiss* = Icel. *heitr,* hot: cf. Goth. *heito,* fever, and E. *heat.*] Having or communicating heat, esp. in a high degree; as, a *hot* stove, coffee too *hot* to drink; carrying a high voltage current; as, a *hot* wire; very warm, as weather or climate; having a sensation of great bodily heat, as from nearness to fire, or from heavy clothing, vigorous exercise, or fever; attended with or producing such a sensation, as a blush or fever; having an effect of burning on the tongue, skin, etc., as pepper, mustard, or a blister; peppery, biting, pungent, acrid. Having or showing intense feeling; ardent or fervent; passionate, vehement, or fiery, as persons, temper, or words; inflamed; as, *hot* with rage; violent, furious, intense; strong or fresh, as a scent or trail. *Slang,* excited about, highly enthusiastic for; as, *hot* for Mozart; wild, unrestrained; as, a *hot* time; passionate or very sexy; as, a *hot* number; showing luck or skill; as, not so *hot* in today's game; stolen or ill-gotten; as, a *hot* necklace; uncomfortable or unpleasant, as: His opponents made the town too *hot* for him.—adv. Also **hot·ly.**

hot air, n. *Slang.* Empty, pretentious talk or writing; boastful exaggeration.

hot·bed, hot′bed″, n. Hort. a glass-covered bed of earth heated by fermenting compost or electrical cables, used for growing plants out of season. Atmosphere which produces rapid growth or development, esp. of something undesirable; as, a *hotbed* of rebellion.

hot-blood·ed, hot′blud′id, a. Excitable; impulsive; passionate; irritable; adventurous.

hot·box, hot′boks″, n. Rail. a journal bearing that has become overheated due to friction.

hotch·pot, hoch′pot″, n. [Fr. *hochepot,* shakepot, < *hocker,* to shake and *pot,* a pot or dish.] A hodgepodge or mixture; *law,* a commixture of property for equality of division; also *hotchpotch.*

hotch·potch, hoch′poch″, n. [For *hotchpot.*] A stew of a variety of ingredients; *Brit.* a hodgepodge; *law,* hotchpot.

hot cross bun, n. A roll marked with a cross in frosting, esp. prepared to be eaten during Lent.

hot dog, n. A cooked frankfurter or sausage, esp. as served in a split roll.

ho·tel, hō·tel′, n. [Fr. *hôtel* < O.Fr. *hostel.*] A building or establishment which provides living accommodations for transient visitors and sometimes long-term residents, and which often offers other facilities such as meeting rooms, restaurants, entertainment, and shops, available to its guests or the general public.

Ho·tel, hō·tel′, n. A communications code word to designate the letter *H.*

hot flash, n. A sudden feeling of bodily warmth symptomatic of menopause in women.

hot·foot, hot′fut″, n. pl. **hot·foots.** Colloq. the prank which involves lighting a match secretly inserted in a victim's shoe between the sole and the upper.—v.i. Colloq. to go in haste, often followed by *it.*—adv. Colloq. with great speed in going.

hot·head, hot′hed″, n. A rash, impetuous person.—**hot·head·ed,** hot′hed′id, a. Violent or fiery in spirit or temper; passionate; emotional.—**hot·head·ed·ly,** adv.—**hot·head·ed·ness,** n.

hot·house, hot′hous″, n. An artificially heated greenhouse for the cultivation of tender plants.—a. Pertaining to a plant raised in a greenhouse; *fig.* tender; overly delicate.

hot line, n. An open telephone line between the heads of state of two nations, maintained to assure a free line of communication for emergency use, esp. to prevent accidental war.

hot pep·per, n. A pungent, thin-walled fruit in the genus *Capsicum,* belonging to the nightshade family, having various shapes and colors; a plant, *Capsicum frutescens,* bearing such fruits.

hot plate, n. A simple, portable appliance for cooking, heated by gas burners or by electricity; a meal, hot and confined to one plate.

hot·press, hot′pres″, n. A machine which applies heat and mechanical pressure to express oil or to produce a smooth, glassy surface on paper or cloth.—v.t.

hot rod, n. *Slang,* a usu. old automobile, stripped of nonessential equipment, with the engine adjusted for greater acceleration and speed.—**hot rod·der,** *slang,* a driver of a hot rod.

hot seat, n. *Slang.* The electric chair; a difficult situation or an embarrassing position.

hot·shot, hot′shot″, n. *Slang.* A successful and important person, as in business; a person displaying skill, as in a game; a fast, nonstop train.

hot spring, n. A natural, warm-water spring with temperatures of 98° F. or more.

hot war, n. *Slang,* actual war with severe fighting, in contrast to the threats and tensions of cold war.

hot wa·ter, n. Colloq. Serious difficulty; a condition of distress, usu. preceded by *in.*

hound, hound, n. [O.E. *hund* = D. *hond* = G. *hund* = Icel. *hundr* = Goth. *hunds,* dog: cf. L. *canis,* Gr. *kyōn,* Skt. *çvan,* dog.] A dog, now esp. one of various breeds trained to hunt by scent or sight. A mean, despicable fellow; an addict; a hobbyist.—v.t. To pursue or drive relentlessly.—**hound·er,** n.

hound's-tongue, houndz′tung, ′n. A weed, *Cynoglossum officinale,* in the borage family, having coarse, hairy, tongue-shaped leaves, reddish-purple flowers, and fruits in the form of prickly nutlets; any species of the genus *Cynoglossum.*

hound's-tooth check, houndz′tŏth chek′, n. A textile pattern of interrupted checks. Also **hound's tooth.**

hour, our, ou′ér, n. [O.Fr. *ure, ore, hore* (Fr. *heure*), < L. *hora,* < Gr. *hōra,* time, season, hour; akin to E. *year.*] A space of time equal to the 24th part of a mean solar or civil day; 60 minutes; a particular or specific time; any definite time of day; the time indicated by a timepiece; the present time; as, the man of the *hour*; the distance which can be traveled in one hour; as, living an *hour* from the nearest hospital; a regular or customary time; as, the cocktail *hour*; *astron.* a unit of measure of right ascension representing 15 degrees, or the 24th part of a great circle. *Educ.* the length of one class period; one unit measure of academic credit.

hour·glass, our′glas″, our′gläs″, ou′ér·-glas″, ou′ér·gläs″, n. A horological device having two bulbous glass vessels joined by a narrow passage through which a quantity of sand or mercury descends within a specific time.—a.

hou·ri, hur′ē, hour′ē, n. pl. **hou·ris.** A beautiful virgin maiden presented to a devout Muslim who has achieved Paradise.

hour·ly, our′lē, ou′ér·lē, a. Recurring or performed every hour; frequent; continual; calculated in terms of hour units.—adv. At every hour or during each hour; frequently; continually.

house, hous, n. pl. **hous·es,** hou′ziz. [O.E. *hūs* = D. *huis* = G. *haus* = Icel. and Goth. *hūs,* house; perhaps akin to E. *hide.*] A building where people live; a habitation, esp. of a single family; a structure used for any purpose, as worship, entertainment, assemblage, eating, storage, keeping animals, or growing plants; an audience. The building in which a legislative body of government meets; (*cap.*) the body itself; as, the *House* of Representatives, the *House* of Commons; a quorum of such a body. A place of occupation or trade; a business establishment; a place for gambling. (*Often cap.*) a family consisting of ancestors and descendants; as, the *House* of Hapsburg. An advisory group for an institution or organization, as a church, college, or university; a dormitory or other residential hall; the inhabitants of such a residence. *Brit.* a lotto or bingo type of game; a college within an English university. *Astrol.* an equal twelfth part of the celestial sphere; a sign of the Zodiac that is considered the base of a planet's greatest influence.

house, houz, v.t.—housed, housing. [O.E. *hūsian.*] To put or receive into a house; provide with a house; to give shelter to; harbor; lodge; *carp.* to fix into a socket or the like.—v.i. To take shelter; dwell.—a. Relating to or suitable for a house.

house ar·rest, n. Detention of an arrested individual in quarters other than a prison, as in a hospital or at home.

house·boat, hous′bōt″, n. A boat fitted for use as a dwelling, esp. one having a flat bottom and a houselike structure built on the deck.

house·break·er, hous′brā″kér, n. One who breaks into a house with a felonious intent; a burglar. *Brit.* a person or a company that razes old buildings; someone who buys usable parts of old houses.—**house·-break·ing,** n.

house·bro·ken, hous′brō″ken, a. Trained, as dogs or cats, to excrete only in the proper place.—**house·break,** v.t.—past *housebroke,* pp. *housebroken,* ppr. *housebreaking.*

house charge, n. *Brit.* cover charge.

house·clean, hous′klēn′, v.i. To maintain cleanliness and order in living quarters, an institution, or an organization.—v.t. To submit, as a house and its furnishings, to a cleaning; to reorganize, as an institution or organization, by altering methods or dismissing personnel considered undesirable.—**house·clean·ing,** n.

house·coat, hous′kōt″, n. A woman's garment, usu. with a long full skirt, worn informally in her own home.

house·fly, hous′flī″, n. pl. **house·flies.** A two-winged insect, *Musca domestica,* common in dwellings.

house·ful, hous′ful″, n. pl. **house·fuls.** A number or quantity sufficient to fill a house.

house·hold, hous′hōld″, hous′ōld″, n. Those who dwell under the same roof and comprise a family; any group living under the same domestic government; house; family.—a. Pertaining to the house and family; referring to housekeeping and maintenance needs; domestic. Occurring frequently; common.

house·hold·er, hous′hōl″dér, hous′ōl″dér, n. The head of a household; the owner or occupant of a home.

house·hold troops, n. pl. Troops assigned to attend the sovereign and the royal family and to guard the palace.

house·keep·er, hous′kē″pér, n. One who maintains a home, in the manner of a housewife; a person employed to care for a home or institution.—**house·keep·ing,** n. The maintenance of a household, institution or organization.—**house·keep,** v.i.

house·leek, hous′lēk″, n. A succulent-leaved herb, *Sempervivum tectorum,* of the orpine family, having pink flowers and leaves forming dense rosettes; any species of the genus *Sempervivum.*

house·lights, hous′līts″, n. pl. Lights of the part of a theater in which the audience is seated, in contrast to those that illuminate the stage or screen.

house·maid, hous′mād″, n. A female servant employed in a household to do housework.

house·maid's knee, n. *Pathol.* an acute or chronic inflammation of the bursa over the kneecap: so called because of its supposed prevalence among housemaids who do much of their work while kneeling.

house·man, hous′man″, hous′man, n. pl. **house·men.** A male servant employed to do general work, as in a home or hotel; also **house·boy.** A resident representative of the management, as in a gambling house.

house·moth·er, hous′muŦH′ér, n. The female head of a number of young persons living together, as in a student residence, who serves as chaperon, hostess, and sometimes as housekeeper.

House of Com·mons, n. The chamber of the legislature in the British and Canadian parliaments whose members are elected by the constituents of the counties and boroughs they represent.

house of cor·rec·tion, n. An institution intended for the confinement of youthful offenders, those found guilty of minor offenses, and others considered capable of rehabilitation.

House of Del·e·gates, n. The lower legislative body of Maryland, Virginia, and West Virginia.

House of Lords, n. The nonelective chamber in the British Parliament in which the members are hereditary or appointed peers and peeresses: it is also the final court of appeal for civil and criminal cases.

House of Rep·re·sen·ta·tives, n. The larger branch of the U.S. Congress and of most state legislatures, whose members represent election districts determined by population.

house or·gan, n. A periodical publication issued by a business firm to inform its employees or patrons of news and activities.

house par·ty, n. Entertainment of guests at a host's home, in a beach or country house, or in a fraternity or sorority, usu. for several days.

house phy·si·cian, n. A resident physician in a hospital or other institution.

house-proud, hous′proud″, a. Pertaining to a woman who bases her self-esteem upon the excellence of her housekeeping and pride in her home.

house-rais·ing, hous′rā″zing, n. A gathering of friends and neighbors, usu. in a rural area, to help with the building of a house for a family of the community.

house·room, hous′rōm″, hous′rụm″, n. Space or accommodation in a house; lodging.

house·top, hous′top″, n. The top or roof of a house.—**cry** or **shout from the house·-tops,** of news or publicity, to disseminate widely; broadcast.

house·warm·ing, hous′war″ming, n. A gathering or party to celebrate moving into a new house.

house·wife, hous′wīf″, n. pl. **house·wives.** A homemaker; a wife, specif. in the capacity of manager of domestic affairs. *Chiefly Brit.* a little box for needles, thread, scissors, and the like.—**house·wife·li·ness,** n.—**house·wife·ly,** a., adv.—**house·wif·-er·y,** n.

house·work, hous′wụrk″, n. The tasks involved in housekeeping, as cooking, cleaning, and otherwise maintaining and managing a house.

hous·ing, hou′zing, n. The act of one who houses or puts something under shelter; the providing of dwellings for a community; shelter, as in a house; lodging; houses collectively. Something serving as a shelter or covering; a niche for a statue; *carp.* the space or cavity made in one piece of wood or the like for the insertion of another; *naut.* the part of a mast which is below deck; *mach.* a frame, plate, or the like that supports a part of a machine.

hov·el, huv′el, hov′el, n. [M.E. *hovel, hovyl*; origin uncertain.] An open shed, as a shelter for cattle or tools; a small, mean dwelling; a wretched hut.—v.t.—*hoveled, hoveling, Brit. hovelled, hovelling.* To shelter or lodge as in a hovel.

hov·er, huv′ér, hov′ér, v.i [Perhaps < O.E. *hove,* to abide, to linger.] To hang fluttering in the air, as a bird in suspended flight; to be in doubt, uncertainty, hesitation, or irresolution; to move to and fro near something threateningly or vigilantly. —n. An act or state of hovering.—**hov·-er·er,** n.—**hov·er·ing,** a. Suspended; wavering.—**hov·er·ing·ly,** adv.

Hov·er·craft, huv′ér·kraft″, huv′ér·kräft″, n. A vehicle which travels a few feet above relatively level terrain or waters by being buoyed or supported by a column of air pressure supplied by fans beneath its chassis. (Trademark.)

how, hou, adv. [O.E. *hū,* instrumental case of *hwā, hwæt,* who, what; really the same word as *why.*] In what manner; by what means or method; to what extent; by what measure; to qualify an adverb or adjective of degree or quantity, as: *How* big? *How* many tickets? *How* far? *How* long? *How* much? In what condition, state, or plight; at what price, as: *How* is wheat going now? For what reason; why, as:

How could you want this? *Colloq.* As a greeting or in response to an introduction: *How* do you do? In reference to one's health or affairs, as: *How* have you been? *How*'s everything? *How*'s business?—*n.* A method, mode, or procedure; as, the *how* of it, or, the know-*how*.—*interj.* An exclamation of surprise, as: *How* now! An exclamation of reaffirmation; as, and *how*! —*conj.* However; that.

how·dah, hou′da, *n.* [Hind. and Ar. *haudah*.] A large, usu. elegantly appointed and canopied chair-seat for two or more persons which is strapped on an elephant's back: used in East Indian countries.

how·ev·er, hou·ev′ẽr, *adv.* In whatever manner or degree; in whatever state; notwithstanding; yet; still; but; on the other hand; *colloq.* how; how on earth: used in questions.—*conj.* In whatever manner or degree.

how·itz·er, hou′it·sẽr, *n.* [< G. *haubitze*, < Czech. *houfnice*, orig. a slingshot.] A short-barreled cannon firing a heavy shell at a high angle, designed for use against targets that cannot be reached by flat trajectories.

howl, houl, *v.i.* [M.E. *houlen* = D. *huilen* = G. *heulen*, howl; imit.] To utter a loud, prolonged, mournful cry, as that of a dog or wolf; to utter or make a similar sound, as the wind or a person in distress; wail.—*v.t.* To utter with howls; to drive or force by howls.—*n.* The prolonged, mournful cry of a dog, wolf, man, or other animal; a loud cry or wail, as of pain or rage; a prolonged sound like wailing, as of the wind; *electron.* an audible, undesirable high-pitched tone produced by electrical or acoustic feedback in a receiver.

howl·er, hou′lẽr, *n.* One who or that which howls; any of the large tropical American monkeys, genus *Alouatta*, notable for their loud howling cries; *colloq.* a comical mistake or blunder, esp. a verbal one.

how·so·ev·er, hou″sō·ev′ẽr, *adv.* In whatever way or manner; to whatever extent or degree.

hoy, hoi, *n.* [D. and G. *heu*; Dan. *höy*.] A heavy barge; formerly a small coastal vessel or tender.

hoy, hoi, *interj.* A call to attract attention.

hoy·den, hoi·den, hoid′en, *n.* [O.D. *heiden*, a heathen, a gypsy, a vagabond.] A boisterous, bold girl; tomboy.—**hoy·den·ish,** *a.*—**hoy·den·ish·ness, hoy·den·ism,** *n.*

Hoyle, hoil, *n.* [From Sir Edmund *Hoyle*, 1672-1769.] A book of recognized authority giving the rules for card games and other games.—**ac·cord·ing to Hoyle,** as prescribed by rule; fairly; correctly.

hua·ra·che, wa·rä′chē, *Sp.* wä·Rä′che, *n.* pl. **hua·ra·ches,** wa·rä′chēz, *Sp.* wä·Rä′ches. A Mexican sandal whose upper part is made of interlaced leather straps. Also **hua·ra·cho,** pl. **hua·ra·chos,** wa·rä′chōs, *Sp.* wä·Rä′chas.

hub, hub, *n.* [Origin obscure: cf. *hob*.] The central part of a wheel, into which the spokes are inserted; the central part of a propeller or fan to which the blades are secured; a center of great importance or activity; as, the *hub* of the universe; a steel punch used in the making of dies for coins or disks.

hub·ble-bub·ble, hub′l-bub′l, *n.* [Varied redupl. of *bubble*.] A tobacco pipe in which the smoke passes through water with a bubbling sound; also *hookah*. A bubbling or gurgling sound; confusion or noise.

hub·bub, hub′ub, *n.* [Imitative of confused noise.] A noise of many confused voices; a tumult; uproar.

hu·bris, hū′bris, hö′bris, *n.* Insolence or arrogance caused by inordinate pride; exaggerated self-confidence. Also *hybris*.

huck·a·back, huk′a·bak″, *n.* [Orig. linen *hawked* or *huckstered* by being carried on the *back*.] A coarse, absorbent cloth of linen or cotton, used principally for towels. Also **huck.**

huck·le·ber·ry, huk′l·ber″ē, *n.* pl. **huck·le·ber·ries.** [Appar. a corruption of *hurtleberry*.] The dark-blue or black edible berry of any of various shrubs, genus *Gaylussacia*, of the heath family; a shrub yielding such a berry.

huck·ster, huk′stẽr, *n.* [M.E. *huccster*, *hokester*, huckster (of either sex): cf. D. *heukster*, fem. of *heuker*, retail dealer, D. *heuken*, M.L.G. *hōken*, G. *höken*, to retail goods, also E. *hawker*.] A peddler, esp. in agricultural produce; a hawker. *Colloq.* someone in the advertising business: usu. derogatory; anyone using especially aggressive or dramatic sales techniques to persuade; as, political *hucksters*.—*v.i.* To deal in small articles or in petty bargains.—*v.t.* To retail or peddle.—**huck·ster·ess, huck·stress,** *n.* A female huckster.

hud·dle, hud′le, *v.i.*—**huddled, huddling.** [Same word as G. *hudeln*, Dan. *hutle*, D. *hoetelen*, to bungle; akin *hustle*.] To crowd together in a group; to hunch one's body together, as if fearful or cold; to come together in order to confer; *football*, to gather in a close group for instructions. —*v.t.* To crowd together without order; to hunch together, as one's body, often with *up*; *Brit.* to produce in a hurried manner. —*n.* A crowd or confused mass; *football*, a gathering of players behind the line of scrimmage for instructions; a private conference.—**hud·dler,** *n.*

Hu·di·bras·tic, hū″di·bras′tik, *a.* Pertaining to or resembling the style of Samuel Butler's *Hudibras*, a 17th century mock-heroic satirical poem consisting of iambic tetrameter couplets; mock-heroic.

Hud·son seal, *n.* Muskrat fur treated to resemble sealskin.

hue, hū, *n.* [O.E. *hīw*, *heow*, appearance; Sw. *hȳ*, color: Goth. *hiwi*, shape, show.] Color; a shade, tint, or gradation of a color; that attribute or quality of a specific color which fixes that color's spectrum position and classifies it as blue, green, red, or yellow.— **hued,** hūd, *a.* Having a color, usu. used in combination; as, rosy-*hued*.—**hue·less,** *a.*

hue and cry, *n.* [Fr. *huer*, to hoot, to shout; akin *hoot*.] Any public protest or outcry; formerly, a shouting or clamor raised as an alarm when a felony was committed.

huff, huf, *n.* [Imit.] A feeling of petulant anger or offended dignity; as, to be in a *huff*.—*v.t.* To make angry or offend; *checkers*, to remove, as a playing piece, from the board as forfeit.—*v.i.* To puff or pant; to take offense.

huff·ish, huf′ish, *a.* Petulant; angry; sulky.—**huff·ish·ly,** *adv.*—**huff·ish·ness,** *n.*

huff·y, huf′ē, *a.*—**huffier, huffiest.** Easily offended; touchy; offended or irritated.— **huff·i·ly,** *adv.*—**huff·i·ness,** *n.*

hug, hug, *v.t.*—**hugged, hugging.** [Origin doubtful; cf. Icel. *hugga*, to soothe, to comfort; D. *hugen*, to coax; Dan. *huge*, to squat.] To press or embrace closely with the arms, esp. affectionately; to clasp to the breast; to grasp or grip, as in wrestling; to cherish in the mind; as, to *hug* one's illusions; to keep close to; as, to *hug* the shore when sailing.—*v.i.* To embrace.—*n.* A close embrace; a clasp with the arms, as in wrestling; a bear's grip.—**hug·ger,** *n.*

huge, hūj, ūj, *a.*—**huger, hugest.** [O.E. *huge*, also *hogge*; cf. O.Fr. *ahuge*, huge; origin unknown.] Having an immense bulk; very large in area; enormous; very great in any respect. Also **huge·ous,** hū′jus.—**huge·ly,** **huge·ous·ly,** *adv.*—**huge·ness,** *n.*

hug·ger-mug·ger, hug′ẽr·mug″ẽr, *n.* [Compare *hug*, to lie close; obsolete *hugger*, to lurk; Norw. *mugg*, secrecy.] A jumbled or disordered state; confusion; secrecy. Also **hug·ger-mug·ger·y,** pl. **hug·ger-mug·ger·ies.**—*a.* Clandestine; sly; confused; disordered.—*v.t.* To hush up; to conceal. —*v.i.* To act clandestinely, secretly, or stealthily.

Hu·gue·not, hū′ge·not″, *n.* [Fr., earlier *eiguenot*, appar. < G. *eidgenoss*, confederate, < *eid*, oath, and *genoss*, companion, associate.] A member of the Reformed or Calvinistic communion of France in the 16th and 17th centuries; a French Protestant.—*a.* Also **Hu·gue·not·ic,** hū″ge·not′ik.—**Hu·gue·not·ism,** *n.*

hu·la, hö′la, *n.* [Native name.] A traditional Hawaiian dance telling a story through graceful swaying movements, usu. accompanied by drums and chanting. Also **hu·la-hu·la,** hö′la·hö′la.

hulk, hulk, *n.* [Same word as D. *hulk*, G. *hulk*, *holk*, Sw. *holk*, a kind of ship, < L.L. *hulca*, *olca*, < Gr. *holkas*, a ship of burden, < *helkō*, to draw.] The body of an old ship laid by as unfit for service; something or someone bulky or unwieldy; the deserted shell of any old or wrecked structure; *usu. pl.* an old or dismantled ship used for storage and formerly as a prison.—*v.i.* To come into view or appear in a massive form, usu. with *up*; *Brit. dial.* to act or move in an ungainly way.—**hulk·ing,** *a.*— **hulk·y,** *a.*—*hulkier, hulkiest.* Large and clumsy of body; unwieldy; ungainly.

hull, hul, *n.* [O.E. *hulu*, akin to *helan*, cover, hide.] The husk, shell, or outer covering of a seed or fruit, as in grains; the calyx of certain fruits, as the strawberry and raspberry; any covering or envelope.—*v.t.* To remove the hull of.—**hull·er,** *n.*—**hull·less,** *a.*

hull, hul, *n.* [Origin uncertain.] The frame or body of a ship, exclusive of superstructure such as masts, yards, sails, and rigging; that part of a flying boat's fuselage which rests upon the water; the main structure or body of a rigid or semi-rigid airship or dirigible.—*v.i.* Of a ship, to float or drift on the water, without power or sails.—*v.t.* To strike or pierce the hull of.

hul·la·ba·loo, hul′a·ba·lö″, *n.* [Imit. of confused noise.] Uproar; loud, noisy confusion.

hull down, *adv.*, *a.* Pertaining to a ship so far away that the hull is below the horizon and only the superstructure may be seen.

hul·lo, hu·lō′, *interj.* Hello. Also **hul·loo,** *Brit.* **hul·loa.**

hum, hum, *v.i.*—**hummed, humming.** [Imit. of sound; cf. G. *hummen*, *summen*, D. *hommelen*, to hum. *Humblebee*, *humbug*, *humdrum* are connected.] To make a prolonged sound like that of a bee; to drone; to murmur; to utter a similar sustained sound with the lips closed; to sing in this manner; to emit steady, mingled sounds of activity; as, a workshop *humming* with activity.—*v.t.* To sing or utter with a humming sound and without articulation; have an effect on by humming.—*n.* Any inarticulate, murmuring sound.—*interj.* A sound, as in clearing the throat, implying doubt and deliberation; a humming sound prompted by surprise or contemplation.—**hum·mer,** *n.*

hu·man, hū′man, ū′man, *a.* [Fr. *humain*, L. *humanus*, < *homo*, *hominis*, a man; akin to *humus*, the ground; also to O.E. *guma*, a man.] Pertaining to, belonging to, or having the qualities of mankind; composed of men; having the qualities or attributes of man. —*n.* A human being.—**hu·man·ness,** *n.*

hu·mane, hū·mān′, ū′mān, *a.* [Same word as *human*.] Kind; benevolent; tender; merciful; tending to civilize or refine.— **hu·mane·ly,** *adv.*—**hu·mane·ness,** *n.*

hu·man en·gi·neer·ing, *n.* The applied science of designing equipment and analyzing working conditions to fit the needs and skills of the worker.

hu·man·ism, hū′ma·niz″um, ū′ma·niz″um, *n.* Any system or mode of thought or action in which human and secular interests predominate; the study of the humanities; humanitarianism; (*sometimes cap.*) the renewed interest in the literature and ideas of the Renaissance humanists, which often de-emphasized religion.—**hu·man·ist,** *n.,* *a.*—**hu·man·is·tic,** *a.*

hu·man·i·tar·i·an, hū·man″i·târ′ē·an, ū·man″i·târ′ē·an, *a.* Tending to promote the welfare of mankind; philanthropic.—*n.* One who professes or practices humanitarian doctrines.

hu·man·i·tar·i·an·ism, hū·man″i·târ′ē·a·niz″um, *n.* Humanitarian principles; *ethics,* the doctrine which holds that mankind's chief obligation is to work for the welfare of human beings.

hu·man·i·ty, hū·man′i·tē, ū·man′i·tē, *n. pl.* **hu·man·i·ties.** [Fr. *humanité,* L. *humanitas,* < *humanus.*] Mankind; people collectively; the quality of being human; the quality of being humane; kindness. *Pl.* the fields of learning including the arts, history, literature, and philosophy, excluding the sciences, usu. used with *the.*

hu·man·ize, hū′ma·nīz″, ū′ma·nīz″, *v.t.* —*humanized, humanizing.* To render human or humane; to attribute human qualities to. —*v.i.* To become kind, compassionate, or civilized; to become human.—**hu·man·i·za·tion,** *n.*—**hu·man·iz·er,** *n.*

hu·man·kind, hū′man·kīnd″, hū′man·kīnd′, ū′man·kīnd″, ū′man·kīnd′, *n.* Mankind.

hu·man·ly, hū′man·lē, ū′man·lē, *adv.* In a human manner; within human understanding or ability; according to feelings or judgments of human beings.

hu·man·oid, hū′ma·noid″, ū′ma·noid″, *a.* Of undoubted human characteristics, in contrast to anthropoid which refers to both manlike and apelike qualities.—*n.*

hum·ble, hum′bl, um′bl, *a.*—*humbler, humblest.* [Fr. *humble* < L. *humilis* < *humus,* the earth.] Not proud or arrogant; modest; meek; submissive; low in rank or conditions.—*v.t.*—*humbled, humbling.* To render humble; to bring down the pride or vanity of; to reduce the power, status, or independence of; to abase.—**hum·ble·ness,** *n.*—**hum·bler,** *n.*—**hum·bly,** *adv.*

hum·ble·bee, hum′bl·bē″, *n.* [< old *humble,* to hum, < *hum*; compare G. *hummel,* Dan. *humle-bi,* Sw. *humla,* humblebee; < the humming sound it makes; whence also *bumblebee.*] A bumblebee.

hum·ble pie, *n.* Formerly, a pie made of the entrails or heart, liver, and kidneys, of the deer.—**eat hum·ble pie,** to apologize, or humiliate oneself; to be forced to admit error.

hum·bug, hum′bug″, *n.* [Origin unknown.] A deluding trick, hoax, fraud, or pretense; a quality or attitude of deception; a person who seeks to deceive others, as a cheat or imposter; something foolish or nonsensical; *Brit., Canadian,* a hard mint candy.—*v.t., v.i.*—*humbugged, humbugging.* To deceive; to/trick or delude.—**hum·bug·ger,** *n.*—**hum·bug·ger·y,** hum′bug″e·rē, *n.*

hum·ding·er, hum′ding′ẽr, *n. Slang,* a person or thing that is remarkable or outstandingly excellent.

hum·drum, hum′drum″, *a.* [< *hum* and *drum*; orig. droning, monotonous.] Commonplace, dull, monotonous.—*n.* The quality of being commonplace, routine, or workaday, or something having this quality. —**hum·drum·ness,** *n.*

hu·mec·tant, hū·mek′tant, *n.* A substance, as glycerol or sorbitol, which furthers moisture retention.—

hu·mer·al, hū′mẽr·al, *a.* [L. *humerus,* the shoulder.] *Anat.* pertaining to the humerus or the shoulder.

hu·mer·al veil, *n. Rom. Cath. Ch.* a scarflike vestment which covers the shoulders and hands, sometimes worn during High Mass.

hu·mer·us, hū′mẽr·us, *n. pl.* **hu·mer·i,** hū′me·rī″. *Anat.* the long, cylindrical bone of the arm of man, extending from shoulder to elbow; *zool.* the forelimb correspondingly located in other vertebrates.

hu·mic, hū′mik, *a.* Obtained from or relating to humus.

hu·mid, hū′mid, ū′mid, *a.* [L. *humidus, umidus,* < *humeo, umeo,* to be moist (akin *uvidus,* moist, *uva,* a grape); whence also *humor.*] Moist; damp; characterized by much moisture.—**hu·mid·ly,** *adv.*

hu·mid·i·fi·er, hū·mid′i·fī″ẽr, ū·mid′i·fī″ẽr, *n.* A piece of equipment for increasing or regulating the amount of moisture in the air of a building, room, or other area.

hu·mid·i·fy, hū·mid′i·fī″, ū·mid′i·fī″, *v.t.*—*humidified, humidifying.* To moisten; to make humid, as the air of a room.— **hu·mid·i·fi·ca·tion,** *n.*

hu·mid·i·stat, hū·mid′i·stat″, *n.* An instrument that automatically controls or maintains the degree of humidity.

hu·mid·i·ty, hū·mid′i·tē, ū·mid′i·tē, *n.* The state of being humid; moistness; dampness.—**rel·a·tive hu·mid·i·ty,** the percentage of water vapor in the air compared with that which is required to saturate it at the same temperature.

hu·mi·dor, hū′mi·dạr″, *n.* A container in which a suitable humidity is maintained, esp. one for storing cigars or tobacco.

hu·mil·i·ate, hū·mil′ē·āt″, ū·mil′ē·āt″, *v.t.*—*humiliated, humiliating.* [L. *humilis, humiliatum,* < *humilis,* humble.] To reduce the dignity or pride of; to humble; to disgrace.—**hu·mil·i·at·ing,** *a.* Humbling; mortifying.—**hu·mil·i·a·tion,** *n.*

hu·mil·i·ty, hū·mil′i·tē, ū·mil′i·tē, *n.* [L. *humilitas.*] The state of being humble; one's feeling of deference to another.

hum·ming·bird, hum′ing·bụrd″, *n.* A tiny, new-world, nonpasserine bird of the family *Trochilidae,* characterized by a long, narrow bill for sipping nectar from flowers, brilliant plumage of the male, and by narrow wings whose rapid vibration creates a humming sound.

hum·mock, hum′ok, *n.* [Prob. a dim. form of *hump.*] A rounded knoll; a protuberance on an ice field. A wooded ridge of land adjacent to a marsh or swamp; also *hammock.*—**hum·mock·y,** hum′o·kē, *a.*

hu·mor, *Brit.* **hu·mour,** hū′mẽr, ū′mẽr, *n.* [Fr. *humeur*; L. *humor,* moisture, liquid, < *humeo,* to be moist.] That quality in speech, writing, or action which tends to excite laughter, the capacity for perceiving the amusing or ludicrous; anything, as speech, writing, or action, intended to be comical; disposition or characteristic emotional state; temperament; frame of mind; as, to be in a good *humor. Zool.* any functioning fluid of an animal; as, the aqueous *humor; medieval med.* one of the four main fluids of the human body, blood, phlegm, yellow bile, and black bile, thought to determine bodily health and temperament.— **out of hu·mor,** displeased.—*v.t.* To comply with the humor or inclination of; to soothe by compliance; to gratify; to adapt oneself to.

hu·mor·al, hū′mẽr·al, ū′mẽr·al, *a. Physiol.* pertaining to or proceeding from the humors or fluids of the body.

hu·mor·esque, hū″mo·resk′, ū″mo·resk′, *n.* [G. *humoreske,* < L. *humor,* E. *humor.*] A musical composition of humorous or playful character.

hu·mor·ist, hū′mẽr·ist, ū′mẽr·ist, *n.* One who possesses a sense of humor; one who

uses humor skillfully, as a professional storyteller.—**hu·mor·is·tic,** *a.*

hu·mor·ous, hū′mẽr·us, ū′mẽr·us, *a.* Full of humor; exciting laughter; comical; funny; expressing humor; jocular; witty; amusing. —**hu·mor·ous·ly,** *adv.*—**hu·mor·ous·ness,** *n.*

hump, hump, *n.* [Origin uncertain: cf. D. *homp,* lump, chunk, L.G. *hump,* heap, hill, stump.] A rounded protuberance, esp. on the back, as that due to abnormal curvature of the spine in man, or that normally present in certain animals, as the camel and bison; a mound or low hill; *rail.* a mound for switching cars by gravity; *Brit. slang,* a fit of ill humor or gloomy dissatisfaction; (*cap.*) an eastern range of the Himalayas; *fig.* a critical or trying point or phase, as: We are over the *hump* now.—*v.t.* To raise, as the back, in a hump; *colloq.* to exert, as oneself; *rail.* to move by using the switching system on a hump.—*v.i. Colloq.* to hurry or exert oneself.—**hump·back,** *n.* A back with a hump; one who has such a back; also *hunchback.* A whale of the genus *Megaptera,* with a humplike dorsal fin.—**hump·backed,** *a.*—**hump·i·ness,** *n.*—**hump·y,** *a.*—*humpier, humpiest.*

humph, humf, *interj.* A sound or grunt expressing doubt, irritation, or contempt.

hu·mus, hū′mus, ū′mus, *n.* [L. earth, ground.] The organic constituent of soil, produced by the partial decomposition of plant and animal matter and essential for plant nutrition.

Hun, hun, *n.* [L.L. *Hunni,* pl.] One of an Asiatic race of warlike nomads who overran and devastated much of Europe in the 5th century, led by their king, Attila; (*often l.c.*) an uncivilized or barbarous devastator.—**Hun·nish,** *a.*—**Hun·nish·ness,** *n.*

hunch, hunch, *v.t.* [Origin obscure: cf. *hump.*] To thrust out or up in a hump.—*v.i.* To lunge or push oneself ahead jerkily; to be in a bent posture while sitting or standing. —*n.* A protuberance or hump; a lump or thick piece; *colloq.* a premonition or suspicion.

hunch·back, hunch′bak″, *n.* A back deformed by a convex curvature of the spine; one who has such a back. Also *humpback.* —**hunch·backed,** *a.*

hun·dred, hun′drid, *n. pl.* **hun·dreds, hun·dred.** [O.E. *hundred* = Icel. *hundrath*; Dan. *hundrede,* D. *honderd,* G. *hundert*; < *hund,* cog. with L. *centum,* Skt. *catam,* a hundred, and a termination akin to E. *read,* and to Goth. *garathjan,* to reckon.] The cardinal number between 99 and 101; a symbol representing it, as *100* or *C*; any collection of 100 units; formerly, a subdivision of a county in England, presently such a subdivision in Delaware.—*a.*— **hun·dredth,** hun′dridth, hun′dritth, *n., a.*

hun·dred-per·cent·er, hun′drid·pẽr·sen′tẽr, *n.* One who totally supports the national policy.

hun·dred·weight, hun′drid·wāt″, *n. pl.* **hun·dred·weights, hun·dred·weight.** A unit of weight equal to 100 pounds in the United States; *Brit.* a unit equalling 112 pounds. Abbr. *cwt.*

Hun·gar·i·an, hung·gâr′ē·an, *a.* Of or pertaining to the central European country of Hungary, its language, or its people. —*n.* A native or inhabitant of Hungary; the language of the Hungarian people. Also *Magyar.*

hun·ger, hung′gẽr, *n.* [O.E. *hunger, hungor* = G. Dan. and Sw. *hunger,* Icel. *hungr.* Goth. *huhrus,* hunger.] An uneasy sensation or weakened physical condition caused by a lack of food; a craving for food; any strong or eager desire.—*v.i.* To feel hunger; to crave food; to desire eagerly.—*v.t.* To cause hunger in; starve.

hun·ger strike, *n.* A protest, in the form of a refusal to eat, against treatment or conditions considered unsatisfactory or unjustifiable.

hung o·ver, *a. Slang,* suffering from the effects of excessive consumption of alcohol.

hun·gry, hung′grē, *a.—hungrier, hungriest.* [O.E. *hungrig.*] Feeling hunger; having a need or craving for food; having a strong desire; poor or unproductive, as soil.—**hun·gri·ly,** *adv.—***hun·gri·ness,** *n.*

hunk, hungk, *n.* [A form of *hunch.*] *Colloq.* a large lump or portion; *slang,* a virile man.

hun·ker, hung′kẽr, *v.i.* [Origin obscure: cf. *huck.*] To squat on one's haunches.—**hun·kers,** *n. pl. Sc. colloq.* the haunches.—**on one's hun·kers,** in a squatting posture.

hunks, hungks, *n. pl., sing. or pl. in construction.* [Origin obscure.] A disagreeable person; a covetous man; a miser.

hunk·y-do·ry, hung′kē·dōr′ē, *a. Slang.* All right; very satisfactory; comfortable. Also **hunk·y.**

hunt, hunt, *v.t.* [O.E. *huntian,* prob. akin to *hentan,* seize, E. *hent.*] To chase or search for, as game, for the purpose of catching or killing; to pursue with force or hostility, often followed by *down;* to search for or seek; endeavor to obtain or find, often followed by *up;* to scour, as a region, in pursuit of game; to search thoroughly; to use or manage, as a horse, in the chase.—*v.i.* To engage in hunting animals as a sport or to obtain food; make a search or quest, often followed by *for.—n.* The act or practice of hunting game; the chase; the act of seeking something; a search; a body of persons associated for the purpose of hunting; an association of huntsmen; a region utilized for hunting.—**hunt·a·ble,** *a.*

hunt·er, hun′tẽr, *n.* One who hunts game; a huntsman; a horse or a dog used in hunting; one who searches or seeks for something; as, a fortune *hunter.*

hunt·ing, hun′ting, *n.* The act of one who or that which hunts; the pursuing of game; the chase; *electron.* an unstable condition, as in an automatic-control system, caused by excessive feedback.—*a.*

hunt·ress, hun′tris, *n.* A woman who hunts or follows the chase; a female horse used in hunting.

hunts·man, hunts′man, *n. pl.* **hunts·men.** One who hunts or practices hunting; a person who manages the chase and oversees the hounds.—**hunts·man·ship,** *n.*

hur·dle, hẽr′dl, *n.* [O.E. *hyrdel,* akin to D. *horde,* G. *hürde,* hurdle, Icel. *hurdh,* Goth. *haurds,* door, L. *crātis,* wickerwork, Gr. *kurtos,* basket, cage.] An obstacle or barrier, man-made or natural, which must be jumped over or vaulted in certain competitive sports such as track and horse-racing; *pl. but sing. in constr.* a race in which such barriers are used; *fig.* any barrier or problem to be overcome. *Brit.* a movable rectangular frame of interlaced twigs, crossed bars, or the like, as for a temporary fence; a frame or sledge on which criminals in England formerly were drawn to the place of execution.—*v.t.* —*hurdled, hurdling.* To jump over, as in racing; to overcome or conquer, as a handicap or difficulty; to construct or enclose with hurdles.—*v.i.* To leap over a hurdle.—**hur·dler,** *n.*

hur·dy-gur·dy, hẽr′dē·gụr′dē, hẽr′dē·gụr″dē, *n. pl.* **hur·dy-gur·dies.** [Intended to suggest its sound.] Any of various instruments operated by a hand crank, esp. a barrel organ; a stringed musical instrument which produces tones by the rotating friction of a resined wheel acting as a bow against four strings.

hurl, hẽrl, *v.t.* [M.E. *hurlen;* origin uncertain: cf. *hurtle.*] To pitch, drive, throw, or fling away forcefully; to utter with vehemence; as, to *hurl* a tirade of abuse.—*v.i.* To throw a missile; *baseball,* to pitch. —*n.* A forcible or violent throw; a fling.—**hurl·er,** *n.*

hurl·ing, hẽr′ling, *n.* A traditional Irish sport, similar to field hockey, played on a 140-yard field by two opposing teams, each having 15 players.

hurl·y, hẽr′lē, *n. pl.* **hurl·ies.** Hubbub; turmoil.

hurl·y-burl·y, hụr′lē·bụr′lē, hụr′lē·bur′lē, *n. pl.* **hurl·y-burl·ies.** [Appar. a reduplicated formation < *hurl:* cf. Fr. *hurluberlu,* a harebrained person.] Commotion; tumult; bustle; confusion.—*a.* Noisy; uproarious, tumultuous.

hur·rah, hu·rä′, hu·rạ′, *interj.* [Compare E. *huzza,* G. *hurrah,* Dan. and Sw. *hurra,* Pol. *hura.*] An exclamation expressive of joy, applause, or encouragement.—*v.i.* To utter a hurrah.—*n.* Commotion; excitement; a joyous or encouraging exclamation. Also **hur·ray,** hu·rā′.

hur·ri·cane, hụr′i·kān″, hụr′i·kãn″, *Brit. also* hur′i·kạn, *n.* [Sp. *huracán;* < Carib.] A violent, tropical, cyclonic storm with winds greater than 75 miles per hour; *fig.* anything suggesting such a storm.

hur·ri·cane deck, *n.* A light upper deck, as on passenger steamers.

hur·ri·cane lamp, *n.* A lamp or candlestick having a glass chimney as protection against wind.

hur·ried, hụr′ēd, hur′ēd, *a.* Pushed or impelled to hurry; moving rapidly; characterized by or done with hurry, as actions or work; hasty.—**hur·ried·ly,** *adv.—***hur·ried·ness,** *n.*

hur·ry, hụr′ē, hur′ē, *v.t.—hurried, hurrying.* [Akin to G. *hurren,* to move hastily.] To impel to greater speed or haste; to urge to act or proceed hastily; to cause to be performed with great or undue rapidity; to hasten.—*v.i.* To move or act with haste, often followed by *up.—n.* The act of hurrying; urgency; bustle; confusion.—**hur·ry·ing·ly,** *adv.*

hur·ry-scur·ry, hur·ry-skur·ry, hụr′ē·skur′ē, hur′ē·skur′ē, *n.* Headlong, disorderly haste; hurry and confusion.—*adv.* With disorderly haste, bustle, and confusion; in disorderly flight or haste.—*a.* Characterized by disorderly flight or haste—*v.i.—hurry-scurried, hurry-scurrying, hurry-skurried, hurry-skurrying.* To rush; to act hastily.

hurt, hẽrt, *v.t.—hurt, hurting.* [O.Fr. *hurter,* Mod. Fr. *heurter,* to knock against; perh. of Celtic origin; cf. W. *hwyrdd,* a push, a thrust, a blow. Hence *hurtle,* *hurl.*] To cause physical or mental pain to; to wound or bruise painfully; to offend or wound the feelings of; to harm; to impair; to damage.—*v.i.* To feel or cause physical or mental pain; to cause harm.—*n.* A wound, bruise, or the like; anguish; loss; damage.

hurt·ful, hẽrt′ful, *a.* Harmful, injurious.—**hurt·ful·ly,** *adv.—***hurt·ful·ness,** *n.*

hur·tle, hẽr′tl, *v.i.—hurtled, hurtling.* To move rapidly and sometimes noisily; to rush; to strike forcibly or collide, with *against* or *together.—v.t.* To fling or dash violently; to hurl.

hus·band, huz′band, *n.* [O.E. *hūsbonda,* the master of the house, < Icel. *hūsūndi,* Dan. *huusbond,* Sw. *husbonde.*] A married man. —*v.t.* To administer or manage with prudence and economy; to conserve. *Archaic,* to cultivate or till; to secure a husband for; to mate.—**hus·band·er,** *n.* —**hus·band·less,** *a.*

hus·band·man, huz′band·man, *n. pl.* **hus·band·men.** One who specializes in agriculture or farm husbandry; farmer.

hus·band·ry, huz′ban·drē, *n.* Agricultural cultivation, production of crops, and the breeding of animals for food, esp. through scientific control and management; frugal and thrifty conservation; household management.

hush, hush, *v.t.* [Akin to *hist, whist, hiss;* G. *hush,* Dan. *hys, hyst,* a sound made to enjoin silence.] To still; to silence; to make quiet; to allay or calm, as fears; to suppress or keep concealed, as news, used with *up.—v.i.* To be or become silent.—*n.* Stillness; quiet.—*interj.* A word used to enjoin silence.

—hush mon·ey, a bribe paid to prevent disclosure of facts.

hush-hush, hush′hush″, *a.* Highly confidential; secret.

hush·pup·py, hush′pup″ē, *n. pl.* **hush·-pup·pies.** *South. U.S.* a cornmeal mixture formed into a small ball and deep-fat fried.

husk, husk, *n.* [Akin to D. *hulze,* G. *hülse,* a husk; equiv. to E. *hull,* a husk, with *sk* as a termination.] The external covering of certain fruits or seeds of plants; glume; hull; chaff; an outer frame or shell.—*v.t.* To deprive of the husk; as, to *husk* corn.

husk·er, *n.* One who or a machine that husks.—**husk·y,** *a.* Abounding with husks; husklike or covered with husks.

husk·ing, hus′king, *n.* The act of removing husks, esp. those of corn; a husking bee. —**husk·ing bee,** a gathering of persons to assist in husking corn.

husk·y, hus′kē, *a.—huskier, huskiest.* [Allied to *hoarse;* O.E. *hwōsta,* Sc. *hoast,* a cough.] Rough in tone, as the voice; hoarse or voice, as or as if caused by emotion.— **husk·i·ly,** *adv.—***husk·i·ness,** *n.*

husk·y, hus′kē, *a.—huskier, huskiest.* Burly; powerful; robust; large in stature.—*n. pl.* **husk·ies.** One who is large and robust.— **husk·i·ness,** *n.*

husk·y, hus′kē, *n. pl.* **husk·ies.** [Said to be a corruption of *Eskimo.*] (*Sometimes cap.*) An Eskimo dog; *Canadian, colloq.* an Eskimo; the Eskimo language.

hus·sar, hụ·zär′, *n.* [Hung. *huszár.*] A member of any of various lightly-armed units maintained in some European armies, often distinguished by showy dress uniforms; originally one of the 15th century light Hungarian cavalry.

Huss·ite, hus′īt, *n.* [From John *Huss,* Bohemian religious nationalist and reformer, burned as a heretic in 1415.] Referring to the doctrines of John Huss.—*a.* —**Huss·it·ism,** *n.*

hus·sy, hus′ē, huz′ē, *n. pl.* **huss·ies.** [Contr. < *huswife, housewife.*] A disreputable, brazen woman; a pert, saucy wench; minx.

hus·tings, hus′tings, *n. pl., sing. or pl. in constr.* [O.E. *hūsting,* < Scand.: cf. Icel. *hūsthing,* 'house assembly,' council summoned by a king or leader.] *Brit.* an ancient court of London, still infrequently held; the temporary platform from which Parliamentary candidates were formerly nominated and addressed the electors. In general, an electioneering platform; election proceedings.—**hus·tings court,** a local court in various cities of Virginia.

hus·tle, hus′el, *v.t.—hustled, hustling.* [D. *husselen,* freq. of *hutsen,* shake, jog.] To push or shove along; to jostle; to force roughly or hurriedly, as into, out of, or through a place; *colloq.* to hurry. *Slang,* to sell or obtain aggressively or by questionable tactics; to seek clients as a prostitute.—*v.i.* To push or force one's way; to proceed or work rapidly or energetically.—*n.* The act of one who hustles; energetic activity, as in work or business.—**hus·tler,** *n. Slang,* a prostitute.

hut, hut, *n.* [Same word as D. *hut,* G. *hütte,* Dan. *hytte,* Sw. *hydda,* a hut; cf. W. *cwt,* a hovel.] A dwelling, usu. small and simply constructed; shack; cabin; a structure for temporary housing of troops.—*v.t.—hutted, hutting.* To place in or furnish with a hut. —*v.i.* To take lodging in huts.

hutch, huch, *n.* [O.Fr. Fr. *huche*, < M.L. *hutica*, chest; perh. < Teut.] A pen or enclosed coop for confining small animals; as, a rabbit *hutch*; a cupboard or case with open shelves to display dishes; a chest, box, or compartment for storing things.

hut·ment, hut'ment, *n.* A group or encampment of huts, as for troops.

huz·zah, huz·za, hu·zä', *interj.* An expression of appreciation, joy, or approval.

hy·a·cinth, hī'a·sinth, *n.* [L. *hyacinthus* < Gr. *hyakinthos,* kind of flower, also a gem: cf. *jacinth.*] *Bot.* any of various bulbous plants of the lily family, genus *Hyacinthus,* esp. *H. orientalis,* characterized by fragrant spikes of bell-shaped flowers; the bulb of this plant. *Gr. antiq.* a plant formerly identified as gladiolus, iris, or larkspur, and believed to spring from the blood of *Hyacinthus,* accidentally killed by Apollo. *Mineral.* a reddish-orange or brownish zircon; also *jacinth.* A bluish gem of the ancients.—**hy·a·cin·thine,** hī''a·sin'thin, hī''a·sin'thīn, *a.*

Hy·a·des, hī'a·dēz'', *n. pl.* [Gr. *hyades* < *hyō,* to rain.] *Astron.* a cluster of stars in the constellation Taurus, formerly thought to indicate rain when they rose with the sun. *Mythol.* the daughters of Atlas, whom Zeus placed among the stars. Also **Hy·ads,** hī'adz.

hy·ae·na, hī·ē'na, *n.* Hyena.

hy·a·line, hī'a·lēn'', hī'a·lin, *n.* [L.L. *hyalinus* < Gr. *hyalinos* < *hyalos,* glass.] Something glassy or transparent. *Biochem.* any of various nitrogenous substances, esp. that which is the main component of hydatid cysts; also **hy·a·lin.**—hī'a·lin, hī'a·lin'', *a.*

hy·a·line car·ti·lage, *n. Anat.* the typical translucent form of cartilage, containing little fibrous tissue.

hy·a·lite, hī'a·līt'', *n.* [Gr. *hyalos,* glass.] *Mineral.* a colorless variety of opal, sometimes transparent like glass, and sometimes whitish and translucent.

hy·a·loid, hī'a·loid'', *a.* Resembling glass; vitriform; transparent.

hy·al·o·plasm, hī·al'o·plaz''um, hī'a·lō·plaz''um, *n.* [Gr. *hyalos,* glass, and *plasma,* E. *plasma,* plasm.] *Biol.* the clear, pellucid part of the protoplasm of a cell, as distinguished from the granular and reticular parts.

hy·a·lu·ron·ic ac·id, hī'a·lụ·ron'ik as'id, hī''a·lụ·ron'ik as'id, *n. Biochem.* a polymer which apparently holds cells together and lubricates joints, found in animal tissues, esp. skin, vitreous humor, and synovial fluid.

hy·a·lu·ron·i·dase, hī'a·lụ·ron'i·dās'', hī''a·lụ·ron'i·dāz'', *n. Biochem.* an enzyme which breaks down the molecular structure of hyaluronic acid, thus increasing the permeability of animal tissues.

hy·brid, hī'brid, *n.* [L. *hybrida, hibrida.*] The offspring of two animals or plants of different races, varieties and, rarely, species and genera; anything derived from heterogeneous sources or composed of elements of different or incongruous kinds; a word composed of elements belonging to different languages.—*a.*—**hy·brid·ism,** hī'bri·diz''um, *n.*—**hy·brid·i·ty,** hi·brid'i·tē, *n.*

hy·brid·ize, hī'bri·dīz'', *v.t.*—*hybridized, hybridizing.* To cause to produce hybrids; to cross, interbreed; to form in a hybrid manner, as words.—*v.i.* To cause the production of hybrids by crossing different varieties or races; to produce hybrids.—**hy·brid·i·za·tion,** hī''bri·di·zā'shan, *n.*—**hy·brid·iz·er,** *n.*

hy·brid per·pet·u·al rose, *n. Hort.* a hardy and fragrant variety of rose, developed from the Bourbon rose and noted for its nearly continuous blooming.

hy·brid tea rose, *n. Hort.* any of many cultivated varieties of *Rosa odorata* or *R.*

chinensis, grown for their usu. recurrent season of bloom.

hy·bris, hī'bris, *n.* Hubris.

hy·da·thode, hī'da·thōd, *n. Bot.* an outer structure located at the leaf apex, for water exudation in higher plants. See *guttation.*

hy·da·tid, hī'da·tid, *n.* [Gr. *hydatis,* a vesicle, < *hydōr,* water.] *Pathol.* a fluid-filled cyst formed in the bodies of men and certain animals by the tapeworm larva; an encysted tapeworm larva.—*a.* Also **hy·da·tid·i·nous,** hī''da·tid'i·nus.

hy·dra, hī'dra, *n. pl.* **hy·dras, hy·drae,** hī'drē. [L. *hydra* < Gr. *hydra,* water serpent, < *hydōr,* water.] *Zool.* any of the fresh-water polyps constituting the genus *Hydra;* (*cap.*), *astron.* a southern constellation represented as a serpent; (*cap. or l.c.*), *class. mythol.* a monstrous serpent slain by Hercules and represented as having nine heads, each of which, when severed, was replaced by two unless the wound was cauterized. *Fig.* any persistent problem or evil arising from many sources or difficult to extirpate.

hy·drac·id, hī·dras'id, *n. Chem.* an acid which contains no oxygen, as hydrochloric acid.

hy·dran·gea, hī·drān'ja, hī·drān'jē·a, hī·dran'ja, hī·dran'jē·a, *n.* [Gr. *hydōr,* water, and *angeion,* a vessel, from the shape of its capsules.] *Bot.* a shrub of the genus *Hydrangea,* cultivated for its clustered pink, white, or blue flowers.

hy·drant, hī'drant, *n.* [Gr. *hydraino,* to irrigate, < *hydōr,* water.] An upright pipe with valves and an outlet from which water is drawn and discharged for fighting fires and watering streets; also *fireplug.* A large water faucet.

hy·dranth, hī'dranth, *n.* [N.L. *Hydra,* genus of polyps, and Gr. *anthos,* flower.] *Zool.* the nutritive region of a hydroid polyp, in which the mouth, tentacles, and stomach area are located.

hy·drate, hī'drāt, *n.* [Gr. *hydōr,* water.] *Chem.* any of a class of compounds produced when certain substances, as metallic salts, unite with water; a hydroxide.—*v.t., v.i.*—*hydrated, hydrating.* To combine chemically with water; to form into a hydrate.—**hy·dra·tion,** hī·drā'shan, *n.*—**hy·dra·tor,** *n.*

hy·drau·lic, hī·drạ'lik, hī·drol'ik, *a.* [L. *hydraulicus,* < Gr. *hydraulikos,* < *hydraulis,* hydraulic organ, < *hydōr,* water, and *aulos,* flute, pipe.] Pertaining to water or other liquid in motion, or to hydraulics; operated by or employing water; operated by means of pressure produced by forcing a liquid, as oil or water, though a narrow opening or pipe; hardening under water, as a cement. —**hy·drau·li·cal·ly,** *adv.*

hy·drau·lic ram, *n.* A pump device by which the energy of descending water is utilized to raise a part of the water to a height greater than that of the source.

hy·drau·lics, hī·drạ'liks, hī·drol'iks, *n. pl., sing. or pl. in constr.* The science dealing with water or other liquid in motion, its uses in engineering, and the laws governing its action.

hy·dra·zine, hī'dra·zēn'', hī'dra·zin, *n.* [< *hydrogen* and *azote.*] *Chem.* A colorless, fuming liquid, H_2NNH_2, used primarily in rocket and jet engine fuels and as a reducing agent; a derivative of this compound formed when one or more of the hydrogen atoms are replaced by an organic group.

hy·dric, hī'drik, *a.* [Gr. *hydōr,* water.] Pertaining to, containing, or needing much moisture; *chem.* of, pertaining to, or containing hydrogen.—**hy·dri·cal·ly,** *adv.*

hy·dride, hī'drīd, hī'drid, *n. Chem.* a compound of hydrogen and another element or radical, usu. a more electropositive one.

hy·dri·od·ic ac·id, hī''drē·od'ik as'id, *n. Chem.* a water solution of hydrogen oxide, HI, a colorless or very light yellow liquid acid, used in medicine.

hy·dro, hī'drō, *n. Brit.* an establishment offering mineral water cures; a spa. *Canadian,* hydroelectric power or the power plant producing it.

hy·dro·air·plane, hī''drō·âr'plān'', *n.* An airplane equipped with floats, or with a boatlike underpart, enabling it to alight upon or ascend from water. Also *seaplane, hydroplane.*

hy·dro·bomb, hī'drō·bom'', *n.* An aerial torpedo which is driven by a rocket engine upon entering water.

hy·dro·bro·mic ac·id, hī''drō·brō'mik as'id, *n. Chem.* hydrogen bromide, HBr, in aqueous solution, sometimes used for sedative purposes.

hy·dro·car·bon, hī''drō·kär'bon, *n. Chem.* any one of the compounds consisting of hydrogen and carbon only, as benzene or methane.—**hy·dro·car·bo·na·ceous, hy·dro·car·bon·ic, hy·dro·car·bo·nous,** *a.*

hy·dro·cele, hī'drō·sēl'', *n.* [Gr. *hydōr,* water, and *kēlē,* a tumor.] *Pathol.* a collection of serous fluid in a saccular body cavity, esp. the scrotum.

hy·dro·ceph·a·lus, hī''drō·sef'a·lus, *n.* [Gr. *hydōr,* water, and *kephalē,* the head.] *Pathol.* an accumulation of serous fluid within the cavity of the cranium, esp. in infancy, causing enlargement of the head. Also **hy·dro·ceph·a·ly.**—**hy·dro·ce·phal·ic,** hī''drō·se·fal'ik, *n., a.*—**hy·dro·ceph·a·lous,** *a.*

hy·dro·chlo·ric ac·id, hī''drō·klōr'ik as'id, *n. Chem.* an aqueous solution of hydrogen chloride, HCl, a strong, fuming, highly corrosive acid used in industry, research, and medicine. Also *muriatic acid.*

hy·dro·chlo·ride, hī''drō·klōr'īd, hī''drō·klōr'id, *n. Chem.* a salt formed by combining hydrochloric acid with an organic base such as an amine.

hy·dro·col·loid, hī''drō·kol'oid, *n.* A gelatinous colloid used in dentistry for making elastic impressions of teeth.—**hy·dro·col·loi·dal,** hī''drō·ko·loid'al, *a.*

hy·dro·cor·ti·sone, hī''drō·kạr'ti·sōn'', hī''drō·kạr'ti·zōn'', *n. Pharm.* an adrenal cortical steroid hormone, $C_{21}H_{30}O_5$, used in medicine as an anti-inflammatory aid in treating arthritis and other conditions. Also *cor·ti·sol.*

hy·dro·cy·an·ic ac·id, hī''drō·sī·an'ik as'id, *n. Chem.* hydrogen cyanide, HCN, in aqueous solution, a weak, oily acid that is extremely volatile and poisonous, used chiefly in the manufacture of fumigants. Also *prussic acid.*

hy·dro·dy·nam·ic, hī''drō·dī·nam'ik, hī''drō·di·nam'ik, *a.* [Gr. *hydōr,* water, and *dynamis,* power.] Pertaining to the force, pressure, or motion of water; hydrokinetic. Also **hy·dro·dy·nam·i·cal.**—**hy·dro·dy·nam·i·cal·ly,** *adv.*

hy·dro·dy·nam·ics, hī''drō·dī·nam'iks, *n. pl., sing. or pl. in constr.* That branch of science dealing with the application of forces to fluids, especially when producing motion in fluids; hydrokinetics. Also **hy·dro·me·chan·ics,** hī''drō·me·kan'iks.

hy·dro·e·lec·tric, hī''drō·i·lek'trik, *a.* Pertaining to the production of electric current by the energy of moving water.—**hy·dro·e·lec·tric·i·ty,** hī''drō·i·lek·tris'i·tē, hī''drō·ē''lek·tris'i·tē, *n.*

hy·dro·flu·or·ic ac·id, hī''drō·flō·ạr'ik as'id, hī''drō·flō·or'ik as'id, *n.* An aqueous solution of hydrogen fluoride, HF, which is extremely corrosive and poisonous, used esp. in polishing, etching, and frosting glass.

hy·dro·foil, hī'drō·foil'', *n.* A foil or surface, attached to a boat or hydroplane, designed to provide support in moving water; a boat equipped with hydrofoils, which lift the hull above water level as it travels.

hy·dro·form·ing, hī′dro·fạr″ming, n. A process for forming high-octane motor fuel or aromatics from naphthas, using hydrogen.

hy·dro·gen, hī′dro·jen, n. [Fr. *hydrogène,* < Gr. *hydōr,* water, and *gen–,* bear, produce (from its generating water by combining with oxygen).] *Chem.* a colorless, odorless, flammable gaseous element, the lightest of the known elements. Sym. H, at. no. 1, at. wt. 1.008.—**hy·drog·e·nous,** hī·droj′e·nus, a.

hy·dro·gen·ate, hī′dro·je·nāt″, hī·droj′e·nāt″, v.t.—*hydrogenated, hydrogenating.Chem.* to combine, expose to, or treat with hydrogen.—**hy·dro·gen·a·tion,** hī″dro·je·nā′shan, hī·droj″e·nā′shan, n.

hy·dro·gen bomb, n. A bomb that uses the fusion of light nuclei, as hydrogen isotopes, under very high temperature, to produce a powerful explosion. Also *fusion bomb, H-bomb.*

hy·dro·gen i·on, n. *Chem.* hydrogen which has been ionized, being the positive ion in acid solutions. Sym. H⁺.

hy·dro·gen per·ox·ide, n. *Chem.* a colorless, unstable, oily liquid, H_2O_2, the aqueous solution of which is used chiefly as a bleaching and oxidizing agent and as a mild antiseptic. Also *peroxide.*

hy·dro·gen sul·fide, n. *Chem.* a colorless, flammable, poisonous gas, H_2S, with the odor of rotten eggs, used esp. in laboratory analysis and metallurgy.

hy·drog·ra·phy, hī·drog′ra·fē, n. [Gr. *hydōr,* water, and *graphō,* to describe.] The scientific measurement, charting, and description of rivers, lakes, seas, and other waters; those sections on a map representing bodies of water.—**hy·drog·ra·pher,** n. —**hy·dro·graph·ic, hy·dro·graph·i·cal,** hī″dro·graf′ik, a.—**hy·dro·graph·i·cal·ly,** adv.

hy·droid, hī′droid, a. *Zool.* pertaining to or resembling the hydras or the hydrozoans, specif. pertaining to that form of hydrozoan which is asexual and grows into branching colonies by budding.—n. A hydrozoan, specif. the polyp form of a hydrozoan.

hy·dro·ki·net·ic, hī′drō·ki·net′ik, hī″drō·ki·net′ik, a. Pertaining to the motion of fluids or to the forces causing such motion. —**hy·dro·ki·net·ics,** n. pl. but sing. in constr. The branch of science which deals with the theories and laws concerning the motions of liquids. Also *hydrodynamics.*

hy·drol·o·gy, hī·drol′o·jē, n. [Gr. *hydōr,* water, and *logos,* discourse.] The science that treats of the properties, laws, and distribution of water underground, on the earth's surface, and in the atmosphere. —**hy·dro·log·ic, hy·dro·log·i·cal,** hī″dro·loj′ik, a.—**hy·dro·log·i·cal·ly,** adv. —**hy·drol·o·gist,** n.

hy·drol·y·sis, hī·drol′i·sis, n. pl. **hy·drol·y·ses,** hī·drol′i·sēz″. *Chem.* chemical decomposition in which a compound is divided into other compounds by taking up the elements of water.—**hy·dro·lyte,** hī′dro·līt″, n. *Chem.* a compound subjected to hydrolysis.—**hy·dro·lyt·ic,** hī″dro·lit′ik, a.

hy·dro·lyze, hī′dro·līz″, v.i., v.t.—*hydrolyzed, hydrolyzing.* To go through or cause to go through the process of hydrolysis.— **hy·dro·lyz·a·ble,** a.—**hy·dro·ly·za·tion,** hī″dro·li·zā′shan, n.—**hy·dro·lyz·er,** n.

hy·dro·man·cy, hī′dro·man″sē, n. [Gr. *hydōr,* water, and *manteia,* divination.] A method of divination by water.—**hy·dro·manc·er,** n.

hy·dro·mel, hī′dro·mel″, n. [Fr. < Gr. *hydōr,* water, and *meli,* honey.] A liquor

consisting of honey diluted in water which forms mead when fermented.

hy·dro·met·al·lur·gy, hī″drō·met′a·-lur″jē, n. The process of extracting metals by leaching ores with aqueous solutions.

hy·dro·me·te·or, hī″drō·mē′tē·ėr, n. *Meteor.* any of the various forms produced by condensation of atmospheric water vapors, as hail, rain, or fog.—**hy·dro·me·te·or·ol·o·gy,** hī″drō·mē″tē·o·rol′o·-jē. n.

hy·drom·e·ter, hī·drom′i·tėr, n. [Gr. *hydōr,* water, and *metron,* a measure.] A device for measuring specific gravity of fluids, consisting of a weighted tube that floats vertically, determining the specific gravity by comparison of a graduated scale on the tube with the liquid level.—**hy·dro·met·ric, hy·dro·met·ri·cal,** hī″dro·-me′trik, a.—**hy·drom·e·try,** n.

hy·drop·a·thy, hī·drop′a·thē, n. [Gr. *hydōr,* water, and *pathos,* affection.] The empirical treatment of disease by the use of water externally or internally; water cure. —**hy·dro·path·ic,** hī″dro·path′ik, a.

hy·dro·phane, hī′dro·fān″, n. [Gr. *hydōr,* water, and *phainō,* to show.] *Mineral.* a partially translucent variety of opal that becomes more nearly transparent by immersion in water.

hy·dro·phil·ic, hī″dro·fil′ik, a. *Chem.* Having an affinity or attraction for water; having the ability of uniting with or dissolving in water. Also **hy·dro·phile,** hī′dro·fīl.

hy·droph·i·lous, hī·drof′i·lus, a. *Bot.* pollinated by the agency of water.—**hy·droph·i·ly,** n.

hy·dro·pho·bi·a, hī″dro·fō′bē·a, n. [Gr. *hydōr,* water, and *phobos,* fear.] An abnormal fear of water. *Pathol.* rabies, an infectious disease of certain animals caused by a virus and transmitted to man by the bite of the infected animal.—**hy·dro·pho·bic,** a. *Pathol.* pertaining to hydrophobia. *Chem.* having no affinity for water.—**hy·dro·pho·bic·i·ty,** hī″dro·fō·bis′i·tē, n.

hy·dro·phone, hī′dro·fōn″, n. Any of various devices for locating causes or sources of sound under water, as for determining the presence and position of submarines from the noise made by their engines. *Med.* an instrument used in auscultation, whereby sounds are conveyed through a column of water.

hy·dro·phyte, hī′dro·fīt″, n. [Gr. *hydōr,* water, and *phyton,* a plant.] *Bot.* a plant which lives and grows in water or very wet soil.—**hy·dro·phyt·ic,** hī″dro·fit′ik, a.

hy·dro·plane, hī′dro·plān″, n. A seaplane; an attachment to an airplane enabling it to glide on the water; a kind of motorboat provided with a plane or planes by means of which it can reduce its displacement at high speed or skim along the surface of the water; a horizontal rudder for submerging or elevating a submarine boat.—v.i.—*hydroplaned, hydroplaning.* To move swiftly over the water with the hull above water level; to travel in or operate a hydroplane.

hy·dro·pon·ics, hī″dro·pon′iks, n. pl. but sing. in constr. A method of growing plants by rooting them in chemical solutions instead of soil.—**hy·dro·pon·ic,** a.—**hy·dro·pon·i·cal·ly,** adv.

hy·dro·qui·none, hī″drō·kwi·nōn′, hī″dro·kwin′ōn, n. *Chem.* a white, sweetish crystalline compound, $C_6H_4(OH)_2$, formed by the reduction of quinone and used in photographic development. Also **hy·dro·quin·ol,** hī″dro·kwin′ōl.

hy·dro·scope, hī′dro·skōp″, n. An optical apparatus which enables the observer to view objects below the surface of the sea.— **hy·dro·scop·ic,** hī″dro·skop′ik, a.

hy·dro·ski, hī′drō·skē″, n. A hydrofoil, sometimes retractable, affixed to the

bottom of a seaplane's fuselage in order to speed up takeoffs and simplify landings.

hy·dro·some, hī′dro·sōm″, n. [N.L. *hydrosoma,* < *Hydra,* genus of polyps, and Gr. *sōma,* body.] *Zool.* the entire body or colony of a compound hydrozoan.

hy·dro·sphere, hī′dro·sfēr″, n. The water on the surface of the globe, encompassing oceans, lakes, and all other waters; the water vapor in the atmosphere.

hy·dro·stat, hī′dro·stat″, n. An electrical device which detects the presence of water, as from leakage or overflow; a device used to prevent damage to a steam boiler from low water level.

hy·dro·stat·ics, hī″dro·stat′iks, n. pl. but sing. in constr. The study of fluids at rest, esp. concentrating on the equilibrium and pressure of liquids.—**hy·dro·stat·ic, hy·dro·stat·i·cal,** a.—**hy·dro·stat·i·cal·ly,** adv.

hy·dro·sul·fide, hy·dro·sul·phide, hī″dro·sul′fīd, hī″dro·sul′fid, n. *Chem.* a compound formed when one of the hydrogen atoms of hydrogen sulfide, H_2S, has been replaced by a more strongly electropositive element or radical; as, sodium *hydrosulfide,* NaHS.

hy·dro·sul·fite, hy·dro·sul·phite, hī″dro·sul′fīt, n. *Chem.* A salt of hyposulfurous acid; hyposulfite.

hy·dro·tax·is, hī″dro·tak′sis, n. *Biol.* a reflex movement by an organism in the direction of or away from water.—**hy·dro·tac·tic,** a.

hy·dro·ther·a·py, hī″dro·ther′a·pē, n. *Med.* the scientific treatment of disease by means of water.—**hy·dro·ther·a·pist,** n.

hy·dro·ther·mal, hī″dro·thėr′mal, a. [Gr. *hydōr,* water, and *thermos,* hot.] Referring to heated water, esp. to the action of heated water that either dissolves or redistributes minerals in the crust of the earth.—**hy·dro·ther·mal·ly,** adv.

hy·dro·tho·rax, hī″dro·thōr′aks, n. [N.L. < Gr. *hydōr,* water, and *thorax,* chest.] *Pathol.* the presence of excess serous fluid in one or both pleural cavities.—**hy·dro·tho·ra·cic,** hī″drō·tho·ras′ik, a.

hy·drot·ro·pism, hī·dro′tro·piz″um, n. [Gr. *hydōr,* water, and *trepo,* turn.] *Biol.* a curving or growing toward or away from moisture.—**hy·dro·trop·ic,** hī″dro·trop′ik, a.—**hy·dro·trop·i·cal·ly,** adv.

hy·drous, hī′drus, a. [Gr. *hydōr,* water.] Containing water; *chem.* containing water in some kind of chemical union as in hydrates or in hydroxides.

hy·drox·ide, hī·drok′sīd, hī·drok′sid, n. [Gr. *hydōr,* water, *oxys,* acid.] *Chem.* a compound formed by the union of an element or radical with one or more hydroxyl groups.

hy·drox·ide i·on, n. *Chem.* the anion containing single atoms of hydrogen and oxygen, with a charge. Also **hy·drox·yl i·on.**

hy·drox·y, hī·drok′sē, a. *Chem.* hydroxyl.

hy·drox·y·a·cet·ic ac·id, hī·drok′sē·-a·sē′tik as′id, hī·drok′sē·a·set′ik as′id, hī·drok″sē·a·sē′tik as′id, hī·drok″sē·a·set′ik as′id, n. *Chem.* glycolic acid, $CH_2OHCOOH$, a colorless crystal derived from chloroacetic acid and used in dyeing.

hy·drox·y ac·id, n. *Chem.* an organic acid composed of a hydroxyl group and a carboxyl group, as lactic acid; any one of a group of organic acids which contain the hydroxyl group and exhibit characteristics of an acid and an alcohol.

hy·drox·yl, hī·drok′sil, n. [(*hydr*)ogen and (*ox*)ygen and *-yl.*] *Chem.* a univalent radical or group, OH, containing hydrogen and oxygen, found in hydroxides, organic acids, and alcohols. Also **hy·drox·yl group.** —a. Also *hydroxy.*—**hy·drox·yl·ic,** hī″drok·sil′ik, a.

hy·drox·yl·a·mine, hĭ·drok″sil·*a*·mēn′, hĭ·drok″sil·am′in, *n. Chem.* a crystalline basic compound, NH_2OH, resembling ammonia in chemical properties, and used as a reducing agent.

hy·dro·zo·an, hī″dro·zō′an, *n.* [N.L. < *Hydra*, genus of polyps, and Gr. *zōion*, animal.] Any of the *Hydrozoa*, a class of coelenterate aquatic, mostly marine animals, simple or compound, including the hydras and other polyps and the small jellyfishes.—*a.*

hy·e·na, hī·ē′na, *n.* [L. *hyaena,* < Gr. *hyaina,* a hyena, < *hys,* a hog, from its hoglike back.] A large, powerful, carnivorous animal of Asia and Africa, feeding chiefly on carrion, and of nocturnal habits, recognized by its piercing cry. Also **hy·ae·na.**—**hy·e·nic,** *a.*—**hy·e·noid,** hī·ē′noid, *a.*

hy·e·tal, hī′ĭ·tal, *a.* [Gr. *hyetos,* rain.] Relating to rain, or its distribution with reference to different regions.

hy·giene, hī′jēn, hī′jē·ēn′, *n.* [Fr. *hygiène,* < Gr. *hygieinos,* healthy, wholesome.] The system or practice of principles or rules designed for promotion and maintenance of health and cleanliness.—**hy·gi·en·ic,** hī″jē·en′ik, hī·jē′nik, *a.*—**hy·gi·en·i·cal·ly,** *adv.*—**hy·gien·ist,** hī·jē′nist, hī·jen′ist, hī′jē·nist, hī′jē·en′ist, *n.*

hy·gi·en·ics, hī″jē·en′iks, hī·jē′niks, *n. pl. but sing. in constr.* The science of health and cleanliness; hygiene.

hy·gro·graph, hī′gro·graf″, hī′gro·gräf″, *n.* [Gr. *hygros,* moist, and *graphō,* I write.] An instrument which registers automatically the variations of moisture content of the atmosphere.

hy·grom·e·ter, hī·grom′i·tėr, *n.* An instrument for measuring the degree of moisture of the atmosphere.—**hy·gro·met·ric,** hī″gro·me′trik, *a.*—**hy·grom·e·try,** hī·grom′i·trē, *n.*

hy·gro·phyte, hī′gro·fīt″, *n.* [Gr. *hygros,* moisture, and *phyton,* a plant.] A hydrophyte.—**hy·gro·phyt·ic,** hī″gro·fit′ik, *a.*

hy·gro·scope, hī′gro·skōp″, *n.* An instrument for indicating the presence and approximate amount of moisture in the atmosphere.

hy·gro·scop·ic, hī″gro·skop′ik, *a.* Pertaining to the hygroscope; capable of absorbing moisture from the atmosphere. —**hy·gro·scop·i·cal·ly,** *adv.*—**hy·gro·scop·ic·i·ty,** hī″gro·skō·pis′i·tē, *n.*

hy·gro·ther·mo·graph, hī″gro·thėr′mo·graf″, hī″gro·thėr′mo·gräf″, *n. Meteor.* an instrument registering both relative humidity and temperature on one chart.

hy·la, hī′la, *n. Zool.* The tree frog; the genus *Hyla.*

hy·lo·zo·ism, hī″lo·zō′iz·um, *n. Philos.* the doctrine, orig. proposed by early Greek philosophers, that all matter possesses life, or that life and matter are inseparably connected.—**hy·lo·zo·ist,** *n.*—**hy·lo·zo·is·tic,** hī″lo·zō·is′tik, *a.*

hy·men, hī′men, *n.* [Gr. *hymēn,* a skin, a membrane; *Hymēn,* the god of marriage.] *Anat.* a mucous membrane, situated at the entrance of the vagina.

hy·me·ne·al, hī″me·nē′al, *a.* Pertaining to marriage or a wedding.—*n.* A wedding song.—**hy·me·ne·al·ly,** *adv.*

hy·me·nop·ter·on, hī″me·nop′tėr·on, *n. pl.* **hy·me·nop·ter·a,** hī″me·nop′tėr·a. Any member of the highly developed *Hymenoptera* order of insects having four membranous wings, as the bee, wasp, ant, and ichneumon fly. Also **hy·me·nop·ter.**—**hy·me·nop·ter·an,** *n., a.*—**hy·me·nop·ter·ous,** *a.*

hymn, him, *n.* [L. *hymnus,* < Gr. *hymnos,* song of praise.] A song or ode in adoration of God or a deity; a religious lyric of benediction, glorification and laudation; doxology.—*v.t.* To worship or praise in a hymn.—*v.i.* To sing hymns in homage.

hym·nal, him′nal, *n.* A book of religious hymns compiled for worship services. Also **hymn·book, hym·na·ry,** pl. **hym·na·ries.**

hym·no·dy, him′no·dē, *n.* The vocalizing or composition of hymns; the collective hymns representative of a specific denomination, era, or locality.—**hym·nod·i·cal,** him·nod′i·kal, *a.*—**hym·no·dist,** *n.*

hym·nol·o·gy, him·nol′o·jē, *n.* A field of study specializing in the classification and history of hymns; the composition of hymns; hymns collectively.—**hym·no·log·ic, hym·no·log·i·cal,** him″no·loj′ik, *a.*—**hym·no·log·i·cal·ly,** *adv.*—**hym·nol·o·gist,** *n.*

hy·oid, hī′oid, *a.* [Gr. *hyoeidēs,* shaped like the letter *u* or *y.*] *Anat.* referring to a U-shaped movable bone between the root of the tongue and the larynx.—**hy·oid bone,** *n.*

hy·os·cine, hī′o·sēn″, hī·o·sin, *n.* Scopolamine.

hy·os·cy·a·mine, hī″o·sī′a·mēn″, hī″o·sī′a·min, *n.* [L. *Hyoscyamus* < Gr. *hyoskyamos,* henbane, lit. 'hog's bean,' < *hys,* hog, and *kyamos,* bean.] *Pharm.* a poisonous alkaloid obtained from henbane and other solanaceous plants, used as a sedative, mydriatic, antispasmodic, and analgesic.

hy·pae·thral, hy·pe·thral, hi·pē′thral, hi·pē′thral, *a.* [Gr. *hypaithros,* under the sky—*hypo,* under, and *aithēr,* ether.] *Arch.* Not covered by a roof; having an open central space or court, as certain classical temples.

hy·pan·thi·um, hi·pan′thē·um, hī·pan′thē·um, *n.* pl. **hy·pan·thi·a,** hi·pan′thē·a, hi·pan′thē·a. [Gr. *hypo,* under, and *anthos,* flower.] *Bot.* the cuplike receptacle that may enlarge and on whose rim rest the stamens, petals, and sepals of certain flowers. Also **ca·lyx tube.**—**hy·pan·thi·al,** *a.*

hy·per·a·cid·i·ty, hī″pėr·a·sid′i·tē, *n.* Excessive acidity, as of the gastric juice.—**hy·per·ac·id,** hī″per·as′id, *a.*

hy·per·ac·tive, hī″pėr·ak′tiv, *a.* Overly or abnormally active; as, a *hyperactive* sense of fear.—**hy·per·ac·tion, hy·per·ac·tiv·i·ty,** hī″pėr′ak·tiv′i·tē, *n.*

hy·per·bar·ic cham·ber, hī″pėr·bar′ik chäm′bėr. *Med.* the airtight chamber through which oxygen is forced under pressure to reach the heart and lungs of a patient, as in open-heart surgery.

hy·per·bo·la, hi·pėr′bo·la, *n.* [N.L. < Gr. *hyperbolē,* hyperbola, lit. 'a throwing beyond.'] *Geom.* a curve consisting of two distinct and similar branches, formed by the intersection of a plane with two similar right circular cones placed apex to apex.

hy·per·bo·le, hi·pėr′bo·lē, *n.* [L. < Gr. *hyperbolē,* a throwing beyond, excess.] *Rhet.* Deliberate exaggeration used for effect; an extravagant statement not intended to be understood in the literal sense.—**hy·per·bol·ic,** hī″pėr·bol′ik, *a.* —**hy·per·bo·list,** *n.*

hy·per·bol·ic, hī″pėr·bol′ik, *a. Math.* Of or relating to a hyperbola; referring to functions analogous to the trigonometric functions but based on distances to the origin and coordinate axes from a point on a hyperbola; as, *hyperbolic* sine.

hy·per·bo·lize, hi·pėr′bo·līz″, *v.i.*—*hyperbolized, hyperbolizing.* To use hyperbole; exaggerate.—*v.t.* To represent or express with hyperbole or exaggeration.

hy·per·cat·a·lec·tic, hī″pėr·kat″a·lek′tik, *a.* [Gr. *hyper,* beyond, and *katalēxis,* termination.] *Pros.* having an extra syllable beyond the final regular foot in a line of verse. Also *hypermetric.*—**hy·per·cat·a·lex·is,** *n.*

hy·per·chro·mic a·ne·mi·a, hī″pėr·kro′mik *a*·nē′mē·a, *n. Med.* an anemia characterized by an increase of hemoglobin in each red blood cell and a general decrease in the number of red blood cells.

hy·per·crit·ic, hī″pėr·krit′ik, *n.* [Gr. *hyper,* beyond, and *kritikos,* critical.] One who is highly critical.—**hy·per·crit·i·cism,** hī″pėr·krit′i·siz″um, *n.*

hy·per·crit·i·cal, hī″pėr·krit′i·kal, *a.* Overcritical; excessively exact.—**hy·per·crit·i·cal·ly,** *adv.*

hy·per·es·the·sia, hy·per·aes·the·sia, hī·pėr·is·thē′zha, hī″per·is·thē′zhē·a, hī″pėr·is·thē′zē·a, *n. Pathol.* an extreme sensitivity to pain, touch, cold, or heat.—**hy·per·es·thet·ic,** hī″pėr·is·thet′ik, *a.*

hy·per·fo·cal dis·tance, hī′pėr·fō′kal dis′tans, *n. Photog.* the closest distance on which a lens may focus in order to obtain a sharp image from that point to infinity.

hy·per·gol·ic, hī″pėr·ga′lik, hī″pėr·gol′ik, hī″pėr·gō′lik, *a. Aerospace,* referring to a rocket propellant which is self-igniting upon contact with an oxidizer.—**hy·per·gol,** hī′pėr·gol″, *n.* A hypergolic propellant.

hy·per·ir·ri·ta·bil·i·ty, hī·pėr·ir″i·ta·bil′i·tē, *n.* Abnormally excessive reaction to stimulation.—**hy·per·ir·ri·ta·ble,** hī″pėr·ir′i·ta·bl, *a.*

hy·per·ker·a·to·sis, hī″pėr·ker″a·tō′sis, *n. Med.* excessive development of the horny tissue of the skin; *veter. pathol.* a disease resulting in thickening of the hide in cattle, caused by contacting or eating substances high in chlorinated naphthalene.—**hy·per·ker·a·tot·ic,** hī″pėr·ker″a·tot′ic, *a.*

hy·per·me·ter, hi·pėr′mi·tėr, *n.* [L.L. < Gr. *hypermetros,* beyond measure, beyond the meter, < *hyper,* beyond, and *metron,* measure.] *Pros.* a verse or line having one or more syllables in addition to those proper to the meter.—**hy·per·met·ric, hy·per·met·ri·cal,** hī″pėr·me′trik, *a.* Also *hypercatalectic.*

hy·per·on, hī′pe·ron″, *n. Phys.* any subatomic particle with a mass greater than that of a neutron. Also *baryon.*

hy·per·o·pi·a, hī″pe·rō′pē·a, *n. Ophthalm.* A defect of the eyesight in which the focus for all objects falls behind the retina with the result that distant objects are seen more sharply than those nearby; far-sightedness. Also **hy·per·me·tro·pia,** hī″pėr·mi·trō′pē·a,—**hy·per·ope, hy·per·met·rope,** hī′pe·rōp″, hī″pėr·me′trōp, *n.*

hy·per·os·mi·a, hī″pe·roz′mē·a, *n.* [N.L. < Gr. *hyper,* over, and *osmē,* smell.] *Med.* an abnormally acute sense of smell.

hy·per·phys·i·cal, hī″pėr·fiz′i·kal, *a.* Beyond what is merely physical; supernatural. —**hy·per·phys·i·cal·ly,** *adv.*

hy·per·pi·tu·i·ta·rism, hī″pėr·pi·tŏ′i·ta·riz″um, hī″pėr·pi·tū′i·ta·riz″um, *n. Pathol.* Extreme activity of the pituitary gland, with an excessive number of growth hormones produced; the resultant irregularity, as giantism.—**hy·per·pi·tu·i·tar·y,** *a.*

hy·per·ploid, hī′pėr·ploid″, *a. Genetics,* having or indicating a chromosome number which is greater than, but not an exact multiple of, the monoploid number, as $n + 1$ or $2n + 1$.—*n.*—**hy·per·ploid·y,** *n.*

hy·per·py·rex·i·a, hī″pėr·pi·rek′sē·a, *n. Pathol.* an excessive degree of fever.—**hy·per·py·ret·ic,** hī″pėr·pi·ret′ik, *a.*

hy·per·sen·si·tive, hī″pėr·sen′si·tiv, *a.* Excessively sensitive. *Pathol.* reacting abnormally to a drug or other substance; allergic.—**hy·per·sen·si·tive·ness, hy·per·sen·si·tiv·i·ty,** hī″pėr·sen″si·tiv′i·tē, *n.*

hy·per·son·ic, hī″pėr·son′ik, *a.* Referring to speed which is at least five times the speed of sound in the air.

hy·per·sthene, hī′pėr·sthēn″, *n.* [Gr. *hyper,* over, and *sthenos,* strength.] *Mineral.* a native silicate of iron and magnesium, usu. of a grayish or greenish-black color.—**hy·per·sthen·ic,** hī″pėr·sthen′ik, *a.*

hy·per·ten·sion, hī″pėr·ten′shan, *n. Pathol.* a condition characterized by high blood pressure, esp. in the arteries.—**hy·per·-ten·sive**, hī″pėr·ten′siv, *a.*

hy·per·thy·roid·ism, hī″pėr·thī′roi·-diz′um, *n. Pathol.* Excessive activity of the thyroid′gland; the resulting abnormal conditions, as rapid heartbeat and increased metabolism.—**hy·per·thy·roid**, *a., n.*

hy·per·ton·ic, hī″pėr·ton′ik, *a. Pathol.* having an excessive degree of tone or tension, esp. of the muscles. *Chem.* referring to a solution having a greater osmotic pressure than a standard or other solution used for comparison. —**hy·per·to·nic·i·ty**, hī″pėr·tō·nis′i·tē, *n.*

hy·per·tro·phy, hī·pėr′trō·fē, *n.* pl. **hy·-per·tro·phies**. [Gr. *hyper*, above, and *trophē*, nutrition.] *Pathol.* an abnormal growth of tissue due to enlargement of each of the cellular parts without an increase in the number of cells; *fig.* any marked increase in size or complexity.—*v.t., v.i.*—*hypertrophied, hypertrophying.*—**hy·-per·troph·ic**, hī″pėr·trof′ik, *a.*

hyp·es·the·sia, hyp·aes·the·sia, hip″is·-thē′zha, hip″is·thē′zhē·a, hip″is·thē′zē·a, *n.* [N.L.] *Pathol.* diminished capacity for sensation.

hy·pe·thral, hi·pē′thral, hī·pē′thral, *a.* Hypaethral.

hy·pha, hī′fa, *n.* pl. **hy·phae**, hī′fē. [Gr. *hypē*, a web.] *Bot.* one of the many branching filaments that make up the body or mycelium of most fungi.—**hy·phal**, *a.*

hy·phen, hī′fen, *n.* [L.L. *hyphen*, < Gr. *hyphen*, a sign for joining syllables, < phrase *hyph′ hen*, under one, in one, together.] A short line (-) used to connect the parts of a compound word or the parts of a word divided for any purpose.—*v.t.* To hyphenate.

hy·phen·ate, hī′fe·nāt″, *v.t.*—*hyphenated, hyphenating.* To join by a hyphen; write with a hyphen.—**hy·phen·at·ed**, hī′fe·-nā″tid, *a.* Joined by a hyphen. Noting U.S. citizens of foreign birth or descent as designated by a hyphenated term, as German-American: often used opprobriously to imply questionable allegiance to their adopted country.—**hy·phen·a·tion**, hī″fe·nā′shan, *n.*

hy·phen·ize, hī′fe·nīz″, *v.t.*—*hyphenized, hyphenizing.* To hyphenate.—**hy·phen·i·-za·tion**, hī″fe·ne·zā′shan, *n.*

hyp·na·gog·ic, hyp·no·gog·ic, hip″na·-goj′ik, *a.* Relating to the condition of drowsiness which precedes sleep.

hyp·no·a·nal·y·sis, hip″nō·a·nal′i·sis, *n. Psychoanal.* treatment conducted while the subject is under hypnosis.

hyp·no·gen·e·sis, hip″nō·jen′i·sis, *n.* Induction of the hypnotic state.—**hyp·no·-ge·net·ic**, hip″nō·je·net′ik, *a.*—**hyp·no·-ge·net·i·cal·ly**, *adv.*

hyp·noi·dal, hip·noid′al, *a. Psychol.* referring to a mental condition similar to light hypnosis, but usu. caused by some means other than hypnotism. Also **hyp·-noid**, hip′noid.

hyp·no·pae·di·a, hip′nō·pē″dē·a, *n.* A teaching procedure designed so that a person can learn while asleep by listening to specially adapted recording devices.

hyp·no·pom·pic, hip″no·pom′pik, *a.* Referring to the state of drowsiness associated with awakening from sleep.

hyp·no·sis, hip·nō′sis, *n.* pl. **hyp·no·ses**. [N.L. < Gr. *hypnoun*, put to sleep, < *hypnos*, sleep.] A condition or state, allied to normal sleep, which can be artificially induced and is characterized by marked susceptibility to suggestion, and considerable loss of will power and sensation; hypnotism.

hyp·no·ther·a·py, hip″nō·ther′a·pē, *n.* Treatment of mental or physical disease by hypnotism.

hyp·not·ic, hip·not′ik, *a.* [L.L. *hypnoticus*, < Gr. *hypnōtikos, hypnoun*, put to sleep.] Pertaining to hypnosis or hypnotism; susceptible to hypnotism, as a person; inducing sleep.—*n.* An agent or drug that produces sleep; a sedative; a person under the influence of hypnotism; one subject to hypnotic influence.—**hyp·not·i·cal·ly**, *adv.*

hyp·no·tism, hip′no·tiz″um, *n.* The induction of hypnosis; the science dealing with the induction of hypnosis; hypnosis. **hyp·no·tist**, *n.* One who hypnotizes.

hyp·no·tize, hip′no·tīz″, *v.t.*—*hypnotized, hypnotizing.* To put into a hypnotic state; *fig.* to sway, charm, or frighten.—*v.i.* To practice hypnotism.—**hyp·no·tiz·a·ble**, *a.* —**hyp·no·ti·za·tion**, hip″no·ti·zā′shan, *n.* —**hyp·no·tiz·er**, *n.*

hy·po, hī′pō, *n. Photog.* sodium thiosulfate, formerly known as sodium hyposulfite, a fixing agent in developing film. *Colloq.* a hypodermic syringe or injection; *fig.* any stimulus providing the effect of a hypodermic injection; *slang*, a hypochondriac.—*v.t. Colloq.* to stimulate.

hy·po·blast, hī′po·blast″, *n. Embryol.* the endoderm.

hy·po·cen·ter, hī″pō·sen′tėr, *n.* That spot on the surface of the earth which is located below the mean position of a nuclear bomb when it is exploded.

hy·po·chlor·ite, hī″po·klōr′īt, *n. Chem.* a salt of hypochlorous acid.—**hy·po·chlo·-rous ac·id**, *chem.* an acid, HClO, whose solutions have marked bleaching properties.

hy·po·chon·dri·a, hī″po·kon′drē·a, *n.* [L.L. *hypochondria*, < Gr. *hypochondria*, neut. pl. of *hypochondrios*, under the cartilage (of the breast-bone).] A morbid condition, characterized by depressed spirits and fancies of ill health; melancholy. Also *hypochondriasis.*

hy·po·chon·dri·ac, hī″po·kon′drē·ak, *a.* [Gr. *hypochondriakós*.] A person suffering from or subject to hypochondria.—*a.* Pertaining to or afflicted with hypochondria; also **hy·po·chon·dri·a·cal**, hī″pō·kon·-drī′a·kal. Pertaining to the hypochondria, the parts of the abdomen left and right of the epigastrium and above the lumbar regions.—**hy·po·chon·dri·a·cal·ly**, *adv.*

hy·po·chon·dri·a·sis, hī″pō·kon·drī′a·-sis, *n.* [N.L.] *Pathol.* An abnormal concern for one's health, accompanied by imaginary ailments; hypochondria.

hy·poc·o·rism, hī·pok′o·riz″um, hi·pok′o·-riz″um, *n.* The use of a term of fondness, as a diminutive or pet name; the pet name itself; some speech form simulating baby talk, usu. when used by an adult.—**hy·po·-co·ris·tic**, hī″po·co·ris·ti·cal, *a.*—**hy·-po·co·ris·ti·cal·ly**, *adv.*

hy·po·cot·yl, hī″po·kot′il, *n.* [Gr. *hypo*, under, and *(cotyl)*edon.] *Bot.* in seedlings, that portion of tissue beneath the cotyledons. —**hy·po·cot·y·lous**, *a.*

hy·poc·ri·sy, hi·pok′ri·sē, *n.* pl. **hy·poc·-ri·sies**. [Fr. *hypocrisie*, L. *hypocrisis*, Gr. *hypokrisis*, a playing a part on the stage, simulation, < *hypokrinomai*, to play a part, to feign—*hypo*, and *krino*, to separate, discern.] The act or practice of simulating or feigning feelings or beliefs, esp. the false appearance of piety and virtue; dissimulation; insincerity.

hyp·o·crite, hip′o·krit, *n.* [Fr. *hypocrite*, Gr. *hypokritēs*.] One who practices hypocrisy.—*a.*—**hyp·o·crit·i·cal**, hip″o·krit′i·-kal, *a.*—**hyp·o·crit·i·cal·ly**, *adv.*

hy·po·derm, hī′po·dėrm″, *n.* Hypodermis; *embryol.* hypoblast.—**hy·po·der·mal, hy·-po·der·mous**, hipo·dėr′mal, *a.*

hy·po·der·mic, hī″po·dėr′mik, *a.* [Gr. *hypo*, under, and *derma*, skin.] Pertaining to parts under the skin; characterized by the introduction of medical preparations under the skin; lying under the skin, as

tissue; *fig.* having a stimulating effect.—*n.* A hypodermic injection; a hypodermic syringe.—**hy·po·der·mi·cal·ly**, *adv.*

hy·po·der·mic in·jec·tion, *n.* The forceful implanting of fluid by inserting a syringe under the skin.

hy·po·der·mic nee·dle, *n.* The hollow needle that is part of a hypodermic syringe.

hy·po·der·mic sy·ringe, *n.* A device comprised usu. of a hollow glass barrel and a hollow needle used to inject fluid into or under the skin.

hy·po·der·mis, hī″po·dėr′mis, *n.* [N.L.] *Biol.* a layer of tissues or cells lying under the outer integument of certain invertebrates, as arthropods, or of plants. Also **hy·po·der·ma**.

hy·po·gas·tri·um, hī″po·gas′trē·um, *n.* pl. **hy·po·gas·tri·a**, hī″po·gas′trē·a. [Gr. *hypo*, under, and *gastēr*, the belly.] *Anat.* the frontal lower and middle part of the abdomen.—**hy·po·gas·tric**, hī″po·gas′trik, *a.*

hy·po·ge·al, hī″po·jē′al, *a.* [Gr. *hypo*, beneath, *gē*, the earth.] Subterranean; *bot.* pertaining to parts of plants which grow beneath the surface of the earth; *geol.* beneath the surface layer of the earth. Also **hy·po·ge·ous**, hī″po·jē′us, hip″o·jē′us.— **hy·po·ge·al·ly**, *adv.*

hy·po·gene, hī′po·jēn″, hip′o·jēn″, *a.* [Gr. *hypo*, under, and root, *gen*, to produce.] *Geol.* Formed under the surface of the earth, as crystalline rocks; referring to deposits of ore or minerals which result from rising currents of subterranean water.

hy·pog·e·nous, hi·poj′e·nus, hi·poj′e·nus, *a. Bot.* growing beneath, or on the under surface, as fungi on leaves.

hy·po·glos·sal, hī″po·glos′al, hī″po·-glä′sal, *a.* [Gr. *hypo*, under, and *glōssa*, tongue.] *Anat.* situated under the tongue, wholly or in part; as, a *hypoglossal* nerve, either of the pair of cranial nerves which give rise to the movements of the tongue. —*n.*

hy·pog·na·thous, hī·pog′na·thus, *a. Zool.* having the lower jaw of greater length than the upper, hence protruding; *anthropol.* pertaining to this condition in man.

hy·pog·y·nous, hī·poj′i·nus, hi·poj′i·nus, *a.* [Gr. *hypo*, under, and *gynē*, woman, female.] *Bot.* of a condition in which the pistil of the flower surmounts the receptacle and in which sepals, petals, and stamens are attached below the pistil.

hy·po·ma·ni·a, hī″po·mā′nē·a, hī″po·-mǎn′ya, *n. Psychiatry*, a mild degree of mania.—**hy·po·man·ic**, hī″po·man′ik, *a.*

hy·po·morph, hī′po·mǎrf″, *n.* A mutant gene, less effective than its equivalent ancestral gene.—**hy·po·mor·phic**, hī″po·-mǎr′fik, *a.*

hy·po·ni·trite, hī″pō·nī′trīt, *n. Chem.* a salt of hyponitrous acid.

hy·po·ni·trous ac·id, hī″pō·nī′trus as′id, *n. Chem.* $H_2N_2O_2$, a weak crystalline acid.

hy·po·phos·phate, hī″po·fos′fāt, *n. Chem.* a salt of hypophosphoric acid.

hy·po·phos·phite, hī″po·fos′fīt, *n. Chem.* an ester or salt of hypophosphorous acid.

hy·po·phos·phor·ic ac·id, hī″po·fos′·fär′ik as′id, hī″po·fos·for′ik as′id, *n. Chem.* a tetrabasic acid, $H_4P_2O_6$, produced by the slow oxidation of phosphorus in moist air.

hy·po·phos·phor·ous ac·id, hī″po·-fos′fėr·us as′id, hī″po·fos·fōr′us as′id, *n. Chem.* the monobasic acid, H_3PO_2, used as a reducing agent.

hy·po·pla·si·a, hī″po·plā′zha, hī″po·-plā′zhē·a, hī″po·plā′zē·a, *n. Biol., pathol.* arrested growth of an organ or part, causing it to be undersized or immature. —**hy·po·plas·tic**, hī·po·plas′tik, *a.*

hy·po·sen·si·tize, hī″po·sen′si·tīz″, *v.t.* —*hyposensitized, hyposensitizing.* To lessen sensitivity of; reduce the allergic reaction to.

---

hy·pos·ta·sis, hī·pos′ta·sis, hi·pos′ta·sis, *n.* pl. **hy·pos·ta·ses,** hī·pos′ta·sēz″, hi·-pos′ta·sēz″. [L.L. < Gr. *hypostasis,* substance, nature, essence, also sediment, < *hyphistasthai,* stand under, subsist, < *hypo,* under, and *histanai,* cause to stand.] *Metaph.* foundation; the essential part of anything, as opposed to attributes; substance, essence, or essential principle; a hypothetical substance; a phenomenon or state of things conceived of as a real substance. *Theol.* one of the three real and distinct subsistences in the one undivided substance or essence of God; a person of the Trinity; the one personality of Christ in which His two natures, human and divine, are united. *Med.* a sediment or deposit, as from urine; the settling of a fluid, as blood, in a bodily part. **—hy·po·stat·ic, hy·po·stat·i·cal,** hī″po·-stat′ik, *a.***—hy·po·stat·i·cal·ly,** *adv.*

hy·pos·ta·tize, hi·pos′ta·tīz′, hi·pos′ta·-tīz″, *v.t.***—**hypostatized, hypostatizing. To treat or regard as a distinct substance or reality.**—hy·pos·ta·ti·za·tion,** hī·pos″-ta·ti·zā′shan, *n.*

hy·po·style, hī′po·stīl, hip′o·stīl″, *a.* [Gr. *hypo,* under, and *stylos,* a pillar.] *Arch.* having the roof supported by rows of pillars.**—***n.*

hy·po·sul·fite, hy·po·sul·phite, hī″po·-sul′fīt, *n. Chem.* a salt of hyposulfurous acid; as, sodium *hyposulfite,* a crystalline compound, $Na_2S_2O_3$, used in photography; sodium thiosulfate.

hy·po·sul·fur·ous ac·id, hī″po·sul·-fūr′us as′id, hī″po·sul′fẽr·us as′id, *n.* A monobasic acid, H_2SO_4, occurring only in solution and salts. Also **hy·dro·sul·-fur·ous ac·id.**

hy·po·tax·is, hī″po·tak′sis, *n.* [N.L. < Gr. *hypotaxis,* subjection, < *hypotassein,* place under, < *hypo,* under, and *tassein,* arrange.] *Gram.* the arrangement of sentence parts whereby one construction, usu. a clause, is dependent upon another, as a subordinate clause.**—hy·po·tac·tic,** hī″po·tak′tik, hip″-o·tak′tik, *a.*

hy·po·ten·sion, hī″po·ten′shan, *n. Pathol.* a condition marked by unusually low blood pressure.**—hy·po·ten·sive,** *a., n.*

hy·pot·e·nuse, hī·pot′e·nōs″, hī·pot′e·-nūs, *n.* [Gr. *hypoteinousa***—***hypo,* under, and *teinō,* to stretch.] *Geom.* that side of a right triangle which is opposite the right angle. Also **hy·poth·e·nuse.**

hy·po·thal·a·mus, hī″po·thal′a·mus, *n.* pl. **hy·po·thal·a·mi,** hī″po·thal′a·mī.″ *Anat.* that part of the posterior section of the forebrain, or diencephalon, which composes the floor of the third ventricle.**—hy·po·tha·lam·ic,** hī″pō·tha·lam′ik, hip″ō·tha·lam′ik, *a.*

hy·poth·e·cate, hī·poth′e·kāt″, hi·poth′e·-kāt″, *v.t.***—**hypothecated, hypothecating. To pledge in security for a debt, but without transfer; to mortgage. To theorize; also *hypothesize.***—hy·poth·e·ca·tion,** hī·poth″-e·kā′shan, *n.***—hy·poth·e·ca·tor,** *n.*

hy·poth·e·sis, hī·poth′i·sis, hi·poth′i·sis, *n.* pl. **hy·poth·e·ses,** hī·poth′i·sēz, hi·-poth′i·sēz. [N.L. < Gr. *hypothesis,* supposition, postulate, < *hypotithenai,* put under, lay down, suppose.] A proposition put forth as a basis for reasoning; a supposition formulated from proved data and presented as a temporary explanation of an occurrence, as in the sciences, in order to establish a basis for further research; a supposition; often, a mere assumption or guess.**—hy·poth·e·size,** *v.i.***—**hypothesized, hypothesizing. To form a hypothesis or hypotheses.**—***v.t.* To assume by hypothesis. Also *hypothecate.*

hy·po·thet·i·cal, hī″po·thet′i·kal, *a.* [Gr. *hypothetikos.*] Referring to an idea or a statement unsupported by fact or evidence; theorized; assumed; not actual; as, a hypothetical example. *Logic,* involving a syllogism with a conditional premise; tentative, as a proposition. Also **hy·po·-thet·ic.—hy·po·thet·i·cal·ly,** *adv.*

hy·po·thet·i·cal im·per·a·tive, *n. Kantianism,* a doctrine formulating the conduct or action essential to a desired result.

hy·po·ton·ic, hī″po·ton′ik, *a. Pathol.* having an inadequate degree of tone or tension, as the muscles; *chem.* of a solution, possessing a lower osmotic pressure than another solution used for comparison.**—hy·po·to·nic·i·ty,** hī″pō·tō·nis′i·tē, *n.*

hy·po·xan·thine, hī″po·zan′thēn, hī″po·-zan′thin, *n. Chem.* a crystalline nitrogenous compound, $C_5H_4N_4O$, related to xanthine, and found in animal and vegetable tissues.**—hy·po·xan·thic,** *a.*

hy·pox·i·a, hī·pok′sē·a, *n.* The condition of insufficient oxygen in bodily tissues, due to improper functioning of respiratory mechanisms or an absence of environmental oxygen.**—hy·pox·ic,** hī·pok′sik, *a.*

hyp·sog·ra·phy, hip·sog′ra·fē, *n.* The science dealing with the form or relief of the earth's surface, esp. the measuring and mapping of differences of elevation; topographic relief.**—hyp·so·graph·ic, hyp·so·graph·i·cal,** hip″so·graf′ik, *a.*

hyp·som·e·ter, hip·som′i·tẽr, *n.* [Gr. *hypsos,* height, and *metron,* measure.] An instrument for measuring altitude by determining the boiling point of a liquid at the given height; any of various triangulation instruments used to determine the height of trees.

hyp·som·e·try, hip·som′i·trē, *n.* The measuring of altitudes or elevations, esp. as related to sea level.**—hyp·so·met·ric, hyp·so·met·ri·cal,** hip″so·me′trik, *a.***—hyp·som·e·trist,** *n.*

hy·rax, hī′raks, *n.* pl. **hy·rax·es, hy·ra·ces,** hī′ra·sēz″. [N.L. < Gr. *hyrax,* shrewmouse.] Any small animal of the genus *Procavia,* comprising small, timid, rabbit-like hoofed mammals of Asia and Africa, which live mostly in rocky places; any animal belonging to the same order, *Hyracoidea; Bib.* the coney. See *daman.*

hy·son, hī′son, *n.* [Chinese *hsi-ch′un,* lit. 'first crop.'] A variety of green China tea.

hys·sop, his′op, *n.* [L. *hyssopus,* < Gr. *hyssōpos,* kind of aromatic plant.] An aromatic herb of the mint family, *Hyssopus officinalis,* usu. with blue flowers; *Bib.* a plant of uncertain kind, the twigs of which were used in ceremonial sprinkling.

hys·ter·ec·to·my, his″te·rek′to·mē, *n.* pl. **hys·ter·ec·to·mies.** [Gr. *hystera,* the uterus, *ektomē,* a cutting out or off.] *Surg.* the removal of the uterus.

hys·ter·e·sis, his″te·rē′sis, *n.* [N.L. < Gr. *hysterēsis,* < *hysterein,* be behind, come late, < *hysteros,* latter, later.] *Phys.* the tendency of a substance to resist changes in its magnetization; the lag in the effect on a substance of a changing magnetizing force. The influence of a previous treatment of a gel upon its present behavior.**—hys·ter·et·ic,** his″te·ret′ik, *a.***—hys·ter·et·i·cal·ly,** *adv.*

hys·te·ri·a, hi·stẽr′ē·a, hi·ster′ē·a, *n.* [N.L. < Gr. *hystera,* uterus, because the disorder was formerly attributed to disturbances of the uterus.] A psychoneurotic disorder characterized variously by violent emotional outbreaks, irrationality, simulated bodily symptoms due to autosuggestion, and impairment of motor and sensory functions; any emotional frenzy.**—hys·ter·ic,** *n.* One subject to hysteria.**—hys·ter·i·cal, hys·ter·ic,** *a.***—hys·ter·i·cal·ly,** *adv.*

hys·ter·ics, hi·ster′iks, *n. pl.,* sing. or pl. in constr. [L. *hystericus,* < Gr. *hysterikos,* pertaining to or suffering in the uterus, < *hystera,* uterus.] A fit of hysteria; an uncontrollable outburst.

hys·ter·o·gen·ic, his″tẽr·o·jen′ik, *a.* Producing hysteria.**—hys·ter·og·e·ny,** his″-te·roj′e·nē, *n.*

hys·ter·oid, his′te·roid″, *a.* Resembling hysteria. Also **hys·ter·oi·dal,** his″te·roid′al.

hys·ter·on prot·er·on, his′te·ron″ prot′e·-ron″, *n.* [Gr. *hysteron,* last, and *proteron,* first.] *Rhet.* a figure of speech involving an inversion of the natural or logical order in words; *logic,* an inverting of the logical order of reasoning by using as a premise that which is to be proved.

hys·ter·ot·o·my, his″te·rot′o·mē, *n.* pl. **hys·ter·ot·o·mies.** [N.L. *hysterotomia,* < Gr. *hystera,* uterus, and *-tomia,* E. *-tomy.*] *Surg.* The operation of cutting into the uterus; a caesarean operation.

I

I, i, ī, *n.* The ninth letter and the third vowel of the English alphabet, representing several vowel sounds; the symbol *I* or *i* in written or printed form; that which is shaped in the form of the letter I, as an I-beam; the Roman numeral for 1; (*cap.*), *chem.* the symbol for iodine.

I, ī, *pron.***—**sing. nom. *I,* poss. *my* or *mine,* obj. *me;* pl. nom. *we,* poss. *our* or *ours,* obj. *us;* intens. and refl. *myself.* [O.E. *ic,* D. *ik,* Goth. *ik,* G. *ich,* Icel. *ek,* Dan. *jeg,* L. *ego,* Gr. *egō,* Skt. *aham,* W. *ym,* Armor. *em***—**I.] The nominative case of the pronoun of the first person singular, by which a speaker or writer denotes himself.**—***n.* pl. **I's.** The pron. *I* conceived of or used as a noun, as: Every sentence began with an *I. Philos.* the conscious subject or ego.

i·amb, ī′am, ī′amb, *n.* pl. **i·ambs.** [Gr. *iambos,* < *iaptō,* to assail; the iamb being much used in satiric poetry.] *Usu. pl., pros.* a metrical foot of two syllables, the first short and the last long, or the first unaccented and the last accented, as in *delight.* Also **i·am·-bus,** ī·am′bus, pl. **i·am·bi, i·am·bus·es,** ī·am′bī.**—i·am·bic,** ī·am′bik, *a., n.*

i·at·ric, i·a′trik, ē·a′trik, *a.* [Gr. *iātrikos,* < *iātros,* physician, < *iasthai,* to heal.] Pertaining to a physician or to medicine. Also **i·at·ri·cal,** ī·at′ri·kal.

i·at·ro·gen·ic, ī·a″tro·jen′ik, ē·a″tro·jen′ik, *a.* Caused by the mannerisms or treatment of a physician, as imaginary illness of the patient brought about by the physician.**—i·at·ro·ge·nic·i·ty,** ī·a″trō·je·nis′i·tē, ē·a″trō·je·nis′i·tē, *n.*

I-beam, ī′bēm″, *n. Constr.* a steel crossbeam or girder having an I-shaped cross section.

I·be·ri·an, ī·bēr′ē·an, *a.* [From the *Iberian* peninsula, where Spain and Portugal are located, or ancient *Iberia,* in southwest Asia between the Black Sea and the Caspian Sea.] Referring to the Iberian peninsula or its early inhabitants; of or pertaining to the ancient Caucasoid peoples of Iberia; referring to the language of the ancient Iberians of Europe.**—***n.*

i·bex, ī′beks, *n.* pl. **i·bex·es, ib·i·ces, i·bex,** ī′bi·sēz, ib′i·sēz. [L.] Any of various large mountain goats of Europe and Asia with large recurved horns, esp. the Alpine ibex, *Capra ibex.*

i·bi·dem, ib′i·dem, i·bī′dem, L. i·bē′dem, *adv.* [L.] In the same place; in that part of a literary work just mentioned: used in footnotes. Abbr. **ibid.**

i·bis, ī′bis, *n.* pl. **i·bis·es, i·bis,** ī′bi·siz. [L. < Gr. *ibis.*] Any of various large wading birds of the family *Threskiornithidae,* allied to the herons and storks, esp. *Threskionis aethiopica* of Africa, a sacred bird of the ancient Egyptians; the wood ibis, *M. americana,* of southern U.S.

I·car·i·an, i·kâr′ē·an, i·kâr′ē·an, *a.* [From *Icarus,* who, according to Greek legend, flew so high that the sun melted the wax of his artificial wings, causing him to fall into the sea.] Pertaining to or characteristic of Icarus; *fig.* presumptuously ambitious, venturesome, or foolhardy; as, an *Icarian* undertaking.

ice, īs, *n.* [O.E. *īs* = D. *ijs* = G. *eis* = Icel. *īss,* ice.] The solid form of water, produced by freezing; the frozen surface of a body of water; a substance resembling this; cake icing; a dessert made of water and fruit juice, sweetened and frozen. *Slang,* jewels, esp. diamonds; a bribe; protection money paid to authorities to permit operation of an illegal enterprise. *Brit.* a portion of ice cream.—**break the ice,** to begin something, esp. to initiate conversation socially.—**on ice,** *slang.* Set aside, as for safekeeping; having every probability of success.—**on thin ice,** in a state involving some hazard.—**ice-cold,** īs′kōld′, *a.* Very cold.

ice, īs, *v.t.*—*iced, icing.* To cover with ice; to convert into ice; to freeze. To refrigerate with ice; cool with ice, as a drink; deprive of warmth of feeling. To cover with icing; frost.—*v.i.* To turn to ice; to freeze, often followed by *over* or *up.*

ice age, *n. Geol.* the Pleistocene glacial epoch, a period during which extensive glaciation occurred.

ice bag, *n.* A waterproof bag for ice, applied to cool the body or to relieve pain.

ice·berg, īs′bụrg, *n.* D. *ijsberg,* G. *eisberg,* Sw. *isberg,* Dan. and Norw. *isbjerg,* 'ice mountain.'] A large floating mass of ice, detached from a glacier and carried out to sea; *colloq.* a person lacking emotional warmth.

ice·blink, īs′blingk″, *n.* A luminous appearance near the horizon or under a cloud, due to the reflection of light from distant formations of ice.

ice·boat, īs′bōt″, *n.* A strong boat that can break a passage through ice; an icebreaker; a boatlike frame equipped with metal runners and usu. propelled by sails, for riding on the surface of ice.

ice·bound, īs′bound″, *a.* Surrounded with ice so as to be immovable or inaccessible; as, an *icebound* trawler.

ice·box, īs′boks″, *n.* A box or chest for containing ice to cool and preserve food; any kind of refrigerator. *Slang,* a solitary confinement cell in a prison.

ice·break·er, īs′brā″kẽr, *n.* Anything serving to break up ice; a tool or machine for breaking ice into small pieces; a boat for breaking channels through ice; a structure of masonry or timber for protection of a pier against moving ice; a game or device to overcome reserve at social gatherings.

ice·cap, īs′kap″, *n.* A permanent cap or covering of ice over an area sloping on all sides from an elevated center; a glacier such as that which covers a large part of Greenland. *Med.* a bag containing ice for application to the head.

ice cream, *n.* A frozen dessert food made of sweetened cream or milk, beaten and with various fruits or flavors added.—**ice-cream,** īs′krēm″, *a.* Of a color corresponding to that of vanilla ice cream.—**ice-cream cone,** a hollow conical wafer for holding ice cream; this wafer filled with ice cream.

ice field, *n.* A large sheet of sea ice whose limits cannot be seen. Fragments of glaciers and pack ice which have joined and frozen together; also *ice pack.*

ice floe, *n.* A large sheet of floating ice.

ice foot, *n.* [Dan. *isfod.*] A belt or fringe of ice that forms around arctic shores.

ice·house, īs′hous″, *n.* A repository in which ice is stored.

Ice·lan·dic, īs·lan′dik, *a.* [From *Iceland,* an island between Scandinavia and Greenland.] Of or pertaining to Iceland or its

inhabitants.—*n.* The language of Iceland, the oldest of the Scandinavian languages.—**Ice·land·er,** īs′lan″dẽr, īs′lan·dẽr, *n.* A native or inhabitant of Iceland.

Ice·land moss, *n.* An edible lichen, *Cetraria islandica,* of arctic regions, used to some extent in medicine.

Ice·land pop·py, *n. Bot.* a perennial poppy, *Papaver nudicaule,* native to subarctic regions: grown ornamentally, having basal, finely-divided foliage and pastel-colored flowers borne on wiry, leafless stalks.

Ice·land spar, *n. Mineral.* a transparent, double-refractive variety of calcite used extensively for optical purposes because of its ability to polarize light.

ice lol·ly, *n. Brit.* a frozen, sweet-flavored confection on a stick.

ice·man, īs′man″, *n. pl.* **ice·men.** A man engaged in the industry of gathering and storing ice, or in selling and delivering it to customers; a man skilled in traveling over ice; a man in charge of the ice on a skating pond.

ice nee·dle, *n.* One of a type of thin ice crystals which are visible floating in the air in clear cold weather.

I·ce·ni, i·sē′nī, *n. pl.* An ancient British tribe whose queen, Boadicea, revolted against the Romans in 61 A.D.—**I·ce·ni·an,** I·ce·nic, *a.*

ice pack, *n.* A large floating mass of ice formed from separate ice sections joined over a period of years; also *pack ice. Med.* a tub of ice in which a patient is immersed as a form of shock treatment; an ice bag.

ice pick, *n.* A pick or small awllike tool for chipping ice.

ice plant, *n.* A low-growing, succulent-leafed herb, *Cryophytum crystallinum,* in the carpet weed family, native to S. Africa, the Mediterranean, and California, grown for the showy, frosty appearance of the large, glistening vesicles or dots on the foliage.

ice sheet, *n.* A broad, thick sheet of ice covering an extensive area for a long period of time; a continental glacier.

ice skate, *n.* One of a pair of leather shoes with metal blades which enable the wearer to glide upon ice.—**ice-skate,** īs′skāt″, *v.i.*—*ice-skated, ice-skating.* To glide along by means of skates upon ice.—**ice skat·er,** *n.*

ice storm, *n.* A storm of rain turning to hail or ice, usu. causing an ice glaze to form on surfaces. Also **sil·ver storm.**

ice wa·ter, *n.* Water obtained from or cooled by ice. Also *Brit.* **iced wa·ter.**

ich·neu·mon, ik·nō′mon, ik·nū′mon, *n.* [L. < Gr. *ichneumōn,* lit. 'tracker,' < *ichneuein,* to track, < *ichnos,* track, trace.] A slender carnivore of the genus *Herpestes,* a weasellike animal which feeds on rodents and snakes; a mongoose native to Africa; the ichneumon fly.

ich·neu·mon fly, *n.* Wasplike insects of the family *Ichneumonidae,* usu. parasitic on other insects, esp. caterpillars.

ich·nite, ik′nīt, *n.* [Gr. *ichnos,* a footprint.] *Paleon.* a fossil footprint. Also **ich·no·lite.**

ich·nog·ra·phy, ik·nog′ra·fē, *n. pl.* **ich·nog·ra·phies.** [Gr. *ichnos,* a footstep, and *grapho,* to describe.] The ground plan of a structure; the study or art of drawing ground plans.—**ich·no·graph·ic, ich·no·graph·i·cal,** ik″na·graf′ik, *a.*—**ich·no·graph·i·cal·ly,** *adv.*

ich·nol·o·gy, ik·nol′o·jē, *n.* The study of fossil footmarks of animals.—**ich·no·log·i·cal,** ik″no·loj′i·kal, *a.*

i·chor, ī′kẽr, ī′kẽr, *n.* [Gr.] *Class. mythol.* an ethereal fluid believed to flow in the veins of the ancient Greek gods. *Pathol.* a watery, acrid discharge from an ulcerated wound.—**i·chor·ous,** *a.*

ich·thy·oid, ik′thē·oid″, *a.* Having fishlike characteristics. Also **ich·thy·oi·dal,** ik″-thē·oi′dal.—*n.* A fishlike organism.

ich·thy·ol·o·gy, ik″thē·ol′o·jē, *n.* A branch of zoology that studies fishes.—**ich·thy·o·log·i·cal,** ik″thē·o·loj′i·kal, *a.*—**ich·thy·ol·o·gist,** *n.*

ich·thy·oph·a·gous, ik″thē·of′a·gus, *a.* Eating or subsisting on fish.

ich·thy·or·nis, ik″thē·ạr′nis, *n.* [Gr. *ornis,* a bird.] An extinct genus of birds with vertebrae like those of fish, and with teeth.

ich·thy·o·saur, ik′thē·o·sạr″, *n.* [Gr. *sauros,* a lizard.] An immense marine reptile of the extinct order *Ichthyosauria,* having paddlelike flippers, fins, a long snout, and tapering, fishlike body.—**ich·thy·o·sau·ri·an,** ik″thē·o·sạr′ē·an, *a., n.*

ich·thy·o·sis, ik″thē·ō′sis, *n.* A hereditary skin disorder marked by a thick, scaly skin surface.—**ich·thy·ot·ic,** ik″thē·ot′ik, *a.*

i·ci·cle, ī′si·kl, *n.* [O.E. *īs-gicel,* < *īs,* ice and *gicel,* an icicle; akin to Icel. *jokull,* icicle, *jaki,* a piece of ice.] A pendent, conical mass of ice formed by the freezing of water as it drips; a person who exhibits cold, unfeeling reactions.

i·ci·ly, ī′si·lē, *adv.* In an icy manner; superciliously; coldly, without warmth.

i·ci·ness, ī′sē·nis, *n.* The state of being icy or very cold; *fig.* a distant manner.

ic·ing, ī′sing, *n.* A sugary preparation for frosting cakes and other pastries; also *frosting.* Atmospheric moisture which has frozen on an aircraft surface.

ic·ing, ī′sing, *n. Ice hockey,* the act of illegally shooting the puck from within the player's own defensive zone to behind the opponent's goal line.

i·con, ī′kon, *n.* [Gr. *eikōn,* an image, < *eiko,* to resemble.] An image, representation, or picture; a religious image, considered sacred by members of the Eastern Orthodox Church; an idol. Also **ei·kon,** *ikon.*—**i·con·ic,** i·kon′ik, *a.* Pertaining to icons; *art,* in a style which is dictated by conventional or traditional precepts. Also **i·con·i·cal.**—**i·con·i·cal·ly,** *adv.*—**i·co·nic·i·ty,** ī″ko·nis′i·tē, *n.*

i·con·o·clast, ī·kon′o·klast″, *n.* [Gr. *eikon,* and *klastēs,* a breaker, < *klao,* to break.] One who makes attacks on cherished beliefs or institutions; one who destroys or opposes the veneration of religious images.—**i·con·o·clasm,** ī·kon′o·klaz″um, *n.* The acts, principles, or practices of an iconoclast.—**i·con·o·clas·tic,** ī·kon″o·klas′tik, *a.*

i·co·nog·ra·phy, ī″ko·nog′ra·fē, *n. pl.* **i·co·nog·ra·phies.** The art of symbolic representation, using pictures and images; the study or analysis of this art; the representation of religious or sacred subjects by fixed symbols or images.—**i·con·o·graph·ic,** ī·kon′o·graf″ik, *a.*

i·co·nol·a·ter, ī″ko·nol′a·tẽr, *n.* One who worships images.—**i·co·nol·a·try,** *n.*

i·co·nol·o·gy, ī″ko·nol′o·jē, *n.* The study of the art of symbolic representation; the study of iconography.—**i·con·o·log·i·cal,** ī·kon″o·loj′i·kal, ī″ko·no·loj′i·kal, *a.*

i·co·no·scope, i·kon′o·skōp″, *n.* A cathode ray tube in a television camera which converts the light rays of the televised image into electrical signals.

i·co·sa·he·dron, ī·ko″sa·hē′dron, ī·kos″a·hē′dron, *n. pl.* **i·co·sa·he·drons, i·co·sa·he·dra,** ī·kō″sa·hē′dra, ī·kos″a·hē′dra. [Gr. *eikosi,* twenty, and *hedra,* seat, side.] *Geom.* a solid having twenty plane faces.—**i·co·sa·he·dral,** *a.*

ic·ter·ic, ik·ter′ik, *a.* [L. *icterus,* jaundice.] Affected with or relating to jaundice. Also **ic·ter·i·cal.**

ic·ter·us, ik′tẽr·us, *n.* [N.L., < Gr. *ikteros,* jaundice.] *Pathol.* jaundice; *bot.* a yellow appearance of certain plants when exposed to excess moisture and cold.

ic·tus, ik′tus, *n. pl.* **ic·tus·es, ic·tus.** [L., < *ico,* to strike.] *Pathol.* a seizure, stroke, or fit. *Pros.* the stressing or accenting of syllables; metrical stress.

i·cy, ī′sē, *a.*—*icier, iciest.* Pertaining to, composed of, resembling, or abounding in ice; slippery; very cold; freezing; *fig.* characterized by coldness or aloofness in manner; frigid.

id, *n.* [L., 3rd person neut. demonst. pron.] *Psychoanal.* a part of the psyche, constituting the unconscious, which is the source of instinctual or libidinal energy.

I'd, īd. Contraction of I would, I should, or I had.

ID, I.D. Abbr. for identification, identity.

i·de·a, ī·dē′a, ī·dēa′, *n.* [L. < Gr. *idea,* form, look, semblance, kind, sort, idea, < *idein,* see.] A thought, conception, or notion; an impression; a conviction or opinion; a plan of action; an intention or design; a mental picture, sometimes merely imagined without corresponding reality; vague knowledge; inkling; a fleeting thought or whim. *Philos.* the Platonic concept of an archetype or pattern, of which the individual objects in any natural class are imperfect copies and from which they derive their being; the absolute ideal; generally, the concept of anything in its highest perfection. *Mus.* a theme, phrase, or figure.—**i·de·a·ful, i·de·a·less,** *a.*

i·de·al, ī·dē′al, ī·dēl′, *a.* [L.L. *idealis.*] Achieving a standard of perfection or excellence; referring to or representing a mental image or conception rather than a material object; not real or practical; visionary. *Philos.* referring to or existing as a Platonic idea or archetype; regarding ideas as the only real entities; pertaining to or of the nature of idealism.—*n.* A conception or standard of something in its highest perfection; a person or thing regarded as realizing such a conception or conforming to such a standard, and taken as a model for imitation; an ultimate object or aim to be realized, esp. one of high or noble character.—**i·de·al·ness,** *n.*

i·de·al·ism, ī·dē′a·liz′um, *n.* The practice of idealizing; the tendency to represent things in an ideal form, or as they might be rather than as they are; the cherishing or pursuit of ideals, as for attainment; *fine arts,* the imaginative treatment of subjects involving selectivity and refinement of details according to preconceived standards of beauty, proportion, and form: opposed to *realism; philos.* any system or theory which maintains that the real is of the nature of thought or ideas, or that the object of external perception consists of ideas: opposed to *realism.*

i·de·al·ist, ī·dē′a·list, *n.* One who holds some form of philosophical idealism; one who represents things as they might be rather than as they are; one who cherishes or pursues ideals to be attained; a visionary or impractical person; a writer or artist who treats subjects imaginatively.—*a.* Idealistic.

i·de·al·is·tic, ī·dē′a·lis′tik, ī″dē·a·lis′tik, *a.* Pertaining or proper to an idealist; characterized by idealism. Also **i·de·al·is·ti·cal.**—**i·de·al·is·ti·cal·ly,** *adv.*

i·de·al·i·ty, ī″dē·al′i·tē, *n.* pl. **i·de·al·i·ties.** Ideal quality or character; the ability to conceive of perfection or excellence in people, governments, or the arts. *Philos.* existence only in the mind; that which exists only in the imagination.

i·de·al·ize, ī·dē′a·līz, *v.t.*—*idealized, idealizing.* To represent in an ideal form or character; to exalt to perfection or excellence; to represent in accordance with preconceived perfection.—*v.i.* To represent something in the form of imagined perfection; to imagine or form an ideal.—**i·de·al·i·za·tion,** *n.* The attribution of flawlessness to a person or thing.—**i·de·al·iz·er,** *n.*

i·de·al·ly, ī·dē′a·lē, *adv.* In accordance with imagined perfection; perfectly; in the imagination or mind; theoretically.

i·de·al point, *n. Projective geom.* the direction of a given set of parallel lines or the point in infinity where parallel lines would meet and cross.

i·de·ate, ī′dē·āt″, ī·dē′āt, *v.t.*—*ideated, ideating.* To form in idea or thought; imagine; conceive.—*v.i.* To form ideas; think.—ī′dē·āt″, ī·dē′it, *n. Philos.* the object which corresponds to the idea, the object being considered distinct from the idea.—**i·de·a·tive,** *a.*

i·de·a·tion, ī″dē·ā′shan, *n.* The faculty of the mind for forming ideas; the establishment of a distinct mental representation or image of an object.—**i·de·a·tion·al, i·de·a·tive,** ī″dē·ā′sha·nal, *a.*—**i·de·a·tion·al·ly,** *adv.*

i·dem, ī′dem, id′em, *pron., a.* [L.] The same as previously given: used to avoid repetition. Abbr. *id.*

i·den·tic, ī·den′tik, ī·den′tik, *a.* [M.L. *identicus,* irreg. < L. *idem,* same.] Identical; *diplomacy,* applied to actions or notes which are identical in form, as when two or more governments deal simultaneously with another government.

i·den·ti·cal, ī·den′ti·kal, ī·den′ti·kal, *a.* The same, or being the same one, as: He is the *identical* man we saw here last week. Of the same kind, nature, or meaning; agreeing exactly; as, *identical* experiences; *logic,* expressing identity, as a proposition.—**i·den·ti·cal·ly,** *adv.*—**i·den·ti·cal·ness,** *n.*

i·den·ti·cal twin, *n.* Either of a pair of twins originating from a single fertilized ovum, each being of the same sex and having the same hereditary features: distinguished from *fraternal twin.*

i·den·ti·fi·a·ble, ī·den′ti·fī″a·bl, ī·den′·ti·fī″a·bl, *a.* Capable of being recognized or identified.—**i·den·ti·fi·a·bly,** *adv.*

i·den·ti·fi·ca·tion, ī·den″ti·fi·kā′shan, ī·den″ti·fi·kā′shan, *n.* The act of identifying; something that identifies a person or thing, as a card, passport, or tag; *psychol.* a mental process in which a person attributes to himself the feelings or qualities of another person or group.

i·den·ti·fy, ī·den′ti·fī″, ī·den′ti·fī″, *v.t.*—*identified, identifying.* [M.L. *identificare,* < *identicus,* same, and L. *facere,* make.] To recognize or establish as being a particular person or thing; to attest or prove to be as purported or asserted; to determine, as the name of a person or a plant; to make, represent to be, or regard or treat as the same or identical; *psychol.* to associate, as oneself, with another or others through the process of identification.—*v.i.* To become one or the same; to associate in feeling, interest, or action, as with a party or cause.—**i·den·ti·fi·er,** *n.*

i·den·ti·ty, ī·den′ti·tē, ī·den′ti·tē, *n.* pl. **i·den·ti·ties.** [L.L. *identitas,* irreg. < L. *idem,* same.] The state or fact of being the same one; the state or fact of remaining the same one, as under varying aspects or conditions; the condition of being oneself or itself, and not another; the condition or character that distinguishes a person or a thing; individuality; sameness in nature or qualities; exact likeness.

id·e·o·gram, id′ē·o·gram″, ī′dē·o·gram″, *n.* A pictorial or graphic symbol representing an object or idea without the use of phonetic sounds; a symbol representing an idea rather than a word, as +, −, $, 3, or the like. Also *ideograph.*

id·e·o·graph, id′ē·o·graf″, id′ē·o·gräf″, ī′dē·o·graf″, ī′dē·o·gräf″, *n.* Ideogram.—**id·e·o·graph·ic,** id″ē·o·graf′ik, ī′dē·o·graf′ik, *a.*—**id·e·o·graph·i·cal·ly,**

adv.—**id·e·og·ra·phy,** id″ē·og′ra·fē, ī″dē·og′ra·fē, *n.* Writing in ideographic characters or symbols.

i·de·o·log·i·cal, ī″dē·o·loj′i·kal, id″ē·o·loj′i·kal, *a.* Pertaining to ideology; relating to ideas; speculative. Also **i·de·o·log·ic.**—**i·de·o·log·i·cal·ly,** *adv.*

i·de·ol·o·gist, ī″dē·ol′o·jist, id″ē·ol′o·jist, *n.* A specialist in ideology; a supporter of a particular ideology; one who indulges in visionary ideas or theories.

i·de·ol·o·gy, ī″dē·ol′o·jē, id″ē·ol′o·jē, *n.* pl. **i·de·ol·o·gies.** A particular system of ideas, esp. on social or political subjects; the science of ideas or their understanding; a system of philosophy which derives ideas exclusively from sensation; abstract speculation, esp. of a visionary or impractical nature.

i·de·o·mo·tor, ī″dē·o·mō′tèr, id″ē·o·mō′tèr, *a. Psychol.* pertaining to involuntary and nonreflexive muscular movement which is the result of complete engrossment by an idea, as opposed to *sensorimotor.*

ides, īdz, *n. pl., sing. or pl. in constr.* [L. *idus,* the ides, < *iduo,* to divide.] In the ancient Roman calendar the 13th of January, February, April, June, August, September, November, and December, and the 15th of March, May, July, and October.

id·i·o·blast, id′ē·o·blast″, *n. Bot.* a cell which differs greatly from the surrounding cells or tissue; *biol.* one of the hypothetical ultimate elements of living protoplasm.—**id·i·o·blast·ic,** *a.*

id·i·o·cy, id′ē·o·sē, *n.* pl. **id·i·o·cies.** The condition of being an idiot; mental deficiency; *fig.* senseless folly.

id·i·o·glos·si·a, id″ē·o·glos′ē·a, id″ē·o·glǎ′sē·a, *n. Pathol.* a condition marked by defective and generally unintelligible speech, garbled so that it sounds like a foreign language; also **id·i·o·la·li·a.** A private or invented language.

id·i·o·graph·ic, id″ē·o·graf′ik, *a. Psychol.* pertaining to the study of individual case histories.

id·i·o·lect, id′ē·o·lekt″, *n. Ling.* the speech pattern or language of a person at a given time in his life span.

id·i·om, id′ē·om, *n.* [L.L. *idioma* < Gr. *idiōma,* a peculiarity, property, idiom, < *idiousthai,* make one's own, < *idios,* own.] A form of expression peculiar to one language; an expression whose understood meaning is not expressed by the exact meanings of the individual words, as *to get along with*; the language peculiar to a people; a variety or form of a language; a dialect; the individual terminology or manner of expression characteristic of a certain group, profession, or the like.—**id·i·o·mat·ic,** id″ē·o·mat′ik, *a.* Peculiar to or characteristic of a particular language; exhibiting the characteristic modes of expression of a language.—**id·i·o·mat·i·cal·ly,** *adv.*—**id·i·o·mat·i·cal·ness,** *n.*

id·i·o·mor·phic, id″ē·o·mȯr′fik, *a. Mineral.* retaining its own typical crystalline form in a rock, not modified by any other constituents of the rock.—**id·i·o·mor·phi·cal·ly,** *adv.*—**id·i·o·mor·phism,** *n.*

id·i·op·a·thy, id″ē·op′a·thē, *n.* pl. **id·i·op·a·thies.** [Gr. *idios,* proper, peculiar, and *pathos,* suffering.] *Pathol.* A disease of unknown or obscure cause; a primary or spontaneous disease.—**id·i·o·path·ic,** id″ē·a·path′ik, *a.*

id·i·o·syn·cra·sy, id″ē·o·sing′kra·sē, *n.* pl. **id·i·o·syn·cra·sies.** [Gr. *idiosynkrasia, idios,* proper, *syn*–, with, and *krasis,* temperament.] A personal peculiarity of constitution, temperament, or manner; a quirk; a mental or moral characteristic belonging to and distinguishing an individual; an unusual way of thinking or feeling.—**id·i-o·syn·crat·ic**, id″ē·ō·sin·krat′ik, a.—**id·i·o·syn·crat·i·cal·ly**, adv.

id·i·ot, id′ē·ot, n. [L. idiota, < Gr. idiōtēs, a private, vulgar, unskilled person, idios, private, peculiar to oneself.] One who suffers from mental retardation in one of its most severe forms, having a mental age of three years or less; an extremely incompetent or foolish person.—**id·i·ot sav·ant**, id′ē·ot sa·vänt′, id′ē·ot sav′ant, Fr. ē·dyō sä·vän, pl. **id·i·ot sa·vants**, Fr. **id·i·ots sa·vants**, ē·dyō sä·vän′, a mentally retarded person who possesses a high degree of some special ability.

id·i·ot box, n. Slang, a television set.

id·i·ot card, n. Slang, TV, a card or other visual prompter, off camera, upon which lines of words are shown to assist the memory of a television performer.

id·i·ot·ic, id″ē·ot′ik, a. Like or relating to an idiot; foolish; utterly absurd. Also **id·i·ot·i·cal**.—**id·i·ot·i·cal·ly**, adv.—**id·i·ot·i·cal·ness**, n.

id·i·ot·ism, id′ē·o·tiz″um, n. Idiocy.

i·dle, ī′dl, a.—idler, idlest. [O.E. īdel, vain, empty, idle = D. ijdel, G. eitel, idle; Dan. idel, mere; from root meaning to shine (Skt. idh, Gr. aithō, to burn).] Not engaged in any occupation; doing nothing; slothful; averse to labor or employment; lazy; useless, ineffectual, or fruitless; as, idle rage; trifling or irrelevant; as, idle talk.—v.i.—idled, idling. To lose or spend time inactively or without being employed.—v.t. To spend in idleness, usu. followed by away; to run without producing power, as a machine.—**i·dle·ness**, n.—**i·dler**, n.—**i·dly**, adv.

i·dler pul·ley, n. Mach. a guide pulley used to keep the drive belt or chain securely in place. Also **i·dle pul·ley**.

i·dler wheel, n. Mach. a wheel placed between two others so as to transfer the motion from one axis to the other without change of direction. Also **i·dle wheel**.

I·do, ē′dō, n. An artificial language, made up of excerpts of common languages, intended as an international medium; a revised and simplified form of Esperanto.

i·do·crase, ī′do·krās″, id′o·krās″, n. [Gr. eidos, form, and krasis, mixture of forms its crystals display.] Mineral. vesuvianite.

i·dol, ī′dol, n. [Fr. idole, L. idolum, < Gr. eidōlon, an image, form, phantom, idol < eidos, form.] An image, representation, or symbol of a deity made or consecrated as an object of worship, esp. among pagans; a false or pagan god; fig. the object of excessive attachment, admiration, or infatuation. A fallacy or misconception.

i·dol·a·ter, ī·dol′a·tẽr, n. [Fr. idolatre, L. idololatres, Gr. eidōlolatrēs, an idol worshiper.] A worshiper of idols; an excessively devoted admirer.

i·dol·a·trous, ī·dol′a·trus, a. Characterized by, pertaining to, or participating in, the worship of idols; blindly or excessively devoted.—**i·dol·a·trous·ly**, adv.—**i·dol·a·trous·ness**, n.

i·dol·a·try, ī·dol′a·trē, n. pl. **i·dol·a·tries**. [Fr. idolatrie, L. idololatria, Gr. eidōlolatreia—eidōlon, idol, and latreuō, to worship.] The worship of idols; excessive admiration or veneration.

i·dol·ize, ī·d′o·līz″, v.t.—idolized, idolizing. To worship as an idol; to make an idol of; to love to excess; to love or reverence to the point of adoration.—v.i. To practice worship or extreme devotion.—**i·dol·iz·er**, n.—**i·dol·i·za·tion**, ī″do·li·zā′shan, n.

i·dyll, **i·dyl**, īd′il, n. [L. idyllium, Gr. eidyllion, eidos, form.] An elaborately structured short poem or narrative prose work, usu. describing idealized scenes or events from rustic life; a picturesque or charmingly simple scene; a romantic or

pastoral interlude; mus. a serene composition suggestive of pastoral repose.—**i·dyl·lic**, ī·dil′ik, a.—**i·dyl·lic·al·ly**, adv.—**i·dyl·list**, īd′i·list, n. One who composes idylls.

if, if, conj. [O.E. gif = D. of = G. ob = Icel. ef, if, whether, = Goth. ibai, whether, lest; prob. akin to O.H.G. iba, condition, stipulation, doubt, Icel. if, ef, doubt.] In case that; granting or supposing that; on condition that, as: If it doesn't rain, we'll go. Even though; as, an imaginative if impractical procedure; whether, as: She asked if I remembered. Used to introduce a wishful sentiment, as: If only it wouldn't rain. Used in elliptical constructions, as: I'll go if permitted.—n. A supposition.

if·fy, if′ē, a. Slang. Of contingent quality; unresolved or conditional; problematic and uncertain.

ig·loo, **ig·lu**, ig′lö, n. pl. **ig·loos**. [Eskimo.] An Eskimo hut, dome-shaped, and built of blocks of hard snow or ice; an excavation made by a seal in the snow over its breathing hole in the ice. Milit. a dome-shaped storage building for munitions.

ig·ne·ous, ig′nē·us, a. [L. igneus, < ignis, fire.] Geol. produced by fire or intense heat within the earth, as rocks of volcanic origin; pertaining to or of the nature of fire.

ig·nes·cent, ig·nes′ent, a. [L. ignescens (-ent), ppr. or ignescere, take fire, < ignis, fire.] Bursting into flame; emitting sparks of fire, as certain stones when struck with steel.—n. An ignescent substance.

ig·nis fat·u·us, ig′nis fach′o·us, n. pl. **ig·nes fat·u·i**, ig′nēz fach′o·ī″. [N.L., 'foolish fire.'] A flitting phosphorescent light seen at night, chiefly over marshy ground, and supposed to be due to spontaneous combustion of gas from decomposed organic matter; also jack-o'-lantern, will-o'-the wisp, friar's lantern. Something deluding or misleading.

ig·nite, ig·nīt′, v.t.—ignited, igniting. [L. ignitus, pp. of ignire, < ignis, fire.] To set on fire, kindle; to make intensely hot; chem. to cause to glow with heat.—v.i. To take fire; to begin to burn.—**ig·nit·er**, n. One who or that which ignites. Electron. in an internal-combustion engine, a device for producing an electric spark which ignites the charge of gas or vapor in the cylinder; also **ig·ni·tor**.—**ig·nit·a·ble**, **ig·nit·i·ble**, a.—**ig·nit·a·bil·i·ty**, **ig·nit·i·bil·i·ty**, ig·nit″a·bil′·i·tē, n.

ig·ni·tion, ig·nish′an, n. The act of igniting or the state of being ignited; a kindling or burning; in an internal-combustion engine, the igniting of the charge in the cylinder; the device which ignites.

ig·ni·tron, ig·nī′tron, ig′ni·tron, n. Electron. a type of mercury arc tube widely used as a starting mechanism and to control the rectification of alternating current in several motor, welding, and electrochemical processes.

ig·no·ble, ig·nō′bl, a. [L. ignobilis.] Mean, worthless, dishonorable, base; of low birth or family; not noble or illustrious.—**ig·no·bil·i·ty**, **ig·no·ble·ness**, ig″nō·bil′i·tē, n.—**ig·no·bly**, adv.

ig·no·min·i·ous, ig″no·min′ē·us, a. [L. ignominiosus.] Shameful; dishonorable; infamous; despicable.—**ig·no·min·i·ous·ly**, adv.—**ig·no·min·i·ous·ness**, n.

ig·no·min·y, ig′no·min″ē, n. pl. **ig·no·min·ies**. [L. ignominia—in-, not, and gnomen, nomen, name.] Public disgrace; shame; dishonor; infamy.

ig·no·ra·mus, ig′no·rā′mus, ig″no·ram′us, n. [< L. ignoro.] An ignorant person.

ig·no·rant, ig′nẽr·ant, a. [L. ignorans, ignorantis, ppr. of ignoro, to be ignorant.] Deficient in knowledge of either general information or a specific field; as, ignorant of physics; uninformed; untaught; un-

enlightened.—**ig·no·rant·ly**, adv.—**ig·no·rance**, ig′nẽr·ans, n. [L. ignorantia.] The state of being ignorant, or of lacking knowledge; the condition of not being cognizant or aware of.

ig·nore, ig·nōr′, v.t.—ignored, ignoring. [L. ignoro, to be ignorant of, < ignarus, not knowing—in-, not, and gnarus, knowing, < root of gnosco, to know.] To disregard; to refuse to notice, consider, or recognize; law, to dismiss or reject for lack of evidence, as a bill of indictment.—**ig·nor·a·ble**, a.—**ig·nor·er**, n.

i·gua·na, i·gwä′na, n. [Sp. < Carib. name.] Any lizard of the genus Iguana, of tropical America, esp. I. iguana an edible herbivorous species five feet or more in length.

i·guan·o·don, i·gwä′no·don″, i·gwan′o·don″, n. [Iguana and Gr. odous, odontos, a tooth, from its serrated teeth.] Paleon. an enormous, powerful, herbivorous dinosaur of the Cretaceous period, genus Iguanodon, characterized by a large, weighty tail which provided support for the animal's upright stance.—**i·guan·o·dont**, n., a.

IHS. A contraction or abbreviation of the Greek for Jesus. Sometimes, a representation of L. Iesus Hominum Salvator, Jesus, Saviour of Men or of L. In Hoc Signo (vinces), in this sign (shalt thou conquer).

i·kon, ī′kon, n. Icon.

i·lang-i·lang, ē′läng·ē′läng, n. Ylang-ylang.

il·e·i·tis, il″ē·ī′tis, n. Pathol. inflammation of the ileum.

il·e·um, il′ē·um, n. pl. **il·e·a**, il′ē·a. [Gr. eilō, to roll, from its convolutions; L. ilia, intestines.] Anat. the lower third of the small intestine located between the jejunum and the cecum.—**il·e·al**, **il·e·ac**, a.

il·e·us, il′ē·us, n. [N.L. < L. ileos, < Gr. eilein, roll up, pack close.] Pathol. severe colic, due to intestinal obstruction.

i·lex, ī′leks, n. [L. ilex, the holm oak, N.L. Ilex, the holly genus.] Bot. the genus Ilex, to which the holly and other shrubs belong.

il·i·ac, il′ē·ak, a. [L. iliacus, < ilia, the flank, the groin, the intestines.] Pertaining to the ilium. Also **il·i·al**.

Il·i·ad, il′ē·ad, n. [L. Ilias (Iliad-), < Gr. Ilias (Iliad-) < Ilion, Ilium, Troy.] A Greek epic poem attributed to Homer, describing the siege of Ilium (Troy) by the Greeks. (Sometimes l.c.) a long narrative of heroic deeds; a prolonged series of sorrows and hardships.—**Il·i·ad·ic**, il″ē·ad′ik, a.

il·i·um, il′ē·um, n. pl. **il·i·a**, il′ē·a. [Properly os ilium, bone of the ilia or flank.] Anat. a bone that forms the upper portion of the innominate bone; the hipbone.

ilk, ilk, n. [O.E. ilca.] Family, class, kind, or breed; as, Jones and his ilk.—**of that ilk**, Sc. dial. of the same family name or estate.

ill, il, a.—worse, worst. [From the Scandinavian; Icel. illr, ill; Icel. and Sw. illa, ill; a contracted form of evil; worse and worst are from a different root.] Suffering from disease or sickness; sick or indisposed; unwell; producing evil or misfortune; calamitous or unfortunate; as, an ill end; hostile; cross, surly, or peevish; as, an ill temper; adverse; bad or evil; wicked; as, ill repute; not proper; rude or unpolished; as, ill manners; incorrect; not skillful.—**ill at ease**, nervous or not comfortable.—**ill turn**, an unkind or injurious act.

ill, il, n. Wickedness; evil; misfortune; injury; disease; that which impairs happiness or prevents success.

ill, il, adv.—worse, worst. Not well; uncomfortably; poorly; not easily; with pain or difficulty; as: He is ill able to sustain the burden. In an unfriendly way; harshly.

I'll, il. Contraction of I will or I shall.

ill-ad·vised, il′ad·vīzd′, a. Badly informed; resulting from bad counsel or from lack of

---

ch- chain, G. nacht; **th-** THen, thin; **w-** wig, hw as sound in whig; **z-** zh as in azure, zeal. Italicized vowel indicates schwa sound.

good counsel; injudicious; imprudent.—
ill·ad·vis·ed·ly, il″ad·vī′zid·lē, *adv.*

il·la·tion, i·lā′shan, *n.* [L. *illatio.*] The act of inferring from premises or reasons; inference; deduction or conclusion.—**il·la·tive**, il′a·tiv, i·lā′tiv, *a.* Capable of being inferred or of inferring; denoting an inference, as: *Therefore* is an *illative* word.—*n.*—**il·la·tive·ly**, *adv.*

il·laud·a·ble, il·lạ′da·bl, *a.* Not worthy of praise.—**il·laud·a·bly**, *adv.*

ill-be·ing, il′bē′ing, *n.* A less than satisfactory condition of health and solvency.

ill-bod·ing, il′bō′ding, *a.* Foretelling misfortune; unlucky.

ill-bred, il′bred′, *a.* Badly brought up; impolite; vulgar.

ill-con·sid·ered, il′kon·sid′ėrd, *a.* Unwise; injudicious; insufficiently planned.

ill-dis·posed, il′di·spōzd′, *a.* Unfavorably or adversely disposed toward a person or idea; having an unfriendly temperament.—**ill-dis·pos·ed·ly**, *adv.*

il·le·gal, i·lē′gal, *a.* Contrary to official rules; unlawful; illicit.—**il·le·gal·i·ty**, il″ē·gal′i·tē, *n.*—**il·le·gal·ly**, *adv.*

il·leg·i·ble, i·lej′i·bl, *a.* Incapable of being read; poorly written; obscure or defaced so that the words cannot be deciphered.—**il·leg·i·bil·i·ty**, il·leg·i·ble·ness, *n.*—**il·leg·i·bly**, *adv.*

il·le·git·i·mate, il″i·jit′i·mit, *a.* Not legitimate; illegal; unauthorized or unwarranted; irregular or improper; not in accordance with good usage. Born out of wedlock. *Logic*, not in accordance with the laws of reasoning; as, an *illegitimate* inference.—**il·le·git·i·ma·cy**, *n.* pl. **il·le·git·i·ma·cies.**—**il·le·git·i·mate·ly**, *adv.*

ill-fat·ed, il′fā′tid, *a.* Predestined to evil or misfortune; doomed; unlucky.

ill-fa·vored, il′fā′vėrd, *a.* Having an unattractive appearance; ugly; displeasing or offensive.

ill-got·ten, il′got′en, *a.* Gained by unfair, unlawful, or improper means; dishonestly acquired.

ill hu·mor, *Brit.* **ill hu·mour,** *n.* Ill temper; surliness; irascibility.—**ill-hu·mored,** *Brit.* **ill-hu·moured,** *a.* Cross; irritable.—**ill-hu·mored·ly,** *Brit.* **ill-hu·moured·ly,** *adv.*

il·lib·er·al, i·lib′ėr·al, i·lib′ral, *a.* Not liberal; of narrow mind or opinions; not generous; stingy; penurious.—**il·lib·er·al·i·ty**, **il·lib·er·al·ness**, i·lib″ėr·al′i·tē, *n.*—**il·lib·er·al·ly**, *adv.*

il·lic·it, i·lis′it, *a.* [L. *illicitus.*] Not permitted, sanctioned, or allowed by law, or by tradition; prohibited; unlawful.—**il·lic·it·ly**, *adv.*—**il·lic·it·ness**, *n.*

il·lim·it·a·ble, i·lim′i·ta·bl, *a.* Incapable of being limited or bounded; immeasurable.—**il·lim·it·a·bly**, *adv.*—**il·lim·it·a·bil·i·ty**, **il·lim·it·a·ble·ness**, *n.*

il·lin·i·um, i·lin′ē·um, *n. Chem.* formerly the name of the element promethium.

il·lit·er·ate, i·lit′ėr·it, *a.* [L. *illiteratus.*] State of being unable to read or write; uneducated; exhibiting a lack of knowledge of a certain field, as: He is scientifically *illiterate.*—*n.*—**il·lit·er·a·cy**, i·lit′ėr·a·sē, *n.* pl. **il·lit·er·a·cies.** The state of being illiterate; an error in speech or writing.—**il·lit·er·ate·ly**, *adv.*—**il·lit·er·ate·ness**, *n.*

ill na·ture, *n.* Evil nature or disposition; unpleasant temper; crossness.—**ill-na·tured,** *a.*—**ill-na·tured·ly**, *adv.*—**ill-na·tured·ness**, *n.*

ill·ness, il′nis, *n.* The state or condition of being sick, whether in body or mind; an ailment or sickness.

il·log·i·cal, i·loj′i·kal, *a.* Contrary to logic and its rules; ignorant or negligent of sound reasoning; not sensible.—**il·log·ic**, *n.*—**il·log·i·cal·i·ty**, i·loj″i·kal′i·tē, *n.*—**il·log·i·cal·ly**, *adv.*

ill-sort·ed, il′sạr′tid, *a.* Not well-matched; not suited.

ill-starred, il′stärd′, *a.* Unfortunate or unlucky, as though having an evil star presiding over one's destiny; ill-fated.

ill tem·per, *n.* A surly or irritable mood; ill humor.—**ill-tem·pered,** *a.*—**ill-tem·pered·ly**, *adv.*—**ill-tem·pered·ness**, *n.*

ill-timed, il′tīmd′, *a.* Badly timed, inopportune, or unseasonable.

il·lu·mi·na·ble, i·lö′mi·na·bl, *a.* Capable of being illuminated.—**il·lu·mi·na·bil·i·ty,** *n.*

il·lu·mi·nance, i·lö′mi·nans, *n. Phys.* illumination, or the measure of its luminous flux.

il·lu·mi·nant, i·lö′mi·nant, *n.* An agent or substance which illuminates or gives light.

il·lu·mi·nate, i·lö′mi·nāt″, *v.t.*—*illuminated, illuminating.* [L. *illumino, illuminatum.*] To light up; to enlighten; to throw light on; to make clear and understandable; to make eminent; to decorate with lights; to adorn, as a manuscript, with gilded and colored decorations. *Radiology*, to submit to radiation.—*v.i.* To become lighted or illuminated.—**il·lu·mi·nat·ing**, *a.*

il·lu·mi·na·ti, i·lö″mi·nä′tī, i·lö″mi·nä′tē, *n. pl.* [L.] Persons possessing, or alleging to possess, superior enlightenment; (*cap.*) a name for various sects or societies which claim to possess superior enlightenment.

il·lu·mi·na·tion, i·lö″mi·nā′shan, *n.* [L. *illuminatio, illuminationis.*] The act of illuminating, or state of being illuminated; a source of light; a festive display of lights; an ornament or illustration in colors and gilding, as in books or manuscripts; intellectual or spiritual enlightenment. *Phys.* illuminance.

il·lu·mi·na·tive, i·lö′mi·nā″tiv, i·lö′mi·na·tiv, *a.* Having the power of illuminating; enlightening.

il·lu·mi·na·tor, i·lö′mi·nā″tėr, *n.* One who or that which illuminates; a person who enlightens; one who decorates books or manuscripts; a device for concentrating or diffusing light.

il·lu·mine, i·lö′min, *v.t., v.i.*—*illumined, illumining.* To illuminate.

il·lu·mi·nism, i·lö′mi·niz″um, *n.* [Fr. *illuminisme,* < *illuminer,* E. *illumine.*] The doctrines or claims of Illuminati; a doctrine advocating enlightenment.—**il·lu·mi·nist,** *n.*

ill-use, il′ūz′, *v.t.*—*ill-used, ill-using.* To use badly; treat unjustly or cruelly.—il′ūs′, *n.* Unjust or cruel treatment; also **ill-us·age.**

il·lu·sion, i·lö′zhan, *n.* [O.Fr. Fr. *illusion,* < L. *illusio(n-),* < *illudere.*] A false impression or belief; a delusion; false perception or conception of some object of sense; a perception of a thing which misrepresents it, or gives it qualities not present in reality; something that deceives by producing a false impression. A very thin, delicate kind of tulle used for veils. *Obs.* the act of deceiving as by legerdemain.—**il·lu·sion·al**, **il·lu·sion·ar·y**, i·lö′zha·ner″ē, *a.*

il·lu·sion·ism, i·lö′zha·niz″um, *n. Philos.* a theory or doctrine that the material world is an illusion. *Art,* the use of a technique that causes illusionary effects.—**il·lu·sion·ist**, *n.* One subject to illusions; one who produces illusions, as by sleight of hand; an adherent of illusionism.

il·lu·sive, i·lö′siv, *a.* Deceiving by false show; illusory.—**il·lu·sive·ly**, *adv.*—**il·lu·sive·ness**, *n.*

il·lu·so·ry, i·lö′so·rē, i·lö′zo·rē, *a.* [L.L. *illusorius,* < L. *illudere.*] Causing illusion; deceptive; of the nature of an illusion; unreal; fancied or visionary.—**il·lu·so·ri·ly**, *adv.*—**il·lu·so·ri·ness**, *n.*

il·lus·trate, il′a·strāt″, i·lus′trāt, *v.t.*—*illustrated, illustrating.* [L. *illustro, illus-*

tratum, to light up, to illuminate.] To make clear, intelligible, or obvious; throw light on by examples, comparisons, or the like; to ornament or elucidate by means of pictures, drawings, diagrams, or the like; to serve to ornament or clarify.—*v.i.* To supply an example.—**il·lus·tra·tion**, il″a·strā′shan, *n.* The act of illustrating; that which illustrates; a particular case or example intended to throw light on one's meaning; a picture or the like, as one accompanying the text of a book, which clarifies or decorates.—**il·lus·tra·tive**, i·lus′tra·tiv, il′a·strā″tiv, *a.*—**il·lus·tra·tive·ly**, *adv.*—**il·lus·tra·tor**, il′a·strā″tėr, i·lus′trā·tėr, *n.*

il·lus·tri·ous, i·lus′trē·us, *a.* [< L. *illustris,* lighted up, clear, distinguished.] Distinguished or esteemed among men; renowned; accomplished; worthy of recognition; commanding respect; eminent; of actions, deserving honor or glory.—**il·lus·tri·ous·ly**, *adv.*—**il·lus·tri·ous·ness**, *n.*

il·lu·vi·a·tion, i·lö″vē·ā′shan, *n.* [< L. *illuvies,* flood.] The addition of soil materials to a lower layer of soil, due to the chemical process of leaching.—**il·lu·vi·al**, i·lö′vē·al, *a.*

ill will, *n.* An attitude of malice; enmity.

il·ly, il′ē, il′lē, *adv.* Ill.

il·men·ite, il′me·nīt″, *n.* [From the *Ilmen* Mountains in Russia.] An opaque black mineral, $FeTiO_3$, a composite of iron, titanium, and oxygen.

I'm, īm. Contraction of I am.

im·age, im′ij, *n.* [Fr. < L. *imago,* an image, likeness, apparition, < stem of *imitor,* to imitate.] A representation of any person or thing, sculptured, painted, or otherwise made visible; an effigy; idol; that which forms a counterpart or likeness of something else; embodiment; semblance; a picture drawn by the memory or imagination; the mental picture created in a poem or story by descriptive wording; the composite public impression of a person, organization, or company due to its known procedures, philosophy, values; *psychol.* the representation in the mind of something once perceived and not now present; *opt.* the figure or appearance of an object made by reflection or refraction.—*v.t.*—*imaged, imaging.* To represent by an image; to reflect the image or likeness of; to mirror; to represent to the mental vision, as by descriptive language; to form a likeness of in the mind.—**im·age·a·ble**, *a.*—**im·ag·er**, *n.*

im·age·ry, im′ij·rē, im′ij·e·rē, *n.* pl. **im·age·ries.** Images in general or collectively; the imagination's process or the resulting mental images; the formation of pictorial images or the images themselves; the use of figures of speech, usu. by writers and speakers; figurative language or description.—**im·a·ge·ri·al**, im″a·jēr′e·al, *a.*

im·ag·i·na·ble, i·maj′i·na·bl, *a.* Capable of being imagined or conceived.—**im·ag·i·na·ble·ness**, *n.*—**im·ag·i·na·bly**, *adv.*

im·ag·i·nal, i·maj′i·nal, *a. Entom.* referring to an imago. Pertaining to the imagination or to imagery.

im·ag·i·nar·y, i·maj′i·ner″ē, *a.* [L. *imaginarius.*] Existing only in imagination or fancy; conceived by the imagination; not real; fancied.—*n.* pl. **im·ag·i·nar·ies.** *Math.* an imaginary number.—**i·mag·i·nar·i·ly**, *adv.*—**i·mag·i·nar·i·ness**, *n.*

im·ag·i·nar·y num·ber, *n. Math.* The positive square root of a negative number; a complex number having the form $a + bi$, with a and b as real numbers, b not equaling zero, and i equaling $\sqrt{-1}$.

im·ag·i·na·tion, i·maj″i·nā′shan, *n.* [O.Fr. Fr. *imagination,* < L. *imaginatio(n-),* < *imaginari.*] The action of imagining, or of forming mental images or concepts of what is not actually present to the senses; the faculty of forming such images or concepts; the power of the mind to reproduce images or concepts stored in the memory under the suggestion of associated images, or of recombining former experiences in the creation of new images; the faculty of producing ideal creations consistent with reality, as in poetical or literary composition; the product of imagining; a conception or mental creation, sometimes a baseless or fanciful one.—**i·mag·i·na··tion·al**, *a.*

im·i·na·tive, i·maj′i·na·tiv, i·maj′i·nā″tiv, *a.* [O.Fr. Fr. *imaginatif*, < L.L. *imaginativus*.] Given to imagining; having exceptional powers of imagination; fanciful; pertaining to or concerned with imagination; characterized by or bearing evidence of imagination.—**i·mag·i·na·tive·ly**, *adv.* —**i·mag·i·na·tive·ness**, *n.*

im·ag·ine, i·maj′in, *v.t.—imagined, imagining.* [O.Fr. Fr. *imaginer*, < L. *imaginari*, picture to oneself, fancy, imagine, < *imago*.] To form a mental image of, as of something not actually present to the senses; represent to oneself in imagination; conceive; to assume or suppose; conjecture or guess; think, believe, or fancy.—*v.i.* To form mental images of things not present to the senses; exercise the imagination; suppose. —**i·mag·in·er**, *n.*

im·ag·ism, im′a·jiz″um, *n. Liter.* a movement in poetic technique originating around 1909, marked by its use of clear, concrete images rather than symbolism, and free verse as opposed to the more restricted, traditional, metric forms.—**im·ag·ist**, *n., a.* —**im·ag·is·tic**, im″a·jis′tik, *a.*

i·ma·go, i·mā′gō, *n.* pl. **im·a·goes**, i·ma·gi·nes**, i·maj′i·nēz″. [L. an image.] *Entom.* the adult, sexually mature insect. *Psychoanal.* an idealized conception of a parent or other person loved in childhood, the unaltered concept being retained in adulthood.

i·mam, i·mäm′, *n.* [Ar. *imām*, < *amma*, to walk before, to preside.] A minister or priest who performs the regular service of the mosque among the Mohammedans. (*Cap.*) a title given to the successors of Mohammed. A Muslim ruler or spiritual leader. Also **i·maum**, i·mäm′, i·mam′.

i·mam·ate, i·mä′māt, *n.* The office or authority of an imam; the region that is ruled by an imam.

i·ma·ret, i·mä′ret, *n.* [Turk.] In Turkey, a kind of hospice for pilgrims and other travelers.

im·bal·ance, im·bal′ans, *n.* A lack of equilibrium or equality; *physiol.* faulty coordination of glands or muscles, as in the ocular muscles; *sociol.* lack of numerical proportion between men and women in a population unit.

im·be·cile, im′bi·sil, im′bi·sil, *Brit.* im′-bi·sēl″, *n.* [L. *imbecillis, imbecillus*, feeble in body or mind.] One who is mentally deficient; a fool; *psychol.* a person having an intelligence quotient between 25 and 50 or a mental age of about seven.—*a.* Mentally feeble; with mental faculties greatly impaired; foolish. Also **im·be·cil·ic**, im″bi··sil′ik.—**im·be·cile·ly**, *adv.*

im·be·cil·i·ty, im″bi·sil′i·tē, *n.* pl. **im··be·cil·i·ties.** [L. *imbecillitas.*] The condition or quality of being imbecile; fatuity; a foolish act or remark.

im·bed, im·bed′, *v.t.—imbedded, imbedding.* Embed.

im·bibe, im·bīb′, *v.t.—imbibed, imbibing.* [L. *imbibo—im-* for *in-*, in, into, and *bibo*, to drink, whence also *beverage*.] To drink in; to absorb; to receive or admit into the mind and retain.—*v.i.* To drink; to absorb.— **im·bib·er**, *n.*—**im·bi·bi·tion**, im″bi··bish′an, *n.* The act of imbibing; *chem.*

absorption of a fluid by a colloidal dispersion or gel.

im·bit·ter, im·bit′er, *v.t.* Embitter.

im·bos·om, im·buz′om, im·bö′zom, *v.t.* Embosom.

im·bri·cate, im′bri·kit, im′bri·kāt″, *a.* [L. *imbricatus*, < *imbrex, imbricis*, a hollow tile for a roof, < *imber*, a shower equiv. to Gr. *ombros*, rain.] Lapping over each other in a regular pattern, as tiles on a roof, scales of fish or reptiles, or leaves in a bud; embellished with a design of overlapping leaves or tiles. Also **im·bri·ca·tive**—im′bri·kāt, *v.t., v.i.—imbricated, imbricating.* To overlap.—**im·bri·cate·ly**, *adv.*—**im·bri·ca··tion**, im″bri·kā′shan, *n.*

im·bro·glio, im·brōl′yō, *n.* pl. **im·bro··glios.** [It. < *imbrogliare*, confuse, = E. *embroil.*] An intricate and perplexing state of affairs; a complicated or difficult situation; a misunderstanding or disagreement of a complicated nature, as between persons or nations; a confused heap.

im·brown, im·broun′, *v.t., v.i.* Embrown.

im·brue, im·brö′, *v.t.—imbrued, imbruing.* [O.Fr. *embreuver, embrevrer*, give to drink, wet.] To soak or drench in a fluid, esp. blood. Also *embrue.*—**im·brue·ment**, *n.*

im·brute, im·bröt′, *v.t., v.i.—imbruted, imbruting.* To degrade or sink to the state of a brute. Also **em·brute.**—**im·brute··ment**, *n.*

im·bue, im·bū′, *v.t.—imbued, imbuing.* [L. *imbuo*, allied to *imber*, a shower; Skt. *ambu*, water.] To soak, steep, or saturate with moisture or dye; *fig.* to inspire, impress, or impregnate, as with emotions or opinions.

im·id·az·ole, im″id·az′ōl, im″id·a·zōl′, *n. Chem.* a colorless, crystalline compound, soluble in water, alcohol and ether, $C_3H_4N_2$. Also **gly·ox·a·line.**

im·ide, im′īd, im′id, *n.* [Varied form of *amide.*] *Chem.* an organic compound derived from ammonia, in which the bivalent radical NH is combined with a bivalent acid radical.—**im·i·do**, *a.*

i·mine, i·mēn′, im′in, *n. Chem.* an organic compound derived from ammonia, in which the bivalent radical NH is combined with a nonacid radical.—**i·min·o**, *a.*

im·i·ta·ble, im′i·ta·bl, *a.* Capable of being imitated or copied.

im·i·tate, im′i·tāt, *v.t.—imitated, imitating.* [L. *imitor, imitatus*, from a root which gives also *imago*, image.] To follow as a model, pattern or example; to copy in actions, manner, or the like; to mimic; to produce a likeness of; to counterfeit.—**im·i·ta·tor**, *n.*

im·i·ta·tion, im″i·tā′shan, *n.* [L. *imitatio, imitationis.*] The act of imitating; that which is made or produced as a copy; a likeness; a counterfeit; *biol.* mimicry; *psychol.* the process of being stimulated to act by the observation of another's performance; *liter.* a work which is patterned after another author's style; *mus.* the repetition of a melodic idea by different parts or voices in a composition.—*a.* Made to resemble that which is genuine, original, or superior; as, *imitation* jewelry. Also **im·i·ta·tion·al.**

im·i·ta·tive, im′i·tā″tiv, *a.* Inclined to imitate or copy; characterized by imitation; counterfeit; *ling.* onomatopoeic.—**im·i··ta·tive·ly**, *adv.*—**im·i·ta·tive·ness**, *n.*

im·mac·u·late, i·mak′ū·lit, *a.* [L. *im-maculatus.*] Free from spot or stain; spotlessly clean, as linen; free from moral blemish or impurity; without flaw or error. *Biol.* without spots or colored marks; unicolor.—**im·mac·u·la·cy**, **im·mac·u··late·ness**, *n.*—**im·mac·u·late·ly**, *adv.*

Im·mac·u·late Con·cep·tion, *n. Rom. Cath. Ch.* a dogma, proclaimed in 1854, that the Virgin Mary was conceived free from original sin.

im·mane, i·mān′, *a.* [L. *immanis.*] Monstrous; huge; prodigious; monstrously cruel or savage.

im·ma·nent, im′a·nent, *a.* [L.L. *im-manens.*] Remaining within; indwelling; inherent. *Philos.* taking place entirely within the mind; subjective. *Theol.* of God, pervading the universe.—**im·ma·nence**, **im·ma·nen·cy**, *n.*—**im·ma·nent·ly**, *adv.*

im·ma·nent·ism, im′a·nent·iz″um, *n.* Any of the theories stating that God, or an abstract power, is totally immanent in the world.—**im·ma·nent·ist**, *n.*—**im·ma··nent·is·tic**, im″a·nen·tis′tik, *a.*

im·ma·te·ri·al, im″a·tēr′ē·al, *a.* Of no essential consequence; unimportant. Not consisting of matter; incorporeal.— **im·ma·te·ri·al·ly**, *adv.*—**im·ma·te·ri··al·ness**, *n.*—**im·ma·te·ri·al·i·ty**, im″-a·tēr″ē·al′i·tē, *n.* Something immaterial; quality of being immaterial.

im·ma·te·ri·al·ism, im″a·tēr′ē·a·liz″um, *n.* The doctrine that there is no material world, but that it exists only in the mind.— **im·ma·te·ri·a·list**, *n.*

im·ma·te·ri·al·ize, im″a·tēr′ē·a·līz″, *v.t.* —*immaterialized, immaterializing.* To make immaterial or incorporeal.

im·ma·ture, im″a·tụr′, im″a·tūr′, im″a··chụr′, *a.* [L. *immaturus*, unripe.] Not mature or ripe; unripe; not brought to a completed state. *Geol.* still in the process of developing; young; as, an *immature* mountain range.—*n.*—**im·ma·ture·ly**, *adv.*— **im·ma·ture·ness**, **im·ma·tu·ri·ty**, *n.*

im·meas·ur·a·ble, i·mezh′er·a·bl, *a.* Incapable of being measured; boundless.— **im·meas·ur·a·ble·ness**, *n.*—**im·meas··ur·a·bly**, *adv.*

im·me·di·a·cy, i·mē′dē·a·sē, *n.* pl. **im··me·di·a·cies.** The condition or quality of being immediate; immediateness; proximity; *usu. pl.* that which is immediate or which pertains to the moment. *Philos.* the presentation to the mind of an object of knowledge directly without inference, interpretation, or reasoning; knowledge gained by intuition rather than as a product of thought or reasoning.

im·me·di·ate, i·mē′dē·it, *a.* Occurring or done without separation by an interval of space or time; as, in the *immediate* area, an *immediate* reaction; instant; related to the present time; as, the *immediate* future; in closest relation; as, the *immediate* members of the family. Acting or occurring without a medium, or without an intervening cause, means, or condition; as, the *immediate* source of the problem; direct.—**im·me··di·ate·ness**, *n.* Immediacy.

im·me·di·ate·ly, i·mē′dē·it·lē, *adv.* Without delay; instantly; at once; forthwith. Without the intervention of any space, object, or medium; directly.—*conj.* As soon as; the instant or second that.

im·med·i·ca·ble, i·med′i·ka·bl, *a.* [L. *immedicabilis.*] Incapable of being healed; incurable.—**im·med·i·ca·bly**, *adv.*

Im·mel·mann turn, im′el·män″ tụrn′, im′el·man tụrn′, *n.* [From Max *Immelmann*, German World War I flyer.] *Aeron.* an airplane turn designed to allow a plane to ascend while switching directions and consisting of a half loop followed by a half roll.

im·me·mo·ri·al, im″e·mōr′ē·al, *a.* [L.] Beyond memory; extending beyond the reach of record or tradition; existing or occurring in the far distant past.—**im··me·mo·ri·al·ly**, *adv.*

im·mense, i·mens′, *a.* [L. *immensus.*] Vast in extent or bulk; very great; very large; boundless; huge; enormous. *Colloq.* extremely good; pleasing; excellent.—**im··mense·ly**, *adv.*—**im·mense·ness**, *n.*

im·men·si·ty, i·men′si·tē, *n.* pl. **im··men·si·ties.** [L. *immensitas.*] The condition or quality of being immense; vastness; that which is immense; an extent not to be measured; infinity.

im·men·su·ra·ble, i·men′shụ·ra·bl, i·men′sẽr·a·bl, *a.* Not to be measured; immeasurable.

im·merge, i·mẽrj′, *v.i.*—*immerged, immerging.* [L. *immergo.*] To plunge into or under, esp. into or under a fluid; to disappear by entering into any medium.—*v.t. Archaic,* to immerse.—**im·mer·gence,** *n.*

im·merse, i·mẽrs′, *v.t.*—*immersed, immersing.* [L. *immergo, immersum.*] To plunge into anything that covers or surrounds, as into a fluid; to dip; *fig.* to engage deeply or involve; as, to *immerse* oneself in business.—**im·mer·sion,** i·mẽr′zhan, i·mẽr′shan, *n.* [L. *immersio, immersionis.*] The act of immersing, or state of being immersed; *relig.* baptism by submerging the whole body under water; *astron.* the disappearance of a celestial body by passing either behind another or into its shadow, causing an eclipse: as opposed to *emersion.*—**im·mer·sion·ist,** *n.* One who holds that immersion is essential to Christian baptism.

im·mersed, i·mẽrst′, *a.* Being submerged; baptized by immersion. *Bot.* growing beneath and entirely covered by water. *Zool.* embedded wholly or partially in surrounding tissue, as an organ.

im·mer·sion heat·er, *n.* A small, waterproof, electric unit used to heat a beverage by being immersed in it.

im·mesh, i·mesh′, *v.t.* Enmesh.

im·me·thod·i·cal, im″e·thod′i·kal, *a.* Not methodical; without system.—**im·me·thod·i·cal·ly,** *adv.*

im·mi·grant, im′i·grant, *n.* One who or that which immigrates, esp. a person who migrates into a country of which he is not a native for permanent residence.—*a.* Immigrating; of or relating to immigrants and immigrating.

im·mi·grate, im′i·grāt″, *v.i.*—*immigrated, immigrating.* [L. *immigro.*] To remove into a country of which one is not a native for the purpose of permanent residence.—*v.t.* To send in or cause to enter as immigrants; as, to *immigrate* new settlers.—**im·mi·gra·tor,** *n.*—**im·mi·gra·tion,** im″i·grā′shan, *n.* Act of immigrating; a body of immigrants; the total number of immigrants during a specific period.—**im·mi·gra·tion·al, im·mi·gra·to·ry,** im′i·gra·tōr″ē.

im·mi·nent, im′i·nent, *a.* [L. *imminens, imminentis,* ppr. of *imminere,* to hang over.] Impending; threatening to fall or occur; near at hand; usu. threatening evil.—**im·mi·nence,** *n.* Something which is imminent; an impending or threatening evil; quality or condition of being imminent. Also **im·mi·nen·cy.**—**im·mi·nent·ly,** *adv.*—**im·mi·nent·ness,** *n.*

im·min·gle, i·ming′gl, *v.t., v.i.*—*immingled, immingling.* To mingle in; intermix or blend.

im·mis·ci·ble, i·mis′i·bl, *a.* Incapable of being mixed: used esp. in referring to liquids, as oil with water.—**im·mis·ci·bil·i·ty,** *n.*—**im·mis·ci·bly,** *adv.*

im·mit·i·ga·ble, i·mit′i·ga·bl, *a.* [L.L. *immitigabilis.*] Not to be mitigated, softened, or made more mild.—**im·mit·i·ga·ble·ness,** *n.*—**im·mit·i·ga·bly,** *adv.*

im·mix, i·miks′, *v.t.* To mix; to mingle; to blend.—**im·mix·ture,** i·miks′chẽr, *n.*

im·mo·bile, i·mō′bil, i·mō′bēl, *a.* [L. *immobilis.*] Immovable; not able to move; fixed.—**im·mo·bil·i·ty,** im″ō·bil′i·tē, *n.*

im·mo·bi·lize, i·mō′bi·līz″, *v.t.*—*immobilized, immobilizing.* To make immovable. *Med.* to restrain movement of, as the body or a bodily part, as part of a surgical or corrective procedure. *Milit.* to make incapable of action, as troops. *Finance,* to

withdraw, as coined money, from circulation in order to build a financial reserve; to change, as circulating capital, into fixed capital.—**im·mo·bi·li·za·tion,** *n.*—**im·mo·bi·liz·er,** *n.*

im·mod·er·a·cy, i·mod′ẽr·a·sē, *n.* pl. **im·mod·er·a·cies.** Absence of moderation. Also **im·mod·er·a·tion.**

im·mod·er·ate, i·mod′ẽr·it, *a.* [L. *immoderatus.*] Without desirable restraint; excessive.—**im·mod·er·ate·ly,** *adv.*—**im·mod·er·ate·ness,** *n.*

im·mod·est, i·mod′ist, *a.* Lacking modesty or propriety; boldly assertive.—**im·mod·est·ly,** *adv.*—**im·mod·es·ty,** *n.*

im·mo·late, im′o·lāt″, *v.t.*—*immolated, immolating.* [L. *immolo, immolatum,* to sacrifice.] To kill, esp. by fire, as a victim offered in sacrifice; to kill or destroy as in war; to sacrifice or renounce, as oneself, for a cause.—**im·mo·la·tion,** im″o·lā′shan, *n.* The act of immolating; a sacrifice offered.—**im·mo·la·tor,** *n.*

im·mor·al, i·mạr′al, *a.* Not moral; not conforming to accepted patterns of what is considered right and wrong behavior in a culture. Licentious, wicked.—**im·mor·al·ist,** *n.*—**im·mo·ral·i·ty,** im″o·ral′i·tē, *n.* pl. **im·mo·ral·i·ties.** Wickedness; an immoral act or practice.—**im·mor·al·ly,** *adv.*

im·mor·tal, i·mạr′tal, *a.* [L. *immortalis.*] Not mortal; not liable or subject to death; remembered or celebrated through all time; not liable to perish or decay; imperishable; everlasting; perpetual, lasting, or constant; pertaining to immortal beings or immortality.—*n.* An immortal being; a person, esp. an author, of enduring fame. *Pl. (usu. cap),* the gods of classical mythology; *(cap.)* the French Academy's 40 members, usu. preceded by *the.*—**im·mor·tal·ly,** *adv.*

im·mor·tal·i·ty, im″ạr·tal′i·tē, *n.* [L. *immortalitas.*] The condition or quality of being immortal; unending life or existence; enduring fame.

im·mor·tal·ize, i·mạr′ta·līz″, *v.t.*—*immortalized, immortalizing.* To make immortal; perpetuate; bestow enduring fame upon.—**im·mor·tal·iz·er,** *n.*

im·mor·telle, im″ạr·tel′, *n.* [Fr. prop. fem. of *immortel,* < L. *immortalis,* E. *immortal.*] A flower which retains its shape and color when dried. See *everlasting.*

im·mo·tile, i·mōt′il, *a.* Not motile; *biol.* incapable of spontaneous movement.—**im·mo·til·i·ty,** *n.*

im·mov·a·ble, i·mö′va·bl, *a.* Incapable of being moved; stationary; not subject to change; motionless; unalterable; incapable of being moved from one's purpose or opinion; incapable of being affected with feeling; emotionless; impassive. *Law,* not liable to be moved because of its own nature; real, as distinguished from personal.—*n. pl., law.* Immovable property; lands and appurtenances thereof, as trees, buildings.—**im·mov·a·bil·i·ty,** *n.*—**im·mov·a·bly,** *adv.*

im·mov·a·ble feast, *n. Relig.* a feast, as Christmas, which is fixed for a certain date and unchanged from year to year, as opposed to *movable feast.*

im·mune, i·mūn′, *a.* [L. *immunis, in-,* not, and *-munis,* bound, under obligation, akin *munis,* duties, functions, *munus,* service, duty.] Exempt; free from; not susceptible to; *med.* protected against a disease, poison, or the like, usu. by inoculation.—*n.*

im·mu·ni·ty, i·mū′ni·tē, *n.* pl. **im·mu·ni·ties.** [L. *immunitas.*] Exemption from obligation, service, or duty; freedom from liability to taxation or jurisdiction. *Eccles.* the exemption of ecclesiastical persons and things from secular or civil liabilities, duties, and burdens; a particular exemption of this kind. *Med.* the state of being immune from or insusceptible to a disease.

im·mu·nize, im′ū·nīz″, i·mū′nīz, *v.t.*—*immunized, immunizing.* To render immune.—**im·mu·ni·za·tion,** *n.* The condition of being immunized; the act of immunizing.—**im·mu·niz·er,** *n.*

im·mu·no·chem·is·try, im″ū·nō·kem′i·strē, *n.* A part of the study of immunology dealing with its chemical aspects.

im·mu·no·ge·net·ics, im″ū·nō·je·net′iks, i·mū″nō·je·net′iks, *n. pl. but sing. in constr.* The study of the genetic aspects of immunity; the study of biological relationships by comparison of serological reactions.—**im·mu·no·ge·net·ic,** *a.*—**im·mu·no·ge·net·i·cal,** *a.*

im·mu·no·gen·ic, im″ū·nō·jen′ik, i·mū″no·jen′ik, *a.* Producing immunity to a particular disease.—**im·mu·no·gen·i·cal·ly,** *adv.*—**im·mu·no·ge·nic·i·ty,** im″ū·nō·je·nis′i·tē, i·mū″nō·je·nis′i·tē, *n.*

im·mu·nol·o·gy, im″ū·nol′o·jē, *n.* That branch of medical science which deals with immunity from disease and the production of such immunity.—**im·mu·no·log·ic, im·mu·no·log·i·cal,** i·mū″no·loj′ik, *a.*—**im·mu·no·log·i·cal·ly,** *adv.*—**im·mu·nol·o·gist,** *n.*

im·mu·no·sup·pres·sive, i·mū″nō·sa·pre′siv, *a. Med.* relating to that which is capable of inhibiting immune responses, such as the rejection by an individual of a transplanted organ.

im·mu·no·ther·a·py, i·mū″nō·ther′a·pē, *n.* The prevention or cure of disease through the use of antigens.

im·mure, i·mūr′, *v.t.*—*immured, immuring.* [O.Fr. *emmurer* < L. *in-,* and *murus,* a wall.] To enclose or imprison within walls; to confine; to inter within a wall.—**im·mure·ment,** *n.*

im·mu·ta·ble, i·mū′ta·bl, *a.* [L. *immutabilis.*] Not mutable; unchangeable; unalterable; changeless.—**im·mu·ta·bil·i·ty, im·mu·ta·ble·ness,** *n.*—**im·mu·ta·bly,** *adv.*

imp, imp, *n.* [Orig. a shoot or scion, < L.L. *impotus,* a graft or scion, < Gr. *emphytos,* engrafted—*en-,* in, and *phyō,* to grow, to produce; similarly Sw. *ymp,* Dan. *ympe,* twig, shoot, scion.] A small devil; a mischievous child; a little malignant spirit.—*v.t.* To graft; to strengthen or enlarge by something inserted or added; *falconry,* to mend, as a deficient wing, by the insertion of a feather.

IMP, *n.* [(*I*)nterplanetary (*M*)onitoring (*P*)latform.] An unmanned satellite designed to explore regions beyond the magnetic field of the earth, and to help plan measures for protecting astronauts from the dangers of radiation in space.

im·pact, im′pakt, *n.* [L. *impactus,* pp. of *impingere,* drive in, strike against.] The striking of one body against another; a collision or impinging; effect or influence; the force of a collision or impingement.—im·pakt′, *v.t.* To drive or press closely or firmly into something; to pack in something; to impinge on; to collide with.

im·pact·ed, im·pak′tid, *a.* Wedged or packed in tightly; *dentistry,* of a tooth, so firmly held by the jawbone that it cannot emerge from the gum.—**im·pac·tion,** *n.*

im·pair, im·pâr′, *v.t.* [Fr. *empeirier* < M.L. *impejorare.*] To make worse; to lessen in quality, quantity, value, excellence, or strength; to deteriorate.—**im·pair·er,** *n.*—**im·pair·ment,** *n.*

im·pal·a, im·pal′a, im·pä′la, *n.* pl. **im·pal·as, im·pal·a.** *Zool.* an antelope native to Africa, *Aepyceros melampus,* noted for its spreading ringed horns and leaping ability.

im·pale, im·pāl′, *v.t.*—*impaled, impaling.* [Fr. *empaler,* < M.L. *impalare.*] To fix upon a sharpened stake or the like; pierce with a sharpened stake thrust up through the body, as for torture or punishment; to fix upon, or pierce through with, anything pointed; *fig.* to render helpless as if pierced through. *Rare*, to enclose or surround with or as with pales or stakes; fence in.—**im·pale·ment**, *n.*—**im·pal·er**, *n.*

im·pal·pa·ble, im·pal′pa·bl, *a.* Not to be felt; incapable of being distinguished or perceived by the touch; not easily apprehended or grasped by the mind; intangible.—**im·pal·pa·bil·i·ty**, *n.*—**im·pal·pa·bly**, *adv.*

im·pan·el, *Brit.* also **im·pan·nel**, im·pan′el, *v.t.*—*impaneled, impaneling.* [A.Fr. *empaneller*, < *em-* (< L. *in-*, in) and *panel*, panel.] To enter on a panel or list for jury duty; to select, as a jury, from the panel. Also *empanel.*—**im·pan·el·ment**, *n.*

im·par·i·ty, im·par′i·tē, *n.* pl. **im·par·i·ties.** [< L. *impar*, unequal—*im-*, not, and *par*, equal.] Inequality; disproportion; disparity.

im·park, im·pärk′, *v.t.* [O.Fr. *emparquer*, < *em-* (< L. *in*, in) and *parc*, E. *park*.] To shut up, as in a park; to enclose as a park.—**im·par·ka·tion**, *n.*

im·part, im·pärt′, *v.t.* [O.Fr. *impartir*, < L. *impartio, impertio*—*im-* for *in-*, and *partio*, to divide, < *pars, partis*, a part.] To make known; to communicate the knowledge of; to give, grant, confer, or communicate; to bestow a part, share, or portion of.—**im·part·a·ble**, *a.*—**im·par·ta·tion**, **im·part·ment**, *n.*—**im·part·er**, *n.*

im·par·tial, im·pär′shal, *a.* Not partial; not favoring one party more than another; unprejudiced; equitable; just.—**im·par·ti·al·i·ty**, im·par·tial·ness, im·pär″shē·al′i·tē, *n.*—**im·par·tial·ly**, *adv.*

im·part·i·ble, im·pär′ti·bl, *a.* Not partible; not subject to partition; indivisible.—**im·part·i·bly**, *adv.*

im·pass·a·ble, im·pas′a·bl, im·pä′sa·bl, *a.* Not passable, as heavy undergrowth; incapable of being passed over, through, or along; not able to be overcome.—**im·pass·a·bil·i·ty**, **im·pass·a·ble·ness**, *n.*—**im·pass·a·bly**, *adv.*

im·passe, im′pas, im·pas′, *Fr.* aN·päs′, *n.* pl. **im·pass·es.** *Fig.* A position from which there is no escape; a deadlock. A road having no way out; a blind alley; a cul-de-sac.

im·pas·si·ble, im·pas′i·bl, *a.* [L. *impassibilis*—*im-* for *in-*, not, and *passibilis*, capable of feeling, < *patior, passus*, to suffer.] Incapable of pain, passion, or suffering; not to be moved to passion or sympathy; not exhibiting or without emotion.—**im·pas·si·bil·i·ty**, **im·pas·si·ble·ness**, *n.*—**im·pas·si·bly**, *adv.*

im·pas·sion, im·pash′an, *v.t.* To move or affect strongly with passion.—**im·pas·sioned**, im·pash′and, *a.* Actuated or animated by passion, ardor, or warmth of feeling; animated; excited; as, an *impassioned* orator.—**im·pas·sioned·ly**, *adv.*—**im·pas·sioned·ness**, *n.*

im·pas·sive, im·pas′iv, *a.* Without emotion; apathetic; unmoved; not subject to suffering; insensible or unconscious; inanimate; not susceptible to injury.—**im·pas·sive·ly**, *adv.*—**im·pas·sive·ness**, **im·pas·siv·i·ty**, im″pa·siv′i·tē, *n.*

im·paste, im·pāst′, *v.t.*—*impasted, impasting.* [It. *impastare*, < *im-* (< L. *in*, in) and *pasta*, < L.L. *pasta*, E. *paste*.] To cover with or enclose in a paste; to form into a paste; to lay on thickly, as paint.—**im·pas·ta·tion**, im″pa·stā′shan, *n.*

im·pas·to, im·pas′tō, im·pä′stō, *n.* *Painting.* The laying on of colors or paint thickly; the color so laid on.

im·pa·tience, im·pā′shens, *n.* The condition or quality of being impatient; restlessness; anxious anticipation; intolerance of delay.

im·pa·ti·ens, im·pā′shē·enz″, *n.* pl. **im·pa·ti·ens.** Garden and wild flowers of the genus *Impatiens*, in the balsam family, having irregular, spurred, orange to red-colored flowers and pods which burst when touched. Also *touch-me-not, jewelweed.*

im·pa·tient, im·pā′shent, *a.* Not patient; uneasy and eager for change; intolerant; followed by *with, of, at, for, under*; prompted by impatience; exhibiting or expressing impatience; as, an *impatient* gesture.—**im·pa·tient·ly**, *adv.*—**im·pa·tient·ness**, *n.*

im·peach, im·pēch′, *v.t.* [O.Fr. *empechier* (Fr. *empecher*), hinder, < L.L. *impedicare*, catch, entangle, < L. *in-*, in, and *pedica*, fetter, < *pes*, foot.] To bring an accusation against; charge with wrongdoing; to accuse, as a public official before a tribunal, of misconduct in office; to call in question or cast an imputation upon; as, to *impeach* a person's motives; to challenge the credibility of; as, to *impeach* a witness.—*n.*—**im·peach·a·ble**, im·pē′cha·bl, *a.*—**im·peach·ment**, *n.*

im·pec·ca·ble, im·pek′a·bl, *a.* [L. *impeccabilis*, without fault.] Faultless or irreproachable; flawless; perfect; as, *impeccable* manners or dress; not liable to sin; exempt from the possibility of doing wrong.—**im·pec·ca·bil·i·ty**, *n.*—**im·pec·ca·bly**, *adv.*

im·pec·cant, im·pek′ant, *a.* Not sinful; faultless; unerring.—**im·pec·can·cy**, *n.*

im·pe·cu·ni·ous, im″pe·kū″ne·us, *a.* [Prefix *im-* for *in-*, not, and *pecunia*, money.] Not having money; without funds; indigent.—**im·pe·cu·ni·os·i·ty**, im″pe·kū″nē·os′i·tē, *n.*—**im·pe·cu·ni·ous·ly**, *adv.*—**im·pe·cu·ni·ous·ness**, *n.*

im·ped·ance, im·pēd′ans, *n.* *Elect., phys.* the ratio between a varying quantity, esp. a force such as voltage, and another quantity, esp. a velocity such as current, which measures the response of a system to the application of the force. Sym. Z.

im·pede, im·pēd′, *v.t.*—*impeded, impeding.* [L. *impedire* (pp. *impeditus*), entangle, hamper, orig. the feet.] To obstruct; to hinder.—**im·ped·er**, *n.*—**im·pe·di·ent**, im·pē′dē·ent, *a., n.*

im·ped·i·ment, im·ped′i·ment, *n.* [L. *impedimentum*, < *impedire*, E. *impede*.] An obstacle; a hindrance; a handicap, esp. a physical defect which prevents distinct speech. *Law*, bar to a legal marriage.—**im·ped·i·men·tal**, im·ped″i·men′tal, **im·ped·i·men·ta·ry**, *a.*

im·ped·i·men·ta, im·ped″i·men′ta, *n. pl.* [L.] Things which impede progress, as baggage or other burdens; *milit.* supplies carried with an army.

im·pel, im·pel′, *v.t.*—*impelled, impelling.* [L. *impello*.] Drive or urge forward; press on; excite to motion or action.

im·pel·lent, im·pel′ent, *a.* Having the quality of impelling.—*n.* A power or force that impels.

im·pel·ler, **im·pel·lor**, im·pel′ẽr, *n.* One who or that which impels; *mech.* a device which imparts motion to air, a fluid, or another substance; a rotor.

im·pend, im·pend′, *v.i.* [L. *impendeo*—*im-* for *in-*, in, on, over, and *pendeo*, to hang.] To threaten from near at hand; to be imminent; to be ready to happen; to be in suspension, usu. with *over*.—**im·pend·ent**, **im·pend·ing**, *a.* Imminent.—**im·pen·dence**, **im·pen·den·cy**, *n.*

im·pen·e·tra·bil·i·ty, im·pen″i·tra·bil′i·tē, im″pen·i·tra·bil′i·tē, *n.* The condition of being impenetrable, impervious; *phys.* that property of matter which prevents two bodies from occupying the same space at the same time.

im·pen·e·tra·ble, im·pen′i·trabl, *a.* Not penetrable; incapable of being penetrated or pierced; impermeable; inaccessible; incomprehensible; inscrutable; *phys.* pre-venting any other substance from occupying the same place at the same time.—**im·pen·e·tra·bly**, *adv.*—**im·pen·e·tra·ble·ness**, *n.*

im·pen·i·tent, im·pen′i·tent, *a.* Not penitent; not repenting of sin; obdurate.—*n.*—**im·pen·i·tence**, *n.*—**im·pen·i·tent·ly**, *adv.*

im·per·a·tive, im·per′a·tiv, *a.* [L. *imperativus*, < *imperare*, command.] Not to be avoided or evaded; urgent and necessary; obligatory; of the nature of or expressing a command; peremptory; *gram.* noting or pertaining to that mood of the verb which expresses command, exhortation, advice, or entreaty.—*n.* Something imperative; a command; *gram.* the imperative mood or a verb form belonging to it.—**im·per·a·ti·val**, im·per″a·tī′val, *a.*—**im·per·a·tive·ly**, *adv.*—**im·per·a·tive·ness**, *n.*

im·pe·ra·tor, im″pe·rä′tẽr, *n.* [L.] A Roman emperor; formerly, a Roman military commander; an absolute or supreme ruler.—**im·per·a·to·ri·al**, im·per″a·tōr′ē·al, *a.*

im·per·cep·ti·ble, im″per·sep′ta·bl, *a.* [M.L. *imperceptibilis*.] Very slight; gradual; subtle; not perceptible; not discernible by the senses or the mind.—**im·per·cep·ti·bil·i·ty**, *n.*—**im·per·cep·ti·bly**, *adv.*

im·per·cep·tive, im″per·sep′tiv, *a.* Not perceptive; lacking perception or vision.—**im·per·cep·tive·ness**, *n.*

im·per·fect, im·pur′fikt, *a.* [L. *imperfectus*.] Not perfect; incomplete; defective; *bot.* relating to a flower having either stamens or pistils but not both; *gram.* denoting incomplete action or state, esp. in past time; *mus.* referring to a cadence which ends on the dominant.—*n. Gram.* the imperfect tense of a verb form.—**im·per·fect·ly**, *adv.*—**im·per·fect·ness**, *n.*

im·per·fect fun·gus, *n.* A class of fungi, thought to reproduce only asexually, that causes certain diseases such as ringworm or athlete's foot.

im·per·fec·tion, im″per·fek′shan, *n.* [L.L. *imperfectio(n-)*.] Lack of completion; imperfect condition or character; defectiveness; a defect or fault.

im·per·fo·rate, im·pur′fẽr·it, im·pur′fo·rāt″, *a.* Not perforated or pierced; as, an *imperforate* sheet of stamps; having no openings or pores.—*n.* A stamp which is not perforated.

im·pe·ri·al, im·pēr′ē·al, *a.* [O.Fr. *imperial* (Fr. *impérial*), < L. *imperialis*, < *imperium*, empire.] Of or pertaining to an empire, or to an emperor or empress; of the nature or rank of an emperor or supreme ruler; supreme in authority; of a commanding quality, manner, or aspect; majestic; domineering or imperious; magnificent; of special size or quality, as various products, commodities, etc.; of weights and measures, conforming to the standards of Great Britain.—**im·pe·ri·al·ly**, *adv.*

im·pe·ri·al, im·pēr′ē·al, *n.* A member of an imperial party or of imperial troops; an emperor or empress; a Russian gold coin worth 15 rubles, in circulation prior to 1917; the top of a carriage, esp. of a stagecoach; a case for luggage carried there; any of various articles of special size or quality; a small pointed beard beneath the under lip, as worn by the emperor Napoleon III.

im·pe·ri·al·ism, im·pēr′ē·a·liz″um, *n.* Imperial government; an imperial system of government; advocacy of imperial interests; specif. the policy of extending the rule or authority of an empire or nation over foreign countries either by direct acquisition of territory, or by indirect control of economic and political life; the policy of acquiring and holding colonies and dependencies; in British history, the policy of so uniting the separate parts of an empire with separate governments as to secure for certain purposes virtually a single state.—**im·pe·ri·al·ist**, *n.*, *a.*—**im·pe·ri·al·is·tic**, *a.*—**im·pe·ri·al·is·ti·cal·ly**, *adv.*

im·pe·ri·al moth, *n.* A large yellow moth, *Eacles imperialis*, having spotted wings with pinkish-brown marginal markings, the larvae of which feed on trees and shrubs.

im·per·il, im·per′il, *v.t.*—*imperiled*, *imperiling*, Brit. *imperilled*, *imperilling*. To bring into peril; to endanger.—**im·per·il·ment**, *n.*

im·pe·ri·ous, im·pēr′ē·us, *a.* [L. *imperiosus*, < *imperium*, empire.] Giving orders or commands in an arbitrary or absolute manner; dictatorial; haughty; arrogant; domineering; urgent or pressing; as, an *imperious* necessity.—**im·pe·ri·ous·ly**, *adv.*—**im·pe·ri·ous·ness**, *n.*

im·per·ish·a·ble, im·per′i·sha·bl, *a.* Not perishable; not subject to decay; indestructible; enduring permanently.—**im·per·ish·a·bil·i·ty**, **im·per·ish·a·ble·ness**, *n.*—**im·per·ish·a·bly**, *adv.*

im·pe·ri·um, im·pēr′ē·um, *n.* pl. **im·pe·ri·a**. [L.] Command; supreme power; empire; *law*, the right to command the power of the state in order to enforce the law.

im·per·ma·nent, im·pur′ma·nent, *a.* Not permanent; not enduring; transient.—**im·per·ma·nence**, **im·per·ma·nen·cy**, *n.*—**im·per·ma·nent·ly**, *adv.*

im·per·me·a·ble, im·pur′mē·a·bl, *a.* [L.L. *impermeabilis*.] Not permeable; impassable; of substances, not permitting the passage of a fluid through the pores or interstices.—**im·per·me·a·bil·i·ty**, **im·per·me·a·ble·ness**, im·pur″mē·a·bil′i·tē, *n.*—**im·per·me·a·bly**, *adv.*

im·per·mis·si·ble, im″pėr·mis′a·bl, *a.* Not permissible; not allowable; forbidden.—**im·per·mis·si·bil·i·ty**, *n.*

im·per·son·al, im·pur′so·nal, *a.* [L.L. *impersonalis*.] Without personal reference or connection; having no personality; as, an *impersonal* deity. *Gram.* of pronouns, indefinite; of verbs, having the nonpersonal or nonspecific subject *it* expressed or understood, as: *It* rains.—**im·per·son·al·i·ty**, im·pur″so·nal′i·tē, *n.* pl. **im·per·son·al·i·ties**. Absence of personal quality; an impersonal being or thing.—**im·per·son·al·ize**, im·pur′so·na·līz″, *v.t.*—**im·per·son·al·ly**, *adv.*

im·per·son·ate, im·pur′so·nāt″, *v.t.*—*impersonated*, *impersonating*. [L. *in-*, in, and *persona*, E. *person*.] To assume the appearance, mannerisms, and speech of someone; to represent; to personate, esp. on the stage.—**im·per·so·nit**, im·pur′so·nāt″, *a.* Embodied in a person; invested with personality.—**im·per·son·a·tion**, im·pur″so·nā′ shan, *n.*—**im·per·son·a·tor**, *n.*

im·per·ti·nence, im·pur′ti·nens, *n.* Rudeness of behavior or speech, esp. to a superior; insolence; unmannerly intrusion or presumption; something impertinent; irrelevance; an incongruity; a triviality; a rude or insolent act or speech. Also **im·per·ti·nen·cy**.

im·per·ti·nent, im·pur′ti·nent, *a.* [L.L. *impertinens (-ent-)*.] Rude, intrusive, or presumptuous, as persons or their actions or speech; insolent or saucy; not pertinent or relevant.—*n.*—**im·per·ti·nent·ly**, *adv.*

im·per·turb·a·ble, im″pėr·tur′ba·bl, *a.* Not easily perturbed or agitated; calm; cool.—**im·per·turb·a·bil·i·ty**, **im·per·turb·a·ble·ness**, im″ pėr·tur″ba·bil′i·tē, *n.*—**im·per·turb·a·bly**, *adv.*

im·per·vi·ous, im·pur′vē·us, *a.* Not pervious; incapable of being passed through, as by a liquid; *fig.* incapable of being emotionally affected or influenced by argument.—**im·per·vi·ous·ly**, *adv.*—**im·per·vi·ous·ness**, *n.*

im·pe·ti·go, im″pi·tī′gō, *n.* [L. < *impeto*, to assail.] *Pathol.* a contagious skin disease, esp. of children, which manifests itself in pustules and eruptions.—**im·pe·tig·i·nous**, im″pi·tij′i·nus, *a.*

im·pe·trate, im′pi·trāt″, *v.t.*—*impetrated*, *impetrating*. [L. *impetratus*, pp. of *impetrare*, < *im-*, in, and *patrare*, bring to pass.] To obtain by entreaty; to entreat or ask for urgently.—**im·pe·tra·tion**, *n.*

im·pet·u·ous, im·pech′ū·us, *a.* [L. *impetuosus*, < *impetus*, an attack.] Rashly impulsive; hasty; furious in motion; forcible.—**im·pet·u·os·i·ty**, im·pech″ū·os′i·tē, im″pe·chŏ·os′i·tē, *n.*—**im·pet·u·ous·ly**, *adv.*—**im·pet·u·ous·ness**, *n.*

im·pe·tus, im′pi·tus, *n.* pl. **im·pe·tus·es**. [L. < *impetere*, rush upon, attack, < *im-*, in, on, and *petere*, fall on, rush at, seek.] The force with which a moving body tends to maintain its velocity and overcome resistance; energy of motion; anything that is an incentive to action; stimulus.

im·pi, im′pē, *n.* pl. **im·pies**, **im·pis**. [< Zulu.] A brigade or large body of soldiers.

im·pi·e·ty, im·pī′i·tē, *n.* pl. **im·pi·e·ties**. [L. *impietas*.] Lack of piety; want of reverence for God; an impious or irreligious act or practice; lack of dutifulness or respect, as toward parents.

im·pinge, im·pinj′, *v.i.*—*impinged*, *impinging*. [L. *impingere* (p.p. *impactus*), drive in or at, strike against, < *in-*, in, on, and *pangere*, fix, drive in.] To strike or dash, used with *on*, *upon*, or *against*; collide; to encroach or infringe, used with *on* or *upon*.—**im·pinge·ment**, *n.*—**im·ping·er**, *n.*

im·pi·ous, im′pē·us, *a.* [L. *impius*.] Wanting in reverence for God, religious observances or symbols; profane; lacking in respect, as for one's parents.—**im·pi·ous·ly**, *adv.*—**im·pi·ous·ness**, *n.*

imp·ish, im′pish, *a.* Like or characteristic of an imp; mischievous.—**imp·ish·ly**, *adv.*—**imp·ish·ness**, *n.*

im·plac·a·ble, im·plak′a·bl, im·plā′ka·bl, *a.* Not placable; not to be appeased or pacified; inexorable; stubborn; constant in enmity.—**im·plac·a·bil·i·ty**, **im·plac·a·ble·ness**, *n.*—**im·plac·a·bly**, *adv.*

im·plant, im·plant′, *v.t.* To instill or inculcate firmly in the mind, as truths or principles; to plant or insert deeply or firmly; to plant or embed, as living tissue in grafting.—im′plant″, im·plänt″, *n.* That which is implanted. *Med.* tissue grafted into the body; a filled tube, as one containing radium, placed in an organ or tissue for treatment.—**im·plan·ta·tion**, im″plan·tā′ shan, *n.*—**im·plant·er**, *n.*

im·plau·si·ble, im·plā′zi·bl, *a.* Not plausible; not having the appearance of truth or credibility.—**im·plau·si·bly**, *adv.*—**im·plau·si·bil·i·ty**, im·plą″zi·bil′i·tē, *n.*

im·plead, im·plēd′, *v.t. Law*, To prosecute a suit against in court; to sue at law.

im·ple·ment, im′ple·ment, *n.* [L.L. *implementum*, lit. 'what accomplishes,' < L. *implēre*, to fill up.] An instrument, tool, or utensil; an article assisting in carrying on manual labors; *fig.* any person or means serving as an instrument in the accomplishing of something; as, an *implement* of divine justice.—im′ple·ment″, *v.t.* To fulfill or satisfy the conditions of; to perform; to put into effect; to supplement; provide or equip with implements.—**im·ple·men·tal**, *a.*—**im·ple·men·ta·tion**, *n.*

im·pli·cate, im′pli·kāt″, *v.t.*—*implicated*, *implicating*. [L. *implicatus*, pp. of *implicare*, enfold, entangle, involve.] To imply as a necessary circumstance, or as something to be inferred or understood; to involve as being concerned in a matter, affair, or condition; as, to be *implicated* in a crime or a scandal.

im·pli·ca·tion, im″pli·kā′shan, *n.* [L. *implicatio(n-)*.] The act of implying, or the state of being implied; as, to admit a thing by *implication* rather than by express statement; something implied, or suggested as naturally to be inferred; the act of involving or the state of being involved in some matter or condition of affairs; the act of implicating or the resulting condition.—**im·pli·ca·tive**, im′pli·kā″tiv, im·plik′a·tiv, *a.*—**im·pli·ca·tive·ly**, *adv.*—**im·pli·ca·tive·ness**, *n.*

im·plic·it, im·plis′it, *a.* [L. *implicitus*, < *implico*, *implicitum*, and *implicatum*, to enfold.] Understood, though not expressed in words; implied; inherent, though not expressed or readily seen; free from doubt or questioning; absolute; deep-rooted; as, *implicit* faith in his word.—**im·plic·it·ly**, *adv.*—**im·plic·it·ness**, *n.*

im·plode, im·plōd′, *v.i.*—*imploded*, *imploding*. To burst inward.—*v.t. Phon.* to produce sounds by implosion.—**im·plo·sion**, *n. Phon.* the sudden stoppage of the breath stream in pronouncing the speech sound, tsk, tsk.—**im·plo·sive**, *a.*, *n.*

im·plore, im·plōr′, *v.t.*—*implored*, *imploring*. [L. *imploro*.] To call upon or for, in supplication; to beseech; to pray earnestly; to entreat; to beg; as, to *implore* forgiveness. —*v.i.* To entreat; to beg.—**im·plo·ra·tion**, *n.*—**im·plor·a·to·ry**, im·plōr′a·tōr″ē, *a.*—**im·plor·er**, *n.*—**im·plor·ing·ly**, *adv.*—**im·plor·ing·ness**, *n.*

im·ply, im·plī′, *v.t.*—*implied*, *implying*. [< L. *implico*.] To involve or contain as an essential part or as a consequence, as: An effect *implies* a cause. To indicate more than the words plainly say; to hint; signify.

im·pol·i·cy, im·pol′i·sē, *n.* pl. **im·pol·i·cies**. Bad policy; inexpediency.

im·po·lite, im″po·līt′, *a.* Not polite; uncivil; rude.—**im·po·lite·ly**, *adv.*—**im·po·lite·ness**, *n.*

im·pol·i·tic, im·pol′i·tik, *a.* Not politic; unwise; imprudent; indiscreet; injudicious.—**im·pol·i·tic·ly**, *adv.*—**im·po·lit·i·cal**, im·po·lit′i·kal, *a.*—**im·po·lit·i·cal·ly**, *adv.*

im·pon·der·a·ble, im·pon′dėr·a·bl, *a.* Not ponderable; that cannot be weighed, measured, or evaluated.—*n.* Anything imponderable.—**im·pon·der·a·bil·i·ty**, **im·pon·der·a·ble·ness**, *n.*—**im·pon·der·a·bly**, *adv.*

im·port, im·pōrt′, *v.t.* [L. *importare*, bring in, bring about, occasion, cause. Some E. senses come through Fr. *importer*, be of consequence, matter, signify.] To bring in; introduce from without or abroad, esp. to bring in from a foreign country, as merchandise or commodities for sale or use. To convey as meaning or implication, as by words, statements, or actions; to mean, signify, betoken, or imply; to make known or express.—im′pōrt, *n.* The act of importing or bringing in; importation, as of merchandise from abroad; that which is imported from abroad; an imported commodity or article. Meaning, implication, or purport; significance; consequence or importance; as, matters of great *import*.—**im·port·a·ble**, *a.*—**im·port·er**, *n.*

im·por·tance, im·pȧr′tans, *n.* [Fr. *importance*, < M.L. *importantia*.] The quality or fact of being important; significance, consequence, or moment; notable character; important position or standing; personal or social consequence; consequential air or manner.

im·por·tant, im·pȧr′tant, *a.* [Fr. *important*, < M.L. *importans (-ant-)*, ppr. of *importare*, be of consequence, L. bring in, cause.] Of much significance or consequence; memorable; prominent; meriting special consideration or attention; of

im·por·ta·tion, im″pôr·tā′shan, im″par·-tā′shan, n. The act of importing or bringing in; the bringing in of merchandise or commodities from foreign countries for sale or use; something imported.

im·por·tu·nate, im·pâr′cha·nit, a. [L. importunus.] Urgent or persistent in solicitation; pertinacious, as solicitations or demands; troublesome.—**im·por·tu·-nate·ly**, adv.—**im·por·tu·na·cy**, im·-pâr′cha·na·sē, im·por·tu·nate·ness, n.

im·por·tune, im″pâr·tön′, im″par·tūn′, im·pâr′chan, v.t. [O.Fr. Fr. importun, < L. importunus, unfit, inconvenient, troublesome.] To harass or beset with solicitations; to beg or beg for urgently or persistently.—v.i. To make urgent or persistent solicitations.—a. Importunate.—**im·por·tune·ly**, adv.—**im·por·tun·er**, n.

im·por·tu·ni·ty, im″par·tö′ni·tē, im″par·-tū′ni·tē, n. pl. **im·por·tu·ni·ties**. State of being importunate; persistence; pl. importunate solicitations or demands.

im·pose, im·pōz′, v.t.—imposed, imposing. [O.Fr. Fr. imposer, but associated with derivatives of L. imponere.] To put or set by or as by authority; as, to impose a name on a place; to lay on, inflict, or set, as something to be borne, endured, obeyed, or fulfilled; as, to impose taxes; to obtrude or thrust upon others; as, to impose oneself on another; pass or palm off fraudulently or deceptively; foist. Print, to arrange in proper order on an imposing stone or the like and secure in a chase for printing.—v.i. To take undue advantage of; to presume, as upon patience, hospitality, or good humor; to pass off something fraudulent.—**im·pos·er**, n.—**im·pos·a·ble**, a.

im·pos·ing, im·pō′zing, a. Making an impression on the mind, as by great size, stately appearance, or dignity; impressive; grand.—**im·pos·ing·ly**, adv.

im·po·si·tion, im″po·zish′an, n. [L. im-positio(n-), < imponere, place or put upon, impose.] The act of imposing by authority; the laying on of something as a burden or obligation; something imposed, as a tax; the act of taking undue advantage; the act of imposing fraudulently or deceptively on others; a fraud, deception, or imposture. Eccles. the ceremonial laying on of hands, as in confirmation.

im·pos·si·ble, im·pos′i·bl, a. [L. impos-sibilis.] Not possible; not capable of being or being done; incapable of being accomplished, thought, or endured; as, an impossible idea or situation; colloq. objectionable or intolerable.—**im·pos·si·ble·ness**, n.—**im·pos·si·bil·i·ty**, im·pos″i·bil′i·tē, im″pos·i·bil′i·tē, n. pl. **im·pos·si·bil·i·ties**.—**im·pos·si·bly**, adv.

im·post, im′pōst, n. [O.Fr. impost, Fr. impôt, L. impositum, < impono, impositum, to lay upon.] That which is imposed; a tax, tribute, or duty; arch. the point where an arch rests on a wall or column.

im·pos·tor, **im·pos·ter**, im·pos′tēr, n. [L. impostor, < impono.] A person who assumes the character or name of another individual for the purpose of deception; one who imposes dishonestly on others.

im·pos·ture, im·pos′chēr, n. [L. impostura, < impono, impositium.] The act of an impostor; fraud, imposition, or deception, esp. under a false identity.—**im·pos·-trous**, **im·pos·tur·ous**, im·pos′trus, a.

im·po·tent, im′po·tent, a. [L. impotens, impotentis—im- for in-, not, and potens, able, potent.] Entirely wanting power, strength, or vigor of body or mind; deficient in capacity; weak; feeble; specif. in the male, completely powerless to perform sexual intercourse.—**im·po·tent·ly**, adv.—**im·po·tence**, **im·po·ten·cy**, n.

im·pound, im·pound′, v.t. To shut up in a pound, as a stray animal; confine within an enclosure or within limits; as, to impound water in a reservoir; to seize and retain in custody of the law, as a document for evidence.—**im·pound·a·ble**, a.—**im·pound·-ment**, **im·pound·age**, n.

im·pov·er·ish, im·pov′ēr·ish, im·pov′rish, v.t. [Prefix im-, intens., and Fr. pauvre, poor.] To make poor; to reduce to poverty; to exhaust the strength, richness, or fertility of, as of the soil.—**im·pov·er·ish·er**, n.—**im·pov·er·ish·ment**, n.

im·prac·ti·ca·ble, im·prak′ti·ka·bl, a. Not practicable; unfeasible; not to be performed or effected by human means or by the means at hand; not useful for an intended purpose; unmanageable, as a stubborn person.—**im·prac·ti·ca·bil·i·-ty**, im·prak·ti·ca·ble·ness, im·prak″ti·-ka·bil′i·tē, n.

im·prac·ti·cal, im·prak′ti·kal, a. Not practical; not taking a common sense view of things; not workable; nonutilitarian.

im·pre·cate, im′pre·kāt″, v.t.—imprecated, imprecating. [L. imprecor, imprecatus—im- for in, on, and precor, to pray.] To call down, as a curse, calamity, or punishment, by prayer; to invoke some calamity upon; to curse.—**im·pre·ca·tion**, im″pre·ka′shan, n. The act of imprecating; a prayer that a curse or calamity may fall on anyone.—**im·pre·ca·tor**, n.—**im·pre·ca·to·ry**, im′-pre·ka·tōr″ē, im′pre·ka·tär″ē, a.

im·pre·cise, im″pri·sīs′, a. Not precise; vague; inaccurate.—**im·pre·cise·ly**, adv.—**im·pre·cise·ness**, **im·pre·ci·sion**, im″-pri·sizh′an, n.

im·preg·na·ble, im·preg′na·bl, a. [O.Fr. imprenable (the g being inserted as in pregnable)—im- for in-, not, and prendre, to take.] Not able to be taken or conquered by force; not to be moved, impressed, or shaken.—**im·preg·na·bil·i·ty**, **im·preg·-na·ble·ness**, im·preg″na·bil′i·tē, n.—**im·preg·na·bly**, adv.

im·preg·na·ble, im·preg′na·bl, a. Able to be impregnated.

im·preg·nate, im·preg′nāt, im′preg·nāt, v.t.—impregnated, impregnating. [L.L. im-praegno, impraegnatum—L. im- for in-, in, and praegnans, pregnant.] To make pregnant or with young; to fertilize; to fill or saturate with, or cause to absorb, some substance; to transmit or infuse an active principle into; to imbue, as with ideas.—im·preg′nit, im·preg′nāt, a. Made pregnant; fertilized.—**im·preg·na·tion**, im″-preg·nā′shan, n.—**im·preg·na·tor**, n.

im·pre·sa·ri·o, im″pri·sär′ē·ō″, im″pri·-sâr′ē·ō″, It. ēm″prē·sä′Rya, n. pl. **im·pre·-sa·rios**, It. **im·pre·sa·ri**, ēm″prē·sä′Rē. [It.] One who organizes, manages, or conducts a company of operatic or other musical performers; one who arranges or produces entertainment.

im·pre·scrip·ti·ble, im·pri·skrip′ti·bl, a. Inalienable; not subject to prescription; of rights, not legally to be withdrawn or revoked.—**im·pre·scrip·ti·bly**, adv.

im·press, im·pres′, v.t. [L. impressus, pp. of imprimere, < im-, in, on, and premere, press.] To press into or on something; as, to impress a seal into wax; to apply or produce with pressure, esp. so as to leave a mark; to stamp or imprint; to cause, affect, or invest with a quality or characteristic; as, a literature strongly impressed with the national characteristics; to fix firmly on the mind or memory; to urge; to subject to or mark or indent by pressure with something; to affect deeply or strongly in mind or feelings; to make an impression on; to influence in opinion. Elect. to introduce into a circuit or conductor by means of an outside source of energy.—im′pres, n. The act of impressing; a mark made by pressure; a stamp or imprint; fig. a distinctive character or effect imparted.—**im·press·er**, n.

im·press, im·pres′, v.t. To press or force into public service, as seamen; to seize or take for public use; to take into service or use by force, as in an emergency.—im′pres, n. Impressment, as into service.

im·press·i·ble, im·pres′i·bl, a. Capable of being impressed; sensitive to impressions; impressionable.—**im·press·i·bil·i·ty**, im·-pres″i·bil′i·tē, n.

im·pres·sion, im·presh′an, n. [O.Fr. Fr. impression, < L. impressio(n-), < imprimere.] The act of impressing, or the state of being impressed; a mark, indentation, or figure produced by pressure; the effect produced by any agency or influence, as: Time has left its impression on the structure. An effect produced on the senses or mind; a strong effect produced on the intellect, feelings, or conscience; a notion, remembrance, or belief, often one that is vague or indistinct. Print. the process or result of printing from type or plates; a printed copy from type, a plate, or an engraved block; the aggregate of copies, as of a book, printed at one time; one of a number of printings made at different times from the same plate or unaltered type: opposed to an edition. Dentistry, an imprint of the teeth and adjacent tissues taken in a plastic or semisoft material.—**im·pres·sion·al**, a.

im·pres·sion, im·presh′an, n. An imitation, often in caricature, of a famous person, performed for entertainment purposes.—**im·pres·sion·ist**, n.

im·pres·sion·a·ble, im·presh′a·na·bl, im·presh′na·bl, a. Susceptible; sensitive; capable of being impressed or influenced.—**im·pres·sion·a·bil·i·ty**, **im·pres·sion·-a·ble·ness**, im·presh″a·na·bil′i·tē, im·-presh″na·bil′i·tē, n.—**im·pres·sion·a·-bly**, adv.

im·pres·sion·ism, im·presh′a·niz″um, n. (Usu. cap.) a late 19th-century school and method of painting in which scenes and objects are represented in their immediate and momentary effect, without strict attention to details, characterized esp. by short dabs of primary colors. A corresponding mode of treatment in literature in which scene, character, and emotion are depicted through the author's or character's impressions rather than by strict objective detail; a method of musical composition diverging markedly from classical techniques and employing varied harmonies and other devices to express impressions or emotions.—**im·pres·sion·ist**, n.—**im·pres·sion·is·tic**, im·presh″a·nis′tik, a.—**im·pres·sion·is·ti·cal·ly**, adv.

im·pres·sive, im·pres′iv, a. Making or tending to make an impression; exciting attention and feeling, esp. admiration.—**im·pres·sive·ly**, adv.—**im·pres·sive·ness**, n.

im·press·ment, im·presment, n. The act or practice of seizing men or property for public service or use.

im·prest, im′prest, n. An advance of money, esp. for use in public business.

im·pri·ma·tur, im″pri·mä′tēr, im″pri·-mä′tēr, im″pri·mä′tēr, im″prī·mā′tēr, n. [L., 'let it be printed.'] A license to print or publish, esp. one printed in a book that has been censored and approved by the Rom. Cath. Ch.; any sanction or authorization.

im·pri·mis, im·prī′mis, adv. [L. imprimis, in primis, in or among the first.] In the first place; first.

im·print, im·print′, v.t. [O.E. emprent, Fr. empreint, pp. of empreindre, to imprint.] To mark by pressure; to stamp; to print; to fix indelibly or permanently; to impress.—im′print, n. Whatever is impressed or printed; bibliog. the name of the printer or publisher of a book, with the place and date of publication.—**im·prin·ter**, *n.*

im·print·ing, im·prin′ting, *n. Psychol.* the learning of filial responses to a maternal object, occurring during a short, impressionable period in the infancy of members of social species, as the pursuit of the mother or a surrogate by a precocial chick upon emergence from the egg.

im·pris·on, im·priz′on, *v.t.* To put into a prison; to incarcerate; to confine; to restrain.—**im·pris·on·er**, *n.*—**im·pris··on·ment**, *n.*

im·prob·a·ble, im·prob′a·bl, *a.* Not probable; not likely to be true; unlikely.—**im·prob·a·bil·i·ty**, **im·prob·a·ble·ness**, im·prob″a·bil′i·tē, im″prob·a·bil′i·tē, *n.*—**im·prob·a·bly**, *adv.*

im·pro·bi·ty, im·prō′bi·tē, im·prob′i·tē, *n.* [L. *improbitas.*] Lack of integrity or principle; dishonesty.

im·promp·tu, im·promp′tö, im·promp′tū, *a.* [L. *in promptu*, in readiness, < *promptus*, readiness.] Offhand; done without previous study; prepared on the spur of the moment; improvised.—*n.* Anything done or said without previous thought or preparation.—*adv.* Offhandedly; extemporaneously; without previous study or preparation.

im·prop·er, im·prop′ėr, *a.* Not proper; not adapted or suited; unbecoming; indecent; erroneous; not regular or normal.—**im·prop·er·ly**, *adv.*—**im·prop·er·ness**, *n.*

im·prop·er frac·tion, *n.* A fraction whose numerator is greater than its denominator.

im·pro·pri·ate, im·prō′prē·āt″, *v.t.*—*impropriated, impropriating.* [L. *im-* for *in-*, and *proprio, propriatum*, to appropriate, < *proprius*, one's own.] *Eccles.* to place, as the profits or revenue of church property, in the hands of a layman.—im·prō′prē·it, im·prō′prē·āt″, *a.* Devolved into the hands of a layman.—**im·pro·pri·a·tion**, *n.*—**im·pro·pri·a·tor**, *n.*

im·pro·pri·e·ty, im″pro·prī′i·tē, *n.* pl. **im·pro·pri·e·ties.** [Fr. *impropriété*, < L. *improprius*, improper.] The quality of being improper; an unsuitable act or expression; incorrect usage in speaking or writing.

im·prove, im·pröv′, *v.t.*—*improved, improving.* [A.Fr. *emprouer*, < *em-* (< L. *in-*, in) and O.Fr. *prou, pro, prod*, profit: cf. L. *prodesse*, be of profit.] To bring to a more desirable or excellent condition; to ameliorate; to better; to make, as land or real estate, more profitable by cultivation or construction; to make more useful; as, to improve a road by resurfacing.—*v.i.* To become better; to convalesce; to increase in value or excellence.—**im·prov·er**, *n.* A person or thing which improves; a preservative or other substance added to improve food.—**im·prov·a·bil·i·ty**, *n.* Capability for improvement.—**im·prov·a·ble**, *a.*

im·prove·ment, im·pröv′ment, *n.* Act of improving; increase in value or excellence; betterment; amelioration; enhancement; a building, sidewalk, or other valuable addition to real property.

im·prov·i·dent, im·prov′i·dent, *a.* Not provident; lacking in foresight; needing to make provision for the future; thriftless; thoughtless; rash.—**im·prov·i·dence**, *n.*—**im·prov·i·dent·ly**, *adv.*

im·prov·i·sa·tion, im·prov″i·zā′shan, im″pro·vi·zā′shan, *n.* The act of improvising; something impromptu, as music or verse.—**im·prov·i·sa·tion·al**, *a.*—**im·prov·i·sa·tor**, *n.*—**im·prov·i·sa·to·ri·al**, **im·prov·i·sa·tor·y**, im″pro·vī′za·tor″ē, im″pro·viz′i·tōr″ē, *a.*—**im·prov·i·sa·to··ri·al·ly**, *adv.*

im·pro·vise, im′pro·vīz″, *v.t.*—*improvised, improvising.* [Fr. *improviser*, < It. *improvvisare, improvviso*, < L. *improvisus*, unforeseen, unexpected.] To compose, as

music or verse, on the spur of the moment; to play, sing, or recite extemporaneously; to produce, provide, or prepare offhand or hastily; to extemporize.—*v.i.* To compose, perform, or provide anything extemporaneously.—**im·pro·vis·er**, *n.*

im·pru·dent, im·prōd′ent, *a.* [L. *imprudens.*] Not prudent; lacking prudence or discretion; indiscreet; injudicious; rash; heedless.—**im·pru·dence**, *n.*—**im·pru·dent·ly**, *adv.*

im·pu·dent, im′pū·dent, *a.* [L. *impudens, impudentis*, without shame.] Offensively forward in behavior; intentionally treating others without due respect; impertinent; bold; disrespectful; flippant.—**im·pu·dence**, *n.*—**im·pu·dent·ly**, *adv.*

im·pu·dic·i·ty, im″pū·dis′i·tē, *n.* [Fr. *impudicité.*] Shamelessness; immodesty.

im·pugn, im·pūn′, *v.t.* [O.Fr. Fr. *impugner*, < L. *impugnare.*] To assail by words or arguments, esp. statements, opinions, motives, or veracity; to call in question; to challenge as false.—**im·pugn·a·ble**, *a.*—**im·pug·na·tion**, **im·pugn·ment**, *n.*—**im·pugn·er**, *n.*

im·pu·is·sance, im·pū′i·sans, im″pū·is·ans, im·pwis′ans, *n.* Weakness; impotence.—**im·pu·is·sant**, *a.*

im·pulse, im′puls, *n.* [L. *impulsus*, < *impellere*, E. *impel.*] An impelling action of force, driving onward or inducing motion; the effect of an impelling force; motion induced, impetus; the inciting influence of a particular feeling or mental state; as, a sympathetic *impulse*; a sudden involuntary inclination prompting to action; *physiol.* a stimulating or inhibiting wave transferred through nerve fibers; *mech.* the product obtained by multiplying force and time, being the number equal to the change in the object's momentum.

im·pul·sion, im·pul′shan, *n.* [O.Fr. Fr. *impulsion*, < L. *impulsio(n-), impellere*, E. *impel.*] The act of driving onward or the resulting state or effect; impulse; impetus; a constraining or inciting action on the mind or conduct; the inciting influence of some feeling or motive; mental impulse.

im·pul·sive, im·pul′siv, *a.* [M.L. *impulsivus.*] Having the power or effect of impelling; driving onward or inducing motion; tending to act or decide impetuously; inciting to action; actuated by mental impulse instead of reflection; swayed by emotional or involuntary impulses. *Mech.* acting momentarily.—**im·pul·sive·ly**, *adv.*—**im·pul·sive·ness**, *n.*

im·pu·ni·ty, im·pū′ni·tē, *n.* [Fr. *impunité*, < L. *impunitas*, < *impunis*, unpunished.] Exemption from punishment or penalty; freedom or exemption from injury, suffering, or loss.

im·pure, im·pūr′, *a.* [L. *impurus.*] Not pure; containing some extraneous matter, esp. of an inferior or contaminating nature; foul; marked by foreign, unsuitable, or objectionable elements or characteristics, as a style of art; not morally pure; unchaste; corrupt.—**im·pure·ly**, *adv.*—**im·pure·ness**, *n.*—**im·pu·ri·ty**, *n.* pl. **im·pu·ri·ties.**

im·pu·ta·ble, im·pū′ta·bl, *a.* That may be imputed; attributable; ascribable.—**im·pu·ta·bil·i·ty**, *n.*—**im·pu·ta·bly**, *adv.*

im·pu·ta·tion, im″pū·tā′shan, *n.* [L.L. *imputatio(n-).*] The act of imputing; an attribution; an ascription; an insinuation or accusation of something discreditable.

im·pute, im·pūt′, *v.t.*—*imputed, imputing.* [O.Fr. Fr. *imputer*, < L. *imputare*, bring into the reckoning, < *in-*, in, and *putare*, reckon.] To attribute or ascribe, usu. something discreditable, to a person; to charge a person with, as a fault; *theol.* to attribute vicariously, as righteousness or guilt.—**im·pu·ta·tive**, *a.*—**im·pu·ta·tive·ly**, *adv.*

—**im·put·a·tive·ness**, *n.*—**im·put·ed·ly**, *adv.*—**im·put·er**, *n.*

in, in, *prep.* [O.E. *in* = D. and G. *in* = Icel. *i* = Goth. *in*, in; akin to L. *in*, Gr. *en*, in.] A particle or function word expressing inclusion or presence within limits of place, time, or circumstances; as, *in* the city, dressed *in* white, *in* politics; an expression of inclusion within or occurrence during the course of a period of time; as, *in* ancient times, to do a task *in* an hour; an indication of situation, action, manner, relation, or respect; as, *in* darkness, *in* sickness, *in* debt, *in* crossing the river, to tell *in* confidence, to write *in* French; an indication of object or purpose; as, *in* honor of the event; into; as, put *in* operation.

in, in, *adv.* [O.E. *inn, in.*] In or into some place, position, state, or relationship; on the inside; within; in one's house, office, or customary location; as, to remain *in* during bad weather; toward the inside; in office or power; in season or in fashion; into something so as to become part of it; as, to stir *in* the sugar; at a point of completion or availability; as, as soon as the bills are *in*.—*a.* That is in; internal; inward; incoming; *colloq.* up-to-date or socially acceptable or desirable; as, the *in* thing to do.—*n.* One of those who are in power, as a member of the political party in office; a vantage point, esp. a position of favor with an influential person or group; as, an *in* with the manager.

in·a·bil·i·ty, in″a·bil′i·tē, *n.* The state of being unable; want of the necessary power, means, capacity, or ability.

in·ac·ces·si·ble, in″ak·ses′i·bl, *a.* Not accessible; not to be reached, obtained, or approached.—**in·ac·ces·si·bil·i·ty**, **in·ac·ces·si·ble·ness**, *n.*—**in·ac·ces·si·bly**, *adv.*

in·ac·cu·ra·cy, in·ak′yėr·a·sē, *n.* pl. **in·ac·cu·ra·cies.** The state of being inaccurate; an inaccurate statement; an error.

in·ac·cu·rate, in·ak′yėr·it, *a.* Not accurate, exact, or correct; containing incorrect statements; not according to truth; erroneous.—**in·ac·cu·rate·ly**, *adv.*—**in·ac·cu·rate·ness**, *n.*

in·ac·tion, in·ak′shan, *n.* State of being inactive; idleness.

in·ac·ti·vate, in·ak′ti·vāt″, *v.t.*—*inactivated, inactivating.* To render inactive; *med.* to arrest the activity of, as of a serum by means of heat.—**in·ac·ti·va·tion**, *n.*

in·ac·tive, in·ak′tiv, *a.* Not active; inert; idle; out of use; indolent; sluggish; *milit.* not mobilized.—**in·ac·tive·ly**, *adv.*—**in·ac·tiv·i·ty**, *n.*

in·ad·e·qua·cy, in·ad′e·kwi·sē, *n.* pl. **in·ad·e·qua·cies.** The quality, condition, or an instance of being inadequate; a defect. Also **in·ad·e·quate·ness.**

in·ad·e·quate, in·ad′e·kwit, *a.* Not adequate; not equal to the purpose; insufficient; inept.—**in·ad·e·quate·ly**, *adv.*

in·ad·mis·si·ble, in″ad·mis′i·bl, *a.* Not admissible; not proper to be admitted, allowed, or received.—**in·ad·mis·si·bil·i·ty**, *n.*—**in·ad·mis·si·bly**, *adv.*

in·ad·vert·ence, in″ad·vėr′tens, *n.* The quality of being inadvertent; an oversight, mistake, or fault which proceeds from heedlessness. Also **in·ad·vert·en·cy**, pl. **in·ad·vert·en·cies.**

in·ad·vert·ent, in″ad·vėr′tent, *a.* [L. prefix *in-*, not, and *advertens, advertentis*, ppr. of *adverto*, to attend to.] Not paying strict attention; failing to notice or observe; heedless. Unintentional; as, an *inadvertent* remark.—**in·ad·vert·ent·ly**, *adv.*

in·ad·vis·a·ble, in″ad·vī′za·bl, *a.* Not advisable; unwise; inexpedient.—**in·ad·vis·a·bil·i·ty**, *n.*

in·al·ien·a·ble, in·āl′ya·na·bl, in·ā′lē·a··na·bl, *a.* Incapable of being alienated, taken away, or transferred to another.—**in·al·ien·a·bil·i·ty**, *n.*—**in·al·ien·a·bly**, *adv.*

in·al·ter·a·ble, in·al'tėr·a·bl, *a.* Not alterable; unalterable.—**in·al·ter·a·bil·i·ty**, **in·al·ter·a·ble·ness**, *n.*—**in·al·ter·a·bly**, *adv.*

in·am·o·ra·ta, in·am′o·rä′ta, in″am·o·rä′ta, *n.* pl. **in·am·o·ra·tas.** [It. *innamorata*, fem. of *innamorato*.] A female lover; a woman with whom one is in love; a sweetheart.

in-and-in, in′and·in′, *adv.* Repeatedly within the same limits, as of family or strain; as, to breed stock *in and in*.

in·ane, i·nän′, *a.* [L. *inanis*, empty.] Empty; foolish; fatuous; void of sense or meaning.—*n.* That which is void or empty; the infinite void of space.—**in·ane·ly**, *adv.*—**in·ane·ness**, **in·an·i·ty**, *n.* pl. **in·an·i·ties.**

in·an·i·mate, in·an′i·mit, *a.* Not animate; destitute of life or animation; without vivacity or briskness; dull; inactive; sluggish.—**in·an·i·mate·ly**, *adv.*—**in·an·i·mate·ness**, *n.*

in·a·ni·tion, in″a·nish′an, *n.* [L.L. *inanitio(n-)*, < L. *inanire*, make empty, < *inanis*, empty, E. *inane*.] The condition of being empty; exhaustion from lack of nourishment; deficiency of vigor; sluggishness or lethargy.

in·an·i·ty, i·nan′i·tē, *n.* pl. **in·an·i·ties.** [L. *inanitas*.] The state of being inane; something inane, as a silly remark; lack of sense or ideas; senselessness or silliness.

in·ap·peas·a·ble, in″a·pē′za·bl, *a.* Not appeasable; unrelenting.

in·ap·pe·tence, in·ap′i·tens, *n.* Lack of appetite, desire, or concern. Also **in·ap·pe·ten·cy.**—**in·ap·pe·tent**, *a.*

in·ap·pli·ca·ble, in·ap′li·ka·bl, *a.* Not applicable; irrelevant; unsuitable; not suitable to the purpose.—**in·ap·pli·ca·bil·i·ty**, **in·ap·pli·ca·ble·ness**, *n.*—**in·ap·pli·ca·bly**, *adv.*

in·ap·po·site, in·ap′o·zit, *a.* Not apposite or suitable; not pertinent.—**in·ap·po·site·ly**, *adv.*—**in·ap·po·site·ness**, *n.*

in·ap·pre·ci·a·ble, in″a·prē′shē·a·bl, in″a·prē′sha·bl, *a.* Negligible; so small as hardly to be noticed or estimated.—**in·ap·pre·ci·a·bly**, *adv.*

in·ap·pre·ci·a·tive, in″a·prē′shē·ā″tiv, in″a·prē′sha·tiv, *a.* Not appreciative; wanting in appreciation; lacking or not showing gratitude.—**in·ap·pre·ci·a·tive·ly**, *adv.*—**in·ap·pre·ci·a·tive·ness**, *n.*

in·ap·proach·a·ble, in″a·prō′cha·bl, *a.* Not approachable; inaccessible; unrivaled.

in·ap·pro·pri·ate, in″a·prō′prē·it, *a.* Not appropriate; unsuitable; not proper.—**in·ap·pro·pri·ate·ly**, *adv.*—**in·ap·pro·pri·ate·ness**, *n.*

in·apt, in·apt′, *a.* Not apt; unsuitable; inappropriate. Without aptitude or capacity; inept; unskillful; awkward.—**in·ap·ti·tude**, in·ap′ti·töd″, in·ap′ti·tūd″, *n.*—**in·apt·ly**, *adv.*—**in·apt·ness**, *n.*

in·arch, in·ärch′, *v.t. Hort.* to graft by uniting a shoot to the stock without separating it from its parent tree.

in·ar·tic·u·late, in″är·tik′ū·lit, *a.* [L.L. *inarticulatus*.] Not articulate; not uttered in the distinct forms of spoken language; unintelligible; unable to use clear or understandable speech; dumb; unable to use speech to convey ideas; not expressed in speech; as, *inarticulate* sorrow. *Zool.* without joints or segments.—**in·ar·tic·u·late·ly**, *adv.*—**in·ar·tic·u·late·ness**, *n.*

in·ar·ti·fi·cial, in·är″ti·fish′al, *a.* Not artificial; natural; simple; artless.—**in·ar·ti·fi·cial·ly**, *adv.*

in·ar·tis·tic, in″är·tis′tik, *a.* Not artistic; not executed tastefully or according to the principles of art; lacking artistic apprecia-

tion; not informed on the principles of art.—**in·ar·tis·ti·cal·ly**, *adv.*

in·as·much as, in″az·much′ az″, *conj.* Insofar as, or to such a degree as; in view of the fact that; seeing that; since.

in·at·ten·tion, in″a·ten′shan, *n.* Want of attention; heedlessness.

in·at·ten·tive, in″a·ten′tiv, *a.* Not attentive; not fixing the mind on something; neglectful; heedless.—**in·at·ten·tive·ly**, *adv.*—**in·at·ten·tive·ness**, *n.*

in·au·di·ble, in·a′di·bl, *a.* Incapable of being heard.—**in·au·di·bil·i·ty**, *n.*—**in·au·di·bly**, *adv.*

in·au·gu·ral, in·a′gūr·al, in·a′gėr·al, *a.* [Fr. *inaugural*, < *inaugurer*, < L. *inaugurare*.] Of or pertaining to an inauguration; relating to or designating a beginning; first.—*n.* An inaugural address, as of a governor or president; ceremony marking induction into office; inauguration.

in·au·gu·rate, in·a′gū·rāt″, in·a′ga·rāt″, *v.t.*—*inaugurated, inaugurating.* [L. *inauguratus*, pp. of *inaugurare*, consecrate or install with augural ceremonies, < *in-*, in, and *augurare*, take auguries.] To induct into office with formal ceremonies; install; to make a formal beginning of; introduce into public use by a formal ceremony; to initiate; commence or begin.—**in·au·gu·ra·tion**, *n.*—**in·au·gu·ra·tor**, *n.*

In·au·gu·ra·tion Day, *n.* The day on which the President of the United States is inaugurated, being Jan. 20th of every year next after a year whose number is divisible by four.

in·aus·pi·cious, in″a·spish′us, *a.* Ill-omened; unlucky; unfavorable.—**in·aus·pi·cious·ly**, *adv.*—**in·aus·pi·cious·ness**, *n.*

in·board, in′bōrd″, *a., adv. Naut.* within the hull or interior, or toward the center, of a ship or boat; as, an *inboard* motor. *Aeron.* near the fuselage or center of an airplane.

in·born, in′barn″, *a.* Innate; inherent; implanted by nature.

in·bound, in′bound″, *a.* Inward bound; as, an *inbound* vessel.

in·breathe, in′brēTH″, in·brēTH′, *v.t.*—*inbreathed, inbreathing.* To breathe in; inhale.

in·bred, in′bred″, *a.* Bred within; innate; natural, brought about by inbreeding.

in·breed, in′brēd″, in·brēd′, *v.t.*—*inbred, inbreeding.* To cross or mate closely related individuals.

in·breed·ing, in′brē″ding, *n. Biol.* the mating of closely related plants or animals, esp. in order to increase homogeneity in the offspring, and resulting in time in the production of a purebred line: inbreeding may in time become deleterious. Restriction to a limited scope of thought or opinion, esp. by the practice of hiring graduates or trainees of a school or firm to instruct others within the same institution.

In·ca, ing′ka, *n.* One of the dominant groups of S. Americans Indians who built an empire in Peru prior to the Spanish conquest; the chief ruler of the Incaic empire or a member of the royal family.—**In·can**, *a., n.*—**In·ca·ic**, ing·kä′ik, *a.*

in·cal·cu·la·ble, in·kal′kya·la·bl, *a.* Beyond calculation; too great to be counted or measured; unpredictable.—**in·cal·cu·la·bil·i·ty**, *n.*—**in·cal·cu·la·bly**, *adv.*

in·ca·les·cent, in″ka·les′ent, *a.* [L. *incalesco*, to grow warm.] Growing warm; increasing in heat; becoming ardent.—**in·ca·les·cence**, *n.*

in·can·desce, in″kan·des′, *v.t., v.i.*—*incandesced, incandescing.* [L. *incandescere*, grow hot, glow.] To glow or cause to glow with heat.—**in·can·des·cence**, *n.* The emission of light by a hot material.

in·can·des·cent, in″kan·des′ent, *a.* Glowing or white with heat; intensely bright; brilliant; pertaining to an incandescent

lamp or light. *Fig.* glowing, as with vitality; strikingly brilliant or lucid.—**in·can·des·cent·ly**, *adv.*

in·can·des·cent lamp, *n.* A lamp whose light is due to the glowing of some special heated material; most common is the electric lamp, which contains a conducting filament in a vacuum, rendered luminous by an electric current; less common, a gas lamp which uses a mantle.

in·can·ta·tion, in″kan·tā′shan, *n.* [L. *incantatio, incantationis*, < *incanto*, to chant a magic formula over one.] The speaking or singing of certain words for the purpose of raising spirits or performing magical actions; the form of words so used; a magical spell, charm, or ceremony.—**in·can·ta·tion·al**, **in·can·ta·to·ry**, in·kan′ta·tōr″ē, *a.*

in·ca·pa·ble, in·kā′pa·bl, *a.* Not capable; possessing inadequate power or ability for a particular purpose; incompetent; as, an *incapable* assistant; not admitting or susceptible due to type or condition, used only with *of*; as, a gas *incapable* of being reduced to a liquid; unable; as; *incapable* of working hard. *Law*, unqualified or disqualified; not having the ability, understanding, or other qualification for certain legal matters.—*n.* One physically or mentally unable to act with effect; an inefficient or incompetent person; one mentally defective.—**in·ca·pa·bil·i·ty**, **in·ca·pa·ble·ness**, *n.*—**in·ca·pa·bly**, *adv.*

in·ca·pac·i·tate, in″ka·pas′i·tāt″, *v.t.*—*incapacitated, incapacitating.* To deprive of capacity or natural power; to render or make unable or unfit; to disqualify; *law*, to render ineligible.—**in·ca·pac·i·ta·tion**, *n.*

in·ca·pac·i·ty, in″ka·pas′i·tē, *n.* Lack of capacity, power, or ability; inability; incompetency; *law*, disqualification in regard to some legal act.

in·car·cer·ate, in·kär′se·rāt″, *v.t.*—*incarcerated, incarcerating.* To imprison; to confine in a jail; to shut up or enclose.—**in·car·cer·a·tion**, *n.*

in·car·na·dine, in·kär′na·dīn″, in·kär′na·din, in·kär′na·dēn″, *a.* [Fr. *incarnadin*, < It. *incarnatino*, < *incarnato*, flesh-colored, < L.L. *incarnatus*.] Flesh-colored; pink; blood-red.—*v.t.*—*incarnadined, incarnadining.* To redden; to cause to become incarnadine.—*n.* An incarnadine color.

in·car·nate, in·kär′nāt, *v.t.*—*incarnated, incarnating.* [L.L. *incarnatus*, pp. of *incarnare*.] To embody in flesh; invest with a bodily, esp. human, form; to put into or represent in concrete form, as an idea; to be the embodiment or type of, as of a quality or an idea.—in·kär′nit, in·kär′nāt, *a.* Embodied in flesh; personified; as, evil *incarnate*. Flesh-colored or red; incarnadine.

in·car·na·tion, in″kär·nā′shan, *n.* [L.L. *incarnatio(n-)*.] The act of incarnating, or the state of being incarnate, esp. assumption of human form or nature, as by a divine being; an incarnate being or form; a person or thing representing or exhibiting something, as a quality or idea, in typical form; the personification or embodiment of an idea, quality, spirit, or god.

in·case, in·kās′, *v.t.*—*incased, incasing.* Encase.

in·cau·tion, in·ka′shan, *n.* Want of caution; heedlessness; carelessness; imprudence.—**in·cau·tious**, in·ka′shus, *a.*—**in·cau·tious·ly**, *adv.*—**in·cau·tious·ness**, *n.*

in·cen·di·a·ry, in·sen′dē·er″ē, *a.* [L. *incendiarius*, < *incendium*, a burning, fire, < *incendere*.] Of or pertaining to the malicious or criminal setting on fire of buildings or other property; used or adapted for setting property on fire; as, *incendiary* bombs; tending to arouse strife, sedition, riot, or rebellion; inflammatory.—*n.* pl.

in·cen·di·a·ries. One who maliciously sets fire to property; one who stirs up strife or mob violence; an agitator; an incendiary bomb.—**in·cen·di·a·rism,** in·sen'dē·a·-riz"um, *n.*

in·cense, in'sens, *n.* [O.Fr. Fr. *encens,* < L.L. *incensum,* incense, prop. pp. neut. of L. *incendere.*] An aromatic gum or other substance producing a sweet odor when burned, used esp. in religious ceremonies; the perfume or smoke arising from such a substance when burned; any pleasant perfume or fragrance; homage or adulation.—*v.t. incensed, incensing.* [O.Fr. Fr. *encenser.*] To burn incense for; perfume with incense.—*v.i.* To burn or offer incense.

in·cense, in·sens', *v.t.—incensed, incensing.* [L. *incensus,* pp. of *incendere,* set on fire, kindle, inflame.] To inflame with wrath; make angry; enrage.

in·cen·tive, in·sen'tiv, *n.* [L. *incentivus,* setting the tune, later inciting, < *incinere,* sing, sound.] That which incites to action; a motive; a stimulus or incitement. *Com.* any special inducement offered by a business firm to promote sales, productivity, or extra effort by personnel.—*a.* Inciting, as to action; stimulating; provocative.

in·cept, in·sept', *v.t.* [L. *inceptus,* pp. of *incipere,* begin, commence.] *Biol.* To take in; intussuscept; engulf.—*v.i. Brit.* to embark upon a vocation.—**in·cep·tor,** *n.*

in·cep·tion, in·sep'shan, *n.* [L. *inceptio(n-).*] Beginning; commencement; origin; an act of incepting.

in·cep·tive, in·sep'tiv, *a.* Beginning; initial; *gram.* expressing the beginning of action, as verbs ending in *-esce,* as in *coalesce.*—*n. Gram.* an inceptive verb or form.—**in·cep·tive·ly,** *adv.*

in·cer·ti·tude, in·sur'ti·tōd″, in·sur'ti·tūd, *n.* [Fr. *incertitude,* < M.L. *incertitudo,* < L. *incertus,* uncertain.] Uncertainty; doubtfulness; want of assurance or confidence; doubt; insecurity.

in·ces·sant, in·ses'ant, *a.* Continuing without interruption; unceasing; uninterrupted; continual.—**in·ces·sant·ly,** *adv.*—**in·ces·san·cy,** *n.*

in·cest, in'sest, *n.* [Fr. *inceste,* L. *incestum,* unchastity, incest, < *incestus,* unchaste.] The act of sexual intercourse or marriage between close blood relations; the criminal offense of marriage or sexual intercourse between blood relations where prohibited by law.—**in·ces·tu·ous,** in·ses'chō·us, *a.* Guilty of incest; involving the crime of incest.—**in·ces·tu·ous·ly,** *adv.*—**in·ces·tu·ous·ness,** *n.*

inch, inch, *n.* [O.E. *ynce,* < L. *uncia,* twelfth part, inch, ounce.] A measure of length, the twelfth part of a foot, or 2.54 centimeters; a small measure or amount. *Meteor.* the amount of water or snow which would cover a surface to the depth of one inch; a degree of pressure which balances the weight of a vertical column of mercury or other liquid one inch in height in a manometer or barometer.—*v.t., v.i.* To move slowly by inches or small degrees.

inch·meal, inch'mēl″, *adv.* Inch by inch; slowly; gradually.

in·cho·ate, in·kō'it, *a.* [L. *inchoa, inchoatum,* to begin.] Just begun; incipient; rudimentary; incomplete; unorganized.—**in·cho·ate·ly,** *adv.*—**in·cho·ate·ness,** *n.*

in·cho·a·tive, in·kō'a·tiv, *a.* Expressing the beginning. *Gram.* inceptive; indicating the start of an action or circumstance.—*n. Gram.* an inceptive verb.—**in·cho·a·tive·ly,** *adv.*

inch·worm, inch'wurm, *n.* Measuring-worm.

in·ci·dence, in'si·dens, *n.* The fact or manner of being incident; falling upon, affecting, or befalling; the range of occurrence or influence of a thing or the extent of its effects; as, the *incidence* of a disease. *Phys.* the falling, or manner of falling, of a ray of light or projectile on a surface; see *angle of incidence.*

in·ci·dent, in'si·dent, *n.* [L. < *incidens (-ent),* ppr. of *incidere,* fall on, befall.] A distinct occurrence or event; something that occurs casually in connection with something else; an event or matter of accessory or subordinate character; a distinct episode within a story or play; a seemingly minor occurrence likely to touch off more serious consequences, as in international relations.—*a.* Liable or apt to happen; naturally appertaining; conjoined or attaching, esp. as subordinate to a principal thing; befalling; falling or striking, as of rays of light on a surface.

in·ci·den·tal, in″si·den'tal, *a.* Occurring or liable to occur in connection with something else; happening in fortuitous or subordinate conjunction with something else; casual or accidental; liable to happen or naturally appertaining to.—*n.* Something incidental, as a circumstance; *pl.* incidental items, esp. expenses.—**in·ci·den·tal·ly,** *adv.*

in·cin·er·ate, in·sin'e·rāt″, *v.t.—incinerated, incinerating.* [M.L. *incineratus,* pp. of *incinerare.*] To burn or reduce to ashes; cremate.—**in·cin·er·a·tion,** in·sin'e·rā'shan, *n.*—**in·cin·er·a·tor,** *n.* A furnace or apparatus for incinerating.

in·cip·i·ent, in·sip'ē·ent, *a.* [L. *incipiens, incipientis,* ppr. of *incipio,* to begin.] In the beginning stage; commencing; beginning to appear.—**in·cip·i·en·cy, in·cip·i·ence,** *n.*—**in·cip·i·ent·ly,** *adv.*

in·cise, in·sīz', *v.t.—incised, incising.* [Fr. *inciser,* < L. *incido, incisum.*] To cut into; to cut on a surface, as figures and inscriptions; to carve; to engrave.

in·cised, in·sīzd', *a.* Cut; made by cutting; *bot.* having deep and uneven cuts, as in some leaves.

in·ci·sion, in·sizh'an, *n.* That which is produced by cutting or incising; a cut, particularly one made in surgery; a gash; a notch. *Fig.* sharpness; keenness.

in·ci·sive, in·sī'siv, *a.* [Fr. *incisif,* incisive.] Cutting; sharply and clearly expressive; biting; trenchant; as, *incisive* humor.—**in·ci·sive·ly,** *adv.*—**in·ci·sive·ness,** *n.*

in·ci·sor, in·sī'zèr, *n.* A foretooth used for cutting; in humans, one of eight such cutting teeth, located between the canines.

in·cite, in·sīt', *v.t.—incited, inciting.* [L. *incito.*] To move to action; to stir up; to stimulate, urge, provoke, spur on.—**in·ci·ta·tion, in·cite·ment,** in″si·tā'shan, *n.* The act of inciting; that which stimulates action or motivates; incentive.—**in·cit·er,** *n.*

in·ci·vil·i·ty, in″si·vil'i·tē, *n. pl.* **in·ci·vil·i·ties.** [L.L. *incivilitas,* < L. *incivilis,* uncivil.] The quality of being uncivil; discourtesy; rudeness; an uncivil act.

in·clem·ent, in·klem'ent, *a.* Severe; harsh; unkind; without mercy. *Meteor.* rough; stormy; tempestuous.—**in·clem·ent·ly,** *adv.*—**in·clem·en·cy,** *n.*

in·clin·a·ble, in·klī'na·bl, *a.* [O.Fr. *inclinable,* < L. *inclinabilis.*] Inclining, tending; favorably disposed.

in·cli·na·tion, in″klī·nā'shan, *n.* [O.Fr. Fr. *inclination,* < L. *inclinatio(n-).*] A disposition more favorable to one thing or person than to another; propensity; preference. The act or an act of leaning, bending, or bowing; state of being inclined; deviation or amount of deviation from the horizontal or vertical; a slanted surface; tendency, esp. of the mind or will. Also **in·clin·ing.** *Geom.* the angle formed by the intersection of two lines or planes; the difference of direction of the lines or planes as measured by the angle. *Astron.* the angle

formed by the intersection of a planet's orbital plane with the plane of the ecliptic; the angle formed by the intersection of the equatorial plane and the orbital plane of a planet.

in·cline, in·klīn', *v.t.—inclined, inclining.* [O.Fr. Fr. *incliner,* < L. *inclinare,* incline.] To cause to lean or bend in a particular direction; bow, as the head; give a slanting direction or position to; turn toward a speaker in order to listen attentively; give a particular tendency to, as to the mind, heart, or will; dispose or influence in mind, will, or habit.—*v.i.* To lean; bend; deviate from the vertical or horizontal; slant; to tend in course or character; have a mental tendency; be disposed.—in'klīn, in·klīn', *n.* An inclined surface; a slope or plane.—**in·clin·er,** *n.*

in·clined, in·klīnd', *a.* Deviating in direction from the horizontal or vertical; sloping; slanting; having a direction making an angle with something else. Disposed, esp. favorably.

in·clined plane, *n.* Any plane surface obliquely angled toward the horizon, or forming with a horizontal plane any angle except a right angle; a simple machine based on an inclined ramp.

in·cli·nom·e·ter, in″klī·nom'i·tèr, *n.* An instrument with a magnetic needle, used to indicate the direction of the earth's magnetic force in relation to the plane of the horizon. *Aeron.* an apparatus used to measure the tilt or angle of an aircraft with relation to the horizontal.

in·close, in·klōz', *v.t.* Enclose.—**in·clo·sure,** in·klō'zhèr, *n.* Enclosure.

in·clude, in·klōd', *v.t.—included, including.* [L. *includere* (pp. *inclusus*), shut in.] To hold or put within limits; to place in an aggregate, class, or category; to contain, embrace, or comprise, as a whole does parts or any part or element; contain as a subordinate element; involve as a factor.—**in·clud·ed,** *a.* Enclosed; embraced; comprised; *bot.* not projecting beyond the mouth of the corolla, as stamens or a style.—**in·clud·a·ble, in·clud·i·ble,** *a.*

in·clu·sion, in·klō'zhan, *n.* [L. *inclusio(n-).*] The act of including; the state of being included; that which is included; *mineral.* a body of gas or liquid or a crystal enclosed within the mass of a mineral; *biol.* a nonliving particle within the cytoplasm of a cell.

in·clu·sion bod·y, *n. Pathol.* a stainable foreign particle contained in a virus-infected cell.

in·clu·sive, in·klō'siv, *a.* Comprising, encompassing, embracing; comprehensive; including a great deal, or everything concerned; covering the specified limits; as, from 1960 to 1965 *inclusive.*—**in·clu·sive·ly,** *adv.*—**in·clu·sive·ness,** *n.*

in·co·er·ci·ble, in″kō·ur'si·bl, *a.* Not coercible; difficult or impossible to restrain, confine, or compress; *phys.* resistant to change or compression, as a gas.

in·cog·i·ta·ble, in·koj'i·ta·bl, *a.* Not cogitable; incapable of being conceived by the mind.—**in·cog·i·tant,** *a.* Inconsiderate; thoughtless.

in·cog·ni·to, in·kog'ni·tō″, in″kog·nē'tō, *fem.* **in·cog·ni·ta,** in·kog'ni·ta, in″kog·-nē'ta, *a.* [It. < L. *incognitus,* unknown.] Unknown; having a concealed or assumed identity, as an assumed name, usu. to escape notice or attention.—*adv.* With the real name or identity concealed; as, to travel *incognito.*—*n. pl.* **in·cog·ni·tos.** One who is incognito; the state of being incognito; the disguise used.

in·cog·ni·zance, in·kog'ni·zans, *n.* Failure to recognize, know, or apprehend.—**in·cog·ni·zant,** *a.* Not having awareness or knowledge of; unacquainted with.

in·co·her·ence, in″kō·hēr′ens, *n*. The state of being incoherent; something incoherent. Also **in·co·her·en·cy**, *pl*. **in·co·her·en·cies**.

in·co·her·ent, in″kō·hēr′ent, *a*. Not coherent; without physical cohesion, unconnected, or loose, as matter; without unity or harmony of elements; disorganized or uncoordinated, as a system; without logical connection, disjointed, or rambling, as thought or language; characterized by such thought or language, as a person.—**in·co·her·ent·ly**, *adv*.

in·com·bus·ti·ble, in″kom·bus′ti·bl, *a*. Not combustible; incapable of being burned or consumed by fire.—*n*. An incombustible substance.—**in·com·bus·ti·bil·i·ty**, **in·com·bus·ti·ble·ness**, *n*.—**in·com·bus·ti·bly**, *adv*.

in·come, in′kum, *n*. Receipts or benefits, usu. monetary, periodically accruing from labor, business, property, or investments.

in·come ac·count, *n*. A financial statement of profit and loss for a particular period.

in·come tax, *n*. A tax levied on incomes, usu. with specified deductions and on incomes exceeding specified amounts.

in·com·ing, in′kum″ing, *a*. Coming in; entering; arriving; beginning or taking a new post or position.—*n*. The act of coming in.

in·com·men·su·ra·ble, in″ko·men′shėr·a·bl, in″ko·men′sėr·a·bl, *a*. [M.L. *incommensurabilis*.] Not commensurable; having no common measure or standard of comparison; utterly disproportionate; *math*. having no common measure.—*n*.—**in·com·men·su·ra·bil·i·ty**, **in·com·men·su·ra·ble·ness**, *n*.—**in·com·men·su·ra·bly**, *adv*.

in·com·men·su·rate, in″ko·men′shėr·it, in″ko·men′sėr·it, *a* Insufficient; not adequate or of sufficient amount; disproportionate; incommensurable.—**in·com·men·su·rate·ly**, *adv*.

in·com·mode, in″ko·mōd′, *v.t.*—*incommoded, incommoding*. [Fr. *incommoder*, < L. *incommodo*, to be troublesome to.] To inconvenience; give inconvenience to by hindering; trouble.—**in·com·mo·di·ous**, in″ko·mo′dē·us, *a*. Not commodious; inconvenient; uncomfortable; tending to incommode.—**in·com·mo·di·ous·ly**, *adv*.—**in·com·mo·di·ous·ness**, *n*.

in·com·mod·i·ty, in″ko·mod′i·tē, *n*. *pl.* **in·com·mod·i·ties**. [O.Fr. *incommodite* (Fr. *incommodité*), < L. *incommoditas*, < *incommodus*.] Inconvenience; disadvantage; discomfort.

in·com·mu·ni·ca·ble, in″ko·mū′ni·ka·bl, *a*. Not communicable; incapable of being expressed, told, or imparted to others; ineffable; taciturn.—**in·com·mu·ni·ca·bil·i·ty**, **in·com·mu·ni·ca·ble·ness**, *n*.—**in·com·mu·ni·ca·bly**, *adv*.

in·com·mu·ni·ca·do, in″ko·mū″ni·kä′dō, *a*. Without access to or restrained from communication, as: In solitary confinement, the prisoner is *incommunicado*.—*adv*.

in·com·mu·ni·ca·tive, in″ko·mū′ni·kā″tiv, *a*. Not communicative; not inclined to impart information; not disposed to talk.—**in·com·mu·ni·ca·tive·ness**, *n*.

in·com·mut·a·ble, in″ko·mū′ta·bl, *a*. Not commutable; unalterable; incapable of being exchanged.—**in·com·mut·a·bil·i·ty**, **in·com·mut·a·ble·ness**, *n*.—**in·com·mut·a·bly**, *adv*.

in·com·pa·ra·ble, in·kom′pėr·a·bl, in·kom′pra·bl, *a*. Not comparable; not able to be compared with others because of dissimilar natures or qualities. Without a match, rival, or peer; unequaled.—**in·com·pa·ra·bil·i·ty**, **in·com·pa·ra·ble·ness**, *n*.—**in·com·pa·ra·bly**, *adv*.

in·com·pat·i·ble, in″kom·pat′a·bl, *a*. Not compatible; unable to coexist in harmony;

discordant; inconsistent; not able to be held by one person at the same time, as: The two offices are *incompatible*. *Med*. undesirable or dangerous when combined; *logic*, incongruous or contradictory in nature, as two propositions.—*n*.—**in·com·pat·i·bil·i·ty**, **in·com·pat·i·ble·ness**, *n*.—**in·com·pat·i·bly**, *adv*.

in·com·pe·tent, in·kom′pi·tent, *a*. Not competent; lacking adequate strength, power, capacity, means, or qualifications; unable; incapable; inadequate. *Law*, lacking necessary legal or constitutional qualifications; not permissible or admissible.—*n*. One who is incompetent.—**in·com·pe·tence**, **in·com·pe·ten·cy**, *n*.—**in·com·pe·tent·ly**, *adv*.

in·com·plete, in″kom·plēt′, *a*. Not complete; not finished; not having all parts or sections to comprise a whole; imperfect; defective due to lack of full development.—**in·com·plete·ly**, *adv*.—**in·com·plete·ness**, *n*.

in·com·ple·tion, in″kom·plē′shan, *n*. Lack of completion; incomplete state; *football*, a forward pass which is not caught in accordance with the rules of the game.

in·com·pli·ant, in″kom·plī′ant, *a*. Unyielding; unaccommodating.—**in·com·pli·ance**, **in·com·pli·an·cy**, *n*.—**in·com·pli·ant·ly**, *adv*.

in·com·pre·hen·si·ble, in″kom·pri·hen′si·bl, *a*. [L. *incomprehensibilis*.] Not to be grasped by the mind; not to be understood; unintelligible.—**in·com·pre·hen·si·bil·i·ty**, **in·com·pre·hen·si·ble·ness**, *n*.—**in·com·pre·hen·si·bly**, *adv*.

in·com·pre·hen·sion, in″kom·pri·hen′shan, *n*. Want of comprehension or understanding.

in·com·press·i·ble, in″kom·pres′i·bl, *a*. Not able to be pressed together, reduced, or lessened.—**in·com·press·i·bil·i·ty**, *n*.—**in·com·press·i·bly**, *adv*.

in·com·put·a·ble, in″kom·pū′ta·bl, *a*. Not calculable; incapable of being computed or reckoned.—**in·com·put·a·bly**, *adv*.

in·con·ceiv·a·ble, in″kon·sē′va·bl, *a*. Unimaginable; unthinkable; incredible.—**in·con·ceiv·a·bil·i·ty**, **in·con·ceiv·a·ble·ness**, *n*.—**in·con·ceiv·a·bly**, *adv*.

in·con·clu·sive, in″kon·klō′siv, *a*. Indeterminate; indefinite; indecisive; not resolving doubtful questions; not producing a final result.—**in·con·clu·sive·ly**, *adv*.—**in·con·clu·sive·ness**, *n*.

in·con·den·sa·ble, **in·con·den·si·ble**, in″kon·den′sa·bl, *a*. Not condensable; incapable of being condensed.—**in·con·den·sa·bil·i·ty**, **in·con·den·si·bil·i·ty**, *n*.

in·con·dite, in·kon′dit, in·kon′dīt, *a*. [L. *inconditus*, < *conditus*, pp. of *condere*, put together.] Poorly constructed; crude.

in·con·form·i·ty, in″kon·fạr′mi·tē, *n*. Nonconformity.

in·con·gru·ent, in·kong′grö·ent, *a*. [L. *incongruus*.] Incongruous; inharmonious; inconsistent.—**in·con·gru·ence**, *n*.

in·con·gru·i·ty, in″kong·grö′i·tē, *n*. *pl.* **in·con·gru·i·ties**. The quality of being incongruous; that which seems awkward or out of place.

in·con·gru·ous, in·kong′grö·us, *a*. [L. *incongruus*.] Inharmonious in character; inconsonant; inconsistent; out of place; inappropriate; unbecoming; lacking harmony of parts.—**in·con·gru·ous·ly**, *adv*.—**in·con·gru·ous·ness**, *n*.

in·con·sec·u·tive, in″kon·sek′ū·tiv, *a*. Not consecutive; disconnected; not successive.—**in·con·sec·u·tive·ly**, *adv*.—**in·con·sec·u·tive·ness**, *n*.

in·con·se·quent, in·kon′se·kwent″, *a*. [L. *inconsequens*(-*ent*-).] Not following from the premises; illogical; inconsistent; irrelevant; disconnected; of persons, characterized by

lack of logical sequence in thought, speech, or action. Of no consequence; insignificant.—**in·con·se·quence**, **in·con·se·quent·ness**, *n*.—**in·con·se·quent·ly**, *adv*.

in·con·se·quen·tial, in″kon·se·kwen′shal, in·kon″se·kwen′shal, *a*. Of no consequence; trivial; unimportant. Inconsequent; illogical; irrelevant.—**in·con·se·quen·ti·al·i·ty**, *n*.—**in·con·se·quen·tial·ly**, *adv*.

in·con·sid·er·a·ble, in″kon·sid′ėr·a·bl, *a*. Not worthy of consideration or notice; unimportant; small; trivial; insignificant.—**in·con·sid·er·a·bly**, *adv*.—**in·con·sid·er·a·ble·ness**, *n*.

in·con·sid·er·ate, in″kon·sid′ėr·it, *a*. [< L. *inconsideratus*.] Not considerate; not acting with due regard for the feelings of others; thoughtless; heedless; without sufficient deliberation or thought.—**in·con·sid·er·ate·ly**, *adv*.—**in·con·sid·er·ate·ness**, **in·con·sid·er·a·tion**, *n*.

in·con·sist·ent, in″kon·sis′tent, *a*. Not consistent; lacking agreement; at variance; discrepant; incongruous; lacking harmony between the different parts or elements; self-contradictory; acting at variance with professed principles or former conduct; not consistent in conduct or principles; erratic.—**in·con·sist·ent·ly**, *adv*.—**in·con·sist·ence**, *n*.—**in·con·sist·en·cy**, *n*. *pl.* **in·con·sist·en·cies**.

in·con·sol·a·ble, in″kon·sō′la·bl, *a*. Incapable of being consoled; brokenhearted.—**in·con·sol·a·ble·ness**, *n*.—**in·con·sol·a·bly**, *adv*.

in·con·so·nant, in·kon′so·nant, *a*. Not consonant; not in harmony or accord; discordant.—**in·con·so·nance**, *n*.—**in·con·so·nant·ly**, *adv*.

in·con·spic·u·ous, in″kon·spik′ū·us, *a*. Not conspicuous or readily noticed; not easily perceived.—**in·con·spic·u·ous·ly**, *adv*.—**in·con·spic·u·ous·ness**, *n*.

in·con·stant, in·kon′stant, *a*. Not constant; subject to change of opinion, inclination, or purpose; unsteady; fickle; capricious; variable.—**in·con·stan·cy**, *n*. *pl.* **in·con·stan·cies**.—**in·con·stant·ly**, *adv*.

in·con·sum·a·ble, in″kon·sō′ma·bl, *a*. Incapable of being consumed. *Econ*. pertaining to those useful products which, like machinery, are not consumed or depleted.—**in·con·sum·a·bly**, *adv*.

in·con·test·a·ble, in″kon·tes′ta·bl, *a*. Not to be disputed; too clear to be controverted.—**in·con·test·a·bil·i·ty**, *n*.—**in·con·test·a·bly**, *adv*.

in·con·ti·nent, in·kon′ti·nent, *a*. Not restraining the passions or appetites, particularly the sexual appetite; *med*. unable to restrain natural bodily discharges.—*adv*.—**in·con·ti·nence**, **in·con·ti·nen·cy**, *n*.—**in·con·ti·nent·ly**, *adv*.

in·con·trol·la·ble, in″kon·trō′la·bl, *a*. Uncontrollable; not governable; delinquent; unmanageable.

in·con·tro·vert·i·ble, in″kon·tro·vėr′ta·bl, *a*. Not arguable; too clear or certain to admit of dispute or controversy.—**in·con·tro·vert·i·bil·i·ty**, **in·con·tro·vert·i·ble·ness**, *n*.—**in·con·tro·vert·i·bly**, *adv*.

in·con·ven·ience, in″kon·vēn′yens, *n*. The quality of being inconvenient; something that gives trouble or uneasiness. Also **in·con·ven·ien·cy**, *pl.* **in·con·ven·ien·cies**.—*v.t.*—*inconvenienced, inconveniencing*. To put to inconvenience; to disturb.

in·con·ven·ient, in″kon·vēn′yent, *a*. Giving trouble or discomfort; wanting due facilities; causing embarrassment; inopportune.—**in·con·ven·ient·ly**, *adv*.

in·con·vert·i·ble, in″kon·vụr′ta·bl, *a*. Incapable of being converted or exchanged; of paper money, not capable of being converted into coined money; of a currency, not exchangeable for that of another country.—in·con·vert·i·bil·i·ty, in·con·vert·i·ble·ness, in″kon·vur″ti·bil′i·tē, n.—in·con·vert·i·bly, adv.

in·con·vin·ci·ble, in″kon·vin′si·bl, a. Incapable of being convinced.—in·con·vin·ci·bil·i·ty, in″kon·vin″ci·bil′i·tē, n.—in·con·vin·ci·bly, adv.

in·co·or·di·nate, in″kō·ar′di·nit, a. Not coordinated. Also in·co·or·di·nat·ed, in″kō·ar′di·nā·tid.—in·co·or·di·na·tion, in″kō·ar″di·nā′shan, n. Physiol. inability to coordinate voluntary muscular movements.

in·cor·po·rate, in·kar′pō·rāt″, v.t.—incorporated, incorporating. [L.L. incorporatus, pp. of incorporare, < L. in-, in, and corporare, embody.] To form into a society or legal corporation; to admit as a member of an association or corporation; to combine into one body or uniform substance, as ingredients; introduce into a body or mass as an integral part or parts; to take in or include as a part, as the body or mass does; to embody or give material form to.—v.i. To form a corporation; to unite or combine so as to form one body.—in·kar′po·rit, in··kar′prit, a. Constituted as a corporation; combined into one body, or substance. Also incorporated.—in·cor·po·ra·ble, a.—in·cor·po·ra·tion, n.—in·cor·po·ra·tive, a. —in·cor·po·ra·tor, n.

in·cor·po·rate, in·kar′pėr·it, in·kar′prit, a. [L.L. incorporatus.] Not embodied; incorporeal.

in·cor·po·rat·ed, in·kar′po·rā″tid, a. Constituted as a legal corporation; combined, blended, or united.

in·cor·po·re·al, in″kar·pōr′ē·al, a. [L. incorporeus.] Not corporeal; immaterial; pertaining to spiritual beings. Law, without material existence, but existing in contemplation of law, as a franchise or a right of way.—in·cor·po·re·al·i·ty, in·cor·po··re·i·ty, in″kar·pōr″ē·al′i·tē, in″kar·po··rē′i·tē, n.—in·cor·po·re·al·ly, adv.

in·cor·rect, in″ko·rekt′, a. Not correct; not exact; erroneous; not according to fact; improper or unsuitable.—in·cor·rect·ly, adv.—in·cor·rect·ness, n.

in·cor·ri·gi·ble, in·kar′i·ji·bl, in·kor′i··ji·bl, a. Incapable of being corrected or amended; bad beyond correction or reform. —n.—in·cor·ri·gi·bil·i·ty, in·cor·ri··gi·ble·ness, in·kar′i·ji·bil′i·tē, in·kor′··i·ji·bil′i·tē, n.—in·cor·ri·gi·bly, adv.

in·cor·rupt, in″ko·rupt′, a. [L. incorruptus.] Above the influence of corruption or bribery; not depraved; without errors, as a text.—in·cor·rupt·ness, n.—in·cor·rupt··ly, adv.—in·cor·rupt·ed, a.

in·cor·rupt·i·ble, in″ko·rup′ti·bl, a. Incapable of corruption, decay, or dissolution; incapable of being bribed; inflexibly upright.—n.—in·cor·rupt·i·bil·i·ty, in··cor·rupt·i·ble·ness, in″ko·rup″ti·bil′i·tē, n.—in·cor·rup·ti·bly, adv.

in·cras·sate, in·kras′āt, v.t.—incrassated, incrassating. [L.L. incrassatus, pp. of incrassare, < L. in-, in, and crassare, thicken, < crassus, thick.] Phar. to make thicker by addition of another substance or by evaporation, as a liquid.—in·kras′āt, in·kras′āt, a. Bot., entom. thickened or swollen. Also in··cras·sat·ed.—in·cras·sa·tion, in″kras·a′shan, n.—in·cras·sa·tive, a.

in·crease, in·krēs′, v.i.—increased, increasing. [Prefix in- or en-, and O.Fr. creser, L. crescere, to grow, allied to creare, to create.] To become greater; to grow; to multiply by the production of young. Astron. to show a gradually enlarging luminous surface; to wax, as the moon.— v.t. To make greater or larger; to augment in bulk, quantity, amount, or degree; to add to.—in·creas·er, n.—in·creas·ing, a.— in·creas·ing·ly, adv.

in·crease, in′krēs, n. Augmentation; a growing greater or larger; something which

is added; the amount by which anything is augmented; increment; interest earned by money.—in·creas·a·ble, a.

in·cred·i·ble, in·kred′i·bl, a. Too extraordinary and improbable to be believed.— in·cred·i·bil·i·ty, in·cred·i·ble·ness, in·kred″i·bil′i·tē, n.—in·cred·i·bly, adv.

in·cred·u·lous, in·krej′u·lus, a. Not given to unquestioning acceptance or ready belief; skeptical; expressing or showing disbelief.—in·cre·du·li·ty, in·cred·u·lous·ness, in″kri·dö′li·tē, in″kri·dū′li·tē, n. —in·cred·u·lous·ly, adv.

in·cre·ment, in′kre·ment, ing′kre·ment, n. [L. incrementum, < incresco, to increase.] Act or process of increasing; augmentation or growth; something added; increase; profit; math. a change, positive or negative, in the value of a quantity.—in·cre·men·tal, in″kre·men′tal, ing″kre·men′tal, a.

in·cres·cent, in·kres′ent, a. [L. increscens, increscentis, ppr. of incresco, to increase.] Increasing, as the moon; growing; augmenting; swelling.

in·cre·tion, in·krē′shan, n. Physiol. a substance secreted internally by an endocrine gland; the process of this secretion.

in·crim·i·nate, in·krim′i·nāt″, v.t.—incriminated, incriminating. [L.L. incrimino, incriminatum—L. in-, and crimino, to accuse one of a crime, < crimen, criminis, a charge.] To charge with a crime or fault; to accuse; to implicate in a wrongdoing.—in·crim·i··na·tion, in·krim″i·nā′shan, n.—in·crim·i·na·tor, n.—in·crim·i·na·to·ry, in·krim′i·na·tōr″ē, in·krim′i·na·tär″ē, a.

in·crust, in·krust′, v.t. [L. incrusto—in-, in, on, and crusta, crust.] To cover with a crust or hard coat; to form a crust on the surface of. Also encrust.—in·crus·ta·tion, in″kru·stā′shan, n. The act of incrusting; the condition of being incrusted; a crust or hard coating, esp. as a decoration.

in·cu·bate, in′kū·bāt″, ing′kū·bāt″, v.t.— incubated, incubating. [L. incubatus, pp. of incubare, lie on, sit or rest on.] To sit upon, as eggs, for the purpose of hatching; hatch by artificial heat, as in an incubator; maintain, as bacterial cultures or embryos, in a controlled environment most suitable for development; brood; produce as if by hatching.—v.i. To sit upon eggs; brood; undergo incubation.—in·cu·ba·tion, in″kū·bā′··shan, ing″kū·bā′shan, n. The act or process of incubating; pathol. the period of development of a disease between infection and the appearance of symptoms.—in·cu·ba·tion··al, a.—in·cu·ba·tive, a.

in·cu·ba·tor, in′kū·bā″tėr, ing′kū·bā″tėr, n. An apparatus for hatching eggs by artificial heat; an apparatus for maintaining suitable temperature, humidity, and oxygen for babies born prematurely or otherwise physically subnormal; an apparatus for incubating bacteriological cultures; one who or that which incubates.

in·cu·bus, in′kū·bus, ing′kū·bus, n. pl. in·cu·bus·es, in·cu·bi, in′kū·bī, ing′kū·· bī″. [L., < incubo, to lie on.] Nightmare; an imaginary being or demon, formerly supposed to be the cause of a nightmare, and believed to have sexual intercourse with women in their sleep; something that weighs heavily on the mind or feelings like a nightmare; an encumbrance of any kind.

in·cul·cate, in·kul′kāt, in·kul·kāt″, v.t.— inculcated, inculcating. [L. inculco, inculcatum.] To impress by frequent admonitions; to teach and enforce by frequent repetitions. —in·cul·ca·tion, in″kul·kā′shan, n.—in·cul·ca·tor, n.—in·cul·ca·to·ry, in·kul′··ka·tōr″ē, in·kul′ka·tär″ē, a.

in·cul·pa·ble, in·kul′pa·bl, a. Not culpable; not guilty; blameless.—in·cul·pa··bil·i·ty, in·cul·pa·ble·ness, in·kul′pa··bil′i·tē, n.—in·cul·pa·bly, adv.

in·cul·pate, in·kul′pāt, in′kul·pāt″, v.t.—

inculpated, inculpating. [L.L. inculpo, inculpatum.] To show to be at fault; to accuse of crime; to impute guilt to; to incriminate: opposed to exculpate.—in·cul·pa·tion, in″··kul·pā′shan, n.—in·cul·pa·to·ry, in·kul′··pa·tōr″ē, in·kul′pa·tar″ē, a.

in·cum·bent, in·kum′bent, a. [L. incumbens, incumbentis, ppr. of incumbo, to lie.] Lying or resting upon; resting upon a person, as a duty or obligation to be performed; filling a post or political office.—n. A person in possession of a political office, ecclesiastical benefice, or other position.— in·cum·ben·cy, n. pl. in·cum·ben·cies. The state of being incumbent; what is incumbent; the term of office or area of responsibilities of an incumbent.—in··cum·bent·ly, adv.

in·cum·ber, in·kum′bėr, v.t. Encumber.

in·cu·nab·u·la, in″kū·nab′ū·la, n. pl., sing. in·cu·nab·u·lum, in″kū·nab′ū·lum. [L. incunabula, swaddling clothes, birthplace, origin, < cunae, a cradle.] Books printed before 1500, in the early stages of European printing; earliest endeavors or beginnings of anything.

in·cur, in·kur′, v.t.—incurred, incurring. [L. incurro, to run against.] To become responsible for or subject to, as some undesirable consequence or inconvenience; become liable to; contract, as a debt.— in·cur·rence, in·kur′ens, in·kur′ens, n.

in·cur·a·ble, in·kur′a·bl, a. Not curable; beyond medical help or skill.—n. A person diseased beyond the possibility of cure.— in·cur·a·bil·i·ty, in·cur·a·ble·ness, in·· kūr″a·bil′i·tē, n.—in·cur·a·bly, adv.

in·cu·ri·ous, in·kur′ē·us, a. Not curious or inquisitive; indifferent.—in·cu·ri·ous·ly, adv.—in·cu·ri·os·i·ty, in·cu·ri·ous·· ness, in″kur·ē·os′i·tē, n.

in·cur·rent, in·kur′ent, in·kur′ent, a. Having an inward-flowing current.

in·cur·sion, in·kur′zhan, in·kur′shan, n. [L. incursio, incursionis, < incurro.] A hostile, often sudden, invasion of a territory; inroad; raid; foray. An entering or running in.—in·cur·sive, a. Making an attack.

in·cur·vate, in′kur·vāt″, in·kur′vāt, v.t.— incurvated, incurvating. [L. incurvatus, pp. of incurvare.] To make curved; turn from a straight line or course; curve, esp. to curve inward.—in′kur·vāt, in·kur′vit, a. Curved, esp. inward.—in·cur·va·ture, in·cur·va··tion, in·kur′va·chėr, in″kur·vā′shan, n.

in·curve, in·kurv′, v.t., v.i.—incurved, incurving. [L. incurvare.] To curve inward.— in′kurv″, n. Baseball, a pitched ball which curves inward as it approaches the batter.

in·cus, ing′kus, n. pl. in·cu·des, in·cus, in·kū′dēz. [L., an anvil.] A bone of the middle ear of mammals shaped like an anvil; pl. in·cu·des. Meteor. the top part of a cumulonimbus cloud, shaped like an anvil; pl. in·cus.—in·cu·date, in·cu·dal, ing′kū·dāt″, ing′kū·dit, in′kū·dāt″, in′kū·· dit, ing′kū·dal, in′kū·dal, a.

in·cuse, in·kūz′, in·kūs′, v.t.—incused, incusing. [L. incusus, pp. of incudere, forge with a hammer.] To impress by striking or stamping, as a coin.—a. Hammered or stamped in, as a figure on a coin.—n. An incuse figure or impression.

in·da·ba, in·dä′bä, n. [Zulu.] A conference or consultation between or with South African natives.

in·da·mine, in′da·mēn″, in′da·min, n. [< indigo and amine.] Chem. any of a certain series of basic organic compounds which form bluish and greenish salts, used in the manufacture of dyes.

in·debt·ed, in·det′id, a. Being under or having incurred a debt; required to repay a loan; beholden; obliged by something received, for which gratitude or restitution is due.—in·debt·ed·ness, n.

in·de·cent, in·dē′sent, a. [L. *indecens*, unseemly.] Offensive to modesty and good taste; immodest; lacking propriety; vulgar; unseemly.—**in·de·cen·cy**, n. pl. **in·de·cen·cies.**—**in·de·cent·ly**, adv.

in·de·cid·u·ous, in″di·sij′ö·us, a. *Bot.* Not deciduous; evergreen.

in·de·ci·pher·a·ble, in″di·sī′fẽr·a·bl, a. Not decipherable.

in·de·ci·sion, in″di·sizh′an, n. Want of decision; a wavering of the mind.

in·de·ci·sive, in″di·sī′siv, a. Not decisive; unable to make decisions; irresolute; vacillating; hesitating; not clearly defined.—**in·de·ci·sive·ly**, adv.—**in·de·ci·sive·ness**, n.

in·de·clin·a·ble, in″di·klī′na·bl, a. *Gram.* Not declinable; not varied by inflected endings.

in·dec·o·rous, in·dek′ẽr·us, in″di·kōr′us, in″di·kạr′us, a. Not decorous; violating decorum or propriety; unseemly; unbecoming.—**in·dec·o·rous·ly**, adv.—**in·dec·o·rous·ness**, n.—**in·de·co·rum**, in″di·kōr′um, in″di·kạr′um, n. Want of decorum; impropriety of behavior.

in·deed, in·dēd′, adv. In reality; in truth; in fact: used to emphasize a previous statement, to intimate a concession or admission, or, interrogatively, to request a confirmation.—*interj.* An expression of surprise or disbelief.

in·de·fat·i·ga·ble, in″di·fat′i·ga·bl, a. [L. *indefatigabilis*, from *in-*, not, and *defatigo*, to tire completely—*de-*, intens., and *fatigo*, to fatigue.] Incapable of being fatigued; not yielding to fatigue.—**in·de·fat·i·ga·bil·i·ty**, **in·de·fat·i·ga·ble·ness**, in″di·fat″i·ga·bil′i·tē, n.—**in·de·fat·i·ga·bly**, adv.

in·de·fea·si·ble, in″di·fē′zi·bl, a. Not defeasible; not to be defeated or made void.—**in·de·fea·si·bil·i·ty**, in″di·fē″zi·bil′i·tē, n.—**in·de·fea·si·bly**, adv.

in·de·fect·i·ble, in″di·fek′ti·bl, a. Not defectible; not liable to defect or failure; unfailing; not liable to fault or imperfection; faultless.—**in·de·fect·i·bil·i·ty**, in″di·fek″ti·bil′i·tē, n.—**in·de·fect·i·bly**, adv.

in·de·fen·si·ble, in″di·fen′si·bl, a. Not defensible; incapable of being excused, vindicated, or justified; incapable of being defended, as a fort or military position.—**in·de·fen·si·bil·i·ty**, in″di·fen″si·bil′i·tē, n.—**in·de·fen·si·bly**, adv.

in·de·fin·a·ble, in″di·fī′na·bl, a. Incapable of being defined; not able to be described or analyzed.—**in·de·fin·a·bil·i·ty**, **in·de·fin·a·ble·ness**, in″di·fī″na·bil′i·tē, n.—**in·de·fin·a·bly**, adv.

in·def·i·nite, in·def′i·nit, a. [L. *indefinitus*.] Not definite; without fixed or specified limit; unlimited; not clearly defined or determined; not precise; vague. *Gram.* not specifying precisely; as, the *indefinite* article *a*, or an *indefinite* pronoun, *any*, *some*, or the like. *Bot.* very numerous or not easily counted, as stamens; indeterminate growth, as of an inflorescence.—**in·def·i·nite·ly**, adv.—**in·def·i·nite·ness**, n.

in·def·i·nite in·te·gral, n. *Math.* any function having a derivative which is the given function.

in·de·his·cent, in″di·his′ent, a. *Bot.* Not dehiscent; not opening spontaneously when ripe, as a fruit.—**in·de·his·cence**, n.

in·del·i·ble, in·del′i·bl, a. [L. *indelebilis*—*in-*, not, and *deleo*, to delete.] Incapable of being canceled or obliterated; making marks difficult or impossible to efface.—**in·del·i·bil·i·ty**, **in·del·i·ble·ness**, in·del″i·bil′i·tē, n.—**in·del·i·bly**, adv.

in·del·i·cate, in·del′i·kit, a. Wanting delicacy; offensive to modesty or propriety; tending toward indecency; showing no regard for the sensitivities of others; having no tact.—**in·del·i·ca·cy**, **in·del·i·cate·ness**, n.—**in·del·i·cate·ly**, adv.

in·dem·ni·fy, in·dem′ni·fī″, v.t.—*indemnified*, *indemnifying*. [L. *indemnis*, free from loss or injury, and *facio*, to make.] To secure against loss, damage, or penalty; to reimburse for expenditures made or damages suffered.—**in·dem·ni·fi·ca·tion**, in·dem″ni·fi·kā′shan, n.—**in·dem·ni·fi·er**, n.

in·dem·ni·ty, in·dem′ni·tē, n. pl. **in·dem·ni·ties.** [Fr. *indemnité*, < L. *indemnitas*, < *indemnis*, uninjured.] Security or exemption from damage, loss, injury, or punishment; compensation or equivalent for loss, damage, or injury sustained.—**in·dem·ni·tee**, in·dem″ni·tē′, n. One who is indemnified.—**in·dem·ni·tor**, in·dem′ni·tẽr, n. One who indemnifies.

in·de·mon·stra·ble, in″di·mon′stra·bl, in·dem′on·stra·bl, a. [L. *indemonstrabilis*.] Not demonstrable; incapable of being demonstrated. — **in·de·mon·stra·bil·i·ty**, in″di·mon″stra·bil′i·tē, in″dem″on·stra·bil′i·tē, n.—**in·de·mon·stra·bly**, adv.

in·dent, in·dent′, v.t. [L.L. *indentare*, O.Fr. *endenter*, < L. *in-*, in, and *dens*, *dentis*, a tooth.] To begin, as a line of type, farther in from the margin than the rest of the paragraph; to notch, jag, or cut into points like a row of teeth. *Law*, to divide or cut, as a document having several copies, in an irregular fashion so that the pieces can be fitted together for authentication; to cut or rip, as a document having several copies, in an irregular fashion along the edge; to prepare, as a legal document, in multiple exact copies. To indenture. *Brit.* to draw up an order from; to place an order for.—*v.i.* To begin a line of type or writing farther in from the margin than other lines; to form or be cut into notches or jags; *chiefly Brit.* to prepare an order or requisition in duplicate.—in′dent, in·dent′, n. The blank space at the beginning of the first line of a paragraph; indention; a notch or indentation; an indenture; a certificate issued at the end of the Revolutionary War by the U.S. government for principal or interest on the public debt; *chiefly Brit.* an order for goods, esp. one from a foreign country.

in·dent, in·dent′, v.t. To drive or force into so as to form a dent; to make a dent or depression in.—in′dent, in·dent′, n. A dent or depression in the surface of anything, as from a blow.

in·den·ta·tion, in″den·tā′shan, n. The act of indenting; a notch or an angular recess, as in a river bank; a series of notches along an edge, as the margin of leaves; an indention.—**in·dent·ed**, in·den′tid, a. Having notches or points like teeth on the margin; toothed.—**in·den·tion**, n. *Print.* The setting in or indenting of type at the left margin of a sheet; the space left by this indenting.

in·den·ture, in·den′chẽr, n. *Law*, a deed or contract under seal, entered into between two or more parties, each party having a duplicate; such a document having copies that are jaggedly cut, or indented, for authentication. *Usu. pl.* a contract by which one person is bound to another under certain conditions and for a specified length of time, as servant and master in an apprenticeship. An official list, as an inventory, that has been legalized; an indentation.—*v.t.* —*indentured*, *indenturing*. To bind by indentures, as in apprenticeship.

in·de·pend·ence, in″di·pen′dens, n. Freedom from subjection to the influence or control of others; the state of being independent. Also *independency*.—**In·de·pend·ence Day**, *U.S.* an annual legal holiday on July 4th, commemorating the adoption of the Declaration of Independence on July 4, 1776. Also *the Fourth;* **Fourth of Ju·ly.**

in·de·pend·en·cy, in″di·pen′den·sē, n. pl. **in·de·pend·en·cies.** The state of being

independent; a territory or state that is not controlled by another nation. (*Cap.*), *eccles.* a doctrine or movement which holds that an individual church congregation is subject only to the covenant of God and not to any external ecclesiastical power.

in·de·pend·ent, in″di·pen′dent, a. Not dependent; not subject to the control of others; not relying on others, with *of* before an object; acting and thinking for oneself; not swayed by bias or influence; self-directing; not associated with or relying upon a larger unit or group; *polit.* not committed to a particular party, esp. in voting. Possessing or constituting a competence; as, an *independent* fortune; *gram.* of a clause, capable of standing alone as a sentence. (*Cap.*), *eccles.* pertaining to the Independents or Congregationalists.—*n. Polit.* one not bound by a party. (*Cap.*), *eccles.* one who maintains that every congregation is autonomous and is not subject to any external ecclesiastical power; in England, a 16th century sect that gave rise to the Independents and Congregationalists.—**in·de·pend·ent of**, irrespective of; without regard to.—**in·de·pend·ent·ly**, adv.

in·de·scrib·a·ble, in″di·skrī′ba·bl, a. Not describable; beyond or transcending description.—**in·de·scrib·a·bil·i·ty**, **in·de·scrib·a·ble·ness**, in″di·skrī″ba·bil′i·tē, n.—**in·de·scrib·a·bly**, adv.

in·de·struct·i·ble, in″di·struk′ti·bl, a. Not destructible; incapable of being destroyed.—**in·de·struct·i·bil·i·ty**, **in·de·struct·i·ble·ness**, in″di·struk″ti·bil′i·tē, n.—**in·de·struct·i·bly**, adv.

in·de·ter·mi·na·ble, in″di·tẽr′mi·na·bl, a. Incapable of being determined, ascertained, or fixed; not able to be decided or ended.—**in·de·ter·mi·na·ble·ness**, n.—**in·de·ter·mi·na·bly**, adv.

in·de·ter·mi·na·cy prin·ci·ple, n. Uncertainty principle.

in·de·ter·mi·nate, in″di·tẽr′mi·nit, a. Not determinate; not settled or fixed; not definite; uncertain; not precise; *bot.* of an inflorescence, having flowers arising from auxiliary buds along the axis so that further growth is possible at the apex. *Math.* of a problem, having an indefinite number of solutions; undefined, as a quantity.—**in·de·ter·mi·nate·ly**, adv.—**in·de·ter·mi·nate·ness**, **in·de·ter·mi·na·cy**, n.—**in·de·ter·mi·na·tion**, n. Want of determination; an unsettled or wavering state, as of the mind.

in·de·ter·min·ism, in″di·tẽr′mi·niz″um, n. *Philos.* the theory maintaining that not all human actions and decisions are determined or conditioned by external causes or motives. —**in·de·ter·min·ist**, n., a.—**in·de·ter·min·is·tic**, a.

in·de·vout, in″di·vout′, a. Not devout; irreligious.—**in·de·vout·ly**, adv.

in·dex, in′deks, n. pl. **in·dex·es**, **in·di·ces**, in′di·sēz″. [L. *index* (*indic-*), < *indicare*, point out, show.] An alphabetical or classified list, as one placed at the end of a book, for facilitating reference to material within the body of the text; anything used to indicate or point out, as a pointer or an indicator in a scientific instrument; the forefinger or index finger; something that serves to direct attention to a fact or condition; an indication, as: The face is an *index* of the heart. *Print.* a mark used to indicate a particular note or paragraph; also *fist*, *hand. Alg.* an exponent; *science*, a number or formula expressing some attribute, as a ratio; (*cap.*), *relig.* an official list, published by the Rom. Cath. Ch., of books condemned for objectionable religious or moral content.—*v.t.* To provide with an index, as a book; enter in an index, as a word; to serve to indicate.—**in·dex·er**, n.—**in·dex·i·cal**, in·dek′si·kal, a.

in·dex fin·ger, *n.* Forefinger.

in·dex fos·sil, *n. Geol.* the fossil of a species which was native to many areas but existed over a narrow span of time, used to establish the age of surrounding geological formations.

in·dex num·ber, *n. Statistics,* a number which indicates change in a factor, as the cost of living, from one year or reference point chosen arbitrarily to another specified time.

in·dex of re·frac·tion, *n. Opt.* the ratio of the speed of light or other form of radiation in a vacuum, or in a given medium, to its speed in a different medium. Also *refractive index.*

In·di·a, in'dē·a, *n.* A communications code word to designate the letter I.

In·di·a ink, *n.* A black pigment, consisting of lampblack mixed with a binding material and molded into sticks or cakes; a liquid ink prepared from this pigment and used in drawing and lettering. Also **Chi·nese ink.**

In·di·a·man, in'dē·a·man, *n.* pl. **In·di·a·men.** A large merchant ship, esp. a sailing vessel formerly used by the East India Company in trade with India.

In·di·an, in'dē·an, *a.* Belonging or pertaining to the American Indians or to India, a S. Asian republic, or the East Indies; pertaining to the language or languages of the American Indians.—*n.* A member of the aboriginal race of N. and S. America, excluding the Eskimos; also *American Indian, Amerindian, Red Indian.* A member of any of the native races of India or the East Indies; a European, esp. an Englishman, who resides or has resided in India or the East Indies; the language or languages of the American Indians.

In·di·an club, *n.* A bottle-shaped wooden club used in gymnastic exercises.

In·di·an corn, *n. U.S.* the maize plant, *Zea mays,* native to the Americas and cultivated extensively by the Indians, having fruits or kernels borne tightly together on an ear or cob, the forerunner of modern hybrid corn; a variety of corn with variegated colored kernels grown for ornament. *Brit.* sweet corn on the cob; corn eaten at the table. Also *maize.*

In·di·an file, *n.* A single line; single file.

In·di·an giv·er, *n. Colloq.* one who takes back a gift he has given or expects a gift in return for one.—**In·di·an giv·ing,** *n.*

In·di·an hemp, *n. Bot.* a tall, perennial, herbaceous, N. American plant of the dogbane family, *Apocynum cannabium,* having tough stem fibers, utilized by the Indians for bowstrings and nets, and yielding a milky juice used experimentally as a possible source of rubber. Also *dogbane.*

In·di·an lic·o·rice, *n.* An East Indian shrub, *Abrus precatorius,* having red and black seeds used as beads in making rosaries and the like, and roots yielding a licorice-like essence. Also **Ro·sa·ry Pea,** *jequirity.*

In·di·an meal, *n.* Corn meal.

In·di·an paint·brush, *n.* Any of various herbaceous plants in the genus *Castilleja,* of the figwort family, mostly of western U.S., attractive because of their brightly-colored yellow to red bracts which surround the flowers. Also **paint·ed cup.** See *paintbrush.*

In·di·an pipe, *n. Bot.* a parasitic or saprophytic, leafless, waxy-white, herbaceous plant, *Monotropa uniflora,* of N. Amer. and Asia, having one nodding flower, the entire plant resembling a tobacco pipe. Also **ghost plant, corpse plant.**

In·di·an pud·ding, *n.* A sweet baked pudding made with milk, molasses, and corn meal.

In·di·an red, *n.* A light-red earth pigment made from iron oxide and used as a coloring agent in watercolors, other painting media, and in cosmetics; a fine-grained

polishing agent: also synthetically derived from copperas.

In·di·an sum·mer, *n.* Unusually temperate weather during the late fall or early winter. *Fig.* a period of fruition and ease, esp. in the later years of life.

In·di·an to·bac·co, *n.* Any of three N. American herbaceous plants: *Lobelia inflata* a plant having loose spikes of light blue flowers and an inflated calyx; *Nicotiana rustica,* a tobacco cultivated by the Indians; *Antennaria plantaginifolia,* a plant having tight clusters of white to pink flowers.

In·di·an tur·nip, *n.* The jack-in-the-pulpit, *Arisaema atrorubens,* or its root.

In·di·a pa·per, *n.* A thin, soft, buff or cream-colored, absorbent paper, made chiefly in China and Japan and used for the first or finest impressions of engravings; a thin, tough, opaque printing paper, used for Bibles and prayer books.

In·di·a rub·ber, *n.* Caoutchouc, a highly elastic substance obtained from the latex or milky juice of tropical plants, as *Hevea brasiliensis,* the treated product used for making elastic bands and erasers; *(l.c.)* anything made of rubber. See *rubber.*

In·dic, in'dik, *a.* Of or pertaining to India; Indian; relating to Indian cultural life, customs, and languages.—*n.* A comprehensive term indicating the many divisions of modern, as well as ancient, Indo-European languages, including Sanskrit and Hindi.

in·di·can, in'di·kan, *n.* [< *indigo.*] *Chem.* a glucoside occurring in the leaves of the indigo plants, *Indigofera tinctoria* and *I. suffruticosa,* and yielding the commercial indigo dye.

in·di·cant, in'di·kant, *n.* That which indicates.

in·di·cate, in'di·kāt", *v.t.*—*indicated, indicating.* [L. *indico, indicatum, index, indicis.*] To point out; to suggest; to show or signify, as a symptom; to imply; to express briefly.—**in·di·ca·tion,** in"di·kā'shan, *n.*

in·dic·a·tive, in·dik'a·tiv, *a.* [L.L. *indicativus.*] Serving to indicate; pointing out. *Gram.* stating or expressing something actual, not merely possible or desirable, as a mood of the verb used in stating or questioning an objective fact.—*n.* A verb in the indicative mood.—**in·dic·a·tive·ly,** *adv.*

in·di·ca·tor, in'di·kā"tĕr, *n.* One who or that which indicates; a device for pointing, as a needle pointer on an instrument; an instrument for recording the pressure of steam in the cylinder of an engine; a speedometer; a device which makes information available, but in which there is no provision for storage of such information; as, a radar *indicator*; a recording instrument of various kinds. *Chem.* a substance which shows visually the presence or conditions of the constituents.—**in·dic·a·to·ry,** in·dik'-a·tŏr"ē, in·dik'a·tär"ē, in'di·ka·tŏr"ē, in'-dik·a·tär"ē, *a.*

in·di·ci·a, in·dish'ē·a, *n. pl.* [L., pl. of *indicium,* < *index.*] Indications; signs, tokens, or symptoms, esp. printed markings on envelopes to replace stamps in sending bulk mail.—**in·di·cial,** in·dish'al, *a.*

in·dict, in·dīt', *v.t.* [O.Fr. *inditer, indicter,* < L. *indico, indictum,* to declare publicly—*in-,* and *dico,* to say, to speak.] *Law,* to accuse or charge with a crime or misdemeanor in due form of law; to accuse of an offense.—**in·dict·a·ble,** in·dī'ta·bl, *a.* —**in·dict·er,** in·dict·or, *n.*—**in·dict·ment,** *n. Law,* a formal accusation or charge against a person. Any accusation.

in·dic·tion, in·dik'shan, *n.* [L. *indictio(n-),* < *indicere,* declare, appoint.] The recurring fiscal period of 15 years in the ancient Roman Empire, at the beginning of which time property was assessed and its value fixed for taxation; a tax based on such

valuation; the 15-year cycle; a specified year in this period.

in·dif·fer·ence, in·dif'ĕr·ens, in·dif'rens, *n.* Want of interest or concern; apathy; unimportance; as, a matter of complete *indifference* to us; mediocre quality.

in·dif·fer·ent, in·dif'ĕr·ent, in·dif'rent, *a.* [L. *indifferens, indifferentis.*] Without interest or concern; not caring; apathetic; not making a difference either way; of no significance; mediocre; neither good nor bad; impartial or unbiased; *biol.* not differentiated.—**in·dif·fer·ent·ism,** *n.* Systematic indifference, esp. the belief that differences in religion are unimportant.—**in·dif·fer·ent·ist,** *n.*—**in·dif·fer·ent·ly,** *adv.*

in·di·gence, in'di·jens, *n.* The condition of being indigent; privation; poverty.

in·di·gene, in'di·jĕn", *n.* [L. *indigena.*] One originating from a particular country or region; a native animal or plant.

in·dig·e·nous, in·dij'e·nus, *a.* Originating or produced in a country or region; innate; natural; native.—**in·dig·e·nous·ly,** *adv.*—**in·dig·e·nous·ness,** *n.*

in·di·gent, in'di·jent, *a.* [L. *indigens, indigentis,* < *indigeo,* to want—*ind-,* a form of *in-,* and *egeo,* to be in want.] Wanting the means of subsistence; needy; impoverished; poor.—*n.*—**in·di·gent·ly,** *adv.*

in·di·gest·ed, in"di·jes'tid, in"dī·jes'tid, *a.* Not digested; shapeless or unformed; not well thought out; chaotic or disordered.

in·di·gest·i·ble, in"di·jes'ti·bl, in"dī·jes'ti·bl, *a.* Not digestible; digested with difficulty.—**in·di·gest·i·bil·i·ty, in·di·gest·i·ble·ness,** in"di·jes"ti·bil'i·tē, in"dī·jes"ti·bil'i·tē, *n.*

in·di·ges·tion, in"di·jes'chan, in"dī·jes'chan, in"di·jesh'chan, in"dī·jesh'chan, *n.* Incapability of or difficulty in digesting food; dyspepsia.—**in·di·ges·tive,** in"di·jes'tiv, in"dī·jes'tiv, *a.*

in·dig·nant, in·dig'nant, *a.* [L. *indignans, indignantis,* ppr. of *indignor,* to consider as unworthy; to disdain.] Exhibiting displeasure or outrage at what seems unjust, unworthy, or base.—**in·dig·nant·ly,** *adv.*

in·dig·na·tion, in"dig·nā'shan, *n.* [L. *indignatio, indignationis.*] Displeasure at what seems unworthy or base; anger, mingled with contempt, disgust, or abhorrence; righteous scorn.

in·dig·ni·ty, in·dig'ni·tē, *n. pl.* **in·dig·ni·ties.** [L. *indignitas.*] Any act which shows contempt for a person, does injury to his dignity, or is humiliating; an insult; an outrage.

in·di·go, in'di·gō", *n. pl.* **in·di·gos, in·di·goes.** [Sp. and It. *indigo,* < L. *indicum,* indigo, < *Indicus,* Indian, India.] A deep violet blue; any of several blue dyes, now usu. synthesized from hydrocarbons, but orig. obtained from various plants, genus *Indigofera,* native to the Indies.—**in·di·goid,** in'di·goid", *a.* Referring to a class of dyes, similar in structure to indigo.—*n.*

in·di·go blue, *n.* The color indigo. A dark-blue powder, $C_{16}H_{10}N_2O_2$, crystalline in structure and having a copper luster which is the coloring principle of indigo and can be synthesized; also *indigotin.*

in·di·go bunt·ing, *n.* A small bird, *Passerina cyanea* of N. America, so named for the indigo coloring of the male. Also **in·di·go bird, in·di·go finch.**

in·di·go snake, *n.* A nonpoisonous, deep blue snake of the southern U.S., *Drymarchon corais,* which attacks small animals in their burrows. Also *gopher snake.*

in·dig·o·tin, in·dig'o·tin, in"di·gōt'in, *n.* See *indigo blue.*

in·di·rect, in"di·rekt', in"dī·rekt', *a.* Not direct; deviating from a direct line or course; circuitous; not open and straightforward; underhanded; deceitful.—**in·di·rec·tion,** *n.* Roundabout methods; deceit.—**in·di·rect·ly,** *adv.*—**in·di·rect·ness,** *n.*

in·di·rect light·ing, *n.* A type of illumination in which the light emitted is diffused and reflected, usu. by a ceiling surface, to minimize glare and shadows.

in·di·rect ob·ject, *n. Gram.* a word that usu. follows a verb of telling, asking, or giving, and indicates the receptor, as: Bake me a cake.

in·di·rect pri·ma·ry, *n. Polit.* an election in which delegates to a convention are chosen by party members; the convention selecting the party's candidates.

in·di·rect tax, *n.* A tax which is ultimately paid for by another, as a customs duty which results in higher consumer prices.

in·dis·cern·i·ble, in″di·sèr′ni·bl, in″di·zèr′ni·bl, *a.* Not discernible; imperceptible; barely recognizable.—**in·dis·cern·i·ble·ness, in·dis·cern·i·bil·i·ty,** in″di·sèr″ni·bil′i·tē, in″di·zèr″ni·bil′i·tē, *n.*—**in·dis·cern·i·bly,** *adv.*

in·dis·cov·er·a·ble, in″di·skuv′er·a·bl, *a.* Incapable of being discovered; undiscoverable.

in·dis·creet, in″di·skrēt′, *a.* Not discreet; lacking sound judgment or discretion; injudicious; imprudent.—**in·dis·creet·ly,** *adv.*—**in·dis·creet·ness,** *n.*

in·dis·crete, in″di·skrēt′, in·dis′krēt, *a.* [L. *indiscretus.*] Not discrete; not consisting of distinct parts.

in·dis·cre·tion, in″di·skresh′an, *n.* The condition or quality of being indiscreet; want of discretion; an indiscreet act; an ill-judged act; an imprudence.

in·dis·crim·i·nate, in″di·skrim′i·nit, *a.* Not discriminate; selecting in a random manner; without making a distinction; lacking perception; confused; promiscuous.—**in·dis·crim·i·nate·ly,** *adv.*—**in·dis·crim·i·nate·ness,** *n.*—**in·dis·crim·i·nat·ing,** in″di·skrim′i·nā″ting, *a.*—**in·dis·crim·i·na·tion,** in″di·skrim′i·nā′shan, *n.*

in·dis·pen·sa·ble, in″di·spen′sa·bl, *a.* Not dispensable; unable to be foregone; absolutely necessary; essential.—**in·dis·pen·sa·bil·i·ty, in·dis·pen·sa·ble·ness,** in″di·spen″sa·bil′i·tē, *n.*—**in·dis·pen·sa·bly,** *adv.*

in·dis·pose, in″di·spōz′, *v.t.*—*indisposed, indisposing.* [Fr. *indisposer.*] To render averse; to disincline; to make unwilling; to render unfit or ill-suited; to disqualify; to cause to become sick.—**in·dis·posed,** *a.* Mildly ill; unwilling.—**in·dis·po·si·tion,** in″dis·po·zish′an, *n.*

in·dis·put·a·ble, in″di·spū′ta·bl, in·dis′pū·ta·bl, *a.* Incapable of being disputed; incontrovertible; incontestable.—**in·dis·put·a·bil·i·ty, in·dis·put·a·ble·ness,** in″di·spū″ta·bil′i·tē, *n.*—**in·dis·put·a·bly,** *adv.*

in·dis·sol·u·ble, in″di·sol′ū·bl, *a.* Not capable of being dissolved or decomposed; not capable of being broken or rightfully violated; perpetullay binding or obligatory; firm; stable.—**in·dis·sol·u·bil·i·ty, in·dis·sol·u·ble·ness,** in″di·sol″ū·bil′i·tē, *n.*—**in·dis·sol·u·bly,** *adv.*

in·dis·tinct, in″di·stingkt′, *a.* [L. *indistinctus.*] Not distinct; not readily distinguishable; blurred; obscure to the mind; not clear; confused; imperfect or dim; as, *indistinct* vision.—**in·dis·tinct·ly,** *adv.*—**in·dis·tinct·ness,** *n.*

in·dis·tinc·tive, in″di·stingk′tiv, *a.* Not distinctive; without distinctive character or characteristics; vague.—**in·dis·tinc·tive·ly,** *adv.*—**in·dis·tinc·tive·ness,** *n.*

in·dis·tin·guish·a·ble, in″di·sting′gwi·sha·bl, *a.* Incapable of being distinguished; unidentifiable.—**in·dis·tin·guish·a·ble·ness,** *n.*—**in·dis·tin·guish·a·bly,** *adv.*

in·dite, in·dīt′, *v.t.*—*indited, inditing.* [O.Fr. *inditer.*] To compose or write.—**in·dite·ment,** *n.*—**in·dit·er,** *n.*

in·di·um, in′dē·um, *n.* [< the *indigo* lines

in its spectrum.] *Chem.* a rare metallic element, silver-white, malleable, and easily fusible, found in sphalerite and various ores. Sym. In, at. no. 49, at. wt. 114.82. See Periodic Table of Elements.

in·di·vid·u·al, in″di·vij′ö·al, *a.* [Fr. *individuel,* L. *individuus,* indivisible—*in-,* not, and *dividuus,* divisible.] Subsisting as one indivisible entity or distinct being; single; pertaining to one only; peculiar to or characteristic of a particular person or thing; marked by special qualities or distinctive characteristics.—*n.* A being or thing forming one of its kind; a single person, animal, or thing, as distinct from a group; a particular person; an entity.—**in·di·vid·u·al·ly,** *adv.*

in·di·vid·u·al·ism, in″di·vij′ö·a·liz″um, *n.* A social theory advocating the liberty, rights, or independent action of the individual; the principle or habit of individual or independent thought or action; the pursuit of individual rather than common or collective interests; egoism; self-interest; individual character; individuality.

in·di·vid·u·al·ist, in″di·vij′ö·a·list, *n.* A person who is markedly independent in thought and action; an advocate of individualism.—**in·di·vid·u·al·is·tic,** in″di·vij″ö·a·lis′tik, *a.*—**in·di·vid·u·al·is·ti·cal·ly,** *adv.*

in·di·vid·u·al·i·ty, in″di·vij″ö·al′i·tē, *n.* pl. **in·di·vid·u·al·i·ties.** The condition of having a distinct and separate existence; a distinctive or independent character; the sum of the characteristics or traits peculiar to an individual.

in·di·vid·u·al·ize, in″di·vij′ö·a·līz″, *v.t.* —*individualized, individualizing.* To mark as an individual; to distinguish by peculiar or distinctive characteristics; to treat as an individual.—**in·di·vid·u·al·i·za·tion,** *n.*

in·di·vid·u·a·tion, in″di·vij″ö·ā′shan, *n.* Individual existence; individuality; the act or state of being individuated. *Philos.* the particularization of the individual from the whole. *Zool.* the emergence of specific units in a compound organism.—**in·di·vid·u·ate,** in″di·vij′ö·āt′, *v.t.*—*individuated, individuating.* To form into a single, distinct entity.

in·di·vis·i·ble, in″di·viz′i·bl, *a.* Not divisible; not separable into parts.—*n.*—**in·di·vis·i·bil·i·ty, in·di·vis·i·ble·ness,** in″di·viz″i·bil′i·tē, *n.*—**in·di·vis·i·bly,** *adv.*

In·do-Ar·y·an, in′dō·âr′ē·an, in′dō·âr′yan, in′dō·ar′ē·an, in″dō·ar′yan, in″dō·är′yan, *a.* Referring to or typical of Indo-Aryans: Asian Indians who speak an Indo-European language and have mainly Caucasoid physical attributes.—*n.*

In·do-Chi·nese, in′dō·chī·nēz′, in′dō·chī·nēs′, *a.* Of or pertaining to Indochina, the southeastern peninsula of Asia; designating the peoples or the languages of Indochina; pertaining to the language family comprising these, the Tibetan, and the Chinese groups of languages.—*n. pl.* **In·do-Chi·nese.**

in·doc·ile, in·dos′il, *a.* [L. *indocilis,* unteachable.] Not docile or teachable; difficult to control or train.—**in·do·cil·i·ty,** in″dō·sil′i·tē, *n.*

in·doc·tri·nate, in·dok′tri·nāt″, *v.t.*—*indoctrinated, indoctrinating.* To instruct in any doctrine; to imbue with certain, usu. partisan, principles; to inculcate.—**in·doc·tri·na·tion,** *n.*—**in·doc·tri·na·tor,** *n.*

In·do-Eu·ro·pe·an, in′dō·ūr″o·pē′an, *a.* Referring to the largest language family, made up of most languages spoken in Europe and in countries colonized by Europeans, also including Sanskrit and the related languages of India and Persia.—*n.*

In·do-Ger·man·ic, in′dō·jẻr·man′ik, *a., n.* Indo-European.

In·do-Hit·tite, in′dō·hit′īt, *a.* Referring to a family of languages which includes the Indo-European and Anatolian groups; pertaining to the theoretic parent language of Anatolian and Indo-European.—*n.*

In·do-I·ra·ni·an, in′dō·i·rä′nē·an, *a.* Referring to a subdivision of the Indo-European language family including Indic and Iranian groups of languages.—*n.*

in·dole, in′dōl, *n.* [< *indigo.*] *Chem.* a white or yellow crystalline compound, C_8H_7N, produced in the intestines as a decomposition of protein, or obtained from indigo or coal tar and used in perfumery and medicine, and as a flavoring agent and chemical reagent. Also **in·dol.**

in·dole·a·ce·tic ac·id, in′dōl·a·sē′tik as′id, in′dōl·a·set′ik as′id, in″dōl·a·sē′tik as′id, in″dōl·a·set′ik as′id, *n. Chem.* one of the most important plant auxins, $C_8H_6NCH_2COOH$: used to promote rooting and growth of plants.

in·dole·bu·tyr·ic ac·id, in′dōl·bū·tir′ik as′id, in″dōl·bū·tir′ik as′id, *n. Chem.* a plant auxin, $C_{10}H_{10}NCH_2COOH$, similar to indoleacetic acid.

in·do·lent, in′do·lent, *a.* [Fr. *indolent.*] Habitually idle or indisposed to labor; lazy; sluggish; *med.* causing little or no pain; as, an *indolent* tumor.—**in·do·lence,** in′do·lens, *n.* Sloth; laziness.—**in·do·lent·ly,** *adv.*

in·dom·i·ta·ble, in·dom′i·ta·bl, *a.* Not to be tamed or subdued; unconquerable; unyielding.—**in·dom·i·ta·bil·i·ty, in·dom·i·ta·ble·ness,** in·dom″i·ta·bil′i·tē, *n.*—**in·dom·i·ta·bly,** *adv.*

In·do·ne·sian, in″do·nē′zhan, in″do·nē′shan, in″do·nē′zē·an, in″dō·nē′zhan, in″dō·nē′shan, in″dō·nē′zē·an, *a.* [Gr. *indos,* Indian, and *nesos,* island.] Of or pertaining to the Malay Archipelago or Indonesia.—*n.* An inhabitant of the Malay Archipelago, the Philippines, or the Republic of Indonesia; the language of these peoples.

in·door, in′dōr′, in·dōr′, *a.* Occurring, used, or belonging in a house or building, rather than out-of-doors; as, *indoor* amusements; referring to the interior of a house or building.—**in·doors,** in·dōrz′, in·darz′, *adv.* In or into a house or building.

in·do·phe·nol, in″dō·fē′nōl, in″dō·fē′nol, *n.* Any of a series of quinone-derived dyes resembling indigo in appearance.

in·dorse, in·dars′, *v.t.* Endorse.

in·dox·yl, in·dok′sil, *n. Chem.* a compound, C_8H_7NO, used to synthesize indigo.

in·draft, *Brit.* **in·draught,** in′draft″, in′dräft″, *n.* A pulling or drawing inward; an inward current or stream, as of water or air.

in·drawn, in′dran″, *a.* Drawn in, as a breath; preoccupied, reserved or introspective.—**in·draw·al,** *n.*—**in·draw·ing,** *a.*

in·du·bi·ta·ble, in·dö′bi·ta·bl, in·dū′bi·ta·bl, *a.* [L. *indubitabilis.*] Certain; too obvious to admit of doubt; unquestionable.—**in·du·bi·ta·ble·ness, in·du·bi·ta·bil·i·ty,** in·dō″bi·ta·bil′i·tē, in·dū″bi·ta·bil′i·tē, *n.*—**in·du·bi·ta·bly,** *adv.*

in·duce, in·dös′, in·dūs′, *v.t.*—*induced, inducing.* [L. *induco, inductum.*] To lead or prevail on by persuasion or argument; to bring on, produce, or cause; as, to *induce* labor in a pregnant woman. *Logic,* to reason by inference from particulars. *Phys.* to produce by induction, as electric current.—**in·duce·ment,** *n.* The act of inducing; a motive or incentive.—**in·duc·er,** *n.*—**in·duc·i·ble,** *a.*

in·duct, in·dukt′, *v.t.* [L. *induco, inductum.*] To introduce; to initiate; to bring in as a member; to install, as in a benefice or office; to call into military service, as a draftee.—**in·duct·ee,** *n.*

in·duct·ance, in·duk′tans, *n. Elect.* the property of an electric circuit, or two neighboring circuits, by which an electromotive force is produced in one of them by a change of current in either circuit.

in·duc·tile, in·duk'til, a. Not ductile; not malleable or pliable; unyielding.—**in·duc·til·i·ty**, in"duk·til'i·tē, n.

in·duc·tion, in·duk'shan, n. The act of inducting; introduction or initiation; installation into office or benefice; the act of causing or bringing about; the act of presenting, as facts or evidence; *logic*, the method or result of inferring a general principle or conclusion from particular facts; *phys*. the property by which one body, having electrical or magnetic polarity, induces electromotive, electrostatic or magnetic force in another body without direct contact; *math*. proof of a property of a given set of numbers by proving it true of the first integer and assuming that if it is true of all preceding integers, it must also be true of the integer in question; *embryol*. the influence of an embryonic cell on the differentiation process of other embryonic cells. An introduction to a literary work; *archaic*, a preface.

in·duc·tion coil, n. An electrical device in which interruptions in the direct current running through a primary coil produces an induced current of high voltage in a surrounding secondary coil.

in·duc·tive, in·duk'tiv, a. Inducing; bringing about or leading; introductory; *elect*. referring to, involving, or producing induction; operating by induction; *embryol*. pertaining to the interaction between an embryonic cell and adjacent inductive cells.—**in·duc·tive rea·son·ing**, *logic*, reasoning by inference from particulars.—**in·duc·tive·ly**, adv.—**in·duc·tive·ness**, n.—**in·duc·tor**, in·duk'tẽr, n.

in·due, in·dū', in·dū', v.t. Endue.

in·dulge, in·dulj', v.t.—indulged, indulging. [L. *indulgere* (ppr. *indultus*), be kind, yield, grant.] To yield to or gratify the wishes or whims of; to humor; to satisfy as a personal inclination, followed by *in*; as, to *indulge* oneself *in* overeating; to grant special privileges to in matters of religion; *com*. to grant, as an extension of time for payment or performance.—v.i. To indulge oneself; to yield to an inclination or impulse, often followed by *in*; as, to *indulge in* a sneer.—**in·dul·ger**, n.—**in·dulg·ing·ly**, adv.

in·dul·gence, in·dul'jens, n. [L. *indulgentia*.] The act or practice of indulging; that which is indulged in; *Rom. Cath. Ch.* a remission of the temporal punishment still due for sin after sacramental absolution; *com*. the granting of an extension of time for payment or performance. Also **in·dul·gen·cy**, n. pl. **in·dul·gen·cies**.—v.t. indulgenced, indulgencing. To confer an indulgence on.—**in·dul·gent**, a. Characterized by or inclined toward indulgence; permissive, as a parent.—**in·dul·gent·ly**, adv.

in·du·line, in'dū·lēn", in'dū·lin, in'du·lēn", n. [< *indigo*.] One of a large series of synthetic aniline dyes yielding blue to purple colors similar to true indigo.

in·dult, in·dult', n. [L.L. *indultum*, indulgence, permission, favor, prop. neut. of L. *indultus*, pp. of *indulgēre*.] *Rom. Cath. Ch.* a favor from the Holy See, a local bishop, or other ecclesiastical superior, granting some privilege not authorized by the common law of the church.

in·du·pli·cate, in·dö'pli·kit, in·dö'pli·kāt", in·dū'pli·kit, in·dū'pli·kāt", a. *Bot*. having the edges bent or rolled inward, as petals or leaves in a bud. Also **in·du·pli·ca·tive**.—**in·du·pli·ca·tion**, n.

in·du·rate, in'dụ·rāt", in'dū·rāt", v.i. indurated, indurating. [L. *induro, induratum*.] To grow or become hard.—v.t. To make hard; to harden; to make unfeeling or stubborn; to make hardy; to accustom; to establish firmly.—in'dū·rit, in'dū·rit, in·dụr'it, in·dūr'it, a. Hardened; callous or

stubborn. Also **in·du·rated**.—**in·du·ra·tion**, n.—**in·du·ra·tive**, a.

in·du·si·um, in·dō'zē·um, in·dö'zhē·um, in·dū'zē·um, in·dū'zhē·um, n. pl. **in·du·si·a**, in·dö'zē·a, in·dö'zhē·a, in·dū'zē·a, in·dū'zhē·a. [L. a woman's undergarment, < *induo*, to put on.] *Bot*. the covering of the capsules or spore cases in ferns; *zool*. the case or covering of a larva; *anat*. the amnion or enclosing membrane.—**in·du·si·al**, a.

in·dus·tri·al, in·dus'trē·al, a. [M.L. *industrialis*.] Characteristic of, referring to, or resulting from industry or productive labor; engaged in or connected with industries; having many well-developed industries; pertaining to those who work in industries; noting to a form of life insurance for the working classes, with inexpensive policies and weekly premiums.—n. A worker in some industry, esp. manufacturing; a company involved in industrial production; *pl*. the stocks and bonds of industrial enterprises.—**in·dus·tri·al·ly**, adv.—**in·dus·tri·al·ness**, n.

in·dus·tri·al arts, n. pl. but sing. in constr. A course of study, taught in technical and secondary schools, which trains students in such technical skills as the use of tools and machinery.

in·dus·tri·al·ism, in·dus'trē·a·liz"um, n. An economic system in which industrial interests predominate, as opposed to the interests of agriculture or foreign trade.

in·dus·tri·al·ize, in·dus'trē·a·līz", v.t.—industrialized, industrializing. To organize large industries in; as, to *industrialize* the South; to introduce the economic system of industrialism into; as, to *industrialize* a new nation.—v.i. To become industrialized.—**in·dus·tri·al·i·za·tion**, n.

in·dus·tri·al school, n. A school for teaching one or more branches of industry; a school for educating neglected children committed to its care and training them in some form of industry.

in·dus·tri·al un·ion, n. A labor union with membership open to all workers in an industry, regardless of occupation, skill, or craft; a vertical union, as opposed to *craft union*.

in·dus·tri·ous, in·dus'trē·us, a. [L. *industrius*, < *indu*, old form of *in*, and *struo*, to fabricate.] Characterized by industry; diligent in business or study; hardworking.—**in·dus·tri·ous·ly**, adv.

in·dus·try, in'du·strē, n. pl. **in·dus·tries**. [L. *industria*, < *industrius*.] Trade or manufacturing in general; specif. that concerned with a particular business; as, the automobile *industry*, the steel *industry*; diligence in employment; steady attention to work or business; assiduity.—**in·dus·tri·al·ist**, n. A person who manages or owns an industry.

in·dwell, in·dwel', v.t.—indwelt, indwelling. To exist or abide within, as an evil spirit; to occupy.—v.i. To reside or exist within someplace.—**in·dwel·ler**, n.

in·e·bri·ant, in·ē'brē·ant, i·nē'brē·ant, n. [L. *inebrians, inebriantis*, ppr. of *inebrio*.] Anything that intoxicates.—a.

in·e·bri·ate, in·ē'brē·āt", i·nē'brē·āt", v.t.—inebriated, inebriating. [L. *inebrio, inebriatum*—*in-*, intens., and *ebrio*, to intoxicate, < *ebrius*, drunk.] To make drunk; intoxicate; to excite or confuse.—n. A habitual drunkard.—a. Also **in·e·bri·at·ed**.—**in·e·bri·a·tion**, in·e·bri·e·ty, in"i·brī'i·tē, n. Drunkenness; intoxication.

in·ed·i·ble, in·ed'i·bl, a. Not edible; unsuitable for eating; not useful as food.

in·ed·it·ed, in·ed'i·tid, a. Not edited; unpublished; published without changes; unabridged.

in·ed·u·ca·ble, in·ej'ụ·ka·bl, in·ed'ū·ka·bl, a. Not educable; incapable of being educated.

in·ef·fa·ble, in·ef'a·bl, a. [L. *ineffabilis*.] Incapable of being expressed in words; unutterable; unspeakable; indefinable; too holy or lofty to be spoken.—**in·ef·fa·bil·i·ty**, in·ef·fa·ble·ness, n.—**in·ef·fa·bly**, adv.

in·ef·face·a·ble, in"i·fā'sa·bl, a. Incapable of being effaced; difficult or impossible to eradicate or erase; ineradicable.—**in·ef·face·a·bil·i·ty**, in"i·fā"sa·bil'i·tē, n.—**in·ef·face·a·bly**, adv.

in·ef·fec·tive, in"i·fek'tiv, a. Not producing desired or required results; incompetent; inefficient.—**in·ef·fec·tive·ly**, adv.—**in·ef·fec·tive·ness**, n.

in·ef·fec·tu·al, in"i·fek'chö·al, a. Not effectual; unable or unwilling to produce a required or desired result; fruitless; futile.—**in·ef·fec·tu·al·i·ty**, in·ef·fec·tu·al·ness, n.—**in·ef·fec·tu·al·ly**, adv.

in·ef·fi·ca·cious, in"ef·i·kā'shus, a. Not efficacious; of inadequate force, power, or means to produce an intended effect, as a medicine.—**in·ef·fi·ca·cious·ly**, adv.—**in·ef·fi·ca·cious·ness**, in·ef·fi·cac·i·ty, in"ef·i·kas'i·tē, n.

in·ef·fi·ca·cy, in·ef'i·ka·sē, n. Lack of the means, power, or force to achieve required or desired results; ineffectiveness.

in·ef·fi·cient, in"i·fish'ent, a. Lacking competence; not effecting required or desired results economically; functioning in a wasteful or profitless manner, usu. characterized by a misuse of time and materials.—**in·ef·fi·cien·cy**, n. pl. **in·ef·fi·cien·cies**.—**in·ef·fi·cient·ly**, adv.

in·e·las·tic, in"i·las'tik, a. Not elastic; unyielding; inflexible; unadaptable.—**in·e·las·tic·i·ty**, in"i·la·stis'i·tē, n.

in·el·e·gant, in·el'e·gant, a. [L. *inelegans* (-ant-).] Not elegant; not in accordance with good taste; unrefined; crude; vulgar.—**in·el·e·gance**, in·el·e·gan·cy, n. pl. **in·el·e·gan·ces**.—**in·el·e·gant·ly**, adv.

in·el·i·gi·ble, in·el'i·ji·bl, a. Not eligible; not qualified or fit to be elected or adopted; not worthy of being chosen or preferred.—**in·el·i·gi·bil·i·ty**, in·el'i·ji·bil'i·tē, n.—**in·el·i·gi·bly**, adv.

in·el·o·quent, in·el'o·kwent, a. Not eloquent; not apt, fluent, or persuasive in speech or writing.—**in·el·o·quence**, n.—**in·el·o·quent·ly**, adv.

in·e·luc·ta·ble, in"i·luk'ta·bl, a. [L. *ineluctabilis*.] That cannot be escaped from or avoided; inevitable.—**in·e·luc·ta·bil·i·ty**, n.—**in·e·luc·ta·bly**, adv.

in·e·lud·i·ble, in"i·lö'di·bl, a. Not eludible; inescapable.—**in·e·lud·i·bil·i·ty**, n.—**in·e·lud·i·bly**, adv.

in·e·nar·ra·ble, in"i·nar'a·bl, a. Indescribable; not narratable.

in·ept, in·ept', i·nept', a. [L. *ineptus*.] Not apt or suitable; inappropriate; absurd or foolish; incompetent, awkward, or inefficient.—**in·ept·i·tude**, in·ep'ti·töd", in·ep'ti·tūd", i·nep'ti·töd", i·nep'ti·tūd", n.—**in·ept·ly**, adv.—**in·ept·ness**, n.

in·e·qual·i·ty, in"i·kwol'i·tē, n. pl. **in·e·qual·i·ties**. [L. *inæqualitas*, < *inæqualis*, unequal.] The condition of being unequal; disparity; lack of proportion, as in distribution; unevenness, as of surface; injustice or social disparity in power and privilege. *Math*. an expression of two unequal quantities connected by either of the signs of inequality, > or <; as, $a > b$, 'a is greater than b'; $a < b$, 'a is less than b.'

in·eq·ui·ta·ble, in·ek'wi·ta·bl, a. Not equitable; not just or fair.—**in·eq·ui·ta·bly**, adv.—**in·eq·ui·ty**, n. pl. **in·eq·ui·ties**.

in·e·qui·valve, in·ē'kwi·valv", a. Having valves unequal in form or size, as in some bivalve mollusks.

in·e·rad·i·ca·ble, in"i·rad'i·ka·bl, a. Not eradicable; that cannot be rooted out or removed.—**in·e·rad·i·ca·bly**, adv.

in·er·ra·ble, in·er′a·bl, in·ur′a·bl, a. [L. *inerrabilis*.] Incapable of erring; infallible.—**in·er·ra·bil·i·ty**, n.—**in·er·ra·bly**, adv.

in·er·rant, in·er′ant, in·ur′ant, a. [L. *inerrans* (-ant-), < *in-*, not, and *errans*, ppr. of *errare*, wander, err.] Not erring; free from error.—**in·er·ran·cy**, n.—**in·er·rant·ly**, adv.

in·ert, in·urt′, i·nurt′, a. [L. *iners* (inert-), unskilled, idle, inert.] Having no inherent power of action, motion, or resistance; as, *inert* matter; inactive, inanimate, or without life; *pharm.* without active properties, as a drug; *chem.* not likely or not able to react chemically to form compounds. Of an inactive or sluggish habit or nature.—**in·ert·ly**, adv.—**in·ert·ness**, n.

in·er·tia, in·ur′sha, i·nur′sha, n. [L.] Passiveness; inactivity; sluggishness; *phys.* the property of matter by which it retains its state of rest or of uniform rectilinear motion so long as no external cause acts to change that state.—**in·er·tial**, a.

in·er·tial guid·ance, n. *Aeron.* an automatic system of navigation for aircraft, missiles, and space vehicles; instruments independent of outside control which note and interpret data and automatically adjust to maintain a predetermined flight path. Also **in·er·tial guid·ance sys·tem**.

in·es·cap·a·ble, in″e·skā′pa·bl, a. That cannot be escaped; unavoidable.

in·es·sen·tial, in″i·sen′shal, a. Not essential; not necessary; unsubstantial or immaterial.

in·es·ti·ma·ble, in·es′ti·ma·bl, a. [L. *inæstimabilis*.] Incapable of being estimated or computed; too valuable, great, or excellent to be rated or fully appreciated; incalculable.—**in·es·ti·ma·bly**, adv.

in·ev·i·ta·ble, in·ev′i·ta·bl, a. [L. *inevitabilis*.] Unavoidable; unalterable; admitting of no escape or evasion; certain to befall.—**in·ev·i·ta·bil·i·ty**, **in·ev·i·ta·ble·ness**, n.—**in·ev·i·ta·bly**, adv.

in·ex·act, in″ig·zakt′, a. Not exact; not precisely accurate or true.—**in·ex·act·i·tude**, **in·ex·act·ness**, n.—**in·ex·act·ly**, adv.

in·ex·cus·a·ble, in″ik·skū′za·bl, a. Incapable of being excused or justified; unpardonable; indefensible.—**in·ex·cus·a·bil·i·ty**, **in·ex·cus·a·ble·ness**, n.—**in·ex·cus·a·bly**, adv.

in·ex·haust·i·ble, in″ig·zas′ti·bl, a. Not exhaustible; incapable of being exhausted or spent; unfailing; tireless.—**in·ex·haust·i·bil·i·ty**, **in·ex·haust·i·ble·ness**, n.—**in·ex·haust·i·bly**, adv.

in·ex·ist·ence, in″ig·zis′tens, n. Absence of existence; nonexistence.—**in·ex·ist·ent**, a. Not existent; having no existence.

in·ex·o·ra·ble, in·ek′sėr·a·bl, a. Unyielding; unbending; implacable; incapable of being moved by entreaty or prayer.—**in·ex·o·ra·bil·i·ty**, **in·ex·o·ra·ble·ness**, n.—**in·ex·o·ra·bly**, adv.

in·ex·pe·di·ent, in″ik·spē′dē·ent, a. Not expedient; inappropriate; unsuitable to time and place; not advisable.—**in·ex·pe·di·ence**, **in·ex·pe·di·en·cy**, n.—**in·ex·pe·di·ent·ly**, adv.

in·ex·pen·sive, in″ik·spen′siv, a. Not expensive; reasonably priced.—**in·ex·pen·sive·ly**, adv.—**in·ex·pen·sive·ness**, n.

in·ex·pe·ri·ence, in″ik·spēr′ē·ens, n. [L.L. *inexperientia*.] Want of experience, or of knowledge or skill gained from experience.—**in·ex·pe·ri·enced**, a.

in·ex·pert, in·eks′pėrt, a. Not expert; not skilled.—**in·ex·pert·ly**, adv.—**in·ex·pert·ness**, n.

in·ex·pi·a·ble, in·eks′pē·a·bl, a. Incapable of being expiated; not to be atoned for; unpardonable.—**in·ex·pi·a·ble·ness**, n.—**in·ex·pi·a·bly**, adv.

in·ex·plain·a·ble, in″ik·splā′na·bl, a. Inexplicable; not to be explained.

in·ex·pli·ca·ble, in·eks′pli·ka·bl, a. Incapable of being explained or interpreted; unaccountable; that cannot be disentangled; mysterious.—**in·ex·pli·ca·bil·i·ty**, **in·ex·pli·ca·ble·ness**, n.—**in·ex·pli·ca·bly**, adv.

in·ex·plic·it, in″ik·splis′it, a. Not explicit; not clearly stated; vague or general.—**in·ex·plic·it·ly**, adv.—**in·ex·plic·it·ness**, n.

in·ex·press·i·ble, in″ik·spres′i·bl, a. Not expressible; not to be uttered; unspeakable; indescribable.—**in·ex·press·i·bil·i·ty**, **in·ex·press·i·ble·ness**, n.—**in·ex·press·i·bly**, adv.

in·ex·pres·sive, in″ik·spres′iv, a. Not expressive; wanting in expression and meaning.—**in·ex·pres·sive·ly**, adv.—**in·ex·pres·sive·ness**, n.

in·ex·pug·na·ble, in″ik·spug′na·bl, a. [L. *inexpugnabilis*.] That cannot be taken by storm or overcome by force; impregnable; unconquerable.—**in·ex·pug·na·bil·i·ty**, **in·ex·pug·na·ble·ness**, n.—**in·ex·pug·na·bly**, adv.

in·ex·ten·si·ble, in″ik·sten′si·bl, a. Not capable of being extended.—**in·ex·ten·si·bil·i·ty**, **in·ex·ten·sion**, n.

in·ex·tin·guish·a·ble, in″ik·sting′gwi·sha·bl, a. Not to be extinguished, quenched, suppressed, or brought to an end; as, *inextinguishable* laughter.—**in·ex·tin·guish·a·bly**, adv.

in·ex·tri·ca·ble, in·eks′tri·ka·bl, a. [L. *inextricabilis*.] Incapable of being freed or extricated from; unsolvable; hopelessly intricate, involved or perplexing; unable to be untangled, undone, or loosed, as a knot.—**in·ex·tri·ca·bil·i·ty**, **in·ex·tri·ca·ble·ness**, n.—**in·ex·tri·ca·bly**, adv.

in·fal·li·ble, in·fal′i·bl, a. [M.L. *infallibilis*.] Not fallible; exempt from liability to error or failure; absolutely trustworthy or sure; as, an *infallible* cure; certain or indubitable. *Rom. Cath. Ch.* not liable to error on doctrines of faith or morals, as the Pope when speaking in his official capacity.—**in·fal·li·bil·i·ty**, **in·fal·li·ble·ness**, n.—**in·fal·li·bly**, adv.

in·fa·mous, in′fa·mus, a. [O.Fr. *infameux*, < M.L. *infamosus*, for L. *infamis*, infamous.] Of evil fame or repute; deserving of a bad reputation; notoriously bad or vile; scandalous; *law*, referring to a crime punishable by imprisonment in a penitentiary or state prison.—**in·fa·mous·ly**, adv.—**in·fa·mous·ness**, n.

in·fa·my, in′fa·mē, n. pl. **in·fa·mies**. [L. *infamia*, < *infamis*.] Evil or shameful notoriety, or public reproach; infamous character or behavior; an infamous act or circumstance; *law*, the loss of rights caused by conviction of an infamous offense.

in·fan·cy, in′fan·sē, n. pl. **in·fan·cies**. [L. *infantia*.] The state or period of being an infant; babyhood; early childhood; the corresponding period in the existence of anything; infants collectively; *law*, the period of life to the age of majority, generally 21 years of age; minority.

in·fant, in′fant, n. [L. *infans* (infant-), young child, *lit.* 'not speaking.'] A child during the earliest period of its life; a baby; a beginner or novice; *law*, a minor.—*a.* Being in infancy or babyhood; being in the earliest period or stage; incipient, nascent, or of recent origin; of or pertaining to infants or infancy; *law*, minor.—**in·fant·hood**, n.—**in·fant·like**, a.

in·fan·te, in·fan′tā, n. [Sp. and Pg. < L. *infans*, E. *infant*.] A royal prince of Spain or Portugal, not heir to the throne.—**in·fan·ta**, in·fan′ta, n. Fem. of infante.

in·fan·ti·cide, in·fan′ti·sīd″, n. [L. *infanticidium*, the crime, *infanticida*, the perpetrator—*infans*, and *cædo*, to kill.] The murder of an infant; the murderer of an infant.—**in·fan·ti·cid·al**, a.

in·fan·tile, in′fan·til″, in′fan·til, a. [L. *infantilis*.] Of or pertaining to infants; characteristic of or befitting an infant; babyish or childish; infantlike; being in the earliest stage of development. Also **in·fan·tine**, in′fan·tīn″, in′fan·tin.—**in·fan·til·i·ty**, n.

in·fan·tile pa·ral·y·sis, n. Poliomyelitis.

in·fan·ti·lism, in′fan·ti·liz″um, in′fan·ti·liz″um, in·fan′ti·liz″um, n. Abnormal persistence or recurrence of childish characteristics, physical, emotional, or mental, in an adult, often accompanied by a failure to mature sexually; a lack of mature emotional development.

in·fan·try, in′fan·trē, n. pl. **in·fan·tries**. [Fr. *infanterie*, < It. *infanteria*, < *infante*, infant, youth, foot soldier, < L. *infans*. Troops regularly serving on foot and carrying small arms, esp. rifles; a military unit composed of such men.—**in·fan·try·man**, in′fan·trē·man, n. pl. **in·fan·try·men**. A soldier of the infantry; a foot soldier.

in·farct, in·färkt′, n. [L. *infarctus*, *infartus*, pp. of *infarcire*, stuff in, < *in-*, in, and *farcire*, stuff.] *Pathol.* a dying portion of tissue whose blood supply has been cut off by the presence of an obstruction, usu. an embolus.—**in·farct·ed**, a.—**in·farc·tion**, n.

in·fat·u·ate, in·fach′ū·āt″, v.t.—*infatuated*, *infatuating*. [L. *infatuatus*, pp. of *infatuare*, < *in-*, in, and *fatuus*, foolish, E. *fatuous*.] To inspire or possess with a foolish, irrational, or blind passion, as of love, admiration, enthusiasm; as, to be *infatuated* with a girl, or with an idea.—**in·fat·u·at·ed**, a.—**in·fat·u·at·ed·ly**, adv.—**in·fat·u·a·tion**, in·fach″ū·ā·shan, n.

in·fea·si·ble, in·fē′zi·bl, a. Not feasible; impracticable.—**in·fea·si·bil·i·ty**, **in·fea·si·ble·ness**, n.

in·fect, in·fekt′, v.t. [L. *infectus*, pp. of *inficere*, put in, dye, imbue, infect.] To affect, infuse, or contaminate with disease-producing germs, as a person or wound; to taint or pollute; to corrupt, to affect morally; to inspire; to influence; to imbue with an opinion, attitude, or belief.—*a.*—**in·fect·ed·ness**, n.—**in·fect·er**, **in·fec·tor**, n.

in·fec·tion, in·fek′shan, n. [L.L. *infectio*(n-).] The penetration of body tissue by disease-producing organisms; a disease or injury resulting from pathogenic organisms; the area affected by the injurious organisms; an epidemic. Transmission of ideas and impulses; moral contamination.

in·fec·tious, in·fek′shus, a. Causing or carrying infection; communicable by infection, as diseases; tending to spread from one to another, as feelings or actions; contagious; catching.—**in·fec·tious·ly**, adv.—**in·fec·tious·ness**, n.—**in·fec·tive**, a.

in·fec·tious hep·a·ti·tis, n. *Pathol.* an acute liver inflammation caused by a virus and marked by jaundice, nausea, and abdominal pain.

in·fec·tious mon·o·nu·cle·o·sis, n. *Pathol.* an acute, contagious, viral disease in which fever and sore throat occur, the lymph nodes enlarge, and mononuclear white blood cells increase abnormally in number. Also **glan·du·lar fe·ver**.

in·fe·cund, in·fē′kund, in·fek′und, a. [Prefix *in-*, not, and *fecund*; L. *infecundus*.] Not fecund; unfruitful; barren.—**in·fe·cun·di·ty**, in″fi·kun′di·tē, n.

in·fe·lic·i·ty, in″fe·lis′i·tē, n. pl. **in·fe·lic·i·ties**. [L. *infelicitas*, < *infelix*, unhappy.] The state of being unhappy; ill fortune; an unfortunate circumstance; inaptness or inappropriateness, as of expression or style.—**in·fe·lic·i·tous**, a. Inappropriate; not fortunate or happy.—**in·fe·lic·i·tous·ly**, adv.

in·fer, in·fụr′, v.t.—**inferred, inferring.** [L. *inferre* (pp. *illatus*), to bring in or on, infer.] To derive by reasoning; to conclude or judge from premises or evidence; as, to *infer* a conclusion; to deduce; to indicate as a conclusion, or imply.—v.i. To draw a conclusion, as by reasoning.—**in·fer·a·ble, in·fer·i·ble, in·fer·ri·ble,** a.—**in·fer·a·bly,** adv.—**in·fer·rer,** n.

in·fer·ence, in′fẽr·ens, in′frens, n. [M.L. *inferentia*.] The act or process of inferring; that which is inferred; a conclusion drawn from premises or evidence; a deduction; a conjecture which may or may not be backed up by proper premises.—**in·fer·en·tial,** in″fe·ren′shal, a.—**in·fer·en·tial·ly,** adv.

in·fe·ri·or, in·fẽr′ē·ẽr, a. [L. compar. of *inferus*, being below, under, nether: cf. *under*.] Lower in station, rank, degree, or grade, usu. followed by *to*; lower in place or position; of lower grade or poorer quality; *bot.* situated below the insertion of sepals and petals, as in an *inferior* ovary; *print.* lower than the main line of type, as the figures in chemical formulae.—n. One inferior to another or others, as in rank, merit, or some specified particular; *print.* an inferior letter or figure.—**in·fe·ri·or·i·ty,** in·fẽr″ē·ạr′i·tē, n.—**in·fe·ri·or·ly,** adv.

in·fe·ri·or·i·ty com·plex, n. *Psychol.* a condition in which extreme feelings of inferiority, often derived from childhood frustrations, manifest themselves either in the form of aggression or withdrawal and reticence.

in·fer·nal, in·fụr′nal, a. [O.Fr. Fr. *infernal*, < L.L. *infernalis*, < L. *infernus*, being below, of the lower regions, < *inferus*.] Hellish; fiendish; diabolical; *colloq.* execrable or outrageous; *class. mythol.* of or pertaining to the lower world or regions of the dead.

in·fer·nal ma·chine, n. An explosive mechanical apparatus, usu. concealed, intended to destroy life or property.

in·fer·no, in·fụr′nō, n. pl. **in·fer·nos.** [It., hell (esp. as the subject and title of a part of Dante's *Divina Commedia*), < L. *infernus*.] An infernal or helllike region; a place of hellish torment; anything that resembles hell in some way, as a burning building.

in·fer·tile, in·fẽr′til, *Brit.* in·fẽr′til, a. Not fertile; not fruitful or productive; sterile; barren.—**in·fer·til·i·ty,** in″fẽr·til′i·tē, n.

in·fest, in·fest′, v.t. [L. *infestare*, < *infestus*, disturbed, unsafe, hostile.] To overrun in great numbers or in a troublesome manner, as: Swarms of mosquitoes *infest* the jungle. To be numerous in, as anything troublesome.—**in·fes·ta·tion,** in″fe·stā′shan, n. —**in·fest·er,** n.

in·fi·del, in′fi·del, n. [L. *infidelis*, faithless, unbelieving.] A disbeliever; one who has no religious faith; an atheist; one who is not a follower of the predominant faith; to Christians, any unbeliever, esp. a Muslim; to Muslims, any unbeliever, esp. a Christian.

in·fi·del·i·ty, in″fi·del′i·tē, n. pl. **in·fi·del·i·ties.** [Fr. *infidélité*; L. *infidelitas*.] Want of faith or belief; skepticism; unfaithfulness in married persons, adultery; atheism or disbelief in God or in a particular religion; unfaithfulness to a charge or moral obligation; treachery; deceit.

in·field, in′fēld″, n. *Baseball*, the square or diamond portion of a playing field marked off by four bases; collectively, the shortstop and three basemen. *Racing*, the area within a race track.—**in·field·er,** n. One of the four baseball players in the infield.

in·fight·ing, in′fī″ting, n. Fighting at close quarters, esp. in boxing; a struggle within an organization, as for leadership or power in a political party.—**in·fight·er,** n.

in·fil·trate, in·fil′trāt, in′fil·trāt″, v.t.—**infiltrated, infiltrating.** To join secretly or take a position in, as a government or organization, for the purpose of spying or taking control; to cause to pass in by, or as by, filtering; to filter into or through; to permeate.—v.i.. To pass in or through a substance by, or as by, filtering; to permeate. —n. One who or that which infiltrates. *Pathol.* an accumulation or an abnormal growth of cells in the tissues.—**in·fil·tra·tion,** in″fil·trā′shan, n. The act or process of infiltrating, or the state of being infiltrated; permeation. *Geol.* the absorption of mineral deposits in porous rocks when permeated by waters. *Milit.* dispatching troops at intervals without being detected by the enemy; a method of attack in which small groups of men penetrate into the enemy's lines at various weak points, in order to bring fire eventually upon the enemy's flanks or rear.— **in·fil·tra·tive,** in″fil·trā″tiv, in·fil′tra·tiv, a.

in·fi·nite, in′fi·nit, a. [L.*infinitus*.] Not finite; without limits; not limited or circumscribed, esp. with reference to time, space, or God; exceedingly great in excellence, degree, and capacity; boundless; limitless; immeasurable; *math.* without a limit or bound.—n. That which is limitless, absolute, or perfect; a boundless space or extent; the Infinite Being; the Almighty.— **in·fi·nite·ly,** adv.—**in·fi·nite·ness,** n.— **fin·i·tude,** in·fin′i·töd″, in·fin′i·tūd″, n.

in·fin·i·tes·i·mal, in″fin·i·tes′i·mal, a. [Fr. *infinitésimal*] Infinitely or immeasurably small; less than any assignable quantity.—n. *Math.* an infinitely small quantity, or one less than any assignable quantity.— **in·fin·i·tes·i·mal·ly,** adv.

in·fin·i·tes·i·mal cal·cu·lus, n. Differential and integral calculus.

in·fin·i·tive, in·fin′i·tiv, n. [L. *infinitivus*, unlimited, indefinite.] *Gram.* a verb form which expresses the meaning of the verb without specifying person or number and which may function as a noun, usu. preceded by *to*, as: *To err* is human. Or as a verb, usu. with auxiliary verbs, as: They must be there.—a. Not limited or restricted as to person or number: opposed to *finite*; *gram.* referring to or having an infinitive.— **in·fin·i·ti·val,** in′fin·i·tī′val, a. Of or belonging to the infinitive.—**in·fin·i·tive·ly,** adv.—**split in·fin·i·tive,** gram. an infinitive phrase in which the function word *to* and the infinitive are separated by a modifier, as *to* swiftly *run*.

in·fin·i·ty, in·fin′i·tē, n. pl. **in·fin·i·ties.** [O.Fr. *infinite* (Fr. *infinité*), < L. *infinitas*, boundlessness.] The state or quality of being infinite; that which is boundless; an unlimited extent, amount, or number; that which can never be completely counted or whose termination can never be reached. *Math.* an infinite quantity or magnitude; the understood limit which is' never reached. *Geom.* infinite distance; an infinitely distant part of space. *Photog.* a camera lens setting for focusing on objects at or beyond a distance so great that light coming from the object to the lens may be considered parallel.

in·firm, in·fụrm′, a. [L. *infirmus*.] Feeble or weak in body or health, esp. from age; not firm, solid, or strong; not steadfast or resolute; *law*, unsound or not valid, as a witness or his testimony.—**in·firm·ly,** adv. —**in·firm·ness,** n.

in·fir·ma·ry, in·fụr′ma·rē, n. pl. **in·fir·ma·ries.** [M.L. *infirmaria*.] A small hospital or dispensary for the care of the sick, injured, or infirm, usu. in a school or institution.

in·fir·mi·ty, in·fụr′mi·tē, n. pl. **in·fir·mi·ties.** [L. *infirmitas*.] The state of being infirm; feebleness; debility; a physical or moral malady; a defect or flaw.

in·fix, in·fiks′, in′fiks, v.t. [L. *infigo, infixum*, to fix.] To fix or fasten in; to insert; to instill; to inculcate, implant, or fix, as principles or thoughts.—in′fiks, n. *Ling.* a letter or syllable similar to a prefix or suffix, but inserted in the body of a word, which changes its meaning.

in·flame, in·flãm′, v.t.—**inflamed, inflaming.** [O.Fr. *enflamer* (Fr. *enflammer*), < L. *inflammare*.] To set aflame, ablaze, or afire; to kindle; to excite violent passion, feeling, or emotion in; to rouse, intensify, or increase, as anger; to produce inflammation in; to cause swelling, fever, or soreness in.—v.i. To burst into flame; to take fire; to become aroused or excited; to become inflamed.—**in·flam·er,** n.

in·flam·ma·ble, in·flam′a·bl, a. Capable of being set on fire; easily kindled; flammable; combustible; easily excited to anger.—**in·flam·ma·bil·i·ty,** in·flam″a·bil′i·tē, **in·flam·ma·ble·ness,** n. The state or quality of being inflammable.—**in·flam·ma·bly,** adv.

in·flam·ma·tion, in″fla·mā′shan, n. [L. *inflammatio*.] The act of inflaming; *pathol.* a redness and swelling of any part of the body, attended with heat and pain.

in·flam·ma·to·ry, in·flam′a·tõr″ē, a. Tending to inflame or to excite anger, animosity, or disorder; *med.* tending to cause inflammation, usu. accompanied by heat.—**in·flam·ma·to·ri·ly,** in·flam″a·tõr′i·lē, in·flam′a·tõr″i·lē, adv.

in·flate, in·flãt′, v.t.—**inflated, inflating.** [L. *inflatus*, pp. of *inflare*.] To distend with air or gas; as, to *inflate* a balloon; to distend, swell, or puff out; to dilate; to puff up with pride, self-importance, or satisfaction; to elate. *Econ.* to expand unduly, as currency or prices; raise above the usual or proper amount or value.—v.i. To become inflated. —**in·flat·a·ble,** a.—**in·flat·ed,** a. Distended with air or gas; swollen; puffed up, as with pride; turgid or bombastic, as language; *econ.* unduly expanded, as currency. *Bot.* having a cavity within; dilated; as, an *inflated* calyx around a fruit.— **in·flat·ed·ness,** n. **in·flat·er, in·fla·tor,** n.

in·fla·tion, in·flã′shan, n. The act of inflating, or the state of being inflated; distension, as with air or gas; pomposity or pretentiousness; self-importance. *Econ.* an expansion of the volume of currency and bank credit, out of proportion to available goods and services, and resulting in a considerable and prolonged rise in prices, wages, and other costs; expansion or increase of the currency of a country by the issuing of paper money, esp. paper money not redeemable in specie or insufficiently secured by precious metal.—**in·fla·tion·ar·y,** a.—**in·fla·tion·ism,** n.—**in·fla·tion·ist,** n.

in·fla·tion·ar·y spi·ral, n. A continuing upward trend in the general price level, resulting chiefly from the interaction of rising costs and rising wages.

in·flect, in·flekt′, v.t. [L. *inflectere* (pp. *inflexus*).] To modulate, as the voice; *gram.* to vary in form, as a word, to indicate number, case, mood, or tense; decline or conjugate. To bend; to turn aside from a straight course.—**in·flec·tion,** *Brit.* also **in·flex·ion,** in·flek′shan, n. Modulation of the voice; a bend or angle; *math.* a change in a curve from convex to concave, or the reverse; *gram.* the process of inflecting; an inflected form of a word; a suffix or other element used in inflecting.— **in·flec·tion·al,** *Brit.* also **in·flex·ion·al,** a.—**in·flec·tion·al·ly,** *Brit.* also **in·flex·ion·al·ly,** adv.—**in·flec·tion·less,** *Brit.* also **in·flex·ion·less,** a.—**in·flec·tive,** a.— **in·flec·tor,** n.

in·flexed, in·flekst′, a. [L. *inflexus*, pp. of *inflecto*.] Curved; bent.—**in·flexed leaf,**

bot. a leaf curved downward or inward toward the axis.

in·flex·i·ble, in·flek′si·bl, *a.* [L. *inflexibilis,* that cannot be bent.] Incapable of being bent; firm in purpose; immovable; rigid, unyielding or stubborn; unalterable. **—in·flex·i·bil·i·ty, in·flex·i·ble·ness,** in·flek″si·bil′i·tē, *n.***—in·flex·i·bly,** *adv.*

in·flict, in·flikt′, *v.t.* [L. *infligo, inflictum.*] To cause to bear or suffer from; to bring about; to cause to feel; as, to *inflict* pain to impose on, as punishment.**—in·flict·a·ble,** *a.***—in·flict·er, in·flic·tor,** *n.***—in·flic·tion,** *n.***—in·flic·tive,** *a.*

in·flo·res·cence, in″flō·res′ens, in″flo·res′ens, *n.* [< L. *inflorescens,* ppr. of *infloresco,* to begin to blossom.] *Bot.* the flowering part of a plant; the manner of arrangement of a cluster of flowers on a common axis or stalk; a cluster of flowers; *rare,* a single flower.**—in·flo·res·cent,** *a.*

in·flow, in′flō′, *n.* The act of flowing in; that which flows in.

in·flu·ence, in′flö·ens, *n.* [O.Fr. Fr. *influence,* < M.L. *influentia,* lit. 'a flowing in,' < L. *influens, influent.*] Exertion of spiritual power or moral persuasion; power of affecting others through the use of authority, money, or social position; power of producing effects by invisible or intangible means; a person or thing that exerts force by intangible means; *astrol.* a supposed radiation from the stars said to affect human destinies; such powers from the stars.**—***v.t.*—*influenced, influencing.* To exert influence; to affect by intangible means; to move, impel.**—in·flu·ence·a·ble,** *a.***—in·flu·enc·er,** *n.***—in·flu·en·tial,** in″flö·en′shal, *a.***—in·flu·en·tial·ly,** *adv.*

in·flu·ent, in′flö·ent, *a.* [L. *influens (-ent-),* ppr. of *influere,* flow in.] Flowing in.**—***n.* A tributary that flows into a larger body of water; *biol.* a species that influences the balance of nature in an area.

in·flu·en·za, in″flö·en′za, *n.* [It. *fluenza,* lit. 'influence.'] An acute, infectious, and highly contagious disease affecting the respiratory tract, producing symptoms not unlike a severe cold, such as fever, muscular pain, intestinal disorders, and general prostration, and caused by viruses: frequently epidemic.**—in·flu·en·zal,** *a.***—in·flu·en·za·like,** *a.*

in·flux, in′fluks″, *n.* [L. *influxus,* a flowing in, < *influo.*] The act of flowing in; inflow; the point at which one stream runs into another or into the sea.

in·fold, in·fōld′, *v.t.* Enfold.**—in·fold·er,** *n.***—in·fold·ment,** *n.*

in·form, in·farm′, *v.t.* [Fr. *informer,* to apprise, L. *informo,* to shape, to describe.] To communicate knowledge to; to tell or apprise; to make aware of. To inspire and give life to; to animate.**—***v.i.* To give information.**—in·form a·gainst,** to communicate incriminating facts about.**—informed,** *a.*

in·for·mal, in·far′mal, *a.* Not in the regular or usual form; unofficial; without ceremony; casual or relaxed; pertaining to casual but educated conversation, as opposed to *formal* writing or discourse.**—in·for·mal·i·ty,** in″far·mal′i·tē, *n.***—in·for·mal·ly,** *adv.*

in·form·ant, in·far′mant, *n.* One who supplies information, as to police; an informer; *ling.* whose speech is studied by linguists for analysis of his native language.

in·for·ma·tion, in″fer·mā′shan, *n.* [L. *informatio.*] News or intelligence communicated by word or in writing; facts or data; knowledge derived from reading or instruction, or gathered in any way; *law,* an accusation of a criminal offense, presented by a public officer rather than a grand jury. A quantity which measures the possible numerical uncertainty in the outcome of

a particular experiment.**—in·for·ma·tion·al,** *a.***—in·for·ma·tive,** in·far′ma·tiv, *a.***—in·for·ma·tive·ly,** *adv.***—in·for·ma·tive·ness,** *n.***—in·for·ma·to·ry,** in·far′ma·tōr″ē, *a.***—in·form·er,** in·far′mer, *n.* One who informs; one who gives incriminating evidence against others.

in·for·ma·tion the·o·ry, *n. Math.* the statistical study of the processes and efficiency of transmitted messages, as in computers or telecommunications.

in·fract, in·frakt′, *v.t.* To break, as rules or laws; to violate; to infringe.**—in·frac·tor,** *n.*

in·frac·tion, in·frak′shan, *n.* [L. *infractio, infractionis,* breaking in pieces, < *infringo, infractum.*] The act of infringing; violation; breaking. *Med.* an incomplete break in a bone.

in·fra dig, in′fra dig′, *a. Latin,* beneath one's dignity. Also **in·fra dig·ni·ta·tem,** in′fra dig″ni·tā′tem.

in·fra hu·man, in″fra·hū′man, *a.* Subhuman.**—***n.*

in·fran·gi·ble, in·fran′ji·bl, *a.* Unbreakable; not to be violated.**—in·fran·gi·bil·i·ty, in·fran·gi·ble·ness,** in·fran″ji·bil′i·tē, *n.***—in·fran·gi·bly,** *adv.*

in·fra·red, in″fra·red′, *a.* Below the red, as the invisible rays of the spectrum lying outside the red end of the visible spectrum; pertaining to these rays.

in·fra·red ra·di·a·tion, *n.* Radiation which is emitted by warm substances and heats substances which absorb it; radiation with wavelengths longer than visible light and shorter than microwave radiation. *Phys.* electromagnetic radiation in the wavelength interval from 2 to 2000 microns; *chem.* such radiation in the interval from 2 to 200 microns.

in·fra·son·ic, in″fra·son′ik, *a.* Having a frequency lower than the auditory capacity of the human ear. See *subsonic.*

in·fra·struc·ture, in′fra·struk″chĕr, *n.* A foundation; *milit.* the permanent structures of a military organization, esp. those of the North Atlantic Treaty Organization.

in·fre·quent, in·frē′kwent, *a.* [L. *infrequens.*] Seldom; rare; not common or habitual; placed at wide intervals; occasional.**—in·fre·quen·cy,** *n.***—in·fre·quent·ly,** *adv.*

in·fringe, in·frinj′, *v.t.*—*infringed, infringing.* [L. *infringo.*] To break, as laws or contracts; to violate; to transgress; to impair or encroach on.**—***v.i.* To encroach; followed by *on* or *upon.***—in·fringe·ment,** *n.***—in·fring·er,** *n.*

in·fun·dib·u·lum, in″fun·dib′ū·lum, *n.* pl. **in·fun·dib·u·la,** in″fun·dib′ū·la. [L. *funnel,* < *infundere,* pour in.] *Anat.* The funnel-shaped portion of the third ventricle in the brain leading to the pituitary gland; an area in the right ventricle where the pulmonary artery arises; cone-shaped areas in the lungs where the bronchial tubes end; the funnel-shaped opening of a Fallopian tube.**—in·fun·dib·u·lar, in·fun·dib·u·late,** in·fun·dib′ū·li·form, in″fun·dib′ū·lāt″, in″fun·dib′ū·lit, in″fun·dib′ū·li·farm, *a.* Having the form of a funnel; *bot.* having a funnel-shaped flower.

in·fu·ri·ate, in·fūr′ē·āt″, *v.t.*—*infuriated, infuriating.* [M.L. *infuriatus,* pp. of *infuriare.*] Render furious; enrage.**—in·fu·ri·ate,** in·fūr′ē·it, *a. Rare.* Infuriated; enraged.**—in·fu·ri·ate·ly, in·fu·ri·at·ing·ly,** in·fūr′ē·ā″ting·lē, *adv.***—in·fu·ri·a·tion,** in·fūr′ē·ā′shan, *n.*

in·fus·cate, in·fus′kāt, *a.* [L. *infuscatus,* pp. of *infuscare,* darken, < *in-,* in, and *fuscus,* E. *fuscous.*] *Entom.* darkened with a fuscous or brownish-gray color, as the wings of insects. Also **in·fus·cat·ed.**

in·fuse, in·fūz′, *v.t.*—*infused, infusing.* [Fr. *infuser,* < L. *infunder, infusum,* to pour into.] To pour into or in; introduce, usu. by

pouring; to inculcate; instill, as: The politician's social fervor *infuses* the masses with hope. To steep in a liquid without boiling to separate the soluble from the insoluble components; macerate.**—in·fus·er,** *n.***—in·fus·i·bil·i·ty,** in·fū″zi·bil′i·tē, *n.***—in·fus·i·ble,** *a.***—in·fu·sive,** in·fū′siv, *a.*

in·fu·sion, in·fū′zhon, *n.* [L. *infusio(n)-,* < *infundere.*] The act of infusing; that which is infused; an introduced element or admixture; a liquid extract obtained from a substance by steeping or soaking it in water; any liquid containing organic matter; *med.* the introduction of a saline or other solution into a vein.

in·fu·so·ri·an, in″fū·sōr′ē·an, in″fū·sar′ē·an, *n. Zool.* any of a class of ciliated protozoans.**—***a.***—in·fu·so·ri·al,** *a.*

in·gath·er, in′gaTH·ĕr, in·gaTH′ĕr, *v.t.* To gather; collect; bring in, as a harvest.**—***v.i.* To assemble or collect.**—in·gath·er·ing,** in′gaTH″ĕr·ing, *n.***—in·gath·er·er,** *n.*

in·gem·i·nate, in·jem′i·nāt″, *v.t.*—*ingeminated, ingeminating.* [L. *ingemino, ingeminatum—in-,* intens., and *gemino,* to double.] To double or repeat.**—in·gem·i·na·tion,** in·jem″i·nā′shan, *n.*

in·gen·er·ate, in·jen′er·it, *a.* [L. *ingenero, ingeneratum,* < *in-,* and *genero,* to generate.] Not generated. *Archaic,* inborn; innate.**—**in·jen′e·rāt″,*v.t.*—*ingenerated, ingenerating. Archaic,* to generate or produce.**—in·gen·er·ate·ly,** *adv.***—in·gen·er·a·tion,** *n.*

in·gen·ious, in·jēn′yus, *a.* [L. *ingeniosus,* able, ingenious, < *ingenium,* ability, cleverness.] Possessed of cleverness, resourcefulness, or inventiveness; clever or original in conception or design.**—in·gen·ious·ly,** *adv.***—in·gen·ious·ness,** *n.*

in·gé·nue, an′zhe·nö″, an′zhe·nū″, Fr. aN·zhā·nY′, *n.* pl. **in·ge·nues,** an′zhe·nöz″, an′zhe·nūz″, Fr. an·zhe·nY′. [Fr.] An innocent or ingenuous girl, esp. as represented on the stage; an actress who plays such a part.

in·ge·nu·i·ty, in″je·nöi′i·tē, in″je·nū′i·tē, *n.* pl. **in·ge·nu·i·ties.** [Fr. *ingenuite,* L. *ingenuitas,* < *ingenuus.*] Inventiveness; the quality of being resourceful or clever; cleverness or originality in idea or construction; an ingenious device or act.

in·gen·u·ous, in·jen′ū·us, *a.* [L. *ingenuus,* inborn, freeborn, ingenious, < *in-,* and root *gen,* to produce.] Innocent; artless; naïve; candid; straightforward and free from reserve.**—in·gen·u·ous·ly,** *adv.***—in·gen·u·ous·ness,** *n.*

in·gest, in·jest′, *v.t.* [L. *ingestus,* pp. of *ingerere,* < *in-,* in, and *gerere,* bear.] To put or take, as food, into the body.**—in·ges·tion,** *n.* [L.L. *ingestio(n)-.*]**—in·ges·tive,** *a.*

in·ges·ta, in·jes′ta, *n. pl.* [L.] Substances ingested.

in·gle, ing′gel, *n.* [Orig. Sc.; origin obscure.] *Brit.* Fire; a fire burning upon a hearth; a fireplace.

in·gle·nook, ing′gel·nuk″, *n. Brit.* a nook or corner by the fire.

in·gle·side, ing′gel·sīd″, *n. Brit.* a fireside.

in·glo·ri·ous, in·glōr′ē·us, *a.* [L. *inglorius.*] Bringing disgrace rather than honor; shameful; ignominious.**—in·glo·ri·ous·ly,** *adv.***—in·glo·ri·ous·ness,** *n.*

in·got, ing′got, *n.* [M.E. *ingot,* molded metal, perhaps < O.E. *in-,* in and *gēotan,* pour.] A mass of metal molded into a convenient shape for storage, shipment, or further processing.

in·got i·ron, *n.* Iron having a high degree of purity, used for making special steels; a special steel of high ductility and rust resistance; *Brit.* mild steel.

in·graft, in·graft′, in·gräft′, *v.t.* Engraft.

in·grain, in·grān′, in′gran″, *v.t.* To fix deeply and firmly, as in the character or mind; to infuse; as, to *ingrain* a habit. Also **en·grain.—in'grān**, *a.* Dyed in the yarn, or in a raw state, before manufacture; firmly fixed; innate.—**in'grān**, *n.* An article dyed with fast colors before manufacture.—**in·grained**, in·grānd', in'grānd", *a.*—**in··grain·ed·ly**, *adv.*

in·grate, in'grāt, *n.* [Fr. *ingrat*, < L. *ingratus*, ungrateful.] An ungrateful person.—*a.* Archaic, ungrateful.—**in·grate·ly**, *adv.*

in·gra·ti·ate, in·grā'shē·āt", *v.t.*—*ingratiated, ingratiating.* To deliberately seek the favor or good graces of others, usu. followed by *with.*—**in·gra·ti·at·ing**, *a.* Pleasing or agreeable; flattering.—**in·gra·ti·at·ing·ly**, *adv.*—**in·gra·ti·a·tion**, in·grā"shē·ā'shan, *n.*—**in·gra·ti·a·to·ry**, in·grā'shē·a·tōr"ē, in·grā'shē·a·tar"ē, *a.*

in·grat·i·tude, in·grat'i·tōd", in·grat'i·tūd", *n.* Want of gratitude; insensibility to favors or kindnesses; unthankfulness.

in·gra·ves·cent, in"gra·ves'ant, *a.* [L. *ingravescens* (-ent-), ppr. of *ingravescere*, grow heavier.] *Pathol.* increasing in severity, as a disease.—**in·gra·ves·cence**, *n.*

in·gre·di·ent, in·grē'dē·ent, *n.* [L. *ingrediens, ingredientis*, ppr. of *ingredior*, to go in—*in-*, into, and *gradior*, to go.] An element of any mixture; a component part or any compound or combination.

in·gress, in'gres, *n.* [L. *ingressus*, < *ingredi*, go in, enter.] The act of going in or entering; entrance; the right to go in; as, to have free *ingress* to a place; a means or place of going in; an entrance.—**in·gres·sion**, in·gresh'on, *n.* [L. *ingressio(n-)*, < *ingredi*.] A going in or entering; entrance.—**in·gres··sive**, *a.* Entering; pertaining to entrance; *gram.* inceptive.—**in·gres·sive·ness**, *n.*

in·group, in'grōp", *n.* *Sociol.* a group whose members are homogeneous and cohesive to the point of excluding others.

in·grow·ing, in'grō"ing, *a.* Growing within or inward; of a nail, growing into the flesh.—**in·grown**, in'grōn", *a.*—**in·growth**, in'grōth", *n.*

in·gui·nal, ing'gwi·nal, *a.* [L. *inguinalis*, < *inguen, inguinis*, the groin.] Pertaining to or located in the groin.

in·gulf, in·gulf', *v.t.* Engulf.

in·gur·gi·tate, in·gur'ji·tāt", *v.t.*—*ingurgitated, ingurgitating.* [L. *ingurgito, ingurgitatum*, to gorge.] To swallow eagerly or in great quantity.—*v.i.* To guzzle; to swill.—**in·gur·gi·ta·tion**, in·gur"ji·tā'shan, *n.*

in·hab·it, in·hab'it, *v.t.* [L. *inhabito*.] To live or dwell in; to occupy as a place of settled residence; to exist within.—**in·hab·it·a·ble**, *a.*—**in·hab·i·ta·tion**, in··hab'i·tā'shan, *n.*—**in·hab·it·er**, *n.*—**in·hab·it·ed**, *a.* Populated.

in·hab·it·an·cy, in·hab'i·tan·sē, *n.* pl. **in·hab·it·an·cies**. Residing or inhabiting; the condition of being inhabited; occupancy; residency. Also **in·hab·it·ance**.

in·hab·it·ant, in·hab'i·tant, *n.* [L. *inhabitans, inhabitantis*, ppr. of *inhabita*.] One who inhabits; a permanent resident.

in·hal·ant, in·hā'lant, *a.* Inhaling; used for inhaling.—*n.* An apparatus or a medicine used for inhaling; as, a nasal *inhalant.*—**in·ha·la·tion**, in"ha·lā'shan, *n.*—**in·ha·la·tion·al**, *a.*

in·ha·la·tor, in'ha·lā"tar, *n.* A device used to aid breathing, or to administer a medicine in vapor form.

in·hale, in·hāl', *v.t.*—*inhaled, inhaling.* To breathe in; draw in by or as by breathing; as, to *inhale* air.—*v.i.* To breathe in, as when smoking a cigarette.—**in·hal·er**, *n.* An apparatus used in inhaling medicinal vapors; a respirator; one who inhales.

in·har·mon·ic, in"här·mon'ik, *a.* Not harmonic; discordant.—**in·har·mo·ni·ous**, in"här·mō'nē·us, *a.*—**in·har·mo·ni-**

ous·ly, *adv.*—**in·har·mo·ni·ous·ness**, in·har"mo·nē, *n.*

in·haul, in'hal", *n. Naut.* a rope for hauling in a sail or spar. Also **in·haul·er**.

in·here, in·her', *v.i.*—*inhered, inhering.* [L. *inhaereo, inhaesum—in-*, and *haereo*, to stick.] To exist or be fixed in; to belong intrinsically, as attributes or qualities, to a subject; to be innate, usu. followed by *in.*—**in·her·ence**, **in·her·en·cy**, in·hēr'ens, in·her'ens, *n.* pl. **in·her·en·cies**.

in·her·ent, in·hēr'ent, in·her'ent, *a.* [L. *inhaerens, inhaerentis*, ppr. of *inhaereo*.] Forming an essential or intrinsic element of; existing inseparably within an object or person; innate.—**in·her·ent·ly**, *adv.*

in·her·it, in·her'it, *v.t.* [O.Fr. *enheriter*, L.L. *inhereditare*, to inherit.] To receive or obtain, as property, rights, or duties, from an ancestor or predecessor; to derive or acquire, as traits or characteristics, through heredity.—*v.i.* To receive or take an inheritance.—**in·her··i·tor**, *n.* An heir; one who inherits.—**in·her·i·tress, in·her·i·trix**, in·her'i·tris, in·her'i·triks, *n. Fem.* an inheritor.

in·her·it·a·ble, in·her'i·ta·bl, *a.* Capable of being inherited or being transmitted from parent to child; heritable.—**in·her·it·a·bil·i·ty, in·her·it·a·ble·ness**, in·her"i·ta·bil'i·tē, *n.*

in·her·it·ance, in·her'i·tans, *n.* That which is or may be inherited; a legacy; a heritage; property, title, or position derived from one's ancestors or predecessors; traits of one's ancestors genetically transmitted; the process of receiving property or traditions from one's progenitors; an endowment from nature; as, our *inheritance* of mountains, rivers, etc.

in·her·it·ance tax, *n.* A tax on an inherited property.

in·he·sion, in·hē'zhan, *n.* [L.L. *inhæsio* (n-).] The state or fact of inhering or becoming a permanent part of something; inherence.

in·hib·it, in·hib'it, *v.t.* [L. *inhibeo, inhibitum*, to restrain—*in-*, in, and *habeo*, to have.] To restrain; to hinder; to prohibit, forbid, or check.—**in·hib·i·tive, in·hib··i·to·ry**, *a.*—**in·hib·i·tor, in·hib·it·er**, *n.* Anything that inhibits; *chem.* a substance that slows, interferes with, or stops a chemical reaction.

in·hi·bi·tion, in"i·bish'an, in"hi·bish'an, *n.* [L. *inhibitio.*] The act of inhibiting; prohibition; restraint; *psychol.* a process that checks or restrains a nervous impulse involving actions or thoughts; *chem.* the slowing or complete stoppage of a chemical reaction.

in·hos·pi·ta·ble, in·hos'pi·ta·bl, in"ho··spit'a·bl, *a.* Not hospitable; not friendly or generous to guests; of a region, climate, or the like, not offering favorable conditions for visitors or travelers; barren or uninviting.—**in·hos·pi·ta·ble·ness**, *n.*—**in·hos·pi·ta·bly**, *adv.*—**in·hos·pi·tal·i·ty**, in"hos··pi·tal'i·tē, in·hos"pi·tal'i·tē, *n.*

in·hu·man, in·hū'man, in·ū'man, *a.* [L. *inhumanus.*] Not human; monstrous; destitute of natural human sympathy for others; brutal; cruel.—**in·hu·man·ly**, *adv.*—**in·hu·man·i·ty**, in"hū·man'i·tē, in"ū·man'i·tē, *n.* pl. **in·hu·man·i·ties**.

in·hu·mane, in"hū·mān', in"ū·mān', *a.* Lacking in humanity, kindness, or sympathy for the suffering of others; cruel.—**in·hu·mane·ly**, *adv.*

in·hume, in·hūm', *v.t.*—*inhumed, inhuming.* [Fr. *inhumer*, L. *inhumo, inhumatum—in-*, in, and *humus*, the ground.] To bury; to inter, as a dead body.—**in·hu·ma·tion**, in"hū·mā'shan, *n.*

in·im·i·cal, i·nim'i·kal, *a.* [L. *inimicus—in-*, not, and *amicus*, friendly.] Unfriendly; hostile; adverse; harmful; as, an action

inimical to commerce. Also **in·im·i·ca·ble**—**in·im·i·cal·ly**, *adv.*—**in·im·i·cal·ness**, **in·im·i·cal·i·ty**, i·nim"i·kal'i·tē, *n.*

in·im·i·ta·ble, i·nim'i·ta·bl, *a.* Incapable of being imitated or copied; surpassing imitation; matchless.—**in·im·i·ta·bil·i·ty, in·im·i·ta·ble·ness**, i·nim"i·ta·bil'i·tē, *n.*—**in·im·i·ta·bly**, *adv.*

in·iq·ui·ty, i·nik'wi·tē, *n.* pl. **in·iq·ui·ties**. [O. Fr. *iniquite* (Fr. *iniquité*), < L. *iniquitas*, < *iniquus*, unequal, unjust, < *in-*, not, and *aequus*, equal.] Gross injustice; wickedness; sin; a wicked act.—**in·iq··ui·tous**, *a.*—**in·iq·ui·tous·ly**, *adv.*—**in··iq·ui·tous·ness**, *n.*

in·i·tial, i·nish'al, *a.* [L. *initialis*, < *initium*, beginning, < *ineo, initum*, to go in.] Placed at the beginning; of or pertaining to the beginning; beginning; incipient.—**in·i·tial·ly**, *adv.*—**in·i·tial·ness**, *n.*

in·i·tial, i·nish'al, *n.* The first letter of a word; the first letters in order of a proper name; an enlarged letter often with ornamentation which introduces a chapter, paragraph, portion of a book, or embroidered on clothes, as a monogram. *v.t.*—*initialed, initialing, initialled, initialling.* To put one's initials on or to.

in·i·tial teach·ing al·pha·bet, *n.* A system for teaching reading in which the basic speech sounds of English are represented by 44 symbols formed by combining letters or phonetic symbols. Abbr. *i.t.a., i/t/a, I.T.A., ITA*.

in·i·ti·ate, i·nish'ē·āt", *v.t.*—*initiated, initiating.* [L. *initio, initiatum*, < *initium*.] To begin or enter upon; to set going; to guide or direct by instruction in rudiments or principles; to introduce or admit into a fraternity, society, or other organization, esp. by sharing secret knowledge.—*a.* Initiated; introduced to the knowledge of something.—*n.* One who has been initiated, esp. one who has been newly initiated.—**in·i·ti·a·tion**, i·nish"ē·ā'shan, *n.* The act or process of initiating; the formal rites by which one is admitted to a group or society.—**in·i·ti·a·tive**, i·nish'ē·a·tiv, i·nish'i··tiv, *a.* Serving to initiate; initiatory.—*n.* An introductory act or step; power or ability to take the lead or originate action. *Govt.* the power to originate legislation; the right of the voters to propose legislation for approval by the legislature or by referendum.—**in·i·ti·a·tor**, *n.*—**in·i·ti·a·to·ry**, i·nish'ē·a·tōr"ē, i·nish'ē·a·tar"ē, *a.*

in·ject, in·jekt', *v.t.* [L. *injectus*, pp. of *injicere*, throw or put in.] To force a fluid into a passage, cavity, or tissue; as, to *inject* a drug into the body with a syringe; to introduce something new and different into a situation or subject, as a remark; to interject.—**in·ject·a·ble**, *a.*—**in·jec·tion**, *n.* The act of injecting; a liquid injected into the body, as for medicinal purposes; a shot. *Aerospace*, the act of placing a man-made satellite or spacecraft into orbit.—**in··jec·tor**, *n.* One who or that which injects; a device for forcing water into a steam boiler.

in·ju·di·cious, in"jō·dish'us, *a.* Acting without sound judgment or discretion; unwise; imprudent.—**in·ju·di·cious·ly**, *adv.*—**in·ju·di·cious·ness**, *n.*

in·junc·tion, in·jungk'shan, *n.* [L. *injunctio, injunctionis*, < *injungo*, to enjoin.] The act of ordering or directing; a command, admonition, or precept; *law*, a writ requiring a person to refrain from doing certain acts.—**in·junc·tive**, *a.*—**in·junc·tive·ly**, *adv.*

in·jure, in'jėr, *v.t.*—*injured, injuring.* [Fr. *injurier*, L. *injurior, injuriari*, < *injuria*, injury, *injurius*, injurious.] To do harm to; to hurt or wound; to impair the excellence, value, or strength of; to damage; to offend or be unjust to, as another's feelings.—

in·jured, in·jur′er, *n.*—in·ju·ri·ous, in·ju′re·us, *a.*—in·ju·ri·ous·ly, *adv.*—in·ju·ri·ous·ness, *n.*

in·ju·ry, in′jŭ·rē, *n.* pl. **in·ju·ries.** Harm or damage occasioned; a wrong received; *law,* damage or violation of another's person, property, rights, or reputation.

in·jus·tice, in·jus′tis, *n.* [L. *injustitia*.] Want of fairness or equity; violation of another's rights; a wrong or unjust act.

ink, ingk, *n.* [O.E. *enke, inke,* O.Fr. *enque,* Fr. *encre,* < L.L. *encaustum,* purple ink used by the Roman emperors, < Gr. *enkaustos,* burned in.] A colored liquid used for writing, printing, and drawing; a dark fluid secreted by certain cephalopods, for protective purposes, as the squid.—*v.t.* To blacken, color, or daub with ink.—ink·er, *n.*—ink·i·ness, *n.*—ink·y, *a.*—*inkier, inkiest.*

ink·ber·ry, ingk′ber″ē, ingk′be·rē, *n.* pl. **ink·ber·ries.** *Bot.* a N. American shrub of the holly family, *Ilex glabra,* having evergreen glabrous leaves and black berries; the berry itself. Also *winterberry.*

ink·blot, ingk′blot″, *n.* Blot drawing, used in psychological tests. See *Rorschach test.*

ink·horn, ingk′harn″, *n.* A small container made of horn or other material, formerly used for holding ink.—*a.* Ostentatiously erudite; as, an *inkhorn* term.

in·kle, ing′kl, *n.* [Origin uncertain.] A kind of linen tape; the linen thread or yarn from which this tape is made.

ink·ling, ingk′ling, *n.* [M.E. *inclen,* to hint.] A hint or whisper; an intimation; a vague rumor; uncertain or incomplete knowledge of.

ink·well, ingk′wel″, *n.* An ink container. *Brit.* **ink·pot.**

ink·wood, ingk′wụd″, *n.* A tropical tree, *Exothea paniculata,* found in the W. Indies and Florida, with hard, reddish-brown wood.

in·laid, in′lād″, *a.* Laid or set in the surface of a thing; as, an *inlaid* decorative design in wood; decorated or made with a design set in the surface; as, an *inlaid* table or box, or *inlaid* work.

in·land, in′land, *a.* Interior; away from the sea; *Brit.* carried on within a country; domestic, not foreign; confined to a country; drawn and payable in the same country; as, an *inland* bill of exchange.—in′land″, in′land, *adv.* In or toward the interior of a country.—in′land″, in′land, *n.* The interior part of a country.—in·land·er, *n.* One who lives in the interior of a country.

in-law, in′lạ″, *n. Colloq.* a person connected with one by marriage; as, a father-*in-law.*

in·lay, in′lā″, in″lā′, *v.t.*—*inlaid, inlaying.* To insert for ornamentation into a surface, as precious stones, gold, ivory, or fine woods.—in′lā″, *n.* pl. **in·lays.** An inlaid surface or decoration; *dentistry,* a filling of metal or porcelain cemented into a tooth cavity.—in·lay·er, *n.*

in·let, in′let, in′lit, *n.* A narrow passage or strip of water between islands; a recess in a shore; an entrance or orifice; something put in or inserted.—in′let″, in·let′, *v.t.*—*inlet, inletting.* To put in; to insert.

in·li·er, in′li″ẽr, *n. Geol.* a rock formation completely surrounded by strata of a later date.

in·mate, in′māt″, *n.* An occupant of an asylum, prison, or hospital.

in me·mo·ri·am, in me·mōr′ē·am, *prep., adv.* [L.] In memory of, or as a memorial to, often used to introduce a commemorative inscription.

in·most, in′mōst″, *Brit.* in′mạst, *a.* [O.E. *innemest,* a double superlative of the prep. or adv. in.] Farthest within; innermost; remotest from the surface or external part; secret or intimate, as thoughts or feelings.

---

inn, in, *n.* [O.E. *inn,* a chamber, a house, an inn; Icel. *inni,* a house.] A public house for the lodging and entertainment of travelers; a small hotel or restaurant; a tavern; *Brit.* formerly, a student residence.—**Inn of Court,** *Brit.* one of four legal societies in London which admit candidates to practice at the English bar.

in·nards, in′ẽrdz, *n. pl. Colloq.* The internal organs or parts of a body, machine, or structure; entrails; the interior.

in·nate, i·nāt′, in′āt, *a.* [L. *innatus.* Inborn; belonging to the body or mind by nature; native; inherent; derived from the constitution of the mind, as opposed to being derived from experience; as, an *innate* fear.—in·nate·ly, *adv.*—in·nate·ness, *n.*

in·ner, in′ẽr, *a.* [O.E. *innera,* compar. of *in.*] Interior or internal; farther inward than something else; not obvious; private or intimate; as, *inner* feelings; of the mind or the spirit.—in·ner·ly, *a.*

in·ner-di·rect·ed, in′ẽr·di·rek′tid, in′ẽr·di·rek′tid, *a. Psychol.* of or referring to a person whose reactions are guided by his own value system rather than by external norms.

In·ner Light, *n.* In Quaker belief, the guiding influence of Christ's presence in man's soul.

in·ner·most, in′ẽr·mōst″, *Brit.* in′ẽr·mạst, *a.* Farthest inward; inmost.—*n.* The innermost part.—in·ner·most·ly, *adv.*

in·ner·sole, in′ẽr·sōl″, *n.* The permanently attached lining of a shoe; the removable inner sole of a shoe. Also *insole.*

in·ner space, *n.* The ocean depths, esp. as a frontier of exploration and scientific investigation: opposed to *outer space.*

in·ner tube, *n.* A flexible ring-shaped tube, usu. of rubber, and inflated by air pressure to hold out the casing of a pneumatic tire.

in·ner·vate, i·nụr′vāt, in′ẽr·vāt″, *v.t.*—*innervated, innervating.* To supply with nerves; to communicate nervous energy to; stimulate through nerves.—in·ner·va·tion, in″ẽr·vā′shan, *n. Physiol.* the communicating of nervous energy by means of nerves; the stimulation of some part or organ through its nerves. *Anat.* the disposition of nerves in an animal body or some part of it.

in·nerve, i·nụrv′, *v.t.*—*innerved, innerving.* To supply with nervous energy; invigorate; animate.

in·ning, in′ing, *n.* [Lit. 'the state of being *in*'; a sort of verbal noun.] *Baseball,* a division of the game in which each team has the opportunity to score while at bat; *fig.* a turn or opportunity; *pl., sing. or pl. in constr.* a division in a cricket match. Land reclamation, esp. from the sea.

inn·keep·er, in′kē″pẽr, *n.* One who manages or owns an inn.

in·no·cence, in′o·sens, *n.* [L. *innocentia.*] The quality of being innocent; also **in·no·cen·cy,** pl. **in·no·cen·cies.** *Bot.* a rock garden herb, *Houstonia caerula,* having light blue, four-petalled flowers with a yellow eye; also *bluet.*

in·no·cent, in′o·sent, *a.* [L. *innocens, innocentis,* harmless.] Free from sin, guilt, malice, or guile; free from the guilt of a particular crime or evil action; without worldly knowledge; simple; unsophisticated; lawful, not prohibited; lacking something; simple-minded; ignorant.—*n.*—in·no·cent·ly, *adv.*

in·noc·u·ous, i·nok′ū·us, *a.* [L. *innocuus.*] Producing no ill effect; inoffensive; insipid; as, an *innocuous* play.—in·noc·u·ous·ly, *adv.*—in·noc·u·ous·ness, *n.*

in·nom·i·nate, i·nom′i·nit, *a.* [L. *innominatus.*] *Law,* of commutative contracts, untitled. Anonymous; unnamed.

---

in·nom·i·nate bone, *n.* Either of the two bony masses consisting of the fused iliac, ischial, and pubic bones that make up the sides of the pelvis.

in·no·vate, in′o·vāt, *v.t.*—*innovated, innovating.* [L. *innovo, innovatum,* to renew.] To change or alter by introducing something new.—*v.i.* To introduce novelties; to make changes in anything established, used with *on* or *in;* as, to *innovate* on established customs.—in·no·va·tion, in″o·vā′shan, *n.* Act of changing or the change made in established laws, customs, rites, and practices by the introduction of something new.—in·no·va·tive, in·no·va·to·ry, in′ō·va·tōr″ē, in′ō·vā″to·rē, *a.* Introducing or tending to introduce change.—in·no·va·tor, *n.*

in·nu·en·do, in″ū·en′dō, *n.* pl. **in·nu·en·dos, in·nu·en·does.** [L. 'intimating,' 'meaning' (in legal documents, used to introduce explanatory matter), abl. of *innuendum,* gerund of *innuere,* give a nod, intimate.] An indirect intimation, usu. of a derogatory nature, about a person or thing; an insinuation. *Law,* a parenthetic explanation, esp. in slander or libel action, of an injurious word or expression introduced in the case.

in·nu·mer·a·ble, i·nö′mẽr·a·bl, i·nū′·mẽr·a·bl, *a.* [L. *innumerabilis—in-,* not, and *numerabilis,* < *numero,* to number.] Countless; too many to count; incapable of being enumerated. Also **in·nu·mer·ous.**—in·nu·mer·a·ble·ness, *n.*—in·nu·mer·a·bly, *adv.*

in·nu·tri·ent, in″nö′trē·ent, in″nū′trē·ent, *a.* Not nutrient or nourishing; innutritious.—in·nu·tri·tion, in″nö·trish′an, in″nū·trish′an, *n.* Lack of nutrition; failure of nourishment.—in·nu·tri·tious, *a.* Not nutritious.—in·nu·tri·tive, in″nö′tri·tiv, *a.* Not nutritive.

in·ob·serv·ance, in″ob·zụr′vans, *n.* [L. *inobservantia.*] Failure to observe or heed; inattention; intentional disregard, as of a rule or custom.—in·ob·serv·ant, *a.*—in·ob·serv·ant·ly, *adv.*

in·oc·u·lant, i·nok′ū·lant, *n.* Inoculum.

in·oc·u·late, i·nok′ū·lāt″, *v.t.*—*inoculated, inoculating.* [L. *inoculatus,* pp. of *inoculare,* ingraft, implant, < *in-,* in, and *oculus,* eye, bud.] To implant, as virus or bacteria, within a human body to cause a mild disease and thus ensure immunity from that disease; to introduce, as microorganisms, into surroundings suitable to their growth, esp. into living organisms; to impregnate, as soil or seed, with bacteria, to induce nitrate formation; to imbue, as a person, with ideas.—*v.i.* To perform inoculation.—in·oc·u·la·tion, i·nok″ū·lā′shan, *n.* The act of inoculating; the injection, esp. of serum.—in·oc·u·la·tive, i·nok″ū·lā″tiv, i·nok′ya·la·tiv, *a.*—in·oc·u·la·tor, *n.*

in·oc·u·lum, i·nok′ū·lum, *n.* The prepared material for injections, usu. composed of bacteria or viruses. Also *inoculant.*

in·of·fen·sive, in″o·fen′siv, *a.* Giving no offense or provocation; harmless; doing no injury.—in·of·fen·sive·ly, *adv.*—in·of·fen·sive·ness, *n.*

in·op·er·a·ble, in·op′ẽr·a·bl, *a.* Not practicable or workable; *med.* unsuitable for surgical operation; as, an *inoperable* tumor.

in·op·er·a·tive, in·op′ẽr·a·tiv, in·op′e·rā″tiv, *a.* Not operative; not working; producing no effect.—in·op·er·a·tive·ness, *n.*

in·op·por·tune, in·op″ẽr·tön′, in·op′ẽr·tün′, *a.* Happening at an inconvenient or inappropriate time; unseasonable.—in·op·por·tune·ly, *adv.*—in·op·por·tune·ness, in·op·por·tu·ni·ty, *n.*

in·or·di·nate, in·ạr′di·nit, *a.* [L. *inordinatus,* not well-ordered.] Excessive;

---

immoderate; not restrained by rules prescribed or limited to usual bounds; disorderly.—**in·or·di·nate·ness,** *n.*—**in·or·di·nate·ly,** *adv.*

in·or·gan·ic, in″ȧr·gan′ik, *a.* Nonliving; lacking in the organization or structure of living organisms; composed of inanimate matter; artificial. *Chem.* pertaining to compounds which do not contain hydrocarbon, but include the oxides and sulfides of carbon.—**in·or·gan·i·cal·ly,** *adv.*

in·os·cu·late, in·os′kū·lāt″, *v.i.,* *v.t.*—*inosculated, inosculating.* [L. *in-,* and *osculor, osculatus,* to kiss.] To unite or cause to unite into a continuous tract by joining open ends, as arteries and nerve fibers; to run into one another, or to cause to blend.—**in·os·cu·la·tion,** in·os″kū·lā′shan, *n.*

in·o·si·tol, i·nō′si·tōl″, i·nō′si·tȧl, i·nō′si·tol, *n.* [Gr. *is* (*in-*), muscle, fiber.] *Chem.* a compound, $C_6H_6(OH)_6$, a vitamin of the B complex essential to growth, found in plant and animal tissues.

in·pa·tient, in′pā″shent, *n.* A patient who is lodged and fed as well as treated in a hospital or the like: opposed to *outpatient.*

in per·so·nam, in·pėr·sō′nam, *adv., a. Law,* referring to legal action which is against a person, not against specific things.

in·phase, in′fāz″, *a. Elect.* of currents, in the same phase.

in·pour, in·pōr′, in·pȧr′, *v.t., v.i.* To cause, as liquid, to flow into a container; to pour in.

in·put, in′pu̇t″, *n.* That which is put in; the amount of power, energy, current, or voltage supplied to a machine or electric circuit. *Computer,* coded information ready for computer processing; the process of feeding information to the computer.—*a.* Of or pertaining to data or equipment for input, esp. to a computer.—*v.t., v.i. inputted, inputting. Computer,* to supply or cause to be supplied, as with data, for processing.

in·quest, in′kwest, *n.* [O.Fr. *enqueste* (Fr. *enquête*), < L. *inquirere* (pp. *inquisitus*).] A legal or judicial inquiry, esp. before a jury; a post mortem investigation made by a coroner; persons holding such an investigation, esp. a coroner's jury; their final verdict.

in·qui·e·tude, in·kwī′i·tōd, in·kwī′i·tūd, *n.* [L. *inquietudo.*] Uneasiness; restlessness; *pl.* anxious thoughts.

in·qui·line, in′kwi·lin″, in′kwi·lin, *n.* [L. *inquilinus,* lodger, < *in-,* in, and *colere,* inhabit.] *Zool.* an animal that shares a habitation with another animal; *fig.* a guest.—*a.*—**in·qui·lin·i·ty,** in″kwi·lin′i·tē, *n.*—**in·qui·li·nous,** in″kwi·li′nus, *a.*

in·quire, in·kwīr′, *v.t.*—*inquired, inquiring.* [O.Fr. *enquerre* (Fr. *enquérir*), < L. *inquirere* (pp. *inquisitus*), < *in-,* in, and *quaerere,* seek.] To ask for information about; as, to *inquire* one's name.—*v.i.* To make an investigation or search, with *into;* to seek information by questioning. Also *enquire.*—**in·quire af·ter,** to ask about, as one's health.—**in·quir·er,** *n.*—**in·quir·ing·ly,** *adv.*

in·quir·y, in·kwīr′ē, in′kwi·rē, *n. pl.* **in·quir·ies.** A seeking for truth, information, or knowledge; investigation; research; the act of inquiring; interrogation; a question or query. Also *enquiry.*

in·qui·si·tion, in″kwi·zish′an, *n.* [L. *inquisitio, inquisitionis,* < *inquiro, inquisitum,* to seek after.] The act of investigating; an inquiry, esp. severe or prolonged; *law,* an inquest. (*Cap.*), *Rom. Cath. Ch.* a court or tribunal, active from the 13th to the 19th century, established for the examination and punishment of heretics.—**in·qui·si·tion·al,** *a.*

in·quis·i·tive, in·kwiz′i·tiv, *a.* Inclined to

seek information; eager for learning; given to prying; overly curious.—**in·quis·i·tive·ly,** *adv.*—**in·quis·i·tive·ness,** *n.*

in·quis·i·tor, in·kwiz′i·tėr, *n.* One who inquires and examines, officially or not; a member of the Inquisition.—**in·quis·i·to·ri·al,** in·kwiz″i·tōr′ē·al, *a.* Pertaining to inquisition, esp. to the Court of Inquisition; making strict or searching inquiry.—**in·quis·i·to·ri·al·ly,** *adv.*

in·road, in′rōd″, *n.* [A *road,* or rather a *raid* or riding into a country.] *Usu. pl.* a harmful encroachment; as, to make *inroads* on my savings. A sudden raid or invasion.

in·rush, in′rush″, *n.* An influx; a rushing in.—**in·rush·ing,** *n., a.*

in·sal·i·vate, in·sal′i·vāt″, *v.t.*—*insalivated, insalivating.* To mix with saliva.—**in·sal·i·va·tion,** in·sal″i·vā′shan, *n.*

in·sa·lu·bri·ous, in″sa·lö′brē·us, *a.* Unfavorable to health; unhealthy; unwholesome.—**in·sa·lu·bri·ous·ly,** *adv.*—**in·sa·lu·bri·ty,** in″sa·lö′bri·tē, *n.*

in·sane, in·sān′, *a.* [L. *insanus.*] Not sane or of sound mind; mentally deranged; mad; characteristic of one mentally deranged; utterly senseless; pertaining to a place where mentally deranged persons are confined and treated; as, an insane asylum.—**in·sane·ly,** *adv.*—**in·sane·ness,** *n.*

in·san·i·tar·y, in·san′i·ter″ē, *a.* Not hygienic; unclean; injurious to health.—**in·san·i·tar·i·ness,** *n.*—**in·san·i·ta·tion,** in·san″i·tā′shan, *n.* Want of sanitation or sanitary regulation; unhygienic condition.

in·san·i·ty, in·san′i·tē, *n. pl.* **in·san·i·ties.** [L. *insanitus.*] The condition of being insane; more or less permanent derangement of one or more psychical functions. Extreme folly or an instance of it. *Law,* such unsoundness of mind as affects legal responsibility or capacity.

in·sa·tia·ble, in·sā′sha·bl, in·sā′shē·a·bl, *a.* [L. *insatiabilis.*] Incapable of being satisfied or appeased. Also *insatiate.*—**in·sa·tia·bil·i·ty,** in·sa·tia·ble·ness, in·sā″sha·bil′i·tē, in·sā″shē·a·bil′i·tē, *n.*—**in·sa·tia·bly,** *adv.*

in·sa·ti·ate, in·sā′shē·it, *a.* [L. *insatiatus.*] Insatiable.—**in·sa·ti·ate·ly,** *adv.*—**in·sa·ti·ate·ness, in·sa·ti·e·ty,** in″sa·tī′i·tē, in·sā′shi·tē, in·sā′shē·i·tē, *n.*

in·scribe, in·skrīb′, *v.t.*—*inscribed, inscribing.* [L. *inscribo, inscriptum—in-,* and *scribo,* to write.] To write down or engrave; to etch, as a motto, name, or dedication, into something durable; to address or dedicate, as a book or poem; to imprint deeply on the mind; to enroll; to write, as characters, in code. *Geom.* to draw or delineate, usu. as a lined surface, within another figure so that the boundaries of the two are in contact at certain points.—**in·scrib·a·ble,** *a.*—**in·scrib·a·ble·ness,** *n.*—**in·scrib·er,** *n.*

in·scrip·tion, in·skrip′shan, *n.* [L. *inscriptio, inscriptionis.*] The act of inscribing or anything inscribed; a word or words engraved on stone, metal, or other hard substance for public inspection; the dedication of a book or poem to a person as a mark of respect; *numis.* the words in the middle of the reverse side of some coins or medals.—**in·scrip·tion·al,** *a.*—**in·scrip·tion·less,** *a.*

in·scrip·tive, in·skrip′tiv, *a.* Of the character of or pertaining to an inscription.—**in·scrip·tive·ly,** *adv.*

in·scroll, in·skrōl′, *v.t.* Enscroll.

in·scru·ta·ble, in·skrö′ta·bl, *a.* [Fr. *inscrutable,* L. *inscrutabilis—in-,* not, and *scrutor,* to search.] Incapable of being searched into and understood; unable to be easily accounted for or explained; opaque; impenetrable.—**in·scru·ta·bly,** *adv.*—**in·scru·ta·bil·i·ty,** in·skrö″ta·bil′i·tē, *n.*—**in·scru·ta·ble·ness,** *n.*

in·seam, in′sēm″, *n.* An inside seam of a piece of clothing or footwear.

in·sect, in′sekt, *n.* [L. *insectum,* something cut in (from their shape), < *inseco,* *insectum,* to cut into.] One of a class of small arthropods characterized in maturity by a body divided into a head, thorax, and abdomen, by three pairs of legs, and usu. by two pairs of wings. A contemptible person.—*a.* Resembling an insect; of a person, mean or contemptible.

in·sec·tar·y, in′sek·ter″ē, *n. pl.* **in·sec·tar·ies.** A laboratory used for the breeding and study of live insects, esp. their habits and responses. Also **in·sec·tar·i·um.**

in·sec·ti·cide, in·sek′ti·sīd″, *n.* A substance or preparation used for killing insects; the killing of insects.—**in·sec·ti·cid·al,** in·sek″ti·sīd′al, *a.*

in·sec·ti·fuge, in·sek′ti·fūj″, *n.* A substance used for repelling insects.

in·sec·tile, in·sek′til, *a.* Of or resembling an insect; composed of insects, as certain animal food.

in·sec·ti·vore, in·sek′ti·vōr″, *n.* An insectivorous animal or plant; one of the *Insectivora,* an order of small mammals including the shrews, moles, and hedgehogs.—**in·sec·tiv·o·rous,** in″sek·tiv′ėr·us, *a.* Insect-eating, as certain animals or insect-digesting, as certain plants; belonging or pertaining to the order *Insectivora.*

in·se·cure, in″si·kūr′, *a.* Prone to fear or anxiety; not sufficiently strong or guarded; unsafe; precarious.—**in·se·cure·ly,** *adv.*—**in·se·cure·ness,** *n.*—**in·se·cu·ri·ty,** in″si·kūr′i·tē, *n.*

in·sem·i·nate, in·sem′i·nāt″, *v.t.*—*inseminated, inseminating.* [L. *inseminatus,* pp. of *inseminare,* < *in-,* in, and *seminare,* sow, E. *seminate.*] To inject, as seed, into something; implant, as ideas; impregnate, esp. with semen.—**in·sem·i·na·tion,** in·sem″i·nā′shan, *n.*

in·sen·sate, in·sen′sāt, in·sen′sit, *a.* [L.L. *insensatus.*] Lacking feeling, sensitivity, sympathy, or comprehension; gross; devoid of sense; without sensation; as, *insensate* rock.—**in·sen·sate·ly,** *adv.*—**in·sen·sate·ness,** *n.*

in·sen·si·ble, in·sen′si·bl, *a.* [L. *insensibilis.*] Unconscious; numb to pain; unable to perceive or understand; not susceptible to emotion or passion; indifferent; gradual; as, *insensible* stages in a process.—**in·sen·si·ble·ness, in·sen·si·bil·i·ty,** in·sen″si·bil′i·tē, *n. pl.* **in·sen·si·bil·i·ties.**—**in·sen·si·bly,** *adv.*

in·sen·si·tive, in·sen′si·tiv, *a.* Not sensitive; without physical sensation or feeling; not susceptible to agencies or influences; lacking sensibility or feeling.—**in·sen·si·tive·ness, in·sen·si·tiv·i·ty,** in·sen″si·tiv′i·tē, *n.*—**in·sen·si·tive·ly,** *adv.*

in·sen·ti·ent, in·sen′shē·ent, in·sen′shent, *a.* Not sentient; lacking sensation or feeling; inanimate.—**in·sen·ti·ence, in·sen·ti·en·cy,** *n.*

in·sep·a·ra·ble, in·sep′ėr·a·bl, in·sep′ra·bl, *a.* [L. *inseparabilis.*] Incapable of being parted or disjoined.—*n. Usu. pl.* indivisible qualities or objects; close friends usu. spending much time together.—**in·sep·a·ra·bil·i·ty,** in·sep″ėr·a·bil′i·tē, *n.*—**in·sep·a·ra·bly,** *adv.*

in·sert, in·surt′, *v.t.* [L. *insertus,* pp. of *inserere.*] To put or set in; to place in a hole or space, or between parts; to introduce into the body of something, as an advertisement into a newspaper.—in′surt, *n.* Something inserted or to be inserted; an extra leaf or leaves, as of illustrations or charts, inserted between the pages of text in a book before it is bound; a circular or the like placed inside a book or periodical which is to be mailed; a cut-in.—**in·sert·er,** *n.*

in·ser·tion, in·sur′shan, *n.* [L.L. *insertion-.*] The act of inserting; that which is inserted, as lace ornamentation sewn to pieces of material, or a map into a page of text. *Biol.* manner or place of attachment, as of an organ or muscle.—**in·ser·tion·al,** *a.*

in·ses·so·ri·al, in″se·sõr′e̱·al, in″se·s̲a̲r′-e̱·al, *a.* [N.L. *Insessores,* pl., the perching birds, < L. *insidere,* sit in or on.] Habitually perching, as a bird; adapted for perching, as a bird's foot.

in·set, in·set′, *v.t.—inset, insetting.* To insert or place in, as material in a garment.—in′set″, *n.* The act of setting in; something set in, as a pictorial representation within a larger illustration, or a section of material inserted into a garment, like a panel in a dress or a gusset in a sleeve.

in·sheathe, in·s̲h̲ē̲t̲h̲′, *v.t.* Ensheath.

in·shore, in′shõr′, in′s̲h̲a̲r′, *a., adv.* Near or toward the shore.

in·shrine, in·shrīn′, *v.t.* Enshrine.

in·side, in′sīd′, *n.* An inner side, surface, or part; a favorable position that allows one an advantage; *pl.* the inner body parts, as the stomach and intestines.—in″sīd′, in′sīd′, *a.* Situated or being on or in the inside; within; interior; internal; originating, suitable for, acting, employed, or done within a building or place; known to a few; confidential.—in″sīd′, *adv.* On the inside; within; within a space or period.—in″sīd′, in′sīd′, *prep.* Within.—**in·side of,** within.—**in·sid·er,** in″sī′dẽr, *n.* A member of an organization or society; a person whose position allows him an advantage or special information.

in·side track, *n.* The shortest lane of a race track, being the closest to the guard rail. *Colloq.* a vantage point, esp. one due to a favorable position or inside knowledge.

in·sid·i·ous, in·sid′e̱·us, *a.* [L. *insidiosus,* < *insidiae,* ambush, artifice, < *insidere,* sit in or on.] Seeking or intended to entrap or beguile; stealthily treacherous or deceitful; operating or proceeding inconspicuously but with grave effect; as, an *insidious* poison.—**in·sid·i·ous·ly,** *adv.*—**in·sid·i·ous·ness,** *n.*

in·sight, in′sīt″, *n.* The act or power of grasping or intuitively understanding the essence of something; discernment; penetration; perception.—**in·sight·ful,** *a.*

in·sig·ni·a, in·sig′ne̱·a, *n. pl.* [L. pl. of *insigne,* a mark, neut. of *insignis,* remarkable.] Badges or distinguishing marks of office, honor, or membership. *Sing.* in *constr.* a badge, emblem, or mark denoting rank, honor, or membership; pl. **in·sig·ni·as.**

in·sig·nif·i·cant, in″sig·nif′i·kant, *a.* Having little importance; negligible; petty; of a person, lacking importance, influence, character, or the like.—**in·sig·nif·i·cant·ly,** *adv.*—**in·sig·nif·i·cance, in·sig·nif·i·can·cy,** *n. pl.* **in·sig·nif·i·can·cies.**

in·sin·cere, in″sin·sẽr′, *a.* [L. *insincerus.*] Not honest in the expression of actual feeling; deceitful.—**in·sin·cere·ly,** *adv.*—**in·sin·cer·i·ty,** in″sin·ser′i·tē, *n. pl.* **in·sin·cer·i·ties.**

in·sin·u·ate, in·sin′ū·āt″, *v.t.—insinuated, insinuating.* [L. *insinuo, insinuatum—in-,* and *sinuo,* to wind, < *sinus,* a bending, curve, bosom.] To introduce by concealed or guarded means; to hint or suggest subtly; to ingratiate, esp. by calculated remarks or action.—*v.i.* To intimate or imply, usu. something unfavorable. *Archaic,* to creep or wind.—**in·sin·u·at·ing, in·sin·u·a·tive,** in·sin′ū·ā″tiv, in·sin′ū·a·tiv, *a.* Given to or characterized by intimation; subtly winning favor.—**in·sin·u·at·ing·ly,** *adv.*—**in·sin·u·a·tor,** *n.*

in·sin·u·a·tion, in·sin″ū·ā′shan, *n.* [L. *insinuatio, insinuationis.*] An indirect suggestion, esp. a derogatory or unfavorable one; an innuendo; the act of suggesting indirectly. The subtle pursuit of favor, usu.

by ingratiating remarks or actions; such a remark or action.

in·sip·id, in·sip′id, *a.* [L. *insipidus—in-,* not, and *sapidus,* savory, < *sapio,* to taste.] Tasteless; wanting interest, spirit, life, or animation; dull, heavy, or uninteresting.—**in·si·pid·i·ty, in·sip·id·ness,** in″si·pid′i·tē, *n.*—**in·sip·id·ly,** *adv.*

in·sist, in·sist′, *v.i.* [L. *insisto—in-,* and *sisto,* to stand.] To demand firmly, with *on* or *upon;* as, to *insist on* locking the windows; to assert an opinion or resolution emphatically, with *on* or *upon;* to repeatedly or persistently dwell on something, with *on* or *upon.*—*v.t.* To contend or assert absolutely; as, to *insist* that the story is untrue; to demand emphatically, as: I *insist* that you leave.—**in·sist·ence, in·sist·en·cy,** in·-sis′tens, *n.* pl. **in·sist·en·cies.—in·sist·ent,** *a.*—**in·sist·ent·ly, in·sist·ing·ly,** *adv.*—**in·sist·er,** *n.*

in si·tu, in sīt′ū̲, in sit′ū̲, *adv., a.* Latin, in its original position.

in·snare, in·snâr′, *v.t.* Ensnare.—**in·snare·ment,** *n.*—**in·snar·er,** *n.*

in·so·bri·e·ty, in″so·brī′i·tē, *n.* Intemperance; drunkenness.

in·so·ci·a·ble, in·sō′sha·bl, *a.* Not sociable; taciturn.—**in·so·ci·a·bly,** *adv.*—**in·so·ci·a·bil·i·ty,** in·sō″sha·bil′i·tē, *n.*

in·so·far, in″so·fär′, in″sō·fär′, *adv.* To this degree or to such an extent, usu. followed by *as.*

in·so·late, in′sō·lāt″, *v.t.—insolated, insolating.* [L. *insolo, insolatum—in-,* and *sol,* the sun.] To dry or prepare in the sun's rays; to expose to the heat of the sun.—**in·so·la·tion,** in″sō·lā′shan, *n.*

in·sole, in′sōl, *n.* The inner sole of a shoe or boot; a removable thickness of warm or waterproof material used as an inner sole in a shoe.

in·so·lent, in′so·lent, *a.* [L. *insolens, insolentis,* contrary to custom, immoderate, haughty, insolent.] Of a person, saucily disrespectful; of language or conduct, rudely overbearing.—*n.* A rudely disrespectful person.—**in·so·lence,** *n.* Extreme discourtesy; impudence.—**in·so·lent·ly,** *adv.*

in·sol·u·ble, in·sol′ū·bl, *a.* [Prefix *in-,* not, and *soluble.*] Incapable of being dissolved, particularly by a liquid; not to be solved or explained.—**in·sol·u·bil·i·ty,** in·sol″ū·bil′i·tē, **in·sol·u·ble·ness,** *n.*—**in·sol·u·bly,** *adv.*

in·solv·a·ble, in·sol′va·bl, *a.* [Prefix *in,* not, and *solvable.*] Not to be solved or explained; not admitting solution.

in·sol·vent, in·sol′vent, *a.* Not solvent; without the money, goods, or estate sufficient to pay all debts; of or pertaining to insolvency or insolvents.—*n.* A person with debts he cannot pay.—**in·sol·ven·cy,** *n.*

in·som·ni·a, in·som′ne̱·a, *n.* [L. < *insomnis,* sleepless, < *in-,* not, and *somnus,* sleep.] Inability to sleep, esp. when chronic; sleeplessness.—**in·som·ni·ac,** in·som′ne̱·ak″, *n., a.*—**in·som·ni·ous,** *a.*

in·so·much, in″sō·much′, *adv.* To such a degree; so, usu. followed by *that* or *as.*—**in·so·much as,** inasmuch as.

in·sou·ci·ant, in·sō′se̱·ant, Fr. aN·sō·-syäN′, *a.* [Fr. < *in-,* not, and *souciant,* ppr. of *soucier,* refl., concern oneself, care, < L. *sollicitare,* disturb, E. *solicit.*] Free from concern or care; without anxiety; carefree.—**in·sou·ci·ant·ly,** *adv.*—**in·sou·ci·ance,** in·sō′se̱·ans, Fr. aN·sō·syäns′, *n.*

in·soul, in·sōl′, *v.t.* Ensoul.

in·spect, in·spekt′, *v.t.* [L. *inspicio, inspectum.*] To examine or view carefully or closely; to view for the purpose of discovering errors; to examine officially, as troops or buildings.

in·spec·tion, in·spek′shan, *n.* The act of inspecting; a critical examination or careful viewing; an official review or examination, as of troops.—**in·spec·tive,** *a.*

in·spec·tor, in·spek′tẽr, *n.* A person who reviews or examines critically; the overseer of a polling place; a police official, ranking below superintendent, in command of several precincts.—**in·spec·tor·ate,** in·spek′tẽr·it, *n.* A body of inspectors or overseers. Their duties or office of investigation; also **in·spec·tor·ship.** The area under the administration of an inspector.—**in·spec·to·ral, in·spec·to·ri·al,** in″spek·tõr′e̱·al, *a.*

in·sphere, in·sfẽr′, *v.t.* Ensphere.

in·spi·ra·tion, in″spi·rā′shan, *n.* [L. *inspiratio.*] A prompting, esp. to creative action, that arises within the mind; an illumination; the act of inspiring; state of being inspired; *theol.* the divine influence by which sacred writers were instructed, esp. in scriptural writing; any source or agent of inspiration; *biol.* breathing.—**in·spi·ra·tion·al,** *a.* Referring to that which produces or is influenced by inspiration.—**in·spi·ra·tion·al·ly,** *adv.*—**in·spir·a·to·ry,** in·spīr′a·tõr″ē, in·spīr′a·t̲a̲r″ē, *a.* Referring to or assisting in inhalation.

in·spire, in·spīr′, *v.t.—inspired, inspiring,* [L. *inspiro.*] To influence; to prompt, as creative action or thought; to stir or animate; to cause, or arouse, as thought or feeling; to generate; *theol.* to guide or animate by divine influence; *biol.* to draw into the lungs.—*v.i.* To breathe or inhale; to communicate inspiration.—**in·spir·a·ble,** *a.*—**in·spir·er,** *n.*

in·spir·it, in·spir′it, *v.i.* To enliven, animate, or encourage; invigorate; enspirit.

in·spis·sate, in·spis′āt, *v.t., v.i.—inspissated, inspissating.* [L. *inspisso, inspissatum.*] To make thick by evaporation.—**in·spis·sa·tion,** in″spi·sā′shan, *n.*—**in·spis·sa·tor,** in′spi·sā″tẽr, *n.*

in·sta·ble, in·stā′bl, *a.* [L. *instabilis.*] Unstable.—**in·sta·bil·i·ty,** in″sta·bil′i·tē, *n.* Lack of a stable temperament; inconstancy; want of reliability; want of firmness in construction.

in·stall, *Brit. also* **in·stal,** in·stal′, *v.t.* [Fr. *installer—in-,* in, and O.H.G. *stal,* a place, E. *stall.*] To set up or adjust for use or service; as, to *install* a heating system; to appoint to an office or post, usu. with formal ceremony; to settle or establish in a position, as in a chair.—**in·stal·la·tion,** in″sta·lā′shan, *n.* Any mechanical device or apparatus set up or adjusted for use; the act of establishing or installing; any military post or camp equipped for official activity.—**in·stall·er,** *n.*

in·stall·ment, *Brit. also* **in·stal·ment,** in·stal′ment, *n.* Any of the specified parts of a debt or sum due at set intervals over a stated time period; one of a number of parts, as of a story, issued at fixed intervals. An installation; the act of installing; state of being installed.

in·stall·ment plan, *n.* A system of credit for goods and services with fixed payments distributed over a specific time period. *Brit.* hire-purchase; never-never plan.

in·stance, in′stans, *n.* [O.Fr. Fr. *instance,* < L. *instantia,* < *instans.*] An example, esp. one given as an illustration or proof; one event in a series; *law,* a suit, proceeding, or precedent.—*v.t.—instanced, instancing.* To cite as an instance or example.—**in·stan·cy,** *n.* Urgency, pressing nature; immediateness.

in·stant, in′stant, *a.* [O.Fr. Fr. *instant,* < L. *instans* (*instant-*), ppr. of *instare,* stand upon, insist, be at hand.] Immediate; imminent; current; pressing; urgent; *colloq.* of foods, readily prepared, usu. by adding water.—*n.* The point of time now present; an infinitesimal or very short space of time; a particular moment; *colloq.* a readily prepared food.—*adv.* Instantly; at once.

in·stan·ta·ne·ous, in″stan·tā′nē·us, *a.* Occurring, accomplished, or completed within an imperceptible amount of time; immediate; referring to or existing at a given instant.—**in·stan·ta·ne·ous·ly,** *adv.* —**in·stan·ta·ne·ous·ness,** *n.*

in·stan·ter, in·stan′tėr, *adv.* [L.] Immediately; without delay; at once.

in·stant·ly, in′stant·lē, *adv.* Immediately; at once. *Archaic,* urgently.—*conj.* As soon as.

in·stant re·play, *n. TV,* an almost immediate rebroadcast of videotaped material, esp. of a segment of a live broadcast of a sports event.

in·star, in′stär, *n. Entom.* an insect in any phase of development between molts.

in·state, in·stāt′, *v.t.*—*instated, instating.* To install or place in a particular position or office.—**in·state·ment,** *n.*

in·stead, in·sted′, *adv.* [Orig. two words, *in stead.*] In the place; rather than, with *of,* as: She chose the trip *instead of* the money. In lieu; as an alternative or substitute, with *of,* as: They sent me a replacement *instead of* a refund.

in·step, in′step″, *n.* [Formerly *instop, instup,* perh. < *in-* and *stoop,* lit. 'the bend in.'] *Anat.* The arched part of the upper side of the human foot; that part of a shoe or stocking which covers the instep; the part of the hind leg of a horse extending from the hock to the pastern joint.

in·sti·gate, in′sti·gāt, *v.t.*—*instigated, instigating.* [L. *instigatus,* pp. of *instigare,* < *in-,* in, on, and *-stigare,* akin to *-stinguere,* prick, and prob. to *stimulus,* goad.] To spur on or incite to some action or course; to bring about by incitement or persuasion; to foment.—**in·sti·ga·tion,** in″sti·gā′shan, *n.* The act of instigating; incitement.—**in·sti·ga·tive,** *a.*—**in·sti·ga·tor,** *n.*

in·still, in·stil, in·stil′, *v.t.*—*instilled, instilling.* [L. *instillare, in-,* in, and *stillare,* drop, drip, < *stilla,* a drop.] To introduce drop by drop; to infuse by degrees into the mind; to inject something; to cause to enter gradually; to insinuate or inculcate.—**in·stil·la·tion,** in″sti·lā′shan, *n.* [L. *instillatio* (*n-*).] The act of instilling; something instilled.—**in·stil·ler,** *n.*—**in·still·ment, in·stil·ment,** *n.*

in·stinct, in′stingkt, *n.* [L. *instinctus,* pp. of *instinguere,* instigate, impel, < *in,* in, on, and *-stinguere,* prick.] *Psychol.* an innate, automatic impulse, in humans and animals, to satisfy basic biological needs, leading to behavior that is purposeful and directive; an involuntary tendency or drive to act in a specific way under given conditions. A natural aptitude or gift for something.— in·stingkt′, *a. Archaic,* imbued or pervaded with something, usu. followed by *with;* as, a sermon *instinct with* feeling.—**in·stinc·tu·al,** *a.* Pertaining to, or of, the nature of instinct; prompted by, or resulting from, instinct.—**in·stinc·tive,** *a.* Spontaneous, unlearned.—**in·stinc·tive·ly,** *adv.*

in·sti·tute, in′sti·tōt″, in′sti·tūt″, *v.t.*— *instituted, instituting.* [L. *institutus,* pp. of *instituere,* < *in-,* in, on, and *statuere,* set up, set, establish.] To set up or establish; to bring into use or practice; to set in operation, as an investigation or legal proceeding; inaugurate or initiate, as a program; to establish in an office or a position; *eccles.* assign to or invest with a spiritual charge.—*n.* A society or organization for carrying on a particular work, as of literary, scientific, or educational character; the building occupied by such a society; something instituted, as an established principle, law, or custom; *pl., law,* an elementary digest of principles of jurisprudence. *Educ.* a brief concentrated program of instruction or sequence of lectures offered to a group having some specialized occupation; a school, often within a university, specializing in technical studies; a center, usu. affiliated with a university, for research and instruction at the postgraduate level in some highly specialized subject.—**in·sti·tut·er,** **in·sti·tu·tor,** *n.*

in·sti·tu·tion, in″sti·tō′shan, in″sti·tū′-shan, *n.* [L. *institutio*(*n-*).] The act of instituting; establishment; foundation; an established law, custom, practice, or organization; *colloq.* any familiar practice or object. An organization or establishment instituted for some public, educational, or charitable purpose; the building devoted to its work; a place of confinement; as, a penal *institution;* a fundamental behavioral pattern of a culture; as, the *institution* of marriage; *eccles.* the establishment of the Eucharist by Jesus Christ.—**in·sti·tu·tion·al,** *a.* Pertaining to or of the nature of an institution; characterized by the drabness and conformity associated with large institutions.—**in·sti·tu·tion·al·ly,** *adv.*

in·sti·tu·tion·al·ism, in″sti·tō′sha·na·liz″um, in″sti·tū′sha·na·liz″um, *n.* Strong attachment to established institutions, as of religion; the system of institutions or organized societies for public, charitable, or educational purposes.—**in·sti·tu·tion·al·ist,** *n.*

in·sti·tu·tion·al·ize, in″sti·tō′sha·na·liz″, in″sti·tū′sha·na·liz″, *v.t.*—*institutionalized, institutionalizing.* To render institutional; make into or treat as an institution. —**in·sti·tu·tion·al·i·za·tion,** *n.*

in·struct, in·strukt′, *v.t.* [L. *instruo, instructum—in-,* and *struo,* to join together, to pile up.] To teach; to educate; to impart knowledge or information to; to train; to direct, order, or command.—**in·struc·ted,** *a.*

in·struc·tion, in·struk′shan, *n.* [L. *instructio.*] The act of instructing or teaching; information; an order, mandate, or direction; *computers,* data which, when coded, directs a computer to perform specific operations.—**in·struc·tion·al,** *a.*

in·struc·tive, in·struk′tiv, *a.* Conveying knowledge; serving to enlighten or inform. **in·struc·tive·ly,** *adv.*—**in·struc·tive·ness,** *n.*

in·struc·tor, in·struk′tėr, *n.* [L.] One who instructs; a teacher; a college teacher who ranks below assistant professor.— **in·struc·tor·ship,** *n.*—**in·struc·tress,** in·struk′tris, *n.* Fem. of instructor.

in·stru·ment, in′stru·ment, *n.* [L. *instrumentum,* < *instruo,* to prepare.] A tool, implement, or utensil; a means by which something is performed or effected; any contrivance from which music is produced; a person used to execute a plan or purpose, as a dupe; an agency; as, an executive *instrument* of government; a device for precise measurement, as an altimeter or speedometer; *law,* a legal paper, as a deed. —*v.t.* To provide with instruments; as, to *instrument* a guided missile.—**in·stru·men·tal,** in″stru·men′tal, *a.* Conducive as a means to some end; pertaining to instruments, esp. musical instruments.—*n.* A musical arrangement played by one or more instruments.—**in·stru·men·tal·ly,** *adv.* By use of an instrument, esp. instruments of music.

in·stru·men·ta·list, in″stru·men′ta·list, *n.* One who plays upon a musical instrument; *philos.* a believer in the doctrine of instrumentalism.

in·stru·men·tal·ism, in″stru·men′ta·liz″um, *n. Philos.* the pragmatic doctrine that action should follow from knowledge and ideas whose authenticity is established by their usefulness.

in·stru·men·tal·i·ty, in″stru·men·tal′i·tē, *n. pl.* **in·stru·men·tal·i·ties.** The con-dition of being instrumental anything that helps to achieve a goal; an agency; a means.

in·stru·men·ta·tion, in″stru·men·tā′shan, *n.* The art of arranging music for a number of instruments; the music for a number of instruments; execution of music on an instrument; the science concerned with the manufacture and usage of instruments for industry, science, etc.

in·stru·ment fly·ing, *n. Aeron.* navigation of a plane, depending solely on instruments for guidance.

in·stru·ment land·ing, *n.* A landing made in poor visibility, using only aircraft instruments and directive ground devices.

in·stru·ment pan·el, *n.* A panel or board containing instruments and gauges, esp. in an airplane or automobile.

in·sub·or·di·nate, in″su·bȧr′di·nit, *a.* Not submitting to authority; willfully disrespectful or disobedient; rebellious.—*n.* —**in·sub·or·di·nate·ly,** *adv.*—**in·sub·-or·di·na·tion,** *n.*

in·sub·stan·tial, in″sub·stan′shal, *a.* [M.L. *insubstantialis.*] Lacking substance; slight; imaginary or unreal.—**in·sub·stan·-ti·al·i·ty,** *n.*

in·suf·fer·a·ble, in·suf′ėr·a·bl, *a.* Not to be suffered, borne, or endured; intolerable; unendurable.—**in·suf·fer·a·ble·ness,** *n.*—**in·suf·fer·a·bly,** *adv.*

in·suf·fi·cient, in″su·fish′ent, *a.* [L.L. *insufficiens* (*-ent-*).] Not sufficient; deficient; inadequate.—**in·suf·fi·cience, in·suf·fi·cien·cy,** *n. pl.* **in·suf·fi·cien·cies.**—**in·-suf·fi·cient·ly,** *adv.*

in·suf·flate, in·suf′lāt, in′su·flāt″, *v.t.*— *insufflated, insufflating.* [L.L. *insufflatus,* pp. of *insufflare.*] To blow or breathe in; to breathe upon, as in baptizing; *med.* to blow, as air or a medicinal substance, into some opening or upon some part of the body; to treat by insufflation.—**in·suf·fla·tion,** *n.*— **in·suf·fla·tor,** *n.*

in·su·lar, in′su·lėr, ins′ū·lėr, *a.* [L.L. *insularis,* < L. *insula,* island.] Of or pertaining to an island or islands; dwelling or situated on an island; forming an island; detached, or standing alone; narrow, provincial, or illiberal; as, *insular* prejudices. *Med.* referring to a separate group of tissues or cells, as the islets of Langerhans in the pancreas.—**in·su·lar·ism,** *n.*—**in·su·lar·i·ty,** in″su·lar′i·tē, ins″ū·lar′i·tē, *n.*

in·su·late, in′su·lāt″, ins′ya·lāt″, *v.t.*— *insulated, insulating.* [L. *insulatus,* made into an island, < *insula,* island.] To place in detachment; to isolate; to cover, surround, or separate with nonconducting material to prevent or lessen the passage of electricity, heat, or sound.—**in·su·la·tion,** *n.* The act of insulating, or the resulting state; a nonconducting material.—**in·su·la·tor,** *n.* A nonconductor; *elect.* a contrivance of nonconducting material for supporting and insulating a conductor.

in·su·lin, in′su·lin, ins′yu·lin, *n.* [L. *insula,* island: with reference to the islands of the pancreas.] *Biochem.* a hormone secreted by the islets of Langerhans in the pancreas, essential to the regulation of carbohydrate metabolism; *med.* a preparation of this hormone used in the treatment of diabetes.

in·su·lin shock, *n. Med.* an abnormal condition, likely to cause collapse, which occurs when an overdose of insulin causes a sudden reduction of sugar in the blood.

in·sult, in′sult, *n.* [Fr. *insulte;* L. *insultus,* < *insilio, insultum,* to leap on.] Any gross affront or indignity offered to another, either by words or action; an act or speech of insolence or contempt.—in·sult′, *v.t.* To treat with gross abuse, insolence, or contempt.—**in·sult·a·ble,** *a.*—**in·sult·er,** *n.*—**in·sult·ing·ly,** *adv.*

in·su·per·a·ble, in·sö′pėr·a·bl, a. [L. *insuperabilis*.] Incapable of being overcome or surmounted, as obstacles or difficulties. —**in·su·per·a·bil·i·ty**, in·sö″pėr·a·bil′i·tē, n.—**in·su·per·a·bly**, adv.

in·sup·port·a·ble, in″su·pōr′ta·bl, a. Not to be supported; unjustifiable; unbearable; insufferable, intolerable.—**in·sup·port·a·ble·ness**, n.—**in·sup·port·a·bly**, adv.

in·sup·press·i·ble, in″su·pres′i·bl, a. Incapable of being suppressed or concealed. —**in·sup·press·i·bly**, adv.

in·sur·a·ble, in·shur′a·bl, a. Capable of being insured, as against the risk of loss or harm; proper to be insured.—**in·sur·a·bil·i·ty**, in·shur″a·bil′i·tē, n.

in·sur·ance, in·shur′ans, n. The act of insuring; the act, system, or business of insuring property, life, or person against loss or harm arising in specified contingencies, as fire, accident, death, etc., in consideration of a payment proportionate to the risk involved; the contract thus made, set forth in a written or printed agreement or policy; the sum paid for insuring anything; the amount for which anything is insured.—**in·sur·ant**, n. The person who takes out an insurance policy.

in·sure, in·shur′, v.t.—*insured, insuring*. [Var. of *ensure*.] To guarantee against risk of loss or harm; to secure indemnity to or on, in case of loss, damage, or death; to issue or procure an insurance policy on.—v.i. To issue or procure an insurance policy.—**in·sured**, n. The person insured. —**in·sur·er**, in·shur′ėr, n. The person or company writing the insurance policy.

in·sur·gent, in·sur′jent, a. [L. *insurgens* (-ent-), ppr. of *insurgere* (pp. *insurrectus*), rise on or up.] Actively revolting against existing government; rebellious.—n. A rebel. *U.S. politics*, a member of a political party who revolts against the party program.—**in·sur·gence**, **in·sur·gen·cy**, n. —**in·sur·gent·ly**, adv.

in·sur·mount·a·ble, in″sėr·mount′ta·bl, a. Incapable of being surmounted, passed over, or overcome.—**in·sur·mount·a·bly**, adv.

in·sur·rec·tion, in″su·rek′shan, n. [L.L. *insurrectio(n-)*, < L. *insurgere*: *insurgent*.] The act of rising in open resistance against established authority; a revolt; an incipient rebellion.—**in·sur·rec·tion·ar·y**, n. pl. **in·sur·rec·tion·ar·ies**. Insurgent; a rebel. —a. Also **in·sur·rec·tion·al**.—**in·sur·rec·tion·al·ly**, adv.—**in·sur·rec·tion··ism**, n.—**in·sur·rec·tion·ist**, n.

in·sus·cep·ti·ble, in″su·sep′ta·bl, a. Not susceptible; not capable of being affected or impressed, usu. followed by *of* or *to*.—**in·sus·cep·ti·bil·i·ty**, in·su·sep″ti·bil′i·tē, n.—**in·sus·cep·ti·bly**, adv.

in·tact, in·takt′, a. [L. *intactus*.] Untouched or unaffected by anything that might harm or impair; remaining uninjured, unaltered, sound, or whole.—**in·tact·ness**, n.

in·tagl·io, in·tal′yō, in·täl′yō, It. ēn·tä′lyạ, n. pl. **in·tagl·ios**, It. **in·ta·gli**, ēn·tä′lyē. [It. < *intagliare*, to carve—*in-*, and *tagliare*, to cut, Fr. *tailler*.] Any figure engraved or cut into a substance so as to form a hollow; a gem with a figure or design that is sunk below the surface; *print.* a reproduction process using a plate into which the letters and other characters are sunk. See *gravure*.

in·take, in′tāk″, n. The point at which a fluid or gas enters a channel or pipe; the act of taking in; that which is taken in; the quantity taken in; the quantity of energy taken into a mechanical system; a narrowing or contraction, as in a tube.

in·tan·gi·ble, in·tan′ji·bl, a. Not tangible; incapable of being perceived by the sense of touch, as incorporeal or immaterial things; not to be grasped mentally, or not

definite or clear to the mind; vague.—n. Anything intangible, esp. a business asset such as good will.—**in·tan·gi·bil·i·ty**, in·tan″ji·bil′i·tē, **in·tan·gi·ble·ness**, n.—**in·tan·gi·bly**, adv.

in·tar·si·a, in·tär′sē·a, n. A wooden mosaic, esp. of Renaissance Italy, inlaid into a surface; the technique of ornamenting a surface in such a manner.—**in·tar·si·ate**, in·tär′sē·āt″, in·tär′sē·it, a.

in·te·ger, in′ti·jėr, n. [L. *integer*, untouched, whole, entire, sound, pure, upright.] *Math.* a whole number, as distinguished from a fraction or a mixed number. A complete entity.

in·te·gra·ble, in′te·gra·bl, a. *Math.* having the capacity to be integrated, as a differential equation.—**in·te·gra·bil·i·ty**, in″te·gra·bil′i·tē, n.

in·te·gral, in′te·gral, a. Whole; entire; complete; belonging to or forming a necessary part of a whole. *Math.* pertaining to a whole number or undivided quantity; not fractional; pertaining to integration.—n. A whole; an entire thing; *math.* a Riemann integral.—**in·te·gral·i·ty**, in″te·gral′i·tē, n.—**in·te·gral·ly**, adv.

in·te·gral cal·cu·lus, n. *Math.* a branch of mathematical analysis concerned with integrals and their use in the solution of differential equations and problems involving lengths, volumes, and areas.

in·te·grand, in′te·grand″, n. [L. *integrandus*, gerundive of *integrare*.] *Math.* the expression to be integrated.

in·te·grant, in′te·grant, a. Making part of a whole; integral.—n. A component part.

in·te·grate, in′te·grāt″, v.t.—*integrated, integrating*. [L. *integratus*, pp. of *integrare*, make whole, < *integer*.] To make up or complete as a whole, as parts do; to bring together, as parts, into a whole; to unite; to indicate the total amount or the mean value of; *math.* to find the integral of. To make equally available, as educational facilities or residences, to members of all races, religions, and ethnic groups.—v.i. To become integrated.

in·te·grat·ed cir·cuit, n. A miniaturized electronic circuit formed by processing a very small block of a semiconductor, usu. crystalline silicon.

in·te·grat·ed in·dus·try, n. An industry in which the manufacturer controls production from raw materials to finished goods.

in·te·gra·tion, in″te·grā′shan, n. [L. *integratio(n-)*.] The act of integrating; the act of combining into an integral whole; unification of diverse elements into a complex whole or a harmonious relation; harmonization; behavior, as of the individual, in harmony with the environment; the act of making equally available, as organizations, services, or places of business, to members of all races, religions, and ethnic groups. *Psychol.* organization of the components of one's personality into a well-balanced behavior pattern. *Math.* the operation of finding the integral of a function or equation; the inverse of differentiation.

in·te·gra·tion·ist, in″te·grā′sha·nist, n. A person who advocates equal opportunities for members of all races, religions, and ethnic groups in education, employment, housing, and like areas.

in·te·gra·tor, in′te·grā″tėr, n. One who or that which integrates, esp. an instrument for indicating the total amount or mean value, as of area or temperature.

in·teg·ri·ty, in·teg′ri·tē, n. pl. **in·teg·ri·ties**. [L. *integritas*, < *integer*.] Unimpaired moral principles; honesty; soundness; the quality of being whole or undivided.

in·teg·u·ment, in·teg′ū·ment, n. [L. *integumentum*, < *integere*, cover.] A cover-

ing, esp. of an animal or plant body; a skin, shell, rind, or husk.—**in·teg·u·men·ta·ry**, in·teg·u·men·tal, in·teg″ū·men′ta·rē, a.

in·tel·lect, in′te·lekt″, n. [L. *intellectus*, < *intelligo*, to understand—*inter*, between, and *lego*, to choose or pick.] Mental capacity to comprehend ideas and relationships and to exercise judgment; the power to learn and to think; a person of exceptional mental abilities; the collective mentalities of a group.—**in·tel·lec·tion**, in″te·lek′shan, n. The act of understanding; a specific instance of this.—**in·tel·lec·tive**, a. Pertaining to the intellect.—**in·tel·lec·tive·ly**, adv.

in·tel·lec·tu·al, in″te·lek′chö·al, a. Relating to the intellect and the exercise of mental faculties; demanding the employment of one's intelligence; rational; highly intelligent; engaged in creative thinking. —**in·tel·lec·tu·al·ism**, n. Dedication to intellectual interests.—**in·tel·lec·tu·al·ist**, n.—**in·tel·lec·tu·al·is·tic**, in″te·lek″chö·a·lis′tik, a.—**in·tel·lec·tu·al·i·ty**, in″te·lek″chö·al′i·tē, n.—**in·tel·lec·tu·al·ize**, in″te·lek′chö·a·līz″, v.t. To make rational; to regard intellectually.

in·tel·li·gence, in·tel′i·jens, n. [L. *intelligentia*.] The faculty or ability for comprehending and reasoning with facts, truths, or propositions; intellectual power; knowledge imparted or acquired; the collecting of information; information communicated, as news or notices; secret enemy information; an agency that seeks to secure such information; an intelligent or spiritual being having no physical body; *Christian Science*, the eternal quality with reference to God.

in·tel·li·gence quo·tient, n. *Psychol.* a technique for stating a person's general intelligence, reached by dividing his mental age, as determined through intelligence tests, by his chronological age, then multiplying by 100. Abbr. *IQ*, *I.Q.*—**in·tel·li·gence test**, *psychol.* one or more standardized graded tests, aimed at measuring an individual's general intelligence or mental ability.

in·tel·li·gent, in·tel′i·jent, a. [L. *intelligens, intelligentis*, ppr. of *intelligo*.] Having the faculty of understanding and reasoning; rational; having a good intellect; having high intellectual capacities; showing good judgment; well-informed.—**in·tel·li·gen·tial**, in·tel′i·jen′shal, a.—**in·tel·li·gent·ly**, adv.

in·tel·li·gent·si·a, in·tel′i·jent′sē·a, in·tel′i·gent′sē·a, n. pl. Intellectuals; the broadly educated; that group which forms a social, artistic, or political elite.

in·tel·li·gi·ble, in·tel′i·ji·bl, a. [L. *intelligibilis*.] Capable of being understood or comprehended; clear; *philos.* able to be apprehended by the mind rather than the senses.—**in·tel·li·gi·bil·i·ty**, in·tel″i·ji·bil′i·tē, n. The quality or state of being intelligible; clarity.—**in·tel·li·gi·ble·ness**, n.—**in·tel·li·gi·bly**, adv.

in·tem·per·ance, in·tem′pėr·ans, in·tem′prans, n. [L. *intemperantia*, want of moderation.] Lack of moderation or due restraint; excess of any kind; habitual or excessive indulgence in alcoholic liquors.—**in·tem·per·ate**, in·tem′pėr·it, in·tem′prit, a.—**in·tem·per·ate·ly**, adv.—**in·tem·per·ate·ness**, n.

in·tend, in·tend′, v.t. [O.Fr. Fr. *entendre*, < L. *intendere* (pp. *intentus*, also *intensus*), stretch out, extend, direct, attend, purpose, intend, < *in-*, in, on, and *tendere*, stretch, E. *tend*.] To have in mind as something willed to be done or brought about; to design or mean for a particular purpose, use, recipient, or destiny; to express, indicate, or mean, as: What did you *intend* by that last speech? *Archaic*, to direct, turn, or aim.—*v.i.* To have a purpose or design, as: He may *intend* otherwise.—**in·tend·er**, *n.*

in·tend·ance, in·ten′dans, *n.* [Fr.] Superintendence; a department of the public service, as in France, or the officials in charge of it.—**in·tend·an·cy**, *n.* pl. **in·tend·an·cies**. The office or function of an intendant; a body of intendants; *S. Amer.* a district under the charge of an intendant.—**in·tend·ant**, in·ten′dant, *n.* [Fr. < L. *intendens (-ent-)*, ppr. of *intendere*.] A supervisor or administrator of public business, esp. of a province, as in France, Mexico, or S. America.

in·tend·ed, in·ten′did, *a.* Intentional or designed; as, to produce the *intended* effect; prospective, as one's future husband or wife.—*n. Colloq.* one who is betrothed.—**in·tend·ed·ly**, *adv.*—**in·tend·ed·ness**, *n.*

in·tend·ment, in·tend′ment, *n.* [O.Fr. Fr. *entendement*, < *entendre*, E. *intend*.] *Law.* The true or correct intention and meaning of the law; the legal meaning of a word.

in·tense, in·tens′, *a.* [O.Fr. Fr. *intense*, < L. *intensus*, stretched tight, intense, pp. of *intendere*.] Existing or occurring in a high or extreme degree; having characteristic qualities in a high degree; performed diligently, earnestly, or strenuously, as an activity; very great, strong, or vehement, as sensations or emotions; having or showing great strength or vehemence of feeling, as a person, the face, language, or the like.—**in·tense·ly**, *adv.*—**in·tense·ness**, *n.*

in·ten·si·fy, in·ten′si·fī′, *v.t.*—*intensified, intensifying.* To render intense or more intense; increase, strengthen, or make more acute; *photog.* to heighten contrast and density of, as a negative.—*v.i.* To become intense or more intense.—**in·ten·si·fi·ca·tion**, in·ten′si·fi·kā′shan, *n.*—**in·ten·si·fi·er**, in·ten′si·fī′ẽr, *n.*

in·ten·sion, in·ten′shan, *n.* [L. *intensio(n-)*, < *intendere*.] Intensity; intensification; connotation; *logic.* the sum of the attributes contained in a concept or connoted by a term.—**in·ten·sion·al**, *a.*—**in·ten·sion·al·ly**, *adv.*

in·ten·si·ty, in·ten′si·tē, *n.* pl. **in·ten·si·ties**. The state of being intense; relative degree, as of heat or color; vigor, energy, or activity; keenness, as of feeling; *phys.* the amount of energy with which a force operates per unit of surface or volume.

in·ten·sive, in·ten′siv, *a.* [Fr. *intensif*, < L. *intendere*.] Of, pertaining to, or characterized by intensity; intensifying; concentrated; *med.* increasing in intensity or degree. *Agric.* more laborious, expensive, or concentrated methods of land cultivation, planned to secure the highest possible yield from each acre: opposed to *extensive*. *Gram.* expressing increase of intensity; giving force or emphasis.—*n.* Something that intensifies; *gram.* an intensive word or prefix.—**in·ten·sive·ly**, *adv.*—**in·ten·sive·ness**, *n.*

in·tent, in·tent′, *a.* [L. *intentus*, stretched, strained, attentive, intent, pp. of *intendere*.] Fixed with strained or earnest attention, as the gaze or mind, used with *on* or *upon*; as, to be *intent on* gain; earnest; having the mind, gaze, or thoughts fixed on some object or with some purpose in view.—*n.* The action of intending, as to commit some act; a particular intention or design; *law*, design or state of mind with regard to one's actions; as, assault with *intent* to kill; meaning or import.—**to all in·tents and pur·pos·es**, for all practical purposes; practically.—**in·tent·ly**, *adv.*—**in·tent·ness**, *n.*

in·ten·tion, in·ten′shan, *n.* [O.Fr. *entencion* (Fr. *intention*), < L. *intentio(n-)*, < *intendere*.] The act or fact of intending or proposing; as, to do a thing without intention; a determination upon some action or result; a purpose or design; *pl.* purposes with respect to a proposal of marriage. The end or object intended; meaning or import, as of words or statements; *med.* a manner or process of healing; *logic*, a general concept.—**in·ten·tion·al**, *a.*—**in·ten·tion·al·i·ty**, in·ten″sha·nal′·i·tē, in·ten″sha·nal′i·tē, *n.*—**in·ten·tion·al·ly**, *adv.*—**in·ten·tioned**, *a.* Having intentions; as, well-*intentioned*.—**in·ten·tion·less**, *a.*

in·ter, in·tur′, *v.t.*—*interred, interring.* [Fr. *enterrer—en*, and *terre*, L. *terra*, the earth.] To bury; to inhume.—**in·ter·ment**, *n.*

in·ter·act, in″tẽr·akt′, *v.i.* To act on each other.—**in·ter·ac·tant**, *n.*—**in·ter·ac·tion**, *n.* Mutual or reciprocal action.—**in·ter·ac·tion·al**, *a.*—**in·ter·ac·tive**, *a.*

in·ter·brain, in′tẽr·brān″, *n.* The diencephalon.

in·ter·breed, in″tẽr·brēd′, *v.t.*—*interbred, interbreeding.* To breed by crossing one variety of animal or plant with another; crossbreed.—*v.i.* To mate in such a manner.

in·ter·ca·lar·y, in·tur′ka·ler″ē, in″tẽr·kal′a·rē, *a.* [L. *intercalarius—inter-*, between, and *calo*, to call or proclaim.] Introduced or interpolated among others; inserted in a calendar, as the odd day, February 29th, in a leap year; of a year, having such an insertion.—**in·ter·ca·late**, in·tur′ka·lāt′, *v.t.*—*intercalated, intercalating.* To insert between others; to insert between other days or other portions of time.—**in·ter·ca·la·tion**, in·tur″ka·lā′shan, *n.*

in·ter·cede, in″tẽr·sēd′, *v.i.*—*interceded, interceding.* [L. *intercedo*, to pass between.] To act between parties with a view to reconciling their differences or points of contention; mediate; to plead or interpose on behalf of another.—**in·ter·ced·er**, *n.*

in·ter·cel·lu·lar, in″tẽr·sel′ū·lẽr, *a. Biol.* lying between cells.

in·ter·cept, in″tẽr·sept′, *v.t.* [Fr. *intercepter*; L. *intercipio, interceptum—inter-*, between, and *capio*, to take.] To take or stop while on the way; to interrupt the journey or passage of, as a messenger or letter; to obstruct the progress of. *Math.* to intersect; to cut off or mark off a line, plane, or solid.—in′tẽr·sept″, *n. Math.* the part of a line, plane, or solid intercepted.—**in·ter·cep·tor**, **in·ter·cept·er**, in″tẽr·sep′tẽr, *n.* One who or that which intercepts; *milit.* a fighter aircraft with high speed and high rate of climb, used to meet and engage enemy aircraft.—**in·ter·cep·tion**, *n. Sports*, a pass caught by a member of the defensive team, but intended for an offensive player.—**in·ter·cep·tive**, *a.*

in·ter·ces·sion, in″tẽr·sesh′an, *n.* [L. *intercessio*.] The act of interceding; mediation; entreaty, prayer, or petition in behalf of another.—**in·ter·ces·sion·al**, *a.*—**in·ter·ces·sor**, in″tẽr·ses′ẽr, in″tẽr·ses′ẽr, *n.*—**in·ter·ces·so·ry**, in″tẽr·ses′o·rē, *a.*

in·ter·change, in″tẽr·chānj′, *v.t.*—*interchanged, interchanging.* To change reciprocally; to put each in the place of the other; to transpose; to cause to succeed alternately; to exchange.—*v.i.* To change reciprocally; to alternate.—in′tẽr·chānj″, *n.* The act or process of mutually giving and receiving; an exchange; alternate succession; an intersection of highways where automobiles can enter or depart without crossing or obstructing the flow of traffic.—**in·ter·change·a·ble**, in″tẽr·chān′ja·bl, *a.*—**in·ter·change·a·bil·i·ty**, **in·ter·change·a·ble·ness**, in″tẽr·chānj″a·bil′i·tē, *n.*—**in·ter·change·a·bly**, *adv.*

in·ter·clav·i·cle, in″tẽr·klav′i·kl, *n. Anat.* a bone between the clavicles and in front of the breastbone, in many vertebrates.

in·ter·col·le·gi·ate, in″tẽr·ko·lē′jit, in″-

tẽr·ko·lē′jē·it, *a.* Between colleges; pertaining to or involving participation by two or more colleges; as, *intercollegiate* competition.

in·ter·co·lum·ni·a·tion, in″tẽr·ko·lum″nē·ā′shan, *n. Arch.* The space between two columns measured at the lowest part of their shafts; the system used for spacing columns.—**in·ter·co·lum·nar**, in″tẽr·ko·lum′nar, *a.*

in·ter·com, in′tẽr·kom″, *n. Colloq.* intercommunication system.

in·ter·com·mu·ni·cate, in″tẽr·ko·mū′ni·kāt′, *v.i.*—*intercommunicated, intercommunicating.* To communicate mutually; to exchange messages or information.—**in·ter·com·mu·ni·ca·tion**, in″tẽr·ko·mū′ni·kā′shan, *n.*

in·ter·com·mu·ni·ca·tion sys·tem, *n.* A system of two-way communication within a limited space or area, consisting essentially of a microphone and loudspeaker at each point, as used by a pilot and bombardier in an aircraft or between offices in a suite. Also *intercom.*

in·ter·com·mun·ion, in″tẽr·ko·mūn′yan, *n.* Mutual participation; rapport; *eccles.* a communion service participated in by members of various denominations.

in·ter·com·mu·ni·ty, in″tẽr·ko·mū′ni·tē, *n.* pl. **in·ter·com·mu·ni·ties**. The quality or condition of being shared equally by, or common to, two or more parties.

in·ter·con·nect, in″tẽr·ko·nekt′, *v.t., v.i.* To connect with or between one another.—**in·ter·con·nec·tion**, *n.*

in·ter·con·ti·nen·tal, in″tẽr·kon″ti·nen′tal, *a.* Between continents; extending, traveling, or able to travel between continents; pertaining to two or more continents.

in·ter·cool·er, in′tẽr·kö″lẽr, *n.* A device which cools fluids, used in alternation with heating processes.

in·ter·con·ver·sion, in″tẽr·kon·vur′zhan, in″tẽr·kon·vur′shan, *n.* Reciprocal conversion; interchange of form or constitution.—**in·ter·con·vert**, *v.t.*—**in·ter·con·vert·i·ble**, *a.*—**in·ter·con·vert·i·bil·i·ty**, in″tẽr·kon·vurt′i·bil′i·tē, *n.*

in·ter·cos·tal, in″tẽr·kos′tal, in″tẽr·ka′stal, *a.* [N.L. *intercostalis*, < L. *inter*, between, and *costa*, rib.] *Anat.* situated between the ribs; pertaining to muscles or parts between the ribs.—*n.* An intercostal muscle or part.—**in·ter·cos·tal·ly**, *adv.*

in·ter·course, in′tẽr·kōrs″, in′tẽr·kạrs″, *n.* [L. *intercursus*.] Reciprocal dealings or communication between persons, groups of persons, or nations; interchange of thought and feeling; sexual union; copulation.

in·ter·crop, in″tẽr·krop′, *v.t.*—*intercropped, intercropping. Agric.* to plant, as a crop, alternately between rows of another crop.—*v.i. Agric.* to plant a crop alternately between the rows of another.

in·ter·cross, in″tẽr·krạs′, in″tẽr·kros′, *v.t.* To cross, as one with another; to cross, as streets do; to cross in interbreeding.—*v.i.* To cross each other; to interbreed.—in′tẽr·krạs″, in′tẽr·kros″, *n.* An instance of interbreeding or the resulting hybrid.

in·ter·cul·tur·al, in″tẽr·kul′chẽr·al, *a.* Pertaining to or taking place between two or more cultures.

in·ter·cur·rent, in″tẽr·kur′ent, in″tẽr·kur′ent, *a.* [L. *intercurrens, intercurrentis*.] Running between; intervening; *pathol.* referring to a disease which occurs during the course of another disease.—**in·ter·cur·rence**, *n.*—**in·ter·cur·rent·ly**, *adv.*

in·ter·de·nom·i·na·tion·al, in″tẽr·di·nom″i·nā′sha·nal, *a.* Occurring between or shared by religious denominations.—**in·ter·de·nom·i·na·tion·al·ism**, *n.*

in·ter·den·tal, in″tẽr·den′tal, *a.* [L. *inter*, between, and *dens (dent-)*, tooth.] Between the teeth; *phon.* produced by placing the tip of the tongue between the upper and lower front teeth.—**in·ter·den·tal·ly**, *adv.*

in·ter·de·part·men·tal, in″tėr·dē″pärt·men′tal, in″tėr·di·pärt·men′tal, *a.* Involving or occurring between two or more departments, as of a commercial enterprise or an institution of learning.—**in·ter·de·part·men·tal·ly**, *adv.*

in·ter·de·pend·ent, in″tėr·di·pen′dent, *a.* Mutually dependent; reciprocally dependent.—**in·ter·de·pend**, *v.i.*—**in·ter·de·pend·ence**, **in·ter·de·pend·en·cy**, *n.*—**in·ter·de·pend·ent·ly**, *adv.*

in·ter·dict, in″tėr·dikt′, *v.t.* [L. *interdico, interdictum—inter*, between, and *dico*, speak.] To debar, forbid, or prohibit; to restrain by an interdict.—in′tėr·dikt″, *n.* A prohibition; a prohibiting order or decree; *Rom. Cath. Ch.* a prohibition of the performance of divine service and the administration or receipt of certain religious rites.—**in·ter·dic·tion**, in″tėr·dik′shan, *n.* The act of interdicting; prohibition.—**in·ter·dic·tive**, **in·ter·dic·to·ry**, in″tėr·dik′to·rē, *a.*—**in·ter·dic·tor**, *n.*

in·ter·dig·i·tate, in″tėr·dij′i·tāt″, *v.i., v.t.*—*interdigitated, interdigitating.* [L. *inter*, between, and *digitus*, finger, E. *digit*.] To interlock, as the fingers of both hands.—**in·ter·dig·i·ta·tion**, in″tėr·dij″i·tā′shan, *n.*

in·ter·dis·ci·pli·nar·y, in″tėr·dis′i·pli·ner″ē, *a.* Involving more than one area of academic pursuit.

in·ter·est, in′tėr·ist, in′trist, *n.* [For earlier *interess*, < M.L. *interesse*, noun use of L. *interesse*, be between, make a difference, concern, < *inter*, between, and *esse*, be.] The feeling of attentiveness or curiosity aroused by something; a particular feeling of this kind; as, varied intellectual *interests*; the power or quality in something which arouses such feeling; the position of being affected by something either to advantage or detriment; benefit or advantage; regard for one's own profit or advantage; self-interest; *sometimes pl.* behalf or welfare; as, to labor in the *interests* of peace. A right or title to or a share in the ownership of property or a commercial enterprise; a business or cause in which one is involved; a number or group of persons having an interest in the same field, industry, or cause; as, the banking *interest*; money paid for the use of money borrowed; *fig.* something added above an exact equivalent; as, an evil act returned with *interest*.

in·ter·est, in′tėr·ist, in′trist, *v.t.* To induce to participate in an undertaking; to engage in something; to concern, as a person, in something, esp. through its bearing on personal welfare; to involve; to engage or arouse the attention or curiosity of.

in·ter·est·ed, in′tėr·i·stid, in′tri·stid, in′te·res″tid, *a.* Feeling or showing curiosity, attention, or involvement in something; having an interest or share in; monetarily involved; influenced by self-interest or personal motives; biased.—**in·ter·est·ed·ly**, *adv.*

in·ter·est group, *n.* A group of people who have in common a special interest, concern, or desire, which often leads to deliberate and unified action.

in·ter·est·ing, in′tėr·i·sting, in′tri·sting, in′te·res″ting, *a.* That interests; exciting or engaging the attention or curiosity; holding the interest or attention.—**in·ter·est·ing·ly**, *adv.*—**in·ter·est·ing·ness**, *n.*

in·ter·est in·ven·to·ry, *n. Psychol.* a complete and formal listing of activities and objects, which attract a person's concern, attention, and curiosity: used in vocational guidance and personality diagnosis.

in·ter·face, in′tėr·fās″, *n.* A surface regarded as the common boundary of two bodies or spaces.—**in·ter·fa·cial**, in″tėr·fā′shal, *a.* Included between two faces; pertaining to an interface.

in·ter·faith, in″tėr·fāth′, *a.* Including persons of different religions.

in·ter·fere, in″tėr·fēr′, *v.i.*—*interfered, interfering.* [O.Fr. *entreferir*, refl., strike each other, < L. *inter*, between, and *ferire*, strike.] To come into opposition, as one thing with another, with the effect of hampering action; clash, obstruct, or impede; to intervene or interpose in another's concerns, esp. intrusively or without warrant; to meddle; *phys.* to act on one another to modify the natural effect, as of sound waves; *sports*, to illegally obstruct an opponent's play; *football*, to block and impede opponents for the protection of the ball carrier.—**in·ter·fer·er**, *n.*—**in·ter·fer·ing·ly**, *adv.*

in·ter·fer·ence, in″tėr·fēr′ens, *n.* The act of interfering or that which interferes; opposing or hampering action; meddling; intervention; *phys.* the reciprocal action of waves, as of light or sound, when meeting, by which they reinforce or neutralize each other. *Elect.* the disturbance of a desired sound, as in radio, by other sounds or by static; the cause of this disturbance. *Sports*, the illegal obstruction of an opponent's play; *football*, the blocking or impeding of opposing players.—**in·ter·fe·ren·tial**, in″tėr·fe·ren′shal, *a.*

in·ter·fer·om·e·ter, in″tėr·fe·rom′i·tėr, *n.* An instrument for measuring small distances and comparing wavelengths by means of the interference of two rays of light.—**in·ter·fer·o·gram**, in″tėr·fēr′o·gram, *n.* A photographic record of optical interference phenomena.—**in·ter·fer·o·met·ric**, in″tėr·fėr″o·me′trik, *a.*—**in·ter·fer·o·met·ri·cal·ly**, *adv.*—**in·ter·fer·om·e·try**, *n.*

in·ter·fer·tile, in″tėr·fur′til, *a.* Having the capacity to interbreed.—**in·ter·fer·til·i·ty**, in″tėr·fur·til′i·tē, *n.*

in·ter·flu·ent, in″tėr·flō′ent, *a.* [L. *interfluens, interfluus—inter*, between, and *fluo*, to flow.] Intermingling or flowing into each other.—**in·ter·flu·ence**, *n.*

in·ter·fruit·ful, in″tėr·frōt′ful, *a. Bot.* capable of two successive cross-pollinations in which the plant which receives the pollen in the first cross-pollination supplies it in the second.—**in·ter·fruit·ful·ness**, *n.*

in·ter·fuse, in″tėr·fūz′, *v.t.*—*interfused, interfusing.* [L. *interfusus*, pp. of *interfundere*, pour between.] To bend or fuse, one with another; to intersperse or intermingle; to permeate; to pervade; to diffuse throughout. —*v.i.* To become blended or fused, one with another.—**in·ter·fu·sion**, in″tėr·fū′zhan, *n.*

in·ter·ga·lac·tic, in″tėr·ga·lak′tik, *a. Astron.* occurring or located in the vast spaces between the galaxies of the heavens.

in·ter·gla·cial, in″tėr·glā′shal, *a. Geol.* formed or occurring between two periods of glacial action.

in·ter·grade, in″tėr·grād′, *v.i.*—*intergraded, intergrading.* To pass or merge gradually, one into another, as different species in the evolutionary process.—in′tėr·grād″, *n.* An intermediate grade or stage.—**in·ter·gra·da·tion**, in″tėr·grā·dā′shan, *n.*—**in·ter·gra·da·tion·al**, *a.*

in·ter·growth, in′tėr·grōth″, *n.* Growth or growing together; the product of such mutual growth.

in·ter·im, in′tėr·im, *n.* [L. in the meantime, < *inter*, between.] An intervening time; the meantime; a temporary arrangement.—*a.* Pertaining to an intervening time period; temporary; as, an *interim* plan.

in·te·ri·or, in·tėr′ē·ėr, *a.* [L. inner, compar. adj. < *inter*, between.] Inner; pertaining to the inside; situated inland; as, the *interior* part of a country; internal or domestic; private or secret; mental; spiritual.—*n.* The inside or internal part; the interior or inland parts of a region or country; the internal or domestic affairs of a country or state; as, the U.S. Department of the *Interior*; the inner or inward nature or character of anything; the inside of a building or room, esp. with reference to artistic effect; a pictorial representation of a building, room, or similar structure.—**in·te·ri·or·i·ty**, in″tėr″e·ar′i·te, *n.*—**in·te·ri·or·ly**, *adv.*

in·te·ri·or dec·o·ra·tion, *n.* The art of designing, decorating, and furnishing interiors of homes, offices, apartments, and other internal areas; the business of professional decorating; the materials used in room décor.

in·ter·ject, in″tėr·jekt′, *v.t.* [L. *interjicio, interjectum*.] To throw between; to interrupt, interpose.—**in·ter·jec·tion**, in″tėr·jek′shan, *n.* [L. *interjectio*.] The act of throwing between; an interruption; an interposition; an expression of emotion or passion; *gram.* an exclamatory word in a sentence without grammatical connection and sometimes considered as one of the eight parts of speech, as *oh!*—**in·ter·jec·tion·al·ly**, *adv.*—**in·ter·jec·to·ry**, in″tėr·jek′to·rē, *a.*—**in·ter·jec·to·ri·ly**, *adv.*

in·ter·knit, in″tėr·nit′, *v.t., v.i.*—*interknitted* or *interknit, interknitting.* To knit together, one with another; intertwine.

in·ter·lam·i·nate, in″tėr·lam′i·nāt″, *v.t.* —*interlaminated, interlaminating.* To interlay or intersperse something between laminae.—**in·ter·lam·i·na·tion**, in″tėr·lam″i·nā′shan, *n.*

in·ter·lard, in″tėr·lärd′, *v.t.* [Fr. *entrelarder*, < *entre-* (< L. *inter*, between) and *larder*, E. *lard*, v.] To diversify or vary by the addition of irrelevant items or ideas; as, to *interlard* applause with catcalls; intersperse, interject, or interpolate.—**in·ter·lar·da·tion**, in″tėr·lär·dā′shan, *n.*

in·ter·lay·er, in′tėr·lā″ėr, *n.* A thickness or layer located between other layers.

in·ter·leaf, in′tėr·lēf″, *n.* pl. **in·ter·leaves**, in′tėr·lēvz″. A sheet of paper, usu. blank, which has been bound or inserted between two regular pages of a book.—*v.t.* Interleave.

in·ter·leave, in″tėr·lēv′, *v.t.*—*interleaved, interleaving.* [Prefix *inter*, and *leaf*.] To insert blank pages in, esp. for notes in a book; to interlaminate.

in·ter·line, in″tėr·lin′, *v.t.*—*interlined, interlining.* To mark or inscribe between the lines; to write or insert between lines of writing or print.—**in·ter·lin·e·a·tion**, in″tėr·lin″ē·ā′shan, *n.*

in·ter·line, in″tėr·lin″, *v.t.*—*interlined, interlining.* To provide, as a garment, with an inner lining inserted between the ordinary lining and the outer fabric.

in·ter·lin·e·ar, in″tėr·lin′ē·ėr, *a.* [M.L. *interlinearis*, < L. *inter*, between, and *linea*, E. *line*.] Inserted between the lines; containing interpolated lines, as of translation.—**in·ter·lin·e·ar·ly**, *adv.*

in·ter·lin·ing, in′tėr·li″ning, in″tėr·li′ning, *n.* An inner lining put between the outer material and the usual lining; the fabric which lines a garment, in″tėr·li′ning. Interlineation; an insertion between written or printed lines, in″tėr·li′ning.

in·ter·link, in″tėr·lingk′, *v.t.* To link, one with another.—in′tėr·lingk″, *n.* A connecting link.

in·ter·lock, in″tėr·lok′, *v.i.* To interlace; to be linked together; to be locked together by a series of connections; *rail.* to function together in a prearranged sequence.—*v.t.* To lock one in another firmly; *rail.* to arrange the operation of particular mechanisms so that they function in a desired sequence, as signals.—in″tẽr·lok″, *n.*—in··tẽr·lock·er, in″tẽr·lok′ẽr, *n.*

in·ter·lo·cu·tion, in″tẽr·lo·kū′shan, *n.* [L. *interlocutio(n-)*, < *interloqui*, speak between.] Interchange of speech; conversation; a dialogue or colloquy.

in·ter·loc·u·tor, in″tẽr·lok′ū·tẽr, *n.* One who takes part in a conversation or dialogue; one who enters into conversation with, or questions, another; the middle performer in a line of minstrels, who converses with the end men; the middleman.

in·ter·loc·u·to·ry, in″tẽr·lok′ū·tōr″ē, in″tẽr·lok′ū·tạr″ē, *a.* Of the nature of, pertaining to, or occurring in conversation or dialogue; spoken intermediately; as, *interlocutory* conversations; interjected into the main course of speech. *Law.* Pronounced during the course of an action, as a decision or order; not finally decisive of a case; pertaining to a provisional decision.—in··tẽr·loc·u·to·ri·ly, *adv.*

in·ter·lop·er, in′tẽr·lō″pẽr, *n.* [Origin uncertain, akin D. *loopen*, run, and E. *landloper.*] An intruder; a trespasser.—in·ter·lope, in″tẽr·lōp′, *v.i.*—*interloped, interloping.* To intrude into some region or field of trade without a proper license; to thrust oneself into the domain or affairs of others.

in·ter·lude, in′tẽr·lōd″, *n.* [M.L. *interludium*, < L. *inter*, between, and *ludere*, play.] An interval; a temporary pause or lull during some other activity; an intervening episode or period. *Theatr.* the pause between acts of a play; the short, usu. humorous, drama presented during this time. *Mus.* an instrumental passage or piece of music rendered between parts of a song, church service, or drama.—in·ter··lu·di·al, in″tẽr·lō′dē·al, *a.*

in·ter·lu·nar, in′tẽr·lō″nẽr, *a.* Pertaining to the moon's monthly period of invisibility between the old moon and the new. Also **in·ter·lu·na·ry.**

in·ter·mar·ry, in″tẽr·mar′ē, *v.i.*—*intermarried, intermarrying.* To become connected by marriage, as two families, tribes, castes, or religions; to marry within the limits of the family or of near relationship.—**in·ter·mar·riage,** *n.*

in·ter·med·dle, in″tẽr·med′l, *v.i.*—*intermeddled, intermeddling.* [Prefix *inter*, and *meddle.*] To meddle officiously; interfere in another's concerns.—**in·ter·med·dler,** *n.*

in·ter·me·di·ar·y, in″tẽr·mē′dē·er″ē, *a.* [= Fr. *intermediaire*, < L. *intermedius.*] Being between; intermediate; acting between persons or parties.—*n.* pl. **in·ter··me·di·ar·ies.** An intermediate agent or agency; a go-between; a medium or means.

in·ter·me·di·ate, in″tẽr·mē′dē·it, *a.* [= Fr. *intermediat*, < M.L. *intermediatus*, < L. *intermedius.*] Being, situated, or occurring between two points, stages, or things; acting between others; intervening.—*n.* Something intermediate; an intermediary. *Chem.* a substance halfway through its progress from raw material to finished product.—**in·ter·me·di·ate·ly,** *adv.*—**in·ter·me·di·ate·ness,** *n.*—**in·ter·me·di·a·cy,** *n.*

in·ter·me·di·ate, in″tẽr·mē′dē·āt′, *v.i.*—*intermediated, intermediating.* To act as an intermediary; to intervene; to mediate.—**in·ter·me·di·a·tion,** in″tẽr·mē″dē·ā′shan, *n.*—**in·ter·me·di·a·tor,** *n.*—**in·ter·me·di·a·to·ry,** in″tẽr·mē′dē·a·tōr″ē, *a.*

in·ter·me·di·ate host, *n. Biol.* an organism on which a young parasite subsists, until ready to leave and multiply sexually elsewhere.

in·ter·me·din, in″tẽr·mē′din, *n. Biol.* a

---

pituitary hormone which causes expansion of the chromatophores in certain cold-blooded vertebrates, as fish or frogs.

in·ter·mez·zo, in″tẽr·met′sō, in″tẽr··med′zō, *It.* ēn″tẽr·med′dza, *n.* pl. **in·ter·mez·zi,** in″tẽr·met′sē, in″tẽr·med′zē, *It.* ēn″tẽR·med′dzē. [It. < L. *intermedius.*] A short musical composition introduced between main divisions of an extended musical work; a short independent musical composition.

in·ter·mi·na·ble, in·tûr′mi·na·bl, *a.* [L. *interminabilis* < *in-*, not, and *terminus*, a bound or limit.] Boundless; unending; wearisomely prolonged.—**in·ter·mi·na··ble·ness,** *n.*—**in·ter·mi·na·bly,** *adv.*

in·ter·min·gle, in″tẽr·ming′gl, *v.t., v.i.*—*intermingled, intermingling.* To mix together or be intermixed.—**in·ter·min·gle·ment,** *n.*

in·ter·mis·sion, in″tẽr·mish′an, *n.* [L. *intermissio(n-)*, < *intermittere.*] The act of intermitting; a temporary cessation; a pause; a space of time between periods of action or activity; an interval between the acts of a play or other public performance.—**in·ter·mis·sive,** in″tẽr·mis′iv, *a.*

in·ter·mit, in″tẽr·mit′, *v.t.*—*intermitted, intermitting.* [L. *intermitto*, to let go between, to interrupt < *inter*, and *mitto*, to send.] To cause to cease for a time; to stop; to suspend or discontinue.—*v.i.* To cease for a time or at intervals, as a fever.—**in·ter·mit·tence, in·ter·mit·ten·cy,** *n.*—**in·ter·mit·tent,** *a.*—**in·ter·mit·tent·ly,** *adv.*—**in·ter·mit·ting·ly,** *adv.*

in·ter·mit·tent cur·rent, *n. Elect.* a current that stops flowing at intervals but never reverses its direction of flow.

in·ter·mix, in″tẽr·miks′, *v.t., v.i.* To mix together; to intermingle.—**in·ter·mix·ture,** *n.*

in·ter·mo·lec·u·lar, in″tẽr·mo·lek′ū·lẽr, in″tẽr·mō·lek′ū·lẽr, *a.* Occurring between molecules.—**in·ter·mo·lec·u·lar·ly,** *adv.*

in·tern, in·terne, in′tûrn, *n.* [Fr. *interne*, < L. *internus*, < *in-*; cf. *extern.*] A recent medical graduate acting as assistant in a hospital for the purpose of clinical training; an advanced student in other fields gaining practical experience under supervision.—*a. Archaic*, internal.—**in·tern·ship,** *n.*

in·tern, in·tûrn′, *v.t.* [Fr. *interner*, < *interne.*] To confine within a prescribed area, esp. in a war; to impound until the end of a war, as a ship in a neutral country.—*v.i.* To act as an intern or serve an internship.—*n.* One who is interned. See *internee.*

in·ter·nal, in·tûr′nal, *a.* [L. *internus.*] Of or pertaining to the inside or inner part; interior; *anat.* inner; occurring near the body's axis or away from its surface. Intrinsic or inherent; as, *internal* evidence; occurring within a country, domestic; as, *internal* affairs; existing in the mind; subjective. *Pharm.* To be taken orally.—**in·ter·nal·i·ty,** in·tûr′nal′i·tē, *n.*—**in·ter·nal·ly,** *adv.*

in·ter·nal-com·bus·tion en·gine, *n.* A heat engine of one or more working cylinders in which the combustion process occurs within the cylinders of the engine.

in·ter·nal·ize, in·tûr′na·līz′, *v.t.*—*internalized, internalizing.* To make internal or subjective; to adopt or incorporate, as cultural patterns or values.—**in·ter·nal·i·za·tion,** in·tûr″na·li·zā′shan, *n.*

in·ter·nal med·i·cine, *n. Med.* that branch of medicine concerned with the diagnosis and treatment of nonsurgical diseases, usu. of adults.

in·ter·nal rev·e·nue, *n.* Total governmental income collected entirely from domestic sources, not including taxes on imports and customs.

in·ter·nal rhyme, *n. Pros.* a rhyme

---

between two words in the same line of poetry; a rhyme between two words within different lines of poetry, neither word appearing at the end of a line.

in·ter·nal se·cre·tion, *n.* A hormone.

in·ter·na·tion·al, in″tẽr·nash′a·nal, *a.* Between or among nations; pertaining to the relations between nations; as, *international* law; affecting or participated in by different nations; having members in several countries, as a group or an organization.—*n.* (*Cap.*) any one of a number of international socialist and communist groups organized in the late 19th and early 20th centuries; (*sometimes cap.*) a labor union which has members in several nations.—**In·ter·na·tio·nale,** aN·tẽR·nä··syạ·näl′, *n.* [Fr.] A revolutionary workers' and Communists' song, orig. sung in France in 1871.—**in·ter·na·tion·al·i·ty,** in″tẽr··nash′a·nal′i·tē, *n.*—**in·ter·na·tion·al·ly,** *adv.*

in·ter·na·tion·al date line, *n.* A theoretical line. See *date line.*

in·ter·na·tion·al·ism, in″tẽr·nash′a·na··liz″um, *n.* International character, relations, outlook, or control; the principle of cooperation among nations to promote their common good, as contrasted with *nationalism*, or devotion to the interests of a particular nation; (*cap.*) the principles or methods advocated by any socialistic association known as an International.—**in·ter·na·tion·al·ist,** *n.*

in·ter·na·tion·al·ize, in″tẽr·nash′a·na··liz″ *v.t.*—*internationalized, internationalizing.* To make international; to bring under international control, as a territory.—**in·ter·na·tion·al·i·za·tion,** in″tẽr·nash″·a·na·li·zā′shan, *n.*

in·ter·na·tion·al law, *n.* A set of rules which control the conduct of nations toward each other in peace or war.

in·ter·na·tion·al pitch, *n. Mus.* a standard of pitch used for tuning, with A above middle C at 440 vibrations per second.

in·ter·na·tion·al re·la·tions, *n. pl. but sing. in constr.* A division of political science dealing with foreign policy and the relationships between nations.

In·ter·na·tion·al Sci·en·tif·ic Vo·cab·u·lar·y, *n.* A specialized scientific vocabulary consisting of words common to two or more languages.

in·ter·ne·cine, in″tẽr·nē′sēn, in″tẽr·nē′sīn, in″tẽr·nes′ēn, in″tẽr·nes′īn, *a.* [L. *internecinus*, < *internecio*, slaughter, destruction, < *internecare*, destroy.] Mutually destructive: applied esp. to war or strife within a group; characterized by great slaughter; deadly; destructive. Also **in·ter·ne·cive,** in″tẽr·nē′siv, in″tẽr·nes′iv.

in·tern·ee, in·tûr·nē′, *n.* A person who has been interned as a prisoner of war.

in·ter·neu·ron, in″tẽr·nụr′on, in″tẽr··nūr′on, *n. Anat.* a neuron that connects a sensory to a motor neuron.—**in·ter·neu··ro·nal,** *a.*

in·tern·ist, in′tûr·nist, in·tûr′nist, *n. Med.* a physician who treats internal diseases; a specialist in internal medicine.

in·tern·ment, in·tûrn′ment, *n.* The act of interning, or the state of being interned or confined.—**in·tern·ment camp,** a confinement camp for prisoners of war, enemy aliens, and the like, during wartime.

in·ter·node, in′tẽr·nōd″, *n.* [L. *internodium.*] *Anat.* a portion of a nerve fiber between two nodes; *bot.* the area on a stem between two nodes.—**in·ter·no·dal,** in″tẽr·nōd′l, *a.*

in·ter·nun·cial, in″tẽr·nun′shal, *a.* Serving as a link between nerve fibers of the brain or spinal cord; pertaining or relating to an internuncio.

in·ter·nun·ci·o, in″tẽr·nun′shē·ō″, in″tẽr·nun′sē·ō″, *n.* pl. **in·ter·nun·ci·os.** [It.

---

now *internunzio,* < L. *internuntius,* < *inter,* between, and *nuntius,* messenger.] A papal ambassador ranking next below a nuncio.

in·ter·o·cep·tor, in"tẽr·ō·sep'tẽr, *n. Physiol.* a sensory receptor which responds to stimuli originating inside the body.—**in·-ter·o·cep·tive,** *a.*

in·ter·of·fice, in"tẽr·a'fis, in"tẽr·of'is, *a.* Operating or communicating between offices of a company.

in·ter·os·cu·late, in"tẽr·os'kū·lāt", *v.i.—interosculated, interosculating.* To intermix; interpenetrate; to form a connecting link.

in·ter·pel·late, in"tẽr·pel'āt, in·tûr'pe·-lāt", *v.t.—interpellated, interpellating.* [L. *interpellatus,* pp. of *interpellare,* interrupt in speaking.] To call formally upon, as a member of the government, for an explanation of official action or governmental policy.—**in·ter·pel·la·tion,** in"tẽr·pe·lā'shan, in·tûr"pe·lā'shan, *n.—**in·ter·pel·-la·tor,** in"tẽr·pe·lā'tẽr, in·tûr"pe·lā'tẽr, *n.*

in·ter·pen·e·trate, in"tẽr·pen'i·trāt", *v.t. —interpenetrated, interpenetrating.* To penetrate between the parts of; to penetrate thoroughly and reciprocally.—*v.i.* To penetrate between things or parts; to penetrate each other.—**in·ter·pen·e·tra·tion,** in"tẽr·pen"i·trā'shan, *n.—**in·ter·pen·e·tra·-tive,** *a.*

in·ter·plan·e·tar·y, in"tẽr·plan'i·ter"ē, *a.* Situated or existing between the planets, or between the sun and a planet.

in·ter·plant, in"tẽr·plant', in"tẽr·plänt', *v.t.* To plant, as a crop, with or between another crop, one acting as a nurse crop.

in·ter·play, in"tẽr·plā", *n.* Reciprocal play, action, or influence; interaction.—in"tẽr·plā", *v.i.* To interact.

in·ter·plead, in"tẽr·plēd', *v.i.* [A.Fr. *enterpleder.*] *Law,* to litigate with each other in order to determine which is the rightful claimant against a third party.—**in·ter·-plead·er,** *n. Law,* a proceeding by which two parties making the same claim against a third party go to trial to determine judicially which is the rightful claimant.

in·ter·po·late, in·tûr'po·lāt", *v.t.—interpolated, interpolating.* [L. *interpolatus,* pp. of *interpolare,* furbish, alter, falsify.] To alter, as a text, by the insertion of new matter, esp. deceptively or without authorization; to insert, as new or spurious matter; interject; interpose; intercalate; *math.* to insert or find intermediate terms in, as a series or sequence.—*v.i.* To make interpolations.—**in·ter·po·la·tion,** in·tûr"po·lā'shan, *n.—**in·ter·po·la·tive,** *a.—**in·ter·po·la·tor,** *n.*

in·ter·pose, in"tẽr·pōz', *v.t.—interposed, interposing.* [Fr. *interposer,* < L. *inter,* between, and *poser,* put, but associated with derivatives of L. *interponere.*] To put between; as, to *interpose* the hand between the eye and a light; to cause to intervene in place, time, or order; put or bring in an objection or delay; to bring influence or action to bear between parties, or on behalf of a party or person; to put in a remark or statement in the midst of a conversation, discourse, or the like.—*v.i.* To come or lie between; to bring one's influence or action to bear between parties at variance, or on behalf of a party or person; to intervene as a mediator or intercessor.—**in·ter·pos·er,** *n.* —**in·ter·pos·ing·ly,** *adv.*

in·ter·po·si·tion, in"tẽr·po·zish'an, *n.* The act of interposing; intervention. *Law,* the doctrine by which the individual state may, through the assertion of its sovereignty, oppose any federal mandate which violates the rights of the state or citizens.

in·ter·pret, in·tûr'prit, *v.t.* [L. *interpretari,* < *interpres* (*interpret-*), agent, broker, interpreter: cf. *inter-* and Skt. *prath-,* spread out.] To set forth the meaning of; to clarify or explain, as oracles, omens, or obscure passages; explain; elucidate; translate; sometimes, to understand; as, to *interpret* a person's expression; to construe or understand in a particular way; as, to *interpret* a reply as favorable; to bring out the meaning of a dramatic work or part, musical score, or artistic conception, by performance or execution; render or present in a revealing manner; of things, to express, indicate, or reveal.—*v.i.* To give an explanation; to translate what is said in a foreign language.—**in·ter·pret·a·bil·i·ty,** in·tûr"prit·a·bil'i·tē, *n.—**in·ter·pret·a·-ble,** *a.—**in·ter·pret·er,** *n.—**in·ter·pre·-tive,** *a.—**in·ter·pre·tive·ly,** *adv.*

in·ter·pre·ta·tion, in·tûr"pri·tā'shan, *n.* [L. *interpretatio(n-).*] The act of interpreting; the meaning ascribed to words or actions as a result of interpreting; an explanation, elucidation, or translation; a rendition, as of a drama, which attempts to bring out the idea of its meaning.—**in·-ter·pre·ta·tion·al,** *a.—**in·ter·pre·ta·-tive,** in·tûr'pre·tā"tiv, *a.*

in·ter·ra·cial, in"tẽr·rā'shal, *a.* Regarding or involving persons of unlike races.

in·ter·reg·num, in"tẽr·reg'num, *n.* pl. **in·ter·reg·nums,** **in·ter·reg·na,** in"tẽr·reg'na. [L.] The time between the death or abdication of a sovereign and the accession of his successor; the interval between the cessation or interruption of one government and the establishment of another; any lapse or interruption in continuity.—**in·ter·reg·-nal,** *a.*

in·ter·re·late, in"tẽr·ri·lāt', *v.t., v.i.—interrelated, interrelating.* To bring into or have reciprocal relation.—**in·ter·re·la·-tion,** *n.—**in·ter·re·la·tion·ship,** *n.*

in·ter·ro·gate, in·ter'o·gāt", *v.t.—interrogated, interrogating.* [L. *interrogo, interrogatum—inter,* between, and *rogo,* to ask.] To examine by asking questions, esp. officially or in a formal, systematic way.

in·ter·ro·ga·tion, in·ter"o·gā'shan, *n.* The act of questioning; a question. *Radio, radar,* the signal pulses of an interrogator; the transmission of such signals.—**in·ter·ro·-ga·tion·al,** *a.*

in·ter·ro·ga·tion point, *n.* Question mark (?) at the end of a sentence, used to indicate a question.

in·ter·rog·a·tive, in"te·rog'a·tiv, *a.* [L. *interrogativus.*] Denoting a question; expressed in the form of a question; inquisitive; *gram.* used in forming a question. —*n. Gram.* a word used in asking questions, as *who? what? which?*—**in·ter·rog·a·-tive·ly,** *adv.*

in·ter·ro·ga·tor, in·ter'o·gā"tẽr, *n.* One who asks questions. *Radio, radar,* a transmitter that sends a signal to set off an automatic response in a transponder.

in·ter·rog·a·to·ry, in"te·rog'a·tōr"ē, in"-te·rog'a·tạr"ē, *n.* pl. **in·ter·rog·a·to·ries.** A question; an interrogation; *law,* a written, formal question or series of questions. —*a.* Interrogative.

in·ter·rupt, in"te·rupt', *v.t.* [L. *interruptus,* pp. of *interrumpere,* < *inter,* between, and *rumpere,* break.] To make a break in, as in an otherwise continuous course; to break off or cause to cease, in the midst or course of; as, to *interrupt* one's work; hinder the continuation of, esp. temporarily; to stop, as a person, in the midst of doing or saying something, esp. by an interjected remark.—*v.i.* To cause a break or discontinuance; to interrupt action or speech. —**in·ter·rupt·er,** **in·ter·rup·tor,** *n.* One who or that which interrupts; *elect.* a device for interrupting or periodically making and breaking a circuit.—**in·ter·rup·tion,** *n.—**in·ter·rup·tive,** *a.*

in·ter·scho·las·tic, in"tẽr·sko·las'tik, *a.* Between schools; as, *interscholastic* games.

in·ter·sect, in"tẽr·sekt', *v.t.* [L. *interseco,* intersectum.*] To cut into or between; to cut or pass across; to divide into parts by crossing or passing through.—*v.i.* To meet and cross each other.

in·ter·sec·tion, in"tẽr·sek'shan, *n.* [L. *intersectio.*] The act or place of intersecting; a point of crossing; as, a street or road *intersection; geom.* the set of points which two configurations have in common.

in·ter·sex·u·al, in"tẽr·sek'shō·al, *a. Biol.* Occurring between the sexes; having sexual traits intermediate between the two sexes.—**in·ter·sex,** in'tẽr·seks", *n. Biol.* an individual with intersexual characteristics.—**in·ter·sex·u·al·i·ty,** in"tẽr·sek"-shō·al'i·tē, *n.—**in·ter·sex·u·al·ly,** *adv.*

in·ter·space, in'tẽr·spās", *n.* A space between things; an intervening space, or interval, of time.—in"tẽr·spās', *v.t.—interspaced, interspacing.* To put a space between; to occupy or fill the space between. —**in·ter·spa·tial,** in"tẽr·spā'shal, *a.—**in·-ter·spa·tial·ly,** *adv.*

in·ter·sperse, in"tẽr·spûrs', *v.t.—interspersed, interspersing.* [L. *interspergo, interspersum—inter,* between, and *spargo,* to scatter.] To scatter or set here and there among other things; to diversify by scattering objects.—**in·ter·spers·ed·ly,** *adv.* **in·ter·sper·sion,** in"tẽr·spûr'zhan, *Brit.* in"tẽr·spûr'shan, *n.*

in·ter·state, in"tẽr·stāt', *a.* Between states; between or jointly involving states of the U.S.; as, *interstate* commerce.

in·ter·stel·lar, in"tẽr·stel'ẽr, *a.* Occurring or situated among the stars.

in·ter·stice, in·tûr'stis, *n.* [L. *interstitium,* < *intersistere,* stand between.] An intervening space; a small or narrow space between things or parts; a small chink, crevice, or opening; an interval; *biol.* a small opening, hole, or space in a tissue, a series of tissues, or an organ.—**in·ter·-sticed,** *a.*

in·ter·sti·tial, in"tẽr·stish'al, *a.* Pertaining to, situated in, or forming interstices; *anat.* situated between the cellular elements of a structure or part; as, *interstitial* tissue.—**in·ter·sti·tial·ly,** *adv.*

in·ter·sub·jec·tive, in"tẽr·sub·jek'tiv, *a. Philos.* understood by or relating to two or more persons, as a language.—**in·ter·sub·-jec·tive·ly,** *adv.—**in·ter·sub·jec·tiv·i·ty,** in"tẽr·sub·jek·tiv'i·tē, *n.*

in·ter·tes·ta·men·tal, in"tẽr·tes"te·-men'tal, *a.* Pertaining to the period of about two centuries between the writing of the last book of the Old Testament and the writing of the New Testament.

in·ter·tid·al, in"tẽr·tīd'al, *a.* Relating or belonging to that part of the coastal or littoral zone between low tide and high tide marks.

in·ter·trop·i·cal, in"tẽr·trop'i·kal, *a.* Situated between the tropics of Cancer and Capricorn. Also **in·ter·trop·ic.**

in·ter·twine, in"tẽr·twīn', *v.t., v.i.—intertwined, intertwining.* To twine, as one with another.—**in·ter·twine·ment,** *n.—**in·-ter·twin·ing·ly,** *adv.*

in·ter·twist, in"tẽr·twist', *v.t., v.i.* To twist, as one with another.—*n.* An intertwisting; an intertwisted mass.—**in·ter·-twist·ing·ly,** *adv.*

in·ter·ur·ban, in"tẽr·ûr'ban, *a.* Between cities.—*n.* A system of transportation between cities; an interurban railway or bus line.

in·ter·val, in'tẽr·val, *n.* [O.Fr. Fr. *intervalle,* < L. *intervallum,* interval, orig. space between palisades.] An intervening period of time; as, an *interval* of 11 days; a pause or cessation; a gap; a space intervening between things, points, or limits; *Brit.* a pause or intermission between acts of a play; *math.* a set of numbers consisting of all the numbers between two given

---

ch- chain, G. na*ch*t;   **th-** THen, thin;   **w-** wig, hw as sound in whig;   **z-** zh as in azure, zeal.   *Italicized vowel* indicates schwa sound.

numbers in which one or both are included or excluded; *mus.* the difference in pitch between two tones.

in·ter·val·om·e·ter, in″tẽr·va·lom′i·tẽr, *n.* A device which operates a camera shutter at ordered intervals.

in·ter·vene, in″tẽr·vēn′, *v.i.*—*intervened, intervening.* [L. *intervenire* (pp. *interventus*).] To come between in action; to intercede or interfere; to come or be between places, times, or events, as: A period of peace *intervened* between the wars. To occur incidentally so as to modify a result, as: The game was fun until the snow *intervened.* To enter into an affair between parties as for the purpose of adjusting differences or aiding one party; *law,* to interpose in a lawsuit.—**in·ter·ven·er, in·ter·ve·nor,** *n.* —**in·ter·ven·tion,** in″tẽr·ven′shan, *n.*

in·ter·ven·tion·ist, in″tẽr·ven′sha·nist, *n.* One who favors federal interference in the political affairs of another state or country, or in economic affairs in his own country.— **in·ter·ven·tion·ism,** *n.*

in·ter·view, in′tẽr·vū′, *n.* [Fr. *entrevue,* < *entrevoir,* refl., see (each other).] A meeting of persons, as for a formal conference or evaluation; as, a job *interview*; a meeting between a representative of the press and a person from whom information is sought for publication; the conversation at such a meeting, or the published report of it.—*v.t.* To have an interview with.—**in·ter·view·er,** *n.*

in·ter·vo·cal·ic, in″tẽr·vō·kal′ik, *a.* Between vowels; as, an *intervocalic* consonant.

in·ter·weave, in″tẽr·wēv′, *v.t.*—past *interwove, interweaved,* pp. *interwoven, interweaved,* ppr. *interweaving.* To weave together, interlace, or intertwine; *fig.* to combine as if by weaving; as, to *interweave* truth with fiction.—*v.i.* To become woven together, interlaced, or intermingled.— in′tẽr·wēv″, *n.*—**in·ter·weave·ment,** *n.*— **in·ter·wo·ven,** *a.*

in·tes·tate, in·tes′tāt, in·tes′tit, *a.* [L. *intestatus—in-,* not, and *testatus,* having made a will, pp. of *testor,* to make a will.] Without having made a valid will; not disposed of by will.—*n.* A person who dies without having made a valid will.—**in·tes·ta·cy,** in·tes′ta·sē, *n.*

in·tes·ti·nal for·ti·tude, *n.* [Guts.] Courage; pluck; stamina.

in·tes·tine, in·tes′tin, *n.* [L. *intestinus,* inward, *intestinum,* an intestine.] *Often pl.* the lower part of the alimentary canal, extending from the pylorus to the anus. See *large intestine, small intestine.*—**in·tes·ti·nal,** in·tes′ti·nal, *Brit.* in″tes·tin′al, *a.*—**in·tes·ti·nal·ly,** *adv.*

in·tes·tine, in·tes′tin, *a.* [L. *intestinus,* < *intus,* within.] Internal with regard to a community, state, or country; domestic.

in·ti·ma, in′ti·ma, *n.* pl. **in·ti·mae,** in′ti·mē″. [N.L. prop. fem. of L. *intimus,* inmost, superl. of *interior.*] *Anat.* the innermost membrane, coat, or lining of some organ or part, esp. of an artery, a vein, or a lymphatic.—**in·ti·mal,** *a.*

in·ti·mate, in′ti·mit, *a.* [< L.L. *intimatus,* pp., but with sense of L. *intimus,* inmost.] Characterized by, involving, or arising from close personal connection or experience; as, an *intimate* friend, *intimate* knowledge; very private or closely personal; pertaining to, or maintaining, sexual relations; pertaining to the inmost or essential nature; intrinsic; as, the *intimate* structure or constitution of something; pertaining to or existing deep within the mind; as, *intimate* beliefs or convictions; inmost; deep within; as, the most *intimate* recesses of the heart; *chem.* characterized by close union or combination of particles or elements.—*n.* An intimate friend or associate.—**in·ti·mate·ly,** *adv.*

in·ti·mate, in′ti·māt′, *v.t.*—*intimated, intimating.* [L. *intimo, intimatum,* to publish or make known, < *intimus,* inmost.] To hint, indicate, or suggest. *Archaic,* to announce; to make known.—**in·ti·mat·er,** *n.*—**in·ti·ma·tion,** *n.*

in·tim·i·date, in·tim′i·dāt′, *v.t.*—*intimidated, intimidating.* [M.L. *intimidatus,* pp. of *intimidate.*] To make timid or fill with fear; to overawe; to cow; to force into or deter from an action by inducing fear; as, to *intimidate* a witness.—**in·tim·i·da·tion,** *n.*—**in·tim·i·da·tor,** *n.*

in·tinc·tion, in·tingk′shan, *n.* [L.L. *intinctio(n-),* < L. *intingere,* dip in.] *Eccles.* a dipping of the eucharistic bread in the wine in order to administer both together in a Communion service.

in·ti·tle, in·tīt′l, *v.t.* Entitle.

in·tit·ule, in·tit′ūl, *v.t.*—*intituled, intituling.* [O.Fr. Fr. *intituler,* < L.L. *intitulare.*] *Brit.* To give a title to, as a legislative act; entitle.—**in·tit·u·la·tion,** *n.*

in·to, in′tö, in′tụ, in′to, *prep.* [Orig. two words, *in* and *to.*] A function word expressing motion or direction toward the inner part of a place or thing; as, going *into* a house; against or to a point or touching; as, walk *into* a closed door; an indication of insertion; as, screwing a fuse *into* the socket; an indication of entrance or inclusion; as, welcomed *into* the community; to the condition, circumstance, relation, or occupation of; as, fell *into* confusion, went *into* teaching; an indication of an extension of space or time; as, lasting far *into* the night; an indication of division, as: Two *into* eight equals four.

in·tol·er·a·ble, in·tol′ẽr·a·bl, *a.* [L. *intolerabilis.*] Not to be tolerated; unendurable; insufferable.—**in·tol·er·a·bil·i·ty, in·tol·er·a·ble·ness,** *n.*—**in·tol·er·a·bly,** *adv.*

in·tol·er·ant, in·tol′ẽr·ant, *a.* [L. *intolerans, intolerantis.*] Refusing to tolerate others' opinions, rights, religious beliefs, etc.; bigoted; prejudiced; not able to endure, usu. followed by *of.*—*n.* Bigot; an intolerant individual.—**in·tol·er·ant·ly,** *adv.*—**in·tol·er·ance,** *n.* The quality of being intolerant; want of capacity to endure or tolerate.

in·tomb, in·tŏm′, *v.t.* Entomb.

in·to·nate, in′tō·nāt′, in′to·nāt, *v.t.*—*intonated, intonating.* [L. *in-,* in, and *tonus,* tone.] To pronounce with a certain tone or modulation; to intone.—**in·to·na·tion,** *n.* The change in pitch of the voice in speaking, often modifying meanings, characterizing dialects, or registering emotional reaction; the manner of producing tones in playing, singing, or speaking; the act of intoning or intonating; something which is intoned; the opening notes or phrases of a plainsong or a Gregorian chant.—**in·to·na·tion·al,** *a.*

in·tone, in·tōn′, *v.t.*—*intoned, intoning.* [L. *in-,* in, and *tonus,* tone.] To utter in a singing voice or tone, as in a liturgical service; chant; recite in monotone.—*v.i.* To speak or recite in a singing voice, esp. in monotone; utter sonorous tones.—**in·ton·er,** *n.*

in·tort, in·tart′, *v.t.* [L. *intorqueo, intortum.*] To twist inward; to curl.—**in·tor·sion, in·tor·tion,** *n.* A winding or twisting, usu. inward, around an axis, as of a plant stem around a pole.

in·tox·i·cant, in·tok′si·kant, *n.* That which intoxicates, as an intoxicating liquor or drug.—*a.* Intoxicating or exciting; as, an *intoxicant* atmosphere.

in·tox·i·cate, in·tok′si·kāt″, *v.t.*—*intoxicated, intoxicating.* [L.L. *intoxico, intoxicatum*—L. *in-,* and *toxicum,* poison = Gr. *toxikon,* a poison in which arrows were dipped, < *toxon,* a bow.] To inebriate; to make drunk, as with alcoholic liquor. *Fig.*

to excite the spirits to a very high pitch; to elate with enthusiasm or frenzy. *Med.* to poison, as by a serum or drug.—*v.i.* To have the power of intoxicating.—**in·tox′si·kit,** in·tok′si·kāt″, *a.*—**in·tox·i·cat·ed,** *a.*—**in·tox·i·cat·ed·ly,** *adv.*—**in·tox·i·cat·ing,** in·tok′si·kā″ting, *a.*—**in·tox·i·cat·ing·ly,** *adv.*

in·tox·i·ca·tion, in·tok″si·kā′shan, *n.* Inebriation; frenzied enthusiasm.

in·tra·cel·lu·lar, in″tra·sel′ū·lẽr, *a.* [L. *intra,* within, *cellula,* a little cell.] *Biol.* occurring within a cell.

in·trac·ta·ble, in·trak′ta·bl, *a.* [L. *intractabilis.*] Not tractable; not to be governed or managed; perverse; obstinate; difficult to manipulate or work with, as metals; difficult to treat or cure, as illnesses.—**in·trac·ta·bil·i·ty, in·trac·ta·ble·ness,** *n.*—**in·trac·ta·bly,** *adv.*

in·tra·cu·ta·ne·ous, in″tra·kū·tā′nē·us, *a. Anat.* intradermal.—**in·tra·cu·ta·ne·ous test,** a test for allergic sensitivity made by injecting a diluted antigen into the skin. —**in·tra·cu·ta·ne·ous·ly,** *adv.*

in·tra·der·mal, in″tra·dụr′mal, *a. Anat.* within the skin or between the layers of the skin, as an injection. Also **in·tra·der·mic.** —**in·tra·der·mal·ly, in·tra·der·mi·cal·ly,** *adv.*

in·tra·dos, in′tra·dos″, in′tra·dōs″, in·trä′dos, in·trä′dōs, *n.* pl. **in·tra·dos, in·tra·dos·es.** [Fr. < L. *intra,* within, and *dorsum,* back.] *Arch.* the interior curve of an arch.

in·tra·mo·lec·u·lar, in″tra·mo·lek′ū·lẽr, in″tra·mō·lek′ū·lẽr, *a.* Occurring or existing within the molecule.—**in·tra·mo·lec·u·lar·ly,** *adv.*

in·tra·mu·ral, in″tra·mūr′al, *a.* [L. *intra,* within, and *murus,* wall.] Existing within the limits of an institution or community; pertaining to competition or events within a school; as, an *intramural* swimming meet; *anat.* within the substance of a wall, as of an organ or cavity of the body.—**in·tra·mu·ral·ly,** *adv.*

in·tra·mus·cu·lar, in″tra·mus′kū·lẽr, *a.* Occurring within, or affecting the interior of a muscle.—**in·tra·mus·cu·lar·ly,** *adv.*

in·tran·si·gent, in·tran·si·geant, in·tran′si·jent, *a.* [Fr. *intransigeant,* < L. *in-,* not, and *transigo,* to transact, to come to a settlement.] Refusing to agree or to come to a settlement; irreconcilable; uncompromising; unbending.—*n.*—**in·tran·si·gence, in·tran·si·gen·cy,** *n.* —**in·tran·si·gent·ist,** *n.*—**in·tran·si·gent·ly,** *adv.*

in·tran·si·tive, in·tran′si·tiv, *a.* Referring to the nature of an intransitive verb.— **in·tran·si·tive verb,** *gram.* a verb which in itself completes the subject and does not require or take a direct object.—**in·tran·si·tive·ly,** *adv.*—**in·tran·si·tive·ness,** *n.*

in·trant, in′trant, *n.* [L. *intrans, intrantis,* ppr. of *intro,* to go into, to enter.] An entrant, esp. one who enters an organization, an institution of learning, or a holy order.

in·tra·psy·chic, in″tra·sī′kik, *a. Psychol.* arising or occurring within the psyche, mind, or self, as conflicting motives within the same person.—**in·tra·psy·chi·cal,** *a.*— **in·tra·psy·chi·cal·ly,** *adv.*

in·tra·spe·cif·ic, in″tra·spi·sif′ik, *a. Biol.* occurring among members of the same species.

in·tra·state, in″tra·stāt′, *a.* Occurring or carried on within a single state.

in·tra·u·ter·ine, in″tra·ū′tẽr·in, in″tra·ū′te·rīn, *a.* Occurring or situated within the uterus.—**in·tra·u·ter·ine de·vice,** a means of continuous contraception placed within the uterus, as a plastic coil. Abbr. *IUD.*

in·tra·ve·nous, in″tra·vē′nus, *a.* Occurring or introduced within a vein or veins, esp.

by means of injection; as, *intravenous* feeding.—**in·tra·ve·nous·ly**, *adv.*

in·tra·vi·tam, in'tra·vī'tam, *a. Biol.* Happening during life; used upon a living subject, as a stain which will not kill living cells. Also **in·tra·vi·tal**, in"tra·vīt'al.

in·tra·zon·al, in"tra·zōn'al, *a. Agric.* relating to a major group of soils whose characteristics are changed little by environmental factors of climate and vegetation.

in·trench, in·trench', *v.t.* Entrench.

in·trep·id, in·trep'id, *a.* [L. *intrepidus—in*, not, and *trepidus*, alarmed.] Fearless; bold; brave; undaunted.—**in·tre·pid·i·ty**, **in·-trep·id·ness**, *n.*—**in·trep·id·ly**, *adv.*

in·tri·cate, in'tri·kit, *a.* [L. *intricatus*, pp. of *intrico*, to entangle—*in*, into, and *tricoe*, trifles, hindrances.] Entangled; involved; difficult to unravel; complicated; difficult to understand.—**in·tri·ca·cy**, in'tri·ka·sē, *n.* pl. **in·tri·ca·cies.** A winding or complicated arrangement; entanglement; something which is intricate.—**in·tri·cate·ly**, *adv.*—**in·tri·cate·ness**, *n.*

in·tri·gant, in·tri·guant, in'tri·gant, *Fr.* aN·tRē·gäN', *n.* [Fr. *intrigant*, It. *intrigante*, ppr. of *intrigare*.] One who practices intrigue; intriguer.—**in·tri·gante**, **in·tri·-guante**, in'tri·gant', *Fr.* aN·tRē·gäNt', *n.* Fem. of intrigant, intriguant.

in·trigue, in·trēg', *v.t.*—*intrigued*, *intriguing.* [Fr. *intriguer*, < It. *intrigare*, < L. *intricare*, entangle, perplex.] To excite the curiosity or interest of; to beguile; to cause to puzzle or ponder; to bring about by trickery or underhanded methods.—*v.i.* To use underhanded methods; to plot or scheme craftily; to carry on a clandestine love affair.—**in·trēg'**, in'trēg, *n.* The use of underhanded machinations or crafty dealings; an instance of this; plot; scheme; a clandestine or illicit love affair; the series of complications forming the plot of a play.—**in·tri·guer**, *n.*—**in·tri·guing**, *a.*—**in·tri·guing·ly**, *adv.*

in·trin·sic, in·trin'sik, in·trin'zik, *a.* [L. *intrinsecus—intra*, inward, *in*, in, and *secus*, beside.] Inherent; essential; innate; belonging to the thing in itself; *anat.* belonging entirely to or being within a given bodily part, as certain muscles. Also **in·trin·si·cal**,—**in·trin·si·cal·ly**, *adv.*—**in·trin·si·cal·ness**, *n.*

in·trin·sic fac·tor, *n.* An element of normal gastric and intestinal mucous membranes or mucosae, essential to the absorption of vitamin B_{12} by the body.

in·tro·duce, in"trō·dōs', in"trō·dūs', *v.t.*—*introduced*, *introducing.* [L. *introduco.*] To make acquainted; to present, as a person or persons, to others; to bring before an audience, the public or the like, for the first time; to bring forward for official attention, as a resolution or a bill; to lead or bring to a knowledge of, for the first time, followed by *to*; to institute or launch; as, to *introduce* a new company policy; to begin or open, as a topic or speech; to put into or insert.—**in·tro·duc·er**, *n.*

in·tro·duc·tion, in"trō·duk'shan, *n.* [L. *introductio.*] The act of introducing, bringing in, or making persons acquainted; a formal presentation of a person, bill, or idea; that which is introduced; that part of a book, discourse, musical work, or the like, which precedes the main work; a preface or preliminary discourse; an elementary or preliminary treatise; as, an *introduction* to biology.

in·tro·duc·to·ry, in"trō·duk'to·rē, *a.* Serving as an introduction; prefatory; preliminary. Also **in·tro·duc·tive.**—**in·-tro·duc·to·ri·ly**, *adv.*

in·tro·it, in'trō·it, in'troit, *n.* [L. *introitus*, an entrance.] (*Often cap.*), *Rom. Cath. Ch.* the first of the variable parts of the Mass,

including an antiphon, a psalm verse, and the Gloria Patri. A musical composition designed for the opening of church services.

in·tro·ject, in"trō·jekt', *v.t. Psychoanal.* to incorporate (external influences and esp. the characteristics of other individuals) into one's own pattern of behavior.—**in·tro·-jec·tion**, *n.*

in·trorse, in·trors', *a.* [L. *introrsus*, toward the inside.] *Bot.* turned or facing inward, as anthers which open toward the center of the flower: opposed to *extrorse.*—**in·trorse·ly**, *adv.*

in·tro·spect, in"trō·spekt', *v.t.* [L. *introspectus*, pp. of *introspicere*.] To look into or examine, as one's own feelings or thoughts. —*v.i.* To look within; to practice self-observation and examination.—**in·tro·spec·tion**, *n.* The observation or examination of one's own mental states or processes. —**in·tro·spec·tion·al**, **in·tro·spec·tive**, *a.*—**in·tro·spec·tive·ness**, *n.*—**in·tro·spec·tive·ist**, *n.*—**in·tro·spec·tive·ly**, *adv.*

in·tro·ver·sion, in"trō·vur'zhan, in"trō·-vur'shan, in'trō·vur"zhan, in'trō·vur"shan, *n.* The act of introverting; an introverted state; *psychol.* concern and interest directed inward toward oneself, rather than toward the outer external world: opposed to *extroversion.*—**in·tro·ver·sive**, in"trō·vur'siv, *a.*—**in·tro·ver·sive·ly**, *adv.*

in·tro·vert, in"trō·vurt', *v.t.* [L. *intro*, within, and *vertere* (pp. *versus*), turn.] To turn inward; *psychol.* to direct, as the mind, inward or upon oneself; *zool.* to ensheathe a part within another part; invaginate.— in'trō·vurt", *n. Psychol.* one characterized by introversion; broadly, one who is shy and reserved. *Zool.* a part that is or can be introverted.—*a.*—**in·tro·vert·ed**, *a.*

in·trude, in·trōd', *v.i.*—*intruded*, *intruding.* [L. *intrudo.*] To thrust oneself into any place or company without welcome or invitation; to force oneself upon others; to encroach.—*v.t.* To thrust in or cause to enter without right or welcome; *geol.* to cause to penetrate by intrusion.—**in·-trud·er**, *n.*—**in·tru·sion**, in·trō'zhan, *n.* The act of intruding; unwarrantable entrance; *law*, an unlawful entry into lands and tenements owned by another. *Geol.* the forcible penetration of molten rock into fissures or other rock formations; the intruded material when solidified.—**in·-tru·sive**, *a.*—**in·tru·sive·ly**, *adv.*—**in·-tru·sive·ness**, *n.*

in·trust, in·trust', *v.t.* Entrust.

in·tu·bate, in'tų·bāt", in'tū·bāt", *v.t.*—*intubated*, *intubating.* [L. *in-*, in, and *tubus*, E. *tube.*] *Med.* to insert a tube into (a hollow organ or orifice), as into the larynx to aid breathing.—**in·tu·ba·tion**, *n.*

in·tu·it, in·tö'it, in·tū'it, in'tö·it, in'tū·it, *v.t.*, *v.i.* [L. *intuitus*, pp. of *intueri*, look upon, regard.] To know by intuition.— **in·tu·it·a·ble**, *a.*

in·tu·i·tion, in"tö·ish'an, in"tū·ish'an, *n.* [< L. *intueor*, *intuitus*, to look upon, to contemplate.] Knowledge discerned directly by the mind without reasoning or analysis; a truth or revelation arrived at by insight; the power or capacity to perceive truth without apparent reasoning or concentration.— **in·tu·i·tion·al**, *a.*

in·tu·i·tion·ism, in"tö·ish'a·niz"um, in"-tū·ish'a·niz"um, *n. Philos.* the doctrine that fundamental truths are perceived intuitively rather than rationally; *ethics*, the doctrine that moral principles and judgments are intuitively acquired; *metaph.* the doctrine that intuition reveals the reality of perceived objects. Also **in·tu·i·tion·al·ism.**—**in·-tu·i·tion·ist**, *n.*, *a.*

in·tu·i·tive, in·tö'i·tiv, in·tū'i·tiv, *a.* Perceived by the mind immediately without the intervention of reasoning; known or obtained by intuition; having the power of

discovering truth without reasoning.— **in·tu·i·tive·ly**, *adv.*—**in·tu·i·tive·ness**, *n.*

in·tu·mesce, in"tų·mes', in"tū·mes', *v.i.*—*intumesced*, *intumescing.* [L. *intumesco—in-*, and *tumesco*, to begin to swell, incept. of *tumeo*, to swell.] To enlarge or expand, as with heat; to swell.—**in·tu·mes·cence**, *n.* —**in·tu·mes·cent**, *a.*

in·tus·sus·cept, in"tus·su·sept', *v.t.* [L. *intus*, within, and *suscipere* (pp. *susceptus*), receive.] To take within, as one part of the intestine into an adjacent part; invaginate. —**in·tus·sus·cep·tion**, *n.* [L. *intus* and *susceptio(n-)*, E. *susception.*] A taking within; *physiol.* the taking in of foreign matter, as nutriment, by a living organism and its conversion into living tissue. *Bot.* the growth of a cell wall by the incorporation of new particles between the existing particles of the wall. *Pathol.* the reception of one part within another, as when a part of the intestine is introduced into an adjacent part, usu. causing obstruction; invagination.—**in·tus·sus·cep·tive**, *a.*

in·u·lase, in'ū·lāz", *n. Biochem.* an enzyme which converts inulin into fructose, but has no effect on starch.

in·u·lin, in'ū·lin, *n.* [L. *inula*, elecampane.] *Biochem.* a white polysaccharide, obtained from the roots of certain plants as the Jerusalem artichoke and dahlia, which upon hydrolysis yield fructose.

in·unc·tion, in·ungk'shan, *n.* [L. *in-unctio(n-)*, < *inunguere*, anoint.] The act of anointing; *med.* the rubbing in of an oil or ointment.

in·un·dant, in·un'dant, *a.* Inundating; overflowing.

in·un·date, in'un·dāt", in'un·dāt", in·-un'dāt, *v.t.*—*inundated*, *inundating.* [L. *inundo*, *inundatum—in-*, and *undo*, to overflow (also in *abound*), < *unda*, a wave.] To overflow, deluge, or flood; to overwhelm with an abundance or superfluity, as: The post office was *inundated* with holiday mail.—**in·un·da·tion**, *n.*—**in·un·da·tor**, *n.*—**in·un·da·to·ry**, in·un'da·tōr"ē, *a.*

in·ur·bane, in"ur·bān', *a.* [L. *inurbanus.*] Not urbane; lacking in courtesy or suavity; rude.—**in·ur·ban·i·ty**, in"ur·ban'i·tē, *n.*

in·ure, in·ūr', i·nųr', *v.t.*—*inured*, *inuring.* [Prefix *in-*, in, and obs. *ure*, operation, work, < O.Fr. *eure*, Mod.Fr. *œuvre*, < L. *opera*, work.] To accustom, esp. to something undesirable or painful; as, *inure* oneself to toil and hardship; to habituate.— *v.i.* To become effectual or useful. Also *enure.*—**in·ure·ment**, *n.*

in·urn, in·urn', *v.t.* To put in an urn, esp. a funeral urn, as cremation ashes; to bury; to entomb.—**in·urn·ment**, *n.*

in·u·tile, in·ū'til, *a.* [O.Fr. Fr. *inutile*, < L. *inutilis.*] Useless; of no use or service; unprofitable.—**in·u·til·i·ty**, *n.* pl. **in·-u·til·i·ties.** [L. *inutilitas.*] Uselessness; a useless thing or person.

in va·cu·o, in vak'ū·ō", *L.* in wä'kų·ō", *adv.* [L.] Within a vacuum.

in·vade, in·vād', *v.t.*—*invaded*, *invading.* [L. *invadere* (pp. *invasus*).] To enter, as a country or region, with armed force for conquest or destruction; make a hostile incursion into; to enter as an enemy; as, disease *invades* the system; enter as if to take possession or overrun; to permeate; intrude upon, as privacy or thoughts; entrench, encroach, or infringe upon.—*v.i.* To undertake an invasion.—**in·vad·er**, *n.*

in·vag·i·nate, in·vaj'i·nāt", *v.t.*—*invaginated*, *invaginating.* [L. *in-*, in, and *vagina*, sheath.] To insert or receive as into a sheath; sheathe; to fold or draw, as a tubular organ, back within itself; introvert; intussuscept.—*v.i.* To become invaginated; undergo invagination.—**in·vaj'i·nit**, in·vaj'i·nāt", *a.* Invaginated; folded in upon itself.—**in·vag·i·na·tion**, in·vaj″i-nā′shan, *n*. The act or process of invaginating, or the resulting state; an invaginated part; *pathol*. intussusception, as of a portion of the intestine; *embryol*. the drawing inward of a portion of the wall of a blastula in the formation of a gastrula.

in·va·lid, in′va·lid, *n*. [Fr. *invalide*, < L. *invalidus*.] A person suffering from prolonged ill health or from some disabling injury; one who is incapacitated by old age or illness; one disabled for active service, as a soldier or sailor.—*a*. Impaired in health; sick or infirm; of or for invalids.—*v.t*. To make an invalid of; *Brit*. to remove from active military service because of illness or disability.—*v.i*. To become an invalid.

in·val·id, in·val′id, *a*. [L. *invalidus*, < in-, not, and *validus*, strong, powerful, effective.] Not valid; having no force, weight, or cogency, as an argument; without legal force, or void, as a contract.—**in·va·lid·i·ty**, in″va·lid′i·tē, *n*.—**in·val·id·ly**, *adv*.

in·val·i·date, in·val′i·dāt″, *v.t*.—*invalidated, invalidating*. To render invalid, or of no force or effect; to deprive of legal force or efficacy.—**in·val·i·da·tion**, in·val″i·dā′shan, *n*.—**in·val·i·da·tor**, *n*.

in·va·lid·ism, in′va·liz·diz″um, *n*. The condition of prolonged ill health.

in·val·u·a·ble, in·val′ū·a·bl, *a*. Of inestimable value; priceless.—**in·val·u·a·ble·ness**, *n*.—**in·val·u·a·bly**, *adv*.

In·var, in·vär′, *n*. [< *invariable*.] An alloy of steel and 35.5 percent nickel which is useful in precision manufacturing due to its minimal expansion at high temperatures. (Trademark.)

in·var·i·a·ble, in·vâr′ē·a·bl, *a*. Not variable; constant; always uniform; incapable of varying.—*n. Math*. An invariable quantity; a constant.—**in·var·i·a·bil·i·ty**, **in·var·i·a·ble·ness**, in·vâr″ē·a·bil′i·tē, *n*.—**in·var·i·a·bly**, *adv*.

in·var·i·ant, in·vâr′ē·ant, *a*. Not variant; invariable; constant.—*n. Math*. an entity or quantity unaffected throughout certain mathematical procedures.—**in·var·i·ance**, **in·var·i·an·cy**, *n*.—**in·var·i·ant·ly**, *adv*.

in·va·sion, in·vā′zhan, *n*. [L.L. *invasio(n)-*, < L. *invadere*.] The act of invading; the entering of a country by an enemy force, as for conquest; a hostile incursion; the entrance or advent of anything troublesome or harmful, as disease; infringement by intrusion; as, *invasion* of rights.—**in·va·sive**, *a*. Characterized by invasion, offense, or intrusion.—**in·va·sive·ness**, *n*.

in·vec·tive, in·vek′tiv, *n*. [Fr. < L. *invectivus*, abusive, < *inveho*, to inveigh.] An abusive or violent utterance; vituperation; a severe, formal censure, either oral or written.—*a*. Containing invectives; abusive.—**in·vec·tive·ly**, *adv*.—**in·vec·tive·ness**, *n*.

in·veigh, in·vā′, *v.i*. [L. *invehor*, to attack with words, to inveigh against—*in*, into, against, and *veho*, to carry.] To utter strong protests; to exclaim against someone or something; to rail, used with *against*.—**in·veigh·er**, *n*.

in·vei·gle, in·vā′gl, in·vē′gl, *v.t*.—*inveigled, inveigling*. [O.Fr. *avogler* (Fr. *aveugler*), to blind, < *avogle*, blind, < L. *ab*, from, and *oculus*, eye.] To induce or beguile by flattery, often with *into*; to win over or acquire by beguilement or flattery.—**in·vei·gle·ment**, *n*.—**in·vei·gler**, *n*.

in·vent, in·vent′, *v.t*. [Fr. *inventer*, < L. *invenio, inventum*, to come upon, to find.] To originate; to contrive, devise, or construct, as something that did not exist before; to construct by use of imagination; to concoct; to fabricate.—**in·vent·i·ble**, *a*.—**in·vent·a·ble**, *a*.

in·ven·tion, in·ven′shan, *n*. [L. *inventio, inventionis*.] The act of inventing; a contrivance or device which did not before

exist; origination; something invented or devised; the power of inventing; that faculty by which a poet or novelist produces plots, characters, etc.—**in·ven·tion·al**, *a*.

in·ven·tive, in·ven′tiv, *a*. Able to invent; quick at invention or contrivance; imaginative; ingenious.—**in·ven·tive·ly**, *adv*.—**in·ven·tive·ness**, *n*.

in·ven·to·ry, in′ven·tōr″ē, in′ven·tṛr″ē, *n*. pl. **in·ven·to·ries**. [L. *inventarium*, an inventory, < *invenio*, invent.] A list of goods, usu. with a description and valuation; a merchant's list of merchandise on hand, prepared annually; any catalogue or account of particular things.—*v.t*.—*inventoried, inventorying*. To list, catalogue, or schedule, as goods; to insert or register in an account book or the like.—**in·ven·to·ri·al**, in″ven·tōr′ē·al, in″ven·tṛr′ē·al, *a*.—**in·ven·to·ri·al·ly**, *adv*.

in·ve·rac·i·ty, in″ve·ras′i·tē, *n*. pl. **in·ve·rac·i·ties**. Lack of veracity; untruthfulness; an untruth.

in·ver·ness, in″vêr·nes′, *n*. [From *Inverness*, county and seaport in Scotland.] (*Sometimes cap*.) An overcoat with a long removable cape; the cape itself.

in·verse, in·vûrs′, in′vûrs, *a*. [L. *inversus*, pp. of *inverto*—*in*, on, to, and *verto*, to turn, as in *advert, convert, revert, subvert*.] Opposite in order or relation; inverted; turned upside down or inside out; *math*. opposite in nature and effect, as: Subtraction is *inverse* to addition, division to multiplication.—*n*. A direct opposite; *math*. a reciprocal.—**in·verse pro·por·tion**, any proportion which contains a reciprocal ratio; a proportion such that one term is greater than the norm, as another is less than the norm.—**in·verse·ly**, *adv*.

in·ver·sion, in·vûr′zhan, in·vûr′shan, *n*. [L. *inversio, inversionis*, < *inverto, inversum*.] The act of inverting; a change of order or position so that what was after is now before, and vice versa; *gram., rhet*. transposition of words so that they are out of their natural order, as "wise was Solomon" for "Solomon was wise"; *mus*. change or reversal of position, as of the elements comprising an interval or chord; *math*. a change in the order of the terms of a proportion or the change of each term in a proportion to its reciprocal form; *chem*. a rearranging of the molecules in a compound, as sucrose, causing the formation of two different isomers, the mixture of which rotates the plane of polarized light in a direction opposite to the direction of rotation produced by the original compound. *Meteor*. a condition where the temperature of the air increases instead of decreases with an increase of altitude.—**in·ver·sive**, *a*.

in·vert, in·vûrt′, *v.t*. [L. *inverto*.] To turn upside down; to invaginate or turn inside out; to put in reverse order or position.—in′vûrt, *n*. One that is inverted or affected by inversion; a homosexual.—*a*. Altered chemically by inversion; as, *invert* sugar.—**in·vert·i·bil·i·ty**, in·vûrt″i·bil′i·tē, *n*.—**in·vert·i·ble**, *a*.

in·ver·tase, in·vûr′tās, *n*. *Biochem*. an enzyme, found in some plants and in an animal's digestive tract, which causes the inversion of cane sugar into two simple sugars, glucose and fructose.

in·ver·te·brate, in·vûr′te·brit, in·vûr′te·brāt″, *a*. [N.L. *invertebratus*.] Not vertebrate; without a backbone; of or pertaining to animals without a vertebral column; *fig*. without strength of character.—*n*. An invertebrate animal; *fig*. a person lacking strength of character.—**in·ver·te·bra·cy**, *n*.—**in·ver·te·brate·ness**, in·vûr′te·bra·sē, *n*.

in·vert·ed, in·vûr′tid, *a*. Turned to a contrary direction; turned upside down; changed in order.—**in·vert·ed arch**, an arch

with its curve turned downward, as in a sewer or in foundations.—**in·vert·ed com·ma**, *Brit*. A comma turned upside down to mark the beginning of a quotation, the end being indicated by an apostrophe; quotation mark.

in·vert·er, in·vûr′tẽr, *n*. Something or someone that inverts; *elect*. a converter.

in·vert sug·ar, *n*. A mixture of glucose and fructose formed naturally in fruits or artificially by the inversion of cane sugar.

in·vest, in·vest′, *v.t*. [L. *investio—in*, and *vestio*, to clothe, < *vestis*, a garment.] To clothe, to dress, to array; to envelop or surround; to place in possession of an office, rank, or dignity; to install; to clothe or furnish, often with authority; as, to *invest* certain powers in the president; to give to or endow with a trait or quality; *milit*. to enclose or surround for the purpose of besieging. To put, as money or capital, into some type of property, with the purpose of getting a profitable return; to spend or commit in the hope of future benefit; as, to *invest* years of study.—*v.i*. To make an investment.—**in·vest·a·ble**, *a*.—**in·ves·tor**, *n*.

in·ves·ti·gate, in·ves′ti·gāt″, *v.t*.—*investigated, investigating*. [L. *investigo, investigatum—in*, and *vestigo*, to follow a track, to search, < *vestigium*, a track.] To search into; to research; inquire into and examine with care.—*v.i*. To make an examination or inquiry.—**in·ves·ti·ga·tion**, in·ves″ti·gā′shan, *n*.—**in·ves·ti·ga·tive**, in·ves′ti·gā·tọ·rē, in·ves′ti·ga·tōr″ē, *a*.—**in·ves·ti·ga·tor**, *n*.

in·ves·ti·ture, in·ves′ti·chẽr, *n*. The act of investing; the act of confirming or bestowing office, authority, rank, or title; that which invests or covers.—**in·ves·ti·tive**, *a*.

in·vest·ment, in·vest′ment, *n*. That in which money is invested; the act of investing; the laying out of money for profit in the purchase of some type of property; money laid out for profit; investiture, as with office; *milit*. a siege by an armed force; *biol*. an outer layer or integument of a part of an animal or plant.

in·vet·er·ate, in·vet′ẽr·it, *a*. [L. *inveteratus*, pp. of *invetero*, to render old—*in*, in, and *vetus*, old.] Deep-rooted or ingrained; firmly fixed by time or habit; as, an *inveterate* disease or custom; confirmed in any given habit or attitude; as, an *inveterate* smoker.—**in·vet·er·a·cy**, *n*.—**in·vet·er·ate·ly**, *adv*.

in·vi·a·ble, in·vī′a·bl, *a*. Not viable; unable to remain alive, particularly due to genetic make-up.—**in·vi·a·bil·i·ty**, in·vī″a·bil′i·tē, *n*.

in·vid·i·ous, in·vid′ē·us, *a*. [L. *invidiosus*, < *invidia*, ill will, E. *envy*.] Calculated to excite ill will or resentment; offensive; as, *invidious* remarks; producing or causing to produce envious dislike; unfairly discriminating; as, an *invidious* comparison; harmful or injurious.—**in·vid·i·ous·ly**, *adv*.—**in·vid·i·ous·ness**, *n*.

in·vig·i·late, in·vij′i·lāt″, *v.i*.—*invigilated, invigilating*. [L. *invigilatus*, pp. of *invigilare*, < *in*, in, on, and *vigilare*, watch.] *Brit*. to keep watch over students at an examination.—**in·vig·i·la·tion**, in·vij″i·lā′shan, *n*.—**in·vig·i·la·tor**, *n*.

in·vig·or·ate, in·vig′o·rāt″, *v.t*.—*invigorated, invigorating*. [L. *in*, intens., and *vigor*, strength.] To give life and energy to; to strengthen.—**in·vig·or·ant**, in·vig′ẽr·ant, *n*.—**in·vig·or·a·tion**, in·vig″o·rā′shan, *n*.—**in·vig·or·a·tor**, *n*.

in·vin·ci·ble, in·vin′si·bl, *a*. [L. *invincibilis—in*, not, and *vincibilis*, conquerable.] Incapable of being conquered or subdued; incapable of being overcome; unconquerable.—**in·vin·ci·bil·i·ty**, **in·vin·ci·ble·ness**, in·vin″si·bil′i·tē, *n*.—**in·vin·ci·bly**, *adv*.

in·vi·o·la·ble, in·vī′o·la·bl, *a.* [L. *in-violabilis*—*in*, not, and *violabilis*, that may be violated, < *violo*, to violate.] Not to be violated; not to be profaned or treated with irreverence; not to be broken or infringed, as an agreement or secrecy; not to be injured or tarnished, as chastity or honor; secure from hurt or destruction.—**in··vi·o·la·bil·i·ty, in·vi·o·la·ble·ness**, in··vī″o·la·bil′i·tē, *n.*—**in·vi·o·la·bly**, *adv.*

in·vi·o·late, in·vī′o·lit, in·vī′o·lāt″, *a.* [L. *inviolatus*.] Not violated or desecrated; unprofaned; pure; unbroken.—**in·vi·o··late·ly**, *adv.*—**in·vi·o·late·ness**, *n.*

in·vis·i·ble, in·viz′i·bl, *a.* [L. *invisibilis*.] Incapable of being seen; imperceptible; concealed; not open to public knowledge; not published in a financial statement or included in statistics.—*n.*—**in·vis·i·bil·i··ty, in·vis·i·ble·ness**, in·viz″i·bil′i·tē, *n.* —**in·vis·i·bly**, *adv.*

in·vi·ta·tion, in″vi·tā′shan, *n.* [L. *invitatio(n-)*, < *invitare*.] The act of inviting; a request to come to a place or gathering, or to do something; a form of spoken or written words, esp. a formal, printed one, in which such a request is conveyed; inducement or enticement.—**in·vi·ta··tion·al**, *a.*

in·vi·ta·to·ry, in·vī′ta·tōr″ē, *a.* [L.L. *invitatorius* (as n.), M.L. *invitatorium*, < L. *invitare*.] Serving to invite; conveying an invitation.—*n. pl.* **in·vi·ta·to·ries.** An invitation, esp. a psalm, as used in church service.

in·vite, in·vīt′, *v.t.*—*invited, inviting.* [L. *invitare* (pp. *invitatus*); origin uncertain.] To ask, as a person, to come to a place or gathering, or to do something; request politely or formally; to act so as to bring on or render probable; as, to *invite* disaster; give occasion for; as, a subject which *invites* few remarks; to attract or tempt.—*v.i.* To give invitation; offer attractions or inducements.—**in′vīt**, *n. Slang*, an invitation.—**in·vit·er**, *n.*—**in·vit·ing**, *a.*—**in·vit·ing·ly**, *adv.*

in vi·tro, in vē′trō, *adv., a. Biol.* occurring outside a living organism and in an artificial environment, as tissues cultivated in a test tube.

in vi·vo, in vē′vō, *adv., a. Biol.* occurring within a living organism.

in·vo·ca·tion, in″vo·kā′shan, *n.* [L. *invocatio, invocationis.*] The act of invoking or addressing in prayer; the form or act of calling for the assistance or presence of any being, particularly of some divinity; a prayer said at the opening of a ceremony or service; the summoning of a spirit, or an incantation used for this; a calling upon a legal or moral standard or right.—**in·vo··cate**, in′vo·kāt″, *v.i.*—*invocated, invocating.* [L. *invoco*, to call, < *vox*, voice.] *Archaic*, to invoke.—**in·vo·ca·tion·al**, *a.*—**in··voc·a·to·ry**, in·vok′a·tōr″ē, *a.*

in·voice, in′vois, *n.* [Appar. < Fr. *envois*, pl. of *envoi*, a message, a thing sent.] A list of items of merchandise shipped or sent to a purchaser with corresponding prices, other charges, and terms; the merchandise or shipment itself; a bill.—*v.t.*—*invoiced, invoicing.* To make an invoice of; to enter in an invoice.

in·voke, in·vōk′, *v.t.*—*invoked, invoking.* [O.Fr. Fr. *invoquer*, < L. *invocare* (pp. *invocatus*), < *in*, in, on, and *vocare*, call.] To call upon, as a divine spirit, in prayer; to appeal to, as for aid or protection; to call for earnestly; as, to *invoke* mercy; to call upon as applicable and binding, as a law; to summon, as a spirit, by incantation; conjure; to make supplication for; to give rise to or bring about.—**in·vok·er**, *n.*

in·vo·lu·cel, in·vol′ū·sel″, *n.* [N.L. *involucellum*, dim. of L. *involucrum*.] *Bot.* A secondary involucre; a small involucre

often at the base of an individual flower or a small cluster of flowers.—**in·vol·u·cel··late, in·vol·u·cel·lat·ed**, in·vol″ū·sel′it, *a.* Having involucels.

in·vo·lu·cre, in′vo·lö″kėr, *n.* [Fr. *involucre*, < L. *involucrum*, wrapper, covering.] A covering, esp. a membranous one; *bot.* one or more whorls of leaflike bracts which surround the base of a flower or cluster of flowers below the calyx or calyxes.—**in··vo·lu·cred**, in·vo·lu·crate, *a.* Having an involucre.—**in·vo·lu·cral**, *a.*—**in·vo·lu··cri·form**, *a.*

in·vo·lu·crum, in″vo·lö′krum, *n. pl.* **in··vo·lu·cra**, in″vo·lö′kra. An enveloping or enclosing sheath; an involucre.

in·vol·un·tar·y, in·vol′un·ter″ē, *a.* Not voluntary; not able to act or not acting according to will or choice; as, an *involuntary* agent; independent of will or choice; unintentional; as, an *involuntary* movement; not proceeding from choice; not done willingly; unwillingly; *physiol.* operating or acting independently of will or conscious control; as, an *involuntary* response.—**in·vol·un·tar·i·ly**, in·vol′un··ter″i·lē, in·vol″un·târ′i·lē, *adv.*—**in·vol··un·tar·i·ness**, *n.*

in·vol·un·tar·y mus·cle, *n.* Smooth muscle.

in·vo·lute, in′vo·löt″, *a.* [L. *involutus*, pp. of *involvo*.] Involved; complicated; intricate; curled in a spiral; *bot.* rolled inward from the edges, as a leaf or petal; *zool.* pertaining to a shell having tightly coiled whorls.—in″vo·löt′, in′vo·löt″, *v.i.*—*involuted, involuting.* To become involute; curl inward; to return to a previous state or condition.—in′vo·löt″, *n. Math.* a curve traced by any point of a taut string when it is unwrapped from a given curve.—**in··vo·lute·ly**, *adv.*

in·vo·lu·tion, in″vo·lö′shan, *n.* [L. *involutio(n-)*, < *involere.* INVOLVE.] The act of involving, or the state of being involved; entanglement or complication; something complicated; a complicated arrangement of words in a sentence, usu. having clauses or phrases intervening between subject and predicate. *Physiol.* a retrograde change, as the return of an organ to its normal size after enlargement; degeneration; the bodily changes and loss of vigor associated with aging. *Biol.* a rolling up or folding in upon itself, or a part formed in this way; *embryol.* the inward turning of cells to form a gastrula; *math.* the raising of a quantity or expression to any given power.—**in·vo·lu··tion·al, in·vo·lu·tion·ar·y**, *a.*

in·volve, in·volv′, *v.t.*—*involved, involving.* [L. *involvere* (pp. *involutus*), roll in or on, enwrap, involve, < *in*, in, on, and *volvere*, roll.] To include as a necessary circumstance, condition, or consequence; imply; entail; affect; to include, contain, or comprehend within itself or its scope; to cause to be inextricably associated or concerned; implicate; to engross or occupy absorbingly; to combine inextricably, entangle; to bring into an intricate or complicated form; to roll or wrap; to swallow up; engulf; overwhelm; *math.* to raise to a given power.—**in·volve·ment**, *n.*—**in··volv·er**, *n.*

in·volved, in·volvd′, *a.* Intricate; complicated; not easily understood.—**in·volv··ed·ly**, in·vol′vid·lē, in·volvd′lē, *adv.*—**in·volv·ed·ness**, *n.*

in·vul·ner·a·ble, in·vul′nėr·a·bl, *a.* [L. *invulnerabilis*.] Not vulnerable; incapable of being wounded or of receiving injury; unassailable; unconquerable.—**in·vul·ner··a·bil·i·ty, in·vul·ner·a·ble·ness**, in·vul″nėr·a·bil′i·tē, *n.*—**in·vul·ner·a·bly**, *adv.*

in·wall, in·wạl′, *v.t.* To enclose with or within a wall.—in′wạl, *n.* An interior wall, esp. of a blast furnace.

in·ward, in′wėrd, *adv.* [O.E. *inweard.*] Near or toward the inside, interior, or center; toward the mind or soul. Also **in·wards**.—*a.* Located on the inside or interior; within the body; internal; inner; of the mind or soul; mental; spiritual; proceeding or directed toward the inside. —*n.* That which is on the inside; an internal part. *Pl.* internal parts of the body; also *innards*.—**in·ward·ly**, *adv.*

in·ward·ness, in′wėrd·nis, *n.* The state of being inward or internal; depth of thought or feeling; a tendency to examine one's own thoughts and feelings; occupation with what concerns man's inner nature; spirituality; the intrinsic character or essence of a thing; inner meaning.

in·weave, in·wēv′, *v.t.*—past *inwove*, *in-weaved*, pp. *inwoven, inweaved*, ppr. *in-weaving.* To weave together; to intertwine or combine by weaving, as in a fabric. Also **in·weave**.

in·wrought, in·rạt′, *a.* [Prefix *in*, and *wrought*.] Worked into or combined with other things; embellished with decorative ornamentation; worked into or on something, as a design or engraving.

i·o·date, ī′o·dāt″, *n. Chem.* a salt of iodic acid.

i·o·date, ī′o·dāt″, *v.t.*—*iodated, iodating.* To combine, impregnate, or treat with iodine.—**i·o·da·tion**, ī″o·dā′shan, *n.*

i·od·ic, ī·od′ik, *a.* Of or containing iodine; as, *iodic* acid.

i·od·ic ac·id, *n.* An acid, HIO_3, formed by the action of oxidating agents on iodine.

i·o·dide, ī′o·dīd″, ī′o·did, *n. Chem.* A compound of iodine with an element or radical; a salt of hydriodic acid; as, hydrogen *iodide.*

i·o·dine, ī′o·dīn″, ī′o·din, ī′o·dēn″, *n.* [Gr. *iodēs*, violetlike, < *ion*, violet, and *eidos*, form.] A nonmetallic element occurring, at ordinary temperatures, as a grayish-black crystalline solid, which changes to a dense violet vapor when heated: used in medicine and photography. Sym. I, at. no. 53, at. wt. 126.904. Also **i·o·din**, ī′o·din. See Periodic Table of Elements.—**i·o·dism**, ī′o·diz″um, *n. Pathol.* poisoning due to the use of iodine or its compounds.—**i·o·dize**, ī′o·dīz″, *v.t.*—*iodized, iodizing.* To treat or impregnate with iodine.

i·o·do·form, ī·ō′do·fạrm″, ī·od′o·fạrm″, *n. Chem.* a yellowish crystalline compound, CHI_3, resembling chloroform and used as an antiseptic.

i·o·dol, ī′o·dōl″, ī′o·dạl″, ī′o·dol″, *n. Chem.* a crystalline compound containing iodine and used as an antiseptic.

i·o·dop·sin, ī″o·dop′sin, *n.* A visual violet pigment occurring in retinal cones and important to daylight vision.

i·o·dous, ī·ō′dus, ī·od′us, *a. Chem.* Of, referring to, or containing iodine; containing iodine in its trivalent form.

i·o·lite, ī′o·līt″, *n.* [Gr. *ion*, a violet, and *lithos*, stone.] A mineral of a violet-blue color; cordierite.

I·o moth, ī′ō mạth″, *n. Entom.* one of the N. American giant silkworm moths, *Automeris io*, identified by its large pink and blue eyespots, one on each hind wing, and in the larval stage by its conspicuous spines.

i·on, ī′on, ī′on, *n.* [Gr. *ion*, ppr. neut. of *ienai*, go.] *Phys., chem.* an electrified atom or group of atoms, having either a positive or negative charge, which has increased or decreased its number of electrons after electrolysis.—**i·on·ic**, ī·on′ik, *a.*

i·on ex·change, *n.* A chemical process during which a mutual transfer of ions between a solid and a liquid occurs, leaving the solid almost unaltered.—**i·on ex··chang·er**, *n.*

I·o·ni·an, ī·ō′nē·an, *a.* [From *Ionia*, an ancient region on the western coast of

Asia Minor.] Pertaining to Ionia; pertaining to a branch of the Greek race named from Ion, the legendary founder; designating or pertaining to a group of Greek Islands in the Mediterranean off the coast of Greece; pertaining to a sea forming the part of the Mediterranean between Greece, Italy, and Sicily.—*n.* A member of a Hellenic people who came to Greece in the 12th century B.C.; an Ionian Greek.

I·on·ic, ĭ·on′ĭk, *a.* Pertaining to the Ionians; *arch.* noting or pertaining to one of the Greek orders, distinguished by the volute, spiral scroll of its capital; *pros.* noting or employing a foot consisting of two long syllables followed or preceded by two short syllables.—*n. Pros.* a verse or meter composed of Ionic feet; an Ionic foot. The Ionian dialect of ancient Greek, the form used by Homer; (*sometimes l.c.*), *print.* a style of type.

i·on·i·za·tion cham·ber, *n. Phys.* a gas-filled tube containing two electrodes and used in detecting the amount of radio-activity in an object by measuring the conductivity, or the degree of ionization, between the electrodes.

i·on·ize, ī′o·nīz″, *v.t.*—*ionized, ionizing.* To separate into ions; produce ions in.—*v.i.* To be converted into an ion form.—**i·on·i·za·tion,** *n.*—**i·on·iz·er,** *n.* A device for ionizing a gas.

i·o·none, ī′o·nōn″, *n. Chem.* a colorless to light-yellow liquid, $C_{13}H_{20}O$, having a woody violet odor: used in chemical synthesis and the manufacture of flavorings and perfumes.

i·on·o·sphere, ī·on′o·sfēr″, *n.* An ionized region of the atmosphere, located beyond the stratosphere at distances beginning 50 miles above the earth's surface and extending upward about 200 miles.

i·o·ta, ī·ō′ta, *n.* [Gr. *iōta*; hence *jot*.] The ninth letter of the Greek alphabet; a very small quantity; a jot.

IOU, ī′ō·ū′, *n.* [A phonetic equivalent of *I owe you.*] An acknowledgment of a debt, esp. a paper having on it these letters, followed by a sum, and duly signed.

ip·e·cac, ip′e·kak″, *n.* [< Pg. and S. Amer. Indian.] A shrub of tropical S. America, *Cephaelis ipecacuanha,* in the madder family; the dried roots of this shrub; the alkaloid obtained from these roots and used as an emetic and expectorant. Also **ip·e·cac·u·an·ha,** ip″e·kak″ū·an′a.

ip·so fac·to, ip′sō fak′tō, *adv.* [L.] Literally, by the fact itself; by the very nature of the act, as: Such a deed makes one a criminal, *ipso facto.*

IQ, I.Q. Abbr. for intelligence quotient.

i·ra·cund, ī′ra·kund″, *a.* [L. *iracundus,* < *ira,* anger, E. *ire.*] Prone to anger; irascible.—**i·ra·cun·di·ty,** *n.*

I·ra·ni·an, i·rā′nē·an, ī·rā′nē·an, *a.* [From *Iran,* a region of southwest Asia.] Pertaining to Iran, its language, or its inhabitants.—*n.* A resident or native of Iran; a branch of certain Indo-European languages, including Persian, Kurdish, and other cognate languages.

I·ra·qi, i·rak′ē, *Pers.* ē·Rä′kē, *a.* [From *Iraq,* a country in southwest Asia.] Of or pertaining to Iraq, its language, or its inhabitants.—*n.* The Arabian dialect spoken in Iraq; a native of Iraq.

i·ras·ci·ble, i·ras′i·bl, ī·ras′i·bl, *a.* [L. *irascibilis,* < *irascor,* to be angry, < *ira,* anger, whence also *ire, irate.*] Quick-tempered; readily aroused to anger; cranky or irritable; characterized or caused by anger.—**i·ras·ci·bil·i·ty, i·ras·ci·ble·ness,** *n.*—**i·ras·ci·bly,** *adv.*

i·rate, ī′rāt, ī·rāt′, *a.* [L. *iratus,* pp. of *irasci,* grow angry, < *ira,* anger, E. *ire.*] Angry; incensed; enraged; characterized or caused by anger.

ire, īer, *n.* [O.Fr. < L. *ira,* wrath.] Anger; wrath; keen resentment.—**ire·ful,** *a.*—**ire·ful·ly,** *adv.*—**ire·ful·ness,** *n.*

i·ren·ic, i·ren′ik, i·rē′nik, *a.* [Gr. *eirēnikos,* < *eirēnē,* peace.] Peaceful; pacific; tending to promote peace. Also **i·ren·i·cal.**—**i·ren·i·cal·ly,** *adv.*

ir·i·da·ceous, ir″i·dā′shus, ī″ri·dā′shus, *a.* [N.L. *Iris* (*Irid-*), the iris genus.] Belonging to the *Iridaceae,* or iris family of plants, which includes the iris, crocus, gladiolus, and freesia; similar to those plants of the iris family.

ir·i·des·cent, ir″i·des′ent, *a.* Giving out or displaying colors like those of the rainbow, as mother-of-pearl.—*n.* A substance or material which is iridescent.—**ir·i·des·cence,** *n.* The condition of being iridescent; a display of gleaming and shimmering colors.—**ir·i·des·cent·ly,** *adv.*

i·rid·ic, i·rid′ik, ī·rid′ik, *a. Chem.* containing, derived from, or pertaining to iridium.

i·rid·i·um, i·rid′ē·um, ī·rid′ē·um, *n.* [From the iridescent colors it exhibits when dissolving in hydrochloric acid.] A hard but brittle silvery metallic element resembling platinum: one of the heaviest substances known. Sym. Ir, at. no. 77, at. wt. 192.20.

ir·i·dos·mine, ir″i·doz′min, ir″i·dos′min, ī″ri·doz′min, ī″ri·dos′min, *n.* A native compound of iridium and osmium, often containing some platinum and rhodium, used to make points for fountain pens. Also **ir·i·dos·mi·um,** *osmiridium.*

i·ris, ī′ris, *n.* pl. **i·ris·es, ir·i·des,** ir′i·dēz″, ī′ri·dēz″. [L. *Iris,* the goddess *Iris, iris* (*irid-*), rainbow, kind of plant, < Gr. *Iris, Iris, iris* (*irid-*), rainbow, iris of the eye, iris plant.] *Anat.* the contractile circular diaphragm forming the colored portion of the eye and containing the pupil in its center. *Bot.* any plant of the genus *Iris,* having sword-shaped leaves and handsome flowers; the flower itself; also *fleur-de-lis, flag.* (*Cap.*), *class. mythol.* the goddess of the rainbow and messenger of the gods. A rainbow; a combination or play of colors; iridescence; *TV, motion pictures,* a device for fading pictures in or out.

i·ris di·a·phragm, *n. Opt., photog.* a diaphragm that can be adjusted to control the amount of light entering through a lens, as in the human eye or a camera.

I·rish, ī′rish, *a.* [M.E. *Irisc,* < O.E. *Iras,* pl., the Irish: cf. O.Ir. *Eriu,* Erin, Ireland.] Of, pertaining to, or characteristic of Ireland or its people.—*n.* The inhabitants of Ireland and their descendants elsewhere; the Celtic language of Ireland. *Slang,* temper; as, to get one's *Irish* up.—**I·rish·ism,** ī′ri·shiz″um, *n.* An Irish peculiarity, as of speech.—**I·rish·man,** *n.* pl. **I·rish·men.** —**I·rish·wom·an,** *n.* pl. **I·rish·wom·en.**

I·rish cof·fee, *n.* A drink made of hot sweetened coffee and Irish whiskey, with whipped cream topping.

I·rish moss, *n. Bot.* a seaweed of the coastal Atlantic, a red alga, *Chondrus crispus,* having cartilaginous tissues from which a carbohydrate emulsifier is obtained and used in foods.

I·rish po·ta·to, *n.* pl. **I·rish po·ta·toes.** The common white potato, *Solanum tuberosum.*

I·rish set·ter, *n.* A deep reddish or mahogany brown breed of bird dog, comparable to the English setter except in color.

I·rish stew, *n.* A stew made of beef, lamb, or mutton with potatoes, onions, and other vegetables.

I·rish ter·ri·er, *n.* A small breed of terrier with wiry, reddish hair.

I·rish wa·ter span·iel, *n.* A retriever dog developed in Ireland with a heavy, curly, water-resistant coat.

I·rish wolf·hound, *n.* A tall, powerful breed of dog with a wiry coat varying in color from white to black.

irk, urk, *v.t.* [The same word as Sw. *yrka,* to urge, enforce, press, from root of *work, wreak,* and *urge.*] To annoy; to distress; to irritate.—**irk·some,** *a.* Annoying; aggravating; wearisome; burdensome.—**irk·some·ly,** *adv.*—**irk·some·ness,** *n.*

i·ron, ī′ern, *n.* [O.E. *iren, isen,* Goth. *eisarn,* Icel. *járn* (< older *isarn*), Dan. *jern,* O.H.G. *isarn,* G. *eisen;* D. *ijer;* akin Skt. *ayas,* W. *haiarn.*] *Chem.* a metallic element, silver-white, malleable, and ductile, widely found in combination, strongly attracted by magnets, and easily oxidized: widely used in the form of steel for making building materials, machinery, tools, and many other products. Sym. Fe, at. no. 26, at. wt. 55.847. Anything that is inflexible, unyielding, strong, or firm; an instrument or utensil made of iron, such as a branding iron; an appliance that, when heated, is used for pressing cloth; *golf,* one of nine golf clubs with a metal head; *slang,* a gun. *Pl.* fetters; chains; manacles; handcuffs.—*a.* Consisting of iron; resembling iron, either actually or metaphorically; harsh, rude, severe; capable of great endurance; firm; robust; inflexible.—*v.t.* To smooth with an iron; to fetter or handcuff; to furnish or arm with iron.—*v.i.* To press clothing, etc., with a heated iron.—**have man·y i·rons in the fire,** to be engaged in many undertakings.—**i·ron out,** *colloq.* smooth out; to straighten out or remove problems or disagreements.—**i·ron·er,** ī′er·nêr, *n.*

I·ron Age, *n.* The cultural time period after the Bronze Age, distinguished by the use of iron, as in tools and weapons; (*l.c*), *mythol.* the final and worst age of the earth, marked by toil, selfishness, and corruption.

i·ron·bark, ī′ern·bärk″, *n.* Any of certain Australian eucalypti with a hard bark and wood, the latter valuable in construction work. Also **i·ron·bark tree.**

i·ron·bound, ī′ern·bound′, *a.* Bound with iron; edged or surrounded with rocks, as a coast; rugged, unyielding, or stern.

i·ron·clad, ī′ern·klad′, *a.* Covered or clothed with iron; armorplated; strict; fixed; as, an *ironclad* contract.—*n.* A 19th century warship covered with thick iron plates.

i·ron cur·tain, *n.* A barrier to information and communication, existing between countries which differ in military, ideological, and political beliefs; as, the *iron curtain* between the Soviet bloc and noncommunist countries.

i·ron gray, *n.* The dark gray color of newly broken iron.—**iron-gray,** *a.*

i·ron·hand·ed, ī′ern·han′did, *a.* Exerting strict or rigorous control; despotic; severe or harsh.

i·ron-heart·ed, ī′ern·här′tid, *a. Colloq.* Hard-hearted; unfeeling; unsympathetic.

i·ron horse, *n. Colloq.* a locomotive.

i·ron·ic, ī·ron′ik, *a.* [Gr. *eirōnikos.*] Pertaining to, of the nature of, or characterized by irony; using, or addicted to, irony. Also **i·ron·i·cal.**—**i·ron·i·cal·ly,** *adv.* —**i·ron·i·cal·ness,** *n.*

i·ron·ing, ī′er·ning, *n.* The process or instance of pressing clothing or other materials with an iron which is heated; items which need pressing or have been freshly pressed.—**i·ron·ing board,** a flat board or similar surface, usu. padded and on legs, on which clothes are ironed.

i·ro·nist, ī′ro·nist, *n.* One who uses irony with great frequency esp. in creating a literary style.

i·ron lung, *n.* A sealed chamber placed over or around the chest of a patient, which forces respiration by rhythmic changes in air pressure, thus acting as a substitute for normal lung action.

a- fat, fāte, fär, fâre, fạll; **e-** met, mē, mēre, hèr; **i-** pin, pīne; **o-** not, nōte, mŏve; **u-** tub, cūbe, bụll; **oi-** oil; **ou-** pound.

i·ron·mas·ter, ī′ẽrn·mä″stẽr, *n. Brit.* the master of an ironworks or foundry.

i·ron·mong·er, ī′ẽrn·mung″gẽr, ī′ẽrn·mong″gẽr, *n. Brit.* a dealer in ironware.— **i·ron·mong·er·y,** *n. Brit.* The goods, shop, or business of an ironmonger; a hardware store.

i·ron py·rites, *n. pl.* Pyrite.

i·ron·smith, ī′ẽrn·smith″, *n.* A worker in iron, as a blacksmith or locksmith.

i·ron·stone, ī′ẽrn·stōn″, *n.* Iron ore; any rock or mineral which contains iron.— **i·ron·stone chi·na,** a hard opaque pottery.

i·ron·ware, ī′ẽrn·wâr″, *n.* Utensils, tools, and other lightweight articles made from iron; hardware.

i·ron·weed, ī′ẽrn·wēd, *n.* A fall-blooming, N. American herb of the genus *Vernonia,* in the composite family, having purple to pink clustered flowers.

i·ron·wood, ī′ẽrn·wu̇d″, *n.* A small N. American tree, *Ostrya virginiana,* having strong, hard wood; also **hop·horn beam.** A tropical wood of the genus *Condalia,* one of the heaviest woods known.

i·ron·work, ī′ẽrn·wu̇rk, *n.* Any object made of iron; *pl., sing. or pl. in constr.* a factory where iron is produced.—**i·ron·work·er,** *n.*

i·ro·ny, ī′ro·nē, ī′ẽr·nē, *n. pl.* **i·ro·nies.** [L. *ironia,* < Gr. *eirōneia,* < *eirōn,* dissembling speaker, < *eirein,* say, speak.] A figure of speech in which the literal meaning is the opposite of the intended meaning: used in ridicule, contempt, or humor. *Liter.* a technique often used in writing satire; a method of expression in which the author veils his real meaning behind plot or character development which portrays the opposite. An outcome opposed to that which one has been led to expect.—**dra·ma·tic i·ro·ny,** *theatr.* a technique in which the audience understands what is happening on the stage, while the performers pretend not to.— **So·cra·tic i·ro·ny,** *philos.* simulated ignorance, used as an argumentative technique.

Ir·o·quoi·an, ir′o·kwoi′an, *a.* Pertaining to or characteristic of the Iroquois or their language.—*n.* The N. American Indian language family of the Iroquois, Hurons, Eries, Cherokees, and others; a member of any one of these tribes.

Ir·o·quois, ir′o·kwoi″, ir′o·kwoiz″, *a.* Pertaining or belonging to the Iroquois.— *n. pl.* **Ir·o·quois.** A member of an early Indian confederation composed of Cayugas, Mohawks, Oneidas, Onondagas, Senecas, and later the Tuscaroras, referred to as the Five Nations; collectively, these tribes.

ir·ra·di·ance, i·rā′dē·ans, *n.* That which is emitted, as a ray or beam of light; luster; splendor. *Phys.* the rate of flow of radiant energy per unit area. Also **ir·ra·di·an·cy.** —**ir·ra·di·ant,** *a.*

ir·ra·di·ate, i·rā′dē·āt″, *v.t.*—**irradiated,** *irradiating.* [L. *irradio, irradiatum.*] To illuminate or shed light upon; to enlighten spiritually or intellectually; to penetrate by radiation; to treat or heal by radiation; to use radiant energy in the heating of.— **ir·ra·di·at·ing·ly,** *adv.*—**ir·ra·di·a·tive,** *a.*—**ir·ra·di·a·tor,** *n.*

ir·ra·di·a·tion, i·rā″dē·ā′shan, *n.* The act of irradiating; the condition of being irradiated; illumination; brightness emitted; a ray; spiritual and intellectual enlightenment; radiation exposure and treatment; *opt.* apparent enlargement of an object strongly illuminated, because of the vivid impression of light on the retina; *phys.* the rate of flow of radiant energy per unit area.

ir·rad·i·ca·ble, ir″rad′i·ka·bl, *a.* Impossible to erase.—**ir·rad·i·ca·bly,** *adv.*

ir·ra·tion·al, i·rash′a·nal, *a.* Void of reason; absurd; mentally unstable. *Math.* denoting a nonrational number not capable of being expressed by an integral number or a quotient of an integer; referring to an algebraic function in which the variable, or variables, emerge irreducibly under a radical sign. *Gr. and L. pros.* referring to a foot other than one in the metrical pattern; pertaining to a foot having such a substitution.—**ir·ra·tion·al·i·ty, ir·ra·tion·al·ness,** i·rash″a·nal′i·tē, *n.*—**ir·ra·tion·al·ly,** *adv.*

ir·ra·tion·al·ism, i·rash′a·na·liz″um, *n.* Irrational belief, thought, or behavior. *Philos.* a system which rejects reason in favor of instinct, intuition, and faith; rejection of reason as a ruling force over the world.—**ir·ra·tion·al·ist,** *n., a.*—**ir·ra·tion·al·is·tic,** *a.*

ir·re·claim·a·ble, ir″i·klā′ma·bl, *a.* Incapable of being reclaimed or reformed.— **ir·re·claim·a·bil·i·ty, ir·re·claim·a·ble·ness,** *n.*—**ir·re·claim·a·bly,** *adv.*

ir·rec·on·cil·a·ble, i·rek′on·sī″la·bl, i·rek″on·sī′la·bl, *a.* Not to be reconciled; implacable, incapable of being made to agree or be consistent.—*n.* One who is not to be reconciled.—**ir·rec·on·cil·a·bil·i·ty, ir·rec·on·cil·a·ble·ness,** *n.*—**ir·rec·on·cil·a·bly,** *adv.*

ir·re·cov·er·a·ble, ir″i·kuv′ẽr·a·bl, *a.* Incapable of being recovered or regained; not capable of being restored, remedied, or made good.—**ir·re·cov·er·a·ble·ness,** *n.* —**ir·re·cov·er·a·bly,** *adv.*

ir·re·cu·sa·ble, ir″i·kū′za·bl, *a.* [L.L. *irrecusabilis,* < L. *in-,* not, *recusare,* object to.] Not to be excepted, objected to, or rejected; as, *irrecusable* evidence.—**ir·re·cu·sa·bly,** *adv.*

ir·re·deem·a·ble, ir″i·dē′ma·bl, *a.* Not redeemable; incapable of restitution, reparation, or reclamation; indicating loss of nominal value, as with depreciation of paper currency; incapable of being saved; hopeless; delinquent.

ir·re·den·ta, ir″i·den′ta, *n.* [It.] Any region whose people are tied ethnically, and/or historically to one country, but who are unwillingly subject to the political administration and jurisdiction of another state.

ir·re·den·tist, ir″i·den′tist, *n. (Usu. cap.)* a member of an Italian political party, formed in 1878, advocating the incorporation by Italy of some neighboring Italian-speaking regions. Anyone advocating such a policy.—*a.*—**ir·re·den·tism,** *n.*

ir·re·duc·i·ble, ir″i·dö′si·bl, ir″i·dū′si·bl, *a.* Not reducible; incapable of being reduced or simplified.—**ir·re·duc·i·bil·i·ty, ir·re·duc·i·ble·ness,** *n.*—**ir·re·duc·i·bly,** *adv.*

ir·ref·rag·a·ble, i·ref′ra·ga·bl, *a.* [Prefix *ir-* for *in,* not, and L. *refragor,* to withstand or gainsay—*re-,* back, and root of *frango,* to break.] Incapable of being refuted or overthrown; incontestable; undeniable; incontrovertible.—**ir·ref·ra·ga·bil·i·ty,** *n.* —**ir·ref·ra·ga·bly,** *adv.*

ir·re·fran·gi·ble, ir″i·fran′ji·bl, *a.* Not to be broken or violated; inviolable; not refrangible; incapable of being refracted.— **ir·re·fran·gi·bly,** *adv.*—**ir·re·fran·gi·bil·i·ty, ir·re·fran·gi·ble·ness,** *n.*

ir·ref·u·ta·ble, i·ref′ū·ta·bl, ir″i·fū′ta·bl, *a.* Not refutable; incapable of being refuted or disproved.—**ir·ref·u·ta·bly,** *adv.*—**ir·ref·u·ta·bil·i·ty,** *n.*

ir·re·gard·less, ir″i·gärd′lis, *a., adv.* Nonstandard form of regardless.

ir·reg·u·lar, i·reg′ū·lẽr, *a.* Not regular; lacking symmetry; uneven; occurring in no regular time pattern or interval; as, an *irregular* heartbeat; not in accordance with rules, established principles, or customs; not conformable to the usual operation of natural laws; *gram.* deviating from the common form, esp. with respect to inflectional endings; *geom.* applied to a figure whose sides as well as angles are not all equal and similar among themselves; *bot.* exhibiting floral parts which vary in size or form or are not arranged with symmetry. Referring to a flawed manufactured product.—*n.* A flawed manufactured product; *milit.* one not conforming to regulations, esp. a soldier not in regular service.—**ir·reg·u·lar·i·ty,** i·reg″ū·lar′i·te, *n.* State or character of being irregular.— **ir·reg·u·lar·ly,** *adv.*

ir·rel·a·tive, i·rel′a·tiv, *a.* Not relative; without relationship; irrelevant.—**ir·rel·a·tive·ly,** *adv.*—**ir·rel·a·tive·ness,** *n.*

ir·rel·e·vant, i·rel′e·vant, *a.* Not applicable or pertinent.—**ir·rel·e·vance, ir·rel·e·van·cy,** *n.*—**ir·rel·e·vant·ly,** *adv.*

ir·re·li·gion, ir″i·lij′an, *n.* Lack of religion or contempt for it; impiety.—**ir·re·li·gion·ist,** *n.*—**ir·re·li·gious,** *a.* Not religious; disregarding or disliking religion; profane; impious.—**ir·re·li·gious·ly,** *adv.* —**ir·re·li·gious·ness, ir·re·lig·i·os·i·ty,** ir″i·lij″ē·os′i·tē, *n.*

ir·re·me·di·a·ble, ir″i·mē′dē·a·bl, *a.* Incapable of being remedied or cured; incurable; irreparable.—**ir·re·me·di·a·ble·ness,** *n.*—**ir·re·me·di·a·bly,** *adv.*

ir·re·mis·si·ble, ir″i·mis′a·bl, *a.* Not remissible; unpardonable; inexcusable; required, as a duty or obligation.—**ir·re·mis·si·bil·i·ty, ir·re·mis·si·ble·ness,** *n.*—**ir·re·mis·si·bly,** *adv.*

ir·re·mov·a·ble, ir″i·mö′va·bl, *a.* Not removable; inflexible; fixed.—**ir·re·mov·a·bil·i·ty, ir·re·mov·a·ble·ness,** *n.*— **ir·re·mov·a·bly,** *adv.*

ir·rep·a·ra·ble, i·rep′ẽr·a·bl, *a.* Not reparable; incapable of being remedied or repaired.—**ir·rep·a·ra·bil·i·ty, ir·rep·a·ra·ble·ness,** *n.*—**ir·rep·a·ra·bly,** *adv.*

ir·re·peal·a·ble, ir″i·pē′la·bl, *a.* Impossible to repeal or to revoke.

ir·re·place·a·ble, ir″i·plā′sa·bl, *a.* Not able to be replaced.

ir·re·plev·i·sa·ble, ir″i·plev′i·sa·bl, *a. Law,* pertaining to what may not be regained by a writ for replevin.

ir·re·press·i·ble, ir″i·pres′i·bl, *a.* Incapable of being repressed, restrained, or kept under control.—**ir·re·press·i·bil·i·ty, ir·re·press·i·ble·ness,** *n.*—**ir·re·press·i·bly,** *adv.*

ir·re·proach·a·ble, ir″i·prō′cha·bl, *a.* Incapable of being reproached; innocent; faultless; unblemished.—**ir·re·proach·a·ble·ness, ir·re·proach·a·bil·i·ty,** *n.*— **ir·re·proach·a·bly,** *adv.*

ir·re·sist·i·ble, ir″i·zis′ti·bl, *a.* Not resistible; incapable of being successfully resisted or opposed; lovable; romantically appealing; tempting.—*n.*—**ir·re·sist·i·bil·i·ty, ir·re·sist·i·ble·ness,** *n.*—**ir·re·sist·i·bly,** *adv.*

ir·res·o·lu·ble, ir″i·zol′ū·bl, i·rez′ol·ū·bl, *a.* Incapable of resolution; insoluble; not able to be relieved or settled.

ir·res·o·lute, i·rez′o·löt″, *a.* Not resolute; not firm or constant in purpose; undecided; wavering; doubtful; hesitant; vacillating. —**ir·res·o·lute·ly,** *adv.*—**ir·res·o·lute·ness,** *n.*—**ir·res·o·lu·tion,** i·rez″o·lö′shan, *n.* Want of resolution or decision; a fluctuation of mind; vacillation.

ir·re·solv·a·ble, ir″i·zol′va·bl, *a.* Incapable of being resolved or analyzed.—**ir·re·solv·a·bil·i·ty, ir·re·solv·a·ble·ness,** *n.*

ir·re·spec·tive, ir″i·spek′tiv, *a.* Having no relation to particular conditions; without regard to certain circumstances; leaving out of account, usu. followed by *of.*—**ir·re·spec·tive·ly,** *adv.*

ir·re·spir·a·ble, ir″i·spïẽr′a·bl, i·res′pi·ra·bl, *a.* Unfit for breathing.

ir·re·spon·si·ble, ir″i·spon′si·bl, *a.* Unreliable; incapable of or unqualified for responsibility.—**ir·re·spon·si·bly**, *adv.*—**ir·re·spon·si·bil·i·ty**, **ir·re·spon·si·ble·ness**, *n.*

ir·re·spon·sive, ir″i·spon′siv, *a.* Unable or not inclined to respond or react to a stimulus.—**ir·re·spon·sive·ness**, *n.*

ir·re·ten·tion, ir″i·ten′shan, *n.* Lack of retention; inability to retain.—**ir·re·ten·tive**, *a.* Not retentive; lacking power to retain, esp. mentally; having a poor memory.—**ir·re·ten·tive·ness**, *n.*

ir·re·triev·a·ble, ir″i·trē′va·bl, *a.* Not retrievable; irrecoverable.—**ir·re·triev·a·bil·i·ty**, **ir·re·triev·a·ble·ness**, *n.*—**ir·re·triev·a·bly**, *adv.*

ir·rev·er·ence, i·rev′ér·ens, *n.* [L. *irreverentia.*] Lack of reverence or veneration; irreverent conduct, action, or words.

ir·rev·er·ent, i·rev′ér·ent, *a.* [L. *irreverens.*] Exhibiting or marked by irreverence; lacking in respect, esp. to superiors.—**ir·rev·er·ent·ly**, *adv.*

ir·re·vers·i·ble, ir″i·vur′si·bl, *a.* Not reversible; incapable of being reversed or altered.—**ir·re·vers·i·bly**, *adv.*—**ir·re·vers·i·bil·i·ty**, **ir·re·vers·i·ble·ness**, *n.*

ir·rev·o·ca·ble, i·rev′o·ka·bl, *a.* Not to be recalled or revoked; incapable of being reversed, repealed, or annulled; irreversible.—**ir·rev·o·ca·bil·i·ty**, **ir·rev·o·ca·ble·ness**, *n.*—**ir·rev·o·ca·bly**, *adv.*

ir·ri·ga·ble, ir′i·ga·bl, *a.* Able to be irrigated.—**ir·ri·ga·bly**, *adv.*

ir·ri·gate, ir′i·gāt″, *v.t.*—**irrigated, irrigating.** [L. *irrigo, irrigatum*—*ir-* for *in*, and *rigo*, to water.] *Agric.* to water, as land, by artificial means such as channels, sprinklers, or flooding. Sprinkle; to freshen or revive, as if by watering. *Med.* to cleanse or flush, as a wound, with a stream or spray of liquid.—**ir·ri·ga·tion**, *n.*—**ir·ri·ga·tive**, **ir·ri·ga·tion·al**, *a.*—**ir·ri·ga·tor**, *n.*

ir·ri·ta·bil·i·ty, ir″i·ta·bil′i·tē, *n.* pl. **ir·ri·ta·bil·i·ties.** The state of being irritable; *physiol.* the attribute of organisms and protoplasm to become aroused to distinctive action following a certain stimulus.

ir·ri·ta·ble, ir′i·ta·bl, *a.* [L. *irritabilis.*] Capable of being irritated; readily provoked or exasperated; of a fiery temper; *physiol.* susceptible to, responding to, or being acted upon by stimuli; *pathol.* subject to excessive reaction or inflammation following certain stimuli or irritants.—**ir·ri·ta·ble·ness**, *n.*—**ir·ri·ta·bly**, *adv.*

ir·ri·tant, ir′i·tant, *a.* [L. *irritans.*] Irritating; causing irritation.—*n.* Anything that irritates; *med.* something producing irritation, as a poison or chemical agent.—**ir·ri·tan·cy**, *n.*

ir·ri·tate, ir′i·tāt″, *v.t.*—**irritated, irritating.** [L. *irrito, irritatum*, to incite, stir up, provoke; perh. < *hirrire*, to snarl.] To excite anger in; to provoke; to vex; to cause displeasure to; to inflame; *physiol.* to excite, as a bodily part, to a particular function or action; to cause to exhibit irritation.—*v.i.* To cause displeasure, anger, or irritation.—**ir·ri·tat·ing·ly**, *adv.*—**ir·ri·tat·ed**, *a.* Inflamed; annoyed.

ir·ri·ta·tion, ir″i·tā′shan, *n.* [L. *irritatio, irritationis.*] The act of irritating or state of being irritated; annoyance; *pathol.* a condition of inflammation or unusual sensitivity in a bodily part.

ir·ri·ta·tive, ir′i·tā″tiv, *a.* Serving to excite or irritate; produced by an irritant or irritation.—**ir·ri·ta·tive·ness**, *n.*

ir·rupt, i·rupt′, *v.i.* [L. *irruptus*, pp. of *irrumpere*, < *ir-*, in, and *rumpere*, break.] To break in; rush in violently or forcibly; to increase suddenly, as an animal population, due to a decrease in deaths.—**ir·rup·tion**, *n.* A bursting or breaking in; a violent incursion or invasion.—**ir·rup·tive**, *a.* Characterized by or pertaining to irruption; *geol.* intrusive.—**ir·rup·tive·ly**, *adv.*

is, iz, *v.i.* [O.E. *is*—Goth. *ist*, L. *est*, Gr. *esti*, Skt. *asti*, is.] The third person sing., present indicative of the verb *be.*

i·sa·gog·ic, ī″sa·goj′ik, *a.* [Gr. *eisagōgikos*, < *eisago*, to introduce.] Introductory, esp. to the study of the Bible.—**i·sa·gog·ics**, *n. pl. but sing. in constr.* A division of theological study introductory to critical interpretation of sacred writings.

is·al·lo·bar, i·sal′o·bär″, *n. Meteor.* a line drawn on a chart or weather map joining the points which reveal equal barometric pressure changes within a specific period of time.—**is·al·lo·bar·ic**, *a.*

i·sa·tin, ī′sa·tin, *n.* [N.L. *Isatis*, genus of plants including woad, < Gr. *isatis*, woad.] *Chem.* an orange-red compound, $C_8H_5NO_2$, used primarily in dye-making.

is·che·mi·a, **is·chae·mi·a**, i·skē′mē·a, *n. Pathol.* localized anemia of tissue, often due to a blood vessel which contracts, thus restricting arterial inflow.—**is·che·mic**, **is·chae·mic**, i·skē′mik, i·skem′ik, *a.*

is·chi·um, is′kē·um, *n. pl.* **is·chi·a**, is′kē·a. [Gr. *ischion.*] *Anat.* the posterior and inferior part of the pelvic arch at the hip joint.—**is·chi·al**, **is·chi·a·tic**, is′kē·al, is″kē·at′ik, *a.*

Ish·ma·el·ite, ish′mē·e·līt″, ish′mā·e·līt″, ish′ma·līt″, *n.* [From *Ishmael*, a Biblical outcast, Gen. xvi. 12.] A descendant of Ishmael; a wanderer; one at war with society.—**Ish·ma·el·it·ish**, *a.*—**Ish·ma·el·it·ism**, *n.*

i·sin·glass, ī′zen·glas″, ī′zen·gläs″, ī′zing·glas″, ī′zing·gläs″, *n.* [Corrupted from D. *huizenblas*—*huizen*, a sturgeon, and *blas*, a vesicle, a bladder.] A gelatinous substance from air bladders of certain fishes, used in clarifying liquors and as a cement. Thin sheets of mica.

Is·lam, is′lam, iz′lam, is·läm′, *n.* [Ar. < *salama*, to be free, safe, or devoted to God.] *Relig.* The Muslim faith, as set forth by the prophet Mohammed, taught from the writings of the Koran, and having as its major premise complete submission to one omniscient god, Allah; collectively, the followers of the Muslim faith.—**Is·lam·ism**, *n.*—**Is·lam·ic**, is·lam′ik, is·lä′mik, iz·lam′ik, iz·lä′mik, *a.*—**Is·lam·i·tic**, is″la·mit′ik, iz″la·mit′ik, *a.*—**Is·lam·ite**, *n.*

is·land, ī′land, *n.* [< O.E. *īgland*, lit. 'island-land,' *īg* (= Icel. *ey*, Dan. and Sw. *ō*), an island, and *land*, land; the *s* is due to erroneous connection with L. *insula*, O.Fr. *isle.*] A tract of land surrounded by water, whether of the sea, a river, or a lake; anything resembling an island. A raised pedestrian platform surrounded by traffic; also *traffic island. Naut.* a superstructure above the deck of a ship; *rail.* a raised platform between different sets of tracks; *anat.* a section of tissue which differs structurally from encircling tissue.—*v.t.* To cause to become or appear like an island; to isolate; to dot, as with islands.

is·land·er, ī′lan·dèr, *n.* An inhabitant of an island.

is·land u·ni·verse, *n. Astron.* a galaxy other than the Milky Way.

isle, īl, *n.* [O.Fr. *isle, ile* Fr. *ile*, < L. *insula*, island.] An island, esp. a small island.—*v.t.*—**isled, isling.** To make into or as into an isle; to place on or as on an isle.—*v.i.* To dwell or remain on an isle.

is·let, ī′lit, *n.* [Dim. of *isle.*] A small island.

is·lets of Lang·er·hans, ī′lits ov läng′èr·häns. [From Paul *Langerhans*, a German physician, 1847–1888.] *Anat.* clusters of endocrine cells, scattered through the tissues of the pancreas, which secrete insulin. Also **is·lands of Lang·er·hans.**

ism, iz′um, *n.* [Noun use of *-ism.*] A distinctive doctrine, theory, system, or practice, often used disparagingly; as, confused by the *isms* of the day.

isn't, iz′ont. Contraction of is not.

i·so·ag·glu·ti·na·tion, ī″sō·a·glöt″i·nā′shon, *n.* The clumping or grouping of red blood cells which occurs when one animal receives a transfusion from another animal of a like species.—**i·so·ag·glu·ti·na·tive**, ī″sō·a·glöt′i·nā″tiv, ī″sō·a·glöt′i·na·tiv, *a.*

i·so·ag·glu·ti·nin, ī″sō·a·glöt′i·nin, *n. Biochem.* an antibody or clotting agent from one organism which is effective in the cells of other individuals in the same species.

i·so·al·lox·a·zine, ī″sō·a·lok′sa·zēn, *n.* A natural yellow pigment, $C_{10}H_6N_4O_2$, source of riboflavin and flavin enzymes, found in many plants and animals.

i·so·bar, ī′so·bär″, *n.* [Gr. *isos*, equal, and *baros*, weight.] *Meteor.* a line drawn on a map connecting places at which the barometric pressure is the same; *phys.* one of two or more atoms with equal atomic weights, but different atomic numbers.—**i·so·bar·ic**, ī″so·bar′ik, *a.*

i·so·bath, ī′so·bath″, *n.* [Gr. *isos*, and *bathos*, depth.] A line, imaginary or drawn on a map, connecting points that have the same depth below sea level; a similar line which indicates depth beneath the earth's surface.—**i·so·bath·ic**, ī″so·bath′ik, *a.*

i·so·cheim, ī′so·kīm″, *n.* [Gr. *isos*, equal, and *cheima, cheimōn*, winter.] A line drawn on a map through places having the same mean winter temperature. Also **i·so·chime.**—**is·o·chei·mal**, is·o·chi·mal, *a.*

i·so·chro·mat·ic, ī″so·krō·mat′ik, ī″sō·kro·mat′ik, *a.* [Gr. *isos*, equal, and *chrōma*, color.] *Opt.* having the same tint or color; *photog.* orthochromatic.

i·soch·ro·nal, i·sok′ro·nal, *a.* [Gr. *isos*, equal, and *chronos*, time.] Uniform in time; of equal time; performed in or during equal periods of time, as oscillations of pendulums. Also **i·so·chron·ic**, **i·soch·ro·nous.**—**i·soch·ro·nal·ly**, *adv.*—**i·soch·ro·nism**, *n.*

i·soch·ro·ous, i·sok′rō·us, *a.* [Gr. *isos*, equal, and *chroa*, color.] Of the same color throughout.

i·so·cli·nal, ī″so·klin′al, ī″sō·klin′al, *a.* [Gr. *isos*, equal, and *clinein*, incline.] Of or pertaining to equal inclination; inclining or dipping in the same direction; noting or pertaining to an isoclinic line. *Geol.* noting or pertaining to a fold of strata which is of the nature of an isocline. Also **i·so·clin·ic**, ī″sō·klin′ik, ī″sō·klin′ik.—*n.* An isoclinic line. Also **i·so·clin·ic.**

i·so·cline, ī′so·klin″, *n. Geol.* a fold of strata so tightly compressed that the parts on each side of the axis dip in the same direction.

i·so·clin·ic line, *n.* A line on a map drawn through points at which the dip of the magnetic needle is the same. Also *isoclinal, isoclinic.*

i·soc·ra·cy, i·sok′ra·sē, *n. pl.* **i·soc·ra·cies.** [Gr. *isocratia*, < *isos*, equal, and *cratein*, rule.] Equality of rule or power; a government in which all possess equal political power.—**i·so·crat**, ī′so·krat″, *n.*—**i·so·crat·ic**, *a.*

i·so·di·a·met·ric, ī″so·dī″a·me′trik, *a.* Having equal diameters or axes; *bot.* having the diameter similar throughout, as a cell; *crystal.* having equal lateral axes, as tetragonal and hexagonal crystals.

i·so·di·mor·phism, ī″sō·dī·mar′fiz·um, *n. Crystal.* isomorphism between the forms of two or more dimorphous substances.—**i·so·di·mor·phous**, *a.*

i·so·dy·nam·ic, ī″sō·dī·nam′ik, ī″sō·dī·nam′ik, *a.* Distinguished by or related to equality of power or force. Pertaining to a line connecting points at which the intensity of the terrestrial magnetism is equal.

i·so·e·lec·tric, ī″sō·i·lek′trik, *a.* Exhibiting no difference in electric potential. *Chem.* denoting the *p*H at which colloidal proteins and related compounds exhibit minimum conductivity or minimum ionization.

i·so·e·lec·tron·ic, ī″sō·i·lek·tron′ik, ī″sō·ē″lek·tron′ik, *a. Phys.* relating to or denoting electron configurations which are similar.—**i·so·e·lec·tron·i·cal·ly,** *adv.*

i·so·gam·ete, ī″so·gam′ēt, ī″sō·ga·mēt′, *n. Biol.* a sex cell, or gamete, that cannot be distinguished from a similar gamete, with which it pairs and is capable of uniting to form a zygote.—**i·so·ga·met·ic,** ī″sō·ga·met′ik, *a.*

i·sog·a·mous, ī·sog′a·mus, *a.* [Gr. *isos,* equal, and *gamos,* marriage.] *Biol.* having two similar gametes in which no differentiation of sex, size, or structure can be distinguished, and reproducing by the union of such gametes: opposed to *heterogamous.*—**i·sog·a·my,** *n.*

i·so·ge·o·therm, ī″sō·jē′o·thurm″, *n.* An imaginary line under the earth's surface which passes through points having the same mean temperature.—**i·so·ge·o·ther·mal, i·so·ge·o·ther·mic,** *a.*

i·so·gloss, ī′so·glas″, ī′so·glos″, *n.* A line on a map which separates regions according to linguistic differences in language, dialect, or syntax.—**i·so·glos·sal,** *a.*

i·so·gram, ī′so·gram″, *n. Meteor.* a line on a map or chart showing all points having constant value in relation to any climatic variable; also *isoline.* Geographic areas or points which exhibit equal and constant value in relation to a physical condition or climatic variable whose change is measured and calculated for a specific period of time.

i·so·hel, ī′so·hel″, *n.* [Gr. *heliēs,* sun.] *Meteor.* a line drawn on a map through places having the same amount of sunshine.

i·so·hy·et, ī″so·hī′et, *n. Meteor.* a line on a map or chart connecting those locations having the same rainfall.—**i·so·hy·et·al,** *a.*

i·so·late, ī′so·lāt″, is′o·lāt″, *v.t.*—*isolated, isolating.* [Fr. *isoler,* It. *isolare,* < *isola* = L. *insula,* an island.] To place apart; to cause to be alone; to cut off from all contact with others; *elect.* to insulate; *chem., bact.* to obtain, as a pure substance, free from all its combinations; *med.* to quarantine.

i·so·la·tion, ī″so·lā′shan, is″o·lā′shan, *n.* State of being isolated; *med.* the separation from others of a person with an infectious or contagious disease.—**i·so·la·ble,** ī′so·la·bl, is′o·la·bl, *a.* Capable of being isolated.

i·so·la·tion·ism, ī″so·lā′sha·niz″um, is″o·lā′sha·niz″um, *n.* A doctrine or policy based on the premise that a nation serves its own welfare best by concentrating upon its own internal affairs, refusing political, military, or economic alliances or entanglements with other nations.—**i·so·la·tion·ist,** *n., a.*

i·so·leu·cine, ī″so·lö′sēn, ī″so·lö′sin, *n. Biochem.* an amino acid, $C_6H_{13}NO_2$, considered essential in the diet of men and animals.

i·so·line, ī′so·lin″, *n.* Isogram.

i·sol·o·gous, ī·sol′o·gus, *a. Chem.* pertaining to a series of hydrocarbons of similar molecular structure, each member of which has two hydrogen atoms less than the one above it.—**i·so·logue, i·so·log,** ī′so·log″, *n.*

i·so·mag·net·ic, ī″sō·mag·net′ik, *a.* Noting or pertaining to an imaginary line on the earth's surface, or a corresponding line on a map, connecting places which have the same magnetic elements.—*n.* An isomagnetic line.

i·so·mer, ī′so·mér, *n.* [Gr. *isos,* equal, and *meros,* part.] *Chem.* a compound or nuclide isomeric with one or more others. *Phys.* one of a group of nuclides with individual energy characteristics but having the same atomic and mass numbers.

i·so·mer·ic, ī″so·mer′ik, *a. Chem.* of compounds or nuclides composed of the same elements in the same proportions by weight, and having the same molecular weight, but differing in one or more properties as a result of different spatial arrangements of the atoms within the molecule.—**i·so·mer·i·cal·ly,** *adv.*—**i·som·er·ism,** ī·som′e·riz″um, *n.* The fact or condition of being isomeric.

i·som·er·ize, ī·som′e·rīz″, *v.i., v.t.*—*isomerized, isomerizing. Chem.* to change, as an organic compound, so that the atoms are rearranged, creating a compound with slightly different properties.

i·som·er·ous, ī·som′ér·us, *a.* Having an equal number of parts, markings, etc.; *bot.* of a flower, having the same number of members in each whorl.

i·so·met·ric, ī″so·me′trik, *a.* Pertaining to or having equality of measure; *crystal.* pertaining to that system of crystallization which is characterized by three equal axes at right angles to one another. Also **i·so·met·ri·cal.**—**i·so·met·ri·cal·ly,** *adv.*

i·so·met·ric ex·er·cise, *n.* Physical exertion which does not involve motion, muscle tone being achieved by setting one muscle against another muscle or against a fixed object, as pushing against the stomach or a wall with one's hands. Also **i·so·met·rics,** *n. pl. but sing. in constr.*

i·so·met·ric line, *n.* A map line showing temperature and pressure changes while holding volume constant; a line representing a constant value.

i·so·met·ric pro·jec·tion, *n.* The projection of an object upon a plane with equally inclined faces so that dimensions are represented in their true proportions.

i·so·me·tro·pi·a, ī″sō·me·trō′pē·a, *n.* [N.L.] *Optics,* a condition in which the refraction is the same in the two eyes.

i·so·morph, ī′so·marf″, *n.* [Gr. *isos,* equal, and *morphe,* form.] An isomorphous substance; an organism or substance similar to or isomorphic with another.—**i·so·mor·phic,** *a.* Isomorphous. *Biol.* being of the same or of like form; different in ancestry but alike in appearance.

i·so·mor·phism, ī″so·mar′fiz·um, *n. Math.* a one-to-one relationship between objects within two sets; *chem.* the occurrence of similar crystalline forms in related substances; *biol.* similarities in organisms of different groups. The state or property of being isomorphous or isomorphic.

i·so·mor·phous, ī″so·mar′fus, *a. Chem.* referring to the ability of a compound or element to crystallize in a form similar to that of another element or compound.

i·son·o·my, ī·son′o·mē, *n.* Equality by law; equal distribution of rights and privileges.

i·so·oc·tane, ī″sō·ok′tān, *n. Chem.* $(CH_3)_2$·CHCH$_2$C(CH$_3$)$_2$, the standard octane used for rating liquid motor fuels.

i·so·pi·es·tic, ī″sō·pī·es′tik, *a.* Pertaining to or indicating equal pressure. Also *isobaric.*—*n.* An isobar.

i·so·pleth, ī′so·pleth″, *n.* An isogram; *meteor.* a special kind of isogram, showing the frequency of a meteorological phenomenon in relation to two variables. On a chart or graph, a line of constant value of a given quantity with respect to either space or time.

i·so·pod, ī′so·pod″, *n.* One of an order of crustaceans, having seven pairs of legs and flattened bodies; a member of the genus *Isopoda.*—*a.*—**i·sop·o·dan, i·sop′o·dan, a**¦, *n.*

i·so·prene, ī′so·prēn″, *n. Chem.* A colorless liquid hydrocarbon, C_5H_8, which polymerizes easily and is synthetically obtained, used primarily for the manufacture of synthetic rubber; the structural unit of natural rubber.—**i·so·pre·noid,** *a., n.*

i·so·pro·pyl, ī″so·prō′pil, *n. Chem.* a significant constituent of several organic compounds, $(CH_3)_2CH$.—*a.*

i·so·pyre, ī′so·pīer″, *n. Mineral.* a variety of opal mixed with impurities.

i·sos·ce·les, ī·sos′e·lēz″, *a. Geom.* having two equal sides; as, an isosceles triangle.

i·so·seis·mal, ī″so·sīz′mal, ī″so·sīs′mal, *a.* Noting or relating to equal earthquake disturbances; pertaining to the imaginary lines on a map or on the earth's surface connecting points where such earthquakes occurred. Also **i·so·seis·mic.**

i·sos·ta·sy, ī·sos′ta·sē, *n.* Equilibrium when there is pressure from all sides; *geol.* the equilibrium of the earth's crust, a condition in which the forces tending to elevate balance those tending to depress.—**i·so·stat·ic,** ī″so·stat′ik, *a.*

i·so·there, ī′so·thēr″, *n. Meteor.* A line on a weather chart passing through points having the same mean summer temperature.—**i·soth·er·al,** ī·soth′ér·al, *a.*

i·so·therm, ī′so·thurm″, *n.* A line on a chart or map passing through places having a corresponding temperature at any particular time. *Phys.* a line indicating pressure or volume changes at the same temperature; also **i·so·ther·mal line.**—**i·so·ther·mal,** ī″so·thur′mal, *a.*

i·so·ton·ic, ī″so·ton′ik, *a.* Characterized by equal osmotic pressure. *Physiol.* noting or pertaining to a solution containing just enough salt to prevent the destruction of the red corpuscles when added to the blood; noting or pertaining to a contraction of a muscle when under a constant tension. *Mus.* pertaining to or characterized by equal tones.—**i·so·ton·i·cal·ly,** *adv.*—**i·so·to·nic·i·ty,** ī″so·tō·nis′i·tē, *n.*

i·so·tope, ī′so·tōp″, *n.* [Gr. *isos,* equal, and *topos,* place.] *Chem., phys.* any of two or more forms of the same element having the same atomic number and nearly the same chemical properties but with different atomic weights.—**i·so·top·ic,** *a.*—**i·so·to·pi·cal·ly,** *adv.*—**i·sot·o·py,** ī·sot′o·pē, ī′so·tō″pē, *n.* Isotopic character.

i·so·trop·ic, ī″so·trop′ik, *a. Phys.* having the same properties in all directions, as elasticity or conduction; *biol.* lacking well-defined axes, as in certain eggs.—**i·sot·ro·py,** *n.*

Is·rae·li, iz·rā′lē, *a.* [From *Israel,* a southwest Asian republic.] Of or pertaining to modern Israel, its culture, or an inhabitant of modern Israel.—*n. pl.* **Is·rae·lis, Is·rae·li.** An inhabitant or native of modern Israel.

Is·ra·el·ite, iz′rē·e·līt″, iz′rā·e·līt″, *n.* A descendant of Jacob; an inhabitant of the kingdom of Israel in ancient times; a member of a group considered to be God's chosen people.—*a.* Of or pertaining to ancient Israel.—**Is·ra·el·it·ish, Is·ra·el·it·ic,** iz″rē·e·lit′ik, *a.*

Is·sei, ēs′sā″, *n. pl.* **Is·sei, Is·seis.** A Japanese person who has immigrated to the U.S.—*a.*

is·su·a·ble, ish′ö·a·bl, *a.* Open to debate; able to be issued; *law,* admitting of litigation.—**is·su·a·bly,** *adv.*

is·su·ance, ish′ö·ans, *n.* The act of issuing; issue.

is·sue, ish′ö, *Brit.* is′ū, *n.* [O.Fr. *issue, eissue* (Fr. *issue*), < *issir, eissir,* < L. *exire,* go out, come forth, issue, < *ex-,* out of, and *ire,* go.] A going, coming, passing, or flowing out; the process of coming out, distributing or putting forth; egress; outflow; a place or means of outflow; that which comes out, as an outflowing stream; offspring or progeny; descendant or descendants; *law*, the yield or profit from land or other property. Something proceeding from any source; the ultimate result, event, or consequence of a preceding affair; as, to await the *issue* of a contest; a point in question or dispute, as between contending parties in any controversy; a point, the decision of which determines a matter; a point at which a matter is ready for decision; as, to bring or put a case to an *issue*; a point or matter, the decision of which is of special or public importance; a quantity issued at one time; as, an *issue* of stamps, coins, or bonds. *Med.* a discharge of blood, pus, or the like; an incision or ulcer emitting such a discharge.—**at is·sue**, in controversy; in question.—**join is·sue**, to submit an issue jointly for legal decision; to join in controversy.—**take is·sue**, to join in controversy; take a contrary view; disagree.

is·sue, ish′ŏ, *Brit.* is′ū, *v.i.—issued, issuing.* To go, pass, or flow out; come forth; emerge. *Law*, to proceed, as offspring, or be born or descended; to come as a yield or profit, as from land. To proceed from any source; to arise as a result or consequence; to result or end; to be sent or asserted publicly or authoritatively, as a writ or money; to be published, as a book.—*v.t.* To send out, discharge, or emit; as, to *issue* water, smoke, or heat; to put forth authoritatively, formally, or publicly; as, to *issue* invitations or to *issue* bonds; publish, as a book or periodical; to distribute officially, as supplies.

isth·mi·an, is′mē·an, *a.* Of or pertaining to an isthmus; (*cap.*) of or pertaining to the Isthmus of Corinth or the Isthmus of Panama. Also **isth·mic.**—*n.* A native or inhabitant of an isthmus.

isth·mus, is′mus, *n.* pl. **isth·mus·es, isth·mi**, is′mī. [L. < Gr. *isthmos*, narrow passage, neck, isthmus, < *ienai*, go.] A narrow strip of land, bordered on both sides by water, connecting two larger bodies of land; *anat.* a connecting part, organ, or passage joining structures or cavities larger than itself; as, the *isthmus* of the fauces.

is·tle, ist′lē, *n.* [Mex. *ixtle*.] A fiber obtained from various tropical American plants, esp. *Bromelia sylvestris*, used in making bagging and carpets.

it, it, *pron.—sing.* nom. *it*, poss. *its* or obs. or prov. *it*, obj. *it*; pl. nom. *they*, poss. *their* or *theirs*, obj. *them*; intens. and refl. *itself*. [O.E. *hit* (gen. *his*, dat. *him*, acc. *hit*), neut. of *hē*, he.] The third person singular neuter pronoun, corresponding to *he* and *she*; a substitute for a neuter noun or a noun representing something possessing sex when sex is not particularized or considered; a reference to some matter expressed or understood, or some thing or abstract idea not definitely conceived; a reference to the subject of inquiry or attention, whether impersonal or personal, as: What was *it*?, *It* is I., *It* is they who are at fault. The grammatical subject of a clause of which the logical subject is a phrase or clause regarded as in apposition with *it*, as: *It* is hard to believe that., *It* is believed that he is dead. An impersonal subject which expresses an action or condition without referring to a specific agent, as:*It* snows. An object of indefinite force following certain verbs; as, to foot *it*.—*n.* The person who, in children's games, performs an action different from that of the other players, as the person who finds the other players in hide and seek; the general trend or state of events, as: How did *it* go for you last year?

it·a·col·u·mite, it″a·kol′ū·mīt″, *n.* [From *Itacolumi*, mountain in Brazil.] A rock consisting of interlocking quartz grains, talc, and mica scales, found mainly in Brazil and North Carolina, and remarkable for its flexibility when in thin slabs.

I·tal·ian, i·tal′yan, *a.* [L. < Gr. *Italia*, Italy, a south European country.] Of or pertaining to Italy, its people, or their language.—*n.* An inhabitant of Italy; the Romance language of Italy.—**I·tal·ian·ate**, i·tal′ya·nāt″, *v.t.—Italianated, Italianating.* To Italianize.—**i·tal′ya·nāt**, i·tal′ya·nit, *a.* Characteristic of or conforming to Italian style or custom.

I·tal·ian hand, *n.* A distinctive modern type face based on the flowing script popular in 15th century Italy. Subtle craftiness or cunning, usu. preceded by *fine*, as: He often makes use of his *fine Italian hand*.

I·tal·ian·ize, i·tal′ya·nīz″, *v.i.—Italianized, Italianizing.* To assume the characteristics of Italian custom, style, or form.—*v.t.* To render Italian; to give Italian characteristics to. Also *Italianate.*—**I·tal·ian·i·za·tion**, *n.*

I·tal·ian son·net, *n.* Petrarchan sonnet.

i·tal·ic, i·tal′ik, i·tal′ik, *n.* [L. *Italicus*, < Gr. *Italikos*.] Usu. pl. a style of printing in which the letters slope to the right, used to indicate emphasis, a foreign word or expression, and titles of books; as, *esprit de corps, Gulliver's Travels*. (*Cap.*) a subfamily of the Indo-European languages.—*a.* Of or pertaining to italics or that style of printing type. (*Cap.*) of or pertaining to ancient Italy or its tribes; specif. pertaining to parts of Italy other than Rome.

i·tal·i·cize, i·tal′i·sīz″, i·tal′i·sīz″, *v.t.—italicized, italicizing.* To print in italic type; to underscore, as a word or words, with a single line to indicate italics.—*v.i.* To use italics.—**i·tal·i·ci·za·tion**, *n.*

itch, ich, *v.i.* [M.E. *icchen*, < O.E. *giccan* = D. *jeuken* = G. *jucken*, itch.] To have or feel a peculiar irritation of the skin which causes a desire to scratch the part affected; to cause such an irritation; to have an uneasy desire, as for something or to do something.—*v.t.* To cause to itch; to irk or irritate.

itch, ich, *n.* The sensation of itching; *fig.* an uneasy or restless desire or longing; as, an *itch* for travel; *pathol.* a contagious disease caused by the itch mite, which burrows under the skin, usu. preceded by *the*.—**itch·y**, ich′ē, *a.*—**itch·i·ness**, *n.*

i·tem, ī′tem, *n.* A separate article or particular in an enumeration; a single particular or detail of any list; a separate piece of information or news, as in a newspaper or newscast.—*adv.* Likewise; also: used in introducing the separate articles or particulars of an enumeration.

i·tem·ize, ī′te·mīz″, *v.t.—itemized, itemizing.* To set down by items, as to take inventory; specify the items or particulars of, as an account; to set down or enter as an item in an enumeration, as in a bill; to list.—**i·tem·i·za·tion**, *n.*—**i·tem·iz·er**, *n.*

it·er·ant, it′ĕr·ant, *a.* [L. *iterans* (*-ant-*), ppr.] Characterized by iteration or repetition.—**it·er·ance**, it′ĕr·ance, *n.*

it·er·ate, it′e·rāt″, *v.t.—iterated, iterating.* [L. *itero, iteratum*, to do again, to repeat, *iterum*, again; akin Skt. *itara*, another.] To utter or repeat, as for a second time.—**it·er·a·tion**, *n.*—**it·er·a·tive**, it′e·rā″tiv, it′ĕr·a·tiv, *a.*

ith·y·phal·lic, ith″i·fal′ik, *a.* [L. *ithyphallicus*, < Gr. *ithyphallikos*, < *ithyphallos*, < *ithys*, straight, and *phallos*, E. *phallus*.] Pertaining to the phallus, as carried in ancient festivals of Bacchus; pertaining to the meter employed in hymns sung in phallic processions. Lustful;

obscene; lewd.—*n.* A poem in ithyphallic meter; a poem of indecent character.

i·tin·er·an·cy, i·tin′ẽr·an·sẽ, i·tin′ẽr·an·sẽ, *n.* A passing from place to place; the traveling from place to place in the discharge of official duty. Also **i·tin·er·a·cy**, i·tin′ẽr·a·sẽ, i·tin′ẽr·a·sẽ.

i·tin·er·ant, i·tin′ẽr·ant, i·tin′ẽr·ant, *a.* [L.L. *itinerans, itinerantis*, traveling, < L. *iter, itineris*, a way or journey.] Passing or traveling about a country or district; as, an *itinerant* preacher; wandering, esp. within a circuit; not settled; strolling.—*n.* One who travels from place to place.—**i·tin·er·ant·ly**, *adv.*

i·tin·er·a·ry, i·tin′e·rer″ē, i·tin′e·rer″ē, *n.* pl. **i·tin·er·a·ries.** [L.L. *itinerarium*.] A travel route; the plan of a journey.—*a.* Traveling; pertaining to a journey.

i·tin·er·ate, ī·tin′e·rāt″, i·tin′e·rāt″, *v.i.—itinerated, itinerating.* To travel from place to place, particularly for the purpose of preaching.—**i·tin·er·a·tion**, *n.*

it'll, it′il. Contraction of it will or it shall.

its, its, *pronominal a.* Possessive case of the pronoun *it*, used attributively, as: The bird called *its* mate. *Its* sole thought was of survival.

it's, its. Contraction of it is or it has.

it·self, it·self′, *pron.* A reflexive or emphatic form of the third pers. sing. neut. pron., as: The dog saw *itself* in the mirror. A denotation of its usual or customary state, as: The cat hasn't been *itself* since the accident.

I've, īv. Contraction of I have.

i·vo·ry, ī′vo·rē, ī′vrē, *n.* pl. **i·vo·ries.** [O.Fr. *ivurie*, Fr. *ivoire*, < L. *eboreus*, made of ivory, < *ebur*, ivory; akin Skt. *ibha*, an elephant.] The substance obtained from the tusks of elephants and walruses, a hard, smooth-textured, creamy-white dentine; the dentine from the teeth of any animal; a product made from the tusks of these animals; a yellow to creamy-white color. *Pl.*, *slang*, piano keys; dice; teeth. A substance resembling true ivory obtained from the seeds of a palm tree; also *vegetable ivory*.—*a.* Consisting of or made of ivory; of the color of ivory.

i·vo·ry black, *n.* A fine black pigment, prepared from ivory dust by calcination.

i·vo·ry nut, *n.* The seed of the tropical American ivory palm which is the source of vegetable ivory; a substitute for true ivory, used in the manufacture of buttons, chessmen, and inlays. Also **ta·gua nut.**

i·vo·ry palm, *n.* A low-growing tropical American palm, *Phytelephas macrocarpa*, bearing drupelike fruits containing bony seeds which are the source of vegetable ivory.

i·vo·ry tow·er, *n.* Fig. A place of seclusion; a spiritual sanctuary; a place to withdraw to from worldly matters.

i·vy, ī′vē, *n.* pl. **i·vies.** [O.E. *īfig*; akin to G. *epheu*, O.G. *ebeheu, ebah*, ivy.] The true or English ivy, *Hedera helix*, a prostrate or climbing plant, with evergreen leaves and aerial rootlets, which is widely cultivated; the Boston ivy, *Parthenocissus tricuspidata*, with three-lobed, deciduous leaves. See *ground ivy*.—**i·vied**, ī′vēd, *a.* Covered or overgrown with ivy.

I·vy League, *n.* A group of U.S. universities and colleges, situated in the Northeast, which are known for social prominence and high scholastic accomplishment.—*a.* (Sometimes *l.c.*) relating to the northeastern schools or their students, esp. their manners and clothing; as, *ivy league* sophistication, or an *ivy league* shirt.—**I·vy Lea·guer**, *n.*

ix·i·a, ik′sē·a, *n.* [N.L. (with reference to the juice), < Gr. *ixos*, bird-lime.] *Bot.* any spring-blooming, bulbous plant of the genus *Ixia*, in the iris family, native to S. Africa, having grassy leaves and spikes of small colorful flowers.

ix·tle, iks′tlē, ist′lē, *n.* Istle.

iz·ard, iz′ẽrd, *n.* [Fr. *isard*.] *Zool.* a chamois, in the deer family, which inhabits the Pyrenees.

iz·zard, iz′ẽrd, *n.* [Cf. *zed*.] *Dial.* a name for the letter Z.

J

J, j, jā, *n.* The tenth letter of the English alphabet and the seventh consonant; a counterpart in speech of the letter J, usu. a voiced affricative stop; tenth in a series; something designated by or having the shape of the letter J or j; a printer's graphic device used for reproducing the letter J or j; (*usu. cap.*), *phys.* joule.

jab, jab, *v.t.—jabbed, jabbing.* [Var. (orig. Sc.) of *job*.] To strike or thrust at, as with something sharp; to punch sharply.—*v.i. n.* A sharp, direct blow or thrust, as in boxing.—**jab·bing·ly**, *adv.*

jab·ber, jab′ẽr, *v.i.* [A form equivalent to *gabble*, Sc. *gabber*, freq. of *gab*, to talk much or pertly.] To talk rapidly, indistinctly, or nonsensically; chatter; babble. —*v.t.* To utter rapidly; as, to *jabber* French.—*n.* Rapid, indistinct talk.—**jab·ber·er**, *n.*—**jab·ber·ing·ly**, *adv.*

Jab·ber·wock·y, jab′ẽr·wok″ē, *n.* pl. **Jab·ber·wock·ies.** [A poem in Lewis Carroll's *Through the Looking Glass.*] A poem characterized by nonsense syllables and meaningless speech; an imitation of this style in writing or speech; gibberish.—*a.* Characterized by or comprised of the lack of sense typical of Jabberwocky.

jab·i·ru, jab′i·rö″, *n.* [Brazil.] A large white wading bird, *Jabiru mycteria*, of the stork family, inhabiting the warmer parts of America; any of various similar birds of Africa, the East Indies, and Australia.

jab·o·ran·di, jab″o·ran′dē, *n.* [Brazil.] Any of various S. American shrubs belonging to the genus *Pilocarpus*; the dried leaves of some of these shrubs that yield pilocarpine.

ja·bot, zha·bō′, *Brit.* zhab′ō, *n.* [Fr., bird's crop.] A ruffle, frill, or other arrangement of lace or embroidery, worn by women at the center front of a blouse or dress bodice; a lace arrangement formerly worn by men on a shirt front.

ja·bot·i·ca·ba, zha·böt″i·käb′a, *n.* A shrubby tropical tree of the myrtle family, *Myrciaria cauliflora*, yielding an edible fruit resembling the grape, and cultivated in California, Florida, and other warm regions.

ja·cal, ha·käl′, *n.* [Mex. Sp.] A small house or hut found in the southwestern U.S. and Mexico, whose walls consist of rows of thin vertical poles filled in and plastered with mud.

jac·a·mar, jak′a·mär″, *n.* [Brazil.] Any of the sharp-billed, usu. brilliantly colored, insectivorous birds of tropical America constituting the family *Galbulidae.*

ja·ça·na, zhä″sa·nä′, *n.* [Brazil.] Any small aquatic bird of the family *Jacanidae*, resembling the plovers and usu. having long, straight claws or toes adapted for walking on the floating leaves of aquatic plants. Also **lil·y-trot·ter.**

jac·a·ran·da, jak″a·ran′da, *n.* [Brazil.] Any of the tall tropical American trees constituting the genus *Jacaranda*; the fragrant ornamental wood of such a tree; any of various related or similar trees or their wood.

ja·cinth, jā′sinth, jas′inth, *n.* See *hyacinth.*

jack, jak, *n.* [From *Jack*, in general use as a familiar equivalent of *John*, man's name, and possibly a var. of *John*, but commonly explained as < O.Fr. *Jaques* (Fr. *Jacques*), < L.L. *Jacobus*, Jacob, James.] A fellow or man; a workman, usu. in combination; as, a steeple*jack*, lumber*jack*; (*often cap.*) a sailor. *Mech.* a machine for raising weights short distances; *playing cards*, a card picturing a boy or knave. *Naut.* a small flag flown at the bow of a ship, usu. to indicate nationality; an iron support at the head of a topgallant mast. Any instrument useful in some task, as a device for turning a roasting spit, often in combination; as, a boot*jack*; *slang*, money. One of the small stones or six-pointed metal pieces used in the game of jacks; also **jack·stone.** *Pl. but sing in constr.* a children's game in which a player simultaneously bounces a small ball and picks up or moves jacks or jackstones; also **jack·stones.** A pin or ball set up as a target in lawn bowling; a mechanism in a harpsichord or similar instrument for striking the string; *elect.* connecting apparatus used to complete a circuit.—*a.* Used, sometimes in combination, to denote the male of a species; as, a *jack*ass.—**eve·ry man jack**, every one without exception.

jack, jak, *v.t.* To lift or move with or as with a jack, used with *up*; *colloq.* to raise or increase, used with *up*; as, to *jack* up prices. To seek at night, as fish or game, with a jacklight.—*v.i.* To hunt or fish with a jacklight.—**jack·er**, *n.*

jack·al, jak′al, jak′ạl, *n.* [Turk. *chakāl*, < Pers. *shaghāl*.] Any of several species of wild dogs, genus *Canis*, of Asia and Africa, which hunt in packs at night; one who does debasing or servile work for another; one who serves the shameful or dishonest purposes of another.

jack·a·napes, jak′a·nāps, *n.* An impertinent fellow; an impudent child.

jack·ass, jak′as″, *n.* A male donkey or ass; a foolish or stupid person.—**jack·ass·er·y**, *n.* An act of folly or stupidity.

jack bean, *n.* A dense, tropical plant, *Canavalia ensiformis*, cultivated in America as an ornamental and for the edible bean.

jack·boot, jak′böt″, *n.* A heavy military boot reaching up over the knee.

jack·daw, jak′dạ″, *n.* A European black bird, *Corvus monedula*, in the crow family. Also *daw.*

jack·et, jak′it, *n.* [Fr. *jaquette*, dim. of *jaque*, a coat of mail, a jacket.] A short outer garment, usu. with a front opening, a protective outer covering, as of cloth, paper, metal, or the like; as, a record or book *jacket*; an open envelope for documents; the skin of a potato.—*v.t.* To cover or furnish with a jacket.—**jack·et·ed**, *a.*—**jack·et·less**, *a.*—**jack·et·like**, *a.*

Jack Frost, *n.* Frost or freezing weather personified.

jack·fruit, jak′fröt″, *n.* An Asiatic tree, *Artocarpus heterophyllus*, widely cultivated in the tropics for its large fruit, both the pulp and seeds of which are edible. Also **jak.**

jack·ham·mer, jak′ham″ẽr, *n.* A machine tool for drilling rock, powered by compressed air.

jack-in-the-box, jak′in·THe·boks″, *n.* pl. **jack-in-the-box·es, jacks-in-the-box.** A toy box from which a clownlike figure springs when the lid is released. Also **jack-in-a-box.**

jack-in-the-pul·pit, jak′in·THe·pul′pit, *n.* pl. **jack-in-the-pul·pits, jacks-in-the-pul·pit.** A common N. American plant of the arum family, which has an upright flower cluster partly

hooded by a leaflike covering. Also *Indian turnip.*

Jack Ketch, *n.* [From *John Ketch*, an English hangman.] *Brit. slang*, an executioner.

jack·knife, jak′nīf″, *n.* pl. **jack·knives.** A large, strong pocketknife. A front dive in which the diver bends his body at the waist and touches his hands to his feet, then straightens just before entering the water headfirst.—*v.t.—jackknifed, jackknifing.* To use a jackknife for cutting, or to cause to jackknife.—*v.i.* To bend or double from the middle like a jackknife; as, two trucks which *jackknife* in a collision.

jack·leg, jak′leg″, *a.* Deficient in training or skill; amateur; employing questionable practices; dishonest; below professional standards; makeshift.

jack·light, jak′līt″, *n.* A light for hunting or fishing at night.—*v.i.* To hunt or fish with a light.—**jack·light·er**, *n.*

jack mack·er·el, *n.* A food fish of the genus *Trachurus*, found chiefly along the coast of California.

jack-of-all-trades, jak″ov·ạl′trädz′, *n.* pl. **jacks-of-all-trades.** A man handy with tools; a man possessing a superficial skill in several trades.

jack-o′-lan·tern, jak′o·lan″tẽrn, *n.* A lantern made from a hollowed pumpkin carved to resemble a face. A phosphorescent light that appears in marshlands; *ignis fatuus.*

jack pine, *n.* A pine tree, *Pinus banksiana*, which grows mainly in barren or rocky areas of N. America.

jack plane, *n.* A plane about 18 inches long used by carpenters for coarse surfacing.

jack·pot, jak′pot″, *n. Poker*, the stakes which accumulate during play until one player, sometimes qualified by having been dealt two jacks or more valuable cards, opens the betting; the highest prize in any contest involving cumulative stakes.—**hit the jack·pot**, *slang.* To win the biggest prize or a desired reward; to achieve a remarkable success.

jack rab·bit, *n.* A hare, with long ears and hind legs longer than forelegs, which belongs to the genus *Lepus* and is indigenous to western N. America.

jack·screw, jak′skrö″, *n.* A jack for lifting heavy objects a limited distance, operated by a screw.

jack·shaft, jak′shaft″, jak′shäft″, *n.* Countershaft; a mine shaft.

jack·smelt, jak′smelt″, *n.* pl. **jack·smelt, jack·smelts.** A big fish of the silversides family, *Atherinopsis californiensis*, found off the Pacific seaboard of the U.S.

jack·snipe, jak′snip″, *n.* pl. **jack·snipe, jack·snipes.** A small species of snipe, *Capella gallinago*, of N. America. Also **Wil·son′s snipe.**

Jack·so·ni·an, jak·sō′nē·an, *a.* [From Andrew *Jackson*, seventh U.S. President, 1767–1845.] Pertaining to or characteristic of Andrew Jackson's policies, political principles, or the term of his presidency, 1829–1837.—*n.* A follower of Andrew Jackson.

jack stay, jak′stā″, *n. Naut.* a rope or rod on a yard or gaff, for bending a sail to; a rod or rope running up and down on the forward side of a mast, for a yard to travel on.

jack·straw, jak′strạ″, *n.* One of a set of straws or strips of wood used in a game in which they are dropped in a confused pile and picked up singly without disturbing the rest of the pile. *Pl. but sing. in constr.* the game itself; also **pick-up-sticks.** A scarecrow; a worthless person.

jack-tar, jak′tär″, *n.* A sailor. Also **Jack Tar.**

jack tow·el, *n.* A long towel with the ends sewed together, for hanging on a roller.

Jac·o·be·an, jak″o·bē′an, *a.* [L. *Jacobus*, James, < Heb. *Jacob*.] Of or pertaining to first month of the year, having 31 days.

James I, King of England in the early 17th century, or the period of his reign; pertaining to the modified Elizabethan style of architecture and furnishings prevailing in the age of James I.—*n.* A writer, statesman, or leading figure of this period.

Ja·cob's-lad·der, jă′kŏbz·lad′ẽr, *n.* [From the ladder seen by the patriarch *Jacob* in a dream: Gen. xxviii. 12.] A common garden plant of the phlox family, *Polemonium caeruleum,* whose leaves have a ladderlike arrangement; any of certain related species. *Naut.* a rope ladder with wooden or iron rungs; also **Ja·cob's lad·der, jack lad·der, pi·lot lad·der.**

jac·o·net, jak′ŏ·net″, *n.* [From *Jagannāth* (or Puri), in Orissa, India.] A soft, light cotton fabric.

jac·quard, jak′ärd, ja·kärd′, Fr. zhä·kär′, *n.* (*Often cap.*) a fabric having a fancy or figured weave, and produced on a Jacquard loom; the weave itself. Also **Jac·quard weave.**

Jac·quard loom, *n.* [From *Jacquard,* of Lyons, who died in 1834.] A loom which is guided by punched paper or cards in weaving patterned textiles.

jac·ta·tion, jak·tā′shan, *n.* [L. *jactatio*(n-), < *jactare,* throw, toss, agitate, discuss, boast, freq. of *jacere,* throw.] Boasting or bragging. *Pathol.* jactitation.

jac·ti·ta·tion, jak″ti·tā′shan, *n.* [M.L. *jactitatio*(n-), < L. *jactitare,* bring forward in public, utter, freq. of *jactare.*] *Law,* a false boast or statement which is detrimental to another; *pathol.* a restless tossing of the body in disease.

jac·u·late, jak′ū·lāt″, *v.t.*—*jaculated, jaculating.* [L. *jaculor, jaculatus,* to throw the javelin, < *jaculum,* javelin, *jacio,* to throw.] To hurl; to throw outwards.—**jac·u·la·tion,** *n.*

jade, jād, *n.* [Fr. *jade,* < Sp. (*piedra de*) *ijada,* '(stone of) colic,' so called from its supposed medicinal virtue (Sp. *ijada,* flank, pain in the side, colic, < L. *ilia,* flanks).] A hard gemstone, either nephrite or jadeite, often green in color, and highly regarded as an ornament; an ornament carved from jade; jade green.

jade, jād, *n.* [Sc. *yaud, jaud,* an old mare; Icel. *jalda,* a mare.] A worthless, uncontrollable, or worn-out horse; a disreputable, loose, or bad-tempered woman; a young woman: used in humor or slight contempt. —*v.t.*—*jaded, jading.* To drive severely; to weary or wear out, as by overwork or excessive use.—*v.i.* To become weary; to lose spirit.—**jad·ish,** *a.*—**jad·ish·ly,** *adv.*—**jad·ish·ness,** *n.*

jad·ed, jā′did, *a.* Worn-out; fatigued; dulled or cloyed; sated or dissipated.— **jad·ed·ly,** *adv.*—**jad·ed·ness,** *n.*

jade green, *n.* The color usu. associated with jade, a light green tinged with blue.

jade·ite, jā′dīt, *n. Mineral.* a valuable form of jade which consists essentially of a silicate of sodium and aluminum and ranges from pale to emerald green in color.

jae·ger, yā′gẽr, *n.* A hunter; formerly, one of a group of German or Austrian soldiers trained in sharpshooting. Also **ja·ger, jä·ger,** *yager.*

jae·ger, yā′gẽr, jā′gẽr, *n.* Any of various sea birds of the family *Stercorariidae,* which force weaker birds to relinquish their prey.

jag, jag, *v.t.*—*jagged, jagging.* [Origin doubtful; cf. W. and Gael. *gag,* a cleft or chink; Gael. *gag,* to notch.] To notch; to cut, tear, or slash into points or teeth like those of a saw.—*n.* A notch or denticulation; a sharp protuberance or indentation.— **jag·ged,** *a.* Having notches or teeth; zigzag; ragged; unevenly edged or surfaced. —**jag·ged·ly,** *adv.*—**jag·ged·ness,** *n.*

jag, jag, *n. Slang,* a condition of intoxication,

usu. from liquor; a bout, spree, or binge; as, a smoking *jag,* a crying *jag.*

jag·ger·y, jag′e·rē, *n.* [Hind. *jagrī.*] A coarse, brown sugar made from the sap of palm trees. Also **jag·gar·y, jag·gher·y.**

jag·gy, jag′ē, *a.*—*jaggier, jaggiest.* Jagged; uneven.

jag·uar, jag′wär, *n.* [Brazil. *jaguara.*] A large, powerful, black-spotted feline, *Panthera onca,* of Central and S. America.

ja·gua·run·di, jä′gwa·run′dē, *n. pl.* **ja··gua·run·dis.** A slim, short-legged member of the wildcat family, *Felis eyra,* found in tropical America. Also **ja·gua·ron·di.**

Jah·veh, Jah·ve, yä′ve, *n.* Yahweh. Also **Jah·weh, Jah·we.**—**Jah·vism, Jah·wism,** yä′viz·um, yä′wiz·um, *n.* Yahwism.— **Jah·vist, Jah·wist,** yä′vist, yä′wist, *n.* Yahwist.

jai a·lai, hī′lī″, hī′a·lī″, hī″ a·lī′, *n.* A game similar to handball, in which players catch and throw a small ball with a curved, wicker racket fastened to the wrist.

jail, *Brit.* **gaol,** jāl, *n.* [Fr. *geole,* O.Fr. *gaiole,* a prison; L.L. *gabiola,* < L. *cavea,* a cage, coop, den, < *cavus,* hollow.] A prison; a building for the confinement of persons held in legal custody, esp. those judged guilty of minor offenses.—*v.t.* To imprison.

jail·bird, jāl′bẽrd″, *n.* A prisoner or former prisoner, esp. a habitual or frequent lawbreaker.

jail·break, jāl′brāk″, *n.* A prison escape achieved through force.

jail de·liv·er·y, *Brit.* **gaol de·liv·er·y,** *n.* An escape from prison; a forcible freeing of prisoners; *Brit. law,* the process of clearing a jail by trying the prisoners.

jail·er, jail·or, *Brit.* **gaol·er,** jā′lẽr, *n.* One who oversees or has charge of a jail or its inmates.

Jain·ism, jī′niz·um, *n.* A very ancient religion of India given its final shape in the 6th century B.C., which opposed Brahmanism and exhibited much in common with Buddhism, stressing asceticism, respect for wisdom, and reverence for all life.—**Jain,** jīn, *n.* One who believes in Jainism.—*a.* Also **Jai·na, Jai·nist.**

jal·ap, jal′ap, *n.* [Sp. *jalapa;* so called from *Jalapa,* city in southeastern Mexico.] A purgative drug obtained from the tuberous roots of *Ipomoea purga,* a Mexican plant, or of any of various other convolvulaceous plants; any of these plants.—**ja·lap·ic,** ja·lap′ik, *a.*—**jal·a·pin,** *n.* A resin which is one of the purgative principles of jalap.

ja·lop·y, ja·lop′ē, *n. pl.* **ja·lop·ies.** [Origin uncertain.] *Slang,* an old, decrepit, or unpretentious automobile.

jal·ou·sie, jal′o·sē″, *Brit.* zhal′u·zē″, *n.* [Fr., lit. 'jealousy.'] A window blind with adjustable horizontal louvers which permit ventilation and light but protect from rain and direct sun rays; a window having louvers of glass with a similar function.— **jal·ou·sied,** *a.*

jam, jam, *v.t.*—*jammed, jamming.* [Perhaps imit.: cf. *champ.*] To press or squeeze tightly between bodies or surfaces so that motion or extrication is made difficult or impossible; to bruise or crush by squeezing; to cause, as a movable part, to become wedged, caught, or displaced so that it cannot work; to render unworkable, as a machine, by such wedging, catching, or displacement; to press, push, or thrust violently, as into a confined space or against some object, as, esp. in applying the brakes of an automobile; to fill or block up, as a passageway, by crowding. *Radio,* to interfere with, as signals, by sending out others of approximately the same wavelength; *naut.* to direct the course of, as a sailboat, windward.—*v.i.* To become wedged or fixed; stick fast; of a machine, to become

unworkable as through the wedging or displacement of a part; to press or push violently, as into a confined space or against one another. *Mus.* to enliven a musical score by improvisations; to be in a jam session.—*n.* The act of jamming or the state of being jammed; a condition of being crowded together so closely as to prevent or hinder motion or progress; as, a traffic *jam;* the mass of objects so pressed or crowded together; an obstruction; *colloq.* a predicament or an embarrassing involvement.—**jam·mer,** *n.*

jam, jam, *n.* [Prob. from *jam, v.t.;* related to *champ.*] *Cooking,* a preserve of a fruit or fruits which have been cooked with sugar and water until thick, used as a spread.

Ja·mai·ca gin·ger, *n.* Ginger grown in Jamaica; an extract of ginger used for flavoring; ginger root in powdered form, used medicinally.

Ja·mai·can, ja·mā′kan, *a.* Of or relating to Jamaica, an island in the West Indies, or to its people.—*n.* A native or resident of Jamaica.

Ja·mai·ca rum, *n.* A dark, heavy-bodied rum made from molasses in Jamaica.

jamb, jambe, jam, *n.* [Fr. *jambe,* a leg, a jamb.] The side or vertical piece of an opening in a wall; as, a door *jamb,* a window *jamb.* A jambeau.

jam·ba·lay·a, jum″ba·lī′a, *n.* A Creole dish of rice cooked with vegetables, herbs, and any of various kinds of meat or fish, usu. ham or shrimp.

jam·beau, jam′bō, *n. pl.* **jam·beaux,** jam′bōz. A medieval piece of armor designed to protect the lower leg; a jambe. Also **greave,** grēv.

jam·bo·ree, jam″bo·rē′, *n.* A boy scout assembly of national or international scope. *Colloq.* a noisy gathering or festivity.

James·i·an, James·e·an, jām′zē·an, *a.* Relating to or characteristic of the writings of Henry James, an Anglo-American novelist; pertaining to the theories of his brother, William James, an American philosopher and psychologist.

jam ses·sion, *n. Jazz,* an impromptu performance by musicians, usu. for their own enjoyment.

Jane Doe, *n.* A feminine name used in examples or hypotheses, esp. in legal proceedings where the name of the woman involved is either unknown or of no importance.

jan·gle, jang′gl, *v.i.*—*jangled, jangling.* [O.Fr. *jangler,* chatter, babble, tattle; prob. ult. imit.] To sound harshly or discordantly; to dispute or speak angrily.—*v.t.* To cause to sound harshly or discordantly; to cause to become tense or angry.—*n.* Harsh or discordant sound; a quarrel or dispute.—**jan··gler,** jang′glẽr, *a.*

Jan·is·sar·y, Jan·i·sar·y, jan′i·ser″ē, *n. pl.* **Jan·is·sar·ies, Jan·i·sar·ies.** [Turk. *yeni,* new, and *tcheri,* militia, soldiers.] (*Often l.c.*) A soldier in an elite unit of Turkish infantry, consisting orig. of captured Christians and used primarily as the Sultan's guard from about the 14th century until its abolition in 1826; in general, a Turkish soldier; a member of a loyalist or subservient group. Also *Janizary.*

jan·i·tor, jan′i·tẽr, *n.* [L., < *janua,* a door.] A person hired to clean and maintain an office, school, apartment, or other building; a caretaker of a building; doorkeeper.—**jan·i·to·ri·al,** jan″i·tōr′ē·al, *a.* —**jan·i·tress,** jan′i·tris, *n.* A female janitor.

Jan·i·zar·y, jan′i·zer″ē, *n. pl.* **Jan·i·zar··ies.** Janissary.

Jan·u·ar·y, jan′ū·er″ē, *n.* [L. *Januarius,* from *Janus,* ancient Roman deity.] The first month of the year, having 31 days.

ja·pan, ja·pan', n. [From *Japan*, country of the Far East.] Any of various hard, durable varnishes orig. from Japan, used for coating wood, metal, and the like; a hard, glossy black varnish containing asphalt; Japanese ornamental work, esp. work varnished and figured in the Japanese manner.—a.—v.t.—japanned, japanning. To varnish with japan; to lacquer; to coat with any material which gives a hard, black glossy finish.—**ja·pan·ner**, n.

Ja·pan clo·ver, n. A hardy bush clover of Asiatic origin, *Lespedeza striata*, grown in the southern U.S. as a forage crop. Also **Jap·an·ese clo·ver**.

Jap·a·nese, jap″a·nēz′, jap″a·nēs′, a. Pertaining to Japan, a country consisting of four large islands and numerous small ones, located off the east coast of Asia; concerning the inhabitants of Japan or their language or culture.—n. pl. **Jap·a·nese**. A native, citizen, or inhabitant of Japan; the language of Japan.

Jap·a·nese an·drom·e·da, jap″a·nēz′ an·drom′i·da, n. An Asian ornamental evergreen shrub of the heath family, *Pieris japonica*, which bears clusters of white flowers. Also **an·drom·e·da**.

Jap·a·nese bee·tle, n. A small green and brown beetle, *Popillia japonica*, introduced into the U.S. about 1916, which is destructive to grasses and to many crops in both its larval and adult stages.

Jap·a·nese mil·let, n. A coarse grass, *Echinochloa crus-galli frumentacea*, introduced into the U.S. for its forage and whose seeds are used in bird feed.

Jap·a·nese per·sim·mon, n. An Asian tree, *Diospyros kaki*, grown in the U.S. for its edible orange or red fruits; the fruit itself.

Jap·a·nese quince, n. A scarlet-flowered spiny shrub of the rose family, *Chaenomeles lagenaria*, which bears a yellow-green fruit used in preserves; the fruit itself.

Jap·a·nese spurge, n. A small, ground-covering perennial herb of the box family, *Pachysandra terminalis*, with spikes of white flowers.

Jap·a·nize, jap′a·nīz, v.t. To render Japanese; to make to conform to Japanese usages or ideas.—**Jap·a·ni·za·tion**, n.

Ja·pan wax, n. A yellow, waxy solid derived from the berries of certain Japanese and Chinese sumacs, esp. *Rhus succedanea*, and used in manufacturing floor and furniture polishes. Also **Ja·pan tal·low**, **su·mac wax**.

jape, jāp, v.t.—japed, japing. [M.E.: cf. O.Fr. *japer*, yelp, and *gaber*, mock.] To trick; to mock.—v.i. To jest; to joke; to gibe.—n. A trick; a jest; a gibe.—**jap·er**, n. —**jap·er·y**, n.—**jap·ing·ly**, adv.

ja·pon·i·ca, ja·pon′i·ka, n. A camellia, *Camellia japonica*; the Japanese quince, *Chaenomeles japonica*.

Jap·o·nism, jap′o·niz″um, n. [Fr. *japonisme*, from *Japon*, Japan.] Adherence to Japanese methods or styles, as in art; any trait, mannerism, or the like which is characteristic of the Japanese. Also **Ja·pan·ism**, ja·pan′iz·um.

jar, jär, n. [Fr. *jarre*, Sp. *jarra*, a jar, < Ar. *jarra*, a water pot.] A broad-mouthed vessel of glass or earthenware, usu. cylindrical in shape; the contents of a jar. —**jar·ful**, n.

jar, jär, v.i.—jarred, jarring. [Also found in forms *chur*, *jur*, and imitative of sound.] To give out a harsh or discordant sound; to grate; to have an annoying or unpleasant effect, used with *on*; to jolt or shake from an unexpected contact; to clash; to quarrel or dispute.—v.t. To cause to give out a harsh or discordant sound; to cause to shake or tremble.—n. A rattling vibration of sound;

a harsh sound; clash of opinions; discord; shock; jolt.

jar·di·niere, jär″di·nēr′, n. [Fr., a female gardener, a gardener's wife.] An ornamental stand or pot for plants and flowers; a garnish made of cooked and diced vegetables for serving with meat.

jar·gon, jär′gon, jär′gon, n. [O.Fr. Fr. *jargon*; origin uncertain.] The terminology or phraseology used by a particular class, trade, or profession; as, legal *jargon*; a barbarous or rude language or dialect, esp. one resulting from a mixture of languages, as pidgin English; a kind of speech abounding in unfamiliar or pretentious words; unintelligible speech or writing; gibberish. —v.i. To speak or write in a jargon.— **jar·gon·al**, **jar·gon·is·tic**, a.

jar·gon, jär′gon, n. [Fr. *jargon*, < It. *giargone*, properly a yellow stone, < Pers. *zargun*, gold-colored.] *Mineral.* a smoky or colorless variety of zircon, the colorless forms resembling the diamond. Also **jar·goon**, jär·gōn′.

jar·gon·ize, jär′go·nīz″, v.i.—jargonized, jargonizing. To talk or write jargon.—v.t. To translate into jargon; to express by means of jargon.

jarl, yärl, n. [Icel.] *Scand. hist.* A chieftain or viceroy; an earl.

jas·mine, **jas·min**, jaz′min, jas′min, n. [Fr. *jasmin*, < Ar. *yasmīn*, Pers. *yasmīn*.] Any of the fragrant-flowered shrubs of the genus *Jasminum* in the olive family; any of various similar plants with scented flowers, as yellow jasmine, cape jasmine, and red jasmine; the fragrance resembling that of these flowers; a pale, soft-yellow color. Also *jessamine*.

jas·per, jas′pėr, n. [O.Fr. *jaspre*, Fr. *jaspe*, L., Gr. *iaspis*, Ar. *yashb*, Heb. *yashpheh*.] An opaque, colored quartz, which takes an elegant polish, often used for vases and jewelry.—**jas·per·ware**, n. A high-fired, quality ceramic having a white body colored with metallic lusters, originated by Wedgwood.

JATO, **jato**, **Jato**, jā′tō, n. [(*J*)et-(*A*)ssisted-(*T*)ake-(*O*)ff.] A takeoff of an aircraft helped by rocket engines or other jet-propulsion devices which provide additional lifting power. The assisting apparatus itself; also **ja·to un·it**.

jaun·dice, jạn′dis, jän′dis, n. [O.Fr. Fr. *jaunisse*, < *jaune*, yellow, < L. *galbinus*, greenish-yellow, yellowish.] *Pathol.* an abnormal physical condition due to bile pigments in the blood, characterized by yellowness of the skin and sclera of the eye, and by lassitude and loss of appetite; also *icterus*. *Fig.* a state of biased views and warped judgment due to bitterness or envy.— v.t.—jaundiced, jaundicing. To affect with jaundice; *fig.* to distort through envy.

jaun·diced, jạn′dist, jon′dist, a.

jaunt, jạnt, jänt, v.i. [Origin obscure.] To make a short journey, esp. for pleasure.—n. A short pleasure trip; an excursion.

jaunt·ing car, n. A light, open, two-wheeled cart, popular in Ireland, having two seats, one on each side, set back to back or facing each other, and a perch in front for the driver.

jaun·ty, jạn′tē, jän′tē, a.—jauntier, jauntiest. [O.E. *gent*, Sc. *genty*, elegant, pretty; < *gentle*, genteel, but modified by *jaunt*.] Having a breezy manner; brisk; sprightly; perky.—**jaun·ti·ly**, adv.—**jaun·ti·ness**, n.

Ja·va, jä′va, n. An Indonesian island; a variety of coffee; a black or black and white speckled chicken; (*l.c.*), *slang*, coffee.—**Jav·a·nese**, jav″a·nēz′, jav″a·nēs′, a. Relating to Java, its inhabitants, or their language. —n. A native of or the language of Java.

Ja·va man, n. *Anthropol.* a prehistoric hominid, genus *Pithecanthropus*, whose skull fragments were discovered in Java in 1891.

Ja·va spar·row, n. A finchlike bird, *Padda oryzivora*, native to Java, often a cage bird. Also **Jav·a·nese spar·row**, ricebird.

jave·lin, jav′lin, jav′e·lin, n. [Fr. *javeline*, It. *giavelina*, Sp. *jabalina*.] A light spear thrown in ancient warfare and hunting; *sports*, a spearlike, metal-tipped shaft of wood about 8½ feet long, used in distance-throwing contests. A distance-throwing contest using a javelin; also **jave·lin throw**.—v.t. To strike or wound with a javelin.

Ja·velle wa·ter, **Ja·vel wa·ter**, zha·vel′ wạt′ėr, zha·vel′ wot′ėr, n. A solution of sodium hypochlorite in water, used for bleaching and disinfecting.

jaw, jạ, n. [M.E. *jawe*, *jowe*; prob. akin to E. *chew*.] One of the two bones or structures, upper and lower, which form the framework of the mouth; *often pl.* the mouth parts collectively. One of two or more mechanical parts which grasp something; *pl.* the two sides of a narrow pass or gorge. *Slang*, insolent or offensive talk.—v.i. *Slang.* To talk; to gossip; to use abusive language.—v.t. *Slang.* To scold; to address abusively.

jaw·bone, jạ′bōn″, n. A bone of the jaw, esp. the lower jaw or mandible.

jaw·break·er, jạ′brā″kėr, n. *Colloq.* a word that is hard to pronounce; an extremely hard candy. A machine for crushing ore; also **jaw crush·er**.

jay, jā, n. [O.Fr. *jai*, *gai* (Fr. *geai*); origin uncertain.] Any of numerous noisy, corvine birds of the family *Corvidae*, known for their colorful plumage and marauding instincts, as the European jay, *Garrulus glandarius*, the blue jay, and the Canada jay. *Slang*, a simple-minded or gullible person; a yokel; a chatterer.

Jay·cee, jā′sē′, n. [From *J.C.*, for (*J*)unior (*C*)hamber of Commerce.] One who belongs to a junior chamber of commerce.

jay·hawk·er, jā′hạ″kėr, n. [Of disputed origin.] (*Cap.*) a nickname for a resident or native of Kansas. A marauder; (*sometimes cap.*) an antislavery guerrilla fighter in Kansas, Missouri, and other states before and during the Civil War.

jay·walk, jā′wạk″, v.i. To cross a street carelessly and away from a regular crossing place, often amid traffic.—**jay·walk·er**, n.

jazz, jaz, n. [Origin obscure; said to have been long used by Negroes of the southern U.S., esp. those of Louisiana, and to be of African origin.] A kind of music, improvised or arranged, and marked by its rhythmic emphasis, syncopation, and harmonic and melodic variations. *Slang*, liveliness; spirit; nonsensical, idle, or empty talk.—a. Of the nature of or pertaining to jazz; as, a *jazz* band.—**jazz·ist**, n.—**jazz·man**, jaz′man″, jaz′man, n.

jazz, jaz, v.i. To play jazz music; to dance to such music.—v.t. To play in the manner of jazz. *Slang*, to accelerate or infuse with liveliness or excitement, usu. with *up*.

jazz band, n. A band devoted to the playing of jazz, which typically uses the trumpet, trombone, saxophone, clarinet, piano, bass, and drums.

jazz·y, jaz′ē, a.—jazzier, jazziest. *Slang.* Pertaining to or reminiscent of jazz music; unrestrained; lively; flashy.—**jazz·i·ly**, adv.—**jazz·i·ness**, n.

jeal·ous, jel′us, a. [O.Fr. *gelos* (Fr. *jaloux*), < M.L. *zelosus*, < L. *zelus*, < Gr. *zelos*.] Feeling envious resentment at the success or advantages of another; proceeding from suspicious fears or envious resentment; as, *jealous* pride; inclined to or troubled by suspicions or fears of rivalry; as, a *jealous* lover; anxiously or suspiciously watchful; solicitous or vigilant in maintaining or guarding something; as, a nation *jealous* of its liberties; intolerant of unfaithfulness or rivalry; as, a *jealous* god.—**jeal·ous·ly**, *adv.*—**jeal·ous·ness**, *n.*

jeal·ous·y, jel'o·sē, *n. pl.* **jeal·ous·ies.** [O.Fr. *gelosie* (Fr. *jalousie*).] Mental uneasiness due to suspicion or fear of rivalry; envious resentment against a successful rival or the possessor of any coveted advantage; an instance of jealous feeling.

jean, jēn, *Brit.* jān, *n.* [Prob. from *Genoa.*] *Pl.* casual trousers or slacks made of denim or jean; also *denims.* A strong, twilled fabric, usu. cotton, used in the manufacturing of casual and work clothing; also *denim. Pl., slang,* slacks.

jeep, jēp, *n.* [From (*G*)eneral (*P*)urpose Vehicle.] A small, sturdy military automobile with four-wheel drive, orig. used during the Second World War by the U.S. Army.

jeer, jēr, *v.i.* [Perhaps < O.Fr. *girer,* It. *girare,* L. *gyrare,* to turn in a circle.] To say or shout mockingly or derisively; to scoff.—*v.t.* To ridicule or scoff at; to deride.—*n.* A taunting or derisive sound or remark; a gibe.—**jeer·er**, *n.*—**jeer·ing·ly**, *adv.*

Jef·fer·so·ni·an, jef"ĕr·sō'nē·an, *a.* [From Thomas *Jefferson,* third U.S. president, 1743–1826.] Of or referring to Jefferson, or his political teachings, which upheld the rights of the states as opposed to a strong central government.—*n.* A supporter of Thomas Jefferson or his political ideas.—**Jef·fer·so·ni·an·ism**, *n.*

Je·ho·vah, ji·hō'va, *n.* An Old Testament name of the Supreme Being, believed to be an erroneous transcription of the Hebrew *Yahveh* or *Yahweh;* God.—**Je·ho·vic**, ji·hō'vik, *a.*

Je·ho·vah's Wit·ness·es, *n. pl.* Members of a Christian sect who believe in an imminent millenium and the establishment of God's theocratic rule.

je·june, ji·jōn', *a.* [L. *jejunus,* fasting, empty, dry, barren, poor.] Lacking in nutritive or substantial qualities, as food or soil; vapid; dull; as, a *jejune* composition; immature; inexperienced.—**je·june·ly**, *adv.*—**je·june·ness**, **je·ju·ni·ty**, ji·jō'ni·tē, *n.*

je·ju·num, ji·jō'num, *n.* [L. < *jejunus,* hungry or empty.] *Anat.* the portion of the small intestine located between the duodenum and the ileum.—**je·ju·nal**, *a.*

jell, jel, *v.i.* [Back formation from *jelly.*] To assume the consistency of jelly; congeal; *fig.* crystallize; to become definite in shape or form, as: The project has not begun to *jell* yet.—*v.t.* To cause to take definite shape.

jel·li·fy, jel'i·fī, *v.t., v.i.*—**jellified, jellifying.** To make or turn into jelly.—**jel·li·fi·ca·tion**, *n.*

jel·lo, jel'ō, *n.* A gelatin dessert with sugar and fruit flavoring. (Formerly trademark.)

jel·ly, jel'ē, *n. pl.* **jel·lies.** [Fr. *gelee,* < *geler,* L. *gelo,* to freeze.] A soft, gelatinous food product made with boiled fruit juice and sugar; any substance having a similar consistency.—*v.t., v.i.*—**jellied, jellying.** To congeal or become congealed.—**jel·lied**, jel'ēd, *a.* Brought to the consistency of jelly.—**jel·ly·like**, *a.*

jel·ly·bean, jel'ē·bēn", *n.* A bean-shaped, sugar coated candy with a jellylike center.

jel·ly·fish, jel'ē·fish", *n. pl.* **jel·ly·fish, jel·ly·fish·es.** Any of several marine invertebrates of a jellylike substance, esp. those with umbrella-shaped bodies and long tentacles, as the medusa; *fig.* one who is weak-willed or lacking in stamina.

jel·ly roll, *n.* A rectangular sheet of sponge cake covered with jelly and then rolled up. Also *Brit.* **Swiss roll.**

jem·a·dar, jem'a·där", *n.* [Hind. and Pers. *jamadār.*] Any of various officials, esp. police, in the Indian government; the head of a body of servants; an officer in an

army regiment, corresponding in rank to a lieutenant.

jem·my, jem'ē, *n. pl.* **jem·mies.** [From *James.*] *Brit.* a short, stout crowbar used by burglars for opening doors or windows; also *jimmy.* A sheep's head cooked for food.—*v.t.*—**jemmied, jemmying.** *Brit.* to jimmy open.

jen·net, jen'it, *n.* [Fr. *genette,* Sp. *ginete,* from the name of a Berber tribe who supplied the Moorish sultans of Grenada with cavalry.] A small Spanish horse; a female donkey. Also *genet.*

jen·ny, jen'ē, *n. pl.* **jen·nies.** [From *Jenny,* for *Jane,* woman's name.] The female of certain animals, used esp. attributively or in composition; as, *jenny* ass, *jenny* wren; a spinning jenny.

jeop·ar·dy, jep'ĕr·dē, *n.* [O.E. *jupartie,* < Fr. *jeu parti,* lit. 'a divided game'; L.L. *jocus partitus,* an even chance.] Exposure to death, loss, or harm; hazard; danger; peril; *law,* the risk of punishment to which a person on trial is exposed.—**jeop·ar·dize**, *v.t.*—**jeopardized, jeopardizing.** To expose to loss or injury; to put in danger; to risk, chance, or hazard. Also **jeop·ard.**—**jeop·ard·ous**, jep'ĕr·dus, *a.*

je·quir·i·ty, je·kwir'i·tē, *n.* [Brazil.] The Indian licorice plant, *Abrus precatorious,* whose black and scarlet seeds or beans contain abrin, a potent poison released when the seeds are broken open; the beans collectively. Also *Indian licorice,* **je·quir·i·ty beans, jum·ble beans.**

jer·bo·a, jĕr·bō'a, *n.* [N.L. < Ar.] Any of various mouselike rodents, as of the genus *Dipus,* with long hind legs used for jumping. Also **jer·bo·a mouse.**

jer·e·mi·ad, jer"e·mi'ad, *n.* [Fr. *jérémiade* < *Jérémie,* Jeremiah. From *Jeremiah,* a Biblical prophet.] A lamentation; a prolonged doleful utterance; a lugubrious complaint.

jerk, jurk, *v.t.* [Cf. O.E. and Sc. *yerk,* a quick, smart lash or blow; provinc. *girk,* a rod.] To thrust with a sudden effort; to give a sudden pull; to twitch; to throw with a sudden, quick motion; to concoct, esp. ice cream sodas.—*v.i.* To make a sudden motion; to give a start; to speak haltingly or in a spasmodic manner.—*n.* A short sudden thrust, push, or twitch; a jolt; a sudden spring; a start; a leap or bound. *Slang,* an ineffectual, dumb person, usu. male. *Pl., physiol.* reaction of a reflex to a stimulus; tic; chorea; *pl., slang,* tremblings, as delirium tremens; *Brit. slang,* physical education.—**jerk·er**, *n.*—**jerk·i·ly**, *adv.*—**jerk·i·ness**, *n.*—**jerk·y**, *a.*—**jerkier, jerkiest.**

jerk, jurk, *v.t.* [Chilian, *charqui.*] To cut, as beef, into long, thin pieces and dry in the sun.—*n.* Meat which has been cured by jerking. Also **jerk·y.**

jer·kin, jur'kin, *n.* [Dim. of D. *jurk,* a frock.] A sleeveless, collarless jacket of hip length with a snug, belted waist.

jerk·wa·ter, jurk'wŏ"tĕr, jurk'wot"ĕr, *a. Colloq.* minor, insignificant, or remote; as, a *jerkwater* town.—*n. Colloq.* a train that does not run on a main line but serves a branch line.

jer·o·bo·am, jer"o·bō'am, *n.* [From *Jeroboam,* a Hebrew king.] A large bottle for wines.

Jer·ry, jer'ē, *n. pl.* **Jer·ries.** *Chiefly Brit., slang,* a German, esp. a soldier.

jer·ry·build, jer'ē·bild", *v.t.*—**jerrybuilt, jerrybuilding.** To build cheaply and flimsily.—**jer·ry·build·er**, *n.*—**jer·ry·built**, jer'ē·bilt", *a.* Built quickly, cheaply, and flimsily, of poor materials.

jer·sey, jur'zē, *n.* [From *Jersey,* an island located in the English Channel.] A knitted fabric of wool, nylon, cotton, or silk, usu. soft and elastic; a close-fitting knit dress, shirt, or sweater; (*cap.*) a breed of dairy cattle developed on Jersey Island and noted for rich milk.

Je·ru·sa·lem ar·ti·choke, *n.* [*Jerusalem* is here a corruption of the It. *girasole.*] A type of sunflower, *Helianthus tuberosus,* valued for its edible underground tubers; the tuber of such a plant. See *girasol.*

Je·ru·sa·lem cher·ry, *n.* The plant, *Solanum pseudo-capsicum,* characterized by orange, red, or yellow berries and valued for ornamentation.

jess, jes, *n.* [O.Fr. *ges, gest, get,* < L.L. *jactus,* a jess, < L. *jacio, jactum,* to throw.] *Falconry,* a short strap of leather fastened around each of the legs of a hawk, to which the falcon's leash is attached.—*v.t.*

jes·sa·mine, jes'a·min, *n.* Jasmine.

jest, jest, *n.* [O.E. *geste,* a jest, a tale, < L. *gestum,* something done, a deed, a feat, < *gero,* to do, whence *gesture,* etc.] A joke; a witty, mocking, or bantering act or remark; the object of laughter; a laughing-stock.—*v.i.* To speak or act playfully, amusingly, or facetiously; to trifle; to joke; to jeer or deride.—*v.t.* To deride or mock.—**in jest,** in the spirit of fun; not in earnest.—**jest·er**, *n.* One who jests; a person retained in a medieval court to amuse a ruler; a professional fool or buffoon.—**jest·ing**, *a., n.*—**jest·ing·ly**, *adv.*

Jes·u·it, jezh'ō·it, jez'ū·it, *n.* [N.L. *Jesuita,* < L. *Jesus,* Jesus.] A member of a Roman Catholic religious order, the Society of Jesus, founded by Ignatius Loyola in 1534. (*Usu. l.c.*) a conniving person; a schemer, used disparagingly.—**Jes·u·it·i·cal**, *a.*—**Jes·u·it·i·cal·ly**, *adv.*—**Jes·u·it·ism**, *n.*

Je·sus, jē'zus, *n.* [Gr. *Iēsous,* < Heb. *Yēshūa,* 'help of *Jehovah.*'] The founder of Christianity; also *Christ,* **Je·sus Christ, Je·sus of Naz·a·reth.** *Christian Science,* the highest incarnation of the divine idea in human form.

jet, jet, *n.* [Fr. *jet,* a throw, a jet, a fountain, < L. *jactus,* a throwing, < *jacio,* to throw.] A shooting forth or spouting; that which issues or streams forth from a narrow opening or orifice, as water or other fluid, gas or flame; the vent or nozzle of a pipe or hose through which gas, liquid, or flame gushes; a jet engine; a jet plane.—*v.i.*—**jetted, jetting.** To issue in a jet; to shoot out; to move swiftly; to travel by jet plane or jet propulsion.—*v.t.* To emit; to spout forth, as water.—*a.* Of or pertaining to jet propulsion or jet plane travel.

jet, jet, *n.* [Old forms *jeat, jayet,* O.Fr. *jayet, gayet,* < Gr. *gagatēs,* from *Gagae,* a town and river in Lycia, where it was obtained.] A hard black mineral, allied to coal, which, when highly polished, is used for making deep, lustrous black jewelry, ornaments, and buttons.—*a.* Similar to or made of jet.

je·té, zhe·tā', *n. pl.* **je·tés**, zhe·tāz', *Fr.* zhe·tā'. *Ballet,* a sharp jump or leap.

jet en·gine, *n.* An engine, used chiefly in aircraft, which achieves its fast forward propulsion by discharging its oxidized fuel as hot air and gases through one or more rear exhausts. Also **jet mo·tor.**

jet·lin·er, jet'lī"nèr, *n.* A jet plane used by commercial airlines.

jet plane, *n.* Any airplane propelled by one or more jet engines. Also *jet,* **jet air·plane.**

jet·port, jet'pŏrt", *n.* An airport used chiefly or exclusively by jet planes.

jet·pro·pelled, jet'pro·peld", *a.* Moved by the power of a jet engine or rocket engine, as an airplane; *fig.* moving swiftly and strongly, as if driven by jet power.

jet pro·pul·sion, *n.* Propulsion by means of a jet of gas or fluid; *aeron.* propulsion by means of a jet engine.

jet·sam, jet'sam, *n.* [< *jettison.*] Goods thrown overboard to lighten a vessel in distress, esp. such goods when washed ashore; *fig.* anything thrown away. Also **jet·som.**

---

a- fat, fāte, fär, fâre, fall;   **e-** met, mē, mère, hėr;   **i-** pin, pīne;   **o-** not, nōte, möve;   **u-** tub, cūbe, bụll;   **oi-** oil;   **ou-** pound.

jet set, *n.* A cosmopolitan group of wealthy, sophisticated, and socially prominent people who travel by jet from one fashionable resort to another.

jet stream, *n.* A strong, high-speed wind current, moving from west to east around the poles of the earth, contained in a narrow stream high in the earth's atmosphere; a trailing stream of fluid or gas exhaust from a rocket or jet engine.

jet·ti·son, jet′i·son, jet′i·zon, *n.* [O.Fr. *getaison,* L. *jactatio,* a throwing, < *jacio,* to throw.] The act of sacrificing the cargo of a ship or aircraft in an emergency to lighten or stabilize the vessel; abandonment; the goods thrown overboard; jetsam.—*v.t.* To throw, as goods or cargo, from an aircraft or ship; to discard as a burden or unnecessary encumbrance.—**jet·ti·son·a·ble,** *a.*

jet·ty, jet′ē, *n. pl.* **jet·ties.** [O.Fr. *jetee* (Fr. *jetée*), < *jeter,* throw.] A pier or structure of stones or piles, projecting from shore into a body of water to protect a harbor or divert the flow of water; a wharf or landing pier; the protective structure of wood framing a pier; a projecting or overhanging part of a building.—*v.t.*—*jettied, jettying.* To construct or furnish with an overhang.—*v.i.* To project outward; to jut.

jet·ty, jet′ē, *a.* Consisting of or resembling jet; black as jet.

Jew, jō, *n.* [O. Fr. *Juieu* < L. *Judaeus* < Gr. *Ioudaios* < Heb. *Yehūdāh,* Judah.] One whose faith is Judaism; a descendant of the Hebrews; orig., one of the tribe or kingdom of Judah.—**Jew·ess,** *n.* Fem. of *Jew.*

jew·el, jō′el, *n.* [O.F. *jouel, joiel* (Fr. *joyau*), jewel; origin uncertain: cf. M.L. *jocalia,* jewels, < L. *jocus* (Fr. *jeu*), jest, sport.] A costly article of personal adornment, esp. one of gold or gems; a gem or precious stone; a precious stone or substitute used as a watch bearing; a bit of glass, enamel, or other material, simulating a gem, used decoratively, as on clothing; a thing or person of great worth or rare excellence; a precious possession.—*v.t.*—*jeweled, jeweling, jewelled, jewelling.* To set or adorn with jewels or as with jewels.—**jew·el·ly,** *a.*

jew·el·er, *Brit.* **jew·el·ler,** jō′e·lėr, *n.* One who makes, repairs, or deals in jewelry and watches.

jew·el·ry, *Brit.* **jew·el·ler·y,** jō′el·rē, *n.* Jewels; articles made of gold, silver, precious stones, or similar materials for personal ornament.

jew·el·weed, jō′el·wēd″, *n.* Any of several N. American herbs of the genus *Impatiens,* having irregular yellow or yellow-orange flowers.

jew·fish, jō′fish″, *n. pl.* **jew·fish, jew·fish·es.** Any of various large fish, esp. *Epinephelus itajara* and other members of the sea bass family, found in the tropical waters of the Atlantic Ocean.

Jew·ish, jō′ish, *a.* Of or pertaining to the Jews, their culture, or the Judaic religion.—*n. Colloq.* Yiddish.—**Jew·ish·ness,** *n.*

Jew·ish cal·en·dar, *n.* The lunisolar calendar in use among Jewish people, reckoned from 3761 B.C., and having a year that begins in early fall and consists of 12 or 13 months, each having 29 or 30 days.

Jew·ry, jō′rē, *n.* [O.Fr. *juirie,* Fr. *juiverie.*] Jewish people collectively.

jew's-harp, jews'-harp, jōz′härp″, *n.* A small lyre-shaped musical instrument held between the teeth, and played by plucking a flexible metal tongue.

Jez·e·bel, jez′e·bel″, jez′e·bel, *n.* [From *Jezebel,* wife of Ahab, king of Israel.] (*Often l.c.*) A shameless or daring woman.

jib, jib, *n.* [< Dan. *gibbe,* D. *gijpen,* to turn suddenly, said of sails.] *Naut.* the foremost sail of a ship, triangular in shape and extended from the outer end of a jib boom. The projecting arm or boom of a crane.—**cut of one's jib,** *colloq.* one's overall appearance.

jib, jib, *v.i.*—*jibbed, jibbing.* [O.Fr. *giber,* to struggle; *regibber,* to kick.] To pull against the bit, as a horse; to move restively sideways or backward; to indicate a refusal to move forward; to balk.—*n.* One who jibs; a horse that jibs. Also **jib·ber.**

jib boom, *n. Naut.* a spar serving as a continuation of the bowsprit and to which the jib is attached.

jibe, jīb, *v.i.*—*jibed, jibing.* [Cf. D. *gijben,* Dan. *gibbe,* Sw. *gippa,* jibe.] *Naut.* To shift from one side to the other when running before the wind, as a fore-and-aft sail or its boom; to alter the course so that the sail shifts in this manner.—*v.t. Naut.* to cause to jibe, as a sail or boom.—*n. Naut.* The motion of a sail or boom when jibing; the change of course which results in jibing. Also **gibe, gybe,** *jib.*

jibe, jīb, *v.i.*—*jibed, jibing.* [Origin uncertain.] *Colloq.* To be in harmony or accord; to agree.

jif·fy, jif′ē, *n. pl.* **jif·fies.** [Provinc. E. *jiffle,* to be restless; cf. *jib,* to turn suddenly.] *Colloq.* A moment; an instant. Also **jiff.**

jig, jig, *n.* [Appar. imit.] A rapid, lively, irregular dance, usu. in triple rhythm; the music for a jig; also **gigue.** *Mech.* a device which guides a mechanical tool or holds firm the material being worked; a device used in fishing to attract the fish, esp. a cluster of metal hooks or a spoon-shaped piece of shiny metal; *min.* an apparatus for separating ore, esp. a sieve immersed in water.—*v.t., v.i.*—*jigged, jigging.* To dance, as a jig or any lively dance; to play music fast and lively, like a jig; to move with a jerky or bobbing motion; to hold material or guide a tool with a jig; to fish with a jig; *min.* to separate, as ore, by shaking in a jig.—**the jig is up,** *slang.* There is no further chance; all hope is gone.

jig·ger, jig′ėr, *n.* A person or thing that jigs; a kind of potter's wheel; a jig for separating ore; a gadget or mechanical device; *colloq.* any contrivance, article, or part that one cannot name more precisely. *Naut.* a light tackle used around the deck of a ship; a small sail set on a jiggermast in the stern; the jiggermast. *Billiards,* a bridge; *golf,* an iron-headed club. A measure for liquor containing about one and one-half ounces.

jig·ger, jig′ėr, *n.* [Corruption of *chigoe.*] Any of the small red larvae of various mites found in Africa and southern U.S., which fasten themselves to the skin of human beings and other vertebrates, causing itching and irritation. Also *chigger,* **chi·goe.**

jig·ger·mast, jig′ėr·mast, *n. Naut.* a small mast for the jigger, in the stern of a canoe, yawl, or ketch; the aftermost mast of a four-masted ship.

jig·gle, jig′l, *v.t., v.i.*—*jiggled, jiggling.* [Freq. of *jig.*] To move up and down or back and forth with short, quick jerks.—*n.* A jiggling movement.—**jig·gly,** *a.*

jig saw, *n.* A narrow saw mounted vertically in a frame and operated with an up-and-down motion, used for cutting curved or irregular lines.—**jig·saw,** *v.t.*—*past jigsawed,* pp. *jigsawed* or *jigsawn,* ppr. *jigsawing.*—*a.*

jig·saw puz·zle, *n.* A puzzle consisting of variously shaped pieces of cardboard, wood, or similar material which form a picture when properly assembled.

jil·lion, jil′yan, *n.* An imaginary number which suggests an enormous amount.—*a.*

jilt, jilt, *v.t.* [Akin Sc. *jillet.*] To discard or cast off, as a fiancé, lover, or sweetheart.—*n.* A woman who casts off a lover.—**jilt·er,** *n.*

Jim Crow, jim′krō′, *n.* The practice of discrimination against Negroes, as segregation of public places.—**Jim-Crow,** *a.* (*Sometimes l.c.*)—**Jim Crow·ism,** *n.*

jim-dan·dy, jim′dan′dē, *a. Colloq.* excellent, admirable, or superior; as, a *jim-dandy* speedboat.—*n.*

jim·jams, jim′jamz″, *n. pl.* [Cf. *gimcrack.*] *Slang.* A feeling of nervousness; the jitters; delirium tremens.

jim·my, jim′ē, *n. pl.* **jim·mies.** [From *Jimmy,* for *James,* man's name.] A short crowbar used by burglars.—*v.t.*—*jimmied, jimmying.* To force open, as a door or window, by means of a jimmy or similar tool. Also *Brit.* **jemmy.**

jim·son weed, jim′son wēd, *n.* [Orig. *Jamestown weed;* from *Jamestown,* Va.] A species of datura, *Datura stramonium,* in the nightshade family, a coarse, ill-smelling annual weed with white flowers and poisonous, narcotic leaves. Also **Jim·son weed.**

jin·gal, jin·gall, gin·gal, gin·gall, jin′gal, *n.* [Hind. *jangal.*] A large musket or cannon fired from a rest, usu. swiveled and sometimes mounted on a carriage, formerly used by natives in India and China.

jin·gle, jing′gl, *v.i.*—*jingled, jingling.* [Prob. imitative, like *jangle, chink,* G. *klingeln.*] To make a tinkling metallic sound; to clink, as bells; to rhyme repetitiously or have repetitive rhythm, as verse or music.—*v.t.* To cause to make a tinkling metallic sound.—*n.* A clinking sound, as of metal; something that jingles; a correspondence of sound in rhymes or rhythms, as alliteration in poetry; a short catchy tune or poem; a carriage with two wheels and a roof, used chiefly in Australia and Ireland.—**jin·gler,** *n.*—**jin·gly,** *a.*

jin·go, jing′gō, *n. pl.* **jin·goes.** A professed patriot who advocates an aggressive, warlike foreign policy.—*a.* Relating to a jingo or jingoism.—**by jin·go,** *colloq.* a mild oath, or an exclamation of astonishment or strong conviction.—**jin·go·ism,** *n.*—**jin·go·ist,** *n.*—**jin·go·is·tic, jin·go·ish,** *a.*

jink, jingk, *v.i.* [Perhaps imit.] *Sc.* To move nimbly; to make a quick, elusive turn.—*n. Sc.* a quick elusive turn. *Pl.* pranks or frolicsome behavior; as, high *jinks.*

jinn, jin, *n. pl.* **jinns, jinn.** [Ar. *jinn,* pl. of *jinnī.*] *Moslem mythol.* one of a class of spirits lower than the angels, capable of appearing in human and animal forms, and exercising influence over mankind for good and evil. Also *genie,* **jin·ni,** ji·nē′, jin′ē.

jin·rik·i·sha, jin·rik′shạ, jin·rik′shä, *n.* [Japanese.] A small two-wheeled vehicle drawn by one or more men, used in the Orient. Also **jin·rick·sha, jin·rick·shaw, jin·rik·sha,** *rickshaw, ricksha.*

jinx, jingks, *n. Colloq.* something which brings bad luck.—*v.t. Colloq.* to cause or bring bad luck to.

jit·ney, jit′nē, *n. pl.* **jit·neys.** [Origin obscure.] A small bus or automobile which carries passengers, orig. charging a fare of five cents; *slang,* a five-cent piece.

jit·ter, jit′ėr, *v.i.* To behave nervously.—**jit·ters,** *n. pl. Slang.* Excessive nervousness; a feeling of uneasiness or fear, as: *The horror movie gave me the jitters.*—**jit·ter·y,** jit′e·rē, *a.* Strained or tense.

jit·ter·bug, jit′ėr·bug″, *n.* A popular dance of the 1940's characterized by quick steps, splits, and twirls; one who does this dance.—*v.i.*—*jitterbugged, jitterbugging.* To do the jitterbug.

jiu·jit·su, jiu·jut·su, jō·jit′sō, *n.* Jujitsu.

jive, jīv, *n.* Swing or jazz music; the dancing to swing music; jargon used by jazz enthusiasts and musicians; misleading talk.—*v.i.* To perform or dance to such music.—*v.t. Slang.* To tease; to fool or confuse.

jo, joe, jō, *n. pl.* **joes.** [Obs. form of *joy.*] *Sc.* a sweetheart.

job, job, *n.* [Origin uncertain.] A piece of work, esp. an individual piece of work done in the routine of one's occupation or trade, or for a fixed price; anything one has to do; a duty; responsibility; post of employment; an affair, matter, or state of affairs; a piece of public or official business carried through with a view to improper private gain; the object worked on; a task which demands uncustomary exertion; the process involved in accomplishing a task. *Slang,* a criminal deed, as a theft or robbery.—*a.* Pertaining to or hired for the job or particular piece of work; sold or bought together.—**job·less,** job'lis, *a.*—**job·less·ness,** *n.*

job, job, *v.i.*—*jobbed, jobbing.* To work at jobs or odd pieces of work; work by the piece; to buy and sell as a broker, middleman, or jobber; to turn public business improperly to private gain.—*v.t.* To buy in large quantities, then sell to dealers in smaller lots; to let out, as work, in separate portions, as among different contractors or workmen; to manipulate corruptly for private gain; *slang,* to deceive or swindle.

job·ber, job'ẽr, *n.* One who deals in goods or merchandise as a wholesaler; one who does piecework or one who does work by the job; *Brit.* a middleman among stock brokers.

job·ber·y, job'e·rĕ, *n. pl.* **job·ber·ies.** Dishonest manipulation of an official or public office for private gain; graft.

job·hold·er, job'hōl"dẽr, *n.* A person working at a steady job; an employee of a government.

job-hop·ping, job'hop"ing, *n.* The act or habit of changing jobs frequently, usu. for improvement of one's salary or wages.—**job-hop·per,** *n.*

job lot, *n.* A miscellaneous collection of merchandise sold in a single dealing, usu. at a lower price, to a retailer; a miscellaneous group or collection, usu. of inferior quality.

Job's com·fort·er, jōbz' kum"fẽr·tẽr, *n.* [From *Job,* O.T.] One whose ostensible efforts to comfort, aggravate the distress of a sufferer.

Job's-tears, jōbz'tẽrz', *n. pl. but sing. in constr. Bot.* A tropical grass, *Coix lacryma-jobi,* bearing small ovoid fruits or grains that have a fanciful resemblance to tears, and are used as food and for ornamental purposes, as necklaces, rosaries, or mats.

job work, *n.* Work done by the job; *print.* miscellaneous work, as the printing of cards, circulars, and posters.

jock, jok, *n.* Jockey; jockstrap; *slang,* an athlete.

jock·ey, jok'ē, *n. pl.* **jock·eys.** [For *Jackey,* dim. of *Jack,* for *John; Jockey* and *Jock* being N. English forms.] One whose profession is to ride horses in horse races; *colloq.* one who drives, pilots, or guides; as, a car *jockey.*—*v.t.*—*jockeyed, jockeying.* To ride in a race; to maneuver; as, to *jockey* for position; to drive or pilot; guide; to cheat; to trick; to deceive; to manipulate.—*v.i.* To maneuver for gain; to act deceitfully or dishonestly.

jock·ey club, *n.* An association or group of racing officials and horse owners which promotes horse racing and formulates rules for it; an area of a race track reserved for club members and consisting of box seats, a restaurant, and lounges.

jock·o, jok'ō, *n. pl.* **jock·os.** [Fr. *jocko;* from W. Afr. name.] Orig. the chimpanzee; now, a name for any monkey or ape.

jock·strap, jok'strap", *n.* An elastic waist band and groin pouch worn esp. by male athletes for genital protection and support. Also **ath·let·ic sup·port·er.**

jo·cose, jō·kōs', *a.* [L. *jocosus,* < *jocus,* a joke.] Given to jokes and jesting; tending to elicit laughter; merry or playful.—**jo·cos·-**

i·ty, jō·kos'i·tē, *n. pl.* **jo·cos·i·ties.** The quality of being jocose; a humorous act or saying.—**jo·cose·ly,** *adv.*—**jo·cose·ness,** *n.*

joc·u·lar, jok'ū·lẽr, jok'ya·lẽr, *a.* [L. *jocularis,* < *jocus.*] Joking; witty; humorous; playful.—**joc·u·lar·i·ty,** jok"ū·lar'i·tĕ, jok"ya·lar'i·tĕ, *n. pl.* **joc·u·lar·i·ties.** The quality or state of being mirthful; a witty comment or deed.—**joc·u·lar·ly,** *adv.*

joc·und, jok'and, jō'kand, *a.* [L.L. *jocundus,* for L. *jucundus,* pleasant, agreeable, < *juvare,* help, please.] Cheerful; gay; merry.—**jo·cun·di·ty,** jō·kun'di·tĕ, *n.* A jocund state or quality.—**joc·und·ly,** *adv.*

jodh·pur, jod'pẽr, jōd'pẽr, *n.* [From *Jodhpur,* India.] *Pl.* riding breeches, styled wide at the hips, that narrow at the knees and fit tightly to the ankles, usu. with stirruplike foot straps. A riding shoe, made esp. for these breeches, that reaches the ankle and is tied by a strap that loops around the ankle and fastens at the side; also **jodh·pur boot, jodh·pur shoe.**

joe, jō, *n. Slang,* a man, as: He is a great *joe. Sc.* a sweetheart; also *jo.*

joe-pye weed, jō"pī' wēd, *n.* [Origin obscure.] A tall wild flower, *Eupatorium purpureum,* in the composite family, having clusters of pink to purple flowers and blooming in late summer.

jo·ey, jō'ē, *n. pl.* **jo·eys.** [Native Australian.] *Aust.* A young kangaroo; any young animal; a young child.

jog, jog, *v.t.*—*jogged, jogging.* [Perhaps a form of *jag,* or allied to W. *gogi,* to shake.] To push or shake slightly and suddenly; to nudge; to arouse, as the memory, by an idea or a reminder; to cause to move or work, as an engine, with a momentary jerk or a series of jerks; to pace, as a horse, at a regular gait; *print.* to cause the edges of, as cards or papers, to fall into alignment by carefully jarring against a surface, as by a *jogging* machine.—*v.i.* To move in a jolting or jerky manner; to move at a slow trot, as a form of mild exercise; to walk or travel idly or slowly, with little progress, usu. followed by *on* or *along.*—*n.* The act, motion, or space of jogging; a push, nudge, or slight shake; a shake or push intended to give notice or awaken attention; *carp., masonry,* a usu. right-angled notch; *mech.* a sudden, irregular change in alignment.—**jog·ger,** *n.*

jog·gle, jog'l, *v.t.*—*joggled, joggling.* [Freq. of *jog.*] To shake slightly; to give a sudden but slight push; to cause to become unstable or insecure by a sudden or unexpected contact; to unite or close; to shift a fitting part until it falls in place; *carp.* to join or match by jogs or notches so as to prevent slippage.—*v.i.* To shake; to totter.—*n.* A joint made by means of jogs or notches; a joint held in place by means of pieces of stone or metal; the piece of metal or stone used in such a joint.—**jog·gler,** *n.*

jog trot, *n.* A slow, easy trot, usu. interspersed with periods of brisk walking, used for physical fitness; a slow gait, usu. of a horse; a slow routine of daily duty to which one persistently adheres.—**jog-trot,** *a.* Monotonous; easygoing; humdrum.

john, jon, *n. Slang.* A toilet; a washroom or lavatory.

John Bar·ley·corn, *n.* A comical personification of liquor, esp. malt or corn liquor.

John Bull, *n.* [From a satire, *The History of John Bull,* by John Arbuthnot.] A personification of England, the English people, or an individual Englishman.—**John Bull·ish,** *a.*—**John Bull·ish·ness,** *n.*—**John Bull·ism,** *n.*

John Doe, *n.* A name used in legal procedure to indicate an unnamed, unidentified, or imaginary person; a name used to denote the average man.

John Han·cock, jon han'kok, *n.* [From the exceptionally large and legible signature of *John Hancock* on the Declaration of Independence.] *Colloq.* one's signature.

John Hen·ry, jon hen'rē, *n. Colloq.* one's signature.

John·ny, jon'ē, *n. pl.* **John·nies.** *U.S. and Brit. colloq.* a young man; a dandy. (*l.c.*), *colloq.* a short hospital gown without a collar used by bed patients.

john·ny·cake, jon'ē·kāk", *n.* Bread or cake of corn meal, salt, water, shortening, and eggs, made on a griddle.

John·ny-jump-up, jon'ē·jump'up", *n.* The wild pansy; any of several spring violets native to America.

John·ny-on-the-spot, jon'ē·on·THe·spot', *n. Colloq.* an individual who is present and willing when he can be of help, or when an opportunity exists.

John·ny Reb, jon'ē reb, *n. Colloq.* a soldier of the Confederate army.

John·son·ese, jon"so·nēz', jon"so·nēs', *n.* [From Dr. Samuel *Johnson,* 1709-1784.] The language or literary style of Dr. Johnson, characterized by pompous phraseology and Latinate vocabulary; in general, pompous or ponderous style.—**John·so·ni·an,** jon·sō'nē·an, *a.* Of, pertaining to, or characteristic of Dr. Johnson's writings or his style.—*n.* One who imitates Dr. Johnson's style; an admirer or student of Dr. Johnson and his writings.—**John·so·ni·an·ism,** *n.*

John·son grass, jon'son gras, *n.* A tall perennial grass, *Sorghum halepense,* used for horse and cattle feed.

join, join, *v.t.* [Fr. *joindre,* < L. *jungere, junctum,* to join, same root as Skt. *yuj,* to join; E. *yoke.*] To connect or bring together; to place in contiguity; to combine; to associate with; to become connected with; to unite with; to enter or become a member of; to unite through marriage; to adjoin; *geom.* to connect by line or lines.—*v.i.* To be contiguous or in contact; to unite or become associated.—*n.* A seam or joint.—**join·a·ble,** *a.*

join·der, join'dẽr, *n.* [Fr. *joindre,* inf., used as noun.] The act of joining. *Law.* The joining of causes of action in a suit; the joining of parties in a suit; the acceptance by a party to an action of an issue tendered.

join·er, joi'nẽr, *n.* One who joins; a carpenter, esp. one who does the woodwork of houses; a member of many clubs and organizations.—**join·er·y,** joi'nẽ·rĕ, *n.*

joint, joint, *n.* [Fr. *joint,* < *joindre,* pp. *joint,* to join.] The place or part at which two separate things are joined or united; as, a building *joint* or a metal *joint;* the mode of connection of two things; junction; *anat.* the joining of two or more bones, as in the elbow; *biol.* a junction connecting two body segments, as the head and thorax of a lobster; *bot.* the part of a plant stem from which a leaf or branch originates; a node; *geol.* a fissure at parallel angles to the rock stratification. *Slang.* A place or establishment of low character or reputation; a marijuana cigarette. *Brit.* a piece of meat for roasting; as, a *joint* of lamb.—*a.* Shared by two or more; as, a *joint* savings account; united or combined; as, a *joint* force or *joint* efforts; *law,* united in liability or interest; as, *joint* defendants; *govt.* relating to two or more governments united in action; as, a *joint* peace pact.—*v.t.* To form or unite with a joint or joints; to cut or divide into joints or pieces; as, to *joint* a turkey.—*v.i.* To unite by joints.—**out of joint,** dislocated, as a shoulderbone; relating to confusion and disorder, as: Her usual efficiency seemed *out of joint.*—**joint·ed,** *a.*—**joint·ed·ly,** *adv.*—**joint·ed·ness,** *n.*—**joint·er,** *n.* One that joints, as a tool or machine used to make joints.—**joint·ly,** *adv.*

joint res·o·lu·tion, *n.* A resolution approved by both houses of a legislature, which becomes law when signed by the chief executive.

joint·ress, join′tris, *n. Law,* a woman on whom an estate has been settled, effective after her husband's death.

joint re·turn, *n.* A tax report of the income of both husband and wife, the total of which both parties may be held individually liable for.

joint stock, *n. Stock market,* stock held in common.—**joint-stock com·pa·ny,** *stock market,* an unincorporated association of individuals, who jointly contribute funds for the purpose of carrying on a specified business or undertaking, of which the shares are transferable by each owner without the consent of the other partners.

joint ten·an·cy, *n.* Common ownership of property by two or more persons, with the property passing on to the surviving person or persons in case of the death of one co-owner.

join·ture, join′chėr, *n.* [O.Fr. Fr. *jointure,* < L. *junctura,* < *jungere,* join: see *join,* and cf. *juncture.*] *Law,* property settled on a woman in consideration of marriage, to become hers fully after her husband's death.—*v.t.*—*jointured, jointuring.* To settle a jointure, as upon a woman.—**join·ture of com·mand,** the combined command of an amphibious landing force which is transferred from the navy commander to the army commander at a certain point in the development of the landing operation.

joint·worm, joint′wųrm″, *n.* The larva of certain injurious insects, esp. of the genus *Harmolita,* which feeds near the joints of stalks of grain.

joist, joist, *n.* [O.Fr. *giste,* Fr. *gite,* a bed, a place to lie on, L.L. *gista,* < L. *jacitum,* pp. of *jacēre,* to lie.] *Building trades,* any of the horizontal timbers, running parallel from wall to wall, that support the boards of a floor or the laths of a ceiling.—*v.t.* To fit or furnish with joists.

joke, jōk, *n.* [L. *jocus,* Fr. *jeu,* It. *giuoco,* a jest; same root as *jacio,* to throw.] A thing said or an action performed to evoke laughter; the absurd or ridiculous side of something; a matter of small importance; a trifle.—*v.i.*—*joked, joking.* To act or speak in a mirthful or mischievous way; to jest.—*v.t.* To make fun of; to make merry with; to tease.—**prac·ti·cal joke,** a prank or playful trick in which the victim is subjected to an embarrassing situation.—**joke·ster,** jōk′stėr, *n.* A joker.—**jok·ing·ly,** *adv.*

jok·er, jō′kėr, *n.* A person who jokes or teases; an extra playing card added to a deck allowing special privileges; *slang,* an obnoxious individual; *law,* a seemingly harmless word, phrase, or clause in a legal document that greatly alters its meaning or purpose.

jol·ly, jol′ē, *a.*—*jollier, jolliest.* [O.Fr. *joli, jolif,* Fr. *joli,* gay, merry, from the Scand., and orig. referring to the festivities of Christmas; from Icel. *jol,* Sw. and Dan. *jul,* E. *yule,* Christmas.] Merry; gay; lively; full of life and mirth; jovial; expressing mirth; exciting mirth or gaiety. *Brit. colloq.* delightful; remarkable.—*adv. Brit. colloq.* extremely; unusually; very.—*v.i.*—*jollied, jollying.* To participate in friendly banter.—*v.t. Colloq.* to try to induce a pleasant, agreeable state of mind in.—**jol·li·fi·ca·tion,** *n.* Festivity, merry-making.—**jol·li·ty,** *n.* Mirth.

jol·ly boat, *n.* [*Jolly* here is same as Dan. *jolli,* D. *jol,* a yawl, a jolly boat.] *Naut.* a ship's boat, about 12 feet in length, with a bluff bow.

Jol·ly Rog·er, *n.* A flag used by pirates and marked by a white skull and crossbones on a black background.

jolt, jōlt, *v.t.* [Appar. for earlier *jot,* perhaps influenced by *jowl.*] To jar or shake as by a sudden rough thrust; shake up roughly; to deliver a blow to, as in boxing; to upset suddenly, psychologically or emotionally; to interrupt or intrude upon abruptly or roughly.—*v.i.* To move with a shock or jerk, or a succession of shocks or jerks.—*n.* A sudden blow, shock, or movement; a sudden psychological or emotional upset; the cause of such an upset.—**jolt·er,** *n.*—**jolt·y,** *a.*—**jolt·ing·ly,** *adv.*

Jo·nah, jō′na, *n.* [From *Jonah,* the Hebrew prophet who was thrown overboard to allay a tempest at sea.] A person or thing supposed to bring ill luck.

jon·gleur, jong′glėr, *Fr.* zhaɴ·glœR, *n.* [Fr. *jongleur,* O.Fr. *jogleor.*] *Medieval hist.* an itinerant minstrel or entertainer who sang songs, sometimes of his own composition, and told stories.

jon·quil, jong′kwil, jon′kwil, *n.* [Fr. *jonquille;* It. *giunchiglia,* dim. < L. *juncus,* a rush.] A species of narcissus, *Narcissus jonquilla,* similar to the daffodil, with long leaves and fragrant white or yellow flowers.

Jon·so·ni·an, jon·sō′nē·an, *a.* [From Ben *Jonson,* English poet and dramatist, 1573?-1637.] Referring to Ben Jonson or his works.

Jor·dan al·mond, jȧr′dan ä′mond, *n.* [Prob. < Fr. *jardin,* garden.] A large almond, grown in Málaga, Spain, which is often sugared and widely used as a confection.

jo·rum, jōr′um, *n.* [Perh. a corruption of *jordan,* a vessel in which pilgrims brought home water from the *Jordan* river.] *Colloq.* A large bowl or drinking vessel; its contents.

jo·seph, jō′zef, jō′sef, *n.* [Prob. in allusion to *Joseph's* coat of many colors.] A coat or habit formerly worn by women equestrians or travelers.

Jo·seph's-coat, jō′zefs·kōt′, jō′sefs·kōt′, *n.* An herbaceous plant, *Amaranthus tricolor,* in the pigweed family, grown for its variegated red foliage and used esp. in window boxes and terraria.

josh, josh, *v.t.* [Origin uncertain.] *Slang.* To chaff; banter in a teasing way.—*v.i. Slang,* to join in banter.—*n. Slang,* a good-natured remark, banter, or joke.—**josh·er,** *n.*

Josh·u·a tree, josh′o̅o̅·a trē″, *n.* A small tree, *Yucca brevifolia,* which has short leaves and greenish-white clusters of flowers, found in southwestern U.S.

joss, jos, *n.* [Pidgin-English corruption of Pg. *deos,* < L. *deus,* god.] A Chinese deity or idol.—**joss stick,** Chinese incense in stick form burnt in worship.

jos·tle, jos′l, *v.t.*—*jostled, jostling.* [Earlier *justle,* freq. of *just.*] To bump, strike, or push roughly or rudely against; to drive or force, by or as by pushing or shoving.—*v.i.* To bump, collide, or push, as in passing or in a crowd, usu. followed by *against* or *with.*—*n.* A jostling, a collision, shock, or push. Also **jus·tle.**—**jos·tle·ment,** *n.*—**jos·tler,** *n.*

jot, jot, *n.* [< *iota,* the smallest letter in the Greek alphabet.] An iota; a point; a tittle; the least quantity assignable.—*v.t.*—*jotted, jotting.* To write down quickly or hurriedly, as in a diary or memorandum book; to make a memorandum of.—**jot·ting,** *n.* A memorandum.

joule, jōl, joul, *n.* [From James P. *Joule,* British scientist, 1819-1889.] *Phys.* that amount of energy or work, an mks (meter-kilogram-second) unit, which is equal to the energy required to exert a force of one newton over a distance of one meter, and equal to 10 million ergs. Abbr. *J, j.*

jounce, jouns, *v.i., v.t.*—*jounced, jouncing.* [M.E., origin obscure.] To move violently up and down; to bounce.—*n.* A bounce; a jolt.—**joun·cy,** *a.*

jour·nal, jųr′nal, *n.* [Fr. < L. *diurnalis, diurnal,* < *dies,* a day.] A diary; an account of daily transactions and events, or the book containing such an account; a record of the transactions of an organization or legal body; a newspaper or other periodical published daily; any periodical or magazine, esp. one published for a specific profession; as, a medical *journal. Bookkeeping,* a daybook; a book which contains the entries from a daybook and is used to aid subsequent entering in a ledger. *Naut.* a daily register of a ship's course and distance, the winds, weather, and other occurrences; a logbook; *mach.* that part of an axle or shaft which rests and moves in the bearings.

jour·nal box, *n. Mach.* a metal enclosure which houses a journal and bearing.

jour·nal·ese, jųr″na·lēz′, jųr′na·lēs′, *n.* A style or manner of writing usu. ascribed to newspaper reporters; a sensational, trite, or poorly phrased form of expression.

jour·nal·ism, jųr′na·liz″um, *n.* The occupation of conducting a news medium, including publishing, editing, writing, or broadcasting; an academic field concerned with the procedures involved in conducting a news medium; a type of writing ideally characterized by objectivity, but sometimes written to appeal to current public taste; reportage.—**jour·nal·ist,** *n.* The conductor of a news medium, as a newspaper editor or regular contributor; one who maintains a journal.—**jour·nal·is·tic,** *a.*—**jour·nal·is·ti·cal·ly,** *adv.*

jour·nal·ize, jųr′na·līz″, *v.t.*—*journalized, journalizing.* To enter in a journal; to give the form of a journal to.—*v.i.* To maintain or keep a journal.—**jour·nal·iz·er,** *n.*

jour·ney, jųr′nē, *n.* [Fr. *journée,* a day, a day's work, a day's journey, < L. *diurnus,* daily, < *dies,* a day.] Travel from one place to another; the distance or time traveled; a trip.—*v.i., v.t.* To travel.—**jour·ney·er,** *n.*

jour·ney·man, jųr′nē·man, *n.* pl. **jour·ney·men.** Any skilled workman who has completed his apprenticeship.

jour·ney·work, jųr′nē·wųrk″, *n.* A journeyman's work; any routine task.

joust, joust, just, jōst, *n.* [O.Fr. *juste, jouste, joste, jousting,* < O.Fr. *juster, jouster, joster,* to tilt; < L. *juxta,* near to, nigh.] A combat between two mounted knights clad in armor and bearing lances; *Medieval hist.* such a combat at a tournament; *pl.* a tournament.—*v.i.* To take part in a joust; to tilt.—**joust·er,** *n.*

Jove, jōv, *n.* [L. *Jovis, Diovis,* the old name of *Jupiter;* same root as *deus,* a god.] The chief divinity of the Romans; Jupiter.—**by Jove,** an exclamation of surprise or emphasis.—**Jo·vi·an,** jō′vē·an, *a.*

jo·vi·al, jō′vē·al, *a.* [L.L. *Jovialis,* because the planet Jupiter was believed to make those born under it of a jovial temperament.] Gay; merry; joyous; jolly; good-humored; (*cap.*) of or referring to Jove.—**jo·vi·al·i·ty,** **jo·vi·al·ness,** jō″vē·al′i·tē, *n.*—**jo·vi·al·ly,** *adv.*

jowl, joul, jōl, *n.* [M.E. *chawl, chavel,* < O.E. *ceafl,* jaw, akin to D. *kevel,* gum, G. *kiefer,* jaw, chap, Icel. *kjaptr,* mouth, jaw.] A jaw, esp. the under jaw; the cheek; a fold of flesh hanging from the jaw, as of a fat person; the dewlap of cattle; the wattle of fowls; the head and adjacent parts of fish.—**jowled, jowl·y,** *a.*

joy, joi, *n.* [O.Fr. *joye, joie, goie,* Fr. *joie,* It. *gioja,* < L. *gaudium,* joy, *gaudere,* to rejoice; seen also in *gaudy, rejoice, jewel.*] Excitement or pleasurable feeling caused by the acquisition or expectation of good; gladness; pleasure; delight; exultation; exhilaration of spirits; the cause of satisfaction and happiness.—*v.i.* To rejoice; to be glad; to exult.

joy·ance, joi′ans, n. *Archaic*, enjoyment.

Joyc·e·an, joi′sē·an, a. Of, referring to, or typical of the Irish novelist James Joyce (1882–1941) or his writings.—n.

joy·ful, joi′ful, a. Full of joy; glad; joyous. —**joy·ful·ly**, adv.—**joy·ful·ness**, n.

joy·less, joi′lis, a. Destitute of joy; giving no pleasure or gladness.—**joy·less·ly**, adv. —**joy·less·ness**, n.

joy·ous, joi′us, a. Gay; joyful; jubilant. —**joy·ous·ly**, adv.—**joy·ous·ness**, n.

joy ride, n. *Colloq.* A pleasure ride in an automobile, esp. when the car is driven recklessly or used without the owner's permission; an incident similar to a joy ride in its brevity, excitement, and danger.— **joy rid·er**, n.—**joy rid·ing**, n.

joy stick, n. *Colloq.* the control lever for an airplane.

ju·ba, jŏ′ba, n. [Negro word.] A lively dance of plantation negroes in the southern U.S., accompanied by hand clapping.

jub·bah, jub′ba, n. [Ar. *jubbah:* akin *jupe.*] A long outer garment with sleeves, worn in Muslim countries by both men and women.

ju·be, jŏ′bē, n. [Fr. *jubé*, < L. *jube,* 'bid thou,' the first word of a formula spoken from the gallery above the rood screen in a church.] *Arch.* a rood loft or choir loft above the large crucifix which surmounts the altar of a church.

ju·bi·lant, jŏ′bi·lant, a. [L. *jubilans,* ppr. of *jubilo,* to shout for joy, < *jubilum,* a shout of joy; not connected with *jubilee.*] Rejoicing; exhibiting joy; triumphant; exultant.—**ju·bi·lance**, **ju·bi·lan·cy**, n.— **ju·bi·lant·ly**, adv

ju·bi·la·tion, jŏ″bi·lā′shan, n. [L. *jūbilā-tiō.*] A rejoicing; a triumph; an exultation; a joyful or festive celebration.—**ju·bi·late**, jŏ′bi·lāt″, v.i.—**jubilated**, jubilating. To rejoice; to exult; to triumph.—**ju·bi·la·to·ry**, a.

ju·bi·lee, jŏ′bi·lē″, jŏ″bi·lē′, n. [O.Fr. *jubile* (Fr. *jubilé*), < L.L. *jubilæus,* Gr. *iobelaios,* < Heb. *yōbēl,* ram, ram's horn, used as a trumpet: Lev. xxv. 9; not connected with *jubilate.*] The celebration of any of certain anniversaries; as, the 25th silver *jubilee* or 50th golden *jubilee;* the completion of the 50th year of any continuous course or period, as of existence or activity, or its celebration; any season or occasion for rejoicing or festivity; rejoicing or jubilation. *Rom. Cath. Ch.* An appointed year, now ordinarily every 25th year, in which remission from the penal consequences of sin is granted upon repentance and the performance of certain religious acts. Among the ancient Hebrews, a celebration to be observed every 50th year and to be announced by the blowing of trumpets, during which the fields were to be left untilled, alienated lands to be restored, and Hebrew slaves to be set free.

Ju·da·ism, jŏ′dē·iz″um, jŏ′dā·iz″um, n. The religion of the Jewish people as prescribed in the Old Testament and in the rabbinical commentaries of the Talmud, characterized by a belief in one God and conformity to Jewish rites and ceremonies; the traditional, religious, and ethical beliefs and customs of the Jewish people. —**Ju·da·ic**, **Ju·da·i·cal**, jŏ·dā′ik, a. Pertaining to the Jewish people or Judaism. —**Ju·da·ist**, jŏ′dē·ist, jŏ′dā·ist, n. An adherent to or supporter of Judaism.—**Ju·da·is·tic**, a. Relating or pertaining to Judaism.

Ju·da·ize, jŏ′dē·īz″, jŏ′dā·īz″, v.i.—*Judaized, Judaizing.* To conform to the religious doctrines and rites of the Jewish people; to assume the manners or customs of the Jewish people.—v.t. To bring into conformity with what is Jewish.—**Ju·da·i·za·tion**, n.—**Ju·da·iz·er**, n.

Ju·das, jŏ′das, n. [From *Judas* Iscariot, the disciple who betrayed Jesus: see Mat.

xxvi. 47–49.] One treacherous enough to betray a friend; one who disguises treachery as friendship. *(l.c.)* a peephole; also **ju·das hole**, **ju·das trap.**—a.

Ju·das tree, n. [From *Judas* Iscariot, the disciple who betrayed Jesus, who is believed to have hanged himself on this kind of tree.] A purple-flowered tree, *Cercis siliquastrum* and *C. Canadensis,* of Europe and Asia; any of various other trees of the same genus; also *American redbud.*

Ju·de·an, jŏ·dē′an, a. Of or relating to Judea, a region in ancient Palestine.—n. A native or inhabitant of Judea.

judge, juj, n. [O.Fr. Fr. *juge,* < L. *judex* (*judic-*), < *jus,* right, law, and *dicere,* say.] A public officer authorized to hear and determine causes in a court of law; one who gives judgment or passes sentence; an appointed person who pronounces a decision in a dispute or contest, as an arbiter; one qualified to pass a critical judgment; an administrative officer at the head of the Hebrew nation in the period between Joshua's death and Saul's coming to the throne.—**judge·ship**, n. The office or term of a judge.

judge, juj, v.t.—*judged, judging.* [O.Fr. *jugier* (Fr. *juger*), < L. *judicare,* judge, decide, adjudge, < *judex.*] To hear, critically examine, and decide, as a court case; to try; to pass sentence on, as a person; to decide or decree judicially or authoritatively; to form an opinion or estimate of; to infer, think, or hold an opinion; to govern, as of ancient Hebrew leaders of tribes.—v.i. To act as a judge; decide; to form an opinion or estimate; make a mental judgment.—**judg·er**, n.

judge ad·vo·cate, n. *Milit.* a legal advisor, esp. the staff officer appointed to prosecute before a court-martial.—**judge ad·vo·cate gen·er·al**, *milit.* supervising legal officer.

judg·mat·ic, juj·mat′ik, a. [Irreg. < *judge* and *-matic* as in dogmatic.] Exercising or showing good judgment; judicious. Also **judg·mat·i·cal.**—**judg·mat·i·cal·ly**, adv.

judg·ment, *Brit.* **judge·ment**, juj′ment, n. [Fr. *jugement.*] The act of judging, as the act of deciding or passing decision on something; the act or faculty of judging truly, wisely, or skillfully; good sense; discernment; understanding; opinion or notion formed by judging or considering; *logic,* the act or mental faculty by which man compares ideas and ascertains the relations of terms and propositions; a determination of the mind so formed, producing a proposition when expressed in words. *Law,* the sentence pronounced on a case by the judge or court by which it is tried; the obligation, esp. debt, imposed by a negative court decision; the certificate indicating the verdict of the case and served to the obligor, usu. the debtor. A calamity regarded as inflicted by God for the punishment of sinners; the final trial of the human race.—**judg·men·tal**, *Brit.* **judge·men·tal**, a.

Judg·ment Day, n. *Theol.* the last day, when final judgment will be pronounced on all men.

ju·di·ca·ble, jŏ′di·ka·bl, a. [L. *judicabilis,* < *judico,* to judge, < *judex,* a judge.] Capable of being judged or tried.— **ju·di·ca·tive**, jŏ′di·kā″tiv, a. Having ability or power to judge; judging.—**ju·di·ca·to·ry**, jŏ′di·ka·tōr″ē, jŏ′di·ka·tar″ē, a. Relating to the administration of or passing of justice.—n. A court of justice; a group having judicial authority; processes involved in administering justice.—**ju·di·ca·ture**, jŏ′di·kā″chēr, n. The administration of law and justice; the power of judicial administration; judicial procedures; a court of justice; judges or courts collectively.

ju·di·cial, jŏ·dish′al, a. [L. *judicialis,* < *judicium,* a trial, a judicial inquiry, judgment, discernment, < *judex, judicis,* a judge.] Relating to judicial administration; relating to courts of justice or judges; decreed by a court; in accordance with the concept of a judge; having the tendency to judge, discriminate, or criticize; serving to determine or decide; participating in a judgment; *theol.* referring to a judgment from God.—**ju·di·cial·ly**, adv.

ju·di·ci·ar·y, jŏ·dish′ē·er″ē, jŏ·dish′e·rē, a. [L. *judiciarius.*] Referring to the judgments of law courts, the courts themselves, or judges.—n. The governmental branch engaged in judicial concerns; the court system of a country; judges taken collectively. Also *Brit.* **ju·di·ca·ture**, jŏ′di·kā″chēr.

ju·di·cious, jŏ·dish′us, a. [Fr. *judicieux,* < L. *judicium,* judgment.] Relating to the use of good judgment; wise; prudent. —**ju·di·cious·ly**, adv.—**ju·di·cious·ness**, n.

ju·do, jŏ′dō, n. A method of defense originating from jujitsu and similar to it in its reliance upon body movement and leverage rather than weapons, but differing from it in its elimination of dangerous blows; a popular sport, similar in style to wrestling.

ju·do·gi, jŏ·dō′gē, n. A loosely fitted white cotton costume, worn by judo wrestlers, consisting of a jacket, pants, and a cloth belt whose color indicates the wearer's grade and skill.

jug, jug, n. [Perhaps < *Jug,* for *Joan,* or *Joanna,* woman's name.] A vessel in various forms for holding liquids, commonly having a handle, often a spout or lip, and sometimes a lid; a pitcher; a deep vessel, usu. earthenware, with a handle and a narrow neck stopped by a cork; the contents of any such vessel; *slang,* a prison or jail.—v.t.—*jugged, jugging.* To put into a jug; cook in a jug; *slang,* to imprison.— **jug·ful**, jug′ful, n. pl. **jug·fuls.** A quantity sufficient to fill a jug.

ju·gal, jŏ′gal, a. [L. *jugalis,* < *jugum,* a yoke.] *Anat.* of or pertaining to the bony arch of the cheek.

ju·gate, jŏ′gāt, jŏ′git, a. [L. *jugum,* a yoke, a ridge or summit.] *Bot.* coupled together, as the pairs of leaflets in compound leaves; *biol.* paired.

jugged hare, n. *Brit.* a rabbit stew cooked in an earthenware pot.

jug·ger·naut, jug′er·nat″, n. [Hindi, *Jagan-nāth,* lord of the world.] Any overpowering and terrible force; any idea, custom, or loyalty demanding blind devotion or terrible sacrifice; *(cap.)* an incarnation of Vishnu, the Hindu god, whose idol so excited worshippers during religious rites that they hurled themselves under the wheels of the enormous cart it was hauled on and were crushed.

jug·gle, jug′l, v.i.—*juggled, juggling.* [O.Fr. *jogler, jugler,* < L. *joculari,* to jest, joke < *joculus,* dim. of *jocus,* E. *joce.*] To perform feats of manual or bodily dexterity, such as tossing up and keeping in continuous motion a number of balls, plates, or knives; to use artifice or trickery.—v.t. To toss up and keep in motion continuously, as several balls, plates, or knives; to handle in an unsteady manner; to manipulate by artifice or trickery; as, to *juggle* accounts.—n. An act of juggling; a trick; a deception.

jug·gler, jug′lẽr, n. [O.Fr. *jogleor* (Fr. *jongleur*), < L. *joculator,* jester, < *joculari.*] One who performs juggling feats, as with balls or knives; one who deceives by trickery; a trickster.—**jug·gler·y**, jug′le·rē, n.

ju·glan·da·ceous, jŏ″glan·dā′shus, a. [L. *juglans* (*jugland-*), walnut.] Belonging to the *Juglandaceae,* or walnut family of trees including walnuts and hickories, having pinnately compound leaves and nut fruits.

Ju·go·slav, ū'gō·släv″, ū'gō·slav″, *a.* [Slav. *jug,* south.] Yugoslav. Also **Ju·go·slav·ic.**

jug·u·lar, jug'ū·lėr, jŏ'gū·lėr, *a.* [N.L. *jugularis,* < L. *jugulum,* collarbone, throat, dim. of *jugum,* a yoke.] *Anat.* of or pertaining to the throat or neck; relating to certain veins in the neck. *Ichth.* of a fish, having the ventral fins at the throat, in advance of the pectoral fins; denoting a ventral fin on the throat.—*n.* A jugular vein, one of the two large veins of the neck returning blood from the neck, face, and brain to the heart.

ju·gu·late, jŏ'gū·lāt″, *v.t.*—*jugulated, jugulating.* [L. *jugulatus,* pp. of *jugulare,* < *jugulum,* throat.] To check or suppress, as disease and the like, by extreme measures; to slit the throat of.—**ju·gu·la·tion,** *n.*

ju·gum, jŏ'gum, *n. Entom.* the posterior region at the base of an insect's forewing which, in some instances, locks the forewings and hindwings together during flight.

juice, jŏs, *n.* [O.E. *jows,* Fr. *jus,* < L. *jus,* broth, soup; cogn. Skt. *yusha,* broth.] The fluid part of animal substances, fruits, or vegetables, esp. those which can be extracted; natural body fluids; as, digestive *juices;* essential or vital element. *Slang,* electricity; fuel, esp. gasoline; intoxicating liquor.—*v.t.*—*juiced, juicing.* To obtain juice from.—**juice·less,** *a.*

juic·er, jŏ'sėr, *n.* An appliance for the extraction of fruit and vegetable juices; an electrical technician who designs the lighting or perfects the electrical circuiting for television, movie, or stage sets.

juic·y, jŏ'sē, *a.* Abounding with juice; succulent; interesting; colorful, esp. when racy or spicy.—**juic·i·ly,** *adv.*—**juic·i·ness,** *n.*

ju·jit·su, jŏ·jit'sŏ, *n.* [Japan.] A style of Japanese wrestling in which agility, leverage, and a knowledge of muscular action are utilized to disable the opponent. Also **jiu·jit·su, jiu·jut·su, ju·jut·su** jŏ·jut'sŏ, jŏ·jut'sŏ.

ju·ju, jŏ'jŏ, *n.* pl. **ju·jus.** [W. Afr.: cf. Fr. *joujou,* plaything.] Among native tribes of western Africa, some object venerated superstitiously and used as a fetish or amulet; the magical power attributed to such an object; a ban or interdiction effected by it.—**ju·ju·ism,** *n.*

ju·jube, jŏ'jŏb, *n.* [Fr. *jujube,* a jujube, < L. *ziziphum,* Gr. *zizyphon,* Ar. *zizuf,* the jujube tree.] The fruit of a spiny Mediterranean shrub or small tree, genus *Zizyphus;* the tree itself; a confection, gelatin, sweetened and flavored to resemble the jujube fruit.

juke·box, jŏk'boks″, *n.* An automatic, usu. coin-operated record player, in a brightly illuminated cabinet which permits pushbutton record selection.

juke joint, *n. Slang.* An establishment which usu. offers food, drinks, and dancing to jukebox music; a roadhouse.

ju·lep, jū'lip, *n.* [Fr. *julep,* Ar. *julāb,* < Pers. *gulāb,* rose-water—*gul,* rose, and *āb,* water.] A sweet drink. *Phar.* sweetened drink serving as a vehicle for medicine. A mixture containing bourbon whiskey, sugar, crushed ice, and mint; also *mint julep.*

Jul·ian, jŏl'yan, *a.* [From *Julius* Caesar: Roman general, statesman, and historian, 100–44 B.C.] Pertaining to or derived from Julius Caesar.—**Jul·ian Cal·en·dar,** *n.* A calendar introduced by Julius Caesar in 46 B.C. and later revised by the Gregorian Calendar.

ju·li·enne, jŏ″lē·en', Fr. zhy·lyen', *a.* [Fr.] Sliced in long thin strips, as vegetables or other food.—*n.* A clear soup made from meat stock and containing julienne vegetables.

Ju·li·et, jŏ'lē·et, jŏ″lē·et', *n.* A communications code word to designate the letter J.

Ju·ly, jū·lī', ju·lī', *n.* The seventh month of the year, containing 31 days.

jum·ble, jum'bl, *v.t.*—*jumbled, jumbling.* [O.E. *jombre, jumbre, jumpre,* to agitate, to shake together; akin to *jump,* and to Dan. *gumpe,* to jolt.] To mix in a confused mass; to put or throw together without order; to confuse in the mind.—*v.i.* To meet, mix, or unite in a confused manner.—*n.* Confused mixture, mass, or collection; disorder; confusion. A small circular sweet cake; also **jum·bal.**

jum·bo, jum'bō, *n.* pl. **jum·bos.** [Cf. *mumbo-jumbo.*] A big person, animal, or thing.—*a.* Unusually large; as, the *jumbo* size detergent.

jum·buck, jum'buk, *n. Aust.* a native sheep.

jump, jump, *v.i.* [Appar. imit.] To spring clear of the ground or other support by a sudden muscular effort; throw oneself in any direction from the ground or other support; leap; to move or go suddenly or abruptly, as with a leap; to start, as from nervous excitement; to be thrown up or moved with a sudden jerk; to rise suddenly in amount or price; to pass abruptly, as if by a leap; as, to *jump* to a conclusion; *checkers,* to capture an opponent's piece. To be bustling with activity; to move with eagerness and energy.—*v.t.* To pass over by a leap; leap over. *Checkers,* to capture, as an opponent's piece, by passing a piece over it to the square beyond. To skip or pass over. *Slang,* to abscond from, or evade by absconding; as, to *jump* bail; to get on board; as, *jump* a freight. To spring off or leave, as: A train *jumps* a track. To pounce on; come down upon violently or suddenly; seize upon by sudden, unexpected action; to seize, as a mining claim; to cause to jump or rise; to promote, as in rank.—*n.* An act of jumping; a spring from the ground or other support by a sudden muscular effort; a leap; a space or obstacle cleared in a leap; a sudden start, as from nervous excitement. *Pl.* a physical condition characterized by such starts; anxiety or restlessness. A sudden upward or other movement of an inanimate object; a sudden rise in amount or price; an abrupt change of level; an abrupt transition from one point or thing to another, with omission of what intervenes; a parachute descent; a brief journey; a sports event featuring competitive jumping.—**jump all o·ver some·one,** to rebuke, criticize, or scold. Also **jump down one's throat.**—**jump at,** *slang,* embrace or accept with eagerness.—**jump on the band·wag·on,** to support or join something or someone already successful.—**jump ship,** *naut.* to desert a ship.—**jump the gun,** to begin prematurely.—**get the jump on,** *slang,* to possess an advantage or head start.—**jump·ing,** *a.*—**jump·i·ness,** *n.*—**jump·y,** *a.*

jump bid, *n. Bridge,* a bid which exceeds the minimum bid required to overcall a previous bid.

jump·er, jum'pėr, *n.* One who or that which jumps, as a skydiver or a horse; a long iron chisel pointed with steel used to prepare a hole, as for blasting; a kind of loose-fitting jacket; a sleeveless dress esp. one-piece, usu. worn over a blouse; *elec.* a piece of wire across a broken circuit; *Brit.* a pullover sweater.

jump·ing bean, *n. Bot., zool.* the seed of the Mexican genera *Sebastiania* and *Sapium,* in the spurge family, which is parasitized by a moth larva whose movements cause the seed to jump about.

jump·ing jack, *n.* A loosely jointed toy man, manipulated by sticks and strings to perform various gyrations. *Usu. pl.,* a common calisthenic involving jumping and coordinated arm movements.

jump·ing mouse, *n.* Any of the mouselike N. American rodents of the family *Zapodidae,* with kangaroolike hind legs and long tails, as the deer mouse.

jump·ing-off place, *n.* An out-of-the-way or remote place; the farthermost limits, as of civilization; a place of embarkation.

jump-off, jump'af″, jump'of″, *n.* The onset of a battle or a race.

jump pass, *n. Football, basketball,* a pass thrown by a player while in the act of jumping.

jump seat, *n.* A movable or folding extra seat, as in a taxicab.

jump shot, *n. Basketball,* a shot in which a player aims and shoots the ball at the basket while at the highest point of a leap.

jump suit, *n.* A one-piece uniform worn for parachute jumping; a similarly styled article of feminine clothing.

jun·ca·ceous, jung·kā'shus, *a.* [L. *juncus,* a rush.] Belonging to the *Juncaceae,* or rush family of plants, grasslike and thriving in wet ground.

jun·co, jung'kō, *n.* pl. **jun·cos, jun·coes.** [Sp. *junco,* a rush, < L. *juncus,* a rush.] *Ornith.* a small, slate-gray bird, *Junco hyemalis,* of the finch family, having conspicuous white outer tail feathers and wintering in the northern U.S. Also *snowbird.*

junc·tion, jungk'shan, *n.* [< L. *junctiō,* < *jungo,* to join.] The act or operation of joining; the state of being joined; the place or point of union; joint; juncture; the place where two or more railroads meet; a crossing or merging of two roads.—**junc·tion·al,** *a.*

junc·ture, jungk'chėr, *n.* [L. *junctūra.*] The line or point at which two bodies are joined; a point of time, esp. one rendered critical or important by a combination of circumstances; *phon.* the transition from one sound to another or a termination of a flow of speech.

June, jūn, *n.* [L. *Junius,* perhaps from *Junius* Brutus; same root as *junior,* L. *juvenis,* a youth; E. *young.*] The sixth month of the year, containing 30 days.

June·ber·ry, jŏn'ber″ē, jŏn'be·rē, *n.* A small, light gray, smooth-barked tree, *Amelanchier canadensis,* whose white flowers bloom profusely in early spring, and which produces edible purple berries. Also *shadbush, service berry.*

june bug, *n.* A large brown beetle of the genus *Phyllophaga,* appearing in early summer, and whose larvae are white grubs which feed on plant roots. Also **june bee·tle,** may **bee·tle.**

jun·gle, jung'gl, *n.* [Hind. *jangal,* forest, jungle.] A wild tropical forest of rank vegetation and dense undergrowth; any coarse, rank vegetation; a jumbled mass; a bafflement; an area, as in business, of merciless competition or struggle for success; *slang,* a place where hoboes congregate.—**jun·gled, jun·gly,** *a.*

jun·gle fe·ver, *n.* A disease prevalent in the East Indies and other tropical regions; a severe variety of remittent fever.

jun·gle fowl, *n.* Any species of gallinaceous or scratching birds, native to the E. Indies, and the ancestor of our domestic fowl.

jun·gle·gym, jung'gl·jim″, *n.* A skeleton structure comprised of many horizontal and vertical rods upon and through which children climb for exercise and play. (Trademark.)

jun·gle rot, *n.* Any skin disease or affliction, as a fungus, prevalent in tropical climates.

jun·ior, jŏn'yėr, *a.* [L. contracted < *juvenior,* comparative of *juvenis,* young.] Younger; applied to distinguish the younger of two persons, usu. father and son, bearing the same name; intended for youth; lower or younger in standing; later in date; of or denoting the third year of a four year course of study.—*n.* A person younger than another; one of newer or inferior standing, as in his profession; a clothing size or range of sizes for girls and women who have slight figures; a student in the year preceding his final or senior year. Abbr. *jr.*,*Jr.*

jun·ior col·lege, *n.* A two-year institution of learning following high school and offering a general curriculum.

jun·ior high school, *n.* An intermediary school comprised of the seventh, eighth, and sometimes the ninth grades.

jun·ior miss, *n.* A young, teenage girl; a clothing size for girls and women who have slight figures.

ju·ni·per, jŏ'nĭ·pẽr, *n.* [L. *juniperus.*] *Bot.* a tree or shrub of the evergreen genus *Juniperus,* esp. a shrub, *J. communis,* having blue berrylike cones used in medicine and in the flavoring of gin. *Bot.* a tree, *J. virginiana,* both native and cultivated, whose wood is of commerical importance; also *red cedar.*—**ju·ni·per oil,** *n.* The volatile oil obtained from the sweet pulp of the juniper berry and used in making gin.

junk, jungk, *n.* [Origin uncertain: cf. M.E. *jonke,* < O.Fr. *jonc,* < L. *juncus,* a rush.] Old or discarded material, as metal, paper, or rags; anything that is regarded as worthless or mere trash; old cable or cordage used for making gaskets, swabs, or oakum; *naut.* hard salted meat used for food on shipboard. *Slang,* narcotics.—*v.t. Colloq.* to cast aside; to discard as no longer of use.—**junk·man,** *n.*—**junk·y,** *a.*

junk, jungk, *n.* [Fr. *jonque,* Sp. and Pg. *junco,* < Malay *ajong,* a large ship.] A flat-bottomed ship used in China and Japan, having large sails and a high stern.

junk art, *n.* A statue, collage, or similar three-dimensional art work which is made from discarded articles of little value, as machine parts, building materials, or driftwood.—**junk art·ist,** *n.*

Jun·ker, yung'kẽr, *n.* [G., < M.H.G. *junc herre,* young gentleman: cf. *younker.*] A member of the aristocratic party in Prussia; a military or government official of Germany regarded as narrow-minded, haughty, or overbearing; formerly, a young German noble.—**Jun·ker·dom,** *n.* The group of Junkers; the spirit or policy of the Junkers. —**Jun·ker·ism,** yung'ke·riz"um, *n.*

jun·ket, jung'kit, *n.* [M.E. *jonket,* basket made of rushes, *joncate,* curded food made in a vessel of rushes; ult. < L. *juncus,* a rush.] A dish made of milk curdled with rennet, sweetened, and flavored. A feast; a picnic; a pleasure excursion; a trip made ostensibly for official business, enjoyed at public expense.—*v.i.* To feast; picnic; go on a trip or pleasure excursion.—**jun·ket·-ter, jun·ke·teer,** jung"ki·tẽr', *n.*

junk·ie, jung'kē, *n. Slang,* one who is addicted to drugs.

Ju·no, jŏ'nō, *n. pl.* **Ju·nos.** [L.] A woman of imposing figure. *Astron.* one of the brightest of the minor planets or asteroids.— **Ju·no·esque,** jŏ"nō·esk', *a.* Pertaining to a large woman of stately appearance.

jun·ta, hŭn'ta, hŏn'ta, jun'ta, hun'ta, *n.* [Sp. < L. *juncta,* fem. of *junctus,* pp. of *jungere,* join.] A deliberative or administrative council, esp. in Spain and Latin America; an interim government formed by a committee following a revolution; a group of persons united for a common goal, often for intrigue. Also **jun·to.**

Ju·pi·ter, jŏ'pi·tẽr, *n.* [L., the main god in Roman mythology.] *Astron.* the largest of the major planets, being the fifth in order from the sun. *Aerospace,* an early U.S. ballistic missile of intermediate range.

ju·pon, jŏ'pon, jŏ·pon', Fr. zhY·pạN', *n.* [Fr. < Sp. *jupon,* < Ar. *jubbah,* an outer garment.] A tight-fitting military garment without sleeves, formerly worn over armor. Also **gi·pon.**

ju·ral, jur'al, *a.* [L. *jus* (*jur-*), right, law.] Pertaining to law; legal; pertaining to rights and obligations.—**ju·ral·ly,** *adv.*

Ju·ras·sic, ju·ras'ik, *a.* [Fr. *jurassique* < Jura Mountains.] *Geol.* of or pertaining to the geological period which precedes the Cretaceous and follows the Triassic; the system of rocks of that period.—*n.* The Jurassic period or system; also **Ju·ra.** See Geological Time Scale.

ju·rat, jur'at, *n.* [Fr. < L. *juratus,* sworn, < *juro,* to swear.] *Law,* a statement on an affidavit describing when, where, before whom, and by whom the affidavit was made.

ju·ra·to·ry, jur'a·tōr"ē, *a. Law,* expressed in, relating to, or constituting an oath.

ju·rel, hŏ·rel', *n.* [Sp.] Any of certain carangid foodfishes of the genus *Caranx,* as *C. latus,* a species of the West Indies.

ju·rid·i·cal, ju·rid'i·kal, *a.* [L. *juridicus* —*jus, juris,* law, and *dico,* to pronounce.] *Law,* of or pertaining to the law, to judges, or to the administration of justice. Also **ju·rid·ic.**—**ju·rid·i·cal·ly,** *adv.*

ju·ris·con·sult, jur"is·kon'sult', jur"is·-kon'sult, *n.* [L. *juris consultus—jus, juris,* law, and *consultus,* < *consulo,* to consult.] One who gives his opinion in cases of law; anyone learned in jurisprudence, esp. public and international law; a jurist.

ju·ris·dic·tion, jur"is·dik'shan, *n.* [L. *jurisdictio*(*n-*), < *juris,* gen. of *jus,* right, law, *dictio*(*n-*), saying.] The right or power of administering law or justice; judicial authority; power or authority in general; rule; control; the extent or range of judicial or other authority; the territory over which authority is exercised; a judicial organization; a court, or system of courts, of justice.—**ju·ris·dic·tion·al,** *a.*—**ju·ris·-dic·tion·al·ly,** *adv.*

ju·ris·pru·dence, jur"is·prŏd'ens, *n.* [L. *jurisprudentia—jus, juris,* law, and *prudentia,* skill.] The science of law; the formal principles upon which laws are based; a body of court decisions; a department of law; as medical *jurisprudence.*—**ju·ris·-pru·den·tial,** jur"is·prŏ·den'shal, *a.*—**ju·-ris·pru·den·tial·ly,** *adv*

ju·ris·pru·dent, jur"is·prŏd'ent, *a.* Understanding law.—*n.* One learned in the law; a jurist.

ju·rist, jur'ist, *n.* [O.Fr. Fr. *juriste,* < M.L. *jurista,* < L. *jus* (*jur-*), right, law.] A lawyer; a judge; one versed in law, esp. civil law; a writer on law.—**ju·ris·tic,** ju·ris'tik, *a.*—**ju·ris·ti·cal·ly,** *adv.*

ju·ror, jur'ẽr, *n.* [A.Fr. *jurour,* O.Fr. *jureor,* < L. *jurator,* swearer, < *jurāre,* swear.] One of a body of persons sworn to deliver a verdict in a legal case submitted to them; a member of any jury; one who has taken an oath; one who serves on a panel judging a contest.

ju·ry, jur'ē, *n. pl.* **ju·ries.** [O.Fr. *jurie,* Fr. *jurer,* L. *jurare,* to swear; same origin as *jūs, jūris,* right, law, *jūstus,* just, < root meaning to bind, seen in *jungo,* to join, and in E. *yoke.*] A certain number of persons selected according to law and sworn to inquire into or to determine facts, and to arrive at a verdict according to the evidence legally adduced; a committee selected to adjudge prizes, as at a fair, beauty contest, or other public exhibition.—**ju·ry·man,** jur'ē·man, *n.* One who is impaneled on a jury, or who serves as a juror.

ju·ry, jur'ē, *a.* [Origin uncertain; perh. < Pg. *ajuda,* help.] *Naut.* A term applied to a thing temporarily replacing a missing item; as, a *jury* rudder; makeshift.

ju·ry-rigged, jur'ē·rigd", *a. Naut.* rigged or equipped temporarily.

jus·sive, jus'iv, *a.* [L. *jūssus,* pp. of *jubēre,* bid, command.] *Gram.* expressing a command.—*n.* A jussive form or construction.

just, just, *a.* [Fr. *juste,* L. *jūstus,* what is according to *jūs,* the rights of man.] Acting in accordance with what is right; equitable; impartial; fair; merited; as, *just* reward; proper; legal; as, *just* debts.—*adv.* Exact in time; as, *just* now; closely in place; as, *just* by; exactly; as, *just* as they were; a moment before; as: She *just* arrived.— **just·ly,** *adv.*—**just·ness,** *n.*

just, just, *n.* Joust.—*v.i.*

jus·tice, jus'tis, *n.* [O.Fr. Fr. *justice,* < L. *jūstitia,* < *jūstus,* E. *just.*] Equitableness; unprejudiced adjudication of conflicting interests on the basis of legal or moral principles; lawfulness; what is rightly due; governmental judiciary department; as, the U.S. Department of *Justice;* a judge; as, *justice* of the U.S. Supreme Court.— **jus·tice·less,** *a.*—**jus·tice·like,** *a.*

jus·tice of the peace, *n.* A local civil officer who may fine or even imprison in certain minor cases, conduct preliminaries in more serious cases, perform marriages, and administer oaths.

jus·ti·ci·a·ble, ju·stish'ē·a·bl, *a.* [Fr. *justiciable.*] Able to be settled by court action or by law; subject to jurisdiction.— **jus·ti·ci·a·bil·i·ty,** *n.*

jus·ti·ci·ar, ju·stish'ē·ẽr, *n.* [L. *justiciarius.*] *Hist.* the chief officer, both political and judicial, of England during the reign of the Normans and Plantagenets.— **jus·ti·ci·ar·y,** ju·stish'ē·er"ē, *a.* Of or relating to the administration of justice.— *n. Law,* a chief judicial officer.

jus·ti·fi·a·ble, jus"ti·fī'a·bl, jus"ti·fī'a·bl, *a.* [Fr. *justifiable.*] Capable of being defended or shown to be just or right; defensible.— **jus·ti·fi·a·bil·i·ty,** **jus·ti·fi·a·ble·ness,** *n.*—**jus·ti·fi·a·bly,** *adv.*

jus·ti·fi·ca·tion, jus"ti·fi·kā'shan, *n.* [L.L. *justificatio*(*n-*).] The act of justifying; the state of being justified; a fact or circumstance that justifies; *theol.* the act whereby man is made or accounted just, or freed from the guilt or penalty of sin.—**jus·ti·-fi·ca·tive, jus·ti·fi·ca·to·ry,** jus'ti·fi·kã"-tiv, ju·stif'i·ka·tōr"ē, jus'ti·fi·kã'to·rē, *a.*

jus·ti·fy, jus'ti·fī", *v.t.*—*justified, justifying.* [O.Fr. Fr. *justifier,* < L.L. *justificāre,* < L. *jūstus,* just, and *facere,* to make.] To prove to be guiltless or blameless; vindicate; show to be just, right, or warranted, as: They *justify* their conduct. To furnish a reason or excuse for, as: The end *justifies* the means. *Law.* to declare guiltless; to acquit; to absolve. *Printing,* to adjust to the correct length by spacing, as lines of type; *theol.* to make just or righteous, free from the guilt or penalty of sin.—*v.i. Printing,* to be correctly spaced, as lines of type; *law,* to show a satisfactory reason for something done.—**jus·ti·fi·er,** *n.*—**jus·ti·fy·ing·ly,** *adv.*

jut, jut, *v.i.*—*jutted, jutting.* [A different spelling of *jet.*] To project beyond the main body.—*n.* That which juts; a projection.

jute, jŏt, *n.* [Hind. *jût.*] A fiber obtained from the plants of the genus *Corchorus* of the linden family, native to India and the East Indies, and used in the manufacture of gunny sacks, burlap, and other coarse cloths; the plant itself.

Jute, jŏt, *n.* [O.E. *Eōtas, Iōtas,* pl.] A member of a Low German tribe, said to have come from Jutland, Denmark, that invaded and settled in Britain in the 5th century.—**Jut·ish,** *a.*

ju·ve·nes·cent, jŭ"ve·nes'ent, *a.* [L. *juvenescens,* ppr. of *juvenesco,* to grow young.] Becoming young.—**ju·ve·nes·cence,** jŭ"ve·-nes'ens, *n.* The state of being juvenescent.

ju·ve·nile, jōo′ve·nil, jō′ve·nil, jō′ve·nil″, *a.* [L. *juvenilis*, < *juvenis*, young; cogn. Skt. *yuvan*, young, E. *young*.] Young; youthful; immature; pertaining or suited to youth; as, *juvenile* games.—*n.* A young person or youth; a children's book; a race horse two years of age; *theatr.* one who enacts youthful parts.—**ju·ve·nil·ism**, *n.*

ju·ve·nile court, *n.* A court exercising jurisdiction in cases concerning children under 18 who are neglected, dependent, or delinquent.

ju·ve·nile de·lin·quen·cy, *n.* The antisocial actions or legal violations of a minor, subject to the jurisdiction of a juvenile court.—**ju·ve·nile de·lin·quent**, *n.*

ju·ve·nile of·fic·er, *n.* A police officer who investigates, prosecutes, and looks after juvenile delinquents.

ju·ve·nil·i·a, jōo′ve·nil′ē·a, jō′ve·nil′ya, *n. pl.* Artistic works, such as writings, produced while young; writings or other artistic works intended for the young.

ju·ve·nil·i·ty, jōo′ve·nil′i·tē, *n. pl.* **ju·ve·nil·i·ties**. Youthfulness; an instance of childishness; immature behavior.

jux·ta·pose, juk″sta·pōz′, *v.t.*—**juxtaposed**, **juxtaposing**. [L. *juxta*, near, and E. *pose*.] To place near or next to; place side by side, often for comparing or contrasting.—**jux·ta·po·si·tion**, juk″sta·po·zish′an, *n.* The act of juxtaposing; state of being juxtaposed; proximity.—**jux·ta·po·si·tion·al**, *a.*

K

K, k, kā, *n.* The eleventh letter of the English alphabet, and the eighth consonant; the counterpart in speech of the letter K; something designated by or having the shape of the letter K or k; a printer's graphic device used for reproducing the letter K or k.

K, kā. *Games*, king; *computer*, the number 1000; *phys.* the Kelvin temperature scale; *chem.* potassium.

k., k, kā. Karat; kilogram; knight; *elect.* capacity; *math.* a constant or fixed quantity.

Kaa·ba, kä′ba, kä′a·ba, *n.* [Ar. *ka′bah*, < *ka′b*, cube.] A small cube-shaped building in the Great Mosque at Mecca, containing a sacred stone said to have been turned black by the tears of repentant pilgrims or by the sins of those who have touched it; this stone which Muslims face when praying; the destination of Islamic pilgrimages.

kab·a·la, kab′a·la, ka·bä′la, *n.* Cabala. Also **kab·ba·la**.

ka·bob, ka·bob′, *n.* Meat cut into cubes, usu. marinated, and broiled on a skewer with vegetables such as mushrooms, tomatoes, and onions. Also *kebab, kebob*.

ka·bu·ki, kä·bōo′kē, ka·bōo′kē, kä′bōo·kē, *n.* Drama popular in Japan, with dancing and singing performed in a manner which is highly stylized.

Kad·dish, kä′dēsh, kä′dish, *n.* [Aram. *qaddîsh*, 'holy.'] In Jewish ritual, a doxology recited during the daily prayers in the synagogue, esp. by mourners on behalf of the dead.

kaf·fee klatsch, kä′fä kläch″, kä′fä klach″, kä′fē kläch″, *n.* [G., 'coffee gossip.'] An informal gathering to drink coffee and chat. Also *coffee klatch*.

kaf·ir, kaf·fir, kaf′ẽr, kä′fẽr, *n.* A type of grain sorghum, cultivated in dry areas, with stout, leafy stalks used for fodder. (*Cap.*) a member of a S. African Bantu tribe.

kai·nite, kī′nīt, kā′nīt, *n.* [Gr. *kainos*, recent.] A mineral, consisting of hydrated magnesium sulfate and potassium chloride, that is used as a fertilizer and a source of potassium and magnesium.

kai·ser, kī′zẽr, *n.* [M.E. *kaiser, caisere* (O.E. *casere*), = G. *kaiser*, < L. *Caesar*, Caesar.] An emperor. (*Cap.*) title of the Holy Roman Emperors; title of Austrian emperors from 1804 to 1918; title of German rulers from 1871 to 1918.—**kai·ser·dom**, *n.*—**kai·ser·ism**, kī′ze·riz″um, *n.* Autocratic rule or government, as that of a kaiser.

ka·ka, kä′ka, *n.* [Maori.] Any of certain New Zealand parrots of the genus *Nestor*, with a chiefly olive-brown coloration.

ka·ka·po, kä″kä·pō′, *n. pl.* **ka·ka·pos**, kä″kä·pōz′. [Maori.] A large nocturnal parrot, *Strigops habroptilus*, of New Zealand with brownish-green coloration, which has well-developed wings but is practically flightless.

kale, kail, kāl, *n.* [Var. of *cole*.] One of several varieties of cabbage, *Brassica oleracea*, with curled leaves that do not form a head; *Sc.* any type of cabbage; *slang*, money.

ka·lei·do·scope, ka·lī′do·skōp″, *n.* [Gr. *kalos*, beautiful, *eidos*, form, and *skopeō*, to view.] An instrument which exhibits, by means of mirror reflection, a variety of beautiful colors and symmetrical forms, consisting in its simplest form of a tube containing two reflecting surfaces inclined at angles to each other and having loose pieces of colored glass inside; a changing or complex design or scene; as, the *kaleidoscope* of the election years.—**ka·lei·do·scop·ic**, **ka·lei·do·scop·i·cal**, *a.*—**ka·lei·do·scop·i·cal·ly**, *adv.*

kal·ends, kal′endz, *n.* Calends.

kale·yard school, kail·yard school, kāl′yärd″ skōl, *n.* A school of writers of the late 19th century, including J. M. Barrie and Ian Maclaren, who wrote of Scottish life in a sentimental manner, with heavy use of dialect.

kal·mi·a, kal′mē·a, *n.* [From Peter *Kalm*, a botanist.] *Bot.* one of several N. American evergreen shrubs of the genus *Kalmia*, in the heath family, having purple, pink, or white flowers in umbellike clusters. Also *mountain laurel*.

kal·so·mine, kal′so·mīn″, kal′so·min, *n.* Calcimine.

ka·ma·la, ka·mä′la, kam′a·la, *n.* [Of Asiatic origin.] A powdery substance obtained from an East Indian tree, used as a vermifuge and a dyestuff.

kame, kām, *n.* [Sc. var. of *comb*.] *Sc.* a comb for the hair. *Geol.* a ridge or mound of detrital material, esp. one left by a retreating ice sheet; an esker.

kam·ik, käm′ik, *n. Canada*, a boot, knee-high in length, made of sealskin and worn mostly in the eastern arctic regions.

ka·mi·ka·ze, kä″mi·kä′zē, *n.* A Japanese pilot of World War II who flew a suicidal mission by heading an airplane laden with explosives into an enemy ship or other target; the airplane used on such a mission.

kam·pong, käm′pang, käm′pong, käm-pang′, käm·pong′, *n.* A local village or group of dwelling places in countries which speak Malay.

kan·ga·roo, kang″ga·rō′, *n. pl.* **kan·ga·roos**, kan·ga·roo. Any of certain marsupials of Australia, with long powerful hind legs for leaping, small short forelegs, and a long broad tail.

kan·ga·roo court, *n.* A court, irregular in procedure and without official authorization, where the law is deliberately misinterpreted or totally disregarded; a mock court which parodies legal procedure.

Kant·i·an, kan′tē·an, *a.* Relating to the German philosopher Immanuel Kant, or to his ideas.—*n.* One who follows Kant.—**Kant·i·an·ism**, *n.* The philosophy of Kant.

ka·o·lin, ka·o·line, kā′o·lin, *n.* [Chinese *kau-ling*, high ridge, the name of a hill where it was found.] A mineral clay that remains white after firing, used in manufacturing high grade porcelain, paper, cloth, window shades, paint, and soaps.

ka·o·lin·ite, kā′o·li·nīt″, *n.* A mineral, $Al_2Si_2O_5(OH)_4$, that is the main ingredient of kaolin.

Ka·pell·meis·ter, kä·pel′mī″stẽr, *n. pl.* **Ka·pell·meis·ter**. [G.] The director of an orchestra, choir, or band.

ka·pok, kā′pok, *n.* [Malay *kãpoq*.] The silky mass which covers the seeds of a silk-cotton tree, *Ceiba pentandra*, of the East Indies, Africa, and tropical America: used esp. in stuffing pillows, sleeping bags, and for insulation. Also **Ja·va cot·ton**.

kap·pa, kap′a, *n.* [Gr.] The tenth letter of the Greek alphabet, K, k, equivalent to English K, k.

ka·put, kä·pŏot′, kä·pŏt′, ka·pŏot′, ka·pŏt′, *a. Slang.* Done for; dead; not in working order; having no possibility of success.

kar·a·bi·ner, car·a·bi·ner, kar″a·bē′nẽr, *n.* A steel ring used by mountain climbers which is inserted into a piton to carry a rope.

kar·a·kul, kar′a·kul, *n.* A breed of sheep native to central Asia which has black fleece in infancy and brown or gray fleece in adulthood. The curly black fleece of the newborn karakul lamb, valuable as a fur; also *caracul*.

kar·at, kar′at, *n.* A measure of the fineness of gold determined by the weight of pure gold in a twenty-fourth part of an alloy; a measure of weight for precious gems. Abbr. *k., kt.* See *carat*.

ka·ra·te, ka·rä′tē, *n.* A method of combat, developed in Japan, in which the hands, feet, knees, and elbows are used to inflict quick, damaging blows on an opponent.

kar·ma, kär′ma, *n.* [Skt., act, fate.] *Hinduism, Buddhism*, the quality of a person's actions in one existence which determines his destiny in the next; destiny, fate.—**kar·mic**, *a.*

ka·ross, ka·ros′, *n. Southern Africa.* A garment worn by the natives, made by sewing animal skins together in the shape of a square; a rug made of animal skins.

kar·roo, ka·roo, ka·rō′, *n.* [Hottentot *karusa*, hard, < the hardness of their soil under drought.] A large arid tableland of South Africa.

kar·y·o·ki·ne·sis, kar″ē·ō·ki·nē′sis, kar″ē·ō·kī·nē′sis, *n.* [Gr. *karyon*, a nut, *kinēsis*, movement.] *Biol.* Mitosis; changes within the nucleus of a live cell during division.—**kar·y·o·ki·net·ic**, *a.*

kar·y·o·lymph, kar′ē·o·limf″, *n. Biol.* the transparent substance which surrounds the nucleus of a cell.

kar·y·o·plasm, kar′ē·o·plaz″um, *n. Biol.* the substance of the nucleus of a cell.—**kar·y·o·plas·mic**, *a.*

kar·y·o·some, kar′ē·o·sōm″, *n. Biol.* a chromatin mass in the nucleus of a cell.

kar·y·o·type, kar′ē·o·tīp″, *n. Genetics*, the total characteristics of a cell's nucleus, esp. its size, form, and chromosome number.

Kas·bah, kaz′ba, kaz′bä, käz′ba, käz′bä, *n.* Casbah.

Kash·mir goat, kash′mẽr gōt, *n.* A goat indigenous to India, raised for its soft delicate wool from which cashmere goods are made.

Kash·mir·i·an, kash·mẽr′ē·an, *a.* [From *Kashmir*, a region in southwest Asia.] Pertaining to or characteristic of Kashmir or the Kashmiri.—*n.*—**Kash·mir·i**, *n.* An inhabitant or native of Kashmir; the language spoken by the people of Kashmir.

ch- chain, G. na*ch*t; **th-** *TH*en, *th*in; **w-** *w*ig, h*w* as sound in *wh*ig; **z-** *zh* as in a*z*ure, *z*eal. *Italicized vowel* indicates schwa sound.

ka·thar·sis, ka·thär′sis, *n.* Catharsis.

ka·ty·did, kā′tē·did, *n.* [Imit. of the sound made.] *Entom.* any of several pale-green, long-horned grasshoppers of the family *Tettigoniidae,* with stridulating organs on the wings which produce shrill sounds.

katz·en·jam·mer, kat″sen·jam′ér, *n.* [G., lit. 'cats' sickness.'] Indisposition following intoxication; a feeling of worry, uneasiness, or nervousness.

kau·ri, kou′rē, *n.* pl. **kau·ris.** [Native name.] A coniferous tree of New Zealand, yielding valuable resin used in varnish, and timber used in construction; any of the other trees of the genus *Agathis.*

ka·va, kä′va, *n.* A Polynesian shrub of the pepper family; an intoxicating beverage made from this shrub.

kay·ak, kai·ak, kī′ak, *n.* [Eskimo name.] A fishing boat or canoe of arctic America, made of sealskins stretched around a wooden frame, with a circular opening in the middle for the occupant. Also *kyak, kyack.*

kay·o, kā′ō′, *n.* pl. **kay·os.** *Boxing,* a knock-out.—*v.t.* To knock out, as an opponent, in boxing.

ka·zoo, ka·zö′, *n.* pl. **ka·zoos.** A toy musical device having a tube open at both ends and a hole in the side containing a membrane through which the player hums or sings to produce a buzzing sound. Also **ga·zoo.**

ke·a, kā′a, kē′a, *n.* [Maori.] A large, greenish, New Zealand parrot, *Nestor notabilis.*

ke·bab, ke·bob, kā′bob, ke·bob′, *n.* Kabob.

kedge, kej, *v.t.*—*kedged, kedging.* [Softened form of *keg;* Icel. *kaggi,* a keg, a cask fastened as a float to an anchor, hence, the anchor itself.] To move or haul, as a ship, by pulling a rope attached to a dropped anchor.—*v.i.* To put into motion by being warped or kedged.—*n.* A small anchor used to keep a ship steady when riding in a harbor or river, or to assist in warping her; also **kedge an·chor.**

keek, kēk, *v.i.* [M.E. *kiken* = D. *kijken* = L.G. *kieken,* peep.] *Sc., North. E.* to peep, peek; as, to *keek* through a hole.

keel, kēl, *n.* [Prob. partly < M.D. *kiel* = O.E. *cēol,* ship, boat, partly < Scand. Cf. Icel. *kjolr,* keel of a vessel.] A longitudinal structure extending along the middle of the bottom of a vessel from stem to stern and supporting the whole frame; a corresponding part in some other structure, as in a dirigible balloon. *Biol.* a longitudinal ridge, as on a leaf or bone; a carina. (*Cap.*), *astron.* the constellation Carina.—**keel·less,** *a.*

keel, kēl, *v.t., v.i.* To turn over or become turned, with the keel uppermost.—**keel o·ver,** to fall bringing the wrong side uppermost; to fall over or faint suddenly.

keel·age, kē′lij, *n.* The fee charged for mooring a ship in port.

keel·boat, kēl′bōt″, *n.* A shallow freight boat or barge, built with a keel, used mainly on rivers of the western U.S.—**keel·boat·man,** kēl′bōt″man, *n.*

keel·haul, kēl′hạl″, *v.t. Naut.* to punish by dropping into the sea on one side of a ship and hauling up on the other; *fig.* to sternly punish or reproach.

keel·son, kel′son, kēl′son, *n.* [Dan. *kjolsviin,* Sw. *kolsvin,* G. *kielschwein,* lit. 'keelswine'; akin *pig* of lead.] *Naut.* an internal beam laid on the middle of the floor timbers over the keel.

keen, kēn, *a.* [O.E. *cēne* = D. *koen* = G. *kühn,* bold, = Icel. *kaenn,* wise, skillful.] So shaped as to cut or pierce substances readily; as, a *keen* blade; sharp, piercing, or biting, as wind or cold; characterized by strength and distinctness of perception, as hearing, sight, or sense of smell; having or showing great mental penetration or acumen; as, *keen* reasoning; animated by or showing strong feeling or desire; as, *keen* competition; intense, as feeling or desire;

ardent, eager; cutting or stinging, as satire; *slang,* extremely good, excellent.—**keen·ly,** *adv.*—**keen·ness,** *n.*

keen, kēn, *v.i.* [< Ir.: cf Ir. *caoinim,* I lament.] To wail in lamentation over the dead.—*n.* A wailing lament for the dead.—**keen·er,** *n.*

keep, kēp, *v.t.*—*kept, keeping.* [O.E. *cēpan,* observe, heed, regard, await, take; origin and connections unknown.] Possess or have; fulfill, as a promise; support, as a family; care for; maintain, as records or a journal; protect, as: God *keep* us. Detain, as: I am sorry to *keep* you so long. Continue; employ, as: She *keeps* a full-time maid. Retain; restrain; withhold; to stock; as: He *keeps* silks and woolens on hand. Entertain; save; prevent, usu. with *from;* manage; preserve, as: This plastic wrap *keeps* vegetables for several days. To maintain or conduct the activities of; as, to *keep* a shop; to hold in custody or under guard, as a prisoner; to observe with formalities or rites, as a holiday; to maintain one's position in or on, as: *Keep* your seat.

keep, kēp, *v.i.*—*kept, keeping.* To remain or stay, as: *Keep* off. Continue or persist in a position, state, action, or course; to continue unimpaired or without spoiling; as, milk that will *keep;* to admit of being reserved for a future occasion; as, news that will *keep.*—**keep in with,** *colloq.* to keep oneself in favor or friendly relations with, as a person.—**keep to one·self,** to hold aloof from the society of others; to maintain a secret.

keep, kēp, *n.* Keeping, maintenance, or support, or the means of keeping; care; the most secure tower in a medieval castle; a dungeon.—**for keeps,** with complete seriousness; permanently.—**keep·a·ble,** *a.*

keep back, *v.t.* To reserve, or withhold, as money or information; to restrain or prevent.—*v.i.* To stop oneself from advancing or approaching near.

keep·er, kē′pér, *n.* Someone who guards, maintains, or exercises responsibility for a person, place, or thing; a person who observes or has respect for a requirement, as one who conforms to the law or abides by his word; a mechanism for holding a thing in place, as a latch, guard ring, or clasp; something that resists spoiling, as a fruit or vegetable.

keep·ing, kē′ping, *n.* Possession or charge; just proportion; harmony or conformity; support or maintenance.—**be in keep·ing with,** accord or harmonize with; be consistent with.

keep off, *v.t.* To avert or fend off, as an attack.—*v.i.* To remain at a distance or stay back.

keep·sake, kēp′sāk″, *n.* Anything kept or given to be kept as a souvenir or as a remembrance of the giver; a token of friendship; a memento.

keep up, *v.t.* To continue, persist in, or sustain; to prevent from falling.—*v.i.* To remain even or equal to; as, to *keep up* with the neighbors; to stay well-informed; to go on without interruption.

keet, keat, kēt, *n. Ornith.* guinea fowl, esp. a fledgling.

kef, kāf, *n.* [Ar. *kaif,* undisturbed.] A dreamy and tranquil state; a narcotic, as hemp, which when smoked produces such a state. Also **keef, kief,** *kif.*

keg, keg, *n.* [Formerly *kag;* Icel. *kaggi,* Sw. *kagge,* a keg.] A small cask or barrel, usu. having a capacity of 5 to 10 gallons; a unit for measuring the weight of nails which equals 100 pounds.

keg·ler, keg′lér, *n.* [G.] *Slang.* One who bowls; a bowler.

ke·loid, kē′loid, *n. Pathol.* a fibrous growth originating in the connective skin tissue. Also **che·loid.**—**ke·loi·dal,** *a.*

kelp, kelp, *n.* [Origin unknown.] Any of various large seaweeds, chiefly of the families *Fucaceæ* and *Laminariaceæ,* such as are burned to obtain the carbonate of soda and iodine that they contain; the ash of such seaweeds.

kel·pie, kel·py, kel′pē, *n.* pl. **kel·pies.** [Perh. connected with *yelp,* < his bellowing.] In Scottish folklore, an evil water sprite, taking the shape of a horse, and often thought to cause or foretell drownings.

kel·pie, kel′pē, *n.* A medium-sized breed of sheepherding dog, developed in Australia by crossing various British breeds of sheep-dogs with the dingo.

Kel·tic, kel′tik, *a.* Celtic.—**Kelt,** *n.* Celt.

Kel·vin, kel′vin, *a.* [From Lord *Kelvin,* British physicist, 1824–1907.] *Phys.* pertaining to the scale used to measure absolute temperature, zero being equal to −459.4 Fahrenheit.

kemp, kemp, *n.* [Cf. Icel. *kampr,* beard, whiskers of an animal.] A coarse hairlike fiber used mainly in carpeting.—**kemp·y,** *a.*

ken, ken, *v.t.*—*kenned, kenning.* [O.E. *cennan* = Goth. *kannjan,* make known, = Icel. *kenna,* make known, know (cf. later E. senses), = G. *kennen,* know; orig. a causative of the verb represented by E. *can.*] *Sc.* to know; be acquainted with; recognize. *Archaic,* descry or see.—*v.i. Sc., Brit. dial.* to have knowledge of something. —*n.* Knowledge or cognizance; mental perception, as: The concept is beyond his *ken.*

ke·naf, ke·naf′, *n.* A plant of the mallow family, *Hibiscus cannabinus,* native to the E. Indies, which yields a fiber used in cordage. Also **am·ba·ry.**

Ken·dal green, ken′dal grēn, *n.* [From *Kendal,* in Westmorland, England, where it was made.] A green woolen cloth of coarse texture; the green color of this cloth, produced by a process employing the woad-waxen plant.

ken·nel, ken′el, *n.* [Norm. Fr., < *ken,* Fr. *chien,* a dog, < L. *canis,* a dog.] A shelter for dogs; a doghouse; *often pl.* a place where dogs are bred or boarded. A pack of dogs; the lair or den of a wild animal, usu. a fox; vile living quarters.—*v.i.*—*kenneled, kenneling, kennelled, kennelling.* To live in a kennel, as a dog.—*v.t.* To keep or confine in a kennel.

ken·nel, ken′el, *n.* [A form of *channel, canal.*] The watercourse of a street; a gutter.

Ken·nel·ly-Heav·i·side lay·er, ken′e-lē·hev′ē·sīd″ lā′ér, *n.* E layer, Heaviside layer.

ken·ning, ken′ing, *n.* [Partly < *ken,* v., partly < the related Icel. *kenning,* descriptive name, appellative.] Just enough to be recognized or perceived; a very small amount. In Old Norse, Anglo-Saxon, and early Teutonic poetry, a descriptive poetical name used for, or in addition to, the usual name of a person or thing, as 'a wave traveler' for 'a boat.'

Ken·ny meth·od, ken′ē meth′od, *n. Med.* a procedure for the treatment of poliomyelitis involving both hot applications and exercise.

ke·no, kē′nō, *n.* [Cf. Fr. *quine,* row of five numbers at lotto; < L. *quini,* five each, distributive of *quinque,* five.] A game of chance, adapted from lotto for gambling purposes.

Kent·ish, ken′tish, *a.* Of or pertaining to the English county of Kent or its inhabitants; of or pertaining to the former English kingdom of Kent, its inhabitants, or the Old English or Middle English dialects spoken there.

kent·ledge, kent′lij, *n.* Pig iron used for permanent ballast in a ship.

Ken·tuck·y blue·grass, *n.* [From its jointed, bluish-green stem.] One of the blue grasses, *Poa pratensis*, growing in tufts and having bluish-green stems, a favorite pasture and lawn grass in central U.S. Also **June grass.**

Ken·tuck·y cof·fee tree, *n.* A tree in the legume family, *Gymnocladus dioica*, having thick, woody pods whose seeds were once used as a coffee bean substitute.

kep·i, kā′pē, kep′ē, *n.* A visored military cap with a flat top, used by the French army.

ker·a·tin, ker′a·tin, *n.* [Gr. *keras, keratos,* horn.] *Biochem.* an insoluble albumoid, containing sulfur, present in horns, hair, and nails.

ker·a·to·plas·ty, ker′a·tō·plas″tē, *n.* [Gr. *keras,* horn, cornea, and *-plasty.*] *Surg.* the operation by which damaged corneal tissue is replaced by healthy corneal tissue.—**ker·a·to·plas·tic**, *a.*

ker·a·to·sis, ker″a·tō′sis, *n. pl.* **ker·a·to·-ses**, ker″a·tō′sēz. *Pathol.* a growth of horny tissue on the skin. Also **ker·a·to·der·ma, ker·a·to·ma.**—**ker·a·to·sic, ker·a·tot·ic,** ker″a·tot′ik, *a.*

kerb, kẽrb, *n. Brit.* curb.

ker·chief, kẽr′chif, *n. pl.* **ker·chiefs, ker·chieves**, kẽr′chēvz. [O.E. *coverchief,* O.Fr. *couvrechef*—Fr. *couvrir,* to cover, and *chef,* the head.] A cloth to dress or cover the head or shoulders; a loose cloth worn about the neck; a handkerchief.—**ker·chiefed, ker·chieft,** *a.*

kerf, kẽrf, *n.* [O.E. *cyrf,* a cutting, < *ceorfan,* cut, E. *carve.*] The cut or incision made by a saw or other cutting instrument; the place at which a tree or branch is or has been cut across; something which is or has been cut off; a cutting.—*v.t.* To make a cut or kerf in.

ker·mes, kẽr′mēz, *n.* [Ar. and Pers. *kermes, kirmis,* < Skt. *krimi,* a worm; *crimson, carmine,* are derivatives.] A scarlet dyestuff consisting of the dried bodies of the female insect, *Kermes ilices,* found on various species of oak around the Mediterranean.

ker·mis, ker·mess, kir·mess, kẽr′mis, *n.* [D. *kermis,* earlier *kermisse, kerkmisse,* 'church mass' on the anniversary of the dedication of a church.] In the Low Countries, an annual fair or festival with sports and merrymaking; an entertainment, usu. for charitable purposes.

kern, kẽrn, *n.* [Fr. *carne,* projecting angle, < L. *cardo,* hinge.] *Print.* a part of the face of a type projecting beyond the body or shank. —*v.t.* To form or furnish with a kern.

kern, kerne, kẽrn, *n.* [O.Gael. and Ir. *cearn,* a man.] *Archaic,* a lightly armed foot soldier or band of soldiers of ancient Ireland and the Highlands of Scotland. A boorish fellow of Scotland and Ireland.

ker·nel, kẽr′nel, *n.* [O.E. *cyrnel,* a little corn, a kernel, dim. of *corn,* a grain.] The usu. edible substance contained in the shell of a nut, in a seed, or in the stone of a fruit; a grain of corn or wheat; the main or essential part of a matter; core; gist.—*v.t.*— *kerneled, kerneling, Brit. kernelled, kernel-ling.* To ripen into kernels.—**ker·nel·ly,** *a.*

ker·o·sene, ker·o·sine, ker′o·sēn″, kar′o·-sēn″, ker″o·sēn′, kar′o·sēn′, *n.* [Gr. *keros,* wax.] A liquid hydrocarbon distilled from coals, bitumen, or petroleum and extensively used in lamps and stoves as a fuel, and as a cleaning agent or solvent. Also *coal oil; Brit.* **par·af·fin** or **par·af·fin oil.**

ker·ri·a, ker′ē·a, *n. Bot.* a shrub of the rose family, *Kerria japonica,* native to Japan, and having ridged, green stems and single or double yellow flowers.

Ker·ry, ker′ē, *n. pl.* **Ker·ries.** [From the Irish county of *Kerry.*] One of a breed of small, black, dairy cattle raised in the southwest of Ireland.

Ker·ry blue ter·ri·er, *n.* A terrier, native to Ireland, long-headed, and bluish-gray in color.

ker·sey, kẽr′zē, *n. pl.* **ker·seys.** [Said to be from *Kersey,* in Suffolk, England.] A coarse woolen or woolen and cotton cloth used primarily for outer wear and other rugged garments.—*a.*

ker·sey·mere, kẽr′zi·mēr, *n.* A cloth made of fine wool in a twill weave; cassimere.

ke·ryg·ma, ki·rig′ma, *n. pl.* **ke·ryg·ma·ta,** ki·rig′ma·ta. The apostolic preaching about the life and teachings of Jesus as the Christ.—**ker·yg·mat·ic,** ker″ig·mat′ik, *a.*

kes·trel, kes′trel, *n.* [Cf. O.Fr. *cresserele* (Fr. *crécerelle*), kestrel.] A common small European falcon inhabiting moors, coasts, and farmland, and noted for hovering in the air with its head to the wind.

ketch, kech, *n.* [Earlier *catch,* appar. < *catch, v.*] A fore-and-aft rigged vessel with two masts, a large mainmast toward the bow, and a smaller mizzenmast toward the stern but in front of the rudder.

ketch·up, kech′up, kach′up, *n.* [Malay *kēchap,* a kind of East Indian pickle.] A sauce for meat and fish, made from mushrooms or unripe walnuts, or tomatoes; usu. a thick, seasoned tomato sauce. Also *catchup, catsup.*

ke·tene, kē′tēn, *n. Chem.* a poisonous, colorless gas, $H_2C=C=O$, with a penetrating odor, obtained from the pyrolysis of acetone or acetic anhydride; any of a class of related compounds.

ke·to, kē′tō, *a. Chem.* pertaining to or containing a ketone.

ke·to·gen·e·sis, kē″tō·jen′i·sis, *n. Med.* the production, within the body, of ketone bodies, esp. in diabetics.—**ke·to·ge·net·ic,** kē″tō·je·net′ik, *a.*

ke·tol, kē′tol, *n. Chem.* an organic compound including both an alcohol and a ketone group.

ke·tone, kē′tōn, *n.* [G. *keton,* < *aceton,* acetone.] *Chem.* any of a class of organic compounds, as acetone, each consisting of a carbonyl group united to one bivalent or two monovalent hydrocarbon radicals, and often used as solvents in industry.— **ke·ton·ic,** ki·ton′ik, *a.*—**ke·to·sis,** ki·tō′-sis, *n. Pathol.* an abnormal accumulation of ketones in the body.

ke·tone bod·y, *n. Biochem.* Acetone body; any acetone, beta-hydroxybutyric acid, or acetoacetic acid present in the blood or urine, esp. of diabetics.

ke·tose, kē′tōs, *n. Chem.* a monosaccharide having a ketone group.

ket·tle, ket′l, *n.* [O.E. *cetel* = D. *ketel* = G. *kessel* = Icel. *ketill* = Goth. *katils,* kettle: cf. L. *catillus,* dim. of *catinus,* bowl, pot.] A vessel, usu. of metal, for boiling liquids, esp. a teakettle; a pot.—**ket·tle hole,** *n.* A pothole.

ket·tle·drum, ket′l·drum″, *n.* A drum consisting of a hollow hemisphere of brass or copper, with a head of parchment whose pitch may be adjusted.

ket·tle of fish, *n.* An awkward situation; a mess; a matter being considered.

key, kē, *n.* [O.E. *cǣg* = O.Fries. *kei, kai,* key.] An instrument for fastening or opening a lock by moving its bolt; something that secures or controls entrance to a place; a means of attaining, understanding, or solving; a book or the like containing the solutions of mathematical or other problems presented elsewhere as exercises; a taxonomic listing of the characteristics of a group of organisms for purposes of identification and comparison; explanatory notes on the abbreviations or symbols used on a map or graph; matter inserted in an advertisement in a magazine or the like, to enable the advertiser to identify the source of replies to it; a pin, bolt, wedge, or other piece inserted in a hole or space to lock or hold parts of a mechanism or structure together; a cotter; *arch.* a keystone. A con-

trivance for grasping and turning a bolt or nut; a hand-operated switch which opens or closes an electric circuit, as in telegraphy; *carp.* a wedge of hardwood used to strengthen a joint; a rough texture on a surface which improves its adhesive qualities, as for plaster or glue. One of a set of levers or parts pressed in operating a piano, organ, flute, telegraph, typewriter, or other mechanism; (*cap.*), *pl.* a body of twenty-four representatives constituting the lower or elective branch of the legislature of the Isle of Man; *bot.* a samara; *mus.* a scale or system of notes or tones based on a particular note; the sum of relations, melodic and harmonic, existing between the tones of such a system; tonality. Tone or pitch, as of voice; as, to speak in a high *key;* strain, or characteristic style, as of expression or thought; degree of intensity, as of feeling or action; *photog.* the tonal quality which dominates a photograph.—*a.* Acting or operating like a key; controlling; of chief or critical importance; pivotal; fundamental; as, the *key* industries of a nation.

key, kē, *v.t.* To lock with or as with a key; to fasten, secure, or adjust with a key, wedge, or the like, as parts of a mechanism; insert the keystone in, as an arch; to regulate the key or pitch of; to adjust as if to a particular key; to bring to a particular degree of intensity of feeling, excitement or energy, usu. followed by *up;* to provide with a key or keys; insert a key in, as an advertisement.

key, kē, *n.* A reef or islet, esp. one formed of coral. Also *cay.*

key·board, kē′bōrd″, *n.* The series of keys in a musical instrument, as a piano or organ, or in a typewriter or typesetting machine.

key club, *n.* A nightclub where members are given door keys upon payment of a set fee.

keyed, kēd, *a.* Having a key or keys; marked with symbols, as a map and its caption; adjusted, harmonized; *mus.* in a specific key.

key·hole, kē′hōl″, *n.* A hole into which a key is inserted, as in a lock; *basketball,* the area on the court from behind which free throws may be made.

key·hole, kē′hōl″, *a.* Pertaining to information of a very private or intimate nature, esp. such information gained by spying.

key·note, kē′nōt″, *n. Mus.* the note or tone on which a key, or system of tones, is founded; the tonic. The determining principle of a speech, thought, action, or program.—*v.t.*—*keynoted, keynoting.* To establish the keynote of; to declare publicly the principles of, as of a political convention.—**key·not·er,** *n.* The person making a keynote address.

key·note address, *n.* A speech, as at a political convention, to present the basic issues of the party or its candidates, and to arouse enthusiasm. Also **key·note speech.**

key punch, *n. Computer,* a keyboard-activated machine which, by systematically punching holes in cards, codes information for use in data processing.

key ring, *n.* A ring, usu. metal, on which keys are kept.

key sig·na·ture, *n. Mus.* the sharps or flats which follow the clef sign and denote the key.

key·stone, kē′stōn″, *n. Arch.* the stone at the apex of an arch which locks the whole. A part of something on which the other parts depend.

key·way, kē′wā″, *n.* An aperture for the reception of a key; *mach.* a groove or slot cut in a shaft or wheel hub for the reception of a key.

key word, *n.* A word of special significance in relation to other words, phrases, or the like; a word that precisely expresses the meaning of a written or spoken text; a word that unlocks a puzzle such as a cryptogram.

---

ch- chain, G. na*ch*t; **th-** THen, thin; **w-** wig, hw as sound in whig; **z-** zh as in azure, zeal. *Italicized vowel* indicates schwa sound.

khad·dar, kä′dẽr, *n. India,* a cloth made of homespun cotton. Also **kha·di**, kä′dē.

khak·i, kak′ē, kä′kē, *n. pl.* **khak·is.** [Hind. *khākī,* dusty, < *khāk,* dust.] A stout, twilled cotton cloth of a yellowish-brown or olive-brown color, much used for military uniforms; a similar fabric of wool; a dull yellowish-brown color; *often pl.* clothing, esp. a military uniform, made of khaki.—*a.* Dust-colored; dull yellowish-brown; made of khaki.

kha·lif, ka·lēf′, kā′lif, kal′if, *n.* Caliph. Also **kha·li·fa.**

kham·sin, kam′sin, kam·sēn′, *n.* [Ar. *khamsin,* fifty, because it blows about fifty days.] A hot southerly wind in Egypt. Also **kham·seen, kam·sin.**

khan, kän, kan, *n.* [Tatar and Turk. *Khān.*] The sovereign of China and the Tatar tribes in the Middle Ages; the title held by descendants of Genghis Khan, the Mongol conqueror; a term of respect for officials or dignitaries in parts of central Asia.—**khan·ate,** *n.* The dominion or jurisdiction of a khan.

khan, kän, kan, *n.* [Pers. *khān,* a house.] In some Oriental countries, an inn; a caravansary.

khed·a, ked·dah, ked′a, *n.* [Hind. *kheda.*] In India, an enclosure constructed to trap wild elephants.

khe·dive, ke·dēv′, *n.* The title given to a Turkish viceroy in Egypt during the late 19th and early 20th centuries.—**khe·di·val, khe·di·vi·al,** *a.*

ki·ang, ky·ang, kē·ang′, *n.* [Tibetan.] A wild variety of ass, *Equus hemionus kiang,* inhabiting Tibet and Mongolia.

kib·ble, kib′l, *n.* [Cf. G. *kübel,* tub, bucket.] *Brit.* a large bucket for hoisting ore in the shaft of a mine.

kib·butz, ki·buts′, ki·böts′, *n. pl.* **kib··but·zim,** ki·but·sēm′. An Israeli settlement or farm operating under a collectivist system.

kibe, kīb, *n.* [M.E. *kybe;* perh. < Welsh.] A chapped or ulcerated chilblain, esp. on the heel.

kib·itz·er, kib′it·sẽr, *n.* [Yiddish < G. *kiebitzen,* to look on < *kiebitz,* a bothersome spectator.] *Colloq.* one who gives unwanted advice, esp. such a person looking on at a card game.—**kib·itz,** kib′its, *v.i.*

ki·bosh, kī′bosh, ki·bosh′, *n. Slang,* that which tends to arrest or squelch; *archaic,* nonsense.—**put the ki·bosh on,** *slang,* to squelch or stop.

kick, kik, *v.t.* [M.E. *kiken;* perh. imit.] To give a blow to with the foot; to strike in return, as firearms; to drive or force by or as by a kick with the foot; as, to *kick* the chair away; *football,* to score, as a field goal, by kicking the ball.—*v.i.* To strike out with the foot; to have the habit of striking out; as, a colt which playfully *kicks;* to recoil, as a firearm when fired; *colloq.* to object or complain; as, to *kick* about doing chores.— **kick a·round,** *slang.* To use harshly; to discuss all phases and possibilities of.— **kick in,** *slang.* To pay one's share; to contribute, esp. money; to die.—**kick out,** *colloq.* to oust or dismiss forcefully.—**kick the buck·et,** *slang,* to die.—**kick·er,** *n.*

kick, kik, *n.* An act of kicking; a blow or thrust with the foot; a recoil, as of a gun; the indentation in the bottom of a glass bottle; *football,* an occurrence of kicking the ball; *colloq.* an objection or complaint. *Slang,* a stimulating or intoxicating quality in alcoholic drink; a thrill or exciting sensation; as, to get a big *kick* from winning; a new interest or activity; as, skin diving, her latest *kick;* vigor and energy; as, plenty of *kick* left in the old man; *pl., slang,* enjoyment or fun.

kick·back, kik′bak″, *n. Slang.* The return of a portion of a commission or payment in accordance with a secret agreement; a sudden recoil or reaction.

kick·off, kik′ạf, kik′of″, *n.* The initial play, esp. kicking the ball in a football or soccer game, repeated after scoring and after half-time; *fig.* the start or beginning. Also **kick off.**

kick off, *v.i. Colloq.* to kick a ball to start play; *slang,* to die.—*v.t. Colloq.* to begin or initiate, as: He will *kick off* the festivities. *Sports, slang,* to remove or dismiss, esp. an amateur player, from a team in competitive sports.

kick·shaw, kik′shạ″, *n.* [Orig. *kickshaws,* as a sing. noun, < Fr. *quelque chose,* something.] Something of little value, as a trinket; a light, unsubstantial dish; a delicacy.

kick turn, *n. Skiing,* a stationary half-turn executed by placing one ski at an angle to the other, and then adjusting the other ski to a position parallel to the first.

kick·up, kik′up″, *n. Colloq.* a disturbance or quarrel.

kick up, *v.t.* To elevate by kicking; *colloq.* to cause to occur; as, to *kick up* a disturbance.—*v.i.* To furnish evidence of disturbance or malfunction; as, an ulcer which *kicks up* periodically.

kid, kid, *n.* [Scand.: cf. Icel. *kidh,* Sw. and Dan. *kid,* and G. *kitze,* kid.] A young goat, or its flesh; the skin of a young goat, or leather made from it; *pl.* gloves or shoes of this leather. *Colloq.* a child or young person. —*v.t., v.i.*—*kidded, kidding.* Of a goat, to give birth to.—**kid·dish·ness,** *n.*—**kid·like,** *a.*

kid, kid, *v.t.*—*kidded, kidding.* [Appar. < *kid, n.*] *Slang.* To tease, jest with, or banter; to deceive or fool; to make good-natured fun of.—*v.i.* To speak or act deceptively in jest; jest.—**kid·der,** *n.*— **kid·ding·ly,** *adv.*

Kid·der·min·ster, kid′ẽr·min″stẽr, *n.* [From *Kidderminster,* town in Worcestershire, England.] A type of ingrain, two-ply carpet with the colors appearing reversed on either side.

Kid·dush, kid′ush, *Heb.* ki·dösh′, *n. Heb.* the prayer or blessing said over the wine at the evening meal, esp. on the eve of the Sabbath or a festival.

kid glove, *n.* A smooth dress glove of kidskin or a material similar in appearance to kidskin.—**with kid gloves,** *fig.* With tender or special regard; with tact.—**kid·gloved,** *a.* Wearing kid gloves; *fig.* considered refined, delicate, or gracious in action or manner.

kid·nap, kid′nap, *v.t.*—*kidnaped, kidnaping, kidnapped, kidnapping.* [Slang E. *kid,* a child, and *nap* for *nab,* to steal.] To seize and forcibly carry away, as a person, usu. for ransom.—**kid·nap·er, kid·nap·per,** *n.*

kid·ney, kid′nē, *n. pl.* **kid·neys.** [M.E. *kidenei;* origin obscure.] In man, either of a pair of glandular organs, about four inches in length, in the back part of the abdominal cavity, which excrete urine; a corresponding organ in other vertebrate animals, or an organ of like function in invertebrate animals; an animal kidney which is eaten by man as food. *Fig.* constitution or temperament.—**float·ing kid·ney,** *pathol.* a kidney which has become loose and displaced in the abdomen.—**kid·ney·like,** *a.*

kid·ney bean, *n.* The common bean plant, *Phaseolus vulgaris,* or its kidney-shaped seed.

kid·skin, kid′skin″, *n.* Leather processed from the hide of a young goat.—*a.*

kier, kēr, *n.* [Cf. Icel. *ker,* vessel, tub.] A large boiler or vat used in bleaching and dyeing.

kie·sul·guhr, kē′zel·gụr, *n.* [G. < *kiesel,* flint, and *guhr,* earthy deposit.] A fine siliceous earth composed chiefly of diatomaceous remains, and commercially valuable as an absorbent or polishing powder; diatomaceous earth.

kif, kif, *n.* Kef.

kil·der·kin, kil′dẽr·kin, *n.* [M.D. *kindeken;* origin uncertain: cf. *firkin.*] A cask holding half a barrel; a measure of capacity of this amount.

kill, kil, *v.t.* [M.E. *cullen, kyllen;* origin uncertain.] To deprive of life in any manner; cause the death of; slaughter; to destroy; put an end to; as, to *kill* sound; defeat or veto, as a legislative bill; *print.* to cancel or delete, as a word, paragraph, or item. To destroy or neutralize the active qualities of; as, to *kill* land in farming; to bring to a stop; as, to *kill* the engine; to stem; as, *kill* the circuit; spoil the effect of, as: General laughter *killed* the speaker's lofty climax. To while away, as time; to tire to the point of exhaustion; *sports,* to powerfully hit, as a ball. *Slang,* to overcome completely or with irresistible effect; as, jokes that *kill* me; to consume totally, as a drink.—*v.i.* To inflict or cause death; to commit murder.

kill, kil, *n.* The act of killing; an animal killed, as by a hunter or by a beast of prey.

kill, kil, *n.* [D. *kil.*] A channel; a creek; a stream: used esp. as an element in place names, as Catskill.

kill·deer, kil′dẽr″, *n. pl.* **kill·deers, kill··deer.** [Imit., from its clear, plaintive cry.] A plover of fields and pastures, having two black breast bands, an orange-red rump, and a characteristic cry 'kill-dee.' Also **kill··dee, kill·deer plov·er.**

kill·er, kil′ẽr, *n.* One who or that which kills; a person or an animal that is given to killing; *slang,* a person or thing making a strong impression.

kill·er whale, *n.* Grampus.

kil·lick, kil′ik, *n.* [Origin obscure.] A small anchor or weight for mooring a boat, sometimes consisting of a stone secured by pieces of wood. Also **kil·lock.**

kil·li·fish, kil′ē·fish″, *n. pl.* **kil·li·fish, kil·li·fish·es.** [Appar. < *kill.*] Any of various fishes of the family *Cyprinodontidae,* esp. the genus *Fundulus,* found in bays, channels, and rivers of N. America.

kill·ing, kil′ing, *n.* The act of one who or that which kills; a slaying; *fig.* an unusually large profit.—*a.* That pertains to killing; as, a *killing* frost; *slang,* irresistibly amusing. —**kill·ing·ly,** *adv.*

kill·joy, kil′joi″, *n.* A person who spoils the joy or enjoyment of others.

kiln, kil, kiln, *n.* [O.E. *cylene, cyln,* perh. < L. *culina,* a kitchen.] A type of oven used to bake, dry, or burn objects such as bricks, pottery, lime, or cement.—*v.t.* To bake in such an oven.

kil·o, kil′ō, kē′lō, *n. pl.* **kil·os.** A kilogram; a kilometer. An authorized communications or code word for the letter *k.*

kil·o·cal·o·rie, kil′o·kal″o·rē, *n. pl.* **kil··o·cal·o·ries.** *Phys.* the large calorie equal to one thousand gram calories. See *calorie.*

kil·o·cy·cle, kil′o·sī″kl, *n.* A thousand cycles; *radio,* a thousand cycles per second. Abbr. *kc.*

kil·o·gram, kil·o·gramme, kil′o·gram″, *n.* [Fr. *kilogramme* < Gr. *chilioi,* a thousand, and Fr. *gramme.*] A measure of mass and weight in the metric system, equaling 1000 grams or 2.2046 pounds avoirdupois. See Metric System table.

kil·o·gram-me·ter, kil′o·gram″mē′tẽr, *n.* A unit of work, or the amount taken to raise one kilogram one meter, about 7.23 foot-pounds.

kil·o·li·ter, *Brit.* **kil·o·li·tre**, kil′o·lē″tẽr, *n.* See Metric System table.

kil·o·me·ter, *Brit.* **kil·o·me·tre**, kil′o·mē″tẽr, ki·lom′i·tẽr, *n.* See Metric System table.

kil·o·par·sec, kil'o·pär"sec", *n. Astron.* one thousand parsecs. Abbr. *kpc.*

kil·o·ton, kil'o·tun", *n.* A thousand tons; the explosive force of a thousand tons of TNT.

kil·o·var, kil'o·vär", *n. Elect.* 1000 vars (volt-ampere-reactive); a unit of power in a kilovolt ampere which is caused by reactance. Abbr. *kVAr, kvar.*

kil·o·volt, kil'o·vōlt", *n. Elect.* a unit of electromotive force equal to 1000 volts. Abbr. *kV, kv.*

kil·o·volt-am·pere, kil'o·vōlt"am'pēr", *n. Elect.* a unit of power equal to 1000 volt-amperes. Abbr. *kVA, kva.*

kil·o·watt, kil'o·wot", *n. Elect.* a unit of power equivalent to 1000 watts or to 1.34 horsepower. Abbr. *kw.*

kil·o·watt-hour, kil'o·wot"our', kil'o·wot"ou'ér, *n. Elect.* a unit consumed or transferred equivalent to the power of one kilowatt working for one hour.

kilt, kilt, *n.* [A Scandinavian word; *cf.* Icel. *kilting,* a skirt, *kjalta,* a person's lap; Dan. *kilte,* to tuck up or kilt.] A knee-length pleated skirt, usu. made of a tartan cloth, regarded as the national dress of the Scottish Highlander, and often worn by Scottish regiments in the British Army.

kilt·er, kil'tèr, *n.* [Origin obscure.] *Colloq.* Good condition; order; as, to be out of *kilter.* Also *Brit.* **kel·ter.**

kilt·ie, kilt·y, kil'tē, *n. pl.* **kilt·ies.** One wearing a kilt; a kilted Highland soldier.

ki·mo·no, ko·mō'no, ko·mō'nō, *n.* [Jap.] A loose, robelike garment with wide sleeves and a sash, worn by both Japanese men and women; a woman's dressing gown.

kin, kin, *n.* [O.E. *cynn, cyn,* Icel. *kyn,* Goth. *kuni,* O.H.G. *chunni,* kin, kind, family, race; compare *kind, n.* and *a., king;* D. and G. *kind,* a child; L. *genus,* Gr. *genos,* race, offspring.] Relatives collectively; clan; kindred; a relative—*a.* Related; similar.

kin·aes·the·sia, kin"is·thē'zha, *n.* Kinesthesia. Also **kin·aes·the·sis.—kin·aes·thet·ic,** kin"is·thet'ik, *a.*

ki·nase, ki'nās, kin'ās, *n. Biochem.* a substance capable of changing a zymogen into an enzyme.

kind, kind, *n.* [O.E. *gecynd, gecynde.*] The nature or determining character; a particular variety or sort.—**in kind,** in the particular or equivalent kind or sort of thing; as, to make payment *in kind,* to retaliate *in kind.*—**kind of,** *colloq.* after a fashion; to some extent; somewhat, as: The room was *kind of* dark.—**of a kind,** of the same kind; alike; as, two *of a kind.*

kind, kind, *a.* [O.E. *gecynde,* < *gecynd.*] Of a good or benevolent nature or disposition; as, a *kind* master, a *kind* heart; proceeding from a good-natured readiness to benefit or please others; as, *kind* actions, *kind* words; beneficent, helpful, friendly, or cordial; as, my *kind* regards; pleasant, agreeable, or favorable; as, the *kind* wind.

kin·der·gar·ten, kin'dèr·gär"ten, kin'dèr·gär"den, *n.* [G., 'children's garden.'] A pre-primary school for furthering the mental, social, and physical development of young children by means of such games and occupations that make use of their natural tendency to express themselves in action.—**kin·der·gart·ner,** kin'dèr·gärt"nèr, kin'dèr·gärd"nèr, *n.*

kind·heart·ed, kind'här'tid, *a.* Having much kindness; characterized by kindness, generosity.—**kind·heart·ed·ly,** *adv.*—**kind·heart·ed·ness,** *n.*

kin·dle, kin'dl, *v.t.*—**kindled, kindling.** [Allied to or derived from Icel. *kynda,* to kindle, *kyndill,* a torch or candle; perhaps < L. *candela,* E. *candle.*] To set on fire; to light; to inflame, rouse, or excite, as the passions.—*v.i.* To take fire; to begin burning; to become aglow; to grow animated; to be roused or excited.

kind·less, kind'lis, *a. Poet.* unkind, cruel, heartless.—**kind·less·ly,** *adv.*

kin·dling, kind'ling, *n.* Materials for lighting a fire, as sticks of dry wood; the act of one who kindles.

kind·ly, kind'lē, *adv.* Obligingly; cordially.—*a.*—**kindlier, kindliest.** Of a kind disposition or character; sympathetic; congenial; benevolent.—**kind·li·ness,** *n.*

kind·ness, kind'nis, *n.* The state or quality of being kind; benevolence; a kind act; an act of good will.

kin·dred, kin'drid, *n.* [O.E. *kinrede,* kindred, < *kin,* and term. *-red,* as in hatred: the *d* is inserted, as in gender, thunder.] Relatives by blood, sometimes by marriage; affinity. —*a.* Allied by blood; related in origin, nature, or the like; similar; allied by the same beliefs or tastes; congenial; as, a *kindred* soul.

kin·e·mat·ics, kin"e·mat'iks, ki"ne·mat'-iks, *n. pl. but sing. in constr.* [Gr. *kinēma,* movement, < *kineō,* to move.] *Phys.* that aspect of the science of dynamics which deals with motion, without reference to the forces producing it.—**kin·e·mat·ic, kin·e·mat·i·cal,** *a.*—**kin·e·mat·i·cal·ly,** *adv.*

kin·e·scope, kin'i·skōp", *n.* [< Gr. *kinein,* move, and *scope.*] The cathode ray tube used in a television receiver, having a fluorescent screen at one end on which images are reproduced by electron beams; a recording on film made from a television program.—*v.t.*—**kinescoped, kinescoping.** To record, as a television program, on film.

ki·ne·sics, ki·nē'siks, ki·nē'siks, *n. pl. but sing. in constr.* A study of the relationship between nonverbal body motion, as a shrug, and communication.—**ki·ne·sic,** *a.*—**ki·ne·si·cal·ly,** *adv.*

ki·ne·si·ol·o·gy, ki·nē"sē·ol'o·jē, ki·nē"-zē·ol'o·jē, ki·nē"sē·ol'o·jē, ki·nē"zē·ol'o·jē, *n.* [< Gr. *kinēsis,* motion.] The science which investigates anatomy and organic processes in reference to human motion.

kin·es·the·sia, kin"is·thē'zha, *n.* [N.L., < Gr. *kinein,* move, and *aisthesis,* perception.] The sense of muscular effort or movement; muscle sense. Also *kinaesthesia,* **kin·es·the·sis.—kin·es·thet·ic,** kin"is·thet'ik, *a.*

ki·net·ic, ki·net'ik, ki·net'ik, *a.* Referring to motion; produced by motion; being in motion; as, *kinetic* sculpture.—**ki·net·ic en·er·gy,** the energy possessed by a body by virtue of its being in motion.

ki·net·ic art, *n.* A type of modern, abstract art which attempts to indicate or present a sense of motion.

ki·net·ics, ki·net'iks, ki·net'iks, *n. pl. but sing. in constr.* The branch of the science of dynamics which treats of forces causing or changing the motion of masses.

ki·net·ic the·o·ry, *n.* The theory that all matter is made up of minute particles which are constantly in random motion, and that the temperature of a given body is a direct function of the average kinetic energy of the atoms or molecules comprising that body.

ki·ne·to·scope, ki·nē'to·skōp", *n.* An early form of the motion picture in which a series of pictures passed rapidly beneath a small opening or peephole for direct viewing.—**ki·ne·to·scop·ic,** ki·nē"to·skop'ik, *a.*

kin·folk, kin'fōk", *n. pl.* Family; relatives. Also *kinsfolk,* **kin·folks.**

king, king, *n.* [O.E. *cyning,* < *cyn,* kin, race, term, and *-ing,* one of, descendant (as in *atheling*); D. *koning,* Icel. *konungr,* Dan. *konge,* G. *könig,* king.] The male sovereign of a nation, tribe, or country; a monarch; a ruler; one preeminent or highly successful in his field; as, a uranium *king*; a playing card having the picture of a king; the chief piece in the game of chess; a crowned man in the game of checkers. (*Cap.*) God;

Christ. (*Cap.*), *pl. but sing. in constr.* title of two books in the Old Testament, relating to the Hebrew kings after King David.—**king·like,** *a.*

king·bird, king'burd", *n.* Any of various North American birds of the flycatcher family, genus *Tyrannus.*

king·bolt, king'bōlt", *n.* A vertical bolt connecting the body of a vehicle with the fore axle, or the body of a railroad car with a truck. Also *kingpin.*

King Charles span·iel, *n.* A small, black-and-tan toy spaniel popularized by Charles II of England.

king crab, *n.* The horseshoe crab; any of several large, edible crabs of the genus *Paralithodes.*

king·craft, king'kraft", king'kräft", *n.* The art of governing as a reigning monarch; the techniques used by a king; the profession of a king.

king·cup, king'kup", *n. Chiefly Brit.* Any of a number of common buttercups; a marsh marigold.

king·dom, king'dom, *n.* The territory or country subject to a king; the dominion of a king or monarch; domain or realm in a general sense; (*often cap.*) the spiritual realm of God or the sphere of God's influence; *nat. hist.* one of the three extensive divisions into which natural objects are classified: the animal, plant, and mineral *kingdoms.*—**king·dom·less,** *a.*

king·fish, king'fish", *n. pl.* **king·fish, king·fish·es.** Any of certain American fishes of the genus *Menticirrhus,* as *M. saxatilis,* a food fish of the Atlantic coast; the cero; *colloq.* one whose leadership or power is unquestioned.

king·fish·er, king'fish"ér, *n.* Any of various usu. crested, bright-colored birds of the family *Alcedinidae,* found worldwide, having short tails and long, stout bills, and feeding on fish and insects.

King James Ver·sion, *n.* A revised English translation of the Bible authorized by King James I and published in 1611. Also *Authorized Version,* **King James Bi·ble.**

king·let, king'lit, *n.* Any of several tiny birds of the genus *Regulus,* similar to the warbler, esp. the golden-crowned or ruby-crowned kinglet. A weak king or one of little importance.

king·ly, king'lē, *a.*—**kinglier, kingliest.** Belonging or pertaining to a king or kings; royal; monarchical; befitting a king; august; splendid.—*adv.* With an air of royalty; as befitting a king.—**king·li·ness,** *n.*

king·mak·er, king'mā"kèr, *n.* One who has sufficient influence to select a candidate for a position of political authority.—**king·mak·ing,** *n., a.*

king·pin, king'pin", *n. Bowling,* the number five pin or the headpin. A kingbolt; *slang,* the leader or chief person.

king post, *n. Carp.* a vertical post between the apex of a triangular roof truss and the tie beam.

King's Coun·sel, *n. Brit. law,* a barrister of distinction appointed to serve as counsel to the crown.

king's Eng·lish, *n.* English usage or speech considered the standard for correct or pure language. Also **queen's Eng·lish.**

king's e·vil, *n.* [From the belief in a king's healing touch.] *Pathol.* scrofula.

king·ship, king'ship, *n.* Royalty; the state, office, or dignity of a king; royal government; a monarchy; (*cap.*) a title referring to a king's person, preceded by *his* or *your.*

king-size, king'sīz", *a.* Larger or longer than standard size; exceptionally large. Also **king-sized.**

king snake, *n. Zool.* any of certain large, non-poisonous snakes, genus *Lampropeltis,* found in the southern U.S., that feed on rodents.

king truss, *n.* A truss for a roof framed with a king post.

king·wood, king'wụd", *n.* A Brazilian wood with violet-tinted streaks, used in cabinetwork; the tree yielding this wood, *Dalbergia cearensis.*

kink, kingk, *n.* [D., G., and Sw. *kink,* a twist or coil in a cable.] A twist or tight curl, as in a hair, rope, or thread; a mental whim or quirk; a crotchet or eccentricity; a muscular cramp; an imperfection that impedes the successful functioning of something; as, a *kink* in a plan or machine.—*v.t.* To cause a kink in.—*v.i.* To form or wind into a kink.—**kink·y,** *a.*—*kinkier, kinkiest.*Twisted or tightly curled; frizzy; having kinks.

kin·ka·jou, king'ka·jō", *n.* [Canadian Fr.; orig. the same word as *carcajou.*] A nocturnal, arboreal carnivore, *Potos caudivolvulus,* related to the raccoon and inhabiting Mexico and Central and S. America. Also **hon·ey bear.**

kin·ni·kin·nick, kin·ni·ki·nic, kin"i·ki·nik', *n.* [N. Amer. Ind., lit. 'mixture.'] A mixture used by the North American Indians for smoking, consisting of dried leaves, bark, and occasionally tobacco; any of various plants used for this purpose, as the kinnikinick sumac and dogwood, *Cornus amomum.*

ki·no gum, kē'nō gum, *n.* [W. Afr.] *Bot.* the dried resinous juice of several tropical trees of the genera *Pterocarpus, Butea,* and *Eucalyptus,* used in throat medicines and in tanning. Also **ki·no.**

kins·folk, kinz'fōk", *n. pl.* Kinfolk.

kin·ship, kin'ship, *n.* Relationship; common blood; familial bond.

kins·man, kinz'man, *n. pl.* **kins·men.** One related by blood, esp. a male relative.—**kins·wom·an,** kinz'wụm"an, *n.* A female relation.

ki·osk, kē·osk', kĭ'osk, *n.* [= Fr. *kiosque,* < Turk. *kiūshk,* < Pers. *kūshk.*] A kind of open pavilion or summerhouse common in Turkey and Persia and imitated elsewhere; a similar structure often used as a bandstand or a newsstand.

kip, kip, *n.* [Origin uncertain.] The hide of a young or small beast; a bundle or set of such hides. *Com.* a measure of deadweight equal to 1000 pounds and used to compute shipping charges.

kip·per, kip'ẽr, *n.* [O.E. *cypera,* spawning salmon, prob. < *coper,* copper, the color.] A herring or salmon which has been kippered; a male salmon at or directly after the spawning season.—*v.t.* Of fish, to cure by splitting open, cleaning, salting, and smoking or drying.

kirk, kụrk, *Scot.* kirk, *n.* [The old form of *church;* O.E. *cyrc.*] A church; *(cap.)* the Church of Scotland or Presbyterian Church, as opposed to the Episcopal Church of Scotland or the Church of England.

Kir·man, kir·män', *n.* A kind of Persian rug with elaborate floral designs and subdued colors. Also **Kir·man·shah, Ker·man·shah,** kir·män'shä.

kir·mess, kụr'mis, *n.* Kermis.

kirsch, kẽrsh, *n.* [G., *kirsche,* cherry.] A brandy made from the distillation of fermented black cherry juice. Also **kirsch·was·ser,** kẽrsh'vä"sẽr.

kir·tle, kụr'tl, *n.* [O.E. *cyrtel,* Icel. *kyrtill,* Dan. *kjortel;* akin to *short.*] *Archaic.* A woman's gown or petticoat; a man's coat or tunic.—**kir·tled,** *a.*

kis·met, kiz'mit, kis'mit, *n.* [Pers. *kusmut.*] A Mohammedan expression for fate or destiny.

kiss, kis, *v.t.* [O.E. *cyssan,* < *coss,* a kiss; Icel. and Sw. *kyssa,* Dan. *kysse,* G. *küssen,* to kiss; the corresponding nouns being Icel. *koss,* Dan. *kys,* G. *kuss.*] To touch or con-

tact with the lips in salutation or as a mark of affection; to make light contact, as: The leaf *kissed* the windowpane.—*v.i.*—*n.* A touch or caress effected with the lips in various manners and signifying various emotions or intents. A kind of confection, usu. bite-size.—**kiss off,** *slang,* to reject or send away.—**kiss·a·ble,** *a.*—**kiss·er,** *n.* One who kisses; *slang,* the face, esp. the mouth.

kiss·ing bug, *n. Zool.* a blood-sucking insect, *Reduvius personatus,* which may inflict painful bites in the area of the mouth and cheek.

kit, kit, *n.* [M.E. *kyt, kitt:* cf. M.D. *kitte,* vessel made of hooped staves.] A set or collection of tools, supplies, or other objects for a special purpose; as, a traveler's *kit,* a first-aid *kit;* the case which contains these objects or the case and contents together; a collection of parts to be assembled; as, a model train *kit. Brit.* a group of supplies, esp. for a soldier; a wooden tub or pail, usu. circular.—**kit and ca·boo·dle,** *colloq.* all of the people or things, as: The whole *kit and caboodle* went to the dance.

kit, kit, *n.* Shortened form of *kitten.*

kit, kit, *n.* [Origin uncertain.] *Mus.* a kind of small violin characterized by its soft muted tones, previously used by dancing masters for rhythm instruction.

kitch·en, kich'en, *n.* [O.E. *cycene,* < L. *coquina,* kitchen, orig. fem. of *coquinus,* pertaining to cooks, < *coquus,* E. *cook, n.*] A room or place appropriated to cooking; the culinary department.—*a.* Employed in or belonging to a kitchen; as, a *kitchen* knife.

kitch·en cab·i·net, *n.* A wooden or metal cupboard, often with drawers, used for storage, as for cooking utensils or imperishable food; an unofficial body of advisers which influences a government head.

kitch·en·ette, kich"e·net', *n.* [Dim. of *kitchen.*] A small area functioning as a kitchen; any small kitchen.

kitch·en gar·den, *n.* A garden in which vegetables, herbs, and fruit are grown, esp. for home consumption.—**kitch·en gar·den·er,** *n.*

kitch·en mid·den, *n. Anthropol.* a mound consisting of bones, shells, and other refuse, marking the site of a prehistoric human habitation.

kitch·en po·lice, *n. pl. Milit.* men assigned to assist the cooks of a military unit. Abbr. *K.P.*

kitch·en·ware, kich'en·wâr", *n.* Pots, pans, dishes, and other utensils used in the kitchen.

kite, kīt, *n.* [O.E. *cyta.*] A light frame covered with paper or cloth, constructed to fly in the wind at the end of a long string. *Ornith.* one of several species of hawks inhabiting the southern U.S., resembling falcons in the shape of their long pointed wings, but soaring and gliding like gulls. *Naut.* any of the highest and lightest sails of a ship.—*v.t.—kited, kiting. Com.* To draw against a fictitious bank balance, with the hope that sufficient funds will be deposited; to force, as stock prices, to unjustifiably high levels.

kith, kith, *n.* [O.E. *cytth,* knowledge, relationship, native country, < *cuth,* known, pp. of *cunnan,* to know.] *Archaic,* acquaintances or friends collectively.—**kith and kin,** friends and relatives, now usu. only relatives.

kithe, kythe, kīTH, *v.t. Sc.* to show or make known.—*v.i.* To appear or become known.

kitsch, kich, *n.* Pretentious and gaudy literature or art of questionable merit, intended to appeal to a mass market.

kit·ten, kit'en, *n.* [Dim. of *cat.*] A young cat, or the young of the cat.—*v.i.* To bring forth young, as a cat.—**have kit·tens,** *slang,* to vent anger.

kit·ten·ish, kit'e·nish, *a.* Like a kitten; fond of playing; coyly playful.—**kit·ten·ish·ly,** *adv.*—**kit·ten·ish·ness,** *n.*

kit·ti·wake, kit'ē·wāk", *n.* [From its cry.] An ocean gull, *Rissa tridactyla,* ranging from New Jersey to the Arctic, distinguished from the common herring gull by its solid black wing tips and black legs.

kit·tle, kit'l, *v.t.—kittled, kittling.* [M.E. *kytylle* = Icel. *kitla* = D. *kittelen* = G. *kitzeln,* tickle.] *Brit., Sc.* To tickle; to rouse; to perplex.—*a.* Ticklish.

kit·ty, kit'ē, *n. pl.* **kit·ties.** [Origin uncertain.] An accumulation, usu. small, of money or objects; in card games, a fund into which the players put money for a specific purpose, or cards remaining after dealing a hand, and utilized by the high bidder. *Brit.* a prison or jail.

kit·ty, kit'ē, *n. pl.* **kit·ties.** A kitten; a name for a pet cat.

kit·ty-cor·ner, kit'ē·kạr"nẽr, *a., adv.* Catty-corner.

ki·va, kē'va, *n.* [N. Amer. Ind.] A large Pueblo Indian ceremonial chamber, often wholly or partly underground.

Ki·wa·nis, ki·wä'nis, *n.* A service organization of men's clubs chartered throughout U.S. and Canada to promote ethical standards in business and the professions.—**Ki·wa·ni·an,** *a., n.*

ki·wi, kē'wē, *n.* [Maori.] A flightless bird of New Zealand, of the genus *Apteryx. Slang,* a nonflying air officer; a student pilot who has not flown solo.

Klan, klan, *n.* [Shortened form of *Ku Klux Klan.*] A unit of the secret organization, Ku Klux Klan.—**Klan·ism,** *n.*—**Klans·man,** klanz'man, *n. pl.* **Klans·men.** A member of the Ku Klux Klan.

klatch, klatsch, klach, kläch, *n.* A social gathering devoted to gossip and light conversation.

Kleen·ex, klē'neks, *n.* A soft paper used as a handkerchief or cleansing tissue. (Trademark.)

klep·to·ma·ni·a, clep·to·ma·ni·a, klep"to·mā'nē·a, klep"to·mān'ya, *n.* [Gr. *klepto,* to steal, and *mania,* madness.] *Psychol.* an irresistible impulse to steal, usu. for no economic reason.—**klep·to·ma·ni·ac,** klep"to·mā'nē·ak", *n.* One affected with kleptomania.

klieg eyes, kleig eyes, klēg īz, *n.* Watering and inflammation of the eyes caused by immoderate exposure to very bright lights.

klieg light, kleig light, klēg līt, *n.* [From Anton and John *Klieg,* American inventors.] A very bright arc lamp employed in floodlighting motion picture and television studios.

klip·spring·er, klip'spring"ẽr, *n.* [S. Afr. D., 'cliff springer.'] A small, active African antelope of the mountainous regions.

kloof, klöf, *n.* [D., cleft: cf. *clove.*] *S. Afr.* A deep mountain cleft; a ravine; a gorge.

Kly·stron, klis'tron, klī'stron, *n. Elect.* an electron tube using electrical current oscillations to generate and amplify ultrahigh frequencies, as television signals. (Trademark.)

knack, nak, *n.* [Imit. of sound, like D. *knak,* Dan. *knaek,* G. *knack,* a crack, a snap; orig. a snap of the fingers, then a trick or way of doing a thing as if with a snap.] An ability or aptitude; as, a *knack* for repairing electrical things; adroitness or dexterity.

knack·er, nak'ẽr, *n.* [< Icel. *hnakkr,* a saddle, orig. a saddler and harness maker.] *Brit.* One who purchases and slaughters diseased or useless horses; one who salvages and sells building materials from old houses or other structures.

knap, nap, *v.t.—knapped, knapping.* [= D. *knappen,* to crack, to munch, to lay hold of; G. *knappen,* to crack, to snap.] *Brit. dial.* To bite off; to break short; to snap; to rap sharply.—*n. Brit. dial.* A short sharp noise; a snap.—**knap·per,** *n.*

knap, nap, *n.* [O.E. *cnaep*: cf. Icel. *knappr,* knob, and E. *knop.*] *Brit. dial.* The top of a hill; summit; a hillock or knoll.

knap·sack, nap'sak", *n.* [L.G. *knappsack,* D. *knapzak,* G. and D. *knappen,* to snap, to eat, and *sack*—lit. 'a provision sack.'] A bag of leather or strong cloth strapped to the back of travelers, esp. soldiers and hikers, used for holding supplies; rucksack.

knap·weed, nap'wēd", *n.* Any of several perennial weedy species of the genus *Centaurea,* in the composite family, having purple to pink flowers in knoblike heads, introduced from Europe and now classed as noxious weeds in many states. Also **Rus·sian knap·weed.**

knar, när, *n.* A knot in wood.—**knarred, knar·ry,** *a.*

knave, nāv, *n.* [O.E. *cnapa* or *cnafa,* a boy, a youth, a son; D. *knaap,* G. *knabe,* a boy or young man, Icel. *knapi,* a servant boy; root doubtful; cf. *knight.*] A rascal; a dishonest man or boy; the jack in a pack of playing cards. *Archaic,* a man or boy servant.—**knav·er·y,** *n.*—**knav·ish,** nā'vish, *a.*—**knav·ish·ly,** *adv.*—**knav·ish·ness,** *n.*

knead, nēd, *v.t.* [O.E. *cnedan, cnaedan;* D. *knedan,* G. *kneten,* Icel. *knotha,* to knead; akin Slav. *gneta, gnesti,* to press, to knead.] To work into a mass with pressing and folding movements of the hands; to massage.—**knead·a·bil·i·ty,** *n.*—**knead·a·ble,** *a.*

knee, nē, *n.* [O.E. *cneow* = D. and G. *knie* = Icel. *kne* = Goth. *kniu,* knee; akin to L. *genu,* Gr. *gónu,* Skt. *jānu,* knee; cf. *kneel.*] *Anat.* the joint or region in man between the thigh and the lower part of the leg; the corresponding or similar joint or region of other vertebrates, as in the leg of a bird or the hind limb of a horse; a joint or region likened to this but not homologous with it, as the tarsal joint of a bird, or the carpal joint in the fore limb of the horse or cow; something resembling this joint, esp. when bent, as a piece of timber with an angular bend; the part of a garment covering the knee.—*v.t.*—**kneed, kneeing.** To strike or touch with the knee.—**kneed,** *a.*

knee ac·tion, *n.* In an automobile, the suspension system allowing independent vertical motion of each front wheel.

knee·cap, nē'kap", *n.* The movable bone covering the knee joint in front; the patella; a protective covering for the knee, esp. of a horse.

knee-deep, nē'dēp', *a.* So deep as to reach the knees, as: The snow lay *knee-deep.* Sunk as far as the knees; *fig.* deeply involved or engaged.

knee-high, nē'hī', *a.* Reaching as high as the knees.

knee·hole, nē'hōl", *n.* An opening for the knees, as in a desk.

knee jerk, *n. Physiol.* a sudden reflex or involuntary kick of the knee caused by a blow on the patellar tendon.

kneel, nēl, *v.i.*—**knelt** or **kneeled, kneeling.** [O.E. *kneole, kneoli,* < *knee;* corresponding to D. *knielen,* Dan. *knaele,* to kneel. Compare *handle,* < *hand.*] To bend the knee; to genuflect; to fall on the knees; to rest on the knees.—**kneel·er,** nē'lẽr, *n.* One who kneels.

knee·pan, nē'pan", *n.* The kneecap or patella.

knell, nel, *n.* [O.E. *cnyll,* a sound of a bell; *cnyallan,* to sound a bell; compare G. *knellen, knallen,* to make a loud noise; and D. *knal,* Sw. *knall,* a loud sound; Icel. *knylla,* to beat, *gnella,* to scream; imitative of sound; *knoll* is akin.] The sound of a bell rung slowly at a funeral; a bell announcing death or extinction; a doleful sound.—*v.i.* To sound in order to announce a death, funeral, failure, or disaster; to sound as an omen or warning.—*v.t.* To summon by, or as by, a knell.

Knes·set, knes'et, *n.* [Heb.] The Israeli parliament.

knick·ers, nik'ẽrz, *n. pl.* [Properly Dutch breeches, shortened from Washington Irving's character Diedrich *Knickerbocker,* as representative of a Dutchman.] Loose breeches reaching just below the knee, where they are gathered in so as to clasp the leg. Also **knick·er·bock·ers.**

knick·knack, nik'nak", *n.* [A reduplication of *knack;* compare *click-clack, tip-top, ding-dong,* etc.] A trifle or toy; any small article more for ornament than practical use.

knife, nif, *n. pl.* **knives.** [O.E. *cníf* = M.L.G. *kníf* = Icel. *knífr* = Sw. *knif* = Dan. *kniv,* knife.] A cutting instrument consisting essentially of a thin blade, usu. of steel and with a sharp edge, attached to a handle; a knifelike weapon; a dagger; a short sword; a blade for cutting, as in a tool or machine.—*v.t.*—**knifed, knifing.** To apply a knife to; cut or stab with a knife. *U.S. slang,* to strike at secretly; try to defeat in an underhand way.—*v.i.* To cut through something, as with a knife.—**knife·like,** *a.*—**un·der the knife,** undergoing a surgical operation.

knife edge, *n.* The edge of a knife; anything very sharp; a wedge upon which a scale beam or pendulum oscillates.—**knife-edged,** nif'ejd", *a.*

knife switch, *n. Elect.* a switch consisting of one or more metal strips which can be pushed between metallic clips and thus close a circuit.

knight, nīt, *n.* [O.E. *cniht,* a boy, a servant, a military follower; D. and G. *knecht,* a male servant, Dan. *knegt,* a fellow, the knave at cards: perhaps < root of *kin* or of *knave.*] *Medieval hist.* a tenant who served as a mounted soldier; a man admitted to a certain military rank after service as page and squire. *Brit.* one holding a non-hereditary dignity conferred by the sovereign and conveying the title *Sir.* A chivalrous person; a champion. *Chess,* a playing piece, usu. the figure of a horse's head.—*v.t.* To dub a knight; to confer the honor of knighthood, as upon someone.

knight-er·rant, nīt'er'ant, *n. pl.* **knights-er·rant.** *Medieval hist.* a knight who traveled in search of adventures to exhibit his prowess.—**knight-er·rant·ry,** nīt'er'-an·trē, *n.* The role, character, or practice of a knight-errant.

knight·hood, nīt'hụd, *n.* The rank, vocation, or character of a knight; knights collectively.

knight·ly, nīt'lē, *a.* Pertaining to a knight; befitting a knight; constituted by knights.—*adv.* In a manner becoming a knight.—**knight·li·ness,** *n.*

knit, nit, *v.t.*—**knitted** or **knit, knitting.** [O.E. *cnyattan,* to knit, to tie, < *cnotta,* a knot; Icel. *knyta,* < *knutr,* a knot; Dan. *knytte,* to knit, to knot.] To weave or form by looping or knotting a continuous thread by means of needles; to tie together; to join closely; to cause to grow together; to contract into folds or wrinkles, as the brow.—*v.i.* To make a fabric by interlooping yarn or thread by means of needles. To become united; to grow together; to become contracted into folds or wrinkles.—*n.* A knitted fabric or garment.—**knit·ted,** *a.*—**knit·ter,** *n.*—**knit·ting,** *n.* The method, action, or product of one who knits.

knit·wear, nit'wâr", *n.* Clothes made from a knitted fabric.

knob, nob, *n.* [Older form *knop;* cf. O.E. *cnoep,* a top, a knob, D. *knop, knoop,* G. *knopf,* Icel. *knappr,* Dan. *knop, knap,* a knob, button, bud; also W., Ir., and Gael. *cnap,* a knob.] A hard rounded protuberance; a round ball at the end of anything; a more or less ball-shaped handle, as for a door; a domelike mountain or hill. *Arch.* a boss; a knot of foliage carved or cast for ornament.—*v.i.*—**knobbed, knobbing.** To grow into knobs; to bunch.—*v.t.* To provide with a knob. *Masonry,* to chip off protruding nodes to prepare a stone for use.—**knobbed,** *a.* Containing knobs; covered with knobs.—**knob·by,** *a.*—**knobbier, knobbiest.**

knob·ker·rie, nob'ker"ē, *n.* [S. Afr. D. *knopkiri,* < *knop,* knob, and Hottentot *kiri,* stick, club.] A short, heavy stick or club with a knob on one end, used as both a striking and a throwing weapon by natives of southern Africa.

knock, nok, *v.i.* [O.E. *cnocian, cnucian,* = Icel. *knoka,* knock, thump; imit.] To strike a sounding blow with the fist, knuckles, or anything hard, esp. on a door, gate, or window, as in seeking admittance, calling attention, or giving a signal; to rap, beat, or pound; to strike in collision, as: His knees *knocked* together. To make a noise as of striking or pounding, as the motor of a car; *slang,* to make harsh or querulous criticisms.—*v.t.* To give a forcible blow to; hit, strike, or beat; to drive or force by a blow or blows; as, to *knock* a man senseless; to strike, as a thing, against something else; bring into collision; *slang,* to criticize harshly; *Brit. slang,* to amaze or leave an excellent impression.—*n.* The act or the sound of knocking; a rap, as at a door; a blow or thump; *slang,* an ill-natured criticism or adverse comment.—**knock·less,** *a.*

knock·a·bout, nok'a·bout", *a.* Rough, boisterous, noisy; suitable for rough use.—*n.* Something suitable or designed for rough use; a slapstick theatrical performance or performer; an aimless wanderer; *naut.* a small, easily handled yacht with a jib and mainsail but no bowsprit.

knock·down, nok'doun", *n.* A striking down or felling; that which strikes down; something constructed to be assembled or disassembled easily.—*a.* Forceful enough to strike down or overwhelm; constructed to be assembled or disassembled easily.—**knock-down-drag-out,** *a. Slang,* characterized by unremitting violence.

knock down, *v.t.* To disassemble or take apart; to reduce, as in price; to indicate, as a sale, at an auction by a blow of the auctioneer's mallet; *slang,* to earn as salary.

knock·er, nok'ẽr, *n.* One that knocks; a contrivance fastened to a door to use for knocking; *slang,* one who persistently finds fault.

knock-knee, nok'nē", *n.* Inward curvature of the legs, causing the knees to knock together in walking; *pl.* knees that knock together in this way.—**knock-kneed,** *a.*

knock off, *v.t. Colloq.* to stop, as what one is doing, esp. work; to accomplish or produce routinely or rapidly; to deduct or delete; to finish. *Slang,* to kill or murder; to rob.—**knock it off,** *slang,* stop immediately.

knock out, *v.t. Boxing,* to defeat by striking a blow that causes the match to be ended. To render unconscious or useless. *Slang,* to overwork, exhaust; to make or do hastily.—**knock·out,** nok'out", *n.* The act of rendering unconscious or putting out of action; a blow that knocks someone out; *slang,* an unusually attractive person or thing, esp. a woman.—*a.*

knock up, *v.t.* To abuse or damage; to hurt or wound; *slang,* to impregnate. *Brit. colloq.* to wake up; to rouse; to exhaust.

knoll, nōl, *n.* [O.E. *cnoll,* a knoll, a summit; N. *knoll,* Dan. *knold,* a knoll; G. *knolle, knollen,* a lump; cf. W. *cnol,* the top, a round hillock.] A small hill or elevation.—**knoll·y,** *a.*

knop, nop, *n.* A knob, often ornamental.

---

knot, not, *n.* [O.E. *cnotta,* a knot = D. *knot,* Icel. *knútr,* Sw. *knut,* G. *knoten,* a knot; cogn. L. *nodus,* that is, *gnodus,* whence *node.*] The intertwining of a flexible material, such as rope, to form a knob which fastens or binds this material to another or to an object; the resulting lump; a bow, usu. of ribbon, for ornamentation; an assemblage of people or objects; a difficult or perplexing situation or problem; a bond or connection, as in marriage; *anat., zool.* a lump occurring in a tissue. *Bot.* a node or swelling on a part of a plant, such as the stem; any of assorted tree diseases in which such protuberances occur; the location on a tree in which a branch grows from the trunk; this section seen in lumber. *Naut.* a division on a log line which is used in determining the speed of a ship; a nautical mile or hourly nautical mile.—*v.t.*—**knotted,** *knotting.* To tie in a knot or knots; to form a knot on; to entangle; to unite closely.—*v.i.* To become knotted; to form knots or joints, as in plants.—**knot·less,** *a.*—**knot·like,** *a.*—**knot·ter,** *n.*—**knot·ty,** *a.* Full of knots; difficult, intricate, or involved; as, a *knotty* problem.

knot, not, *n.* [Said to be named after King Canute (*Cnut*), who was very fond of it.] A red-breasted shore bird, *Calidris canutus,* which breeds in Arctic regions and winters in S. America.

knot·hole, not′hōl″, *n.* A hole in a board, formed by the falling out of a knot.

knot·ted, not′id, *a.* Twisted with or into knots; full of knots or snarled; decorated with knots; intricate or puzzling; gnarled; *bot.* having knobs or nodelike swellings.

knot·ty pine, *n.* Pine lumber having circular or oval knots distributed throughout, which represent buried basal portions of branches, and considered undesirable except when used for ornamental panelling.

knot·weed, not′wēd″, *n.* Any of several plants of the genus *Polygonum* in the buckwheat family, having short internodes which appear as a series of small knots, as the common, prostrate, bluish-green weed, *P. aviculare.* Also **knot·grass.**

knout, nout, *n.* [Russ. *knute.*] A whip with leather thongs, used formerly in Russia to punish criminals.—*v.t.* To punish or flog with the knout.

know, nō, *v.t.*—past *knew,* pp. *known,* ppr. *knowing.* [O.E. *cnawan* (*gecnawan*) = O.H.G. -*cnaan,* know, = Icel. *kna* (pres. ind.), know how, can; akin to L. *gnoscere, noscere,* Gr. *gignōskein,* Skt. *jna-,* know; the same root as E. *can* and *ken.*] To perceive or understand as fact or truth, or apprehend with clearness and certainty; to have fixed in the mind or memory; as, to *know* a lesson, or to *know* a poem by heart; to be cognizant or aware of; as, to *know* the cause of; be familiar or conversant with, as a subject, method, or ethnic group; to be acquainted with, as a thing, place, or person, usu. by sight, experience, or report; to recognize, as: You will *know* him by his red hat. To be able to distinguish or differentiate; *archaic,* to have sexual intercourse with.—*v.i.* To have knowledge, or clear and certain perception, as of fact or truth; to be cognizant or aware, as of some fact, circumstance, or occurrence; to have information, as about something.—**know·a·ble,** nō′a·bl, *a.*—**know·er,** *n.*—**in the know,** *colloq.* unusually well informed; having inside or confidential information.

know-how, nō′hou″, *n.* Special experience and useful knowledge applicable to a complex operation, particularly a technical one.

know·ing, nō′ing, *n.* The act or process of learning or perceiving something.—*a.* Sagacious; astute; expressive of the possession of inside information or secret knowledge; as, a *knowing* expression; conscious; intentional.—**know·ing·ly,** *adv.*—**know·ing·ness,** *n.*

know-it-all, nō′it·al″, *n. Colloq.* a person boastfully confident of knowing everything.—*a.*

knowl·edge, nol′ij, *n.* [M.E. *knaulage, knauleche, knowleche,* ult. < O.E. *cnāwan,* know (perhaps through M.E. *cnawlechen, knowlechen,* v., acknowledge, confess, recognize), with suffix of uncertain origin.] Acquaintance with facts, truths, or principles, as from study or investigation; familiarity or conversance, as with a subject, language, or branch of learning; acquaintance with a thing, place, person, as by sight, experience, or report; the fact or state of knowing; perception of fact or truth; clear and certain mental apprehension; the state of being cognizant or aware, as of a fact or circumstance; cognizance of facts, or range of cognizance; practical understanding of an art or skill; the sum of what is known; that which is or may be known; the body of truths or facts accumulated by mankind in the course of time; *archaic,* sexual intercourse.—**knowl·edge·a·ble,** **knowl·edg·a·ble,** nol′i·ja·bl, *a.*—**knowl·edge·a·ble·ness,** **knowl·edg·a·ble·ness,** *n.*—**knowl·edge·a·bly,** **knowl·edg·a·bly,** *adv.*

know-noth·ing, nō′nuth″ing, *n.* An ignorant person; an agnostic. (*cap.*), *U.S. hist.* a member of a political party, active from 1853 to 1856, which aimed at keeping the power of the government in the hands of native-born citizens, in opposition to recent immigrants: so called because members claimed to know nothing of their party's activity.—*a.* Grossly ignorant; agnostic. (*cap.*), *U.S. hist.* of, pertaining to, or resembling the Know-Nothings.

knuck·le, nuk′l, *n.* [M.E. *knokel* = D. *kneukel* = G. *knochel,* knuckle; dim. of a form represented by D. *knok,* G. *knochen,* bone.] A joint of a finger, esp. one of the joints at the roots of the fingers; the rounded prominence of such a joint when the finger is bent; a joint of meat, consisting of the parts about the carpal or tarsal joint of a quadruped; a cylindrical, projecting part on a hinge, through which an axis or pin passes; the joint of a hinge.—*v.t.* To strike, tap, or touch with the knuckles.—*v.i.* To hold the knuckles close to the ground in playing marbles.—**knuck·le down,** to apply oneself vigorously or earnestly.—**knuck·le un·der,** to yield or submit.—**knuck·ly,** *a.*

knuck·le ball, *n. Baseball,* a slow pitch with irregular trajectory achieved by grasping the ball between the knuckles and thumb. Also **knuck·ler,** nuk′lėr.

knuck·le·bone, nuk′l·bōn″, *n.* A bone forming the knuckle of the finger; the rounded end of the fingerbone at a joint; a leg bone in quadrupeds, having a knobbed end; a joint of meat in which there is a knucklebone; a metacarpal or metatarsal bone of a sheep.

knuck·le-dust·er, nuk′l·dus″tėr, *n.* Brass knuckles, used in lethal fisticuffs.

knuck·le·head, nuk′l·hed″, *n. Slang,* an inept or stupid person.—**knuck·le·head·ed,** *a.*

knuck·le joint, *n.* A joint forming a knuckle; *mach.* a flexible joint formed by two abutting links.

knur, nur, *n.* [Var. of *knar.*] A knot on a tree or in wood; a knotty lump or growth.

knurl, nurl, *n.* A knob or protuberance; a ridge, usu. small and one of a series, wrought on an object such as a thumbscrew or coin.—*v.t.* To make ridges on. Also *nurl.*—**knurled,** nurld, *a.*—**knurl·y,** nur′lē, *a.*

K O, *n.* pl. **K O's.** *Boxing.* a knockout.—*v.t.*—*KO′d, KO′ing.* To knock out, as an opponent, in boxing. Also **K.O., k.o.**

ko·a·la, kō·ä′la, *n.* [Native name.] A marsupial animal of Australia, *Phascolarctos cinereus,* arboreal in habit, with gray fur, large ears, and no tail.

ko·bold, kō′bold, kō′bōld, *n.* A domestic spirit or elf found in German folklore.

Ko·dak, kō′dak, *n.* A hand-held camera. (Trademark.)

Ko·di·ak bear, kō′dē·ak″ bâr, *n.* A brown bear of great size, *Ursus middendorffi,* native to Kodiak Island, coastal Alaska, and British Columbia. Also **Ka·di·ac bear.**

Koh·i·noor, kō′i·nur″, *n.* [< Pers. *kōhinūr,* mountain of light.] A diamond, discovered in India and famous for its size, now among the British crown jewels.

kohl, kōl, *n.* A black powder which is prevalent in the East and used as a cosmetic to darken and enhance eyelids.

kohl·ra·bi, kōl·rä′bē, kōl′rä″bē, *n.* pl. **kohl·ra·bies.** [G. < *kohl,* kale, and L. *rapa,* a turnip; kale or cabbage turnip.] A variety of cabbage, *Brassica caulorapa,* distinguished by an edible enlargement of the stem immediately above the ground.

koi·ne, koi·nā′, *n. Ling.* any regional language or dialect which becomes the standard language of a larger region. (*Cap.*) a language composed primarily of Greek dialects and commonly used in the Middle East during the Roman and Hellenistic periods.

ko·kan·ee, kō·kan′ē, *n. Canada,* a small sockeye salmon.

kok-sa·ghyz, kōk″sa·gēz′, *n.* An Asian dandelion, *Taraxacum kok-saghyz,* which yields a milky juice from which a commercial rubber is made.

ko·la, kō′la, *n.* [W. Afr. *kola* (N.L. Cola).] The kola nut; the tree producing this nut; an extract prepared from the kola nut.

ko·la nut, *n.* The bitter brownish nut or seed of an African tree, *Cola acuminata,* also often cultivated in the West Indies and Brazil, and used as a stimulant and tonic.—**ko·la tree,** *n.* See *cola.*

ko·lin·sky, ko·lin·ski, kō·lin′skē, *n.* pl. **ko·lin·skies.** [Russ. *Kolinski,* of Kola, in northern Russia.] Any of various Asian minks, esp. *Mustela siberica*; the fur of such an animal.

kol·khoz, kol·chaz′, *n.* pl. **kol·kho·zy, kol·khoz·es.** *U.S.S.R.,* a collective farm.

koo·doo, ku·du, kö′dö, *n.* [Native name.] A striped African antelope having long horns, spirally twisted.

kook, kök, *n. Slang.* A person considered odd, peculiar, or eccentric; one who is insane.—**kook·y,** kö′kē, *a.*—**kookier, kooki·est.**

kook·a·bur·ra, kuk″a·bur′a, *n.* An Australian bird, *Dacelo gigas,* related to the kingfisher and having a loud laughing cry.

Ko·ran, kō·rän′, kō·ran′, *n.* [Ar. *qur′ān,* reading, recitation, < *qara′a,* read.] The sacred book of the Mohammedans, containing the professed revelations of Allah to Mohammed.—**Ko·ran·ic,** kō·ran′ik, *a.*

Ko·re·an, kō·rē′an, *a.* Of or pertaining to Korea, a peninsula off the east coast of China.—*n.* A native of Korea; the language of Korea.

ko·sher, kō′shėr, *a.* [Heb. *kosher,* fit, proper, lawful.] Right, lawful, or clean according to Jewish dietary laws, esp. used in reference to food, food containers, and kitchen utensils made ritually proper for use; conforming to Jewish dietary laws. *Slang,* proper; authentic.—*v.t.* To make kosher; also **ka·sher.**

ko·to, kō′tō, *Jap.* ka′ta″, *n.* pl. **ko·tos,** *Jap.* **ko·to.** [Jap.] A Japanese musical instrument having thirteen strings stretched over a sounding box, and played with both hands.

kou·mis, kö′mis, *n.* Kumiss.

kow·tow, kou′tou′, kou′tou″, kō′tou′, kō′tou″, *v.i.* [Chinese.] To kneel, bend, and touch the ground with the forehead as an act of deep reverence or respect; to act in a servile manner.—*n*. The performance of kowtowing.

kraal, kräl, *n*. [S. Afr. D., < Pg. *curral* = Sp. *corral*, enclosure.] A S. African native village surrounded by a stockade; the inhabitants of such a village; an enclosure for cattle.—*v.t*. To enclose in a kraal.

kraft, kraft, kräft, *n*. [G., strength.] A sturdy, brown wrapping paper pressed from wood pulp and used in the making of paper bags.

krait, krīt, *n*. [Hind. *karait*.] Any of a number of poisonous Asian snakes, genus *Bungarus*.

kra·ken, krä′ken, *n*. A legendary Scandinavian sea monster.

kra·ter, cra·ter, krā′tèr, *n*. A bowl or wide-necked vase used by the ancient Greeks to mix water with wine.

K ra·tion, *n*. *Milit*. an emergency package of food rations developed during W.W. II.

kraut, krout, *n*. Sauerkraut; (*often cap*.), *slang*, a disparaging term for a German, esp. a soldier.

Krem·lin, krem′lin, *n*. [Fr. *kremlin*, < Russ. *kreml*, citadel.] The Soviet government; the citadel of Moscow, including within its walls the chief office of the government of the Soviet Union; (*l.c.*) the citadel of a Russian town or city.

Krem·lin·ol·o·gy, krem″li·nol′o·jē, *n*. The study of the governmental policies and practices of the Soviet Union.—**Krem··lin·ol·o·gist**, *n*.

krieg·spiel, krēg′spēl″, *n*. [G. *kriegsspiel*, 'war game.'] A game designed to teach military science by means of blocks which represent armies, guns, and other military equipment and which are moved about on maps or model battlefields.

krill, kril, *n*. *pl*. **krill**. A type of small crustacean inhabiting open oceanic waters, constituting the basic food of some whales.

krim·mer, crim·mer, krim′ér, *n*. [G. *krimmer*, < *Krim*, Crimea.] A lambskin from the Crimean region, dressed as a fur, with wool in loose, soft curls and usually whitish or pale gray.

kris, krēs, *n*. Creese.

Krish·na·ism, krish′na·iz″um, *n*. [From *Krishna*, an avatar of Vishnu and a popular Hindu deity.] A common form of Hindu worship, based on the teachings of the *Bhagavad-Gita*.

Kriss Krin·gle, kris′ kring′gl, *n*. Santa Claus.

kryp·ton, krip′ton, *n*. [N.L., < Gr. *krypton*, neut. or *kryptos*, hidden.] *Chem*. a rare inert gaseous element, used in high-power electric light bulbs. Sym. Kr, at. no. 36, at. wt. 83.80. See Periodic Table of Elements.

ku·chen, kö′*chen*, *n*. One of several varieties of sweetened yeast-dough coffeecakes usu. made with fruit.

ku·dos, kö′dōz, kö′dōs, kö′dos, kū′dōz, kū′dōs, kū′dos, *n*. *pl. but sing. in constr*. [Gr.] Glory; renown; recognition.

kud·zu, kụd′zō, *n*. *Bot*. a leguminous prostrate to climbing vine, *Pueraria thunbergiana*, native to China and Japan, cultivated for its fibers, for erosion control, and as a forage crop. Also **kud·zu vine**.

Ku Klux Klan, kö′ kluks′ klan′, *n*. A secret society formed in the southern U.S. in post-Civil War years to promote white supremacy by means of violence and terrorism; a secret fraternal group formed in 1915, consisting solely of white, American-born Protestants, and hostile to all other groups, esp. Negroes, Jews, and Catholics.—**Ku Klux·er**, *n*.—**Ku Klux·ism**, *n*.

ku·lak, kụ·läk′, kö′läk, *n*. A well-to-do 19th century Russian peasant opposed to the Soviet policy of collectivization of farms.

Kul·tur, G. kụl·tör, *n*. [G., < L. *cultura*,

E. *culture*.] Culture; civilization, esp. the assumed cultural superiority of the Germans of W.W.II.

ku·miss, kö′mis, *n*. [= Fr. *koumis* = G. *kumys*, < Russ. *kumys*; from Tatar.] Fermented mare's or camel's milk used as a beverage by Asiatic nomads; a similar drink prepared from cow's milk and used for dietetic and medicinal purposes. Also *koumis*, **kou·miss, kou·myss**.

küm·mel, kim′el, G. k ̄ym′el, *n*. [G. *kümmel*, caraway.] A liqueur made in Germany and Russia, which is flavored with caraway seeds and cumin.

kum·quat, cum·quat, kum′kwot, *n*. [From Chinese name meaning 'golden orange.'] *Bot*. A round to oblong, yellow-orange citrus fruit of the genus *Fortunella*, with an acid pulp and a sweet rind used for preserves; the tree bearing this fruit.

kunz·ite, kụnts′īt, *n*. [From G. F. *Kunz*, Amer. expert in precious stones.] A transparent lilac variety of spodumene found in California, and used as a gem.

kur·ra·jong, cur·ra·jong, kụr′a·jong″, *n*. [Native Aust.] *Bot*. an Australian tree, *Brachychiton populneum*, which is grown as an ornamental and which yields a strong fiber for cordage. Also **bot·tle tree**.

kur·to·sis, kụr·tō′sis, *n*. *Statistics*, the pointedness or flatness around the mode of a frequency curve.

kvass, kväs, *n*. [Russ. *kvas*.] A Russian fermented drink, usu. made from an infusion of rye, barley, and malt. Also **quass**, kväs, kwäs.

ky·ack, kī′ak, *n*. Two connected saddle bags hung on either side of a packhorse; a kayak.

ky·ak, kī′ak, *n*. Kayak.

ky·a·nite, kī′a·nīt″, *n*. *Min*. an aluminosilicate, used as a refractory, usu. occurring in blue crystals and crystal aggregates. Also **cy·a·nite**.

ky·mo·gram, kī′mo·gram, *n*. A record plotted by a kymograph.

ky·mo·graph, cy·mo·graph, kī′mo·graf″, kī′mo·gräf″, *n*. [Gr. *kyma*, a wave, *grapho*, I write.] *Med*. an instrument for graphically recording variations in motion or pressure, esp. blood pressure; *aeron*. a device that graphs an airplane's oscillations.—**ky·mo··graph·ic**, kī″mo·graf′ik, *a*.—**ky·mog·ra··phy**, kī·mog′ra·fē, *n*.

Kym·ric, kim′rik, *n*. [From *Kymry*, or *Cymry*, a Celtic branch of peoples among which the Welsh are included.] The Welsh language. Also **Cym·ric**.—*a*. Of or pertaining to the Kymry. Also **Cym·ric**.

ky·pho·sis, ki·fō′sis, *n*. *Pathol*. an abnormal backward curving of the spine; hunchback. —**ky·phot·ic**, ki·fot′ik, *a*.

kyte, kīt, *n*. *Sc*. The stomach; the belly. Also **kite**.

kythe, kīTH, *v.t., v.i*. Kithe.

L

L, l, el, *n*. The twelfth letter and ninth consonant of the English alphabet; an utterance or sound represented by this letter; an ell or something having the shape of the capital letter L, as a dining ell; a printer's device for reproducing this letter; that which is twelfth in order or series; the Roman numeral for 50.

L, L., l, l. (*Cap*.) abbr. for Latin, longitude, and the British pound or pounds; (*l.c.*) abbr. for left, length, lira or lire, liter or liters.

la, lä, *n*. *Mus*. The syllable used for the sixth tone of a major scale; the tone A.

la, lạ, lä, *interj*. An expression of surprise.

lab, lab, *n*. *Colloq*. a laboratory.

lab·a·rum, lab′ér·rum, *n. pl*. **lab·a·ra**, lab′ér·a. [L.L. Etym. doubtful.] *Eccles*. a banner bearing the first two letters, XP, of the Greek word for Christ, which is the monogram of Christianity.

lab·da·num, lab′da·num, *n*. A resin obtained from rockroses belonging to the genus *Cistus*, and used in medicine, perfumes, and fumigants. Also *ladanum*.

lab·e·fac·tion, lab″e·fak′shan, *n*. [L. *labefactiō*, < *labefaciō—labo*, to totter, and *facio*, to make.] A weakening or decay, as of a civic authority; downfall.

la·bel, lā′bel, *n*. [O.Fr. *label, lambel*, a rag, a tatter, a shred; of Germanic or Celtic origin.] A slip of paper or other printed material which is affixed to an object to indicate its owner, contents, or nature; a word or phrase used to identify or describe persons or ideas; a trademark or brand; *arch*. a projecting molding over doors and windows; *her*. a design placed across the top of a shield to indicate the eldest son.—*v.t*. —*labeled, labeling, esp. Brit*. *labelled, labelling*. To attach or affix a label to; to identify, describe, or designate by means of a label; to classify.—**la·bel·er, la·bel·ler**, *n*.

la·bel·lum, la·bel′um, *n. pl*. **la·bel·la**, la·bel′a. [L., a little lip, dim. of *labrum*, a lip.] *Bot*. the liplike, often prominent, petal of an orchid situated between the two lateral petals.—**la·bel·late**, *a*.—**la·bel··loid**, *a*.

la·bi·al, lā′bē·al, *a*. [L. *labium*, a lip.] Pertaining to the lips; of a labium; *phon*. formed chiefly by the lips, as *b, m, p*, or *ō* and *oo; mus*. creating tones by the impact of air on a sharp edge, as in the flue pipes of an organ.—*n*. *Phon*. any labial sound. A flue pipe in an organ.—**la·bi·al·ly**, *adv*.

la·bi·al·ize, lā′bē·a·līz″, *v.t*.—*labialized, labializing*. To give a labial sound or character to; to round; to utter labially.— **la·bi·al·i·za·tion**, lā″bē·a·li·zā′shan, *n*.

la·bi·ate, lā′bē·āt″, *a*. [N.L. *labiatus*.] Having a labium or labia; lipped. *Bot*. having one or more liplike parts; bilabiate; belonging to the *Labiatae* or mint family of plants, most of whose members have bilabiate corollas.—*n*. *Bot*. a labiate plant.

la·bile, lā′bil, *Brit*. lā′bīl, *a*. [L.L. *labilis*, < L. *labi*, fall, slide; cf. *lapse*.] *Biol*. apt to lapse or change; *chem., phys*. unstable; *med*. pertaining to a mode of application in electrotherapy in which the active electrode is moved over the part to be acted upon.—**la·bil·i·ty**, la·bil′i·tē, *n*.

la·bi·o·den·tal, lā″bē·ō·den′tal, *a*. *Phon*. produced by touching the lower lip to the upper teeth, as the *f* or *v* sounds.—*n*. A sound formed in this manner.

la·bi·o·ve·lar, lā″bē·ō·vē′lér, *a*. *Phon*. articulated by partially rounding and closing the lips while the back of the tongue is near or touching the velum, as the *w* sound.—*n*. A sound formed in this manner.

la·bi·um, lā′bē·um, *n. pl*. **la·bi·a**, lā′bē·a. [L., lip, akin to *labrum*.] A lip or liplike part; *entom*. the lower liplike part of the mouth of an insect; *anat*. any of the outer or inner folds of the vulva; *bot*. the lower lip of a bilabiate corolla.

la·bor, *Brit*. **la·bour**, lā′bér, *n*. [M.E. *labour*, < O.Fr. *labor, labour* (Fr. *labeur*), < *labor*, toil, trouble, distress.] Persistent exertion of body or mind; bodily toil for the sake of gain or economic production; those engaged in such toil considered as a group or class; as, the claims and rights of *labor*; work or a task done or to be done; the product or result of toil; the process of childbirth.—*v.i*. To perform labor; exert one's powers of body or mind; work; toil; to move with effort or difficulty; roll or pitch heavily, as a ship; to be burdened,

---

ch- chain, G. na*ch*t;   **th-** THen, thin;   **w-** wig, hw as sound in whig;   **z-** zh as in azure, zeal.   *Italicized vowel* indicates schwa sound.

troubled, or distressed; to be in travail or childbirth.—*v.t.* To work out in detail; elaborate.—**la·bor·er**, *n.*—**la·bor·ing·ly**, *adv.*—**la·bor·less**, *a.*

lab·o·ra·to·ry, lab'ro·tôr″ē, lab'ēr·a·tōr″ē, *Brit.* la·bor'a·to·rē, la·bor'a·trē, *n.* pl. **lab·o·ra·to·ries**. [L.L. *laboratorium*, < L. *labor*, labor.] A building or room designed for scientific or technical investigation or experimentation; a situation or place providing the means for study, observation, or experimentation; a place where chemicals or medicines are prepared.—*a.* Referring to or suggestive of work done or functions performed in a laboratory.

la·bor camp, *n.* A colony of prisoners who are forced into labor; a camp for migrant farm workers.

La·bor Day, *n.* In most parts of the U.S. and Canada, the first Monday in September, observed as a legal holiday to honor labor.

la·bored, *Brit.* **la·boured**, lā'bērd, *a.* Produced with labor; heavy; bearing the marks of constraint and effort; as, a *labored* speech.

la·bo·ri·ous, la·bōr'ē·us, *a.* [L. *laboriosus.*] Requiring labor; toilsome; not easy; diligent in work or service; industrious; assiduous.—**la·bo·ri·ous·ly**, *adv.*—**la·bo·ri·ous·ness**, *n.*

la·bor·ite, *Brit.* **la·bour·ite**, lā'bo·rīt″, *n.* One who promotes the interests, theories, and practices of labor organizations; (*cap.*) one belonging to a political party which is devoted primarily to labor interests.

la·bor-sav·ing, *Brit.* **la·bour-sav·ing**, lā'bēr·sā″ving, *a.* Adapted to supersede or diminish manual labor.

la·bor un·ion, *Brit.* **la·bour un·ion**, *n.* A trade union; an organization of wage earners designed to advance the economic interests and general working conditions of its members.

lab·ra·dor·ite, lab'ra·da·rīt″, lab″ra·dạr'īt, *n.* A mineral which is a kind of plagioclase feldspar, distinguished by its iridescence.

Lab·ra·dor re·triev·er, *n.* A retriever, originally bred in Newfoundland, characterized by a broad head and chest and a short, thick coat, usu. black.

la·bret, lā'bret, *n.* [L. *labrum*, lip.] An ornament worn by certain primitive peoples, consisting of a piece of bone, wood, or the like, inserted through a pierced lip.

la·brum, lā'brum, lab'rum, *n.* pl. **la·bra**. [L. *lip*; akin to E. *lip*: cf. *labellum* and *labium*.] A lip or liplike part; *zool.* the upper part of the mouth of an insect or crustacean; *conch.* the outer margin of the aperture of a gastropod's shell; *anat.* a rim of cartilage ringing the bony portion of a joint.

la·bur·num, la·bur'nam, *n.* [L.] *Bot.* an ornamental small tree, *Laburnum anagyroides*, in the legume family, grown for its pendulous racemes of yellow flowers. Also **gold·en-chain tree**.

lab·y·rinth, lab'i·rinth, *n.* [L. *labyrinthus*; Gr. *labyrinthos*.] A place with intricate winding passages; a maze; a bewildering arrangement of things or circumstances. *Anat.* the inner ear, including the bony and fluid-filled structures.

lab·y·rin·thine, lab″i·rin'thin, lab″i·rin'thēn, *a.* Pertaining to or like a labyrinth; full of windings; intricate. Also **lab·y·rin·thi·an**, **lab·y·rin·thic**, lab″i·rin'thē·an.—**lab·y·rin·thi·cal·ly**, *adv.*

lac, lak, *n.* [Hind. *lākh* = Pers. *lāk*: cf. *lake* and *lacquer*.] A resinous substance deposited on trees by the lac insect, *Laccifer lacca*, of southern Asia, and used as a basis for shellac and varnish, and in the production of a red coloring matter.

lac·co·lith, lak'o·lith, *n. Geol.* a body of igneous rock which has intruded itself between beds of overlying strata, causing the formation of domes. Also **lac·co·lite**.

lac·co·lith·ic, **lac·co·lit·ic**, lak″o·lith'ik, lak″o·lit'ik, *a.*

lace, lās, *n.* [O.Fr. *las* < L. *laqueus*, a noose, a snare; akin *lasso*, *latchet*.] A string or cord used for fastening boots, shoes, or a garment; a delicate kind of network or fabric, either man-made or machine-woven; a braid for ornamenting uniforms or hats.—*v.t.* To fasten with lace or string through eyelet holes or hooks; to constrict or compress by drawing laces tightly; to intertwine; to adorn with lace; to add a small amount of liquor to, as to another liquid; to streak with color; *colloq.* to strike or beat.—*v.i.* To be fastened or tied by a lace; to have a lace. —**lace in·to**, *colloq.* Thrash; scold.—**laced**, *a.*—**lace·like**, *a.*—**lac·er**, *n.*—**lac·y**, *a.*

lac·er·ate, las'e·rāt″, *v.t.*—*lacerated*, *lacerating*. [L. *lacero, laceratum*, to tear, < *lacer*, mangled, torn.] To tear; to rend; to make a ragged wound or gash in by violence or tearing; *fig.* to torture; to harrow.—**las'e·rāt**, las'ēr·it, *a.* Rent; torn; tortured; *bot.* having the appearance of being torn, as a leaf. Also **lac·er·at·ed.**—**lac·er·a·ble**, *a.*—**lac·er·a·tive**, las'e·rā″tiv, las'er·a·tiv, *a.*

lac·er·a·tion, las″e·rā'shan, *n.* An act of tearing; a jagged wound or tear caused by lacerating.

lac·er·til·i·an, las″ēr·til'ē·an, las″ēr·til'yan, *a.* [L. *lacerta*, a lizard.] Belonging or referring to the family of lizards. Also **la·cer·tian**, la·sur'shan, la·sur'shē·an.—*n.*

lace·wing, lās'wing″, *n.* Any of various neuropterous insects, esp. of the genera *Chrysopa* and *Hemerobius*, with lacelike wings and bright eyes, whose larvae prey on plant lice.

lach·es, lach'iz, *n.* pl. **lach·es**. [Norm. Fr. *lachesse*, remissness, lit. < O.Fr. *lasche*, < L. *laxus*, lax, slow.] *Law*, negligence or inexcusable delay in carrying out a duty or claiming a legal right.

lach·ry·mal, **lac·ri·mal**, lak'ri·mal, *a.* [L. *lachryma, lacryma, lacrima*, a tear; cog. with Gr. *dakry*, a tear, and E. *tear*.] Pertaining to or characterized by tears; as, a *lachrymal* mood. *Anat.* of, relating to, or near those organs which produce tears; as, a *lacrimal* bone.—*n.* A lachrymatory. *Anat.* organ which secretes and produces tears; also **lach·ry·mal gland**.

lach·ry·ma·to·ry, lak'ri·ma·tōr″ē, *n.* pl. **lach·ry·ma·to·ries**. *Rom. antiq.* a small vase found in tombs, and believed to have contained tears collected from mourners. Also *lachrymal*.

lach·ry·mose, lak'ri·mōs″, *a.* Given to crying; tearful; tending to provoke tears; mournful; as, a *lachrymose* novel. Also **lac·ri·mose.**—**lach·ry·mose·ly**, *adv.*

lac·ing, lā'sing, *n.* The act of fastening with a lace; a cord or lace used in drawing tight or fastening together, as in a shoe; a braid or trimming, often of silver or gold; a dash or sprinkling of liquor in a beverage or food; *colloq.* a beating or flogging.

la·cin·i·ate, la·sin'ē·āt″, la·sin'ē·it, *a.* [L. *lacinia*, a flap, fringe, or border.] Fringed; *bot.* notched; slashed into deep, pointed lobes, as a leaf or petal. Also **la·cin·i·at·ed.** —**la·cin·i·a·tion**, *n.*

lack, lak, *n.* [M.E. *lak* = M.L.G. *lak*, defect, fault, blemish: cf. Icel. *lakr*, lacking, defective.] A deficiency or absence of something necessary, desirable, or customary; that which is wanted or needed.—*v.t.* To be deficient in or wanting; as, to *lack* funds; to fall short in respect to; as, to *lack* the necessary votes.—*v.i.* To be absent, wanting, or deficient, often followed by *in*.—**lack·ing**, *a., prep.*

lack·a·dai·si·cal, lak″a·dā'zi·kal, *a.* Listless; lethargic; lacking in vigor or zest.—**lack·a·dai·si·cal·ly**, *adv.*—**lack·a·dai·si·cal·ness**, *n.*

lack·a·day, lak'a·dā″, *interj.* [Contr. for *alack, the day*.] *Archaic*, exclamation of sorrow or regret.

lack·ey, lak'ē, *n.* [Fr. *laquais*, < Sp. and Pg. *lacayo, alacayo*.] An attending male servant; a footboy or footman; any servile follower.—*v.t., v.i.*—*lackeyed, lackeying*. To act as a lackey; to attend servilely. Also **lac·quey.**

lack·lus·ter, *Brit.* **lack·lus·tre**, lak'lus″tēr, *a.* Without luster, brightness, or vitality; dull.—*n.* Want of luster.

la·con·ic, la·kon'ik, *a.* [Fr. *laconique*, L. *laconicus*, < *Lacones*, the Spartans.] Short; brief; terse; expressing a great deal in few words.—**la·con·i·cal·ly**, *adv.*—**lac·o·nism**, lak'o·niz″um, *n.*

lac·quer, lak'ēr, *n.* [Obs.Fr. *lacre*, < Pg. *laca*, lac, < Hind. *lākh*, E. *lac*.] A varnish consisting of resins dissolved in a volatile solvent, occasionally with pigments added, and used as a protective or decorative coating; a natural varnish from the Asiatic tree, *Rhus vernicifiua*, producing a hard, glossy finish, esp. on wood. Any wooden article, often inlaid, coated with lacquer; also **lac·quer ware.**—*v.t.* To coat with or as with lacquer; *fig.* to smooth over, as with words.—**lac·quer·er**, *n.*

lac·ri·ma·tor, **lach·ry·ma·tor**, lak'ri·mā″tēr, *n.* An irritant which causes tears, as tear gas.

la·crosse, la·krạs', la·krọs', *n.* [Fr.] A game which originated with North American Indians, played with two ten-man teams, the object of the game being to advance downfield and score by throwing a small ball into the opponent's goal with a crosse or lacrosse stick.

lac·tal·bu·min, lak″tal·bū'min, *n. Biochem.* a protein, belonging to the albumin class, found in milk and obtained from the residue whey, used principally in preparation of some foods, adhesives, and varnishes.

lac·tase, lak'tās, *n.* [L. *lac* (*lact-*) milk.] *Biochem.* an enzyme in intestinal juices and certain yeasts that catalyzes the production of glucose and galactose from lactose.

lac·tate, lak'tāt, *n. Chem.* a salt of lactic acid.—*v.i.*—*lactated, lactating*. To produce or secrete milk.

lac·ta·tion, lak·tā'shan, *n.* In mammals, the production of milk; the time period of milk production; the act of nursing or suckling young.—**lac·ta·tion·al**, *a.*—**lac·ta·tion·al·ly**, *adv.*

lac·te·al, lak'tē·al, *a.* Relating to, producing, or resembling milk; milky. Also **lac·te·an**, **lac·te·ous**, lak'tē·us.—*n. Anat.* one of numerous, minute lymphatic vessels which absorb or take up lymph from the alimentary canal and convey it to the thoracic duct.—**lac·te·al·ly**, *adv.*

lac·tes·cent, lak·tes'ent, *a.* [L. *lactescens* (*-ent-*), ppr. of *lactescere*, become milky, < *lactere*, be milky, < *lac* (*lact-*), milk.] Becoming or being milky; producing milk; concerned with the secretion of milk; *entom.* secreting a milky fluid; *bot.* forming a milky juice.—**lac·tes·cence**, *n.*—**lac·tes·cen·cy**, *n.*

lac·tic, lak'tik, *a.* [Fr. *lactique*.] Pertaining to or produced from milk.

lac·tic ac·id, *n. Biochem.* a syruplike acid, $CH_3CHOHCOOH$, which is present naturally in sour milk, produced commercially by synthesis or bacterial fermentation of carbohydrates, and utilized in food processing, medicine, and industry.

lac·tif·er·ous, lak·tif'ēr·us, *a.* [L. *lactifer.*] Producing or conveying milk or a milky liquid.

lac·to·ba·cil·lus, lak″tō·ba·sil'us, *n.* pl. **lac·to·ba·cil·li**, lak″tō·ba·sil'ī. Any of the rod-shaped bacteria, genus *Lactobacillus*, which produce lactic acid in the fermentation of milk and carbohydrates.

---

a- fat, fāte, fär, fåre, fạll;   **e-** met, mē, mēre, hẽr;   **i-** pin, pīne;   **o-** not, nōte, möve;   **u-** tub, cūbe, bụll;   **oi-** oil;   **ou-** pound.

lac·to·gen·ic, lak″to·jen′ik, *a.* Causing lactation.

lac·tone, lak′tōn, *n.* [< *lactic.*] *Chem.* any of a class of anhydrides derived from hydroxy acids.—**lac·ton·ic,** lak·ton′ik, *a.*

lac·tose, lak′tōs, *n. Biochem.* a sugar obtained from milk, $C_{12}H_{22}O_{11}$, which is a white, odorless, disaccharide used as a sweetening agent in baby feedings and other foods. Also *milk sugar*, **sug·ar of milk.**

la·cu·na, la·kū′na, *n.* pl. **la·cu·nas, la·cu·nae.** [L., hole, cavity, gap, pool, pond, < *lacus.* Cf. *lagoon.*] A gap or hiatus, as in a manuscript; a pit or cavity; *biol.* an interstitial or intercellular space in plant or animal tissue; *anat.* one of the numerous minute cavities in the substance of bone. Any space, depression, or cavity.—**la·cu·nal, la·cu·nar, la·cu·nar·y,** lak′ū·nėr″e, la·kū′na·rē, *a.*

la·cu·nar, la·kū′nėr, *n.* pl. **la·cu·nars, lac·u·nar·i·a,** lak″ū·nâr′e·a. [L., < *lacuna.*] *Arch.* A vault or ceiling having recessed panels or coffers; one of these panels.—*a.*

la·cus·trine, la·kus′trin, *a.* [L. *lacus,* E. *lake.*] Of or pertaining to a lake; living or occurring on or in lakes, as various animals and plants; formed at the bottom of lakes, as geological strata.

lad, lad, *n.* [Of doubtful origin; cf. W. *llawd,* Ir. *lath,* a lad, a youth.] A young man or boy; a familiar term applied to any male; fellow; comrade.—**lad·dish,** *a.*—**lad·hood,** *n.*

lad·a·num, lad′a·num, *n.* Labdanum.

lad·der, lad′ėr, *n.* [O.E. *hlaedder* = O.Fris. *hladder,* D. *ladder,* O.H.G. *hleitra, hleitara,* Mod.G. *leiter,* a ladder; cogn. L. *clathri,* a trellis or grate.] A frame of wood, metal, or rope, consisting of two long sidepieces connected by crosspieces at suitable distances, forming steps by which persons may ascend or descend a structure; something similar to a ladder; a means of rising to eminence; a series of gradations with reference to status or position. *Brit.* a run or hole in a woman's stocking.—**lad·der·less,** *a.*—**lad·der·like,** *a.*—**lad·der·y,** *a.*

lad·der-back, *a.* Referring to the back of a chair which has horizontal pieces between the two vertical posts.—**lad·der back,** *n.* A chair so constructed.

lad·die, lad′e, *n. Chiefly Sc.* lad.

lade, lād, *v.t.*—past **laded,** pp. **laden** or **laded,** ppr. *lading.* [O.E. *hladan,* load, take up (liquid), = D. and G. *laden* = Icel. *hladha* = Goth. *-hlathan,* load: cf. *ladle* and *last.*] To load, as with a burden or cargo; to put on or in, as a burden, load, or cargo; to load oppressively, or burden; to lift out or dip, as with a ladle.—*v.i.* To take on a load or cargo; to lade a liquid.

lad·en, lād′en, *a.* Loaded, weighed down; burdened or oppressed.—*v.t.* To lade.

la-di-da, lä′de·dä′, *a. Colloq.* Affectedly genteel or refined; foppish; pretentious; as, *la-di-da* speech.—*interj.* An expression of ridicule aimed at pretentious or affected refinement.—*n.* One who is affectedly genteel, foppish, or pretentious; behavior considered characteristic of affected refinement or pretentious gentility. Also **la-de-da, lah-di-dah.**

la·dies' man, la·dy's man, *n.* A man who is attractive to women and who persistently seeks out their attentions.

lad·ing, lā′ding, *n.* The act of one who or that which lades; that with which something, as a ship, is laden; load; freight; cargo.

La·di·no, la·dē′nō, *Sp.* lä·dē′na̱, *n.* In South America, one of mixed Spanish and Indian descent; a mestizo; the Spanish language of the 15th century written in Hebrew characters, which was brought to the Balkan countries by the Jews who left Spain at the time of the Inquisition.

la·dle, lād′l, *n.* [O.E. *hlædel,* < *hladan,* E. *lade.*] A long-handled utensil with a cuplike bowl for dipping or conveying liquids.—*v.t.*—**ladled, ladling.** To dip or convey with or as with a ladle.—**la·dler,** *n.*

la·dy, lā′dē, *n.* pl. **la·dies.** [O.E. *hlæfdīge,* perhaps orig. meaning 'loaf-kneader,' < *hlaf,* loaf, and *-dige,* akin to *dāh,* E. *dough.*] A woman of good family or social position, or of good breeding or refinement; a polite term for any woman; the mistress of a household; a woman who is the object of chivalrous devotion; a wife or consort; (*cap.*) the Virgin Mary; as, 'our *Lady*'; a title of women of a certain rank; a less formal substitute for marchioness, countess, viscountess, and baroness; a title used before the Christian name and surname of the daughters of dukes, marquises, and earls, and before the husband's Christian name and surname in the case of the wife of one who holds a courtesy title in which *Lord* precedes the Christian name; a title used before the surname of the wife of a baronet or knight.—*a.* Having the qualities of a lady; ladylike.

la·dy bee·tle, lā′dē bēt′l, *n.* Ladybug.

la·dy·bird, lā′dē·bṷrd″, *n.* Ladybug.

la·dy·bug, lā′dē·bug″, *n.* Any of various beneficial beetles of the family *Coccinellidae* that are small, usu. brightly colored, and feed chiefly on plant lice. Also *lady beetle, ladybird.*

la·dy chap·el, *n.* (*Often cap.*), *chiefly Brit.* a chapel dedicated to the Virgin Mary and adjoining a church or cathedral, usu. at the east end of the chancel.

La·dy Day, *n.* Formerly, one of various days celebrated in honor of the Virgin Mary, now only the feast of the Annunciation, March 25th.

la·dy·fin·ger, lā′dē·fing″gėr, *n.* A small sponge cake shaped like a finger. Also **la·dys·fin·ger.**

la·dy-in-wait·ing, lā′dē·in·wā′ting, *n.* pl. **la·dies-in-wait·ing.** A lady who is in attendance upon a queen or princess.

la·dy·kin, lā′dē·kin, *n.* A little lady.

la·dy·like, lā′dē·līk″, *a.* Like or befitting a lady; of a man, effeminate or foppish.—**la·dy·like·ness,** *n.*

la·dy·love, lā′dē·luv″, *n.* A lady who is loved; a mistress or sweetheart.

la·dy·ship, lā′dē·ship″, *n.* The condition or rank of a lady; (*often cap.*) the form used in speaking of or to a woman having the title of *Lady,* used with *her* or *your.*

la·dy's-slip·per, lā′dēz·slip″ėr, *n. Bot.* any species of orchid belonging to the genus *Cypripedium,* whose flowers have a protruding labellum somewhat resembling a slipper. Also **la·dy-slip·per, moc·ca·sin flow·er.**

la·dy's-smock, lā′dēz·smok″, *n.* A brassicaceous plant, *Cardamine pratensis,* with white or purple flowers; any of certain related species. Also *cuckooflower,* **la·dy smock.**

lag, lag, *v.i.*—**lagged, lagging.** [Origin obscure.] To fall behind; to hang back; to develop or move comparatively slowly; to fail to reach maximum development; to decrease gradually; in marbles or billiards, to decide the order of play by a toss of a marble to the line, or a shot of the cue ball to the cushion.—*n.* A retardation or falling behind; the interval of time between connected events; the last one; in marbles or billiards, the lagging action; *elect.* an alternating-current circuit, the phase delay between voltage peak and current peak.

lag, lag, *n.* [Cf. Sw. *lagg,* stave of a cask.] One of the staves or strips which form the outside of a wooden drum; the casing of a steam cylinder.—*v.t.*—**lagged, lagging.** To cover with lags or lagging.

lag, lag, *v.t.*—**lagged, lagging.** *Slang.* To send to prison; to arrest.—*n. Slang.* A sentence in prison; a convict.

lag·an, lag′an, *n.* [O.Fr. perh. < Scand. or L.G., < the root of E. *lie.*] *Maritime law,* anything sunk in the sea, but attached to a buoy or the like in order that it may be recovered. Also *ligan.*

la·ger, lä′gėr, *n.* A beer originated in Germany, which is aged after being brewed. Also **la·ger beer.**

lag·gard, lag′ėrd, *a.* Lagging; backward; slow.—*n.* One who lags behind; a dilatory person; a loiterer.—**lag·gard·ly,** *adv.*—**lag·gard·ness,** *n.*

lag·ging, lag′ing, *n.* The insulation of a boiler or an oil tank with asbestos or other material; the covering formed or the material used. *Constr.* wooden frames or planking used to support arches under construction or to retain excavations.

la·gniappe, la·gnappe, lan·yap′, lan′yap, *n.* [Creole Fr. < Amer. Sp. *la ñapa,* the lagniappe.] In Louisiana and southeastern Texas, a small present given by a storekeeper to a customer; an extra; a dividend or tip.

lag·o·morph, lag′o·mȧrf, *n.* Any gnawing mammal of the order *Lagomorpha,* identified by an additional pair of upper incisors, as a rabbit, hare, or pika.—**lag·o·mor·phic, lag·o·mor·phous,** *a.*

la·goon, la·gōn′, *n.* [It. and Sp. *laguna,* < L. *lacuna,* < *lacus,* a lake.] A shallow body of water usu. connected with the sea, a lake, or a river. Also *la·gune.*—**la·goon·al,** *a.*

la·ic, lā′ik, *a.* [L. *laicus,* < Gr. *laikos,* < *laos,* people.] Belonging to the laity or people, as distinguished from the clergy. Also **la·i·cal.**—*n.* A layman.—**la·i·cal·ly,** *adv.*

la·i·cism, lā′i·siz″um, *n.* A political or governmental system which is free from ecclesiastical jurisdiction or influence.

la·i·cize, lā′i·sīz″, *v.t.*—**laicized, laicizing.** To secularize; remove from the jurisdiction of the clergy; as, to *laicize* the educational system; to permit the introduction of secular elements into that which is exclusively clerical.—**la·i·ci·za·tion,** *n.*

laid pa·per, lād pā′pėr, *n.* Paper marked with close parallel lines or watermarks.

lair, lâr, *n.* [O.E. *leger* = D. *leger* = O.H.G. *legar* = Goth. *ligrs,* couch, bed; < the root of E. *lie.*] The resting place or den of a wild beast; a place to lie in, as a couch or bed.—*v.i.* To go to, lie in, or have a lair.—*v.t.* To place in a lair; to serve as a lair for.

laird, lârd, *Sc.* lārd, *n.* [A form of *lord.*] *Sc.* a landowner or house proprietor.—**laird·ly,** *a.*

lais·sez faire, lais·ser faire, les″ā fâr′, *Fr.* le·sā feR′, *n.* [Fr. *laisser,* leave, let, and *faire,* to do.] The policy of noninterference or minimal interference by government in the economic affairs of industry and private enterprise; noninterference with personal freedom.—**lais·sez-faire,** *a.*

la·i·ty, lā′i·tē, *n.* Lay persons collectively, as distinguished from the clergy; people outside of any profession as distinguished from those in it.

lake, lāk, *n.* [Fr. *lac,* < L. *lacus,* lake; cogn. *loch.*] A substantial body of water wholly surrounded by land and often having no direct communication with the sea; a sizable body of any liquid.

lake, lāk, *n.* [Var. of *lac.*] A red pigment prepared from lac or cochineal by combination with a metallic compound; a red or crimson color; any of various pigments prepared from animal, vegetable, or coal-tar coloring matters by union with metallic compounds.

lake dwell·er, *n.* An inhabitant of a lake dwelling.—**lake dwell·ing,** a dwelling, esp. of prehistoric times, built on piles in a lake.

lake her·ring, *n.* A whitefish, *Leucichthys artedi*, of the Great Lakes. Also *cisco*.

Lake·land ter·ri·er, *n.* A variety of small dogs bred in northwestern England esp. for fox hunting.

lak·er, lā'kẽr, *n.* One connected with lakes; a fish of or taken from a lake, esp. a lake trout; a vessel used or suited for lake navigation.

lake trout, *n.* Any of various species of trout, esp. *Salvelinus namaycush*, found in northern U.S. and Canadian lakes.

Lal·ly col·umn, lä'lē kol'um, *n. Constr.* a tubular, concrete-filled, steel column. (Trademark.)

lam, lam, *v.t.*—*lammed, lamming.* [Cf. Icel. *lemja*, beat, thrash, lit. 'make lame'; akin to E. *lame.*] *Slang*, to beat or thrash.—*v.i. Slang.* To run quickly; run off or away.—*n. Slang*, an escape, esp. from the police.—**on the lam**, running away.—**take it on the lam**, to flee.

la·ma, lä'ma, *n.* [Tibetan.] A Lamaist priest or monk.—**La·ma·ism**, *n.* A variety of Buddhism prevailing in Tibet and Mongolia, distinguished by a belief in Shamanism and a complex monastic hierarchy.—**La·ma·is·tic**, *a.*—**La·ma·ist**, *n.*

La·marck·i·an, la·mär'kē·an, *a. Biol.* of or pertaining to the French naturalist Jean de Lamarck (1744–1829), or his theory of organic evolution.—*n.* One who holds the Lamarckian theory.—**La·marck·i·an·the·o·ry, La·marck·ism**, *n.* The theory of organic evolution which holds valid the principle of the inheritance of acquired characteristics.

la·ma·ser·y, lä'ma·ser"ē, *n. pl.* **la·ma·ser·ies.** A monastery of lamas.

lamb, lam, *n.* [O.E., Goth., Icel., and O.H.G. *lamb*; D. and Dan. *lam*, G. *lamm*, lamb.] A young sheep, or the meat derived from it; an innocent or very meek person; one who is naive and easily duped, esp. in matters of financial speculation.—*v.i.* To bear or give birth, as a ewe.

lam·baste, lam·bāst', *v.t.*—*lambasted, lambasting.* [Appar. < *lamb* and *baste.*] *Slang.* To beat or thrash; to issue an abrasive written or verbal attack on. Also **lam·bast.**

lamb·da, lam'da, *n.* [Gr. *lambda.*] The eleventh letter of the Greek alphabet, equivalent to the English *l.*

lam·bent, lam'bent, *a.* [L. *lambens* (*lambent-*), ppr. of *lambere*, lick, lap.] Running or moving lightly over a surface, as a flame; playing lightly or brilliantly over a subject; as, *lambent* wit; softly bright, as light.—**lam·ben·cy**, *n.*—**lam·bent·ly**, *adv.*

lam·bert, lam'bẽrt, *n.* [From J. H. *Lambert*, G. physicist.] *Opt.* the luminance of a perfectly diffusing white surface receiving an illuminance of one lumen per square centimeter.

lam·bre·quin, lam'brē·kin, lam'bẽr·kin, *n.* [Fr. < Flemish.] A protective scarf worn over the helmet in medieval times; a hanging or drapery covering the upper part of a door or window, or suspended from a shelf.

lamb·skin, lam'skin, *n.* The skin of a lamb, usu. dressed with the fleece on; leather made from a lamb's skin.

lamb's-quar·ters, *n. pl., sing. or pl. in constr. Bot.* goosefoot.

lame, lām, *a.*—*lamer, lamest.* [O.E. *lama* = D., Dan., and Sw. *lam*, G. *lahm*, lame; Icel. *lama*, a lame person; akin provinc. E. *lam*, to beat.] Crippled or physically disabled in one or more limbs, esp. the lower extremities; impaired; disabled; imperfect or defective; unsound, weak; as, a *lame* excuse.—*v.t.*—*lamed, laming.* To make lame; to cripple or disable.—**lame·ly**, *adv.*—**lame·ness**, *n.*

lame, lām, *Fr.* läm, *n. pl.* **lames**, lāmz, *Fr.* läm. *Medieval hist.* a thin plate, usu. metal,

which attaches to and overlaps like plates thus forming flexible pieces of armor.

la·mé, la·mā', *Fr.* lä·mā', *n.* A fabric of metallic, esp. gold and silver, threads interwoven with various other fibers.

lame duck, *n. Colloq.* A political official serving out his term prior to the inauguration of his recently elected successor; a person who is weak or ineffectual. *Slang*, a speculator in stocks who has lost a considerable amount of money. *Milit. slang*, a disabled aircraft.—**lame-duck**, *a.*

la·mel·la, la·mel'a, *n. pl.* **la·mel·lae**, la·mel'las, la·mel'ē. [Dim. of *lamina.*] A thin plate or scale; one of the thin plates which compose the gills of certain mollusks. *Bot.* one of the scalelike parts or gills on the underside of a mushroom cap; the middle membrane between two plant cells.—**la·mel·lar**, la·mel'ẽr, lam'e·lẽr, *a.*—**lam·el·late**, lam·el·lat·ed, lam'e·lāt", lam'e·lit, la·mel'āt, la·mel'it, *a.*

la·mel·li·branch, la·mel'i·brangk", *n.* [N.L. *Lamellibranchia*, pl., < L. *lamella*, thin plate, and Gr. *branchia*, gills.] Any of the *Lamellibranchiata*, a class of mollusks, including the oyster, clam, and mussel, having lamellate gills and a bivalved calcareous shell.—*a.*—**la·mel·li·bran·chi·ate**, la·mel'i·brang'kē·āt", la·mel'i·brang'kē·it, *n.*, *a.* Also **pe·lec·y·pod.**

la·mel·li·corn, la·mel'i·kạrn", *a.* [L. *lamella*, a plate, and *cornu*, a horn.] *Entom.* having antennae, the three last joints of which are platelike and disposed somewhat like the teeth of a comb: said of many beetles, as the cockchafers, scarabs, and other members of the superfamily *Lamellicornia.*—*n.* A lamellicorn beetle.

la·mel·li·form, la·mel'i·fạrm", *a. Entom.* being thin or scalelike, as a lamella.

la·ment, la·ment', *v.i.* [L. *lamentor*, to wail, < *lamentum*, a wail; same root as *latrare*, to bark, an onomatopoetic word.] To mourn; to weep or wail; to express grief or sorrow; to regret deeply.—*v.t.* To mourn for; to deplore.—*n.* Lamentation; an elegy.—**lam·en·ta·ble**, lam'en·ta·bl, la·men'ta·bl, *a.*—**lam·en·ta·ble·ness**, *n.*—**lam·en·ta·bly**, *adv.*—**la·ment·ed**, la·men'tid, *a.*

lam·en·ta·tion, lam"en·tā'shan, *n.* [L. *lamentatio.*] The act of lamenting; a wailing; expression of sorrow.

la·mi·a, lā'mē·a, *n. pl.* **la·mi·as**, la·mi·ae**, lā'mē·ē". [L. < Gr. *lámia.*] *Class. mythol.* a monster having the head and breast of a woman and the body of a snake, fabled to suck the blood of children. A vampire; a female demon.

lam·i·na, lam'i·na, *n. pl.* **lam·i·nae**, **lam·i·nas**, lam'i·nē". [L. a thin plate or lamina.] A flat, thin plate, sheet, or scale, as of metal, wood, or animal tissue; such a layer or coat lying over another. *Bot.* the upper broad part of the petal; the blade of a leaf.—**lam·i·nal**, **lam·i·nar**, *a.*

lam·i·nar flow, lam'i·nẽr flō, *n.* The smooth flow of a glutinous material, different layers of which move parallel at slightly varying rates.

lam·i·nate, lam'i·nāt", *v.t.*—*laminated, laminating.* To form, as metal or wood, into a lamina by compressing or rolling; to divide or separate into thin layers; to cover with laminae; to construct by placing layer upon layer.—*v.i.* To split into thin layers.—**lam'i·nāt"**, lam'i·nit, *a.* Laminated; having laminae.—**lam'i·nāt"**, lam'i·nit, *n.* That which is laminated.—**lam·i·nat·ed**, lam'i·nā"tid, *a.*—**lam·i·na·tion**, lam"i·nā'shan, *n.*

lam·mer·gei·er, lam·mer·gey·er, lam'ẽr·gī"ẽr, *n.* [G. *lämmergeier*—*lämmer*, pl. of *lamm*, a lamb and *geier*, a vulture.] Europe's largest bird of prey in the vulture family,

having a mustache of hanging feathers, and inhabiting mountains from Spain to Asia. Also **beard·ed vul·ture.**

lamp, lamp, *n.* [Fr. *lampe*, L. and Gr. *lampas*, < Gr. *lampō*, to shine; akin *lantern.*] A device, often decorative, used to hold light bulbs and direct their light; any contrivance providing light, as by electricity, gas, or inflammable liquid; an apparatus emitting radiation or heat; as, a sun *lamp*; *fig.* a source of spiritual or intellectual enlightenment; *pl., slang*, the eyes.—*v.t. Slang*, to see or look at.—**lamp·less**, *a.*

lamp·black, lamp'blak", *n.* A fine, black soot of nearly pure carbon, formed by the condensation of the smoke of burning gas, oil, or pitch, and used for pigmentation in paints and printing inks.

lam·per eel, lam'pẽr el, *n.* Lamprey.

lamp·light·er, laınp'lī"tẽr, *n.* One who lights street lamps; a device for lighting lamps, as a torch or a spill.

lam·poon, lam·pōn', *n.* [Fr. *lampon*, a drinking or scurrilous song, < *lamper*, to drink, to guzzle; akin *lap*, to lick.] A keen, often abusive satire in prose, verse, or art which mocks an individual or situation.—*v.t.* To satirize or ridicule in a lampoon.—**lam·poon·er**, *n.*—**lam·poon·er·y**, *n.*

lamp·post, lamp'pōst", *n.* A post or pillar used to support a lamp which lights a street, park, entranceway, or the like.

lam·prey, lam'prē, *n. pl.* **lam·preys.** [Fr. *lamproie*, It. *lampreda*, < L.L. *lampetra*—L. *lambo*, to lick, and *petra*, a stone, from their habit of attaching themselves to stones by their mouths.] An eellike animal, of the class *Cyclostomata*, with a suctorial mouth which preys on fresh- and salt-water fish. Also **lam·prey eel**, *lamper eel.*

lam·ster, lam'stẽr, *n. Slang.* A person on the lam; one fleeing, as from the law. Also **lam·is·ter.**

la·na·i, lä·nä'ē, la·nī', *n. pl.* **la·na·is.** Hawaiian. A patio; veranda.

la·nate, lā'nāt, *a.* [L. *lanatus.*] Woolly; covered with a growth or substance resembling wool. Also *lanose.*

Lan·cas·tri·an, lang·kas'trē·an, *a. Eng. hist.* of or pertaining to the English royal house of Lancaster, the reigning members of which were Henry IV, V, and VI.—*n. Eng. hist.* an adherent or member of the house of Lancaster. One who lives in or is from Lancaster or Lancashire.

lance, lans, läns, *n.* [O.Fr. Fr. *lance*, < L. *lancea*, lance.] A long shaft with a sharp-pointed iron or steel head, used by mounted soldiers in a charge; a soldier armed with this weapon; lancer; some similar weapon or implement, as a fish spear; a lancet.—*v.t.*—*lanced, lancing.* To pierce with or as with a lance; to make an incision in with a lancet.—**lance·like**, *a.*

lance cor·po·ral, *n. Milit.* a U.S. Marine Corps enlisted man with a rank over private first class and under corporal; *Brit. milit.* a private designated to act temporarily as a corporal without official change of rank or a pay increase.

lance·let, lans'lit, läns'lit, *n.* [Dim. of *lance.*] Any of various small, limbless, fish-like marine animals of the genus *Brachiostoma*, characterized by a thin, transparent body pointed at both ends, and usu. found in sand beneath shallow waters. Also **am·phi·ox·us**, am"fē·ok'sus.

Lan·ce·lot, Laun·ce·lot, lan'se·lot, lan'se·lot", län'se·lot, län'se·lot", *n.* A valiant knight in Arthurian legend.

lan·ce·o·late, lan'sē·o·lāt", lan'sē·o·lit, *a.* [L. *lanceolatus*, < *lanceola*, dim. of *lancea*, E. *lance.*] Shaped like the head of a lance; *bot.* of leaves, much longer than broad, widening above the base and tapering to the apex.—**lan·ce·o·late·ly**, *adv.*

---

a- fat, fāte, fär, fâre, fạll;   **e-** met, mē, mēre, hẽr;   **i-** pin, pīne;   **o-** not, nōte, mōve;   **u-** tub, cūbe, bụll;   **oi-** oil;   **ou-** pound.

lanc·er, lan'sẽr, län'sẽr, *n.* [Fr. *lancier,* < *lance,* E. *lance.*] A mounted soldier armed with a lance; *pl. but sing. in constr.* a form of quadrille, or music for it.

lan·cet, lan'sit, län'sit, *n.* [Fr. *lancette,* dim. of *lance.*] A small surgical instrument, sharp-pointed and generally two-edged, used in opening veins, tumors, or abscesses; *arch.* a lancet arch; a lancet window.—**lan·cet·ed,** lan'si·tid, län'si·tid, *a. Arch.* characterized by lancet arches or lancet windows.

lan·cet arch, *n.* An arch characterized by a sharply pointed apex.

lan·cet win·dow, *n. Arch.* a narrow window with a sharply pointed apex.

lance·wood, lans'wụd, läns'wụd, *n.* [So named from its being suitable for making the shafts of lances.] Any of several trees of the American tropics, esp. *Oxandra lanceolata,* which yields a tough, elastic wood used for archery bows, fishing rods, and cabinet wood.

lan·ci·nate, lan'si·nāt″, *v.t.* of *lancinated, lancinating.* [L. *lancinatus,* pp. of *lancinare,* tear, rend, lacerate.] To tear or rend; stab or pierce.—**lan·ci·na·tion,** *n.*

land, land, *n.* [O.E. *land, lond,* = D., G., Icel., Sw., Dan., and Goth. *land,* land.] The solid substance of the earth's surface; as, dry *land;* the exposed part of the earth's surface, as distinguished from that covered by water; as, to travel by *land;* ground or soil, esp. as considered with reference to quality, character, or use; as, poor *land;* rural countryside as opposed to an urban area; a part of the earth's surface marked off by natural or political boundaries; a region or country; the people of a country; a realm or domain; as, the *land* of the Vikings; ground considered as a subject of possession, with its appurtenances, such as trees, water, and buildings; *law,* any interest or estate owned in land; *econ.* natural resources as related to economic production. One of the strips into which a field is divided by plowing; a surface between grooves, as on the inner surface of a rifle barrel.—**land·less,** *a.*—**land·like,** *a.*

land, land, *v.t.* To set on or cause to go on land or shore; as, to *land* passengers or cargo from a vessel; disembark; to bring down upon land or water, as an airplane; set down from a train or the like; to bring into, or cause to arrive in, any place or situation; as, an action that *landed* him in trouble; *angling,* to pull, as a fish, out of water with a hook or a net; *colloq.* to capture, gain, or win.—*v.i.* To come to land or shore, as a vessel; reach; go or come ashore from a ship or boat; to come down upon the surface, as an airplane; alight upon the ground, as from an airplane or a train, or after a jump or the like; to come to rest or arrive in any place, position, or condition; arrive.—**land on,** to castigate; rebuke.

lan·dau, lan'dạ, lan'dou, *n.* [From *Landau,* a town in Germany, where first made.] A carriage having four wheels and a divided top, either part of which may be lowered; an automobile with a convertible top over the rear seat.

lan·dau·let, lan'dạ·let', *n.* A small landau; an automobile with a roofed or open seat for the driver in front, and a top in the rear which can be lowered or folded back.

land·ed, lan'did, *a.* Having an estate in land; consisting of real estate or land; as, *landed* property.

land·fall, land'fạl', *n.* The first sighting of land on a journey by sea or air; the first land sighted or arrived at after a journey; a landslip.

land grant, *n.* Public land granted by the government to be used for some special purpose such as railroads, colleges, or roads.

land·grave, land'grāv″, *n.* [G. *landgraf,* 'land count.'] Orig. a count in medieval Germany having jurisdiction over a designated territory; the title of various German princes.—**land·gra·vi·ate,** land·grā've·it, land·grā've·āt″, *n.* The office, jurisdiction, or territory of a landgrave.

land·hold·er, land'hōl″dẽr, *n.* A holder, owner, or proprietor of land.—**land·hold·ing,** *n.*

land·ing, lan'ding, *n.* The act of coming ashore or settling on the ground; a place where persons or goods are landed, as from a ship or airplane; any place to land at or on. *Arch.* the floor at the head or foot of a flight of stairs; a platform between flights of stairs.

land·ing craft, *n. Nav.* a type of flat-bottomed vessel used for putting men and materiel ashore.

land·ing field, *n.* A cleared, level field where airplanes can land and take off.

land·ing gear, *n. Aeron.* the understructure of an aircraft including wheels, floats, or skis and their supporting frame.

land·ing strip, *n.* An airstrip or that part of an airstrip where the airplanes actually touch the surface in landings or takeoffs; an auxiliary runway.

land·la·dy, land'lā″dē, *n. pl.* **land·la·dies.** [Cf. *landlord.*] A woman who owns and rents apartments, buildings, or other property; the mistress of an inn or boarding house; a female landlord.

land·locked, land'lokt″, *a.* Enclosed or encompassed by land; restricted to fresh water; as, *landlocked* salmon.

land·lord, land'lạrd″, *n.* The owner of land or of real estate, esp. one who has tenants; the proprietor of an inn or lodginghouse; innkeeper.

land·lord·ism, land'lạr·diz″um, *n.* The conduct, practices, and actions characteristic of landlords; the belief that advocates the predominance of landed interests; the economic system by which land is leased by a landlord to a tenant.

land·lub·ber, land'lub″ẽr, *n. Naut.* a landsman or inexperienced person aboard a ship. A contemptuous term for a new seaman.—**land·lub·ber·ly,** *a.*

land·mark, land'märk″, *n.* Any fixed, conspicuous object that distinguishes a locality, guides travelers or ships at sea, or defines the boundary of a territory; an event that marks an era; a turning point.

land mass, *n.* A continent, or other large body of land.

land meas·ure, *n.* Any unit of measurement used in giving the area of land, as an acre; a system of square measure used in measuring land.

land of·fice, *n.* A government office in which the sales of public lands are recorded.—**land-of·fice busi·ness,** *colloq.* a rushing, profitable business.

land·own·er, land'ō″nẽr, *n.* One who owns land.—**land·own·ing,** *n., a.*—**land·own·er·ship,** *n.*

land plas·ter, *n.* Gypsum rock finely ground for use as a fertilizer and soil conditioner.

land-poor, land'pụr″, *a.* Owning considerable land but unable to meet immediate financial obligations, esp. those incurred by owning the land, as taxes.

land re·form, *n.* A program, usu. sponsored by a government, to redistribute agricultural lands more equitably.

land·scape, land'skāp″, *n.* [D. *landschap,* Dan. *landskab,* equivalent to *land-shape.*] An extensive natural scene or vista of land forms, viewed from one position; a picture representing a tract of country with the various objects it contains; such pictures in general, or the painting of such pictures.—*v.t.*—**landscaped, landscaping.** To design and develop by landscape gardening.—*v.i.* To work as a landscape gardener.—**land·scap·er,** *n.* Landscape gardener.

land·scape ar·chi·tect, *n.* One trained in the profession of modifying the natural features of the landscape so as to improve its beauty.—**land·scape ar·chi·tec·ture,** *n.*

land·scape gar·den·er, *n.* One having special ability or training in the planning and ornamental planting of gardens, parks, and the like.—**land·scape gar·den·ing,** *n.*

land·side, land'sīd″, *n. Agric.* the flat side of a plow, opposite the moldboard, that presses against the unplowed ground and acts as a guide.

land·slide, land'slīd″, *n.* The slipping or sliding of a considerable portion of soil or rock from a higher to a lower level; the material which slides or slips; also *Brit. landslip. Fig.* a conspicuous and impressive election victory; an overwhelming number of votes.

land·slip, land'slip″, *n. Chiefly Brit.* landslide.

lands·man, landz'man, ländz'man, *n. pl.* **lands·men.** One who lives on the land; a compatriot; an inexperienced seaman. Also **land·man.**

land·ward, land'wẽrd, *a.* Lying, facing, or being in the direction of the land.—*adv.* Toward the land. Also **land·wards.**

Land·wehr, länt'vãR″, *n.* [G., 'land defense.'] A military reserve force trained for wartime service.

lane, lān, *n.* [O.E. *lane* = D. *laan,* lane.] A narrow way or passage between hedges, fences, walls, or houses; any narrow or well-defined passage, track, channel, or course; a portion of a highway, usu. indicated by pavement markings, which is intended for one line of vehicles; a fixed route pursued by ocean steamers; in racing events, each of the parallel paths which mark the courses of competitors; one of the parallel paths in a bowling alley.

lang·lauf, läng'louf″, *n.* Hiking or racing cross-country on skis.—**lang·lauf·er,** läng'loi″fẽr, *n.*

lan·grage, lang'grij, *n.* [Origin unknown.] A kind of cannon shot consisting of bolts and nails, fastened together or enclosed in a case, formerly used to destroy sails and rigging in naval battles.

Lang·shan, lang'shan, *n.* [From *Langshan,* near Shanghai, China.] A type of large, black or white domestic fowl native to China.

lang·syne, lang″zīn', lang″sīn', *n.* [Sc. *lang,* long, and *syne,* since.] *Sc.* the time long ago.—*adv.*

lan·guage, lang'gwij, *n.* [Fr. *langage,* < *langue,* L. *lingua,* the tongue.] A system of communication between humans through written and vocal symbols; speech peculiar to an ethnic, national, or cultural group; words esp. employed in any art, branch of knowledge, or profession; a person's characteristic mode of speech; diction; linguistics; by extension, the articulate or inarticulate expression of thought and feeling by living creatures.

langue d'oc, läng dạk', *n.* [O.Fr. 'language of *oc*' (Pr. *oc,* yes), that is, the language in which the Pr. affirmative *oc,* rather than the O.Fr. *oil* (Fr. *oui*), is used.] The form of Romance language spoken in southern France in the Middle Ages which evolved into modern Provençal.

langue d'oïl, läng dạ·ēl', läng dạ·ē, läng doil, *n.* [O.Fr. 'language of *oïl*' (O.Fr. *oil,* Fr. *oui,* yes).] The form of Romance language spoken in northern France in the Middle Ages which evolved into modern French.

lan·guet, lang'gwet, *n.* [Fr. *languette,* dim. of *langue,* < L. *lingua,* tongue.] Any of various small tongue-shaped parts, processes, or projections.

lan·guid, lang'gwid, *a.* [L. *languidus,* < *langueo,* to droop or flag.] Flagging; drooping; weak; listless; sluggish; indisposed to exertion; slow; without animation. —**lan·guid·ly,** *adv.*—**lan·guid·ness,** *n.*

lan·guish, lang'gwish, *v.i.* [Fr. *languir,* ppr. *languissant,* < L. *langueo,* to languish; akin to *lax, lag, slack.*] To be or become dull, feeble, or spiritless; to pine; to droop or fade; to be no longer vigorous in health; to live through a period of suffering and unhappy circumstances; as, to *languish* in exile; to adopt a look of wistful tenderness. —*n.* Act of pining; a wistful and tender look.—**lan·guish·er,** *n.*—**lan·guish·ing,** *a.*—**lan·guish·ing·ly,** *adv.*—**lan·guish··ment,** *n.*

lan·guor, lang'gẽr, *n.* [L. *languor.*] Physical exhaustion or lassitude; feebleness; faintness; listlessness; a state of dreaminess; oppressive stillness.—**lan·guor·ous,** *a.*—**lan··guor·ous·ly,** *adv.*

lan·gur, lung·gụr', *n.* [Hind. *langūr.*] Any of certain large, slender, long-limbed, long-tailed Asiatic monkeys of the genus *Presbytis.*

la·ni·ar·y, lā'nē·er″ē, lan'ē·er″ē, *n.* pl. **la·ni·ar·ies.** [L. *laniarius,* pertaining to a butcher, < *lanius,* a butcher.] One of the canine teeth, esp. of carnivorous animals.— *a.* Of teeth, suited for lacerating or tearing flesh.

la·nif·er·ous, la·nif'ẽr·us, *a.* [L. *lanifer, laniger,* < *lana,* wool, and *-ferous,* bearing.] Wool-bearing; woolly. Also **la·nig·er·ous,** la·nij'ẽr·us.

lank, langk, *a.* Lean, tall, and bony; long and limp, as hair; of plants, ungracefully tall and slender.—**lank·ly,** *adv.*—**lank··ness,** *n.*

lank·y, lang'kē, *a.*—*lankier, lankiest.* Awkwardly thin and tall.—**lank·i·ly,** *adv.*—**lank·i·ness,** *n.*

lan·ner, lan'ẽr, *n.* [O.Fr. Fr. *lanier,* appar. a noun use of O.Fr. *lanier,* cowardly: cf. O.Fr. *lanier,* wool-worker, L. *lanarius,* pertaining to wool, < *lana,* wool.] A falcon, *Falco biarmicus,* of southern Eurasia and northern Africa; the female of this species, larger than her mate.—**lan·ner·et,** lan'e·· ret″, *n.* [O.Fr. Fr. *laneret.*] *Falconry,* the male lanner.

lan·o·lin, lan'o·lin, *n.* [L. *lana,* wool, and *oleum,* oil.] An oily or greasy substance obtained from unwashed wool, said to be beneficial in skin ointments or lotions. Also **lan·o·line.**

la·nose, lā'nōs, *a.* [L. *lanosus,* < *lana,* wool.] Woolly; lanate, or covered with fine, woolly hairs.

lans·que·net, lans'ke·net″, *n.* [Fr., < G. *landsknecht,* < *land,* land, country, and *knecht,* manservant: see *knight.*] A mercenary foot soldier, armed with a pike or lance, formerly employed in various European armies; a game of cards, originating in Germany. Also **lands·knecht,** G. länts'knecht″.

lan·ta·na, lan·tã'na, lan·tä'na, *n.* [N.L.] *Bot.* any of the plants of the mostly tropical genus *Lantana,* in the verbena family, including species cultivated for their aromatic yellow, orange, lilac, or white flowers.

lan·tern, lan'tẽrn, *n.* [O.Fr.Fr. *lanterne,* < L. *lanterna,* < Gr. *lamptēr,* a light, torch, lantern, < *lampein,* shine.] A usu. portable case which is transparent or translucent, for enclosing a light and protecting it from wind or rain; the chamber at the top of a lighthouse surrounding the light; *arch.* an upright structure erected on a roof, forming the upper part of a tower or surmounting a dome, to admit light or air, or for decoration.

lan·tern fly, *n.* Any of various tropical homopterous insects of the family *Fulgor-*

idae, once supposed to emit light in the dark.

lan·tern jaw, *n.* A long, thin, projecting lower jaw, in man.—**lan·tern-jawed,** lan'tẽrn·jạd″, *a.*

lan·tern wheel, *n.* A wheel used like a pinion, consisting essentially of two parallel disks or heads whose peripheries are connected by a series of bars which engage the teeth of another wheel. Also **lan·tern pin·ion,** *trundle.*

lan·tha·nide se·ries, lan'tha·nīd″ sẽr'ēz, lan'tha·nid sẽr'ēz, *n.* The series of rare-earth metals starting with lanthanum and ending with lutetium. See Periodic Table of the Elements.

lan·tha·num, lan'tha·num, *n.* [Gr. *lanthanō,* I lie hid: because its existence long remained unknown.] A metallic element of the rare-earth series, having a valence of three, and allied to aluminum. Sym. La, at. no. 57.

la·nu·gi·nose, la·nö'ji·nōs″, la·nū'ji·nōs″, *a.* [L. *lanuginosus,* < *lanugo,* down, < *lana,* wool.] Downy; covered with down or fine soft hair. Also **la·nu·gi·nous,** la·nö'ji·nus, la·nū'ji·nus.—**la·nu·gi·nous·ness,** *n.*

la·nu·go, la·nö'gō, la·nū'gō, *n.* pl. **la·nu·· gos.** [L., < *lana,* wool.] *Biol.* A woolly or downy growth, as on the surface of a leaf or on the body of an insect; the coat of delicate downy hairs covering the human fetus.

lan·yard, lan·iard, lan'yẽrd, *n.* [For earlier *lanyer,* < O.Fr. *lasniere* (Fr. *laniere*), thong, *lasne,* thong: cf. L. *lacinia,* lappet, strip.] *Naut.* a short rope or line for securing or holding something, esp. rigging. A cord or string used for securing or holding objects around the neck or on the belt, as pistols, knives, or whistles. *Milit.* a cord with a small hook at one end, used in firing certain kinds of cannon; a cord, usu. colored, worn over the shoulder and signifying an award.

Lao, lou, *n.* The language spoken by the people of Laos, a country in southeastern Asia.—*a.*—**La·o·tian,** lä·ō'shan, *n.* A member of a group of the Thai race inhabiting Laos.—*a.* Pertaining to the people of Laos or their language.

la·oc·o·on, lä·ok'ō·on″, *n.* [From *Laocoon,* an ancient priest of Greek legend who struggled unsuccessfully against two serpents.] (*Often cap.*), *fig.* a person struggling against overwhelming difficulties.

La·od·i·ce·an, lä·od″i·sē'an, lā″o·di·· sē'an, *a.* Like the Christians of ancient Laodicea, a city in Asia Minor; lukewarm in religion.—*n.* A person who is indifferent, esp. toward his professed faith.

lap, lap, *n.* [O.E. *laeppa*; D. and Dan. *lap,* Sw. *lapp,* G. *lappen,* a lap, a loose flap, *lappen,* to hang loose; akin to *label, lobe.*] The surface of the upper part of the legs when one is in a sitting position; the clothing over the upper thighs when one is in a sitting position; *fig.* an area of influence, responsibility, or power; as, in the *lap* of providence, problems tossed in one's *lap.*

lap, lap, *v.t.*—*lapped, lapping.* [< O.E. *wlap,* to wrap.] To wrap or twist around; to enfold; to fold; to double over; to lay partly above; overlap.—*v.i.* To be spread or laid; to be turned over; to lie over something in part, as slates on a roof. *Sports,* to move ahead of someone by one or more laps in a race.—**lap·per,** *n.*

lap, lap, *n.* The overhanging portion of an object placed on top of another; the folding over of a pliable material; one complete round on a racetrack; a revolving disk of soft metal used for the polishing and cutting of gems and glass.

lap, lap, *v.i.*—*lapped, lapping.* [O.E. *lapian, lappian,* O.D. *lappen, lapen,* L.G. *lappen,* to

lap or lick up; allied to L. *lambo,* Gr. *lapto*— to lap or lick.] To take up liquid or food with the tongue; to feed or drink by licking up; to make a sound like that produced by taking up water by the tongue.—*v.t.* To take into the mouth with the tongue; to lick up.—*n.* A lick, as with the tongue; a sound made in this way; a sound as of water washing against the beach.—**lap·per,** *n.*

lap·a·rot·o·my, lap″a·rot'o·mē, *n.* pl. **lap·a·rot·o·mies.** *Surg.* cutting of the abdominal wall.

lap·board, lap'bōrd″, *n.* A thin, flat board to be held on the lap for use as a table or writing surface.

lap dog, *n.* A small pet dog such as may be held in the lap.

la·pel, la·pel', *n.* [Dim. < *lap,* part of a garment.] An outward fold of the front facings of a garment extending from the collar down over the chest.

lap·ful, lap'fụl, *n.* pl. **lap·fuls, laps·ful.** As much as the lap can contain.

lap·i·dar·y, lap'i·der″ē, *n.* pl. **lap·i·dar·· ies.** [L. *lapidarius,* < *lapis, lapidis,* a stone; akin Gr. *lepas,* a rock.] A craftsman who cuts, polishes, and engraves gems or precious stones; the art and technique of cutting stones. An expert or dealer in precious stones; also **la·pid·ar·ist,** la··pid'ẽr·ist.—*a.* Of or pertaining to the art of cutting, polishing, and engraving precious stones. Inscribed on stone; also **lap·i·· dar·i·an,** lap″i·der'ē·an.

lap·i·date, lap'i·dāt″, *v.t.*—*lapidated, lapidating.* [L. *lapidatus,* pp. of *lapidare,* < *lapis* (*lapid-*), a stone.] To pelt with stones; to stone to death.—**lap·i·da·tion,** *n.*

la·pil·lus, la·pil'us, *n.* pl. **la·pil·li,** la·· pil'ī. [L. *lapillus,* a little stone, contr. of *lapidulus,* dim. of *lapis,* a stone.] A glassy volcanic fragment ejected during an eruption.

lap·in, lap'in, *Fr.* lä·paN', *n.* A rabbit; the fur of a rabbit, often dyed in imitation of costlier furs.

lap·is laz·u·li, lap'is laz'ụ·lē, lap'is laz'ū·li, *n.* [L. *lapis,* a stone, and L.L. *lazulum,* this mineral; same origin as *azure.*] A semiprecious stone of a rich blue color, consisting of lazurite and other minerals, and used for jewelry, ornaments, and pigmentation; the azure color of this stone. Also *lazuli.*

lap joint, *n.* *Carp.* a joint in which two pieces or ends are overlapped and bolted together.—**lap-joint·ed,** *a.*

Lapp, lap, *n.* A member of a Scandinavian people of Mongoloid descent, chiefly inhabiting northern Norway, Sweden, and Finland; also **Lap·land·er.** Any of several Finno-Ugric languages spoken by the Lapps; also *Lappish.*—**Lap·pish,** *a.*

lap·pet, lap'it, *n.* [Dim. of *lap,* a loose part, etc.] A little lap or flap, as on a dress, esp. on a headdress; a cotton fabric with imitation embroidery, as dotted Swiss; *ornith.* the wattle of a bird.

lap robe, *n.* A fur robe or a heavy blanket, used to cover the lap and legs when sitting in the cold, as in a sports stadium, in a car, or on a ship.

lapse, laps, *n.* [L. *lapsus,* < *labi, lapsus,* to slide, to fall (as in *collapse, elapse, relapse,* etc.); akin *lap* (*n.*), *lobe.*] A slip or error, usu. trivial; an unnoticed passage of time; a slipping or gradual falling downward into disuse or failure; apostasy; backsliding; cessation of insurance coverage due to nonpayment of premiums; a denial or failure due to neglect; as, a *lapse* of justice. *Law,* forfeiture of a right or privilege through failure to exercise it within a stipulated time, or through some other contingency.

lapse, laps, *v.i.*—*lapsed, lapsing.* To err; to deviate from duty, moral integrity, or an established standard; to slip into decay or ruin; to slip gradually; to cease to exist; of time, to pass or elapse; *law*, to pass from one person to another through omission or negligence; *insurance*, to become void.— **laps·er**, *n.*

lap·strake, lap′strāk″, *a. Naut.* of a boat, built with each streak or course of planking overlapping the one below it; clinker-built. —*n.* A lapstrake boat. Also **lap·streak.**

La·pu·tan, la·pū′tan, *a.* Of or pertaining to Laputa, a flying island in Swift's *Gulliver's Travels*, whose inhabitants undertook farfetched, absurd projects; *fig.* impractical.— *n.* A visionary.

lap·wing, lap′wing″, *n.* [O.E. *hleápewince*, *lapwinke*, equiv. to *leapwink*; from its leaping or jerking mode of flight.] A large, crested plover, *Vanellus vanellus*, having a chest crossed by a wide black band.

lar, lär, sing. of *lares*.

lar·board, lär′bōrd″, *naut.* lär′bėrd, *n.* [Perhaps < M.E. *ladeborde*, the loading side.] *Naut.* port: opposed to *starboard.*—*a.*

lar·ce·ny, lär′se·nē, *n.* pl. **lar·ce·nies.** [Contr. for *latrociny*, < L. *latrocinium*, < *latro*, a robber.] The unlawful seizure of any article or articles with the intention of depriving the legal owner; theft.—**lar·ce·-ner, lar·ce·nist,** *n.*—**lar·ce·nous,** *a.* Pertaining to or having the character of larceny; guilty of or inclined to larceny.—**lar·ce·-nous·ly,** *adv.*

larch, lärch, *n.* [G. *lärche*, < L. *larix* (*laric-*), larch.] One of the deciduous, coniferous trees of the genus *Larix*, in the pine family, having needle-like leaves borne in whorl-like clusters at the ends of short spur branches, as *L. decidua*, commonly seen in parks, and *L. laricina*, native and common in swamps of the northern U.S.

lard, lärd, *n.* [Fr. *lard*, L. *lardum*, *laridum*, allied to Gr. *larinos*, fat, < *laros*, dainty.] The fat of hogs after rendering.—*v.t.* To cover or dress with lard, as meat; to stuff with pieces of bacon, as in cooking fowl; to embellish, as literary works.—**lar·don, lar·doon,** lär′don, lär·dön′, *n.* [Fr.] A strip of lard or bacon.

lar·der, lär′dėr, *n.* [O.Fr. *lardier*.] A room for storing food; a pantry.

lar·es, lâr′ēz, lā′rēz, *n. pl.* [Related to L. *larva*, a specter.] Household gods regarded by the ancient Romans as spirits of deceased ancestors.—**lar·es and pe·na·tes,** the household or domestic gods of the ancient Romans; *fig.* cherished belongings, esp. household belongings.

large, lärj, *a.*—*larger, largest.* [Fr. *large*, L. *largus*, abundant, large.] Being of great size, extent, or capacity; great in quantity or number; big by comparison with like objects or operations; having wide range or broad scope; as, *large* concepts; *naut.* of a wind, favorable.—*adv.* In a greater than usual size; as, to write *large; naut.* with the wind blowing over the stern toward the bow.—**at large,** without restraint or confinement; fully; with all details; elected by the whole rather than by a part or subdivision; as, congressman *at large.*—**large·ly,** *adv.* Mainly; generally; in a large manner.—**large·ness,** *n.*

large cal·o·rie, *n. Phys.* an amount of heat 1,000 times as great as a gram calorie. Also *kilocalorie, calorie.*

large-heart·ed, lärj′här′tid, *a.* Generous; magnanimous; sympathetic.—**large-heart·-ed·ness,** *n.*

large in·tes·tine, *n. Anat.* the shorter and wider portion of the intestine which prepares the feces for discharge by dehydrating the digestive residues, and which includes the cecum, colon, and rectum.

large-mind·ed, lärj′mīn′did, *a.* Characterized by broad, tolerant views or liberal ideas.—**large-mind·ed·ly,** *adv.*—**large-mind·ed·ness,** *n.*

large-scale, lärj′skāl′, *a.* Of great size or extent; of great range; in accordance with a scale permitting much detail, as a map or model.

lar·gess, lar·gesse, lär·jes′, lär′jis, *n.* [Fr. *largesse*, < L. *largitio*, a bounty, < *largiri*, to bestow, < *largus*, large.] Charitable or generous giving; a present, gift, or donation given unselfishly.

Large White, *n.* A type of British-bred hogs with long, white bodies.

lar·ghet·to, lär·get′ō, *a., adv.* [It.] *Mus.* slow, but not as slow as largo.—*n.* pl. **lar·ghet·tos.** A musical movement or passage having a moderately slow tempo.

larg·ish, lär′jish, *a.* Quite large.

lar·go, lär′gō, *a., adv.* [It.] *Mus.* slow, with breadth and dignity.—*n.* pl. **lar·gos.** A musical movement or passage having a slow tempo.

lar·i·at, lar′ē·at, *n.* [Sp. *la reata*, 'the rope.'] A long rope with a noose used for catching horses, cattle, or other grazing animals; lasso; a rope or cord for picketing grazing animals.

lark, lärk, *n.* [O.E. *lāwerce* = D. *leeuwerik* = G. *lerche*, lark.] Any of various European and Asian singing birds of the family *Alaudidae*, esp. the skylark, *Alauda arvensis*; any of various similar birds of other families, as the meadowlark.

lark, lärk, *n.* [< O.E. *lac*, Icel. *leikr*, Goth. *laiks*, sport, play.] Merriment; frolic; sport; a capricious adventure; prank.—*v.i.* To sport; frolic; to behave impishly.

lark·spur, lärk′spur′, *n. Bot.* any of several annual, herbaceous plants of the genus *Delphinium*, in the crowfoot family, cultivated for their blue, pink, or white flowers, produced in loose racemes.

lar·ri·gan, lar′i·gan, *n.* (*Often cap.*), *Canada*, a high, soft soled leather moccasin.

lar·ri·kin, lar′i·kin, *n. Aust. slang.* A streetcorner rough; a rowdy.—*a.* Disorderly; rough.

lar·rup, lar′up, *v.t. Colloq.* to whip or flog.— *n.* A whipping; a blow.

lar·um, lar′um, *n.* An alarm.

lar·va, lär′va, *n.* pl. **lar·vae,** lär′vē. [L. *larva*, a mask, a specter.] *Entom.* the stage which follows the egg in the life cycle of an insect, known variously as worm, grub, or caterpillar; *zool.* a free-living or detached embryo, usu. strikingly different in appearance from the adult, occurring in several phyla of the animal kingdom.—**lar·val,** *a.*

lar·vi·cide, lär′vi·sīd″, *n.* A chemical preparation used for killing larvae.—**lar·-vi·cid·al,** *a.*

la·ryn·ge·al, la·rin′jē·al, la·rin′jel, lar″-in·jē′al, *a.* Pertaining to the larynx.—*n.* A sound made in the larynx.—**la·ryn·ge·al·-ly,** *adv.*

lar·yn·gi·tis, lar″in·jī′tis, *n.* [Term. -*itis* denotes inflammation.] An inflammation of the larynx.—**lar·yn·git·ic,** lar″in·jit′ik, *a.* Pertaining to or characteristic of laryngitis.

lar·yn·gol·o·gy, lar″ing·gol′o·jē, *n. Med.* the study of the larynx and its diseases. —**la·ryn·go·log·i·cal,** la·ring″go·loj′i·kal, *a.*—**lar·yn·gol·o·gist,** *n.*

la·ryn·go·scope, la·ring′go·skōp″, *n.* A reflecting instrument for examining the larynx.—**la·ryn·go·scop·ic, la·ryn·-go·scop·i·cal,** la·ring″go·skop′ik, *a.* —**la·ryn·go·scop·i·cal·ly,** *adv.*—**la·ryn·-gos·co·pist,** lar″ing·gos′ko·pist, *n.*—**lar·-yn·gos·co·py,** *n.*

lar·yn·got·o·my, lar″ing·got′o·mē, *n. pl.* **lar·yn·got·o·mies.** *Surg.* a cutting into the larynx.

lar·ynx, lar′ingks, *n. pl.* **la·ryn·ges, lar·-ynx·es,** la·rin′jēz. [N.L. < Gr. *larynx, laryng-*.] *Anat.* the cartilaginous structure at the upper end of the human trachea which contains and supports the vocal cords

and associated structures; *zool.* a corresponding structure in other vertebrates.

las·car, las′kėr, *n.* [Hind. and Pers. *lashkar*, army, camp.] A native East Indian seaman. Also **lash·kar.**

las·civ·i·ous, la·siv′ē·us, *a.* [L. *lascivia*, lewdness, *lascivus*, wanton.] Lewd; lustful; exciting sensual emotions.—**las·civ·i·-ous·ly,** *adv.*—**las·civ·i·ous·ness,** *n.*

la·ser, lā′zėr, *n.* [(*l*)ight (*a*)mplification by (*s*)timulated (*e*)mission of (*r*)adiation.] A device for amplifying light radiation, in which a beam of light is shot through a crystal causing the crystal to emit an intense, direct light beam that is useful in micromachining, surgery, and computer design.

lash, lash, *n.* [Akin to G. *lasche*, a flap, a thong, a latchet, a scarf joint; D. *lasch*, a piece joined on, a joining; Dan *laske*, Sw. *laska*, to scarf.] The flexible end of a whip; a whip; a blow with a whip or anything flexible and tough; a sharp, cutting, or ridiculing remark; a violent impact against something, as of rain or wind; an eyelash.— *v.t.* To whip or beat; to goad or incite, as by an emotional appeal; to attack or ridicule severely in words; to strike forcefully against; to switch or flick suddenly, as: The cow *lashed* her tail.—*v.i.* To attack or strike with or as with a whip; to censure in sharp terms, followed by *out*; to wriggle or move suddenly or quickly, as a snake or an animal's tail.—**lash·er,** *n.*—**lash·ing,** *n.* A physical or verbal whipping or beating; the act of lashing.

lash, lash, *v.t.* To tie or bind; to fasten with chain, rope, or cord.—**lash·er,** *n.*—**lash·-ing,** *n.* A piece of rope or the like used for tying or binding; the action of lashing.

lash·ings, lash′ingz, *n. pl. Brit.* a large quantity or an abundance, usu. followed by *of.*

lass, las, *n.* [A contr. for *ladess*, fem. of *lad*, or a contr. of W. *llodes*, a lass.] A young woman, usu. unmarried; a girl; a sweetheart.—**las·-sie,** las′ē, *n.* [Dim. of *lass*.] A young girl.

las·si·tude, las′i·tōd″, las′i·tūd″, *n.* [L. *lassitudo*, < *lassus*, weary; same root as *late*.] A feeling of weariness or weakness; listlessness of body or mind.

las·so, las′ō, las′ö, *n.* pl. **las·sos, las·soes.** [Sp. *lazo*, Pg. *laço*, < *laqueus*, a noose.] A long rope, usu. woven of hemp or rawhide, with a running noose, used to catch cattle and horses; a lariat.—*v.t.* To catch with a lasso.—**las·so·er,** *n.*

last, last, läst, *a., irreg. superl. of late.* [O.E. *last*, a contr. for *latost*, latest; cf. *best* for *betst*.] Happening or coming after all the others; final; latest; hindmost; remaining; next before the present; conclusive; utmost; extreme; lowest; as, *last* on the list; farthest of all from possessing a given quality, character, use, or the like; most unlikely, as: You are the *last* man I should consult.—*adv.* On the last occasion; at the time before the present; after all others; lastly; finally.—*n.* Someone or something that comes last; the concluding part; the final reference, appearance, or instance.—**at last,** after a long time.—**breathe one's last,** die.

last, last, läst, *v.i.* [O.E. *laestan*, to follow, to observe or perform, to last, to endure; Goth. *laistjan*, to trace footsteps, to follow, < O.E. *last*, Goth. *laists*, a footstep.] To continue in time; to endure; to remain in existence; to hold out; to be sufficient in quantity; as, provisions to *last* for a week; to continue unimpaired; not to decay or perish.—**last·er,** *n.*

last, last, läst, *n.* [O.E. *lást, laest*, D. *leest*, Dan. *laest*, a last; Goth. *laists*, footstep; Icel. *leistr*, the foot below the ankle, a short sock.] A mold or form of the human foot, made of wood or metal, and on which shoes are formed or repaired.—*v.t.* To form on or shape by a last.—**stick to one's last,** remain

in the trade or field that one knows best.—
last·er, *n.* One who works on lasts.

last, last, läst, *n.* [O.E. *hlaest,* < *hladan,* to lade; D., Dan., and G. *last,* Icel. *lest,* a load.] A load; a certain weight or measure which varies for different articles but is generally estimated at 4,000 lbs.

Las·tex, las'teks, *n.* (*Sometimes l.c.*) an elastic yarn whose core of latex is covered with threads of cotton, silk, or synthetic fiber. (Trademark.)

last·ing, las'ting, lä'sting, *a.* Enduring; durable; permanent; of long continuance. —*n.* A durable fabric used in construction of the uppers of certain shoes.—**last·ing·ly,** *adv.*—**last·ing·ness,** *n.*

last·ly, last'lē, läst'lē, *adv.* Finally; in the last place.

Last Sup·per, *n.* The last meal shared by Christ and His disciples prior to His crucifixion and at which He instituted the sacrament of the Holy Eucharist.

last word, *n.* The final comment in a discussion or argument; a conclusive or decisive work, as: His biography is the *last word* on the life of Bernard Shaw. *Colloq.* the most recent fashion, style, or trend.

Lat·a·ki·a, lat"a·kē'a, *n.* [From *Latakia,* a Syrian seaport.] A fine variety of Turkish tobacco.

latch, lach, *n.* [M.E. *lacche,* appar. < *lacchen,* E. *latch.*] A device for securing a door or gate, usu. consisting of a bar which slips into a notch on a doorjamb or gate; a device for locking a window; sometimes, a spring lock.—*v.i., v.t.* To secure or fasten by means of a latch.— **latch on·to,** *colloq.* get possession of; as, to *latch onto* a job.

latch·et, lach'it, *n.* [Fr. *lacet,* a lace or string.] *Archaic,* a lace or thong that fastens a shoe or sandal onto the foot.

latch·key, lach'kē", *n.* A key used to raise the latch of an outside door. Also *passkey.*

latch·string, lach'string", *n.* A string passed through a hole in a door, for raising the latch from the outside.

late, lāt, *a.*—*later* or *latter, latest* or *last.* [O.E. *laet,* D. *laat,* Icel. *latr,* Dan. *lad,* Sw. *lat,* late, slow, tardy; Goth. *lats,* sluggish; G. *lass,* wearied; akin L. *lassus* (for *ladtus*); the root is that of *let.*] Coming or happening after the usual time; slow; tardy; long delayed; far advanced toward the end or close; as, a *late* hour, the *late* 17th century; existing or happening not long ago, but not now; deceased; departed; last or recent, as in time or position.—*adv.* After the usual time, or the time appointed; after delay; not long ago; lately; far into the night, day, week, or other particular period.—**of late,** lately, recently. —**late·ly,** *adv.*—**late·ness,** *n.*—**lat·ish,** lā'tish, *a.* Somewhat late.

lat·ed, lā'tid, *a.* [< *late, a.*] *Liter.* belated.

la·teen sail, la·tēn' sāl, *n.* [Fr. (*voile*) *latine* 'Latin (sail).'] *Naut.* a triangular sail extended by a long yard at an angle of about 45° to the mast, common on the Mediterranean.—**la·teen-rigged,** la·tēn'-rigd", *a.* Having a lateen sail or sails.

Late Greek, *n.* The Greek used from approximately 300 to 700 A.D.

Late Lat·in, *n.* The written Latin used in the Western Roman Empire from approximately 300 to 700 A.D.

La Tène, *Fr.* lä ten', *a. Archaeol.* referring to the later part of the Iron Age, the artifacts of which were found in the shallows of Lake Neuchâtel, Switzerland.

la·ten·si·fy, lā·ten'si·fī", *v.t.*—*latensified, latensifying. Photog.* to intensify, as a latent image on photographic film or plate, by treatment with developing fluids or by exposure to dim light.—**la·ten·si·fi·ca·tion,** lā·ten"si·fi·kā'shan, *n.*

la·tent, lāt'ent, *a.* [L. *latens, latentis,* <

lateo, to lurk; allied to Gr. *lanthanō, lathein,* to escape notice.] Not visible or apparent although present; not manifested; *psychol.* present in a concealed form but capable of becoming manifest; as, a *latent* homosexual; *bot.* undeveloped or dormant, as a hidden bud.—**la·ten·cy,** lāt'en·sē, *n.* —**la·tent·ly,** *adv.*

la·tent con·tent, *n. Psychoanal.* the real or unconscious meaning of a dream.

la·tent heat, *n. Phys.* heat required to change the state of a body without changing its temperature, as that absorbed by a unit mass of a solid in converting to a liquid at its melting point, heat of fusion, or that absorbed by a unit mass of a liquid in converting to a gas at its boiling point, heat of vaporization.

la·tent pe·ri·od, *n. Med.* the period in a disease between the moment of infection and the appearance of symptoms; *physiol.* the time between stimulation and reaction. Also *latency.*

la·ter, lā'ter, *a.* [Compar. of *late.*] More late. —*adv.* Late in a greater degree; to stay *later* than usual; subsequently; afterward; as, Prince Hal, *later* King Henry V of England.

lat·er·al, lat'ėr·al, *a.* [L. *lateralis,* < *latus* (*later-*), side.] Of or pertaining to the side; situated at, proceeding from, or directed toward a side; as, a *lateral* move; *phon.* articulated in such a manner that the breath passes over the side or sides of the tongue.— *n.* A lateral part or extension, as a branch or shoot; *phon.* a lateral sound.—**lat·er·al·ly,** *adv.*

lat·er·al pass, *n. Football,* a pass thrown in a direction backward from the passer or parallel to the goal line: opposed to *forward pass.*

lat·er·ite, lat'e·rīt", *n.* [L. *later,* a brick.] A porous reddish-colored tropical soil bearing heavy concentrations of iron and aluminum hydroxides, formed by decomposition of underlying rocks; any soil produced by such decomposition.—**lat·er·it·ic,** lat"e·rit'ik, *a.*

la·tex, lā'teks, *n.* pl. **lat·i·ces, la·tex·es,** lat'i·sēz. [L., a liquid.] *Bot.* a milky juice occurring in special cells of certain plants, as milkweed, euphorbia, poppies, and plants yielding India rubber, which coagulates on exposure to the air and is the source of natural rubber; *chem.* any of various thermoplastics produced by emulsion polymerization and used in paints, adhesives, coated fabrics, and coated papers.

lath, lath, läth, *n.* [O.E. *laetta,* D. and G. *latte,* whence Fr. *latte,* It. *latta,* a lath, a pole, etc. Akin *lattice, latten.*] A thin narrow board or slip of wood nailed to the rafters of a building to support roofing material; a thin narrow slip of wood, perforated metal, or wire mesh nailed to a wall to support plaster, tile, or the like; such materials collectively; any similar piece of metal or wood.—*v.t.* To cover or line with laths.— **lath·er,** lath'ėr, lä'thėr, *n.* One who applies laths.—**lath·ing,** lath'ing, lä'thing, *n.* Lath materials; lath work on a wall; work of putting on lath materials.

lathe, lāth, *n.* [Prob. < Scand.: cf. Dan. *dreielad,* turning lathe.] A machine for shaping wood, metal, or the like by rotating it rapidly against a fixed cutting tool; a small form of potter's wheel.—*v.t.*—*lathed, lathing.* To cut, shape, or otherwise treat on a lathe.

lath·er, laTH'ėr, *n.* [O.E. *lēathor* = Icel. *laudhr,* washing soda, foam.] Foam or suds made from soap or synthetic detergent agitated with water; foam or froth formed in profuse sweating, as of a horse.—*v.t.* To apply lather to; cover with lather; *colloq.* to beat or flog.—*v.i.* To form a lather; to become covered with lather, as a horse.— **lath·er·er,** *n.*—**lath·er·y,** laTH'é·rē, *a.*

lath·y, lath'ē, lä'thē, *a.*—*lathier, lathiest.* Lathlike; long and slender; thin.

lat·i·cif·er·ous, lat"i·sif'ėr·us, *a.* [L. *latex,* sap, and *fero,* to bear.] *Bot.* containing or secreting latex.

lat·i·fun·di·um, lat"i·fun'dē·um, *n.* pl. **lat·i·fun·di·a,** lat"i·fun'dē·a. An extensive farm or estate, as in Rome in the period from the 1st century B.C. to the 4th century A.D., which resembled an early English baronial manor.

Lat·in, lat'in, lat'in, *n.* [L. *Latinus,* < *Latium,* Latium.] The language of the Roman Empire; a native of Latium, a country in ancient Italy; a member of any of the Latin peoples, as of Italy, Spain, or France; a native of a Latin-American country; a member of the Roman Catholic Church, as distinct from the Eastern Orthodox Church.—*a.* Referring to those peoples, as the Italians, French, and Spanish, or esp. the Latin Americans, using languages derived from that of ancient Rome; pertaining to the language of the ancient Romans, or its later forms; pertaining to ancient Latium and its inhabitants.

Lat·in-A·mer·i·can, lat'in·a·mer'i·kan, *a.* Pertaining to the western hemisphere countries south of the U.S., in which languages derived from Latin are spoken.— **Lat·in A·mer·i·can,** *n.* A native or inhabitant of any of these countries.

Lat·in·ate, lat'i·nāt", *a.* Pertaining to a style of written or spoken English evidencing Latin origin of words and sentence structures; resembling Latin.

Lat·in cross, *n.* An upright bar crossed near the top by a shorter transverse piece.

Lat·in·ism, lat'i·niz"um, *n.* An idiom or sentence structure borrowed from Latin.

Lat·in·ist, lat'i·nist, *n.* One learned in Latin or in the culture of the ancient Romans.

La·tin·i·ty, la·tin'i·tē, *n.* [L. *latinitas.*] Use of the Latin language; a Latin style or idiom.

Lat·in·ize, lat'i·nīz", *v.t.*—*Latinized, Latinizing.* To cause to conform to the customs and practices of the Latins or of the Roman Catholic Church; to translate into Latin.— *v.i.* To use Latin words, idioms, and quotations.—**Lat·in·i·za·tion,** lat"i·ni·-zā'shan, *n.*

Lat·in Quar·ter, *n.* A district in Paris on the south side of the Seine, known for its student and artist residents.

Lat·in square, *n.* Any square arrangement of letters or other symbols wherein each element appears once and only once in each row and column: used in the statistical design of experiments.

lat·i·tude, lat'i·töd", lat'i·tūd", *n.* [L. *latitudo,* breadth, < *latus,* broad.] *Geog.* the angular distance north or south of the equator of a point on the earth's surface, measured in degrees on the meridian of the point; a place or region as marked by its latitude. *Astron.* the angular distance of a heavenly body from the ecliptic. Freedom from narrow restrictions; permitted freedom of choice or action.—**lat·i·tu·di·nal,** lat"i·töd'i·nal, lat"i·tūd'i·nal, *a.*—**lat·i·tu·di·nal·ly,** *adv.*

lat·i·tu·di·nar·i·an, lat"i·töd'i·nâr'ē·an, lat"i·tūd"i·nâr'ē·an, *a.* Permitting free thought or conduct, esp. in matters of religion.—*n.* A person who is liberal or tolerant in his views, esp. in religion; any of the 17th century Anglican churchmen who were not in favor of strict adherence to established church doctrines.—**lat·i·tu·-di·nar·i·an·ism,** *n.*

la·trine, la·trēn', *n.* [L. *latrina,* a bath, < *lavo,* to wash.] A toilet; something used as a toilet, esp. in a military camp or barracks.

lat·ten, lat'en, lat'en, *n.* [O.Fr. *laton* (Fr. *laiton*); perh. < Teut. and akin to *lath.*] A brasslike alloy, commonly made in thin sheets, formerly much used for church utensils;

iron plate tinned over; tin plate; any metal in thin sheets.

lat·ter, lat′ẽr, *a., irreg. compar. of late.* More recent; nearer the end; as, the *latter* part of the week; pertaining to or being the second of two, as opposed to *former.*—**lat·ter-day,** lat′ẽr·dā′, *a.* Of a later time; of the present; modern.—**lat·ter·ly,** *adv.*

Lat·ter-day Saint, *n.* One who is a Mormon.

lat·tice, lat′is, *n.* [Fr. *lattis,* < *latte,* lath.] A structure of wood or metal made by crossing laths, rods, or bars, and forming open reticulated work, often in a diagonal pattern; a window or gate made of such laths or strips crossing one another. *Phys.* a space lattice; in a nuclear reactor, a structure of fissionable and nonfissionable material in a regular geometrical arrangement.—*v.t.*—*latticed, latticing.* To give the form or appearance of a lattice to; to furnish with a lattice.—**lat·ticed,** *a.*—**lat·tice·like,** *a.*

lat·tice gird·er, *n.* A girder in which the central portion consists of pieces arranged like latticework.

lat·tice·work, lat′is·wᵾrk″, *n.* Any lattice or work made of crossed strips in the pattern of a lattice.

Lat·vi·an, lat′vē·an, *a.* Referring to Latvia, a formerly independent European country on the eastern Baltic coast which is now part of the Soviet Union, to its people, or to any of the Baltic dialects; pertaining to the Baltic or Lettish language spoken here which is one of the languages of the Baltic branch of the Indo-European chain.—*n.* An inhabitant of Latvia or his language.

laud, lạd, *v.t.* [L. *laudo,* to praise, < *laus, laudis,* praise; *allow* is a derivative.] To praise in words alone, or with words and singing; to extol; acclaim.—*n.* A song or hymn of praise. *Pl., sing. or pl. in constr., Rom. Cath. Ch.* a series of psalms of praise which, when recited with the matins, comprises the first in a series of seven canonical hours recited throughout the day.—**laud·er, lau·da·tor,** lạ′dā·tẽr, *n.*

laud·a·ble, lạ′da·bl, *a.* [L. *laudabilis.*] Praiseworthy; commendable.—**laud·a·bil·i·ty, laud·a·ble·ness,** *n.*—**laud·a·bly,** *adv.*

lau·da·num, lạd′a·num, lạd′num, *n.* [N.L. (used by Paracelsus), appar. a var. of L. *ladanum.*] Tincture of opium.

lau·da·tion, lạ·dā′shan, *n.* [L. *laudatio(n-),* < *laudare,* E. *laud,* v.] The act of lauding; praise; tribute.

laud·a·to·ry, lạ′da·tōr″ē, *a.* [L.L. *laudatorius.*] Containing or expressing praise. Also **laud·a·tive.**—**laud·a·to·ri·ly,** *adv.*

laugh, laf, läf, *v.i.* [O.E. *hlehhan, hlihhan,* to laugh; cf. Goth. *hlahjan,* O.H.G. *hlahhan,* Icel. *hlæja,* D. *lagchen,* to laugh.] To express merriment, amusement, ridicule, nervousness, or the like, with a vocal outburst or chuckling noise and usu. with accompanying facial and bodily manifestations; to be merry, amused, or scornful; to appear gay or bright.—*v.t.* To express by laughing; to coerce or compel with or as with laughter.—*n.* The inarticulate sound expressing sudden amusement that is peculiar to man; *colloq.* something laughable.—**laugh at,** to ridicule; to treat with some degree of contempt. —**laugh a·way,** to banish or minimize by laughter.—**have the last laugh,** to succeed after predicted or apparent defeat.—**laugh up one's sleeve,** to laugh to oneself or so as not to be observed.—**laugh off,** to dismiss, reject, or scorn by laughter. —**laugh on the oth·er** or **wrong side of one's mouth,** to feel vexation or disappointment after exhibiting a boastful or exultant attitude.—**laugh·er,** *n.*—**laugh·ing·ly,** *adv.*

laugh·a·ble, laf′a·bl, lä′fa·bl, *a.* Exciting or eliciting laughter; comical; ludicrous.—**laugh·a·ble·ness,** *n.*—**laugh·a·bly,** *adv.*

laugh·ing gas, *n.* Nitrous oxide.

laugh·ing jack·ass, *n.* An Australian bird, the kookaburra, so named for its raucous, braying song.

laugh·ing·stock, laf′ing·stok″, lä′fing·- stok″, *n.* A person or thing that is an object of ridicule; a butt for laughter or jokes.

laugh·ter, laf′tẽr, läf′tẽr, *n.* [O.E. *hleahtor,* Icel. *hlair,* O.H.G. *hlahtar.*] The act, distinctive sound, or physical manifestation, esp. facial, that expresses merriment; appearance or expression of mirth or delight.

launce, lans, läns, *n.* Sand launce.

launch, lạnch, länch, *v.t.* [Also written *lanch,* a form of *lance;* Fr. *lancer,* O.Fr. *lanchier,* to throw or dart.] To propel, drive, or precipitate in flight; to move or cause to slide from the land into the water; to set afloat, as a newly built boat, for the first time; to put into operation; initiate; to inaugurate on a course or mode of operation, as a person or organization; to throw, as a lance.—*v.i.* To set a vessel on the water, often with *out* or *forth;* to enter into a new field of activity; to rush headlong or plunge with enthusiasm, usu. followed by *into;* to set out, often with *on.*—*n.* The setting afloat of a ship or boat; a kind of motorboat, long, low, and usu. open; *aerospace,* the blast-off of a rocket, missile, or space vehicle.

launch·er, lạnch′ẽr, länch′ẽr, *n.* A mechanical device which discharges a projectile, as a rocket installation or rifle part for firing grenades.

launch·ing pad, *n.* The heat-resistant platform upon which a guided missile or rocket rests before firing. Also **launch pad.**

laun·der, lạn′dẽr, län′dẽr, *v.t.* [Contr. of earlier *lavender,* < O.Fr. *lavandier,* masc., *lavandiere,* Fr. *lavandiere,* fem. < L. *lavandus,* gerundive of *lavare,* wash.] To wash, as clothes; to wash and iron.—*v.i.* To wash and iron; to submit to washing and ironing; as, a dress that *launders* well.— *n. Mining,* a conveyor used for washing ore residues.—**laun·der·er,** *fem.* **laun·dress,** lạn′dris, län′dris, *n.*

laun·der·ette, lạn″de·ret′, län″de·ret′, lạn′de·ret′, län′de·ret′, *n.* Laundromat.

Laun·dro·mat, lọn′dro·mat″, län′dro·mat″, *n.* A business establishment consisting of coin-operated automatic laundry equipment. (Trademark.)

laun·dry, lạn′drē, län′dre, *n. pl.* **laun·dries.** A place or establishment where washing and ironing is done; a utility area set apart in a kitchen, basement, or other location in a home or residence hall for laundering; articles to be washed or already washed.

laun·dry·man, lạn′drē·man″, län′drē·- man″, *n. pl.* **laun·dry·men.** An employee or manager of a laundry; one who picks up and returns laundry.—**laun·dry·wom·an,** lạn′drē·wᵾm″an, län′drē·wᵾm″an, *n. pl.* **laun·dry·wom·en.**

lau·ra, lạ′ra, *n. pl.* **lau·ras,** L. **lau·rae.** [L.L., < L.Gr. *laura,* laura, Gr. alley, lane.] In the early Eastern Church, a monastic community.

lau·ra·ceous, lạ·rā′shus, *a.* [L. *laurus,* laurel.] Belonging to the *Lauraceae,* or laurel family of plants.

lau·re·ate, lạr′ē·it, *a.* [L. *laureatus,* < *laurea,* laurel tree, crown of laurel, < *laurus,* laurel.] Recognized or deserving of distinction, esp. for poetic achievement or merit; crowned or decked with laurel as an honor or mark of distinction; of or pertaining to a poet, esp. a poet laureate; consisting of laurel, as a crown or wreath.—*n.* One crowned with laurel; a poet laureate.—

v.t.—*laureated, laureating.* To crown with laurel, in token of honor; as, to *laureate* a victor; to appoint as poet laureate.— **lau·re·ate·ship,** *n.*

lau·rel, lạr′el, lor′el, *n.* [O.Fr. Fr. *laurier,* < L. *laurus,* laurel.] A small lauraceous evergreen tree, *Laurus nobilis,* of southern Europe; any of various trees similar to the true laurel; a branch or wreath of it; the foliage of this tree as an emblem of victory or distinction. *Pl.* honor won, as by achievement; as, to win one's *laurels.*—*v.t.* —*laureled, laureling,* Brit. *laurelled, laurelling.* To adorn or wreathe with laurel; to honor with marks of distinction.—**look to one's lau·rels,** to guard one's honors against rivals.—**rest on one's lau·rels,** to rest contentedly and confidently on honors already won.

Lau·ren·tian, lạ·ren′shan, *a.* [L.L. *Laurentius,* Lawrence.] Referring to, pertaining to, or of the St. Lawrence River; *geol.* noting or pertaining to a series of rocks of the Archaean system, occurring in Canada near the St. Lawrence River and the Great Lakes.

lau·ric ac·id, lạr′ik as′id, lor′ik, *n. Chem.* a white crystalline acid existing in vegetable fats as a glyceride, $CH_3(Ch_2)_{10}COOH$, used in making cosmetics, soaps, and lauryl alcohol. Also **do·dec·a·no·ic ac·id.**

lau·rus·ti·nus, lạr″a·stī′nus, *n. pl.* **lau·rus·ti·nus·es.** [N.L., < L. *laurus,* laurel, and *tinus,* kind of plant.] An evergreen garden shrub, *Viburnum tinus,* native to southern Europe, with white or pinkish flowers. Also **lau·rus·tine.**

lau·ryl al·co·hol, lạr′il al′ko·hạl″, lor′il al′ko·hạl″, *n. Chem.* a liquid or crystalline solid compound, $CH_3(CH_2)_{10}CH_2OH$, derived from the fatty acids in coconut oil, and used for producing detergents.

la·va, lä′va, lav′a, *n. pl.* **la·vas.** [It., orig. 'stream,' < L. *lavare,* wash.] The molten or fluid rock which issues from a volcano or volcanic vent; a variety of this substance caused by hardening of lava under variable conditions.

la·va·bo, la·vä′bō, la·vä′bō, *n. pl.* **la·va·boes.** [L., 'I will wash.'] (*Often cap.*), *eccles.* the ritual washing of the celebrant's hands after the offertory in the mass or eucharistic service in the Rom. Cath. and Anglican churches; the verses recited accompanying the ceremony; the small towel or the basin used in the washing; the basin and tank construction found in medieval monasteries. A simulated basin and tank used as a wall fixture or planter.

lav·age, la·väzh′, lav′ij, *n. pl.* **lav·a·ges,** la·vä′zhiz, lav′i·jiz, *Fr.* lä·väzh′. [Fr., < *laver,* wash.] A washing; *med.* the process of cleansing, as by injection, esp. the washing out of the stomach.

la·va-la·va, lä″va·lä′va, *n.* A printed cotton waistcloth or loincloth worn by Pacific Island natives.

lav·a·liere, lav·a·lier, Fr. **la·val·lière,** lav″a·lēr′, läv′va·lēr′, Fr. lä·vä·lyeʀ′, *n.* [From the Duchesse de *La Vallière* (1644– 1710), mistress of Louis XIV of France.] A pendant, usu. of jewels, suspended on a chain that is worn around the neck.

la·va·tion, la·vä′shan, lä·vä′shan, *n.* [L. *lavatio.*] A washing or cleansing.—**la·va·tion·al,** *a.*

lav·a·to·ry, lav′a·tōr″ē, *n. pl.* **lav·a·to·ries.** [M.L. *lavatorius,* as *n.,* L.L. *lavatorium,* < L. *lavare,* wash.] A room with means for washing the hands and face, and often with toilet conveniences; a place where washing is done; a vessel for washing or bathing purposes.

lave, lāv, *v.t.*—*laved, laving.* [O.Fr. Fr. *laver,* < L. *lavare,* pp. *lavatus, lautus,* or *lotus,* wash: cf. *launder, lava,* and *lotion.*] *Liter.* To wash or bathe; of a river or the sea, to wash or flow against; to pour or ladle.

lav·en·der, lav′en·dẻr, n. [M.L. *lavendula, lavandula*; origin uncertain; commonly referred to L. *lavare*, wash, from its use with freshly washed linen or in baths or toilet water.] Any of the European menthaceous plants belonging to the genus *Lavandula*, with spikes of pale purple flowers, and yielding a fragrant oil; the dried flowers or other parts of these plants, esp. of *L. officinalis*, used in sachets and as a preservative; a pale purple color.—*a.* Pale, delicate purple.—*v.t.* To scent with lavender.—**lav·en·der wa·ter,** a toilet water or perfume made with oil of lavender.

la·ver, lā′vẻr, n. A basin placed in the court of the ancient Jewish tabernacle for ceremonial cleansing before sacrifices; anything which provides a spiritual cleansing, esp. the baptismal water and font.

la·ver, lā′vẻr, n. [L., kind of water plant.] Any of several edible seaweeds, esp. of the genus *Porphyra*.

lav·ish, lav′ish, a. [M.E. *lavas, lavage*, a., lavish, *lavas*, n., extravagant outpouring: cf. O.Fr. *lavasse, lavache*, deluge of rain, L. *lavare*, wash.] Using, expending, or bestowing in great abundance; prodigal, often with *of*; exceedingly liberal; extravagant; done with profusion or prodigality.—*v.t.* To expend, bestow, or spend in great abundance or without stint.—**lav·ish·er,** n.—**lav·ish·ly,** adv.—**lav·ish·ment,** n.—**lav·ish·ness,** n.

law, lạ, n. [O.E. *lagu*, < same root as *lie, lay, low*; cogn. Sw. *lag*, Icel. *lag, log*, Dan. *lov*, a law; the root is also in L. *lex*, a law (whence *legal*).] The body of rules or principles, prescribed by authority or established by custom, which a state, community, society, or the like recognizes as binding on its members; one of the individual rules belonging to such a body; the controlling influence of such rules, or the condition of society brought about by their observance; as, to maintain *law* and order; rules of this class collectively as an institution or authority in human life; as, courts of *law*; the department of knowledge or study concerned with such rules or system of rules; a body of such rules concerned with a particular subject; as, commercial *law*, labor *law*; a body of such laws derived from a particular source; as, statute *law*, common *law*; the rules and principles employed in the common law courts as distinguished from equity courts; the legal profession; as, the practice of *law*; legal action or judicial remedy; as, to take it to *law*; any rule or injunction that must be obeyed; as: Good table manners are the *law* at home. A binding rule or principle of conduct viewed as an expression of the divine will or as derivable from conscience, reason, or nature; as, the *law* of God, the *law* of nature; an enforcer of law, as a policeman; a controlling force, instinctive and usu. spontaneous; as, the *law* of survival; any governing force in business, art, games, language, or the like; as, the *law* of supply and demand, the *laws* of chess; *philos., phys.* a statement of a relation or sequence of phenomena invariable under the same conditions; as, the *law* of gravitation; *math.* a rule on which something depends, as the construction of a curve. *Bib.* any revelation or commandment from God. *Brit. sports,* the allowance of distance or time given to the game in an animal hunt or to the competition in a race.—*v.t., v.i.* To prosecute; to take to law.—**be a law un·to one·self,** to act against conformity; to act according to personal desires regardless of established ways and methods.—**lay down the law,** to state authoritatively one's wishes, views, or instructions.—**take the law in·to one's own hands,** to try to achieve justice through

means other than normal legal processes, as: The lynchers wanted to *take the law into their own hands.*—**law·like,** a.

law-a·bid·ing, lạ′a·bī″ding, a. Observant of the law; obeying the law.—**law-a·bid·ing·ness,** n.

law·break·er, lạ′brā″kẻr, n. One who violates the law.—**law·break·ing,** n., a.

law·ful, lạ′ful, a. Allowed by law; agreeable or conformable to law; legitimate, rightful. —**law·ful·ly,** adv.—**law·ful·ness,** n.

law·giv·er, lạ′giv″ẻr, n. One who gives, makes, or promulgates a law or a code of laws; a legislator.—**law·giv·ing,** n., a.

law·less, lạ′lis, a. Not founded on, governed by, or conforming to law; not checked or controlled by law; illegal; disorderly.— **law·less·ly,** adv.—**law·less·ness,** n.

law·mak·er, lạ′mā″kẻr, n. A legislator or lawgiver.—**law·mak·ing,** a., n.

law mer·chant, n. The body of principles and rules, determined largely by custom, that regulates commerce; commercial law.

lawn, lạn, län, n. [O.E. *laund, lawnde*, a clear space in a forest, a wild shrubby or woody tract, < W. *llan*, an enclosed space, or < Fr. *lande*, a heath or wild tract.] A space of ground covered with grass, and kept neatly mown, generally in front of or around an estate or house.—**lawn·y,** a.— *lawnier, lawniest.*

lawn, lạn, län, n. [M.E. *laun, launde*; prob. from *Laon*, city in northern France.] A thin or sheer linen or cotton fabric, plain or printed.—**lawn·y,** a.—*lawnier, lawniest.*

lawn bowl·ing, n. A game played on closely-cut grass where a player rolls wooden balls trying to land them as near as possible to a small white ball.

lawn mow·er, n. A machine for mowing lawns, propelled by hand or by a motor.

lawn ten·nis, n. Tennis played outdoors on a prepared court, esp. one of grass.

Law of Mo·ses, n. The Pentateuch, or first five books of the Old Testament; Torah.

law of na·tions, n. International law.

law·ren·ci·um, lạ·ren′sē·um, lo·ren′sē·um, n. [After Ernest O. Lawrence, U.S. physicist, 1901–1958, inventor of the cyclotron.] A radioactive metallic element of the actinide series. Sym. Lw, at. no. 103. See Periodic Table of Elements.

law·suit, lạ′sõt″, n. A suit at law; an action or a prosecution of a claim in a court of justice.

law·yer, lạ′yẻr, loi′ẻr, n. [M.E. *lawyere, lawiere.*] A person trained in the law; one whose profession is to conduct lawsuits in a court or to give legal advice and aid; attorney-at-law.—**law·yer·ly,** a.

lax, laks, a. [L. *laxus*, loose, slack, prob. akin to *languere*, E. *languish*, and perhaps to E. *slack.*] Loose or slack; as, a *lax* cord; not tense, rigid, or firm; lacking in tone or vigor; as, a *lax* constitution, *lax* mental powers; relaxed, as the limbs; open or not retentive, as the bowels; having the bowels unduly open, as a person; not close or tight, as an attachment or connection; of a loose texture; as, *lax* tissue, *lax* soil; open or not compact, as a panicle of a plant; lacking in strictness or severity; as, *lax* discipline, *lax* morals; careless or negligent; not rigidly exact or precise; as, *lax* ideas of a subject.—**lax·ly,** adv.—**lax·ness,** n.

lax·a·tion, lak·sā′shan, n. [L. *laxatio(n-)*, < *laxare*, loosen, relax, < *laxus*, E. *lax.*] A loosening or relaxing, or the state of being loosened or relaxed. *Med.* defecation.

lax·a·tive, lak′sa·tiv, a. [Fr. *laxatif.*] Having the quality of loosening the intestines and relieving constipation.—*n.* A medicine that acts as a gentle purgative.—**lax·a·tive·ly,** adv.—**lax·a·tive·ness,** n.

lax·i·ty, lak′si·tē, n. [Fr. *laxité*, < L. *laxitas.*] The state or quality of being lax or loose; looseness.

lay, lā, v.t.—*laid, laying.* [O.E. *lecgan* = D. *leggen* = G. *legen* = Icel. *leggja* = Goth. *lagjan*, lay; causative of the Teut. verb represented by E. *lie.*] To put or place in a position of rest or recumbency; as, to *lay* a book on a desk; to bring or throw down from an erect position; as, to *lay* a person low; to place, set, or cause to be in a particular situation, state, or condition; as, to *lay* bare the land; to dispose or place in proper position or in an orderly fashion; as, to *lay* bricks; to bury; as, *lay* him in a quiet churchyard; devise or arrange, as a plan; bring forth and deposit, as an egg or eggs; to deposit, as a wager; bet; to make, as a wager or bet; place before a person, or bring to a person's notice or consideration; set, as a snare; place or locate, as a scene; to present, bring forward, or prefer, as a claim or charge; impute, attribute, or ascribe, as: The theft was *laid* to him. To impose as a burden, duty, penalty, or the like; set, as a table; form by twisting strands together, as a rope; place on or over a surface, as paint; cover or spread with something else; as, a brick wall *laid* with plaster; to cause to subside, as dust; to appease or suppress, as doubts or anger; *naut.* to shift into a specific position or direction; *milit.* to bring to firing position, as a cannon; *slang*, have sexual intercourse with.—*v.i.* To lay eggs; to wager or bet; to deal or aim blows, usu. followed by *on, at, about*; to apply oneself vigorously; *dial.* to plan or scheme, often followed by *out; naut.* to put or bring oneself into a specified position; as, to *lay* aloft; *nonstandard, lie*; as, to *lay* down.—*n.* The way or position in which a thing is laid or lies; as, the *lay* of the ground; a share of profits, as in a whaling voyage; the manner in which a rope is formed; *chiefly Brit. slang*, a plan or line of activity; *slang*, the act of, or the female partner in, sexual intercourse.— **lay by** or **a·way,** to put aside; to put away for future use; lay up in reserve; save.— **lay down,** impose, as regulations; concede defeat.—**lay for,** *slang*, to await, as in ambush.—**lay hold of** or **on,** to grasp; seize; catch.— **lay low,** *slang.* Thrash soundly; disable; defeat; reprimand; stay hidden.—**lay off,** to put aside; to discontinue; to dismiss, esp. temporarily, as a workman; to mark or plot off.—**lay on the ta·ble,** in parliamentary use, to table or postpone consideration of, as a proposal or resolution.—**lay out,** to extend at length; spread out in order; specif., to prepare, as a body, for burial; to plot or plan out; to expend, as money, for a particular purpose; *colloq.* to exert, as oneself, to produce a good effect; as, *lay* onself *out* to be agreeable; *slang*, to knock-out or kill.—**lay up,** to put away in a place of safety, as for future use; store up; to cause to remain in bed or indoors through illness; *naut.* to put, as a ship, in a dock or other place of safety.

lay, lā, a. [O.Fr. Fr. *lai*, < L.L. *laicus.*] Belonging to, pertaining to, or performed by the people or laity, as distinguished from the clergy; not belonging to, connected with, or proceeding from a particular profession; esp. law or medicine; as, a *lay* magistrate, a *lay* opinion on a medical matter; nonprofessional.—**lay broth·er,** a man who has taken the vows of a religious order, but is employed chiefly in manual labor.—**lay sis·ter,** a woman who occupies a similar position in a female religious order.

lay, lā, n. [O.Fr. *lai*, < Celtic; Ir. and Gael. *laoi*, a verse, hymn, poem; same root as in G. *lied*, a song.] A song; a ballad; a narrative poem.

lay day, n. Com. one of a certain number of days allowed by a charter party for loading or unloading a vessel without paying additional charges; *naut.* any day a ship is held up in port.

lay·er, lā'ẽr, *n.* A thickness of some material laid on or spread over a surface; a stratum; one who or that which lays; *hort.* a shoot or twig attached to the living stock for the purpose of propagation.—*v.t.*, *v.i.* Make a layer of; *hort.* to propagate by layers.—**lay·-ered**, *a.*

lay·er·age, lā'ẽr·ij, *n. Hort.* the practice of propagating plants by layering.

lay·ette, lā·et', *n.* [Fr.] Clothing, blankets, and other necessities for a newborn child.

lay fig·ure, *n.* [With *lay*- as in obs. *layman*, < D. *leeman*, lay-figure, < *led* (now *lid*), limb, joint, and *man*, man.] A jointed model of the human body used by artists to show the correct effect of drapery; a mere puppet or nonentity.

lay in, *v.t.* To set aside for later; to stow, as provisions.

lay·man, lā'man, *n. pl.* **lay·men.** Any man not a clergyman; one of the laity; one not professionally or specially knowledgeable in a specified area; as, a political *layman.*

lay·off, lā'ạf', lā'of', *n.* Discharge, as of workmen; a period of closing down; as, a factory *layoff*; the act of laying off.

lay·out, lā'out', *n.* Plan or arrangement, as of a newspaper; the arrangement of equipment and materials, as in an office or shop. *Colloq.* a place or establishment; a setup.

lay·o·ver, lā'ō'vẽr, *n.* A postponement; deferment; a short halt, esp. during a journey; a stopover.—**lay o·ver**, *v.t.* To postpone or defer, as an action.—*v.i.* To make a stopover.

lay read·er, *n.* A layman in the Anglican church authorized to conduct portions of the public worship service.

lay-up, lā'up″, *n. Basketball*, a short, one-handed jump shot aimed so that the ball bounces into the basket from the backboard.

lay·wom·an, lā'wụm″an, *n. pl.* **lay·wom·-en.** A female member of the laity.

laz·ar, laz'ẽr, lā'zẽr, *n.* [O.Fr. *lazare*, from *Lazarus* of the New Testament (Luke, xvi. 20).] A leper; any person infected with a repulsive disease.

laz·a·ret·to, laz″a·ret'ō, *n. pl.* **laz·a·ret·-tos.** [Sp. *lazareto*, It. *lazzeretto*, Fr. *lazaret.*] A hospital for persons afflicted with contagious diseases; a ship or hospital used for quarantine purposes; *naut.* a small storage space, usu. for provisions, in a ship. Also **laz·a·ret, laz·a·rette.**

laze, lāz, *v.i.*—*lazed, lazing.* [< *lazy.*] To be lazy; to idle or lounge lazily.—*v.t.* To pass, as time, lazily, used with *away.*—*n.* A process or period of lazing.

laz·u·li, laz'ụ·lē, laz'ụ·lī″, laz'ū·lē, laz'ū·-lī, lazh'ụ·lē, lazh'ụ·lī″, *n.* Lapis lazuli.—**laz·u·line**, laz'a·lēn″, laz'a·līn″, laz'ū·lēn″, laz'ū·līn″, lazh'a·lēn″, lazh'a·līn″, *a.*

laz·u·lite, laz'a·līt″, laz'ū·līt″, lazh'a·līt″, *n.* Blue spar; an azure blue crystalline solid, a phosphate of aluminum, magnesium, and iron.—**laz·u·lit·ic**, laz″ū·lit'ik, *a.*

la·zy, lā'zē, *a.*—*lazier, laziest.* [Origin doubtful; perh. for *late-sy* (< *late*), with term, as in tricksy, tipsy; or O.Fr. *lasche*, lax, slow, remiss, < L. *laxus.*] Reluctant to work or exert oneself in any way; indolent; moving slowly, heavily, or apparently with labor; sluggish; placed on its side, as a livestock brand.—**la·zi·ly**, *adv.*—**la·zi·ness**, *n.*—**la·zy·ish**, *a.*

la·zy·bones, lā'zē·bōnz″, *n. pl., sing. or pl. in constr. Colloq.* a lazy person.

la·zy Su·san, *n.* A large, circular, revolving tray for food or condiments.

la·zy tongs, *n. pl. but sing. in constr.* A kind of extensible tongs for grasping objects at a distance, consisting of a series of pairs of crossing pieces, each pair pivoted together in the middle and connected with the next pair at the extremities.

lea, lē, lā, *n.* [Also written *lay*, < O.E. *leáh*, untilled land, pasture; Dan. dial. *lei*, fallow; D. *leeg*, empty, fallow.] *Poet.* a meadow or grassy plain. Farmland which is temporarily used for hay or pasturage. Also **ley**, lā, lē.

lea, lē, *n.* [M.E. *lee*; origin uncertain.] A unit of length used in measuring yarn, and which varies with the type of yarn.

leach, lēch, *v.t.* [Cf. O.E. *leccan*, moisten, wet, also E. *leak.*] To cause, as water, to percolate through something; to rid, as laundry, of solubles by percolation; to draw, as solubles, from a material by percolation; extract.—*v.i.* To percolate, as water; to undergo the action of percolating water, as ashes.—*n.* A leaching; the material leached; a vessel for use in leaching.—**leach·a·bil·i·ty**, *n.*—**leach·a·ble**, *a.*—**leach·ing**, *n.*

lead, led, *n.* [O.E. *lead* = D. *lood*, lead, = G. *lot*, plummet.] *Chem.* a heavy, soft, malleable, bluish-gray metal, commonly found in combination as galena. Sym. Pb, at. no. 82, at. wt. 207.19: see Periodic Table of Elements. A plummet suspended by a line, as for taking soundings; frames of lead in which panes are fixed, as in stained glass windows; bullets or shot. *Print.* a thin strip of type metal less than type-high, for increasing the spaces between lines of type; black lead or graphite, or a small stick of it used in pencils. *Pl.* lead roofing material.— *a.* Made of lead or one of its alloys.—*v.t.* To cover, line, or weight, as with lead; to fix in position with lead, as glass in a window frame; to glaze, as pottery, with a lead compound; *print.* to insert leads between the lines of; *chem.* to add or to mix with lead, as oxygen or sulfur.—**red lead**, red oxide of lead, a heavy, granular powder used in making paints, cements, and glass.—**white lead**, a white carbonate of lead, used as a pigment in paints.—**lead·less**, *a.*—**lead·en**, *a.* Like lead in color or weight.

lead, lēd, *v.t.*—*led, leading.* [O.E. *laeden*, to lead, < *lad*, a course, < *lithan*, to go or travel; D. *leiden*, Icel. *leitha*, Dan. *lede*, to lead.] To guide or conduct by showing the way, route, course; to command, govern, direct; to hold first place in order, rank, position; to induce or influence; to initiate and guide, as conversation or proceedings; to compel to motion, as with a rein or by the hand; to direct, as the playing of music; to pass or live through, as a life of gaiety; to cause to spend or endure, as: He *led* his wife a sad life.—*v.i.* To go before and show the way; to have precedence or pre-eminence; to take the first place; to have a position of authority; to be chief, commander, or director; to conduct, bring, draw, induce; *shooting*, to aim ahead of an object in motion.

lead, lēd, *n.* The act or function of leading; guidance; direction; precedence; the first or foremost place; position in advance of others, or the extent of advance; something that leads; an open channel through a field of ice; a conductor conveying electricity; a guiding indication. *Cards*, the initiation of play, or first card played. *Naut.* the course of a rope; *mining*, a lode or deposit in an old river bed; *theatr.* the principal part in a play, or the person who plays it; *journ.* the first paragraph of a news story.—*a.*

lead ac·e·tate, led as'í·tāt″, *n. Chem.* a poisonous, water-soluble, white crystalline solid, Pb (C₂H₃O₂)₂·3H₂O, often used in dyeing cotton. Also **sug·ar of lead, salt of Sat·urn.**

lead ar·se·nate, led är'se·nāt″, *n. Chem.* an extremely poisonous, white crystalline, acidic salt, Pb₃(AsO₄)₂ used as a constituent of insecticides.

lead col·ic, led kol'ik, *n.* Severe abdominal pain caused by lead poisoning. Also **paint·er's col·ic.**

lead·en, led'en, *a.* [O.E. *leaden.*] Consisting or made of lead; as, a *leaden* coffin; heavy, or hard to lift; oppressive, as the air; sluggish; dull, spiritless, or gloomy; of a dull gray color; of a base or inferior nature.— **lead·en·ly**, *adv.*—**lead·en·ness**, *n.*

lead·er, lē'dẽr, *n.* One who or that which leads; a guide or conductor; a guiding or directing head, as of an army, party, movement; one foremost or esp. eminent in position, influence; as, *leaders* of society; one first in a line or procession; a horse harnessed at the front of a team; a principal or important editorial article, as in a newspaper; a principal article of trade, esp. one offered at a low price to attract customers; a pipe for conveying water; a tendon; *fishing*, a length of silkworm, gut, or the like, to which the snell of a fly is attached. *Mus.* a conductor or director, as of an orchestra, band, or chorus; the player at the head of the first violins in an orchestra; the principal cornetist in a band; the principal soprano in a chorus. *Pl., print.* a row of dots or short lines to lead the reader's eye across a space.—**lead·er·less**, *a.*—**lead·er·ship**, *n.* The position, function, or guidance of a leader; ability to lead.

lead·er of the op·po·si·tion, *n. Brit. politics*, the principal member of the party not in power who directs opposition to the government in the House of Commons.

lead glass, led glas, *n.* A refractive glass made with lead oxide and used to make lenses. Also *flint glass.*

lead-in, lēd'in″, *n. Radio, TV.* A wire connector joining the antenna to a receiving or transmitting set; an introduction or transition to a commercial.—*a.*

lead·ing, lē'ding, *a.* Guiding; conducting; preceding. Chief; principal; most influential.

lead·ing ar·ti·cle, *n. Journ.* the article most conspicuously placed or displayed, as in a newspaper or periodical. *Brit. journ.* the main editorial or leader.

lead·ing la·dy, *n.* An actress assigned to play the major feminine role in a dramatic production.

lead·ing man, *n.* An actor assigned to play the major male role in a dramatic production.

lead·ing ques·tion, *n.* A question which suggests the answer or guides the answerer.

lead·ing tone, *n. Mus.* the seventh tone of the major or minor scale, leading upward a half step to the tonic.

lead line, led līn, *n. Naut.* sounding line.

lead·off, lēd'ạf, lēd'of″, *n.* An action or move that begins something, as a game; a player who is the first to begin. *Baseball*, the first batter in the line-up; also **lead·off man.**

lead off, lēd' ạf″, *v.t.*, *v.i.* To begin; to open; *baseball*, to be the first batter in the line-up.

lead on, lēd on, *v.t.* To persuade to follow a course that may not be advantageous.

lead pen·cil, led pen'sil, *n.* An instrument for drawing or writing, made by enclosing graphite in a casing of wood or metal.

lead·plant, led'plant″, led'plänt″, *n.* A native shrub, *Amorpha canescens*, in the legume family, cultivated for its dark to blue-violet flowers and its white, downy leaflets.

lead poi·son·ing, led poi'zo·ning, *n. Pathol.* an acute, toxic condition found among persons, esp. children, whose tissues have absorbed lead; a chronic condition among workers who are in contact with paint or other lead products. Also **plumb·ism.**

leads·man, ledz'man, *n. pl.* **leads·men.** *Naut.* the man who drops a line weighted with lead to measure the water's depth.

lead time, lēd tīm, *n.* The amount of time required to produce a project, job, or product from its planning to its completion; the time between the ordering of a product and its delivery.

lead up, lēd up, *v.i.* To advance toward something gradually or indirectly, usu. followed by *to*; to pave the way, usu. followed by *to*.

lead-up, lēd′up″, *n.* That which paves the way or leads up to something.

lead work, led wurk, *n.* An article made out of lead; work done using lead.

lead·wort, led′wurt, *n. Bot.* any plant of the genus *Plumbago*, woody, tropical, and having spikes of blue, white, or purplish showy flowers. Also *plumbago.*

lead·y, led′ē, *a.—leadier, leadiest.* Containing lead; resembling lead.

leaf, lēf, *n. pl.* **leaves.** [O.E. *lēaf* = D. *loof* = G. *laub* = Icel. *lauf* = Goth. *laufs*, leaf.] *Bot.* one of the lateral outgrowths of a stem, often broad and flat and usu. green, which produce food photosynthetically; the leaves of some plants, as tobacco or tea, as a commercial product; foliage. Something resembling a foliage leaf, being broad and flat; a thin sheet of metal; a lamina or layer; a layer of fat, esp. that about the kidneys of a hog; a single thickness of paper, as in a book, comprising two pages of print arranged back to back; a sliding, hinged, or detachable flat part, as of a door, shutter, or table top; one layer of a leaf spring.— **leaf·less,** *a.—*leaf·like, *a.*

leaf, lēf, *v.i. Bot.* to produce leaves, as a bush. To flip or turn over papers or pages, as: He *leafed* through the files.—*v.t.* To flip or turn, as pages.

leaf·age, lē′fij, *n.* Leaves; foliage.

leaf bud, *n.* A bud which develops into a leafy shoot consisting of a stem and leaves, as distinguished from a flower bud.

leafed, lēft, *a. Bot.* possessing leaves: used chiefly in combination; as, three-*leafed.*

leaf fat, *n.* Animal fat found in the abdominal cavity of hogs, usu. around the kidneys.

leaf·hop·per, lēf′hop″ėr, *n. Entom.* any of the small, leaping, homopterous insects with sucking mouth parts, feeding on plants, and belonging to the family *Cicadellidae.*

leaf lard, *n.* Lard prepared from the leaf or internal fat of the hog.

leaf·let, lēf′lit, *n.* A small flat or folded sheet of printed matter, as for distribution; *bot.* one of the several blades or divisions of a compound leaf.

leaf min·er, *n. Entom.* one of numerous insects, represented by species of moths, beetles, and flies, that feeds during the larval stage between the lower and upper surfaces of a leaf, producing a characteristic configuration.

leaf mold, *n.* A mixture of dead and decaying leaves and other vegetable matter contributing to the fertility of the soil.

leaf spring, *n. Mech.* a metal catch or spring consisting of a series of superimposed leaves, lamina, or plates fastened together.

leaf·stalk, lēf′stak″, *n. Bot.* the slender stemlike structure by which a leaf is usu. attached to the stem. Also *petiole.*

leaf·y, lē′fē, *a.—leafier, leafiest.* Abounding in, covered with, or consisting of leaves or foliage.—**leaf·i·ness,** *n.*

league, lēg, *n.* [Fr. *ligue*, It. *lega*, L.L. *liga*, < L. *ligo*, to bind.] A combination of parties for promotion of their mutual interests and goals, as of states for military aid or defense; the covenant or compact by which these parties are joined; an association of athletic teams united by mutual interests and competing among themselves; any group, class, or category.—*v.t.—leagued, leaguing.* To combine or unite in a league.

league, lēg, *n.* [O.Fr. *legue*, Fr. *lieue*, < L.L. *leuca, leuga*, etc.] Any of several measures of distance varying in different countries, the English land league being three statute miles, the nautical league nearly three and one-half.

lea·guer, lē′gėr, *n.* One who belongs to a league.

leak, lēk, *v.i.* [Prob. < Scand.: cf. Icel. *leka*, M.L.G. and G. *lecken*, D. *lekken*, leak.] To let air, water, light, or the like enter or escape, usu. unintentionally; to pass in or out in this manner, as: Gas may *leak* from that pipe. *Fig.* to become known, sometimes unintentionally, often followed by *out*, as: Rumors will *leak* out.—*v.t.* To let leak in or out.

leak, lēk, *n.* A hole, crack, or opening by which water, air, light, or the like enters or escapes without design; the act of leaking; *fig.* any avenue or means of unintended entrance or escape, or the entrance or escape itself; *colloq.* a means for the escape of a secret, or the escape itself; *elect.* a point where current escapes from a conductor because of poor insulation, or the escape itself.

leak·age, lē′kij, *n.* The act of leaking; that which leaks in or out; the amount of leakage; *com.* an allowance for loss by leaking.

leak·y, lē′kē, *a.—leakier, leakiest.* Having a leak or leaks; allowing water, air, light, or the like to leak in or out.—**leak·i·ness,** *n.*

lean, lēn, *v.i.—leaned, leaning,* Brit. leaned or *leant, lent, leaning.* [O.E. *hlaenan*, to make to lean, *hlinian*, to lean; O.H.G. *hlinen*, G. *lehnen*, D. *leunen*, to lean; cogn. with Gr. *klino*, to make to bend, and L. *clino, inclino*, to bend, to *incline.*] To slope or incline from a straight or perpendicular position or line; to slant; to incline in feeling or opinion; to tend toward; to rest, as for support; to depend for consolation and comfort, used with *on.—v.t.* To cause to lean; to incline; to support or rest.—*n.* Inclination.

lean, lēn, *a.* [O.E. *hlaene.*] Not plump or fat; as, *lean* cattle; thin; spare; containing little or no fat; meager; poor; unremunerative, as work; marked by scarcity; as, *lean* years; *fig.* lacking in substantiality, richness, fullness, quantity; as, a *lean* diet, *lean* soil. —*n.* The lean part of anything; specif. that part of flesh which consists of muscle rather than fat.—**lean·ly,** *adv.—*lean·ness, *n.*

lean·ing, lē′ning, *n.* Inclination; bias; tendency.—*a.* On a slant; inclining.

lean-to, lēn′tö″, *a.* Having rafters pitched against or leaning on another building or a wall.—*n. pl.* **lean·tos.** A structure, as a shed or building extension, whose roof slopes in only one direction, specif. away from the support, as a post or wall; the roof itself.

leap, lēp, *v.i.—leaped* or *leapt, leaping.* [O.E. *hleápan*, to leap, to run, past, *hleóp*; Sc. *loup*, D. *loopen*, to run; Icel. *klaupa*, Dan. *löbe*, Goth. *hlaupan*, G. *laufen*; allied to Gr. *kraipnos, karpalimos*, swift.] To spring or rise from the ground with feet in the air; to move with springs or bounds. *Fig.* to act or react on impulse; to make a sudden transition, as from one job to one of much higher rank, or from one idea to another far removed.—*v.t.* To pass over by leaping; to cause to leap, as one's riding horse; to make to pass over by leaping, as sheep.—*n.* The act of leaping; the space passed over or cleared by leaping; a jump; a spring; a bound; a sudden transition, as in rank, thoughts, or the like.— **a leap in the dark,** a rash or risky act of any kind.—**by leaps and bounds,** very swiftly.— **leap·er,** lē′pėr, *n.*

leap·frog, lēp′frog″, lēp′frag″, *n.* A game in which one player places his hands on the back or shoulders of another player who is in a stooping posture, and leaps over him.— *v.t.—leapfrogged, leapfrogging.* To leap over, as a person or object; to go around, as an obstacle.—*v.i.* To move forward in the manner of the game of leapfrog.

leap year, *n.* A year containing 366 days, or one more day, February 29, than an ordinary year: a device in the Gregorian calendar to offset the difference in length between the ordinary year and the astronomical year; every year whose number is exactly divisible by 4, as 1968, except centenary years, which must be exactly divisible by 400, as 2000; an intercalary year in any calendar.

learn, lurn, *v.t.—learned* or *learnt, learning.* [O.E. *leornian*, to learn, to teach; akin to *laeran*, to teach, *lár*, learning, lore; akin to G. *lernen*, to learn, *lehren*, to teach; D. *leeren*, Icel. *laera*, to teach, to learn; Goth. *laisjan*, to teach; allied to O.E. *lesan*, Icel. *lesa*, to gather.] To gain or acquire understanding or knowledge of, or skill in; to acquire by study; to memorize.—*v.i.* To gain or receive knowledge, information, or intelligence.—**learn·a·ble,** *a.—*learn·er, *n.*

learn·ed, lur′nid, *a.* Having a great store of information obtained by study; erudite; characterized by scholarship or study; as, a *learned* book. Gained by learning, lurnd, lurnt.—**learn·ed·ly,** *adv.—*learn·ed·ness, *n.*

learn·ing, lur′ning, *n.* Knowledge or skill acquired by study in any field; the process of obtaining skill or knowledge.

lease, lēs, *n.* [Norm. *lees, leez*, a lease, L.L. *lessa*; < L. *laxare*, to loosen, relax, < *laxus*, lax.] A contract authorizing the use and possession of land and/or buildings for a fixed time and fee, usu. payable in installments; property or a building that is rented by contract; the specified time for rental; an opportunity or good fortune that favors an enjoyment or continued enjoyment of life; as, a new *lease* on life.—*v.t.— leased, leasing.* To grant by lease; to let, usu. for a specified rent; to hold or occupy under a lease.—*v.i.* To rent by contract; to confer a formal agreement.—**lease·hold,** lēs′hōld″, *a.* Held by contract.—*n.* A tenure by contract; land so held.—**lease·hold·er,** *n.* A tenant under a lease.

leash, lēsh, *n.* [Fr. *laisse*, O.Fr. *lesse*, a leash, < L.L. *laxa*, a loose cord, < L. *laxus*, loose.] A thong or line by which a dog, hawk, or other animal is held; esp. in hunting, three animals of any kind, as greyhounds; control or restraint.—*v.t.* To hold, as by a leash; *fig.* to restrain, as anger.

least, lēst, *a., irreg. superl. of little.* [O.E. *laest*, superl. of *laessa*, E. *less.*] Smallest in size, amount, degree, or the like; slightest; lowest in consideration or dignity.—*n.* That which is least; the least amount, quantity, or degree.—*adv.* To the least extent, amount, or degree.—**at least,** at the least or lowest estimate; at any rate; in any case. —**in the least,** in the smallest degree.— **least·wise,** *adv. Colloq.* At least; at any rate. Also *dial.* **least·ways.**

least squares, *n. pl. Statistics,* a method of fitting a line or curve to statistical data so that the sum of the squares of the distances between the points and the line is the least possible.

leath·er, leтн′ėr, *n.* [O.E. *lether* = L.G. *ledder, lier*, Icel. *lethr*, Dan. *læder, lær*, G. and D. *leder*; root unknown.] The skin of animals, esp. of cattle, dressed and prepared for use by tanning or similar processes; tanned hide.—*a.* Pertaining to or consisting of leather.—*v.t.* To furnish or cover with leather.—**leath·ern,** leтн′ėrn, *a.—*leath·er·y, leтн′e·rē, *a.* Pertaining to or resembling leather; tough.

leath·er·back, leтн′ėr·bak″, *n.* A large marine turtle, *Dermochelys coriacea,* with a leathery, flexible carapace.

Leath·er·ette, leTH′e·ret′, *n.* A manufactured material that resembles leather in appearance and other qualities, used for bookbinding, upholstery, and similar purposes. (Trademark.)

leath·er·neck, leTH′ėr·nek″, *n. Slang,* a member of the U.S. Marine Corps, so called because of the high, leather-lined collar of the original uniform.

Leath·er·oid, leTH′e·roid″, *n.* An artificial leather consisting mostly of vegetable fiber, as paper stock, variously treated. (Trademark.)

leath·er·wood, leTH′ėr·wu̇d″, *n.* An Amer. shrub, *Dirca palustris,* with a tough bark.

leave, lēv, *v.t.—left, leaving.* [O.E. *laefan* = O.H.G. *leiben* = Icel. *leifa* = Goth. *-laibjan,* leave; a causative form < a root meaning in Teut. 'remain'; cf. O.E. *belifan* and G. *bleiben,* remain; Skt. *lip-,* smear, stick; cf. Gr. *liparos,* oily, *liparas,* persistent.] To go away from, depart from, or quit, as a place, person, or thing; to allow to remain in the same place or condition; to let remain in a position to do something without interference, as: *Leave* me alone to think. To go away from or quit permanently; separate or withdraw from; as, to *leave* a church or a society; to allow to rest or remain for action or decision, as: *Leave* the matter to me. To result in or have as an aftermath, as: The acid *leaves* a stain in cloth. To have remaining after death, as: He *leaves* a widow and two children. To bequeath by will; to have as a remainder after subtraction, as: Two from four *leaves* two. Let remain without being removed, consumed, used, dealt with, as: The robbers *left* nothing of any value. To let stay or be as specified; as, to *leave* a thing unsaid; to deposit, or give in charge or safekeeping for one's return; as, to *leave* provisions in a cache; to station to remain behind; as, to *leave* a person on guard; to give for use after one's departure; as, to *leave* orders or a message; have remaining in a particular condition upon quitting, as: He *left* the place as he found it. To stop, abandon, or cease to wear or use, now only with *off;* as, to *leave off* one's sweater or coat, to *leave off* smoking; to omit or exclude, often followed by *out; nonstandard,* to allow, used as a substitute for let, as: *Leave* him stay.—*v.i.* To go away, depart or set out, as: We *leave* for Europe tomorrow.—**leav·er,** *n.*

leave, lēv, *n.* [O.E. *léaf, geleaf,* leave, permission; same as the *-lieve* in *believe;* akin D. *-lof* in *oorlof,* permission; Icel. *leyfi,* permission, *lof,* praise, permission; G. (*er*)*lauben,* to permit.] Liberty granted to act; permission, esp. to be absent for a period; the duration of the absence granted; a formal parting or farewell, usu. preceded by *take.*—**leave-tak·ing,** *n.* The act of taking leave; a bidding good-bye.

leave, lēv, *v.i.—leaved, leaving.* [< *leaf.*] To put forth leaves; leaf.—**leaved,** *a.* Having leaves; leafed; as, a four-*leaved* clover.

leav·en, lev′en, *n.* [O.Fr. Fr. *levain,* < L. *levamen,* that which raises, < *levare,* raise, cf. *lever.*] A substance, as yeast or a mass of fermented dough, used to produce fermentation in dough; *fig.* an agent which works to produce a gradual change or modification; as, the *leaven* of reform. Also **leav·en·ing.**—*v.t.* To raise, as a dough, by means of leaven; *fig.* to permeate with a modifying or transforming influence.

leav·ing, lē′ving, *n.* That which is left; residue; *pl.* remains or refuse.

Leb·a·nese, leb″a·nēz′, leb″a·nēs′, *a.* [From *Lebanon,* a southwest Asian republic bordering on the eastern Mediterranean.] Of, pertaining to, or characteristic of Lebanon or its inhabitants.—*n.* pl. **Leb·a·nese.** An inhabitant or native of Lebanon.

le·bens·raum, lā′bens·roum″, lā′benz·- roum″, *n.* [G. *leben,* life, living, and *raum,* space.] (*Often cap.*) additional land claimed by a nation for economic and political expansion.

lech·er, lech′ėr, *n.* [O.Fr. *lecheor,* gourmand, sensualist, < *lechier,* lick, live in gluttony or sensuality, Fr. *lecher;* lick; < Teut., akin to E. *lick.*] A man immoderately given to sexual indulgence.—**lech·er·ous,** *a.*—**lech·er·ous·ly,** *adv.*—**lech·er·ous·- ness,** *n.*—**lech·er·y,** *n.* pl. **lech·er·ies.** [O.Fr. *lecherie.*] Unrestrained indulgence in sex.

lec·i·thin, les′i·thin, *n.* [Gr. *lékithos,* egg yolk.] *Biochem.* a fatty substance consisting of fatty acids, choline, phosphoric acid, and glycerol, found in the cells of plants and animals, and utilized in the food, cosmetic, drug, and textile industries.

lec·tern, lek′tėrn, *n.* [O.Fr. *lectrin;* L.L. *lectrinum,* < *lectrum,* pulpit, Gr. *lektron,* a couch.] A desk or stand from which parts of a church service are read; a stand upon which a speaker or lecturer may rest notes or books.

lec·tion, lek′shan, *n.* [L. *lectio,* < *lego,* to read.] A lesson or portion of Scripture read at a church service; a variant reading of a passage in a manuscript or book.—**lec·- tion·ar·y,** lek′sha·ner″ē, *n.* pl. **lec·tion·- ar·ies.** A book containing portions of Scripture to be read on particular days in the Church calendar.

lec·tor, lek′tėr, *n.* [L. < *legere,* read.] *Rom. Cath. Ch.* one ordained to the second of the four minor orders; one who reads lessons from the Scripture in a church service. In certain European universities, one who lectures.

lec·ture, lek′chėr, *n.* [Fr. *lecture,* < L. *lectura,* a reading, < *lego,* to read, whence also *legend, lesson, legible.*] A discourse read or delivered before an audience or class, usu. for the purpose of instruction; a reprimand or formal reproof.—*v.t.—lec- tured, lecturing.* To give a lecture or sequence of lectures to; to reprimand or reprove.— *v.i.* To deliver lectures, esp. for instruction. —**lec·tur·er,** lek′chėr·ėr, *n.* One who lectures; a college teacher, usu. below the rank of assistant professor, who delivers lectures.—**lec·ture·ship,** *n.*

le·der·ho·sen, lā′dėr·hō″zen, *n.* pl. Knee-length trousers made of leather, worn esp. in Germany.

ledge, lej, *n.* [M.E. *legge,* prob. < *leggen,* E. *lay.*] Any relatively narrow, projecting part forming a horizontal, shelflike surface; a shelflike projection on the side of a mountain or cliff; a reef, ridge, or line of rocks in the sea. *Mining,* a layer or mass of rock underground; a lode or vein.

ledg·er, lej′ėr, *n.* [Perh. lit. 'a book that rests on a *ledge* or shelf'; in any case < the same stem; akin to old *leger, ledger,* resting in a place; D. *legger,* one that lies; akin to *lie,* to rest.] *Bookkeeping,* the principal book of accounts containing the final entries of debits and credits. A large, supporting timber secured horizontally to the upright timbers of a scaffold; a flat slab of stone laid horizontally over a grave or tomb.

ledg·er board, *n.* The horizontal board which forms the top of a fence or the railing of a staircase.

ledg·er line, *n. Mus.* a short line added above or below the staff for a note too high or too low to be placed on the staff. Also **leg·er line.**

lee, lē, *n.* [O.E. *hlēo,* shelter, = Icel. *hlé,* naut. lee.] Shelter, esp. the side or part that is sheltered or turned away from the wind. —*a. Naut.* Of or pertaining to the lee, as opposed to *weather;* in the same direction as the wind.

lee·board, lē′bōrd″, *n.* A long flat piece of wood attached to the lee side of a vessel to prevent it from drifting leeward.

leech, lēch, *n.* [O.E. *læce, lýce,* = M.D. *lake, lieke,* leech.] Any of the bloodsucking or carnivorous, usu. aquatic worms of the class *Hirudinea,* certain freshwater species of which were formerly used by physicians for bloodletting; an instrument used for drawing blood; *fig.* a person who clings to another, esp. with a view to gain.—*v.t.* To apply leeches to; to bleed.—*v.i.* To cling to, as a leech.

leek, lēk, *n.* [O.E. *leac* = D. *look* = G. *lauch* = Icel. *laukr,* leek.] A liliaceous herb, *Allium porrum,* allied to the onion but with a cylindrical bulb and flat leaves which are used in cooking.—**leek-green,** lēk′grēn′, *a.* Of the dull bluish-green color of the leek.

leer, lēr, *n.* [O.E. *hlēor,* face, cheek.] A sidelong glance expressive of malignity, lasciviousness, or slyness.—*v.i.* To cast a sly, malicious, or lascivious look.—**leer·ing·ly,** *adv.*

leer·y, lēr′ē, *a.—leerier, leeriest.* Wary; suspicious, followed by *of.* Also **lear·y.**

lees, lēz, *n. pl.* [Fr. *lie,* Walloon *lizi,* L.L. *liæ;* origin unknown.] The sediments of a liquid, esp. liquor or wine; the dregs.

lee shore, *n.* A shore toward which the wind blows and may drive a ship.

lee tide, *n.* A tide running in the same direction in which the wind is blowing.

lee·ward, lē′wėrd, *Naut.* lō′ėrd, *a.* Pertaining to the part or side, as of a boat, which is sheltered or away from the wind; downwind: opposed to *windward.*—*n.* The sheltered side.—*adv.*

lee·way, lē′wā″, *n.* A degree of freedom of thought or action; additional time and space within which to function. *Naut.* the lateral drift of a ship in motion to leeward.

left, left, *a.* [O.E. *left, lyft,* weak, = North Fries. *leeft,* M.D. *luft, lucht,* M.L.G. *lucht,* left.] Belonging, pertaining to, or located on the side of a person or thing which is turned toward the west when one faces north; (*often cap.*) belonging to or pertaining to the political Left.—*n.* The left side, or what is on the left side. (*Cap.*) the complex of groups and individuals advocating radical change in the established economic and political order. (*Usu. cap.*) in continental Europe, that part of a legislative assembly which sits on the left side of the chamber as viewed by the president, a position customarily assigned to representatives holding more liberal or radical views.—**left·ist,** *n.,* *a.* (*Sometimes cap.*)

left field, *n. Baseball.* The left area of the outfield, as viewed from home plate; the position of the player who defends this area. —**out in left field,** *slang,* completely mistaken.—**left field·er,** *n.*

left-hand, left′hand′, *a.* On or to the left; of, for, or with the left hand.—**left-hand·ed,** left′han′did, *a.* Using the left hand more easily than the right; preferably using the left hand; adapted to or performed by the left hand; moving or rotating from right to left; counter-clockwise; as, a *left-handed* screw; clumsy or awkward; as, a *left-handed* method of proceeding; ambiguous or insincere; as, a *left-handed* compliment; morganatic, as a marriage.—*adv.* Also **left·hand·ed·ly.**—**left-hand·ed·ness,** *n.*—**left-hand·er,** left′han′dėr, left′han″dėr, *n.* A left-handed person; *colloq.* a left-handed punch.

left·o·ver, left′ō″vėr, *n.* Something left over or remaining; an unconsumed remnant of food, as from a meal.—*a.*

left wing, *n.* A political party, faction, or group which advocates leftist principles.— **left·wing, left-wing,** *a.*—**left-wing·er,** *n.*

leg, leg, *n.* [< Scand.: cf. Icel. *leggr,* Sw. *lagg,* leg, Dan. *laeg,* calf of the leg.] One of the members or limbs which support and move the human or animal body; specif. that part of the limb between the knee and the ankle; that part of a garment, such as a stocking, trousers, or the like, which covers the leg; something resembling or suggesting a leg in use, position, or appearance; one of the supports of a piece of furniture; a projection which acts as a support to a structure; a projection of an L-beam; the haunch or loin or similar portion of a meat animal. *Math.* one of the sides of a pair of dividers or compasses; one of the sides of a triangle other than the base or the hypotenuse. *Naut.* the course or run made by a sailing vessel on one tack; one of the series of straight runs which make up the zigzag course of a sailing vessel proceeding to windward. *Aeron.* the straight flight portion of a zigzag pattern. *Fig.* one of the distinct portions or stages of any course or journey; as, the last *leg* of the trip. *Radio, TV,* a relay station between networks of distant stations. *Electron.* a forking circuit; hi-fi component; antenna branch. *Sports,* that portion of a tournament to be completed by a contestant; a lap of a relay race. *Bridge,* a partial score toward a game. *Cricket,* the part of the field to the left of and behind a right-handed batsman and vice versa; the fielder occupying this part of the field.—*v.i.*—*legged, legging. Colloq.* to walk or run, usu. followed by the indefinite *it,* as: We'll *leg it* together.—**give a leg up,** to boost or help mount; to give assistance to.—**not have a leg to stand on,** to have no valid premise or justification.—**on one's last legs,** almost depleted in energy, purpose, or ambition; near death.—**pull one's leg,** to deceive; to tantalize or tease.—**shake a leg,** *slang,* to hasten.—**stretch one's legs,** to activate oneself after prolonged inactivity.—**leg ∙ less,** *a.*

leg. Abbr. for legal, legate, legato, legend, legislation, legislative, legislature.

leg ∙ a ∙ cy, leg′a·sē, *n.* pl. **leg ∙ a ∙ cies.** [< L. *legatum,* a legacy, < *lego,* to bequeath, to appoint.] *Law,* a bequest; a particular thing or certain sum of money given by the last will or testament. Anything handed down by an ancestor or predecessor.

le ∙ gal, lē′gal, *a.* [L. *legalis,* < *lex (leg-),* law.] Of or pertaining to law; connected with the law or its administration; characteristic of the profession of the law; as, a *legal* mind; appointed, established, or authorized by law; deriving authority from law; determined by or conforming to the law; as, *legal* incapacity, a *legal* infant; recognized or acknowledged by law rather than by equity; permitted by law, or lawful. *Theol.* pertaining to the Mosaic law; of or pertaining to the doctrine of salvation by good works rather than through grace.—**le ∙ gal ∙ ly,** *adv.*

le ∙ gal, lē′gal, *n. Often pl.* selected securities in which the funds of such publicly regulated investors as savings banks and trustees may legally be placed.

le ∙ gal cap, *n.* White, ruled writing paper measuring 8½ × 13 inches, used esp. by lawyers.

le ∙ gal hol ∙ i ∙ day, *n.* A day designated by law on which official business transactions are restricted.

le ∙ gal ∙ ism, lē′ga·liz″um, *n.* Strict adherence, or the principle of strict adherence; salvation by good works or strict adherence to precise religious regulations of conduct and not by grace.—**le ∙ gal ∙ ist,** *n.*—**le ∙ gal ∙ is ∙ tic,** lē″ga·lis′tik, *a.*—**le ∙ gal ∙ is ∙ ti ∙ cal ∙ ly,** *adv.*

le ∙ gal ∙ i ∙ ty, lē·gal′i·tē, *n.* pl. **le ∙ gal ∙ i ∙ ties.** The state or quality of being legal or in conformity with the law; lawfulness; attachment to or observance of law; often, insistence on the letter of the law; *theol.* reliance on good works for salvation, rather than on free grace. *Pl.* obligations required by law.

le ∙ gal ∙ ize, lē′ga·līz″, *v.t.*—*legalized, legalizing.* To make legal; authorize; sanction.— **le ∙ gal ∙ i ∙ za ∙ tion,** lē″ga·li·zā′shan, *n.*

le ∙ gal re ∙ serve, *n.* A sum of money which banks and insurance companies are legally required to put aside for security purposes.

le ∙ gal ten ∙ der, *n.* A legally approved currency to be given in payment of a debt and which must be accepted by the creditor.

leg ∙ ate, leg′it, *n.* [O.Fr. *legat,* Fr. *légat,* < L. *legatus,* < *legare,* send, depute, appoint, bequeath, < *lex, (leg-),* law.] An ecclesiastic delegated by the Pope as his representative; a deputy, envoy, or ambassador. *Rom. hist.* a deputy or lieutenant of a general or of a governor of a province; a governor of a province.—**leg ∙ ate ∙ ship,** *n.*

leg ∙ a ∙ tee, leg′a·tē′, *n.* [< L. *legatum,* a legacy.] One to whom a legacy is bequeathed.

leg ∙ a ∙ tine, leg′a·tin, leg′a·tīn″, *a.* Pertaining to a legate; having the authority of a legate.

le ∙ ga ∙ tion, li·gā′shan, *n.* [L. *legatio, (n-),* < *legare,* send, depute.] A diplomatic minister and his assistants when the minister is not of the highest, or ambassadorial rank; the official residence of such a minister; the status of a legate; the act of sending a legate; the commission entrusted to a legate. —**le ∙ ga ∙ tion ∙ ar ∙ y,** li·gā′sha·ner″ē, *a.*

le ∙ ga ∙ to, le·gä′tō, *It.* le·gä′tạ, *a., adv.* [It., tied, < L. *ligare,* to tie.] *Mus.* played, sung, or directed in an even, smooth manner, one note gliding directly into the next.

le ∙ ga ∙ tor, li·gā′tẽr, leg″a·tạr′, *n.* [L., < *legare,* bequeath.] One who bequeaths; a testator.—**leg ∙ a ∙ to ∙ ri ∙ al,** leg″a·tōr′ē·al, *a.*

leg ∙ end, lej′end, *n.* [O.Fr. *legende,* Fr. *légende,* < M.L. *legenda,* lit. 'something to be read,' orig. neut. pl. gerundive of L. *legere,* read.] A story or account, nonhistorical or unverifiable, which is handed down by tradition from earlier times and popularly accepted as factual; any stories of this kind dealing with objects or people; as, the *legend* of the canon or the *legend* of the Druids; a collection of stories of any admirable person; as, the *legend* of Robin Hood; an individual or object that is the subject of such accounts; a caption or inscription, as on a coat of arms or monument; a list which defines or explains, as symbols on a map.—**leg ∙ end ∙ ar ∙ y,** lej′en·der″ē, *a.* Pertaining to or of the nature of a legend; celebrated or described in legend. —*n.* pl. **leg ∙ end ∙ ar ∙ ies.** A collection or book of legends.—**leg ∙ end ∙ ry,** lej′en·drē, *n.* Legends collectively.

leg ∙ er ∙ de ∙ main, lej″ẽr·de·mān′, *n.* [Fr. *léger de main,* light of hand—*léger,* L.L. *leviarius,* < L. *levis,* light (whence *levity*), and *main,* L. *manus,* hand.] Sleight of hand; a deceptive performance which depends on dexterity of hand, usu. magic or juggling; trickery; deception.—**leg ∙ er ∙ de ∙ main ∙ ist,** *n.* One who practices sleight of hand; a juggler or magician.

leg ∙ ged, leg′id, legd, *a.* Having legs: usu. used in compounds; as, bandy-*legged.*

leg ∙ ging, leg′ing, *n.* A covering or protection for the leg, worn in different lengths, and made of cloth, canvas, or leather, as chaps, overalls, or gaiters. *Usu. pl.* pants worn over trousers, usu. with suspenders, foot straps, and a matching jacket, and donned by young children for outdoor winter wear. Also **leg ∙ gin,** leg′in.

leg ∙ gy, leg′ē, *a.*—*leggier, leggiest.* Having long shapely legs; having overly long legs; of or noting plants with spindly stalks.

leg ∙ horn, leg′hạrn″, leg′ẽrn, *n.* (*Usu. cap.*) a Mediterranean breed of domestic chickens known for their prolific egg-laying, leg′ẽrn, leg′hạrn″. A variety of straw plait obtained from an Italian wheat; a hat or bonnet made of this straw, leg′harn.

leg ∙ i ∙ ble, lej′i·bl, *a.* [L. *legibilis,* < *lego,* to read.] Capable of being read; consisting of

that which can be readily noted; as, *legible* annoyance.—**leg ∙ i ∙ bil ∙ i ∙ ty,** lej″i·bil′i·tē, *n.* —**leg ∙ i ∙ bly,** *adv.*

le ∙ gion, lē′jon, *n.* [L. *legio,* < *lego,* to collect.] An ancient Roman infantry unit consisting of 3000 to 6000 with a complement of cavalry; a large body of troops; a great number.—*a.* Innumerable: used predicatively.—**A ∙ mer ∙ i ∙ can Le ∙ gion,** an association of former American servicemen.

le ∙ gion ∙ ar ∙ y, lē′ji·ner″ē, *a.* Belonging to a legion or legions.—*n.* pl. **le ∙ gion ∙ ar ∙ ies.** One of a legion; a soldier belonging to a legion.

le ∙ gion ∙ naire, lē″ji·nâr′, *n.* A legion member. (*Usu. cap.*) an American Legion member.

Le ∙ gion of Hon ∙ or, *n.* An order instituted in France by Napoleon I as a reward for merit, both civil and military.

Le ∙ gion of Mer ∙ it, *n. Milit.* a decoration awarded to American and foreign personnel for distinguished service to the U.S. in time of war or peace.

leg ∙ is ∙ late, lej′is·lāt″, *v.i.*—*legislated, legislating.* [Back formation from *legislation* or *legislator.*] To exercise the function of legislation; to make or enact laws.—*v.t.* To effect by legislation, usu. with *into* or *out.*

leg ∙ is ∙ la ∙ tion, lej″is·lā′shan, *n.* The procedure of making or enacting laws; laws enacted.

leg ∙ is ∙ la ∙ tive, lej′is·lā″tiv, *a.* Empowered to legislate; related to lawmaking; as, the *legislative* process; related to the operation of the legislature; authorized by legislation or the legislature; as, a *legislative* provision. —*n.* The branch of government which makes and repeals laws.—**leg ∙ is ∙ la ∙ tive ∙ ly,** *adv.*

Leg ∙ is ∙ la ∙ tive As ∙ sem ∙ bly, *n.* The unicameral legislature of a Canadian province.

leg ∙ is ∙ la ∙ tive coun ∙ cil, *n.* (*Often cap.*), *Brit.* in a bicameral legislature, the upper house.

leg ∙ is ∙ la ∙ tor, lej′is·lā″tẽr, *n.* A lawmaker; a member of a national or state legislature.—**leg ∙ is ∙ la ∙ to ∙ ri ∙ al,** lej″is·la·- tōr′ē·al, *a.*—**leg ∙ is ∙ la ∙ to ∙ ri ∙ al ∙ ly,** *adv.*— **leg ∙ is ∙ la ∙ tor ∙ ship,** *n.*—**leg ∙ is ∙ la ∙ tress,** **leg ∙ is ∙ la ∙ trix,** lej′is·lā″tris, lej″is·lā′tris, lej·is·lā″triks, *n.* pl. **leg ∙ is ∙ la ∙ trix ∙ es,** **leg ∙ is ∙ la ∙ tri ∙ ces,** lej″is·lā′tri·sēz, lej″is·- la·tri′sēz. Feminine of legislator.

leg ∙ is ∙ la ∙ ture, lej′is·lā″chẽr, *n.* The officially empowered elected body of persons who make, repeal, and amend laws; *U.S. govt.* the lawmaking branch, as distinguished from the executive and judicial branches.

le ∙ gist, lē′jist, *n.* One who is skilled and knowledgeable in the law.

le ∙ git, le·jit′, *a. Slang,* legitimate or lawful. —*n. Slang,* the legitimate theater or stage, as distinguished from movies, television plays, burlesques, and vaudeville.

le ∙ git ∙ i ∙ ma ∙ cy, li·jit′i·ma·sē, *n.* The state or quality of being legitimate.

le ∙ git ∙ i ∙ mate, li·jit′i·mit, *a.* [M.L. *legitimatus,* pp. of *legitimare,* < L. *legitmus,* lawful, < *lex, leg-,* law.] According to law; lawful; in accordance with established rules or principles; conforming to accepted standards; born of parents legally married; as, a *legitimate* child; of the normal or regular type or kind; genuine, or not spurious; resting on or ruling by the principle of hereditary right; in accordance with the laws of reasoning; as, a *legitimate* conclusion; logical.—li·jit′i·māt″, *v.t.*— *legitimated, legitimating.* To show or declare to be legitimate or proper; to authorize or justify; to invest, as a bastard, with the rights of one lawfully born.—li·jit′i·mit, *n.* The professional theater or stage, usu. preceded by *the.*—**le ∙ git ∙ i ∙ mate ∙ ly,** *adv.*— **le ∙ git ∙ i ∙ mate ∙ ness,** *n.*—**le ∙ git ∙ i ∙ ma ∙ tion,** li·jit″i·mā′shan. *n.*

le·git·i·ma·tize, li·jit′i·ma·tiz″, *v.t.—legitimatized, legitimatizing.* To legitimate.

le·git·i·mist, li·jit′i·mist, *n.* One who supports legitimate authority; one who believes in the sacredness of hereditary monarchies or the doctrine of divine right.—*a.* Of, relating to, or upholding legitimate authority. Also **le·git·i·mis·tic.—le·git·i·mism,** *n.*

le·git·i·mize, li·jit′i·miz″, *v.t.—legitimized, legitimizing.* To legitimate.—**le·git·i·mi·za·tion,** *n.*

leg·man, leg′man″, leg′man, *n. Journ.* a newsman assigned to the gathering of information and the reporting of incidents as soon as they occur. An aide or assistant employed to gather information, run errands, and perform other minor tasks.

leg-of-mut·ton, leg′o·mut′on, leg′ov·mut′on, *a.* Having the triangular shape of a leg of mutton; as, a *leg-of-mutton* sail.

leg·ume, leg′ūm, li·gūm′, *n.* [Fr. *legume,* < L. *legumen,* legume, pulse, lit. 'something gathered (or picked),' < *legere,* gather.] *Bot.* A simple, dry, dehiscent, podlike fruit which splits along two seams, as a pea pod; any plant of the legume family, *Leguminosae,* the species of which have such fruits; *usu. pl.* plants of this family used for fodder and fertilizer.

le·gu·min, li·gū′min, *n.* [< *legume.*] *Biochem.* a protein resembling casein, obtained from the seeds of leguminous plants.

le·gu·mi·nous, li·gū′mi·nus, *a.* [N.L. *leguminosus,* < L. *legumen.*] *Bot.* pertaining to plants of the legume family, *Leguminosae,* characterized by irregular sweet-pea shaped flowers and legume fruits; of, relating to, or having legumes.

le·hu·a, lā·hö′ä, *n. Bot.* A hardwood, tropical tree of the genus *Metrosideros,* in the myrtle family, having bright red flowers borne in large clusters; the flower of this tree, the state flower of Hawaii.

le·i, lā′ē, lā, *n. pl.* **le·is.** [Hawaiian.] In the Hawaiian Islands, a wreath of flowers or leaves for the neck or head.

Leices·ter, les′tėr, *n.* [From *Leicestershire,* England, where these sheep were orig. bred.] Any of a mutton type of sheep characterized by their large size and long wool.

leis·ter, lē′stėr, *n.* [Icel. *ljostr,* Sw. *ljustra,* a leister.] A barbed instrument having at least three prongs and used for spearing fish.—*v.t.* To spear by using a leister.

lei·sure, lē′zhėr, lezh′ėr, *n.* [O.Fr. *leisir* (Fr. *loisir*), noun use of *leisir,* inf., < L. *licere,* be permitted.] Opportunity or time afforded by freedom from immediate occupation or duty; free or unoccupied time; ease.—*a.* Free or unoccupied; as, *leisure* hours; leisured; as, the *leisure* class.—**at lei·sure,** with free or unrestricted time; as, to proceed *at leisure;* without haste; unoccupied or disengaged; as, to be *at leisure.*—**at one's lei·sure,** when one has leisure; at one's convenience, as: Let me hear from you *at your leisure.*—**lei·sured,** lē′zhėrd, lezh′ėrd, *a.* Having or characterized by leisure.—**lei·sure·less,** *a.*

lei·sure·ly, lē′zhėr·lē, lezh′ėr·lē, *a.* Acting, proceeding, or done without hurrying; as, a *leisurely* person, speaker, or speech; showing or suggesting ample leisure; unhurried; as, a *leisurely* manner; deliberate.—*adv.*—**lei·sure·li·ness, lei·sure·ness,** *n.*

leit·mo·tif, līt′mō·tēf″, *n.* [G., 'leading motive.'] *Mus.* a motif or theme associated throughout an opera or music drama with a particular person, situation, or idea.

lem·ma, lem′a, *n. pl.* **lem·mas** or **lem·ma·ta.** [L. < Gr. *Lemma,* assumption, premise, thesis, theme, < *Lambanein,* take.] A subsidiary proposition introduced in proving some other proposition, as in mathematics; an argument, theme, or subject; a phrase, word, or heading in a glossary. *Bot.* the outer bract of the flowers of grasses.

lem·ming, lem′ing, *n.* [Norw.] Any of various small, arctic, mouselike rodents of the genera *Lemmus, Dicrostonyx, Phenacomys,* and *Synaptomys,* which migrate in great numbers in search of food and often perish in the sea.

lem·nis·cus, lem·nis′kus, *n. pl.* **lem·nis·ci,** lem·nis′ī, lem·nis′kē. *Anat.* a longitudinal band of nerve fibers in the brain. Also *fillet.*

lem·on, lem′on, *n.* [O.Fr. Fr. *limon,* < M.L. *limo(n)-,* < Ar. and Pers. *limun, lemon.*] *Bot.* the yellow, acid fruit of the subtropical tree, *Citrus limon,* in the rue family; the tree itself; a light yellow color, as that of the lemon. *Slang,* something that is inferior to, or does not meet, one's expectations.—*a.* Possessing the flavor, color, or odor of a lemon.

lem·on·ade, lem″o·nād′, *n.* A drink made of lemon juice, water, and sweetening.

lem·on balm, *n.* A fragrant, bushy perennial mint, *Melissa officinalis,* having lemon-flavored foliage.

lem·on ver·be·na, *n.* A subtropical garden shrub, *Aloysia triphylla,* in the verbena family, native to S. America and cultivated for its panicles of white flowers and lemon-scented leaves.

le·mur, lē′mėr, *n.* [N.L. < L. *lemures,* pl., ghosts, specters.] Any of various small, arboreal, nocturnal mammals of the genus *Lemur,* of Madagascar, closely related to monkeys and characterized by a foxlike head and woolly fur; any of various similar mammals, as the loris.—**lem·u·roid,** lem′ū·roid″, lem′ya·roid″, *n.* A lemur.—*a.* Similar to or resembling a lemur.

lem·u·res, lem′ū·rēz″, lem′ya·rēz″, L. lem′u̇·Res″, *n. pl.* [L.: cf. *lemur.*] *Rom. relig.* The spirits of the departed; ghosts.

Le·nard rays, lā′närd rāz, G. lā′närt räz, *n. pl.* [From P. *Lenard,* 1862–1947, German physicist.] *Phys.* cathode rays issued from a Lenard tube.—**Le·nard tube,** a special form of vacuum tube containing a diaphragm or window of aluminum through which Lenard rays are emitted.

lend, lend, *v.t.—lent, lending.* [O.E. *laenan,* to lend, < *laen,* a loan, (< *lihan* = G. *leihen,* to lend); cf. D. *leenen,* Dan. *laane,* Icel. *lana,* to lend.] To grant to another for temporary use; to furnish on condition of the thing or its equivalent in kind being returned; to afford, grant, or furnish in general, as assistance.—*refl.* to accommodate; to adapt so as to be of assistance, as: He *lent* himself to the scheme.—*v.i.* To make a loan.—**lend a hand,** to assist.—**lend·er,** *n.*

lend-lease, lend′lēs′, *n.* The supplying of war materials and services by the U.S. to its allies during World War II, as specified under the conditions of the Lend-Lease Act; the lending of material to combatants under the conditions of the Lend-Lease Act.—*v.t.* To lend, as war materials, as specified by the Lend-Lease Act.

Lend-Lease Act, *n.* An act, passed by Congress on March 11, 1941, permitting the U.S. government to furnish war materials and services to allies during World War II, with the stipulation that repayment in kind be made after the conflict.

length, lengkth, length, *n.* [O.E. *length,* < *lang,* long; akin *strength,* < *strong.*] The longest measure of any object, in distinction from depth, thickness, breadth, or width; linear measure from end to end; extent from start to finish, as of a word, book, or time period; one of the three dimensions of space; distance to a place; a portion of space considered as measured lengthwise; some definite long measure; as, to cut a rope into *lengths;* long continuance; the state of being long; duration of any extent in time; detail or amplification in language; extent, degree, or height in conduct or action; as, to go to great *lengths;* extent of progress; measure of distance in racing, as: The horse won by two *lengths. Phon.* the duration or stress of a sound.—**at length,** at or in the fullest extent; with amplitude of detail; at last; after a long period; at the end or conclusion.

length·en, lengk′then, leng′then, *v.t.* To make long or longer; to extend in length.—*v.i.* To grow longer.—**length·en·er,** *n.*

length·wise, lengkth′wiz″, length′wiz″, *adv., a.* In the direction of the length; in a longitudinal direction. Also **length·ways.**

length·y, lengk′thē, leng′thē, *a.—lengthier, lengthiest.* Long or moderately long; protracted; as, a *lengthy* discourse.—**length·i·ly,** *adv.*—**length·i·ness,** *n.*

le·ni·en·cy, lē′nē·en·sē, lēn′yen·sē, *n. pl.* **le·ni·en·cies.** The quality of being lenient; clemency. Also **le·ni·ence,** lē′nē·ens, lēn′yens.

le·ni·ent, lē′nē·ent, lēn′yent, *a.* [L. *leniens,* < *lenio,* to soften, < *lenis,* soft, mild; akin *lentus,* slow.] Mild; acting without rigor or severity; merciful; clement; gentle.—**le·ni·ent·ly,** *adv.*

Len·in·ism, len′i·niz″um, *n.* Marxist principles as interpreted and expounded by Vladimir Ilyich Lenin, 1870–1924, Russian revolutionary leader and premier of the U.S.S.R.—**Len·in·ist,** len′in·ist, *a.* Pertaining to the doctrines of Lenin.—*n.* A follower of Leninism. Also **Len·in·ite,** len′i·nīt″.

le·nis, lē′nis, lā′nis, *n. pl.* **le·nes,** lē′nēz, lā′nēz. A weakly articulated consonant.—*a.* Produced by weak articulation and pressure with very little expiration, as b, d, g, compared to the fortis consonants p, t, k.

len·i·tive, len′i·tiv, *a.* Having the quality of softening or mitigating, as medicines; assuasive; emollient.—*n.* A soothing medicine or application.

len·i·ty, len′i·tē, *n. pl.* **len·i·ties.** [L. *lenitas.*] Gentleness; clemency; tenderness; mercy; the state of being lenient.

lens, lenz, *n. pl.* **lens·es.** [L. *lens* (*lent-*), a lentil (which is shaped like a convexo-convex lens).] A piece of transparent substance, usu. glass, having two opposite surfaces, either both curved or one curved and one plane, used for changing the direction of light rays, as in magnifying, or in correcting errors of vision; a combination of such pieces; some analogous device, as for affecting sound waves. *Anat.* that part of the eye which focuses light rays on the retina; also *crystalline lens.*

Lent, lent, *n.* [O.E. *lencten,* spring, *lenctenfassten,* spring fast, Lent; D. *lente,* G. *lenz,* spring; perh. connected with *long,* the days becoming longer in spring.] A 40-day period of self-denial, fasting, and penitence, beginning at Ash Wednesday and continuing until Easter, observed in the Christian Church in commemoration of Christ's 40-day fast.—**Lent·en,** *a.* (Sometimes *l.c.*) pertaining to Lent or referring to the austerity of Lent; as, plain *Lenten* fare.

len·ta·men·te, len″ta·men′tä, *It.* len″tä·men′te, *adv.* [It. < *lento.*] *Mus.* slowly.

len·tan·do, len·tän′dō, *It.* len·tän′da̱, *a.* [It., gerund of *lentare,* slacken, < L. *lentus,* slow.] *Mus.* In a slackening manner; getting slower.

len·tic, len′tik, *a.* Of or living in ponds, swamps, or other still water.

len·ti·cel, len′ti·sel, *n.* [Fr. *lenticelle,* dim. < L. *lens* (*lent-*), a lentil.] *Bot.* a pore, often lenticular in shape, in the bark of woody stems through which the exchange of gases occurs.

len·tic·u·lar, len·tik′ū·lėr, len·tik′ya·lėr, *a.* [L. *lenticularis.*] Having the form of a double-convex lens; of or relating to a lens; resembling a lentil in size or form.—**len·tic·u·lar·ly,** *adv.*

len·tic·u·late, len·tik′ū·lāt″, len·tik′ya·lāt″, *v.t.*—**lenticulated, lenticulating.** *Photog.* to impress, as film, with microscopic lenses.

len·ti·go, len·tī′gō, *n.* pl. **len·tig·i·nes,** len·tij′i·nēz″. [L., < *lens* (*lent*-), a lentil.] *Med.* A freckle; a freckly condition.—**len·tig·i·nous,** len·tij′i·nus, *a.*

len·til, len′til, *n.* [O.Fr. Fr. *lentille,* < L. *lenticula,* dim. of *lens* (*lent*-), a lentil.] An annual plant of the legume family, *Lens culinaris,* having flattened, biconvex, edible seeds; the seed of the plant.

len·tis·si·mo, len·tis′i·mō″, *It.* len·tēs′sē·ma̱, *a. Mus.* very slow.—*adv. Mus.* very slowly.

len·to, len′tō, *It.* len′ta̱, *a.* [It. < L. *lentus,* slow.] *Mus.* slow.—*adv. Mus.* slowly.—*n. Mus.* a slowly played passage.

len·toid, len′toid, *a.* Lens-shaped.—*n.* A lens-shaped body.

Le·o, lē′ō, *n.* [L., a lion.] *Astron.* the Lion, a constellation in the northern hemisphere whose brightest star is Regulus; *astrol.* the fifth sign of the zodiac.

Le·o·nid, lē′o·nid, *n.* pl. **Le·o·nids, Le·on·i·des,** lē·on′i·dēz″. *Astron.* any of a shower of meteors occurring yearly about November 15th, appearing to shoot from the constellation Leo.

le·o·nine, lē′o·nīn″, *a.* [L. *leoninus.*] Pertaining to or resembling a lion.

leop·ard, lep′ėrd, *n.* [O.Fr. *leopard, lepart* (Fr. *leopard*), < L.L. *leopardus,* Gr. *leopardos,* < *leōn,* lion, and *pardos,* pard.] A large, ferocious, nocturnal Asiatic or African mammal, *Panthera pardus,* of the cat family, characterized by a tawny coat with black markings; any of various related animals, as the jaguar, snow leopard, panther, and cheetah; the fur of the leopard. *Her.* a representation of a lion from the side view with the head facing forward.—**leop·ard·ess,** *n.* A female leopard.

le·o·tard, lē′o·tärd″, *n.* A one-piece, stretchable, skin-tight garment worn by dancers, acrobats, or the like.

lep·er, lep′ėr, *n.* [Orig. meant the disease, being < Fr. *lepre,* L. *lepra,* < Gr. *lepra,* leprosy, < *lepros,* scaly, connected with *lepos,* a husk.] A ′person affected with leprosy; *fig.* an outcast.

le·pid·o·lite, li·pid′o·līt″, lep′i·do·līt″, *n.* [Gr. *lepis* (*lepio*), scale, and *lithos,* stone.] A variety of mica containing lithium, commonly occurring in lilac, rose-colored, or grayish-white scaly masses.

lep·i·dop·ter·an, lep″i·dop′tėr·an, *n.* [N.L. *Lepidoptera,* pl., < Gr. *lepis,* (*lepio*), scale, and *pteron,* wing.] Any lepidopterous insect, as a butterfly, moth, or skipper. Also **lep·i·dop·ter·on,** pl. **lep·i·dop·ter·a.**—*a.* Lepidopterous.

lep·i·dop·ter·ous, lep″i·dop′tėr·us, *a.* Of or pertaining to the *Lepidoptera,* an order of insects comprising the butterflies, moths, and skippers, which in the adult stage have four membranous wings covered with small scales. Also **lep·i·dop·ter·al.**

lep·i·do·si·ren, lep″i·dō·sī′ren, *n.* [N.L. < Gr. *lepis* (*lepid*-), scale, and *seiren,* E. *siren.*] *Zool.* an eel-shaped lungfish of the genus *Lepidosiren,* native to the Amazon River.

lep·i·dote, lep′i·dōt″, *a.* [Gr. *lepidōtos,* scaly, < *lepis,* a scale.] *Bot.* Covered with scurfy, scaly spots; scurfy.

lep·o·rine, lep′o·rīn″, lep′o·rin, *a.* [L. *leprinus,* < *lepus, leporis,* a hare.] *Zool.* pertaining to or having the qualities of a hare.

lep·re·chaun, lep′re·kạn″, lep′re·kọn″, *n.* [Ir.] *Ir. folklore,* a mischievous elf, usu. in the form of an old man, who, it is believed, will reveal where treasure is hidden if caught.

lep·ro·sar·i·um, lep″ro·sâr′ē·um, *n.* pl. **lep·ro·sar·i·ums, lep·ro·sar·i·a,** lep″ro·sâr′ē·a. [M.L. < L.L. *leprosus.*] A hospital or asylum for lepers.

lep·rose, lep′rōs, *a.* [L.L. *leprosus.*] *Pathol.* pertaining to or resembling leprosy; *bot.* scurfy or scaly, as certain lichens.

lep·ro·sy, lep′ro·sē, *n. Pathol.* an infectious, chronic disease due to a microorganism, *Mycobacterium leprae,* and variously characterized by ulcerations, tubercular nodules, loss of fingers and toes, and anaesthesis in certain nerve regions. Also *Hansen's disease.*—**lep·rot·ic,** le·prot′ik, *a.*

lep·rous, lep′rus, *a.* [L.L. *leprosus,* < L. *lepra,* leprosy.] Affected with leprosy; of or like leprosy. *Bot.* scaly or scurfy; leprose.—**lep·rous·ly,** *adv.*—**lep·rous·ness,** *n.*

lep·ton, lep′ton, *n.* pl. **lep·ta,** lep′ta. *Phys.* a particle, small in mass, as an electron, positron, neutrino, antineutrino, or mumeson.

lep·to·some, lep′to·sōm″, *a.* Ectomorphic; asthenic. Also **lep·to·som·ic, lep·to·so·mat·ic,** lep″tō·so·mat′ik.—*n.* Also **lep·to·som.**

lep·to·spi·ra, lep″to·spī′ra, *n.* pl. **lep·to·spi·rae, lep·to·spi·ras,** lep″to·spī′rē. *Bact.* any of the thin-coiled, aerobic bacteria, genus *Leptospira,* some of which infect man. —**lep·to·spi·ral,** *a.*

les·bi·an, lez′bē·an, *a.* [From *Lesbos,* a Greek island in the Aegean Sea.] Of or pertaining to lesbians or lesbianism; (*cap.*) pertaining to Lesbos or its inhabitants.—*n.* (*Sometimes cap.*) a female homosexual; (*cap.*) an inhabitant of Lesbos.—**les·bi·an·ism,** *n.* Homosexual relations between females.

lese maj·es·ty, lēz maj′i·stē, *n.* [< *Fr. lèse-majesté,* < M.L. *læsa majestas,* 'injured majesty' (*læa,* pp. fem. of L. *lædere*).] *Law,* any crime or offense against the sovereign power in a state, or the dignity of the sovereign; also **leze maj·es·ty.** An assault against any widely revered belief or institution. Also **lèse ma·jes·té.**

le·sion, lē′zhan, *n.* [O.Fr. lesion (Fr. *lesion*), < L. *læsio(n*-), < *lædere* (pp. *læsus*), hurt, injure.] An injury; a wound; *pathol.* an abnormal, localized change in the structure of an organ or tissue, resulting from disease or injury.

les·pe·de·za, les″pi·dē′za, *n. Bot.* any one of several herbs or shrubs of the genus *Lespedeza,* in the legume family, cultivated as forage or as a soil binder.

less, les, *a.* irreg., *compar. of little.* [O.E. *laes(sa)* = O.Fries. *lessa,* less: a compar. form (positive lacking, superl. E. *least*) associated with the unrelated E. *little.*] Fewer or smaller in size, amount, or degree; lower in consideration, dignity, or importance; with *than.*—*n.* A smaller amount or quantity.—*adv.* To a lesser extent, amount, or degree.—*prep.* Lacking; minus; without.

les·see, le·sē′, *n.* The person to whom a lease is given.

less·en, les′en, *v.t.* To make smaller or less; to disparage.—*v.i.* To become smaller; to decrease or diminish.

less·er, les′ėr, *a., compar. of little.* [A double compar. < *less.*] Less; smaller; less important.

les·son, les′on, *n.* [O.Fr. Fr. *lecon,* < L. *lectio(n*-), a reading, E. *lection.*] Reading or dictation assigned to a pupil for study; a period or division of instruction; as, a music *lesson;* something to be learned; an instructive experience or example; a reprimand or punishment intended to teach one better ways; a portion of Scripture or other sacred writing read at religious services.—*v.t.* To give a lesson to; teach or instruct; admonish or reprove.

les·sor, les′ạr, le·sạr′, *n.* One who leases to a tenant.

lest, lest, *conj.* [O.E. *leste,* for *les the,* shortened < O.E. *thý, læs the,* the, less that, lest—*thý,* by that = *the* in the more, etc., *læs = less, the,* indeclinable relative.] For fear that; in case.

let, let, *v.t.*—*let, letting.* [O.E. *laetan, letan* = D. *laten,* Icel. *lats* Goth. *letan,* G. *lassen;* allied to E. *late,* and L. *lassus,* weary.] To permit; to allow; to permit to enter, pass, or go; to rent or lease; to make or cause, as: *Let* me hear you sing. Used in the imperative mood as an auxiliary to express a proposal, command, suggestion, or warning, as: Let me go! *Let's* accept. *Let* him try to resist.—*v.i.* To be or become rented.—**let down,** to disappoint or betray.—**let off,** to excuse; to permit to avoid punishment.—**let on,** to pretend; to reveal.—**let up,** to abate; to cease.

let, let, *n.* In certain games, as tennis, an interference with the course of the ball on account of which the stroke or point must be played over again. *Archaic,* hindrance or obstruction; an impediment or obstacle.

let·down, let′doun″, *n.* A disappointment or disenchantment; a lessening, lowering, or decrease; *aeron.* the gliding descent of an airplane from a cruising altitude preparatory to the approach and landing.

le·thal, lē′thal, *a.* [L. *lethalis, letalis,* mortal, < *letum,* death.] Causing or able to cause death; deadly; mortal; fatal.—**le·thal·i·ty,** *n.*—**le·thal·ly,** *adv.*

le·thal gene, *n. Genetics,* a dominant or recessive gene that may affect an organism at any stage of its life, causing death. Also **le·thal fac·tor.**

le·thar·gic, le·thär′jik, *a.* Affected with lethargy; inclined to sleep; dull; sluggish; pertaining to lethargy. Also **le·thar·gi·cal.** —**le·thar·gi·cal·ly,** *adv.*

leth·ar·gy, leth′ėr·jē, *n.* pl. **leth·ar·gies.** [L. *lethargia,* < Gr. *lēthargia,* oblivion, *lēthargos,* forgetful, < *lēthē,* oblivion.] Unnatural sleepiness; dullness; inaction; inattention; drowsiness; *pathol.* profound sleep, from which a person can scarcely be awakened.—**leth·ar·gize,** leth′ėr·jīz″, *v.t.* —*lethargized, lethargizing.*

Le·the, lē′thē, *n.* [Gr. *lēthē,* forgetfulness; akin L. *lateo,* to lie hid.] *Gr. mythol.* One of the streams of Hades which contained waters that induced oblivion in the drinker; oblivion; forgetfulness.—**Le·the·an,** li·thē′an, lē′thē·an, *a.*

let's, lets. Contraction of let us.

let·ter, let′ėr, *n.* [Fr. *lettre,* < L. *litera,* a letter.] A symbol or character used to represent a sound; a character standing for a vowel or consonant; a written or printed message; an award for participation in some school activity, often athletic in nature. *Print.* a single type or character; a specific type style; types collectively; *Pl.* learning; erudition; as, a man of *letters;* literature in general.—*v.t.* To write letters on; inscribe. —*v.i.* To be awarded a letter for participation in a school activity.—**the let·ter,** the literal or verbal meaning.—**let·ter·er,** *n.* An artist or craftsman who does lettering.

let·ter car·ri·er, *n.* A postman.

let·tered, let′ėrd, *a.* Learned; versed in literature; belonging to learning; marked or designated with letters.

let·ter·head, let′ėr·hed″, *n.* A printed heading on a piece of stationery, usu. one giving the name and address of a business concern or an institution; a sheet of paper with such a heading.

let·ter·ing, let′ėr·ing, *n.* The process or act of engraving, stamping with, or forming letters; the letters produced by this process.

let·ter·man, let′ėr·man″, let′ėr·man, *n.* pl. **let·ter·men.** A person awarded a letter, usu. the initial of his school, for exceptional accomplishment in scholastic or athletic activity.

let·ter of cred·it, *n.* A bank letter or certificate entitling the person named therein to a specified amount of money which he may withdraw from that bank or any of its affiliates; a bank letter which grants a named person a specific amount of credit against a guarantee to repay that sum.

let·ter of marque, *n. Hist.* a governmental license or written authority issued to a private citizen as permission to seize and plunder an enemy's merchant ships. Also **let·ters of marque, let·ter of marque and re·pri·sal.**

let·ter-per·fect, *let'ẽr·pur'fikt, a.* Knowing perfectly one's part, lesson, or the like; verbatim; precise.—*adv.* Of writing or memorizing, precisely or perfectly.

let·ter·press, *let'ẽr·pres", n. Printing,* words impressed by raised type; *Brit.* print or printed matter as differentiated from illustrations.

let·ters of ad·min·is·tra·tion, *n. Law,* a court authorization which charges a particular person with the administration of a deceased person's estate.

let·ters of cre·dence, *n.* Credentials furnished to an envoy or diplomatic agent for presentation to a foreign country, affirming his authority to represent his country. Also **let·ter of cre·dence.**

let·ters pat·ent, *n. Law,* a governmental document granting exclusive rights and authority to some act, usu. the sole right of manufacturing and selling a given product or invention.

let·ters tes·ta·men·ta·ry, *n. Law,* a written court directive authorizing the executor of a will to proceed.

Let·tish, *let'ish, a.* Pertaining to the Letts or their language.—*n.* The language of the Letts. Also *Latvian.*—**Lett,** *n.* One of a people living on and near the eastern coast of the Baltic Sea; their language.

let·tuce, *let'is, n.* [M.E. *letuse* = O.Fr. Fr. *laitue* (pl. *laitues*), < L. *lactuca,* lettuce, so called from its milky juice, < *lac* (*lact*-), milk.] A common vegetable, *Lactuca sativa,* of the composite family, having edible leaves often used in salads; any species of *Lactuca. Slang,* paper money.

let·up, *let'up", n. Colloq.* a cessation, pause, or lessening.—**let up,** *v.i.*

leu·cine, *lö'sēn, lö'sin, n.* [Gr. *leucos,* white.] *Chem.* a white, crystalline, amino acid, $C_6H_{13}NO_2$, formed in various ways, esp. by the pancreatic digestion of proteins in the body. Also **leu·cin.**

leu·cite, *lö'sīt, n.* [Gr. *leucos,* white.] A whitish or grayish mineral, $KAlSi_2O_6$, consisting of a silicate of aluminum and potassium, found in certain igneous or volcanic rocks.—**leu·cit·ic,** *lö·sit'ik, a.*

leu·co·ma·ine, *lö·kō'ma·ēn", lö·kō'ma·in, lö'ko·mān", n. Biochem.* one of several often poisonous nitrogen compounds present in animal tissue as a by-product of metabolism.

leu·co·plast, *lö'ko·plast", n. Bot.* a colorless plastid which functions as a starch formation center in many types of plant cells.

leu·ke·mi·a, *lö·kē'mē·a, n.* [Gr. *leukos,* white, *kytos,* a cell, and *haima,* blood.] *Pathol.* A fatal disease of the blood, in which there is a pronounced increase in the number of leukocytes; cancer of the blood. Also **leu·cae·mi·a,** *lö·sē'mē·a.*—**leu·ke·mic,** *a.*

leu·ko·cyte, leu·co·cyte, *lö'ko·sīt", n. Physiol.* A white blood corpuscle; a colorless blood cell active in the defense against infection and bacteria, and occasionally found in body tissues.—**leu·ko·cyt·ic, leu·co·cyt·ic,** *lö"ko·sīt'ik, a.*

leu·ko·cy·to·sis, leu·co·cy·to·sis, *lö"kō·sī·tō'sis, n. Physiol.* a temporary increase in the number of leukocytes in the blood, usu. caused by an infection, and not indic-

ative of leukemia.—**leu·ko·cy·tot·ic,** *lö"ko·sī·tot'ik, a.*

leu·ko·ma, leu·co·ma, *lö·kō'ma, n.* [Gr. *leukōma,* < *leukos,* white.] *Pathol.* a white opacity of the cornea of the eye.

leu·ko·pe·ni·a, leu·co·pe·ni·a, *lö"ko·pē'nē·a, n. Physiol.* an acute decrease of leukocytes in the blood. Also **leu·ko·cy·to·pe·ni·a,—leu·ko·pe·nic,** *a.*

leu·kor·rhe·a, *lö"ko·rē'a, n. Pathol.* a whitish discharge emanating from the vagina, usu. resulting from congestion. Also **leu·kor·rhoe·a, leu·cor·rhe·a, leu·cor·rhoe·a.—leu·kor·rhe·al, leu·kor·rhoe·al,** *a.*

leu·ko·sis, leu·co·sis, *lö·kō'sis, n. Veter. pathol.* any of several diseases afflicting production of leukocytes.—**leu·kot·ic,** *lö·kot'ik, a.*

Le·val·loi·si·an, *lev"a·loi·zē'·an, lev"a·loi'zhan, a. Anthropol.* of or having to do with a delineated cultural tradition described as Middle Paleolithic and distinguished by a particular technique for producing tools from flint. Also **Le·val·lois,** *le·val'wä.*

Le·vant, *li·vant', n.* [It. *levante,* the east, the direction of sunrise, < L. *levare,* to raise, *se lavare,* to rise.] The countries adjoining the eastern Mediterranean and Aegean shores, including Syria, Egypt, and Israel; (*l.c.*) levanter. (*Usu. cap.*) a type of high quality morocco leather with prominent grain, orig. produced in the Levant regions; also **Le·vant mo·roc·co.**

le·vant, *li·vant', v.i.* [Sp. *levantar,* to raise, to remove; *levantar la casa,* to break up house, < L. *levare,* to raise.] *Brit.* to run away secretly, esp. without paying a debt.—**le·vant·er,** *n.* One who avoids paying a debt.

le·vant·er, *li·van'tẽr, n.* A forceful wind blowing in an easterly direction in the area of the Mediterranean; (*cap.*) a Levantine.

Le·van·tine, *lev'an·tīn", lev'an·tēn", li·van'tin, li·van'tīn, a.* Pertaining to the Levant, the region and countries bordering the eastern Mediterranean.—*n.* A native of the Levant.—**Lev·an·tin·ism,** *n.*

le·va·tor, *li·vā'tẽr, li·vā'tar, n. pl.* **lev·a·to·res,** *lev"a·tōr'ēz.* [L., < *levare,* raise.] *Anat.* a muscle that raises some part of the body; *surg.* an instrument used to raise a depressed part of the skull.

lev·ee, *lev'ē, n.* [Fr. *levee,* < *lever,* raise.] An embankment for preventing the overflowing of a river; a landing place for vessels; a quay; a series of small terraces or ridges, for confining the flow of water in irrigation.—*v.t., v.i.*—**leveed, leveeing.**

lev·ee, *lev'ē, le·vē', n.* [Fr. *leve,* also *lever,* a rising (from bed), reception of visitors by a great personage on rising; < *lever,* rise.] A morning reception held by a prince or great personage; a reception; as, a presidential *levee* at the White House; formerly, a reception of visitors held by a highly ranked person on rising from bed; *Brit.* a public court assembly for men only, held in the early afternoon.

lev·el, *lev'el, n.* [O.Fr. *livel* (Fr. *niveau*), < L. *libella,* dim. of *libra,* a balance, level.] A device for determining the horizontal plane, used esp. by surveyors and carpenters; a spirit level; a measuring of differences in elevation with such an instrument; a horizontal condition; the horizontal line or plane in which anything is situated, with reference to its elevation; as, flying at the *level* of the clouds; a flat or horizontal surface, esp. land; a rating, status, or value; as, a social *level;* extent or degree; as, *level* of education.—*a.* Having no part higher than another; having an even surface; being in a plane parallel to the plane of the horizon; horizontal; being in the same horizontal plane with another or others;

even or equable; as, *level* abilities; uniform or evenly distributed; *colloq.* calm or mentally well-balanced, often used in compounds; as, *level-headed.*—*v.t.*—**leveled, leveling, levelled, levelling.** To make level, smooth, flat, or even, as a surface; to demolish, raze, or destroy; to raise or lower to a particular level or horizontal plane; *fig.* to raise or lower to a particular position, high or low; to bring to a common level; remove or reduce inequalities, as of social rank or of adjoining pieces of ground; to make even or uniform, as coloring; to aim, direct, or point at a mark, as a weapon; *surv.* to find the relative elevation of, as different pieces of land, esp. with a surveyor's level.—*v.i.* To be on a level or plane, usu. followed by *with;* to bring things or persons to a common level; to aim, esp. a weapon; *slang,* to be truthful, straightforward. *Surv.* to take levels; use a surveyor's level.—**find its lev·el, find one's lev·el,** to arrive at the natural or proper level or position, high or low, as: Water always finds its *level.*—**one's lev·el best,** one's very best; one's utmost.—**on the lev·el,** *slang,* honest or reliable.—**lev·el·ly,** *adv.*—**lev·el·ness,** *n.*

lev·el cross·ing, *n. Brit.* grade crossing.

lev·el·er, *Brit.* **lev·el·ler,** *lev'e·lẽr, n.* One who or that which levels, usu. one who would bring all men to a common level, or abolish social or other distinctions.

lev·el-head·ed, *lev'el·hed'id, a.* Characterized by sound judgment; having common sense; sensible.—**lev·el-head·ed·ness,** *n.*

lev·el·ing rod, *n.* A graduated rod or staff used for measuring heights in connection with a surveyor's level.

lev·er, *lev'ẽr, lē'vẽr, n.* [O.Fr. Fr. *leveur,* lit. 'raiser,' < *lever,* raise, also rise, < L. *levare,* lighten, lift, raise, < *levis,* light.] A bar used for lifting or prying; a bar or rigid piece, rotating about a fixed axis or fulcrum, which lifts or sustains weight at one point by means of applied force at a second point.—*v.t., v.i.* To move with or apply a lever.—**lev·er·age,** *n.* The action of a lever; the mechanical advantage or power gained by using a lever; increased power of acting, as: He wielded enough *leverage* to get the bill passed.

lev·er·et, *lev'ẽr·it, n.* [Fr. *levrette,* dim. of O.Fr. *levre* (now *lievre*), a hare, < L. *lepus, leporis,* a hare.] A hare in its first year of life.

le·vi·a·than, *li·vī'a·than, n.* [L.L., < Heb. *livyāthān.*] A sea monster mentioned in the Old Testament; any huge marine animal, as the whale; anything, esp. a ship, of huge size.—*a.*

lev·i·gate, *lev'i·gāt", v.t.*—**levigated, levigating.** [L. *lævigo,* < *lævis,* smooth.] To make a smooth paste of; to rub or grind to a fine powder, with or without the use of a liquid.—*a. Bot.* glabrous.—**lev·i·ga·tion,** *n.*—**lev·i·ga·tor,** *n.*

lev·i·rate, *lev'ẽr·it, lev'e·rāt", lē'vẽr·it, lē'vi·rāt", n.* [L. *levir,* a husband's brother; akin Gr. *daēr.*] The ancient Jewish law according to which a childless widow married her husband's brother; the resulting marriage.—**lev·i·rat·ic, lev·i·rat·i·cal,** *lev"i·rat'ik, lē"vi·rat'ik, a.*

Le·vis, *lē'vīz, n.* [From *Levi* Strauss, Amer. manufacturer.] Heavy, close-fitting denim pants which are strengthened at the strain points with rivets. (Trademark.)

lev·i·tate, *lev'i·tāt", v.i.*—**levitated, levitating.** [L. *levitas,* lightness, E. *levity:* cf. *gravitate.*] To rise or float in the air, allegedly through some supernatural power that overcomes the force of gravity.—*v.t.* To cause to rise or float in the air.—**lev·i·ta·tion,** *lev"i·tā'shan, n.*

lev·i·ty, *lev'i·tē, n.* [L. *levitas,* < *levis,* light; akin to E. *light,* G. *leicht,* easy, slight,

Gr. *elachys*, small. L. *levis*, gives, *lever*, *levy*, *elevate*, *alleviate*, *relieve*, etc.] Inappropriate or excessive frivolity; lack of suitable seriousness; fickleness. Buoyancy; lightness of weight.

le·vo·ro·ta·tion, lē″vō·rō·tā′shan, *n.* Rotation toward the left or in a counterclockwise direction; *opt.*, *crystal*. the rotation of the plane of polarization of light to the left.—**le·vo·ro·ta·to·ry**, lē″vō·rō′ta·tōr″ē, *a.* Also **le·vo**, lē′vō.

lev·u·lose, lev′ū·lōs″, lev′ya·lōs″, *n.* [L. *laevus*, left.] *Chem.* fructose.

lev·y, lev′ē, *n.* pl. **lev·ies**. [O.Fr. *levee* (Fr. *levee*), < *lever*, raise.] A raising or collecting, as of money or troops, by authority or force; that which is raised, as a tax, assessment, or a body of troops.—*v.t.*—**levied**, **levying**. To make a levy of; collect, as taxes or contributions; impose, as an assessment; to raise or enlist, as troops, for service; to get going or start.—*v.i.* To make a levy.—**lev·i·a·ble**, lev′ē·a·bl, *a.*—**lev·i·er**, *n.*

lewd, lōd, *a.* [O.E. *lǣwede*, lay; origin uncertain.] Inclined to, characterized by, or inciting to lust or lechery; lascivious; sexually unchaste; obscene or indecent, as language or song.—**lewd·ly**, *adv.*—**lewd·ness**, *n.*

lew·is, lō′is, *n.* [Origin uncertain.] *Constr.* a kind of tenon, in sections, fitted into a dovetail recess or mortise in a block of stone, and used to attach the block to a derrick for lifting and moving. Also **lew·is·son**, **lew·is·i·ron**.

lew·is·ite, lō′i·sīt″, *n.* [From Winford Lee *Lewis*, U.S. chemist, 1878–1943.] A heavy, oily liquid, developed during World War I for use in chemical warfare, causing burns and tissue destruction.

lex, leks, *n.* pl. **le·ges**, lē′jēz, L. le′ges. Law. Abbr. for lexical, lexicon.

lex·i·cal, lek′si·kal, *a.* [Gr. *lexikós*, of or for words, (*lexikón*, neut., word book), < *léxis*, speech, phrase, word, < *légein*, speak.] Pertaining to the words or vocabulary of a language, as differentiated from its syntax or grammar; pertaining to or of the nature of a lexicon; pertaining to lexicography.—**lex·i·cal·i·ty**, *n.*—**lex·i·cal·ly**, *adv.*

lex·i·cal mean·ing, *n.* The literal meaning or definition of a word or morpheme, as compared to the meaning a word or morpheme assumes in combination with other words and morphemes.

lex·i·cog·ra·pher, lek″si·kog′ra·fèr, *n.* An author or compiler of a dictionary.

lex·i·cog·ra·phy, lek″si·kog′ra·fē, *n.* The act of compiling or writing a dictionary; the occupation of composing dictionaries.—**lex·i·co·graph·ic**, **lex·i·co·graph·i·cal**, lek″si·kō·graf′ik, lek″si·ko·graf′ik, *a.*—**lex·i·co·graph·i·cal·ly**, *adv.*

lex·i·con, lek′si·kon″, lek′si·kon, *n.* pl. **lex·i·ca**, **lex·i·cons**, lek′si·ka. [Gr. *lexicon*, < *lexis*, a speaking, speech, a word, < *legō*, to speak.] A dictionary, usu. one of Greek, Hebrew, or Latin; the particular vocabulary associated with a profession, activity, or field of interest; *ling.* all the morphemes in any given language.

Ley·den jar, līd′en jär, *n.* [So named from having been invented at *Leyden*, Holland.] *Elect.* a glass jar coated inside and outside, usu. with tinfoil, to within a third of the top, so that it may be readily charged with static electricity.

li, lē, *n.* pl. **li**. A Chinese linear measure equivalent to about one third of a mile.

li·a·bil·i·ty, lī″a·bil′i·tē, *n.* pl. **li·a·bil·i·ties**. The state or fact of being legally responsible or under obligation; the extent to which one is liable, as for a debt; the state of being liable or subject to something possible or probable; as, *liability* to disease; a hindrance or drawback. Usu. *pl.* debts or pecuniary obligations; *accounting*, balance sheet entries representing debts: opposed to *assets*.

li·a·ble, lī′a·bl, *a.* [Either < the verb to *lie*, with the sense of lying open or subject to, or < Fr. *lier*, to bind, and hence akin to *ally*, *lien*. Cf. *rely*, *reliable*.] Answerable for consequences; under obligation legally to make good a loss; responsible; apt or likely to incur something undesirable; susceptible; subject or exposed to; as, *liable* to disease; *colloq.* likely; as, *liable* to rain.

li·ai·son, lē″ā·zaN′, lē″a·zon″, lē′a·zon, lē·ā′zon, lē·ā′zon, Fr. lye·zaN′, *n.* [Fr., < L. *ligatio(n-)*, < *ligare*, bind.] *Milit.* the connection or cooperative relationship maintained between armed forces units to ensure concerted action; a similar connection to be maintained between the divisions of any organization; as, a manufacturers' *liaison*; an illicit affair between a man and a woman; *phonet.* the joining in pronunciation of a usu. silent final consonant to a following word that begins with a vowel sound; *cooking*, a thickening, as of beaten eggs and cream, used for sauces.

li·a·na, lē·ä′na, lē·an′a, *n.* [Fr. *liane*, < *lier*, L. *ligare*, to bind; akin *lien*.] A climbing and twining plant, rooted in the ground, that, when woody grows in tropical forests, and when herbaceous is found in temperate zones. Also **li·ane**, lē·än′.—**li·a·noid**, *a.*

li·ar, lī′èr, *n.* [O.E. *lēogere*.] One who lies, or purposely makes false statements.

Li·as, lī′as, *n.* [O.Fr. *liois* (Fr. *liais*), a compact kind of limestone.] *Geol.* the lowest division of the European Jurassic series of rocks.—**Li·as·sic**, **li·as·ik**, *a.*

li·ba·tion, lī·bā′shan, *n.* [L. *libatio(n-)*, < *libare*, pour out as a libation.] A pouring out of wine or other liquid in honor of a deity, esp. the ceremonial practice of the ancient Greeks and Romans in offering sacrifice; the liquid poured out; humorously, an alcoholic or other strong beverage, esp. when served and enjoyed on festive occasions.—**li·ba·tion·al**, **li·ba·tion·ar·y**, *a.*

li·bel, lī′bel, *n.* [Fr. *libelle*, L. *libellus*, a libel or lampoon, lit. 'a little book,' dim. of *liber*, the inner bark or rind of a tree used for paper, and hence a book; akin *library*.] A defamatory writing or representation. *Law*, a malicious writing or representation which brings its object into contempt or exposes him to public derision; the act of publishing such a writing; the writ containing a plaintiff's allegations.—*v.t.*—**libeled**, **libeling**, **libelled**, **libelling**. To publish a libel against; to defame by libel; to lampoon.

li·bel·ant, *Brit.* **li·bel·lant**, lī′be·lant, *n. Law*, one who brings a libel suit in court.

li·bel·ee, *Brit.* **li·bel·lee**, lī″be·lē′, *n. Law*, the defendant against whom a lawsuit involving libel has been instituted.

li·bel·er, *Brit.* **li·bel·ler**, lī′be·lèr, *n.* One guilty of libel or of publishing a libel.

li·bel·ous, *Brit.* **li·bel·lous**, lī′be·lus, *a.* Of a slanderous, defamatory nature; given to libel.—**li·bel·ous·ly**, *Brit.* **li·bel·lous·ly**, *adv.*

li·ber, lī′bèr, *n. Bot.* the inner fibrous bark, a part of the phloem.

lib·er·al, lib′èr·al, lib′ral, *a.* [L. *liberalis*, < *liber*, free; akin to *libet*, *lubet*, it pleases, it is agreeable, Skr. *lubh*, to desire. L. *liber* gives also *liberate*, *liberty*, *libertine*, *livery*, *deliver*.] Pertaining to the liberal arts; given generously and bountifully; not literal or strict, as a translation; tolerant or open-minded, esp. in religion or politics; pertaining to liberalism as a political movement.—*n.* One who is tolerant in religious and political matters; one who is not constrained by orthodoxy or tradition; (*often cap.*) a member of a reformist political party.—**lib·er·al·ly**, *adv.*—**lib·er·al·ness**, *n.*

lib·er·al arts, *n. pl.* A general course of study including natural and social sciences, the arts, and humanities, as opposed to a practical, technical course of study.

lib·er·al·ism, lib′èr·a·liz″um, lib′ra·liz″um, *n.* The disposition to change or reform what is established, as in religion or politics; (*often cap.*) specific principles and practices developed by advocates of political change; *econ.* a theory advocating individual freedom from governmental control and a market which is self-regulating.—**lib·er·al·ist**, *n.*, *a.*—**lib·er·al·is·tic**, *a.*

lib·er·al·i·ty, lib″e·ral′i·tē, *n. pl.* **lib·er·al·i·ties**. [L. *liberalitas*; Fr. *liberalité*.] The quality of being liberal or broadminded; generosity or munificence; a generous gift.

lib·er·al·ize, lib′èr·a·līz″, lib′ra·līz″, *v.t.*—**liberalized**, **liberalizing**. To render liberal.—*v.i.* To become liberal.—**lib·er·al·i·za·tion**, *n.*—**lib·er·al·iz·er**, *n.*

lib·er·ate, lib′e·rāt″, *v.t.*—**liberated**, **liberating**. [L. *libero*, *liberatum*, < *liber*, free.] To set at liberty, as from restraint or bondage; to free; to disengage; to release from combination, as in a chemical compound.—**lib·er·a·tion**, *n.*—**lib·er·a·tor**, *n.*

Li·be·ri·an, lī·bēr′ē·an, *a.* Of or pertaining to Liberia, a country on the western coast of Africa, colonized in 1822 by freed American slaves and made a republic in 1847.—*n.* A native or inhabitant of Liberia.

lib·er·tar·i·an, lib″èr·târ′ē·an, *n.* One who maintains the doctrine of the freedom of the will; one who advocates liberty, esp. with regard to thought or conduct.—*a.*—**lib·er·tar·i·an·ism**, *n.*

lib·er·ti·cide, li·bur′ti·sīd″, *n.* [*Liberty*, and L. *caedo*, to kill.] Destruction of liberty; a destroyer of liberty.—**li·ber·ti·cid·al**, *a.*

lib·er·tin·age, lib′èr·tē″nij, lib′èr·tin·ij, *n.* Libertinism.

lib·er·tine, lib′èr·tēn″, lib′èr·tin, *n.* [L. *libertinus*, a freedman, < *liber*, free.] One who is lacking in moral or sexual restraint; one who leads a dissolute, licentious life; a rake; a freethinker concerning religion. *Rom. hist.* a freed Roman slave.—*a.* Licentious; dissolute.—**lib·er·tin·ism**, lib′èr·tē·niz″um, lib′èr·ti·niz″um, *n.* The conduct of a libertine or rake. Also *libertinage*.

lib·er·ty, lib′èr·tē, *n. pl.* **lib·er·ties**. [O.Fr. *liberte* (Fr. *liberte*), < L. *libertas*, *liber*, free.] Freedom or release from slavery, captivity, or restraint; freedom from arbitrary or oppressive government or control; independence from external or foreign rule; power or right of doing, thinking, or speaking according to choice; the right to various political, social, or economic privileges; freedom to occupy or use a locale, usu. followed by *of*; an immunity, privilege, or right enjoyed by grant or prescription; specif. leave granted to a sailor to go ashore; unwarranted or impertinent freedom in action or speech.—**at lib·er·ty**, free; unoccupied or disengaged; unemployed.—**take lib·er·ties** or **a lib·er·ty**, act or speak in a manner too free or familiar.

lib·er·ty cap, *n.* A soft, brimless, conical cap used as a symbol of liberty; a cap of this kind given to a freedman in ancient Rome at his manumission. Also **Phryg·ian cap**.

li·bid·i·nous, li·bid′i·nus, *a.* [L. *libidinosus*, < *libido*, *lubido*, lust, < *libet*, *lubet*, it pleases.] Having a strong sexual desire; lustful.—**li·bid·i·nous·ly**, *adv.*—**li·bid·i·nous·ness**, *n.*

li·bi·do, li·bē′dō, li·bī′dō, *n.* [L. *libido*, pleasure, lust, < *libet*, it is pleasing; akin to E. *lief*, love.] The sexual instinct. *Psychoanal.* those instincts and drives activating human action.—**li·bid·in·al**, li·bid′i·nal, *a.*—**li·bid·i·nal·ly**, *adv.*

Li·bra, li′bra, lē′bra, *n.* pl. **Li·brae.** [L., a balance.] *Astron.* the Balance, a constellation; *astrol.* the seventh sign in the zodiac.

li·brar·y, li′brer″ē, li′bre·rē, li′brē, *n.* pl. **li·brar·ies.** [O.Fr. *librairie*, library (Fr. bookseller's shop); < M.L. *libraria*, library, L. bookseller's shop, prop. fem. of L. *librarius*, pertaining to books, < *liber*, book.] A place set apart to contain books and other literary material for reading, study, or reference, as a room, set of rooms, or building for the use of members of a society or the general public. A commercial establishment devoted to the lending of books; also *rental library.* A collection of books or the like for reading, study, or reference; a series of books of similar character, size, binding, or the like, issued by a single publishing house.—**li·brar·i·an**, li·brâr′ē·an, *n.* One who has studied library science; one in charge of a library.—**li·brar·i·an·ship**, *n.*

li·brar·y card, *n.* A card distributed by a library giving the holder the privilege of borrowing books and other materials. Also *Brit.* **li·brar·y tick·et.**

li·brar·y paste, *n.* A white, thick adhesive made from starch and used on paper and cardboard.

li·brar·y sci·ence, *n.* The study of the administration and organization of libraries.

li·bra·tion, li·brā′shan, *n.* The act of balancing or hovering; *astron.* a real or apparent oscillation of a celestial body, esp. the moon.—**li·brate**, li′brāt, *v.i.*—*librated, librating.* To oscillate.—**li·bra·to·ry**, li′bra·tōr″ē, *a.*

li·bret·to, li·bret′ō, *n.* pl. **li·bret·tos**, **li·bret·ti.** [It., dim. of *libro*, < L. *liber*, book.] The text or words of an opera or other extended musical composition; a book or booklet containing such a text.—**li·bret·tist**, *n.* The writer of a libretto.

li·bri·form, li′bri·fârm″, *a. Bot.* having the form of or resembling phloem fibers.

Lib·y·an, lib′ē·an, *a.* Of or pertaining to Libya, a country of northern Africa; pertaining to a branch of the Hamitic family of languages spoken in ancient Libya.—*n.* A native or inhabitant of Libya; any of the Libyan languages.

li·cense, esp. *Brit.* **li·cence**, li′sens *n.* [O.Fr. *licence*, < L. *licentia*, < *licere*, be permitted.] Formal permission or authorization to do or forbear some act; formal permission from a constituted authority to do something, as to marry; a certificate of such permission; an official permit; freedom of action, speech, thought, permitted or conceded; disregard of legal or moral restraints; sometimes, licentiousness; intentional deviation from rule, convention, or fact, as for the sake of literary or artistic effect; as, poetic *license.*—*v.t.*—*licensed, licensing, Brit. licenced, licencing.* To give permission or license to do something; to authorize; to give leave to depart; to allow freedom of action.—**li·cens·a·ble**, *a.*—**li·cen·see**, *Brit.* **li·cen·cee**, li″sen·sē′, *n.* An individual to whom a license has been given.—**li·cens·er**, *n.*

li·cense plate, *n.* A metal plate, bearing numerals and/or letters to indicate official registration, designed for attachment to an automobile. Also *Brit.* **num·ber plate.**

li·cen·ti·ate, li·sen′shē·it, li·sen′shē·āt″, *n.* [M.L. *licentiatus*, pp. of *licentiare*, license, < L. *licentia*, E. *license.*] One who has received a license, as from a university, to practice an art or profession; a university degree intermediate between bachelor and doctor in some European universities.—**li·cen·ti·ate·ship**, *n.*

li·cen·tious, li·sen′shus, *a.* [L. *licentiosus*, < *licentia*, E. *license.*] Unrestrained by law or morality, esp. in sexual behavior; lascivious; lewd.—**li·cen·tious·ly**, *adv.*—**li·cen·tious·ness**, *n.*

li·chee, lē′chē′, *n.* Litchi.

li·chen, li′ken, *n.* [L., < Gr. *leikhen*, lichen.] *Bot.* any of a group of compound plants made up of fungi in symbiotic union with algae, having a thallus or body not differentiated into stem and leaf, and growing in greenish, gray, yellow, brown, or blackish crustlike patches on rocks, trees, and the like; *pathol.* any of various eruptive skin diseases, resembling lichens in appearance.—*v.t.* To cover with lichens.—**li·chen·ous**, **li·chen·ose**, li′ke·nus, *a.*

lich gate, **lych gate**, lich′ gāt″, *n.* [Lit. 'corpse gate,' < O.E. *lic*, Icel. *lik*, Goth. *leik*, form, body; G. *leiche*, a corpse. Akin *like.*] A churchyard gate, with a roof under which a bier might stand during the first part of a funeral service.

li·chi, lē′chē, *n.* Litchi.

lic·it, lis′it, *a.* [L. *licitus*, lawful, < *liceo*, to be permitted.] Lawful.—**lic·it·ly**, *adv.*

lick, lik, *v.t.* [O.E. *liccian* = D. *likken* = G. *lecken*, lick; akin to L. *lingere*, Gr. *leikhein*, lick: cf. *electuary* and *lecher.*] To pass the tongue over the surface of; as, to *lick* a spoon; take with the tongue, usu. with *up*, *off*, *from*; as, *licking up* the spilled milk; render or bring by strokes of the tongue; as, to *lick* the platter clean; to pass or play lightly over, as waves or flames. *Colloq.* to beat, thrash, or whip, as for punishment; overcome in a fight; outdo or surpass.—*n.* An act of licking, as with the tongue; a stroke of the tongue over something; a small quantity, such as might be taken up by the tongue; a place to which wild animals resort to lick salt occurring naturally there. *Colloq.* a blow; a brief or brisk stroke of activity; a spurt, as in running or racing.—**a lick and a prom·ise**, superficial or hasty work, as if with a promise of doing better later.—**lick in·to shape**, bring into appropriate form or condition; as, *lick* a manuscript into shape for printing.—**lick one's chops**, eagerly anticipate, as food.—**lick·er**, *n.*

lick·e·ty-split, lik′i·tē·split′, *adv. Slang.* Very quickly; in great haste.

lick·ing, lik′ing, *n. Colloq.* a beating or thrashing; a defeat. The act of one who or that which licks.

lick·spit·tle, lik′spit″l, *n.* One who seeks favor through servile behavior; a flatterer; a despicable sycophant.

lic·o·rice, **li·quo·rice**, lik′o·ris, lik′ēr·ish, lik′rish, *n.* [O.Fr. *licorece*, also *ricolice* (Fr. *réglisse*), < L.L. *liquiritia*, corruption of L. *glycyrrhiza*, < Gr. *glykyrriza*, licorice, < *glykys*, sweet, and *rhiza*, root.] A European leguminous plant, *Glycyrrhiza glabra*; the sweet-tasting dried root of this plant, or an extract made from it, used in medicine or as flavoring in confectioneries.

lic·o·rice stick, *n.* A stick of candy flavored with licorice; *slang*, clarinet.

lic·tor, lik′ter, *n.* [L., < *ligare*, to bind.] A Roman officer whose insignia of office was the fasces, and who attended the chief magistrates during public appearances.

lid, lid, *n.* [O.E. *hlid* = D. and G. *lid*, lid.] A movable piece, whether separate or hinged, for closing the opening of any container; a movable cover; an eyelid; *slang*, a hat; *colloq.* means of repression or restraint, as on prices.—**lid·ded**, *a.*—**lid·less**, lid′lis, *a.*

li·dar, li′där, *n. Meteor.* a radar system of advanced concept using laser light beams.

li·do, lē′dō, *It.* lē′dạ, *n.* A chic bathing resort; (*cap.*) an Italian island in the Adriatic Sea, located near Venice.

lie, li, *v.i.*—past *lay*, pp. *lain*, ppr. *lying.* [O.E. *licgan* = D. *liggen* = G. *liegen* = Icel. *liggja* = Goth. *ligan*, lie; akin to L. *lectus*, Gr. *lechos*, bed.] To be in a recumbent or prostrate position, as on a bed; to assume such a position; as, to *lie* down on a couch; to rest in a horizontal or flat position, as an inanimate object; to be placed or situated; as, land *lying* along the coast; to be in or have a specified direction, as a road or course; to be or remain in a position or state of inactivity or concealment; as, to *lie* in ambush; to remain unused; to be interred, as in a tomb; to be inherent or to exist, usu. followed by *in*; to extend or continue; to rest, press, or weigh, followed by by *on* or *upon*; *law*, to be sustainable or admissible, as an action or appeal; *archaic*, to pass the night, lodge, or sojourn.—*n.* The manner, relative position, or direction in which something lies; the place where a bird, beast, or fish is accustomed to lie or lurk.—**lie low**, to remain hidden.

lie, li, *v.i.*—lied, lying. [O.E. *lēogan* = D. *liegen* = G. *lügen* = Icel. *ljūga* = Goth. *liugan*, lie.] To speak falsely or utter untruth knowingly, as with intent to deceive; to express what is false or convey a false impression.—*v.t.* To bring or put by lying; as, to *lie* oneself out of a difficulty.—*n.* A false statement made with intent to deceive; an intentional untruth; something intended or serving to convey a false impression; the charge or accusation of lying.—**give the lie to**, to charge with lying; to contradict flatly; *fig.* to imply or show to be false, as: His actions *gave the lie to* his professions.—**lie in one's throat** or **teeth**, to lie in blatant contradiction of truth.

lie by, *v.i.* To remain in a state of inactivity or rest.

lied, lēd, *G.* lēt, *n.* pl. **lied·er.** [G.] A German song, lyric, or ballad.

Lie·der·kranz, lē′dèr·kränts″, lē′dèr·krants″, *n.* A soft, pungent cheese akin to Limburger. (Trademark.) A German club or society of choral singers, esp. one composed of men only. Also **lie·der·kranz.**

lie de·tec·tor, *n.* A device which detects and records tracings of physical changes, such as blood pressure, pulse rate, and the like, of a subject under questioning, as a means of determining the truth or falsity of his answers.

lie down, *v.i.* To take a short rest; to neglect or fail in one's duty; to give in to reverses or abuse.

lief, lēf, *a.* [O.E. *leof* = D. *lief* = G. *lieb* = Icel. *ljufr* = Goth. *liufs*, dear; < the root of E. *love.*] *Archaic.* Beloved or dear; glad or willing.—*adv.* Gladly; willingly.

liege, lēj, *a.* [O.Fr. *lige*, liege, free, exempt, appar. < O.H.G. *ledig*, free.] Owing allegiance and service, as a feudal vassal to his lord; entitled to allegiance and service, as a feudal lord; pertaining to the relation between vassal and lord; loyal; faithful.—*n.* A liege lord; a vassal; a subject, as of a ruler; also **liege·man.**

lie in, *v.i.* To be confined in childbed.

lien, lēn, lē′en, *n.* [Fr. *lien* < L. *ligamen*, < *ligo*, to bind.] *Law.* A legal claim; the right of one man to retain or sell the property of another as security, payment, or satisfaction of a claim.

li·en·ter·y, li′en·ter″ē, *n.* [Gr. *leienteria—leios*, smooth, and *enteron*, an intestine.] *Pathol.* a type of diarrhea, in which the food is discharged undigested.—**li·en·ter·ic**, *a.*

lie o·ver, *v.i.* To await future action.

li·erne, lē·ųrn′, *n.* [Fr., appar. < *lier*, < L. *ligare*, bind: cf. *liane* and *lien.*] *Arch.* a short connecting rib in Gothic vaulting.

lie to, *v.i. Naut.* to lie comparatively stationary, with the head of the vessel as near the wind as possible.

lieu, lö, *n.* [Fr., < L. *locus*, place.] *Archaic.* Place; stead.—**in lieu of**, in place of; instead.

lieu·ten·an·cy, lö·ten′an·sē, *n.* pl. **lieu·ten·an·cies.** The rank, office, commission, or authority of a lieutenant.

lieu·ten·ant, lö·ten′ant, *Brit.* except *navy,* lef·ten′ant, *n.* [Fr., composed of *lieu,* L. *locus,* place, and *tenant,* L. *tenens,* holding.] An officer, civil or military, who takes the place of a superior in his absence; a commissioned officer in the army, ranking next below a captain; a commissioned naval officer, ranking next below lieutenant commander.

lieu·ten·ant colo·nel, *n.* A military officer next in rank below a colonel.

lieu·ten·ant com·mand·er, *n.* A navy officer who ranks immediately below a commander.

lieu·ten·ant gen·er·al, *n.* A military officer next in rank below a general.

lieu·ten·ant gov·er·nor, *n.* An elected state official ranking next below a governor, who assumes the governor's duties in the event of his absence, resignation, or death; *Brit.* deputy governor.

lieu·ten·ant jun·ior grade, *n.* pl. **lieu·ten·ants jun·ior grade.** A commissioned navy officer ranking next below a lieutenant.

life, lif, *n.* pl. **lives.** [O.E. *lif,* Icel. *lif,* Dan. *liv,* D. *lijf,* Goth. *libains,* life.] That state of an animal or a plant in which its organs are capable of performing their functions, or in which the performance of functions has not permanently ceased; animate existence or vitality; the time during which such a state continues; the period from birth to death; spiritual existence after death; period during which anything continues to exist or be useful; as, the *life* of the machine; a person's condition or circumstances; mode, manner, or course of living; social surroundings and characteristics; as, high or low *life;* that which makes alive or lively; as, the *life* of the party; a particular aspect or phase of living; as, social *life,* adult *life;* animating or inspiring principle; animation or vivacity; energy; the living form or nature itself, as opposed to a copy or imitation; a prison sentence for the rest of the prisoner's existence; a living person; collectively, human beings in any number; as, a great loss of *life;* narrative of a person's life; a biography or memoir; human affairs; course of things in the world, as: Well, that's *life.—a.* Lifelong; of or relating to vital existence; as, *life* forces; working from a living model; as, a *life* drawing.—**bring to life,** to make animate; to recall in lifelike detail.—**for dear life,** with the most extreme effort or speed.—**for life,** until death.

life belt, *n. Naut.* a type of life preserver which resembles a belt.

life·blood, lif′blud″, *n. Fig.* that which is essential to existence, as: Electricity is the *lifeblood* of industry.

life·boat, lif′bōt″, *n.* A boat constructed, equipped, and stocked for saving persons from drowning; such a boat carried on board a ship for emergency use.

life buoy, *n.* A buoyant device, in various forms, to enable persons in the water to keep afloat until rescued.

life cy·cle, *n.* The complete series of activities or processes which an organism undergoes during its life. Also **life history.**

life ex·pect·an·cy, *n.* The number of years that a person is likely to live, as projected by statistical probability.

life·giv·ing, lif′giv″ing, *a.* Bestowing or communicating life; being able to impart life; invigorating.

life·guard, lif′gärd″, *n.* A skilled swimmer employed at a pool or beach to save bathers from drowning.

life his·to·ry, *n. Biol.* all the phenomena shown by an organism in its development from egg or spore, through its embryonic stages, maturity, reproduction, and death. Also **life cycle.**

life in·sur·ance, *n.* A sum of money contracted to be paid to a named beneficiary upon the death of the insured, or to be paid to an insured person who lives to a specified age; the policy or contract covering the terms of such protection; the business of providing life insurance.

life·less, lif′lis, *a.* Deprived of life; dead; inanimate; inorganic; destitute of life or spirit; dull; heavy; inactive.—**life·less·ly,** *adv.*—**life·less·ness,** *n.*

life·like, lif′lik″, *a.* Resembling or simulating life; giving the impression of real life; as, a *lifelike* picture or statue, a *lifelike* description.—**life·like·ness,** *n.*

life line, *n.* A rope projected to a foundering ship or to a drowning person; a line used to bring up or lower a diver; a line for protecting life, esp. a line acting as a ship's guardrail; any indispensable transportation route used to carry vital supplies, esp. to isolated areas; *palmistry,* a curved diagonal line across the palm of one's hand which allegedly reveals information about the length and events of one's life.

life·long, lif′lang″, lif′long″, *a.* Lasting or continuing through life.

life net, *n.* A strong net or similar device held by firemen or others to catch persons jumping from a burning building.

life of Ri·ley, *n. Slang,* an enjoyable, carefree style of life.

life peer, *n.* An appointed member of the House of Lords, not a hereditary title.—**life peer·age,** *n.*

life pre·serv·er, *n.* A buoyant jacket, belt, or other similar device for saving persons in the water from sinking and drowning. *Brit. slang,* a short, heavy stick used as a weapon; a blackjack or bludgeon.

lif·er, li′fér, *n. Slang,* one given or serving a sentence of life imprisonment.

life raft, *n.* A raft used for emergencies, as when the passengers or crew must abandon ship.

life·sav·er, lif′sā″vér, *n.* One who saves another from death, as from drowning; *fig.* one who or that which aids in time of need; *chiefly Brit.* a lifeguard.—**life·sav·ing,** *n., a.*

life-size, lif′siz′, *a.* Of the size of the original object or living person; as, a *life-size* picture. Also **life-sized.**

life·time, lif′tim″, *n.* The period of time that life continues.

life·work, lif′wurk′, *n.* The work, labor, or task of a lifetime.

lift, lift, *v.t.* [Icel. *lypta,* lift, raise, orig. into the air; akin to Icel. *lopt,* O.E. *lyft,* the air.] To move or bring upward from the ground or other support into the air or to a higher position by the use of strength or power; to raise to a higher position; as, to *lift* the eyes; to hold up or display; to raise in rank, dignity, condition, or estimation; to elevate or exalt; to elate, often with *up;* to send up audibly or loudly; as, *lift* a cry; to pay off, as a mortgage. *Surg.* to perform facial surgery on, for removing wrinkles and minimizing signs of age; to subject, as the face, to such surgery. To unearth; as seedlings; to stop or cancel, as a ban, blockade, or artillery fire. *Golf,* to relocate, as a ball; raise the arc of, as a golf shot. *Colloq.* to steal or rob; to plagiarize.—*v.i.* To move upward or rise; to rise and disperse, as clouds or fog; to arrive at a better state; as, a mood that *lifted;* to pull or strain in the effort to lift something; to rise into view above the horizon when approached, as land seen from the sea.—*n.* The act or an act of lifting, raising, or rising; the distance through which something is lifted; lifting or raising force; the weight or load lifted; *fig.* a helping upward or onward; as, a *lift* to one's fortunes. A ride in a vehicle, esp. one given to aid a pedestrian; exaltation or uplift, as in feeling; a holding up of the head; a rise or elevation of ground; a device or apparatus for lifting; *chiefly Brit.* an elevator or dumbwaiter, or the shaft in which either moves. One of the layers of leather forming the heel of a boot or shoe; a layer of ore that is mined in a single operation; that part of the aerodynamic force that maintains an aircraft aloft; *colloq.* an instance of theft.—**lift·er,** *n.* One who or that which lifts.

lift-off, lift′af″, lift′of″, *n.* The action of a rocket vehicle as it separates from its launch pad in a vertical ascent; an act or instance of lifting an airplane off the ground, applied esp. to helicopters; the instant at which an airplane or space vehicle becomes airborne.

lift pump, *n.* Any pump which lifts or raises a liquid and does not eject it forcibly under pressure: distinguished from *force pump.*

lift truck, *n.* A motorized or hand-driven truck or dolly designed for unloading, lifting, and moving loads.

lig·a·ment, lig′a·ment, *n.* [L. *ligamentum,* < *ligo,* to bind (whence also *ligation, ligature, lien, league, -ly* in *ally*).] *Anat.* a band of strong fibrous tissue connecting bones at a joint, or serving to hold in place and support body organs. What ties or unites one thing or part to another; a bond.—**lig·a·men·tous,** lig″a·men′tus, *a.* Of the nature of or being part of a ligament. Also **lig·a·men·tal, lig·a·men·ta·ry.**

li·gan, li′gan, *n.* [Contr. for L. *ligamen,* a band, < *ligo,* to bind.] Lagan.

li·gate, li′gāt, *v.t.*—*ligated, ligating.* [L. *ligatus,* pp. of *ligare,* bind, tie.] To bind, as with a ligature; tie up, as a bleeding artery.

li·ga·tion, li·gā′shan, *n.* [L. *ligatio, ligationis,* < *ligo,* to bind.] The act of ligating or binding; a bond; a ligature.—**lig·a·tive,** lig′a·tiv, *a.*

lig·a·ture, lig′a·chér, lig′a·chur, *n.* [L. *ligatura,* < *ligo,* to bind.] The act of binding; anything that binds; a cord, thong, band, or bandage; a ligament; *mus.* a slur or the notes connected by it; *print.* a type consisting of two or more letters or characters cast on the same body, as *æ, fi,* or *fl; surg.* a thread, wire, or the like for tying blood vessels to prevent hemorrhage, or for removing tumors by strangulation.—*v.t.*—*ligatured, ligaturing.* To bind or tie up, as with a ligature; to ligate.

light, lit, *n.* [O.E. *lēoht* = D. and G. *licht,* akin to Icel. *ljōs* and Goth. *liuhath,* light, also to L. *lux* and *lumen,* light, *lucere,* shine, *luna,* moon, Gr. *leukós,* light, bright, white, *àmphilúke,* twilight, Skt. *ruc-,* shine.] That which makes things visible or affords illumination. *Phys.* a form of radiant energy which acts on the organs of sight and moves with a velocity of about 186,300 miles per second by undulations or waves which vary in length from 4000 to 7700 angstroms; a similar form of radiant energy, as ultraviolet or infrared, which does not affect the retina. An illuminating agent or source, as the sun, a lamp; the light, radiance, or illumination from a particular source; as electric *light;* the illumination from the sun, or daylight; daybreak or dawn; daytime; illumination; measure or supply of light; as, a wall which cuts off *light;* the sensation produced by stimulation of the organs of sight; a particular illumination in which an object takes on a certain appearance; as, viewing a portrait in various *lights;* the effect of light falling on an object or scene as represented in a picture; the aspect in which a thing appears or is regarded, as: He viewed the experience in an amiable *light.* The state of being visible, exposed to view, or revealed to public notice or knowledge; as, to bring secret information to *light;* mental or spiritual illumination or enlightenment; as, the *light* of knowledge; a person who is an illuminating or shining example; as, a *light* of the legal profession; a luminary; *pl.* information, ideas, or mental capacities possessed; as, to act according to one's *lights*. A gleam or sparkle, as in the eyes; a means of igniting, as a spark, flame, or match; a window, or a pane or compartment of a window; a traffic signal; a lighthouse; *archaic*, eyesight.—*a.* Having light or illumination; as, the *lightest* room in the house; pale, whitish, or not deep or dark in color; as, a *light* green.—**bring to light, come to light,** to reveal or be revealed.—**in light of,** with awareness of; considering, as: *In light of* the circumstances, his decision appears correct.—**see the light,** to come into existence; to be made public; to become aware of or understand.

light, lit, *v.i.*—*lighted* or *lit, lighting.* [O.E. *līhtan* = D. *lichten* = G. *leuchten* = Goth. *liuhtan,* shine.] To take fire or become kindled; as, kindling which would *light* easily; to set afire a pipe, cigar, or cigarette for smoking, usu. used with *up*; to become bright, as with light or color, used with *up*; to brighten with animation or joy, used with *up*, as: Their faces *light up* with happiness. —*v.t.* To kindle or ignite, as a fire, candle, match, or cigar; to turn on, as a lamp; to furnish with light or illumination; as, to *light* a house with electricity; to make bright, as with light or color, or to animate, often with *up*, as: Happiness *lit up* her face. To show, conduct, or guide with a light, as: This lantern will *light* you on your way.

light, lit, *a.* [O.E. *lēoht, līht,* = D. *licht* = G. *leicht* = Icel. *lēttr* = Goth. *leihts,* light: cf. L. *levis,* light, Gr. *elachys,* small, Skt. *laghu,* swift, light, also E. *lung.*] Of little weight; not heavy; as, a *light* load; of little weight in proportion to bulk, or of low specific gravity; as, a *light* metal, liquid, or gas; of less than usual or average weight; as, *light* clothing, *light* artillery; of less weight than the proper or standard amount; of little density; as, a *light* vapor or haze; of small amount, force, or intensity; as, a *light* rain, *light* sleep; requiring little mental effort; not profound, serious, or heavy; as, *light* reading, *light* opera, a *light* comedy; easy to endure, deal with, or perform; as, *light* afflictions, *light* taxes, *light* duties; trifling, trivial, or of little moment or importance; as, a loss which was a *light* matter; free from sorrow or care; as, a *light* heart; buoyantly cheerful, gay, or jesting; as, a *light* laugh; well-leavened or spongy, as bread; low in alcohol, as beer or wine; easily digested, as food; of soil, porous and sandy; slight, gentle, or restrained; as, a *light* combing, a *light* drinker; slender or delicate in appearance; as, a *light*, graceful figure; airy or buoyant in movement; as, *light* as a bubble; nimble or agile; as, a *light* leap; easily swayed or changing; as, to be *light* of love or purpose; affected with a sensation of dizziness or giddiness; as, to be *light*-headed; wanton or unchaste; as, a *light* woman; adapted by small weight and built for swift movement; as, a *light* sailing vessel; *milit.* simply armed or equipped; as, *light* cavalry; *phon.* of a soft or unstressed vowel or syllable; *poker,* owing money to the pot; as, to be *light* the bet.—*adv.* Lightly; with little or no cargo or weight of any sort; as, walking *light* since his confession, to travel *light.*

light, lit, *v.i.*—*lighted* or *lit, lighting.* [O.E. *lihtan,* to descend, alight, < *lēoht,* light, not heavy: to *alight* from horseback or a vehicle is to make it lighter by relieving it of weight.] To descend, as from a horse, vehicle, roof, or the like; dismount; alight; to come to rest or settle down on something; land; to come by chance or happen to find or hit, usu. with *on* or *upon*; as, to *light on* a good deal; to fall unexpectedly, as a blow.—**light in·to,** *colloq.* to abuse or

attack physically or verbally.—**light out,** *slang,* to depart or flee quickly.

light ad·ap·ta·tion, *n. Ophthalm.* pupillary contraction of the eye when exposed to intensified light, enabling it to function efficiently and involving change in the number of functioning cones and rods within the retina.

light air, *n. Meteor.* a wind with a velocity of one to three miles per hour, as measured by the Beaufort scale.

light breeze, *n. Meteor.* a wind with a velocity of four to seven miles per hour, as measured by the Beaufort scale.

light·en, lit'en, *v.i.* To become lighter or less dark; grow brighter; to flash; give out flashes of lightning; to shine or gleam.— *v.t.* To make light or clear; dissipate darkness from; illuminate; to brighten; to cause, as a color, to become lighter.

light·en, lit'en, *v.t.* To make lighter or less heavy; to relieve of weight; to lessen; to make less burdensome or oppressive; to alleviate; as, to *lighten* his worries; to cheer or make glad.—*v.i.* To become lighter in weight; to become less oppressive or severe; to become more cheerful in mood or manner.

light·er, li'tèr, *n.* One who or that which lights, illuminates, or ignites; a mechanical or electrical means for igniting something; as, a cigarette *lighter.*

light·er, li'tèr, *n.* A shallow barge used to load and unload ships, and to transport cargo short distances.—*v.t.* To haul, as cargo, in a lighter.

light·er·age, li'tèr·ij, *n.* The hauling of cargo or the loading and unloading of vessels by lighter; the charge for such service.

light·er-than-air, li'tèr·THan·âr', *a. Aeron.* Of less specific gravity than the air, as balloons or dirigibles; of or pertaining to such aircraft.

light·face, lit'fās", *n. Print.* a typeface that is distinguishable by its light, thin lines.— **light·faced,** lit'fāst", *a.*

light·fast, lit'fast", lit'fäst", *a.* Relatively colorfast when exposed to sunlight or artificial lighting, usu. said of fabrics or paint; unharmed by exposure to light.— **light·fast·ness,** *n.*

light-fin·gered, lit'fing'gèrd, *a.* Having light or nimble fingers; dexterous with the fingers, esp. in picking pockets or in other forms of petty theft; thievish.—**light-fin·gered·ness,** *n.*

light-foot·ed, lit'fut'id, *a.* Nimble; springy of step; light of foot; graceful.—**light-foot·ed·ly,** *adv.*—**light-foot·ed·ness,** *n.*

light-hand·ed, lit'han'did, *a.* Having a light touch; dexterous; short-handed, as lacking in help.—**light-hand·ed·ly,** *adv.*—**light-hand·ed·ness,** *n.*

light-head·ed, lit'hed'id, *a.* Dizzy; delirious; frivolous; thoughtless in attitude.— **light-head·ed·ly,** *adv.*—**light-head·ed·ness,** *n.*

light-heart·ed, light·heart·ed, lit'här'tid, *a.* Free from grief or anxiety; gay; cheerful; optimistic.—**light-heart·ed·ly, light·heart·ed·ly,** *adv.*—**light-heart·ed·ness, light·heart·ed·ness,** *n.*

light heav·y·weight, *n.* A boxer weighing between 161 and 175 pounds; a wrestler weighing between 175 and 191 pounds.

light·house, lit'hous", *n.* A tower or other lofty structure with a powerful light, erected as a guide or warning of danger to navigators.

light·house·keep·ing, *n.* Household chores limited to the less difficult duties, as dusting and sweeping; housekeeping in a room or small quarters with minimal cooking facilities.

light·ing, li'ting, *n.* Illumination; the device or system which provides illumination; the

arrangement of light or lighting; as, soft *lighting* in a living room, stage *lighting*; the effect, usu. in contrast, of pale and dark colors in a painting or photograph.

light·less, lit'lis, *a.* Without light; dark; not receiving light; not giving out light.— **light·less·ness,** *n.*

light·ly, lit'lē, *adv.* [O.E. *lēohtlīce.*] In a light manner; with little weight, force, or intensity; slightly or gently; as, to tap *lightly* on the door; to a small amount or degree; as, *lightly* salted food; easily, or without trouble or effort; airily or buoyantly; nimbly; as, to dance *lightly*; cheerfully, or with cheerful unconcern; as, to converse *lightly*; indifferently or slightingly; as, to be *lightly* concerned; frivolously; without due consideration or reason, often with a negative; as, an offer *not lightly* to be refused.

light me·ter, *n.* Exposure meter.

light-mind·ed, lit'mīn'did, *a.* Characterized by levity; frivolous.—**light-mind·ed·ly,** *adv.*—**light-mind·ed·ness,** *n.*

light·ness, lit'nis, *n.* The condition or quality of being light, bright, or illuminated; pale shade or color; a lack of darkness.

light·ness, lit'nis, *n.* The condition or quality of being light in weight; agility, nimbleness, or grace; as, the *lightness* of his step; joy, or gaiety of mood or manner; levity; lack of seriousness, as: The *lightness* of his speech hid his seriousness.

light·ning, lit'ning, *n.* [From the verb to *lighten.*] A discharge of atmospheric electricity from the highly negative portion of a cloud to the earth or to another cloud, resulting in a flash of light; the flash of light. —*a.* Resembling lightning, esp. with regard to its velocity or suddenness; as, a *lightning* attack, with *lightning* speed.—*v.i.*—*lightninged, lightning.* To release a spark or flash of lightning, usu. with *it* as the subject, as: *It lightninged* last night.

light·ning ar·rest·er, *n. Elect.* an apparatus for safeguarding an electrical appliance, TV, or such, from lightning or other high-voltage surges by grounding them.

light·ning bug, *n.* Firefly.

light·ning rod, *n.* A metallic rod attached to buildings, vessels, and other structures to protect them from lightning by conducting the electric charge into the earth or water.

light-o'-love, lit'o·luv', *n.* A woman inconstant in love; a wanton coquette; a prostitute.

light op·er·a, *n.* Operetta.

light·proof, lit'prŏf, *a.* Incapable of being penetrated by light.

light quan·tum, *n. Phys.* photon.

lights, lits, *n. pl.* Lungs, esp. of sheep, hogs, and other animals, used for food.

light·ship, lit'ship", *n.* A moored ship equipped with warning lights to guide vessels away from a dangerous area.

light·some, lit'som, *a.* Light, esp. in form, appearance, or movement; airy, buoyant, nimble; cheerful or gay; frivolous.—**light·some·ly,** *adv.*—**light·some·ness,** *n.*

light·some, lit'som, *a.* Giving off light; luminous; well-lighted; bright; illuminated. —**light·some·ness,** *n.*

light-struck, lit'struk", *a. Photog.* injured or fogged by accidental exposure to light, as film or a sensitized plate.

light·weight, lit'wāt", *n.* One of less than average weight; a boxer intermediate in weight between a featherweight and welterweight, weighing not over 135 pounds; *colloq.* a person of little mental capacity or of slight influence or importance.—*a.* Relating to someone or something lightweight; unimportant or trivial.

light·wood, lit'wụd", *n. Southern U.S.* Wood used in lighting a fire; a resinous coniferous wood.

light-year, lit'yēr", lit'yèr', *n. Astron.* the distance traversed by light in one year, about 5,880,000,000,000 miles, being about 63,000 times the distance of the earth from the sun: used as a unit in measuring stellar distances. Abbr. *lt.-yr.*

lig·ne·ous, lig′nē·us, *a.* [L. *ligneus,* < *lignum,* wood.] Made of, consisting of, or resembling wood; woody.

lig·ni·fy, lig′ni·fī″, *v.t.—lignified, lignifying.* [L. *lignum,* wood, and *facio,* to make.] To convert into wood.—*v.i.* To become wood; become woody.—**lig·ni·fi·ca·tion,** lig″-ni·fi·kā′shan, *n.*

lig·nin, lig′nin, *n. Bot.* an organic substance associated with cellulose in the cell walls, esp. of the xylem or wood of many plants.

lig·nite, lig′nīt, *n.* A usu. brownish-black coal, mineralized to a certain degree, but retaining a distinct woody texture. Also *brown coal.*—**lig·nit·ic,** lig·nit′ik, *a.*

lig·no·cel·lu·lose, lig″nō·sel′ū·lōs″, lig″-nō·sel′ya·lōs″, *n. Bot.* an association of lignin and cellulose that forms the essential part of woody cell walls and fibrous tissue in plants.—**lig·no·cel·lu·los·ic,** lig″nō-sel′ū·los·ik, lig″nō·sel′ya·los·ik, *a.*

lig·num vi·tae, lig′num vī′tē, *n. pl.* **lig·num vi·taes.** [L., wood of life, from its hardness and durability.] *Bot.* The hard, heavy, green-brown wood of either of two tropical American trees of the genus *Guaiacum, G. officinale* or *G. sanctum,* which is used in making furniture, pulley blocks, bowling balls, and instruments; either tree.

lig·ro·in, lig′rō·in, *n.* [Origin obscure.] A volatile inflammable liquid, a petroleum distillate intermediate between naphtha and benzine, used esp. as a solvent.

lig·u·la, lig′ū·la, lig′ya·la, *n. pl.* **lig·u·lae,** lig′ū·las, lig′ū·lē, lig′ya·lē. [L. *ligula,* a strap, < *ligo,* to bind.] *Bot.* the corolla of a ray flower in the composite family, as in the sunflower, where the fused petals produce a strap-shaped structure; a thin scarious projection from the summit of the sheath in grasses. *Biol.* any strap-shaped part or organ; *entom.* the distal part of the labium, or lower lip, of an insect. Also **lig·ule.**—**lig·u·late,** *a.* Shaped like a strap; having a ligula. Also **lig·u·la·ted,** *lingulate.*

lig·ure, lig′ūr, *n.* [Gr. *linggourion, ligurion.*] *O.T.* a kind of precious stone, believed to be the jacinth. Ex. xxviii.19.

like, līk, *a.* [M.E. *lic, liche,* < O.E. *gelīc* = D. *gelijk* = G. *gleich* = Icel. *glīkr* = Goth. *galeiks,* like, lit. 'of the same body, or form'; from a Teut. prefix (O.E. *ge-,* together) and a noun meaning 'body.'] Of the same form, appearance, kind, character, or amount; as, a *like* instance; corresponding or agreeing in general or in some noticeable respect; similar; resembling, used in compounds; as, water*like. Dial.* likely, as: It's *like* to rain tomorrow. *Dial.* about, as: She seemed *like* to cry.—*n.* A counterpart, match, or equal; as, they and their *like;* something of a similar nature, preceded by *the;* as, oranges, lemons, and *the like.*

like, līk, *prep.* In a similar manner with; similarly to; in the manner characteristic of; as, runs *like* a deer; resembling or similar to, as: I never saw anything *like* it. Characteristic of, as: It would be *like* him to come without notice. Giving promise or indication of, as: It looks *like* rain. Disposed or inclined to, used with *feel;* as, *feel like* going to bed; such as; as, places *like* France, England, or Spain.—*adv. Colloq.* likely or probably; as, *like* enough, as *like* as not.—*conj.* Nonstandard, just as or as, as: It was *like* we thought. *Nonstandard,* as if; as, *like* he was afraid.—**like . . . like . . .,** *colloq.* as . . . so . . ., used to express resemblance or similarity between the one and the other; as, 'like mother, *like* daughter' for 'as the mother (is), so the daughter (is).'—**like to, liked to,** *nonstandard,* came near, as: He *liked to* have choked.

like, līk, *v.t.—liked, liking.* [O.E. *līcian* = D. *lijken* = Icel. *līka* = Goth. *leikan,* please; appar. orig. meaning 'conform,' 'suit,' and from the same Teut. noun as E. *like.*] To take pleasure in, or find agreeable to one's taste; to regard with favor, or have a kindly or friendly feeling for; to want, as: He would *like* a new hat.—*v.i.* To feel inclined, or wish, as: Come when you *like. Archaic,* to be pleasing, or suit the tastes or wishes.—*n. Usu. pl.* a liking, favorable feeling, or preference; as, *likes* and dislikes.—**lik·a·ble, like·a·ble,** *a.*—**like·a·ble·ness,** *n.*

like·li·hood, līk′lē·hụd″, *n.* Probability; state or condition of being probable; something which is probable.

like·ly, līk′lē, *a.—likelier, likeliest.* Like the truth; credible; probable, as: He forecast a *likely* increase in grain production. Suitable, well-adapted, or convenient for some purpose; capable of succeeding; promising; as, a *likely* candidate; personally charming or attractive; as, a *likely* young woman.—*adv.* Probably; as may be expected or reasonably thought.

like·mind·ed, līk′mīn′did, *a.* Having the same or similar belief, opinion, or purpose.—**like·mind·ed·ly,** *adv.*—**like·mind·ed·ness,** *n.*

lik·en, lī′ken, *v.t.* To compare; to represent as resembling.

like·ness, līk′nis, *n.* The condition or quality of being like; semblance, guise, or form; that which closely resembles or represents something else, esp. a portrait.

like·wise, līk′wīz″, *adv.* In like manner; also; moreover; too.

lik·ing, lī′king, *n.* Feeling of inclination or attraction; favor or fancy; pleasure or taste; friendly feeling.

li·lac, lī′lak, *n.* [Sp. *lilac,* < Ar. *līlak,* < Pers. *līlak,* var. of *nīlak,* bluish, < *nīl,* blue, indigo, < Skt. *nīla,* dark blue.] Any of the shrubs of the olive family constituting the genus *Syringa,* as *S. vulgaris,* the common garden lilac, with large clusters of fragrant flowers in white or various shades of purple; a light purple color.—*a.* Having a purple color, as that of lilacs.—**li·la·ceous,** li·lā′shus, *a.* Of the color of the lilac.

lil·i·a·ceous, lil·ē·ā′shus, *a.* [L.L. *liliaceus,* < L. *lilium,* E. *lily.*] Of or like the lily; belonging to the lily family of plants.

lil·ied, lil′ēd, *a.* Abounding in, covered by, or adorned with lilies.

Lil·li·pu·tian, lil″i·pū′shan, *a.* [From *Lilliput,* a fictitious country inhabited by very small people, described in Jonathan Swift's *Gulliver's Travels.*] Of or pertaining to Lilliput or its fictional six-inch-tall inhabitants; tiny; diminutive; petty.—*n.* An inhabitant of Lilliput; a small person; a person of petty ideas.

lilt, lilt, *n.* [M.E. *lulten;* origin obscure.] Rhythmic swing or cadence; a springing movement or step; a buoyant, sprightly song or tune.—*v.t., v.i.* To sing, play, speak, or move in a light, cheerful, or rhythmic manner.—**lilt·ing,** *a.*—**lilt·ing·ly,** *adv.*—**lilt·ing·ness,** *n.*

lil·y, lil′ē, *n. pl.* **lil·ies.** [O.E. *lilie,* < L. *lilium,* < Gr. *leirion,* lily.] Any plant of the genus *Lilium,* comprising scaly-bulbed herbs with showy funnel-shaped or bell-shaped flowers of various colors, as *L. candidum,* the Madonna lily; the flower or the bulb of such a plant; any of various related or similar plants or their flowers, as the mariposa lily or the day lily.—*a.* Like or suggestive of a white lily; as, a *lily* hand; white as a lily; delicately fair; pure or unsullied; as, the *lily* truth; sometimes, pale or fragile.

lil·y-liv·ered, lil′ē·liv′ẽrd, *a.* Cowardly.

lil·y of the val·ley, *n. pl.* **lil·ies of the val·ley.** An herb, *Convallaria majalis,* with

a raceme of drooping, bell-shaped, fragrant white flowers.

lil·y pad, *n.* The large, floating leaf of a water lily.

lil·y-white, lil′ē·hwīt′, lil′ē·wīt′, *a.* White as a lily; as, *lily-white* hands; pure; uncorrupt; of or pertaining to groups which exclude Negroes, esp. political factions.

Li·ma, lē′ma, *n.* A communications code word to designate the letter L.

li·ma bean, lī′ma bēn, *n.* [From *Lima,* capital of Peru.] A kind of bean, esp. *Phaseolus limensis,* with a broad, flat, edible seed; the seed, a common vegetable.

lim·a·cine, lim′a·sin″, lim′a·sin, lī′ma-sin″, lī′ma·sin, *a.* [L. *limax (limac-),* slug, snail.] *Zool.* pertaining to or having a resemblance to a slug.

li·man, li·män′, *n.* A muddy bay or shallow lagoon at a river's mouth.

limb, lim, *n.* [O.E. *lim,* Icel. *limr,* Dan. and Sw. *lem,* a limb. The *b* is added as in crumb or thumb.] One of the jointed appendages of the human or animal body, as an arm or leg; a large or main branch of a tree; a representative, branch, or member of a group or organization; *colloq.* a mischievous, playful child.—**out on a limb,** *colloq.* in a vulnerable position.—**limbed,** limd, *a.*

limb, lim, *n.* [L. *limbus,* a border, edging, or fringe.] The graduated edge of a circle or arc within an astronomical or surveying instrument; *astron.* the border or outermost edge of the sun, moon, or other celestial body; *bot.* the border or upper spreading part of a sympetalous corolla, or of a petal or sepal.

lim·bate, lim′bāt, *a. Bot.* bordered, as a leaf or flower having one color surrounded by an edging of another.

lim·ber, lim′bẽr, *a.* [Closely allied to *limp,* pliant, flaccid.] Easily bent; flexible; pliant; being able to move or bend one's body with ease; supple.—*v.t.* To render limber, usu. followed by *up.*—*v.i.* To render oneself limber, followed by *up.*—**lim·ber·ly,** *adv.*—**lim·ber·ness,** *n.*

lim·ber, lim′bẽr, *n.* [Really a pl. form < Icel. *limar,* limbs, branches of a tree; akin to *limb.*] *Milit.* a vehicle having two wheels, which may be used to tow a caisson or gun.—*v.t.* To attach a limber to.—*v.i.* To connect a limber and gun together, usu. followed by *up.*

lim·bers, lim′bẽrz, *n. pl.* [Cf. Fr. *lumière,* light, opening, hole.] *Naut.* a series of holes or channels for the passage of water to the pump well.

lim·bo, lim′bō, *n.* [It., < L. *limbus,* a hem or edge.] (*Often cap.*), *theol.* a supposed region bordering hell, considered the abode for the souls of unbaptized children and virtuous people who lived before the time of Christ. A place, state, or condition of people and things forgotten or no longer wanted; a prison or other place of confinement; a suspended state of mind, usu. between alternatives; an intermediate place or condition.

lim·bo, lim′bō, *n. pl.* **lim·bos.** A West Indian dance in which each participant dances his way under a rod which is held up horizontally and lowered each time the dancers have successfully passed under it.

Lim·burg·er, lim′bụr″gẽr, *n.* A soft cheese, usu. white and creamy, with a pungent odor and sharp flavor.

lim·bus, lim′bus, *n. pl.* **lim·bi,** lim′bī. [L. and M.L.: cf. *limb,* border.] *Zool., anat.* a border or edge.

lime, līm, *n.* [O.E. *līm* = D. *lijm* = G. *leim* = Icel. *līm,* lime, glue: cf. L. *limus,* slime, mud, *linere,* smear, and E. *loam.*] Calcium oxide, CaO, a white caustic solid prepared by calcining limestone or other calcium carbonate substances, and used in making mortar and cement; also **caus·tic lime,**

quicklime. Birdlime.—*v.t.*—*limed, liming*. To treat with lime; to smear with birdlime; to catch, as birds, with birdlime.—*a.*—**lim·y,** *a.*—*limier, limiest.*

lime, lim, *n.* [Formerly *line,* < O.E. *lind,* D. and G. *linde,* Dan. Sw. Icel. *lind,* the tree.] A European tree. See **linden.**

lime, lim, *n.* [Fr. *lime,* < Sp. *lima,* lime; < Ar., and akin to E. *lemon*.] A greenish-yellow acid fruit, smaller than the lemon, borne by the subtropical tree, *Citrus aurantifolia;* the tree itself.—**lime·like,** *a.*

lime·ade, lim″ād′, *n.* A beverage made with lime juice, water, and a sweetener.

lime glass, *n.* Glass made with a large amount of lime, and used in manufacturing commercial products such as bottles and window glass.

lime·kiln, lim′kil″, lim′kiln′, *n.* A kiln in which limestone or sea shells are exposed to a strong heat and reduced to lime.

lime·light, lim′lit″, *n.* A powerful light produced by an oxyhydrogen flame on a piece of lime, formerly used as a stage spotlight; a center of public interest; spotlight.—*v.t.* —**lime·light·er,** *n.* A showoff.

li·men, li′men, *n.* pl. **li·mens, lim·i·na,** lim′i·na. [L., threshold.] *Psychol.* the threshold.

lim·er·ick, lim′ėr·ik, *n.* An amusing verse composed of five predominantly anapestic lines, with lines one, two, and five having three feet and rhyming, lines three and four having two feet and rhyming.

lime·stone, lim′stōn′, *n.* A rock consisting wholly or chiefly of calcium carbonate, $CaCO_3$, originating principally from the calcareous remains of organisms, and yielding lime when heated.

lime·sul·fur, lim′sul″fėr, *n. Chem.* a product composed of lime, sulfur, and water which have been boiled together: used as an insecticide and fungicide.

lime twig, *n.* A twig smeared with birdlime to catch birds; *fig.* a trap or snare.

lime·wa·ter, lim′wą″tėr, lim′wot″ėr, *n.* A water solution of calcium hydroxide, used in medicine and in the chemical industry; natural water containing calcium carbonate or calcium sulfate.

lim·ey, li′mē, *n.* pl. **lim·eys.** *Slang.* A British sailor; an Englishman.

li·mic·o·line, li·mik′o·lin″, li·mik′o·lin, *a.* [L.L. *limicola,* a dweller in mud, < L. *limus,* mud, and *colere,* inhabit.] Shore-inhabiting; of or pertaining to the families of birds, *Charadriidae* and *Scolopacidae,* including the plovers, snipes, and sandpipers.

lim·i·nal, lim′i·nal, li′mi·nal, *a.* [L. *limen,* threshold.] Referring to or located at the limen.

lim·it, lim′it, *n.* [O.Fr. Fr. *limite,* < L. *limes,* (*limit*-), boundary.] The final or furthest bound or point as to extent, amount, continuance, or procedure; as, the *limit* of vision; a boundary or bound, as of a country, tract, or district; *usu. pl.* a tract or area within boundaries; as, the *limits* of the school; *math.* a fixed value or form which a variable quantity or form may approach indefinitely but can never reach; *cards,* in some games such as poker, the highest amount allowable per bet, hand, or game. A previously determined maximum or minimum; as, the *limit* placed on the number of fish caught. *Colloq.* the utmost or the worst; an individual or object which elicits an extreme reaction, usu. of exasperation, preceded by *the,* as: He is *the limit* in his actions.—*v.t.* To restrict by or as by fixing limits, often with *to;* as, to *limit to* fifty minutes; to confine or keep within limits; as, to *limit* the number of students; *law,* to fix or assign definitely or specifically.—**lim·it·a·ble,** *a.*—**lim·i·ta·tive,** lim′i·tā″tiv, *a.*—**lim·it·er,** *n.*—**lim·it·ing,** *a.*—**lim·it·less,** *a.*

lim·i·tar·y, lim′i·ter″ē, *a.* Of, pertaining to, or serving as a limit; limited; limiting.

lim·i·ta·tion, lim″i·tā′shan, *n.* [L. *limita-tio(n-).*] That which limits; a limit or bound; restriction; a limiting condition, circumstance, or restriction; as, permission subject to various *limitations;* the act of limiting; the state of being limited; *law,* the assignment, as by statute, of a period of time within which an action must be brought, or the period of time assigned; as, a statute of limitations.

lim·it·ed, lim′i·tid, *a.* Confined within limits; restricted, narrow, or circumscribed; as, *limited* space, *limited* resources; restricted with reference to governing powers by limitations prescribed in a constitution or law; as, a *limited* monarchy; referring to a lack of imagination, experience, or intelligence in an individual; of a train or bus, restricted in number of passengers and stops; restricted as to amount of liability; as, a *limited* company.—**lim·it·ed·ly,** *adv.* —**lim·it·ed·ness,** *n.*

lim·it·ed war, *n.* A war which is limited or confined in one or more respects, as in the objectives sought, the weapons employed, or the locations involved, as: The two countries were involved in a *limited war* in which nuclear weapons were not used.

lim·net·ic, lim·net′ik, *a.* [Gr. *limnetes,* living in marshes, < *limne,* marsh, pool, lake.] Living in open fresh water; pertaining to fresh-water organisms; as, *limnetic* worms.

lim·nol·o·gy, lim·nol′o·jē, *n.* The scientific study of the interrelationships between organisms in a body of fresh water and their physical, geographical, biological, and chemical environment.—**lim·no·log·i·cal,** lim″no·loj′i·kal, *a.*—**lim·no·log·i·cal·ly,** *adv.*—**lim·nol·o·gist,** *n.*

Li·moges, li·mōzh′, *Fr.* lē·mązh′, *n.* A translucent porcelain of high quality made in the French city so named. Also **Li·moges ware.**

lim·o·nene, lim′o·nēn″, *n.* [N.L. *limonum,* lemon.] *Chem.* A liquid terpene occurring in three optically different forms: the dextrorotatory, which is present in essential oils of lemon and orange and in celery seeds; the levorotatory, which is synthesized from needle oils of certain pine and fir trees; the racemic, which occurs in the essential oil of wormseed.

lim·o·nite, li′mo·nīt″, *n.* [Gr. *leimōn,* meadow.] An abundant, medium grade iron ore, composed of oxygen, water, and iron, that varies in color from dark brown to yellow, and colors many soils and brown rocks.—**li·mo·nit·ic,** li″mo·nit′ik, *a.*

lim·ou·sine, lim′o·zēn″, lim″o·zēn′, *n.* [From *Limousin,* an old French province.] A closed automobile with the chauffeur partitioned off from the passengers; a large vehicle for shuttling passengers to and from airport or train terminals; any expensively equipped, large automobile.

limp, limp, *v.i.* [O.E. *limp-halt, lemp-healt,* limping-halt, lame; cf. L.G. *lumpen,* to limp; Icel. *limpa,* weakness; allied to *limp, limber,* and prob. to *lame.*] To walk lamely, usu. due to an injured leg; to proceed or progress unsteadily, esp. with labored and irregular movements.—*n.* The act of limping; a halt in one's gait; unsteady movement. —**limp·er,** *n.*—**limp·ing·ly,** *adv.*

limp, limp, *a.* [Origin obscure: cf. limp and limber.] Lacking stiffness or firmness, as of substance, fiber, structure, or bodily frame; drooping; flabby; flaccid; flexible. *Fig.* without firmness or force, as of mind or character; lacking energy.—**limp·ly,** *adv.*— **limp·ness,** *n.*

lim·pet, lim′pit, *n.* [O.Fr. *limpine,* a limpet; cf. Gr. *lepas, lepados,* a limpet.] A univalve,

marine, and littoral mollusk or shellfish of the class *Gastropoda,* having a conical shell opening widely on the bottom with a flat-soled foot for creeping and clinging to rocks. *Fig.* someone who sticks or clings stubbornly to a person or thing.

lim·pid, lim′pid, *a.* [L. *limpidus;* allied to Gr. *lampō,* to shine, hence akin to *lamp.*] Characterized by clearness or transparency, as water, mica, or glass; translucent; tranquil; serene; lucid; intelligible in form or style.—**lim·pid·i·ty,** lim·pid′i·tē, **lim·-pid·ness,** *n.*—**lim·pid·ly,** *adv.*

limp·kin, limp′kin, *n.* A strident-voiced, large, wading bird, *Aramus guarauna,* that inhabits the warmer swampy regions of America and the West Indies. Also **cour·lan.**

lim·u·lus, lim′ū·lus, lim′ya·lus, *n.* pl. **lim·u·li.** [N.L. *Limulus,* < L. *limulus,* dim. of *limus,* sidelong.] Horseshoe crab; a king crab of the genus *Limulus.*

lin·age, li′nij, *n.* The number of printed lines on a page; the payment for articles and advertisements calculated in lines printed; alignment. Also *lineage.*

lin·al·o·ol, li·nal′ō·ōl″, li·nal′ō·ol″, lin″a·löl′, *n.* A terpenic, unsaturated alcohol, $C_{10}H_{17}OH$, having a distinctive odor and used in oils, soaps, and perfumes.

linch·pin, linch′pin″, *n.* [Lit. 'axle-pin,' < O.E. *lynis,* an axletree; D. *luns, lens,* G. *lünse,* a linchpin.] A pin used to prevent a wheel from sliding off an axletree.

Lin·coln·esque, ling″ko·nesk′, *a.* [From Abraham *Lincoln,* 1809–1865, U.S. statesman and president.] Characteristic of or similar to Abraham Lincoln.—**Lin·coln·i·an,** ling″kō′nē·an, *a.* Referring to a feature, policy, mannerism, or attitude similar to that of Abraham Lincoln.

lin·dane, lin′dān, *n.* A crystalline, white powdery substance, almost entirely the gamma isomer of benzene hexachloride, used as an herbicide and insecticide.

lin·den, lin′den, *n.* [Orig. a., O.E. *linden; lind* = D. and G. *linde* = Icel., Sw., and Dan. *lind,* the linden.] Any of the trees of the genus *Tilia,* which have yellowish or cream-colored flowers and heart-shaped leaves, as *T. europæa,* a common European species, also called lime, and *T. americana,* a large American species, also called basewood, both often cultivated as a shade tree; the wood of such trees.

line, lin, *n.* [In part, O.E. *line,* rope, line, row, < L. *linea,* thread, string, stroke, line, < *lineus,* a., of flax, linen, < *linum,* flax, E. *line;* in part, O.Fr. *ligne,* < L. *linea.*] A mark or stroke long in proportion to its breadth, made with a pen, pencil, or tool on a surface. *Math.* a continuous extent of length, straight or curved, without breadth or thickness; the trace of a moving point. Something resembling a traced line, as a band of color, a seam, a furrow, or marks of rock stratification; a furrow or wrinkle of the face or neck; one of the furrows or marks on the palm of the hand supposed in palmistry to indicate one's fortune or character; as, the life *line;* a row or series; as, a *line* of trees; a row of written or printed letters or words; as, ten *lines* in a paragraph; a verse of poetry; *usu. pl.* the spoken words of a play or actor's part. A short written message, as: Drop a *line* to a friend. A course of action, procedure, or thought; as a *line* of policy; a position of uniformity or agreement; a bit of knowledge or information, followed by *on;* as, to get a *line* on his whereabouts; *slang,* ingratiating or persuasive speech, as: His *line* gained her sympathy. One's field of experience, interest, or taste, as: That's out of my *line.* A kind of occupation or business and the merchandise peculiar to it; as, a man in the hardware *line* selling a *line* of household goods; a real or imaginary boundary or limit; as, the equatorial *line*, the *line* between right and wrong; a course or direction; as, the *line* of march; a continuous chronological succession of people, plants, or animals, esp. in family descent; as, a *line* of emperors or a *line* of hybrids; specialization of part production and assemblage; as, an assembly *line*; a path, usu. straight, between something observed and the observer; as, a *line* of vision; a thread, string, cord, or rope; as, a fishing *line*; a system of public conveyances; as, a bus *line*; the wire or wires connecting points or stations, as for telegraph, telephone, and television; one of the straight, horizontal, parallel strokes of the musical staff, or those placed above or below it; outline, contour, or shape; as, the *line* of my features. *Milit.* a disposition of ships or tanks, all abreast; the group of officers in charge of fighting troops; *often pl.* a distribution and entrenchment of troops for defense purposes; as, within the enemy's *lines*. *Sports*, ten bowling frames; the seven football players who stand abreast of the line of scrimmage. *Bridge*, a horizontal mark on the scorepad that differentiates points earned toward game, below the line, from points earned by setting contracts, having honors, or making overtricks, above the line.—**hold the line**, to take a firm position; maintain existing conditions, as: The government will *hold the line* against inflation.—**in line**, straight; conforming to standards; in control, as: The rowdy soldiers were kept *in line*.—**in line for**, next to receive or achieve; as: He was *in line for* a salary raise.—**on the line**, directly, frankly, or promptly; as, to lay it *on the line*, deliver cash *on the line*.—**out of line**, not complying with proper practices or standards, as: Shouting is *out of line* in a hospital.—**read be·tween the lines**, to discover a meaning not explicitly expressed.—**toe the line**, to meet responsibility; to strictly comply with an order or rule, as: All army privates must *toe the line*.—**lin·a·ble, line·a·ble**, *a.*—**line·less**, *a.*—**line·like**, *a.*

line, līn, *v.t.*—*lined, lining.* To trace by a line or lines; sketch; delineate; as, to *line* a person's silhouette; to mark with a line or lines; as, to *line* a graph; to bring into a line, often followed by *up*; as, to *line up* the markers for surveying; to form or arrange a line along; as, to *line* the road with houses; to secure or obtain, esp. a position or a needed item, followed by *up*; *archaic*, to measure or test with a line.—*v.i.* To take a position in a line; form a line, often followed by *up*; as, to *line up* for the march; to hit a line drive in a baseball game.

line, līn, *v.t.*—*lined, lining.* [O.E. *line*, to double a garment with *linen*.] To cover on the inside; to protect by a layer on the inside, as a garment; to fill or stuff, as with cash; to back or face, as a book.—*n.* A thickness of mucilage, usu. in wood layers.

lin·e·age, lin′ē·ij, *n.* [Fr. *lignage*, < *ligne*, L. *linea*, a line.] Descendants in a line from a common progenitor; line of descent from an ancestor; race; family.

line·age, lī′nij, *n.* Linage.

lin·e·al, lin′ē·al, *a.* [L.L. *linealis*, < L. *linea*, E. *line*.] Being in the direct line, as a descendant or ancestor; hereditary; transmitted by direct or continuous descent; linear.—**lin·e·al·ly**, *adv.*

lin·e·a·ment, lin′ē·a·ment, *n.* [L. *lineamentum*.] *Usu. pl.* The outline or contour of a body or figure, particularly of the face; distinctive or characteristic features.—**lin·e·a·men·tal**, lin″ē·a·men′tal, *a.*—**lin·e·a·men·ta·tion**, lin″ē·a·men·tā′shan, *n.*

lin·e·ar, lin′ē·ér, *a.* [L. *linearis*, < *linea*, E. *line*.] Of or pertaining to a line or lines; resembling a line or thread; narrow and elongated; consisting of or involving lines;

as, *linear* design; extended in a line; as, a *linear* series; pertaining to length, or involving measurement in one direction only; as, *linear* measure; *math.* of the first degree, as an equation. Pertaining to artwork in which movement and rhythm of line are the chief concern.—**lin·e·ar·ly**, *adv.*

lin·e·ar ac·cel·er·a·tor, *n. Phys.* a device for accelerating charged particles in a straight path by employing alternate electrode gaps and field-free regions so placed that particles passing through them receive successive increases of energy.

lin·e·ar meas·ure, *n.* A system of measuring length, as contrasted with area or volume; a unit in a linear measuring system, as an inch or meter.

lin·e·ar per·spec·tive, *n.* A technique, used esp. in art work, for representing perspective and an illusion of space on a flat surface by drawing lines that converge at a set horizon point.

lin·e·ar pro·gram·ming, *n. Math.* the theory or methodology of locating and determining the minimum or maximum value of a linear function, the variables of which are subject to certain linear constraints, as linear equalities.

lin·e·a·tion, lin″ē·ā′shan, *n.* [L. *lineatio* (n-).] A marking with or tracing by lines; a division into lines; a line or outline; an arrangement or group of lines.—**lin·e·ate, lin·e·at·ed**, lin′ē·it, lin′ē·āt″, *a.*

line·back·er, lin′bak″ér, *n. Football*, a player positioned behind the linemen who plays either as a defensive lineman or as a defender against passes or running plays.—**line·back·ing**, *n.*

line·breed·ing, lin′brē″ding, *n. Biol.* inbreeding to develop and maintain desirable characteristics of individuals in the same ancestral line.—**line-breed**, lin′brēd, *v.i., v.t.*—*line-bred, line-breeding.*

line cut, *n.* An engraving composed of lines and solid areas. Also **line·block.**

line draw·ing, *n.* A drawing composed of lines and solid unshaded areas, suitable for reproduction by a line cut.

line drive, *n.* A baseball forcefully batted in a line approximately parallel to the ground. Also *liner.*

line en·grav·ing, *n.* A kind of engraving made with a metal plate that has incised lines of varying thickness and density; the engraved plate used; a print made with the plate.—**line en·grav·er**, *n.*

line gauge, *n.* A ruler showing printing point sizes, usu. marked off in picas, agates, and other measurements.

line haul, *n.* The moving of freight between depots, as distinguished from loading and unloading.

line·man, lin′man, *n. pl.* **line·men.** A repairman who works on electric power, telephone, or telegraph lines; also *linesman.* A railway employee who inspects the tracks; *surv.* one who handles the line for marking distances; *football*, one who plays forward, as a guard, tackle, or center.

lin·en, lin′en, *n.* [Properly an a. signifying made of flax, < O.E. *lin*, flax, L. *linum*, Gr. *linon*, flax; cf. Armor. *lin*, W. *llin*, flax.] Cloth, thread, or yarn of flax; *usu. pl.* articles previously made of linen, but now often made of cotton; as, table *linens.*—*a.* Made of flax or flax yarn; linen textured.

line of·fic·er, *n. Milit.* an officer commissioned in a combat unit.

line of force, *n. Phys.* a theoretical line in an electric or magnetic field which corresponds to the direction and force of that field.

line of scrim·mage, *n. Football*, the imaginary line, running through the football and paralleling the goal lines, at which the players are positioned before a scrimmage.

line of sight, *n.* An imaginary line extending from the viewer's eye to the distant

object upon which sight or an observing device is focused; also **line of vi·sion.** The hypothetical straight line obtained by aligning the sights of a firearm with the target; the direct path, when unimpeded by the horizon, joining radio transmitting and receiving antennas.

line·o·late, lin′ē·o·lāt″, *a.* [L. *lineola*, dim. of *linea*, E. *line*.] *Biol.* Marked with minute lines; finely lineate. Also **lin·e·o·lat·ed.**

line out, *v.i. Baseball*, to hit a line drive which is caught by an opposing player.—*v.t.* To indicate or describe with lines; to outline; to mark, as a passage, for deletion.

lin·er, lī′nér, *n.* One who or that which traces by or marks with lines; one of a line of steamships or airplanes; a grease pencil or other cosmetic preparation, as of liquid or paste, used to accentuate the eyes; *baseball*, a line drive.

lin·er, lī′nér, *n.* One who fits or provides linings; something serving as a lining; a backing; a coat lining which may be zipped in or out of a coat; a part that fits into another unit; as, a helmet *liner.*

lines·man, linz′man, *n. pl.* **lines·men.** A lineman. *Sports*, an official employed to watch the lines which mark out the field, as in tennis; an official, as in football, who marks the distances gained and lost in the progress of the play and otherwise assists the referees and field judges.

line squall, *n.* A squall or thunderstorm, or a series of storms building up on a cold front, characterized by a change in wind direction and usu. a drop in temperature.

line storm, *n.* A violent rain storm raging at or about the time of the equinox. Also *equinoctial storm.*

line-up, line·up, lin′up″, *n.* The formation of persons or things into a line, or into position for action; the persons or things themselves, esp. a line of suspects assembled by the police for identification; a grouping of those with similar interests or purpose; *sports*, a schedule of the positions of players.

ling, ling, *n. pl.* **ling, lings.** [D. *ling*; Dan. and N. *lange*; G. *leng, langfisch*, so named from being *long.*] An elongated food fish of the cod family, found in the N. Atlantic; any of several related fish, esp. the burbot.

ling, ling, *n.* [Icel. and Dan. *lyng*, heather.] Common heather, *Calluna vulgaris.*

lin·gam, ling′gam, *n.* A phallic symbol in Hinduism, used in the worship of the god Siva. Also **lin·ga**, ling′ga.

ling·cod, ling′kod″, *n. pl.* **ling·cod, ling·cods.** A large food fish, *Ophiodon elongatus*, of the N. Pacific, similar to the common greenling. Also *cultus.*

lin·ger, ling′gér, *v.i.* [M.E. *lenger*, freq. of *leng*, tarry, < O.E. *lengan*, prolong, delay, < *lang*, E. *long.*] To remain or stay on in a place longer than is usual or expected, as if from reluctance to leave it; tarry; dawdle or loiter; to dwell in contemplation, thought, or enjoyment; to be tardy in action; to delay or procrastinate; to die slowly; to continue, remain, or persist, although tending to cease or disappear.—*v.t.* To pass in a leisurely or tedious manner, as time or life, usu. followed by *away* or *out*; as, to *linger away* the hours; *archaic*, to drag out or protract.—**lin·ger·er**, *n.*—**lin·ger·ing·ly**, *adv.*

lin·ge·rie, län″zhe·rā′, lan′zhe·rē″, län″je·rā′, lan′je·rē′, Fr. laNzh·e·Rē′, *n.* [Fr.] Women's underwear and sleepwear; feminine intimate apparel.

lin·go, ling′gō, *n. pl.* **lin·goes.** [L. *lingua*, the tongue.] *Colloq.* Language; speech; a contemptuous or humorous term for language one does not understand; the specialized vocabulary or speech of a particular field, profession, or group.

lin·gua, ling'gwa, *n.* pl. **lin·guae**, ling'gwē. The tongue or any part that resembles the tongue.

lin·gua fran·ca, ling'gwa frang'ka, *n.* pl. **lingua fran·cas**, **lin·guae fran·cae**, ling'gwē fran'sē. A compound language spoken along the Mediterranean coast, made up of words from French, Italian, Spanish, Arabic, and modern Greek, serving as a common medium of communication; any language, often hybrid, serving as a means of communication, esp. in commerce and trade, between peoples of different tongues.

lin·gual, ling'gwal, *a.* [M.L. *lingualis*, < L. *lingua*, O.L. *dingua*, tongue, speech, language.] Of or pertaining to the tongue or some tonguelike part; pertaining to the use of the tongue in speaking; pertaining to languages; *phon.* of speech sounds, uttered with the aid of the tongue, as *d* and *t.*—*n. Phon.* a lingual sound.—**lin·gual·ly**, *adv.*

lin·guist, ling'gwist, *n.* A person skilled in languages, esp. one who knows several languages; a polyglot; a linguistics specialist.

lin·guis·tic at·las, *n.* A series of maps representing areal speech variations. Also **di·a·lect at·las.**

lin·guis·tic form, *n.* Any understandable unit of speech, as a sentence, word, suffix, or the like.

lin·guis·tic ge·og·ra·pher, *n.* One who studies the geography of dialects. Also **di·a·lect ge·og·ra·pher.**

lin·guis·tic ge·og·ra·phy, *n.* The science of language and dialectic distribution and movement among regions and peoples. Also **di·a·lect ge·og·ra·phy.**

lin·guis·tics, ling·gwis'tiks, *n. pl., sing.* or *pl. in constr.* The science dealing with the origin, structure, history, regional variations, and phonetic attributes of language. —**lin·guis·tic**, *a.*—**lin·guis·ti·cal**, *a.*— **lin·guis·ti·cal·ly**, *adv.*

lin·gu·late, ling'gū·lāt", ling'gya·lāt", *a.* Shaped like the tongue or a strap; ligulate.

lin·i·ment, lin'i·ment, *n.* [L.L. *linimentum*, < L. *linire, linere*, smear.] A liquid preparation, usu. oily, for rubbing on or applying to the skin, as for sprains or bruises.

li·nin, li'nin, *n.* [L. *linum*, flax, E. *line*.] *Biol.* the substance forming the netlike structure which connects the chromatin granules in the nucleus of a cell.

lin·ing, li'ning, *n.* A layer of material on the inner side of something; as, a silk *lining* in a garment, or a brick *lining* in a furnace; the act of lining something.

link, lingk, *n.* [M.E. *link, lenk*; < Scan.: cf. Icel. *hlekkr*, Sw. *länk*, link.] One of the rings or separate pieces of which a chain is composed; one of the 100 wire rods forming the divisions of a surveyor's chain, used as a unit of length equaling 7.92 inches; one of the parts of any chainlike arrangement, as one of a number of sausages in a chain; anything serving to connect one part or thing with another; a bond or tie; a device used to fasten cuffs; *mach.* a short, movable connecting rod for transmitting motion or power.—*v.t., v.i.* To join by or as by a link or links; unite.—**link·er**, *n.*

link, lingk, *n.* [Origin, uncertain; perh. equiv. to *lint*, the first part of *linstock*.] A torch usu. made of tow with tar or pitch.

link·age, ling'kij, *n.* The act of linking; the state or manner of being linked; a system of links; *chem.* the way in which two or more atoms or radicals are united in a molecule; *elect.* a relationship between the number of turns of a coil and the coil's magnetic flux, each turn of the coil being linked to one unit of flux; *genetics*, location on the same chromosome of two or more genes of different traits, usu. resulting in the inheritance of these traits as an inseparable

---

unit; *art*, any of various mathematical or drawing devices, as a pantograph.

link·boy, lingk'boi", *n.* A boy formerly employed to carry a torch to light a person's way through dark streets. Also *linkman.*

linked, lingkt, *a.* Connected; *genetics*, exhibiting linkage.

link·ing verb, *n. Gram.* a verb which serves to connect the subject and predicate of a sentence without indicating action, as *be, become, feel, seem.*

link·man, lingk'man, *n.* pl. **link·men.** Linkboy.

links, lingks, *n. pl.* [O.E. *hlinc*, rising ground; same root as L. *clivus*, sloping.] A golf course; *Sc.* a stretch of flat or slightly rolling sandy ground along the seashore.— **links·man**, lingks'man, *n.* pl. **links·men.** A golfer.

link·work, lingk'wurk", *n.* Work composed of links, as a chain; a linkage; *mech.* a mechanism or device in which motion is transmitted by rods or links.

Lin·ne·an, Lin·nae·an, li·nē'an, *a.* Of or pertaining to the Swedish botanist, Karl von Linné, 1707–78 (Latinized name, Carolus Linnaeus), who established the binomial system of scientific nomenclature.

lin·net, lin'it, *n.* [O.Fr. *linette* (so called from its feeding on flaxseed), < *lin*, < L. *linum*, flax, E. *line*.] A small Old World finch, *Acanthus cannabina.*

li·no·cut, li'no·kut", *n.* A print produced from a design cut into a piece of wood-mounted linoleum.

lin·o·le·ic acid, lin"o·lē'ik as'id, li·nō'lē·ik as'id, *n. Chem.* a liquid acid of unsaturated fats, $C_{18}H_{32}O_2$, found in linseed oil and other vegetable oils, and used chiefly as a drier in varnishes and paints.

li·no·le·um, li·nō'lē·um, *n.* [L. *linum*, flax, and *oleum*, oil.] A floor covering made by pressing a preparation of oxidized linseed oil and ground cork on canvas or burlap.

Lin·o·type, li'no·tip", *n.* [A 'line of type.'] *Print.* a machine for setting and casting a complete line of type on a metal slug by the operation of a keyboard. (Trademark.)— *v.i., v.t. (l.c.)* to set type or set into type by means of such a machine.—**lin·o·typ·er**, **lin·o·typ·ist**, *n.*

lin·sang, lin'sang, *n.* [Javanese.] Any of the carnivorous catlike mammals constituting the genus *Prionodon* of the East Indies or the related genus *Poiana* of Africa.

lin·seed, lin'sēd", *n.* [O.E. *linsǣd.*] Flaxseed. —**lin·seed oil**, the oil obtained by pressing flaxseed, used for its drying qualities in making paints, printing inks, and the like.

lin·sey-wool·sey, lin'zē-wul'zē, *n.* pl. **lin·sey-wool·seys.** A stout, once popular coarse fabric with a warp of linen or cotton and a woof or filling of wool.

lin·stock, lin'stok", *n.* [For *lintstock, luntstock*, < D. *lont*, Dan. *lunte*, a match, and *stock*, a stick.] A staff with a fork at one end to hold a lighted match, formerly used in firing a cannon.

lint, lint, *n.* [O.E. *linet*, L. *linteum, linteus*, < *linum*, flax.] Fluff or fuzz consisting of yarn or fabric ravelings; a soft substance made by scraping linen, used for dressing wounds; the hairy fibers of cotton seeds.— **lint·less**, *a.*—**lint·y**, lin'tē, *a.*—*lintier, lintiest.*

lin·tel, lin'tel, *n.* [O.Fr. *lintel*, Fr. *linteau*, < L.L. *limitellus*, dim. < L. *limes, limitis*, a limit.] The horizontal structure over a door, window, or similar opening used to support the weight above it.

lint·er, lin'tėr, *n.* A machine for removing fibers which remain on cotton seeds after the initial ginning; *pl.* the fibers themselves.

lint·white, lint'hwit", lint'wit", *n.* [O.E. *linetwige.*] *Sc.* the linnet.

---

li·on, li'on, *n.* [O.Fr. Fr. *lion*, < L. *leo* (*leon*-), < Gr. *leōn*, lion; cf. *Leo*.] A large, tawny, carnivorous animal, *Panthera leo*, of the cat family, native in Africa and southern Asia, the male of which has a full, flowing mane; this animal as the national emblem of Great Britain; a man of great strength or courage; a celebrated or prominent person. (*Cap.*), *astron.* the zodiacal constellation or sign Leo; the northern constellation Leo Minor.—**li·on·ess**, li'o·nis, *n.* A female lion.—**li·on·like**, *a.*

li·on·heart·ed, li'on·här"tid, *a.* Brave; courageous.

li·on·ize, li'o·niz", *v.t.*—*lionized, lionizing.* To treat as a celebrity, as: He was *lionized* at many parties after his success. *Brit.* to visit or exhibit the objects of interest of, as of a place.—*v.i. Brit.* to visit objects of interest or see the sights.—**li·on·i·za·tion**, *n.*—**li·on·iz·er**, *n.*

li·on's share, *n.* The largest portion; a large, unfair share.

lip, lip, *n.* [O.E. *lippa* = D. *lip* = G. *lippe*, lip; akin to L. *labium* and *labrum*, lip.] Either of two fleshy parts or folds forming the margins of the mouth and performing an important function in speech; a liplike part or structure; the edge of an opening or cavity; the margin or edge of a vessel, esp. a projecting edge as of a pitcher; any edge or rim; *slang*, impudent talk; *bot.* either of the two parts, upper and lower, into which the corolla or calyx of certain plants, esp. those of the mint family, is divided; *biol.* a labellum; *conch.* the outer or the inner margin of the aperture of a gastropod's shell.—*a.* Applied or relating to the lip or lips; labial; insincere.—*v.t.*—*lipped, lipping.* To touch with the lips; to utter, esp. softly; to use the lips in playing, as a musical wind instrument; *golf*, to hit, usu. putt, the ball around the rim of, as: He *lipped* the cup at the ninth hole.—**lip·like**, *a.*—**lipped**, *a.*

li·pase, li'pās, lip'ās, *n.* [Gr. *lipos*, fat.] *Biochem.* an enzyme, occurring in the pancreas, liver, and certain seeds, which is capable of breaking down fats into fatty acids and glycerin.

lip·id, lip'id, lip'id, *n. Biochem.* any of a group of organic substances, including fats, sterols, and waxes, insoluble in water but able to be metabolized. Also **li·pide**, li'pid, li'pid, lip'id, lip'id.

lip·oid, lip'oid, li'poid, *a. Biochem.* resembling fat. Also **lip·oi·dal.**—*n.* A substance similar to fat, as wax.

li·pol·y·sis, li·pol'i·sis, *n.* [Gr. *lipos*, fat.] *Chem.* the breaking down of fats into fatty acids and glycerin, as by the action of lipase.—**lip·o·lyt·ic**, lip"o·lit'ik, *a.*

li·po·ma, li·pō'ma, *n.* pl. **li·po·mas, li·po·ma·ta**, li·pō'ma·ta. [Gr. *lipos*, fat, *oma*, a tumor.] *Pathol.* a fatty tumor.—**li·pom·a·tous**, li·pom'a·tus, *a.*

lip·o·phil·ic, lip"o·fil'ik, *a. Physical chem.* With a marked affinity for lipids, esp. fats; aiding the absorption or solubility of lipids.

lip·o·pro·tein, lip"o·prō'tēn, lip"o·prō'tē·in, li"po·prō'tēn, li"po·prō'tē·in, *n. Biochem.* one of the class of proteins containing a simple protein in combination with a lipid.

lip·o·trop·ic, lip"o·trop'ik, lip"o·trō'pik, li"po·trop'ik, li"po·trō'pik, *a. Biochem.* tending to promote the utilization of fat and thus prevent excessive fat deposits in the liver.

lip·py, lip'ē, *a.*—*lippier, lippiest. Slang*, impudent in speech.

lip-read, lip'rēd", *v.t.*—*lip-read, lip-reading.* To understand, as speech, by watching a speaker's lips forming words one does not hear.—**lip-read·er**, *n.*

lip read·ing, *n.* The reading or understanding, as by a deaf person, of the movements of another's lips forming words.

---

ch- chain, G. na*ch*t;   **th-** T*H*en, thin;   **w-** wig, hw as sound in whig;   **z-** zh as in azure, zeal.   *Italicized vowel* indicates schwa sound.

lip serv·ice, *n.* Service expressed in words alone; insincere declaration of devotion or good will.

lip·stick, lip'stik″, *n.* A cosmetic, usu. contained in a small tube, for coloring the lips.

lip sync, *n. Movies, TV,* lip synchronization, the technique of synchronizing lip movement with sounds of speech and singing, esp. when action and sound are recorded at separate times.—**lip-sync,** lip'singk′, *a.*

li·quate, lī'kwāt, *v.t., v.i.—liquated, liquating.* [L. *liquo, liquatum.*] *Metal.* to separate or become separated from a less fusible metal by the application of just sufficient heat to melt the more easily liquefiable.—**li·qua·tion,** lī·kwā'shan, lī·kwā'zhan, *n.*

liq·ue·fa·cient, lik″we·fā'shent, *n.* [L. *liquefaciens (-ent-),* ppr. of *liquefacere.*] A liquefying agent, as a drug that causes the liquefaction of solid deposits.

liq·ue·fac·tion, lik″we·fak'shan, *n.* [L. *liqueo,* to be fluid, and *facio,* to make.] The act of making liquid or the process of becoming liquid; the state of being liquid or melted.

liq·ue·fied pe·tro·le·um gas, *n.* A condensed, liquefied gas containing combustible hydrocarbons, used esp. as a fuel or for chemical synthesis.

liq·ue·fy, lik'we·fī″, *v.t., v.i.—liquefied, liquefying.* To convert or be converted from a solid form to that of a liquid.—**liq·ue·fi·a·ble,** lik″we·fī'a·bl, *a.* Capable of being liquefied.—**liq·ue·fi·er,** *n.*

li·ques·cent, li·kwes'ent, *a.* [L. *liquesco,* to melt.] Melting; becoming liquid or fluid.—**li·ques·cence,** *n.*

li·queur, li·kur′, *Brit.* li·kūr′, *Fr.* lē·kŒR′, *n.* [Fr.] Any of a class of alcoholic liquors, usu. strong, sweet, and highly flavored, as curaçao or crème de menthe; a cordial.

liq·uid, lik'wid, *a.* [O.Fr. Fr. *liquide,* < L. *liquidus,* liquid, fluid, clear, < *liquere,* be liquid.] Able to flow like water; composed of particles or molecules which move freely among themselves but do not tend to separate as those of gases do; neither gaseous nor solid; clear, transparent, or bright; as, *liquid* eyes; sounding smoothly or agreeably; flowing easily and smoothly, as certain consonant sounds; of movement, facile; in cash, or easily convertible into cash, as assets; of or pertaining to liquids; as, *liquid* measure.—*n.* A fluid substance that is not a gas; *phon.* a smoothly flowing consonant sound, as of *l, m, n,* and *r.*—**li·quid·i·ty,** liq·uid·ness, li·kwid'i·tē, *n.*—**liq·uid·ly,** *adv.*

liq·uid air, *n.* The intensely cold, transparent, liquid product, used chiefly as a refrigerant, formed when air is greatly compressed and then cooled.

liq·uid·am·bar, lik'wid·am″bẽr, *n.* [N.L. < L. *liquidus,* liquid, and M.L. *ambar,* amber.] Any tree of the genus *Liquidambar,* esp. the sweet gum, a large American tree having star-shaped leaves; the fragrant balsamic liquid of this tree, storax, which is used in medicine.

liq·ui·date, lik'wi·dāt″, *v.t.—liquidated, liquidating.* [M.L. *liquidatus,* pp. of *liquidare,* < L. *liquidus,* E. *liquid.*] To settle or pay, as a debt or claim; to reduce, as accounts, to order; to determine the amount of, as indebtedness or damages; to turn into cash; as, *liquidate* securities; to settle the accounts and distribute the assets of, in winding up affairs; to do away with; *slang,* to murder.—*v.i.* To liquidate debts or accounts; go into liquidation.—**liq·ui·da·tion,** lik″wi·dā'shan, *n.*

liq·ui·da·tor, lik'wi·dā″tẽr, *n.* One who liquidates; a person appointed to conduct the winding up of the affairs of a firm or estate.

liq·uid crys·tal, *n.* A liquid, as ammonium oleate, which has certain crystalline properties, as anisotropy.

liq·uid·ize, lik'wi·dīz″, *v.t.—liquidized, liquidizing.* To make liquid; *fig.* to stir or stimulate, as the imagination.

liq·uid meas·ure, *n.* The system of units of capacity ordinarily used in measuring liquid commodities. See Measures and Weights table.

liq·uor, lik'ẽr, lik'war, *n.* [O.Fr. *licur* (Fr. *liqueur*), < L. *liquor,* liquid state, a liquid, < *liquere,* be liquid.] A distilled alcoholic beverage, as brandy or whisky, as distinguished from a fermented beverage, as wine or beer; any liquid substance; a solution of a substance, esp. a concentrated one used in the industrial arts, lik'ẽr. *Phar.* a solution of a medicinal substance in water, lik'war.—lik'ẽr, *v.t. Slang,* to ply with liquor, often with *up.*—*v.i.* To drink liquor, often with *up.*

liq·uo·rice, lik'o·ris, lik'o·rish, lik'rish, *n.* Licorice.

lir·i·o·den·dron, lir″ē·ō·den'dron, *n. pl.* **lir·i·o·den·drons, lir·i·o·den·dra.** [N.L. < Gr. *leirion,* lily, and *dendron,* tree.] Any tree of the genus *Liriodendron,* esp. the tulip tree, *L. tulipifera.*

lisle, lil, *n.* A kind of twisted thread made of cotton; material, usu. knitted, made of this thread.

lisp, lisp, *v.i., v.t.* [O.E. *wlisp, wlips,* lisping; D. *lispen,* Dan. *laespe,* Sw. *laspa,* to lisp; G. *lispeln,* to whisper, to lisp.] To pronounce imperfectly, as by giving the sound of *th* or *dh* to the sibilant letters *s* and *z*; to speak imperfectly, as a child.—*n.* The habit or act of lisping; the habitual utterance of *th* for *s.*—**lisp·ing·ly,** *adv.*

lis pen·dens, lis pen'denz, *n. Law.* A suit that is pending; a rule giving the court jurisdiction or control over disputed property pending a verdict.

lis·some, lis·som, lis'om, *a.* [< *lithesome.*] Supple; flexible; lithe; nimble; agile.—**lis·some·ly,** *adv.*—**lis·some·ness,** *n.*

list, list, *n.* [Fr. *liste,* list, roll, orig. border, band, strip, < O.H.G. *lista.*] A record consisting of a series of names, words, or the like; a number of names of persons or things set down one after another; a roll; a register; a catalog.—*v.t.* To set down together in a list, or make a list of; enter in a list with others; to set down or enter in a formal or official list or register; *archaic,* to enlist, as for military or naval service.—*v.i.* To be presented for sale at a specific price, as in a catalog; *archaic,* to enlist, as for military or naval service.—**list·er,** *n.*

list, list, *n.* [O.E. *līste* = D. *lijst* = O.H.G. *lista,* G. *leiste,* border: cf. *list,* and *listel.*] A border, strip, or band of anything, esp. cloth; a selvage; a ridge of earth thrown up by a lister or plow; *carp.* a strip from the edge of a plank.—*a.* Made of selvages or strips of cloth; as, *list* carpet.—*v.t.* To border or edge; to produce furrows and ridges in by means of a lister or plow; *carp.* to cut a strip, as of wood, from the edge of.

list, list, *v.i.* [Origin uncertain: cf. *list.*] *Naut.* to careen or incline to one side, as a ship.—*v.t.* To cause to lean to one side.—*n.* A careening or leaning to one side, as of a ship.

list, list, *v.i.* [Orig. form of *listen,* which is a lengthened form < O.E. *hlystan,* to listen, < *hlyst,* hearing.] *Archaic,* to listen.—*v.t. Archaic,* to listen to.

list·ed, lis'tid, *a.* Set down or entered in a list, as a telephone number; of securities, entered in or admitted to a stock exchange.

lis·ten, lis'en, *v.i.* To give close attention in order to hear; to give ear; to hear and attend to.—*n.*—**lis·ten·er,** *n.*

lis·ten in, *v.i.* To attend to a discussion or communication; as, to *listen in* to a broadcast; to eavesdrop.

lis·ten·ing post, *n. Milit.* a post or position, as in advance of a defensive line, established for the purpose of listening, in order to detect the enemy's movements. Any position maintained for the purpose of obtaining information.

list·er, lis'tẽr, *n.* A plow with a double moldboard used to prepare the soil for planting by producing furrows and ridges. Also **list·er plow.**

list·er plant·er, *n.* A lister plow with attachments for dropping and covering seeds. Also **list·er drill.**

list·ing, lis'ting, *n.* The act or process of putting together a list; an entry on a list; a list, catalog, or directory.

list·less, list'lis, *a.* [O.E. *list,* O.E. *lyst,* desire, pleasure.] Characterized by a lack of interest or energy; languid and indifferent; spiritless.—**list·less·ly,** *adv.*—**list·less·ness,** list'lis·nis, *n.*

list price, *n.* The published or suggested retail price of a commodity, and the figure from which a discount is reckoned.

lit·a·ny, lit'a·nē, *n. pl.* **lit·a·nies.** [Fr. *litanie;* Gr. *litaneia,* < *litaneuō,* to pray, *litē,* a prayer.] A type of ceremonial or liturgical prayer comprising a series of solemn invocations and their fixed responses; *(cap.)* a collection of short supplications taking this form in the *Book of Common Prayer,* usu. preceded by *the.* Any recitation similar to a litany.

li·tchi, lē'chē, *n. pl.* **li·tchis.** A sweet, thin-shelled fruit yielded by a tree of China; the litchi tree. Also *lichee, lychee.*

li·ter, lē'tẽr, *n.* [< Gr. *litra,* a pound.] Metric measure of capacity, a cubic decimeter of 61.025 cu. in., and equivalent to 1.0567 U.S. liquid quarts. See Metric System table.

lit·er·a·cy, lit'ẽr·a·sē, *n.* The state of being literate, esp. of possessing the skills of reading and writing.

lit·er·al, lit'ẽr·al, *a.* [L. *literalis,* < *litera,* a letter.] According to the letter or verbal expression; not figurative or metaphorical; following the letter or exact words; as, a *literal* translation; tending to interpret statements factually or unimaginatively; consisting of or expressed by letters.—**lit·er·al·i·ty,** lit·er·al·ness, lit″e·ral'i·tē, *n.*—**lit·er·al·ly,** *adv.*

lit·er·al·ism, lit'ẽr·a·liz″um, *n.* The act or practice of adhering to the letter or strict sense, as in translating; a mode of interpreting literally or realistically, as in literature or art.—**lit·er·al·ist,** *n.*—**lit·er·al·is·tic,** lit″ẽr·a·lis'tik, *a.*

lit·er·al·ize, lit'ẽr·a·līz″, *v.t.—literalized, literalizing.* To interpret or translate literally.

lit·er·ar·y, lit'e·rer″ē, *a.* [L. *literarius.*] Pertaining to or dealing with letters or literature; well-read; engaged in the writing profession.—**lit·er·ar·i·ly,** *adv.*—**lit·er·ar·i·ness,** *n.*

lit·er·ate, lit'ẽr·it, *a.* [L. *literatus.*] Having the ability to read and write; educated; learned; lettered.—*n.*—**lit·er·ate·ly,** *adv.*

lit·e·ra·ti, lit″e·rä'tē, lit″e·rä'tī, *n. pl.* [It. *litterato.*] Literary men; scholars; intellectuals.

lit·e·ra·tim, lit″e·rä'tim, *adv.* [M.L. < L. *littera, litera,* E. *letter.*] Letter for letter; literally; as, to reproduce a text *literatim.*

lit·er·a·tor, lit'e·rä″tẽr, *n.* [L.] A literary man; a litterateur.

lit·er·a·ture, lit'ẽr·a·chẽr, lit'ẽr·a·chur″, li'tra·chẽr, li'tra·chur″, *n.* [L. *litteratura.*] The class of writings in which imaginative expression, aesthetic form, universality of ideas, and permanence are characteristic features, as fiction, poetry, romance, and drama; literary productions collectively; the literary productions upon a given subject, or a particular branch of knowledge; the collective writings of a country or period; the occupation of an author or writer; *colloq.* any printed material, as: Have you any *literature* on India?

lith·arge, lith'ärj, li·thärj', *n.* [O.Fr. *litarge* (Fr. *litharge*), < L. *lithargyrus*, < Gr. *litharguros*, < *lithos*, stone, and *arguros*, silver.] A yellowish-red oxide of lead, used for glazing earthenware, making lead glass, and preparing pigments.

lithe, līTH, *a.* [O.E. *lithe*, gentle; G. *linde*, *gelind*, Dan. *lind*, Icel. *linr*, soft, mild; allied to L. *lentus*, pliant, *lenis*, mild (whence *lenity*).] Easily bent; pliant; flexible; limber. Also **lithe·some.—lithe··ly,** *adv.***—lithe·ness,** *n.*

li·the·mi·a, li·thae·mi·a, li·thē'mē·a, *n.* [N.L. < Gr. *lithos*, stone, and *aima* blood.] *Pathol.* a condition in which there is an excess of uric acid in the blood.—**li·the·-mic, li·thae·mic,** *a.*

lith·i·a, lith'ē·a, lith'ya, *n.* [N.L. < Gr. *lithos*, stone.] A white oxide of lithium, Li₂O.

li·thi·a·sis, li·thī'a·sis, *n.* [N.L. < Gr. *lithiasis*, < *lithos*, stone.] *Pathol.* the formation of stony solids in any part of the body, as in the bladder.

lith·i·a wa·ter, *n.* A mineral water, natural or artificial, containing lithium salts.

lith·ic, lith'ik, *a.* Pertaining to or consisting of stone; *pathol.* pertaining to stony formations in the body, esp. in the bladder; *chem.* of or relating to lithium.—**lith·i·-cal·ly,** *adv.*

lith·i·um, lith'ē·um, *n.* A metallic element, soft and silver-white, the lightest metal known. Sym. Li, at. no. 3, at. wt. 6.939. See Periodic Table of Elements.

lith·o·graph, lith'o·graf", lith'o·gräf", *n.* A print produced by lithography.—*v.t.* To produce or copy by lithography.—**li·thog·-ra·pher,** li·thog'ra·fer, *n.*—**lith·o·graph·-ic,** lith"o·graf'ik, *a.*—**lith·o·graph·i·cal·-ly,** *adv.*

li·thog·ra·phy, li·thog'ra·fē, *n.* The art or process of producing a picture, writing, or the like, on a flat, specially prepared stone, and of taking ink impressions from this as in ordinary printing; a similar process in which a substance other than stone, as aluminum or zinc, is used.

lith·oid, lith'oid, *a.* [Gr. *lithoeides*.] Stone-like; stony. Also **li·thoi·dal,** li·thoi'dal.

li·thol·o·gy, li·thol'o·jē, *n.* The science dealing with the mineral composition of rock specimens usu. as observed with the naked eye; *med.* the science treating of calculi in the human body.—**lith·o·log·ic,** **lith·o·log·i·cal,** lith"o·loj'ik, *a.*—**lith·o·-log·i·cal·ly,** *adv.*

lith·o·marge, lith'o·märj", *n.* [N.L. *lithomarga*, < Gr. *lithos*, stone, and L. *marga*, marl.] Any of several compact clays, esp. kaolin, usu. in an impure state.

lith·o·phyte, lith'o·fīt", *n. Zool.* a polyp with a hard or stony structure, as a coral; *bot.* any plant growing on the surface of rocks.—**lith·o·phyt·ic,** lith"o·fit'ik, *a.*

lith·o·pone, lith'o·pōn", *n.* A pigment composed of zinc sulfide and barium sulfate, used primarily in paint and linoleum manufacturing.

lith·o·sphere, lith'o·sfēr", *n.* The crust or outer part of the solid earth.

li·thot·o·my, li·thot'o·mē, *n. pl.* **li·thot·-o·mies.** The surgical operation of removing stones from the bladder.—**lith·o·tom·ic,** **lith·o·tom·i·cal,** lith"o·tom'ik, *a.*—**li·-thot·o·mist,** *n.*

li·thot·ri·ty, li·tho'tri·tē, *n. pl.* **li·thot·-ri·ties.** [= Fr. *lithotritie*, < Gr. *lithos*, stone, and L. *terere* (pp. *tritus*), rub.] *Surg.* the operation of crushing stone in

---

the bladder into particles that may be voided.—**li·thot·ri·tist,** *n.*

Lith·u·a·ni·an, lith"ö·ā'nē·an, *a.* Of or pertaining to Lithuania, a country on the Baltic Sea, its inhabitants, or their language. —*n.* A native of Lithuania; the Baltic language of Lithuania.

lit·i·ga·ble, lit'i·ga·bl, *a.* Capable of being litigated; subject to a lawsuit.

lit·i·gant, lit'i·gant, *a.* Engaged in a lawsuit.—*n.*

lit·i·gate, lit'i·gāt", *v.t.*—litigated, litigating. [L. *litigo, litigatum—lis, litis,* strife, dispute, and *ago,* to carry on.] To bring before a court of law for decision; to make the subject of a lawsuit.—*v.i.* To carry on a suit by judicial process.—**lit·i·ga·tor,** *n.*

lit·i·ga·tion, lit"i·gā'shan, *n.* The act or process of litigating; the proceedings in a suit at law; a lawsuit.

li·ti·gious, li·tij'us, *a.* [L. *litigiosus,* < *litigium,* a dispute.] Of or relating to litigation; fond of litigation; given to bringing lawsuits; contentious.—**li·ti·gious·ly,** *adv.* —**li·ti·gious·ness, li·ti·gi·os·i·ty,** li·-tij"ē·os'i·tē, *n.*

lit·mus, lit'mus, *n.* [< G. *lackmus,* D. *lakmoes—lack,* lacker, and *mus, moes,* pulp, pap.] A blue coloring matter procured from certain lichens, used as a test for acids.— **lit·mus pa·per,** paper colored with litmus that turns red in acids and blue again in alkalies.

li·to·tes, lī'to·tēz", lī'tō·tēz", lit'o·tēz", li·-tō'tēz, *n.* [N.L. < Gr. *litotes,* < *litos,* plain, simple.] *Rhet.* a figure in which an affirmative meaning is expressed by denying its opposite, as in 'an artist of no small stature.'

li·tre, lē'ter, *n.* Liter.

lit·ter, lit'er, *n.* [Fr. *litière,* < L.L. *lectaria,* < L. *lectus,* a bed; same root as *lie, lay.*] Articles scattered in a slovenly manner; scattered rubbish; a condition of disorder; the young produced at one birth by a multiparous mammal; a stretcher; a portable, often canopied couch or bed carried on a shafted frame; straw, hay, or other soft substance used as a bed for animals or as plant protection.—*v.t.* To make untidy, as a place, with scattered articles; to scatter in a careless manner; to furnish, as animals, with litter or bedding; to spread straw for; to give birth to, as: The cat *littered* kittens.—*v.i.* To scatter matter about in a careless or slovenly manner; to bring forth a litter, as: The rabbit *littered* in its small nest.—**lit·ter·y,** lit'e·rē, *a.* Strewn with litter; very messy.

lit·te·rae hu·ma·ni·o·res, lit'e·rē" hū·-man"ē·ōr'ēz, *n. pl.* The humanities.

lit·te·ra·teur, lit"er·a·tur', Fr. lē·tā·rä·-tœr', *n.* [Fr.] An author of literary works.

lit·ter·bug, lit'er·bug", *n. Slang,* one who strews refuse or trash on public property or roads.

lit·tle, lit'l, *a.*—littler or less or lesser, littlest or least. [O.E. *lytel,* D. *luttel,* Icel. *litill,* Sw. *liten,* Dan. *liden, lille,* Goth. *leitile,* little.] Small or relatively small in size or extent; not great or large; short in duration; small in amount; having a small amount of dignity, power, importance, or status; of small force or weight; slight; trivial; small in mind; petty, mean, or narrow; appealing, pleasing, or amusing; as, her *little* way of flirting.—*n.* That which is little or insignificant; a short time or distance; a small quantity, space, degree, or the like.—*adv.*—less, least. In a small quantity or degree; infrequently; not at all, used before a verb, as: He *little* understands the situation.—**lit·tle by lit·tle,** by degrees; gradually.—**make lit·tle of,** treat as insignificant or of little consequence.

Lit·tle A·mer·i·ca, *n.* The U.S. base set up in 1929 on the Ross Ice Shelf in Antarctica by Admiral Richard E. Byrd.

Lit·tle Bear, *n. Astron.* Ursa Minor.

lit·tle·neck, lit'l·nek", *n.* A quahog clam, *Venus mercenaria,* when young and of a size preferred for eating raw.

lit·tle of·fice, *n.* (*Sometimes cap.*), *Rom. Cath. Ch.* a set of prayers, like but shorter than the divine office, in honor of the Blessed Virgin.

lit·tle slam, *n. Bridge,* the winning of all except one of the tricks in one hand. Also *small slam.*

lit·tle the·a·ter, *n.* A nonprofessional acting group, or the theater in which it performs; experimental drama, usu. played to a relatively small audience.

lit·to·ral, lit'er·al, *a.* [L. *littoralis,* < *littus, littoris,* the shore.] Of or pertaining to a shore.—*n.* The shore of a sea or lake and the country lying near it.

li·tur·gi·ol·o·gy, li·tur"jē·ol'o·jē, *n.* The science or study of liturgies; liturgics.— **li·tur·gi·o·log·i·cal,** li·tur"jē·o·loj'i·kal, *a.*—**li·tur·gi·ol·o·gist,** *n.*

lit·ur·gist, lit'er·jist, *n.* An authority on liturgies; a compiler of a liturgy or liturgies; one who uses or favors the use of a liturgy.

lit·ur·gy, lit'er·jē, *n. pl.* **lit·ur·gies.** [Gr. *leitourgia—leitos,* public, < *laos, leōs,* the people, and *ergon,* work.] The ritual or established formulas for public worship, as the Mass in the Roman Catholic Church. —**li·tur·gic, li·tur·gi·cal,** li·tur'jik, *a.* Pertaining to a liturgy or to public prayer and worship.—**li·tur·gics,** *n. pl. but sing. in constr.* The art or operation of leading public worship; the science or study of various liturgies.

liv·a·ble, live·a·ble, liv'a·bl, *a.* Endurable; habitable or suitable for living in, as a house; agreeable or companionable, as a person, usu. followed by *with.*—**liv·a·ble·-ness, live·a·ble·ness, liv·a·bil·i·ty, live·-a·bil·i·ty,** liv"a·bil'i·tē, *n.*

live, liv, *v.i.—lived, living.* [O.E. *lifian,* to live or dwell; L.G. and D. *leven,* Icel. *lifa,* Dan. *leve,* G. *leben,* Goth. *liban,* to live.] To have life; to be capable of performing the vital functions; to continue; to remain effective; not to perish; to pass or spend life in a particular manner; to conduct oneself in life; to regulate one's life; to abide, dwell, reside; to feed or subsist, with *on;* as, to *live on* insects; to acquire a livelihood; *scrip.* to be exempt from spiritual death.—*v.t.* To pass or spend; as, to *live* a life of ease; to illustrate by example; as to *live* one's principles.—**live and let live,** to practice tolerance toward the conduct or beliefs of others.—**live down,** to live so as to atone for an error, scandal, or the like.— **live up to,** to rise to an expectation; to satisfy an aim or standard; to fulfill an obligation.

live, līv, *a.* [Shortened form of *alive,* but, unlike *alive,* commonly used attributively.] Being in life, living, or alive; of or pertaining to life or living beings; as, *live* weight; characterized by or indicating the presence of living creatures; full of life, energy, or activity; alert, wide-awake,' or up-to-date; of present interest, as a question or issue; burning or glowing, as a coal; vivid or bright, as color; flowing freely; as, a *live* spring; still in use or to be used, as type set up or copy for printing; moving or imparting motion or power; as, a *live* axle; loaded or unexploded, as a cartridge or shell; charged with or carrying a current of electricity; as, a *live* wire; in the native or pure state, as a mineral; not mined or quarried, as a rock; being still in play; as, a *live* ball; pertaining to a performance or appearance in person, as contrasted with a recording or film; as, a *live* concert.

live-bear·ing, līv'bâr"ing, *a.* Producing living young; viviparous, as the guppy.

---

ch- chain, G. na*ch*t;   th- THen, thin;   w- wig, hw as sound in whig;   z- zh as in azure, zeal.   *Italicized vowel* indicates schwa sound.

lived, līvd, *a.* Having life or a life as specified, usu. used in compounds; as, long-*lived*.

live-for·ev·er, liv′fèr·ev″èr, *n.* Sedum.

live·li·hood, liv′lē·hụd″, *n.* [Corrupted < O.E. *liflode*, *livelode*, O.E. *lif-lāde*, lit. 'life-leading, lead or course of life'; < *lif*, life, and *lād*, a leading, as in *lode, lode*stone.] Means of maintaining life; support of life; maintenance.

live load, *n. Engin.* the variable weight, as traffic or persons, supported by a structure, apart from the weight of the structure itself.

live·long, liv′lảng″, liv′lȯng″, *a.* Lasting a long time; enduring; entire, esp. when seemingly slow in passing; as, the *livelong* day.

live·ly, līv′lē, *a.*—**live·li·er, live·li·est.** Brisk; vivacious; rousing; active; animated; spirited; strong, energetic, keen; as, a *lively* mind; full of activity; as, a *lively* nightspot; fresh; resilient; bright, as colors.—*adv.* In a lively manner.—**live·li·ly,** *adv.*—**live·li·ness,** *n.*

liv·en, lī′ven, *v.t.* [< *life*.] To put life into; to rouse or cheer, often with *up.*—*v.i.* To become more lively; brighten, usu. with *up.*—**liv·en·er,** *n.*

live oak, *n.* A species of evergreen oak, *Quercus virginiana,* native to the United States and yielding durable, hard wood.

liv·er, liv′èr, *n.* [O.E. *lifer* = D. *lever* = G. *leber* = Icel. *lifr*, liver.] *Anat.* a large, reddish-brown, glandular organ, situated in the upper right-hand side of the abdominal cavity, divided by fissures into several lobes, and which secretes bile and performs various metabolic functions. A similar or analogous organ in other animals; such an organ, or the flesh of one, used as food.

liv·er, liv′èr, *n.* One who lives in a certain manner; as, a frugal *liver*; a resident.

liv·er fluke, liv′èr flōk, *n.* Any of several parasitic worms invading the liver and bile ducts of man and some domestic animals.

liv·er·ied, liv′e·rèd, liv′rèd, *a.* Clad in livery, as servants.

liv·er·ish, liv′èr·ish, *a.* Like liver in color; having a disordered liver; ill-tempered.—**liv·er·ish·ness,** *n.*

liv·er·wort, liv′èr·wụrt″, *n.* Any of the cryptogamic plants of the class *Hepaticae*, comprising mosslike or thalloid plants which grow mainly on damp ground or on tree trunks.

liv·er·wurst, liv′èr·wụrst″, *n.* Liver sausage.

liv·er·y, liv′e·rē, liv′rē, *n. pl.* **liv·er·ies.** [Fr. *livrée*, a giving out, something given out or delivered over, < *livré*, pp. of *livrer*, to deliver, < L. *libero*, to liberate.] The distinctive uniform or attire worn by male servants; the distinctive uniform or other dress worn by officials or members of an organization or group; characteristic covering or outward appearance; as, the *livery* of grief; the care and feeding of horses at a certain rate; the stable which affords such care; *law*, formal delivery, as of property.

liv·er·y, liv′e·rē, *a.* Liverish.

liv·er·y com·pa·ny, *n.* One of several trade associations in London, England, that sprang from the medieval guilds.

liv·er·y·man, liv′e·rē·man, liv′rē·man, *n. pl.* **liv·er·y·men.** *Brit.* one who is entitled to wear a livery, esp. a freeman of the City of London. An owner or employee of a livery stable.

liv·er·y sta·ble, *n.* A stable where horses and carriages are tended or kept for hire.

live steam, *n.* Steam coming fresh from the boiler and with full power for work.

live·stock, liv′stok″, *n.* Domestic animals, as cattle and hogs, bred or kept on a farm for use and commercial profit.

live wire, *n.* A wire carrying a current of electricity; *slang*, an energetic, alert person.

liv·id, liv′id, *a.* [L. *lividus,* < *liveo,* to be black and blue.] Black and blue, as bruised flesh; of a lead or ashen color, as the face; discolored by contusion, as flesh. *Colloq.* enraged; furious.—**li·vid·i·ty, liv·id·ness,** *n.*—**liv·id·ly,** *adv.*

liv·ing, liv′ing, *n.* The act or condition of one who or that which lives; manner or course of life; as, holy *living*; means of maintaining life or livelihood; as, to earn one's *living*; an ecclesiastical office or cure, as a rectory, with revenues included; those alive, preceded by *the.*—*a.* Alive; not dead; in actual existence or use; as, *living* languages; active, vigorous, or strong; as, a *living* faith; burning or glowing, as a coal; lifelike, as a picture; of or pertaining to living beings; as, within *living* memory; pertaining to or sufficient for living; as, *living* conditions, a *living* wage.—**liv·ing·ly,** *adv.*—**liv·ing·ness,** *n.*

liv·ing death, *n.* A life completely emptied of happiness and satisfaction.

liv·ing room, *n.* A room for general family use and social activity; a sitting room; a parlor.

liv·ing wage, *n.* An income sufficient for a wage earner to support himself and his dependents at or above minimum standards.

lix·iv·i·ate, lik·siv′ē·āt″, *v.t.*—**lixiviated, lixiviating.** [L. *lixivium.*] To treat with a lixivium; to leach.—**lix·iv·i·al,** *a.*—**lix·iv·i·a·tion,** *n.*

lix·iv·i·um, lik·siv′ē·um, *n. pl.* **lix·iv·i·ums, lix·iv·i·a.** [L., prop. neut. of *lixivius,* made into lye, < *lix,* ashes, lye.] The solution, containing alkaline salts, obtained by leaching wood ashes; lye; any solution obtained by leaching.

liz·ard, liz′èrd, *n.* [O.Fr. *laisart,* masc., *laisarde,* fem. (Fr. *lézard, lézarde*), < L. *lacertus,* masc., *lacerta,* fem., lizard.] Any of numerous four-legged reptiles of the suborder *Lacertilia,* with an elongated body, tapering tail, and scaly or granular skin, including various allied limbless forms; any of certain similar reptiles, esp. of large size, as the crocodiles or dinosaurs; leather or lizard skin, used for bags, shoes, and the like; (*cap.*), *astron.* the northern constellation Lacerta.

lla·ma, lä′ma, *n.* [Sp.; < Peruvian.] A woolly-haired S. American ruminant mammal of the genus *Lama,* allied to the alpaca, probably a domesticated variety of the guanaco, related to the camel but smaller and without a hump, and used as a beast of burden; the soft, fleecy wool of the llama or a textile made of it.

lla·no, lä′nō, *Sp.* yä′nạ, *n. pl.* **lla·nos,** lä′nōz, *Sp.* yä′nạs. [Sp., a plain, as adj. flat, level, < L. *planus.*] An extensive treeless plain.

Lloyd's, loidz, *n.* [Because the headquarters of the underwriters was orig., from 1688, *Lloyd's* coffeehouse.] A society of underwriters in London, England, at first issuing maritime insurance, and now underwriting various other insurance policies.

lo, lō, *interj.* [O.E. *lá.*] Look; see; behold; observe.

loach, lōch, *n.* [Fr. *loche,* a loach, origin unknown.] A small, fresh-water fish of the family *Cobitidæ,* related to the carp family.

load, lōd, *n.* [Orig. the same word as *lode* (O.E. *lad,* way, course, carrying), but now differentiated in spelling and sense and associated with *lade.*] That which is laid on or placed in anything for conveyance, a burden; the quantity that can be or usu. is carried, as in a cart; this quantity taken as a unit of measure or weight; anything supported or sustained; as, the *load* of fruit on a tree; something that weighs down or oppresses like a burden; the charge of a firearm; *slang,* a sufficient

quantity of liquor drunk to intoxicate. *Mech.* the weight supported by a structure or part; as, a live *load,* a dead *load*; the external resistance overcome by an engine, dynamo, or the like, under a given condition, measured by the power required. *Pl.,* slang, a great quantity or number.—*v.t.* To put a load on or in; to supply abundantly or excessively with something; to weigh down, burden, or oppress; overwhelm with abuse; to charge, as a firearm; to add weight to, as with lead; as, to *load* dice; to place on or in something for conveyance; to heap or pile on something; to take on as a load; as, a vessel *loading* coal.—*v.i.* To put on or take on a load; to load a firearm; to become loaded, burdened, or weighted, as: The bus will *load* quickly.—**load·er,** *n.*

load·ed, lō′did, *a.* Full or weighted down; weighted, as trick or fraudulent dice; containing a charge, as of ammunition; having emotional, irrational overtones, as: Communism is a *loaded* word. Leading; as, a *loaded* question. *Slang,* intoxicated; rich or wealthy.

load·ing, lō′ding, *n.* The act of one who or that which loads; that with which something is loaded; a load; a burden; a charge; *insurance,* a charge added to a premium to permit profit by covering expenses and contingencies.

load line, *n. Naut.* any of several marks on a ship's sides which indicate the proper draft under certain conditions, as the water's salinity and temperature. Also **Plim·soll line,** *Plimsoll mark.*

load·star, lōd′stär″, *n.* Lode star.

load·stone, lōd′stōn″, *n.* Lodestone.

loaf, lōf, *n. pl.* **loaves,** lōvz. [O.E. *hlaf* = G. *laib* = Icel. *hleifr* = Goth. *hlaifs,* loaf, bread.] Bread or cake baked in a mass of definite form; a shaped or molded mass of other food, as of sugar or chopped meat; as, a meat *loaf.*

loaf, lōf, *v.i.* [The verb < the noun *loafer,* G. *läufer,* D. *looper,* one that runs or gads about.] To lounge; to idle away one's time.—*v.t.* To pass or spend in idleness, as time; to spend lazily.—**loaf·er,** lō′fèr, *n.* A lazy person; idler; a shoe for casual wear, similar to a moccasin.

loam, lōm, *n.* [O.E. *lám*; D. *leem,* G. *lehm,* loam, clay, allied to E. *lime,* and prob. L. *limus,* slime, mud.] A rich soil compounded of sand, clay, and organic matter; a mixture of sand, clay, and straw used for molding in iron founding and in plastering; *archaic,* earth or soil.—*v.t.* To cover with loam.—**loam·y,** *a.*

loan, lōn, *n.* [O.E. *lan* (?), *laen,* a loan, < *lihan,* to lend; Icel. *lán,* Dan. *laan,* D. *leen,* a loan; same root as L. *linguo,* to leave.] The act of lending or condition of being lent; that which is lent, esp. a sum of money lent at interest; anything given with return expected.—*v.t., v.i.* To lend.

loan shark, *n. Colloq.* a money lender who charges exorbitant, usu. illegal, rates of interest.

loan trans·la·tion, *n.* The process or procedure of forming compound words and expressions by directly translating from one language to another; as, the German *Überwelt* becomes the American *other-worldly*; any word so derived.

loan word, *n.* [Tr. G. *lehnwort.*] A word borrowed or adopted from another language, as, *gourmet* from the French.

loath, loth, lōth, lōTH, *a.* [O.E. *lath* hateful, odious; Icel. *leithr,* Dan. and Sw. *led,* O.H.G. *leit,* odious.] Very averse; reluctant; unwilling.—**loath·ness,** *n.*

loathe, lōTH, *v.t.*—**loathed, loathing.** [O.E. *láthian,* to hate.] To feel disgust for; to have an extreme aversion toward; to dislike greatly; to abhor.—**loath·er,** *n.*

loath·ful, lōTH'ful, *a. Rare*, loathsome.— **loath·ful·ly**, *adv.*—**loath·ful·ness**, *n.*

loath·ing, lō'THing, *n.* Extreme disgust or aversion; abhorrence, detestation.—**loath·ing·ly**, *adv.*

loath·some, lōTH'som, lōth'som, *a.* Exciting disgust; odious; detestable.—**loath·some·ly**, *adv.*—**loath·some·ness**, *n.*

lob, lob, *v.t.*—*lobbed, lobbing.* [Prob. vaguely imit., as suggesting something thick and heavy.] To throw, hit, or toss in a high arc or curve.—*v.i.* To move heavily or clumsily; to lob an object, as a ball.—*n. Tennis*, a ball struck high to the back of the opponent's court; *cricket*, a slow ball thrown underhand.

lo·bar, lō'bėr, lō'bär, *a.* Of or pertaining to a lobe, as of the lungs.

lo·bate, lō'bāt, *a.* [N.L. *lobatus*.] Having a lobe or lobes; lobed; sometimes, having the form of a lobe; *ornith.* noting or pertaining to a foot in which the individual toes have membranous flaps or lobes along the sides. Also **lo·bat·ed**.—**lo·bate·ly**, *adv.*—**lo·ba·tion**, lō·bā'shan, *n.* Lobate formation; lobe.

lob·by, lob'ē, *n. pl.* **lob·bies.** [L.L. *lobia*, *lobium*, a portico, < O.H.G. *laubja*, G. *laube*, an arbor, < *laub*, a leaf, foliage. *Lodge* is another form of this word.] An entrance hall, a foyer, or an open room used as a waiting room or passageway in a theater, apartment building, or hotel; an anteroom, open to the public, that is connected to a meeting place of a legislature.

lob·by, lob'ē, *n. pl.* **lob·bies.** *U.S. politics*, a person or group of people, representing special interests, who endeavor by personal persuasion to influence legislators' voting policies and other decision making.—*v.i.*—*lobbied, lobbying.* To try to influence legislators.—*v.t.* To influence, as lawmakers; to back or try to secure passage of; as, to *lobby* a bill.—**lob·by·er**, **lob·by·ist**, *n.*—**lob·by·ism**, *n.*

lobe, lōb, *n.* [Fr. *lobe*, < M.L. *lobus*, < Gr. *lobós*, lobe.] A roundish projection or division, as of an organ or leaf; the soft, pendulous lower part of the external ear.—**lobed**, *a.* Having a lobe or lobes; lobate; *bot.* of leaves, having lobes extending from a position at most halfway in from the margin, as a maple leaf.

lo·bel·ia, lō·bēl'ya, *n.* [N.L.; from M. de *Lobel*, 1538–1616, Flem. botanist.] Any of the herbaceous plants of the genus *Lobelia*, in the bluebell family, having irregular blue, red, yellow, or white flowers.

lob·lol·ly, lob'lol"ē, *n. pl.* **lob·lol·lies.** [Cf. *lob* and obs. prov. *lolly*, broth.] *Bot.* loblolly pine; loblolly bay. *Colloq.* a swamp or mudhole.

lob·lol·ly bay, *n.* An ornamental white-flowered shrub or small tree, *Gordonia lasianthus*, of the southern U.S. Also *loblolly*.

lob·lol·ly pine, *n.* A pine, *Pinus taeda*, native to the southeastern U.S., having bright-red fissured bark. Also *loblolly*.

lo·bo, lō'bō, *n. pl.* **lo·bos.** A brownish-gray wolf found in the western U.S.

lo·bot·o·my, lō·bot'o·mē, lō·bot'o·mē, *n. pl.* **lo·bot·o·mies.** *Surg.* a treatment for some psychic disorders involving the cutting of certain nerve fibers in the brain.

lob·scouse, lob'skous, *n.* [Origin obscure: cf. *loblolly*.] *Naut.* a stew made of meat, potatoes, onions, and ship biscuits.

lob·ster, lob'stėr, *n.* [O.E. *loppestre*, < L. *locusta*, lobster, also locust.] Any of various large, edible, marine, stalk-eyed decapod crustaceans of the family *Homaridae* and esp. of the genus *Homarus*, having two enormous claws that are modifications of the first pair of legs; any of various similar crustaceans, as the spiny lobster; the flesh of these crustaceans used as food.

lob·ster New·burg, lob·ster New·burgh, *n.* (*Sometimes l.c.*) a dish consisting of lobster meat cooked with a cream sauce, egg yolks, cayenne, and wine, and usu. poured over hot rice, noodles, or toast.

lob·ster pot, *n.* An oblong trap, usu. with wooden slats for sides, used for catching lobsters.

lob·ster ther·mi·dor, *n.* A dish, combining cooked lobster meat with a seasoned cream sauce, mushrooms, grated cheese, and wine, poured back into a lobster shell, browned, and served.

lob·ule, lob'ūl, *n.* [N.L. *lobulus*, dim. of M.L. *lobus*, E. *lobe*.] A small lobe; a subdivision of a lobe.—**lob·u·lar, lob·u·lose**, *a.*

lob·worm, lob'wụrm", *n.* The lugworm.

lo·cal, lō'kal, *a.* [L. *localis*, < *locus*, a place, seen also in *lieu*, *lieutenant*, *allocate*, *collocate*, *couch*, *allow*, etc.] Pertaining to a particular place; as, a *local* event; limited or confined to a spot, place, or definite district; as, a *local* newspaper; *med.* confined to a particular part or organ; as, a *local* infection. Pertaining to a particular segment of an organization; as, *local* union, chapter one; making a stop at every station along the way; as, a *local* train.—*n.* One living or employed in a particular place or district; a local segment of an organization; a means of conveyance, as a bus or train, that stops at every station on the route; a newspaper item of interest only to those located in a particular district.—**lo·cal·ly**, *adv.*—**lo·cal·ness**, *n.*

lo·cal col·or, *n.* Distinctive characteristics or peculiarities of a place or period, as represented in literature or observed in reality.

lo·cale, lō·kal', lō·käl', *n.* [Fr. *local*, a locality, the *e* being erroneous as in *morale*.] A place, esp. with reference to its characteristics or an event related to it; as, a cooler *locale*; the setting for a drama or for a work of literature or art.

lo·cal gov·ern·ment, *n.* The administration of the local affairs of a town or district by its inhabitants, rather than by the state or country at large.

lo·cal·ism, lō'ka·liz"um, *n.* A local idiom or peculiarity of speech; a local custom; excessive interest in or devotion toward a certain town or area.

lo·cal·i·ty, lō·kal'i·tē, *n. pl.* **lo·cal·i·ties.** A position, situation, place, or district; a geographical place or situation; the fact of being local.

lo·cal·ize, lō'ka·liz", *v.t.*—*localized, localizing.* To fix in or assign to a particular place; to discover or detect the place of; to check, control, or restrict, as an infection from spreading to other areas of the body.—*v.i.*—**lo·cal·i·za·tion**, lō'kal·i·zā'shan, *n.*

lo·cal op·tion, *n.* A right of choice exercised by a minor political division, esp. concerning the sale of liquor within its limits.

lo·cate, lō'kāt, lō·kāt', *v.t.*—*located, locating.* [L. *loco, locatum*.] To set in a particular spot or position; to place; to ascertain the whereabouts of; to pinpoint, as a cause; to point out something, as on a map, chart, or in a book; to ascribe a place to.—*v.i.* To settle; to open and operate a business in a place.

lo·ca·tion, lō·kā'shan, *n.* The act of locating; the place where one settles; a site, with respect to its environment; place taken by; as, one's *location* in line; *motion picture industry*, *TV*, an area extraneous to the studio which provides the setting for a production, preceded by *on*.

loc·a·tive, lok'a·tiv, *a. Gram.* in certain inflected languages, indicating place; as, a *locative* adjective or a *locative* case.—*n.* The locative case; a word so inflected.

lo·ca·tor, lō'kā·tėr, lō·kā'tėr, *n. U.S.* an individual who locates boundaries, as of a mining claim or land. An instrument for determining position of aircraft during flight.

loch, lok, lo*ch*, *n.* [Gael.; allied to *lake*.] *Sc.* A lake; an arm of the sea running into the land, esp. if narrow or almost landlocked.

lock, lok, *n.* [O.E. *locc* = D. and Dan. *lok*, Icel. *lokkr*, G. *locke*, a curl or ringlet.] A tuft of hair; a tress; a ringlet; a tuft of wool, or the like; *pl.* the hair on one's head.

lock, lok, *n.* [O.E. *loc*, fastening; < the root of O.E. *lūcan*, D. *luiken*, Icel. *lūka*, Goth. *galūkan*, shut, close.] A contrivance for fastening or securing something; a device for securing a door, gate, drawer, or the like, in position when closed, and consisting of a bolt or system of bolts propelled and withdrawn by a mechanism operated by a key or other device; also, a contrivance to keep a wheel from rotating, as in descending a hill. The mechanism in a firearm by means of which the charge is exploded; an enclosed portion of a canal or river, with gates at each end, for raising or lowering vessels from one level to another; an airtight chamber, or one of a series of such chambers, used in entering or leaving a compartment in which the air pressure is above normal; any of various grapples or holds in wrestling.—**lock, stock, and bar·rel**, entirely, totally, or completely.—**lock·a·ble**, *a.*—**lock·less**, *a.*

lock, lok, *v.t.* To fasten, as a door or gate, by the operation of a lock; to secure by so fastening doors, gates, or the like; as, to *lock* the building; to shut in a place fastened by a lock, as for security or restraint, often followed by *up*; as, to *lock up* the prisoner; to enclose, surround, or hem in, as: The vessel was *locked* in ice. To hold fast in some condition, as: She was *locked* in sleep. To exclude by or as by a lock, as: He was *locked* out of the house. To join or unite firmly by interlinking or intertwining; as, to *lock* hands together; to embrace closely, as: They were *locked* in each other's arms. To move, as a vessel, by means of a lock or locks, as in a canal.—*v.i.* To become locked, as: This door *locks* with a key. Become fastened, fixed, or interlocked; to go or pass by means of a lock or locks, as a vessel; to build locks for a waterway.

lock·age, lok'ij, *n.* The construction, use, or operation of locks, as in a canal or stream; the passing of a vessel through a lock or locks; the amount of elevation and descent effected by a lock or system of locks; toll paid for passage through a lock or locks.

lock·er, lok'ėr, *n.* A chest, drawer, compartment, closet, or the like, that may be locked; one who or that which locks; *naut.* a chest or compartment in which to stow things.

lock·er room, *n.* A room, as in a gymnasium, with lockers for storing clothes and other belongings.

lock·et, lok'it, *n.* [Fr. *loquet*, latch, catch, dim. of O.Fr. *loc*, lock, < Teut., and akin to E. *lock*.] A small case for holding a miniature portrait, a lock of hair, or other keepsake, and worn as an ornament, often on a necklace.

lock·jaw, lok'ja", *n. Pathol.* a form of tetanus which causes the jaws to become locked together. Also *trismus*.

lock nut, lock·nut, *n. Mach.* A nut so constructed that it cannot work itself loose; a supplementary nut applied to keep a regular nut secure.

lock·out, lok'out", *n.* The closing of a place of work against the workmen on the part of the employers, in order to bring the men to terms as to hours, wages, or the like.—*v.t.* To prevent, as employees, from entering a place of work.

lock·smith, lok′smith″, *n.* A mechanic whose occupation is to make or repair locks.

lock step, *n.* A marching step used by a file of men to keep as close as possible to one another.

lock stitch, *n.* A sewing machine stitch in which two threads are locked together at the beginning and end of each stitch.

lock·up, lok′up″, *n.* The act of locking up, or the state of being locked up; a place for the temporary detention of persons under arrest; a jail; *Brit. colloq.* a rented garage or storage space that can be locked.

lo·co, lō′kō, *a.* [Sp.] *Slang.* Insane; crazy.— *n.* Locoweed; *veter. pathol.* loco disease or locoism.—*v.t.* To poison with locoweed; *slang*, to make crazy.

Lo·co·fo·co, lō″kō·fō′kō, *n.* [A made name for a self-lighting cigar or match, said to be < *loco-* in *locomotive* (erron. supposed to mean 'self-moving') and L. *focus*, hearth, fireplace.]*U.S. hist.* A member of the radical or 'equal rights' faction of the Democratic party in New York State about 1835; any Democrat of that period, used disparagingly.

lo·co·ism, lō′kō·iz″um, *n.* A disease of horses, sheep, and cattle, caused by loco-weed poisoning. Also *loco, lo·co dis·ease.*

lo·co·mo·tion, lō″ko·mō′shan, *n.* [L. *locus*, place, and *motio*, motion.] The act or power of moving from place to place.

lo·co·mo·tive, lō″ko·mō′tiv, *a.* [L. *loco*, abl. of *locus*, place, and M.L. *motivus*, E. *motive*.] Of or pertaining to movement from place to place; as, the *locomotive* faculty, *locomotive* power; serving to produce such movement, or adapted for or used in locomotion; as, *locomotive* organs; moving from place to place by its own powers of locomotion, as an animal; traveling from place to place; moving or traveling by means of its own mechanism, as a machine or vehicle.—*n.* A self-propelled engine used for moving trains. An organized cheer, as at a football or basketball game, which starts slowly and increases progressively in speed.—**lo·co·- mo·tive·ness**, *n.*

lo·co·mo·tor, lō″ko·mō′tèr, *n.* [L. *loco*, abl. of *locus*, place, and *motor*, E. *motor*.] One who or that which has locomotive power.—*a.* Of or pertaining to locomotion. Also **lo·co·mo·to·ry.**

lo·co·mo·tor a·tax·i·a, *n.* *Pathol.* a disease of the spinal cord caused by syphilis, marked by intense pain, difficulty in coordination and walking, and eventually paralysis.

lo·co·weed, lō′kō·wēd″, *n.* Any of various plants of the legume family, genera *Astragalus* and *Oxytropis*, found in southwestern U.S., and producing loco disease. See *locoism.*

loc·u·late, lok′ū·lāt″, lok′ū·lit, *a.* *Biol.* having, composed of, or divided into loculi or cells. Also **loc·u·lat·ed, loc·u·lar.** —**loc·u·la·tion**, lok″ū·lā′shan, *n.*

loc·u·lus, lok′ū·lus, *n.* pl. **loc·u·li**, lok′ū·lī″. *Zool.* a small chamber, cavity, or cell. *Bot.* a chamber of an ovary that contains the seed; a chamber of an anther that contains the pollen of a plant; also **loc·ule.** A recess or small chamber for placing urns or corpses in an ancient catacomb or sepulcher.

lo·cum te·nens, lō′kum tē′nenz, lō′kum ten′inz, *n.* pl. **lo·cum te·nen·tes**, lō′kum tē′nen·tēz. [L.] *Brit.* one who substitutes temporarily, as for a physician or clergyman. Also **lo·cum.**— **lo·cum-te·nen·cy**, lō′kum·tē′nen·sē, lō″kum·ten′en·sē, *n.*

lo·cus, lō′kus, *n.* pl. **lo·ci, lo·ca**, lō′sī, lō′ka. [L., place.] A place; locality. *Math.* a curve or other figure considered as generated by a moving point, line, or surface; the set of or figure consisting of all points, lines, or surfaces that satisfy a given condition. *Genetics*, the location of a gene linearly on a chromosome.

lo·cust, lō′kust, *n.* [L. *locusta*, locust, also lobster: cf. *lobster*.] Any of the grasshoppers with short antennae which constitute the family *Acrididae*, certain species of which migrate in large numbers, destroying vegetation; any of various cicadas, as the seventeen-year locust. *Bot.* a thorny-branched, white-flowered American legume tree, *Robinia pseudo-acacia*, or its durable wood; any of various other trees, as the honey locust, *Gleditsia triacanthos.*—**lo·- cust·like**, *a.*

lo·cu·tion, lō·kū′shan, *n.* [L. *locutio(n-)*, < *loqui*, speak.] A particular form of expression; phrase; a style of speech or verbal expression; phraseology.

lode, lōd, *n.* [O.E. *lād*, way, course, carrying = O.H.G. *leita*, procession, = Icel. *leidh*, way, course; < a Teut. verb, O.E. *līthan*, O.H.G. *līdan*, Icel. *līdha*, Goth. *-leithan*, meaning 'go,' whence also E. *lead.*] *Mineral.* A veinlike metalliferous deposit; any body of ore with more or less definite boundaries separating it from the surrounding rocks.

lo·den cloth, lōd′en klath, *n.* A woolen cloth, thick and waterproof, used for heavy outer wear. Also **lo·den.**

lode·star, lōd′stär, *n.* A star that shows the way, esp. the North Star; something that serves as a guiding principle; that on which the attention is fixed. Also *loadstar.*

lode·stone, lōd′stōn″, *n.* The mineral, magnetite, which possesses magnetic polarity and attracts iron; a piece of this serving as a magnet; *fig.* something that attracts. Also *loadstone.*

lodge, loj, *v.t.*—**lodged, lodging.** [O.Fr. *logier*, Fr. *loger*, < *loge.*] To furnish with a habitation or quarters, esp. temporarily; to furnish with a room or rooms in one's house for payment; to have as a lodger; to serve as a habitation or shelter for; to shelter; to harbor; to put or deposit, as in a place, for storage or keeping; to bring or send into a particular place or position, as: The bullet *lodged* in his heart. To contain or enclose; to vest, as with power; to lay, as information or a complaint, before a court or similar authority; to beat down or lay flat, as vegetation in a storm; to track, as a deer, to its lair.—*v.i.* To have a habitation or quarters, esp. temporarily, as in a house or hotel; to live in hired quarters in another's house; to be fixed or implanted in a place or position.—**lodg·er**, *n.*

lodge, loj, *n.* [O.Fr. Fr. *loge*, orig. 'leafy shelter'; < Teut., and akin to E. *leaf* and *lobby.*] A small or rude shelter or habitation; an American Indian family unit or its habitation; a cabin or hut; a house used as a temporary abode, as in the hunting season; a house or cottage, as in a park or on an estate, occupied by a caretaker, gardener, or the like; a resort inn or hotel; the habitation of an animal, esp. of a beaver or muskrat. The meeting place of a branch of a fraternal or secret society; the members composing the branch; a secret society as a whole.—**lodge·a·ble**, *a.*

lodg·ing, loj′ing, *n.* A place of abode, esp. a temporary one; accommodation in a house, esp. in rooms for hire; *pl.* a room or rooms hired for residence in another's house. Also *Brit. diggings*, **digs.**

lodg·ing house, *n.* A house in which lodgings are rented, esp. a house other than an inn or hotel.

lodg·ment, lodge·ment, loj′ment, *n.* The act of lodging, or the state of being lodged; a lodging place; something lodged or deposited; *milit.* a position or foothold gained from an enemy or an entrenchment made upon it.

lod·i·cule, lod′i·kūl, *n.* [L. *lodicula*, a coverlet.] *Bot.* one of the scales which occur at the base of the fruit of grasses.

lo·ess, lō′es, les, lus, G. lœs, *n.* [G. *löss.*] A loamy deposit formed by wind, yellowish and calcareous, common in Europe, Asia, and the Mississippi valley.—**lo·ess·i·al**, lō·es′ē·al, les′ē·al, lus′ē·al, *a.*

loft, laft, loft, *n.* [O.E. *loft*, from Scand.: cf. Icel. *lopt*, the air, sky, an upper room, and E. *lift.*] A floor or room above another, esp. that directly beneath the roof, as an attic; an apartment over a stable used for storage; a hayloft; a gallery in a church or hall, as for a choir; any upper story of a warehouse, mercantile building, or factory. *Golf*, the slope of the face of a club backward from the vertical, tending to drive the ball upward; the act of driving the ball upward.—*v.t. Golf*, To give loft to, as a golf club; to hit upward, as a golf ball; to go over or clear, as an obstacle.—*v.i.* To hit or propel something upward into the air.—**loft·less**, *a.*

loft·ing i·ron, *n. Golf*, an ironheaded club with a sloped face, used in lofting the ball. Also **loft·er.**

loft·y, laf′tē, lof′tē, *a.*—*loftier, loftiest.* [< *loft, aloft.*] Extremely high; tall; elevated in condition or character; dignified; proud; haughty; elevated in language or style; sublime; stately.—**loft·i·ly**, *adv.*— **loft·i·ness**, *n.*

log, lag, log, *n.* [Icel. *lag*, a felled tree; D., Dan., and G. *log*, the nautical log; akin *lie, lay.*] A bulky piece of unhewed timber either from a branch or tree trunk; *fig.* anything inert or senseless; *naut.* a contrivance for measuring the rate of a ship's velocity through the water. A record or account, as of ship and aircraft travel, motion picture shooting, or radio and television transmission.—*v.t.* To cut or chop into logs; to chop down the timber in; as, to *log* the forest; to record or account for; as, to *log* the night's events. —*v.i.* To chop down and transport trees; as, to *log* in the western mountains.

log, lag, log, *n.* Logarithm.

lo·gan·ber·ry, lō′gan·ber″ē, *n.* pl. **lo·- gan·ber·ries.** [From J. H. *Logan*, 1841– 1928, the originator.] *Bot.* The red fruit of the bramble, *Rubus ursinus* variety *loganobaccus*, related to the blackberry; the plant itself.

log·a·oe·dic, la″ga·ē′dik, log″a·ē′dik, *a.* [L.L. *logaoedicus*, < Gr. *logaoidikós*, < *logós*, speech, prose, and *aóide*, song.] *Pros.* composed of dactyls and trochees or of anapaests and iambs, producing a movement somewhat suggestive of prose; as, *logaoedic* verse.—*n.* A logaoedic verse.

log·a·rithm, la′ga·riTH″um, la′ga·riTH″um, log′a·rith″um, log″a·rith″um, *n.* [N.L. *logarithmus*, < Gr. *lógos*, and *árithmós*, number.] *Math.* the exponent or power to which a fixed number, called the *base*, must be raised in order to produce a given number, called the *antilogarithm*. Also *log*.—**log·a·rith·mic, log·a·rith·mi·cal**, la″ga·riTH′mik, la′ga·rith″mik, log″a·riTH′- mik, log″a·rith′mik, *a.*—**log·a·rith·mi· cal·ly**, *adv.*

log·book, lag′buk″, log′buk″, *n.* A book which contains the record of a journey of a ship or aircraft; any journal of an advancement or achievement.

loge, lōzh, *n.* [Fr.: cf. *lodge.*] A booth or similar enclosure; a box in a theater or opera house; the front section of the first balcony, isolated by a partition or railing.

logged, lạgd, logd, *a.* Referring to something sluggish or weighty which affects movement; permeated with moisture; waterlogged.

log·ger, lạ'gẽr, log'ẽr, *n.* One engaged in logging, a lumberjack; a machine for loading logs; a tractor employed in logging.

log·ger·head, lọ'gẽr·hed", log'ẽr·hed", *n.* [Cf. *log.*] A thickheaded or stupid person; a blockhead; a heated ball of iron with a long handle, used to melt tar or heat liquids; *naut.* a post in the stern of a whaleboat, around which the harpoon line is passed; *zool.* a large-headed marine turtle, *Caretta caretta,* of the Atlantic Ocean. *Ornith.* an American shrike, *Lanius ludovicianus;* also **log·ger·head shrike.—at log·ger·heads,** contending over differences of opinion; engaged in dispute.—**log·ger·head·ed,** *a.*

log·gia, loj'a, lạ'jē·a, *It.* lạd'jä, *n.* pl. **log·gias,** *It.* **log·gie,** *It.* lạd'jē. [It., = E. *lodge.*] A gallery or arcade in a building, open to the air on at least one side.

log·ic, loj'ik, *n.* [O.Fr. *logique,* < M.L. *logica,* < Gr. *logike,* prop. fem. of *logikos,* pertaining to reason, < *logos,* reason.] The science of formal reasoning, using principles of valid inference; a system of reasoning or argumentation; the system or principles of reasoning applicable to a particular branch of knowledge or study; convincing force; as, the irresistible *logic* of facts; the apparently unavoidable cause and effect relationship of events leading to a particular conclusion; reason or sound sense, as in speech or action.—**lo·gi·cian,** *n.* A person skilled in logic.

log·i·cal, loj'i·kal, *a.* Of or pertaining to logic; as, *logical* terms; according to the principles of logic; as, *logical* reasoning; reasonable, or reasonably to be expected, as: War was the *logical* consequence. Reasoning in accordance with the principles of logic.—**log·i·cal·i·ty,** loj"i·kal'i·tē, *n.* —**log·i·cal·ly,** *adv.*—**log·i·cal·ness,** *n.*

log·i·cal pos·i·tiv·ism, *n.* An early 20th century movement in philosophy holding that the only two types of statements that could have a truth value are analytic statements and statements that can in principle be verified by the data of sense perception, and all metaphysical, ethical, and esthetic statements are without truth value. Also **log·i·cal em·pir·i·cism.**

lo·gi·on, lō'gē·on", lō'jē·on", log'ē·on", *n.* pl. **lo·gi·ons,** **lo·gi·a,** lō'gē·a, lō'jē·a, log'ē·a. [Gr. *logion,* announcement, oracle, < *logos,* speech.] A traditional saying or maxim, as of a religious teacher. (*Sometimes cap.*) a saying of Jesus, esp. one contained in collections supposed to have been among the sources of the present Gospels, or a saying ascribed to Jesus but not recorded in the Gospels.

lo·gis·tic, lō·jis'tik, *a.* [Gr. *logisticos,* < *logizesthai,* reckon, calculate, < *logos,* account, reckoning.] Pertaining to reckoning or calculation; pertaining to military logistics. Also **lo·gis·ti·cal.**—**lo·gis·ti·cal·ly,** *adv.*

lo·gis·tics, lō·jis'tiks, *n.* pl. but sing. in constr. The branch of military science concerned with the procurement, transportation, maintenance, and supply of troops, equipment, and facilities.—**lo·gis·ti·cian,** lō"ji·stish'an, *n.*

log·jam, lạg'jam", log'jam", *n.* A group of logs which have wedged together in a river or stream; any barrier, impediment, or deadlock.

log·o·gram, lạ'go·gram", log'o·gram", *n.* A symbol or abbreviation representing a frequently used word or group of words, as ¢ used for *cents.* Also *logograph.*—**log·o·gram·mat·ic,** lạ"go·gra·mat"ik, log"o-

gra·mat'ik, *a.*—**log·o·gram·mat·i·cal·ly,** *adv.*

log·o·graph, lạ'go·graf", lạ'go·gräf", log'-o·graf", log'o·gräf", *n.* Logogram.—**log·o·graph·ic,** lạ"go·graf'ik, log"o·graf'ik, *a.* —**log·o·graph·i·cal·ly,** *adv.*

lo·gog·ra·phy, lō·gog'ra·fē, *n. Print.* the usage of logotypes; also **log·o·typ·y,** lạ'go·tīp"ē. A method of reporting without stenography, each of several reporters in succession taking down a few words.

log·o·griph, lạ'go·grif", log'o·grif", *n.* [Fr. *logogriphe,* < Gr. *logos,* word, and *griphos,* fishing basket, riddle.] A puzzle in which a certain word, and other words formed from any or all of its letters, must be guessed from indications given in a set of verses; an anagram; a puzzle involving anagrams.

lo·gom·a·chy, lō·gom'a·kē, *n.* pl. **lo·gom·a·chies.** [Gr. *logos,* word, and *mache,* contest.] A contention about words; verbal dispute; any of various word formation games.—**lo·gom·a·chist,** *n.*

log·or·rhe·a, lạ"go·rē'a, log"o·rē'a, *n. Pathol.* a condition marked by excessive and incoherent talkativeness.

Lo·gos, lō'gos, lō'gōs, log'os, *n.* [Gr. *logos,* word, speech, also reason, account, reckoning, proportion, < *legein,* speak.] *Theol.* Jesus Christ, the Divine Word (John i. 1–14.), the second person of the Trinity; (*l.c.*), *philos.* the supreme reason that pervades the structure and development of the universe.

log·o·type, lạ'go·tīp", log'o·tīp", *n. Typog.* a single type bearing two or more distinct letters, a syllable, or word.

log·roll, lạg'rōl", log'rōl", *v.t.* [Back formation from *logrolling.*] To promote successfully the passage of, as a bill, by logrolling.—*v.i.* To engage in political logrolling.—**log·roll·er,** *n.*

log·roll·ing, lạg'rō"ling, log'rō"ling, *n.* The practice, esp. among legislators, of trading votes or favors for mutual political profit; the action of rolling logs to a particular place; birling.

log·wood, lạg'wụd", log'wụd", *n. Bot.* the heavy, brownish-red heartwood of a W. Indian and Central American tree, *Hæma, toxylon campechianum,* used in dyeing and histological work.

lo·gy, lō'gē, *a.*—**logier, logiest.** [? < *log,* heavy, inert.] *Colloq.* Heavy; sluggish; dull.

loin, loin, *n.* [O.Fr. *loigne, longe* (Fr. *longe*), < L. *lumbus,* loin.] *Usu. pl.* the part or parts of the body of man or of most quadrupeds, on either side of the vertebral column between the false ribs and the hipbone; in Biblical and poetic use, the part of the body which should be clothed, or which is regarded as the seat of physical strength and generative power. A cut of meat from the loin of an animal, esp. a portion including the vertebrae of such parts.

loin·cloth, loin'klạth", *n.* A piece of cloth worn about the loins or hips, and often passing between the thighs, commonly worn by natives of warm countries as the only garment.

loi·ter, loi'tẽr, *v.i.* [M.E. < Dutch: cf. mod. D. *leuteren,* wabble, trifle, loiter.] To linger idly or aimlessly in or about a place or on one's way; to move or go in a slow or lagging manner; as, to *loiter* along; to waste time or dawdle over work.—*v.t.* To pass, as time, in an idle or aimless manner, usu. followed by *away;* as, to *loiter away* the hours.—**loi·ter·er,** *n.*

loll, lol, *v.i.* [Akin to Icel. *lulla,* to loll, *lalla,* to toddle as a child.] To recline in a lax, lazy manner; to lounge; to hang extended loosely, as the tongue of a dog.—*v.t.* To let hang or droop.—*n.* The act of lounging; one who lolls.

lol·li·pop, lol·ly·pop, lol'ē·pop", *n.* [< *loll,* to protrude the tongue, and *pop,* probably same as *pap,* infants' food.] A hard candy that is sucked rather than chewed, and is on a short stick. Also *sucker.*

lol·lop, lol'op, *v.i.* [Extended form of *loll.*] *Brit. dial.* To loll or lounge; to bob, or go with a bounding motion.

Lom·bard, lom'bẽrd, lom'bärd, lum'bẽrd, lum'bärd, *n.* [O.Fr. Fr. *Lombard,* < L. *Langobardi, Longobardi,* pl.; < Teut.] A member of a 6th century Germanic tribe which settled in Lombardy, a part of northern Italy; one of the descendants of this tribe; a native or inhabitant of Lombardy.—**Lom·bar·dic,** *a.*

Lom·bard Street, *n.* A street in London, England, famous as a financial center; the London money market.

Lom·bard·y pop·lar, lom'bẽr·dē pop'lẽr, lum'bẽr·dē pop'lẽr, *n.* A variety of black poplar, *Populus nigra italica,* with upward-pointing branches lying close to the tapering trunk.

lo·ment, lō'ment, *n. Bot.* a dry indehiscent fruit, occurring in certain legumes, which separates at maturity into segments, each segment containing one seed. Also **lo·men·tum,** lō·men'tụm, pl. **lo·men·ta.**—**lo·men·ta·ceous,** lō"men·tā'shus, *a.* Bearing or pertaining to loments.

lone, lōn, *a.* [Contr. from *alone.*] Solitary; without any companion; unfrequented; not having others near; without a spouse.—**lon·er,** *n.* A person who chooses to be alone.

lone·ly, lōn'lē, *a.*—**lonelier, loneliest.** Unfrequented by man; deserted; not having others near; apart from fellows or companions; sad from want of companionship or sympathy; characterized by sadness, desolation, or the feeling of emptiness; as, a *lonely* beach.—**lone·li·ly,** *adv.*—**lone·li·ness,** *n.*

lone·some, lōn'som, *a.* Depressed or forlorn due to a lack of company; causing such depression; lonely; isolated.—**by one's lone·some,** *colloq.* all by oneself.—**lone·some·ly,** *adv.*—**lone·some·ness,** *n.*

long, lạng, long, *a.* [O.E. *lang, long,* = D. and G. *lang* = Icel. *langr* = Goth. *laggs,* long; akin to L. *longus,* long.] Having considerable extent; not short; as, a *long* distance; unusually great in proportion; as a *long* arm; having considerable or great extent in duration; as, a *long* while; having considerable or great extension from beginning to end; having many items, as a series, enumeration, or the like; not brief; having a specified extension in space, duration, quantity, or the like; as five miles *long;* beyond the normal or standard quantity, space, or duration; as, a *long* ton, a ton of 2240 pounds; extending to a great distance in space or time; as, a *long* memory; lengthy; as, a *long* book; tedious; having a long time to run, as a promissory note; *chiefly law,* distant or remote in time; as, a *long* date; *pros., phon.* occupying a relatively long time in utterance, as the sounds of *a, e, i, o, u* in the words *fate, me, pine, note, lute; gambling,* unlikely to win; as, a *long* chance; *colloq.* tall; *finance,* well supplied, as with some commodity or stock, hence, depending for profit on a rise in prices.—*n.* Something that is long; a long time; as, before *long;* a garment size for tall men; *pros., phon.* a long sound or syllable; *finance,* one who purchases stocks or commodities expecting a rise in prices.—*adv.* For or through a great extent of space or time; as, a reform *long* advocated; for a specified period or time, as: How *long* did he stay? Throughout the entire time; as, all summer *long;* at a point of time far distant from the time indicated; as, *long* before.—**in the long run,** after a long course or experience; in the final result.—**so long as, as long as,** provided that.

long, lạng, long, *v.i.* [O.E. *langian*, to lengthen, to long, < *lang*, long; similarly, Icel. *langa*, G. *verlangen*, to wish for.] To desire earnestly or eagerly, usu. followed by an infinitive, or by *for* or *after.*

long·boat, lạng′bōt″, long′bōt″, *n. Naut.* the largest and strongest boat that was carried by a sailing ship.

long·bow, lạng′bō″, long′bō″, *n.* An old English archer's weapon, measuring about six feet long, and drawn by hand.—**draw the long bow,** to exaggerate; to tell improbable stories.

long dis·tance, *n.* The service handling telephone calls between distant areas.—**long-dis·tance,** lạng′dis′tans, long′dis′-tans, *a., adv.* Connecting far places; over a long way.

long di·vi·sion, *n. Math.* division, usu. by a number having at least two digits, in which all the steps of the arithmetical process are indicated in writing.

long doz·en, *n.* Thirteen.

lon·ge·ron, lon′jẽr·on, *n.* [Fr.] *Aeron.* a main longitudinal brace or support on an airplane.

lon·gev·i·ty, lon·jev′i·tē, *n.* [L. *longaevitas.*] Long life; length or duration of life; length of tenure or duration of service.—**lon·ge·vous,** lon·jē′vus, *a.* Long-lived.

long green, *n. Slang,* paper money.

long·hair, lạng′hâr′, long′hâr′, *n. Colloq.* An intellectual; a performer or devotee of the arts, esp. of classical music; classical music.—*a.* Characteristic of a longhair or what appeals to him; relating to classical music. Also **long-hair, long-haired.**

long·hand, lạng′hand″, long′hand″, *n.* The ordinary written characters used in handwriting, with the words completely written out.—*a.*

long·head, lạng′hed″, long′hed″, *n. Anthropol.* A head having a low cephalic index; a person who is dolichocephalic.—**long·head·ed,** *a. Anthropol.* dolichocephalic. Shrewd; far-seeing; discerning.—**long·head·ed·ly,** *adv.*—**long·head·ed·ness,** *n.*

long·horn, lạng′hạrn″, long′hạrn″, *n.* A type of cattle having long horns, introduced from Spain into southwestern U.S. about the 16th century; also **Tex·as long·horn.** (*Usu. cap.*), *slang,* a Texan.

long·horn, lạng′hạrn″, long′hạrn″, *n.* A Cheddar cheese in the shape of a cylinder.

long-horned bee·tle, lạng′hạrnd″ bēt′l, long′hạrnd″, *n. Entom.* one of the beetles of the family *Cerambycidae,* characterized by long cylindrical antennae and, often, brightly-colored bodies, being voracious woodborers in the larval stage, destructive to fruit and forest trees. Also **long·horn.**

long-horned grass·hop·per, lạng′hạrnd″ gras′hop″ẽr, long′hạrnd″ gräs′hop″ẽr, *n. Entom.* any of the insects belonging to the family *Tettigoniidae,* including the katydids, characterized by their long hairlike antennae, stridulating organs which make them noted singers, and auditory organs located at the base of the front tibia.

long house, *n.* A communal dwelling or council meeting house of the Iroquois or other N. American Indians.

lon·gi·corn, lon′ji·kạrn″, *a.* [N.L. *longicornis,* < L. *longus,* long, and *cornu,* horn.] *Entom.* Having long antennae; belonging to the family *Cerambycidae.*—*n.* A longicorn beetle.

long·ing, lạng′ing, long′ing, *n.* An earnest or persistent desire; a yearning.—*a.* Having or marked by such a desire.—**long·ing·ly,** *adv.*

lon·gi·tude, lon′ji·tōd″, lon′ji·tūd″, *n.* [L. *longitudo* (*longitudin-*), length, < *longus,* long.] *Geog.* distance east or west on the earth's surface, measured by the angle contained between the meridian of a particular place and some prime meridian,

as that of Greenwich, England: expressed in degrees or in hours and minutes. *Astron.* the arc of the ecliptic measured eastward from the vernal equinoctial point to the foot of the circle of latitude drawn through the object, as a star whose position is in question.—**lon·gi·tu·di·nal,** lon″ji·tōd′i·-nal, lon″ji·tūd′i·nal, *a.* Of or pertaining to longitude or length; as, *longitudinal* distance, *longitudinal* measure; extending in the direction of the length of a thing; as, a flag with *longitudinal* stripes; running lengthwise; *zool.* pertaining to or extending along the long axis of the body, or the direction from front to back, or head to tail.—**lon·gi·tu·di·nal·ly,** *adv.*

long jump, *n. Chiefly Brit.* broad jump.

long-leaf pine, lạng′lēf pīn′, long′lēf, *n.* A tall tree, *Pinus palustris,* with orange-brown bark, native to the southern U.S., and a source of lumber and turpentine.

long-lived, lạng′livd′, long′līvd′, lạng′livd′, long′livd′, *a.* Having a long life or existence; lasting long.—**long-lived·ness,** *n.*

long pig, *n.* [From a term used by Maori and Polynesian people.] Human flesh prepared and eaten at a cannibal feast.

long-play·ing, lạng′plā′ing, long′plā′ing, *a.* Indicating a phonograph record which is 10 or 12 inches in diameter and plays at 33⅓ revolutions per minute.

long-range, lạng′rānj′, long′rānj′, *a.* Relating to extended distances or long periods of future time.

long·shore·man, lạng′shōr″man, lạng′-shōr′man, long′shōr″man, long′shōr′man, *n. pl.* **long·shore·men.** A dock laborer employed at loading and unloading freight carried on ships.

long shot, *n.* Any undertaking offering little hope of success but great gains if achieved; *gambling,* a bet, as on a race horse, at great odds, with a poor chance of winning.—**not by a long shot,** *colloq.* Not at all; decidedly out of the question.

long-sight·ed, lạng′sī′tid, long′sī′tid, *a.* Far-sighted; hypermetropic. Having great foresight; foreseeing remote results.—**long-sight·ed·ness,** *n.*

long·some, lạng′som, long′som, *a.* Tiresome on account of length; tedious.—**long·some·ly,** *adv.*—**long·some·ness,** *n.*

long·spur, lạng′spụr″, long′spụr″, *n. Ornith.* any of several species of cold-weather birds belonging to the *Fringillidae* or finch family, characterized by a sparrowlike appearance and a long spurlike hind claw on each foot, and inhabiting the Arctic tundra and prairies of N. America.

long-suf·fer·ing, lạng′suf′ẽr·ing, long′-suf′ẽr·ing, *a.* Bearing injuries or provocation for a long time; patient; not easily provoked.—*n.* Patience or long endurance of adversity or offense. Also *archaic,* **suf·fer·ance.**—**long-suf·fer·ing·ly,** *adv.*

long suit, *n. Cards,* the suit in which one holds the largest number of cards. The quality or activity in which one is superior or especially proficient.

long-term, lạng′tụrm″, long′tụrm″, *a.* Having a relatively long duration; as, a *long-term* contract.

Long Tom, *n.* A long-range field gun; formerly, a long gun or cannon mounted on warships.

lon·gueur, lạng′gụr′, long′gụr′, Fr. lạn̄·-gœr′, *n.* [Fr., lit. 'length,' < *long,* < L. *longus,* long.] A long or tedious passage, as in a book or play.

long-wind·ed, lạng′win′did, long′win′did, *a.* Talking or writing, or continuing to, at a tedious length; capable of prolonged exertion without being out of breath.—**long-wind·ed·ly,** *adv.*—**long-wind·ed·ness,** *n.*

loo, lō, *n.* [Short for *lanterloo.*] A game of cards in which forfeits are paid into a pool; the forfeit or sum paid into the pool.—

v.t.—**looed, looing.** To subject to a forfeit at loo.

loo·fa, loo·fah, lō′fa, *n.* [Ar. *lufah.*] Any gourdlike plant, genus *Luffa,* bearing fibrous fruit used as a filter or sponge.

look, lụk, *v.i.* [O.E. *lōcian,* to look; akin Prov. G. *lugen,* O.H.G. *luogen, luoken,* to look, G. *loch,* a hole.] To employ one's vision; to direct the eyes toward an object; to direct the mind or attention; consider; to have or assume a particular air or manner; as, to *look* upset; to use one's sight for examining, seeking, or watching; to seem or appear to the mind or eye, as: She *looks* familiar to me. To have a particular indicated direction, outlook, or situation; to face or front upon; to give certain indications.—*v.t.* To express or show by a look; to appear in a befitting manner; as, to *look* one's age; to seek, followed by *up;* to examine, often followed by *over.*—*n.* The act of looking or seeing; the aspect of someone or something; an examination or search by eye; *usu. pl.* outward aspect or appearance.—**look af·ter,** to take care of.—**look back,** to recollect or reflect on.—**look down on,** to regard as inferior.—**look for·ward to,** to expect eagerly.—**look in,** to make a brief visit.—**look on,** to consider or judge; to be an onlooker or spectator.—**look out,** to be alert or watchful.—**look the oth·er way,** to ignore or avoid.—**look up to,** to respect or admire.

look·er, lụk′ẽr, *n.* One who looks; *slang,* a person of attractive appearance, often preceded by *good.*

look·er-on, lụk″ẽr·on′, *n. pl.* **look·ers-on.** A spectator or onlooker.

look·ing glass, *n.* A mirror.

look·out, lụk′out″, *n.* The act of looking out; a watch kept, as for something that may happen; a person or party stationed or employed to keep such a watch; a station or place from which a watch is kept. *Brit.* view, prospect, or outlook. *Colloq.* the object of one's care or concern.

loom, lōm, *n.* [M.E. *lome,* < O.E. *gelōma,* tool, implement: cf. *heirloom.*] A machine or apparatus for weaving yarn or thread into a fabric; the art or the process of weaving; *naut.* the part of an oar between the blade and the handle.

loom, lōm, *v.i.* [Origin uncertain.] To appear indistinctly or come into view in indistinct and enlarged form; to rise before one's vision with an appearance of great size; *fig.* to impend or threaten, as: The possibility of an epidemic *loomed* over the city.—*n.* A looming appearance, as of something seen indistinctly at a distance or through a fog; as, the *loom* of an iceberg.

loom, lōm, *n.* [< Scand.] *Brit.* a guillemot or loon.

loon, lōn, *n.* [O.E. *loom,* Dan. *loom,* Icel. *lōmr,* G. *lohme, lomme,* a loon.] *Ornith.* any of several species of diving waterfowl of the genus *Gavia,* characterized by prolonged underwater swimming, a sharp, pointed bill, and a yodeling, laughterlike call.

loon, lōn, *n.* [Same word as O.D. *loen,* a stupid man.] An idle or worthless man; a crazy person; *Sc.* a boy.

loon·y, loon·ey, lun·y, lō′nē, *a.*—**loonier, looniest, lunier, luniest.** [For *luny,* < *lunatic.*] *Slang.* Crazy; insane; extremely foolish.—*n. pl.* **loon·ies, lun·ies.** *Slang,* a lunatic.—**loon·i·ness,** *n.*

loop, lōp, *n.* [M.E. *loupe:* cf. Gael. and Ir. *lub,* loop, bend.] A folding or doubling of a portion of a cord, thread, ribbon, or the like, upon itself, so as to leave an opening between the parts; the portion so doubled; a curved piece or a ring of metal, wood, or the like, used as a fastening device or for the insertion of something, as a handle; anything shaped like a loop, as a line drawn on paper, or a bend in a river.

Phys. the part of a vibrating string of a musical instrument, a column of air in an organ pipe, or the like, between two adjacent nodes; an antinode. *Elect.* a closed circuit; *aeron.* a complete revolution by an airplane moving in an almost vertical plane.—*v.t.* To form into a loop or loops; to make a loop or loops in; to encircle with something arranged in a loop; to fasten by a loop; *aeron.* to make, as an airplane, execute a loop or loops.—*v.i.* To make or form a loop or loops; to move by forming loops, as does a measuring worm.—**loop the loop,** to execute a loop or series of loops in an airplane; to traverse a looplike course or track, as on a roller coaster.—**loop·er,** *n.* One who or that which loops something or forms loops; a measuringworm.

loop, löp, *n.* [M.E. *loupe:* cf. D. *luip,* watch, ambush.] *Archaic,* a small or narrow opening, as in a wall. Also *loophole.*

loop·hole, löp'hōl", *n.* [D. *luipen,* to peep.] A small aperture in a wall for observation, ventilation, or illumination; such an opening in a fortification through which small arms can be fired; an opportunity for escape or evasion, esp. a textual basis in a document or law for escape or evasion of taxes, legal commitments, or obligations.—*v.t.*—*loopholed, loopholing.* To provide with loopholes or make loopholes in.

loop stitch, *n. Sewing,* a type of stitch employing loops, as a chain stitch.

loop·y, lö'pē, *a.*—*loopier, loopiest.* Full of loops. *Slang,* odd; eccentric; crazy. *Sc.* crafty; cunning.

loose, lös, *a.*—*looser, loosest.* [< Scand.; = Icel. *lauss,* loose, free, empty, = D. and G. *los,* loose, free, = O.E. *lēas,* free from, without, = Goth. *laus,* empty, without; akin to E. *loss.*] Free from bonds, fetters, or restraint; as, to get one's hand *loose;* free or released from fastening or attachment; as, a *loose* end; uncombined, as a chemical element; not bound together, as papers or flowers; unpackaged; unemployed or unappropriated; as, *loose* funds; lacking proper control or power of restraint; as, *loose*-tongued; lax, as the bowels; not tight or constricted, as a cough; free from moral restraint, or lax in principle or conduct; wanton or unchaste; as, a *loose* woman; not firmly fixed in place; as, a *loose* tooth; slack, relaxed, or lacking tension; not fitting closely, as garments; not close or compact in structure or arrangement; as, a *loose* weave; having freedom while still being associated; as, a *loose* organization; of earth or soil, not cohering; not strict, exact, or precise; as, *loose* thinking. *Sports,* of a formation, having team members widely spaced; of a ball or puck during play, not controlled by either team.—**loose·ly,** *adv.*—**loose·ness,** *n.*

loose, lös, *v.t.*—*loosed, loosing.* To let loose or free from bonds or restraint; to release, as from constraint, obligation, or penalty; to unfasten, undo, or untie, as a bond, fetter, or knot; to shoot or let fly; to slacken, relax, or make less tight; to render less firmly fixed; loosen; *naut.* to set free from fastening or attachment; as, to *loose* a boat from its moorings.—*v.i.* To let go a hold; to shoot or let fly an arrow or bullet.

loose, lös, *adv.* In a loose manner; loosely.—**cut loose, let loose,** to free; *colloq.* to enjoy oneself in an unrestrained way.

loose end, *n.* Something remaining unattached or hanging loose; as, the *loose end* of a rope; a matter, situation, or detail left unsettled or unfinished.—**at loose ends,** in a confused, undecided, or unsettled state.

loose-joint·ed, lös'join'tid, *a.* Having loose joints, esp. loosely built with joints not firmly articulated; *biol.* marked by limber or supple movement.—**loosejoint·ed·ness,** *n.*

loos·en, lö'sen, *v.t.* To render less firm, tight, or compact; to slacken or relax; as, to *loosen* one's grasp; to relax in strictness or severity, as regulations or discipline; of the bowels, to open or free from constipation; to set free from bonds.—*v.i.* To become loose or looser.—**loos·en·er,** *n.*

loose sen·tence, *n.* A sentence in which the principal clause is first and expresses the essential idea, then is followed by a subordinate clause or other trailing modifiers: distinguished from *periodic sentence.*

loose smut, *n.* A grain disease caused by a fungus of the genus *Ustilago,* in which the grain head becomes a powdery mass of spores.

loose·strife, lös'strīf", *n.* [< *loose,* v., and *strife;* intended as a translation of L. *lysimachia,* taken as < Gr. *lysis,* loose, and *machē,* strife.] Any of various leafy-stemmed herbs of the genus *Lysimachia,* in the primrose family, as the common yellow-flowered species, *L. vulgaris;* any of various herbaceous plants of the genus *Lythrum,* in the loosestrife family.

loot, löt, *n.* [Hind. *lūt.*] Spoils or plunder; taken by pillaging, as in war; booty; anything dishonestly and ruthlessly appropriated; as, a burglar's *loot; slang,* money; *colloq.* accumulation of valued things; as, the child's birthday *loot.*—*v.t.* To plunder or pillage, as a conquered town; rob, as by corrupt practice in public office; to take or carry off, as loot.—*v.i.* To take loot; to plunder.—**loot·er,** *n.*

lop, lop, *v.t.*—*lopped, lopping.* [Akin O.D. *luppen,* to maim.] To remove or cut off the top, extreme, or superfluous parts of anything, usu. with *off;* to trim or clip, as a tree, by cutting off twigs or branches.—*n.* The act of lopping, or the section or parts lopped off.—**lop·per,** *n.*

lop, lop, *v.i.*—*lopped, lopping.* [Allied to *lap.*] To hang loosely or limply; droop; to be pendulous; to sway, move, or go in a droopy or awkward manner.—*v.t.* To allow to hang loosely.—*a.* Drooping; as, *lop* ears.

lope, lōp, *v.i.*—*loped, loping.* [Prob. orig. a var. of *loup* with later use due in part to D. *loopen,* run.] To move or run with bounding steps or a long easy stride.—*v.t.* To cause to lope, as a horse.—*n.* The act or the gait of loping; a long, easy stride.—**lop·er,** *n.*

lop-eared, lop'ērd", *a.* Having ears that lop or hang down; as, a *lop-eared* rabbit.

loph·o·branch, lof'o·brangk", lō'fo·-brangk", *n.* [N.L. *Lophobranchii,* pl., < Gr. *lóphos,* crest, and *brágchia,* gills.] Any of the *Lophobranchii,* a group of teleostean fishes having gills arranged in tufts, as sea horses and pipefishes.—*a.* Belonging or pertaining to the *Lophobranchii.*—**loph·o·bran·chi·ate,** lof"o·brang'kē·it, lof"o·brang'kē·āt", lō"fo·brang'kē·it, lō"-fo·brang'kē·āt", *a., n.*

lop·py, lop'ē, *a.*—*loppier, loppiest.* Hanging loose; droopy; pendulous.

lop·sid·ed, lop'sī'did, *a.* Larger or heavier at one side than the other; lying or inclining to one side; unevenly proportioned; not symmetrical.—**lop·sid·ed·ly,** *adv.*—**lop·sid·ed·ness,** *n.*

lo·qua·cious, lō·kwā'shus, *a.* [L. *loquax, loquacis,* < *loquor,* to speak; Skt. *lap,* to speak, to talk; seen also in *locution, colloquy, eloquent,* and *obloquy.*] Talkative; given to continual or excessive talking; garrulous; verbose.—**lo·qua·cious·ly,** *adv.*—**lo·qua·cious·ness,** *n.*—**lo·quac·i·ty,** lō·kwas'i·tē, *n. pl.* **lo·quac·i·ties.** The quality of or an instance of being loquacious.

lo·quat, lō'kwot, lō'kwat, *n.* [From Chinese name meaning 'rush orange.'] A small evergreen tree, *Eriobotrya japonica,* native to China and Japan but often cultivated elsewhere for ornament and for its yellow, plumlike fruit; the fruit, often eaten in the form of preserves.

lo·ran, lōr'an, *n.* [(*lo*)ng-(*ra*)nge (*n*)avigation.] A method by which a navigator determines the position of his ship or airplane, depending in part on the measurement of the difference in arrival time of radio signals sent out by various ground stations.

lord, lärd, *n.* [O.E. *laverd, lowerd,* etc., O.E. *hlāford,* a lord, < *hlāf,* bread, a loaf, and *weard,* lit. 'keeper of the bread.' *Lady* also has *loaf* as first element.] A person possessing supreme power and authority, as a ruler, governor, monarch, nobleman, or proprietor of a manor; one who is recognized as a master or leader in his field. (*Cap.*) a designation of the Supreme Being; God; Jesus Christ, esp. in the expression our Lord. (*Cap.*), *Brit.* a title given to peers below the rank of duke, as a marquis, earl, viscount, baron, or, by courtesy, to a younger son of a marquis or a duke; a prefix to the title of a bishop, a judge in court, or a high official; as, *Lord* Chancellor, *Lord* Mayor.—*v.i.* To domineer; to rule with arbitrary or despotic sway, followed by *it;* as, to *lord* it over us.—**The Lords,** the peers and bishops who together form one of the two estates constituting the British parliament.

lord·ly, lärd'lē, *a.*—*lordlier, lordliest.* Befitting or suitable for a lord; grand, dignified, or elegant; haughty; pertaining to a lord.—*adv.*—**lord·li·ness,** *n.*

Lord of Mis·rule, *n.* In England, a person formerly chosen to direct revels and sports at Christmas.

lor·do·sis, lär·dō'sis, *n.* [N.L., < Gr. *lordōsis,* < *lordōs,* bent back.] *Pathol.* abnormal inward curvature of the spine.—**lor·dot·ic,** lär·dot'ik, *a.*

Lord's Day, *n.* The Sabbath; Sunday.

lord·ship, lärd'ship, *n.* The authority of a lord; the territory over which a lord has jurisdiction; sovereignty; (*cap.*) in Great Britain, the title accorded a lord, usu. used with *his* or *your.*

Lord's Prayer, *n.* The prayer starting with the words *Our Father,* taught by Jesus to his disciples. Matt. vi. 9–13; Luke xi. 2–4.

Lord's Sup·per, *n.* The Last Supper; the sacrament in commemoration of this; the Eucharist; the Communion or Holy Communion; the Mass.

Lord's ta·ble, *n.* An altar or table for communion services. Also **com·mun·ion ta·ble.**

lore, lōr, *n.* [O.E. *lār,* < stem of *laeran,* to teach; D. *leer,* Dan. *laere,* G. *lehre,* lore.] The store of knowledge which exists regarding a specific subject, esp. traditional knowledge, anecdotes, or popularly held beliefs; learning; erudition.

lore, lōr, *n.* [L. *lorum,* thong.] *Zool.* the space between the eye and the bill of a bird, or a corresponding space in other animals, as serpents.—**lo·re·al,** lōr'ē·al, *a.*

lor·gnette, lärn·yet', *n.* [Fr., < *lorgner,* to spy or peep.] Opera glasses with a handle; eyeglasses with a handle into which they fold.

lor·gnon, *Fr.* lär·nya̱N', *n.* An eyeglass, as a monocle; a pair of eyeglasses, as a pince-nez; a lorgnette.

lo·ri·ca, lō·rī'ka, lo·rī'ka, *n. pl.* **lo·ri·cae,** lō·rī'sē, lo·rī'sē, lō·rī'kē, lō·rī'kē. [L., orig. a corselet of leather thongs, < *lorum,* a thong.] An ancient Roman cuirass or corselet; *zool.* the protective covering with which certain infusorians are provided.—**lor·i·cate, lor·i·cat·ed,** lär'i·kāt", lär'i·kit, lor'i·kāt", lor'i·kit, *a.*

lor·i·keet, lär'i·kēt", lor'i·kēt", lär"i·kēt", lor"i·kēt", *n.* [A dim. of *lory,* plus *parra-* (*keet*).] Any of certain small birds of the parrot family, found in Australia and neighboring S. Pacific areas, and characterized by bright plumage and tongues brushlike at their tips. Also **lory.**

lo·ris, lōr′is, *n. pl.* **lo·ris.** [Fr. and N.L.; said to be < D. *loeris,* booby.] A small, slender, tailless, large-eyed, nocturnal lemur, *Loris gracilis,* a native of southern India and Ceylon; any of various lemurs of the related genus *Nycticebus.*

lorn, lạrn, *a.* [An archaic or poetic pp. of *loss.*] *Poet.* Forsaken; forlorn; abandoned; desolate.

lor·ry, lạr′ē, *n. pl.* **lor·ries.** [Cf. Prov. E. *lurry,* to pull or drag.] A four-wheeled truck, wagon, or railroad car for heavy or bulky loads, usu. without sides. *Brit.* a low, flat wagon drawn by horses; a large motor-driven truck.

lo·ry, lōr′ē, *n. pl.* **lories.** [Malay *lūrī.*] Lorikeet.

lose, lōz, *v.t.*—**lost, losing.** [O.E. *losian,* be lost, perish, also destroy, ruin, < *los,* E. *loss.*] To come to be without, by some chance, and have no hope of finding; as, to *lose* a wallet; to mislay, as: He *lost* his pen. To suffer the loss or deprivation of, as, to *lose* one's life; to be bereaved of by death; as, to *lose* a child; to fail to keep, preserve, or maintain; as, to *lose* one's balance; to forfeit or relinquish, as: He *lost* money on the stock market. To cease to have; as, to *lose* all fear; to bring to destruction or ruin, now used chiefly in the passive, as: The ship and crew were *lost.* To have slip from sight, hearing, or attention; as, to *lose* a face in a crowd; to become separated from or ignorant of; as, to *lose* one's way or aim; to leave far behind in a pursuit or race; to use to no purpose; to waste; to fail to have, get, or catch; to miss; as, to *lose* a meal; to fail to win, as a prize or stake; to be defeated in a game, lawsuit, or battle, as: The lawyer *lost* the case. To cause the loss of, as: The delay *lost* the battle for them. To become bewildered; to become absorbed or engrossed in, to the exclusion of knowledge or consciousness of all else; as, to *lose* oneself in the music; of a doctor, to be unable to save the life of.—*v.i.* To suffer loss; as, to *lose* on a contract; to fail to win, aş in a contest or game; to lessen or depreciate in some way; as, to *lose* in translation.—**los·a·ble·ness,** *n.*—**los·er,** lō′zėr, *n.*

lose out, *v.i. Colloq.* To be unsuccessful in an attempt; to fail to achieve something.

loss, lạs, los, *n.* [O.E. *los,* destruction = Icel. *los,* breaking up; akin to O.E. *lēosan,* lose, E. *loose,* L. *luere,* Gr. *lyein,* loose, Skt. *lū-,* cut.] That which is lost; deprivation of, or a state of being without something that one has had; state of grief caused by death, or death itself; as, mourning the *loss* of a parent; the failure to preserve or maintain; as, *loss* of prestige or speed; failure to make good use of something; as, a *loss* or waste of time; a losing by defeat; as, *loss* of a race or a game; detriment or disadvantage due to an inability to keep, have, or get; as, to bear the *loss* of a robbery; destruction or ruin. *Milit.* the losing of soldiers by casualty; *usu. pl.* the number of soldiers so lost. *Insurance,* damage, death, or other occurrences covered by the stipulations of a policy, guaranteeing indemnity to the insured. *Phys.* that measure of mechanical or electrical power lost, due to resistance or friction in the apparatus.—**at a loss,** in a state of bewilderment or uncertainty; an amount at which the cost of an article or service is greater than the selling price.

loss lead·er, *n.* An article of merchandise, usu. in a retail store, priced below cost as a means of creating more store trade.

loss ra·tio, *n. Insurance,* the amount of money paid out in claims in ratio to

premiums received during a specific period, usu. a year.

lost, lạst, lost, *a.* No longer possessed or retained; as, *lost* powers; no longer to be found; as, *lost* articles; having gone astray, or bewildered as to place or direction, as: The child was *lost.* Not used to good purpose, as opportunities, time, or labor; wasted, as: The day was *lost.* That which one has failed to win; as, a *lost* prize; attended with defeat; as, a *lost* battle; destroyed, eradicated; engrossed, rapt; distraught, bewildered, or hopeless, as: He has the look of a *lost* man.—**lost cause,** a venture which is unsuccessful or doomed to failure.—**lost to,** no longer belonging to; no longer possible or open to; as, an opportunity *lost to* him; insensible to; as, *lost to* all sense of duty.

lot, lot, *n.* [O.E. *hlot,* akin to G. *loos,* Icel. *hlutr,* Goth. *hlauts,* lot,' and O.E. *hlēotan,* cast lots, obtain by lot.] One of a set of specially marked objects used to decide a question, make a decision, or select a winner by random selection; the casting or drawing of such objects as a method of deciding something; as, to choose a person by *lot* for a task; the decision or choice so made; something assigned by or as by the casting or drawing of lots, as a share of property; allotted share or portion; *fig.* the portion in life assigned by fate or providence, or one's fate, fortune, or destiny; as, to have a happy *lot,* happiness beyond the common *lot* of mankind. *Motion pictures,* the studio. A distinct portion or piece of land; a distinct portion or parcel of anything, as of merchandise. *Colloq.* a number of things or persons collectively; a person of a specified sort; as, one who is a bad *lot;* often *pl.* a great many or a great deal, with *of;* as, a *lot of* books, *lots of* money.—*v.t.*—**lotted, lotting.** To cast or draw lots for; to divide or distribute by lot; to assign to one as his *lot;* allot; to divide into lots, as land.—*v.i.* To cast or draw lots.—*adv.* A great many; much, as: He is a *lot* wiser.

lo·ta, lo·tah, lō′ta, *n.* [Hindi.] A spheroidal pot, usu. of brass or copper, used in India for holding water.

loth, lōth, lōTH, *a.* Loath.

Lo·thar·i·o, lō·thâr′ē·ō″, *n. pl.* **Lo·thar·i·os.** [From *Lothario,* one of the characters in Rowe's *The Fair Penitent.*] (*Sometimes l.c.*) A man who seduces women; a rake.

lo·tic, lō′tik, *a.* Referring to or existing in water which is in motion.

lo·tion, lō′shan, *n.* [L. *lotio(n-),* a washing, < *lavare* (pp. *lotus*), wash.] *Pharm.* a liquid for medicinal or cosmetic use which is applied externally to benefit the skin; as, a hand *lotion.*

lot·ter·y, lot′e·rē, *n. pl.* **lot·ter·ies.** [Fr. *loterie.*] A game or method of fund raising, for public, charitable, or private purposes, by sale of numbered tickets which, when drawn by chance, entitle the holders to prizes; any affair or happening that seems determined by lot or chance.

lot·to, lot′ō, *n.* [It. *lotto* (whence Fr. *loto*), orig. lot.] A game played by drawing numbered disks from a bag or the like and covering corresponding numbers on cards, the winner being the first player to fill a row.

lo·tus, lō′tus, *n. pl.* **lo·tus·es.** [L. *lotus, lotos,* < Gr. *lōtos,* name of various plants.] A plant, commonly identified with a species of jujube or of nettletree, referred to in Greek legend as the lotus tree which yielded a fruit that induced a state of dreamy, contented forgetfulness in those who ate it; the fruit itself; any of various nymphaeaceous plants with ornate flowers and large floating leaves, as either of two Egyptian water lilies, *Castalia lotus* and *C. caerulea,* or either of the two species of nelumbo, *Nelumbo nelumbo,* the fragrant sacred lotus,

and *N. lutea,* or water chinkapin, both of India; a representation of such a plant, common in Egyptian and Hindu decorative art; any of the shrubby herbs with red, pink, or white flowers constituting the fabaceous genus *Lotus,* some of which are valued as pasture plants. Also **lo·tos.**

lo·tus-eat·er, lō′tus·ē″tėr, *n. Class. mythol.* one of a race of people in Homer's *Odyssey* who lived an indolent, dreamy existence induced by eating the lotus fruit. *Fig.* anyone who leads a life indifferent to affairs around him; a daydreamer.—**lo·tus-eat·ing,** *n., a.*

loud, loud, *a.* [O.E. *hlūd,* loud; O.Fris. *hlud,* D. *luid,* G. *laut,* loud; cogn. Gr. *klyó,* to hear.] Strongly heard; of great volume or sound intensity, or carrying far; making very audible sounds; clamorous; vociferous. *Colloq.* flashy or showy, as dress; of odors, strong or offensive; vulgar, as manners.—**loud·ly,** *adv.*—**loud·ness,** *n.*

loud·en, loud′en, *v.i., v.t.* To become or make louder; increase in sound.

loud·mouthed, loud·mouthed, loud′-mouTHd″, loud′mouth″, *a.* Loud of voice to the irritation of others; vociferous.—**loud-mouth, loud·mouth,** loud′mouth″, *n.*

loud·speak·er, loud′spē″kėr, *n.* Any of various electric devices for amplifying the sound of a speaker's voice, music, or the like; public-address system; bull horn.

lough, lok, loch, *n.* [Ir. *loch;* cf. *loch.*] *Ir.* a lake; an arm of the sea.

Lou·is Qua·torze, lō′ē ka·tarz′, lō′is ka·tạrz′, *Fr.* lwē kä·tạrz′, *a.* [Fr., Louis Fourteenth.] Pertaining to the period of Louis XIV of France, 1643-1715, or to the styles of architecture, furniture, and décor then prevailing, characterized by a greater use of classical forms and details than in the Louis Treize period and by great richness of ornamentation.

Lou·is Quinze, lō′ē kanz, lō′is kanz, *Fr.* lwē kaNz, *a.* [Fr., Louis Fifteenth.] Pertaining to the period of Louis XV of France, 1715-1774, or to the extremely ornate, rococo styles of architecture, furniture, and décor then prevailing, which showed a disregard for symmetry and a profusion of ornament.

Lou·is Seize, lō′ē sez, lō′is sez, *Fr.* lwē sez, *a.* [Fr., Louis Sixteenth.] Pertaining to the period of Louis XVI of France, 1774-1792, or to the styles of architecture, furniture, and décor then prevailing, which were characterized by a return to greater, classical simplicity than in the Louis Quinze period.

Lou·is Treize, lō′ē trez, lō′is trez, *Fr.* lwē trez, *a.* [Fr., Louis Thirteenth.] Pertaining to the period of Louis XIII of France, 1610-1643, or to the styles of architecture, furniture, and décor then prevailing, which were less light and elegant than those of the earlier Renaissance, and employed forms and features based on the classical.

lounge, lounj, *v.i.*—**lounged, lounging.** [Origin obscure.] To pass time idly and indolently; to recline indolently, loll; to move or go in a leisurely, easy manner.—*v.t.* To pass, as time, in lounging.—*n.* A kind of sofa for reclining, often without a back, and with a headrest at one end; a place for lounging, as in a hotel, train, or airplane; a room open to the public where liquor is served, as in a hotel.—**loung·er,** *n.*—**loung·ing,** loun′jing, *a.*

loup·cer·vier, lō″sėr·vyä′, *n. pl.* **loup·cer·viers, loup·cer·vier.** [Fr., < L. *lupus cervarius,* wolf that hunts the deer (*cervus,* deer).] The Canadian lynx, *Lynx canadensis.*

loupe, lōp, *n.* A small magnifying glass, adapted as an eyepiece or affixed to spectacles, used esp. by jewelers or watchmakers.

louse, lous, *n. pl.* **lice,** līs. [O.E. *lūs,* pl. *lys* = D. *luis,* Dan. *lus,* Icel. *lus,* G. *laus,* perh. < root of *lose.*] The common name of various wingless, flat-bodied insects with biting and sucking mouthparts, as the sucking genus *Anoplura,* the biting genus *Mallophaga,* or the plant louse of the family *Aphididae,* that are parasitic on man, animals, and plants. *Slang,* a mean or despicable person; pl. **lou·ses.**—*v.t.*—**loused,** *lousing.* To delouse or free of lice.—**louse up,** *slang,* to botch or mess up.—**lous·y,** lou'zē, *a.*—**lousier, lousiest.** Infested with lice. *Colloq.* foul or despicable; bad or inferior. *Slang,* well-provided with or having too much of something, followed by *with,* as: He's *lousy with* brains.—**lous·i·ly,** *adv.*—**lous·i·ness,** *n.*

louse·wort, lous'wurt", *n. Bot.* any of the scrophulariaceous herbs constituting the genus *Pedicularis,* as *P. canadensis* or wood betony, with fernlike leaves and reddish-yellow flowers, formerly thought to breed lice because of sheep grazing on it.

lout, lout, *n.* An awkward person; a bumpkin; a clown.—**lout·ish,** lou'tish, *a.* Clownish; rude; awkward.—**lout·ish·ly,** *adv.*—**lout·ish·ness,** *n.*

lout, lout, *v.i.* [O.E. *lūtan,* to bow or stoop; Icel. *luta,* Dan. *lude,* to stoop; same root as *little.*] *Archaic,* to bend, bow, or stoop down in courtesy or submission.

lou·ver, lō'vèr, *n.* [O.Fr. *lover, lovier;* origin obscure.] An arrangement of louver boards or the like covering a window or other opening; a single louver board; a turret or lantern on the roof of a medieval building, that supplies ventilation or light; one of a number of slitlike openings, as in an automobile grill, for ventilating purposes. Also **lou·vre,** lō'vRe.—**lou·ver board, lou·ver board·ing,** one of a series of overlapping, sloping boards or slats, so arranged as to admit air but exclude rain.—**lou·vered,** *a.*

lov·a·ble, love·a·ble, luv'a·bl, *a.* Of such a nature as to attract love; amiable; pleasing.—**lov·a·bil·i·ty, lov·a·ble·ness,** *n.*—**lov·a·bly,** *adv.*

lov·age, luv'ij, *n.* [O.Fr. *levesche* (Fr. *livêche*), < L.L. *levisticum,* for L. *ligusticum,* prop. neut. of *ligusticus,* Ligurian.] A European herb, *Levisticum officinale,* in the parsley family once cultivated as a medicinal home remedy.

love, luv, *n.* [Ó.E. *lufu* = O.H.G. *luba,* love; from a root seen also in E. *lief* and *belief,* and further represented by L. *libet, lubet,* it is pleasing, Gr. *líptesthai,* be eager, Skt. *lubh-,* desire.] A feeling of warm personal attachment or deep affection, as for a friend, parent, or child; a strong or passionate affection for a person of the opposite sex; sexual passion or desire, or its gratification; an object of love or affection, sweetheart; a term denoting affection; a love affair; (*cap.*) a personification of sexual affection, as Eros or Cupid. A strong predilection or liking for anything; as, *love* of books; the object so viewed, as: Music was her *love.* The benevolent affection of God for his creatures, or the reverent affection due God from them; *tennis,* nothing, or no score.—**for love,** without compensation.—**for love or mon·ey,** for any consideration; by any means; as, not to be had *for love or money.*—**for the love of,** for the sake of.—**in love,** enamored of someone or something.—**make love to,** to kiss or caress as lovers.—**no love lost,** no love wasted, as between persons who care little for each other.

love, luv, *v.t.*—**loved, loving.** [O.E. *lufian.*] To have love or deep affection for; to have a strong or passionate affection for, as for one of the opposite sex; to be in love with; to have a strong liking for or to take great pleasure in; as, to *love* music; to express by kissing, or by caressing gestures of love or

devotion for; to flourish in, as a plant or animal in a climate suitable to its needs.—*v.i.* To have love or affection, esp. to be or to fall in love with one of the opposite sex.

love af·fair, *n.* A romantic liaison between two lovers, esp. an illicit one; a current interest in or attachment to something; as, a *love affair* with opera.

love ap·ple, *n.* A name formerly used for a tomato.

love·bird, luv'burd", *n.* Any of various small parrots, esp. of the genera *Agapornis* of Africa, and *Psittacula* of S. America, remarkable for the apparent affection shown between mates.

love feast, *n.* Among the early Christians, a meal eaten in token of brotherly love and charity; an analogous service, held by certain modern religious denominations; a banquet or other gathering of persons, as of members of a political party, to promote good feeling.

love game, *n. Tennis,* a game in which the losing person or team has not scored.

love-in-a-mist, luv'in·a·mist', *n. Bot.* a garden plant, *Nigella damascena,* of the buttercup or crowfoot family, with feathery dissected leaves and whitish or blue flowers.

love-in-i·dle·ness, luv'in·id'l·nis, *n. Bot.* wild pansy, *Viola tricolor.*

love knot, *n.* An ornamental knot serving as a symbol of love; a knot of ribbon given or worn as a token of love.

love·less, luv'lis, *a.* Devoid of or unaccompanied by love; as, a *loveless* marriage; feeling no love; receiving or winning no love.—**love·less·ly,** *adv.*—**love·less·ness,** *n.*

love-lies-bleed·ing, luv'līz"blē'ding, *n. Bot.* A plant, *Amaranthus caudatus,* with spikes of crimson flowers; several other plants of the same genus.

love·lock, luv'lok", *n.* A separate lock of hair; formerly, a long, flowing lock or curl dressed separately from the rest of the hair, worn by courtiers.

love·lorn, luv'lärn", *a.* Forsaken by one's love; without a lover; pining or suffering because of this.—**love·lorn·ness,** *n.*

love·ly, luv'lē, *a.*—**lovelier, loveliest.** [O.E. *luflic.*] Having beauty that appeals to the heart as well as to the eye, as a person or a face; charmingly or exquisitely beautiful, as a flower; of great moral or spiritual beauty; as, a *lovely* character; *colloq.* delightful or highly pleasing, as: We had a *lovely* time.—*adv.* Extremely well.—*n. Colloq.* an attractive woman.—**love·li·ness,** *n.*

love-mak·ing, luv'mā"king, *n.* Courtship; sexual relations between lovers.

lov·er, luv'èr, *n.* One who loves; a friend or well-wisher; one who is enamored of a person of the opposite sex, usu. indicating the man; a paramour; *pl.* two persons in love with each other. One who has a strong predilection or liking for something; as, a *lover* of music.—**lov·er·ly,** *a.* Like or befitting a lover; as, *loverly* attentions.—*adv.*

love seat, *n.* A small-sized sofa or an upholstered double chair.

love set, *n. Tennis,* a set in which the winner does not lose a game.

love·sick, luv'sik", *a.* Sick or languishing with love; expressive of languishing love.—**love·sick·ness,** *n.*

lov·ing, luv'ing, *a.* Fond; affectionate; expressing love or kindness.—**lov·ing·ly,** *adv.*—**lov·ing·ness,** *n.*

lov·ing cup, *n.* A large wine cup, having two or more handles, passed from guest to guest at banquets; a similar cup given as an award or trophy.

lov·ing-kind·ness, luv'ing·kīnd'nis, *n.* Tender, considerate affection.

low, lō, *a.* [M.E. *lowe, lohe,* earlier *lāh,* < Scand.: cf. Icel. *lāgr,* Dan. *lav,* also D. *laag,* G. dial. *lage,* low; < the root of E.

lie.] Of small extent upward; rising slightly from a surface; of less than average or normal height or depth, as a liquid or stream; situated or occurring not far above the ground or floor; not far above the horizon, as a heavenly body; lying or being below the general level; as, *low* ground; designating or pertaining to regions near sea level or near the sea, as opposed to highland or inland regions; prostrate or dead; profound or deep, as a bow; far down in the scale of rank or estimation; lowly, humble, or meek; of inferior quality or character; not advanced in civilization or organization; lacking in dignity or elevation, as thought or expression; groveling or abject; mean or base; coarse or vulgar; dissolute or degraded; cheap; near depletion; as, *low* on food; lacking in strength or vigor; feeble or weak; affording little strength or nourishment, as a diet; small in amount, degree, or force; denoted by a low number; being situated close to the equator; as, a *low* latitude; assigning or attributing no great amount, value, or excellence; produced by relatively slow vibrations, as sounds; not loud; depressed or dejected; *phon.* of a vowel sound, uttered with a wide space between the tongue and palate.—*adv.* In or to a low position, point, degree; near the ground, floor, or base; not aloft; humbly; cheaply; at or to a low pitch; in a low tone; softly; quietly; relatively late or recent, as a date.—**low·ness,** *n.*

low, lō, *n.* That which is low; a low position; *meteor.* a low-pressure atmospheric area. *Cards,* the lowest card in the trump suit; that score which is lowest in value among participants in a game. *Mech.* the lowest gear transmission ratio of drive shaft speed to engine crankshaft speed which produces maximum development of torque or force.

low, lō, *v.i.* [O.E. *hlōwan* = D. *loeien,* Icel. *hloa,* O.H.G. *hlojan,* to low.] To bellow, as an ox or cow.—*n.* The sound uttered by a bovine animal; a moo. Also **low·ing.**

low·born, lō'bärn, *a.* Of humble or lowly birth.

low·boy, lō'boi, *n.* A low chest of drawers supported by short legs.

low·bred, lō'bred', *a.* Of a low or inferior breed; characterized by or characteristic of low or vulgar breeding.

low·brow, lō'brou", *n. Slang,* a person who is uninterested in cultural matters or one who has vulgar tastes.—lō'brou', *a. Slang,* of or pertaining to those of uncultivated tastes.

Low Church, *a.* Pertaining or belonging to a party within the Anglican Church which does not stress church authority and ritual but does emphasize evangelism.—**Low Church·man,** *n.*

low com·e·dy, *n.* Comedy characterized by physical action, extremely absurd situations, and coarse humor, as burlesque.

low-down, low·down, lō'doun', *a.* Mean; sneaking; contemptible.—lō'doun", *n. Slang.* The facts in the case; the truth.

low·er, lō'ér, *a., compar. of low.* In a position or condition considered inferior to other values or ranks; located beneath something; as, the *lower* peg. (*Usu. cap.*), *geol.* pertaining to an earlier period of geologic time; situated under the earth's newer upper strata. Farther to the south.

low·er, lō'ér, *v.t.* [< *lower,* compar. of *low;* cf. *linger,* < *long, a.*] To make lower in position; to let down; to take or bring down; to reduce, as in value, amount, pitch, volume, or the like; to humble; to make less high or haughty; to weaken.—*v.i.* To decrease; to descend; to become lower.—*n.* Something located beneath another thing; the *lower* berth.

low·er, lour, lou'èr, lour, *v.i.* [Same word as D. *loeren,* to frown; L.G. *luren,* to look sullen; akin to *leer*.] To frown; to look sullen; to appear dark or gloomy; to threaten a storm.—*n*. A frown; a murky or gloomy sky.—**low·er·ing, lour·ing,** *a*. Threatening a storm; cloudy; overcast; sullen.—**low·er·ing·ly,** *adv*.—**low·er·y, lour·y,** *a*. Cloudy; gloomy.

low·er-case, lō′ĕr·kās′, *a. Print.* of small letters, as opposed to capital letters.—*n*. A lower-case letter. Abbr. *l.c.*—*v.t.*—*lower-cased, lower-casing.* To type, set, or print with small letters.

low·er class, *n*. A class in society below all others in social status.—**low·er-class,** *a*.

low·er-class·man, lō′ĕr·klas′man, lō′ĕr·kläs′man, *n.* pl. **low·er-class·men.** Underclassman; a freshman or sophomore in a college or secondary school.

low·er crit·i·cism, *n*. Criticism of the Bible based on the search for and examination of the language of original texts: differentiated from *higher criticism*.

low·er·most, lō′ĕr·mōst″, *Brit.* lō′ĕr·most, *a*. Lowest.

low·est com·mon de·nom·i·na·tor, *n. Math.* the lowest common multiple of the denominators of a series of fractions, as: 8 is the lowest common denominator of ½, ¼, and ⅛. Also **least com·mon de·nom·i·na·tor.**

low·est com·mon mul·ti·ple, *n. Math.* the smallest number exactly divisible by each number in a given group, as: 12 is the *lowest common multiple* of 3, 4, and 6. Also **least com·mon mul·ti·ple.**

low fre·quen·cy, *n. Radio,* a frequency in the range of 30 to 300 kilocycles.

Low Ger·man, *n*. Any of the German dialects spoken in the northern lowland region of Germany; a group of West Germanic languages including Dutch, Flemish, Frisian, and sometimes English, as well as the dialects of lowland Germany.

low-key, lō′kē′, *a*. Subdued; restrained; limited in vigor or intensity. Also **low-keyed.**

low·land, lō′land, *n*. Land which is lower than the neighboring country; low or level country.—*a*.—**the Low·lands,** the low, level districts of southern and eastern Scotland.—**low·land·er,** *n*. One who lives in or was born in a lowland area; (*cap.*) a person from the Lowlands.

low-lev·el, lō′lev′el, *a*. Of minor rank or importance; close to the ground; as, *low-level* bombing.

low·ly, lō′lē, *a*.—*lowlier, lowliest.* Low or humble in position in life; not lofty or exalted; meek.—*adv*. In a low position, manner, or condition; humbly.—**low·li·ness,** *n*.

Low Mass, *n. Rom. Cath. Ch.* a mass celebrated with simple ceremony by one priest and usu. one altar boy or server.

low-mind·ed, lō′mīn′did, *a*. Having a mean or degraded mind; harboring vulgar or demeaning sentiments.—**low-mind·ed·ly,** *adv*.—**low-mind·ed·ness,** *n*.

lown, loun, *a*. [M.E. *lowne*; < Scand.] *Dial.* Calm; quiet; still.—*n*.—*v*

low-necked, lō′nekt′, *a*. Of a garment, usu. a dress, cut low so as to leave the neck and shoulders exposed; décolleté.

low-pres·sure, lō′presh′ĕr, *a*. Having or exerting a low degree of pressure, as steam or water; without forcefulness.

low-ten·sion, lō′ten′shan, *a. Elect.* performing under a low-voltage current.

low-test, lō′test′, *a*. Reaching a relatively high temperature before boiling, as gasoline.

low tide, *n*. The lowest water level of the tide; the time when this occurs; *fig.* the lowest level of anything.

lox, loks, *n*. [(*l*)iquid and (*ox*)ygen.] Liquid oxygen, used in propellants for rockets.

lox, loks, *n*. A variety of smoked salmon, usu. eaten with bagels and cream cheese.

lox·o·drome, lok′so·drōm″, *n*. Rhumb line.

loy·al, loi′al, *a*. [Fr. *loyal*, O.Fr. *loial*, *leial*, < L. *legalis*, E. *legal*.] Faithful to one's oath, engagements, or obligations; faithful to one's allegiance, as to a sovereign, government, or state; faithful to any person or thing conceived as imposing obligations.—**loy·al·ist,** loi′a·list, *n*.—**loy·al·ly,** *adv*.—**loy·al·ty,** *n.* pl. **loy·al·ties.**

loy·al·ty oath, *n*. An oath in which one affirms loyalty to one's country and government, usu. with the added stipulation that one is not, and has never been, a member of a group declared subversive, as the Communist Party.

loz·enge, loz′inj, *n*. [Fr. *losange,* prob. < Sp. *losa,* a slate or flat stone for paving.] A small tablet of sugar, usu. medicated and originally in the shape of a diamond. *Geom.* an equilateral four-sided figure, having two acute and two obtuse angles; a diamond shape.

LP, el′pē′, *a*. [(*L*)ong (*P*)laying.] Pertaining to a microgroove phonograph record rotating at the speed of 33⅓ revolutions per minute.—*n*. A long-playing record. (Trademark.)

LSD, el′es′dē′, *n*. Lysergic acid diethylamide, a hallucinogenic drug affecting the central nervous system, producing changes in thought, mood, perception, and behavior. Also **LSD-25.**

lu·au, lō·ou′, lō′ou, *n*. A Hawaiian feast, usu. with native entertainment.

lub·ber, lub′ĕr, *n*. An awkward or clumsy individual. *Naut.* one who is unskilled in seamanship; also *landlubber.*—*a*. Clumsy.—**lub·ber·li·ness,** *n*.—**lub·ber·ly,** *a., adv*.

lub·ber line, *n. Navig.* a fixed line on a compass or navigational device indicating a ship or an aircraft's forward direction. Also **lub·ber's line, lub·ber's mark, lub·ber's point.**

lub·ber's hole, *n. Naut.* an opening in the platform at the head of a mast through which sailors may mount and descend without going over the rim.

lube, lōb, *n. Colloq.* lubricant.

lu·bri·cant, lō′bri·kant, *a*. Lubricating.—*n*. A lubricating material, as grease or oil.

lu·bri·cate, lō′bri·kāt′, *v.t.*—*lubricated, lubricating.* [L. *lubricatus,* pp. of *lubricare lubricus,* slippery.] To make slippery or smooth; to apply an oily or greasy substance; to apply such a substance in order to diminish friction; as, to *lubricate* parts of a mechanism.—*v.i.* To apply or serve as a lubricant to something.—**lu·bri·ca·tion,** lō′bri·kā′shan, *n*.—**lu·bri·ca·tive,** *a*.—**lu·bri·ca·tor,** *n*.

lu·bri·cous, lō·brish′us, *a*. [L. *lubricus,* slippery, uncertain, deceitful.] Slippery, as of a surface; of an oily smoothness; unstable or uncertain; shifty or elusive; wanton or lewd. Also **lu·bri·cious.**—**lu·bri·cious·ly,** *adv*.—**lu·bric·i·ty,** lō·bris′i·tē, *n*.

lu·carne, lō·kärn′, *n*. [Fr. *lucarne,* L. *lucerna,* a lamp, < *luceo,* to shine.] A dormer or garret window; a window in a steeple.

lu·cent, lō′sent, *a*. [L. *lucens* (*lucent-*), ppr. of *lucere,* shine, be light or clear.] Shining or luminous; clear, transparent, or translucent.—**lu·cen·cy,** *n*.—**lu·cent·ly,** *adv*.

lu·cerne, lu·cern, lō·sụrn′, *n*. [Fr. *luzerne, luserne*; origin unknown.] *Brit.* alfalfa.

lu·cid, lō′sid, *a*. [L. *lucidus,* < *lucēre.*] Easily understood, clear, or intelligible; characterized by clear perception, thought, or understanding; rational, sane; bright or shining; transparent.—**lu·cid·i·ty, lu·cid·ness,** *n*.—**lu·cid·ly,** *adv*.

Lu·ci·fer, lō′si·fĕr, *n*. [L. *lux, lucis,* light, and *fero,* to bring.] The defiant, ambitious archangel, interpreted as Satan, who was driven out of heaven; the planet Venus when it emerges as the morning star; (*l.c.*)

a match ignitible by friction.—**lu·cif·er·ous,** *a*. Giving light.

lu·cif·er·ase, lō·sif′e·rās″, *n*. [L. *lucifer,* light-bringing.] *Chem.* a substance, probably an enzyme, which is present in the luminous organs of fireflies and the like, and which, acting with luciferin, produces luminosity.

lu·cif·er·in, lō·sif′ĕr·in, *n*. [L. *lucifer,* light-bringing.] *Chem.* an organic substance whose action with luciferase causes luminosity in various organisms.

Lu·cite, lō′sīt, *n*. Any of the transparent thermoplastic acrylic resins used esp. as a glass substitute. (Trademark.)

luck, luk, *n*. [M.E. *lucke* = D. *luk, geluk,* = M.L.G. *lucke, gelucke,* = M.H.G. *gelücke,* G. *glück,* luck, fortune.] Whatever happens to a person, as if by chance, in the course of events; fate; good fortune or success, considered as the result of chance; some object on which good fortune is supposed to depend.—**luck·i·ly,** luk′i·lē, *adv*.—**luck·i·ness,** *n*.

luck·y, luk′ē, *a*.—*luckier, luckiest.* Favored by luck; fortunate; meeting with or resulting in success; believed capable of bringing success; favorable.

lu·cra·tive, lō′kra·tiv, *a*. [Fr. *lucratif,* < L. *lucrativus,* < *lucror,* to profit, < *lucrum,* gain; same root as G. *lohn,* reward.] Yielding profit or gain; profitable; moneymaking.—**lu·cra·tive·ly,** *adv*.—**lu·cra·tive·ness,** *n*.

lu·cre, lō′kĕr, *n*. [Fr. *lucre,* L. *lucrum*.] Money; monetary profit; as, filthy *lucre*.

lu·cu·brate, lō′kū·brāt′, *v.i.*—*lucubrated, lucubrating.* [L. *lucubro, lucubratum,* to study by candlelight, < obs. a. *lucuber,* bringing light, < *lux,* light.] To write in a scholarly manner; to write or study arduously, esp. at night.—**lu·cu·bra·tion,** lō″kū·brā′shan, *n*.—**lu·cu·bra·tor,** *n*.

lu·cu·lent, lō′kū·lent, *a*. [L. *luculentus,* < *lux* (*luc-*), light.] Full of light; luminous; clear or lucid, as arguments or explanations; convincing.—**lu·cu·lent·ly,** *adv*.

Lu·cul·lan, lō·kul′an, *a*. Pertaining to Lucullus, a wealthy Roman famous for luxury, esp. at the table; as, a *Lucullan* feast. Also **Lu·cul·le·an, Lu·cul·li·an.**

lu·di·crous, lō′di·krus, *a*. [L. *ludicrus,* < *ludus,* sport or game; seen also in *allude, delude, elude, illusion, prelude.*] Producing laughter; comical; very ridiculous.—**lu·di·crous·ly,** *adv*.—**lu·di·crous·ness,** *n*.

lu·es, lō′ēz, *n*. [L.] Syphilis.—**lu·et·ic,** lō·et′ik, *a*.—**lu·et·i·cal·ly,** *adv*.

luff, luf, *n*. [Cf. O.Fr. *lof,* a contrivance for altering a ship's course, later, as also D. *loef,* the weather side.] *Naut.* The sailing of a ship with its head closer to the wind; the forward edge of a fore-and-aft sail; the fullest and broadest part of a ship's bow.—*v.i. Naut.* To bring a ship's head closer into the wind, with sails shaking; of a sail, to shake, from being brought close to wind.—*v.t. Naut.* to bring the head, as of a vessel, closer to the wind.

Luft·waf·fe, luft′väf″e, *n*. [G., *luft,* air, and *waffe,* weapon.] The German air force in the Nazi regime.

lug, lug, *v.t.*—*lugged, lugging.* [O.E. *geluggian,* to lug; Sw. *lugga,* to draw, to haul, *lugg,* N. *lug,* the forelock or hair of the head; cf. O.E. *lyccan,* Dan. *luge,* to pluck.] To haul; to drag; to pull along or carry, as something heavy and moved with difficulty; *colloq.* to bring unreasonably into a discussion.—*v.i.* To pull or tug.—*n*. A projecting part of an object resembling the human ear, as an handle; a loop on a harness which the shaft goes through; *slang,* a dull or clumsy person.

lug, lug, *n*. Lugworm.

lug·gage, lug′ij, *n*. [< *lug.*] Baggage, as of a traveler; suitcases.

lug·ger, lug′ẽr, n. [A vessel having *lug*sails; Dan. *lugger*, D. *logger*.] A vessel, usu. small, carrying either two or three masts with lugsails.

lug·sail, lug′sāl″, *Naut.* lug′sal, n. *Naut.* a quadrilateral sail bent upon a yard that crosses the mast obliquely. Also **lug**.

lu·gu·bri·ous, lụ·gö′brē·us, lụ·gū′brē·us, a. [L. *lugubris*, mournful, < *lugeo*, to weep; akin to Gr. *lygros*, sad.] Mournful; doleful; esp. in a particularly exaggerated or ludicrous manner.—**lu·gu·bri·ous·ly**, adv. —**lu·gu·bri·ous·ness**, **lu·gu·bri·os·i·ty**, lụ·gö″brē·os′i·tē, lụ·gū″brē·os′i·tē, n.

lug·worm, lug′wụrm, n. Any marine worm with tufted gills, genus *Arenicola*, which burrows in the sand of the seashore and is much used for bait. Also **lob·worm**, **lug**.

luke·warm, lök′wạrm′, a. [O.E. *luke*, lukewarm, D. *leuk*, O.E. *wlaec*, lukewarm; O.E. *lewe* G. *lau*, lukewarm.] Moderately warm; tepid; not ardent or zealous; indifferent.—**luke·warm·ly**, adv.—**luke··warm·ness**, n.

lull, lul, v.t. [Dan. *lulle*, Sw. *lulla*, G. *lullen*, to sing badly; prob. an imitation of the sound; cf. L. *lallo*, to sing lullaby.] To cause to rest or sleep by gentle, soothing means; to quiet; to quiet or calm down by deception.—v.i. To subside; to become calm.—n. A temporary quiet before or after a storm, tumult, confusion, or great activity.

lull·a·by, lul′a·bī″, n. pl. **lull·a·bies**. A song to lull or quiet babies; any lulling music.—v.t.—**lullabied, lullabying**. To calm with a lullaby.

lu·lu, lö′lö, n. *Slang*, anything or anyone outstanding or extraordinary, as in difficulty, scope, or loveliness.

lum, lum, n. [Origin uncertain.] *Sc.*, *Brit.* a chimney.

lum·ba·go, lum·bā′gō, n. [L., < *lumbus*, loin.] Rheumatism or rheumatic pains affecting the lumbar region of the back.

lum·bar, lum′bẽr, lum′bär, a. [L. *lumbus*, loin.] Of or pertaining to the loin or loins.— n. A lumbar vertebra, artery, or the like.

lum·ber, lum′bẽr, v.i. [M.E. *lomeren*: cf. Sw. dial. *lomra*, resound.] To move clumsily or heavily, esp. because of great or ponderous bulk; to make a rumbling noise.

lum·ber, lum′bẽr, n. [Orig. a pawnbroking establishment, from the *Lombards*, who were famed as pawnbrokers or money-lenders.] Timber or logs sawed or split into various sizes for use as beams, boards, or planks; *Brit.* castoff articles, as old furniture or similar household items stored or thrown aside.—v.t. To convert, as logs, into lumber; *Brit.* to clutter or obstruct with useless articles.—v.i. To cut or saw into lumber for marketing.— **lum·ber·er**, **lum·ber·man**, lum′bẽr·man, n.—**lum·ber·less**, a.

lum·ber·ing, lum′bẽr·ing, a. Clumsy or awkward; moving awkwardly or heavily.— **lum·ber·ing·ly**, adv.—**lum·ber·ing··ness**, n.

lum·ber·ing, lum′bẽr·ing, n. Logging; the business or occupation of felling, cutting, or preparing timber for commercial use.

lum·ber·jack, lum′bẽr·jak″, n. One who cuts or transports timber; a logger; a straight wool or leather jacket, usu. hiplength and belted, resembling a logger's jacket; *Canadian*, the Canada jay.

lum·ber·yard, lum′bẽr·yärd″, n. An area where a supply of lumber or wood is stored; a commercial establishment for storing and selling wood products.

lum·bri·coid, lum′bri·koid, a. Of or similar to a common earthworm.

lu·men, lö′men, n. pl. **lu·mi·na**, lö′mi·na. [L. light, window, opening.] *Opt.* a unit

expressing luminous flux, being equal to the light which falls on an area of one square centimeter from one candle placed at a distance of one centimeter; *anat.* a duct or canal in a tubular organ, as an artery; *bot.* the cavity within the walls of a cell, left by the disappearance of the protoplast; *med.* the bore of a tube, as a catheter.

Lu·mi·nal, lö′mi·nal, n. Phenobarbital. (Trademark.)

lu·mi·nance, lö′mi·nans, n. The condition or quality of being luminous; the measure of luminous intensity or brightness of an illuminated surface or source of light.

lu·mi·nar·y, lö′mi·ner″ē, n. pl. **lu·mi·nar·ies**. [O.Fr. *luminarie* (Fr. *luminaire*), < L.L. *luminare*, a light, lamp, heavenly body, L. window, < L. *lumen*, light.] A person of eminence in a particular field; a body or thing that gives light, esp. a celestial body, as the sun or moon.—a.

lu·mi·nes·cence, lö″mi·nes′ens, n. [L. *lumen* (*lumin-*), light.] An emission of light not due directly to incandescence and occurring at a temperature below that of incandescent bodies, as is the case in phosphorescence and fluorescence; the light so produced.—**lu·mi·nesce**, v.i.— *luminesced, luminescing*.—**lu·mi·nes·cent**, a.

lu·mi·nif·er·ous, lö″mi·nif′ẽr·us, a. [L. *lumen* (*lumin-*), light, and *ferre*, bear.] Producing or conveying light.

lu·mi·nos·i·ty, lö″mi·nos′i·tē, n. pl. **lu·mi·nos·i·ties**. The quality of being luminous; the intensity of light in a color; something luminous.

lu·mi·nous, lö′mi·nus, a. [L. *luminosus*, < *lumen*, light.] Radiating or reflecting light; shining; bright; lighted up or illuminated; intellectually brilliant; enlightening; clear, or readily intelligible.—**lu·mi·nous·ly**, adv.—**lu·mi·nous·ness**, n.

lu·mi·nous en·er·gy, n. Light visible to the human eye; electromagnetic radiation in the wavelength range between 3800 and 7600 angstrom units.

lu·mi·nous flux, n. The time rate of transmission of visible energy from a particular source, usu. stated in lumens.

lu·mi·nous paint, n. A paint that can glow in the dark because of a phosphorescent ingredient as barium sulfide.

lum·mox, lum′uks, n. A dull-witted, awkward person.

lump, lump, n. [M.E. *lumpe*: cf. D. *lomp*, lump, rag, Sw. *lump*, clod.] A piece or mass of solid matter without regular shape, or of no particular shape; a protuberance or swelling; as, a *lump* on the head; an aggregation, collection, or mass. *Colloq.* a dull, stolid person; a big, sturdy person.— a. In the form of a lump or lumps; including all of a number of items taken together; as, a *lump* sum.—v.t. To make into a lump or lumps; to raise into or cover with lumps; to unite into one aggregation, collection, or mass; deal with in the lump or mass.—v.i. To form a lump or lumps; to rise in a lump or lumps; to move heavily.— **a lump in one's throat**, a tightening of the throat, as from an emotion.—**in the lump**, in the mass; as a whole; in gross; wholesale. —**lump·ing·ly**, adv.

lump, lump, v.t. [Cf. *glump*.] *Colloq.* To regard or endure with displeasure; put up with as a disagreeable necessity, as: If you don't like it, *lump* it.

lum·pen, lum′pen, a. Characterized by or relating to groups or individuals who have been uprooted or dispossessed, specif. from their normal social or economic status.

lump·fish, lump′fish″, n. pl. **lump·fish**, **lump·fish·es**. [Appar. < *lump*.] A clumsy fish, *Cyclopterus lumpus*, of the N. Atlantic, having a high ridged back and rounded bony nodules on the skin.

lump·ish, lum′pish, a. Like a lump; heavy and clumsy; dull or stupid.—**lump·ish·ly**, adv.—**lump·ish·ness**, n.

lump·y, lum′pē, a.—*lumpier, lumpiest*. Full of lumps; covered with lumps, as a surface; like a lump, as in being heavy or clumsy; rough or choppy, as water.— **lump·i·ly**, adv.—**lump·i·ness**, n.

lump·y jaw, n. *Pathol.*, *veter. pathol.* an infectious disease, esp. of cattle, due to parasites, and causing lumpy tumors, esp. around the jaw. Also **ac·ti·no·my·co·sis**, ak″ti·nō·mi·kō′sis.

Lu·na, lö′na, n. [L. *luna*, moon, crescent.] The moon, personified by the Romans as a goddess.

lu·na·cy, lö′na·sē, n. pl. **lu·na·cies**. [< L. *lunaticus*, lunatic, moon-struck, < *luna*, the moon (lunatics being at one time supposed to be affected by the moon), for *lucna*, < root of *luceo*, to shine.] The height of folly or extravagant conduct; insanity; formerly, insanity which is broken by intervals of lucidity; *law*, any form of unsoundness of mind, usu. not including idiocy.

lu·na moth, n. [L. *luna*, moon, crescent: with reference to the spots on the wings.] A large N. American silkworm moth, *Actias luna*, with greenish wings, the hind ones having long tails, and each wing having a crescent-shaped spot. Also **Lu·na moth**.

lu·nar, lö′nẽr, a. [L. *lunaris*, < *luna*, the moon.] Pertaining to or of the moon; measured by the revolutions of the moon; as, a *lunar* calendar; moonlike in shape; *astrol.* under the moon's influence. Of or relating to silver.

lu·nar caus·tic, n. *Chem.* silver nitrate, $AgNO_3$, a compound used in medicine, esp. as a cauterizing agent.

lu·nar e·clipse, n. A partial or total darkening of the moon when it enters the darkest part of the earth's shadow.

lu·nate, lö′nāt, a. Having a form like that of the half-moon; crescent-shaped. Also **lu··nat·ed**.—**lu·nate·ly**, adv.

lu·na·tic, lö′na·tik, n. An insane person; a zany character.—a. Insane; mad; extremely irrational or reckless; zany; for use by the insane; as, a *lunatic* asylum. Also **lu·nat·i·cal**.

lu·na·tic fringe, n. An extremist or fanatical minority group in any organization, esp. a political or social one.

lu·na·tion, lö·nā′shan, n. The time from one new moon to the following, averaging 29½ days. Also **lu·nar month**, **syn·od·ic month**.

lunch, lunch, n. [Short form for *luncheon*.] A light meal, esp. one served between breakfast and dinner; the food for a lunch.—v.i. To eat lunch.—v.t. To provide lunch for.— **lunch·er**, n.

lunch·eon, lun′chon, n. A midday meal, usu. a formal one.

lunch·eon·ette, lun″cho·net′, n. See *lunchroom*.

lunch·room, lunch′röm″, lunch′rụm″, n. A room where lunch may be eaten. A restaurant where light or quickly prepared meals are served; also *luncheonette*.

lune, lön, n. [Fr. *lune*, < L. *luna*, moon, M.L. a fit of lunacy.] Anything shaped like a crescent or a half-moon; a crescent-shaped figure on a plane or sphere bounded by two arcs of circles; *pl.* fits of lunacy.

lu·nette, lö·net′, n. [Fr. dim. of *lune*.] Any of various objects of crescentlike or semicircular outline or section. *Arch.* a space of this shape in a vaulted ceiling or wall; a painting filling such a space; an arched or rounded aperture or window, as in a vault; *fort.* a work consisting of a projecting angle with two flanks.

lung, lung, n. [O.E. *lunge*, pl. *lungan*, Icel. *lunga*, D. *long*, D. and G. *lunge*, a lung.]

Either of the two saclike respiratory organs in man and other vertebrates that are air-breathing; a similar respiratory organ found in certain invertebrates. A mechanical breathing device; as, an iron *lung*.—**lunged,** *a.* Having lungs; having a certain number or kind of lungs; as, weak-*lunged*.

lunge, lunj, *n.* [For obs. *allonge,* < Fr. *allonge,* < *allonger,* lengthen, extend, lunge.] A thrust, as in fencing; any sudden forward movement; a plunge; a lurch.—*v.i.*—**lunged,** *lunging.* To make a lunge or thrust; move with a lunge.—*v.t.* To thrust; cause to move with a lunge.

lunge, longe, lunj, *n.* [Fr. *longe,* halter, lunge, < L. *longus,* long.] A long rope or rein used to guide a horse during training or exercise.—*v.t.*—**lunged,** *lunging,* **longed,** *longeing.* To train or exercise, as a horse, by the use of a lunge or rope.

lung·er, lung'ẽr, *n. Slang.* A person affected with pulmonary tuberculosis; a consumptive.

lung·fish, lung'fish", *n.* pl. **lung·fish, lung·fish·es.** Any fish of the group *Depnoi* having lungs as well as gills for breathing.

lung·wort, lung'wụrt", *n.* A European blue-flowered plant of the borage family, *Pulmonaria officinalis,* with spotted leaves; a N. American blue-flowered plant, *Mertensia virginica,* of the same family.

lu·ni·so·lar, lõ"ni·sõ'lẽr, *a.* Pertaining to or depending upon the mutual relations or joint action of the moon and sun.

lu·ni·tid·al, lõ"ni·tĩd'al, *a.* Pertaining to that part of the tidal movement dependent on the moon.

lu·ni·tid·al in·ter·val, *n.* The interim between the moon's passage over a particular meridian and the following lunar high tide.

lunk·er, lungk'ẽr, *n. Colloq.* something large, esp. a game fish of large size.

lunk·head, lungk'hed", *n.* [Var. of *lumphead.*] *Colloq.* A thickheaded or stupid person; a blockhead.—**lunk·head·ed,** *a.*

lu·nu·la, lõ'nũ·la, *n.* pl. **lu·nu·lae,** lõ'nũ·lē. [Dim. of L. *luna,* the moon.] Something in the shape of a crescent, as the white crescent at the base of a fingernail. Also **lu·nule,** lõ'nũl.—**lu·nu·late, lu·nu·lat·ed,** *a.*

Lu·per·ca·li·a, lõ"pẽr·kā'lē·a, lõ"pẽr·kal'ya, *n.* pl. **Lu·per·ca·li·a, Lu·per·ca·li·as.** [L., prop. neut. pl. of *Lupercalis,* a. < *Lupercus,* appar. < *lupus,* wolf.] *Often pl. in constr.* an ancient Roman fertility festival celebrated annually on February 15th in honor of Lupercus, a Roman deity.—**Lu·per·ca·li·an,** *a.*

lu·pine, lõ'pin, *a.* [L. *lupus,* a wolf; cogn. with E. *wolf.*] Like a wolf; wolfish; ravenous.

lu·pine, lu·pin, lõ'pin, *n.* [L. *lupinus, lupinum:* cf, *lupine.*] Any plant of the fabaceous genus *Lupinus;* a European herb with edible seeds cultivated since ancient times; a wild species with blue, pink, or white flowers common in sandy soil in the eastern U.S.; *pl.* the seeds of this plant.

lu·pu·lin, lõ'pū·lin, *n.* [L. *lupulus,* hops.] A fine, yellow powder obtained from the fruits of hops, and used in medicine as a sedative.

lu·pus, lõ'pus, *n.* [L., wolf.] *Pathol.* any of various diseases caused by the tubercle bacillus and resulting in lesions of the skin and mucous membranes. Also **lu·pus vul·ga·ris.**

lurch, lụrch, *v.i.* [Origin not certain.] To roll or heave suddenly to one side, as a ship at sea; to stagger to one side, as a drunk man.—*n.* A sudden roll of a ship; a stagger.

lurch, lụrch, *n.* [O.Fr. *lourche,* It. *lurcio,* G. *lurz, lurtsch,* a lurch at cribbage.] A thorough defeat, esp. in the game of cribbage.—**in the lurch,** in a hopeless or embarrassing situation.

lurch·er, lụr'chẽr, *n. Archaic,* a sneak thief; a poacher. *Brit.* a poacher's dog trained to hunt silently.

lure, lụr, *n.* Fr. *leurre,* < M.H.G., *luodẽr,* a lure, G. *luder,* carrion, a bait for wild beasts.] An enticement through the prospect of pleasure or advantage; an artificial bait or decoy used in capturing animals, esp. one used in angling, or one used in falconry to bring back the falcon.—*v.t.*—**lured,** *luring.* To entice; to attract; to attract by a lure or to a lure.—**lure·ment,** *n.*—**lur·er,** *n.*—**lur·ing·ly,** *adv.*

lu·rid, lụr'id, *a.* [L. *luridus,* pale-yellow, wan, ghastly.] Glaringly vivid or sensational; conspicuous or terrible because of fiery intensity, fierce passion, or wild unrestraint; as, *lurid* crimes; glaring in brightness or color; lighted up or shining with an unnatural or fiery glare; wan, pallid, or ghastly in hue.—**lu·rid·ly,** *adv.*—**lu·rid·ness,** *n.*

lurk, lụrk, *v.i.* [Akin to Norw. *luska,* Dan. *luske,* to lurk, to skulk; Dan. *lur,* G. *lauer,* an ambush or watching.] To lie in wait; to move furtively; to remain inconspicuous; to be concealed or unobserved.—**lurk·er,** *n.*—**lurk·ing·ly,** *adv.*

lus·cious, lush'us, *a.* [Origin uncertain: cf. obs. *licius* for *delicious.*] Highly pleasing to the taste or smell; pleasurable to the senses, feelings, or mind; strong in sensuous or voluptuous appeal; ornately attractive. **lus·cious·ly,** *adv.*—**lus·cious·ness,** *n.*

lush, lush, *a.* [< *luscious.*] Having luxuriant foliage; marked by extravagance, opulence, or abundance; fresh, succulent, juicy.—**lush·ly,** *adv.*—**lush·ness,** *n.*

lush, lush, *n.* [Origin obscure.] *Slang,* one who habitually drinks liquor to excess.—*v.t., v.i.* To drink, as liquor.

lust, lust, *n.* [O.E., D., G., and Sw. *lust,* Icel. and Dan. *lyst,* Goth. *lustus,* desire.] Sexual appetite; depraved or unlawful sexual craving or appetite; intense longing or passionate desire; an eagerness to possess or enjoy; as, *lust* for money.—*v.i.* To have carnal desire; to desire eagerly, with *after* or *for.*

lus·ter, *Brit.* **lus·tre,** lus'tẽr, *n.* [Fr. *lustre,* < L. *lustrum,* purificatory sacrifice < stem of *luceo,* to shine.] A shining by reflected light; sheen; brightness or brilliance; splendor or distinction, as of achievement; fame; a chandelier or the like ornamented with drops or pendants of cut glass; glossy surface of porcelain or pottery; fabric with a sheen; *mineral.* a variation in the nature of the reflecting surface of minerals.—*v.t.* To furnish with a gloss.—*v.i.* To be lustrous; to become glossy.—**lus·ter·less,** *a.*

lus·ter, *Brit.* **lus·tre,** lus'tẽr, *n.* A five-year period. See *lustrum.*

lus·ter·ing, lus'tẽr·ing, *n.* [Fr. *lustrine,* It. *lustrino,* < *lustro,* luster, gloss.] A finishing process for giving a luster to cloth. Also *Brit.* **lus·tring.**

lus·ter·ware, lus'tẽr·wâr", *n.* Pottery which has a glossy and often iridescent finish.

lust·ful, lust'ful, *a.* Having or marked by strong desires; full of lewd sexual desire or appetite; libidinous.—**lust·ful·ly,** *adv.*—**lust·ful·ness,** *n.*

lus·tral, lus'tral, *a.* [L. *lustralis,* < *lustro,* to purify, < *lustrum,* a purificatory sacrifice, < stem of *luo, lavo,* to wash.] Pertaining to or used in a rite of purification; happening every five years.

lus·trate, lus'trāt, *v.t.*—**lustrated,** *lustrating.* [L. *lustro, lustratum,* to cleanse.] To purify by rites or ceremonies.—**lus·tra·tion,** lus·trā'shan, *n.*—**lus·tra·tive,** lus'tra·tiv, *a.*

lus·trous, lus'trus, *a.* Characterized by luster or sheen; luminous; bright; shining;

noted or illustrious.—**lus·trous·ly,** *adv.*—**lus·trous·ness,** *n.*

lus·trum, lus'trum, *n.* pl. **lus·trums, lus·tra.** [L.] In ancient Rome, the purification of the people performed at the end of every five years, following the census. A period of five years; also *luster, Brit. lustre.*

lust·y, lus'tē, *a.*—**lustier, lustiest.** [< *lust* = D. and G. *lustig,* D. *lystig,* merry, jovial.] Characterized by life, spirit, vigor, or health; robust or hearty, as a drink or dinner.—**lust·i·ly,** *adv.*—**lust·i·ness,** *n.*

lu·sus na·tu·rae, lõ'sus na·tụr'ē, lõ'sus na·tūr'ē, *n.* An abnormally formed person, animal, or plant; a freak.

lu·tan·ist, lõt'a·nist, *n.* A performer on the lute. Also **lu·ten·ist,** *lutist.*

lute, lõt, *n.* [Fr. *luth,* lut, Sp. *laud,* < Ar. *al ûd,* the wood (*al* being the definite article).] A stringed musical instrument, having a pear-shaped body and long, fretted, sharply angled neck.—*v.i., v.t.*—**luted,** *luting.* To play on a lute.

lute, lõt, *n.* [L. *lutum,* mud, clay, < *luo,* to wash.] A claylike cement or sealing compound used for packing joints or waterproofing porous surfaces. Also *luting.*—*v.t.*—**luted,** *luting.* To close or coat with lute.

lu·te·al, lõ'tē·al, *a.* Of or concerning the corpus luteum.

lu·te·in, lõ'tē·in, *n.* A yellowish or orange compound occurring in many plants and in egg yolk, animal fat, and corpora lutea, used in certain biochemical studies; also *xanthophyll.* A hormone preparation from corpora lutea.

lu·te·in·ize, lõ'tē·i·nīz", *v.t.*—**luteinized,** *luteinizing.* To cause the formation of corpora lutea in.—*v.i.* To become changed into corpora lutea.—**lu·te·in·i·za·tion,** *n.*

lu·te·in·iz·ing hor·mone, *n.* A secretion of the pituitary gland that stimulates the activities of the reproductive organs of vertebrate animals.

lu·te·o·lin, lõ'tē·o·lin, *n.* [L. *luteolus,* yellowish, dim. of *luteus,* E. *luteous.*] *Chem.* a deep yellow compound, $C_{15}H_{10}O_6$, used esp. in dyeing silk.

lu·te·ous, lõ'tē·us, *a.* [L. *luteus,* < *lutum,* a plant used in dyeing yellow.] Having a greenish-yellow color.

lute·string, lõt'string, *n.* [Appar. a corruption of *lustring.*] A glossy silk fabric formerly used for women's dresses. A glossy, narrow, heavy ribbon.

lu·te·ti·um, lu·te·ci·um, lõ·tē'shē·um, *n. Chem.* a metallic element of the rare-earth series. Sym. Lu, at. no. 71, at. wt. 174.97. See Periodic Table of Elements.

Lu·ther·an, lõ'thẽr·an, *a.* Of or pertaining to Martin Luther, 1483-1546, a German religious reformer, or his doctrines; belonging to the Lutheran church.—*n.* One who follows Luther or adheres to his doctrines; a member of the Lutheran Church.—**Lu·ther·an·ism, Lu·ther·ism,** *n.*

lut·ing, lõ'ting, *n.* A claylike cement. See *lute.*

lut·ist, lõ'tist, *n.* A lute player; a lute maker.

lux, luks, *n.* pl. **lux·es, lu·ces,** lõ'sēz. [L., light.] *Opt.* a unit of illumination, equivalent to one lumen per square meter. Also **me·ter·can·dle.**

lux·ate, luk'sāt, *v.t.*—**luxated,** *luxating.* [L. *luxo, luxatum,* < *luxus,* dislocated, Gr. *loxos,* slanting.] *Anat.* To put out of joint, as a limb; to dislocate.—**lux·a·tion,** luk·sā'shan, *n.*

luxe, lõks, luks, *n. Fr.* lyks, *n.* [Fr., < L. *luxus,* luxury.] Luxury; elegance.

lux·u·ri·ant, lug·zhụr'ē·ant, luk·shụr'ē·ant, *a.* [L. *luxurians* (-*ant*-), ppr. of *luxuriare.*] Exuberant in growth, as vegetation or foliage; growing freely and abundantly; richly abundant, profuse, or

---

a- fat, fāte, fär, fâre, fall;   **e-** met, mē, mẽre, hẽr;   **i-** pin, pīne;   **o-** not, nõte, mõve;   **u-** tub, cūbe, bụll;   **oi-** oil;   **ou-** pound.

superabundant; florid, as imagery or ornamentation.—**lux·u·ri·ance, lux·u·ri·an·cy,** *n.*—**lux·u·ri·ant·ly,** *adv.*

lux·u·ri·ate, lug·zhụr′ē·āt, lug·shụr′ē·āt, *v.i.*—*luxuriated, luxuriating.* [L. *luxurio,* to be rank or luxurious, to be wanton.] To indulge or revel without restraint, followed by *in;* to grow exuberantly; to live luxuriously; to find pleasure; as, to *luxuriate* in praise.—**lux·u·ri·a·tion,** *n.*

lux·u·ri·ous, lug·zhụr′ē·us, lug·shụr′ē·us, *a.* [L. *luxuriosus.*] Marked by abundance or plentiful supply; opulent; characterized by indulgence in or love of luxury; ministering to luxury; furnished with luxuries; overelaborate; as, a *luxurious* style of writing.—**lux·u·ri·ous·ly,** *adv.*—**lux·u·ri·ous·ness,** *n.*

lux·u·ry, luk′shạ·rē, lug′zhạ·rē, *n.* pl. **lux·u·ries.** [L. *luxuria.*] Any nonessential, usu. costly or scarce, which is personally gratifying; free or constant indulgence in such nonessentials; any pleasure indulged in.

ly·can·thro·py, lī·kan′thrọ·pē, *n.* A kind of insanity in which the patient supposes himself to be a wolf; the fabled transformation of a human being into the form of a wolf.—**ly·can·thrope,** lī′kan·thrōp″, lī·kan′thrōp, *n.* One who exhibits symptoms of lycanthropy; a werewolf.—**ly·can·throp·ic,** lī′kan·throp′ik, *a.*

ly·cée, lē·sā′, *n.* [Fr., < L. *Lyceum.*] In France, a secondary school which prepares students for university education and is maintained by the state.

ly·ce·um, lī·sē′um, *n.* [L. *Lyceum,* Gr. *Lykeion,* from a temple dedicated to Apollo *lykeios,* Apollo the wolfslayer, < *lykos,* a wolf.] An organization or a building used for the purpose of popular education through plays, lectures, concerts, and discussions; a lycée; (*cap.*) a garden with covered walks in Athens, where Aristotle held his school of philosophy.

ly·chee, lī′chē, *n.* Litchi.

lych gate, *n.* Lich gate.

lych·nis, lik′nis, *n.* [L., < Gr. *lychnis,* kind of plant with a red flower, akin to *lychnos,* lamp.] *Bot.* any of various showy plants constituting the genus *Lychnis,* as *L. coronaria* and *L. calcedonica,* common in flower gardens and having crimson to scarlet flowers.

ly·co·po·di·um, lī′kō·pō′dē·um, *n.* [N.L., < Gr. *lykos,* wolf, and *poys* (*pod-*), foot.] *Bot.* any plant of the genus *Lycopodium,* as the club moss and ground pine, having a creeping or erect stem with mosslike evergreen leaves, and formerly used for decorative Christmas wreaths. Also **ly·co·pod,** lī′kō·pod″.—**ly·co·po·di·um pow·der,** a fine yellow powder consisting of the spores of lycopodium, used in pharmacology and in the manufacture of fireworks.

lydd·ite, lid′īt, *n.* [From *Lydd,* in Kent, Eng., where first made.] *Chem.* an explosive prepared from picric acid.

lye, lī, *n.* [O.E. *lēag* = D. *loog* = G. *lauge,* lye.] The alkaline solution obtained by leaching wood ashes; any strong alkaline solution, as of potassium or sodium hydroxide, used chiefly in washing or in making soap.

ly·gus bug, *n.* *Entom.* any of various species of pestilent leaf bugs of the genus *Lygus,* in the order *Hemiptera,* which feed on plant juices.

ly·ing, lī′ing, *n.* Intentional untruthfulness.—*a.*

ly·ing-in, lī′ing·in′, *n.* pl. **ly·ings-in, ly·ing-ins.** A woman's confinement during and following childbirth.—*a.* Pertaining to childbirth.

lymph, limf, *n.* [L. *lympha,* water, perh. akin to *limpidus,* E. *limpid.*] *Physiol.* a clear, coagulable, bodily fluid, composed of plasma and white corpuscles, and carried in the lymphatic vessel system; any of similar fluids emitted from inflamed areas.—**lym·phoid,** lim′foid, *a.*

lym·phad·e·ni·tis, lim·fad″e·nī′tis, lim″fa·de·nī′tis, *n.* *Pathol.* inflammation of lymph nodes or glands.

lym·phat·ic, lim·fat′ik, *a.* [N.L. *lymphaticus.*] *Anat.* pertaining to, containing, or conveying lymph. Characterized by sluggishness of thought and action.—*n.* *Anat.* a lymphatic vessel.—**lym·phat·i·cal·ly,** *adv.*

lymph cell, *n.* A cell found in lymph; lymphocyte. Also **lymph cor·pus·cle.**

lymph gland, *n.* One of the numerous glandular masses of lymphatic tissue, scattered through the lymph system, which produces lymphocytes. Also **lymph node.**

lym·pho·blast, lim′fo·blast″, *n.* *Physiol.* an immature cell which becomes a lymphocyte.—**lym·pho·blas·tic,** *a.*

lym·pho·cyte, lim′fo·sīt″, *n.* *Physiol.* a leukocyte, one of the white blood corpuscles, which develops in the lymphatic tissues.—**lym·pho·cyt·ic,** lim″fo·sit′ik, *a.*

lym·pho·cy·to·sis, lim″fo·sī·tō′sis, *n.* *Pathol.* a condition of the blood involving an excessive number of lymphocytes.—**lym·pho·cy·tot·ic,** lim″fō·sī·tot′ik, *a.*

lym·pho·gran·u·lo·ma, lim″fo·gran″u·lō′ma, *n.* pl. **lym·pho·gran·u·lo·mas, lym·pho·gran·u·lo·ma·ta.** *Pathol.* The inflammation of a lymph node; a venereal disease marked by swollen lymphatic tissue.—**lym·pho·gran·u·lo·ma·to·sis,** *n.*

lym·pho·ma, lim·fō′ma, *n.* pl. **lym·pho·mas, lym·pho·ma·ta.** *Pathol.* a tumor which is found in the lymphoid tissue.—**lym·pho·ma·toid,** *a.*—**lym·pho·ma·to·sis,** *n.*—**lym·pho·ma·tous,** *a.*

lym·pho·poi·e·sis, lim″fo·poi″ē′sis, *n.* *Pathol.* the formation of lymphoid tissue.—**lym·pho·poi·et·ic,** *a.*

lyn·ce·an, lin·sē′an, *a.* [L. *lynceus,* < Gr. *lynkeios,* < *lygx,* E. *lynx.*] Pertaining to a lynx; lynx-eyed; sharp-sighted.

lynch, linch, *v.t.* To put to death by mob action, esp. by hanging or burning, without authority or due process of law.—**lynch·er,** *n.*—**lynch·ing,** *n.*

lynx, lingks, *n.* pl. **lynx, lynx·es.** [L., < Gr. *lynx,* lynx.] Any of various medium-sized cats of the genus *Lynx,* inhabiting Europe, Asia, and N. America, characterized by relatively long legs, a very short tail, tufted ears and cheek ruffs, esp. *L. canadensis,* the Canadian lynx, and *L. rufus,* the bobcat; (*cap.*), *astron.* a minor northern constellation between Ursa Major and Auriga.

lynx-eyed, lingks′īd″, *a.* Sharp-sighted.

ly·on·naise, lī″o·nāz′, *Fr.* lē·ạ·nez′, *a.* [From *Lyons,* France.] *Cookery,* prepared with onions; as, *lyonnaise* potatoes.

ly·o·phil·ic, lī″o·fil′ik, *a.* *Chem.* denoting a colloid which cannot be readily precipitated because of a strong affinity for the dispersion medium.

ly·oph·i·li·za·tion, lī·of″i·li·zā′shạn, *n.* *Biochem.* the process of drying by freezing biological materials in a vacuum.—**ly·oph·i·lize,** lī·of′i·līz″, *v.t.*—*lyophilized, lyophilizing.*

ly·o·pho·bic, lī″o·fō′bik, lī″o·fob′ik, *a.* *Chem.* noting a weak affinity between colloidal particles and the suspension medium.

ly·rate, lī′rāt, lī′rit, *a.* [N.L. *lyratus.*] *Zool.* lyre-shaped, as the tail of certain birds; *bot.* of a leaf, divided transversely into several lobes, the smallest at the base. Also **ly·rat·ed.**

lyre, līer, *n.* [O.Fr. *lire* (Fr. *lyre*), < L. *lyra,* < Gr. *lyra,* lyre.] A harplike musical instrument of ancient Greece, used for accompanying the voice in singing and recitation, and consisting typically of a hollow body with two curving arms connected near the top by a crosspiece from which strings are stretched to the body; (*cap.*), *astron.* the northern constellation Lyra.

lyre·bird, līer′bụrd″, *n.* One of two Australian songbirds, genus *Menura,* so named because the male displays a lyrate tail during courtship.

lyr·ic, lir′ik, *a.* [Fr. *lyrique,* < L. *lyricus,* < Gr. *lyrikos, lyra,* E. *lyre.*] *Poetry,* having the form and musical quality of a song; expressing ardent personal feelings. *Mus.* having a lightness of voice, as a tenor or soprano; pertaining, adapted, or sung to the lyre, or composing poems to be sung to the lyre.—*n.* A lyric poem; *usu. pl.* the text of a song.—**lyr·i·cal,** *a.*—**lyr·i·cal·ly,** *adv.*—**lyr·i·cal·ness,** *n.*

lyr·i·cism, lir′i·siz″um, *n.* Songlike character or style, as in poetry; artistic expression of personal feeling.—**lyr·i·cist,** lir′i·sist, *n.* A lyric poet; a writer of song lyrics.

lyr·ism, lir′iz·um, *n.* [Fr. *lyrisme,* < *lyrique,* E. *lyric.*] Lyricism; musical performance.

lyr·ist, līer′ist, lir′ist, *n.* [= Fr. *lyriste,* < L. *lyristes,* < Gr. *lyristes.*] One who plays on the lyre, līer′ist. A lyric poet, lir′ist.

lyse, līs, *v.t.*—*lysed, lysing. Biochem.* to cause the dissolution of cells by lysins.—*v.i. Biochem.* to undergo such dissolution.

Ly·sen·ko·ism, li·seng′kō·iz″um, *n.* [From T. *Lysenko,* Russ. agronomist and biologist, 1898– .] *Biol.* a theory maintaining that acquired characteristics are inherited by the influence of environmental factors on chromosomes and genes: opposed to orthodox genetic theory.

ly·ser·gic ac·id, li·sụr′jik as′id, lī·sụr′jik as′id, *n.* An acidic crystalline solid which is an ergot derivative and the base of LSD.

ly·sin, lī′sin, *n. Biochem.* any of a class of substances acting as antibodies and capable of causing the dissolution or destruction of bacteria, blood corpuscles, and other cellular elements.

ly·sine, lī′sēn, lī′sin, *n.* A basic amino acid, $NH_2(CH_2)_4CH(NH_2)COOH$, necessary to animal nutrition.

ly·sis, lī′sis, *n.* [N.L., < Gr. *lysis,* a loosing, solution, dissolution, < *lyein,* loose.] *Med.* the gradual recession of a disease; *biochem.* the dissolution or destruction of cells by lysins.

Ly·sol, lī′sōl, lī′sol, *n.* A disinfectant and antiseptic containing phenol derivatives saponified for solubility in water. (Trademark.)

ly·so·zyme, lī′so·zīm″, *n. Biochem.* an enzyme capable of disintegrating bacteria, found in the latex of some plants, in tears and mucus, and in leukocytes.

lyt·ic, lit′ik, *a.* [Gr. *lytikos,* able to loose, < *lyein,* loose.] *Physiol.* pertaining to or producing lysis.

lyt·ta, lit′a, *n.* pl. **lyt·tas, lyt·tae,** lit′ē. [L. < Gr. *lytta, lyssa,* rabies.] A long, wormlike cartilage in the tongues of dogs and other carnivorous animals, once thought to be capable of causing rabies.

M

M, m, em, *n.* pl. **M's, Ms, m's, ms.** The thirteenth letter and tenth consonant of the English alphabet, representing a labially articulated nasal sound; a graphic delineation of this letter; the spoken sound represented by M or m; something like the letter M in shape; the Roman numeral for 1,000. *Print.* a device for printing the letter M or m; an em.

ma, mä, *n.* Childish or colloquial form of mamma or mother.

M.A. Abbr. for Master of Arts, an advanced academic degree.

ma'am, mam, mäm, mam, *n.* [Contr. of madam.] *Colloq.* madam; *Brit.* a courteous form used to address the Queen or a princess.

mac, mak, *n.* (*Often cap.*), *slang*, a form of address for a man whose name is unknown; *Brit. colloq.* a mackintosh.

ma·ca·bre, ma·ca·ber, ma·kab′re, ma·kab′re, *a.* [Fr. *macabre*, death.] Ghastly; hideous; gruesome; suggesting or dwelling on the frightening, ugly aspect of death.—**ma·ca·bre·ly,** *adv.*

ma·ca·co, ma·kä′kō, ma·kä′kō, *n. pl.* **ma·ca·cos.** [= Fr. *mococo*: cf. Fr. *maki*, lemur, < Malagasy *maka*.] Any of various species of lemur.

mac·ad·am, ma·kad′am, *n.* [From J. L. *McAdam*, 1756–1836, Sc. inventor.] Macadamized roadway; the material used for making it.—**mac·ad·am·ize,** ma·kad′a·mīz″, *v.t.*—*macadamized, macadamizing.* To make or cover, as a road, by the laying down and pressing together of layers of small broken stones, often held together with tar or asphalt.—**mac·ad·am·i·za·tion,** *n.*

mac·a·da·mi·a nut, mak″a·dā′mē·a nut, *n.* The hard-shelled, edible nut produced by the tree, genus *Macadamia*, of Australia.

ma·caque, ma·käk′, *n.* [Fr. < Pg. *macaco*, said to be of African origin.] Any of various monkeys of the genus *Macaca*, found chiefly in Asia, having cheek pouches and a short tail.

mac·a·ro·ni, mac·ca·ro·ni, mak″a·rō′nē, *n. pl.* **mac·a·ro·nis, mac·a·ro·nies.** [Fr. and Provinc. It. *macaroni*, It. *maccheroni*, orig. a mixture of flour, cheese, and butter.] A dough of fine wheat flour dried in tubular form; formerly a fop or dandy.

mac·a·ron·ic, mak″a·ron′ik, *a.* [M.L. *macaronicus,* < It. *maccaroni* (orig. a mixture of flour, cheese, and butter), E. *macaroni.*] Pertaining to a mixture of Latin or Greek with words from another language; combining non-Latin words with Latin endings as a kind of burlesque verse; involving a mixture of languages; *fig.* mixed or jumbled.—*n. Usu. pl.* macaronic composition, poem or verse; language macaronic in nature.—**mac·a·ron·i·cal·ly,** *adv.*

mac·a·roon, mak″a·rön′, *n.* A small sweet cooky, made of egg white and sugar, and containing almond meal or shredded coconut.

ma·caw, ma·kạ′, *n.* [Brazil.] Any of various large, long-tailed parrots, chiefly of the genus *Ara*, inhabiting tropical and subtropical America, and notable for their brilliant plumage and harsh voices.

Mac·ca·bees, mak′a·bēz″, *n. pl., but sing. in constr. O.T.* the books treating of Jewish history under the Maccabean princes, included in the Apocrypha. *Pl. in constr.* the family of Jewish priests and patriots, descended from Mattathias and his sons, who began the revolution against the Syrians for national and religious freedom in 168 B.C.—**Mac·ca·be·an,** mak″a·bē′an, *a.*

mac·ca·boy, mak′a·boi″, *n.* [From *Macouba*, town in Martinique.] A kind of snuff, usu. rose-scented. Also **mac·co·boy, mac·ca·baw.**

mace, mās, *n.* [O.Fr. *mace* (Fr. *masse*): cf. L. *mateola*, mallet.] A medieval weapon of war consisting of a heavy staff or club, often with a spiked metal head; any club-like weapon or implement; a staff borne before or by certain officials as a symbol of office; the bearer of such a staff; a light stick with a flat head, formerly used in place of a cue in playing billiards.—**mace·bear·er,** mās′bâr″ĕr, *n.*

mace, mās, *n.* [Fr. *macis*, It. *mace*, L. *macis, macir,* Gr. *maker,* an Indian spice.] A spice, the dried covering of the seed of the nutmeg, usu. ground, and used in cooking or in pickling.

Mace, mās, *n.* A chemical spray with a range of up to thirty feet, which will render a person docile on contact and is sometimes used by police to subdue unmanageable persons. (Trademark.)—**mace,** *v.t.*—*maced, macing.* To spray with Mace.

mac·é·doine, mas″i·dwän′, *Fr.* mä·sä·dwän′, *n. pl.* **mac·é·doines,** mas″i·dwänz′, *Fr.* mä·sä·dwän′. [Fr., early meaning, Macedonian parsley.] A sauce, jellied salad, or simple mixture of small or diced vegetables or fruits; any mixture or combination.

Mac·e·do·ni·an, mas″i·dō′nē·an, *a.* [From *Macedonia*, an ancient country north of Greece, now a region comprising parts of Bulgaria, Greece, and Yugoslavia.] Of or relating to the ancient or modern region of Macedonia, its language, or people.—*n.* One born or living in ancient or modern Macedonia; the Slavic language spoken in modern Macedonia; the now extinct language of ancient Macedonia.

mac·er·ate, mas′e·rāt″, *v.t.*—*macerated, macerating.* [L. *maceratus,* pp. of *macerare,* soften, macerate.] To soften or separate the parts of, as a substance, by steeping in a liquid, with or without heat; to steep in order to extract soluble constituents; to soften or break up, as food, by the digestive process; to cause to grow lean or waste away.—*v.i.* To undergo maceration.—**mac·er·a·tion,** *n.*—**mac·er·a·tor,** *n.*

mach, mäk, mak, *G.* mäch, *n.* [From Ernst *Mach*, 1838–1916, Austrian physicist.] (*Sometimes cap.*) the ratio or relation of the speed of a moving body or a part thereof to the speed of sound in the medium in which it moves, indicated by a number; as, *mach* 1, a speed equal to that of sound. Also **mach num·ber.**

mach an·gle, *n.* The acute angle between a mach line and the line of flight of a moving body.

ma·chet·e, ma·shet′ē, ma·chet′ē, *Sp.* mä·chä′tä, *n. pl.* **ma·chet·es.** [Sp.] A large knife or cutlass, used esp. in Central and South America as a tool or a weapon.

Mach·i·a·vel·li·an, mak″ē·a·vel′ē·an, *a.* Pertaining to Niccolò Machiavelli, 1469–1527, an Italian writer and statesman; in conformity with Machiavelli's principles; crafty and deceitful in seeking and maintaining political power; marked by unscrupulous cunning or guile.—*n.* One who adopts the principles of Machiavelli.—**Mach·i·a·vel·li·an·ism,** *n.*

ma·chic·o·la·tion, ma·chik″o·lā′shan, *n.* [Fr. *mâchicoulis, mâchecoulis;* origin doubtful.] *Arch.* The floor opening in a projecting gallery or parapet through which molten lead or missiles were dropped upon the enemy; a structure with such openings.—**ma·chic·o·late,** ma·chik′o·lāt,*v.t.*—*machicolated, machicolating.*

mach·i·nate, mak′i·nāt″, *v.t., v.i.*—*machinated, machinating.* [L. *machinatus,* pp. of *machinari,* contrive, < *machina,* machine.] To contrive or devise, esp. artfully or with evil purpose; to plot.—**mach·i·na·tion,** mak″i·nā′shan, *n.* [L. *machinatio(n-).*] The act or process of machinating; artful or evil contrivance; *often pl.* a crafty scheme, evil design, or plot.—**mach·i·na·tor,** *n.*

ma·chine, ma·shēn′, *n.* [Fr. *machine,* < L. *machina,* < Gr. *mēchanē,* contrivance, machine, < *mēchos,* means, expedient.] An apparatus, consisting of interrelated parts with separate functions, and used in the performance of some kind of work; a me-

chanical apparatus or contrivance; something operated by a mechanical apparatus, as an automobile or a bicycle; a contrivance, esp. in the ancient theater, for producing stage effects; an incident or feature introduced for effect into a literary composition; the human or animal frame considered as a mechanical apparatus; a person acting like a mere mechanical apparatus; any complex agency or operating system; as, the *machine* of government; the body of persons conducting and controlling the activities of a political party or other organization; a device which transmits and modifies force or movement, as the lever, wedge, wheel and axle, pulley, screw, and inclined plane. See *simple machine.*—*v.t.*—*machined, machining.* To make, prepare, or finish with a machine or mechanical apparatus.—**ma·chin·a·bil·i·ty,** *n.*—**ma·chin·a·ble, ma·chine·a·ble,** *a.*—**ma·chine·like,** *a.*

ma·chine gun, *n.* An automatic weapon, using small-arms ammunition, capable of delivering a rapid and continuous round of gunfire.—**ma·chine-gun,** *v.t.*—*machine-gunned, machine-gunning.* To shoot or fire at, employing a machine gun.—**ma·chine gun·ner,** *n.*

ma·chine lan·guage, *n.* Instructions or information expressed in the form of a code which can be directly processed by a computer.

ma·chin·er·y, ma·shē′ne·rē, *n. pl.* **ma·chin·er·ies.** Any collection or functioning unit of machines or mechanical apparatus; the parts of a machine, collectively; any combination or system of agencies by which action is maintained; as, the *machinery* of government; a group of contrivances for producing stage effects; *liter.* plot devices, esp. those involving supernatural beings or events.

ma·chine shop, *n.* A workshop in which materials, chiefly metals, are cut and shaped by machine tools.

ma·chine tool, *n.* A power-driven machine for cutting or shaping wood, metals, or the like, as a lathe or planer.

ma·chin·ist, ma·shē′nist, *n.* One who operates machinery or machine tools; one who makes, assembles, or repairs machines; *U.S. Navy,* a warrant officer who serves under an engineer officer.

mach line, *n.* A theoretical line representing the backsweep of a cone-shaped shock wave made by an assumed infinitesimally small particle moving at the same speed and along the same flight path as that of an actual body or particle: used in defining effects resulting from supersonic speeds.

mach·me·ter, mäk′mē″tĕr, mak′mē″tĕr, *n.* A special indicator which measures airspeed relative to the speed of sound, and indicates the speed which an airplane using the mach-meter cannot exceed without encountering damage due to compressibility or mach effects. See *mach.*

mach wave, *n.* A species of shock wave theoretically formed by an infinitesimally small particle moving at supersonic speed, the same as that of an actual body, the wave forming a mach angle with the line of flight of the body. See *mach.*

mack, mak, *n. Brit. colloq.* mackintosh. Also *mac.*

mack·er·el, mak′ĕr·el, mak′rel, *n. pl.* **mack·er·el, mack·er·els.** [O.Fr. *maquerel* (Fr. *maquereau*); origin unknown.] An edible fish, *Scomber scombrus,* of the N. Atlantic, distinguished by dark blue stripes on its back and a silvery underside; any of various fishes of the scombroid family.

mack·er·el sky, *n.* A sky spotted with small, white, fleecy clouds.

Mack·i·naw, mak′i·nạ″, *n.* A short coat of a thick blanketlike, often plaid, woolen material. Also **Mack·i·naw coat.**

Mack·i·naw blan·ket, *n.* A thick blanket often woven with bars of color, formerly worn in the northern and western U.S. by Indians, lumbermen, traders, and the like.

Mack·i·naw boat, *n.* A flat-bottomed boat with sharp prow and square stern, propelled by oars and sometimes sails.

mack·in·tosh, mac·in·tosh, makʹinˑtosh″, *n.* [From Charles *Mackintosh*, 1766–1843, the inventor.] A cloth coat made waterproof by means of India rubber; the cloth itself; any waterproof coat.— **mack·in·toshed,** *a.*

mack·le, makʹl, *n.* [Fr. *macule*, < L. *macula*, spot.] A blur in printing, as from a double impression. Also *macule.*—*v.t., v.i.* —*mackled, mackling.* To blur or become blurred. Also *macule,* makʹūl.

ma·cle, makʹl, *n.* [Fr. L. *macula*, a spot, the mesh of a net.] A double crystal, particularly a flat, double crystal of a diamond.

mac·ra·mé, makʹraˑmā″, *n.* [Ar. *migramah*, embroidered veil, Turk. *makrama*, kerchief.] Trimming, fringe, or heavy lace of knotted thread, usu. in geometrical patterns. Also **mac·ra·me lace.**

mac·ro·ce·phal·ic, makʺrōˑseˑfalʹik, *a.* [Gr. *macrocephalos*, < *macros*, long, large, and *cephlē*, head.] Having an abnormally large head or cranial capacity. Also **mac·ro·ceph·a·lous,** makʺrōˑsefʹaˑlus.— **mac·ro·ceph·a·ly,** makʺrōˑsefʹaˑlē, *n.*

mac·ro·cosm, makʹroˑkoz″um, *n.* [Fr. *macrocosme*, < M.L. *macrocosmus*, < Gr. *macro*, long, large, and *cosmos*, world.] The great world, or universe: opposed to *microcosm.* The whole complex set up; as, the *macrocosm* of poverty, a large scale model of a smaller unit.— **mac·ro·cos·mic,** makʺroˑkozʹmik, *a.*— **mac·ro·cos·mi·cal·ly,** *adv.*

mac·ro·cyte, makʹroˑsīt″, *n.* A red blood cell which is abnormally large.— **mac·ro·cyt·ic,** makʺroˑsitʹik, *a.*— **mac·ro·cy·to·sis,** makʺroˑsīʹtōʹsis, *n.*

mac·ro·ev·o·lu·tion, makʺrōˑevʺoˑlōʹshan, *n.* A sudden, complex mutation or inherited change in animals or plants above the level of a species. Also **sal·ta·tion ev·o·lu·tion.**—**mac·ro·ev·o·lu·tion·ar·y,** *a.*

mac·ro·gam·ete, makʹrōˑgamʹēt, makʺrōˑgaˑmēt′, *n. Biol.* the larger of two gametes in conjugation, usu. the female reproductive cell. Also *megagamete.*

mac·ro·graph, makʹroˑgraf″, makʹroˑgräf″, *n.* A photograph or drawing either life-sized or larger.

ma·crog·ra·phy, maˑkrogʹraˑfē, *n.* The investigation of something by use of the naked eye, as opposed to *micrography;* the use of very large characters in handwriting, or the writing itself.

ma·cron, māʹkron, makʹron, *n.* [N.L., < Gr. *makron,* neut. of *makros,* long.] A short horizontal line placed over a vowel to indicate the pronunciation is long, as *ā* in *cave.*

mac·ro·nu·cle·us, makʺroˑnöʹklēˑus, makʺroˑnūʹklēˑus, *n. Zool.* the larger nucleus in a ciliate protozoan.—**mac·ro·nu·cle·ar, mac·ro·nu·cle·ate,** *a.*

mac·ro·phage, makʹroˑfāj″, *n. Biol.* a large phagocytic cell found in connective tissues.— **mac·ro·phag·ic,** makʺroˑfajʹik, *a.*

mac·rop·ter·ous, maˑkropʹtĕrˑus, *a. Zool.* large-winged or finned.—**mac·rop·ter·y,** *n.*

mac·ro·scop·ic, makʺroˑskopʹik, *a.* [Cf. *microscopic.*] Visible to the naked eye, as opposed to *microscopic.* Also **mac·ro·scop·i·cal.**—**mac·ro·scop·i·cal·ly,** *adv.*

ma·cru·run, maˑkrürʹan, *a.* Of or pertaining to crustaceans of the suborder *Macrura,* including the lobster, prawn, crayfish, and shrimp, marked by their having large abdomens and long tails. Also **ma·cru·ral, ma·cru·roid.**—*n.*

ma·cru·rous, maˑkrürʹas, *a.* Long-tailed; pertaining to crustaceans of the suborder *Macrura.*

mac·u·la, makʹūˑla, *n.* pl. **mac·u·lae,** makʹūˑlē. [L., a spot.] A spot or stain, esp. a discolored spot on the skin. Also *macule.*— **ma·cu·lar,** *a.*

mac·u·late, makʹūˑlāt, *v.t.*—*maculated, maculating.* [L. *maculatus,* pp. of *maculare,* < *macula,* a spot.] To mark with a spot or spots; to stain; to pollute.—makʹūˑlit, *a.* Spotted; stained; defiled or impure.— **mac·u·la·tion,** makʺūˑlāʹshan, *n.* A spotting or a spotted condition; a marking of spots, as on an animal or a plant; a disfiguring spot or stain; defilement.

mac·ule, makʹūl, *n.* Mackle; macula.— *v.t., v.i.*—*maculed, maculing.* Mackle.

mad, mad, *a.*—*madder, maddest.* [M.E. *madd,* < O.E. *gemædd, gemæded,* pp. of a verb < *gemād,* mad; akin to Icel. *meidha,* hurt, maim, Goth. *maidjan,* change, corrupt.] Insane; mentally deranged; foolish or imprudent; affected with or characterized by wild excitement; frenzied or frantic; as, *mad* cries, *mad* haste; wild with eagerness, fondness, or desire; infatuated; furious with anger; wildly gay; furious in violence; as, the *mad* tempest; abnormally furious or violent; as, a *mad* bull; affected with rabies; rabid.—*v.t., v.i.*—*madded, madding.*—*n.* A period or interval of bad temper; anger.—**like mad,** *slang,* frantically; with much haste or enthusiasm.—**mad as a hat·ter,** quite crazy.—**mad·ly,** *adv.*

mad·am, madʹam, *n.* pl. **mes·dames,** māˑdam′, māˑdäm′, *Fr.* meˑdäm′, **mad·ams.** [O.Fr. Fr. *madame,* orig. *ma dame,* 'my lady.'] A term of address used orig. to a woman of rank or authority, but now as a conventional courtesy to any woman; pl. **mes·dames.** A woman who manages a household, as: Is the *madam* of the house at home? A woman who operates a brothel; pl. **mad·ams.**

mad·ame, madʹam, maˑdam′, maˑdäm′, maˑdam′, maˑdäm′, *Fr.* mäˑdäm′, *n.* pl. **mes·dames,** māˑdam′, māˑdäm′, *Fr.* meˑdäm′. A French title of respect, used to or of a married woman who is not of English or American nationality. Abbr. *Mme.*

mad·cap, madʹkap″, *a.* Rash, impulsive, or reckless; flighty or harebrained.—*n.*

mad·den, madʹen, *v.t.* To make mad; to craze; to enrage.—*v.i.* To become mad; to act as if mad.—**mad·den·ing,** madʹeˑning, *a.*—**mad·den·ing·ly,** *adv.*

mad·der, madʹĕr, *n.* [O.E. *mædere* = Icel. *madhra,* madder.] A European plant, *Rubia tinctorum,* in the madder family, once widely cultivated for its roots which yield a scarlet dye; the dye itself; the color, turkey red, produced by the dye; any of various other plants of the genus *Rubia.*

mad·ding, madʹing, *a.* Acting madly; behaving senselessly; inducing madness.

made, mād, *a.* Fashioned or constructed, not naturally existing; fabricated or invented; as, a *made* word; specially prepared from various ingredients; as, a *made* gravy, a *made* dish; assured of success or fortune; as, a *made* man.—**have it made,** *slang,* to be fortunately situated, or certain to be successful.

Ma·dei·ra, maˑdērʹa, maˑderʹa, *Port.* mäˑdeʹRa, *n.* A dessert wine, similar to sherry, made on the Portuguese islands of Madeira.

mad·e·moi·selle, madʺeˑmoˑzel′, madʺmwoˑzel′, *Fr.* mädˑmwäˑzel′, *n.* pl. **mad·e·moi·selles, mes·de·moi·selles,** madʺeˑmoˑzelz′, madʺmwoˑzelz′, mäʺdeˑmoˑzel′, mädʹmwoˑzel′, *Fr.* mädˑmwäˑzel′. [Fr., orig. *madamoisele,* 'my noble lady.'] The conventional French title of respect for a girl or unmarried woman who is not of English or American nationality (see

madame), used separately or, like *Miss,* prefixed to the name. Abbr. *Mlle.,* pl. *Mlles.*

made-up, mādʹup′, *a.* Concocted, fabricated, or invented; assembled; resolute or determined; as, a *made-up* mind; wearing facial cosmetics or make-up.

mad·house, madʹhous″, *n.* A confused or chaotic situation or place; a hospital or asylum for the mentally disturbed.

mad·man, madʹman″, madʹman, *n.* pl. **mad·men.** A lunatic; a maniac.

mad·ness, madʹnis, *n.* The state or quality of being mad; insanity; extreme enthusiasm or excitement; folly. Rabies.

Ma·don·na, maˑdonʹa, *n.* [It. *ma donna,* < L. *mea domina,* my lady.] The Virgin Mary, usu. with *the;* a statue or picture depicting the Virgin Mary.

Ma·don·na lil·y, *n.* A common, hardy, outdoor lily, *Lilium candidum,* with clear waxy white flowers. Also **An·nun·ci·a·tion lil·y.**

mad·ras, madʹras, maˑdras′, maˑdräs′, *n.* [From *Madras,* India.] A cotton cloth of fine thread and close weave, having woven stripes or patterns, used for garments; a light, open-weave drapery fabric patterned or striped with heavier yarns; a large cotton kerchief.

mad·re·pore, madʹreˑpōr″, *n.* [Fr. *madrépore,* < It. *madrepora,* < *madre,* mother, and Gr. *pŏros,* a kind of stone.] *Zool.* a common variety of branching, stonelike reef coral.—**mad·re·po·ri·an, mad·re·por·ic, mad·re·po·rit·ic,** madʺreˑpōrʹēˑan, madʺreˑparʹik, madʺreˑporʹik, madʺreˑpoˑritʹik, maˑdrepʺoˑritʹik, *a.*

mad·ri·gal, madʹriˑgal, *n.* [It. *madrigale,* earlier *madriale, mandriale,* appar. orig. a pastoral song, < *mandra,* < L. *mandra,* stall, herd, < Gr. *mandra,* enclosed space, fold.] A short amatory or pastoral lyric poem adaptable to musical accompaniment, popular, esp. during the 16th century; a part song without instrumental accompaniment, usu. for five or six voices, and using contrapuntal imitation; any part song; a song.—**mad·ri·gal·ist,** madʹriˑgaˑlist, *n.* A composer or a singer of madrigals.

mad·ri·lène, madʹriˑlen″, madʹriˑlän″, *Fr.* mäˑdRēˑlen′, *n.* A clear, tomato-flavored soup, often served chilled.

ma·dro·ño, maˑdrōnʹyō, *n.* pl. **ma·dro·ños,** *Bot.* an ornamental evergreen shrub, *Arbutus menziesii,* in the heath family, native to western N. America, having smooth red bark, shining leaves, and orange-red berries. Also **ma·dro·ña, ma·dro·ne,** maˑdrōnʹya, maˑdrōʹne.

ma·du·ro, maˑdụrʹō, *n.* A dark cigar of strong flavor.—*a.*

mad·wort, madʹwụrt″, *n.* A prickly-stemmed plant, *Asperugo procumbens,* of the borage family; a yellow-flowered plant of the genus *Alyssum,* in the mustard family; gold-of-pleasure.

Mae·ce·nas, mēˑsēʹnas, mīˑsēʹnas, *n.* [From Gaius Cilnius *Maecenas,* 70–8 B.C., Roman patron of letters, and friend of Virgil and Horace.] A generous patron, esp. of literature or art.

mael·strom, mālʹstrom, *n.* [Dutch *malen,* to grind, *stroom,* a stream.] Any great or forceful whirlpool; a turbulent and agitated state or condition, as of affairs or emotions; (*cap.*) a whirlpool off the coast of Norway.

mae·nad, mēʹnad, *n.* [L. *Mænas (Mænad-),* < Gr. *mainas (mainad-),* < *mainesthai,* rage, be mad.] A bacchante; a frenzied or raging woman. Also *menad.*—**mae·nad·ic,** mēˑnadʹik, *a.*—**mae·nad·ism,** *n.*

ma·es·to·so, mīˑstōʹsō, *It.* mäʺesˑtạʹsạ, *a., adv.* [It.] *Mus.* with majesty or stateliness: a musical direction.

maes·tro, mīʹstrō, *It.* mäˑesʹtRạ, *n.* pl. **maes·tros,** *It.* mäˑesˑtrī, *It.* mäˑesˑtRē. [It., < L. *magister,* a master.] A master of music, as a conductor, composer, or performer; a master of any art.

Mae West, *n.* [From *Mae West*, American stage and screen actress.] An inflatable rubber jacket for use as a life preserver.

Ma·fi·a, mä´fē·a, *n.* A secret organization in Sicily which disregards laws and enforces its own code, often by terrorism; similar and perhaps related organizations in the U.S. and other countries, alleged to be engaged in large-scale criminal activities, as gambling and traffic in narcotics; also **Maf·fi·a.** (*l.c.*) the spirit of hostility to law in Sicily.

mag·a·zine, mag´´a·zēn´, mag´a·zēn´´, *n.* [Fr. *magasin*, It. *magazzino*, storehouse, < Ar.] A periodical publication, usu. with a paper cover, containing miscellaneous articles, and often illustrations and photographs; a building or room for keeping military stores, as arms, ammunition, and provisions; a room or place for keeping gunpowder and other explosives, as in a fort or on a warship; a storehouse or warehouse; a stock of goods; a chamber in a rifle or shotgun from which cartridges are automatically fed; a removable box which holds the film in some cameras.—**mag·a·zin·ist,** mag´´a·zē´nist, *n.* A member of the staff of a magazine.

mag·da·len, mag´da·len, *n.* [From Mary *Magdalene*, St. Luke vii. 36–50.] A reformed prostitute; a house or refuge established for the purpose of reforming prostitutes. Also **mag·da·lene,** mag´da·lēn´´, mag´da·lē´nē.

Mag·da·le·ni·an, mag´da·lē´nē·an, *a.* Of or referring to a culture of the Upper Paleolithic period characterized by the highest industrial and artistic accomplishments attained by Cro-Magnon man.

Mag·el·lan·ic cloud, maj´´e·lan´ik kloud, *n.* [From Ferdinand *Magellan*, Portuguese explorer, 1480?–1521.] *Astron.* either of two tracts of nebulous stars in the southern heavens, the nearest galaxies to the Milky Way.

Ma·gen Da·vid, mä·gän´ dä·vēd´, mä´gen dä´vid, *n.* Star of David.

ma·gen·ta, ma·jen´ta, *n.* [From *Magenta*, in northern Italy, where a battle was won by French and Sardinians over Austrians in 1859, the year when the dye was discovered.] Fuchsin; a purplish-red color.

mag·got, mag´ot, *n.* [W. *magiad*, a maggot or grub, < *magu*, to breed.] The legless, wormlike larva of many dipterous insects, esp. that found in decaying animal matter. —**mag·got·y,** *a.*

Ma·gi, mä´jī, *n. pl.*, *sing.* **Ma·gus.** [L., < Gr. *Mágos*; < Pers]. The three wise men who came to Jerusalem paying homage to the infant Jesus; (*sometimes l.c.*) the Zoroastrian priestly caste in ancient Media and Persia, traditionally reputed to have practiced supernatural arts; (*l.c.*) magicians, sorcerers, or astrologers.—**Ma·gi·an,** mä´jē·an, *n.*, *a.*—**Ma·gi·an·ism,** *n.*

mag·ic, maj´ik, *n.* [L. *magicus*, pertaining to sorcery, < *magia*, Gr. *mageia*, the theology of the Magians, magic.] The art of producing effects by seemingly superhuman control over the powers of nature; sorcery; enchantment; any power or influence that proves irresistible or extraordinary; the use of legerdemain to create illusions or perform tricks.—*a.*—**mag·i·cal,** maj´i·kal, *a.*—**mag·i·cal·ly,** maj´ik lē, *adv.*

ma·gi·cian, ma·jish´an, *n.* One skilled in magic; an entertainer performing tricks of illusion and deception; an enchanter.

mag·ic lan·tern, *n.* An early model of a slide projector.

Ma·gi·not line, mazh´i·nō´´ lin, *Fr.* mä·zhē·nō´, *n.* [From André *Maginot*, 1877–1932, Fr. minister of war.] The vast series of French fortifications which the German army outflanked in 1940. *Fig.*

any situation, arrangement, or institution that provides an illusion of security; any defensive system that fails to protect.

mag·is·te·ri·al, maj´´i·stēr´ē·al, *a.* [L. *magisterius*, < *magister*, a master.] Belonging to a master or ruler; pertaining to a magistrate or his office; authoritative; arrogant; pompous.—**mag·is·te·ri·al·ly,** *adv.*—**mag·is·te·ri·al·ness,** *n.*

mag·is·tral, maj´i·stral, *a.* [L. *magistralis*, < *magister*, E. *master*.] *Phar.* prescribed or prepared for a particular person or occasion; *fort.* principal or chief; as, a *magistral* line.

mag·is·trate, maj´i·strāt´´, maj´i·strit, *n.* [L. *magistratus*, a magistrate, < *magister*, a master.] A civil officer in the executive branch of the government; a low-ranking judicial officer with limited jurisdiction, as a justice of the peace or police court judge. —**mag·is·tra·cy,** maj´i·stra·sē, *n.* pl. **mag·is·tra·cies.** The office or dignity of a magistrate; the district of a magistrate; a body of magistrates. Also **mag·is·tra·ture,** maj´i·strā´´chèr.

mag·ma, mag´ma, *n.* pl. **mag·mas, mag·ma·ta,** mag´ma·ta. [L., < Gr. *magma*, < *massein*, knead.] Any soft, pasty mass of mineral or organic matter; *geol.* molten material within or beneath the earth's crust, from which igneous rock is formed; *phar.* a suspension of matter in a small amount of liquid.—**mag·mat·ic,** mag·mat´ik, *a.*

Mag·na Char·ta, Mag·na Car·ta, mag´na kär´ta, *n.* [M.L., 'great charter.'] The great English charter of personal and political liberty, obtained from King John by the English barons at Runnymede on June 15, 1215; any constitution guaranteeing fundamental, personal, or other rights.

mag·na cum lau·de, mäg´na kụm lou´dä, mäg´na kụm lou´de, mäg´na kụm lou´dē, mag´na kụm la´dē, *adv.* [L., lit. 'with great praise.'] With high honor or distinction: used to denote academic excellence. See *cum laude, summa cum laude.*

mag·na·nim·i·ty, mag´´na·nim´i·tē, *n.* pl. **mag·na·nim·i·ties.** The quality of being magnanimous; nobility or dignity of soul or character; an act which is magnanimous.

mag·nan·i·mous, mag·nan´i·mus, *a.* [L. *magnanimus—magnus*, great, and *animus*, mind.] Exhibiting nobleness of soul and generosity of mind; rising above ignoble motives and resentment; suggesting an elevated spirit.—**mag·nan·i·mous·ly,** *adv.* —**mag·nan·i·mous·ness,** *n.*

mag·nate, mag´nāt, mag´nit, *n.* [L. *magnates* (pl.), powerful persons, the great, < *magnus*, great.] A person of rank, influence, or power in a given field; a person of distinction in any area.

mag·ne·sia, mag·nē´zha, mag·nē´sha, *n.* [M.L. (in alchemy), N.L. manganese oxide, also magnesium oxide (in this sense appar. associated with L. *magnes*, magnet); prop. fem. of L. *Magnesius*, pertaining to Magnesia (district in Thessaly).] Magnesium oxide, MgO, a white tasteless substance used in manufacturing, and in medicine as an antacid and mild laxative.—**mag·ne·sian,** *a.*

mag·ne·site, mag´ni·sīt´´, *n.* A mineral consisting of magnesium carbonate, MgCO₃, usu. occurring in compact white masses, and used esp. in making materials for lining furnaces.

mag·ne·si·um, mag·nē´zē·um, mag·nē´zhum, mag·nē´shē·um, *n.* *Chem.* a light, malleable, ductile, silver-white metallic element that burns with a dazzling light, used in lightweight alloys. Sym. Mg, at. no. 12, at. wt. 24.312.

mag·net, mag´nit, *n.* [O.Fr. *magnete*, < L. *magnes* (*magnet-*), lodestone, magnet, < Gr.

Mágnes (*líthos*), '(stone) of Magnesia (in Thessaly),' lodestone.] A body, as a piece of iron or steel, which possesses the property of attracting certain substances, esp. iron, and which, in the form of a freely suspended needle or bar, tends to assume a north and south position; lodestone; any person or thing that attracts or draws, as by some inherent power or charm.—**mag·net·ic,** mag·net´ik, *a.*—**mag·net·i·cal·ly,** *adv.*

mag·net·ic e·qua·tor, *n.* An irregular imaginary line approximately parallel to and near the earth's equator, representing all points at which a magnetic needle has no inclination or dip. Also *aclinic line.*

mag·net·ic field, *n.* Any space or region in which magnetic forces are present, as the space or region in or around a piece of magnetized steel, or in or around an electrical current.

mag·net·ic flux, *n.* The amount of magnetic force or induction passing through a given plane within a magnetic field, expressed in maxwells.

mag·net·ic mo·ment, *n.* *Phys.* the product of the pole strength of a magnet and the distance between its poles.

mag·net·ic nee·dle, *n.* A thin steel magnetic bar which, when freely suspended in a horizontal plane, indicates the presence of the earth's magnetic forces and their direction, and which is the principal component of a compass.

mag·net·ic north, *n.* The direction indicated by a magnetic compass as north, generally different from that considered true north.

mag·net·ic pole, *n.* Either of two areas or poles on a magnet where the magnetic force is the greatest; either of two slightly shifting places on the earth's surface, each exerting an opposite magnetic pull, one located in the Arctic and one in the Antarctic.

mag·net·ic re·cord·ing, *n.* A process in which data, esp. sound, is recorded using magnetic tape, wire, or other magnetized materials; a recording made by this process.

mag·net·ic storm, *n.* A temporary disruption of the normal condition of the earth's magnetic field, occurring nearly simultaneously with sunspot activity, and affecting compasses and radio and wire transmission.

mag·net·ic tape, *n.* A ribbon of paper, metal, or plastic coated with material which is sensitive to electromagnetic impulses: used in making magnetic recordings.

mag·net·ism, mag´ni·tiz´´um, *n.* The characteristic properties possessed by the magnet; the agency producing magnetic phenomena. The science dealing with magnetic phenomena; also **mag·net·ics.** Magnetic or attractive power or charm.

mag·net·ite, mag´ni·tīt´´, *n.* A black native oxide of iron, Fe₃O₄, which is strongly attracted by a magnet.—**mag·net·it·ic,** mag·ni·tit´ik, *a.*

mag·net·ize, mag´ni·tīz´´, *v.t.*—*magnetized, magnetizing.* To communicate magnetic properties to; *fig.* to exert an attracting or compelling influence upon; *archaic,* to mesmerize.—**mag·net·iz·a·ble,** *a.* —**mag·net·i·za·tion,** mag´´ni·tī·zā´shan, *n.*—**mag·net·iz·er,** *n.*

mag·ne·to, mag·nē´tō, *n.* pl. **mag·ne·tos.** A magnetoelectric machine, esp. a small electric generator with permanent magnets, used to produce the alternating current which provides the ignition spark in an internal-combustion engine. Also **mag·ne·to·e·lec·tric gen·er·a·tor, mag·ne·to·gen·er·a·tor.**

mag·ne·to·e·lec·tric, mag·nē´´tō·i·lek´trik, *a.* Noting or pertaining to the induction of electric current by means of magnets. Also **mag·ne·to·e·lec·tri·cal.— mag·ne·to·e·lec·tric·i·ty,** *n.*

mag·ne·to·hy·dro·dy·nam·ics, mag·nē″tō·hī′drō·di·nam′iks, mag·nē″tō·hī″drō·di·nam′iks, *n. pl., sing. or pl. in constr. Phys.* the study of the interaction that exists between a magnetic field and an electrically conducting fluid.—**mag·ne·to·hy·dro·dy·nam·ic,** *a.*

mag·ne·tom·e·ter, mag″ni·tom′i·tėr, *n.* An instrument for measuring magnetic forces.—**mag·ne·to·met·ric,** mag″nē·tō·me′trik, *a.*—**mag·ne·tom·e·try,** *n.*

mag·ne·to·mo·tive, mag·nē″tō·mō′tiv, *a.* Producing magnetic effects; pertaining to such production.—**mag·ne·to·mo·tive force,** the force which gives rise to magnetic flux, equaling the magnetic flux multiplied by the reluctance.

mag·ne·ton, mag′ni·ton″, *n.* [< *magnetic.*] *Phys.* a unit used in measuring the magnetic moment of atomic particles.

mag·ne·to·sphere, mag·nē′to·sfēr″, *n. Phys.* a belt of ionized particles in the atmosphere, held there by the magnetic field of the earth, and extending about 40,000 miles beyond the exosphere.—**mag·ne·to·spher·ic,** *a.*

mag·ne·to·stric·tion, mag·nē″tō·strik′shan, *n. Phys.* the dimensional change in a ferromagnetic body when under the control of a magnetic field.—**mag·ne·to·stric·tive,** mag″nē″tō·strik′tiv, *a.*

mag·ne·tron, mag′ni·tron″, *n. Electron.* a vacuum tube in which the electron flow is under the control of a magnetic field external to the tube: used to produce radio waves of short frequencies.

Mag·nif·i·cat, mag·nif′i·kat″, mäg·nif′i·kät″, män·yif′i·kät″, *n.* [L., 'doth magnify': the first word of the hymn in the Vulgate.] The hymn of the Virgin Mary in Luke 1.46–55, beginning "My soul doth magnify the Lord," used as a canticle at evensong or vespers; a musical setting for this.

mag·ni·fi·ca·tion, mag″ni·fi·kā′shan, *n.* [L.L. *magnificatio(n-).*] The act of magnifying, or the state of being magnified; the degree of magnifying power; a magnified reproduction.

mag·nif·i·cent, mag·nif′i·sent, *a.* [O.Fr. *magnificent,* < L. *magnificent-* (recorded in compar., superl., and other forms), for *magnificus.*] Making a splendid appearance or show, as a house, dress, or jewels; fine in a way that commands admiration or awe; extraordinarily fine, or superb; impressive, noble, or sublime; (*usu. cap.*) great in deeds or achievement, used as a title; as, Lorenzo the *Magnificent.*—**mag·nif·i·cence,** *n.*—**mag·nif·i·cent·ly,** *adv.*

mag·nif·i·co, mag·nif′i·kō″, *n. pl.* **mag·nif·i·coes.** [It., < L. *magnificus.*] A Venetian nobleman; a lordly or distinguished person.

mag·ni·fy, mag′ni·fī″, *v.t.*—*magnified, magnifying.* [Fr. *magnifier,* < L. *magnificare.*] To make great or greater; enlarge; to increase the apparent dimensions of, as by use of a lens; to represent as greater than reality; to dramatize; to exaggerate; *archaic,* to extol or exalt.—*v.i.* To enlarge or be able to enlarge the apparent dimensions of objects.—**mag·ni·fi·a·ble,** *a.*—**mag·ni·fi·er,** *n.*

mag·nil·o·quent, mag·nil′o·kwent, *a.* Speaking in a lofty, pompous, or bombastic manner; having a high-flown or grandiose style; grandiloquent.—**mag·nil·o·quence,** *n.*—**mag·nil·o·quent·ly,** *adv.*

mag·ni·tude, mag′ni·töd″, mag′ni·tūd″, *n.* [L. *magnitudo,* < *magnus,* great; akin to Gr. *mégas,* great, and E. *mickle, much.*] Greatness, or great size, amount, extent, or importance; size, amount, or extent, without reference to greatness or smallness; as, to determine the *magnitude* of an angle;

greatness of moral character; *math.* a given number used as a basis for comparing quantities of the same or similar class. *Astron.* the brightness of a star expressed according to the numerical system used by astronomers, the brightest stars being of the first magnitude, and the least bright, of the sixth magnitude; also **vis·u·al mag·ni·tude.**

mag·no·lia, mag·nōl′ya, mag·nō′lē·a, *n.* [Named for Pierre *Magnol,* 1638–1715, French botanist.] *Bot.* Any ornamental tree or shrub of the genus *Magnolia,* native to eastern North America and Asia, having showy terminal flowers often appearing before the leaves; the blossom of such a tree, esp. *Magnolia grandiflora,* the State flower of Mississippi and Louisiana.—**mag·no·li·a·ceous,** mag·nō″lē·ā′shus, *a. Bot.* belonging to the family *Magnoliaceae,* whose floral parts are arranged spirally, and which includes the magnolia and tulip trees.

mag·num, mag′num, *n.* [L., a large thing.] A large-sized wine bottle with a capacity of about 51 liquid ounces.

mag·num o·pus, *n.* [L.] A great work; the major work or masterpiece of an author or artist.

mag·pie, mag′pī″, *n.* [From *Mag,* for *Margaret,* woman's name, and *pie.*] *Ornith.* any of several species of large, black-and-white corvine birds of the genus *Pica,* native to Europe and N. America, with wedge-shaped tails longer than the body, and noted for their mischievousness and noisy, harsh voices; *fig.* a talkative or chattering person.

mag·uey, mag′wā, ma·gā′, *Sp.* mä·ge′ē, *n.* [Sp.; prob. < Haitian.] *Bot.* The true maguey, *Agave cantala,* an Asiatic plant grown for its fibers which are used in cordage; a Mexican plant, *Agave atrovirens,* the juice of which is used in making the Mexican beverages pulque and mescal; any plants of the related genus *Furcraea;* any of the various fibres from such plants.

Ma·gus, ma′gus, *n. pl.* **Ma·gi.** See *Magi.*

Mag·yar, mag′yär, *Hung.* ma′dyoR, *n.* [Hung.] A member of the Finno-Ugric ethnic group, which forms the predominant element of the population of Hungary; the language of this race; a Hungarian.—*a.* Of or pertaining to the Magyars or their language; Hungarian.

ma·ha·ra·jah, ma·ha·ra·ja, mä″ha·rä′ja, *Hind.* ma·hä′Rä′ja, *n.* [Skt. *maha,* great, and *raja,* a prince or king.] The title assumed by some Indian princes ruling over a native state or much territory.—**ma·ha·ra·nee, ma·ha·ra·ni,** mä″ha·rä′nē, *Hind.* ma·hä′Rä′nē, *n.* [Skt., great queen or princess.] A female Indian ruler; the wife of a maharajah.

ma·hat·ma, ma·hät′ma, *n.* [Skt. *mahà,* great, *âtmâ,* mind, soul.] Esp. in India a highly esteemed, saintly, wise person; *theos.* a name for certain Asiatic holy men said to have occult powers.—**ma·hat·ma·ism,** *n.*

Ma·ha·ya·na, mä″ha·yä′na, *Hind.* ma·hä′yä′na, *n.* A system of Buddhist thought emphasizing universal salvation and compassion, practiced primarily in China, Japan, Tibet, and Mongolia.

Mah·di, mä′dē, *n. pl.* **Mah·dis.** [Ar. *mahdī,* lit. 'the guided or directed one.'] The title of an expected spiritual and temporal Muslim ruler destined to establish a reign of righteousness throughout the world; any of various claimants to this title, esp. Mohammed Ahmed who successfully led the Sudanese forces against British-held Khartoum in 1885.—**Mah·dism,** mä′diz·um, *n.* The doctrine of the coming of the Mahdi; adherence to or support of a claimant to this title.—**Mah·dist,** *n.*

Ma·hi·can, ma·hē′kan, *n. pl.* **Ma·hi·can, Ma·hi·cans.** A tribe of the Algonquian

Indian stock formerly living in the northern Hudson Valley; a member of this tribe. Also *Mohican.*

mah-jongg, mah-jong, mä′jang′, mä′jong′, mä′zhang′, mä′zhong′, *n.* [Corruption of Chinese *ma-ch′iao,* sparrow (lit. 'hemp-bird'): referring to the bird pictured on the first tiles of one of the suits.] A game of Chinese origin, usu. played by 4 persons with 144 dominolike pieces marked in suits, each player adding to and discarding from his tiles in order to form a winning set.

mahl·stick, maul·stick, mäl′stik″, mal′stik″, *n.* [G. and D. *malen,* to paint, and E. *stick.*] A stick used by painters to steady and support the hand in working.

ma·hog·a·ny, ma·hog′a·nē, *n. pl.* **ma·hog·a·nies.** [Prob. W. Ind.] An evergreen, tropical tree, *Swietenia mahogani,* native to Central America and the W. Indies and introduced into other tropical countries; the reddish-brown, strong, hard, heavy wood obtained from this tree; a substitute mahogany, *Cariniana pyriformis,* native to Columbia; a reddish-brown color.—*a.* Being mahogany in color.

ma·hout, ma·hout′, *n.* [Hind.] In India and the E. Indies, an elephant driver and keeper.

Mah·rat·ta, ma·rat′a, *n.* One of a race of Hindus inhabiting southwest and central India. Also *Maratha.*

maid, mād, *n.* [Short for *maiden.*] A female servant; a young unmarried woman; a virgin.

maid·en, mād′en, *n.* [O.E. *maegden,* dim. of *maegeth,* a maiden, Goth. *magaths,* G. *magd,* maid; akin O.E. *magu,* Goth. *magus,* Icel. *mōgr,* a boy, a son; allied to Gael. *mac,* a son.] A young unmarried woman; an instrument of capital punishment similar to the guillotine; a racehorse that has not yet won a race.—*a.* Befitting or pertaining to a maiden; unmarried, as a woman; made, used, or appearing for the first time; as, a *maiden* voyage; virgin; fresh, unused.—**maid·en·ov·er,** *cricket,* a scoreless turn or over.

maid·en·hair, mād′en·hâr″, *n. Bot.* a common native N. American fern, *Adiantum pedatum,* often cultivated, and having dark, glossy stalks and triangular-shaped pinnules arranged in a semicircular frond.

maid·en·head, mād′en·hed″, *n.* The hymen; virginity.

maid·en·hood, mād′en·hud″, *n.* The time or state of being a maiden; the state of an unmarried female; virginity. Also **maid·hood.**

maid·en·li·ness, mād′en·lē·nis, *n.* Behavior that becomes a maiden; modesty.—**maid·en·ly,** *a.*

maid·en name, *n.* A woman's surname prior to her marriage.

maid-in-wait·ing, mād′in·wā′ting, *n. pl.* **maids-in-wait·ing.** An unmarried woman appointed to wait upon or attend a queen or princess; a lady-in-waiting.

maid of hon·or, *n.* An unmarried woman who is a bride's principal attendant at a wedding; an unmarried woman, usu. of the nobility, who attends a queen or princess.

maid·ser·vant, mād′sur″vant, *n.* A female servant.

ma·ieu·tic, mā·ū′tik, *a.* [Gr. *maieutikos, maieuesthai,* act as midwife; < *maia,* midwife.] Pertaining to the Socratic method of bringing out ideas latent in the mind. Also **ma·ieu·ti·cal.**

mai·gre, mā′gėr, *Fr.* me′gRe, *a.* [Fr.] Containing neither flesh nor its juices, as kinds of food permissible on days of religious abstinence.

mail, māl, *n.* [Fr. *malle,* O.Fr. *male,* a bag, a mail; either < Armor. *mal,* Ir. and Gael. *mala,* a bag, or < O.H.G. *malaha,* a wallet; Icel. *malr,* a knapsack.] Letters, papers, and packages which are sent and delivered through the post office; a collection of postal matter sent at a specified time; as, the daily *mail*; a conveyance for transporting postal matter; the postal system.—*v.t.* To send through the mail; to put in a post office or mailbox for delivery.—*a.*

mail, māl, *n.* [Fr. *maille*, the mesh of a net, a link of mail; < L. *macula*, a spot, a mesh.] Armor made of pliable metal plates; any defensive covering, as the shell of a lobster.—*v.t.* To put on mail or armor.—**mailed,** *a.* Covered with mail or armor; *zool.* protected by an external covering of scales or hard substance.

mail·a·ble, mā′la·bl, *a.* Capable of being carried in the mail; legally approved as mail.—**mail·a·bil·i·ty,** *n.*

mail·bag, māl′bag″, *n.* A bag in which the public mail is carried; a large sack used to transport mail in bulk.

mail·box, māl′boks″, *n.* A box for deposited mail awaiting collection and delivery; a box which receives private mail, as at a residence.

mailed fist, *n.* Superior and threatening force, esp. among nations.

mail·er, mā′lêr, *n.* One who mails; a container for sending something in, as a cardboard tube. A mechanical device for addressing letters and packages.

mail·lot, mä·yō′, ma·yō′, *Fr.* mä·yō′, *n.* pl. **mail·lots,** mä·yōz′, *Fr.* mä·yō′. A close-fitting garment worn by acrobats, dancers, and gymnasts; a woman's one-piece bathing suit; a jersey knit shirt.

mail·man, māl′man″, *n.* pl. **mail·men.** One who is a carrier and a deliverer of mail; a postman.

mail or·der, *n.* An order sent by mail for goods to be shipped to the buyer; the goods received.—**mail-or·der house,** a firm whose business is primarily conducted through mail orders.

maim, mām, *v.t.* [O.E. *main*, to hurt or maim; < O.Fr. *mechaigner*, Pr. *maganhar*, *magagnare*, to maim; origin doubtful.] To deprive of the use of a limb; to mutilate, cripple, or disable; to render defective.—**maim·er,** *n.*

main, mān, *a.* [Icel. *megn*, *meginn*, main, strong, mighty; *megin*, might, main, main part; O.E. *maegn*, *maegen*, power, strength; same root as *may*, *might*.] Principal, chief, or most eminent; foremost in importance, rank, or size; pertaining to a vast expanse; as, the *main* river; sheer, mighty, or utmost, as strength or force.—*n.* All one's strength; violent effort; as, with might and *main*; the chief portion; most important point; a principal gas or water conduit as distinguished from the smaller ones supplied by it; *liter.* the ocean or the high seas.—**in the main,** for the most part; speaking generally.

main·land, mān′land″, mān′land, *n.* A great land mass; the principal section of a country or continent as compared with an island near it.—**main·land·er,** *n.*

main·ly, mān′lē, *adv.* In the main; chiefly.

main·mast, mān′mast″, mān′mäst″, *Naut.* mān′mast, *n. Naut.* The principal mast in a ship or other vessel; the after mast in a two-masted vessel; the middle mast on a ship having three masts.

mains, mānz, *n.* pl. but sing. in constr. Brit. the home farm of an estate.

main·sail, mān′sāl″, *Naut.* mān′sal, *n. Naut.* the principal sail in a ship.

main·sheet, mān′shēt″, *n. Naut.* a rope at one or both of the lower corners of a mainsail to keep it properly secured.

main·spring, mān′spring″, *n.* The principal spring of any mechanical part, as in a watch; *fig.* the main cause of any action.

main·stay, mān′stā″, *n. Naut.* the stay extending from the top of the mainmast to the deck, used to secure the mast; *fig.* the chief support.

main stem, *n.* The principal course, line, or trunk, as of a stream, railroad, or tree. *Slang,* the principal street of a town or city; main drag.

main·stream, mān′strēm″, *n.* The main channel of a river that has many tributaries; the principal current or prevailing trend of opinion or activity.

main·tain, mān·tān′, *v.t.* [Fr. *maintenir*—*main,* L. *manus,* the hand, and Fr. *tenir,* L. *teneo,* to hold.] To preserve or keep in any particular state or condition; to support; to keep possession of; to continue; to furnish sustenance for; provide the expenses of; to uphold; to defend, as against attack; to vindicate or justify, as one's right or cause; to assert.—**main·tain·a·ble,** *a.*

main·te·nance, mān′te·nans, *n.* The act of maintaining or being maintained; the preservation and upkeep of buildings, roads, and machinery; means of or provision for support; *law,* intermeddling in a suit by one who is not legally involved.

mai·son·ette, mai·son·nette, mā″zo-net′, *n. Chiefly Brit.* A self-contained apartment in a private home; a house of small size.

maî·tre d′, mā″têr dē′, mā″tre dē′, *n.* pl. **maî·tre d′s.** *Colloq.* maître d'hôtel.

maî·tre d'hôtel, mā″têr dō·tel′, mā″tre dō·tel′, *Fr.* me″tre dō·tel′, *n.* pl. **mai·tres d'hô·tel.** A hotel steward or headwaiter in a restaurant; a hotel manager or owner; also *maître d'.* A sauce prepared with lemon juice, melted butter, and minced parsley.

maize, māz, *n.* Indian corn; a yellow color similar to the color of ripe corn.

maj·es·ty, maj′i·stē, *n.* pl. **maj·es·ties.** [L. *majestas,* < *majus,* compar. form of *magnus,* great.] Grandeur or dignity of rank, character, or manner; supreme authority; imposing loftiness of person or mien; stateliness; (*usu. cap.*) a title of emperors, kings, and queens, preceded by *his, her,* or *your.*—**ma·jes·tic, ma·jes·ti·cal,** ma·jes′tik, *a.*—**ma·jes·ti·cal·ly,** *adv.*

ma·jol·i·ca, ma·jol′i·ka, ma·yol′i·ka, *n.* [It. *maiolica;* said to be from an old form of the name of the Spanish island of *Majorca.*] Italian pottery coated with enamel and usu. richly decorated; any pottery similar to this. Also **ma·iol·i·ca.**

ma·jor, mā′jer, *a.* [L. *major,* greater, larger, superior, older, compar. of *magnus,* great.] Greater, as in size, amount, extent, importance, or rank; having great or primary importance or rank; of or relating to the majority; of full legal age; *logic,* broader or more extensive; as, the *major* term of a syllogism. *Mus.* of an interval, being greater by a half step than the corresponding minor interval; as, a *major* third, which consists of two whole steps, where a minor third consists of a step and a half; of a chord, having a major third between the root and the note next above it; of a tone, distant by a major interval from a given tone; pertaining to a scale, mode, or key whose third tone is major in relation to the fundamental tone.

ma·jor, mā′jer, *n.* One of superior rank in a specified area; the subject or course of academic study pursued by a student as his area of specialization; the student; as, an English *major;* an individual of legal age; *logic,* the principal term or premise; *mus.* a major interval, chord, key, or scale; *milit.* a commissioned officer ranking next below a lieutenant colonel and next above a captain; *pl., sports,* the major leagues.—*v.i.* To pursue a principal course of study, followed by *in;* as, to *major* in English.

ma·jor-do·mo, mā″jer·dō′mō, *n.* pl. **ma·jor-do·mos.** [It. *maggiordomo*—L. *major,* greater, and *domus,* a house.] The chief steward who manages a large household, as a palace; a butler or steward.

ma·jor·ette, mā″jo·ret′, *n.* One of a group of female marchers, esp. a baton twirler, usu. accompanying a band on parade.

ma·jor gen·er·al, *n.* A military officer next in rank below a lieutenant general and above a brigadier general.

ma·jor·i·ty, ma·jar′i·tē, ma·jor′i·tē, *n.* pl. **ma·jor·i·ties.** [Fr. *majorité,* < M.L. *majoritas,* < L. *major.*] The greater part or number; the number which is over half of a particular total; a number of voters or votes, jurors, or others in agreement, constituting the greater part or more than half of the total number; the excess whereby the greater number, as of votes, surpasses the remainder: contrasted with *plurality;* a group, as a political party, with the most votes; the state or time of being of full legal age; as, to attain one's *majority;* the military rank or office of a major.

ma·jor·i·ty rule, *n.* A precept in politics by which a majority decision applies to the whole, the majority vote usu. consisting of at least one more than half the total.

ma·jor league, *n. Sports.* One of the two principal leagues in professional baseball; a league of similar importance in other sports, as football or basketball.

ma·jor-med·i·cal, mā″jer·med′i·cal, *a. Insurance,* being or pertaining to a type of coverage which is intended to pay partially or totally the medical bills incidental to treatment for a major illness, usu. after the insured has initially paid a certain designated amount.

ma·jor or·der, *n.* One of the three clerical gradations in the Roman Catholic Church, priesthood, diaconate, or subdiaconate; a similar clerical rank in other religious denominations, as the Eastern and Episcopal Churches.

ma·jor par·ty, *n.* A powerful political party within a governmental system, as the Republican or Democratic Party in the U.S., having sufficient strength to win an election for control of the government or provide the major opposition to any other party in control.

ma·jor prem·ise, *n. Logic,* in a syllogism, the premise containing the major term.

ma·jor suit, *n. Bridge,* either of two suits, spades or hearts, esp. with regard to their higher scoring value compared to diamonds and clubs.

ma·jor term, *n. Logic,* in a syllogism, the term which is the predicate of the conclusion.

ma·jus·cule, ma·jus′kūl, maj′u·skūl″, *a.* [Fr., < L. *majusculus,* somewhat greater or larger, dim. of *major.*] Large, as letters, whether capital or uncial; written in such letters: opposed to *minuscule.*—*n.* A majuscule letter, as a capital or uncial.—**ma·jus·cu·lar,** *a.*

make, māk, *v.t.*—**made, making.** [O.E. *macian* = O.Fries. *makia* = O.S. *macōn* = O.H.G. *mahhōn,* G. *machen,* make, O.H.G. also fit together; appar. < a Teut. a. stem meaning 'fit, suitable.'] To bring into existence by shaping a portion of matter or by combining parts or ingredients; as, to *make* a dress or a cake; form or fashion; frame or construct; manufacture or produce; prepare, as food; compose, as a poem; draw up, as a legal document; be sufficient to constitute; serve for; become by development, as: A lawyer *makes* the best legislator. To produce by any action or causative agency; as, to *make* a mark, to *make* trouble; give rise to, or cause; fix or establish, as rules; enact, as laws; to score, as in games; create by appointment; as, to *make* a manager; to form in the mind, as a judgment, an estimate, or a plan; entertain mentally, as doubt; judge or infer as to the truth, nature, or meaning of something, as:

What do you *make* of his statement? Judge or estimate to be, as: I *make* the distance ten miles. To produce, earn, or get for oneself, as by work or actions; as, to *make* a living; acquire, gain, or win; to bring into a certain form or condition, or convert; as, to *make* clay into bricks; prepare for use; as, to *make* a bed; train, as a dog; assure the success or fortune of; to cause to be or become as specified; as, to *make* a vessel airtight; render; constitute or appoint; to cause or compel to do something; as, to *make* a horse go; to do, perform, execute, or effect; as, to *make* a movement; put forth or deliver; as, to *make* a speech; accomplish by traveling; as, to *make* five miles an hour; to arrive at or reach; as, to *make* a port; *elect.* to complete, as a circuit.—*v.i.* To make something; to bring about, effect, or operate, usu. with *for* to cause something or someone to be as specified; as, to *make* ready; show oneself in action or behavior; as, to *make* bold; start to do, or as if to do, something; to direct or pursue the course, or go; as, to *make* for home; to rise, as the tide; increase in size, depth, or volume.—**make be·lieve**, pretend.—**make good**, make satisfactory; fulfill, as a promise; succeed.—**make love**, neck; participate in sexual intercourse.—**make off**, to leave, often in haste.—**make out**, *slang*, succeed, as in sexual endeavor.—**make o·ver**, transfer a title or property; remodel.—**make pub·lic**, disclose.—**make sail**, *naut.* To initiate or extend the spread of the sails; embark.—**make sure**, ascertain the truth of.—**make the cards**, to shuffle a deck of playing cards.—**make time**, to hurry; travel at a set pace; flirt.—**make tracks**, move swiftly.—**make up**, become reconciled after quarreling; compensate or make amends for; compose; consist of; put on cosmetics or dress, as for a part; to flatter or make advances to.—**make wa·ter**, urinate; *naut.* leak.—**make way**, give room for passing; give place; advance.—**mak·a·ble**, *a.*

make, māk, *n.* Style or manner of being made; form or build; structure; constitution; disposition, character, or nature; the act or process of making; production with reference to the maker, or to the place or time of making; as, of our own *make*; that which is made; yield or output; *colloq.* the making or seeking of gain or profit at the expense of another; *cards*, the act of naming the trump, or the suit named as trump. *Elect.* the completing of a circuit; the passage of the current through a circuit.—**on the make**, *colloq.* Intent on personal gain; seeking sexual activity.

make-be·lieve, māk'bi·lēv", *n.* Pretense; fiction; also **make-be·lief**. A pretender.—*a.* Unreal; pretended.

make do, *v.i.* To manage or carry on with minimal or substitute materials.

make-do, māk'dö", *n.* A stopgap or substitute, usu. temporary or inferior.—*a.* Of a makeshift or temporary nature.

ma·ker, mā'kėr, *n.* One who makes; (*cap.*) God. *Law*, a person who makes, executes, or signs a legal instrument, as a promissory note; *cards*, the person who first declares the successful bid in bridge.

make-read·y, māk'red"ē, *n. Print.* the operation of making a form ready for printing by using overlays and underlays to produce a distinct impression.

make·shift, māk'shift", *n.* A temporary substitute or contrivance, usu. for some emergency.—*a.* Having the nature of a substitute; also **make·shift·y**.—**make·shift·ness**, *n.*

make-up, māk'up", *n.* Cosmetics, such as lipstick, which women use on their faces; cosmetics applied to other areas of the body; the cosmetics which an actor uses to

ready himself for a specific role; the way in which an actor does this; the manner of being made up or put together; as, the *make-up* of the student body; physical or mental constitution; *print.* the arrangement of set type and illustrations into columns or pages; *colloq.* a second examination administered to students who are absent from or fail the original test. Also **make-up**.

make·weight, māk'wāt", *n.* Something put on a scale to complete a required weight; *fig.* anything added to supply a deficiency.

make weight, *v.i. Sports*, to reduce one's weight, as a boxer or wrestler, in order to qualify to compete in a certain class.

mak·ing, mā'king, *n.* The act of one who or that which produces, forms, effects, evolves, or makes; the process of being made; structure, constitution, or make-up; means or cause of the successful formation of character or advancement, as: Discipline is the *making* of a good student. *Usu. pl.* the materials of which something may be made; as, the *makings* of a meal; qualifications for becoming something; as: He has the *makings* of a fine man. Something which is or has been made; the quantity made at one time.—**in the mak·ing**, in the process of being made.

Ma·lac·ca cane, ma·lak'a kān, *n.* [From *Malacca*, in the Malay Peninsula.] A cane or walking stick made of the brown, often mottled or clouded stem of an East Indian rattan palm of the genus *Calamus*.

ma·la·ceous, ma·lā'shus, *a.* [L. *malus*, apple tree.] Belonging to a subfamily of the *Rosaceae*, which includes the apple, pear, quince, loquat, and hawthorn trees.

mal·a·chite, mal'a·kīt", *n.* [Fr. *malachite*, < L. *malache*, < Gr. *malachē*, *molochē*, mallow (with reference to the color of the leaf).] *Mineral.* A green basic carbonate of copper, $Cu_2CO_3(OH)_2$, used for making ornamental articles; a copper ore.

mal·a·cos·tra·can, mal'a·kos'tra·kan, *a.* [N.L. *Malacostraca*, pl., < Gr. *malakostrakos*, soft-shelled, < *malakos*, soft, and *ostrakon*, shell.] Belonging to the *Malacostraca*, a subclass of crustaceans including the lobsters, shrimps, and crabs.—*n.* A malacostracan crustacean. Also **mal·a·cos·tra·cous**.

mal·a·dapt·ed, mal'a·dap'tid, *a.* Not suited to a specific condition or situation.

mal·ad·just·ment, mal'a·just'ment, *n.* [Prefix *mal*, bad.] An unsatisfactory or inadequate adjustment; *psychol.* a lack of harmony between an individual's desires or capacities and his external situation.—**mal·ad·just·ed**, mal'a·just'tid, *a.*

mal·ad·min·is·ter, mal'ad·min'i·stėr, *v.t.* [Prefix *mal*, bad.] To administer or conduct inefficiently or dishonestly.—**mal·ad·min·is·tra·tion**, *n.*

mal·a·droit, mal'a·droit', *a.* [Prefix *mal*, bad.] Not adroit or dexterous; awkward, inept, or tactless.—**mal·a·droit·ly**, *adv.* —**mal·a·droit·ness**, *n.*

mal·a·dy, mal'a·dē, *n.* pl. **mal·a·dies**. [Fr. *maladie*, < *malade*, O.Fr. *malabde*, ill, < L. *male*, *habitus*, in bad condition.] Any disease of the human body; an ailment; *fig.* any undesirable condition, as a moral, mental, or social disorder.

Mal·a·ga, mal'a·ga, *n.* A sweet white wine imported from Málaga, Spain; the white, sweet, grape from which the wine is made, grown also in California.

Mal·a·gas·y, mal'a·gas'ē, *a.* Of or pertaining to Madagascar or the Malagasy Republic; pertaining to the Malagasy people or their language.—*n. pl.* **Mal·a·gas·y**, **Mal·a·gas·ies**. A native of Madagascar or the Malagasy Republic; the language spoken there, belonging to the Malayo-Polynesian family.

ma·laise, ma·lāz', *Fr.* mä·lez', *n.* [Fr.] A condition of unlocalized bodily uneasiness, debility, or discomfort, often a preliminary symptom of disease; an indefinite feeling of morbid discontent and ill-being.

mal·a·mute, **mal·e·mute**, mal'a·mūt", *n.* Alaskan malamute.

mal·a·prop·ism, mal'a·prop·iz"um, *n.* [From Mrs. *Malaprop* in Richard Sheridan's play, *The Rivals*, noted for her misuse of words.] A ludicrous misuse of words, esp. through incorrect choice of a word with a sound similar to the correct one; an instance or example of this.—**mal·a·prop**, *a., n.*—**mal·a·prop·i·an**, *a.*

mal·ap·ro·pos, mal"ap·ro·pō', *a.* [Fr. *mal à propos*, 'ill to purpose.'] Inappropriate; inopportune; as, a *malapropos* remark.—*adv.* Inappropriately.

ma·lar, mā'lėr, *a.* [< L. *mala*, the cheekbone, the jaw.] *Anat.* pertaining to the cheek or cheekbone.—*n. Anat.* the cheekbone. Also **ma·lar bone**.

ma·lar·i·a, ma·lâr'ē·a, *n.* [It., for *mala aria*, 'bad air.'] *Pathol.* a febrile disease, usu. intermittent or remittent, and characterized by attacks of chills, fever, and sweating, formerly supposed to be due to swamp exhalations, but now known to be caused by parasitic protozoans, transferred to the blood by mosquitoes, and which occupy and destroy the red blood corpuscles.—**ma·lar·i·al, ma·lar·i·an, ma·lar·i·ous**, *a.*

ma·lar·key, **ma·lar·ky**, ma·lär'kē, *n. Colloq.* deceptive, insincere, or nonsensical talk.

mal·ate, mal'āt, mā'lāt, *n. Chem.* a salt or ester of malic acid.

Ma·lay, mā'lā, ma·lā', *a.* [From *Malay* Peninsula in southeast Asia.] Of or pertaining to the Malays or their country or language; noting or pertaining to a brown-skinned people, characterized by short stature, short broad skull, large mouth, prominent cheekbones, and straight black hair.—*n.* A member of the dominant people of the Malay Peninsula and adjacent islands; the language spoken by this people; a member of the Malaysian hypothetical subrace. One of a breed of domestic fowls.

Ma·lay·an, ma·lā'an, *a.* Belonging to the Malays or to their country.—*n.* A native of the Malay Peninsula; the language of the Malays.

mal·con·tent, mal'kon·tent", *a.* Dissatisfied, discontented, or rebellious; specif. discontented with the government or the existing order.—*n.*

male, māl, *a.* [O.Fr. *male*, *masle*, *mascle* (Fr. *mâle*), < L. *masculus*, male.] Belonging to the sex which produces sperm, fertilizes the female, and begets young; pertaining to or characteristic of this sex; masculine; consisting of men; as, a *male* choir. *Bot.* designating or pertaining to any reproductive structure which produces or contains elements that bring about the fertilization of the female element; staminate, as in seed plants. *Mech.* designating a part which fits into a corresponding part.—*n.* A male human being; a man or boy; any animal of the male sex. *Bot.* a staminate plant; the stamen of a flower and the pollen it produces.—**male·ness**, *n.*

male al·to, *n.* An unusually high adult male voice, generally employing falsetto; a male voice part above the range of tenor; one who performs such a part. Also **coun·ter·ten·or**, koun"tėr·ten'ėr.

mal·e·dict, mal'i·dikt, *a.* [L. *maledictus*, pp. of *maledicere*, < *male*, ill, and *dicere*, say.] *Archaic.* accursed.—*v.t.* To curse.—**mal·e·dic·tion**, mal'i·dik'shan, *n.* The utterance of a curse against an individual; a curse.—**mal·e·dic·to·ry**, mal"i·dik'to·rē, *a.*

mal·e·fac·tion, mal''e·fak'shan, n. [L. *malefactio(n)-,* < *malefacere,* do evil.] An evil deed; an offense; crime.—**mal·e·fac·tor,** mal'e·fak''ter, n. An evildoer; an offender against the law; a criminal; one who does evil to another.—**mal·e·fac·tress,** n. A female malefactor.

male fern, n. A fern, *Dryopteris filix-mas,* whose roots and stalks yield an oleoresin used to expel tapeworms.

ma·lef·ic, ma·lef'ik, a. [L. *maleficus,* that does ill.] Effecting evil; having an injurious influence; baleful.

ma·lef·i·cent, ma·lef'i·sent, a. Doing evil; harmful.—**ma·lef·i·cence,** n.

ma·lev·o·lent, ma·lev'o·lent, a. [L. *malevolens, malevolentis.*] Possessing an evil disposition toward another or others; exhibiting ill will; sinister; rancorous; malicious; *astrol.* pertaining to evil influence.—**ma·lev·o·lent·ly,** adv.—**ma·lev·o·lence,** n.

mal·fea·sance, mal·fē'zans, n. [Fr. *malfaisance.*] *Law,* illegal, unjustified, or detrimental conduct, esp. in the performance of public or official duties.—**mal·fea·sant,** a., n.

mal·for·ma·tion, mal''fôr·mā'shan, n. Abnormal structure, esp. of a bodily part; irregular or defective formation.—**mal·formed,** mal·fârmd', a.

mal·func·tion, mal·fungk'shan, n. Failure to function either partially or totally.— v.i.

mal·ic ac·id, mal'ik as'id, mā'lik as'id, n. *Chem.* a colorless, highly water-soluble, crystalline substance, $C_4H_6O_5$, having a pleasant sour taste and found in apples, grapes, and rhubarb.

mal·ice, mal'is, n. [O.Fr. Fr. *malice* < L. *malitia,* badness, spite, malice, < *malus,* bad.] Desire to inflict injury or suffering on another; active or vindictive ill will; *law,* evil intent on the part of one who commits a wrongful act injurious to others.— **ma·li·cious,** ma·lish'us, a.—**ma·li·cious·ly,** adv.—**ma·li·cious·ness,** n.

ma·lign, ma·lin', v.t. [L. *malignus,* for *maligenus,* of an evil nature. Cf. *benign,* with exactly the opposite sense.] To speak evil of; traduce; defame; slander.—a. Of an evil nature, disposition, or character; malicious; pernicious; tending to injure or produce evil effects.—**ma·lign·er,** n.— **ma·lign·ly,** adv.

ma·lig·nan·cy, ma·lig'nan·sē, n. pl. **ma·lig·nan·cies.** The quality or condition of being malignant; a tumor which is malignant. Also **ma·lig·nance.**

ma·lig·nant, ma·lig'nant, a. [L. *malignans,* < *maligno,* to act maliciously.] Having extreme malevolence or enmity; malicious; exerting pernicious influence. *Pathol.* increasing in danger and size, as a tumor; not benign; virulent; tending to cause death. —**ma·lig·nant·ly,** adv.

ma·lig·ni·ty, ma·lig'ni·tē, n. pl. **ma·lig·ni·ties.** [L. *malignitas.*] State or quality of being malign; malice; rancor; virulence; malignancy; an instance of malignancy.

ma·lines, ma·lēn', Fr. mä·lēn', n. pl. **ma·lines.** [From *Malines* (or Mechlin), city in Belgium.] Mechlin lace. A very fine, tullelike net used for millinery; also **ma·line.**

ma·lin·ger, ma·ling'gèr, v.i. [Fr. *malingre,* sickly, weakly; < *mal,* ill and O.Fr. *hingre, heingre,* feeble, nasalized form of L. *aeger,* sick.] To feign illness in order to avoid duty or work.—**ma·lin·ger·er,** n.

mall, mal, mäl, mal, n. [Fr. *mail,* It. *maglio, malleo,* L. *malleus,* a hammer.] A landscaped public area for walking; an area surrounded with shops or other buildings and closed to vehicular traffic; a planted or paved strip separating lanes of traffic.

mall, mal, mäl, mal, v.t., n. Maul.

mal·lard, mal'èrd, n. pl. **mal·lards, mal·lard.** [O.Fr. *malard,* Prov. Fr. *maillard,* < *maille* (L. *macula*), a spot on a bird's feather, from the iridescent spot on the wing.] *Ornith.* a wild duck, *Anas platyrhynchos,* the male having an all green head, common in the northern hemisphere and the ancestor of the domestic duck.

mal·le·a·ble, mal'ē·a·bl, a. [O.Fr. *malleable* (Fr. *maléable*); < L. *malleare,* beat with a hammer.] Capable of being extended or shaped by hammering or by pressure with rollers; *fig.* pliable, adaptable, or tractable.—**mal·le·a·bil·i·ty, mal·le·a·ble·ness,** n.

mal·lee, mal'ē, n. [Aust.] Any of various dwarf Australian species of eucalyptus, as *Eucalyptus dumosa* and *E. oleosa,* which sometimes form large tracts of brushwood; the brushwood made up of these trees.

mal·le·muck, mal'e·muk'', n. [D. *mallemok.*] Any of various oceanic birds, as the albatross and the fulmar.

mal·let, mal'it, n. [O.Fr. *maillet,* dim. of *mail.*] A hammer, usu. of wood, used chiefly for driving another tool, as a chisel; the wooden implement used to strike the ball in the game of croquet; the long-handled stick used to drive the ball in polo.

mal·le·us, mal'ē·us, n. pl. **mal·le·i,** mal'ē·ī''. [L. hammer.] *Anat.* the outermost of three small bones in the middle ear of man and other mammals, so called from its hammerlike shape.

mal·low, mal'ō, n. [O.E. *mealwe,* < *malva,* mallow.] Any herbaceous plant of the genus *Malva,* naturalized from the Old World, and characterized by round-toothed leaves and white, purple, or rose flowers, as *Malva rotundifolia;* any malvaceous plant.

malm, mäm, n. [O.E. *mealm,* Goth. *malma,* sand; akin to *meal,* < root meaning to grind.] A soft, grayish limestone, easily crumbled; a soil containing clay and chalk, found in southeastern England; a clay and chalk mixture used in making bricks.

malm·sey, mäm'zē, n. [O.E. *malvesie,* Fr. *malvoisie;* < Napoli di *Malvasia,* in the Morea, peninsula forming part of Greece; the white and red wines produced there first received the name.] A strong sweet wine made in the Madeira Islands; the grape used to make this wine. Also *malvasia, malvoisie.*

mal·nour·ished, mal'nur'isht, mal''nur'isht, a. Poorly or insufficiently nourished.

mal·nu·tri·tion, mal''nŏ·trish'an, mal''nū·trish'an, n. Insufficient or otherwise faulty nutrition.

mal·oc·clu·sion, mal''o·klö'zhan, n. *Dentistry.* Faulty occlusion; imperfect closing or meeting, as of the opposing teeth of the upper and the lower jaws.

mal·o·dor, mal·ō'dèr, n. An offensive odor; stench.

mal·o·dor·ous, mal·ō'dèr·us, a. Having an offensive odor; foul-smelling.—**mal·o·dor·ous·ly,** adv.—**mal·o·dor·ous·ness,** n.

Mal·pigh·i·an cor·pus·cle, mal·pig'ē·an kâr'pu·sl, mal·pig'ē·an kâr'pus·el, n. [From Marcello *Malpighi,* 1628-1694, Italian anatomist.] *Anat.* A small round body in the cortical substance of the kidney; also **Mal·pigh·i·an bod·y.** A nodule of lymphoid tissue in the spleen.

Mal·pigh·i·an lay·er, n. *Anat.* a layer of cells lying deep within the epidermis, which provides replacements for the outer cells of the epidermis.

Mal·pigh·i·an tube, n. *Entom.* one of a group of appendages of the alimentary canal of insects, serving as excretory organs. Also **Mal·pigh·i·an ves·sel.**

mal·po·si·tion, mal''po·zish'an, n. *Pathol.* faulty or wrong position, esp. of a part or organ of the body or of a fetus in the uterus.

mal·prac·tice, mal·prak'tis, n. Improper, neglectful, or illegal performance of duty by one in a public or professional position, as a lawyer, physician, or public servant, esp. when resulting in injury or loss.— **mal·prac·ti·tion·er,** n.

malt, malt, n. [O.E. *mealt* (Icel., Sw., and Dan. *malt,* D. *mout,* G. *malz*), < *meltan,* to melt.] Grain, usu. barley, steeped in water, germinated, dried in a kiln, and then used in brewing and distilling; a beverage produced from malt, as beer, ale, or whisky.—v.t. To make into malt; to mix or process with malt extract or malt.—v.i. To be converted into malt; to convert grain into malt.—**malt·y,** a.— *maltier, maltiest.*

Mal·ta fe·ver, mal'ta fē'vèr, n. Brucellosis.

malt·ase, mal'tās, n. *Biochem.* an enzyme that transforms maltose into glucose by hydrolysis.

malt·ed milk, mal'tid milk', n. A dissolvable powder made from dried milk and malted cereals. The beverage made from this powder and milk or other liquid, usu. with ice cream and flavoring; also **malt·ed.**

Mal·tese, mal·tēz', mal·tēs', a. Of or relating to Malta, a group of Mediterranean islands, or to the inhabitants or natives or their Arabic dialect.—n. pl. **Mal·tese.**

Mal·tese cat, n. A bluish-gray variety of the domestic cat.

Mal·tese cross, n. A cross having four equal arms that expand in width from the place of meeting outward, each arm terminated by a cleft or two short-pointed branches: used as a symbol by the Knights of Malta. *Bot.* an herbaceous garden flower, *Lychnis chalcedonica,* in the pink family, having scarlet, two-cleft petals similar to the cleft branches of a Maltese cross; also **scar·let lych·nis.**

mal·tha, mal'tha, n. [Gr., a mixture for caulking ships.] A viscous bituminous substance with a consistency somewhere between petroleum and asphalt. Also **mal·thite.**

Mal·thu·si·an, mal·thö'zē·an, a. Relating to T. R. Malthus, English economist, or his theory that the population increases in a geometric ratio while subsistence increases arithmetically and that unless natural catastrophes, war, or sexual restraint control population increase, world-wide famine or war will follow.—n. One who adheres to Malthusian doctrines.—**Mal·thu·si·an·ism,** n.

malt liq·uor, n. One of the alcoholic beverages prepared from malt, as beer.

malt·ose, mal'tōs, n. *Chem.* A white crystalline sugar, $C_{12}H_{22}O_{11} \cdot H_2O$, formed by the action of diastase, as in malt, on starch and used primarily as a sweetener. Also **malt sug·ar.**

mal·treat, mal·trēt', v.t. To treat roughly or severely; to abuse.—**mal·treat·ment,** n.

malt·ster, malt'stèr, n. A man whose occupation is to make malt or deal in it.

mal·va·ceous, mal·vā'shus, a. [L. *malva,* mallow.] Pertaining to the plants of the mallow family, *Malvaceae,* as hibiscus, rose-of-sharon, and hollyhock.

mal·va·si·a, mal''va·sē'a, n. The sweet grape used in making malmsey, a Madeira wine; the wine itself. Also *malmsey, malvoisie.*—**mal·va·si·an,** a.

mal·ver·sa·tion, mal''vèr·sā'shan, n. [Fr. < *malverser,* < L. *male,* ill, and *versari,* occupy oneself.] Improper or corrupt behavior in an office or a position of trust; corrupt administration, as of justice or of funds.

mal·voi·sie, mal'voi·zē, mal'vo·zē, n. Malmsey.

mam·ba, mäm'bä, n. [S. Afr.] A long, slender, arboreal South African serpent, *Dendraspis angusticeps,* which has a deadly bite.

mam·bo, măm′bō, *n.* pl. **mam·bos.** A fast dance originating in Haiti, similar to but more complex than the cha-cha and rumba; the music associated with this dance.—*v.i.* To dance a mambo.

Mam·e·luke, măm′e·lōōk″, *n.* [Ar. *mamlūk,* slave.] A member of a Turkish military body in Egypt, orig. recruited from slaves, which held the throne from about 1250 until 1517 and remained the ruling class until 1811; (*l.c.*) in Islamic countries, a slave. Also **Mam·a·luke, Mam·luk.**

mam·ma, mam′a, *n.* pl. **mam·mae,** mam′ē. [L., the female breast, from root meaning to swell, to swell with juice.] The breast; the organ in mammals that secretes the milk.

mam·ma, ma·ma, mä′ma, ma·mä′, *n.* [A repetition of the infantile utterance *ma, ma.*] Mother: a term of address implying familiarity and tenderness, used chiefly by young persons in reference to mother.

mam·mal, mam′al, *n.* [N.L. *Mammalia,* prop. neut. pl. of L.L. *mammalis,* a. < L. *mamma.*] *Zool.* any animal or animal group of the highest vertebrate class, *Mammalia,* which is characterized by suckling of the young, the presence of hair, and viviparous births.—**mam·ma·li·an,** ma·mā′lē·an, ma·māl′yan, *a., n.*

mam·mal·o·gy, ma·mal′o·jē, *n. Zool.* the science of mammals.—**mam·mal·o·gist,** *n.*—**mam·ma·log·i·cal,** mam″ma·loj′i·kal, *a.*

mam·ma·ry, mam′a·rē, *a.* Referring to or resembling a mamma or the mammae.

mam·ma·to-cu·mu·lus, ma·mā″tō·kū′mū·lus, *n.* pl. **mam·ma·to-cu·mu·li,** mam·ma·to-cu·mu·lus, ma·mā″tō·kū′mū·li. *Meteor.* a cumulus cloud with hanging, breast-shaped formations.

mam·mer, mam′er, *v.i.* [Prob. imit.] *Brit.* To mutter; to stammer; to hesitate in speech or thought.

mam·mil·la, ma·mil′a, *n.* pl. **mam·mil·lae,** ma·mil′ē. [L. *mammilla, mamilla,* dim. of *mamma.*] *Anat.* The nipple of the breast or mamma; any nipplelike process or protuberance; papilla.—**mam·mil·lar·y,** mam′i·ler″ē, *a.* Pertaining to or resembling a nipple; studded with nipplelike protuberances.—**mam·mil·late,** mam′i·lāt″, *a.* Formed like a nipple; having small nipplelike protuberánces. Also **mam·mil·lat·ed.—mam·mil·la·tion,** mam″i·lā′shan, *n.*

mam·mon, mam′on, *n.* [L. *mammona,* Gr. *mammōnas,* mammon, riches.] *N.T.* riches considered as an evil; avarice or greed. (*Cap.*) the personification of avarice.—**mam·mon·ism,** mam′o·niz″um, *n.*—**mam·mon·ist, mam·mon·ite,** *n.*—**mam·mon·ish, mam·mon·is·tic,** *a.*

mam·moth, mam′oth, *n.* [Russ. *mamant, mamont,* < Tartar, *mamma,* the earth.] An extinct species of Pleistocene elephant with long tusks and covered with dense, shaggy hair, the remains of which are found buried in Europe, Asia, and N. America.—*a.* Very large; enormous; gigantic.

mam·my, mam′ē, *n.* [Cf. *mam* and *mamma.*] *Colloq.* mother. A Negro female nurse or old family servant in the southern U.S.

man, man, *n.* pl. **men.** [O.E. *man, mann, man,* person = D., O.H.G., and Sw. *man,* G. *mann,* Icel. *mathr, mannr,* Dan. *mand,* Goth. *manna* < root *man,* to think, seen in Skt. *man,* to think, *manas,* mind, *manushya,* man.] A human being, particularly a male adult; the human species, as: *Man* is the dominant species. *Anthropol., zool.* a member of the family *Hominidae* which is characterized by a large brain, speech, and an erect stance; the only extant species of *Hominidae, Homo sapiens.* An adult male having marked masculine attributes; a male servant; an adult male in some person's employ; a

husband; any human individual; a piece with which a game, as chess or checkers, is played.—*interj. Slang,* an exclamation of surprise or enthusiasm.

man, man, *v.t.*—*manned, manning.* To supply with men; to furnish with a sufficient force or complement of men; to assume one's position or station at, on, or in, as: *Man* the lifeboats! To infuse with courage; *falconry,* to cause, as a hawk, to become tractable to men.

ma·na, mä′nä, *n.* [Polynesian.] *Anthropol.* a belief held by Polynesians that a power of supernatural origin may reside in a person or an object.

man·a·cle, man′a·kl, *n.* [Fr. *manicle,* L. *manicula,* dim. of *manica,* a manacle, < *manus,* the hand.] An instrument of iron for fastening the hands. *Often pl.* handcuffs; shackles.—*v.t.*—*manacled, manacling.* To put handcuffs or other fastenings upon; to shackle.

man·age, man′ij, *v.t.*—*managed, managing.* [Fr. *manège,* the management of a horse, management or guidance in general; It. *maneggiare,* to handle, to manage; < L. *manus,* the hand.] To control and direct, as a person or enterprise; to conduct, carry on, guide, administer; to succeed or contrive, often in spite of difficulty; to move or use in the manner desired; to treat, as a person, with caution or judgment.—*v.i.* To direct or conduct affairs; to carry on a concern or business.

man·age·a·ble, man′i·ja·bl, *a.* Capable of being managed; easily made subservient to one's views or designs.—**man·age·a·bil·i·ty, man·age·a·ble·ness,** *n.*—**man·age·a·bly,** *adv.*

man·age·ment, man′ij·ment, *n.* The act of managing, treating, directing, carrying on, or using for a purpose; administration; cautious handling or treatment; the body of directors or managers of any business, concern, or interest collectively.

man·ag·er, man′i·jer, *n.* One who manages; one who has the guidance or direction of anything; one who is directly at the head of an undertaking.—**man·ag·er·ship,** *n.*—**man·ag·er·ess,** *n. Chiefly Brit.* feminine of manager.

man·a·ge·ri·al, man″i·jēr′ē·al, *a.* Of or belonging to a manager.—**man·a·ge·ri·al·ly,** *adv.*

man·a·kin, man′a·kin, *n.* Any of various songless passerine birds of the family *Pipridae,* small and brilliantly colored, found in Central and S. America. Manikin.

ma·ña·na, ma·nyä′na, *Sp.* mä·nyä′nä, *n.* [Sp., < L. *mane,* morning, in the morning.] Tomorrow; a future time; often used to imply easygoing procrastination.—*adv.*

man ape, *n.* A name sometimes applied to any of the anthropoid apes, as the gorilla, orangutan, chimpanzee, or gibbon; a fossil having characteristics common to both the ape and to early man, and being a possible ancestor to both.

man-at-arms, man′at·ärmz′, *n.* pl. **men-at-arms.** A soldier; a heavily armed soldier of the Middle Ages.

man·a·tee, man″a·tē″, man″a·tē′, *n.* [Haitian.] *Zool.* an aquatic, seaweed-eating mammal belonging to the order *Sirenia,* characterized by a large spindle-shaped body, paddlelike fore limbs, absence of hind limbs, and native to the warm seas and rivers of Florida, West Indies, and Brazil. Also *sea cow.*—**man·a·toid,** man′a·toid″, *a.*

man·chi·neel, man″chi·nēl′, *n.* [It. *mancinello,* Fr. *manzanille,* Sp. *manzanillo,* < *manzana,* an apple, < L. *malum Matianum,* a kind of apple.] A euphorbiaceous tree of the West Indies and Central America, *Hippomane mancinella,* yielding an acrid, highly poisonous juice and a wood which is sometimes used for cabinetmaking.

Man·chu, man·chō′, *n.* pl. **Man·chus, Man·chu.** One of a Mongolian people inhabiting Manchuria who conquered China in 1644 and set up a dynasty that lasted until 1912; a language spoken by the Manchus belonging to the Tungusic subfamily of the Uralic-Altaic language group. —*a.* Of or pertaining to the Manchus, their country, or their language.

man·ci·ple, man′si·pl, *n.* [O.Fr. *mancipe,* L. *manceps,* one who purchases anything at a public sale—*manus,* the hand, and *capio,* to take.] A steward; a purveyor, particularly of a college or monastery.

Man·dae·an, Man·de·an, man·dē′an, *a.* [Mandæan *mandā,* knowledge.] Of or pertaining to members of an ancient Gnostic sect surviving in south Iraq, or to the Aramaic dialect used in their writings. —*n.*

man·da·la, mun′da·la, *n.* A graphic cosmic symbol shown as a square within a circle bearing representations of deities arranged symmetrically and used as a meditation aid by Buddhists and Hindus; in the terminology of the Swiss psychologist Carl Jung, 1875–1961, a symbol depicting the endeavor to reunite the self.

man·da·mus, *n.* [L., lit. 'we command.'] *Law,* a command or writ issued by a superior court and directed to a person, corporation, or lower court, requiring them to do a specified act.

man·da·rin, man′da·rin, *n.* [Pg. *mandarim,* through Malay and Hind. < Skt. *mantrin,* counselor, < *mantra,* thought, counsel.] A member of any of the nine ranks of officials during the Chinese Empire. (*Cap.*) the chief dialect of China, esp. of the northern parts and centering around Peking; the official dialect promoted by the government as the national language. A small, flattish orange of Chinese origin, or the tree, *Citrus reticulata,* producing it; also **man·da·rin or·ange.**

man·da·ta·ry, man′da·ter″ē, *n.* pl. **man·da·ta·ries.** [L.L. *mandatarius,* < L. *mandatum,* E. *mandate.*] A nation or individual having a mandate.

man·date, man′dāt, man′dit, *n.* [L. *mandatum,* pp. neut. of *mandare,* commit, enjoin, command.] A command, order, or injunction; a command from a superior court or official to an inferior one; *Rom. Cath. Ch.* an order issued by the Pope, esp. one commanding the preferment of a certain person to a benefice; *politics,* the instruction as to policy given by the electorate to a representative. *Law,* orig., a contract by which one person requested another to act for him gratuitously; later, any contract of agency. *International politics,* a commission given to one nation by an associated group of nations to administer the government and affairs of a people or territory; the territory under such charge.—*v.t.*—*mandated, mandating.* To consign, as a territory, to a particular nation under a mandate.—**man·da·tor,** man·dā′ter, *n.* One issuing a mandate.

man·da·to·ry, man′da·tōr″ē, *a.* [L.L. *mandatorius.*] Pertaining to, of the nature of, or containing a mandate; obligatory by reason of a command; having received a mandate, as a nation.—*n.* pl. **man·da·to·ries.** A person or nation to whom a mandate is given.—**man·da·to·ri·ly,** *adv.*

man·di·ble, man′di·bl, *n.* [L. *mandibulum,* the jaw, < *mando,* to chew.] The under jaw bone in vertebrates; the upper or lower bill of a bird; one of a pair of lateral anterior jaws of an arthropod.—**man·dib·u·lar,** man·dib′ū·ler, *a.* Noting or pertaining to a mandible. Also **man·dib·u·lar·y.—man·dib·u·late,** man·dib′ū·lit, man·dib′ū·lāt″, *a.* Provided with mandibles, as many insects.—*n.*

Man·din·go, man·ding′gō, *a.* Of or pertaining to any of a number of Negroid peoples forming an extensive linguistic group in western Africa; of or pertaining to their language.—*n. pl.* **Man·din·gos, Man·din·goes.**

man·do·lin, man′do·lin, man″do·lin′, *n.* [Fr. *mandoline,* < It. *mandolino,* dim. of *mandola.*] A musical instrument of the lute class, having a deep, pear-shaped, sound box, fretted neck, and usu. four pairs of metal strings.—**man·do·lin·ist,** *n.*

man·drag·o·ra, man·drag′ĕr·a, man″dra·gōr′a, *n.* [L. and Gr. *mandragoras,* the mandrake.] Mandrake.

man·drake, man′drāk, man′drik, *n.* [< *mandragora.*] *Bot.* a European herb, *Mandragore officinarum,* in the nightshade family, yielding powerful extracts and whose forked roots were formerly the subject of superstitious folklore; also *mandragora.* May apple.

man·drel, man′drel, *n.* [Origin obscure.] *Mach.* A spindle, arbor, or bar to which an object is secured while being worked upon; the live spindle of a lathe; a rod or core around which metal or the like is cast or shaped. Also **man·dril.**

man·drill, man′dril, *n.* [Fr. *mandrille,* from the West African name.] A rather large, vicious baboon, *Mandrillus sphinx,* native to West Africa, identified by its red and blue ribbed facial features.

mane, mān, *n.* [O.E. *manu* = G. *mahne* = Icel. *mön;* mane; akin to L. *monile,* Gr. *mannos,* necklace, Skt. *manya,* nape of neck.] The long hair growing on the back of or about the neck and nearby parts of some animals, as the horse and the lion; *fig.* a person's hair when long and abundant.—**maned,** *a.*

man-eat·er, man′ē″tĕr, *n.* A cannibal; any animal, as a tiger, lion, or shark, that sometimes devours human beings.—**man-eat·ing,** *a.*

ma·nège, ma·nezh′, ma·nāzh′, *n.* [Fr. *manege,* < It. *maneggio,* management.] The art of breaking, training, and riding horses; the precision exercises of a horse; a school for training horses and teaching horsemanship. Also **ma·nege.**

ma·nes, mā′nēz, *L.* mä′nes, *n. pl.* [L. < O.L. *manus,* good, benevolent.] (*Often cap.*) Among the Romans, the spirits or souls of deceased persons; *sing. in constr.* the spirit of a particular individual.

ma·neu·ver, *Brit.* **ma·noeu·vre,** ma·nö′vĕr, *n.* [Fr. *manoeuvre*—*main,* L. *manus,* the hand, and *oeuvre,* L. *opera,* work.] A regulated movement, particularly in an army or navy; *pl.* large tactical movements of troops imitating actual combat conditions Adroit management.—*v.i.* To perform maneuvers, as military or naval maneuvers; to employ intrigue or stratagem to effect a purpose.—*v.t.* To cause to perform maneuvers; to handle skillfully.—**ma·neu·ver·a·bil·i·ty,** *n.*—**ma·neu·ver·a·ble,** *a.*—**ma·neu·ver·er,** *n.*

man Fri·day, *n.* A male employee who acts as an efficient administrative assistant.

man·ful, man′ful, *a.* Bold; brave; resolute. —**man·ful·ly,** *adv.*—**man·ful·ness,** *n.*

man·ga·nate, mang′ga·nāt″, *n. Chem.* a salt of manganic acid.

man·ga·nese, mang′ga·nēs″, mang′ga·nēz″, *n.* [By metathesis from *magnesium,* the name first given to it.] *Chem.* a hard grayish-white metallic element used as an alloying agent to give steel toughness. Sym. Mn, at. no. 25, at. wt. 54.93.— **man·ga·ne·sian,** *a.*—**man·ga·nous,** *a.*

man·ga·nese spar, *n.* Rhodonite; rhodochrosite.

man·gan·ic, man·gan′ik, *a. Chem.* of or pertaining to the content of manganese, esp. trivalent manganese.

man·gan·ic ac·id, *n. Chem.* an instantaneous acid, H_2MnO_4, that occurs only in solution or in the form of salts.

man·ga·nite, mang′ga·nīt″, *n. Chem.* A gray or black manganese hydroxide, $MnO(OH)$; any of several salts containing manganese in the quadrivalent state.

mange, mānj, *n.* [O.Fr. *manjue,* itch, < *mangier* (Fr. *manger*), eat, < L. *manducare,* chew.] Any of various skin diseases affecting animals and sometimes man, characterized by loss of hair and by scabby eruptions, and usu. caused by parasitic mites.

man·gel-wur·zel, mang′gel·wur̨′zel, *n.* [G., lit. 'want-root,' but the proper form is *mangold-wurzel*—G. *mangold,* beet, and *wurzel,* root = beetroot.] *Chiefly Brit.* a variety of beet, *Beta vulgaris, perennis,* cultivated as food for cattle. Also **man·gel, man·gold wur·zel.**

man·ger, mān′jèr, *n.* [Fr. *mangeoire,* < *manger,* < L. *manducare,* to eat.] A trough or box in which fodder is laid for horses or cattle.

man·gle, mang′gl, *v.t.*—*mangled, mangling.* [Perh. < L. *mancus,* maimed, through L.L. *mangulare,* to mangle; cf. O.E. *bemancian,* to maim; L.G. *mank,* mutilated; D. *mank,* lame; G. *mangel,* a defect; *mangeln* to be wanting.] To cut or crush by repeated blows; to mutilate; to spoil; to destroy or badly damage.

man·gle, mang′gl, *n.* [D. and G. *mangel,* < O.Fr. *mangonel,* Gr. *manganon,* a war engine, the axis of a pulley.] A machine used to smooth or iron cotton fabrics by running them through rollers which are heated.—*v.t.*—*mangled, mangling.* To smooth cloth with a mangle.—**man·gler,** mang′glèr, *n.* One who uses a mangle.

man·go, mang′gō, *n. pl.* **man·goes, man·gos.** [Pg. *manga;* from Tamil.] An aromatically-flavored edible fruit of the tropical tree, *Mangifera indica,* in the sumac or cashew family; the tree itself.

man·go·steen, mang′go·stēn″, *n.* [Malay *mangustan.*] The juicy edible fruit of an East Indian tree, *Garcinia mangostana;* the tree itself.

man·grove, mang′grōv, man′grōv, *n.* [Malay *manggi-manggi.*] A tropical tree, *Rhizophora mangle,* growing on the banks of rivers and on the seacoast, remarkable for giving off adventitious roots from the stem and branches, and useful as a source of tannin; any of numerous similar plants.

man·gy, mān′jē, *a.*—*mangier, mangiest.* Having, due to, or resembling the mange; contemptible or mean; squalid or shabby.— **man·gi·ly,** *adv.*—**man·gi·ness,** *n.*

man·han·dle, man′han″dl, man·han′dl, *v.t.*—*manhandled, manhandling.* To handle roughly; to move by human force.

man·hat·tan, man·hat′an, *n.* A cocktail made of whiskey and vermouth, sometimes with bitters added.

man·hole, man′hōl, *n.* A circular, often covered hole through which a man can enter an underground or closed structure, such as a drain, cesspool, or steam boiler, for cleaning or repairing.

man·hood, man′hud, *n.* The state of being a man or adult male person; manly character or qualities; virility; men collectively; the state of being human.

man-hour, man′our″, man′ou″èr, *n.* An hour of work by one man, used as a time unit in industry for estimating costs and wages.

man·hunt, man′hunt″, *n.* An organized, extensive search for a person, esp. a criminal or suspect.—**man·hunt·er,** *n.*

ma·ni·a, mā′nē·a, mān′ya, *n.* [L., < Gr. *mania,* madness, < *mainesthai,* rage, be mad.] Intense excitement or enthusiasm; a vehement passion or desire; a rage or craze. *Psychiatry,* a form of insanity characterized by great excitement, with or without delusions, and by violence in its acute stage.—**man·ic,** man′ik, mā′nik, *a.*

ma·ni·ac, mā′nē·ak″, *n.* [M.L. *maniacus.*] A raving or wildly insane person; a lunatic.—*a.* Raving with insanity; mad.— **ma·ni·a·cal,** ma·nī′a·kal, *a.*—**ma·ni·a·cal·ly,** *adv.*

man·ic-de·pres·sive, man′ik·di·pres′iv, *a. Psychiatry,* pertaining to a mental disorder characterized by marked emotional shifts from great excitement and high spirits to deep depression.—*n.* One afflicted with this disorder.

man·i·cure, man′i·kūr, *n.* [L. *manus,* hand, *cura,* care.] The care of the nails and the hands.—*v.t.*—*manicured, manicuring.* To trim or care for, as the fingernails; give a manicure to.—**man·i·cur·ist,** man′i·kūr″ist, *n.* A person who provides professional hand care.

man·i·fest, man′i·fest″, *a.* [L. *manifestus,* lit. 'that may be laid hold of by the hand'— *manus,* the hand, and root seen in obs. *fendo,* to dash against (as in *offend*).] Clearly visible to the eye or obvious to the understanding; not obscure or difficult to be seen or understood; evident.—*n.* A transporter's document containing such information as the cargo, destination, and passenger list for a vessel or airplane.—*v.t.* To disclose to the eye or to the understanding; to show plainly; to prove; to display; to exhibit.— **man·i·fes·ta·tive,** man″i·fes′ta·tiv, *a.*— **man·i·fest·er,** *n.*—**man·i·fest·ly,** *adv.*

man·i·fes·ta·tion, man″i·fe·stā′shan, *n.* The act of manifesting; a making evident to the eye or the understanding; the exhibition of anything by clear evidence; display; that which displays or reveals; an indication; the appearance in bodily form of a spirit; a public demonstration, as by a political party.—**man·i·fes·tant,** man″i·fes′tant, *n.* One who participates in or starts a public demonstration.

man·i·fest con·tent, *n. Psychoanal.* the happenings or images taking place within a dream.

Man·i·fest Des·ti·ny, *n.* The doctrine, held by expansionists in the U.S. during the 19th century, that the U.S. was predestined to extend its influence and territory over the entire N. American continent; (*l.c.*) such a doctrine as applying to any country or people in relation to a geographic area, regardless of its existing national boundaries.

man·i·fes·to, man″i·fes′tō, *n. pl.* **man·i·fes·tos, man·i·fes·toes.** [It.] A public declaration of principles, objectives, or opinions, usu. by a government or political faction.

man·i·fold, man′i·fōld″, *a.* [O.E. *manigfeald.*] Having many different parts, elements, features, or forms; multifarious; numerous and varied; as, *manifold* duties; having or operating many units of one type.—*n.* That which is manifold; a copy or facsimile, as of writing, made by manifolding; *mech.* a pipe with a number of inlets or outlets, as for exhaust.—*v.t.* To make manifold; to multiply; to make copies of, as with carbon paper.—**man·i·fold·er,** *n.* A contrivance for making manifolds or copies, as of writing.— **man·i·fold·ly,** *adv.*—**man·i·fold·ness,** *n.*

man·i·kin, man·a·kin, man·ni·kin, man′i·kin, *n.* [M.D. *manneken,* dim. of *man, man:* cf. *mannequin.*] A mannequin; a model of the human body for demonstrating anatomy or surgical operations; a little man; a dwarf.

ma·nil·a, ma·nil·la, ma·nil′a, *a.* [From *Manila,* city in Philippine Islands.] Composed of abaca plant fibers; (*cap.*) manufactured from Manila hemp.—*n.*

Ma·nil·a hemp, *n.* An elastic, strong fiber obtained from a Philippine plant, *Musa textilis,* related to the banana, used in the manufacture of cordage, marine cables, and fabrics. Also *abaca, manila.*

ma·nil·a pa·per, *n.* A strong, buff-colored or light brown paper formerly made exclusively of Manila hemp.

man in the street, *n.* The average man; the ordinary citizen.

man·i·oc, man′ē·ok″, mä′nē·ok″, *n.* [Pg. and Sp. *mandioca.*] *Bot.* a spurge, *Manihot esculenta,* having starchy edible roots. Also *cassava.*

man·i·ple, man′i·pl, *n.* [L. *manipulus,* handful, company of soldiers.] A subdivision of the Roman legion, consisting of 60 or 120 men; *eccles.* one of the eucharistic vestments, consisting of an ornamental band or stripe worn on the left arm near the wrist.—**ma·nip·u·lar,** ma·nip′ū·lẽr, *a.* Pertaining or relating to a Roman maniple; of or relating to manipulation.

ma·nip·u·late, ma·nip′ū·lāt″, *v.t.*—*manipulated, manipulating.* [Appar. < Fr. *manipuler,* manipulate (chemical or pharmaceutical substances).] To handle, manage, or use, esp. with skill, in some process of treatment or performance; to manage or influence by artful skill, often by unfair tactics; to adapt or change, as financial statements or operations, to suit one's purpose or advantage.—**ma·nip·u·lat·a·ble, ma·nip·u·la·ble,** ma·nip′ū·la·bl, *a.*—**ma·nip·u·la·tive, ma·nip·u·la·to·ry,** ma·nip′ū·la·tõr″ē, *a.*

ma·nip·u·la·tion, ma·nip″ū·lā′shan, *n.* [Cf. Fr. *manipulation.*] The act or art of manipulating; the state or fact of being manipulated; manual or mechanical treatment or operation; skillful or artful management; fraudulent management for one's advantage.

ma·nip·u·la·tor, ma·nip′ū·lā″tẽr, *n.* One who manipulates; a mechanical aid in handling materials under conditions which do not permit touching the materials or being in their immediate presence.

man·i·tou, man·i·tu, man·i·to, man′i·tö, *n.* Among Algonquian Indians, a spirit that governs nature.

man·kind, man″kind′, man′kind″, *n.* The human race or humans collectively, man″kind′. The males of the human race, man′kind″.

man·like, man′lik″, *a.* Resembling a man or mankind.

man·ly, man′lē, *a.*—*manlier, manliest.* Pertaining to or becoming a man; having the attributes of a man, as self-reliance, bravery.—*adv.*—**man·li·ness,** *n.*

man-made, man′mād, *a.* Formed or manufactured by man; produced by man rather than nature; as, a *man-made* lake; synthetic, as fibers or textiles.

man·na, man′a, *n.* [L., < Gr. *mánna,* < Heb. *mān.*] *O.T.* the food miraculously supplied to the children of Israel in the wilderness. Divine or spiritual food; anything likened to the manna of the Israelites. A sweetish exudation from a species of ash, *Fraxinus ornus,* used as a mild laxative; a similar product obtained from other plants.

manned, mand, *a.* Operated by or containing a man or men; as, a *manned* spacecraft.

man·ne·quin, man′e·kin, *n.* [A corruption of *manikin.*] A life-sized model of the human figure used for dressmaking, tailoring, or displaying clothes; a jointed model, often made of wood, used by artists; a person employed as a fashion model.

man·ner, man′ẽr, *n.* [< Fr. *manière,* manner, O.Fr. *manier,* belonging to the hand, < L. *manus,* the hand—properly, the method of handling a thing.] The way in which anything is done or occurs; one's way of performing or behaving; one's characteristic conduct or deportment; a characteristic artistic style or form; *pl.* social conduct or behavior currently considered as polite or impolite, pleasing or displeasing; *sing.* but *pl.* in *constr.* sorts or kinds; as, all *manner* of things.—**by all man·ner of means,** certainly.—**in a man·ner,** in a certain degree or to a certain extent; somewhat.—**man·nered,** *a.* Having manners of a stated kind, usu. used in compounds; as, well-*mannered*; having a stilted or affected style in writing or art.—**man·ner·less,** *a.* Without good manners.

man·ner·ism, man′e·riz″um, *n.* A characteristic trait, style, or mode of speech or behavior; an affectation or specific eccentricity; (*usu. cap.*) a 16th century European art form characterized by exaggerated form and intense color.—**man·ner·ist,** *n.*—**man·ner·is·tic,** *a.*

man·ner·ly, man′ẽr·lē, *a., adv.* Showing good manners; without rudeness.—**man·ner·li·ness,** *n.*

man·nish, man′ish, *a.* Characteristic of or resembling a man; as applied to a woman, masculine; unwomanly.—**man·nish·ly,** *adv.*—**man·nish·ness,** *n.*

man·nite, man′īt, *n.* Mannitol.—**man·nit·ic,** ma·nit′ik, *a.*

man·ni·tol, man′i·tōl″, man′i·tol″, *n. Chem.* a white, slightly sweet, crystalline alcohol, $C_6H_8(OH)_6$, occurring in three optically different forms, the common one being found in the manna of the ash, *Fraxinus ornus,* and in other plants: used to manufacture resins, plasticizers, and laxatives.

man·nose, man′ōs, *n. Chem.* a sweetish compound of the sugar class, $C_6H_{12}O_6$, produced by the oxidation of mannitol.

man-of-war, man′ov·war′, *n.* pl. **men-of-war.** A boat employed for the purposes of war; warship. See *Portuguese man-of-war.*

ma·nom·e·ter, ma·nom′i·tẽr, *n.* An instrument for measuring the pressure of gases, vapors, or liquids.—**man·o·met·ric,** man·o·met′rik, *a.*—**man·o·met·ri·cal,** man″o·me′trik, *a.*—**man·o·met·ri·cal·ly,** *adv.*

man·or, man′ẽr, *n.* [O.Fr. *maneir* (Fr. *manoir*), noun use of *maneir,* < L. *manēre,* remain.] In England, a landed estate or territorial unit, orig. of the nature of a feudal lordship, consisting of a lord's demesne and of lands within which he has the right to exercise certain privileges and exact certain fees; in colonial America, a tract of land within which the proprietor had similar rights; the mansion of a lord with the land belonging to it; a mansion.—**man·or house,** the house or mansion of the lord of a manor.—**ma·no·ri·al,** ma·nõr′ē·al, *a.*—**ma·no·ri·al·ism,** *n.*

man·pow·er, man′pou″ẽr, *n.* The power of a man; specif. a unit assumed to be equal to the rate at which a man can do mechanical work, commonly taken as one tenth of a horsepower; rate or work in terms of this unit. Power in terms of men available or required; as, the *manpower* of an army.

man·rope, man′rōp″, *n. Naut.* one of the ropes serving as a handrail on each side of a gangway or hatchway.

man·sard, man′särd, *n.* [From the inventor, François *Mansart,* French architect, died 1666.] *Arch.* A curb roof with the lower slope approaching the vertical and the higher slope nearly horizontal; a room possessing this style of roof.

manse, mans, *n.* [L.L. *mansus, mansum,* a residence, < L. *maneo, mansum,* to stay, to dwell.] The dwelling of a clergyman; *archaic,* manor house.

man·serv·ant, man′sur″vant, *n.* pl. **men·serv·ants.** A male servant.

man·sion, man′shan, *n.* [L. *mansio, mansionis,* < *maneo, mansum,* to dwell (seen also in *manor, menial, remain, remnant*).] A dwelling or residence of considerable size and pretension.

man-sized, man′sīzd″, *a. Colloq.* Large; suitable in size or kind for a man. Also **man-size.**

man·slaugh·ter, man′slạ″tẽr, *n. Law.* The unlawful killing of a person, without malice aforethought; homicide.

man·slay·er, man′slā″ẽr, *n.* One who kills a human being.—**man·slay·ing,** *n., a.*

man·sue·tude, man′swi·töd″, man′swi·tūd″, *n.* [L. *mansuetudo.*] *Archaic.* Tameness; gentleness; mildness.

man·ta, man′ta, *Sp.* män′tä, *n.* [Sp., < M.L. *mantum,* cloak: cf. *mantle.*] *Spain, Sp. America,* a cloak or wrap, esp. in Spanish America, a kind of wrap worn by women. *Zool.* any one of a group of large rays found in the waters of tropical America; also **de·vil·fish.**

man·teau, man′tō, man·tō′, *Fr.* män·tō′, *n.* pl. **man·teaus,** *Fr.* **man·teaux,** man′tōz, man·tōz′, *Fr.* män·tō′. [Fr.] *Obs.* a mantle or cloak, esp. one worn by women.

man·tel, man′tel, *n.* [O.Fr. *mantel,* Fr. *manteau*—same as *mantle.*] The ornamental work surrounding and above a fireplace. A narrow shelf or slab above a fireplace; also **man·tel·shelf.** Also *chimney piece,* **man·tel·piece.**

man·tel·et, man′te·let″, mant′lit, *n.* [Dim. of *mantle.*] A short cape or mantle; *milit., hunting,* a type of protective shelter or shield used in combat, or by hunters. Also **mant·let.**

man·tel·let·ta, man″te·let′a, *n.* [It. dim. of *mantello,* < L. *mantellum,* E. *mantle.*] *Rom. Cath. Ch.* a sleeveless vestment of silk or wool reaching to the knees, worn by cardinals, bishops, abbots, and other dignitaries.

man·tic, man′tik, *a.* [Gr. *mantikos,* < *mantis,* a prophet.] Relating to prophecy or divination; prophetic.—**man·ti·cal·ly,** *adv.*

man·ti·core, man′ti·kõr″, *n.* A mythical beast with a lion's body, a man's head, and a dragon's or scorpion's tail.

man·til·la, man·til′a, man·tē′a, *n.* [Sp., same origin as *mantle.*] A Spanish woman's scarf, often of lace, covering the head and shoulders; a light cloak or cape.

man·tis, man′tis, *n.,* pl. **man·tis·es, man·tes,** man′tēz. [Gr., a prophet; an insect.] A carnivorous insect belonging to the family *Mantidae,* having a lengthened prothorax, and forelimbs in a position resembling that of a person's hands in prayer. Also **pray·ing man·tis, man·tid, pray·ing man·tid, prey·ing man·tid.**

man·tis·sa, man·tis′a, *n.* [L., addition, increase.] *Math.* the decimal part of a logarithm. Compare *characteristic.*

man·tle, man′tl, *n.* [O.Fr. *mantel* (Fr. *manteau*), < L. *mantellum, mantelum,* cloak, cloth, napkin.] A loose, sleeveless cloak; something that covers, envelops, or conceals; a chemically prepared, incombustible network hood for a gas jet, which, when the jet is lighted, becomes incandescent and gives a brilliant light; *zool.* the inner protective membrane fold of a mollusk; *ornith.* the back and folded wings of a bird taken together when of the same color. The outer covering used as a protective device in blast furnaces; a mantel.

man·tle, man′tl, *v.t.*—*mantled, mantling.* To cover with or as with a mantle; envelop; conceal.—*v.i.* To spread over the surface; spread like a mantle, as a blush over the face; to be or become covered with a coating; *ornith.* to spread out first one wing and then the other over the corresponding outstretched leg, as a hawk or other bird does.

man·tle rock, *n.* The covering of uncombined fragments of rock, soil, and other materials that forms the earth's surface layer.

man-trap, man′trap″, *n.* A snare, esp. to catch trespassers; *colloq.* a means of captivating a man, as a seductress.

man·tu·a, man′chö·a, *n.* [Either a corruption of Fr. *manteau*, a mantle, or from *Mantua* in Italy.] A loose-fitting gown or mantle worn by women, esp. in the 17th and 18th centuries.

man·u·al, man′ū·al, *a.* [O.Fr. Fr. *manuel*, < L. *manualis*, < *manus*, hand.] Of or pertaining to the hand or hands; performed, made, operated, or used by the hand or hands; requiring or utilizing human energy; of the nature of a manual or handbook.—*n.* A small book, esp. one designed for ready reference; a handbook; *mus.* an organ keyboard; *milit.* a prescribed exercise in the handling of a rifle or other weapon.—**man·u·al·ly,** *adv.*

man·u·al al·pha·bet, *n.* A form of communication among the deaf in which various positions of the hand and fingers represent letters of the alphabet. Also *dactylology*, **fin·ger·spell·ing.**

man·u·al train·ing, *n.* A course of instruction emphasizing hand skills and practical arts, as carpentry and metalwork.

ma·nu·bri·um, ma·nö′brē·um, ma·nū′brē·um, *n.* pl. **ma·nu·bri·ums, ma·nu·bri·a.** [L. a handle, < *manus*, the hand.] *Anat.* a handle-shaped cell or bone; the upper segment of the sternum or handle-shaped section of the malleus. *Zool.* the tubular mouth of the medusa.—**ma·nu·bri·al,** *a.*

man·u·fac·ture, man″ū·fak′chẽr, *n.* [Fr. *manufacture*, < L. *manu*, abl. of *manus*, hand, and *facere*, make.] The making of goods or wares by manual labor or by machinery, esp. on a large scale; any article or material which is manufactured.—*v.t.*—*manufactured, manufacturing.* To make or produce by hand or machinery, esp. on a large scale; to work up, as material, into form for use. *Fig.* to produce as if by mere mechanical industry; produce artificially; invent fictitiously; as, to *manufacture* an alibi.—**man·u·fac·tur·a·ble,** *a.*—**man·u·fac·tur·al,** *a.*—**man·u·fac·tur·er,** *n.*

man·u·mit, man″ū·mit′, *v.t.*—*manumitted, manumitting.* [L. *manumitto*—*manus*, hand, and *mitto*, to send.] To release from slavery; to free, as a slave; to emancipate.—**man·u·mis·sion,** man″ū·mish′an, *n.*—**man·u·mit·ter,** *n.*

ma·nure, ma·nụr′, ma·nūr′, *v.t.*—*manured, manuring.* [O.Fr. *manuvrer, manovrer*, work by hand (Fr. *manoeuvrer*, manipulate, work, maneuver), < *manuevre*, handwork, manual labor.] To treat with fertilizing matter; apply manure to.—*n.* Any natural or artificial substance for fertilizing the soil, esp. dung or refuse.—**ma·nu·ri·al,** *a.*—**ma·nur·er,** *n.*

ma·nus, mā′nus, *n.* pl. **ma·nus.** [L., the hand.] *Anat.* The hand; the part of an animal's forelimb corresponding to the hand in man.

man·u·script, man′ū·skript″, *n.* [L. *manuscriptum*, written with the hand—*manus*, the hand, and *scribo, scriptum*, to write.] An author's handwritten or typewritten work from which the printed copy is produced; a book or paper written by hand; a writing of any kind, in contradistinction to what is printed. Abbr. *ms, MS, ms., MS.*—*a.* Written with the hand; not printed.

man·ward, man′wẽrd, *adv.* Toward man.—*a.* Also **man·wards.**

man·wise, man′wïz″, *adv.* According to the manner or nature of men.

Manx, mangks, *a.* Of or pertaining to the Isle of Man in the Irish Sea, its inhabitants,

or their language.—*n.* The inhabitants of the Isle of Man taken together; the nearly extinct native Celtic language of the inhabitants.—**Manx·man,** *n.* pl. **Manx·men.** A native of the Isle of Man.

Manx cat, *n.* A domestic cat, originating in the Isle of Man, and characterized by a rudimentary tail and hind legs longer than forelegs.

man·y, men′ē, *a.*—*more, most.* [O.E. *manig* = D. *menig* = G. *manch* = Goth. *manags*, many.] Constituting a large number; numerous; being one of a large number, followed by *a* or *an*; as, *many* a day.—*pron. pl. in constr.* A considerable number of people or things.—*n. pl. in constr.* A great or considerable number.—**as man·y,** equal in number.—**the man·y,** the multitude.

man·y·plies, men′ē·plïz″, *n.* *Zool.* the omasum.

man·y-sid·ed, men′ē·sï′did, *a.* Having many sides; having many aspects, capabilities, or talents; as, a *many-sided* man.—**man·y·sid·ed·ness,** *n.*

man·za·ni·ta, man″za·nē′ta, *n.* [Sp., dim. of *manzana*, apple.] Any of various shrubs of the genus *Arctostaphylos*, in the heath family, native to western U.S.; the berries from these shrubs.

map, map, *n.* [L. *mappa*, a napkin—*mappa mundi*, a map of the world.] A graphic representation or charting of the whole or part of the earth's surface, the heavens, or one of the heavenly bodies; anything which resembles a map in appearance or function.—*v.t.*—*mapped, mapping.* To delineate in a map, as the figure of any portion of land; to represent in detail; to program or devise for the future.—**off the map,** out of existence; declining, as a community.—**map·per,** *n.*

ma·ple, mā′pl, *n.* [O.E., in *mapeltrēow*, maple tree.] Any tree or shrub of the genus *Acer*, native to the northern hemisphere, having oppositely arranged, fan-lobed leaves and a dry, double-winged fruit, economically important for lumber and syrup, and as an ornamental shade tree; the wood, esp. of the hard maple, *Acer saccharum*, which is light brown, strong, and often beautifully grained, used for furniture, musical instruments, and flooring.

ma·ple leaf, *n.* A fan-lobed leaf of the maple tree, genus *Acer*; the symbol or emblem of Canada, usu. a red leaf set against a white background.

ma·ple sug·ar, *n.* Sugar from the sugar maple tree, *Acer saccharum*, obtained by boiling down the sap taken from the trunk of the tree in early spring.

ma·ple syr·up, *n.* A syrup prepared by partially concentrating the natural sap in maple trees; a prepared syrup that simulates true maple syrup.

ma·quette, ma·ket′, ma·ket′, *n.* *Arch., fine arts,* a small, three-dimensional, scale model of a projected design.

ma·qui, mä′kē, *n.* An ornamental shrub of Chile, *Aristotelia macqui*; a medicinal wine made from the berries of that plant.

ma·quis, mä·kē′, *n.* pl. **ma·quis.** Shrubby evergreen underbrush common in the Mediterranean region frequented by bandits and refugees. (*Usu. cap.*) the French Resistance in World War II; a member of the Resistance.

mar, *v.t.*—*marred, marring.* [O.E. *myrran, merran, amyrran, ammerran,* to hinder, to spoil.] To injure in any way; to spoil, impair, deface, deform.—*n.*

mar·a·bou, mar′a·bö″, *n.* [Fr. *marabout*, orig. a Mohammedan marabout.] *Ornith.* either of two large carrion-eating storks, *Leptoptilos crumeniferus* of Africa and *L. dubius* of the East Indies, having under the wings and tail white, fluffy feathers used in

millinery and for making furlike trimming or material; the trimming made from such feathers. A special type of dyed raw silk from which the gum has not been removed. Also *marabout.*

mar·a·bout, mar′a·böt″, mar′a·bö, *n.* [Fr. *marabout*, < Pg. *marabuto*, < Ar. *murâbit*, marabout.] *N. Afr.* one of a class of Mohammedan holy men venerated as saints and exercising great influence in religious and secular affairs; the tomb of such a holy man, serving as a shrine. *Ornith.* marabou.

ma·rac·a, ma·rä′ka, ma·rak′a, *n.* A rhythm instrument consisting of a gourd, or a rattle shaped like a gourd, that contains seeds or pebbles.

mar·a·schi·no, mar″a·skē′nō, mar″a·shē′nō, *n.* [It., < *marasca, amarasca*, a kind of sour cherry, < L. *amarus*, bitter.] A kind of liqueur made from sour cherries—**mar·a·schi·no cher·ry,** a cherry flavored with, or preserved in, imitation maraschino and used as a garnish.

ma·ras·mus, ma·raz′mus, *n.* [Gr. *marasmos*, < *marainō*, to cause to pine or waste away.] *Pathol.* a wasting of flesh without fever or apparent disease, esp. in infants.—**ma·ras·mic, ma·ras·moid,** *a.*

Ma·ra·tha, ma·rä′ta, *n.* Mahratta.

Ma·ra·thi, ma·rä′tē, ma·rat′ē, *n.* The Indic language of the Mahratta, a Hindu people of central India. Also **Mah·rat·ti.**

mar·a·thon, mar′a·thon″, mar′a·thon, *n.* [From the feat of the Greek runner who in 490 B.C. bore the news of victory from *Marathon* to Athens, some 20 miles away.] A long-distance race, esp. a foot race of about 26 miles; any contest requiring great stamina.—*a.*—**mar·a·thon·er,** *n.*

ma·raud, ma·rạd′, *v.i.* [Fr. *marauder*, to beg, play the rogue, < *maraud*, a rogue.] To rove in quest of plunder.—*v.t.* To raid.—**ma·raud·er,** *n.*

mar·ble, mär′bl, *n.* [Fr. *marbre*, < L. *marmor*, marble, Gr. *marmaros*.] A metamorphosed limestone varying in color, sometimes mottled, whose texture may be granular or compact enough to take a high polish; a block or piece of sculpture of this material; a little ball of glass, or other hard substance, used by children in play; *pl.* a game played with such balls of glass.—*a.* Composed of marble; stained or veined like marble; *fig.* hard or insensible like marble.—*v.t.*—*marbled, marbling.* To stain or vein like marble. Also **mar·ble·ize,** mär′be·lïz″.—*marbleized, marbleizing.*—**mar·bled, mar·bly,** mär′blē, *a.*—**mar·bler,** *n.*

mar·ble cake, *n.* A cake of light and dark batter, swirled so that the coloration suggests marble.

mar·bling, mär′bling, *n.* Any marking resembling that of veined marble; the process of coloring in imitation of marble; the marblelike markings decorating a book's edges or binding.

marc, märk, Fr. mär, *n.* [Fr.] The refuse matter which remains after the pressing of fruit such as grapes or apples; a brandy produced from this matter.

mar·ca·site, mär′ka·sīt″, *n.* [Fr. *marcassite,* a word of Arabic origin.] Iron pyrites or bisulfide of iron, nearly of the color of tin, used for industrial or ornamental purposes; a product or ornament made of this substance.—**mar·ca·sit·i·cal,** mär″ka·sit′i·kal, *a.*

mar·cel, mär·sel′, *v.t.*—*marcelled, marcelling.* [From *Marcel* Grateau, a French hairdresser who introduced the process.] To wave, as the hair, in a particular style by means of special irons, producing the effect of regular, continuous waves extending over the head.—*n.* A marcelling.—**mar·cel·ler,** *n.*

mar·ces·cent, mär·ses′ent, *a.* [L. *marcescens, marcescentis*, ppr. of *marcesco*, to fade.] *Bot.* withering, but persisting until the ripening period or after, as in grass leaves.—**mar·ces·cence,** *n.*

march, märch, *v.i.* [Fr. *marcher*; It. *marciare*: < Fr. *marche*, a boundary.] To walk with a steady and measured pace, often rhythmically, as soldiers in an organized group; to walk in a dignified, often formal, fashion; to advance steadily.—*v.t.* To cause to march.—*n.* The measured and uniform walk of a body of men, as soldiers, moving simultaneously and in order; a stately and deliberate walk; a steady or labored progression; an advance of soldiers from one point to another; the distance passed over; progressive advancement; progress; as, the *march* of intellect; *mus.* a composition rhythmically suited to accompany the movement of marching.—**march·er,** *n.*

march, märch, *n.* [O.E. *mearc*, a mark, sign, boundary; Icel. *mark*, O.H.G. *marcha* (whence Fr. *marche*, boundary).] A frontier or boundary of a territory; *pl.* the areas at the borders of England and Scotland or England and Wales.—*v.i.* To be contiguous; to be situated next, with a boundary line between.

March, märch, *n.* [O.Fr. *march*, < L. *Martius*, pertaining to Mars, the god of war; *Martius mensis*, Mars' month.] The third month of the year, having 31 days. Abbr. *Mar.*

mar·che·sa, mär·ke′zä, *n. pl.* **mar·che·se,** mär·ke′zē. *It.* the spouse or widow of a marchese; the Italian equivalent to the rank of marchioness.—**mar·che·se,** mär·ke′ze, *n. pl.* **mar·che·si,** mär·ke′zē. The Italian equivalent of marquis.

mar·chion·ess, mär′sha·nis, mär″sha·nes′, *n.* [< L.L. *marchio*, a marquis.] The wife or widow of a marquis; a female having the rank of a marquis.

march·pane, märch′pän″, *n.* [O.Fr. *marcepain*, It. *marzapane*, L.Gr. *maza*, a barley cake, and L. *panis*, bread.] Marzipan.

Mar·cion·ism, mär′sha·niz″um, *n.* A Gnostic ascetic movement of the 2nd to 7th centuries A.D., rejecting the Old Testament and repudiating the belief in Christ as God incarnate.—**Mar·cion·ite,** *n.*

Mar·co·ni, mär·kō′nē, *It.* mär·ką′nē, *a.* [From the Italian electrical engineer, Guglielmo *Marconi*, who invented wireless telegraphy.] (*Sometimes l.c.*) pertaining to wireless telegraphy, as developed by Marconi.

Mar·co·ni rig, *n. Yachting*, a rig having triangular sails and a broad rake. Also *Bermuda rig.*

Mar·di gras, mär′dē grä″, mär′dē grä′, [Fr., 'fat Tuesday.'] Shrove Tuesday; the last day of a carnival, celebrated in Paris, New Orleans, and other cities with parades and special festivities.

mare, mâr, *n.* [O.E. *mere*, *miere*, a mare, fem. of *mear*, *mearh*, a horse; Icel. *mar*, a horse, *merr*, a mare, G. *mähre*, a mare, O.H.G. *marah*, *march*, a horse; allied to Ir. *marc*, W. *march*, a horse.] The female of the horse, donkey, or zebra, esp. when mature.

ma·re, mär′ä, mâr′e, *n. pl.* **ma·ri·a,** mär′ē·a, mâr′ē·a. *Astron.* one of the larger depressions on the surface of the moon.

ma·re clau·sum, mâr′ē klą′sum, *L.* mä′Re klou′sum, *n.* [L. 'a closed sea.'] A body of water controlled by one nation.

ma·re li·be·rum, mâr′ē lib′er·um, *L.* mä′Re lē′be·Rum″, *n.* [L. 'a free sea.'] A body of water open to all nations for navigation.

ma·rem·ma, ma·rem′a, *n. pl.* **ma·rem·me,** ma·rem′ē. [It.] Marshy coastland, esp. in Italy, characterized by a mephitic odor.

mare's-nest, mârz′nest″, *n.* A discovery or accomplishment that is found to be bogus or worthless; a greatly disordered or confused place or state of affairs.

mare's-tail, mârz′tāl″, *n.* A long, thin, and graceful cirrus cloud; *bot.* a common marsh plant, *Hippuris vulgaris*, having densely whorled leaves on long shoots.

mar·gar·ic ac·id, mär·gar′ik as′id, mär·gär′ik as′id, *n.* [Fr. *margarique*, < Gr. *margaron*, pearl.] *Chem.* a white fatty acid resembling stearic acid, and derived from lichens or formed synthetically.

mar·ga·rine, mär′jer·in, mär′je·rēn″, märj′rin, *n.* A substitute for butter consisting of a mixture of prepared edible fats extracted from vegetable oils, and treated with lactic acid bacilli. Also *oleomargarine,* **mar·ga·rin,** mär′jer·in, märj′rin.

mar·ga·rite, mär′ga·rīt″, *n. Chem.* hydrated aluminum calcium silicate; *geol.* a crystalline structure appearing in igneous rocks in which tiny spherical crystals are grouped in a beadlike pattern.

mar·gay, mär′gä, *n.* [Fr.; < Brazilian name.] A small spotted wild cat, *Felis tigrina*, native to tropical America.

mar·gin, mär′jin, *n.* [L. *margo* (*margin-*), border, edge.] A border or edge; the space surrounding the main body of writing or printing on a page; a limit, or a condition, beyond which something ceases to exist or be possible; as, the *margin* of consciousness; an amount allowed or available beyond what is actually necessary. *Com.* the difference between the cost and the selling price; the smallest return necessary for a business enterprise to remain profitable. *Finance*, security, as a percentage in money, deposited with a broker as a provision against loss on transactions on behalf of his principal.—*v.t.* To provide with a margin or border; to furnish with marginal notes, as a document; to enter in the margin, as of a book. *Finance*, to deposit a margin upon; secure by a margin.

mar·gi·nal, mär′ji·nal, *a.* [N.L. *marginalis*.] Pertaining to a margin; situated on the border or edge; characterized by the intermingling but incomplete acceptance of the values and norms of two cultures; written or printed in the margin of a page; close to minimal requirements, value, or quality; as, *marginal* talent; *econ.* barely showing a profit.—**mar·gi·na·li·a,** *n. pl.* Marginal notes.—**mar·gin·al·i·ty,** *n.*—**mar·gin·al·ly,** *adv.*

mar·gin·al u·til·i·ty, *n. Econ.* the additional usefulness or utility the consumer gains from the final unit of some economic service or commodity.

mar·gin·ate, mär′ji·nāt″, *v.t.*—**marginated, marginating.** [L. *marginatus*, pp. of *marginare*, < *margo*, E. *margin*.] To furnish with a margin; to border.—*a.* Having a definite margin. Also **mar·gin·at·ed.**—**mar·gin·a·tion,** *n.*

mar·grave, mär′grāv, *n.* [Fr. *margrave*, < D. *markgraaf*, G. *markgraf*—*mark*, a march, or border, and *graf*, an earl or count.] Originally, a lord or keeper of the marches or border provinces in Germany; a title of nobility in Germany corresponding to a British marquis.—**mar·gra·vate,** *n.* The territory or jurisdiction of a margrave.—**mar·gra·vi·al,** *a.*—**mar·gra·vine,** *n.* The wife of a margrave.

mar·gue·rite, mär′ge·rēt′, *n.* [Fr., < L. *margarita*, pearl.] *Bot.* any of several cultivated flowers of the composite family, as *Chrysanthemum frutescens* and *Anthemis tinctoria.*

Mar·i·an, mâr′ē·an, *a.* [L.L. *Maria*, Mary.] Of or pertaining to the Virgin Mary; of or pertaining to some other Mary, as Mary Tudor, Queen of England, or Mary, Queen of Scots.—*n.* One who especially venerates the Virgin Mary; a supporter or

follower of Mary Tudor or of Mary, Queen of Scots; a specific lunar crater.

mar·i·cul·ture, mär″i·kul′chèr, *n.* The cultivation of undersea plants and animals.

mar·i·gold, mar′i·gōld″, *n.* [From *Mary* (the Virgin) and *gold*.] *Bot.* Any of the various strong-scented, golden-flowered, garden plants in the composite family, genus *Tagetes*; the pot marigold, *Calendula officinalis*, in the composite family, the heads of which are sometimes used as flavoring in cooking.

ma·ri·jua·na, ma·ri·hua·na, mar″i·wä′na, mar″i·hwä′na, mär″i·wä′na, mär″i·hwä′na, *n.* [Amer. Sp., native word.] A narcotic, cannabin, obtained from the dried leaves and flower heads of the pistillate plant, *Cannabis sativa*, and usu. smoked in cigarettes; the plant itself. See *hemp.*

ma·rim·ba, ma·rim′ba, *n.* [W.Afr.] A xylophonelike musical instrument of African origin, popularized and perfected in Central America, made from a number of wooden strips of various sizes yielding different tones when struck by a hammer or stick, and having resonators beneath to reinforce the sound.

ma·ri·na, ma·rē′na, *n.* [Sp.] A small boat basin where moorings, supplies, and repair service are available.

mar·i·nade, mar″i·nād′, *n.* [Fr., < *mariner*.] A pickle or brine usu. of vinegar or wine seasoned with herbs and spices, in which one steeps meat or fish before cooking to improve the flavor; a dish of meat or fish thus steeped.—mar′i·nād″, *v.t.*—*marinaded, marinading.* To marinate.

mar·i·nate, mar′i·nāt″, *v.t.*—*marinated, marinating.* [Fr. *mariner*, put in brine or pickle, < *marin*, E. *marine*.] To steep or soak in a marinade.—**mar·i·na·tion,** *n.*

ma·rine, ma·rēn′, *a.* [O.Fr. Fr. *marin* (fem. *marine*), < L. *marinus*, < *mare*, sea.] Of or pertaining to the sea; existing in the sea; produced by the sea; adapted for use at sea; as, a *marine* barometer; pertaining to navigation or shipping; nautical; naval; maritime; serving on shipboard, as soldiers. —*n.* One of a class of naval troops serving both on shipboard and on land, esp. a member of the U.S. Marine Corps; shipping in general; seagoing vessels collectively, esp. with reference to nationality or class; the department of a government having to do with naval affairs; a picture with a marine subject.

ma·rine glue, *n.* A water-insoluble compound used to coat previously caulked crevices on a ship's deck.

mar·i·ner, mar′i·nèr, *n.* [Fr. *mariner*.] One whose occupation is to navigate or assist in navigating ships; seaman; sailor. (*Cap.*), *aeron.* one of several unmanned U.S. spacecrafts used for exploratory flights to other planets, specif. Venus and Mars.

mar·i·ner's com·pass, *n. Navig.* a compass comprised of several magnetic needles running parallel and fastened to a marked card which indicates direction.

Mar·i·ol·a·try, mâr″ē·ol′a·trē, *n.* [L. *Maria*, Mary, the Virgin Mary, and Gr. *latreia*, service, worship.] The idolatrous veneration of the Virgin Mary; excessive idealization of woman having its root in the adoration of the Virgin Mary.—**Mar·i·ol·a·ter,** *n.*—**Mar·i·ol·a·trous,** *a.*

Mar·i·ol·o·gy, mâr″ē·ol′o·jē, *n.* The complete body of religious doctrine and belief about the Virgin Mary.—**Mar·i·ol·o·gist,** *n.*

mar·i·on·ette, mar″ē·o·net′, *n.* [Fr. for *Mariolette*, a dim. of *Mariole*, a little figure of the Virgin *Mary*.] A jointed puppet moved by strings.

mar·i·po·sa lil·y, mar″i·pō′sa lil′ē, mar″i·pō′za lil′ē, *n.* [Sp. *mariposa*, butterfly.] One of several liliaceous plants of N.

America, genus *Calochortus*, with snowy white, yellow, or lilac flowers often spotted and opening wide in the shape of a globe. Also **mar·i·po·sa tu·lip.**

Mar·ist, mâr'ist, *n.* [Fr. *Mariste*, < L.L. *Maria*, Mary.] A member of the Roman Catholic religious order which originated in 1816 at Lyons, France, devoted to missionary and educational work, and dedicated to the Virgin Mary.—*a.* Belonging or pertaining to the Marists.

mar·i·tal, mar'i·tal, *a.* [L. *maritalis*, < *maritus*, husband, as a. married, pertaining to marriage.] Of or pertaining to marriage; matrimonial; connubial; as, *marital* harmony.—**mar·i·tal·ly,** *adv.*

mar·i·time, mar'i·tīm", *a.* [L. *maritimus*, < *mare*, sea.] Bordering on the sea; living near the sea; of or pertaining to the sea; connected with the sea in relation to navigation or shipping; as, *maritime* law; characteristic of a seaman; nautical.

mar·jo·ram, mär'jer·am, *n.* [G. *marjoran*, It. *marjorana*, L.L. *marjoraca*, < L. *amaracus*, Gr. *amarakos*, marjoram.] *Bot.* either of two perennial mint plants, *Majorana hortensis*, a sweet and savory herb, or *Origanum vulgare*, pot marjoram, both used for flavoring in cooking.

mark, märk, *n.* [O.E. *mearc*, boundary, landmark, sign, = G. *mark*, boundary, march, = Goth, *marka*, boundary; akin to L. *margo*, border, E. *margin*, and to E. *march*.] A visible trace or impression, as a cut, dent, stain, stamp, or bruise; a symbol, letter, or number used to indicate the degree of achievement or conduct, as of pupils in a school; a symbol to indicate origin, ownership, comparative merit, standard of excellence, or distinction; as, a trade*mark*; a distinctive property, character, or trait; as, the *mark* of a gentleman; a badge, brand, or other visible sign assumed or imposed; a recognized standard; as, below the *mark*; a symbol used in writing or printing; as, a punctuation *mark*; a target; a goal; a notice; a cross made by a person who cannot write. *Naut.* one of the pieces of leather or cloth on a lead line to indicate depth in fathoms; *sports*, *track*, the starting line; *bowling*, a spare or strike; *slang*, a dupe; *archaic*, a boundary or frontier.—*v.t.* [O.E. *mearcian*.] To make marks on; to set the boundaries of; to establish limits often with *out*; to indicate or designate by or as by marks; to evidence; to grade; to record, as a score; to be a distinguishing feature of; to single out or be destined; as, *marked* for success; to notice or observe; to give attention to.— *v.i.* To be attentive; to consider.—**leave a mark,** to make an impression.—**mark down,** to lower the price.—**mark time,** to move the feet as in marching, without advancing. *Fig.* to stop action or progress for a time; to bide one's time.—**mark up,** to raise prices.—**on your mark,** be ready to start, esp. a race.—**wide of the mark,** far from the target; inaccurate.

marked, märkt, *a.* Furnished with a mark or marks; affixed; as, the *marked* price of goods; distinguished or singled out; as, a *marked* man; strikingly noticeable, conspicuous.—**mark·ed·ly,** mär'kid·lē, *adv.*

mark·er, mär'ker, *n.* One who or that which marks; one who records, as a grader; something used as a mark or indication; a counter, as in a game; anything used for marking locations, as a beacon from a radio station.

mar·ket, mär'kit, *n.* [O.Fr. *markiet*, It. *marcato*, L. *mercatus*, < *mercor*, to buy, < *merx*, *mercis*, merchandise.] Traffic in certain goods or services; as, the cigarette *market*; country or place of sale; as, the U.S. *market*, the foreign *market*; those for whom a commodity or service is made available; as, the teenage *market*; a public place where goods are exposed for sale, whether a building or open space; a shop; purchase or sale, or rate of purchase or sale; those formally conducting a sale; as, the stock *market*; demand for commodities; the field of business; as, the worst on the *market*; an occasion on which goods are publicly exposed for sale and buyers assemble to purchase; a fair.—*v.i.* To deal in a market; to purchase provisions for a household.—*v.t.* To offer for sale in a market; to vend; to sell.—**mar·ket·er,** *n.*

mar·ket·a·ble, mär'ki·ta·bl, *a.* Capable of being sold; very saleable; noting or pertaining to buying or selling.—**mar·ket·a·bil·i·ty,** mär"ki·ta·bil'i·tē, *n.*

mar·ket gar·den, *n. Chiefly Brit.* truck farm, or place where vegetables are produced for local markets.

mar·ket in·dex, *n. Business,* a gauge of an industry's activity or the ability of a given region to consume certain goods or services.

mar·ket·ing, mär'ki·ting, *n.* Trading in a market; buying or selling; the entire process of storing, shipping, advertising, and selling which promotes and actualizes a sales transaction.

mar·ket let·ter, *n.* A report issued periodically by brokerage and investment firms containing opinions and advice on the current markets, used to increase business and to supply existing customers with fresh ideas.

mar·ket or·der, *n.* An instruction to a broker to purchase or sell in the market at the current price.

mar·ket·place, mar·ket place, mär'kit·plās", *n.* A place, esp. an open space in a town, where a market is held; the sphere of commerce; *fig.* the world as the place or realm where ideas, values, or works struggle for acceptance.

mar·ket price, *n.* The price at which anything is currently sold; current value. Also *market value.*

mar·ket re·search, *n.* The collection and organization of data concerning the preferences and buying habits of consumers.

mar·ket val·ue, *n.* The price of services, commodities, or securities in the open market; market price.

mark·ing, mär'king, *n.* The act of making a mark; a mark or series of marks upon something; *often pl.* characteristic arrangement of natural coloring; as, the *markings* on a bird's egg.

marks·man, märks'man, *n.* pl. **marks·men.** One who is skillful at hitting a mark; one who shoots well; *milit.* the lowest passing grade attainable in the U.S. army for target shooting.—**marks·man·ship,** *n.*

marl, märl, *n.* [O.Fr. *marle*, < M.L. *margila*, dim. of L. *marga*, marl.] A soil or earthy deposit consisting of clay and calcium carbonate, used as a fertilizer; any of various other soft or crumbly deposits, as a mixture of green sand and clay also used as a fertilizer; *poet.* earth.—*v.t.* To fertilize with or as with marl.—**mar·la·cious,** mär·lā'shus, *a.*—**mar·ly,** *a.*—*marlier, marliest.*

marl, märl, *v.t.* [D. *marlen*, appar. < *marren*, tie.] *Naut.* to wind, cover, or fasten with marline or twine, each turn being secured by a hitch.

mar·lin, mär'lin, *n.* Any one of a number of oceanic game fish, included in the genus *Makaira*, and related to the sailfish and spearfish.

mar·line, mär'lin, *n.* [D. *marling, marlijn—marren*, to tie, to moor, and *lijn*, a line, a cord.] *Naut.* a small line composed of two strands loosely twisted, used for winding around ropes to prevent their being chafed. Also **mar·lin, mar·ling,** mär'ling.

mar·line·spike, mar·lin·spike, mär'lin·spīk", *n. Naut.* an iron spike used to sepa-rate the strands of a rope in splicing. Also **mar·ling·spike,** mär'ling·spīk".

marl·ite, mär'līt, *n.* A variety of marl which is unaffected by exposure to air.— **mar·lit·ic,** mär·lit'ik, *a.*

mar·ma·lade, mär'ma·lād", mär"ma·lād', *n.* [Fr. *marmelade*; Pg. *marmelada, marmelo*, a quince; < L. *melimelum*, Gr. *melimēlon*, lit. 'a sweet apple'—*meli*, honey, and *melon*, an apple, peach, orange.] A preserve containing small pieces of fruit and rind, and made by boiling the pulp and rind of a citrus or other fruit with sugar.

mar·mo·re·al, mär·mōr'ē·al, mär·mar'·ē·al, *a.* Resembling, pertaining to, or made of marble. Also **mar·mo·re·an.**—**mar·mo·re·al·ly,** *adv.*

mar·mo·set, mär'mo·zet", *n.* [O.Fr. Fr. *marmouset*, grotesque little figure or creature; origin uncertain.] Any of the rather small, squirrellike monkeys in the family *Callithricidae*, with long, hairy, nonprehensile tails, inhabiting the Amazonian region.

mar·mot, mär'mot, *n.* [Fr. *marmotte*; It. *marmotta, marmontana*, < L. *mus* (*muris*) *montanus*, mountain mouse.] Any of several species of short-legged, short-tailed rodents of the genus *Marmota*, native to northern latitudes and hibernating in burrows, as the eastern woodchuck, *Marmota monax.*

ma·roon, ma·rön', *v.t.* [Fr. *marron*, runaway, < Sp. *cimarron*, wild, unruly, < *cima*, the top of a hill; Cuba, *cimarron*, a runaway slave.] To put ashore and leave on a desolate island with punitive intent; to leave abandoned and helpless; to strand.— *n.* Any of the descendants of the 17th and 18th century fugitive slaves now inhabiting the mountainous regions of the West Indies and Guiana.

ma·roon, ma·rön', *n.* [Fr. *marron* = It. *marrone*, chestnut; origin unknown.] A very dark purplish-red or claret color; a kind of small firework often used as a warning signal.—*a.* Having a dark purplish-red or claret color.

mar·plot, mär'plot", *n.* One who, by his officious interference, mars or defeats a plan or plot.

mar·quee, mär·kē', *n.* [Fr. *marquise*, a marchioness, a marquee.] A rooflike projection over an outer doorway, walk, or terrace used for protection and advertising, as of a theater; a signboard. A large tent erected outdoors for temporary purposes; a canopy; an officer's field tent; also *marquise.*

Mar·que·san, mär·kā'zan, mär·kā'san, *n.* A native of the Marquesas Islands in French Polynesia; the language of the inhabitants of the Marquesas islands.—*a.*

mar·quess, mär'kwis, *n.* Marquis.

mar·que·try, mär'ki·trē, *n.* pl. **mar·que·tries.** [Fr. *marqueterie*, < *marqueter*, to spot, to inlay, < *marque*, a mark.] Inlaid work consisting of fine woods and other materials used for a decorative effect on furniture and floorings. Also **mar·que·te·rie.**

mar·quis, mär'kwis, mär·kē', Fr. mär·kē', *n.* pl. **mar·quis·es, mar·quis,** mär·kēz', Fr. mär·kē'. [Fr. *marquis*, It. *marchese*, L.L. *marchisus, marchensis*, a prefect of the *marches* or border territories.] A title of dignity in Britain next in rank to that of duke, the second of the five orders of English nobility. Also *marquess.*—**mar·quis·ate,** mär'kwi·zit, *n.* The rank, dignity, or territory of a marquis.

mar·quise, mär·kēz', Fr. mär·kēz', *n.* pl. **mar·quis·es,** mär·kē'ziz, Fr. mär·kēz'. [Fr.] The wife or widow of a marquis, or a lady holding the rank equal to that of a marquis. *Jewelry*, a gem, oval in shape, with pointed ends; *arch.* a marquee.

mar·qui·sette, mär"ki·zet', mär"kwi·zet', *n.* A loosely woven fabric of either cotton, silk, rayon, or nylon, chiefly used for curtains and garments.

Mar·ra·no, ma·rä′nō, *n. pl.* **Mar·ra·nos.** Any Spanish Jew who publicly converted to Catholicism under pressure of the Spanish Inquisition in the late Middle Ages, but secretly followed the Jewish faith.

mar·riage, mar′ij, *n.* [O.Fr. Fr. *mariage* < *marier*, E. *marry.*] The social institution by which a man and woman are legally united and establish a new family unit; wedlock; the state of being married; the relation between husband and wife; the action or act of marrying; the ceremony of marrying; a wedding; any intimate union.—**mar·riage·a·ble**, mar′i·ja·bl, *a.*—**mar·riage·a·bil·i·ty, mar·riage·a·ble·ness,** *n.*

mar·riage of con·ven·ience, *n.* A marriage entered into for monetary or social gain.

mar·ried, mar′ēd, *a.* United in wedlock; wedded; pertaining to marriage or married persons; as, *married* life; closely united.

mar·ron, mar′on, ma·rōn′, *Fr.* mä·ʀaN′, *n.* A chestnut, candied or preserved, esp. as used in cookery.

mar·row, mar′ō, *n.* [O.E. mearh, mearg = D. marg, merg, Dan. marv, Icel. mergr, G. mark, marrow; cf. O.E. mearu, D. murw, tender, soft.] The tissue, of soft and vascular structure, present in bone cavities. *Fig.* the essence; pith; vitality.—**mar·row·y,** *a.*

mar·row, mar′ō, *Sc.* maʀ′o, *n.* [M.E.; origin obscure.] *Sc., Brit. dial.* A companion, partner, or associate; a mate.

mar·row·bone, mar′ō·bōn″, *n.* A bone containing marrow that is eatable. *Pl.* the knees: used facetiously.

mar·row·fat, mar′ō·fat″, *n.* A kind of garden pea with large seeds; the seed itself.

mar·ry, mar′ē, *v.t.*—**married, marrying.** [O.Fr. Fr. *marier*, < L. *maritare,* < *maritus,* husband, *adj.* married, pertaining to marriage, < *mas* (*mar-*), male, a male.] To join as husband or wife; to take in marriage, to unite in wedlock; to give in marriage; to unite intimately; *naut.* to join together, as two ropes, end to end without increasing the diameter.—*v.i.* To enter into the conjugal state; take a husband or wife.

Mars, märz, *n.* [L.] *Astron.* the major planet next above the earth, being the fourth in order from the sun. The Roman god of war.

mar·seille, mär·sāl′, *n.* [From *Marseilles,* city in France.] A thick cotton fabric woven in figures or stripes, with an embossed or quilted effect. Also **mar·seilles,** mär·sālz′.

marsh, märsh, *n.* [O.E. mersc, for merisc (=mere-ish), a marsh or bog, an adj. form < mere, a mere.] A tract of low and very wet land; a fen; swamp.

mar·shal, mär′shal, *n.* [O.Fr. mareschal (Fr. maréchal) = M.L. marescalcus, < O.H.G. marahscalh, 'horse servant,' < marah, horse, and scalh, servant.] A general officer of high or the highest rank in various European or other armies; a person charged with the arrangement or regulation of ceremonies; any of various former or present law enforcement officials; an administrative officer of a U.S. judicial district who performs duties similar to those of a sheriff; a high officer of a royal household or court.—*v.t.*—*marshaled, marshaling, esp. Brit.* marshalled, marshalling. To arrange or place in due or proper order; array, draw for battle, or review; to usher or lead. *Her.* to combine to form a complete heraldic composition.—**mar·shal·cy, mar·shal·ship,** *n.*

marsh el·der, *n.* Any of the herbaceous or shrubby composite plants, genus *Iva,* with thick leaves and small, nodding greenish flowers, native to eastern N. America, and inhabiting salt marshes or wasteland; also **sump·weed.**

marsh gas, *n.* Methane, an inflammable gas resulting from decomposition of vegetation, esp. in marshy land.

marsh hawk, *n.* An American hawk found in meadows and marshes, *Circus cyaneus hudsonius,* identified by its white rump, and preying on small animals, as rodents, frogs, and snakes.

marsh hen, *n. Ornith.* A bird of the rail family, *Rallus longirostris,* inhabiting the salt marshes along the Atlantic and Gulf coasts; a coot.

marsh mal·low, *n. Bot.* a European herb, *Althaea officinalis,* of the mallow family, naturalized in N. America, and noted for its abundant blue to rose-colored blossoms.

marsh·mal·low, märsh′mel″ō, märsh-mal′ō, *n.* A sweet confection made from sugar, gelatin, corn syrup, and albumin, coated with powdered sugar, and used as a snack and in desserts and salads; a mucilaginous substance obtained from roots of the marsh mallow plant, and used in medicine and confectionery.

marsh mar·i·gold, *n.* An early blooming marsh herb, *Caltha palustris,* of the buttercup family, with bright yellow flowers and glossy leaves. Also *cowslip.*

marsh·y, mär′shē, *a.*—**marshier marshiest.** Pertaining to or of the nature of a marsh or swamp; swampy; produced in marshes.—**marsh·i·ness,** *n.*

mar·su·pi·al, mär·sō′pē·al, *a.* [N.L. marsupialis, < L. marsupium.] Pertaining to, resembling, or having a marsupium or pouch; of or pertaining to the marsupials.—*n.* Any of the *Marsupialia,* an order of nonplacental mammals which includes the kangaroo, opossum, and koala, most of which have a marsupium or pouch on the abdomen of the female containing the mammary glands and serving as a receptacle for the young.

mar·su·pi·um, mär·sō′pē·um, *n. pl.* **mar·su·pi·a,** mär·sō′pē·a. [L., pouch, < Gr. marsupion, marspion, dim. of marsipos, bag, pouch.] The pouch or fold of skin on the abdomen of a female marsupial which encloses the nipples and functions as a receptacle for carrying the young, as in the opossum; a similar pouch for carrying eggs in certain fishes, as the male sea horse.

mart, märt, *n.* [Contr. < market.] A place where buying and selling are actively carried on; market; trading center.

mar·tel·lo tow·er, mär·tel′ō tou′ėr, *n.* [From *Mortella* in Corsica, where a tower of this kind made a strong resistance to an English naval force in 1794.] (*Sometimes cap.*) a small circular fort, with very thick walls, built chiefly to defend a coast.

mar·ten, mär′ten, mär′tin, *n. pl.* **mar·tens, mar·ten.** [Older martern, Fr. martre, < D. marter, G. marder, a marten.] A N. American, bushy-tailed mammal, *Martes americana,* of the weasel family, inhabiting northern forests, and valuable for its fur. The dark brown fur of this animal; also **baum mar·ten.**

mar·ten·site, mär′ten·zīt″, *n. Metal.* a primary constituent of hardened steel, composed of carbon and iron, and present in steel during the process of transforming austenite.—**mar·ten·sit·ic,** mär′ten·zit′ik, *a.*

mar·tial, mär′shal, *a.* [L. martialis, < Mars, Martis, the god of war.] Pertaining to war; suited to war; military; given to war.—**mar·tial·ism,** *n.*—**mar·tial·ist,** *n.*—**mar·tial·ly,** *adv.*—**mar·tial·ness,** *n.*

mar·tial law, *n.* A temporary military rule imposed in times when civil authority is unable to maintain law and order.

Mar·tian, mär′shan, *a.* Pertaining to Mars, god of war, or to the planet Mars.—*n.* An imaginary inhabitant of Mars.

mar·tin, mär′tin, mär′tin, *n.* [From the proper name *Martin;* cf. *robin*-redbreast.] *Ornith.* any of various species of swallows, esp. the largest of the swallows, *Progne subis,* well known for its attraction to multicelled nesting boxes, and the only swallow in which the male is of a uniformly iridescent blue-black color; also **pur·ple mar·tin.** A European swallow, *Delichon urbica;* also **house mar·tin.**

mar·ti·net, mär″ti·net′, mär′ti·net″, *n.* [From General *Martinet,* a very strict French officer in the reign of Louis XIV.] A military officer who is an excessively strict disciplinarian; one who lays stress on discipline and a rigid adherence to rules and regulations.—**mar·ti·net·ish,** *a.*—**mar·ti·net·ism,** *n.*

mar·tin·gale, mär′tin·gāl″, *n.* [Fr.; origin uncertain.] A strap of a horse's harness passing from the bit or headgear, between the forelegs, to the girth, to prevent the animal from tossing its head. *Naut.* a short perpendicular spar under the end of a bowsprit, or a stay extending from such a spar to the jib boom. A gambling system in which the stakes are doubled after each loss.

mar·ti·ni, mär·tē′nē, *n. pl.* **mar·ti·nis.** A cocktail generally mixed in the proportion three parts gin or vodka to one part dry vermouth, and served with a lemon peel or an olive.

mart·let, märt′lit, *n.* [Appar. for obs. martinet, < Fr. martinet, martin, < Martin, man's name.] A European martin; *her.* a bird represented without feet.

mar·tyr, mär′tėr, *n.* [Gr. martyr, a martyr, a form of martyrs, a witness.] One who goes to his death rather than renounce his faith or religious beliefs; one who endures intense suffering for adherence to any principle or belief; one who suffers greatly; one who exaggerates his suffering to enlist the sympathy of others.—*v.t.* To put to death for adherence to a belief, principle, or loyalty to a cause; to persecute; to torment or torture. Also **mar·tyr·ize**—*martyrized, martyrizing.*—**mar·tyr·dom,** *n.*

mar·tyr·ol·o·gy, mär″ti·rol′o·jē, *n. pl.* **mar·tyr·ol·o·gies.** That branch of ecclesiastical history that deals with the lives of religious martyrs; a detailed account of an individual's martyrdom; such accounts in general; a list of Christian martyrs.—**mar·tyr·o·log·ic, mar·tyr·o·log·i·cal,** *a.*—**mar·tyr·ol·o·gist,** *n.*

mar·tyr·y, mär′ti·rē, *n. pl.* **mar·tyr·ies.** A shrine built in tribute to a martyr.

mar·vel, mär′vel, *n.* [Fr. merveille; It. maraviglia; < mirabilia, wonderful things, < mirabilis, wonderful, < mirar, to wonder.] A wonder; an object of great astonishment.—*v.i.*—marveled, marveling, Brit. marvelled, marvelling. To be struck with surprise or astonishment; to wonder.—*v.t.* To be filled with wonder at or about, usu. with a clause as an object.

mar·vel·ous, *Brit.* **mar·vel·lous,** mär′ve·lus, *a.* Exciting wonder; astonishing; surpassing belief; partaking of the miraculous. *Colloq.* first rate, excellent; as, a marvelous dinner.—**mar·vel·ous·ly,** *Brit.* **mar·vel·lous·ly,** *adv.*—**mar·vel·ous·ness,** *Brit.* **mar·vel·lous·ness,** *n.*

Marx·ism, märk′siz·um, *n.* [From Karl Marx, 1818–1883, German socialist.] The economic, social, and political theories formulated by Karl Marx and Friedrich Engels, stressing the doctrines of dialectical materialism, class struggle, the labor theory of value, and the inevitable decay of capitalism, leading to the goal of a classless society.—**Marx·ist,** märk′sist, *a., n.*—**Marx·i·an,** mark′sē·an, *a.*

Marx·ism-Len·in·ism, märk′siz″um-len′-i·niz″um, *n.* A form and practice of communism devised by Lenin from the basic teachings of Karl Marx.

Mar·y, mâr′ē, *n.* Jesus' mother. Also *Virgin Mary.*

Mar·y Mag·da·lene, *n. N.T.* Mary from Magdala, a woman exorcised by Jesus, identified with the contrite sinner to whom Jesus granted forgiveness.

mar·zi·pan, mär′zi·pan″, *n.* [G.] A candy composed of almond paste, sugar, and egg whites. Also *marchpane.*

mas·car·a, ma·skar′a, *n.* [Sp., mask.] A cosmetic preparation for darkening the eyelashes.

mas·cot, mas′kot, mas′kot, *n.* [Fr. *mascotte.*] A thing, animal, or person thought to bring good luck.

mas·cu·line, mas′kū·lin, *a.* [L. *masculinus,* < *masculus,* male, < *mas, maris,* a male; of same origin as *marry, marital, male.*] Of the male sex; not female; strong; robust; powerful; manly; virile; said of a woman, coarse, bold, mannish; *gram.* denoting or pertaining to the gender of words which are esp. applied to male beings or things regarded grammatically as male.—*n. Gram.* The masculine gender; a word or form of this gender.—**mas·cu·line·ly,** *adv.*—**mas·cu·line·ness, mas·cu·lin·i·ty,** mas″kū·lin′i·tē, *n.*

mas·cu·lin·ize, mas′kū·li·nīz″, *v.t.*—*masculinized, masculinizing.* To infuse a male character into. *Med.* to cause male secondary sex characteristics to develop, as in a female.

ma·ser, mā′zėr, *n.* [(m)icrowave (a)mplification by (s)timulated (e)mission of (r)adiation.] Any one of several devices used to amplify electromagnetic waves by utilizing energy emitted upon the stimulation of an excited atomic or molecular system.

mash, mash, *n.* [O.E. *masc-, max-* (recorded in compounds), = G. *meisch,* mash.] A soft, pulpy mass; a pulpy state or condition; crushed malt or meal of grain mixed with hot water to form wort; a mess of grain, bran, or meal fed dry or moistened to livestock and poultry.—*v.t.* To mix, as crushed malt, with hot water to form wort; to reduce to a soft, pulpy mass, as by beating or pressure; to crush.—**mash·er,** *n.* One who or that which mashes. *Slang,* a man who makes advances to women, esp. to those who are strangers to him.

mash·ie, mash·y, mash′ē, *n.* [Cf. Fr. *massue,* club.] *Golf,* a club having a short iron head with a sloping face for making lofting shots of medium distance. Also **num·ber five i·ron.**

mask, mask, mäsk, *n.* [Fr. *masque:* cf. M.L. *mascus, masca,* mask, specter, *masca,* witch, It. *maschera,* Sp. *máscara,* mask, all of uncertain origin and relations.] A covering for the face, worn for disguise, protection, safety, and the like; a figure of a face or head worn by ancient Greek and Roman actors; a false face; a likeness of a person's face, as in marble, or as molded in plaster, wax, or such; as, a death *mask;* anything that disguises or conceals; a disguise; a pretense; a covering; a person wearing a mask; a masquerade or revel; a masque or dramatic composition; *arch.* a representation of a face or head, generally grotesque, used as an ornament; *milit.* a screen, as of earth or brush, for concealing or protecting a battery or any military operation; *photog.* an opaque material, tape or paper, used to change or block out part of a picture being printed. A dog or a fox's head.—**mask·er, mas·quer,** *n.* One who dons a mask; one who plays in a masque.—**mask·like,** *a.*

mask, mask, mäsk, *v.t.* [Fr. *masquer.*] To cover with a mask; to disguise or conceal; to render indistinct. *Milit.* to conceal, as a battery or any military operation, from the enemy; to hinder, as an army, from con-

ducting an operation, as by a superior force.—*v.i.* To put on a mask; disguise oneself; take part in a masque or masquerade.

masked, maskt, mäskt, *a.* Wearing, or provided with, a mask or masks; disguised; concealed; as, a *masked* intention; of an illness, latent; as, *masked* walking pneumonia. *Zool.* marked on the face or head as if wearing a mask; *entom.* having the wings, legs, or other characteristics of the future imago indicated in outline beneath the integument, as certain insect pupae.

mas·och·ism, mas′o·kiz″um, maz′o·kiz″-um, *n.* [From Leopold von Sacher-*Masoch,* 1836–95, Austrian novelist, who described it.] *Psychol.* A form of sexual perversion in which the victim takes pleasure in physical abuse; propensity to derive pleasure from emotional or physical pain; pathological self-destruction.—**mas·och·-ist,** *n.*—**mas·och·is·tic,** mas″o·kis′tik, maz″o·kis′tik, *a.*

ma·son, mā′son, *n.* [O.Fr. Fr. *macon,* < M.L. *macio(n-), machio(n-), mattio(n-);* origin uncertain.] A builder or worker in stone; one who builds with brick, artificial stone, or the like; one who molds cement or concrete in imitation of stonework; (*often cap.*) a Freemason.—*v.t.* To construct of, or strengthen with masonry.—**ma·son·ic,** ma·son′ik, *a.* Having to do with masons or masonry; (*often cap.*) related to Freemasons.

Ma·son-Dix·on line, mā′son-dik′son lin, *n.* The boundary between Pennsylvania and Maryland, partly surveyed by Charles Mason and Jeremiah Dixon between 1763 and 1767, and noted before the extinction of slavery as a line of demarcation between the free and the slave states. Also **Ma·son and Dix·on's line.**

Ma·son·ite, mā′so·nīt″, *n.* A fiberboard made from steam-treated wood fiber pressed into sheets. (Trademark.)

Ma·son jar, *n.* A glass jar with a tight-fitting metal top, used for home canning and preserving of foodstuffs.

ma·son·ry, mā′son·rē, *n.* pl. **ma·son·ries.** [Fr. *maçonnerie.*] The art or occupation of a mason; the work produced by a mason; (*cap.*) the mysteries, principles, and practices of Freemasons.

ma·son wasp, *n.* Any of numerous solitary wasps that build mud nests.

Mas·o·ret·ic, mas″o·ret′ik, *a.* Relating to the Masora, the traditional Jewish guide to the Old Testament.—**Ma·so·ra, Ma·so·-rah,** ma·sōr′a, *n.*

masque, mask, mask, mäsk, *n.* [Fr.] A dramatic performance popular with courtly audiences in 16th and 17th century England, orig. consisting of pantomime and dancing, but later characterized by elaborate staging and costuming, the use of dance and song, and the participation of amateur as well as professional actors; a work composed for such a performance; a masquerade.

mas·quer·ade, mas″ke·rād′, *n.* [Fr. *mascarade,* < It. *mascherata* (= Sp. *mascarada*), < *maschera,* mask.] A festive gathering of costumed individuals wearing masks and other disguises; a disguise worn at such a gathering. A disguise or false outward show; a going about under false pretenses.—*v.i.*—*masqueraded, masquerading.* To take part in a masquerade; disguise oneself; to go about under false pretenses; assume a false character.—**mas·quer·ad·er,** *n.*

mass, mas, *n.* [O.Fr. Fr. *masse,* < L. *massa,* mass, lump: cf. Gr. *maza,* barleycake, *mas-sein,* knead.] A body of coherent matter, usu. of indefinite shape and often of considerable size; as, a *mass* of dough; a gathering of incoherent particles, parts, or objects regarded as forming one body; as, a *mass* of flowers; an aggregation; a considerable

number or quantity; as, a *mass* of information; the main body, bulk, or greater part of anything; bulk, size, or massiveness. *Paint.* an expanse, as of color, light, or shade; *phys.* that property of a body to which its inertia is ascribed, being a measure of its acceleration upon application of a given force.—*a.*—*v.t.* To gather into or arrange in a mass or masses; assemble.—*v.i.* To form a mass or masses.—**the mass·es,** the great body of ordinary people.

Mass, mas, *n.* [O.E. *maesse,* Fr. *messe,* Dan. and G. *messe,* L.L. *missa,* mass, < *Ite, missa est,* "Go, you are dismissed."] The celebration or liturgy of the Eucharist in Roman Catholic, Greek, or Anglican churches; (*sometimes l.c.*) a musical setting for certain portions of this service. See *High Mass, Low Mass.*

mas·sa·cre, mas′a·kėr, *n.* [Mod.Fr. < O.Fr. *macecler,* butcher, < *mache-col-macher,* smash, and *col,* neck.] The indiscriminate killing of human beings; a brutal murder; slaughter; *colloq.* a resounding defeat, as in sports.—*v.t.*—*massacred, massacring.*—**mas·sa·crer,** mas′a·krėr, *n.*

mas·sage, ma·säzh′, ma·säj′, *Brit.* mas′äzh, *n.* [Fr., < *masser,* to massage: cf. Pg. *amassar,* knead, < *massa,* dough.] The act or art of treating the body by rubbing or kneading to stimulate circulation or increase suppleness.—*v.t.*—*massaged, massaging.* To treat by massage.—**mas·sag·er, mas·sag·ist,** *n.*

mas·sa·sau·ga, mas″a·sa′ga, *n.* A small rattlesnake found in areas between southern Texas and the Great Lakes region.

mass de·fect, *n. Phys.* the difference between the mass number of a nucleus and the greater total mass of its constituting particles, being equal to the energy release in the nucleus formation.

mas·sé, ma·sā′, *Brit.* mas′ē, *n.* [Fr., pp. of *masser,* strike by a massé, < *masse,* kind of cue, = E. *mace.*] *Billiards,* a stroke made by hitting the cue ball with the cue held almost or quite perpendicularly. Also **mas·sé shot.**

mass-en·er·gy e·qua·tion, *n.* The equation, $E = mc^2$, which expresses the relationship between energy and mass, in which energy is E, mass is m, and the velocity of light is c.

mas·se·ter, ma·sē′tėr, *n.* [Gr. *masētēr, massētēr,* lit. 'a chewer,' from *massaomai,* to chew.] The thick muscle which raises the lower jaw thus assisting chewing.—**mas·-se·ter·ic,** mas″i·ter′ik, *a.*

mas·seur, ma·sụr′, *Fr.* ma·sœʀ′, *n.* [Fr.] A man who practices massage.—**mas·-seuse,** ma·sös′, ma·söz′, *Fr.* mä·sœz′, *n.* pl. **mas·seus·es,** ma·sö′siz, ma·sö′ziz, *Fr.* mä·sœz′. A female masseur.

mas·si·cot, mas′i·kot″, *n.* [Fr.; origin obscure.] Lead monoxide, PbO, in the form of a yellow powder, used as a pigment and drier.

mas·sif, mas′if, *Fr.* mä·sēf′, *n.* [Fr., noun use of *massif,* E. *massive.*] *Geol.* A compact portion of a mountain range, containing one summit or a number of summits, and surrounded more or less completely by depressions which give it the appearance of an independent whole; a band or zone of the earth's crust, raised or depressed as a unit, and bounded by faults.

mas·sive, mas′iv, *a.* [Fr. *massif,* < *masse,* E. *mass.*] Consisting of or forming a large mass; bulky and heavy; consisting of or marked by great masses, as a style of architecture; large, impressive; as, a *massive* brow; solid, substantial, or imposing; broad in scope; of great magnitude, as a sensation; *med.* affecting a large continuous mass of bodily tissue, as a disease; *mineral.* not having an outward crystalline form, although sometimes crystalline in structure; *geol.* homogeneous.—**mas·sive·-ly,** *adv.*—**mas·sive·ness,** *n.*

mass meet·ing, *n.* A large or public meeting called for a hearing on or discussion of some specific cause.

mass num·ber, *n. Phys.* the integer nearest the atomic weight of any isotope of an element, equal to the sum of the protons and neutrons in the nucleus.

mass-pro·duce, mas'pro·dōs', mas'pro·dụs', *v.t.*—*mass-produced, mass-producing.* To produce, as goods, in great number, usu. by machine.—**mass-pro·duc·er,** *n.* —**mass pro·duc·tion,** *n.*

mass spec·tro·graph, *n. Phys.* a device which uses magnetic and electrical fields to record the mass spectrum of a stream of charged particles.

mass·y, mas'ē, *a.*—*massier, massiest.* Massive.—**mass·i·ness,** *n.*

mast, mast, mäst, *n.* [O.E. *maest* = D., G., Sw., and Dan. *mast*, a mast.] A long, round piece of timber or a hollow pillar of iron or steel standing upright in a vessel, and supporting the yards, sails, and rigging; any large vertical pole, as one which supports an antenna.—*v.t.* To fix a mast or masts in; to erect the masts of.

mast, mast, mäst, *n.* [O.E. *maest*, G. *mast*; akin to *meat*.] The fruit of the oak and beech or other forest trees, frequently used as feed for hogs.

mas·ta·ba, mas·ta·bah, mas'ta·ba, *n.* [Ar., 'bench.'] An ancient Egyptian tomb, rectangular in plan, with sloping sides and a flat roof; in Mohammedan countries, a bench or seat.

mas·tec·to·my, ma·stek'to·mē, *n. pl.* **mas·tec·to·mies.** The surgical removal of a breast. Also **mam·mec·to·my.**

mas·ter, mas'tẽr, mä'stẽr, *n.* [O.E. *maister, maistre,* O.Fr. *maistre,* < L. *magister,* master, < root *mag,* seen in L. *magnus,* great: same root as *may, might,* much.] One who rules, governs, or directs; one who has others, esp. workers or servants, under his immediate control; an employer; a crafts-man skillful or experienced enough to train others and to independently pursue his own trade; one who has possession of something and the power of controlling or using it at pleasure; the person entrusted with the command of a merchant ship; captain; an artist, sculptor, thinker, or architect whose accomplishments rank far above those of his contemporaries; a philosophical or religious leader with a following; one eminently skilled in any pursuit, accomplishment, art, or science; *chiefly Brit.* a male school teacher. One who is proficient or adept; as, a *master* of sarcasm; a title of respectful address used before a person's name, often that of a boy or young gentleman; a title of dignity; a degree in colleges and universities; as, *Master* of Arts; the title of the head of some societies or corporations; the title of a legal functionary who assists a judge in various ways.—*v.t.* To become the master of; to overpower; to subdue; to become adept at or expert in.—*a.* Belonging to a master; chief; principal; controlling; de-scriptive of a mechanism which controls other similar mechanisms.—**mas·ter·dom, mas·ter·hood,** *n.*—**mas·ter·li·ness,** *n.*—**mas·ter·ly,** *a., adv.* Of or exhibiting the style, skill, ability, or other characteristics of a master.

mas·ter-at-arms, mas'tẽr·at·ärmz', mä'-stẽr·at·ärmz', *n. pl.* **mas·ters-at-arms.** *Nav.* a petty officer whose duties include maintaining order on a ship and keeping custody of prisoners.

mas·ter chief pet·ty of·fic·er, *n. Nav.* an enlisted man of the highest noncom-missioned grade.

mas·ter·ful, mas'tẽr·ful, mä'stẽr·ful, *a.* Decisive or authoritative in manner; im-perious or arbitrary; displaying great skill or mastery.—**mas·ter·ful·ly,** *adv.*—**mas·-ter·ful·ness,** *n.*

mas·ter key, *n.* A key that will open a number of locks, proper keys of which cannot be interchanged.

mas·ter·mind, mas'tẽr·mīnd', mä'stẽr·-mīnd", *v.t.* To adeptly plan, devise, or execute as a project or undertaking.—*n.*

mas·ter of cer·e·mo·nies, *n.* A person who acts as chairman, moderator, or host at a formal, theatrical, or public event. Also *emcee.* Abbr. M.C.

mas·ter·piece, mas'tẽr·pēs", mä'stẽr·pēs", *n.* One's highest achievement; that work of a craftsman qualifying him for mastership in a guild or trade organization; anything extraordinary in kind or quality; anything done or made with superior skill.

mas·ter race, *n.* A people or nation who believe themselves superior to others and therefore fitted to conquer, enslave, or rule.

mas·ter ser·geant, *n. Milit.* A noncom-missioned officer of the next to highest enlisted grade in the Army and Marine Corps; a noncommissioned rank officer in the Air Force who is in one of the three highest enlisted grades.

mas·ter·ship, mas'tẽr·ship", mä'ster·ship", *n.* The power, duty, or office, of a master; mastery; masterly skill, experience, pro-ficiency, or knowledge.

mas·ter·sing·er, mas'tẽr·sing"ẽr, mä'stẽr·-sing"ẽr, *n.* Meistersinger.

mas·ter stroke, *n.* A masterly achievement or action.

mas·ter·work, mas'tẽr·wụrk", mä'stẽr·-wụrk", *n.* Principal performance; master-piece.

mas·ter·y, mas'te·rē, mä'ste·rē, *n. pl.* **mas·ter·ies.** The act of mastering; the state of having control over something; superiority in competition; victory; eminent skill or thorough knowledge.

mast·head, mast'hed", mäst'hed", *n. Naut.* the top of a ship's mast, esp. of the lower mast. That part of a periodical, appearing in each issue, and listing the name, editors, staff members, and owners of the periodi-cal.—*v.t. Naut.* To send to the masthead, as a punishment; to raise to the masthead, as a flag.—*a.*

mas·tic, mas'tik, *n.* [Fr. *mastic,* L. *mastiche, mastichum,* Gr. *mastichē,* from *mastax,* the jaws.] An aromatic resin exuding from a tree, *Pistacia lentiscus,* native to southern Europe, and used to make varnish and as a flavoring in liquors; the tree which yields this resin. A preparation used as an adhe-sive or seal; a type of cement used to fill holes in plaster or masonry.

mas·ti·cate, mas'ti·kāt", *v.t., v.i.*—*masti-cated, masticating.* [L.L. *masticatus,* pp. of *masticare,* chew: cf. *mastic,* Gr. *mastax,* jaw.] To grind with the teeth in preparation for swallowing; chew; to reduce to a pulp by crushing or kneading, as rubber.— **mas·ti·ca·ble,** mas'ti·ka·bl, *a.*—**mas·-ti·ca·tion,** mas"ti·kā'shan, *n.*—**mas·ti·-ca·tor,** *n.*—**mas·ti·ca·to·ry,** mas'ti·ka·-tōr"ē, *a.* Of, pertaining to, or used in mastication.—*n. pl.* **mas·ti·ca·to·ries.** *Pharm.* a medicinal substance chewed to promote the secretion of saliva.

mas·tiff, mas'tif, mä'stif, *n.* [< a hypo-thetical Fr. *mastif,* < G. *masten,* to fatten, O.H.G. *mastjan,* to feed, < *mast,* food, mast (acorns, etc.).] One of a variety of hunting dogs, an old English breed, large and very stoutly built, with pendulous lips and drooping ears.

mas·ti·goph·o·ran, mas"ti·gof'ẽr·an, *n.* Any protozoan of the class *Mastigophora,* having one or several flagella. Also **mas·-ti·go·phore.**—*a.*—**mas·ti·goph·o·rous,** *a.*

mas·ti·tis, ma·stī'tis, *n.* [Gr. *mastos,* the breast, and term. *-itis,* denoting inflamma-tion.] *Pathol.* inflammation of the breast; *veter. pathol.* inflammation of the udder, esp. in cows.—**ma·stit·ic,** ma·stit'ik, *a.*

mas·to·don, mas'to·don", *n.* [Gr. *mastos,* breast, mammilla, and *odous,* a tooth.] Any of several extinct species of mammals, genus *Mammut,* resembling the elephant but larger, and named from the mammillary projections on its molar teeth.—**mas·to·-don·ic,** mas"to·don'ik, *a.*

mas·toid, mas'toid, *a. Anat.* of or denoting the process or projection of the temporal bone behind the ear and parts connected with it.—*n.*

mas·toid·ec·to·my, mas"toi·dek'to·mē, *n. pl.* **mas·toid·ec·to·mies.** The surgical removal of mastoid cells or part of the mastoid process.

mas·toid·i·tis, mas"toi·dī'tis, *n. Pathol.* inflammation of any of the various parts of the mastoid process.

mas·tur·bate, mas'tẽr·bāt", *v.i.*—*mastur-bated, masturbating.* To engage in the act of masturbation.—*v.t.* To perform masturba-tion upon.

mas·tur·ba·tion, mas"tẽr·bā'shan, *n.* [L. *masturbatio(n-),* < *masturbari,* practice masturbation.] The handling or stimulation, usu. by oneself, of the genital organs; onanism.—**mas·tur·ba·tion·al,** *a.*—**mas·-tur·ba·tor,** *n.*

ma·su·ri·um, ma·sụr'ē·um, *n. Chem.* the hypothetical metallic element resembling manganese, now replaced on the periodic table by technetium. Sym. Ma.

mat, mat, *n.* [O.E. *matt,* < L. *matta,* mat (of rushes).] A piece of fabric made of plaited or woven rushes, straw, hemp, or other fiber, or a similar article made of some other material, often used to lie on, to cover a floor, or to wipe shoes on; a smaller piece of material, often ornamental, set upon a table, and often under a dish of food, a lamp, or a vase; a thick covering, as of padded canvas, laid on a floor in various sports or gymnastics; a sack made of mat-ting, as for coffee or sugar; a thickly growing or tangled mass, as of hair or weeds.—*v.t.*—*matted, matting.* To cover with or as with mats or matting; to form into a mat, as by interweaving; to entangle in a thick mass.—*v.i.* To become entangled.

mat, matt, matte, mat, *a.* [Fr. *mat* = G. *matt,* dull.] Without luster; dull; as, *mat* gold.—*n.* A dull surface or finish, as in metal; a tool for producing it.—*v.t.*—*matted, matting.* To finish with a dull surface.

mat, mat, *n.* [Origin uncertain.] A frame-like piece of pasteboard or other material placed around a picture and extending to the outer frame or acting as a frame itself; *print.* the impression from which a plate is cast for printing.—*v.t.*—*matted, matting.* To supply, as a picture, with a mat.

mat·a·dor, mat'a·dạr", *n.* [Sp., lit. 'a killer,' < *matar,* L. *mactare,* to kill, to sacrifice.] The bullfighter appointed to kill the bull in bullfights; in some card games, a high trump; *(cap.), milit.* a U.S. un-manned guided missile.

match, mach, *n.* [O.E. *gemæcca,* mate, fellow.] A person or thing that equals or closely resembles another in some respect; a person or thing that is an exact counter-part of another; a corresponding or suitably associated pair; one's equal in age, station, or ability; an engagement for a contest or game; the contest or game itself; a matri-monial compact or alliance; a suitable or potential partner in marriage.—**match·-a·ble,** *a.*—**match·less,** *a.*—**match·less·-ness,** *n.*

match, mach, *v.t.* To equal or be equal to; to be the match or counterpart of; to correspond to; to adapt or make to correspond; to pair or assort, as persons or things, with a view to equality or correspondence; to fit together, as two things; to place in opposition or conflict; to provide with an adversary or competition of equal power; to compare with respect to superiority; to unite in marriage or procure a matrimonial alliance for.—*v.i.* To be equal or suitable; to correspond in some respect; to ally oneself in marriage.—**match·er,** *n.*

match, mach, *n.* [O.Fr. *meiche* (Fr. *mèche*); origin uncertain.] A short, slender piece of wood or other material tipped with a chemical substance, which produces fire when rubbed on a rough or chemically prepared surface; a wick or cord, prepared to burn at a uniform rate, formerly used to fire cannon.

match·board, mach'bōrd", *n.* A wooden board having one edge notched and a protruding tongue on the opposite edge, which provides a tight joint when two such boards are joined and used for floors, siding, or other construction purposes.

match·book, mach'buk", *n.* A paper folder in which paper matches are fastened in rows.

matched or·der, *n.* A prohibited stock market practice in which orders both to buy and sell a specific stock are placed at the same time by one individual with different brokers.

match·lock, mach'lok", *n.* Orig. the lock of a musket using a match or wick for firing; a musket or handgun fired by a match.

match·mak·er, mach'māk̇ér, *n.* One who makes, or seeks to bring about, matrimonial matches; one who makes or arranges matches, as for boxing contests.—**match·-mak·ing,** *n., a.*

match play, *n. Golf,* a play in which the score is determined by counting the holes won by each team or individual, not the number of strokes: distinguished from *medal play.*

match point, *n.* The final point which determines the winner in a match of tennis, badminton, squash, and other games, mach' point'. *Duplicate bridge,* an additional point or half point awarded for exceeding or tying scores of opposing partnerships, mach' point".

match·wood, mach'wud", *n.* Wood suitable, or cut into pieces of the proper size, for matches; splinters.

mate, māt, *n.* [A form of old *make,* a mate, and also of *match* (an equal); O.D. *maet,* D. *maat,* companion, mate; same root as *mete,* to measure.] One of a pair; a companion; often used in combination; as, play*mate;* an equal; a match; an officer in a ship whose duty is to assist the master or other officer; a husband or wife; one of a pair of animals which associate for propagation.—*v.t.* —*mated, mating.* To match; to marry; to join or pair, as animals; to join appropriately.—*v.i.* To marry; pair for breeding; associate; match.—**mate·less,** *a.*

mate, māt, *n., v.t., interj. Chess,* checkmate.

ma·té, ma·te, mä'tā, mat'ā, *n.* [Sp. *mate,* prop. the vessel in which the beverage is made, < Peruvian *mati,* calabash.] *Bot.* a small holly tree, *Ilex paraguariensis,* native to southern Brazil, Paraguay, and Argentina. An aromatic, tealike beverage made from the leaves of this tree; also **Par·a·guay tea,** *yerba.*

mat·e·lote, mat'e·lōt", *Fr.* mät·e·lat', *n.* [Fr., < *matelot,* sailor.] A highly seasoned stew of fish, onions, and wine.

ma·ter, mā'tér, *n.* pl. **ma·ters, ma·tres,** mā'trēz. *Brit. colloq.* mother.

ma·ter·fa·mil·i·as, mā"tėr·fa·mil'ē·as, *n.* [L.] The mother of a family.

ma·te·ri·al, ma·tēr'ē·al, *n.* [L.L. *materialis,* < L. *materia,* matter.] The substance or substances of which a thing is made or composed; any constituent element of a thing; anything serving as crude or raw matter for working upon or developing; something, such as a body of facts or ideas, which is utilized as the foundation for a literary work, as a report or novel; a textile fabric; *pl.* articles of any kind requisite for making or doing something; as, writing *materials.*—*a.* Formed or consisting of matter; physical; corporeal; as, the *material* world; relating to, concerned with, or involving matter; as, *material* force; concerned or occupied unduly with corporeal things or interests; pertaining to the physical rather than the spiritual or intellectual aspect of things; as, a *material* civilization; of substantial import; of much consequence; important; pertinent or essential; *law,* of evidence, of such significance as to be likely to influence the determination of an issue; *philos.* of or pertaining to matter as distinguished from form.—**ma·te·ri·al·ly,** *adv.*

ma·te·ri·al·ism, ma·tēr'ē·a·liz"um, *n. Philos.* the philosophical theory which regards matter and its motions as constituting the universe, and all phenomena, including those of the mind, as due to material agencies. Any opinion or tendency based on purely material interests; devotion to material rather than spiritual objects and considerations.—**ma·te·ri·al·ist,** *n.*—**ma·te·ri·al·is·tic,** *a.*—**ma·te·ri·al·is·ti·cal·ly,** *adv.*

ma·te·ri·al·i·ty, ma·tēr"ē·al'i·tē, *n.* pl. **ma·te·ri·al·i·ties.** The quality of being material; something considered relevant or important to the correct disposition of an issue. Also **ma·te·ri·al·ness,** *n.*

ma·te·ri·al·ize, ma·tēr'ē·a·līz", *v.t.* —*materialized, materializing.* To give material form to; invest with material attributes; make physically perceptible; to render materialistic; to cause to become a reality. —*v.i.* To assume material or bodily form; to come into perceptible existence; become an actual fact.—**ma·te·ri·al·i·za·tion,** ma·tēr"ē·a·li·zā'shan, *n.*—**ma·te·ri·al·iz·er,** *n.*

ma·te·ri·a med·i·ca, ma·tēr'ē·a med'i·ka, *n.* [L.] That branch of medical science which treats of the drugs employed in medicine; collectively, all the curative substances employed in medicine.

ma·té·ri·el, ma·tēr"ē·el', *n.* [Fr., 'material.'] The aggregate of things used or needed in carrying on any business, undertaking, or operation, as military supplies and equipment: distinguished from *personnel.*

ma·ter·nal, ma·tụr'nal, *a.* [O.Fr. Fr. *maternel,* < L. *maternus,* of a mother, < *mater,* mother.] Of, pertaining to, befitting, having the qualities of, or being a mother; derived from a mother; related through a mother.—**ma·ter·nal·ism,** *n.*—**ma·ter·nal·is·tic,** ma·tụr"na·lis'tik, *a.*—**ma·ter·nal·ly,** *adv.*

ma·ter·ni·ty, ma·tụr'ni·tē, *n.* pl. **ma·ter·ni·ties.** The state or character of being a mother; motherhood; motherliness.—*a.* Fashioned for or pertaining to the period of a woman's pregnancy and the birth of her child; as, *maternity* clothes.

mat·ey, mā'tē, *a. Brit. colloq.* Chummy; friendly; sociable.—*n. Brit. colloq.* companion, friend, chum.

math, math, *n. Colloq.* mathematics.

math·e·mat·i·cal, math"i·mat'i·kal, *a.* [L. *mathematicus.*] Pertaining to mathematics; according to the principles of mathematics; *fig.* precise. Also **math·e·mat·ic.**—**math·e·mat·i·cal·ly,** *adv.*

math·e·mat·i·cal log·ic, *n.* Symbolic logic.

math·e·ma·ti·cian, math"e·ma·tish'an, *n.* One who is well versed in mathematics; a specialist in mathematics.

math·e·mat·ics, math"e·mat'iks, *n.* pl. *but sing. in constr.* [L. *mathematica,* Gr. *mathematikē* (*technē,* art, understood), < stem of *manthanō, mathēsomai,* to learn.] The science dealing with quantity, form, measurement, and arrangement and in particular with the methods for discovering by concepts and symbols, the properties and interrelationships of quantities and magnitudes. Abbr. *math.*

ma·tin, mat'in, mat'in, *a.* [Fr. *matin,* < L. *matutinus,* pertaining to the morning.] Pertaining to the morning; used in the morning.—*n. Pl., usu. sing. in constr., eccles.* morning worship, prayers, or songs; time of morning service; the first of seven canonical hours; in the Anglican Church, the morning public prayer; also *Brit.* **mat·tins.** *Poet.* a song of the morning, as of birds.—**mat·in·al,** *a.* Relating to the morning or to matins.

mat·i·née, mat·i·nee, mat'i·nā', *Brit.* mat'i·nā, *n.* [Fr., < *matin,* morning.] An entertainment, esp. a dramatic or musical performance, held in the daytime, usu. in the afternoon.

ma·tri·arch, mā'trē·ärk", *n.* [L. *mater,* mother, and E. *-arch* as in *patriarch.*] A woman holding a ruling position analogous to that of a patriarch, as in a family or tribe.—**ma·tri·ar·chal,** *a.*—**ma·tri·ar·chal·ism,** *n.*—**ma·tri·ar·chate,** mā'trē·är"kit, mā'trē·är"kāt, *n.* A matriarchal system or community.—**ma·tri·ar·chy,** mā'trē·är"kē, *n.* pl. **ma·tri·ar·chies.** The matriarchal system; a form of social organization in which the mother is head of the family, and in which kinship and descent are reckoned through the female line.

mat·ri·cide, ma'tri·sīd", mā'tri·sīd", *n.* [L. *matricidium,* the crime, *matricida,* the perpetrator—*mater, matris,* mother, and *caedo,* to slay.] The killing or murder of one's mother; one who murders or kills his mother.

ma·tric·u·lant, ma·trik'ū·lant, *n.* One who matriculates; a candidate for matriculation.

ma·tric·u·late, ma·trik'ū·lāt", *v.t.*—*matriculated, matriculating.* [L. *matricula,* a public register, dim. of *matrix,* a womb, a parent stem, a register, < *mater,* a mother.] To admit to membership, as a student in a college or university.—*v.i.* To be entered or enrolled.—ma·trik'ū·lit, *n.* One who is matriculated.—**ma·tric·u·la·tion,** *n.* The act of matriculating.—**ma·tric·u·la·tor,** *n.*

ma·tri·lin·e·al, ma"tri·lin'ē·al, mā"tri·lin'ē·al, *a.* Pertaining to or based on the maternal line of descent.—**ma·tri·lin·e·al·ly,** *adv.*

mat·ri·mo·ni·al, ma"tri·mō'nē·al, *a.* [L. *matrimonialis.*] Pertaining to matrimony or marriage.—**mat·ri·mo·ni·al·ly,** *adv.*

mat·ri·mo·ny, ma'tri·mō"nē, *n.* pl. **mat·ri·mo·nies.** [O.Fr. *matrimonie, matrimoine,* < L. *matrimonium,* < *mater,* mother.] The ceremony of marriage; the married state; a game of cards, played by any number of persons; the combination of a king and a queen in this and certain other games.

ma·tri·mo·ny vine, *n.* Boxthorn.

ma·trix, mā'triks, ma'triks, *n.* pl. **ma·tri·ces, ma·trix·es,** mā'tri·sēz, ma'tri·sēz. [L., breeding animal, L.L. womb, source, also public register, < L. *mater,* mother.] That which originates, develops, or encloses anything; the electroformed mold of a disk or phonograph record used to duplicate an orig. recording in mass production; *zool.* the intercellular substance of a tissue; *anat.* a formative cell, as the corium beneath a fingernail; *geol.* the rock or main substance in which a crystal, mineral, or fossil is embedded and the impression remaining; *min.* gangue; *print.* a die, stamp, mold, or form impression utilized in stereotype, linotype, and type founding; *math.* an array of elements in rows and columns, as the coefficients of a set of linear equations, treated as a unit using special algebraic laws in facilitating the study of relations between the elements.

ma·tron, mā′trŏn, *n.* [Fr. *matrone,* L. *matrona,* < *mater,* mother.] A mature married woman, esp. one who has children; a female nurse, guard, or attendant, as in a school or rest room; a female superintendent of an institution, as a women's prison.—**ma·tron·age,** mā′trō·nĭj, mā′-trō·nĭj, *n.* The state of being a matron.—**ma·tron·ize,** mā′trō·nīz″, *v.t.*—*matronized, matronizing.* To cause to be a matron or take on matronlike qualities; to chaperone.

ma·tron·ly, mā′trŏn·lē, *a.* Of, like, or pertaining to a matron. Also **ma·tron·al,** mā′trō·nal, ma′tro·nal.

ma·tron of hon·or, *n.* A married woman chosen by the bride to serve as her principal attendant at the wedding.

mat·ro·nym·ic, ma″trō·nĭm′ĭk, *n.* A name taken from one's mother or a maternal ancestor. Also *metronymic.*

matt, matte, mat, *a., n., v.t.* Mat.

matte, mat, *n.* [Fr., origin uncertain.] *Metal.* an unfinished metallic product of the smelting of certain sulfide ores, esp. those of copper.

mat·ter, mat′ĕr, *n.* [O.Fr. *matere* (Fr. *matière*), < L. *materia,* stuff, material, matter, subject.] The substance or substances of which physical objects are composed; constituent substance or stuff; material; a particular kind of substance; as, coloring *matter;* some substance excreted by a living body, esp. pus; physical or corporeal substance in general, whether solid, liquid, or gaseous, esp. as distinguished from incorporeal substance, as spirit or mind, or from qualities or actions; whatever occupies space; the material with which thought is concerned; the material or substance of a discourse or book; things or something of a specified kind or in a specified connection; as, a *matter* of record; ground, reason, or cause; as a *matter* of complaint; a thing, affair, or business; as, a *matter* of life and death; an amount or extent reckoned approximately; as, a *matter* of ten miles; something of consequence or significance; trouble or difficulty, usu. preceded by *the,* as: What is *the matter? Philos.* that out of which anything is made.

mat·ter, mat′ĕr, *v.i.* To be of significance or importance; to signify. *Pathol.* to form or exude pus.

mat·ter-of-course, mat′ĕr·ov·kōrs′, mat′-ĕr·ov·kạrs′, *a.* Happening or proceeding as if in the natural sequence of events; taking things in stride.

mat·ter-of-fact, mat′ĕr·ov·fakt′, *a.* Treating of facts or realities; not fanciful, imaginative, or idealistic; adhering to facts; prosaic.—**mat·ter-of-fact·ly,** *adv.*—**mat·ter-of-fact·ness,** *n.*

mat·ting, mat′ing, *n.* A coarse, woven fabric of rushes, grass, straw, or hemp used for covering floors and for wrapping articles; material for mats; mat weaving.

mat·ting, mat′ing, *n.* A dull finish or surface, as on metalwork; also *matte.* A mat or border used in picture framing.

mat·tock, mat′ok, *n.* [O.E. *mattuc.*] A kind of pick used for loosening the soil, with an arm or blade like that of an adz, and commonly with another arm which is either pointed or like a narrow ax blade.

mat·tress, ma′trĭs, *n.* [O.Fr. *materas* (Fr. *matelas*); < Ar.] A case, usu. cloth, filled with foam rubber, straw, cotton, or other resilient material, usu. quilted or fastened together at intervals, used as or on a bed; a mat or mass of interwoven brushwood or poles, used in building or protecting dikes and other structures; such a mat or mass placed on soft ground as a foundation.

mat·u·rate, mach′ụ·rāt″, mat′ū·rāt′, *v.i., v.t.*—*maturated, maturating.* [L. *maturo, maturatum,* to make ripe, < *maturus,* ripe.] To ripen or bring to ripeness; mature.

mat·u·ra·tion, mach″ụ·rā′shan, mat″ū-·rā′shan, *n.* [L. *maturatio.*] The process of maturing or ripening; *biol.* the final phase in the formation of mature gametes, or reproductive cells, during which they undergo certain changes in structure and physiology, esp. reduction in chromosome numbers.—**mat·u·ra·tion·al,** *a.*—**ma·-tur·a·tive,** ma·chụr′a·tiv, mach′ụ·rā″tiv, mat′ū·rā″tiv, *a.*

ma·ture, ma·tụr′, ma·tūr′, ma·chụr′, *a.* [L. *maturus,* ripe.] Ripe; brought by a natural process to a complete state of development; completely developed physically or mentally; of or characteristic of a state of full physical or emotional development; as, *mature* appearance, *mature* judgment; completely elaborated or perfected, as a plan; *med.* having reached the stage of final development; *com.* having reached the time fixed for payment; *geol.* having been fully developed by erosion, as topographical features.—*v.t.*—*matured, maturing.* [L. *maturo.*] To make mature; to ripen; to make complete or ready for any special use.—*v.i.* To become mature or ripe; reach completion; *com.* to reach the time fixed for payment.—**ma·ture·ly,** *adv.*—**ma·ture·ness,** *n.*

ma·tu·ri·ty, ma·tụr′i·tē, ma·tūr′i·tē, ma·chụr′i·tē, *n.* The state or quality of being mature; ripeness; a state of perfection, full development, or completeness; *com.* the time when a note or bill of exchange becomes due.

ma·tu·ti·nal, ma·töt′i·nal, ma·tūt′i·nal, *a.* [L. *matutinus,* pertaining to the morning.] Pertaining to or happening in the morning; early.—**ma·tu·ti·nal·ly,** *adv.*

mat·zo, mät′sa, mät′sō, *n. pl.* **mat·zoth,** **mat·zos,** mät′sōt, mät′soz, mät′sōs. [< Heb.] A type of unleavened bread, usu. shaped in large, flat wafers, eaten esp. at the Jewish Passover. Also **mat·za, mat·zah, mat·zoh.**

mat·zo ball, *n.* A dumpling made of unleavened meal and served in soup.

maud·lin, mạd′lin, *a.* [From *Maudlin,* Mary *Magdalen,* who is pictured with eyes swollen and red with weeping.] Tearful, emotional as a result of intoxication; over-emotional; excessively sentimental.—**maud·lin·ly,** *adv.*—**maud·lin·ness,** *n.*

maul, mall, mạl, *n.* [Same as *mall.*] A kind of large hammer or mallet used esp. in driving piles.—*v.t.* To beat with a maul, or as with a maul; to batter; to maltreat; to split, as a log, using a maul and wedges.—**maul·er,** *n.*

maul·stick, mạl′stik, *n.* Mahlstick.

maund, mạnd, *n.* A measure of weight in India and other Asiatic countries, varying from 20 to 160 pounds according to locality; the official Indian weight of 82.286 pounds.

maun·der, mạn′dĕr, *v.i.* [O.E. *mand, mond,* a basket < old *maunder,* a beggar who carries a basket.] To wander in talking, as a drunk or confused person; to act in a confused way.—**maun·der·er,** *n.*

maun·dy, mạn′dē, *n.* [O.Fr. *mande,* < L. *mandatum,* a command, mandate.] A ceremony of washing the feet of the poor on Maundy Thursday, performed as a religious rite by a sovereign or ecclesiastic; alms distributed at the ceremony or on this day.

—**Maun·dy Thurs·day,** the Thursday before Good Friday.

mau·so·le·um, mạ″so·lē′um, mạ″zo·lē′-um, *n. pl.* **mau·so·le·ums, mau·so·le·a.** [Gr. *mausōleion,* from *Mausolus,* king of Caria, to whom Artemisia, his widow, erected a stately monument.] A magnificent tomb or stately burial monument.—**mau·so·le·an,** *a.*

mauve, mōv, *n.* [Fr., mallow, L. *malva,* a mallow with petals having purple markings.] A light bluish-purple; a coal-tar dye obtained from aniline, reddish-violet in color.

mav·er·ick, mav′ĕr·ik, mav′rik, *n.* [Said to be named from Samuel *Maverick,* a Texas cattle raiser who neglected to brand his cattle.] In cattle raising regions, an animal found without an owner's brand, esp. a calf separated from its mother; *colloq.* one who departs from the customs or beliefs of his group.

ma·vour·neen, ma·vour·nin, ma·vụr′-nēn, ma·vōr′nēn, ma·vạr′nēn, *n.* [Ir. *mo muirnín.*] *Ir.* my darling.

maw, mạ, *n.* [O.E. *maga* = D. *maag* = G. *magen* = Icel. *magi,* maw.] The mouth, gullet, or stomach, esp. of a carnivorous animal; a bird's crop; *fig.* any gaping, dark opening that threatens to swallow one up.

mawk·ish, mạ′kish, *a.* [< old *mawk,* a maggot.] Lacking a pleasing flavor, or slightly nauseating in flavor; characterized by sickly sentimentality.—**mawk·ish·ly,** *adv.*—**mawk·ish·ness,** *n.*

max·i·foot·ball, mak′si·fụt″bạl, *n. Aerospace,* an elliptical orbit of a command ship, designed to maintain a path at a fixed maximum distance from an accompanying vehicle.

max·il·la, mak·sil′a, *n. pl.* **max·il·lae,** mak·sil′ē. [L., a dim. form akin to *mala,* cheekbone, jaw.] A jaw or jawbone, esp. a bone of the upper jaw; one of the paired appendages immediately behind the mandibles of insects and other arthropods, usu. serving as accessory jaws.—**max·il·lar·y,** *n., a.*

max·il·li·ped, mak·sil′i·ped″, *n.* In lobsters, crabs, and other crustaceans, one of the small appendages situated directly behind the maxillae, and used in eating. Also **max·il·li·pede,** mak·sil′i·pēd″.—**max·il·li·ped·a·ry,** mak″sil·i·ped′a·rē, *a.*

max·im, mak′sim, *n.* [Fr. *maxime,* < L. *maxima* (*sententia,* opinion, understood), the greatest or chief opinion; *maximus,* superl. of *magnus,* great.] An established principle or general truth; a principle or formula embodying a rule of conduct, as a proverb.

max·i·mal, mak′si·mal, *a.* Pertaining to or being a maximum; highest; largest; most; greatest possible.—**max·i·mal·ly,** *adv.*

Max·i·mal·ist, mak′si·ma·list, *n.* Formerly, in Russian politics, a member of an extremist or radical group or faction of socialists, as in the Social Revolutionary Party; (*l.c.*) a member of a group or faction elsewhere having similar views.

max·i·mize, mak′si·mīz″, *v.t.*—*maximized, maximizing.* To make as great as possible; to raise to the maximum.—**max·i·miz·er,** *n.*

max·i·mum, mak′si·mum, *n. pl.* **max·i·mums, max·i·ma.** [L., neut. of *maximus,* greatest, superl. of *magnus,* great.] The greatest quantity or amount possible, assignable, allowable, or the like; the highest amount, value, or degree attained or recorded: opposed to *minimum.*—*a.*

ma·xi·xe, ma·shēsh′, mäk·sēks′, ma·-shē′shä, *n.* A Brazilian ballroom dance of the early 20th century, similar to a two-step.

max·well, maks′wel, maks′wel, *n.* [From J. C. *Maxwell,* Sc. physicist.] *Elect.* A unit of the rate of flow of magnetic energy passing through one square centimeter of a regular cross section of a magnetic field measuring one gauss; the centimeter-gram-second unit of electromagnetic flux measured by the above procedure.

may, mā, *aux. v.*—pres. sing. *may, may* or archaic *mayest* or *mayst, may*; pres. pl. *may*; past *might*. [O.E. *mæg,* 1st and 3rd pers. sing. pres. ind. of *magan* = O.H.G. *magan* (G. *mögen*) = Icel. *mega* = Goth. *magan,* be able.] Used to express permission or opportunity, as: You *may* enter. Used to express possibility, as: We *may* be late. Used to express wish or prayer, as: *May* you live long. Used to express contingency, esp. in clauses expressing condition, concession, purpose, or result, as: He fought so that others *may* have peace.

May, mā, *n.* [Fr. *mai,* Pr. *mai,* May, < L. *Maius,* < the goddess *Maia,* a goddess of growth or increase.] The fifth month of the year, having 31 days.

ma·ya, mā′yä, mä′ya, *n.* [Skt. *māyā.*] *Hindu philos.* illusion or deceptive appearance.

Ma·ya, mä′ya, *n. pl.* **Ma·yas, Ma·ya.** *Coll.* the Amerindian descendants of an advanced pre-Columbian civilization still comprising the majority of the populace of the Yucatan Peninsula; a member of the Mayan tribe; the Mayan language, both ancient and modern.

Ma·yan, mä′yan, *a.* Of or referring to Mayas, their language, or their culture.—*n.* A Mayan Indian; an extensive stock of Central American and Mexican languages.

May ap·ple, *n. Bot.* an American perennial herb in the barberry family, *Podophyllum peltatum,* having a single, nodding, white flower between two large umbrella-shaped leaves and lemonlike edible fruit. Also *mandrake.*

may·be, mā′bē, *adv.* [< 'it *may* be.'] Perhaps; possibly.

May Day, *n.* The first day of May, traditionally celebrated with gay outdoor festivals, and recently in some countries by parades and political demonstrations.— **May·ing,** mā′ing, *n.* (*sometimes l.c.*) the celebrating of May Day.

May·day, mā′dā″, *n.* The international signal word of ships and airplanes in distress, usu. sent by radiotelephone.

may·flow·er, mā′flou″ėr, *n.* Any of several flowers that bloom in May, esp. the trailing arbutus, *Epigaea repens,* the Canada mayflower, *Maianthemum canadense,* and the hepatica, *Hepatica americana; Brit.* any of the hawthorns of the genus *Crataegus;* (*cap.*) the ship which brought the Pilgrims from England to America in 1620.

may·fly, May fly, mā′flī″, *n. pl.* **may·flies.** Any of various insects of the order *Ephemeroptera* with transparent wings, of which the forewings are larger, its life consisting of a long nymphal or larval stage and a short adult stage; an artificial fly resembling a mayfly which is used in sport fishing.

may·hem, mai·hem, mā′hem, mā′em, *n. Law,* the act of intentionally maiming a person, or inflicting a disabling, mutilating, or crippling wound, impairing his ability to defend himself. A situation involving violent or destructive behavior; the manifestations of such a situation.

may·on·naise, mā″o·nāz′, mā′o·nāz″, *n.* [Fr., origin uncertain.] A salad dressing composed of yolks of eggs beaten with vegetable or olive oil until thick, and seasoned with vinegar or lemon juice, salt, pepper, sugar, or other flavoring.

may·or, mā′ėr, mâr, *n.* [Fr. *maire,* Sp. *mayor,* < L. *major,* greater, compar. of *magnus,* great.] The chief executive of a city, town, or borough; the chief officer of a municipal corporation.—**may·or·al,** *a.*

may·or·al·ty, mā′ėr·al·tē, mâr′al·tē, *n. pl.* **may·or·al·ties.** The office of a mayor; the time of his service.

may·or·ess, mā′ėr·is, mâr′is, *n.* The wife of a mayor; a woman mayor. *Brit.* a woman elected by the mayor to perform the official duties of mayor's wife.

May·pole, mā′pōl″, *n.* (*Often l.c.*) a pole wreathed with flowers and ribbons, around which dances and sports events are held on May Day.

may·pop, mā′pop″, *n.* [Origin uncertain.] The passionflower, *Passiflora incarnata,* a strong, perennial vine having large flowers with white petals and large pink to purple-colored centers, and producing edible yellow fruits; the fruit itself, a large many-seeded berry.

May queen, *n.* A young woman crowned with spring flowers and honored as queen at the games or pageants held on May Day.

May·time, mā′tīm″, *n.* The month of May. Also **May·tide,** mā′tīd″.

maze, māz, *n.* [Akin to provinc. E. *mazle,* to wander as if stupefied; Icel. *masa,* to chatter or prattle; Dan. *mase,* to have trouble; cf. also W. *masu,* to swoon. *Amaze* is from this.] A confusing network of paths or passages; a labyrinth; a winding and turning; confusion of thought; perplexity.—*v.t.*—*mazed, mazing.*

ma·zel tov, ma·zal tov, mä′zel tȧv″, mä′zel tȧf″, mä′zel tōv″, *interj.* [< Heb., 'good luck.'] A Yiddish phrase expressing congratulations.

ma·zer, mā′zėr, *n.* [Orig. a cup made of maple or spotted wood, < O.Fr. *mazre,* spotted wood, or O.E. *maser,* a maple (from being spotted); O.H.G. *masar,* G. *maser,* a knur, a spot in wood, G. *mase,* a spot; akin *measles.*] A drinking bowl or large goblet, generally of valuable material, formerly made of hardwood.

ma·zur·ka, ma·zur′ka, *n.* A lively Polish round dance in three-quarter time; the music written for this dance.

ma·zy, mā′zē, *a.*—*mazier, maziest.* Having the character of a maze; intricate; confusing. —**ma·zi·ly,** *adv.*—**ma·zi·ness,** *n.*

maz·zard, maz′ėrd, *n.* A wild cherry, *Prunus avium,* used as a rootstock to cultivate sweet cherries.

Mc·Car·thy·ism, ma·kär′thē·iz″um, *n.* [From Joseph *McCarthy,* 1909–1957, U.S. Senator.] The practice of publicly accusing a person or persons of procommunist activity, corruption, or disloyalty to the government, such charges being made usu. without substantiating evidence, or on hearsay; unethical investigative techniques.

Mc·Coy, ma·koi′, *n.* [From Kid *McCoy,* an American boxer.] The genuine article or person, preceded by *the* or *the real.*

me, mē, *pron.* [O.E. *mé, mec* (accusative), *mé* (dat.), G. *mich* (acc.), *mir* (dat.), Icel. *mik, mér,* Goth. *mik, mis,* L. *me, mihi,* Gr. *eme, emoi,* Skt. *mâm, mahyam,* me, to me.] The objective case of *I:* used as the direct object, or accusative, and as the indirect object, or dative, of a verb, and as the object of a preposition.

mead, mēd, *n.* [O.E. *medu* = D. *mede,* Icel. *mjȯthr,* Dan. *miȯd,* Sw. *mjȯd,* W. *medd,* Ir. *meadh,* mead; Gr. *methy,* wine; Lith. *medus,* Rus. *med,* Skt. *madhu,* honey.] A fermented liquor made from honey, water, malt, and yeast, and flavored with spices; any of several nonalcoholic drinks.

mead·ow, med′ō, *n.* [O.E. *maedu,* a meadow, shorter form *maed,* a mead, allied to *math* (after-*math*) and *mow.*] A level tract of land under grass, usu. mowed for hay or used for grazing; a piece of grassland in general.

mead·ow beau·ty, *n. Bot.* any of several herbaceous plants of the genus *Rhexia,* native to the sands and pine barrens of

eastern N. America, having flowers with four lopsided, drooping, pinkish-red petals and large curved anthers.

mead·ow fes·cue, *n. Bot.* an important meadow and pasture grass, *Festuca elatior,* native to Europe but now widely cultivated in the U.S. Also **tall fes·cue.**

mead·ow grass, *n.* Any of several grasses growing in a meadow and used either as pasture or for hay, esp. *Poa pratensis,* the Kentucky bluegrass.

mead·ow·lark, med′ō·lärk″, *n.* A N. American brownish songbird, *Sturnella magna,* in the blackbird family, inhabiting fields and meadows and recognized by its bright yellow breast crossed by a black V, and white outer tail feathers; any of several other songbirds, genus *Sturnella.*

mead·ow mouse, *n.* Any of various small, short-tailed rodents of the genus *Microtus,* that inhabit fields and meadows; a field mouse.

mead·ow mush·room, *n.* A common edible gill mushroom, *Agaricus campestris,* of fields and lawns, cultivated commercially in the U.S.

mead·ow rue, *n.* Any of several herbaceous plants of the buttercup family, genus *Thalictrum,* with slender terminal clusters of small drooping flowers and trilobate leaves.

mead·ow saf·fron, *n.* A liliaceous herb, *Colchicum autumnale,* whose rootlike corms and seeds contain the alkaloid, colchicine, which is used in the treatment of rheumatism and gout, and in plant breeding experiments to induce polyploidy. Also *autumn crocus.*

mead·ow·sweet, med′ō·swēt″, *n. Bot.* a low, semiwoody shrub, *Spiraea latifolia,* of the rose family, native to eastern N. America, and characterized by a terminal, steeple-shaped cluster of white to pink flowers.

mea·ger, *Brit.* **mea·gre,** mē′gėr, *a.* [Fr. *maigre,* < L. *macer,* lean.] Scanty; small; lacking in quality or quantity; wanting richness, fertility, strength; having little flesh; thin; lean.—**mea·ger·ly,** *Brit.* **mea·gre·ly,** *adv.*—**mea·ger·ness,** *Brit.* **mea·gre·ness,** *n.*

meal, mēl, *n.* [O.E. *mael,* time, portion, repast; D. and Dan. *maal,* G. *mahl, mal,* Icel. *mál,* part, repast, time; < root seen in *measure, mete, moon.* It is the termination seen in piece*meal,* etc.] A portion of food prepared, served, or taken at one of the regular times for eating; occasion of taking food; a repast.—**meal·time,** mēl′tīm″, *n.* The usual time of eating meals.

meal, mēl, *n.* [O.E. *melu* = D. *meel,* = G. *mehl,* = Icel. *mjȯl,* meal; < a root meaning 'grind,' whence also L. *molere.*] The edible part of any grain, and of certain leguminous plants, coarsely ground and unsifted, as corn meal, oatmeal, peanut meal, soybean meal, and the like; any ground or powdery substance resembling this. Compare *flour.*

meal·ie, mē′lē, *n.* [S. Afr. D. *milje,* < Pg. *milho,* millet, maize, < L. *milium,* millet.] *Afr.* An ear of maize or Indian corn; usu. *pl.* Indian corn.

meal·worm, mēl′wurm″, *n.* The beetle larva, *Tenebrio molitor,* which infests and contaminates meal, flour, or grain, often raised for fishing bait and as food for some animals and birds.

meal·y, mē′lē, *a.*—*mealier, mealiest.* Having the qualities of meal, or resembling meal; containing meal; flecked; powdery, as meal; overspread with something that resembles meal; mealy-mouthed; pale or sallow.—**meal·i·ness,** *n.*

meal·y·bug, mē′lē·bug″, *n.* Any of various insects of the family *Pseudococcidae,* having oval bodies covered with a powderlike secretion, and causing plant destruction, esp. in greenhouses.

meal·y-mouthed, mē′lē·mouᴛʜd′, mē′-lē·mouᴛʜt′, *a.* Unwilling or hesitating to tell the truth in plain language; inclined to speak euphemistically; not sincere.

mean, mēn, *v.t.*—*meant*, ment, *meaning.* [O.E. *maenan,* to mean, to intend; D. *meenan,* Dan. *mene,* G. *meinen,* to think, to mean.] To have in the mind; to view or contemplate; to intend; as, to *mean* to fix something; to purpose or design; to signify or intend to signify; as, a word that *means* many things; to import; to denote.— *v.i.* To be minded or disposed; to intend; as, to *mean* well; to be of a stated significance, as: His wife *means* everything to him.

mean, mēn, *a.* [O.E. *maene,* mean, false, bad, < *mán,* evil, wickedness; Icel. *meinn,* mean; cf. D. and Dan. *gemeen,* Goth. *gamains,* G. *gemein,* common.] Of little value; inferior; of small consequence; low in rank or birth; humble; ignoble or base; miserly; contemptible; shabby. *Colloq.* selfish; vexatious, troublesome; physically indisposed; ashamed; ill-tempered, vicious. *Slang,* excellent, skillful; as, to play a *mean* guitar.—**mean·ly,** *adv.* In a mean manner; in a low conditon; poorly; sordidly.— **mean·ness,** *n.* The state or quality of being mean; want of dignity or rank; want of spirit or honor; mean or base conduct or action.

mean, mēn, *a.* [O.Fr. *meien, moien,* Fr. *moyen,* Pr. *meian,* < L. *medianus,* middle, < *medius,* middle.] Occupying a middle position; middle; midway between extremes; intermediate; *math.* having an intermediate value between two extremes; as, *mean* distance, *mean* motion.—*n.* What is midway or intermediate between two extremes; the middle rate or degree; moderation. *Math.* a quantity having an intermediate value between several others; the simple average formed by adding the quantities together and dividing by their number being called the *arithmetical mean*; see *geometric mean. Pl. but sing. in constr.* the medium or what is used to accomplish or reach an end; measure or measures adopted; agency; instrumentality; as, by this *means,* a *means* to an end. *Pl.* income; revenue; resources; estate.—**by all means,** certainly; on every consideration.—**by no means,** not at all; certainly not.

me·an·der, mē·an′dėr, *n.* [L. *Maeander,* Gr. *Maiandros,* a river in Asia Minor proverbial for its windings.] A roundabout journey. *Usu. pl.* a winding course; a labyrinth.—*v.i.* To wind or turn; to have an intricate or winding course; to roam aimlessly; to ramble, as a conversation.— **me·an·der,** *n.*—**me·an·der·ing·ly,** *adv.* —**me·an·drous,** mē·an′drus, *a.*

mean de·vi·a·tion, *n. Statistics,* the arithmetic average of the absolute values of the individual deviations in a distribution from a central value, usu. the average or mean. Also *average deviation.*

mean dis·tance, *n. Astron.* the arithmetic average of the distances from the farthest and nearest points of a satellite or planet to the object about which it revolves.

mean·ing, *n.* mē′ning, *n.* The intention of a verbal expression, a gesture, or an act; aim or purpose; what is to be understood; signification, as of words; significance or import; as, the *meaning* of a dream.—*a.* Having intention, usu. used in compounds; as, a well-*meaning* gesture; significant or expressive; as, a *meaning* look.—**mean·ing·-ly,** *adv.*—**mean·ing·ness,** *n.*

mean·ing·ful, mē′ning·ful, *a.* Of significance; of value; filled with meaning.— **mean·ing·ful·ly,** *adv.*—**mean·ing·ful·-ness,** *n.*

mean·ing·less, mē′ning·lis, *a.* Without value or purpose; having no meaning.—

mean·ing·less·ly, *adv.*—**mean·ing·less·-ness,** *n.*

mean so·lar day, *n.* A day of 24 hours, measured from midnight to midnight and defined as the interval between two successive transits of a mean sun over the same meridian. Also **civ·il day.**

mean so·lar time, *n.* Time that is based upon the rotation of the earth relative to the mean sun. Also **civ·il time, mean time.**

mean square, *n. Statistics,* the mean of the squares of a group of numbers.

mean square de·vi·a·tion, *n. Statistics.* Variance; standard deviation.

means test, *n.* An inquiry to determine a person's eligibility for aid, esp. from public funds.

mean sun, *n. Astron.* an imaginary sun whose transit along the celestial equator is uniform: used as an aid in computing time.

mean·time, mēn′tīm″, *n.* The interval between one specified period and another.— *adv.* During the interval; at the same moment or time.

mean·while, mēn′hwīl″, mēn′wīl″, *adv., n.* Meantime.

mea·sled, mē′zeld, *a.* Infected with larval tapeworms or measles, as swine or other livestock.

mea·sles, mē′zelz, *n. pl., sing. or pl. in constr.* [Lit. 'the spots or spotted sickness'; D. *mazelen,* G. *masern,* pl. of *maser* (also *mase, masel*), O.G. *masa, masar,* a spot.] *Med.* an infectious disease occurring principally in children and characterized by a widespread red rash. See *German measles. Veter. pathol.* a disease affecting swine and other animals caused by the larvae of tapeworms; *pl. in constr.* the larvae themselves.

mea·sly, mē′zlē, *a.*—*measlier, measliest.* Infected with measles; having larval tapeworms, as meat. *Slang,* very slight or scanty; as, a *measly* portion; very unsatisfactory; as, a *measly* production.

meas·ur·a·ble, mezh′ėr·a·bl, *a.* Referring to that which may be measured; limited.— **meas·ur·a·bil·i·ty, meas·ur·a·ble·ness,** mezh″ėr·a·bil′i·tē, *n.*—**meas·ur·a·bly,** *adv.*

meas·ure, mezh′ėr, *n.* [Fr. *mesure,* < L. *mensura,* < *metior, mensus,* to measure.] The extent of a thing in length, breadth, and thickness, in circumference, capacity, or in any other respect; a standard of measurement, as a foot, pound, quart, or the like; a fixed unit of measurement; the instrument by which extent or capacity is ascertained; any criterion or measuring rod for comparing or judging; the act of measurement; a certain definite quantity; as, a *measure* of wine; that which is allotted or dealt out to one; moderation or just degree; as, beyond *measure*; an indefinite quantity or degree; as, in some *measure* erroneous; a decree or act of a legislature; as, a house *measure*; often *pl.* something done with a view to the accomplishment of a purpose; as, *measures* taken to avoid punishment. *Mus.* that division by which notes are grouped according to the regular recurrence of primary accents; that section of music marked off by two bar lines; a bar. *Pros.* the arrangement of the syllables in each line with respect to quantity and accent; a metrical foot. *Print.* the width of a printed page or column. *Pl.,* *geol.* strata or beds; as, coal *measures.*— **for good meas·ure,** as an addition; as something extra.—**have** or **take one's meas·ure,** size up or estimate another's character, ability, or actions.

meas·ure, mezh′ėr, *v.t.*—*measured, measuring.* To ascertain the extent, dimensions, or capacity of, esp. against some standard; to judge the greatness or import of; to value; to proportion; to allot or distribute by

measure, often with *out* or *off*; to serve as a measure; as, fidelity *measuring* love; to pass over or traverse; to compare; as, to *measure* my love with his.—*v.i.* To take a measurement or measurements; to result in or have a given measurement.—**meas·ure one's length,** to fall or be thrown down.— **meas·ure swords,** to fight with swords; to compete or contend with.—**meas·ure up,** to be qualified; to be equal to a standard.— **meas·ure·less,** *a.*—**meas·ur·er,** *n.*

meas·ured, mezh′ėrd, *a.* Apportioned, often according to size or extent; judged by a standard; deliberate or carefully chosen; slow and uniform; rhythmical; restricted or moderate.

meas·ure·ment, mezh′ėr·ment, *n.* The act of measuring; the amount or size ascertained by measuring; a system of measuring.

meas·ur·ing·worm, mezh′ėr·ing·wurm″, *n.* A small caterpillar, the larva of a moth of the family *Geometridae,* which moves by drawing up the rear end of its body to form a loop and then advancing the front end. Also *inchworm, looper, spanworm.*

meat, mēt, *n.* [O.E. *mete* = D. met, Icel. *matr.* D. *mad,* Sw. *mat,* Goth. *mats,* food; further connections doubtful.] Flesh of animals, usu. mammals, used as food; the edible portion of something; as coconut *meat;* food in general or anything eaten as nourishment; *fig.* the gist, essence, or vital points, as of a discourse or written work; *slang,* something enjoyed, as: Baseball is his *meat.*—**meat·less,** *a.*

meat-and-po·ta·toes, *n. pl., sing. or pl. in constr. Colloq.* The basic part; the essential content or foundation of something; that which accounts for the major source of trade or profit in a business.—*a.* Having a fundamental or pragmatic quality, as contrasted with that which is amusing or artistic.

me·a·tus, mē·ā′tus, *n.* pl. **me·a·tus·es, me·a·tus.** [L. < *meo,* to go.] *Anat.* a foramen, passage, or duct of the body, as the opening of the nose or ear.

meat·y, mē′tē, *a.*—*meatier, meatiest.* Of or like meat; abounding in meat, as a sauce or casserole; *fig.* full of substance, or pithy.— **meat·i·ness,** *n.*

mec·ca, mek′a, *n.* [From *Mecca,* the Arabian city, birthplace of Mohammed, to which the Mohammedans turn in prayer and resort in pilgrimage.] A place attracting many pilgrims or visitors; the goal of one's greatest desires or aspirations.

me·chan·ic, me·kan′ik, *n.* [L. *mechanicus* < Gr. *mechanikos,* < *mechane,* E. *machine.*] A worker skilled in the construction, operation, and repair of machinery, motors, or tools; a machinist.—*a.* Mechanical.

me·chan·i·cal, me·kan′i·kal, *a.* Pertaining to or concerned with the use of tools, or the construction of machines or mechanisms; involving machinery; exhibiting skill in the use of tools and the like; acting or operated by mechanical means; produced by such means; performed as if by machinery, without spontaneity, spirit, or individuality; of or pertaining to the material forces of nature acting on bodies or masses; of or relating to the subject matter of mechanics; in accordance with the laws of mechanics; pertaining to, or controlled or effected by physical forces that are not chemical. Explaining certain phenomena as due to mechanical action or the physical forces of the universe.—**me·chan·i·cal·ly,** *adv.*—**me·chan·i·cal·ness,** *n.*

me·chan·i·cal ad·van·tage, *n. Mech.* the ratio of the force producing work in a mechanism, or output force, to the force applied to a mechanism, or input force.

me·chan·i·cal draw·ing, *n.* The art or act of drawing, as machinery or structures,

UNIT		Avoirdupois	Troy	Apothecaries'
short ton	WEIGHT	20 short hundredweight, 2000 lbs.		
long ton		20 long hundredweight, 2240 lbs.		
short hundredweight		100 lbs., 0.05 short tons		
long hundredweight		112 lbs., 0.05 long tons		
pound (lb.)		16 oz., 7000 gr.	12 oz., 240 pennyweight, 5760 gr.	12 oz., 5760 gr.
ounce (oz.)		16 drams, 437.5 gr.	20 pennyweight, 480 gr.	8 drams, 480 gr.
pennyweight			24 gr., 0.05 oz.	
dram		27.343 gr., 0.0625 oz.		
scruple				3 scruples, 60 gr.
grain (gr.)		0.036 drams, 0.002285 oz.	0.042 pennyweight, 0.002083 oz.	20 gr., 0.333 drams
				0.05 scruples, 0.002083 oz.

UNIT		U.S. liquid measure	U.S. dry measure	British liquid and dry measure
bushel	CAPACITY		4 pecks (2150.42 in.³)	4 pecks (2219.36 in.³)
peck			8 quarts (537.605 in.³)	2 gallons (554.84 in.³)
gallon		4 quarts (231 in.³)		4 quarts (277.420 in.³)
quart		2 pints (57.75 in.³)	2 pints (67.200 in.³)	2 pints (69.355 in.³)
pint		4 gills (28.875 in.³)	½ quart (33.600 in.³)	4 gills (34.678 in.³)
gill		4 fluidounces (7.218 in.³)		5 fluidounces (8.669 in.³)
fluidounce		8 fluidrams (1.804 in.³)		8 fluidrams (1.7339 in.³)
fluidram		60 minims (0.225 in.³)		60 minims (0.216734 in.³)
minim		1/60 fluidram (0.003759 in.³)		1/60 fluidram (0.003612 in.³)

UNIT		Volume	Area	Length
cubic yard	DIMENSION	27 ft.³, 46,656 in.³		
cubic foot		1728 in.³, 0.0370 yd.³		
cubic inch		0.00058 ft.³, 0.000021 yd.³		
square mile			640 acres, 102,400 rods²	
acre			4840 yd.², 43,560 ft.²	
square rod			30.25 yd.², 0.006 acres	
square yard			1296 in.², 9 ft.²	
square foot			144 in.², 0.111 yd.²	
square inch			0.007 ft.², 0.00077 yd.²	
mile				320 rods, 1760 yd., 5280 ft.
rod				5.50 yd., 16.5 ft.
yard				3 ft., 36 in.
foot				12 in., 0.333 yd.
inch				0.083 ft., 0.027 yd.

UNIT		METRIC	UNIT		METRIC
short ton	METRIC	0.907 metric tons	gill	METRIC	0.118 l. (U.S.)
long ton		1.016 metric tons			0.142 l. (Brit.)
short hundredweight		45.359 kg.	fluidounce		29.573 ml. (U.S.)
long hundredweight		50.802 kg.			28.416 ml. (Brit.)
pound		0.453 kg. (avdp.)	fluidram		3.696 ml. (U.S.)
		0.373 kg. (troy and apoth.)			3.552 ml. (Brit.)
ounce		28.349 g. (avdp.)	minim		0.0616 ml. (U.S.)
		31.103 g. (troy and apoth.)			0.0592 ml. (Brit.)
pennyweight		1.555 g. (troy)	cubic yard		0.765 m.³
dram		1.771 g. (avdp.)	cubic foot		0.028 m.³
		3.887 g. (apoth.)	cubic inch		16.387 cm.³
scruple		1.295 g. (apoth.)	square mile		2.590 km.²
grain		0.0648 g. (avdp., troy, and apoth.)	acre		0.405 hectares, 4047 m.²
bushel		35.238 l. (U.S.)	square rod		25.293 m.²
		36.368 l. (Brit.)	square yard		0.836 m.²
peck		8.809 l. (U.S.)	square foot		0.093 m.²
		9.092 l. (Brit.)	square inch		6.451 cm.²
gallon		3.785 l. (U.S.)	mile		1.609 km.
		4.546 l. (Brit.)	rod		5.029 m.
quart		0.946 l. (U.S.)	yard		0.914 m.
		1.136 l. (Brit.)	foot		30.480 cm.
pint		0.473 l. (U.S.)	inch		2.540 cm.
		0.568 l. (Brit.)			

by using special instruments, as scales, compasses, and rulers; a drawing made in this manner.

mech·a·ni·cian, mek″a·nish′an, *n.* One skilled in building, repairing, or operating tools or machines; a mechanic.

me·chan·ics, me·kan′iks, *n. pl.* The functional, mechanical, or routine details of something. *Sing. in constr.* that area of physics concerned with motion and the effect of forces on material bodies, and including kinematics, kinetics, and statics; the application, both practical and theoretical, of this study to the designing, repairing, assembling, and operating of machines.

mech·a·nism, mek′a·niz″um, *n.* [Gr. *mechane*.] The structure or arrangement of parts of a machine or similar device; such parts collectively; a piece of machinery; anything like a machine in its structure or operation; the machinery, or the agencies, means, or procedures, by which a particular effect is produced or a purpose is accomplished; machinery or mechanical appliances in general; mechanical execution or technique, as in painting or music; *philos.* the theory that everything in the universe is produced by mechanical or material forces; *biol.* the machinelike chemical or physical processes which are responsible for many natural phenomena; *psychol.* a conscious or unconscious mental process which motivates emotional and behavioral responses.

mech·a·nist, mek′a·nist, *n. Philos.* one who believes in mechanism. A machinist; a mechanician.

mech·a·nis·tic, mek″a·nis′tik, *a.* Pertaining to mechanists or mechanism, or to mechanics, or to mechanical theories in philosophy; determined mechanically; as, a *mechanistic* society.—**mech·a·nis·ti·cal·ly**, *adv.*

mech·a·nize, mek′a·niz″, *v.t.*—*mechanized, mechanizing.* To render mechanical; to operate or perform by or as if by machinery; introduce machinery into, as an industry or business; *milit.* to furnish with armed tanks and vehicles.—**mech·a·ni·za·tion**, *n.*—**mech·a·niz·er**, *n.*

Mech·lin lace, mek′lin lās′, *n.* [From *Mechlin*,, Belgium, where orig. made.] A type of bobbin lace with raised designs. Also **Mech·lin**, *malines.*

me·cop·ter·an, me·kop′tèr·an, *n. Entom.* any carnivorous insect of the order *Mecoptera*, which includes scorpion flies.—**me·cop·ter·ous**, *a.*

med·al, med′al, *n.* [Fr. *médaille*, It. *medaglia*, < L. *metallum*, Gr. *metallon*, metal.] A decorative piece of metal, often coin-shaped, issued as an award to honor a person or to mark an event; a similar object bearing a design of religious significance.—*v.t.*—*medaled, medaling, Brit. medalled, medalling.* To award or present a medal to.—**me·dal·lic**, me·dal′ik, *a.*

med·al·ist, *Brit.* **med·al·list**, med′a·list, *n.* A manufacturer, engraver, or collector of medals; one who receives an award consisting of a medal; *golf*, the player in a tournament who qualifies with the lowest score.

me·dal·lion, me·dal′yan, *n.* [Fr. *medaillon*.] A large medal; a circular or oval design used as a motif on fabrics, wallpaper, and the like.

Med·al of Hon·or, *n.* The highest military decoration awarded by the U.S., presented usu. by the President in the name of Congress to a member of the U.S. armed forces who, while engaged in conflict with an enemy of the U.S., distinguishes himself at the risk of life by gallantry and intrepidity above and beyond the call of duty. Also *Congressional Medal of Honor.*

med·al play, *n. Golf*, a competition in which the score is tabulated by counting the total number of strokes taken to complete the round: distinguished from *match play.*

med·dle, med′l, *v.i.*—*meddled, meddling.* [O.E. *medlen*, to mix, < O.Fr. *medler, mesler* (Fr. *méler*), to mix, *se mesler de*, to mix oneself up with; < L.L. *misculare*, < L. *misceo*, to mix.] To interfere or take part in a matter in an officious, impertinent, or offensive manner.—**med·dler**, *n.*

med·dle·some, med′l·som, *a.* Given to meddling; officiously intrusive.—**med·dle·some·ness**, *n.*—**med·dle·some·ly**, *adv.*

me·di·a, mē′dē·a, *n.* pl. **me·di·ae**, mē′dē·ē″. [A plural of *medium*.] *Anat.* the intermediate layer in the wall of an artery or lymphatic vessel; *phon.* a medial or voiced stop.

me·di·a·cy, mē′dē·a·sē, *n.* The state of being mediate.

me·di·ad, mē′dē·ad″, *adv. Anat., zool.* in the direction of the central line or plane.

me·di·al, mē′dē·al, *a.* [L.L. *medialis*, < L. *medius*, middle.] Situated in or pertaining to the middle; median; intermediate; pertaining to a mean or average; average; ordinary; *phon.* of a letter, syllable, or sound, neither the first nor the last.—*n. Phon.* A medial letter, syllable, or sound; one of the voiced stops (*b, d, g*) seen as a group of intermediate sounds falling between the tenues (*k, p, t*) and the aspirates (*bh, dh, gh, ph, th*).—**me·di·al·ly**, *adv.*

me·di·an, mē′dē·an, *a.* [L. *medianus*, < *medius*, middle.] Situated in or pertaining to the middle; medial; noting or pertaining to a plane dividing something into two equal parts, esp. one dividing an animal into right and left halves; *arith., statistics*, noting or pertaining to the middle number or value in a given series, as: 4 is the *median* number in the series 1, 3, 4, 8, 9. *Geom.* referring to a line drawn from a triangle's vertex to the opposite side's midpoint.—*n.* —**me·di·an strip**, a narrow piece of land separating opposite lanes on a highway.—**me·di·an·ly**, *adv.*

me·di·ant, mē′dē·ant, *n.* [It. *mediante*.] *Mus.* the third tone above the keynote on the diatonic scale.

me·di·as·ti·num, mē″dē·a·sti′num, *n.* pl. **me·di·as·ti·na**. [L. *mediastinus*, in the middle, < *medius*, middle.] *Anat.* The division of the chest cavity from the sternum backward, dividing the cavity into two parts and enclosing all the thoracic organs but the lungs; a septum.—**me·di·as·ti·nal**, *a.*

me·di·ate, mē′dē·it, *a.* [L. *medio, mediatum*, to be in the middle, < *medius*, middle.] Being between two extremes; acting as a means or agent; not direct or immediate; effected by the intervention of an agency.—mē′dē·āt″, *v.i.*—*mediated, mediating.* To interpose between parties at variance with a view to effecting agreement or reconciliation; to be in a middle or intermediate place.—*v.t.* To effect by mediation or interposition between parties; as, to *mediate* a peace; to serve as the intermediary in bringing about or in conveying.—**me·di·ate·ly**, *adv.*—**me·di·ate·ness**, *n.*

me·di·a·tion, mē″dē·ā′shan, *n.* The act of or an instance of mediating; *labor, international law*, friendly intervention to help find a solution to a dispute.—**me·di·a·tive**, mē′dē·ā″tiv, mē′dē·a·tiv, *a.*

me·di·a·tize, mē′dē·a·tiz″, *v.t.*—*mediatized, mediatizing.* [Fr. *médiatiser*, or G. *mediatisieren*, < L.L. *mediatus*, pp.] To annex, as a principality, to another state, while allowing certain rights to the former sovereign.—**me·di·a·ti·za·tion**, *n.*

me·di·a·tor, mē′dē·ā″tèr, *n.* One who mediates or interposes between parties at variance for the purpose of reconciling them.—**me·di·a·to·ri·al**, mē″dē·a·tōr′ē·al, *a.*—**me·di·a·tress, me·di·a·trice**,

me·di·a·trix, mē″dē·ā″tris, mē″dē·a·trix, *n.* Feminine of mediator.

me·di·a·to·ry, mē′dē·a·tōr″ē, mē′dē·a·tär″ē, *a.* Pertaining to mediation; having the function of mediating.

med·ic, med′ik, *n.* [L. *medicus*, pertaining to healing, medical, as *n.* a physician, < *mederi*, heal, cure. Cf. *remedy*.] *Colloq.* a medical practitioner, medical corpsman, or medical student.

med·ic, med′ik, *n.* [Gr. *mēdikē*, lit. 'a plant of *Media*.'] Any of certain leguminous plants, genus *Medicago*, yielding fodder and allied to clover. Compare *alfalfa.*

med·i·ca·ble, med′i·ka·bl, *a.* [L. *medicabilis*, < *medicare*.] Susceptible of medical treatment; curable.—**med·i·ca·bly**, *adv.*

med·i·caid, med′i·kād″, *n. (Often cap.)* a medical aid program sponsored jointly by federal, state, and local governments for the disabled or needy of any age who are not eligible for social security benefits: distinguished from *medicare.*

med·i·cal, med′i·kal, *a.* [L.L. *medicalis*, < L. *medicus*, medical, *medeor*, to heal, to cure.] Pertaining to or connected with medicine or physicians; medicinal; tending to cure.—**med·i·cal·ly**, *adv.*

med·i·cal ex·am·in·er, *n.* A medically trained public official appointed to make post-mortem examinations of the bodies of victims of suicide, homicide, or other unnatural circumstances, in order to determine the cause of the death; a physician appointed by a firm or insurance company to examine employees or applicants.

med·i·cal ju·ris·pru·dence, *n.* See *jurisprudence.*

me·dic·a·ment, me·dik′a·ment, med′i·ka·ment, *n.* [L. *medicamentum*.] Any substance used for healing wounds or treating diseases; a healing application.—**med·i·ca·men·tal**, **med·i·ca·men·ta·ry**, **med·i·ca·men·tous**, med″i·ka·men′tal, *a.*

med·i·care, med′i·kâr″, *n (Often cap.)* a U.S. government insurance program, financed by social security, that provides hospital and medical care for certain persons, esp. the aged.

med·i·cate, med′i·kāt″, *v.t.*—*medicated, medicating.* [L. *medicatus*, pp. of *medicare, medicari*, < *medicus*.] To treat with medicine or medicaments; to impregnate with a medicinal substance.—**med·i·ca·tion**, med″i·kā′shan, *n.* The act or process of medicating; a medicinal preparation used to treat or cure an ailment.—**med·i·ca·tive**, med′i·kā″tiv, *a.* Medicinal.

Med·i·ce·an, med″i·sē′an, med″i·chē′an, *a.* Of or pertaining to the Medici, an illustrious Florentine family of great power and wealth which flourished in the 15th and 16th centuries.

me·dic·i·nal, me·dis′i·nal, *a.* [L. *medicinalis.*] Pertaining to or having the properties of a medicine; curative; remedial; as *medicinal* substances.—*n.*—**me·dic·i·na·ble**, *a.*—**me·dic·i·nal·ly**, *adv.*

med·i·cine, med′i·sin, *esp. Brit.* med′sin, *n.* [O.Fr. *medicine* (Fr. *médecine*), < L. *medicina*, < L. *medicus*.] Any substance used in treating disease or relieving pain; medicament; remedy; the art or science of restoring or preserving health or physical condition, often divided into medicine proper, surgery, and obstetrics; the science of treating disease with drugs or curative substances, as distinguished from *surgery* and *obstetrics*; the medical profession; any object or practice regarded by N. American Indians as of magical efficacy.—*v.t.*—*medicined, medicining.* To administer medicine to.—**give some·one a taste of his own med·i·cine**, repay someone in kind for a hurt or injury inflicted.—**take one's med·i·cine**, to accept suffering or punishment, particularly when oneself is the cause.

med·i·cine ball, *n.* A heavy ball, large and usu. leather-covered, lifted, rolled, or thrown for exercise.

med·i·cine man, *n.* Among the American Indians and other primitive tribes, any man whom they suppose to possess supernatural powers of healing or invoking spirits; a patent medicine saleman, esp. one prevalent in the U.S. prior to 1900.

med·i·cine show, *n.* In the 19th century, a traveling group of entertainers who drew potential customers for the remedies and medicines that were offered for sale.

med·i·co, med′i·kō″, *n.* [It. and Sp. < L. *medicus.*] *Colloq.* A doctor; a medical student.

me·di·e·val, me·di·ae·val, mē′dē·ē′val, med′ē·ē′val, mid′ē·ē′val, mid·ē′val, *a.* [L. *medius,* middle, and *ævum,* age.] Relating to the Middle Ages or the period between the 8th and the middle of the 15th century. **—me·di·e·val·ism, me·di·ae·val·ism,** *n.* The spirit or principles of the Middle Ages, or devotion to them.**—me·di·e·val·ist, me·di·ae·val·ist,** *n.* One versed in or devoted to the history, culture, art, or study of the Middle Ages.**—me·di·e·val·ly, me·di·ae·val·ly,** *adv.*

me·di·o·cre, mē′dē·ō′kėr, mē′dē·ō″kėr, *a.* [Fr. *médiocre,* < L. *mediocris,* middling.] Of moderate degree or quality; average, ordinary; barely adequate; inferior.**— me·di·oc·ri·ty,** mē″dē·ok′ri·tē, *n.* pl. **me·di·oc·ri·ties.** [L. *mediocritas.*] The quality or state of being mediocre; moderate to low proficiency or value; a person of moderate talents or abilities of any kind.

med·i·tate, med′i·tāt″, *v.i.*—*meditated, meditating.* [L. *meditor, meditatus,* to meditate.] To dwell on anything in thought; to cogitate.—*v.t.* To contemplate doing; to plan or intend; as, to *meditate* murder; to think on.**—med·i·tat·ing·ly,** *adv.*—**med·i·ta·tor,** *n.*

med·i·ta·tion, med″i·tā′shan, *n.* [L. *meditatio.*] The act of meditating; close or continued thought; the revolving of a subject in the mind.**—med·i·ta·tive,** med′i·tā″tiv, *a.* Inclined to meditation; pertaining to meditation.**—med·i·ta·tive·ly,** *adv.* **—med·i·ta·tive·ness,** *n.*

med·i·ter·ra·ne·an, med″i·te·rā′nē·an, *a.* [L. *mediterraneus*—*medius,* middle, and *terra,* land.] Surrounded by or in the midst of land; inland; (*cap.*) pertaining to, situated on, or near the Mediterranean Sea between Africa, Europe, and Asia.

me·di·um, mē′dē·um, *n.* pl. **me·di·a, me·di·ums,** mē′dē·a. [L. *medium,* the middle, midst, a means.] Something placed or ranked between other things; a mean between two extremes; that by or through which anything is accomplished, conveyed, or carried on; an agency or instrumentality, as: Television is a communications and advertising *medium.* The element that surrounds or pervades; environment; *biol.* the culture in which organisms grow, or the substances in which they are preserved for study. A person who is said to be capable of communicating with the spirits of the deceased; the liquid vehicle with which dry colors are ground and prepared for painting; the form or material used by an artist. —*a.* Middle; middling.

me·di·um fre·quen·cy, *n.* Any radio wave frequency ranging between 300 and 3000 kilocycles per second. Abbr. *mf.*

me·di·um·is·tic, mē″dē·u·mis′tik, *a.* Relating to or having the characteristics of a spiritualistic medium.

me·di·um of ex·change, *n.* Any article or substance accepted as a measure of value exchangeable for merchandise or service.

med·lar, med′lẽr, *n.* [O.Fr. *meslier, mesler, medler,* < L. *mespilus,* Gr. *mespilon,* medlar.] A small European tree of the rose

family that bears fruit resembling the crab apple; the fruit itself.

med·ley, med′lē, *n.* pl. **med·leys.** [O.Fr. *medlee, meslee* (Fr. *mêlée*), < *medler, mesler.*] A mixture, esp. of heterogeneous elements; a jumble; a piece of music combining airs or passages from various sources; *sports,* a relay contest, as running, in which each of the members of a team races a different distance, or swimming, in which each member does a different stroke.—*a.*

Mé·doc, mā·dok′, *Fr.* mā·dạk′, *n.* A wine-producing region in the department of Gironde in southwestern France; claret produced in this region.

me·dul·la, mi·dul′a, *n.* pl. **me·dul·las, me·dul·lae,** mi·dul′ē. [L., marrow, pith, < *medius,* middle.] *Anat.* the marrow of bones; the medulla oblongata; the soft inner substance of an organ or part, as of a kidney. *Bot.* the pith of plants.**—med·ul·lar·y,** med′a·lẽr″ē, mej′a·lẽr″ē, mi·dul′a·•rē, *a.*

me·dul·la ob·lon·ga·ta, mi·dul′a ob″lang·gä′ta, *n.* pl. **me·dul·la ob·lon·ga·tas, me·dul·lae ob·lon·ga·tae,** mi·dul′ē ob″lang·gä′tē. [N.L., 'prolonged medulla.'] *Anat.* the lowest or hindmost part of the brain, continuous with the spinal cord.

me·du·sa, me·dō′sa, me·dō′za, me·dū′sa, me·dū′za, *n.* pl. **me·du·sas, me·du·sae,** me·dō′sē, me·dō′zē, me·dū′sē, me·dū′zē. [Gr. *Medousa,* originally the fem. of *medōn,* a ruler.] *Zool.* a jellyfish. (*Cap.*), *mythol.* one of the three Gorgons who had her hair changed into serpents and was killed by Perseus. **me·du·san,** *a., n.*— **me·du·soid,** *a.*

meek, mēk, *a.* [Same as Sw. *miuk,* Icel. *mjúkr,* soft, meek; Dan. *myg,* pliant, supple; Goth. *muks,* soft, meek.] Mild of temper; gentle; not easily provoked or irritated; submissive; lacking courage.— **meek·ly,** *adv.*—**meek·ness,** *n.*

meer·schaum, mēr′sham, mēr′sham, mēr′-shoum, *n.* [G., lit. 'seafoam'—*meer,* the sea, and *schaum,* foam; from having been found on the seashore in lumps resembling petrified sea foam.] A heat-resistant silicate of magnesium, occurring in fine claylike masses mainly in Asia Minor and used to make pipe bowls and ornamental carvings; also *sepiolite.* A tobacco pipe.

meet, mēt, *v.t.*—*met, meeting.* [O.E. mē:an, gemētan, < mōt, gemōt, meeting: see *moot.*] To come upon or encounter; come face to face with or into the presence of; go to the place of arrival of; as, to *meet* a train; come into the company of, as in intercourse, dealings, and the like; come into personal acquaintance with, as by formal presentation; to come into contact, junction, or connection with; as, when hand *meets* hand; to come before or to; as, to *meet* the eye or ear; to face directly or without avoidance; to encounter in opposition or conflict; as, to *meet* a person in a duel; to oppose; as, to *meet* charges with countercharges; cope or deal effectively with, as an objection; satisfy, as obligations; come into conformity with, as expectations; to encounter in experience; as, to *meet* one's fate; receive; as, to *meet* one's deserts.—*v.i.* To come together, face to face, or into company; assemble, as for action or conference; become personally acquainted; to come into contact or form a junction, as lines; to be conjoined or united; as, qualities that seldom *meet* in one person; concur or agree; to come together in opposition or conflict, as adversaries.—*n.* A gathering or meeting for a sports event; those assembled at such a meeting; the place of meeting.**—meet with,** to come across; light upon; to encounter in experience; to confer with; experience or undergo; receive, as praise.**—meet·er,** *n.*

meet, mēt, *a.* [O.E. *gemet,* fit, proper, < *metan,* to measure; Icel. *maetr,* meet, worthy.] Fit; suitable; proper; appropriate.**—meet·ly,** *adv.*—**meet·ness,** *n.*

meet·ing, mē′ting, *n.* A coming together; an assembly for some common purpose, or the persons present; an assembly of Quakers for religious worship; junction.

meet·ing house, *n.* A building or place used for public meetings; a Quaker house of worship.

meg·a·ce·phal·ic, meg″a·se·fal′ik, *a.* [Gr. *megas,* large, and *kephalē,* head.] Large-headed; *craniom.* having a skull with a cranial capacity exceeding the mean. Also **meg·a·ceph·a·lous,** meg″a·sef′a·lus.— **meg·a·ceph·a·ly,** *n.*

meg·a·city, meg′a·sit″ē, *n.* pl. **meg·a·cit·ies.** A city with 1,000,000 or more inhabitants.

meg·a·cy·cle, meg′a·sī″kl, *n.* [Gr. *megas,* great, and *kyklos,* circle.] A unit used to measure the frequency of electromagnetic waves, equal to 1,000,000 cycles per second; a million cycles.

meg·a·ga·mete, meg″a·ga·mēt′, meg″-a·gam′ēt, *n.* Macrogamete.

meg·a·lith, meg′a·lith, *n. Archaeol.* a stone of great size, esp. in ancient construction work and primitive monumental remains.**—meg·a·lith·ic,** *a.*

meg·a·lo·ma·ni·a, meg″a·lō·mā′nē·a, *n.* [N.L.] *Psychiatry,* a form of mental disorder characterized by extreme overestimation of one's abilities or importance. An obsession for grandiose action.— **meg·a·lo·ma·ni·ac,** meg″a·lō·mā′nē·ak″, *a., n.*—**meg·a·lo·ma·ni·a·cal,** *a.*

meg·a·lop·o·lis, meg″a·lop′o·lis, *n.* A far-reaching metropolitan area in which any number of cities are geographically linked by contiguous suburbs. Also **me·gap·o·lis,** me·gap′o·lis.—**meg·a·lo·pol·i·tan,** meg″a·lō·pol′i·tan, *a., n.*—**meg·a·lo·pol·i·tan·ism,** *n.*

meg·a·lo·saur, meg′a·lo·sạr″, *n.* [Gr. *megas, megalē,* great, and *sauros,* a lizard.] *Paleon.* a carnivorous dinosaur, 40 to 50 feet long, that existed during the Jurassic period.

meg·a·phone, meg′a·fōn″, *n.* A large funnel-shaped instrument for magnifying sound, or for directing it in increased volume, usu. used in addressing a large audience out of doors or in calling some distance.—*v.t., v.i.*—*megaphoned, megaphoning.*—**meg·a·phon·ic,** meg″a·fon′ik, *a.*—**meg·a·phon·i·cal·ly,** *adv.*

meg·a·spo·ran·gi·um, meg″a·spō·ran′jē·um, meg″a·spạ·ran′jē·um, *n.* pl. **meg·a·spo·ran·gi·a,** meg′a·spō·ran′jē·a. [N.L.] *Bot.* a sporangium or spore case that produces megaspores.

meg·a·spore, meg′a·spōr″, *n. Bot.* One of the larger of the two kinds of reproductive spores produced within a megasporangium; a spore that develops into the embryo sac of a seed-bearing plant.**—meg·a·spor·ic,** *a.*—**meg·a·spor·o·gen·e·sis,** meg′a·spōr·o·jen′e·sis, *n.*

meg·a·spo·ro·phyll, meg′a·spōr′i·fil, *n. Bot.* a modified leaf that functions reproductively by producing only megasporangia.

meg·a·there, meg′a·thẽr′, *n.* [N.L. *megatherium.*] *Paleon.* any of the huge ground sloths, mammals of the extinct genus *Megatherium,* living during Pleistocene times and inhabiting the Americas. Also **meg·a·the·ri·um.—meg·a·the·ri·an,** *a.*

meg·a·ton, meg′a·tun″, *n.* A unit of explosive force equal to 1,000,000 tons of TNT. Abbr. *MT.*

meg·a·watt, meg′a·wot″, *n. Elect.* one million watts of power. Abbr. *Mw.*

me·gilp, ma·gilp′, me·gilp′, *n.* A combination of linseed oil and mastic varnish which artists employ as a vehicle for oil pigments. Also **me·gilph,** me·gilf'.

meg·ohm, meg'ōm″, *n. Elect.* a resistance unit equal to 1,000,000 ohms. Abbr. *meg, MΩ.*

mei·o·sis, mī·ō'sis, *n. Biol.* the process resulting in the formation of the mature reproductive cells and consisting of the reduction of the chromosome number by one half, from the diploid to the haploid. *Liter.* an understatement; presentation of something as less important than it actually is, esp. litotes.—**mei·ot·ic,** mī·ot'ik, *a.*—**mei·ot·i·cal·ly,** *adv.*

Meis·ter·sing·er, mī'stėr·sing″ėr, mī'stėr·zing″ėr, *n.* [G., 'mastersinger.'] A merchant or craftsman belonging to guilds established during the 14th, 15th, and 16th centuries in the principal cities of Germany, for the cultivation of poetry and music. Also *mastersinger.*

mel·a·mine, mel'a·mēn″, mel″a·mēn', *n.* The nitrogen compound, $C_3N_3(NH_2)_3$, which is a high-melting, white crystalline organic base primarily used in the production of melamine resins and in organic synthesis.

mel·a·mine res·in, *n. Chem.* any thermosetting resin produced by the reaction of formaldehyde with melamine and primarily used as a coating for plastics, fabrics, and paper, and as an adhesive agent for laminated or molded goods.

mel·an·cho·li·a, mel″an·kō'lē·a, mel″an·kōl'ya, *n.* [L.L.] *Psychiatry,* a mental disease characterized by great depression, brooding, gloomy forebodings without apparent reason, a marked inaccessibility to most external stimuli, and often, real or imagined physical ailments.—**mel·an·cho·li·ac,** mel″an·kō'lē·ak″, *a., n.*

mel·an·chol·y, mel'an·kol″ē, *n. pl.* **mel·an·chol·ies.** [Gr. *melancholia,* excess of black bile, melancholy madness—*melas, melaina,* black, and *cholē,* bile.] A state of despondency, esp. frequent or lengthy despondency; somber contemplation.—*a.* Characterized by prolonged depression; causing dejection or gloom; contemplative orsoberly reflective. Also **mel·an·chol·ic,** mel′an·kol'ik.—**mel·an·chol·i·cal·ly, mel·an·chol·i·ly,** *adv.*—**mel·an·chol·i·ness,** *n.*

Mel·a·ne·sian, mel″a·nē'zhan, mel″a·nē'shan, *a.* [< *Melanesia,* < Gr. *melas* (*melan*), black, and *nesos,* island.] Of or pertaining to Melanesia, one of the principal island groups of the southwest Pacific, its inhabitants, or their languages.—*n.* An inhabitant of Melanesia; any of the Austronesian languages or dialects spoken there.

mé·lange, *Fr.* mä·länzh', *n. pl.* **mé·lange** mä·länzh'. [Fr., < *méler,* to mix.] A mixture; an assortment; a medley.

mel·a·nin, mel'a·nin, *n. Biochem.* any of various dark pigments present in the hair, epidermis, or eyes of men and animals, sometimes produced in excess by certain diseases.—**mel·a·noid,** mel'a·noid″, *a., n.*

mel·a·nism, mel'a·niz″um, *n. Physiol.* an excessive development of black or dark pigment in the skin, hair, and eyes of a human being, or in the skin, coat, or plumage of an animal.—**me·lan·ic,** me·lan′ik, *a.*—**mel·a·nis·tic,** mel″a·nis'tik, *a.*

mel·a·nite, mel'a·nīt″, *n.* An andradite garnet which is black in color.—**mel·a·nit·ic,** mel″a·nit'ik, *a.*

mel·a·no·ma, mel″a·nō'ma, *n. pl.* **mel·a·no·mas, mel·a·no·ma·ta,** mel″a·nō'ma·ta. *Pathol.* a tumor, usu. malignant, composed of cells containing dark pigment.

mel·a·no·sis, mel″a·nō'sis, *n. pl.* **mel·a·no·ses.** [N.L., < Gr. *melanōsis,* a becoming black, < *melas* (*melan*), black.] *Pathol.* The deposition or development of black or dark pigment in the tissues, sometimes leading to the production of malignant pigmented tumors; a discoloration caused by this.—**mel·a·not·ic,** mel″a·not'ik, *a.*

mel·a·nous, mel'a·nus, *a.* [Gr. *melas* (*melan*), black.] Black-haired and dark-complexioned.

mel·a·phyre, mel'a·fīėr″, *n.* [Fr. *mélaphyre,* < Gr. *melas,* black, and Fr. (*por*) *phyre,* porphyry.] Any of various dark-colored igneous rocks of porphyritic texture.

Mel·ba toast, mel'ba tōst″, *n.* Crisply toasted bread in thin, small slices.

meld, meld, *v.t.* [G. *melden,* announce.] *Cards,* to announce and display, as a counting combination of cards in one's hand, for a score.—*v.i.*—*n. Cards.* An act of melding; any counting combination of cards to be melded.

meld, meld, *v.t., v.i.* To blend; to unite.

me·lee, mā'lā, mā·lā', mel'ā, *n.* [Fr., a participial substantive, < *méler,* to mix.] A confused, all-out, hand-to-hand fracas; an affray.

mel·ic, mel'ik, *a.* [Gr. *melikos,* < *melos,* song.] Meant for singing; lyric; noting or relating to an ornate form of lyric poetry of ancient Greece.

mel·i·lot, mel'i·lot″, *n.* [Gr. *melilōton, melilōtus—meli,* honey, and *lōtos,* lotus.] A leguminous annual or biennial herb of the clover genus, *Melilotus,* cultivated for fodder and pasture; sweet clover.

mel·i·nite, mel'i·nit″, *n. Chem.* a high explosive, the basis or chief ingredient of which is picric acid.

mel·io·rate, mel'ya·rāt″, mē'lē·o·rāt″, *v.t., v.i.—meliorated, meliorating.* [L. *melioro, melioratum,* < *melior,* better, compar. of *bonus,* good.] To make better; to improve; to ameliorate.—**mel·io·ra·ble,** *a.*—**mel·io·ra·tion,** mēl″ya·rā′shan, mē″lē·a·rā′shan, *n.*—**mel·io·ra·tive,** mēl'ya·rā″tiv, mēl'yėr·a·tiv, mē'lē·a·rā″tiv, mē'lē·ėr·a·tiv, *a.*—**mel·io·ra·tor,** *n.*

mel·io·rism, mēl'ya·riz″um, mē'lē·a·riz″um, *n.* The view or doctrine that the natural tendency of the world is toward improvement and that human effort can aid the process.—**mel·io·rist,** *a., n.*—**mel·io·ris·tic,** mēl″ya·ris'tik, mē″lē·a·ris'tik, *a.*

mel·lif·er·ous, me·lif'ėr·us, *a.* [L. *mellifer —mel, mellis,* honey, and *fero,* to bear.] Producing honey.

mel·lif·lu·ous, me·lif'lö·us, *a. Fig.* sweet-sounding, as the voice. Flowing as with honey; sweetly flowing. Also **mel·lif·lu·ent.**—**mel·lif·lu·ous·ly,** *adv.*—**mel·lif·lu·ous·ness,** *n.*

mel·low, mel'ō, *a.* [Allied to Prov. G. *möll,* soft, ripe, *mölich,* mellow, *mollig,* soft, L. *mollis,* Gr. *malakos,* Skt. *mridu,* tender, soft, and to E. *meal,* < root *mar,* to grind or crush.] Soft with ripeness; rich or delicate to the eye, ear, or palate, as color, sound, or flavor; toned down by the lapse of time; softened or matured by length of years; genial. *Colloq.* made good humored by liquor; somewhat intoxicated.—*v.t., v.i.* To soften by ripeness or age; to render or become mellow.—**mel·low·ly,** *adv.*—**mel·low·ness,** *n.*

me·lo·de·on, me·lō'dē·on, *n.* [< *melody,* Gr. *melōdia.*] A wind instrument with metallic free reeds and a keyboard similar to the harmonium; a small organ with metal reeds. Also **A·mer·i·can or·gan.**

mel·o·dist, mel'o·dist, *n.* A composer or singer of melodies.

mel·o·dize, mel'o·dīz″, *v.t.—melodized, melodizing.* To make melodious; to compose the melodies or music for.—*v.i.* To make a melody; to blend in a harmonious manner.—**mel·o·diz·er,** *n.*

mel·o·dra·ma, mel'o·drä″ma, mel'o·dram″a, *n.* [Gr. *melos,* a song, and *drama,* drama.] An extravagantly sentimental or emotionally exaggerated drama or play; formerly, a romantic play interspersed with music.—**mel·o·dra·mat·ic,** mel″o·dra·-mat'ik, *a.*—**mel·o·dra·mat·i·cal·ly,** *adv.*—**mel·o·dra·mat·ics,** *n.*—**mel·o·dram·a·tist,** mel″o·dram'a·tist, mel″o·drä'ma·tist, *n.*

mel·o·dy, mel'o·dē, *n. pl.* **mel·o·dies.** [Gr. *melōdia,* a tune, choral song—*melos,* a limb, a part, and *ōdē,* a song, an ode.] An agreeable succession of sounds; sweetness of sound; sound highly pleasing to the ear. *Mus.* a succession of tones, usu. produced by a single voice or instrument: distinguished from rhythm and harmony; the particular air or tune of a musical piece. A melic poem.—**me·lod·ic,** me·lod'ik, *a.*—**me·lod·i·cal·ly,** *adv.*—**me·lo·di·ous,** me·lō'dē·us, *a.*—**me·lo·di·ous·ness,** *n.*

mel·oid, mel'oid, *a.* Of or pertaining to any of the beetles of the family *Meloidae,* including oil beetles and blister beetles.—*n.*

mel·on, mel'on, *n.* [O.Fr. *melon,* < L.L. *melo*(n-), for L. *melopepo,* < Gr. *melopepon,* apple-shaped melon, < *melon,* apple, and *pepon.*] The fruit of any of various cucurbitaceous plants, as the muskmelon or the watermelon; the vine itself; *slang,* an accumulation of profits, exceeding ordinary dividends, for distribution among the stockholders of a company.

melt, melt, *v.t.*—past *melted,* pp. *melted* or *molten,* ppr. *melting.* [O.E. *meltan,* allied to *malt, mellow.*] To reduce from a solid to a liquid or flowing state by heat; to liquefy; to cause to fade or dissolve; to cause to fuse or blend. *Fig.* to soften in attitude; render gentle or susceptible.—*v.i.* To become liquid; to dissolve; to pass by imperceptible degrees, often followed by *away;* to blend or to shade, often followed by *into; fig.* to become tender, mild, or gentle.—*n.* Something that is melted; a melting process or melted state; the quantity in a single operation of melting.—**melt·a·bil·i·ty,** mel″ta·bil'i·tē, *n.*—**melt·a·ble,** *a.*—**melt·er,** mel'tėr, *n.*

melt·ing point, *n.* The degree of heat at which a solid will melt or fuse.

melt·ing pot, *n.* A crucible; a container in which substances can be melted; *fig.* a country, city, or society containing many cultures and ethnic groups.

mel·ton, mel'ton, *n.* [From *Melton* Mowbray, Eng.] A smooth strong wool having a short nap, used for overcoats or other outdoor garments.

melt·wa·ter, melt'wȧ″tėr, melt'wot″ėr, *n.* That water resulting from melted ice or snow.

mem·ber, mem'bėr, *n.* [O.Fr. *membre,* < L. *membrum,* limb, part.] A part or organ of an animal body, esp. a limb, as a leg; a constituent part of any structural or composite whole, as a subordinate architectural feature of a building, a clause of a sentence, either side of an algebraic equation, a component of a mathematical set, or one proposition of a logical syllogism; each of the persons composing a society, party, community, or other body; each of the persons included in the membership of a legislative body, as the British House of Commons or the U.S. House of Representatives.—**mem·bered,** *a.*—**mem·ber·less,** *a.*

mem·ber·ship, mem'bėr·ship″, *n.* The state of being a member, as of a society or organization; the status of a member; the total number of members belonging to a body; as, a church with a large *membership.*

mem·brane, mem'brān, *n.* [L. *membrana,* a thin skin, parchment, < *membrum,* a limb.] *Biol.* A thin tissue of the animal body which covers organs, lines cavities or canals, or joins adjacent parts; similar tissue in plants.—**mem·bra·ceous,** **mem·bra·nous,** mem″bra·nã′shus, mem′-bra·nus, a.

mem·brane bone, n. Anat. a bone that originates in membranous tissue rather than cartilage.

mem·bra·nous lab·y·rinth, n. Anat. the part of the inner ear composed of membranous structures, as the cochlea.

me·men·to, me·men′tō, n. pl. **me·men·tos, me·men·toes.** [L., remember, be mindful, < memini, to remember.] Anything that reminds one of what is past; a souvenir; something serving to remind or warn; (cap.), Rom. Cath. Ch. in the canon of the Mass, either of two prayers, one for the living and one for the dead.

me·men·to mo·ri, me·men′tō mōr′ī, me·men′tō mar′ī, me·men′tō mōr′ē, n. [L.] An emblematic reminder of mortality, as a death's head.

mem·o, mem′ō, n. Colloq. memorandum.

mem·oir, mem′wär, mem′war, n. [Fr. mémoire, < L. memoria, memory, < memor, mindful.] A record or written statement of something noteworthy; a scholarly report; a biography. Usu. pl. an account of events typically drawn from recollections of one's life and observations; an autobiography; a report of the transactions of a learned society.

mem·o·ra·bil·i·a, mem″ēr·a·bil′ē·a, mem″ēr·a·bil′ya, n. pl. [L.] Things and occasions worthy of remembrance or record.

mem·o·ra·ble, mem′ēr·a·bl, a. [L. memorabilis.] Worthy to be remembered; notable; distinguished; remarkable.— **mem·o·ra·ble·ness,** n.—**mem·o·ra·bly,** adv.

mem·o·ran·dum, mem″o·ran′dum, n. pl. **mem·o·ran·dums, mem·o·ran·da.** [L., something to be remembered.] A note used in aiding the memory; a brief record; an informal communication about office matters sent among the staff of a company; law, a brief containing terms of contract agreement, transaction, or points of law; diplomacy, a summary of the state of a question, or a justification of a decision adopted; bus. a statement transferring the title on goods, allowing the buyer to return the goods if desired. Also memo.

me·mo·ri·al, me·mōr′ē·al, a. [L. memorialis, < memoria, E. memory.] Of or pertaining to the memory; preserving the memory of a person or thing; commemorative.—n. Something designed or adapted to preserve the memory of a person, an event, or anything belonging to past time, as a monument or periodic observance; a record; a written statement of facts presented to a sovereign or legislative body, as the basis of, or expressed in the form of, a petition or remonstrance.—**me·mo·ri·al·ist,** me·mōr′ē·a·list, n.—**me·mo·ri·al·ly,** adv.

Me·mo·ri·al Day, n. A day, May 30, set apart in most of the States of the U.S. to honor the dead of American wars; also Dec·o·ra·tion Day; April 26, May 10, or June 3, similarly observed in various southern States.

me·mo·ri·al·ize, me·mōr′ē·a·līz′, v.t.— memorialized, memorializing. To commemorate; to present a memorial to.—**me·mo·ri·al·i·za·tion,** me·mōr″ē·a·li·zā′shan, n.—**me·mo·ri·al·iz·er,** n.—**me·mo·ri·al·ly,** adv.

me·mo·ri·al park, n. A cemetery.

me·mo·ri·ter, me·mōr′i·tér, me·mōr′i·ter, adv., a. [L.] From memory.

mem·o·rize, mem′o·rīz″, v.t.—memorized, memorizing. To commit to memory; learn by heart.—**mem·o·riz·a·ble,** a.—**mem·o·ri·za·tion,** mem″o·ri·zā′shan, n.—**mem·o·riz·er,** n.

mem·o·ry, mem′o·rē, n. pl. **mem·o·ries.** [O.Fr. memorie (Fr. mémoire), < L. memoria, memory, period of remembrance, historical account, record, memorial, < memor, mindful, remembering; akin to Gr. merimna, care, martur, witness, martyr, Skt. smar-, remember.] The mental capacity or faculty of retaining and reviving impressions, or of recalling previous experiences; this capacity as possessed by a particular individual; as, to have a good memory; the totality of things retained by a person; a person or thing remembered; the length of time over which recollection extends; as, an event within recent memory; the repute of a person or thing among those remembering; reputation, esp. after death; the state or fact of being remembered; as, to remain in perpetual memory; commemorative remembrance; commemoration; as, a monument erected in memory of a person; the component in a computer that stores pertinent information for ready access.

mem·sa·hib, mem′sä″ib, mem′sä″ēb, mem′sä″hib, mem′sä″hēb, n. [= ma'am sahib.] In India, a native's term of respect for a European lady.

men·ace, men′is, v.t.—menaced, menacing. [Fr. menacer, < L. minax, threatening, mina, a threat, < root min, seen in mineo, to project (in prominent, eminent).] To threaten, as with harm, evil, or death.— v.i. To behave in a threatening way; to voice threats.—n. A threat; indication of a probable evil to come; a person who is a threat; a source of worry; a nuisance.

me·nad, mē′nad, n. Maenad.

mé·nage, mā·näzh′, Fr. mā·näzh′, n. [Fr. ménage, a household; O.Fr. mesnage, L.L. mansionaticum, < L. mansio, a dwelling.] A household; housekeeping; household management.

me·nag·er·ie, me·naj′e·rē, me·nazh′e·rē, n. [Fr. ménagerie.] A collection of animals, esp. wild or foreign animals, for exhibition; a place where such a collection is kept.

mend, mend, v.t. [For amend.] To make whole or sound by repairing, as something broken, worn, or otherwise damaged; as, to mend broken china, shoes or clothes, a fence or a road; to remove or correct, as faults in manners or morals; to reform; restore to due condition by any suitable action; as, to mend sails by adjusting them properly; to set right; as, to mend matters.—v.i. To become better or improve; of a sick person, to progress toward recovery.

mend, mend, n. The act or fact of mending; improvement; the way to recovery; as, to be on the mend; a repair; a mended place. —**mend·a·ble,** a.

men·da·cious, men·dā′shus, a. [L. mendax, mandacis, lying, < stem of mentior, to lie.] Lying; false; given to telling untruths.— **men·da·cious·ly,** adv.—**men·da·cious·ness,** n.

men·dac·i·ty, men·das′i·tē, n. pl. **men·dac·i·ties.** The quality of being mendacious; a falsehood; a lie.

men·de·le·vi·um, men″de·lē′vē·um, n. A synthetic radioactive element. Sym. Md or Mv, at. no. 101. See Periodic Table of Elements.

Men·de·li·an, men·dē′lē·an, men·dēl′yan, a. [From Gregor Johann Mendel, 1822–1884, an Austrian monk and scientific investigator.] Pertaining to Mendel or to Mendelism.—n. Also **Men·de·li·an·ist, Men·del·ist.**

Men·del·ism, men′de·liz″um, n. A theory or doctrine of heredity based upon Mendel's experiments with peas. Also **Men·de·li·an·ism,** men·dē′lē·a·niz″um.—**Men·del's laws,** the principles or laws concerning the inheritance of characteristics in animals and plants, according to which there occurs, in the second and later generations of hybrids, every possible combination of the characters of the original parent animals or plants, each combination in a definite proportion of individuals; also particulate inheritance.

men·di·cant, men′di·kant, a. [L. mendicans, mendicantis, ppr. of mendico, to beg, < mendicus, a beggar (akin to menda, a fault).] Practicing begging; of or denoting one who begs; denoting one who begs as part of religious discipline; as, a mendicant friar.—n. A beggar; a member of a begging order; a begging friar.—**men·di·can·cy,** men·dic·i·ty, men·dis′i·tē, n.

men·ha·den, men·hād′en, n. [N. Amer. Ind.] A marine fish, Brevoortia tyrannus, having the appearance of a herring, common along the eastern coast of the U.S., and used for bait and for making oil and fertilizer.

men·hir, men′hir, n. [W. maen, a stone, and hir, long.] Archaeol. a tall monument of rude stone, of unknown antiquity, standing singly or in groups.

me·ni·al, mē′nē·al, a. [O.E. meyneal, etc., O.Fr. meignial, < meignee, maisgnee, a household, L.L. masnata; same origin as mansion.] Pertaining to household or domestic servants; servile; low.—n. A domestic servant; one who is servile.— **me·ni·al·ly,** adv.

Mé·nière's dis·ease, mān·yârz′ di·zēz′, n. [From Ménière, Fr. physician, who first described it.] Pathol. a disorder of the labyrinth of the ear marked by dizziness, ringing in the ears, and more or less complete deafness.

me·nin·ges, mi·nin′jēz, n. pl., sing. **me·ninx,** mē′ningks. [Gr. mēningx, mēningos, a membrane.] Anat. three membranes, the dura mater, pia mater, and arachnoid, that envelop the brain and spinal cord.—**me·nin·ge·al,** mi·nin′jē·al, a.

men·in·gi·tis, men″in·ji′tis, n. Pathol. inflammation of the membranes of the brain or spinal cord, esp. inflammation of the pia mater and arachnoid.—**men·in·git·ic,** men″in·jit′ik, a.

me·nis·cus, mi·nis′kus, n. pl. **me·nis·cus·es, me·nis·ci,** mi·nis′ī. [N.L., < Gr. meniskos, crescent, dim. of mēnē, moon.] A crescent or crescent-shaped body; opt. a lens with a crescent-shaped section; phys. the convex or concave upper surface of a column of liquid, caused by capillarity; anat. a disk of cartilage located in a joint between the surfaces of the articulating bones.—**me·nis·coid,** mi·nis′koid, a.

Men·non·ite, men′o·nīt″, n. [From Menno Simon, the founder, 1492–1559.] A member of an evangelical Christian sect opposed to the baptism of infants, military service, taking of oaths, and holding public office.— **Men·no·nit·ism,** n.

me·nol·o·gy, mi·nol′o·jē, n. pl. **me·nol·o·gies.** [Gr. mēn, a month, logos, account.] A calendar marking the feast days of the saints with brief biographies; a calendar marking the months.

me·no mos·so, mā′nō ma′sō, It. me′na mas′sa, adv., a. Mus. slower, less hurriedly.

men·o·pause, men′o·paz″, n. [Gr. mēn, month, pausis, a stopping.] Physiol. The natural and permanent cessation of menstruation normally between the ages of 45 and 50; woman's change of life.— **men·o·pau·sal,** a.

me·nor·ah, me·nōr′a, me·nar′a, n. [Heb.] A nine-armed candelabrum used in the celebration of the Jewish holiday of Hanukkah; a candelabrum, often with seven arms, symbolic of the Creation, used in Jewish religious ceremonies.

men·or·rha·gi·a, men″o·rā′jē·a, men″o·rā′ja, n. [Gr. mēn, mēnos, a month, and rheō, to flow.] Pathol. A profuse or prolonged menstrual discharge; hemorrhage from the uterus.—**men·or·rhag·ic,** men″o·raj′ik, *a.*

men·sal, men′sal, *a.* [L. *mensis,* a month; same root as Gr. *mēn,* a month.] Occurring once a month; monthly.

men·sal, men′sal, *a.* [L.L. *mensalis,* < L. *mensa,* table.] Of, pertaining to, or used at the table.

mense, mens, *n. Brit. dial.* decorum.—*v.t. Brit. dial.* to ornament or grace.—**mense·ful,** *a.*—**mense·less,** *a.*

men·ses, men′sēz, *n. pl., sing. or pl. in constr. Physiol.* menstruation.

Men·she·vik, men′she·vik, *Russ.* men″she·vēk′, *n. pl.* **Men·she·viks, Men·she·vik·i,** men′she·vik″ē, men′she·vē″kē, *Russ.* men″she·vi·kē′ [Russ., < *menshe,* less: with allusion to the minority (Russ. *menshinstvo*) or smaller faction of the party.] *Russ. politics,* a member of the less radical faction of the Social Democratic party, as distinguished from *Bolshevik.* Also **Men·she·vist.**—**Men·she·vism,** men′she·viz″um, *n.*

men·stru·al, men′strō·al, men′stral, *a.* [L. *menstrualis,* monthly.] *Physiol.* pertaining to the menses of females. Also **men·stru·ous**

men·stru·a·tion, men″strō·ā′shan, *n. Physiol.* the uterine discharge of blood and mucous occurring, on an average, every 28 days from puberty to menopause; the act or time of menstruation. Also *menses, period.*—**men·stru·ate,** men′strō·āt″, *v.i.*—**menstruated, menstruating.**

men·stru·um, men′strō·um, *n. pl.* **men·stru·a, men·stru·ums.** [< L. *menstruus,* monthly, < *mensis,* a month; < an old belief of the alchemists about the influence of the moon.] Any fluid which dissolves a solid; a solvent.

men·sur·a·ble, men′shèr·a·bl, *a.* [L. *mensurabilis,* < *mensuro,* to measure, < *mensura,* measure.] Capable of being measured; measurable.—**men·sur·a·bil·i·ty,** *n.*

men·su·ral, men′shèr·al, *a.* Pertaining to measure.

men·su·ral mu·sic, *n. Mus.* polyphonic music developed in the 13th century and characterized by each note having an assigned rhythmic value. Also **men·sur·a·ble mu·sic**

men·su·ra·tion, men″shu·rā′shan, *n.* The act or process of measuring or taking the dimensions of anything; measurement; *geom.* the science of determining the length of a figure, its area, or its volume.—**men·su·ra·tion·al,** *a.*

men·tal, men′tal, *a.* [L.L. *mentalis,* < L. *mens* (*ment-*), mind.] Of or pertaining to the mind; pertaining to the totality of an individual's intellectual and emotional processes; intellectual rather than emotional or physical; of, pertaining to, or afflicted by a disorder of the mind; for the treatment or care of persons afflicted by such disorders; as, a *mental* institution; performed by or existing in the mind, esp. without the use of written figures; as, *mental* arithmetic.—**men·tal·ly,** *adv.*

men·tal, men′tal, *a.* [L. *mentum,* chin.] Of or pertaining to the chin.

men·tal age, *n. Psychol.* the age which corresponds to the level of an individual's mental ability, as: A four-year-old child, whose test performance equals that of an average six-year-old, has a *mental age* of six.

men·tal de·fi·cien·cy, *n. Psychol.* failure in the development of intelligence, as in moronism, imbecility, and idiocy, characterized by an individual's inability to function adequately in society.

men·tal·i·ty, men·tal′i·tē, *n. pl.* **men·tal·i·ties.** Mental capacity or endowment; intellectuality; mind.

men·tha·ceous, men·thā′shus, *a.* [L. *mentha,* E. *mint.*] Belonging to the *Menthaceae* or mint family of plants, including the horsemint, peppermint, and pennyroyal.

men·thene, men′thēn, *n.* [L. *mentha,* E. *mint.*] *Chem.* an oily hydrocarbon, $C_{10}H_{18}$, derived from menthol.

men·thol, men′thōl, men′thal, men′thol, *n.* [G., < L. *mentha,* E. *mint.*] *Chem., pharm.* a white, crystalline compound, $CH_3C_6H_9(C_3H_7)OH$, obtained from oil of peppermint or synthesized, and used in medicine, in perfumes, and in confections.—**men·tho·lat·ed,** men′tho·lā″tid, *a.*

men·ti·cide, men′ti·sīd″, *n.* The methodical attempt to alter radically an individual's beliefs and value systems through the employment of such techniques as torture, use of drugs, and sustained questioning; brainwashing.

men·tion, men′shan, *n.* [L. *mentio, mentionis,* < same root as *mens,* mind, Skt. *man,* to think.] A brief notice or remark with regard to something; a casual speaking of; a reference to; a recognition for achievement.—*v.t.* To note briefly; to refer to in passing; to recognize for notable achievement.—**men·tion·a·ble,** *a.*—**men·tion·er,** *n.*

men·tor, men′tèr, *n.* [From *Mentor,* the counselor of Telemachus, according to Homer.] A wise and faithful adviser or tutor.

men·u, men′ū, mã′nū, *n.* [Fr., lit. 'minute or detailed list,' < L. *minutus,* minute.] A bill of fare; a list of meals that can be served; a list of the dishes to be served at a meal; a meal.

me·ow, mi·aou, mi·aow, mē·ou′, myou, *n.* [Imit.] A sound made by a cat.—*v.i.* To make such a sound. Also *mew.*

me·per·i·dine, me·per′i·dēn″, me·per′i·din, *n. Pharm.* a man-made narcotic, $C_{15}H_{21}NO_2·HCl$, employed as an analgesic and sedative.

Meph·is·to·phe·li·an, Meph·is·to·phe·le·an, mef″i·stō·fē′lē·an, *a.* Having diabolic qualities, as the prominent fictional character, Mephistopheles; fiendish; relentlessly evil; crafty; coldly cynical.

me·phi·tis, me·fī′tis, *n.* [L. *mephitis,* a pestilential exhalation.] A noxious or offensive exhalation arising from substances in the earth, as poisonous chemicals; a foul stench.—**me·phit·ic,** me·fit′ik, *a.* Pertaining to mephitis; having an offensive smell; noxious.—**me·phit·i·cal·ly,** *adv.*

me·pro·ba·mate, me·prō′ba·māt″, mep″rō·bam′āt, *n. Pharm.* a powder, $C_9H_{18}N_2O_4$, used as a tranquilizer and antispasmodic.

mer·bro·min, mèr·brō′min, *n. Pharm.* a compound, $C_{20}H_8Br_2HgNa_2O_6$, having the form of a green powder which, when mixed with water, produces a red solution employed as an antiseptic and germicide. Also *Mercurochrome.*

mer·can·tile, mur′kan·tēl″, mur′kan·til″, mur′kan·til, *a.* [Fr. *mercantile,* < It. *mercantile,* < L. *mercans* (*mercant-*), ppr. of *mercari,* trade.] Of or pertaining to merchants, trade, or commerce; commercial; *pol. econ.* of or pertaining to the mercantile system.

mer·can·tile sys·tem, *n. Pol. econ.* a system, developing with the rise of the modern nation state, which aimed at the acquisition of an ever increasing amount of precious metals by establishing a favorable balance of trade and exporting far more goods than those imported, and by setting up colonies as a source of needed goods and revenue and as a market. Also *mercantilism.*

mer·can·til·ism, mur′kan·ti·liz″um, mur′kan·tē·liz″um, mur′kan·tī·liz″um, *n.* Mercantile system; mercantile principles or practices; the mercantile spirit.—**mer·can·til·ist,** *n., a.*

mer·cap·tan, mèr·kap′tan, *n.* [G., < M.L. *mercurius,* mercury, and L. *captans* (*captant-*), ppr. of *captare,* strive to take.] *Chem.* any of a class of sulfur-containing compounds analogous to the alcohols and combining readily with mercury, esp. the most important member of this class, C_2H_5SH, ethyl mercaptan, a colorless liquid, with a pungent, garliclike odor.

Mer·ca·tor pro·jec·tion, *n.* [From Gerardus *Mercator* (Gerhard Kremer, 1512–1594), Flemish cartographer.] *Cartography,* a projection of the globe or part of it as a rectangular plane surface, the meridians being equidistant parallel straight lines, and the distance between the parallels of latitude increasing from the equator toward the pole, resulting in serious distortion of areas in the highest latitudes. Also **Mer·ca·tor's pro·jec·tion.**

mer·ce·nar·y, mur′se·ner″ē, *a.* [Fr. *mercenaire,* L. *mercenarius,* < *merces,* reward, wages.] Motivated by reasons of gain; obtained by hire: said only of soldiers serving a foreign state.—*n. pl.* **mer·ce·nar·ies.** One who is hired; a soldier hired into foreign service.—**mer·ce·nar·i·ly,** mur″se·nâr′i·lē, mur′se·ner″i·lē, *adv.*—**mer·ce·nar·i·ness,** *n.*

mer·cer, mur′sèr, *n.* [O.Fr. Fr. *mercier,* < L. *merx* (*merc-*), goods, wares.] *Brit.* a dealer in textile fabrics, esp. silks and other expensive cloths.—**mer·cer·y,** mur′se·rē, *n. pl.* **mer·cer·ies.** *Brit.* A mercer's fabrics; his shop.

mer·cer·ize, mur′se·rīz″, *v.t.*—**mercerized, mercerizing.** [From John *Mercer,* the originator.] To apply, as to cotton fabrics, caustic soda under stress or tension, in order to increase strength and sheen, and improve retention of dyes.

mer·chan·dise, mur′chan·dīz″, mur′chan·dīs″, *n.* [O.Fr. Fr. *marchandise,* < *marchand,* E. merchant.] Goods; wares, esp. manufactured products.—**mer·chan·dize,** *v.i., v.t.*—**merchandised, merchandising.** To carry on business activity; to buy or sell; to organize and conduct a campaign for the sale of. Also **mer·chan·dize.**—**mer·chan·dis·er, mer·chan·diz·er,** *n.*

mer·chant, mur′chant, *n.* [O.Fr. *mercheant,* later (also Fr.) *marchand,* < M.L. *mercatare,* freq. of L. *mercari,* trade, deal, buy, < *merx* (*merc-*), goods, wares.] One who buys and sells commodities for profit; retail dealer; shopkeeper; *Brit.* wholesale dealer. —*a.* Pertaining to trade or commerce; pertaining to the merchant marine.—**mer·chant·a·ble,** *a.* Marketable.

mer·chant·man, mur′chant·man, *n. pl.* **mer·chant·men.** A trading ship.

mer·chant ma·rine, *n.* The commercial ships belonging to a nation; the crew and officers on such ships.

Mer·cian, mur′shē·an, mur′shan, *a.* [From *Mercia,* an ancient Anglian kingdom in the central part of England.] Of or pertaining to Mercia, its inhabitants, or the dialect of Anglo-Saxon spoken there.—*n.* A native or inhabitant of the ancient kingdom of Mercia; any of the dialects spoken there.

mer·cu·rate, mur′kū·rāt″, *n. Chem.* a salt containing bivalent mercury. Also **mer·cu·ri·ate.**—*v.t.*—**mercurated, mercurating.** To mix or act on with mercury.—**mer·cu·ra·tion,** *n.*

mer·cu·ri·al, mèr·kur′ē·al, *a.* [L. *mercurialis.*] Lively; sprightly; fickle. (*Often cap.*) of or relating to the planet Mercury or the god Mercury. Containing or consisting of quicksilver or mercury.—*n.* A preparation of mercury used as a drug.—**mer·cu·ri·al·ly,** *adv.*—**mer·cu·ri·al·ness,** *n.*

mer·cu·ric, mèr·kur′ik, *a. Chem.* of or containing mercury, esp. bivalent mercury.

—mer·cu·rous, *a. Chem.* containing mercury in its univalent state.

Mer·cu·ro·chrome, mẽr·kūr′o·krōm″, *n.* Merbromin. (Trademark.)

mer·cu·ry, mụr′kū·rē, *n.* pl. **mer·cu·ries**. [L. *Mercurius*, the god, also the planet, M.L. *mercurius*, metallic mercury, prob. < L. *merx, merc-,* goods, wares; cf. *merchant*.] A heavy, silver-white metallic element remarkable for its liquid state at ordinary temperatures; quicksilver; a column of this substance used in a thermometer to indicate temperature, or in a barometer, to indicate air pressure. Sym. Hg, at. no. 80, at. wt. 200.59. See Periodic Table of Elements. Any herb of the genus *Mercurialis,* esp. the poisonous weed *M. perennis. (Cap.)* a Roman deity, messenger of the gods, and god of commerce, dexterity, eloquence, and thievery; the smallest planet in the solar system and nearest to the sun.

mer·cu·ry chlo·ride, *n.* An acrid, crystalline, highly poisonous compound, $HgCl_2$, produced by the sublimation of sulfate of mercury and sodium chloride, and used as an antiseptic, fungicide, disinfectant, and preservative, and in photography and chemical analysis. Also **mer·cu·ric chlo·ride**.

mer·cu·ry-va·por lamp, *n.* A lamp containing a tube of mercury vapor through which an electric discharge passes, emitting light chiefly in the ultraviolet region.

mer·cy, mụr′sē, *n.* pl. **mer·cies**. [Fr. *merci,* < L. *merces, merecedis,* pay, recompense, in L.L. mercy, < stem of *mereo,* to deserve.] Benevolence, mildness, or tenderness of heart; a disposition that tempers justice and leads to the infliction of a lighter punishment than law or justice will warrant; clemency; an act or exercise of benevolence or favor; a blessing; compassion or pity, or the power to display either.—**at one's mercy,** completely in one's power.—**mer·ci·ful,** mụr′si·fụl, *a.*—**mer·ci·ful·ly,** *adv.*—**mer·ci·ful·ness,** *n.*—**mer·ci·less,** mụr′si·lis, *a.*—**mer·ci·less·ly,** *adv.*—**mer·ci·less·ness,** *n.*

mer·cy seat, *n. O.T.* The covering of the ark of the covenant; God's throne.

mere, mēr, *a.—merest.* [O.Fr. *mier,* L. *merus,* pure, unmixed.] This or that and nothing else; simple; absolute; entire; utter; as, *mere* folly.—**mere·ly,** *adv.* Solely; simply; only; for this and no other purpose.

mere, mēr, *n.* [O.E. *mere,* lake, sea, = G. *meer* = Icel. *marr,* sea; akin to L. *mare,* sea.] *Poet.* A lake; a pond.

mer·e·tri·cious, mer″i·trish′us, *a.* [L. *meretricius,* < *meretrix, meretricis,* a prostitute, < *mereo,* to earn.] Having a gaudy but alluring appearance; showy, but in bad taste; insincere or deceptive; archaic, pertaining to prostitutes.—**mer·e·tri·cious·ly,** *adv.*—**mer·e·tri·cious·ness,** *n.*

mer·gan·ser, mẽr·gan′sẽr, *n.* [L. *mergo,* to dive, and *anser,* a goose.] Any of several species of diving ducks of the genus *Mergus,* having a narrow bill with serrated upper edges, and subsisting on fish.

merge, mụrj, *v.t.—merged, merging.* [L. *mergo,* to dip, to dive; seen also in *emerge, immersion, submerge.*] To cause to unite; to combine; blend so that individuality is obscured.—*v.i.* To be absorbed; to be incorporated; to be blended.—**mer·gence,** *n.*

merg·er, mụr′jẽr, *n.* The legal combination of corporations in which their assets are transferred to the resulting successor corporation; any combination of two or more businesses resulting in a single successor corporation or enterprise; a combination; a uniting.

me·rid·i·an, me·rid′ē·an, *n.* [O.Fr. *meridien* (Fr. *méridien),* < L. *meridianus,* < *meridies,* midday, the south, < *medius,*

middle, and *dies,* day.] *Geog.* a great circle of the earth passing through the poles and any given point on the earth's surface; the half of such a circle included between the poles. *Astron.* the great circle of the celestial sphere which passes through its poles and the observer's zenith. A point or period of highest development or greatest prosperity.—*a.* Of or pertaining to a meridian; of or pertaining to midday or noon; pertaining to a period of greatest elevation, prosperity, or splendor, as: Athens reached its *meridian* glory in the age of Pericles.

me·rid·i·o·nal, me·rid′ē·o·nal, *a.* [O.Fr. *meridional* (Fr. *méridional)* < L.L. *meridionalis,* < L. *meridies.*] Pertaining to a meridian; southern or southerly; characteristic of the south or of the people inhabiting the south of a country or continent.—*n.* An inhabitant of the south, esp. of the south of France.—**me·rid·i·o·nal dis·tance,** the distance east or west of a given meridian.—**me·rid·i·o·nal·ly,** *adv.*

me·ringue, me·rang′, *n.* A light mixture made of the beaten whites of eggs and sugar, usu. baked or browned, and used as a topping for pies and cakes, as a shell for ice cream or fruit, or as a small cake.

me·ri·no, me·rē′nō, *n.* pl. **me·ri·nos.** [Sp. *merino,* moving from pasture to pasture, < *merino,* an inspector of sheep walks, < L.L. *majorinus,* < L. *major,* greater.] A breed of sheep first raised in Spain, with long, fine wool; the wool of merino sheep; a soft, twilled wool, or wool and cotton fabric or yarn.—*a.* Made from the wool, fabric, or yarn of merino sheep.

mer·i·stem, mer′i·stem″, *n.* [< Gr. *meristós,* divided, < *merizein,* divide, < *méros,* part.] *Bot.* Embryonic tissue; undifferentiated, growing, actively dividing cells.—**mer·i·ste·mat·ic,** mer″i·ste·mat′ik, *a.*—**mer·i·ste·mat·i·cal·ly,** *adv.*

me·ris·tic, me·ris′tik, *a. Biol.* Separated into segments; divided; changing in number or shape by dividing.—**me·ris·ti·cal·ly,** *adv.*

mer·it, mer′it, *n.* [Fr. *mérite,* L. *meritum,* what is deserved, < *mereo,* to earn or deserve.] Excellence deserving honor or reward; worth; something that deserves a reward or punishment; *sometimes pl.* the state or fact of deserving; as, to treat a person according to his *merits. Pl.* the rights or wrongs of a case or question.—*v.t.* To be worthy of; to deserve.—**mer·i·ted,** mer′i·tid, *a.*—**mer·it·ed·ly,** *adv.*—**mer·it·less,** *a.*

mer·i·to·ri·ous, mer″i·tōr′ē·us, *a.* [L. *meritorius.*] Possessing or having merit; deserving reward or praise; praiseworthy. —**mer·i·to·ri·ous·ly,** *adv.*—**mer·i·to·ri·ous·ness,** *n.*

mer·it sys·tem, *n.* The system whereby U.S. civil service employees receive appointment and promotion on the basis of ability rather than by political pressure or patronage.

merle, merl, mụrl, *n.* [Fr. *merle,* a blackbird.] The European blackbird, *Turdus merula.*

mer·lin, mụr′lin, *n.* [Fr. *émerillon,* < L. *merula,* a blackbird, meaning blackbird hawk.] A small European falcon, *Falco columbarius aesalon;* the pigeon hawk, a closely related American bird.

mer·lon, mụr′lon, *n.* [Fr. *merlon,* < It. *merlone,* aug. of *merlo,* merlon.] In a battlement, the solid part between two embrasures or crenels.

mer·maid, mụr′mād″, *n.* [*Mer* is same as *mere,* a lake.] A fabled marine creature with the head and upper body of a woman and a fish's tail; a proficient female swimmer.— **mer·man,** *n.* pl. **mer·men.** The male counterpart of a mermaid.

mer·o·blas·tic, mer″o·blas′tik, *a. Biol.* of or denoting egg cells that only partially undergo subdivision or cleavage: opposed to *holoblastic.*—**mer·o·blas·ti·cal·ly,** *adv.*

mer·ri·ment, mer′i·ment, *n.* Gaiety; laughter; mirth; hilarity.

mer·ry, mer′ē, *a.—merrier, merriest.* [O.E. *myrie, murie,* pleasant; cf. Ir. and Gael. *maer,* Gael. *mir,* merry.] Cheery and full of fun; gay and noisy; mirthful; festive.— **make mer·ry,** to be jovial; to be festive.— **mer·ri·ly,** *adv.*—**mer·ri·ness,** *n.*

mer·ry-an·drew, mer″ē·an′drö, *n.* [From *Andrew* Borde, a physician to Henry VIII, who attracted attention by his facetious speeches.] A buffoon or clown.

mer·ry-go-round, mer′ē·gō·round″, *n.* A revolving machine, as a circular platform fitted with hobby-horses, on which persons, esp. children, ride for amusement; carousel; *fig.* any whirl or rapid round, as of business or social life. Also *carousel.*

mer·ry·mak·er, mer′ē·mā″kẽr, *n.* One who participates in a gay festivity; an entertainer; a reveler.

mer·ry·mak·ing, mer′ē·mā″king, *n.* A convivial entertainment; a festival; the participating in or contributing to a gay celebration.—*a.*

mer·ry·thought, mer′ē·thạt″, *n. Brit.* wishbone.

Mer·thi·o·late, mẽr·thī′o·lāt″, *n. Pharm.* thimerosal, a germicidal and antiseptic mercurial compound. (Trademark.)

me·sa, mā′sa, *Sp.* me′sä, *n.* [Sp., < L. *mensa,* table.] A comparatively small, high tableland or plateau with the sides descending steeply to the surrounding land, common in the southwestern U.S.

mé·sal·li·ance, mā″za·li′ans, mā·zal′ē·ans, *Fr.* mā·zäl·yäNs′, *n.* pl. **mé·sal·li·an·ces.** [Fr.] A marriage to a person of an inferior social rank.

mes·arch, mez′ärk, mes′ärk, mē′zärk, mē′särk, *a. Bot.* denoting a condition in which the primary xylem or wood tissue differentiates both toward the center and outside of the stems or other organs. Compare *endarch, exarch.*

mes·cal, me·skal′, *n.* [Sp. *mezcal;* < Mex.] An intoxicating spirit distilled from the fermented juice of certain species of agave; any agave yielding this spirit; either of two species of cactus, *Lophophora williamsii* and *L. lewinii,* of Texas and northern Mexico, whose buttonlike tops, mescal buttons, are dried and used as a stimulant, esp. by the Indians.

mes·ca·line, mes′ka·lēn″, mes′ka″lin, *n. Pharm.* a white, crystalline alkaloid, $C_{11}H_{17}NO_3$, which is produced from mescal buttons and can cause hallucinations.

mes·dames, mā·däm′, mā·dam′, *Fr.* mā·däm′, pl. of *madame* or *madam.* Abbr. *Mmes.*

mes·de·moi·selles, mā″de·mo·zel′, mäd″mwo·zel′, *Fr.* mäd·mwä·zel′, pl. of *mademoiselle.* Abbr. *Mlles.*

me·seems, me·sēmz′, *v. impers.*—past *meseemed. Archaic,* it seems to me.

me·sem·bry·an·the·mum, me·zem″brē·an′the·mum, me·zem″brē·ant′the·mum, *n. Bot.* any of several species of succulent, herbaceous plants of the genus *Mesembryanthemum,* native to southern Africa and a favorite ornamental of rock gardens.

mes·en·ceph·a·lon, mes″en·sef′a·lon″, mez″en·sef′a·lon″, *n.* [Gr. *mesos,* middle, and *enkephalos,* the brain.] The middle or central portion of the brain.—**mes·en·ce·phal·ic,** mes″en·se·fal′ik, *a.*

mes·en·chyme, mes′eng·kīm″, mez′eng·kīm″, *n. Biol.* the cells of the mesodermic layer of tissue that develop into certain structures such as the heart, blood and lymphatic vessels, cartilage, and bone.—

mes·en·chy·mal, mes·en·chym·a·tous, mes″eng·kim′a·tus, *a.*

mes·en·ter·on, mes·en′te·ron″, mez·en′-te·ron″, *n.* pl. **mes·en·ter·a,** mes·en′tèr·a, mez·en′tèr·a. [N.L.] *Embryol.* the early stages of the intestinal canal, bounded by endoderm.—**mes·en·ter·on·ic,** *a.*

mes·en·ter·y, mes′en·ter″ē, mez′en·ter″ē, *n.* pl. **mes·en·ter·ies.** [N.L. *mesenterium,* < Gr. *mesentérion,* < *mésos,* middle, and *enteron,* intestine.] *Anat.* a fold or duplicate of peritoneum investing and attaching to the posterior wall of the abdomen, a part or parts of the intestines or other abdominal viscera; *zool.* one of the membranous partitions which divide the digestive cavity in certain invertebrates. Also **mes·en·te·ri·um,—mes·en·ter·ic,** *a.*

mesh, mesh, *n.* [Cf. M.D. *masche, maesche,* D. *maas,* Gr. *masche,* Icel. *möskvi,* mesh, O.E. *max,* net.] An arrangement of interlaced or interlocked strands or wires uniformly spaced; netted or netlike work; one of the open spaces of network or a net. *Pl.* the threads that bind such spaces; the means of catching or holding fast; as, caught in the *meshes* of the law. *Mach.* the entanglement of gear teeth; *elect.* a set of branches within a network being such that removal of a branch opens the circuit; *metal.* a term designating the fineness of a powder determined by passing the powder through screens of a set gauge.—*v.t.* To catch or entangle in or as in the meshes of a net; enmesh; to form with meshes, as a net; to cause to interlock or match; *mach.* to engage, as gear teeth.—*v.i.* To become enmeshed; to interlock or match; *mach.* to become engaged, as the teeth of one wheel with those of another.—**mesh·work,** *n.* Meshed work; network.

me·shu·ga, me·shug·ga, me·shug′a, *a.* [Yiddish.] *Slang.* Insane; crazy.

me·si·al, mē′zē·al, mē′sē·al, mez′ē·al, mes′ē·al, *a.* [Gr. *mesos,* middle.] Middle; median.—**me·si·al plane,** an imaginary plane dividing the body longitudinally into symmetrical halves.—**me·si·al·ly, me·sal·ly,** *adv.*

me·sic, mez′ik, mes′ik, mē′zik, mē′sik, *a.* Having a medium amount of moisture.—**mes·i·cal·ly,** *adv.*

me·sit·y·lene, mi·sit′i·lēn″, mes′it·i·lēn″, *n. Chem.* a hydrocarbon, $C_6H_3(CH_3)_3$, having the form of a clear liquid, derived from coal tar or prepared synthetically, and used as a solvent.

mes·mer·ism, mez′me·riz″um, mes′me·riz″um, *n.* [From F. A. *Mesmer,* 1733–1815, German physician, who propounded the doctrine.] The doctrine of the induction of a hypnotic state through an influence or emanation transmitted from the operator to the subject; the induction, influence, or state concerned; in general, hypnotism.—**mes·mer·ic,** mez·mer′ik, mes·mer′ik, *a.*—**mes·mer·i·cal·ly,** *adv.*—**mes·mer·ist,** *n.*

mes·mer·ize, mez′me·rīz″, mes′me·rīz″, *v.t.*—**mesmerized, mesmerizing.** To hypnotize; to subject to spellbinding influence.—**mes·mer·i·za·tion,** mez″me·ri·zā′shan, mes″me·ri·zā′shan, *n.*—**mes·mer·iz·er,** *n.*

mesne, mēn, *a.* [Norm. *mesne,* middle, < *medianus,* middle *a.,* middle.] *Law,* middle or intermediate.

mesne lord, *n.* A feudal lord who holds the land of a superior but is, in turn, a landlord to a lesser tenant.

mes·o·blast, mez′o·blast″, mes′o·blast″, mē′zo·blast″, mē′so·blast″, *n.* [Gr. *mesos,* middle, and *blastos,* a bud.] *Embryol.* the middle layer of the primitive embryo which later becomes the mesoderm.—**mes·o·blas·tic,** *a.*

mes·o·carp, mez′o·kärp″, mes′o·kärp″, mē′zo·kärp″, mē′so·kärp″, *n.* [Gr. *mesos,* middle, and *karpos,* fruit.] *Bot.* the

middle part or layer of the pericarp, as the fleshy layer of some fruits.

mes·o·derm, mez′o·durm″, mes′o·durm″, mē′zo·durm″, mē′so·durm″, *n.* [Gr. *mesos,* middle, and *derma,* skin.] *Zool.* the middle layer of tissue between the ectoderm and the endoderm in the embryo of multicellular animals.—**mes·o·der·mal, mes·o·der·mic,** *a.*

Mes·o·lith·ic, mez″o·lith′ik, mes″o·lith′ik, mē″zo·lith′ik, mē″so·lith′ik, *a. Anthropol.* of or relating to the period of cultural transition dividing the Paleolithic period from the Neolithic.

mes·o·morph, mez′o·marf″, mes′o·marf″, mē′zo·marf″, mē′so·marf″, *n.* A muscular type of body structure developed by the relative dominance of tissues derived from the mesoderm, the middle of the three cell layers of the embryo; a person having this type of body structure.—**mes·o·mor·phic,** mez″o·mar′fik, mes″o·mar′fik, mē″zo·mar′fik, mē″so·mar′fik, *a.* Of, pertaining to, or characteristic of mesomorphs; *phys.* pertaining to a form intermediate between liquid and crystalline.—**mes·o·mor·phism,** *n.*—**mes·o·mor·phy,** *n.*

me·son, mē′zon, mē′son, mez′on, mes′on, *n. Phys.* any of a group of subatomic particles with variable masses between those of the electron and proton, neutral or carrying a positive or negative charge, and all of which being extremely short-lived. Also **mes·o·tron.**

mes·o·neph·ros, mez″o·nef′ros, mes″o·nef′ros, mē″zo·nef′ros, mē″so·nef′ros, *n.* pl. **mes·o·neph·roi,** mez″o·nef′roi, mes″o·nef′roi, mē″zo·nef′roi, mē″so·nef′roi. [N.L. (Gr. *nephros,* kidney).] *Embryol.* the central part of the embryonic renal organ of vertebrates.—**mes·o·neph·ric,** *a.*

mes·o·phyll, mez′o·fil, mes′o·fil, mē′zo·fil, mē′so·fil, *n. Bot.* the chlorophyll containing leaf tissues between the epidermal layers.—**mes·o·phyl·lic, mes·o·phyl·lous,** mez″o·fil′ik, mes″o·fil′ik, mē″zo·fil′ik, mē″so·fil′ik, *a.*

mes·o·phyte, mez′o·fīt″, mes′o·fīt″, mē′zo·fīt″, mē′so·fīt″, *n. Bot.* a plant, intermediate between a hydrophyte and a xerophyte, which grows in soil containing moderate amounts of moisture.—**mes·o·phyt·ic,** mez″o·fit′ik, mes″o·fit′ik, mē″zo·fit′ik, mē″so·fit′ik, *a.*

mes·o·sphere, mez′o·sfēr″, mes′o·sfēr″, mē′zo·sfēr″, mē′so·sfēr″, *n. Meteor.* The area from about 20 to 50 miles above the earth's surface, between the stratosphere and the thermosphere; an atmospheric layer located above the ionosphere, about 250 miles above the earth's crust.—**mes·o·spher·ic,** mez″o·sfer′ik, mes″o·sfer′ik, mē″zo·sfer′ik, mē″so·sfer′ik, *a.*

mes·o·the·li·um, mez″o·thē′lē·um, mes″o·thē′lē·um, mē″zo·thē′lē·um, mē″so·thē′lē·um, *n.* pl. **mes·o·the·li·ums, mes·o·the·li·a.** [N.L. (with *-thelium* as in *epithelium*).] *Embryol., anat.* That portion of the mesoderm which lines the primitive coelom of the embryo; epithelium having its origin in the mesoderm.—**mes·o·the·li·al,** *a.*

mes·o·tho·rax, mez″o·thôr′aks, mes″o·thôr′aks, mē″zo·thôr′aks, mē″so·thôr′aks, *n.* pl. **mes·o·tho·rax·es, mes·o·tho·ra·ces.** [N.L.] *Entom.* the middle one of the three divisions of an insect's thorax, bearing the first pair of wings and the middle pair of three pairs of legs.—**mes·o·tho·rac·ic,** mez″o·thō·ras′ik, mez″o·tha·ras′ik, mes″o·thō·ras′ik, mes″o·tha·ras′ik, mē″zo·thō·ras′ik, mē″zo·tha·ras′ik, mē″so·thō·ras′ik, mē″so·tha·ras′ik, *a.*

mes·o·tho·ri·um, mez″o·thôr′ē·um, mes″o·thôr′ē·um, mē″zo·thôr′ē·um, mē″so·thôr′ē·um, *n. Chem.* an isotope of either radium or actinium, both products of the disintegration of thorium.

Mes·o·zo·ic, mez″o·zō′ik, mes″o·zō′ik, mē″zo·zō′ik, mē″so·zō′ik, *a.* [Gr. *mesos,* middle, and *zoë,* life.] *Geol.* Noting or pertaining to an era between Paleozoic and Cenozoic times, marked by the appearance of flowering plants, and dominated by dinosaurs; pertaining to the group of rocks whose fossils represent forms of life of this era.—*n.*

mes·quite, mes·quit, me·skēt′, mes′kēt, *n.* [Sp. *mezquite;* < Mex.] A leguminous tree or shrub, *Prosopis glandulosa,* of the southwestern U.S. and Mexico, whose beanlike pods are rich in sugar and are used for livestock feed; any species of *Prosopis,* as the screw bean.

mess, mes, *n.* [O.Fr. *mes,* a dish, a course of dishes at table; It. *messo;* properly that which is sent, < L. *missus,* pp. of *mitto,* to send.] A disorderly mixture; a state of dirt and disorder; a situation of confusion or embarrassment; a muddle; a dish or quantity of food; food for a person at one meal; a number of persons who eat together, esp. in the military; the place where they eat; a sloppy or unappetizing preparation of food.—*v.i.* To make a dirty or untidy mess; to bungle; to meddle in; to busy oneself in an unorganized or confused way; to take meals in common with others, as one of a mess. —*v.t.* To cause to be untidy; to make a mess of, as one's affairs; to meddle in; to serve up or dish out food for; to supply with meals.—**mess·i·ly,** mes′i·lē, *adv.*—**mess·i·ness,** *n.*—**mess·y,** *a.*—*messier, messiest.*

mes·sage, mes′ij, *n.* [O.Fr. Fr. *message,* < M.L. *missaticum,* < L. *mittere,* pp. *missus,* send.] An oral, written, or signaled communication sent from a person or persons to another or others, as information, advice, tidings, direction, or the like; a telegram; an official communication, as from a chief executive to a legislative body; the point or significance of an utterance, novel, play, musical work, or the like; the business, errand, or mission of a messenger; an inspired communication to be delivered to the world; as, the *message* of a prophet; *computers,* a word or words taken as a single unit.

mes·sa·line, mes″a·lēn′, mes′a·lēn″, *n.* [Fr.] A thin, soft silk fabric with a twilled or satin weave.

mes·sen·ger, mes′en·jèr, *n.* [O.E. *messager,* Fr. *messager.* The *n* has intruded as in *passenger.*] One who delivers a message or does an errand; one who conveys dispatches from one government or official body to another; an envoy; courier; *archaic,* a harbinger or herald.

Mes·si·ah, mi·sī′a, *n.* [Heb. *mashiach,* anointed, < *māshach,* to anoint.] The deliverer and savior promised to the Jewish people; Jesus, regarded in the Christian religion as the savior; also **Mes·si·as.** (*Usu. l.c.*) a promised liberator; an ardent leader.—**Mes·si·ah·ship,** *n.*—**Mes·si·an·ic,** mes″ē·an′ik, *a.*

mes·sieurs, mes′èrz, Fr. mā·syœ′, pl. of *monsieur.* Abbr. *MM.*

mess jack·et, *n.* A man's waist-length jacket for semiformal occasions, also worn by waiters and bellhops as part of their uniform.

mess kit, *n.* A compact set of eating utensils, including plate, cup, knife, fork, and spoon, used esp. by soldiers and campers. Also **mess gear.**

Messrs., mes′èrz, *n. pl.* See *mister.*

mes·suage, mes′wij, *n.* [O.Fr. *messuage, mesnage,* L.L. *messuagium, mansionaticum,* < L. *mansio,* a dwelling.] *Law,* a dwelling house with the adjacent buildings and lands used by the household.

mes·ti·zo, me·stē′zō, mi·stē′zō, *n.* pl. **mes·ti·zos, mes·ti·zoes.** [Sp. *mestizo,*

L. *mixtus*, pp. of *misceo*, to mix.] The off-spring of a Caucasian and a person of some other race; an individual of mixed blood; in western U.S. and Spanish America, a person of Spanish and Indian ancestry.—**mes·ti·za**, *n.* A female mestizo.

me·tab·o·lism, me·tab'o·liz"um, *n.* [Gr. *metabole*, a change, < *metaballein*, to change, < *meta* (denoting change) and *ballein*, throw.] *Physiol.* the sum of the chemical changes in living organisms and cells by which food is converted into living protoplasm, *anabolism*, and by which protoplasm is used and broken down into simpler compounds and waste by liberation of energy, *catabolism*.—**met·a·bol·ic**, **met·a·bol·i·cal**, met"a·bol'ik, *a.*—**met··a·bol·i·cal·ly**, *adv.*

me·tab·o·lite, me·tab'o·lit", *n. Physiol.* anything produced by metabolic activity.

me·tab·o·lize, me·tab'o·liz", *v.t.*—*metabolized, metabolizing.* To subject to or alter by metabolism.

met·a·car·pal, met"a·kär'pal, *a.* Of or pertaining to the metacarpus.—*n.* A metacarpal bone.

met·a·car·pus, met"a·kär'pus, *n.* pl. **met·a·car·pi**, met"a·kär'pi. [N.L.] *Anat.* the part of a hand or forelimb, esp. its bony structure, included between the wrist or carpus and the fingers or phalanges.

met·a·cen·ter, *Brit.* **met·a·cen·tre**, met'a·sen"tẽr, *n.* [Fr. *métacentre*, < Gr. *meta*, after, and *kentron*, E. *center*.] *Nav. arch.* the point where the vertical line passing through the center of buoyancy of a ship or other floating body, in its normal upright position, meets the vertical line passing through the new center of buoyancy when the floating body is in a slightly inclined position: the stability of the floating body depending on this point being above the center of gravity of the body.—**met·a··cen·tric**, met"a·sen'trik, *a.*

met·a·gal·ax·y, met"a·gal'ak·sē, *n.* pl. **met·a·gal·ax·ies**. *Astron.* the entire universe, including all galaxies.—**met·a··ga·lac·tic**, met"a·ga·lak'tik, *a.*

met·a·gen·e·sis, met"a·jen'i·sis, *n. Zool.* reproduction characterized by the alternation of a sexual generation and a generation which reproduces asexually: occurring in the 'Coelenterates. Also *digenesis, heterogenesis*.—**met·a·ge·net·ic**, met"a·je·net'ik, *a.*—**met·a·ge·net·i·cal·ly**, *adv.*

met·al, met'al, *n.* [O.Fr. *metal*, Fr. *métal*, L. *metallum*, mine, mineral, metal, Gr. *metallon*, mine.] Any of a class of elementary substances as gold, silver, copper, and the like, many of which are characterized by opacity, ductility, conductivity, and a particular luster; an alloy or mixture composed wholly or partly of such substances; an object made of such material; formative material or mettle; as, candidates of comparable *metal*; glass in a state of fusion; *chiefly Brit.* material for roads, as broken stone; *print.* type metal.—*v.t.*—*metaled, metaling, metalled, metalling.* To cover or provide with metal.

met·al·ize, **met·al·lize**, met'al·liz", *v.t.*—*metalized, metalizing, metallized, metallizing.* To form into or unite with metal; to give metallic properties to.

me·tal·lic, me·tal'ik, *a.* [L. *metallicus*.] Pertaining to, resembling, or consisting of metal; having the qualities of metal.—**me·tal·li·cal·ly**, *adv.*

met·al·lif·er·ous, met"a·lif'ẽr·us, *a.* Containing, producing, or yielding metal.

met·al·line, met'al·lin, met'a·lin", *n.* Having or containing at least one metal or metallic salt; metallic; metallike.

met·al·log·ra·phy, met"a·log'ra·fē, *n.* The science or description of metals, esp. the study of metals and alloys by micro-scope; a process of printing using a metal plate in place of a stone.—**met·al·log··ra·pher**, *n.*—**met·al·lo·graph·ic**, me··tal"o·graf'ik, *a.*

met·al·loid, met'a·loid", *n.* Any of certain elements having some but not all of the properties of a metal, as bismuth and silicon.—*a.* Like a metal and a nonmetal; having the form, appearance, or properties of a metalloid. Also **met·al·loi·dal**.

met·al·lur·gy, met'a·lụr"jē, *Brit.* me··tal'ẽr·jē, *n.* [Gr. *ergon*, work.] The technical and scientific study of metals; the process of separating them from other materials in the ore; smelting, refining, shaping, and otherwise developing them.—**met·al·lur·gic**, **met·al·lur·gi·cal**, *a.*—**met·al·lur·gi·cal·ly**, *adv.*—**met·al·lur·gist**, met'a·lụr"jist, me·tal'ẽr·jist, *n.*

met·al·work, met'al·wụrk", *n.* Work, esp. artistic work, in metal; anything made of metal; shaping or forming of metal.—**met··al·work·er**, *n.*—**met·al·work·ing**, *n.*

met·a·mere, met'a·mẽr", *n.* [Gr. *meta*, with or among, and *meros*, a part.] In segmented animals, one of the segments; a somite.—**met·a·mer·ic**, met"a·mer'ik, *a.*—**met·a·mer·i·cal·ly**, *adv.*—**me·tam··er·ism**, me·tam'e·riz"um, *n.*

met·a·mor·phic, met"a·mạr'fik, *a.* [Gr. *meta-* (denoting change) and *morphē*, form.] Related to metamorphosis; characterized by change in structure or form. *Geol.* exhibiting metamorphism.

met·a·mor·phism, met"a·mạr'fiz·um, *n.* Change of form; metamorphosis; *geol.* a change in the structure or constitution of a rock due to natural agencies, as pressure and heat, esp. when the rock becomes harder and more crystalline.

met·a·mor·phose, met"a·mạr'fōz, met"·a·mạr'fōs, *v.t.*—*metamorphosed, metamorphosing.* To change into a different form; to change the shape or character of; to transform.—*v.i.* To be able to be, or to be transformed in character or shape.

met·a·mor·pho·sis, met"a·mạr'fo·sis, *n.* pl. **met·a·mor·pho·ses**, met"a·mạr'fo·sēz. [L., < Gr. *metamorphoun*, transform, < *meta-*, (denoting change) and *morphē*, form.] Change of form, structure, or substance; transformation by magic or witch-craft; any complete change in appearance, character, or circumstance; a form resulting from any such change; *zool.* a marked change in the form, and usu. the habits, of an animal in its development after the embryonic stage, as the transformation of a tadpole into a frog; *bot.* the structural or functional modification of a plant organ or structure during the course of its development; *pathol.* a change, as in structure, of an organ or tissues.

met·a·neph·ros, met"a·nef'ros, *n.* pl. **met·a·neph·roi**, met"a·nef'roi. [Gr. *meta*, after, *nephros*, a kidney.] *Biol.* in the embryonic stage of higher vertebrates, the third of three successive renal organs, developing into the kidney.—**met·a·neph··ric**, met·a·ne·phrit·ic, met"a·ne·frit'ik, *a.*

met·a·phase, met'a·fāz", *n. Biol.* that stage in the process of mitosis which is followed by the anaphase, and in which the separated chromosomes are arranged and attached at the spindle's equator.

met·a·phor, met'a·fạr", met'a·fẽr", *n.* [Fr. *métaphore*, < L. *metaphora*, < Gr. *meta-phora*, < *metapherein*, transfer, < *meta-* (denoting change) and *pherein*, bear.] A figure of speech in which a term or phrase is applied to something to which it is not literally applicable, in order to suggest a resemblance, as: She is the flower of my life.—**met·a·phor·ic**, **met·a·phor·i·cal**, met"a·fạr'i·kal, met"a·for'i·kal, *a.*—**met··a·phor·i·cal·ly**, *adv.*

met·a·phos·phate, met"a·fos'fāt, *n. Chem.* a salt or ester of metaphosphoric acid.

met·a·phos·phor·ic ac·id, met"a·fos··fạr'ik as'id, met"a·fos·for'ik as'id, *n. Chem.* HPO_3, a colorless acid obtained from phosphorous pentoxide, often used in dentistry and chemical analysis.

met·a·phys·ic, met"a·fiz'ik, *n.* [M.L. *metaphysica*, n. pl., < Gr. *meta*, after, and *physika*, things pertaining to nature (neut. pl. of *physikos*); orig. with reference to writings of Aristotle.] Metaphysics.

met·a·phys·ics, met"a·fiz'iks, *n. pl. but sing. in constr.* That branch of philosophy which treats of first principles, including ontology, the science of being, and cosmology, the science of universal order, and closely connected with epistemology, the science or theory of knowledge; in general, philosophy, esp. of the most speculative or esoteric nature.—**met·a·phys·i·cal**, *a.*—**met·a·phy·si·cian**, met"a·fi·zish'an, met"a·fiz'i·sist, *n.*

met·a·pla·sia, met"a·plā'zha, met"a·plā'zhē·a, *n.* [N.L., < Gr. *metaplassein*, form differently, < *meta-* (denoting change) and *plassein*, form, mold.] *Physiol.* the change of one kind of tissue into another kind.

met·a·plasm, met'a·plaz"um, *n.* [Gr. *metaplasmos*, transformation—*meta*, over, and *plasso*, to form.] *Gram.* a change in a word or sentence by adding, transposing, or removing a syllable, letter, or word. *Biol.* in the protoplasm of a cell, the starches, pigments, and other nonliving matter.—**met·a·plas·mic**, met"a·plaz'mik, *a.*

met·a·pro·tein, met"a·prō'tēn, met"a··prō'tē·in, *n. Biochem.* any product resulting from the action of an acid or alkali on a protein substance, and differing from the protein in solubility and usu. in composition.

met·a·psy·chol·o·gy, met"a·sī·kol'o·jē, *n.* The speculative study concentrating on the nature and function of the mind and the relation between the mental and physical processes.—**met·a·psy·cho·log·i·cal**, met"a·sī"ko·loj'i·kal, *a.*

met·a·so·ma·tism, met"a·sō'ma·tiz"um, *n.* [Gr. *meta-* (denoting change) and *soma* (*somat-*), body.] *Geol.* the process by which the chemical composition and texture of a rock is altered, usu. by replacement of one mineral with another. Also **met·a·so·ma·to·sis**, met"a·sō"ma·tō'sis.—**met·a·so·mat·ic**, met"a·sō·mat'ik, *a.*

me·ta·sta·ble, met'a·stā"bl, met"a·stā'bl, *a.* Having only a small degree of stability; *metal.* not subject to spontaneous change but chemically unstable; *phys.* a state of fine balance or equilibrium, which can be changed by altering certain conditions slightly to induce stability.

me·tas·ta·sis, me·tas'ta·sis, *n.* pl. **me··tas·ta·ses**, me·tas'ta·sēz". [L.L. < Gr. *metastasis, metistanas*, remove, change, < *meta*, denoting change, and *istanas*, cause to stand.] A transformation; a rapid transition, as from one subject to another; *pathol.* the transference, as through the blood or lymphatics, of diseased or disease-producing cells from one part of the body to another and the condition resulting from the transfer of such; *phys.* a basic change of position or orbit of a particle.—**met·a·stat·ic**, met"a·stat'ik, *a.*—**met·a·stat·i·cal·ly**, *adv.*

me·tas·ta·size, me·tas'ta·sīz", *v.i.*—*metastasized, metastasizing. Pathol.* of diseased or disease-producing cells, to transfer or extend to another part of the body.

met·a·tar·sal, met"a·tär'sal, *a.* Belonging to the metatarsus.—*n.* A bone of the metatarsus.—**met·a·tar·sal·ly**, *adv.*

met·a·tar·sus, met"a·tär'sus, *n.* pl. **met··a·tar·si**, met"a·tär'sī. [N.L.] *Anat., zool.* The part of a foot of a hind limb, esp. of its bony structure, included between the tarsus and the toes or phalanges.

me·tath·e·sis, me·tath′i·sis, *n. pl.* **me·-tath·e·ses,** me·tath′i·sēz″. [L.L. < Gr. *metathesis, metatithenai,* transpose, < *meta,* denoting change, and *titenai,* set.] The transposition of letters, syllables, or sounds in a word; a reversal of conditions; *chem.* a double decomposition, as when two compounds react with each other to form two other compounds.—**met·a·thet·ic, met·-a·thet·i·cal,** met″a·thet′ik, met″a·thet′i·kal, *a.*

met·a·tho·rax, met″a·thōr′aks, *n. pl.* **met·a·tho·rax·es, met·a·tho·ra·ces,** met″a·thōr′a·sēz, met″a·thar′a·sēz″. [N.L.] The posterior division of an insect's thorax, bearing the third pair of legs and the second pair of wings.—**met·a·tho·-ra·cic,** met″a·thō·ras′ik, *a.*

met·a·zo·an, met″a·zō′an, *n.* [N.L. *metazoön,* < Gr. *meta,* after, and *zoön,* animal.] Any of a large zoological division, *Metazoa,* comprising all the multicellular animals: distinguished from *Protozoa.*—*a.*—**met·a·-zo·al, met·a·zo·ic,** *a.*

mete, mēt, *v.t.*—**meted, meting.** [O.E. *metan* = D. *meten,* Goth. *mitan,* G. *messen,* to measure; Icel. *meta,* to value; < root of L., *modus,* a measure; Gr. *metron,* a measure; Skt. *mâ,* to measure.] To divide by measure; to allot, usu. followed by *out;* as, to *mete* out reward.

mete, mēt, *n.* [M.E. < M.Fr. < O.Fr. < L. *mēta,* goal.] A mark indicating a limit; a boundary.

met·em·pir·i·cal, met″em·pir′i·kal, *a.* [Gr. *meta,* beyond, and *empeiria,* experience, < *en,* in, and *peira,* trial, experiment.] Beyond or outside of experience; not based on experience; transcendental. Also **met·-em·pir·ic.**—**met·em·pir·i·cism, met·-em·pir·ics,** *n.*—**met·em·pir·i·cist,** *n.*

me·tem·psy·cho·sis, me·tem″si·kō′sis, me·temp″si·kō·sis, met″em·si·kō′sis, *n. pl.* **me·tem·psy·cho·ses,** me·tem″si·kō′sēz, me·temp″si·kō·sēz, met″em·si·kō′sēz. [Gr. *meta,* denoting change, *en,* in, and *psyche,* soul.] Transmigration; the passing of the soul of a man after death into some other human or animal body.—**met·em·psy·-chic, me·tem·psy·cho·sic, me·tem·psy·-cho·si·cal,** met″em·si′kik, *a.*

met·en·ceph·a·lon, met″en·sef′a·lon″, *n. pl.* **met·en·ceph·a·lons, met·en·ceph·-a·la,** met″en·sef′a·la. [N.L.] *Anat.* The posterior segment of the brain, practically coextensive with the medulla oblongata; the afterbrain; the epencephalon.—**met·en·-ce·phal·ic,** met″en·se·fal′ik, *a.*

me·te·or, mē′tē·ėr, *n.* [< Gr. *meteoros,* raised on high—*meta,* beyond, and *aeiro,* to raise.] *Astron.* a meteoroid white with heat from its terrific velocity upon entering the earth's atmosphere, and seen as a streak of light.

me·te·or·ic, mē″tē·ar′ik, mē″tē·or′ik, *a.* Pertaining to a meteor or meteors; relating to phenomena of the atmosphere; meteorological; *fig.* transiently brilliant.—**me·te·-or·ic i·ron,** iron as found in meteoric stones.—**me·te·or show·er, me·te·or·ic show·er,** the phenomenon observed when several meteors at once enter the earth's atmosphere, seeming to radiate out of a common point.—**me·te·or·ic stones,** aerolites that fall to the surface of the earth, usu. consisting of metallic iron and certain silicates.—**me·te·or·i·cal·ly,** *adv.*

me·te·or·ite, mē′tē·o·rīt″, *n.* A meteor which has reached the earth's crust without being completely consumed.—**me·te·or·-it·ic, me·te·or·it·i·cal, me·te·or·it·al,** mē″tē·o·rit′ik, mē″tē·o·rit′al, *a.*

me·te·or·it·ics, mē″tē·o·rit′iks, *n. pl. but sing. in constr.* The science of meteors.

me·te·or·o·graph, mē″tē·ar′o·graf″, mē″-tē·ar′o·gräf″, *n.* An apparatus which records or registers various meteorological phenomena simultaneously.—**me·te·or·-**

o·graph·ic, *a.*—**me·te·o·rog·ra·phy,** mē″tē·o·rog′ra·fē, *n.*

me·te·or·oid, mē′tē·o·roid″, *n. Astron.* any of the many small bodies which travel through interplanetary space and which, when entering the earth's atmosphere, become meteors or shooting stars.

me·te·or·o·log·i·cal el·e·ments, *n.* Any of the phenomena which are the objects of meteorological observation, esp. those conditions which largely determine the weather of a locality at a specific time, such as air temperature, humidity, wind velocity, cloud cover, and the like.

me·te·or·ol·o·gy, mē″tē·o·rol′o·jē, *n.* [Gr. *meteorologia.*] The science concerned with atmospheric phenomena, esp. in relation to weather and climate; the atmospheric phenomena and weather of a locality.—**me·te·or·o·log·ic, me·te·or·o·log·i·cal,** mē″tē·ėr·o·loj′ik, mē″tē·ėr·o·loj′i·cal·ly, *adv.*—**me·te·or·ol·o·gist,** *n.*

me·ter, me·tre, mē′tėr, *n.* [O.Fr. *metre* (Fr. *mètre*), < L. *metrum,* poetic meter, verse, < Gr. *metron,* measure, due measure, meter, verse; akin to L. *metiri,* to measure; Skt. *mā-,* measure, and perhaps ult. to E. *mete.*] *Pros.* poetic measure; arrangement of words in measured or rhythmic lines or verses; a particular form of such arrangement, based on the kind and number of feet constituting the verse; verse or poetry. *Mus.* the rhythmic element as measured by division into parts of equal time value.

me·ter, me·tre, mē′tėr, *n.* [Fr. *mètre,* < Gr. *metron,* measure.] *Metric system,* the fundamental unit of length, intended to be, and being very nearly, equal to one tenmillionth of the distance from the equator to the pole measured on a meridian, but actually being equal to the distance between two lines on a platinum-iridium bar preserved at the International Bureau of Weights and Measures, near Paris: equivalent to 39.37 inches. See Metric System table.

me·ter, mē′tėr, *n.* An instrument that measures, esp. one that automatically measures and records the quantity of gas, water, electricity, or the like, passing through it or actuating it.—*v.t.* To measure by means of a meter.

me·ter-kil·o·gram-sec·ond, mē′tėr-kil′o·gram″sek′ond, *a.* Of or relating to a measuring system in which the units of mass, length, and time are the kilogram, the meter, and the second.

me·ter maid, me·ter·maid, *n.* A woman authorized by the city to issue tickets for parking violations.

met·es·trus, met″es′trus, *n. Zool.* the time of regression in the estrous cycle of the female mammal.

meth·ac·ry·late, meth·ak′ri·lāt″, *n. Chem.* an ester or salt obtained from methacrylic acid.

meth·a·cryl·ic ac·id, meth′a·kril′ik as′id, meth″a·kril′ik as′id, *n. Chem.* a colorless synthetic acid, $C_4H_6O_2$, whose esters are the basis of many plastics.

meth·a·done, meth′a·dōn″, *n.* A synthetic, habit-forming drug used to induce sleep and dull pain. Also **meth·a·don,** meth′a·don″.

meth·ane, meth′ān, *n.* [< *methyl.*] *Chem.* a colorless, odorless, flammable gas, CH_4, the first member of a homologous series of hydrocarbons, occurring in the emanations from marshes and the firedamp of coal mines, and obtained from natural gas.

meth·ane se·ries, *n. Chem.* a homologous series of saturated aliphatic hydrocarbons, C_nH_{2n+2}. Also **al·kane se·ries, par·af·fin se·ries.**

meth·a·nol, meth′a·nōl″, meth′a·nal″, meth′a·nol″, *n. Chem.* a flammable watersoluble, volatile, highly toxic, liquid

alcohol, CH_3OH, used in chemical synthesis and as an antifreeze, fuel, solvent, and denaturant for ethyl alcohol. Also *methyl alcohol, wood alcohol.*

met·he·mo·glo·bin, met·hae·mo·glo·bin, met·hē′mo·glō′bin, met·hem′o·glō″bin, met·hē″mo·glō′bin, met·hem″o·glō′bin, *n. Biochem.* a brownish compound, a combination of oxygen and hemoglobin, formed in the blood, occurring in the use of certain drugs.

me·the·na·mine, me·thē′na·mēn″, me·thē′na·min, *n. Chem.* a hydrocarbon, $C_6H_{12}N_4$, used as an antiseptic and a vulcanizing accelerator. Also *hexamethylenetetramine.*

me·thinks, mi·thingks′, *v. impers.*—past *methought. Archaic,* it seems to me.

me·thi·o·nine, me·thi′o·nēn″, me·thi′o·nin, *n.* [< *me(thyl)* and *thio-* and *-ine.*] *Biochem.* a natural or synthetic amino acid, $C_5H_{11}O_2NS$, used in warding off or treating certain diseases of the liver.

meth·od, meth′od, *n.* [Fr. *méthode,* L. *methodus,* < Gr. *methodos*—*meta,* after, and *hodos,* a way.] A manner of procedure, esp. a systematic or clearly defined way of accomplishing an end; plan; system or order in thought or action; the plan of procedure characteristic of a discipline; logical or scientific arrangement.—**the meth·od,** a theory of acting technique developed by Constantin Stanislavski emphasizing the value of an actor's own emotional experience in his efforts to understand and convincingly recreate the motives and behavior of his character. Also **the Meth·od,** *the Stanislavski method, the Stanislavski system.*—**me·thod·i·cal, me·thod·ic,** me·thod′i·kal, me·thod′ik, *a.* Marked by systematic behavior; painstaking; in systematic order.—**me·thod·i·cal·ly,** *adv.*—**me·thod·i·cal·ness,** *n.*

Meth·od·ist, meth′o·dist, *n.* A follower or member of the sect of Christians founded by John Wesley, so called from the regularity of their lives and their strict observance of religious duties; (*l.c.*) one characterized by strict adherence to method.—*a.*—**Meth·od·ism,** meth′o·diz″um, *n.* The doctrines and worship of the Methodists.—**Meth·od·is·tic,** meth″od·is′tik, *a.*

meth·od·ize, meth′o·dīz″, *v.t*—*methodized, methodizing.* To reduce to method; to prepare by following a method.—**meth·-od·iz·er,** *n.*

meth·od·ol·o·gy, meth″o·dol′o·jē, *n. pl.* **meth·od·ol·o·gies.** The system of methods or of classification as it is applied by a science or art; *logic,* the study of procedures fundamental to the organization of a science or a field of study.—**meth·-od·o·log·i·cal,** meth″o·do·loj′i·kal, *a.* —**meth·od·o·log·i·cal·ly,** *adv.*—**meth·-od·ol·o·gist,** *n.*

meth·ox·ide, meth·ok′sīd, meth·ok′sid, *n.* Methylate.

me·thox·y·chlor, me·thok′si·klôr″, *n.* An insecticide, less toxic than DDT, consisting of a white crystalline solid, Cl_3CCH-$(C_6H_4OCH_3)_2$. Also **DMDT, me·thox·y DDT.**

Me·thu·se·lah, me·thō′ze·la, me·thōz′la, *n. O.T.* a patriarch who lived 969 years. Gen. v. 27. *Fig.* one who lives to an extraordinarily great age.

meth·yl, meth′il, *n.* [Gr. *meta,* after, with, and *hylē,* wood.] *Chem.* a univalent hydrocarbon radical, CH_3.—**me·thyl·ic, me·-thil′ik,** *a.*

meth·yl·al, meth″i·lal′, meth′i·lal″, *n. Chem.* a colorless, volatile liquid compound, $CH_3OCH_2OCH_3$, with a pleasant odor, obtained by the oxidation of methyl alcohol, and used in organic synthesis, perfumes, adhesives, and protective coatings.

---

ch- chain, G. na*ch*t; **th-** THen, thin; **w-** wig, hw as sound in whig; **z-** zh as in azure, zeal. *Italicized vowel* indicates schwa sound.

meth·yl al·co·hol, *n.* Methanol.

meth·yl·a·mine, meth″*i·*la·mēn′, meth″-il·am′in, *n. Chem.* a flammable, colorless gas, CH_3NH_2, characterized by its penetrating ammoniacal odor and used primarily in industry, esp. in tanning and pharmaceuticals.

meth·yl·ate, meth′*i·*lāt″, *n. Chem.* a methyl alcohol derivative in which the hydrogen of the hydroxyl group has been replaced by a metal. Also *methoxide.—v.t.—methylated, methylating.* To combine with methyl; mix with methyl alcohol.—**meth·yl·a·tion,** meth″*i·*lā′shan, *n.*—**meth·yl·a·tor,** *n.*

meth·yl·at·ed spir·it, *n.* Ethyl alcohol denatured with wood alcohol, which renders it unfit for human consumption. Also **meth·yl·at·ed spir·its.**

meth·yl bro·mide, *n. Chem.* a highly poisonous gas or liquid, CH_3Br, used esp. in organic synthesis, and as a refrigerant, fumigant, or solvent. Also **bro·mo·meth·ane.**

meth·yl·ene, meth′*i·*lēn″, *n. Chem.* a bivalent hydrocarbon radical, CH_2, occurring in many compounds.

meth·yl·ene blue, *n. Chem., pharm.* a compound, $C_{16}H_{18}N_3ClS·3H_2O$, used as a chemical indicator in oxidation-reduction reactions, a stain in bacteriology and biology, and an antidote in cyanide poisoning. Also **meth·yl·thi·o·nine chlo·ride,** meth″*il·*thi′o·nēn″ klôr′īd, meth″*il·*thi′o·nin.

me·tic·u·lous, me·tik′ū·lus, *a.* [Fr. *méticuleux,* L. *metus,* fear.] Overly scrupulous concerning small details; exceedingly careful or fastidious.—**me·tic·u·lous·ly,** *adv.*—**me·tic·u·lous·ness, me·tic·u·los·i·ty,** me·tik″ū·los′i·tē, *n.*

mé·tier, mā′tyā, mā·tyā′, *n.* [Fr.] Profession; occupation; specialty; an activity for which a person is particularly skilled or trained.

mé·tis, mā·tēs′, mā·tē′, *n. pl.* **mé·tis,** mā·tēs′, mā·tēz′. [Fr., an analogy of mestizo.] (*Often cap.*) One of racially mixed heritage; in Canada, a person of American Indian and French-Canadian parentage.

Me·tol, mē′tōl, mē′tal, mē′tol, *n.* [G.] *Photog.* a soluble white powder used as a developer. (Trademark.)

Me·ton·ic cy·cle, mi·ton′ik sī′kl, *n.* [From *Meton,* a 5th century B.C. astronomer.] The cycle of synodic months, equivalent to nineteen years, in which the phases of the moon return to the pattern they assumed at the cycle's start with relation to the days of the year.

me·ton·y·my, me·ton′i·mē, *n.* [Gr. *metōnymia—meta,* denoting change, and *onoma,* a name.] *Rhet.* a figure by which one word is substituted for another on account of some actual relation between the things signified, as when we say, "We read Virgil," that is, his *poems* or *writings.*—**met·o·nym,** met′o·nim, *n.*—**met·o·nym·i·cal,** met″o·nim′i·kal, *a.*

me-too, mē′tö′, *a.* Characterized by the attempt to imitate policies or tactics used successfully by rivals, esp. in politics.—**me-too·er,** *n.*—**me-too·ism,** *n.*

met·o·pe, met′o·pē″, met′ōp, *n.* [Gr. *metopē,* < *meta,* between, and *opē,* opening, hole.] *Arch.* one of the square spaces, either decorated or plain, between triglyphs in the Doric frieze. Also **in·ter·tri·glyph.**

me·top·ic, me·top′ik, *a.* [Gr. *metōpon,* forehead.] *Anat.* Of or pertaining to the forehead; frontal.

Met·ra·zol, me′tra·zōl″, me′tra·zạl″, me′tra·zol″, *n. Pharm.* a stimulant, pentylenetetrazol, $C_6H_{10}N_4$, used in treating certain heart conditions and some mental disorders. (Trademark.)

met·ric, me′trik, *n.* A standard or method for measuring; *pl. but sing in constr.* the branch of prosody concerned with meter.

met·ric, me′trik, *a.* Pertaining to a measurement system using the meter as a basis. Also *metrical.*

met·ri·cal, me′tri·kal, *a.* Pertaining to rhythm or meter; consisting of poetic meter; of or relating to measurement. Also *metric.*—**met·ri·cal·ly,** *adv.*—**met·rist,** me′trist, mē′trist, *n.* A composer of verses.

met·ric sys·tem, *n.* A widely used decimal system of weights and measures, employing the gram and the meter as its basic units. See Metric System table.

met·ric ton, *n.* See Metric System table.

met·ri·fy, me′tri·fī″, *v.t.—metrified, metrifying.* [O.Fr. *metrifier,* < M.L. *metrificare,* < L. *metrum,* meter, verse.] To put into meter or compose in verse.—**met·ri·fi·ca·tion,** me″tri·fi·kā′shan, *n.*—**met·ri·fi·er,** *n.*

met·ro, me′trō, *n. pl.* **met·ros.** (*Often cap.*) In European cities, esp. London and Paris, an underground railway; subway. Also *Fr.* **mé·tro,** mā·trō′.

me·trol·o·gy, mi·trol′o·jē, *n. pl.* **me·trol·o·gies.** [Fr. *métrologie.*] The science of measures and weights; a system of measures. See Measures and Weights table.—**met·ro·log·i·cal,** me″trō·loj′i·kal, *a.*—**met·ro·log·i·cal·ly,** *adv.*—**me·trol·o·gist,** *n.*

met·ro·nome, me′trō·nōm″, *n.* [Gr. *metron,* measure, and *nómos,* law.] An instrument operated either mechanically or electrically for marking exact time, used esp. in music practice.—**met·ro·nom·ic,** me″trō·nom′ik, *a.*—**met·ro·nom·i·cal·ly,** *adv.*

me·tron·o·scope, me·tron′o·skōp″, *n.* A mechanical device employing timed intervals of printed matter, used to test or develop reading speeds.

me·tro·nym·ic, me″trō·nim′ik, me″trō·nim′ik, *n., a.* Matronymic.

me·trop·o·lis, me·trop′o·lis, *n. pl.* **me·trop·o·lis·es.** [L.L., < Gr. *mētropolis, mētēr,* mother, and *polis,* city.] The chief city, though not necessarily the capital, of a country, state, or region; a central or principal point of urban activity; as, a commercial *metropolis;* the mother city or state of an ancient Greek colony; the chief see of an ecclesiastical province.

met·ro·pol·i·tan, me″trō·pol′i·tan, *a.* [L.L. *metropolitanus.*] Pertaining to or constituting a metropolis or chief city; as, a *metropolitan* city; characteristic of a metropolis or chief city, or of its inhabitants; pertaining to or constituting a mother country; pertaining to an ecclesiastical metropolis; as, a *metropolitan* bishop.—*n.* An inhabitant of a metropolis; one having metropolitan manners; a citizen of the mother city or parent state of a colony; the bishop or similar-ranking cleric presiding over the bishops of an ecclesiastical province.—**met·ro·pol·i·tan·ism,** *n.*

met·tle, met′l, *n.* [An altered spelling of *metal,* which was formerly used in the same sense.] Characteristic temperament; spirit; courage; ardor.—**put a man on his met·tle,** to stimulate a man to do his utmost.—**met·tle·some,** met′l·som, *a.* Spirited; courageous; ardent. Also **met·tled.**

mew, mū, *v.i.* [Imit. Cf. W. *mewian,* G. *miauen,* to mew.] To cry as a cat.—*n.* The cry of a cat. Also *meow.*

mew, mū, *n.* [O.E. *mœw,* a gull or mew.] A sea gull, esp. *Larus canus,* the common European gull.

mew, mū, *n.* [Fr. *mue,* a molting, a mew or cage, < L.L. *muta,* a mew, < L. *mutare,* to change.] A cage for hawks or other birds while molting; a place of confinement, retirement, or concealment.

Pl. but sing. or pl. in constr., chiefly Brit. stables or coach houses, usu. with living quarters, situated around a court, alley, or back street; the lane, alley, or street lined by stables or mews.—*v.t.* To shut up, enclose, or confine, as in a cage.

mewl, mūl, *v.i.* [Imit.; compare *miaul,* Fr. *miauler.*] To cry feebly, as a child.

Mex·i·can, mek′si·kan, *a.* Of or pertaining to Mexico or the people of Mexico.—*n.* A native or inhabitant of Mexico.

Mex·i·can bean bee·tle, *n.* A ladybug with spotted wings, *Epilachna varivestis,* that feeds on the foliage of bean plants.

Mex·i·can hair·less, *n.* Any of the breed of virtually hairless, small dogs indigenous to Mexico.

me·zu·zah, me·zuz′a, *Heb.* me·zö·zä′, *n. pl.* **me·zu·zahs,** *Heb.* **me·zu·zoth,** *Heb.* me·zö·zạt′.[Heb.,doorpost.]*Judaism,*a piece of parchment inscribed on one side with the passages Deut. vi. 4–9 and xi. 13–21, and on the other with the word 'Shaddai,' a name applied to God, and so placed in a case that the divine name is visible from the outside, the case being attached to the doorpost of a house in fulfillment of the injunction in each of the passages.

mez·za·nine, mez′a·nēn″, mez′a·nēn′, *n.* [It. *mezzanino,* < *mezzo,* middle.] *Arch.* a story situated between two main ones; an entresol. The lower theater balcony or the first rows of balcony seats.

mez·za vo·ce, met′sa vō′chā, mez′a vō′chä, *It.* med′dzä va̧′che, *a., adv. Mus.* at half the possible vocal power: used as a direction to the vocalist.

mez·zo, met′sō, mez′ō, *It.* med′dzạ, *a.* [It., < L. *medius,* middle.] Middle; medium; half.

mez·zo for·te, met′sō fạr′tā, mez′ō fạr′tä, *It.* med′dzạ fạr′te, *a., adv. Mus.* Medium loud; halfway between soft and loud: used as a vocal or instrumental direction.

mez·zo pi·a·no, met′sō pē·ä′nō, mez′ō pē·ä′nō, *It.* med′dzạ pyä′na̧, *a., adv. Mus.* medium soft but not as soft as piano: used as a vocal or instrumental direction.

mez·zo-so·pran·o, met′sō·so·pran′ō, met′sō·so·prä′nō, mez′ō·so·pran′ō, mez′ō·so·prä′nō, *n. pl.* **mez·zo-so·pran·os, mez·zo-so·pran·i,** met′sō·so·prä′nē, mez′ō·so·prä′nē. [It.] *Mus.* A voice or voice part intermediate in range between soprano and contralto; a person having such a voice.

mez·zo·tint, met′sō·tint″, mez′ō·tint″, *n.* [It. *mezzotinto,* half-tint.] A style of metal engraving in which the roughened surfaces of copper or steel plates are smoothed or scraped, by burnishing or other hand tooling, to delineate dark and light shades; a print from such an engraving.—*v.t.* To engrave in mezzotint.—**mez·zo·tint·er,** *n.*

mho, mō, *n.* [Reversed spelling of *ohm.*] *Elect.* a unit of conductivity, equal to the conductivity of a body whose resistance is one ohm.

mi, mē, *n. Mus.* The syllable used for the third tone of the scale, as E in the major scale of C; the tone E.

mi·aow, mē·ou′, myou, *v.t., n.* Meow.

mi·as·ma, mi·az′ma, mē·az′ma, *n. pl.* **mi·as·mas, mi·as·ma·ta,** mi·az′ma·ta, mē·az′ma·ta. [N.L. < Gr. *miasma,* pollution, < *miainein,* stain, pollute.] A threatening, poisonous, or morbid element of the atmosphere; foul-smelling emanations from decaying organic matter, formerly believed poisonous.—**mi·as·mal, mi·as·mat·ic, mi·as·mic,** mi″az·mat′ik, *a.*

mi·ca, mi′ka, *n.* [L. *mico,* to glitter.] *Mineral.* a silicate of layered structure, consisting of thin flexible laminae or scales which easily separate, and having a shining, almost metallic luster. See *isinglass.*—**mi·ca·ceous,** mi·kā′shus, *a.*

METRIC SYSTEM

Linear Measure

Unit	Number of meters	U.S. equivalent
micron (μ)	0.000001	0.00003937 inch, 0.03937 mil
millimeter (mm)	0.001	0.03937 inch, 39.37 mils
centimeter (cm)	0.01	0.3937 inch
decimeter (dm)	0.1	3.937 inches
meter (m)	1	39.37 inches
dekameter (dkm)	10	10.93 yards, 32.81 feet
hectometer (hm)	100	109.36 yards, 328.1 feet
kilometer (km)	1000	0.6214 mile

Area

Unit	Number of centares	U.S. equivalent
square millimeter (mm²)	0.000001	0.00155 square inch
square centimeter (cm²)	0.0001	0.155 square inch
centare (ca) or square meter (m²)	1	10.76 square feet
deciare (da)	10	11.96 square yards
aretare (a) or square dekameter (dkm²)	100	119.60 square yards
dekare (dka)	1,000	0.247 acre
hectare (ha) or square hectometer (hm²)	10,000	2.471 acres
square kilometer (km²)	1,000,000	0.386 square mile

Capacity

Unit	Number of liters	Metric equivalent cubic centimeters	U.S. equivalent cubic	U.S. equivalent dry	U.S. equivalent liquid
milliliter (ml)	0.001	1	0.061 cubic inch	0.0018 pint	0.034 fluidounce
centiliter (cl)	0.01	10	0.61 cubic inch	0.018 pint	0.338 fluidounce
deciliter (dl)	0.1	100	6.10 cubic inch	0.18 pint	3.381 fluidounces
liter (l)	1	1,000	61.02 cubic inch	0.908 quart	1.057 quarts
dekaliter (dkl)	10	10,000	0.35 cubic foot	1.14 pecks	2.643 gallons
hectoliter (hl)	100	100,000	3.53 cubic feet	2.84 bushels	26.425 gallons
kiloliter (kl)	1,000	1,000,000	1.31 cubic yards	28.38 bushels	264.25 gallons

Volume

Unit	Number of steres	U.S. equivalent
cubic millimeter (mm³)	0.000000001	0.000061 cubic inch, 0.016 minim
cubic centimeter (cm³ or cc)	0.000001	0.061 cubic inch
cubic decimeter (dm³)	0.001	61.02 cubic inches
decistere (ds)	0.1	3.53 cubic feet
stere (s) or cubic meter (m³)	1	1.308 cubic yards, 35.31 cubic feet
dekastere (dks)	10	13.079 cubic yards
cubic dekameter (dkm³)	1,000	1,307.943 cubic yards

Mass and Weight

Unit	Number of grams	U.S. equivalent (Avoirdupois weight)
milligram (mg)	0.001	0.0154 grain
centigram (cg)	0.01	0.154 grain
decigram (dg)	0.1	1.543 grains
gram (g or gm)	1	0.0353 ounce, 15.43 grains
dekagram (dkg)	10	0.353 ounce
hectogram (hg)	100	3.527 ounces
kilogram (kg)	1,000	2.205 pounds
metric ton (MT or t)	1,000,000	1.102 tons, 2,204.6 pounds

mi·celle, mi·sel′, *n. Chem.* an aggregate of molecular structural units joined chemically and existing in some colloidal solutions; *biol.* an ultramicroscopic structural unit of protein or other material within the protoplasm of a cell.—**mi·cel·lar**, *a.*

Mich·ael·mas, mik′el·mas, *n.* [*Michael*, and *mass*, a feast.] *Brit.* The feast honoring St. Michael, the archangel, celebrated on the 29th of September; one of England's quarter days, when rents or other quarterly payments are due.

Mich·ael·mas dai·sy, *n.* Any of various species of aster blooming at the time of Michaelmas.

Mick·ey Finn, mik′ē fin, *n.* (*Sometimes l.c.*), *slang*, a drink of liquor, or other beverage, to which a drug has secretly been added to render the unsuspecting drinker unconscious. Also **mick·ey, mick·y**.

mi·cro·anal·y·sis, mī″krō·a·nal′i·sis, *n. Chem.* analysis of extremely minute amounts of material.

mi·cro·bar·o·graph, mī′kro·bär′o·graf″, mī″kro·bär′o·gräf″, *n.* A barograph for recording extremely small fluctuations of atmospheric pressure.

mi·crobe, mī′krōb, *n.* [Gr. *mikros*, small, *bios*, life.] A microscopic organism, as a bacterium, esp. a pathogenic species; microorganism.—**mi·cro·bi·al, mi·cro·bi·an, mi·cro·bic**, *a.*

mi·cro·bi·ol·o·gy, mī″krō·bī·ol′o·jē, *n.* The science and study of microscopic organisms.—**mi·cro·bi·o·log·ic, mi·cro·bi·o·log·i·cal**, mī″krō·bī′o·loj′i·kal, *a.* —**mi·cro·bi·o·log·i·cal·ly**, *adv.*—**mi·cro·bi·ol·o·gist**, *n.*

mi·cro·cli·mate, mī′kro·klī′mit, *n.* The climate of a particular site or small area, as a cave, forest, or habitat: opposed to *macroclimate*.—**mi·cro·cli·mat·ic**, mī″krō·klī·mat′ik, *a.*—**mi·cro·cli·ma·to·log·i·cal**, mī″krō·klī″ma·to·loj′i·kal, *a.*—**mi·cro·cli·ma·tol·o·gy**, mī″krō·klī″ma·tol′o·jē, *n.*

mi·cro·cline, mī′kro·klīn″, *n.* [G. *mikroklin*, < Gr. *micrós*, small, and *klinein*, incline.] A multicolored mineral of the feldspar family, similar to orthoclase but of the triclinic system, and used in making glass and enamelware, glazing pottery, and in electrical insulators.

mi·cro·coc·cus, mī″kro·kok′us, *n.* pl. **mi·cro·coc·ci**, mī″kro·kok′sī. [N.L., < Gr. *micrós*, small, and N.L. *coccus*.] Any species of the genus *Micrococcus*, comprising globular or oval bacterial organisms of which certain species cause disease, and others produce fermentation.

mi·cro·cop·y, mī′kro·kop″ē, *n.* pl. **mi·cro·cop·ies.** A photographic reduction of a printed page, document, or other graphic material.—*v.t., v.i.—microcopied, microcopying.*

mi·cro·cosm, mī′kro·koz″um, *n.* [Fr. *microcosme*, < M.L. *microcosmus*, < Gr. *mikrós*, small, and *kósmos*, world.] A little world; anything regarded as a world in miniature; often, man viewed as an epitome of the great world or universe. Also **mi·cro·cos·mos**, mī″kro·koz′mos, mī″kro·koz′mōs.—**mi·cro·cos·mic, mi·cro·cos·mi·cal**, *a.*—**mi·cro·cos·mi·cal·ly**, *adv.*

mi·cro·cos·mic salt, *n. Chem.* a phosphate of sodium and ammonium, $NaNH_4HPO_4·4H_2O$, used as a reagent in tests for metallic oxides and certain salts.

mi·cro·crys·tal·line, mī″krō·kris′ta·lin, mī″krō·kris′ta·līn″, *a.* Minutely crystalline; composed of microscopic crystals.—**mi·cro·crys·tal·lin·i·ty**, mī″krō·kris″ta·lin′i·tē, *n.*

mi·cro·cyte, mī′kro·sīt″, *n. Pathol.* one of the dwarfed or abnormally small red corpuscles of the blood occurring in certain forms of anemia.—**mi·cro·cyt·ic**, mī″kro·sit′ik, *a.*

mi·cro·e·lec·tron·ics, mī″krō·i·lek·tron′iks, mī″krō·ē″lek·tron′iks, *n. pl. but sing. in constr.* The area of miniaturization in the electronics field, esp. the application of subminiature elements in electronic systems, as solid-state transistors.

mi·cro·film, mī′kro·film″, *n.* Film containing a photographic copy of printed or graphic material, greatly reduced in size but able to be enlarged by viewing through a special enlarger, having the advantage of permanency and of occupying small space. —*v.t.*

mi·cro·gam·ete, mī″krō·gam′ēt, mī″krō·ga·mēt′, *n. Biol.* the male and smaller gamete of an organism which has unlike gametes.

mi·cro·gram, mī′kro·gram″, *n.* A unit of weight equaling one millionth of one gram; a micrographic photograph or drawing.

mi·cro·graph, mī′kro·graf″, mī′kro·gräf″, *n.* An instrument for executing extremely minute writing or engraving; a photograph or a drawing of an object as seen through a microscope.—**mi·cro·graph·ic**, mī″kro·graf′ik, *a.*—**mi·crog·ra·phy**, mī·krog′ra·fē, *n.* The art of writing in very small characters; the description or depiction of microscopic objects; examination with the microscope.

mi·cro·groove, mī′kro·grōv″, *n.* A closely spaced groove cut on long-playing phonograph records for the purpose of including more material on a single disk.

mi·cro·me·te·or·ite, mī″krō·mē′tē·o·rīt″, *n.* A meteorite or meteoritic particle less than one millimeter in diameter, small enough to pass through the earth's atmosphere without being destroyed by heat.

mi·cro·me·te·or·oid, mī″krō·mē′tē·o·roid″, *n. Aerospace*, a minute meteoroid such as those encountered by space probes or satellites.

mi·crom·e·ter, mī·krom′i·tėr, *n.* [Gr. *mikros*, small, and *metron*, a measure.] An instrument or device fitted to a telescope or microscope for measuring very small distances, diameters, or angles.—**mi·crom·e·try**, *n.*

mi·crom·e·ter cal·i·per, *n.* A gauge or caliper with a spindle moved by a micrometer screw: used for making accurate measurements.

mi·crom·e·ter screw, *n.* A screw with fine threading and a calibrated head used primarily in micrometers.

mi·cro·mi·cron, mī″krō·mī′kron, *n.* A unit of length equal to one millionth part of a micron.

mi·cro·mil·li·me·ter, mī″krō·mil′i·mē″tėr, *n.* A millionth part of a millimeter; a millimicron.

mi·cron, mi·kron, mī′kron, *n.* pl. **mi·crons, mi·cra**. [Gr. *mikron*, small.] A unit of length equal to one millionth of a meter or one thousandth of a millimeter. Sym. μ, mu.

Mi·cro·ne·sian, mī″kro·nē′zhan, mī″kro·nē′shan, *a.* [< *Micronesia*, < Gr. *mikrós*, small, and *nesos*, island.] Of or pertaining to Micronesia, a cluster of small islands in the western Pacific, its inhabitants, or languages.—*n.* A native of Micronesia, which is inhabited by a mixture of peoples, chiefly Polynesian; any of the languages or dialects spoken there.

mi·cro·nu·cle·us, mī″krō·nö′klē·us, mī″krō·nū′klē·us, *n.* pl. **mi·cro·nu·cle·i**. *Biol.* the smaller nucleus of the two produced by some ciliated one-celled organisms, and the one which is the source of gametes.—**mi·cro·nu·cle·ar**, *a.*

mi·cro·nu·tri·ent, mī″krō·nö′trē·ent, mī″krō·nū′trē·ent, *n. Biochem.* a nutrient needed only in small amounts to promote growth and health.—*a.* Pertaining to such nutrients; a trace element.

mi·cro·or·gan·ism, mi·cro·or·gan·ism, mī″krō·ạr′gạ·niz″um, *n. Biol.* a microscopic organism, as a protozoan or bacterium.

mi·cro·pa·le·on·tol·o·gy, mī″krō·pā″lē·on·tol′o·jē, *n.* The study and identification of microscopic fossils or fossil fragments.—**mi·cro·pa·le·on·to·log·i·cal, mi·cro·pa·le·on·to·log·ic**, mī″krō·pā″lē·on″to·loj′i·kal, mī″krō·pal″ē·on″to·loj′i·kal, *a.*—**mi·cro·pa·le·on·tol·o·gist**, *n.*

mi·cro·par·a·site, mī″krō·par′a·sīt″, *n.* Any parasitic plant or animal of microscopic size.—**mi·cro·par·a·sit·ic**, mī″krō·par″a·sit′ik, *a.*

mi·cro·phone, mī′kro·fōn″, *n.* [Gr. *mikros*, small, and *phōnē*, sound.] An instrument for converting sound waves into electrical waves for transmitting, recording, or intensifying such sounds as speech or music: used in broadcasting, telephony, motion pictures, public address systems, and the like.—**mi·cro·phon·ic**, mī″kro·fon′ik, *a.*

mi·cro·phon·ics, mī″kro·fon′iks, *n. pl. but sing. in constr.* The noise in electronic circuitry caused by a component's mechanical vibrations which alter the electrical response.

mi·cro·pho·to·graph, mī″kro·fō′to·graf″, mī″kro·fō′to·gräf″, *n.* Microfilm; a photographic representation of microscopic size. A photograph of microscopic objects; also *photomicrograph*.—**mi·cro·pho·to·graph·ic**, *a.*—**mi·cro·pho·tog·ra·phy**, mī″krō·fo·tog′ra·fē, *n.*

mi·cro·phys·ics, mī″kro·fiz′iks, *n. pl. but sing. in constr.* Physics as concerned with minute masses or the ultimate particles and structure of matter.

mi·cro·print, mī′kro·print″, *n.* A microphotograph that can be read with the aid of an enlarging viewer.—*v.t., v.i.*

mi·cro·pyle, mī′kro·pil″, *n.* [Gr. *mikros*, small, *pylē*, gate.] *Bot.* the opening by which a pollen tube enters the ovule; *zool.* an opening through which the spermatozoa enter an ovum.—**mi·cro·py·lar**, *a.*

mi·cro·read·er, mī″krō·rē″dėr, *n.* A projective device used to show the enlarged image or close-up of microfilm or a microphotograph.

mi·cro·scope, mī′kro·skōp″, *n.* [Gr. *mikros*, small, and *skopeō*, to view.] An optical instrument consisting of a lens or combination of lenses which render minute objects distinctly visible.

mi·cro·scop·ic, mī″kro·skop′ik, *a.* Visible only by the aid of a microscope; minute or tiny; pertaining to or resembling a microscope; made by, or as by, the aid of a microscope; as, *microscopic* observations. Also **mi·cro·scop·i·cal**.—**mi·cro·scop·i·cal·ly**, *adv.*

mi·cros·co·py, mī·kros′ko·pē, mī′krō·skō″pē, *n.* The use of the microscope; investigation by means of the microscope.—**mi·cros·co·pist**, mī·kros′ko·pist, mī″kro·skō′pist, *n.*

mi·cro·sec·ond, mī′kro·sek″ond, *n.* One millionth of one second.

mi·cro·seism, mī′kro·sī″zum, mī′kro·sī″sum, *n.* A weak, recurrent earth tremor or vibration generally caused by earthquakes.—**mi·cro·seis·mic**, mī″kro·sīz′mik, mī″kro·sīs′mik, *a.*

mi·cro·some, mī′kro·sōm″, *n.* [N.L. *microsoma*.] *Biol.* one of the minute granules in the protoplasm of animal and plant cells.—**mi·cro·so·mi·al, mi·cro·so·mic**, *a.*

mi·cro·spo·ran·gi·um, mī″krō·spō·ran′jē·um, mī″krō·spa·ran′jē·um, *n.* pl. **mi·cro·spo·ran·gi·a**. [N.L.] *Bot.* a sporangium, or spore case, containing microspores.

mi·cro·spore, mĭ′krō·spōr″, *n. Bot.* One of the smaller of the two kinds of spores produced asexually by seed plants; the pollen grain or male element.—**mi·cro··spor·ic, mi·cro·spor·ous,** mĭ″krō··spär′ik, mĭ″krō·spor′ik, mĭ″krō·spōr′us, mĭ″krōs′pĕr·us, *a.*

mi·cro·struc·ture, mĭ′krō·struk″chĕr, *n. Metal.* the detailed and precise formation of a metal as shown by microscopic examination.

mi·cro·tome, mĭ′krō·tōm″, *n.* An instrument for cutting very fine sections of organic tissue for microscopic study.— **mi·cro·tom·ic, mi·cro·tom·i·cal,** mĭ″krō·tom′ik, *a.*

mi·cro·wave, mĭ′krō·wāv″, *n.* An extremely short electromagnetic wave having a very high frequency range generally regarded as being between a wavelength of 1 millimeter and 30 centimeters.

mid, mid, *a.* [O.E. *mid,* mid, in the middle; Goth. *midjis,* Icel. *midr* (*mithr*); cogn. L. *medius;* Gr. *mesos,* Skt. *madhyas,* middle.] Being at a point approximately equal in distance from extremes; as, *mid*winter; having the central position; as, the *mid*-Victorian era; intervening. *Phonet.* pertaining to a vocalic made with the tongue arched in an intermediate position.— *prep. Poet.* amid.—*adv.* In the middle.

mid·brain, mid′brān″, *n.* Mesencephalon.

mid·day, mid′dā″, *n.* The midpoint of the day; noon.—*a.*

mid·dle, mid′l, *a.* [O.E. *middel* = D. *middel* = G. *mittel,* middle.] Equally distant from limits or extremes; as, the *middle* point of a road; intervening or intermediate; as, the *middle* distance; medium; as, a man of *middle* size; (*usu. cap.*) in the history of a language, intermediate between periods classified respectively as Old and New or Modern; as, *Middle* English; *gram.* the intermediate verb construction in some languages, as Greek, which parallels reflexive construction in English; (*sometimes cap.*), *geol.* denoting the principal intermediate division of a period; as, the *Middle* Devonian.—*n.* The point or part equidistant from extremes or limits; the waist, or middle part of the human body; something intermediate; a mean.— *v.t., v.i.*—*middled, middling.* To situate in the center; *naut.* to fold in the center.

mid·dle-aged, mid′l·ājd′, *a.* Intermediate in age between youth, or the earlier period of adult life, and old age: approximately between 45 and 65 years old; characteristic of or suitable for middle-aged people. —**mid·dle age,** *n.*

Mid·dle Ag·es, *n. pl.* The period extending from the classical period to the Renaissance, or from the 6th to the 16th century.

mid·dle·brow, mid′l·brou″, *n.* One who exhibits a moderate or limited interest in intellectual pursuits; a person whose cultural tastes tend to reflect those most widely accepted by the general public.— *a.* Also **mid·dle·browed.**

mid·dle C, *n. Mus.* the note C which falls approximately midway between the highest and lowest note on a piano keyboard and is notated by the use of a ledger line directly above the bass staff and directly below the treble staff.

mid·dle class, *n.* The class of people intermediate between the classes of higher and lower social rank or standing; that class of people considered to have average social rank, educational background, financial status, and living standards; an intermediate class. *Brit.* the class socially and conventionally intermediate between the aristocratic class and the laboring class.

mid·dle-class, mid′l·klas′, mid′l·kläs′, *a.* Belonging, pertaining to, or characteristic of a middle class, esp. the social middle class; bourgeois.

mid·dle dis·tance, *n. Art,* the space between the foreground and the background in a painting or photograph; *track,* a race distance ranging between 880 yards and 4500 yards.

mid·dle ear, *n. Anat.* the area between the outer ear and inner ear made up of the tympanic membrane and a cavity containing the malleus, stapes, and incus.

Mid·dle Eng·lish, *n.* The English language in the second major stage of its development, roughly comprising the period from 1150 to 1475, represented in the works of Chaucer, Gower, and Malory, and marked by the loss of the synthetic structure of Old English and by the entry of large numbers of French and Latin words into the language.

Mid·dle French, *n.* The French language of the period from about 1300 to 1500.

Mid·dle Greek, *n.* The Greek language of the Middle Ages, from about 700 to 1500. Also **Me·di·e·val Greek.**

Mid·dle High Ger·man, *n.* The High German language of the period from about 1100 to 1500.

Mid·dle Low Ger·man, *n.* The Low German language of the period from about 1100 to 1500.

mid·dle·man, mid′l·man″, *n. pl.* **mid··dle·men.** An intermediary between two parties; a person, as a broker, agent, merchant, or retailer, who intervenes between the producer and the consumer of goods; *theatr.* that performer in a minstrel troupe who converses and banters with the end men.

mid·dle·most, mid′l·mōst″, *a.* Being in or near the middle; midmost.

mid·dle term, *n. Logic.* That term of a categorical syllogism with which the two other terms are separately compared, and by means of which they are brought together in the conclusion; that term of a syllogism which appears twice in the premises, but is eliminated from the conclusion.

mid·dle·weight, mid′l·wāt″, *n.* A person having an average weight; a boxer or wrestler weighing more than 147 pounds but less than 160 pounds.—*a.*

mid·dling, mid′ling, *a.* Medium in size, quality, grade, or rank; mediocre; ordinary; *slang,* in fairly good health.—*adv. Slang,* moderately, fairly.—**mid·dlings,** *n. pl.* Any of various products or commodities of intermediate quality, condition, or grade; the coarser particles of ground wheat mingled with bran. A term used chiefly in the southern and central U.S. referring to salt pork or bacon; also **mid·dling meat.**—**mid·dling·ly,** *adv.*

mid·dy, mid′ē, *n. pl.* **mid·dies.** *Colloq.* a midshipman. A loose blouse with a sailor collar, often extending below the waistline to terminate in a broad band or fold, worn by children and young girls; also **mid·dy blouse.**

midge, mij, *n.* [O.E. *mycg* = D. *mug* = G. *mücke,* midge.] Any of numerous small, dipterous insects, esp. species of the family *Chironomidae* which are mosquitolike in appearance; a gnat; *fig.* a small person.

midg·et, mij′it, *n.* [Dim. of *midge.*] A person or thing of unusually small size but with normal proportions.—*a.* Very small.

mid·i·ron, mid′ī″ĕrn, *n. Golf.* A steel-headed club whose face has a medium degree of slope; a number two iron.

mid·land, mid′land, *a.* Being in the interior region of a country; inland.—*n.* The interior of a country. (*Cap.*) the dialect of English prevalent in central England; the dialect of English prevalent in some interior regions of the U.S.

mid·line, mid′līn″, *n.* A line of balance, as a median line.

mid·most, mid′mōst″, *a.* In the very middle; middlemost.—*adv.*

mid·night, mid′nīt″, *n.* The middle of the night; twelve o'clock at night.—*a.* Being or occurring in the middle of the night; very dark.—**burn the mid·night oil,** to continue to work late into the night.— **mid·night·ly,** *a., adv.*

mid·night sun, *n.* The sun visible at midnight in arctic or antarctic regions during their summer.

mid·noon, mid′nōn′, *n.* The middle of the day; noon.

mid-o·cean ridge, *n.* A mountain chain rising from the floor of the ocean and believed to be a sign of convection currents that carry and deposit magma from the interior of the earth.

mid·point, mid-point, mid′point″, *n.* A point located at the middle or center, as of a discussion.

mid·rash, mid′räsh, *Heb.* mē·DRÄSH′, *n. pl.* **mid·rash·im, mid·rash·oth,** mid·rä′shim, *Heb.* mē″DRÄ·shĕm′, mid·rä′shōs, *Heb.* mē″DRÄ·shät′. [Heb.] An explanation of the Old Testament; (*cap.*) the body of traditional Scriptural interpretations written between 500 B.C. and 1200 A.D.—**mid··rash·ic,** mid·räsh′ik, *a.*

mid·rib, mid′rib″, *n. Bot.* the middle vein of a leaf.

mid·riff, mid′rif, *n.* [O.E. *midhrif*—*mid,* and *hrif,* belly.] The diaphragm; the area of the body between the chest and waist; the section of a garment covering this area; a garment that bares the midriff.

mid·sec·tion, mid′sek″shan, *n.* The central or middle part of anything; *colloq.* the midriff.

mid·ship, mid′ship″, *a.* Being in or belonging to the middle of a ship.

mid·ship·man, mid′ship″man, mid·ship′-man, *n. pl.* **mid·ship·men.** [So called from the midshipman's former place of duty aboard ship.] A student officer of the U.S. Naval Academy, Coast Guard Academy, or similar officer training institution, holding a rank below a warrant officer and above a master chief petty officer; rank held by such a student prior to graduation as an ensign. *Brit. Navy,* an officer of the rank held by young men on graduation from the government naval schools; formerly, one of a class of young men who performed duties aboard ship and constituted the group from which officers were selected.

mid·ships, mid′ships″, *adv.* Amidships.

midst, midst, *n.* [M.E. *middest,* for *middes* (with advbl. genit. *-es*), as in *in middes, on middes,* for O.E. *on middan,* in the middle.] The middle point, part, or stage; the position of anything surrounded by other things or parts, occurring in the middle of a period of time, or during a course of action; as, in the *midst* of their travels; middle.—*prep.* Amid, amidst.

mid·sum·mer, mid′sum′ĕr, mid′sum″ĕr, *n.* The middle of summer.

Mid·sum·mer Day, *n.* The 24th day of June, a quarter day in England celebrating the birthday of St. John the Baptist. Also **St. John's Day.**

mid·term, mid′tŭrm″, *n.* The point halfway through a school term or term of office. *Often pl., colloq.* an examination or set of examinations given at the halfway point of a school term.

mid-Vic·to·ri·an, mid′vik·tōr′ē·an, *a.* Of, pertaining to, or characteristic of the middle portion of the reign or period of Queen Victoria, who reigned 1837–1901 in England; as, *mid-Victorian* writers, literature, art, or ideas.—*n.* A person, as a writer, belonging to the mid-Victorian time; a person of mid-Victorian ideas or tastes.

mid·way, mid′wā″, n. At a fair or amusement park, the area along which side shows and similar exhibitions are located; the middle of the way or distance.—mid′wā′, adv., a. In the middle of the way or distance; halfway.

mid·week, mid′wēk″, n. The middle of the week; (cap.) among the Quakers, Wednesday.—a. Occurring in the middle of the week.—**mid·week·ly,** a., adv.

Mid·west, mid′west′, n. The geographical portion of the U.S. bounded by the Rocky Mountains on the west and the Allegheny Mountains on the east, with the Ohio River and the southern borders of Missouri and Kansas forming the south boundary. Also **Mid·dle West.**—**Mid·west·ern,** a.—**Mid·west·ern·er,** n.

mid·wife, mid′wīf″, n. pl. **mid·wives.** [< O.E. mid, with (G. mit), and wife.] A woman who assists a mother in childbirth.—**mid·wife·ry,** mid′wī″fe·rē, mid′wīf″rē, n. The art or practice of a midwife.

mid·win·ter, mid′win′tẽr, n. The middle of winter.

mid·year, mid′yẽr″, n. The middle of the year; often pl., colloq. an examination or set of examinations given at the middle of an academic year.—a.

mien, mēn, n. [Var. of demean.] External manner of a person; look; bearing; appearance.

miff, mif, n. [Origin obscure: cf. G. muff, sullenness.] Colloq. An unpleasant mood; a petty quarrel.—v.t. To offend; cause to be ill-humored or annoyed.—**miff·y,** a.—miffier, miffiest. Touchy.

Mig, mig, n. [From (Mi)koyan and (G)urevich, Russian aeronautical engineers.] Any one of a series of Russian fighter aircraft, as the Mig-15, a jet fighter used in the Korean War, and the Mig-21, a jet fighter used by the North Vietnamese in the Vietnam conflict.

might, mīt, n. [O.E. miht, meaht, = D. and G. macht = Goth. mahts, might.] Ability or power to do or accomplish; effective power or force of any kind; as, the might of intellect, or of public opinion; bodily strength; powerful influences, agencies, or resources; superior power or strength; as, the doctrine that might makes right.—**with might and main,** with all the power or strength possessed; with great force or vigor.

might, mīt, v. Past tense of may.

might·y, mī′tē, a.—mightier, mightiest. [O.E. mihtig.] Possessing, characterized by, or showing might or power; having, showing, or requiring great bodily strength; of great size; as, a mighty rock; great in amount, extent, degree, or importance.—adv. Colloq. to a great extent or degree; as, a mighty long time.—**might·i·ly,** mīt′i·lē, adv. In a mighty manner; powerfully; vigorously; to a great extent or degree, or very much; as, to be mightily pleased.—**might·i·ness,** n.

mi·gnon, min·yon′, min·yun′, min′yon, Fr. mē·nyaɴ′, a. [Fr., origin uncertain.] Small and pretty; delicately pretty.—**mi·gnonne,** min·yon′, min′yon, Fr. mē·nyaɴ′, a. Fem. form of mignon.

mi·gnon·ette, min″ya·net′, n. An herbaceous plant, Reseda odorata, having small yellowish-green flowers, common in gardens where it is cultivated for its fragrance.

mi·graine, mī′grān, n. A recurring headache marked by severe pain, usu. limited to a single side of the head, and often with attendant nausea. Also **hem·i·cra·ni·a.**

mi·grant, mī′grant, a. Migrating; migratory.—n. One who or that which migrates, as a migratory worker.

mi·grate, mī′grāt, v.i.—migrated, migrating. [L. migratus, pp. of migrare, migrate.] To move from one place to another; to travel from one country, region, or domicile to settle in another; to go to a new habitat or to shift periodically from one region to another, as certain diseases or symptoms.—**mi·gra·tor,** n.

mi·gra·tion, mī·grā′shan, n. The act of migrating; a migratory movement; a number of persons or animals migrating together; chem. the shift in position of atoms in a molecule.—**mi·gra·tion·al,** a.

mi·gra·to·ry, mī′gra·tōr″ē, a. Pertaining to or characterized by periodic migration; migrating; roving or nomadic.

mi·ka·do, mi·kä′dō, n. pl. **mi·ka·dos.** [Jap. venerable one.] (Often cap.) the emperor of Japan.

mike, mīk, n. Colloq. microphone.

Mike, mīk, n. A communications code word used to designate the letter M.

mil, mil, n. [L. mille, thousand.] A unit of length equal to .001 of an inch, used in measuring the diameter of wires; a milliliter, or cubic centimeter; a military unit of angular measurement, 1/6400 of 360 degrees, used in gunnery and in the launching of bombs and guided missiles.

mi·la·dy, mi·lā′dē, n. pl. **mi·la·dies.** An English noblewoman; a fashionable or stylish woman.

milch, milch, a. [O.E. melc, milch, giving milk.] Giving milk: applied to domesticated animals; as, a milch cow.

mild, mīld, a. [O.E. milde = D. and G. mild = Icel. mildr = Goth. -milds, mild.] Gentle or temperate in feeling or behavior toward others; characterized by or showing such gentleness, as one's manner or words; not harsh, fierce, or stern; gentle or moderate in force or effect; soft, pleasant; not cold, severe, or extreme, as air, weather, or climate; not acute, as disease; not sharp, pungent, nor strong, as food or perfume; moderate in intensity, degree, or character; Brit. dial. easily worked, as soil, stone, or wood.—**mild·ly,** adv.—**mild·ness,** n.

mil·dew, mil′dō″, mil′dū″, n. [O.E. mildēaw, < mil-, mele-, honey, and dēaw, E. dew.] Any of numerous minute parasitic fungi producing a whitish coating or discoloration on plants; the coating, discoloration, or the disease produced by such fungi; any similar discoloration due to fungi, as on cotton and linen fabrics, paper, or leather, when exposed to dampness.—v.t. To affect with mildew.—v.i. To become affected with mildew.—**mil·dew·y,** a.

mile, mīl, n. [O.E. mīl, < L. milia, millia, pl. of mille, thousand, as of paces or steps.] A unit of linear measure in the U.S. and other English-speaking nations equivalent to 5,280 feet. Also **stat·ute mile.**—**ge·o·graph·i·cal** or **nau·ti·cal mile,** a unit of linear measure equivalent to one minute of a great circle of the earth: officially fixed in Great Britain at 6,080 feet, and formerly in the U.S. as 6,080.27 feet.—**in·ter·na·tion·al nau·ti·cal mile,** a measure of distance by air or sea equaling 6,076.115 feet, now used officially in the U.S.

mile·age, mil·age, mī′lij, n. Distance in miles; as, the track mileage of a railroad; the aggregate number of miles made or traveled in a given time; an allowance for traveling expenses at a fixed rate per mile; a fixed charge per mile, as for railroad transportation; the miles a vehicle can travel on a certain amount of fuel; colloq. durability, use, or value, as: She got a lot of mileage out of the dress.

mile·post, mīl′pōst″, n. A post set up to mark distance by miles, as along a highway.

mil·er, mī′lẽr, n. A man or horse trained to run in competitive one-mile races.

mi·les glo·ri·o·sus, mī′lēz glōr″ē·ō′sus, L. mē′les glō″Rē·ō′sṵs, n. pl. **mi·li·tes glo·ri·o·si,** mil′i·tēz″ glōr″ē·ō′sī, L. mē′li·tes″ glō″Rē·ō′sē. [L. 'boastful soldier.'] L. formerly, a standard character in comedies who portrayed a military braggart.

mile·stone, mīl′stōn″, n. A stone or post set up to mark distance by miles, as along a highway or other line of travel; fig. an event worth noting in the development of a lifetime, a career, or an endeavor.

mil·foil, mil′foil″, n. [Fr. mille-feuille, < L. millefolium, lit. 'thousand-leaf.'] The yarrow plant, Achillea millefolium.

mil·i·ar·i·a, mil″ē·âr′ē·a, n. [N.L., prop. fem. of L. miliarius, E. miliary.] Pathol. An inflammatory disease of the skin, located about the sweat glands, marked by the formation of vesicles or papules resembling millet seeds; prickly heat.

mil·i·ar·y, mil′ē·er″ē, mil′ya·rē, a. [L. miliarius, < milium, millet.] Resembling a millet seed or seeds. Pathol. characterized by spots or vesicles resembling millet seeds, as in miliaria.

mi·lieu, mil·ū′, mēl·ū′, Fr. mē·lyœ′, n. pl. **mi·lieus,** Fr. **mi·lieux.** [Fr., < O.Fr. mi, middle, and lieu, place.] Environment; setting.

mil·i·tant, mil′i·tant, a. [L. militans (-ant-), ppr. of militare.] Engaged in warfare; forcible in action or disposition; as, the militant church; combative; aggressive.—n. One engaged in warfare or strife; one using vigorous or violent methods to advance his cause.—**mil·i·tan·cy, mil·i·tant·ness,** n.—**mil·i·tant·ly,** adv.

mil·i·ta·rism, mil′i·ta·riz″um, n. Military spirit or policy; the ideals characteristic of the armed forces or military class; the tendency to regard military efficiency as the supreme ideal of the state, and to subordinate all other interests to those of the military organization; a militaristic program of aggressive preparedness.—**mil·i·ta·rist,** mil′i·tẽr·ist, n. One who is proficient in the ways and strategies of war; one who is imbued with militarism.—**mil·i·ta·ris·tic,** mil″i·ta·ris′tik, a.—**mil·i·ta·ris·ti·cal·ly,** adv.

mil·i·ta·rize, mil′i·ta·rīz″, v.t.—militarized, militarizing. To equip with or provide military supplies and the like; to arm; to imbue with militarism.—**mil·i·ta·ri·za·tion,** mil″i·tẽr·i·za′shan, n.

mil·i·tar·y, mil′i·ter″ē, a. [L. militaris, < miles, milit-, soldier.] Of or pertaining to soldiers, the army, armed forces, the affairs of war, or the state of war; befitting or characteristic of a soldier; following the life of a soldier.—n. Military personnel; armed forces, esp. officers.—**mil·i·tar·i·ly,** mil″i·târ′i·lē, mil′i·ter″i·lē, adv.

mil·i·tar·y po·lice, n. The branch or service of the army which performs police duties. Abbr. MP.

mil·i·tate, mil′i·tāt″, v.i.—militated, militating. [L. milito, militatum, to fight.] To oppose; to fight or act for or against; to manifest weight or influence, usu. followed by against.—**mil·i·ta·tion,** n.

mi·li·tia, mi·lish′a, n. [L., military service, soldiery.] An organization of men enrolled and trained as military reserves for the defense of a nation in time of emergency. U.S. the organized militia of the individual states, or National Guard; Army, Navy, Air Force, or Marine organized reserves; all able-bodied men not already in the armed forces, legally liable to call for military duty.—**mi·li·tia·man,** mi·lish′a·man, n. pl. **mi·li·tia·men.**

mil·i·um, mil′ē·um, n. pl. **mil·i·a,** mil′ē·a. [L., millet.] Pathol. a small white or yellowish nodule resembling a millet seed, produced in the skin by the retention of a fatty secretion.

milk, milk, *n.* [O.E. *milc, meolc,* = D. *melk* = G. *milch* = Icel. *mjölk* = Goth. *miluks,* milk; akin to L. *mulgere,* Gr. *amelgein,* to milk.] An opaque white or bluish-white liquid secreted by the mammary glands of female mammals for the nourishment of their young; in the case of the cow, goat, and some other animals, this liquid used for food or as a source of dairy products; any liquid resembling this, as the liquid within a coconut, the juice or sap of certain plants, or various pharmaceutical preparations.—*v.t.* [O.E. *milcian, meolcian,* < *milc, meolc.*] To press or draw milk from the udder of, as a cow or goat; to extract something from, as if by milking; drain the contents, strength, information, or wealth from; exploit; elicit.—*v.i.* To draw milk, as from a cow; to yield milk, as a cow.—**cry o·ver spilt milk,** regret something that is already over or done, and can no longer be changed.—**milk·er,** *n.*

milk-and-wa·ter, milk'an·wạ'tèr, milk'- an·wot'ẽr, *a.* Tasteless; insipid; wishy-washy.

milk fe·ver, *n. Pathol.* a fever, caused by infection, appearing with the onset of lactation following childbirth. *Veter. pathol.* a similar condition in dairy cows following calving, symptomized by drowsiness and paralysis.

milk leg, *n. Pathol.* phlebitis; inflammation of the veins in the leg which causes pain and swelling, often occurring in women after childbirth.

milk-liv·ered, milk'liv'ẽrd, *a.* Cowardly; timorous.

milk·maid, milk'mād', *n.* A woman or girl who milks cows or is employed in a dairy.

milk·man, milk'man', *n.* pl. **milk·men.** A man who sells or delivers milk, eggs, and other dairy products.

milk of mag·ne·sia, *n.* A milky aqueous liquid, Mg(OH)$_2$, containing magnesium hydroxide in suspension: used as a counteraction for stomach acidity or as a laxative.

milk punch, *n.* A beverage made of milk, with whiskey or other liquor, sugar, and nutmeg, and often served iced.

milk shake, *n.* A drink consisting of cold milk, flavoring syrup, and usu. ice cream, blended in a hand shaker or mechanical mixer.

milk sick·ness, *n.* A disease brought about by the consumption of dairy products or of the meat of cattle that have grazed on certain poisonous plants.

milk snake, *n.* A harmless snake, *Lampropeltis doliatus triangulus,* common in N. America, identified by an arrow-shaped spot at the back of the head, and erroneously thought to invade dairies to drink milk. Also **house snake.**

milk·sop, milk'sop', *n.* An effeminate man or boy; one devoid of manliness; a sissy.

milk sug·ar, *n.* Lactose.

milk tooth, *n.* One of the first, or temporary, teeth in young mammals, later replaced by permanent ones. Also **ba·by tooth, de··cid·u·ous tooth.**

milk vetch, *n.* [So called from an old belief that these plants increased the secretion of milk in goats feeding on them.] Any of various plants of the leguminous genus *Astragalus,* or of certain allied genera.

milk·weed, milk'wēd', *n.* Any of various plants, mostly with milky juice, of the family *Asclepiadaceae,* esp. those of the genus *Asclepias,* as *A. syriaca,* the common milkweed, an herb with downy stems and leaves.

milk·wort, milk'wụrt', *n.* Any of the herbs and shrubs constituting the genus *Polygala,* formerly reputed to increase the secretion of milk in women; a primulaceous seaside plant, known as the sea milkwort, *Glaux maritima.*

milk·y, mil'kē, *a.*—**milkier, milkiest.** Of or like milk; abounding in or yielding milk or a milklike liquid; white as milk; mild, meek, tame, or spiritless.—**milk·i·ness,** *n.*

Milk·y Way, *n. Astron.* The faintly luminous band or tract stretching across the heavens, composed of innumerable stars too faint for unassisted vision; the galaxy, or Milky Way galaxy, including our solar system.

mill, mil, *n.* [O.E. *miln, mylen, myln,* < L. *molina,* a mill, < *mola,* a mill or millstone, < *molo,* to grind.] A building containing machinery which grinds grain into flour; any of various machines for processing materials by cutting, planing, grinding, polishing, or stamping.—*v.t.* To grind in a mill; to pass through a mill; to form grooves, as on the edge of a coin.—*v.i.* To move in a circular fashion, as a herd of cattle; *slang,* to fight with the fists.

mill, mil, *n.* [L. *mille,* a thousand.] A monetary unit of the U.S., having the value of one thousandth of a dollar; one tenth of a cent. Abbr. *mi., M., m.*

mill·board, mil'bōrd', *n.* A thick and strong material produced in paper mills, used for making cartons and in bookbinding; pasteboard.

mill·dam, mil'dam', *n.* A dam crossing a river or other watercourse and raising the water to a level sufficient to turn a mill wheel; *Sc.* a millpond.

milled, mild, *a.* Having undergone the operation of a mill; having the edge transversely grooved, as a dime or the head of a screw that is to be turned by the fingers.

mil·le·nar·i·an, mil'e·nâr'ē·an, *a.* [L. *millenarius,* containing a thousand, < *mille,* a thousand.] Consisting of a thousand, esp. a thousand years; pertaining to the millennium.—*n.* One who believes in the millennium.—**mil·le·nar·i·an·ism,** *n.*

mil·le·nar·y, mil'e·ner'ē, *a.* Consisting of a thousand, esp. one thousand years; millenarian; millennial.—*n.* pl. **mil·le··nar·ies.** The space of a thousand years; a thousandth anniversary; millenarian.

mil·len·ni·um, mi·len'ē·um, *n.* pl. **mil··len·ni·ums, mil·len·ni·a.** [L. *mille,* a thousand, and *annus,* a year.] An aggregate of a thousand years; the thousand years mentioned in the Bible during which millenarians believe Christ will reign on earth with his saints. Rev. xx. 1–5. A period of perfection, peace, and happiness on earth to occur at some unspecified time.—**mil·len··ni·al,** mi·len'ē·al, *a.* Pertaining to the millennium, or to a thousand years.—**mil·len··ni·al·ly,** *adv.*—**mil·len·ni·al·ism,** *n.*—**mil·len·ni·al·ist,** *n.*

mil·le·pore, mil'e·pōr', *n.* [L. *mille,* a thousand, and *porus,* a pore.] One of the large, branching, reef-building corals, genus *Milipora,* so named from their numerous minute pores.

mill·er, mil'ẽr, *n.* One who keeps or operates a mill, esp. a grain mill; a milling machine; *entom.* any of various moths which appear to be powdered with flour.

mill·er·ite, mil'e·rīt', *n.* Nickel sulfide, NiS, a crystalline, brassy-colored mineral.

mill·er's-thumb, mil'ẽrz·thum', *n.* Any of various small, spiny-finned fresh-water fishes, esp. of the genus *Cottus.*

mil·les·i·mal, mi·les'i·mal, *a., n.* [L. *millesimus,* < *mille,* a thousand.] Thousandth.—**mil·les·i·mal·ly,** *adv.*

mil·let, mil'it, *n.* [Fr. *millet,* dim. of *mil,* < L. *milium,* millet; < *√* root meaning to grind as in *mill.*] A common name for various species of grass or small grain cultivated in many parts of Europe, Asia, and Africa as food for humans, and in the U.S. primarily as fodder; various allied forage grasses; the seed of any of these grains and grasses.

mil·li·am·pere, mil"ē·am'pēr, *n. Elect.* a one-thousandth part of an ampere, a unit of electric current.

mil·liard, mil'yẽrd, mil'yärd, *n.* [Fr.] *Brit.* a thousand millions; a billion in the U.S.

mil·li·ar·y, mil'ē·er"ē, *a.* [L. *milliarus,* < *mille,* a thousand.] Pertaining to the ancient Roman mile of a thousand paces.

mil·li·bar, mil'i·bär', *n.* A unit of air pressure, equaling one thousandth of a bar. Abbr. *mb.*

mil·li·cur·ie, mil'i·kūr"ē, mil'i·kū·rē", *n.* One thousandth of a curie, a unit expressing radioactivity, esp. of radium. Abbr. *mCi, mc.*

mil·lier, mēl·yā', *n.* [Fr. < L. *mille,* thousand.] In the metric system, a unit of weight equal to 1,000,000 grams, or 2,204.6 pounds avoirdupois; a metric ton.

mil·li·far·ad, mil'i·far"ad, mil'i·far"ad, *n. Elect.* one thousandth of a farad, a unit measuring the electrical capacity of a condenser. Abbr. *mF, mf.*

mil·li·gal, mil'i·gal", *n. Phys.* one thousandth of a gal, a unit measuring acceleration. Abbr. *mGal.*

mil·li·gram, *Brit.* **mil·li·gramme,** mil'i·gram", *n.* The thousandth part of a gram, equal to a cubic millimeter of water or .0154 of a grain.

mil·li·hen·ry, mil'i·hen"rē, *n.* pl. **mil·li··hen·ries, mil·li·hen·rys.** *Elect.* one thousandth part of a henry, an inductance unit. Abbr. *mH, mh.*

mil·li·lam·bert, mil'i·lam"bẽrt, *n. Opt.* one thousandth part of a lambert, a measure of brightness. Abbr. *mL.*

mil·li·li·ter, *Brit.* **mil·li·li·tre,** mil'i·lē"tẽr, *n.* [Fr. *millilitre.*] In the metric system, a unit of capacity equal to one thousandth of a liter, or 0.061 cubic inch, or 0.27 U.S. fluid dram.

mil·li·me·ter, *Brit.* **mil·li·me·tre,** mil'i·mē"tẽr, *n.* The thousandth part of a meter, 0.03937 of an inch.—**mil·li·met··ric,** mil"i·me'trik, *a.*

mil·li·mi·cron, mil'i·mī"kron *n.* pl., **mil·li·mi·crons, mil·li·mi·cra.** The millionth part of a millimeter, or the thousandth part of a micron, a unit of length. Also **micromillimeter.**

mil·line, mil'līn", mil·līn', *n.* A measure of advertising space equal to a one-column width of one agate line published in one million copies of a magazine or newspaper.

mil·li·ner, mil'i·nẽr, *n.* [Thought to be for *Milaner,* from *Milan,* in Italy, famous for its silks and ribbons.] A designer, maker, trimmer, or seller of women's hats.

mil·li·ner·y, mil'i·ner"ē, mil'i·ne·rē, *n.* The business or occupation of a milliner; the articles made or sold by milliners.

mill·ing, mil'ing, *n.* The act of subjecting something to the operation of a mill or milling machine; the process of finishing the edge of something, as a coin, with fine notches or transverse grooves; the notches or grooves themselves.

mill·ing cut·ter, *n.* A revolving steel cutting tool which shapes or cuts metals.

mill·ing ma·chine, *n.* Any of a class of machines used for holding a rotating cutter and shaping, cutting, or otherwise dressing metal surfaces.

mil·lion, mil'yon, *n.* pl. **mil·lions** or, when after a numeral, **mil·lion.** [O.Fr. Fr. *million,* < L. *mille,* thousand.] The number of ten hundred thousand, or a thousand thousand; often, the amount of a thousand thousand pecuniary units; a very sizeable number; *pl.* the multitude or the mass of the common people, used with *the.*—*a.*—**mil·lionth,** mil'yonth, *a., n.*

mil·lion·aire, mil·lion·naire, mil"ya··nâr', *n.* [Fr. *millionnaire.*] A person worth a million or millions, as of dollars, pounds, or francs.—**mil·lion·air·ess,** *n.* Feminine of millionaire.

mil·li·pede, mil′i·pēd″, n. [L. millepeda.] A myriapod of the class Diplopoda, characterized by two pairs of legs for each of the segments of the body. Also **mil·le·pede**, mil′li·pēd, mil′i·pēd.

mil·li·sec·ond, mil′i·sek″ond, n. One thousandth of a second.

mill·pond, mil′pond″, n. A pond or reservoir which supplies water to turn a mill wheel.

mill·race, mil′rās″, n. The stream of water that turns a mill wheel, or the channel in which it runs.

mill·run, mil′run″, n. A millrace; a test to determine the mineral content of rock or ore samples; minerals thus extracted; a sawmill's marketable production; in general a mill's output or goods of average quality; the common or ordinary, said of persons or things.—**mill-run**, a. Coming from a mill, usu. ungraded.

mill·stone, mil′stōn″, n. One of the stones for grinding grain in a mill; stone or rock from which such stones are made; fig. a personal burden or problem.

mill·stream, mil′strēm, n. The flowing water which turns a mill wheel; millrace.

mill wheel, n. A water wheel used to drive a mill.

mill·wright, mil′rīt″, n. A person whose occupation it is to design, construct, or maintain mills or the machinery of mills.

mi·lo, mī′lō, n. pl. **mi·los**. Any of several grain sorghums with slender stalks and heads of yellow or white seeds, cultivated for grain and forage.

mi·lord, mi·lard′, n. A Continental rendering of the English my lord, used in speaking to or of an English lord or gentleman.

milt, milt, n. [O.E. milte, Dan. milt, Icel. milti, G. milz, the spleen; D. milt, the spleen, the milt of fishes; same root as melt.] The seminal fluid of male fish; the organs producing the seminal fluid, esp. when full.—**milt·er**, n. [D. milter.] A male fish having the time of spawning.

Mil·ton·ic, mil·ton′ik, a. Resembling or relating to John Milton or his poetry. Also **Mil·to·ni·an**, mil·tō′nē·an.

mim, mim, a. [Imit.: cf. mum.] Brit. dial. Primly silent or restrained; affectedly modest; demure.

mime, mīm, mēm, n. [L. mimus, < Gr. mimos, imitator, actor, mime, or farce, akin to mimeisthai, imitate.] A mimic; an actor or comedian specializing in pantomime or mimicry; the art of narration or portrayal of character, idea, or mood by bodily movements; pantomime; a kind of farce popular among the ancient Greeks and Romans in which actual persons and events were represented in a ludicrous way; a player in this kind of farce.—v.t.—mimed, miming. To mimic.—v.i. To play a part by mimicry, esp. without words.—**mim·er**, n.

mim·e·o·graph, mim′ē·o·graf″, mim′ē·o·gräf″, v.t. To duplicate by means of a mimeograph.—n. A device for copying, usu. typewritten material, by using an inked stencil. Also **Mim·e·o·graph**. (Trademark.)

mi·me·sis, mi·mē′sis, mī·mē′sis, n. [Gr.] Rhet. imitation of the manner or speech of another; biol. mimicry.

mi·met·ic, mi·met′ik, mī·met′ik, a. Inclined to imitate; pertaining to, characterized by, or exhibiting mimicry; makebelieve.—**mi·met·i·cal·ly**, adv.

mim·ic, mim′ik, v.t.—mimicked, mimicking. [L. mimicus, Gr. mimikos.] To imitate or copy closely; to imitate in action or speech, esp. in derision; to resemble or copy through biological imitation.—n. One who imitates or mimics; a professional imitator, as an actor or performer;

an imitation or copy.—a. Of or pertaining to mimicry; imitative; simulated or mock. —**mim·i·cal**, a.—**mim·ick·er**, n.

mim·ic·ry, mim′ik·rē, n. pl. **mim·ic·ries**. The act, instance, practice, or result of mimicking; biol. the superficial resemblance of organisms to other organisms, or to a given environment, serving to protect or conceal.

mi·mo·sa, mi·mō′sa, mi·mō′za, n. [N.L., < L. mimus, E. mime: so called from the seeming mimicry of animal life by the sensitive plant.] Any plant of the genus Mimosa, native to tropical regions, and comprising trees, shrubs, and herbs, having usu. bipinnate and often sensitive leaves and small flowers in globular heads or cylindrical spikes.—**mim·o·sa·ceous**, mim″o·sā′shus, mī″mo·sā′shus, a. Belonging to the genus Mimosa.

mi·na, mī′na, n. pl. **mi·nas**, **mi·næ**, mī′nē. [L., < Gr. mnā; < Semitic: cf. Heb. māneh.] An ancient unit of weight and value equal to the sixtieth part of a talent.

min·a·ble, **mine·a·ble**, mī′na·bl, a. Capable of being mined; as, minable ores.

min·a·ret, min″a·ret′, min′a·ret″, n. [Fr. minaret, Sp. minarete, < Ar. mānārah, a lighthouse, a minaret, < nār, to shine.] The slender, lofty turret or tower adjacent to a mosque, usu. with one or more projecting balconies, used by a muezzin for summoning Moslems to daily prayer.— **min·a·ret·ed**, a.

min·a·to·ry, min′a·tōr″ē, min′a·tąr″ē, a. [L. minatorius, < minator, a threatener, mina, a threat.] Threatening; menacing.— **min·a·to·ri·ly**, adv.

mince, mins, v.t.—minced, mincing. [O.E. minsian, < min, small; also O.Fr. mincer, < mince, fine, small.] To cut or chop into very small pieces; as, to mince onions; to diminish in speaking; to extenuate; to palliate; as, to mince matters; to pronounce with affected elegance.—v.i. To walk with short steps; to affect delicacy in manner; to speak with affected elegance.—**minc·er**, min′sėr, n.—**minc·ing**, a.—**minc·ing·ly**, adv.

mince·meat, mins′mēt″, n. Meat chopped fine; a chopped mixture of raisins, apples, other fruit, spices, suet, and usu. meat.— **mince pie**, a pie made of mincemeat.

mind, mīnd, n. [O.E. mynd, gemnyd, mind, thought, intention; Dan. minde, Icel. minni, memory; < root man, to think, seen also in mean, to intend; L. mens, mentis, mind (whence mental); Gr. menos, mind.] The unconscious and conscious processes that perceive, conceive, comprehend, evaluate, and reason; the cognitive and intellectual faculty; rational or sound mental state; sanity; state of thought and feeling; mental disposition; opinion; viewpoint; attention; intention; inclination; memory; recollection; a person of superior intellectual power.—v.t. To pay attention to; to heed; to obey; to attend to; to take care of; concerning; to feel concern about; to be averse to; object to; to notice; to remember. —v.i.—give some·one a piece of one's mind, rebuke.—have a good mind to, have a strong inclination.—on one's mind, occupied with worrisome thoughts.—be of two minds, be in doubt or undecided.— **Di·vine Mind**, Christian Science, the Divine Being.—**mind·er**, mīnd′dėr, n. Chiefly Brit. one who minds or watches over; as, a baby-minder.—**mind·ful**, mīnd′ful, a. Attentive; bearing in mind; heedful. —**mind·ful·ly**, adv.—**mind·ful·ness**, n. Attention.—**mind·less**, mīnd′lis, a. Destitute of mind; stupid; unthinking; inattentive; heedless; careless.—**mind·less·ly**, a. —**mind·less·ness**, n.—**mind·ed**, a. Having a mind of a given kind; as, weak-minded.

mind-bod·y prob·lem, n. Philos. the question of the relationship between mind and body.

mind read·er, n. One who professes the power to read another's mind.—**mind read·ing**, reading or discerning the thoughts in the minds of others, esp. by some alleged supernatural power.

mind's eye, n. Imagination; memory.

mine, mīn, pronominal adjective. [O.E. min, genit. or a. corresponding to me = Dan. and Sw. min, Icel. minn, Goth. meina, D. mijn, G. mein. My is a shortened form.] Possessive of I; belonging to me; as, mine is a brown hat; my; once regularly used before nouns beginning with a vowel; as, mine eyes; now generally used similarly to hers, ours, yours, theirs, as equivalent to my followed by a noun and serving either for a nominative or an objective case.

mine, mīn, n. [Fr. a mine, miner, to form a mine.] A pit or excavation in the earth, from which coal, metallic ores, or other mineral substances are taken by digging; the location, buildings, and equipment of such an excavation. Milit. a contrivance floating on, or near, the surface of the sea to destroy ships by explosion; a similar device used on land against personnel and vehicles; a passage dug under a fortification, in which a quantity of explosives may be lodged for blowing up the works. Fig. a rich source or store of wealth or of anything highly valued.—v.i. To dig a mine; to burrow.—v.t. To dig away the foundation from; to undermine; to sap.— **min·er**, mī′nėr, n.

mine·field, mīn′fēld″, n. Milit. An area of land or water throughout which mines have been laid; the mines in such an area.

mine·lay·er, mīn′lā″ėr, n. A naval ship, esp. constructed and equipped to lay floating mines.

min·er·al, min′ėr·al, min′ral, a. [Fr. minéral, < Med. L. mineralis, < minera, < O.Fr. miniere, mine, < mine, E. mine.] Obtained from mines; of the nature of a mineral; pertaining to minerals; impregnated with a mineral or minerals; as, mineral water; neither animal nor plant; as, the mineral kingdom; inorganic.—n. A substance obtained by mining; specif., any of a class of substances occurring in nature, usually comprising inorganic substances, as quartz or feldspar, of definite chemical composition, but sometimes including aggregations of such substances, more correctly called rocks; certain natural products of organic origin, as asphalt or coal. Mining, ore. Sometimes, any substance neither animal nor plant. Pl., Brit. mineral water.

min·er·al·ize, min′ėr·a·līz″, min′ra·līz″, v.t.—mineralized, mineralizing. To convert into a mineral substance; to transform, as a metal, into an ore; to impregnate or supply with mineral substances; petrify.— v.i. To search for or to study minerals. —**min·er·al·i·za·tion**, n.—**min·er·al·iz·er**, n.

min·er·al·o·gy, min″e·rol′a·jē, min″e·ral′a·jē, n. pl. **min·er·al·o·gies**. The science concerned with minerals; a treatise on mineral science.—**min·er·al·og·i·cal**, min″ėr·a·loj′i·kal, a.—**min·er·al·og·i·cal·ly**, adv.—**min·er·al·o·gist**, n.

min·er·al oil, n. Any of a class of oils of mineral origin, as petroleum and its derivatives, consisting of mixtures of hydrocarbons, and used as illuminants, fuels, and in certain medicines, as a laxative.

min·er·al pitch, n. Asphalt.

min·er·al wa·ter, n. Water which is either naturally or artificially impregnated with gases, carbonates, sulfates or iron, often used for medicinal purposes; pl., Brit. slang, carbonated soft drinks.

a- fat, fāte, fär, fâre, fạll; **e-** met, mē, mēre, hėr; **i-** pin, pīne; **o-** not, nōte, mōve; **u-** tub, cūbe, bụll; **oi-** oil; **ou-** pound.

min·er·al wax, *n.* Ozocerite.

min·er·al wool, *n.* A glassy, woollike substance used as insulation, produced by sending a blast of hot air or steam through molten slag. Also *rock wool*.

min·e·stro·ne, min″i·strō′nē, *It.* mē″ne·-strᾳ′ne, *n.* [It., aug. < *minestra*, soup, < L. *ministrare*, E. *minister*, *v.*] A favorite Italian soup containing vegetables, herbs, and vermicelli in a broth of chicken or meat.

mine·sweep·er, mīn′swē″pẽr, *n. Nav.* a small ship used for dragging a body of water in order to remove or detonate mines laid by an enemy.—**mine·sweep·ing**, *n.*

Ming, ming, *n.* A Chinese dynasty, ruling from 1368 to 1644, during which time earlier institutions were restored and the arts, esp. porcelains, were brought to a high degree of excellence.—*a.* (*Usu. cap.*) characteristic of the Ming dynasty or the art objects it produced; as, *Ming* porcelain.

min·gle, ming′gl, *v.t.*—*mingled, mingling.* [< O.E. *mengan*, to mix, with freq. term. *-le*; D. *mengen, mengelen*, G. *mengen, mengeln*, Icel. *menga*, to mingle; G. *menge*, multitude.] To mix up together so as to form one whole; to blend; to join in social affairs.—*v.i.* To become mixed; to become united; to join; as, to *mingle* with or in a crowd.

ming tree, *n.* A conifer tree, artificially dwarfed, grown in a small pot. See *bonsai*.

min·i·a·ture, min′ē·a·chẽr, min′a·chẽr, *n.* [It. *miniatura*, orig. a design such as that on the margins of old manuscripts, < *miniare*, to write with *minium* or red lead, this pigment being much used in the illuminating of old manuscripts.] A representation or image of anything on a very small scale; a painting, esp. a portrait, of small dimensions, often executed on ivory or vellum; the art of producing such paintings; a small scale; as, shown in *miniature.*—*a.* On a small scale.

min·i·a·tur·ize, min′ē·a·cha·rīz″, min′a·cha·rīz″, *v.t.*—*miniaturized, miniaturizing.* To produce a copy of on a greatly reduced scale; *electron.* to achieve reduction in the size of a product by introducing transistors or other space-saving components.—**min·i·a·tur·i·za·tion**, *n.*

min·i·cab, min′i·kab″, *n.* [(*mini*)ature (*cab*).] A very small car, often of European make, serving as a taxi.

min·i·cam, min′i·kam″, *n.* A miniature camera.

Min·ié ball, min′ē bᾳl″, min′ē·ᾳ″, *Fr.* mē·-nyᾳ′, *n.* [From C. E. Minié, 1804–1879, Fr. inventor.] A conical bullet with a hollow base, expanding, when fired, to fit the rifling of the bore.

min·i·foot·ball, min′i·fut″bᾳl, *n. Aerospace*, an elliptical orbit of a command ship, designed to maintain a path at a fixed minimum distance from an accompanying vehicle.

min·i·fy, min′i·fī″, *v.t.*—*minified, minifying.* [< L. *minor*, less, and E. *-fy*.] To make less; to represent as less than in reality.—**min·i·fi·ca·tion**, *n.*

min·im, min′im, *n.* The smallest liquid measure, equal to one drop or one-sixtieth of a fluidram. See Measures and Weights table. The least of anything; that which is tiny or insignificant. *Chiefly Brit., mus.* a half note.—*a.* Very small; smallest.

min·i·mal, min′i·mal, *a.* Pertaining to or being a minimum; least possible; smallest; very small.—**min·i·mal·ly**, *adv.*

Min·i·mal·ist, min′i·ma·list, *n.* (*Sometimes l.c.*) a member of a less radical group or faction of socialists, esp. such a socialist formerly active in Russian politics.

min·i·mize, min′i·mīz″, *v.t.*—*minimized, minimizing.* To reduce to a minimum; to treat as of the least import or of the smallest

proportion or part.—**min·i·mi·za·tion**, *n.*—**min·i·miz·er**, *n.*

min·i·mum, min′i·mum, *n.* pl. **min·i·mums, min·i·ma.** [L.] The smallest amount or degree; least quantity assignable in a given case, as opposed to *maximum*; an amount arbitrarily fixed by a restaurant or similar establishment designating the smallest charge for food or drink per person. *Math.* a certain functional value which is smaller than any value in the immediate area.—*a.* Made up of or indicating the lowest or least size, degree, or amount possible or attainable; pertaining to a certain minimum.

min·i·mum wage, *n.* A wage level that is established, either by law or by union negotiation, as the least amount to be paid employees for performing certain work.

min·ing, mīn′ing, *n.* The act or work of one who mines, esp. the action, process, or industry of extracting ores from mines; *milit.* the laying of explosive underwater or land mines.

min·ion, min′yon, *n.* [Fr. *mignon*, a darling.] An unworthy favorite; a servile dependent; an official of subordinate authority; a small printing type.

min·is·ter, min′i·stẽr, *n.* One authorized to conduct religious services, as a pastor or clergyman; one to whom the executive head of a government entrusts the direction of certain affairs of state; as, *Minister* of War; a diplomatic representative below ambassadorial rank; one who acts under the authority of another; a servant; an attendant.—*v.t.* To administer, as medicine; to apply.—*v.i.* To act as a religious minister; to perform service; to give things that are needed; to furnish; as, to *minister* to one's needs.

min·is·te·ri·al, min″i·stẽr′ē·al, *a.* Pertaining to ministry or to a minister; pertaining to ministers of state or the performance of service; invested with or pertaining to authority delegated by law.—**min·is·te·ri·al·ist**, min″i·stẽr′ē·a·list, *n. Brit. politics*, one who supports the ministry in office.—**min·is·te·ri·al·ly**, *adv.*

min·is·ter plen·i·po·ten·ti·ar·y, *n.* Plenipotentiary.

min·is·trant, min′i·strant, *a.* [L. *ministrans, ministrantis*.] Performing service; acting as minister or attendant.—*n.* An individual who ministers.

min·is·tra·tion, min″i·strā′shan, *n.* [L. *ministratio*.] The act of ministering or performing service; ecclesiastical function; *often pl.* service or assistance given.—**min·is·tra·tive**, *a.*

min·is·try, min′i·strē, *n.* pl. **min·is·tries.** The act of ministering; the office or functions of a minister, civil or religious; duration of the office of a minister, civil or religious; the clergy; the body of ministers of a state or the chief officials of a government. (*Usu. cap.*) a department of government headed by a minister; the building in which this ministry is housed.

min·i·track, min′i·trak″, *n.* (*Sometimes cap.*), *aerospace*, an electronic tracking system comprised of receiving stations on the ground, which determines the path of an earth satellite by picking up radio waves sent out by a transmitter in the payload.

min·i·um, min′ē·um, *n.* [L. Hence *miniature*.] Red oxide of lead; red lead, Pb_3O_4.

min·i·ver, min′i·vẽr, *n.* [O.Fr. *menu vair*, 'small vair.'] A fur used in the Middle Ages for lining and trimming robes of state, variously described as a white and gray fur, a white fur adorned with pieces of dark fur, or a plain white fur; the winter fur of the ermine.

mink, mingk, *n.* pl. **mink, minks.** A semiaquatic carnivorous mammal, genus *Mustela*, with a slender, weasellike body, esp. *M. vison*, a common N. American species;

the soft, thick, valuable fur of the mink; apparel made of this fur.

min·ne·sing·er, min′i·sing″ẽr, *n.* [O.G. *minne*, love, and *singer*, a singer.] A German lyric poet and singer of the 12th and 13th centuries.

min·now, min′ō, *n.* [M.E. *menow*, appar. < O.E. *myne*, kind of fish.] A small, orig. European fish, *Phoxinus phoxinus*, in the family *Cyprinidae*; a fish used for fishing bait.

Mi·no·an, mi·nō′an, *a.* Referring to the Bronze Age of Cretan culture which flourished from about 3000 to 1100 B.C.—*n.* An inhabitant of ancient Crete.

mi·nor, mī′nẽr, *a.* [L. *minor* (neut, *minus*), less, smaller, inferior, younger, a compar. form (with superl. *minimus*) associated with *parvus*, little.] Lesser, as in size, extent, or importance, or being the lesser of two; as, the *minor* group in a divided deliberative body; of a less important or secondary class or kind; as, *minor* poets, *minor* faults or considerations; under legal age; *logic*, less broad or extensive; as, the *minor* term of a syllogism, or the *minor* premise. *Mus.* of an interval, smaller by a half step than the corresponding major interval; of a chord, having a minor third between the root and the second note; of a tone, distant by a minor interval from a given tone; denoting a scale, mode, or key whose third tone is minor in relation to the fundamental tone.—*n.* One of inferior rank or importance in a specified class; *educ.* a subject or a course of study subordinate or supplementary to a major or principal subject or course. A person under legal age; *logic*, the minor term or premise; *mus.* a minor interval, chord, or scale; (*cap.*) a Minorite or Franciscan friar.—*v.i. U.S.* to pursue a minor subject or course of study, usu. followed by *in.*

Mi·nor·ca, mi·nẽr′ka, *n.* [From the Mediterranean island of *Minorca*.] One of a breed of domestic fowls of large size, notable for prolific laying of eggs.

Mi·nor·can, mi·nᾳr′kan, *a.* Of or relating to Minorca, one of the Balearic islands.—*n.* A native of Minorca.

Mi·nor·ite, mī′no·rīt″, *n.* One of the Franciscan friars.

mi·nor·i·ty, mi·nᾳr′i·tē, mi·nor′i·tē, mī·-nᾳr′i·tē, mi·nor′i·tē, *n.* pl. **mi·nor·i·ties.** [Fr. *minorité*, M.L. *minoritas*, < L. *minor*.] The state or period of being a minor or under legal age; the smaller part or number, or a number forming less than half of the whole; a portion of the population differing from the majority in race, religion, national origin, or political affiliation, esp. when subject to discrimination; a smaller party or group opposed to a majority, as in voting or other action.—*a.*

mi·nor league, *n. U.S.* any professional sports association, as in baseball, aside from the major leagues.—*a.*

mi·nor or·der, *n. Rom. Cath. Ch.* any of the four degrees in the process of becoming a priest, namely porter, lector, acolyte, and exorcist.

mi·nor prem·ise, *n. Logic*, the proposition in a syllogism that involves the subject of the argument's conclusion.

mi·nor suit, *n. Bridge*, clubs or diamonds.

mi·nor term, *n. Logic*, the term, in the minor premise of a syllogism, that becomes the subject of the argument's conclusion.

Min·o·taur, min′o·tᾳr″, *n.* [L. *Minotaurus*, < Gr. *Minōtauros*, < *Minōs*, Minos (king of Crete, for whom the labyrinth was built), and *tauros*, bull.] A monster of Greek mythology, half bull and half man, confined in the Cretan labyrinth and fed with human flesh until slain by Theseus; (*often l.c.*) any devouring or destroying agency.

min·ster, min'stẽr, n. [O.E. mynster, (like G. munster, D. monster), < L. monasterium, a monastery.] The church of a monastery; a cathedral or other important church, often used in combination; as, Westminster.

min·strel, min'strel, n. [O.Fr. menestrel, < L.L. ministrellus, a harper, one who ministered to the amusement of the rich by music or jesting; a dim. < L. minister, a servant.] In the Middle Ages, a roaming musician who subsisted by reciting verse and singing, usu. accompanied by a harp; a singer, musical performer, or poet; a member of the troupe of a minstrel show.—**min·strel·sy,** min'strel·sē, n. The art or occupation of minstrels; a body of songs or ballads; a group of minstrels.

min·strel show, n. A performance consisting of songs, dances, and jokes, given by comedians, musicians, and singers made up in blackface.

mint, mint, n. [O.E. mynet, coin, < L. moneta, mint, money, < Moneta, lit. 'adviser,' surname of Juno, in whose temple Roman money was coined, < monere, remind, advise.] A place in which currency is manufactured by the authority of the government; a place where something is made or fabricated; a very great amount or number of anything, esp. of money.—v.t. To make, as coins, by stamping metal; to coin; fig. to make or fabricate as if by coining; as, to mint words or phases.—a. In unused or original condition; as, a car in mint condition.—**mint·age,** min'tij, n. The act or process of minting; coinage; fabrication; the product or result of minting; the output of a mint; a word, phrase, or the like minted or coined; a stamp or character impressed; the charge for or cost of minting or coining.—**mint·er,** n.

mint, mint, n. [O.E. minte, < L. menta, mentha, < Gr. mintha, mint.] Any plant of the mint family, esp. of the genus Mentha, comprising aromatic herbs with opposite leaves and small vertically arranged flowers, as the spearmint and peppermint; a candy or cooky flavored with mint.

mint ju·lep, n. See julep.

min·u·end, min'ū·end′, n. [L. minuendus, to be lessened, minuo, to lessen.] Math. the number from which another number is to be subtracted.

min·u·et, min'ū·et′, n. [Fr. menuet, very small (with reference to the small steps taken in the dance), dim. of menu, small.] A slow, stately dance of French origin in triple meter, dating back to the 17th century; the music to which a minuet is performed, or is in minuet rhythm.

mi·nus, mi'nus, prep. [L., a., neut. of minor.] Less by the subtraction of, or decreased by; as, 10 minus 3, gross earnings minus cost; wanting or without; as, a book minus its title page, to escape minus hat and coat.—n. The minus sign; a minus quantity; a deficiency or loss.—a. Less; involving or denoting subtraction; as, a minus quantity, the minus sign; negative.

mi·nus·cule, min'u·skūl″, mi·nus'kūl, a. [Fr. < L. minusculus, rather small, dim. of minor.] Very small. Paleography, small, as lower-case letters; written in such letters: opposed to majuscule.—n. A minuscule letter, as distinguished from a capital; the small cursive script developed in the 7th century from the uncial, which it afterward superseded.—**mi·nus·cu·lar,** a.

mi·nus sign, n. Math. a mark or sign (−) indicating the operation of subtraction or a negative quantity.

min·ute, min'it, n. [O.Fr. Fr. minute, < M.L. minuta, small part or division, prop. fem. of L. minutus, E. minute.] The sixtieth part of an hour, or sixty seconds;

an indefinitely short space of time; as, wait a minute; a point of time, or an instant or moment, as: Come here this minute. The sixtieth part of a degree; a rough draft, as of a document; a short note or memorandum; pl. the official record of the proceedings at a meeting of a society, board, committee, council, or other body.—v.t.—minuted, minuting. To time exactly, as movement or speed; to make a draft of, as a document; to record in a memorandum; note down; to enter in the minutes of a society or other body.

mi·nute, mī·nōt′, mī·nūt′, mi·nōt′, mi·nūt′, a.—minuter, minutest. [L. minutus, pp. of minuere, make smaller, akin to minor, less, smaller.] Extremely small, as in size, amount, extent, or degree; as minute portions, differences, or variations; of very small scope or individual importance; attentive to or concerned with very small details or particulars; as, minute inquiries, a minute report.—**mi·nute·ly,** adv.—**mi·nute·ness,** n.

min·ute gun, min'it, n. A gun which is fired at intervals of a minute, as an expression of mourning at a military funeral or as a sign or signal of distress.

min·ute hand, min'it, n. The hand that indicates the minutes on a clock or watch.

min·ute·man, min'it·man″, n. pl. **min·ute·men.** One of the American militiamen just before and during the Revolutionary War who held themselves in readiness for instant military service; aerospace, an intercontinental three-stage ballistic missile with solid-propellant engines. One who belongs to a small conservative secret organization in the United States which consists of armed groups prepared to combat a communist invasion through guerrilla warfare.

min·ute steak, n. A thin cut of beef that requires little cooking time.

mi·nu·ti·a, mi·nō'shē·a, mi·nō'sha, mi·nū'shē·a, mi·nū'sha, n. pl. **mi·nu·ti·ae.** [L. < minutus, small.] Usu. pl. Small or minor details; trifles.

minx, mingks, n. An impudent or forward girl; a flirt.—**minx·ish,** a.

Mi·o·cene, mi'o·sēn″, a. [Gr. meiōn, less, and kainos, recent.] Geol. Relating to or denoting the fourth epoch of the Tertiary period, coming between the Pliocene and Oligocene epochs, and characterized by the development of modern mammals; the strata of this epoch. See Table of Geologic Time.—n. The Miocene epoch or strata.

mir, mēr, n. [Russ.] A Russian commune or peasant community under the Czars.

mir·a·cle, mir'a·kl, n. [Fr. miracle, < L. miraculum, something wonderful, < miror, to wonder.] A wonder; a marvelous thing; something which seems to go beyond the known laws of nature and is held to be the act of a supernatural being; a supernatural event; an indication of a very high standard; as, a miracle of endurance.

mir·a·cle play, n. A dramatic representation, developed in the Middle Ages, which dealt with the lives of the saints or Biblical events.

mi·rac·u·lous, mi·rak'ū·lus, a. Of the nature of a miracle; with the power to effect miracles; effected by the direct agency of supernatural power; exceedingly surprising or wonderful.—**mi·rac·u·lous·ly,** adv.—**mi·rac·u·lous·ness,** n.

mir·a·dor, mir″a·dôr′, n. Sp. arch. a feature of a building such as a window or balcony, intended to provide a view.

mi·rage, mi·räzh′, n. [Fr., < mirer, look at (oneself) in a mirror, see reflected, < M.L. mirare.] An optical illusion, due to atmospheric densities, by which reflected images of distant objects are seen, often inverted; any illusion.

mire, mīer, n. [Same as Icel. mȳrr, mȳri,

Sw. myra, N. myre, a swamp, fen.] Wet, swampy soil; mud; a marsh.—v.t.—mired, miring. To fix or sink in mire, as an automobile; to cause to become fixed in mire; to entangle; to soil or daub with mud.—v.i. To sink in mud; to be unable to advance.—**mir·y,** a.—mirier, miriest.

mirk, mụrk, n., a. Murk.—**mirk·y,** a.—mirkier, mirkiest. Murky.

mir·ror, mir'ẽr, n. [Fr. miroir, a mirror, < mirer, to look at, < L. miror, to admire.] Any polished surface that reflects images of objects; a lookingglass; something depicting a true image; an exemplar.—v.t. To reflect as in a mirror; to provide a true image of.

mirth, mụrth, n. [O.E. myrgth, mirhth, < mirig, merg, merry.] Merriment; gaiety; humorous amusement, usu. accompanied by laughter.—**mirth·ful,** a.—**mirth·ful·ly,** adv.—**mirth·ful·ness,** n.—**mirth·less,** a.

mir·za, mụr'za, Pers. mēr'zä, n. [Persian for emirzadeh, son of the prince—emir, prince, and zadeh, son.] A Persian title of honor, often used to denote a prince.

mis·ad·ven·ture, mis″ad·ven'chẽr, n. An unfortunate event; misfortune or mischance, as an accident or mishap; bad luck.

mis·ad·vise, mis″ad·vīz′, v.t.—misadvised, misadvising. To give bad or erroneous advice to.

mis·al·li·ance, mis″a·lī'ans, n. Any improper alliance or association, esp. an improper connection by marriage; mésalliance.

mis·an·thrope, mis'an·thrōp″, miz'an·thrōp″, n. [Gr. misanthrōpos—miseo, to hate, and anthrōpos, man.] A hater of mankind; one who harbors distrust of human character in general. Also **mi·an·thro·pist,** mis·an'thro·pist, miz·an'thro·pist.—**mis·an·throp·ic,** **mis·an·throp·i·cal,** mis″an·throp'ik, miz″an·throp'ik, a.—**mis·an·throp·i·cal·ly,** adv.—**mis·an·thro·py,** mis·an'thro·pē, miz·an'thro·pē, n.

mis·ap·ply, mis″a·plī′, v.t.—misapplied, misapplying. To apply incorrectly; to use wrongfully.—**mis·ap·pli·ca·tion,** mis″ap·la·ka'shan, n.

mis·ap·pre·hend, mis″ap·ri·hend′, v.t. To misunderstand.—**mis·ap·pre·hen·sion,** mis″ap·ri·hen'shan, n.

mis·ap·pro·pri·ate, mis″a·prō'prē·āt″, v.t.—misappropriated, misappropriating. To appropriate wrongly; to put to a wrong or dishonest use.—**mis·ap·pro·pri·a·tion,** mis″a·prō'prē·ā′shan, n.

mis·be·come, mis″bi·kum′, v.t.—past misbecame, pp. misbecome, ppr. misbecoming. Not to be suitable for; to be unfit for; to be unbecoming to.

mis·be·got·ten, mis″bi·got'en, a. Unlawfully begotten; illegitimate. Also **mis·be·got.**

mis·be·have, mis″bi·hāv′, v.i.—misbehaved, misbehaving. To behave poorly.—v.t. To act badly or improperly; as, to misbehave oneself at a lecture.—**mis·be·hav·er,** n.—**mis·be·ha·vior,** Brit. **mis·be·ha·viour,** mis″bi·hāv'yẽr, n.

mis·be·lief, mis″bi·lēf′, n. False or erroneous belief or opinion.—**mis·be·lieve,** v.i., v.t.—misbelieved, misbelieving.—**mis·be·liev·er,** n.

mis·brand, mis·brand′, v.t. To label falsely; to brand incorrectly; to misrepresent the brand name of.

mis·cal·cu·late, mis·kal'kū·lāt″, v.t.—miscalculated, miscalculating. To judge erroneously; to make a wrong guess or estimate of.—**mis·cal·cu·la·tion,** mis″kal'kū·lā'shan, n.—**mis·cal·cu·la·tor,** n.

mis·call, mis·kạl′, v.t. To call by a wrong name; to name improperly.—**mis·call·er,** n.

mis·car·riage, mis·kar′ij, *n.* The premature expulsion of a nonviable fetus; lack of success at bringing about an expected, just, or proper result; as, a *miscarriage* of justice; the failure of mail, freight, or the like to reach its proper destination.

mis·car·ry, mis·kar′ē, *v.i.—miscarried, miscarrying.* To fail to reach its destination, as a letter; to fail to attain the intended effect; not to succeed; as, the project *miscarried*; to abort.

mis·cast, mis·kast′, mis·käst′, *v.t.—miscast, miscasting.* To cast, as a theatrical production, inappropriately; to select or fill a role with an actor unsuited to the part; to give, as an actor, an unsuitable part or role.

mis·ce·ge·na·tion, mis″i·je·nā′shan, mi·-sej″e·nā′shan, *n.* [L. *miscere,* mix, and *genus,* race.] Mixture of races by sexual union; interbreeding between different races.—**mis·ce·ge·net·ic,** *a.*

mis·cel·la·ne·a, mis″e·lā′nē·a, *n. pl.* [L. neut. pl. of *miscellaneus,* E. *miscellaneous.*] A miscellaneous collection, esp. of literary compositions.

mis·cel·la·ne·ous, mis″e·lā′nē·us, *a.* [L. *miscellaneus,* < *misceo,* to mix.] Consisting of different elements, types, or things intermingled; diversified; many-sided.—**mis·cel·la·ne·ous·ly,** *adv.*—**mis·cel·la·ne·ous·ness,** *n.*

mis·cel·la·ny, mis′e·lā″nē, *Brit.* mi·sel′a·nē, *n. pl.* **mis·cel·la·nies.** [Fr. *miscellanées.*] A mixture of various kinds; a collection of written compositions by several authors on various subjects; *pl.* a collection of separate compositions, treatises, or extracts.—**mis·cel·la·nist,** *n.* One who writes miscellanies.

mis·chance, mis·chans′, mis·chäns′, *n.* Bad luck; misfortune; mishap; misadventure.

mis·chief, mis′chif, *n.* [O.Fr. *mescheif, meschef,* mischief; < Fr. *mes,* Sp. and Pg. *menos* = L. *minus,* less, and *chef* = L. *caput,* the head.] Behavior, often playful, that causes vexation, slight annoyance or minor difficulty; some such specific act; a tendency to vex, tease, or upset; one who or that which is a source of vexation, trouble, or annoyance; harm, injury, or damage attributed to a specific source, as: Rising tides often occasion *mischief.*

mis·chief-mak·er, mis′chif·mā″kėr, *n.* One who makes mischief; one who excites or instigates quarrels or discord.—**mis·chief-mak·ing,** *a., n.*

mis·chie·vous, mis′chi·vus, *a.* Harmful; injurious; fond of mischief; annoying or troublesome in conduct; teasing; playful.—**mis·chie·vous·ly,** *adv.*—**mis·chie·vous·ness,** *n.*

mis·ci·ble, mis′i·bl, *a.* [Fr. *miscible,* < L. *misceo,* to mix.] Capable of being mixed.—**mis·ci·bil·i·ty,** mis″i·bil′i·tē, *n.*

mis·con·ceive, mis″kon·sēv′, *v.t., v.i.—misconceived, misconceiving.* To receive a false notion or opinion of anything; to misunderstand.—**mis·con·ceiv·er,** *n.*—**mis·con·cep·tion,** mis″kon·sep′shan, *n.*

mis·con·duct, mis·kon′dukt, *n.* Immoral conduct, esp. adultery in a legal sense; wrong or bad conduct; misbehavior; mismanagement, esp. by a government official or military personnel.—mis″kon·dukt′, *v.t.* To manage improperly or badly; to misbehave: used reflexively.

mis·con·strue, mis″kon·strö′, *Brit.* mis·-kon′strö, *v.t.—misconstrued, misconstruing.* To interpret erroneously; to take in a wrong sense; to misunderstand.—**mis·con·struc·tion,** mis″kon·struk′shan, *n.*

mis·count, mis·kount′, *v.t., v.i.* To count erroneously; to miscalculate.—*n.* An erroneous counting or numbering; a miscalculation.

mis·cre·ant, mis′krē·ant, *n.* [O.Fr. *mescreant—mes,* less, and *creant,* believing, < L. *credo,* to believe.] A vile wretch; a scoundrel; a villain; *archaic,* an infidel or heretic.—*a.* Wicked, vicious, degenerate.

mis·cre·ate, mis″krē·āt′, *v.t., v.i.—miscreated, miscreating.* To create or shape improperly; misform.—**mis·cre·at·ed,** *a.*

mis·cue, mis·kū′, *n.* Billiards, a slip of the cue, causing it to strike the ball improperly; *colloq.* an error or mistake.—*v.i.—miscued, miscuing.* Billiards, to make a miscue; *theatr.* to miss a cue or answer an incorrect one.

mis·date, mis·dāt′, *v.t.* To date wrongly; affix an incorrect date to.—*n.* An erroneous date.

mis·deal, mis·dēl′, *n.* Cards. A wrong deal; a deal in which each player does not receive his proper cards or his proper number of cards.—*v.t., v.i.—misdealt, misdealing.* To deal cards incorrectly.

mis·deed, mis·dēd′, *n.* An evil or wicked deed; an immoral act.

mis·de·mean, mis″di·mēn′, *v.t., v.i.* To behave improperly.—**mis·de·mean·ant,** mis″di·mē′nant, *n.* One who is guilty of misbehavior; *law,* one convicted of a misdemeanor.—**mis·de·mean·or,** *Brit.* **mis·de·mean·our,** mis″di·mē′nėr, *n.* Misbehavior; a misdeed; *law,* any indictable offense not amounting to a felony.

mis·di·rect, mis″di·rekt′, *v.t.* To give a wrong direction to; to direct to a wrong person or place.—**mis·di·rec·tion,** mis″-di·rek′shan, *n.* A wrong direction; *law,* an error in the charge given by the judge to a jury.

mis·do, mis·dö′, *v.t., v.i.—past misdid, pp. misdone, ppr. misdoing.* To do wrongly; do amiss.—**mis·do·er,** *n.*—**mis·do·ing,** *n.*

mise, mēz, mīz, *n.* [O.Fr., Fr. *mise,* < *mettre,* put, set, < L. *mittere,* send.] A settlement or agreement; *law,* the issue in a writ of right.

mis·em·ploy, mis″em·ploi′, *v.t.* To employ to no purpose, or to a bad or improper purpose.—**mis·em·ploy·ment,** *n.*

mi·ser, mī′zėr, *n.* [L. *miser,* wretched, unhappy, sick, bad.] One who lives in wretched circumstances in order to save and hoard money; a greedy hoarder of wealth; a niggardly, avaricious person.—**mi·ser·li·ness,** *n.*—**mi·ser·ly,** *a.*

mis·er·a·ble, miz′ėr·a·bl, miz′ra·bl, *a.* [O.Fr. *miserable* (Fr. *misérable*), < L. *miserabilis,* pitiable, < *miserari,* pity, < *miser,* wretched.] Being in a state of misery, or in wretched circumstances; wretchedly poor; wretchedly unhappy, uneasy, or uncomfortable. *Colloq.* being in poor health, or ailing. Attended with or causing misery; as, a *miserable* existence; manifesting misery; pitiable or deplorable; as, a *miserable* failure; of bad character; contemptible; of wretched quality; extremely inadequate.—**mis·er·a·ble·ness,** *n.*—**mis·er·a·bly,** *adv.*

Mis·e·re·re, miz″e·râr′ē, miz″e·rēr′ē, *n.* [L., 'have pity,' 'have mercy': the first word of the psalm.] The 51st psalm, or 50th in the Vulgate; a musical setting for this penitential psalm. (*l.c.*) a prayer or expression asking for mercy; the misericord of a church stall.

mis·er·i·cord, mis·er·i·corde, miz″ėr·i·kard′, mi·zer′i·kard″, *n.* [O.Fr. *misericorde* (Fr. *miséricorde*), < L. *misericordia,* < *misericors,* compassionate, < *misereri,* to have pity, and *cor,* heart.] A relaxation of a monastic rule, or a room in a monastery where such relaxations are permitted; a small projection on the under side of a hinged seat of a church stall, which, when the seat is thrown back, gives support to a person standing in the stall and leaning against it; a kind of medieval dagger used

to give the death blow to a fallen adversary.

mis·er·y, miz′e·rē, *n. pl.* **mis·er·ies.** [O.Fr. *miserie,* Fr. *misère,* L. *miseria,* < *miser,* wretched.] Wretchedness of condition or circumstances; wretchedness or distress caused by privation or poverty; great distress of mind; extreme unhappiness; extreme bodily discomfort or pain; a cause or source of wretchedness.

mis·es·ti·mate, mis·es′ti·māt″, *v.t.—misestimated, misestimating.* To estimate wrongly.—mis·es′ti·mit, *n.* An incorrect estimate.—**mis·es·ti·ma·tion,** *n.*

mis·fea·sance, mis·fē′zans, *n.* [O.Fr. *mesfaisance.*] *Law.* The wrongful performance of a lawful act; the wrongful and injurious exercise of lawful authority.—**mis·fea·sor,** *n.*

mis·file, mis·fīl′, *v.t.—misfiled, misfiling.* To file improperly.

mis·fire, mis·fīėr′, *v.i.—misfired, misfiring.* To fail to fire or explode at the proper time or in the proper manner; as, a weapon that *misfired*; to fail to ignite properly; as, an engine that *misfired*; to fail to gain or reach an intended or desired end, as: The plan *misfired.—n.*

mis·fit, mis·fit′, *v.t., v.i.—misfitted, misfitting.* To fit poorly.—mis·fit′, mis′fit, *n.* A wrong or bad fit; *fig.* one who does not or cannot adjust to his situation or surroundings.

mis·for·tune, mis·fär′chan, *n.* Ill fortune; ill luck; calamity; mishap.

mis·giv·ing, mis·giv′ing, *n. Often pl.* a feeling of doubt, distrust, or apprehension.

mis·gov·ern, mis·guv′ėrn, *v.t.* Tó govern or manage badly.—**mis·gov·ern·ment,** *n.*

mis·guide, mis·gīd′, *v.t.—misguided, misguiding.* To guide wrongly; mislead.—**mis·guid·ance,** *n.*—**mis·guid·ed,** mis·gī′did, *a.* Misled; misdirected; erring.—**mis·guid·ed·ly,** *adv.*—**mis·guid·er,** *n.*

mis·han·dle, mis·han′dl, *v.t.—mishandled, mishandling.* To handle or manage badly; to maltreat.

mis·hap, mis′hap, mis·hap′, *n.* Mischance; a lamentable accident; misfortune.

mish·mash, mish′mash″, mish′mäsh″, *n.* [Varied redupl. of *mash.*] A hodgepodge; a jumble.

Mish·nah, Mish·na, mish′na, *Heb.* mish′-nä′, *n. pl.* **Mish·na·yoth, Mish·noth,** mish′na·yōt″, *Heb.* mish·nä′yạt′. [Heb. *mishnāh,* instruction.] *Judaism.* The collection of precepts that forms the basis of the Talmud, assembled about A.D. 200 by Rabbi ha-Nasi; any article of this collection; any collection of the traditional or oral doctrine of Judaism.—**Mish·na·ic, Mish·nic, Mish·ni·cal,** mish·nā′ik, *a.*

mis·in·form, mis″in·fąrm′, *v.t.* To give incorrect or misleading information to.—**mis·in·form·ant, mis·in·form·er,** *n.*—**mis·in·for·ma·tion,** mis″in·fėr·mā′shan, *n.*

mis·in·ter·pret, mis″in·tụr′prit, *v.t.* To interpret erroneously; to understand or explain in a wrong sense.—**mis·in·ter·pre·ta·tion,** mis″in·tụr″pre·tā′shan, *n.*—**mis·in·ter·pret·er,** *n.*

mis·join·der, mis·join′dėr, *n. Law.* A joining, in one suit or action, of causes or of parties that ought not to be so joined.

mis·judge, mis·juj′, *v.t., v.i.—misjudged, misjudging.* To judge erroneously; to form false or unjust opinions or notions.—**mis·judg·ment,** *Brit.* **mis·judge·ment,** *n.*

mis·lay, mis·lā′, *v.t.—mislaid, mislaying.* To lay in a place not recollected; to lay wrongly, as: He *mislaid* the tile.

mis·lead, mis·lēd′, *v.t.—misled, misleading.* To lead astray; to guide into error; to deceive.—**mis·lead·er,** *n.*—**mis·lead·ing,** mis·lē′ding, *a.*

mis·man·age, mis·man′ij, *v.t.—mismanaged, mismanaging.* To manage or administer poorly, improperly, or dishonestly.—**mis·-man·age·ment**, *n.*

mis·mar·riage, mis·mar'ij, *n.* A marriage between a man and woman who are unsuited to one another, incompatible, or unhappy with one another.

mis·match, mis·mach', *v.t.* To match badly or unsuitably, as boxers.—*n.*

mis·mate, mis·māt', *v.t.*—*mismated, mismating.* To mate or match unsuitably.

mis·name, mis·nām', *v.t.*—*misnamed, misnaming.* To call by the wrong name.

mis·no·mer, mis·nō'mèr, *n.* [Prefix *mis-*, < Fr. prefix *mes-*, wrong and *nommer*, to name.] A mistaken or inapplicable name or designation; an incorrect naming, esp. on a legal document.

mi·sog·a·mist, mi·sog'a·mist, mī·sog'a·-mist, *n.* [Gr. *miseō*, to hate, and *gamos*, marriage.] A hater of marriage.—**mi·sog·-a·my**, mi·sog'a·mē, mī·sog'a·mē, *n.* Hatred of marriage.

mi·sog·y·ny, mi·soj'i·nē, mī·soj'i·nē, *n.* [Gr. *miseō*, to hate, and *gynē*, woman.] Hatred of women.—**mi·sog·y·nic**, mi·-sog·y·nous, *a.*—**mi·sog·y·nist**, *n.*

mi·sol·o·gy, mi·sol'o·jē, mī·sol'o·jē, *n.* [Gr. *misologia*, < *misein*, hate, and *logos*, reason.] Hatred of reason or reasoning.—**mi·sol·o·gist**, *n.*

mis·o·ne·ism, mis″ō·nē'iz·um, mī″sō·-nē'iz·um, *n.* [It. *misoneismo*, < Gr. *misein*, hate, and *neos*, new.] Hatred or dislike of a change or what is new.—**mis·o·ne·ist**, *n.*—**mis·o·ne·is·tic**, *a.*

mis·pick·el, mis'pik″el, *n.* [G.] Arsenopyrite.

mis·place, mis·plās', *v.t.*—*misplaced, misplacing.* To put in a wrong or unrecollected place; put, as trust or faith, in an improper, unwise, or unfitting idea, person, or thing.—**mis·place·ment**, *n.*

mis·play, mis·plā', *n. Games, sports,* a wrong or inept play, or one that is against the rules.—*v.t.* To break the rules or make an error on or with.

mis·print, mis·print', *v.t.* To make a mistake in printing; to print wrongly.—**mis'-print″**, mis·print', *n.* A mistake in printing; a deviation from the original copy.

mis·pri·sion, mis·prizh'an, *n.* [< Fr. prefix *mes* (= L. *minus*, less), and L. *prehensio*, a taking, < *prehendo*, to take.] *Law.* Malfeasance by a public official; failure of any citizen to reveal to the authorities knowledge of a crime, esp. of treason or a felony, or failure to attempt to prevent its commission.

mis·prize, **mis·prise**, mis·prīz', *v.t.*—*misprized, misprizing, misprised, misprising.* [O.Fr. *mespriser*, (Fr. *mépriser*), to despise—prefix *mes*, mis = L. *minus*, less, and *priser* = L. *pretiare*, to prize, < *pretium*, price.] To scorn or undervalue; to despise.

mis·pro·nounce, mis″pro·nouns', *v.t., v.i.*—*mispronounced, mispronouncing.* To pronounce erroneously or incorrectly.—**mis·-pro·nun·ci·a·tion**, mis″pro·nun″sē·ā'-shan, *n.*

mis·quote, mis·kwōt', *v.t., v.i.*—*misquoted, misquoting.* To quote erroneously; to cite incorrectly.—**mis·quo·ta·tion**, mis″kwō·-tā'shan, *n.*

mis·read, mis·rēd', *v.t.*—*misread, mis·red', misreading.* To read incorrectly; to interpret wrongly.

mis·reck·on, mis·rek'on, *v.t., v.i.* To reckon or compute incorrectly; miscalculate.

mis·re·mem·ber, mis″ri·mem'bèr, *v.t., v.i.* To remember incorrectly.

mis·re·port, mis″ri·pōrt', *v.t.* To report erroneously or incorrectly.—*n.* An erroneous report.

mis·rep·re·sent, mis″rep·ri·zent', *v.t.* To give a false or erroneous representation of; to represent in an inadequate manner; as,

to *misrepresent* one's country.—**mis·rep·-re·sen·ta·tion**, *n.*—**mis·rep·re·sen·ta·-tive**, *a.*—**mis·rep·re·sent·er**, *n.*

mis·rule, mis·rōl', *n.* Bad rule; unjust government; disorder; lawless confusion.—*v.t.*—*misruled, misruling.* To rule unjustly; to govern unwisely or oppressively.

miss, mis, *v.t.* [O.E. *missan*, to miss = D. and G. *missen*, Icel. *missa*, Dan. *miste*, to miss; closely akin to Teut. prefix *mis*; same root as O.E. *mithan*, to conceal, avoid; G. *meiden*, to avoid.] To fail to hit or reach; as, to *miss* a target; to fail to meet; as, to *miss* a plane; to fail to obtain or find; as, to *miss* a path; to fail to perceive or understand; as, to *miss* the point; to discover the absence of; as, to *miss* one's keys; to feel or perceive the absence of, mourn the loss of; as, to *miss* a friend; to omit; as, to *miss* a meal; to avoid; as, to *miss* injury; to fail to be present at; as, to *miss* a meeting; to let slip; as, to *miss* one's chance.—*v.i.* To fail to hit or strike what is aimed at; as, an arrow that *missed*; to be unsuccessful; *colloq.* to misfire.—*n.* A failure to hit, reach, obtain, do, or the like; loss; want.—**miss·ing**, *a.* Absent from the place where it was expected to be found; not to be found; wanting; lost.

miss, mis, *n.* pl. **miss·es**. [Contr. < *mistress.*] An unmarried female; a young lady; a girl; (*cap.*) a title of address prefixed to the name of an unmarried female; (*often cap.*) a term of address used in speaking to a young woman, as: Come here, Miss.

mis·sal, mis'al, *n.* [L.L. *missale, liber missalis*, < *missa*, the mass.] The Roman Catholic liturgical book containing the office of the mass; any prayer book.

mis·sel, mis'el, *n.* [< its feeding on the mistletoe; cf. G. *mistel-drossel*, mistletoe thrush.] A large thrush, *Turdus viscivorous*, common to Europe, which subsists largely on the berries of the mistletoe. Also **mis·sel thrush**, **mis·tle thrush**.

mis·send, mis·send', *v.t.*—*missent, missending.* To send to a wrong place or person.

mis·shape, mis·shāp', *v.t.*—*past misshaped, pp. misshaped* or *misshapen, ppr. misshaping.* To shape poorly; to give a wrong form to; to deform.—**mis·shap·en**, mis·shā'pen, *a.* Badly formed; deformed.—**mis·shap·en·-ly**, *adv.*—**mis·shap·en·ness**, *n.*

mis·sile, mis'il, *Brit.* mis'īl, *a.* [L. *missilis*, < *mitto, missum*, to send, to throw.] Capable of being thrown or projected from the hand or from any instrument or engine; designed for throwing or firing missiles.—*n.* A weapon or projectile thrown or to be thrown, as a lance, arrow, or bullet; a self-propelled unmanned weapon; as, a guided *missile* or rocket.

mis·sile·man, mis'il·man, *n.* pl. **mis·-sile·men**. A person skilled in designing, building, or operating missiles. Also **mis·sil·eer**.

mis·sile·ry, mis'il·rē, *n.* The science of manufacturing and operating guided missiles. Also **mis·sil·ry**.

miss·ing link, *n.* Something lacking for the completion of a series or sequence of any kind; a hypothetical form of animal assumed to have constituted a connecting link between the anthropoid apes and man.

mis·sion, mish'an, *n.* [L. *missio*, a sending < *mitto, missum*, to send.] A person or group of persons acting as an envoy; the tasks or objectives of those acting as envoys; the sending of an individual or group by an authority to perform a specific service; as, a religious *mission*, diplomatic *mission*, military *mission*; the building, such as an embassy, church, or mission house, which houses the operations of an envoy; a religious congregation without a resident clergyman; a special vocation or calling, as: Medicine was his life's *mission.*—*v.t.* To

assign a mission to, as a person or persons; to organize or establish a mission amidst or in.—*a.* Of or relating to a mission; of or denoting the style of the early Spanish missions of the American Southwest; as, *mission* furniture, *mission* architecture.

mis·sion·ar·y, mish'a·ner″ē, *n.* pl. **mis·-sion·ar·ies**. Anyone under church sponsorship sent to an area to spread religion or carry on educational or charitable activities; one who tries to convert others to a system or belief which he strongly favors; anyone sent on a mission. Also **mis·sion·er**.—*a.* Pertaining to or devoted to missions; possessing or denoting the desire to convert others; characteristic of missionaries.

mis·sis, mis'iz, mis'is, *n. Slang*, wife, as: I gave it to the *missis. Dial.* mistress, as a woman in charge of a household. Also **mis·sus**.

Mis·sis·sip·pi·an, mis″i·sip'ē·an, *a.* Of or pertaining to the State of Mississippi or the Mississippi River; *geol.* denoting or pertaining to a geological subdivision or a layer of rocks which comprises the lower or earlier portion of the Carboniferous period in N. America.—*n.* A native or inhabitant of Mississippi; *geol.* the Mississippian subdivision.

mis·sive, mis'iv, *n.* [Fr. *missive*, a letter, < L. *missus*, sent.] A letter sent, esp. one from some authoritative or official source.—*a.* Sent or proceeding from; intended to be sent.

mis·spell, mis·spel', *v.t., v.i.*—*misspelled* or *misspelt, misspelling.* To spell wrongly or incorrectly.—**mis·spell·ing**, *n.*

mis·spend, mis·spend', *v.t.*—*misspent, misspending.* To spend amiss or to no purpose; to waste; to spend for wrong uses.

mis·state, mis·stāt', *v.t.*—*misstated, misstating.* To state wrongly; to make an erroneous statement of.—**mis·state·ment**, *n.*

mis·step, mis·step', *n.* An erroneous step; a mistake in behavior.

miss·y, mis'ē, *n.* pl. **miss·ies**. *Colloq.*, dim. Miss; young girl.

mist, mist, *n.* [O.E. *mist*, gloom, cloud = L.G., D., and Sw. *mist*, Icel. *mistr*, mist; akin G. *mist*, dung; < root seen in Skt. *mih*, to sprinkle.] Visible watery vapor suspended in the atmosphere at or near the surface of the earth; aqueous vapor condensed on the surface of something, blurring it; *meteor.* a haze in which horizontal visibility is more than one kilometer but less than two. Something which dims or darkens, and obscures or intercepts vision; a film in front of the eyes; a cloud of particles, as of dust, resembling a mist.—*v.t.* To cover with mist; to cloud.—*v.i.* To be misty; to become misty; to drizzle.—**mist·i·ly**, *adv.*—**mist·i·ness**, *n.*

mis·take, mi·stāk', *v.t.*—*past mistook, pp. mistaken, ppr. mistaking.* To err in identifying; to select wrongly; to regard otherwise than as the facts warrant; to misjudge, misinterpret, or misevaluate.—*v.i.* To be under a misapprehension or misconception; to be in error.—*n.* An error in opinion, judgment, or perception, due to inadequate knowledge, carelessness, inattention, or the like; a wrong act done unintentionally.—**mis·tak·a·ble**, mi·stā'ka·bl, *a.* Capable of being mistaken or misconceived.—**mis·-tak·en**, mi·stā'ken, *a.* Erroneous; incorrect; having made, or laboring under, a mistake; wrong; founded on or springing from an error.—**mis·tak·en·ly**, *adv.*—**mis·tak·-en·ness**, *n.*—**mis·tak·er**, *n.*

Mis·ter, mis'tèr, *n.* [Var. of *master.*] The conventional title of respect for a man, prefixed to the name and to certain official designations; title of address for all naval officers below commander, and for military warrant officers, flight officers, and cadets;

(*l.c.*) sir: used in direct address without the surname. Abbr. *Mr.*

mist·flow·er, mist'flou″ẻr, *n.* A N. American asteraceous plant, *Eupatorium coelestinum,* with heads of blue flowers.

mis·think, mis·thingk′, *v.i.—misthought, misthinking. Archaic,* to think mistakenly.—*v.t. Archaic,* to think ill or unfavorably of.

mis·time, mis·tīm′, *v.t.—mistimed, mistiming.* To time wrongly; to speak or act at an inappropriate moment.

mis·tle·toe, mis′l·tō″, *n.* [O.E. *misteltān,* Icel. *mistel-teinn.*] A European plant, *Viscum album,* growing parasitically on trees, with thick yellowish-green leaves and flowers and, in winter, small white berries: used as a Christmas decoration. A related American plant, *Phoradendron flavescens,* Oklahoma's State flower.

mis·tral, mis′tral, mi·sträl′, *n.* [Pr. < L. *magistralis,* lit. 'the master-wind.'] A violently cold, northerly wind common to southern France and nearby areas.

mis·treat, mis·trēt′, *v.t.* To treat improperly; to maltreat.—**mis·treat·ment,** *n.*

mis·tress, mis′tris, *n.* [O.Fr. *maistresse* (Fr. *maitresse*), fem. corresponding to *maistre,* L. *magister,* a master.] A woman who has authority, command, or ownership, esp. the female head of a family, household, estate, or school; a woman exercising supremacy over anything; as, *mistress* of his money; a woman cohabiting unlawfully with a man, esp. when the man supports her financially; a female owner of an animal or formerly a slave; anything regarded as feminine that rules or commands; a female who has attained mastery in a field; *chiefly Brit.* a female teacher.

mis·tri·al, mis·trī′al, mis·trīl′, *n. Law.* A trial vitiated by some error; an inconclusive trial, as where the jury cannot agree.

mis·trust, mis·trust′, *n.* Want of confidence or trust; suspicion.—*v.t.* To suspect; to doubt.—*v.i.* To be doubtful or suspicious. —**mis·trust·ful,** *a.*—**mis·trust·ful·ly, mis·trust·ing·ly,** *adv.*—**mis·trust·ful·ness,** *n.*

mist·y, mis′tē, *a.—mistier, mistiest.* Clouded or covered with mist; made up of or characterized by mist; indefinite; indistinct.

mis·un·der·stand, mis″un·dėr·stand′, *v.t., v.i.—misunderstood, misunderstanding.* To misconceive or misinterpret; to mistake; to take in a wrong sense.

mis·un·der·stand·ing, mis″un·dėr·stan′ding, *n.* Misconception; mistake of meaning; error; disagreement; dissension.

mis·us·age, mis·ū′sij, mis·ū′zij, *n.* Improper or incorrect use or employment, esp. of words; abuse.

mis·use, mis·ūz′, *v.t.—misused, misusing.* To treat or use improperly; to use to a bad purpose; to abuse; to maltreat.—mis·ūs′, *n.* Improper use; employment in a wrong way or to a bad purpose; abuse.—**mis·us·er,** mis·ū′zẻr, *n.* An individual who misuses; *law,* abuse of a franchise, benefit, privilege, office, or the like.

mis·val·ue, mis·val′ū, *v.t.—misvalued, misvaluing.* To value wrongly.

mis·ven·ture, mis·ven′chẻr, *n.* An unfortunate venture; a misadventure.

mis·write, mis·rīt′, *v.t.—past miswrote,* pp. *miswritten,* ppr. *miswriting.* To write in an incorrect way.

mite, mīt, *n.* [O.E. *mīte* = D. *mijt,* L.G. *mite,* Dan. *mide,* G. *miete—*mite; < root seen in Icel. *meita,* Goth. *maita,* to cut.] Any of numerous small, usu. minute animals, order *Acarina,* including many which live as parasites on animals, plants, and foods.

mite, mīt, *n.* [D. *mijt,* a small coin; perh. lit. 'something cut small,' the origin being same as *mite,* a small insect.] A small coin or a small amount of money; a very small particle, quantity, object, or contribution.

mi·ter, *Brit.* **mi·tre,** mī′tẻr, *n.* [O.Fr. Fr. *mitre,* < L. *mitra,* < Gr. *mitra,* belt, girdle, headband, headdress.] The tall, official headdress of a bishop in the Western Church, deeply cleft crosswise, the outline of the front and back resembling a pointed arch; bishopric; a headband worn in ancient times by Greek women; the official headdress of the ancient Jewish high priest; a miter joint.—*v.t.—mitered, mitering, Brit. mitred, mitring.* To bestow a miter upon, or raise to a rank entitled to it.

mi·ter box, mi·tre box, *n. Carp.* a narrow box or trough having on the sides vertical kerfs which are used to cut the angle pieces for a miter joint.

mi·ter joint, mi·tre joint, *n.* A joint in which the plane of the abutting surfaces bisects the angle formed by the pieces.— **mi·ter, mi·tre,** *v.t.—mitered, mitering, Brit. mitred, mitring.* To construct or join by a miter joint.

mi·ter square, *n.* A measuring tool used in the construction of miter joints consisting of a pair of straight edges either fixed at a 45° angle or adjustable to any angle.

mith·ri·date, mith′ri·dāt″, *n.* [M.L. *mithridātum,* < L. *Mithridātēs,* name of a king of Pontus who is said to have rendered himself immune to poisons by taking them in small doses.] *Old pharm.* a substance which was believed to be a universal antidote against poison.—**mith·ri·dat·ic,** mith″ri·dat′ik, *a.*

mith·ri·da·tism, mith′ri·dā″tiz·um, *n.* The production of immunity against the action of a poison by taking the poison in gradually increased doses.

mit·i·cide, mit′i·sīd″, *n.* A chemical agent that kills mites.—**mit·i·cid·al,** *a.*

mit·i·gate, mit′i·gāt″, *v.t.—mitigated, mitigating.* [L. *mitigo, mitigatum,* to mitigate, < *mitis,* mild.] To alleviate or render less painful, rigorous, intense or severe; to assuage, lessen, abate.—*v.i.* To become milder; diminish in severity.— **mit·i·ga·ble,** mit′i·ga·bl, *a.*—**mit·i·ga·tion,** *n.*—**mit·i·ga·tive,** *a.*—**mit·i·ga·tor,** *n.*—**mit·i·ga·to·ry,** mit′i·ga·tōr″ē, *a.*

mi·tis, mī′tis, mē′tis, *n.* [L. *mitis,* mild.] A malleable iron produced by fusing wrought iron with a small amount of aluminum, the aluminum rendering the product fluid enough to cast. Also **mi·tis met·al, mi·tis i·ron.**—*a.*

mi·to·chon·dri·on, mī″to·kon′drē·on, mit″o·kon′drē·on, *n. pl.* **mi·to·chon·dri·a,** mī″to·kon′drē·a, mit″o·kon′drē·a. *Biol.* one of the minute, threadlike, granular bodies in the cytoplasm of the cell that is thought to function in phases of cellular metabolism. Also *chondriosome.*—**mi·to·chon·dri·al,** *a.*

mi·to·sis, mī·tō′sis, *n. pl.* **mi·to·ses,** mī·tō′sēz″. [N.L., < Gr. *mitos,* a thread.] *Biol.* the usual method of cell division, characterized typically by the resolving of the chromatin of the nucleus into a threadlike form, which separates into segments or chromosomes, each of which in turn separates longitudinally into two parts, one part of each chromosome being retained in each of two new cells resulting from the orig. cell. Compare *amitosis.*—**mi·tot·ic,** mī·tot′ik, *a.*—**mi·tot·i·cal·ly,** *adv.*

mi·tral, mī′tral, *a.* Of, pertaining to, or resembling a miter. *Anat.* noting or pertaining to a valve in the heart which prevents the blood in the left ventricle from returning to the left auricle.

mitt, mit, *n.* [Abbr. of *mitten.*] A mitten; a laced glove without fingers, worn by women and sometimes extending as far as or beyond the elbow; *baseball,* a large, rounded, heavily padded glove worn for hand protection. *Slang,* a hand; a boxing glove.

mit·ten, mit′en, *n.* [Fr. *mitaine,* < *mite,* mitten.] A covering for the hand, differing from a glove in not having a separate cover for each finger, only the thumb being separate; a mitt.

mit·ti·mus, mit′i·mus, *n.* [L., we send.] *Law.* A warrant of commitment to prison; a writ for removing records from one court to another.

mix, miks, *v.t.—mixed or mixt, mixing.* [First in *mixed,* pp., for older *mixt,* < L. *mixtus,* pp. of *miscēre,* mix; akin to Gr. *mignynai,* Skt. *mic-,* mix.] To put together, as various substances, into one mass or compound by blending all ingredients thoroughly; to put together haphazardly, often with *up;* to jumble or confuse; to join, associate, or unite with in company; to put in an extra ingredient; as, to *mix* a little flour with the gravy; to form by combining ingredients; as, to *mix* a martini; to crossbreed.—*v.i.* To become mixed; to associate in company; as, to *mix* well with strangers; to be crossbred.—*n.* The product or result of mixing; a combination of ingredients prepared, packaged, and sold commercially as a time- or work-saving preparation, usu. requiring the addition of a liquid; as, a cake *mix,* cement *mix;* the proportioned ingredients or formula of a mixture; as, a *mix* of four to one; an often carbonated beverage, as ginger ale, which is added to alcoholic liquors; *colloq.* a muddle or mess. —**mix it, mix it up,** *slang.* To fight or argue; fisticuff.—**mix up,** to confuse; to mistake a person or object with another.— **mix·a·bil·i·ty, mix·a·ble·ness,** miks″a·bil′i·tē, *n.*—**mix·a·ble, mix·i·ble,** *a.*

mixed, mikst, *a.* Put together or formed by mixing; composed of different constituents or elements; as, a *mixed* chorus of both male and female voices; of different kinds combined; as, *mixed* candies, *mixed* emotions; comprising persons of different status, character, races, sexes, opinions; as, *mixed* society, *mixed* foresome; *colloq.* mentally confused; *phon.* noting central articulation of a vowel; *law,* applying to or made up of two or more types or classes of issue or action.—**mixed up,** completely confused.

mixed bud, *n. Bot.* a bud that contains the embryonic structures for both leaves and flowers.

mixed farm·ing, *n.* The raising of various crops and livestock on a farm, both for sale and for consumption by the farmer and his family.

mixed num·ber, *n.* A number consisting of a whole number and a fraction, as $4\frac{1}{2}$.

mix·er, mik′sẻr, *n.* One who or that which mixes; a kitchen appliance used to beat, blend, or mix food. *Slang,* a person with a capacity for mixing sociably with others; a gathering, often a dance, held to acquaint people with one another. *Radio, TV,* a system used in combining or blending sounds from more than one source; the technician who operates such a system.

mix·ture, miks′chẻr, *n.* [L. *mixtura,* < *miscere.*] The act of mixing, or the state of being mixed; a product of mixing; an assemblage of ingredients mixed together but not chemically combined; a fabric woven of yarns combining various colors; any combination of differing elements, kinds, or qualities; an added element or ingredient; an admixture.

mix-up, miks′up″, *n.* A confused state of things; a muddle; *colloq.* a fight.

miz·zen, miz′en, *n.* [Fr. *misaine,* < It. *mezzana,* prop. fem. of *mezzano,* middle, < L. *medianus,* E. *median*] *Naut.* The aftermost fore-and-aft sail of a three-masted

---

ch- chain, G. na**ch**t;   **th-** **TH**en, thin;   **w-** wig, hw as sound in whig;   **z-** zh as in azure, zeal.   *Italicized vowel* indicates schwa sound.

vessel, set abaft the mizzenmast; the sail on the mizzenmast of a ketch, yawl, or the like; a mizzenmast.—**miz·zen·mast,** *n.* *Naut.* The aftermost mast of a three-masted vessel; in a ketch, yawl, or the like, the mast nearest the stern.—**miz·zen·top,** *n. Naut.* a platform at the head of the lower mizzenmast.

miz·zle, miz'l, *v.i.*—*mizzled, mizzling.* [Origin obscure.] *Brit. slang,* to disappear suddenly; run off. To drizzle.

mne·mon·ics, nē·mon'iks, ni·mon'iks, *n. pl. but sing. in constr.* [Gr. *mnēmonikos,* pertaining to memory, < *mnēmōn,* mindful, *mnasthai,* to remember; same root as in E. *mind.*] The art or system of memory training. Also **mne·mo·tech·nics,** nē″mō·tek′niks.—**mne·mon·ic,** nē·mon'ik, ni·mon'ik, *a.* Pertaining to mnemonics; assisting or training the memory.—**mne·mon·i·cal·ly,** *adv.*

mo·a, mō'a, *n.* [Maori.] Any of various extinct, large, flightless, birds of New Zealand, constituting the family *Dinornithidæ,* resembling an ostrich in general appearance.

Mo·ab·ite, mō'a·bīt″, *a.* [From *Mōab,* one of the sons of Lot, Gen. xix. 37.] Of or pertaining to the Moabites, their kingdom, or their language. Also **Mo·a·bit·ic, Mo·a·bit·ish,** mō'a·bit'ik, mō'a·bī″tish. —*n.* An inhabitant of the kingdom of Moab; a language of the Moabite people.— **Mo·a·bit·ess,** mō'a·bī″tis, *n.* Feminine of Moabite.

moan, mōn, *v.i.* [O.E. *mone, moone,* etc., O.E. *maenān,* to moan; perh. an imit. word.] To utter a low dull sound from grief or pain; to make lamentations.—*v.t.* To mourn or lament; to express mournfully.—*n.* A low dull sound due to grief or pain; a sound resembling that made by a person moaning.

moat, mōt, *n.* [Fr. *mote,* L.L. *mota,* the mound of earth dug from a trench.] A ditch or deep trench, often filled with water, surrounding the rampart of a castle or other fortified place to serve as a defense.—*v.t.* To surround with or as with a ditch for defense.

mob, mob, *n.* [Abbr. < L. *mobile vulgus,* the fickle crowd, < *mobilis,* movable, fickle, < *moveo,* to move.] A riotous or disorderly crowd; a lawless crowd; rabble; the lower classes or common people; the masses; *colloq.* a group of criminals.—*v.t.*—*mobbed, mobbing.* To overcrowd; to attack by crowding.—**mob·bish,** *a.*

mob·cap, mob'kap″, *n.* A large, loose, full-crowned cap, usu. tied beneath the chin, formerly worn indoors by women. Also **mob.**

mo·bile, mō'bil, *a.* [Fr. *mobile,* L. *mobilis,* fickle, mobile, movable, < *moveo,* to move.] Capable of being easily moved; moving; fast-flowing; changeable; varying in goal, emotion, or appearance; readily adaptable; responsive; an individual's or group's ability to move from one social level to another; equipped to move easily; of or pertaining to a mobile.—**mo·bil·i·ty,** mō·bil'i·tē, *n.* [Fr. *mobilité,* L. *mobilitas.*] The state, quality, or condition of being mobile.

mo·bile, mō'bēl, *Brit.* mō'bīl, *n.* A structure made of several balanced parts, often of metal wire, the parts capable of independent motion when in contact with air currents or a mechanical force.

mo·bile home, *n.* Trailer; a large trailer-like home capable of being readily moved to new locations.

mo·bi·lize, mō'bi·līz″, *v.t.*—*mobilized, mobilizing.* [Fr. *mobiliser.*] To put in a state of readiness for active military service; to organize, as resources or industry, for use in time of national emergency; to marshal,

as one's energies, for use or action.—*v.i.* To undergo preparation or organization for use or action.—**mo·bi·li·za·tion,** *n.*

mob·oc·ra·cy, mob·ok'ra·sē, *n. pl.* **mob·-oc·ra·cies.** Rule or political control by a mob; the mob as a controlling power.— **mob·o·crat,** mob'o·krat″, *n.* One who advocates mobocracy; a leader of the mob. —**mob·o·crat·ic, mob·o·crat·i·cal,** *a.*

mob·ster, mob'stẽr, *n. Slang.* One who belongs to a criminal group; a gangster.

moc·ca·sin, mok'a·sin, mok'a·zin, *n.* [< Algonquian Indian.] A kind of soft shoe with a low heel and no laces, resembling a slipper; a heelless shoe, made of deerskin or other soft leather, similar to that once worn by American Indians; any of several venomous snakes of the genus *Agkistrodon,* found in southern U.S.

moc·ca·sin flow·er, *n.* A cypripedium; a lady's slipper.

mo·cha, mō'ka, *n.* [From *Mocha (Mokha),* seaport of Arabia near the mouth of the Red Sea.] A choice variety of coffee, originally coming from Mocha, Arabia; a coffee, or coffee-chocolate flavoring; a light chocolate-brown color; a very fine, soft, glove leather made from the skin of African sheep.—*a.*

mock, mok, *v.t.* [Fr. *moquer,* in *se moquer,* to mock, flout; origin doubtful; cf. It. *mocca,* a grimace; also Gr. *mokos,* mockery.] To imitate or mimic, esp. in contempt or derision; to deride; ridicule; treat with scorn; to disappoint; to deceive; to defy.— *v.i.* To use ridicule; to gibe; scoff; jeer.—*a.* False; counterfeit; imitation.—*n.* An act of derision or scorn; the object of such an act; a copy or imitation.—**mock·er·y,** mok′e·rē, *n. pl.* **mock·er·ies.** The act of mocking; ridicule; the object of ridicule; a vain or unsuitable effort; fraudulent or contemptible pretense.—**mock·ing·ly,** *adv.*— **mock·er,** *n.*

mock-he·ro·ic, mok'hi·rō'ik, *a.* Burlesquing or satirizing the heroic manner, character, or attitude.—*n.* A poem, play, or other literary work in mock-heroic style. —**mock-he·ro·i·cal·ly,** *adv.*

mock·ing·bird, mok'ing·bẽrd″, *n.* A N. American bird, *Mimus polyglottos,* remarkable for its faculty of imitating the songs of other birds; any of several related birds in the mockingbird family.

mock or·ange, *n.* A cultivated shrub of the genus *Philadelphus,* with creamy white flowers which somewhat resemble the blossoms of the orange tree in appearance and fragrance; the syringa.

mock tur·tle soup, *n.* A soup prepared from calf's head, veal, or other meat, and seasoned to resemble the flavor of turtle soup.

mock-up, mok'up″, *n.* A model, usu. full size, of any object made for purposes of testing, display, or instruction.

mod·al, mōd'al, *a.* [M.L. *modalis.*] Of or pertaining to mode, manner, or form; *gram.* denoting or pertaining to mood; *mus.* relating to or performed in a mode; *philos.* relating to a thing's mode or form, and not its substance or attributes; *logic,* exhibiting modality.—**mo·dal·i·ty,** mō·dal'i·tē, *n. pl.* **mo·dal·i·ties.** [M.L. *modalitas.*] The state of being modal; modal quality or relation; a modal attribute or circumstance; *logic,* a proposition in relation to its expressing necessity or contingency; *med.* the applying of a therapeutic, or physiotherapic, agent.— **mod·al·ly,** *adv.*

mod·al aux·il·ia·ry, *n.* Any auxiliary verb that is used with another verb to indicate mood, as *can, do, may, might, must,* and *shall.*

mode, mōd, *n.* [O.Fr. Fr. *mode,* manner, way, usage, later vogue, fashion, < L.

modus, measure, due measure, manner, form.] Manner of acting or doing; a method; a way; customary or conventional usage in manners or dress; the latest style or fashion; *philos.* the manner, form, state, or existence of a basic substance. *Gram.* the distinctive form of a verb indicating whether the act or state predicted is conceived as a certainty, a contingency, or a command; any of the groups of forms of a verb serving to indicate this; as, the indicative, subjunctive, or imperative *mode;* also *mood. Logic,* the form of a proposition with reference to necessity, contingency, possibility, or impossibility of its content; also *mood. Mus.* any of various arrangements of the diatonic tones of an octave, differing from one another in the order of the whole steps and halfsteps. *Statistics,* the value in a frequency distribution which occurs most frequently.

mod·el, mod'el, *n.* [Fr. *modèle,* < It. *modello,* dim. < L. *modus,* E. *mode.*] A standard for imitation or comparison; a pattern; an exemplar; a representation, generally in miniature, to show the construction or serve as a copy of something; an image in clay, wax, paper, etc., to be reproduced in more durable material; anything that serves as an artist's pattern; a person who poses for artists; one employed to put on articles of apparel and display them to customers; mode of structure or formation; a typical form or style.—*a.* Serving as a model; worthy to serve as a model; exemplary.—*v.t.*—*modeled, modeling, Brit. modelled, modelling.* To form or plan according to a model; to give shape or form to, esp. in clay, wax, paper, etc.; to make a model or representation of; to wear for display or sale, as clothes and accessories.— *v.i.* To make models; to assume a typical or natural appearance, or an appearance of natural relief, as the parts of a drawing in progress; to be employed for displaying apparel.—**mod·el·er,** *Brit.* **mod·el·ler,** *n.*

mod·er·ate, mod'ẽr·it, mod'rit, *a.* [L. *modero,* and *moderor, moderatus,* to limit, moderate, < *modus,* a measure.] Not extreme or excessive; temperate in opinions, views, or behavior; inclined toward the average in size, extent, or quality; mediocre; avoiding the more radical extremes of political and social opinion.—*n.* One who holds moderate rather than extreme or radical opinions.—mod'e·rāt″, *v.t.*—*moderated, moderating.* To reduce in intensity or severity; to restrain from excess; to act as president or chairman of, as of a discussion or meeting.—*v.i.* To become less violent or intense; to preside as a moderator. —**mod·er·ate·ly,** *adv.*—**mod·er·ate·ness,** *n.*

mod·er·ate breeze, *n. Meteor.* the Beaufort scale designation for a wind moving at 13 to 18 miles per hour.

mod·er·ate gale, *n. Meteor.* the Beaufort scale designation for a strong wind moving at 32 to 38 miles per hour.

mod·er·a·tion, mod'e·rā'shan, *n.* [L. *moderatio.*] The act of moderating, tempering, or restraining; the state or quality of being moderate; the act of presiding as a moderator; *pl., Brit.* at Oxford University, the first public examination for degrees.—**in mod·er·a·tion,** temperately; not excessively.

mod·e·ra·to, mod″e·rä′tō, *a., adv.* [It.] *Mus.* Moderate; in moderate time.

mod·er·a·tor, mod'e·rā″tẽr, *n.* [L.] One who or that which moderates; a presiding officer; an arbitrator; *phys.* a moderating substance for a nuclear reactor, used to retard the speed of neutrons.—**mod·er·a·tor·ship,** *n.*

mod·ern, mod'ẽrn, *a.* [Fr. *moderne,* < L.L. *modernus,* modern, belonging to the

present mode, < L. *modus*, mode, manner.] Pertaining to the present time; recent; not ancient; pertaining to or characteristic of the current period, esp. of contemporary forms of art, music, literature, and architecture; (*usu. cap.*) characteristic of or pertaining to the latest period in the development of a language; as, *Modern* German.—*n.* A person of modern times; a person whose tastes, opinions, and styles are characteristic of the present times; *print.* a kind of type face distinguished by heavy downward strokes and thin serifs.

Mod·ern He·brew, *n.* The Hebrew language as used in 20th century Israel.

mod·ern·ism, mod′ẽr·niz″um, *n.* The thought and action characteristic of modern life; sympathy with or the exercise of thought and action characteristically modern; a usage, practice, or quality characteristically modern; (*often cap.*), *theol.* an early 20th century Roman Catholic humanistic movement that reinterpreted church teaching in conformity with developments in modern science and philosophy, declared heretical in 1907 by Pope Pius X; a similarly liberal movement in 20th century Protestantism.—**mod·ern·ist,** *n.*—**mod·ern·ist·ic,** mod″ẽr·nis′tik, *a.*

mod·ern·ize, mod′ẽr·niz″, *v.t.*—*modernized, modernizing.* To give a modern character to; to adapt to, as modern styles, opinions, and tastes.—*v.i.* To adopt or conform to modern ideas or style.—**mod·ern·iz·er,** *n.*—**mod·ern·i·za·tion,** mod″ẽr·ni·zā′shan, *n.*

mod·est, mod′ist, *a.* [Fr. *modeste,* L. *modestus,* < *modus,* a limit.] Characterized by a moderate estimation of oneself or one's capabilities; restrained by a sense of propriety; not forward or bold; unpretentious; moderate; not excessive, extreme, or extravagant.—**mod·est·ly,** *adv.*—**mod·es·ty,** *n.* pl. **mod·es·ties.**

mod·i·cum, mod′i·kum, *n.* [L., a small or moderate quantity, < *modicus,* moderate, < *modus,* measure.] A little; a small quantity.

mod·i·fi·ca·tion, mod″i·fi·kā′shan, *n.* The act or state of being modified; the altered result; an alteration in form, appearance, or character; *biol.* a change in an organism which results from its own environment or activity and is not inherited by its descendants; *gram.* the qualification or limitation of a word, phrase, or sentence by another.—**mod·i·fi·ca·tive, mod·i·fi·ca·to·ry,** mod′i·fi·kā″to·rē, *a.*

mod·i·fy, mod′i·fī″, *v.t.*—*modified, modifying.* [Fr. *modifier,* < L. *modifico*—*modus,* limit, manner, and *facio,* to make.] To partially change external qualities; to vary; to alter in some respect; to moderate; to qualify. *Gram.* to limit or qualify the intention of.—**mod·i·fi·a·ble,** *a.*—**mod·i·fi·er,** *n.*

mo·dil·lion, mō·dil′yon, mo·dil′yon, *n.* [Fr. *modillon,* < L. *modulus,* a model, dim. of *modus,* a measure.] *Arch.* one of a series of blocks or brackets carved in ornamental form and placed under the cornice in the Corinthian and other orders.

mod·ish, mō′dish, *a.* [< *mode.*] According to the mode or fashion; fashionable.—**mod·ish·ly,** *adv.*—**mod·ish·ness,** *n.*

mo·diste, mō·dēst′, *Fr.* ma·dēst′, *n.* [Fr. *modiste,* a milliner, < *mode,* fashion.] A woman who deals in articles of ladies' dress; a milliner; a dressmaker.

mod·u·late, moj′u·lāt″, *v.t.*—*modulated, modulating.* [L. *modulor, modulatus,* < *modus,* limit, measure, mode.] To control, temper, or modify; to vary or inflect the sound or tone, as of the voice, in such a manner as to give expressiveness to what is uttered; *mus.* to change the key of in the course of a composition; *tele-*

communications, to alter the frequency, phase, intensity, or amplitude, as of a signal or carrier wave, in radio, telephony, or television.—*v.i. Mus.* to pass from one key into another.—**mod·u·la·tion,** moj″u·lā′shan, mod″ū·lā′shan, *n.* The act of modulating; the condition of being modulated; *mus.* the change from one scale or mode to another in the course of a composition. An inflection of the voice that gives expression to an utterance.—**mod·u·la·tor,** moj′u·lā″tẽr, mod′ū·lā″tẽr, *n.*—**mod·u·la·to·ry,** moj′u·la·tōr″ē, mod′ū·la·tōr″ē, *a.*—**mod·u·la·bil·i·ty,** *n.*

mod·ule, moj′ōl, mod′ūl, *n.* [L. *modulus,* dim. of *modus,* measure, E. *mode.*] A standard or unit for measuring, esp. a unit of measurement by which prefabrication of building materials can be standardized; the semidiameter of a column's base taken as a measuring unit for classical architecture.—**mod·u·lar,** *a.*—**mod·u·lar·i·ty,** moj″u·lar′i·tē, mod″ū·lar′i·tē, *a.*

mod·u·lus, moj′u·lus, mod′ū·lus, *n.* pl. **mod·u·li,** moj′u·lī, mod′ū·lī. *Phys.* a coefficient or quality which expresses the measure of a property, force, or effect; as, the *modulus* of elasticity; *math.* absolute value.—**mod·u·lo,** moj′u·lō″, mod′ū·lō″, *prep.*

mo·dus o·pe·ran·di, mō′dus op″e·ran′dī, *L.* mō′dus o″pe·Rän′dē, *n.* [L.] A way of operating or working.

mo·dus vi·ven·di, mō′dus vi·ven′dī, *L.* mō′dus wē·wen′dē, *n.* [L.] Mode of living; way of getting along; a temporary arrangement between persons or parties pending a settlement of matters in debate.

mo·fette, mō·fet′, *Fr.* ma·fet′, *n.* [Fr., < It. *mofetta,* < L. *mephitis,* noxious exhalation.] A noxious emanation, chiefly carbon dioxide, escaping from the earth in regions of nearly extinct volcanic activity; one of the openings or fissures from which this emanation issues. Also **mof·fette.**

Mo·gen Da·vid, ma′gen da′vid, ma′gen dä′vid, *n.* Star of David. Also *Magen David.*

Mo·gul, mō′gul, mō′gul, mō·gul′, *n.* [Ar. and Pers. *Mughul,* Mongol.] A Mongol or Mongolian, esp. one of the Mongol conquerors of India in the 16th century; one of their descendants; (*l.c.*) any great personage.—*a.* Of or pertaining to the Moguls or the Mongol empire of Hindustan; as, *Mogul* architecture.—**the Great Mo·gul,** an emperor of the Hindustan or Delhi empire.

mo·hair, mō′hâr′, *n.* [< Ar. *mukhayyar,* a kind of camlet or haircloth.] The hair of the Angora goat; cloth made of this hair, or clothing made from it.

Mo·ham·med·an, mō·ham′i·dan, *a.* Pertaining to Mohammed or the Islam religion founded by him. Also **Mo·ham·mad·an,** *Muhammadan, Muhammaden.*—*n.* A follower of Mohammed; one who professes Mohammedanism.—**Mo·ham·med·an·ism,** mō·ham′i·da·niz″um, *n.* The religion of Mohammed, contained in the Koran.

Mo·hawk, mō′hak, *n.* pl. **Mo·hawks, Mo·hawk.** A trible of North American Indians, one of the Iroquois Five Nations, once living in what is now New York State; the language of the tribe.

Mo·he·gan, mō·hē′gan, *n.* pl. **Mo·he·gans, Mo·he·gan.** One of a tribe of Algonquian Indians who inhabited southeastern Connecticut; Mahican; Mohican.

Mo·hi·can, mō·hē′kan, *n.* pl. **Mo·hi·cans, Mo·hi·can.** A Mahican.

Mo·hock, mō′hok, *n.* One of a class of ruffians, often aristocrats, who attacked people on London streets in the 18th century.

Mohs′ scale, mōz′ skāl″, *n. Mineral.* a scale of mineral hardness developed by the mineralogist, Friedrich Mohs, orig. listing 10 minerals, but later revised to 15 and based

on the minerals' susceptibility to scratching:

1. talc	9. topaz
2. gypsum	10. garnet
3. calcite	11. fused zirconia
4. fluorite	12. fused alumina
5. apatite	13. silicon carbide
6. feldspar	14. boron carbide
7. vitreous pure silica	15. diamond
8. quartz	

moi·e·ty, moi′e·tē, *n.* pl. **moi·e·ties.** [Fr. *moitié,* < L. *medietas,* < *medius,* middle.] The half; one of two equal parts; a portion or a share. *Anthropol.* one of two fundamental divisions of a tribe.

moil, moil, *v.t.* To wet; to soil, as with moisture; daub.—*v.i.* To work hard; toil; drudge; to work in wet and mire.—*n.* Toil or drudgery; confusion, turmoil, or trouble.—**moil·er,** *n.*—**moil·ing·ly,** *adv.*

moi·ré, mwä·rā′, môr′ā, mar′ā, *Fr.* mwä·Rā′, *n.* A wavelike pattern or finish, as on silk or metal; a rippled or wavy fabric, as of silk or rayon.—*a.* Having a wavelike pattern. Also **moire,** mwär, môr, mar.

moist, moist, *a.* [O.Fr. *moiste,* < L. *mucidus,* slimy.] Moderately wet; damp; humid; tearful.—**mois·ten,** moi′sen, *v.t.* To make moist or damp.—*v.i.* To become moist.—**moist·en·er,** *n.*—**moist·ly,** *adv.*—**moist·ness,** *n.*—**mois·ture,** mois′chẽr, moish′chẽr, *n.* Diffused wetness or condensed liquid.

mois·tur·ize, mois′che·rīz″, moish′che·rīz″, *v.t.*—*moisturized, moisturizing.* To make moist.—**mois·tur·iz·er,** *n.*

moke, mōk, *n. Brit. slang,* a donkey.

mol, mole, mōl, *n.* [G. *mol, molekül,* molecule.] *Chem.* The molecular weight of a substance expressed in grams; gram molecule.—**mo·lal,** mō′lal, *a.* Denoting or relating to a gram molecule; denoting a solution with a concentration of one mol of solute in each liter of solvent.—**mo·lal·i·ty,** mō·lal′i·tē, *n.* pl. **mo·lal·i·ties.**

MOL, mol, *n.* [(M)anned (O)rbiting (L)aboratory.] An orbiting space laboratory for the study of outer space and its possible application to military use.

mo·la, mō′la, *n.* pl. **mo·la, mo·las.** *Ichth.* Any of the fishes of the family *Molidae;* the ocean sunfish.

mo·lar, mō′lẽr, *n.* [L. *molaris,* < *mola,* millstone; same root as *meal.*] A tooth with a broad surface for grinding, located in back of the canines and incisors in mammals.—*a.* Relating to such a tooth; grinding.

mo·lar, mō′lẽr, *a.* [L. *moles,* mass.] *Phys.* pertaining to a mass or to a body as a whole, as differentiated from molecular or atomic; *chem.* characterizing a solution made up of one mol of solute per one liter of solution.—**mo·lar·i·ty,** mō·lar′i·tē, *n.*

mo·las·ses, mo·las′iz, *n.* [Pg. *melaço* or Sp. *melaza,* < L. *mel,* honey.] Any of several dark-colored, thick syrups, as that produced during the refining of sugar or sorghum. Also *Brit. treacle.*

mold, *Brit.* **mould,** mōld, *n.* [O.E. *molde* = O.H.G. *molta* = Icel. *mold* = Goth. *mulda,* mold, dust; akin to E. *meal.*] Loose, friable earth, esp. such earth rich in organic matter and favorable to the growth of plants.

mold, *Brit.* **mould,** mōld, *n.* [Fr. *moule, molle* (with *d* added), also *modle,* < L. *modulus,* dim. of *modus,* a measure.] The matrix in which anything is cast and receives its form; something shaped in or by a mold; a hollow tool for producing a form by percussion or compression; a distinctive type or example; cast; form; shape; character; *arch.* a molding or a number of moldings.—*v.t.* To form into a particular shape; to shape; to fashion; to influence.—**mold·a·ble,** *a.*—**mold·er,** *n.*

mold, *Brit.* **mould,** mōld, *n.* [M.E. *mowlde,* appar. < *mowled, mouled,* pp. of *moulen.*

earlier *muwlen*, grow moldy, akin to Icel. *mygla*, Sw. *mogla*, Dan. *mugle*, grow moldy.] *Bot.* A growth of minute fungi forming on vegetable or animal matter, commonly as a downy or furry coating, and associated with decay; any of the fungi that produce such a growth.—*v.t.*, *v.i.* To become or make moldy.

mold·board, *Brit.* **mould·board**, mōld'-bōrd", mōld'bạrd", *n.* The curved metal plate of a plow, which turns over the soil; the blade attached to the front of a bulldozer to push aside loose material; a board which forms a mold for casting concrete.

mold·er, mōl'dẽr, *v.i.* [< *mold*, earth, mustiness; lit. 'to turn to mold.'] To turn to dust by natural decay; to waste away by gradual separation of the component particles; to crumble.—*v.t.* To cause to decay or waste away.

mold·ing, mould·ing, mōl'ding, *n.* The act or process of one who or that which molds; something molded. *Arch.* a decorative variety of contour or outline given to cornices, jambs, or strips of woodwork; a shaped member introduced into a structure to afford such variety or decoration; shaped material in the form of a strip, used for supporting pictures, covering electric wires, or finishing.

mold·y, *Brit.* **mould·y**, mōl'dē, *a.*— *moldier, moldiest.* Overgrown with mold; musty, as from age or decay.—**mold·i·ness**, *n.*

mole, mōl, *n.* [O.E. *māl*, a blot, a spot = O.D. *mael*, Dan. *maal*, G. *mal*, a spot; cogn. L. *macula*, a spot.] A spot, or small, discolored, congenital mark on the human body; nevus; birthmark.

mole, mōl, *n.* [Same word as *mold*, earth, being abbreviated from the fuller name *moldwarp*, *mouldwarp*, lit. 'earth-caster,' < *mold*, and *warp*, to cast.] *Zool.* a small, insectivorous mammal of the family *Talpidae*, usu. living underground, and having small eyes, soft fur, and strong fossorial forefeet with which it digs burrows just under the surface of the ground.

mole, mōl, *n.* [Fr., < L. *moles*, a mass, a dam, a mole; same root as *magnus*, great.] A massive barricade or breakwater formed to enclose a harbor or anchorage and protect it from the waves; the harbor created by a mole.

mole, mōl, *n.* [Fr. *môle*, < L. *mola*, lit. 'millstone.'] *Pathol.* a mass of fleshy matter occurring in the uterus, usu. as the result of an abortive conception.

mole, mōl, *n.* Mol.

mole crick·et, *n.* Any of various crickets, esp. those constituting the genus *Gryllotalpa*, having large fossorial forelegs adapted for burrowing in the ground, as *G. vulgaris*, the common European species, or *G. borealis*, of N. America.

mo·lec·u·lar, mō·lek'ū·lẽr, mo·lek'ū·lẽr, *a.* Pertaining to or consisting of molecules.— **mo·lec·u·lar·i·ty**, mō·lek"ū·lar'i·tē, mo·-lek"ū·lar'i·tē, *n.*—**mo·lec·u·lar·ly**, *adv.*

mo·lec·u·lar e·lec·tron·ics, *n. pl. but sing. in constr.* That branch of electronics dealing with the production of complex electronic circuits in microminiature form by producing semiconductor devices and circuit elements integrally; the utilization of such properties in place of vacuum tubes or solid state electronics in amplifying and regulating devices, being esp. significant in reducing the size of electronic equipment used in space research vehicles. Also **mo·lec·tron·ics.**

mo·lec·u·lar for·mu·la, *n. Chem.* a formula indicating the kind and number of each atom comprising a molecule of a substance.

mol·e·cule, mol'e·kūl, *n.* [Fr. *molécule*, <

N.L. *molecula*, dim. of L. *moles*, mass.] *Chem., phys.* the smallest particle of an element or compound that is capable of existing separately without loss of any original chemical properties; *fig.* any very small particle.

mole·hill, mōl'hil", *n.* A small mound or ridge of earth raised by a mole; something insignificant.

mole·skin, mōl'skin", *n.* The soft, fragile pelt of a mole; a strong, twilled, soft-nap cotton cloth, used in making work and hunting clothes; *usu. pl.* garments made of this fabric.

mo·lest, mo·lest', *v.t.* [Fr. *molester*, < L. *molestus*, troublesome, < *moles*, trouble, a great mass.] To annoy, disturb, or meddle; to make improper or illicit advances.— **mo·les·ta·tion**, mō"le·stā'shan, mol"e·-stā'shan, *n.*—**mo·lest·er**, *n.*

moll, mol, *n.* [From *Moll*, for *Mary*, woman's name: cf. *molly*.] *Slang.* The female companion of a thief or gangster; a prostitute.

mol·li·fy, mol'i·fī", *v.t.*—*mollified, mollifying.* [O.Fr. *mollifier*, L. *mollificare*—*mollis*, soft, and *facio*, to make.] To alleviate, as pain or irritation; to pacify; to appease; to soothe the disposition of.—**mol·li·fi·ca·tion**, *n.*—**mol·li·fi·er**, *n.*—**mol·li·fy·ing·ly**, *adv.*—**mol·li·fi·a·ble**, *a.*

mol·lus·coid, mo·lus'koid, *a.* Resembling a mollusk; having to do with the phylum *Molluscoidea*, which includes the brachiopods.—*n.*

mol·lusk, mol·lusc, mol'usk, *n.* [Fr. *mollusque*, < N.L. *mollusca*, pl., < L. *molluscus*, soft (applied to a thin-shelled nut), < *mollis*, soft.] Any of the *Mollusca*, a large phylum of invertebrate animals having soft, unsegmented bodies usu. covered with a hard shell of one, two, or more pieces, as snails, mussels, oysters, clams, squids, octopuses, and the like.— **mol·lus·can**, mo·lus'kan, *a.*, *n.*

mol·ly, mol·lie, mol'ē, *n. pl.* **mol·lies.** Any of several brightly colored tropical fish belonging to the genus *Molliensia*, frequently kept in aquariums.

mol·ly·cod·dle, mol'ē·kod"l, *n.* A man or boy accustomed to being coddled; a milksop; an effeminate man.—*v.t.*—*mollycoddled, mollycoddling.* To coddle or pamper.

Mo·lo·tov cock·tail, mol'o·tof"kok'tāl", *n.* [From V. M. *Molotov*, Russian statesman.] A simple incendiary bomb, constructed principally of a bottle filled with a liquid that is flammable.

molt, *Brit.* **moult**, mōlt, *v.t.*, *v.i.* [M.E. *mouten*, < L. *mutare*, change.] *Biol.* to shed, as feathers or skin, to be ready for a new growth.—*n.*—**molt·er**, *n.*

mol·ten, mōl'ten, *a.* Liquefied by heat; in a state of fusion; produced by melting and casting.—**mol·ten·ly**, *adv.*

mol·to, mōl'tō, *It.* maًl'ta, *adv. Mus.* very, much; as, *molto* allegro.

mo·ly, mō'lē, *n. pl.* **mo·lies.** [Gr. *mōly*.] A magic herb spoken of by Homer in the *Odyssey* as a gift from Hermes to Odysseus to protect him from the enchantress Circe.

mo·lyb·date, mo·lib'dāt, *n. Chem.* a salt of molybdic acid, esp. the acid, H_2MoO_4.

mo·lyb·de·nite, mo·lib'de·nīt", mol"ib·-dē'nīt, *n.* A soft, graphitelike native sulfide of molybdenum, MoS_2, a major ore of molybdenum.

mo·lyb·de·num, mo·lib'de·num, mol"-ib·dē'num, *n.* A silver-white metallic element mainly used in alloy steel. Sym. Mo, at. no. 42, at. wt. 95.94. See Periodic Table of Elements.—**mo·lyb·dic**, mo·-lib'dik, *a.*—**mo·lyb·dous**, *a.*

mom, mom, *n.* (*Sometimes cap.*), *colloq.* mother.

mo·ment, mō'ment, *n.* [O.Fr. Fr. *moment*, < L. *momentum*, movement, moment of

time, weight, influence, importance, < *movere*, E. *move.*] An indefinitely short space of time; an instant; as, to wait a *moment*; the present or other particular instant or point of time; as, to be busy at the *moment*; the present or current brief space of time; as, supplies sufficient for the *moment*; a period, usu. brief, of greatness, happiness, distinction; as, to have one's *moment*; the precise instant of opportunity; as, to improve the *moment*; weight, importance, or consequence; as, matters of *moment*; a definite stage in the course of events, esp. a particular point in logical or historical development; as, a great *moment* in American history. *Philos.* an essential or constituent element; an aspect or modality of a thing. *Phys.* the result of the multiplication of a quantity, such as a force, by its perpendicular distance from a point or axis; a tendency to produce motion, such as rotation about an axis; a quantifying of such a tendency. *Statistics*, the arithmetic mean of the products of the powers of random variables in a probability distribution.

mo·men·tar·y, mō'men·ter"ē, *a.* [L. *momentarius.*] Lasting but a moment; as, a *momentary* glimpse, a *momentary* impulse; of very short duration; very brief, short-lived, or ephemeral; occurring or present every moment; as, *momentary* interruptions; constant; occurring at any moment; as, to live in fear of *momentary* exposure.— **mo·men·tar·i·ly**, mō"men·târ'i·lē, mō'-men·ter"i·lē, *adv.*—**mo·men·tar·i·ness**, *n.*

mo·ment·ly, mō'ment·lē, *adv.* Every moment, or from moment to moment; at any moment; for a moment; momentarily.

mo·men·tous, mō·men'tus, *a.* Of great moment, importance, or consequence; involving serious or far-reaching consequences, as events, issues, or decisions.— **mo·men·tous·ly**, *adv.*—**mo·men·tous·ness**, *n.*

mo·men·tum, mō·men'tum, *n. pl.* **mo·men·ta, mo·men·tums.** [L.] Impetus, as of a moving body; *mech.* the quantity of motion of a moving body, being equivalent to the product of its mass and velocity. *Philos.* a moment; an essential or constituent element.

mom·ism, mom'iz·um, *n.* (*Sometimes cap.*) a social phenomenon of excessive popular worship of mothers and motherhood, usu. characterized by sentimentality and reflecting maternal domination of the home: first used by U.S. author Philip Wylie.

mon·a·chal, mon'a·kal, *a.* [L. *monachus*, Gr. *monachos*, a monk, < *monos*, alone.] Pertaining to monks or monastic life; monastic.

mon·a·chism, mon'a·kiz"um, *n.* [Fr. *monachisme.*] Monasticism.

mon·ac·id, mon·as'id, *a. Chem.* capable of combining with one molecule of a monobasic acid. Also *monoacid.*—*n.*

mon·ad, mon'ad, mō'nad, *n.* [L.L. *monas*, (*monad-*), < Gr. *monas*, (*monad-*) < *monos*, alone, single.] Unity; an indivisible unit; *philos.* an absolutely simple metaphysical entity, conceived as the ultimate unit of being; *biol.* any simple, single-celled organism, often a flagellate amoeba; *chem.* an element, atom, or radical having a valence of one.—**mo·nad·ic, mo·nad·i·cal, mo·nad·al**, mo·nad'ik, *a.*—**mo·nad·i·cal·ly**, *adv.*

mon·a·del·phous, mon"a·del'fus, *a.* [Gr. *monos*, single, and *adelphos*, brother.] *Bot.* Having stamens united into one bundle or set by their filaments; of stamens, so united.

mon·ad·ism, mon'a·diz"um, mō'nad·iz"-um, *n. Philos* the doctrine of monads as ultimate units of being, proposed by the German philospher, G. W. von Leibnitz. Also **mon·ad·ol·o·gy**, mon″a·-dol′o·jē, mō″na·dol′o·jē.—**mon·ad·is·tic**, a.

mo·nad·nock, mo·nad′nok, n. [From Mount *Monadnock*, in New Hampshire.] *Geog.* an isolated hill or mountain of resistant rock standing over a peneplain.

mo·nan·drous, mo·nan′drus, a. [Gr. *monandros*.] Having one husband at a time; pertaining to or characterized by monandry. *Bot.* referring to a flower having only one stamen, or a plant having such flowers.

mo·nan·dry, mo·nan′drē, n. The practice of having one husband at a time.

mo·nan·thous, mo·nan′thus, a. *Bot.* producing but one flower.

mon·arch, mon′ark, n. [L. *monarcha*, < Gr. *monárchēs*, a monarch, *monarchos*, ruling alone.] A sole ruler; the hereditary ruler of a state whose power is limited under a constitution, as an emperor, king, queen, or prince; something or someone superior to others of the same kind. *Entom.* a large butterfly, *Danaus plexippus*, orange and brown in color with black markings; also **milk·weed but·ter·fly.**—**mo·nar·chal, mo·nar·chi·al**, mo·när′kal, mo·när′kē·al, a.—**mo·nar·chal·ly**, adv.

Mo·nar·chi·an·ism, mo·när′kē·a·niz″-um, n. *Theol.* a theory advanced in the 2nd and 3rd centuries by certain groups in the Christian church, denying the doctrine of the Trinity.—**Mo·nar·chi·an**, a., n.

mo·nar·chi·cal, mo·när′ki·kal, a. Pertaining to a monarchy or monarch; ruled by or advocating rule by a monarch. Also **mo·nar·chic.**—**mo·nar·chi·cal·ly**, adv.

mon·ar·chism, mon′ėr·kiz″um, n. The principles of monarchy; advocacy of a monarchy or a monarch.—**mon·ar·chist**, n., a.—**mon·ar·chist·ic**, a.

mon·ar·chy, mon′ėr·kē, n. pl. **mon·ar·chies.** [Gr. *monarchia*.] A state or country in which the supreme power is either actually or nominally placed in the hands of a king, queen, or other monarch; the system of government in which power is vested in a monarch.

mon·as·ter·y, mon′a·ster″ē, n. pl. **mon·as·ter·ies.** [L.L. *monasterium*, < Gr. *monastērion*, < *monastēs*, a solitary, *monazō*, to be alone, < *monos*, alone, sole.] A building which houses those under religious vows and in seclusion: usu. applied to the houses for monks; the community of individuals living in such an environment.—**mon·as·te·ri·al**, a.

mo·nas·tic, mo·nas′tik, a. [Gr. *monastikos*.] Pertaining to monasteries; pertaining to individuals, esp. to monks and their commitment to religious matters; pertaining to a life of seclusion, religious or otherwise. Also **mo·nas·ti·cal.**—n. A member of a monastery; a monk.—**mo·nas·ti·cal·ly**, adv.—**mo·nas·ti·cism**, mo·nas′ti·siz″um, n. Monastic life; the monastic system or condition.

mon·a·tom·ic, mon″a·tom′ik, a. *Chem.* Having one atom in the molecule; containing one replaceable atom or group of atoms; univalent.

mon·au·ral, mon·är′al, a. Of or pertaining to sound which is perceived through only one ear. *Electron.* pertaining to a type of sound reproduction heard as if it emanated from a single source or direction; also *monophonic.*—**mon·au·ral·ly**, adv.

mon·ax·i·al, mon·ak′sē·al, a. Having but one axis; *bot.* uniaxial.

mon·a·zite, mon′a·zīt″, n. [G. *monazit*, < Gr. *monazein*, be alone.] A rare, crystalline, reddish-brown mineral consisting of a phosphate of cerium or other lanthanide metals.

Mon·day, mun′dē, mun′dā, n. [O.E.

mónandaeg—mónan, genit. of *móna*, the moon, and *daeg*, day.] The second day of the week; the day following Sunday.—**Mon·days**, adv.

mo·ne·cious, mo·nē′shus, mō·nē′shus, a. Monoecious.

mon·e·tar·y, mon′i·ter″ē, mun′i·ter″ē, a. [L. *moneta*, money.] Pertaining to money or currency; pecuniary.—**mon·e·tar·i·ly**, mon″i·târ′i·lē, mon′i·ter″i·lē, mun″i·târ′i·lē, mun′i·ter″i·lē, adv.

mon·e·tar·y u·nit, n. The standard unit of a currency system.

mon·e·tize, mon′i·tīz″, mun′i·tīz″, v.t.—*monetized, monetizing.* To make legal as money; to form into coin or money.—**mon·e·ti·za·tion**, n.

mon·ey, mun′ē, n. pl. **mon·eys, mon·ies.** [O.Fr. *moneie, monnoie*, Fr. *monnaie*, < L. *moneta*, the mint, money.] Coin; gold, silver, or other metal, stamped by public authority and used as the medium of exchange; any equivalent for commodities, and for which individuals readily exchange their goods or service, as money orders or checks; a circulating medium; wealth; property having pecuniary value.—**in the mon·ey**, *slang.* Possessing a large amount of money; affluent.—**put mon·ey on**, *slang*, to bet on.

mon·ey·chang·er, mun′ē·chān″jėr, n. One whose business it is to change money, as from one nation's currency to another's, at fixed rates; a coin dispenser.

mon·eyed, mon·ied, mun′ēd, a. Representing wealth; rich.

mon·ey·mak·er, mun′ē·mā″kėr, n. A person who successfully accumulates money; a business, product, or scheme which is lucrative.—**mon·ey·mak·ing**, a., n.

mon·ey or·der, n. An order granted upon payment of a sum and a small commission, by one post office, bank, or telegraph company, and payable at another.

mon·ey·wort, mun′ē·wųrt″, n. A creeping primulaceous herb, *Lysimachia nummularia*, with roundish leaves and yellow flowers.

mon·ger, mung′gėr, mong′gėr, n. [O.E. *mangere*, a dealer, < *mangian*, to traffic; Icel. *mangari, mang*, traffic, O.D. *mangher*, O.H.G. *mangari*, a merchant; perh. < L. *mango*, dealer.] *Chiefly Brit.* a trader, a dealer: now chiefly in combination. One who occupies himself with contemptible things; as, a scandal*monger.*—v.t.—**mon·ger·ing**, n., a.

Mon·gol, mong′gol, mong′gol, mong′gōl, mon′gol, mon′gol mon′gōl, n. One of a pastoral Asiatic people now residing chiefly in Mongolia; any of the languages of these people; Mongolian; Mongoloid.—a. Mongolian.—**Mon·go·li·an**, mong·gō′lē·an, mon·gō′lē·an, a. Pertaining or related to, or characteristic of the Mongols or their languages; pertaining to Mongolia; Mongoloid.—n. A Mongol; the language or group of languages of the Mongols; (*usu. l.c.*), *pathol.* one afflicted with Mongolism.—**Mon·gol·ic**, mong·gol′ik, mon·gol′ik, a. Of or pertaining to the Mongols; Mongolian.—n. The Mongolian language.

Mon·gol·ism, mong′go·liz″um, mon′go·liz″um, n. A congenital mental deficiency in a child characterized by slanting eyes and a broad skull, face, and hands. Also **mon·go·li·an·ism, mon·go·li·an id·i·o·cy**, *mongoloid*, mong·gō′lē·a·niz″um, mon·gō′lē·a·niz″um.

Mon·gol·oid, mong′go·loid″, mon′go·loid″, a. Mongol. *Anthropol.* pertaining to or comprising a major racial division of mankind constituted principally of the yellow-skinned, slant-eyed peoples of Asia; like the Mongols. (*Usu. l.c.*) *pathol.* characteristic of an individual afflicted with mongolism.—n.

mon·goose, mong′gōs″, mon′gōs″, n. pl. **mon·goos·es.** [E. Ind.] A slender carnivorous mammal, *Herpestes nyula*, of India, of the same genus as the common ichneumon of Egypt, and resembling the ferret in form and habits; any animal of the same genus or of related genera.

mon·grel, mung′grel, mong′grel, n. [M.E. *mengrell*, prob. < O.E. *mengan*, mix.] Any plant or animal resulting from the crossing of different breeds; a dog of no definable breed; the product of any incongruous mixture.—a. Of mixed breed, race, origin, or nature; as, a *mongrel* pup.—**mon·grel·ly**, adv.—**mon·grel·ize**, v.t.—*mongrelized, mongrelizing.*

mon·i·ker, mon·ick·er, mon′i·kur, n. *Slang*, a name, usu. a nickname.

mo·nil·i·form, mō·nil′i·fạrm″, a. [L. *monile*, necklace.] Resembling the shape of a string of beads; *biol.* characterized by a series of beadlike swellings alternating with contractions, as certain roots, stems, and of nuclei in the class *Infusoria.*—**mo·nil·i·form·ly**, adv.

mon·ism, mon′iz·um, mō′niz·um, n. [Gr. *monos*, alone, single.] *Philos.* The metaphysical theory that one substance or principle is the basis of all reality; the metaphysical theory that universal reality is a unitary whole; the epistemological theory that posits the identity of the object and the concept of the object; theoretical explanation of a diversity in terms of a single principle.—**mon·ist**, n.—**mo·nis·tic**, mo·nis·ti·cal, mo·nis′tik, mō·nis′tik, a.—**mo·nis·ti·cal·ly**, adv.

mo·ni·tion, mō·nish′an, mo·nish′an, n. [O.Fr. Fr. *monition*, < L. *monitio(n-)*, < *monere*, remind, advise.] Admonition or warning; an official or legal notice; a formal notice from a bishop requiring the amendment of some ecclesiastical offense; *law*, a legal summons or order of a court.

mon·i·tor, mon′i·tėr, n. [L.] One who maintains discipline and enforces rules of conduct; anything that reminds or cautions; a student chosen to help with classroom duties, as assisting in roll taking; a device for a nozzle that can easily direct the flow of water, used in fighting fires or in mining; any of certain large lizards, family *Varanidae*, popularly believed to give warning of the presence of crocodiles; a former class of heavily-armed, iron-clad, naval steam vessels riding low in the water: so called from the name of the first American vessel of its kind. *TV*, an apparatus, as a receiver, used to check transmission or quality of a broadcast.—v.t.,v.i. To oversee, as a monitor; to listen to or view, as a broadcast; to check transmission and quality.—**mon·i·to·ri·al**, mon″i·tōr′ē·al, a.—**mon·i·tor·ship**, n.—**mon·i·to·ry**, mon′i·tōr″ē, mon′i·tạr″ē, a. Giving admonition.—**mon·i·tress**, mon′i·tris, n. A female monitor.

monk, mungk, n. [O.E. *monec, munec*, < L.L. *monachus*, Gr. *monachos*, one who lives alone, < *monos*, alone.] One of a community of males inhabiting a monastery and bound by vows to celibacy, poverty, and religious obedience; a religious ascetic.—**monk·hood**, mungk′hud, n. Character, condition, or routine of a monk.—**monk·ish**, a.—**monk·ish·ly**, adv.—**monk·ish·ness**, n.

monk·er·y, mung′ke·rē, n. pl. **monk·er·ies.** A monastery; *pl.* monastic beliefs or practices: used disparagingly.

mon·key, mung′kē, n. pl. **mon·keys.** [Origin uncertain; cf. Fr. (obs.) *monne*, Sp. *mona*, female monkey.] Any member, except man, lemurs, and apes, of the highest order of mammals, *Primates*, as baboons, marmosets, guenons, and capuchins; a person likened to such an animal,

Country	Currency	Unit	
Afghanistan	Afghani	100 puls	AFS
Albania	Lek	100 quintars	Lk.
Algeria	Dinar	100 centimes	D.A.
Andorra	Sp. Peseta	100 centimos	Ptas.
	Fr. Franc	100 centimes	F.
Argentina	Peso	100 centavos	M$N
Australia	Dollar	100 cents	$A.
Austria	Schilling	100 groschen	S.
Bahamas	Dollar	100 cents	Bah. $
Barbados	Dollar	100 cents	E.C.$
Belgium	Franc	100 centimes	B.F.
Bermuda	Pound	100 cents	£
Bolivia	Peso	100 centavos	$B.
Botswana	So. Af. Rand	100 cents	R.
Brazil	New Cruzeiro	100 centavos	N.Cr.$
Bulgaria	Lev	100 stotinki	Lev
Burma	Kyat	100 pyas	K.
Burundi	Franc	100 centimes	BFU
Cambodia	Riel	100 sen	J
Cameroon	Franc	100 centimes	CFA F.
Canada	Dollar	100 cents	Can.$
Central African Rep.	Franc	100 centimes	Fr. CFA
Ceylon	Rupee	100 cents	Rs.
Chad	Franc	100 centimes	CFA F.
Chile	Escudo	100 centesimos = 1,000 ps.	Esc.
China, Nationalist	Dollar	100 cents	N.T.$
People's Rep.	Yuan	10 tsjad = 100 fyng	Yuan
Colombia	Peso	100 centavos	Col.$
Congo cap. Brazzaville	Franc	100 centimes	CFA Frs.
cap. Kinshasa	Zaire	100 makuta = 10,000 sengi	Z.
Costa Rica	Colon	100 centimos	C
Cuba	Peso	100 centavos	P.
Cyprus	Pound	1000 mils	C£
Czechoslovakia	Crown	100 heller	Kcs.
Dahomey	Franc	100 centimes	CFA Frs
Denmark	Krone	100 ore	D.Kr.
Dominican Rep.	Peso	100 centavos	R.D.$
Ecuador	Sucre	100 centavos	S/.
El Salvador	Colon	100 centavos	C.
Equatorial Guinea	Sp. Peseta	100 centimos	Ptas.
Ethiopia	Dollar	100 cents	E.$
Fiji	Dollar	100 cents	F.$
Finland	Markka	100 pennia	F.Mk.
France	Franc	100 centimes	F.
Gabon	Franc	100 centimes	CFA F.
Gambia	Pound	100 pennies	£G
Germany Demo. Rep.	Mark	100 pfennige	M.
Federal Rep.	Deutsche Mark	100 pfennige	DM
Ghana	New Cedi	100 pesewas	N¢
Greece	Drachma	100 lepta	Drs.
Guatemala	Quetzal	100 centavos	Q
Guinea	Franc	100 centimes	Fr.
Guyana	Dollar	100 cents	G.$
Haiti	Gourde	100 centimes	Gde.
Honduras	Lempira	100 centavos	Lps.
Hong Kong	Dollar	100 cents	H.K.$
Hungary	Forint	100 filler	Ft.
Iceland	Krona	100 aurar	Kr.
India	Rupee	100 paisa	Re.
Indonesia	Rupiah	100 sen	Rp.
Iran	Rial	100 dinars	Rls.
Iraq	Dinar	1000 fils	ID.
Ireland	Pound	100 pennies	£
Israel	Pound	100 agorot	I.£
Italy	Lira	100 centesimi	Lit.
Ivory Coast	Franc	100 centimes	CFA Frs.
Jamaica	Dollar	100 cents	J.$
Japan	Yen	100 sen	Y
Jordan	Dinar	1000 fils	JD.
Kenya	Shilling	100 cents	K.Shs.
Korea Demo. Rep.	Won		
Republic	Won		
Kuwait	Dinar	KD 1 = 1000 fils	KD.
Laos	Kip	100 at	Kip
Lebanon	Pound	100 piasters	L.L.
Lesotho	So. Af. Rand	100 cents	R.
Liberia	Dollar	100 cents	L$
Libya	Pound	1000 milliemes	L.£
Liechtenstein	Sw. Franc	100 centimes	S.Frs.
Luxembourg	Franc	100 centimes	L.Frs.
Malagasy Rep.	Franc	100 centimes	F.M.G.
Malawi	Pound	100 pennies	M.£
Malaysia	Dollar	100 cents	M.$
Maldive Islands	Rupee		
Mali	Franc	100 centimes	F.M.
Malta	Pound	20 shillings = 240 pence	M.£
Mauritania	Franc	100 centimes	CFA Frs
Mauritius	Rupee	100 cents	Rs.
Mexico	Peso	100 centavos	P.
Monaco	Franc	100 centimes	F.
Mongolia	Tughrik	100 mongo	
Morocco	Dirham	100 Moroccan francs	DH.
Nauru	Austr. Dollar	100 cents	$A
Nepal	Rupee	100 paisa	Re.
Netherlands	Guilder (Florin)	100 cents	FL.
New Zealand	Dollar	100 cents	NZ$
Nicaragua	Cordoba	100 centavos	C$
Niger	Franc	100 centimes	CFA Frs.
Nigeria	Pound	20 shillings = 240 pence	£N.
Norway	Krone	100 ore	N.Kr.
Pakistan	Rupee	100 paisa	Pak.Rs.
Panama	Balboa	100 centesimos	B/.
Paraguay	Guarani	100 centimos	G.
Peru	Sol	100 centavos	S/.
Philippines	Peso	100 centavos	P
Poland	Zloty	100 groszy	Zl.
Portugal	Escudo	100 centavos	Esc.
Rhodesia	Dollar	100 cents	Rhod.$
Rumania	Leu	100 banai	Leu
Rwanda	Franc	100 centimes	F.R.W.
San Marino	It. Lira	100 centesimi	Lit.
Saudi Arabia	Riyal	20 quirsh	S.RLS.
Senegal	Franc	100 centimes	C.F.A.
Sierra Leone	Leone	100 cents	LE
Singapore	Dollar	100 cents	S.$
Somalia	Shilling	100 cents	So.Shs.
South Africa	Rand	100 cents	R.
Southern Yemen	Dinar	1000 fils	
Spain	Peseta	100 centimos	Ptas.
Sudan	Pound	100 piasters = 1000 milliemes	£S.
Swaziland	So. Af. Rand	100 cents	R.
Sweden	Krona	100 ore	S Kr.
Switzerland	Franc	100 centimes	S. Frs.
Syria	Pound	100 piasters	£ S.
Tanzania	Shilling	100 cents	E.A.Shs.
Thailand	Baht (Tical)	100 satang	Bht.
Togo	Franc	100 centimes	CFA Frs.
Tonga	Pa'ang	100 seniti	T$
Trinidad & Tobago	Dollar	100 cents	T.T.$
Tunisia	Dinar	10 dirham	D.
Turkey	Lira	100 kurus	TL.
Uganda	Shilling	100 cents	U.Sh.
Union of Soviet Socialist Rep.	Ruble	100 kopecks	Rbl.
United Arab Rep. (Egypt)	Pound	100 piasters = 1,000 milliemes	L.E.
United Kingdom	Pound	100 pennies	£
United States	Dollar	100 cents	$
Upper Volta	Franc	100 centimes	CFA Frs.
Uruguay	Peso	100 centesimos	$
Vatican City	It. Lira	100 centesimi	Lit.
Venezuela	Bolivar	100 centimos	Bs.
Vietnam Demo. Rep.	Dong	100 sau	
Republic	Piastre		V.N.$
Western Samoa	Tala		
Yemen	Riyal	40 bugshahs	
Yugoslavia	Dinar	100 paras	Din.
Zambia	Kwacha	100 newee	K

as a mischievous child or a mimic; any of various mechanical devices, as the hammerlike weight of a pile-driving apparatus.—**make a mon·key out of**, to make, as a person, seem ridiculous.—**have one's mon··key up**, *Brit. slang*, to be irritated or angry.

mon·key, mung′kē, *v.t.*—*monkeyed, monkeying.* To imitate, as a monkey does; to mimic; to mock.—*v.i.* To play or trifle idly; fool, often with *with*.

mon·key bread, *n.* The gourdlike edible fruit of the baobab; the tree itself.

mon·key bus·i·ness, *n. Slang.* Deceitful behavior; mischievous, high-spirited, or frivolous conduct.

mon·key dog, *n.* Affenpinscher.

mon·key jack·et, *n.* A short, close-fitting jacket or coat, much worn by sailors.

mon·key puz·zle, *n.* A South American evergreen tree, *Araucaria araucana*, with twisted branches, sharp-pointed leaves, and edible nuts.

mon·key·shine, mung′kē·shīn″, *n. Sometimes pl., slang.* A foolish trick or prank; monkey business.

mon·key suit, *n. Slang.* Any uniform; any regimental or formal suit of clothes for men; a full-dress uniform of the army or navy: used disparagingly, as an allusion to the costume worn by an organ grinder's monkey.

mon·key wrench, *n.* A wrench with an adjustable jaw; *slang*, anything which interferes with proper functioning, as: He threw a *monkey wrench* into the project.

monk's cloth, *n.* A sturdy cotton material in a basket weave, used esp. for draperies and bedspreads.

monks·hood, mungks′hụd″, *n.* A poisonous plant of the genus *Aconitum*, esp. *A. napellus*, with a large, arched, hoodlike sepal; aconite.

mon·o·ac·id, mon″ō·as′id, *a. Chem.* characterizing an alcohol or base with one replaceable hydroxyl radical that can react with one acid group to yield a salt. Also **mon·a·cid·ic**, mon″a·sid′ik.—*n.* An alcohol or base with one such hydroxyl group. Also *monacid.*

mon·o·ba·sic, mon″ō·bā′sik, *a. Chem.* of an acid, having but one atom of hydrogen replaceable by a basic atom or radical.—**mon·o·ba·sic·i·ty**, mon″ō·bā·sis′i·tē, *n.*

mo·no·car·box·yl·ic, mon″ō·kär·bok′si·lik, *a. Chem.* containing one group of the univalent radical carboxyl, COOH.

mon·o·carp, mon′o·kärp″, *n.* [Gr. *monos*, single, and *karpos*, fruit.] *Bot.* a plant that perishes after having once borne fruit.

mon·o·car·pel·lar·y, mon″o·kär′pe·ler″ē, *a. Bot.* having only a single carpel.

mon·o·car·pic, mon″o·kär′pik, *a. Bot.* Producing fruit merely once and then dying; of the nature of a monocarp.—**mon·o·car·pous**, mon″o·kär′pus, *a. Bot.* Having a gynœcium which forms only a single ovary; monocarpic.

mon·o·chord, mon′o·kȯrd″, *n.* [Gr. *monochordon*.] An acoustical instrument of ancient invention, consisting of a sounding board with a single string, used for the mathematical determination of musical intervals.

mon·o·chro·mat, mon″o·krō′mat, *n. Ophthalm.* an individual who is totally colorblind. Also **mon·o·chro·mate**.

mon·o·chro·mat·ic, mon″o·krō·mat′ik, mon″ō·kro·mat′ik, *a.* Consisting of one color or one hue; consisting of a single wavelength or of wavelengths of a limited range; of or relating to monochromatism.—**mon·o·chro·mat·i·cal·ly**, *adv.*—**mon·o··chro·ma·tic·i·ty**, mon″o·krō″ma·tis′i·tē, *n.*

mon·o·chro·ma·tism, mon″o·krō′ma··tiz″um, *n.* Color blindness.

mon·o·chrome, mon′o·krōm″, *n.* A painting in one color or shades of one color; the art of producing this kind of painting. Also *monotint.*—**mon·o·chro·mic**, mon″o·krō′mik, **mon·o·chro·mi·cal**, *a.*—**mon·o·chro·mi·cal·ly**, *adv.*—**mon·o··chrom·ist**, *n.*—**mon·o·chro·my**, *n.*

mon·o·cle, mon′o·kl, *n.* A single eyeglass.—**mon·o·cled**, *a.*

mon·o·cli·nal, mon″o·klīn′al, *a. Geol.* Dipping in one direction, as strata; pertaining to strata which dip in the same direction.—*n.* A monocline.—**mon·o·cline**, mon′o·klīn, *n. Geol.* a monoclinal structure or fold.—**mon·o·cli·nal·ly**, *adv.*

mon·o·clin·ic, mon″o·klin′ik, *a.* [Gr. *monos*, single, and *klinein*, incline.] *Crystal.* noting or pertaining to that system of crystallization in which the crystals have three unequal axes, with one oblique intersection.—**mon·o·clin·ic sys·tem**, *n.*

mon·o·cli·nous, mon″o·klī′nus, mon′o··klī″nus, *a. Bot.* having both stamens and pistils in one flower.—**mon·o·cli·nism**, *n.*

mon·o·coque, mon′o·kōk″, mon′o·kok″, *n.* A type of airplane construction in which the skin of the fuselage bears the primary stresses arising in the fuselage. An airplane so constructed, such as the Messerschmitt 109.

mon·o·cot·y·le·don, mon″o·kot″i·lēd′on, *n. Bot.* a plant belonging to the class *Monocotyledonae* which produces an embryo bearing only one cotyledon and is characterized by leaves with parallel veining. Also **mon·o·cot**, **mon·o·cot·yl**, mon′o··kot″.—**mon·o·cot·y·le·don·ous**, *a.*

mo·noc·ra·cy, mō·nok′ra·sē, mo·nok′ra·sē, *n. pl.* **mo·noc·ra·cies.** Rule by one person; autocracy.—**mon·o·crat**, mon′o··krat″, *n.*—**mon·o·crat·ic**, mon″o·krat′ik, *a.*

mo·noc·u·lar, mo·nok′ū·lėr, *a.* Used by one eye; one-eyed.

mon·o·cul·ture, mon′o·kul″chėr, *n.* The cultivation of only one crop on an area of land.—**mon·o·cul·tur·al**, *a.*

mon·o·cy·cle, mon′o·sī″kl, *n.* A cycle having only one wheel; unicycle: opposed to bicycle.

mon·o·cy·clic, mon″o·sī′klik, mon″o·sik′lik, *a.* Possessing one cycle; *bot.* arranged in one whorl, as certain flower parts; *Chem.* containing a single ring in the molecular diagram.—**mon·o·cy·cly**, *n.*

mo·no·cyte, mon′o·sīt″, *n. Anat.* a large leukocyte, the nucleus of which is horseshoe-shaped.

mon·o·dac·ty·lous, mon″o·dak′ti·lus, *a.* [Gr. *monos*, single, and *daktylos*, finger.] *Zool.* having only one finger, toe, or claw. Also **mon·o·dac·tyl**.

mo·nod·ic, mo·nod′ik, *a.* [Gr. *monoōsikōs*.] Of, pertaining to, or of the nature of a monody; *mus.* pertaining to or of the nature of monody.—**mo·nod·i·cal·ly**, *adv.*

mon·o·dra·ma, mon′o·drä″ma, mon′o··dram″a, *n.* A drama performed or intended for performance by a single person.—**mon·o·dra·mat·ic**, mon″o·dra·mat′ik, *a.*—**mon·o·dram·a·tist**, *n.*

mon·o·dy, mon′o·dē, *n. pl.* **mon·o·dies.** [L.L. *monodia*, < Gr. *monoīdia*, < *monos*, alone, and *aeidein*, sing.] An ode in Greek tragedy sung by a single voice; a mournful song or dirge; a poem in which one person laments another's death. *Mus.* A solo song developed in 17th century opera consisting of a vocal line similar to recitative and accompanied by a figured bass; homophony.—**mo·nod·ic**, mo·nod′ik, *a.*—**mon·o·dist**, mon′o·dist, *n.* One who writes or composes monodies.

mo·noe·cious, mo·nē′shus, *a.* [Gr. *monos*, one, and *oikos*, a house.] *Bot.* having male and female flowers on the same plant. *Zool.* having male and female organs of reproduction in the same individual; hermaphroditic. Also **mo·ne·cious**, **mo··noi·cous**.—**mo·noe·cious·ly**, *adv.*—**mo··noe·cism**, mo·noe·cy, *n.*

mon·o·fil·a·ment, mon″o·fil′a·ment, *n.* A single synthetic filament. Also **mon·o··fil**, mon′a·fil″.—*a.* Made of a single filament.

mo·nog·a·mous, mo·nog′a·mus, *a.* Upholding or practicing monogamy; relating to monogamy. Also **mon·o·gam·ic**, mon″a·gam′ik.—**mo·nog·a·mist**, mo··nog′a·mist, *n.*—**mo·nog·a·mis·tic**, *a.*—**mo·nog·a·mous·ly**, *adv.*—**mo·nog··a·mous·ness**, *n.*

mo·nog·a·my, mo·nog′a·mē, *n.* The practice or principle of being married to only one person at a time: opposed to *bigamy* or *polygamy*; *zool.* the pairing with only a single mate.

mon·o·gen·e·sis, mon″o·jen′i·sis, *n. Biol.* The theoretical descent of all living things from a single cell; the theoretical descent of the whole human race from a single pair; asexual reproduction. Also **mo·nog·e·ny**, mo·noj′e·nē.—**mon·o·ge··net·ic**, mon″ō·je·net′ik, *a.* Of or pertaining to monogenesis or monogenism; *geol.* resulting from one genetic process, as in the development of a group of mountains.—**mo·nog·e·nism**, mo·noj′e·niz″um, *n.*—**mo·nog·e·nist**, *n.*

mon·o·gram, mon′o·gram″, *n.* [L.L. *monogramma*, < Gr. *monos*, single, and *gramma*, character, letter, < *graphein*, write.] A character consisting of two or more letters combined or interlaced, commonly the initials of a person's name placed on personal items for decoration or identification.—*v.t.*—*monogramed, monograming, monogrammed, monogramming.* To adorn or inscribe with a monogram.—**mon·o··gram·mat·ic**, mon″o·gra·mat′ik, *a.*—**mon·o·grammed**, *a.*

mon·o·graph, mon′o·graf″, mon′o·gräf″, *n.* [Gr. *monos*, single, and *graphē*, description.] A scholarly dissertation or study of a limited subject or field; an account or description of a single thing or class of things.—*v.t.* To author a monograph about.—**mo·nog·ra·pher**, mo·nog′ra·fėr, *n.*—**mon·o·graph·ic**, mon″o·graf′ik, *a.*

mo·nog·y·nous, mo·noj′i·nus, *a.* Having but one wife at a time; characterized by or pertaining to monogyny; as, a *monogynous* culture. *Bot.* of a flower, having only one pistil; of a plant, having such flowers.—**mo·nog·y·ny**, mo·noj′i·nē, *n.* The practice or the condition of having but one wife at a time.

mo·nol·a·try, mo·nol′a·trē, *n.* [Gr. *monos*, single, and *latpeīa*, worship.] The worship of one god, esp. when other gods are recognized as existing.—**mo·nol·a·trous**, *a.*

mon·o·lay·er, mon″o·lā′ėr, *a. Chem.* a monomolecular layer.

mon·o·lin·gual, mon″o·ling′gwal, *a.* Speaking only a single language: opposed to *multilingual.*

mon·o·lith, mon′o·lith, *n.* A single stone block, usu. of great size, esp. one employed in sculpture or architecture; a pillar, column, or the like formed of a single great stone; a menhir. *Fig.* something characterized by massiveness and homogeneity; as, a bureaucratic *monolith.*

mon·o·lith·ic, mon′o·lith′ik, *a.* Of or relating to a monolith; formed of a single stone; consisting of monoliths. *Fig.* characterized by massiveness and uniformity.—**mon·o·lith·i·cal·ly**, *adv.*

mon·o·logue, **mon·o·log**, mon′o·lag″, mon′o·log″, *n.* [Fr. *monologue*.] A discourse, dramatic sketch, or poem delivered by one performer; soliloquy; an extended speech that monopolizes conversation; a humorous dissertation or series of short funny stories delivered by a lone comedian.—**mon·o·log·ist, mon·o·logu·ist,** mon'o·lạg″ist, mon'o·log″ist, mo·nol'o·jist, n.

mon·o·ma·ni·a, mon″o·mā'nē·a, măn'yo·mā'nē·a, n. That mental disorder in which the patient is obsessed by one idea, or is irrational on one subject only; excessive enthusiasm for one idea, object, or project.—**mon·o·ma·ni·ac,** n., a.—**mon·o·ma·ni·a·cal,** mon″o·ma·nī'a·kal, a.

mon·o·mer, mon'o·mėr, n. Chem. a molecule with low molecular weight, able to react with other molecules of low weight to create a polymer.—**mon·o·mer·ic,** mon'o·mer'ik, a.

mo·nom·er·ous, mo·nom'ėr·us, a. Comprised of one part; bot. of flowers, having one member in each whorl.

mon·o·met·al·lism, mon″o·met'a·liz″um, n. The employment of only one metal as a standard in the coinage of a country; the rationale for a single metallic standard.—**mon·o·me·tal·lic,** mon″ō·me·tal'ik, a.—**mon·o·met·al·list,** n.

mo·nom·e·ter, mo·nom'i·tėr, n. Pros. a line of poetry having one metrical foot.—**mon·o·met·ri·cal,** mon″o·me'tri·kal, a.

mo·no·mi·al, mō·nō'mē·al, mo·nō'mē·al, n. [Gr. monos, sole, and onoma, a name.] Alg. an expression composed of a single term; biol. a taxonomic name of a plant or animal consisting of a single word.—a. Biol. pertaining to a one-word name; alg. consisting of a single term.

mon·o·mo·lec·u·lar, mon″ō·mo·lek'ū·lėr, a. Having or pertaining to a thickness of a single molecule.

mon·o·mor·phic, mon″o·mạr'fik, a. Biol. having only one form. Of the same or of an essentially similar type of structure.—**mon·o·mor·phism,** mon″o·mạr'fiz·um, n.—**mon·o·mor·phous,** a.

mon·o·nu·cle·ar, mon″o·nō'klē·ėr, mon″o·nū'klē·ėr, a. Having a single nucleus.

mon·o·nu·cle·o·sis, mon″o·nō″klē·ō'sis, mon″o·nū″klē·ō'sis, n. A virus disease of the blood, characterized by the existence of too many monocytes. Also infectious mononucleosis.

mo·noph·a·gous, mo·nof'a·gus, a. Zool. feeding on only one particular kind of animal or plant.

mon·o·phon·ic, mon″o·fon'ik, a. Electron. of or pertaining to sound reproduction consisting of only one sound source or output signal: opposite of stereophonic; also monaural. Mus. characterized by only one melodic line, unaccompanied or with only light accompaniment.—**mo·noph·o·ny,** mo·nof'o·nē, n. Music in a monophonic style.

mon·oph·thong, mon'of·thạng″, mon'of·thong″, n. [Gr. monos, sole, and phthongos, sound.] A single vowel sound; two or more written vowels pronounced as one.—**mon·oph·thon·gal,** a.

mon·o·phy·let·ic, mon″ō·fī·let'ik, a. Genetics. Of or pertaining to a single tribe or stock; developed from a single ancestral type, as a group of animals.

mon·o·phyl·lous, mon″o·fil'us, a. Bot. having one leaf only, or formed of one leaf.

Mo·noph·y·site, mo·nof'i·sīt″, n. [L., Gr. monophysitēs.] One holding that there is in Christ but a single nature, a divine one, or one composite nature, partly divine and partly human, as believed by the Coptic Church of Egypt.—**Mon·o·phy·sit·ic,** mon″ō·fī·sit'ik, a.—**Mo·noph·y·sit·ism,** n.

mon·o·plane, mon'o·plān″, n. An airplane having only one main lifting surface or wing, usu. divided into two segments by the fuselage.

mon·o·ple·gi·a, mon″o·plē'jē·a, mon″-o·plē'ja, n. [N.L. < Gr. monos, single, and plegia, as in paraplegia, E. paraplegia.] Pathol. paralysis affecting only one limb or one part of the body.—**mon·o·ple·gic,** a.

mon·o·pode, mon'o·pōd″, a. [= Fr. monopode, < Gr. monopous (monopod-).] Having but one foot.—n. A creature having but one foot, esp. one of a mythical race of men having one leg. Bot. a monopodium.

mon·o·po·di·um, n. pl. **mon·o·po·di·a.** Bot. an inflorescence or flower cluster having one primary axis or stalk and producing floral offshoots to right and left beneath the apex. Also monopode.—**mon·o·po·di·al,** a.

mo·nop·o·list, mo·nop'o·list, n. One who has a monopoly; an advocate of monopoly.—**mo·nop·o·lis·tic,** mo·nop'o·lis'tik, a.—**mo·nop·o·lis·ti·cal·ly,** adv.

mo·nop·o·lize, mo·nop'o·līz″, v.t.—monopolized, monopolizing. To acquire, have, or exercise a monopoly of; to engross; to obtain exclusive possession of; to keep entirely to oneself.—**mo·nop·o·li·za·tion,** mo·nop″o·li·zā'shan, n.—**mo·nop·o·liz·er,** n.

mo·nop·o·ly, mo·nop'o·lē, n. pl. **mo·nop·o·lies.** [L. monopolium, < Gr. monopolion, < monos, alone, single, and polein, sell.] Exclusive control of a commodity or service in a particular market, esp. control that makes possible the manipulation of prices; anything that is the subject of a monopoly; a corporation or the like having a monopoly; an exclusive trading or manufacturing privilege; exclusive possession of or control of anything.

mon·o·pro·pel·lant, mon″ō·pro·pel'ant, n. Aerospace, a liquid rocket propellant consisting of a mixture of fuel and oxidizer, as alcohol and hydrogen peroxide, ready for burning in the combustion chamber. Also **mon·o·fu·el.**—a.

mo·nop·so·ny, mo·nop'so·nē, n. pl. **mo·nop·so·nies.** Econ. a market situation when there is a single buyer.—**mo·nop·so·nist,** n.—**mo·nop·so·nis·tic,** mo·nop″so·nis'tik, a.

mon·o·rail, mon'o·rāl″, n. [Gr. monos, one, and rail.] A railway whose cars run on or are suspended from a single rail; the rail itself.

mon·o·sep·al·ous, mon″o·sep'a·lus, a. [Gr. monos, one, and E. sepal.] Bot. composed of a single sepal, as a calyx.

mon·o·so·di·um glu·ta·mate, mon″o·sō'dē·um glö'ta·māt″, n. Chem. a crystalline sodium salt, $C_5H_8O_4NaN$, used as a seasoning to enhance flavor, esp. of meat. Abbr. MSG.

mon·o·stich, mon'o·stik″, n. [L.L. monostichum, < Gr. monostichon, neut. of monostichos, consisting of one line.] A poem or epigram of a single metrical line.

mon·o·sty·lous, mon″o·stī'lus, a. Bot. having one style only, as a flower.

mon·o·syl·lab·ic, mon″o·si·lab'ik, a. Consisting of one syllable; using, uttering, or consisting of words of only one syllable; brief; terse.—**mon·o·syl·lab·i·cal·ly,** adv.

mon·o·syl·la·ble, mon'o·sil″a·bl, n. A word of one syllable.

mon·o·sym·met·ric, mon″o·si·me'trik, a. Biol. zygomorphic; having bilateral symmetry. Crystal. monoclinic. Also **mon·o·sym·met·ri·cal.**—**mon·o·sym·met·ry,** mon″o·sim'i·trē, n.

mon·o·the·ism, mon'o·thē·iz″um, n. [Gr.] The doctrine of, or belief in, the existence of one God only.—**mon·o·the·ist,** n.—**mon·o·the·is·tic,** mon″o·thē·is'tik, a.—**mon·o·the·is·ti·cal·ly,** adv.

mon·o·tint, mon'o·tint″, n. Monochrome.

mon·o·tone, mon'o·tōn″, a. [= Fr. monotone, < L.Gr. monotonos, of one tone.] Continuing in one tone, as utterance; monotonous; of one tone or color.—n. A continuation of the same tone, as in speaking; tone unvaried in pitch; any unvaried sound or repetition of sounds; sameness of style, as in composition or writing; something characterized by such sameness or monotony; a single tone or color; a picture or print in one tone or color.—v.t., v.i.—monotoned, monotoning. To recite in monotone.—**mon·o·ton·ic,** mon″o·ton'ik, a.

mo·not·o·nous, mo·not'o·nus, a. [L.Gr. monotonos.] Uttered or continuing in the same tone, or on one note; unvarying in any respect; lacking in variety; tiresomely uniform.—**mo·not·o·nous·ly,** adv.—**mo·not·o·nous·ness,** n.

mo·not·o·ny, mo·not'o·nē, n. [L.Gr. monotonia.] Sameness of tone or pitch, as in music or talking; monotone; boring repetition of the same or similar activities, conversation, or other interests.

mon·o·treme, mon'o·trēm″, n. [Gr. monos, single, trēma, aperture.] One of the Monotremata, the lowest order of mammals, oviparous, with a single outlet for the feces and the products of the urinary and generative organs, comprising only the duckbills and echidnas.

mon·o·type, mon'o·tīp″, n. Biol. the sole representative of its group, as a single species constituting a genus. Print. a print from a metal plate on which a picture is painted; the method of producing such a print. (Cap.), print. a device for casting and setting type in separate units, as opposed to Linotype; (trademark).—**mon·o·typ·er,** n.—**mon·o·typ·ic,** a.

mon·o·va·lent, mon″o·vā'lent, n. [Gr. monos, single, and L. valens, valentis, ppr. of valeo, to be worth.] Chem. pertaining to an elementary substance, one atom of which enters into combination with a single atom of another elementary substance; univalent; bact. having a single type of antibody specific to a single type of cell or bacterium.—**mon·o·va·lence, mon·o·va·len·cy,** n.

mon·ox·ide, mon·ok'sīd, mo·nok'sīd, n. Chem. an oxide containing one oxygen atom to the molecule.

Mon·roe Doc·trine, mon·rō' dok'trin, n. [From U.S. President James Monroe, based on statements issued to Congress on December 2, 1823.] The policy holding that any attempt by a European country to colonize or enter into the internal affairs of a Spanish-American country would be considered an unfriendly act toward the U.S. government.

mon·sei·gneur, mạN·se·nyœr', n. pl. **mes·sei·gneurs,** mā·se·nyœr'. [Fr.] A French title of honor given to princes, bishops, and other high dignitaries; a person with such a title.

mon·sieur, mo·syœ', n. pl. **mes·sieurs,** mes'ėrz, Fr. mā·syœ'. [Fr., contr. of monseigneur.] The common title of courtesy and respect in France, corresponding to the English sir and Mr. Abbr. Mons., M.; pl. Messrs., MM.

Mon·si·gnor, mon·sē'nụr, It. mạn″sē·nyạr', n. pl. **mon·si·gnors,** It. **mon·'si·gno·ri,** mạn″sē·nya'Rē. [It., < Fr. monseigneur.] (Sometimes l.c.), Rom. Cath. Ch. A title conferred upon priests who have received certain papal honors; a priest bearing this title. Abbr. Monsig., Msgr. Also It. **Mon·si·gno·re.**—**mon·si·gno·ri·al,** a.

mon·soon, mon·sön', n. [Pg. monção, < Ar. mawsim, time, season.] A seasonal wind of the Indian Ocean and southern Asia, blowing from the southwest from April to October and from the northeast during the rest of the year; the season during which this wind blows from the southwest, commonly marked by heavy rains; any wind whose direction is reversed periodically.—**mon·soon·al,** a.

a- fat, fāte, fär, fåre, fạll; **e-** met, mē, mēre, hėr; **i-** pin, pīne; **o-** not, nōte, möve; **u-** tub, cūbe, bụll; **oi-** oil; **ou-** pound.

mon·ster, mon'stèr, *n.* [Fr. *monstre,* < L. *monstrum,* a marvel, a monster, < *moneo,* to admonish.] A plant or an animal of abnormal or hideous structure or appearance; a creature exhibiting malformation of important organs or parts; a person or thing which inspires horror because of extraordinary crimes, heinousness, depravity, deformity, or power to do harm; an imaginary or mythical creature such as a sphinx, centaur, or griffin; any huge or unnatural person or thing.—*a.* Of inordinate size or numbers; monstrous.

mon·strance, mon'strans, *n.* [L.L. *monstrantia,* < L. *monstro,* to show.] *Rom. Cath. Ch.* the receptacle in which the consecrated Host is presented for the adoration of the people. Also **os·ten·so·ri·um.**

mon·stros·i·ty, mon·stros'i·tē, *n. pl.* **mon·stros·i·ties.** The state of being monstrous; that which is monstrous, esp. in form or growth; something abnormal or unnatural; a freak.

mon·strous, mon'strus, *a.* [L. *monstosus.*] Unnatural in form or character; out of the common course of nature; possessing the appearance or qualities of a monster; enormous; huge; extraordinary; shocking; frightful; horrible.—**mon·strous·ly,** *adv.*—**mon·strous·ness,** *n.*

mons ve·ne·ris, monz' ven'èr·is, *n. pl.* **mon·tes ve·ne·ris.** [L., 'mount of Venus.'] *Anat.* a rounded eminence of fatty tissue over the pubic symphysis of the human female.

mon·tage, mon·tazh', *Fr.* mạn·täzh', *n.* [Fr., mounting, putting together.] The art or process of combining many pictorial elements in one photographic composition; a composition produced by this process. *Motion Pictures, TV,* a rapid succession of images illustrating a number of related ideas; juxtaposition or superimposition of shots to produce a single image. Any combination of heterogeneous elements in an artistic, literary, or musical composition to create a single image or unified whole.

mon·tane, mon'tān, *a.* [L. *montanus,* < *mons* (*mont-*).] Pertaining to or inhabiting mountains.—*n.* The lower belt of mountain vegetation.

mon·tan wax, mon'tan waks, *n.* A hard wax obtained by extraction from lignite, and used in making polishes, paints, pastes, and carbon paper.

mont-de-pié·té, mạnd·e·pyä·tā', *n. pl.* **monts-de-pié·té,** mạnd·e·pyä·tā'. [Fr., < It. *monte di pietà,* lit. 'mountain of pity.'] A public pawnbroking establishment which lends money on reasonable terms, esp. to the poor.

mon·te, mon'tē, mōn'tā, *Sp.* mạn'te, *n.* [Sp., the stack of cards which remains after each player has received his share, < L. *mons,* a mountain.] A Spanish gambling game played with cards, in which a player bets that one of his cards will be matched in suit before the other players' cards. Also **mon·te·bank.**

Mon·tes·so·ri meth·od, mon''ti·sōr'ē meth'od, *It.* mạn''tes·sạ'rē, *n.* A system for training and instructing young children, originated by Maria Montessori in Rome in 1907, having as its fundamental aims the self-education of the children, substituting guidance for control, and emphasizing the training of the senses. Also **Mon·tes·sor·i sys·tem.**—**Mon·tes·so·ri·an,** *a.*

month, munth, *n.* [O.E. *mōnath* = G. *monat* = Icel. *mānudhr* = Goth. *mēnōths,* month.] The period, called a 'lunar month,' of a complete revolution of the moon with regard to some point, usu. the interval from one new moon to the next, called a 'synodical month,' and equivalent to 29 days, 12 hours, 44 minutes, and 2.7 seconds; the twelfth part of a solar year, called a 'solar month'; any one of the twelve parts, as January, February, and so on, into which the calendar year is divided, called a 'calendar month'; the time from any day of one calendar month to the corresponding day of the next; a period of four weeks or of thirty days.

month·ly, munth'lē, *a.* Pertaining to a month or to each month; done, happening, or appearing, once a month or every month; continuing or lasting for a month.—*n. pl.* **month·lies.** A periodical published once a month. *Pl.* Menstruation; the period of menstruating.—*adv.* Once a month; by the month.

mon·ti·cule, mon'ti·kūl'', *n.* [L. *monticulus,* dim. of *mons, montis,* a mountain.] A little mount; a small hill; a lesser volcanic cone.—**mon·tic·u·late, mon·-tic·u·lous,** mon·tik'ū·lit, *a.*

mon·u·ment, mon'ū·ment, *n.* [L. *monumentum,* < *moneo,* to remind, to warn.] Anything by which the memory of a person, period, or event is perpetuated; a memorial, esp. something built or erected in memory of events, actions, or persons; any enduring or notable example, esp. an archaeological historic building or ruin, as the pyramids of Egypt; art, literature, and the like, considered to have enduring value; a stone or shaft establishing a boundary of a given area or property; an area of natural beauty or historical significance which is maintained for public use by a government, as the Grand Canyon or Gettysburg National Park; an exemplar or personification of abstract quality, as: Albert Schweitzer is a *monument* to man's devotion to his fellow-man.—*v.t.* To commemorate by building a monument to; to establish a memorial on. Also **mon·u·men·tal·ize,** mon''ū·men'ta·līz''—**monumentalized, monumentalizing.**

mon·u·men·tal, mon''ū·men'tal, *a.* [L.L. *monumentalis.*] Of or pertaining to a monument or monuments; of the nature of, resembling, or serving as a monument; massive or imposing; substantial and important, as a literary work; historically prominent; as, a *monumental* figure or event; conspicuously great or gross; as, a *monumental* fraud, *monumental* stupidity. *Fine arts,* larger than life-size.—**mon·u·men·tal·ly,** *adv.*

moo, mö, *v.i.* To bellow, as a cow.—*n.* A mooing sound or utterance.

mooch, mouch, möch, *v.i. Slang.* To skulk or sneak; to hang or rove about, esp. with the idea of picking up what one can.—*v.t. Slang.* To steal (a small amount); to appropriate surreptitiously; pilfer.—**mooch·er,** *n.*

mood, möd, *n.* [O.E. *mōd,* mind, passion, disposition = D. *moed,* Icel. *módr* (*mōthr*), Dan. and Sw. *mod,* Goth. *mods,* G. *muth,* mood, spirit, passion, courage.] A temporary disposition or state of mind; a particular or characteristic emotional quality; a predominating attitude; *archaic,* a fit of temper or sullenness.—**in the mood,** favorably disposed.

mood, möd, *n.* [Fr. *mode,* L. *modus*; merely a different spelling of *mode.*] *Gram.* a special form of verbs expressing certainty, contingency, possibility, or command; *logic,* modality. Also **mode.**

mood·y, möd'ē, *a.*—**moodier, moodiest.** [O.E. *mōdig,* angry.] Subject to or indulging in gloomy moods or moroseness; fretful; out of humor; sullen; melancholy; expressing or indicating such ill humor; as, *moody* looks. —**mood·i·ly,** *adv.*—**mood·i·ness,** *n.*

moo·la, moo·lah, mö'la, *n. Slang.* money.

moon, mön, *n.* [O.E. *mōna* (masc.) = Icel. *máni,* Dan. *maane,* D. *maan,* G. *mond,* Goth. *mena,* Lith. *menu,* Gr. *mēnē,* Skt. *mas*; < root *ma,* to measure: the moon being early adopted as a measurer of time. *Month* is a derivative.] The heavenly body which revolves around the earth; a satellite of any planet; as, the *moons* of Jupiter; the period of a revolution of the moon; *poet.* a month. Something in the shape of a moon or crescent.—*v.i. Colloq.* to wander or gaze idly or moodily.—*v.t. Colloq.* to spend idly, as time.

moon·beam, mön'bēm'', *n.* A ray of light from the moon.

moon blind·ness, *n.* Poor vision at night; nyctalopia. *Veter. pathol.* an intermittent eye inflammation of horses, usu. resulting in blindness; mooneye.—**moon-blind,** mön'blīnd'', *a.*

moon·calf, mön'kaf'', mön'käf'', *n. pl.* **moon·calves.** A congenital idiot; a stupid or simple person.

moon·eye, mön'ī'', *n. Veter. pathol.* Moon blindness; the eye so afflicted.—**moon·-eyed,** *a.*

moon·fish, mön'fish'', *n. pl.* **moon·fish, moon·fish·es.** Any of various salt-water fish with relatively round, flat, moon-shaped bodies, esp. fishes of the genus *Vomer,* having a deep, compressed silvery or yellowish body, found in the waters off both coasts.

moon·flow·er, mön'flou'èr, *n.* A night-blooming, self-entwining, tropical American morning glory, *Calonyction aculeatum,* with fragrant white flowers; any of several allied plants.

moon gar·den, *n. Aeron.* one of the projects in which scientists, in their studies of food problems facing future spacemen in orbit, grow ordinary vegetables under reduced air pressure.

moon·ish, mö'nish, *a.* Like the moon in shape or other characteristic; influenced by or due to the moon; changeable as the moon; fickle.—**moon·ish·ly,** *adv.*

moon·let, mön'lit, *n.* A small moon; an artificial satellite.

moon·light, mön'līt'', *n.* The light afforded by the moon.—*a.* Illuminated by the moon; occurring during or by moonlight; moonlit.

moon·light·er, mön'lī''tèr, *n. Colloq.* a person who holds a second job in addition to his normal, full-time occupation.—**moon·light,** *v.i.*—**moon·light·ing,** *n.*

moon·lit, mön'lit'', *a.* Lighted or illuminated by the moon.

moon·rise, mön'rīz'', *n.* The appearance of the moon above the visible horizon; the time when the moon appears.

moon·scape, mön'skāp'', *n.* The actual appearance of the moon's topography or a description or representation of it.

moon·seed, mön'sēd'', *n.* Any of the climbing herbs of the genus *Menispermum,* as *M. canadense,* with panicles of greenish-white flowers, black fruit, and crescent moon-shaped seeds.

moon·set, mön'set'', *n.* The sinking of the moon below the visible horizon; the time when the moon so disappears.

moon·shine, mön'shin'', *n.* The light of the moon; foolish or unrealistic talk; ideas without substance; *colloq.* illicitly distilled or smuggled liquor, usu. liquor made from corn.—**moon·shin·er,** mön'shi''nèr, *n. Colloq.* one who pursues an illegal trade usu. at night, esp. a distiller of illicit liquor.

moon·stone, mön'stōn'', *n.* A translucent variety of feldspar, specif. an adularia with a pearly luster, used as a gem.

moon·struck, mön'struk'', *a.* Affected mentally, supposedly by the moon's influence; dazed; lunatic; excessively romantic or sentimental. Also **moon·-strick·en,** mön'strik''en.

moon·y, mö'nē, *a.*—**moonier, mooniest.** Pertaining to or characteristic of the moon; resembling the moon; round; crescent-shaped; illuminated by moonlight; resembling moonlight; mooning.

---

ch- chain, G. na*ch*t; **th-** THen, thin; **w-** wig, hw as sound in whig; **z-** zh as in azure, zeal. *Italicized vowel* indicates schwa sound.

listless, silly; dreamy.—**moon·i·ly**, *adv.*—**moon·i·ness**, *n.*

moor, mụr, *n.* [O.E. *mōr* = Icel. *mór*, a heath; D. *moer*, a morass; Dan. *mor*, a moor, a marsh; G. *moor*, a marsh, a moor.] A tract of waste land, esp. when covered with heath; a bog; a tract of ground on which game is preserved for hunting.—**moor·ish**, *a.* Abounding with moors; like a moor.

moor, mụr, *v.t.* [D. *marren, maren*, to tie, to moor; same word as E. *mar*, O.E. *merran*, to hinder, to mar, O.H.G. *marrjan*, to stop.] To confine or secure, as a boat, ship, aircraft, or the like, in a particular station by cables, anchors, chains, or the like; to fix firmly.—*v.i.* To be anchored or made secure with cables or chains; to secure a ship in such a manner.—**moor··age**, mụr'ij, *n.* A place for mooring; the amount charged for mooring; the act of mooring or the state of being moored.—**moor·ing**, *n. Naut.* the act of one who moors. *Pl.* that by which a ship is moored; the place where a ship is moored.

Moor, mụr, *n.* [O.Fr. Fr. *More, Maure*, < L. *Maurus*, < Gr. *Mauros*.] One of the ancient inhabitants of northwestern Africa; a Mohammedan of the mixed Berber and Arab race inhabiting this region, esp. Morocco; one belonging to the group of this race which in the 8th century invaded and conquered Spain.—**Moor·ish**, *a.*

moor·hen, *n.* The gallinule or water hen of Europe; the female of the red grouse.

moose, mös, *n. pl.* **moose**. [Algonquian.] A large animal, *Alces americanus*, of the deer family, inhabiting forested regions of Canada and the northern U.S., the male of which has enormous palmate antlers; a similar species, *A. gigas*, found in Alaska; the European elk, *A. machlis*.

moot, mōt, *a.* [O.E. *mōt, gemōt*, meeting, assembly; akin to Icel. *mōt*, M.L.G. *mōte, gemōte*, D. *gemoet*, meeting.] Subject to argument or discussion; debatable or doubtful; as, a *moot* point; impractical or insignificant; theoretical.—*n.* An early English assembly of the people, exercising political, administrative, and judicial powers; an argument or discussion, esp. of a hypothetical legal case.—*v.t.* To bring forward for discussion; to make insignificant or theoretical.—**moot·ness**, *n.*

moot court, *n.* A mock court which tries hypothetical legal cases as practice for law students.

mop, mop, *n.* [M.E. *mappe*: cf. L. *mappa*, napkin, cloth, E. *map*.] An implement made of a bundle of yarn or other absorbent material fastened to a stick or handle, and used esp. for cleaning floors; something suggesting a mop; as, a *mop* of hair.—*v.t.*—*mopped, mopping*. To wipe away; to clean with a mop, as a floor.

mop, mop, *n.* [Compare D. *moppen*, to pout, to make a sulky face.] A wry mouth; a grimace.—*v.i.* To make a wry face.

mop·board, mop'bōrd″, *n.* A baseboard.

mope, mōp, *v.i.*—*moped, moping*. [Origin uncertain.] To act in a listless, dispirited manner; to be sunk in listless apathy or dull dejection.—*v.t.* To make dispirited or dejected.—*n.* A mopish person; *pl.* low spirits.—**mop·er**, *n.*—**mop·ing·ly**, *adv.*—**mop·ish**, mō'pish, *a.*—**mop·ish·ly**, *adv.*—**mop·ish·ness**, *n.*

mop·pet, mop'it, *n.* [Dim. of *mop*.] A small child; youngster.

mop up, *v.t. Colloq.* To defeat decisively; to clear away or dispose of after a confrontation involving thorough defeat.—*v.i. Colloq.* to finish off or clean up the remnants of, esp. a group defeated by military force.

mop-up, mop'up″, *n. Slang*, a brutal defeat or trouncing; *colloq.* the final clearing, as of the battlefield after a military victory.

mo·quette, mō·ket', *n.* [Fr.] A thick, velvety fabric used for carpets and upholstery.

mo·ra, mōr'a, mạr'a, *n. pl.* **mo·rae**, **mo·ras**, mōr'ē, mạr'ē. [L., delay.] *Pros.* the unit of time or meter equivalent to the ordinary or normal short sound or syllable.

mo·ra·ceous, mō·rā'shus, mạ·rā'shus, *a.* [L. *morus*, mulberry tree.] *Bot.* belonging to the *Moraceæ* or mulberry family of plants, which includes the mulberry, breadfruit, fig, hemp, hop, and Osage orange.

mo·raine, mo·rān', *n.* [Fr., akin to It. *mora*, a heap of stones.] An accumulation of stones, rocks, gravel, and other debris carried and deposited by a glacier.—**mo·rain·al, mo·rain·ic**, *a.*

mor·al, mạr'al, mor'al, *a.* [Fr. *moral*, < L. *moralis*, < *mos, moris*, manner, *mores*, manners, morals (seen also in *demoralize, demure, morose*).] Of or concerned with the principles of right and wrong in conduct and character; teaching or upholding standards of good behavior; conforming to the rules of right conduct; sexually virtuous; judged by one's conscience to be ethical or approved; capable of distinguishing between right and wrong; not proven but sufficient for practical purposes; as, *moral* certainty; of or affecting the intellect, emotions, and conduct; as, a *moral* victory.—*n.* The lesson taught by a fable, parable, or story. *Pl.* ethics; principles and mode of life; behavior as to right or wrong, esp. in relation to sexual matters.—**mor·al·ly**, mạr'a·lē, mor'a·lē, *adv.*

mo·rale, mo·ral', *n.* [An erroneous spelling of Fr. *moral*, used in same sense.] Mental attitude, as of soldiers, expressing courage, zeal, hope, or confidence.

mor·al haz·ard, *n. Insurance*, the risk to an insurance company based on the possible dishonesty of the insured.

mor·al·ism, mạr'a·liz″um, mor'a·liz″um, *n.* The habit of moralizing; moral counsel; the practice of morality, as distinct from religion.

mor·al·ist, mạr'a·list, mor'a·list, *n.* One who teaches morals; a writer or lecturer on ethics; one who practices morality.—**mor·al·is·tic**, *a.*

mo·ral·i·ty, mo·ral'i·tē, mạ·ral'i·tē, *n. pl.* **mo·ral·i·ties**. [O.Fr. *moralite* (Fr. *moralité*), L.L. *moralitas*.] Moral quality or character; the quality of conforming to the principles of good conduct; moral or virtuous conduct; sexual virtue; morals or ethics; moral instruction; a moral lesson or precept; a moralizing discourse or utterance.

mo·ral·i·ty play, *n.* A kind of allegorical drama of the 15th and 16th centuries, employing personifications of virtues, vices, or other abstractions as characters.

mor·al·ize, mạr'a·liz″, mor'a·liz″, *v.t.*—*moralized, moralizing*. [O.Fr. Fr. *moraliser*, M.L. *moralizare*, < L. *moralis*.] To explain in a moral sense; to draw a moral from; to give a moral quality or character to; to improve the morals of.—*v.i.* To make moral reflections.—**mor·al·i·za·tion**, *n.*—**mor·al·iz·er**, *n.*—**mor·al·iz·ing·ly**, *adv.*

mor·al phi·los·o·phy, *n.* Ethics.

mo·rass, mo·ras', *n.* [Same as D. *moeras*, < *moer*, a moor; Sw. *moras*, G. *morast*.] A tract of low, soft, wet ground; a marsh; a swamp. *Fig.* something that entraps or delays.

mor·a·to·ri·um, mạr″a·tōr'ē·um, mạr″a·tạr'ē·um, *n. pl.* **mor·a·to·ri·a, mor·a·to·ri·ums**. [L. *moratorius*, < *mora*, delay.] A special period of delay granted by law to debtors; the period of such a delay; any temporary suspension of activity.

mor·a·to·ry, mạr'a·tōr″ē, mạr'a·tạr″ē, mor'a·tōr″ē, mor'a·tạr″ē, *a.* [L.L. *moratorius*, delaying, < L. *morari*, delay.] *Law*, denoting an authorized delay of payment.

Mo·ra·vi·an, mō·rā'vē·an, mạ·rā'vē·an, *a.* Pertaining to Moravia, its inhabitants, or the Moravian Church.—*n.* A native of Moravia; any of the dialects spoken by the Moravian population; one of a religious sect, also called United Brethren, tracing its origin to John Huss, and adhering to evangelical principles.

mo·ray, mōr'ā, mạr'ā, *n.* [Cf. Pg. *moréia*, < L. *murœna*.] Any of numerous voracious eels with porelike gills constituting the family *Murœnidæ*, esp. those of the genus *Murœna*, as *M. helena*, a species common in the Mediterranean and valued as a food-fish, or *Gymnothorax moringa*, a species common in West Indian waters.

mor·bid, mạr'bid, *a.* [L. *morbidus*, < *morbus*, disease.] Affected by or characteristic of disease; as, *morbid* tissues, discharges, or symptoms; pertaining to diseased parts; as, *morbid* anatomy; being in or suggesting an unhealthy mental state; unwholesomely gloomy, sensitive, or extreme.—**mor·bid·ly**, *adv.*—**mor·bid·ness**, *n.*

mor·bid·i·ty, mạr·bid'i·tē, *n.* A morbid state or quality; the proportion of death, sickness, or disease in a given locality.

mor·da·cious, mạr·dā'shus, *a.* [L. *mordax, mordacis*, < *mordeo*, to bite.] Biting; sarcastic.—**mor·dac·i·ty**, mạr·das'i·tē, *n.*—**mor·da·cious·ly**, *adv.*

mor·dant, mạr'dant, *a.* [O.Fr. Fr. *mordant*, ppr. of *mordre*, < L. *mordēre*, to bite.] Pungent, acrid, or corrosive, as substances; sharp, as pain; caustic, sarcastic, or cutting, as speech, speakers, or wit. Having the property of fixing colors, as in dyeing.—*n.* A substance used in dyeing to fix the coloring matter, esp. a metallic compound, as an oxide or hydroxide, which combines with the organic dyestuff and forms an insoluble colored compound or lake in the fiber; an acid or other corrosive substance used in etching to eat out the lines.—*v.t.* To impregnate or treat with a mordant.—**mor·dan·cy**, *n.* The quality of being sharp or caustic; pungency.—**mor·dant·ly**, *adv.*

mor·dent, mạr'dent, *n.* [It. *mordente*, prop. ppr. of *mordere*, < L. *mordēre*, to bite.] *Mus.* a melodic embellishment consisting of a rapid alternation of a principal tone with a supplementary tone a half-step below it, called *single* or *short* when the supplementary tone occurs but once, and *double* or *long* when this occurs twice or oftener.—**in·vert·ed mor·dent**, pralltriller.

more, mōr, mạr, *a., compar. of many or much* with *most* as the *superl.* [O.E. *māra* = O.H.G. *mēro* = Icel. *meiri* = Goth. *maiza*, more, greater.] In greater quantity, amount, measure, degree, or number; additional or further.—*n.* A greater quantity, amount, or number; something of greater importance; a greater number of a class specified, or the greater number of persons.—*adv., compar. of much* with *most* as the *superl.* In or to a greater extent or degree: in this sense much used before adjectives and adverbs, esp. before those of two or more syllables, to form comparative phrases; as, *more* curious, *more* wisely; in addition; further; longer; again.—**more or less**, to an indefinite extent or measure.

mo·reen, mo·rēn', *n.* [Connected with *mohair*, Fr. *moire*.] A heavy, woolen, or woolen and cotton fabric, often embossed, used for curtains, clothing, and the like.

mo·rel, mo·rel', *n.* [Fr. *morille*, < O.H.G. *morhila*.] An edible mushroom belonging to the genus *Morchella*, esp. *M. esculenta*.

mo·rel·lo, mo·rel'ō, *n. pl.* **mo·rel·los**. [It. *morello*, dark-colored.] A kind of cultivated cherry distinguished by dark red skin and juice.

---

a- fat, fāte, fär, fâre, fạll;   **e-** met, mē, mēre, hėr;   **i-** pin, pīne;   **o-** not, nōte, möve;   **u-** tub, cūbe, bụll;   **oi-** oil;   **ou-** pound.

more·o·ver, mōr·ō'vėr, mōr'ō"vėr, *adv.* Beyond what has been said; further; besides; also.

mo·res, mōr'āz, mō'rēz, *n. pl.* [L.] Customs; manners; ways; specif., customs prevailing among a people or a social group and accepted as right and obligatory.

Mo·resque, mo·resk', *a.* [Fr., < It. *moresco*, < *Moro*, L. *Maurus*, a Moor.] Moorish; in the Moorish style, as architecture, decoration, or motif.

Mor·gan, mạr'gan, *n.* One of a superior breed of American trotting horses descended from a stallion owned by Justin Morgan, 1747–1798, of Vermont.

mor·ga·nat·ic, mạr"ga·nat'ik, *a.* [M.L. (*matrimonium ad*) *morganaticam*, 'marriage with morning gift' (in lieu of a share in the husband's possessions), < O.H.G. *morgan*, morning.] Designating or pertaining to a marriage in which a man of high or noble rank takes as wife a woman of lower station, with the stipulation that neither she nor children of the marriage will have any claim to his rank or property.—**mor·ga·nat·i·cal·ly**, *adv.*

mor·gan·ite, mạr'ga·nīt", *n.* A rose-colored variety of the mineral beryl and used as a semiprecious gem.

mor·gen, mạr'gen, *n.* [D. and G.] A land measure equal to about two acres, formerly used in Holland and the Dutch colonies, still used in South Africa; a land measure equal to about two thirds of an acre, formerly used in Prussia, Norway, and Denmark.

morgue, mạrg, *n.* [Fr. Origin unknown.] A place where the bodies of dead people, particularly accident victims, are kept until identified or buried; the reference files or library in a newspaper or magazine office; any information or records stored for possible use in the future; any place where these are stored.

mor·i·bund, mạr'i·bund", mōr'i·bund", *a.* [L. *moribundus*, < *mori*, to die.] Dying; deathlike; in an inactive state; nearing extinction; as, a *moribund* venture. —**mor·i·bun·di·ty**, *n.*

mo·ri·on, mōr'ē·on", mạr'ē·on", *n.* [Fr. *morion*, < Sp. *morrion*, a morion; origin doubtful.] A kind of metal helmet having a high crest, worn during the 16th and part of the 17th centuries.

mo·ri·on, mōr'ē·on", mạr'ē·on", *n.* [For L. *mormorion.*] A variety of smoky quartz of a dark brown or nearly black color.

Mo·ris·co, mo·ris'kō, *n. pl.* **Mo·ris·cos**, **Mo·ris·coes**. [Sp. *morisco*, Moorish, < *Moro*, a Moor.] A Moor, particularly of Spain.—*a.*

Mor·mon, mạr'mon, *n.* A member of that religious body properly known as the Church of Jesus Christ of Latter-day Saints; a 4th century prophet who, according to Mormon tradition, was the author of the Book of Mormon which Joseph Smith published in 1830.—*a.* Pertaining to Mormons or the Mormon religion.— **Mor·mon·ism**, *n.*

morn, mạrn, *n.* [Contr. < O.E. *morwen*, morning, whence also *morrow.*] *Poet.* The first part of the day; morning.

morn·ing, mạr'ning, *n.* [O.E. *morwening*, *morgen* (D., Dan., and G. *morgen*, Icel. *morginn*, Goth. *maurgins*) by common change of *g* to *w*, with the *-ing* of verbal nouns. The root is seen in Lith. *mirgu*, to glimmer, to gleam.] The first part of the day; dawn; the part of the day beginning at twelve o'clock at night, or dawn, and extending to twelve at noon; *fig.* the first or early part, as of life.

morn·ing-glo·ry, mạr'ning·glōr"ē, mạr'-ning·glạr"ē, *n. pl.* **morn·ing-glo·ries**. Any of various convolvulaceous plants, esp. of the genus *Ipomoea*, as *I. purpurea*, a

twining plant with cordate leaves and funnel-shaped flowers of various colors.

Morn·ing Prayer, *n.* A morning prayer service conducted in Anglican churches.

morn·ing sick·ness, *n.* Nausea occurring in the early part of the day, characteristic of the first months of pregnancy.

morn·ing star, *n.* A bright planet, Venus, seen in the east before sunrise.

Mo·ro, mōr'ō, *n. pl.* **Mo·ro**, **Mo·ros**. [Sp., a Moor.] A member of any of various tribes of Mohammedan Malays in the southern Philippine Islands; the language of these people.

Mo·roc·can, mo·rok'an, *n.* A native or inhabitant of Morocco, a kingdom in northwest Africa.—*a.*

mo·roc·co, mo·rok'ō, *n.* A fine, supple, pebbled leather orig. made in Morocco from goatskins tanned with sumac; any leather made to resemble morocco. Also **mo·roc·co leath·er.**

mo·ron, mōr'on, *n.* [Gr. *mōrós*, dull, foolish.] An adult with retarded intellectual development whose mentality corresponds to that of a normal child from 8 to 12 years of age; *slang*, one who is stupid or foolish.— **mo·ron·ic**, mo·ron'ik, *a.*—**mo·ron·i·cal·ly**, *adv.*—**mo·ron·ism**, **mo·ron·i·ty**, mo·ron'i·tē, *n.*

mo·rose, mo·rōs', *a.* [L. *morosus*, wayward, peevish, morose, < *mos*, *moris*, a custom, habit.] Of a sullen disposition; gloomy.—**mo·rose·ly**, *adv.*—**mo·rose·ness**, mo·ros'i·ty, mo·ros'i·tē, *n.*

morph, mạrph, *n. Ling.* a minimal sequence of phonemes which carries a meaning and cannot be subdivided into a smaller connotational grouping.

mor·phal·lax·is, mạr"fa·lak'sis, *n. pl.* **mor·phal·lax·es**, mạr"fa·lak'sēz". *Biol.* a type of regeneration which depends upon reorganization of cells rather than upon cell proliferation. Compare *epimorphosis.*

mor·pheme, mạr'fēm, *n. Ling.* the smallest structural unit of a language which carries a meaning and consists of allomorphic groups having semantic similarities and definable features of distribution.—**mor·phem·ic**, *a.*—**mor·phem·i·cal·ly**, *adv.*

mor·phem·ics, mạr'fem'iks, *n. pl. but sing. in constr. Ling.* the study of morphemic combinations in the formation and structure of words.

mor·phi·a, mạr'fē·a, *n.* Morphine.

mor·phine, mạr'fēn, *n.* [Fr. *morphine*, < L. *Morpheus.*] *Pharm.* a bitter crystalline alkaloid, $C_{17}H_{19}NO_3 \cdot H_2O$, the most important narcotic principle of opium, used in medicine, usu. in the form of a sulfate or other salt, to dull pain or induce sleep. Also *morphia.*—**mor·phin·ic**, mạr'fin'ik, *a.*

mor·phin·ism, mạr'fi·niz"um, *n. Pathol.* A morbid condition induced by the habitual use of morphine; the habit inducing it. —**mor·phi·no·ma·ni·a**, *n. Pathol.* uncontrollable craving for morphine.—**mor·phi·no·ma·ni·ac**, *n.*

mor·pho·gen·e·sis, mạr"fo·jen'i·sis, *n.* The changes in form or structure in the development of an organism or part of an organism.—**mor·pho·ge·net·ic**, **mor·pho·gen·ic**, mạr"fo·je·net'ik, *a.*

mor·phol·o·gy, mạr·fol'o·jē, *n.* [G. *mor-phologie*, < Gr. *morphe*, form, and *-logia*, < *legein*, speak.] *Biol.* the study of the form and structure of plants and animals, without regard to functions; the form and structure of a plant or an animal. *Ling.* the form of words as affected by inflection, derivation, and composition; the study of word formation. *Geol.* the study of the features of the earth's surface; also *geomorphology*, *physiography.*—**mor·pho·log·ic**, **mor·pho·log·i·cal**, mạr"fo·loj'ik, *a.*—**mor·pho·log·i·cal·ly**, *adv.*—**mor·phol·o·gist**, *n.*

mor·pho·pho·ne·mics, mạr"fō·fo·nē'-miks, mạr"fō·fō·nē'miks, *n. pl. but sing. in constr. Ling.* the science dealing with phonemic changes and variations occurring when morphemes combine to form words or larger structures.

mor·ris, mạr'is, mor'is, *n.* [Fr. *moresque*, < Sp. *morisco*, < *Moro*, a Moor.] A folk dance formerly common in England, particularly in the May games, where the performers were costumed to represent various folkloric characters. Also **mor·ris dance.**

Mor·ris chair, *n.* A comfortable armchair with an adjustable back and cushions that can be removed.

mor·ro, mōr'ō, mor'ō, *Sp.* mạr'Rạ, *n.* [Sp., something round.] A rounded hill.

mor·row, mor'ō, *n.* The next day after the present or after some other specified day.

Morse code, mạrs kōd, *n.* [From S. F. B. Morse, 1791–1872, American inventor.] A system of dots, dashes, and spaces, or the corresponding sounds or signals, used in telegraphy and signaling to represent letters of the alphabet or numerals.

mor·sel, mạr'sel, *n.* [Fr. *morceau* < L. *morsus*, bite.] A bite; a small piece of food; a fragment; a little piece of anything.—*v.t.* —morseled, morseling, morselled, morselling. To separate into small pieces.

mort, mạrt, *n.* [Fr. *mort*, death.] *Hunting*, a flourish sounded on a horn signaling the death of game. *Brit. dial.* a great quantity.

mor·tal, mạr'tal, *a.* [L. *mortālis*, < *mors*, *mortis*, death: same root as Skt. *mri*, to die, *mrita*, dead.] Subject to death, as man; deadly; causing death; fatal; pertaining to death; as, *mortal* pain; extreme; dire; human; pertaining to man's ephemerality; *colloq.* conceivable or imaginable. *Theol.* incurring the penalty of spiritual death or divine condemnations; not venial; as, a *mortal* sin. *Colloq.* tiresome and prolonged; as, ten *mortal* hours.—*n.* A being subject to death; a human being.—**mor·tal·ly**, *adv.*

mor·tal·i·ty, mạr·tal'i·tē, *n. pl.* **mor·tal·i·ties**. [L. *mortālitās.*] The state of being mortal; frequency of death; the number of deaths in proportion to a population; death in large numbers resulting from wars, plagues, or other disasters; the human race; humanity.

mor·tal·i·ty ta·ble, *n.* A table of statistics, compiled by insurance companies, showing the average life expectancy of persons of a given age or population group, usu. over a period of several years.

mor·tal mind, *n. Christian Science*, the viewpoint that life and intelligence are derived from, and dependent on, matter.

mor·tar, mạr'tėr, *n.* [O.E. *mortere*, vessel and O.Fr. Fr. *mortier*, vessel, cannon, < L. *mortarium*, vessel in which substances are pounded, or one in which mortar is made.] A vessel of hard material having a bowl-shaped cavity in which drugs are reduced to powder with a pestle; any of various mechanical appliances in which substances are pounded or ground; a cannon, short in proportion to its bore, for throwing shells at high angles; some similar contrivance, as for throwing pyrotechnic bombs or a life line.

mor·tar, mạr'tėr, *n.* [O.Fr. Fr. *mortier*, < L. *mortarium*, mortar, also a vessel in which it is made.] A mixture of quicklime or cement combined with sand and water and used for binding together stones or bricks.—*v.t.* To bind together or fix with mortar.

mor·tar·board, mạr'tėr·bōrd", *n.* A board, usu. square, used by masons to hold mortar; *fig.* a cap with a tassel affixed to a stiff, cloth-covered square crown, worn at high school and college commencement exercises.

mort·gage, mạr'gij, n. [O.Fr. morgage (Fr. mort-gage), < mort, dead, and gage, pledge, E. gage.] Law. A conditional transfer of property to a creditor as security for the repayment of money; the deed by which such a transaction is effected; the rights conferred by it, or the state of the property conveyed.—v.t.—mortgaged, mortgaging. To convey or place under a mortgage; as, to mortgage land; fig. to pledge; as, to mortgage one's future for a present advantage.—mort·ga·gee, mạr'ga·jē', n. One to whom property is mortgaged.—mort·ga·ger, mort·ga·gor, mạr'ga·jẽr, n. One who mortgages property.

mor·tice, mạr'tis, n., v.t.—morticed, morticing. Mortise.

mor·ti·cian, mạr·tish'an, n. [L. mors (mort-), death, with termination as in E. physician.] An undertaker.

mor·ti·fi·ca·tion, mạr''ti·fi·kā'shan, n. The subduing of the passions and appetites by penance or abstinence; humiliation and shame; chagrin; a source of shame. Pathol. the death or decay of part of a living organism; gangrene.

mor·ti·fy, mạr'ti·fī'', v.t.—mortified, mortifying. [Fr. mortifier—L. mors, mortis, death, and facio, to make.] To subdue or bring into subjection, as passions, by abstinence or rigorous severities; to humiliate; to chagrin; pathol. to affect with gangrene or decay.—v.i. To observe rigorous self-discipline; pathol. to become gangrenous.

mor·tise, mạr'tis, n. [Fr. mortaise, a mortise; origin unknown.] A hole or notch cut in a piece of material, as wood, to fit a corresponding projecting piece, called a tenon, on another piece in order to join the two together.—v.t. mortised, mortising. To cut a mortise in; to join securely. Also mortice.

mort·main, mạrt'mān'', n. [Fr. mort, dead, and main, hand.] Law. Inalienable possession of lands or buildings by a religious corporation; holding of land in perpetuity, esp. by a charitable trust.

mor·tu·ar·y, mạr'chö·er''ē, n. pl. mor·tu·ar·ies. [L.L. mortuarium, < L. mortuus, dead, < mori, to die.] A place for the temporary reception of the dead; a funeral home.—a. Pertaining to the burial of the dead.

mor·u·la, mạr'ụ·la, mạr'ū·la, n. pl. mor·u·las, mor·u·lae, mạr'ụ·lē'', mạr·ū·lē'. [Dim. of L. morum, mulberry, from the appearance of the mass of cells.] Embryol. the mass of cells resulting from the division of a cell or ovum during the cleavage stage.—mor·u·lar, a.—mor·u·la·tion, n.

mo·sa·ic, mō·zā'ik, n. [Fr. mosaïque, < It. mosaico, musaico, < L. Gr. mousaikos, belonging to the Muses, < Mousa, a Muse.] A type of artistic composition created by inlaying small pieces of variously colored enamel, glass, precious stones, or the like, in a mortar of cement so as to form a design or picture; the process of making such an object; any arrangement or design similar to a mosaic; photog. a series of aerial photographs of the terrain pieced together to make one composite photograph; arch. a systematic patterning of various areas and features of a building; bot. a virus disease characterized by green and yellow blotches on the foliage; TV, the part of a television camera tube which is coated with tiny photosensitive globules that produce electric charges.—a. Like or pertaining to a mosaic.—v.t.—mosaicked, mosaicking.—mo·sa·i·cal·ly, adv.—mo·sa·i·cist, mō·zā'i·sist, n. One who makes mosaics.

Mo·sa·ic, mō·zā'ik, a. Relating to Moses, the Hebrew lawgiver, or to his writings and institutions.

mo·sa·ic gold, n. An alloy of copper and zinc used as a pigment in paint for gilding pictures, etc; ormolu; artificial gold; chem. stannic sulfide.

Mo·sa·ic Law, n. The civil, moral, and religious laws of the Hebrews, originally given to Moses by God and incorporated in the Pentateuch, the first five books of the Bible.

Mo·selle, mō·zel', n. A light, white French or German wine, made in the Moselle River valley.

mo·sey, mō'zē, v.i.—moseyed, moseying. Slang. To move, or go along or away; to move leisurely; as, to mosey along.

Mos·lem, moz'lem, mos'lem, n. [Ar. moslem, muslim, a true believer, < salama, to resign oneself to God.] One who adheres to Islam and surrenders to the will of Allah.—a. Of or pertaining to the customs, laws, and religion of Islam. Also Muslim, Muslem.

mosque, mosk, mạsk, n. [M.Fr. mosqué, It. moschea, Sp. mezquita, < Ar. masjid, the place of adoration, < sajad, to adore.] A Moslem temple or place of worship.

mos·qui·to, mo·skē'tō, n. pl. mos·qui·toes, mos·qui·tos. [Sp., dim. of mosca, < L. musca, a fly.] Any of various dipterous insects of the family Culicidae, the females having a long proboscis with which they puncture the skin of animals, including man, to suck blood, some species transmitting such diseases as malaria and yellow fever.—mos·qui·to·ey, a.

mos·qui·to hawk, n. Dial. A nighthawk; a dragonfly.

mos·qui·to net, n. A screen, curtain, or canopy of gauze or fine net for keeping out mosquitoes.

moss, mạs, mos, n. [D., O.G., and Dan. mos, L. muscus, moss.] A small, simple, bryophytic plant of the class Musci, which usu. grows in dense stands forming carpets of vegetation on the ground, rocks, or tree bark, and having a stemlike axis with leaflike structures, but lacking vascular tissues, flowers, and seeds.—v.t. To cover with moss.—moss·like, moss·y, a.—mossier, mossiest.

moss·back, mạs'bak'', mos'bak'', n. A very old turtle having a growth of algae on its shell; an old fish having a similar mossy growth; a wild bull or cow; fig. a very conservative person.

moss-grown, mạs'grön'', mos'grön'', a. Overgrown with moss; antiquated.

moss pink, n. A low phlox, Phlox subulata of the eastern U.S., with showy pink, purple, or white flowers.

most, mōst, a., irreg. superl. of many and much. [O.E. mæst.] Greatest in any way; greatest in number, amount, or extent; amounting to a majority; as, most people.—adv. In the greatest or highest degree, quantity, or extent, often used before adjectives and adverbs to form the superlative degree; very; as, most kind; colloq. almost.—n., pl. in constr. The greatest number; the majority; the greatest amount, degree, or advantage.—at most, at the most, at the utmost extent.—for the most part, mostly.—make the most of, to use fully.—the most, colloq. The greatest; the best.

most·ly, mōst'lē, adv. For the most part; chiefly; mainly.

Most Rev·er·end, n. A title of courtesy used for high church officials, esp. an archbishop or bishop.

mot, mō, n. [Fr. mot, a word, a motto, L.L. muttum, < L. muttio, to mutter.] A pithy or witty saying; a bon mot.

mote, mōt, n. [O.E. mot, a mote; cf. D. mot, dust, sweepings.] A small particle; a speck.

mo·tel, mō·tel', n. [(mo)tor and ho(tel).] A lodging place, esp. designed for motorists, characterized by separate outside entrances to individual sleeping accommodations, and close-by parking. Also motor court, tourist court.

mo·tet, mō·tet', n. [Fr. motet, < It. mottetto, a dim. of motto.] Mus. a sacred polyphonic choral composition, usu. unaccompanied.

moth, mạth, moth, n. pl. moths. [O.E. moththe = D. mot = G. motte = Icel. motti, moth.] Any of the numerous, usu. nocturnal, insects of the order Lepidoptera, whose larvae feed on clothes, fabrics, furs, and vegetation, and are distinguished from the butterflies by their stouter bodies, smaller wings, and less colorful appearance; a clothes moth of the family Tineidae.

moth·ball, mạth'bal'', moth'bạl, n. A ball, usu. of small size, of camphor or naphthalene, used for, repelling moths from stored clothing.

moth-ball, mạth'bạl'', moth'bạl'', a. Milit. in protective storage or reserve, as naval vessels, airplanes, tanks, and the like.—v.t. To put in storage.

moth-eat·en, mạth'ēt''en, moth'ēt''en, a. Eaten or damaged by or as if by moths; worn out.

moth·er, muTH'ẽr, n. [O.E. mōdor = D. moeder = G. mutter = Icel. modhir, mother; akin to L. mater, Gr. mētēr, Skt. mātar-, mother.] The female who gives birth to a child; a female parent; one's nearest female ancestor; colloq. a mother-in-law, stepmother, or adoptive mother; fig. something that gives rise to, or exercises protective care over something else; as, necessity, the mother of invention. A woman looked upon as a mother, or exercising control or authority like that of a mother; the head or superior of a female religious community; a term of familiar address for an old or elderly woman; the qualities characteristic of a mother.—a. Being a mother; as, a mother bird; bearing a relation like that of a mother; as, a mother plant or cell; pertaining to or characteristic of a mother; as, mother love; derived from one's mother, or native; as, mother tongue, mother wit.—v.t. To be the mother of; give origin or rise to; to care for or protect as a mother does; to acknowledge oneself the mother of; acknowledge oneself the author of; to assume as one's own; to provide with a mother.—moth·er·less, a.—moth·er·less·ness, n.

moth·er, muTH'ẽr, n. [L.G. moder, D. modder, Dan. mudder, G. mutter—dregs, mud, slime, etc.; allied to mud.] A thick slimy substance composed of bacteria that gathers on the surface of fermenting liquids and produces fermentation, esp. in changing wine or cider to vinegar.—moth·er·y, a.

Moth·er Car·ey's chick·en, n. Any of various small petrels, esp. the stormy petrel.

moth·er·hood, muTH'ẽr·hụd'', n. The state of being a mother; maternity; the qualities or spirit of a mother; mothers collectively.

moth·er house, n. The convent which houses the Mother Superior in a religious community; the first convent erected in a religious community.

Moth·er Hub·bard, n. [From the old woman in a familiar nursery rhyme.] A kind of full, loose gown worn by women.

moth·er-in-law, muTH'ẽr·in·lạ'', n. pl. moth·ers-in-law. The mother of one's husband or wife.

moth·er·land, muTH'ẽr·land'', n. One's native country; the land of one's ancestors.

moth·er·ly, muTH'ẽr·lē, a. Pertaining to or befitting a mother; like a mother; tender and affectionate.—adv.—moth·er·li·ness, n.

moth·er-of-pearl, muTH'ẽr·ov·pụrl'', n. A hard, iridescent substance which forms the inner layer of certain shells, as that of the pearl oyster; nacre.—*a.*

Moth·er's Day, *n.* A day in honor of or remembrance of mothers, observed annually in the U.S. on the second Sunday in May.

moth·er tongue, *n.* One's native language; a language to which other languages owe their origin.

mo·tif, mō·tēf′, *n.* [Fr.] A passage or theme that reappears in varying form throughout a musical composition; the prevailing idea an artist or writer has endeavored to express; a central and recurring idea or theme of any kind; a repeated design, as in lace.

mo·tile, mōt′il, mō′til, *a.* [L. *movere* (pp. *motus*), E. *move.*] *Biol.* moving, or capable of moving, spontaneously; as, *motile* cells or spores.—*n. Psychol.* one in whose mind motor images are predominant or especially distinct.—**mo·til·i·ty,** mō·til′i·tē, *n.*

mo·tion, mō′shan, *n.* [O.Fr. *motion,* < L. *motio(n),* < *movēre,* E. *move.*] The process of moving or changing place or position; a movement or gesture; the power of movement, as of the body; the manner of moving; action, activity, or active operation; as, to set a plan in *motion;* an inward prompting, impulse, or inclination; as, undertaken of his own *motion;* a suggestion or proposal formally made to a deliberative assembly; as, a *motion* to adjourn; *mus.* melodic progression, as the change of a voice part from one pitch to another; *law,* an application made to a court or a judge for an order, ruling, or the like; *mech.* a piece of mechanism with a particular action or function.—*v.t.* To direct by a significant motion or gesture.—*v.i.* To make a significant motion or gesture.—**mo·tion·al,** *a.*—**mo·tion·less,** mō′shan·lis, *a.*—**mo·tion·less·ly,** *adv.*—**mo·tion·less·ness,** *n.*

mo·tion pic·ture, *n.* A series of photographs printed on a band of clear film and usu. projected by light on a screen in rapid succession, giving the illusion of continuous movement of the object photographed; a play, performance, event, or demonstration presented by this method. *Pl.* the business of creating, producing, or marketing a motion picture.—**mo·tion-pic·ture,** *a.*—**mo·tion-pic·ture the·a·ter,** cinema.

mo·tion sick·ness, *n.* Discomfort, often including dizziness and nausea, which some people suffer in moving vehicles.

mo·ti·vate, mō′ti·vāt″, *v.t.*—*motivated, motivating.* To furnish with a motive; to impel; to induce.—**mo·ti·va·tion,** mō″ti·vā′shan, *n.*—**mo·ti·va·tion·al,** *a.*—**mo·ti·va·tive,** *a.*

mo·tive, mō′tiv, *n.* [Fr. *motif,* a motive, L.L. *motivus,* moving, < L. *moveo, motum,* to move.] That which incites to action; that which determines the choice or moves the will; cause; object; inducement; the theme in a piece of music; the prevailing idea in the mind of an artist; motif.—*a.* Causing motion; inducing action; forming a motive. —*v.t.* To supply a motive to or for; to prompt; to relate to the theme or prevailing idea.

mo·tive pow·er, *n.* Any power or force that produces motion or transmits mechanical energy; *rail.* all the locomotives of a railroad.

mo·tiv·i·ty, mō·tiv′i·tē, *n.* The ability to move or to produce motion.

mot juste, mō zhyst′, *n.* pl. **mots justes.** *Fr.* The most precise word; the expression that fits perfectly.

mot·ley, mot′lē, *a.* [W. *mudliw,* a changing color, a motley color—*mud,* change, and *lliw,* a stain, a hue; akin to *mottle.*] Consisting of different colors, or parti-colored; exhibiting a combination of discordant elements; heterogeneous; dressed in a garment of several colors.—*n.* A heterogeneous, often discordant collection; a many-colored garment, esp. that characteristically worn by a jester or fool; a woolen, English-made fabric of several colors worn from the 14th to 17th century.

mo·to·neu·ron, mō″to·nụr′on, mō″to-nūr′on, *n. Anat., physiol.* a neuron which excites or inhibits the action of a gland or muscle.

mo·tor, mō′tėr, *n.* [L. < *movēre,* E. *move.*] That which imparts motion; a prime mover, as a steam engine, which receives and modifies energy from some natural source in order to utilize it in driving machinery; a machine, similar to a dynamo, for converting electric energy into rotary motion; a comparatively small and powerful engine, esp. an internal-combustion engine in an automobile, motorboat, or the like; a motorcar.—*a.* Causing or imparting motion; pertaining to or operated by a motor; *physiol.* conveying an impulse that results or tends to result in motion, as a nerve; of or pertaining to such nerves; *psychol.* pertaining to or involving consciousness of action; as, *motor* images.— *v.i.* To drive, ride, or travel in an automobile.—*v.t.* To convey in an automobile.

mo·tor ar·e·a, *n. Physiol.* the area in the cerebrum where impulses for movement of the skeletal muscles are initiated and transmitted to the lower centers of the nervous system.

mo·tor·bike, mō′tėr·bīk″, *n.* A bicycle propelled by a motor; a small, lightweight motorcycle.

mo·tor·boat, mō′tėr·bōt″, *n.* A boat driven by an internal-combustion engine or an electric motor. Also *power boat.*

mo·tor·bus, mō′tėr·bus″, *n.* A public passenger vehicle propelled by an internal-combustion or diesel engine, or other motive power. Also **mo·tor coach.**

mo·tor·cade, mō′tėr·kād″, *n.* A public procession of motorcars or other motor vehicles.

mo·tor·car, mō′tėr·kär″, *n.* Automobile. *Rail.* a passenger or freight car having its own motor; also **mo·tor car.**

mo·tor court, *n.* Motel.

mo·tor·cy·cle, mō′tėr·sī″kl *n.* A two-wheeled vehicle propelled by an internal-combustion engine, having seats for one or two persons and sometimes carrying a sidecar for an additional person or for parcels.—*v.i.*—*motorcycled, motorcycling.*—**mo·tor·cy·clist,** mō′tėr·sī″klist, *n.*

mo·tor·drome, mō′tėr·drōm″, *n.* An enclosed, circular track where motorcycles or automobiles are raced or tested.

mo·tor ho·tel, *n.* A motel, frequently located in a business section, offering all the services of a hotel in addition to providing immediately adjacent parking space.

mo·tor·ing, mō′tėr·ing, *n.* Driving or traveling in an automobile, esp. as a form of recreation.—**mo·tor·ist,** mō′tėr·ist, *n.* One who drives in an automobile.

mo·tor·ize, mō′to·rīz″, *v.t.*—*motorized, motorizing.* To provide with a motor or with motor-powered equipment.—**mo·tor·i·za·tion,** *n.*

mo·tor·man, mō′tėr·man, *n.* pl. **mo·tor·men.** A man who operates an electric-powered vehicle, as a streetcar, subway train, or electric locomotive.

mo·tor pool, *n.* A number of cars owned by the military, a single company, or a government agency and made available for necessary staff use.

mo·tor scoot·er, *n.* A scooterlike vehicle usu. having two wheels separated by a low footboard, and equipped with a motor and a seat for the driver.

mo·tor truck, *n.* See *truck.*

mo·tor ve·hi·cle, *n.* Any conveyance powered by a motor and equipped with rubber tires to travel on roads.

mot·tle, mot′l, *v.t.*—*mottled, mottling.* [< *motley.*] To diversify with spots or blotches of a different color or shade.—*n.* A diversifying spot or blotch of color; mottled coloring or pattern.—**mot·tled,** *a.* Spotted or blotched in coloring.—**mot·tler,** *n.*—**mot·tling,** *n.* Mottled coloring.

mot·tled e·nam·el, *n. Dentistry,* tooth enamel that has become spotted or stained by excessively fluoridated drinking water.

mot·to, mot′ō, *n.* pl. **mot·toes, mot·tos.** [It.] A sentence, phrase, or word attached to or inscribed on anything as indicative of, or appropriate to its purpose or character; as, the *motto* appended to a coat of arms; a maxim adopted as expressing one's guiding idea or principle; a short passage, usu. a quotation, prefixed to a literary work or one of its parts as illustrative of the contents.

moue, mö, *n.* pl. **moues.** [Fr.] A pouting grimace.

mouf·lon, mouf·flon, möf′lon, *n.* [Fr. *mouflon;* said to be < Sardinian name.] A wild sheep, *Ovis musimon,* inhabiting the mountainous regions of Sardinia, Corsica, and Greece, the male of which has large curving horns; any of various similar wild sheep; the wool of the mouflon.

mouil·lé, mö·yā′, *a.* [Fr. pp. of *mouiller,* wet, moisten.] *Phon.* pronounced with a following *y* sound, as *l* (*ll, gl*) and *n* (*gn, n*) in Sp. *llama,* It. *imbroglio,* E. *million,* *minion,* Fr. *mignon,* Sp. *canon,* and also applied to *l* and *ll* in certain positions in modern French pronunciation, where only the *y* sound now remains, as in *bouillon.*

mou·jik, mö·zhik′, mö′zhik, *n.* Muzhik.

mou·lage, mö·läzh′, *n.* A mold of an object made to aid identification or preserve evidence in criminal investigation; a mold or cast of a part of the body used to guide medical treatment or surgery; the making of such molds.

mou·lin, mö·laN′, *n.* [Fr. *moulin,* L.L. *molinus,* < L. *mola,* a mill.] A deep cylindrical hole in a glacier, formed by water and debris from the surface draining into it.

mound, mound, *n.* [O.E. and G. *mund,* a defense; same root as *mount.*] A man-made elevation of earth, rocks, gravel, or the like; a natural hillock or knoll; any pile or heap; as, a *mound* of discarded clothes; an earthwork used as a burial place or fortification, such as those of the Indian Mound Builders who once inhabited the Mississippi River and Great Lakes regions; *baseball,* the elevation on which the pitcher stands when delivering the ball.—*v.t.* To fortify or enclose with a mound; to pile up into a mound.

mount, mount, *n.* [O.E. *munt,* Fr. *mont,* < L. *mons, montis,* a hill, < root seen in *eminent, prominent.*] A hill; a mountain; now chiefly poetical, or used in proper names; as, *Mount Sinai.* The cardboard or other material on which a picture is mounted; the setting of a gem; a hinge used by collectors to affix stamps; a slide used to support objects prepared for microscopic examination; an animal, esp. a horse, used for riding; the manner of mounting an animal or an instance of it.—**mount·a·ble,** *a.*—**mount·er,** *n.*—**mount·less,** *a.*

mount, mount, *v.i.* [Fr. *monter,* < *mont,* a hill.] To increase; as, the cost of food *mounts* up; to place on high; to go up; to ascend; to get on or upon anything, esp. to get on a horse.—*v.t.* To ascend; to climb up to or upon; to place oneself upon; to furnish with a horse or horses; to raise up; to lift onto a horse. To put on a support; as, to *mount* a map; to prepare for use; as, to *mount* a specimen on a slide for microscopic examination; to be equipped with; as, a fort that *mounts* a hundred cannons; to do guard duty; as, to *mount* guard; to start; as, to *mount* an attack.

moun·tain, moun'tin, *n.* [O.Fr. *muntaine, montaigne,* Fr. *montagne,* < L.L. *montaneus,* mountainous, < L. *mons, montis,* a mountain.] A mass of earth rising higher than a hill above the level of the adjacent land; something great in size; a great amount; a large pile.—*a.* Characterizing mountains; inhabiting a mountain; similar to a mountain, as in size.

moun·tain ash, *n.* A species of tree, *Sorbus americana,* having pinnate leaves, white corymbose flowers, and red berries; any of certain related trees, as the European rowan tree; an Australian eucalyptus tree.

moun·tain cran·ber·ry, *n. Bot.* a type of dwarf cowberry, *Vaccinium vitis-idaea,* with persistently green leaves, red or pink flowers, and dark red berries.

moun·tain dew, *n. Slang,* bootleg whiskey, esp. corn whiskey, made in an illegal still in a mountainous area.

moun·tain·eer, moun"ta·nēr', *n.* An inhabitant of a mountainous district; a climber of mountains.—*v.i.* To climb mountains.

moun·tain goat, *n.* A goat, *Oreamnos americanus,* native to the mountainous regions of the northwestern U.S. and Canada. Also **Rock·y Moun·tain goat.**

moun·tain lau·rel, *n.* An evergreen shrub, *Kalmia latifolia,* of N. America with deep pink, rose, or white flowers.

moun·tain li·on, *n.* A puma. Also *cougar, panther, catamount.*

moun·tain ma·hog·a·ny, *n.* Any of the various shrubs, genus *Cercocarpus,* in the rose family and native to western N. America.

moun·tain·ous, moun'ta·nus, *a.* Full of mountains; large as a mountain; huge.—**moun·tain·ous·ly,** *adv.*—**moun·tain·ous·ness,** *n.*

moun·tain sick·ness, *n. Pathol.* an illness caused by air rarefaction, usu. at altitudes above 10,000 feet, and characterized by nausea, difficulty in breathing, and weakness.

moun·tain·side, moun'tan·sīd", *n.* One of the inclined surfaces of a mountain.

Moun·tain Stand·ard Time, *n. (Sometimes l.c.)* see *Standard Time.* Abbr. *MST, m.s.t., M.S.T.* Also **moun·tain time.**

moun·tain·top, moun'tan·top", *n.* A mountain summit or peak.—*a.*

moun·tant, moun'tant, *n.* An adhesive used to secure a drawing to a mount.

moun·te·bank, moun'te·bangk", *n.* [It. *montimbanco, montambanco—montare,* to mount, and *banco,* bench.] Formerly, one who mounts a bench or stage in the market or other public place to sell medicines which he represents as infallible remedies. A quack doctor; any boastful and false pretender; a charlatan.—**moun·te·bank·er·y,**

Moun·tie, Moun·ty, moun'tē, *n. Colloq.* one of the Royal Canadian Mounted Police.

mount·ing, moun'ting, *n.* The act of ascending; that with which an article is mounted, set off, or finished for use, as the setting of a gem; the cardboard on which a picture or art print is pasted.

mourn, mōrn, mȧrn, *v.i.* [O.E. *murnan* = Icel. *morna,* O.H.G. *mornēn,* Goth. *maurnan,* to grieve.] To express grief or sorrow; to grieve; to be sorrowful; to lament; to wear the dress or appearance of grief.—*v.t.* To grieve for; to lament; to deplore; to bewail; to voice in a sorrowful way.—**mourn·er,** *n.*—**mourn·ful,** *a.* Expressing sorrow; exhibiting the appearance of grief; doleful; causing sorrow; sad; calamitous; sorrowful; feeling grief.—**mourn·ful·ly,** *adv.*—**mourn·ful·ness,** *n.*—**mourn·ing,**

mōr'ning, mär'ning, *n.* The act of expressing grief; lamentation; the dress or customary habit worn by mourners; the time during which one grieves.—*a.* Employed to express grief; as, a *mourning* ring.—**mourn·ing·ly,** *adv.*

mourn·ing cloak, *n.* A handsome purplish brown butterfly, *Nymphalis antiopa,* having wings bordered with yellow, brown, and blue, and found in both Europe and N. America.

mourn·ing dove, *n.* A small, wild dove, *Zenaidura macroura,* found in N. America, having a plaintive coo.

mouse, mous, *n.* pl. **mice,** mīs. [O.E. *mūs* pl. *mȳs* = D. *muis* = G. *maus* = Icel. *mūs,* mouse; akin to L. *mūs,* Gr. *mûs,* Skt. *mush,* mouse, Skt. *mush-,* steal.] Any of various small rodents of the family *Muridae;* any similar animal. *Slang,* a term of affection for a girl or child; a black eye; a timid individual. *Naut.* a mousing.—*mouz, v.i.*—**moused, mousing.** To hunt for or catch mice; to seek or search stealthily or watchfully, as if for prey; to prowl.—*v.t.* To hunt out, as a cat does mice; to handle or treat as a cat does a mouse; *naut.* to secure by a mousing.

mouse-ear chick·weed, mous'ēr" chik'wēd", *n.* A naturalized herb, *Cerastium vulgatum,* in the pink family, having hairy, sticky leaves and stems, and small white flowers with deeply cleft petals.

mouse-ear hawk·weed, mous'ēr" hȧk'wēd", *n.* A European herbaceous plant, *Hieracium pilosella,* in the composite family, having white, woolly, basal leaves and yellow blossoms resembling small dandelions and naturalized in the U.S.

mous·er, mou'zèr, *n.* A cat or other animal good at catching mice; one who prowls about.

mouse·trap, mous'trap, *n.* A small trap with a metal spring, for catching mice.

mous·ing, mou'zing, *n.* The hunting and killing of mice. *Naut.* a wrapping, as of rope yarn, around the shank end or the point of a hook, to secure the load.

mousse, mōs, *n.* [Fr. *mousse,* froth; < Teut., and akin to E. *moss.*] *Cooking.* A dessert made of whipped cream, beaten eggs, and gelatin variously prepared and sometimes frozen; a dish of fish, meat, or vegetables stabilized with gelatin.

mousse·line, mōs·lēn', *n.* [Fr.] A sheer fabric similar to muslin.—**mousse·line de laine,** mōs·lēn de len', *n.* [Fr., 'muslin of wool.'] A thin woolen fabric, often having a printed pattern.—**mousse·line de soie,** mōs·lēn de swä', *n.* [Fr., 'muslin of silk.'] A thin silk or synthetic fabric resembling muslin.

mous·tache, mus'tash, mu·stash', *n.* Mustache.

Mous·te·ri·an, mö·stēr'ē·an, *a. Anthropol.* of or pertaining to the culture of Neanderthal man during the Middle Paleolithic age in western Europe.

mous·y, mous·ey, mou'sē, mou'zē, *a.*—*mousier, mousiest.* Resembling or characteristic of a mouse; timid; quiet; colorless or drab; infested with mice.

mouth, mouth, *n.* pl. **mouths,** mouTHz. [O.E. *mūth* = D. *mond* = G. *mund* = Goth. *munths,* mouth.] *Anat., zool.* the opening through which man or animals take in food; the cavity containing the parts used in chewing and tasting food. *Fig.* a person or animal requiring food; as, another *mouth* to feed. Source of vocal utterance; talk, esp. idle talk; a grimace made with the mouth; something providing entrance or exit; as, the *mouth* of a river or the *mouth* of a bottle; the opening between the jaws of a vise. *Mus.* the opening of an organ pipe, flute, or wind instrument through which air is blown to produce

sound.—mouTH, *v.t.* To speak in a pompous manner; to speak without understanding or sincere feeling; to enunciate carelessly; to put into the mouth; to rub with the mouth or lips; to accustom, as a horse, to the bit.—*v.i.* To speak oratorically; to grimace with the lips.—**mouthed,** mouTHd, moutht, *a.*—**mouth·er,** mou'THèr, *n.*

mouth·breed·er, mouth'brē"dèr, *n.* Any of several small fishes, frequently kept in a home aquarium, which are distinguished by the practice of carrying eggs and young in their mouths.

mouth·ful, mouth'fu̇l", *n.* pl. **mouth·fuls.** As much as a mouth can hold; as much as is taken into the mouth at one time; a small quantity; *colloq.* a speech sound or succession of sounds difficult to utter.—say a **mouth·ful,** *slang,* to make a wise or important observation.

mouth or·gan, *n.* Harmonica; panpipe.

mouth·piece, mouth'pēs", *n.* A piece forming the mouth of an object; that part of an apparatus which is held against, close to, or in the mouth, as of a musical instrument, telephone, or horse's bit; an agency or person expressing the sentiments or views of another or a group; a spokesman; *slang,* a criminal lawyer.

mouth-to-mouth meth·od, mouth'tö--mouth' meth'od, *n.* A type of artificial respiration consisting of air being blown directly into the mouth and lungs of the patient by another person at short, regular intervals.

mouth·wa·ter·ing, mouth'wȧ"tèr·ing, mouth'wot"èr·ing, *a.* Of foods causing the secretion of saliva into the mouth because of their appealing flavor, odor, or appearance.

mouth·y, mou'THē, mou'thē, *a.*—*mouthier, mouthiest.* Loud-mouthed; ranting; bombastic.

mou·ton, mö'ton, *n.* Sheepskin which has been treated to resemble seal or beaver fur.

mou·ton·née, möt"o·nā', *a. Geol.* of rocks, rounded like a sheep's back.

mov·a·ble, move·a·ble, mö'va·bl, *a.* [O.Fr. *movable, mouvable.*] Capable of being moved; changing from one date to another; as, a *movable* feast; not stationary in one position or place. *Law,* relating to personal property, such as can be changed with regard to place.—*n.* Often *pl.* anything capable of being moved, as goods, wares, commodities, furniture; *pl., law,* a piece of personal property.—**mov·a·ble·ness, move·a·ble·ness, mov·a·bil·i·ty,** *n.*—**mov·a·bly, move·a·bly,** *adv.*

mov·a·ble feast, *n. Rom. Cath. Ch.* a feast in the ecclesiastical calendar, the date of which, like Easter, varies from year to year.

move, möv, *v.t.*—*moved, moving.* [O.Fr. *mover, mouver,* Mod.Fr. *mouvoir,* L. *movēre, motum,* to move.] To carry, convey, or draw from one place to another; to cause to change place or posture; to set in motion; to excite into action; to influence; to rouse or excite the feelings of; to touch the tender emotions; to expel from the bowels; to force or dislodge; to effect advancement. *Chess, checkers,* to change the position of, as a piece. *Com.* to transfer, as goods, by sale. *Parl.* to offer, as a formal proposal, for consideration by a deliberative assembly.—*v.i.* To change place or posture; to stir; to pass or go; to walk; to carry or bear oneself; to change residence; to take action; to begin to act; to function, as a machine; to live or be active in a particular environment; to progress; to initiate action; as, to *move* on the project.—*n.* Proceeding; action taken; the moving of a piece in playing chess; a change of abode.—**on the move,** *colloq.* to be busy or active.—**move·less,** *a.*—**move·less·ly,** *adv.*—**move·less·ness,** *n.*—**mov·er,** *n.*

move·ment, mōv′ment, *n.* The act of moving; the course, process, or result of change, esp. change involving location or position; motion; an individual act or manner of motion. *Milit.* a tactical or strategic relocation of troops. A loosely organized body of individuals or groups working toward some general goal; the activities of such a body. The tendency or trend of events. A change in the market price of some stock or commodity. *Liter., fine arts,* the representation or suggestion of motion. *Mech.* the moving parts of a mechanism. *Mus.* a detached and independent portion of a composition; rhythm; tempo. The voiding of the bowels; the matter voided.

mov·ie, mō′vē, *n. Colloq.* a motion picture. *Pl.* the industry that produces motion pictures; motion pictures as a form of entertainment or an art, usu. preceded by *the*; a showing of one or more motion pictures.

mov·ing, mō′ving, *a.* Capable of or characterized by movement or action; causing to move or act; impelling; exciting the feelings; touching; pathetic; affecting. **—mov·ing·ly,** *adv.*

mov·ing pic·ture, *n.* Motion picture.

mov·ing stair·case, *n.* Escalator. Also **mov·ing stair·way.**

mow, mou, *n.* [O.E. *mūga,* a heap, a mow, N. *mūgi,* a heap of hay.] A pile of hay or sheaves of grain deposited in a barn; the part of a barn where they are stored.

mow, mō, *v.t.*—past *mowed,* pp. *mowed* or *mown,* ppr. *mowing.* [O.E. *māwan;* akin, Icel. *mūgr, mūgi,* a swathe.] To cut down with a scythe or mowing machine, as grass; to cut the grass from; to cut down indiscriminately, or in great numbers or quantity, as men in a battle.—*v.i.* To cut grass; to use the scythe or mowing machine. **—mow·er,** *n.* One who mows; a mowing machine.—**mow·ing ma·chine,** an agricultural machine with blades for cutting down grass, clover, grain, and the like.

mox·a, mok′sa, *n.* [Chin.] A soft downy substance prepared in China and Japan from the young leaves of certain plants, used as a counterirritant for the gout or similar afflictions, by burning it on the skin; any substance used in this way as a counterirritant.

mox·ie, mok′sē, *n. Slang.* Courage; vigor, energy; aggressiveness.

moz·zet·ta, moz·zet·ta, mō·zet′a, *It.* mȧt·tset′tȧ, *n.* [It.] *Rom. Cath. Ch.* a short cape which covers the shoulders and can be buttoned over the breast, to which a hood is attached, worn by the pope and by cardinals, archbishops, bishops, and abbots.

mu, mū, mö, *n.* [Gr. *mu.*] The twelfth letter of the Greek alphabet.

much, much, *a.*—*more, most.* [Shortened form of old *mochel, muchel,* much, < O.E. *mycel, micel,* much, great, many; akin Icel. *mjog, mjok,* much, *mikill,* great; Goth. *mikils,* O.H.G. *mihhil;* same root as L. *magnus,* great, E. *may.*] Great in quantity or amount; abundant; as, *much* water.—*adv.* To a great amount or extent, greatly: used esp. with comparatives and past participles; as, *much* better, *much* surprised; nearly; as, *much* as it was.—*n.* A great quantity; a great deal; a noteworthy or important thing.—**much as,** even though.—**make much of,** to treat something as very important; to treat someone with consideration.—**much·ness,** *n.*

mu·cic ac·id, mū′sik as′id, *a.* [L. *mucus,* mucus.] *Chem.* a dibasic crystalline acid, $C_6H_{10}O_8$, obtained by oxidizing certain carbohydrates with nitric acid.

mu·cid, mū′sid, *a.* [L. *mucidus,* < *mucere.*] Moldy; musty; slimy.**—mu·cid·i·ty,mu·cid·ness,** *n.*

mu·cif·er·ous, mū·sif′er·us, *a.* Mucus-producing; secreting mucus.

mu·ci·gen, mū′si·jin, mū′si·jen″, *a. Biochem.* a substance which can be easily converted by the body into mucin. Also **mu·cin·o·gen.**

mu·ci·lage, mū′si·lij, *n.* [L. *mucilago* < *mucus,* slime, mucus.] Any preparation of glue or gummy substance used for adhesion; any of several gummy, gelatinous substances secreted by plants. Also *gum.* **—mu·ci·lag·i·nous,** mū″si·laj′i·nus, *a.*— **mu·ci·lag·i·nous·ly,** *adv.*

mu·cin, mū′sin, *n.* [L. *mucus,* mucus.] *Biochem.* any of a group of nitrogenous substances found in mucous secretions, varying in composition according to its source.**—mu·ci·nous,**mū′si·nus,*a.*—**mu·cin·oid,** *a.*

muck, muk, *n.* [Prob. < Scand.: cf. Icel. *myki,* dung.] Farmyard dung, or decaying vegetable matter, in a moist state; manure; filth; dirt; anything foul or disgusting. *Min.* earth, rock, or other useless matter to be removed in order to get out the mineral or other substance sought.—*v.t.* To manure; to dirty or soil; to remove muck from.— **muck a·bout,** *Brit. slang,* to potter or go aimlessly.**—muck·y,** muk′ē, *a.*

muck·luck, muk′luk, *n.* Mukluk.

muck·rake, muk′rāk″, *v.i.*—*muckraked, muckraking.* To expose corruption, real or alleged, esp. in politics; defame.**—muck·rak·er,** *n.*

mu·co·cu·ta·ne·ous, mū″kō·kū·tā′nē·us, *a. Anat.* pertaining to an area where mucous membrane and the skin come together, as in the nose, mouth, vagina, and anus.

mu·coid, mū′koid, *n.* [< *mucin* and *-oid.*] *Biochem.* any of a group of substances resembling the mucins, occurring in connective tissue and in cysts.—*a.*

mu·co·pro·tein, mū″ko·prō′tēn, mū″ko·prō′tē·in, *n. Biochem.* any of various proteins containing polysaccharides, found in the body's fluids and connective tissues.

mu·co·sa, mū·kō′sa, *n.* pl. **mu·co·sae,** mū·kō′sē. [N.L., fem. of L. *mucosus,* E. *mucous.*] *Anat.* a mucous membrane.— **mu·co·sal,** *a.*

mu·co·se·rous, mū″ko·sēr′us, *a. Anat.* pertaining to a fluid that contains serum or plasma with a considerable amount of mucus.

mu·cous, mū′kus, *a.* [L. *mucosus.*] Pertaining to or resembling mucus; slimy; ropy; secreting a slimy substance.**—mu·cos·i·ty,** mū·kos′i·tē, *n.*

mu·cous mem·brane, *n.* A membrane that lines all the cavities of the body which open externally, such as the mouth, nose, or intestines, and which secretes mucus.

mu·cro, mū′krō, *n.* pl. **mu·cro·nes,** mū·krō′nēz. [L.] *Biol.* A sharp point or tip; a spinelike part; a short point projecting abruptly, as at the end of a leaf.—**mu·cro·nate, mu·cro·nat·ed,** mū′krō·nit, mū′krō·nāt″, *a.*—**mu·cro·na·tion,** *n.*

mu·cus, mū′kus, *n.* [L., mucus from the nose.] *Biol.* a viscid fluid secreted by the mucous membranes.

mud, mud, *n.* [Allied to L.G. *mod, mudde,* D. *modder,* Dan. *mudder,* Sw. *modd,* mud; mire; Icel. *mod,* dust.] Wet and soft earth; earthy matter, as in a puddle; mire; *colloq.* an abusive charge or remark.—*v.t.*— *mudded, mudding.* To smear with or as with mud; to stir up the muddy sediment of.

mud daub·er, *n.* Any of numerous wasps of the family *Sphecidae,* which construct nests of mud.

mud·dle, mud′l, *v.t.*—*muddled, muddling.* [< *mud.*] To make muddy or turbid, as water; to confuse mentally; to confuse with drink; to make unclear; to mix up or jumble together in a confused or bungling way; to bring into a mess; to waste, as time or money, in a stupid or unthinking manner; to mix or stir, as a cocktail.—*v.i.* To think or act in a confused, ineffective way, with *through.*—*n.* A muddled condition; a confused mental state; a confused, disordered, or embarrassing state of affairs; a mess; confusion in thought or action.

mud·dle·head·ed, mud′l·hed″id, *a.* Mentally confused; inept; stupid.**—mud·dle·head·ed·ness,** *n.*

mud·dy, mud′ē, *a.*—*muddier, muddiest.* Abounding in mud; cloudy, as color; confused or vague, as in expression or thought; dull or unclear, as the mind.—*v.t.* —*muddied, muddying.* To soil with mud; to cloud or make dull.—*v.i.* To become soiled with mud.**—mud·di·ly,** *adv.*—**mud·di·ness,** *n.*

mud·guard, mud′gärd″, *n.* A cover attached over the wheel of a bicycle, car, truck, or other vehicle to stop flying mud.

mud·pup·py, mud′pup″ē, *n.* pl. **mud·pup·pies.** An aquatic salamander of the genus *Necturus,* having external gills and short, well-developed legs.

mud·sill, mud′sil″, *n.* The lowest sill of a structure, usu. placed in or on the ground.

mud·sling·ing, mud′sling″ing, *n.* The act of defaming; the casting of derogatory personal slurs at a person, esp. a political rival.**—mud·sling·er,** *n.*

mud·stone, mud′stōn″, *n.* A clayey rock of nearly uniform texture throughout, with little or no lamination, which can easily decompose into mud.

mud tur·tle, *n.* A name of the soft-shelled turtles of the family *Kinosternidae,* found in South, Central, and North America.

mud vol·ca·no, *n.* A cone-shaped hill built around an opening in the earth by mud which is brought to the earth's surface by escaping gas.

muen·ster, mun′stēr, mun′stēr, min′stēr, myn′stēr, *n.* [From *Munster,* France.] A bland, semisoft, white cheese processed from whole milk; a European sharp cheese. Also **mün·ster.**

mu·ez·zin, mū·ez′in, mö·ez′in, *n.* [A *muezzin,* < *azzana,* to inform, < *azana,* to hear.] An Islamic crier who, from a mosque, summons the faithful to prayers five times a day.

muff, muf, *n.* [Dan. *muffe,* D. *mof,* L.G. *muffe, muff,* a muff, akin to O.H.G. *mouwa,* D. *mouw,* a long sleeve.] A tubular cover, usu. made of fur, into which both hands are placed to keep them warm; a collection of feathers on the sides of the head or legs of some birds; any failure or inept action; *sports,* a bungled catch.—*v.t., v.i. Colloq.* To bungle; to miss a chance.

muf·fin, muf′in, *n.* A quick bread baked in individual cup-shaped molds; a drop biscuit.

muf·fle, muf′l, *n.* [Fr. *mufle;* origin unknown.] An oven or arched chamber in a furnace or kiln, used for heating substances without direct contact with the fire; a furnace containing such a chamber. Something that muffles, esp. something that deadens sound. The thick, bare part of the upper lip and nose of some animals.

muf·fle, muf′l, *v.t.*—*muffled, muffling.* [O.E. *muffle,* akin to *muff;* cf. D. *muffel,* a muff; Fr. *moufle,* a mitten.] To enfold or wrap so as to conceal from view or protect from the weather; to deaden the sound of; as, to *muffle* an oar or a drum; to deaden, as sound, by or as by wrappings; to keep from seeing or speaking by wrapping up the head; to wrap (oneself) up in clothing.

muf·fler, muf′lēr, *n.* Anything used for muffling, esp. a scarf or wrapping worn around the neck or throat for warmth; any of various devices for deadening such sound as that of the escaping gases of an internal-combustion engine.

muf·ti, muf′tē, *n.* pl. **muf·tis.** [Ar.] An official expounder of the Mohammedan law; in Turkey the official head of the state religion or one of his deputies.

muf·ti, muf′tē, *n.* [Orig. Anglo-Ind.; perh. for *mufti dress.*] Civilian dress as opposed to military or other uniform, or as worn by one who usually wears a uniform.

mug, mug, *n.* [Cf. Sw. *mugg*, Norw. *mugge*, mug.] A drinking vessel, usu. cylindrical and commonly with a handle; the quantity it holds; the face; the mouth; a grimace; a facial photograph; a thug or ruffian.—*v.t.* —*mugged, mugging. Slang.* To photograph, as a person's face, often for criminal records; to assault, usu. with the intent of robbing.—*v.i. Slang.* To grimace; to overact or assume a funny or exaggerated face.

mug·ger, mug′ẽr, *n.* [Hindi *magar.*] A man-eating crocodile, *Crocodilus palustris,* of southeast Asia, growing to about 12 feet in length.

mug·ger, mug′ẽr, *n.* One who assaults or mugs, usu. with the intent of robbing; one who assumes a funny face or who overacts to attract attention.

mug·gy, mug′ē, *a.*—**muggier, muggiest.** [Prov. E. *mug,* mist; Icel. *mugga,* mugginess, drizzle; cf. Gael. *mugach,* cloudy; W. *mwg,* smoke.] Damp and close, as the weather; warm and humid.—**mug·gi·ly,** *adv.*—**mug·gi·ness,** *n.*

mug·wump, mug′wump″, *n.* [Algonquian *mugquomp,* leader.] A Republican at the time of the presidential campaign of 1884 who refused to support the party nominee, James G. Blaine; any independent voter, who may or may not be a member of a regular party; one who espouses both sides of a controversial question; a fence-straddler; one with pretensions of political superiority.—**mug·wump·er·y, mug·-wump·ism,** *n.*—**mug·wump·i·an,** *a.*—**mug·wump·ish,** *a.*

Mu·ham·mad·an, mṳ·ham′i·dan, *a., n.* Mohammedan. Also **Mu·ham·med·an.**

muk·luk, muk′luk, *n.* [Eskimo] A kind of boot made of sealskin or reindeer skin, usu. lined with fur, and worn by Eskimos; a similar moccasin-type shoe with a soft sole. Also **muckluck.**

mu·lat·to, mu·lat′ō, mū·lat′ō, *n.* pl. **mu·lat·toes.** [Sp. *mulato,* < *mulo,* a mule.] The offspring of parents of whom one is Caucasian and the other Negro; loosely, any individual of mixed Caucasian and Negro blood; the light brown color of a mulatto.—*a.* Like a mulatto in color.

mul·ber·ry, mul′ber″ē, mul′be·rē, *n.* pl. **mul·ber·ries.** [For *murberry*; O.E., *murberie,* a mulberry, also, *múr, mór,* < *morus,* a mulberry tree.] The usu. dark red or purple edible fruit or berry of a tree of the genus *Morus*; the tree itself, one variety of which has leaves that are used for silkworm culture; a dark red or purplish color.

mulch, mulch, *n.* [Akin to *mols* in O.E. *molsnian,* to rot, G. *mulsch, molsch,* rotten; D. *molsemen,* to molder.] *Hort.* a loose covering of an organic material, such as peat moss, straw, or manure, spread on the ground around plantings to improve the soil and to check freezing, erosion, evaporation, and weed growth.—*v.t. Hort.* to cover or to protect(herbs or young trees) with mulch.

mulct, mulkt, *n.* [L. *mulcta, multa,* a fine.] A fine or penalty imposed on a person guilty of some offense or misdemeanor.—*v.t.* To punish by fine or forfeiture; to defraud; to swindle.

mule, mūl, *n.* [O.E. *mūl,* Fr. *mule,* < L. *mulus,* a mule.] A hybrid mammal, the offspring of an ass and a mare, or of a horse and a she-ass; any animal produced by a

mixture of different species; a hybrid; a hybrid plant; the offspring of a canary and a related finch; a spinning machine combining the drawing rollers of Arkwright and the jenny of Hargreaves. *Colloq.* a stubborn person.

mule, mūl, *n.* A backless slipper.

mule skin·ner, *n. Colloq.* a driver of mules.

mu·le·teer, mū″le·tẽr′, *n.* [Fr. *muletier.*] One who drives mules.

mu·ley, mul·ley, mū′lē, mul′ē, *a.* Pertaining to cows, esp. those without horns; bald.—*n.* pl. **mu·leys.** A hornless cow; any cow.

mu·li·eb·ri·ty, mū″lē·eb′ri·tē, *n.* [L. *muliebritas,* < *muliebris,* womanly, womanish, < *mulier,* a woman.] Womanhood; femininity.

mul·ish, mū′lish, *a.* Like a mule; sullen; stubborn.—**mul·ish·ly,** *adv.*—**mul·ish·-ness,** *n.*

mull, mul, *v.i. Colloq.* To study or ruminate, often followed by *over.*—*v.t.* To make a failure of. *Archaic, Brit.* to fumble, as a ball in rugby or other sports.

mull, mul, *n.* [Hind. *mulmul,* muslin.] A sheer, soft muslin; a thin fabric of silk or rayon.

mull, mul, *v.t.* To heat, sweeten, and flavor with spices, as wine.

mul·lah, mul′a, mul′a, mö′la, *n.* [Turk., Pers., and Hind. *mullā,* < Ar. *mawlā.*] In Mohammedan countries, a title of respect for one who is learned in, teaches, or expounds the sacred law.

mul·lein, mul·len, mul′en, *n.* [A.Fr. *moleine,* perh. < O.Fr. *mol,* < L. *mollis,* soft.] A stout weed of the figwort family, *Verbascum thapsus,* with coarse woolly leaves and dense spikes of usu. yellow flowers; any of various similar plants.

mul·lein pink, *n. Bot.* an herb, *Lychnis coronaria,* in the pink family, having deep rose or white flowers and dense, white, woolly hairs covering the stems and leaves. Also **dust·y mill·er, rose cam·pion.**

mull·er, mul′ẽr, *n.* [O.Fr. *moulleur,* < *moulre, mouldre* (Fr. *moudre*), L. *molere,* to grind, < *mola,* a millstone.] A sort of flat-bottomed pestle used for grinding such things as paints or pigments; any of several mechanical grinding instruments.

mul·let, mul′it, *n.* pl. **mul·lets, mul·let.** [O.Fr. Fr. *mulet,* dim. < L. *mullus,* red mullet.] Any of the fishes of the genus *Mullus,* or the family *Mullidae,* having two long barbels at the mouth, and red coloration; any fish of the genus *Mugil,* or of the family *Mugilidae,* which includes various species with a cylindrical body and gray coloration.

mul·li·gan, mul′i·gan, *n. Colloq.* a stew of meat and vegetables; also **mul·li·gan stew.** *Golf,* an unscored extra shot allowed in unofficial but not tournament play.

mul·li·ga·taw·ny, mul″i·ga·ta̤nē, *n.* [Tamil *milagutannir,* lit. 'pepper water.'] An East Indian curry soup.

mul·lion, mul′yon, *n.* [For *munnion,* a word equiv. to Fr. *moignon,* Sp. *muñon,* a stump, the mullion of a window being the stump below the tracery.] *Arch.* A vertical division between the lights of windows, screens, or doors; a division between the panels in wainscoting.—*v.t. Arch.* to equip with or separate by mullions.—**mul·-lioned,** *a.*

mull·ite, mul′īt, *n.* A synthesized aluminum silicate, $Al_6Si_2O_{13}$, capable of withstanding high temperatures and resisting corrosion.

mul·tan·gu·lar, mul·tang′gū·lẽr, *a.* Having many angles; polygonal.

mul·ti·cel·lu·lar, mul″ti·sel′ū·lẽr, *a.* Having or made up of a number of cells.

mul·ti·col·or, mul′ti·kul″ẽr, *n.* A varicolored design or arrangement.—*a.* Of many colors; *print.* pertaining to a press

able to print more than one color in one operation.—**mul·ti·col·ored,** mul″ti·kul′-ẽrd, mul′ti·kul″ẽrd, *a.* Of two or more colors.

mul·ti·di·men·sion·al, mul″ti·di·men′-shan·al, *a.* Having several dimensions; more than one dimension.

mul·ti·far·i·ous, mul″ti·fâr′ē·us, *a.* [L. *multifarius,* manifold—*multus,* many, and *farius.*] Having great multiplicity, diversity, or variety; made up of many different parts. —**mul·ti·far·i·ous·ly,** *adv.*—**mul·ti·far·i·ous·ness,** *n.*

mul·ti·fid, mul′ti·fid, *a.* [L. *multifidus.*] *Bot.* divided into several parts or lobes by clefts; as, a *multifid* leaf.—**mul·ti·fid·ly,** *adv.*

mul·ti·flo·ra rose, mul′ti·flōr′a rōz, mul″-ti·flạr′a, *n.* A thorny climbing rose, *Rosa multiflora,* having clustered, fragrant flowers.

mul·ti·flo·rous, mul″ti·flōr′us, *a.* [L. *multus,* many, *flos, floris,* a flower.] *Bot.* Many-flowered; having many flowers.

mul·ti·fold, mul′ti·fōld″, *a.* Manifold; many and varied.

mul·ti·form, mul′ti·fạrm″, *a.* [L. *multiformis.*] Having many forms, shapes, kinds, or appearances.—**mul·ti·for·mi·ty,** mul″-ti·fạr′mi·tē, *n.*

mul·ti·lat·er·al, mul″ti·lat′ẽr·al, *a.* Having many sides; polygonal; having three or more parties or nations as participants.— **mul·ti·lat·er·al·ly,** *adv.*

mul·ti·lin·gual, mul″ti·ling′gwal, *a.* Polyglot.—*n.*

mul·ti·mil·lion·aire, mul″tē·mil″ya·-nâr′, mul″ti·mil″ya·nâr′, *n.* A very wealthy individual; one whose wealth is measured in the millions.

mul·tip·a·ra, mul·tip′ẽr·a, *n.* pl. **mul·tip·a·rae,** mul·tip′a·rē″. [N.L.] *Obstet.* a woman who has borne two or more children, or who is delivering or near to giving birth the second time.—**mul·tip·a·rous,** *a.* [N.L. *multiparus.*] Producing many, or more than one, at a birth. *Bot.* of a cyme, having many lateral axes.

mul·ti·par·tite, mul″ti·pär′tīt, *a.* Divided into several or many parts; *bot.* more deeply cleft than multifid ; *govt.* multi-lateral.

mul·ti·ped, mul′ti·ped″, *n.* An animal that has many feet, as a centipede. Also **mul·-ti·pede,** mul′ti·pēd″.—*a.* Many-footed.

mul·ti·phase, mul′ti·fāz″, *a.* Showing many phases.—**mul·ti·pha·sic,** *a.*

mul·ti·ple, mul′ti·pl, *a.* [M.L. *multiplus.*] Consisting of, having, or involving many individuals, parts, elements, or relations; repeated; manifold; *bot.* of a fruit, collective.—*n. Math.* a number into which another number may be divided without a remainder, as: 12 is a *multiple* of 3; a common multiple of two or more numbers, as a number that can be divided by each of them without a remainder. *Elect.* denoting a circuit wired in parallel.

mul·ti·ple-choice, mul′ti·pl·chois′, *a.* Pertaining to a question or group of questions for which one must select the correct answer from the several choices given.

mul·ti·ple fac·tors, *n.* pl. *Genetics,* groups of genes which may act together to produce certain quantitative alterations in hereditary characteristics.

mul·ti·ple scle·ro·sis, *n.* A serious disease in which parts of the brain and spinal cord harden, causing tremors, muscular weakness, and other debilitating symptoms.

mul·ti·ple shop, *n. Brit.* A store which is a member of a group of similar stores, usu. under single ownership and management; a chain store. Also **mul·ti·ple store.**

mul·ti·ple star, *n. Astron.* a group of several adjacent stars apparently rotating about a single gravitational center.

mul·ti·plet, mul'ti·plet", mul'ti·plit, n. Phys. a line of the spectrum composed of several lines of similar wavelengths.

mul·ti·ple vot·ing, n. The voting by one person in more than one district in one election when this may be done legally, as before the 1918 election reforms in Great Britain; this action performed illegally.

mul·ti·plex, mul'ti·pleks, a. [L.] Manifold; multiple; telecommunications, designating a system for sending several messages simultaneously over the same wire or channel.—v.t., v.i. To transmit, as signals, using a multiplex system.—n. An electronic multiplex circuit or system.

mul·ti·pli·a·ble, mul'ti·plī'a·bl, a. Capable of being multiplied. Also **mul·ti·plic·a·ble**, mul"ti·plik'a·bl.

mul·ti·pli·cand, mul"ti·pli·kand', n. [L. multiplicandus.] Arith. the number to be multiplied by another, which is called the multiplier.

mul·ti·pli·cate, mul'ti·pli·kāt", a. [L. multiplicatus, pp. of multiplicare.] Multiple; manifold.

mul·ti·pli·ca·tion, mul"ti·pli·kā'shan, n. [L. multiplicatio, multiplicationis.] The act or process of multiplying; the state of being multiplied; arith., alg. the operation by which any given number or quantity may be added to itself any number of times.—**mul·ti·pli·ca·tion ta·ble**, a table containing the product of all the simple digits multiplied by each other, to some assumed limit, as to 12 times 12.—**mul·ti·pli·ca·tive**, mul'ti·pli·kā"tiv, mul"ti·plik'a·tiv, a. Tending to multiply; having the power to multiply.—**mul·ti·pli·ca·tive·ly**, adv.

mul·ti·plic·i·ty, mul"ti·plis'i·tē, n. [L. multiplicitas, < multiplex.] The state of being multiplex, numerous, or various; an extensive aggregate of individuals of the same kind; a great number.

mul·ti·pli·er, mul'ti·plī"ẽr, n. One who or that which multiplies; the number in arithmetic by which another is multiplied; phys. an instrument or device for increasing the strength or range of an effect.

mul·ti·ply, mul'ti·plī", v.t.—multiplied, multiplying. [Fr. multiplier, < L. multiplicare, < multiplex.] To increase in number; to make more by natural reproduction or by addition; arith. to add to itself any given number of times.—v.i. To grow or increase in number, or to become more numerous by reproduction; to extend; to spread; arith. to arrive at the product by the process of multiplication.—mul'ti·plē, adv.—**mul·ti·pli·a·ble**, a.

mul·ti·ply, mul'ti·plī", a. Composed of many layers or plies.

mul·ti·stage, mul'ti·stāj", a. Having several stages of power which operate in succession, as a rocket or missile.

mul·ti·sto·ry, mul"ti·stōr'ē, a. Arch. having many levels, floors, or stories. Also **mul·ti·sto·ried**.

mul·ti·tude, mul'ti·tōd", mul'ti·tūd", n. [L. multitudo, < multus, much, many.] The state of being many; a great number, collectively; a great many, indefinitely; a crowd, throng, or gathering of people.—**the mul·ti·tude**, the populace, or the mass of men without reference to an assemblage.—**mul·ti·tu·di·nous**, mul"ti·tōd'i·nus, mul"ti·tūd'i·nus, a. Pertaining or belonging to a multitude; consisting of a multitude.—**mul·ti·tu·di·nous·ly**, adv.—**mul·ti·tu·di·nous·ness**, n.

mul·ti·va·lent, mul"ti·vā'lent, mul·tiv'a·lent, a. Chem. with a valence of three or higher; having more than one degree of valence. Characterized by having several meanings, values, or attractions.—**mul·ti·va·lence**, n.

mul·ti·ver·si·ty, mul"ti·vur'si·tē, n. pl. **mul·ti·ver·si·ties**. Any very large uni-

versity with numerous colleges and departments, and a huge faculty staff engaged in a variety of teaching and research activities.

mum, mum, a. [Imit. of a low sound made with the lips closed, like L. and Gr. mu; akin mumble.] Silent; not speaking.—interj. Be silent; hush.—**mum's the word**, say nothing about it.

mum, mum, v.i.—mummed, mumming. [Of Dutch or German origin; cf. G. mummen, to mask, D. mommen, to mask.] To act in a mask or disguise.

mum, mum, n. [G. mumme, from Christian Mumme, who first brewed it at Brunswick, Germany, in 1492.] A type of malt liquor.

mum, mum, n. Chrysanthemum.

mum·ble, mum'bl, v.i., v.t.—mumbled, mumbling. [Freq. < mum; like D. mommelen, Dan. mumle, G. mummeln, to mumble.] To mutter; to speak unintelligibly or indistinctly; to chew or bite softly, as with no teeth.—n.—**mum·bler**, n.—**mum·bling·ly**, adv.

mum·ble·ty·peg, mum'bl·tē·peg". A game in which a knife is flipped into the ground in various manners from different hand positions. Also **mum·ble-the-peg**.

Mum·bo Jum·bo, mum'bō jum'bō, n. A god of certain African tribes. (l.c.) any senseless object of popular idolatry; any involved yet meaningless ritual or incantation. (l.c.), slang, contrived, ostentatious, or unintelligible language; gobbledygook.

mum·mer, mum'ẽr, n. A masked celebrant, esp. at holiday festivals; an actor, esp. in a pantomime.—**mum·mer·y**, mum'e·rē, n. A masking or masquerade; a farcical show; hypocritical ceremony.

mum·mi·fy, mum'i·fī", v.t.—mummified, mummifying. To make into a mummy; to embalm and dry, as a mummy.—**mum·mi·fi·ca·tion**, n. The act of mummifying; the process of becoming a mummy.

mum·my, mum'ē, n. pl. **mum·mies**. [Fr. mumie, momie, Sp. momia, It. mummia, < Ar. mūmiyah, < mūm, wax.] A dead human body embalmed and dried after the manner of those found in Egyptian tombs; a human body dried up and preserved, either artificially or by accident; something which resembles a mummy.—v.t.—mummied, mummying. To embalm; mummify.

mump, mump, v.t. [An imit. word, allied to mumble and munch.] Brit. dial. To mumble or mutter, as in sulkiness; to nibble; to chew; to munch.—v.i. Brit. dial. To sulk; to grin.

mumps, mumps, n. pl. but sing. in constr. Pathol. A disease consisting of an inflammation of the salivary glands, with swelling along the neck; parotiditis.

munch, munch, v.t., v.i. To chew, sometimes audibly.—**munch·er**, n.

mun·dane, mun·dān', mun'dān, a. [L. mundanus, < mundus, the world.] Of or relating to the world; earthly; routine; ordinary; unexalted.—**mun·dane·ly**, adv.

mun·go, mung'gō, n. pl. **mun·gos**. A cloth of short wool fibers which have been reclaimed from old woolen fabrics; a fabric similar to shoddy.

mu·nic·i·pal, mū·nis'i·pal, a. [L. municipalis, < municipium, a town governed by its own laws—munia, official duties, and capio, to take.] Pertaining to local self-government; pertaining to the corporation of a town or city, or to the citizens of a municipality.—**mu·nic·i·pal·ly**, adv.

mu·nic·i·pal·i·ty, mū-nis"i·pal'i·tē, n. A town, city, or borough which has local self-government; a community under municipal jurisdiction.

mu·nic·i·pal·ize, mū·nis'i·pa·līz", v.t.—municipalized, municipalizing. To incorporate as a city or other municipal entity; to place under local self-government and control.—**mu·nic·i·pal·i·za·tion**, n.

mu·nif·i·cent, mū·nif'i·sent, a. Giving with great generosity or liberality.—**mu·nif·i·cence** n.—**mu·nif·i·cent·ly**, adv.

mu·ni·ment, mū'ni·ment, n. [O.Fr. muniment, < L. munimentum, fortification, defense, < munire.] Pl., law, a document by which rights or privileges are defended or maintained, as a title deed or charter.

mu·ni·tion, mū·nish'an, n. [Fr. munition, < L. munitio(n-), fortifying, a fortification, defense, < munire, wall, fortify, strengthen, < moenia, walls.] Usu. pl. Materials used in war for defense or attack; material or equipment for carrying on any undertaking.—a. Pertaining to munitions; as, a munition ship.—v.t. To provide with munitions.

mun·tin, mun'tin, n. Arch. a vertical support within the framing of a window, screen, or door.

munt·jac, munt'jak, n. [Jav.] Any of various small deer constituting the genus Muntiacus, of southern and eastern Asia and the adjacent islands, esp. M. muntjac, of Java and India; any of the small deer of the related genus Elaphodus, of China and Tibet.

mu·ral, mur'al, a. [L. muralis, < murus, a wall.] Pertaining to or resembling a wall; affixed or applied to a wall.—n. A painting executed directly on a wall or ceiling; a wallpaper design used to simulate a mural.—**mu·ral·ist**, mur'a·list, n.

mur·der, mur'dẽr, n. [O.E. morthor, morther, < morth, death; Goth. maurthr, D. moord, Dan., Sw., and G. mord, Icel. morth; < root mar, to crush, whence also L. mors, death (E. mortal); Skt. mri, to die.] The act of unlawfully killing a human being by another human with premeditated malice.—v.t. To kill, as a human being, with premeditated malice; to slay feloniously; fig. to abuse or violate grossly; as, to murder the queen's English.—v.i. To commit murder.—**mur·der·er, mur·der·ess**, n.

mur·der·ous, mur'dẽr·us, a. Pertaining to murder; guilty of murder; accompanied or marked by murder; capable of or intending murder; deadly; bloody.—**mur·der·ous·ly**, adv.—**mur·der·ous·ness**, n.

mure, mūr, v.t.—mured, muring. To immure.

mu·rex, mūr'eks, n. pl. **mu·ri·ces, mu·rex·es**, mūr'i·sēz". [L.] Any of several gastropod mollusks belonging to the genus Murex, native to tropical waters, and yielding a purple dye valued by the ancients; the dye itself.

mu·ri·at·ic ac·id, mūr'ē·at'ik as'id, n. A commercial term for hydrochloric acid.

mu·ri·cate, mūr'i·kāt", a. [L. muricatus, murex, the point of a rock.] Full of sharp points. Also **mu·ri·cat·ed**.

mu·rine, mur'īn, mur'in, a. [L. murinus, < mus (mur-), mouse.] Relating to a mouse or rat; belonging or pertaining to the Muridae, the family of rodents containing the mice and rats, or to the Murinae, the subfamily including the domestic species. Also **mu·rid**.—n. A murine rodent.

murk, mirk, murk, n. [O.E. murc, mirce, dark, Icel. myrkr, Dan. and Sw. mörk, dark.] Darkness or gloom.—a.

murk·y, mur'kē, a.—murkier, murkiest. Dark; obscure; gloomy; thick, as a fog.—**murk·i·ly**, adv.—**murk·i·ness**, n.

mur·mur, mur'mẽr, n. [Fr. murmure, < L. murmur, a reduplication of an imit. syllable mur, seen in G. murren, D. morren, Icel. murra, Dan. murre, to murmur.] A low, continuous or continually repeated sound, as that of a stream; a low indistinct sound or hum; a complaint uttered in a low, muttering voice; a grumble or mutter; med. a sound emitted by the heart which is a sign of an abnormality.—v.i. To utter or give out a murmur or hum; to grumble; to utter complaints; to mutter.—*v.t.* To utter indistinctly; to mutter.—**mur·mur·er,** *n.*—**mur·mur·ing,** *n., a.*—**mur·mur·ous,** *a.*—**mur·mur·ly,** *adv.*

Mur·phy bed, mụr'fē bed, *n.* [From W. L. *Murphy,* 20th century U.S. inventor.] A bed that can be swung back behind a closet or cabinet door when not being used.

mur·rain, mụr'in, *n.* [O.Fr. *morine,* < L. *morior,* to die.] *Pathol.* any of several diseases that affect cattle, as hoof-and-mouth disease.

murre, mụr, *n.* pl. **murres, murre.** [Etym. doubtful.] *Ornith.* a ducklike bird, *Uria aalge,* with a slender pointed bill, short neck, black upper parts, and white under parts and found along the Atlantic coast from the Arctic south to Nova Scotia. Also **At·lan·tic murre, com·mon murre.**

mur·rey, mụr'ē, *n.* [O.Fr. *morée,* a dark-red color, < L. *morum,* a mulberry.] A dark purplish-red or mulberry color.—*a.*

mu·sa·ceous, mū·zā'shus, *a.* [From *Musa,* the typical genus.] *Bot.* belonging or pertaining to the *Musaceae,* the family of plants that includes the banana.

mus·ca·dine, mus'ka·din, mus'ka·dīn″, *n.* A grape vine, *Vitis rotundifolia,* growing in the southern U.S. and bearing a thick-skinned purple fruit having a strong musk flavor.

mus·cæ vo·li·tan·tes, mus'ē vol″i·tan'·tēz, *n.* [N.L., 'flies flying about.'] Specks that seem to dance in the air before the eyes, due to defects in the vitreous humor of the eye or to other causes.

mus·ca·rine, mus'kẽr·in, mus'ka·rēn″, *n. Chem.* a poisonous alkaloid, $C_8H_{19}NO_3$, found in some fungi.—**mus·ca·rin·ic,** mus″ka·rin'ik, *a.*

mus·cat, mus'kat, mus'kat, *n.* [Fr. < Pr. *muscat,* M.L. *muscatus,* having the flavor of musk, musky, < L.L. *muscus, musk.*] Any of several varieties of grape, usually of light color, and having the flavor or odor of musk: grown for making wine and raisins; the wine so made. Also *muscatel,* **mus·kat.**

mus·ca·tel, mus″ka·tel', mus'ka·tel″, *n.* [O.Fr. *muscatel, muscadel,* dim. < Pr. *muscat.*] A strong, rich sweet wine made from muscat grapes; the muscat grape. Also *muscat,* **mus·ca·del, mus·ca·delle.**

mus·cle, mus'l, *n.* [Fr. *muscle,* < L. *musculus,* a little mouse, a mussel, a muscle, dim. of *mus,* a mouse—probably from the appearance under the skin.] A tissue consisting of elongated fibers which contract on stimulation and produce bodily motion; a contractive organ, consisting of muscle tissue; physical strength; effective force; as, put *muscle* into the orders.—*v.i.*—*muscled, muscling. Slang,* to gain one's way or encroach using force or threats, usu. followed by *in.*—*v.t. Slang,* to force or threaten. To strengthen.

mus·cle-bound, mus'l-bound″, *a.* Having the muscles enlarged, overstrained, and inelastic, as by overexercise.

mus·cle sense, *n.* Kinaesthesia.

mus·co·va·do, mus″ko·vä'dō, mus″ko·vä'dō, *n.* [Sp. (*azucar*) *masacabado,* Pg. (*açucar*) *mascavado* (sugar) of inferior quality.] Raw or unrefined sugar, obtained by evaporating the juice of the sugar cane and draining off the molasses. Also **mus·ca·va·do.**

Mus·co·vite, mus'ko·vīt″, *n.* A native or inhabitant of Muscovy, the former principality of Moscow, and by extension, of Russia generally; a Russian; (*l.c.*) the common light-colored variety of mica.—*a.* Of or pertaining to Muscovy or its inhabitants; pertaining to Russia generally; Russian.

Mus·co·vy duck, mus'ko·vē duk, *n.* [Erro. for *musk duck.*] A large wild duck, *Cairina moschata,* of Central America,

extensively raised in its domesticated variety. Also **musk duck.**

mus·cu·lar, mus'kū·lẽr, *a.* Pertaining to or consisting of muscles; performed by or dependent on muscles; as, *muscular* exertion; having well-developed muscles; strong or brawny; strong or forceful, esp. with the suggestion of a lack of grace or subtlety.—**mus·cu·lar·i·ty,** mus″kū·lar'i·tē, *n.*—**mus·cu·lar·ly,** *adv.*

mus·cu·lar dys·tro·phy, *n. Pathol.* a disease which results in progressive deterioration and atrophy of muscle tissue.

mus·cu·la·ture, mus'kū·la·chẽr, *n.* [= Fr. *musculature,* < L. *musculus, muscle.*] *Anat.* The system of muscles; the muscle arrangement in an organ.

Muse, mūz, *n.* [Fr. *muse,* L. *musa,* < Gr. *mousa,* a muse.] (*Sometimes l.c.*) the spirit or power which is said to inspire artistic creation. *Class. mythol.* any of nine sister goddesses who presided over the arts, as Calliope over epic poetry and Erato over lyric poetry; any goddess who presides over one of the arts.

muse, mūz, *v.i.*—*mused, musing.* [Fr. *muser,* to muse, dawdle, loiter.] To think or meditate in silence; to say thoughtfully.—*v.t.* To think or meditate on.—*n.*—**muse·ful,** *a.*—**muse·ful·ly,** *adv.*—**mus·ing·ly,** *adv.*

mu·sette, mū·zet', Fr. mY·zet', *n.* [Fr. dim. of O.Fr. *muse,* bagpipe: cf. *Muse* and *music.*] A small French bagpipe with wind produced by means of a bellows, popular in the 17th century; a soft pastoral melody imitating a bagpipe air; a small woodwind instrument, forerunner of the oboe. A small bag with a shoulder strap used esp. by the military; also **mu·sette bag, field bag.**

mu·se·um, mū·zē'um, *n.* [L., < Gr. *mouseion,* orig. a temple of the Muses.] A building or area used for exhibiting interesting objects connected with literature, art, science, history, or nature.

mush, mush, *Dial.* mụsh, *n.* [Prob. var. of *mash.*] Meal, usu. cornmeal, boiled in water or milk until it becomes thick and soft; any thick, soft matter or mass; anything unpleasantly lacking in firmness, force, or dignity; *colloq.* maudlin sentiment or sentimental language.

mush, mush, *v.i.* [Fr. *marchons,* a starting order.] *Colloq., Canada, northern U.S.* to journey on foot, particularly over snow, by dog team and sled.—*n.* Such a trip.—*interj.* The call to start a team of dogs.

mush·room, mush'rōm, mush'rụm, *n.* [O.Fr. *mosseron* (Fr. *mousseron*), < *mosse* (Fr. *mousse*), moss.] Any of various rapidly growing, fleshy fungi such as toadstools and morels; any of certain edible species belonging to the family *Agaricaceæ,* typically having a stalk with an umbrella-like cap; anything of similar shape or of correspondingly rapid growth.—*a.* Of, pertaining to, or made of mushrooms; resembling or suggesting a mushroom in shape; of rapid growth and often short duration.—*v.i.* To gather mushrooms; to have or assume the shape of a mushroom; to sprout, multiply, or develop quickly.

mush·y, mush'ē, *Dial.* mụsh'ē, *a.*—*mushier, mushiest.* Mushlike; soft; thick; yielding; pulpy; *fig.* weakly sentimental.—**mush·i·ly,** *adv.*—**mush·i·ness,** *n.*

mu·sic, mū'zik, *n.* [Fr. *musique,* L. *musica,* < Gr. *mousikē* (*technē,* art, understood), music, art, culture.] The art of organizing or arranging sounds into meaningful patterns or forms, usu. involving pitch, harmony, and rhythm; a musical piece or composition; the sound of a musical composition when it is performed; the written or printed score of a composition; a pleasing sound or sounds; euphony.

—**ab·so·lute mu·sic,** instrumental elements such as text, narrative, or description: opposed to *program music.*—**a·le·a·to·ry mu·sic,** music in which elements of the performance are either left up to the performer's decision or allowed to be governed by chance; also **chance mu·sic·e·lec·tron·ic mu·sic,** music which includes sound produced electronically in a laboratory and recorded on magnetic tape.—**pro·gram mu·sic,** music composed in reference to an extramusical idea or ideas such as narrative, description, or text: opposed to *absolute music.*—**face the mu·sic,** to accept, acknowledge, or take the consequences of one's actions or mistakes.

mu·si·cal, mū'zi·kal, *a.* [O.Fr. Fr. *musical,* < M.L. *musicalis.*] Of, pertaining to, or producing music; as, a *musical* instrument; of the nature of or resembling music; set to or accompanied by music; as, a *musical* comedy; fond of or skilled in music.—*n.* Musical comedy; a musicale.—**mu·si·cal·ly,** *adv.*—**mu·si·cal·i·ty, mu·si·cal·ness,** *n.*

mu·si·cal chairs, *n.* pl. but sing. in constr. A game for any number of players, who walk to music around a line of chairs, one fewer in number than the players, with the object of finding a seat when the music ceases.

mu·si·cal com·e·dy, *n.* A humorous play or film with a plot that is interspersed with songs and dances.

mu·si·cale, mū″zi·kal', *n.* [Fr., fem. of *musical.*] A social entertainment featuring music.

mu·si·cal saw, *n.* A handsaw whose curved blade is held between the player's knees and is struck with a drumstick or played by a violin bow. Also **sing·ing saw.**

mu·sic box, *n. Mus.* a box enclosing a small instrument, having a barrel with tuned teeth operated by pins, which plays one or more tunes mechanically.

mu·sic dra·ma, *n. Mus.* a type of opera developed by Richard Wagner in which the plot is uninterrupted by arias or recitatives, and the music, incorporating leitmotifs, is subservient to the dramatic action.

mu·sic hall, *n.* A hall for musical entertainments; *Brit.* a theater licensed for vaudeville and variety shows.

mu·si·cian, mū·zish'an, *n.* A person whose profession is music; one who is skilled in the composition or performance of music.—**mu·si·cian·ly,** *adv.*—**mu·si·cian·ship,** *n.*

mu·sic of the spheres, *n.* The inaudible harmony believed by ancient Pythagoreans to be produced by the movement of celestial bodies.

mu·si·col·o·gy, mū″zi·kol'o·jē, *n.* The study of the history, theory, and physics of music.—**mu·si·co·log·i·cal,** mū″zi·ko·loj'i·kal, *a.*—**mu·si·co·log·i·cal·ly,** *adv.* —**mu·si·col·o·gist,** *n.*

mus·ing, mū'zing, *a.* Absorbed in thought; meditative.—*n.* Meditation.—**mus·ing·ly,** *adv.*

musk, musk, *n.* [O.Fr. Fr. *musc,* < L.L. *muscus,* L.Gr. *moschos,* < Pers. *mushk,* musk: cf. Skt. *muska,* testicle.] A substance secreted in a glandular sac under the skin of the abdomen of the male musk deer, having a strong, lasting odor, and much used in perfumery; a similar secretion of other animals; an artificial imitation of the substance; the odor, or some similar odor; the musk deer.

musk deer, *n.* A small deer without horns, *Moschus moschiferus,* of central Asia, the male of which secretes musk.

mus·keg, mus'keg, *n.* [Cree Ind.] *Canada,* a bog or swamp.—*a.* Relating to a swampy place; as, the wildlife in a *muskeg* valley.

mus·kel·lunge, mus´ke·lunj″, *n. pl.* **mus·-kel·lunge**. [Amer. Ind.] A large variety of pike, *Esox masquinongy*, found in the lakes and rivers of northern U.S. and Canada. Also **mus·kie**, **mus·ky**.

mus·ket, mus´kit, *n.* [Fr. *mousquet*, O.Fr. *mousket*, *moschet*, orig. a sparrow hawk, lit. 'fly-hawk,' < L. *musca*, a fly.] A large-caliber, smoothbore firearm, first developed in the 16th century.

mus·ket·eer, mus″ki·tēr´, *n.* A soldier armed with a musket. Also *Fr.* **mous·-que·taire**, mös″ke·târ´.

mus·ket·ry, mus´ki·trē, *n.* Muskets collectively; musketeers collectively; the art or science of firing small arms.

musk·mel·on, musk´mel″on, *n.* A cultivated, herbaceous, trailing vine, *Cucumis melo*, in the gourd family, with a fleshy, edible fruit; the fruit itself, globular or oblong, often furrowed or warty, with a musky-odored rind and sweet, aromatic, yellow to green flesh; cantaloupe.

Mus·ko·ge·an, **Mus·kho·ge·an**, mus·-kō´gē·an, *n.* A linguistic stock of N. American Indians of the southeastern U.S., including the Choctaw, Creek, Seminole, Yazoo, and other tribes.

musk ox, *n.* An even-toed, hoofed mammal of the bovine family, *Ovibos moschatus*, now living only in the arctic regions of N. America, characterized by a mass of long shaggy hair covering a woolly undercoat, down-curved horns, and a very short tail: named from its musky odor.

musk·rat, musk´rat″, *n. pl.* **musk·rat**, **musk·rats**. A large, essentially aquatic, fur-bearing, N. American rodent, *Ondatra zibethica*, with a long, scaly, sparsely-haired tail, partially webbed hind feet, and a musky odor; the brown fur of this animal. Also *musquash*.

musk rose, *n.* A climbing shrub, *Rosa moschata*, native to the Mediterranean region, having large white flowers with the odor of musk.

musk tur·tle, *n.* Any of the small aquatic turtles found in N. America, genus *Sternotherus*, which emits a musky secretion in self-defense.

musk·y, mus´kē, *a.*—*muskier*, *muskiest.* Having the odor or taste of musk.—**musk·-i·ness**, *n.*

Mus·lem, muz´lem, mŏoz´lem, mŭs´lem, *n.* Moslem.

Mus·lim, muz´lim, mŏoz´lim, mŭs´lim, *n.* Moslem.

mus·lin, muz´lin, *n.* [Fr. *mousseline*, < It. *mussolina*, muslin, < *Mussolo*, Mosul, town in Iraq.] A thin cotton fabric made in various degrees of sheerness or fineness, and often printed, woven, or embroidered in patterns; a heavier cotton cloth, bleached or unbleached.

mus·quash, mus´kwosh, *n.* A muskrat. *Brit.* the fur of the muskrat.

muss, mus, *n.* [Origin uncertain; in later use associated with *mess*.] *Colloq.* A disorderly struggle, fracas, or row; a state of disorder, or an untidy or dirty mess.—*v.t. Colloq.* To put into disorder; make untidy or messy; rumple.

mus·sel, mus´el, *n.* A bivalve mollusk, in particular the edible marine mollusk of the family *Mytilidae*; a clawlike freshwater mollusk of the family *Unionidae*.

Mus·sul·man, mus´ul·man, *n. pl.* **Mus·-sul·mans**. [Corrupted < *Muslimun*, pl. of *Moslem*.] A Moslem or Mohammedan.—*a.*

muss·y, mus´ē, *a.*—*mussier*, *mussiest.* [< *muss.*] *Colloq.* Untidy; messy; rumpled.—**muss·i·ly**, *adv.*—**muss·i·ness**, *n.*

must, must, *aux. v.* [O.E. *mõste*; similar forms in Goth., D., Sw., and G.] To be

obliged, bound, or compelled to by moral principle, law, order, command, threat of physical force, logical necessity, or natural law; to be supposed, as: It *must* be very late. To be certain, as: Peace *must* follow.—*n. Colloq.* Anything necessary; an essential.—*a.* Necessary; essential.

must, must, *n.* Mold; moldiness.

must, must, *n.* [L. *mustum*, new wine, < *mustus*, new, fresh.] Unfermented juice pressed from grapes or other fruits.

mus·tache, mus´tash, mu·stash´, *n.* [Fr. *moustache*, < It. *mostaccio*, < Gr. *mystax*, upper lip, mustache: cf. *mastax*, mouth, < *masasthai*, chew.] The hair growing on the upper lip or on either half of the upper lip of men; hairs or bristles growing near the mouth of an animal; a stripe of color suggestive of a mustache on the head or neck of a bird. Also *moustache*, *mustachio*.

mus·ta·chio, mu·stä´shō, mu·stä´shē·ō″, mu·stash´ō, mu·stash´ē·ō″, *n. pl.* **mus·-ta·chios**. [It. *mostaccio* or Sp. *mostacho*.] A mustache.—**mus·ta·chioed**, *a.*

mus·tang, mus´tang, *n.* [Sp. *mesteño*, belonging to the *mesta*, or body of graziers.] The small wild horse of western N. America, a descendant of horses imported from Spain.

mus·tard, mus´têrd, *n.* [O.Fr. *moustarde* (Fr. *moutarde*), orig. a condiment of powdered mustard seed mixed with must, < L. *mustum*, must.] Any of several herbaceous plants of the genus *Brassica*, in the mustard family, the seeds of some of the species yielding the commercial mustard condiment; the paste or powder prepared from the seeds of *B. alba* and *B. nigra*, used as a food spice and medicinally for poultices and as a counterirritant.

mus·tard gas, *n.* An agent of chemical warfare, $(ClCH_2CH_2)_2S$, causing destruction of tissue, blindness, and death, first used by the Germans in World War I. Also **di·chlo·ro·di·eth·yl sul·fide**.

mus·tard plas·ter, *n. Med.* a compress used to apply powdered mustard and flour; a piece of adhesive fabric coated with a solution of pulverized black mustard which acts as a counterirritant on contact.

mus·te·line, mus´te·lin″, mus´te·lin, *a.* [L. *mustelinus*, < *mustela*, a weasel.] Pertaining to the weasel, skunk, and kindred animals of the family *Mustelidae*.

mus·ter, mus´têr, *v.t.* [O.Fr. *moustrer*, *mostrer*, *monstrer*, to exhibit, < L. *monstrare*, to show, *monstrum*, a monster.] To collect, as troops, for service, review, parade, or exercise; to assemble or bring together, as information.—*v.i.* To assemble or meet in one place, as soldiers.—*n.* An assembling of troops for review or for service; the act of assembling; an assemblage. Also **mus·ter roll**.—**pass mus·ter**, to pass without censure, as one among a number on inspection.—**mus·ter in** or **out**, to join or be released from military service.

musth, must, *n.* [Hind. *mast*: cf. Skt. *matta*, intoxicated.] The state of sexual, nervous frenzy and dangerous irritability occurring periodically in male elephants and accompanied by an oily secretion around the eyes and mouth.—*a.* Also *must*.

mus·ty, mus´tē, *a.*—*mustier*, *mustiest.* [Probably connected with *moist*, or with L. *mucidus*, moldy; cf. Sp. *mustio*, musty.] Tasting or smelling moldy; fusty; spoiled by age; antiquated; stale; dull.—**mus·ti·ly**, *adv.*—**mus·ti·ness**, *n.*

mu·ta·ble, mū´ta·bl, *a.* [L. *mutabilis*, < *muto*, to change; akin to *moveo*, to move.] Capable of being altered; subject to change; inconstant in mind or feelings; fickle. —**mu·ta·bil·i·ty**, mū″ta·bil´i·tē, **mu·-ta·ble·ness**, *n.*—**mu·ta·bly**, *adv.*

mu·ta·gen·ic, mū″ta·jen´ik, *a. Genetics*, able to produce mutations, as x-rays.—**mu·ta·gen·i·cal·ly**, *adv.*

mu·tant, mūt´ant, *n. Biol.* a form which is undergoing mutation or which has resulted from mutation.—*a.*

mu·tate, mū´tāt, *v.t.*—*mutated*, *mutating.* [L. *mutatus*, pp. of *mutare*, change.] To change; alter; *phon.* to change by mutation or by umlaut.—*v.i.* To change; undergo mutation.

mu·ta·tion, mū·tā´shan, *n.* [L. *mutatio(n-).*] The act or process of changing; a change or alteration, as in form, qualities, or nature; *phon.* a subtle shift in the formative position of a vowel or consonant in anticipation of some other sound or as a result of a preceding sound. *Biol.* a sudden inheritable change appearing in the offspring of a parent organism due to an alteration in a gene or chromosome, or an increase in the number of chromosomes; the process by which this change occurs; the resultant species or individual.—**mu·ta·tion·al**, **mu·ta·tive**, mū´ta·tiv, *a.* —**mu·ta·tion·al·ly**, *adv.*

mute, mūt, *a.* [L. *mutus*, silent, dumb.] Silent, or refraining from speech or utterance; not emitting or having sound of any kind; incapable of speech; dumb; temporarily bereft of speech; as, *mute* with astonishment; unaccompanied by speech or sound; unspoken; as, a *mute* plea. *Law,* making no response when arraigned, as a prisoner. *Phon.* silent; plosive.—**mute·ly**, *adv.*—**mute·ness**, *n.*—**mut·ism**, *n.*

mute, mūt, *n.* A person without the power of speech; an actor whose part is confined to pantomime. *Law,* a prisoner who makes no response when arraigned. *Phon.* a silent letter; a plosive. *Mus.* a device to deaden or muffle the sound of an instrument.

mute, mūt, *v.t.*—*muted*, *muting.* To deaden or muffle the sound, as of a musical instrument. To soften the intensity, as of a color.

mu·ti·cate, mū´ti·kāt″, *a. Bot.* having no awn; *zool.* without defense structures, as claws. Also **mu·ti·cous**.

mu·ti·late, mūt´i·lāt″, *v.t.*—*mutilated*, *mutilating.* [L. *mutilo*, *mutilatum*, to lop, < *mutilus*, maimed; akin Gr. *mitylos*, docked.] To cut off a limb or essential part from; to maim; to remove any material part from so as to render imperfect.—**mu·ti·la·tion**, *n.*—**mu·ti·la·tor**, *n.*

mu·ti·neer, mūt″i·nēr´, *n.* One guilty of mutiny.

mu·ti·nous, mūt´i·nus, *a.* Engaged in, disposed to, or characteristic of mutiny.—**mu·ti·nous·ly**, *adv.*—**mu·ti·nous·ness**, *n.*

mu·ti·ny, mūt´i·nē, *n. pl.* **mu·ti·nies.** [< Fr. *mutin*, O.Fr. *meutin*, mutinous, riotous, *meute*, a revolt, an *emeute*, < L.L. *mota*, a body of men raised for an expedition, < L. *moveo*, *motus*, to move.] Revolt against constituted authority; resistance of soldiers or seamen against the authority of their commanders.—*v.i.*—*mutinied*, *mutinying.* To engage in mutiny; to rise against military or naval officers.

mutt, mut, *n. Slang.* A mongrel dog; a dull, stupid individual.

mut·ter, mut´êr, *v.i.* [An imit. word; cf. G. *muttern*, L. *muttire*, to mutter, *mu*, the sound produced by closing the lips.] To utter words with a low voice and compressed lips; to grumble; to murmur; to sound with a low rumbling noise.—*v.t.* To utter in a low indistinct manner.—*n.* Murmur; obscure utterance.—**mut·ter·er**, *n.*—**mut·ter·ing·ly**, *adv.*

mut·ton, mut´on, *n.* [M.E. *motoun*, sheep.] The flesh of mature sheep, raw or cooked for food.—**mut·ton·y**, *a.*—**mut·ton chops**, *n. pl.* Side whiskers that broaden at the lower jaw.

mu·tu·al, mū´chŏo·al, *a.* [Fr. *mutuel*, < L.L. *mutualis*, < L. *mutuus*, mutual, < *muto*, to change.] Reciprocally given and received; pertaining alike or reciprocally to both sides; interchanged; equally relating to, affecting, or proceeding from two or more together; common to two or more combined; shared alike.—**mu·tu·al·ly,** adv.

mu·tu·al fund, n. An investment company which sells its own stock and purchases a diversified portfolio of securities with the proceeds. Also **o·pen-end fund.**

mu·tu·al·ism, mū′chö·a·liz″um, n. Biol. an association between two or more dissimilar organisms from which all benefit; sociol. the doctrine that both the individual and society profit from mutual dependence.—**mu·tu·al·ist,** n.—**mu·tu·al·is·tic,** a.

mu·tu·al·i·ty, mū″chö·al′i·tē, n. The state or quality of being mutual; interdependence.

mu·tu·al·ize, mū′chö·a·līz″, v.t.—mutualized, mutualizing. To make mutual. Econ. to place ownership of the majority of the stock of a corporation in the hands of its employees or customers.—v.i. To become mutual.—**mu·tu·al·i·za·tion,** n.

mu·tu·el, mū′chö·al, n. Usu. pl. pari-mutuel

mu·zhik, mö·zhik′, mö′zhik, n. [Russ.] A Russian peasant. Also **moujik, mu·jik, mu·zjik.**

muz·zle, muz′l, n. [O.Fr. musel (Mod.Fr. museau), dim. of O.Fr. muse, L.L. musus, a mouth, < L. morsus, a bite, < mordeo, morsum, to bite.] The projecting mouth and nose of an animal; the open end of a gun or pistol; a restrictive harness for an animal's mouth which prevents biting or eating.—v.t.—muzzled, muzzling. To put a muzzle on; to restrain, as opinion.—**muz·zler,** n.

muz·zle·load·er, muz·zle-load·er, muz′l·lō″dẽr, n. A gun loaded from the muzzle.—**muz·zle·load·ing, muz·zle-load·ing,** a.

muz·zy, muz′ē, a.—muzzier, muzziest. [Akin to muse, to be absent-minded.] Slang. Absent-minded; bewildered; confused.—**muz·zi·ly,** adv.—**muz·zi·ness,** n.

my, mī, pronominal a. [Contr. < mine, O.E. min.] The possessive case of I, used as an attributive; as, my face.—interj. Expressing surprise, as: My, what a long book!

my·al·gi·a, mī·al′jē·a, mī·al′ja, n. [N.L., < Gr. mys, muscle, and algos, pain.] Pathol. Pain in the muscles; muscular rheumatism.—**my·al·gic,** a.

my·as·the·ni·a, mī″as·thē′nē·a, n. [N.L.] Pathol. muscular debility.—**my·as·then·ic,** mī″as·then′ik, a.

my·ce·li·um, mī·sē′lē·um, n. pl. **my·ce·li·a,** mī·sē′lē·a. [Gr. mykēs, a fungus, and helōs, wart.] Bot. the mass of hyphae, filamentous structures forming the body of a true fungus.—**my·ce·li·al,** a.—**my·ce·li·oid,** mī·sē′lē·oid″, a.

My·ce·nae·an, My·ce·ni·an, mī″si·nē′an, a. Of or pertaining to the ancient city of Mycenae; pertaining to the civilization which flourished in the Aegean area during its Bronze Age, c. 1400–1100 B.C.

my·ce·to·zo·an, mī·sē″to·zō′an, n. [N.L., < Gr. mykēs, fungus, and zoon, animal.] A fungus, member of the order Mycetozoa, possessing both animal and plant characteristics; slime mold.—a. Characterizing the Mycetozoa.

my·col·o·gy, mī·kol′o·je, n. [Gr. mykēs, and logos.] Bot. The study of fungi; the fungi of a region; characteristics and life processes of a kind of fungus.—**my·co·log·ic, my·co·log·i·cal,** mī″ko·loj′i·kal, a.—**my·co·log·i·cal·ly,** adv.—**my·col·o·gist,** mī·kol′o·jist, n.

my·cor·rhi·za, my·co·rhi·za, mī″kō·rī′za, mī″ka·rī′za, n. pl. **my·cor·rhi·zae, my·cor·rhi·zas.** [Gr. mykēs, a fungus, and rhiza, a root.] Bot. the symbiotic rela-

tionship of a fungus with the roots of certain plants, as pines, oaks, and orchids, in which the mycelium of the fungus forms an intricate mass surrounding, and sometimes invading, the root tissues.—**my·cor·rhi·zal, my·co·rhi·zal,** a.

my·co·sis, mī·kō′sis, n. [N.L., < Gr. mykēs, fungus.] Pathol. The presence of parasitic fungi in or on the body; a disease caused by such a fungus, as ringworm.—**my·cot·ic,** mī·kot′ik, a.

my·dri·a·sis, mi·drī′a·sis, mī·drī′a·sis, n. [L., < Gr. mydriasis.] Excessive dilatation of the pupil of the eye, as the result of disease or drugs.—**myd·ri·at·ic,** mid″rē·at′ik, a. Pertaining to or producing mydriasis.—n. A mydriatic drug.

my·e·len·ceph·a·lon, mī″e·len·sef′a·lon″, n. pl. **my·e·len·ceph·a·lons, my·e·len·ceph·a·la.** [N.L., < Gr. myelos, narrow, and N.L. encephalon.] Anat. the posterior area of the hindbrain from which the medulla oblongata develops.—**my·e·len·ce·phal·ic,** mī″e·len·se·fal′ik, a.

my·e·lin, mī′e·lin, n. [G., < Gr. myelos, narrow.] Anat. a soft, white, fatty substance encasing the axis cylinder of certain nerve fibers.—**my·e·lin·ic,** a.—**my·e·lin·i·za·tion,** n. Anat. the process by which the myelin sheath is formed. Also **my·e·li·na·tion.**

my·e·lin sheath, n. Anat. the medullary case enclosing certain nerve fibers.

my·e·loid, mī′e·loid″, a. Anat. Resembling marrow; having to do with the spinal cord.

my·na, mī′na, n. [Hindu mainā.] Any of numerous Asian starlings, particularly the genus Gracula, certain varieties of which are domesticated and taught to imitate speech. Also **my·nah.**

Myn·heer, mīn·hâr′, mīn·hēr′, n. [D. mijnheer, < mijn, my, and heer, lord, gentleman.] The Dutch term of address and title of respect corresponding to 'sir' and 'Mr.'; (l.c.) a Dutchman.

my·o·car·di·o·graph, mī″o·kär′dē·o·graf″, mī″o·kär′dē·o·gräf″, n. An instrument which records the action of the muscles of the heart.

my·o·car·di·um, mī″o·kär′dē·um, n. pl. **my·o·car·di·a,** mī″o·kär′dē·a. [N.L. (Gr. kardia, heart).] Anat. the muscular substance of the heart.—**my·o·car·di·al,** a.

my·o·gen·ic, mī″o·jen′ik, a. Having its origin in muscle. Also **my·o·ge·net·ic.**

my·o·glo·bin, mī″o·glō′bin, mī′o·glō″bin, n. Biochem. hemoglobin in the muscles, similar to blood hemoglobin, but carrying less carbon monoxide and more oxygen.

my·o·graph, mī′o·graf″, mī′o·gräf″, n. An instrument used to measure muscular activity.

my·ol·o·gy, mī·ol′o·je, n. The science of muscles; the branch of anatomy that treats of muscles.—**my·o·log·ic, my·o·log·i·cal,** a.

my·o·ma, mī·ō′ma, n. pl. **my·o·mas, my·o·ma·ta.** [N.L., < Gr. mys, muscle.] Pathol. a tumor composed of muscular tissue.—**my·om·a·tous,** mī·om′a·tus, mī·ō′ma·tus, a.

my·o·neu·ral, mī″o·nur′al, mī″o·nūr′al, a. Of or concerning both muscle and nerve.

my·o·pi·a, mī·ō′pē·a, n. [N.L.] Pathol. A condition of the eye in which images are focused in front of the retina, objects being seen distinctly only when near to the eye; nearsightedness; lack of foresight.—**my·ope,** mī′ōp, n.—**my·op·ic,** mī·op′ik, a.—**my·op·i·cal·ly,** adv.

my·o·so·tis, mī″o·sō′tis, n. [L., < Gr. myosōtis, < myos, gen. of mys, mouse, and oys (ōt-), ear.] Any plant of the genus Myosotis, as the common forget-me-not.

myr·i·ad, mir′ē·ad, n. [Gr. myrias, myriados, < myria, ten thousand, innumerable.]

Ten thousand; an indefinite, immense number; a multitude of things or people.—a. Innumerable, multitudinous but indefinite.

myr·i·a·pod, mir′ē·a·pod″, n. [Gr. myria, ten thousand, and pous, podos, a foot.] Zool. an elongated, segmented, wormlike arthropod, belonging to either the class Chilopoda, the centipedes, which have one pair of legs to each segment, or the class Diplopoda, the millipedes, which have two pair of legs to each segment. Also **myr·i·o·pod.**—a.—**myr·i·ap·o·dous,** mir″ē·ap′o·dus, a.

myr·me·col·o·gy, mur″me·kol′o·je, n. Entom. the study of ants.—**myr·me·co·log·i·cal,** mur″me·ko·loj′i·kal, a.—**myr·me·col·o·gist,** n.

myr·me·coph·a·gous, mur″me·kof′a·gus, a. Adapted to feeding on ants, as jaws of anteaters.

myr·mi·don, mur′mi·don″, mur′mi·don, n. A follower or soldier who willingly executes unscrupulous commands; (cap.) in Greek legend, a member of a warlike people of Thessaly who followed their king, Achilles, into war with Troy.

myr·ob·a·lan, mi·rob′a·lan, mi·rob′a·lan, n. [L. myrobalanum, Gr. myrobalanos—myron, unguent, and balanus, a nut.] A dried fruit of certain East Indian plants, genus Terminalia, used by dyers, tanners, and ink manufacturers.

myrrh, mur, n. [O.E. myrre, < L. myrrha, murra, < Gr. myrra: cf. Ar. murr, bitter.] Valuable gum resin obtained from small, spiny trees native to Arabia and E. Africa, esp. from Commiphora myrrha, used medicinally as a tonic and in dentifrices; C. erythraea, the myrrh of antiquity, still used in incense and perfume.

myr·tle, mur′tl, n. [O.Fr. mirtile, myrtle berry (Fr. myrtille, bilberry), dim. < L. myrtus, < Gr. myrtos, myrtle.] Bot. an evergreen cultivated shrub, Myrtus communis, in the myrtle family, native to the Mediterranean region, having fragrant white flowers and aromatic berries; the classical myrtle used as an emblem of love and held sacred to Venus. An evergreen, ornamental, trailing vine, native to the Old World and a favorite ground cover and window-box plant, Vinca minor, in the dogbane family, having pale blue or white flowers; also periwinkle.

my·self, mī·self′, pron. pl. **our·selves.** Used to intensify 'I,' as: I myself am responsible. Used reflexively as a form of 'me,' functioning as the direct or indirect object of a verb or as the object of a preposition, as: I hit myself with the rake handle, gave myself a gift, I thought only of myself. My natural or usual state, as: After a time, I was myself again.

mys·ta·gogue, mis′ta·gag″, mis′ta·gog″, n. [Gr. mystagōgos—mystēs, one initiated in mysteries, and agōgos, a leader.] One who instructs in or interprets mysteries.—**mys·ta·go·gy,** mis′ta·gō″je, n. The practice or doctrines of a mystagogue; the interpretation of mysteries.—**mys·ta·gog·ic,** mis′ta·goj′ik, a.—**mys·ta·gog·i·cal·ly,** adv.

mys·te·ri·ous, mi·stēr′ē·us, a. Partaking of or containing mystery; not revealed or explained; unintelligible; beyond human comprehension; occult; enigmatical—**mys·te·ri·ous·ly,** adv. In a mysterious manner.—**mys·te·ri·ous·ness,** n.

mys·ter·y, mis′te·rē, mis′trē, n. pl. **mys·ter·ies.** [L. mysterium, < Gr. mystērion, < mystēs, one initiated, < myein, initiate into mysteries, < myein, close (the lips).] Anything that is kept secret or remains unexplained or unknown; a puzzling or inexplicable matter or occurrence; any affair, thing, or person not fully explained

---

a- fat, fāte, fär, fâre, fall;   **e-** met, mē, mēre, hėr;   **i-** pin, pīne;   **o-** not, nōte, möve;   **u-** tub, cūbe, bull;   **oi-** oil;   **ou-** pound.

and therefore arousing curiosity or suspense; a story or dramatic representation of such an affair, object, or person; obscurity, as of something unexplained or puzzling; an obscure, puzzling, or mysterious quality or character. *Christian relig.* a sacramental rite, esp. the Eucharist; *pl.* the Eucharistic elements; *sing.* an incident or scene in connection with the life of Christ regarded as of special significance. A miracle play, sometimes restricted to one based on Biblical subjects; *theol.* any truth unknowable except by divine revelation. *Pl.* in ancient pagan religions, certain rites to which only the initiated were admitted; rites or secrets known only to those esp. initiated; as, the *mysteries* of the fraternity.

mys·tic, mis'tik, *a.* [L. *mysticus,* Gr. *mystikos,* < *mystēs,* one initiated.] Hidden from or obscure to human knowledge or comprehension; involving some secret meaning, often religious; mysterious; occult; pertaining to the ancient mysteries; pertaining to mystics or mysticism.—*n.* A believer in mysticism; one who professes to have mystical religious experiences; one initiated or admitted to occult rites.

mys·ti·cal, mis'ti·kal, *a.* Beyond the scope of human experience; pertaining to a spiritual event, intuition, or insight which defies comprehension; related to a spiritual communication or contact with God.—**mys·ti·cal·ly,** *adv.*—**mys·ti·cal·i·ty, mys·ti·cal·ness,** mis"ti·kal'i·tē, *n.*

mys·ti·cism, mis'ti·siz"um, *n.* The theory or belief that man can intuitively know God or religious truth, through the inward perception of the mind, a more immediate and direct method than that of ordinary understanding or sense perception; any seeking to solve the mysteries of existence by internal illumination or special revelation; a dreamy contemplation or speculation on ideas that have no foundation in human experience.

mys·ti·fy, mis'ti·fī, *v.t.*—*mystified, mystifying.* [Coined < *mystic,* and *-fy,* Fr. *-fier,* L. *facere,* to make.] To perplex purposely; to play on the credulity of; to bewilder; to obscure.—**mys·ti·fi·ca·tion,** mis"ta·fa·kā'shun, *n.*

mys·tique, mi·stēk', *n.* A collection of vaguely mystical beliefs, feelings, or attitudes associated with a person, organization, profession, or the like; an unusual viewpoint, often a mystical one, characterizing a particular religious or other group; a highly developed skill or esoteric quality.

myth, mith, *n.* [Gr. *mythos,* a word, a fable, a legend.] A fable or legend embodying the convictions of a people as to their gods or other divine personages, their own origin and early history and the heroes connected with it, or the origin of the world; in a looser sense, any invented story; something or someone having no existence in fact.—**myth·ic, myth·i·cal,** mith'i·kal, *a.* Relating to myths; described in a myth; fictitious; fabled.—**myth·i·cal·ly,** *adv.*

myth·i·cize, mith'i·sīz", *v.t.*—*mythicized, mythicizing.* To change into a myth; to deal with or interpret as a myth.—**myth·i·ciz·er,** *n.*

my·thog·ra·pher, mi·thog'ra·fèr, *n.* One who collects or writes about myths. Also **my·thog·ra·phist.**

myth·o·log·i·cal, mith"o·loj'i·kal, *a.* Relating to mythology or myths. Also **myth·o·log·ic.**—**myth·o·log·i·cal·ly,** *adv.*

my·thol·o·gist, mi·thol'o·jist, *n.* One versed in mythology. Also **my·thol·o·ger.**

my·thol·o·gize, mi·thol'o·jīz", *v.i.*—*mythologized, mythologizing.* To relate or construct myths; to explain myths.—*v.t.* To interpret in relation to mythology; to make into or explain as a myth.—**my·thol·o·giz·er,** *n.*

my·thol·o·gy, mi·thol'o·jē, *n.* pl. **my·thol·o·gies.** [L.L. *mythologia,* < Gr. *mythologia, mythos,* myth and *legein,* speak.] The study of myths; myths collectively; often, a body of myths relating to a particular person, or describing the legendary deeds of gods and men; as, Greek *mythology,* Teutonic *mythology.*

myth·o·ma·ni·a, mith"o·mā'nē·a, *n. Psychiatry,* a marked propensity for falsehood and exaggeration.—**myth·o·ma·ni·ac,** *n., a.*

myth·o·poe·ic, mith"o·pē'ik, *a.* [Gr. *mythopoios,* making myths, < *mythos,* myth, and *poiein,* make.] Pertaining to the making of myths.—**myth·o·poe·ism,** *n.*—**myth·o·poe·ist,** *n.*

my·thos, mith'os, *n.* pl. **my·thoi.** The embodiment in myth of a people's beliefs and fears arising out of past experience; myth; mythology.

myx·o·ma, mik·sō'ma, *n.* pl. **myx·o·mas, myx·o·ma·ta.** [N.L., < Gr. *myxa,* mucus.] *Pathol.* a tumor consisting of mucous and connective tissue.—**myx·o·ma·to·sis,** mik"sō·ma·tō'sis, *n.*—**myx·om·a·tous,** mik·som'a·tus, *a.*

N

N, n, en, *n.* The fourteenth letter and the eleventh consonant of the English alphabet; the voiced nasal sound represented by *n;* anything shaped like this letter; a representation of *N* or *n* printed or written; a printing type that reproduces *N* or *n;* (*cap.*), *chem.* the symbol for nitrogen; (*l.c.*), *math.* an indefinite number.

nab, nab, *v.t.*—*nabbed, nabbing.* [Same as Dan. *knappe,* Sw. *knappa,* to snatch; cf. D. and G. *knappen,* to snap.] *Colloq.* To catch or seize suddenly or unexpectedly; to arrest.

na·bob, nā'bob, *n.* [Corruption of Hind. *nawwâb,* < Ar. *nuwwâb,* pl. of *nâyib,* a deputy, < Ar. *nâba,* to take one's turn.] A governor of a province or commander of an army in India under the Mogul empire; also *nawab.* A person of great power or wealth.

na·celle, na·sel', *n.* [Fr. < L.L. *navicella,* dim. of L. *navis,* ship.] The streamlined housing or enclosure on an airplane usu. sheltering the engine; the enclosed part of an airplane, dirigible, or balloon in which passengers, crew, or cargo are carried.

na·cre, nā'kèr, *n.* [Fr. *nacre,* Sp. *nacar,* < Pers. *nakar,* an ornament of different colors.] Mother-of-pearl.—**na·cred,** nā'kèrd, *a.* Similar to or having a lining of nacre.—**na·cre·ous,** nā'krē·us, *a.* Consisting of or resembling nacre; having a pearly sheen.

Na-De·ne, Na·de·ne, nä·dā'nē, nä"dā·nā', *n.* A linguistic subdivision which includes the Tlingit, Haida, and Athapaskan subfamilies of languages spoken by groups of Indians in western N. America.—*a.*

na·dir, nā'dèr, nā'dēr, *n.* [Fr. *nadir,* Ar. and Pers. *nadir, nazîr,* the nadir, < *nazara,* to correspond, to be opposite.] That point on the imaginary celestial sphere directly opposite to the zenith and directly under a given place or person. *Fig.* the lowest point; the time of greatest depression.

nag, nag, *n.* [Same as Sc. *naig,* D. *negge,* a pony; perh. akin to *neigh.*] A small horse, or in informal language, any horse; an inferior race horse; an aged, worthless horse.

nag, nag, *v.i.*—*nagged, nagging.* [Norse and Sw. *nagga,* to gnaw, irritate, scold = G. *nagen,* to gnaw.] To scold; to find fault constantly; to be the cause of pain or discomfort; as, a headache that *nags.*—*v.t.* To

harass; to discomfort, as a bad conscience.—*n.* The act of nagging.—**nag·ger,** *n.*—**nag·ging,** *a.*—**nag·ging·ly,** *adv.*

na·ga·na, na·gä'na, *n.* [Native word.] A disease caused by flies, primarily of horses in tropical Africa, due to a microscopic parasite introduced by the bite of the tsetse fly.

Na·hua·tl, nä'wät·l, *n.* pl. **Na·hua·tl, Na·hua·tls.** People of early Indian origin of the southern part of Mexico and Central America; the Uto-Aztecan language of these people.—*a.* Of or pertaining to these people, their language, or living area.—**Na·hua·tlan,** nä'wät·lan, *n., a.*

nai·ad, nā'ad, nä'ad, nī'ad, nī'ad, *n.* pl. **nai·ads, nai·a·des,** nā'a·dēz", nī'a·dēz". [Gr. *naias, naiados,* a naiad, < *naō,* to flow.] *Mythol.* a water nymph; a female deity that presides over rivers and springs. A female swimmer; *bot.* any of the aquatic plants of the genus *Naias; entom.* the aquatic stage in the life of some insects.

na·ïf, na·if, nä·ēf', *a.* [Fr.] Naïve.

nail, nāl, *n.* [O.E. *nægel* = D. and G. *nagel* = Icel. *nagl,* nail.] A slender piece of metal, usu. with one end pointed and the other enlarged, for driving into or through wood or other materials to hold separate pieces together. *Biol.* a thin, horny plate, consisting of modified epidermis, growing on the upper side of the end of a finger or toe; something resembling it, as the horny part at the end of the bill of a duck. A measure of length for cloth, equal to two and one-quarter inches.—**hit the nail on the head,** do or express something precisely.

nail, nāl, *v.t.* [O.E. *næglian.*] To fix or fasten with a nail or nails; to enclose within something by driving nails in, usu. followed by *up. Fig.* to make fast or keep firmly in one place or position, as: Surprise *nailed* him to the spot. To settle decisively, as a bargain, usu. followed by *down. Colloq.* to arrest or seize; to catch in some difficulty or lie; to detect and expose, as a lie. *Slang,* to hit; as, to *nail* him with a left hook.—**nail·er,** *n.*

nail file, *n.* A small file used for shaping the fingernails.

nail·head, nāl'hed", *n.* The head or enlarged end of a nail; an ornament resembling the head of a nail, as on a dress, a belt, or the like; a small projection in architectural work.—**nail·head·ed,** *a.*

nail set, *n.* A steel punch used to drive a nailhead below or level with the surface of wood or the like. Also **nail·set.**

nain·sook, nān'suk, nan'suk, *n.* [Hind.] A kind of lightweight muslin, plain or striped, originally made in India.

na·ïve, na·ive, nä·ēv', *a.* [Fr. *naïf,* fem. *naïve,* < L. *nativus,* native; latterly also rustic, simple.] Having or displaying a simple or trusting nature; lacking experience; lacking careful judgment or analysis; unsophisticated; ingenuous; credulous.—**na·ïve·ly,** *adv.*—**na·ïve·ness,** *n.*—**na·ïve·té, na·ïve·ty,** nä·ēv·tā', nä·ēv'tē, *n.*

na·ked, nā'kid, *a.* [O.E. *nacod* = D. *naakt* = G. *nackt* = Icel. *nökvidhr* = Goth. *naqaths,* naked; all being orig. pp. and akin to L. *nudus,* nude.] Bare of clothing or covering; nude; destitute of adequate or sufficient clothing; bare of any covering, overlying matter, vegetation, or foliage; as, *naked* fields; bare, stripped, or destitute of something specified; as, *naked* trees without leaves; without a sheath or covering, as a sword; without armor or weapons; defenseless or unprotected; as, *naked* to attack; exposed to view or plainly revealed; as, *naked* emotions; without carpets, hangings, or furnishings, as rooms or walls; undisguised, unadorned, or plain; as, facts or *naked* truth; plain-spoken or blunt; not accompanied or supplemented by anything else; bare or mere; as, a *naked* outline of facts; unassisted by an eyeglass, microscope, telescope, or other instrument; as, visible with the *naked* eye. *Bot.* of seeds, not enclosed in an ovary; of flowers, without a calyx or corolla; of stalks or branches, without leaves; without hairs or pubescence. *Law*, unsupported, as by authority or consideration; as, a *naked* promise.—**na·ked·ly,** *adv.*—**na·ked·ness,** *n.* The state of being naked; nudity; bareness; plainness.

nam·a·ble, name·a·ble, nā′ma·bl, *a.* Capable of being named; deserving mention.

nam·ay·cush, nam′i·kush′, nam′ā·kush″, *n.* A large spotted trout, *Cristivomer namaycush*, of N. American lakes. Also **Mack·i·naw trout, Great Lakes trout,** lake trout.

nam·by-pam·by, nam′bē·pam′bē, *a.* [Contemptuously formed from the name of *Ambrose* Phillips, a rather weak poet of Addison's time.] Affectedly timid; weakly sentimental; insipid; vapid.—*n.* A person lacking in strength of character.—**nam·by·pam·bi·ness,** *n.*

name, nām, *n.* [O.E. *nama*, Goth. *namo*, Icel. *nafn*, Dan. *navn* (for *namn*), Sw. *namn*, all cogn. with L. *nomen*, for *gnomen* (whence E. *noun*), Skt. *nâman*, for *jnâman* or *gnâman*, a name; < same root as *know*.] That by which a person or thing is called or designated, in distinction from other persons or things; title or appellation; reputation or character; as, one's good or bad *name*; renown or fame; as, to make a *name* in politics; the mere word by which anything is called, as distinguished from *reality*; persons having a certain name; a family; (*cap.*) the sacred title or name of the divinity.—**Chris·tian** or **giv·en name,** a personal name preceding the family name, and usually bestowed at baptism, as distinguished from a *surname*. —**in the name of,** on behalf of.

name, nām, *v.t.*—*named, naming.* To give a name to; to mention by name; to nominate; to designate for any purpose by name; to identify by giving the name of; to specify; to speak of or mention as.—**name for** or **af·ter,** to give the same name as.—**nam·er,** *n.*

name, nām, *a.* Famous; known; as, a *name* brand; giving its title or name to, as an art collection.

name day, *n.* That day which is the feast day of the saint after whom one is named.

name-drop, nām′drop″, *v.i.*—*name-dropped, name-dropping.* To refer to prominent persons in a familiar manner in order to impress listeners. — **name-drop·per,** *n.* — **name-drop·ping,** *n.*

name·less, nām′lis, *a.* Without a name; anonymous; not known to fame; obscure; without family or legal name; that cannot or ought not to be named.—**name·less·ly,** *adv.*—**name·less·ness,** *n.*

name·ly, nām′lē, *adv.* To mention by name; that is to say.

name·plate, nām′plāt″, *n.* A plaque bearing the title or name of a company or person; *journ.* the title or name of a publication displayed on the cover or front page.

name·sake, nām′sāk″, *n.* An individual with the same name as another, esp. one named for someone in particular.

na·nism, nā′niz·um, nan′iz·um, *n.* [Fr. *nanisme*, < L. *nanus*, < Gr. *nanos*, a dwarf.] Abnormally small size or stature; dwarfism.

nan·keen, nan·kēn′, *n.* A cloth orig. made at Nanking, China, of natural, yellowish-buff cotton; an imitation cotton cloth dyed that color; a yellowish-buff color; *pl.* clothes made from this material; (*cap.*) Chinese porcelain with a design in blue on white. Also **nan·kin,** nan′kin.

nan·ny, nan′ē, *n.* pl. **nan·nies.** *Brit.* a child's governess or nursemaid. *Slang*, a female goat; also *nanny goat.*

nan·ny goat, *n.* A female goat.

na·no·sec·ond, nā′no·sek″ond, nan′o·-sek″ond, *n.* One billionth of a second.

nap, nap, *v.i.*—*napped, napping.* [O.E. *hnappian, hnaeppian,* to take a nap, to doze.] To have a short sleep; to drowse; to be caught unprepared.—*v.t.* To sleep through, as a morning.—*n.* A short sleep.—**nap·per,** nap′ér, *n.*

nap, nap, *n.* [O.E. *hnoppa*, the nap of cloth = D. *nop, noppe*, Dan. *noppe*, L.G. *nobbe, nap*; allied to *knob* or *knop*, from the little tufts on coarse cloth.] The woolly substance on the surface of cloth; the pile, as of a rug; a downy substance, as on some plants. —*v.t.*—*napped, napping.* To raise or put a nap on.—**nap·less,** *a.*—**napped,** *a.*—**nap·per,** nap′ér, *n.* A person who or a machine which raises nap on fabric or leather.

na·palm, nā′päm, *n. Milit.* a highly flammable jellylike substance used with gasoline to make incendiary bombs, flame-throwers, and the like.

nape, nāp, nap, *n.* [Same as O.E. *cnaep*, a top.] The back part of the neck.

na·per·y, nā′pe·rē, *n.* [Fr. *napperie*, < *nappe*, a towel, < L. *mappa*, a towel, whence also *map*.] A collective term for linen cloths used for domestic purposes, esp. for the dining table.

naph·tha, naf′tha, nap′tha, *n.* [L., < Gr. *naphtha*.] A colorless, volatile liquid, a petroleum distillate, a product intermediate between gasoline and benzine, used as a solvent or fuel; any of various similar liquids distilled from other products.

naph·tha·lene, naf′tha·lēn″, nap′tha·lēn″, *n. Chem.* a white, odorous, crystalline hydrocarbon, $C_{10}H_8$, usu. prepared from coal tar and used in making dyes and moth balls. Also **naph·tha·line, naph·tha·lin.—naph·tha·len·ic,** naf″tha·len′ik, nap″tha·len′ik, *a.*

naph·thene, naf′thēn, nap′thēn, *n. Chem.* any of several saturated ring hydrocarbons, CnH_2n, that occur in some petroleums.— **naph·the·nic,** naf·thē′nik, naf·then′ik, nap·thē′nik, nap·then′ik, *a.*

naph·thol, naf′thōl, naf′thal, naf′thol, nap′thōl, nap′thal, nap′thol, *n. Chem.* either of two isomers, $C_{10}H_7OH$, which are derivatives of naphthalene and have a white or yellow color: used in the manufacture of dyes and found naturally in coal tar; any of several hydroxy derivatives of naphthalene. Also **naph·tol.**

Na·pier·i·an log·a·rithm, na·pēr′ē·an lạ′ga·riTH″um, *n. Math.* a natural logarithm.

na·pi·form, nā′pi·fạrm″, *a.* [L. *napus*, a turnip, and *forma*, form.] Having the shape of a turnip; as, a napiform root.

nap·kin, nap′kin, *n.* [M.E. *napekyn*, dim. < O.Fr. *nape* (Fr. *nappe*), tablecloth, cloth, < L. *mappa*, napkin, cloth: cf. *map*.] A square piece of linen, cotton, or paper used at meals to wipe the lips and hands, and to protect the clothes; *Brit.* a square or oblong linen or cotton cloth, as a diaper. A sanitary napkin.—**nap·kin ring,** a ring, often of metal, wood, or plastic, for holding a table napkin, folded and rolled up when not in use.

na·po·le·on, na·pō′lē·an, na·pōl′yan, *n.* [After *Napoleon* I.] A rich oblong pastry consisting of puff paste layers and a cream or custard filling; *Fr.* a 20-franc gold coin of the Napoleonic era. *Cards*, a game in which the trump is named by the highest bidder; a bid in this game to take all tricks.

Na·po·le·on·ic, na·pō″lē·on′ik, *a.* Having the same manner as, or characteristic of Napoleon I of France, 1769–1821, or his dynasty.—**Na·po·le·on·i·cal·ly,** *adv.*

nap·py, nap′ē, *n* pl. **nap·pies.** [Origin obscure.] A small serving dish, often of glass.

na·prap·a·thy, na·prap′a·thē, *n.* [< Czech *naprava*, correction.] A system of treatment of disease based on the belief that illness is caused by disordered connective or ligamental tissues, and using massage, manipulation, and adjustment of joints and muscles as therapy.— **nap·ra·path,** nap′ra·path″, *n.* One who practices naprapathy.

nar·cis·sism, när′si·siz″um, *n.* Self-love; excessive admiration of or fascination with oneself. *Psychoanal.* an early stage in psychosexual development in which the self is the focus of erotic interest; the arrestment of psychosexual development at this stage. Also **nar·cism,** när′siz·um.—**nar·cis·sist, nar·cist,** *n.*—**nar·cis·sis·tic, nar·cis·tic,** *a.*

nar·cis·sus, när·sis′us, *n.* pl. **nar·cis·sus, nar·cis·si, nar·cis·sus·es,** när·sis′ē, när·sis′ī. [L., < Gr. *narkissos*, < *narkē*, torpor; from the narcotic properties of the plants.] *Bot.* popular, ornamental, spring-blooming, bulbous plants of the genus *Narcissus*, in the Amaryllis family, having white, yellow, or orange flowers with a cuplike crown, and including the jonquil and daffodil; (*cap.*), *class. mythol.* a handsome youth who died from hopeless love of his own reflection, and was transformed into a narcissus.

nar·co·lep·sy, när′ko·lep″sē, *n.* An illness characterized by the frequent, sudden, uncontrollable need for deep, but brief sleep. —**nar·co·lep·tic,** *a.*, *n.*

nar·co·ma·ni·a, när″ko·mā′nē·a, *n.* [N.L., < Gr. *narcē*, numbness, and E. *mania.*] *Pathol.* an abnormal craving for a narcotic drug.—**nar·co·ma·ni·ac,** när″ko·mā′nē·ak″, *n.*—**nar·co·ma·ni·a·cal,** när″kō·ma·nī′a·kal, *a.*

nar·co·sis, när·kō′sis, *n.* [N.L., < Gr. *narcōsis*, < *narcoun*, benumb, < *narcē*, numbness, torpor.] The production of stupor or insensibility by a narcotic drug; a state of drowsiness or insensibility.

nar·cot·ic, när·kot′ik, *n.* [Gr. *narkōtikos*, < *narkoō*, to render torpid, < *narkē*, torpor.] A substance which relieves pain, induces sleep, and in large doses brings on stupor, coma, and even death, as opium or morphine; an addict. Something which sooths or numbs.—*a.* Having the properties of a narcotic; inducing narcosis; relating to or induced by narcotics; relating to addicts or treatment for addiction.—**nar·cot·i·cal·ly,** *adv.*

nar·co·tize, när′ko·tīz″, *v.t.*—*narcotized, narcotizing.* To bring under the influence of a narcotic; to numb the awareness of.—*v.i.* To perform, as a narcotic, as: The remedy *narcotized* rather than cured.—**nar·co·ti·za·tion,** *n.*

nard, närd, *n.* [L. *nardus*, < Gr. *nardos*, Heb. and Pers. *nard*, nard.] A medicinal, aromatic ointment obtained from the rhizomes of an East Asian plant, *Nardostachys jatamansi*, used by the ancients and of limited use today. Also *spikenard.*

nar·ghi·le, nar·gi·leh, nar·gi·le, när′gi·lē, när′gi·lä″, *n.* [Pers. and Turk name.] A kind of tobacco pipe or smoking apparatus, used by Orientals, in which the smoke passes through water; a hookah.

nar·is, nâr′is, *n.* pl. **nar·es,** nâr′ēz. [L.] *Anat.* The nostril; the nasal passage or opening.

nark, närk, *n. Brit. slang.* An informer; a stool pigeon.—*v.i. Brit. slang*, to spy, esp. on behalf of the police.

nar·rate, nar′rāt, na·rāt′, *v.t.*—*narrated, narrating.* [L. *narro, narratum*, to relate, for *gnarro*, from root *gna*, seen also in E. *know*; cf. *gnarus*, knowing.] To tell; to relate, as a story.—*v.i.* To recount particulars of a happening.—**nar·ra·tor,** *n.*

nar·ra·tion, na·rā′shan, *n.* The act of narrating; that which is related; a narrative; a chronological recounting of events; an explanation accompanying a visual presentation; *rhet.* a discourse which recites the time, manner, or consequences of an action.—**nar·ra·tion·al,** *a.*

nar·ra·tive, när′a·tiv, *n.* That which is narrated; the technique or act of narration in speech or writing.—*a.* Pertaining to narration; consisting of a narrative.—**nar·ra·-tive·ly,** *adv.*

nar·row, när′ō, *a.* [O.E. *nearu, naru,* narrow.] Of little breadth or width; limited in extent or space; limited in range or scope; limited in amount; small; meager; straitened, as circumstances; barely sufficient or adequate; lacking breadth of view or sympathy; illiberal; close, careful, or minute, as a scrutiny, search, or inquiry; nearly disastrous; as, a *narrow* escape. *Brit. dial.* parsimonious; stingy. *Phon.* uttered with a slight opening of the vocal organs.—*n.* A narrow part, place, or thing; a narrow part of a valley, passage, or road; *pl.* a narrow part of a strait, river, or sound.—*v.t.* To make narrower; limit or restrict; make illiberal.—*v.i.* To become narrower; decrease in breadth.—**the Nar·-rows,** a strait at the entrance of New York harbor.—**nar·row·ly,** *adv.*—**nar·row·-ness,** *n.*

nar·row-mind·ed, när′ō-mīn′did, *a.* Having or showing an illiberal mind, as persons, opinions, utterances; devoid of breadth of view or sympathy; intolerant.—**nar·row-mind·ed·ly,** *adv.*—**nar·row-mind·ed·-ness,** *n.*

nar·thex, när′theks, *n.* [Gr.] *Arch.* a vestibule that lies between the principal entrance of a church and the nave.

nar·whal, när′wal, *n.* [Sw. and Dan. *narhwal* = Icel. *nāhvalr*.] An arctic whale, *Monodon monoceros,* in the mammalian order *Cetacea,* the male having a long, spirally twisted tusk that originates from a tooth in the upper jaw. Also **nar·wal, nar·whale,** när′hwāl, när′wāl″.

nar·y, när′ē, *a.* [Corruption of *ne'er a,* never a.] *Dial.* Never a; not a; not.

na·sal, nā′zal, *a.* [N.L. *nasalis,* < L. *nasus,* nose.] Of or pertaining to the nose. *Phon.* produced by expelling the air column entirely through the nose, as in *m, n,* and *ng,* or partially, as in the French nasal vowels; accompanied by resonance which is produced in the nose; as, a *nasal* voice.—*n. Phon.* a nasal speech sound, as *m, n,* or *ng; anat.* a nasal bone.—**na·sal·i·ty, na·sal·ism,** nā·-zal′i·tē, *n.*—**na·sal·ly,** *adv.*

na·sal·ize, nā′za·līz″, *v.t.*—*nasalized, nasalizing. Phon.* to pronounce, as speech sounds, with nasality.—*v.i. Phon.* to speak with an erroneous nasal overlay on speech sounds which are usu. voiced only.—**na·sal·i·za·tion,** nā″za·li·zā′shun, *n.*

nas·cent, nas′ent, nā′sent, *a.* [L. *nascens, nascentis,* ppr. of *nascor,* to be born.] Beginning to exist or to grow; coming into being; arising; *chem.* having to do with the nascent state.—**nas·cence, nas·cen·cy,** *n.*

nas·tic, nas′tik, *a. Bot.* of, relating to, or showing the direction of a plant's growth as a result of changing cellular pressure.

na·stur·tium, na·stur′shim, na·stur′shim, *n.* [L., kind of cress, < *nasus,* nose, and *torquere,* twist (from its pungency).] Pungent garden herbs of the genus *Tropaeolum,* in the family *Tropaeolaceae,* having peltate-shaped leaves, spurred, funnelform flowers of yellow, orange, and red, and climbing by means of coiled petioles; the generic name of a genus of plants in the mustard family, which includes the watercress.

nas·ty, nas′tē, *a.*—*nastier, nastiest.* [O.E. *nasky,* connected with L.G. *nask,* Sw. *naskug, nasket,* unclean, dirty.] Filthy; dirty; indecent; obscene; disgusting to taste or smell; disagreeable; troublesome; mean; as, a *nasty* disposition; serious, as an accident.—**nas·ti·ly,** *adv.*

na·tal, nāt′al, *a.* [L. *natalis,* < *natus,* birth, < *nasci,* be born.] Of or pertaining to one's birth; as, one's *natal* day; presiding over or affecting one at birth; as, *natal* stars or influences; of places, native.—**na·tal·i·ty,** nā·tal′i·tē, *n. pl.* **na·tal·i·ties.** Birth rate.

na·tant, nāt′ant, *a.* [L. *natans* (*natant-*), ppr. of *natare,* swim, float, freq. of *nare,* swim.] Swimming; floating; *bot.* floating on water, as a leaf of an aquatic plant.—**na·ta·tion,** nā·tā′shan, na·tā′shan, *n.* [L. *natatio(n-),* < *natare.*] The act or art of swimming.—**na·ta·tor,** *n.* A swimmer.

na·ta·to·ri·al, nā″ta·tōr′ē·al, nat″a·tōr′-ē·al, *a.* Pertaining to, adapted for, or characterized by swimming; as, *natatorial* powers or organs in *natatorial* birds. Also **na·ta·to·ry,** na′ta·tōr″ē.

na·ta·to·ri·um, nā″ta·tōr′ē·um, nat″a·-tōr′ē·um, *n. pl.* **na·ta·to·ri·ums, na·ta·-to·ri·a.** A swimming pool, particularly one indoors.

na·tes, nā′tēz, *n. pl.* The buttocks.

na·tion, nā′shan, *n.* [L. *natio,* < *natus,* born, *nascor,* to be born.] A people inhabiting a certain territory and united by common political institutions; the country or territory itself; an aggregation of persons speaking the same or a cognate language and usu. sharing a common ethnic origin; an Indian tribe belonging to a confederation of tribes.—**na·tion·hood,** *n.*—**na·tion·less,** *a.*

na·tion·al, nash′a·nal, *a.* [Fr. *national,* < *nation.*] Of, pertaining to, or characteristic of a nation or people; as, a *national* language or literature; of, pertaining to, or maintained by a nation as an organized whole or independent political unit; as, *national* politics; involving an entire nation, as a crisis; devoted to one's own nation, interests, and welfare; patriotic.—*n.* In diplomatic use, a citizen or subject of a particular nation.—**na·tion·al·ly,** *adv.*

na·tion·al bank, *n.* A bank associated with the finances of a nation; a bank chartered by the federal government and required to be a member of the Federal Reserve System and the Federal Deposit Insurance Corporation.

Na·tion·al Guard, *n.* The militia organized and maintained in part by a state, paid by the federal government, and available to serve the state or to be made a part of the U.S. army.

na·tion·al in·come, *n. Econ.* the aggregate earnings from all factors in the production of goods and services in a nation during a specified period of time, usu. one year, including employee compensations, income from rentals and interest, and business profits after taxes. See *gross national product, net national product.*

na·tion·al·ism, nash′a·na·liz″um, *n.* National spirit or aspirations; devotion to the interests of one's own nation; desire for national advancement or independence.

na·tion·al·ist, nash′a·na·list, *n.* One inspired with nationalism; an advocate of national independence.—*a.* Relating to or advocating nationalism.—**na·tion·al·is·-tic,** nash″an·al·is′tik, *a.*—**na·tion·al·is·-ti·cal·ly,** *adv.*

na·tion·al·i·ty, nash″a·nal′i·tē, *n. pl.* **na·tion·al·i·ties.** National quality or character; the fact or relation of belonging to a particular nation or country, or origin with respect to a nation; devotion to one's own nation; nationalism; existence as a distinct nation; national integrity or independence; a nation or people; as, the various *nationalities* of the Balkan Peninsula.

na·tion·al·ize, nash′a·na·līz″, *v.t.*—*nationalized, nationalizing.* To make national, esp. to bring under the control or ownership of a nation, as industries or land; to admit or establish as part of a nation, as persons; naturalize; to make into a nation,

as a colony.—*v.i.* To become naturalized.—**na·tion·al·i·za·tion,** nash″a·nal·a·zā′-shun, *n.*—**na·tion·al·iz·er,** *n.*

na·tion·al park, *n.* An area of land noted for its scenic beauty, historical interest, or scientific importance, and set aside and maintained by the national government for public study or recreational purposes.

na·tion·al prod·uct, *n.* See *gross national product, net national product.*

Na·tion·al So·cial·ism, *n.* The totalitarian policies and practices of the Nazi party under Adolph Hitler, dictator of Germany from 1933 to 1945.—**Na·tion·al So·cial·-ist,** *n., a.*

na·tion·wide, nā′shan·wīd″, *a.* Extending throughout the nation.

na·tive, nā′tiv, *a.* [L. *nativus,* born, innate, natural, native, < *nascor, natus,* to be born.] Pertaining to the place or circumstances of one's birth; being the scene of one's origin; conferred by birth; belonging to one's nature or constitution; simple, artless; not artificial or acquired; indigenous to a particular region; occurring in nature pure or unmixed with other substances, as iron or silver when found almost pure.—*n.* One born in a place or country, and not a foreigner or immigrant; something indigenous to a region.—**na·tive·ly,** *adv.* By birth; naturally.—**na·tive·ness,** *n.*

na·tiv·ism, nā′ti·viz″um, *n.* The policy of protecting the interests of native inhabitants against those of immigrants; the policy or practice of favoring natives above naturalized citizens, as in elections or in appointments to political office. *Philos.* the doctrine of innate ideas.—**na·tiv·ist,** *n.*—**na·tiv·is·tic,** na″ti·vis′tik, *a.*

na·tiv·i·ty, na·tiv′i·tē, nā·tiv′i·tē, *n. pl.* **na·tiv·i·ties.** [O.Fr. *nativite* (Fr. *nativité*), < L.L. *nativitas.*] Birth, esp. birth with reference to place or attendant circumstances; *astrol.* a horoscope established when one is born. (*Cap.*) the birth of Christ; the church festival, Christmas, commemorating the birth of Christ; a representation of the birth of Christ, as in art.

nat·ro·lite, na′tro·līt″, nā′tro·līt″, *n.* A mineral, a hydrous silicate of sodium and aluminum, occurring sometimes in white, often needle-shaped crystals.

na·tron, nā′tron, *n.* [Fr. and Sp. *natron,* < Ar. *natrun,* native carbonate of soda: same word as *niter.*] Native carbonate of soda, $Na_2CO_3.10H_2O$, found in solution in some lakes and mineral springs.

nat·ter, nat′ér, *v.i. Brit.* to gripe or complain. *Brit., Aust.* to chatter. *Canadian,* to gossip.—*n. Brit.* a chat. *Canadian,* gossip.

nat·ty, nat′ē, *a.*—*nattier, nattiest.* [Akin *neat.*] Neatly dressed; of tidy appearance; spruce.—**nat·ti·ly,** *adv.*—**nat·ti·ness,** *n.*

nat·u·ral, nach′ér·al, nach′ral, *a.* [L. *naturalis.*] Pertaining to nature; produced by nature, not artificial; in conformity with the laws of nature; happening in the ordinary course of things; consistent with nature, normal; connected with the existing physical system of things, not spiritual; pertaining to the essence of a thing; without affectation or artificiality; related by birth, not by adoption; born out of wedlock; in a state of nature; unregenerated; based on innate beliefs or convictions. *Mus.* neither sharped nor flatted, as a note; without accidentals, as in the scale of C; without valves, as a horn or trumpet.—*n. Colloq.* a person with inherent ability in a certain area. *Mus.* the symbol or sign which, when assigned to a note, cancels the effect of its previous alteration; a note affected by a natural sign.—**nat·u·ral·ly,** *adv.*—**nat·u·-ral·ness,** *n.*

nat·u·ral child·birth, *n.* Childbirth for which the mother has been physically and psychologically prepared by prenatal exercise and education resulting in reduced pain and tension so that drugs are unnecessary.

nat·u·ral gas, *n.* A combustible gas formed naturally in the earth, esp. in petroleum regions, and consisting typically of methane with varying amounts of other gases: used as a fuel and as a raw material for making acetylene, carbon black, and other products.

nat·u·ral his·to·ry, *n.* The study or description of nature in its widest sense, esp. from a popular or amateur approach; the biological and earth sciences collectively; zoology and botany; a treatise on some subject of natural science.

nat·u·ral·ism, nach'ĕr·a·liz″um,nach′ra·-liz″um, *n.* Action arising from or based on natural instincts and desires alone; adherence or attachment to what is natural. *Art, liter.* close adherence to nature or reality; realism, specif. the view of the 19th and 20th century realistic writers, including French author, Emile Zola, who aimed to present a photographic picture of modern life, objective, detached, and detailed, emphasizing the importance of economic and social factors over free will. *Philos.* the view of the world which takes account only of natural elements and forces, or scientific laws, excluding the supernatural, spiritual or teleological arguments; *theol.* the doctrine that all religious truth is derived from a study of nature, and not from revelation.

nat·u·ral·ist, nach'ĕr·a·list, nach′ra·list, *n.* One versed in natural history or natural science; one who makes a study of animals and plants; an adherent of naturalism.—**nat·u·ral·is·tic,** nach″ĕr·a·lis′tik, nach″ra·lis′tik, *a.* Pertaining to naturalists or natural history; pertaining to naturalism, esp. in art and literature; pertaining to or in accordance with nature.—**nat·u·ral·is·ti·cal·ly,** *adv.*

nat·u·ral·ize, *Brit.* **nat·u·ral·ise,** nach′ĕr·a·līz″, nach′ra·līz″, *v.t.*—*naturalized, naturalizing.* To confer the rights and privileges of a native citizen upon; to accustom, as flora or fauna, to a climate or a place; to adopt as native or vernacular; as, to *naturalize* foreign words; to regard as resulting from a natural instead of supernatural agency or cause; to cause to conform to nature.—*v.i.* To adapt; to study the natural sciences.—**nat·u·ral·i·za·tion,** *n.*

nat·u·ral law, *n.* A rule of conduct founded on the natural ethics of man, religion, or nature, and considered to be morally binding on society in the absence of formal law.

nat·u·ral log·a·rithm, *n. Math.* logarithms using *e*, 2.718+, as a base. Also *Napierian logarithm.*

nat·u·ral num·ber, *n. Math.* any positive whole number.

nat·u·ral phi·los·o·phy, *n.* Natural science; physical science.

nat·u·ral re·source, *n. Usu. pl.* The collective developed or potential physical and biological wealth of any country, such as oil, minerals, forests, and water; native ability.

nat·u·ral sci·ence, *n.* Any science, as biology, geology, or chemistry, dealing with objects and phenomena of nature.

nat·u·ral se·lec·tion, *n. Biol.* the theory that nature tends to maintain and perpetuate those species having particular characteristics of genetic origin that best fit them for survival in their environment.

nat·u·ral the·ol·o·gy, *n.* Any system of religion that is developed by a study of the natural world and the use of reason, without revelation.

na·ture, nā′chĕr, *n.* [O.Fr. Fr. *nature,* < L. *natura,* birth, natural constitution or character, nature < *nasci,* be born.] The particular combination of qualities be-

longing to a person or thing by birth or constitution; the instincts or inherent tendencies which determine personal conduct; native or inherent character or disposition; acquired character or disposition, or the person possessing it, as: There goes a stubborn *nature.* Kind or sort; as, a story of that *nature;* the vital powers; as, food sufficient to sustain *nature;* the universe with all its phenomena. (*Sometimes cap.*) the sum total of the forces at work throughout the universe, considered collectively. The material world, esp. as surrounding man and existing independently of his activities; reality, as distinguished from any effect of art; as, true to *nature;* a primitive, wild, or uncultivated condition; a natural, simple state; *theol.* the moral state as unaffected by grace.—**by na·ture,** innately.

na·tur·op·a·thy, nā″cha·rop′a·thē, nach″-a·rop′a·thē, *n.* A method of treating illness or disease without drugs or surgery, using proper foods, heat, exercise, and massage to aid natural healing.—**na·tur·o·path,** nā′-chĕr·o·path″, nach′ĕr·o·path″, *n.*—**na·tur·o·path·ic,** *a.*

naught, nạt, *n.* [O.E. *náht, nóht, náwiht,* lit. 'no whit,' not a whit. *Naught* is the same and *not* is an abbreviated form.] Nothing; nought. *Arith.* zero, cipher.—*a., adv.*

naugh·ty, nạ′tē, *a.*—*naughtier, naughtiest.* Bad; mischievous, or ill-behaved; as, a *naughty* child; not proper; obscene; as, a *naughty* magazine, a *naughty* fellow.—**naugh·ti·ly,** *adv.*—**naugh·ti·ness,** *n.*

nau·se·a, nạ′zē·a, nạ′zha, nạ′sē·a, nạ′sha, *n.* [L. < Gr. *nausia,* < *naus,* a ship.] Stomach sickness or upset, often with an inclination to vomit; loathing; disgust.

nau·se·ate, nạ′zē·āt″, nạ′zhē·āt″, nạ′sē·āt″, nạ′shē·āt″, *v.i.*—*nauseated, nauseating.* [L. *nauseo.*] To feel nausea or disgust; to be inclined to vomit.—*v.t.* To sicken; to affect with disgust.—**nau·se·at·ing,** *a.*—**nau·se·at·ing·ly,** *adv.*

nau·seous, nạ′shus, nạ′zē·us, *a.* Loathsome or disgusting; causing a feeling of nausea; *colloq.* feeling ill with nausea.—**nau·seous·ly,** *adv.*—**nau·seous·ness,** *n.*

nautch, nạch, *n.* [Hind. *nāch.*] In India, an exhibition of dancing by professional dancing girls.

nau·ti·cal, nạ′ti·kal, *a.* [L. *nauticus,* < *nauta,* a seaman, for *navita,* < *navis,* a ship.] Pertaining to seamanship or navigation.—**nau·ti·cal·ly,** *adv.*

nau·ti·cal mile, *n.* See *mile.*

nau·ti·lus, nạt′i·lus, *n.* pl. **nau·ti·lus·es, nau·ti·li.** [Gr. *nautilos,* a sailor, a nautilus, < *naus,* a ship.] Any of a genus, *Nautilus,* of the cephalopods with a pearly chambered spiral shell; also **cham·bered nau·ti·lus, pear·ly nau·ti·lus.** The argonaut; also *paper nautilus.* (*Cap.*) the first submarine powered by nuclear energy and commissioned for the U.S. Navy.

Nav·a·ho, Nav·a·jo, nav′a·hō″, nä′va·hō″, *n.* pl. **Nav·a·hos, Nav·a·hoes, Nav·a·jos, Nav·a·joes.** A tribe or member of the tribe of Indians living, for the most part, on reservations in Arizona, New Mexico, and Utah and now comprising the largest group of Indian peoples of the U.S.; the Navaho language,an Athapaskan dialect.—*a.*

na·val, nā′val,*a.* [L. *navalis,* < *navis,* a ship, whence also *nautical, navigate, navy;* cogn. Gr. *naus,* Skt. *naus;* from a root *nu* for *snu,* meaning to float or flow.] Consisting of ships or of forces fighting in ships; pertaining to a navy or to ships of war; maritime.

nave, nāv, *n.* [Lit. 'ship,' < O.Fr. *nave,* Mod.Fr. *nef,* It. *nave,* < L. *navis,* a ship.] The middle part, lengthwise, of a church, often including a clerestory.

nave, nāv, *n.* [O.E. *nafu, nafa* = D. *nave, naaf,* Dan. *nav,* Icel. *nöf,* G. *nabe,* a nave,

cogn., Skt. *nâbhi,* a nave, a navel. *Navel* is a dim. from this, and *auger* is partly derived from it.] The thick piece in the center of a wheel into which the spokes and axle are inserted; the hub.

na·vel, nā′vel,*n.* [O.E. *nafela* = D. *navel,* = G. *nabel* = Icel. *nafli,* navel; akin to L. *umbilicus,* Gr. *omphalos,* navel, Skt. *nâbhi,* nave, navel.] A scar, usu. a pit or depression, in the middle of the surface of the abdomen at the point of detachment of the umbilical cord; the umbilicus; any similar depression, as in a navel orange; *fig.* the central point or middle of anything or place.

na·vel or·ange, *n.* A variety of orange having at the apex a navellike formation containing a small secondary fruit.

na·vic·u·lar, na·vik′ū·lĕr, *a.* [L. *navicula,* a little ship, < *navis,* a ship.] Shaped like a boat; as, the *navicular* bone of the wrist or ankle.—*n.* The bone of the wrist or ankle so named for its boat shape.

nav·i·ga·ble, nav′i·ga·bl, *a.* Capable of being navigated; affording passage to ships. —**nav·i·ga·bil·i·ty, nav·i·ga·ble·ness,** *n.* —**nav·i·ga·bly,** *adv.*

nav·i·gate, nav′i·gāt″, *v.i.*—*navigated, navigating.* [L. *navigo, navigatum,* < *navis,* a ship, *ago,* to do.] To travel on water in ships or boats; to guide a ship; to sail; to plan or compute the course of a vessel or vehicle.—*v.t.* To travel over in ships; to sail on; to steer or manage the progress of; to ascertain or plot the position or movements of.

nav·i·ga·tion, nav″i·gā′shan, *n.* [L. *navigatio.*] The act of navigating; the science or art of managing ships; the science of determining the location, speed, destination, and direction of airplanes and other craft.—**nav·i·ga·tion·al,** *a.*—**nav·i·ga·tion·al·ly,** *adv.*

nav·i·ga·tor, nav′i·gā″tĕr, *n.* One who navigates, or is trained in the methods of navigation; one who directs the course of a ship or airplane.

nav·vy, nav′ē, *n.* pl. **nav·vies.** [Abbr. of *navigator.*] *Brit.* A laborer employed in construction work; a machine for excavating earth.

na·vy, nā′vē, *n.* pl. **na·vies.** [O.Fr. *navie,* < L. *navis,* a ship.] All of a nation's military vessels; (*often cap.*) the institutions and equipment for the maintenance of sea defenses, such as personnel, ships, navy yards, stores, and naval academies, together with the governmental agency directing them. A dark blue color; also **na·vy blue.**

na·vy bean, *n.* A dried white bean related to the kidney bean, so called from its use by the U.S. Navy.

Na·vy Cross, *n.* A bronze medal in the shape of a cross, awarded to men of the U.S. Navy for exceptionally heroic actions in wartime.

na·vy yard, *n.* A shipyard for the outfitting, building, and repairing of naval vessels, and for the storing of supplies; dockyard.

na·wab, na·wäb′, *n.* A nabob; a viceroy or deputy in India in the old Mogul empire.

nay, nā, *adv.* [Equiv. to *ne aye* (O.E. *ne,* not), that is, not ever; < Icel. and Dan. *nei,* Sw. *nej,* no, nay; compare *nor* for *ne or,* not or; *neither,* for *ne either,* not either.] No: used to express negation or refusal; indeed: used to imply that something more is to be added to an expression; as, asking, *nay,* begging for order.—*n.* Denial; refusal; one who casts a negative vote, or the vote itself.

Naz·a·rene, naz″a·rēn′, naz′a·rēn″, *n.* An inhabitant of Nazareth; a name given to Christ and the early converts to Christianity; a member of the Church of the Nazarene, a Protestant denomination following Wesleyan doctrine.

Naz·a·rite, naz′a·rīt″, n. [Heb. nazir, separated.] A Jew of ancient times who by certain vows and acts devoted himself to the service of Jehovah; incorrectly, a Nazarene. Also **Naz·i·rite**.

Na·zi, nä′tsē, nat′sē, n. pl. **Na·zis**. [G., short for Nationalsozialist, National Socialist.] A member of the National Socialist party of Germany, which in 1933 obtained political control of the country under Adolf Hitler; (often l.c.) one believed to hold to similar beliefs.—a. Of or pertaining to the Nazis.—**na·zi·fi·ca·tion**,nä″tsi·fi·kā′shan, nat′si·fi·kā′shan, n.—**na·zi·fy**, nä′tsi·fī″, nat′si·fī″, v.t.—**Na·zism**, **Na·zi·ism**, nä′tsiz·um, nat′siz·um, nä′tsē·iz″um, nat′sē·iz″um, n.

Ne·an·der·thal, nē·an′dèr·thạl″, nē·an′dèr·tạl″, nē·an′dèr·täl″, nā·än′dèr·täl″, a. Of or resembling Neanderthal man.—n. A Neanderthal man; fig. any coarse-looking, crude, and rough-mannered person. Also **Ne·an·der·thal·er**.

Ne·an·der·thal man, n. A Paleolithic cave dweller of the Late Pleistocene epoch, Homo neanderthalensis, whose bones have been found in Europe and parts of Africa and Asia.

neap, nēp, a. [O.E. nep, neap; akin to Dan. knap, Icel. hneppr, narrow, scanty, and probably to nip.] Low, or not rising high, as the tides that occur after the first and third quarters of the moon.—n. One of the lowest tides, or the time of one: opposite to spring tide. Also **neap tide**.

Ne·a·pol·i·tan ice cream, nē″a·pol′i·tan is′ krēm″, n. A layered brick of ices and ice creams of various flavors.

near, nēr, a. [O.E. neár, compar. of neáh, nigh (nearer being thus a double compar.) = Icel. nær, nærri, Dan. nær, nearer.] Not far distant in place, time, or degree; closely connected by blood; as, a near relation; intimate or familiar; close or literal, as a translation; narrow, as an escape; short, or not circuitous; stingy or miserly; on the left of a horse or vehicle, as opposed to off; as, near foreleg.—adv. Within a short time, distance, or degree; almost; as, near six feet tall; closely; naut. close to the wind.—prep. At no great distance from; close to.—v.i., v.t. To approach; to come near.—**near·ly**, adv.—**near·ness**, n.

near·by, nēr′bī′, a. Close at hand; near; adjacent; neighboring.—adv.

Ne·arc·tic, nē·ärk′tik, nē·är′tik, a. [Gr. néos, new, and articos, arctic.] Zoogeog. belonging to or concerning the temperate and arctic regions of N. America, including Greenland.

near-point, nēr′point″, n. Ophthalm. the shortest distance at which the eye can distinctly see a small object.

near-sight·ed, nēr′sī″tid, a. Short-sighted; seeing clearly at a short distance only.—**near-sight·ed·ly**, adv.—**near-sight·ed·ness**, n.

neat, nēt, a. [Fr. net, nette, < L. nitidus, shining, < niteo, to shine.] Having everything in good order; tidy and clean; being simple and precise in speech, appearance, or form; clever or ingenious; as, a neat solution to the problem; pure or unadulterated, as liquor drunk without a chaser; net, with all deductions made; slang, great, excellent.—**neat·ly**, adv.—**neat·ness**, n.

neat, nēt, n. [O.E. neát (sing. and pl.); Sc. nowt, Icel. naut, Sw. nót, Dan. nód, cattle, an ox; < verbal stem Icel. njóta, O.E. neótan, to use, to enjoy; Goth. niutan, to take.] Animals of the bovine type, as oxen or cows: used either collectively or of one individual.

neath, nēth, nēTH, prep. Dial., poet. beneath. Also **'neath**.

neat's-foot oil, n. A light oil used as a lubricant and softener in the leather industry, made from the bones and feet of cattle. Also **ba·bul·um oil, hoof oil**.

neb·bish, neb′ish, n. [Yiddish.] Slang, a drab, timid, ineffectual person.

neb·u·la, neb′ū·la, n. pl. **neb·u·lae**, **neb·u·las**, neb′ū·lī″. [L. nebula, a cloud; allied to Gr. nephele, a cloud; G. nebel, mist.] Astron. a vast cloudlike interstellar mass, either luminous or dark, consisting of gaseous matter and small quantities of dust; a star enveloped in gaseous matter; a galaxy, esp. a galaxy beyond the Milky Way. Pathol. visual opacity; a small cloudy spot on the cornea; cloudy urine. Med. an oily medication prepared by atomization.—**neb·u·lar**, a.

neb·u·lar hy·poth·e·sis, n. A theory of cosmogenesis formulated by the French astronomer Laplace in 1796, holding that the bodies of the solar system were formed by the solidifying of gaseous matter flung into space in successive orbits by a whirling nebular mass.

neb·u·lize, neb′ū·līz″, v.t.—nebulized, nebulizing. To reduce to fine spray; atomize.—v.i. To become unclear or nebulous.—**neb·u·liz·er**, n.

neb·u·lous, neb′ū·lus, a. [L. nebulosus.] Unclear; indistinct; vague; confused; cloudy; cloudlike; of, concerning, or similar to a nebula; nebular.—**neb·u·los·i·ty**, neb″ū·los′i·tē, n.—**neb·u·lous·ly**, adv.—**neb·u·lous·ness**, n.

nec·es·sar·y, nes′i·ser″ē, a. [L. necessarius; < necesse, unavoidable, indispensable.] Such as must be; happening or existing by necessity; inevitable; acting or proceeding from compulsion or necessity; as, a necessary agent; not free; involuntary; that cannot be dispensed with; indispensable; essential; requisite; needful.—n. pl. **nec·es·sar·ies**. Something necessary, indispensable, or requisite; a requisite; New England dial. a privy or water closet.—**nec·es·sar·i·ly**, adv.—**nec·es·sar·i·ness**, n.

nec·es·sar·y con·di·tion, n. Logic, a proposition which must be valid in order that a second proposition be so.

ne·ces·si·tar·i·an·ism, ne·ses″i·târ′ē·a·niz″um, n. The doctrine of the inevitable determination of the will by antecedent causes, as opposed to freedom of the will. Also **ne·ces·sar·i·an·ism**.—**ne·ces·si·tar·i·an**, ne·ses″i·târ′ē·an, n. One who advocates or believes in this doctrine.—a. Also **nec·es·sar·i·an**.

ne·ces·si·tate, ne·ses′i·tāt″, v.t.—necessitated, necessitating. To make necessary, as: Repairs on the highway necessitated our taking a detour. To compel or force, as: The law necessitated registration of guns.—**ne·ces·si·ta·tion**, n.—**ne·ces·si·ta·tive**, a.

ne·ces·si·tous, ne·ses′i·tus, a. Indigent; destitute; involving necessity; being unavoidable or necessary, as: The theater is closed until necessitous repairs can be made. Urgent, as: Necessitous action is required before the river floods.—**ne·ces·si·tous·ly**, adv.—**ne·ces·si·tous·ness**, n.

ne·ces·si·ty, ne·ses′i·tē, n. pl. **ne·ces·si·ties**. [L. necessitas.] The state of being necessary; condition demanding that something must be; unavoidableness; indispensableness; need; irresistible compulsion; compulsion of circumstances; the absolute determination of the will by motives; that which is requisite; a necessary; extreme indigence; pinching poverty.

neck, nek, n. [O.E. hnecca = Icel. hnakki, nape of the neck, = D. nek, G. nacken, nape, neck.] The part of the body connecting the head and trunk; the part of a garment covering or extending about the neck; the length of the neck of a horse or other animal as a measure in racing; any narrow connecting or projecting part suggesting the neck of an animal; a narrow strip of land, as an isthmus or a cape; a strait or narrow body of water connecting two larger bodies of water; the slender part of a bottle or any similarly shaped object; the long, slender part of a guitar or string instrument extending from the body to the head; geol. a hardened column of lava; print. the part of a type between the face and the shoulder; arch. the lowest part of the capital of a column, immediately above the lower astragal at the head of the shaft; anat. a constricted part of a bone or organ; dentistry, the part of a tooth between the crown and the root.—v.t. To decapitate or strangle.—v.i. Slang, to fondle and kiss amorously.—**break one's neck**, slang, make a supreme effort.—**get it in the neck**, slang, be dismissed or victimized.—**neck and neck**, abreast.—**neck of the woods**, slang, region or locale.—**save one's own neck**, disentangle oneself from danger or difficulties, often at another's expense.—**win by a neck**, slang, to achieve victory by a narrow margin.—**neck·less**, a.—**neck·like**, a.

neck·er·chief, nek′ér·chif, n. [For neck kerchief.] A cloth worn round the neck by women or men.

neck·ing, nek′ing, n. Arch. a molding or group of moldings between the projecting part of a capital of a column and the shaft. Slang, amorous kissing and fondling.

neck·lace, nek′lis, n. [< neck and lace 'string.'] An ornament of precious stones, beads, or the like, worn round the neck.

neck·line, nek′līn″, n. The shape of the part of a woman's garment which outlines the neck; as, a U-shaped neckline.

neck·tie, nek′tī″, n. A band of cloth worn around the neck under the shirt collar and knotted in front; a cravat; any bow or tie which is worn beneath the chin.

ne·crol·o·gy, ne·krol′o·jē, ne·krol′o·jē, n. pl. **ne·crol·o·gies**. A death notice; a register of deaths or obituaries.—**nec·ro·log·ic**, nec·ro·log·i·cal, nek″ro·loj′i·kal, a.—**nec·ro·log·i·cal·ly**, adv.—**ne·crol·o·gist**, n.

nec·ro·man·cy, nek′ro·man″sē, n. [Gr. manteia, divination.] The art of divining or influencing future events through communication with spirits conjured from the dead; black magic; witchcraft; sorcery.—**nec·ro·man·cer**, n.—**nec·ro·man·tic**, nek″ro·man′tik, a.—**nec·ro·man·ti·cal·ly**, adv.

ne·croph·a·gous, ne·krof′a·gus, ne·krof′a·gus, a. [Gr. phagein, to eat.] Feeding on dead bodies or carrion.—**ne·croph·a·gy**, n.

ne·crop·o·lis, ne·krop′o·lis, ne·krop′o·lis, n. pl. **ne·crop·o·lis·es**, **ne·crop·o·les**, ne·krop′o·lēz. [Gr. polis, a city; the city of the dead.] A cemetery, esp. the burial place of an ancient city.

nec·rop·sy, nek′rop·sē, n. pl. **nec·rop·sies**. The examination of a body after death; a post-mortem examination, or autopsy.

ne·cro·sis, ne·krō′sis, ne·krō′sis, n. [Gr. nekrōsis, deadness.] Pathol. death of cellular material or of a section of tissue, due to irreversible injury to nuclear structure; bot. a condition of disease in plants evidenced by the decay or death of cellular tissue, chiefly in leaves and other soft parts.—**ne·crot·ic**, ne·krot′ik, ne·krot′ik, a.—**nec·ro·tize**, nek′ro·tīz, v.t.—necrotized, necrotizing. To produce necrosis, as in an organ or tissue.

nec·tar, nek′tér, n. [Gr.] Class. mythol. the drink of the Greek and Roman gods. A refreshing beverage, often a mixture of fruit juices; bot. a sweet fluid in the flower composed chiefly of sucrose, which serves to attract insects: essential to pollination of plants, and used by bees, in the making of honey.—**nec·tar·ous**, nek′tér·us, a.

nec·tar·ine, nek″ta·rēn′, nek′ta·rēn″, n. Hort. a variety of the common peach, *Prunus persica nectarina*, whose fruit at maturity is smooth like a plum.

nec·ta·ry, nek′ta·rē, n. pl. **nec·ta·ries**. Bot. a nectar-secreting gland situated at the base of a flower and appearing as a protuberance or slight depression; *entom.* a glandular tube in an aphid's body which secretes honeydew.

née, nee, nā, a. [Fr., < L. *natus*, born.] Born: a term placed before a married woman's maiden name to indicate her parentage, as Madame de Staël, *née* Necker.

need, nēd, n. [O.E. *néd* = D. *nood*, Icel. *nauth*, Dan. *nöd*, G. *noth*, Goth. *nauths*, need, necessity.] The lack or sense of the lack of something wanted or required; duty; a state that requires supply or relief; a pressing occasion for something; urgent want; necessity; want of the means of subsistence; poverty; indigence.—v.t. To have necessity or need for; to want, lack, require.—v.i. To be in need; to be obliged to, used as an auxiliary verb.—**need·i·ness**, n.—**need·y**, nē′dē, a.—*needier, neediest*.—**need·ful**, a.—**need·ful·ly**, adv.—**need·ful·ness**, n.

nee·dle, nēd′l, n. [O.E. *nǣdl* = O.H.G. *nādela*, G. *nadel*, = Icel. *nāl* = Goth. *nēthla*, needle.] A small, slender, pointed instrument, usu. of polished steel, with an eye or hole for thread, used in sewing; a slender, rodlike implement used in knitting or one hooked at the end used in crocheting; any of various objects resembling or suggesting a needle; a pointed instrument used in engraving or etching; the slender instrument or stylus in a phonograph, used in the transmission of sound vibrations; a pointer on a compass or gauge; the sharply pointed end of a syringe, as for hypodermic injections; a post, beam, or the like, of wood or metal, used in building; a sharp-pointed mass or pinnacle of rock; an obelisk or tapering, four-sided shaft of stone; *chem.*, *mineral.* a needlelike crystal; *zool.* a slender, sharp spicule; *bot.* a needle-shaped leaf, as of a conifer.—v.t.—*needled, needling*. To sew or pierce with or as with a needle. *Colloq.* to annoy, tease, or embarrass; to incite or goad to action.—v.i. To work with a needle; to form needles in crystallization.—**the nee·dle**, aggravating abuse; nagging, teasing, or badgering.—**nee·dle·like**, a.—**nee·dler**, n.—**nee·dling**, n.

nee·dle·fish, nēd′l·fish″, n. pl. **nee·dle·fish**, **nee·dle·fish·es**. A fish of the family *Belonidae*, having a long jaw and needle teeth; a pipefish of the family *Syngnathidae*.

nee·dle·point, nēd′l·point″, n. Embroidery on canvas, using simple stitches of equal length to make a pattern; a lace made on a paper pattern with a needle only and using buttonhole stitch.—a.

need·less, nēd′lis, a. Not needed or wanted; unnecessary.—**need·less·ly**, adv.—**need·less·ness**, n.

nee·dle·wom·an, nēd′l·wum″an, n. pl. **nee·dle·wom·en**. A woman who works with a needle, as in sewing or embroidery.

nee·dle·work, nēd′l·wurk″, n. Work executed with a needle; the business of one who works with a needle.—**nee·dle·work·er**, n.

need·n't, nēd′ant. Contraction of need not.

needs, nēdz, adv. [An adverbial genitive of *need*.] Of necessity; necessarily, generally with *must*.

ne'er, nâr, adv. Poet. contraction of never.

ne'er-do-well, nâr′dö·wel″, n. A good-for-nothing; a worthless person.—a. Worthless; by-passed by success. Also *Sc.*, *N. Eng.* **ne'er-do-weel**.

ne·far·i·ous, ni·fâr′ē·us, a. [L. *nefarius.* < *nefas*, impious, unlawful.] Wicked in the extreme; villainous; detestably vile.—**ne·far·i·ous·ly**, adv.—**ne·far·i·ous·ness**, n.

ne·gate, ni·gāt′, neg′āt, nē′gāt, v.t., v.i.—*negated, negating*. [L. *negatus*, pp. of *negare*, say no, deny, < *neg-*, *nec-* (for *ne*), not, and a defective verb, pres. indic. *aio*, I say.] To deny; nullify.—**ne·gat·er, ne·ga·tor**, n.

ne·ga·tion, ni·gā′shan, n. [L. *negatio(n-)*, < *negare*.] The act of denying; a denial; the absence or opposite of what is actual, positive, or affirmative; a negative thought or thing; a nonentity.—**ne·ga·tion·al, neg·a·to·ry**, neg′a·tōr″ē, a.—**ne·ga·tion·ist**, n.

neg·a·tive, neg′a·tiv, a. [L. *negativus*, < *negare*.] Expressing or containing negation or denial; as, a *negative* statement, a *negative* proposition; expressing refusal to do something; refusing consent, as to a proposal; prohibitory, as a command or order; characterized by the absence of distinguishing or marked qualities or features; as, a *negative* attitude, a *negative* character or person; lacking positive attributes. Math. denoting a quantity less than zero; involving or denoting subtraction; as, a *negative* quantity; minus. Measured or proceeding in the opposite direction to that which is considered as positive; *logic*, denying that part or all of one category of things is in another category. *Elect.* noting or pertaining to the kind of electricity developed as on resin or amber, when rubbed with flannel; designating a point in a circuit having a lower potential than some other point, the current in the external circuit flowing in a direction toward the point of lower potential. *Med.* not showing signs of the presence of a particular disease or organism; *chem.* of an element or radical, nonmetallic or acid; *photog.* showing light and shade, and right and left, reversed from the conditions in nature.—n. A negative statement, proposition, reply, term, or word; a refusal of assent; a veto; the negative form of a statement; that side of a question which denies what the opposite side affirms; a negative quality or characteristic; a negative quantity or symbol; *elect.* the negative plate or element in a voltaic cell; *photog.* a negative picture, as on a glass plate, used chiefly for printing positive pictures.—v.t.—*negatived, negativing*. To deny, as a statement or proposition; contradict; to prove the contrary of; disprove; to refuse assent or consent to; pronounce against; veto; to neutralize or counteract.—**neg·a·tive·ly**, adv.—**neg·a·tive·ness, neg·a·tiv·i·ty**, neg″a·tiv′i·tē, n.

neg·a·tiv·ism, neg′a·ti·viz″um, n. Any philosophy characterized by skepticism or the challenging of generally accepted precepts; *psychol.* an attitude or behavior marked by contrariness.—**neg·a·tiv·ist**, n.—**neg·a·tiv·is·tic**, neg″a·ti·vis′tik, a.

neg·a·tron, neg′a·tron″, n. An electron.

ne·glect, ni·glekt′, v.t. [L. *neglectus*, pp. of *neglegere, negligere*, < *neg-*, *nec-* (for *ne*), not, and *legere*, gather, pick up.] To pay insufficient attention to; disregard; to fail to perform or to omit through indifference or carelessness.—n. The act or fact of neglecting; disregard; the state of being neglected.—**ne·glect·er, ne·glec·tor**, n.—**ne·glect·ful**, a.—**ne·glect·ful·ly**, adv.—**ne·glect·ful·ness**, n.

neg·li·gee, neg″li·zhā′, neg′li·zhā″, n. [Fr. *négligé*, < *negliger*, to neglect.] A woman's dressing gown, usu. long and flowing; very informal attire, often careless or negligent. Also *Fr.* **neg·li·gée**.

neg·li·gence, neg′li·jens, n. The condition of being negligent or habitually neglectful; a negligent act or lack of proper care. *Law*, unusual or imprudent action, or lack of action, that will likely cause injury or loss to persons or property.

neg·li·gent, neg′li·jent, a. [O.Fr. *negligent* (Fr. *négligent*), < L. *negligēns* (*-ent-*), ppr. of *negligere*.] Guilty of or characterized by

neglect, as of duty; as, *negligent* officials; casual; nonchalant.—**neg·li·gent·ly**, adv.

neg·li·gi·ble, neg′li·ji·ble, a. [L. *negligere*.] So unimportant that it may be safely disregarded.—**neg·li·gi·bly**, adv.—**neg·li·gi·bil·i·ty, neg·li·gi·ble·ness**, neg″li·ji·bil′i·tē, n.

ne·go·ti·a·ble, ni·gō′shē·a·bl, ni·gō′sha·bl, a. Capable of being negotiated; of bills and securities, transferable by delivery, with or without endorsement, according to the circumstances, the title passing to the transferee.—**ne·go·ti·a·bil·i·ty**, ni·gō″shē·a·bil′i·tē, n.

ne·go·ti·ate, ni·gō′shē·āt″, v.i.—*negotiated, negotiating*. [L. *negotiatus*, pp. of *negotiari*, < *negotium*, business, < *neg-*, *nec-* (for *ne*) not, and *otium*, leisure.] To confer or bargain, one with another, in order to reach an agreement, as in business or political affairs.—v.t. Bus. to conduct or manage; as, *negotiate* a merger; to arrange for; to circulate by endorsement; transfer, sell, or assign in exchange for something of similar value. To succeed in moving through, over, or around; as, to *negotiate* a difficult place or situation.—**ne·go·ti·a·tion**, ni·gō″shē·ā′shan, n.—**ne·go·ti·ant**, ne·go·ti·a·tor, ni·gō′shē·ant, n.

Ne·gril·lo, ni·gril′ō, n. pl. **Ne·gril·lo, Ne·gril·los**. [Sp., dim. of *negro*.] A Negrito of the African division.

Ne·gri·to, ni·grē′tō, n. pl. **Ne·gri·tos, Ne·gri·toes**. [Sp., dim. of *negro*.] A member of any of certain dwarfish negroid peoples of southeastern Asia and of Africa, esp. of the Philippine Islands and the East Indies.

Ne·gro, nē′grō, n. pl. **Ne·groes**. [Sp. and Pg. *negro, black*, as *n.*, a black person, Negro, < L. *niger*, black.] A person of Negroid ancestry; a member of the black-skinned ethnic group of mankind.—a.

Ne·groid, nē′groid, a. Anthropol. pertaining to or comprising a major racial division of man principally constituted by the black-skinned peoples of Africa.—n.

ne·gro·phile, nē′grō·fīl″, n. (Often cap.) one who likes and is interested in Negroes.

ne·gro·phobe, nē′grō·fōb″, n. (Often cap.) one who fears or intensely dislikes the black race.—**ne·gro·pho·bi·a**, n.

Ne·gus, nē′gus, n. [Amharic for 'king.'] The title of the Emperor of Ethiopia.

ne·gus, nē′gus, n. [From Col. *Negus* of Queen Anne's time.] A beverage made of wine, hot water, sugar, nutmeg, and lemon.

neigh, nā, v.i. [O.E. *hnaegan*, Icel. *hneggja, gneggja*, Sw. *gnägga*, prob. imit.; compare L. *hinnio*.] To utter the cry of a horse; to whinny.—n.

neigh·bor, Brit. **neigh·bour**, nā′bėr, n. [O.E. *neahbur, neh-bur*, lit. 'a near-dweller,' < *neah*, near, and *bur, gebur*, a dweller, a boor.] One who lives near another; one in close proximity; one's fellow-man; one who is kind or helpful; mister: a term of address.—a. Being in the vicinity; adjoining; next.—v.t. To adjoin; to border on or be near to; to place in proximity to.—v.i. To live close at hand; to have a neighborly association.—**neigh·bor·ing**, Brit. **neigh·bour·ing**, a.—**neigh·bor·ly**, Brit. **neigh·bour·ly**, a.—**neigh·bor·li·ness**, Brit. **neigh·bour·li·ness**, n.

neigh·bor·hood, Brit. **neigh·bour·hood**, nā′bėr·hud″, n. Nearness; proximity; the region near or about some place or thing; the vicinity; a district or locality, often with reference to its character or inhabitants; as, a run-down or a fashionable *neighborhood*; a number of persons living near one another in a particular locality.—**in the neigh·bor·hood of**, approximately.

nei·ther, nē′THėr, nī′THėr, a. [M.E. *neither*, var. of *nauther*, < O.E. *nāhwæther*.] Not either; not the one or the other, as: *Neither* statement is true.—pron. Not the one or the other, as: *Neither* was present.—*conj.* Not either, preceding a series of two or more alternative words connected by nor; as, *neither* you nor I; nor yet.

nek·ton, nek'ton, *n.* [G., < Gr. *nektón*, neut. of *nektós*, swimming, < *néktein*, swim.] The aggregate of free-swimming organisms in the middle depths of the sea, moving independently of wave patterns and currents. See *plankton.*—**nek·ton·ic,** *a.*

nel·son, nel'son, *n. Wrestling,* a hold in which pressure is applied to the back of the opponent's head, neck, and arms.—**full nel·son,** a similar hold in which both arms of the opponent are gripped.

nem·a·thel·minth, nem"a·thel'minth, *n.* [N.L. *Nemathelminthes,* pl., < Gr. *nama-*(*namat-*), thread, and *helmins* (*helminth-*), worm.] Any of the *Nemathelminthes,* a phylum or group of worms including the nematodes, characterized by an elongated, unsegmented cylindrical body.

nem·a·to·cyst, nem'a·to·sist, ni·mat'o·-sist, *n.* [Gr. *nêma, nêmatos,* a thread, and *kystis,* a bag.] *Zool.* a thread cell or stinging apparatus of coelenterate animals, used in killing its prey and for protection.—**nem·a·to·cys·tic,** *a.*

nem·a·tode, nem'a·tōd", *a.* [N.L. *Nematoda,* pl. < Gr. *nematodeis,* threadlike, *nema(nemat-)*, thread, and *eidos,* form.] Belonging to the phylum, *Nematoda,* of thin, unsegmented, cylindrical, parasitic worms, whose hosts may be domestic plants, animals, or man.—*n.*—**nem·a·tol·o·gy,** nem"a·tol'o·jē, *n.* The branch of zoology that treats of nematodes.

Nem·bu·tal, nem'bū·tal, *n.* Sodium pentobarbital. (Trademark.)

ne·mer·te·an, ni·mur'tē·an, *n.* [N.L. *Nemertea,* pl., < Gr. *Nemertes,* name of a Nereid.] Any of the *Nemertea* or *Nemertinea,* a phylum of worms usu. living in or near the sea, and often brilliantly colored. Also **nem·er·tine, nem·er·tin·e·an, nem·er·toid.**—*a.*

nem·e·sis, nem'i·sis, *n.* pl. **nem·e·ses.** [L., < Gr. *Némesis,* < *némein,* deal out, distribute.] An agent of retribution or punishment; an invincible opponent; an insuperable obstacle; (*cap.*), *class. mythol.* the goddess of retribution or vengeance.

ne·o·ars·phen·a·mine, nē"ō·ärs·fen'a·-mēn", nē"ō·ärs·fi·nam'in, *n.* A yellow medicinal powder, $C_{13}H_{13}As_2N_2NaO_4S$, made from arsphenamine, but not as toxic.

ne·o·clas·sic, nē"ō·klas'ik, *a.* Of or pertaining to a revival of classic style, as in art or literature. Also **ne·o·clas·si·cal.**—**ne·o·clas·si·cism,** nē"ō·klas'i·siz"um, *n.*

ne·o·Dar·win·ism, nē"ō·där'wi·niz"um, *n. Biol.* Darwin's theory as developed by later students who believed natural selection is the basis for evolution and therefore rejected that part of his theory concerned with the inheritance of acquired characteristics as an evolutionary force.—**Ne·o·Dar·win·i·an,** *n.,* *a.*—**Ne·o·Dar·win·ist,** *n.*

ne·o·dym·i·um, nē"ō·dim'ē·um, *n. Chem.* a rare earth, trivalent, metallic element. Sym. Nd, at. no. 60, at. wt. 144.24. See Periodic Table of the Elements.

ne·o·im·pres·sion·ism, nē"ō·im·presh'a·niz"um, *n.* The theory and practice of a small group of late 19th century painters associated with the impressionists in virtue of their interest in portraying the ephemerality of natural phenomena with maximal truth, but much more concerned than these artists with systematic and esp. pointillism or divisionist techniques in the use of color and form.—**ne·o·im·pres·sion·ist,** *a., n.*

Ne·o·La·marck·ism, nē"ō·la·mär'kiz·um, *n.* [Gr. *neos,* new, and *Lamarck,* an eminent French naturalist.] *Biol.* Lamarckism as qualified by later students who postulated that evolution is caused by the

interaction of natural selection and acquired characteristics.

Ne·o·Lat·in, nē"ō·lat'in, *n.* New Latin, as used since c. 1500 in scientific writing and taxonomy.

ne·o·lith, nē'o·lith, *n.* [Gr. *neos,* new and *lithos,* stone.] A neolithic stone implement; a person belonging to the neolithic period.—**ne·o·lith·ic,** nē"ō·lith'ik, *a.* (*Sometimes cap.*), *anthropol.* noting or pertaining to the last part of the Stone Age, characterized by the use of highly finished or polished stone implements and by the development of basic agriculture.

ne·ol·o·gism, nē·ol'o·jiz"um, *n.* A new word or phrase; the new usage or meaning of old words; the use or introduction of new words; new doctrines, esp. the new interpretation of religious writings or doctrines.—**ne·ol·o·gist,** *n.*—**ne·ol·o·gis·tic, ne·ol·o·gis·ti·cal,** *a.*

ne·ol·o·gy, nē·ol'o·jē, *n.* pl. **ne·ol·o·gies.** Neologism.—**ne·o·log·i·cal,** nē"o·loj'i·kal, *a.*—**ne·o·log·i·cal·ly,** *adv.*

ne·o·my·cin, nē"ō·mī'sin, *n. Pharm.* an antibiotic, developed from the micro-organism *Streptomyces fradiae,* which inhibits or destroys a broad range of bacteria, used esp. in treating skin infections.

ne·on, nē'on, *n.* [Gr. *neon,* new.] *Chem.* a colorless, inert gaseous element comprising 0.0012 percent of normal air: used in the electronics industry. Sym. Ne, at. no. 10, at. wt. 20.183.—*a.* Relating to neon; pertaining to neon, as electrical advertising displays. See Periodic Table of the Elements.

ne·o·na·tal, nē"ō·nāt'al, *a.* Affecting or pertaining to a newborn infant.—**ne·o·na·tal·ly,** *adv.*—**ne·o·nate,** nē'o·nāt", *n.*

ne·o·or·tho·dox·y, nē"ō·ar'tho·dok"sē, *n.* A Protestant movement of the 20th century, reacting against liberalism and stressing Reformation theology.—**ne·o·or·tho·dox,** *a.*

ne·o·phyte, nē'o·fīt", *n.* [Gr. *neos,* new, and *phyton,* a plant, < *phyō,* I grow.] A new convert or proselyte; a novice; one newly admitted to the order of priest; a tyro; a beginner.—**ne·o·phyt·ic,** nē"o·fit'ik, *a.*—**ne·o·phyt·ism,** nē'·o·fi·tiz"um, *n.*

ne·o·plasm, nē'o·plaz"um, *n. Pathol.* Any new and abnormal growth of body tissue; a tumor.—**ne·o·plas·tic,** *a.*

ne·o·plas·ti·cism, nē"ō·plas'ti·siz"um, *n.* (*Often cap.*), *art,* the practice and theory of the de Stijl group, lead by Mondrian, emphasizing simple geometric shapes with spatial relations restricted to movement along the vertical and horizontal axes, using only primary colors together with grey, black, or white. Also **ne·o·Plas·ti·cism, Ne·o·plas·ti·cism, Ne·o·Plas·ti·cism.**—**ne·o·plas·tic,** *a.*

Ne·o·pla·to·nism, nē"ō·plāt'o·niz"um, *n.* A philosophical and religious system originated in the 3rd century, composed chiefly of elements of Platonism and Oriental mysticism, later influenced by Christianity. Also **Ne·o·Pla·to·nism.**—**Ne·o·pla·ton·ic, Ne·o·Pla·ton·ic,** nē"-ō·pla·ton'ik, *a.*—**Ne·o·pla·to·nist, Ne·o·Pla·to·nist,** *n.*

ne·o·prene, nē'o·prēn", *n. Chem.* a synthetic, oil resistant rubber formed by polymerization of chloroprene, and used in crepe soles, paints, and putties.

Ne·o·Scho·las·ti·cism, nē"ō·sko·las'ti·siz"um, *n.* The revival, extension, and modern application of the Scholasticism of Thomas Aquinas, beginning in the 19th century, advanced during the pontificate of Pope Leo XIII, and carried on in the 20th century, esp. by Catholic lay existentialist theologians.—**Ne·o·Scho·las·tic,** *a.*

ne·ot·e·ny, nē·ot'e·nē, *n. Zool.* the attainment of sexual maturity by a larva.—**ne·ot·e·nic,** *a.*

Nep·a·lese, nep"a·lēz', nep"a·lēs', *n.* pl. **Nep·a·lese.** A native of Nepal.—*a.* Characterizing or relating to the kingdom, people, or language of Nepal.

ne·pen·the, ni·pen'thē, *n.* [Gr. *nepenthes*—*nē,* not, and *penthos,* grief.] A potion believed in classical times to erase the memory of physical suffering and sorrow; anything capable of bringing forgetfulness of pain or care. Also **ne·pen·thes,** ni·pen'thēz.—**ne·pen·the·an,** *a.*

neph·e·line, nef'e·lin, *n.* [Fr. *nepheline,* < Gr. *nephele,* cloud.] A mineral, (Na_3,K)-$(AlSiO_4)_4$, a silicate of sodium, occurring in various volcanic rocks. Also **neph·e·lite.**—**neph·e·lin·ic,** *a.*

neph·e·lin·ite, nef'e·li·nit", *n.* A heavy, dark-colored rock of volcanic origin, essentially a basalt containing nepheline but no feldspar and little or no olivine.

neph·e·lom·e·ter, nef"e·lom'i·tėr, *n. Phys.* an instrument used to measure the size or quantity of particles suspended in a liquid by measuring light reflected from them.—**neph·e·lo·met·ric, neph·e·lo·met·ri·cal,** nef"e·lo·me'trik, *a.*—**neph·e·lo·met·ri·cal·ly,** *adv.*—**neph·e·lom·e·try,** *n.*

neph·ew, nef'ū, *Brit.* nev'ū, *n.* [O.Fr. Fr. *neveu,* < L. *nepos* (*nepot-*), grandson, nephew; akin to Gr. *népodes,* offspring, Skt. *napāt,* grandson, O.E. *nefa,* nephew: cf. *niece.*] A son of one's brother or sister or a son of one's sister-in-law or brother-in-law; an illegitimate son of an ecclesiastic, used euphemistically.

neph·o·gram, nef'o·gram", *n. Meteor.* a photograph of a cloud or clouds.—**neph·o·graph,** nef'o·graf", nef'o·gräf", *n.* An instrument for photographing clouds.—**ne·phol·o·gy,** ne·fol'o·jē, *n.* The branch of meteorology dealing with clouds.—**neph·o·log·i·cal,** nef"o·loj'i·kal, *a.*

neph·o·scope, nef'o·skōp", *n.* An instrument for determining the altitude of clouds and the velocity and direction of their motion.—**neph·o·scop·ic,** *a.*

ne·phrid·i·um, nē·frid'ē·um, *n.* pl. **ne·phrid·i·a,** ne·frid'ē·a. [N.L., dim. < Gr. *nephros,* kidney.] *Zool.* a primitive excretory organ in annelids, mollusks, and other invertebrates, similar to a kidney and also functioning in some cases in reproduction.—**ne·phrid·i·al,** *a.*

neph·rite, nef'rīt, *n.* [Gr. *nephrites.*] A white to dark green variety of actinolite: a type of jade.

ne·phri·tis, ne·frī'tis, *n.* [Gr. term. *-itis,* signifying inflammation.] *Pathol.* inflammation of the kidneys.—**ne·phrit·ic,** ne·frit'ik, *a. Pathol.* pertaining to the kidneys or to nephritis.

nep·o·tism, nep'o·tiz"um, *n.* [Fr. *nepotisme,* < L. *nepos,* nephew.] Favoritism shown to relatives, usu. in the form of patronage, and based upon the relationship rather than merit.—**ne·pot·ic, nep·o·tis·tic, nep·o·tis·ti·cal,** ne·pot'ik, *a.*—**nep·o·tist,** *n.*

Nep·tune, nep'tōn, nep'tūn, *n.* [L. *Neptunus.*] *Astron.* the planet which is eighth in order from the sun, has two satellites, a mean diameter in miles of 31,000, a distance from the sun in millions of miles of 2,790, and a period of sidereal revolution of 165 years. *Rom. mythol.* the god of the sea; the sea.—**Nep·tu·ni·an,** nep·tō'nē·an, nep·tū'nē·an, *a.* Pertaining to the planet Neptune, the god, or the sea; (*often l.c.*), *geol.* relating to a theory which refers the formation of all rocks and strata to the agency of water.

nep·tu·ni·um, nep·tō'nē·um, nep·tū'nē·um, *n. Chem.* a radioactive element produced artificially by neutron bombardment and decaying of plutonium. Sym. Np, at. no. 93, at. wt. 237. See Periodic Table of the Elements.

---

ch- chain, G. nacht; **th-** THen, thin; **w-** wig, hw as sound in whig; **z-** zh as in azure, zeal. *Italicized vowel* indicates schwa sound.

ne·rit·ic, ne·rit′ik, *a.* Of or pertaining to the strip of shallow water immediately adjacent to a seacoast.

ner·o·li oil, ner′o·lē oil″, nēr′o·lē, *n.* [From the name of an Italian princess, its discoverer.] The fragrant essential oil made from the flowers of the orange tree and used in the manufacture of perfume and cologne.

Ne·ro·ni·an, nēr·ō′nē·an, *a.* Of, pertaining to, or suggestive of the Roman emperor Nero, reigned A.D. 54–68, noted for his profligacy, cruelty, and tyranny. Also **Ne·ron·ic.**

ner·va·tion, nur·vā′shan, *n.* The arrangement or distribution of nerves. *Bot.* the distribution of the veins of leaves; venation.

nerve, nurv, *n.* [L. *nervus,* a sinew, strength, vigor < root *snar* (with initial *s*), seen in E. *snare.*] One of the whitish fibers which proceed from the brain and spinal cord or from the central ganglia of animals, and spread through all parts of the body, and whose function is to convey sensation and originate motion through all parts of the body; courage or steadiness, esp. under trying circumstances; strength or power. *Colloq.* impudence, arrogance; *bot.* one of the ribs or principle veins in a leaf. *Pl.* emotional stability; as, *nerves* like iron; nervousness; as, a shaking bundle of *nerves.* —*v.t.*—**nerved, nerving.** To give nerve, strength, or vigor to.—**get on one's nerves,** to make one nervous or irritable.

nerve cell, *n.* Any of the cells constituting the cellular element of nervous tissue, esp. one of the essential cells of a nerve center.

nerve cen·ter, *n.* A group of nerve cells closely connected with one another and acting together in the performance of some function.

nerve fi·ber, *n.* One of the primary threadlike fibers or processes known as axons or dendrites of a neuron or nerve cell.

nerve gas, *n. Chemical warfare,* a gas which damages or impairs the central nervous system resulting in extreme weakness or paralysis.

nerve im·pulse, *n. Physiol.* transmission of a wave of sensation along a nerve fiber which activates or inhibits a nerve cell, gland, or muscle.

nerve·less, nurv′lis, *a.* Not nervous under stress; calm, esp. in emergencies; destitute of nerve, strength, or vigor; feeble; weak; lacking firmness or courage; spiritless; *anat.* without nerves.—**nerve·less·ly,** *adv.*—**nerve·less·ness,** *n.*

nerve-rack·ing, nerve-wrack·ing, nurv′-rak″ing, *a.* Extremely annoying or irritating.

nerv·ous, nur′vus, *a.* Pertaining to or having nerves; originating from or affecting the nerves; easily agitated; tense or anxious.—**nerv·ous·ly,** *adv.*—**nerv·ous·ness,** *n.*

nerv·ous break·down, *n.* Nervous exhaustion or infirmity; an emotional or mental weakness, usu. resulting from prolonged mental strain; nervous prostration; neurasthenia.

nerv·ous Nel·lie, *n. Slang,* an ineffectual, fearful, and indecisive person.

nerv·ous sys·tem, *n. Physiol., zool.* the elaborate network of nerve cells making up the ganglia, spinal cord, nerves, and brain, esp. of vertebrate animals and man, and whose function is to receive and transmit impulses from the brain and sense organs.

ner·vure, nur′vūr, *n. Bot.* a vein of a leaf; *entom.* one of the tubes which help to expand an insect's wing. Also **ner·vule.**

nerv·y, nur′vē, *a.*—**nervier, nerviest.** *Colloq.* arrogant or insolent; bold or courageous. *Brit.* nervous, jittery.—**nerv·i·ness,** *n.*

nes·cience, nesh′ens, nesh′ē·ens, *n.* [L. *nescientia,* < *nescio,* not to know—*ne,* not, and *scio,* to know.] Lack or want of knowledge; ignorance; agnosticism.—**nes·cient,** *a.*

ness, nes, *n.* [O.E. *naes,* Icel. *nes,* Dan. *naes,* a ness; prob. a form of *nose.*] A promontory; a cape or headland.

Nes·sel·rode, nes′el·rōd″, *n.* [From a proper name.] A mixture used in making desserts, consisting of preserved fruits, nuts, rum, and other ingredients.

nest, nest, *n.* [O.E. *nest* = D. and G. *nest; nest;* akin to L. *nidus,* nest, Skt. *nīda,* resting place, nest.] A structure formed or a place used by a bird for the incubation of its eggs and the rearing of its young; a place used by insects, fish, turtles, rabbits, or the like, for depositing their eggs or young; a number of birds or other animals inhabiting one nest; a snug home, retreat, or resting place; a place where something bad is fostered or flourishes; as, a *nest* of crime; the occupants or frequenters of such a nest; an assemblage of things lying or set close together; a set or series of boxes, baskets, tables, cups, or other articles, such that the smaller fit within the larger.—*v.i.* To build or have a nest; to settle or lodge in or as in a nest; to fit within another or one another; to search for nests.—*v.t.* To settle or place in or as in a nest; to provide with a nest; to fit or place, one within another, to form a nest, as boxes, cups, or other articles.

nest egg, *n.* A sum of money laid up as the beginning of a fund or as a reserve; a natural or artificial egg left in a nest to induce a hen to continue laying eggs there.

nest·er, nes′tėr, *n.* One who or that which nests; *western U.S. slang,* formerly, a farmer who established a farm, either by homesteading or squatting, on land that was open range for cattle and sheep.

nes·tle, nes′l, *v.i.*—**nestled, nestling.** [Freq. < *nest.*] To lie close and snug; to be sheltered or situated in a pleasant spot; *archaic,* to make or occupy a nest—*v.t.* To house, shelter, or settle as in a nest; to place or press closely.—**nes·tler,** *n.*

nest·ling, nest′ling, nes′ling, *n.* [A dim. < *nest.*] A young bird in the nest; *fig.* a child that is young.

Nes·to·ri·an, ne·stōr′ē·an, ne·star′ē·an, *n.* A follower of Nestorius, patriarch of Constantinople in the 5th century, who believed that there were two distinct natures in Christ, the human and the divine; one of the Christians of Persia and India who constitute the modern Nestorian sect.—*a.*—**Nes·to·ri·an·ism,** *n.*

net, net, *n.* [O.E. *net* = D. *net* = G. *netz* = Icel. *net* = Goth. *nati,* net.] A bag or other contrivance of strong thread or cord made into an open, meshed fabric, for catching fish, birds, or other animals; anything serving to catch or ensnare; a piece of meshed fabric for any purpose; as, a tennis *net,* a hair *net;* a lacelike fabric or material with uniform meshes, used in dressmaking or millinery, or forming the groundwork of many kinds of lace; any network or reticulated system of filaments, lines, veins, or the like; in sports such as tennis, badminton, or volleyball, a ball struck into the net.—*v.t.* —**netted, netting.** To catch or ensnare with or as with a net; to cover, screen, or enclose with a net or netting; to strike, as a ball, against the net; to make with meshes in the manner of network.—**net·ta·ble,** *a.*—**net·like,** *a.*

net, net, *a.* [Fr. *net,* clean, clear.] Left after all deductions for taxes, charges, expenses, allowances, discounts, and the like have been deducted, as opposed to *gross;* as, *net* profit, *net* prices. Final or fundamental, as: The *net* effect was good.—*n.* Net income, profits, weight, score, or the like.—*v.t.*—**netted, netting.** To gain or yield as clear profit.

neth·er, neTH′ėr, *a.* [O.E. *nither, nithor, neothra,* compar. of *nithe,* under, downward; root seen in Skt. *ni,* downward.] Lower; lying or being beneath or in the lower part.—**neth·er·most,** *a.* Lowest.

neth·er world, *n.* The world of punishment awaiting sinners after death; hell; Satan's domain; the hereafter in general.

net in·come, *n.* An individual's gross income minus those expenses and taxes incurred in acquiring this income; in income taxation, an individual's gross income less certain allowable deductions. See *gross income.*

net na·tion·al prod·uct, *n. Econ.* a country's gross national product less deduction for the depreciation and consumption of capital goods. Abbr. *NNP.* See *gross national product, national income.*

net prof·it, *n.* The actual or remaining profit of a business or transaction after all costs, operating expenses, and taxes have been deducted from the total receipts. See *gross profit.*

ne·tsu·ke, net′skē, net′skä, *Jap.* ne′tsö·ke′, *n.* [Jap.] In Japanese use, a small ornamental knob or button attached to a man's sash, from which a tobacco pouch or other article is suspended.

net·ting, net′ing, *n.* The process of making nets; the process of fishing with the use of a net; any piece of network.

net·tle, net′l, *n.* [O.E. *netele* = D. *netel* = G. *nessel,* nettle.] Any plant of the genus *Urtica,* comprising widely distributed herbs with stinging hairs; any of various allied or similar plants.—*v.t.*—**nettled, nettling.** *Fig.* to irritate, provoke, or vex. To sting as a nettle does.

net·tle rash, *n. Pathol.* urticaria, an eruption upon the skin caused by the sting of a nettle or other allergic factor.

net·tle·some, net′l·som, *a.* Easily irritated; vexing, annoying.

net·work, net′wurk″, *n.* An interlacement of threads, wires, or strings into a fabric or web; a net; a complicated intermingling of lines, passages, or the like; as, a *network* of railroads; an undercover group whose members are separated but in communication; *TV, radio,* a series of broadcasting stations working as a unit.

Neuf·châ·tel, nö″sha′tel′, nö′sha·tel″, *Fr.* nœ·shä·tel′, *n.* [From *Neufchâtel*-en-Bray, a town in northern France, where produced.] A soft, white cheese made from milk with or without the cream. Also **Neuf·châ·tel cheese.**

neume, nöm, nūm, *n. Mus.* any of several symbols used in notating Gregorian chant.—**neu·mat·ic,** nö·mat′ik, nū·mat′ik, *a.*

neu·ral, nur′al, nūr′al, *a.* [Gr. *neuron,* a nerve; akin to L. *nervus.*] Pertaining to the nerves or nervous system.—**neu·ral·ly,** *adv.*

neu·ral·gia, nu·ral′ja, nū·ral′ja, *n.* [N.L. < Gr. *neuron,* nerve, and *algos,* pain.] *Pathol.* pain that is usu. sharp and paroxysmal, along the course of a nerve.—**neu·ral·gic,** *a.*

neu·ral tube, *n. Embryol.* a hollow tubular formation of nerve tissue in the embryo of vertebrates made of joined ectodermal folds on each side of the neural plate and developing at one end into the brain.

neu·ras·the·ni·a, nur″as·thē′nē·a, nūr″-as·thē′nē·a, *n.* [Gr. *neuron,* nerve, *astheneia,* weakness.] *Med.* a condition, as from prolonged emotional tension or overwork, characterized by excessive mental and physical fatigue and sometimes by obscure physical complaints or phobias.—**neu·ras·then·ic,** nur″as·then′ik, nūr″as·then′ik, *a., n.*—**neu·ras·then·i·cal·ly,** *adv.*

neu·ri·lem·ma, nur″i·lem′a, nūr″i·lem′a, *n.* [N.L., < Gr. *neuron,* nerve, and *lemma,* husk, skin.] *Anat.* the delicate membranous sheath of a nerve fiber.—**neu·ri·lem·mal, neu·ri·lem·mat·ic, neu·ri·lem·ma·tous,**

nŭr″*i*·li·mat′ik, nūr″*i*·li·mat′ik, nŭr″*i*·lem′*a*·tus, nūr″*i*·lem′*a*·tus, *a*.

neu·ri·tis, nŭ·rī′tis, nū·rī′tis, *n. Pathol.* inflammation of a nerve causing impaired reflexes or paralysis.—**neu·rit·ic,** nŭ·rit′ik, nū·rit′ik, *a*., *n*.

neu·ro·cir·cu·la·to·ry, nŭr″ō·sŭr′kū·la·tōr′ē, *a.* Pertaining to the nervous and circulatory systems of the body.

neu·ro·crine, nŭr′ō·krin, nūr′ō·krin, nŭr′o·krin″, nūr′o·krin″, nūr′o·krēn″, nūr′o·krēn″, *a.* Pertaining or related to a hormone that influences nerve activity.—**neu·ro·crin·ism,** *n*.

neu·ro·fi·bril, nŭr″o·fī′bril, nūr″o·fī′bril, *n. Anat.* any of the minute fibrils in the nerve cells, regarded as conducting elements.—**neu·ro·fi·bri·lar,** *a*.

neu·ro·gen·ic, nŭr″o·jen′ik, nūr″o·jen′ik, *a. Med.* beginning in nerve tissue or in a nerve. Also **neu·rog·e·nous,** nŭ·roj′e·nus, nū·roj′e·nus.—**neu·ro·gen·i·cal·ly,** *adv*.

neu·rog·li·a, nŭ·rog′lē·a, nū·rog′lē·a, *n*. [N.L. < Gr. *neuron,* nerve, and *glia,* glue.] *Anat.* the delicate connective tissue which supports and binds together the essential elements of nervous tissue, esp. in the central nervous system.—**neu·rog·li·al, neu·rog·li·ac, neu·rog·li·ar, neu·rog·lic,** nŭ·rog′lē·ak″, nū·rog′lē·ak″, *a*.

neu·rol·o·gist, nŭ·rol′o·jist, nū·rol′o·jist, *n.* A physician specializing in diagnosis and treatment of diseases of the nerves or nervous system.

neu·rol·o·gy, nŭ·rol′o·jē, nū·rol′o·jē, *n.* The science of the nerves or the nervous system and its diseases or disorders.—**neu·ro·log·i·cal,** nŭr″o·loj′i·kal, nūr″o·loj′i·kal, *a*.

neu·ro·ma, nŭ·rō′ma, nū·rō′ma, *n.* pl. **neu·ro·mas, neu·ro·ma·ta.** *Pathol.* a tumor that is comprised of nerve tissue.—**neu·rom·a·tous,** nŭ·rom′a·tus, nū·rom′a·tus, *a*.

neu·ron, nŭr′on, nūr′on, *n.* [Gr. *neûron,* nerve.] *Anat.* the basic functional and structional element of the nervous system consisting of a nerve cell with all its processes. Also **neu·rone,** nŭr′ōn, nūr′ōn.—**neu·ron·ic,** nŭ·ron′ik, nū·ron′ik, *a*.

neu·rop·a·thy, nŭ·rop′*a*·thē, nū·rop′*a*·thē, *n.* Disease of the nervous system.—**neu·ro·path·ic,** nŭr″o·path′ik, nūr″o·path′ik, *a.*—**neu·ro·path·i·cal·ly,** *adv*.

neu·rop·ter·an, nŭ·rop′tẽr·an, nū·rop′tẽr·an, *n.* [N.L. *Neuroptera,* pl. Gr. *neuron,* nerve, and *pteron,* wing.] Any insect of the order *Neuroptera,* as the lacewings, dobsonflies, and antlions, characterized by two pairs of membranous wings with netlike nervation. Also **neu·rop·ter, neu·rop·ter·on.**—*a.*—**neu·rop·ter·oid, neu·rop·ter·ous,** *a*.

neu·ro·sis, nŭ·rō′sis, nū·rō′sis, *n.* pl. **neu·ro·ses,** nŭ·rō′sēz, nū·rō′sēz. A functional nervous or emotional disorder, less serious than a psychosis, marked by severe anxiety, depression, and the like, without any apparent physical origin. Also *psychoneurosis*.

neu·rot·ic, nŭ·rot′ik, nū·rot′ik, *a.* Affected by or relating to a neurosis; *pathol.* of or relating to the nerves.—*n.* One who has a neurosis, or whose behavior suggests one.—**neu·rot·i·cal·ly,** *adv*.

neu·ro·tox·ic, nŭr″ō·tok′sik, nūr″ō·tok′sik, *a.* Poisonous to nerves or to nerve tissue such as the brain.

neu·ter, nō′tẽr, nū′tẽr, *a.* [L., not either, not one nor the other—compounded of *ne* and *uter,* either of two.] *Gram.* neither masculine nor feminine; neither active nor passive; intransitive; as, a *neuter* verb. *Zool.* without fully developed sexual organs; *bot.* of a flower having neither stamens nor pistils.—*n. Gram.* a word or inflectional form of the neuter gender; the neuter

gender itself. *Zool.* an animal incapable of propagation; an animal after castration. *Bot.* a flower which has neither stamens nor pistils.

neu·tral, nō′tral, nū′tral, *a.* [L. *neutralis,* < *neuter*.] On neither side in a dispute or armed conflict; of no particular kind or characteristic; indefinite; of a color, without a decided hue, or combining well with most other colors. *Biol.* neuter; *chem.* neither acid nor alkaline, as pure water; *elect.* neither positive nor negative.—*n.* A person or nation that remains neutral; a person, aircraft, or vessel belonging to a nation remaining neutral in an armed conflict; *mach.* the position of gears when force is not being transmitted from the motor to the working parts, usu. preceded by *in* or *at; phon.* the vowel sound made with the tongue in a relaxed, central position, as the *a* in *about*.—**neu·tral·i·ty,** nō·tral′i·tē, nū·tral′i·tē, *n.*—**neu·tral·ly,** *adv*.

neu·tral·ism, nō′tra·liz″um, nū′tra·liz″um, *n.* The maintaining or the advocating of a neutral attitude or a policy of nonalignment in foreign affairs.—**neu·tral·ist,** *n., a.*—**neu·tral·is·tic,** *a*.

neu·tral·ize, nō′tra·līz″, nū′tra·līz″, *v.t.*—**neutralized, neutralizing.** To make neutral; declare neutral, as in time of war, or invest with neutrality; render ineffective or counteract. *Chem.* to render neutral by adding either acid or base to, until equivalent amounts are reached; to render inert the peculiar properties of. *Elect.* to cause to be electrically or magnetically inert.—*v.i.* To become neutral; to undergo a process of neutralization.—**neu·tral·i·za·tion,** nō″tra·li·zā′shan, nū″tra·li·zā′shan, *n.*—**neu·tral·iz·er,** *n*.

neu·tral spir·its, *n.* Ethyl alcohol, C_2H_5OH, which is 190 proof, 95 percent pure, used for blending with whiskies, and in the making of liqueurs and cordials.

neu·tri·no, nō·trē′nō, nū·trē′nō, *n.* [(neutr)on and -*ino*: little neutron.] *Phys.* an uncharged elementary particle with a mass nearing zero.

neu·tron, nō′tron, nū′tron, *n.* [(neutr)al electr(*on*).] An uncharged particle in the nucleus of an atom with a mass nearly the same as that of the proton.

né·vé, nā·vā′, *n.* [Fr., < L. *nix (niv-),* snow.] Granular snow accumulated on high mountains and subsequently compacted into glacial ice; a field of such snow. Also *firn*.

nev·er, nev′ẽr, *adv.* [The neg. of *ever;* O.E. *naefre,* < *ne,* not, and *aefre,* ever; cf. *neither, either*.] Not ever; at no time; in no degree; absolutely not.

nev·er·more, nev″ẽr·mōr′, *adv.* Never again; at no future time.

nev·er-nev·er, nev′ẽr-nev′ẽr, *a.* Imaginary, fanciful, as: Theatrical ballet often depicts a *never-never* world.—**nev·er-nev·er land,** an imaginary or euphoric place or condition; any remote, unpopulated, barren area.—**nev·er-nev·er plan,** *Brit. slang.* installment buying; also *hire-purchase*.

nev·er·the·less, nev″ẽr·THe·les′, *adv.* [The *the* is the old instrumental case of the demonst. used before comparatives; O.E. *thý læs,* the or by that less.] Not the less; however; notwithstanding; in spite of.

ne·vus, nae·vus, nē′vus, *n.* pl. **ne·vi,** nē′vī. [L.] A congenital mark, blemish, or mole on the skin of a person; a birthmark.

new, nō, nū, *a.* [O.E. *niwe, neowe,* new = D. *nieuw,* Goth. *niujis,* G. *neu;* cogn. W. *newydd,* Ir. *nuadh,* L. *novus,* Gr. *neos,* Skt. *navas*.] Recently made, invented, produced, or come into being; lately discovered or experienced; unfamiliar; recently brought into a particular location, situation, condition, or relationship; not habituated or accustomed; never in existence or use

before; novel; starting afresh; different from a former or older condition; replacing something older; fresh; repeated; modern, contemporary; refreshed, strengthened. (*Cap.*) modern, with reference to a language.—**new·ly.**—*n.* Something new.—**new·ish,** *a.*—**new·ness,** *n*.

new·born, nō′barn′, nū′barn′, *n.* pl. **new·born, new·borns.** A recently born infant.—*a.* Recently or only just born; *fig.* born anew or reborn; as, a *newborn* interest.

New·burg, nō′bŭrg, nū′bŭrg, *a.* Made with a sauce of butter, egg yolks, cream, and wine; as, lobster *Newburg*.

New Church, *n.* The church of the New Jerusalem, being the denomination composed of the followers of Emanuel Swedenborg.

new·com·er, nō′kum″ẽr, nū′kum″ẽr, *n.* One who has lately come; new arrival.

new crit·i·cism, *n.* (*Often cap.*) a modern, mainly American movement in literary criticism emphasizing textual explication rather than historical or biographical study in the analysis and evaluation of a work.

New Deal, *n.* The economic recovery measures and the reform legislation advocated by Franklin D. Roosevelt; the period of his administration.—**New Deal·er,** *n*.

new·el, nō′el, nū′el, *n.* [O.Fr. *noel, noiel* (Fr. *noyau*), fruit stone, kernel, newel, < L.L. *nucale,* neut. of *nucalis,* of or like a nut, < L. *nux (nuc-),* nut.] A central pillar or upright from which the steps of a winding stair radiate. A post at the head or foot of a stair, supporting the handrail; also **new·el post**.

new·fan·gled, nō′fang′geld, nū′fang′geld, *a.* New-fashioned; of the newest design; fond of anything novel.

new-fash·ioned, nō′fash′and, nū′fash′and, *a.* Made in a new fashion; lately come into fashion.

New·found·land, nō′fond·land″, nō′fond·land″, nō′fon·land″, nō′fon·land″, nū′fond·land″, nū′fond·land″, nū′fon·land″, nū′fon·land″, *n.* One of a breed of large, usu. black, shaggy dogs, orig. from the island of Newfoundland, noted for their intelligence, docility, and swimming ability.

new·ly, nō′lē, nū′lē, *adv.* Lately; freshly; recently; anew; afresh; with a new form or manner.

new·ly·wed, nō′lē·wed″, nū′lē·wed″, *n.* A recently married person.

new·mar·ket, nō′mär″kit, nū′mär″kit, *n.* [From *Newmarket,* town in England.] A kind of card game. In the 19th century, a man's long, close-fitting outdoor coat, or a similar coat for women; also **New·mar·ket coat**.

new moon, *n.* The period of time when the moon is in a direct line between the sun and the earth so that its illuminated side is not visible from the earth; the moon shortly after this phase when it is visible as a crescent.

news, nōz, nūz, *n.* pl. but sing. in constr. [< *new;* prob. the old genit. of *new,* < such phrases as O.E. *hwæt niwes?* what news?] Current information about something that has taken place, or about something not known before; recent intelligence regarding any event, esp. as presented by a news media such as the papers, radio, or television; anything or anyone regarded by a news media as a subject worthy of treatment; a newspaper or news broadcast.

news·a·gen·cy, *n.* A firm which gathers or collects news items for periodicals, newspapers, and other subscribers; a newspaper retailer.

news·boy, nōz′boi″, nūz′boi″, *n.* A boy who sells or delivers newspapers.

news·break, nōz′brāk″, nūz′brāk″, *n.* Any newsworthy occurrence, incident, or event.

---

ch- chain, G. na*ch*t;   **th-** THen, thin;   **w-** wig, hw as sound in whig;   **z-** zh as in azure, zeal.   *Italicized vowel* indicates schwa sound.

news·cast, nōz′kast″, nōz′käst″, nŭz′kast″, nŭz′käst″, *n.* A broadcast of current events on either television or radio.—**news·· cast·er**, *n.*

news con·fer·ence, *n.* A meeting for reporters called by a press agent, celebrity, or government official to release information and respond to reporters' questions.

news·let·ter, nōz′let″ẽr, nŭz′let″ẽr, *n.* A letterlike report or analysis of a specialized nature, printed for periodic distribution to subscribers.

news·man, nōz′man″, nŭz′man″, *n.* pl. **news·men.** One who collects, reports, or interprets the news; one who delivers or sells newspapers and magazines.

news·mon·ger, nōz′mung″gẽr, nōz′mong″- gẽr, nŭz′mung″gẽr, nŭz′mong″gẽr, *n.* A gossip; a teller of idle tales.

news·pa·per, nōz′pā″pẽr, nŭz′pā″pẽr, *n.* A publication issued daily or weekly including news, opinions, features, and advertisements; the organization that composes, publishes, and distributes newspapers; one copy of a news publication; newsprint.— **news·pa·per·man**, *n.*

news·print, nōz′print″, nŭz′print″, *n.* An inexpensive paper manufactured from wood pulp, machine-finished, and used mostly for newspapers.

news·reel, nōz′rēl″, nŭz′rēl″, *n.* A brief motion picture depicting news events.

news·stand, nōz′stand″, nŭz′stand″, *n.* A booth or stand where newspapers and periodicals are sold. Also *Brit.* **news stall.**

New Style, *a.* According to or pertaining to the Gregorian calendar.

news·wor·thy, nōz′wụr″THē, nŭz′wụr″THē, *a.* Of enough importance or interest to merit reporting.

news·y, nō′zē, nŭ′zē, *a.*—**newsier, newsiest.** *Colloq.* full of news.—*n.* pl. **news·ies.** *Colloq.* a newsboy.

newt, nōt, nŭt, *n.* [M.E. *newte*, for *ewte* (an *ewte* being taken as a *newte*), < O.E. *efete*, E. *eft*.] Any of various small, colorful, semi-aquatic salamanders belonging to the genus *Triturus*, and found in N. America, Europe, and Asia.

New Tes·ta·ment, *n.* Those books of the Bible written by the early Christian church fathers between A.D. 40 and 100, and comprising the four Gospels, 21 Epistles, Acts of the Apostles, and the Apocalypse of St. John the Evangelist.

new·ton, nōt′on, nŭt′on, *n. Phys.* in the meter-kilogram-second system, a standard unit of force equivalent to the force necessary to accelerate a one-kilogram mass one meter per second per second, a force of 100,000 dynes.

New·to·ni·an, nō·tō′nē·an, nŭ·tō′nē·an, *a.* Pertaining to Sir Isaac Newton, or to his principles and discoveries in physics, optics, and other fields; as, the *Newtonian* telescope.

New World, *n.* Western Hemisphere including N. America and S. America: opposed to *Old World* of Europe, Asia, Africa, and Australia.

new year, *n.* The year approaching or newly begun; (*cap.*) the first day or days of a year.—**New Year's Day**, the first day of the year, January 1st by the Gregorian calendar.

next, nekst, *a.* [O.E. *néhst, néhsta*, superl. of *néh, neáh*, nigh.] Nearest in place, time, rank, or degree; directly following; adjacent.—*adv.* At the time or turn nearest or immediately succeeding.—*prep.* Adjoining or nearest to.

next friend, *n. Law*, a person other than a legal guardian who acts, as in a suit at law, for the benefit of an infant or other person under legal disability.

next of kin, *n.* Closest of kin; a person's nearest blood relative or relatives; *law*, the blood relatives of an intestate entitled to share in his estate.

next to, *prep.* Immediately following; adjacent to.—*adv.* Practically; as, *next to* impossible.—**get next to some·one**, *slang.* To ingratiate oneself with; to become the friend, confidant, or intimate of; to become sexually intimate with.

nex·us, nek′sus, *n.* pl. **nex·us.** [L.] Tie; connection; connector; a linked series.

ni·a·cin, nī′a·sin, *n. Biochem.* nicotinic acid.

ni·ag·a·ra, nī·ag′ra, nī·ag′ẽr·a, *n.* [From *Niagara* Falls.] A cataract; a deluge; a torrent.

nib, nib, *n.* The bill or beak of a bird; the point of anything, esp. of a pen; any pointed tip.—*v.t.*—**nibbed, nibbing.** To supply with a nib; to mend or make sharp the nib of, as a pen.

nib·ble, nib′l, *v.t.*—**nibbled, nibbling.** [A freq. < *nib*, or < *nip*.] To bite a little at a time; to eat in small bits.—*v.i.* To bite gently, usu. followed by *at*.—*n.* A little morsel; the act of nibbling.—**nib·bler**, nib′lẽr, *n.*

nib·lick, nib′lik, *n. Golf*, an iron club with a wide face at a sharp angle, used to lift the ball high into the air. Also **num·ber nine i·ron.**

nibs, nibz, *n. Slang*, one who is overbearing or haughty, usu. preceded by *his* or *her*.

nic·co·lite, nik′o·līt″, *n.* [N.L. *niccolum*, nickel.] A mineral of a pale copper-red color and metallic luster, consisting essentially of nickel arsenide, NiAs, and usu. occurring massive. Also **cop·per nick·el.**

nice, nīs, *a.*—*nicer, nicest.* [O.Fr. *nice, nisce*, simple, < L. *nescius*, < *ne*, not, *scio*, to know.] Pleasing or agreeable; kind; respectable; refined; fitting or proper; as, not too *nice* an observation; skillful; as, a *nice* shot at the basket; tactful; as, a *nice* maneuver; subtle or minute; as, a *nice* distinction; highly accurate or precise; as, a *nice* measurement; attractive and delicious; as, a *nice* meal; fastidious or finicky.—**nice·ly**, *adv.*—**nice·ness**, *n.*

Ni·cene Creed, nī·sēn′ krēd, nī′sēn krēd, *n.* A statement of Christian belief adopted by the initial Nicene Council, A.D. 325, to oppose Arianism, later revised and now accepted by the Roman Catholic and most Protestant churches. Also **Ni·cae·an Creed.** —**Ni·cene**, *a.*

ni·ce·ty, nī′si·tē, *n.* pl. **ni·ce·ties.** [O.Fr. *nicete*.] *Usu. pl.* a delicate or precise point; a minute difference or fine distinction; as, the *niceties* of his book on Shakespeare; a refined or elegant feature; as, the *niceties* of living abroad. The quality of being nice; precision; excess of delicacy or fastidiousness; delicacy requiring careful management; as, a matter of the utmost *nicety*.— **to a ni·ce·ty**, precisely.

niche, nich, *n.* [Fr. *niche*, < It. *nicchia*.] A recess or hollow, as in a wall, for a statue or other decorative object; a place or position suitable or appropriate for a person or thing. —*v.t.*—**niched, niching.** To place in a niche.

nick, nik, *n.* [Cf. G. *knick*, a flaw; also E. *notch*, O.D. *nocke*, a notch.] A notch, chip, or concavity in a surface or border; *print.* a notch in the shank of a type to guide the typesetter.—*v.t.* To make a nick or notch in; to record or count by making notches in; *slang*, to rob or cheat.—**in the nick of time**, at the final critical moment.—**nick·er**, *n.*

nick·el, nik′el, *n.* [Sw. *nickel*, nickel; a name connected with *nick*, the evil spirit, and given to this metal because its copper-colored ore deceived the miners by giving no copper.] A hard silver-white metallic element, malleable and ductile, much used in alloys. Sym. Ni, at. no. 28, at. wt. 58.71. See Periodic Table of Elements. *U.S.* the five-cent coin composed of copper and nickel.—*v.t.*—**nickeled, nickeling**, *esp. Brit.* **nickelled, nickelling.** To coat with nickel

plating.—**nick·el·ic**, ni·kel′ik, nik′e·lik, *a.* Pertaining to or containing nickel, esp. trivalent nickel.—**nick·el·if·er·ous**, nik″e·lif′ẽr·us, *a.* Containing nickel.—**nick·el·ous**, nik′e·lus, *a.* Having bivalent nickel.— **nick·el-plat·ing**, nik′el·plat′ing, *n.* The coating or plating of metals with nickel.— **nick·el sil·ver**, an alloy composed of copper, zinc, and nickel; also **Ger·man sil·ver.**

nick·el·o·de·on, nik″e·lō′dē·an, *n.* An early jukebox; formerly, a theater with an admission charge of a nickel.

nick·er, nik′ẽr, *v.i.* [Imit.] To neigh; to laugh; to snicker.—*n.* A neigh; a laugh; a snicker.

nick·nack, nik′nak″, *n.* Knickknack.

nick·name, nik′nām″, *n.* [M.E. *nekename*, for *ekename* (an *ekename* being taken as a *nekename*): cf. *eke*.] A familiar form of a proper name, as *Jim* for *James*; a name added to or substituted for the proper name of a person or place, as in ridicule or familiarity. —*v.t.*—**nicknamed, nicknaming.** To give a nickname to, or call by a specified nickname; to call by an incorrect or improper name; misname.

ni·co·ti·a·na, ni·kō″shē·ā′na, ni·kō″shē··an′a, ni·kō″shē·ä′na, *n. Bot.* any of the plants belonging to the genus *Nicotiana*, esp. *N. tabacum* and *N. alata*, popular ornamental plants.

nic·o·tin·a·mide, nik″o·tin′a·mīd″, nik″-o·tin′a·mid, *n. Biochem.* $C_5H_4NCONH_2$, a part of the vitamin B complex, used in treating or warding off pellagra, or in veterinary medicine. Also **ni·a·cin·a·mide**, nī″a·sin′a·mīd″.

nic·o·tine, nik′o·tēn″, nik′o·tin, nik″o·tēn′, *n.* A highly poisonous, volatile alkaloid, $C_{10}H_{14}N_2$, derived from tobacco.—**nic·o··tin·ic**, nik″o·tin′ik, *a.*

nic·o·tin·ic ac·id, *n.* One of the vitamins in the B complex, consisting of a crystalline compound formed from the oxidation of nicotine, and used esp. in the prevention of pellagra.

nic·ti·tate, nik′ti·tāt″, *v.i.*—*nictitated, nictitating.* [L. *nicto, nictatum*, to wink.] To wink. Also **nic·tate.**—**nic·ti·tant**, *a.*— **nic·ti·ta·tion**, *n.*

nic·ti·tat·ing mem·brane, *n.* A thin, movable membrane forming a third eyelid at the inner corner of the eye, in birds, reptiles, and amphibians. Also **nic·tat·ing mem·brane.**

ni·dic·o·lous, nī·dik′o·lus, *a. Ornith.* reared in the nest for some time; compare *nidifugous*. Sharing the nest of an animal of another kind.

nid·i·fi·cate, nid′i·fi·kāt″, *v.i.*—*nidificated, nidificating.* [L. *nidifico*, < *nidus*, a nest, *facio*, to make.] To make a nest.—**nid·i··fi·ca·tion**, *n.*—**nid·i·fi·ca·tion·al**, *a.*

ni·dif·u·gous, nī·dif′ū·gus, *a. Ornith.* designating a bird which leaves the nest soon after it is hatched, as the domestic chicken. Compare *nidicolous*.

ni·dus, nī′dus, *n.* [L.] A nest, esp. one in which insects or spiders deposit their eggs; a spot in an organism which is a center of infection; *fig.* a place of origin or source of development.—**ni·dal**, *a.*

niece, nēs, *n.* [Fr. *nièce*, O.Fr. *niepce*, < L. *neptis*, a granddaughter; allied to *nepos, nepotis*, a nephew.] The daughter of a brother or sister or of a brother-in-law or sister-in-law.

ni·el·lo, nē·el′ō, *n.* pl. **ni·el·los**, *It.* **ni·el·li**, nē·el′ē. [It., < L. *nigellus*, blackish, dim. of *niger*, black.] The art of producing ornamental silver plates with incised designs filled with a black metallic composition; the composition, consisting of silver, copper, lead, and sulfur, used in this art; ornamental work so produced; a specimen of such work.—*v.t.*—**nielloed, nielloing.**—**ni·el·list**, *n.*

nif·ty, nif′tē, a.—*niftier, niftiest.* [Origin obscure.] *Slang.* Smart; stylish; fine.—*n.*

nig·gard, nig′ẽrd, n. [< Icel. *knöggr,* Sw. *njugg,* niggardly, with term. -*ard.*] A miser; a meanly covetous person; one who is extremely stingy.—*a.*—**nig·gard·li·ness,** n.—**nig·gard·ly,** a., adv.

nig·gle, nig′l, v.i.—*niggled, niggling.* [Appar. < Scand.] To trifle; work ineffectively; work with excessive care for minor or petty details.—**nig·gler,** n.—**nig·gling,** nig′ling, a. Trifling; petty; finical; excessively elaborate.—*n.*—**nig·gling·ly,** adv.

nigh, nī, adv. [O.E. *nēah, nēh,* = D. *na* = G. *nahe* = Icel. *nā*- = Goth. *nehw,* nigh: cf. *near* and *next.*] *Archaic, dial.* Near in space, time, or relation; nearly or almost.—*prep. Archaic, dial.* Near to; near.—*a. Archaic, dial.* Being near; not distant; near in relationship; with reference to animals or vehicles, left or near; short or direct; parsimonious.—*v.t., v.i. Archaic, dial.* To draw near to; approach.

night, nīt, n. [O.E. *niht, neaht* = Goth. *nahts,* L. *nox, noctis,* Gr. *nyx, nyktos,* Skt. *nakti, nakta*—night; < root *nak,* to vanish, to perish.] That part of the natural day when the sun is beneath the horizon, or the time from sunset to sunrise; a state or time of darkness, depression, misfortune, or the like; a state of ignorance, obscurity; the darkness of death or the grave; a time of sadness or sorrow.—*a.*

night blind·ness, n. A condition of the eyes in which one can see well by daylight but poorly or not at all by night or dim light.—**night-blind,** a.

night-bloom·ing ce·re·us, nīt′blö″ming sēr′ē·us, n. Any of several species of nocturnally blooming cactus of the genus *Selenicereus,* esp. *S. pteranthus,* marked by its large, fragrant, white flowers.

night·cap, nīt′kap″, n. A cap worn in bed; *colloq.* an alcoholic drink taken before going to bed.

night clothes, n. pl. Clothes worn in bed.

night club, n. A café or restaurant serving liquor and food and presenting entertainment from night until early morning. Also **night·club.**

night crawl·er, n. *Colloq.* an earthworm, esp. a large nocturnal one.

night·dress, nīt′dres″, n. Nightgown.

night·fall, nīt′fal″, n. The fall of night; the close of the day; evening.

night·gown, nīt′goun″, n. A loose gown worn in bed. Also *nightdress.*

night·hawk, nīt′hak″, n. A N. American species of the goatsucker family, *Chordeiles minor,* a relative of the whipporwill; the nightjar; *colloq.* a person up and about during the night.

night her·on, n. Any of certain nocturnal herons of the genus *Nycticorax,* and allied species, as *N. nycticorax,* found in the Old World and in the U.S.

night·in·gale, nīt′in·gāl″, nī′ting·gāl″, n. [O.E. *nihtegale,* lit. 'the night-singer,' < *niht,* night, *galan,* to sing.] A migratory bird, genus *Luscinia,* belonging to the thrush family, esp. the European species, *L. megarhynchos,* well known for the sweet singing of the male at night.

night·jar, nīt′jär″, n. [*Jar* or *churr* is from the sound of its voice.] *Ornith.* any of the common European goatsuckers, esp. *Caprimulgus europaeus.*

night latch, n. A spring latch for a door which opens from without by a key and from within by a knob.

night let·ter, n. A telegram sent at night for delivery the following morning at a lower rate than a straight telegram.

night·light·er, nīt′lī″tẽr, n. *Canada,* a game hunter, usu. of deer, who illegally uses a bright light to startle the prey into standing still.

night·long, nīt′lang″, nīt′long″, a. Lasting the entire night.—*adv.* Throughout the entire night.

night·ly, nīt′lē, a. Occurring or happening at night; occurring or happening every night; relating to or characteristic of the night.—*adv.* By night; every night.

night·mare, nīt′mâr″, n. [*Night,* and O.E. and Icel. *mara,* G. *mahr,* incubus, nightmare; Pol. *mara,* nightmare, phantom.] A fearful or terrifying dream causing intense anxiety and feelings of oppression and helplessness; a thought, experience, or situation producing the terror or anxiety characteristic of a fearful dream; an evil spirit once believed to suffocate or oppress people as they slept.—**night·mar·ish,** nīt′mâr″ish, a.

night owl, n. *Colloq.* a person given to staying up late at night. See *nighthawk.*

night ra·ven, n. A bird that cries in the night, esp. the night heron.

night·rid·er, nīt′rī″dẽr, n. *South. U.S.* one of a band of mounted men committing deeds of violence at night, as for intimidation or vengeance.—**night·rid·ing,** n.

nights, nīts, adv. During the night; at night.

night·shade, nīt′shād″, n. [O.E. *nihtscada,* lit. 'the shade or shadow of night'; so D. *nachtschade,* G. *nachtschatten,* the nightshade.] Any of the members of the family *Solanaceae,* which includes the potato, tomato, and black nightshade; specif. any of the genus *Solanum,* which includes the deadly nightshade and the bittersweet nightshade.

night·shirt, nīt′shụrt″, n. A long pullover or tailored sleeping shirt worn usu. by men and boys.

night soil, n. Human waste collected and used as manure.

night stick, n. A heavy stick or long club carried by a policeman. Also *Brit.* **trun·cheon.**

night·time, nīt′tīm″, n. The time between evening and morning.

night·walk·er, nīt′wạ″kẽr, n. A person who roams in the night, esp. for criminal purposes.

ni·gres·cent, nī·gres′ent, a. [L. *nigrescens* (-*ent*-), ppr. of *nigrescere,* become black, < *niger,* black.] Blackish; somewhat black.—**ni·gres·cence,** n.

nig·ri·tude, nig′ri·tōd″, nig′ri·tūd″, nī′-gri·tŏd″, nī′gri·tūd″, n. [L. *nigritudo.*] Blackness; complete darkness.—**nig·ri·tu·di·nous,** nig″ri·tŏd′i·nus, nig″ri·tūd′i·-nus, a.

ni·gro·sine, nī′grō·sēn″, nī′grō·sin″, n. *Chem.* any of the blue-black dyes which are derivatives of aniline and are used commercially as coloring or dyeing agents. Also **ni·gro·sin,** nī′grō·sin.

ni·hil·ism, nī′i·liz″um, nē′i·liz″um, n. [= Fr. *nihilisme,* < L. *nihil,* nothing.] Nothingness or nonexistence. *Philos.* an extreme form of skepticism, denying all real existence; total disbelief in religion or moral principles and obligations, or in established laws and institutions. (*Sometimes cap.*) the principles of a Russian revolutionary party, active in the latter half of the 19th century, holding that existing social and political institutions must be destroyed in order to clear the way for a new state of society, and in its extreme measures employing terrorism and assassination. Any revolutionary activity or propaganda promoting terrorism.—**ni·hil·ist,** n., a.—**ni·hil·is·tic,** a.

ni·hil·i·ty, nī·hil′i·tē, nē·hil′i·tē, n. [L. *nihil,* nothing.] Nothingness.

ni·hil ob·stat, nē′hil ob′stat, n. Official Roman Catholic approval to publish a book or work after examination shows it contains nothing contrary to the faith or morals of that religion.

Ni·ke, nī′kē, n. [Gr. *Nikē,* goddess of victory.] A ground-to-air rocket missile, guided electronically, and able to intercept and destroy bombers at high altitudes.

nil, nil, n. [L.] Nothing, as: His liabilities were over $5000 and his assets *nil.*

Nile green, nīl′ grēn′, n. [From the river *Nile,* in Egypt.] A pale green. Also **Nile.**

nill, nil, v.t., v.i. *Archaic,* to be averse or unwilling.

nim·ble, nim′bl, a.—*nimbler, nimblest.* [O.E. *nemel,* capable, O.E. *numol,* capable, catching, < *niman,* to take = Icel. *nema,* D. *nemen,* G. *nehmen,* Goth. *niman,* to take; akin *numb, benumb.*] Light and quick in motion; moving with ease and agility; quick-witted; clever.—**nim·ble·ness,** n.—**nim·bly,** adv.

nim·bo·stra·tus, nim″bō·strā′tus, nim″-bō·strat′us, n. pl. **nim·bo·stra·tus.** *Meteor.* a low, dark gray cloud or layer of clouds, often bringing prolonged rain or snow.

nim·bus, nim′bus, n. pl. **nim·bi, nim·-bus·es,** nim′bī. [L., a cloud.] A luminous aura believed to surround a divine or holy personage, or an artistic representation of it; an atmosphere, as of luxury or romance, emanating from a person or thing; formerly, a dense rain cloud.—**nim·bused,** a.

ni·mi·e·ty, ni·mī′i·tē, n. pl. **ni·mi·e·ties.** [L. *nimietās,* < *nimius,* excessive, < *nimis,* too much.] Excess; redundancy.

nim·i·ny-pim·i·ny, nim′i·nē·pim′i·nē, a. Effeminate; affectedly refined; mincing.

Nim·rod, nim′rod, n. [From *Nimrod,* described in Gen. x. 9 as "a mighty hunter before the Lord."] (*Often l.c.*) anyone expert in or devoted to hunting.

nin·com·poop, nin′kom·pöp″, ning′kom·-pöp″, n. [A corruption of L. *non compos,* not of sound mind.] A fool; a blockhead; a simpleton.—**nin·com·poop·er·y,** n.—**nin·com·poop·ish,** a.

nine, nīn, n. [O.E. *nigon* = L.G. and D. *negen,* G. *neun,* Goth. *niun,* Icel. *niu,* Sw. *niu,* Dan. *ni;* cogn. W. *naw,* Ir. *naov,* L. *novem,* Gr. *ennéa,* Skt. *navam*—nine.] The cardinal number between eight and ten; a symbol representing it; a set of nine persons or things; *sports,* a baseball team; (*cap.*) the nine Muses.—*a.* One more than eight in number.

nine·pins, nīn′pinz″, n. pl. but sing. in constr. A bowling game similar to tenpins, played with nine large wooden pins.

nine·teen, nīn′tēn″, n. [O.E. *nigontyne,* i.e. *nine ten.*] The cardinal number which follows 18; a symbol representing this number; a set of 19 persons or things.—*a.* One more than 18 in number.—**nine·teenth,** nīn′tēnth′, a. Following the eighteenth; being the ordinal of 19; being one of 19 equal parts.—*n.* One of 19 equal parts; that which follows the eighteenth in a series.

nine·ty, nīn′tē, n. pl. **nine·ties.** [O.E. *nigontig*—*nigon,* nine, and *tig,* ten.] The cardinal number which follows 89; nine times ten; a symbol representing this number; a set of 90 persons or things.—*a.* One more than 89 in number.—**nine·ti·eth,** nīn′tē·ith, a. Following the eighty-ninth; being the ordinal of 90; being one of 90 equal parts.—*n.* One of 90 equal parts; that which follows the eighty-ninth in a series.

nin·ny, nin′ē, n. pl. **nin·nies.** [A contr. for *nincompoop,* or < It. *ninno,* Sp. *niño,* a child.] A fool; a simpleton. Also **nin·ny·ham·mer,** nin′ē·ham″ẽr.

ni·non, nē·nạn′, n. A sheer fabric, as chiffon, used for curtains, draperies, and women's clothing.

ninth, ninth, a. Following the eighth; being the ordinal of nine; being one of nine equal parts into which anything is divided.—*n.* One of nine equal parts; that which follows the eighth in a series; *mus.* an interval

---

ch- chain, G. na*ch*t; **th-** THen, thin; **w-** wig, hw as sound in whig; **z-** zh as in azure, zeal. *Italicized vowel* indicates schwa sound.

containing an octave and a tone.—**ninth·ly,** *adv.*

ni·o·bi·um, nī·ō′bē·*um, n.* [From *Niobe.*] *Chem.* a rare, plantinum-gray metallic element, formerly named columbium, similar to tantalum in properties and used mainly as an alloy in special steels. Sym. Nb, at. no. 41, at. wt. 92.906.—**ni·o·bic,** nī·ō′bik, nī·ob′ik, *a.* See Periodic Table of the Elements.

ni·o·bous, nī·ō′bus, *a.* Of, containing, or pertaining to trivalent niobium.

nip, nip, *v.t.*—*nipped, nipping.* [M.E. *nyppen:* cf. D. *knippen,* clip, snip, snap, catch.] To compress sharply between two surfaces or points; pinch; bite suddenly; to take off by pinching, biting, or snipping, usu. followed by *off*; as, to *nip off* buds or shoots from a plant; to check in growth as if by taking off buds; to affect sharply and painfully or injuriously, as cold does; irritate or vex keenly; *colloq.* to snatch or take suddenly or quickly, used with *away* or *up.*—*v.i. Brit. colloq.* to move or go suddenly or quickly, followed by *off* or *away.*—*n.* The act of nipping; a pinch; a biting quality, as in cold or frosty air; a sharp or biting remark; a sharp taste or tang.—**nip and tuck,** with one competitor equaling the speed or efforts of the other; extremely close, as: They ran *nip and tuck* for five miles.—**nip in the bud,** to check or stop in the early stages.

nip, nip, *n.* [Dan. *nip,* a sip, *nippe,* D. and G. *nippen,* to nip; akin *nipple.*] A sip or small amount of anything, esp. of some alcoholic beverage.—*v.t., v.i.*—*nipped, nipping.* To drink in sips; to sip.

ni·pa, nē′pa, nī′pa, *n.* [Malay *nīpah.*] A fruit-bearing palm, *Nipa fruticans,* of the East Indies, the Philippines, and Australia, whose foliage is much used for thatching, mat-making, and basketry; the liquor made from this fruit-bearing palm.

nip·per, nip′ẽr, *n.* One who or that which nips; *usu. pl.* a device for nipping, as pincers or forceps; *pl., slang,* handcuffs. One of the great claws of a crustacean; one of the incisors of a horse; *Brit. colloq.* a small boy; *naut.* a rope or clamp used with an anchor or for anchoring.

nip·ping, nip′ing, *a.* Pertaining to or being that which nips or pinches; sharp or biting, as cold or wind; cutting or sarcastic; as, *nipping* speeches.—**nip·ping·ly,** *adv.*

nip·ple, nip′l, *n.* [Formerly also *nibble,* and *neble*; origin uncertain.] A protuberance on the female breast with an opening through which the milk ducts discharge; anything resembling a nipple in shape or function, as the mouthpiece of a nursing bottle; a short piece of threaded pipe used as a coupling.

Nip·pon·ese, nip″o·nēz′, nip″o·nēs′, *a.* Of or pertaining to Nippon or Japan; Japanese. —*n. pl.* **Nip·pon·ese.** A Japanese.

nip·py, nip′ē, *a.*—*nippier, nippiest.* Inclined to nip; sharp; biting, as chilly weather. *Brit. colloq.* agile; quick.

nir·va·na, nir·vä′na, nir·van′a, nẽr·vä′na, nẽr·van′a, *n.* [Skt. *nir,* out, and *vāna,* blown; lit. 'blown out.'] (*Often cap.*), *Buddhism,* the emancipation of the soul, achieved through extinction of the self and characterized by cessation of all suffering and pain, and esp. cessation of the successive cycles of transmigration. Freedom, as from passion or suffering.

Ni·sei, nē′sā′, *n. pl.* **Ni·sei, Ni·seis.** A son or daughter born in the U.S. of immigrant Japanese parents.

ni·si, nī′sī, *conj.* [L.] *Law,* unless: used as after *decree* or *order,* to indicate that it will become effective on a specified date unless modified or made invalid by some contingency.

Nis·sen hut, nis′en hut′, *n.* A prefabricated, long, half-cylindrical metal structure,

similar to a Quonset hut, used esp. by the military for housing or for storage.

ni·sus, nī′sus, *n.* pl. **ni·sus.** [L., < *niti,* strive.] Effort; endeavor; striving; an impulse, esp. an instinctive one.

nit, nit, *n.* [O.E. *hnitu*; D. *neet,* Icel. *nitr.* Dan. *gnid,* Sw. *gnet,* G. *niss,* a nit; cogn. Gr. *konis,* a nit.] The egg of a louse or similar parasitic insect; a louse in the immature stage.—**nit·ty,** *a.*—*nittier, nittiest.*

ni·ter, *Brit.* **ni·tre,** nī′tẽr, *n.* [Fr. *nitre,* L. *nitrum,* Gr. *nitron,* < some oriental source.] Potassium nitrate or sodium nitrate. Also *saltpeter.*

nit·id, nit′id, *a.* [L. *nitidus.*] Bright; shining.—**ni·tid·i·ty,** ni·tid′i·tē, *n.*

nit-pick, nit′pik″, *v.i. Slang,* to be overly critical or excessively involved with unimportant details.

ni·trate, nī′trāt, *n. Chem.* a salt or ester of nitric acid; *agric.* potassium nitrate or sodium nitrate, employed as a fertilizer.—*v.t.*—*nitrated, nitrating.* To treat with nitric acid or a nitrate; to convert into a nitrate.—**ni·tra·tion,** nī″trā′shan, *n.*—**ni·tra·tor,** *n.*

ni·tric, nī′trik, *a. Chem.* Of or pertaining to nitrogen; specif. pertaining to a compound in which the nitrogen has a higher valence than in a corresponding nitrous compound.

ni·tric ac·id, *n. Chem.* a corrosive liquid, HNO_3, with powerful oxidizing properties, used in the manufacture of dyes, explosives, metal products, and medicines. Also *aqua fortis.*

ni·tric ox·ide, *n. Chem.* a colorless, gaseous compound, NO, formed when certain metals, as copper, are dissolved in nitric acid.

ni·tride, nī′trīd, nī′trid, *n. Chem.* a compound of nitrogen with another, more electropositive element or radical, as phosphorus, boron, or a metal.

ni·tri·fy, nī′tri·fī″, *v.t.*—*nitrified, nitrifying.* To oxidize, as ammonia compounds, to nitrites or nitrates, esp. by bacterial action; impregnate, as soil, with nitrates; to unite with nitrogen or nitrogen compounds.— **ni·tri·fi·ca·tion,** nī″tri·fi·kā′shan, *n.*— **ni·tri·fi·er,** *n.*

ni·trile, nī′tril, nī′trīl, *n.* [< *nitrogen.*] *Chem.* any of a class of compounds regarded as cyanides of hydrocarbon radicals and having the general formula $RC \equiv N$.

ni·trite, nī′trīt, *n. Chem.* a salt of nitrous acid.

ni·tro, nī′trō, *a. Chem.* containing the group NO_2.

ni·tro·bac·te·ri·a, nī″trō·bak·tēr′ē·a, *n. pl.* Certain bacteria of the soil involved in nitrifying processes.

ni·tro·ben·zene, nī″trō·ben′zēn, nī″trō·ben·zēn′, *n. Chem.* a poisonous, oily benzene derivative, $C_6H_5NO_2$, yellow in color, used in the manufacture of aniline.

ni·tro·cel·lu·lose, nī″trō·sel′ū·lōs″, *n. Chem.* any one of several highly flammable, thermoplastic polymers obtained by treating cellulose with nitric acid or a mixture of nitric and sulfuric acids, different chemical proportions and procedures producing materials of different characteristics, such as guncotton, fast-drying lacquers, and rocket propellants.—**ni·tro·cel·lu·los·ic,** nī″trō·sel′ū·lō′sik, *a.*

ni·tro·gen, nī′trō·jen, *n.* [< Gr. *nitron,* niter, and root *gen,* to produce.] A gaseous element, possessing neither color, odor, nor taste, that constitutes about four-fifths of the atmosphere and is essential to life. Sym. N, at. no. 7, at. wt. 14.0067.—**ni·trog·e·nous,** nī·troj′e·nus, *a.* Relating to or containing nitrogen. See Periodic Table of Elements.

ni·tro·gen bal·ance, *n.* Equality in the intake and loss of nitrogen in an organism or in the soil. Also **ni·tro·gen e·qui·lib·ri·um.**

ni·tro·gen cy·cle, *n.* An ever-recurring

process in which the nitrogen present in the atmosphere and soil is changed, as by nitrogen fixation, into matter usable by plants, then animals, and then, by decay or denitrification, sent back into the air or soil.

ni·tro·gen fix·a·tion, *n.* The process of converting atmospheric nitrogen to various nitrogenous compounds by certain soil bacteria, thereby making the nitrogen available to the bacterial host plant; the industrial process of converting free nitrogen to nitrogen compounds for use as explosives and fertilizers.—**ni·tro·gen·fix·ing,** *a.*

ni·tro·gen·ize, nī′trō·je·nīz″, nī·troj′e·-nīz″, *v.t.*—*nitrogenized, nitrogenizing.* To impregnate or combine with nitrogen.

ni·tro·gen mus·tard, *n. Chem.* any of a class of toxic, blistering compounds, important in the treatment of some diseases.

ni·tro·glyc·er·in, nī″trō·glis′ẽr·in, *n. Chem.* a highly flammable, explosive liquid, $CH_2NO_3CHNO_3CH_2NO_3$, produced by the action of nitric and sulfuric acids on glycerol, used primarly in making dynamites or rocket propellants, and in medicine for relaxing or dilating blood vessels. Also **ni·tro·glyc·er·ine,** glyc·er·yl tri·ni·trate, nī″trō·glis′ẽr·in, nī″trō·glis′e·rēn″.

ni·tro·par·af·fin, nī″trō·par′a·fin, *n. Chem.* any organic derivative of paraffin hydrocarbons where one or more hydrogen atoms have been replaced by a nitro group.

ni·trous, nī′trus, *a. Chem.* obtained from or containing nitrogen: applied to compounds containing less oxygen than those called nitric.

ni·trous ac·id, *n. Chem.* an acid, HNO_2, which is unstable and occurs only in solution.

ni·trous bac·te·ri·a, *n. pl. Chem.* soil bacteria that, by oxidation, change compounds of ammonia into nitrates.

ni·trous ox·ide, *n. Chem.* a combination of nitrogen and oxygen, N_2O, which sometimes produces an exhilarating effect upon inhaling, used as an anesthetic during dental work and surgery. Also *laughing gas.*

nit·ty grit·ty, nit′ē grit′ē, *n. Slang,* the essence; as, the *nitty gritty* of life.

nit·wit, nit′wit″, *n.* A dull-witted or stupid person.

ni·val, nī′val, *a.* [L. *nivalis,* < *nix (niv-),* snow.] Of or pertaining to snow; of plants, growing in or near the snow.

niv·e·ous, niv′ē·us, *a.* [L. *niveus,* < *nix (niv-),* snow.] Like snow, esp. in color; snow-white.

nix, niks, *n.* [G. *nichts,* nothing.] *Slang,* nothing.—*adv. Slang,* no.—*interj. Slang,* stop it: an exclamation of warning.—*v.t. Slang.* To differ with; to prevent or prohibit; as, to *nix* our plans.

nix, niks, *n.* [G. *nix,* masc.] *Teut. mythol.* a water spirit, usu. small, and either good or bad.—**nix·ie,** nik′sē, *n.* [G. *nixe,* fem.] *Teut. mythol.* a female water spirit.

ni·zam, ni·zäm′, ni·zam′, *n.* [Hind. and Turk. *nizam,* < Ar. *nazama,* arrange, govern.] The soldiers, or one of the soldiers, of the Turkish regular army; (*cap.*) the hereditary title of the rulers of Hyderabad, India, from the 18th century to 1950.

no, nō, *adv.* [O.E. *nā, nō* (= Icel. *nei*), < *ne,* not, and *ā, ō,* ever.] Nay: used to express dissent, denial, or refusal, as in response to a query, or to give emphasis to another negative; as, *no,* never again; not in any degree, not at all: used with a comparative; as, working *no* faster; not; as, whether or *no.*—*n. pl.* **noes, nos.** A denial or refusal; an utterance of the word 'no,' as : *No* was his response. A negative vote or voter; as, 50 *noes.*

no, nō, *a.* [M.E. *no,* reduced form of *non,* E. *none.*] Not any; as, of *no* use; not at all, very far from being, as: He is *no* genius.— **no one,** nobody.

no, noh, nō, *n.* (*Sometimes cap.*) the traditional classic drama of Japan characterized by heroic, tragic themes, elaborate costumes, and formalized singing and dancing. Also **nō, Nō, No·ga·ku,** na̠'ga·kō'.

No·a·chi·an, nō·ā'kē·an, *a.* Of or pertaining to the patriarch Noah or his time; as, the *Noachian* deluge. Also **No·ach·ic, No·ach·i·cal, No·ah·ic,** nō·ā'ik.

nob, nob, *n.* [Prob. = *knob.*] *Slang,* the head; *cribbage,* the jack of the same suit as the card turned up, counting one to the holder.

nob, nob, *n.* [Of uncertain origin.] *Brit. slang,* one having wealth, class distinction, or influence.

nob·ble, nob'l, *v.t.*—*nobbled, nobbling.* [Origin uncertain.] *Brit. slang.* To tamper with, as a horse, by drugging or otherwise disabling, in order to destroy its chance of winning a race; to win over by illicit or underhand means; to acquire dishonestly; to swindle; to seize, catch, or capture, as a person for arrest.—**nob·bler,** *n.*

nob·by, nob'ē, *a.*—*nobbier, nobbiest.* [< *nob.*] *Brit. slang.* Smart, fashionable, or elegant; first-rate.—**nob·bi·ly,** *adv.*

No·bel·ist, nō·bel'ist, *n.* A Nobel prize winner.

No·bel·i·ty, nō·bel'i·tē, *n.* The fraternity of Nobel prize winners; a collective name for all those who have been awarded the Nobel prize.

no·be·li·um, nō·bē'lē·um, *n. Chem.* a radioactive, synthetic, element in the actinoid series, produced first at the Nobel Institute of Physics by the high-speed bombardment of curium with a carbon 13 isotope. Sym. No, at. no. 102, at. wt. 253. See Periodic Table of the Elements.

No·bel prize, nō·bel' prīz, *n.* One of five annual awards provided for by the will of the Swedish industrialist, Alfred Nobel, and given for outstanding contributions in the fields of chemistry, physics, medicine, literature, and the advancement of peace.

no·bil·i·ar·y, nō·bil'ē·er"ē, *a.* [Fr. *nobiliaire,* < L. *nobilis,* E. *noble.*] Of or pertaining to the nobility.

no·bil·i·ty, nō·bil'i·tē, *n.* pl. **no·bil·i·ties.** [O.Fr. *nobilite,* < L. *nobilitas.*] The body of persons forming a class of society with special hereditary titles, ranks, and privileges; the aristocracy; *Brit.* the peerage. The state or quality of being noble; noble birth or rank; exalted moral excellence; admirable dignity; majesty or augustness.

no·ble, nō'bl, *a.*—*nobler, noblest.* [O.Fr. Fr. *noble,* < L. *nobilis,* well-known, famous, highborn, noble, from the stem of *noscere,* know.] Famous, illustrious, or great, as persons or their achievements; distinguished by birth, rank, or title, or pertaining to persons so distinguished; belonging to or constituting the aristocracy; of an exalted moral character or excellence; admirable in dignity of conception, or in the manner of expression, execution, or composition; imposing or fine in appearance; stately or magnificent; of an admirably high quality, type, or class; fine, choice, or notably superior; of metals or minerals, precious or valuable; *chem.* inert.—*n.* A person of noble birth or rank; a nobleman; *Brit.* a peer. An old English gold coin, formerly worth six shillings, eight pence.—**no·ble·man,** nō'bl·man, *n.*—**no·ble·ness,** *n.*—**no·ble·wom·an,** nō'bl·wu̇m"an, *n.*—**no·bly,** nō'blē, *adv.*

no·blesse, nō·bles', *Fr.* na̠·bles', *n.* [Fr. *noblesse,* L.L. *nobilitia,* < L. *nobilis.*] The nobility; persons of noble rank collectively.

no·blesse o·blige, nō·bles' ō·blēzh', *Fr.* na̠·bles' a̠·blēzh', *n.* The obligation of people of wealth and social position to behave with honor and generosity; broadly, the duty to behave honorably.

no·bod·y, nō'bod"ē, nō'bo·dē, *pron.* No person; no one.—*n.* pl. **no·bod·ies.** A person of no standing or position.

no·cent, nō'sent, *a.* [L. *nocens* (nocent-), ppr. of *nocere,* harm, hurt: cf. *innocent.*] Hurtful, harmful, or injurious; *archaic,* guilty.

nock, nok, *n.* [M.E. *nocke,* bow tip: akin D. *nok* (naut.).] A piece at the butt end of an arrow with a notch for the bowstring; the notch itself; either of the notches at the ends of the bow horn which secure the bowstring.—*v.t.* To furnish with a nock, as a bow or an arrow; to adjust, as an arrow, to the bowstring, in readiness to shoot.

noc·tam·bu·la·tion, nok·tam″bū·lā'shan, *n.* [L. *nox, noctis,* night, and *ambulo,* to walk.] Somnambulism; sleepwalking. Also **noc·tam·bu·lism,** nok·tam'bū·liz″um.—**noc·tam·bu·list,** *n.*

noc·ti·lu·ca, nok″ti·lö'ka, *n.* pl. **noc·ti·lu·cae,** nok″ti·lö'sē. [L., something that shines by night, < *nox* (noct-), night, and *lucere,* shine.] A marine flagellate protozoan of the genus *Noctiluca,* notable for its phosphorescence.

noc·turn, nok'turn, *n.* [O.Fr. Fr. *nocturne,* < L. *nocturnus.*] (*Often cap.*), *Rom. Cath. Ch.* an office forming a part of matins.

noc·tur·nal, nok·tur'nal, *a.* Pertaining or belonging to the night; done or occurring at night; *zool.* active by night; *bot.* of flowers, closing during the day and blooming during the night.—**noc·tur·nal·i·ty,** nok″tēr·nal'i·tē, *n.*—**noc·tur·nal·ly,** *adv.*

noc·turne, nok'turn, *n.* [Fr.] *Mus.* a dreamy or pensive composition, variable in form; a serenade concerning the night. *Paint.* a work depicting a night scene.

noc·u·ous, nok'ū·us, *a.* Injurious; harmful; noxious.—**noc·u·ous·ly,** *adv.*—**noc·u·ous·ness,** *n.*

nod, nod, *v.i.*—*nodded, nodding.* [Allied to O.H.G. *nuoton, knoton,* to shake; Gael. *nodadh,* a wink or nod.] To let the head sink from sleep; to make an inclination of the head, as in assent, command, beckoning, or salutation; to make a mistake in a heedless moment; to bend or incline the top or to sway, as plumes or flowers.—*v.t.* To incline, as the head; to signify by a nod; to beckon by a nod.—*n.* A quick downward motion of the head as a sign of assent, salutation, or from drowsiness.—**nod·der,** *n.*

nod·dle, nod'l, *n.* [Formed < *nod.*] *Colloq.* the head.—*v.t., v.i.*—*noddled, noddling.* To nod a little; to nod often.

nod·dy, nod'ē, *n.* pl. **nod·dies.** [Prob. < *nod,* and equivalent to sleepyhead; cf. *noodle.*] A simpleton; a fool. A large dark-colored tern of the subfamily *Sterninae,* genus *Anous,* found on warm sea coasts, and so called from its tameness being considered as stupidity.

node, nōd, *n.* [L. *nodus* (for *gnodus*), a knot; cogn. *knot, noddle.*] A knot; a knob; a protuberance; *pathol.* a swelling; *bot.* a joint or knot on a stem where leaves arise; *phys.* an area in a vibrating body marked by little or no vibration; *geom.* a point on a curve to which two tangents can be drawn; *astron.* one of the points at which the orbit of a satellite intersects the ecliptic.—**nod·al** nōd'al, *a.*—**no·dal·i·ty,** *n.*

nod·i·cal, nod'i·kal, nō'di·kal, *a. Astron.* relating to nodes.

no·dose, nō'dōs, nō·dōs', *a.* [L. *nodosus.*] Knotted; knobby.—**no·dos·i·ty,** nō·dos'i·tē, *n.*

nod·ule, noj'öl, *n.* [L. *nodulus,* dim. < *nodus,* a knot.] A little knot or lump. *Bot.* a small woody body found in bark; a tubercle.—**nod·u·lar,** noj'u·lẻr, *a.* Pertaining to or in the form of a nodule.—**nod·u·lose, nod·u·lous,** noj'u·lōs", noj″u·lōs', noj'u·lus, *a.* Having little knots or nodules; knotty.

no·dus, nō'dus, *n.* pl. **no·di.** A difficult or complicated situation; a knotty point.

no·el, nō·el', *n.* [Fr. < L. *dies natalis,* birthday of Christ.] A Christmas song or carol. (*Cap.*) Christmas day; yuletide.

no·et·ic, nō·et'ik, *a.* [Gr. *noētikós* < *noein,* perceive, think, < *noos, nous,* mind.] Of or pertaining to the mind or intellect; originating in the mind independent of the senses.

nog, nog, *n.* [Var. of obs. or prov. *knag,* M.E. *knagge,* spur, projection, peg.] A wooden peg, pin, or block; a brick-shaped piece of wood built into a wall as a backing for nails.—*v.t.*—*nogged, nogging.* To secure by a nog or peg; to fill, as the open spaces in a wooden framework, with small stones or brick.

nog, nog, *n.* [Origin obscure.] Eggnog; *chiefly Brit.* a kind of strong ale or beer. Also **nogg.**

nog·gin, nog'in, *n.* [Ir. *noigin,* Gael. *noigean,* a noggin.] A small mug or wooden cup; a measure of liquor equivalent to a gill, or one-quarter of a pint; *colloq.* the head.

nog·ging, nog'ing, *n.* Brickwork serving to fill the spaces in a wooden frame; a piece of wood built into a wall, as for a backing for nails.

no-hit·ter, nō'hit'ẻr, *n. Baseball,* a game in which the pitcher, working the whole game without relief, permits the opposing team no hits.

no·how, nō'hou″, *adv. Dial.* Not in any way; not at all.

noil, noil, *n.* [Origin uncertain.] A short fiber of wool, cotton, or silk separated from the long fiber in combing.

noise, noiz, *n.* [O.Fr. *noise,* noise, uproar, Fr. quarrel; of disputed origin.] A sound or sounds of a loud, confused, or discordant kind; a din; a sound of any kind; as, the *noises* of the meadow; *electron.* unwanted sound or disturbances causing interference in a communications system.—*v.t.*—*noised, noising.* To spread the report or rumor of.—*v.i.* To make a noise, outcry, or clamor; to talk much or publicly.

noise·less, noiz'lis, *a.* Making or attended with no noise; silent; quiet.—**noise·less·ly,** *adv.*—**noise·less·ness,** *n.*

noise·mak·er, noiz'mā″kẻr, *n.* A person or thing which produces noise, esp. a device made for that purpose to be used at parties.

noi·some, noi'som, *a.* [< M.E. *noy,* annoyance, with term. *-some.*] Offensive, esp. to the sense of smell; fetid; noxious; harmful.—**noi·some·ly,** *adv.*—**noi·some·ness,** *n.*

nois·y, noi'zē, *a.*—*noisier, noisiest.* Making much noise; abounding in or attended with noise.—**nois·i·ly,** *adv.*—**nois·i·ness,** *n.*

no·li me tan·ge·re, nō'li mē tan'je·rē, *L.* nō'lē me täng·ge·Re″, *n.* [L. *noli me tangere,* 'touch me not.'] A warning that someone or something must not be touched or interfered with; a picture representing Christ appearing to Mary Magdalene after his resurrection; *bot.* the touch-me-not.

nol·le pros·e·qui, nol'ē pros'e·kwī″, *n.* [L. to be unwilling to prosecute.] *Law,* an entry in a legal record that a plaintiff or prosecutor wishes to halt proceedings, in whole or part, in an action he has begun.

no·lo con·ten·de·re, nō'lō kon·ten'de·rē, *n. Law,* a plea by the defense which is not a confession of guilt but is so taken by the court, and allows the defendant the right to deny the charges in any further action.

nol-pros, nol'pros', *v.t.*—*nol-prossed, nol-prossing. Law,* to enter a nolle prosequi on the legal record to denote the discontinuance of legal action by prosecutor or plaintiff against one or more defendants or one or more counts in a suit.

no·mad, nō'mad, nom'ad, *n.* [Gr. *nomas, nomados,* living on pasturage, < *nemō,* to feed, to pasture.] One of those people who shift their residence according to the state of the pasture, supply of food, or seasonal factors, and have no permanent abode; a wanderer.—*a.* Nomadic.—**no·mad·ic,** nō·-

---

mad′ik, *a.* Pertaining to or like nomads; wandering; pastoral.—**no·mad·i·cal·ly,** *adv.*—**no·mad·ism,** *n.*

no man's land, *n.* Unclaimed or uninhabited land; a field of human endeavor marked by uncertainty and danger; *milit.* ground between hostile forces.

nom·arch, nom′ärk, *n.* [Gr. *nomarchēs,* < *nomos,* nome, and *árchein,* lead, rule.] The governor of an ancient Egyptian province or of a nomarchy.—**nom·ar·chy,** nom′är·kē, *n. pl.* **nom·ar·chies.** [Gr. *nomarchía.*] One of the provinces into which modern Greece is divided.

nom de guerre, nom″ de gâr′, *Fr.* nọN de geʀ′, *n. pl.* **noms de guerre,** nomz″ de gâr′, *Fr.* nọN de geʀ′. [Fr., 'name of war.'] An assumed name under which one pursues a profession or other undertaking.

nom de plume, nom″ de plöm′, *Fr.* nọN de plȳm′, *n. pl.* **noms de plume,** nomz″ de plȳm′, *Fr.* nọN de plȳm′. [Fr.] Pen name.

no·men, nō′men, *n. pl.* **nom·i·na,** nom′i·na. [L.] The second of three names of a citizen of ancient Rome, indicating his gens or family group. See *praenomen, cognomen, agnomen.*

no·men·cla·tor, nō′men·klā″tẽr, *n.* [L., < *nōmen,* name, and *calo,* to call (seen in *calendar*).] A person who invents names for things, as in science or the arts.

no·men·cla·ture, nō′men·klā″chẽr, nō·men′kla·chẽr, *n.* A system of names; the systematic naming of things; the vocabulary of names or technical terms which are appropriated to a science, art, or other field.—**no·men·cla·tur·al,** *a.*—**no·men·cla·to·ri·al,** nō″men·kla·tō′ri·al, *a.*

nom·i·nal, nom′i·nal, *a.* [L. *nōminālis,* < *nōmen* (*nōmin-*), name.] Of, pertaining to, or consisting of a name or names; containing or bearing a name or names; assigned to a person by name; being something in name only; of a price or a consideration, named as a mere matter of form, being trifling in comparison with the actual value. *Gram.* relating to a noun; of the nature of a noun or nouns.—**nom·i·nal·ly,** *adv.*

nom·i·nal·ism, nom′i·na·liz″um, *n. Philos.* a theory of medieval philosophy revived and restated in branches of contemporary logical positivism, and holding that universals are mere names corresponding to nothing in objective reality.

nom·i·nal price, *n. Com.* an estimated price given on days when no real sale has taken place, derived by averaging the closing bid quotation with the closing asked quotation: most often used in commodity trading.

nom·i·nal wag·es, *n. pl. Econ.* wages estimated in terms of money received without relationship to their purchasing power. Compare *real wages.*

nom·i·nate, nom′i·nāt″, *v.t.*—*nominated, nominating.* [L. *nomino, nominatum.*] To designate for an office or duty; to propose or offer the name of, as a candidate for an office or place.—**nom·i·nit,** *a.* Having a certain name.—**nom·i·na·tion,** nom″i·nā′shan, *n.* The act of nominating; the act of naming for an office; the state of being nominated.—**nom·i·na·tor,** *n.* One that nominates.

nom·i·na·tive, nom′i·na·tiv, nom′i·nā″tiv, nom′na·tiv, *a.* [L. *nominatus,* naming.] Proposed by nomination or so appointed; *gram.* a term applied to that form of a noun or pronoun which is used when the noun or pronoun is the subject of a sentence.—*n.* The nominative case; a nominative word.

nom·i·nee, nom′i·nē′, *n.* A person nominated; one proposed to fill a place or office.

no·mism, nō′miz″um, *n.* Conduct based on religious and moral laws.—**no·mis·tic,** nō·mis′tik, *a.*

nom·o·gram, nom′o·gram″, nō′mo·gram″,

n. A graph using three parallel lines or curves representing three variables and graduated in such a way that a straight line connecting any two values will give the related value of the third at the point where the line intersects that variable. Also **nom·o·graph.**—**no·mog·ra·phy,** nō·mog′ra·fē, *n.*

no·mol·o·gy, nō·mol′o·jē, *n.* The science of law or of the formulation of law; the science dealing directly with the laws of reason; that branch of a science which formulates laws from the general principles derived from experimentation, as in psychology.—**nom·o·log·i·cal,** nom″o·loj′i·kal, *a.*—**no·mol·o·gist,** *n.*

nom·o·thet·ic, nom″o·thet′ik, *a.* [Gr. *nomothetikos,* < *nomos,* law, and *tithenai,* set.] Lawgiving; legislative; founded on law or a system of laws; involved in the process or study of law formation.

non·a·bra·sive, non″a·brā′siv, non″a·brā′ziv, *a.* Not causing wear or scraping away by friction.

non·ab·sorb·ent, non″ab·sar′bent, non″ab·zar′bent, *a.* Not sucking up or not capable of sucking up liquids; *chem.* not capable of absorbing by molecular or chemical processes.

non·ac·cept·ance, non″ak·sep′tans, *n.* Failure to accept; a refraining from acceptance.

non·ad·he·sive, non″ad·hē′siv, *a.* Not having the quality of adhering or of causing to stick together.

non·ad·ja·cent, non″a·jā′sent, *a.* Not adjoining or contiguous.

non·ad·min·is·tra·tive, non″ad·min′i·strā″tiv, *a.* Neither of nor pertaining to the executive function or staff of an organization.

non·age, non′ij, nō′nij, *n.* [L. *non,* not, and E. *age.*] The time before a person becomes legally of age; period of immaturity in general.

non·a·ge·nar·i·an, non″a·je·nâr′ē·an, nō″na·je·nâr′ē·an, *n.* [L. *nonagenarius,* < *nonageni,* ninety each, *nonaginta,* ninety, *novem,* nine.] A person who is ninety, or between 90 and 100 years old.—*a.* Being between 90 and 100 years old.

non·ag·gres·sion, non″a·gresh′an, *n.* Abstention, as by international agreement, from military attack.

non·a·gon, non′a·gon″, *n.* [L. *nonus,* ninth, and Gr. *gonia,* an angle.] A geometric figure having nine sides and nine angles. Also *enneagon.*

non·al·co·hol·ic, non″al·ko·ha̱′lik, non″al·ko·hol′ik, *a.* Not containing alcohol, as a beverage.

non·ap·pear·ance, non″a·pēr′ans, *n.* A failure to appear; default.

non·be·liev·er, non″bi·lē′vẽr, *n.* One who does not believe; one who denies religious teachings; one without faith in God.

non·bel·lig·er·ent, non″be·lij′ẽr·ent, *n.* A person or a nation not officially engaged in war, but aiding one of those so engaged. —*a.* Not officially at war.

nonce, nons, *n.* [Same as *once,* with an initial *n* belonging to the old dative of the article.] Present occasion or purpose: used mainly in the phrase *for the nonce.*

non·cha·lant, non″sha·länt′, non′sha·lant, *a.* [Fr., < *non,* not, *chaloir,* to care for, < L. *calere,* to be warm or ardent.] Indifferent; casual; coolly unconcerned.— **non·cha·lance,** non″sha·läns′, non′sha·lans, *n.* The condition of being nonchalant; casual indifference.—**non·cha·lant·ly,** *adv.*

non·col·le·gi·ate, non″ko·lē′jit, non″ko·lē′jē·it, *a.* Not belonging to a college. Of a university, not composed of colleges. *Brit.* belonging to the body of students in a university not attached to any particular college or hall.

non·com, non′kom″, *n. Colloq.* a noncommissioned officer.

non·com·bat·ant, non·kom′ba·tant, non″kom·bat′ant, *n.* A member of a military force whose direct responsibility does not involve actual fighting, as a chaplain or a medical corpsman; a civilian during a period of war.

non·com·bus·ti·ble, non″kom·bus′ti·bl, *a.* Not easily ignitable.—*n.*

non·com·mis·sioned of·fi·cer, *n.* A subordinate officer who is selected from the ranks of the enlisted men and who may hold one of several grades, as corporal or sergeant.

non·com·mit·tal, non″ko·mit′al, *a.* Not indicating or involving commitment.— **non·com·mit·tal·ly,** *adv.*

non·com·mu·ni·cant, non″ko·mū′ni·kant, *n.* One who is not a communicant; one who does not take communion, as at a religious service.

non·com·pli·ance, non″kom·pli′ans, *n.* Neglect, refusal, or failure to comply; insurgency; disobedience.—**non·com·pli·ant,** *n.*

non com·pos men·tis, non kom′pos men′tis, *L.* nōn kŏm′pōs men′tis, *n.* [L., 'not having control of one's mind.'] *Law.* Not of sound mind; not capable, mentally, of managing one's own affairs.

non·con·duc·tor, non″kon·duk′tẽr, *n.* A substance which resists or conducts with difficulty such forces as electricity, heat, or sound.—**non·con·duc·ting,** *a.*

non·con·form, non″kon·farm′, *v.i.* To deviate from conventional rules of behavior.

non·con·form·ist, non″kon·far′mist, *n.* One who does not conform to the prevalent norms of thought or behavior; (*often cap.*) one who refuses to conform to an established church, particularly the Church of England. —**non·con·form·i·ty,** non″kon·far′mi·tē, *n.* Neglect or failure to conform; want of agreement; neglect or refusal to unite with an established church in its rites and mode of worship; (*often cap.*) the position of Protestant dissenters in England.

non·con·ta·gious, non″kon·tā′jus, *a. Med.* Of disease, not transmissible by contact; noncommunicable.

non·co·op·er·a·tion, non″kō·op″e·rā′shan, *n.* Failure or refusal to cooperate with an individual, party, or organization; *specif.* the practice or policy, followed for political or revolutionary ends, of refraining from cooperating in activities instituted or maintained by the government; as, the movement of *noncooperation* conducted by Gandhi and his followers in opposing the British rule of India. See *civil disobedience, passive resistance.*—**non·co·op·er·a·tion·ist,** *n.*—**non·co·op·er·a·tive,** non″kō·op′ra·tiv, *a.*—**non·co·op·er·a·tor,** *n.*

non·cor·ro·sive, non″ko·rō′siv, *a.* Not having the power of corroding, as certain acids.

non·com·mu·ni·ca·ble, non″ka·mū′ni·ka·bl, *a.* Not capable of transmission, as information; not transmissible through personal contact, as a disease.

non·de·duct·i·ble, non″di·duk′ti·bl, *a.* Not subtractable, as: Gifts to relatives are *nondeductible* from taxable income.

non·de·liv·er·y, non″di·liv′e·rē, *n. pl.* **non·de·liv·er·ies.** Failure to deliver or distribute; that which is not delivered according to contract or expectation.

non·de·script, non″di·skript′, *a.* Defying description or classification; amorphous. —*n.* A person or thing not easily classed or described.

non·de·struc·tive, non″di·struk′tiv, *a.* Not causing destruction, mutilation, or ruin.

non·dis·junc·tion, non″dis·jungk′shan, *n. Biol.* the failure of paired chromosomes to separate normally during the first stage of meiosis, leaving one daughter cell with both chromosomes and the other with none.

non·dis·tinc·tive, non″di·stingk′tiv, *a.* Not distinctive; *phon.* having a slight articulatory variation that carries no phonemic value, as seen in the slight difference between the *p* in pose and the *p* in repose.— **non·dis·tinc·tive·ly,** *adv.*

none, nun, *pron. sing. or pl. in constr.* [M.E. *non*, < O.E. *nān*.] No one; not one; not any, as of something indicated; no part.— *adv.* To no extent; in no way; not at all, as: The supply is *none* too great.

non·ef·fec·tive, non″i·fek′tiv, *a.* Not efficacious; without the power to cause or produce effect; *milit.* unfit for active duty.— *n.* A noneffective person in the army or navy.

non·e·go, non·ē′gō, non·eg′ō, *n.* [L., not I.] *Metaph.* That which is external to consciousness; the objective world.

non·en·ti·ty, non·en′ti·tē, *n. pl.* **non·en·ti·ties.** [L.L. *nonentitas*.] Nonexistence; a thing not existing or existing only in fantasy; a person or thing utterly without consequence or importance.

nones, nōnz, *n. pl.* (*Often cap.*), *eccles.* the fifth canonical hour, observed each day at 3 P.M., or the prescribed prayers for it.

nones, nōnz, *n. pl.* [L. *nonae*, < *nonus*, for *novenus*, ninth, < *novem*, nine.] In the Roman calendar, the fifth day of the months January, February, April, June, August, September, November, and December, and the seventh day of March, May, July, and October: so called as falling on the *ninth* day before the ides, both days included.

non·es·sen·tial, non″i·sen′shal, *a.* Not essential; not absolutely necessary.—*n.* A person or thing that is not absolutely necessary.

none·such, nun′such″, *n.* A person or thing with no equal, and which cannot be compared to another; nonpareil. Also *nonsuch.*—*a.*

none·the·less, nun″THe·les′, *adv.* Nevertheless; however. Also **none the less.**

non-Eu·clid·e·an, non″ū·klid′ē·an, *a.* Not included in or not in conformity with the system of geometry established by Euclid. Also **non-Eu·clid·i·an.**

non·ex·empt, non″ig·zempt′, *a.* Not subject to an exemption; not exempt from liability.

non·ex·ist·ence, ríon″ig·zis′tens, *n.* Absence of existence; a thing that has no existence.—**non·ex·ist·ent,** *a.* Not existent; having no existence.

non·ex·por·ta·tion, non″eks·pōr·tā′shan, *n.* Failure or refusal to export.

non·fat·ten·ing, non′fat′en·ing, *a.* Not fattening; not high in calories; as, proteins are generally *nonfattening.*

non·fea·sance, non·fē′zans, *n. Law,* failure to perform a duty required of one: compare with *malfeasance, misfeasance.*

non·fer·rous, non·fer′us, *a.* Containing little or no iron; referring to metals other than iron.

non·fic·tion, non·fik′shan, *n.* Any prose work that is not fictional, as essays, biographies, and histories.

non·he·red·i·tar·y, non″he·red′i·ter″ē, *a.* Not transmitted from parent to child; not descended by inheritance from an ancestor to an heir.

no·nil·lion, nō·nil′yan, *n.* [L. *nonus*, nine, and E. *million*.] *Arith.* In the U.S. and France, a number followed by 30 zeros; in Great Britain and Germany, a unit followed by 54 zeros.—*a.*

non·im·por·ta·tion, non″im·pōr·tā′shan, *n.* Failure or refusal to import.

non·in·duc·tive, non″in·duk′tiv, *a.* *Elect.* having little or no inductance.—**non·in·duc·tive·ly,** *adv.*—**non·in·duc·tiv·i·ty,** non″in·duk·tiv′i·tē, *n.*

non·in·flam·ma·ble, non″in·flam′a·bl, *a.* Not combustible; not flammable; not easily set on fire.

non·in·ter·ven·tion, non″in·tèr·ven′shan, *n.* Abstention from intervening; *polit.* a policy of not interfering in the affairs of another nation or nations.—**non·in·ter··ven·tion·al,** *a.* **non·in·ter·ven·tion·al··ist,** *n.*—**non·in·ter·ven·tion·ist,** *n., a.*

non·in·tox·i·cant, non″in·tok′si·kant, *n.* A beverage or drug that does not intoxicate.

non·join·der, non·join′dèr, *n. Law,* omission to join, as of one who should have been a party to an action.

non·jur·ing, non·jur′ing, *a.* [L. *non*, not, and *juro*, to swear.] Not swearing allegiance: applied esp. to clergymen of the Church of England who would not swear allegiance to the English government after the Revolution of 1688.—**non·ju·rant,** non·ju′ror, non·jur′ant, non·jur′èr, *n.*

non·le·gal, non·lē′gal, *a.* Having no legal aspect: distinguished from *illegal.*

non·met·al, non′met″al, *n. Chem.* An element not having the character of a metal, as carbon, nitrogen, or halogens; an element with properties more acid than basic, and unable to form cations in solution.—**non··me·tal·lic,** non″me·tal′ik, *a.*

non·mor·al, non·mar′al, non·mor′al, *a.* Having no relation to morality; having no moral aspect: distinguished from *immoral.* —**non·mo·ral·i·ty,** non″ma·ral′i·tē, *n.*

non·ob·jec·tive, non″ob·jek′tiv, *a. Fine arts.* Not attempting to represent objects as they are in nature; nonrepresentational; abstract.—**non·ob·jec·tiv·ism,** *n.*—**non··ob·jec·tiv·ist,** *n.*—**non·ob·jec·tiv·i·ty,** non″ob·jek″tiv′i·tē, *n.*

non·ob·serv·ance, non″ob·zur′vans, *n.* The act of defying or neglecting to comply, as with an official edict; failure to observe, as a religious holiday.

non·pa·reil, non″pa·rel′, *n.* [Fr. < *non*, not or no, and *pareil*, equal, < L. *par*, equal.] A person or thing of peerless excellence; a finch of the southern U.S.; *print.* a small printing type.—*a.* Without equal.

non·par·ti·san, non·pär′ti·zan, *a.* Not bound by ties or obligations to a regular political party; objective.—*n.*—**non·par··ti·san·ship,** *n.*

non·plus, non·plus′, non′plus, *v.t.*—*nonplused, nonplusing, esp. Brit. nonplussed, nonplussing.* [L. *non-*, not, and *plus*, more, further.] To make completely confused; to utterly baffle.—*n.* A condition of complete perplexity; an inability to say or do more, usu. preceded by *at* a or *in* a.

non·pro·duc·er, non″pro·dō′sèr, non″·pro·dū′sèr, *n. Econ.* one who does not contribute his labor or capital to the production of goods of exchangeable value.

non·pro·duc·tive, non″pro·duk′tiv, *a.* Producing nothing; not directly making goods, as a segment of the labor force; not progressing; failing to produce.—**non·pro·duc·tive·ly,** *adv.*—**non·pro·duc·tive·ness, non·pro··duc·tiv·i·ty,** non″prō·duk·tiv′i·tē, *n.*

non·prof·it, non·prof′it, *a.* Not for profit; the legal purpose and activities of such tax exempt entities as churches, charities, hospitals, or foundations.

non·pro·lif·er·a·tion, non″prō·lif″e·rā′shan, *n.* The act of regulating the expansion of nuclear weapons to nations not possessing them, esp. through a treaty or other international agreement.—*a.*

non pro·se·qui·tur, non prō·sek′wi·tèr, *n.* [L., 'he does not pursue (prosecute).'] *Law,* a judgment rendered against the plaintiff when he does not appear in court to prosecute an action he has started. Also **non pros.** —**non-pros,** non″pros′, *v.t.*—*non-prossed, non-prossing.*

non·re·fill·a·ble, non″rē·fil′a·bl, *a.* Of certain containers, esp. liquor bottles, not legally refillable with contents to be offered for sale; *med.* pertaining to prescriptions which may be filled only once.

non·re·mov·a·ble, non″ri·mö′va·bl, *a.* Not capable of being removed; as, the *nonremovable* grass stains, the *nonremovable* shelving.

non·re·new·a·ble, non″ri·nö′a·bl, non″·ri·nū′a·bl, *a.* Not offering an option to renew on the same terms, as a contract, lease, insurance policy, or magazine subscription.

non·rep·re·sen·ta·tion·al, non″rep·ri·zen·tā′sha·nal, *a. Art.* Not depicting nature as it is; abstract; nonobjective.—**non··rep·re·sen·ta·tion·al·ism,** *n.*

non·res·i·dent, non·rez′i·dent, *a.* Not resident in a particular place, esp. not residing where official duties require one to reside.—*n.* One who is nonresident.— **non·res·i·dence,** *n.*—**non·res·i·den·cy,** *n. pl.* **non·res·i·den·cies.**

non·res·i·den·tial, non″rez·i·den′shal, *a.* Pertaining to a neighborhood where people do not have homes, as: Factories are located in *nonresidential* areas.

non·re·sis·tance, non″ri·zis′tans, *n.* The policy of submission without opposition to authority, power, or usurpation.—**non·re·sis·tant,** *a., n.*

non·re·stric·tive, non″ri·strik′tiv, *a.* Not restrictive; non-confining; free. *Gram.* pertaining to a descriptive word or phrase, as an adjective clause, which does not limit or modify its antecedent and may be omitted without changing the essence of the thought, as the phrase 'who wore green' in the sentence, 'The Irish, who wore green, won the game.'

non·re·turn·a·ble, non″ri·tur′na·bl, *a.* Pertaining to merchandise which may not be returned for refund of the purchase price; denoting containers, esp. bottles, on which no deposit is collected and which need not be returned after use.

non·rig·id, non·rij′id, *a.* Not rigid; *aeron.* pertaining to a type of airship having a flexible gas container without a supporting structure, and held in shape by internal pressure.

non·sched·uled, non·skej′öld, *Brit.* non··shed′ūld, *a.* Not having a prearranged plan involving time or place of action; not entered on a schedule; of or pertaining to an airline authorized to fly without schedules.

non·sec·tar·i·an, non″sek·târ′ē·an, *a.* Not having an affiliation with any particular religious group.

non·seg·re·gat·ed, non·seg′re·gā′tid, *a.* Not segregated; integrated.

non·sense, non′sens, *n.* Words or ideas that lack meaning or are absurd; foolish or meaningless actions or behavior; anything of little importance or utility.—**non·sen··si·cal,** non·sen′si·kal, *a.*—**non·sen·si··cal·ly,** *adv.*—**non·sen·si·cal·ness,** *n.*

non se·qui·tur, non sek′wi·tèr, *L.* nōn se′kwi·tuṛ″, *n.* [L., 'it does not follow.'] An inference or a conclusion which does not follow from the premises.

non·sked, non·sked′, *n. Colloq.* a nonscheduled airline.

non·skid, non·skid′, *a.* Corrugated or with special tread or ridges to resist skidding, as a vehicle tire.

non·smok·er, non·smō′kèr, *n.* One who does not smoke, esp. tobacco.

non·stand·ard, non′stan′dèrd, *a.* Not standard; denoting written or spoken language which does not conform to usage generally accepted as correct.

non·stop, non′stop′, *a., adv.* With no stops on the way.

non·stri·at·ed, non·strī′ā·tid, *a.* Not striated.—**non·stri·at·ed fi·ber,** the fiber constituting the involuntary muscles.

non·such, non'such", *n.* Nonesuch.

non·suit, non"söt', *n.* [A.Fr. *nounsute*, < O.Fr. *non*, not, and *sieute*, suit.] *Law*, a judgment given against a plaintiff who neglects to prosecute, fails to show a legal cause of action, or to present sufficient evidence.—*v.t.* To subject to a nonsuit.

non·sup·port, non"su·pôrt', *n. Law*, failure to support a legal dependent as required by a court order.

non·sym·met·ri·cal, non"si·me'tri·kal, *a.* Not symmetrical; not harmoniously proportioned; not well-balanced.

non·tax·a·ble, non·tak'sa·bl, *a.* Of a business, property, or income which is specifically exempt from taxation.

non·trans·fer·a·ble, non·trans'fèr·a·bl, *a.* Not subject to transfer of ownership, as titles, securities, or other property.

non trop·po, non trop'ō, *It.* nạn trạp'pạ, *adv., a.* [It.] *Mus.* Moderately fast; not too rapidly.

non·un·ion, non·ūn'yan, *a.* Not belonging to, or not in accordance with the rules of a trade union; not recognizing or favoring trade unions; not maintained or manufactured by union workers.—*n. Med.* an imperfect healing of a broken bone.—**non·un·ion·ism**, non·ūn'ya·niz"um, *n.*—**non·un·ion·ist**, *n.*

non·us·er, non·ū'zèr, *n. Law*, failure to use a right or privilege.

non·ver·bal, non·vụr'bal, *a.* Involving or needing little or no language; being deficient in the understanding or use of words; pertaining to that which is other than verbal: opposed to *verbal*.

non·vi·a·ble, non·vī'a·bl, *a.* Being inadequately fitted to live, develop, or perform.

non·vi·o·lence, non·vī'o·lens, *n.* The practice or principle of abstaining from all forms of violence; the use of passive resistance as a technique of protest.—**non·vi·o·lent**, *a.*—**non·vi·o·lent·ly**, *adv.*

non·vol·a·tile, non'vol'a·til, non·vol'a·til, *Brit.* non·vol'a·tīl", *a.* Not readily vaporized; unchangeable.

non·vot·er, non·vō'tér, *n.* One who fails to vote; one who is disenfranchised.

non·white, non·hwīt', non·wīt', *n.* One of any race other than Caucasian.—*a.*

noo·dle, nöd'l, *n.* Dried unleavened egg dough or paste, usu. shaped in flat strips, often boiled and served in casseroles and soups; *slang*, the head. *Slang*, a dolt or simpleton; also **noo·dle·head**.

nook, nụk, *n.* [Cf. Sc. *neuk*, Ir. *niuc*, a nook.] A corner; a recess; a secluded retreat.

noon, nön, *n.* [O.E. *nôn*, L. *nona* (*hora*), the ninth hour; orig. 3 P.M., the time of eating the chief meal, but afterward the term became applied to the midday hour.] The middle of the day; the time when the sun is in the meridian; twelve o'clock. *Fig.* the time of greatest brilliancy or power; the prime. Also **noon·day**, nön'dā".—*a.* Pertaining to midday.—**noon·tide**, nön'tīd", *n.* The time of noon; midday; one's best time or greatest point.—**noon·time**, nön'tīm", *n.*

no one, *pron.* Nobody; no person. Also **no-one**, nō'wun".

noose, nös, *n.* [Ult. < L. *nodus*, knot.] A loop with a running knot, as in a snare, lasso, or hangman's halter, which tightens as the rope is pulled; *fig.* a tie, bond, or snare.—*v.t.*—*noosed, noosing*. To secure by or as by a noose; ensnare with or catch with a noose; to put to death by hanging; *fig.* to make fast by the marriage tie. To make a noose with or in, as a rope.

no·pal, nō'pal, *n.* [Mex. *nopalli*.] A cactus plant, *Nopalea cochinellifera*, cultivated as food for cochineal insects; the prickly pear.

no-par, nō'pär", *a.* Having no definite face value: applied chiefly to a certain class of capital stock certificates. Also **no-par val·ue**.

nope, nōp, *adv. Slang*, no.

nor, nạr, *unstressed* nèr, *conj.* [*Or* with the neg. particle *ne*, *n-* prefixed: old forms were *nother*, *nouther*.] A word used to render negative the second or a subsequent member or a clause or sentence, specif. as a correlative to *neither* and with other negatives for emphasis; equivalent to *and not* and in this case not always corresponding to a foregoing negative, as: He is happy, *nor* need we be concerned.

Nor·dic, nạr'dik, *a. Anthropol.* of or related to that division of the Caucasian race characterized by fair skin, blond hair, and elongated skull; of or related to the blond peoples from northern Europe, particularly the Scandinavians.—*n.* An individual with Nordic characteristics or of Nordic origin.

Nor·folk jack·et, nạr'fok jak'it, *n.* [From *Norfolk*, county in eastern England.] A belted, single-breasted jacket or coat with box pleats in both front and back. Also **Nor·folk coat.**

no·ri·a, nōr'ē·a, nạr'ē·a, *n.* [Sp.] A wheel with buckets around its circumference used in Spain, the Middle East, and Asia for raising water; a Persian wheel.

nor·land, nạr'land, *n.* (*Often cap.*) Area or territory in the north; northland.

norm, nạrm, *n.* [L. *norma*, a carpenter's square, a rule, for *gnorima*, < root *gno*, to know.] A rule; a pattern; a model; *psychol.* an authoritative standard in a test taken from the average achievement of a group.

nor·mal, nạr'mal, *a.* [L. *normalis*.] According to a rule, principle, or norm; conforming with a type or standard considered usual; natural; not abnormal; regular; *geom.* perpendicular. *Psychol.* sane; average; as, of *normal* intelligence.—*n.* The common or usual condition; the standard; *geom.* a straight line at right angles to the tangent or tangent plane at any point of a curve or curved surface.—**nor·mal·i·ty**, nạr·mal'i·tē, *n.*—**nor·mal·ly**, nạr'ma·lē, *adv.*

nor·mal curve, *n. Statistics*, a graph or curve in the shape of a bell, exhibiting the distribution of the several values of a variable. Also **Gauss·i·an curve.**

nor·mal·cy, nạr'mal·sē, *n.* Normality; the state or condition of being normal.

nor·mal dis·tri·bu·tion, *n. Statistics*, a frequency distribution having the characteristics of a normal curve.

nor·mal·ize, nạr'ma·līz", *v.t.*—*normalized, normalizing*. To make normal; to reduce to a standard or norm.—*v.i.* To become normal once again.—**nor·mal·i·za·tion**, nạr"ma·li·zā'shan, *n.*—**nor·mal·iz·er**, *n.*

nor·mal school, *n.* [Fr. *ecole normale*, lit. 'a school that serves as a model.'] A school in which teachers are trained.

Nor·man, nạr'man, *n.* A native or inhabitant of Normandy.—*a.* Pertaining to Normandy or the Normans.—**Nor·man ar·chi·tec·ture**, the round-arched style of architecture, a variety of the Romanesque. —**Nor·man French**, the language of the Normans at the time of the Norman Conquest; the French dialect of Normandy. —**Nor·man-French**, *a.*

nor·ma·tive, nạr'ma·tiv, *a.* Relating to or establishing norms; based on a standard; as, *normative* conduct, *normative* grammar.— **nor·ma·tive·ly**, *adv.*—**nor·ma·tive·ness**, *n.*

Norse, nạrs, *n. pl. but sing. in constr.* The ancient Scandinavians, esp. the West Scandinavians; the Norwegians; *sing.* the language of Norway.—*a.* Belonging to ancient Scandinavia; Norwegian.—**Norse·man**, nạrs'man, *n. pl.* **Norse·men.** A native of ancient Scandinavia.

north, nạrth, *adv.* [O.E. *north* = D. *noord* = G. *nord* = Icel. *nordhr* = Norw., Sw., and Dan. *nord*, north.] In the direction which is to the right of a person facing the setting sun or west; toward or in the north; from the north, as with reference to wind.—*n.* A cardinal point of the compass lying in the plane of the meridian and to the right of a person facing the setting sun or west; the direction in which this point lies. (*Cap.*) a quarter or territory situated in this direction; that part of the U.S. which in general lies north of Maryland, the Ohio River, and Missouri.—*a.* Lying toward or situated in the north; directed or proceeding toward the north; coming from the north, as a wind.

north·bound, nạrth'bound", *a.* Moving in a northerly direction.

north by east, *n.* On a mariner's compass, a direction one point to the right or east of due north: N 11° 15' E.

north by west, *n.* The compass point that is one point to the left or west of due north: N 11° 15' W.

north·east, nạrth'ēst', *Naut.* nạr"ēst', *n.* [O.E. *northēast*.] The point on the mariner's compass or the general direction midway between north and east; a region in this direction.—*a.* Situated in the northeast; directed toward the northeast; as, to take a *northeast* course; coming from the northeast, as the wind.—*adv.* From, toward, or in the northeast.

north·east by east, *n.* A point on the compass indicating a direction north of due east by three points.

north·east by north, *n.* A point on the compass indicating a direction east of due north by three points.

north·east·er, nạrth"ē'stėr, *Naut.* nạr"ē'stėr, *n.* A blustery wind or gale from the northeast, often with cold heavy rain or snow, and popularly supposed to continue for three days.

north·east·er·ly, nạrth"ē'stėr·lē, *Naut.* nạr"ē'stėr·lē, *a.* Toward, in, or from the northeast.—*adv.* Toward or from the northeast.

north·east·ern, nạrth"ē'stėrn, *Naut.* nạr"ē'stėrn, *a.* Pertaining to or being in the northeast, or in a northeast direction.

north·east·ern·er, nạrth"ē'stėr·nėr, *n.* (*Often cap.*) an inhabitant or native of a northeastern region, as of northeastern U.S.

north·east·ward, nạrth"ēst'wėrd, *Naut.* nạr"ēst'wėrd, *adv., a.* In the direction of or toward the northeast.—*n.* The northeast. Also **north·east·ward·ly**, **north·east·wards.**

north·er, nạr'THér, *n.* A strong wind or storm from the north, esp. a fall or winter gale which blows across the southwestern region of the U.S.

nor·ther·ly, nạr'THér·lē, *a.* Of or pertaining to the north; directed toward or located in the north; northern; proceeding from the north, as the wind.—*adv.* In the direction of or from the north.—*n. pl.* **nor·ther·lies**. A wind moving from the north.—**north·er·li·ness**, *n.*

north·ern, nạr'THérn, *a.* Toward the north; proceeding from the north; located in the north; (*often cap.*) characteristic of the inhabitants of a region that is situated toward the north, esp. of the U.S. Native to the north; as, a *northern* variety of a plant; *astron.* located to the north of the celestial equator.—*n.* An inhabitant of a northern region.—**north·ern·most**, *a.*—**north·ern·ness**, *n.*

North·ern Cross, *n. Astron.* the six stars of the constellation Cygnus, formed in the shape of a cross.

North·ern Crown, *n. Astron.* a constellation of stars, Corona Borealis.

north·ern·er, nạr'THér·nér, *n.* (*Sometimes cap.*) a native or inhabitant of the north, esp. in the U.S.

North·ern Hem·i·sphere, *n.* That half of the earth north of the equator.

north·ern lights, *n. pl.* Aurora borealis.

North Ger·man·ic, *n.* A sub group of Germanic languages that includes Norwegian, Swedish, Danish, Icelandic, and Faroese.—*a.*

north·ing, nạr'thing, nạr'THing, *n.* The distance of a planet from the equator northward; *astron.* north declination; *naut.* the difference of latitude northward from the last point of reckoning.

north·land, nạrth'land, *n.* [O.E. *northland.*] The land or region in the north; the northern part of a country. (*Cap.*), *Canadian,* the territories lying north of the Provinces in Canada; the far north. The land or lands of the Northmen or Scandinavians.—**north·land·er,** *n.*

North·man, nạrth'man, *n. pl.* **North·men.** A member of the Scandinavian peoples, noted for their seafaring skills, daring, and piracies who, from about A.D. 700 to 1000 raided, made settlements, and ruled parts of the European mainland from Russia to France, as well as parts of Great Britain, Ireland, Iceland, Greenland, and who made explorations to North America. Also *Norseman.*

north-north·east, nạrth'nạrth″ēst', *Naut.* nạr'nạr″ēst', *n.* The direction on the mariner's compass halfway between north and northeast, situated 22° 30' east of north.—*a., adv.* From or toward this direction.

north-north·west, nạrth'nạrth″west', *Naut.* nạr'nạr″west', *n. Naut.* the direction on the mariner's compass halfway between north and northwest, situated 22° 30' west of north.—*a., adv.* From or toward this direction.

North Pole, *n. Astron.* that point of the heavens toward the north determined by extending the earth's vertical axis, thereby cutting the northern celestial sphere with the point of intersection occurring 1° 20' from Polaris; *geog.* the northern extremity of the earth's axis; (*l.c.*) that pole of a magnet which seeks the northern magnetic pole of the earth.

North Star, *n.* Polaris.

north·ward, nạrth'wẹrd, *Naut.* nạr'THẹrd, *adv.* [O.E. *northweard.*] Toward the north. —*a.* Moving toward, in, to, near, or facing the north.—*n.* The northern part, region, or point.—**north·wards,** *adv.*—**north·ward·ly,** *a., adv.*

north·west, nạrth″west', *Naut.* nạr″west', *n.* The direction between the north and the west; the compass point midway between north and west; (*cap.*) a region lying in this direction.—*a.* Proceeding from or directed toward the northwest.—*adv.* Toward or from the northwest.

north·west by north, *n.* The compass point 11° 15' or one point north of northwest: N 33° 45' W.

north·west by west, *n.* The compass point 11° 15' or one point west of northwest: N 56° 15' W.

north·west·er, nạrth″wes'tẹr, *Naut.* nạr″wes'tẹr, *n.* A strong wind or storm from the northwest. See *nor'wester.*

north·west·er·ly, nạrth″wes'tẹr·lē, *Naut.* nạr″wes'tẹr·lē, *a., adv.* Toward the northwest; from the northwest, as the wind.

north·west·ern, nạrth″wes'tẹrn, *a.* Pertaining to or being in a region designated northwest; coming from this point, as the wind.

north·west·ern·er, nạrth″wes'tẹr·nẹr, *n.* (*Often cap.*) an inhabitant or native of a northwestern region, as of northwestern U.S.

north·west·ward, nạrth″west'wẹrd, *Naut.* nạr″west'wẹrd, *adv., a.* Toward the northwest. Also **north·west·ward·ly.**—*n.* The northwest.—**north·west·wards,** *adv.*

Nor·we·gian, nạr·wē'jan, *a.* [From *Nor-*

way, after M.L. *Norvegia,* Norway.] Of or pertaining to Norway, its inhabitants, or their language.—*n.* A native or inhabitant of Norway; the language of Norway, belonging to the Scandinavian group.

nor'west·er, nạr·wes'tẹr, *n.* A strong wind or gale from the northwest; also *northwester.* A seaman's heavy outer garment worn during severe weather; an oilskin hat.

nose, nōz, *n.* [O.E. *nosu,* akin to *nasu,* G. *nase,* Icel. *nōs,* nose; also to L. *nasus,* nose, *nares,* nostrils, Skt. *nas,* nose, *nōsā,* nostrils, nose.] The human facial feature which contains the nostrils; the organ that includes the nasal cavities, the nostrils, and olfactory nerve endings, and which functions in speech, respiration, and smelling; the sense of smell; the organ of smell found in vertebrates; a faculty for perceiving or detecting; something regarded as resembling the nose of an animal or person; a projecting part of anything; the forward end of a ship or aircraft; *fig.* the human nose as an instrument for prying or meddling.—*v.t.—nosed, nosing.* To perceive or detect by or as by the nose or sense of smell; to nudge or push with the nose, as: The mare *nosed* her colt away from the fence. To touch or rub with the nose; approach the nose to, as in smelling or examining; sniff; to defeat in a close contest, followed by *out*; move ahead. —*v.i.* To smell or sniff; pry or meddle, followed by *about, into*; advance.—**by a nose,** *slang,* by a slight margin.—**count nos·es,** *colloq.* to count the persons in a group or party. —**cut off one's nose to spite one's face,** to harm one's own cause by being spiteful toward another.—**fol·low one's nose,** to go straight ahead; be guided by one's sense of smell or instinct.—**lead by the nose,** *fig.* to control or subjugate completely.—**look down one's nose at,** *slang,* to regard condescendingly or disdainfully.—**nose to the grind·stone,** engaged in unrelenting work. —**on the nose,** *slang,* precisely.—**pay through the nose,** to pay an exorbitant price.—**put some·one's nose out of joint,** to displace one in favor of others in a mortifying way.—**turn up one's nose at,** to scorn.—**un·der one's nose,** easily observed.—**nose·less,** *a.*—**nose·like,** *a.*

nose·band, nōz'band″, *n.* That part of a bridle or halter which passes over the animal's nose.

nose·bleed, nōz'blēd″, *n.* Bleeding from the nose. Also *epistaxis.*

nose cone, *n. Aeron.* a cone-shaped, heat-resistant section of a missile or rocket, located at the front end of the vehicle, and capable of accommodating instruments, cargo, or passengers.

nose dive, *n.* Of an airplane, a headlong dive with the 'nose' of the machine pointing downward; any sudden, steep drop.—**nose·dive,** *v.i.*—past *nose-dived* or *nose-dove,* pp. *nose-dived,* ppr. *nose-diving.*

nose·gay, nōz'gā″, *n.* A small bunch of flowers; a bouquet; a posy.

nose·piece, nōz'pēs″, *n.* A piece, as on a helmet, covering the nose; the piece on eyeglasses that rests on the nose; the piece of a microscope to which the object lens fastens; a noseband.

no-show, nō'shō', *n.* One who neither cancels nor claims a reservation he has made for a seat on an airplane, train, or the like.

nos·ing, nō'zing, *n. Arch.* The projecting edge of a molding or stair tread; a projecting molding.

no·sol·o·gy, nō·sol'o·jē, *n. pl.* **no·sol·o·gies.** [Gr. *nosos* and *logos.*] A systematic classification or description of diseases; the branch of medical science concerned with the classification of diseases.—**no·so·log·ic, nos·o·log·i·cal,** nos″o'loj'ik, *a.*—**no·sol·o·gist,** *n.*

nos·tal·gia, no·stal'ja, no·stal'jē·a, no-

stal'ja, no·stal'jē·a, *n.* [Gr. *nostos,* return, and *algos,* pain.] A longing to return to a past time or to irrecoverable circumstances; homesickness.—**nos·tal·gi·cal·ly,** *adv.*

nos·tril, nos'tril, *n.* [O.E. *nosethril, nosethirl, nósthyrl,* lit. 'nose hole,' *thyrl* or *thyrel* meaning a hole, whence *thyrlian,* to bore.] One of the two apertures of the nose which give passage to air.

nos·trum, nos'trum, *n.* [L. *nostrum,* ours, *i.e.* a medicine belonging to us alone.] A private remedy; a quack medicine; any scheme or device proposed as a remedy for existing ills in any department; a cure-all.

nos·y, nos·ey, nō'zē, *a.*—*nosier, nosiest. Colloq.* Prying; inquisitive.—**nos·i·ly,** *adv.* —**nos·i·ness,** *n.*

not, not, *adv.* [Older *nat,* contr. < *naught,* nought, and equiv. to *ne aught.*] In no way at all; to no extent: used to show negation, denial, refusal, or prohibition, or to express the negative, reverse, or complete lack of something, as: It is *not* an easy step to take, you may *not* drive.

no·ta·bil·i·ty, nō″ta·bil'i·tē, *n. pl.* **no·ta·bil·i·ties.** The quality of being notable; a notable or distinguished person or thing.

no·ta·ble, nō'ta·bl, *a.* [Fr. *notable,* L. *notabilis,* < *noto,* to mark or note, < *nota,* a mark, for *gnota,* < *notus, gnotus,* known.] Worthy of notice; remarkable; memorable; famous or distinguished.—*n.* A person or thing of note or distinction; (*usu. cap.*), *Fr. hist.* one of the nobles or notable men selected by the king to form a parliament before the revolution.—**no·ta·ble·ness,** *n.*—**no·ta·bly,** *adv.*

no·tar·i·al, nō·târ'ē·al, *a.* Pertaining to a notary; done or taken by a notary.—**no·tar·i·al·ly,** *adv.*

no·ta·rize, nō'ta·rīz″, *v.t.*—*notarized, notarizing.* To authenticate or certify, or to cause to be certified, as a deed or contract, through the services of a notary public.—**no·ta·ri·za·tion,** *n.*

no·ta·ry, nō'ta·rē, *n. pl.* **no·ta·ries.** [L. *notarius,* < *nota,* a note.] A person authorized by law to attest documents, administer oaths, and authenticate deeds and contracts. Also **no·ta·ry pub·lic.**—*v.t.* To certify; attest; notarize.

no·ta·tion, nō·tā'shan, *n.* [L. *notātiō(n-),* < *notāre,* E. *note, v.*] The act of noting, marking, or setting down in writing; a record, note, or jotting; the process of noting or setting down by means of a special system of signs or symbols, or the particular method or the system of signs used; as, an algebraic *notation,* a chemical *notation.*—**no·ta·tion·al,** *a.*—**no·tate,** *v.t.*

notch, noch, *n.* [Softened form of old *nock,* a notch = O.D. *nock,* O.Sw. *nocka,* a notch; akin *nick.*] A cut, hollow, or V-shaped nick on a surface or edge; a nick carved into a gunstock, stick, or similar object, as for tallying or recording; a narrow mountain pass or defile; *colloq.* a step, unit, or degree; as, falling a *notch* behind his class.—*v.t.* To cut a notch or notches in; to tally or record by notching; to score; as, *notching* his first victory.—**notched,** *a.*

note, nōt, *n.* [Fr. *note,* < L. *nota,* a mark, sign, character, *notus,* known, for *gnotus,* < *gnosco, nosco,* to know.] *Often pl.* a memorandum or short summary intended to assist the memory, or for reference or further development; *pl.* a summary of observations or impressions. A statement of an explanatory or critical nature added to the text of a book or other manuscript; a short statement giving pertinent information; a brief, informal letter; a diplomatic or official communication in writing; a written promise to pay an acknowledged debt; as, a promissory *note;* a negotiable government or bank certificate. Reputation or distinction; as, a lecturer of *note*; notice or heed; as, taking *note* of his remarks; a distinguishing mark or indicative sign which makes some element or condition known; as, the *note* of anxiety in her voice. *Mus.* a written character which represents a sound of particular duration or pitch; a vocal or instrumental tone; a piano key. A musical sound, as a bird call; any distinctive call or sound of a bird or animal; a sign or character used in printing or writing to indicate punctuation or to point out something.—*v.t.*—*noted*, *noting*. To observe carefully; to heed or attend to; to make particular mention of; to set down in writing or make a memorandum of; to designate or signify; to annotate; to notate in musical symbols.—**not·er**, *n.*

note·book, nōt′bu̇k″, *n.* A blank book in which notes or memoranda are written; an account book for recording promissory notes.

not·ed, nō′tid, *a.* Much known by reputation or report; notable; celebrated; marked with musical notes or notations.—**not·ed·ly**, *adv.*—**not·ed·ness**, *n.*

note·less, nōt′lis, *a.* Not attracting notice; not conspicuous; not distinguished.

note of hand, *n.* Promissory note.

note·pap·er, nōt′pā″pẽr, *n.* Paper of a small size for writing notes or letters.

note·wor·thy, nōt′wụr″T͟He, *a.* Significant; worthy of observation or notice.—**note·wor·thi·ly**, *adv.*—**note·wor·thi·ness**, *n.*

noth·ing, nuth′ing, *n.* [Orig. two words, *no thing.*] No thing, not anything, or naught; as, to see, do, or say *nothing*; no part, share, or trace of, as: There is *nothing* of his father about him. That which is nonexistent; as, to create a world out of *nothing*, to reduce something to *nothing*; something of no importance or significance; a trifling action, matter, circumstance, or thing; a person of no importance; a nobody or nonentity. *Arith.* that which is without quantity or magnitude; a zero or naught (o). —*adv.* In no respect or degree; not at all, as: It was *nothing* like what we expected.—**noth·ing do·ing**, *colloq.* Absolutely no; definitely not.

noth·ing·ness, nuth′ing·nis, *n.* The state of being nothing; nonexistence or that which is nonexistent; unconsciousness; utter insignificance, emptiness, or worthlessness; triviality, as of speech or writing; something insignificant or trivial; a mere nothing.

no·tice, nō′tis, *n.* [Fr. *notice*, < *notitia*, notice, < *nosco*, *notum*, to know.] The act of noting, observing, or remarking; attention; as, a play worthy of *notice*; cognizance; information; direction; order; a written announcement; warning; intimation beforehand; a printed bulletin, a sign, or a poster; attention; courtesy; a formal statement of the termination of a contract or agreement; a brief critical review.— *v.t.*—*noticed*, *noticing.* To take cognizance of; to perceive; become aware of; to observe; to mention or make observations on; to treat with attention and civility.— **no·tice·a·ble**, nō′ti·sa·bl, *a.*—**no·tice·a·bly**, *adv.*

no·ti·fi·ca·tion, nō″ti·fi·kā′shan, *n.* The act of notifying or giving notice; notice given in words or writing; anything which communicates information, as a letter, a telegram, or an advertisement.

no·ti·fy, nō′ti·fī″, *v.t.*—*notified*, *notifying.* [Fr. *notifier*, L. *notificare*, < *notus*, known, and *facio*, to make.] To give notice to; to inform by words or writing. *Chiefly Brit.* to declare; to make known.—**no·ti·fi·er**, *n.*

no·tion, nō′shan, *n.* [L. *nōtiō(n-)*, a becoming acquainted, conception, notion, < *nōscere*, know.] A general concept; a vague or imperfect concept; an opinion, view, or belief; an intention; as, the *notion* to go to

town; a fanciful or foolish idea or whim; a device, contrivance, or ingenious article; *pl.* small useful articles such as pins, needles, and ribbons, esp. as displayed for sale.

no·tion·al, nō′sha·nal, *a.* Of, referring to, or expressing ideas, concepts, or notions; imaginary; abstract or speculative; indulging in whims or foolish ideas. *Semantics,* pertaining to a word which expresses a complete and distinct concept; presentive, as opposed to *symbolic. Grammar,* based upon the expressed meaning of the linguistic form; having complete lexical, as opposed to *relational*, meaning.—**no·tion·al·i·ty**, nō″sha·nal′i·tē, *n.*—**no·tion·al·ly**, *adv.*

no·to·chord, nō′to·kård″, *n.* [Gr. *nōton*, back, and *chordē*, string.] *Biol.* a rodlike embryonic structure which is the primitive backbone of the higher vertebrates, but which persists throughout life in certain of the lower forms, as the amphioxus.— **no·to·chord·al**, *a.*

no·to·ri·ous, nō·tōr′ē·us, nō·tạr′ē·us, *a.* [L.L. *notorius*, < L. *notoria*, *notorium*, an indictment, *notor*, a voucher, *notare*, to mark.] Publicly or generally known but regarded with disapproval; widely known. —**no·to·ri·ous·ly**, *adv.*—**no·to·ri·ous·ness**, *n.*—**no·to·ri·e·ty**, nō″to·rī′i·tē, *n.* pl. **no·to·ri·e·ties.**

no-trump, nō′trump′, *n. Bridge,* a bid or declaration in which no suit is designated as trump.—*a.* Pertaining to a bid or contract to be played without any suit being trump.

not·with·stand·ing, not″wiT͟H·stan′ding, not″with·stan′ding, *prep.* In spite of; without being prevented by, as: He went fishing *notwithstanding* the rainy weather.— *adv.* Nevertheless; anyway; however, as: He will go *notwithstanding.*—*conj.* Although; in spite of the fact that.

nou·gat, nō′gat, nō′gä, *n.* [Fr.] A chewy confection made of sugar, honey, or corn syrup containing chopped nuts and/or fruit pieces.

nought, nạt, *n.*, *a.*, *adv.* Naught.

nou·me·non, nō′me·non″, nou′me·non″, *n.* pl. **nou·me·na.** [Gr., the thing perceived, < *noeō*, to perceive, < *nous*, the mind.] *Philos.* The ground of a phenomenon, inaccessible to sense knowledge, but necessarily postulated by practical reason; the thing itself in contrast to the phenomenon; according to Immanuel Kant, the object of a pure, nonsensual intuition.— **nou·me·nal**, *a.*

noun, noun, *n.* [O.Fr. *noun, non, nom,* Mod. Fr. *nom,* < L. *nomen,* name.] *Gram.* a word that denotes a person, place, thing, condition, action, or quality and functions mainly as the subject of a sentence or clause, an appositive, or the object of a verb or preposition.

nour·ish, nụr′ish, nur′ish, *v.t* [O.Fr. *nurrir, norrir,* Mod.Fr. *nourrir,* < L. *nutrire,* to nourish.] To feed and cause to grow; to supply with nutriment; to rear; to support. *Fig.* to encourage, foster, or cherish; to comfort; to promote.—**nour·ish·er**, *n.*—**nour·ish·ing**, *a.*

nour·ish·ment, nụr′ish·ment, nur′ish·ment, *n.* Food, sustenance, nutriment; the act of nourishing; nutrition; *fig.* that which promotes any kind of growth or development; as, intellectual *nourishment.*

nous, nös, nous, *n.* [Gr. *nous,* contr. of *noos,* mind, prob. akin to *gignōskein,* know, and E. *know.*] *Gr. philos.* mind or intellect, esp. intellectual apprehension and intuition, as opposed to sensible apprehension; *Neoplatonism,* the divine reason.

nou·veau riche, nō′vō rēsh′, *Fr.* nō·vō rēsh′, *n.* pl. **nou·veaux riches.** [Fr. (fem. *nouvelle riche*), 'new rich.'] One who has newly become rich; a wealthy parvenu: usu. used disparagingly.

no·va, nō′va, *n.* pl. **no·vae**, **no·vas**, nō′vē. [N.L., prop. fem. of L. *novus,* new.] *Astron.* a star which suddenly increases its intensity and then after several weeks grows gradually fainter.

no·vac·u·lite, nō·vak′ū·līt″, *n.* [L. *novācula,* sharp knife, razor, < *novare,* renew.] *Petrog.* a hard, compact, siliceous rock, probably sedimentary in origin, used for hones.

no·va·tion, nō·vā′shan, *n.* [L. *novātiō(n-),* < *novāre.*] *Law,* the substitution of a new obligation for an old one, usu. by the substitution of a new debtor or of a new creditor.

nov·el, nov′el, *n.* [O.Fr. *novele,* something new, news, Fr. *nouvelle* and It. *novella,* story, also L.L. *novella* (in Rom. law).] *Liter.* a fictitious prose narrative of considerable length, portraying characters, actions, and scenes representative of real life in a plot of more or less intricacy.—*a.* [O.Fr. *novel* (Fr. *nouveau*), < L. *novellus,* dim. of *novus,* new.] Of a new kind or different from anything seen or known before; unusual or strange, esp. in a notable or interesting way.—**nov·el·ist**, nov′e·list, *n.*—**nov·el·is·tic**, nov″e·lis′tik, *a.*

nov·el·ette, nov″e·let′, *n.* A short novel. Also *novella.*

nov·el·ize, nov′e·līz″, *v.t. novelized*, *novelizing.* To organize or put into the form of a novel.—**nov·el·i·za·tion**, *n.*

no·vel·la, nō·vel′a, *It.* nạ·vel′lä, *n.* pl. **no·vel·las**, *It.* **no·vel·le**, nō·vel′ā, *It.* nạ·vel′le. *Liter.* A short narrative in prose, often satiric or moralizing, as the stories in the *Decameron* of Boccaccio; a novelette.

nov·el·ty, nov′el·tē, *n.* pl. **nov·el·ties.** [O.Fr. *novelte* (Fr. *nouveauté*), < L.L. *novellitās,* < L. *novellus,* novel.] Novel character, newness, or strangeness; something novel or new; a novel experience or proceeding; an innovation; a new or novel article of trade, esp. comic or decorative, usu. having temporary appeal.

No·vem·ber, nō·vem′bẽr, *n.* [L., < *novem,* nine; the ninth month, according to the ancient Roman year, which began in March.] The eleventh month of the year, containing 30 days; the month following October.

No·vem·ber, nō·vem′bẽr, *n.* A communications code word to designate the letter N.

no·vem·de·cil·lion, nō″vem·di·sil′yan, *n.* A very large cardinal number which, in America and France, is written as 1 followed by 60 zeros, and in England and Germany as 1 followed by 114 zeros. —*a.*

no·ve·na, nō·vē′na, no·vē′na, *n.* pl. **no·ve·nae**, nō·vē′nē, no·vē′nē. [M.L., prop. fem. of L. *novēnus,* nine each, < *novem,* nine.] *Rom. Cath. Ch.* a devotion of prayers or services on nine consecutive days, or one particular day in nine consecutive months; as, a *novena* of nine first Fridays.

nov·ice, nov′is, *n.* [Fr., < L. *novitius,* new, fresh, < *novus,* new.] One who is new to the circumstances in which he or she is placed; one who is new in any business; a beginner. *Eccles.* one newly converted to the Christian faith; one who has entered a religious house, but has not taken the vow; a probationer.—**no·vi·ti·ate, no·vi·ci·ate**, nō·vish′ē·it, nō·vish′ē·āt″, *n.* The state or time of being a novice; apprenticeship. *Eccles.* a year or other time of probation in a religious order; the house occupied by religious novices.

No·vo·cain, nō′vo·kān″, *n.* [L. *novus,* new, and *cocaine.*] *Pharm.* a local anesthetic, procaine hydrochloride. (Trademark.)

now, nou, *adv.* [O.E. *nū* = D. and G. *nu* = Icel. *nū* = Goth. *nū,* now; akin to L. *nunc,*

Gr. *nu*, *nun*, Skt. *nu*, *nūnam*, now.] At the present time or moment; immediately or at once; at the time or moment only just past; at this time or juncture in some period under consideration or in some course of proceedings described; as, night was *now* approaching; in these present times or nowadays; under the present or existing circumstances or as matters stand; no: used to strengthen a command or entreaty, as: *Now*, please don't!—*conj.* Now that, since, or seeing that.—*n.*—**now and a·gain**, at one time and again at another; now and then.— **now that**, since; seeing that.

now·a·days, nou′a·dāz″, *adv.* At the present time; in these days.

no·way, nō′wā″, *adv.* In no way; in no respect, or degree; not at all. Also **no·ways**.

no·where, nō′hwâr″, nō′wâr″, *adv.* In, at, or to no place; not anywhere; as, a plant found *nowhere* else.—*n.* Also *dial.* **no·-wheres**, nō′hwârz, nō′wârz.

no·whith·er, nō′hwiTH″ẽr, nō′wiTH″ẽr, *adv.* To no place in particular; nowhere.

no·wise, nō′wīz″, *adv.* In no way; not at all.

nox·ious, nok′shus, *a.* [L. *noxius*, < *noxa*, harm, injury, < *nocēre*, to harm, hurt.] Harmful or injurious to health or physical well-being; as, *noxious* vapors; deleterious; unwholesome; morally harmful or pernicious; as, *noxious* teachings.—**nox·ious·ly**, *adv.*—**nox·ious·ness**, *n.*

no·yade, nwä·yäd′, *n.* [Fr. < *noyer*, to drown.] Putting to death by drowning, a method of execution used during the reign of terror in France, esp. at Nantes.

noz·zle, noz′l, *n.* [For *nosle*, a dim. of *nose*.] The projecting spout of something; a terminal pipe or terminal part of a pipe or hose from which something is discharged; *slang*, the nose.

nth, enth, *a.* The last or most extreme of a series; utmost.

nu, nō, nū, *n.* [Gr. *nu*.] The thirteenth letter of the Greek alphabet.

nu·ance, nō′äns, nū′äns, nō·äns′, nū·äns′, *Fr.* nY·äns′, *n.* pl. **nu·anc·es**, nō′än·siz, nū′än·siz, nō·än′siz, nū·än′siz, *Fr.* nY·äns′. [Fr., < *nue*, L. *nubes*, a cloud.] A gradation by which a color passes from its lightest to its darkest shade; shade of color; a subtle or delicate degree of meaning, tone, or feeling.

nub, nub, *n.* [= *knub*.] A knob or protuberance; a lump or small piece; also **nub·ble**, nub′l. *Colloq.* the point or gist of anything.—**nub·bly**, nub′lē, *a.*—*nubblier*, *nubbliest*.

nub·bin, nub′in, *n.* [Cf. *nub*.] A small lump or piece; *bot.* a small or imperfect ear of corn, or an undeveloped fruit.

Nu·bi·an, nō′bē·an, nū′bē·an, *a.* Of or pertaining to Nubia, a region of Africa south of Egypt and bordering on the Red Sea; the inhabitants or the language of the region.—*n.* One of a negroid people, of mixed descent, inhabiting Nubia; the language spoken by this people; a Nubian or negro slave; a Nubian horse.

nu·bile, nō′bil, nū′bil, *a.* [L. *nubilis*, < *nubo*, to marry.] Of an age or stage of physical maturity suitable for marriage: said of a girl or young woman.—**nu·bil·i·ty**, nū·bil′it·ē, *n.*

nu·bi·lous, nō′bi·lus, nū′bi·lus, *a.* [L. *nubilus*, < *nubes*, a cloud.] Cloudy; foggy; vague; indefinite.

nu·cel·lus, nō·sel′us, nū·sel′us, *n.* pl. **nu·cel·li**, nō·sel′ī, nū·sel′ī. [Dim. of L. for a *kernel*.] *Bot.* the central part of an ovule, containing the embryo sac.—**nu·cel·lar**, *a.*

nu·cha, nō′ka, nū′ka, *n.* pl. **nu·chae**, nō′kē, nū′kē. [M.L.; < Ar.] The nape of the neck.—**nu·chal**, *a.* Pertaining to the nape or back of the neck; *entom.* situated on the hind part of the thorax, as certain markings.—*n.*

nu·ci·form, nō′si·fạrm″, nū′si·fạrm″, *a. Bot.* Resembling a nut; nut-shaped.

nu·cle·ar, nō′klē·ẽr, nū′klē·ẽr, *a. Biol.* of, pertaining to, or comprising a nucleus. *Phys.* referring to the uses or action of the atomic nucleus; as, *nuclear* fission; that which operates with atomic energy; as, a *nuclear* power station; referring to, entailing the use of, or the possession of atomic weapons. Also **nu·cle·al**.

nu·cle·ar en·er·gy, *n.* See *atomic energy*.

nu·cle·ar force, *n.* The powerful and explosive interaction between nucleons which holds together atomic nuclei.

nu·cle·ar phys·ics, *n.* The branch of physics which studies atomic nuclei, their properties, structure, and constituent parts, and the energies resulting from nuclear changes.—**nu·cle·ar phys·i·cist**, *n.* Also **a·tom·ic phys·i·cist**.

nu·cle·ase, nō′klē·ās″, nū′klē·ās″, *n. Biochem.* an enzyme which breaks down or hydrolyzes nucleic acids.

nu·cle·ate, nō′klē·it, nō′klē·āt″, nū′klē·it, nū′klē·āt″, *v.i.*—*nucleated*, *nucleating*. [L. *nucleatus*, having a kernel or stone, < *nucleus*, nucleus.] To form into a nucleus.—*v.i.* To form, or gather round, a nucleus.—*a.* Having a nucleus.—**nu·cle·a·tion**, nō″klē·ā′shạn, nū″klē·ā′shan, *n.*

nu·cle·a·tion par·ti·cles, *n. pl.* Microscopic salt grains and other particles in the atmosphere which form a nucleus around which raindrops form.

nu·cle·ic ac·id, nō·klē′ik as′id, nū·klē′ik, *n.* A complex organic compound important in the heredity and the control of the metabolism of all living cells, composed of phosphoric acids, bases from purines or pyrimidines, and carbohydrates, esp. sugars.

nu·cle·in, nō′klē·in, nū′klē·in, *n.* [< *nucleus*.] *Biochem.* any of a class of phosphorus-containing protein substances in cell nuclei.—**nu·cle·ic**, nō·klē′ik, nū·klē′ik, *a.*

nu·cle·o·lus, nō·klē′o·lus, nū·klē′o·lus, *n.* pl. **nu·cle·o·li**, nō·klē′o·lī″, nū·klē′o·lī″. [L., little nut, dim. of *nucleus*.] *Biol.* an organized, conspicuous, round body in the nucleus of a cell, other than a chromosome. Also **nu·cle·ole**, nō′klē·ōl″, nū′klē·ōl″.—**nu·cle·o·lar**, **nu·cle·o·loid**, *a.*—**nu·cle·o·late**, **nu·cle·o·lat·ed**, nō′klē·o·lāt″, nū′klē·o·lāt″, *a.*

nu·cle·on, nō′klē·on″, nū′klē·on″, *n. Phys.* An elementary particle in the atomic nucleus, esp. a proton or a neutron.— **nu·cle·on·ics**, nō″klē·on′iks, nū″klē·on′iks, *n. pl. but sing. in constr.* The science dealing with the practical application of nuclear physics.

nu·cle·o·plasm, nō′klē·o·plaz″um, nū′klē·o·plaz″um, *n. Biol.* Protoplasm of a cell nucleus; karyoplasm.—**nu·cle·o·plas·mat·ic**, **nu·cle·o·plas·mic**, nō″klē·ō·plaz·mat′ik, nū″klē·ō·plaz·mat′ik, *a.*

nu·cle·o·pro·tein, nō′klē·o·prō′tēn, nō″klē·o·prō′tē·in, nū″klē·o·prō′tēn, nū″klē·o·prō′tē·in, *n.* [< *nucleus* and *protein*.] *Biol.* A conjugated protein, combining a protein and a nucleic acid, and occurring in living cells; an essential constituent of genes and viruses. Also *nuclein*.

nu·cle·o·side, nō′klē·o·sīd″, nū′klē·o·sīd″, *n. Biochem.* a compound with a pyrimidine or purine base, a phosphoric group, and pentose nucleic acid.

nu·cle·o·tide, nō′klē·o·tīd″, nū′klē·o·tīd″, *n. Chem.* a phosphorylated ester or derivative of a nucleoside.

nu·cle·us, nō′klē·us, nū′klē·us, *n.* pl. **nu·cle·i**, **nu·cle·us·es**, nō′klē·ī″, nū′klē·ī″. [L., nut, kernel, fruit stone, dim. < *nux* (*nuc-*), nut.] A central part or thing about which other parts or things are grouped; anything constituting a central part, foundation, or beginning; a source, basis,

or center of development or growth; kernel; *biol.* a complex, usu. round mass of protoplasm present in the interior of all living cells and essential to vital cell activities such as growth, metabolism, assimilation, and reproduction; *anat.* a mass of gray matter consisting of nerve cells, located in the brain and spinal cord; *astron.* the more condensed portion of a nebula, galaxy, or head of a comet; *phys.* the central, densest part of an atom, positively charged, around which are grouped electrons with a corresponding negative charge; *chem.* an arrangement or group of atoms, such as the benzene ring, which combines with other atoms to form compounds without losing its original structure.

nu·clide, nō′klīd, nū′klīd, *n. Phys.* an individual atom of given atomic number, mass number, and energy content, which exists for a measurable length of time and has a distinct nuclear structure.

nude, nōd, nūd, *a.* [L. *nudus*, naked (seen also in *denude*); same root as *naked*.] Naked; not covered with clothes or drapery; bare; being nude in color; *law*, indicating the absence of some legal requirement.—*n.* A naked figure depicted in an art form; an unclothed human being; the fact of being naked; the color of the skin.—**nude·ly**, *adv.* —**nude·ness**, *n.*—**nu·di·ty**, nō′di·tē, nū′di·tē, *n.* pl. **nu·di·ties**. The state of being naked; nakedness; an uncovered part.

nudge, nuj, *n.* [Allied to Prov.G. *knütschen*, Dan. *knuge*, to squeeze.] A jog or gentle poke, as with the elbow.—*v.t.*—*nudged*, *nudging*. To give a hint or signal by a usu. furtive, touch with the hand, elbow, or foot. —**nudg·er**, *n.*

nu·di·cau·lous, nō″di·ḳạ′lus, nū″di·ḳạ′lus, *a.* [L. *nudus*, naked, and *caulis*, stem.] *Bot.* having leafless stems. Also **nu·di·caul**, nō′di·ḳạl″, nū′di·ḳạl″.

nud·ism, nō′diz·um, nū′diz·um, *n.* The practice of going naked as a means of healthful living.—**nud·ist**, *n, a.*

nu·ga·to·ry, nō′ga·tōr″ē, nū′ga·tōr″ē, *a.* [L. *nugatorius*, < *nugor*, *nugatus*, to trifle, < *nugae*, trifles.] Trifling; worthless; of no force; futile; inoperative.

nug·get, nug′it, *n.* [Appar. a dim. of *nug*.] A lump of something, esp. a lump of native gold.—**nug·get·y**, *a.*

nui·sance, nō′sans, nū′sans, *n.* [O.Fr. *nuisance*, *noidance*, < *nuisir*, *noisir*, Mod.Fr. *nuire*, L. *nocere*, to annoy.] Something or someone annoying or obnoxious; that which is offensive or irritating; a pest; *law*, an annoyance which interferes with the legal rights of an individual or a community.

nui·sance tax, *n.* Any small tax levied on consumer products and services.

null, nul, *a.* [Fr. *nul*, < L. *nullus*, not any, no, none, < *ne*, not, and *ullus*, any, dim. < *unus*, one.] Of no legal or binding force; invalid; void; of no effect, consequence, significance, or value; lacking distinctive character or individuality; expressionless; being zero; nonexistent.—**null and void**, of no legal or binding force.

nul·lah, nul′a, *n. Anglo-Ind.* A dry bed of a rivulet; a rivulet; a ravine.

nul·li·fi·ca·tion, nul″i·fi·kā′shan, *n.* [L.L. *nullificātiō(n-)*.] The act of nullifying; the state of being nullified; *U.S. hist.* the action of a State in declaring a federal law inoperative within its limits, under the assumption of absolute State sovereignty.— **nul·li·fi·ca·tion·ist**, *n.*

nul·li·fy, nul′i·fī″, *v.t.*—*nullified*, *nullifying*. [L.L. *nullificare*, < L. *nullus*, E. *null*, and *facere*, make.] To make null; render or declare legally void or inoperative; to make ineffective, futile, or of no consequence.— **nul·li·fi·er**, *n.*

nul·li·ty, nul′i·tē, *n.* pl. **nul·li·ties**. The state or fact of being null; nothingness; invalidity; something null, specif. that which has no legal force or validity.

numb, num, *a.* [Lit. 'taken,' < O.E. *numen*, pp. of *niman*, O.E. *nim*, Goth. *niman*, to seize.] Without physical sensation or feeling; not able to move.—*v.t.* To make numb.—**numb·ly**, *adv.*—**numb·ness**, *n.*—**numb·ing**, *a.*—**numb·ing·ly**, *adv.*

num·ber, num′bẽr, *n.* [O.Fr. Fr. *nombre*, < L. *numerus*, number, aggregate, class, musical measure, verse; akin to Gr. *nemein*, deal out.] The sum, total, or aggregate of a collection of units; a word, symbol, or a combination of words or symbols used in counting or to denote a total; a numeral; the concept associated with a symbol of a numerical system; the particular numeral assigned to anything in order to fix its place in a series; as, the license *number* of an automobile; one of a series of things distinguished by numerals; the full count of a collection or company; a quantity of individuals; a certain collection, company, or quantity not exactly determined but usu. large, as: She has a *number* of hats. Quantity as composed of units, as: The difference between many and few is a matter of *number*. A single issue of a periodical or a serial section of a book; any of a collection of poems or songs; a distinct part of an extended musical work; a single part of a program made of several parts. *Theatr.* a single performance or routine in a stage presentation; a musical or choreographic arrangement. Rhythm, as in verse or music. *Slang*, an article or line of merchandise; a person, esp. a young woman, as: His girl is a cute *number*. Mathematics as a system of thought; *sometimes pl.* numerical strength or superiority; *gram.* the property of language which serves to indicate whether a word refers to one, two, or more than two, and in English which serves to indicate whether a word refers to one or more than one. *Pl.* a multitude; a considerable collection of people or things.

num·ber, num′bẽr, *v.t.* [O.Fr. Fr. *nombrer*, < L. *numerare*, < *numerus*: cf. numerate.] To ascertain the number of; reckon; to count over one by one; enumerate; to fix, limit, or reduce the number of; to include as one of a group; to mark with or distinguish by a number or numbers; to live or have lived, as: Grandfather *numbered* 87 years in this valley. To have or comprise in number, as: The city *numbers* a million inhabitants. To amount to in number, as: The crew *numbers* 50 men.—*v.i.* To count; to be numbered or included, followed by *with* or *among*; to call out or count off, usu. followed by *off*.—**any num·ber of**, many; a large amount.—**get one's num·ber, have one's num·ber**, *slang*, to have identified hidden aspects of a person and his motives. —**num·ber one**, (*often cap.*), *slang*, oneself. —**one's num·ber is up**, *slang*. To be without luck or good fortune; to be about to fail or die.—**with·out num·ber, be·yond num·ber**, innumerable.—**num·ber·a·ble**, *a.*—**num·ber·er**, *n.*—**num·ber·less**, *a.*

num·bers, num′bẽrz, *n. pl. but sing. in constr.* Slang, an illegal lottery in which one bets on the appearance of particular numbers in a daily newspaper, as in a stock market quotation or other statistical list. Also **num·bers game, num·bers pool**.

numb·fish, num′fish″, *n. pl.* **numb·fish, numb·fish·es**. An electric ray fish, so called from its power of numbing its prey by means of electric shocks.

numb·skull, num′skul″, *n.* Numskull.

nu·men, nō′min, nū′min, *n. pl.* **nu·mi·na**, nō′mi·na, nū′mi·na. A divine spirit, esp. one thought to dwell within an object or one locally presiding.

nu·mer·a·ble, nō′mẽr·a·bl, nū′mẽr·a·bl, *a.* [L. *numerabilis*, < *numerus*, number.] Ca-

pable of being numbered or counted.—**nu·mer·a·ble·ness**, *n.*—**nu·mer·a·bly**, *adv.*

nu·mer·al, nō′mẽr·al, nū′mẽr·al, *a.* [L. *numeralis*.] Pertaining to or consisting of number; expressing number; representing number.—*n.* A figure, character, or group of figures used to express a number; a word or combination of words expressing a number; *pl.* the numbers designating the graduating year of a high school, college, or other class. —**num·er·al·ly**, *adv.*

nu·mer·ate, nō′me·rāt″, nū′me·rāt″, *v.t.*— numerated, numerating. [L. *numero, numeratum.*] To count; enumerate; to read in words, as a numerical symbol or expression.

nu·mer·a·tion, nō″me·rā′shan, nū″me·rā′shan, *n.* [L. *numeratio*.] The act or art of numbering or calculating; the art of expressing in numerical figures any number expressed in words; expression in words of any numerical figure.

nu·mer·a·tor, nō′me·rā″tẽr, nū′me·rā″tẽr, *n.* The term or number above the line in a fraction indicating the number of units taken of the denominator; one who numbers; as, a census *numerator*.

nu·mer·i·cal, nō·mer′i·kal, nū·mer′i·kal, *a.* Pertaining to, denoted by, or denoting a number or numbers; expressed by or consisting of numbers rather than letters; *math.* designating an absolute value.

nu·mer·ol·o·gy, nō″me·rol′o·jē, nū″me·rol′o·jē, *n.* Belief in the occult influence of numbers upon the life of an individual.

nu·mer·ous, nō′mẽr·us, nū′mẽr·us, *a.* [L. *numerōsus*, < *numerus*, E. *number*, *n.*] Consisting of a great number of units or individuals; very many.—**nu·me·ros·i·ty**, nū″me·ros′i·tē, *n.*—**nu·mer·ous·ness**, nō″me·ros′i·tē, nū″me·ros′i·tē, *n.*—**nu·mer·ous·ly**, *adv.*

nu·mi·nous, nō′mi·nus, nū′mi·nus, *a.* Of, pertaining to, or resembling a numen; holy; spiritual; supernatural; infused with the divine; evoking reverence, wonder, or awe; mysterious; inscrutable.

nu·mis·mat·ic, nō″miz·mat′ik, nō″mis·mat′ik, nū″miz·mat′ik, nū″mis·mat′ik, *a.* [Fr. numismatique, < L. *numisma, nomisma*, coin, medal, < Gr. *nomisma*, current coin, < *nomizein*, use customarily, < *nomos*, custom, law.] Of, pertaining to, or consisting of, coins, medals, and similar objects; pertaining to numismatics. Also **nu·mis·mat·i·cal.**—**nu·mis·mat·i·cs**, *n. pl. but sing. in constr.* The study and/or collecting of rare coins, medals, and related objects.—**nu·mis·mat·i·cal·ly**, *adv.*—**nu·mis·ma·tist**, nō·miz′ma·tist, nō·mis′ma·tist, nū·miz′ma·tist, nū·mis′ma·tist, *n.*

num·ma·ry, num′a·rē, *a.* Relating to or dealing in coins.

num·mu·lar, num′ū·lẽr, *a.* [L. *nummulus*, dim. of *nummus*, coin.] Coin-shaped; of or relating to coins, money, and similar objects; nummary.

num·skull, num′skul″, *n.* [Numb and skull.] A dunce; a stupid person. Also **numbskull**.

nun, nun, *n.* [O.E. *nunne*, < Eccles. L. *nonna*, a nun, *nonnus*, a monk, L.Gr. *nonna, nonnos*, < Coptic or Egypt. *nane, nanu*, good, beautiful.] A woman devoted to a religious life who lives in a convent or nunnery, under vows of perpetual chastity, obedience, and poverty; *ornith.* any of several varieties of pigeons.

nun·ci·o, nun′shē·ō″, *n. pl.* **nun·ci·os**. [Sp. nuncio, It. nunzio, < *nuncius*, a messenger, for *noventius*, < *novus*, new.] A papal ambassador to a country with which the Vatican has permanent diplomatic relations. See *apostolic delegate, legate.*—**nun·ci·a·ture**, nun′shē·a·chẽr, *n.* The office or term of appointment of a nuncio.

nun·cu·pa·tive, nung′kū·pā″tiv, nung·kū′pa·tiv, *a.* [L.L. *nuncupativus*, < L. *nuncupare*, call by name, declare, < *nomen*,

name, and *capere*, take.] *Law.* oral, rather than written, esp. wills and other binding legal agreements.

nun·ner·y, nun′e·rē, *n. pl.* **nun·ner·ies**. A convent in which nuns reside.

nup·tial, nup′shal, *a.* [L. *nuptialis, nuptiæ*, marriage, < *nubo, nuptum*, to marry; akin *nubes, nimbus*, a cloud, from the veiling of the bride.] Pertaining to marriage; describing wedding rituals or customs.—*n. Usu. pl.* a wedding or marriage.—**nup·tial·ly**, *adv.*

nup·tial plum·age, *n. Ornith.* the more colorful male plumage of some species of birds during the mating season. Also **breed·ing plum·age**.

nurse, nurs, *n.* [Fr. *nourrice*, < L. *nutrix, nutricis*, a nurse, < *nutrio*, to nourish.] One who tends or takes care of the sick or infirm, esp. one who has undergone appropriate training; a female who has the care of another's child or children; a woman engaged to suckle an infant; as, a wet *nurse*; *fig.* one who cares for, nurtures, cherishes, or protects; *entom.* an insect whose role is to tend the young of the colony.—*v.t.*— nursed, nursing. To feed and tend in infancy; to suckle; to rear; to nurture; to tend in sickness or infirmity; to promote growth or vigor in; to foster; to manage with care and economy, with a view to increase; as, to *nurse* one's slender resources; to try to cure; as, to *nurse* an indisposition; to handle with care; to keep in mind; as, to *nurse* a grievance; *billiards*, to keep the balls grouped for a series of caroms.—*v.i.* To carry out the duties of a nurse; to suckle; to feed from the breast.—**nurs·er**, nur′sẽr, *n.*

nurse·maid, nurs′mād″, *n.* A maidservant employed in taking care of children. Also **nurs·er·y·maid**.

nurs·er·y, nur′se·rē, *n. pl.* **nurs·er·ies**. An area set apart for children; a nursery school; *hort.* a place where trees, shrubs, and flowering plants are raised from seed or otherwise in order to be transplanted or sold.

nurs·er·y·man, nur′se·rē·man, *n. pl.* **nurs·er·y·men**. One who owns or works in a nursery for cultivating plants.

nurs·er·y rhyme, *n.* A tale for children written in rhyming verse.

nurs·er·y school, *n.* A school for children not old enough for kindergarten.

nurs·ing bot·tle, *n.* A bottle which has a rubber nipple, used for feeding milk and other liquids to infants.

nurs·ing sta·tion, *n. Canada*, a small emergency hospital with nurses in attendance and a visiting doctor.

nurs·ling, nurs′ling, *n.* [Nurse, and dim. term. *-ling*.] One who or that which is nursed; a newborn child or animal. Also **nurse·ling**.

nur·ture, nur′chẽr, *n.* [Fr. *nourriture*, < *nourrir*, to nourish.] The act of nursing or nourishing; education; breeding; that which nourishes; food; *biol.* the nongenetic influences that modify an organism after its conception.—*v.t.*—nurtured, nurturing. To nourish; to educate; to train or bring up.—**nur·tur·er**, *n.*

nut, nut, *n.* [O.E. *hnutu* = D. *noot* = G. *nuss* = Icel. *knot* = Sw. *not* = Dan. *nod*, nut.] *Bot.* a fruit consisting of an edible kernel enclosed in a woody or leathery shell; the kernel itself; a hard, indehiscent, one-seeded fruit, as the chestnut or the acorn. *Fig.* something suggesting a nut that is hard to crack, as a difficult question. *Slang*, the head; a witless or crazy person; a very enthusiastic person; a testicle. A perforated metal block with an internal thread used to screw on the end of a bolt. *Mus.* in instruments of the violin type, the piece, as of ebony, at the upper end of the neck, over which the strings pass; the movable piece at the lower end of the bow by means of which the hairs may be slackened or tightened. *Pl.* nonsense.—*v.i.*—**nutted,** **nutting.** To seek for or gather nuts.

nu·tant, nōt′ant, nūt′ant, *a.* [L. *nūtāns* (*nūtant-*), ppr. of *nutare*, freq. of *-nuere*, nod akin to Gr. *neuein*, nod, incline.] *Bot.* drooping; nodding. *Entom.* sloping.

nu·ta·tion, nō·tā′shan, nū·tā′shan, *n.* [L. *nūtātiō(n-)*, < *nūtāre*, nod.] A nodding of the head, usu. involuntarily; *astron.* a slight oscillation of the earth's axis; *bot.* a side-to-side movement of a plant part during growth.—**nu·ta·tion·al,** *a.*

nut·brown, nut′broun′, *a.* Brown, as a ripe nut.

nut·crack·er, nut′krak″ĕr, *n.* An instrument for cracking hard-shelled nuts; *ornith.* a brown spotted bird of the crow family and the genus *Nucifaga*, as *N. columbiana*, the nutcracker of western N. America.

nut·hatch, nut′hach″, *n.* [M.E. *notehache*, *nuthage, nuthake*: cf. hack.] *Ornith.* any of several chubby tree-climbing birds of the family *Sittidae*, with a long bill and a stubby tail, and which habitually goes head first down a tree trunk feeding on nuts and insects.

nut·let, nut′lit, *n.* A small nut; a small nutlike fruit or seed; the stone of a drupe.

nut·meg, nut′meg, *n.* [M.E. *notemuge*, < *note*, nut, and O.Fr. *muge, mugue*, musk.] The hard, aromatic seed of the fruit of an East Indian tree, *Myristica fragrans*, used as a spice; the tree itself; the similar product of certain other trees of the same genus or other genera.

nut·meg mel·on, *n.* A variety of muskmelon having a rather soft rind with a netted surface, and sweet, green flesh.

nut·pick, nut′pik″, *n.* A small instrument with a sharp point, used for extracting the soft kernel from nuts.

nut pine, *n.* Piñon.

nu·tri·a, nō′trē·a, nū′trē·a, *n.* [Sp. *nutria, lutria*, < L. *lutra*, an otter.] The commercial name for the soft brown fur of the coypu, sometimes dyed to give the appearance of beaver; the coypu.

nu·tri·ent, nō′trē·ent, nū′trē·ent, *a.* [L. *nutrio*, to nourish.] Nourishing, nutritious. —*n.* Any substance which nourishes.

nu·tri·ment, nō′tri·ment, nū′tri·ment, *n.* [L. *nutrimentum*, < *nutrire*.] That which nourishes; food; any matter that, taken into a living organism, serves to sustain its existence, promoting growth and replacing wornout tissues.—**nu·tri·men·tal,** nō″tri·men′tal, nū″tri·men′tal, *a.*

nu·tri·tion, nō·trish′an, nū·trish′an, *n.* [L. *nutritio*, < *nutrio*.] The act or process by which organisms, whether plant or animal, absorb into their systems their proper food; the process of assimilating and converting food into tissue; the study of this process; that which nourishes; nutriment.—**nu·tri·tion·al,** *a.*—**nu·tri·tion·al·ly,** *adv.*—**nu·tri·tion·ist,** *n.* A person who specializes in the science of nutrition.

nu·tri·tious, nō·trish′us, nū·trish′us, *a.* Containing or serving as nutriment; promoting growth, replacing wornout tissues, and supplying energy; nourishing.—**nu·tri·tious·ly,** *adv.*—**nu·tri·tious·ness,** *n.*

nu·tri·tive, nō′tri·tiv, nū′tri·tiv, *a.* Having the quality of nourishing; nutritious; pertaining to nutrition.—**nu·tri·tive·ly,** *adv.* —**nu·tri·tive·ness,** *n.*

nuts, nuts, *a. Slang.* Insane; eccentric; tremendously enthusiastic, followed by *about* or *over*; very much in love, followed by *about* or *over*.—*interj. Slang*, an exclamation expressing disgust, annoyance, scorn, despair, or the like, often followed by *to*. Also **nerts, nertz, nurts.**

nut·shell, nut′shel″, *n.* The hard shell of a nut.—**in a nut·shell,** in short, simple form; briefly.

nut·ty, nut′ē, *a.*—**nuttier, nuttiest.** Producing or containing nuts; tasting of or like nuts. *Slang*; silly; eccentric; crazy.—**nut·ti·ness,** *n.*

nux vom·i·ca, nuks vom′i·ka, *n.* [N.L., 'vomiting nut': L. *nux*, nut; N.L. *vomica*, < L. *vomere*, vomit.] The strychnine-containing seed, used in medicine, of the orangelike fruit borne by an East Indian tree, *Strychnos nuxvomica*, in the family *Loganiaceae*; the tree itself.

nuz·zle, nuz′l, *v.i.*—**nuzzled, nuzzling.** [Freq. of *nose*; to some extent confused with *nestle*.] To burrow or dig with the nose, as an animal does; thrust or push the nose; to nestle, snuggle up to, or cuddle.—*v.t.* To root up with the nose; touch or rub with the nose; thrust the nose against or into something. To cuddle, as a person or thing.

nyc·ta·lo·pi·a, nik″ta·lō′pē·a, *n.* [L.L. < Gr. *nyktalōps*, blind by night, *nyx*(*nykt-*), night, and *alaos*, blind, and *ōps*, eye.] *Ophthalm.* A condition of the eyes in which sight is normal in the day or in a strong light, but is abnormally poor or wholly gone at night or in a dim light; night blindness; a visual condition exactly opposite to hemeralopia or day blindness.—**nyc·ta·lop·ic,** nik″ta·lop′ik, *a.*

nyc·ti·trop·ic, nik″ti·trop′ik, *a.* [Gr. *nyx, nyktos*, night, *tropos*, a turn.] *Bot.* of certain plants, the leaves of which assume positions at night different from those assumed during the daytime.—**nyc·tit·ro·pism,** nik·ti′tro·piz″um, *n.* Night position or 'sleep movements' of the leaves of certain plants.

ny·lon, nī′lon, *n.* [Coined name.] A synthetic, thermoplastic chemical substance made from dicarboxylic acid and diamine, formable into fibers, sheets, bristles, and filaments of extreme toughness, strength, and elasticity: used for yarn, brush bristles, rope, rods, protective coverings, and other applications; *pl.* women's sheer hosiery made of nylon.

nymph, nimf, *n.* [O.Fr. *nimphe* (Fr. *nymphe*), < L. *nympha*, < Gr. *nymphē*, bride, nymph, pupa.] *Class. mythol.* one of a numerous class of inferior divinities, conceived as beautiful maidens inhabiting the sea, rivers, woods, trees, mountains, and meadows, and frequently mentioned as attending a superior deity; *poet.* a beautiful or graceful young woman or maiden; *slang*, a nymphomaniac. *Entom.* an insect in an intermediate stage of development, between a larva and an imago, esp. an immature insect of the orders that undergo only an incomplete metamorphosis and in a form in which the external wing rudiments have become apparent.—**nym·phal,** **nym·phe·an,** nim′fē·an, *a.*

nym·pho·lep·sy, nim′fo·lep″sē, *n.* pl. **nym·pho·lep·sies.** [Gr. *nymphē*, nymph, and *-lmpsia*, seizure, < *lambanein*, take: cf. *epilepsy*.] An ecstasy formerly supposed to be inspired by nymphs; a frenzy of emotion, as for something unattainable.—**nym·pho·lept,** nim′fo·lept″, *n.* [Gr. *nympholēptos*, siezed by nymphs.] One seized with nympholepsy. —**nym·pho·lep·tic,** nim″fo·lep′tik, *a.*

nym·pho·ma·ni·a, nim″fo·mā′nē·a, *n.* [Gr. *nymphē*, a bride, and *mania*, madness.] *Pathol.* abnormal, uncontrollable sexual desire in females.—**nym·pho·ma·ni·ac,** nim″fo·mā′nē·ak″, *n., a.* Also *slang*, **nym·pho,** nim′fō.

O

O, o, ō, *n.* The fourth vowel and fifteenth letter of the English alphabet; the sound represented by the vowel *O*; anything resembling the letter *O* in its rounded shape;

the Arabic cipher zero; a symbol for the fifteenth in a series; printing type for this letter; *chem.* symbol for oxygen; *elect.* ohm.

O, ō, *interj.* A word used before the name in address, esp. in solemn or poetic language, to lend earnestness to an appeal, as: "Praise the Lord, *O* Jerusalem," Ps. cxlvii. 12. An expression of surprise, gladness, longing, pain, as: *O* woe is me.—*n.* The exclamation 'O.'

oaf, ōf, *n.* [< Icel. *álfr*, an elf.] A stupid dolt; a clumsy, dull-witted person.— **oaf·ish,** *a.*—**oaf·ish·ly,** *adv.*—**oaf·ish·ness,** *n.*

oak, ōk, *n.* [O.E. *āc* = D. *eik* = G. *eiche* = Icel. *eik* = Sw. *ek* = Dan. *eg*, oak.] Any tree or shrub of the fagaceous genus *Quercus*, including many large forest trees with hard, durable wood; any of certain other somewhat similar trees or shrubs; the wood of an oak tree.—*a.*—**oak·en,** ō′ken, *a.*

oak ap·ple, *n.* Any of various roundish galls produced on oaks. Also **oak gall.**

oak leaf clus·ter, *n. Milit.* a small bronze or silver emblem of oak leaves and acorns to be worn added to certain decorations and representing an additional award of the original medal.

oa·kum, ō′kum, *n.* [O.E. *ācumba*, tow, oakum, lit. 'matter combed out.'] The substance of old ropes untwisted and pulled into loose fibers, and used for caulking the seams of wooden ships.

oak wilt, *n.* A fungous disease which causes leaves of oak trees to wilt, discolor, or defoliate.

oar, ōr, ạr, *n.* [O.E. *ār* = Icel. *ār* = Dan. *aare*, oar.] A long shaft with a blade at one end used to row, propel, or steer a boat; something resembling this or used for a similar purpose; a paddle; an oarsman.— *v.t.* To propel with or as with oars; to row; to traverse, as the sea, by or as if by rowing.—*v.i.* To row; move or advance as if by rowing.—**oared,** *a.*

oar·fish, ōr′fish″, ạr′fish″, *n. pl.* **oar·fish,** **oar·fish·es.** Any of the deep-sea fishes constituting the genus *Regalecus*, characterized by an oarlike dorsal fin and a compressed, tapelike body from 12 to over 20 feet long

oar·lock, ōr′lok″, ạr′lok″, *n.* [O.E. *ārloc*.] A U-shaped or other device set on a pivot for holding an oar during rowing or steering. Also **row·lock.**

oars·man, ōrz′man, ạrz′man, *n. pl.* **oars·men.** One skilled in the use of oars; a rower; one who rows for exercise or sport, esp. on a racing crew.

o·a·sis, ō·ā′sis, ō′a·sis, *n. pl.* **o·a·ses,** ō·ā′sēz, ō′a·sēz″. [L. and Gr., < Coptic *oueh*, to dwell, and *saa*, to drink.] A fertile tract where there is water located in the midst of a desert; a green spot in the midst of barrenness; *fig.* anything providing relief or refuge; as, a private study that is an *oasis* in a household of children.

oat, ōt, *n.* [O.E. *āte* (pl. *ātan*).] Usu. *pl.* a cereal grass, *Avena sativa*, cultivated for its edible grain, which is used in making oatmeal and as a food for animals; the grain itself. Any species of the same genus, as the common wild oat.—**feel one's oats,** *colloq.* To feel exuberant and lively; feel full of one's own importance.—**sow one's wild oats,** *colloq.* indulge in the follies or adventures common to youth—**oat·en,** *a.*

oat·cake, ōt′kāk″, *n.* A cake, usu. thin and brittle, made of oatmeal.

oat grass, *n.* Any wild species of oat; any of certain oatlike grasses.

oath, ōth, *n. pl.* **oaths,** ōTHz. [O.E. *āth* = D. *eed* = G. *eid* = Icel. *eidhr* = Goth. *aiths*, oath.] A solemn appeal to God or to some revered person or figure, in attestation of the truth of a statement or one's determination to keep a promise; a statement or promise strengthened by such an appeal; a formally affirmed statement or promise accepted as an equivalent; the form of words in which such a statement or promise is made; as, the *oath* of office; a light or blasphemous use of the name of God or anything sacred; any profane expression or expletive; a curse; a mild expression used in ejaculation.

oat·meal, ōt′mēl″, ōt′mēl′, *n.* A cooked cereal made from oatmeal.—*a.*

ob·bli·ga·to, ob″li·gä′tō, *It.* ạb″blē·gä′tạ, *a.* [It., 'obliged.'] *Mus.* Necessary to or indispensable; so important that it cannot be omitted: used as a direction to the performer. Also *obligato.*—*n. pl.* **ob·bli·ga··tos**, *It.* **ob·bli·ga·ti**. *Mus.* An obbligato part or accompaniment; an accompanying instrumental solo of more or less distinct character and independent value. Also *obligato.*

ob·con·i·cal, ob·kon′i·kal, *a. Bot.* Inversely conical; conical, with the pointed end being the base or place of attachment, as in leaves. Also **ob·con·ic**.

ob·cor·date, ob·kọr′dāt, *a. Bot.* inversely heart-shaped, as leaves.

ob·du·rate, ob′dụ·rit, ob′dū·rit, *a.* [L. *obdūrātus*, < *obduro*, to harden—*ob*, intensive, *duro*, to harden, < *dūrus*, hard (seen in *indurate, endure, duration*).] Indifferent to or unmoved by human feelings; persisting obstinately in wrongdoing; stubborn; inflexible; unyielding.—**ob·du·ra·cy**, *n.* —**ob·du·rate·ly**, *adv.*—**ob·du·rate·ness**, *n.*

o·be·di·ence, ō·bē′dē·ens, *n.* [Fr. *obedience*, < *obedientia*, obedience.] The act or habit of obeying; submission; compliance. —**o·be·di·ent**, *a.*—**o·be·di·ent·ly**, *adv.*

o·bei·sance, ō·bā′sans, ō·bē′sans, *n.* [Fr. *obéisance*, < L. *obedientia*.] A bow or curtsy; an act of reverence, or deference; worshipful respect, submission.—**o·bei··sant**, *a.*

ob·e·lisk, ob′e·lisk, *n.* [L. *obeliscus*, < Gr. *obeltkos*, dim. of *obelós*.] A tapering, four-sided shaft of stone, usu. monolithic, having a pyramidal apex and often seen among the monuments of ancient Egypt; something resembling such a shaft. A mark, the obelus, used to indicate those words or passages in ancient manuscripts deemed spurious, corrupt, or doubtful; *print.* the dagger (†) used to make reference to an accompanying note.—**dou·ble ob·e·lisk**, *print.* the double dagger (‡).

ob·e·lize, ob′e·līz, *v.t.*—**obelized, obelizing.** To mark, as a word or passage, with an obelus; to condemn as spurious, corrupt, or doubtful.

ob·e·lus, ob′e·lus, *n. pl.* **ob·e·li**. [L.L., < Gr. *obelós*, spit, pointed pillar, obelus.] A mark, as − or ÷, used in ancient manuscripts to point out spurious, corrupt, doubtful, or superfluous words or passages; *print.* the obelisk or dagger.

o·bese, ō·bēs′, *a.* [L. *obesus*, fat—*ob*-, intens., and *edo, esum*, to eat.] Excessively corpulent; fat; overweight.—**o·bese·ness**, **o··bes·i·ty**, ō·bē′si·tē, *n.*—**o·bese·ly**, *adv.*

o·bey, ō·bā′, *v.t.* [Fr. *obéir*, < L. *obedio, obedire*, to obey, O.L. *obœdire.*] To comply with the commands of; to be under the government of; to be ruled by; to submit to the direction or control of; as, to *obey* one's sense of fitness.—*v.i.* To submit to commands or authority; to do as one is bid.— **o·bey·er**, *n.*

ob·fus·cate, ob·fus′kät, ob′fu·skät″, *v.t.* *obfuscated, obfuscating.* [L. *obfusco, obfuscatum*—prefix *ob*, and *fusco*, to obscure, < *fuscus*, dark.] To darken or obscure; to bewilder, confuse, or muddle.—**ob·fus·· ca·tion**, *n.*—**ob·fus·ca·to·ry**, *a.*

o·bi, ō′bē, *Jap.* ạ′bē, *n. pl.* **o·bis**, *Jap.* **o·bi**. [Jap.] A long, broad sash tied over a kimono and worn by Japanese women and children.

o·bi, ō′bē, *n.* A practice of magical rituals among the negroes of British West Indies, the southeastern U.S., and the Guianas of northern S. America; a charm or fetish used in the rituals. Also **o·be·ah**, ō′bē·a.

o·bit, ō′bit, ob′it, *n.* [L. *obitus*, death, < *obeo, obitum*, to die.] A record of the date of a person's decease; an obituary.

ob·i·ter dic·tum, ob′i·tėr dik′tum, *n. pl.* **ob·i·ter dic·ta**. [L., 'something said by the way.'] *Law,* an incidental opinion of a judge, not part of his judicial decision and not binding. Any incidental opinion; a passing remark.

o·bit·u·ar·y, ō·bich′ọ·er″ē, *n. pl.* **o·bit·· u·ar·ies**. [Fr. *obituaire*.] A published death notice, often including a brief biographical sketch of the deceased's life.—*a.* Relating to or recording the decease of a person.

ob·ject, ob′jikt, ob′jekt, *n.* [L. *objectum*, lit. 'something thrown before or against.'] That toward which the mind is directed in any of its states or activities; what is thought about, believed, seen, or felt; some visible and tangible thing; that to which efforts are directed; as, the *object* of intensive research; aim; end; ultimate purpose. *Gram.* a noun or noun substitute on which the action expressed by a transitive verb is exercised; a noun or noun substitute which follows a preposition in a prepositional phrase.— **ob·ject·less**, ob′jikt·lis, *a.*

ob·ject, ob·jekt′, *v.t.* [Fr. *objecter*, L. *objicio, objectum*.] To bring forward as a matter of reproach, or as an adverse ground or reason; to state or urge in opposition; to state as an objection.—*v.i.* To oppose in words or arguments; to be adverse to something or someone; to voice disapproval.— **ob·jec·tor**, *n.*

ob·ject ball, *n. Billiards.* The ball which the player aims to hit with the cue ball; any ball except the striker's; the ball first struck by the cue ball.

ob·ject glass, *n.* In a telescope or microscope, the lens or combination of lenses which first receives the rays from the object and forms the image viewed through the eyepiece; objective.

ob·jec·ti·fy, ob·jek′ti·fī″, *v.t.*—*objectified, objectifying.* [M.L. *objectum*, an object.] To present in concrete form; to render objective; externalize.—**ob·jec·ti·fi·ca·tion**, *n.*

ob·jec·tion, ob·jek′shan, *n.* The act of objecting; that which is said or felt in opposition or disagreement; the reason or cause for disapproving, disagreeing, or disputing; an adverse reason, argument, or charge.

ob·jec·tion·a·ble, ob·jek′sha·na·bl, *a.* Provoking protest or disapproval; reprehensible, offensive, or insulting.—**ob·jec·· tion·a·bil·i·ty, ob·jec·tion·a·ble·ness**, *n.* —**ob·jec·tion·a·bly**, *adv.*

ob·jec·tive, ob·jek′tiv, *a.* [M.L. *objectivus*.] Being the object of perception or thought; belonging to the object of thought rather than to the thinking subject: opposed to *subjective*; intent upon or dealing with things external to the mind rather than thoughts or feelings, as a person or a book; being the object of one's endeavors or actions; as, an *objective* point; perspective, being or pertaining to the object whose perspective delineation is required; as, an *objective* plane. *Gram.* noting the case in declension in English that indicates the grammatical object; being in or pertaining to this case.—*n.* An object glass; an end toward which efforts are directed; something aimed at; an objective point; *gram.* the objective case, or a word in that case. —**ob·jec·tive·ly**, *adv.*—**ob·jec·tive·ness**, *n.*

ob·jec·tive com·ple·ment, *n. Gram.* one or several words, usually a noun, pronoun, or adjective, which correctly must follow in the predicate after the use of a factitive verb indicating the result of a process implicit in the verb, as captain, in: 'They elected him captain.'

ob·jec·tiv·ism, ob·jek′ti·viz″um, *n.* A tendency to stress the objective or external elements of cognition. *Philos.* that doctrine which postulates that reality exists externally, independent of the mind; the ethical doctrine which maintains the existence of a moral order independent of subjective judgement; the tendency to deal with things external to the mind rather than with thoughts or feelings, as in a writer or artist.—**ob·jec·tiv·ist**, *n., a.*—**ob·jec·ti·· vis·tic**, *a.*

ob·jec·tiv·i·ty, ob″jek·tiv′i·tē, *n.* The character or quality of being objective; intentness on objects independent of the mind; reality outside the mind.

ob·ject les·son, *n.* A lesson in which a material object, a performance, or an experience is made the basis of instruction; something that illustrates a principle in a concrete form.

ob·jet d'art, *Fr.* ạb·zhe där′, *n.* Any valuable article or object of art; a curio.

ob·jur·gate, ob′jėr·gāt″, ob·jur′gāt, *v.t., v.i.* —*objurgated, objurgating.* [L. *objurgo, objurgatum*.] To scold, reprove, or censure; to chastise harshly.—**ob·jur·ga·tion**, *n.*— **ob·jur·ga·to·ry**, *a.*

ob·lan·ce·o·late, ob·lan′sē·ọ·lit, ob·lan′· sē·ọ·lāt″, *a. Bot.* of a leaf shaped like the head of a lance, with the broadest part above the middle.

ob·last, ob′last, ob′läst, *Russ.* ạb′läst, *n. pl.* **ob·lasts**, *Russ.* **ob·las·ti**, ạb′läs·tē. An administrative region of the U.S.S.R.

ob·late, ob′lāt, o·blāt′, *a.* [L. *oblātus*, thrust forward (i.e. at the equator), also offered, devoted.] *Geom.* of a sphere, flattened or depressed at the poles so that the greatest width of its diameter lies midway between them. Also **ob·late sphe·roid.**—**ob·late·· ness**, *n.*—**ob·late·ly**, *adv.*

ob·late, ob′lāt, o·blāt′, *n. Rom Cath. Ch.* A lay person admitted into a monastery, without taking vows or submitting to full rule; (*cap.*) a member of a lay community devoted to religious and charitable work.

ob·la·tion, o·blā′shan, *n.* [L. *oblātiō*, an offering.] The act of making an offering to God, as the presentation in the Eucharist of the elements of bread and wine; a gift offered to God, as the Eucharistic elements; any gift made as an expression of piety or charity.—**ob·la·tion·al, ob·la·to·ry**, ob′· la·tọr″ē, *a.*

ob·li·gate, ob′li·gāt″, *v.t.*—*obligated, obligating.* [L. *obligātus*, pp. of *obligāre*.] To bind morally or legally to fulfill certain conditions.—ob′li·git, ob′li·gāt″, *a.* Bound; constrained. *Biol.* restricted to a particular host, as certain parasites: opposed to *facultative.*

ob·li·ga·tion, ob″li·gā′shan, *n.* [L. *obligātiō(n-)*, < *obligare.*] The act of binding oneself by promise or contract; the binding force of a contract or promise; anything imposing a moral or legal duty; the state or fact of being indebted for a benefit or service, as a debt of gratitude. *Law,* an agreement that may be enforced by law; *com.* a liability, as a contract, bond, or promissory note.

ob·li·ga·to, ob″li·gä′tō, *It.* ạb″blē·gä′tạ, *a., n. pl.* **ob·li·ga·tos**, *It.* **ob·li·ga·ti**. Obbligato.

ob·lig·a·to·ry, o·blig′a·tọr″ē, ob′li·ga·· tọr″ē, *a.* [L.L. *obligātōrius*.] Binding morally or legally; required as a matter of obligation; compulsory, imperative; creating or recording an obligation; as, an *obligatory* record.—**ob·lig·a·to·ri·ly**, *o·blig'a·tōr"-i·lē*, *ob'li·ga·tōr"i·lē*, *o·blig"a·tōr'i·lē*, *ob"li·ga·tōr'i·lē*, *adv.*—**ob·lig·a·to·ri·ness**, *n.*

o·blige, *o·blīj'*, *v.t.*—*obliged, obliging.* [Fr. *obliger*, < L. *obligo*, to bind, to oblige.] To constrain by any force, physical, moral, or legal; to compel; to bind by any restraint; to bind by some favor done; to lay under obligation of gratitude; to perform a service for.—**o·bliged**, *a.* Having received some accommodation or favor; laid under obligation; indebted.—**o·blig·er**, *n.*

ob·li·gee, *ob"li·jē'*, *n. Law*, one to whom another is bound by legal agreement; one to whom a bond is given. Morally, one who is under obligation for a benefit or favor received.

o·blig·ing, *o·blī'jing*, *a.* Disposed to oblige, do favors, or perform services; accommodating; willing; kind.—**o·blig·ing·ly**, *adv.*—**o·blig·ing·ness**, *n.*

ob·li·gor, *ob"li·gar'*, *ob'li·gar*, *n. Law.* One who is legally bound to discharge an obligation; one who gives a bond.

ob·lique, *o·blēk'*, *Milit.* *o·blīk'*, *a.* [L. *oblīquus*.] Neither perpendicular nor parallel; slanting; sloping; not straightforward; indirectly expressed; devious; indirectly aimed at or accomplished. *Geom.* pertaining to a solid, esp. a cone or cylinder whose axis is not perpendicular to its base. *Naut.* navigating a ship in a direction other than toward one of the cardinal points of the compass. *Bot.* having the base of the leaf slanting.—*n. Anat.* of certain muscles of the eye and the abdomen, running at an angle and not laterally.—*adv. Milit.* at an angle of 45 degrees, esp. in marching.—*v.i. obliqued, obliquing.*—**ob·lique·ly**, *adv.*—**ob·lique·ness**, *n.*

ob·lique an·gle, *n.* An angle other than a right angle, as an acute or obtuse angle.

ob·lique case, *n. Gram.* any case except the nominative and vocative.

ob·liq·ui·ty, *o·blik'wi·tē*, *n.* pl. **ob·liq·ui·ties.** The state of being oblique; divergence from moral standards; mental deviation or an instance of it; obscurity, esp. intentional obscurity, in writing or speech; a confusing statement; an inclination or the degree of inclination. *Astron.* the angle between the plane of the earth's orbit and that of the earth's equator, equal to 23° 26′ 40″.16, diminishing at the rate of 47″ per century; also **ob·liq·ui·ty of the e·clip·tic.**—**ob·liq·ui·tous**, *a.*

ob·lit·er·ate, *o·blit'e·rāt"*, *v.t.*—*obliterated, obliterating.* [L. *oblitero*, to blot out, to cause to be forgotten.] To efface, erase, or blot out, as writing; to destroy any indication or sign of; to cancel.—**ob·lit·er·a·tion**, *o·blit"e·rā'shan*, *n.*—**ob·lit·er·a·tive**, *o·blit'e·rā"tiv*, *o·blit'ér·a·tiv*, *a.*

ob·liv·i·on, *o·bliv'ē·an*, *n.* [L. *oblīviō*, *oblīviōnis*, < *obliviscor*, to forget.] The condition or instance of forgetting; the condition or instance of being forgotten; an official pardon; heedless disregard.

ob·liv·i·ous, *o·bliv'ē·us*, *a.* [L. *oblīviōsus*.] Forgetful; without memory of; causing forgetfulness; without consciousness of; mentally absent; unaware, usu. followed by *of* or *to.*—**ob·liv·i·ous·ly**, *adv.*—**ob·liv·i·ous·ness**, *n.*

ob·long, *ob'lạng"*, *ob'long"*, *a.* [L. *oblongus*, oblong—*ob*, against, inversely, and *longus*, long.] Rectangular, and having the length greater than the breadth; longer than broad.—*n.* An oblong figure.—**ob·long·ness**, *n.*

ob·lo·quy, *ob'lo·kwē*, *n.* pl. **ob·lo·quies.** [L. *obloquium*, < *obloquor*.] Censorious, reproachful, or defamatory language; denunciation of a man or his deeds; the odium and disgrace arising from public blame or vilification.

ob·nox·ious, *ob·nok'shus*, *a.* [L. *obnoxius*.] Reprehensible; censurable; odious; hateful; offensive; unpopular.—**ob·nox·ious·ly**, *adv.*—**ob·nox·ious·ness**, *n.*

o·boe, *ō'bō*, *n.* [It., < Fr. *hautbois*.] *Mus.* A wooden wind instrument in the form of a slender tapering tube, in which the tone is produced by a double reed; the reed stop on the organ having a tone similar to that of the oboe.—**o·bo·ist**, *ō'bō·ist*, *n.*

ob·o·vate, *ob·ō'vāt*, *a. Bot.* In outline, inversely ovate; having the narrow end downward.—**ob·o·void**, *ob·ō'void*, *a. Bot.* of an ovoid body, being attached at the smaller end.

ob·scene, *ob·sēn'*, *a.* [L. *obscēnus*, *obscænus*, of evil omen, offensive, disgusting.] Objectionable or repugnant to acceptable standards of decency or morality; indecent; pornographic; offensive in language or action; tending to incite lust or depravity.—**ob·scene·ly**, *adv.*—**ob·scene·ness**, *n.*

ob·scen·i·ty, *ob·sen'i·tē*, *ob·sē'ni·tē*, *n.* pl. **ob·scen·i·ties.** Obscene quality or character; indecency; something obscene; as, *obscene* language.

ob·scu·rant, *ob·skūr'ant*, *n.* One who obscures, esp. one who opposes the progress of knowledge, or attempts to prevent inquiry or reform.—*a.* Of or pertaining to obscurants. Also **ob·scu·ran·tic**, *ob"skū·-ran'tik.*—**ob·scu·ra·tion**, *ob"skū·rā'shan*, *n.*

ob·scu·rant·ism, *ob·skūr'an·tiz"um*, *ob"-skū·ran'tiz·um*, *n.* The principles or practice of obscurants; opposition to inquiry and learning; intentional obscurity or vagueness.—**ob·scu·rant·ist**, *n.*, *a.*

ob·scure, *ob·skūr'*, *a.*—*obscurer, obscurest.* [Fr. *obscur*, < L. *obscūrus.*]Not easily understood; not expressed with clarity; not clear or distinct to any sense; removed or remote from worldly or important activities; unnoticed, or unknown to fame; lacking illumination; gloomy or dim; *phon.* having a neutral, unstressed vowel quality as represented by a schwa.—*v.t.*—*obscured, obscuring.* To make dark or dim; to make less intelligible, legible, or visible; to prevent from being seen or known; *phon.* to neutralize, as a vowel, to the sound usu. heard in an unstressed syllable as signified by schwa.—*n.*—**ob·scur·ed·ly**, **ob·scure·-ly**, *ob·skūr'id·lē*, *adv.*—**ob·scure·ness**, *n.*

ob·scu·ri·ty, *ob·skūr'i·tē*, *n.* pl. **ob·scu·-ri·ties.** [L. *obscūritās.*] The quality or state of being obscure; ambiguity in meaning; the condition of a thing or person unknown or undistinguished; darkness or dimness.

ob·se·qui·ous, *ob·sē'kwē·us*, *a.* [L. *obse-quiōsus*, obsequious, < *obsequium*, compliance, < *obsequor*, to follow.] Excessively obedient or submissive to the will of another; compliant; servile.—**ob·se·qui·ous·ly**, *adv.*—**ob·se·qui·ous·ness**, *n.*

ob·se·quy, *ob'se·kwē*, *n.* pl. **ob·se·quies.** [L.L. *obsequiæ*, pl., for L. *exsequiæ*, *exequiæ*, funeral rites.] *Usu. pl.* a funeral rite or ceremony.

ob·serv·a·ble, *ob·zur'va·bl*, *a.* Capable of being observed; worthy of observation.—**ob·serv·a·bil·i·ty**, **ob·serv·a·ble·ness**, *ob·zérv"a·bil'i·tē*, *n.*—**ob·serv·a·bly**, *adv.*

ob·ser·vance, *ob·zur'vans*, *n.* [O.Fr. Fr. *observance*, < L. *observantia.*] The action of observing, conforming to, following, or keeping; as, *observance* of laws, rules, customs, or methods; a keeping or celebrating by appropriate procedure, as ceremonies; a procedure, ceremony, or rite, as for a particular occasion or use; as, patriotic *observances*; attention; a pious or religious rule or discipline.

ob·ser·vant, *ob·zur'vant*, *a.* Making quick or careful observation; taking notice; attentive to duties or commands; adhering to in practice, often with *of*; as, *observant of* duties.—*n.*—**ob·ser·vant·ly**, *adv.*

ob·ser·va·tion, *ob"zur·vā'shan*, *n.* [L. *observātiō.*] The act, power, or habit of observing; a taking notice or paying attention. *Science*, the act of taking notice of particular phenomena as they occur in the course of experiments or nature; the observing of some phenomenon, often by the assistance of an instrument, as planets observed by means of a telescope; information gained by such an act. A remark or judgment based on what has been observed; notice.—**ob·ser·va·tion·al**, *a.*

ob·ser·va·to·ry, *ob·zur'va·tōr"ē*, *n.* pl. **ob·ser·va·to·ries.** A place used for making observations of natural phenomena, esp. a building for astronomical observations; a place providing a good view.

ob·serve, *ob·zurv'*, *v.t.*—*observed, observing.* [L. *observo.*] To look on without actively participating; to regard attentively; to watch; to notice; to perceive; to detect; to discover; to remark in words; to mention; to keep, as a holiday, with due ceremonies; to celebrate; to keep or adhere to in practice; to comply with; to obey.—*v.i.* To attend or watch without joining in; to perceive; to remark; to comment.—**ob·serv·ed·ly**, *ob·zur'vid·lē*, *adv.*—**ob·serv·ing·ly**, *adv.*

ob·ser·ver, *ob·zur'vér*, *n.* A person or instrument which observes. *Milit.* a person who observes artillery targets and directs firing; a person assigned to watch and usu. report on military activities. A person who celebrates a ceremony or rite, as a holiday; a person delegated to audit an event but not take part in it.

ob·sess, *ob·ses'*, *v.t.* [L. *obsideo*, to besiege.] To occupy a person's thoughts to an unusual degree; preoccupy the mind; to harass or vex through a persistent, usu. undesirable or unwanted thought or emotion.—**ob·ses·sive**, *a.*—**ob·ses·sive·ly**, *adv.*

ob·ses·sion, *ob·sesh'an*, *n.* An act of obsessing; a thought or emotion which comes strongly to mind with unwanted persistency; the thought itself.—**ob·ses·sion·al**, *a.*—**ob·ses·sion·al·ly**, *adv.*

ob·sid·i·an, *ob·sid'ē·an*, *n.* [L. *Obsidiānus*, from *Obsidius* or *Obsius*, its alleged discoverer.] *Mineral.* a glassy rock of volcanic origin, usu. of a black color, somewhat transparent in thin sections, and used in making costume jewelry.

ob·so·lesce, *ob"so·les'*, *v.i.*—*obsolesced, obsolescing.* To be or become obsolete.

ob·so·les·cent, *ob"so·les'ent*, *a.* [L. *obsolescēns*, ppr. of *obsolescere.*] Becoming obsolete; passing out of use, as a word; tending to become out of date, or being no longer of the most modern type or kind, as machinery; *biol.* gradually disappearing, or imperfectly developed, as organs or marks.—**ob·so·les·cence**, *n.*—**ob·so·les·cent·ly**, *adv.*

ob·so·lete, *ob"so·lēt'*, *ob'so·lēt"*, *a.* [L. *obsolētus*, pp. of *obsolescere*, fall into disuse.] Fallen into disuse or no longer in use; as, an *obsolete* custom, an *obsolete* word; of a discarded type; as, an *obsolete* battleship; out-of-date. *Biol.* imperfectly developed; indistinct, esp. in comparison with the corresponding characteristic in other individuals, as of the opposite sex or of a related species.—*v.t.* To cause to be obsolete by a more recent or better replacement.—**ob·so·lete·ly**, *adv.*—**ob·so·lete·ness**, *n.*

ob·sta·cle, *ob'sta·kl*, *n.* [Fr. *obstacle*, < L. *obstāculum*, < *obsto*, to withstand.] Anything that stands in the way of progress; an obstruction or impediment of any sort.

ob·sta·cle course, *n. Milit.* a difficult route in a training area, including walls, fences, ditches, hurdles and other obstacles which must be overcome.

ob·stet·ric, ob·ste′trik, _a._ [L. _obstetrix,_ a midwife—_ob,_ before, and _sto,_ to stand.] Pertaining to obstetrics or to the care of a woman in pregnancy, labor, birth, and the postnatal period. Also **ob·stet·ri·cal.**—**ob·stet·ri·cal·ly,** _adv._

ob·ste·tri·cian, ob″sti·trish′an, _n._ A physician in obstetrics.

ob·stet·rics, ob·ste′triks, _n. pl. but sing. in constr._ That branch of medical science which includes prenatal care and childbirth.

ob·sti·na·cy, ob′sti·na·sē, _n. pl._ **ob·sti·na·cies.** The state, instance, or quality of being obstinate; an obstinate viewpoint, feeling, or act.

ob·sti·nate, ob′sti·nit, _a._ [L. _obstinātus,_ pp. of _obstino, obstinatum,_ to resolve, < _obsto,_ to stand against.] Pertinaciously adhering to an opinion or purpose; fixed firmly in resolution; not yielding to reason or argument, stubborn; not yielding to medical care; not easily subdued or overcome.—**ob·sti·nate·ly,** _adv._—**ob·sti·nate·ness,** _n._

ob·strep·er·ous, ob·strep′ĕr·us, _a._ [L. _obstreperus,_ < _obstrepo,_ to roar.] Unruly, noisy, or boisterous; resisting control, direction, or advice in a noisy or willfully unruly way.—**ob·strep·er·ous·ly,** _adv._—**ob·strep·er·ous·ness, ob·strep·e·ros·i·ty,** ob·strep″e·ros′i·tē, _n._

ob·struct, ob·strukt′, _v.t._ [L. _obstruo, obstructum._] To block or close, as a street or channel, with obstacles or impediments that prevent passing; to hinder or impede the passage, progress, or operation of; to stand in the way of, so as to block the view. —**ob·struc·tive,** _a., n._—**ob·struc·tor,** _n._

ob·struc·tion, ob·struk′shan, _n._ The act or a case of obstructing; anything that clogs or closes a way, passage, or channel; an obstacle or impediment to passage, progress, or activity; the delaying by contrivances of official business before a deliberative assembly.

ob·struc·tion·ist, ob·struk′sha·nist, _n._ One who intentionally obstructs, esp. one who delays or hinders action on the business before a deliberative assembly by parliamentary or legalistic maneuvers.—**ob·stru·ction·ism,** _n._—**ob·struc·tion·is·tic,** _a._

ob·stru·ent, ob′strö·ent, _a._ [L. _obstruēns,_ ppr. of _obstruo._] _Phon._ momentarily constricting the air passage in the articulation of a speech sound.—_n. Med._ a substance that blocks the natural passages of the body; _phon._ an obstruent articulation.

ob·tain, ob·tān′, _v.t._ [L. _obtineo._] To gain possession of; to gain, procure, receive, get, acquire.—_v.i._ To be in customary or common use, as: The custom still _obtains._ —**ob·tain·a·ble,** ob·tā′na·bl, _a._—**ob·tain·er,** _n._ One who obtains.—**ob·tain·ment,** _n._

ob·tect, ob·tekt′, _a._ [L. _obtectus._] _Entom._ covered with a hard chitinous shell, as the pupa of some insects. Also **ob·tect·ed.**

ob·test, ob·test′, _v.t._ [L. _obtestor._] To call upon as a witness; to entreat; implore; to supplicate.—_v.i._ To protest.—**ob·tes·ta·tion,** _n._

ob·trude, ob·tröd′, _v.t._—obtruded, obtruding. [L. _obtrudo._] To thrust forward; to force into any place or state unduly or without solicitation; as, to obtrude oneself upon a person's privacy; to offer with importunity.—_v.i._ To obtrude oneself; to enter when not invited.—**ob·trud·er,** _n._ —**ob·tru·sion,** ob·trö′zhan, _n._—**ob·tru·sive,** ob·trö′siv, _a._ Disposed to obtrude; forward; instrusive.—**ob·tru·sive·ly,** _adv._—**ob·tru·sive·ness,** _n._

ob·tund, ob·tund′, _v.t._ [L. _obtundere_ (pp. _obtusus_), < _ob,_ to, against, and _tundere,_ beat.] To blunt; dull; deaden.—**ob·tund·ent,** _a., n._ Dulling sensibility, as of nerves.—_n._—**ob·tund·ent a·gent,** _dentistry,_ an anesthetic for the nerves of teeth.

ob·tu·rate, ob′tu·rāt″, ob′tū·rāt′, _v.t._—obturated, obturating. [L. _obtūrātus,_ pp. of _obtūrāre,_ stop up.] To stop up; to close.— **ob·tu·ra·tion,** _n._—**ob·tu·ra·tor,** _n._ Something that closes an opening, as the shutter of a camera, or a surgical plate for closing an abdominal opening.

ob·tuse, ob·tös′, ob·tūs′, _a._ [L. _obtusus._] Not pointed or acute; blunt; not having acute sensibility; stupid; dull, as pain.— **ob·tuse·ly,** _adv._—**ob·tuse·ness,** _n._—**ob·tuse an·gle,** an angle larger than a right angle but less than 180°.

ob·verse, ob·vʉrs′, ob′vʉrs, _a._ [L. _obversus,_ pp. of _obvettere._] Turned toward or facing one; corresponding to something else, as a counterpart; having the base narrower than the top, as a leaf.—_n._ That side of a coin, medal, or the like, which bears the principal design, as opposed to _reverse;_ the front or principal face of anything; a counterpart. _Logic,_ a proposition formed by the obversion of another.—**ob·verse·ly,** _adv._

ob·ver·sion, ob·vʉr′zhan, ob·vʉr′shan, _n._ _Logic,_ a form of inference in which a negative proposition is inferred from an affirmative, or an affirmative from a negative, as: "All men are mortal" becomes by _obversion_ "No men are immortal." The action or an example of obverting; that which is obverted.

ob·vert, ob·vʉrt′, _v.t._ [L. _obvertere_ (pp. _obversus._)] To turn to expose a different side; _logic,_ to derive, as a proposition, by obversion.

ob·vi·ate, ob′vē·āt″, _v.t._—obviated, obviating. [L. _obvio, obviātum,_ to meet.] To counter, eliminate, or prevent, as difficulties or objections, by forethought; to overcome; to clear out of the way.— **ob·vi·a·tion,** _n._—**ob·vi·a·tor,** _n._

ob·vi·ous, ob′vē·us, _a._ [L. _obvius,_ in the way.] Easily discovered, seen, or understood; perfectly plain or evident.—**ob·vi·ous·ly,** _adv._—**ob·vi·ous·ness,** _n._

ob·vo·lute, ob′vo·löt″, _a._ [L. _ob-,_ against, and _volūtus,_ rolled.] Rolled or turned inward; _bot._ having the margins of leaves overlapping.

oc·a·ri·na, ok″a·rē′na, _n._ [Prob. dim. of It. _oca,_ goose, with reference to the shape.] A simple musical instrument shaped somewhat like an elongated egg, with finger holes and a whistlelike mouthpiece. Also _colloq. sweet potato._

oc·ca·sion, o·kā′zhan, _n._ [L. _occāsiō, occāsiōnis,_ < _occido, occasum,_ to fall.] The time of an occurrence, incident, or event, or the event itself; an important or significant event or time; an opportune or convenient time; as, putting it off until the right _occasion;_ the incidental cause, motive, or reason for a particular action; as, the _occasion_ for my discharge; a demand or requirement; as, having no _occasion_ for it.— _v.t._ To cause incidentally; to produce or bring about.

oc·ca·sion·al, o·kā′zha·nal, _a._ Occurring at times, but not regularly or systematically; made or suitable for a specific occasion; as, _occasional_ verse; intended for use, as a chair or table, as the need arises.—**oc·ca·sion·al·ly,** _adv._ Sometimes but not often.

oc·ca·sion·al·ism, o·kā′zha·na·liz″um, _n._ _Philos._ the doctrine that the interaction of mind and matter is not to be explained as resulting from a causal connection but by the supposition that God takes an act of the will as the occasion of producing a corresponding movement of the body, and a state of the body as the occasion of producing a corresponding mental state.—**oc·ca·sion·al·ist,** _n._

oc·ci·dent, ok′si·dent, _n._ [O.Fr. Fr. _occident,_ < L. _occidens_ (_occident-_), the west

(where the sun sets), prop. ppr. of _occidere,_ fall, go down, set.] The west; the western regions. (_Cap._) the western countries; the western hemisphere, as opposed to the _Orient;_ Europe, as opposed to Asia.— **oc·ci·den·tal,** ok″si·den′tal, _a._ [O.Fr. Fr., _occidental,_ < L. _occidentālis._] Of the occident or west; western; (_usu. cap._) of, pertaining to, or characteristic of the Occident.—_n._ (_Usu. cap._) a native or inhabitant of the Occident.—**oc·ci·den·tal·ism,** _n._ (_Usu. cap._) occidental character or characteristics.—**oc·ci·den·tal·ist,** _n._ (_Usu. cap._) a student or an advocate of Occidental institutions.—**oc·ci·den·tal·ize,** _v.t._—_occidentalized, occidentalizing._ To render Occidental.—**oc·ci·den·tal·ly,** _adv._

oc·cip·i·tal, ok·sip′i·tal, _a._ [M.L. _occipitālis._] _Anat._ Of or pertaining to the occiput; of the posterior part of the head or skull.—_n._ The occipital bone.—**oc·cip·i·tal·ly,** _adv._ **oc·cip·i·tal bone,** _n._ _Anat._ a compound bone which forms the posterior part of the skull.

oc·ci·put, ok′si·put″, ok′si·put, _n._ pl. **oc·cip·i·ta, oc·ci·puts.** [L.] _Anat._ the hinder part of the head or skull.

oc·clude, o·klöd′, _v.t._—occluded, occluding. [L. _occlūdere_ (pp. _occlusus_), < _ob,_ to, and _cludere, claudere,_ shut, close.] To close, shut, or stop up, as a passage; to shut in, out, or off. _Chem._ of certain metals and other solids, to absorb and retain, as gases. —_v.i. Dentistry,_ to meet closely or fit into each other, as opposing teeth in the upper and lower jaw.—**oc·clud·ent,** _a._—**oc·clu·sive,** o·klö′siv, _a._

oc·clud·ed front, _n._ _Meteor._ the front formed when a warm air mass is forced away from the earth's surface by a cold front or mass of cold air.

oc·clu·sion, o·klö′zhan, _n._ The act of occluding, or the state of being occluded; _chem._ the retention of gases in the pores of a metal; _dentistry,_ the meeting closely of opposing teeth in the upper and the lower jaw.

oc·cult, o·kult′, ok′ult, _a._ [L. _occultus,_ pp. of _occulere,_ cover over, conceal.] Not disclosed; kept secret; communicated only to the initiated; beyond the bounds of ordinary or natural knowledge; mysterious; transcendental. _Early science,_ not apparent on mere inspection but discoverable by experimentation; of a nature not understood, as physical qualities; dealing or experimenting with such qualities; as, _occult_ science. Of or pertaining to certain so-called sciences, as magic or astrology, involving the alleged knowledge or employment of secret or mysterious agencies; having to do with such sciences; as, an _occult_ philosopher.— _n._—**oc·cult·ly,** _adv._ **oc·cult·ness,** _n._

oc·cult, o·kult′, ok′ult, _v.t._ [L. _occultare_ (pp. _occultatus_), freq. of _occulere._] To hide; shut off, as an object, from view, by interposing something between the object and the eye. _Astron._ to eclipse, as a heavenly body; hide by occultation.—_v.i._ To become hidden or shut off from view, as an intermittent beam of light from a lighthouse.— **oc·cult·er,** _n._

oc·cul·ta·tion, ok″ul·tā′shan, _n._ [L. _occultātio(n-)._] _Astron._ the hiding of one heavenly body by another passing between it and the observer, esp. the eclipse of a star or planet by the moon; the act of shutting off from view, or the resulting obscured state. _Fig._ disappearance from view or notice.

oc·cult·ism, o·kul′tiz·um, _n._ The doctrine, study of, or belief in the supernatural and communication with it.—**oc·cult·ist,** _n._ One who believes or is versed in occultism.

oc·cu·pan·cy, ok′kū·pan·sē, _n. pl._ **oc·cu·pan·cies.** The act of occupying; a holding in possession; the term during which one is an occupant; _law,_ the act of occupying or taking possession of unowned real estate to acquire title thereto.—**oc·cu·-pant,** *n.*

oc·cu·pa·tion, ok″ū·pā′shan, *n.* [L. *occu-pātiō*.] One's principal employment, busi-ness, vocation, trade, or other means of livelihood; the act of occupying or taking possession, as of land or buildings; seizure and control of a foreign country or territory by military invasion.—**oc·cu·pa·tion·al,** *a.* Of or relating to occupation; pertaining to a trade or vocation, as guidance.—**oc·-cu·pa·tion·al·ly,** *adv.*

oc·cu·pa·tion·al ther·a·py, *n.* *Med.* a method of treatment of convalescents utilizing light work for diversion, physical exercise, or vocational training.

oc·cu·py, ok′ū·pī″, *v.t.*—*occupied, occupy-ing.* [L. *occupo*, to take possession of, possess—prefix *ob*, and *capio*, to take.] To take and keep possession of, as by military conquest; to take up, as room or time; to employ or use, as one's time or attention; to fill, as a post or office; to inhabit or be a dweller in.—**oc·cu·pi·a·ble,** *a.*—**oc·cu·-pi·er,** *n.*

oc·cur, o·kur′, *v.i.*—*occurred, occurring.* [L. *occurro*.] To suggest or come to the mind, imagination, or memory; to befall; to happen; to take place; to exist so as to be found or seen.—**oc·cur·rence,** o·kur′ens, o·kur′ens, *n.* The act of occurring or taking place; any incident or event.—**oc·cur·rent,** *a.*

o·cean, ō′shan, *n.* [O.Fr. *occean* (Fr. *océan*), < L. *ōceanus*, < Gr. *Ōkeanos*, the ocean, orig. the great stream supposed to en-compass the earth, and personified as a god, Oceanus.] The immense body of salt water covering more than 70 percent of the earth's surface; any of the geographical divisions of this body, usu. given as the Atlantic, Pacific, Indian, Arctic, and Ant-arctic oceans; *fig.* a great expanse or amount; as, the undulating *ocean* of grass. —*a.* Of or pertaining to the ocean.

o·cean·ar·i·um, ō′sha·nâr′ē·um, *n.* A large tank, or the building housing it, used for the study or display of marine life.

o·ce·an·ic, ō′shē·an′ik, *a.* Pertaining to the ocean; occurring in or produced by the ocean, as distinguished from smaller seas; vast, extensive.

o·ce·a·nog·ra·phy, ō″shē·a·nog′ra·fē, ō″she·nog′ra·fē, *n.* The science and study of oceanic phenomena; the science dealing with undersea space and the conducting of research in such areas as underwater trans-portation, communication, geography, and engineering.—**o·ce·a·nog·ra·pher,** *n.*—**o·ce·a·no·graph·ic, o·ce·a·no·graph·i·-cal,** ō″shē·a·no·graf′ik, ō″she·no·graf′ik, *a.*—**o·ce·a·no·graph·i·cal·ly,** *adv.*

o·cean sun·fish, *n.* Any of several large fish, esp. the *Mola mola*, of tropical and temperate seas, with short bodies and very long fins. Also **head·fish.**

oc·el·lat·ed, os′e·lā″tid, ō·sel′ā·tid, *a.* Having ocelli or simple eyes; having eyelike spots or markings. Also **oc·el·late,** os′e·-lāt″, ō·sel′it, ō·sel′āt.—**oc·el·la·tion,** os″-e·lā′shan, *n.* An eyelike spot or marking.

o·cel·lus, ō·sel′us, *n.* pl. **o·cel·li,** ō·sel′ī. [L., dim of *oculus*, eye.] *Entom.* a simple eye of an insect or other arthropod, present in both the larval and adult stages; *usu. pl.* a pigmented, eyelike area on the wings of some butterflies and moths. *Ornith.* the brilliantly colored, eyelike spot on the tail feathers of a peacock.—**o·cel·lar,** *a.*

o·ce·lot, ō′se·lot″, o′se·lot″, *n.* [Fr. from Mex. name, meaning 'field tiger.'] A spotted, leopardlike cat, *Felis pardalis*, ranging from Texas through S. America, being nocturnal and arboreal.

o·cher, o·chre, ō′kėr, *n.* [L. *ōchra*, Gr. *ochra*, < *ochros*, pale, pale yellow.] Any of

various clays containing iron oxide, and varying in color from pale yellow to brownish-red, much used as pigments in paints; the color itself.—**o·cher·ous, o·-chre·ous, o·cher·y,** *a.*

och·loc·ra·cy, ok·lok′ra·sē, *n.* pl. **och·-loc·ra·cies.** [Gr. *ochlos*, the multitude, and *kratos*, power.] Rule by the multitude or common people; mob rule.—**och·lo·crat,** ok′lo·krat″, *n.*—**och·lo·crat·ic,** *a.*

och·lo·pho·bia, ok″lo·fō′bē·a, *n.* *Psychol.* morbid fear of crowds or mobs.

o'clock, o·klok′, *adv.* Of or by the clock: used in specifying the hour of the day; as, one *o'clock.*

o·co·til·lo, ō″ko·tēl′yō, *Sp.* a″ka·tē′ya, *n.* pl. **o·co·til·los,** ō″ko·tēl′yōz, *Sp.* a″ka·tē′yas. [Mex. Sp., dim. of *ocote*, kind of pine.] *Bot.* a native, desert shrub of Mexico and south-western U.S., *Fouquieria splendens*, in the candlewood family, characterized by thorny, stout stems and showy, red flowers, and cultivated as a landscape subject.

oc·re·a, ok′rē·a, ō′krē·a, *n.* pl. **oc·re·ae,** ok′rē·ē″, ō′krē·ē″. [L. *ocrea*, a greave or legging.] *Bot.* a sheath, located at the node of a stem and which is the result of the fusion of two stipules. Also **och·re·a.**—**oc·re·ate,** ok′rē·it, ok′rē·āt″, ō′krē·it, ō′krē·āt″, *a. Bot.* furnished with ocreae.

oc·ta·chord, ok′ta·kard″, *n.* [Gr. *oktō*, eight, and *chorde*, a string.] *Mus.* A musical instrument having eight strings; any standard scale of eight notes.

oc·ta·gon, ok′ta·gon″, ok′ta·gon, *n.* [Gr. *oktō*, eight, and *gōnia*, angle.] *Geom.* a figure with eight sides and eight angles. Also **oc·tan·gle.**—**oc·tag·o·nal,** ok·tag′o·nal, *a.* Having eight sides and eight angles.—**oc·tag·o·nal·ly,** *adv.*

oc·ta·he·dron, ok′ta·hē′dron, *n.* pl. **oc·-ta·he·drons, oc·ta·he·dra.** [Gr. *oktō*, eight, *hedra*, a base.] *Geom.* a solid with eight faces.—**oc·ta·he·dral,** *a.* In the form of an octahedron.

oc·tam·er·ous, ok·tam′ėr·us, *a.* [Gr. *oktameres*.] Consisting of or divided into eight parts; *bot.* of flowers, having eight members in each whorl, as eight stamens.

oc·tam·e·ter, ok·tam′i·tėr, *n.* A verse of eight feet or measures.—*a.*

oc·tane, ok′tān, *n.* [Gr. *octō*, eight (with reference to the atoms of carbon).] *Chem.* a hydrocarbon, C_8H_{18}, of the methane series.—**oc·tane num·ber,** a fuel value that increases with antiknock qualities.

oc·ta·nol, ok′ta·nol, *n.* Any of the four alcohols, $C_8H_{17}OH$, obtained from octane: used chiefly as an antifoaming agent, solvent, or ingredient for perfume.

oc·tant, ok′tant, *n.* [L. *octāns*, an eighth part, < *octo*, eight.] The eighth part of a circle; *navig.* an instrument resembling a sextant or quadrant in principle, but having an arc equal to one-eighth of a circle or 45°; *astron.* the position of a celestial body when 45° away from another; *geom.* any one of the eight partitions formed when space has been divided by three coordinate planes.

oc·tave, ok′tiv, ok′tāv, *n.* [O.Fr. Fr. *octave*, < L. *octava*, fem. of *octavus*, eighth, < *octō*, eight.] The eighth of a series, or a series or group of eight. *Eccles.* the eighth day from a feast day counted as the first; the period of eight days beginning with a feast day. *Mus.* a tone on the eighth degree from a given tone; the interval between such tones; the harmonic combination of such tones; a series of tones, or of keys of an instrument, extending through this interval; in a diatonic scale, the eighth tone from the bottom, with which the repetition of the scale begins; in organ building, a stop whose pipes give tones an octave above the normal pitch of the keys used. *Fencing,* the eighth in a series of eight parries; *pros.* a

group or a stanza of eight lines, as the first eight lines of a sonnet.—*a.* Consisting of eight lines or parts.

oc·ta·vo, ok·tā′vō, ok·ä′vō, *n.* The size of one leaf of a sheet or paper folded so as to make eight leaves. Abbr. *8vo*, *8°.* A book having eight leaves to each sheet; a page usu. 6 × 9½ inches; a book with pages this size.—*a.*

oc·tet, oc·tette, ok·tet′, *n.* A musical com-position for eight voices or instruments; a company of eight singers or players; any group of eight. *Pros.* a group of eight lines of verse, esp. the first eight lines of a sonnet; an octave.

oc·til·lion, ok·til′yan, *n.* [Fr. *octillion*, < L. *octō*, eight, and Fr. *(m)illion*, million.] In Britain and Germany, the eighth power of a million, represented by 1 followed by 48 zeros; in the U.S. and France, a thousand septillions, represented by 1 fol-lowed by 27 zeros.—*a.*—**oc·til·lionth,** *a.*, *n.*

Oc·to·ber, ok·tō′bėr, *n.* [L. < *octō*, eight: the eighth month of the primitive Roman year, which began in March.] The tenth month of the year in the Gregorian calen-dar, with 31 days; *Brit.* ale or cider made in October.

oc·to·de·cil·lion, ok″tō·di·sil′yan, *n.* In the American and French numbering systems, a cardinal number represented by a 1 preceding 57 zeros; 10 to the 57th power. *Brit.*, *G.* the cardinal number, 1, preceding 108 zeros.—*a.* Equaling one octodecillion in number.

oc·to·dec·i·mo, ok″tō·des′i·mō″, *n.* [N.L. in *octōdecimō*, 'in eighteenth.'] The page size, 4 × 6½ inches, of a book in which each leaf is one-eighteenth of a whole sheet of paper; a volume of this size. Abbr. *18mo* or *18°.* —*a.* In octodecimo; having pages this size.

oc·to·ge·nar·i·an, ok″tō·je·nâr′ē·an, *n.* [L. *octōgēnārius*, < *octōgēnī*, eighty, *octō*, eight.] A person eighty years of age, or between eighty and ninety.—*a.*—**oc·tog·-e·nar·y,** ok·toj′e·ner″ē, *a.*, *n.* pl. **oc·tog·-e·nar·ies.**

oc·to·pod, ok′to·pod″, *n.* [N.L. *Octopoda*, pl., < Gr. *octōpous* (*octōpod-*), eight-footed, < *octō*, eight, and *pous* (*pod-*), foot.] *Zool.* any cephalopod of the order *Octopoda*, having eight arms, propelled by a funnel-like siphon and which may or may not have an external shell, including the octopus, chambered nautilus, and paper nautilus.—*a.* Having eight feet or arms and belonging to the *Octopoda.*—**oc·top·o·dan,** ok·top′-o·dan, *a.*, *n.*—**oc·top·o·dous,** *a.*

oc·to·pus, ok′to·pus, *n.* pl. **oc·to·pus·es, oc·to·pi,** ok′to·pī″. [N.L., < Gr. *octōpus*, eight-footed.] Any cephalopod of the genus *Octopus*, having eight arms provided with suckers, large eyes, and a naked body with a small, internal shell; also *devilfish. Fig.* a far-reaching and powerful organization.

oc·to·roon, ok″to·rön′, *n.* [< *octo-* and *-roon* as in *quadroon*.] A person having one-eighth negro blood, as the offspring of a quadroon and a white person.

oc·to·syl·lab·ic, ok″tō·si·lab′ik, *a.* Con-sisting of eight syllables.—*n.* Octosyllable.

oc·to·syl·la·ble, ok′to·sil″a·bl, *n.* An eight syllable line, verse, or word.

oc·troi, ok′troi, *Fr.* ak·trwä′, *n.* [Fr., < *octroyer*, grant, < M.L. *auctorizāre*, E. *authorize.*] In France and elsewhere, a local tax levied on certain articles brought into a city; the place at which the tax is collected; the officials charged with collecting it.

oc·tu·ple, ok′tu·pl, ok·tū′pl, ok′tö′pl, ok·tū′pl, *a.* [L. *octuplus.*] Eightfold; having eight effective units or elements; eight times as great.—*v.t.*—*octupled, octupling.* To make eight times as great.—**oc·tup·let,** ok·tup′lit, ok·tö′plit, ok·tū′plit, ok′tu·-plit, ok·tū·plit, *n.* A series or group of eight of a kind. *Mus.* an octet; a group of eight notes to be rendered in the time of six of like value.—**oc·tu·ply,** *adv.*

oc·u·lar, ok'ū·lẽr, *a.* [L.L. *oculāris,* < L. *oculus,* eye: cf. *eye,* also *optic.*] Of or pertaining to the eye; as, *ocular* movements; of the nature of an eye; as, an *ocular* organ; performed by the eye or eyesight; as, *ocular* inspection; perceived by the eye or eyesight; as, *ocular* demonstration; derived from actual sight; as, *ocular* proof; actually seeing; as, an *ocular* witness.—*n.* The eyepiece of an optical instrument.—**oc·u·lar·ly,** *adv.*

oc·u·list, ok'ū·list, *n.* [L. *oculus,* eye.] One trained and skilled in the examination and treatment of the eye; an ophthalmologist.

oc·u·lo·mo·tor, ok″ū·lō·mō'tẽr, *a.* [L. *oculus,* eye, and *motor,* E. *motor.*] *Anat.* Moving the eyeball; connected to or pertaining to the eyeball movement.

oc·u·lo·mo·tor nerve, *n. Anat.* either of the pair of cranial nerves supplying most of the muscles moving the eyeball.

od, od, ōd, *n.* [Arbitrary name, given by Baron Karl von Reichenbach, 1788–1869.] A hypothetical force once thought to pervade all nature and to manifest itself in magnetism, mesmerism, and chemical action. Also **od·ic force, od·yl, od·yle,** od'il, ō'dil.—**od·ic,** od'ik, ō'dik, *a.*

o·da·lisque, ōd'a·lisk, *n.* [Fr. *odalisque,* < Turk. *ōdalik,* < *ōdah,* chamber.] A concubine or female slave in a harem. Also **o·da·lisk.**

odd, od, *a.* [M.E. *odde,* < Scand.: cf. Icel. *odda-* (as in *odda-madhr,* odd man), < *oddi,* point, triangle, odd number.] Differing in character from what is ordinary or usual; singular, peculiar, or strange; remaining over after a division into pairs, groups, or parts; not forming part of any particular group, set, or class; as, an *odd* lot of books; being part of a pair, set, or series of which the rest is missing; as, an *odd* glove; being a surplus, esp. a small one, over a definite quantity or sum; as, two dollars and some *odd* cents; leaving a remainder of one when divided by two, as a number: opposed to *even*; occasional or casual; as, *odd* jobs; out-of-the-way or secluded; as, *odd* corners of the city.—*n.* That which is or appears to be odd. *Golf,* one stroke over an opponent's score; *Brit.* a stroke subtracted from a player's score, giving him an advantage.—**odd·ly,** *adv.*—**odd·ness,** *n.*

odd·ball, od'bạl″, *n. Slang,* someone or something which behaves in an eccentric, curious, or nonconforming manner.—*a.* Unusual or eccentric.

odd·i·ty, od'i·tē, *n.* pl. **odd·i·ties.** A singular person, thing, or occurrence; the state or quality of being odd, unusual, or eccentric; a peculiarity.

odd lot, *n. Stock market,* a quantity of securities smaller than the amount common in business transactions, as a lot of stocks numbering less than 100 shares, or a lot of bonds representing less than $1,000 face value. Also **broken lot.**

odd·ment, od'ment, *n.* An odd article or one left over. *Print.* any part or copy for a book other than the text, as the index.

odds, odz, *n. pl., sing. or pl. in constr.* The probability ratio for or against something occurring or being so; in a contest, the difference in favor of one over another; amount by which one wager exceeds that of another; an allowance awarded the weaker of two opponents to equalize them.

odds and ends, *n. pl.* Miscellaneous matters or articles; remnants; scraps.

odds-on, odz'on′, odz'ạn″, *a.* Considered as having a better than an even chance to win or reach a goal; as, an *odds-on* favorite in a horse race.

ode, ōd, *n.* [L. *ode,* Gr. *ōdē,* song or poem, < *aoidē,* a song; seen in *parody, prosody.*] A poem of irregular metrical structure, usu. expressing the poet's intense personal feelings; a poem to be set to music or to be sung. —**od·ic,** ō'dik, *a.*

o·de·um, ō·dē'um, *n.* pl. **o·de·a.** [L. *odeum,* Gr. *ōideion,* < *ōdē,* a song.] A theater for musical or dramatic presentations; in ancient Greece and Rome, a music hall. Also **ode·on.**

o·di·ous, ō'dē·us, *a.* [L. *odiōsus,* < *odium,* hatred, *odi,* I hate; same root as O.E. *atol,* hateful, horrible.] Arousing hatred, repugnance, or extreme dislike.—**o·di·ous·ly,** *adv.*—**o·di·ous·ness,** *n.*

o·di·um, ō'dē·um, *n.* [L.] Intense hatred or dislike, esp. of something despicable; disgrace associated with something hateful; the quality that provokes hatred.

o·do·graph, ō'do·graf″, ō'do·gräf″, *n.* An instrument used to record the distance and course traveled by a vehicle; an instrument used to record the frequency, length, and number of steps taken by a pedestrian.

o·dom·e·ter, ō·dom'i·tẽr, *n.* [Gr. *odometron,* < *odos,* way, and *metron,* measure.] A device attached to a wheeled vehicle for recording the number of revolutions of a wheel and thus indicating the distance traveled, as on an automobile; a similar instrument for measuring distances in surveying. Also **ho·dom·e·ter.**—**o·dom·e·try,** *n.*

o·don·to·blast, ō·don'to·blast″, *n. Anat.* one of a layer of cells which line the pulp chamber of a tooth and form dentin.—**o·don·to·blas·tic,** ō·don″to·blas'tik, *a.*

o·don·to·glos·sum, ō·don″to·glos'um, *n.* [Gr. *odous, odontos,* a tooth, and *glōssa,* a tongue.] *Bot.* favorite greenhouse, epiphytic orchids of the genus *Odontoglossum,* native to tropical America, having large showy flowers which bear crests on the liplike petal.

o·don·toid, ō·don'toid, *a.* [Gr. *odontoeidēs,* < *odous(odont-),* tooth, and *eidos,* form.] Resembling a tooth; *anat.* related to the odontoid process.—*n. Anat.* the odontoid process.

o·don·toid proc·ess, *n. Anat.* a prominent toothlike process of the axis, or second cervical vertebra, upon which the atlas rotates.

o·don·tol·o·gy, ō″don·tol'o·jē, od″on·tol'o·jē, *n.* That branch of anatomical science which relates to the teeth, their health, growth, structure, and diseases.—**o·don·to·log·i·cal,** ō·don″to·loj′i·kal, *a.* —**o·don·tol·o·gist,** *n.*

o·dor, *Brit.* **o·dour,** ō'dẽr, *n.* [L. *odor,* a smell; allied to Gr. *ozō,* to smell; akin *olfactory.*] That quality perceived through the sense of smell; effect of stimulation of the olfactory organ; scent. *Fig.* a suggestive property; reputation. *Archaic,* incense or perfume.—**o·dored,** *a.*—**o·dor·less,** *a.*

o·dor·ant, ō'dẽr·ant, *n.* A substance bearing an odor, as that added to natural gas as a warning identification.

o·dor·if·er·ous, ō″do·rif'ẽr·us, *a.* [L. *odoriferus.*] Giving off odor or scent, esp. an agreeable fragrance; ill smelling; *fig.* suggestive of moral offense.—**o·dor·if·er·ous·ly,** ō″dẽr·if′ẽr·us·lē, *adv.*—**o·dor·if·er·ous·ness,** *n.*

o·dor·ous, ō'dẽr·us, *a.* Having or emitting an odor; sweet of scent; fragrant.— **o·dor·ous·ly,** *adv.*—**o·dor·ous·ness,** *n.*

od·ys·sey, od'i·sē, *n.* A long journey marked by wanderings, adventures, and hardships; (*cap.*), *class. mythol.* the poem in which Homer recounts the wanderings and return of Odysseus or Ulysses, from Troy to his home in Ithaca.—**Od·ys·se·an,** od″i·sē'an, *a.*

Oed·i·pus com·plex, ed'i·pus kom'pleks, ē'di·pus kom'pleks, *n. Psychoanal.* the

desire, most readily expressed in sexual terms, of a son for his mother with a consequential rivalry between the son and his father, a complex which may appear later in life as seeking a mother image in relations with other women.—**oed·i·pal,** ed'i·pal, ē'di·pal, *a.* Of or pertaining to Oedipus complex.

oe·nan·thic es·ter, ē·nan'thik es'tẽr, *n.* [Gr. *oinos,* wine, and *anthos,* a flower.] An oily liquid which is believed to be the primary agent in providing the distinctive aroma of wines.

oe·nol·o·gy, ē·nol'o·jē, *n.* Enology, the science of winemaking.

oe·no·mel, ē'no·mel″, en'o·mel″, *n.* A beverage of ancient Greece, composed of wine and honey; anything combining strength and sweetness.

o'er, ōr, ạr, *adv., prep.* Over, usu. poetical.

oer·sted, ụr'sted, *n.* [After H. C. Oersted, the Dan. physicist.] The centimeter-gram-second electromagnetic unit of magnetic intensity, equal to a mechanical force of one dyne exerted on a unit magnetic pole.

of, uv, ov, *unstressed* ov, *prep.* [O.E. *of* = Icel., Sw., Dan., and D. *af,* Goth. *af,* G. *ab*; cogn. L. *ab,* Gr. *apo,* Skt. *apa,* from, away from.] At a distance from; as, within a mile *of* home; produced by or tracing its source to; as, the novels *of* Hemingway, an animal *of* mixed breed; on the part of; as, generous *of* her; due to or because of; as ,*of* his own choice, dead *of* starvation; composed of or holding; as, a chain *of* gold, a tub *of* water; identified as; as, the city *of* New York; with reference to; as, Jim, skipper *of* the vessel; from the aggregate of; as, some *of* us; concerning, relating to, about, as: He spoke little *of* his childhood. Belonging to or over; as, top *of* a bottle, King *of* Siam; relating to or indicating; as, state *of* mind, manufacture *of* soap; on, in, in the course of, or noting time; as, *of* an evening, *of* late; before; as, five minutes *of* six; pivoted at or directed toward; as, love *of* the theater; so as to be free of or wanting; as, relieved *of* worry.

off, ạf, of, *adv.* Away, as: The child scampered *off.* From or away by removal or separation; as, cut *off* from old associates, the button that came *off*; no longer continuing; as, negotiation broken *off*; absent from duty or work; as, time *off*; into existence, as: The wedding did not come *off.* Completely; as, to kill *off* one's chances; to, at, or in relation to time; as, to put *off* the party; to, at, or in relation to space; as, to pace *off* a distance; from a fixed price; as, a dollar *off*; so as to be out of operation, as: Turn the lights *off.* Thus divided; as, cut *off* in sections. *Naut.* in a direction opposite land, a ship, or the wind; sailing obliquely.—*a.* Denoting one's circumstances; as, well *off*; no longer operating; as, an understanding that is *off*; not true to facts; as, a reckoning that is *off*; free from duty; as, *off* hours; away; as, *off* on vacation; of lessened activity; as, the *off* season; distant; of riding or driving, on the right-hand side: opposed to *near*; eccentric, odd; as, a bit *off*. *Cricket,* pertaining to the side of the field opposite which the batsman stands.—*prep.* So as to be removed from or separated, as: Take if *off* the floor. Leading away from; as, *off* the boulevard; away from; as, *off* the job; below what is taken as normal or standard; as, a dollar *off* the price, *off* one's luck; by means of; as, to live *off* investments; no longer engaged in, as: Since his injury, he is *off* football. *Naut.* away from and seaward of; as, the collision *off* Cape Hatteras.— *interj.* Go away; be off.

off, ạf, of, *v.i.* To go, usu. as an imperative. *Naut.* to move out to sea.

of·fal, ạ'fal, of'al, *n.* [Lit. 'off-fall'; so D.

afval, Icel. *affall*, G. *abfall*, with similar meanings.] The entrails or trimmings of a butchered animal normally not consumed by humans; waste; refuse; garbage; by-products of milling.

off and on, *adv.* Intermittently. Also **on and off.**

off·beat, af′bēt″, of′bēt″, *n. Mus.* a secondary, unaccented beat.—af′bēt′, of′bēt′, *a. Slang.* Unusual; unconventional; unexpected; out-of-step; mistaken or questionable.

off·cast, af′kast″, af′käst″, of′kast″, of′käst″, *a.* Cast off; rejected.—*n.* One who or that which is cast off or rejected. Also **cast·off.**

off-col·or, *Brit.* **off-col·our,** af′kul′ér, of′kul′ér, *a.* Varying from the standard or desired color; varying from normal propriety or decency; risqué; not in proper health. Also **off-col·ored.**

of·fence, ə′fens, of′ens, *n.* Offense.

of·fend, ō·fend′, *v.t.* [L. *offendo*.] To displease or annoy; to make angry; to insult; to be disagreeable to; to cause discomfort to; to hurt; to be offensive to, as the sense of taste, smell, or sight.—*v.i.* To offend or be offensive; to transgress the moral or divine law; to commit a sin or crime.—**of·fend·er,** *n.*

of·fense, ō·fens′, ə′fens, of′ens, *n.* [Fr. *offense,* < L. *offēnsa,* an offense, < *offendo, offensum,* to strike against.] Something that is offending or displeasing; any wrongdoing, as a violation of divine or human law; a crime or sin; a misdemeanor; an act of mounting an attack; assault; the attempt to score, as in certain sports.—**take offense,** to become angry or feel resentment at something said or done.—**of·fense·less,** ō·fens′lis, *a.*

of·fen·sive, ō·fen′siv, ə′fen·siv, of′en·siv, *a.* [Fr. *offensif*.] Causing displeasure, anger, or resentment; giving a disagreeable sensation; repugnant; disgusting; pertaining to or relating to attack: opposed to *defensive.*—*n.* An attack or aggressive movement; the act of attacking.—**of·fen·sive·ly,** *adv.*—**of·fen·sive·ness,** *n.*

of·fer, ə′fér, of′ér, *v.t.* [O.E. *offrian,* and Fr. *offrir* (j′*offre,* I offer), < L. *offerre,* to offer.] To present for acceptance or rejection; to propose for consideration, notice, or action; to indicate an intention; to volunteer; as, to *offer* to go first; to suggest, promise, or give, as: This plan *offers* the best chance of success. To inflict or make, or to threaten to inflict; as, to *offer* resistance; to present as an act of worship, to sacrifice, often followed by *up*; to bid, as a price or payment; to put forward for sale; tender; proffer.—*v.i.* To present itself; as, going to see her every time an opportunity *offers*; to make an attempt or suggestion; to make a marriage proposal; to sacrifice or present an offering in worship.—*n.* The act of offering; that which is proposed or suggested; a marriage proposal; the act of bidding a price, or the sum bid.—**of·fer·er,** **of·fer·or,** *n.*

of·fer·ing, ə′fér·ing, of′ér·ing, *n.* The act of a person who offers; that which is offered, esp. a contribution of money to a church; a sacrificial gift dedicated to a deity.

of·fer·to·ry, ə′fér·tōr″ē, ə′fér·tar″ē, of′-ér·tōr″ē, of′ér·tar″ē, *n.* pl. **of·fer·to·ries.** [L.L. *offertorium,* place to which offerings were brought, also offering, oblation, < L. *offerre*.] *Eccles.* the verses, anthem, or music said, sung, or played while the offerings of the congregation are received at a religious service; that part of a service at which offerings are made; the offerings themselves. *Rom. Cath. Ch.* the oblation of the unconsecrated elements made by the celebrant at this part of the Eucharistic service.—**of·fer·to·ri·al,** *a.*

off·hand, af′hand′, of′hand′, *adv.* Without

preparation or study; extemporaneously; brusquely. Also **off·hand·ed·ly.**—*a.* Made or done without study or hesitation; casual or curt. Also **off·hand·ed.**—**off·-hand·ed·ness,** *n.*

of·fice, ə′fis, of′is, *n.* [Fr. *office,* < L. *officium,* duty, office, < *ob* and *facio,* to do, or < *opem,* aid (opulence), and *facio* (fact).] The place where an individual or organization conducts its business, or those who work there; a commercial or professional firm; as, the company's Chicago *office,* a dentist's *office.* (*Cap.*), *U.S.* a federal agency beneath a department in rank; (*cap.*), *Brit.* a department in the national government. A position in a corporate or governmental organization, esp. one entailing authority, responsibility, or trust; the duty or function entrusted to a person; as, handling the *office* of counselor; *often pl.* an act, usu. a favor or service, done for another; as, with the help of his good *offices; eccles.* a prescribed form of devotion, or a service for a particular occasion, esp. one for the dead; *pl.,* *Brit.* the service parts of a house or farm, such as the kitchen, laundry, barn, or stable.

of·fice boy, *n.* A boy or young man who performs odd jobs in an office.

of·fice·hold·er, ə′fis·hōl″dér, of′is·hōl″-dér, *n.* An individual holding a position with the government.

of·fic·er, ə′fi·sér, of′i·sér, *n.* A person holding a title, office, or post of authority in any public or private institution; a policeman; a commissioned individual in the armed forces; the captain or any of the mates in charge of a passenger or merchant ship.—*v.t.* To furnish with officers; to appoint officers over; to direct or command.

of·fi·cial, ō·fish′al, *a.* [L. *officiālis.*] Pertaining to an office of trust or public duty; derived from the proper office or officer, or from the proper authority; as, *official* permission; communicated by virtue of authority; formed; as, the *official* opening of the store.—*n.* One invested with an office of a public nature.—**of·fi·cial·ly,** *adv.*

of·fi·cial·dom, ō·fish′al·dom, *n.* Collectively, all officials; officials as a class; the behavior or viewpoints of officials; the concern or responsibility of an official.

of·fi·cial·ism, ō·fish′a·liz″um, *n.* An official system, attitude, or condition characterized by rigid adherence to regulations and procedures; officials considered as a group.

of·fi·ci·ant, ō·fish′ē·ant, *n.* [M.L. *officiāns* (-*ant-*), ppr. of *officiāre.*] One who officiates at a religious service or ceremony.

of·fi·ci·ar·y, ō·fish′ē·er″ē, *a.* [M.L. *officiārius,* < L. *officium.*] Pertaining to or derived from an office, as a title or rank; having a title, rank, or dignity derived from an office.—*n.* pl. **of·fi·ci·ar·ies.** An officer or official; officers collectively.

of·fi·ci·ate, ō·fish′ē·āt″, *v.i.*—*officiated, officiating.* To perform official duties; to conduct a religious service; *sports,* to perform the duties of umpire or referee.—*v.t.* To judge, as an event, according to its rules; to act as priest or minister for; to fulfill, as an office.—**of·fi·ci·a·tor,** *n.*—**of·fi·ci·a·tion,** *n.*

of·fic·i·nal, ō·fis′i·nal, *a.* [< L. *officīna,* a shop; same origin as *office.*] *Pharm.* Stocked by a pharmacy; securable without a prescription: opposed to *magistral*; sanctioned by a pharmacopoeia.—*n. Pharm.* a drug available without a prescription.—**of·fic·i·nal·ly,** *adv.*

of·fi·cious, ō·fish′us, *a.* [L. *officiōsus,* dutiful, obliging, < *officium,* an office.] Excessively forward in kindness; offering or performing services not wanted; annoy-

ingly eager to oblige or assist; meddling.—**of·fi·cious·ly,** *adv.*—**of·fi·cious·ness,** *n.*

off·ing, ə′fing, of′ing, *n.* The more distant part of the sea as seen from the shore, beyond the anchoring ground; a position at sea at a considerable distance from shore.—**in the off·ing,** near or in sight. *Fig.* likely to occur; happening soon.

off·ish, ə′fish, of′ish, *a. Colloq.* Inclined to keep aloof; distant in manner.—**off·ish·ly,** *adv.*—**off·ish·ness,** *n.*

off·print, af′print″, of′print″, *n.* A reprint in separate form of an article which originally appeared as part of a larger publication.—*v.t.* To reprint separately.

off·scour·ing, af′skour″ing, af′skou″ér·ing, of′skour″ing, of′skou″ér·ing, *n. Often pl.* refuse; garbage. A person who is outcast and despised.

off·set, af′set′, of′set′, *v.t.*—*offset, offsetting.* To equalize or counterbalance; as, to *offset* one thing against another; to compensate, as: The gains *offset* the losses. *Mech.* to bend in a short jog, as a pipe or rod; *arch.* to indent, as a wall or surface, causing a ledge. *Print.* to print by offset lithography; to smear or transfer, as ink, undesirably from one sheet or surface to another.—*v.i.* To project, as an offshoot or branch; to make an offset.—af′set″, of′set″, *n.* A start or outset; any offshoot; a spur of a mountain range; a branch from a family or race; something which counterbalances or compensates; *mech.* a short bend in a rod, pipe, or surface. *Arch.* the ledge formed from a reduction in thickness of a wall. *Surv.* a short distance measured perpendicularly from a main line, usu. to determine the area of an irregular section. *Print.* the inadvertent smearing or transfer of ink from one printed surface to another; offset lithography.—*a.*

off·set li·thog·ra·phy, *n.* A printing process which transfers the inked design or other copy from a lithographic plate, originally a stone, to a rubber surface, usu. a roller which in turn sets the design off onto the sheet or object to be printed.—**pho·to-off·set,** *n.* An offset printing process when the metal lithographic plate is produced photomechanically.

off·shoot, af′shōt″, of′shōt″, *n.* A lateral shoot from a main stem, as of a plant; anything conceived as springing or proceeding from a main stock or source; a branch or a descendant of a family or race.

off·shore, af′shōr′, of′shōr′, *adv.* Off or away from the shore; at a distance from the shore.—*a.* Moving or tending away form the shore; being or operating at a distance from the shore.

off·side, af′sīd′, of′sīd′, *a. Sports,* esp. football and ice hockey, referring to a player or a play in illegal territory, or ahead of the ball or puck.—*adv.*

off·spring, af′spring″, of′spring″, *n.* pl. **off·spring, off·springs.** [O.E. *ofspring.*] Children or young born of a particular parent or progenitor; a descendant; descendants collectively; a child or an animal in relation to its parent or parents; *fig.* the product, result, or effect of something.

off·stage, af′stāj′, of′stāj′, *n.* The area of a stage not seen by the audience; backstage; the wings.—*a.,* *adv.* Away from or out of the audience's view.

off-the-cuff, af′тне·kuf′, of′тне·kuf′, *a. Slang.* Not prepared in advance; impromptu; extemporaneous; improvised, as statements or actions.

off-white, af′hwit′, af′wit′, of′hwit′, of′wit′, *n.* Any shade of white with a tint of some other color, esp. gray or yellow.—*a.*

off year, *n.* A year in which some aspect of production or activity is below normal; a year in which there is no major election.—**off-year,** *a.*

oft, äft, oft, *adv.* [O.E., Icel., and G. *oft,* Dan. *ofte,* Sw. *ofta,* Goth. *ufta,* oft, often; *often* is a later form; akin to *over.*] *Poet.* often.

of·ten, ȧ′fen, of′en, ȧf′ten, of′ten, *adv.* Frequently; many times; repeatedly.

of·ten·times, ȧ′fen·tīmz″, of′en·tīmz″, ȧf′ten·tīmz″, of′ten·tīmz″, *adv.* Frequently; often; many times. Also **oft·times.**

og·do·ad, og′dō·ad″, *n.* [L.L. *ogdoas* (*ogdoad-*), < Gr. *ogdoas* (*ogdoád-*), < *oktō,* eight.] The number eight; a group of eight.

o·gee, ō·jē′, ō′jē, *n.* [Fr. *ogive, augive;* etymology doubtful.] A double curve formed by uniting a concave and a convex line. *Arch.* a molding or arch produced by combining a convex and concave line to form an S or inverted S profile. Abbr. *O.G., o.g.* Also **cyma, gu·la.**

og·ham, og′am, ȧ′gam, *n.* [Ir. *ogham,* O.Ir. *ogam.*] An alphabet of twenty characters used by the ancient Irish; an inscription in such characters; any of the characters. Also **og·am—og·ham·ic, og·am·ic,** *a.*— **og·ham·ist, og·am·ist,** *n.*

o·give, ō′jīv, ō·jīv′, *n.* [Fr.] *Arch.* a Gothic or pointed arch; the diagonal rib of such an arch. *Statistics,* the distribution curve of a frequency. The nose of a rocket or projectile.

o·gle, ō′gl, *v.t.*—*ogled, ogling.* [Same as L.G. *oegeln,* to eye, G. *äugeln,* to ogle, < *auge,* D. *oog,* the eye.] To look or stare at boldly, amorously, or with the aim of attracting notice; to eye.—*v.i.* To look boldly, amorously, or flirtatiously; to stare. —*n.* A provocative or flirtatious side glance or look.—**o·gler,** *n.*

o·gre, ō′gẽr, *n.* [Fr. *ogre,* < L. *Orcus,* the god of the infernal regions, hell.] A hideous and cruel monster of popular legends and fairy tales who devoured human flesh; an evil, barbarous, or terrifying person.— **o·gre·ish, o·grish,** ō′gẽr·ish, ō′grish, *a.*— **o·gress,** ō′gris, *n.* A female ogre.

oh, ō, *interj.* An expression of surprise, pain, disapprobation, or desire; in direct address, an expression used to gain someone's attention.—*n.* pl. **oh's, ohs.** The exclamation 'oh.'

ohm, ōm, *n.* [From G. S. Ohm, 1787–1854, German physicist.] *Elect.* the unit of resistance equivalent to the resistance of a conductor in which one volt, the unit difference of potential, produces a current of one ampere.—**ohm·ic,** ō′mik, *a.*

ohm·age, ō′mij, *n. Elect.* electrical resistance expressed in ohms.

ohm·me·ter, ōm′mē″tẽr, *n. Elect.* an instrument for measuring in ohms electrical resistance.

oil, oil, *n.* [O.Fr. *oile* (Fr. *huile*), < L. *oleum,* oil, olive-oil; akin to Gr. *elaiov,* olive-oil, *elaia* (L. *olea*), olive tree.] Any of a large class of substances typically unctuous, viscous, combustible, liquid at ordinary temperatures, and soluble in ether or alcohol but not in water, used for food, anointing, perfuming, lubricating, illuminating, heating, smoothing waves at sea in a storm, and many other purposes; some substance of similar consistency; an oil color; sometimes, an oil painting; petroleum; an oilskin garment; *slang,* wheedling, fawning insincerity, or flattery.—*v.t.* Anoint with oil; moisten, smear, or lubricate with oil; to supply with oil; to convert into oil by melting, as butter. *Fig.* to bribe; make oily or smooth, as in speech; as, to *oil* the tongue.—*a.* Resembling or related to oil; derived from, utilizing, or providing oil.

oil bee·tle, *n.* Any blister beetle belonging to the genus *Meloe,* which gives off an oily liquid from its leg joints.

oil cake, *n.* A mass of seeds or pulp remaining after the extraction of oil from cotton-seed, linseed, or coconut fruits, used to feed livestock or as fertilizer.

oil·cloth, oil′klȧth″, oil′kloth″, *n.* Cloth waterproofed with oil and coloring agents, used as a covering for tables, shelves, and the like.

oil col·or, *Brit.* **oil col·our,** *n. Fine Arts,* paint made by grinding a pigment in oil, most often linseed oil.

oil·er, oi′lẽr, *n.* One who oils; a worker employed to oil engines or machinery; any apparatus for lubricating machinery with oil; a can with a spout, used for oiling; a ship propelled by oil; oil tanker; an oilskin coat.

oil field, *n.* An area, usu. under either land or water, rich in petroleum deposits.

oil of vit·ri·ol, *n. Chem.* sulfuric acid.

oil paint, *n.* Any paint in which a drying oil is the medium.

oil paint·ing, *n.* The art of painting with oil colors; a picture in oil colors.

oil palm, *n.* A cultivated West African palm whose fruit yields palm oil.

oil pan, *n.* The part of the crankcase in internal-combustion engines where the lubricating oil is contained.

oil·seed, oil′sēd″, *n.* Any seed that is grown as a source of oil, such as linseed, castor bean, or soybean.

oil·skin, oil′skin″, *n.* A cotton fabric waterproofed with oil, used for raincoats and hats. *Pl.* a suit or raincoat made of this material.—*a.*

oil slick, *n.* A slick or smooth film on the surface of water, due to the presence of oil.

oil·stone, oil′stōn″, *n.* A fine-grained whetstone, whose rubbing surface is lubricated with oil, used to sharpen some cutting tools.

oil well, *n.* A well drilled to obtain petroleum.

oil·y, oi′lē, *a.*—*oilier, oiliest.* Pertaining to oil; of the nature of or consisting of oil; resembling oil; full of or containing oil; smeared or covered with oil, or greasy; smooth, as in manner or speech; bland; unctuous.—**oil·i·ness,** *n.*

oint·ment, oint′ment, *n.* [< Fr. *oindre,* pp. *oint,* to anoint, < L. *ungere.*] Any soft unctuous substance, usu. medicated, applied to the skin for medicinal and cosmetic purposes; an unguent; a salve.

oi·ti·ci·ca, oi″ti·sē′kä, *n.* A S. American tree, *Licania rigida,* in the rose family, whose seeds are the source of an oil used in paints and varnishes.

O·jib·wa, ō·jib′wä, ō·jib′wa, *n.* pl. **O·jib-was, O·jib·wa.** An American Indian tribe, one of the Algonquians; the language of these Indians. Also *Chippewa,* **O·jib·way.**

O.K., ō′kā′, *a., adv.* [Origin variously explained; said to be from Choctaw Indian *okeh,* 'it is so.'] All right; correct: usu. used to express approval.—ō′kā′, *v.t.*—*O.K.'d, O.K.'ing.* To endorse; as, to *O.K.* a bill; agree; approve. —ō′kā′, *n.* Agreement; endorsement; approval. Also **OK, o·kay, o·keh.**

o·ka, ō′ka, *n.* (*Usu. cap.*) a specially cured cheese which is made in Quebec by Trappist monks.

o·ka·pi, ō·kä′pē, *n.* pl. **o·ka·pis, o·ka·pi.** [Afr.] An African mammal, *Okapia johnstoni,* related to the giraffe but differing in having a shorter neck, being purplish-maroon in color, and marked by black and white striped limbs and rump.

oke, ōk, *n.* An Egyptian, Greek, and Turkish unit of weight equal to about 2¾ pounds. Also **o·ka,** ō′ka.

o·kie, ō′kē, *n. Slang.* A migrant farm worker, usu. from Oklahoma; sometimes derogatorily, a native or inhabitant of Oklahoma.

o·kou·me, ō″ko·mä′, *n.* Gaboon.

o·kra, ō′kra, *n.* [Afr.] A tall malvaceous plant, *Hibiscus esculentus,* native to Africa, and cultivated in the East and West Indies and southern U.S. for its edible, mucilaginous pods, which are used as a vegetable and in soups and stews; the pods of this plant; gumbo.

old, ōld, *a.*—*older, oldest; elder, eldest.* [O.E. *ald, eald,* = D. *oud* = G. *alt,* old; orig. pp., and akin to Icel. *ala,* nourish, bring up, Goth. *alan,* grow up, and L. *alere,* nourish.] Having lived, existed, been made, or originated long ago; pertaining to persons advanced in years or having characteristics associated with age; stating a specified age, or length of time; as, a three-year-*old* child, a month-*old* magazine; deteriorated through age or long use, stale; as, *old* clothes, *old* jokes; belonging to remote times; as, *old* coins; familiar or beloved; as, *old* England, *old* fellow; skilled and experienced; as, an *old* hand at intrigue; (*often cap.*) being the earlier or earliest of two or more things of the same kind; as, the *Old* Testament, the *Old* World. *Colloq.* used as an intensive; as, any *old* time. *Geol.* of streams and land contours, at the stage of development when the forces have lessened in vigor.—*n.* An earlier time.—**old·en,** ōl′den, *a.*—**old·ish,** ōl′dish, *a.*

Old Bai·ley, ōld′ bā′lē, *n.* The seat of the central criminal court of London, England.

old coun·try, *n.* A name given by immigrants, esp. Europeans, to the country of their origin.

Old Eng·lish, *n.* The English language in use during the period 450 to about 1150 A.D. *Print.* black letter.

old·fan·gled, ōld′fang′geld, *a.* Old-fashioned; not modern or current.

old-fash·ioned, ōld′fash′ond, *a.* Characterized by antiquated fashions, ideas, behavior, or methods; out-of-date; related to or derived from a former era; adhering to traditional or conservative ways and customs.—**old-fash·ioned·ly,** *adv.*—**old-fash·ioned·ness,** *n.*

old fash·ioned, *n.* (*Sometimes cap.*) an alcoholic beverage made with bitters, water, sugar, whiskey, and fruit.

Old French, *n.* The language of France from the 9th to the 15th century, having descended from Vulgar Latin. Abbr. *O.Fr., O.F., OF.*

Old Glo·ry, *n.* The flag of the United States.

old gold, *n.* A brownish-yellow color.

old guard, *n.* (*Sometimes cap.*) the members of a community, group, or political party who are conservative in thought or action; (*cap.*) the imperial guard of Napoleon I, established in 1804.

old hand, *n.* One who is experienced in or has extensive knowledge of a subject, situation, or procedure; a veteran.

Old High Ger·man, *n.* An antecedent form of modern High German, and used in southern Germany between 800 and 1100 A.D., later becoming the basis of Middle High German. Abbr. *O.H.G., OHG.*

old-line, ōld′lin, *a.* Clinging to old ideas or customs; conservative; traditional; as, an *old-line* family.

old maid, *n.* An elderly or confirmed spinster; an excessively prudish and fastidious person; a game of cards which ends with the holder of the odd queen being the loser. —**old-maid·ish,** ōld′mā′dish, *a.*

old man, *n. Colloq.* Father; husband; a man, such as a boss or employer, who is in an authoritative position; a masculine form of address, implying warm regard, as: Hello, *old man.*

old mas·ter, *n.* An artist of a former period, whose work is generally acclaimed, esp. one of the renowned painters of the 13th to the 18th centuries.

Old Nick, *n.* The devil; Satan.

Old Norse, *n.* The language of Scandinavia, esp. Norway, Denmark, and Iceland, spoken from the 8th to the 14th centuries A.D., and derived from the North Germanic language group.

old rose, *n.* A rose color tinged with varying degrees of purple or gray.—*a.*

Old Sax·on, *n.* The Low German dialect of the Saxons as spoken before the 12th century.—*a.*

old school, *n.* Persons having the character, manners, or opinions of a former age.—**old-school,** ōld′skōl′, *a.*

old school tie, *n.* A necktie showing the colors of one of the exclusive, fee-paying schools known in Britain as public schools; a tendency to uphold established institutions and upper class interests thought to be typical of those who have attended these schools; snobbishness and exclusiveness based on social class.

old-shoe, ōld′shō′, *a. Colloq.* Comfortably familiar; easy; informal.—**old shoe,** *n.*

old squaw, *n. Ornith.* a sea duck, *Clangula hyemalis,* ranging from the Arctic to the Great Lakes, and having a white body with dark wings. Also *oldwife.*

old·ster, ōld′stèr, *n.* [Formed to correspond to *youngster.*] An old person; an experienced person. *Brit. navy,* a midshipman of four years standing.

old style, *n. Print.* a typeface which, unlike modern type, used slanted serifs and little difference in the thickness of strokes. (*Cap.*) the date reckoned according to the Julian Calendar in contrast to the New Style date which came into use when the Gregorian Calendar was adopted.—*a. Print.* describing Arabic numerals part of which descend below the base of a line of old style type.—**old-style,** ōld′stīl′, *a.*

Old Tes·ta·ment, *n.* The books constituting the Hebrew Bible, including the Mosaic Law and histories, the Prophets, and the Hagiographa; the teachings of these books indicating the covenant made between God and man on Mount Sinai, securing the foundation for the Jewish religion. Abbr. *OT, O.T.*

old-time, ōld′tīm′, *a.* Part of or a mark of old or former times; as, a revival of the *old-time* songs; long-lasting; as, an *old-time* custom.—**old-tim·er,** ōld′tī′mèr, *n. Colloq.* One whose residence, membership, or experience dates back a long time; a veteran; one who is old; one who adheres to old-fashioned ideas or ways.

old·wife, old′wīf′, *n.* pl. **old·wives.** *Ichth.* alewife; menhaden. *Ornith.* old squaw.

old wives' tale, *n.* A story or a notion often grounded in superstition and passed down from generation to generation.

Old World, *n.* The Eastern Hemisphere, comprising the land masses of Africa, Asia, and Europe; Europe.

old-world, ōld′wurld′, *a.* Of the ancient world; belonging to or characteristic of a former period; of or relating to the Old World as contrasted to the New World or the Americas.

o·le·ag·i·nous, ō″lē·aj′i·nus, *a.* [Fr. *oléagineux,* oily, < L. *oleaginus,* of the olive, < *olea,* olive.] Having the nature or qualities of oil; containing oil; producing oil; *fig.* unctuous.—**o·le·ag·i·nous·ly,** *adv.*—**o·le·ag·i·nous·ness,** *n.*

o·le·an·der, ō′lē·an′dèr, ō″lē·an′dèr, *n.* [Fr. *oléandre,* < M.L. *oleander;* origin uncertain.] *Bot.* an evergreen, leathery-leaved shrub, *Nerium oleander,* in the dogbane family, native to the Mediterranean region, and cultivated in the South and grown as a house plant in the North, for its fragrant, double, white- and red-colored flowers.

o·le·as·ter, ō″lē·as′tèr, *n.* [L., < *olea,* olive.] *Bot.* The wild variety of the olive, *Olea europœa* var. *oleastra.* A shrub or small tree, *Elæagnus angustifolia,* native to southern Europe and western Asia, with fragrant yellow flowers and silver-green foliage: planted in the U.S. as an orna-

mental and in shelter belts; also *Russian olive,* **Treb·i·zond date,** treb′i·zond″ dāt.

o·le·ate, ō′lē·āt″, *n. Chem.* a salt or ester of oleic acid; as, mercury *oleate; pharm.* an ointment or medical preparation containing oleic acid.

o·le·ic, ō·lē′ik, ō′lē·ik, *a.* [L. *oleum,* oil.] *Chem.* pertaining to or derived from oil; as, *oleic* acid.

o·le·ic ac·id, *n. Chem.* An unsaturated fatty acid, $C_{17}H_{33}COOH$, found in natural fats and oils as a glyceride, and used in compounding many products, as cosmetics and soap.

o·le·o, ō′lē·ō, *n.* Oleomargarine.

o·le·o·graph, ō′lē·o·graf″, ō′lē·o·gräf″, *n.* A kind of chromolithograph printed in oil colors on cloth in imitation of an oil painting.—**o·le·o·graph·ic,** ō″lē·o·graf′ik, *a.*—**o·le·og·ra·phy,** ō″lē·og′ra·fē, *n.*

o·le·o·mar·ga·rine, ō″lē·ō·mär′ja·rin, ō′lē·ō·mär′ja·rēn″, ō″lē·ō·märj′rin, ō″lē·ō·märj′rēn, *n.* [L. *oleum,* and E. *margarin.*] A substitute for butter made from animal fat or vegetable oils, boiled and churned with milk. Also **o·le·o·mar·ga·rin,** *margarine,* oleo.

o·le·o·res·in, ō″lē·ō·rez′in, *n.* A natural mixture of an essential oil and a resin; *pharm.* a preparation containing an oil holding resin in solution.—**o·le·o·res·in·ous,** ō″lē·ō·rez′i·nus, *a.*

ol·er·i·cul·ture, ol′èr·i·kul″chèr, *n.* [L. *olus* (*oler-*), potherb, and *cultura,* culture.] *Hort.* the science of vegetable culture for home use, storage, and for marketing.

ol·fac·tion, ol·fak′shan, *n.* [L. *olfacere* (pp. *olfactus*), smell, < *olere,* emit a smell, and *facere,* make.] The act of smelling; the sense of smell.—**ol·fac·to·ry,** ol·fak′to·rē, ol·fak′trē, *a.,* *n.* pl. **ol·fac·to·ries.**

ol·fac·to·ry nerve, *n. Anat.* either of two nerves which consist of sensory fibers and conduct impulses from the olfactory organ in the nose to the brain. Also *olfactory.*

ol·fac·to·ry or·gan, *n. Anat.* an organ composed of membranes in the nasal cavity, sensitive to the stimuli of odors. Also *olfactory.*

o·lib·a·num, ō·lib′a·num, *n.* [L.L.] Frankincense.

ol·i·gar·chy, ol′i·gär″kē, *n.* pl. **ol·i·gar·chies.** [Gr. *oligarchia.*] A form of government in which the power is exercised by or vested in a few; a state so governed; the ruling few or class collectively.—**ol·i·gar·chic,** ol·i·gar·chi·cal, ol″i·gär′kik, *a.* —**ol·i·garch,** ol′i·gärk″, *n.*

Ol·i·go·cene, ol′i·gō·sēn, *a.* [Gr. *oligos,* little, and *kainos,* new.] *Geol.* noting or pertaining to the third oldest epoch of the Tertiary period or system.—*n.* The Oligocene epoch of the Tertiary. See Table of Geological Time.

ol·i·go·chaete, ol′i·gō·kēt″, *n. Zool.* any of a class, *Oligochaeta,* of aquatic or terrestrial annelids such as earthworms, having no special appendages on the head, and a number of small bristlelike parts for locomotion.—*a.* Also **ol·i·go·chae·tous.**

ol·i·go·clase, ol′i·gō·klās″, *n.* [Gr. *oligos,* little, and *klásis,* fracture.] *Mineral.* a kind of feldspar containing sodium and calcium, commonly occurring in whitish crystals, sometimes shaded with gray, green, or red.

ol·i·goph·a·gous, ol″i·gof′a·gus, *a. Biol.* feeding on only a limited assortment of foods, as many insects.—**ol·i·goph·a·gy,** *n.*

ol·i·gop·o·ly, ol″i·gop′o·lē, *n. Econ.* the state of a market controlled by few producers, sellers, or stock holders, in relation to many buyers.

ol·i·gop·so·ny, ol″i·gop′so·nē, *n. Econ.* the state of a market controlled by few

buyers in relation to many sellers or producers.

ol·i·go·sac·cha·ride, ol″i·gō·sak′a·rīd″, ol″i·gō·sak′èr·id, *n. Chem.* a carbohydrate or saccharide containing monosaccharides in small numbers.

ol·i·go·troph·ic, ol″i·gō·trof′ik, *a.* Of or pertaining to a lake having insufficient nutrients to support abundant plant and animal life, and therefore having a high oxygen content.

o·li·o, ō′lē·ō′, *n.* pl. **o·li·os.** [Sp. *olla,* pot, stew.] A dish of many ingredients; any mixture of heterogeneous elements; a medley or potpourri of musical or literary pieces; a miscellany. *Theatr.* the vaudeville portion of a minstrel or burlesque show; a vaudeville number usu. performed between acts or during set changes.

ol·ive, ol′iv, *n.* [O.Fr. Fr. *olive,* < L. *olīva,* akin to Gr. *elaia,* olive tree, olive.] An evergreen tree, *Olea europaea,* of the Mediterranean and other warm regions, cultivated chiefly for its fruit; the fruit, a small oval drupe, esteemed as a relish, and valuable as a source of oil; the wood of this tree, valued for ornamental work; any of various related or similar trees; the foliage of the tree, a wreath of it, or an olive branch used as an emblem of peace; an olive color, tint, or tinge. Any of the gastropod mollusks of the family *Olividae,* with an elongated, oval shell, numerous in tropical seas.—*a.* Of the dull, yellowish-green color of the unripe olive fruit.—**ol·i·va·ceous,** ol″i·vā′shus, *a.* [N.L. *olīvāceus.*] Of an olive hue or tint.

ol·ive drab, *n.* Any of various shades of an olive-toned mixture of green and brown; a woolen fabric of this color used for U.S. Army uniforms. The uniform itself; also **ol·ive drabs.**—*a.*

ol·ive-green, ol′iv·grēn′, *n.* Green with a yellowish or brownish tinge.—*a.*

o·liv·en·ite, ō·liv′e·nīt″, ol′i·ve·nīt″, *n.* [< G. *olivenerz,* 'olive ore.'] A mineral consisting of arsenate of copper, occurring in crystals and in masses, usually olive-green in color.

ol·ive oil, *n.* An oil expressed from the pulp of olives, used with food, in medicine, and for various other purposes.

ol·i·vine, ol′i·vēn″, ol″i·vēn′, *n.* [L. *olīva,* olive.] An olive-green mineral, some varieties of which are used as semiprecious gemstones. Also *chrysolite.*—**ol·i·vin·ic,** ol·i·vin·it·ic, ol″i·vin′ik, ol″i·vi·nit′ik, *a.*

o·lla, ol′a, *Sp.* a′lyä, a′yä, *n.* [Sp., pot, stew, < L. *olla,* pot, jar.] An earthen pot or jar used as a container for water or for cooking in southwestern U.S. A kind of stew; see *olla-podrida.*

ol·la-po·dri·da, ol″a·po·drē′da, *Sp.* a″-lyä pa·drē′dä, a″ya pa·dre′dä, *n.* [Sp. 'rotten pot.'] A Spanish stew of various highly seasoned meats and vegetables; also *olla.* Any incongruous mixture or miscellaneous collection; see *olio.*

o·lym·pi·ad, ō·lim′pē·ad″, *n.* [Gr. *Olympias*(-*ad*-).] (*Often cap.*) a period of four years between celebrations of the Olympic games, by which the ancient Greeks computed time from 776 B.C.; a celebration of the modern Olympic games.

O·lym·pi·an, ō·lim′pē·an, *a.* Pertaining to or dwelling on Mount Olympus, as the greater gods of Greece; pertaining to Olympia, a plain in Ellis, Greece; godlike; lofty or majestic; Olympic.—*n.* An Olympic deity; a contender in an Olympic contest.

O·lym·pic, ō·lim′pik, *a.* Pertaining to the Olympic games; relating to Olympia, Greece; relating to Mount Olympus; majestic; Olympian.—**O·lym·pics,** *n. pl.* The Olympic games.

O·lym·pic games, *n. pl.* An international competition in numerous sports, held every four years, each time in a different country, and named for an ancient Greek festival; the greatest festival of ancient Greece, the celebration of which included many athletic events, held every four years on the plain of Olympia. Also **O·lym·pi·an games,** *Olympics.*

o·ma·sum, ō·mā′sum, *n.* pl. **o·ma·sa,** ō·mā′sa. [L.] The third stomach of ruminating animals. Also *manyplies, psalterium.*

om·ber, om·bre, om′bẽr, *n.* [Fr. *ombre, hombre,* < Sp. *hombre,* lit. 'man,' < L. *homo,* man.] A game of cards, fashionable in the 17th and 18th centuries, played, usu. by three persons, with forty cards; the player who undertakes to win the pool in this game. Also **hom·bre.**

om·buds·man, ảm′bŏdz·man″, *n.* pl. **om·buds·men.** In New Zealand and some Scandinavian countries, an appointed official charged with investigating reports and complaints of malfeasance by government agencies or officials against private citizens.

o·me·ga, ō·mē′ga, ō·mā′ga, ō·meg′a, ō′meg·a, *n.* [Gr. *ō,* and *méga,* great, lit. 'the great or long *o.*'] The twenty-fourth and last letter of the Greek alphabet. The last; the ending.

om·e·let, om·e·lette, om′e·lit, om′lit, *n.* [Fr. *amelette, omelette.*] Beaten eggs fried, at times with cheese, mushrooms, or other foods, until set.

o·men, ō′men, *n.* [L. *omen,* older *osmen,* < *os, oris,* the mouth, or connected with *auris,* the ear.] A circumstance or occurrence thought to portend future good or evil; a sign or augury.—*v.t.* To foretell or find out, as by omens.

o·men·tum, ō·men′tum, *n.* pl. **o·men·ta,** ō·men′ta. [L.] *Anat.* a fold or duplication of the peritoneum passing between certain of the viscera.—**great·er o·men·tum,** that attached to and hanging down from the stomach and the transverse colon.—**less·er o·men·tum,** the omentum found between the stomach and the liver.—**o·men·tal,** *a.*

om·i·cron, om′i·kron″, ō′mi·kron″, *n.* [L.Gr. *ō mikrón,* 'small *o.*'] The fifteenth letter of the Greek alphabet.

om·i·nous, om′i·nus, *a.* [L. *ōminōsus.*] Betokening, foreboding, or threatening evil; inauspicious; having the nature of a portent or sign.—**om·i·nous·ly,** *adv.*—**om·i·nous·ness,** *n.*

o·mis·sion, ō·mish′an, *n.* [L. *omissiō.*] The act of leaving out or omitting, or the condition of being omitted or left out; neglect or failure to do something that should have been done; something omitted or left out.—**o·mis·si·ble,** ō·mis′i·bl, *a.* Capable of being, or permitted to be, omitted.

o·mis·sive, ō·mis′iv, *a.* Leaving out; not including.—**o·mis·sive·ly,** *adv.*

o·mit, ō·mit′, *v.t.*—omitted, omitting. [L. *omitto,* to neglect, disregard, say nothing of—prefix *ob-,* and *mitto,* to send.] To pass over or neglect; to fail to do or to use; to leave out; not to insert, as part of a communication.—**o·mit·ter,** *n.*

om·ma·te·um, om″a·tē′um, *n.* pl. **om·ma·te·a,** om″a·tē′a. [N.L., < Gr. *omma* (*ommat-*), eye, < *om-,* see.] *Zool.* a compound eye, as in insects and crustaceans.—**om·ma·te·al,** *a.*

om·ma·tid·i·um, om″a·tid′ē·um, *n.* pl. **om·ma·tid·i·a,** om″a·tid′ē·a. [N.L., dim. < Gr. *omma* (*ommat-*), eye.] *Zool.* one of the radial elements or segments which make up the compound eye of insects, crustaceans, and other arthropods.—**om·ma·tid·i·al,** *a.*

om·ni·bus, om′ni·bus″, om′ni·bus, *n.* pl. **om·ni·bus·es.** [L., 'for all,' dat. pl. of *omnis,* all.] A bus, as a vehicle for public transportation; a collection of writings having the same theme, or by the same author.—*a.* Pertaining to or covering

numerous objects or items at once; as, an *omnibus* bill or resolution.

om·ni·di·rec·tion·al, om″nē·di·rek′-sha·nal, *a. Elect.* sending, radiating, or receiving radio signals equally well in all directions.

om·ni·far·i·ous, om″ni·fâr′ē·us, *a.* [L. *omnifārius.*] Of all forms, varieties, or kinds.—**om·ni·far·i·ous·ly,** *adv.*—**om·ni·far·i·ous·ness,** *n.*

om·nif·ic, om·nif′ik, *a.* [L. *omnis,* all, and *facio,* to make.] All-creating.—**om·nif·i·cent,** om·nif′i·sent, *a.* Having complete creative power; creating every thing.

om·nip·o·tence, om·nip′o·tens, *n.* [L. *omnipotēns,* omnipotent—*omnis,* all, and *potens,* powerful.] Unlimited or infinite power as an attribute of God; (*cap.*) God. Very great power or influence.—**om·nip·o·tent,** om·nip′o·tent, *a.* Almighty or all-powerful as a god or deity.—**the Om·nip·o·tent,** God.—**om·nip·o·tent·ly,** *adv.*

om·ni·pres·ent, om″ni·prez′ent, *a.* [M.L. *omnipraesens* (*-ent-*), < L. *omnis,* all, and *praesens,* present.] Present everywhere at the same time.—**om·ni·pres·ence,** *n.*—**om·ni·pres·ent·ly,** *adv.*

om·ni·range, om′ni·rānj″, *n.* A radio navigation system consisting of transmitters which emit signals for each degree of the compass, allowing aircraft to determine their positions relative to the location of the transmitter. Also **om·ni·di·rec·tion·al ra·di·o range.**

om·nis·cience, om·nish′ens, *n.* [L. *omnis,* all, and *scientia,* knowledge.] The faculty of knowing everything; knowledge unbounded or infinite: an attribute of God.—**om·nis·cient,** om·nish′ent, *a.* Having knowledge of all things; infinitely knowing.—**the Om·nis·cient,** God.—**om·nis·cient·ly,** *adv.*

om·ni·vore, om′ni·vōr″, *n.* An omnivorous animal or person.

om·niv·o·rous, om·niv′ẽr·us, *a.* [L. *omnivorus—omnis,* all, and *voro,* to eat.] Eating both plant and animal foods; eating food of every kind indiscriminately; *fig.* absorbing everything avidly; as, an *omnivorous* tourist.—**om·niv·o·rous·ly,** *adv.*—**om·niv·o·rous·ness,** *n.*

o·mo·pha·gia, ō″mo·fā′ja, ō″mo·fā′jē·a, *n.* [L.L., < Gr. *ōmophagia.*] The eating of raw flesh or raw food.—**o·mo·phag·ic,** ō′moph·a·gous, ō″o·faj′ik, ō·mof′a·gus, *a.*—**o·moph·a·gist,** ō·mof′a·jist, *n.*

on, on, *prep.* [O.E. *on, an,* on, in, to, D. *aan* = G. *an* = Icel. *ā* = Goth. *ana;* akin to Gr. *ana,* up, upon.] Positioned above and in contact with a supporting surface; as, *on* the table; in the immediate proximity; as, Stratford-*on*-Avon, to border *on* absurdity; situated or placed; as, a scar *on* the face, *on* the map, *on* a jury; supported by, suspended by, or dependent on; as, *on* wheels or *on* foot, hanging *on* a nail, to live *on* one's family, *on* my honor; in a state, condition, course, process; as, *on* fire, *on* the march, *on* strike; grounded or based; as, *on* this account, *on* purpose, a duty *on* silk, profit *on* sales; at the risk of; as, *on* pain of death; at the time or occasion of; as, *on* Sunday, *on* our arrival; directed or moving toward; as, to go *on* one's way, to march *on* the capital; encountering; as, to happen *on* a person or thing; aiming at or directed toward; as, to gaze *on* a scene, to seize *on* an excuse, bent *on* mischief, to tell *on* one; with reference or respect to; as, a poem *on* spring, views *on* public matters.

on, on, an, *adv.* On or into a position of support, contact, or attachment; as, put the coffee *on,* put coal *on;* on oneself or itself; as, to put one's coat *on,* to take *on* polish or color; attached to a thing, as for support; as, to catch or hold *on;* forward, onward, or along, as in any course or process; as, come *on,* get *on* in the world,

further *on;* with continuous procedure; as, to work *on;* into or in active operation or performance; as, turn *on* the gas, war is *on.*—**be on to,** to be fully aware of or alive to, as an attempt, scheme, or situation.

on, on, an, *a.* Being in action or application; situated nearer; near; planned, as: What is *on* after dinner? *Cricket,* noting that side of the wicket, or of the field, on which the batsman stands.—*n.* The condition or fact of being on; *cricket,* the on side.

on·a·ger, on′a·jẽr, *n.* pl. **on·a·gri, on·a·gers,** on′a·grī″. [L. *onager, onagrus,* < Gr. *ónagros,* < *ónos,* ass, and *agros,* field.] *Zool.* a wild ass of the genus *Equus,* of a rust color with a light dorsal stripe, which travels in herds in Iran, Afghanistan, and northern India. An ancient piece of machinery used in warfare for throwing stones.

o·nan·ism, ō′na·niz″um, *n.* [From *Onan,* son of Judah: see Gen. xxxviii. 9.] Withdrawal during intercourse before ejaculation; masturbation.—**o·nan·ist,** *n.*—**o·nan·is·tic,** *a.*

once, wuns, *adv.* [M.E. *ones, ānes,* adv., orig. genitive, < *on, ān,* one.] A single time; even a single time, at any time, or ever; as, if the facts *once* become known; at one time in the past, or formerly; by one degree or step; as, a cousin *once* removed.—*a.* That *once* was; former.—*conj.* If or when at any time; if ever; whenever.—*n.* One time; a single occasion.—**once and for all,** finally, definitely.—**once in a while,** occasionally, infrequently.—**once up·on a time,** at an indefinite time, usu. long ago.—**all at once,** simultaneously; suddenly.—**at once,** simultaneously; immediately.

once-o·ver, wuns′ō″vẽr, *n. Colloq.* A single or brief look or appraisal; a hasty, superficial job.

on·col·o·gy, ong·kol′o·jē, *n.* [Gr. *onkos,* bulk, mass.] *Med.* the part of medical science that treats and studies tumors.—**on·co·log·ic, on·co·log·i·cal,** ong″ko·loj′ik, *a.*

on·com·ing, on′kum″ing, *n.* The coming on or approaching of something; approach; as, the *oncoming* of winter.—*a.* Coming on; approaching; emergent.

one, wun, *a.* [M.E. *one, on, an,* < O.E. *ān* = D. *een* = G. *ein* = Icel. *einn* = Goth. *ains,* one; akin to L. *ūnus,* one, Gr. *oinē,* ace on dice.] Being but a single object, unit, or individual, in contrast to two or more; as, *one* book, *one* person; being an individual instance of something; as, *one* day of the month; indicating an uncertain or indefinite time; as, he will show up *one* day; single through union or combination; as, responding with *one* cheer; being in agreement or accord; as, of *one* opinion; of a unique kind; nature, or character; undivided; forming a whole; the same, as: It was all *one* and the same to them.

one, wun, *n.* The first cardinal number; the number between zero and two; the figure 1 representing the number; first in a series; a single person or thing; a unit; unity.—**at one,** in a state of agreement or accord; united.—**one and all,** everyone, individually and collectively.—**one by one,** one after another; singly and in succession.

one, wun, *pron.* Any indefinitely indicated person or thing; anyone; anything; a single person or thing of a group already indicated; a certain person or being; someone; anyone of us all.—**one of these days,** some day or some time; before long, as: He'll return *one of these days.*

one an·oth·er, *pron.* Each other.

one-base hit, *n. Baseball.* A safe hit on which the batter reaches first base; a single. Also **one-bag·ger.**

one-egg, wun′eg, *a.* Produced from a single cell.

---

a- fat, fāte, fär, fâre, fạll; **e-** met, mē, mēre, hẽr; **i-** pin, pīne; **o-** not, nōte, mŏve; **u-** tub, cūbe, bụll; **oi-** oil; **ou-** pound.

one-horse, wun′hŏrs′, wun′hɑrs′, *a.* Drawn by a single horse; *colloq.* unimportant; as, a *one-horse* town.

o·nei·ric, ō·nī′rik, *a.* Of or relating to a dream; pertaining to a waking condition which appears dreamlike.

o·nei·ro·crit·ic, ō·nī′rō·krit′ik, *n.* One involved in the explanation and interpretation of dreams.—**o·nei·ro·crit·i·cal,** *a.*—**o·nei·ro·crit·i·cal·ly,** *adv.*

o·nei·ro·man·cy, ō·nī′rō·man″sē, *n.* [Gr. *oneiros,* dream, and *manteia,* divination.] Divination through dreams.—**o·nei·ro·man·cer,** *n.*

one·ness, wun′nis, *n.* The state of being one; singleness; uniqueness; unity; agreement; wholeness.

on·er·ous, on′ẽr·us, ō′nẽr·us, *a.* [O.Fr. *onereus* (Fr. *onéreux*), < L. *onerōsus,* < *onus* (*oner-*), load.] Burdensome, oppressive, or troublesome; as, *onerous* duties or responsibilities; *law,* having or imposing a legal burden or obligation that is disadvantageous. —**on·er·ous·ly,** *adv.*—**on·er·ous·ness,** *n.*

one·self, wun′self′, wunz′self′, *pron.* Someone's own self: used for emphasis, as an object of a verb or proposition, or reflexively. One's usual physical or mental condition; as, not to feel *oneself.* Also **one's self.**

one-shot, wun′shot″, *a.* Nonrecurring; of a single action or attempt, not to be repeated; pertaining to an isolated issue of a periodical, not followed or preceded by other issues.

one-sid·ed, wun′sī′did, *a.* Having but one side; having one side larger or more developed than the other; having the parts all on one side, as an inflorescence; turned or leaning to one side; existing or occurring on one side only. *Fig.* concerned with or considering but one side of a matter or question; partial, unjust; as, a *one-sided* judgment. *Sports,* with one contestant having an overwhelming decision or victory. *Law,* unilateral, as a contract.—**one-sid·ed·ly,** *adv.*—**one-sid·ed·ness,** *n.*

one-step, wun′step″, *n.* A round dance of the early 1920's, danced by couples to a ragtime beat; the ragtime music for this dance.

one-time, wun′tīm″, *a.,* *adv.* Having been so at one time; former; as, his *one-time* partner.

one-track, wun′trak″, *a.* Having but one track; *colloq.* confined to a single interest, activity, or idea.

one-up·man·ship, wun′up′man·ship″, *n.* The tendency to compete, whether in society, business, or sports, by maintaining a constant advantage or margin of superiority.

one-way, wun′wā′, *a.* Moving, permitting movement, or making provision for movement in only one direction; lacking reciprocity; one-sided; as, a *one-way* relationship.

on·go·ing, on′gō″ing, ɑn′gō″ing, *a.* Progressing without interruption; as, separate *ongoing* investigations.

on·ion, un′yon, *n.* [Fr. *oignon, ognon,* < L. *ūniō, uniōnis,* unity, an onion with one bulb, < *unus,* one.] An edible bulb of a garden herb, *Allium cepa,* in the lily family, with a strong characteristic pungent odor and taste; the plant itself.—**on·ion·like,** *a.*—**on·ion·y,** *a.*

on·ion·skin, un′yan·skin″, *n.* A strong, thin, translucent, glossy paper.

on-line, on′līn″, ɑn′līn″, *a.* *Data processing,* operating under direct control of the central computer; *rail.* situated on or taking place on the regular line.

on·look·er, on′lʉk″ẽr, ɑn′lʉk″ẽr, *n.* One who looks on; a spectator.—**on·look·ing,** *a.*

on·ly, ōn′lē, *adv.* [One, with its old pronunciation, and term. *-ly;* O.E. *ānlich.*] For one purpose alone, as: He is going *only* because his parents are there. Neither more

nor less than; merely; simply; just, as: It is *only* a bruise. Alone; solely; exclusively; as, for you *only;* as short a time ago as, as: I told him *only* this morning. In the end, as: You will *only* wish you had never come. Certainly, followed by *too,* as: He was *only too* pleased to go, it was *only too* obvious.— *a.* Single; alone in its class; solitary; as, the *only* child in the family; incomparable; as, there is *only* one Shakespeare.—*conj.* But, as: I would have bought it *only* it was too expensive. Excepting that.

on·o·mas·tic, on″o·mas′tik, *a.* [Gr. *onomastikos,* pertaining to naming, < *onomazein,* to name, < *onoma,* name.] Of, pertaining to, or connected with a name or names, or the naming of something; consisting of names; *law,* noting the signature of a legal document or instrument, the body of which is in the handwriting of another person.

on·o·mas·tics, on″o·mas′tiks, *n. pl. but sing. in constr.* The study of the origin and meaning of proper names.

on·o·mat·o·poe·ia, on″o·mat″o·pē′ɑ, *n.* [Gr. *onomatopoiia*—*onoma, onomatos,* a name, and *poieō,* to make.] The formation of words by imitation of sounds produced by or associated with some object or action, as buzz, hum, boom, cuckoo; a word formed in this manner; *rhet.* the use of such naturally associative words to enhance the rhetorical value of speech or writing.—**on·o·mat·o·poe·ic,** **on·o·mat·o·po·et·ic,** on″o·mat″o·pō·et′ik, *a.*—**on·o·mat·o·poe·i·cal·ly,** **on·o·mat·o·po·et·i·cal·ly,** *adv.*

on·rush, on′rush″, ɑn′rush″, *n.* A powerful rush or flow onward.—**on·rush·ing,** *a.*

on·set, on′set″, ɑn′set″, *n.* An assault or attack; a beginning; outset.—**on·set·ter,** *n.*—**on·set·ting,** *a.*

on·shore, on′shōr′, ɑn′shɑr′, *a.* Proceeding to or maneuvering toward shore or onto the shore; on or close to the shore; happening or done on land.—*adv.* In the direction of, close to, or parallel with the shore; ashore.

on·slaught, on′slɑt″, ɑn′slɑt″, *n.* [Cf. D. *aanslag,* stroke, attempt, M.L.G. *anslach,* attack, onslaught.] An onset, assault, or attack, esp. a vigorous or furious one.

on·to, on′tö, ɑn′tö, *unstressed* on′to, ɑn′to, *prep.* To a place or position on; upon the top of; on; as, to throw the ball *onto* the roof; *colloq.* informed about or alert to, as: I'm *onto* his tactics.

on·tog·e·ny, on·toj′e·nē, *n.* [Gr. *on, ontos,* being, and *genesis*—root *gen,* to produce.] *Biol.* the history of the individual development of an organism.—**on·to·ge·net·ic,** on″tō·je·net′ik, *a.*—**on·to·ge·net·i·cal·ly,** *adv.*

on·tol·o·gy, on·tol′ō·jē, *n.* [Gr. *on, ontos,* being, and *logos,* discourse.] *Philos.* the study of the nature of existence and being in the abstract. See *metaphysics.*—**on·to·log·i·cal,** on″to·loj′i·kal, *a.*—**on·tol·o·gist,** *n.*—**on·to·log·i·cal·ly,** *adv.*

o·nus, ō′nus, *n. pl.* **o·nus·es.** [L.] A burden; an obligation; stigma.

on·ward, on′wẽrd, ɑn′wẽrd, *adv.* Toward a point ahead or in front; forward, as in space or time; at a position or point in advance. Also **on·wards.**—*a.* Directed or moving onward or forward; forward.

on·yx, on′iks, ō′niks, *n.* [Gr. *onyx,* the nail; the color of the gem resembles that of the nail.] A semipellucid travertine with variously colored zones or veins; an agate with layers of chalcedony, sometimes used for cameos; the color black; *med.* a nail on a toe or finger; *pathol.* the condition of pus between the strata of the cornea.—*a.* Black or jet black.

o·o·cyte, ō′o·sīt″, *n.* [Gr. *ōon,* an egg, *kytos,* a cell.] *Biol.* an ovarian egg prior to maturation.

oo·dles, ŏd′lz, *n. pl.* [Provinc. (Ir.) form of *huddle.*] *Slang,* a large quantity; as, *oodles* of money.

OO gauge, *n.* In model railroading, a gauge of track with the rails three-fourths of an inch apart.

o·o·gen·e·sis, ō″o·jen′i·sis, *n.* *Biol.* a series of cell divisions starting with the primordial germ cells in the ovary, and which results in the production of the ovum. Also **o·o·ge·′ny,** ō·oj′e·nē.—**o·o·ge·net·ic,** ō″o·je·net′ik, *a.*

o·o·go·ni·um, ō″o·gō′nē·um, *n. pl.* **o·o·go·ni·a,** **o·o·go·ni·ums,** ō″o·gō′nē·ɑ. [N.L., < Gr. *ōon,* egg, and *-gonium* as in *archegonium.*] *Bot.* a one-celled female sex structure found in thallophytes which produces one or more eggs.

o·o·lite, ō′o·līt″, *n.* [Fr. *oolithe,* < Gr. *ōon,* egg, and *lithos,* stone.] *Geol.* a rock, usu. of calcium carbonate, composed of rounded concretions resembling the roe of a fish.— **o·o·lit·ic,** ō″o·lit′ik, *a.*

o·ol·o·gy, ō·ol′o·jē, *n.* The science that treats of the study of bird eggs, their shape, color, clutch number, and incubation period.—**o·o·log·i·cal,** ō″o·loj′i·kal, *a.*— **o·ol·o·gist,** *n.*—**o·o·log·i·cal·ly,** *adv.*

oo·long, ö′lɑng″, ö′long″, *n.* [Chin. *wu,* black, and *lung,* dragon.] A variety of dark tea partially fermented before being cured.

oo·mi·ak, ö′mē·ak″, *n.* Umiak.

oomph, ʉmf, *n.* Personal glamour; physical attractiveness; sex appeal; vibrance; pep.

o·o·pho·rec·to·my, ō″o·fo·rek′to·mē, *n. pl.* **o·o·pho·rec·to·mies.** *Surg.* the surgical removal of one or both ovaries, the most frequent indication being ovarian pathology such as tumorous growth. Also *ovariectomy.* —**o·o·pho·rec·to·mize,** *v.t.*—*oophorectomized, oophorectomizing.*

ooze, öz, *n.* [In part < O.E. *wōs,* juice, moisture, in part < O.E. *wāse,* mud, with confusion between the derivatives of the two forms.] Soft mud or slime; a marsh or bog; a calcareous mud, chiefly the shells of small organisms, covering parts of the ocean bottom; an infusion of oak or sumac bark, used in tanning; the act of oozing; gentle flow; that which oozes.—*v.i.* *oozed, oozing.* To filter or exude through pores or small openings, as: Water *oozed* out of the marshy ground. To move slowly and almost unnoticed; of a substance, to exude moisture; *fig.* to leak out or pass away slowly or imperceptibly, often followed by *out* or *away,* as: His courage *oozed away* bit by bit.—*v.t.* To make by oozing; to exude slowly, as a trickle of moisture.—**ooz·y,** ö′zē, *a.*— *oozier, ooziest.*

ooze leath·er, *n.* Leather prepared from calfskin or other skin giving it a soft, velvety finish on the flesh side.

o·pac·i·ty, ō·pas′i·tē, *n. pl.* **o·pac·i·ties.** [Fr. *opacité,* < L. *opācitās,* < *opācus,* E. *opaque.*] The state of being opaque; darkness; imperviousness to light or sound; the degree of opaqueness; the capacity of a substance to obstruct the passage of any radiant energy; obscurity of meaning; denseness or stupidity; something opaque; *photog.* the light absorption capacity of the emulsion on a plate or film.

o·pah, ō′pa, *n.* A large and beautiful elliptical sea fish, *Lampris regius,* with edible red flesh.

o·pal, ō′pal, *n.* [L. *opalus,* Gr. *opallios,* an opal; cf. Skt. *upala,* a precious stone.] A hydrous silica of various colors and varieties, neither as hard nor as dense as quartz, the finest characterized by iridescent reflection of light; a gem of such a mineral.

o·pal·es·cence, ō″pa·les′ens, *n.* A play of colors like that of the opal; the reflection of a milky, iridescent light.—**o·pal·es·cent,** *a.*

o·pa·line, ō′pa·lin, ō′pa·līn″, *a.* Pertaining to or like opal; opalescent.—*n.* A semi-translucent glass.

o·paque, ō·pāk′, *a.* [= Fr. *opaque*, < L. *opacus*, shady, darkened.] Impermeable to light; not transparent; dull, not bright; not transmitting sound, heat, or electricity. Not lucid; obscure; unintelligent, dense, stupid. —*n.* Something opaque. *Photog.* an opaque pigment used to block out parts of a print or photographic negative.—*v.t.*—*opaqued*, *opaquing*. *Photog.* to correct, as a photographic negative, esp. when preparing a plate for printing.—**o·paque·ly**, *adv.*—**o··paque·ness**, *n.*

op art, op′ ärt′, *n* The mid 20th century school of abstract painting which employs geometrical figures and, often, vibrant colors in an attempt to produce such visual effects and illusions as movement and three dimensional depth. Also *optical art*.

ope, ōp, *v.t.*, *v.i.*—*oped*, *oping*. *Poet.* open. —*a.*

o·pen, ō′pen, *a.* [O.E. *open* = D. *open* = G. *offen* = Icel. *opinn*, open; prob. from the root of E. *up*.] Not shut, as a door, gate, or window; not closed, covered, or shut up, as a house, car, box, or drawer; exposed or unprotected; not enclosed by or as by barriers or partitions, as a space; that may be entered, used, shared, or competed for by all; as, an *open* session or tournament; accessible or available, often followed by *to*; as, the only course *open to* us; accessible or receptive to appeals, ideas, or offers, often followed by *to*; as, *open to* suggestion; without prohibition as to hunting or fishing, as a season; *colloq.* without or not enforcing legal restrictions; as, an *open* town. Unfilled, as a position; unoccupied, as time; undecided, as a question; liable or subject, followed by *to*; as, *open to* temptation; exposed to general view or knowledge, or existing or carried on publicly; acting without concealment; unreserved, candid, or frank; expanded, extended, or spread out; as, an *open* newspaper; generous or liberal; as, giving with an *open* hand; having openings or apertures, or being perforated or porous; unobstructed, as a passage, country, stretch of water, or view; free from frost, fog, or ice, or being mild and moderate; *print.* widely spaced or leaded, as printed matter. *Mus.* of an organ pipe, not closed at the upper end; of a string, not stopped by a finger; of a note, produced by such a pipe or string; on a wind instrument, without the aid of a slide or key. *Phon.* uttered with a relatively wide opening of the mouth; not closed by a consonant at the end of the syllable, as a vowel; ending in a vowel, as a syllable. Unfortified, unoccupied, and safe under international agreement from enemy attack; as, an *open* city; ready and prepared for business.—**o·pen·ly**, *adv.*—**o·pen·ness**, *n.*

o·pen, ō′pen, *v.t.* [O.E. *openian*.] To move from a shut or closed position so as to admit passage; to give access to, or make accessible or available; to clear of obstructions; to establish for use by the public or customers; to make accessible to knowledge, sympathy, or ideas; to make or force an opening in; to uncover, lay bare, or expose to view; to disclose, reveal, or divulge; to expand, extend, or spread out; to make less compact or close together; to set in action, begin, start, or commence. *Law*, to make the first statement of, as a case, to the court or jury; to recall or revoke, as a judgment or decree, in order to allow further contest or delay. *Naut.* to come in sight of.—*v.i.* To become open, as a door, building, box, or the like; to afford access, followed by *in* or *into*; to have an opening, passage, or outlet, followed by *into*, *upon*, *toward*, or the like; to become receptive to knowledge, sym-

pathy, or ideas, as the mind; to come into view, or become more visible or plain; to become disclosed or revealed; to disclose or reveal one's knowledge, thoughts, or feelings; to spread out or expand; to become less compact or close together; to begin, start, or commence, as a session, term, season, or tour.

o·pen, ō′pen, *n.* An open or clear space; the outdoors; an opening or aperture; an opening or opportunity; the condition or situation of being exposed to public view or knowledge; as, the news is in the *open*; a tournament or contest that may be entered by either professionals or amateurs; as, a golf *open*.

o·pen air, *n.* The unconfined atmosphere; the air out of doors.—**o·pen-air**, *a.* Occurring or existing outdoors.

o·pen-and-shut, ō′pen·an·shut′, *a.* Obvious; resolved with ease.

o·pen chain, *n. Chem.* a series or chain of carbon atoms which are open or not connected at the ends, as that found in organic compounds.—**o·pen-chain**, *a.*

o·pen door, *n.* The policy of admission of all nations to a country upon equal terms, esp. for purposes of trade; free admission or access.—**o·pen-door**, *a.*

o·pen-end, ō′pen·end′, *a.* Having no definite limits; allowing for wide interpretation or freedom of action. *Finance*, permitting additional debt to be incurred; as, an *open-end* mortgage; allowing more shares of capital stock to be issued; as, an *open-end* investment company.

o·pen·er, ō′pe·nẽr, *n.* Someone or something that opens; a device used to open a sealed container; as, a bottle *opener*; the first theatrical or variety number, or sports event, in a series; an opening joke, monologue, or remark, used to gain attention or set a mood; *pl.*, *poker*, the predetermined minimum holding or combination of cards needed by a player to begin the betting.

o·pen-eyed, ō′pen·īd′, *a.* Having the eyes open; watchful; vigilant; aware; amazed.

o·pen-hand·ed, ō′pen·han′did, *a.* Generous; liberal; munificent.—**o·pen-hand·-ed·ly**, *adv.*—**o·pen-hand·ed·ness**, *n.*

o·pen-heart·ed, ō′pen·här′tid, *a.* Candid or frank; sincere; benevolent.—**o·pen-heart·ed·ly**, *adv.*—**o·pen-heart·ed·ness**, *n.*

o·pen-hearth, ō′pen·härth′, *a. Metal.* Referring to a type of furnace used in making steel; designating or pertaining to the process by which steel is made in such a furnace, or to the steel produced by this process.

o·pen-heart sur·ger·y, ō′pen·härt′ sur′je·rē, *n. Surg.* an operation in which a heart is opened for diagnosis or treatment, the blood flow being diverted through a heart-lung machine.

o·pen house, *n.* A time or occasion when a house is hospitably thrown open to all friends who may wish to visit or to enjoy its entertainment; a period during which a naval base, school, or other institution is open to visitors; a dwelling kept open to be shown for sale by the owner or a Realtor.— **keep o·pen house**, to be always ready to entertain visitors.

o·pen hous·ing, *n.* The principle and practice prohibiting the sale or rental of property on a discriminatory basis of race, color, religion, or national origin. Also **fair hous·ing**.—**o·pen-hous·ing**, *a.* Pertaining to nondiscriminatory sale or rental of property; as, an *open-housing* ordinance.

o·pen·ing, ō′pe·ning, *n.* The act of one who or that which opens; a making or becoming open; the act of beginning, starting, or commencing; the first part or initial stage of anything; the beginning or premiere of a performance, season, session, fashion show-

ing, term, tour, or use of something; as, the *opening* of Parliament, an *opening* of a sale; an open space in solid matter; a gap, hole, or aperture; an open or clear space affording entrance or passage; an unobstructed or unoccupied space or place; a tract of land thinly wooded as compared with adjoining forest tracts; a vacancy or vacant position; an opportunity for employment; *law*, the statement of the case made by counsel to the court or jury preliminary to offering evidence; *chess*, *checkers*, a particular mode of beginning a game.—*a.*

o·pen let·ter, *n.* A protest, appeal, criticism, or suggestion written in the form of a letter and addressed to a certain person or group, but released to periodicals or broadcasting media for widespread publicity and readership.—**o·pen-let·ter**, *a.*

o·pen-mind·ed, ō′pen·mīn′did, *a.* Having or showing a mind open to new arguments or ideas; unprejudiced.—**o·pen-mind·-ed·ly**, *adv.*—**o·pen-mind·ed·ness**, *n.*

o·pen-mouthed, ō′pen·mouTHd′, ō′pen·-moutht′, *a.* Having the mouth open; gaping, as with astonishment; noisy, clamorous; greedy, ravenous.—**o·pen-mouth·ed·ly**, *adv.*—**o·pen-mouth·ed·-ness**, *n.*

o·pen or·der, *n. Milit.* a drill or combat formation of troops in which relatively wide intervals separate the individuals. Also **ex·tend·ed or·der**.

o·pen ses·a·me, *n.* [From the use of words to open the door of the robbers' den in the tale of *Ali Baba and the Forty Thieves*, in *Arabian Nights' Entertainments*.] *Fig.* Any password or charm at which doors fly open; any means that remove obstacles to success.

o·pen shop, *n.* A factory, store, or other business establishment where union and nonunion workers are employed without discrimination, although a union may act as bargaining agent for all workers.— **o·pen-shop**, *a.*

o·pen stock, *n.* A quantity of extra items of a set, as china and silverware, kept for sale as replacements.

o·pen syl·la·ble, *n. Phon.* a syllable terminating in a vowel or diphthong sound.

o·pen up, *v.i.* To begin firing or fighting; to begin talking freely; to expand or become revealed; *slang*, to give confidential information about someone.—*v.t.* To cut into; to disclose or reveal; to make accessible or available; to increase the speed of, as an automobile. *Slang*, to perform surgery on.

o·pen·work, ō′pen·wụrk″, *n.* Any kind of ornamental or decorative work, of such material as wood, stone, or lace, having openings through its substance.

o·per·a, op′ẽr·a, op′ra, *n.* [It., < L. *opera*, work; akin to *opus*.] A drama or dramatic composition set to music and sung, acted, and sometimes danced, accompanied by an orchestra; the score, words, or a performance of such a musical drama; the house or theater where opera is performed.—**op·er·at·ic**, op″e·rat′ik, *a.*— **op·er·at·i·cal·ly**, *adv.*

o·per·a, ō′pẽr·a, op′ẽr·a, *n. Chiefly mus.* plural of *opus*.

op·er·a·ble, op′ẽr·a·bl, *a.* Workable; practicable; capable of being treated by surgery.—**op·er·a·bil·i·ty**, op″ẽr·a·bil′-i·tē, *n.*—**op·er·a·bly**, *adv.*

o·pé·ra bouffe, op′ẽr·a böf′, op′ra böf′, *Fr.* a·pä·Rä böf′, *n.* pl. **o·pé·ra bouffes**, **o·pé·ras bouffe**, *Fr.* **o·pé·ras bouffes**, a·pä·Rä böf′. [Fr.] A comic opera, esp. of farcical character. Also *It.* **o·pe·ra buf·fa**, op′ẽr·a bö′fa, op′ra bö′fa, *It.* a′pe·Rä bö′fä.

o·pé·ra co·mique, op′ẽr·a ko·mēk′, op′ra ko·mēk′, *Fr.* a·pä·Rä ka·mēk′, *n.* pl. **o·pé·ra co·miques**, **o·pé·ras co·mique**,

Fr. **o·pé·ras co·miques,** a̧·pä·Rä ka̧·mēk′. [Fr.] A light opera in the nature of a comedy, consisting partly of spoken dialogue; before the 19th century, an opera on any theme having some spoken dialogue.

op·er·a glass, *n.* Small binoculars of low magnifying power, as used in theaters or at concerts. Also **op·er·a glass·es.**

o·per·a hat, *n.* A man's collapsible tall hat, held open or in shape by springs, and usu. made of a black, silky fabric.

op·er·a house, *n.* A theater specif. for the performance of operas.

op·er·ate, op′e·rāt″, *v.i.—operated, operating.* [L. *operor, operātum,* to work, < *opus, operis,* a work.] To work, act, or function; to exert power or influence; to produce a desired effect; to perform a surgical operation; to buy and sell securities or commodities, esp. on speculation or in large quantities; to conduct military operations, usu. followed by *against.—v.t.* To put into operation or cause to continue functioning; to drive or control, as a machine; to effect or accomplish.—**op·er·at·a·ble,** *a.*

op·er·a·tion, op′e·rā′shan, *n.* [L. *operā-tiō(n-).*] The act, process, or manner of operating; a mode of activity; as, a mental *operation*; a process in some form of work or production; a course of productive or industrial activity; as, a building *operation*; a business transaction, esp. one of a speculative nature or on a large scale; as, an *operation* in wheat; *surg.* a process or method of operating on the body of a patient, usu. with instruments; *milit.* a course of warlike proceedings; *math.* the action of working upon a quantity so as to change its value or form, as in addition or subtraction.—**in op·er·a·tion,** in force or action; operational.

op·er·a·tion·al, op′e·rā′sha·nal, *a.* Of or relating to an activity, process, or other operation; in fit condition to be used or employed; functional; *milit.* of or pertaining to military activities on land or sea or in the air, or to the state of readiness of a unit for active, esp. combat, duty, as: The tank unit is *operational.*

op·er·a·tions re·search, *n.* The scientific study of any operation in business or government, with the intention of increasing efficiency. Also **op·er·a·tion·al re·search.**

op·er·a·tive, op′e·rā″tiv, op′ĕr·a·tiv, op′ra·tiv, *a.* Operating; exerting force; active in the production of effects; efficacious; producing the effect; having to do with manual, surgical, or other operations.—*n.* A skilled workman; an artisan; a detective; a secret agent.—**op·er·a·tive·ly,** *adv.*—**op·er·a·tive·ness,** *n.*

op·er·a·tor, op′e·rā″tĕr, *n.* One who manipulates or handles the production operations of a device or machine; as, a sewing machine *operator*; an owner or administrator of a business; as, a real estate *operator*; a broker; *surg.* one who performs operations; *slang,* a shrewd person who gains unexpected or abnormal profit from his labors; *math.* a symbol for a mathematical process.

o·per·cu·lum, ō·pụr′kū·lum, *n.* pl. **o·per·cu·la, o·per·cu·lums,** ō·pụr′kū·la. [L., < *operio,* to close or shut.] *Bot.* a lid or cover produced by a circular dehiscence as in the spore cases of mosses and in the capsule fruits of certain seed plants. *Zool.* a horny covering over the aperture of some gastropod shells when the animal is completely retracted; the bony structure covering the gills of many fishes.—**o·per·cu·late, o·per·cu·lat·ed,** ō·pụr′kū·lit, ō·pụr′kū·lāt″, *a.*—**o·per·cu·lar,** *a., n.*

op·er·et·ta, op″e·ret′a, *n.* [It. dim. of *opera.*] A short, often humorous opera, usu.

having spoken dialogue and a light theme; light opera.—**op·er·et·ist,** *n.*

op·er·ose, op′e·rōs″, *a.* [L. *operōsus < opera,* work.] Laborious or tedious; industrious; hard-working.—**op·er·ose·ly,** *adv.*—**op·er·ose·ness,** *n.*

oph·i·cleide, of′i·klīd″, *n.* [Fr. *ophicléide,* < Gr. *ophis,* serpent, and *kleis (kleid-),* key.] An obsolete musical wind instrument, consisting of a conical metal tube bent double, and usu. having eleven keys.

o·phid·i·an, ō·fid′ē·an, *a.* [Gr. *ophis,* a serpent.] Of, pertaining to, or characteristic of snakes.—*n.* A snake.

oph·i·ol·o·gy, of″ē·ol′o·jē, ō″fē·ol′o·jē, *n.* The branch of zoology which treats of snakes.—**oph·i·o·log·i·cal,** of″ē·o·loj′i·kal, *a.*—**oph·i·ol·o·gist,** *n.*

oph·ite, of′īt, ō′fīt, *n.* [Gr. *ophis,* a serpent.] A green porphyry or serpentine; a diabase.

o·phit·ic, ō·fit′ik, *a.* Pertaining to the rock texture of certain ophites, in which feldspar crystals are embedded in a matrix.

oph·thal·mi·a, of·thal′mē·a, op·thal′mē·a, *n.* [Gr., < *ophthalmos,* the eye, < root *op,* to see, as in *optic.*] *Pathol.* inflammation of the eyelid, the eye, or its membranes.

oph·thal·mic, of·thal′mik, op·thal′mik, *a.* Belonging or pertaining to the eye.

oph·thal·mol·o·gist, of″thal·mol′o·jist, op″thal·mol′o·jist, *n.* A medical doctor whose specialty is ophthalmology.

oph·thal·mol·o·gy, of″thal·mol′o·jē, of″thal·mol′o·jē, of″tha·mol′o·jē, op″thal·mol′o·jē, op″thal·mol′o·jē, op″tha·mol′o·jē, *n. Med.* the science that deals with the anatomy, functions, and diseases of the eye.—**oph·thal·mo·log·ic, oph·thal·mo·log·i·cal,** of·thal″mo·loj′ik, op·thal″mo·loj′ik, *a.*—**oph·thal·mo·log·i·cal·ly,** *adv.*

oph·thal·mo·scope, of·thal′mo·skōp″, op·thal′mo·skōp″, *n.* An instrument for viewing the interior of the eye or examining the retina.—**oph·thal·mo·scop·ic, oph·thal·mo·scop·i·cal,** of·thal″mo·skop′ik, op·thal″mo·skop′ik, *a.*—**oph·thal·mos·co·py,** of″thal·mos′ko·pē, op″thal·mos′ko·pē, *n. pl.* **oph·thal·mos·co·pies.**

o·pi·ate, ō′pē·it, ō′pē·āt″, *n.* [< *opium.*] Any medicine that contains opium or one of its derivatives and has the quality of inducing sleep or alleviating pain. *Colloq.* any narcotic; anything that dulls sensation, quiets the nerves, or causes relaxation.—*a.* Inducing sleep; narcotic; containing opium.—ō′pē·āt″, *v.t.—opiated, opiating.* To administer an opiate to; deaden or depress.

o·pine, ō·pīn′, *v.t.—opined, opining.* [Fr. *opiner,* < L. *opinor,* to think.] To think; to suppose; to hold as an impression or opinion.—*v.i.* To state an opinion.

o·pin·ion, o·pin′yan, *n.* [L. *opinio, opinionis,* < *opinor,* to think; same root as *opto,* to wish, *optimus,* best.] A judgment or belief that is stronger than an impression but less firm than positive knowledge; a judgment or impression of persons or things regarding their character or qualities; a commonly held attitude or sentiment; as, public *opinion*; the official expression of a judgment by a qualified authority; *law,* the statement made by the court setting forth the reasoning and legal principles involved in making a particular decision.

o·pin·ion·at·ed, o·pin′ya·nā″tid, *a.* Conceited or obstinate in opinion; dogmatic.—**o·pin·ion·at·ed·ly,** *adv.*—**o·pin·ion·at·ed·ness,** *n.*

o·pin·ion·a·tive, o·pin′ya·nā″tiv, *a.* Of or relating to opinion; dogmatic; obstinate in beliefs.—**o·pin·ion·a·tive·ly,** *adv.*—**o·pin·ion·a·tive·ness,** *n.*

op·is·thog·na·thous, op″is·thog′na·thus, *a.* [Gr. *opisthen,* behind, and *gnathos,* jaw.] Of a skull or an animal, having receding jaws; of a jaw, receding.—**op·is·thog·na·thism,** *n.*

o·pi·um, ō′pē·um, *n.* [L., < Gr. *opion,* poppy juice, opium, dim. of *opos,* juice.] The dried juice of the unripe fruit of the opium poppy, *Papaver somniferum,* a poisonous, narcotic, addictive alkaloid from which morphine and codeine are derived.

o·pi·um pop·py, *n.* A glaucous, annual herb, *Papaver somniferum,* native to the Orient, but now grown throughout the world for its capsule fruits, from which a milky juice is obtained that yields opium; the white, pink, and red flowers of this plant cultivated as an ornamental.

o·pos·sum, o·pos′um, pos′um, *n.* pl. **o·pos·sums, o·pos·sum.** [N. Amer. Ind.] A marsupial, nocturnal mammal, *Didelphis virginiana,* native to eastern U.S., having a prehensile tail, carrying its young in an abdominal pouch, and noted for feigning death when in danger.

op·po·nent, o·pō′nent, *n.* [L. *opponens, opponentis,* ppr. of *oppono,* to oppose.] One who supports the opposite side in a controversy, argument, game, or the like; an adversary.—*a.* Opposing, antagonistic; opposite in position; *anat.* of a muscle, acting against or limiting the movement of another by bringing parts into opposition.

op·por·tune, op″ĕr·tön′, op″ĕr·tūn′, *a.* [Fr. *opportun,* < L. *opportunis,* lit. 'offering a port or harbor,' < *portus,* a port.] Particularly suitable or appropriate; well-timed; timely or convenient.—**op·por·tune·ly,** *adv.*—**op·por·tune·ness,** *n.*

op·por·tun·ism, op″ĕr·tö′niz·um, op″ĕr·tū′niz·um, *n.* The practice or policy of turning every opportunity to one's own advantage, with relatively small regard for possible consequences or the moral or ethical principles involved; an instance of such behavior.—**op·por·tun·ist,** *n., a.*—**op·por·tun·is·tic,** op″ĕr·tö·nis′tik, op″ĕr·tū·nis′tik, *a.*—**op·por·tun·is·ti·cal·ly,** *adv.*

op·por·tu·ni·ty, op″ĕr·tö′ni·tē, op″ĕr·tū′ni·tē, *n. pl.* **op·por·tu·ni·ties.** [L. *opportunitas.*] An appropriate or convenient time or occasion; a favorable position or chance.

op·pos·a·ble, o·pō′za·bl, *a.* Capable of being opposed or resisted; capable of being opposed or put opposite to something else, as the thumb and forefinger.—**op·pos·a·bil·i·ty,** o·pō″za·bil′i·tē, *n.*

op·pose, o·pōz′, *v.t.—opposed, opposing.* [O.Fr. Fr. *opposer.*] To act against or contend in opposition to; to strive against, resist, or combat; to set as an opponent or adversary, or as a resisting or combating force; to set as an obstacle or hindrance; to stand in the way of; to use or take as being opposite or contrary; to set against in some relation as of offsetting or contrast; as, to *oppose* the advantages to the disadvantages; to set as to face or be opposite; to place in front.—*v.i.* To be or act in opposition.—**op·pos·er,** *n.*—**op·pos·ing·ly,** *adv.*

op·po·site, op′o·zot, op′o·sit, *a.* [O.Fr. Fr. *opposite,* < L. *oppositus,* pp. of *oppōnere,* put before or against, oppose.] Situated on opposed sides of something, as: The houses were on *opposite* sides of the street. Located in a corresponding position but against each other; as: They stood directly *opposite* each other, face to face. Tending or going away counter to one another; as, in the *opposite* direction; contrary or diametrically different; as, black is *opposite* to white; *bot.* situated on opposed sides of an axis, as leaves when there are two growing from one node on a stem.—*n.* One who or that which is contrary or opposite.—*adv.*—*prep.* Facing; in a part complementary to; as, to play *opposite* a famous actor.—**op·po·site·ly,** *adv.*—**op·po·site·ness,** *n.*

op·po·site num·ber, *n.* A counterpart; a comparable person, place, or thing in another place, time, system, or activity, as:

---

ch- chain, G. na**ch**t; **th-** **TH**en, **th**in; **w-** **w**ig, **hw** as sound in **wh**ig; **z-** **zh** as in azure, zeal. *Italicized vowel* indicates schwa sound.

A U.S. army general's *opposite number* in the navy is an admiral, George Washington's *opposite number* in South America was Simon Bolivar.

op·po·si·tion, op"o·zish'an, *n.* [Partly < *oppose,* partly < *opposite.*] The act or condition of opposing, checking, or restraining; the state of being opposed or contrasted; antagonism or resistance; that which opposes, or the collective body of opposers; the political party opposed to the administration or the party in power; a standing or placing over or against something; *astron.* the situation of two heavenly bodies when diametrically opposite to each other, or when their longitudes differ by 180°; *logic,* the relationship between propositions having identical subjects and predicates but being unlike in quantities or qualities, or both.—**op·po·si·tion·al,** *a.*

op·press, o·pres', *v.t.* [O.Fr. Fr. *oppresser,* < M.L. *oppressāre,* freq. of L. *opprimere* (pp. *oppressus*), press against, bear down, subdue, < *ob,* against, and *premere,* press.] To burden with cruel or unreasonable restrictions; to tyrannize; to treat with unjust severity, rigor, or hardship; to subdue; suppress; to weigh down, as weariness does; to lie heavy upon, as care or sorrow; to depress.—**op·pres·si·ble,** *a.* —**op·pres·sor,** *n.*

op·pres·sion, o·presh'an, *n.* The act of oppressing; excessively restrictive authority or power; severity; hardship; cruelty; a sense of heaviness or weight in the mind or body; depression.

op·pres·sive, o·pres'iv, *a.* Unreasonably burdensome; unjustly severe; given to oppression; tyrannical; overpowering; overwhelming.—**op·pres·sive·ly,** *adv.*—**op·pres·sive·ness,** *n.*

op·pro·bri·ous, o·prō'brē·us, *a.* [L.L. *opprobriosus.*] Conveying or expressing opprobrium, as language, epithets, or a speaker; imputing disgrace or shame; abusive; disgraceful or shameful.—**op·pro·bri·ous·ly,** *adv.*—**op·pro·bri·ous·ness,** *n.*

op·pro·bri·um, o·prō'brē·um, *n.* [L.] The disgrace or reproach incurred by conduct considered shameful or wrong; infamy; scornful reproach; a cause or object of such reproach.

op·pugn, o·pūn', *v.t.* [L. *oppugno*—*ob-,* against, and *pugno,* to fight, < *pugnus,* the fist.] To attack by arguments or criticism; to oppose; to question; to exercise hostile reasoning against.—**op·pugn·er,** *n.*

op·so·nin, op'so·nin, *n.* [Gr. *opsōn,* cooked meat.] *Bact.* a constituent of blood serum which causes invading cells or bacteria to become more susceptible to the destructive action of the phagocytes.—**op·son·ic,** op·son'ik, *a.*

opt, opt, *v.i.* [Fr. *opter,* < L. *optare* (pp. *optatus*), choose, wish.] To make a choice; choose. Also **op·tate.**

op·ta·tive, op'ta·tiv, *a.* [L. *optativus,* < *opto,* to desire or wish.] Expressing a desire or wish; *gram.* applied to that mood of the verb in which wish or desire is expressed.— **op·ta·tive·ly,** *adv.*

op·tic, op'tik, *a.* [Fr. *optique,* < M.L. *opticus,* < Gr. *optikos.*] Pertaining to sight or vision; pertaining to or connected with the eye as the organ of sight, or sight as a function of the brain; constructed to assist the sight; acting by means of sight or light; optical.—*n.* Usu. *pl.,* colloq. the eyes.

op·ti·cal, op'ti·kal, *a.* Pertaining to sight; visual; constructed to assist the sight, as devices; acting by means of sight or light, as instruments; related to the eye; pertaining to optics; dealing with or skilled in optics.—**op·ti·cal·ly,** *adv.*

op·ti·cal art, *n.* Op art.

op·ti·cal il·lu·sion, *n.* A deceptive or misleading image or visual impression pre-

sented to the vision; something that deceives by presenting a false impression to the eyes.

op·ti·cal·ly ac·tive, *a.* Characterized by the power to rotate the plane of polarization of light.

op·ti·cal·ly in·ac·tive, *a.* Pertaining to compounds which are optically neutral in plane-polarized light.

op·ti·cal ro·ta·tion, *n. Physical chem.* the power possessed by certain substances to rotate the oscillations of light through an arc to a degree intrinsic in the substance.

op·tic ax·is, *n.* A line or direction through a doubly-refracting crystal along which a ray of light undergoes no double refraction.

op·ti·cian, op·tish'an, *n.* One who makes glasses for remedying defects of vision in accordance with the prescriptions of oculists.

op·tic nerve, *n. Anat.* one of a pair of cranial nerves of sight.

op·tics, op'tiks, *n. pl. but sing. in constr.* The branch of physical science that deals with vision, and the properties and phenomena of light, its origins and effects, and its role as a medium of sight.

op·tic thal·a·mus, *n.* The thalamus.

op·ti·mal, op'ti·mal, *a.* Optimum.

op·ti·mism, op'ti·miz"um, *n.* [< L. *optimus,* best.] An inclination to emphasize the happy aspect of any happening or circumstance. *Phil.* the conviction that the world is good and is building toward the ultimate in excellence.—**op·ti·mist,** op'-ti·mist, *n.*—**op·ti·mis·tic,** op"ti·mis'tik, *a.* —**op·ti·mis·ti·cal·ly,** *adv.*

op·ti·mize, op'ti·miz", *v.i.*—*optimized, optimizing.* To hold or express optimistic views.—*v.t.* To make the best of; to make or arrange something in order to be highly functional or effective. *Computer technology,* to establish a program which will automatically adapt itself to achieve maximum efficiency in the operation of a computer; to revise a program for this purpose.— **op·ti·mi·za·tion,** *n.*

op·ti·mum, op'ti·mum, *n. pl.* **op·ti·ma,** **op·ti·mums,** op'ti·ma. [L., prop. neut. of *optimus,* best (superl. of *bonus,* good), akin to *ops,* power, means, wealth.] The best or most favorable point, degree, or amount for the purpose, as of temperature, light, or moisture for the growth or reproduction of an organism; the best possible result or highest degree which can be obtained given certain conditions.—*a.* Highly favorable, best, most desirable; as, *optimum* circumstances.

op·tion, op'shan, *n.* [L. *optiō,* option, < *opto,* to wish or desire.] The power of choice; the thing chosen or elected; the action of making a choice; a buyer's purchased privilege to decide to buy or sell within an agreed period of time on specified terms; the power of buying something at a future date; the right of the beneficiary of an insurance policy, or the insured person, to determine the intervals and the amount in which the benefits shall be paid.— **op·tion·al,** *a.* Left to one's choice or preference.—**op·tion·al·ly,** *adv.*

op·tom·e·trist, op·tom'i·trist, *n.* One who is skilled in optometry.

op·tom·e·try, op·tom'i·trē, *n.* The measurement and examination of the visual powers; the practice or art of testing the eyes by means of suitable instruments or appliances for defects of vision in order to correct them with glasses.—**op·to·met·ric, op·to·met·ri·cal,** op"to·me'tri·kal, *a.*

op·u·lent, op'ū·lent, *a.* [L. *opulens* (-ent-), *opulentus,* < *ops,* power, means, wealth.] Endowed with wealth or power; yielding riches; richly or abundantly supplied.— **op·u·lent·ly,** *adv.*—**op·u·lence,** op'ū·lens, *n.*

o·pun·ti·a, ō·pun'shē·a, ō·pun'sha, *n.* [N.L., < L. *Opuntius,* pertaining to *Opus,* a town in Locris, Greece.] *Bot.* any of several species of American cacti of the genus *Opuntia,* characterized by flattened to globose, spiny branches, showy yellow to red-colored flowers, and producing edible, pear-shaped fruits. Also *prickly pear.*

o·pus, ō'pus, *n. pl.* **o·pe·ra, o·pus·es,** op'ėr·a. [L. *pl. opera.*] A literary work; a musical composition or collection of a composer's compositions usu. numbered chronologically according to publication. *Colloq.* a play on television or radio; a movie. Abbr. *op.*

o·pus·cule, ō·pus'kūl, *n.* [L. *opusculum,* dim. of *opus.*] A small or insignificant work; a literary or musical work of small size.— **o·pus·cu·lar,** *a.*

or, ar, *unstressed* ėr, *conj.* [M.E. *or,* contr. of *other,* < O.E. *oththe* = O.H.G. *eddo, odo* (G. *oder*), = Goth. *aiththau,* or.] A particle used to connect words, phrases, or clauses representing alternatives; as, this road *or* that; one used to connect alternative or equivalent terms; as, the Hawaiian *or* Sandwich Islands; a word often used in correlation, as in *either ... or, or ... or,* and *whether ... or;* a word used to clarify or correct something just said, as: The previous report, *or* rather rumor, was false.

or, ar, *prep., conj.* [M.E. *or, ar,* var. (due in part to Icel. *ār,* early) of *er,* < O.E. *ǣr,* E. *ere.*] *Archaic.* Before; ere; sooner than or rather than.

or, ar, *n.* [Fr. *or,* < L. *aurum,* gold.] *Heraldry.* The metal or tincture gold; yellow when used to represent gold.—*a.* Of the metal or color gold.

or·ach, or·ache, ar'ach, or'ach, *n.* [Formerly *arrach,* < Fr. *arroche,* orache; origin unknown.] *Bot.* a garden plant, *Atriplex hortensis,* in the goosefoot family, grown for greens, and similar to the spinach.

or·a·cle, ar'a·kl, or'a·kl, *n.* [L. *orāculum,* < *oro,* to speak, to pray, < *os, oris,* the mouth.] A place where hidden knowledge is believed to be revealed, often in ambiguous terms, esp. the shrine of Apollo at Adelphi in ancient Greece; the agency that does the revealing, or what is revealed; a revelation or divine utterance for the guidance of man, or the one who does such revealing; a person whose judgments have great weight. *Bib.* the inner part of the Temple of Solomon; the wisdom of the prophets.—**o·rac·u·lar,** ō·rak'ū·lėr, *a.*— **o·rac·u·lar·i·ty,** ō·rak"ū·lar'i·tē, *n.*— **o·rac·u·lar·ly,** *adv.*

o·ral, ōr'al, ar'al, *a.* [L. *ōs* (*ōr-*), mouth.] Of or pertaining to the mouth; as, the *oral* cavity; done, taken, or administered by the mouth; as, an *oral* contraceptive; uttered by the mouth, or spoken; as, *oral* testimony; employing speech, as teachers or methods of teaching; *zool.* referring to that surface or area of a polyp where the mouth is located; *phon.* articulated through the mouth only, without nasal resonance; *psychoanal.* relating to the initial phase of psychosexual growth during which the oral gratifications of sucking and biting are as yet undifferentiated from sexual gratifications; pertaining to personality patterns or traits which reflect the nature of one's primary libido experiences; as, *oral* aggressiveness.—**o·ral·ly,** *adv.*

or·ange, or'inj, *n.* [O.Fr. *orenge* (Fr. *orange*), < Ar. *nāranj,* < Pers. *nārang,* orange.] The globose, reddish-yellow edible fruit of *Citrus aurantium,* a white-flowered evergreen rutaceous tree cultivated in warm countries; the tree itself, occurring in several varieties, as *Citrus aurantium sinensis,* common sweet orange, and *C. aurantium amara,* bitter orange or Seville orange; any of several other citrus trees,

---

a- fat, fāte, fär, fåre, fall; **e-** met, mē, mēre, hėr; **i-** pin, pīne; **o-** not, nōte, mŏve; **u-** tub, cūbe, bŭll; **oi-** oil; **ou-** pound.

as *C. trifoliata*, trifoliate orange, a hardy Japanese species cultivated widely in the U.S., for hedges; the fruit of such trees; a moraceous tree, the Osage orange, *Maclura pomiferum*, or the fruit; a reddish-yellow color.—*a.* Of or pertaining to the orange; of a reddish-yellow color; made with or flavored like the orange, as a food or beverage.

or·ange·ade, or″inj·ād′, or″in·jād′, *n.* A drink made of orange juice and sweetened water, often carbonated.

or·ange hawk·weed, *n.* A herbaceous plant, *Hieracium aurantiacum*, of the composite family, having orange- to flame-colored flowers, introduced into the U.S. as a garden plant but now naturalized. Also *devil's paintbrush.*

Or·ange·ism, or′in·jiz″um, *n.* The principle of Irish Protestant ascendancy upheld by the Orangemen.—**Or·ange·ist,** *n.*

Or·ange·man, or′inj·man″, *n.* pl. **Or·ange·men.** [From William III of England, Prince of *Orange*, a place now in France.] A member of a secret society instituted in Ireland in 1795 to uphold Protestant ascendancy; a Northern Ireland Protestant.

or·ange pe·koe, *n.* Black tea made from tiny top leaves; high quality tea from India or Ceylon.

or·ange·ry, or′inj·rē, *n.* pl. **or·ange·ries.** [Fr. *orangerie.*] A protected garden or greenhouse where oranges are grown.

or·ange·wood, or′inj·wud″, *n.* The hardwood of orange trees in the genus *Citrus*, used esp. in carvings and lathe work.

o·rang·u·tan, o·rang·u·tan, o·rang-ou·tan, ō·rang′ụ·tan″, ạ·rang′ụ·tan″, *n.* [Malay *orangutan*, lit. 'man of the woods.'] An arboreal, anthropoid ape of the genus *Pongo*, native to Sumatra and Borneo, characterized by extremely long arms for size of body, a mongoloid look, and brownish-red hair. Also **o·rang, o·rang·u·tang, o·rang-ou·tang, o·rang-ou·tang,** ō·rang′ụ·tang″, ạ·rang′ụ·tang″, *o·rang′-ụ·tang″.*

o·rate, ō·rāt′, ōr′āt, *v.i.*—*orated, orating.* To deliver an oration; to speak in an ostentatious or pompous manner.—*v.t.* To declaim.

o·ra·tion, ō·rā′shạn, *n.* [L. *oratio*, < *oro, oratum*, to pray.] A formal discourse carefully prepared and given on a special occasion; a speech, formal in style and delivery.

or·a·tor, ạr′a·tẽr, or′a·tẽr, *n.* [L.] A public speaker; one who delivers an oration; one who is skilled as a speaker; an eloquent man.—**or·a·tor·i·cal,** ạr′a·tạr′i·kạl, or″a·tor′i·kal, *a.*—**or·a·tor·i·cal·ly,** *adv.*

or·a·to·ri·o, ạr″a·tōr′ē·ō″, or″a·tōr′ē·ō″, *n.* pl. **or·a·to·ri·os.** [It., < L.L *oratorium*, E. *oratory*; so named from the musical services in the church of the Oratory of St. Philip Neri, in Rome.] An extended musical composition for solo voices, chorus, and orchestra, with a text more or less dramatic in character usu. based upon a religious theme, and performed without action, costume, or scenery.

or·a·to·ry, ạr′a·tōr″ē, or′a·tōr″ē, *n.* [L. *oratoria*, prop. fem. of *oratorius*, pertaining to an orator or to praying, < *orator.*] The art of an orator; the art of public speaking; the exercise of eloquence; eloquent speaking or language.

or·a·to·ry, ạr′a·tōr″ē, or′a·tōr″ē, *n.* pl. **or·a·to·ries.** [L.L. *oratorium*, place of prayer, prop. neut. of L. *oratorius.*] A place of prayer; a small chapel or a room for private devotions. (*Cap.*) any of certain religious societies of the Rom. Cath. Ch. composed of secular priests, not bound by vows; a house of this society.

orb, ạrb, *n.* [L. *orbis*, circle, disc, orb.] A sphere or globe; the emblem of sovereignty,

being a globe topped by a cross. *Chiefly poet.* any of the heavenly bodies; the eyeball or eye. *Astrol.* the space within which the influence of a planet or star is supposed to act; *archaic*, a circle or something circular. —*v.t.* To form into a circle or sphere; *archaic*, to encircle.—*v.i.* To move in an orbit; to assume the shape of an orb.

or·bic·u·lar, ạr·bik′ū·lẽr, *a.* [L.L. *orbicularis*, < L. *orbiculus*, dim. of *orbis*, E. *orb.*] Like an orb; circular; ringlike; spherical; rounded; *bot.* circular or disc-shaped, as the leaf of the lotus. Also **or·bic·u·late,** ạr·bik′ū·lit, ạr·bik′ū·lāt″.—**or·bic·u·lar·i·ty,** ạr·bik″ū·lar′i·tē, *n.*—**or·bic·u·lar·ly,** *adv.*

or·bit, ạr′bit, *n.* [L. *orbita*, a wheeltrack, a circuit, < *orbis*, an orb.] The curved line which a planet describes in its periodical revolution around its central body; a sphere of activity, or customary range of activity; *phys.* the assumed path described by an electron circling an atomic nucleus; *anat.* the bony cavity in which the eye is situated; *ornith.* the skin which surrounds the eye of a bird.—*v.t.* To project into an orbital path, as a man-made satellite; to circle around, as a planet or satellite.—*v.i.* To travel or move in circles.—**or·bit·al,** **or·bit·ar·y,** *a.*—**or·bit·er,** *n.*

orc, ạrk, *n.* [L. *orca*, kind of whale.] Any of various marine mammals, as the grampus or killer whale; a cetacean.

or·chard, ạr′chẽrd, *n.* [O.E. *ortgeard*, appar. < L. *hortus*, garden, and O.E. *geard*, E. *yard*: cf. Goth. *aurtigards*, Icel. *jurtagardhr*, garden.] A section of land devoted to the raising of fruit trees, usu. enclosed and often near a dwelling; the fruit trees growing on such an area.—**or·char·dist,** ạr′chẽr·dist, *n.* One who cultivates an orchard; also **or·chard·man.**

or·ches·tra, ạr′ki·strạ, *n.* [L., < Gr. *orchēstra*, < *orcheisthai*, dance.] A company of performers on various musical instruments, esp. stringed instruments of the violin class, woodwinds, brass, and percussion, for playing concert music, as symphonies, operas, and other compositions. In the ancient Greek theater, the circular space in front of the stage, allotted to the chorus; in the Roman theater, a similar space reserved for persons of distinction. In a modern theater, the space reserved for the musicians, usually the front part of the main floor; also **or·ches·tra pit.** The entire main floor space for spectators.—**or·ches·tral,** ạr·kes′tral, *a.* Of or pertaining to or suggesting an orchestra; composed for or performed by an orchestra. —**or·ches·tral·ly,** *adv.*

or·ches·trate, ạr′ki·strāt″, *v.t.*—*orchestrated, orchestrating.* [Cf. Fr. *orchestrer.*] To compose or arrange, as music, for performance by an orchestra.—**or·ches·tra·tion,** *n.* The act, art, or result of orchestrating.—**or·ches·tra·tor, or·ches·trat·er,** *n.*

or·chid, ạr′kid, *n.* [Gr. *orchis*, a testicle, hence an orchid, from the form of the root.] Any of certain temperate to tropical plants of the family *Orchidaceae*, either terrestrial or epiphytic, with showy, irregular, colorful flowers; a plant belonging to the orchid family; a light bluish-red to light purple color; *usu. pl., fig.* praise for work well done.—*a.* Light bluish-red to light purple.—**or·chi·da·ceous,** *a.*

or·chis, ạr′kis, *n.* [L., < Gr. *órchis*, orchis (named from the shape of the root), orig. testicle.] Any of various terrestrial, north temperate orchids of the genus *Orchis*, having rose-pink flowers borne in open spikes and growing in boglike habitats; a common name for other orchids.

or·dain, ạr·dān′, *v.t.* [O.Fr. *ordener* (Fr. *ordonner*) < L. *ordināre* (pp. *ordinatus*) order, arrange, appoint, < *ordo* (ordin-).]

Eccles. to invest with ministerial or priestly functions; to confer holy orders upon. To decree, as an edict; to give orders for; to destine or predestine: said of God or fate.— *v.i.* To decree; to order; to command.— **or·dain·er,** *n.*—**or·dain·ment,** *n.*

or·deal, ạr·dēl′, ạr·dē′al, ạr′dēl, *n.* [O.E. *ordel, ordāl*, decision, ordeal, lit. 'out-deal' (like D. *oordeel*, G. *urtheil*, a decision).] Any severe trial, strict test, or trying experience; an ancient form of trial to determine guilt or innocence by causing the accused to face serious physical danger, escape from injury being considered a proof of innocence.

or·der, ạr′dẽr, *n.* [O.Fr. Fr. *ordre*, < L. *ordō* (ordin-), row, series, rank, class, regular arrangement, order.] A state or condition marked by harmony or methodical arrangement; the successive or proper arrangement of things; a social state of established authority and observance of the law; a properly functioning state or condition; the customary mode, procedure, or established usage, esp. the prescribed conduct for debates, legislative bodies, or public meetings; a rank, grade, or class of society; an authoritative direction, injunction, or mandate; a command; a direction or commission to make or provide something; the furnished object; a body or society of persons living by common consent under the same religious, moral, or social regulations; a body of persons of the same occupation or pursuits; as, a clerical *order*; any class, kind, or sort of people or things having a particular rank in a scale or distinguished from others by nature or character; as, talents of high *order*; a monastic society or fraternity: historically, a society or fraternity of knights of combined military and monastic character; as, the Teutonic *Order*; an institution having as its purpose the rewarding of meritorious service by the conferring of a dignity; as, the *Order* of the Golden Fleece; the badge or insignia of such an institution. *Arch.* a column viewed as the characteristic element of an architectural style; any one of the typical styles of classical architecture, as the Doric, Ionic, Corinthian, Tuscan, and Composite. *Law*, a direction of a court or judge made or entered in writing but not included in the judgment; *biol.* a taxonomic category ranking below the class and above the family. *Eccles.* a prescribed form for divine service or administration of a rite; any one of the degrees or grades of the clerical office; *usu. pl.* the rank or status of an ordained Christian minister; the rite or sacrament of ordination. *Math.* a degree of complexity in algebra; *milit.* a rifle position in which the rifle butt is on the ground and the weapon is held vertically against the right side; *theol.* any of the nine ranks of choir of angels.— **in or·der to,** as a means to; with a view to.

or·der, ạr′dẽr, *v.t.* To arrange methodically or in a particular sequence; to regulate, conduct, or manage, as: I had to *order* my travels methodically. To ordain, will, or destine; to give an order for; to direct or command to be done; prescribe; to direct to be made, supplied, or furnished; *eccles.* to invest with clerical rank or authority. To issue orders or instructions, or to give commands; to give an order or commission. —**or·der arms,** to bring a rifle into the order position.—**or·der·er,** *n.*

or·dered, ạr′dẽrd, *a.* Marked by order; having a regular system or pleasing arrangement; having elements or quantities arranged in a specific sequence.

or·dered pair, *n. Math.* two numbers or quantities written or set down in a manner indicating that one of the pair is first or is to be considered or treated before the other.

or·der·ly, ạr'dẽr·lē, *a.* Arranged or disposed in order; characterized by regular sequence or arrangement; observant of or exhibiting order, system, or method, as persons or the mind; characterized by or observant of rule or discipline; not unruly or disorderly; *milit.* pertaining to orders or commands, or charged with the communication or execution of orders.—*adv.* In regular sequence; with proper arrangement; methodically; according to established order or rule.—**or·der·li·ness,** *n.*

or·der·ly, ạr'dẽr·lē, *n.* pl. **or·der·lies.** An army private or a noncommissioned officer who performs menial tasks and carries orders or messages for a superior officer; a hospital attendant who performs nonmedical services.

or·di·nal, ạr'di·nal, *a.* [L. *ordinālis,* < *ordō, ordinis,* a row.] Expressing order or succession; as, the *ordinal* numbers, *first, second, third; biol.* pertaining to an order.— *n.* A number denoting order or degree, as *second, tenth;* also **or·di·nal num·ber.** *Eccles.* a book containing the ordination service.

or·di·nance, ạr'di·nans, *n.* [O.Fr. *ordenance* (Fr. *ordonnance*), < *ordener,* to ordain.] A law, edict, or decree established by authority; a law or provision enacted by a municipal government for local application. *Eccles.* an established rite or ceremony; a decree of God or fate.

or·di·nand, ạr'di·nand″, *n.* [L. *ordinandus,* gerundive of *ordinare.*] *Eccles.* one about to receive holy orders.

or·di·nar·i·ly, ạr'di·nâr'i·lē, ạr'di·ner″- i·lē, *adv.* In the customary or usual way; in ordinary cases; usually; in an ordinary degree or to the usual extent.

or·di·nar·y, ạr'di·ner″ē, *a.* [L. *ordinārius,* < *ordo* (*ordin-*).] Customary, usual, or normal; of the usual kind; not distinguished in any important way from others; often, somewhat inferior or below the average level of quality; pertaining to jurisdiction which is immediate, rather than delegated. —*n.* Something regular, customary, or usual; the commonplace condition or degree; as, out of the *ordinary. Eccles.* an order or form for divine service, esp. that for saying Mass; the service of the Mass exclusive of the canon; one having ordinary or immediate jurisdiction, as a bishop in his diocese. *Hist.* formerly, a clergyman appointed to prepare condemned prisoners for death. In some states of the U.S., a judge of a court of probate. A high bicycle of an early type, with one large and one small wheel. *Brit.* a meal regularly served at a fixed price in an eatinghouse or inn; a place where such meals are served.— **or·di·nar·i·ness,** *n.*

or·di·nate, ạr'di·nāt″, ạr'di·nit, *a.* [L. *ordinātus,* well-ordered.] Regular; methodical.—*n. Math.* the coordinate of a point in a plane Cartesian coordinate system equal to its distance from the x-axis measured along a line parallel to the y-axis.

or·di·na·tion, ạr'di·nā'shan, *n.* [L. *ordinātiō,* regulation, < *ordinō,* to ordain.] *Eccles.* the conferring or the reception of holy orders. The act of settling, arranging, or establishing.

ord·nance, ạrd'nans, *n.* [Same as *ordinance,* Fr. *ordonnance,* arrangement, equipment; orig. it had reference to guns of a particular size or equipment.] Artillery; weapons, ammunition, vehicles, and other military equipment collectively; (*sometimes cap.*), *milit.* the department in charge of arsenals, depots, and the purchase, manufacture, storage, distribution, and development of military equipment.

or·don·nance, ạr'do·nans, Fr. ạʀ·dạ·- näns', *n.* [Fr.] A pleasing or effective arrangement or disposition of parts, as of

a building, a picture, or a literary composition; an ordinance, decree, or law.

Or·do·vi·cian, ạr″do·vish'an, *a.* [L. *Ordovices,* pl., an ancient British tribe in northern Wales.] *Geol.* of or pertaining to a period in the Paleozoic era, between the Cambrian and Silurian periods, beginning about 500 million years ago and ending about 440 million years ago.—*n.* The Ordovician period or rock system. See Table of Geologic Time.

or·dure, ạr'jẽr, ạr'dūr, *n.* [Fr. *ordure,* < O.Fr. *ord,* filthy, L. *horridus,* horrid.] Dung; excrement; feces.

ore, ōr, *n.* [O.E. *ōra* (= D. *oer*), ore; with mod. form prob. due to association with O.E. *ār,* brass.] A metal-bearing mineral or rock, or a native metal, esp. when valuable enough to be mined; a mineral or natural product serving as a source of some nonmetallic substance, as sulfur.

o·re·ad, ōr'ē·ad″, *n.* [Gr. *oreiás, oreiados;* < *óros,* mountain.] *Mythol.* A mountain nymph; any of a group of nymphs of hills and mountains.

ore dress·ing, *n. Metal.* the mechanical technique of separating metal from ore without chemical change, as by crushing.

o·reg·a·no, o·reg'a·nō″, ä·reg'a·nō″, *n.* [Sp.] *Bot.* a perennial herb, *Origanum vulgare,* in the mint family, cultivated for its purple-pink spiked flowers and its aromatic leaves which are used as a condiment. Also **wild mar·jo·ram.**

Or·e·gon grape, or'e·gon grāp', or'e·gon″ *n.* An evergreen shrub, *Mahonia aquifolium,* in the barberry family, native to northwest N. America, having yellow flowers, hollylike leaves and blue berries, and used in the Christmas trade: the state flower of Oregon. Also **ma·ho·nia.**

or·gan, ạr'gan, *n.* [L. *organum,* Gr. *organon,* instrument, tool, bodily organ, musical instrument, < *erg-,* work.] *Mus.* any of various musical instruments, consisting of one or more sets of pipes which produce notes by means of compressed air, played by means of keys arranged in one or more keyboards; one of the independent sets of pipes of such an instrument; a reed organ, harmonium, or American organ; a barrel organ or hand organ. An instrument or means of performance; a means or medium of commmunicating thoughts, opinions; as, a company publication or house *organ;* a newspaper serving as the mouthpiece of a political party; *anat., biol.* a part or member of living organisms, as the heart or a leaf, having some specific function.

or·gan bank, *n.* A place where human or animal organs or tissues are stored for future surgical use as transplants; a supply of such organs and tissues.

or·gan·dy, or·gan·die, ạr'gan·dē, *n.* [Fr. *organdi.*] A fine, translucent, stiff-finished muslin, often printed or dyed, used for dresses, curtains, and other sheer items.

or·gan·elle, ạr″ga·nel', ạr'ga·nel″, *n. Biol.* a part of a cell having a specific function.

or·gan grind·er, *n.* A street musician who plays a hand organ or hurdy-gurdy.

or·gan·ic, ạr·gan'ik, *a.* [L. *organicus,* < Gr. *organikos,* < *organon,* organ.] Pertaining to the organs of an animal or plant; pertaining to the alteration of the structure of an organ; having organs; characterized by the systematic arrangement of parts into a whole; systematic; pertaining to the structure of a thing; constitutional. *Chem.* pertaining to a class of chemical compounds which formerly comprised only those existing in or derived from plants or animals, but which now includes these and all other compounds of carbon. *Law,* pertaining to the framework of laws forming the organization of a government. *Agric.* pertaining to the use of such nonchemical

fertilizers as manure and compost.— **or·gan·i·cal·ly,** *adv.*

or·gan·ic dis·ease, *n. Pathol.* a disease in which there is a structural alteration in the organ involved: opposed to *functional disease.*

or·gan·i·cism, ạr·gan'i·siz″um, *n. Biol.* the theory that the life process is dependent on the interrelated activity of the parts of the organism and not on the separate, individual organs; *pathol.* the doctrine that symptoms and disease are caused by diseased organs only; *sociol.* a view of society as a system of interdependent elements.—**or·gan·i·cist,** *n.*

or·gan·ism, ạr'ga·niz″um, *n.* An individual life form composed of a number of mutually dependent parts; any form of animal or plant life, often used of minute, obscure, or not readily classified forms; as, microscopic *organisms;* any organized body or system analogous to a living being; as, the social *organism.*—**or·gan·is·mic,** ạr'ga·niz'mik, *a.*—**or·gan·is·mi·cal·ly,** *adv.*

or·gan·ist, ạr'ga·nist, *n.* One who plays an organ.

or·gan·i·za·tion, ạr'ga·ni·zā'shan, *n.* The act or process of organizing; the state or the manner of being organized; organic structure; that which is organized; a biologic organism; any organized whole; a body of persons organized for some end or work; the officials, workers, and committees comprising a political party.—**or·gan·i·za-- tion·al,** *a.*—**or·gan·i·za·tion·al·ly,** *adv.*

or·gan·ize, ạr'ga·nīz″, *v.t.*—**organized, organizing.** [= Fr. *organiser,* < M.L. *organizare,* < Gr. *organizein,* organize, < *organon,* organ.] To form as or into a whole consisting of interdependent or coordinated parts, esp. for harmonious or united action; as, to *organize* the industries of a country for service in time of war; arrange in a systematic whole, or systematize; as, to *organize* knowledge or facts; prepare for arranging for various factors or details involved; as, to *organize* an expedition; to enroll, as employees, in a labor union; to unionize the employees of, as a factory.— *v.i.* To assume organic structure; to combine in an organized company, party, or the like.—**or·gan·iz·a·ble,** *a.*—**or·gan·iz·er,** ạr'ga·nī″zẽr, *n.*

or·ga·no·gen·e·sis, ạr″ga·nō·jen'i·sis, ạr·gan″o·jen'i·sis, *n.* [Gr. *organon,* an organ, and *genesis,* birth.] *Biol.* the development of an organ or of organs in plants or animals.—**or·ga·no·ge·net·ic,** ạr″ga·nō-- je·net'ik, ạr·gan″ō·je·net'ik, *a.*—**or·ga-- no·ge·net·i·cal·ly,** *adv.*

or·ga·nog·ra·phy, ạr″ga·nog'ra·fē, *n.* pl. **or·ga·nog·ra·phies.** The technical description of the organs of plants or animals. —**or·ga·no·graph·ic, or·ga·no·graph-- i·cal,** ạr″ga·no·graf'ik, *a.*—**or·ga·nog-- ra·phist,** *n.*

or·ga·nol·o·gy, ạr″ga·nol'o·jē, *n.* The study dealing with organic structure and function in animals or plants.—**or·ga-- no·log·ic, or·ga·no·log·i·cal,** ạr″ga·no·- loj'ik, ạ.—**or·ga·nol·o·gist,** *n.*

or·ga·non, ạr'ga·non″, *n.* pl. **or·ga·na, or·ga·nons,** ạr'ga·na. [Gr. *organon.*] An instrument of thought or knowledge; *philos.* a system of rules or principles to demonstrate or investigate pure knowledge. Also *organum.* (*Cap.*) the title of the treatises on logic by Aristotle.

or·ga·no·ther·a·py, ạr″ga·nō·ther'a·pē, ạr·gan″ō·ther'a·pē, *n.* [Gr. *organon,* and *therapeuō,* I heal.] *Med.* the use of extracts from animal organs, such as kidneys or thyroid glands, for therapeutic purposes. Also **or·ga·no·ther·a·peu·tics,** ạr″ga·- nō·ther'a·pū″tiks, ạr·gan″ō·ther'a·pū″tiks.

or·ga·num, ạr'ga·num, *n.* pl. **or·ga·na, or·ga·nums,** ạr'ga·na. [L.] An organon;

mus. a medieval type of vocal harmony which follows the melody at a consistent 4th or 5th interval; the harmonic part itself; also **di·a·pho·ny.**

or·gan·za, ạr´gan´za, *n.* A sheer, plain woven dress fabric, as of silk or rayon.

or·gan·zine, ạr´gan·zēn″, *n.* [Fr. *organsin*, It. *organzino.*] A silk thread of several strands twisted together; a fabric made of such thread.

or·gasm, ạr´gaz·um, *n.* [Fr. *orgasme*, < Gr. *organ*, swell, be excited.] The ultimate emotional and physical excitement of a sexual act; an instance of such; intense excitement.—**or·gas·mic, or·gas·tic,** ạr·gaz´mik, ạr·gas´tik, *a.*

or·geat, ạr´zhat, *Fr.* ạr·zhä´, *n.* [Fr., < *orge*, < L. *hordeum*, barley.] A syrup or cloudy emulsion flavored with almonds and synthetic flavors, used as an ingredient of a punch and certain cocktails, and as a flavoring in foods; a sweet drink originally made from barley water.

or·gi·as·tic, ạr″jē·as´tik, *a.* Marked by unrestrained revelry; pertaining to the festivals honoring the gods of Greek and Roman mythology.—**or·gi·as·ti·cal·ly,** *adv.*

or·gy, ạr´jē, *n.* pl. **or·gies.** [Fr. *orgie*, < L. *orgia*, pl., < Gr. *órgia*, pl., secret rites, any rites of worship, prob. < *erg-*, do work: cf. *organ.*] A drunken, licentious revelry; any uncontrolled indulgence. *Pl.* the secret rites connected with the worship of certain deities of classic Greece and Rome, esp. Dionysus or Bacchus, characterized by wild singing and dancing.

o·ri·el, ōr´ē·el, *n.* [O.Fr. *oriol*, L.L. *oriolum*, a porch; origin doubtful.] *Arch.* a bay window projecting from an upper story, sometimes supported by a corbel.

o·ri·ent, ōr´ē·ent, ōr´ē·ent″, *a.* [As *a.* L. *oriens* (orient-), ppr. of *oriri*, rise; as *n.*, O.Fr. Fr. *orient* < L. *oriens*, the east (where the sun rises), noun use of *oriens*, ppr.] Fine or precious, as gems, esp. pearls; brilliant, shining.—*n.* The east: contrasted with the occident; the eastern hemisphere; *(cap.)* the countries to the east and southeast of the Mediterranean. The luster or coloring of a pearl.

o·ri·ent, ōr´ē·ent″, *v.t.* [Fr. *orienter*, < *orient*, the east.] To place so as to face the east; build, as a church, with the chief altar to the east and the chief entrance to the west; to place in any definite position with reference to the points of the compass or other points; as, to *orient* a building north and south; to direct to a particular object; adjust with relation to or bring into due relation to surroundings, circumstances, facts; as, to *orient* oneself to a new set of conditions; to ascertain the position of with reference to the points of the compass or other points; to find the bearings of.—*v.i.* To turn eastward or in any particular direction.

o·ri·en·tal, ōr″ē·en´tal, *a.* [O.Fr. Fr. *oriental*, < L. *orientālis*, < *oriens*, the east.] (*Usu. cap.*) of the orient or east; eastern; of, pertaining to, or characteristic of the Orient or East. (*Cap.*), *zoogeog.* belonging to a division comprising southern Asia and the Malay Archipelago as far as and including the Philippines, Borneo, and Java. Indicating a gem that is a variety of corrundum. Referring to a native pearl found esp. in Eastern seas; of gems, precious, bright, of superior quality.—*n.* (*Usu. cap.*) A native or inhabitant of the Orient or East, esp. one belonging to a native race; an Asiatic.—**o·ri·en·tal·ly,** *adv.*

o·ri·en·tal·ism, ōr″ē·en´ta·liz″um, *n.* (*Usu. cap.*) Oriental character or characteristics; an Oriental peculiarity; knowledge of Oriental languages, literature, or culture.—**o·ri·en·tal·ist.**

o·ri·en·tal·ize, ōr″ē·en´ta·līz″, *v.t.*—*orientalized, orientalizing.* To render Oriental.—*v.i.* To take on Oriental characteristics.

O·ri·en·tal pop·py, *n.* A robust poppy, *Papaver orientale*, having stiff-haired stems and dissected leaves, native from the Mediterranean region to Iran, and cultivated for its large showy orange, scarlet, or pink flowers.

O·ri·en·tal rug, *n.* A rug of Asiatic origin, either handwoven or hand-knotted. Also **O·ri·en·tal car·pet.**

o·ri·en·tate, ōr´ē·en·tāt″, ōr″ē·en´tāt, *v.t.*—*orientated, orientating.* [Fr. *orienter.*] To orient.—*v.i.* To face or turn toward the east or in any specified direction; be oriented, as a church.

o·ri·en·ta·tion, ōr″ē·en·tā´shan, *n.* The act or process of orienting, or the state of being oriented; insight into one's status in a given circumstance; a program designed to introduce one into a new situation; *psychol.* awareness of one's place and time and of the identity of other persons; *chem.* the ordering of the atoms in a compound; *zool.* the faculty by which homing pigeons and migratory birds return to a given place.—**o·ri·en·ta·tion·al,** *a.*—**o·ri·en·ta·tive,** *a.*

o·ri·fice, ạr´i·fis, or´i·fis, *n.* [Fr. *orifice*, < L. *orificium*—*os, oris*, the mouth, and *facio*, to make.] The mouth or aperture of a tube, pipe, or similar object; an opening; a vent. *Elect.* an opening in a wave guide through which energy is transmitted.—**or·i·fi·cial,** ạr″i·fish´al, or″i·fish´al, *a.*

or·i·flamme, ạr´i·flam″, or´i·flam″, *n.* [Fr., < L. *aurum*, gold, *flamma*, flame.] Any standard or symbol which rouses the devotion of followers; a red banner, esp. the red silk flag which is the royal standard of France.

o·ri·ga·mi, ạr″i·gä´mē, *n.* pl. **o·ri·ga·mis.** [Jap.] The Japanese art of folding paper into various realistic or decorative shapes; a product of this art.

or·i·gin, ạr´i·jin, or´i·jin, *n.* [Fr. *origine*, < L. *origo, originis*, < *orior*, to rise.] The beginning of anything; the commencement; fountain; source; that from which anything primarily proceeds; parentage; lineage; *anat.* the relatively fixed attachment of a muscle; *math.* the point of intersection of the axes in a Cartesian coordinate system.

o·rig·i·nal, o·rij´i·nal, *a.* [O.Fr. Fr. *original*, < L. *orīginālis*, < *origo* (origin-).] Belonging to or pertaining to the origin, source, or beginning of something; created by one's own thought and imagination independent of the ideas and works of others; novel; capable of fresh thoughts and invention.

o·rig·i·nal, o·rij´i·nal, *n.* That from which a copy, translation, or the like is made; the person upon whom a literary portrait or a stage character is based; an original work as opposed to a copy or imitation; an early form of something; one who is original in his way of thinking; an eccentric person.—**o·rig·i·nal·ly,** o·rij´i·na·lē, *adv.*

o·rig·i·nal·i·ty, o·rij″i·nal´i·tē, *n.* pl. **o·rig·i·nal·i·ties.** The state or quality of being original; first-hand and authentic character, as of a work of art; freshness or novelty, as of an idea, method, or performance; ability to think or act in an independent, individual manner.

o·rig·i·nal sin, *n.* An archetypal conception of some event or action which reduced man from a blissful to a fallen state; *Bib.* a depravity or tendency to evil, held to be innate in mankind and transmitted from Adam to the race in consequence of his sin; *Rom. Cath. Ch.* the privation of sanctifying grace in consequence of Adam's sin.

o·rig·i·nate, o·rij´i·nāt″, *v.t.*—*originated, originating.* To initiate; to give existence

to; to invent.—*v.i.* To arise; to derive from; to begin at a specified point.—**o·rig·i·na·tion,** *n.*—**o·rig·i·na·tor,** *n.*—**o·rig·i·na·tive,** *a.*—**o·rig·i·na·tive·ly,** *adv.*

o·ri·ole, ōr´ē·ōl″, *n.* [Obs. Fr. *oriol*, or N.L. *oriolus*, < L. *aureolus*, golden.] Any of certain American songbirds in the *Icteridae* or blackbird family, the males being fiery orange and black in color, which build elaborate, pendent, basket-shaped nests; an Old World songbird of the family *Oriolidae*, being largely bright yellow and black in color.

O·ri·on, ō·rī´on, ạ·rī´on, *n.* [A celebrated hunter of Greek mythology.] *Astron.* a conspicuous constellation depicted on sky charts as the giant hunter, including the first magnitude stars of Rigel and Betelgeuse, and located in the heavens between Canis Major and Taurus; *class. mythol.* a giant hunter who was placed in the sky after being accidentally killed by Diana, goddess of the moon.

o·ri·son, ạr´i·zon, or´i·zon, *n.* [O.Fr. *orison, oreison*, < L. *oratio*, a prayer, < *oro*, to pray.] A prayer or supplication.

Or·lon, ạr´lon, *n.* (*Sometimes l.c.*) an acrylic fiber used in the manufacture of clothing, house furnishings, and in industry. (Trademark.)

or·mo·lu, ạr´mo·lö″, *n.* [Fr. *ormoulu*—*or*, gold, and *moulu*, pp. of *moudre*, L. *molere*, to grind.] An alloy with a copper base used for decorative purposes; mosaic gold.

or·na·ment, ạr´na·ment, *n.* [O.Fr. Fr. *ornement*, < L. *ornāmentum*, < *ornāre*, equip, deck, adorn.] An accessory, article, or detail used to beautify, or to enrich or improve the appearance or general effect; an adornment, decoration, or embellishment. *Fig.* anything that lends beauty or renders more pleasing or attractive; a person who adds luster, as to surroundings, society, a class, profession, place, or time. The act of adorning or the state of being adorned; adornment or means of adornment; outward display; *eccles.* any accessory, adjunct, or equipment; *mus.* a note or group of notes used as a melodic embellishment.—ạr´na·ment″, *v.t.* To furnish with ornaments or something ornamental; adorn, decorate, or embellish; to be an ornament to; serve to adorn.

or·na·men·tal, ạr″na·ment´tal, *a.* Of the nature of an ornament or of ornamentation; decorative; serving to ornament or adorn, or lend beauty or attractiveness; of or pertaining to ornament.—*n.* Something ornamental; specif., a plant cultivated for ornamental or decorative purposes.—**or·na·men·tal·ly,** *adv.*

or·na·men·ta·tion, ạr″na·men·tā´shan, *n.* The act of ornamenting, or the state of being ornamented; that with which a thing is ornamented; objects or work used to ornament something.

or·nate, ạr·nāt´, *a.* [L. *ornatus*, pp. of *orno*, to adorn.] Adorned; decorated; ornamental; richly and artistically finished; much embellished.—**or·nate·ly,** *adv.*—**or·nate·ness,** *n.*

or·ner·y, ạr´ne·rē, *a.* [Corruption of *ordinary.*] *Colloq.* Ugly in disposition or temper; stubborn; ordinary; common; low or vile.—**or·ner·i·ness,** *n.*

or·nith·ic, ạr·nith´ik, *a.* [Gr. *ornis, ornithos*, a bird.] Of or pertaining to birds.

or·ni·thol·o·gist, ạr″ni·thol´o·jist, *n.* A person expert in ornithology.

or·ni·thol·o·gy, ạr″ni·thol´o·jē, *n.* That branch of zoology which treats of the form, structure, classification, and habits of birds.—**or·ni·tho·log·ic, or·ni·tho·log·i·cal,** ạr″ni·tho·loj´i·kal, *a.*—**or·ni·tho·log·i·cal·ly,** *adv.*

or·ni·thop·ter, ạr″ni·thop´tẽr, *n.* [Gr. *pteron*, wing.] An aircraft designed to be propelled through the air by means of flapping wings.

or·ni·tho·sis, ạr″ni·thō′sis, *n. Veter. pathol.* a disease related to psittacosis found in both wild and domestic fowl, milder in form when contracted by man.**—or·ni·tho·tic,** *a.*

o·rog·e·ny, ō·roj′e·nē, ạ·roj′e·nē, *n.* [Gr. *oros,* mountain.] *Geol.* the formation of mountains by movements of the earth's crust. Also **or·o·gen·e·sis,** ōr″o·jen′i·sis, ạr″o·jen′i·sis.**—or·o·gen·ic, or·o·ge·net·ic,** ạr″o·jen′ik, ōr″o·jen′ik, är″o·je··net′ik, or″o·je·net′ik, *a.*

o·rog·ra·phy, ō·rog′ra·fē, *n.* [Gr. *oros,* mountain.] That branch of physical geography concerned with mountains.**—or·o··graph·ic, or·o·graph·i·cal,** ạr″o··graf′ik, or″o·graf′ik, *a.***—or·o·graph·i·cal·ly,** *adv.*

o·ro·ide, ōr′ō·īd″, *n.* [Fr. *or,* gold, and Gr. *eidos,* resemblance.] An alloy resembling gold in appearance, used in the manufacture of cheap watchcases and trinkets.

o·ro·tund, ōr′o·tund″, *a.* [L. *os, oris,* the mouth, and *rotundus,* round, rotund.] Of the voice, characterized by fullness, richness, and clearness; of a manner of speaking, pompous and ostentatious.**—o·ro··tun·di·ty,** ōr″o·tun′di·tē, *n.*

or·phan, ạr′fan, *n.* [Gr. *orphanós,* orphaned; allied to L. *orbus,* bereaved.] A child bereft through death of one or, more commonly, both parents; a young animal separated from its mother; a waif.**—***a.* Being an orphan; for or pertaining to orphans.**—***v.t.* To reduce to the state of an orphan.**—or·phan·hood,** *n.*

or·phan·age, ạr′fa·nij, *n.* The state of orphanhood; a home or institution for the care of orphans.

or·phrey, ạr′frē, *n. pl.* **or·phreys.** [O.Fr. *orfreis* (Fr. *orfroi*), < M.L. *aurifrigium,* < L. *aurum,* gold, and *Phrygius,* Phrygian.] An ornamental band or border, esp. on an ecclesiastical vestment; gold embroidery; rich embroidery of any sort; a piece of richly embroidered fabric.

or·pi·ment, ạr′pi·ment, *n.* [O.Fr. Fr. *orpiment,* < L. *auripigmentum,* < *aurum,* gold, and *pigmentum,* E. *pigment.*] Arsenic trisulfide, As_2S_3, found as a yellow mineral and prepared artificially: used as a pigment.

or·pine, or·pin, ạr′pin, *n.* [O.Fr. Fr. *orpin,* appar. a shortened form of *orpiment.*] *Bot.* a rock garden herb, *Sedum telephium,* in the orpine family, bearing reddish-purple flowers in late summer.

or·rer·y, ạr′e·rē, or′e·rē, *n. pl.* **or·rer·ies.** [Named for the fourth Earl of *Orrery.*] A machine that represents the movements and phases of the planets and other parts of the solar system.

or·ris, or·rice, ạr′is, or′is, *n.* [Appar. a corruption of *iris.*] Any of certain species of the genus *Iris,* esp. *I. florentina,* cultivated for its flowers and esp. for its fragrant rhizomes.

or·ris·root, ạr′is·röt″, ạr′is·rut″, or′is··röt″, or′is·rut″, *n.* The rhizome of certain species of *Iris,* as *I. florentina,* containing an essential oil used as an ingredient in perfumes and medicine, and as a flavoring substance.

ort, ạrt, *n.* [L.G. *ort,* O.D. *oorete,* remnants of food.] Often *pl.* A scrap of food left after a meal; a fragment.

or·thi·con, ạr′thi·kon″, *n.* A sensitive, television camera electron tube which converts a picture or image into electrical impulses for transmission to the antenna of a receiver. Also **im·age or·thi·con,** **or·thi·con·o·scope,** ạr″thi·kon′o·skōp″.

or·tho, ạr′thō, *a. Chem.* taking up or referring to two adjacent positions in the benzene ring.

or·tho·ce·phal·ic, ạr″thō·se·fal′ik, *a.* [< Gr. *orthós,* straight, upright, right, correct,

and Gr. *kephallē,* head.] Having a medium or intermediate relationship between the height of the skull and the breadth or the length. Also **or·tho·ceph·a·lous,** ạr″thō·sef′a··lus.**—or·tho·ceph·a·ly,** *n.*

or·tho·chro·mat·ic, ạr″thō·krō·mat′ik, ạr″thō·kro·mat′ik, *a. Photog.* Representing accurately the relations of colors or the normal gradations of light and shade, as film; referring to an emulsion that makes a film or plate sensitive to colors other than red. See *isochromatic.*

or·tho·clase, ạr′thō·klās″, ạr′thō·klāz″, *n.* A mineral of the feldspar group, $KAlSi_3O_8,$ which contains potassium, belongs to the monoclinic system, and has two cleavages at right angles to each other.

or·tho·clas·tic, ạr″thō·klas′tik, *a. Crystal.* characterized by cleavages at right angles to each other, as certain feldspars, esp. orthoclase.

or·tho·don·tics, ạr″thō·don′tiks, *n. pl. but sing. in constr.* The branch of dentistry which corrects irregularities or abnormalities of the teeth, usu. by mechanical aids such as braces. Also **or·tho·don·tia,** ạr″thō·don′sha, ạr″thō·don′shē *a.***—or··tho·don·tic,** *a.***—or·tho·don·tist,** *n.*

or·tho·dox, ạr′thō·doks″, *a.* [L.L. *orthodoxus,* < Gr. *orthódoxos,* < *orthós,* right, and *dóxa,* opinion.] Sound or correct in opinion or doctrine, esp. theological or religious doctrine; conforming to the Christian faith as represented in the early church creeds; approved or conventional. (*Cap.*) of or pertaining to the Eastern, or Greek, Orthodox Church; relating to or denoting Orthodox Judaism.**—or·tho··dox·ly,** *adv.***—or·tho·dox·ness,** *n.*

Or·tho·dox Ju·da·ism, *n.* That branch of Judaism which adheres to the Mosaic Laws as interpreted in the Talmud.

or·tho·dox·y, ạr′thō·dok″sē, *n. pl.* **or··tho·dox·ies.** [Gr. *orthodoxía.*] Orthodox character; orthodox belief or practice.

or·tho·e·py, ạr·thō′e·pē, ạr″thō·ep″ē, *n.* [Gr. *orthoépeia—orthos,* right, and *épos,* a word.] The study of the customary or correct pronunciation of words.**—or·tho··ep·ic, or·tho·ep·i·cal,** ạr″thō·ep′ik, *a.***—or·tho·ep·i·cal·ly,** *adv.***—or·tho·e·pist,** *n.***—or·tho·e·pis·tic,** ạr″thō·e·pis′tik, *a.*

or·tho·gen·e·sis, ạr″thō·jen′i·sis, *n.* [Gr. *genesis,* origin.] The view of evolution that all variations of species follow a defined direction, and are not simply a succession of accidental changes; *sociol.* a view that all cultures of man and society go through the same developmental stages in the same order, despite varying external differences. **—or·tho·ge·net·ic,** ạr″thō·je·net′ik, *a.***—or·tho·ge·net·i·cal·ly,** *adv.*

or·tho·gen·ic, ạr″thō·jen′ik, *a.* Orthogenetic. *Psychol.* pertaining to or concerned with treatment of mentally retarded or seriously maladjusted children.

or·thog·na·thous, ạr·thog′na·thus, *a.* [Gr. *orthós,* straight, and *gnathos,* a jaw.] Having a nearly vertical facial profile; having jaws that do not protrude. Also **or·thog··nath·ic,** ạr″thog·nath′ik, ạr″thog·nath′-ik.**—or·thog·na·thism, or·thog·na·thy,** ạr·thog′na·thiz″um, *n.*

or·thog·o·nal, ạr·thog′o·nal, *a.* Pertaining to or involving right angles; rectangular, as the angles of the axes of some crystals.**—or·thog·o·nal·i·ty,** ạr·thog″o·nal′i·tē, *n.***—or·thog·o·nal·ly,** *adv.*

or·tho·graph·ic pro·jec·tion, *n. Cartography,* a projection used in drawing hemispheric maps: the maps are in scale at the center, with distortion increasing away from the center. *Drafting,* representation of a surface of an object by projecting perpendiculars from that surface to the drawing surface; depiction of various views of a building or object on a single drawing

surface by projecting each view orthogonally; also **or·thog·o·nal pro·jec·tion.**

or·thog·ra·phy, ạr·thog′ra·fē, *n. pl.* **or··thog·ra·phies.** [Gr. *orthographia—orthós,* right, and *graphē,* writing.] The art of writing words with the proper letters; standard or correct spelling; the part of grammar which treats of letters and spelling; a system of written symbols to represent language sounds; *drafting, cartography,* orthographic projection.**—or·thog·ra··pher,** *n.***—or·tho·graph·ic, or·tho··graph·i·cal,** ạr″thō·graf′ik, *a.***—or·tho··graph·i·cal·ly,** *adv.*

or·tho·pe·dics, or·tho·pae·dics, ạr″·thō·pē′diks, *n. pl. but sing. in constr.* A branch of surgery dealing with the correction of skeletal deformities and with the treatment of chronic diseases of bones and muscles, esp. of the joints and spine. **—or·tho·pe·dic, or·tho·pae·dic,** *a.***—or·tho·pe·dist, or·tho·pae·dist,** *n.*

or·tho·phos·phate, ạr″thō·fos′fāt, *n. Chem.* an ester or salt of orthophosphoric acid.

or·tho·phos·phor·ic ac·id, ạr″thō·fos··far′ik as′id, ạr″thō·fos·for′ik as′id, *n. Chem.* a thick liquid or a crystalline acid, $H_3PO_4,$ obtainable from oxidation of phosphorus, used in fertilizers as soluble acid phosphates, and in beverages as a flavoring agent and an acidulant.

or·tho·psy·chi·a·try, ạr″thō·si·kī′a··trē, ạr″thō·sī·kī′a·trē, *n.* A branch of psychiatry concerned with behavioral problems and the prevention and early treatment of emotional disorders, esp. among young people.**—or·tho·psy·chi·at·ric, or·tho··psy·chi·at·ri·cal,** ạr″thō·sī″kē·a′trik, *a.* **—or·tho·psy·chi·a·trist,** *n.*

or·thop·ter·on, ạr·thop′ter·on″, *n. pl.* **or·thop·ter·a.** [N.L. *Orthoptera,* pl., < Gr. *orthos,* straight, and *pteron,* wing.] *Entom.* any of the *Orthoptera,* an order of mostly plant-feeding insects including the cricket, grasshopper, katydid, and cockroach.**—or·thop·ter·al, or·thop·ter·ous,** *a.***—or·thop·ter·oid, or·thop·ter·an,** *a., n.*

or·thop·tic, ạr·thop′tik, *a.* Pertaining to or producing normal binocular vision; as, *orthoptic* exercises of the eye muscles to cure certain abnormal conditions, esp. strabismus.**—or·thop·tics,** *n. pl. but sing. in constr.*

or·tho·rhom·bic, ạr″thō·rom′bik, *a. Crystal.* Of or pertaining to a system of crystalization characterized by three unequal axes intersecting at right angles; rhombic; trimetric.

or·tho·scop·ic, ạr″thō·skop′ik, *a.* [Gr. *orthós,* straight, and *skopeō,* to see.] Pertaining to, characterized by, or giving correct vision.

or·tho·trop·ic, ạr″thō·trop′ik, *a.* [Gr. *orthós,* straight, upright, and *tropos,* < *trepein,* turn.] *Bot.* of, pertaining to, or exhibiting a mode of growth which is more or less vertical, either upward or downward. **—or·tho·trop·i·cal·ly,** *adv.***—or·thot··ro·pism,** ạr·tho′tro·piz″um, *n.*

or·thot·ro·pous, ạr·tho′tro·pus, *a. Bot.* pertaining to an erect, straight ovule or seed that has the micropyle at the apex and the hilum at the base.

or·to·lan, ạr′to·lan, *n.* [It. *ortolano,* < L. *hortolānus,* < *hortus,* a garden.] *Ornith.* A European sparrowlike bunting, *Emberiza hortulana,* in the finch family, with a yellow throat and olive-brown head; a name loosely applied to the bobolink and the sora in the U.S.

o·ryx, ōr′iks, ạr′iks, *n. pl.* **o·ryx·es, o·ryx.** [L., < Gr. *oryx,* pickax, oryx, < *oryssein,* dig.] Any of three species of large African antelopes of the genus *Oryx,* having long, straight, heavily-ringed horns and inhabiting the desert regions from Arabia to southwest Africa; the gemsbok, *Oryx gazella.*

os, os, *n.* pl. **os·sa,** os'a. [L. *os* (*oss*-); akin to Gr. *ostéon* and Skt. *asthan,* bone.] *Anat., zool.* a bone.

os, os, *n.* pl. **o·ra,** ōr'a, ạr'a. [L. *os* (*or*-), mouth: cf. *oral.*] *Anat.* A mouth; an opening or entrance.

os, ōs, *n.* pl. **o·sar,** ō'sär. [Sw. *ås* (*pl. åsar*), ridge.] *Geol.* an esker, esp. when of great length.

O·sage or·ange, ō'sāj ạr'inj, ō·sāj' ạr'inj, *n.* A moraceous hedge tree of N. America, *Maclura pomifera,* having spines and yellow wood; its rough-skinned, inedible fruit, similar to an orange. Also **hedge ap·ple.**

Os·car, os'kẽr, *n.* A statuette awarded by the Academy of Motion Picture Arts and Sciences for an outstanding accomplishment in the movie industry.

Os·car, os'kẽr, *n.* A communications code word to designate the letter O.

os·cil·late, os'i·lāt, *v.i.—oscillated, oscillating.* [L. *oscillatus,* pp. of *oscillare,* to swing.] To swing to and fro, as a pendulum does; move to and fro between two points; vibrate; to waver or fluctuate between attitudes, opinions, or purposes. *Phys.* to have, produce, or generate oscillations.— *v.t.* To cause to swing or move to and fro.— **os·cil·la·to·ry,** os'i·la·tōr″ē, *a.*

os·cil·la·tion, os'i·lā'shan, *n.* [L. *oscillatiō(n-).*] The act or fact of oscillating; a single swing, or movement in one direction of an oscillating or vibrating body; a fluctuation or a swaying between various attitudes, purposes, or beliefs. *Phys.* a single backward or forward surge, as of electric current, from the maximum to the minimum values; a periodic or regular change in electromagnetic force.— **os·cil·la·tion·al,** *a.*

os·cil·la·tor, os'i·lā″tẽr, *n.* One who or that which oscillates; a device or machine producing or concerned with oscillations; *electron.* a device producing the oscillations which give rise to electric waves, as the vacuum tube of a radio.

os·cil·lo·gram, o·sil'ō·gram″, *n.* The tracing or record made by an oscilloscope or oscillograph.

os·cil·lo·graph, o·sil'ō·graf″, o·sil'ō·gräf″, *n.* [Gr. *graphein,* to write.] An instrument for measuring and recording alternating-current wave forms.— **os·cil·lo·graph·ic,** o·sil'ō·graf'ik, o·sil'ō·gräf'ik, *a.—* **os·cil·log·ra·phy,** os″i·log'ra·fē, *n.*

os·cil·lo·scope, o·sil'o·skōp″, *n.* An electronic optical device which pictures changes in electric current by means of a cathode ray tube.

os·cine, os'in, os'īn, *a.* [L. *oscen* (*oscin*-), singing bird from which auguries were taken, < *ob*, before, and *canere,* sing.] Of or pertaining to the *Oscines,* a suborder of passerine birds, containing those with the most highly developed vocal organs. Also **os·ci·nine.—***n.*

os·cu·late, os'kū·lāt, *v.i., v.t.—osculated, osculating.* [L. *ōsculor,* to kiss, < *ōsculum,* a kiss, dim. of *os,* the mouth.] To kiss; to touch; to greet, as with a kiss; *geom.* to touch at a point, as two curves coming in contact.— **os·cu·la·tion,** os″kū·lā'shun, *n.* —**os·cu·la·to·ry,** os'kū·la·tōr″ē, *a.*

o·sier, ō'zhẽr, *n.* [Fr. *osier,* Fr. dial. *oisis,* Armor. *ozil,* *aozil,* an osier; cf. Gr. *oisos,* an osier.] *Bot.* Either of two species of willow, *Salix viminalis* or *S. purpurea,* having long pliable twigs, grown for ornament and for use in basketry; a twig from one of these trees; a dogwood, *Cornus stolonifera.—a.* Made of osier.— **o·siered,** *a.*

os·mic, oz'mik, *a. Chem.* related to or containing osmium, esp. in a high valence.

os·mi·rid·i·um, oz″mi·rid'ē·um, *n.* Iridosmine.

os·mi·um, oz'mē·um, *n.* [N.L. < Gr. *'osmē,'* smell, odor; named from the penetrating odor of one of its oxides.] *Chem.* a very hard, brittle, and extremely heavy metallic element of the platinum group, used in alloys with iridium and in the production of electric light filaments. Sym. Os, at. no. 76, at. wt. 190.2. See Periodic Table of Elements.

os·mose, oz'mōs, os'mōs, *v.t.—osmosed, osmosing.* [Gr. *ōsmós,* an impulse, a pushing, < *ōtheō,* to push.] To subject to osmosis or diffusion through a membrane.—*v.i.* To go through or be subjected to osmosis.—*n. Physical chem.* osmosis.

os·mo·sis, oz·mō'sis, os·mō'sis, *n.* [N.L. deriv. of Gr. *ōsmos,* impulse, < *ōtheō,* to push.] *Physical chem.* the tendency, when two solutions of differing concentrations are separated by a semipermeable membrane, for the solution of higher density to pass through the membrane until the two solutions are equalized in pressure; an instance of this passage or diffusion; also *osmose. Fig.* any gradual absorption of knowledge or ideas.— **os·mot·ic,** oz·mot'ik, os·mot'ik, *a.—***os·mot·i·cal·ly,** *adv.*

os·mund, oz'mund, os'mund, *n.* [Fr. *osmonde.*] *Bot.* any fern of the genus *Osmunda,* esp. the royal fern or the cinnamon fern.

os·prey, os'prē, *n.* pl. **os·preys.** [M.E. *ospraie* = Fr. *osfraie,* < L. *ossifraga,* lit. 'bone breaker.'] A large eaglelike hawk, *Pandion haliaetus,* brownish-black above and white below, that dives for fish; also **fish hawk.** A feather plume for hats.

os·se·in, os'ē·in, *n.* [< L. *osseus,* bony, < *os, ossis,* a bone; akin Gr. *osteon,* Skt. *asthi,* a bone.] *Biochem.* the soft gluelike protein substance of bone left after the removal of the mineral matter.— **os·se·ous,** os'ē·us, *a.* Bony; resembling bone.— **os·se·ous·ly,** *adv.*

Os·set·ic, o·set'ik, *a.* [From *Ossetia,* an area in the southern Soviet Union, in Caucasia.] Pertaining to the Ossets, their language, or their country. Also **Os·se·tian,** o·sē'shan.—*n.* An Indo-European dialect of the Iranian group, spoken by the Ossets. —**Os·set,** os'it, *n.* The people of Ossetia. Also **Os·sete, Os·se·tian,** os'ēt.

Os·si·an·ic, os″ē·an'ik, osh″ē·an'ik, *a.* [From *Ossian,* a legendary 3rd century Irish poet and hero.] Of or pertaining to Ossian or his poems; pertaining to or resembling the 18th century prose poems by James Macpherson, which he alleged were translations from the original Gaelic of Ossian.

os·si·cle, os'i·kl, *n.* [L. *ossiculum,* dim. of *os* (*oss*-), bone.] A little bone; a small bony or bonelike part.— **os·sic·u·lar, os·sic·u·late,** o·sik'ū·lẽr, o·sik'ū·lit, *a.*

os·si·fi·ca·tion, os″i·fi·kā'shan, *n.* The act of ossifying; the change or process of changing into a bony substance; bone or bonelike tissue.

os·si·frage, os'i·frij, *n.* [L. *ossifragus,* masc., *ossifraga,* fem., lit. 'bone-breaker,' *os* (*oss*-), bone, and *frangere,* break.] Either of two large birds, the lammergeier or the osprey.

os·si·fy, os'i·fī″, *v.t.—ossified, ossifying.* [L. *os, ossis,* bone, and *facio,* to form.] To form into bone; to change from a soft substance into bone or a substance of the hardness of bones.—*v.i.* To become bone or like bone in hardness and rigidity; *fig.* to become inflexible in outlook or habits.— **os·si·fi·er,** *n.*

os·su·ar·y, osh'ö·er″ē, os'ö·er″ē, *n.* pl. **os·su·ar·ies.** [L. *ossuarium.*] A place or container where the bones of the dead are deposited.

os·te·al, os'tē·al, *a.* [Gr. *osteon,* a bone.]

Consisting of or pertaining to bone; osseous; bonelike.

os·te·i·tis, os″tē·i'tis, *n. Pathol.* inflammation of the bone tissues or bone.

os·ten·si·ble, o·sten'si·bl, *a.* [Fr. *ostensible,* < L. *ostendere,* (pp. *ostentus,* also *ostensus*), show, display, < *ob,* before, and *tendere,* stretch, E. *tend.*] Presented as having a certain character, or outwardly appearing as such; professed or pretended; apparent; open to view, visible.— **os·ten·si·bly,** *adv.*

os·ten·sive, o·sten'siv, *a.* [L.L. *ostensivus,* < L. *ostendere,* show.] Manifestly or clearly demonstrative; ostensible; *logic,* setting forth a general principle manifestly including the proposition to be proved.— **os·ten·sive·ly,** *adv.*

os·ten·ta·tion, os″ten·tā'shan, *n.* [L. *ostentātiō,* < *ostento,* to show off, to display, intens. of *ostendo.*] Pretentious display motivated by vanity or the attempt to impress other people; *archaic,* the act of exhibiting.— **os·ten·ta·tious,** *a.* Characterized by ostentation; showy.— **os·ten·ta·tious·ly,** *adv.—***os·ten·ta·tious·ness,** *n.*

os·te·o·ar·thri·tis, os″tē·ō·är·thrī'tis, *n. Pathol.* a deteriorative disease of the joints, most often afflicting older persons. Also **de·gen·er·a·tive joint dis·ease.**

os·te·o·blast, os'tē·o·blast″, *n. Anat.* a bone-forming cell.— **os·te·o·blas·tic,** os″tē·o·blas'tik, *a.*

os·te·oc·la·sis, os″tē·ok'la·sis, *n.* [N.L. (Gr. *klásis,* fracture).] *Anat.* the breaking down or absorption of osseous tissue; *surg.* the fracturing of a bone to correct deformity.

os·te·o·clast, os'tē·o·klast″, *n.* [Gr. *ostéon,* bone, and *klastós,* broken.] *Anat.* one of the large multinuclear cells found in growing bone and involved in absorption of osseous tissue, as in the formation of canals. *Surg.* an instrument for effecting osteoclasis.— **os·te·o·clas·tic,** os″tē·o·klas'tik, *a.*

os·te·oid, os'tē·oid″, *a.* Bonelike; bony.

os·te·ol·o·gy, os″tē·ol'o·jē, *n.* The branch of anatomy that deals with bones or their structure.— **os·te·o·log·ic,** os″tē·o·log·i·cal,** os″tē·o·loj'ik, *a.—***os·te·ol·o·gist,** *n.*

os·te·o·ma, os″tē·ō'ma, *n.* pl. **os·te·o·mas, os·te·o·ma·ta,** os″tē·ō'ma·ta. [N.L., < Gr. *ostéon,* bone.] *Pathol.* a tumor composed of bony tissue.

os·te·o·ma·la·cia, os″tē·ō·ma·lā'sha, os″tē·ō·ma·lā'shē·a, os″tē·ō·ma·lā'sē·a, *n.* [N.L., < Gr. *ostéon,* bone, and *malakía,* softness, < *malakós,* soft.] *Pathol.* a condition marked by softening of the bones, caused by a lack of certain vitamins and minerals.— **os·te·o·ma·lac·ic,** os″tē·o·ma·las'ik, *a.*

os·te·o·my·e·li·tis, os″tē·ō·mī″e·lī'tis, *n. Pathol.* an inflammatory, suppurative disease of bones, resulting from an infection.

os·te·op·a·thy, os″tē·op'a·thē, *n.* [Gr. *ostéon,* bone, and *pathein,* suffer.] A method of treatment resting upon the supposition that most diseases are due to deformation of some part of the body and can be relieved or cured by manipulation of bones and muscles.— **os·te·o·path,** os'tē·a·path″, *n.—***os·te·o·path·ic,** os″tē·a·path'ik, *a.—***os·te·o·path·i·cal·ly,** *adv.*

os·te·o·phyte, os'tē·o·fīt″, *n.* [Gr. *ostéon,* bone, and *phytón,* a growth plant.] *Pathol.* a small bony excrescence or outgrowth.— **os·te·o·phyt·ic,** os″tē·o·fit'ik, *a.*

os·te·o·plas·ty, os'tē·o·plas″tē, *n. Surg.* the transplanting, rebuilding, or inserting of bone to correct a defect or loss.— **os·te·o·plas·tic,** os″tē·o·plas'tik, *a.* Pertaining to bone formation or to osteoplasty.

os·te·o·tome, os'tē·o·tōm″, *n. Surg.* an instrument for cutting or dividing bone.

os·te·ot·o·my, os″tē·ot'o·mē, *n.* [Gr. *tomē,* a cutting.] *Surg.* the dividing of a bone, or the excision of part of it.

os·ti·na·to, os″ti·nä′tō, *It.* a̱s″tē·nä′ta̱, *n.* pl. **os·ti·na·tos.** *Mus.* a melodic phrase or figure which recurs persistently.

os·ti·ole, os′tē·ōl′, *n.* [L. *ostiolum,* dim. of *ostium,* door.] A small orifice, opening, or pore.—**os·ti·o·lar,** os′tē·o·lẽr, o·stī′o·lẽr, *a.*

ost·ler, os′lẽr, *n.* Hostler.

os·tra·cism, os′tra·siz″um, *n.* [Gr. *ostrakismos,* < *ostrakon,* a shell, a voting tablet.] The act of exiling or excluding; the predicament of being ostracized or exiled; a political measure among the ancient Greeks by which undesirable persons were banished by public vote for a term of years; banishment from the privileges of society by common consent; expulsion.

os·tra·cize, os′tra·sīz″, *v.t.*—*ostracized, ostracizing.* To banish from society by popular decision; to exclude from public or private favor; expatriate; to exile by ostracism.

os·tra·cod, os′tra·kod″, *n. Zool.* any tiny crustacean of the subclass *Ostracoda,* inhabiting both fresh and marine waters, and characterized by a bivalve carapace through which segmented appendages protrude when the crustacean propels itself.—**os··tra·co·dan, os·tra·co·dous,** os″tra·kōd′an, *a.*

os·trich, a̱′strich, os′trich, *n.* pl. **os··trich·es, os·trich.** [O.Fr. *ostruche, ostruce,* Fr. *autruche,* < L. *avis,* a bird, and *strūthio,* Gr. *struthiōn,* an ostrich.] Any of several species of the largest, most swift-footed bird in the world, two-toed and flightless, of the genus *Struthio,* native to the arid sandy regions from Arabia to southern Africa, and having wing and tail feathers much used in millinery; a large flightless bird of the genus *Rhea,* native to S. America, having three toes and erroneously referred to as the American ostrich; *fig.* one who wishes to evade danger by refusing to see it, or one who will not recognize an impending problem.

Os·we·go tea, o·swē′gō tē, *n.* [From *Oswego,* New York.] *Bot.* an aromatic, tall herb, *Monarda didyma,* of the mint family, native to eastern N. America and cultivated for its scarlet-red flowers. Also *bee balm.*

oth·er, uTH′ẽr, *a.* [O.E. *ōther* = O.H.G. G. *ander* = Icel. *annarr* = Goth. *anthar,* other; all compar. forms akin to Skt. *antara,* other, and perhaps to L. *alter* and Gr. *eteros,* other.] Being the remaining one of two or more; as, the *other* hand; being the remaining ones of a number; as, the *other* men; additional or further; as, he and one *other* person; different or distinct from the ones mentioned or implied; as, in this or some *other* city; different in nature or kind; as, to wish a child to be *other* than he is; former; as, to recall the customs of *other* times; second or alternate; as, every *other* year; not long past; as, the *other* morning. —*pron.* The other one; someone or something else or different; as, some child or *other;* another person or thing; as, no *other* in existence, *others* to be considered.—*adv.* Otherwise; differently.—**oth·er·ness,** *n.*

oth·er·wise, uTH′ẽr·wiz″, *adv.* In a different manner; differently; by other causes; given other circumstances; in other respects.—*a.* Other; different; under different circumstances.

oth·er world, *n.* The world of the dead; the world to come.

oth·er·world·ly, uTH′ẽr·wųrld′lē, *a.* Of, pertaining to, or devoted to another, often ideal, world, as the world of mind or imagination or the spiritual world to come; oblivious to the material realm.—**oth·er··world·li·ness,** *n.*

o·tic, ō′tik, ot′ik, *a.* [Fr. *otique,* < Gr. *ous, otos,* the ear.] Belonging or relating to the ear.

o·ti·ose, ō′shē·ōs″, ō′tē·ōs″, *a.* [L. *otiosus,* < *otium,* leisure.] Idle; useless; futile; needless; ineffective.—**o·ti·ose·ly,** *adv.*—**o·ti·ose·ness, o·ti·os·i·ty,** ō″shē·os′i·tē, ō″tē·os′i·tē, *n.*

o·ti·tis, ō·tī′tis, *n.* [Gr. *ous, ōtos,* the ear, and term. *-itis,* signifying inflammation.] *Pathol.* inflammation of the ear.

o·to·cyst, ō′to·sist, *n. Zool.* one of the supposed organs of hearing in many invertebrates, which probably serve chiefly as organs of the sense of direction and equilibrium.—**o·to·cys·tic,** ō″to·sis′tik, *a.*

o·to·lar·yn·gol·o·gy, ō″tō·lar″ing·gol′o·jē, *n.* A branch of medicine which is concerned with the ear, nose, and throat.—**o·to·lar·yn·gol·o·gist,** *n.*

o·to·lith, ōt′o·lith, *n.* [Gr. *lithos,* a stone.] *Anat., zool.* a small calcareous body in the internal ear cavities of vertebrates, or in the otocyst of an invertebrate.—**o·to··lith·ic,** ō·to·lith′ic, *a.*

o·tol·o·gy, ō·tol′o·jē, *n.* That area of medicine which deals with the ear and its diseases.—**o·to·log·i·cal,** ōt″o·loj′i·kal, *a.*—**o·tol·o·gist,** *n.*

o·to·scope, ō′to·skōp″, *n.* An instrument for examining internal parts of the ear; an instrument for auscultation in the ear.—**o·to·scop·ic,** ō″to·skop′ik, *a.*—**o·tos··co·py,** ō·tos′ko·pē, *n.*

ot·ta·va, ō·tä′va, *It.* a̱t·tä′vä, *adv. Mus.* to be played an octave higher or lower than written: a direction placed above or below notes in a score. Abbr. *8va.*

ot·ta·va ri·ma, ō·tä′va rē′ma, *n.* pl. **ot·ta·va ri·mas.** [It., eighth or octuple rhyme.] An Italian stanza consisting of eight lines, of which the first six rhyme alternately and the last two form a couplet, as, ababacc.

Ot·ta·wa, ot′a·wa, *n.* pl. **Ot·ta·was, Ot··ta·wa.** An Indian tribe of Algonquian stock which inhabited the area around Lake Superior and Lake Michigan after the Iroquois had driven them from their homes near Lake Huron; a member of the tribe.

ot·ter, ot′ẽr, *n.* pl. **ot·ters, ot·ter.** [O.E. *oter, otor,* = D. and G. *otter* = Icel. *otr,* otter; akin to Skt. *udra,* otter, Gr. *udra,* water serpent, hydra, *udōr,* water.] Any of several fish-eating, aquatic, playful mammals of the genus *Lutra,* having webbed, clawed feet, bristly whiskers, and a slightly flattened, long, pointed tail, and valued commercially for its smooth, dark brown fur; the fur of this animal.

ot·to, ot′ō, *n.* Attar.

ot·to·man, ot′o·man, *n.* [Fr. *ottomane,* prop. fem. of *ottoman,* E. *Ottoman.*] A divan or sofa; a low cushioned seat without back or arms; a cushioned footstool; a corded rayon or silk fabric with a large transverse cord.

Ot·to·man, ot′o·man, *a.* [Fr. *ottoman;* from the name of the founder of the empire.] Of or pertaining to the Turkish dynasty or empire founded about 1300 by Othman or Osman; Turkish.—*n.* pl. **Ot·to·mans.** A Turk of the family or tribe of Othman; a Turk.

oua·ba·in, wä·bä′in, *n. Chem.* a glycoside, $C_{29}H_{44}O_{12}$, white and crystalline in appearance, obtained principally from a S. African tree, *Strophanthus glaber,* and used as a heart stimulant.

ou·bli·ette, ō″blē·et′, *n.* [Fr., < *oublier,* L. *obliviscor,* to forget.] A dungeon with an opening only at the top.

ouch, ouch, *interj.* An exclamation expressing sudden pain.

ought, a̱t, *aux. v.* [Orig. the preterit of the verb *to owe.*] To have a moral obligation, as: We *ought* to be truthful. To be correct, proper, or advisable, as: You *ought* to answer invitations. To be assumed or anticipated as likely, reasonable, or natural, as: The computer *ought* to give the correct answer.—*n.* Moral obligation.

ought, a̱t, *n.* [A corruption of *nought.*] Aught.

oughtn't, a̱t′ont. Contraction of ought not.

Oui·ja, wē′ja, *n.* [Fr. *oui,* yes, and G. *ja,* yes.] A device consisting of a small planchette which rests on a larger board marked with words, letters, and other characters, and which, by moving over the larger board and touching the words and letters is thought to give answers and telepathic messages. (Trademark.)

ounce, ouns, *n.* [< L. *uncia,* the twelfth part of anything; whence also *inch.*] A unit of weight which is one-twelfth of a pound troy and equal to 480 grains; a unit of weight which is one-sixteenth of a pound avoirdupois and equal to 437.5 grains; abbr. *oz.* Fluid ounce; abbr. *fl. oz.* A small amount; as, an *ounce* of sense.

ounce, ouns, *n.* [Fr. *once,* Sp. *onza,* It. *lonza,* prob. < L.L. *luncea,* a lynx.] Snow leopard.

our, our, ou′ẽr, (unstressed a̱r), *pronominal a.* [O.E. *ūre,* our, contr. for *úser,* our, < *ús,* us = G. *unser,* Goth. *unsar,* our.] Possessive case of the personal pronoun *we,* used as an attributive; as, *our* country, *our* rights.

Our Fa·ther, *n.* Lord's Prayer.

ours, ourz, ou′ẽrz, ärz, *pron.* Pertaining to or belonging to us; possessive form of *we,* used instead of *our* and a noun, as subject, object, or predicate noun, as: *Ours* is the best, they took their papers and *ours,* this book is *ours.*

our·self, a̱r·self′, our·self′, ou″ẽr·self′, *pron.* Myself or ourselves considered as a single individual, used in the regal or formal style, as: We, *ourself,* shall attend the opening session. One's own self, as distinct from others, as: Each of us must decide the question for *ourself.*

our·selves, är·selvz′, our·selvz′, ou″ẽr··selvz′, *pron. pl.* A reflexive or emphatic form of the first person plural pronoun, as: We treated *ourselves* to a good dinner, we *ourselves* prefer modern art. A denotation of our usual or customary state, as: We didn't feel *ourselves* all day.

oust, oust, *v.t.* [O.Fr. *ouster,* Mod.Fr. *ôter,* supposed to be < L.L. *hausto, haustare,* to remove, a freq. < L. *haurio,* to draw out (as in *exhaust.*)] To eject, as from a position or location; to forcibly remove; *law,* to dispossess.—**oust·er,** ou′stẽr, *n.* One who removes; an expulsion or removal; *law,* a dispossession from property legally or rightfully held.

out, out, *adv.* [O.E. *ūt* = D. *uit* = O.H.G. *ūz,* G. *aus,* = Icel. and Goth. *ūt,* out; akin to Skt. *ud-,* up, out.] Forth from, away from, or not in a place, position, or state; as, to rush *out,* *out* of town, *out* of fashion; away from one's home, country; as, on the voyage *out;* away from one's work; as, *out* on account of illness; to nonexistence; as, light going *out;* on strike; as, miners are *out;* from a number, stock, or store; as, to pick *out;* from a source, ground, cause, or material, with *of;* as, *out* of pity, made *out* of scraps; so as to project or extend; as, to stand *out;* from a state of composure, satisfaction, or harmony; as, to feel put *out,* to fall *out* with a friend; a stray from what is correct; as, *out* in one's calculations; so as to deprive or be deprived, with *of;* as, to cheat *out of* money; having used the last, with *of;* as, *out of* coal; to or at an end or conclusion; as, to fight it *out;* with completeness or effectiveness; as, to fit *out,* to dig a hole *out;* into or in existence, activity, or outward manifestation; as, fever breaking *out,* the flowers being *out;* into or in public notice or knowledge; as, the truth coming *out;* into or in society; as, a young girl who came *out* last season; aloud or loudly; as, to speak *out.*—*prep.* Out or forth from; as, *out* the window; outside of, on the exterior of, or beyond; along or out on, as: Go *out* the old road.—*interj.* Begone! Away!—*a.* Left exposed; as, *out* at the elbows; not within normal bounds or limits; as, a ball being *out*; mistaken; as, *out* in your figuring; lacking practice; as, a backhand that is *out*; at a specified financial loss; as, *out* five dollars; lacking or without; as, having bread and then being *out*; senseless or no longer conscious; as, a boxer who was *out* in the second round; removed from or not in effective operation or play, as in a game; as, *out* for the quarter; no longer employed or in office; at an end; as, before the year is *out*; at odds; as, being *out* over the matter of salary; no longer in working order; as, a radio that is *out*; no longer available; extinguished; headed outward; as, the *out* train; not possible; as, a tour that is *out*; unusual; as, an *out* selection; *baseball*, failing to reach the intended base; as, *out* at first, *out* trying to steal.—*n.* A person or thing that is out; a dodge or escape valve; as, to have an *out*; *print.* the omission of a word or words, or that which is omitted; *baseball*, a put-out; *pl.* odds or bad terms; as, on the *outs* with her.—*v.i.* To go or come out; as, murder will *out*; to go away from or out of doors; to utter or come out with, as: *Out* with your speech.—*v.t.* To put out.—**out all out,** completely in full force.—**out and a·way,** by far.—**out and out,** thoroughly, completely; undisguised.—**out from un·der,** relieved of a difficulty or burden.—**out of hand,** out of control.

out·age, ou′tij, *n. Elect.* the failure of a system to act when current is interrupted; the period of interrupted power. A quantity of material lost or lacking, as from a container.

out·bal·ance, out″bal′ans, *v.t.*—*outbalanced, outbalancing.* To outweigh.

out·bid, out″bid′, *v.t.*—*past outbid,* pp. *outbidden, outbid,* ppr. *outbidding.* To bid more than; to go beyond in the offer of a price.—**out·bid·der,** *n.*

out·board, out′bōrd′, *a.* Situated on the outside of a ship or aircraft; situated less close to the centerline of a ship or of a fuselage. Of a machine part, outside a main bearing; of a boat, with an outboard motor.—*adv.* On the exterior, or farther away from the center.—*n.* A boat having an outboard motor, or the motor itself.

out·board mo·tor, *n.* A portable engine having a tiller and propeller, usu. powered by gasoline and mounted on a small boat.

out·bound, out′bound′, *a.* Outward bound; as, an *outbound* vessel, *outbound* traffic.

out·brave, out″brāv′, *v.t.*—*outbraved, outbraving.* To surpass in bravery; to confront or withstand defiantly.

out·break, out′brāk″, *n.* A breaking out; a bursting forth; a sudden manifestation, as of war, anger, disease; a riot or public disorder.

out·breed, out″brēd′, *v.t.*—*outbred, outbreeding.* To breed selectively by mating unrelated individuals; to breed more rapidly than; to eliminate, as an undesirable trait or feature, by selective breeding.—**out·breed·ing,** *n.*

out·build·ing, out′bil″ding, *n.* A detached building subordinate to a main building. Also *outhouse.*

out·burst, out′burst″, *n.* A sudden and forceful breaking or bursting out, as of emotion; a sudden and forceful outflow; a spurt, as of energy or growth.

out·cast, out′kast″, *n.* One who is cast out or expelled; an exile; one driven from home or country; a vagabond.—*a.* Cast out; characteristic of what is cast out; thrown away; rejected.

out·caste, out′kast″, out′käst″, *n.* In India, one who has forfeited membership in his caste; a person of no caste.

out·class, out″klas′, out″kläs′, *v.t.* To surpass in class or grade; be or prove to be of a distinctly higher class.

out·come, out′kum″, *n.* That which comes out of or results from something; the issue; the result; the consequence; the conclusion.

out·crop, out′krop″, *n. Geol.* the exposure of an inclined stratum at the surface of the ground; the part so exposed; basset. An outbreak of any kind.—out″krop′, *v.i.*—*outcropped, outcropping. Geol.* To appear above the surface of the ground; to crop out, as strata.

out·cross, out″kras′, out″kros′, *v.t. Biol.* To mate, as different strains of the one breed, producing a hybrid; to produce by so mating.—out″kras′, out′kros″, *n. Biol.* the act of so mating or the resulting hybrid; also **out·cross·ing,** out′kra″sing, out′-kros″ing.

out·cry, out′krī″, *n. pl.* **out·cries.** A vehement or loud cry; cry of distress, righteous anger, or the like; clamor; noisy opposition; sale at public auction.—out″krī′, *v.t.*—*outcried, outcrying.* To surpass in shouting or crying; to cry louder than.

out·curve, out′kurv″, *n. Baseball,* a pitch that curves outward or away from the batter. Also *outshoot.*

out·date, out″dāt′, *v.t.*—*outdated, outdating.* To put out of date; render antiquated or obsolete.—**out·dat·ed,** *a.*

out·dis·tance, out″dis′tans, *v.t.*—*outdistanced, outdistancing.* To leave far behind; to surpass or outstrip in any competition or career.

out·do, out″dō′, *v.t.*—*past outdid,* pp. *outdone,* ppr. *outdoing.* To excel; to surpass; to perform beyond, as one's normal expectations.—**out·do·er,** *n.*

out·door, out′dōr′, *a.* Being, belonging, or performed in the open air or outside the house; also *outdoors. Chiefly Brit.* pertaining to aid given or activities performed outside the premises of a welfare institution.

out·doors, out″dōrz′, *adv.* Out of the house; in the open air.—*n. pl. but sing.* in constr. The world existing beyond house boundaries; open air.—*a.*

out·er, ou′tèr, *a.* [Compar. of *out.*] Being on the outside; external; farther removed from a central point.—*n.* That part of a target beyond the circles surrounding the bull's-eye; a shot which strikes that part.

out·er·most, ou′tèr·mōst″, *Brit.* ou′tèr·-most, *a.* Being the most distant; farthest from the center.

out·er space, *n.* Space beyond earth's atmosphere; interstellar and interplanetary space.

out·face, out″fās′, *v.t.*—*outfaced, outfacing.* To confront; to defy; to brave; to stare down.

out·fall, out′fal″, *n.* The outlet or place of discharge of a river, drain, sewer, or the like.

out·field, out′fēld″, *n. Baseball,* the part of the field beyond the diamond or infield, or the players stationed in it; *cricket,* the part of the field farthest from the batsman; *agric.* the outlying land of a farm or the like.—**out·field·er,** out′fēl″dèr, *n. Sports,* a player in the outfield.

out·fight·ing, out′fī″ting, *n.* Fighting at a relatively long distance from the main area of dispute or headquarters.

out·fit, out′fit, *n.* The act of fitting out or equipping, as for a voyage, journey, trip, expedition, or for any purpose; an assemblage of articles for fitting out or equipping; as, an explorer's *outfit*; a set of articles for any purpose; as, a cooking *outfit*; a complete ensemble of coordinated clothing. *Colloq.* a body of persons associated as a

unit for any purpose, as an army unit; any party, company, or set.—*v.t.*—*outfitted, outfitting.* To furnish with an outfit; to fit out, as a ship; equip.—*v.i.* To furnish oneself with an outfit.—**out·fit·ter,** *n.*

out·flank, out″flangk′, *v.t.* To go or extend beyond the flank or wing of, as of an opposing regiment or team; to outmaneuver; to get the better of.—**out·flank·er,** *n.*

out·flow, out′flō″, *n.* The act of flowing out; that which is discharged.

out·foot, out″fut′, *v.t.* To surpass in running, walking, dancing, or the like; *naut.* to exceed, as another boat, in speed.

out·fox, out″foks′, *v.t.* To get the better of, as by craftiness; to outsmart.

out·gen·er·al, out″jen′èr·al, *v.t.*—*outgeneraled, outgeneraling, Brit. outgeneralled, outgeneralling.* To exceed in generalship; to gain advantage over by superior maneuvering or other military skill.

out·go, out″gō′, *v.t.*—*past outwent,* pp. *outgone,* ppr. *outgoing.* To advance beyond; to excel; to surpass; *archaic,* to go faster than.—out′gō″, *n. pl.* **out·goes.** A going out; outflow, as of electricity; expenditure.

out·go·ing, out′gō″ing, *a.* Going out; as, an *outgoing* tenant; friendly or responsive.—*n.* The act of going out; that which goes out; *usu. pl., Brit.* outlay or expenditure.

out·grow, out″grō′, *v.t.*—*past outgrew,* pp. *outgrown,* ppr. *outgrowing.* To surpass in growing; grow too large for; as, a child *outgrows* its clothes; grow out of fitness for or sympathy with; as, to *outgrow* early surroundings or friends; put off, leave behind, or lose in the changes incident to development or the passage of time; as, to *outgrow* opinions, habits, or weaknesses.—**out·growth,** out′grōth″, *n.* A growing out or forth; that which grows out; an offshoot; an excrescence; *fig.* a natural development, product, or result.

out·guess, out″ges′, *v.t.* To show oneself smarter than; to anticipate.

out·haul, out′hal″, *n. Naut.* a rope used for hauling out a sail on a boom, yard, or spar.

out·Her·od, out″her′od, *v.t.* [A Shakespearean word; after *Herod,* as represented in the old mystery plays.] To outdo in extravagance or excess, as: She *out-Heroded* Silas Marner in miserliness.

out·house, out′hous″, *n.* A small house or building near the main one; an outside privy.

out·ing, ou′ting, *n.* An excursion, pleasure trip, or the like; an airing; the part of the sea out from the shore.—*a.*

out·ing flan·nel, *n.* A light cotton fabric with a short nap.

out·jock·ey, out″jok′ē, *v.t.*—*outjockeyed, outjockeying.* To get the better of by adroit maneuvering; outwit.

out·land, out′land″, *n.* [O.E. *ūtland.*] *Usu. pl.* remote, outlying sections of a country; *archaic,* foreign land.—out′land″, out′land″, *a.* Remote.—**out·land·er,** *n.* A resident of a remote district or foreign country.

out·land·ish, out″lan′dish, *a.* [O.E. *ūtlændisc,* foreign, < *ūt,* out, and *land,* land.] Strange, alien, in looks or actions; bizarre or extremely ridiculous; as, an *outlandish* idea; foreign; distant or remote.—**out·land·ish·ly,** *adv.*—**out·land·ish·ness,** *n.*

out·last, out″last′, out″läst′, *v.t.* To last longer than; to exceed in duration; to outlive.

out·law, out′la″, *n.* [O.E. *ūtlaga;* < Scand.] A habitual criminal; one excluded from the benefits and protections of the law because of having defied the law; an untamed or untamable horse or other animal—*a.*

out·law, out′la″, *v.t.* [O.E. *ūtlagian.*] To remove from legal jurisdiction or deprive of legal force, as: The debt was *outlawed* by the statute of limitations. To prohibit; to deprive of the benefits and protection of the law, as a person or group; to condemn as an outlaw.—**out·law·ry,** out'lạ"rē, *n.* pl. **out·-law·ries.**

out·lay, out'lā", *n.* A laying out or expending, as of money; that which is laid out or expended; disbursement.—out"lā', *v.t.*—*outlaid, outlaying.* To spend or disburse, as money.

out·let, out'let, out'lit, *n.* The place or opening by which anything is let out, escapes, or is discharged; *elect.* that part in a wiring system from which current may be taken. A medium of self-expression; as, painting as an emotional *outlet;* a marketplace for products, as a store or other facility.

out·li·er, out'lī"ẽr, *n.* One who or that which lies outside; one residing outside the place of his business, duty, or the like; *geol.* a part of a formation left detached through the removal of surrounding rock by denudation or erosion.

out·line, out'līn", *n.* The line, real or apparent, by which a figure or object is defined or bounded; the contour; a drawing or a style of drawing showing only lines of contour, without shading; systematic account of the plan or content of a book, speech, or the like; *sometimes pl.* preliminary account or general sketch of the principal aspects of something being considered, as a project or plan.—*v.t.*—*outlined, outlining.* To draw the outline of, as of a figure or object; to give the main features of; to sketch verbally.

out·live, out'liv', *v.t.*—*outlived, outliving.* To survive longer than; to endure the results of.

out·look, out'lụk", *n.* One's mental view; as, an *outlook* on life; the prospect of a thing or a situation; as, the political *outlook;* the lookout or place from which an observer sees; the view or prospect from a place; the act of looking out or keeping watch.

out·ly·ing, out'lī"ing, *a.* Lying away from the main body or center; remote; being on the exterior or frontier; beyond the boundary or limit.

out·ma·neu·ver, out"ma·nö'vẽr, *v.t.* To surpass by maneuvering; to gain advantage over by more skillful actions.

out·match, out"mach', *v.t.* To be more than a match for; to surpass or outdo.

out·mode, out"mōd', *v.t.*—*outmoded, outmoding.* To make obsolete or cause to become unfashionable.—*v.i.* To pass from style.—**out·mod·ed,** out"mō'did, *a.* No longer in style; obsolete or not usable because of changes in acceptability.

out·most, out'mōst", *Brit.* out'most, *a.* [A superl. of *out.*] Farthest outward; most remote from the middle; outermost.

out·num·ber, out"num'bẽr, *v.t.* To be greater in number.

out-of-date, out'ov·dāt', *a.* Not stylish; obsolete.—**out-of-date·ness,** *n.*

out of sight, *n. Slang.* The ultimate; the greatest.

out-of-the-way, out'ov·the·wā", *a.* Remote from much-traveled ways or frequented or populous regions; unfrequented; secluded; seldom met with; unusual; improper.

out·pa·tient, out'pā"shent, *n.* A patient who receives medical treatment from, but has not been admitted to, a hospital.

out·play, out'plā', *v.t.* To play better than; surpass or defeat in playing.

out·point, out"point', *v.t.* To excel in number of points, as in a competition or contest; *naut.* to sail closer to the wind.

out·port, out'pōrt', *n. Canadian,* a remote fishing village in Newfoundland.

out·post, out'pōst", *n.* A post or station outside the limits of a camp or at a distance from the main body of an army, protecting the latter against unsuspected attack;

the troops placed at such a station; a remote settlement.

out·pour, out'pōr', *v.t.* To pour out; to effuse.—out'pōr', *n.* An outflow. Also **out·pour·ing,** out'pōr"ing.

out·put, out'pụt', *n.* The act of turning out; production; the quantity or amount produced, as in a given time; the product or yield, as of an industry. *Electron.* energy produced by a machine or system to be stored, transformed, or converted. *Computers,* processed data; the device, as magnetic tape or a disk drum, used for taking accumulated data out of a computer; the accumulative records produced by a computer or the technique of producing these records.

out·rage, out'rāj, *n.* [Fr. *outrage,* O.Fr. *oultrage,* < L.L. *ultragium,* L. *ultra,* beyond.] An atrocious act of violence; a wanton transgression of law or decency; a gross violation of morality; an enormous insult.—*v.t.*—*outraged, outraging.* To wantonly abuse; to subject to a gross insult; to rape.

out·ra·geous, out·rā'jus, *a.* Characterized by an outrage; atrocious; violent; indecent or lawless; extravagant; excessive.—**out·-ra·geous·ly,** *adv.*—**out·ra·geous·ness,** *n.*

out·range, out"rānj', *v.t.*—*outranged, outranging.* To possess a longer range than; to move beyond the range of; as, to *outrange* enemy guns.

out·rank, out"rangk', *v.t.* To rank above.

ou·tré, ö·tRā', *a.* [Fr. pp. of *outrer,* push beyond bounds, carry to excess or extremes, < *outre,* beyond, < L. *ultra.*] Passing the bounds of what is usual and considered proper; extravagant; eccentric; bizarre.

out·reach, out"rēch', *v.t.* To reach beyond; exceed; *archaic,* to reach out or extend.—*v.i.* To reach out.—out'rēch", *n.* A reaching out; length of reach.

out·ride, out"rīd', *v.t.*—*past outrode,* pp. *outridden,* ppr. *outriding.* To outdo or outstrip in riding; of a ship, to last through, as: The sturdy vessel *outrode* the storm.

out·ride, out'rīd", *n. Pros.* in sprung rhythm, one to three unaccented syllables that have been appended to the slack of a metrical foot, found often in the poetry of the Englishman, Gerard Manley Hopkins.

out·rid·er, out'rī"dẽr, *n.* An attendant on a motorcycle or on horseback who precedes or accompanies a car or carriage; a person who is a member of an advance guard; a cowboy or scout who rides ahead.

out·rig·ger, out'rig"ẽr, *n.* A framework terminating in a float, extended outward from the side of a canoe to prevent upsetting; a spar rigged out from a ship's mast to extend a sail or rope; a bracket extending outward from the side of a boat or shell to support an oarlock; a frame or part placed to project beyond a main structure and act as a support, as that supporting the rudder of an airplane.

out·right, out'rīt', out'rīt", *adv.* Completely, entirely, or altogether; as, to sell a thing *outright;* without restraint, reserve, or concealment; openly; straight out or ahead, or directly onward; forthwith; at once.—out'rīt", *a.* Complete or total; downright or unqualified; as, an *outright* refusal; directed straight out or on.

out·run, out"run', *v.t.*—*past outran,* pp. *outrun,* ppr. *outrunning.* To exceed in speed or distance in running; to exceed or go beyond; to escape or elude, as: The U-boat *outran* the blockade.

out·sell, out"sel', *v.t.*—*outsold, outselling.* To outdo in selling; sell more than; to be sold in greater number than; as, to *outsell* the next most popular brand.

out·sert, out'sẽrt", *n.* A folded sheet of paper used to wrap around other folded

sheets or sections in a book or other publication. Also *outset, wraparound.*

out·set, out'set", *n.* A setting out; beginning; start; opening. An outsert.

out·shine, out'shin', *v.t.*—*outshone, outshining.* To shine more brightly than; to surpass in luster; to be superior to in excellence, wit, or the like.—*v.i. Archaic,* to shine forth.

out·shoot, out"shöt', *v.t.*—*outshot, outshooting.* To excel in shooting; to shoot beyond; to shoot forth.—*v.i.* To project or shoot out.—out'shöt", *n.* That which shoots out or projects; the act of shooting forth; *baseball,* an outcurving pitch.

out·side, out'sīd', out'sīd", *n.* The external, outer, or exposed parts or surface of an object; the external aspect or features; superficial appearance, mere outward show; the space immediately without or beyond an enclosure or boundary.—out"sīd', out"-sīd', *a.* Pertaining to or being on the outside; external; performed or originating beyond a set limit or enclosure; not from or of a designated group or institution; only remotely possible; as, an *outside* possibility; extreme; as, an *outside* limit; *baseball,* of a pitch, passing too far away from home plate on the side away from the batter.—out"sīd', *adv.* On or toward the outside; toward, near, or on the limits; outdoors.—out"sīd', out'sīd", *prep.* To, toward, or on the external side of; beyond the boundary or boundaries of; *colloq.* except.—**at the out·side,** *colloq.* at the greatest limit, or maximum.—**out·side of,** *colloq.* Other than; besides.

out·sid·er, out"sī'dẽr, *n.* One who is not connected with or admitted to a particular association, set, or group; someone unfamiliar with a particular subject; someone or something outside a wall, boundary, or the like; a contender, esp. a race horse regarded as unlikely to win.

out·sit, out'sit', *v.t.*—*outsat, outsitting.* To sit beyond the time of; to sit longer than.

out·size, out'sīz", *n.* A nonstandard size, esp. one that is unusually large.—*a.* Unusual or abnormal in size, extent, or weight. Also **out·sized.**

out·skirts, out'skurts", *n. pl.* The part or district near the edge or boundary of a city or other area; purlieu; border district; *fig.* the fringes of a designated state; as, on the *outskirts* of aristocracy.

out·smart, out"smärt', *v.t.* Outwit.

out·soar, out"sōr', *v.t.* To soar beyond; to fly higher than.

out·sole, out'sōl", *n.* The outside bottom surface or sole on a shoe or boot.

out·speak, out"spēk', *v.t.*—*past outspoke,* pp. *outspoken,* ppr. *outspeaking.* To excel or exceed in speaking; to speak candidly.—*v.i.* To speak out or freely.—**out·spo·ken,** out'spō'ken, *a.* Free or bold in speech; spoken with candor or boldness.—**out·-spo·ken·ly,** *adv.*—**out·spo·ken·ness,** *n.*

out·stand, out"stand', *v.i.*—*outstood, outstanding. Naut.* to sail out to sea; to leave port. To stand out or protrude.—*v.t.* To withstand.

out·stand·ing, out"stan'ding, *a.* Prominent; eminent; excellent; striking; still existing or unpaid, as a debt; projecting or protruding.—**out·stand·ing·ly,** *adv.*—**out·stand·ing·ness,** *n.*

out·sta·tion, out'stā"shan, *n.* A station remote from a central location; an outlying position or post.

out·stay, out'stā', *v.t.* To stay longer than; to overstay; to excel in staying power.

out·stretch, out"strech', *v.t.* To extend; to stretch or spread out; to expand; to go beyond.

out·strip, out"strip', *v.t.*—*outstripped, outstripping.* To outrun; to advance beyond; to excel; to surpass.

out·turn, out′tŭrn″, *n.* The quantity turned out or produced; the output; the quality of goods produced.

out·ward, out′wĕrd, *a.* [O.E. *úteweard—úte,* out, and *weard,* denoting direction.] Exterior; external; obvious or easily visible; as, *outward* signs of tension; pertaining to the physical as opposed to the mental or spiritual; superficial or ostensible; derived from without; not properly belonging; turned or moving away from the inside or center.—**out·wards,** out′wĕrds, *adv.* Toward the outer parts; visibly or apparently; away from a port or country.—**out·ward·ly,** out′wĕrd·lē, *adv.* Externally; on the outside; in appearance only.—**out·ward·ness,** *n.*

out·wear, out″wâr′, *v.t.*—past *outwore,* pp. *outworn,* ppr. *outwearing.* To last longer than; to outgrow; to outlive; to wear out by using; as, to *outwear* new clothes too quickly; to use up or exhaust.

out·weigh, out″wā′, *v.t.* To exceed in weight; to exceed or surpass in value, influence, or importance.

out·wind, out″wind′, *v.t.* To make breathless.

out·wit, out″wit′, *v.t.*—*outwitted, outwitting.* To defeat or frustrate by superior ingenuity; to prove too clever for; to outsmart; to trick; *archaic,* to have more intelligence than.

out·work, out″wŭrk′, *v.t.*—*outworked* or *outwrought, outworking.* To surpass in working; to work harder or faster than; to complete; *archaic,* to surpass in workmanship.—out′wŭrk″, *n.* A minor fortification outside the main one.—**out·work·er,** *n.* One who works out of doors or outside an office or the like.

ou·zel, ou·sel, ö′zel, *n.* [O.E. *ōsle* = G. *amsel.*] *Ornith.* One of several European birds of the thrush family, esp. the ring ouzel, *Turdus torquatus,* having a white band across the chest; the water ouzel, a bird of a closely related family.

o·va, ō′va, *n.* Plural of *ovum.*

o·val, ō′val, *a.* [Fr. *ovale,* < L. *ovum,* an egg; Gr. *ōon,* an egg.] Of the general shape of the outline of an egg; resembling the longitudinal section of an egg; elliptical.—*n.* An object or figure in the shape of an egg; an elliptical figure.—**o·val·ly,** *adv.*—**o·val·ness,** *n.*

o·var·i·ec·to·my, ō·vâr′ē·ek′to·mē, *n.* pl. **o·var·i·ec·to·mies.** *Surg.* removal of one or both ovaries. Also *oophorectomy.*

o·var·i·ot·o·my, ō·vâr′ē·ot′o·mē, *n.* pl. **o·var·i·ot·o·mies.** *Surg.* incision into or removal of an ovary.

o·va·ri·tis, ō″va·rī′tis, *n.* [N.L.] *Pathol.* inflammation of an ovary. Also **o·o·pho·ri·tis.**

o·va·ry, ō′va·rē, *n.* pl. **o·va·ries.** [Mod. L. *ovarium,* < L. *ovum,* an egg.] One of the pair of female reproductive glands of vertebrates in which ova and sex hormones are formed and developed; this gland in invertebrates, producing ova; *bot.* a case enclosing ovules or young seeds.—**o·var·i·an,** ō·vâr′ē·an, *a.*—**o·var·i·al,** *a.*

o·vate, ō′vāt, *a.* [L. *ovatus.*] Egg-shaped; oval, esp. pertaining to leaves of plants.

o·va·tion, ō·vā′shan, *n.* [L. *ovatio(-n),* < *ovare,* exult, rejoice, hold a triumphal celebration.] An enthusiastic public reception of a person; a burst of enthusiastic and prolonged applause; *Rom. hist.* a lesser form of triumph granted to successful military commanders.

ov·en, uv′en, *n.* [O.E. *ofen* = D. *oven* = G. *ofen* = Icel. *ofn* = Goth. *auhns,* oven.] A chamber or receptacle for baking, heating, or drying.

ov·en·bird, uv′en·bŭrd″, *n.* A N. American warbler, *Seiurus aurocapillus,* similar to a small thrush but striped underneath and having an orange crown: usu. seen walking on the woodland floor where it builds its oven-shaped nest; also **teach·er bird.** Any of several passerine birds of the genus *Furnarius,* of S. America.

o·ver, ō′vĕr, *prep.* [O.E. *ofer* = D. *over* = G. *über* = Icel. *yfir* = Goth. *ufar,* over; akin to L. *super,* Gr. *hyper,* over; Skt. *upari,* above.] Above in place or position; as, the roof *over* one's head; higher up than; reaching higher than, so as to submerge; as, in water *over* one's head; above in authority, power, or rank, so as to govern, control, or conquer; beyond one's ability to understand; as, remarks which were *over* my head; above in degree, quality, or amount; in preference to; in excess of, or more than; as, *over* a mile; on or upon; so as to rest on or cover; here and there, on or in; as, at various places *over* the country; upon; thus altering one's disposition or attitude; as, to see a vast happiness come *over* him; to and fro, on or in; as, to travel all *over* Europe; through all parts of; as, to go *over* a matter; above and to the other side of; as, to leap *over* a wall; from side to side of, or to the other side of, or across; as, to sail *over* a river; from end to end of; as, *over* the wire; on the other side of; as, lands *over* the sea; during the duration of; as, *over* a long term of years; until after the end of; as, to adjourn *over* the holidays; while engaged on or concerned with; as, to fall asleep *over* one's work; in reference to, concerning, or about; as, to quarrel *over* a matter; by means of a mode of communication; as, to tell her *over* the telephone.—*adv.* Past the top or upper surface or edge of something; so as to bring the upper end or side down or under; as, to turn a thing *over;* remaining beyond a certain amount, as: Five goes into seven once, with two left *over.* Once more, or again; as, to do a thing *over;* in repetition; as, twenty times *over;* from an upright to a prone position, as: The vase fell *over.* So as to cover or affect the whole surface; through a region or area; as, to travel all *over;* past the top level or brim; as, beer spilling *over;* from beginning to end, or all through; as, to read a thing *over;* from side to side, or to the other side; as, to sail *over;* across any intervening space; as, coming *over* to see us; from one person or party to another; as, to sign property *over;* on the other side, as of a sea, river, or any space; as, *over* in Europe; from one frame of mind or attitude to another; at some distance, as in a direction indicated; as, *over* by the hill; throughout or beyond a period of time; as, to stay *over* until Monday. *Radio,* on two-way circuits, used to indicate a completed message, with an answer expected.—*a.* Upper; higher up; higher in authority, or power; that which is in excess or addition; remaining; surplus; extra; too great; excessive; completed or past; serving or intended as an outer covering; outer.—*n.* An amount in excess or addition; an extra. *Cricket,* the number of balls, usu. six, delivered between successive changes of bowlers; the part of the game played between such changes. *Milit.* a shot that misses and strikes past the target.—*v.t.* To go or get over; leap over.—**o·ver and a·bove,** in addition to; besides.—**o·ver and o·ver,** repeatedly.—**o·ver there,** *colloq.* in Europe at the scene of war: used in the U.S. during World War I.

o·ver·a·bun·dance, ō′vĕr·a·bun′dans, *n.* Surfeit; a too abundant supply.—**o·ver·a·bun·dant,** *a.*

o·ver·ac·cen·tu·ate, ō″vĕr·ak·sen′chö·āt″, *v.t.*—*overaccentuated, overaccentuating.* To emphasize or accent excessively.

o·ver·act, ō″vĕr·akt′, *v.t., v.i.* To act or perform to excess or with exaggeration.—**o·ver·ac·tion,** *n.*

o·ver·ac·tive, ō″vĕr·ak′tiv, *a.* Needlessly active, or energetic to excess; risking fatigue.—**o·ver·ac·tiv·i·ty,** *n.*

o·ver a·gainst, *prep.* As contrasted with.

o·ver·age, ō′vĕr·āj, *a.* Older than the customary or specified age; as, *overage* for the position.

o·ver·age, ō′vĕr·ij, *n. Com.* an excess of goods or money over and above the amount recorded in stock and sales records.

o·ver·all, ō′vĕr·ạl″, *n. Brit.* a loose smocklike outer garment that covers or protects. *Pl.* loose, stout trousers, usu. with a part extending over the chest and supported by shoulder straps, worn by workmen and others, often over other clothing to protect it; long waterproof leggings.

o·ver·all, ō′vĕr·ạl″, *a.* From one extreme limit of a thing to the other; as, the *overall* length of a bridge or a ship; covering or including everything.—ō′vĕr·ạl′, *adv.*

o·ver·anx·ious, ō′vĕr·angk′shus, ō′vĕr·ang′shus, *a.* Concerned, apprehensive, or desirous to excess.

o·ver·arm, ō′vĕr·ärm″, *a. Sports,* delivered or executed with the arm raised above the shoulder.

o·ver·awe, ō′vĕr·ạ′, *v.t.*—*overawed, overawing.* To restrain by awe, fear, or superior influence.

o·ver·bake, ō″vĕr·bāk′, *v.t., v.i.*—*overbaked, overbaking.* To bake too long.

o·ver·bal·ance, ō″vĕr·bal′ans, *v.t.*—*overbalanced, overbalancing.* To exceed in weight or value; outweigh; to destroy the balance or equilibrium of.—ō″vĕr·bal′ans, *n.* Something more than an equivalent.

o·ver·bear, ō″vĕr·bâr′, *v.t.*—past *overbore,* pp. *overborne,* ppr. *overbearing.* To overcome by physical weight or force; overwhelm; prevail over or overrule, as wishes or objections; to treat in a domineering way.—*v.i.* To be excessively fruitful.

o·ver·bear·ing, ō″vĕr·bâr′ing, *a.* Domineering; dictatorial; haughtily or rudely arrogant.—**o·ver·bear·ing·ly,** *adv.*

o·ver·bid, ō″vĕr·bid′, *v.t.*—past *overbid,* pp. *overbid* or *overbidden,* ppr. *overbidding.* To outbid; to bid more than the value of, as in a card game.—*v.i.* To bid beyond the actual worth or value, as at an auction or in a card game.—ō′vĕr·bid″, *n.* A greater bid.

o·ver·blown, ō″vĕr·blōn′, *a.* More than full-blown, as a flower; excessive; stout, plump, or unusually large; inflated with vanity, pomposity, or conceit; pretentious.

o·ver·board, ō′vĕr·bōrd″, *adv.* Over the side of a ship or boat.—**go o·ver·board,** to be extravagant; to give excessive praise or blame; to act in an exaggerated manner.

o·ver·bor·row, ō″vĕr·bor′ō, ō″vĕr·bạr′ō, *v.t., v.i.* To borrow in excess.

o·ver·bred, ō″vĕr·bred′, *a.* Of plants or animals bred for improvement, having inferior characteristics resulting from the overdevelopment of other selected qualities.

o·ver·build, ō″vĕr·bild′, *v.t.*—*overbuilt, overbuilding.* To build a covering structure on; to construct more buildings than required in, as in an area or town; to erect on too costly or too elaborate a scale.

o·ver·bur·den, ō″vĕr·bŭr′den, *v.t.* To give an excessive weight, work load, or responsibility to.—ō′vĕr·bŭr″den, *n. Mining, geol.* a capping; useless earth and stone above a deposit of mineral. Anything that overburdens.

o·ver·buy, ō″vĕr·bī′, *v.t., v.i.*—*overbought, overbuying.* To buy in unnecessarily large quantities; to buy recklessly, regardless of ability to pay.

o·ver·call, ō′vĕr·kạl″, *n.* A higher bid than previously given; *bridge,* a bid that exceeds the highest previous bid by opponents and that is made before one's partner has either bid or doubled.—ō″vĕr·kạl′, ō′vĕr·kạl″, *v.t., v.i.*

o·ver·cap·i·tal·ize, ŏ″vẽr·kap′i·ta·līz″, *v.t.—overcapitalized, overcapitalizing.* To furnish, as a company or enterprise, with more capital than its prospects warrant; to estimate the nominal capital of a company or enterprise at a higher value than law or sound judgment justify.—**o·ver·cap·i·tal·i·za·tion,** *n.*

o·ver·care·ful, ŏ′vẽr·kâr′ful, *a.* Cautious to a degree inimical to one's ambition, enterprise, or successful accomplishment; timid; tentative.

o·ver·cast, ŏ″vẽr·kast′, ŏ′vẽr·käst′, ŏ′vẽr·kast″, ŏ′vẽr·käst″, *v.t.* To darken; as, clouds that *overcast* the sky; to cover with gloom; *sewing,* to enwrap the rough edges, as of material, with long stitches to check raveling.—*v.i.* To become dark or overcast. —ŏ′vẽr·kast′, ŏ′vẽr·käst′, ŏ′vẽr·kast″, ŏ′vẽr·käst″, *a.* Cloudy; gloomy.—ŏ′vẽr·kast″, ŏ′vẽr·käst″, *n.* A covering, esp. of clouds; *meteor.* a cloud or clouds covering most of the visible sky; *avi.* a cloud covering overhead, opposed to an undercast.

o·ver·cast·ing, ŏ′vẽr·kas″ting, ŏ′vẽr·kä″sting, *n.* The action of sewing long stitches to enwrap rough edges of fabric to check raveling; stitching done in this manner. *Embroidery,* this stitch used to outline designs, sometimes covering a foundation thread.

o·ver·cau·tion, ŏ″vẽr·ka̧′shan, *n.* Excessive caution.—**o·ver·cau·tious,** ŏ″vẽr·ka̧′shus, *a.* Cautious to excess; too cautious.

o·ver·cer·ti·fy, ŏ″vẽr·suŗ′ti·fī″, *v.t.— overcertified, overcertifying.* Banking, to certify, as a check, for a sum in excess of the amount credited to the drawer in his account.

o·ver·charge, ŏ″vẽr·chärj′, *v.t.—overcharged, overcharging.* To charge, as a person, too high a sum or price; to overload; to exaggerate.—*v.i.* To make too high a charge.—ŏ′vẽr·chärj″, *n.* A charge that is excessive.

o·ver·clothes, ŏ′vẽr·klōz″, ŏ′vẽr·klōTHz″, *n. pl.* Garments worn over other clothes, as an overcoat.

o·ver·cloud, ŏ″vẽr·kloud′, *v.t.* To cover or overspread with clouds; to obscure; to spread gloom.—*v.i.* To grow overcast or gloomy.

o·ver·coat, ŏ′vẽr·kōt″, *n.* A coat worn over all other clothing; a topcoat; an extra coat of paint applied to a surface.—ŏ″vẽr·kōt′, ŏ′vẽr·kōt″, *v.t.* To put an extra coat of paint on.

o·ver·come, ŏ″vẽr·kum′, *v.t.—past overcame,* pp. *overcome,* ppr. *overcoming.* To conquer; to vanquish; to get the better of; to surmount, as temptations and obstacles; to lay low or overwhelm emotionally or physically, as does illness, liquor, or fatigue. —*v.i.* To gain the superiority; to be victorious.—**o·ver·com·er,** *n.*

o·ver·com·pen·sa·tion, ŏ″vẽr·kom″pen·-sā′shan, *n. Psychoanal.* the action of making amends for a handicap or disadvantage with greater effort than is immediately required, resulting in the development of a new capability to supplant or balance the deficiency, or in the appearance of a pathological symptom.—**o·ver·com·pen·sate,** ŏ″vẽr·kom′pen·sāt, *v.i., v.t.—overcompensated, overcompensating.*

o·ver·con·cern, ŏ″vẽr·kon·surn′, *n.* Excessive solicitude or worry, esp. when unwarranted.

o·ver·con·fi·dence, ŏ″vẽr·kon′fi·dens, *n.* Too great or excessive confidence; foolhardiness.—**o·ver·con·fi·dent,** ŏ′vẽr·-kon′fi·dent, *a.*

o·ver·cook, ŏ″vẽr·ku̧k′, *v.t.* To cook to excess.

o·ver·crowd, ŏ″vẽr·kroud′, *v.t., v.i.* To fill or crowd to excess.

o·ver·de·vel·op, ŏ″vẽr·di·vel′op, *v.t., v.i.*

To develop to excess, esp. in photography. —**o·ver·de·vel·op·ment,** *n.*

o·ver·do, ŏ″vẽr·dö′, *v.t.—past overdid,* pp. *overdone,* ppr. *overdoing.* To do to excess; to use excessively; to overact; to overtax the strength of; to exaggerate; to cook too much.—*v.i.* To carry to extremes.

o·ver·dose, ŏ′vẽr·dōs″, *n.* Too great a dose. Also **o·ver·dos·age.**—ŏ″vẽr·dōs′, *v.t.—overdosed, overdosing.* To dose excessively.

o·ver·draft, ŏ′vẽr·draft″, ŏ′vẽr·dräft″, *n. Banking,* the action of overdrawing an account at a bank; a draft in excess of one's credit; the amount of the excess. A draft that passes over a fire in a furnace or downward in a kiln.

o·ver·draw, ŏ″vẽr·dra̧′, *v.t.—past overdrew,* pp. *overdrawn,* ppr. *overdrawing.* To withdraw, as from one's bank account, larger sums than are to one's credit; to depict with exaggeration; to draw, as a bow, too far.—*v.i.* To withdraw from an account beyond the amount of one's balance.

o·ver·dress, ŏ″vẽr·dres′, *v.t., v.i.* To dress fussily or elaborately beyond the limits of good taste; to dress too warmly.

o·ver·dress, ŏ′vẽr·dres″, *n.* A dress or garment, as of lace, worn over another dress or gown.

o·ver·drive, ŏ′vẽr·drīv″, *n.* A gear system by means of which the drive shaft turns faster than the engine, thereby reducing power output.—ŏ″vẽr·drīv′, *v.t.—past overdrove,* pp. *overdriven,* ppr. *overdriving.* Drive too hard or too great a distance; to overwork.

o·ver·due, ŏ″vẽr·dö′, ŏ″vẽr·dū′, *a.* Past the time of payment; as, an *overdue* bill; belated, or past the specified arrival time; as, an *overdue* train; delayed or deferred too long; as, *overdue* repairs; more than mature or ready; as, crops *overdue* for harvesting.

o·ver·ea·ger, ŏ″vẽr·ē′gẽr, *a.* Intensely ardent, or impatiently desirous, to an unreasonable degree.—**o·ver·ea·ger·ness,** *n.*

o·ver·eat, ŏ″vẽr·ēt′, *v.i.—past overate,* pp. *overeaten,* ppr. *overeating.* To eat to excess.

o·ver·em·pha·sis, ŏ″vẽr·em′fa·sis, *n.* Excessive emphasis; undue stress.—**o·ver·em·pha·size,** ŏ″vẽr·em′fa·sīz, *v.t.—overemphasized, overemphasizing.*

o·ver·es·ti·mate, ŏ″vẽr·es′ti·māt″, *v.t. —overestimated, overestimating.* To estimate too high; to overvalue.—ŏ″vẽr·es′ti·mit, *n.* —**o·ver·es·ti·ma·tion,** *n.*

o·ver·ex·ert, ŏ″vẽr·ig·zuŗt′, *v.t.* To put forth excessively vigorous action or effort.— **o·ver·ex·er·tion,** *n.*

o·ver·ex·pose, ŏ″vẽr·ik·spōz′, *v.t.—overexposed, overexposing.* To expose too much, as to sunlight; *photog.* to expose too long to light.—**o·ver·ex·po·sure,** ŏ″vẽr·ik·spō′zhẽr, *n.*

o·ver·ex·tend, ŏ″vẽr·ik·stend′, *v.t., v.i.* To expand excessively; to extend beyond safe or reasonable limits.—**o·ver·ex·tend·ed,** *a.*

o·ver·fem·i·nine, ŏ″vẽr·fem′i·nin, *a.* Overly womanly or womanish; having exaggerated feminine grace and manners.

o·ver·fill, ŏ″vẽr·fil′, *v.t.* To fill beyond capacity; fill so as to cause overflowing.— *v.i.* To become so full as to overflow.

o·ver·flight, ŏ′vẽr·flīt″, *n.* Flight by an aircraft over a specific area; flight by an aircraft of one nation in the airspace of another nation, usu. for reconnaissance.—

o·ver·fly, ŏ″vẽr·flī′, *v.t.—past overflew,* pp. *overflown,* ppr. *overflying.*

o·ver·flow, ŏ″vẽr·flō′, *v.t.—past overflowed,* pp. *overflown,* ppr. *overflowing.* To flow or spread over; to inundate; to cause to run over the brim of; to deluge; to overwhelm.—*v.i.* To swell and run over

the brim or banks; to be so full that the contents run over; to abound.—ŏ″vẽr·flō′, ŏ′vẽr·flō, *n.* An inundation; a flowing over; superabundance; an opening to carry off surplus liquid.

o·ver·gar·ment, ŏ′vẽr·gär″ment, *n.* An outer garment.

o·ver·gen·er·ous, ŏ″vẽr·jen′ẽr·us, *a.* Unexpectedly magnanimous; liberal to excess. —**o·ver·gen·er·ous·ness,** *n.*

o·ver·glaze, ŏ′vẽr·glāz″, *n. Ceramics,* a glaze or color applied over previous glaze on pottery.—*a.*—ŏ″vẽr·glāz′, ŏ′vẽr·glāz″, *v.t.—overglazed, overglazing.*

o·ver·grow, ŏ″vẽr·grō′, ŏ′vẽr·grō″, *v.t.— past overgrew,* pp. *overgrown,* ppr. *overgrowing.* To cover with growth; to outgrow.—*v.i.* To grow beyond natural or suitable size.—**o·ver·growth,** ŏ′vẽr·grōth″, *n.* Excessive growth; growth over or on an object, as a tree or a crystal.

o·ver·hand, ŏ′vẽr·hand″, *adv.* With the hand over the object; with the knuckles upward; with the hand raised above the shoulder, as in pitching a ball; *needlework,* with stitches passing successively over an edge. Also **o·ver·hand·ed.**—*a.* Done or delivered overhand.—*n.* An overhand action, as a throw or stroke.—*v.t.* To sew overhand.

o·ver·hand knot, *n.* A simple knot, easily tied and untied.

o·ver·hang, ŏ″vẽr·hang′, *v.t.—overhung, overhanging.* To hang or be suspended over; extend, project, or jut over. *Fig.* to impend or threaten, as danger or evil; hang or rest over, as if ominously. **To** adorn with hangings.—*v.i.* To hang over; project or jut out over something below.— ŏ′vẽr·hang″, *n.* An overhanging; a projection; the extent of projection, as of the bow of a vessel; *aeron.,* the amount by which an upper wing of a biplane projects laterally beyond the lower wing.

o·ver·haul, ŏ″vẽr·ha̧l′, ŏ′vẽr·ha̧l″, *v.t.* To investigate or examine thoroughly, as for repair, revision, or correction; to repair or restore; to gain upon or overtake. *Naut.* to slacken, as a rope; to release the blocks of, as a tackle.—ŏ′vẽr·ha̧l″, *n.* An examination and thorough repair; also **o·ver·haul·ing.** —**o·ver·haul·er,** *n.*

o·ver·head, ŏ′vẽr·hed″, *a.* Aloft; in the sky, esp. near the zenith; above one's head. —ŏ″vẽr·hed′, *adv.* Over; above.—ŏ′vẽr·-hed″, *n.* Business expenses, as rent, office expenses, taxes, or depreciation, which are not directly chargeable to production. Ceiling, esp. in a ship's cabin. *Sports,* as in tennis or badminton, a stroke of the racket making impact above the head; a smash.

o·ver·hear, ŏ″vẽr·hẽr′, *v.t.—overheard, overhearing.* To hear, as a speaker or conversation, though not intended or expected to hear.—**o·ver·hear·er,** *n.*

o·ver·heat, ŏ″vẽr·hēt′, *v.t.* To heat or excite to excess.—*v.i.* To become overheated; to become overexcited or agitated.

o·ver·in·dulge, ŏ″vẽr·in·dulj′, *v.t., v.i.— overindulged, overindulging.* To indulge to excess.—**o·ver·in·dul·gent,** *a.*—**o·ver·in·dul·gence,** *n.*

o·ver·is·sue, ŏ′vẽr·ish″ö, *Brit.* ŏ′vẽr·is″ū, *n.* An excessive issue; an issue, as of stocks, bonds, or bills, in excess of the conditions which should regulate or control it.—*v.t.* To issue in excess, as bank notes or bills of exchange; to issue contrary to prudence, honesty, or authorization.

o·ver·joy, ŏ″vẽr·joi′, *v.t.* To give great or excessive joy to.—**o·ver·joyed,** *a.* Enthusiastically delighted.

o·ver·kill, ŏ′vẽr·kil″, *n. Milit.* The capacity for destruction beyond what is necessary for victory by military weapons, chiefly nuclear; an instance of such action.— *v.t.*

o·ver·land, ō″vẽr·land″, ō′vẽr·land, *a.* By land; made upon or across the land; as, an *overland* journey.—*adv.* Across, upon, or by means of land.

o·ver·lap, ō″vẽr·lap′, *v.t.*—overlapped, *overlapping.* To extend, cover, or fold over; to extend so as to lie, coincide with, or rest upon.—*v.i.* To lap over, upon part of another.—ō′vẽr·lap″, *n.* The lapping of one thing over another; the amount or degree of such overlapping; the place where such overlapping occurs; *geol.* the extension of a superior stratum over an inferior so as to cover and conceal it.

o·ver·lay, ō″vẽr·lā′, *v.t.*—overlaid, *over-laying.* To lay or place over or upon another thing; to cover, overspread, or surmount with something; to finish with a layer or applied decoration of something; as, to *overlay* wood with gold; to lie over or upon; to conceal or obscure as if by covering; *printing,* to put an overlay upon.— ō′vẽr·lā″, *n.* Something laid over something else; a covering; a layer or decoration of something applied; as, an *overlay* of fine wood; *Sc.* a neckcloth or cravat. *Print.* a piece of paper, reinforced at the proper places by shaped pieces, put on the tympan of a press to increase or equalize the impression; a transparent sheet on which instructions for preparing the underlying printing copy are given. A transparent sheet layed over a map on which military information is added to the map.

o·ver·leap, ō″vẽr·lēp′, *v.t.*—overleaped or *overleapt, overleaping.* To leap over; to pass by leaping; to leap too far, as to overreach; to overlook.

o·ver·lie, ō″vẽr·lī′, *v.t.*—past overlay, pp. *overlain,* ppr. *overlying.* To lie over or upon, as a stratum; to smother by lying on, as, the young of some animals.

o·ver·load, ō″vẽr·lōd′, *v.t.* To put too large or too heavy a load on or in.—ō′vẽr·-lōd″, *n.* An excessive burden; *elect.* amperage beyond established safety limits.

o·ver·long, ō′vẽr·lạng′, ō′vẽr·long′, *a.,* *adv.* Too long.

o·ver·look, ō″vẽr·lụk′, *v.t.* To fail to notice, perceive, or consider; as, to *overlook* a misspelled word; to disregard or ignore indulgently, as faults or misconduct; to look over, as from a higher position; to afford a view down·over; as, a hill that *overlooks* the sea; to rise above; to look over in inspection, examination, or perusal; to look after, oversee, or supervise; to look upon with the evil eye, or bewitch.—ō′vẽr·-lụk″, *n.* Land, as a bluff, commanding a view.—**o·ver·look·er,** ō′vẽr·lụk″ẽr, *n.*

o·ver·lord, ō′vẽr·lạrd″, *n.* One who is lord over another; a person with great authority, influence, or power.—*v.t.* To govern or rule domineeringly.—**o·ver·lord·ship,** *n.*

o·ver·ly, ō′vẽr·lē, *adv.* Overmuch; excessively; too much; too.

o·ver·man, ō′vẽr·man, *n.* pl. **o·ver·men.** A man in authority over others; a foreman or overseer; an arbiter or umpire.

o·ver·man, ō′vẽr·man′, *v.t.*—overmanned, *overmanning.* To provide too many men for, as a particular situation.

o·ver·mas·ter, ō″vẽr·mas′tẽr, ō′vẽr·mä′-stẽr, *v.t.* To overpower; to subdue; to vanquish.—**o·ver·mas·ter·ing·ly,** *v.t.*

o·ver·match, ō″vẽr·mach′, *v.t.* To be too skillful or too powerful for; to match against a competitor who is superior in strength, skill, or the like.—*n.* An unequal contest; the superior contestant.

o·ver·mod·est, ō″vẽr·mod′ist, *a.* Excessively modest.—**o·ver·mod·est·y,** *n.*— **o·ver·mod·est·ly,** *adv.*

o·ver·much, ō′vẽr·much′, *a.* Too much; exceeding what is necessary or proper.— *adv.* In too great a degree.—*n.* More than sufficient; an excess.

o·ver·night, ō′vẽr·nīt′, *adv.* Through or during the night; in the course of the night or evening; on the evening before; for the night; suddenly or more quickly than expected, as: Cities sprang up *overnight.*— ō′vẽr·nīt″, *a.* Lasting through the night; performed or happening at night; made for nighttime or limited use; as, an *overnight* bag, an *overnight* pass.—ō′vẽr·nīt″, *n.* An overnight pass.

o·ver·pass, ō″vẽr·pas′, ō′vẽr·päs′, *v.t.* To pass over; to cross; to surpass; to surmount; overlook; transgress.—*v.i.* To pass by or over.

o·ver·pass, ō″vẽr·pas′, ō′vẽr·päs″, *n.* A section of a highway, railroad, or the like that bridges or crosses over another road or highway.

o·ver·pas·sion·ate, ō″vẽr·pash′a·nit, *a.* Ardent, passionate, or emotional to excess. —**o·ver·pas·sion·ate·ly,** *adv.*

o·ver·pay, ō″vẽr·pā′, *v.t.*—overpaid, *over-paying.* To pay, as wages, in excess of the amount due.

o·ver·per·suade, ō″vẽr·pẽr·swād′, *v.t.*— overpersuaded, *overpersuading.* To convince by persuasion, esp. against a person's inclination or intention.—**o·ver·per·sua·-sion,** *n.*

o·ver·play, ō″vẽr·plā′, *v.t.* To play, act, or behave to excess or in an exaggerated manner; to surpass or defeat in playing; to overstress; *golf,* to hit, as the ball, beyond the putting green.—*v.i.* To overemphasize a dramatic part or action.

o·ver·plus, ō′vẽr·plus″, *n.* Surplus; that which remains beyond a specified quantity.

o·ver·pop·u·late, ō″vẽr·pop′ū·lāt′, *v.t.*— overpopulated, *overpopulating.* To fill with too many individuals; to cause the number of people to exceed the capacity to produce sufficient food or other essentials. —**o·ver·pop·u·lat·ed,** *a.*—**o·ver·pop·u·-la·tion,** ō″vẽr·pop″ū·lā′shan, *n.*

o·ver·pow·er, ō″vẽr·pou′ẽr, *v.t.* To vanquish by power or force; to subdue; to affect violently or intensely; as, his emotions *overpowered* him; to furnish with excessive power.—**o·ver·pow·er·ing,** ō″vẽr·pou′ẽr·-ing, *a.*—**o·ver·pow·er·ing·ly,** *adv.*

o·ver·praise, ō″vẽr·prāz′, *v.t.*—over-praised, *overpraising.* To praise to excess or too highly.—*n.*

o·ver·price, ō″vẽr·prīs′, *v.t.*—overpriced, *overpricing.* To set too high a price on.

o·ver·print, ō″vẽr·print′, *v.t.* To print over or stamp over, as a sheet already printed; as, to *overprint* a postage stamp with additional marks.—ō′vẽr·print″, *n.* A stamp printed in this manner; the printing on the stamp.

o·ver·prize, ō″vẽr·prīz′, *v.t.*—overprized, *overprizing.* To value or prize too highly.

o·ver·pro·duce, ō″vẽr·pro·dōs′, ō″vẽr·-pro·dūs′, *v.t., v.i.*—overproduced, *over-producing.*To produce too much, or in excess of the demand.—**o·ver·pro·duc·tion,** *n.*

o·ver·proof, ō′vẽr·prōf′, *a.* Of liquor, containing a greater proportion of alcohol than does proof spirit.

o·ver·pro·por·tion, ō″vẽr·pro·pōr′shan, ō″vẽr·pro·par′shan, *v.t.* To make or portray larger than the correct proportion. —ō′vẽr·pro·pōr′shan, ō′vẽr·pro·par′shan, *n.*—**o·ver·pro·por·tion·ate,** *a.*—**o·ver·-pro·por·tion·ate·ly,** *adv.*

o·ver·pro·tect, ō″vẽr·pro·tekt′, *v.t.* To shelter unduly or with exaggerated concern.—**o·ver·pro·tec·tion,** *n.*—**o·ver·pro·-tec·tive·ness,** *n.*—**o·ver·pro·tec·tive,** *a.* —**o·ver·pro·tec·tive·ly,** *adv.*

o·ver·rate, ō″vẽr·rāt′, *v.t.*—overrated, *over-rating.* To rate too favorably; to regard as having more valuable qualities than is really the case.

o·ver·reach, ō″vẽr·rēch′, *v.t.* To reach or extend over or beyond; to aim at but go beyond; as, to *overreach* the target; to defeat, as oneself, by excessive eagerness or cunning in promoting one's aims; to over-exert by reaching too far; to get the better of; to outwit.—*v.i.* To reach too far; to extend over; to cheat. Of horses, to strike, or strike and injure, the forefoot with the hind foot.—*n.*—**o·ver·reach·er,** *n.*

o·ver·re·fine·ment, ō′vẽr·ri·fīn′ment, *n.* Excessive refinement; refinement with excess of subtlety or affectation of nicety.

o·ver·ride, ō″vẽr·rīd′, *v.t.*—past overrode, pp. overridden, ppr. *overriding.* To ride over; to trample down; to supersede; to annul. *Surg.* to lap over, as the end of a bone, in setting a fracture.—ō″vẽr·rīd′, *n.* A commission; a device installed to check the operation of an automatic device.

o·ver·ripe, ō″vẽr·rīp′, *a.* Too ripe; matured to excess.—**o·ver·ripe·ness,** *n.*

o·ver·rule, ō″vẽr·rōl′, *v.t.*—overruled, over-*ruling.* To exercise rule or controlling influence over: now used chiefly of Providence or God; to prevail over so as to change the purpose or action; to rule or decide against, as a plea, argument, or objection; disallow; to rule against or disallow the arguments of.

o·ver·run, ō″vẽr·run′, *v.t.*—past overran, pp. overrun, ppr. *overrunning.* To ravage or swarm over in great numbers so as to injure or overwhelm; to spread or grow rapidly over, as vines or weeds; to spread rapidly throughout, as a new idea or fashion; to run over or overflow; to run beyond; *fig.* to exceed; *print.* to carry over to the next line, as words.—*v.i.* To run over or overflow; to extend beyond the proper or desired limit; to run beyond the proper or desired limit.—ō″vẽr·run″, *n.* An act of overrunning; a surplus.

o·ver·sand·ed, ō″vẽr·san′did, *a.* Containing sand in excess, as cement.

o·ver·seas, ō″vẽr·sēz′, *adv.* Beyond or across the sea; abroad.—ō′vẽr·sēz′, *a.* Beyond the sea; relating to travel over the sea. Also **over·sea.**

o·ver·see, ō″vẽr·sē′, *v.t.*—past oversaw, pp. *overseen,* ppr. *overseeing.* To superintend; to take charge of; to observe secretly or by accident.—**o·ver·se·er,** ō′vẽr·sē″ẽr, ō′vẽr·sẽr″, *n.*

o·ver·sell, ō″vẽr·sel′, *v.t.*— oversold, over-*selling.* To sell to excess; to sell more, as stock, than can be delivered; to promote excessively—*v.i.* To promote something excessively.

o·ver·sen·si·tive, ō″vẽr·sen′si·tiv, *a.* Unnecessarily sensitive, or sensitive to an extreme.—**o·ver·sen·si·tive·ness,** *n.*

o·ver·set, ō″vẽr·set′, *v.t.*—overset, over-*setting.* To disturb in mind or body; to overthrow.—*v.i. Printing,* to set too much type or supply too much copy for available space. To become disturbed; to be overthrown.—ō′vẽr·set″, *n.*

o·ver·sexed, ō″vẽr·sekst′, *a.* Having or giving evidence of an overly strong sexual urge. Also **o·ver·sex·u·al.**

o·ver·shad·ow, ō″vẽr·shad′ō, *v.t.* To cast a shadow or shade over; make dark or gloomy; to shelter or protect; to dominate; to diminish the importance of or render insignificant by comparison.

o·ver·shoe, ō′vẽr·shō″, *n.* A shoe worn over another; an outer waterproof shoe or boot designed for protection.

o·ver·shoot, ō″vẽr·shōt′, *v.t.*—overshot, *overshooting.* To shoot or go over or beyond, as a point, limit, or target; as, *overshoot* the mark. To drive or force beyond the proper limit; to overreach. *Aeron.* to fly beyond, over, or past, as a planned target, spot, or boundary; to bring down a plane beyond, as a designated spot; to drop a bomb on the far side of, as a target.—*v.i.* To shoot beyond or above the target; to proceed beyond.

---

o·ver·shot, ō″vėr·shot″, *a*. Having the upper jaw projecting beyond the lower; propelled by the weight of water falling from above; as, an *overshot* wheel.

o·ver·shot, ō″vėr·shot″, *n*. A weave distinguished by a pattern of loose threads on the surface of a fabric.

o·ver·sight, ō″vėr·sīt″, *n*. An inadvertent mistake of omission; superintendence; watchful care.

o·ver·sim·pli·fy, ō″vėr·sim′pli·fī″, *v.t.* —oversimplified, oversimplifying. To simplify in such a manner as to alter, distort, or cloud the meaning of.—*v.i.* To be engaged in inordinate simplification.—**o·ver·sim·pli·fi·ca·tion**, ō″vėr·sim″pli·fi·kā′shan, *n*.

o·ver·size, ō″vėr·sīz′, *a*. Of excessive size; of a size larger than is necessary or usual. Also **o·ver·sized**.—ō′vėr·sīz″, *n*. An object which is exceptionally large; a large size.

o·ver·skirt, ō″vėr·skurt″, *n*. An outer skirt; a skirt arranged over or on top of a dress skirt.

o·ver·sleep, ō″vėr·slēp′, *v.i.* —overslept, oversleeping. To sleep beyond the hour for waking.—*v.t.* To sleep beyond or through; to allow, as oneself, to sleep too late.

o·ver·soul, ō″vėr·sōl′, *n*. (*Often cap.*), *philos.* the spiritual unity of all being.

o·ver·spend, ō″vėr·spend′, *v.t.* —overspent, overspending. To spend beyond the limits of—*v.i.* To spend recklessly.

o·ver·spread, ō″vėr·spred′, *v.t.* —overspread, overspreading. To extend or spread over; to cover completely.—*n*.

o·ver·state, ō″vėr·stāt′, *v.t.* —overstated, overstating. To exaggerate; to state in too strong terms.—**o·ver·state·ment**, *n*.

o·ver·stay, ō″vėr·stā′, *v.t.* To stay too long; to stay beyond the limits or duration of; to wear out, as one's welcome. *Finance*, to stay in, as a market, past the time when the greatest profit could have been derived from a sale.

o·ver·step, ō″vėr·step′, *v.t.* —overstepped, overstepping. To step over or beyond; to exceed.

o·ver·stock, ō″vėr·stok′, *v.t.* To stock in excess of what is needed or wanted; to fill too full.—ō′vėr·stok″, *n*.

o·ver·stride, ō″vėr·strīd′, *v.t.* —past overstrode, pp. overstridden, ppr. overstriding. To stride or step over or across; to bestride; to stride beyond or farther than; to surpass; to be superior in power or ability.

o·ver·strung, ō″vėr·strung′, *a*. Too highly strung; hypersensitive; *archery*, referring to a bow which is strung more tightly than necessary.

o·ver·stuff, ō″vėr·stuf′, *v.t.* To fill too full; *furniture*, to provide with a complete covering of deep upholstery.

o·ver·sub·scribe, ō″vėr·sub·skrīb′, *v.t.* —oversubscribed, oversubscribing. To subscribe for in excess of what is available or required.—**o·ver·sub·scrip·tion**, ō″vėr·sub·skrip′shan, *n*.

o·ver·sub·tle, ō″vėr·sut′l, *a*. Too subtle.

o·ver·sup·ply, ō″vėr·su·plī″, *n*. pl. **o·ver·sup·plies**. An excessive supply; a supply in excess of demand.—ō″vėr·su·plī′, *v.t.* —oversupplied, oversupplying.

o·vert, ō·vurt′, ō′vurt, *a*. [O.Fr. *overt*, Fr. *ouvert*, O.Fr. *ouvrir*, to open, < L. *aperire*, to open.] Open to view; public; apparent. *Law*. manifest; criminal; resulting in action.—**o·vert·ly**, *adv*.

o·ver·take, ō″vėr·tāk′, *v.t.* —past overtook, pp. overtaken, ppr. overtaking. To come upon or catch up with in following; to reach or go beyond; as: Demand may *overtake* the supply. To take by surprise.

o·ver·talk·a·tive, ō″vėr·tȧ′kȧ·tiv, *a*. In the habit of talking excessively.—**o·ver·talk·a·tive·ness**, *n*.

o·ver·tax, ō″vėr·taks′, *v.t.* Overburden or oppress with taxes; to make excessive demands on, as one's strength or capabilities.

o·ver-the-coun·ter, ō′vėr·THe·koun′tėr, *a*. Sold in another way than on an organized securities exchange, as stocks; *phar.* legally sold without a prescription.

o·ver·throw, ō″vėr·thrō′, *v.t.* —past overthrew, pp. overthrown, ppr. overthrowing. To cast down, as from a position of power; to upset or overturn; to throw over and beyond, as a baseball over a base.—*v.i.* To throw over and beyond.—ō′vėr·thrō″, *n*. An overthrowing; deposition; defeat.

o·ver·thrust, ō″vėr·thrust″, *n*. *Geol.* an older, orig. lower rock stratum that has subsequently been transposed to a position above a newer formation.

o·ver·time, ō″vėr·tīm″, *n*. Time during which one works before or beyond the regular hours; payment for overtime; time over any specified interval.—*a., adv.* Of, during, or for overtime.—ō″vėr·tīm′, *v.t.* —overtimed, overtiming. *Photog.* overexpose.

o·ver·tone, ō′vėr·tōn″, *n*. *Mus.* one of the secondary sounds of a tone, set higher in pitch, which along with the fundamental produces timbre; a harmonic. The color of light produced by its reflection from a painted surface. A second and usu. less important meaning or implication.

o·ver·top, ō″vėr·top′, *v.t.* —overtopped, overtopping. To assume authority over; to surpass; to rise above the top of.

o·ver·trade, ō″vėr·trād′, *v.i.* —overtraded, overtrading. *Finance*, to speculate beyond one's capital or beyond market requirements.

o·ver·train, ō″vėr·trān′, *v.t., v.i. Athletics*, to train to excess, or to a point of physical reaction.

o·ver·trick, ō″vėr·trik″, *n. Cards*, a trick greater than the number bid or more than needed to make a game.

o·ver·trump, ō″vėr·trump′, ō′vėr·trump″, *v.t., v.i. Cards*, to trump with a higher trump than has already been played.

o·ver·ture, ō″vėr·chėr, ō′vėr·chụr″, *n*. [O.Fr. *overture* (Fr. *ouverture*), < *ouvrir*, open.] *Mus.* an orchestral composition forming the introduction to an opera or oratorio; an independent piece sometimes used as a prelude to a play or concert. An opening of negotiations; a proposal or an offer.—*v.t.* —overtured, overturing. To submit as an overture or proposal; to make an overture or proposal to.

o·ver·turn, ō″vėr·turn′, *v.t.* To turn over; throw over with violence; upset; overthrow; destroy the power of; defeat; bring to ruin.—*v.i.* To turn over on its side or face; upset; capsize.—ō′vėr·turn″, *n*. The act of overturning or the state of being overturned; a commercial transaction or turnover.

o·ver·use, ō″vėr·ūz′, *v.t.* —overused, overusing. To use too much; use too hard or too often.—ō″vėr·ūs′, *n*. Excessive use.

o·ver·warm, ō″vėr·wȧrm′, *a*. Overheated; uncomfortably warm.—*v.t.* To heat to a degree higher than intended.

o·ver·watch, ō″vėr·woch′, ō″vėr·wȧch″, *v.t.* To watch over; to weary of watching.— **o·ver·watch·er**, *n*.

o·ver·wear, ō″vėr·wâr′, *v.t.* —past overwore, pp. overworn, ppr. overwearing. To wear until worn out; to say until commonplace.

o·ver·wea·ry, ō′vėr·wēr′ē, *a*. Excessively wearied; overcome with fatigue.—ō″vėr·wēr′ē, *v.t.* —overwearied, overwearying. To weary to excess.

o·ver·weath·er, ō″vėr·weTH′ėr, *a*. Pertaining to meteorological conditions at a level higher than weather disturbances that may affect aircraft operations.

o·ver·ween·ing, ō″vėr·wē′ning, *a*. Arrogant; conceited; presumptuous; as, an *overweening* individual; inordinate; extreme; as, *overweening* ambition.—**o·ver·ween·ing·ly**, *adv*.—**o·ver·ween·ing·ness**, *n*.

o·ver·weigh, ō″vėr·wā′, *v.t.* To exceed in weight; to outweigh; to oppress.

o·ver·weight, ō″vėr·wāt″, *n*. Extra weight above the legal amount, as for shipping; weight beyond the customary or healthful amount; greater weight; preponderance.—ō′vėr·wāt′, *a*. Weighing more than is permitted or considered normal.

o·ver·whelm, ō″vėr·hwelm′, ō″vėr·welm′, *v.t.* To cover up or bury, as: Volcanic eruptions can *overwhelm* great areas. Submerge; to overcome or crush, as: Misfortunes *overwhelm* us. To defeat; to overthrow; to overcome totally; as, grief that *overwhelms*.—**o·ver·whelm·ing**, ō″vėr·hwel′ming, ō″vėr·wel′ming, *a*.—**o·ver·whelm·ing·ly**, *adv*.

o·ver·wind, ō″vėr·wīnd′, *v.t.* —overwound, overwinding. To wind too far or too much, as a spring; *elec.* to wind enough, as an electromagnet, so that magnetic saturation with a small current is obtained.

o·ver·win·ter, ō″vėr·win′tėr, *v.i.* To spend the winter.

o·ver·word, ō″vėr·wụrd″, *n*. A word or phrase often repeated, as a song refrain.

o·ver·work, ō″vėr·wụrk″, *v.t.* —overworked or overwrought, overworking. To cause to work too much; to use to excess; to excite to the point of frenzy; to decorate with, over the entire surface.—*v.i.* To toil excessively; to do more than the required amount of work.—ō′vėr·wụrk″, *n*. Excessive work; work done beyond the stipulated amount; work that is extra or taxing in character.

o·ver·write, ō″vėr·rīt′, *v.t.* —past overwrote, pp. overwritten, ppr. overwriting. To write in an exaggerated, rhetorical style; to write at length beyond requirements; to write over a surface.—*v.i.* To write in too exaggerated a manner.

o·ver·wrought, ō″vėr·rȧt′, ō′vėr·rȧt′, *a*. Overworked or taxed beyond one's strength; affected or excited to excess; emotionally distressed, as by labor, care, or worry. Overly elaborated.

o·vi·duct, ō′vi·dukt″, *n*. [L. *ductus*, a duct.] *Zool.* a passage which conducts the ovum or egg from an ovary. Also *Fallopian tube*.—**o·vi·duc·tal**, *a*.

o·vine, ō′vin, ō′vīn, *a*. [L. *ovīnus*, < *ovis*, a sheep.] Pertaining to sheep; like sheep.—*n*.

o·vip·a·rous, ō·vip′ėr·us, *a*. [L. *ovum*, an egg, *pario*, to produce.] *Zool.* producing eggs that are hatched after being expelled from the body: opposed to *ovoviviparous*.—**o·vip·ar·ous·ly**, *adv*.—**o·vip·ar·ous·ness**, or **o·vi·par·i·ty**, ō′vi·par′i·tē, *n*.

o·vi·pos·it, ō″vi·poz′it, ō′vi·poz′it, *v.i.* [L. *ovum*, an egg; and E. *posit*.] *Zool.* to deposit eggs through an ovipositor.—**o·vi·po·si·tion**, ō″vi·po·zish′an, *n*.

o·vi·pos·i·tor, ō″vi·poz′i·tėr, *n. Zool.* An organ at the extremity of the abdomen of many insects for depositing their eggs; an organ with a similar function in certain varieties of fish.

o·void, ō′void, *a*. [L. *ovum*, and Gr. *eidos*, form.] Having a shape like an egg; ovate. Also **o·voi·dal**.—*n*. A body which is egg-shaped.

o·vo·lo, ō′vo·lō″, *n*. pl. **o·vo·li**, ō′vo·li″. [It., < L. *ovum*.] *Arch.* a convex molding forming a quarter of an ellipse or circle.

o·vo·vi·vip·a·rous, ō′vō·vī·vip′ėr·us, *a*. [L. *ovum, vivo*, to live, *pario*, to produce.] *Zool.* producing eggs which incubate and hatch within the body but without placentas, as certain fishes and reptiles: opposed to *oviparous*.—**o·vo·vi·vip·ar·ous·ly**, *adv*.—**o·vo·vi·vip·ar·ous·ness**, *n*.

o·vu·late, ō'vū·lāt″, v.i.—ovulated, ovulating. To produce or release an ovum from an ovary.—o·vu·la·tion, n.

o·vule, ō'vūl, n. [Fr. ovule, dim. < L. ovum, egg.] Biol. a little egg; an ovum, esp. when small, immature, or unfertilized. Bot. a rudimentary seed; the body which contains the embryo sac and therefore the female germ cell, which after fertilization develops into a seed.—o·vu·lar, a.

o·vum, ō'vum, n. pl. o·va, ō'va. [L., egg; akin to Gr. ōon, egg.] Biol. an egg, in a broad biological sense; the female reproductive cell of animals, which, usu. only after fertilization, is capable of developing into a new individual; the female reproductive cell or gamete of plants. Arch. an egg-shaped ornament.

owe, ō, v.t.—owed, owing. [O.E. āgan = O.H.G. eigun = Icel. eiga = Goth. aigan, have, possess: cf. own and ought.] To be under obligation to pay, render, or offer, sometimes followed by to; to be in debt or beholden for, because of certain conditions; to cherish a certain feeling toward a person.—v.i. To be in debt.—ow·ing, a. Indebted, owed, or due.—ow·ing to, due to, on account of, or because of.

owl, oul, n. [O.E. ūle = D. uil, Icel. ugla, Dan. ugle, Sw. uggla, G. eule, names imit. of its cry; compare L. ululo, to lament, E. howl.] Ornith. any of various large-headed, nocturnal birds of prey, in the order Strigiformes, with large, forward-directed eyes, facial discs, a hooked bill, and talons; a breed of pigeon with a head resembling an owl. A person who prefers staying awake during the night hours; a person of somber appearance.—a. Available, as a service, during the late night hours.—owl·et, ou'let, n. A young owl.—owl·ish, ou'lish, a.—owl·ish·ly, adv.—owl·ish·ness, n.

own, ōn, a. [O.E. āgen, pp. of āgan, to possess, like Dan. and Sw. egen, Icel. eiginn, D. and G. eigen, own.] Distinctly and emphatically belonging to oneself: usu. used following a possessive pronoun or a noun in the possessive; as, my own idea; pertaining to oneself; as, my own niece.—v.t. [O.E. āgnian (< agen-own, a.), Icel. eigna, Dan. egne, G. eignen, to own.] To hold or possess, esp. property; to acknowledge.—v.i. To admit, used with to or up.—hold one's own, to maintain one's situation; to be equal to the task or the opposition.—own·er, n.—own·er·ship, n.

ox, oks, n. pl. ox·en, ox·es, ok'sn. [O.E. oxa = Icel. oxi, Sw. and Dan. oxe, D.os, G. ochs, ochse, Goth. auhsa, auhsus, an ox; cogn. L. vacca, a cow, Skt. uksha, an ox.] Any animal of the bovine kind; a male bovine animal, castrated and full grown; pl. ox·en. awkward youth or man; pl. ox·es.

ox·a·late, ok'sa·lāt″, n. [Gr. oxalis, sorrel, < oxys, sharp, acid.] Chem. an ester or salt of oxalic acid.

ox·al·ic ac·id, ok·sal'ik as'id, n. A poisonous, white, crystalline acid, $C_2H_2O_4$, obtained from certain plants and produced artificially, used for bleaching, cleaning, and dyeing.

ox·a·lis, ok'sa·lis, ok·sal'is, n. [L., < Gr. oxalis, sorrel, < oxus, sharp, acid.] Bot. any herb of the genus Oxalis, containing oxalic acid. Also wood sorrel.

ox·a·zine, ok'sa·zēn″, ok'sa·sin, n. Chem. any one of a group of compounds with the formula, C_4H_5NO, whose molecules have four carbon atoms, one nitrogen atom, and one oxygen atom in a ring formation.

ox·blood, oks'blud″, n. A deep, dull red color.

ox·bow, oks'bō″, n. A bow-shaped piece of wood placed under and around the neck of an ox, with its upper ends inserted in the bar of the yoke; a geologic feature, as a

bow-shaped bend in a river, or the land embraced by it.—a.

ox·eye, oks'ī″, n. pl. ox·eyes. Bot. an herbaceous daisylike plant, Chrysanthemum leucanthemum, in the composite family, with white ray flowers; also ox·eye dai·sy; an herbaceous sunflowerlike plant, Heliopsis helianthoides, in the composite family, with yellow ray flowers, native to woodlands in temperate N. America. Any of a number of shore birds, as the American dunlin.

ox·ford, oks'fĕrd, n. (Sometimes cap.) a low shoe usu. laced over the instep.

ox·ford cloth, n. A sturdy fabric of cotton or rayon yarn, sometimes in a basket weave, used for shirting and lightweight sportswear.

Ox·ford Group move·ment, n. A movement, founded in 1921 by Frank Buchman, and dedicated to world improvement through public and private morality. Also Mor·al Re-Ar·ma·ment, Buch·man·ism.

Ox·ford move·ment, n. A movement toward High Church principles in the Church of England, which originated at Oxford University about 1833.

ox·heart, oks'härt″, n. A large, heart-shaped variety of cherry.

ox·i·dant, ok'si·dant″, n. Chem. an agent for oxidation.

ox·i·dase, ok'si·dās″, ok'si·dāz″, n. Biochem. one of a number of oxidizing enzymes found in living tissue.—ox·i·da·sic, ok″si·dā'sik, ok″si·dā'zik, a.

ox·i·da·tion, ok″si·dā'shan, n. Chem. The act or process of uniting with oxygen; the resulting state; the process by which an element in a compound gains or loses electrons in forming the compound.—ox·i·da·tive, a.—ox·i·da·tive·ly, adv.

ox·i·da·tion re·duc·tion, n. Chem. a chemical reaction by which electrons are transferred or shared by atoms forming a compound.

ox·ide, ok'sīd, ok'sid, n. [Fr. oxide, now oxyde, < ox(ygène), oxygen, and (ac)ide, acid.] Chem. a compound of oxygen with another element or a radical. Also ox·id, ok'sid.—ox·id·ic, ok·sid'ik, a.

ox·i·dize, ok'si·dīz″, v.t.—oxidized, oxidizing. To convert into an oxide; combine with oxygen; to cover with a coating of oxide, or rust; to take away hydrogen from, as by the action of oxygen; to change, as a compound, so that the valence of the positive element is higher.—v.i. To become oxidized.—ox·i·diz·a·ble, a.—ox·i·diz·er, n.

ox·ime, ok'sēm, ok'sim, n. Chem. a compound containing the group >C=NOH, principally produced by hydroxylamine acting on ketones or aldehydes.

ox·lip, oks'lip″, n. [O.E. oxanslyppe, > oxan, oxen, and slyppe, slime: cf. cowslip.] An herbaceous rock garden or border plant, Primula elatior, cultivated for its fragrant yellow flowers.

Ox·o·ni·an, ok·sō'nē·an, a. [M.L. Oxonia, Oxford.] Of or pertaining to Oxford, England, or Oxford University.—n. A native or inhabitant of Oxford; a member or graduate of Oxford University.

ox·tail, oks'tāl″, n. The tail of an ox; the skinned tail of ox or cattle, used in soup.

ox·tongue, oks'tung″, n. Any of several herbaceous plants of the genus Anchusa, in the borage family, characterized by tongue-shaped leaves covered with stiff rough hairs, esp. the bugloss, Anchusa officinalis.

ox·y·a·cet·y·lene, ok″sē·a·set'i·lēn″, ok″sē·a·set'i·lin, a. Of, pertaining to, or using a mixture of oxygen and acetylene; as, the oxyacetylene torch used in welding.

ox·y·cal·ci·um, ok″si·kal'sē·um, a. Pertaining to or produced by oxygen and calcium, as the calcium light or limelight.

ox·y·gen, ok'si·jen, n. [Fr. oxygène, < Gr.

oxys, sharp, acid, and gen-, bear, produce (from its being regarded as an acid-forming principle).] Chem. a colorless, odorless, gaseous element, occurring as O_2, constituting about one-fifth of the volume of the atmosphere, which supports combustion and plays an essential role in the respiratory process of animals and plants. Sym. O, at. no. 8, at. wt. 15.9994.—ox·y·gen·ic, ok″si·jen'ik, a.—ox·y·gen·ic·i·ty, ok″si·je·nis'e·tē, n.

ox·y·gen ac·id, n. Chem. an inorganic acid with an admixture of oxygen. Also ox·y·ac·id.

ox·y·gen·ate, ok'si·je·nāt″, v.t.—oxygenated, oxygenating. To treat or combine with oxygen.—ox·y·gen·a·tion, n.

ox·y·gen mask, n. A device covering the nose and mouth and supplying oxygen from an adjoining tank.

ox·y·gen tent, n. A protective cover which makes possible delivering and retaining pure oxygen, placed over the head and shoulders of a patient to aid respiration.

ox·y·he·mo·glo·bin, ok'si·hē'mo·glō″bin, ok″si·hem'o·glō″bin, ok″si·hē'mo·glō'bin, ok″si·hem'o·glō'bin, n. Biochem. hemoglobin combined with oxygen, found in arterial blood.

ox·y·hy·dro·gen, ok″si·hī'dro·jen, a. Relating to a combination of oxygen and hydrogen.—n. A combination of oxygen and hydrogen, as utilized in a torch to weld and cut metals.

ox·y·mo·ron, ok″si·mōr'on, n. pl. ox·y·mo·ra, ok″si·mōr'a. [Gr. oxymōron, a smart saying which at first view appears foolish, < oxys, sharp, and mōros, foolish.] Rhet. a figure of speech employing the juxtaposition of two normally contradictory words, as 'cruel kindness.'

ox·y·sul·fide, **ox·y·sul·phide**, ok″si·sul'fīd, ok″si·sul'fid, n. Chem. a sulfide in which part of the sulfur is replaced by oxygen.

ox·y·te·tra·cy·cline, ok″si·te″tra·sī'klin, ok″si·te″tra·si'klin, n. Pharm. an antibiotic, $C_{22}H_{24}N_2O_9 \cdot 2H_2O$, capable of destroying numerous pathogenic microorganisms.

ox·y·to·cic, ok″si·tō'sik, ok″si·tos'ik, a. [N.L., < Gr. oxys, sharp, quick, and tokia, a bringing forth, as in dystokia, E. dystocia.] Accelerating childbirth; stimulating contraction of the muscle of the uterus.—n. An oxytocic medicine.

ox·y·to·cin, ok″si·tō'sin, n. Biochem. a hormone, $C_{43}H_{66}N_{12}O_{12}S_2$, which promotes contraction of smooth muscle of the uterus and release of breast milk.

o·yer and ter·mi·ner, ō'yĕr and tur'mi·nĕr, oi'ér and tur'mi·nĕr, n. [A.Fr., < O.Fr., lit. 'hearing and determining.'] One of various higher criminal courts in some states; Brit. a commission empowering judges on circuit to hold courts to hear and determine offenses.

o·yez, ō'yes, ō'yez, interj. [A.Fr. oyez, 'hear ye,' 2nd pers. pl. impv. of oyer.] Hear! attend! a cry uttered, usu. three times, by a public or court crier to command silence and attention before a proclamation is made.—n. Such a cry. Also o·yes.

oys·ter, oi'stĕr, n. [O.Fr. oistre (Fr. huître), L. ostrea, ostreum, < Gr. óstreon, oyster.] Any of various edible marine bivalve mollusks of the family Ostreidae, with an irregularly shaped shell, found on the bottom or adhering to rocks in shallow water; any of various similar bivalves; the oyster-shaped bit of dark meat in the front hollow of the side bone of a fowl; something from which one may extract or derive advantage, as: The world is the young man's oyster. Slang, an uncommunicative individual.—v.i. To dredge for or otherwise take oysters.

oys·ter bed, *n.* A place where oysters breed or are bred.

oys·ter·catch·er, oi'stẽr·kach″ẽr, *n. Ornith.* any of several very large, dark and white, shore birds of the genus *Haematopus,* esp. *H. palliatus* of N. America, having white wing patches and a red wedge-shaped bill, and feeding on oysters and clams along the Atlantic and Gulf coasts.

oys·ter crab, *n.* A crab, *Pinnotheres ostreum,* living as a commensal within the shell of an oyster.

oys·ter crack·er, *n.* A small cracker, usu. salted, eaten with oysters or soup.

oys·ter·man, oi'stẽr·man, *n.* pl. **oys·ter·men.** One who gathers, breeds, or sells oysters; a boat equipped for oyster fishing. Also **oys·ter·er.**

oys·ter plant, *n.* Salsify.

oys·ter white, *a.* White with a slight gray tint. Also *off-white.*

o·zo·ce·rite, ō·zŏk'e·rīt″, ō·zō'se·rīt″, ō″zō·sẽr'īt, *n.* [Gr. *ozein,* smell, and *keros,* wax.] A waxy mixture of natural hydrocarbons, used in manufacturing electric insulation, rubber products, polishes, and waxes. Also **o·zo·ke·rite,** ō·zō'ke·rīt″, ō″zō·kẽr'īt.

o·zone, ō'zōn, ō·zōn', *n.* [Fr. *ozone,* < Gr. *ozein,* smell.] A form of oxygen, O_3, having three atoms to the molecule, with an odor suggesting that of weak chlorine, produced esp. when an electric spark is passed through oxygen or air, and found in the atmosphere in minute quantities, esp. after a thunderstorm: used as a powerful oxidizing agent, for sterilizing water and in bleaching. Popularly, a supposed bracing element in the air, as in the mountains or at the seaside.—**o·zon·ic,** ō·zon'ik, ō·zō'nik, *a.*—**o·zo·nif·er·ous,** *a.*—**o·zo·nous,** ō'zo·nus, ō'zō·nus, *a.*

o·zo·nide, ō'zo·nīd″, ō'zō·nīd″, *n. Chem.* an unstable organic compound with ozone, often explosive.

o·zon·ize, ō'zo·nīz″, ō'zō·nīz″, *v.t.*—*ozonized, ozonizing.* To charge or impregnate with ozone; to convert, as oxygen, into ozone. —*v.i.* To become ozone.—**o·zon·iz·er,** *n.*

o·zo·no·sphere, ō·zō'no·sfẽr″, *n. Meteor.* a layer in the stratosphere, at a height of approximately 20 miles, which has a high concentration of ozone. Also **o·zone lay·er, o·zone stra·tum.**

P

P, p, pē, *n.* The sixteenth letter and twelfth consonant of the English alphabet; a counterpart in speech of the letter P; the sixteenth in a series; something designated by or having the shape of the letter P or p; a printer's graphic device used for reproducing the letter P or p. *Chem.* symbol for phosphorus.

pa, pä, *n. Colloq.* father.

PABA, paba, pab'a, pē″ā″bē'ā″, *n.* Para-aminobenzoic acid.

pab·u·lum, pab'ū·lum, *n.* Food, esp. in an absorbable solution; *fig.* food for thought.— **pab·u·lar,** *a.*

pa·ca, pä'ka, pak'a, *n.* [Pg. *paca,* < *pak,* the native name.] A large brown, white-spotted rodent of Central and South America. Also **spot·ted ca·vy.**

pace, päs, *n.* [O.Fr. Fr. *pas,* < L. *passus,* a step, pace, lit. 'a stretch' (of the leg), *pandere* (pp. *passus*), spread, stretch, extend.] A single step, as in walking or running; the distance traversed in a step; a linear measure of varying length representing this distance, commonly two and one-half feet; rate of walking or running; rate of movement or progress in general; tempo;

manner of walking or running; gait; any of the various gaits of a horse, specif. a gait of a horse in which the feet on the same side are lifted and put down together.—**put one through one's pac·es,** to cause to demonstrate accomplishments, skills, or capabilities.—**set the pace,** to be an example for emulation; to fix or regulate the speed, as in racing.—**paced,** *a.* Having a specific pace: used in compounds; as, slow-*paced*; measured or counted by paces; regulated by a pacemaker.

pace, päs, *v.t.*—*paced, pacing.* To traverse with paces or steps; to measure by paces; to stride nervously to and fro; to regulate the pace of; to set the pace for, as in racing; to train to a certain pace, as a horse.—*v.i.* To walk with slow, regular steps; to move with paces or steps, often nervously; to amble or go at a pace, as a horse.

pace·mak·er, päs'mā″kẽr, *n.* Someone or something that sets or controls the pace, esp. in a race; a person or thing that serves as an example or model for others; also **pace·set·ter.** *Anat.* the area in the right atrium that controls the heartbeat; *med.* a small electronic device used to stimulate and control heart action in certain pathological conditions; *chem.* a compound whose reaction rate controls the rate of reaction in a series of reactions.—**pace·mak·ing,** *n., a.*

pac·er, pā'sẽr, *n.* One who paces; a horse that paces, or whose natural gait is a pace; a pacemaker.

pa·chi·si, pa·chē'zē, pä·chē'zē, *n.* The game of Parcheesi.

pach·y·derm, pak'i·dụrm″, *n.* [Fr. *pachyderme,* < Gr. *pachydermos,* thick-skinned, < *pachys,* thick, and *derma,* skin.] An artificial classification of certain hoofed, nonruminant mammals, mostly thick-skinned, as the elephant, hippopotamus, and rhinoceros; an elephant; any thick-skinned animal; *fig.* a thick-skinned person who is not sensitive to criticism, ridicule, or rebuff.— **pach·y·der·mal,** *a.*—**pach·y·der·ma·tous,** pak″i·dụr'ma·tus, *a.*—**pach·y·der·mous,** pak″i·dụr'mus, *a.*—**pach·y·der·ma·tous·ly,** *adv.*—**pach·y·der·moid,** pak″i·dụr'-moid, *a.*

pach·y·san·dra, pak″i·san'dra, *n. Bot.* any of several species of evergreen trailing herbs or subshrubs in the box family, genus *Pachysandra,* grown as ground cover, esp. in shady areas.

pa·cif·ic, pa·sif'ik, *a.* [L. *pacificus,* < *pax* (*pac-*), peace, and *facere,* make.] Making or tending to make peace; conciliatory; peaceable, as in disposition or character; not warlike; peaceful, or at peace; tranquil, calm, or quiet. (*Cap.*) designating or pertaining to the ocean between the Americas and Asia and Australia, so named because of its calmness by Ferdinand Magellan, 16th century navigator; of or pertaining to the region bordering on the Pacific Ocean; as, the *Pacific* States, *Pacific* time.—*n.* (*Cap.*) the Pacific Ocean.—**pa·cif·i·cal·ly,** *adv.*

pa·cif·i·ca·tion, pas″i·fi·kā'shan, *n.* The act of pacifying; state or condition of being pacified; appeasement; *milit.* the subduing or overcoming of enemy forces, as guerrillas or other native opposition.—**pa·cif·i·ca·tor,** pa·sif'i·kā″tẽr, *n.*—**pa·cif·i·ca·to·ry,** pa·sif'i·ka·tōr″ē, *a.*

Pa·cif·ic Stand·ard Time, *n.* (*Sometimes l.c.*) see *Standard Time.* Abbr. *PST, p.s.t., P.S.T.*

pac·i·fi·er, pas'i·fī″ẽr, *n.* One who pacifies; a device of plastic, rubber, or the like, resembling a nipple for a baby to suck.

pac·i·fism, pas'i·fiz″um, *n.* [Fr. *pacifisme,* < *pacifique,* < L. *pacificus,* E. *pacific.* For *pacifism* as compared with *pacificism,* cf. *conservatism* (< *conservative*), *idly* (for *idlely*), *simply, mammalogy, symbology,* etc.]

The principle or policy of establishing and maintaining universal peace or such relations among all nations that all differences may be adjusted by peaceful means, or without recourse to war; refusal to bear arms or to kill; sometimes, in a disparaging sense, the spirit, attitude, or procedure of those who insist on peace at any price. Also **pa·cif·i·cism,** pa·sif'i·siz″um.—**pac·i·fist,** pas'i·fist, *n., a.*—**pac·i·fis·tic,** pas″i·fis'tik, *a.*—**pac·i·fis·ti·cal·ly,** *adv.*

pac·i·fy, pas'i·fī, *v.t.*—*pacified, pacifying.* [Fr. *pacifier,* L. *pacificare.*] To make peaceful; to restore peace to; to subdue; to appease; to cause to give up anger or excited feeling; to allay the agitation or excitement of; to calm.—**pac·i·fi·a·ble,** *a.*

pack, pak, *n.* [M.E. *packe, pakke,* prob. < D. or L.G.: cf. D. *pak,* M.L.G. *pak, packe,* G. *pack.*] A quantity of anything wrapped or tied up, as for carrying; a bundle, parcel, or bale, esp. for transport on the back of a man or animal; a fixed quantity of something, wrapped for sale; as, a *pack* of cigarettes; a group of certain animals, as hounds or wolves; the quantity of anything, as a food product, put up or packed at any one time or in one season; a complete set, as of playing cards; a beautifying material; as, a mud *pack*; a wrapping of the body in wet or dry cloths for therapeutic purposes; a mass of floating pieces of ice driven together; a group of things or persons, said in contempt.—*v.t.* To make into a pack; to put together compactly; to put into cans, bottles, or the like, as tomatoes, in suitable form for the market or preservation; to press or crowd together, as into a compact mass or close quarters; to fill, as a box or suitcase, with clothing or the like; to make impervious to water, steam, air, or the like by means of packing material, as a gasket; to cover or envelop with something pressed closely around (the object); to treat with a therapeutic pack; to load, as with a pack; to carry; as, to *pack* a gun; to send off or dismiss summarily.—*v.i.* To pack goods into compact form, as for transportation or storage; admit of compact storing or arrangement; as, goods that *pack* well; to become compacted, as snow or ice; crowd together, as persons; collect into packs as certain animals; to go away, esp. in haste, usu. followed by *off.*—*a.* Used in transporting; as, a *pack* animal; suitable for packing.—**send pack·ing,** to dismiss; send away abruptly.—**pack·a·bil·i·ty,** pak″a·bil'i·tē, *n.*—**pack·a·ble,** *a.*

pack, pak, *v.t.* [Appar. connected with *pact.*] To make up corruptly, as a jury or legislature, so as to further particular interests.

pack·age, pak'ij, *n.* A parcel or bundle, usu. rather small, wrapped or boxed for shipping or mailing; a quantity of anything packed together; a container in which anything is packed, as a box, case, or crate; the packing of goods; an article composed of several parts assembled into a unit ready for use; a group or series of something, as theater tickets or television programs.—*v.t.* To provide with a container; to bundle or wrap into a parcel or unit.—**pack·ag·er,** *n.* One who wraps or packs; one who makes packages.

pack·age deal, *n.* A sales offer consisting of a group of related products or services at a set price for the group, which must be accepted in its entirety; the products or services included in the offer; any agreement where approval of one element involves or rests upon approval of another element, as a labor union contract.

pack·age store, *n.* A retail store selling sealed bottles of alcoholic beverages which may not be consumed on the premises.

pack·er, pak'ẽr, *n.* One who packs; one who owns a meat packing house; one who works in a meat packing house; one involved in the canning or preserving of various types of foods; a wholesale dealer in packed foods; a machine which packs.

pack·et, pak′it, *n.* [Fr. *paquet.*] A small pack, package, or parcel; a parcel of letters. A vessel carrying mail, goods, and passengers on a schedule; also **pack·et boat.**

pack ice, *n.* Ice pack.

pack·ing, pak′ing, *n.* The act of one who or that which packs; any material used for making a tight connection, as in a steam pipe. *Nuclear phys.* the building up of a nucleus from protons and neutrons, resulting in a loss of mass and a formation of energy.

pack·ing house, *n.* An establishment where meats or other foods are prepared and packed for the market. Also **pack·ing plant.**

pack·man, pak′man, *n.* pl. **pack·men.** One who carries a pack, esp. of wares for sale; a peddler.

pack rat, *n.* A large N. American rodent, *Neotoma cinerea*, characterized by a bushy tail and its habit of hoarding small articles often of little value to it. *Colloq.* a person who collects useless things; an aged prospector.

pack·sack, pak′sak″, *n.* A baglike flexible case of leather or woven material designed with straps for carrying objects, usu. on the back of a person or pack animal.

pack·sad·dle, pak′sad″l, *n.* A saddle on which burdens are laid for conveyance by pack animals.

pack·thread, pak′thred″, *n.* Strong thread or twine used for tying parcels and for sewing.—**pack·thread·ed,** *a.*

pact, pakt, *n.* [Fr. *pacte,* L. *pactum,* a bargain (as in *compact*), < *paciscor, pactus,* to fix, bargain, covenant; same root as *pax,* peace.] A contract; an agreement or covenant between persons, groups, or nations.

pad, pad, *n.* [Origin uncertain.] A cushionlike mass of some soft material, as for comfort or protection or for filling out or stuffing; a number of sheets of paper bound together at one edge to form a tablet; a cushion of absorbent material saturated with ink, used to ink a rubber stamp; a launching pad; the large floating leaf of the water lily; a wad of gauze or other dressing material used for medical and surgical purposes; one of the cushionlike protuberances on the under side of the feet of dogs, foxes, and some other animals; the pulvillus of an insect's foot; the handle of certain tools; the socket of a brace; a cushion used as a saddle. *Slang,* place of residence; a bedroom or bed.—*v.t.—padded, padding.* To stuff or fill with padding; to protect with padding; *fig.* to extend with unnecessary wordage, as a speech or writing; *slang,* to expand, as an expense account, in a fraudulent manner.

pad, pad, *n.* [Orig. beggars' and thieves' slang: cf. D. *pad,* path, and E. *path*; in later use, associated with the sound.] A dull sound, as of footsteps on the ground; a road horse; a highwayman; *Brit. dial.* a path or road.—*v.t.—padded, padding.* To travel along, as a road, on foot; to beat down by treading.—*v.i.* To travel on foot; to walk with muffled footsteps.

pad·ding, pad′ing, *n.* The act of one who or that which pads; material, as cotton, synthetic fibers, or straw, used to stuff, fill, or protect something; *fig.* matter used to expand a written article, speech, or expense account.

pad·dle, pad′l, *n.* [M.E. *padell*; origin uncertain.] A short oar with a broad blade at one end or at each end, used without a rowlock for propelling a canoe or similar craft; any of various implements having broad blades, used for stirring, mixing, beating, or the like, in industry, arts, and crafts; a kind of racket with a short handle and rounded blade used in table tennis; a thin board with a short handle used in spanking and hazing; one of the broad boards on the circumference of a paddle wheel or on a water wheel; a paddle wheel, or a vessel propelled by a paddle wheel; the flipper or limb of certain swimming animals, as the whale and turtle; the act of paddling; the act of spanking; swimming with short strokes, as a dog does.—*v.i.—paddled, paddling.* To use a paddle to propel a canoe or the like; propel or travel in a canoe or similar craft by using a paddle; move by means of paddle wheels, as a steamship; row slowly or gently with oars. —*v.t.* To propel by paddling; to convey, as in a canoe, by paddling; to hit, as a ping-pong ball, with the *paddle*; to beat with or as with a paddle; to spank.—**pad·dle your own ca·noe,** make one's way unaided.—**pad·dler,** *n.*

pad·dle, pad′l, *v.i.—paddled, paddling.* [Origin uncertain.] To dabble or play in or as in shallow water.

pad·dle·fish, pad′l·fish″, *n.* pl. **pad·dle·fish·es, pad·dle·fish.** A ganoid fish, *Polyodon spathula*, allied to the sturgeons, about four feet long and with a snout shaped like a paddle: common in the Mississippi River and its tributaries. Also *spoonbill, spoonbill cat.*

pad·dle wheel, *n.* A wheel with paddle boards on its circumference, for propelling a vessel through the water; a boat propelled by paddle wheels.

pad·dock, pad′ok, *n.* [For *parrok,* O.E. *pearroc.*] An area adjacent to a racecourse, used for saddling and mounting of horses; a field enclosed for pasture or for exercising animals; *Aust.* any enclosed field.

pad·dy, pad′ē, *n.* pl. **pad·dies.** [Malay *padi.*] Rice in the husk whether in the field or gathered; the flooded land on which rice is grown.

pad·dy wag·on, *n. Slang,* patrol wagon.

pad·lock, pad′lok, *n.* [M.E. *padlokke*; first element uncertain.] A portable or detachable lock having a pivoted or sliding hasp or shackle which passes through a staple, ring, or the like and is then fastened.—*v.t.* To fasten with or as with a padlock.

pa·dre, pä′drā, pä′drē, *Sp.* pä′THre, *It.* pä′dRe, *n.* pl. **pa·dres,** *It.* **pa·dri,** pä′drāz, pä′drēz, *Sp.* pä′THres, *It.* pä′dRē. [It. *padre,* L. *pater,* father.] Father: a title applied esp. in Spain, Italy, and Spanish American countries to a priest, and in India to any clergyman; *colloq.* a military or naval chaplain.

pa·dro·ne, pa·drō′nē, pa·drō′nā, *It.* pä·dRä′ne, *n.* pl. **pa·dro·nes,** *It.* **pa·dro·ni,** pa·drō′nēz, pa·drō′näz, *It.* pä·dRạ′nē. [It. < L. *patronus,* E. *patron.*] *It.* One who supplies native laborers; a master of a vessel; an innkeeper; an owner or operator of any business.

pad·u·a·soy, paj′ö·a·soi″, *n.* pl. **pad·u·a·soys.** [Appar. a corruption of Fr. *pou-de-soie,* by association with *Padua,* city in Italy.] A smooth, corded, rich silk fabric, much worn by both men and women in the 18th century; a garment made of this fabric.—*a.*

pae·an, pē·an, pē′an, *n.* [Gr.] An ancient Greek hymn in honor of Apollo, who was also called Paean or Paian; a war song before or after a battle; hence, a song of triumph generally; a song of joy or praise.

pae·do·gen·e·sis, pē″dō·jen′i·sis, *n.* [Gr. *pais, paidos,* a child, *genesis,* descent.] *Biol.* precocious reproduction by larval or other immature animals, often parthenogenetically.—**pae·do·ge·net·ic, pa·do·gen·ic,** pē″dō·je·net′ik, *a.*

pae·on, pē′on, *n.* [Gr. *paeon.*] *Class. pros.* a metrical foot, consisting of four syllables, one long and three short; (*cap.*), *mythol.* paean.

pa·gan, pā′gan, *n.* [L. *paganus,* a peasant, < *pagus,* a village or country district; compare origin of *heathen.* Akin *peasant.*] One who worships false gods or subscribes to a polytheistic religion; one who is neither a Christian, a Jew, nor a Mohammedan; a heathen; an idolater; a person with no religion.—*a.* Of or related to pagans; irreligious; heathenish.—**pa·gan·ish,** *a.*

pa·gan·ism, pā′ga·niz″um, *n.* The worship of false gods; heathenism; the condition of being a pagan.

pa·gan·ize, pā′ga·nīz″, *v.t.—paganized, paganizing.* To render heathenish; to convert to paganism.—*v.i.* To become pagan.—**pa·gan·iz·er,** *n.*

page, pāj, *n.* [Fr. *page,* < L. *pāgina,* a page, < stem *pag,* seen in L. *pango,* Gr. *pēgnymi,* to fix; akin *compact* (a.), *pageant.*] One side of the leaf of a book; a leaf of a book; a writing or record, or something noteworthy enough to be recorded; as, a *page* of history. *Print.* type set up for one side of a leaf.—*v.t.—paged, paging.* To number the pages of; *paginate.—v.i.* To go through a book, page by page.—**pag·i·nal,** paj′i·nal, *a.*

page, pāj, *n.* [Fr. *page,* It. *paggio,* a page, < L.L. *pagius,* perh. < Gr. *padion,* or *pais,* child.] A youth or young boy appointed to attend and perform errands for specific persons, including members of a legislative body during its sessions, royalty, simulated royalty in plays or pageants, and the leading figures in such formal functions as a coronation, wedding, or convention; young males employed to perform light chores in a hotel, club, or private residence. *Medieval,* a youth being prepared for knighthood.—*v.t.* To act as a page; to summon a person by calling his name continually.

pag·eant, paj′ent, *n.* [Old forms *pagyn, pagen,* orig. a scaffold or stage, < L. *pagina,* a slab, a page (of a book).] A spectacle or entertainment; a great display or show, as at some public celebration; a theatrical exhibition; anything showy, without stability or duration.

pag·eant·ry, paj′en·trē, *n.* pl. **pag·eant·ries.** A showy exhibition or spectacle; mere show; pageants collectively.

pag·i·nate, paj′i·nāt″, *v.t.—paginated, paginating.* To number the pages of, as of a book.

pag·i·na·tion, paj″i·nā′shan, *n.* An indicating of the sequence of pages, as of a book; the figures which indicate the page numbers.

pa·go·da, pa·gō′da, *n.* [Fr. *pagode,* < Pers. and Hind., *but-gadah—but,* an idol, and *gadah,* a house.] A temple in the Far East, usu. in the form of a pyramid or a tower, with the roof over each story designed to turn upward; a gold or silver coin bearing the figure of a pagoda.

pail, pāl, *n.* [O.Fr. *paile, paele,* < L. *patella,* a pan, < *pateo,* to lie open.] A cylindrical container with a handle, used for carrying liquids and solids; bucket; the amount carried in a full pail.

pail·ful, pāl′ful″, *n.* pl. **pail·fuls.** The quantity that a pail will hold.

pail·lasse, pal·yas′, pal′yas, *n.* [Fr., < *paille,* straw.] *Chiefly Brit.* a mattress filled with straw or wood shavings, used as an under mattress or a pallet. Also *palliasse.*

pail·lon, *Fr.* pä·yäN′, *n.* Metallic foil used in enamel work and gilding.

pain, pān, *n.* [Fr. *peine,* O.Fr. *peine, paine,* etc., < L. *poena,* punishment, and latterly pain, torment.] Physical ache, discomfort, or distress because of injury, overstrain, or illness; emotional or mental affliction or suffering; grief. *Pl.* the throes of travail or childbirth; assiduous or careful effort.

—v.t. To give pain to; to cause to endure physical or mental suffering; to afflict; to distress.—**v.i.** To suffer or give pain.— **on, un·der,** or **up·on pain of,** carrying the penalty or punishment of.—**pain·less,** a.— **pain·less·ly,** adv.—**pain·less·ness,** n.

pain·ful, pān'ful, a. Giving or accompanied by pain; distressing; requiring labor or toil; difficult; demanding diligent effort; vexatious or annoying.—**pain·ful·ly,** adv. —**pain·ful·ness,** n.

pains·tak·ing, pānz'tā"king, pān'stā"king, a. Taking or given to taking pains; done with diligence and carefulness; laborious and careful.—n. The taking of pains; careful labor.—**pains·tak·ing·ly,** adv.

paint, pānt, v.t. [O.Fr. paindre, pp. paint (Fr. peindre), < L. pingere, pictum, to paint.] Fine arts, to make, as a picture, by laying on colors. To describe vividly; to decorate or protect with a coat of paint; to use facial make-up on; to apply, as medication, with a swab.—v.i. To cover something with paint; to make pictures; to use cosmetics.

paint, pānt, n. A pigment, either in dry form or diluted with oil, water, or some other thinner for use in fine arts or as a protective covering for many surfaces, including wood and plaster; a coating of this; a cosmetic, esp. one which adds color.

paint·brush, pānt'brush", n. A brush used for painting buildings, pictures, and other objects. Bot. a N. American prairie wild flower, Castilleja coccinea, in the snapdragon family, with scarlet-tipped bracts surrounding the flowers; also Indian paintbrush.

paint·ed bunt·ing, n. A brilliantly colored N. American bird, Passerina ciris, of the finch family, the male having a blue-violet head, green on the back, red on rump and underparts, and breeding in the Gulf States. Also **paint·ed finch.**

paint·er, pān'tėr, n. One whose occupation is to apply paint to surfaces or walls; an artist who represents objects or abstractions by means of colors or pigments.—**paint·er·ly,** a.

paint·er, pān'tėr, n. [Ir. painteir, a snare, a net.] A rope used to fasten a boat to a ship or other object.

paint·er, pān'tėr, n. [Var. of panther.] American panther, or cougar.

paint·er's col·ic, n. Pathol. a type of lead poisoning marked by a slow pulse and acute pain in the abdomen.

paint·ing, pān'ting, n. A painted surface; the occupation of painting. Fine arts, the art of painting; a picture made through the art of painting; a painting characteristic of a certain style, place, or period.

pair, pâr, n. pl. **pairs, pair.** [Fr. paire, < L. pār, equal, whence also parity.] Two things similar in form, and suited to each other or used together; as, a pair of stockings; a single thing composed of two pieces which work together; as, a pair of scissors; two of a sort; a couple; a brace; a man and his wife; two mated animals; two members of a deliberative body, taking opposite sides, who agree not to vote and so to permit the absence of one or both; the agreement thus reached; two players in competition against similar partnerships. Cards, two cards of one denomination; as, a pair of kings. Mech. two pieces combining to make a unit, as a screw and nut.—v.t. To arrange in couples or pairs; match; mate.—v.i. To join in pairs; to mate; to be one of a pair; to associate oneself with another. To depart from a company in twos, usu. followed by off.

pair-oar, pâr'ōr", n. A boat where two rowers sit one in front of the other, each pulling one oar.—**pair-oared,** a.

pair pro·duc·tion, n. Phys. the instantaneous creation of an electron and positron

from a photon which has passed through a highly intensified electric field.

pais·ley, pāz'lē, a. [From Paisley, Scotland.] (Often cap.) Typically made of woolen material, patterned in bright colors; having the pattern characteristic of paisley.—n. pl. **pais·leys.** (Often cap.) A paisley fabric; an article, as a shawl, made of the fabric.

pa·jam·as, pa·jä'maz, pa·jam'az, n. pl. [Hind.] A loose garment, consisting of jacket and trousers, worn for sleeping or lounging; wide trousers worn in the East by men and women. Also Brit. pyjamas.

pal, pal, n. [Said to be of Gipsy origin.] Slang, an intimate associate or friend.—v.i. —palled, palling. Slang, to associate as a pal or as pals.

pal·ace, pal'is, n. [Fr. palais, < L. Palatium, the house of Augustus, on the hill at Rome, called by this name.] The house in which an emperor, a king, or other distinguished person resides; a splendid residence; a stately mansion; an ornate public place for amusement or entertainment.

pal·a·din, pal'a·din, n. [Fr. paladin, < L. palatinus, attached to the palace, < palatium.] A heroic champion of a noble cause; an eminent hero; any of the 12 knights serving Charlemagne.

Pa·lae·arc·tic, pä'lē·ärk'tik, pal'ē·ärk'tik, a. Referring to a zoogeographical division of the globe, including Europe and the northern regions of Asia, Africa, and Arabia. Also **Pa·le·arc·tic.**

pa·laes·tra, pa·les·tra, pa·les'tra, n. pl. **pa·laes·trae, pa·laes·tras,** pa·les'trē. A school for athletics in ancient Greece; gymnasium.—**pa·laes·tral,** a.—**pa·laes·tri·an,** a.

pal·an·quin, pal"an·kēn', n. [Fr. and Pg. palanquin, < Pali, pâlangki.] A covered conveyance used in India, China, and Japan, borne by poles on the shoulders of men and carrying a single person; a covered litter. Also **pal·an·keen.**

pal·at·a·ble, pal'a·ta·bl, a. Agreeable to the palate or taste; savory; fig. agreeable to the mind or feelings.—**pal·at·a·bil·i·ty, pal·at·a·ble·ness,** n.—**pal·at·a·bly,** adv.

pal·a·tal, pal'a·tal, a. [Fr. palatal.] Anat. of or pertaining to the palate; phon. of speech sounds, uttered with the aid of the palate, as the -ion in onion.—n. Phon. a palatal sound.—**pal·a·tal·ly,** adv.

pal·a·tal·ize, pal'a·ta·līz", v.t.—palatalized, palatalizing. Phon. to render palatal either by assimilation or pronunciation, as the -ture in mature.—**pal·a·tal·i·za·tion,** pal'a·ta·li·zā'shan, n.

pal·ate, pal'it, n. [L. palatum, the palate.] Anat. the roof of the mouth which separates the nasal and oral cavities and consists of an anterior bony arch, the hard palate, and the soft palate, a muscular tissue at the posterior part of the upper mouth. The sense of taste; intellectual taste.

pa·la·tial, pa·lā'shal, a. [< L. palatium, palace.] Pertaining to or like a palace; becoming or suitable for a palace; magnificent. —**pa·la·tial·ly,** adv.—**pa·la·tial·ness,** n.

pal·a·tine, pal'a·tīn", pal'a·tin, a. [Fr. palatin, L. palatinus, < palatium, palace.] Pertaining to a palace, esp. a Roman palace; possessing royal privileges; related to a palatine.—n. A vassal or lord invested with royal privileges and rights within his province or territory; a count palatine; a high official of a royal palace; (cap.) an inhabitant of the Palatinate, an area west of the Rhine in southwest Germany. A fur shoulder cape.—**pal·at·i·nate,** pa·lat'i·nāt", pa·lat'i·nit, n. The province or territory under a palatine; the office of a palatine; (cap.) a region in southwestern Germany formerly belonging to Bavaria.

pal·a·tine, pal'a·tīn", pal'a·tin, a. [Fr. palatin.] Of or pertaining to the palate:

palatal.—n. Anat. either of the two bones, right and left, that form the hard palate.

pa·lav·er, pa·lav'ėr, pa·lä'vėr, n. [Pg. palavra, Sp. palabra, a word, < L. parabola, a parable, in late times a word.] A lengthy talk or conference with some barbaric race; a discussion; superfluous or idle talk; flattery.—v.t. To flatter or persuade.—v.i. To talk idly or profusely.

pale, pāl, a. [O.Fr. pale (Fr. pâle), < L. pallidus, pale.] A whitish color; wan; pallid; as, a pale countenance; low in saturation; as, a pale blue; not bright; dim; feeble.—v.t., v.i.—paled, paling. To cause to be or become pale.—**pal·ish, pal·y,** a.— **pale·ly,** adv.—**pale·ness,** n.

pale, pāl, n. [O.E. pal, Fr. pal < L. palus, a stake, from root seen in page of a book, pageant, pact.] A pointed stake used in fencing; a picket; a barrier which surrounds and encloses an area; the space enclosed; a limit or boundary; a district within a fixed boundary; the bounds within which socially acceptable behavior is confined; as, his manners were beyond the pale. A part of Ireland which was invaded by Anglo-Normans in the 12th century and later came under English jurisdiction; also English Pale, Pale.—v.t.—paled, paling. To enclose with pales; to fence; to encompass.

pa·le·a, pä'lē·a, n. pl. **pa·le·ae,** pä'lē·ē". [L. palea, chaff.] Bot. the upper of two enclosing bracts in the grass flower. Also palet. —**pa·le·a·ceous,** pä"lē·ā'shus, a. Bot. Consisting of chafflike scales; covered with paleae.—**pa·le·al,** a.

pa·le·eth·nol·o·gy, pä"lē·eth·nol'o·jē, pal'ē·eth·nol'o·jē, n. The branch of ethnology that treats of the earliest or most primitive races of mankind.

pale·face, pāl'fās", n. A white person: term supposedly first used by the American Indians.

pa·le·o·bot·a·ny, pa·lae·o·bot·a·ny, pä'lē·ō·bot'a·nē, pal'ē·ō·bot'a·nē, n. The study of plants found in a fossil state. —**pa·le·o·bo·tan·i·cal,** pä"lē·ō·bo·tan'i·kal, pal"ē·ō·bo·tan'i·kal, a.—**pa·le·o·bo·tan·i·cal·ly,** adv.—**pa·le·o·bot·a·nist,** n.

Pa·le·o·cene, Pa·lae·o·cene, pä'lē·o·sēn", pal'ē·o·sēn", a. Geol. of or pertaining to an epoch of the Tertiary Period, occurring about 70,000,000 years ago, before the Eocene Epoch, and characterized by the presence of primitive mammals and modern birds.—n. The Paleocene epoch. See Table of Geologic Time.

pa·le·og·ra·phy, pä"lē·og'ra·fē, pal"ē·og'ra·fē, n. [Gr. graphō, to write.] An ancient manner of writing; ancient writings collectively; the science of deciphering ancient documents or inscriptions.—**pa·le·og·ra·pher,** n.—**pa·le·o·graph·ic, pa·le·o·graph·i·cal,** pä"lē·o·graf'ik, pal"ē·o·graf'ik.—**pa·le·o·graph·i·cal·ly,** adv.

pa·le·o·lith, pä'lē·o·lith, pal'ē·o·lith, n. [Gr. palaios, ancient, and lithos, stone.] A Paleolithic stone implement.

Pa·le·o·lith·ic, pä"lē·o·lith'ik, pal"ē·o·lith'ik, a. Noting or pertaining to that earlier part of the Stone Age, an early culture characterized first by the development of primitive stone implements and later by the appearance of cave paintings and crude sculpture.

pa·le·o·mag·net·ism, pä"lē·ō·mag'ni·tiz"um, n. The geophysical science which investigates the residual magnetization in ancient rocks by determining their intensity and direction when formed.—**pa·le·o·mag·net·ic,** a.

pa·le·on·tol·o·gy, pa·lae·on·tol·o·gy, pä"lē·on·tol'o·jē, pal"ē·on·tol'o·jē, n. pl. **pa·le·on·tol·o·gies.** The science of ancient life; that branch of biological science which treats of fossil remains; a treatise on the

pal·a·tine, pal'a·tīn", pal'a·tin, a. [Fr. palatin.] Of or pertaining to the palate:

subject.—**pa·le·on·to·log·ic, pa·le·on·-to·log·i·cal,** pā″lē·on″to·loj′ik, pal″ē·on″-to·loj′i·kal, *a.*—**pa·le·on·tol·o·gist,** *n.*

Pa·le·o·zo·ic, pā″lē·o·zō′ik, pal″ē·o·zō′-ik, *a.* [Gr. *zōē,* life.] *Geol.* Pertaining to the era preceding the Mesozoic and extending from the Cambrian through the Permain periods, during which fish, primitive insects, reptiles, and seed-bearing ferns appeared and rock systems were formed.—*n.* See Table of Geologic Time.

pa·le·o·zo·ol·o·gy, pā″lē·ō·zō·ol′o·jē, pal″ē·ō·zō·ol′o·jē, *n.* The study of fossil animals, including both invertebrate and vertebrate paleontology.—**pa·le·o·zo·o·-log·i·cal,** pā″lē·ō·zō″o·loj′i·kal, pal″ē·-ō·zō″o·loj′i·kal, *a.*

pal·et, pal′it, *n.* Palea.

pal·ette, pal′it, *n.* [Fr. *palette,* palette, flat-bladed implement, dim. of *pale, pelle,* shovel, < L. *pala,* spade, shovel.] A thin, usually oval or oblong board or tablet with a thumb hole at one end, used by painters to lay and mix colors on; the set of colors on a palette; a selection of colors, as those used by a particular artist; see *pallet. Armor,* a small rounded plate formerly used to protect the front of the armpit; also *pallette.*

pal·ette knife, *n. Painting,* a thin, flexible blade rounded at the end and set in a handle, used for mixing or applying artists' colors.

pal·frey, pal′frē, *n.* pl. **pal·freys.** [O.Fr. *palefrei,* < L.L. *parafredus,* L. *paraveredus,* an extra post horse, < Gr. *para,* beside, and L. *veredus,* a post horse (< *veho,* to carry, and *rheda,* a carriage).] *Archaic.* A riding horse, distinguished from a war horse; a small horse suited to a lady.

pal·imp·sest, pal′imp·sest″, *n.* [Gr. *palimpsestos,* rubbed again—*palin,* again, and *psao,* to rub.] A parchment or other piece of writing material from which one writing has been erased to make room for another, often leaving the first faintly visible, a process to which many ancient manuscripts were subjected.—*a.*

pal·in·drome, pal′in·drōm″, *n.* [Gr. *palin-dromos,* running back—*palin,* again, and *dromos,* a running.] A word, verse, or sentence that is the same when read backward or forward, as 'radar.'

pal·ing, pā′ling, *n.* A fence formed of pales or pickets; the act of building a fence of pales or pickets; an individual pale; pales collectively.

pal·in·gen·e·sis, pal″in·jen′i·sis, *n.* [Gr. *pálin,* back, again, and *genesis,* genesis.] Rebirth; regeneration; reincarnation; *embryol.* the reproducing of ancestral structures during the development of an embryo: opposed to *cenogenesis.*—**pal·in·-ge·net·ic,** pal″in·je·net′ik, *a.*—**pal·in·ge·-net·i·cal·ly,** *adv.*

pal·i·node, pal′i·nōd″, *n.* [Gr. *palinōdia—palin,* again, and *ōdē,* a song.] A poem in which a poet retracts something contained in a former piece; a recantation or retraction in general.—**pal·i·nod·ist,** *n.*

pal·i·sade, pal″i·sād′, *n.* [Fr. *palissade,* < *palisser,* furnish with a paling, < *palis,* paling, < L. *palus,* E. *pale.*] A fence of pales or stakes set firmly in the ground, as for enclosure or defense; a long, strong stake pointed at the top, for fixing firmly in the ground with others like it, in a close row, either vertical or inclined, for a defense, as in fortification; *fig.* something resembling a fence of stakes; *pl.* a line of lofty cliffs.—*v.t.—palisaded, palisading.* To furnish or fortify with a palisade.

pall, pal, *n.* [O.E. *paell,* < L. *pallium,* a cloak, pall.] A large cloth thrown over a coffin or a tomb; an enveloping covering or cloud; an atmosphere of an oppressive nature. *Eccles.* a square of linen, usually stiffened with cardboard, used as a cover for the chalice during Mass; pallium.—*v.t.* To cover with a pall; to shroud.

pall, pal, *v.i.* [W. *pallu,* to fail; *pall,* loss of energy, failure; the verb *appall* was prob. to some extent affected by this word.] To become devoid of interest or attraction; to have a dulling or wearying effect, with *on* or *upon.*—*v.t.* To make vapid; to cloy.

pal·la·di·um, pa·lā′dē·um, *n. Chem.* a silver-white, malleable and ductile, metallic element of the platinum group. Sym. Pd, at. no. 46, at. wt. 106.4. See Periodic Table of Elements.

Pal·la·di·um, pa·lā′dē·um, *n.* [From Pallas or Athena, equiv. to L. *Minerva.*] A statue of the Greek goddess, Athena, on whose preservation the safety of the city of Troy was said to depend. (*l.c.*) a safeguard; something that affords effectual protection for a community or organized group of persons.

pall·bear·er, pal′bâr″ėr, *n.* One of those who attend the coffin at a funeral.

pal·let, pal′it, *n.* [< Fr. *paille,* straw; L. *palea,* chaff.] A small or rude bed; a bed or mattress of straw.

pal·let, pal′it, *n.* [Fr. *palette,* < L.L. *paletta,* dim. < L. *pala,* a spade or shovel.] A broad-bladed, wooden instrument used by potters for forming and rounding their wares; a lip or projection on the point of a pawl engaging the teeth of a wheel, always used with the escapement wheel of a clock or watch; an instrument to take up and apply gold leaf, or to decorate the back of a book; a transportable platform used for the storage or removal of goods; a palette.

pal·let·ize, pal′i·tīz″, *v.t.—palletized, pal-letizing.* To load on pallets for storage or transportation.

pal·lette, pal′it, *n. Armor,* palette.

pal·li·al, pal′ē·al, *a. Zool.* Of or pertaining to the cerebral cortex; pertaining to a pallium, esp. of a mollusk.

pal·liasse, pal·yas′, pal′yas, *n.* Paillasse.

pal·li·ate, pal′ē·āt″, *v.t.—palliated, palliat-ing.* [Fr. *pallier,* to cloak, palliate; < L. *pallium,* a cloak, whence also *pall* (*n.*).] To try to conceal the significance of by excuses and apologies; to mitigate, lessen, or abate. —**pal·li·a·tion,** pal″ē·ā′shan, *n.*—**pal·-li·a·tor,** *n.*—**pal·li·a·tive,** pal′ē·ā″tiv, pal′ē·a·tiv, *a., n.*—**pal·li·a·tive·ly,** *adv.*

pal·lid, pal′id, *a.* [L. *pallidus,* < *palleo,* to become pale.] Pale, wan; deficient in color. —**pal·lid·ly,** *adv.*—**pal·lid·ness,** *n.*

pal·li·um, pal′ē·um, *n.* pl. **pal·li·a, pal·li·ums,** pal′ē·a. [L., cloak, covering.] A voluminous rectangular mantle worn by men in ancient Greece and Rome; *Rom. Cath. Ch.* a narrow circular band of white wool worn over the shoulders, having two 12-inch pendants hanging one in front and one in back, worn in certain services by the pope and archbishops. *Zool.* an outgrowth of the dorsal body wall of many mollusks, forming folds or processes which represent the mantle and other parts; a similar structure in brachiopods. *Anat.* the cerebral cortex of a vertebrate.

pall-mall, pel′mel′, *n.* [O.Fr. *palemail,* < It. *pallamaglio,* < *palla,* a ball (akin E. *ball*), and *maglio,* L. *malleus,* a mallet.] A popular game of 17th century England and France in which a ball was struck with a mallet through a ring elevated upon a pole; the alley where the game was played.— **Pall Mall,** a street in London celebrated for its clubs.

pal·lor, pal′ėr, *n.* [L.] Paleness; wanness.

palm, päm, *n.* [O.E. *palm,* < L. *palma,* palm tree, orig. palm of the hand; from the resemblance of the leaf to the outspread hand.] Any of the tropical or subtropical plants constituting the family *Palmaceae,* the majority of which are trees with a tall, usu. unbranched stem surmounted by a crown of large, palmately cleft, fan-shaped leaves; any of various other trees or shrubs which resemble the palm; a leaf or branch of a palm tree, esp. as formerly borne for an emblem of victory or triumph; a representation of such a leaf or branch, as on a decoration of honor, or as an addition of honor to a military decoration. *Fig.* the victor's reward of honor, or the honor of being victorious or of surpassing others; triumph; success.—**pal·ma·ceous,** pal·-mā′shus, päl·mā′shus, pä·mā′shus, *a.* Belonging to the palm family.—**palm·like,** *a.*

palm, päm, *n.* [O.Fr. *palme* (Fr. *paume*), < L. *palma,* palm, hand, also palm tree; akin to Gr. *palamē,* O.E. *folm,* palm, hand, Skt. *pāni,* hand.] That part of the inner surface of the hand which extends from the wrist to the bases of the fingers; the corresponding part of the forefoot of an animal; the part of a glove covering the palm; an instrument worn over the palm of the hand by sail-makers, corresponding to a thimble; a flat, widened part at the end of an armlike projection; the blade of an oar; the flat, expanded part of the horn or antler of some deer; the inner surface of the fluke of an anchor; a linear measure based on either the breadth of the hand, three to four inches, or its length from wrist to finger tips, seven to nine inches.—*v.t.* To touch or stroke with the palm or hand; handle; hold; shake hands with; to conceal in the palm, as in cheating at cards or dice or in legerdemain; to pick up furtively; to impose fraudulently; *basketball,* to briefly hold, as the ball, while dribbling.—**palm off,** to pass off fraudu-lently or deceptively; as, to *palm off* spurious things as genuine, or to *palm off* a borrowed witticism as one's own.

pal·mar, pal′mėr, päl′mėr, pä′mėr, *a.* [L. *palmaris.*] Pertaining to or situated in the palm of the hand; similar to or of the breadth of the hand.

pal·ma·ry, pal′ma·rē, päl′ma·rē, pä′-ma·rē, *a.* [L. *palmarius.*] Deserving the palm of victory; preeminent; praise-worthy.

pal·mate, pal′māt, pal′mit, päl′māt, päl′-mit, pä′māt, *a.* [L. *palmatus.*] Shaped like a hand with the fingers extended, as a leaf or an antler; of a bird's foot, webbed. *Bot.* pertaining to a leaf divided or lobed in a manner resembling the outstretched hand, with the lobes radiating from the region of the apex of the petiole; pertaining to the arrangement of the main veins in a leaf, which radiate from the apex of the petiole. Also **pal·mat·ed.**—**pal·mate·ly,** *adv.*—**pal·ma·tion,** pal·mā′shan, päl·mā′shan, pä·mā′shan, *n.* Palmate state or formation; a palmate structure.

palm·er, pä′mėr, päl′mėr, *n.* [O.Fr. *palmier, paumier,* < M.L. *palmārius,* < L. *palma,* E. *palm.*] Formerly, a pilgrim who had re-turned from the Holy Land, in token of which he bore a palm branch; an itinerant monk who went from shrine to shrine, under a perpetual vow of poverty; any pilgrim; a palmerworm; a kind of hairy artificial fly used in angling; a hackle.

palm·er·worm, pä′mėr·wurm″, *n.* Any of various caterpillars destructive to vegeta-tion, esp. the larva of an American moth, *Dichomeris ligulella,* which is destructive to fruit trees.

pal·met·to, pal·met′ō, *n.* pl. **pal·met·tos, pal·met·toes.** [Sp. *palmito,* dim. of *palma,* < L. *palma,* E. *palm.*] Any of several species of palm trees in the genus *Sabal,* esp. *S. palmetto,* characterized by fan-shaped leaves whose blades curve down-ward at the tips, native to the coastal dune regions from N. Carolina to Florida, and planted as an ornamental; the State tree represented on the seal of S. Carolina;

(*cap.*) a nickname for the State of S. Carolina.

palm·is·try, pä′mi·strē, *n.* [M.E. *pawmestry*, *palmestrie*, < *paume*, *palme*, E. *palm.*] The art or practice of telling fortunes and interpreting character by the lines and configurations of the palm of the hand.—**palm·ist**, *n.*

pal·mi·tate, pal′mi·tāt″, päl′mi·tāt″, pä′mi·tāt″, *n. Chem.* a salt or ester of palmitic acid.

pal·mit·ic ac·id, pal·mit′ik as′id, päl·mit′ik, pä·mit′ik, *n. Biochem.* a white, crystalline fatty acid occurring in the fats and oils of plants and animals and used primarily in making soap.

pal·mi·tin, pal′mi·tin, päl′mi·tin, pä′mi·tin, *n.* [Fr. *palmitine*, < L. *palma*, E. *palm.*] *Chem.* a colorless crystalline compound, an ester of glycerol and palmitic acid, occurring in palm oil and solid fats: used in soap making.

palm oil, *n.* A vegetable fat obtained from the fruit of a very productive oil palm, *Elaeis guineensis*, native to tropical Africa and now found throughout the tropics, used for food by the natives, but finding its chief use in the making of soap and candles.

Palm Sun·day, *n.* The Sunday next before Easter: so called from the custom in the Roman Catholic Church and in some Anglican churches, of solemnly blessing and distributing palm or other branches and carrying them in procession, in commemoration of Christ's triumphal entry into Jerusalem.

palm·y, pä′mē, *a.*—*palmier*, *palmiest.* Abounding in palms. *Fig.* flourishing; prosperous; as, the *palmy* days of Rome.

pal·my·ra, pal·mī′ra, *n.* [Pg. *palmeira*, < L. *palma*, E. *palm.*] One of the most useful of all palms, *Borassus flabellifer*, of the E. Indies, whose leaf stalk fibers are used in the making of stiff brushes, the fruit and young roots used for food, and whose sap is a source of sugar and wine. Also **pal·my·ra palm**.

pal·o·mi·no, pal″o·mē′nō, *n.* pl. **pal·o·mi·nos.** [Am. Sp.] A golden-coated horse with a white, flaxen, or ivory mane and tail.

palp, palp, *n.* pl. **pal·pi**, pal′pī. Palpus.—**pal·pal**, *a.*

pal·pa·ble, pal′pa·bl, *a.* [Fr. *palpable*, < L. *palpabilis*, < *palpo*, to touch; akin *palpitate.*] Perceptible to the touch; capable of being felt; tangible; easily perceived and detected; plain; obvious.—**pal·pa·bil·i·ty**, *n.*—**pal·pa·bly**, *adv.*

pal·pate, pal′pāt, *v.t.*—*palpated*, *palpating.* [L. *palpātus*, pp. of *palpāre*, touch, feel, stroke.] To examine by the sense of touch. —**pal·pa·tion**, pal·pā′shan, *n.* Examination by touch or feeling, as with the hand, to assist in diagnosing an illness.

pal·pate, pal′pāt, *a. Zool.* having a palpus or palpi.

pal·pe·bral, pal′pe·bral, *a.* [L. *palpebra*, an eyelid.] Pertaining to or situated near the eyelid.

pal·pi·tate, pal′pi·tāt″, *v.i.*—*palpitated*, *palpitating.* [L. *palpito*, *palpitatum*, freq. of *palpo*, to feel.] To pulsate violently: applied particularly to an abnormally rapid and strong beat of the heart, as from fright or disease; to throb; to tremble; to quiver.— **pal·pi·ta·tion**, *n.*—**pal·pi·tant**, pal′pi·tant, *a.*

pal·pus, pal′pus, *n.* pl. **pal·pi**, pal′pī. [Mod. L. *palpus* < L. *palpare*, to stroke, to feel.] *Zool.* An organ of sense extending from the mouth parts of certain insects and crustaceans; a feeler; palp.

pals·grave, palz′grāv, palz′grāv, *n.* [G. *pfalzgraf*, < *pfalz* (contr. < L. *palatium*, palace), and *graf*, an earl.] Formerly, in Germany, a nobleman having judicial powers within his own province. A count or countess palatinate of a county in England or Ireland.

pal·sy, pal′zē, *n.* pl. **pal·sies.** [O.Fr. *paralisie* (Fr. *paralysie*), < L. *paralysis.*] Paralysis, esp. a progressive form of paralysis culminating late in life, characterized by tremors of the limbs, muscular weakness and rigidity, and a peculiar gait and attitude. *Fig.* any condition in which the energies, sensibilities, or powers of resolution are weakened seriously; any palsied or paralyzing influence.—*v.t.*—*palsied*, *palsying.* To affect with or as with palsy; paralyze; render powerless to act, think, or resolve.—**pal·sied**, *a.*

pal·ter, pal′tĕr, *v.i.* [Of same origin as *paltry*, and orig. having reference to the haggling of dealers in old clothes.] To act insincerely; to equivocate; to haggle; to shift; to dodge; to use trickery.—**pal·ter·er**, *n.*

pal·try, pal′trē, *a.*—*paltrier*, *paltriest.* [Same as L.G. *paltrig*, *palterig*, ragged, < *palte*, Fris. *palt*, G. *palte*, Sw. *palta* (plur. *paltor*), Dan. *pialt*, a rag; akin *palter.*] Petty; trivial; inferior; worthless; mean; despicable.—**pal·tri·ness**, *n.*

pa·lu·dal, pa·lōd′al, *a.* [L. *palus*, *paludis*, a marsh.] Pertaining to marshes; generated by marshes; as, *paludal* fever.

pal·u·dism, pal′ū·diz″um, *n.* [L. *palus* (*palud-*), marsh.] *Pathol.* malarial disease.

pal·u·drine, pal′ū·drēn″, pal′ū·drin, pa·lō′drin, *n.* A drug, $C_{11}H_{16}N_5Cl$, used to treat malaria.

pal·y·nol·o·gy, pal″i·nol′o·jē, *n. Bot.*, *paleon.* the study of both extant and fossil pollen grains and spores.—**pal·y·no·log·i·cal**, pal″i·no·loj′i·kal, *a.*—**pal·y·no·log·i·cal·ly**, *adv.*

pam·pas, pam′paz, pam′pas, *Sp.* päm′päs, *n. pl.* [Sp.-Amer.] The immense grassy plains of South America, particularly of Argentina.—**pam·pe·an**, pam·pē′an, pam′pē·an, *a.*

pam·per, pam′pĕr, *v.t.* [M.E. *pampren*: cf. G. *pampen*, cram.] To indulge, as a child, to the full or to excess; to gratify the tastes or desires of; to coddle.—**pam·per·er**, *n.*

pam·pe·ro, päm·pâr′ō, *Sp.* päm·pe′Ra, *n.* pl. **pam·pe·ros.** [Sp.] A cold, strong, dry wind which blows from the Andes over the pampas of South America.

pam·phlet, pam′flit, *n.* [Formerly *paunflet*, *pamfilet*, *pamflet*: < Med. L. *Pamphilet*, name of a popular poem.] A small, unbound publication consisting of a folded sheet of paper, or of a few sheets stapled or otherwise held together; a short treatise or essay, usu. on a current or controversial topic, published by itself.—**pam·phlet·eer**, pam″fli·tēr′, *n.* A writer of pamphlets.— *v.i.* To write and issue pamphlets.

pan, pan, *n.* [O.E. *panne* = D. *pan* = G. *pfanne*, pan.] A vessel, commonly of metal, used for cooking and other domestic purposes; as, a frying *pan*; used in compounds; as, a dish*pan*, a sauce*pan*; any dishlike receptacle or part; as, the *pans* or scales of a balance; any of various open or closed vessels used in industrial or mechanical processes; a vessel in which gold or other precious metal is separated from gravel and waste by agitation with water. A thin fragment of drifting ice formed in bays or near the shore; a natural depression in the ground, as one containing water, mud, or salts; an artificial depression made in the ground for evaporating salt water to make salt; hardpan; formerly, the part of a flintlock of a gun holding the powder; *slang*, the face.—*v.t.*—*panned*, *panning.* To wash, as gravel or sand, in a pan; to separate, as gold, by such washing; *colloq.* to criticize severely.—*v.i.* To wash gravel, sand, or other matter in a pan when searching for gold; to yield gold, as gravel washed in a pan.—**pan out**, *colloq.* to turn out, esp. to succeed, as: How did your trip *pan out*?

pan, pän, *n.* [Hind. *pān.*] The betel leaf; a mixture containing this leaf and used for chewing.

pan, pan, *v.i.*—*panned*, *panning.* To move a camera in a horizontal or vertical plane in order to follow a person or object in motion, to include an entire scene, to achieve a panoramic effect, or to record more than can be viewed from a stationary position; of a camera to be rotated or moved in this way.—*v.t.* To rotate or move, as a camera, in this way; to photograph in this way.

pan·a·ce·a, pan″a·sē′a, *n.* [L., < Gr. *panakeia*, a universal remedy—*pan*, all, and *akeomai*, to cure.] A remedy for all diseases; a cure-all; a solution for any difficulty.—**pan·a·ce·an**, *a.*

pa·nache, pa·nash′, pa·näsh′, *n.* [Fr., < It. *pennacchio*, < *penna*, < L. *penna*, feather.] An ornamental plume or tuft of feathers, esp. one worn on a helmet or cap; an ornate or showy style; verve; dash; flamboyance.

pa·na·da, pa·nä′da, pa·nā′da, *n.* [Fr. *panade*, < L. *panis*, bread.] A food consisting of bread, water or other liquid, and seasonings, boiled to the consistency of pulp.

pan·a·ma, pan′a·mä″, *n.* (*Often cap.*) a finely plaited hat made of the young leaves of the jipijapa, *Carludovica palmata*, a palmlike plant of Central and South America. Also **pan·a·ma hat**.

Pan-A·mer·i·can, pan″a·mer′i·kan, *a.* Of, pertaining to, or embracing all of North, Central, and South America, or all the peoples of these countries.

Pan-A·mer·i·can·ism, pan″a·mer′i·ka·niz″um, *n.* The idea or principle of a cultural, economic, military, and political alliance or union of all the countries of North, Central, and South America; advocacy of, or a movement favoring this principle.

pan·cake, pan′kāk″, *n.* A thin, flat cake of batter cooked in a pan or on a griddle; a griddlecake or flapjack. A make-up or cosmetic in a pressed disk or cake form similar to, and often used as a foundation for, facial powder; also **pan·cake make-up**, **cake make-up**. *Aeron.* a landing made by pancaking an airplane; also **pan·cake land·ing**.—*v.i.*—*pancaked*, *pancaking.* *Aeron.* to make a landing by dropping flat to the ground or coming abruptly down with little or no forward movement.— *v.t. Aeron.* to cause, as an airplane, to pancake.

pan·cake ice, *n.* Thin, flat pieces of floating ice, resembling pancakes, newly formed and too small to hamper navigation.

pan·chro·mat·ic, pan″krō′mat′ik, pan″kro·mat′ik, *a.* [Gr. *pan-*, all, and *chrōma* (*chrōmat-*), color.] Sensitive to light of all colors, as a photographic plate.—**pan·chro·ma·tism**, pan·krō′ma·tiz″um, *n.*

pan·cra·ti·um, pan·krā′shē·um, *n.* pl. **pan·cra·ti·a**, pan·krā′shē·a. [Gr. *pangkration*—*pan*, all, and *kratos*, strength.] A gymnastic contest of ancient Greece consisting of a combination of boxing and wrestling.—**pan·crat·ic**, pan·krat′ik, *a.*

pan·cre·as, pan′krē·as, pang′krē·as, *n.* [N.L., < Gr. *pankreas*, < *pan-*, all, and *kreas*, flesh.] *Anat.*, *zool.* a gland situated near the stomach, secreting an important digestive fluid, pancreatic juice, into the duodenum, and producing insulin.— **pan·cre·at·ic**, pan″krē·at′ik, pang″krē·at′ik, *a.*

pan·cre·at·ic juice, *n. Biochem.* an alkaline fluid containing a mixture of digestive enzymes, discharged by the pancreas into the duodenum.

---

a- fat, fāte, fär, fâre, fạll;   **e-** met, mē, mēre, hėr;   **i-** pin, pīne;   **o-** not, nōte, möve;   **u-** tub, cūbe, bụll;   **oi-** oil;   **ou-** pound.

pan·cre·a·tin, pan′krē·a·tin, pang′krē·-a·tin, n. Biochem. a mixture of digestive enzymes found in the pancreatic juice; med. a preparation made from the pancreas of cattle or hogs, used as a digestive.

pan·da, pan′da, n. pl. **pan·das, pan·da**. A small carnivore, Ailurus fulgens, native to the Himalayas, with reddish-brown fur and conspicuous white face markings; also **bear·cat, les·ser pan·da**. A larger carnivore, Ailuropoda melanoleuca, of Tibet and China, with black-and-white fur and black-ringed eyes; also **gi·ant pan·da**.

pan·da·nus, pan·dā′nus, n. pl. **pan·da·nus·es**. [N.L. < Malay pandan.] Bot. any plant of the genus Pandanus, in the screw-pine family, native to the old-world tropics, having spiral masses of pineapple-like leaves at the apex of the branches. Also screw pine.

pan·dect, pan′dekt, n. [L. pandecta, pandectes, < Gr. pandéctēs, lit. 'all-receiver,' < pan-, all and déchesthai, receive.] A comprehensive treatise or digest; pl. a complete body or code of laws. (Cap.), pl., Rom. law, the Digest.

pan·dem·ic, pan·dem′ik, a. [= Fr. pandémique, < Gr. pándēmos, public, common, < pan-, all and dēmos, people.] Of a disease, prevalent throughout an entire country or continent, or the whole world; general; universal.—n. A pandemic disease.

pan·de·mo·ni·um, pan″de·mō′nē·um, n. [Orig. Pandæmonium, Milton's name for the capital of hell, < Gr. pan-, all and daimōn, E. demon.] Wild lawlessness or uproar; chaos; a place of riotous disorder or lawless confusion. (Often cap.) the abode of all the demons; hell.

pan·der, pan′dėr, n. [For pandar, from Pandare or Pandarus, who is described in medieval romance as lending his aid to bring together Troilus and Cressida. Cf. Shakespeare's Troilus and Cressida, iii. 2.210.] A go-between in love affairs; one who solicits clients for prostitutes or furnishes women for prostitution; a pimp; a procurer; one who caters to or takes advantage of another's weaknesses. Also **pan·der·er**.—v.t. To act as a pander for.—v.i. To act as a pander; to cater basely, used with to.—**pan·der·age, pan·der·ism**, n.—**pan·der·ly**, a.

pan·dit, pun′dit, pan′dit, n. India. A wise or highly respected man; a scholar; a title of respect for such a person.

Pan·do·ra, pan·dōr′a, pan·dạr′a, n. [L., < Gr. Pandora.] Class. myth. the first mortal woman, on whom all the gods and goddesses bestowed gifts.—**Pan·do·ra's box**, class. myth. a box or jar, the gift of Zeus to Pandora, containing all human ills, which escaped when she opened it, leaving only hope.

pan·do·ra, pan·dōr′a, pan·dạr′a, n. Bandore.

pan·dow·dy, pan·dou′dē, n. pl. **pan·dow·dies**. [Origin obscure.] A kind of pudding or deep-dish pie made with apples and usu. sweetened with molasses.

pan·du·rate, pan′dū·rāt″, a. Bot. fiddle-shaped, applied to a leaf. Also **pan·du·ri·form**, pan·dūr′i·färm″, pan·dūr′i·färm″.

pane, pān, n. [O.Fr. Fr. pan-, < L. pannus, a cloth, rag.] One of the compartments of a window or door consisting of a single sheet of glass in a frame; a piece of glass for such a compartment; a panel in a door, ceiling, or the like; a flat section, side, or surface, as one of the sides of a bolthead or a facet of a cut diamond; a sheet or part of a sheet of postage stamps.

pan·e·gyr·ic, pan″i·jir′ik, pan″i·jī′rik, n. [L. panegyricus, < Gr. panegyrikos, a festival oration, prop. a. < panegyris, a general assembly, < pan-, all and agyris, agora, assembly.] An oration, discourse, or writing in praise of a person or thing; a eulogy; a formal or elaborate approbation.—**pan·e·gyr·i·cal**, a.—**pan·e·gyr·i·cal·ly**, adv.

pan·e·gyr·ist, pan″i·jir′ist, pan″i·jī′rist, pan′i·jir″ist, pan′i·jī″rist, n. A eulogist.

pan·el, pan′el, n. [O.Fr. panel (Fr. panneau), < M.L. pannellus, dim. of L. pannus, piece of cloth, E. pane.] A distinct portion or compartment of a wainscot, ceiling, door, or shutter, or of any surface, sunk below or raised above the general level, or enclosed by a frame or border; such a compartment on the side or the back of the binding of a book; a broad strip of the same or another material set vertically, as for ornament, in or on a garment; a thin, flat piece of wood used as a surface for a painting, or a picture painted on such a piece of wood; a large size of photograph of much greater height than width; glass set into a window frame. Law, the list of persons summoned for service as jurors; the body of persons composing a jury. Sc. law, the person or persons indicted and brought to trial. A list or body of persons, as of those selected or employed for some purpose; Brit. the list or body of physicians of a district engaged in and available for the treatment of persons paying for health insurance. Aeron. a section of an airplane wing; a strip of cloth in a parachute gore; a mount of instruments or control devices, as in an aircraft's cockpit. Elect. a control board; min. a section within a coal mine set off from adjacent sections by unusually thick walls.—v.t.—paneled, paneling, Brit. panelled, panelling. To arrange in, divide into, or furnish with panels; ornament with a panel or panels; to set in a frame as a panel; Sc. law, to bring to trial.

pan·el heat·ing, n. Heating of an area by radiation from panels which contain heating units. Also radiant heating.

pan·el·ing, chiefly Brit. **pan·el·ling**, pan′-el·ing, n. Arch. Wood, metal, or other material made into panels; a wall or other surface consisting of panels; panels collectively.

pan·el·ist, pan′el·ist, n. One who is a member of a panel, as for purposes of discussing, judging, or the like.

pan·el truck, n. A small, enclosed truck commonly used for light deliveries.

pan·e·tel·la, pan·e·tel·a, pan″i·tel′a, n. [Sp.] A long, slender cigar pointed at the end intended for the mouth. Also **pan·a·tel·la, pan·a·tel·a**.

pan·fish, pan′fish″, n. pl. **pan·fish·es, pan·fish**. Any small fish suitable for frying whole in a pan.

pang, pang, n. [Origin uncertain.] Often pl. a sudden, brief, sharp pain; a spasm; as, a hunger pang. Fig. a sudden feeling of mental distress.

pan·gen·e·sis, pan·jen′i·sis, n. Biol. the Darwinian theory, now abandoned, that hereditary attributes are transmitted by gemmules that are thrown off into free circulation by individual cells from every part of the organism, and that collect in the reproductive cells or bodies. Compare blastogenesis.—**pan·ge·net·ic**, pan″je·net′-ik, a.—**pan·ge·net·i·cal·ly**, adv.

pan·go·lin, pang·gō′lin, n. [Malay penggōling, roller.] Zool. a horny-scaled mammal of the order Pholidota, native to Africa and southwestern Asia, having a long pointed tail, living primarily on a diet of ants and termites, and capable of rolling into a ball when molested. Also scaly anteater.

pan·han·dle, pan′han·dl, n. The handle of a pan; (sometimes cap.) a narrow projecting strip of land that is not a peninsula, esp. part of a state; as, the Texas Panhandle.

pan·han·dle, pan′han·dl, v.i.—panhandled, panhandling. Colloq. to confront and beg from strangers on the street.—v.t. Colloq. To confront and beg from; to acquire by begging.—**pan·han·dler**, n.

Pan·hel·len·ic, pan″he·len′ik, a. [Gr. pan-, all, and Hellēnikos, Greek, < Hellēnes, the Greeks.] Pertaining to all Greece, or to all the Greek people; referring to Greek-letter fraternities and sororities.

pan·ic, pan′ik, n. [Fr. panique, < Gr. Panikós, pertaining to or caused by Pan, < Pan, E. Pan.] Acute fear or demoralizing terror, often contagious in a group situation; an instance, outbreak, or period of such fear; finance, an outbreak of widespread alarm, often precipitating a real and general financial disaster; slang, an unusually humorous situation or person.—a. Of the nature of panic; fig. to be used in case of a panic; as, panic button; (cap.) of or pertaining to the god Pan.—v.t.—panicked, panicking. To affect with panic; slang, to elicit amusement from.—v.i. To be affected by panic.—**pan·ick·y**, a.

pan·ic grass, n. [L. panicum, a kind of grass.] Any of several species of grass of the genus Panicum, world-wide in distribution, a few cultivated, as the millets, for forage, others weedy, and characterized by panicled inflorescences. See witch grass.

pan·i·cle, pan′i·kl, n. [L. panicula, tuft on plants, dim. of panus, swelling, ear of millet.] Bot. an indeterminate compound raceme with loosely branching flower clusters, in which each flower is borne on a short pedicel or stalk.—**pan·i·cled**, a.—**pa·nic·u·late, pa·nic·u·lat·ed**, pa·nik′-ya·lāt″, pa·nik′ya·lit, a.

pan·ic-strick·en, pan′ik·strik″en, a. Stricken with panic or extreme fear; overwrought from fear. Also **pan·ic-struck**, pan′ik·struk″.

pan·jan·drum, pan·jan′drum, n. [A made word, with prefix pan- and termination simulating Latin: appar. first used by Samuel Foote, 1720-77, the English dramatist and actor.] Any pretentious personage or official.

pan·leu·ko·pe·ni·a, pan·leu·co·pe·ni·a, pan″lö·ko·pē′nē·a, n. Veter. pathol. distemper in cats.

panne, pan, n. [Fr.] A soft, lustrous, lightweight velvet with flattened pile; also **panne vel·vet**. Silk or rayon satin with a lustrous sheen resulting from a special finishing process; also **panne sat·in**.

pan·nier, pan′ier, pan′yėr, pan′ē·ėr, n. [O.Fr. Fr. panier, < L. panarium, breadbasket, < panis, bread.] A basket for carrying on a person's back, or one of a pair to be slung across the back of a beast of burden; a skirt puffed or draped at the hips; a framework formerly used to distend the skirt of a woman's dress.—**pan·niered**, a.

pan·ni·kin, pan′i·kin, n. Chiefly Brit. A small pan or cup.

pa·no·cha, pa·no·che, pa·nō′cha, n. [Mex. Sp.] A coarse grade of sugar made in Mexico; candy made of brown sugar, butter, and milk, usu. with nuts. Also penuche.

pan·o·ply, pan′o·plē, n. pl. **pan·o·plies**. [Fr. panoplie, < Gr. panoplia, < pan-, all, and hóplon, tool, implement, pl. arms: cf. hoplite.] A complete suit of armor; any complete equipment of war or defense; a complete covering or array of something.—**pan·o·plied**, a.

pan·o·ram·a, pan″o·ram′a, pan″o·rä′ma, n. [Gr.] An unobstructed view or prospect over a wide area; a continuously passing or changing scene or series of events; an extended pictorial representation of a landscape or other scene, often as viewed from a central point, and sometimes exhibited a part at a time by being unrolled continuously before spectators; a comprehensive survey, as of a subject.—**pan·o·ram·ic**, a.—**pan·o·ram·i·cal·ly**, adv.

---

pan·pipe, pan′pīp″, n. A primitive wind instrument consisting of a series of pipes of graduated length closed at the lower ends, with tones produced by blowing across the upper ends. Also **Pan's pipes**, **pan·pipes**.

pan·psy·chisn, pan·sī′kiz·um, n. Philos. the metaphysical doctrine that the entire universe, or any least particle of it, has a psychic or mental aspect.—**pan·psy·chist**, pan·sī′kist, n.

pan·sy, pan′zē, n. pl. **pan·sies**. [Fr. pensée, thought, heart's-ease, < penser, to think.] An annual or short-lived perennial, Viola tricolor hortensis, one of the oldest garden varieties of the violet, with variously and richly colored blossoms; also heartsease. Slang, a male homosexual; an effeminate man.

pant, pant, v.i. [O.Fr. pantoier, to pant, to gasp, pantois, a panting; Pr. panteiar, to be breathless.] To breathe quickly or spasmodically, as after exertion or from excitement; to gasp; to throb or heave rapidly or violently; to emit loud puffs of smoke or steam; to yearn or long for.—v.t. To breathe or gasp out.—n. A quick short breath; a gasp; a throb or palpitation; a puff or puffing noise, as from an engine.

pan·ta·lets, **pan·ta·lettes**, pan″ta·lets′, n. pl. [Dim. < pantaloon.] Long loose underpants with a frill or other finish at the bottom of each leg, and usu. extending below the dress or hoopskirt, formerly worn by women and girls; a pair of separate frilled or trimmed pieces for attaching to the legs of women's underpants.

pan·ta·loon, pan″ta·lōn′, n. [Fr. pantalon < It. pantalone, buffoon, < Pantalone, a Venetian, so called from St. Pantaleone, patron of Venice.] Pl. a man's closely fitting garment covering the hips and legs, varying in form during the 18th and 19th centuries; trousers. (Sometimes cap.) an easily deceived, foolish old man, originally characterized in early Italian comedy. In modern pantomime, a man represented as the butt and accomplice of the clown; buffoon.

pan·tech·ni·con, pan·tek′ni·kon″, pan·-tek′ni·kon, n. Brit. A storehouse, usu. for furniture; a furniture moving van.

pan·the·ism, pan′thē·iz″um, n. [Gr. pan-, all, and theós, god.] The doctrine that all aspects of the universe are divinely inspired and that reality is only a manifestation of divine inspiration; the religious belief or philosophical doctrine which identifies the universe with God; the Roman worship of all the gods.—**pan·-the·ist**, n.—**pan·the·is·tic**, **pan·the·is·-ti·cal**, a.—**pan·the·is·ti·cal·ly**, adv.

pan·the·on, pan′thē·on″, pan′thē·on, pan·thē′on, n. [L. < Gr. pántheion, prop. neut. of pántheios, of all gods, < pan-, all, and theós, god.] A temple dedicated to all the gods; a public building containing tombs or memorials of the illustrious dead of a nation. The deities of a people collectively. (Cap.) an ancient Roman temple now serving as a Christian church.—**pan·-the·on·ic**, pan″thē·on′ik, a.

pan·ther, pan′thér, n. [L. panthēra, Gr. pánthēr; cf. Skt. pundarika, a leopard.] A common name applied to two different carnivorous mammals in the cat family, the unspotted puma or cougar, Felis concolor, native to the Americas, and the black phase of the leopard, Panthera pardus, of Asia and Africa; slang, a fierce or violent person.—**pan·ther·ess**, pan′thér·is, n. A female panther.

pan·ties, pan′tēz, n. pl. Short underpants worn by women and children. Also **pant·ie**, **pant·y**.

pan·tile, pan′tīl″, n. [Cf. D. pan, pan, also tile, dakpan, pantile, lit. 'roof tile.'] A roofing tile straight in its length but curved

in its width, either like the letter 'S' or like a half cylinder, and laid so it overlaps an adjoining tile.—**pan·til·ing**, n.

pan·to·fle, **pan·tof·fle**, pan′to·fl, pan·-tof′l, pan·tō′fl, n. [Fr. pantoufle.] A slipper.

pan·to·graph, pan′to·graf″, pan′to·gräf″, n. [Gr. pan, pantos, all, and graphō, to write.] An instrument by means of which drawings, maps, plans, and the like can be copied mechanically on the original scale, or on one reduced or enlarged; elect. a device, as a trolley, for collecting and transferring current.—**pan·to·graph·ic**, pan″to·graf′ik, a.—**pan·tog·ra·phy**, pan·-tog′ra·fē, n.

pan·to·mime, pan′to·mīm″, n. [L. pantomimus, < Gr. pantomimos, < panto-, all (see pan-), and mimos, imitator, < L. mime.] The dramatic technique of communicating through mute gestures; a play or entertainment in which the performers express themselves by mute gestures, often to the accompaniment of music; gesture without speech; Brit. dumb show. Brit. a Christmas theatrical spectacle featuring singing, dancing, and comical skits adapted from fairy tales; also **Christ·mas pan·to·mime**. One who acts in pantomime; also **pan·to·-mi·mist**.—v.t.—pantomimed, pantomiming. To represent or express by pantomime.—v.i. To express oneself by pantomime. —**pan·to·mim·ic**, **pan·to·mim·i·cal**, pan″to·mim′ik, pan″to·mim·i·cal·ly, adv.—**pan·to·mim·ic·ry**, n.

pan·to·then·ic ac·id, pan′to·then′ik as′id, pan″to·then′ik as′id, n. Biochem. an unstable organic compound, $C_9H_{17}NO_5$, part of the vitamin B complex, and considered necessary to the growth of cells.

pan·toum, pan·tōm′, n. [Fr. < Malay pantun.] A poem in a fixed form, consisting of a varying number of stanzas of four lines, with lines rhyming alternately, the second and fourth lines of each stanza being repeated to form the first and third of the succeeding stanza, and the first and third lines of the first stanza forming the second and fourth of the last stanza. Also **pan·tun**, pan·tōn′.

pan·trop·ic, pan·trop′ik, pan·trō′pik, a Existing in all or nearly all parts of the tropics, as certain plants and animals. Also **pan·trop·i·cal**, pan·trop′i·kal.

pan·try, pan′trē, n. pl. **pan·tries**. [Fr. paneterie, a pantry, < L. panis (Fr. pain), bread, whence also pannier.] A room or closet for provisions, silverware, china, glassware, and table linen; a room adjacent to a dining room and kitchen where foods are arranged prior to serving.

pants, pants, n. pl. Trousers; underpants, usu. worn by women or children; Brit. men's drawers.

pants suit, n. A woman's coordinated suit consisting of a jacket and a pair of slacks, usu. for informal wear. Also **pant suit**, slack suit.

pant·y gir·dle, **pant·ie gir·dle**, n. A woman's girdle with a crotch sewn in.

pant·y hose, n. A one-piece skintight garment serving as panties and stockings. Also **pant·i hose**.

pant·y·waist, pan′tē·wāst″, n. A child's shirt and pants outfit buttoned together at the waist. Slang, an effeminate or timid boy or man.—a.

pan·zer, pan′zér, G. pän′tsĕR, a. [G.] Armored; of or relating to a unit of tanks; as, a panzer division.—n. A German tank or other armored vehicle.

pap, pap, n. [Of similar origin to pap, food; cf. L. papilla, the nipple.] Chiefly dial. a nipple of the breast; a teat. Something resembling or shaped like a teat.

pap, pap, n. [M.E. = D. pap = G. pappe.] Soft food for infants or invalids, as bread soaked in water or milk; something lacking

in substance or value, as an idea or piece of writing; slang, profits or favors secured through political or official patronage.

pa·pa, pä′pa, pa·pä′, n. [A reduplication of one of the earliest cries uttered by infants.— Fr., G., D., and Dan. papa, L. papa, pappa, Gr. pappa; cf. mama, mamma.] Father: used chiefly by children.

Pa·pa, pä′pa, pa·pä′, n. A communications code word to designate the letter P.

pa·pa·cy, pā′pa·sē, n. pl. **pa·pa·cies**. [L.L. papatia, the papacy, < L. papa, the pope, lit. 'father.'] Rom. Cath. Ch. The office and dignity of the pope; papal authority and jurisdiction; the popedom; the popes collectively; the term of office of a particular pope; (cap.) the form of government of the Roman Catholic Church.

pa·pa·in, pa·pä′in, pa·pī′in, pā′pa·in, n. [< papaya.] Biochem. a digestive enzyme in the milky juice of the unripe fruit of the papaya tree, Carica papaya, which acts on proteins; pharm. a commercial preparation prepared from this fruit containing a proteolytic enzyme similar to pepsin and used in medicine as an aid to protein digestion.

pa·pal, pā′pal, a. Belonging to the pope, the papacy, or the Roman Catholic Church. —**pa·pal·ly**, adv.

pa·pal cross, n. A type of cross characterized by three crossbars, the longest being at the bottom.

pa·pav·er·ine, pa·pav′e·rēn″, pa·pav′ĕr·-in, pa·pā′ve·rēn″, pa·pā′vĕr·in, n. Pharm. a crystalline alkaloid, $C_{20}H_{21}NO_4$, obtained from the opium poppy, Papaver somniferum, used medicinally to relax muscles and to relieve spasms.

pa·paw, pô′pa, pa·pô′, n. [Sp. papaya, the fruit, papayo, the tree; < Carib.] Bot. A small tree, Asimina triloba, native to temperate N. America, in the family Annonaceae, with large drooping leaves, purple flowers, and edible, oblong-shaped, yellow fruits; the fruit itself. Also pawpaw.

pa·pa·ya, pa·pä′ya, n. [Sp.] Bot. A tropical American tree, Carica papaya, in the family Caricaceae, palmlike in appearance, producing edible, yellow, melonlike fruits, which yield the enzyme, papain; the fruit itself.

pa·per, pā′pér, n. [Fr. papier, It. papiro, < L. papyrus, Gr. papyros, the papyrus.] A substance used for writing, printing, packaging, and wall covering, manufactured principally from rag, wood, or other vegetable fiber reduced to a pulp; a piece, leaf, or sheet of paper; material resembling paper, as papyrus; any written or printed document; collectively, such documents as promissory notes, bills of exchange. Pl. a document serving to establish identity or status; as, citizenship papers, ship's papers. A sample of a student's written work; a newspaper; a journal; an essay or article on some subject. Slang, free passes to an entertainment; an audience admitted free of charge.—v.t. To cover with paper, esp. wallpaper; to fold or enclose in paper; to provide with paper. Slang, to fill, as a place of entertainment, by issuing free tickets.—a. Made out of paper; paperlike; having to do with clerical work; existing only on paper; as, a paper gain; admitted free of charge.—**on pa·per**, in written form; in the planning or theoretical stage.—**pa·-per·y**, pā′pe·rē, a. Having the thinness or consistency of paper.—**pa·per·er**, n.— **pa·per·i·ness**, n.

pa·per·back, pā′pér·bak″, n. A book bound in paper.

pa·per birch, n. A N. American tree, Betula papyrifera, having pendulous catkins, white bark peeling into papery layers, and producing a strong, elastic, uniformly-textured wood used for interior decorating and woodenware. Also **ca·noe birch**.

---

a- fat, fāte, fär, fâre, fạll; **e-** met, mē, mēre, hėr; **i-** pin, pīne; **o-** not, nôte, möve; **u-** tub, cūbe, bụll; **oi-** oil; **ou-** pound.

pa·per·board, pā′pér·bõrd″, *n.* A board made of compressed paper or paper pulp; cardboard.—*a.*

pa·per chase, *n.* The game of hare and hounds.

pa·per cut·ter, *n.* A machine for cutting or trimming a number of sheets of paper at one time; a paper knife.

pa·per·hang·er, pā′pér·hang″ér, *n.* One who is employed to hang wallpaper.— **pa·per·hang·ing,** *n.*

pa·per knife, *n.* A knife for cutting open envelopes or the leaves of books; the cutting edge of a paper cutter.

pa·per mon·ey, *n.* Bank notes or other currency in paper form authorized by a government.

pa·per mul·ber·ry, *n. pl.* **pa·per mul·ber·ries.** A native tree of China and Japan, *Broussonetia papyrifera,* in the mulberry family, having a milky juice, and bark used for papermaking in the Far East.

pa·per prof·it, *n.* A profit able to be realized only through selling, as securities.

pa·per·weight, pā′pér·wāt″, *n.* A small weight laid on loose papers to keep them in place.

pa·per work, *n.* The handling of correspondence, examinations, forms, and written reports necessary to conduct business.

pap·e·terie, pap′i·trē, *Fr.* päp·e·tRē′, *n.* [Fr., < *papetier,* one who makes or sells paper, < *papier,* E. *paper.*] A case or box of paper and other materials for writing.

Pa·phi·an, pā′fē·an, *a.* [From *Paphos,* an ancient city of Cyprus sacred to Aphrodite or Venus, and the site of one of her most celebrated temples.] Of or relating to Paphos or to the goddess of love or beauty; pertaining to love, esp. illicit love or sexual indulgence.—*n.* A native or resident of Paphos; (*sometimes l.c.*) a harlot.

pa·pier-mâ·ché, pā′pér·ma·shā′, *Fr.* pä·pyä′mä·shā′, *n.* [Fr., lit 'masticated paper.'] A material prepared by pulping different kinds of paper into a mass, which is molded into various articles, dried, and japanned.—*a. Fig.* Unreal; pretentious.

pa·pil·i·o·na·ceous, pa·pil″ē·o·nā′shus, *a.* [N.L. *papilionaceus,* < L. *papilio(n-),* butterfly.] *Bot.* pertaining to the flowers of the legume or pea family, which are irregular in shape, having a butterfly appearance consisting of a standard, wings, and a keel.

pa·pil·la, pa·pil′a, *n. pl.* **pa·pil·lae,** pa·pil′ē. [L., dim. of *papula,* E. *papule.*] *Anat.* a nipple, or one of certain small protuberances such as the papillae of the tongue or of the skin of the fingertips, or a process at the root of a hair. *Bot.* a small projection on a plant suggesting a nipple in shape.— **pap·il·lar·y,** pap′i·ler″ē, pa·pil′a·rē, *a.*—**pap·il·late,** pap′i·lāt″, pa·pil′it, *a.*— **pap·il·lose,** pap′i·lōs″, *a.*

pap·il·lo·ma, pap″i·lō′ma, *n. pl.* **pap·il·lo·ma·ta,** pap·il·lo·mas, pap″i·lō′ma·ta. [N.L.] *Pathol.* a benign tumor of the skin or a mucous membrane, as a wart or corn, consisting of a hypertrophied papilla or a group of papillae.

pap·il·lon, pap′i·lon″, *n.* A small spaniel of the breed characterized by conspicuous fringed ears suggestive of the wings of a butterfly.

pap·il·lote, pap′i·lōt″, *n.* [Fr., < *papillon,* < L. *papilio(n-),* butterfly.] An ornamental curled paper used to cover the projecting bone of a chop or cutlet.

pa·pist, pā′pist, *n.* [Fr. *papiste,* < *pape,* pope.] An adherent of the Pope; a member of the Roman Catholic Church: usually in disparagement.

pa·pis·try, pā′pi·strē, *n.* The system, doctrines, or practices of papists; popery: usually in disparagement.

pa·poose, pap·poose, pa·pös′, pä·pös′, *n.*

An infant or young child of N. American Indian parentage.

pap·pus, pap′us, *n. pl.* **pap·pi.** [L., < Gr. *pappos,* the down of plants.] *Bot.* a feathery, bristly, or scalelike appendage borne on the ovary and persisting in the fruit of plants of the composite family, as the dandelion, and often functioning in the wind dispersal of the fruit.—**pap·pose,** **pap·pous,** pap′ōs, pap′us, *a.*

pap·ri·ka, pa·prē′ka, pa·prē′ka, pap′ri·ka, *n.* [Hung.] The fruit of a variety of pepper, *Capsicum frutescens fasciculatum,* native to tropical America but now introduced throughout the world; the dried and ground fruit of this plant used in cooking, esp. as a condiment, as in Hungarian goulash.

Pap smear, *n.* [From George N. *Papanicolaou,* U.S. physician.] *Pathol.* an examination of cells for evidence of uterine cancer or of any condition interpreted as precancerous. Also **Pa·pa·nic·o·laou test,** **pap test,** pä″pa·nē′ko·lou test″.

pap·ule, pap′ūl, *n.* [L. *papula,* pustule, pimple.] *Pathol.* a small, solid, somewhat pointed elevation of the skin, usu. inflammatory but not forming pus.—**pap·u·lar,** *a.*—**pap·u·lif·er·ous,** pap″ya·lif′ér·us, *a.*

pa·py·rus, pa·pī′rus, *n. pl.* **pa·py·ri,** **pa·py·rus·es,** pa·pī′rī. [L., < Gr. *papyros,* the plant papyrus, something made from papyrus: cf. *paper.*] A tall, aquatic, reedlike plant, *Cyperus papyrus,* of the sedge family, native to southern Europe, Syria, and Africa, with fruits borne in umbels; a paper prepared from the stems of this plant by the ancients and used in Egypt as early as 2400 B.C.; an ancient document or manuscript written on this material.

par, pär, *n.* [L. *par,* equal.] An equality in value or standing, or a level of equality, as: The gains and losses are about on a *par.* An average or normal amount, degree, quality, condition, or the like; as, taking 70° as the *par* of indoor temperatures; a commonly accepted standard; *com.* the established value of the monetary unit of one country in terms of that of another using the same metal as a standard of value; as, *par* of exchange; equality between the market value and the nominal or face value of stocks or bonds; as, a stock issued at *par*; *golf,* the number of strokes allowed to a hole or course as representing a hypothetical score made by skillful playing.—*a.* Normal; average; *com.* at or of par.

par·a, par′a, *a. Chem.* indicating a relationship in the benzene ring.

par·a-am·i·no·ben·zo·ic ac·id, par′a·a·mē″nō·ben·zō′ik as′id, par′a·am″e·nō·ben·zō′ik as′id, *n.* The crystalline para isomer derivative of aminobenzoic acid, $H_2NC_6H_4COOH$, a growth factor of folic acids and a part of the vitamin B complex.

par·a·bi·o·sis, par″a·bī·ō′sis, *n. Biol.* fusion of two organisms, sometimes naturally as in the case of Siamese twins, or a union involving surgery, as the fusion of physiological functions.—**par·a·bi·ot·ic,** par″a·bī·ot′ik, *a.*—**par·a·bi·ot·i·cal·ly,** *adv.*

par·a·ble, par′a·bl, *n.* [Fr. *parabole,* < L. *parabola,* Gr. *parabolē,* < *paraballō,* to throw beside, to compare.] Orig. a comparison or similitude; an allegorical story dealing with ordinary life from which a moral message or religious truth is taught. (*Cap.*), *pl.* a collective term for the allegories recounted by Jesus.—**par·a·bol·ic,** par″a·bol′ik, *a.*—**pa·rab·o·list,** pa·rab′o·list, *n.*

pa·rab·o·la, pa·rab′o·la, *n.* [Gr. *parabolē.*] *Geom.* A plane curve produced by the intersection of a cone with a plane parallel to one of its sides; the locus of points in a

plane equidistant from a fixed point and fixed line in the plane.—**par·a·bol·ic,** par·a·bol′ik, *a.*

pa·rab·o·loid, pa·rab′o·loid″, *n. Geom.* The solid generated by the rotation of a parabola about its axis; a parabolic conoid. —**pa·rab·o·loi·dal,** pa·rab″o·loid′al, par″a·bo·loid′al, *a.*

par·a·chute, par′a·shöt″, *n.* [Fr., < *para-* (as in *parasol*) and *chute,* a fall.] An apparatus, used for descending safely through the air, that opens out somewhat like an umbrella and catches the air so as to retard or slow down the speed of descent; the canopy of a parachute or any contrivance that suggests one by its shape, use, or type of operation; *zool.* patagium.—*v.i.*—*parachuted, parachuting.* To jump or cast off from an aircraft and descend to the earth by parachute.—*v.t.* To drop men or supplies by parachute.—**par·a·chut·ic,** *a.*

par·a·chute spin·na·ker, *n. Naut.* on a racing vessel, a large spinnaker which balloons out when sailing before the wind.

par·a·chut·ist, par′a·shö″tist, *n.* One who parachutes, esp. one practiced in the art of jumping from an airborne aircraft; a paratrooper.

par·a·clete, par′a·klēt″, *n.* [Gr. *paraklētos,* < *parakaleō.*] One called to aid or support; (*cap.*) the Holy Spirit.

pa·rade, pa·rād′, *n.* [Fr. *parade,* < Sp. *parada,* a parade, a place for the exercise of troops, < L. *paro, paratus,* to prepare.] An organized march, sometimes featuring floats and instrumental music. *Milit.* a marshaling of troops for inspection; a ceremonial procession of marching personnel. A public walk or promenade; as, an Easter *parade.*

pa·rade, pa·rād′, *v.t.*—*paraded, parading.* To exhibit in a showy manner; to make a show of; to assemble and march in military order.—*v.i.* To assemble in military order; to proceed in military procession; to promenade.—**pa·rad·er,** *n.*

par·a·di·chlor·o·ben·zene, par″a·dī·klör″ō·ben″zēn, par″a·dī·klör″ō·ben·zēn′, *n. Chem.* a white crystalline volatile compound, $C_6H_4Cl_2$, used as a fumigant and insecticide.

par·a·digm, par′a·dim, par′a·dim″, *n.* [Gr. *paradeigma.*] *Gram.* an example of a word, as a noun, adjective, or verb, in its various inflections. An example. A model.— **par·a·dig·mat·ic,** par″a·dig·mat′ik, *a.*

par·a·di·sa·ic, par″a·di·sā′ik, par″a·di·zā′ik, *a.* Paradisiacal.—**par·a·di·sa·i·cal,** *a.*—**par·a·di·sa·i·cal·ly,** *adv.*

par·a·dise, par′a·dīs″, par′a·dīz″, *n.* [L. *paradisus,* < Gr. *paradeisos,* a garden— properly a Pers. word.] The garden of Eden; heaven; a place of bliss; the place where the righteous enjoy eternal bliss after death; a state of rapturous delight.

par·a·di·si·a·cal, par″a·di·sī′a·kal, par″a·di·zī′a·kal, *a.* [L.L. *paradisiacus.*] Of, like, or befitting paradise. Also **par·a·dis·i·ac,** *paradisaic,* **par·a·di·sal,** par″a·dis′ē·ak″, par″a·dis′al.—**par·a·di·si·a·cal·ly,** *adv.*

par·a·dox, par′a·doks″, *n.* [L. *paradoxum,* < Gr. *paradoxon,* neut. of *paradoxos,* contrary to received opinion, incredible.] A statement or proposition seemingly self-contradictory or absurd, and yet explicable as expressing a truth; such statements collectively, or the making of them; as, to indulge in *paradox*; a self-contradictory and false proposition; an argument which through a valid process of deduction arrives at a self-contradictory conclusion; an opinion or statement contrary to received opinion; any person, thing, or act exhibiting apparent contradictions or inconsistencies. —**par·a·dox·i·cal,** par″a·doks′i·kal, *a.* Of the same nature as or involving a paradox; given to paradoxes.—**par·a·dox·i·cal·ly,** *adv.*—**par·a·dox·i·cal·ness,** *n.*

par·aes·the·sia, par"is·thē'zha, par"is·thē'zhē·a, par"is·thē'zē·a, *n.* [N.L.] *Pathol.* abnormal sensation, as prickling or itching. Also *paresthesia,* **par·aes·the·sis.**

par·af·fin, par'a·fin, *n.* [G. *paraffin,* < L. *parum,* too little, and *affinis,* related; from its want of affinity for other substances.] *Chem.* A white or colorless waxy mixture of hydrocarbons not easily acted upon by reagents, and obtained chiefly from petroleum: used for candles, preservative coatings, waterproofing, lubricants, electrical insulation, and in pharmacology and in the manufacture of perfumes and cosmetics; any hydrocarbon of the methane series. Also **par·af·fine,** par'a·fin, par'a·fēn".—*v.t.* *paraffined, paraffining.*—**par·af·fin·ic,** par"·a·fin'ik, *a.*

par·a·gen·e·sis, par"a·jen'i·sis, *n. Geol.* the formation of minerals in close contact, so that one affects another's development.—**par·a·ge·net·ic,** par"a·je·net'ik, *a.*

par·a·go·ge, par'a·gō'jē, *n.* [Gr. *paragōgē.*] The incorrect addition of a letter or syllable to the end of a word, as the *-ted* in nonstandard *hit-ted.*—**par·a·gog·ic,** par"·a·goj'ik, *a.*

par·a·gon, par'a·gon", par'a·gon, *n.* [Fr. *parangon,* < Sp. *paragon, parangon,* model.] A model or pattern of excellence or perfection; a flawless pearl of exceptional size.

pa·rag·o·nite, pa·rag'o·nīt", *n.* [Gr. *paragōn,* ppr. of *paragein,* lead beside, mislead.] A kind of mica analogous to muscovite but containing sodium in place of potassium.—**pa·rag·o·nit·ic,** pa·rag"o·nit'ik, *a.*

par·a·graph, par'a·graf", par'a·gräf", *n.* [O.Fr. Fr. *paragraphe,* < M.L. *paragraphus,* < Gr. *paragraphos,* a line or mark in the margin.] A distinct portion of written or printed matter dealing with a particular point or quoting the words of one speaker and usually beginning with an indentation on a new line; a note, item, or brief article, as in a newspaper, usually forming a distinct, undivided whole.—*v.t.* To divide into paragraphs; to express in a paragraph; to mention in a paragraph; write or publish paragraphs about.—**par·a·graph·ic,** par'·a·graf'ik, *a.*—**par·a·graph·er,** par'a·graf"ēr, par'a·grä"fēr, *n.* One who writes paragraphs or short pieces as for a newspaper; also *esp. Brit.* **par·a·graph·ist.**

par·a·keet, par'a·kēt", *n.* Any of several popular cage birds, esp. *Melopsittacus undulatus,* being a small parrot with a tapering tail, native to Australia and Asia, and capable of mimicking human speech. Also *parrakeet, budgerigar,* **par·a·quet, par·o·quet, par·ro·ket, par·ro·quet.**

par·al·de·hyde, par'al'de·hīd", *n. Chem.* a colorless liquid, $C_6H_{12}O_3$, formed by the polymerization of ordinary aldehyde: used in medicine as a hypnotic.

par·al·lax, par'a·laks, *n.* [Gr. *parallaxis,* < *parallassein,* change, vary, deviate.] The apparent displacement of an object observed, esp. a heavenly body, due to a change or difference in the position of the observer; *astron.* the angular amount of such a displacement of a heavenly body as measured between lines drawn to it from the two different points of observation.—**par·al·lac·tic,** par"a·lak'tik, *a.*

par·al·lel, par'a·lel", *a.* [Fr. *parallèle,* < L. *parallēlus,* < Gr. *parallēlos,* < *para,* beside, and *allelon,* of one another, < *allos,* other.] Pertaining to lines, either straight or curved, to planes, and to curves which are equidistant at all corresponding points; specif., according to non-Euclidean theories, intersecting at infinity, as lines or planes; corresponding, analogous. *Elect.*

having parts connected between like terminals. *Mus.* pertaining to consecutive harmonic intervals which consist of the same number of degrees, or applied to motion in the same numerical intervals.

par·al·lel, par'a·lel", *n.* Anything parallel in direction, course, or tendency; a match, counterpart, or analogy. *Geog.* any of the imaginary circles on the earth's surface, parallel to the equator, by which degrees of latitude north or south of the equator are represented; a line on a map or projection showing this imaginary circle. *Elect.* connection of all negative electrical parts on one conductor and all positive on another. *Milit.* a trench dug in front of a fortress, parallel to its defenses. *Print.* a pair of vertical parallel lines, such as ∥, used as a mark of reference.—*v.t.*—*paralleled, paralleling, parallelled, parallelling.* To make parallel; to furnish a parallel for; find or provide a match for; to equal; to compare. —*adv.*

par·al·lel bars, *n. pl.* A pair of horizontal bars supported by uprights, used in gymnastics.

par·al·lel·e·pi·ped, par"a·lel"e·pī'pid, par"a·lel"e·pip'id, *n.* [Gr. *parallelepipedon, parallelos,* parallel, and *epipedon,* plane surface.] A prism whose six bases are parallelograms. Also **par·al·lel·e·pip·e·don,** par"a·lel"e·pip'i·don", par"a·lel"e·pip'i·don.

par·al·lel forc·es, *n. pl. Phys.* forces which act parallel to each other.

par·al·lel·ism, par'a·lel"iz·um, *n.* The position or relation of parallels; agreement in direction, tendency, or character; the nature of being parallel; correspondence or analogy; a comparison. *Metaph.* the doctrine which states that mental and bodily processes are concomitant, each varying with variation of the other, but that there is no interaction or causal relation between the two series of changes.

par·al·lel·o·gram, par"a·lel'o·gram", *n.* A quadrilateral having its opposite sides parallel and equal.

pa·ral·o·gism, pa·ral'o·jiz"um, *n.* [Gr. *paralogismos.*] A fallacious argument; an instance of false reasoning.—**pa·ral·o·gist,** *n.*—**pa·ral·o·gis·tic,** **pa·ra·log·i·cal,** pa·ral"o·jis'tik, par"a·loj'i·kal, *a.*

pa·ral·y·sis, pa·ral'i·sis, *n. pl.* **pa·ral·y·ses,** pa·ral'i·sēz". [L., < Gr. *paralysis,* < *paralyein,* disable at the side.] *Pathol.* impairment or loss of the power of voluntary motion, or of sensation, in one or more parts of the body; a disease characterized by this. *Fig.* a more or less complete crippling, or arrest of powers and activities; as, a *paralysis* of trade.—**par·a·lyt·ic,** par"a·lit'ik, *a., n.*

pa·ral·y·sis ag·i·tans, pa·ral'i·sis aj'i·tanz", *n. Pathol.* Parkinson's disease.

par·a·lyze, par'a·līz", *v.t.*—*paralyzed, paralyzing.* To affect with paralysis; to destroy the energy and power of. Also *Brit.* **par·a·lyse.**—**par·a·ly·za·tion,** par"a·li·zā'shan, *n.*—**par·a·lyz·er,** *n.*

par·a·mag·net·ic, par"a·mag·net'ik, *a. Phys.* pertaining to substances having magnetic permeabilities exceeding that of empty space but lower than the permeabilities of ferromagnetic materials.—**par·a·mag·net,** par"a·mag'nit, *n.*—**par·a·mag·net·ism,** *n.*

par·a·mat·ta, **par·ra·mat·ta,** par"a·mat'a, *n.* [From *Parramatta,* a town in New South Wales, Australia.] A light twilled dress fabric with a weft of merino wool and a warp of cotton or silk.

par·a·me·ci·um, par"a·mē'shē·um, par"·a·mē'sē·um, *n. pl.* **par·a·me·ci·a.** [N.L. < Gr. *paramēkēs,* oblong *(pará,* beside, and *mēkos,* length).] Any of a group of one-celled, slipper-shaped protozoans of the

genus *Paramecium,* having an oblique oral groove and moving by means of cilia.

par·a·med·ic, par'a·med"ik, *n.* [< *para (chute)* and *medic.*] A medical corpsman or doctor who parachutes into an area of medical need.—**par"a·med'ik,** *a.*—**par·a·med·i·cal,** par"a·med'i·kal, *a.*

par·a·ment, par'a·ment, *n.* An ecclesiastical banner or vestment.

pa·ram·e·ter, pa·ram'i·tēr, *n.* [Gr. *para* beside, and *metron,* measure.] *Math.* In an expression, a constant or variable whose value determines the specific form of the expression; an independent variable other than a coordinate variable in terms of which the coordinate variables may be expressed.—**par·a·met·ric, par·a·met·ri·cal,** par"a·me'trik, *a.*

par·am·ne·sia, par"am·nē'zha, par"am·nē'zhē·a, par"am·nē'zē·a, *n.* [N.L., < Gr.] *Psychiatry,* the sensation or illusion of remembering something which has never been experienced.

par·a·mor·phism, par"a·mar'fiz"um, *n. Mineral.* the process in which a mineral undergoes a change in physical properties without alteration of its chemical composition.—**par·a·mor·phic, par·a·mor·phous,** *a.*

par·a·mount, par'a·mount", *a.* [O.Fr. *par* (L. *per-*), through, completely, and *amont,* above.] Foremost in importance; pre-eminent; highest in rank or order; superior to all others.—*n.* An overlord.—**par·a·mount·cy, par·a·mount·ship,** *n.*—**par·a·mount·ly,** *adv.*

par·a·mour, par'a·mur, *n.* [Fr. *par amour,* with love.] An illicit or unlawful lover, esp. of a wedded person; a lover; a loved one.

pa·rang, pä'räng, *n.* [Malay.] A large, heavy sheath knife used both as a tool and weapon by the Malays.

par·a·noi·a, par"a·noi'a, *n.* [N.L. < Gr. *paránoia.*] *Psychiatry,* a mental disorder characterized chiefly by systematic delusions, esp. of persecution or grandeur. Also **par·a·noe·a.**

par·a·noid, par'a·noid", *a. Psychiatry,* of, like, or characterized by paranoia. Also **par·a·noi·ac.**—*n.* A person affected by paranoia. Also **par·a·noe·ac.**

par·a·noid schiz·o·phre·ni·a, *n. Psychiatry,* a mental disorder similar to paranoia, but often accompanied by hallucinations and behavioral deterioration.

par·a·nor·mal, par"a·nar'mal, *a.* Supernatural; not subject to a scientific explanation.—**par·a·nor·mal·i·ty,** par"a·nar"mal'i·tē, *n.*—**par·a·nor·mal·ly,** *adv.*

par·a·nymph, par'a·nimf", *n.* [LL. *paranymphus* (fem. *paranympha*), < Gr. *paránymphos,* < *pará,* beside, and *nymphē,* bride.] A groomsman or a bridesmaid; in ancient Greece, a friend who accompanied the bridegroom when he went to bring home the bride, or the bridesmaid who escorted the bride to the bridegroom.

par·a·pet, par'a·pit, par'a·pet", *n.* [Fr. *parapet,* It. *parapetto—parare* (Fr. *parer,* E. *parry*), to ward off, to guard, and *petto* (L. *pectus*), the breast.] *Fort.* a wall or rampart to cover soldiers from the attacks of the enemy in front; a breastwork. *Arch.* a low protective wall placed at the edges of platforms and roofs and at the sides of bridges.—**par·a·pet·ed,** *a.*

par·aph, par'af, *n.* [O.Fr. Fr. *paraphe,* < M.L. *paraphus,* for *paragraphus,* E. *paragraph.*] A flourish made after a signature, as in a document, orig. as a precaution against forgery.

par·a·pher·nal·ia, par"a·fēr·nāl'ya, par"a·fe·nāl'ya, *n. pl., sing. or pl. in constr.* [L.L. *paraphernalia,* < Gr. *parapherna,* what a bride has besides her dowry.] Personal property of any kind; apparatus or equipment, esp. for sports; furnishings of an apartment or house; fittings or trappings; ornaments; *law*, formerly, the belongings of a wife over and above her dowry.

par·a·phrase, par′a·frāz″, *n.* [Fr. *paraphrase*, < L. *paraphrasis*, < Gr. *paráphrasis*, < *paraphrázein*, say in other words, < *pará*, beside, and *phrázein*, tell.] A restatement of the sense of a text or passage in other words, as for clearness; a free rendering or translation, as of a passage; the act or process of paraphrasing.—*v.t.*, *v.i.* —*paraphrased*, *paraphrasing*. To render in or make a paraphrase.—**par·a·phras·er,** *n.*

par·a·phras·tic, par″a·fras′tik, *a.* Paraphrasing or forming a paraphrase.—**par·a·phras·ti·cal·ly,** *adv.*

pa·raph·y·sis, pa·raf′i·sis, *n.* pl. **pa·raph·y·ses,** pa·raf′i·sēz″. [N.L. < Gr. *paráphysis*, offshoot, < *paraphýesthai*, grow at the side.] *Bot.* a sterile, usually filamentous outgrowth often occurring among the reproductive organs in many cryptogamous plants.

par·a·ple·gi·a, par″a·plē′jē·a, par″a·plē′ja, *n.* [N.L. < Gr. *paraplegia*, < *parapléssein*, strike on one side.] *Pathol.* paralysis of both legs and the lower trunk.—**par·a·ple·gic,** par″a·plē′jik, par″a·plej′ik, *a.*, *n.*

par·a·psy·chol·o·gy, par″a·sī·kol′o·jē, *n.* The study and investigation of psychic phenomena, such as telepathy, clairvoyance, and extrasensory perception.

par·a·ros·an·i·line, par″a·rō·zan′i·lin, par″a·rō·zan′i·lēn″, *n. Chem.* a crystalline base, $C_{19}H_{19}N_3O$, from which many dyes are derived, esp. a red chloride used as a coloring and as a biological stain.

Pa·rá rub·ber, pä·rä′ rub′ėr, *n.* [From *Pará*, in Brazil.] Rubber prepared from the milky latex of the tree, *Hevea brasiliensis*, in the spurge family, native to the Amazon region of S. America and now obtained from commercial plantations in the tropics of both hemispheres.

par·a·sang, par′a·sang″, *n.* [Gr. *parasangēs*, < Pers. *farsang*, a parasang.] Any of several Persian units of measure, esp. an ancient measure of distance equal to three and three-fourths miles.

par·a·se·le·ne, par″a·si·lē′nē, *n.* pl. **par·a·se·le·nae,** par″a·si·lē′nē. [N.L., < Gr. *pará*, beside, and *selēnē*, moon.] *Meteor.* A bright moonlike spot on a lunar halo; a mock moon.—**par·a·se·le·nic,** par″a·si·lē′nik, par″a·si·len′ik, *a.*

par·a·shah, pär′a·shä″, *n.* pl. **par·a·shoth, par·a·shi·oth,** pär′a·shōt″, pär″a·shē′ōt. [Heb.] (*Sometimes cap.*) A section of the Pentateuch; one of the lessons from the Torah read in the Jewish synagogue on the Sabbath; a selection from a lesson for reading on a holy day.

par·a·site, par′a·sīt″, *n.* [L. *parasitus*, < Gr. *parasītos*, one who eats at the table of another.] *Fig.* one who lives on others without making a fitting return; *biol.* an animal or plant which lives on or in a living organism, often injuring the host.—**par·a·sit·ic, par·a·sit·i·cal,** par″a·sit′ik, *a.* [L. *parasiticus*, < Gr. *parasitikos*.]—**par·a·sit·i·cal·ly,** *adv.*

par·a·sit·i·cide, par″a·sit′i·sīd″, *n.* An agent or preparation that destroys parasites. —**par·a·sit·i·cid·al,** *a.*

par·a·sit·ism, par′a·sī″tiz·um, *n. Pathol.* state of being infested by parasites or suffering disease as a result of infestation.

par·a·si·tize, par′a·si·tīz″, par′a·sī·tīz″, *v.t.*—*parasitized*, *parasitizing.* To invade or live upon, as a parasite.

par·a·sit·ol·o·gy, par″a·sī·tol′o·jē, par″a·si·tol′o·jē, *n.* The branch of science that treats of parasitism, esp. in animal life.

par·a·si·to·sis, par″a·sī·tō′sis, par″a·si·tō′sis, *n.* Parasitism.

par·a·sol, par′a·sạl″, par′a·sol″, *n.* [Fr. *parasol*, < It. *parasole—parare* (L. *parare*, to prepare), to ward off, and *sole* (L. *sol*), the sun.] A woman's umbrella used as a protection against the sun. *Milit.* protection against attack, esp. air attack, given by airplanes actually in the air.

par·a·sym·pa·thet·ic nerv·ous sys·-tem, *n. Anat.* the section of the autonomic nervous system made up of nerves arising in the sacral and cranial regions, which slows the heart beat, contracts the pupils, dilates blood vessels, and in general functions in contrast to the sympathetic nervous system.—**par·a·sym·pa·thet·ic,** par″a·sim″pa·thet′ik, *a.*, *n.*

par·a·syn·the·sis, par″a·sin′thi·sis, *n.* [N.L. < Gr.] *Gram.* a process of combination and derivation in the formation of words: illustrated by *great-hearted*, derived from the combination, *great heart* by means of the suffix *-ed*.—**par·a·syn·thet·ic,** par″a·sin·thet′ik, *a.*

par·a·tax·is, par″a·tak′sis, *n.* [N.L., < Gr.] *Gram.* the arrangement of phrases or clauses one after another without connectives to show the relation between them.—**par·a·tac·tic, par·a·tac·ti·cal,** par″a·tak′tik, *a.*—**par·a·tac·ti·cal·ly,** *adv.*

par·a·thi·on, par″a·thī′on, *n. Chem.* a very poisonous insecticide, $C_{10}H_{14}NO_5PS$.

par·a·thy·roid gland, *n. Anat.* any of four small glands, lying near or embedded in the thyroid gland, which control the calcium content of the blood.—**par·a·thy·roid,** par″a·thī′roid, *a.*

par·a·troop·er, par′a·trö″pėr, *n.* A soldier trained to parachute into battle from an aircraft.—**par·a·troop,** *a.*—**par·a·troops,** *n. pl.*

par·a·ty·phoid, par″a·tī′foid, *n.* [Gr. *para*, beyond, and *typhoid*.] *Pathol.* an infectious bacterial disease with symptoms resembling typhoid fever. Also **par·a·ty·phoid fe·ver.** —*a.*

par·a·vane, par′a·vān″, *n.* A torpedo-shaped machine fitted with an apparatus for severing the moorings of sea mines; a similar machine, equipped with explosives, for attacking submarines.

par·boil, pär′boil″, *v.t.* [Fr. *parbouillir*.] To boil in part; precook; *colloq.* to make unpleasantly hot.

par·buck·le, pär′buk″l, *n.* [Earlier *parbunkel*; origin unknown.] A kind of purchase for raising or lowering a cylindrical object along an inclined plane or a vertical surface, consisting of a rope looped over a post with its two free ends passed around the object; a kind of double sling made with a rope.—*v.t.*—*parbuckled*, *parbuckling.*

par·cel, pär′sel, *n.* [Fr. *parcelle*, < a L.L. *particella*, equivalent to L. *particula*, dim. of *pars*, *partis*, a part.] One or more items wrapped or otherwise packed up; a package; a quantity or number of things put up together, as for a sale; a lot; a collection; a group; a portion of anything taken separately; as, a *parcel* of arable land; a piece.— *v.t.*—*parceled, parceling, Brit. parcelled, parcelling.* To divide into parts or portions, usu. followed by *out*; to make or pack up as a parcel.—*a.* Part.—*adv.* Partly.

par·cel·ing, par·cel·ling, pär′se·ling, *n.* The process of dividing into small parts and dealing out; as, a *parceling* of land.

par·cel post, *n.* The department of a post-office system which conveys and delivers parcels of limited size.

par·ce·nar·y, pär′se·ner″ē, *n.* See *coparcenary.*

par·ce·ner, pär′se·nėr, *n.* Coparcener.

parch, pärch, *v.t.* [Perh. < Fr. *percer*, Fr. dial. *percher*, to pierce, as if to pierce or penetrate with heat, or a corruption of L. *peratesco*, to grow very dry.] To dry or shrivel by exposure to heat or extreme cold;

to cause thirst; to preserve, as corn or peas, by drying.—*v.i.* To become very dry; to thirst from lack of moisture.

Par·chee·si, pär·chē′zē, *n.* A game originating in India, played on a marked board, and similar to backgammon in manner of play. (Trademark.) Also *pachisi,* **par·che·-si, par·chi·si.**

parch·ment, pärch′ment, *n.* [O.Fr. Fr. *parchemin*, < L.L. *pergamena*, parchment, from *Pergamum*, a city in Asia Minor from which parchment was brought.] The skin of sheep, goats, lambs, or calves prepared for use as a writing material; a manuscript or document on such material; a diploma; paper resembling this material.

pard, pärd, *n. Slang.* A partner; a companion.

pard·ner, pärd′nėr, *n. Slang.* Partner; pal.

par·don, pär′don, *v.t.* [O.Fr. *pardoner*, (Fr. *pardonner*), < L.L. *perdonare*, to pardon—L. *per-*, through, quite, and *dono*, to give.] To forgive; to exempt from punishment; to erase guilt for; to make allowances to for a discourtesy.—*n.* Forgiveness; release from the consequences of a wrong act; forbearance for an offense or omission; *law*, the official warrant of a penalty remitted; *Rom. Cath. Ch.* an indulgence.—**par·don·a·ble,** *a.*—**par·don·a·ble·ness,** *n.*—**par·don·a·bly,** *adv.*

par·don·er, pär′do·nėr, *n.* One who pardons; a medieval layman who dispensed ecclesiastical indulgences for a fee.

pare, pâr, *v.t.*—*pared*, *paring.* [Fr. *parer*, to pare, to dress, to curry, < L. *parare*, to prepare.] To cut or trim the covering of; as, to *pare* apples; to trim or cut, often used with *off* or *away*; diminish gradually.

par·e·gor·ic, par″e·gar′ik, par″e·gor′ik, *n. Med.* Camphorated tincture of opium, used to assuage diarrhea; a drug used in cough remedies; an anodyne which relieves pain.

pa·ren·chy·ma, pa·reng′ki·ma, *n.* [Gr. *para*, beside, and *enchyma*, an infusion— *en*, in, and *cheō*, to pour.] *Bot.* a tissue composed of thin-walled cells which usu. store food, as in fruits, pith, and growing point areas of plants; *zool.* loosely formed tissue of lower animals without a coelom, as in the flatworms.—**par·en·chym·a·tous, par·en·chy·mal,** par″eng·kim′a·tus, *a.*—**par·en·chym·a·tous·ly,** *adv.*

par·ent, pâr′ent, par′ent, *n.* [L. *parens*, *parentis*, < *pario, parere*, to bring forth; to beget; akin to *parere*, to appear, *parare*, to prepare.] *Biol.* a father or mother; ancestor; a plant or animal that produces offspring. *Fig.* cause, source.—*a.*—**pa·ren·tal,** pa·ren′tal, *a.*

par·ent·age, pâr′en·tij, par′en·tij, *n.* Ancestry; birth; origin; character or circumstances of parents.

pa·ren·tal gen·er·a·tion, *n. Genetics,* the generation from which parents are selected for crossbreeding to form hybrids.

par·ent com·pa·ny, *n. Finance,* an incorporated company which owns the controlling stock of another company or a number of companies: distinguished from *holding company.*

par·en·ter·al, pa·ren′tėr·al, *a. Med.* Not through or in the intestine; introduced in a way other than through the digestive tract. —**par·en·ter·al·ly,** *adv.*

pa·ren·the·sis, pa·ren′thi·sis, *n.* pl. **pa·ren·the·ses,** pa·ren′thi·sēz″. [Gr. *parenthesis—para*, beside, *en*, in, and *thesis*, a placing, < *tithenai*, to place.] An explanatory or qualifying comment inserted into the midst of a passage, without being grammatically connected with it, and usu. marked off by upright curves (), brackets, commas, or dashes; the upright curves () collectively, or separately, used by printers and writers to mark off an interjected comment or to indicate in mathematics or logic a symbolic unit; interval or interlude.

—**par·en·thet·ic, par·en·thet·i·cal,** par″en·thet′ik, *a.*—**par·en·thet·i·cal·ly,** *adv.*

pa·ren·the·size, pa·ren′thi·sīz″, *v.t.*—*parenthesized, parenthesizing.* To insert a comment as a parenthesis; put between marks of parenthesis; to intersperse with parentheses.

par·ent·hood, pâr′ent·hụd″, par′ent·hụd″, *n.* The relation, rights, or responsibilities of a parent.

pa·re·sis, pa·rē′sis, par′i·sis, *n.* pl. **pa·re·ses,** pa·rē′sēz, par′i·sēz. [N.L. < Gr. *paresis,* < *parienai,* let go, relax, < *para,* from, and *ienai,* send.] *Pathol.* Incomplete paralysis, affecting motion but not sensation.—**pa·ret·ic,** pa·ret′ik, pa·rē′tik, *n., a.*

par·es·the·sia, par″is·thē′zha, par″is·thē′zhē·a, par″is·thē′zē·a, *n.* A spontaneous abnormal sensation such as tingling, itching, burning, or numbness. Also **par·aes·the·sia.**—**par·es·thet·ic,** par″is·thet′ik, *a.*

pa·re·u, pä′rä·ö″, *n.* Lava-lava.

pa·reve, pär′e·ve, *a. Judaism,* containing neither meat nor milk nor any of their derivatives, and permissible under dietary law to be used with both meat and dairy dishes. Also *parve.*

par ex·cel·lence, pär ek′se·läns″, *Fr.* pä Rek·se·läns′, *adv.* [Fr.] Superbly; pre-eminently.—*a.*

par·fait, pär·fā′, *n.* A dessert made of beaten eggs and whipped cream, sweetened, flavored, and frozen without stirring; a sundae made of layers of ice cream, fruit or other flavored sauce, and whipped cream.

par·fleche, pär′flesh, pär·flesh′, *n.* [Appar. Canadian Fr., from N. Amer. Ind.] A hide, esp. of a buffalo, stretched on a frame and dried after the hair has been removed by soaking in water and lye; an article made of such a hide.

par·get, pär′jit, *v.t.*—*pargeted, pargeting,* Brit. *pargetted, pargetting.* [Appar. < O.Fr. *pargeter,* for *pourgeter,* rough-cast, *parget,* lit. 'cast forward or forth' (Fr. *projeter*).] To cover with plaster or parget; decorate with plaster work.—*n.* Plaster or rough cast used as a covering for walls; a kind of mortar made of lime, cow dung and hair, used as a lining for chimneys; gypsum; plaster work used as an ornamental facing, esp. for exterior walls, with raised or indented patterns. Also **par·get·ing, par·get·ting,** pär′ji·ting.

par·he·lic cir·cle, *n. Meteor.* A luminous band which passes through the sun and is parallel to the horizon, which results from the reflections of atmospheric ice prisms. Also **par·he·lic ring.**

par·he·li·on, pär·hē′lē·an, *n.* pl. **par·he·li·a,** pär·hē′lē·a. [N.L. *parhelion,* for L. *parelion,* < Gr. *parēlion, parēlios,* < *para,* beside, and *ēlios,* sun.] A bright circular spot on a solar halo; a mock sun, usu. one of two or more such spots seen on opposite sides of the sun, and often accompanied by additional luminous arcs and bands. Also *sundog.* Compare *paraselene.*—**par·he·li·a·cal, par·he·lic,** pär′hi·lī′a·kal, pär·hē′lik, pär·hel′ik, *a.*

pa·ri·ah, pa·rī′a, par′ē·a, pär′ē·a, *n.* [A Tamil word.] An outcast; one of a low caste of southern India and of Burma; *fig.* one despised by society.

Par·i·an, pâr′ē·an, par′ē·an, *a.* Pertaining to the island of Paros in the Aegean Sea and to the superlatively fine marble which originated there.—*n.* A porcelain clay, resembling this marble, from which unglazed statuettes and vases are made; also **Par·i·an ware.** A person from Paros or resident there.

pa·ri·es, pâr′ē·ēz″, *n.* pl. **pa·ri·e·tes,** pa·rī′i·tēz″. [L., wall.] *Biol.* a wall, as of a hollow organ.

pa·ri·e·tal, pa·rī′i·tal, *a.* [L.L. *parietalis,* < L. *paries,* wall.] *Anat.* pertaining to the pair of bones forming part of the top and sides of the skull; pertaining to parietes or structural walls of hollow organs. *Bot.* referring to attachment to the wall of the ovary, usu. applying to the ovule or placenta of certain plants. Pertaining to or having authority over those within the walls or buildings of a college.—*n.*

pa·ri·e·tal bone, *n. Anat.* either of the two bones forming the top and sides of the part of the skull enclosing the brain. Also *parietal.*

par·i·mu·tu·el, par′i·mū′chō·el, *n.* A system of betting on a horse race in which those who bet on the winning horses divide the total money wagered in proportion to their bet, less a small percentage for the track management; an electronic machine which records and computes pari-mutuel betting.

par·ing, pâr′ing, *n.* The action of paring; a piece pared off; as, a potato *paring.*

Par·is green, par′is grēn′, *n.* An insecticide, pigment, and wood preservative derived from copper acetate and arsenic trioxide.

par·ish, par′ish, *n.* [Fr. *paroisse,* L.L. *paroecia,* < Gr. *pároikia,* a parish, a neighborhood.] *Eccles.* a territorial division of a diocese; the congregation of a church; the geographical area assigned to a specific church. In the state of Louisiana, a county. *Brit.* a civil district which may retain the boundaries of what was originally an ecclesiastical district.—**pa·rish·ion·er,** pa·rish′a·nêr, *n.*

par·i·ty, par′i·tē, *n.* [L.L. *paritas,* < L. *par,* equal.] Equality, as in amount, status, or character; equivalence; correspondence; similarity or analogy. *Finance,* equivalence in value in the currency of another country; equivalence in value at a fixed ratio between moneys of different metals. *Econ.* a system of regulating prices of agricultural commodities, to give U.S. farmers purchasing power equivalent to that which they had in the base period between August, 1909 and July, 1914.

par·i·ty, par′i·tē, *n.* [L. *parere,* bring forth.] *Obstet.* the condition or fact of having borne offspring.

park, pärk, *n.* [Either < Fr. *parc,* L.L. *parcus,* a park (< L. *parcere,* to spare), or < O.E. *pearruc,* a park (whence *paddock*).] An area of land set aside for public recreation or conservation of natural resources, usu. under government control; a stadium or amusement area; *milit.* an area where vehicles and weapons are repaired and stored; *Brit.* an enclosed tract of land where wild game is kept for hunting.—*v.t.* To put temporarily in a place; as, to *park* a car; to enclose, as in parks; to collect and arrange together, as military supplies or artillery; *slang,* to lay down, put, or leave, as: He *parked* his belongings in the corner.—*v.i.* To leave a vehicle standing without the operator; *slang,* to neck in a stationary car. —**park·er,** *n.*

par·ka, pär′ka, *n.* [Russ.] A hooded fur coat, cut like a shirt, worn in northeastern Asia and in Alaska; any similarly styled coat worn as sportswear or for military use in areas of extreme cold.

park·ing lot, *n.* An area used for the outdoor parking of automobiles.

park·ing or·bit, *n.* The initial orbit or orbits of a space vehicle around the earth prior to the firing of booster rockets which will propel it into outer space flight.

par·kin·son·ism, pär′kin·so·niz″um, *n. Pathol.* Parkinson's disease; a group of nervous disorders, including Parkinson's disease, which have similar symptoms.

Park·in·son's dis·ease, pär′kin·sonz di·zēz′, *n. Pathol.* a progressive form of paralysis marked by loss of flexibility in the muscles, tremor, and a jerky gait.

park·way, pärk′wā″, *n.* A wide thoroughfare landscaped with trees and shrubs; a driveway through a park.

par·lance, pär′lans, *n.* [O.Fr., < *parlant,* ppr. of *parler,* to speak.] A way of speaking; idiom; as, military *parlance;* speech.

par·lan·do, pär·län′dō, *a.* [It. gerund of *parlare,* speak.] *Mus.* sung in a speaking or declamatory style.

par·lay, par′lē, pär·lā′, *v.t., v.i.*—*parlayed, parlaying.* To place a bet on one race or contest, the winnings, if any, to be wagered on a subsequent contest; to exploit advantageously, as one's talents.—*n.* A bet of a parlay type.

par·ley, pär′lē, *v.i.*—*parleyed, parleying.* [Fr. *parler,* to speak, O.Fr. *paroler,* < L.L. *parabolare,* to speak, < L. *parabola,* a comparison, later, a word.] To confer or speak with a person on some point of mutual concern; to confer with an enemy, as on an exchange of prisoners, a cessation of arms, or other negotiable matter.—*n.* pl. **par·leys.** Mutual discourse or conversation; a conference with an enemy, as in war.

par·lia·ment, pär′li·ment, *n.* [O.Fr. Fr. *parlement,* < *parler,* speak.] (*Usu. cap.*) the legislature of the United Kingdom, composed of the House of Lords and the House of Commons; the name given to an equivalent legislative body in the British Commonwealth of Nations; a legislative assembly or body, esp. one having different estates. *Fr. hist.* before the Revolution, one of a number of high courts of justice. A meeting or assembly for conference on public or national affairs.

par·lia·men·tar·i·an, pär′li·men·târ′ē·an, *n.* One skilled in parliamentary procedure or debate; (*usu. cap.*), *Eng. hist.* a supporter of the Parliament in opposition to Charles I.

par·lia·men·tar·i·an·ism, pär″li·men·târ′ē·a·niz″um, *n.* The principle of government, established in England, which ensures that the authority of the prime minister and the members of his cabinet is contingent upon the approval of the majority of the legislature. Also **par·lia·men·ta·ry gov·ern·ment.**

par·lia·men·ta·ry, pär″li·men′ta·rē, pär″li·men′trē, *a.* Of or pertaining to a parliament or its members; enacted or established by a parliament; as, *parliamentary* statutes; characterized by the existence of a parliament; in accordance with the rules and usages of parliaments or deliberative bodies.

par·lia·men·ta·ry pro·ce·dure, *n.* The rules and practices by which parliaments or other deliberative assemblies are conducted. Also **par·lia·men·ta·ry law.**

par·lor, Brit. **par·lour,** pär′lêr, *n.* [Fr. *parloir,* < *parler,* to speak.] A room in which guests are received and entertained; a living room; a room in a hotel or club used for conferences or private receptions; a room furnished for business or professional use; as, a beauty *parlor.*

par·lor car, *n.* An extra-fare railroad car fitted with comfortable individual chairs for daytime travel.

par·lor·maid, pär′lêr·mād″, *n.* A maid employed to take care of a parlor, attend to guests, and perform other related duties.

par·lous, pär′lus, *a.* [Var. of *perilous.*] *Archaic.* Perilous or dangerous; clever, shrewd.—*adv. Archaic,* excessively.—**par·lous·ly,** *adv.*

Par·me·san, pär′mi·zan″, pär′mi·zän″, pär′mi·zan, pär″mi·zan′, pär″mi·zän′, *n. Cookery,* a variety of cheese, originally from Parma in Italy, often grated and used with spaghetti and certain soups.

pa·ro·chi·al, pa·rō′kē·al, *a.* [L. *parochia,* corruption < *paroecia,* a parish.] Belonging to a parish; restricted to a parish; limited in range or scope; narrow.—**pa·ro·chi·al·ly,** adv.

pa·ro·chi·al·ism, pa·rō′kē·a·liz″um, n. The state of being parochial; narrowness of mind.

pa·ro·chi·al school, n. A primary or secondary school maintained by a parish, usu. correlating religious instruction with secular subjects.

par·o·dy, par′o·dē, n. pl. **par·o·dies.** [Fr. parodie, < Gr. parōdia—para, beside, and ōdē, an ode.] A literary composition in which the form and expression of serious writings are closely imitated but adapted to a ridiculous subject or a humorous method of treatment; a burlesque imitation of a serious poem; a poor imitation; a travesty.—v.t.—parodied, parodying.—**pa·rod·ic,** pa·rod′ik, a.—**par·o·dist,** par′o·dist, n.

pa·rol, pa·rōl′, par′ol, n. [= parole.] Law. Word of mouth; oral statement; the pleadings in a suit.—a.

pa·role, pa·rōl′, n. [Fr. parole, <L. L. parabola, a word, a parable.] The release of a prisoner to court supervision before having served his full sentence on condition of his future good conduct; the period of a parole. Milit. the pledge of a prisoner of war not to escape, or not to serve against his captors if given his release.—v.t.—paroled, paroling.—a. Of or pertaining to parole or one on parole.—**pa·rol·ee,** n.

par·o·no·ma·sia, par″o·nō·mā′zha, par″o·nō·mā′zhē·a, par″o·nō·mā′zä·a, n. [L., < Gr. paronomasia, < para, beside and onomázein, name, call, < ónoma, name.] Rhet. A playing on words; punning; a pun. —**par·o·no·mas·tic,** par″o·no·mas′tik, a. —**par·o·no·mas·ti·cal·ly,** adv.

par·o·nym, par′o·nim, n. [Fr. paronyme < Gr. parónymos, derivative, < par, beside, and ónyma, name.] A word derived from or related to another word; a derivative or cognate word; also, the form in one language for a word in another, as English 'canal' for Latin 'canalis.'—**pa·ron·y·mous,** pa·ron′i·mus, a. [Gr. parónymos.] Having the same derivation, as words; allied in origin; derived from a word in another language with little or no change in form.— **pa·ron·y·my,** pa·ron′i·mē, n. Paronymous character; the transference of a word from one language to another with little or no change in form.

pa·rot·id gland, pa·rot′id gland, n. [Gr. parōtis, parōtidos—para, beside, and ous, ōtos, the ear.] Anat. either of the two salivary glands on either side of the face, located one in front of each ear.—**pa·rot·id,** a. Of or pertaining to the parotid gland.

pa·rot·i·di·tis, pa·rot′i·dī′tis, n. Pathol. Inflammation of the parotid; mumps. Also **par·o·ti·tis,** par″o·tī′tis.—**par·o·tit·ic,** par″o·tit′ik, a.

Par·ou·sia, pa·rō′zē·a, pa·rō′sē·a, pa·rō′zē·a, pa·rō′sē·a, n. The Second Coming of Christ.

par·ox·ysm, par′ok·siz″um, n. [Gr. paroxysmós—para, in excess, and oxynō, to sharpen, < oxys, sharp.] A sudden and violent access of passion or emotion; a fit; pathol. any sudden onset or intensification of a disease or symptom, esp. one occurring with regularity, as the chills.—**par·ox·ys·mal,** a.

par·ox·y·tone, pa·rok′si·tōn″, a. Gr. gram. characterized by a word having the acute accent on the penultimate syllable.—n.

par·quet, pär·kā′, pär·ket′, n. [Fr. part of a park, enclosure, flooring, dim. of parc, park.] A flooring of parquetry. The main floor of a theater extending back from the orchestra pit.—v.t.—parqueted, parqueting. To construct of parquetry, as a floor.

par·quet cir·cle, n. The seats at the rear of the main floor of a theater or opera house, esp. those under the balconies; parterre.

par·quet·ry, pär′ki·trē, n. [Fr. parqueterie.] Mosaic work of wood, usu. in geometric pattern, used for floors or wainscoting.

parr, pär, n. Young salmon before migration to salt water; the young of several varieties of fishes, as the cod.

par·ra·keet, par′a·kēt″, n. Parakeet.

par·ri·cide, par′i·sīd″, n. [L. parricida, the criminal, parricidium, the crime, < pater, father, and caedo, to kill.] The murder of a parent or immediate relative; a person who murders his father or mother.—**par·ri·cid·al,** a.

par·rot, par′ot, n. [< Fr. Perrot, or Perrette, personal names from Pierre, Peter (like Fr. pierrot, a sparrow, from Pierre); cf. Sp. Perico, a dim. for Pedro, Peter, also a small parrot periquito, a small parrot.] Any of numerous species of birds belonging to the order Psittaciformes, including the parakeet, lovebird, cockatoo, macaw, and others, characterized by a stout hooked bill, two toes in front and two toes behind, and brilliant plumage, some of which are kept as cage birds because of their ability to imitate human speech; fig. a person who repeats by rote what he hears without thought to its meaning.—v.t. To repeat as a parrot; to repeat, as a person, by rote.— **par·rot·like,** a.—**par·rot·y,** a.

par·rot fe·ver, n. Psittacosis. Also **par·rot dis·ease.** See ornithosis.

par·rot·fish, par′ot·fish″, n. Any of several species of tropical fish which are brilliantly colored and have teeth fused into a beak-like structure, belonging to the families Scaridae and Labridae.

par·ry, par′ē, v.t.—parried, parrying. [Fr. parer, It. parare, to ward off, < L. parare, to prepare, keep off.] To ward off, as a blow or a thrust; to turn aside; evade; avoid.—v.i. To ward off a blow or thrust. —n. pl. par·ries. An evasion, esp. a verbal one; a defensive motion made in fencing.

parse, pärs, pärz, v.t. [L. pars, a part, pars ōrātiōnis, a part of a speech: to parse a word is to tell what part of speech it is.] Gram. to analyze or describe grammatically.—v.i. Gram. to show the several parts of speech composing a sentence and their relation to each other by agreement.

par·sec, pär′sek, n. [< (par)allax and (sec)ond.] Astron. a unit of distance corresponding to a heliocentric parallax of one second of arc, being equal to about 200,000 times the distance of the earth from the sun, or about three and one-fourth light-years.

par·si·mo·ny, pär′si·mō″nē, n. [Fr. parsimonie, < L. parsimonia, parcimonia, < parco, parsum, to spare.] Excessive closeness in the use or expenditure of money; extreme frugality; stinginess; miserliness. —**par·si·mo·ni·ous,** pär″si·mō′nē·us, a. —**par·si·mo·ni·ous·ly,** adv.—**par·si·mo·ni·ous·ness,** n.

pars·ley, pärs′lē, n. [O.E. persely, persylle, etc., Fr. persil, < L. petroselīnum, Gr. petroselinon, rock parsley.] A well-known garden herb, Petroselinum crispum, in the parsley family, Umbelliferae, native to Europe and widely cultivated for its leaves which are used as a garnish for foods.—a. Garnished with parsley.

pars·nip, pär′snip, n. [Corrupted < Fr. pastinaque, L. pastinaca, a parsnip, < pastinum.] An herbaceous European biennial, Pastinaca sativa, in the parsley family, cultivated and naturalized in the U.S., having large pinnate leaves, yellowish-green flowers borne in umbels, and an edible thickened white taproot; the root.

par·son, pär′son, n. [O.Fr. persone, < L.L. persona ecclesiæ, the person of the church, L. persona, a person.] One who has the paro-

chial charge of a church parish; a clergyman, minister, or preacher.—**par·son·age,** pär′so·nij, n. The official dwelling of a parson.—**par·son·ic, par·son·i·cal,** pär·son′ik, a.

part, pärt, n. [O.Fr. Fr. part, < L. pars (part-), piece, portion, share, role, region, party.] A portion or division of a whole, separate in reality or in thought; a piece, section, or fragment; a constituent; an essential or integral portion or element, as: She had become part of his life. A division of a novel, play, or poem; a portion, member, or organ of an animal body; an allotted portion; a share; each of a number of equal portions comprising a whole; math. an aliquot part. Usu. pl. a region, quarter, or district; a personal or mental endowment or ability; as, a man of parts. One of the parties or sides in a contest, dispute, or agreement; the dividing line formed in parting the hair; a constituent and distinct piece or member of a machine, either included during manufacture or used as a replacement. Mus. one of the voices or instruments in harmonized music; the melody or score for it. Participation, interest, or concern in something; one's share in some action; a duty, function, or office; a character sustained in a play or real life; a role; the words or lines assigned to an actor in such a character.—**for one's part,** so far as concerns one.—**for the most part,** as concerns the greatest part; mostly.—**in good part,** without offense; good-naturedly. —**in part,** to some extent.—**part and par·cel,** an essential part: used emphatically.—**take one's part,** to espouse one's side or cause; to support one.—**take part,** to participate.

part, pärt, v.t. To divide into parts; break; cleave; to comb, as the hair, away from a dividing line; to dissolve, as a relationship or a connection, by separation of the parts, persons, or things involved; as, to part company; to divide into shares; distribute in parts; apportion; to put or hold apart; separate; as, to part players in a scuffle; to separate, as mixed substances, by mechanical or chemical means.—v.i. To be or become divided into parts; break or cleave; to come or go apart; separate, as two or more things; to go apart from each other or one another, as persons; to be or become separated from something else, usu. followed by from; to go away or depart; to die.—adv. In part; partially.—a. Partial. —**part with,** to give up; relinquish.

par·take, pär·tāk′, v.i.—past partook, pp. partaken, ppr. partaking. [Part and take.] To take a part, portion, or share in common with others, used with of; to have or receive a share or part; to participate, used with in; to have something of the character or nature of, followed by of.—v.t. To have a part in; to share.—**par·ta·ker,** n.

part·ed, pär′tid, a. Divided; separated; bot. cleft into divisions, as a leaf; archaic, deceased.

par·terre, pär·târ′, n. [Fr., < par, on, by, and terre, earth, ground.] An ornamental, patterned arrangement of flower beds and walks; in a theater, the area of the main floor behind the parquet, under the balcony.

par·the·no·car·py, pär′the·nō·kär″pē, n. Bot. the development of a fruit without pollination and fertilization, such fruit often being seedless.—**par·the·no·car·pic,** pär″the·nō·kär′pik, a.—**par·the·no·car·pi·cal·ly,** adv.

par·the·no·gen·e·sis, pär″the·nō·jen′i·sis, n. [Gr. parthenos, virgin, and genesis, genesis.] Biol. the development of an egg into a new individual without fertilization by a sperm, uncommon and occurring usu. in lower plants and invertebrates, sometimes artificially induced by chemicals as in frog eggs: distinguished from *asexual reproduction*. Also **vir·gin birth.—par·-the·no·ge·net·ic,** pär″the·nō′je·net′ik, *a.* **—par·the·no·ge·net·i·cal·ly,** *adv.*

Par·the·non, pär′the·non″, pär′the·non, *n.* [L., < Gr. *Parthenōn,* < *parthénos,* virgin.] The temple of Athene on the Acropolis of Athens, structurally completed about 438 B.C. and regarded as the finest example of Doric architecture.

Par·thi·an, pär′thē·an, *a.* Pertaining to Parthia, an ancient kingdom of western Asia southeast of the Caspian Sea, or to its inhabitants.—*n.* A native or inhabitant of Parthia; an ancient Iranian language.

par-three, pär′thrē′, *a.* Denoting or pertaining to a small-sized golf course in which the par for any one hole does not exceed three strokes, the yardage of the holes averaging about 150 yards.—*n.* Any such course.

par·tial, pär′shal, *a.* [Fr. *partial,* < L. *pars, partis,* a part.] Affecting one part only; not complete or total; prejudiced in favor of one side; having a fondness for, usu. used with *to; bot.* subordinate; as, a *partial* umbel.—**par·tial·ly,** *adv.*

par·tial frac·tion, *n. Alg.* one of the fractions into which a given fraction can be resolved, the sum of such simpler fractions being equal to the given fraction.

par·tial·i·ty, pär·shal′i·tē, pär″shē·al′i·tē, *n. pl.* **par·tial·i·ties.** The state or quality of being partial; bias; favoritism; a special liking or fondness. Also **par·tial·ness.**

par·tial·ly or·dered, *a. Math.* pertaining to a relation within a set which applies to some pairs of the set but not to all.

par·ti·ble, pär′ti·bl, *a.* [L.L. *partibilis.*] That can be parted or divided; divisible. —**par·ti·bil·i·ty,** *n.*

par·tic·i·pant, pär·tis′i·pant, *a.* Sharing; having a share or part.—*n.* One who takes part in or shares in something.

par·tic·i·pate, pär·tis′i·pāt″, *v.i.*—*participated, participating.* [L. *participo, participatum—pars, partis,* a part, and *capio,* to take.] To partake; to take a part or have a share in common with others, usu. followed by *in.—v.t. Rare.* To take part in; receive a part of.—**par·tic·i·pa·tion,** pär·tis″i·pā′shan, *n.*—**par·tic·i·pa·tive,** *a.*—**par·tic·i·pa·tor,** *n.*

par·tic·i·pat·ing, pär·tis′i·pā″ting, *a.* Taking part in, or sharing with another or others, as a golf match, profits, or benefits.

par·ti·cip·i·al, pär″ti·sip′ē·al, *a. Gram.* Pertaining to or having the nature and use of a participle; formed from a participle. —*n.* A participle.—**par·ti·cip·i·al·ly,** *adv.*

par·ti·ci·ple, pär′ti·sip″l, pär′ti·si·pl, *n.* [L. *participium,* < *particeps,* partaking—*pars, partis,* a part, and *capio,* to take; cf. *principle,* < L. *principium.*] *Gram.* a part of speech, so called because it partakes of the character both of a verb and an adjective.

par·ti·cle, pär′ti·kl, *n.* [L. *particula,* dim. of *pars* (*part-*), E. *part,* n.] A minute portion, piece, or degree; as, a *particle* of dust, a *particle* of pride; a clause or article, as of a document. *Rom. Cath. Ch.* a little piece or fragment of the Host; the small Host given to each lay communicant. *Gram.* a minor part of speech, as a conjunction, a preposition, or a monosyllabic adverb; a prefix or a suffix. *Mech.* a portion of matter so minute that, while it possesses mass, it may be treated as a geometrical point.

par·ti·cle, pär′ti·kl, *n. Phys.* fundamental particle.

par·ti-col·ored, pär′tē·kul″ĕrd, *a.* Colored differently in different parts; diversified. Also **par·ty-col·ored.**

par·tic·u·lar, pĕr·tik′ū·lĕr, *a.* [O.Fr. *particuler* (Fr. *particulier*), < L. *particularis,* < *particular,* E. *particle.*] Belonging or pertaining to some one person, thing,

group, class, occasion, or other category, rather than to others or all; special; not general; characteristic; being a definite one, individual, or single, or considered separately; distinguished or different from others or from the ordinary; noteworthy, marked, or unusual; exceptional or special; being such in an exceptional degree; dealing with or giving details, as an account or description of a person; detailed, minute, or circumstantial; careful; fastidious; scrupulous. *Logic,* not general; not referring to the whole extent of a class, but only to some individual or individuals in it: contrasted with *universal. Law,* pertaining to a portion of something; separate; individual; specific.—*n.* An individual or distinct part, as an item of a list or enumeration; *usu. pl.* points, details, or circumstances. *Logic,* a certain group or individual within a general category; a specific proposition.—**in par·-tic·u·lar,** particularly or especially.

par·tic·u·lar·ism, pĕr·tik′ū·la·riz″um, *n.* Exclusive attention or devotion to one's own particular interests or party; *govt.* the principle of leaving each state of a federation free to retain its own laws and promote its own interests; *Theol.* the doctrine that divine grace is provided only for the elect.—**par·tic·u·lar·ist,** *n.*—**par·-tic·u·lar·is·tic,** *a.*

par·tic·u·lar·i·ty, pĕr·tik″ū·lar′i·tē, *n. pl.* **par·tic·u·lar·i·ties.** The quality or fact of being particular; a special, peculiar, or individual character; detailed, minute, or circumstantial character, as of description or statement; attentiveness to details or small points, or special carefulness; fastidiousness; that which is particular; a particular or characteristic feature or trait.

par·tic·u·lar·ize, pĕr·tik′ū·la·rīz″, *v.t. particularized, particularizing.* To make particular; to mention or indicate particularly; state or treat in detail.—*v.i.* To speak or treat particularly or specifically; go into detail on any subject.—**par·tic·u·-lar·i·za·tion,** *n.*

par·tic·u·lar·ly, pĕr·tik′ū·lĕr·lē, *adv.* In a particular manner; specially; individually; in detail, or minutely; in a particular or exceptional degree.

par·tic·u·late, pĕr·tik′ū·lit, pĕr·tik′ū·lāt″, *a.* [L. *particula,* E. *particle.*] Consisting of or pertaining to minute, separate particles.

par·tic·u·late in·her·it·ance, *n.* See *Mendelism.*

part·ing, pär′ting, *a.* Serving to part; dividing; separating; given at separation; as, a *parting* kiss.—*n.* The act of dividing or separating; a division; a separation; leave-taking; *archaic,* death.

par·ti·san, pär′ti·zan, *n.* [Fr., < *parti,* a party, < L. *pars, partis,* a part.] An adherent, esp. a particularly zealous supporter of a party, faction, or person. *Milit.* a member of a group of irregular troops or of a guerrilla band that harasses an occupying enemy.—*a.* Biased in favor of a party or interest; pertaining to military operations carried out by partisans or guerrillas. Also **par·ti·zan.—par·ti·san·ship,** *n.*

par·tite, pär′tīt, *a.* [L. *partitus,* pp. of *partire,* part.] Divided into parts; *entom.* divided to the base, as a wing; *bot.* parted.

par·ti·tion, pär·tish′an, *n.* [Fr. *partition,* < L. *partitio(n-),* < *partire,* part.] The act of parting, or the fact of being parted; division into or distribution in portions or shares; separation, as of two or more things; something that separates; a part, division, or section; an interior wall or barrier dividing a building or enclosure; a septum or dissepiment, as in a plant or animal structure; each of the parts into which a thing is divided, as by boundaries; *law,* a division of property among joint owners, esp. a

division of real property held jointly; *logic,* the separation of a whole into its integrant parts; *math.* a mode of separating a positive whole number into a sum of positive whole numbers.—*v.t.* To make partition of; divide into parts or portions; dismember and distribute; *law,* to divide, as property.— **par·ti·tion·er,** *n.*—**par·ti·tion·ment,** *n.*

par·ti·tive, pär′ti·tiv, *a.* Serving to separate into parts; *gram.* expressing the relation of a part to a whole, as the Latin *partitive* genitive.—*n. Gram.* a word expressing partition.—**par·ti·tive·ly,** *adv.*

part·let, pärt′lit, *n.* A 16th century ruffled garment worn by women around the neck and shoulders.

part·ly, pärt′lē, *adv.* In part; in some measure or degree; not wholly.

part mu·sic, *n. Mus.* vocal music with parts for two or more independent performers. Also *part song.*

part·ner, pärt′nĕr, *n.* [Var. of *parcener,* appar. by association with *part.*] A sharer; an associate in an enterprise; a spouse; one of a couple who dance together; *sports,* a player on the same side; *law,* one who holds a partnership in a business.—*v.t.* To serve as the partner of; to furnish a partner for.

part·ner·ship, *n.* The state of being a partner; participation; joint interest. *Com.* the relation between partners in business; the contract creating this relationship; an association of persons joined as partners in business.

part of speech, *n. Gram.* any of the traditional classes of words differentiated by their meaning and syntactic function in a sentence, as, in English grammar, the noun, pronoun, verb, adverb, adjective, conjunction, preposition, and interjection.

par·tridge, pär′trij, *n. pl.* **par·tridg·es, par·tridge.** [O.Fr. *perdriz* (Fr. *perdrix*), < L. *perdix,* < Gr. *perdix.*] A common name for several scratching, chickenlike game birds of the family *Phasianidae;* a plump European partridge, *Perdix perdix,* gray with a short reddish tail, inhabiting open farming country, and introduced into the U.S.; also **Hun·gar·i·an par·tridge.** A reddish-brown bird, *Bonasa umbellus,* with a ruff around the neck and a fan-shaped tail, native to eastern N. America; also *ruffed grouse.*

par·tridge·ber·ry, pär′trij·ber″ē, *n. pl.* **par·tridge·ber·ries.** An evergreen trailing herb, *Mitchella repens,* in the madder family, native to northeastern N. America, with white to pink flowers borne in pairs at the end of the stems, and producing red berries. Also *checkerberry, twinberry.*

part song, *n.* A song adapted for singing in two or more vocal parts, usu. without instrumental accompaniment; a harmonized or concerted song.

part-time, pärt′tīm″, *a.* Employed or functioning less than the usual or normal number of hours: distinguished from *full-time.*

par·tu·ri·ent, pär·tur′ē·ent, pär·tūr′ē·-ent, *a.* [L. *parturiens, parturientis,* ppr. of *parturio,* < *partus,* birth, *pario,* to bear.] Bringing forth or about to bring forth young; about to bring forth an original thought or other creation.—**par·tu·ri·tion,** pär″tu·rish′an, pär″tū·rish′an, pär″chu·-rish′an, *n.* [L. *parturitio.*] The act of bringing forth young.

par·ty, pär′tē, *n. pl.* **par·ties.** [Fr. *partie,* a party, side, faction, a suitor or litigant.] A person or a number of persons united in purpose or opinion, taking one side of an issue, debate, or contest; a group of persons, united by certain political views, which attempts to have its candidates elected to office; as, the Republican *party;* a social gathering or entertainment of invited guests, as at a private home or elsewhere; a group of persons gathered for a specific purpose; as, a hunting *party*; one who participates in or is concerned with an affair or action, as: He was *party* to the scheme. *Law*, a person or persons involved in a legal matter. A person; a certain individual; as, the *party* you want to see.—*a.*

par·ty line, *n.* A single telephone line serving several subscribers; also *Brit.* **shared line.** A boundary line between adjoining properties; political policies followed by its members, esp. of the Communist party.

par·ty wall, *n.* A wall on the line between adjoining premises, in which each of the respective owners use in common.

pa·rure, pa·rŭr′, *Fr.* pä·RYR′, *n.* [Fr., < *parer*, prepare, adorn.] A set of jewels or ornaments.

par·ve, pär′ve, *a.* Pareve.

par·ve·nu, pär′ve·nö″, pär′ve·nū″, *n.* [Fr. *parvenu*, lit. 'one who has arrived,' < *parvenir*, L. *pervenire*, to arrive.] One who has suddenly acquired wealth or position above his class; but who lacks the social graces appropriate to his new status.—*a.*

par·vis, pär′vis, *n.* [O.Fr. *parevis* (Fr. *parvis*), < L.L. *paradisus*, E. *paradise*.] A vacant enclosed area in front of a church; a colonnade or portico in front of a church; a church porch.

pas, pä, *n.* pl. **pas.** [Fr.] A step or movement in dancing, or a kind of dance; precedence, or right of preceding; as, to yield the *pas*.

Pasch, pask, *n.* [O.Fr. *pasche, pasque* (Fr. *pâque*), < L.L. *pascha*, < Gr. *páscha*, < Heb. *pesakh*, Passover, < *pāsakh*, pass over.] *Archaic.* The Jewish feast of the Passover; the Christian feast of Easter.— **pas·chal**, pas′kal, *a.*

pas·chal lamb, *n.* Among the Jews, the lamb slain and eaten at the Passover; (*caps.*) Christ, of whom the lamb of the Jewish Passover is taken as a figure; any of various symbolical representations of Christ.

pas de deux, *Fr.* pä de dœ′, *n. Ballet,* a dance by two performers, esp. choreographed according to a set form in classical ballet.

pas de trois, *Fr.* pä de tRwä′, *n. Ballet,* a dance for three performers.

pa·se, pä′sä, *n. Bullfighting,* a movement of his cape by the matador to attract the bull and to divert its charge.

pash, pash, *n.* [Origin unknown.] *Brit. dial.* the head.

pa·sha, pa·shä′, pash′a, pä′sha, *n.* [Pers. *pâshâh*, contr. < *padishah*, protector or great king.] A title of courtesy placed after a person's name in Turkey and in Arabic countries, formerly conferred upon military commanders and governors of provinces. Also *bashaw*, **pa·cha.**

pa·sig·ra·phy, pa·sig′ra·fē″, *n.* [Gr. *pasi*, for all (dat. pl. of *pas*, all), and *graphēs*, writing.] Any of various systems of writing proposed for universal use, which employ characters representing ideas instead of words; a kind of writing that may be understood and used by all nations.— **pas·i·graph·ic, pas·i·graph·i·cal**, pas·i·graf′ik, *a.*

pasque·flow·er, pask′flou″ẽr, *n.* [Altered (after *Pasque*) from earlier *passeflower*, < Fr. *passe fleur*, < *passer*, E. pass, and *fleur*, E. *flower*.] An early spring flower, *Anemone patens*, in the buttercup family, having five to seven white to blue, petallike sepals, the entire plant being covered with silky hairs: native to the dry prairies from Illinois to S. Dakota; the State flower of S. Dakota.

pas·quin·ade, pas″kwi·nād′, *n.* [Fr., < It. *pasquinata*.] A lampoon or satire, esp. one publicly displayed. Also **pas·quil**, pas′kwil. —*v.t.*—*pasquinaded, pasquinading.*

pass, pas, päs, *v.i.* [O.Fr. Fr. *passer*, < M.L. *passare*, < L. *passus*, a step.] To go,

move onward, proceed; to be successful in an examination, test, or inspection; to go away or depart; to die, usu. used with *on*; to move past; to elapse or be spent, as: The time *passes* quickly. To happen or occur; as, to know what *passed* in the conference; to make one's or its way, as: The overflow *passed* through the gorge. To undergo alteration or conversion; as, to *pass* from a solid to a liquid state; to circulate; to be accepted, usu. with *for* or *as*; to be exchanged or conveyed; as, rumors *passed* around the campus; to go uncensored or unchallenged; to be voided or excreted; to be enacted or ratified; to give judgment, usu. with *on* or *upon*; *aeron.* to go from subsonic to supersonic speed; *law*, to be conveyed from one to another; *sports*, to make a pass, as in football or hockey; *cards*, to forgo one's opportunity to bid or to play.—*v.t.* To go by or move past; to transcend, exceed, surpass; to cause to go by, march or move past; as, to *pass* troops in review; to undergo successfully; as, an examination or inspection; to cross; to go beyond; to spend; as, to *pass* hours in play; to circulate; as, to *pass* counterfeit money; to leave unmentioned or unnoticed; to omit payment or action upon; to discharge or void body waste; to cause to go from one to another; convey; transfer; pledge; to sanction or approve, as laws; to obtain sanction or approval of; to pronounce judgment; to allow or permit the overcoming of an obstacle or barrier; *law*, to transfer ownership; *football, hockey*, to transfer to a player on the same team, as a ball or puck; *baseball*, to walk, as a batter.—**pass a·way,** to pass out of existence; to die.—**pass mus·ter,** to meet the requirements of an inspection.—**pass off,** to run off, as water on soil; to vanish, as vapor; to circulate deceptively or fraudulently.—**pass the buck,** to put work or responsibility upon someone else.—**pass·er**, pas′ẽr, pä′sẽr, *n.*

pass, pas, päs, *n.* [In part, < *pass, v.*, or O.Fr. Fr. *passe*, < *passer*; in part, < O.Fr. Fr. *pas*, step, passage.] The act of passing; a road, navigable channel, or defile affording passage through an obstructed area; a written permission to enter, leave, or move about in an area requiring control; a free ticket for transportation or admission. *Milit.* the granting of permission for personnel to be absent from duty; the form granting this permission; the period of time granted. The passing of a test or course of studies; *Brit.* passing an examination acceptably but without honors. A motion of the hands along or over an object; a movement of the hand intended to divert, deceive, or cast a spell; manipulation of an object, as by a juggler; a complete process through a machine; *sports*, the passing of a ball or puck from one player to a teammate. *Aeron.* a sweep, movement, or run during aircraft maneuver, esp. if unsuccessful; movement by a fighter plane. *Cards*, the decision to forgo one's turn to bid, wager, double, or redouble; *baseball*, a walk; *fencing*, a thrust or lunge; *slang*, a gesture designed to provoke a response from one of the opposite sex; *archaic*, a sally of wit.

pass·a·ble, pas′a·bl, pä′sa·bl, *a.* [O.Fr. Fr. *passable*.] That may be traveled on, crossed, or traversed; tolerable; acceptable for circulation, as currency; capable of being enacted, as a legislative bill.

pass·a·bly, pas′a·blē, pä′sa·blē, *adv.* Tolerably; fairly; moderately.

pas·sa·ca·glia, pä″sa·käl′ya, pas″a·käl′ya, *n.* [It., < Sp. *pasacalle, pasar*, pass, and *calle*, street (appar. because played in the streets).] An old dance tune of Spanish origin, constructed upon a recurring theme, usu. a ground bass, in three-quarter time; the dance performed to this music.

pas·sa·do, pa·sä′dō, *n.* pl. **pa·sa·dos, pa·sa·does.** [It. *passata*.] *Fencing*, a forward thrust or lunge while one foot advances.

pas·sage, pas′ij, *n.* [O.Fr. Fr. *passage*, < *passer*, pass.] The act of passing; movement, transit, or transition, as from one place or state to another; a traveling from one place to another, esp. by sea, commonly a voyage across the sea from one port to another; the privilege of conveyance as a passenger, esp. on a sea-going vessel; lapse, as of time; progress or course, as of events; an interchange of communications or confidences between persons; an exchange of blows, or an altercation or dispute; an evacuation of the bowels; the passing into law of a legislative measure; the causing of something to pass; transference or transmission; liberty, leave, or right to pass, as through a country; that by which a person or thing passes; a means of passing; a way or route; an avenue; a channel; a pass; a thoroughfare for foot passengers; a hall, corridor, or the like; an indefinite portion of a writing or speech, usu. one of no great length; a paragraph; verse. *Mus.* a phrase or other division of a piece; a scalelike or arpeggiolike series of tones introduced as an embellishment; a run, roulade, or flourish.—*v.i.*—*passaged, passaging.* To make passage; cross; pass; voyage; to have a passage at arms or an encounter; to fence with words.

pas·sage·way, pas′ij·wā″, *n.* A way for passage, as in a building or among buildings; a passage.

pass a·way, *v.i.* To come to an end; to die. —*v.t.* Terminate; to idle, as time.

pass·book, pas′bụk″, päs′bụk″, *n.* A book held by a depositor, in which a bank enters the credits and debits of his account; bankbook.

pas·sé, pa·sä′, pas′ä, *Fr.* pä·sā′, *a.* [Fr.] Past; old-fashioned; past the prime of life.

passed ball, *n. Baseball,* a pitched ball which the catcher fails to stop though it is within his reach, his failure allowing a base runner or base runners to advance.

passe·men·te·rie, pas·men′trē, *Fr.* päs·-mäN·tRē′, *n.* [Fr., < *passement*.] *Millinery,* trimming made of braid, cord, or beads.

pas·sen·ger, pas′en·jẽr, *n.* [O.E. *passager,* one who makes a passage; the *n* being an intrusive element, as in *messenger*.] One who travels on a plane, ship, railroad, bus, taxi, or other conveyance; a wayfarer or traveler; as, a foot *passenger*.

pas·sen·ger pi·geon, *n.* A N. American wild pigeon, *Ectopistes migratorius*, great flocks of which once abounded, esp. in the Mississippi valley, and which was widely hunted as a table delicacy, leading to its extinction in 1914.

pass·er-by, pas′ẽr·bī′, pas′ẽr·bī″, pä′sẽr·bī′, pä′sẽr·bī″, *n.* pl. **pass·ers-by.** One who passes by.

pas·ser·ine, pas′ẽr·in, pas′e·rīn″, pas′e·rēn″, *a.* [L. *passerinus*, < *passer*, sparrow.] *Ornith.* belonging or pertaining to the order, *Passeriformes*, the perching birds, having three toes in front and one toe behind, and including the suborder *Oscines*, or true song birds.—*n.* Any bird of this order as the sparrow, robin, and warbler.

pas seul, *Fr.* pä sœl′, *n.* pl. **pas seuls.** [Fr. lit. 'solo step.'] *Ballet,* a dance by one person.

pas·si·ble, pas′i·bl, *a.* [L. *passibilis*, < *patior, passus*, to suffer.] Capable of suffering; impressionable.—**pas·si·bil·i·ty**, *n.*

pas·sim, pas′im, *adv.* [L., < *passus*, pp. of *pandere*, spread.] Here and there: a reference note indicating that something recurs throughout a piece of writing. Abbr. *pass.*

pass·ing, pas′ing, pä′sing, *a.* Going by; fleeting, transitory; superficial, hasty, cursory; current; as, the *passing* show; acceptable; fulfilling requirements; as, a *passing* grade on an examination.—*n.* The act of one that passes or causes something to pass; a place or mode of passage.—**in pass·ing,** as one proceeds; incidentally.

pass·ing note, *n. Mus.* a note outside the harmony, introduced between two successive harmonic tones in order to produce a melodic transition. Also **pass·ing tone.**

pas·sion, pash′an, *n.* [L. *passio, passionis,* < *patior, passus,* to bear, to suffer; allied to Gr. *pathos,* suffering; cf. *patient, passive, compatible.*] A compelling, intense feeling or emotion; love, ardent affection; amorous desire; lust; violent agitation of mind; violent anger; zeal, ardor; an avid desire; as, a *passion* for fame; a display of deep feeling; as, a *passion* of tears; a pursuit to which one is devoted; the subject of an engrossing pursuit. *Psychol.* an outbreak of violent emotion; formerly, a general term for emotion. (*Usu. cap.*) the last suffering and death of Jesus Christ; a musical setting of those sufferings as recorded in the first four books of the New Testament; a series of pictures, the *Stations of the Cross,* representing those sufferings.—**pas·sion·less,** *a.*

pas·sion·al, pash′a·nal, *n.* A book in which are described the sufferings of saints and martyrs.—*a.* Relating to or produced by passion.

pas·sion·ate, pash′a·nit, *a.* Capable of or characterized by passion or intense feeling; expressing passion or strong feeling; readily moved to anger; fiery; ardent; moved by sexual desire; vehement.—**pas·sion·ate·ly,** *adv.*—**pas·sion·ate·ness,** *n.*

pas·sion-flow·er, pash′an·flow″ėr, *n.* Any of several species of climbing vines of the genus *Passiflora,* mostly native in tropical America, and named from the showy flowers which are said to have the appearance of Christ's wounds and crown of thorns.

Pas·sion play, *n.* A representation in dramatic form of the different scenes in the Passion of Christ.

pas·sive, pas′iv, *a.* [L. *passivus,* < *patior, passus,* to suffer.] Being without response to something normally expected to provoke expressions of emotion or feeling; not active; inert; influenced or incited by an outside agency: distinguished from *active;* incapable of receiving impressions from outside sources; receiving or suffering without resistance; *gram.* noting a verbal inflection indicating that the subject experiences the action of the verb. *Chem.* inactive; resistant to chemical activity. *Med.* pertaining to certain inactive but unhealthy symptoms.—*n. Gram.* The passive voice; the passive verb form and construction in a language.—**pas·sive·ly,** *adv.* —**pas·sive·ness,** *n.*—**pas·siv·i·ty,** *n.*

pas·sive re·sist·ance, *n.* A method of protest which seeks to bring about social and legal change through nonviolent actions, such as noncooperation and civil disobedience: used esp. by minority groups to demonstrate opposition to a government or its laws.

pass·key, pas′kē″, päs′kē″, *n.* pl. **pass·keys.** A key for opening several locks; a master key; a private key; a latchkey.

pass out, *v.t.* To spread, distribute.—*v.i. Colloq.* To lose consciousness; faint; to die.

Pass·o·ver, pas′ō″vėr, päs′ō″vėr, *n.* A seven-day festival of the Jews during which no foods made with leaven may be eaten, occurring in the spring of the year to commemorate the escape of the Hebrews from slavery in Egypt. Also *Pesach.*

pass o·ver, *v.t.* To give little or no consideration; to omit action on; to disregard.

pass·port, pas′pōrt, päs′pärt, *n.* [Fr. *passeport,* a safe-conduct,

orig. permission to enter or leave a port.] A warrant issued to a citizen of a country by the appropriate authority, giving him permission to travel, protection while out of the country, and the right of reentry; a certificate permitting travel or the conveyance of goods through foreign territory; a document authorizing a vessel to proceed, issued esp. in wartime to a neutral merchant ship; something that enables one to pass, to gain entrance, or to attain an object.

pass up, *v.t. Colloq.* To forgo the advantages of; neglect.

pass·word, pas′wurd″, päs′wurd″, *n. Milit.* a secret word by which one having a right to pass is recognized. A watchword.

past, past, päst, *a.* Gone by; ended; over; belonging to a time previous to this; bygone; preceding; not present or future; having served a term in office; as, a *past* president; *gram.* indicating time gone by or former action or state, as designated in verb tense or construction.—*prep.* Beyond in time; after; as, *past* noon; beyond in position; further than; as, the street *past* the stop sign; beyond in number, as: He is *past* seventy. Beyond the scope or influence of.—*n.* A bygone time; a past or former time; as, far back in the *past;* an earlier time in the history, life, or career of a person, thing, or country.—*adv.* So as to pass by or beyond; by.

pas·ta, pä′sta, *n.* [It.] An unleavened paste or dough prepared with flour and eggs and used in making spaghetti, noodles, and macaroni; a dish made of this.

paste, past, *n.* [O.Fr. *paste,* Fr. *pate;* < L. *pasta,* paste, < Gr. *paste,* a mess of barley porridge, < *passo,* to sprinkle.] A kind of adhesive made of various compounds; a dough used in cooking, as for pies or pastry; pasta; any of various mashed, whipped, or ground foods; as, liver *paste;* any composition in which there is sufficient moisture to soften without liquefying the mass; a smooth-textured, semisolid substance; as, tooth*paste;* a compound of rock crystals and alkaline salts colored with metallic oxides, and used for making imitation gems; a moist, pliable clay used in making chinaware, pottery, or porcelain. —*v.t.*—*pasted, pasting.* To fasten or cement with paste; to cover with something applied by means of paste.

paste, past, *v.t.*—*pasted, pasting. Slang.* To strike severely with a blow; to punch, as on the face.—*n.* A hard blow.

paste·board, past′bōrd″, *n.* Paper pulp or layers of treated paper pressure-molded or rolled into rigid sheets; cardboard. *Slang.* theater ticket; playing card.—*a.* Made of or like pasteboard; unsubstantial or flimsy.

pas·tel, pa·stel′, pas′tel, *n.* [Fr., < It. *pastello,* dim. < L.L. *pasta,* E. *paste.*] A soft, pale color; a kind of dried paste made of pigments ground with chalk compounded with gum water; a chalk crayon made with such paste; the art of drawing, or a drawing made with such crayons; a short slight prose study or sketch.—*a.* Pertaining to a pastel; having a subdued, soft, or delicate tint or shade.—**pas·tel·ist, pas·tel·list,** pa·stel′ist, pas′tel·ist, *n.* An artist who draws with pastels.

pas·tern, pas′tėrn, *n.* [O.Fr. *pasturon,* < *pasture,* a shackle for cattle at pasture, < L. *pasco, pastum,* to feed.] The part of a horse's foot between the fetlock and hoof; either of two bones of this area; a hobble for horses and other animals.

pas·teur·ize, pas′che·rīz″, pas′te·rīz″, *v.t.* —*pasteurized, pasteurizing.* [From Louis *Pasteur,* 1822–1895, Fr. chemist.] To subject, as milk, wine, beer, fruit juices, or other liquids to a temperature ranging from 140 to 155°F. for one-half hour, in order to kill the bacteria which cause

fermentation.—**pas·teur·i·za·tion,** *n.*— **pas·teur·iz·er,** pas′che·rī″zėr, pas′te·rī″zėr, *n.* An apparatus used for pasteurizing.

Pas·teur treat·ment, pa·stur′ trēt′ment, *Fr.* pä·stOER′, *n.* A treatment for preventing certain diseases, esp. hydrophobia, by a series of inoculations with a virus of gradually increasing strength.

pas·tiche, pa·stēsh′, pä·stēsh′, *n.* [It., < *pasta,* < L.L. *pasta,* E. *paste.*] A work of art, music, or literature whose design and techniques are taken from other works; a satiric use of these elements; a disorganized mixture of elements; a hodgepodge. Also **pas·tic·cio,** pa·stē′chō, *It.* päs·tēt′cha.

pas·tille, pa·stēl′, pa·stil′, *n.* [Fr. *pastille,* L. *pastillus,* a little roll, < *pastus,* food, *pasco, pastum,* to feed.] A sweetened lozenge, usu. medicated; a troche; a small roll of aromatic paste for burning as a fumigant or disinfectant. Pastel for making crayons; a crayon formed from pastel; see *pastel.* Also **pas·til,** pas′til.

pas·time, pas′tīm″, päs′tīm″, *n.* [*Pass* and *time.*] That which amuses and serves to make time pass agreeably; sport; diversion.

past mas·ter, *n.* One who has occupied the office or dignity of master in a lodge or guild; one who is exceptionally expert in his craft or business.

pas·tor, pas′tėr, *n.* [L. *pastor,* a shepherd, < *pasco, pastum,* to feed; same root as W. *pasg,* a feeding, Armor. *paska,* to feed, Skt. *pā,* to guard.] A minister of the gospel having charge of a church and congregation.—**pas·tor·ship,** pas′tėr·ship″, päs′tėr·ship″, *n.*

pas·to·ral, pas′tėr·al, pä′stėr·al, *a.* [L. *pāstōrālis,* < *pastor.*] Pertaining to shepherds, or to the care of flocks or herds; living as a shepherd or shepherds; as, a *pastoral* people; used for pasture, as land; having the simplicity or charm of farm country, as scenery; pertaining to the country or to life in the country; rustic or rural; portraying the life of shepherds or of the country in an idyllic manner, as a work of literature, art, or music; pertaining to a pastor, minister, or clergyman, or to his labors or duties.—*n.* A poem or play dealing with the life of shepherds, either in a conventional or artificial manner, or with simple rural life generally; a bucolic, pastoral poem or drama, as a form of literature; a pastoral picture or work of art; a pastorale; a treatise on the duties of a minister or clergyman; a letter from a spiritual pastor to his people or flock, esp. one from a bishop to his clergy or people; a pastoral staff or crozier;—**pas·to·ral·ly,** *adv.*—**pas·to·ral·ness,** *n.*—**pas·to·ral·ism,** *n.*

pas·to·rale, pas″to·räl′, pas″to·ral′, pas″to·rä′lē, *It.* päs″ta·rä′lē, *n.* pl. **pas·to·rales,** *It.* päs″to·ra·li, *It.* päs″ta·Rä′lē. [It.] *Mus.* An opera or cantata with a pastoral subject; a piece of music suggestive of pastoral life.

pas·tor·ate, pas′tėr·it, pä′stėr·it, *n.* The office or jurisdiction of a pastor; a body of pastors; a parsonage.

pas·to·ri·um, pas″stōr′ē·um, pä·stōr′ē·um, *n.* pl. **pas·to·ri·ums,** *L.* **pas·to·ri·a.** [N.L., < L. *pastor.*] *Southern U.S.* a parsonage.

past par·ti·ci·ple, *n. Gram.* a participle expressing a state, time, or action completed in the past, just completed, or completed and continuing in its effect. Abbr. *pp.* Also *perfect participle.*

past per·fect, *a. Gram.* pluperfect.—*n.*

pas·tra·mi, pa·strä′mē, *n.* Beef, usu. a shoulder cut, smoked or pickled and highly seasoned.

pas·try, pā′strē, *n.* pl. **pas·tries.** A sweet baked food made of flaky dough, or of which the dough constitutes the principal baked ingredient, as the crust of a pie or tart.

---

a- fat, fāte, fär, fâre, fall;   **e-** met, mē, mēre, hėr;   **i-** pin, pīne;   **o-** not, nōte, möve;   **u-** tub, cūbe, bull;   **oi-** oil;   **ou-** pound.

past tense, *n. Gram.* one of the forms of a verb indicating action or state of being that is past or took place in the past.

pas·ture, pas′chẽr, päs′chẽr, *n.* [O.Fr. *pasture* (Fr. *pâture*), < L. *pastura* < *pasco,* to feed.] Grass for the food of cattle or other animals; ground covered with grass for the food of animals; a grazing ground.—*v.t.*—*pastured, pasturing.* To feed on growing grass, or to supply pasture for. —*v.i.* To graze.—**pas·tur·age,** *n.*—**pas··tur·er,** *n.*

past·y, pas′tē, päs′tē, *n. pl.* **past·ies.** *Brit.* a meat pie covered with a crust.

past·y, pā′stē, *a.*—*pastier, pastiest.* Like paste; of the consistency of paste; pale and unhealthy of complexion.

PA sys·tem, *n.* Public-address system.

pat, pat, *n.* A light stroke or blow with something flat, as an implement or the palm of the hand; a gentle stroke with the hand or fingers, given in affection, kindness, or approbation; a small mass of something, as butter, shaped by patting or other manipulation; a distinct mass of anything; the sound of a light stroke or of light footsteps. —*v.t*—*patted, patting.* To strike lightly with something flat, as an implement, the palm of the hand, or foot; to strike gently with the palm or fingers as an expression of affection, kindness, or approbation; to strike, as the floor, with lightly sounding footsteps.—*v.i.* To strike lightly or gently; to walk or run with light footsteps.

pat, pat, *a.* Apt; opportune; mastered or learned; glib; as, a *pat* answer.—*adv.* Aptly; promptly or readily; perfectly.—**stand pat,** to be unyielding; to stand steadfast or firm; *poker,* to play the hand with the cards originally dealt.—**pat′ness,** *n.*

pa·ta·gi·um, pa·tā′jē·um, *n. pl.* **pat·a··gi·a,** pa·tā′jē·a. [N.L., < L. a gold border on a woman's tunic.] A wing membrane, as of a bat; the extensible fold of skin, as of a flying squirrel; a fold of skin between the body and wing of a bird.

patch, pach, *n.* [= Swiss *patschen,* to patch, to clap on a piece, *batsch,* a patch, a piece.] A piece of cloth sewn on a garment to repair it; any similar piece; a piece of material protecting a wound or injury; as, an eye *patch;* a small piece of ground, often on which a single type of plant is grown; a plot; a scrap; any small area of a surface distinct from its surroundings; a piece of cloth sewn on the sleeve of a garment for ornamental or identification purposes.— *v.t.* To mend with patches or pieces; to repair clumsily; to cover an injury; to make up of pieces and shreds; *fig.* to smooth over or settle, usu. with *up;* as, to *patch up* a quarrel.

patch·ou·li, pach′u̯·lē, pa·chō′lē, *n.* [An Ind. name.] A mint plant of India and China, *Pogostemon cablin,* the leaves of which furnish a fragrant oil; the perfume of this plant. Also **pach·ou·li, patch·ou·ly.**

patch pock·et, *n.* A pocket formed by sewing a piece of material on the outside of a garment.

patch test, *n. Med.* a test for allergic sensitivity, determined by noting the skin reaction when small pads impregnated with the allergen are applied.

patch·work, pach′wu̯rk″, *n.* Work composed of cloth of assorted figures or colors sewn together, esp. used in quilts; anything formed of incongruous parts.

patch·y, pach′ē, *a.*—*patchier, patchiest.* Full of patches; irregular or uneven in texture or quality; as, a *patchy* performance. —**patch·i·ness,** *n.*

pate, pāt, *n.* [Perh. < Ir. *pata, pota,* Sc. *pat,* a pot, the radical meaning being the brainpan or skull.] The head of a person; the top of the head; the brain: used disparagingly or humorously.

pâ·té, pä·tā′, *n. pl.* **pâ·tés,** pä·tāz′, *Fr.* pä·tā′. [Fr.] A meat, fowl, or fish paste, often cooked in pastry as an hors d'oeuvre; a small pie or patty.

pâte, pät, *n.* [Fr.] Paste; *ceram.* the paste used for making earthenware or porcelain.

pâ·té de foie gras, pä·tā′ de fwä″ grä′, *Fr.* pä·tā′ de fwä grä′, *n. pl.* **pâ·tés de foie gras,** pä·tāz′ de fwä″ grä′, *Fr.* pä·tā′ de fwä grä′. [Fr., 'pâté of fat liver.'] A spread made with the livers of specially fattened geese.

pa·tel·la, pa·tel′a, *n. pl.* **pa·tel·lae,** pa·tel′ē. [L. dim. of *patera,* a cup, < *pateo,* to lie open.] *Anat.* a flat, oval-shaped bone covering the anterior surface of the knee; kneecap. *Biol.* any panlike shape. *Archaeol.* a small shallow dish or pan; saucer.—**pa·· tel·lar,** *a.*—**pa·tel·late,** pa·tel′it, pa·tel′- ät, *a.*

pa·tel·li·form, pa·tel′i·farm″, *a.* Having or resembling the form of a patella or saucer.

pat·en, pat′en, *n.* [L. *patina,* a pan, < *pateo,* to lie open.] The round metallic plate on which the bread is placed in the sacrifice of the Lord's supper; also **pat·in,** *patine.* A metallic plate or flat dish.

pat·ent, pat′ent, *esp. Brit.* pā′tent, *a.* [L. *patens* (*patent-*), ppr. of *patere,* lie open; in latter senses, through O.Fr. Fr. *patent* (*lettres patentes,* letters patent).] Open to view or knowledge, manifest, evident, or plain; open to the perusal of all. Open, as a door or a passage; lying open, or not shut in or enclosed, as a place. *Bot.* expanded or spreading. Pertaining to a grant by a government of exclusive rights, esp. to an invention, for a certain term of years; conferred by a patent, as a right or privilege; made the subject of a patent, as a commodity or article; endowed with a patent, as persons; appointed by a patent, as a person, esp. appropriated by a patent to a person or persons for manufacture or sale during a certain term of years, as an invention; of a kind specially protected by a patent; by extension, belonging as if by a proprietary claim.—**pa·ten·cy,** pāt′en·sē, *n.*—**pat·ent·ly,** *adv.*

pat·ent, pat′ent, *esp. Brit.* pā′tent, *n.* An official document conferring some right or privilege, esp. a grant from a government to a person or persons, conferring the exclusive rights to the manufacture or sale of a new invention for a certain term of years; an invention or process which has been patented; a tract of land granted by a patent; *fig.* a token indicating a right to something.—*v.t.* To grant by a patent; grant the exclusive rights by a patent, as an invention; sometimes, to appoint by a patent; to take out a patent on; to obtain the exclusive rights by a patent; *fig.* to originate and establish as one's own.— **pat·ent·a·bil·i·ty,** *n.*—**pat·ent·a·ble,** *a.*

pat·ent·ee, pat″en·tē′, *n.* One to whom a patent is granted.

pat·ent flour, *n.* A high-quality flour prepared from the inner endosperm of wheat.

pat·ent leath·er, *n.* Leather with a finely varnished glossy surface, used for shoes, boots, purses, and other accessories.

pat·ent med·i·cine, *n.* A medicine which is available without a prescription; any medicine whose manufacture and sale are restricted in any way, as by patent or registry of name as a trademark.

pat·ent of·fice, *n.* An agency of a government, in the U.S. being part of the Department of Commerce, which examines applications for and grants patents.

pat·en·tor, pat′en·tẽr, *n.* An official who grants patents.

pat·ent right, *n.* An exclusive right to an invention, granted by a government patent.

pa·ter, pā′tẽr, pat′ẽr, *n.* [L.] (*Often cap.*) the paternoster or Lord's Prayer. A recital of it, pä′tẽr, pat′ẽr. *Brit.* father, pä′tẽr.

pa·ter·fa·mil·i·as, pā″tẽr·fa·mil′ē·as, pä″tẽr·fa·mil′ē·as, pat″ẽr·fa·mil′ē·as, *n.* [L., < *pater,* father, and *familia,* a family.] The father or head of a family; *Roman law,* a person who had his independence.

pa·ter·nal, pa·tu̯r′nal, *a.* [Fr. *paternel,* < L. *paternus,* < *pater,* father.] Of or pertaining to a father; characteristic of or befitting a father; fatherly; as, to speak in a *paternal* manner; related on the father's side; as, one's *paternal* grandmother.— **pa·ter·nal·ly,** *adv.*

pa·ter·nal·ism, pa·tu̯r′na·liz″um, *n.* The principle or practice of an authority in managing or governing the affairs of a country, community, company, or of individuals, in the manner of a father's relationship with his children.—**pa·ter·· nal·ist,** *n., a.*—**pa·ter·nal·is·tic,** *a.*

pa·ter·ni·ty, pa·tu̯r′ni·tē, *n.* [Fr. *paternité.*] Fatherhood; the fact of being a father; derivation from a father; as, the child's *paternity;* origin; authorship.

pa·ter·nos·ter, pā′tẽr·nos′tẽr, pat′ẽr·· nos′tẽr, *n.* [L. *pater noster,* our father: the first words of the prayer in the L. version.] (*Often cap.*) the Lord's Prayer, esp. in the Latin form. A recital of this prayer as an act of worship; any form of words used as a prayer or charm; one of certain beads in a rosary, regularly every eleventh bead, differing in size or material from the rest, and indicating that the Lord's Prayer is to be said; the whole rosary. Also **Pa·ter Nos·ter.**

path, path, päth, *n. pl.* **paths,** paᴛнz, päᴛнz, paths, päths. [O.E. *paeth* = D. and L.G. *pad,* G. *pfad,* a path; perh. < Gr. *patos,* a trodden way, *patein,* to walk.] A way beaten or trodden by the feet of man or beast; a narrow or unimportant road; a footway; a way or route in general; the way or course which an animal or any object follows in the air, in water, or in space; *fig.* course of life, conduct, or procedure.

pa·thet·ic, pa·thet′ik, *a.* [L. *patheticus,* Gr. *pathētikos.*] Causing or arousing pity or sorrow; typified by arousing such emotions; affecting the feelings. Also **pa·thet·i·cal.**— **pa·thet·i·cal·ly,** *adv.*

pa·thet·ic fal·la·cy, *n.* Attribution of human qualities to the inanimate world, as an 'arrogant wind.'

path·find·er, path′fīn″dẽr, päth′fīn″dẽr, *n.* One who finds a path or way, as through a wilderness; one who embarks on new paths, as in art or science.

path·less, path′les, päth′les, *a.* Having no beaten way; untrodden.—**path·less·ness,** *n.*

path·o·gen, path′o·jen, *n.* A disease-producing organism, esp. a microorganism. Also **path·o·gene,** path′o·jēn″.

path·o·gen·e·sis, path″o·jen′i·sis, *n.* The production or development of disease; the mode of production or development of a disease. Also **pa·thog·e·ny,** pa·thoj′e·nē. —**path·o·ge·net·ic,** path″ō·je·net′ik, *a.*— **path·o·gen·ic,** path″o·jen′ik, *a.*

pa·thog·no·mon·ic, pa·thog″no·mon′ik, *a.* [Gr. *pathognomonikós,* skilled in judging of diseases (*gnomon,* a judge).] Indicative or characteristic of a particular disease.

pa·thol·o·gist, pa·thol′o·jist, *n.* One versed in pathology.

pa·thol·o·gy, pa·thol′o·jē, *n. pl.* **pa·· thol·o·gies.** [Gr. *pathos,* suffering, and *logos,* discourse.] The science dealing with the nature of diseases, their causes, symptoms, and effects on the organism; the entire set of circumstances which constitute a diseased condition.—**path·o·· log·ic, path·o·log·i·cal,** path″o·loj′ik, *a.* —**path·o·log·i·cal·ly,** *adv.*

pa·thom·e·ter, pa·thom′i·tẽr, *n.* An instrument which records such physical indications of emotional strain as fluctuating blood pressure, and may be employed as a lie detector. See *polygraph.*

pa·thos, pā′thos, _n._ [Gr. _pathos_, passion, suffering, < stem of _pathein_, to suffer.] The quality, attribute, or element, esp. in the arts, that arouses such emotions as pity, compassion, sorrow, or sympathy; expression of strong or deep feeling.

path·way, path′wā″, päth′wā″, _n._ A path; a narrow way to be passed on foot.

pa·tience, pā′shens, _n._ [Fr. _patience_, < L. _patientia_, < _patiens_, patient.] The quality, capacity, or act of being patient. _Chiefly Brit._ a card game played by one person; solitaire.

pa·tient, pā′shent, _a._ [L. _patiens, patientis_.] Bearing pain or trial without complaining; sustaining afflictions with fortitude, calmness, or submission; waiting with calmness; not hasty; long-suffering; persevering; calmly diligent; able to bear, used with _of_. —_n._ One who or that which is passively affected; a person who is under medical treatment.—**pa·tient·ly**, _adv._

pat·i·na, pat′i·na, _n._ pl. **pat·i·nae**, pat′i·nē. [L. _patina_, a dish, a kind of cake, < _pateo_, to be open.] The fine green rust, considered valuable when found on ancient bronzes, copper coins, or medals. A surface change due to age; also _patine_.

pat·ine, pat′in, _n._ Patina; paten.

pa·ti·o, pat′ē·ō″, pä′tē·ō″, _n._ pl. **pa·ti·os**. [Sp.] A court, as of a house, esp. an inner court open to the sky; a paved area attached to a house, for outdoor enjoyment.

pat·ois, pat′wä, _Fr._ pä·twä′, _n._ pl. **pat·ois**. [Fr.] A dialect differing from the standard language of the country; a provincial or illiterate form of speech; the jargon of a social or professional group.

pa·tri·arch, pā′trē·ärk″, _n._ [L.L. _patriarcha_, < Gr. _patriarches_, < _patria_, family (< _father_), and _archein_, rule.] The father and ruler of a family; the male head of a family or tribal line, as Abraham, Isaac, and Jacob. A person regarded as the father or founder of an order or class; one of the elders or leading older members of a community; a venerable old man.—**pa·tri·ar·chal**, _a._—**pa·tri·arch·ship**, _n._

pa·tri·ar·chal cross, _n._ A cross with two transverse pieces, the upper being shorter than the lower.

pa·tri·ar·chate, pā′trē·är″kit, _n._ [M.L. _patriarchatus_.] The office, dignity, jurisdiction, province, or residence of an ecclesiastical patriach; a patriarchy.

pa·tri·ar·chy, pā′trē·är″kē, _n._ pl. **pa·tri·ar·chies**. [Gr. _patriarchia_.] A form of social organization in which the father is head of the family, clan, or tribe, and in which descent is reckoned in the male line; a family, community, tribe, or country governed by a patriarch or the eldest male; an ecclesiastical patriarchate.

pa·tri·cian, pa·trish′an, _a._ [Fr. _patricien_, < L. _patricius_, pertaining to the _patres_, senators or patricians, < _pater_, father.] Pertaining to the senatorial order in ancient Rome; of noble birth.—_n._ A person of noble birth; a nobleman; a person of high social status.

pa·tri·ci·ate, pa·trish′ē·it, pa·trish′ē·āt″, _n._ The aristocracy or patrician class; the rank of patrician.

pat·ri·cide, pa′tri·sīd, pā′tri·sīd″, _n._ [L. _pater, patris_, father, and _caedo_, kill.] Killing one's father; one who takes the life of his father.—**pat·ri·cid·al**, _a._

pat·ri·lin·e·al, pa″tri·lin′ē·al, pā″tri·lin′ē·al, _a._ Descending from or inheriting through the paternal instead of the maternal line.

pat·ri·mo·ny, pa′tri·mō″nē, _n._ pl. **pat·ri·mo·nies**. [L. _patrimonium_, < _pater, patris_, father.] A right or estate inherited from one's father or ancestors; heritage; a church estate or endowment.—**pat·ri·mo·ni·al**, _a._

pa·tri·ot, pā′trē·ot, pā′trē·ot″, _Brit._ pa′trē·ot, _n._ [Fr. _patriote_, L. _patria_, one's native country, < _pater_, father.] A person who loves his country, and zealously supports and defends it and its interests. —**pa·tri·ot·ic**, pā″trē·ot′ik, _Brit._ pa″trē·ot′ik, _a._—**pa·tri·ot·i·cal·ly**, _adv._— **pa·tri·ot·ism**, pā′trē·o·tiz″um, _Brit._ pa′trē·o·tiz″um, _n._

pa·tris·tic, pa·tris′tik, _a._ [= Fr. _patristique_, < Gr. _patēr_ (_patr-_), or L. _pater_ (_patr-_), father.] Of or pertaining to the fathers of the Christian church or their writings. Also **pa·tris·ti·cal**, **pa·tris·ti·cal·ly**, _adv._

pa·trol, pa·trōl′, _v.i., v.t._—_patrolled, patrolling_. [Fr. _patrouille, patrouiller_, to patrol, also to paddle with the feet, < _patte_, O.Fr. _pate_, a paw = G. _pfote_, D. _poot_, a paw.] To walk around or through, as an area or city, for the purpose of protection. —_n._ One or more policemen or soldiers patrolling an area. _Milit._ a detachment of two or more men engaged in reconnaissance or combat. The act of patrolling; a section of a troop of Boy Scouts or Girl Scouts.— **pa·trol·ler**, _n._

pa·trol·man, pa·trōl′man, _n._ pl. **pa·trol·men**. An individual who patrols; a policeman appointed to a particular district.

pa·trol wag·on, _n._ A vehicle used by the police for the conveyance of prisoners.

pa·tron, pā′tron, _n._ [L. _patronus_, a protector or patron, < _pater_, a father.] A customer or client, particularly on a regular basis, of a store, restaurant, barbershop, or other establishment; one who, through money or influence, supports or protects a person, institution, or cause; a patron saint; among the ancient Romans, a master who, after freeing a slave, continued in a paternal relationship with him.—**pa·tron·ess**, pā′tro·nis, pa′tro·nis, _n._ A female patron.— **pa·tron·al**, _a._

pa·tron·age, pā′tro·nij, pa′tro·nij, _n._ The trade or business given to a commercial establishment; the support, protection, or encouragement of a patron, as given to a person, cause, or institution; the right or power to make political job appointments; the offices or jobs so dispensed; condescension when conferring favor.

pa·tron·ize, pā′tro·nīz″, pa′tro·nīz″, _v.t._— _patronized, patronizing_. To give one's regular trade or patronage to; to show favor in a condescending manner; to act as a patron toward by supporting or encouraging a person, cause, or institution.—**pa·tron·iz·er**, _n._—**pa·tron·iz·ing**, _a._—**pa·tron·iz·ing·ly**, _adv._

pa·tron saint, _n._ Any saint considered the special protector of a country, church, society, trade, or person; as, St. Patrick, _patron saint_ of Ireland.

pat·ro·nym·ic, pa″tro·nim′ik, _n._ [L. _patronymicus_, < Gr. _pater, patros_, a father, and _onoma_, a name.] A surname derived from the name of the male parent or paternal ancestor, usu. by adding a suffix or prefix, as in Johnson, son of John, or McHenry, son of Henry.—_a._

pa·troon, pa·trön′, _n._ [In part, Fr. _patron_ or Sp. _patrón_; in part, D. _patroon_; all < L. _patronus_, E. _patron_.] One who held an estate in land with certain manorial privileges and the right to entail, granted under the old Dutch governments of New York and New Jersey.

pat·sy, pat′sē, _n._ pl. **pat·sies**. _Slang._ One who gets the blame; scapegoat; sucker; a cowardly man.

pat·ten, pat′en, _n._ [Fr. _patin_, a clog, patten, < _patte_, the foot.] A shoe with a protective sole of thick wood.

pat·ter, pat′ėr, _v.t._ [< L. _pater_, father, the first word of the paternoster.] To repeat or say rapidly or glibly; to recite or repeat in a rapid, mechanical way, as prayers.—_v.i._ To talk rapidly, esp. with little regard to content.—_n._ Mere rapid talk; the jargon of any class or group; light, rapidly spoken words, as comedians might use.—**pat·ter·er**, _n._

pat·ter, pat′ėr, _v.i._ [Freq. of _pat_.] To strike or move with a succession of slight tapping sounds; to move in a quick manner.—_v.t._ To cause to patter.—_n._ The act of pattering; the sound made by pattering.

pat·tern, pat′ėrn, _n._ [Same word as _patron_, which has also the sense of _pattern_ in Fr. and Sp., as has L.L. _patronus_.] An original or model proposed for imitation; that which is to be copied or imitated; an ornamental design or decoration, as on fabrics, chinaware, wallpaper, or wrapping paper; anything corresponding in outline to an object that is to be fabricated and serving as a guide for determining shape and dimensions; as, a _pattern_ for a chair; style in literary or musical compositions; a natural arrangement of parts; as, the _pattern_ of a snowflake; distinguishable or perceptible traits or peculiarities of a certain person or persons; as, the behavior _pattern_ of an alcoholic; a sufficient amount of material for a garment; _avi._ the flight path of an airplane on its landing approach; _milit._ the distribution of ammunition hits in a target area.—_v.t._ To make after a pattern.—_v.i._ To make a pattern.—**pat·terned**, _a._

pat·ty, pat′ē, _n._ pl. **pat·ties**. [Fr. _pâté_, pie, pasty.] A small flat cake of ground meat or chopped fish, usu. fried; a small pie; a thin, circular piece of candy.

pat·ty shell, _n._ A small, pie-shaped pastry shell in which foods of various kinds are served; as, a chicken _patty shell_.

pat·u·lous, pach′a·lus, _a._ [L. _patulus_, < _pateo_, to be open.] Expanded; opened widely; _bot._ spreading, as the sepals of a flower or limbs of a tree.—**pat·u·lous·ly**, _adv._—**pat·u·lous·ness**, _n._

pau·ci·ty, pạ′si·tē, _n._ [L. _paucitas_, < _paucus_, few.] Smallness of number; scarcity; scantiness.

pau·low·ni·a, pä·lō′nē·a, _n._ [N.L.; named from Anna _Paulovna_, daughter of the czar Paul I. of Russia.] An ornamental tree, _Paulownia tomentosa_, in the figwort family, a native of China introduced into eastern U.S., and bearing terminal panicles of showy pale violet flowers which blossom in early spring; a genus _Paulownia_.

paunch, pạnsh, pänch, _n._ [O.Fr. _panche_ (Fr. _panse_), < L. _pantex, panticis_, the belly.] The belly and its contents; potbelly; the abdomen; the first and largest stomach of a ruminant, as of a cow.—**paunch·i·ness**, _n._—**paunch·y**, pạn′chē, pän′chē, _a._

pau·per, pạ′pėr, _n._ [L. _pauper_, poor (whence _poverty, poor, impoverish_); akin _paucus_, few.] An extremely poor person; one in a state of poverty, esp. one who lives on public welfare funds.—**pau·per·ism**, pạ′pe·riz″um, _n._—**pau·per·ize**, pạ′pe·rīz″, _v.t._— _pauperized, pauperizing_.

pause, pạz, _n._ [Fr. < L. _pausa_, Gr. _pausis_, a stopping, < _pauo_, to stop.] A temporary cessation; an intermission from action, as of working, singing, or running; a short stop; hesitation proceeding from doubt; delay; a momentary suspension in speech to clarify meaning; _mus._ a symbol indicating a hold. —_v.i._—_paused, pausing_. To make a pause or short stop; to stop speech or action; to wait or linger, used with _on_ or _upon_; to refrain for a time; to hesitate.—**paus·er**, _n._

pav·an, pav′an, _n._ [Fr. _pavane_; origin uncertain.] A stately dance in vogue in Europe during the 16th century; the music for this dance. Also **pav·in**, **pa·vane**, pa·vän′, pa·van′, _Fr._ pä·vän′.

pave, pāv, _v.t._—_paved, paving_. [Fr. _paver_, L.L. _pavare_, < L. _pavire_, to ram, to pave.]

To cover, surface, or lay with concrete, asphalt, brick, gravel, or other material, as a street or sidewalk.—**pave the way**, to make it easier for; to prepare for.—**pav·er**, pā′vėr, n.

pa·vé, pa·vā′, pav′ā, Fr. pä·vā′, n. pl. **pa·vés**, pa·vāz′, pav′āz, Fr. pä·vā′. A pavement. *Jewelry*, a setting in which the gems are placed close together so as to conceal the metal mounting.—*adv.*

pave·ment, pāv′ment, n. [L. *pavimentum*.] A paved walk or road; a surface which is covered with a solid compact paving material; the material with which anything is paved; *Brit.* a sidewalk.

pav·id, pav′id, a. [L. *pavidus*, < *paveo*, to fear.] Timid; fearful.

pa·vil·ion, pa·vil′yon, n. [Fr. *pavillon*, L. *papilio, papilionis*, a butterfly, also a tent, from shape of latter.] An open building, often in a garden or park, used for exhibitions and entertainment; a section which projects from the main part of a building; one of several detached or semidetached units into which a large building, such as a hospital, may be divided; a large tent, often an elaborate or sumptuous one; *jewelry*, the lower part of a faceted gem.—*v.t.* To find shelter in a pavilion; to place within a pavilion.

pav·ing, pā′ving, n. Pavement; the material used for a pavement.

pav·ior, *Brit.* **pav·iour**, pāv′yėr, n. One whose occupation is to pave; a paver.

paw, pạ, n. [< the Celtic: W. *pawen*, Armor. *pav, pao*; cf. D. *poot*, G. *pfote*, a paw.] The foot of animals having claws or nails; *slang*, the human hand.—*v.i., v.t.* To draw or scrape with the forefoot along the ground; *slang*, to handle roughly or rudely.—**paw·er**, n.

pawl, pạl, n. [W. *pawl*, akin to L. *palus*, a stake.] *Mech.* a pivoted bar for catching the teeth of a ratchet wheel so as to keep the wheel moving in one direction only.

pawn, pạn, n. [Fr. *pan*, a piece of a garment, formerly also a pawn or pledge, < L. *pannus*, a cloth, a rag.] The state of being held, as jewels, as security for borrowed money; some article or chattel deposited as a pledge for borrowed money; a hostage; the act of pawning.—*v.t.* To give or deposit in pledge; to pledge for the fulfillment of a promise.—**pawn·a·ble**, a.—**pawn·er**, **pawn·or**, pạ′nėr, pạ′nạr, n.

pawn, pạn, n. [O.Fr. *paon, poon, peon*, prop. a foot soldier.] *Chess*, one of eight men of the lowest rank moving forward square by square but capturing diagonally; a person who is manipulated to serve another's own ends.

pawn·bro·ker, pạn′brō″kėr, n. A person who lends money at interest on personal property deposited as a pledge.

Paw·nee, pạ′nē, n. pl. **Paw·nees**, **Paw·nee**. One of a tribe of the Plains Indians of N. America, of the Caddoan language group, who formerly inhabited the valley region between the Platte and Arkansas rivers in Nebraska, and are now located in northern Oklahoma.

pawn·shop, pạn′shop″, n. An establishment where articles are pawned and redeemed, and where unredeemed items are exhibited and sold.

pawn tick·et, n. A receipt given for articles pawned.

paw·paw, pạ′pạ″, n. Papaw.

pax, paks, n. [L. *pax*, peace.] *Rom. Cath. Ch.* an embrace, exchanged between the celebrants after the Agnus Dei of a High Mass, symbolizing a kiss of peace; peace.

pay, pā, v.t.—*paid, paying.* [O.Fr. *paier* (Fr. *payer*) < L. *pacare*, pacify.] To discharge, as a debt or obligation, by giving or doing something; to compensate, as for goods supplied or services rendered; to satisfy the claims of by giving money due; to defray, as a cost or expense; to yield a recompense or return to, or to be profitable to; to requite, as for good, harm, or offense; to retaliate against or punish, with *on* or *out*; to give or render, as attention, regard, court, or compliments, as if due or fitting; to make, as a call or visit.—*v.i.* To give money or goods that are due; to discharge a debt; to yield a return or profit; to be worthwhile; to give compensation for damage or loss sustained; to suffer or be punished for something.—*n.* Payment, as of wages; wages, salary, or stipend; a source of payment; paid employ; requital, reward, or punishment.—*a.* Relating to payments for services or goods, those who pay, or the goods themselves; having a mechanism for receiving monetary payment, usu. in coin; as, a *pay* phone; pertaining to land, possessing adequate mineral resources for profitable exploitation.

pay·a·ble, pā′a·bl, a. Justly owed and unpaid; capable of being paid; suitable for payment.—**pay·a·bly**, adv.

pay·check, pā′chek″, n. Wages or salary paid in the form of a check; salary; wages.

pay dirt, n. Earth containing a sufficient quantity of metal to be profitably worked by the miner; *colloq.* any source of profit.

pay·ee, pā·ē′, n. The person to whom money is paid or is to be paid.

pay·er, pā′ėr, n. One who pays; the person named in a bill or note who has to pay the holder.

pay·load, pā′lōd″, n. The portion of a load producing revenue, such as passengers, baggage, or freight. *Rocketry, aeron.* in an explosive missile, the warhead and its compartment; the energy yield of a missile warhead or an aircraft bomb load.

pay·mas·ter, pā′mas″tėr, pā′mä″stėr, n. One who is authorized to pay out salaries or wages.

pay·ment, pā′ment, n. The act of paying; whatever is paid; recompense; requital; reward or punishment.

pay·off, pā′ạf″, pā′of″, n. The act or occasion of payment of wages or debts; the moment of reckoning; the outcome; the ending, often unexpected, of a narrative; *slang*, a bribe.

pay off, v.t. To pay all that is owed; to pay and discharge from employment; to exact retribution; *slang*, to bribe; *naut.* to turn or fall off to the leeward.—*v.i.* To give full return for effort.

pay·o·la, pā·ō′la, n. *Slang*, a secret or indirect transaction whereby payment is made in return for a business favor, as paying a disc jockey to promote a record.

pay·roll, pā′rōl″, n. A roll or list of persons to be paid, with the amounts due; the aggregate of these amounts; the money to be disbursed. Also **pay roll**.

pay sta·tion, n. A public telephone, usu. operated by a coin machine.

pay up, v.i., v.t. To give payment in full; to give payment upon demand.

P.D.Q. Instantly; immediately.

pea, pē, n. pl. **peas, pease**. [Assumed sing. of *pease* (orig. sing., but later taken as pl.).] The round, highly nutritious seed of *Pisum sativum*, a hardy leguminous vine in wide cultivation; the plant itself; any of various related or similar plants or the seed; as, the chick*pea* or the cow*pea*; any plant of the leguminous genus *Lathyrus*, as *L. odoratus*, the sweet pea, a climbing annual esteemed for its sweet-scented, variously colored flowers.—**pea·like**, a.

peace, pēs, n. [< O.Fr. *pais* (Fr. *paix*), < L. *pax, pacis*, peace—root *pac*.] A state of quiet or tranquility; calm, quietness, or repose; freedom from war or hostility; a cessation of hostilities; absence of strife; tranquility of mind; harmony; serenity; public tranquility and order.—**at peace**, in a tranquil state; in a state of harmony.—**hold** or **keep one's peace**, to be quiet.

peace·a·ble, pē′sa·bl, a. Tranquil; peaceful; disposed to peace; not quarrelsome.—**peace·a·ble·ness**, n.—**peace·a·bly**, adv.

peace·ful, pēs′ful, a. Characteristic of a period of peace; tranquil; quiet; untroubled; free from noise or tumult; averse to argument or strife.—**peace·ful·ly**, adv.—**peace·ful·ness**, n.

peace·mak·er, pēs′mā″kėr, n. An individual, group, or country that reconciles, or attempts to reconcile, parties at variance.—**peace·mak·ing**, n., a.

peace of·fer·ing, n. Something offered to an offended party to procure peace; an offering made as an expression of thanksgiving to God; *O.T.* a sacrificial offering as prescribed by Levitical law.

peace of·fic·er, n. An officer invested with power to preserve civil peace, as a sheriff, policeman, or constable.

peace pipe, n. The pipe smoked by the N. American Indians in token or ratification of peace. Also *calumet*.

peace·time, pēs′tim″, n. A period of peace, esp. between nations.—*a.*

peach, pēch, n. [O.Fr. *pesche* (Fr. *peche*), < M.L. *persica*, for L. *Persicum*, < Gr. *Persicon*, lit. 'Persian (apple).'] The thick-fleshed, downy, edible, fruit of a small tree, *Prunus persica*, in the rose family, native to China and widely cultivated in north temperate regions; the tree itself; a peach color; *slang*, a person or thing that is greatly admired.

peach·blow, pēch′blō″, n. A purplish-pink color; also **peach·bloom**. A glaze of this color used on Oriental porcelain; an American glassware popular in the late 19th century, being opaque and with varying shades of red, rose, yellow, light blue, and white.

peach·y, pē′chē, a.—**peachier, peachiest**. Peachlike, as in color or appearance. *Slang*, excellent; exquisite; unusually attractive.

pea·cock, pē′kok″, n. pl. **pea·cocks, pea·cock**. [M.E. *pecok*, < O.E. *pēa* (< L. *pavo*), peacock, and *coc*, E. *cock*.] The male of the peafowl, *Pavo cristatus*, a gallinaceous bird native to India but now widely domesticated, distinguished for its long, erectile, ocellated tail coverts with rich iridescent coloring of green, blue, and gold; any peafowl, male or female; *fig.* a vain, pompous, arrogant person.—*v.i.* To make a display like a peacock.—**pea·cock·ish**, a.—**pea·cock·y**, a.

pea·cock blue, n. A variable greenish-blue color as seen in peacock feathers.

pea·fowl, pē′foul″, n. pl. **pea·fowls, pea·fowl**. A gallinaceous bird, *Pavo cristatus*, related to the pheasant, the male being the peacock and the female being the peahen.

pea green, n. A light green with a yellowish tinge.

pea·hen, pē′hen″, n. [M.E. *pehen*: cf. *peacock*.] The female peafowl.

pea jack·et, n. [*Pea* is < D. and L.G. *pije*, coarse, thick cloth; a warm jacket; akin to Goth. *paida*, a garment.] A short, double-breasted, heavy wool coat worn by sailors. Also **pea·coat**, pē′kōt″.

peak, pēk, v.i. [Perh. < *peak*, n., from the sharpened features of sickly persons.] To become emaciated, weak, and sickly.—**peak·ed**, pē′kid, a.—**peak·ed·ness**, n.

peak, pēk, n. [Var. of *pike*.] The pointed top of a mountain; a mountain with a pointed summit; the pointed top of anything; the highest point or degree of development; as, the *peak* of his influence; a projecting point; as, the *peak* of a man's beard; projecting brim or front piece of a cap. *Elect.* the maximum of a curve showing the variations of the load, as of a power station, during a certain period of time; the maximum load during a given interval of time. —*a.*—*v.t.* To form into a peak.—*v.i.* To project in a peak.—**peak·ed**, pēkt, pē′kid, *a.*

peal, pēl, *n.* [A mutilated form of *appeal.*] A loud, prolonged sound or a succession of sounds, as of bells, thunder, or laughter; a set of bells tuned to each other in the major scale; the changes rung on such bells.—*v.i.* To utter or give out a peal.— *v.t.* To cause to ring or sound loudly and sonorously; to ring out.

pea·nut, pē′nut″, *n. Bot.* a widely cultivated subtropical legume, *Arachis hypogaea,* native to Brazil, with edible oily seeds which are borne in slightly constricted pods and develop below the ground; the seed itself; the pod fruit. *Slang,* an unimportant person or thing; *pl.* a small or trifling sum of money.—*a.*

pea·nut but·ter, *n.* A paste made from crushed, roasted peanuts, used as a spread.

pear, pâr, *n.* [O.E. *peru,* < M.L. *pira,* or L. *pirum,* pear.] An edible, fleshy, pome fruit with gritty concretions, typically rounded but elongated and tapering toward the stem, produced by the tree, *Pyrus communis,* in the rose family, and widely cultivated; the tree itself.

pearl, pûrl, *n.* [Fr. *perle,* < L.L. *perula, perla,* a pearl, either for *pirula,* < L. *pirum,* a pear, or for *pilula,* a pill, a globule.] A smooth, rounded nacreous body formed around an irritant, usu. produced by oysters and valued as a gem when perfectly colored and lustrous; something similar in shape and luster; mother-of-pearl; what is precious or best; *print.* a 5-point type. A pale shade of gray with a blue tinge.—*a.* Relating to or made of pearl.—*v.t.* To set or adorn with pearls.—*v.i.* To take the form or appearance of a pearl; to color or shape like pearls; to seek pearls.—**pearl·er**, *n.*

pearl, pûrl, *n., v.t.* Purl.

pearl gray, *n.* A light bluish gray color.

Pearl Har·bor, *n.* An inlet on the Oahu coast near Honolulu, Hawaii; the location of an American naval base, the object of a surprise air attack by Japan, December 7, 1941; that attack, as: "Remember *Pearl Harbor!*"

pearl·ite, pûr′līt, *n. Metal.* an alloy of iron which contains little carbon and is formed into bands of ferrite and cementite in slowly cooled steels; *petrog.* perlite.— **pearl·it·ic**, pûr′lit″ik, *a.*

pearl·ized, pûr′līzd, *a.* Similar in appearance to mother-of-pearl.

pearl mil·let, *n. Bot.* a tall grass, *Pennisetum glaucum,* cultivated in Africa, the Orient, and southern U.S. for its edible seeds and as a forage plant. Also **Af·ri·can mil·let, In·di·an mil·let.**

pearl·y, pûr′lē, *a.*—*pearlier, pearliest.* Containing or embellished with pearls; resembling pearls, as in color or luster; iridescent.

pear-shaped, pâr′shāpt″, *a.* Of an elongated, rounded form tapering toward one end, as in the pear fruit; *mus.* of a voice that is rich, resonant, and strong.

peart, pērt, pyert, *a.* [Var. of *pert.*] *Dial.* In high spirits; lively or brisk; cheerful.— **peart·ly**, *adv.*

peas·ant, pez′ant, *n.* [O.Fr. *paîsant* (Fr. *paysan*), < *pais, pays,* L. *pagus,* a district of country (with *t* affixed as in *tyrant*).] A countryman, esp. in Europe, who is engaged in working on the land as a small farmer or a farm laborer; a rustic; a simple person; *colloq.* a simple-minded, uncouth person.—*a.* Rustic; rural.—**peas·ant·ry,** pez′an·trē, *n.* Peasants collectively.

pease·cod, peas·cod, pēz′kod″, *n.* The pod of the pea; a doublet, having the lower front part so shaped and quilted as to

project from the body, in a fashion in vogue toward the end of the 16th century.

pea·shoot·er, pē′shö″tėr, *n.* A tube, usu. plastic, through which small projectiles, as dried peas, can be blown, used as a child's toy.

pea soup, *n.* A thick soup prepared from dried split peas. *Colloq.* a dense fog; also **pea soup·er.**

peat, pēt, *n.* [For *beat, bete,* < old *bete,* to mend a fire; O.E. *bétan,* to make better; akin *bette boot.*] Partially decayed, highly combustible, dry plant material usu. formed in swamps; a piece of this suitable for fuel. —**peat·y**, pē′tē, *a.*—*peatier, peatiest.*

peat moss, *n.* Any moss of the genus *Sphagnum,* common in bogs.

peau de soie, pō″ de swä′, pō′ de swä″, *n.* [Fr. 'skin of silk.'] A soft silk fabric with little luster, having a satin finish on both sides or on one only.

pea·vey, pē′vē, *n. pl.* **pea·veys.** [From the name of the inventor.] A lumberman's canthook having a strong spike at the end. Also **pea·vy**, *pl.* **pea·vies.**

peb·ble, peb′l, *n.* [O.E. *papolstán,* lit. 'pebble-stone'; etym. unknown.] A small stone worn and rounded by the action of water; a transparent colorless rock crystal used for eyeglass lenses; a lens constructed from it. Leather which has been treated to give a granulated texture; also **peb·ble leath·er.**—*v.t.*—*pebbled, pebbling.* To treat, as leather, so as to give a rough, granulated texture; to pelt with pebbles.—**peb·bly,** peb′lē, *a.*

pe·can, pi·kän′, pi·kan′, pē′kan, *n.* [Fr. *pacane,* Sp. *pacana.*] A very productive nut tree, *Carya illinoensis,* related to the hickory, native to southeastern U.S. and now extensively cultivated for its edible, thin-shelled nuts: the State tree of Texas; the nut itself.

pec·ca·ble, pek′a·bl, *a.* [L.L. *peccabilis,* peccable, < L. *pecco,* to sin.] Liable to sin. —**pec·ca·bil·i·ty,** *n.*

pec·ca·dil·lo, pek″a·dil′ō, *n. pl.* **pec·ca·dil·loes, pec·ca·dil·los.** [Sp. *pecadillo,* dim. of *pecado,* L. *peccatum,* a sin, < *pecco.*] A slight trespass or offense; a petty crime or fault.

pec·cant, pek′ant, *a.* [L. *peccans, peccantis,* ppr. of *pecco.*] Sinning; corrupt; breaking a rule or principle.—**pec·can·cy,** *n.*— **pec·cant·ly,** *adv.*

pec·ca·ry, pek′a·rē, *n. pl.* **pec·ca·ries, pec·ca·ry.** [S. Amer. name.] *Zool.* either of two species of hoofed mammals of the family *Tayassuidae,* related to the pig, the common collared species, *Tayassus angulatus,* native from southwestern U.S. to Argentina, and the rarer white-lipped species, *Tayassus pecari,* limited to the forests of tropical America.

pec·ca·vi, pe·kä′vē, pe·kä′vē, *n. pl.* **pec·ca·vis.** [L., 'I have sinned,' < *pecco,* to sin.] A confession of sin or guilt.

peck, pek, *n.* [Perh. a form of *pack*; but compare Fr. *picotin,* a peck; L.L. *picotus,* a liquid measure.] A fourth of a bushel, a dry measure of eight quarts; a container measuring this amount. See Measures and Weights table. *Slang,* a great amount, as: He has had a *peck* of trouble.

peck, pek, *v.t.* [A form of *pick.*] To strike with the beak, as a bird, or with a pointed object or instrument.—*v.i.* To make holes with a beak or a pointed instrument; to nibble at food; to nag, followed by *at.*—*n.* A sharp stroke, as with a beak; *slang,* a perfunctory kiss.—**peck·er**, pek′ėr, *n.*

peck·ing or·der, *n. Ornith.* among domesticated fowl, esp. chickens, a type of superiority enjoyed by certain hens who peck at others without reprisal. In human society, a hierarchy of prestige or power. Also **peck or·der.**

Peck·sniff·i·an, pek·snif′ē·an, *a.* [From Seth *Pecksniff,* a character in Dickens' *Martin Chuzzlewit.*] Resembling an unctuous or pretentious hypocrite; insincere.

peck·y, pek′ē, *a.*—*peckier, peckiest.* Having pits or grooves caused by fungi decay, as in wood.

pec·tate, pek′tāt, *n. Chem.* a salt of pectic acid.

pec·ten, pek′ten, *n. pl.* **pec·tens, pec·ti·nes**, pek′ti·nēz″. [L. *pecten (pectin-),* a comb, < *pectere,* to comb.] *Zool., anat.* A comblike part or process; a pigmented vascular membrane with parallel folds suggesting the teeth of a comb, projecting into the vitreous humor of the eye in birds and reptiles; a scallop of the genus *Pecten.*

pec·tic ac·id, *n. Chem.* a water-insoluble acid, $C_{17}H_{24}O_{16}$, derived from the methyl ester groups of pectins through hydrolyzation.

pec·tin, pek′tin, *n.* [< *pectic.*] *Biochem.* A complex carbohydrate found in the cell walls of plants, being highly concentrated in certain ripe fruits, as the apple, forming a viscous solution in water, and, when combined with sugar and acid, yielding fruit jelly; a commercial product containing mostly pectin and used in the pharmaceutical trade.—**pec·tic**, pek′tik, *a.* Derived from, or containing pectin.—**pec·ti·na·ceous,** pek″ti·nā″shus, *a.*

pec·ti·nate, pek′ti·nāt″, *a.* [L. *pectinatus.*] Having resemblance to the teeth of a comb; serrated. Also **pec·ti·nat·ed.**— **pec·ti·na·tion**, *n.*

pec·to·ral, pek′tėr·al, *a.* [L. *pectoralis* (as n., *pectorale*), < *pectus (pector-),* breast.] Of or pertaining to the breast or chest; thoracic; good for diseases of the thorax, as a medicine; worn on the breast or chest; proceeding from the heart or inner consciousness.—*n.* An ornament or device, as a breastplate, worn on or over the breast; *med.* a remedy or medicine for an illness of the chest; *anat.* a part of the chest; as, the *pectoral* muscles.

pec·to·ral cross, *n. Eccles.* a cross worn by a prelate of superior rank, esp. a bishop, as an indication of office held.

pec·to·ral fin, *n.* Either of a pair of fins located behind the head of a fish, and corresponding to the forelimbs of higher vertebrates. Compare *ventral fin.*

pec·to·ral gir·dle, *n. Zool., anat.* A bony or cartilaginous arch supporting the forelimbs of a vertebrate; the arch formed by the shoulder blade and collarbone in man. Also **pec·to·ral arch.**

pec·u·late, pek′ū·lāt″, *v.t., v.i.*—*peculated, peculating.* [L. *peculor, peculatus,* to steal, < *peculium,* private property, < *pecu,* cattle, of which wealth orig. consisted; cogn. E. *fee.*] To appropriate, as public money or goods entrusted to one's care; to embezzle. —**pec·u·la·tion,** *n.*—**pec·u·la·tor,** *n.*

pe·cu·liar, pi·kūl′yėr, *a.* [L. *peculiaris,* one's own, peculiar, extraordinary, < *peculium,* one's own property.] Strange; queer, eccentric; unusual or uncommon; different in nature from others of the same kind; belonging characteristically or exclusively to a person, thing, or group.—*n. Brit.* a parish or church which is exempt from customary ecclesiastical jurisdiction. —**pe·cu·liar·ly,** *adv.*

pe·cu·li·ar·i·ty, pi·kū″lē·ar′i·tē, pi·kūl·yar′i·tē, *n. pl.* **pe·cu·li·ar·i·ties.** A characteristic or trait that is eccentric or unusual; the quality of being peculiar; a distinctive characteristic or feature.

pe·cu·ni·ar·y, pi·kū″nē·er″ē, *a.* [Fr. *pecuniaire,* L. *pecuniarius,* < *pecunia,* money, < *pecu,* cattle.] Relating to or connected with money; consisting of money; entailing a money penalty.—**pe·cu·ni·ar·i·ly,** pi·kū″nē·âr′i·lē, *adv.*

ped·a·gog·ics, ped″a·goj′iks, ped″a·gō′-jiks, *n. pl. but sing. in constr.* The science or art of teaching.

ped·a·gogue, ped·a·gog, paed·a·gogue, ped′a·gog″, ped′a·gag″, *n.* [Gr. *paidagōgos* —*pais, paidos*, a child, and *agō*, to lead.] A school teacher; educator, primarily of youth; derogatively, one who is dogmatic or pedantic.—**ped·a·gog·ic, ped·a·gog·i·cal**, ped″a·goj′ik, ped″a·gō′jik, *a.*—**ped·a·gog·i·cal·ly**, *adv.*

ped·a·go·gy, paed·a·go·gy, ped′a·gō″jē, ped′a·gog″ē, *n. pl.* **ped·a·go·gies, paed·a·go·gies.** [Gr. *paidagōgia*.] The function, work, or art of a teacher; the profession or science of teaching.

ped·al, ped′al, *n.* [L. *pedalis*, belonging to the foot, < *pes, pedis*, the foot.] A lever to be pressed down by the foot, as in playing some musical instruments or operating certain mechanisms; a sort of treadle.—*pedaled, pedaling, esp. Brit. pedalled, pedalling.* To drive by pedaling, as a bicycle.—*v.i.* To use the pedal for an effect, as in playing the piano.—*a.*

pe·dal·fer, pi·dal′fèr, *n.* Soil, esp. in humid climates, that is rich in alumina and iron and lacks a layer of carbonate deposits. See *pedocal.*—**ped·al·fer·ic**, *a.*

ped·al point, *n. Mus.* a single tone in a musical text sustained by one of the parts, usu. the bass, while the other parts run through a series of progressions.

ped·al push·ers, *n. pl.* Slacks extending to midcalf, worn by women and girls, orig. for cycling.

ped·ant, ped′ant, *n.* [Fr. *pédant*, It., Sp., and Pg. *pedante*.] A person who displays his learning excessively or unnecessarily; one who lays undue stress on rules and details; one who relies on book learning and neglects practical reasoning.—**pe·dan·tic**, pe·dan′tik, *a.*—**pe·dan·ti·cal·ly**, *adv.*

ped·ant·ry, ped′an·trē, *n. pl.* **ped·ant·ries.** The manners or character of a pedant; ostentatious show of learning; undue adherence to rules or established forms.

ped·ate, ped′āt, *a.* [L. *pedatus*, < *pes, pedis*, the foot.] Having feet; characteristic of a foot. *Bot.* referring to a palmate leaf whose lobes are cleft in two.—**ped·ate·ly**, *adv.*

ped·dle, ped′l, *v.i.*—*peddled, peddling.* [< Prov. E. *ped* or *pad*, a wicker basket, a pannier, akin to *pod.* Hence *pedlar.*] To travel about the country and retail small wares; to go about as a peddler; to be engaged in a small business; to trifle.—*v.t.* To sell or dispense in small quantities while traveling about.—**ped·dler, ped·ler, ped·lar**, ped′lèr, *n.* One who peddles. A hawker.

ped·dling, ped′ling, *a.* Trifling; paltry; piddling.—**ped·dling·ly**, *adv.*

ped·er·as·ty, paed·er·as·ty, ped′e·ras″tē, pē′de·ras″tē, *n.* Sexual relations between males through anal intercourse, esp. between a man and a boy.—**ped·er·ast**, *n.*—**ped·er·as·tic**, *a.*—**ped·er·as·ti·cal·ly**, *adv.*

ped·es·tal, ped′i·stal, *n.* [Sp. *pedestal*, Fr. *piedestal*, It. *piedestallo*, < L. *pes, pedis*, the foot, and G. and E. *stall*.] A support for a column, statue, vase, or table; a foundation or base.—*v.t.*—*pedestaled, pedestaling, pedestalled, pedestalling.* To set on or provide with a pedestal.—**put on a ped·es·tal**, to esteem as a hero or idol; glorify.

pe·des·tri·an, pe·des′trē·an, *n.* [L. *pedestris*, < *pes, pedos*, the foot.] One who walks or journeys on foot; a walker.—*a.* Going on foot; performed on foot; walking. Commonplace, dull, or prosaic; as prose.—**pe·des·tri·an·ism**, pe·des′trē·a·niz″um, *n.*

pe·di·a·tri·cian, pē″dē·a·trish′an, ped″-ē·a·trish′an, *n.* A physician specializing in pediatrics. Also **pe·di·at·rist**, pē″dē·a′trist, ped″ē·a′trist.

pe·di·at·rics, *Brit.* **pae·di·at·rics**, pē″dē·a′triks, ped″ē·a′triks, *n. pl. but sing. in constr.* The science which deals with the medical care and diseases of children.—**pe·di·at·ric**, *a.*

ped·i·cab, ped′i·kab, *n.* A three-wheeled, motorless vehicle, usu. hooded, seating two passengers and pedaled by a driver.

ped·i·cel, ped′i·sel, ped′i·sel″, *n.* [< *pedicellus*, a form equiv. to L. *pediculus*, dim. of *pes, pedis*, the foot.] *Bot.* the stalk that supports an individual flower of an inflorescence or cluster of flowers as distinguished from the peduncle below, which supports all the pedicels of the cluster; *zool.* a footstalk or supportive structure by which certain lower animals are attached. —**ped·i·cel·lar**, ped″i·sel′èr, *a.*—**ped·i·cel·late**, ped″i·sel′it, ped″i·sel′at, ped′i·se·lit, ped′i·se·lāt″, *a.*

ped·i·cle, ped′i·kl, *n.* Pedicel; peduncle.

pe·dic·u·lar, pe·dik′ū·lèr, pe·dik′ya·lèr, *a.* [L. *pediculus*, a louse.] Lousy: being infested with lice.

pe·dic·u·late, pe·dik′ū·lit, pe·dik′ū·lāt″, pe·dik′ya·lit, pe·dik′ya·lāt″, *a.*—Belonging or relating to the order *Pediculati*, a group of teleost fishes characterized by the elongated base of the pectoral fins simulating an arm or peduncle.—*n.*

pe·dic·u·lo·sis, pe·dik″ū·lō′sis, *n.* [N.L., < L. *pediculus*.] *Pathol.* the state of being infested with lice. Also *phthiriasis.*—**pe·dic·u·lous**, pe·dik′ū·lus, *a.*

ped·i·cure, ped′i·kūr″, *n.* [L. *pes, pedis*, foot *cura*, care.] Podiatry; cosmetic care of the feet and toenails; one whose business is the care of the feet.—**ped·i·cur·ist**, *n.*

ped·i·gree, ped′i·grē″, *n.* [O.Fr. *pedegru*, Fr. *pie de grue*, crane's foot; L. *pes*, foot, *de*, of, *grus*, crane.] A line of ancestors; lineage; a genealogy; a table or list tracing the ancestry, as of domesticated animals; pure or distinguished ancestry; the origin or derivation of something.—**ped·i·greed**, ped′i·grēd″, *a.* Of pure or distinguished ancestry.

ped·i·ment, ped′i·ment, *n.* [Earlier *periment*, perh. a corruption of *pyramid*.] *Arch.* a low triangular part resembling a gable, crowning the front of buildings in the Greek style, esp. over a portico, and often ornamented with sculptures; hence, any decorative member of similar outline and position, as over an opening. *Geol.* a gentle rocky slope at the foot of a steep hill or mountain, usu. covered with alluvium.—**ped·i·men·tal**, ped″i·men′tal, *a.* Of, on, or like a pediment.—**ped·i·ment·ed**, ped′i·men″tid, *a.* Having or resembling a pediment.

pe·do·bap·tism, pae·do·bap·tism, pē″dō·bap′tiz·um, *n.* [Gr. *pais, paidos*, a child.] The baptism of infants.

ped·o·cal, ped′o·kal″, *n.* A soil of dry regions that contains a stratified bed of calcium carbonate. See *pedalfer.*—**ped·o·cal·ic**, *a.*

pe·do·don·tia, pē″do·don′sha, pē″do·don′shē·a, *n.* Pedodontics.

pe·do·don·tics, pē″do·don′tiks, *n. pl. but sing. in constr.* The field or practice of dentistry that specializes in child dental care and treatment. Also *pedodontia.*—**pe·do·don·tic**, *a.*

pe·dol·o·gy, pi·dol′o·jē, *n.* The scientific study of the physical, mental, and social growth of children. Also **pai·dol·o·gy.**—**pe·do·log·i·cal**, pēd″o·loj′i·kal, *a.*—**ped·o·log·i·cal·ly**, *adv.*—**pe·dol·o·gist**, *n.*

pe·dol·o·gy, pi·dol′o·jē, *n.* The science that deals with the formation, properties, and utilization of soil.—**pe·do·log·i·cal**, pēd″o·loj′i·kal, *a.*—**ped·o·log·i·cal·ly**, *adv.*—**pe·dol·o·gist**, *n.*

pe·dom·e·ter, pe·dom′i·tèr, *n.* [L. *pes, pedis*, the foot, and Gr. *metron*, a measure.] An instrument, often resembling a watch, by which paces are numbered as a person walks, thus measuring the distance traveled.

pe·dro, pē′drō, pā′drō, *n.* [Sp. *Pedro*, a man's name, Peter.] Any of several varieties of the card game 'all fours' in which the five of trumps, and sometimes the other five of the same color, count at face value for additional points; the five of trumps; the other five of the same color.

pe·dun·cle, pi·dung′kl, *n.* [< L. *pes, pedis*, a foot.] *Bot.* the stalk or stem of a solitary flower of a plant; the main stalk or stem of an inflorescence or cluster of flowers as distinguished from the pedicels or little stalks of each individual flower of the cluster; *zool.* the stalk of certain sessile animals as brachiopods and barnacles; *anat.* a stalklike structure in the brain. —**pe·dun·cled, pe·dun·cu·lat·ed**, *a.*—**pe·dun·cu·late**, pi·dung′kū·lit, pi·dung′kū·lāt″, *a.*—**pe·dun·cu·la·tion**, *n.*

peek, pēk, *v.i.* To look quickly or furtively, esp. through a small hole or from a concealed position; peep.—*n.* A quick, furtive glance; a peep.

peel, pēl, *v.t.* [O.Fr. *peiler* (Fr. *peler*), to peel, < L. *pellis*, the skin.] To strip the skin, bark, or rind from; to strip, as bark or skin, from the surface.—*v.i.* To lose the skin or rind; to fall off or come away, as bark or skin; *slang*, to remove one's clothes. —*n.* The rind or skin of a fruit or vegetable.—**keep one's eyes peeled**, *slang.* To keep a close watch; be alert.

peel, pēl, *n.* [Fr. *pelle*, < L. *pala*, a spade.] A long-handled implement like a shovel, used for putting bread and other foods into an oven for baking and taking them out.

peel·er, pē′lèr, *n.* One who peels; a device which peels.

peel·ing, pē′ling, *n.* That which is peeled from something, as the skin or rind of a fruit.

peel off, *v.i. Aeron.* to swerve sharply away from a flying formation, usu. for diving or when preparing to land.

peen, pein, pēn, *n.* [Cf. Norw. *pen, pænn*, Fr. *panne*, and G. *pinne*.] The wedge-shaped, spherical, or otherwise modified end on the head of a hammer, opposite to the face.—*v.t.* To treat by striking regularly all over with the peen of a hammer.

peep, pēp, *v.i.* [M.E. *pepen*, also *pipen*: cf. O.Fr. Fr. *piper*, L. *pipare*, D. and G. *piepen*, peep, all imit., also E. *pipe*, n.] To utter the shrill little cry of a young bird or a mouse; cheep; squeak; to speak in a thin, weak voice.—*n.* A peeping cry or sound; any of various small sandpipers.

peep, pēp, *v.i.* [Cf. *peek.*] To look through a small aperture or from a hiding place; look slyly, pryingly, or furtively; peek; peer; to come partially into view; begin to appear. —*v.t.* To show or protrude slightly.—*n.* A brief or stealthy look; the first appearance, as of dawn; an aperture for looking through; peephole.

peep·er, pē′pèr, *n.* One that makes a peeping sound; any of a number of frogs that peep.

peep·er, pē′pèr, *n.* One who peeps, esp. in a prying way; a voyeur; *slang*, an eye.

peep·hole, pēp′hōl″, *n.* A hole or gap through which one may peep, as in a door.

Peep·ing Tom, *n.* [In allusion to the man who is said to have peeped at Lady Godiva riding naked through Coventry.] (*Sometimes l.c.*) A prying observer; a voyeur.

peep show, *n.* An exhibition of photographs or pictures, magnified and viewed through a small aperture.

peep sight, *n.* A plate on the rear of a gun barrel, having a small hole through which the gunner peeps in sighting.

peer, pēr, *n.* [Lit. 'an equal'; O.Fr. *peer, per*, *par* (Fr. *pair*), < L. *par*. equal.] One of the

ch- chain, G. na*ch*t; **th-** THen, thin; **w-** wig, hw as sound in whig; **z-** zh as in azure, zeal. *Italicized vowel* indicates schwa sound.

same rank or qualities; an equal, esp. according to the law; a member of one of the five degrees of British nobility: duke, marquis, earl, viscount, baron; a nobleman.

peer, pēr, *v.i.* [Origin uncertain; prob. in part for *appear*.] To look narrowly, as in the effort to discern clearly; to peep out or appear slightly; come into partial view.

peer·age, pēr′ij, *n.* The rank or dignity of a peer; the body of peers; a book which records peers and their genealogies.

peer·ess, pēr′is, *n.* The wife of a peer; a woman having in her own right the rank of a peer.

peer·less, pēr′lis, *a.* Unequaled; having no peer or equal.—**peer·less·ly,** *adv.*—**peer·less·ness,** *n.*

peeve, pēv, *v.t.*—*peeved, peeving.* [Backformation < *peevish.*] To render peevish; irritate.—*n.* A source of annoyance.

peev·ish, pē′vish, *a.* [Cf. Dan. *piaeve,* to cry like a child; Sc. *pew, pyow,* a sound of complaint.] Cross; easily vexed; fretful; querulous.—**pee·vish·ly,** *adv.*—**pee·vish·ness,** *n.*

pee·wee, pe·wee, pē′wē″, *n. Colloq.* an exceptionally small person or thing; *ornith.* pewee.—*a.* Tiny.

pee·wit, pē′wit, pū′it, *n.* Pewit.

peg, peg, *n.* [M.E. *pegge:* cf. L.G. *pigge,* peg, Sw. *pigg,* Dan. *pig,* point, spike.] A pin of wood or other material driven or fitted into something, as to fasten parts together, to hang things on, to make fast a rope or string on, to stop a hole, or to mark some point. *Mus.* a pin of wood or metal to which one end of a string of a musical instrument is fastened, and which may be turned in its socket to adjust the string's tension. *Colloq.* a rank or degree; a leg, sometimes one of wood; a drink of brandy and soda, or whiskey and soda; a throw, as in baseball.—*v.t.*—*pegged, pegging.* To drive or insert a peg into; fasten with or as with pegs; mark with pegs; strike or pierce as with a peg; *colloq.* to aim or throw.—*v.i.* To work persistently; keep on energetically; *colloq.* to aim or throw.—*a.* Tapered near the bottom, as the legs of pants.

Peg·a·sus, peg′a·sus, *n.* [L., < Gr. *Pegasos,* < *pege,* stream, spring.] *Class. myth.* a winged horse; *fig.* poetic inspiration; *astron.* a northern constellation represented as a flying horse located between Cygnus and Aquarius.

peg leg, *n. Colloq.* A wooden leg; one who has a wooden leg.—**peg·legged,** *a.*

peg·ma·tite, peg′ma·tīt″, *n.* [Gr. *pēgma* (*pēgmat-*), something fastened together, < *pēgnynai,* make fast.] A coarse, crystalline granitic or other rock occurring in veins; specif. granite with a graphic texture.—**peg·ma·tit·ic,** peg′ma·tit′ik, *a.*

peg top, *n.* A child's wooden top spun on a metal peg; *pl.* a man's trousers or a woman's skirt cut wide at the hips and gradually narrowing to the ankles.—**peg·top,** peg′top″, *a.*

peign·oir, pān·wär′, pen·wär′, pān′wär, pen′wär, *n.* [Fr. < *peigner,* < L. *pectinare,* to comb, < *pecten,* a comb.] A woman's dressing gown or negligee.

pe·jo·ra·tive, pi·jar′a·tiv, pi·jor′a·tiv, pej′o·rā″tiv, pē′jo·rā″tiv, *a.* Having or indicating a disparaging meaning; depreciative.—*n.* A pejorative form or word.—**pej·o·ra·tion,** pej′o·rā′shan, *n.*—**pe·jo·ra·tive·ly,** *adv.*

Pe·king·ese, pē″king·ēz′, *a.* Of or pertaining to the city of Peking, China.—*n. pl.* **Pe·king·ese.** The Chinese dialect of Peking; a native or inhabitant of Peking.

Pe·king·ese, Pe·ki·nese, pē″ki·nēz′, *n. pl.* **Pe·king·ese.** One of a Chinese breed of small, short-legged dogs having a flat face and a long, silky coat.

Pe·king man, pē′king′ man′, *n. Paleon., anthropol.* a fossil man, *Sinanthropus pekinensis,* of the Pleistocene period, the bones of which were discovered near Peking, China. Also *Sinanthropus.*

pe·koe, pē′kō, *Brit.* pek′ō, *n.* [Chin., lit. 'white down.'] A fine black tea native to India, Ceylon, and Java.

pel·age, pel′ij, *n.* [Fr., < O.Fr. *peil* (Fr. *poil*), < L. *pilus,* hair.] The hair, fur, wool, or other such covering of a mammal.

pe·lag·ic, pe·laj′ik, *a.* [Gr. *pelagos,* the ocean.] Relating to the ocean; of certain plants and animals, inhabiting the open ocean, usu. some distance from the coast.

pel·ar·go·ni·um, pel″är·gō′nē·um, *n.* [< Gr. *pelargos,* a stork—from the shape of the capsules.] *Bot.* Any of various herbs or subshrubs of the genus *Pelargonium,* in the geranium family, native to S. Africa and grown as an ornamental; the geranium cultivated by florists as opposed to the wild geranium. Also *geranium, stork's-bill.*

pel·er·ine, pel″e·rēn′, *n.* [Fr., < *pelerin,* a pilgrim.] A woman's cape, longer in front than in back.

pelf, pelf, *n.* [O.Fr. *pelfre,* spoil, booty, < L. *pilare,* to rob, and *facere,* to make.] Money, riches: often used disparagingly.

pel·i·can, pel′i·kan, *n.* [L.L. *pelicanus pelecanus,* < Gr. *pelekan.*] Any of various large, fish-eating, web-footed, water birds of the genus *Pelecanus,* having a long flat bill with a distensible pouch beneath, used for storing food.

pe·lisse, pe·lēs′, *n.* [Fr. *pelisse,* < L. *pelliceus,* made of skins, < *pellis,* a skin.] A long, loose cloak, often lined or trimmed with fur.

pel·la·gra, pe·lā′gra, pe·lag′ra, pe·lä′gra, *n.* [It. *pellagra,* L. *pellis,* skin, and Gr. *agra,* seizure.] *Pathol.* a disease affecting the skin, digestive system, and nervous system, caused by niacin deficiency.—**pel·la·grous,** pe·lā′grus, pe·lag′rus, pe·lä′grus, *a.*

pel·la·grin, pe·lā′grin, pe·lag′rin, pe·lä′grin, *n. Pathol.* one who is afflicted with pellagra.

pel·let, pel′it, *n.* [O.Fr. Fr. *pelote,* < L. *pila,* ball.] A round or spherical body, esp. one of small size; a little ball, as of food or medicine; a ball, usu. of stone, formerly used as a missile; a bullet; one of a charge of small shot, as for a sportsman's gun; an imitation bullet, as of wax or paper.—*v.t.* To form into pellets; to hit with pellets.

pel·li·cle, pel′i·kl, *n.* [L. *pellicula,* dim. of *pellis,* skin.] A thin skin; membrane; a scum or film on a liquid surface.—**pel·lic·u·lar,** pe·lik′ū·lêr, *a.*—**pel·lic·u·late,** pe·lik′ū·lit, pe·lik′ū·lāt″, *a.*

pel·li·to·ry, pel′i·tōr″ē, pel′i·tar″ē, *n. pl.* **pel·li·to·ries.** [Partly by corruption > L.L. *parietaria,* < L. *paries,* wall; partly for M.E. *peletre* = Sp. *pelitre* = O.Fr. *piretre,* < L. *pyrethrum,* pellitory of Spain.] *Bot.* A greenhouse plant, *Pilea microphylla,* in the nettle family, native to tropical America, having a fine close foliage and discharging its pollen in an artillery-like fashion; also **ar·til·ler·y plant.** A southern European species, *Parietaria officinalis,* forming a mat and growing on old walls. An herbaceous plant, *Anacyclus pyrethrum,* in the composite family, native to southern Europe, whose roots are used in medicine; also **pel·li·to·ry of Spain.**

pell-mell, pell·mell, pel′mel′, *adv.* [Fr. *pêle-mêle,* < *pelle* (L. *paka*), a shovel, and *mêler,* to mix.] In a disordered manner; with confused haste.—*a.* Confused; indiscriminate.—*n.* A disorderly crowd or group; confusion.

pel·lu·cid, pe·lö′sid, *a.* [L. *pellucidus—pel,* for *per,* through, and *lucidus,* bright.] Admitting the passage of light; translucent;

limpid or clear; as, *pellucid* water; expressed in a clear or lucid style; as, a *pellucid* sentence.—**pel·lu·cid·i·ty,** **pel·lu·cid·ness,** pel′ū·sid′i·tē, *n.*—**pel·lu·cid·ly,** *adv.*

pe·lo·ri·a, pe·lōr′ē·a, pe·lar′ē·a, *n.* [Gr. *pelōr,* a monster.] *Bot.* regularity of structure in the flowers of plants which normally bear irregular flowers.—**pe·lor·ic,** pe·lar′ik, pe·lor′ik, *a.*

pe·lo·rus, pe·lōr′us, pe·lar′us, *n. pl.* **pe·lo·rus·es.** *Navig.* an instrument similar to a navigator's compass, used to establish the relative bearings of objects under observation. Also **dumb com·pass.**

pe·lo·ta, pe·lō′ta, *Sp.* pe·lạ′tä, *n. pl.* **pe·lo·tas,** pe·lō′taz, *Sp.* pe·lạ′täs. [Sp., < L. *pila,* ball: cf. *pellet.*] Jai alai; any similar Basque, Spanish, or Spanish-American game; a ball used in these games.

pelt, pelt, *n.* [Shortened from *peltry,* < L. *pellis,* a skin.] The skin of an animal with the hair or wool on it; the untanned hide of an animal; the human skin: used humorously.

pelt, pelt, *v.t.* [O.E. *pulten,* prob. < L. *pultare* to strike or knock, < *pello,* to drive.] To strike successively with something thrown or driven; hurl, fling; to assail verbally.—*v.i.* To continue beating steadily, as with rain or heavy hail; to move with haste and vigor.—*n.* A blow or stroke from something thrown.—**pelt·er,** *n.*

pel·tate, pel′tāt, *a.* [L. *pelta,* a target.] *Bot.* Having the leaf blade attached to its stalk inside the margin, often close to the middle of the lower surface; of leaves, shield-shaped. Also **pel·tat·ed.**—**pel·tate·ly,** *adv.*

pel·try, pel′trē, *n. pl.* **pel·tries.** [Fr. *pelletrie.*] Pelts collectively; the skins of fur-bearing animals in the raw state; a pelt.

pel·vic fin, *n.* One of a pair of fins on the underside of a fish, corresponding to the rear legs of a quadruped. Also *ventral fin.*

pel·vic gir·dle, *n.* In vertebrates, a bony or cartilaginous arch supporting the hind limbs; in man, the arch formed by the two innominate bones. Also **pel·vic arch.**

pel·vis, pel′vis, *n. pl.* **pel·vis·es, pel·ves,** pel′vēz. [L., basin.] *Anat., zool.* The basin-like cavity in the lower part of the trunk of many vertebrates, formed in man by the innominate bones, sacrum, and coccyx; the bones forming this cavity; the basin-like cavity into which the ureter expands at the hilum of the kidney.—**pel·vic,** *a.*

pem·mi·can, pem·i·can, pem′i·kan, *n.* [N. American Ind.] A N. American Indian food preparation exhibiting excellent keeping qualities and consisting of dried, lean venison or buffalo meat and melted fat, sometimes mixed with dried fruit, and pressed into cakes.

pem·phi·gus, pem′fi·gus, pem·fī′gus, *n.* [Gr. *pémphix, pemphigos,* a bubble.] *Pathol.* a disease consisting of an eruption of large watery blisters on the skin and mucous membranes.

pen, pen, *n.* [O.Fr. Fr. *penne,* < L. *penna,* feather, L.L. pen to write with.] Any instrument for writing with ink; a small instrument of steel or other metal, with a split point, used, when fitted into a holder, for writing with ink; the pen and penholder together; a pointed quill used for writing with ink; the pen as the instrument of writing or authorship; the writing profession; style or quality of writing; a writer or author. *Ornith.* a feather of a bird, esp. a large feather of the wing or tail; a quill. *Zool.* an internal, corneous or chitinous, feather-shaped structure in certain cephalopods, as the squid.—*v.t.*—*penned, penning.* To write with a pen; set down in writing; compose with a pen.—**pen·ner,** *n.*

pen, pen, *n.* [O.E. *penn.*] A small enclosure for domestic animals, as hogs, cows, sheep, or poultry; the animals enclosed in a pen;

any place of confinement or safekeeping.—
v.t.—*penned* or *pent*, *penning.* To confine in
or as in a pen.

pen, pen, *n.* A female swan.

pen, pen, *n. Slang,* a penitentiary.

pe·nal, pēn'al, *a.* [Fr. *pénal,* < L. *pœnalis,*
< *pœna,* pain, punishment.] Of or relating
to penalties or punishment; prescribing
punishment; incurring punishment; relating to a place of punishment.—**pe·nal·-
ize,** pēn'a·līz″, pen'a·līz″, *v.t.*—*penalized,*
penalizing. To impose a penalty on, as for
an infraction of the rules in such sports as
football, basketball, or hockey; to declare,
as a deed or action, liable to penalty; to put
at a disadvantage.—**pe·nal·i·za·tion,** *n.*—
pe·nal·ly, *adv.*

pe·nal code, *n. Law,* a code of laws relating
to crimes and the punishment prescribed
for them.

pen·al·ty, pen'al·tē, *n. pl.* **pen·al·ties.** The
punishment for committing a crime, offense,
or trespass; the suffering to which a person
subjects himself by agreement, in case of
nonfulfillment of stipulations; the sum forfeited for breaking an agreement; the disadvantage or hardship associated with an
action or condition; *sports,* a handicap imposed for an infringement of the rules.—*a.*

pen·ance, pen'ans, *n.* [O.Fr. *penance,*
peneance, < L. *pœnitentia,* repentance, <
pœnitens, penitent.] The suffering to which
a person subjects himself as an expression
of repentance for sin; a discipline imposed
by church authorities as an atonement for
sin; a sacrament of the Roman Catholic
Church for remission of sin.

pe·na·tes, pe·nā'tēz, *n. pl.* [L.] The
household gods of the ancient Romans.
See *lares.*

pen·cel, **pen·sil,** pen'sel, *n.* [For *pen-
noncel.*] A small pennon or streamer.

pen·chant, pen'chant, *Fr.* päN·shäN', *n.*
[Fr., < *pencher,* to incline.] Strong inclination; decided taste; liking; bias.

pen·cil, pen'sil, *n.* [O.Fr. *pincel* (Fr.
pinceau), < L. *pencellum,* dim. of *peniculus,*
brush, dim. of *penis,* tail.] An instrument
for marking, drawing, or writing made of a
strip of chalk, graphite, or the like encased
in wood or metal; a similarly shaped instrument used for medicinal, cosmetic, or
theatrical purposes; the characteristic style
or skill of an artist; a set of lines, light rays,
or the like, diverging from or converging
on a point; *archaic,* an artist's paintbrush,
esp. for fine work.—*v.t.*—*penciled, penciling,*
pencilled, pencilling. To write or mark with
or as with a pencil.

pend·ant, **pend·ent,** pen'dant, *n.* [Fr.
pendant, hanging, what hangs, a counterpart, < *pendre,* L. *pendere,* to hang.] Anything hanging down, esp. from the neck,
used for decoration or ornamentation; the
ringed stem of a pocket watch by which it is
fastened to a chain; an apparatus hanging
from a roof or ceiling for giving light; one
of a pair; companion or match; *arch.* a
hanging ornament used in Gothic vaults
and timber roofs; *naut.* pennant.

pend·ent, **pend·ant,** pen'dent, *a.* [L.
pendens, pendentis, hanging, ppr. of *pendere,*
to hang.] Hanging; suspended; overhanging; projecting; not yet determined;
pending.—**pend·en·cy,** *n.*—**pend·ent·ly,** *a.*

pen·den·tive, pen·den'tiv, *n.* [Fr. *pen-
dentif.*] *Arch.* The part of a groined ceiling
springing from one pillar or impost; a
triangular, concave masonry device which
provides a transition from a circular or
polygonal plan, as a dome, to a supporting
construction of another plan, as a rectangle.
—*a.* Assuming the function of a pendentive.

pend·ing, pen'ding, *a.* Remaining undecided; not terminated; impending;
imminent.—*prep.* For the time or the
continuance of; during; until.

pen·drag·on, pen·drag'on, *n.* [W. *pen,* a
head, and *dragon,* a leader.] The ruler or
leader of all the chiefs amongst the ancient
Britons.

pen·du·lous, pen'ja·lus, pen'da·lus, pen'-
dya·lus, *a.* [L. *pendulus,* < *pendeo,* to hang.]
Hanging so as to swing freely; swinging.
Undecided; vacillating.—**pen·du·lous·-
ness,** *n.*—**pen·du·lous·ly,** *adv.*

pen·du·lum, pen'ja·lum, pen'da·lum,
pen'dya·lum, *n.* [Lit. 'what hangs down,' <
L. *pendulus.*] A body so suspended from a
fixed point as to swing to and fro by the
alternate action of gravity and momentum;
the swinging piece in a clock serving as the
regulating power, the wheelwork being
attached to register the number of vibrations, and the weight or spring serving to
counteract the effects of friction and resistance of the air.—**pen·du·lar,** *a.*

pe·ne·plain, pē'ne·plān″, pē″ne·plān', *n.*
[L. *paene,* almost.] An area so denuded by
erosion that it is virtually a plain. Also
pe·ne·plane.

pen·e·tra·ble, pen'i·tra·bl, *a.* [L. *pene-
trabilis.*] Capable of being penetrated or
pierced; susceptible.—**pen·e·tra·bil·i·ty,**
pen″i·tra·bil'i·tē, *n.*—**pen·e·tra·ble·ness,**
n.—**pen·e·tra·bly,** *adv.*

pen·e·tra·li·a, pen″i·trā'lē·a, *n. pl.* [L.,
< *penetralis,* internal.] The innermost
recesses of a building, as of a temple or
palace; a sanctuary; hidden things.

pen·e·trance, pen'i·trans, *n. Genetics,* the
degree to which a gene produces its particular effects on an organism.

pen·e·trate, pen'i·trāt″, *v.t.*—*penetrated,*
penetrating. [L. *penetro, penetratum,* to
penetrate; root *pene,* denoting internality,
and *tra,* to go.] To enter or pierce; to make
way into the interior of; to affect, as the
mind or feelings, deeply; to pierce with the
intellect, so as to reach the inner meaning
of; to permeate.—*v.i.* To enter, pass into,
or diffuse with; to comprehend the meaning of; to have a profound effect upon.—
pen·e·trant, pen'i·trant, *n., a.*

pen·e·trat·ing, pen'i·trā'ting, *a.* Having
the power of entering or piercing; sharp;
acute; discerning.—**pen·e·trat·ing·ly,** *adv.*

pen·e·tra·tion, pen″i·trā'shan, *n.* The act
of penetrating; the extension of influence
into, or the physical infiltration of, one
country or culture by another; the distance or depth a projectile penetrates into a
target or territory; discernment; mental
acuteness.

pen·e·tra·tive, pen'i·trā″tiv, *a.* Able or
tending to penetrate; sharp; actue; discerning.—**pen·e·tra·tive·ly,** *adv.*—**pen·-
e·tra·tive·ness,** *n.*

pen·e·trom·e·ter, pen″i·trom'i·tėr, *n.*
An instrument for measuring the resistance
of semisolids under specific conditions. An
instrument for measuring the strength of
X-rays or other penetrating radiations;
also **pen·e·tram·e·ter,** pen″i·tram'i·tėr.

pen·guin, pen'gwin, peng'gwin, *n.* [= Fr.
pingouin, earlier *penguyn,* auk; of disputed
origin.] *Ornith.* any of several species of
flightless marine birds of the family
Spheniscidae, confined mostly to the antarctic
and subantarctic, having flipperlike wings
well-suited for swimming, and webbed
feet on short legs that act as rudders.

pen·hold·er, pen'hōl″dėr, *n.* A holder into
which a metallic writing tip may be fitted;
a container for pens.

pen·i·cil·late, pen″i·sil'it, pen″i·sil'āt, *a.*
Having or consisting of a brushlike bundle
of short, compact fibers or hairs.—**pen·-
i·cil·late·ly,** *adv.*—**pen·i·cil·la·tion,** *n.*

pen·i·cil·lin, pen″i·sil'in, *n.* An antibiotic
produced from molds of the genus *Penicillium,* effective in inhibiting the growth
of a number of disease-producing bacteria,
esp. cocci.

pen·i·cil·li·um, pen″i·sil'ē·um, *n. pl.*
pen·i·cil·li·a, pen″i·sil'ē·a. Any fungus,
genus *Penicillium,* often found as mold on
ripening cheese or decaying fruit, certain
species being the source of penicillin.

pen·in·su·la, pe·nin'sa·la, pe·nins'ū·la,
n. [L., *pene,* almost, and *insula,* an island.]
A portion of land almost surrounded by
water, connected to the mainland by an
isthmus.—**pen·in·su·lar,** *a.*

pe·nis, pē'nis, *n. pl.* **pe·nes,** **pe·nis·es,**
pē'nēz. [L.] The male copulatory organ
formed primarily of erectile tissue, also
serving in mammals as the male organ of
urination.—**pe·nile, pe·ni·al,** pēn'il, pē'nil,
pē'nē·al, *a.*

pen·i·tence, pen'i·tens, *n.* [Fr. *pénitence,*
< L. *pœnitentia,* repentance. *Penance* is the
same word.] The condition of being penitent; sorrow for one's sins or offenses;
repentance; contrition.

pen·i·tent, pen'i·tent, *a.* [L. *pœnitens,*
repentant.] Suffering or expressing sorrow
for sins or offenses and resolved on amendment; contrite.—*n.* One who is penitent;
an individual who confesses sins and accepts
the penance given by a priest.—**pen·i·-
tent·ly,** *adv.*

pen·i·ten·tial, pen″i·ten'shal, *a.* Of, relating to, or expressing penance or penitence.—*n.* A penitent; a book of church
rules concerning penance.—**pen·i·ten·-
tial·ly,** *adv.*

pen·i·ten·tia·ry, pen″i·ten'sha·rē, *n. pl.*
pen·i·ten·tia·ries. [M.L. *pœnitentiarius.*]
A place for imprisonment and reformatory
discipline; specif. in the U.S., a federal or
state prison. *Rom. Cath. Ch.* an office of the
papal court, presided over by a cardinal
called the 'grand penitentiary,' having
jurisdiction over certain cases of conscience; an officer appointed to deal with
such cases.—*a.* Pertaining to or intended
for penal confinement and discipline; of an
offense, punishable by imprisonment in a
penitentiary; penitential.

pen·knife, pen'nīf″, *n. pl.* **pen·knives.** A
small pocketknife, formerly used in making
and mending quill pens.

pen·man, pen'man, *n. pl.* **pen·men.** A
copyist; a scribe; a penmanship expert;
an author or writer.

pen·man·ship, pen'man·ship″, *n.* The art
or skill of handwriting; the use of the pen;
quality or manner of writing.

pen·na, pen'a, *n. pl.* **pen·nae,** pen'ē. [L.
feather.] *Ornith.* a contour feather, as distinguished from a down plume or feather.—
pen·na·ceous, pe·nā'shus, *a.*

pen name, *n.* A name an author assumes to
sign a work or works; a nom de plume;
pseudonym.

pen·nant, pen'ant, *n.* [Var. of *pendant,*
associated also with *pennon.*] A flag of distinctive form, as long and tapering, short
and swallow-tailed, or triangular, borne on
naval or other vessels and used in signaling
or as a means of identification; any long,
narrow flag or banner, usu. tapering to a
point; a flag serving as an emblem, as of
success in an athletic contest; *mus.* a hook,
or cross stroke, attached to the stem of a
note having shorter time value than a
quarter note.

pen·nate, pen'āt, *a.* Possessing feathers or
wings. Also **pen·nat·ed.**

pen·ni·less, pen'ē·lis, *a.* Impoverished;
destitute.

pen·non, pen'on, *n.* [O.Fr. Fr. *penon,* <
penne, < L. *penna,* feather.] A tapering,
triangular, swallow-tailed flag, orig. borne
on the lance of a knight; a pennant; any
flag or banner; a wing or pinion.

pen·non·cel, **pen·on·cel,** pen'on·sel″, *n.*
Pencel.

pen·ny, pen'ē, *n. pl.* **pen·nies,** *Brit.* **pence.**
[O.E. *penig, pening, pending* = D. *penning,*

Dan. *penge*, Icel. *penningr*, O.H.G. *pfenting*, G. *pfennig*, perh. of same origin as *pawn*, a pledge.] A cent, in the U.S. and Canada; a coin equal to one-twelfth of a shilling in Britain and various Commonwealth countries; a sum of money, as: He made a pretty *penny* on the deal.

pen·ny an·te, *n. Cards*, the game of poker when the amount of the ante is limited to one cent; *slang*, a transaction involving only a small sum of money.

pen·ny ar·cade, *n.* An amusement arcade filled with coin-operated mechanical games and amusements.

pen·ny dread·ful, *n. Brit. colloq.* a magazine or novel, formerly priced at a penny, containing cheap, sensational stories.

pen·ny pinch·er, *n.* One who spends money reluctantly.—**pen·ny-pinch·ing**, *n., a.*

pen·ny·roy·al, pen″ē·roi′al, *n.* [Appar. a corruption of obs. *puliol royal* (O.Fr. *puliol*, dim. < L. *pulegium*, pennyroyal).] *Bot.* a low European mint, *Mentha pulegium*, or an American mint, *Hedeoma pulegioides*, both used medicinally and yielding a pungently aromatic oil.

pen·ny·weight, pen′ē·wāt″, *n.* A troy weight containing 24 grains, one-twentieth of an ounce. Abbr. *dwt., pwt.*

pen·ny-wise, pen′ē·wīz′, *a.* Extremely saving or cautious in trifling matters.

pen·ny·wort, pen′ē·wurt″, *n. Bot.* any of several plants with small roundish leaves, as the navelwort, *Cotyledon umbilicus*, in the orpine family, and the water pennywort, *Hydrocotyle americana*, in the parsley family.

pen·ny·worth, pen′ē·wurth″, *n.* As much as is bought for a penny; a minute quantity; a bargain.

pe·nol·o·gy, poe·nol·o·gy, pē·nol′o·jē, *n.* [Gr. *poine*, punishment, and *logos*, discourse.] The study of crime prevention, prison and reformatory management, and the correction of criminals.—**pe·no·log·i·cal**, pēn″o·loj′i·kal, *a.*—**pe·nol·o·gist**, *n.*

pen·sile, pen′sil, *a.* [L. *pensilis*, < *pendeo*, to hang.] Hanging; suspended; pendulous; having or building a hanging nest.—**pen·sile·ness, pen·sil·i·ty**, *n.*

pen·sion, pen′shan, *Fr.* päN·syǎN, *n. pl.* **pen·sions**, pen·syǎN′. [Fr. *pension*, < L. *pensio, pensionis*, a paying, < *pendo, pensum*, to weigh, to pay (whence *expend*, etc.).] A stated allowance paid regularly to a person on his retirement or to his dependents on his death, in consideration of past services, meritorious work, age, loss, or injury; a regular allowance, pen′shan. A boarding house or school, or payment for room and board, esp. in Europe, *Fr.* päN·syǎN′.—*v.t.* To grant a pension to; to discharge with a pension, usu. followed by *off*.—**pen·sion·a·ble**, *a.*

pen·sion·ar·y, pen′sha·ner·ē, *n. pl.* **pen·sion·ar·ies**. A pensioner; a hireling.—*a.* Receiving a pension; consisting of a pension.

pen·sion·er, pen′sha·nẽr, *n.* One in receipt of a pension; a hireling; a Cambridge University student who pays for his expenses out of his own income.

pen·sive, pen′siv, *a.* [Fr. *pensif*, < *penser*, to think or reflect, < L. *pensare*, to weigh, to consider, a freq. from *pendo, pensum*, to weigh.] Engaged in serious or melancholy thought or reflection; expressing thoughtfulness or a certain sadness.—**pen·sive·ly**, *adv.*—**pen·sive·ness**, *n.*

pen·ste·mon, pen·stē′mon, pen′ste·mon, *n.* [N.L., < Gr. *pénte*, five, and *stēmōn*, warp, thread (with reference to the fifth stamen, usu. rudimentary.] *Bot.* any of several N. American herbs of the genus *Penstemon*, in the figwort family, chiefly grown as ornamentals, and characterized by colorful tubular-shaped flowers. Also **beard·tongue, pent·ste·mon.**

pen·stock, pen′stok″, *n.* [*Pen*, an enclosure, and *stock*.] A trough, tube, or conduit for conveying water to a water wheel; a floodgate or sluice.

pent, pent, *a.* Penned or shut in; closely confined.

pen·ta·chlo·ro·phe·nol, pen″ta·klōr″ō-fē′nōl, pen″ta·klōr″ō-fē′nǎl, pen″ta-klōr″ō-fē′nol, *n. Chem.* the compound, C_6Cl_5OH, a white crystalline powder used chiefly as a disinfectant, fungicide, or wood preservative.

pen·ta·cle, pen′ta·kl, *n.* [L.L. *pentaculum*, < Gr. *pente*, five.] A figure consisting of five straight lines so joined as to form a five-pointed star; formerly a symbol used in magic. Also *pentagram, pentangle.*

pen·tad, pen′tad, *n.* [Gr. *pente*, five.] The number five; an aggregate of five; a period of five years; *chem.* an element or atom with a valence of five.

pen·ta·dac·tyl, pen″ta·dak′til, pen″ta-dak′til, *a.* Having hands or feet with five digits each; having projections formed like five fingers, as on the wings of some primitive birds. Also **pen·ta·dac·ty·late.**—**pen·ta·dac·tyl·ism**, *n.*

pen·ta·gon, pen′ta·gon″, *n.* [Gr. *pente*, five, and *gōnia*, an angle.] *Geom.* a figure of five sides and five angles. (*Cap.*) the central office building of the U.S. Defense Department and military forces; the U.S. military command.—**pen·tag·o·nal**, pen·tag′o·nal, *a.*—**pen·tag·o·nal·ly**, *adv.*

pen·tag·o·noid, pen·tag′o·noid″, *a.* Similar to a pentagon in shape.

pen·ta·gram, pen′ta·gram″, *n.* [Gr. *pente*, five, and *grammē*, a line.] A pentacle.

pen·ta·he·dron, pen″ta·hē′dron, *n. pl.* **pen·ta·he·drons, pen·ta·he·dra**, pen″-ta·hē′dra. [Gr. *pente*, five, and *hedra*, a side or base.] *Geom.* a solid having five faces.—**pen·ta·he·dral**, *a.*

pen·tam·er·ous, pen·tam′ẽr·us, *a.* [Gr. *pente*, five, and *meros*, a part.] Having or divided into five parts; *bot.* having floral whorls composed of five, or a multiple of five, parts.

pen·tam·e·ter, pen·tam′i·tẽr, *n.* [Gr. *pente*, five, and *metron*, measure.] *Pros.* a verse of five feet.—*a.* Having five metrical feet.

pen·tane, pen′tān, *n.* [Gr. *pente*, five (with reference to the atoms of carbon).] *Chem.* a hydrocarbon, C_5H_{12}, of the methane series, existing in three isomeric forms, and present as a colorless fluid in petroleum.

pen·tan·gle, pen′tang·gl, *n.* Pentacle.

pen·tar·chy, pen′tär·kē, *n. pl.* **pen·tar·chies.** [Gr. *pente*, five, and *archē*, rule.] A government ruled by five persons; the rulers of such a government; a union or federation of five states, governed separately but united for a common purpose.—**pen·tar·chi·cal**, *a.*

pen·ta·stich, pen′ta·stik″, *n.* [Gr. *pente*, five, and *stichos*, a verse.] A composition, usu. a poem or stanza, having five lines.

Pen·ta·teuch, pen′ta·tōk″, pen′ta·tūk″, *n.* [Gr. *pente*, five, and *teuchos*, a book.] A collective term for the first five books of the Old Testament.—**Pen·ta·teuch·al**, *a.*

pen·tath·lon, pen·tath′lon, *n.* [Gr. *péntathlon*, < *pente*, five, and *áthlon, áthlos*, contest.] An athletic contest comprising five track and field events, and won by the contestant having the highest total score; a contest in the modern Olympic games consisting of five events: fencing, swimming, shooting, riding, and jumping.

pen·ta·ton·ic scale, pen′ta·ton′ik skäl, pen″ta·ton′ik, *n. Mus.* a scale that comprises only five notes, most commonly one like a major scale but omitting the fourth and seventh tones.

pen·ta·va·lent, pen″ta·vā′lent, pen·tav′-

a·lent, a. Chem. Having a valence of five; quinquevalent.

Pen·te·cost, pen′te·kǎst″, pen′te·kost″, *n.* [L.L. *Pentecoste*, < Gr. *pentecoste*, 'fiftieth (day),'.] A Christian festival on the seventh Sunday after Easter, commemorating the descent of the Holy Ghost upon the apostles; Whitsunday. The Jewish festival Shabuoth, observed on the fiftieth day following the first day of Passover.—**Pen·te·cos·tal**, pen″te·kǎ′stal, pen″te-kos′tal, *a.*

pent·house, pent′hous″, *n.* [Formerly *pentice*, < Fr. *appentis*, a penthouse.—L. *ad*, to, and *pendeo*, to hang.] A dwelling or apartment situated on the roof of a building; a shed or sloping roof projecting from the wall of a building; a rooflike canopy or shelter constructed over a door or window; a structure on the roof of a building which covers a water tank or elevator machinery.

pen·to·bar·bi·tal, pen″to·bär′bi·tal″, pen″to·bär′bi·tǎl″, *n. Pharm.* a barbituric acid, $C_{11}H_{18}O_3N_2$, used as a sedative and hypnotic, esp. in its calcium or sodium salt form, and usu. administered prior to an operation.

pen·tom·ic, pen·tom′ik, *a. Milit.* relating to U.S. Army divisions organized into five self-sustaining battle groups armed with nuclear weapons, and possessing a high degree of ground and air maneuverability.

pen·to·san, pen′to·san″, *n.* [< *pentose*.] *Chem.* any of a class of polysaccharides which yield pentoses upon hydrolysis, and occur in plants and humus.

pen·tose, pen′tōs, *n. Chem.* any of a class of monosaccharides containing five atoms of carbon.

Pen·to·thal, pen′to·thǎl″, *n.* Thiopental. (Trademark.)

pen·tyl, pen′til, *n. Chem.* any of the monovalent isomeric radicals with the formula C_5H_{11}.

pen·tyl·ene·tet·ra·zol, pen″ti·lēn·te′tra·zǎl″, pen″ti·lēn·te′tra·zol″, *n. Pharm.* a white, bitter-tasting, powdery compound, $C_6H_{10}N_4$, used as a stimulant in respiratory and circulatory disorders and to bring about a convulsive state in certain types of mental disease.

pe·nu·che, pe·nu·chi, pe·nō′chē, *n.* Panocha.

pe·nult, pē′nult, pi·nult′, *n.* [L. *paenultima*, prop. fem. of *paenultimus*, last but one, < *paene*, almost, and *ultimus*, last.] That preceding the last of a series, esp. the syllable next to the last in a word. Also **pe·nul·ti·ma**, pi·nul′ti·ma.

pe·nul·ti·mate, pi·nul′ti·mit, *a.* Next to the last; of or pertaining to the penult.—*n.* The penult.

pe·num·bra, pi·num′bra, *n. pl.* **pe·num·brae, pe·num·bras**, pi·num′brē. [N.L., < L. *paene*, almost, and *umbra*, shade, shadow.] The partial or imperfect shadow outside the complete shadow, or umbra, of an opaque body, as a planet, where the light from the source of illumination is only partly cut off; the grayish marginal portion of a sunspot.—**pe·num·bral**, *a.*

pe·nu·ri·ous, pe·nur′ē·us, pe·nūr′ē·us, *a*; Meanly parsimonious or stingy; in a condition of penury or want; poverty-stricken; scanty.—**pe·nu·ri·ous·ly**, *adv.*—**pe·nu·ri·ous·ness**, *n.*

pen·u·ry, pen′ū·rē, *n.* [L. *penuria*, want, scarcity: cf. Gr. *penia*, poverty, need.] Want or destitution; extreme poverty; dearth or insufficiency.

pe·on, pē′on, pē′ŏn, *n.* [Sp. *peon*, a foot soldier, a day laborer, < L. *pes, pedis*, the foot.] A day laborer or unskilled worker, esp. in Latin America. A person kept in servitude to work out a debt. In India and Ceylon, a foot soldier, a native constable, or a messenger.—**pe·on·age**, pē′o·nij, *n.*

The state or condition of a peon; the system by which persons are held in bondage or partial slavery while they work off a debt or are leased out as laborers while serving a prison sentence.

pe·o·ny, pē′o·nē, *n.* pl. **pe·o·nies.** [L. *paeonia*, < Gr. *paiōnia*, < *Paiōn*, Apollo, who used this flower to cure the wounds of the gods.] Any of several species of large perennial herbs or subshrubs of the genus *Paeonia*, in the buttercup family, native to Asia, widely cultivated, and having large flowers of crimson, pink, or white colors.

peo·ple, pē′pl, *n.* pl. **peo·ple, peo·ples.** [O.Fr. *pueple* (F. *peuple*), < L. *populus*, people, populace, multitude.] The whole body of persons constituting a community, tribe, race, or nation; as, the Jewish *people*; the persons of any particular group, company, or number; persons in relation to a superior or leader; as, the king and his *people*; a body of attendants or retainers; one's family or relatives; the members of any group or number to which one belongs; the body of enfranchised citizens of a state; the commonalty or populace, usu. with *the*; persons indefinitely, whether men or women; as: *People* may say what they please. Human beings as distinguished from animals; animals of an indicated kind; as, the monkey *people* of Brazil.—*v.t.*—*peopled, peopling.* To furnish with people; populate; to live in; inhabit.—**peo·pler,** *n.*

Peo·ple's par·ty, *n. Amer. hist.* a national party existing from 1891 to 1904 which propounded the unlimited coinage of silver and gold, the enactment of an income tax, and controls on railroads and other monopolies. Also **Pop·u·list par·ty.**

pep, pep, *n.* [Short for *pepper*.] *Colloq.* Spirit or animation; vigor, energy, or vim. —*v.t.*—*pepped, pepping. Colloq.* to animate or invigorate, usu. followed by *up.*

pep·los, pep′los, *n.* pl. **pep·los·es.** [L. *peplus*, < Gr. *péplos*.] A voluminous outer garment or shawl worn draped in folds by women in ancient Greece. Also **pep·lus.**

pep·lum, pep′lum, *n.* pl. **pep·lums, pep·la,** pep′la. [L.] A short flouncelike section attached to a dress, jacket, or blouse at the waistline.—**pep·lumed,** *a.*

pe·po, pē′pō, *n.* pl. **pe·pos.** [L. melon, pumpkin, < Gr. *pépon*, kind of gourd or melon eaten when ripe, orig. a. ripe.] *Bot.* a large fleshy succulent berry with a thick rind, the characteristic fruit of the gourd family to which the melon and the cucumber belong.

pep·per, pep′ẽr, *n.* [O.E. *pipor, peppor,* < L. *piper,* Gr. *piperi, peperic* a word of Oriental origin.] A pungent spice derived from the dried unripe fruit of the vine, *Piper nigrum*; the fruit ground in its entirety for black pepper and the inner seed for white pepper; any plant belonging to the family *Piperaceae*. The green or red pepper fruits of the garden vegetable, *Capsicum frutescens*, in the family *Solonaceae*, as cayenne.—*v.t.* To sprinkle with pepper; to cover or spatter with dots; to pelt with shot or missiles; to enliven, as a speech, with pungent remarks.—**pep·per·er,** *n.*— **pep·per·ish,** *a.*

pep·per-and-salt, pep′ẽr·an·sạlt, *a* Having a speckled appearance due to a fine intermingling of white or light gray and black hues. Also *salt-and-pepper.*

pep·per·box, pep′ẽr·boks″, *n.* A small container with a perforated top, for sprinkling pepper. Also *pepper pot.*

pep·per·corn, pep′ẽr·kạrn″, *n.* The dried unripe berry or fruit of the pepper plant; an insignificant quantity or trifle.

pep·per·grass, pep′ẽr·gras″, pep′ẽr·gräs″, *n.* Any of many herbaceous species of the genus *Lepidium*. The plant, *L. sativum*,

grown esp. for salad garnishing; also *garden cress.*

pep·per·mint, pep′ẽr·mint″, *n.* A perennial herb, *Mentha piperita*, of the mint family, grown for its leaves which have a pungent oil; the oil itself; a candy or lozenge flavored with this oil; any of several related species of the genus *Mentha.*

pep·per pot, *n.* A West Indian stew consisting of meat or fish, hot peppers, and cassava juice. In parts of the United States, peppery stew of tripe, vegetables, and dumplings; also **Phil·a·del·phi·a pep·per pot.** A pepperbox.

pep·per tree, *n.* A resinous S. American evergreen tree, *Schinus molle*, in the sumac family, introduced into California and Florida as an ornamental, having graceful pendulous branches and rose-colored fruits. Also **Cal·i·for·nia pep·per tree, Pe·ru·vi·an mas·tic tree.**

pep·per vine, *n. Bot.* a woody vine or shrub, *Ampelopsis arborea*, of the southern U.S.

pep·per·y, pep′e·rē, *a.* Noticeably flavored with pepper; having pepperlike qualities, as sharpness or pungency; having a choleric temper.

pep·py, pep′ē, *a.*—*peppier, peppiest. Colloq.* Lively; energetic; animated.—**pep·pi·ness,** *n.*

pep·sin, pep·sine, pep′sin, *n.* [Gr. *pepsis,* digestion, < *peptō,* to digest.] *Biochem.* An enzyme formed in the stomach that reduces proteins to proteoses and peptides; an extract of this enzyme, from the stomachs of hogs, sheep, or cows, used for aiding digestion.

pep·sin·o·gen, pep·sin′o·jen, *n. Biochem.* a zymogen found in the gastric glands which is converted into pepsin in a mild solution of hydrochloric acid.

pep·tic, pep′tik, *a.* Promoting or relating to digestion; relating to pepsin.—*n.* A medicine which promotes digestion.

pep·ti·dase, pep′ti·dās″, *n. Biochem.* one of a group of enzymes that hydrolyzes peptides or peptones into amino acids.

pep·tide, pep′tid, pep′tīd, *n. Biochem.* a compound of amino acids involving the linking of a carboxyl group from one acid to an amino group from another acid.

pep·tize, pep′tīz, *v.t.*—*peptized, peptizing.* To disperse in a colloid.—**pep·tiz·er,** *n.*, **pep·ti·za·tion,** pep″tĭ·zā′shan, *n.*

pep·tone, pep′tōn, *n.* [G. *pepton,* < Gr. *péptein.*] *Biochem.* any of a class of diffusible and soluble substances into which proteins are converted by the action of pepsin or trypsin.—**pep·ton·ic,** pep·ton′ik, *a.*

pep·to·nize, pep′to·nīz″, *v.t.*—*peptonized, peptonizing.* To convert into a peptone; to subject, as food, to an artificial partial digestion by means of pepsin or pancreatic extract as an aid to digestion.—**pep·to·ni·za·tion,** *n.*—**pep·to·niz·er,** *n.*

per, pụr, pẽr, *prep.* Through, by, or by means of; for each; as, five dollars *per* year.

per·ac·id, pẽr·as′id, *n. Chem.* an acid derived from an element in its highest oxidation state, as perchloric acid.

per·ad·ven·ture, pụr″ad·ven′chẽr, per″ad·ven′chẽr, *n.* [Prefix *per-*, by, and *adventure*, Fr. *par aventure*.] Chance, doubt.— *adv. Archaic.* Perhaps; possibly; it may be.

per·am·bu·late, pẽr·am′bū·lāt″, *v.t.*— *perambulated, perambulating.* [L. *perambulo—per-*, and *ambulo*, to walk.] To walk through or over; traverse; to survey the boundaries of while walking.—*v.i.* To walk around; stroll.—**per·am·bu·la·tion,** *n.*

per·am·bu·la·tor, pẽr·am′bū·lā″tẽr, *n.* One who perambulates; odometer. A small carriage for a young child or infant, pushed by hand; also **ba·by car·riage.**

per an·num, pẽr an′um, *adv.* [L.] By the year; for or in each year; annually.

per·bo·rate, pẽr·bōr′āt, pẽr·bạr′āt, *n.* A salt formed by the reaction between a borate and hydrogen peroxide, esp. sodium perborate, $NaBO_3·4H_2O$, used as a disinfecting and bleaching agent and in manufacturing processes. Also **per·ox·y·bo·rate,** pe·rok″sē·bōr′āt, pe·rok″sē·bōr′it, pe·rok″ sē·bạr′āt, pe·rok″sē·bạr′it.

per·cale, pẽr·kāl′, *n.* [Fr.; appar. of E. Ind. origin.] A closely woven, smooth-finished cotton fabric.

per·ca·line, pụr″ka·lēn′, *n.* [Fr., < *percale.*] A fine, lightweight cotton fabric, usu. finished with a gloss and dyed in one color, used esp. for linings.

per cap·i·ta, pẽr kap′i·ta, *adv., a.* [L., 'by the heads.'] For or by each person individually; *law,* distributed between individuals equally, as an inheritance.

per·ceive, pẽr·sēv′, *v.t.*—*perceived, perceiving.* [Fr. *percevoir,* L. *percipio,* to perceive, to comprehend—*per-*, and *capio,* to take.] To have or obtain knowledge or awareness of by the senses; to apprehend with the mind; to discern, know, understand.—**per·ceiv·a·ble,** pẽr·sē′va·bl, *a.*— **per·ceiv·a·bly,** *adv.*—**per·ceiv·er,** *n.*

per·cent, per cent, pẽr·sent′, *n.* pl. **per·cent.** [Prop. *per cent.* (with period), abbr. of L. *per centum,* by the hundred.] A rate determined by the hundred; also *percentage.* A proportion for or of every hundred; as, 25 *percent* of a number; also *per centum.*—*a.* Pertaining to a whole proportioned into 100 equal parts; bearing interest at a predetermined percent. Sym. %. Abbr. *p.c., pct.*— **per·cents,** *n. pl.* Securities having a stated rate of interest; as, the three *percents.*

per·cent·age, pẽr·sen′tij, *n.* A rate or proportion per hundred; also *percent.* An allowance, duty, commission, discount, or rate of interest on a hundred; loosely, a proportion in general. *Colloq.* individual gain; advantage or profit for oneself.

per·cen·tile, pẽr·sen′til, pẽr·sen′tĭl, *n. Statistics,* any of the points dividing a range of data into 100 equal intervals and indicating the percentage of a distribution falling below it.

per cen·tum, pẽr sen′tum, *n.* See *percent.*

per·cept, pụr′sept, *n.* [L. *perceptum,* neut. of *perceptus,* pp. of *percipere,* E. *perceive.*] That which is perceived; the object of perception; the mental result or product of perceiving, as distinguished from the act of perceiving.

per·cep·ti·ble, pẽr·sep′ti·bl, *a.* [L.L. *perceptibilis,* < L. *percipere,* E. *perceive.*] Capable of being perceived; discernible; appreciable.—**per·cep·ti·bil·i·ty,** *n.*— **per·cep·ti·bly,** *adv.*

per·cep·tion, pẽr·sep′shan, *n.* [L. *perceptio(n-),* < *percipere,* E. *perceive.*] The act of perceiving; apprehension with the mind or the senses; an immediate or intuitive recognition, as of a moral or esthetic quality; the faculty of perceiving; the result or product of perceiving, as distinguished from the act of perceiving.— **per·cep·tion·al,** *a.*

per·cep·tive, pẽr·sep′tiv, *a.* [L. *percipere* (pp. *perceptus*), E. *perceive.*] Of or pertaining to perception; having the power or faculty of perceiving; of ready or quick insight, understanding, or perception.— **per·cep·tive·ly,** *adv.*—**per·cep·tive·ness,** *n.*— **per·cep·tiv·i·ty,** pẽr″sep·tiv′i·tē, *n.*

per·cep·tu·al, pẽr″sep′chö·al, *a.* Pertaining to perception.—**per·cep·tu·al·ly,** *adv.*

perch, pụrch, *n.* [O.Fr. Fr. *perche,* < L. *pertica,* pole, measuring rod, measure of land.] A pole or rod fixed horizontally to serve as a roost for birds; any object or place for a bird, or anything else, to alight or rest upon; an elevated position or station; a pole in a carriage or other vehicle connecting the fore and hind running parts; a pole or staff set up in a shallow or other place in water to serve as a mark for navigation; a linear measure equaling one rod; a square rod; a solid measure for stonework, commonly 16½ feet by 1½ feet by 1 foot.—*v.i.* [O.Fr. Fr. *percher.*] To alight or rest upon a perch, as a bird; to settle or rest in some elevated position, as if on a perch.—*v.t.* To set or place on a perch; set in some elevated position, as if on a perch.

perch, pŭrch, *n.* pl. **perch, perch·es.** [O.Fr. Fr. *perche,* < L. *perca,* < Gr. *pérkē,* perch.] A spiny-finned, fresh-water game fish of the genus *Perca,* as *P. fluviatilis* of Europe, or *P. flavescens,* the yellow perch of the U.S., used for food; any of various similar fishes of the same or related families.

per·chance, pĕr·chans', pĕr·chäns', *adv.* [L. *per-,* by, and E. *chance.*] Perhaps; maybe; by chance.

Per·che·ron, pŭr'che·ron", pŭr'she·ron", *n.* [Fr.] One of a breed of draft horses noted for strength and speed, orig. raised in Perche, a district in France.

per·chlo·rate, pĕr·klōr'āt, pĕr·klạr'āt, *n. Chem.* a salt of perchloric acid.

per·chlo·ric ac·id, pĕr·klōr'ik as'id, pĕr··klạr'ik, *n. Chem.* a colorless acid, $HClO_4$, consisting of chloric acid with an added atom of oxygen, chiefly used in analytical chemistry.

per·cip·i·ent, pĕr·sip'ē·ent, *a.* [L. *percipiens,* ppr. of *percipio.*] Perceiving or having the faculty of perception; discerning.—*n.* One that perceives.—**per·cip·i··ence, per·cip·i·en·cy,** *n.*

per·coid, pŭr'koid, *a.* [L. *perca,* perch.] Belonging to the suborder *Percoidea,* a very large natural group of spiny-finned fishes comprising the true perches and related families; resembling a perch. Also **per··coi·de·an,** pĕr·koi'dē·an.—*n.* A percoid fish. Also **per·coi·de·an.**

per·co·late, pŭr'ko·lāt", *v.t.*—*percolated, percolating.* [L. *percolo—per-,* and *colo,* to strain, < *colum,* a sieve.] To strain or filter; to permeate; to make in a percolator, as coffee.—*v.i.* To pass through small interstices or pores; to filter; to seep or ooze.—**per·co·la·tion,** pŭr'ko·lā'shan, *n.*

per·co·la·tor, pŭr'ko·lā'tẽr, *n.* That which percolates or filters; a kind of coffeepot in which boiling water is forced upward and seeps down through the ground coffee.

per con·tra, pĕr kon'tra, L. peR kōn'trä, *adv.* [L.] In contrast; on the other hand.

per·cuss, pĕr·kus', *v.t.* [L. *percussus,* pp. of *percutere,* < *per-,* through, and *quatere,* shake, strike.] To strike sharply; *med.* to strike or tap for diagnostic purposes.

per·cus·sion, pĕr·kush'an, *n.* [L. *percussio(n-).*] The act of percussing; the striking of one body against another with some violence; the shock or vibration so produced; impact; *med.* the striking or tapping of a part of the body for diagnostic purposes. *Mus.* the striking of musical instruments to produce tones; percussion instruments as a group, esp. when considered a section of an instrumental group.—**per·cus··sion·ist,** pĕr·kush'a·nist, *n. Mus.* one who plays percussion instruments.

per·cus·sion cap, *n.* A small metallic cap or cup containing fulminating powder, exploded by percussion: used formerly to fire the charge of a gun.

per·cus·sion in·stru·ment, *n.* A musical instrument that is played by striking, as a drum or piano.

per·cus·sive, pĕr·kus'iv, *a.* Acting by percussion; pertaining to percussion.—**per·cus·sive·ly,** *adv.*—**per·cus·sive·ness,** *n.*

per·die, pĕr·dē', *interj. Archaic,* an oath. Also **par·di,** pär·dē'.

per di·em, pĕr dē'em, pĕr dī'em, *adv.* [L.]

By the day; for each day.—*n.* A daily allowance, as for expenditures incurred when traveling.—*a.*—*n.* Abbr. *p.d.,* *P.D.*

per·di·tion, pĕr·dish'an, *n.* [L.L. *perditio,* < L. *perdo, perditus,* to destroy, to ruin.] The place or state of eternal damnation; hell; spiritual death. *Archaic,* ruin; utter destruction.

per·du, per·due, pĕr·dō', pĕr·dū', per··dō', per·dū', *a.* [Fr. *perdu* (fem. *perdue*), pp. of *perdre,* lose, < L. *perdere.*] Lost to sight; hidden or concealed.—*n. Obs.* a soldier placed in a dangerous position or sent on a hazardous enterprise.

per·dur·a·ble, pĕr·dur'a·bl, pĕr·dūr'a·bl, *a.* [Fr. < L. *perduro—per-,* intens., and *-duro,* to last.] Very durable; lasting; imperishable.—**per·dur·a·bil·i·ty,** *n.*—**per·dur·a·bly,** *adv.*

per·e·gri·nate, per'e·gri·nāt", *v.t.*—*peregrinated, peregrinating.* [L. *peregrinatus,* pp. of *peregrinari,* < *peregrinus.*] To travel over; traverse.—*v.i.* To travel or journey, esp. by walking.—**per·e·gri·na·tion,** per"·e·gri·nā'shan, *n.*

per·e·grine, per'e·grin, per'e·grēn", per'·e·grin", *a.* [L. *peregrinus,* foreign, as n. a foreigner, < *pereger,* being on a journey, or abroad, < *per-,* through, and *ager,* field, land: cf. *pilgrim.*] Foreign; alien; coming from abroad; wandering; migratory.—*n.* The peregrine falcon.

per·e·grine fal·con, *n.* [= M.L. *falco peregrinus,* Fr. *faucon pèlerin,* lit. 'pilgrim falcon.'] A hawk of world-wide distribution, *Falco peregrinus,* noted for its swift flight and its use in falconry, and characterized by long pointed wings, a long narrow tail, and rowing wing strokes; also *peregrine.* The American variety of this falcon, *F. peregrinus anatum*; also **duck hawk.**

per·emp·to·ry, pe·remp'to·rē, per'emp··tōr"ē, per'emp·tạïr"ē, *a.* [L. *peremptorius,* < *perimo, peremptus,* to destroy—*per-,* thoroughly, and *emo,* to take, to buy.] Precluding debate or expostulation; decisive; authoritative; positive in opinion or judgment; dogmatic; imperious. *Law,* final; determinate.—**per·emp·to·ri·ly,** *adv.*—**per·emp·to·ri·ness,** *n.*

per·en·ni·al, pe·ren'ē·al, *a.* [L. *perennis,* < *per-,* through, and *annus,* year.] Lasting or continuing throughout the year, as a spring or stream; lasting for an indefinitely long time; enduring; perpetual; everlasting; *bot.* continuing more than two years.—*n.*—**per·en·ni·al·ly,** *adv.*

per·fect, pŭr'fikt, *a.* [O.Fr. *parfit* (Fr. *parfait*), < L. *perfectus,* pp. of *perficere,* perform, complete, finish.] Carried through to completion in every detail; in a state proper to a thing when completed; having all essential elements or characteristics; lacking in no respect; complete; in a state of complete excellence; without blemish or defect; faultless; of supreme moral excellence; completely skilled or versed; having learned one's lesson or part thoroughly; completely corresponding to a type or description; exact; as, a *perfect* sphere; correct in every detail; as, a *perfect* copy; entire or unqualified; pure or unmixed; as, *perfect* yellow; unmitigated or utter; as, *perfect* fury. *Bot.* a flower which bears both stamens and pistils; monoclinous. *Gram.* denoting an action or state completed at the present time; as, the *perfect* tense. *Mus.* noting the consonances of a normal unison, octave, fifth, and fourth, as distinguished from those of a third and sixth, which are called *imperfect*; noting the intervals, harmonic or melodic, of an octave, fifth, and fourth in their normal form, as opposed to *augmented* and *diminished*; noting a chord or triad involving a perfect fifth and having its fundamental tone in the bass; of

a cadence or period, complete or fully satisfactory.—*n. Gram.* The perfect tense; a verb form in this tense.—*v.t.* pĕr·fekt', pŭr'fikt, *v.t.* To bring to completion or finish; to make perfect or faultless; bring to perfection; loosely, to bring nearer to perfection; improve; to make fully skilled or versed; as, to *perfect* oneself in an art.—**per·fect·er,** *n.* **per·fect·ness,** *n.*

per·fect·i·ble, pĕr·fek'ti·bl, *a.* Capable of becoming or being made perfect.—**per·fect·i·bil·ist,** *n.*—**per·fect·i·bil·i·ty,** *n.*

per·fec·tion, pĕr·fek'shan, *n.* [L. *perfectio(n-),* < *perficere.*] The state or quality of being perfect; flawlessness; the state of completion or maturity; supreme moral excellence; the highest degree of proficiency, as in some art; a perfect embodiment of something; the highest degree of excellence; the highest or most perfect degree of a quality or trait; as, the *perfection* of goodness; the act of perfecting.

per·fec·tion·ism, pĕr·fek'sha·niz"um, *n.* Any of various doctrines maintaining that religious, moral, social, or political perfection is attainable; a personal philosophy demanding perfection.—**per·fec·tion·ist,** pĕr·fek'sha·nist, *n.,* *a.*—**per·fec·tion·is··tic,** pĕr·fek"sha·nis'tik, *a.*

per·fec·tive, pĕr·fek'tiv, *a.* Tending to make perfect; conducive to perfection; *gram.* indicating a verbal inflection which denotes completion.—*n. Gram.* Perfective aspect; a verb in this form or aspect.—**per·fec·tive·ly,** *adv.*—**per·fec·tive·ness, per·fec·tiv·i·ty,** pŭr"fek·tiv'i·tē, *n.*

per·fect·ly, pŭr'fikt·lē, *adv.* In a perfect manner or degree; completely; quite; as, *perfectly* clear.

per·fec·to, pĕr·fek'tō, *n.* pl. **per·fec·tos.** [Sp., lit. 'perfect.'] A thick, medium-sized cigar tapering toward both ends.

per·fect par·ti·ci·ple, *n.* Past participle.

per·fect pitch, *n.* The ability to recognize and name the pitch of a tone without hearing an established pitch as a point of reference. Also *absolute pitch.*

per·fer·vid, pĕr·fŭr'vid, *a.* [L. *perfervidus—per-,* intens., and *fervidus,* fervid.] Very fervid; ardent.—**per·fer·vid·i·ty, per·fer·vid·ness,** *n.*—**per·fer·vid·ly,** *adv.*—**per·fer·vor,** *Brit.* **per·fer·vour,** *n.*

per·fid·i·ous, pĕr·fid'ē·us, *a.* Guilty of or involving perfidy; treacherous; traitorous.—**per·fid·i·ous·ly,** *adv.*—**per·fid·i·ous··ness,** *n.*

per·fi·dy, pŭr'fi·dē, *n.* pl. **per·fi·dies.** [L. *perfidia,* < *perfidus,* faithless—prefix *per-,* and *fidus,* faithful; *per-* having the same force as in *perjure, pervert.*] The act of violating faith or allegiance; breach of faith; treachery; faithlessness.

per·fo·li·ate, pĕr·fō'lē·it, pĕr·fō'lē·āt", *a.* [L. *per-,* through, and *folium,* a leaf.] *Bot.* descriptive of a leaf whose base completely surrounds the stem, the structure seemingly passing through the leaf.—**per·fo·li·a··tion,** *n.*

per·fo·rate, pŭr'fo·rāt", *v.t.*—*perforated, perforating.* [L. *perforo, perforatus*—prefix *per-,* through, and *foro,* to bore.] To bore through; to pierce with a pointed instrument; to make a hole or holes through by boring or punching.—*v.i.* To penetrate.—pŭr'fo·rit, pŭr'fo·rāt", *a.*—**per·fo·ra·ted,** pŭr'fo·rā"tid, *a.*—**per·fo·ra·tor,** *n.*

per·fo·ra·tion, pŭr'fo·rā'shan, *n.* The act of perforating, boring, or piercing; the state of being perforated or pierced; a hole bored; a hole, or one of a series of holes passing through anything.

per·force, pĕr·fōrs', *adv.* [Prefix *per-,* through, by, and *force.*] Of necessity; through circumstances.

per·form, pĕr·fạrm', *v.t.* [O.E. *parforme, parfourne,* < O.Fr. *parfournir,* to perform —prefix *par-,* and *fournir,* to accomplish, to furnish.] To do; to execute; to accomplish; to fulfill or discharge, as a duty; to act or represent, as on the stage.—*v.i.* To act or exhibit talent, esp. before an audience; to fulfill or see through.—**per·form·a·ble,** *a.* —**per·form·er,** *n.*

per·for·mance, pêr·fạr′mạns, *n.* An entertainment presented before an audience; the portrayal of a character on the stage; the act or manner of exhibiting an art, skill, or capacity; the degree to which anything, as a machine, functions as intended; an action, deed, or thing done; the act of performing or condition of being performed.—**per·form·ing,** *a.*

per·fume, pụr′fūm, pêr·fūm′, *n.* [Fr. *parfum,* < L. *per-,* through, and *fumus,* smoke; lit. 'smoke or vapor that disseminates itself.'] A fluid, powder, or other substance that emits an agreeable or pleasing scent; the fragrant odor emitted by such a substance.—pêr·fūm′, *v.t.*—*perfumed, perfuming.* To fill or impregnate with a pleasing odor; to scent.—**per·fum·er,** pêr·fū′mêr, *n.* One who or a thing that perfumes; one whose trade is to make or sell perfumes.—**per·-fum·er·y,** pêr·fū′me·rē, *n.* pl. **per·-fum·er·ies.** Perfumes collectively; the art of preparing perfumes; a business establishment where perfumes are made or sold.

per·func·to·ry, pêr·fungk′to·rē, *a.* [L.L. *perfunctorius*—L. *per-* and *fungor, functus,* to perform, execute.] Done in a half-hearted or careless manner and merely for the sake of getting rid of the duty; careless, slight, or not thorough; indifferent. —**per·func·to·ri·ly,** *adv.*—**per·func·to·ri·ness,** *n.*

per·fuse, pêr·fūz′, *v.t.*—*perfused, perfusing.* [L. *perfusus,* pp. of *perfundere,* < *per-,* through, and *fundere,* pour.] To overspread with moisture, color, or the like; to diffuse, as a liquid, through or over something.— **per·fu·sion,** pêr·fū′zhạn, *n.*—**per·fu·sive,** pêr·fū′siv, *a.*

per·go·la, pụr′go·la, *n.* [It.] An elaborate bower or arbor fully covered by a roof of latticework over which climbing shrubs and vines grow; sometimes such a covering over a walk.

per·haps, pêr·haps′, *adv.* [L. *per-,* by (as in *perchance*), and E. *hap.*] Possibly; maybe.

pe·ri, pēr′ē, *n.* [Pers. *pari,* a fairy.] *Pers. mythol.* a beautiful spiritual being, represented as a descendant of fallen angels, excluded from paradise until the accomplishment of some task imposed as a penance. A beautiful person, esp. a woman.

per·i·anth, per′ē·anth″, *n.* [Gr. *peri,* about, and *anthos,* a flower.] *Bot.* the floral envelope, that is, the sepals and petals considered together: used esp. when there is no clear distinction between them.

per·i·apt, per′ē·apt″, *n.* [Gr. *periapton, peri,* around, and *haptō,* to fasten.] A bracelet, necklace, or other ornament worn as a charm; an amulet.

per·i·car·di·tis, per″i·kär·dī′tis, *n.* [Term. *-itis,* signifying inflammation.] *Pathol.* inflammation of the pericardium.

per·i·car·di·um, per″i·kär′dē·um, *n.* pl. **per·i·car·di·a,** per″i·kär′dē·a. [Gr. *peri-kardion*—*peri,* around, and *kardia,* the heart.] The membranous sac that encloses the heart.—**per·i·car·di·ac, per·i·car·di·al,** per″i·kär′dē·ak, *a.*

per·i·carp, per′i·kärp″, *n.* [Gr. *peri,* about, and *karpos,* fruit.] *Bot.* the wall of a ripened fruit or ovary, consisting of three not always distinguishable layers, epicarp, mesocarp, and endocarp.—**per·i·car·pi·al, per·i·car·pic,** *a.*

per·i·chon·dri·um, per″i·kon′drē·um, *n.* pl. **per·i·chon·dri·a,** per″i·kon′drē·a. [N.L., < Gr. *peri,* around, and *chondros,* cartilage.] *Anat.* the membrane of fibrous

connective tissue covering the surface of cartilages except at the joints.—**per·i·chon·dral, per·i·chon·dri·al,** *a.*

per·i·cline, per′i·klīn″, *n.* [G. *periklin,* < Gr. *periclinēs,* sloping on all sides, < *peri,* around, and *clinein,* incline.] A mineral, a variety of albite, occurring in large white opaque crystals.

pe·ric·o·pe, pe·rik′o·pē″, *n.* pl. **pe·ric·o·pes, pe·ric·o·pae,** pe·rik′o·pē″. An extract, esp. a passage from the Bible read on stated occasions.

per·i·cra·ni·um, per″i·krā′nē·um, *n.* pl. **per·i·cra·ni·a,** per″i·krā′nē·a. [Gr. *peri,* about, and *kranion,* the skull.] The membrane that forms the external covering of the skull.—**per·i·cra·ni·al,** *a.*

per·i·cy·cle, per′i·sī″kl, *n.* [Gr. *peri,* around, and *cyclos,* ring, circle.] *Bot.* the outer layer or tissue of the stele or central cylinder in the root and stem of vascular plants from which branch roots develop.— **per·i·cy·clic,** *a.*

per·i·derm, per′i·dụrm″, *n.* [Gr. *peri,* around, and *derma,* skin.] *Bot.* a collective term for cork and cork cambium formed as secondary tissue in many roots and stems and sometimes developing into bark.— **per·i·der·mal, per·i·der·mic,** *a.*

pe·rid·i·um, pe·rid′ē·um, *n.* pl. **pe·rid·i·a, pe·rid·i·ums,** pe·rid′ē·a. [N.L., < Gr. *pēridion,* dim. of *pēra,* leather pouch, wallet.] *Bot.* the surface layer or coat of the spore-bearing structure in many fungi, as in the puffball.—**pe·rid·i·al,** *a.*

per·i·dot, per′i·dot″, *n.* A precious stone of a yellowish-green color, a variety of olivine.—**per·i·dot·ic,** per″i·dot′ik, *a.*

per·i·do·tite, per′i·dō″tīt, pe·rid′o·tīt″, *n.* Any of a group of igneous rocks of granitic structure, composed chiefly of olivine with an admixture of various other minerals, but nearly or wholly free from feldspar.— **per·i·do·tit·ic,** per″i·dō·tit′ik, pe·rid″o·tit′ik, *a.*

per·i·gee, per′i·jē″, *n.* [Gr. *peri,* about, and *gē,* the earth.] *Astron.* That point of the moon's orbit which is nearest the earth; this same point in the orbit of an artificial satellite: opposed to *apogee.*—**per·i·ge·al, per·i·ge·an,** per″i·jē′al, per″i·jē′an, *a.*

per·i·gon, per′i·gon″, *n.* Round angle.

per·i·he·li·on, per″i·hē′lē·on, per″i·hel′-yon, *n.* pl. **per·i·he·li·a,** per″i·hē′lē·a, per″i·hel′ya. [Gr. *peri,* about, and *hēlios,* the sun.] *Astron.* that point in the orbit of a planet or comet at which it is least distant from the sun opposed to *aphelion.*—**per·i·he·li·al, per·i·he·li·an,** *a.*

per·il, per′il, *n.* [Fr. *péril,* < L. *periculum,* danger, < root seen in *perior, experior,* to try (whence *experiment*).] Danger; risk; jeopardy; exposure of person or property to injury, loss, or destruction.—*v.t.*—*periled, periling,* Brit. *perilled, perilling.* To imperil; expose to danger.—**per·il·ous,** per′i·lus, *a.*—**per·il·ous·ly,** *adv.*—**per·il·ous·ness,** *n.*

per·i·lune, per′i·lön″, *n.* *Aeron.* the low point in the orbit of a spacecraft.

pe·rim·e·ter, pe·rim′i·têr, *n.* [Gr. *peri,* about, and *metron,* measure.] The boundary or circumference of a figure having two dimensions; the sum of all sides of the boundary. *Ophthal.* an instrument which is used to determine the extent of one's field of vision.—**per·i·met·ric, per·i·met·ri·cal,** per″i·me′trik, *a.*—**per·i·met·ri·cal·ly,** *adv.*—**pe·rim·e·try,** *n.*

per·i·morph, per′i·marf″, *n.* [Gr. *peri,* about, and *morphē,* form.] *Mineral.* a mineral or crystal enclosing another mineral or crystal. See *endomorph.*

per·i·ne·um, per″i·nē′um, *n.* pl. **per·i·ne·a,** per″i·nē′a. [N.L., < Gr. *perinaion, perineos.*] *Anat.* The region between the anus and the genital organs; the region

of the body including the passageway for the rectum and genitourinary ducts.—**per·i·ne·al,** *a.*

per·i·neu·ri·um, per″i′nụr′ē·um, per″i·nūr′ē·um, *n.* pl. **per·i·neu·ri·a,** per″i·nụr′ē·a, per″i·nūr′ē·a. [N.L., < Gr. *peri,* around, and *neuron,* nerve.] *Anat.* the sheath of connective tissue which encloses a funiculus or bundle of nerve fibers.

pe·ri·od, pēr′ē·od, *n.* [O.Fr. *periode* (Fr. *période*), < L. *periodus,* < Gr. *periodos,* a going around, circuit, cycle, period < *peri,* around, and *odós,* way.] An indefinite portion of time in history or in a person's life characterized by certain features or conditions; as, a *period* of prosperity; any specified division or portion of time; a round of time marked by the recurrence of some phenomenon or occupied by some recurring process of action; one of the specified portions of time into which a school day is divided; in a game, one of the portions into which playing time is divided; the point of completion or conclusion of any course. *Astron.* the time in which a heavenly body makes a single rotation; the time in which a planet or satellite revolves about its primary. *Phys.* the time of one complete oscillation or cycle of a periodic motion; the interval between a phase and its recurrence. *Geol.* one of the larger divisions of geological time, being a subdivision of an era; *mus.* a division of a composition, usu. a passage of eight or sixteen measures, which is complete in itself, commonly consisting of two or more contrasted or complementary phrases and involving a cadence at the end; *physiol.* the time of each month during which a woman menstruates. The point or character (.) used to mark the end of a complete declarative sentence or to indicate an abbreviation; a full pause such as is made at the end of a complete sentence; a sentence, esp. a well-constructed sentence of several clauses; *class. pros.* a group of two or more cola.—*a.* Of or pertaining to a particular historical period.

pe·ri·od·ic, pēr″ē·od′ik, *a.* Performed at intermittent intervals; happening or returning regularly; recurring; pertaining to a period or to periods; relating to periodic sentences.

per·i·od·ic ac·id, pụr″ī·od′ik as′id, pụr″-ī·od′ik, *n.* A highly oxygenated acid containing iodine in a valence state of +7. Also **met·a per·i·od·ic ac·id.**

pe·ri·od·i·cal, pēr″ē·od′i·kal, *n.* A publication which appears at regular intervals, as a newspaper or magazine.—*a.* Characteristic of periodic publications; regularly published; periodic.—**pe·ri·od·i·cal·ly,** *adv.*

pe·ri·o·dic·i·ty, pēr″ē·o·dis′i·tē, *n.* The state or quality of being periodic.

pe·ri·od·ic law, *n. Chem.* the principle that the properties of elements are periodic functions of their atomic numbers, that is, that the chemical and physical properties recur periodically when the elements are arranged in the order of their atomic numbers.

pe·ri·od·ic sen·tence, *n.* A sentence in which completion of the main clause and thought is delayed until all the subordinate components are included: contrasted with *loose sentence.*

pe·ri·od·ic ta·ble, *n. Chem.* a table illustrating the periodic system, in which the chemical elements, arranged in the order of their atomic numbers, are shown in related groups. See Periodic Table of Elements.

per·i·o·don·tal, per″ē·o·don′tal, *a. Dentistry,* relating to the periodontium or to periodontics.

per·i·o·don·tics, per″ē·o·don′tiks, *n. pl. but sing. in constr.* That division of dentistry

---

ch- chain, G. na*ch*t;   th- THen, thin;   w- wig, hw as sound in whig;   z- zh as in azure, zeal.   *Italicized vowel* indicates schwa sound.

PERIODIC TABLE OF THE ELEMENTS

Group numbers appear above columns in Roman numerals.
Atomic number in the upper left corner of each box.
Element and its symbol in the center of each box.
Atomic weight based on carbon 12.01115 in lower center of each box.
Numbers in the table in parentheses are mass numbers of the most stable isotopes.

I A	II A	III B	IV B	V B	VI B	VII B	VIII	VIII	VIII	I B	II B	III A	IV A	V A	VI A	VII A	Noble gases
1 Hydrogen H 1.00797																1 Hydrogen H 1.00797	2 Helium He 4.0026
3 Lithium Li 6.939	4 Beryllium Be 9.0122											5 Boron B 10.811	6 Carbon C 12.01115	7 Nitrogen N 14.0067	8 Oxygen O 15.9994	9 Fluorine F 18.9984	10 Neon Ne 20.183
11 Sodium Na 22.9898	12 Magnesium Mg 24.312											13 Aluminum Al 26.9815	14 Silicon Si 28.086	15 Phosphorus P 30.9738	16 Sulfur S 32.064	17 Chlorine Cl 35.453	18 Argon Ar 39.948
19 Potassium K 39.102	20 Calcium Ca 40.08	21 Scandium Sc 44.956	22 Titanium Ti 47.90	23 Vanadium V 50.942	24 Chromium Cr 51.996	25 Manganese Mn 54.9380	26 Iron Fe 55.847	27 Cobalt Co 58.9332	28 Nickel Ni 58.71	29 Copper Cu 63.56	30 Zinc Zn 65.37	31 Gallium Ga 69.72	32 Germanium Ge 72.59	33 Arsenic As 74.922	34 Selenium Se 78.96	35 Bromine Br 79.904	36 Krypton Kr 83.80
37 Rubidium Rb 85.47	38 Strontium Sr 87.62	39 Yttrium Y 88.905	40 Zirconium Zr 91.22	41 Niobium Nb 92.906	42 Molybdenum Mo 95.94	43 Technetium Tc (97)	44 Ruthenium Ru 101.07	45 Rhodium Rh 102.905	46 Palladium Pd 106.4	47 Silver Ag 107.87	48 Cadmium Cd 112.40	49 Indium In 114.82	50 Tin Sn 118.69	51 Antimony Sb 121.75	52 Tellurium Te 127.60	53 Iodine I 126.9044	54 Xenon Xe 131.30
55 Cesium Cs 132.905	56 Barium Ba 137.34	57–71 Lanthanide Series (see below)	72 Hafnium Hf 178.49	73 Tantalum Ta 180.948	74 Tungsten W 183.85	75 Rhenium Re 186.2	76 Osmium Os 190.2	77 Iridium Ir 192.20	78 Platinum Pt 195.09	79 Gold Au 196.967	80 Mercury Hg 200.59	81 Thallium Tl 204.37	82 Lead Pb 207.19	83 Bismuth Bi 208.980	84 Polonium Po (209)	85 Astatine At (210)	86 Radon Rn (222)
87 Francium Fr (223)	88 Radium Ra (226)	89–103 Actinide Series (see below)															

Lanthanide Series

57 Lanthanum La 138.91	58 Cerium Ce 140.12	59 Praseodymium Pr 140.907	60 Neodymium Nd 144.24	61 Promethium Pm (145)	62 Samarium Sm 150.35	63 Europium Eu 151.96	64 Gadolinium Gd 157.25	65 Terbium Tb 158.924	66 Dysprosium Dy 162.50	67 Holmium Ho 164.930	68 Erbium Er 167.26	69 Thulium Tm 168.934	70 Ytterbium Yb 173.04	71 Lutetium Lu 174.97

Actinide Series

89 Actinium Ac (227)	90 Thorium Th 232.038	91 Protactinium Pa (231)	92 Uranium U 238.04	93 Neptunium Np (237)	94 Plutonium Pu (239)	95 Americium Am (243)	96 Curium Cm (247)	97 Berkelium Bk (247)	98 Californium Cf (251)	99 Einsteinium Es (254)	100 Fermium Fm (253)	101 Mendelevium Md (252)	102 Nobelium No (253)	103 Lawrencium Lw (257)

Atomic weights corrected to correspond with values of the Commission on Atomic Weights as of 1963.

705

dealing with diseases of the periodontium and their treatment. Also **per·i·o·don·tia,** per″ē·o·don′sha, per″ē·o·don′shē·a.—**per·i·o·don·tic,** a.—**per·i·o·don·tist,** per″ē·o·don′tist, n.

per·i·o·don·ti·um, per″ē·o·don′shum, per″ē·o·don′shē·um, n. pl. **per·i·o·don·tia.** Dentistry, the bone, gum, and connective tissue around a tooth. Also **par·o·don·ti·um.**

per·i·o·nych·i·um, per″ē·ō·nik′ē·um, n. pl. **per·i·o·nych·i·a,** per″ē·ō·nik′ē·a. Anat. the skin adjoining the sides and base of a fingernail or toenail.

per·i·os·te·um, per″ē·os′tē·um, n. pl. **per·i·os·te·a,** per″ē·os′tē·a. [Gr. peri, about, and osteon, bone.] Anat. a vascular membrane investing and nourishing the bones of animals.—**per·i·os·te·al,** a.

per·i·os·ti·tis, per″ē·o·stī′tis, n. Pathol. inflammation of the periosteum.—**per·i·os·tit·ic,** per″ē·o·stit′ik, a.

per·i·ot·ic, per″ē·ō′tik, per″ē·ot′ik, a. [Gr. peri, around, and ons (ōt-), ear.] Anat. Surrounding the ear; noting or pertaining to certain bones or bony elements which form or help to form a protective capsule for the internal ear, being usually confluent or fused, and in man constituting part of the temporal bone.

per·i·pa·tet·ic, per″i·pa·tet′ik, a. [L. peripateticus, < Gr. peripatētikós, walking about (with reference to the practice of Aristotle while teaching), < peripatien, walk about, < peri, about, and patein, tread, walk.] Walking about, perambulating, or itinerant; (cap.) of or pertaining to the philosophy or the followers of Aristotle.—n. One who walks or travels about; (cap.) a disciple of the Aristotelian school of philosophy.—**per·i·pa·tet·i·cal·ly,** adv.—**per·i·pa·tet·i·cism,** n.

pe·riph·er·al, pe·rif′ėr·al, a. Pertaining to, situated in, or constituting the periphery; dealing with the relatively minor or secondary aspects of a situation or thing; as, peripheral comments on the broadcast; anat. relating to the external or outer surface. Also **pe·i·pher·ic,** per″i·fer′ik.—**pe·riph·er·al·ly,** adv.

pe·riph·er·y, pe·rif′e·rē, n. pl. **pe·riph·er·ies.** [L.L. peripheria, < Gr. periphéreia, < peripherein, carry around, < peri, around, and phérein, bear.] The circumference of a circle or the line forming the boundary of any rounded or closed figure; the external boundary of any surface or area; the external surface or outside of a body; the relatively minor or secondary aspects of a situation or thing, as: Initial reports dealt with the periphery of the issue.

pe·riph·ra·sis, pe·rif′ra·sis, n. pl. **pe·riph·ra·ses,** pe·rif′ra·sēz″. [Gr. periphrasis—peri, about, and phrazō, to speak.] A roundabout phrase or expression; circumlocution; the use of more words than are necessary to express the idea. Also **per·i·phrase,** per′i·frāz″.

per·i·phras·tic, per″i·fras′tik, a. Having the character of or characterized by periphrasis; circumlocutory; gram. denoting a construction formed by replacing an inflected form with a phrase, as 'the book of Jim' for 'Jim's book.'—**per·i·phras·ti·cal·ly,** adv.

pe·rique, pe·rēk′. n. [Louisiana Fr.] A rich-flavored tobacco produced in Louisiana.

per·i·sarc, per′i·särk″, n. [Gr. peri, around, and sárx (sarc-), flesh.] Zool. the horny or chitinous outer case or covering with which the soft parts of hydrozoans are often covered.—**per·i·sar·cal,** **per·i·sar·cous,** a.

per·i·scope, per′i·skōp″, n. [Gr. peri, round, skopeō, to look.] A tubular instrument containing a system of mirrors and lenses, used to view objects which are above

the line of direct vision, as when submerged in a submarine or a trench.

per·i·scop·ic, per″i·skop′ik, a. Opt. of a certain kind of lens, giving a clear image of objects viewed obliquely or peripherally. Of, pertaining to, or by means of a periscope. Also **per·i·scop·i·cal.**

per·ish, per′ish, v.i. [Fr. périr, ppr. périssant, to perish, < L. perio, to perish—per, through, and eo, to go.] To lose life, esp. in a violent manner; to die untimely; to be destroyed or ruined; to pass away; decay.

per·ish·a·ble, per′i·sha·bl, a. Liable to perish; subject to destruction or decay.—n. Usu. pl. goods subject to decay, esp. food.—**per·ish·a·bil·i·ty,** **per·ish·a·ble·ness,** n.—**per·ish·a·bly,** adv.

pe·ris·so·dac·tyl, pe·ris″ō·dak′til, pe·ris″ō·dak′til, a. [Gr. perissos, uneven, and daktylos, a finger or toe.] Having feet with an odd number of toes or digits, as the ungulate or hoofed mammals, the rhinoceros, tapir, and horse.—n. Also **pe·ris·so·dac·tyle,** pe·ris″ō·dak′til, pe·ris″ō·dak′til, pe·ris″ō·dak′til.—**pe·ris·so·dac·ty·lous,** a.

per·i·stal·sis, per″i·stal′sis, per″i·stal′sis, n. pl. **per·i·stal·ses,** per″i·stal′sēz, per″i·stal′sēz. Physiol. the automatic movement of constriction and relaxation of a tubelike muscular organ or system as the intestines, which slowly propels the contents forward.—**per·i·stal·tic,** per″i·stal′tik, per″i·stal′tik, a.—**per·i·stal·ti·cal·ly,** adv.

per·i·style, per′i·stīl″, n. [Gr. peri, about, and stylos, a column.] Arch. A series of columns surrounding a courtyard or a building; an open space enclosed by a series of columns.—**per·i·sty·lar,** a.

per·i·the·ci·um, per″i·thē′shē·um, per″i·thē′sē·um, n. pl. **per·i·the·ci·a,** per″i·thē′shē·a, per″i·thē′sē·a. [Gr. peri, around, and thēkē, a theca or case.] Bot. a globose or pear-shaped ascocarp or fructification in certain sac fungi, characterized by a definite small pore, as in the powdery mildew.—**per·i·the·ci·al,** a.

per·i·to·ne·um, per″i·to·nē′um, n. pl. **per·i·to·ne·ums, per·i·to·ne·a.** [Gr. peritonaion—peri, about, and teinō, to stretch.] Anat. a thin, smooth, serous membrane lining the whole internal surface of the abdomen and investing most of its viscera.—**per·i·to·ne·al,** **per·i·to·nae·al,** a.—**per·i·to·ne·al·ly,** **per·i·to·nae·al·ly,** adv.

per·i·to·ni·tis, per″i·to·nī′tis, n. Pathol. an inflammation of the peritoneum.

per·i·wig, per′i·wig″, n. [O.E. perriwig, perewake, perwicke, corrupted < Fr. perruque.] A small wig; a peruke.

per·i·win·kle, per′i·wing″kl, n. [O.E. pervinke, pervenke, Fr. pervenche, < L. pervinca, the periwinkle.] Bot. A creeping, evergreen ground cover, Vinca minor, in the dogbane family, characterized by symmetrical blue or white petals, which have a pinwheel appearance with a tiny star outlined in the center of the flower; any of several species of the genus Vinca. Also myrtle, vinca.

per·i·win·kle, per′i·wing″kl, n. [Origin obscure: cf. O.E. winewinclan, or pinewinclan, or pinewinclan, pl. sea snails, also E. winkle.] Zool. Any of various marine gastropods or sea snails, esp. Littorina littorea, which is used for food in Europe; the shell of these animals.

per·jure, pur′jėr, v.t.—perjured, perjuring. [L. perjuro—per-, and juro, to swear, per-, here conveying a bad sense as in perfidia, perfidy.] Usu. refl. To cause to be false to oaths or solemn promises; to cause to be guilty of perjury, as: The witness perjured himself.—**per·jur·er,** n.

per·ju·ry, pur′ju·rē, n. pl. **per·ju·ries.** The act of willfully making a false oath or

violating an oath or promise; law, the act of knowingly making a false statement on a matter material to the issue in question while under oath in a judicial proceeding—**per·ju·ri·ous,** pėr·jur′ē·us, a.—**per·ju·ri·ous·ly,** adv.

perk, purk, v.i. [W. perc, neat, trim, smart; cf. also pert, spruce, dapper.] To hold up the head jauntily; to regain one's liveliness or spirit, usu. with up; colloq. to percolate.—v.t. To make trim or smart; to raise, as the head, briskly or jauntily.—a. Jaunty.

perk·y, pur′kē, a.—perkier, perkiest. Trim; saucy; jaunty; spirited. Also **perk.**—**perk·i·ly,** adv.—**perk·i·ness,** n.

per·lite, pur′līt, n. Petrog. a form of vitreous rock, usu. occurring as a mass of enamellike globules. Also **pearlite.**—**per·lit·ic,** pėr·lit′ik, a.

per·ma·frost, pur′ma·frŏst″, pur′ma·frŏst″, n. Subsoil that is permanently frozen, occurring primarily in subarctic or arctic areas.

per·ma·nence, pur′ma·nens, n. The state or quality of being permanent; continuance.

per·ma·nen·cy, pur′ma·nen·sē, n. pl. **per·ma·nen·cies.** Permanence; a permanent thing.

per·ma·nent, pur′ma·nent, a. [L. permanens, permanent, < permaneo, to continue—per-, through, and maneo, to remain.] Continuing in the same state, or without any change that destroys the form or nature; durable; lasting; fixed.—**per·ma·nent·ly,** adv.—**per·ma·nent·ness,** n.

per·ma·nent, pur′ma·nent, n. A wave set in the hair by a chemical preparation and lasting for several months. Also **per·ma·nent wave.**

per·ma·ment mag·net, n. A magnet which does not lose its magnetism when removed from a magnetic field.

per·ma·nent press, n. A fabric finish reputed to possess permanent crease resistance; an article of clothing or a fabric possessing this finish.—a. Denoting or characteristic of such a fabric finish.

per·ma·nent tooth, n. Any of the teeth that supplant the milk teeth; in man, one of the 32 teeth that supplant the 20 temporary teeth of babyhood.

per·man·ga·nate, pėr·mang′ga·nāt″, n. [L. per-, intensive, and manganese.] Chem. a dark purple salt containing potassium, manganese, and oxygen, and used in solution as an oxidizer and disinfectant.

per·man·gan·ic ac·id, pur″man·gan′ik as′id, n. Chem. $HMnO_4$, an acid existing only in solution, and a powerful oxidizer.

per·me·a·bil·i·ty, pur″mē·a·bil′i·tē, n. The quality or state of being permeable; phys. the capacity or power of being traversed by magnetic lines of force.

per·me·a·ble, pur′mē·a·bl, a. Capable of or open to being permeated.—**per·me·a·ble·ness,** n.—**per·me·a·bly,** adv.

per·me·ance, pur′mē·ans, n. The act of permeating; permeation; phys. the conducting power of a magnetic circuit for magnetic flux, or the reciprocal of magnetic reluctance.—**per·me·ant,** pur′mē·ant, a. Permeating; penetrating; pervading.

per·me·ate, pur′mē·āt″, v.t.—permeated, permeating. [L. permeatus, pp. of permeare, < per-, through, and meare, go.] To pass through the substance or mass of; penetrate through the pores or interstices of; be diffused through; pervade; saturate.—v.i. To penetrate; diffuse itself.—**per·me·a·tion,** n.—**per·me·a·tive,** a.

Per·mi·an, pur′mē·an, a. [From Perm, in Russia, or that part of Russia which formed the ancient kingdom of Permia, where the series is largely developed.] Geol. Pertaining to the last period of the Paleozoic era in which this system was formed; denoting a system of rocks lying beneath the Triassic rocks, and immediately above the Carboniferous system, and forming the uppermost of the Paleozoic strata.—*n. Geol.* Permian period; Permian rock system. Part of the Finno-Ugric subfamily of Uralic languages, comprising Votyak, Zyrian, and others.

per·mill, pėr·mil′, *adv.* Per thousand. Also **per·mil.—per·mil·lage,** pėr·mil′ij, *n.*

per·mis·si·ble, pėr·mis′a·bl, *a.* That may be permitted; allowable.—**per·mis·si·bil·i·ty, per·mis·si·ble·ness,** *n.*—**per·mis·si·bly,** *adv.*

per·mis·sion, pėr·mish′an, *n.* [L. *permissio.*] The act of permitting or allowing; authorization; formal consent; leave.

per·mis·sive, pėr·mis′iv, *a.* Permitting or allowing; permitted; optional; tolerant of behavior which others would not allow; lenient.—**per·mis·sive·ly,** *adv.*—**per·mis·sive·ness,** *n.*

per·mit, pėr·mit′, *v.t.*—*permitted, permitting.* [L. *permittere* (pp. *permissus*), let go through, let go, let, < *per-,* through, and *mittere,* send.] To allow to do something, as: *Permit* me to explain. To allow to be done or occur, whether by giving express leave or by refraining from prohibiting or hindering, as: The law *permits* the sale of such drugs. To tolerate; to afford opportunity for, or admit of, as: Vents *permit* the escape of gases. To afford opportunity to, as: The weather did not *permit* the boat to land.—*v.i.* To grant leave or permission; allow liberty to do something; afford opportunity or possibility, as: Write when time *permits.* Allow or admit, usu. followed by *of;* as, statements that *permit* of no denial.—pėr′mit, pėr·mit′, *n.* A written order granting leave to do something; an authoritative or official certificate of permission; a license; permission or leave.—**per·mit·ter,** *n.*

per·mu·ta·tion, pėr″mū·tā′shan, *n.* [L. *permutatio(n-),* < *permutare.*] *Math.* the act of changing the order of a number of elements arranged in a particular order, as *abc* into *acb, bac, bca, cab,* or *cba,* or of arranging a number of elements in groups made up of equal numbers of the elements taken in different orders, as *a, b,* and *c* into *ab, ba, ac, ca, bc,* and *cb;* any of the resulting arrangements or groups. The act of permutating; alteration.—**per·mu·ta·tion·al,** *a.*

per·mute, pėr·mūt′, *v.t.*—*permuted, permuting.* [L. *permuto.*] To interchange; to change as regards order or arrangement; *math.* to subject to or undergo permutation.—**per·mut·a·ble,** *a.*

per·ni·cious, pėr·nish′us, *a.* [L. *perniciosus,* < *pernicies,* destruction—*per-,* thoroughly, and stem of *nex, necis,* death (as in *internecine*).] Injurious; destructive; deadly.—**per·ni·cious·ly,** *adv.*—**per·ni·cious·ness,** *n.*

per·ni·cious a·ne·mi·a, *n. Pathol.* a severe type of anemia caused by malformation of red blood cells, and resulting in lesions of the spinal cord, gastrointestinal, muscular, and nervous disturbances, and other complications.

per·o·ne·al, per″o·nē′al, *a.* [Gr. *peronē,* a brooch, also a name of the fibula.] *Anat.* pertaining to or positioned near the fibula.

per·o·rate, per′o·rāt″, *v.i.*—*perorated, perorating.* [L. *peroratus,* pp. of *perorare,* < *per-,* through, and *orare,* speak.] To speak or declaim at length; make a speech; to bring a speech to a close with a formal conclusion.

per·o·ra·tion, per″o·rā′shan, *n.* [L. *peroratio(n-).*] The concluding part of a speech or discourse, in which the speaker or writer sums up and stresses the principal points.—**per·o·ra·tion·al,** *a.*

per·ox·i·dase, pe·rok′si·dās″, pe·rok′si·dāz″, *n. Biochem.* an enzyme which acts as a

catalyst in the oxidation of certain compounds by decomposing organic peroxides.

per·ox·ide, pe·rok′sid, *n. Chem.* That oxide of a given element or radical which contains the greatest, or an unusual amount of oxygen; hydrogen peroxide.—*v.t.*—*peroxided, peroxiding.* To remove color from, as hair, by means of a peroxide.

per·pend, pur′pend, *n.* [Fr. *parpaing, parpain,* < *par,* through, and *pan,* the side of a wall.] A long stone or brick reaching through the thickness of a wall and visible on both sides. Also **par·pen, per·pent.**

per·pen·dic·u·lar, pur″pen·dik′ū·lėr, *a.* [L. *perpendicularis,* < *perpendiculum,* plumb line, < *per-,* through, and *pendere,* hang.] Being at right angles with the plane of the horizon; vertical; upright; sheer or steep, as a mountain side; *geom.* meeting a given line or surface at right angles; (*often cap.*), *arch.* noting or pertaining to a style of architecture, the last stage of English Gothic, in which most of the chief lines of the tracery intersect at right angles.—*n.* A perpendicular line or plane; upright position; an instrument for indicating the vertical line from any point; *geom.* a straight line meeting a given line or surface at right angles.—**per·pen·dic·u·lar·i·ty,** *n.*—**per·pen·dic·u·lar·ly,** *adv.*

per·pe·trate, pur′pi·trāt″, *v.t.*—*perpetrated, perpetrating.* [L. *perpetro—per-,* through, and *patro,* to finish or perform; same root as *pater,* father.] To do, execute, or perform, as a criminal act or a hoax; to be guilty of; to commit.—**per·pe·tra·tion,** *n.*—**per·pe·tra·tor,** *n.*

per·pet·u·al, pėr·pech′ö·al, *a.* [O.Fr. *perpetuel* (Fr. *perpétuel*), < L. *perpetualis,* < *perpetuus,* continuing throughout, appar. < *per-,* through, and *petere,* seek.] Continuing or enduring forever or indefinitely; eternal; permanent; continuing or continued without intermission or interruption; uninterrupted; continuous; *hort.* blooming more or less continuously throughout the season or the year; *phys.* pertaining to the motion of a theoretical mechanism that would operate continuously.—*n.* A hybrid rose of perpetual bloom.—**per·pet·u·al·ly,** *adv.*

per·pet·u·al cal·en·dar, *n.* A calendar covering a long span of years and so devised that the day of the week for any given date may be readily determined.

per·pet·u·ate, pėr·pech′ö·āt″, *v.t.*—*perpetuated, perpetuating.* [L. *perpetuo, perpetuatum.*] To make perpetual; to cause to endure or to be continued indefinitely; to preserve from extinction or oblivion.—**per·pet·u·a·ble,** *a.*—**per·pet·u·a·tion,** *n.*—**per·pet·u·a·tor,** *n.*

per·pe·tu·i·ty, pur″pi·tö′i·tē, pur″pi·tū′i·tē, *n. pl.* **per·pe·tu·i·ties.** [O.Fr. *perpetuite* (Fr. *perpetuité*), < L. *perpetuitas,* < *perpetuus.*] The state or character of being perpetual; endless or indefinitely long duration or existence; something that is perpetual; a perpetual annuity. *Law,* of property, the condition of being inalienable perpetually, or for a period beyond certain limits fixed, or conceived as being fixed, by the general law; property so conditioned.

per·plex, pėr·pleks′, *v.t.* [L. *perplexus,* entangled, confused, < *per-,* through, and *plexus,* pp. of *plectere,* plait, interweave.] To confuse mentally; to cause to be bewildered over what is not understood or certain; to render complicated or confused, as a matter or question; hamper with complications, confusion, or uncertainty.—**per·plex·ing,** *a.*—**per·plex·ing·ly,** *adv.*

per·plexed, pėr·plekst′, *a.* Bewildered or puzzled; at a loss for what to think or do; involved or confused.—**per·plex·ed·ly,** pėr·plek′sid·lē, *adv.*

per·plex·i·ty, pėr·plek′si·tē, *n. pl.* **per·plex·i·ties.** The state of being perplexed, puzzled, or at a loss; a circumstance or thing that perplexes; the state of being intricate or involved.

per·qui·site, pur′kwi·zit, *n.* [M.L. *perquisitum,* prop. neut. of L. *perquisitus,* pp. of *perquirere,* seek diligently for, < *per-,* through, and *quaerere,* seek.] An incidental fee or profit over and above fixed income, salary, or wages; anything customarily supposed to be allowed or left to an employee or servant as an incidental advantage of the position held; something advantageous, claimed as a right.

per·ron, per′on, *Fr.* pe·RAN′, *n.* [Fr. < L.L. *petronus,* a perron, < L. and Gr. *petra,* a stone.] *Arch.* an external platform and stairway by which access is given to the entrance door of a building.

per·ry, per′ē, *n. pl.* **per·ries.** [Fr. *poiré,* perry, < *poire,* L. *pirum,* a pear.] *Chiefly Brit.* a fermented liquor made from the juice of pears and resembling cider.

per·salt, pur′salt″, *n. Chem.* In a series of salts or a given metal or radical, that salt in which the metal or radical has a high, or the highest degree of apparent valence; a salt derived from a peracid.

per se, pėr sē′, pėr sā′, *adv.* [L.] By itself; inherently or intrinsically.

per·se·cute, pur′se·kūt″, *v.t.*—*persecuted, persecuting.* [Fr. *persecuter,* < L. *persequor, persecutus,* to persecute—*per-,* intens., and *sequor,* to follow.] To harass or afflict with repeated acts of cruelty or annoyance; to afflict persistently; to afflict or punish because of particular opinions or adherence to a particular creed or mode of worship.—**per·se·cu·tive,** *a.*—**per·se·cu·tor,** *n.*

per·se·cu·tion, pur″se·kū′shan, *n.* The act or practice of persecuting; the state of being persecuted.

per·se·ver·ance, pur″se·vēr′ans, *n.* [L. *perseverantia.*] The act or habit of persevering; persistence in anything undertaken; *Calvinistic theol.* the continuance in a state of grace of the elect of God.

per·se·vere, pur″se·vēr′, *v.i.*—*persevered, persevering.* [L. *persevero,* < *perseverus,* very severe or strict—*per-,* intens., and *severus,* severe, strict.] To continue resolutely in any enterprise undertaken, despite difficulties encountered; to pursue steadily any design or course begun.—**per·se·ver·ing,** *a.*—**per·se·ver·ing·ly,** *adv.*

Per·sian, pur′zhan, pur′shan, *a.* Pertaining to Persia, a country in southwest Asia now called Iran; referring to the language, culture, or people of Persia.—*n.* The language of, or a native or resident of Persia.

Per·sian cat, *n.* A breed of domestic cat developed in Persia, with long silky hair, a round head, and short legs.

Per·sian lamb, *n.* A lamb of the Asiatic karakul breed of sheep. The shiny, curled fleece of this lamb, used as a fur; also *caracul.*

per·si·flage, pur′si·fläzh″, *Fr.* peR·sē·fläzh′, *n.* [Fr. < *persifler* to quiz—L. *per-,* and *sibilare,* to hiss.] Idle, bantering talk; frivolous treatment of any subject, serious or otherwise.

per·sim·mon, pėr·sim′on, *n.* [Algonquian Ind.] Any of several trees of the genus *Diospyros,* in the ebony family, characterized by a very hard wood and an edible plumlike fruit which is sweet and slightly astringent when ripe, esp. *D. kaki,* the Japanese persimmon, and the N. American species, *D. virginiana,* cultivated in California and the Gulf states; the plumlike fruit.

per·sist, pėr·sist′, pėr·zist′, *v.i.* [Fr. *persister,* L. *persisto—per-,* through, and *sisto,* to stand.] To continue steadily and firmly in the pursuit of any business or course commenced; to continue in the face of some amount of opposition; to persevere;

---

a- fat, fāte, fär, fâre, fall;   **e-** met, mē, mēre, hėr;   **i-** pin, pīne;   **o-** not, nōte, möve;   **u-** tub, cūbe, bull;   **oi-** oil;   **ou-** pound.

to endure; to be insistent; as, to *persist* in one's demands.—**per·sist·er**, *n.*

per·sist·ence, pėr·sis′tens, pėr·zis′tens, *n.* The state of persisting or of being persistent; steady continuance in a course; perseverance; the continuance of an effect after the cause which first gave rise to it is removed. Also **per·sist·en·cy**.

per·sist·ent, pėr·sis′tent, pėr·zis′tent, *a.* Inclined to persist; persevering; tenacious of purpose; continuous; *bot.* remaining after maturity, without withering or falling off; *zool.* continuing to function throughout the life span, as the gills of fish.—**per·sist·ent·ly**, *adv.*

per·snick·et·y, pėr·snik′i·tē, *a. Colloq.* Finicky; extremely fastidious; overly precise; demanding great care and precision. Also **per·nick·et·y**.

per·son, pur′son, *n.* [O.Fr. *persone* (Fr. *personne*), < L. *persona*, actor's mask, character acted, personage, person, M.L. *parson*: cf. *parson*.] A human being, whether man, woman, or child; a human being as distinguished from other animals or a thing; the self or individual personality of a human being; the living body of a human being; the body in its external aspect; as, lovely in face and *person*; a character, part, or role sustained on the stage or in real life; one of the characters in a play or story; as, a *person* of the drama; a human being regarded as inferior; formerly, a personage. *Philos.* a self-conscious or rational being; *law*, an individual human being or a corporate body having rights and duties before the law; *theol.* any of the three hypostases or modes of being in the Trinity; *gram.* the form or inflection of a pronoun or verb that indicates the speaker (first *person*), one spoken to (second *person*), or a person or thing spoken of (third *person*).—**in per·son**, in one's own bodily presence.

per·so·na, pėr·sō′na, *n.* pl. **per·so·nae**, **per·so·nas**, pėr·sō′nē. [L.] *Usu. pl.* the characters represented in a work of fiction, as a play, story, or novel; dramatis personae. *Psychol.* the social role or façade a person assumes in satisfying the requirements of his environment, pl. **per·so·nas**.

per·son·a·ble, pur′so·na·bl, *a.* Having an attractive appearance; having a pleasant personality or disposition.—**per·son·a·ble·ness**, *n.*

per·son·age, pur′so·nij, *n.* A man or woman of distinction; as, an illustrious *personage*; an entity regarded as having an individuality like that of a human being; as, a divine or a mythological *personage*; a character in a fictional or historical work; a person.

per·so·na gra·ta, pėr·sō′na grä′ta, pėr·sō′na grä′ta, L. peR·sō′nä grä′tä, *n.* pl. **per·so·nae gra·tae**, pėr·sō′nē grä′tē, pėr·sō′nē grä′tē, L. peR·sō′nī grä′tī. [L.] An acceptable person; *govt.* a diplomatic envoy whose presence is welcomed by the government of the foreign country to which he is sent.

per·son·al, pur′so·nal, *a.* [L. *personalis.*] Pertaining to a person as distinct from a thing; relating to, characteristic of, or affecting some individual person; private; applying to the person, character, or conduct of an individual, generally in a disparaging manner; as, *personal* remarks; belonging to face and figure; as, *personal* charm; done in person, not by representative; as, a *personal* interview; *law*, pertaining to possessions not fixed or permanent in nature: opposed to *real*; *gram.* denoting or pointing to the person; as, a *personal* pronoun.—*n.* A news item or advertisement concerning a person or persons. Abbr. *pers.*

per·son·al ef·fects, *n.* The private possessions of an individual, as clothing or jewelry.

per·son·al e·qua·tion, *n.* The tendency to bias or error in observation or interpretation, due to differences in individuals.

per·son·al·ism, pur′so·na·liz″um, *n.* A philosophy which emphasizes the person or the personality as the supreme value and the ultimate reality. Also **per·son·al·i·de·al·ism**.—**per·son·al·ist**, *n.*—**per·son·al·is·tic**, *a.*

per·son·al·i·ty, pur″so·nal′i·tē, *n.* pl. **per·son·al·i·ties**. The sum of characteristics that constitute an individual; the state of existing as an intelligent being; a person of distinction; *usu. pl.* a remark, usu. disparaging, reflecting on the conduct, character, or appearance of some person; as, to indulge in *personalities*.

per·son·al·ize, pur′son·al·īz″, *v.t.*—**personalized**, **personalizing**. To make personal; to apply to oneself; to mark with one's initials or name; to personify.

per·son·al·ly, pur′son·al·ē, *adv.* In a personal manner; in person; with respect to an individual; as regards one's personal existence or individuality.

per·son·al pro·noun, *n. Gram.* a pronoun that is inflected for person, gender, number, and case, and that denotes the speaker or speakers, one or more persons spoken to, or one or more persons spoken about, as, *I, you, he, she, we, they.*

per·son·al prop·er·ty, *n. Law.* Things belonging to the person, as money, jewels, or furniture, as distinguished from *real* property such as land and houses; movables; chattels.

per·son·al·ty, pur′so·nal·tē, *n.* pl. **per·son·al·ties.** *Law*, personal property, as distinguished from *realty* or *real property.*

per·so·na non gra·ta, pėr·sō′na non grä′ta, pėr·sō′na non grä′ta, L. peR·sō′nä nōn grä′tä, *n.* pl. **per·so·nae non gra·tae**, pėr·sō′nē non grä′tē, pėr·sō′nē non grä′tē, L. peR·sō′nī nōn grä′tī. [L.] An unacceptable or unwelcome person; *govt.* a diplomatic envoy whose presence is unwelcomed by the government of the foreign country to which he is sent.

per·son·ate, pur′so·nāt″, *v.t.*—**personated**, **personating.** To assume the character or appearance of, whether in real life or on the stage; to represent by an assumed appearance; to personify, as in literature; impersonate. *Law*, to mimic the appearance and mannerisms of, with malicious or fraudulent intent.—**per·son·a·tion**, *n.*—**per·son·a·tive**, *a.*—**per·son·a·tor**, *n.*

per·son·ate, pur′so·nit, pur′so·nāt″, *a.* [L. *personatus*, masked, < *persona*: see *person*.] *Bot.* Masklike, as the bilabiate corolla of some flowers; having the lower lip pushed upward so as to close the opening between the lips, as in the snapdragon.

per·son·i·fi·ca·tion, pėr·son″i·fi·kā′shan, *n.* The act of personifying; that which personifies; a person or thing exemplifying a quality; embodiment; *art*, the representation of inanimate objects or abstract ideas as human beings; *rhet.* attributing human qualities or characteristics to abstract ideas or inanimate objects.

per·son·i·fy, pėr·son′i·fī″, *v.t.*—**personified**, **personifying.** [L. *persona*, and *facio*, to make.] To treat or regard as human; to represent, as an abstract or inanimate thing, as if endowed with the character of a rational being; typify.—**per·son·i·fi·er**, *n.*

per·son·nel, pur″so·nel′, *n.* [Fr., < *personne*, a person.] The body of persons engaged or employed in any occupation, service, or work.—*a.* Of or relating to personnel; as, the *personnel* department.

per·spec·tive, pėr·spek′tiv, *n.* [Fr. *perspectif*, < L. *perspicio, perspectum—per-*, through, and *specio*, to view.] The art or science of drawing or otherwise representing objects or scenes on a plane so that they appear to have their natural dimensions and spatial relations; the appearance of an object with regard to dimensions and spatial position, as affected by distance from the eye; a representation of an object or objects that gives the illusion of space or depth; view or vista; the interrelationships or proportionate significance of facts or information as considered from a particular point of view; the ability to evaluate information, situations, and the like with respect to their meaningfulness or comparative importance.—*a.* Pertaining to the art of perspective; marked by or rendered in perspective.—**aer·i·al per·spec·tive**, a planar representation of distance or depth achieved by modification of light, shade, and color: distinguished from *linear perspective.*—**per·spec·tive·ly**, *adv.*

per·spi·ca·cious, pur″spi·kā′shus, *a.* [L. *perspicax, perspicācis, perspicio*, to look through.] Having keen mental perception or discernment.—**per·spi·ca·cious·ly**, *adv.*—**per·spi·ca·cious·ness**, **per·spi·cac·i·ty**, pur″spi·kas′i·tē, *n.*

per·spi·cu·i·ty, pur″spi·kū′i·tē, *n.* [L. *perspicuitas.*] The quality of being perspicuous; clearness; perspicacity.—**per·spic·u·ous**, pėr·spik′ū·us, *a.* [L. *perspicuus.*] Clear to the understanding; lucid.—**per·spic·u·ous·ly**, *adv.*—**per·spic·u·ous·ness**, *n.*

per·spi·ra·tion, pur′spi·rā′shan, *n.* The process or act of perspiring; the watery fluid or sweat excreted from the pores.—**per·spir·a·to·ry**, pėr·spī′ra·tōr″ē, pėr·spī′ra·tar″e, *a.*

per·spire, pėr·spīėr′, *v.i.*—**perspired**, **perspiring.** [L. *perspiro—per-*, through, and *spiro*, to breathe.] To excrete perspiration through the pores of the skin; to sweat.—*v.t.* To emit or exude through pores.

per·suade, pėr·swād′, *v.t.*—**persuaded**, **persuading.** [L. *persuadeo—per-*, effectively, and *suadeo*, to advise, urge.] To influence, move, or prevail on by argument, advice, or expostulation to a certain belief or course of action; to convince.—**per·suad·a·ble**, *a.*—**per·suad·er**, pėr·swā′dėr, *n.*

per·sua·sion, pėr·swā′zhan, *n.* [L. *persuasio, persuasionis.*] The act or power of persuading; the state of being persuaded; a conviction or belief; a religious creed or system of beliefs; a sect or party adhering to a creed or system of beliefs.—**per·sua·si·ble**, pėr·swā′si·bl, *a.* [L. *persuasibilis.*] Capable of being persuaded; persuadable.

per·sua·sive, pėr·swā′siv, *a.* Having the power of persuading; tending to persuade or influence.—*n.* That which persuades.—**per·sua·sive·ly**, *adv.*—**per·sua·sive·ness**, *n.*

pert, purt, *a.* [Partly < O.Fr. *apert, appert* (as in *malapert*), < L. *apertus*, open; partly < W. *pert, perc*, trim, spruce.] Impertinent or forward; saucy; lively; smart; chic.—**pert·ly**, *adv.*—**pert·ness**, *n.*

per·tain, pėr·tān′, *v.i.* [O.Fr. *partenir*, < L. *pertinere*, extend, reach, relate.] To have reference or relation; to relate; as, documents which *pertain* to the case; to belong or be connected as a part, adjunct, possession, or attribute; to belong properly or fittingly; to be appropriate.

per·ti·na·cious, pur″ti·nā′shus, *a.* [L. *pertinax—per-*, intens., and *teneo*, to hold.] Holding or adhering tenaciously to any opinion, purpose, or design; obstinate; stubborn; perversely persistent.—**per·ti·na·cious·ly**, *adv.*—**per·ti·na·cious·ness**, **per·ti·nac·i·ty**, pur″ti·nas′i·tē, *n.*

per·ti·nent, pur′ti·nent, *a.* [L. *pertinens*, ppr. of *pertineo*, to pertain.] Pertaining to the subject or matter in hand; relevant.—**per·ti·nence**, **per·ti·nen·cy**, *n.*—**per·ti·nent·ly**, *adv.*

per·turb, pėr·tu̟rb′, v.t. [L. perturbo—per-, intens., and turbo, to disturb; < turba, a crowd.] To disturb, esp. in the mind; to disquiet; to agitate; to cause to be disordered or confused; to derange.—**per·-turb·a·ble**, a.

per·tur·ba·tion, pu̟r″tėr·bā′shan, n. [L. perturbatio.] The act of perturbing or state of being perturbed; mental uneasiness or anxiety; something that causes mental disquiet. Astron. a disturbance in the regular motion of a celestial body, the result of a force additional to that which causes the regular motion.—**per·tur·ba·tion·al**, a.

per·tus·sis, pėr·tus′is, n. [L. per-, intens., and tussis, a cough.] Pathol. whooping cough.—**per·tus·sal**, a.

pe·ruke, pe·rŏk′, n. [Fr. perruque, It. perucca, It. dial. pilucca, peruke, < L. pilus, hair. Periwig is a corruption of perruque, and its final syllable has become wig.] A type of wig, esp. that worn by men in the 17th, 18th, and early 19th centuries. Also periwig.

pe·rus·al, pe·rö′zal, n. The act of perusing or reading carefully; a reading; scrutiny.

pe·ruse, pe·röz′, v.t.—perused, perusing. [< prefix per-, intens., and use.] To read with careful attention; to read through; to examine carefully.—**pe·rus·er**, n.

Pe·ru·vi·an bark, pe·rö′vē·an bärk′, n. Cinchona.

per·vade, pėr·vād′, v.t.—pervaded, pervading. [L. pervadere (pp. pervasus), < per-, through, and vadere, go.] To extend presence, activity, or influence throughout; to diffuse or permeate; to go, pass, or spread through, as: Fear pervaded the audience.—**per·vad·er**, n.—**per·va·sion**, pėr·vā′zhan, n.—**per·va·sive**, pėr·vā′siv, a.—**per·va·sive·ly**, adv.—**per·va·sive·ness**, n.

per·verse, pėr·vu̟rs′, a. [L. perversus, < perverto, to pervert, corrupt, overthrow—per-, and verto, to turn.] Purposely deviating from accepted or expected behavior or opinion; contrary; wicked or wayward; stubborn; cross or petulant.—**per·verse·ly**, adv.—**per·verse·ness**, n.

per·ver·sion, pėr·vu̟r′zhan, pėr·vu̟r′shan, n. [L. perversio(n), < pervertere.] The act of perverting; the state of being perverted; a perverted form of something; abnormal sexual instinct, desire, or activity; pathol. a change to what is unnatural or abnormal.

per·ver·si·ty, pėr·vu̟r′si·tē, n. pl. per·ver·si·ties. [L. perversitas.] State or quality of being perverse; an instance of being perverse; perverseness.

per·ver·sive, pėr·vu̟r′siv, a. Tending or having power to pervert.

per·vert, pėr·vu̟rt′, v.t. [O.Fr. Fr. pervertir, < L. pervertere (pp. perversus), turnabout, overturn, corrupt.] To turn away from the right course; to lead astray morally or to corrupt; to lead into mental error or false judgment; to bring over to a religious belief regarded as false or wrong; to turn from the proper to an improper use or purpose; to misapply; to distort; to misinterpret, esp. willfully; to bring to a less excellent state; to debase; to affect with perversion; pathol. to change to what is unnatural or abnormal.—pu̟r′vėrt, n. A sexual deviate; one who has been perverted; one who has been brought over to a religious belief regarded as false or wrong; pathol. one affected with perversion.—**per·vert·ed**, pėr·vu̟r′tid, a. Turned from what is right; wicked; misguided; distorted; affected with or due to perversion; pathol. changed to or being of an unnatural or abnormal kind.—**per·vert·ed·ly**, adv.—**per·vert·ed·ness**, n.—**per·vert·er**, n.—**per·vert·i·bil·i·ty**, n.—**per·vert·i·ble**, a.—**per·vert·i·bly**, adv.

per·vi·ous, pu̟r′vē·us, a. [L. pervius—per-, through, and via, a way.] Capable of being penetrated; permeable; allowing an entrance or a passage through; open to suggestion or argument.—**per·vi·ous·-ness**, n.

pes, pēz, n. pl. **pe·des**, pē′dēz. [L.] Zool. A foot; a part resembling or serving as a foot.

Pe·sach, pä′säch, n. Passover. Also **Pe·sah.**

pes·ky, pes′kē, a.—peskier, peskiest. [Origin uncertain; cf. pest.] Colloq. Troublesome; annoying; vexing.—**pesk·i·ly**, adv.—**pesk·i·ness**, n.

pes·sa·ry, pes′a·rē, n. pl. **pes·sa·ries.** [M.L. pessarium, < L. pessum, Gr. pessos, a small oval stone, a medicated plug.] A device introduced into the vagina to correct uterine displacement; a vaginal suppository. A contraceptive device; also diaphragm.

pes·si·mism, pes′i·miz″um, n. [L. pessimus, the worst.] The tendency to take the most unfavorable view of situations or actions: opposed to optimism. Philos. the belief that man is imperfectible; the attitude that evil and pain are universal in this world and that life is essentially unhappy.—**pes·si·mist**, pes′i·mist, n.—**pes·si·mis·tic**, pes″i·mis′tik, a.—**pes·si·mis·ti·cal·ly**, adv.

pest, pest, n. [Fr. peste, < L. pestis, a plague, a pest (whence pestilent, pestiferous); same root as perdo, to destroy.] Anything very noxious or destructive, as certain insects or plants; a mischievous, annoying, or destructive person; a nuisance; an epidemic or plague.

pes·ter, pes′tėr, v.t. [O.Fr. empestrer, orig. to shackle the feet of a horse at pasture, < L.L. pastorium, foot shackles, < L. pastor, a shepherd.] To annoy persistently with trivialities; to irritate; to bother.

pest·hole, pest′hōl″, n. An insanitary place open to the outbreak and spread of disease.

pest·house, pest′hous″, n. Archaic, a hospital for persons infected with bubonic plague or other pestilential disease.

pest·i·cide, pes′ti·sīd″, n. Any substance, as a chemical poison, used to destroy weeds, insects, rodents, or other noxious plants or animals.—**pes·ti·cid·al**, a.

pes·tif·er·ous, pe·stif′ėr·us, a. [L. pestis, plague, and fero, to produce.] Pestilential; infectious; noxious or evil in any manner; colloq. irritating or bothersome.—**pes·tif·er·ous·ly**, adv.—**pes·tif·er·ous·ness**, n.

pes·ti·lence, pes′ti·lens, n. [L. pestilentia, < pestilens, pestilent, < pestis, plague.] Any contagious disease that is epidemic and usu. deadly, esp. the bubonic plague; fig. anything evil or destructive.

pes·ti·lent, pes′ti·lent, a. [L. pestilens.] Pestilential; infectious; noxious to morals or society; pernicious; troublesome.—**pes·ti·lent·ly**, adv.

pes·ti·len·tial, pes″ti·len′shal, a. Producing or tending to produce infectious disease; having the nature of an infectious and deadly disease; destructive; troublesome.—**pes·ti·len·tial·ly**, adv.

pes·tle, pes′l, pes′tl, n. [O.Fr. pestel, < L. pistillum, < pinsere (pp. pistus), pound, bray.] An instrument for breaking, grinding, or mixing substances in a mortar; any of various mechanical appliances for pounding, stamping, and similar operations.—v.t.—pestled, pestling. To pound or pulverize with or as with a pestle.—v.i. To work with a pestle.

pet, pet, n. [< Ir. peat, Gael. peata, a pet, or perh. < petty, Fr. petit, little.] A tame animal kept for companionship; a favorite child or other pampered or indulged individual; something cherished.—a. Cared for or kept as a pet; favorite; as, a pet theory; personal or particular; as, a pet peeve.—v.t.—petted, petting. To fondle; to indulge; colloq. to kiss and caress.—v.i.

Colloq. to kiss, fondle, or caress in an intimate manner.—**pet·ter**, n

pet, pet, n. [Possibly an abbr. form of petulant or petulance.] A slight fit of peevishness.—v.i.—petted, petting. To fret or sulk.

pet·al, pet′al, n. [< Gr. petalon, a leaf, < petalos, spread out, expanded; same root as in patent.] Bot. one of the leaflike divisions of the inner floral envelope or corolla of a flower, often colored and showy.—**pet·aled**, **pet·alled**, a.—**pet·al·like**, a.

pet·al·oid, pet′a·loid″, a. Bot. Petallike; resembling a petal in shape or appearance.—**pet·al·ous**, pet′a·lus, a. Bot. Having petals; petaled.

pe·tard, pi·tärd′, n. [Fr. pétard, < péter, to break wind, bounce, < L. pedo, peditum, with same sense.] A metal cone filled with explosives and used formerly in times of warfare to blow up a gate or barrier; a type of firecracker.

pet·a·sus, pet′a·sus, n. pl. **pet·a·sus·es.** [Gr. petasos.] A broad-brimmed hat worn in ancient Greece; the winged cap of Mercury. Also **pet·a·sos**, pet′a·sos, pet′a·sos″.

pet·cock, pet′kok″, n. A small cock or faucet, as for draining off water or oil from a cylinder or for releasing excess air pressure from a tank, radiator, or the like. Also **pet cock.**

pe·te·chi·a, pi·tē′kē·a, pi·tek′ē·a, n. pl. **pe·te·chi·ae**, pi·tē′kē·ē, pi·tek′ē·ē. [N.L. < It. petecchia, purple spot in disease.] Pathol. a small purplish spot occurring on the skin or in certain membranes, caused by hemorrhaging.—**pe·te·chi·al**, a.—**pe·te·chi·ate**, pi·tē′kē·it, pi·tē′kē·āt″, pi·tek′ē·it, pi·tek′ē·āt″, a.

pe·ter, pē′tėr, v.i. [Origin unknown.] Colloq. to diminish gradually and then disappear or cease, followed by out.

pe·ter pan col·lar, n. (Often cap.) a round, flat, close-fitting collar used on the clothing of women and children.

Pe·ter's pence, pē′tėrz pens′, n. [From St. Peter, as the first bishop of Rome.] A voluntary contribution made annually to the Pope by Roman Catholics; formerly, an annual tax or tribute, orig. of a penny, paid to the papal see at Rome by each English householder having land of a certain value. Also **Pe·ter pence.**

pet·i·ole, pet′ē·ōl″, n. [Fr., < L. petiolus, a dim. < pes, pedis, a foot.] Bot. a leafstalk; the stalk connecting the blade of the leaf with the branch or stem. Zool. the constricting area or stalklike structure between the thorax and abdomen in some insects, as in the wasp.—**pet·i·o·lar**, pet·i·oled, a.—**pet·i·o·late**, pet·i·o·lat·ed, pet′ē·o·lāt″, a.

pet·i·o·lule, pet′ē·ol·ūl″, pet′ē·ol′ūl, n. [A dim. of petiole.] Bot. the stalk of a leaflet which is a part of a compound leaf.

pet·it, pet′ē, Fr. pe·tē′, a. [Fr., perh. < Celtic: cf. petty.] Law. Small; petty; minor.

pe·tite, pe·tēt′, a. [Fr., fem. of petit.] Little or tiny; small and shapely, esp. a woman or girl.—**pe·tite·ness**, n.

pet·it four, pet′ē fōr′, pet′ē fär′, Fr. pe·tē fōr′, n. pl. **pet·its fours**, **pet·it fours**, pet′ē fōrz′, pet′ē färz′, Fr. pe·tē fōr′. A small piece of cake, iced and decorated.

pe·ti·tion, pe·tish′an, n. [L. petitio, petitionis, < peto, petitum, to seek, attack.] A formal, written request or supplication to a superior authority soliciting some favor, grant, right, or mercy; an entreaty, supplication, or prayer, as to a superior in rank or power or to a deity; something requested or solicited; law, a written application, as for court action in certain legal proceedings.—v.t. To make a petition, request, or supplication to; to solicit.—v.i. To make or present a petition.—**pe·ti·tion·ar·y**, pe·tish′o·ner″ē, a. Resembling or containing a petition.—**pe·ti·tion·er**, n.

pet·it ju·ry, pet′ē jur̄′ē, *n. Law,* a group of citizens, usu. 12, impaneled to decide a civil or criminal case tried in court: distinguished from *grand jury.* Also **pet·ty ju·ry,** *traverse jury, trial jury.*

pe·tit mal, pe·tē′ mal′, *Fr.* pe·tē mäl′, *n. Pathol.* a mild form of epilepsy marked by short periods of unconsciousness and usu. involving no convulsions: distinguished from *grand mal.*

pet·it point, pet′ē point″, *n.* [Fr.] One of a variety of small embroidery stitches, as a tent stitch; needlework of this stitch, usu. done on canvas.

Pe·trar·chan son·net, pi·trär′kan son′it, *n.* [From Francesco *Petrarca* (E. *Petrarch*), It. poet, 1304-1374.] A particular sonnet form, originating in Italy and perfected by Petrarch, characterized by an octave rhyming *abbaabba* and a sestet rhyming variously, usu. *cdecde* or *cdccdc,* with the octave typically presenting the theme or problem and the sestet containing the resolution. Also *Italian sonnet.*

pet·rel, pe′trel, *n.* [Commonly associated with the apostle *Peter,* who "walked on the water" Mat. xiv. 29.] *Ornith.* a little black sea bird with white rump patches, in the family *Hydrobatidae,* sometimes found far out at sea, esp. two species of the eastern N. Atlantic, Leach's petrel and Wilson's petrel, the latter following in the wake of ships. See *storm petrel, stormy petrel.*

pe·tri dish, pe′trē dish″, *n.* [From Julius *Petri,* German bacteriologist, 1852-1922.] (*Sometimes cap.*) a round, shallow glass dish with a cover, used for holding bacterial cultures.

pet·ri·fac·tion, pe″tri·fak′shan, *n.* The act or process of petrifying, or turning to stone; the state of being petrified; something petrified. Also **pet·ri·fi·ca·tion,** pe″tri·fi·kā′shan.—**pet·ri·fac·tive,** *a.*

pet·ri·fy, pe′tri·fī″, *v.t.*—*petrified, petrifying.* [L. *petra* (< Gr. *petra*), a stone or a rock (seen also in *petroleum, pier*), and *facio,* to make.] To convert to stone or stony substance, as by the infiltration and deposit of mineral matter; to turn into a fossil; to make callous or obdurate; to paralyze or stupefy with fear or amazement.—*v.i.* To become stone or of a stony hardness; to become paralyzed with fear.

pe·tro·chem·is·try, pe″trō·kem′i·strē, *n.* [(*petro*)leum and *chemistry.*] The branch of chemistry concerned with petroleum and the chemical products derived from petroleum and natural gas.—**pe·tro·chem·i·cal,** pe″trō·kem′i·kal, *a.*

pet·ro·glyph, pe′tro·glif″, *n.* [Gr. *pétra,* rock, and *glyphē,* carving.] A picture carved on a rock, esp. a prehistoric carving.

pe·trog·ra·phy, pi·trog′ra·fē, *n.* [Gr. *petros,* a stone, and *graphō,* to write.] The scientific classification and description of rocks, one of the branches of petrology. —**pe·trog·ra·pher,** *n.*—**pet·ro·graph·ic,** **pet·ro·graph·i·cal,** pe″tro·graf′ik, *a.*

pet·rol, pe′trol, *n.* [Fr. *petrole,* < M.L. *petroleum.*] *Brit.* gasoline.

pet·ro·la·tum, pe″tro·lā′tum, *n.* [N.L., < M.L. *petroleum.*] A purified, semisolid, unctuous substance obtained from petroleum and used in medical dressings and ointments, in explosives as a stabilizer, and as a rust preventive. Also **pe·tro·le·um jel·ly.**

pe·tro·le·um, pe·trō′lē·um, *n.* [M.L. < L. *petra,* rock, and *oleum,* oil.] An oily, dark-colored, flammable liquid which is a form of bitumen or a mixture of various hydrocarbons, occurring naturally in the upper strata of the earth in various parts of the world, and commonly obtained by drilling: used in its natural state or after treatment as a fuel, or separated by distillation into gasoline, naphtha, benzine, kerosene, or paraffin.

pe·trol·o·gy, pi·trol′o·jē, *n.* [Gr. *petros,* a rock, and *logos,* a treatise.] The branch of geology which determines the composition, structure, and history of rocks.—**pet·ro·log·ic,** **pet·ro·log·i·cal,** pe″tro·loj′ik, *a.*—**pet·ro·log·i·cal·ly,** *adv.*—**pe·trol·o·gist,** *n.*

pet·ro·nel, pe′tro·nel, *n.* [O.Fr. *petrinal, poictrinal,* < L. *pectus, pectoris,* the breast, being discharged with the stock placed against the breast.] A kind of carbine or large pistol used in the 15th century.

pe·tro·pro·tein, pe″trō·prō′tēn, pe″trō·prō′tē·in, *n.* A man-made edible protein obtained from bacteria fed on paraffin derived from petroleum.

pe·tro·sal, pi·trō′sal, *a.* [L. *petrosus.*] *Anat.* relating to the petrous portion of the temporal bone or to a homologous bone.

pet·rous, pe′trus, *a.* [L. *petrosus,* < *petra,* a stone.] Like stone; hard; stony. *Anat.* pertaining to the hard portion of the temporal bone in which the internal organs of hearing are situated; also *petrosal.*

pet·ti·coat, pet′ē·kōt″, *n.* An underskirt, worn by women and children; any skirt-like part or covering. *Elect.* an insulator part resembling a skirt.—*a.* Female or feminine; as, a kind of petticoat council.

pet·ti·fog, pet′ē·fog″, pet′ē·fag″, *v.i.*—*pettifogged, pettifogging.* [*Petty* and Prov. E. *fog,* to seek gain by mean practices.] To be contentious or argumentative over trivialities; to practice law in a deceitful manner. —**pet·ti·fog·ger,** *n.*—**pet·ti·fog·ger·y,** *n.*

pet·tish, pet′ish, *a.* Unpredictably irritable; petulant.—**pet·tish·ly,** *adv.*—**pet·tish·ness,** *n.*

pet·ti·toes, pet′ē·tōz″, *n. pl.* [*Petty* and *toes.*] The feet of a pig served as food. A humorous term for human feet or toes, esp. a child's.

pet·ty, pet′ē, *a.*—*pettier, pettiest.* [Fr. *petit,* little, small, akin to W. *pitw,* small, *pid,* a point.] Trivial; of little consequence; having or showing a narrow scope or outlook; small-minded; spiteful over small things; of secondary rank or office.— **pet·ti·ly,** *adv.*—**pet·ti·ness,** *n.*

pet·ty cash, *n. Bus.* money kept on hand from which minor expenses are met.

pet·ty lar·ce·ny, *n. Law,* theft of goods valued below a specific amount: contrasted with *grand larceny.* Also **pet·it lar·ce·ny.**

pet·ty of·fic·er, *n. Navy,* an enlisted man whose rank corresponds with that of a non-commissioned officer in the army.

pet·u·lance, pech′u·lans, *n.* [L. *petulantia.*] The quality or condition of being petulant; peevishness. Also **pet·u·lan·cy.**

pet·u·lant, pech′u·lant, *a.* [L. *petulans, petulantis,* petulant, < *peto,* to attack.] Showing irritation or impatience, esp. over a trivial matter; peevish.—**pet·u·lant·ly,** *adv.*

pe·tu·ni·a, pe·tö′nē·a, pe·tö′nya, pe·tū′-nē·a, pe·tū′nya, *n.* [N.L., < Fr. *petun,* tobacco; of S. Amer. origin.] *Bot.* any of several highly developed varieties of the annual garden herb, *Petunia hybrida,* in the nightshade family, a popular plant in all temperate regions, and a profuse bloomer with a variety of color patterns to its large funnelform flowers. A reddish-purple color.

pew, pū, *n.* [O.Fr. *pui,* a raised place, < L. *podium,* a balcony, a front balcony in an amphitheater, < Gr. *podion,* < *pous, podos,* the foot.] One of the benchlike seats fixed in a church for use by the congregation; an enclosed compartment in a church containing seats for the use of a family or some other group.

pe·wee, pee′wee, pē′wē, *n.* [Imit. of its note.] *Ornith.* a sparrow-sized flycatcher, *Contopus virens,* of eastern N. America, having an olive-gray back, whitish under-parts, and two conspicuous white wing bars, and singing a plaintive note resembling its name. Also *wood pewee.*

pe·wit, pee·wit, pē′wit, pū′it, *n.* [Imit. of its note.] The lapwing, *Vanellua cristatus;* the European black-headed gull, *Larus ridibundus;* the phoebe; the pewee.

pew·ter, pū′tėr, *n.* [O.Fr. *peutre* (Fr. *peautre*) = Sp. *peltre* = It. *peltro,* pewter.] Any of various alloys in which tin is the chief constituent, usu. one of tin and lead; a vessel or utensil made of such an alloy, used for tableware; such utensils collectively.—*a.* Consisting or made of pewter.— **pew·ter·er,** *n.*

pe·yo·te, pā·ō′tē, pē·ō′tē, *Sp.* pe·ya′te, *n. pl.* **pe·yo·tes,** pā·ō′tēz, pē·ō′tēz, *Sp.* pe·ya′tes. [Sp. < Mex.] A cactus, *Lopho-phora williamsii,* used for centuries for its hallucinatory effects by the Indians of Mexico and southwestern U.S.; one of several alkaloids isolated from this cactus, esp. mescaline, producing dreamlike, intoxicating effects with vivid kaleidoscopic visions. Also *mescal,* **pe·yo·tl,** pā·ōt′l.

pH, pē′āch′, *n. Chem.* the negative of the logarithm of hydrogen ion concentration in aqueous solution: low pH is acid, high pH is alkaline, pH of 7 is neutral.

pha·e·ton, fā′i·ton, *Brit.* fāt′on, *n.* [From *Phaethōn* of Greek mythology, destroyed by Zeus.] An open four-wheeled carriage which was usu. drawn by two horses; later, a touring car.

phag·o·cyte, fag′o·sīt″, *n.* [Gr. *phagein,* to eat, *kytos,* cell.] *Physiol.* a leukocyte that destroys and absorbs harmful bacteria, foreign matter, and inert cells in the blood stream.—**phag·o·cyt·ic,** fag″o·sit′ik, *a.*— **phag·o·cy·to·sis,** fag″o·sī·tō′sis, *n. Physiol.* the absorption and destruction of bacteria, etc. by phagocytes.

phal·ange, fal′anj, fa·lanj′, *n. Anat., zool.* phalanx.

pha·lan·ge·al, fa·lan′jē·al, *a.* Pertaining to a phalanx or the phalanges.

pha·lan·ger, fa·lan′jėr, *n.* [From two of the toes being joined as far as the last *phalange.*] *Zool.* a nocturnal, arboreal marsupial of the genus *Phalanger,* in the family *Phalan-geridae,* native to Australia and New Guinea, having large eyes, close woolly fur and a partly naked prehensile tail. Also *cus·cus.*

phal·an·ster·y, fal′an·ster″ē, *n. pl.* **phal·an·ster·ies.** [Fr. *phalanstère,* < *phalange,* phalanx, and (*mona*)*stère,* monastery.] In Fourierism, the building or buildings occupied by a phalanx or socialistic community; the community itself; any similar association of persons, or the building or buildings occupied by them.

pha·lanx, fā′langks, fal′angks, *n. pl.* **pha·lanx·es,** **pha·lang·es,** fa·lan′jēz. [L., < Gr. *phalagx,* line of battle, phalanx (of troops), body, block, bone of finger or toe.] In ancient Greece, a body of heavily-armed infantry formed in ranks and files close and deep, with shields joined and long spears overlapping; any body of troops in close array; a compact or closely massed body of persons, animals, or things; *fig.* a number of persons united or banded together, as for a common purpose. In Fourierism, a group of persons holding their property in common. *Anat., zool.* any of the digital bones of the hand or foot, pl. **pha·lang·es.** *Bot.* a bundle of stamens, joined by their filaments.

phal·a·rope, fal′a·rōp″, *n.* [< Gr. *phala-ros,* white, and *pous, podos,* a foot.] *Ornith.* any of several species of sandpiperlike birds in the family *Phalaropodidae,* equally at home wading or swimming.

phal·lic, fal′ik, *a.* [Gr. *phallicós.*] Of or pertaining to the phallus.—**phal·li·cism,**

phal′i·siz″um, *n.* Worship of the phallus, as the symbol of creative power. Also **phal·lism**, fal′iz·um.—**phal·li·cist**, *n.*

phal·lus, fal′us, *n. pl.* **phal·li**, **phal·lus·es**, fal′ī. [L., < Gr. *phallós*, penis.] An image of the male reproductive organ, symbolizing in certain ancient religious systems the generative power in nature, esp. that carried in procession in ancient festivals of Dionysus or Bacchus. *Anat.* the penis or clitoris.

phan·er·o·gam, fan′ĕr·o·gam″, *n.* [Gr. *phaneros*, evident, and *gamos*, marriage.] *Bot.* in an older classification of plants, a seed plant or spermatophyte, as opposed to a *cryptogam*.—**phan·er·o·gam·ic**, **phan·er·og·a·mous**, fan″e·rog′a·mus, *a.*

phan·tasm, **fan·tasm**, fan′taz·um, *n.* [Gr. *phantasma*, < *phantazein*, to show, < the stem of *phanainein*, to show.] A creation of the fancy or imagination; an apparition; a deceptive likeness of something; also *phantasma. Philos.* a mental image of an external object.—**phan·tas·mal**, fan·taz′mal.—**phan·tas·mic**, *a.*

phan·tas·ma, fan·taz′ma, *n. pl.* **phan·tas·ma·ta**. Phantasm.

phan·tas·ma·go·ri·a, fan·taz″ma·gŏr′ē·a, fan·taz″ma·gạr′ē·a, *n.* [L. < Gr. *phantasma*, phantasm, and (appar.) *agora*, assembly.] A shifting series of phantasms, illusions, or deceptive appearances, as in a dream or as created by the imagination; a changing scene made up of many elements; an exhibition of optical illusions, as one in which figures increase or diminish in size, dissolve, or pass into each other. Also **phan·tas·ma·go·ry**, fan·taz′ma·gŏr″ē, fan·taz′ma·gạr″ē.—**phan·tas·ma·go·ri·al**, **phan·tas·ma·gor·ic**, *a.*—**phan·tas·ma·go·rist**, *n.*

phan·ta·sy, fan′ta·sē, fan′ta·zē, *n. pl.* **phan·ta·sies**. Fantasy.—**phan·tas·tic**, **phan·tas·ti·cal**, fan·tas′tik, *a.*

phan·tom, **fan·tom**, fan′tom, *n.* [O.Fr. *fantosme* (Fr. *fantôme*), var. of *fantasme*.] An appearance without material substance; an apparition or specter; a thing or person that is little more than an appearance or show, or a mere semblance; an image appearing in a dream or formed in the mind.—*a.* Of the nature of a phantom; illusive; spectral.

phar·aoh, fâr′ō, *n.* [L.L. *Pharao*, < Gr. *Pharaō*, < Heb. *Par′ōh*, < Egypt. *per-′o*, 'great house.'] (*Often cap.*) A title of the ancient Egyptian kings; an Egyptian king.—**phar·a·on·ic**, **phar·a·on·i·cal**, fâr″ā·on′ik, *a.* (*Often cap.*)

phar·aoh ant, *n.* A red ant, *Monomorium pharaonis*, often found in domestic dwellings.

phar·i·sa·ic, far″i·sā′ik, *a.* [L.L. *Pharisaicus*, < Gr. *Pharisaicós*.] Laying great stress on the external observances of religion without regard to the spirit, or on an outward show of morality, and assuming superiority because of this; (*cap.*) of or pertaining to the Pharisees. Also **phar·i·sa·i·cal**.—**phar·i·sa·i·cal·ly**, *adv.*—**phar·i·sa·i·cal·ness**, *n.*

phar·i·sa·ism, far′i·sā·iz″um, *n.* (*Often cap.*) The doctrines and conduct of the Pharisees; rigid observance of external rites and forms of religion without genuine piety; hypocrisy in religion. Also **phar·i·see·ism**, far′i·sē·iz″um.

Phar·i·see, far′i·sē″, *n.* [O.Fr. *pharisee*, < L.L. *Pharisæus*, < Gr. *Pharisaios*, Pharisee; from an Aram. name meaning 'separated,' 'separatist.'] One of an ancient Jewish sect noted for strict interpretation and observance of the written and oral law and for pretensions to superior sanctity; (*l.c.*) a pharisaic, self-righteous, or hypocritical person.

phar·ma·ceu·ti·cal, fär″ma·sō′ti·kal, *a.*

[Gr. *pharmakeutikos*, < *pharmakeuein*, to administer medicine, < *pharmakon*, a drug.] Pertaining to the knowledge or art of pharmacy.—*n.* A medicine or drug product. Also **phar·ma·ceu·tic**.—**phar·ma·ceu·ti·cal·ly**, *adv.*

phar·ma·ceu·tics, fär′ma·sō′tiks, *n. pl. but sing. in constr.* The science of preparing medicines; pharmacy.

phar·ma·cist, fär′ma·sist, *n.* One skilled in or engaged in the practice of pharmacy; a druggist. Also **phar·ma·ceu·tist**, fär′ma·sō′tist.

phar·ma·co·dy·nam·ics, fär″ma·kō·di·nam′iks, *n. pl. but sing. in constr.* The division of pharmacology which deals with the action of drugs and their effect upon the body.—**phar·ma·co·dy·nam·ic**, *a.*—**phar·ma·co·dy·nam·i·cal·ly**, *adv.*

phar·ma·cog·no·sy, fär″ma·kog′no·sē, *n.* That branch of pharmacology which deals with sources, characteristics, and possible uses of medicinal substances in their natural or unprepared state.—**phar·ma·cog·nos·tic**, fär″ma·kog·nos′tik, *a.*

phar·ma·col·o·gy, fär″ma·kol′o·jē, *n.* [Gr. *pharmakon* and *logos*.] The science or knowledge of drugs, or the art of preparing medicines.—**phar·ma·co·log·ic**, **phar·ma·co·log·i·cal**, fär″ma·ko·loj′ik, *a.*—**phar·ma·co·log·i·cal·ly**, *adv.*—**phar·ma·col·o·gist**, fär″ma·kol′o·jist, *n.*

phar·ma·co·poe·ia, fär″ma·ko·pē′a, *n.* [Gr. *pharmakon*, and *poiein*, to make.] A book of directions and requirements for the preparation of medicines, generally published by an authority; a collection or stock of drugs.—**phar·ma·co·poe·ial**, **phar·ma·co·poe·ic**, *a.*

phar·ma·cy, fär′ma·sē, *n. pl.* **phar·ma·cies**. [Fr. *pharmacie*, < Gr. *pharmakeia*, < *pharmakon*.] The art of preparing and compounding medicines, and of dispensing them according to the prescriptions of medical practitioners; the place where medicines are compounded or dispensed; a drugstore.

pha·ros, fâr′os, *n.* (*Cap.*) a lighthouse or tower which stood in ancient times on the isle of Pharos, at the entrance to the Port of Alexandria. Any lighthouse for the guidance of seamen; a beacon.

pha·ryn·ge·al, fa·rin′jē·al, fa·rin′jal, far″in·jē′al, *a.* Of, relating to, or produced in the pharynx. Also **pha·ryn·gal**, fa·ring′gal.

phar·yn·gi·tis, far″in·ji′tis, *n. Pathol.* inflammation of the pharynx.

phar·yn·gol·o·gy, far″ing·gol′o·jē, *n. Med.* the science concerned with the pharynx and its ailments.

phar·ynx, far′ingks, *n. pl.* **phar·yn·ges**, **phar·ynx·es**, fa·rin′jēz. [Gr. *pharynx, pharyngos*; akin to *pharanx*, a chasm.] *Anat.* the muscular tube which connects the cavity of the mouth and the esophagus.

phase, fāz, *n.* [N.L. *phasis*, < Gr. *phásis*, appearance, phase, < *phainein*, show.] Any of the appearances or aspects in which a thing of varying modes or conditions manifests itself to the eye or mind; a stage of change or development. *Astron.* the particular appearance presented by a planet or the moon at a given time, specif. one of the recurring appearances or states of the moon or a planet in respect to the form, or the absence, of its illuminated disk. *Biol.* a distinct stage in mitosis or meiosis; as, the prophase. *Chem.* a homogeneous portion of a nonhomogeneous system, which can be separated mechanically from other portions; as, the gaseous, liquid, and solid *phases* of water. *Phys.* a particular stage or point of advancement in a cycle of periodical changes or movements; the fractional portion of a cycle completed at a given moment, measured from an assumed starting point.—**pha·sic**, *a.*

phase, fāz, *v.t.*—**phased**, **phasing**. To put in the same phase; synchronize; to conduct by phases, as a project; to schedule, as production processes, so that goods are available when required.—**phase in**, to introduce or bring into use gradually or by stages.—**phase out**, to withdraw from use gradually.

phase mi·cro·scope, *n.* A microscope which converts phase differences in light rays reflected by or passed through an object into differences in intensity, thus producing an image in which the details are distinct, despite their refractive indexes being very close. Also **phase-con·trast mi·cro·scope**.

phase mod·u·la·tion, *n. Electron.* modulation of a carrier wave in radio transmission by altering its phase.

Ph.D., *n.* [L.] Doctor of Philosophy: the highest degree awarded in the graduate school of a university.

pheas·ant, fez′ant, *n.* [A.Fr. *fesant*, O.Fr. Fr. *faisan*, < L. *phasianus*, < Gr. *phasianós*, pheasant, < *Phasis*, the river Phasis in Colchis.] Any of various large, long-tailed gallinaceous birds of the genus *Phasianus*, orig. natives of Asia, esp. the ringed-necked pheasant, a game bird which has been introduced into Europe and America.

phel·lem, fel′em, fel′em, *n. Bot.* a layer of cork tissue, formed on the outside of the cork cambium or phellogen, found in stems and roots. See *cork*.

phel·lo·derm, fel′o·durm″, *n. Bot.* secondary tissue formed in roots and stems by the cork cambium or phellogen on its inner surface, and which in early stages often contains chloroplasts.—**phel·lo·der·mal**, *a.*

phel·lo·gen, fel′o·jen, *n. Bot.* a layer of tissue or secondary meristem external to the true cambium and giving rise to cork tissue on the outside and phelloderm on the inside. Also **cork cam·bi·um**.—**phel·lo·ge·net·ic**, **phel·lo·gen·ic**, fel″o·je·net′ik, fel″o·jen′ik, *a.*

phe·na·caine, fē′na·kān″, fen′a·kān″, *n. Chem.* a crystalline compound, $C_{18}H_{22}N_2O_2$, usu. administered in its hydrochloridic form as a local anesthetic, esp. for the eyes.

phe·nac·e·tin, fe·nas′i·tin, *n. Chem.* a compound, $C_{10}H_{13}NO_2$, of coal-tar origin, used to relieve nervous headache, neuralgia, or fever. Also *acetophenetidin*.

phen·a·cite, fen′a·sīt″, *n. Mineral.* the vitreous mineral, beryllium silicate, Be_2SiO_4, whose crystals are sometimes used as gems. Also **phen·a·kite**.

phe·nan·threne, fē·nan′thrēn, *n. Chem.* a crystalline, water-insoluble, coal-tar derivative and anthracine isomer, $C_{14}H_{10}$, used to synthesize dyes and drugs.

phe·na·zine, fen′a·zēn″, fen′a·zin, *n. Chem.* a yellowish crystalline organic compound, $C_6H_4N_2C_6H_4$, some derivatives of which are important dyes.

phen·e·tole, fen′i·tōl″, fen′i·tol″, *n.* [< (*phen*)yl and *et*(*hyl*) and *-ol*.] *Chem.* the ethyl ether of phenol, a colorless, volatile, aromatic liquid, $C_6H_5OC_2H_5$. Also **phen·e·tol**.

phe·no·bar·bi·tal, fē″nō·bär′bi·tal″, fē″nō·bär′bi·tạl″, fē″no·bär′bi·tal″, fē″no·bär′bi·tạl″, *n.* [< *pheno* and *barbit*(*uric acid*) and *-al*.] *Chem.* a crystalline barbiturate, $C_{12}H_{12}N_2O_3$, usu. in white powder form, and used as a hypnotic or sedative.

phe·no·cop·y, fē′no·kop″ē, *n. Genetics,* a noninherited modification of an organism induced by the environment that simulates a variation produced by heredity.

phe·no·cryst, fē′no·krist, fen′o·krist, *n.* [Gr. *phainein*, show, and *krystallos*, crystal.] *Geol.* any of the conspicuous crystals in a porphyritic rock.

phe·nol, fē′nōl, fē′nol, *n. Chem.* Carbolic acid, C_6H_5OH, a coal tar derivative, or a hydroxyl derivative of benzene; any analogous hydroxyl derivative of benzene.— **phe·nol·ic,** fi·nō′lik, fi·na′lik, fi·nol′ik, *a.* **phe·no·late,** fēn′o·lāt″, *n. Chem.* a salt of phenol. Also *phenoxide.*—*v.i.*—**phenolated,** *phenolizing.* To carbolize.

phe·no·lic res·in, *n. Chem.* a resin derived from phenol and an aldehyde and used to make plastics, paint, or adhesives.

phe·nol·o·gy, fi·nol′o·jē, *n.* [Gr. *phaino,* I appear, *logos,* a discourse.] The scientific study of the annual recurrence of plant and animal phenomena as effected by seasonal and other environmental changes.—**phe·no·log·i·cal,** fēn′o·loj′i·kal, *a.*—**phe·no·log·i·cal·ly,** *adv.*—**phe·nol·o·gist,** *n.*

phe·nol·phthal·ein, fē″nōl·thal′ēn, fē″nōl·thal′ē·in, fē″nōl·fthal′ēn, fē″nōl·fthal′ē·in, fē″nol·thal′ēn, fē″nol·thal′ē·in, fē″nol·fthal′ēn, fē″nol·fthal′ē·in, *n. Chem.* a white crystalline compound, $C_{20}H_{14}O_4$, formed by the interaction of phenol and phthalic anhydride, used medicinally and to indicate the presence of alkalis, which turn it red, and of acids, which decolorize.

phe·nol red, *n.* A red crystalline acid-base indicator, $C_{19}H_{14}O_5S$, also used in medical analysis.

phe·nom·e·nal, fi·nom′e·nal, *a.* Connected with, relating to, or constituted by phenomena; so surprising or extraordinary as to arrest the attention; astounding; *philos.* knowable through the senses.— **phe·nom·e·nal·ly,** *adv.*

phe·nom·e·nal·ism, fi·nom′e·na·liz″um, *n.* The philosophical doctrine that denies the knowability, if not the existence, of a reality beyond the world of phenomena, limiting the range of knowledge to possible objects of sensation and phenomena which are the objects of introspection.—**phe·nom·e·nal·ist,** *n.*—**phe·nom·e·nal·is·tic,** *a.*—**phe·nom·e·nal·is·ti·cal·ly,** *adv.*

phe·nom·e·nol·o·gy, fi·nom″e·nol′o·jē, *n.* The science of phenomena: distinguished from *ontology;* the science of being; in the system of Edmund Husserl, German philosopher, the scientific decription of consciousness and its intentional objects in their pure essences, suspending assertions of their existence independent of consciousness.—**phe·nom·e·no·log·i·cal,** fi·nom″e·no·loj′i·kal, *a.*—**phe·nom·e·no·log·i·cal·ly,** *adv.*—**phe·nom·e·nol·o·gist,** *n.*

phe·nom·e·non, fi·nom′e·non″, *n. pl.* **phe·nom·e·na,** **phe·nom·e·nons,** fi·nom′e·na. [Gr. *phainomenon,* what appears, < *phainomai,* I appear.] A visible manifestation or appearance; *philos.* in the philosophy of Immanuel Kant, an object or occurrence presented to our observation either in the external world or in the human mind, in contrast to that object or occurrence as it is in itself. An appearance produced by the action of the different forces upon matter; what strikes us as strange and uncommon; something extraordinary; an exceedingly remarkable thing or personage.

phe·no·type, fē′no·tīp″, *n. Genetics.* Visible composition of an organism; outward characteristics of an organism resulting from the simultaneous influence of genotype and environment; a group of organisms displaying the same phenotypic characteristics: distinguished from *genotype.* —**phe·no·typ·ic,** **phe·no·typ·i·cal,** fē′no·tip′ik, *a.*—**phe·no·typ·i·cal·ly,** *adv.*

phe·nox·ide, fi·nok′sid, *n. Chem.* phenolate.

phen·yl, fen′l, fēn′l, *n.* [Fr. *phényle,* < Gr. *phainein,* shine and *yln,* matter.] *Chem.* a univalent radical, C_6H_5, present in benzene, phenol, and certain other compounds.— **phe·nyl·ic,** fe·nil′ik, *a.*

phen·yl·ene, fen′i·lēn″, fēn′i·lēn″, *n. Chem.* a bivalent organic radical, C_6H_4, which may be regarded as benzene with two of its hydrogen atoms removed.

phi, fī, fē, *n.* [Gr. *phī.*] The twenty-first letter, Φ, φ, of the Greek alphabet which corresponds to the English ph and f.

phi·al, fī′al, *n.* Vial.

Phi Be·ta Kap·pa, *n.* An honorary society, ΦBK, founded in the U.S. and drawing its members from the ranks of university or college undergraduates who have achieved academic distinction; one who has membership in this society.

Phil·a·del·phi·a law·yer, fil″a·del′fē·a lạ′yẽr, *n.* A clever, sharp lawyer well-versed in the fine points of legal technicalities and phraseology.

phil·a·del·phus, fil″a·del′fus, *n. Bot.* a mock orange in the genus *Philadelphus.*

phi·lan·der, fi·lan′dẽr, *v.i.* [From *Philander,* a virtuous youth in Ariosto's *Orlando Furioso.*] To make love to a woman without having serious intentions; flirt.—**phi·lan·der·er,** *n.*

phi·lan·thro·pist, fi·lan′thro·pist, *n.* A person who practices philanthropy; a benefactor.

phi·lan·thro·py, fi·lan′thro·pē, *n. pl.* **phi·lan·thro·pies.** [Gr. *philanthropia,* < *philos,* loving, and *anthrōpos,* a man.] Love of mankind, esp. as shown in practical efforts to promote well-being by donating to needy causes; such benevolent activity or a particular instance of it.—**phil·an·throp·ic,** **phil·an·throp·i·cal,** fil″an·throp′ik, *a.*—**phil·an·throp·i·cal·ly,** *adv.*

phi·lat·e·ly, fi·lat′e·lē, *n.* [Fr. *philatélie,* < Gr. *philos,* loving, and *ateleia,* exemption from taxation.] The collection or study of stamps and other stamped or imprinted materials which pertain to fiscal or postal history.—**phil·a·tel·ic,** **phil·a·tel·i·cal,** fil″a·tel′ik, *a.*—**phil·a·tel·i·cal·ly,** *adv.*— **phi·lat·e·list,** fi·lat′e·list, *n.*

phil·har·mon·ic, fil″här·mon′ik, fil″ẽr·mon′ik, *a.* [Gr. *philos,* loving, and *harmonia,* harmony.] Loving harmony; fond of harmony or music; relating or pertaining to symphonic and other musical organizations. —*n.*

phil·har·mon·ic pitch, *n.* A standard pitch for tuning, establishing A above middle C as 440 vibrations per second.

phil·hel·lene, fil·hel′ēn, *n.* [Fr. *philhellène,* < Gr. *philos,* loving, and *Hellen,* a Greek.] A friend of Greece; one who supports the causes and interests of the Greeks.—*a.* Also **phil·hel·len·ic,** fil″he·len′ik, fil″he·lē′nik.—**phil·hel·len·ism,** fil·hel′e·nizm, *n.*—**phil·hel·len·ist,** fil·hel′e·nist, fil″he·lē′nist, *n.*

Phi·lip·pic, fi·lip′ik, *n.* One of a series of orations by Demosthenes, the Grecian orator, against Philip, king of Macedon; any of the orations of Cicero, ancient Roman orator, against Antony; (*l.c.*) any discourse full of acrimonious invective.

Phil·ip·pine ma·hog·a·ny, fil′i·pēn″ ma·hog′a·nē, *n.* Any of several tropical Philippine hardwoods, genus *Shorea,* having some characteristics of mahogany but cheaper and used in general construction.

Phi·lis·ti·a, fi·lis′tē·a, *n.* [M.L.] A former country on the southwest coast of Palestine occupied by the ancient Philistines; the nation of the Philistines; the class or body of such Philistines.

Phi·lis·tine, fil′i·stēn″, fil′i·stīn″, fi·lis′-tin, fi·lis′tēn, *n.* An inhabitant of Philistia, now a portion of Syria; the English form of Philister, a term applied by German students to any one who has not been trained in a university. *Fig.* a person deficient in liberal culture and aesthetics, and so wanting in sensitivity and taste; a person of narrow views; a prosaic, practical

man.—*a.*—**Phi·lis·tin·ism,** fil′i·stē·niz″um, fil′i·sti·niz″um, fi·lis′ti·niz″um, fi·lis′-tē·niz″um, *n.*

phil·o·den·dron, fil′o·den′dron, *n. pl.* **phil·o·den·drons,** **phil·o·den·dra,** fil′o·den′dra. *Hort.* any of many species of tree-climbing vines of the genus *Philodendron,* in the arum family, native to the American tropics, a few of which are cultivated as an indoor ornamental, esp. for their deep-green, thick, glossy leaves and for their ability to thrive with a minimum of sunlight.

phi·log·y·ny, fi·loj′i·nē, *n.* [Gr. *philos,* loving, and *gynē,* a woman.] Fondness for women.—**phi·log·y·nist,** *n.*—**phi·log·y·nous,** *a.*

phi·lol·o·gy, fi·lol′o·jē, *n.* [Gr. *philologia,* < *phileō,* to love, and *logos,* a word.] The scientific study of written records of literary, social, and cultural history in order to establish authenticity, accuracy, and meaning; linguistics, esp. historical and comparative.—**phi·lol·o·gist,** **phi·lol·o·ger,** **phil·o·lo·gi·an,** fil′o·lō′jē·an, *n.*—**phil·o·log·i·cal,** **phil·o·log·ic,** fil″o·loj′i·kal, *a.*—**phil·o·log·i·cal·ly,** *adv.*

phil·o·mel, fil′o·mel″, *n.* [From *Philomela,* daughter of Pandion, king of Athens, who was changed into a nightingale.] *Poet.* the nightingale. Also **phil·o·me·la,** fil′o·mē′la.

phil·o·pro·gen·i·tive, fil′ō·prō·jen′i·tive, *a.* Fond of children; prolific.— **phil·o·pro·gen·i·tive·ness,** *n.*

phil·o·sophe, fil′o·sof″, fil″o·zof′, *Fr.* fē·la·zaf′, *n.* [Fr.] One of the thinkers or popular philosophers of 18th century France, as Voltaire or Rousseau.

phi·los·o·pher, fi·los′o·fẽr, *n.* [Gr. *philosophos*—*philos,* loving, and *sophos,* wise.] A person who formulates theories on questions of philosophy; a person versed in or devoted to philosophy; one who governs his life by philosophical principles; one who lives wisely or reasonably.

phi·los·o·pher's stone, *n. Alchem.* a legendary substance that supposedly converted base metal to gold ore.

phil·o·soph·i·cal, fil″o·sof′i·kal, *a.* Pertaining to or according to philosophy; proceeding from philosophy; as, an attitude of *philosophical* skepticism; characteristic of a philosopher; based on the rules of practical wisdom; temperate, detached, or calm. Also **phil·o·soph·ic.**—**phil·o·soph·i·cal·ly,** *adv.*

phi·los·o·phize, fi·los′o·fīz″, *v.i.*—*philosophized, philosophizing.* To reason or theorize as a philosopher; to discourse philosophically, esp. in a pedantic, imprecise, or moralistic manner.—**phi·los·o·phiz·er,** *n.*

phi·los·o·phy, fi·los′o·fē, *n. pl.* **phi·los·o·phies.** [O.Fr. Fr. *philosophie,* < L. *philosophia,* < Gr. *philosophia,* < *philósophos.*] The love or pursuit of wisdom; the study or science of the truths or principles underlying all knowledge; any one of the three branches, 'natural philosophy,' 'moral philosophy,' and 'metaphysical philosophy,' accepted as composing this science; the study or science of the principles of a particular branch of knowledge; a system of philosophical doctrine; as, the *philosophy* of Spinoza; a system of principles for guidance in practical affairs; wise composure in dealing with problems.

phil·ter, *Brit.* **phil·tre,** fil′tẽr, *n.* [Fr. *philtre,* L. *philtrum,* < Gr. *philtron,* < *philos,* loving.] A drug or potion supposed to have the power of exciting love magically; any potion supposed to have magical powers.—*v.t.*—*philtered, philtering, Brit. philtred, philtring.* To charm or enchant with a philter.

phiz, fiz, *n.* [A contr. of *physiognomy.*] *Slang,* the face or visage.

phle·bi·tis, fle·bī′tis, n. [Gr. *phelps, phlebos,* a vein.] *Pathol.* inflammation of the inner membrane of a vein.—**phle·bit·ic**, fle·bit′ik, a.

phle·bot·o·my, fle·bot′o·mē, n. pl. **phle·bot·o·mies**. [Gr. *phlebotomia*.] *Surg.* The act or practice of opening a vein for letting blood; bleeding.—**phleb·o·tom·ic**, fleb″o·tom′ik, a.—**phle·bot·o·mist**, fle·bot′o·mist, n. *Surg.* One who opens a vein for letting blood; a blood-letter.—**phle·bot·o·mize**, fle·bot′o·mīz″, v.t.—*phlebotomized, phlebotomizing. Surg.* to bleed by opening a vein.

phlegm, flem, n. [Gr. *phlegma, phlegmatos,* a slimy humor, < *phlegō,* to burn.] *Physiol.* the thick mucus secreted in the respiratory passages. *Anc. physiol.* one of the four humors, supposed to cause apathy and sluggishness. Self-possession; sluggishness; indifference.—**phlegm·y**, a.—*phlegmier, phlegmiest.*

phleg·mat·ic, fleg·mat′ik, a. Sluggish in temperament; apathetic; self-possessed; impassive; producing or resembling the humor phlegm. Also **phleg·mat·i·cal**.—**phleg·mat·i·cal·ly**, adv.

phlo·em, flō′em, n. [G., < Gr. *phlóos, phloiós,* bark.] *Bot.* A complex tissue of vascular anatomy consisting of sieve tubes, companion cells, parenchyma, and fibers, and which functions for the conduction of food; the outer of the two complex tissues in plants, the xylem being the inner one; the inner bark of a woody plant. See *bast.*

phlo·em ne·cro·sis, n. *Bot.* any of several diseases located in the phloem and in which disintegration of the cells takes place, resulting in the clogging of the food-conducting tubes, esp. a virus disease of the American elm.

phlo·em ray, n. *Bot.* a vascular ray or strand of parenchyma cells only one cell thick and extending radially through the secondary phloem, and whose function is the transverse conduction of food.

phlo·gis·tic, flō·jis′tik, a. Pertaining to phlogiston; *med.* inflammatory.

phlo·gis·ton, flō·jis′ton, flō·jis′ton, n. [Gr. *phlogistos,* burnt, < *phlogizō,* to burn, < *phlegō,* to burn.] According to an obsolete theory, the principle of inflammability, a hypothetical element which was thought to be pure fire fixed in combustible bodies.

phlox, floks, n. [L., < Gr. *phlóx,* kind of plant, orig. flame, < *phlégein,* burn.] Any of the herbs constituting the genus *Phlox,* native to N. America, many of which are cultivated for their cymes or panicles of showy flowers of various colors.

phlyc·te·na, **phlyc·tae·na**, flik·tē′na, n. pl. **phlyc·te·nae**, flik·tē′nē. [Gr. *phlyktaina*.] *Pathol.* a small watery pustule or blister.

pho·bi·a, fō′bē·a, n. [Gr. *phobos,* fear.] A persistent, exaggerated, and usu. illogical fear or dread.—**pho·bic**, a.

phoe·be, fē′bē, n. [*Imit.* of its note; with spelling conformed to *Phoebe*.] *Ornith.* any of several gray-brown American flycatchers of the genus *Sayornis,* family *Tyrannidae,* esp. *S. phoebe* of eastern N. America, characterized by an upright posture, a persistent tail-wagging habit, and often building its nest under small bridges. Also **phoe·be bird, bridge bird.**

phoe·nix, **phe·nix**, fē′niks, n. [Gr. *phoinix*.] A beautiful bird of ancient Egyptian legend said to be the only one of its kind and to live 500 or 600 years, then burning itself on a funeral pyre and rising youthful from its ashes: an emblem of immortality; a paragon; a person of distinction or beauty.

phon, fon, n. *Audiology,* a measure of perceived loudness established by comparing a sound to a standard sound, 1000 cycles per second, and adjusting the decibel level of the standard until listeners perceive them to be equal, as: The decibel level of the standard is the *phon* of the sound.

pho·na·tion, fō·nā′shan, n. [Gr. *phōnē,* voice.] The act of uttering vocal sounds.—**pho·nate**, fō′nāt, v.i., v.t.—*phonated, phonating.*

phone, fōn, n. *Colloq.* a telephone.—v.i., v.t.—*phoned, phoning.*

phone, fōn, n. [Gr. *phōnē,* sound, voice.] *Phon.* a simple vocal sound, a primary element of speech.

pho·neme, fō′nēm, n. One of a set of the basic units of speech which, differing with each language or dialect, provide the small changes in sound that differentiate between word meanings, as in the English words *tip* and *pip,* the difference in meaning brought about by forming the *t* and *p* sounds indicating that these speech units are phonemes.

pho·ne·mic, fo·nē′mik, fō·nē′mik, a. Relating to phonemes; relating to phonemics; pertaining to distinctions of speech elements in a language. Also **pho·ne·mat·ic**, fō″ne·mat′ik.—**pho·ne·mi·cal·ly**, adv.

pho·ne·mics, fo·nē′miks, fō·nē′miks, n. pl. but sing. in constr. Linguistic analysis of phonemes and phonemic systems; a phonemic system.—**pho·ne·mi·cist**, fō·nē′mi·sist, n.

pho·net·ic, fo·net′ik, fō·net′ik, a. [Gr. *phōnetikos,* < *phōnē,* voice, sound.] Pertaining to sounds, their physical production, and written representation; concerning pronunciation; describing nondistinctive elements in the speaking of a language, as length or aspiration. Also **pho·net·i·cal**.—**pho·net·i·cal·ly**, adv.

pho·net·ic al·pha·bet, n. A set of characters, one for each distinct speech sound.

pho·ne·ti·cian, fō″ni·tish′an, n. An expert in phonetics.

pho·net·ics, fo·net′iks, fō·net′iks, n. pl. but sing. in constr. *Ling.* The study of speech sounds in respect to how they are produced, transmitted, received, and transcribed; the system of the speech sounds of a particular language.

phon·ic, fon′ik, fō′nik, a. Pertaining to sound or to speech.

phon·ics, fon′iks, fō′niks, n. pl. but sing. in constr. A method of teaching beginning reading, spelling, and pronunciation through phonetic interpretation of words.

pho·no·gram, fō′no·gram″, n. A character or symbol representing a single speech sound, a syllable, or a word.—**pho·no·gram·ic**, **pho·no·gram·mic**, a.—**pho·no·gram·i·cal·ly**, **pho·no·gram·mi·cal·ly**, adv.

pho·no·graph, fō′no·graf″, fō′no·gräf″, n. [Gr. *phōnē,* sound, and *graphō,* to write.] A record player.—**pho·no·graph·ic**, fō″no·graf′ik, a.—**pho·no·graph·i·cal·ly**, adv.

pho·nog·ra·phy, fō·nog′ra·fē, n. The representation of sounds by characters, each of which represents one sound, and always the same sound; phonetic shorthand.

pho·no·lite, fōn′o·līt″, n. A green or gray volcanic rock containing much alkali feldspar and nepheline.—**pho·no·lit·ic**, fōn″o·lit′ik, a.

pho·nol·o·gy, fō·nol′o·jē, fo·nol′o·jē, n. pl. **pho·nol·o·gies**. The study of the sounds of a particular language; the system of sounds used in a language.—**pho·no·log·ic**, **pho·no·log·i·cal**, fōn″o·loj′ik, a.—**pho·no·log·i·cal·ly**, adv.—**pho·nol·o·gist**, fō·nol′o·jist, fo·nol′o·jist, n.

pho·ny, **pho·ney**, fō′nē, a.—*phonier, phoniest.* [Origin uncertain.] *Slang.* Not genuine; spurious, counterfeit, or bogus; fraudulent.—n. pl. **pho·nies**. *Slang.* Something fake or counterfeit; one who is not genuine.—**pho·ni·ness**, n.

phos·gene, fos′jĕn, n. [Gr. *phōs,* light, and root *gen,* to produce.] A heavy, poisonous gas, $COCl_2$, with a choking odor, used in warfare and in the synthesis of organic compounds. Also **car·bon·yl chlo·ride.**

phos·pha·tase, fos′fa·tās″, n. *Biochem.* an enzyme secreted by the liver that hydrolyzes and synthesizes phosphoric acid esters.

phos·phate, fos′fāt, n. [Fr. *phosphate,* < *phosphore, phosphorus.*] *Chem.* a salt of phosphoric acid; a fertilizing material containing such salts. A drink consisting of carbonated water, fruit syrup, and a small quantity of phosphoric acid.—**phos·phat·ic**, fos·fat′ik, a.

phos·phate rock, n. A rock formed primarily of calcium phosphate and used for the manufacture of fertilizer, phosphoric acid, and other phosphorous compounds.

phos·pha·tide, fos′fa·tīd″, fos′fa·tid, n. A phospholipid.—**phos·pha·tid·ic**, fos″fa·tid′ik, a.

phos·pha·tize, fos′fa·tīz″, v.t.—*phosphatized, phosphatizing.* To change to the form of a phosphate; to treat with phosphates.—**phos·pha·ti·za·tion**, fos″fa·ti·zā′shan, n.

phos·phene, fos′fēn, n. [Fr. *phosphène,* < Gr. *phōs,* light, and *phainein,* show.] *Physiol.* a luminous image produced by mechanical stimulation of the retina, as by pressing the eyeball with the finger when the lid is closed.

phos·phide, fos′fīd, fos′fid, n. A compound of a metal with phosphorus.

phos·phite, fos′fīt, n. *Chem.* a salt of phosphorous acid.

phos·pho·cre·a·tine, fos″fō·krē′a·tēn″, fos″fō·krē′a·tin, n. *Biochem.* an organic compound, $C_4H_{10}N_3O_5P$, which is found in muscle tissue and which furnishes the energy for contractions.

phos·pho·lip·id, fos″fō·lip′id, fos″fō·li′pid, n. *Biochem.* one of a group of lipoidal compounds, such as lecithin and cephalin, that are phosphoric esters and are found in living cells throughout nature. Also *phosphatide,* **phos·pho·lip·ide**, fos″fō·lip′īd, fos″fō·lip′id, fos″fō·li′pīd, fos″fō·li′pid.

phos·pho·ni·um, fos·fō′nē·um, n. [N.L., < (*phosph*)*orus* and *amm*(*onium*).] *Chem.* a univalent radical, PH_4, analogous to ammonium, composed of four atoms of hydrogen and one of phosphorus.

phos·phor, fos′fĕr, n. [L. *Phosphorus.*] Any phosphorescent substance, as phosphorus, that glows when exposed to radiation. (*Cap.*) the morning star Venus; also **Phos·phore**, fos′fōr, fos′fạr.

phos·phor bronze, n. An alloy of copper, tin, and some phosphorus, having extreme durability, and used in making various products, as bearings, guns, cutlery, and wire.

phos·pho·resce, fos″fo·res′, v.i.—*phosphoresced, phosphorescing.* To give out a faint light without sensible heat.

phos·pho·res·cence, fos″fo·res′ens, n. The property of being luminous at temperatures below incandescence, from slow oxidation, as in the case of phosphorus, or after exposure to light or other radiation; the luminous appearance of objects having this property.—**phos·pho·res·cent**, fos″fo·res′ent, a. Exhibiting phosphorescence.—**phos·pho·res·cent·ly**, adv.

phos·phor·ic ac·id, fos·fạr′ik as′id, fos·for′ik, n. *Chem.* any one of three oxygen acids of phosphorous: metaphosphoric acid, orthophosphoric acid, or pyrophosphoric acid.

phos·pho·rite, fos′fo·rīt″, n. *Mineral.* A massive form of the mineral apatite; any of various compact or earthy, more or less impure, varieties of native calcium phosphate.—**phos·pho·rit·ic**, fos″fo·rit′ik, a.

phos·pho·rous, fos′fĕr·us, fos·fōr′us, fos·fạr′us, a. *Chem.* pertaining to or containing the element phosphorus, esp. in its lower valence.

phos·pho·rous ac·id, *n.* A crystalline acid of phosphorous, H_3PO_3, used for producing phosphites.

phos·pho·rus, fos'fẽr·us, *n.* pl. **phos·pho·ri,** fos'fe·rī". [L. *Phosphorus,* Phosphor (N.L. *phosphorus,* phosphorus), < Gr. *phôsphóros,* lit. 'light-bringer,' < *phos,* light, and *phérein,* bear.] *Chem.* a solid non-metallic element existing in several allotropic forms: the white or yellow form is poisonous, very flammable, and luminous in the dark, the red form, used in matches, is less flammable and not poisonous. Sym. P, at. no. 15, at. wt. 30.9738. See Periodic Table of Elements.

phot, fot, fōt, *n.* A quantitative measure of illumination, which equals one lumen per square centimeter.

pho·tic, fō'tik, *a.* Pertaining to light or to organisms producing light; describing the depths of the sea to which sunlight penetrates.

pho·to, fō'tō, *n.* pl. **pho·tos.** *Colloq.* shortened form of photograph.

pho·to·bi·ot·ic, fō"tō·bī·ot'ik, *a. Biol.* unable to live or develop without light.

pho·to·cell, fō'tō·sel", *n.* A photoelectric cell.

pho·to·chem·is·try, fō"tō·kem'i·strē, *n.* [Gr. *phôs, phōtos,* light, and E. *chemistry.*] That branch of chemistry concerned with the reaction of chemicals when exposed to light or other radiant energy.—**pho·to·chem·i·cal,** fō"tō·kem'i·kal, *a.*

pho·to·chron·o·graph, fō'tō·kron'o·graf", fō"tō·kron'o·gräf", fō"tō·krō'no·graf", fō"tō·krō'no·gräf", *n.* A device for taking photographs at regular, short intervals of time, as of a bird or other object in motion; a picture taken by such a device; an instrument for recording the transit of a star by means of photography; a chronograph in which the tracing or record is made by the action of a pencil of light on a sensitized surface.

pho·to·com·pose, fō"tō·kom·pōz', *v.t.*—*photocomposed, photocomposing.* To set type photographically.—**pho·to·com·pos·er,** fō"tō·kom·pō"zẽr. *n.* A machine used to photocompose.—**pho·to·com·po·si·tion,** fō"tō·kom"po·zish'an, *n.*

pho·to·con·duc·tiv·i·ty, fō"tō·kon"duk·tiv'i·tē, *n. Phys.* a marked increase in electric conductivity of a substance, as crystals, caused by exposure to light, x-rays, or ultraviolet radiation.—**pho·to·con·duc·tive,** fō"tō·kon·duk'tiv, *a.*

pho·to·cop·y, fō'tō·kop"ē, *n.* pl. **pho·to·cop·ies.** A photographic reproduction of graphic material.—*v.t.*—*photocopied, photocopying.* To make a photocopy; photoduplicate.

pho·to·cur·rent, fō'tō·kur"ent, fō'tō·kur"ent, *n. Phys.* an electric current generated from a photoelectric source.

pho·to·de·tec·tor, fō"tō·di·tek'tẽr, *n.* A semiconductor device that establishes the presence of radiant energy through various photoelectric means: used to observe temperature changes, esp. in solar telescopes.

pho·to·dis·in·te·gra·tion, fō"tō·di·sin"te·grā'shan, *n. Phys.* the breaking up of the nucleus of an atom of deuterium by absorption of a photon.

pho·to·dra·ma, fō'tō·drä"ma, fō'tō·dram"a, *n.* A motion picture; a photoplay; a movie.—**pho·to·dra·mat·ic,** fō"tō·dra·mat'ik, *a.*—**pho·to·dram·a·tist,** fō"tō·dram'a·tist, *n.*

pho·to·du·pli·cate, fō'tō·dö'pli·kāt, fō"tō·dü'pli·kāt, *v.t.*—*photoduplicated, photoduplicating.* To reproduce photographically, as graphic materials.—*n.*—**pho·to·du·pli·ca·tion,** fō"tō·dö"pli·kā'shan, fō"tō·dü"pli·kā'shan, *n.*

pho·to·dy·nam·ics, fō"tō·dī·nam'iks, fō"tō·di·nam'iks, *n.* The science dealing with the energy of light, esp. with light in relation to its effect on plants and animals.—**pho·to·dy·nam·ic,** *a.*—**pho·to·dy·nam·i·cal·ly,** *adv.*

pho·to·e·lec·tric, fō"tō·i·lek'trik, *a.* Of or pertaining to electric light; pertaining to the electricity or electrical effects produced by light; pertaining to photoelectricity; noting or pertaining to apparatus for taking photographs by electric light. Also **pho·to·e·lec·tri·cal.**—**pho·to·e·lec·tric·i·ty,** fō"tō·i·lek·tris'i·tē, fō"tō·ē"lek·tris'i·tē, *n.* Electricity produced or affected by light; the science dealing with electricity or electrical effects produced by light.

pho·to·e·lec·tric cell, *n.* A vacuum tube in which the action of light produces or changes the strength of electric current. Also *photocell.*

pho·to·e·lec·tron, fō"tō·i·lek'tron, *n.* An electron which is released photoelectrically from a metal surface.

pho·to·e·mis·sion, fō"tō·i·mish'an, *n.* The phenomenon of emission of electrons from a surface, due to the absorption of radiation such as light. Also **pho·to·e·lec·tric ef·fect.**—**pho·to·e·mis·sive,** fō"tō·i·mis'iv, *a.*

pho·to·en·grav·ing, fō"tō·en·grā'ving, *n.* A process in which the action of light is used to obtain a picture upon a plate or block, in line or halftone, for subsequent reproduction on a printing press.—**pho·to·en·grave,** fō"tō·en·grāv', *v.t.*—*photoengraved, photoengraving.*—**pho·to·en·grav·er,** *n.*

pho·to fin·ish, *n. Horse racing,* a finish of a race in which the leading horses are so close that a photograph is needed to determine the winner.

pho·to·flash, fō'tō·flash", *n. Photog.* An electrical device which produces a momentary flash of brilliant light; a flash bulb. Also **pho·to·flash bulb, pho·to·flash lamp.**

pho·to·flood, fō'tō·flud", *n. Photog.* an electric lamp which is operated at excess voltage in order to produce a brilliant light. Also **pho·to·flood lamp.**

pho·to·gel·a·tin proc·ess, fō"tō·jel'a·tin pros'es, *n.* Collotype.

pho·to·gene, fō'tō·jēn", *n.* [Gr. *phōs, phōtos,* light, and root *gen,* to produce.] *Ophthalm.* An afterimage; an image of an object persisting on the retina after the object has been withdrawn from the field of vision.

pho·to·gen·ic, fō"tō·jen'ik, *a.* Constituting a favorable subject for photography, particularly an aesthetic subject; *med.* resulting from exposure to light. *Biol.* phosphorescent; luminiferous, as the jellyfish or glowworm.

pho·to·gram, fō'tō·gram", *n.* A silhouette-like photograph resulting from the interception of light by an object placed on light-sensitive paper.

pho·to·gram·me·try, fō"tō·gram'i·trē, *n.* The technique of using aerial photographs in the preparation of maps and surveys.—**pho·to·gram·met·ric,** fō"tō·gra·me'trik, *a.*—**pho·to·gram·me·trist,** *n.*

pho·to·graph, fō'tō·graf", fō'tō·gräf", *n.* A picture obtained by means of photography. —*v.t.* To take a photograph of.—*v.i.* To take photographs; appear in a photograph, as: She *photographs* well.—**pho·tog·ra·pher,** fo·tog'ra·fẽr, *n.* One who is skilled in taking photographs, esp. one who does so as a business.

pho·tog·ra·phy, fo·tog'ra·fē, *n.* [Gr. *phōs, phōtos,* light, and *graphō,* to describe.] The art or the process of obtaining accurate representations of objects by means of the chemical action of light or other kinds of radiant energy on specially treated surfaces.

—**pho·to·graph·ic,** fō"tō·graf'ik, *a.* Of, produced by, or used in photography; resembling a photograph; recording or reproducing with great accuracy. Also **pho·to·graph·i·cal.**—**pho·to·graph·i·cal·ly,** *adv.*

pho·to·gra·vure, fō"tō·gra·vūr', fō"tō·grã'vūr, *n.* [Gr. *phôs, phōtos,* light, Fr. *gravure,* engraving.] A process by which an engraving is produced on a metal plate by light acting on a sensitive surface; a print made by photogravure.

pho·to·he·li·o·graph, fō"tō·hē'lē·o·graf", fō"tō·hē'lē·o·gräf", *n.* A telescope adapted for taking photographs of the sun.

pho·to·ki·ne·sis, fō"tō·ki·nē'sis, fō"tō·kī·nē'sis, *n. Biol.* light-induced movement or activity.—**pho·to·ki·net·ic,** fō"tō·ki·net'ik, fō"tō·kī·net'ik, *a.*

pho·to·lith·o·graph, fō"tō·lith'o·graf", fō"tō·lith'o·gräf", *n.* A picture produced by photolithography.—*v.t.*

pho·to·li·thog·ra·phy, fō"tō·li·thog'ra·fē, *n.* A kind of lithographing in which the printing surface or stone is prepared by a photographic technique. Also **pho·to·lith·o,** fō"tō·lith'ō.—**pho·to·lith·o·graph·ic,** fō"tō·lith"o·graf'ik, *a.*—**pho·to·li·thog·ra·pher,** *n.*

pho·tol·y·sis, fō·tol'i·sis, *n.* The decomposition of materials caused by the action of light.—**pho·to·lyt·ic,** fōt"o·lit'ik, *a.*

pho·to·map, fō'to·map", *n.* An aerial photograph, or a combination of several photographs, marked with grid lines and other data and used as a map.—*v.t.*—*photomapped, photomapping.*

pho·to·me·chan·i·cal, fō"tō·me·kan'i·kal, *a.* Noting or pertaining to any of various processes for printing in ink from plates or surfaces prepared by the aid of photography.—**pho·to·me·chan·i·cal·ly,** *adv.*

pho·tom·e·ter, fō·tom'i·tẽr, *n.* [Gr. *phôs, phōtos,* light, and *metron,* measure.] An instrument that measures the intensity of light.

pho·tom·e·try, fō·tom'i·trē, *n.* The measurement of the intensity of light or the relative intensity of different lights; the science that treats such measurements.—**pho·to·met·ric, pho·to·met·ri·cal,** fō"to·me'trik, *a.*—**pho·to·met·ri·cal·ly,** *adv.* —**pho·tom·e·trist,** *n.*

pho·to·mi·crog·ra·phy, fō"tō·mī·krog'ra·fē, *n.* [Gr. *phōs, phōtos,* light, *mikros,* small, and *graphō,* to write.] The art or process of photographing minute objects when magnified by means of a microscope.—**pho·to·mi·cro·graph,** fō"tō·mī'kro·graf", fō"tō·mī'kro·gräf", *n.*—**pho·to·mi·cro·graph·ic,** fō"to·mī'kro·graf'ik, *a.*

pho·to·mon·tage, fō"tō·mon·täzh', fō"to·man·täzh', *n.* The art or process of joining together several photographs to demonstrate a single theme or for aesthetic effect; the combination so produced.

pho·to·mur·al, fō'to·mūr"al, *n.* A wall-sized photograph used as interior decoration.

pho·ton, fō'ton, *n. Phys.* a quantum of electromagnetic radiation moving at the velocity of light with energy in proportion to its frequency. Also *light quantum.*

pho·to·neg·a·tive, fō'to·neg'a·tiv, *a. Phys.* reacting to increasing radiation with lowered conductivity; *biol.* negative phototropism.

pho·to-off·set, fō"tō·af'set", fō"tō·of'set", *n.* Offset lithography.

pho·to·pe·ri·od, fō"to·pēr'ē·od, *n. Biol.* the period of light exposure in a 24-hour cycle that controls the growth and development of certain plants and animals.—**pho·to·pe·ri·od·ic, pho·to·pe·ri·od·i·cal,** fō"to·pēr"ē·od'ik, *a.*—**pho·to·pe·ri·od·i·cal·ly,** *adv.*—**pho·to·pe·ri·od·ism,** fō"to·pēr'ē·o·diz"um, *n.*

pho·toph·i·lous, fō·tof′i·lus, a. Biol. thriving in light; as, a photophilous plant. Also **pho·to·phil·ic,** fō″tō·fil′ik.—**pho·toph·i·ly,** n.

pho·to·pho·bi·a, fō″to·fō′bē·a, n. [Gr. phōs, phōtos, light, and phobia, dread.] An intolerance or dread of light.—**pho·to·pho·bic,** a.

pho·to·pi·a, fō·tō′pē·a, n. Vision in bright lighting conditions.—**pho·top·ic,** fō·top′ik, fō·tō′pik, a.

pho·to·play, fō′to·plā″, n. A play reproduced as a motion picture; a motion picture screenplay.

pho·to·pos·i·tive, fō″to·poz′i·tiv, a. Referring to a photoelectric substance whose electric conductivity is increased by absorption of electromagnetic radiation.

pho·to·re·cep·tor, fō″tō·ri·sep′tēr, n. Physiol. a nerve receptor that responds to light.—**pho·to·re·cep·tion,** fō″tō·ri·sep′shan, n.

pho·to·re·con·nais·sance, fō″tō·ri·kon′i·sans, n. Aerial reconnaissance to take photographs.

pho·to·sen·si·tive, fō″to·sen′si·tiv, a. Readily affected or changed by light or other radiant energy.—**pho·to·sen·si·tiv·i·ty,** fō″to·sen″si·tiv′i·tē, n.

pho·to·sphere, fō′to·sfēr″, n. [Gr. phōs, phōtos, light, and E. sphere.] A sphere of light; that part of the sun's luminous surface which is visible.—**pho·to·spher·ic,** fō″to·sfer′ik, a.

Pho·to·stat, fō′to·stat″, n. A special camera for making facsimile copies of drawings or documents, directly on sensitized paper without the inversion of ordinary negatives. (Trademark.) (Often l.c.) the copy thus produced.—v.t., v.i. (l.c.) to copy with a Photostat.—**pho·to·stat·ic,** fō″to·stat′ik, a.

pho·to·syn·the·sis, fō″to·sin′thi·sis, n. [Gr. phōs, phōtos, light, synthēsis, a putting together.] Bot. the process by which green plants manufacture a simple sugar from carbon dioxide and water in the presence of light and chlorophyll, with oxygen produced as a by-product.—**pho·to·syn·the·size,** v.i.—photosynthesized, photosynthesizing.—**pho·to·syn·thet·ic,** fō″to·sin·thet′ik, a.—**pho·to·syn·thet·i·cal·ly,** adv.

pho·to·tax·is, fō″to·tak′sis, n. [N.L.] Biol. the property of a cell or organism of exhibiting attraction, positive phototaxis, or repulsion, negative phototaxis, in relation to light. Also **pho·to·tax·y.**—**pho·to·tac·tic,** fō″to·tak′tik, a.

pho·to·te·leg·ra·phy, fō″tō·te·leg′ra·fē, n. Telegraphy by means of light, as with a heliograph; the electric transmission of facsimiles of photographs.—**pho·to·tel·e·graph,** fō″to·tel′e·graf″, fō″to·tel′e·gräf″, n.—**pho·to·tel·e·graph·ic,** fō″to·tel′e·graf′ik, a.

pho·tot·ro·pism, fō·to′tro·piz″um, n. Bot. the tendency to turn or grow in a direction oriented to the stimulus of light.—**pho·to·trop·ic,** fō″to·trop′ik, a. Exhibiting phototropism.

pho·to·tube, fō′to·tōb″, fō′to·tūb″, n. A photoelectric cell.

pho·to·type·set·ting, fō″tō·tīp′set″ing, n. Photocomposition on a keyboard typesetting machine.—**pho·to·type,** n.

pho·to·ty·pog·ra·phy, fō″tō·tī·pog′ra·fē, n. The art of making printing surfaces and reproductions by the use of light or photography.—**pho·to·ty·po·graph·ic,** **pho·to·ty·po·graph·i·cal,** fō″to·tī′po·graf′ik, a.

pho·to·vol·ta·ic, fō″tō·vol·tā′ik, a. Pertaining to the production of an electromotive force by the incidence of radiant energy, esp. light, upon the juncture of two different materials.

pho·to·zin·cog·ra·phy, fō″tō·zing·kog′ra·fē, n. The photographic process of printing from a prepared sensitized zinc plate.—**pho·to·zin·co·graph,** n.

phras·al, frā′zal, a. Gram. of the nature of, or consisting of, a phrase.

phrase, frāz, n. [Gr. phrasis, a phrase (seen also in periphrasis, paraphrase), < phrazō, I speak.] Gram. two or more connected words not including a finite verb with its subject. A characteristic or aphoristic expression; an idiom, or manner or style of expression. Rhet. one or more words spoken in a single breath with a pause before and after, and forming a meaningful unit; mus. a short part of a composition usu. occupying a distinct rhythmical period of from two to four bars; dance, a sequence of movements comprising a unit in a choreographic pattern.—v.t.—phrased, phrasing. To express in a particular manner; as, to phrase a plea badly; to verbalize; rhet. to speak in phrases; mus. to divide, as a piece, into phrases.

phra·se·o·gram, frā′zē·o·gram″, n. A combination of shorthand characters that represent a phrase.

phra·se·ol·o·gist, frā″zē·ol′o·jist, n. One who is concerned with or collects phrases; a coiner of phrases.

phra·se·ol·o·gy, frā″zē·ol′o·jē, n. Manner of expression; choice of words; diction.—**phra·se·o·log·i·cal,** frā″zē·o·loj′i·kal, a.—**phra·se·o·log·i·cal·ly,** adv.

phras·ing, frā′zing, n. The act of forming phrases; wording; phraseology; mus. the rendering of musical phrases.

phra·try, frā′trē, n. pl. **phra·tries.** [Gr. phratria, < phratēr, clansman.] In ancient Greece, a division of the people, orig. based on kinship; a subdivision of a phyle. Any analogous group among primitive races, as the aborigines of Australia or the Americas.

phre·net·ic, fri·net′ik, a. Frenetic. Also **phre·net·i·cal.**

phren·ic, fren′ik, a. [< Gr. phrēn, in sense of diaphragm.] Pertaining to the mind or activity of the mind; anat. pertaining to the diaphragm.

phre·nol·o·gy, fri·nol′o·jē, fre·nol′o·jē, n. [Gr. phren (phren-), mind.] The theory that the mental powers of an individual consist of independent faculties, each of which has its seat in a definite brain region whose size, supposedly indicated by the shape of the skull over it, is commensurate with the development of the particular faculty; the system based on this theory.—**phren·o·log·ic,** **phren·o·log·i·cal,** fren″o·loj′ik, a.—**phren·o·log·i·cal·ly,** adv.—**phre·nol·o·gist,** n.

Phryg·i·an, frij′ē·an, a. [From Phrygia, in Asia Minor.] Pertaining to the ancient country of Phrygia, its inhabitants, or language.—n. The language of Phrygia; a native of Phrygia.

phthal·ein, thal′ēn, thal′ē·in, fthal′ēn, fthal′ē·in, n. Chem. any of a group of compounds, certain derivatives of which yield important dyes, formed by treating phthalic anhydride with phenols.

phthal·ic ac·id, thal′ik as′id, fthal′ik, n. Chem. any of three isomeric benzene-dicarboxylic acids, $C_8H_6O_4$, used in making synthetic dyes, perfumes, and resins.

phthal·in, thal′in, fthal′in, n. Chem. any one of a group of colorless, crystalline compounds formed from the breaking up and reduction of the phthaleins.

phthi·ri·a·sis, thi·rī′a·sis, fthi·rī′a·sis, n. Pathol. pediculosis.

phy·col·o·gy, fī·kol′o·jē, n. [Gr. phykos and logos.] Bot. The study of the green, blue-green, red, and brown algae all constituting a subdivision of the plant phylum Thallophyta. Also algology.—**phy·co·log·i·cal,** fī″ko·loj′i·kal, a.—**phy·col·o·gist,** n.

phy·co·my·cete, fī″kō·mī′sēt, fī″kō·mī·sēt′, n. Bot. Any of the lowest and simplest class of the fungi, the Phycomycetes, akin to the algae but lacking chlorophyll, comprising the bread molds, water molds, and downy mildews.—**phy·co·my·ce·tous,** fī″kō·mī·sē′tus, a.

phy·lac·ter·y, fi·lak′te·rē, n. pl. **phy·lac·ter·ies.** [L.L. phylacterium, < Gr. phylacterion, outpost, safeguard, amulet, phylássein, guard.] Judaism, either of two small leather cases containing slips inscribed with certain texts from the Pentateuch, worn on the left arm and forehead during early morning prayer as a reminder to keep the law: Deut. vi. 8, xi. 18; also tefillin. A reminder; an amulet, charm, or safeguard worn on the person; any early Christian receptacle containing a holy relic.

phy·le, fī′lē, n. pl. **phy·lae,** fī′lē. A large political subdivision in ancient Greece.

phyl·lo·clade, fil′o·klād″, n. [< Gr. phyllon, leaf, and cládos, branch.] Bot. a modified branch or stem, more or less flattened, and functioning as a leaf, as in the Christmas cactus.—**phyl·lo·cla·di·oid,** a.—**phyl·lo·cla·dous,** fi·lok′la·dous, a.

phyl·lode, fil′ōd, n. [Gr. phyllōdēs, leaflike.] Bot. an expanded petiole resembling and having the function of a leaf. Also **phyl·lo·di·um.**—**phyl·lo·di·al,** a.

phyl·lo·di·um, fil·ō′dē·um, n. pl. **phyl·lo·di·a.** Bot. phyllode.

phyl·loid, fil′oid, a. Bot. leaflike.

phyl·lome, fil′ōm, n. [< Gr. phyllon, leaf, and -ome.] Bot. a leaf of a plant, or a structure morphologically corresponding to it.—**phyl·lom·ic,** fi·lom′ik, fi·lō′mik, a.

phyl·lo·pod, fil′o·pod″, n. pl. **phyl·lo·po·da.** [N.L. Phyllopoda, pl., < Gr. phyllon, leaf, and pous (pod-), foot.] Any of the Phyllopoda, an order of crustaceans characterized by leaflike swimming parts.—a.—**phyl·lop·o·dan,** fi·lop′o·dan, a., n.—**phyl·lop·o·dous,** a.

phyl·lo·tax·y, fil′o·tak″sē, n. pl. **phyl·lo·tax·ies.** [N.L.] Bot. The arrangement of leaves on a stem or axis; the study of the principles governing such arrangement. Also **phyl·lo·tax·is,** fil″o·tak′sis.—**phyl·lo·tac·tic,** **phyl·lo·tac·ti·cal,** fil″o·tak′tik, a.

phyl·lox·e·ra, fil″ok·sēr′a, fi·lok′sēr·a, n. pl. **phyl·lox·e·rae,** **phyl·lox·e·ras,** fil″ok·sēr′ē, fi·lok′se·rē″. [Gr. phyllon, a leaf, and xēros, parched.] A plant louse which infests the leaves and roots of oaks and grapevines, one species of which has caused wide damage in wine-producing areas.—**phyl·lox·e·ran,** a., n.

phy·log·e·ny, fī·loj′e·nē, n. [Gr. phyle, a tribe, and genesis, root gen, to produce.] Biol. The origin and evolution of types or species of animal and plant forms; the history of racial origins. Also **phy·lo·gen·e·sis,** fī″lo·jen′i·sis.—**phy·lo·ge·net·ic,** **phy·lo·ge·net·i·cal,** fī″lo·je·net′ik, a.—**phy·lo·ge·net·i·cal·ly,** adv.—**phy·log·e·nist,** n.

phy·lon, fī′lon, n. pl. **phy·la,** fī′la. Biol. a group related genetically, as a family, tribe, or race.

phy·lum, fī′lum, n. pl. **phy·la,** fī′la. [Gr. phylon, a tribe.] Biol. a major division in the classification of animals and plants under which related classes are grouped; ling. a category of various language stocks having certain characteristics in common which indicate their derivation from a common source.—**phy·lar,** a.

phys·i·at·rics, fiz″ē·a′triks, n. pl. but sing. in constr. A division of medicine which deals with the treatment of diseases or injuries by such physical or natural means as massage, manipulation, heat, and mud baths; any kind of physical therapy. See physiotherapy.

phys·ic, fiz′ik, n. [Gr. *physikos*, pertaining to nature, natural, < *physis*, nature, < *phyō*, to bring forth, to spring up.] Any medicine; a medicine that purges; a purge; a cathartic.—*v.t.*—**physicked**, **physicking**. To purge with a cathartic; to remedy.

phys·i·cal, fiz′i·kal, a. [M.E. *physicalis*, < L. and M.L. *physica*.] Pertaining to the body, or bodily; of or pertaining to material nature; pertaining to the properties, processes, laws, or science of nature, or to physics; obvious to the senses.—**phys·i·cal·ly**, *adv.*

phys·i·cal ed·u·ca·tion, n. A course of athletic training and hygiene to develop and care for the body, generally a part of a school program.

phys·i·cal ge·og·ra·phy, n. A branch of geography concerned with the natural features and phenomena of the earth's surface, as land forms, climate, winds, ocean currents, and the like.

phys·i·cal·ism, fiz′i·ka·liz″um, n. *Philos.* in logical positivism, the idea that all meaningful language must be reducible to terms referring to things, events, or properties existing in space and time.—**phys·i·cal·ist**, *n.*—**phys·i·cal·is·tic**, fiz″i·ka·lis′tik, a.

phys·i·cal·i·ty, fiz″i·kal′i·tē, n. pl. **phys·i·cal·i·ties**. The state of being preoccupied with bodily attributes or needs, as opposed to intellectual or social concerns; an individual's physical characteristics, esp. when too fully developed or emphasized.

phys·i·cal sci·ence, n. The observation and interpretation of natural laws, processes, and properties of nonliving matter.

phys·i·cal ther·a·py, n. Physiotherapy.

phy·si·cian, fi·zish′an, n. [O.Fr. *fisicien*, physician (Fr. *physicien*, physicist), < L. and M.L. *physica*.] One legally qualified to practice medicine; a doctor engaged in general medical practice as distinguished from one specializing in surgery; one who is skilled in the art of healing.

phys·i·cist, fiz′i·sist, n. A scientist in the field of physics.

phys·i·co·chem·i·cal, fiz″i·kō·kem′i·kal, a. Both physical and chemical; relating to physical chemistry.—**phys·i·co·chem·i·cal·ly**, *adv.*

phys·ics, fiz′iks, n. pl. but sing. in constr. That branch of science which treats of the laws, properties, and interactions of matter, motion, and energy.

phys·i·o·crat, fiz′ē·o·krat″, n. [Fr. *physiocrate*, < Gr. *physis*, nature, and *-kratia*, < *kratein*, rule.] One of a school of political economists, followers of the French economist François Quesnay, 1694–1774, who recognized an inherent natural order as properly governing society, regarded land as the basis of wealth and taxation, and advocated freedom of industry and trade.—**phys·i·o·crat·ic**, *a.*—**phys·i·oc·ra·cy**, *n.* The doctrine of the physiocrats; government by or in accordance with nature.

phys·i·og·no·my, fiz″ē·og′no·mē, fiz″ē·on′o·mē, n. pl. **phys·i·og·no·mies**. [Properly *physiognomy*, < Gr. *physiognōmonia*—*physis*, nature, and *gnōmōn*, one who knows, < stem of *gignōskō*, to know.] The face or countenance regarded as an indication or revelation of character; the art of discerning character from the features of the body, esp. the face; the external appearance of a thing, esp. as revealing its nature or character.—**phys·i·og·nom·ic**, **phys·i·og·nom·i·cal**, fiz″ē·og·nom′ik, fiz″ē·o·nom′ik, a.—**phys·i·og·nom·i·cal·ly**, *adv.*—**phys·i·og·no·mist**, *n.*

phys·i·og·ra·phy, fiz″ē·og′ra·fē, n. [Gr. *physis*, nature, and *graphō*, to describe.] The description of natural phenomena; physical geography; geomorphology.—**phys·i·og·ra·pher**, *n.*—**phys·i·o·graph·ic**, **phys·i·o·graph·i·cal**, fiz″ē·o·graf′ik, a.

phys·i·o·log·i·cal, fiz″ē·o·loj′i·kal, a. Of or pertaining to physiology; agreeing or in accord with the normal or appropriate functioning of a healthy organism. Also **phys·i·o·log·ic.**—**phys·i·o·log·i·cal·ly**, *adv.*

phys·i·ol·o·gy, fiz″ē·ol′o·jē, n. [L. *physiologia*, < Gr. *physiologia*, natural philosophy, < *physis*, nature, and *légein*, speak.] The science dealing with the normal functions of living plant and animal organisms or their organs; a treatise on this subject; the collective functions and vital processes of living matter; as, the *physiology* of a guinea pig.—**phys·i·ol·o·gist**, fiz″ē·ol′o·jist, *n.*

phys·i·o·ther·a·py, fiz″ē·ō·ther′a·pē, n. The treatment of disease, bodily weaknesses, or defects by physical remedies, such as massage and exercise. Also *physical therapy.*

phy·sique, fi·zēk′, n. [Fr.] The physical or bodily structure, appearance, or constitution.—**phy·siqued**, fi·zēkt′, *a.*

phy·so·stig·mine, fī″sō·stig′mēn, fī″sō·stig′min, n. [N.L. *Physostigma*, < Gr. *physa*, bellows, and *stigma*, E. *stigma*.] *Chem.* a poisonous alkaloid constituting the active principle of the Calabar bean, used in medicine as a myotic in glaucoma. Also **es·er·ine.**

phy·to·gen·ic, fī″to·jen′ik, a. Having its origin in plant life.

phy·to·ge·og·ra·phy, fī″tō·jē·og′ra·fē, n. [Gr. *phyton*, a plant, and E. *geography.*] The science concerned with the geographical distribution and interrelation of plants.

phy·tog·ra·phy, fī·tog′ra·fē, n. [Gr. *phyton*, a plant, and *graphē*, description.] That branch of botany which concerns itself with describing and naming plants.

phy·to·lite, fī′to·līt″, n. The fossil of a plant. Also **phy·to·lith.**

phy·ton, fī′ton, n. The unit formed by a leaf and the portion of the stem associated with it; the smallest portion of a leaf, stem, or root that can, if severed, generate an entire plant.—**phy·ton·ic**, fī′ton′ik, a.

phy·to·pa·thol·o·gy, fī″tō·pa·thol′o·jē, n. The study of plant diseases, their causes and control; plant pathology.—**phy·to·path·o·log·ic**, **phy·to·path·o·log·i·cal**, fī″tō·path″o·loj′ik, a.

phy·toph·a·gous, fī·tof′a·gus, a. [Gr. *phyton*, a plant, *phagō*, to eat.] Eating or subsisting on plants, as certain insects.—**phy·toph·a·gy**, *n.*

phy·to·plank·ton, fī″to·plangk′ton, n. *Bot.* usu. minute floating or drifting aquatic plant organisms, such as diatoms and blue-green algae.—**phy·to·plank·ton·ic.** *a.*

phy·to·so·ci·ol·o·gy, fī″tō·sō″sē·ol′o·jē, fī″tō·sō″shē·ol′o·je, n. That branch of ecology which treats of the origin and composition of plant communities and the interrelations of the floral varieties therein. —**phy·to·so·ci·o·log·ic**, **phy·to·so·ci·o·log·i·cal**, fī″to·sō″sē·o·loj′ik, fī″to·sō″shē·o·loj′ik, a.—**phy·to·so·ci·o·log·i·cal·ly**, *adv.*—**phy·to·so·ci·ol·o·gist**, *n.*

phy·to·tox·ic, fī″to·tok′sik, a. Having a poisonous effect on plants.—**phy·to·tox·ic·i·ty**, fī″tō·tok·sis′i·tē, *n.*

pi, pī, n. [Gr. *pi* (the initial letter of *peripherein*, circumference, E. *periphery*).] The sixteenth letter *Π*, *π*, of the Greek alphabet corresponding to the English P, p; *math.* the Greek letter *Π*, *π* used as the symbol for the ratio of the circumference of a circle to its diameter; the ratio itself, 3.141592. +

pi, **pie**, pī, n. [Origin uncertain.] Printing types mixed together indiscriminately.—*v.t.*—**pied**, **piing** or **pieing.** To reduce, as printing type, to a state of disorder.

pi·al, pī′al, a. Belonging or relating to the pia mater.

pi·a ma·ter, pī′a mā′tėr, n. [M.L. 'tender

mother.'] *Anat.* the delicate, fibrous, and highly vascular membrane forming the innermost of the three coverings enveloping the brain and spinal cord. See *arachnoid* and *dura mater.*

pi·a·nis·si·mo, pē″a·nis′i·mō″, *It.* pyä·nēs′sē·mą, a. [It., superl. of *piano.*] *Mus.* very soft.—*adv. Mus.* very softly.—*n. Mus.* a piece or movement so played.

pi·an·ist, pē·an′ist, pyan′ist, pē′a·nist, n. A performer on the piano, esp. a professional one.

pi·an·o, pē·an′ō, pyan′ō, n. pl. **pi·an·os**. [It. < *pianoforte.*] A musical instrument with a keyboard by means of which metal strings are struck by felt-covered hammers to bring forth musical sounds. Also *pianoforte.*

pi·an·o, pē·ä′nō, *It.* pyä′ną, a., adv. [It., soft, smooth, < L. *planus*, plain.] *Mus.* Soft, softly; a direction to execute a passage softly or with diminished volume.—*n.* A passage performed in this manner.

pi·an·o ac·cor·di·on, n. *Mus.* a hand-held instrument of the reed organ family having bellows and a keyboard of no more than three and one-half octaves.

pi·an·o·forte, pē·an″o·fōr′tē, pē·an″o·fōr′tā, pē·an″o·far′tē, pē·an″o·far′tā, n. [It. *piano*, soft, smooth, and *forte* (L. *fortis*), strong.] A piano.

pi·as·sa·va, pē″a·sä′va, n. [Pg. *piaçaba.*] The fiber of either of two Brazilian palm trees, *Attalea funifera* and *Leopoldinia piassaba*, extensively used in making brooms, brushes, ropes, and the like; either palm tree. Also **pi·as·sa·ba.**

pi·az·za, pē·az′a, pē·ä′za, *Brit.* pē·at′sa, pē·ad′za, *It.* pyät′sä, n. pl. **pi·az·zas**, *It.* **piaz·ze**, *It.* pyät′tse. [It., < L. *platea.*] An open public square in a town or city, esp. in Italy; an arcade, covered walk, or gallery, as around a square or in front of a building; chiefly *U.S.* a veranda of a house.

pi·broch, pē′brOch, n. [Gael. *piobaireachd*, pipe music, ult. < E. *pipe.*] In the Scottish Highlands, a musical piece performed on the bagpipe, comprising a series of variations on a ground theme, usu. martial in character, but sometimes used as a dirge.

pi·ca, pī′ka, n. [Supposed to be < A.L. *pica*, book of rules for church services, appar. the same word as L. *pica*, magpie.] A size of printing type, 12-point; a standard printing measure, equaling the depth of this type size, about one-sixth of an inch; a kind of typewriter type having 10 characters to the linear inch.

pi·ca, pī′ka, n. [N.L., < L. *pica*, magpie (with reference to its omnivorous feeding).] *Med.* an unnatural craving for substances not normally considered food, as chalk or clay.

pi·ca·dor, pik′a·dạr″, *Sp.* pē″kä·THạr′, n. pl. **pi·ca·dors**, *Sp.* **pi·ca·do·res**, *Sp.* pē″kä·THạ′res. [Sp., < *pica*, a pike or lance.] A horseman who excites and irritates the bull in a bullfight and attempts to weaken him by pricking his shoulder muscles with a lance.

pic·a·resque, pik″a·resk′, a. [< Sp.] Pertaining to rogues or picaroons; of or characterized by a fictional narrative, Spanish in origin, describing the adventures or fortunes of a vagabond hero in an episodic literary style; as, a *picaresque* novel.

pic·a·ro, pik′a·rō″, *Sp.* pē″kä·Rą″, n. [Sp.] A rogue, wanderer, or gypsy. Also *picaroon.* —**pic·a·ra**, pik′a·rä″, *Sp.* pē″kä·Rä″, n. Feminine of *picaro.*

pic·a·roon, pik″a·rön′, n. [Sp. *picarón*, augmentative of *picaro*, a rogue.] A rogue or wanderer; also *picaro.* A cheat; a brigand; a pirate; a pirate ship.—*v.i.* to operate as a pirate.

pic·a·yune, pik″ē·yön′, pik″ē·ün′, a. [Fr. *picaillon*, < Pr. *picaioun*, old copper coin of

Piedmont.] *Colloq.* Of little value or account; small; petty; mean. Also **pic·a·-yun·ish.**—*n.* The Spanish half real, a coin formerly in use in a the southern U.S.; any small coin, as a five-cent piece; *colloq.* an insignificant person or thing.

pic·ca·lil·li, pik′a·lil″ē, *n.* A relish of East Indian origin, consisting of various chopped vegetables and pungent spices.

pic·co·lo, pik′o·lō″, *n.* pl. **pic·co·los.** [It. *piccolo*, small.] A small flute with a pitch an octave higher than that of the ordinary orchestral flute; an organ stop reproducing the sound of a piccolo.—**pic·co·lo·ist,** pik′o·lō″ist, *n.*

pic·e·ous, pis′ē·us, pī′sē·us, *a.* [L. *piceus*, < *pix, picis*, pitch.] Of or belonging to pitch; resembling pitch; flammable; black as pitch.

pick, pik, *v.t.* [M.E. *piken, picken*, < an O.E. verb represented in *pīcung*, pricking, and akin to *pīc*, pickax; cf. *peck* and *pique, verb.*] To choose or select carefully; to detach or remove, esp. with the fingers; to pluck or gather; as, to *pick* fruit or flowers; to use a pointed instrument, the fingers, the teeth, or the like on, in order to remove pieces of clinging matter; as, to *pick* a bone; to clear by such action; to prepare for use by removing feathers, hulls, or other parts; as, to *pick* a fowl; to take up, as bits of food, with the bill or teeth; to eat daintily; to pierce, indent, dig into, or break up with a pointed instrument; to form, as a hole, by such action; to separate or pull apart, as fibers; to open, as a lock, with a pointed instrument or the like, esp. for the purpose of robbery; to steal the contents of, as a pocket or purse; to seek and find occasion for; as, to *pick* a quarrel; to seek or find, as flaws. *Mus.* to pluck, as the strings of an instrument; to play, as a stringed instrument, by plucking with the fingers.—*v.i.* To make careful or fastidious selection; to strike with or use a pick, pointed instrument, or the like on something; to pluck or gather something; to eat with small bites or daintily; to pilfer.—*n.* Choice or selection; the right of selection; that which is selected; the choicest or most desirable part or example; an act of picking; a stroke with something pointed; the quantity of a plant crop picked at a particular time.—**pick on,** to select from others, as for special treatment; *colloq.* to harass, torment, or find fault with.—**pick·er,** pik′ẽr, *n.*

pick, pik, *v.t.* [Var. of *pitch*.] *Brit. dial.* to pitch or throw.—*n. Brit. dial.* a cast or throw. *Weaving*, a cast or throw of the shuttle; a single weft thread in cloth.

pick, pik, *n.* [Appar. partly < *pick*, verb, and partly < *pike*.] A tool consisting of a pointed, usu. curved metal head secured to a wooden handle and used for loosening and breaking up soil, rock, and the like; a pickax or mattock; any pointed tool or instrument for picking; as, an ice *pick* or tooth*pick*; a plectrum.

pick·a·back, pik′a·bak″, *adv., a.* [< the older form *pickapack*, a reduplication of *pack*.] Piggyback.

pick·a·nin·ny, pic·a·nin·ny, pik′a·nin″ē, *n.* pl. **pick·a·nin·nies.** [Sp. *pequeño niño*, little infant.] A Negro child: usu. an offensive designation.

pick·ax, pick·axe, pik′aks, *n.* pl. **pick·-ax·es.** [Appar. < *pick* and *ax*, but really a corruption of O.Fr. *picquois*, a pickax, < *picquer*, to pierce.] A pick with a sharp point at one end and a broad blade at the other; also *mattock*. A pick pointed at both ends.—*v.t.*—*pickaxed, pickaxing.* To cut, dig, or loosen with a pickax.—*v.i.* To employ a pickax or to put one to use.

picked, pikt, *a.* Specially chosen or selected, as for excellence or efficiency, or for a particular purpose; cleared or cleaned, as of

refuse, by picking; harvested, as fruit; worked on with a pick or the like.

pick·er·el, pik′ẽr·el, pik′rel, *n.* pl. **pick·-er·el, pick·er·els.** [Dim. of *pike*.] Any of various species of pike, esp. one of the smaller species, as *Esox reticulatus*; the pikeperch; *Brit.* a young pike.

pick·er·el·weed, pik′ẽr·el·wēd″, pik′rel·-wēd″, *n.* Any N. American perennial aquatic herb of the genus *Pontederia*, esp. *P. cordata*, common in ponds and bogs, having arrowhead-shaped leaves and bright blue flowers borne on tall spikes.

pick·et, pik′it, *n.* [Fr. *piquet*, a dim. of *pique*, a pike.] A stake or post that is sharpened or pointed, used to form a fence or to secure a tent or other object; a person posted, as by a labor union, before or near a place of business at the time of a strike in order to discourage or prevent entrance by workers or customers; a protester or demonstrator; *milit.* a detachment of troops stationed ahead of an encampment to guard against a surprise attack.—*v.t.* To fence or fortify with pickets or pointed stakes; to fasten to a picket or stake; to place or post as a guard or picket; to post a guard or picket near or before.—*v.i.* To be stationed as a picket.—**pick·et·er,** *n.*

pick·et line, *n.* A group of persons, as strikers or protesters, standing or marching in a line as pickets.

pick·et ship, *n. Milit.* a ship or aircraft used as a radar picket to supplement early-warning radar.

pick·ing, pik′ing, *n.* The act of someone or something that picks; the thing or the amount that is picked. *Usu. pl.* that which is left to be picked or gleaned; profits or benefits not honestly obtained.

pick·le, pik′l, *n.* [D. and L.G. *pekel,* G. *pōkel, bōkel,* brine.] An item of food, esp. a cucumber, preserved in brine or a vinegar solution; a solution of salt and water or of vinegar in which meat, fish, or vegetables are preserved or marinated; a bath, as a chemical solution, used as an industrial cleaner or preservative. *Colloq.* a state or condition of difficulty or disorder; a plight.—*v.t.*—*pickled, pickling.* To preserve in or treat with brine or vinegar.

pick off, *v.t.* To single out and shoot, as: The riflemen *picked off* the enemy. *Baseball*, to throw or tag out, as a runner caught off base.

pick out, *v.t.* To choose or select carefully; to distinguish from surrounding or accompanying things; to perceive or discover, as sense or meaning; to play, as a tune, one note at a time or by ear.

pick o·ver, *v.t.* To inspect carefully or one at a time for the purpose of making a choice.

pick·pock·et, pik′pok″it, *n.* One who steals, or makes a practice of stealing, from people's pockets.

pick·up, pik′up″, *n.* Acceleration, or the power to accelerate; a truck with a small, open body for carrying light loads. *Tele-communications*, the reception of light or sound waves into a television or radio transmitting set; a receiving device that converts a sound, scene, or other form of intelligence into corresponding electric signals; as, a microphone *pickup*; a television camera *pickup*; the location of the orig. transmission of a broadcast, or the system which connects to a broadcasting studio, a program that originates elsewhere. *Electron.* a device for reproducing sound by converting mechanical vibrations into electric impulses, as that contained in the tone arm of a phonograph; also *cartridge. Colloq.* a person, usu. a stranger of the opposite sex, with whom informal social contact is made, often for sexual purposes; an increase or improvement, esp. in business. *Colloq.* something, as alcohol, that revives or stimulates; also **pick-me-up.**

pick up, *v.t.* To take up, as with the fingers; recover or regain, as courage; to acquire casually or as chance or opportunity offers; as, to *pick up* a livelihood; to take up into a vehicle or along with one, as a person or thing; to increase or accelerate; to receive or bring within scope of the senses; as, to *pick up* a radio signal; to make neat or orderly, as a room. *Colloq.* to make informal social contact with, as one of the opposite sex; to arrest or apprehend, as one who breaks the law.—*v.i.* To improve, increase, or make gains.

Pick·wick·i·an, pik·wik′ē·an, *a.* Of, relating to, or like the blundering simplicity of Mr. Samuel Pickwick, protagonist of Charles Dickens' novel, *Pickwick Papers;* of or pertaining to a sense that is attached to words merely for the occasion, regardless of their actual or literal sense.

pick·y, pik′ē, *a.*—*pickier, pickiest.* Unduly particular or fussy, esp. about trivialities; finicky.

pic·nic, pik′nik, *n.* An outdoor pleasure excursion, usu. one with a meal carried along and shared by the participants; *colloq.* a pleasurable or easy experience or undertaking. The arm and shank sections of pork shoulder, sold fresh, pickled, or cured and smoked; also **pic·nic shoul·der.**—*v.i.*—*picknicked, picnicking.* To have or take part in a picnic.—**pic·nick·er,** *n.*

pic·nom·e·ter, pik·nom′i·tẽr, *n.* Pycnometer.

pic·o·line, pik′o·lēn″, pik′o·lin, *n.* [L. *pix* (*pic-*), pitch, and *oleum*, oil.] *Chem.* any of three isomeric derivatives of pyridine, C_6H_7N, obtained from coal tar as colorless oily liquids with a strong odor, and used as solvents and in medicines.—**pic·o·lin·ic,** pik″o·lin′ik, *a.*

pi·cot, pē′kō, *n.* [Fr. dim. of *pic*, a pick, something pointed.] One of a number of ornamental loops in embroidery or tatting, or along the edge of lace or ribbon.—*v.t., v.i.*

pic·o·tee, pik″o·tē′, *n.* [Fr. *picoté*, pp. of *picoter*, mark with pricks or spots, < *picot*.] A variety of carnation having petals of a light background marked at the outer margin with another color, usu. red.

pic·ric ac·id, pik′rik as′id, *n.* [Gr. *pikros*, bitter, sharp.] *Chem.* a bitter, crystalline, toxic, water-soluble yellow acid, C_6H_3-N_3O_7, used chiefly in explosives, dyes, and medicines, and in leather processing.

pic·ro·tox·in, pik″ro·tok′sin, *n. Chem.* a bitter, highly poisonous, crystalline compound, $C_{30}H_{34}O_{13}$, used in medicines to counteract barbiturate poisoning or to stimulate respiration.—**pic·ro·tox·ic,** *a.*

pic·to·graph, pik′to·graf″, pik′to·gräf″, *n.* [L. *pictus*, pp. of *pingere*, represent pictorially, paint.] A pictorial sign or symbol; a record consisting of pictorial symbols, as hieroglyphics; a chart, diagram, or graph using pictures to represent number or change.—**pic·to·graph·ic,** pik″to·graf′ik, *a.*—**pic·to·graph·i·cal·ly,** *adv.*—**pic·-tog·ra·phy,** pik·tog′ra·fē, *n.*

pic·to·ri·al, pik·tōr′ē·al, pik·tạr′ē·al, *a.* [L.L. *pictorius*, < L. *pictor*, painter, < *pingere*.] Pertaining to, expressed in, or of the nature of a painting or picture; as, records in *pictorial* form; illustrated by or containing pictures; pictographic.—*n.* A periodical in which pictures are an important feature.—**pic·to·ri·al·ly,** *adv.*—**pic·to·ri·al·ness,** *n.*

pic·ture, pik′chẽr, *n.* [L. *pictura*, < *pingere* (pp. *pictus*), represent pictorially, paint.] A painting, drawing, photograph, or other visual representation, as of a person, object, or scene; any visual image, however produced; a mental image; a motion picture; a graphic or vivid description or account; the image or counterpart of, as: He is the *picture* of his father. A representative example of something; a concrete embodiment of some quality; as, the *picture* of health; a tableau; an overall view of a situation or event.—*v.t.*—*pictured, picturing.* To represent in a picture or pictorially; to illustrate; to form a mental image of, or imagine; to depict in words; to describe graphically.

pic·ture hat, *n.* A large, wide-brimmed woman's hat, often trimmed or decorated with plumes or flowers.

pic·tur·esque, pik″cha·resk′, *a.* Quaint and charming enough to form a pleasing picture; suggesting a picture; pictorial; abounding with vivid and striking imagery; graphic.—**pic·tur·esque·ly,** *adv.*—**pic·tur·esque·ness,** *n.*

pic·ture tube, *n.* A cathode ray tube which reproduces images on a television screen. Also *kinescope.*

pic·ture win·dow, *n.* A large window of a single pane which frames a pleasing view.

pic·ture writ·ing, *n.* The art of recording events or expressing ideas by pictures or pictorial symbols; pictorial symbols forming a record or communication.

pic·ul, pik′ul, *n.* [Malay.] In China and elsewhere in the East, a weight equal to 100 catties, or about 133⅓ pounds.

pid·dle, pid′l, *v.i.*—*piddled, piddling.* [A form of *peddle.*] To deal in trifles; to waste time or energy; *colloq.* to urinate.—*v.t.* To dawdle or waste, usu. followed by *away;* as, to *piddle away* time.—**pid·dling,** pid′-ling, *a.* Unimportant, trifling.

pid·dock, pid′ok, *n.* [Origin obscure.] Any of the bivalve marine mollusks of the genus *Pholas,* or others in the family *Pholadidae,* with long ovate shells and often found burrowed in soft rock, wood, or clay.

pidg·in, pij′in, *n.* A composite language developed as a means of communication between speakers of different languages and resulting in a simplification and combination of pronunciation, grammar, and vocabulary of the two languages.

Pidg·in Eng·lish, Pidg·in Eng·lish, *n.* Any of several pidgins based on English which are used in parts of China, Melanesia, western Africa, and northern Australia in dealings between indigenous and English-speaking peoples.

pie, pī, *n.* [M.E. *pie, pye.*] A one- or two-layered crust or pastry filled with fruit, meat, or any of a variety of sweets. *Slang,* anything considered excellent or easily accomplished.

pie, pī, *n.* [Fr. *pie,* < L. *pica,* a magpie.] Magpie.

pie, pī, *n.,* *v.t.*—*pied, pieing.* *Print.* pi.

pie·bald, pī′bạld″, *a.* [< *pie,* a magpie, and *bald,* spotted with white.] Having spots or patches of white and black or other colors; mottled; blotched.—*n.* A mottled or spotted animal, usu. a horse.

piece, pēs, *n.* [Fr. *pièce,* Pr. *peza,* It. *pezza,* < L.L. *petium,* a piece, prob. < the Celtic; W. *peth,* Armor. *pez,* a piece.] A fragment or part of anything separated from the whole; as, a *piece* of cake; a definite quantity or portion or something considered as an entity; as, a *piece* of writing paper; one item of a group, set, or the like; as, a *piece* of flatware; a standard amount or length according to which an item is produced or sold; as, a *piece* of muslin, a *piece* of work; an instance or example; as, a fine *piece* of shooting; an artistic or literary composition; as, a *piece* of pottery; a coin; *games,* a small object, as a disk or figure, used for counting, moving on a board, or the like; *chess,* any figure superior to a pawn; *milit.* a single firearm; *dial.* a certain distance or length of time; as, just a *piece* up the road.—*v.t.*—*pieced, piecing.* To mend or enlarge by the

addition of a piece; to patch; to unite or join.—**a piece of one's mind,** *colloq.* a bluntly expressed criticism or rebuke.—**of a piece, of one piece,** of the same type; in accord.—**speak one's piece,** voice one's opinions or attitudes.—**piec·er,** *n.*

piece-dye, pēs′dī″, *v.t.*—*piece-dyed, piece-dyeing. Textiles,* to dye, as cloth, after weaving: distinguished from *yarn-dye.*—**piece-dyed,** *a.*

piece goods, *n. pl.* Goods generally sold by the piece or by linear measure, as fabrics. Also *yard goods.*

piece·meal, pēs′mēl″, *adv.* [O.E. *maelum,* by parts.] Piece by piece; in pieces; gradually.—*a.* Done in pieces or bit by bit.

piece·work, pēs′wụrk″, *n.* Work done and paid for by the unit, or by the quantity of pieces produced.—**piece·work·er,** *n.*

pie chart, *n. Statistics,* a circular graph divided by radii into sections, illustrating the proportion of individual segments to a series or whole.

pied, pīd, *a.* [< *pie,* magpie.] Parti-colored; variegated; piebald; spotted or blotched with two or more colors; as, *pied* fabric.

pied·mont, pēd′mont, *a.* [< *Piedmont,* It. *Piemonte,* division of northwestern Italy, < L. *pes (ped-),* foot, and *mons (mont-),* mountain.] Lying along or near the foot of a mountain range or mountain; as, a *piedmont* plain, a *piedmont* glacier.—*n.* A region lying along or near the foot of a mountain range.

pie·plant, pī′plant″, pī′plänt″, *n. Dial.* the common garden rhubarb, *Rheum rhaponticum,* so called from its use in pies.

pier, pēr, *n.* [O.Fr. *pere, piere,* a stone (Fr. *pierre*), < L. and Gr. *petra,* a stone.] A wharf or quay resting on columns or piles, projecting from shore into a body of water, and serving as a docking place for ships or as a recreation area; a breakwater or mole; a support for a bridge, arch, or masonry of any kind; a large square pillar or shaft; a gatepost; the solid part between openings in a wall.

pierce, pērs, *v.t.*—*pierced, piercing.* [O.Fr. *percier* (Fr. *percer*), perh. ult. < L. *pertundere* (pp. *pertusus*), *pierce.*] To penetrate or run into or through with a pointed instrument or the like; puncture or stab; to make a hole or opening in; bore into or through; tunnel; perforate; to make, as a hole, by or as by boring or perforating; to force or make a way into or through; as, to *pierce* a wilderness; to penetrate with the eye or mind; see into or through; to affect sharply with some sensation or emotion, as of cold, pain, or grief; to penetrate or sound sharply through, as: A cry *pierced* the air.—*v.i.* To force or make a way into or through something; penetrate.—**pierc·ing,** *a.* Shrill, penetrating; as, a *piercing* whistle.—**pierc·ing·ly,** *adv.*

pier glass, *n.* A tall mirror, esp. one used to fill the pier or space between two windows.

Pi·er·rot, pē″e·rō′, *Fr.* pye·RŌ′, *n.* [Fr., dim. from *Pierre,* man's name, Peter.] A typical male character in French pantomime, having a whitened face and wearing a loose white fancy costume; (*l.c.*) a masquerader or buffoon so made up.

pier ta·ble, *n.* A console or low table designed to stand between two windows, often under a pier glass.

pie·tà, pē″ä·tä′, pyä·tä′, pē·ä′ta, pyä′ta, *n.* [It. piety, pity, sorrow, < L. *pietas.*] (*Sometimes cap.*) a painting or sculpture of the Virgin Mary seated and supporting the dead body of Christ in her arms or on her knees.

Pi·e·tism, pī′i·tiz″um, *n.* [N.L. *Pietismus,* < L. *pietas.*] A 17th century movement begun in the Lutheran churches in Germany which emphasized personal religious involvement and study rather than formal-

ism. (*l.c.*) emphasis on religious feeling; devotion; exaggeration or affectation of piety.—**Pi·e·tist, pi·e·tist,** *n.*—**pi·e·tis·tic, pi·e·tis·ti·cal,** pī′i·tis′tik, *a.*—**pi·e·tis·ti·cal·ly,** *adv.*

pi·e·ty, pī′i·tē, *n.* *pl.* **pi·e·ties.** [O.Fr. *piete* (Fr. *piété*), < L. *pietas,* piety, dutifulness, tenderness, pity, < *pius,* E. *pious:* cf. *pietà* and *pity.*] The quality or fact of being pious; reverence for God or a Supreme Being; regard for or fidelity to religious obligations; devoutness; dutiful respect or regard for parents or others; a pious act, remark, belief, or the like.

pi·e·zo·e·lec·tric·i·ty, pī·ē″zō·i·lek-tris′i·tē, pī·ē″zō·ē″lek·tris′i·tē, *n.* Electricity created by pressure as from compression along an axis of a crystal such as quartz.—**pi·e·zo·e·lec·tric,** pī·ē″zō·i·lek′trik, *a.*—**pi·e·zo·e·lec·tri·cal·ly,** *adv.*

pi·e·zom·e·ter, pī″i·zom′i·tẽr, *n.* [Gr. *piezō,* to press, *metron,* measure.] An instrument for measuring compressibility and pressure, esp. very high pressures.—**pi·e·zo·met·ric, pi·e·zo·met·ri·cal,** pī·ē″zo·me′trik, *a.*—**pi·e·zom·e·try,** pī″i·zom′i·trē, *n.*

pif·fle, pif′l, *n.* [Origin doubtful.] *Colloq.* Silly talk or written matter; nonsense.—*v.i.*—*piffled, piffling. Colloq.* to talk or babble in a nonsensical way.

pig, pig, *n.* [M.E. *pigge:* cf. D. *big,* young pig.] A young swine of either sex; broadly, any swine or hog, wild or domestic; the flesh of swine, used for food; pork; *colloq.* a person or animal of piggish character or habits; as, being a *pig* at the table. *Metal.* an oblong mass of metal, esp. iron, that has been run while molten into a mold of sand or the like; one of the molds for such masses of metal; metal in the form of such masses, esp. pig iron.—*v.i.*—*pigged, pigging.* To bring forth pigs; farrow; to lie or huddle together; to live like pigs.—**pig it,** *Brit.* to live like pigs, esp. crowded together or under poor circumstances.

pig bed, *n. Metal.* a thick layer of sand containing molds for casting pigs of crude iron.

pig·boat, pig′bōt″, *n. Slang,* a submarine.

pi·geon, pij′on, *n.* [O.Fr. *pijon* (Fr. *pigeon*), < L.L. *pipio(n-),* squab, *pipire,* peep, chirp.] Any member of the family *Columbidae,* comprising birds characterized by a compact body and short legs, and existing in several hundred species widely distributed throughout the world; a dove, esp. a domesticated member of this family, as one of the varieties of the rock dove or the domestic pigeon, *Columba livia;* a small slim brown pigeon, the morning dove, with a long pointed tail; *fig.* a simpleton or dupe.

pi·geon breast, *n. Pathol.* a malformation of the chest in which there is abnormal projection of the sternum and the sternal region, often associated with rickets. Also **pi·geon chest, chick·en breast.**—**pi·geon breast·ed,** *a.*

pi·geon hawk, *n.* A small N. American falcon or hawk, *Falco columbarius columbarius,* with pointed wings, the male being bluish-gray above with broad black bands on the tail. See *merlin.*

pi·geon·heart·ed, pij′on·här′tid, *a.* Timid; easily frightened.

pi·geon·hole, pij′on·hōl″, *n.* One of a series of small compartments in a desk, cabinet, or the like, open in front, and used for holding letters and papers; a hole in a dovecote for pigeons to pass in and out; a recess for pigeons to nest in.—*v.t.*—*pigeonholed, pigeonholing.* To place or file in a pigeonhole; to put away in a proper place for later reference; assign to a definite place in some orderly system; put aside, esp. with the intention of ignoring or forgetting.

pi·geon pea, *n. Bot.* A valuable leguminous shrub, *Cajanus cajan*, widely cultivated in the tropics, having trifoliate leaves and yellow flowers, and grown for its seeds that are used in human food and as a forage crop for animals; the seed itself.

pi·geon-toed, pij′on-tōd″, *a.* Having the toes or feet turned inward.

pi·geon·wing, pij′on-wing″, *n.* A winglike figure in skating; a kind of fancy dance step, involving a jump and a kicking of the feet together in midair.

pig·fish, pig′fish″, *n. pl.* **pig·fish, pig-·fish·es.** A grunt, *Orthopristis chrysopterus*, a food fish of the southern Atlantic coast of the U.S.

pig·ger·y, pig′e·rē, *n. pl.* **pig·ger·ies.** *Chiefly Brit.* A place where pigs are kept; a pigpen; a pigsty.

pig·gin, pig′in, *n.* [Gael. *pigean*, Ir. *pigin*, an earthen pitcher.] *Brit. dial.* A small, pail-like wooden vessel with an erect handle, for milking or to drink from.

pig·gish, pig′ish, *a.* Like or befitting a pig; hoggish; greedy; selfish; unclean or filthy. —**pig·gish·ly,** *adv.*—**pig·gish·ness,** *n.*

pig·gy·back, pig′ē-bak″, *adv., a.* On the back or shoulders, like a pack; astride the shoulders or back; also pickaback. Of the shipping of one carrier on another; as, truck trailers or automobiles traveling *piggyback* on railroad flatcars.—*a.*

pig·gy bank, *n.* A savings bank for coins in the form of a pig; any coin bank.

pig·head·ed, pig′hed″id, *a.* Stupidly obstinate; perverse; stubborn.—**pig·head-·ed·ly,** *adv.*—**pig·head·ed·ness,** *n.*

pig i·ron, *n.* Crude, impure iron cast in the form of oblong ingots called pigs; crude iron as a material, whether molten or in pigs.

pig lead, *n.* Lead in the form of ingots or pigs.

pig·ment, pig′ment, *n.* [L. *pigmentum*, < *pingere*, paint.] A coloring matter or substance; specif. a dry substance, usu. pulverized, which when mixed with a liquid in which it is somewhat insoluble becomes a paint; ink, or the like; *biol.* any substance whose presence in the tissues or cells of animals or plants colors them.—*v.t.* To color.—**pig·men·tar·y,** pig′men·ter″ē, *a.*

pig·men·ta·tion, pig″men·tā′shan, *n. Biol.* coloration with or deposition of pigment, esp. excessive deposition of skin pigment.

Pig·my, pig′mē, *a.* Pygmy.

pig·nut, pig′nut″, *n.* The nut of the hickory, *Carya glabra*, a N. American tree; the tree itself; the tuber of a European plant, *Conopodium denudatum*, fed to hogs.

pig·pen, pig′pen″, *n.* An enclosed area for keeping pigs or hogs; a pigsty; also *Brit.* piggery. *Fig.* any untidy place.

pig·skin, pig′skin″, *n.* The skin of a pig or hog; leather made from it. *Colloq.* a football; a jockey's saddle.

pig·stick, pig′stik″, *v.i.* To hunt and spear wild boar while on horseback.—**pig-·stick·er,** *n.*—**pig·stick·ing,** *n.*

pig·sty, pig′stī″, *n. pl.* **pig·sties.** A sty or pen for pigs. Also *pigpen*.

pig·tail, pig′tāl″, *n.* The hair in a tight braid; tobacco twisted into a roll or into strands.—**pig-tailed,** *a.* Wearing the hair braided in a pigtail.

pig·weed, pig′wēd″, *n.* Any of several weeds of the genus *Amaranthus*, esp. *A. retroflexus*. Any of certain members of the goosefoot family, *Chenopodiaceae*.

pi·ka, pī′ka, *n.* [Native Siberian.] Any of various small mammals allied to the rabbits and inhabiting alpine regions of the northern hemisphere, as *Ochotona princeps*, of N. America.

pike, pīk, *n. pl.* **pikes, pike.** [Prob. another use of *pike*, from the pointed snout.] Any of various large, slender, voracious fresh-water fishes of the genus *Esox*, having a

long snout, esp. *E. lucius*, of the northern hemisphere; any related fish, as the muskellunge; any of various similar appearing fishes, as *Stizostedion vitreum*, the walleyed pike or pikeperch.

pike, pīk, *n.* [Abbr. of *turnpike*.] A turnpike; the toll paid at a tollgate.

pike, pīk, *n.* [Fr. *pique*, akin to *pic*, a pick, and *piquer*, prick.] A long staff having a pointed head of iron or steel, formerly much used as a weapon of the infantry.— *v.t.*—*piked, piking.* To pierce, wound, or kill with or as with a pike.

pike, pīk, *n.* [O.E. *pīc*, a pick or pickax: cf. O.Fr. Fr. *pic*, a pick, Fr. also peak, Sp. *pico*, beak, pick, peak.] A sharp point; a spike; the pointed end of anything, as of an arrow or a spear; *Brit. dial.* the pointed summit of a hill or mountain, or a hill or mountain with such a summit.

pike·man, pīk′man, *n. pl.* **pike·men.** A soldier armed with a pike.

pike·perch, pīk′purch″, *n. pl.* **pike·perch, pike·perch·es.** Any of several pikelike fishes of the perch family, as *Stizostedion vitreum*, the walleyed pikeperch of N. America, or *S. canadense*; the sauger. See *pike*.

pik·er, pī′kėr, *n. Slang.* One who gambles or speculates in a small, cautious way; one who does anything in a contemptibly small or cheap way.

pike·staff, pīk′staf″, pīk′stäf″, *n. pl.* **pike-·staves,** pīk′stāvz″. The shaft of a pike; a long staff with a sharp pike at the lower end of it, once carried by foot travelers.

pi·laf, pi·laff, pi·läf′, pē′läf, *n.* [Pers. and Turk.] An oriental dish consisting of rice steamed in stock and flavored with spices and often combined with meat or poultry. Also **pi·lau,** pi·lou′, pē·lạ′.

pi·las·ter, pi·las′tėr, *n.* [Fr. *pilastre*, It. *pilastro*, < L. *pila*, a pile.] An architectural feature in the form of a rectangular pillar or column projecting from and constituting part of a wall.

pil·chard, pil′chėrd, *n.* [Prob. a Cornish word; cf. Ir. *pilseir*, a pilchard; W. *pilcod*, a minnow.] A food fish, *Sardina pilchardus*, resembling the herring but smaller, found primarily in the Mediterranean and the European Atlantic waters; any of certain related fishes found off the eastern and western coasts of N. America.

pile, pīl, *n.* [O.E. *pīl*, shaft, stake, < L. *pilum*, javelin.] A heavy stake or beam of timber, usu. pointed at the lower end, driven vertically into the ground or the bed of a river, to support a superstructure or form part of a wall; any pillar or upright member, as of iron or concrete, similarly used; *her.* a bearing in the form of a wedge, usu. extending from the top of the escutcheon with its point downward; *archery*, an unedged arrowhead.—*v.t.*—*piled, piling.* To furnish, strengthen, or support with piles; to drive piles into.

pile, pīl, *n.* [O.Fr. Fr. *pile*, < L. *pila*, pillar, pier, mole.] An assemblage of things laid or lying one upon another; a mass of any matter, rising to some height; a heap; a funeral or sacrificial pyre; a lofty or large structure, building, or mass of buildings. *Colloq.* a large number, quantity, or amount of anything; a large accumulation of money. *Phys.* a reactor; *elect.* a series of plates of two dissimilar metals, as copper and zinc, arranged alternately with layers of cloth or paper moistened with an acid solution and placed between them for producing an electric current.—*v.t.*—*piled, piling.* To lay or dispose in a pile, often with *up*; to accumulate or amass, with *up*; to cover or load with a pile or piles.—*v.i.* To gather or rise in a pile or piles, as snow; to accumulate, or mount up, as money, interest, debts, or evidence; to move in a

body and more or less confusedly, with *in, into, out, off,* or *down*.

pile, pīl, *n.* [L. *pilus*, a hair, the hair.] Hair; soft fine hair or down; wool, fur, or pelage; the nap of a fabric, esp. a soft, thick nap such as that on velvet, plush, and many carpets; a piled fabric, carpet, or the like.—**piled,** pīld, *a.*

pile, pīl, *n.* [Cf. L. *pila*, ball.] *Usu. pl.* A swelling, often inflamed or bleeding, at the anus, formed by the dilatation of a blood vessel; a hemorrhoid.

pi·le·at·ed, pī′lē·ā″tid, pil′ē·ā″tid, *a.* [< L. *pileus*, a cap.] *Ornith.* having a large crest similar to a cap on the back of the head; as, the *pileated* woodpecker; *bot.* having a pileus or cap, as the mushroom. Also **pi·le·ate,** pī′lē·it, pī′lē·āt″, pil′ē·it, pil′ē·āt″.

pile driv·er, *n.* A machine or contrivance for driving in piles, either a steam hammer or a heavy weight which is dropped from a height on the head of a pile.

pi·le·um, pī′lē·um, pil′ē·um, *n. pl.* **pi·le·a.** [N.L., < L. *pileum, pilleum*.] *Ornith.* the entire top of the head of a bird, from the base of the bill to the nape.

pi·le·us, pī′lē·us, pil′ē·us, *n. pl.* **pi·le·i,** pī′lē·ī″, pil′ē·ī″. [L. *pileus*, better *pilleus*, also *pilleum*, felt cap, akin to *pilus*, hair, and Gr. *pilos*, felt, felt cap.] *Bot.* a cap or cap-like part, as of a mushroom. A kind of skullcap of felt worn by the ancient Romans and Greeks.

pile·wort, pil′wurt″, *n.* [So called from its reputed efficacy against *piles*.] *Bot.* a N. American herb, *Erechtites hieracifolia*, of the composite family, having a cluster of brush-shaped flowers with no rays, and commonly found in clearings and burned-over areas. Also **fire-weed.**

pil·fer, pil′fėr, *v.i., v.t.* [O.Fr. *pelfrer*, to plunder, < *pelfre*, goods, spoil, booty.] To steal in small quantities; to practice petty theft.—**pil·fer·age,** pil′fėr·ij, *n.*—**pil·fer-·er,** *n.*

pil·gar·lic, pil·gär′lik, *n.* [Peeled garlic.] One who is mockingly pitied; *obs.* a bald-headed man.

pil·grim, pil′grim, *n.* [O.Fr. *peligrin, pellegrin* (Fr. *pèlerin*), < M.L. *peregrinus*, pilgrim, L. foreigner.] One who journeys, esp. a long distance, to some sacred place as an act of devotion; a traveler or wanderer, esp. in foreign lands. (*Cap.*) one of the English colonists who founded the colony of Plymouth, Massachusetts, in 1620; also **Pil·grim Fa·ther.**

pil·grim·age, pil′gri·mij, *n.* [O.Fr. *peligrinage* (Fr. *pèlerinage*).] A journey, esp. a long one, made to some sacred place as an act of devotion; a long journey, esp. one made to visit a place held in honor.— *v.i.*—*pilgrimaged, pilgrimaging.* To go on a pilgrimage.

pil·ing, pī′ling, *n.* Piles collectively; a structure composed of piles.

pill, pil, *n.* [Prob. < O.Fr. *pile*, pill, < L. *pila*, ball.] A small usu. globular or rounded mass of medicinal substance, to be swallowed hole; *fig.* something unpleasant that has to be accepted or endured; *slang*, a disagreeable or annoying person; *sports slang*, a ball, esp. a golf ball or baseball.—*v.t.* To dose with pills; to shape into pills; *slang*, to blackball.—**the pill,** an oral contraceptive in pill form.

pil·lage, pil′ij, *v.t.*—*pillaged, pillaging.* [Fr. *pillage*, < *piller*, to rob.] To strip of money or goods by open violence; plunder; to take as plunder.—*v.i.* To take, loot, or plunder.—*n.* The act of plundering; that which is taken by open force; plunder; spoil.—**pil·lag·er,** *n.*

pil·lar, pil′ėr, *n.* [O.Fr. *piler* (Fr. *pilier*), < M.L. *pilare*, < *pila*, pillar, pile.] An upright shaft or structure, as of stone, brick, or other material, relatively slender in proportion to its height, and of any shape in section, used as a support, or standing alone, as for a monument; an upright supporting part; a post; anything having similar shape or function; a person who is a chief supporter of a state, institution, or cause; a person, principle, or fact that is a main support of something.—*v.t.* To provide or support with pillars.—**from pil·lar to post**, from one situation to another; hither and thither.

pil·lar box, *n. Brit.* a short, hollow pillar set up in a public place, containing a receptacle for mail to be collected by postmen. Also **pil·lar post.**

pill·box, pil′boks, *n.* A box for holding pills; a small concrete blockhouse, formerly used in Europe as a machine gun emplacement; a small round-shaped hat having no brim, esp. such a hat for women.

pill bug, *n.* Any of various small terrestrial isopods, esp. of the genus *Armadillo*, which can roll themselves up into a small ball.

pil·lion, pil′yon, *n.* [< the Celtic; W. *pilyn*, Ir. *pillin*, Gael. *pillean*, a pillion, a packsaddle, < root of L. *pilus*, hair (whence *pile*, of cloth).] A cushion or pad placed behind the saddle on a horse for another rider, esp. a woman; on a motorcycle, an extra seat behind that of the driver.—*adv.* On a pillion; as, to ride *pillion.*

pil·lo·ry, pil′o·rē, *n. pl.* **pil·lo·ries.** [Fr. *pilori*, a pillory, Pr. *espitlori*, L.L. *pilorium*, *spilorium*, a pillory; origin uncertain.] A wooden frame erected on a post or pole, with holes for holding securely the head and hands, once used to punish an offender by holding him up to public scorn.—*v.t.*—*pilloried, pillorying.* To place in a pillory; to subject to public ridicule or contempt.

pil·low, pil′ō, *n.* [O.E. *pyle, pylu*, < L. *pulvinus*, pillow, cushion.] A support for the head during sleep or rest, specif. a bag or case filled with feathers, sponge rubber, or other soft material; a decorative cushion; a cushion or pad, as the cushion on which pillow lace is made; a supporting piece or part, as the block on which the inner end of a bowsprit rests.—*v.t.* To rest on or as on a pillow; support with pillows; to serve as a pillow for.—*v.i.* To rest as on a pillow.

pil·low block, *n. Mach.* a steel block or similar device used as support for a journal or shaft.

pil·low·case, pil′ō·kās″, *n.* A removable case, usu. of cotton, drawn over a pillow. Also **pil·low·slip**, pil′ō·slip″.

pil·low lace, *n.* Handmade lace worked on a small pillow or cushion with threads wound on bobbins. Also **bob·bin lace.**

pil·low sham, *n.* An ornamental cover laid over a bed pillow not in use.

pi·lose, pī′lōs, *a.* [L. *pilosus*, < *pilus*, hair (whence *pile*, of cloth).] Covered with hair, usu. soft, downy hair.—**pi·los·i·ty**, pī·los′i·tē, *n.*

pi·lot, pī′lot, *n.* [< O.D. *pijloot*, a pilot, < *pijlen*, to sound the depth, and *loot*, the sounding lead.] The operator of an aircraft or spacecraft; a person qualified and usu. licensed to conduct ships in and out of harbors or through hazardous waters; the helmsman of a vessel; guide, director. *Mach.* the lesser part of a tool or machine that guides the activity of a different or larger part; a pilot light. *Rail.* cowcatcher.—*v.t.* To act as the pilot of; to guide through dangers or difficulties.—*a.* Pertaining to something that leads or shows the way; as, a *pilot* model.—**pi·lot·less**, *a.*

pi·lot·age, pī′lo·tij, *n.* The occupation, act, or capability of piloting vessels or aircraft; the remuneration of a pilot; air navigation by references to check points or other ground features.

pi·lot bal·loon, *n. Meteor.* a small, free balloon sent aloft and observed to determine the direction and speed of the wind. Also *track balloon.*

pi·lot bis·cuit, *n.* Hardtack. Also **pi·lot bread.**

pi·lot burn·er, *n.* A pilot light.

pi·lot en·gine, *n.* A locomotive engine sent on in advance of a train to clear the way.

pi·lot·fish, pī′lot·fish″, *n.* A marine fish, *Naucrates ductor*, which often accompanies sharks; a white fish found in N. American waters.

pi·lot·house, pī′lot·hous″, *n. pl.* **pi·lot·hous·es**, pī′lot·hou″ziz. *Naut.* an enclosed place or house on the deck of a vessel, sheltering the steering gear and the pilot or helmsman.

pi·lot light, *n.* A small gas jet kept burning continuously, as in a gas stove, to ignite any of the main or ordinary gas burners when desired.

Pilt·down man, pilt′doun man″, *n.* A hypothetical man, formerly believed to be a very early type of man, whose existence was inferred from fragments of a skull discovered at Piltdown, England, in 1912, and exposed in 1954 as a hoax.

pil·u·lar, **pil·lu·lar**, pil′ū·lėr, *a.* [L. *pilula*, a pill.] Pertaining to pills; pill-like.—**pil·ule, pil·lule**, pil′ūl, *n.* A little pill.

pi·ma cot·ton, pē′ma kot′on, *n.* A variety of fine, strong cotton developed from Egyptian stock and orig. grown in the southwestern U.S.; the cloth woven from it. Also **Pi·ma cot·ton, Pi·ma.**

pi·men·to, pi·men′tō, *n. pl.* **pi·men·tos.** [Sp. *pimenta*, pepper, *pimiento*, capsicum, < M.L. *pigmentum*, spice, L. pigment.] A tropical American tree, *Pimenta dioica*, from whose small, unripe berries allspice is prepared; allspice. Sweet pepper; also *pimiento.*

pi·men·to cheese, *n.* A cheese made by processing Neufchâtel, Cheddar, and cream cheeses with ground pimiento. Also **pi·mien·to cheese.**

pi me·son, pī′ mē′zon, *n. Phys.* a meson, believed to be the binding force in atomic nuclei, which has a mass about 270 times that of an electron and which decays in 24 billionths of a second into a mu meson and a neutrino. Also *pion.*

pi·mien·to, pi·myen′tō, *n. pl.* **pi·mien·tos.** [Sp.] One variety of the red pepper, *Capsicum frutescens*, used as a relish or garnish; a paprika source. See *pimento.*

pimp, pimp, *n.* [A nasalized form of *pipe* (pr. *pimpa*, a pipe), a pimp being as it were one who whistles for females like a call bird.] One who procures customers for a prostitute, usu. in exchange for a percentage of her earnings; procurer; pander.—*v.i.* To pander; to solicit for prostitutes.

pim·per·nel, pim′pėr·nel″, pim′pėr·nel, *n.* [O.Fr. *pimprenele* (Fr. *pimprenelle*); origin uncertain.] *Bot.* an herb, *Anagallis arvensis*, in the primrose family, with scarlet, purple, or white flowers that close at the approach of bad weather. Also **scar·let pim·per·nel, poor man's weath·er glass.**

pimp·ing, pim′ping, *a.* [Origin uncertain.] *Colloq.* Little; insignificant; petty; weak or sickly.

pim·ple, pim′pl, *n.* [A nasalized form of L. *papula*, a pimple; or < W. *pwmp, pwmpl*, a knob.] A small elevation or swelling of the skin, with an inflamed base; pustule.—**pim·pled**, pim′ply, pim′peld, pim′plē, *a.*

pin, pin, *n.* [Same as D. *pin*, Dan. *pind*, G. *pinn*, W. *pin*. a pin, a peg, etc., L. *penna* or *pinna*, a feather, a pen.] A piece of metal, wood, or the like, used for fastening separate articles together, or used as a support from which a thing may be hung; a small piece of wire pointed at one end and with a rounded head at the other, often used as a cheap and ready means of fastening cloth or paper materials; something like a pin in shape or use, as a hair*pin* or clothes*pin*; a peg; a bolt; a bar used as a support for adjacent parts in a machine; a badge or ornament attached to a pin; anything of little value; a trifle; a peg in stringed musical instruments for increasing or diminishing the tension of the strings; a wood club used as a target in bowling and similar games; a small flag pole marking a hole in golf; a fall in wrestling; *naut.* a thole; *pl. colloq.* legs.—*v.t.*—*pinned, pinning.* To fasten with a pin or pins of any kind; to transfix or penetrate with a pin; to clutch; to hold fast; to gain a fall in wrestling; *colloq.* to hang or rest, as: He *pinned* his hopes on a final effort.—**on pins and nee·dles**, *slang*, nervous, anxious, or uneasy.—**pin down**, to force to decide on or reveal an intention or position.—**pin on**, to accuse, as of a crime.

pi·na·ceous, pī·nā′shus, *a.* [L. *pinus*, pine.] *Bot.* belonging to the pine family, *Pinaceae*, evergreen needle-leafed trees and shrubs including the pine, spruce, fir, hemlock, and larch.

pi·ña cloth, pēn′ya klạth″, *Sp.* pē′nyä, *n.* [Sp. *piña*, the pineapple.] A delicate, soft, transparent cloth made from the fibers of the pineapple leaf.

pin·a·fore, pin′a·fōr″, pin′a·fạr″, *n.* [Because it is or was *pinned* on *before*.] A child's sleeveless apron that encircles and protects clothing; a woman's low-necked, sleeveless garment which may be worn on top of a blouse.

pi·nas·ter, pī·nas′tėr, pi·nas′tėr, *n.* [L., < *pinus*, pine.] A species of pine, *Pinus pinaster*, growing in the south of Europe.

pi·ña·ta, pēn·yä′ta, pin·yä′ta, *Sp.* pē·nyä′tä, *n.* A pot or figure, usu. of pottery and brightly decorated, filled with gifts and candies, hung from ceilings in Mexican and Central American homes, to be broken by children during the Christmas holidays. Also **pi·na·ta.**

pin·ball, pin′bạl″, *n.* A mechanical game in which a spring propelled ball rolls down a slightly inclined surface having holes, targets, and various obstacles and electrically scores certain points for the player if the ball drops through any of the holes or strikes any of the targets.

pince-nez, pans′nā″, pins′nā″, *Fr.* paNs-nā′, *n. pl.* **pince-nez.** [Fr., 'pinch-nose.'] A pair of eyeglasses kept in place by a spring which pinches the bridge of the nose.

pin·cers, pin′sėrz, *n. pl. but sing. in constr.* [< Fr. *pincer*, to pinch (whence *pince, pincers*).] A tool with two handles and jaws for gripping, pulling, or clipping something; *zool.* a gripping organ, as the claw of a crayfish. Also *pinchers*, **pinch·er.—pin·cer·like**, *a.*

pinch, pinch, *v.t.* [Fr. *pincer*, It. *pizzare*, Sp. *pizcar, pinchar*, to pinch; of doubtful origin.] To squeeze between the fingers, the teeth, claws, or the parts of an instrument; to compress or cramp painfully; to cause to shrink or contract, as from pain or stress; to cause to become drawn or thin; to subject to sharp physical discomfort, as hunger or cold; to restrict in funds or circumstances; to nip. *Slang*, to steal; to arrest. *Mach.* to move, as a heavy object, by levering it with a pinch bar. To sail, as a boat, close-hauled.—*v.i.* To squeeze or press painfully; hurt; to be unduly frugal; to be stingy; *min.* of a vein or ore, to thin out or disappear.—*n.* The act of pinching; a nip or squeeze; the quantity of a material that can be held by a finger and thumb; a small quantity; a time of urgent need or emergency; hardship. *Slang*, an arrest; a theft.—**pinch pen·nies**, to be very frugal or stingy.—**pinch·er**, *n.*

pinch bar, *n.* A kind of crowbar or lever with a projection which serves as a fulcrum.

pinch·beck, pinch′bek″, *n.* [From the name of the inventor, a London watchmaker of the last century.] An alloy of copper and zinc, resembling gold, and sometimes used for cheap jewelry; anything sham or spurious.—*a.*

pinch·cock, pinch′kok″, *n.* A clamp for compressing a flexible pipe, as a rubber tube, in order to regulate or stop the flow of a fluid.

pinch·ers, pin′chẽrz, *n. pl. but sing. in constr.* Pincers.

pinch hit·ter, *n. Baseball,* a substitute who, at some critical moment of the game, takes the turn at bat of a weaker or less reliable batsman. One who substitutes for another person, esp. in emergencies.—**pinch-hit,** pinch′hit′, *v.i.*—**pinch-hit,** *pinch-hitting.*—**pinch hit,** *n.*

pin curl, *n.* A curl that is moistened and secured with a clip or bobby pin.

pin·cush·ion, pin′ku̇sh″on, *n.* A small cushion or pad in which pins are stuck for keeping.

Pin·dar·ic, pin·dar′ik, *n.* An ode in imitation of the odes of Pindar, the Greek lyric poet, metrically complex but regular, consisting of the similarly structured strophe and antistrophe and a contrasting epode. Also **Pin·dar·ic ode, reg·u·lar ode.**—*a.* After the style and manner of Pindar.

pind·ling, pind′ling, *a.* [Origin uncertain.] *Dial.* puny, sickly, or delicate.

pine, pīn, *n.* [O.E. *pīn,* < L. *pinus,* pine.] *Bot.* any tree or shrub of the genus *Pinus,* having evergreen, needle-shaped leaves and woody cones, used as an ornamental, and yielding turpentine, resin, and lumber; the wood of any such tree. *Colloq.* the pineapple. —**pine·like,** *a.*—**pin·y, pine·y,** pī′nē, *a.*—*pinier, piniest.*

pine, pīn, *v.i.*—*pined, pining.* [O.E. *pinian,* to pain, to pine; same word as *pain.*] To long intensely and painfully, often with *for;* to lose vigor and health from grief, regret, or longing, often followed by *away;* to languish.—*v.t. Archaic,* to feel anguish over.

pin·e·al, pin′ē·al, *a.* [Fr. *pinéal,* < L. *pinea,* pine cone, < *pinus,* pine.] Resembling a pine cone in shape; *anat.* pertaining to the pineal body.

pin·e·al bod·y, *n.* A small, usu. cone-shaped body in the brain of vertebrates having no proven function but believed variously to be a vestigial sense or endocrine organ. Also **pin·e·al gland,** *epiphysis.*

pine·ap·ple, pīn′ap″l, *n.* [M.E. *pinappel,* pine cone.] The edible juicy fruit of a tropical plant, *Ananas comosus,* a large collective fruit developed from a spike or head of flowers, and surmounted by a crown of leaves; the plant itself, having a short stem and rigid, spiny-margined, recurved leaves; also *pine. Milit. slang,* a fragmentation grenade, pineapplelike in shape.

pine·drops, pīn′drops″, *n. pl., sing. or pl. in constr. Bot.* a parasitic and saprophytic plant, *Pterospora andromedea,* with a leafless stalk and small, white, drooping flowers, native to the pine regions of northeastern U.S. and southeastern Canada. Also **gi·ant's bird nest.**

pi·nene, pī′nēn, *n.* [L. *pinus,* pine.] *Chem.* a liquid, isomeric terpene, $C_{10}H_{16}$, forming the principal constituent of oil of turpentine and occurring also in other essential oils.

pine nut, *n.* An edible pine seed, esp. from the western pine, *Pinus edulis,* which after roasting and salting is used in cooking.

pin·er·y, pī′ne·rē, *n. pl.* **pin·er·ies.** A hothouse or open field in which pineapples are raised; a forest where pine trees grow, esp. for commercial purposes.

pine·sap, pīn′sap″, *n. Bot.* a parasitic and saprophytic, leafless plant, *Monotropa*

hypopitys, with yellow or red nodding flowers, native in northeastern N. America.

pine sis·kin, *n. Ornith.* a small, brown finch, *Spinus pinus,* found in N. America, having streaked feathers and yellow-marked wings and tail. Also **pine finch.**

pine tar, *n.* A thick tar derived from pine wood which is used in roofing and in the manufacture of soaps, remedies for skin infection, paints, expectorants, and disinfectants.

pi·ne·tum, pī·nē′tum, *n. pl.* **pi·ne·ta,** pī·nē′ta. [L., a pine plantation.] A plantation or collection of pine and other coniferous trees, esp. one for scientific purposes.

pin·feath·er, pin′feᴛʜ″ẽr, *n. Ornith.* a newly emerging, undeveloped feather, before the web portions have expanded.—**pin·feath·ered,** *a.*—**pin·ɾeath·er·y,** *a.*

pin·fish, pin′fish″, *n. pl.* **pin·fish, pin·fish·es.** Any of several spiny-finned marine fishes related to the porgy, esp. the small dark green species, *Lagodon rhomboides,* found off the Atlantic coast of southern U.S.

pin·fold, pin′fōld″, *n.* [O.E. *pyndan,* to pound, to shut in, and *fold.*] An enclosure for stray animals, esp. cattle; a pound or pen.—*v.t.* To restrain by a barrier, as within a pinfold.

ping, ping, *n.* [Imit.] A brief, high-pitched, ringing sound, as that produced by a sharp rap of metal on metal.—*v.i.*

Ping-Pong, ping′pong″, *n.* Table tennis. (Trademark.)

pin·head, pin′hed″, *n.* The head of a pin; something very small or insignificant; *slang,* a person having little intelligence.—**pin·head·ed,** *a. Slang,* dull or stupid.—**pin·head·ed·ness,** *n.*

pin·hole, pin′hōl″, *n.* A small hole or perforation made by or as by a pin.

pin·ion, pin′yon, *n.* [O.Fr. *pignon,* feather = *penon,* E. *pennon.*] The distal or terminal segment of a bird's wing, which includes the carpus, metacarpus, and phalanges; the wing of a bird, or the flight feathers collectively; a feather; a quill.—*v.t.* To cut one pinion off or bind the wings of, as a bird, so as to prevent it from flying; to disable or restrain in this way; to bind, as a person's arms or hands, so as to deprive him of the use of them; to disable in this way, or shackle; to bind or hold fast, as to a thing.

pin·ion, pin′yon, *n.* [Fr. *pignon,* pinion, O.Fr. battlement, < L. *pinna,* pinnacle.] A small gearwheel, or cogwheel, engaging with a larger one or with a rack.

pin·ite, pin′īt, pī′nīt, *n.* [G. *pinit;* named from the *Pini* mine in Saxony.] A mineral consisting essentially of a hydrous silicate of aluminum and potassium.

pink, pingk, *v.t.* [Perh. a nasalized form of *pick.*] To pierce with a rapier or the like; stab; to punch, as cloth or leather, with small holes or figures for ornament; to finish the edge of, as fabric, with a scalloped, notched, or other pattern for ornament or to inhibit raveling; *Brit.* to deck or adorn.

pink, pingk, *n.* [D. and Dan.] A sailing ship with a very narrow stern. Also **pink·ie, pink·y,** ping′kē.

pink, pingk, *n.* [Cf. D. *pinken,* to twinkle with the eyes, to wink—some of them are marked with eyelike spots.] *Bot.* A large plant family, *Caryophyllaceae;* any of several species of garden flowers in this family, esp. of the genus *Dianthus,* often having pink- to rose-colored showy flowers, as the sweet william, carnation, and garden pink.

pink, pingk, *n.* [Origin uncertain.] A pale reddish color of various shades; the highest form or degree; as, in the *pink* of condition; the highest type or example of excellence; the color scarlet, as worn by fox hunters; a scarlet hunting coat; *pl.* formerly, army officers' trousers of a light tan color with a

pinkish hue. *Slang,* one whose political or economic opinions are regarded as leftist, or moderately radical.—*a.* Pertaining to the color pink; *slang,* having somewhat radical political views.—**pink·ish,** ping′kish, *a.*

pink·eye, pingk′ī″, *n. Pathol.* Contagious inflammation of the mucous membranes of the eyelids, affecting humans and certain animals; acute conjunctivitis.

pink·ie, pink·y, ping′kē, *n. Colloq.* the smallest finger.

pink·ing shears, *n. pl.* Scissors having serrated blades, used to cut a notched, nonfraying edge on fabrics.

pink la·dy, *n.* A mixture of grenadine, gin, egg white, and lemon juice well shaken with ice, strained, and served as a cocktail.

pink·o, ping′kō, *n. pl.* **pink·os, pink·oes.** *Slang,* a person holding leftist but not extremely radical political opinions.

pink·root, pingk′rōt″, pingk′ru̇t″, *n.* A root of any of various plants of the genus *Spigelia,* esp. *S. marilandica* of the U.S., used as a vermifuge; a plant having such a root. Also *wormwood.*

pin mon·ey, *n.* Any small amount of money reserved for minor expenditures; an allowance of money made by a husband to his wife for her private expenditures.

pin·na, pin′a, *n. pl.* **pin·nae, pin·nas,** pin′ē. [L. *pinna, penna,* a feather, a wing, a fin.] *Bot.* a leaflet of a pinnate fern leaf. *Zool.* the wing or feather of a bird; the fin of a fish. *Anat.* the auricle, or external ear. —**pin·nal,** *a.*

pin·nace, pin′is, *n.* [Fr. *pinasse,* Sp. *pinaza,* Pg. *pinaça,* It. *pinaccia, pinazza,* a pinnace, < L. *pinus,* a pine tree.] *Naut.* A small sailing vessel formerly used as a tender or scout; any of several varieties of ship's boats.

pin·na·cle, pin′a·kl, *n.* [Fr. *pinacle,* L.L. *pinnaculum,* < L. *pinna,* a feather.] A high peak; the highest point or apex, as of power or achievement; *arch.* a small structure, usu. ending in a cone or pyramid, which rises above the roof of a building or crowns a buttress or tower.—*v.t.*—*pinnacled, pinnacling.* To put a pinnacle or pinnacles on; to put on or as on a pinnacle.

pin·nate, pin′āt, pin′it, *a.* [L. *pinnatus* < *pinna,* a feather or fin.] Shaped, formed, or branching like a feather, esp. in the arrangement of like parts on opposite sides of an axial part.—**pin·nate leaf,** *bot.* a compound leaf in which the leaflets are placed on either side of the rachis.—**pin·nate·ly,** *adv.*—**pin·na·tion,** pi·nā′shan, *n.*

pin·nat·i·fid, pi·nat′i·fid, *a.* [L. *pinna,* and *findo,* to cleave.] *Bot.* of a simple leaf, cleft or parted in a pinnate rather than palmate way, with the divisions extending approximately halfway to the midrib.—**pin·nat·i·fid·ly,** *adv.*

pin·nat·i·sect, pi·nat′i·sekt″, *a.* [L. *seco, sectum,* to cut.] *Bot.* divided pinnately down to the midrib.

pin·ner, pin′ẽr, *n.* One who or that which pins; a woman's headdress, with long flaps hanging down each side, worn in the 17th and 18th centuries.

pin·ni·ped, pin′i·ped″, *a.* [L. *pinna,* feather, fin, and *pes (ped-),* foot.] Belonging to the *Pinnipedia,* a suborder of carnivorous mammals with limbs adapted to an aquatic life, including the seals and walruses.—*n.* A pinniped animal.

pin·nu·la, pin′ya·la, *n. pl.* **pin·nu·lae,** pin′ya·lē″. [L., dim. of *pinna,* feather, fin.] A pinnule; *ornith.* a barb of a feather.

pin·nule, pin′ūl, *n. Zool.* a part or organ resembling the barb of a feather, or a fin; a small detached finlike appendage in certain fishes, as the mackerel. *Bot.* a secondary pinna; one of the pinnately disposed divisions of a pinna of a bipinnate fern leaf.—**pin·nu·lar,** pin′ya·lẽr, *a.*—**pin·nu·late,**

pin·nu·lat·ed, pin'ū·lāt", *a.* Having pinnules.

pi·noch·le, pi·noc·le, pē'nuk·l, pē'nok·l, *n.* [G. *pinochel, binochel*; origin uncertain.] A card game played by two, three, or four persons, with two decks of 24 cards each; the combination of the queen of spades and the jack of diamonds in this game. Also **pe·nuch·le, pe·nuck·le**.

pi·no·le, pi·nō'lē, *Sp.* pē·nạ'le, *n.* [Sp.; < Mex.] Maize or wheat, dried, ground, and sweetened, usu. with the flour of mesquite beans added.

pi·ñon, pin'yon, pēn'yōn, *Sp.* pē·nyạn, *n. pl.* **pi·ñons**, *Sp.* **pi·ño·nes**. [Sp. *piñón*, < *piña*, < L. *pinea*, pine cone, < *pinus*, pine.] *Bot.* Any of several pines, esp. *Pinus edulis*, native to the Rocky Mountain and Pacific regions whose large seeds are edible; the seed itself. Also **nut pine, pine nut, pin·yon**.

pin·point, pin'point", *n.* The pointed end of a pin; a tiny or insignificant object or matter.—*v.t.* To locate with a pin, as on a map; define, describe, or locate precisely. —*a.* Precise, fine, or exact.

pin·prick, pin'prik", *n.* A puncture made with or as with a pin; a minor nuisance or irritation.—*v.t., v.i.*

pins and nee·dles, *n. pl. but sing. in constr.* A sensation of prickling or tingling as a result of previous numbness.—**on pins and nee·dles**, in a mood or state of anticipation or uneasiness.

pin·set·ter, pin'set"ẽr, *n. Bowling*, a device which removes fallen pins or resets all pins for a new frame. Also **pin·spot·ter**, pin'spot"ẽr.

pin stripe, *n.* A very narrow stripe used as a fabric design; a pattern or garment with these stripes.—**pin-striped**, *a.*

pint, pīnt, *n.* [D. *pint*, Fr. and G. *pinte*, a pint, Sp. *pinta*, a mark, also a pint (a quantity marked), < L. *pingo, pinctum*, to paint.] A measure of capacity containing one half of a quart. See Measures and Weights table.

pin·tail, pin'tāl", *n. pl.* **pin·tail, pin·tails**. A N. American surface-feeding marsh duck, *Anas acuta*, having a long slim neck with a white line extending its length, and a long needle-pointed tail.—**pin-tailed**, *a.*

pin·tle, pin'tl, *n.* [Dim. of *pin*.] A pin or bolt, usu. vertical, esp. one that serves as an axis; *naut.* an iron bolt by which the rudder is hung to the sternpost.

pin·to, pin'tō, pēn'tō, *a.* [Sp., 'painted.'] Piebald; mottled; spotted.—*n. pl.* **pin·tos, pin·toes**. A pied or spotted horse. A spotted bean; also **pin·to bean**.

Pintsch gas, pinch gas, *n.* [From Richard *Pintsch*, G. inventor.] A gas made by cracking petroleum or shale oil, formerly used for illumination.

pint-size, pīnt'sīz", *a. Colloq.* small or short. Also **pint-sized**.

pin-up, pin'up", *n.* A wall accessory, or something hung on or otherwise attached to a wall, as a lamp. *Colloq.* a picture or photograph of a glamorous, often voluptuous girl, hung on an admirer's wall; the girl herself; also **pin·up girl**.—*a.* Designed to be hung on or attached to a wall; *colloq.* pertaining to or having the attributes of a pinup girl. Also **pin-up**.

pin·wale, pin'wāl", *a.* Of fabrics, having very narrow wales or ridges; as, *pinwale* corduroy.

pin·weed, pin'wēd", *n.* Any of several species of small N. American herbs of the genus *Lechea*, in the rockrose family, so called from its slender stems and minute flowers and seed pods.

pin·wheel, pin'hwēl", pin'wēl", *n.* A child's toy consisting of paper or plastic spokes or vanes fastened by a pin to a stick so as to revolve in the wind or when blown; a wheel-shaped firework which revolves

rapidly and shoots off colored fire when ignited.

pin·work, pin'wurk", *n.* In needlepoint lace, the stitches raised from the design surface, producing a light effect.

pin·worm, pin'wurm", *n.* A small nematoid worm, *Enterobius vermicularis*, infesting the intestine and rectum, esp. of children.

pin wrench, *n.* A wrench with a protruding pin which is used for insertion into a head, as of a bolt, in order to maintain a secure hold.

pinx·ter flow·er, pink·ster flow·er, *n.* pingk'stẽr flow'ẽr, *n.* An eastern N. American shrub, *Rhododendron nudiflorum*, in the heath family, with large pink to white clusters of flowers appearing in early spring in advance of the leaves. Also **pink a·zal·ea**.

pi·on, pī'on, *n. Phys.* a pi meson.

pi·o·neer, pī"o·nẽr', *n.* [Fr. *pionnier*, pioneer, O.Fr., *peonier*, foot soldier, < *peon*, foot soldier.] One of those who first enter or settle in a region, opening it for occupation and development by others; *fig.* one of those who are first or earliest in any field of inquiry, enterprise, or progress; as, *pioneers* in electronics. Formerly, one of a unit of foot soldiers detailed to make or repair roads and the like; *biol.* an animal or plant that enters and survives in an ecologically unfavorable region.—*v.t.* To go before and prepare, as a way.—*v.i.* To act as a pioneer; to clear the way.—*a.* Earliest; noting or characteristic of a pioneer; like a pioneer.

pi·os·i·ty, pī·os'i·tē, *n.* Overdrawn or excessive piety; a show of piousness.

pi·ous, pī'us, *a.* [L. *pius*, dutiful, devout, tender, kind: cf. *piety* and *pity*.] Having or showing a dutiful spirit of reverence for God or an earnest regard for religious obligations; as, *pious* people, *pious* actions; sacred, as differentiated from secular; devout; religious; godly; practised or used from religious motives, real or pretended, or for some good object; as, a *pious* fraud, a *pious* deception.—**pi·ous·ly**, *adv.*—**pi·ous·ness**, *n.*

pip, pip, *n.* [Earlier *peep*; origin unknown.] One of the spots on dice, playing cards, or dominoes; each of the small segments into which the surface of a pineapple is divided; a rootstock, as of lilies of the valley, or a portion of a rootstock, as of peonies. A star indicating rank, worn by a British army officer.

pip, pip, *n.* [D. *pip*, L.G. *pipp*, Fr. *pipie*, < L.L. *pipita*, for L. *pituita*, phlegm, the pip.] *Veter. pathol.* a disease of fowl, marked by a secretion of thick mucus in the throat and mouth or by a formation of scaly crust on the tongue. Any minor human disorder: used humorously.

pip, pip, *n.* [Fr. *pipin*, a kernel; derivation uncertain.] The seed of a fleshy fruit, as an orange. *Slang*, anything or anyone extraordinary or admirable

pip, pip, *v.i.*—*pipped, pipping*. [An imit. word, differing slightly in form < *peep* = Dan. *pipe*, Sw. *pipa*, G. *pipen*, to pip.] To chirp or peep, as a chicken.—*v.t.* To crack or break through, as an eggshell, during the process of hatching.

pip, pip, *n.* A mechanically or electronically produced image or signal, as on a radarscope.

pip·age, pipe·age, pī'pij, *n.* Conveyance, as of water, oil, or gas, by means of pipes; the pipes so used; the sum charged for the conveyance.

pi·pal, pī'pal, *n.* [Hind. *pīpal*, < Skt. *pippala*.] A species of fig tree, *Ficus religiosa*, of India, yielding a kind of resin. Also **pee·pal, pee·pul**.

pipe, pīp, *n.* [O.E. *pīpe* = O.Fries. *pīpe* = O.H.G. *pfífa* (G. *pfeife*), < M.L. *pipa*, a

pipe, < L. *pipare*, peep, chirp (imit.). In the sense of a tubular vessel, O.Fr. Fr. *pipe*, from the same L. source.] A hollow cylinder of wood, metal, concrete, or other material, for the conveyance of water, gas, steam, or for some other purpose; a tube; material formed into a tube or tubes; piping or tubing; any of various tubular or cylindrical objects, parts, or formations; the tubular part of a key; a tubular organ or passage in an animal body; *pl.* the respiratory passages. A tube used as, or to form an essential part of, a musical wind instrument; a wind instrument consisting of a single tube of straw, reed, wood, or other material, as a flageolet, flute, or oboe. *Usu. pl.* a bagpipe. A boatswain's whistle, or the sounding of it as a call; one of the tubes from which the tones of an organ are produced; *pl.* the voice, esp. as used in singing. The note or call of a bird. *Geol.* a cylindrical vein of ore; one of the vertical cylindrical masses of bluish rock or 'blue ground,' of eruptive origin, in which diamonds are found embedded in South Africa. A tube with a small bowl at one end, used for smoking tobacco or some other substance; a quantity, as of tobacco, that fills the bowl and is smoked at one time. A large wine cask of varying capacity; such a cask with its contents; such a cask as a measure of capacity for wine, equal to 4 barrels, 2 hogsheads, or half a tun, and containing 126 wine gallons. *Slang*, a simple, easily accomplished task.—**pipe·less**, *a.*—**pipe·like**, *a.*

pipe, pīp, *v.i.*—*piped, piping*. To play on a pipe; to make or utter a shrill sound like that of a pipe; whistle, as the wind.—*v.t.* To play, as music, on a pipe; to sing, as a bird; to attract or lead by playing on a pipe; summon or order by sounding the boatswain's pipe or whistle; to supply with pipes; to convey by means of pipes; to trim or finish, as a garment, with piping.— **pipe down**, *slang*. To stop making noise; cease talking; be silent.—**pipe up**, to start to sing or to play, as an instrument; to speak forcefully.

pipe clay, *n.* A fine white clay used for making tobacco pipes, molds, and other articles, and for cleaning white leather.— **pipe-clay**, pīp'klā", *v.t.* To whiten with pipe clay.

pipe clean·er, *n.* A fabric-covered wire used to clean the stem and bowl of a pipe for smoking.

pipe dream, *n. Colloq.* Any fantastic notion; an unrealistic goal or desire.

pipe·fish, pīp'fish", *n.* Any of the *Syngnathidæ*, a family of lophobranch fishes with an elongated tubular snout and a slender body encased in bony rings; needlefish.

pipe·fit·ter, pīp"fit'ẽr, *n.* A person who works at installing or repairing pipes, as for a heating or ventilating system.

pipe·fit·ting, pīp"fit'ing, *n.* Any of various shaped pieces of pipe used for connecting two or more pipes together; the occupation of, or work of, joining pipes together.

pipe·ful, pīp'fụl, *n. pl.* **pipe·fuls**. A quantity, as of tobacco, sufficient to fill the bowl of a pipe.

pipe·line, pīp'līn", *n.* A conduit of pipe through which oil is forced by pumping from an oil region to the market or refinery; a similar system for transporting water, gases, or semisolids; a direct way or means for conveying information.—*v.t.*— *pipelined, pipelining.* To convey by a pipeline; provide with a pipeline.

pipe ma·jor, *n.* The marching leader of a bagpipe band.

pipe of peace, *n.* A peace pipe; a calumet.

pipe or·gan, *n. Mus.* an organ constructed of pipes of various lengths with both pedal and manual keyboards.

pip·er, pī'pėr, *n.* One who plays on a pipe; a bagpiper.

pi·per·a·zine, pi·per'*a*·zēn″, pi·per'*a*·zin, pī·per'*a*·zēn″, pī·per'*a*·zin, pip'ėr·a·zēn″, pip'ėr·a·zin, *n.* [< (*piper*)*idine* and (*az*)*ote* and *-ine.*] *Chem.* a deliquescent crystalline compound, $C_4H_{10}N_2$, obtained by the action of ammonia on ethylene bromide or chloride, and used chiefly in medicine, pharmaceuticals, and agricultural chemicals.

pi·per·i·dine, pi·per'i·dēn″, pi·per'i·din, pī·per'i·dēn″, pī·per'i·din, pip'ėr·i·dēn″, pip'ėr·i·din, *n.* [< *piperine.*] *Chem.* a volatile liquid alkaloid, $C_5H_{11}N$, with a strong pepperlike odor, obtained from piperine.

pip·er·ine, pip'e·rēn″, pip'ėr·in, *n.* [L. *piper*, pepper.] *Chem.* a white crystalline alkaloid, $C_{17}H_{19}NO_3$, obtained from pepper and other plants of the pepper family *Piperaceae*, and prepared synthetically.

pipe·stone, pīp'stōn″, *n.* A reddish argillaceous stone used by N. American Indians for making tobacco pipes.

pi·pette, pi·pet, pī·pet', pi·pet', *n.* [Fr., a small pipe.] A small tube, usu. graduated, terminating in a perforated point, used for measuring or transferring liquids.—*pipetted, pipetting, v.t.*

pipe wrench, *n.* A large wrench used by plumbers or pipefitters to turn a metal pipe.

pip·ing, pī'ping, *n.* The act of one who or that which pipes; the music of pipes; a shrill sound; material formed into a pipe or pipes; pipes collectively. A kind of tubular band of fabric, sometimes containing a cord, used for trimming garments along the edges and seams; a cordlike ornamentation made of icing, used on pastry.—*a.* Playing on a musical pipe; characterized by the music of the peaceful pipe rather than the martial fife or trumpet; emitting a shrill sound.—**pip·ing hot**, so hot as to hiss.

pip·it, pip'it, *n.* [Imit. of its note.] Any of several birds of the genus *Anthus*, esp. the American pipit, *A. spinoletta rubescens*, distinguished by its habit of wagging its tail and walking instead of hopping, which breeds in the Arctic and winters in open country from the Atlantic coast to the Mississippi valley.

pip·kin, pip'kin, *n.* [Dim. of *pipe.*] A small, earthen, potlike container.

pip·pin, pip'in, *n.* [Perh. because grown from the *pips* or seeds.] Any of several varieties of apples; a seed; see pip. *Slang*, anything or anyone extraordinary or admirable.

pip·sis·se·wa, pip·sis'e·wa, *n.* [N. American Ind.] Any of several species of evergreen herbs of the genus *Chimaphila*, in the family *Pyrolaceae*, native to the northern hemisphere, having waxy, white to pink flowers and whose shiny, toothed leaves have been used for their tonic and diuretic properties. Also **prince's-pine**, prin'siz·pīn″.

pip-squeak, pip'skwēk″, *n. Colloq.* one who is small or inconsequential.

pi·quant, pē'kant, pē'känt, *a.* [Ppr. of Fr. *piquer*, to prick, to sting, to pique; of same origin as *pick, pike, peak*, etc.] Being agreeably sharp or pungent to the taste; interesting or stimulating; having an intriguing character; lively.—**pi·quan·cy, pi·quant·ness**, *n.*—**pi·quant·ly**, *adv.*

pique, pēk, *n.* [Fr., *piquant.*] An offense taken; a sense of resentment, irritation.—*v.t.*—*piqued, piquing.* [Fr. *piquer.*] To nettle; to irritate; to stimulate, as one's interest; to touch with envy, jealousy, or other passion.—*v.i.* To cause irritation.

pi·qué, pi·kā', pē·kā', *Fr.* pē·kā', *n.* [Fr., stitched, quilted, pp. of *piquer.*] A cotton, silk, or rayon fabric woven with a quilted effect, commonly with narrow transverse ribs or raised stripes.

pi·quet, pic·quet, pi·ket', pi·kā', *n.* [< Fr. *pique*, a pike, a lance, a spade at cards.] A game of cards played by two persons with a deck excluding all cards below the seven.

pi·ra·cy, pī'ra·sē, *n. pl.* **pi·ra·cies**. The act, practice, or crime of robbery on the high seas; the profession of a pirate; literary theft or any infringement of copyright law.

pi·ra·gua, pi·rä'gwa, pi·rag'wa, *n.* Pirogue.

pi·ra·nha, pi·rän'ya, pi·ran'ya, *n.* [Sp.] Any small voracious S. American freshwater fish of the subfamily *Serrasalminae* of the family *Characinidae* which will attack any sized animal, including man. Also *caribe*, **pi·ra·ña**, pi·rä·ya.

pi·rate, pī'rat, *n.* [Fr. *pirate*, L. *pirata*, < Gr. *peiratēs*, < *peiraō*, to attempt, *peira*, a trial.] A robber or person who takes by violence the property of another on the high seas; an armed ship or vessel engaged in piracy; a person who appropriates the literary work or invention of another without compensation or permission.—*v.t.* *pirated, pirating.* To commit an act of piracy upon; to appropriate by piracy; to publish without right or permission.—*v.i.* To commit piracy.—**pi·rat·i·cal**, pī·rat'i·kal, *a.*—**pi·rat·i·cal·ly**, *adv.*

pirn, pụrn, pirn, *n.* [M.E. *pyrne*; origin obscure.] *Brit. dial.* The bobbin, spool, or reel of a spinning wheel; a fishing reel.

pi·rogue, pi·rōg', *n.* [Fr. *pirogue*, Sp. *piragua*; orig. a W. Ind. word.] A kind of canoe made from a single trunk of a tree hollowed out; a dugout boat. Also *piragua*.

pir·ou·ette, pir″ö·et', *n.* [Fr., top, whirligig, whirl: cf. It. *pirolo, peg.*] A whirling about on one foot or on the points of the toes, as in dancing; a quick, short turn or whirl of a horse.—*v.i.*—*pirouetted, pirouetting.* To perform a pirouette; whirl, as on the toes; move in pirouette.

pis·ca·ry, pis'ka·rē, *n. pl.* **pis·ca·ries.** [M.L. *piscaria*, prop. fem. of L. *piscarius*, pertaining to fish, < *piscis*, fish.] *Law*, the right or privilege of fishing in particular waters. A place where fish may be caught.

pis·ca·to·ry, pis'ka·tōr″ē, pis'ka·tạr″ē, *a.* [L. *piscatorius.*] Of, pertaining to, or relying upon fishermen or fishing. Also **pis·ca·to·ri·al**, pis″ka·tōr'ē·al, pis″ka·tạr'ē·al.—**pis·ca·to·ri·al·ly**, *adv.*

Pis·ces, pis'sēz, pis'ēz, *n. pl.* [L., pl. of *piscis*, fish.] The Fishes, a zodiacal constellation; the twelfth sign of the zodiac; the class *Pisces*, of animals that includes the true fishes.

pis·ci·cul·ture, pis'i·kul″chėr, *n.* [L. *piscis*, a fish, and *cultura*, culture.] The breeding, rearing, preservation, and feeding of fish by artificial means; fish culture.

pis·ci·na, pi·sī'na, pi·sē'na, *n. pl.* **pis·ci·nae**, pi·sī'nē, pi·sē'nē. [L., orig. fish pond, < *piscis*, fish.] *Eccles.* a basin with a drain, in old churches usu. in a niche in the wall near the altar, used for certain ablutions.—**pis·ci·nal**, *a.*

pis·cine, pis'īn, pis'ēn, pis'in, *a.* Pertaining to fish or fishes.

pis·civ·o·rous, pi·siv'ėr·us, *a.* [L. *piscis*, and *voro*, to eat.] Feeding on fish.

pish, psh, pish, *interj.* An exclamation expressing disdain or repudiation. Also **pish and tush**.—*v.t., v.i.* To use this expression.

pi·si·form, pī'si·fạrm″, *a.* [N.L. *pisiformis*, < L. *pisum*, pea, and *forma*, form.] Having the form of a pea; as, the *pisiform* bone of the wrist; composed of small, rounded masses like peas; as, *pisiform* iron ore.

pis·mo clam, piz'mō klam, *n.* (*Often cap.*) a clam with a thick shell, *Tivela stultorum*, found along the southern California coast and valued as food.

pi·so·lite, pī'so·līt″, piz'o·līt″, *n.* [Gr. *pisos*, pea, and *lithos*, stone.] Limestone composed of rounded concretions about the size of a pea. Compare *oolite.*—**pis·o·lit·ic**, pis″o·lit'ik, *a.*

pis·soir, pē·swär', *n. Fr.* a street urinal in a low enclosure, common in some European cities.

pis·ta·chi·o, pi·stash'ē·ō″, pi·stä'shē·ō″, *n. pl.* **pis·ta·chi·os**. [It. *pistacchio*, < L. *pistacium*, < Gr. *pistácion*, the nut, < *pistácē*, the tree; < Pers.] *Bot.* one of several species of small trees of the genus *Pistacia*, in the cashew family, esp. *P. vera*, native to the Mediterranean and Asia Minor and now cultivated in southern U.S. for its nut; the nut itself, used as a confection; a flavoring prepared from this nut. A light green color. Also **pis·tache**, pi·stash'.

pis·til, pis'til, *n.* [L. *pistillum*, a pestle, a dim. < *pinso, pistum*, to pound, to beat in a mortar; akin *pestle, piston.*] *Bot.* The female reproductive organ in a flowering plant comprised of the ovary with its contained ovules, the style, and the stigma: two or more of such organs being a compound pistil; the female element of a flower which is destined to produce seeds. See *gynoecium.*

pis·til·late, pis'ti·lit, pis'ti·lāt″, *a. Bot.* Of a flower, having pistils and no functional stamens; female.

pis·tol, pis'tol, *n.* [Fr. *pistole*, < It. *pistola*, a pistol; orig. a dagger made at *Pistola* or *Pistoia*, near Florence. From dim. poniards the name came to be given to miniature firearms.] A small firearm designed to be fired with one hand only.—*v.t.*—*pistoled, pistoling*, Brit. *pistolled, pistolling.* To shoot with a pistol.

pis·tole, pi·stōl', *n.* [Fr. *pistole*, same as *pistol*, so named as being orig. a half crown, a dim. of the crown.] An old gold coin of Spain; any of various old European gold coins.

pis·tol grip, *n.* A grip or handle, esp. of a saw, resembling the butt of a pistol.

pis·tol-whip, pis'tol·hwip″, pis'tol·wip″, *v.t.*—*pistol-whipped, pistol-whipping.* To deliver repeated blows with the barrel of a pistol.

pis·ton, pis'ton, *n.* [Fr. *piston*, < It. *pistone*, piston, var. of *pestone*, large pestle, ult. < L. *pinsere* (pp. *pistus*), pound, bray.] A movable disk or short cylinder fitting closely within a tube or hollow cylinder, and capable of being driven alternately forward and backward in the tube by pressure, as in a steam engine, thus imparting reciprocatory motion to a piston rod attached to it on one side, or of being driven thus by the rod, as in a pump; *mus.* a sliding valve used to change the pitch in a cornet or the like.

pis·ton pin, *n.* A wrist pin.

pis·ton ring, *n.* A metallic ring, usu. one of a series, and split so as to be expansible, placed around a piston in order to maintain a tight fit, as inside the cylinder of an internal-combustion engine.

pis·ton rod, *n.* A rod which connects a piston to a point outside the cylinder, and either moves the piston or is moved by it.

pit, pit, *n.* [O.E. *pytt*, pit, hole, < L. *puteus*, well, pit, shaft.] A hole or cavity in the ground, whether natural or made by digging; an excavation made in digging for some mineral deposit; the shaft of a coal mine or the mine itself; a covered or concealed excavation in the ground, that serves as a trap for animals or men; the abode of evil spirits and lost souls; hell, used with *the*; in general, a hollow or indentation in a surface; a natural hollow or depression in the body; as, the *pit* of the stomach; the slight depression in the surface of the body below the lower end of the breastbone; a small depressed scar such as those left on the skin after smallpox. An enclosure for combats, as of dogs or cocks; a section of a theater, orig. the entire part of the floor of the house behind the musicians, but now the sunken area nearest the stage that is occupied by the orchestra; that part of the floor of a commodity exchange devoted to a special kind of business; as, the grain *pit.*—*v.t.*—*pitted, pitting.* To place or bury in a pit; to set animals in a pit or enclosure to fight, hence to set in active opposition, as one against another; match in a conflict or contest; to mark with pits or depressions.—*v.i.* To become marked with pits or depressions; to retain for a time the mark of pressure, as the skin.

pit, pit, *n.* [Cf. D. *pit,* kernel.] *Bot.* the stone of a fruit, as of a cherry, peach, or plum.—*v.t.* To remove, as the stones, from; as, to *pit* prunes.

pi·ta, pē′ta, *n.* [Sp., < Peruvian.] A fiber obtained from the century plant, *Agave americana,* the istle or yucca; the plant itself.

pit·a·pat, pit′a·pat″, *adv.* [A redupl. of *pat,* a slight blow.] In a flutter; with palpitation or quick succession of beats.—*n.* A light quick step.—*v.i.* To move with short, rapid steps.

pitch, pich, *n.* [O.E. *pic,* < L. *pix (pic-),* akin to Gr. *pissa,* pitch.] Any of various dark-colored tenacious or viscous substances used for covering the seams of wooden vessels after calking or for making pavements, as the residuum, 'coal-tar pitch,' left after the distillation of coal tar, or 'wood pitch' derived similarly from wood tar; any of certain bitumens; as, mineral *pitch;* asphalt; any of various resins; the sap or crude turpentine which exudes from the bark of pines.—*v.t.* To smear or cover over with or as with pitch.—**pitch·like,** *a.*

pitch, pich, *v.t.* [M.E. *picchen;* origin uncertain; perh. related to *pick.*] To set up or erect, as a tent, camp, or the like; in general, to put, set, or plant in a fixed or definite place or position; as, a roof having rafters *pitched* against an adjoining building; to set in order, or arrange; as a *pitched* battle; to set at a certain point, degree, or level; to set at a particular pitch, or determine the key or keynote of, as a tune; in certain card games, to lead, as a card of a particular suit, thereby fixing that suit as a trump; to throw, fling, hurl, or toss; as, to *pitch* a harpoon; *baseball,* to deliver or serve, as the ball, to the batter; *golf,* to loft, as the ball, so that it alights with little roll. *Mech.* to engage; interlock.—*v.i.* To fix a tent or temporary habitation; encamp; to take up a position; settle; to fix or decide, with *on* or *upon,* often casually or without particular consideration; to throw or toss; to plunge or fall forward or headlong, specif. to plunge with alternate fall and rise of bow and stern, as a ship: opposed to *roll;* in general, to lurch; to slope downward, or dip. *Baseball,* to deliver or serve the ball to the batter; fill the position of pitcher. *Mech.* to engage; interlock.—**pitch in·to,** to attack; to start with fervor; as, *pitch into* one's work.

pitch, pich, *n.* The act or manner of pitching; a throw or toss; a plunge forward or headlong, or a lurch; the pitching movement, or a plunge forward, of a ship or plane; *slang,* an aggressive sales talk; *cards,* a variety of seven-up, in which the trump suit for a deal is determined by the first card led. Something that is pitched; a quantity of something pitched or placed somewhere; a place of pitching, encamping, or positioning; a spot where a person or thing is placed or stationed; point, position, or degree, as in a scale; as, a *pitch* of ecstasy; *mus.* degree of highness or acuteness, or

of lowness or graveness of a tone or of sound, depending upon the relative rapidity of the vibrations by which it is produced; a particular tonal standard with which given tones may be compared in respect to their relative height; as, concert *pitch,* French *pitch;* height in general; as, the *pitch* of an arch; the height to which any bird rises in the air. Downward inclination or slope; a sloping part or place; the inclination of a bed or vein, as of ore, from the horizontal; the slope or steepness of a roof. *Mech.* the distance between two things, esp. in a series; the distance between the centers of two adjacent teeth in a toothed wheel or rack, measured on the pitch circle or pitch line.—*a.*—**full pitch,** *cricket,* a bowl so directed that the ball hits the wicket without first hitting the ground.

pitch, pich, *n. Aerospace,* the variation in flight from horizontal to vertical: one of the three axes, along with roll and yaw, on which the altitude of a space vehicle may be controlled.

pitch-black, pich′blak′, *a.* Completely or extremely dark; utterly black, as pitch.

pitch·blende, pich′blend″, *n.* [= G. *pechblende.*] A mineral consisting largely of uranium oxide, occurring in black or brown pitchlike masses: a principal source of uranium and radium.

pitch-dark, pich′därk′, *a.* Dark as pitch; very dark.

pitch·er, pich′ér, *n.* [O.Fr. *pichier,* < M.L. *picarium, bicarium;* perh. akin to E. *beaker.*] A container in various forms and sizes, with a handle ar.d a spout or lip, for holding and pouring liquids. *Bot.* a pitcherlike modification of the leaf of certain plants.

pitch·er, pich′ér, *n.* One who pitches; *baseball,* the player who throws the ball to the batter.

pitch·er plant, *n.* Any of various plants having pitcherlike leaves usu. filled with water, esp. *Sarracenia purpurea,* found in bogs in eastern N. America, whose leaves trap and digest insects.

pitch·fork, pich′fạrk″, *n.* A fork used in · lifting or throwing hay or sheaves of grain. —*v.t.* To lift or throw with a pitchfork.

pitch in, *v.i. Colloq.* to add one's efforts in support of a group venture.

pitch·out, pich′out″, *n. Baseball,* a pitch thrown outside or above the batter's reach so the catcher can stop a suspected attempt to steal a base; *football,* a lateral pass between two backs, thrown while they are behind the line of scrimmage.

pitch pipe, *n.* A small musical pipe having one or more fixed tones, blown to give the pitch for group singing or for tuning an instrument.

pitch·stone, pich′stōn″, *n.* A glassy igneous rock having a resinous luster and in appearance resembling hardened pitch and obsidian.

pitch·y, pich′ē, *a.*—*pitchier, pitchiest.* Full of or abounding in pitch; smeared with pitch; of the nature of or resembling pitch; dark as pitch.

pit·e·ous, pit′ē·us, *a.* [O.Fr. *pitos, piteus* (Fr. *piteux*), < M.L. *pietosus,* pitiful, < L. *pietas.*] Exciting or deserving pity or sympathy; pathetic.—**pit·e·ous·ly,** *adv.*—**pit·e·ous·ness,** *n.*

pit·fall, pit′fạl″, *n.* A concealed pit prepared as a trap for animals or men; *fig.* any trap or danger for the unwary.

pith, pith, *n.* [O.E. *pitha,* pith: cf. D. *pit,* pith, marrow, kernel.] *Bot.* the central cylinder of spongy cellular tissue in the stems of dicotyledonous plants; *zool.* the soft interior of a part, as of a feather or bone. The important inner part; the essential part; center, essence, substance, or gist; as, the *pith* of the matter; substantial

quality, weight, or importance; as, a speech with *pith;* bone and spinal cord marrow.—*v.t.* To take the pith from, as from a plant; to pierce, sever, or destroy the spinal cord of; slaughter, as cattle, by severing the spinal cord.

pit·head, pit′hed″, *n.* The entrance to a mine or coal shaft, or the adjacent structures and grounds.

pith·e·can·thro·pus, pith″e·kan′thro·pus, pith″e·kan·thrō′pus, *n. pl.* **pith·e·can·thro·pi.** [N.L., < Gr. *pithēkos,* ape, and *ánthrōpos,* man.] The extinct genus of a prehistoric hominid having two species, *P. erectus* and *P. robustus,* of manlike apes or apelike men and proposed by German anthropologist Haeckel as being the 'missing link' joining men and apes in evolution. —**pith·e·can·thro·poid,** *a., n.*

pith·y, pith′ē, *a.*—*pithier, pithiest.* Terse and striking; forceful; having meaning and substance; consisting of pith; of, containing, or abounding in pith.—**pith·i·ly,** *adv.*—**pith·i·ness,** *n.*

pit·i·a·ble, pit′ē·a·bl, *a.* [O.Fr. *piteable* (Fr. *pitoyable*).] Deserving to be pitied; exciting or arousing pity; lamentable; deplorable; exciting a contemptuous pity; contemptible, miserable, or pitiful.—**pit·i·a·ble·ness,** *n.*—**pit·i·a·bly,** *adv.*

pit·i·er, pit′ē·ér, *n.* One who pities.

pit·i·ful, pit′i·ful, *a.* Deserving pity; arousing compassion; miserable; paltry; insignificant; contemptible.—**pit·i·ful·ly,** *adv.*—**pit·i·ful·ness,** *n.*

pit·i·less, pit′ē·lis, pit′i·lis, *a.* Without pity; hardhearted; merciless.—**pit·i·less·ly,** *adv.*—**pit·i·less·ness,** *n.*

pit·man, pit′man, *n. pl.* **pit·men, pit·mans.** One who works in a pit, as in coal mining; *pl.* **pit·men.** *Mach.* a rod connecting a rotating with a reciprocating part; a connecting rod; *pl.* **pit·mans.**

pi·ton, pē′ton, pē′tôn, *Fr.* pē·tạn′, *n.* A metal spike, usu. with an eye for a rope in one end, driven into a rock or ice crevice as a support in mountain climbing.

Pi·tot-stat·ic tube, pē′tō·stat′ik töb″, pē·tō′stat′ik töb″, *n. Aeron.* an instrument consisting of a modified Pitot tube often joined to an airspeed indicator, and used to indicate the speed of an aircraft in flight.

Pi·tot tube, pē′tō töb″, pē·tō′, *n.* [From Henri *Pitot,* 1695-1771, French physicist and engineer.] *Hydraulics,* an instrument for determining velocity of moving fluids.

pit·saw, pit saw, pit′sạ″, *n.* A handsaw operated by two men, one on the log and the other below it, often in a pit.

pit·tance, pit′ans, *n.* [Fr. *pitance,* a monk's mess, < L.L. *pietantia, pitantia,* a monk's allowance, < L. *pietas,* piety.] A small allowance; any very small portion allowed or assigned.

pit·ted, pi′tid, *a.* Having pits or indentations, as pockmarks on the face.

pit·ter-pat·ter, pit′ér·pat″ér, *n.* [Varied reduplication of *patter.*] A rapid succession of light beats or taps, as of rain.—*v.i.* To make such a sound.—*adv.* With this sound.

pit·ting, pi′ting, *n.* The function or process that makes pits, such as the hollows left by smallpox; such pits collectively.

pi·tu·i·tar·y, pi·tō′i·ter″ē, pi·tū′i·ter″ē, *a.* [L. *pituita,* phlegm.] *Anat.* of or pertaining to the pituitary gland; describing a form of giantism resulting from glandular malfunction.—*n. pl.* **pi·tu·i·tar·ies.** The pituitary gland; *med.* any of several hormone extracts taken from the pituitary gland.

pi·tu·i·tar·y gland, *n. Anat.* a small, oval-shaped endocrine gland situated at the base of the brain and secreting hormones with a broad range of effects on growth, metabolism, maturation, reproduction, and other bodily functions.

---

ch- chain, G. na*ch*t; **th-** THen, thin; **w-** wig, hw as sound in whig; **z-** zh as in azure, zeal. *Italicized vowel* indicates schwa sound.

Pit·u·i·trin, pi·tö′i·trin, pi·tū′i·trin, *n. Med.* an extraction of the pituitary gland, usu. of cattle. (Trademark.)

pit vi·per, *n.* Any of the venomous snakes constituting the family *Crotalidae,* as the rattlesnake and moccasin, characterized by a pit or depression between the nostril and each eye.

pit·y, pit′ē, *n.* pl. **pit·ies.** [Fr. *pitié,* O.Fr. *pité,* < L. *pietas,* piety, < *pius,* pious.] The suffering of one person excited by the distresses of another; commiseration; compassion; mercy; the ground or subject of pity; cause of grief; a thing to be regretted. —*v.t.*—*pitied, pitying.* [O.Fr. *pitoyer,* to pity.] To feel pity or compassion toward; to feel pain or grief for; to have sympathy for.—*v.i.* To feel compassion or pity.— **pit·y·ing,** *a.*—**pit·y·ing·ly,** *adv.*

pit·y·ri·a·sis, pit″i·rī′a·sis, *n.* [Gr. *pityron,* bran.] A skin disease occurring in humans and some domestic animals, consisting of irregular branlike scaly patches shed by the epidermis.

più, pū, *adv.* [It.] *Mus.* more: an indication for performers; as, *più lento,* more slowly.

piv·ot, piv′ot, *n.* [Fr. *pivot;* origin uncertain.] A pin or short shaft on the end of which something rests and turns, or upon and about which something rotates or oscillates; the end of a shaft or arbor, resting and turning in a bearing; that on which something turns, hinges, or depends; the person upon whom a line, as of troops, wheels about; a quick turning around on one foot; the act of pivoting.—*v.t.* To mount on, attach by, or provide with a pivot or pivots.—*v.i.* To turn on or as on a pivot.—**piv·ot·al,** piv′o·tal, *a.* Of, pertaining to, or serving as a pivot; of critical importance.—**piv·ot·al·ly,** *adv.*

piv·ot tooth, *n.* A replacement crown connected by a pivot to the root of a tooth.

pix·i·lat·ed, pik′si·lā″tid, *a.* Slightly unbalanced mentally; eccentric. *Slang,* intoxicated; drunk.—**pix·i·la·tion,** *n.*

pix·y, pix·ie, pik′sē, *n.* pl. **pix·ies.** [Perh. for *pucksy,* < *Puck.*] A fairy, esp. one who is mischievous.—*a.* Mischievous; roguish. —**pix·y·ish,** pik′sē·ish, *a.*

piz·za, pēt′sa, *n.* [It.] A spicy Italian dish, consisting of cheese and tomatoes, with sausage, anchovies, or various additions, spread on a layer of bread dough and baked.

piz·ze·ri·a, pēt″se·rē′a, *n.* An establishment where pizzas are baked and sold for consumption on the premises or for taking home.

piz·zi·ca·to, pit″zi·kä′tō, *It.* pēt″tsē·kä′ta, *a.* [It., pp. of *pizzicare,* pinch, pick.] *Mus.* played by plucking the strings with the finger instead of using the bow, as on a violin.—*n.* pl. **piz·zi·ca·ti,** pit″si·kä′tē, *Mus.* a note or passage so played.—*adv.*

plac·a·ble, plak′a·bl, plā′ka·bl, *a.* [L. *placabilis,* < *placo,* to soothe, pacify; akin to *placeo,* to please.] Capable of being easily appeased or pacified: opposed to *implacable.*—**plac·a·bil·i·ty,** plā″ka·bil′i·tē, plā″ka·bil′i·tē, *n.*—**plac·a·bly,** *adv.*

plac·ard, plak′ärd, plak′ėrd, *n.* [Fr., < *plaque,* a plate, from the Teut.; cf. D. *plak,* a flat piece of wood, a slice, *plakbriefje,* a placard; L.G. *plakke,* a piece of turf.] A written or printed paper posted in a public place; a poster; a small tag or plate bearing information.—*v.t.* To post placards on; to inform by means of a placard.

pla·cate, plā′kāt, plak′āt, *v.t.*—*placated, placating.* To appease, pacify, or conciliate. —**pla·cat·er,** *n.*—**pla·ca·tion,** plā·kā′shan, *n.*—**pla·ca·tive,** pla·ca·to·ry, plā′ka·tiv, plak′a·tiv, plā″ka·tōr′ē, plak′a·tōr″ē, *a.*

place, plās, *n.* [Fr. *place,* a place, post, position, an open space in a town; < L. *platea,* a street, an area, < Gr. *plateia,* < *platys,* flat, broad.] An indefinite expanse or region; as, a faraway *place;* a site or other locality; a city or village; a broad way or open square in a city; any portion of space marked off by its use or character; as, an eating or parking *place;* a house, room, or other dwelling; a passage in a book or piece of music; an order of proceedings; as, in the first *place;* rank; social class or station; order of priority or importance; an office, appointment, or job; a duty or right; as, it is not his *place* to say; ground or occasion, as: A party is no *place* for gloom. Room or stead, with the sense of substitution; as, to act in *place* of another; position in a sequence or scale, as of numbers or musical notes; the original or natural position of something; as, each in its proper *place;* a position won in a race or competition; as, to win first *place; astron.* the position in the sky of a heavenly body at any time; *colloq.* a state of success or achievement, as: He will get some *place. Sports,* one of the leading positions at the finish line in a race; in U.S. horse racing, the position of second at the finish line.—*v.t.*—*placed, placing.* To locate; arrange in position; to appoint, induct, or establish in an office or job; to put or set into a particular rank, state, or condition; to fix in a period of time, as: History *places* him at the time of Plato. Entrust or bestow; as, to *place* confidence in a friend; recognize or identify; as, to *place* a face or accent; to arrange for the disposition of; as, to *place* an order; to present for deliberation; as, to *place* the problem before the board; to control the physical projection and resonance, as of the voice, for maximum effect in speaking or singing, as: Vocal lessons helped to *place* his voice correctly.—*v.i.* To earn a certain standing; as, to *place* high in a competition or examination; *sports,* to be among the first three at the finish line; to come in second at a horse race.—**take place,** come to pass.—**in place of,** as a substitute for; instead of.—**give place,** to make way, yield. —**place·a·ble,** *a.*—**place·less,** *a.*

pla·ce·bo, pla·sē′bō, *n.* pl. **pla·ce·bos, pla·ce·boes.** [L., 'I shall be pleasing (or acceptable).'] *Rom. Cath. Ch.* the vespers of the office for the dead; *med.* a preparation with little or no therapeutic value given merely to please the patient, or given as a control in experiments testing the effectiveness of a genuine drug. Anything intended to gratify or humor.

place hit·ter, *n. Baseball,* a player who can control the direction of balls he hits.

place kick, *n. Football,* a kick in which the ball is kicked over the opponents' goal post, the ball being placed on the ground and held in position for kicking by a teammate.—**place-kick,** plās′kik″, *v.t.*—**place kick·er,** *n.*

place·ment, plās′ment, *n.* The act of placing, or the state of being placed; location; arrangement; the placing of a person in suitable employment; *football,* the placing of the ball on the ground in attempting to kick a goal from the field of play by means of a place kick.

place-name, plās′nām″, *n.* A name of a place or locality; any geographical name.

pla·cen·ta, pla·sen′ta, *n.* pl. **pla·cen·tas, pla·cen·tae,** pla·sen′tē. [L., a cake, = Gr. *plakous* (*plakount*), flat cake, contr. < *plakoeis* (*plakoent-*), flat.] *Zool., anat.* the organ by which the fetus of most mammals is attached to the wall of the uterus and through which the fetus receives nourishment and voids waste matter; *bot.* that part of the ovary of flowering plants which bears the ovules.—**pla·cen·tal, plac·en·tar·y,** plas′en·ter″ē, pla·sen′te·rē, *a.*

plac·en·ta·tion, plas″en·tā′shan, *n. Anat., zool.* the attachment or means of attachment of a fetus to the wall of the uterus; the

manner of the disposition or construction of a placenta. *Bot.* the disposition or arrangement of a placenta in seed plants.

plac·er, plā′sėr, *n.* One who places, sets, or arranges; one of the winning contestants in a race, either a person or an animal.

plac·er, plas′ėr, *n.* [Sp., sandbank, akin to *plaza.*] *Min.* A glacial or alluvial deposit containing particles of gold or other valuable minerals; a place where alluvial and glacial deposits are washed to obtain such minerals.

place set·ting, *n.* A complete set of the dishes and utensils needed to serve one person at a meal.

pla·cet, plā′sit, *n.* [L. 'it pleases.'] An expression of assent or sanction; a vote of assent.

plac·id, plas′id, *a.* [L. *placidus,* < *placeo,* to please.] Gentle; quiet; undisturbed; equable; serene; mild; unruffled.—**pla·cid·i·ty,** pla·sid′i·tē, *n.*—**plac·id·ly,** *adv.*

plack·et, plak′it, *n.* [< Fr. *plaquer,* to lay or clap on.] The opening or slit in a petticoat or skirt. *Archaic,* a woman; a placket.

plac·oid, plak′oid, *a.* [Gr. *pláx* (*plac-*), something flat, tablet.] Platelike, as the spiny scales of dermal investments of sharks or other elasmobranch fish.—*n.* A fish with placoid scales.

pla·fond, pla·fon′, *Fr.* plä·fᴀɴ′, *n.* [Fr., < *plat,* flat, and *fond,* bottom.] *Arch.* a ceiling, whether flat or arched, of decorative character, formed by the underside of the floor above.

pla·gal, plā′gal, *a.* [M.L. *plagalis,* < *plaga,* plagal mode, < Gr. *plágios,* oblique, < *plágos,* side.] *Gregorian mus.* having the final tone or keynote in the middle of the compass, as a mode.—**pla·gal ca·dence,** *modern mus.* noting a cadence in which the chord of the tonic is preceded by that of the subdominant.

pla·gia·rism, plā′ja·riz″um, plā′jē·a·riz″-um, *n.* [L. *plagiarius,* plunderer, later kidnapper, plagiarist, perh. < *plaga,* net, snare.] The appropriating and putting forth as one's own the ideas, language, or designs of another; something appropriated and put forth in this manner.—**pla·gia·rist,** *n.*—**pla·gia·ris·tic,** plā″ja·ris′tik, *a.*

pla·gia·rize, *Brit.* **pla·gia·rise,** plā′ja·rīz″, plā′jē·a·rīz″, *v.t.*—*plagiarized, plagiarizing.* To appropriate by plagiarism; to appropriate ideas or passages from, by plagiarism.—*v.i.* To commit plagiarism.— **pla·gia·riz·er,** *n.*

pla·gia·ry, plā′ja·rē, plā′jē·a·rē, *n.* pl. **pla·gia·ries.** [L. *plagiarius.*] A plagiarist; plagiarism.

pla·gi·o·clase, plā′jē·o·klās″, *n.* [G. *plagioklas,* < Gr. *plágios,* oblique, and *klásis,* fracture.] Feldspar of the soda-lime class, with two prominent cleavage directions at oblique angles, and triclinic crystals.— **pla·gi·o·clas·tic,** plā″jē·o·klas′tik, *a.*

pla·gi·o·trop·ic, plā″jē·o·trop′ik, *a.* [Gr. *plágios,* oblique, and *-tropos,* < *trépein,* turn.] *Bot.* noting, pertaining to, or exhibiting a mode of growth which is more or less divergent from the vertical.—**pla·gi·o·trop·i·cal·ly,** *adv.*—**pla·gi·ot·ro·pism,** plā″jē·o′tro·piz″um, *n.*

plague, plāg, *n.* [Same as D. *plaag,* Dan. and G. *plage,* Icel. *plaga,* Pr. *plaga,* O.Sp. *plaga,* the plague; all < L. *plaga,* a blow, stroke, calamity.] A widespread disease with a high mortality rate; pestilence; *specif.* a virulent, infectious, and febrile disease caused by the bacillus, *Pasteurella pestis,* primarily a rodent disease, but transmitted to men by fleas, and occurring in several forms: bubonic, pneumonic, and septicemic; a great affliction, disaster, or evil; a cause of annoyance or trouble; nuisance.—*v.t.*—*plagued, plaguing.* To harass or trouble; annoy or vex; to afflict with disease, calamity, or evil.—**pla·guer,** *n.*

pla·guy, pla·guey, plā′gē, *a. Colloq.* Causing vexation; annoying; troublesome. —*adv.* Annoyingly or excessively.—**pla·gui·ly,** *adv.*

plaice, plās, *n. pl.* **plaice.** [O.Fr. *plais,* < L.L. *platessa,* flatfish, prob. < Gr. *platús,* broad, flat.] A European flatfish, *Pleuronectes platessa,* an important food fish sometimes weighing more than 10 pounds; any of various American flatfishes or flounders.

plaid, plad, *n.* [Gael. *plaide,* < *peallaid,* a sheepskin, < *peall,* a skin or hide.] A large rectangular outer garment or wrap, frequently of tartan, worn by Highlanders and others in Scotland; a fabric woven in a tartan pattern; such a cross-barred pattern.— *a.* Having such a pattern.—**plaid·ed,** plad′id, *a.* Wearing a plaid.

plain, plān, *a.* [Fr. *plain,* Pr. *plan,* < L. *planus,* plain (same root as *plango,* to beat). *Plan* and *plane* are the same word.] Without elevations or depressions; as, a *plain* landscape; level, flat, even, or smooth; without ornament or embellishment; as, a *plain* dress; homely or unattractive; as, a *plain* girl; without disguise, cunning, or affectation; as, *plain* talk; unrefined or unsophisticated; as, *plain* people; evident, absolute, or unmistakable, as: The answer was *plain* to me. Without difficulties or intricacies; simple, as opposed to rich or luxurious; as, *plain* furnishings; not highly seasoned; as, *plain* food; *cards,* being other than a face card or a trump; sheer, mere, or downright; as, *plain* foolishness.—*adv.* Clearly or simply, as: He is *plain* stupid.—*n.* An area of level land; *geog.* the general term for all those parts of the dry land which cannot properly be called hilly or mountainous.—**plain·ly,** *adv.*—**plain·ness,** *n.*

plain·chant, plān′chant″, plān′chänt″, *n.* Plainsong.

plain·clothes man, plān′klōz′ man″, plān′-klōтнz′, *n.* A police detective who does not wear a uniform while on duty. Also **plain·clothes·man.**

plain-laid, plān′lād′, *a.* Pertaining to rope, made by laying three left-handed strands together with a right-handed twist.

plain sail·ing, *n.* Sailing on water that is calm and free from hazard. *Fig.* an unhindered course of action; progress without difficulties.

Plains In·di·an, *n.* A member of one of the Indian tribes which formerly inhabited the vast plains and prairies of N. America, having a variety of language stocks, yet possessing common cultural traits because of their contact in their nomadic life pursuing the buffalo.

plains·man, plānz′man, *n. pl.* **plains·men.** A man or inhabitant of the plains.

plain·song, plān′sang″, plān′song″, *n. Mus.* the simple, grave, and unadorned chant in which the services of the Roman Catholic Church have been rendered from a very early age; the simple notes of an air without ornament or variation. *Fig.* a plain unexaggerated statement.

plain-spo·ken, plān′spō′ken, *a.* Plain or frank in speech; forthright; candid; blunt; outspoken.

plaint, plānt, *n.* [Fr. *plainte,* a complaint, < *plaindre,* to complain, < L. *plango, planctum,* to beat the breast, to lament, akin to *plaga,* a blow, Gr. *plēssō,* strike.] Lamentation; complaint; audible expression of sorrow; *law,* a form of action, esp. one asking a court for redress of a grievance.

plain·tiff, plān′tif, *n. Law.* The person who brings a suit before a tribunal; the person who complains in any litigation: opposed to *defendant.*

plain·tive, plān′tiv, *a.* Expressive of sorrow;

voicing melancholy.—**plain·tive·ly,** *adv.*— **plain·tive·ness,** *n.*

plait, plāt, plat, *n.* [O.Fr. *ploit, pleit,* < L. *plicatus,* folded, < *plicare,* to twist, whence *ply.*] A fold or pleat. A braid, as of hair or straw; also *plat.*—*v.t.* To fold; to double in narrow strips; to braid; to interweave the locks or strands of; as, to *plait* the hair.— **plait·er,** *n.*—**plait·ing,** plā′ting, *n.*

plan, plan, *n.* [Fr. *plan,* < L. *planus,* plain, flat, level.] A devised scheme; a way of executing an act; a method or arrangement; an aim or project; the representation of anything drawn on a plane and forming a map or chart; the representation of a horizontal section of a building, showing the extent, division, and distribution of its area into apartments and passages; *graphics,* one of many planes at right angles to the line of sight between the viewer and the object.— *v.t.*—*planned, planning.* To invent or contrive for construction; to scheme; to devise; to form in design.—*v.i.*—**plan·less,** *a.*— **plan·less·ly,** *adv.*—**plan·less·ness,** *n.*— **plan·ner,** plan′ėr, *n.*

pla·nar, plā′nėr, *a.* Lying in a plane; flat; relating to a plane.

pla·na·tion, plā·nā′shan, pla·nā′shan, *n.* [L.L. *planare* (pp. *planatus*), make level.] *Geol.* the process of erosion and deposit by which a nearly level land surface is produced.

planch·et, plan′chit, *n.* [Dim. of *planch.*] A flat piece of metal for stamping as a coin; a coin blank.

plan·chette, plan·chet′, *n.* [Fr., dim. of *planche,* E. *planch.*] A small heart-shaped or triangular board supported on two casters and a vertical pencil, which is said to trace lines, words, or sentences without conscious effort on the part of persons whose fingers are lightly resting on the board. See *Ouija.*

plane, plān, *n.* A carpenter's hand tool with an oblique cutting blade, used in trimming, leveling, smoothing, or shaping a piece of wood or wood surface.—*v.t.*—*planed, planing.* To make smooth, esp. by the use of a plane.—*v.i.* To work with a plane; to work as a plane.—**plan·er,** plā′nėr, *n.* A power machine with rotating blades that smoothes or finishes metal or wood surfaces; a thing that or one who planes.

plane, plān, *n.* [< L. *planus.*] A smooth or level surface; a part of something having a level surface. *Aeron.* any supporting surface of an airplane; an airplane. A surface such that if any two points in it be joined by a straight line, the whole of the straight line will be in the surface; a certain position of achievement, development, living, or the like.—*a.* Without elevations or depressions; even; level; flat; concerned with level surfaces; as, *plane* geometry.

plane, plān, *v.i.*—*planed, planing.* To soar, as a glider; to skim across water, as a speedboat; to go by plane.

plane an·gle, *n.* An angle contained between two straight lines diverging from a single point or between two planes diverging from a single straight line.

plane ge·om·e·try, *n.* The geometry of figures all in the same plane. Compare *solid geometry.*

plan·er tree, *n.* [From J. J. *Planer,* 1743-1789, G. botanist.] A small tree, *Planera aquatica,* in the elm family, growing in moist ground in the southern U.S. and bearing a small, ovoid, nutlike fruit.

plan·et, plan′it, *n.* [O.Fr. *planete* (Fr. *planète*), < L.L. *planeta,* < Gr. *planētēs,* planet, lit. 'wanderer,' < *planan,* cause to wander.] Any one of the heavenly bodies revolving about the sun and shining by reflected light: Mercury, Venus, Earth, Mars, Jupiter, Saturn, Uranus, Neptune, and Pluto; orig. a star moving in an orbit,

as distinguished from a fixed star, formerly applied also to the sun; *astrol.* a heavenly body regarded as exerting influence on mankind and events.

plane ta·ble, *n.* A surveying instrument fixed on a tripod, and used for charting maps in the field.

plan·e·tar·i·um, plan″i·târ′ē·um, *n. pl.* **plan·e·tar·i·ums, plan·e·tar·i·a,** plan″i·târ′ē·a. An astronomical mechanism which, by the movement of its parts, represents the motions and orbits of the planets and other heavenly bodies on a doomed ceiling; the building in which this mechanism is housed.

plan·e·tar·y, plan′i·ter″ē, *a.* [Cf. L.L. *planetarius,* an astrologer.] Of, pertaining to, or resembling a planet or the planets; terrestrial or mundane; wandering or erratic; *astrol.* pertaining to a planet or the planets as exerting influence on mankind and events; *mach.* noting or pertaining to a form of transmission consisting of an epicyclic train of gears.

plan·e·tes·i·mal, plan″i·tes′i·mal, *a.* [< *planet,* with *-esimal* as in *infinitesimal.*] *Astron.* of or pertaining to minute bodies in space.—*n.* One of these minute bodies.

plan·e·tes·i·mal hy·poth·e·sis, *n. Astron.* a hypothesis that the planets and satellites of the solar system were formed by the gradual massing together of countless numbers of minute particles in space.

plan·e·toid, plan′i·toid″, *n. Astron.* any of a numerous group of very small planets between the orbits of Mars and Jupiter; an asteroid.—**plan·e·toi·dal,** *a.*

plane tree, *n.* [O.Fr. Fr. *plane,* < L. *platanus,* < Gr. *plátanos,* < *platus,* broad (with reference to the broad leaves).] A large, massive-trunked, deciduous American tree, *Platanus occidentalis,* with chalky-white, irregular patched bark, and fruit heads in the form of conspicuous pendent balls; also *sycamore, buttonball, buttonwood.* A similar species, *P. acerifolia,* common as a street tree in European cities; also **plane, plat·an,** plat′an.

plan·et-struck, plan′it·struk″, *a.* Supposedly influenced by planets; stricken with panic or terror. Also **plan·et-strick·en,** plan′it·strik″en.

plan·et wheel, *n.* Any of the wheels in an epicyclic train, whose axes revolve around the common center. Also **plan·et gear.**

plan·gent, plan′jent, *a.* [L. *plangens, plangentis,* ppr. of *plango,* to beat.] Beating, dashing, as a wave; loud sounding, esp. a metallic or plaintive sound.—**plan·gen·cy,** *n.*—**plan·gent·ly,** *adv.*

pla·ni·form, plā′ni·fạrm″, plan′i·fạrm, *a.* Having a flat surface, as the wings of some insects.

pla·nim·e·ter, pla·nim′i·tėr, *n.* [L. *planus,* plain, and Gr. *metron,* a measure.] An instrument for measuring the area of any plane figure.—**pla·nim·e·try,** pla·nim′i·trē, *n.*—**plan·i·met·ric, plan·i·met·ri·cal,** plan″i·me′trik, *a.*

plan·ish, plan′ish, *v.t.* [< *plane.*] To make smooth, as wood; to condense, smooth, and toughen, as a metallic plate, by light blows of a hammer; to polish.—**plan·ish·er,** *n.*

plan·i·sphere, plan′i·sfēr″, *n.* [= Fr. *planisphère,* < L. *planus,* flat, plane, and *sphæra,* E. *sphere.*] A projection or representation of the whole or a part of a sphere on a plane, esp. a map of half or more of the celestial sphere with a device for indicating the part of the heavens visible at a given time.—**plan·i·spher·ic,** plan″i·sfer′ik, *a.*

plank, plangk, *n.* [O.Fr. *planke,* var. of *planche* (Fr. *planche*), < L. *planca,* plank, board, slab: cf. *planch.*] A long, flat piece of timber thicker than a board; timber in such pieces; something to stand on or to cling to for support; an article in a platform of political or other principles.—*v.t.*

TABLE OF PLANETS

Planet	Symbol	Distance from Sun (in millions of miles)	Distance from Sun (in AU)	Orbital Period	Rotation Period	Diameter	Mean Density gm/cm³	Mass in terms of Earth's Mass	Surface Gravity in terms of Earth's	Escape Velocity (M./s)	Number of Satellites
Mercury	☿	36	0.387	88 d.	58.65 d.	3,025 M.	5	0.054	0.38	2	0
Venus	♀	67	0.723	225 d.	244 d. Rg	7,526 M.	5	0.81	0.87	6	0
Earth	⊕	92.9557	1.00	365.25 d.	23 h 56 m 04 s	7,927 M.	5	1.00	1.00	7	1
Mars	♂	142	1.52	687 d.	24 h 37 m 23 s	4,218 M.	4	0.11	0.39	3	2
Jupiter	♃	483	5.20	11.9 y.	9 h 50 m 30 s	88,700 M.	1.3	318	2.65	37	12
Saturn	♄	886	9.55	29.5 y.	10 h 14 m	75,100 M.	0.7	95	1.17	22	9
Uranus	♂ or ♅	1,780	19.20	84.0 y.	10 h 49 m	29,200 M.	1.3	15	1.05	13	5
Neptune	♆	2,790	30.09	165 y.	14 h ?	27,700 M.	2.2	17	1.23	15	2
Pluto	♇	3,670	39.5	248 y.	6.387 d.	3,600 M. ?	5	0.07 ?	0.5 ?	?	0

Abbreviations: R| = retrograde; AU = astronomical units; M. = miles; y. = years; d. = days; h = hours; m = minutes; s = seconds

To lay, cover, or furnish with planks; to broil or bake, and serve on a board, as meats or fish. *Colloq.* to place or set down with emphasis; to pay instantly, with *down.* —**walk the plank,** to be compelled as prisoners of pirates, to walk off a plank extending over the water from a ship's side.

plank·ing, plang′king, *n.* The act of laying or covering with planks; planks collectively, as in a floor.

plank·ter, plangk′tẽr, *n.* Any organism that is a component of plankton.

plank·ton, plangk′ton, *n.* [Gr. *plagkton,* wandering.] The mass of small organisms, plant and animal, floating or drifting in a body of water.—**plank·ton·ic,** plangk′·ton′ik, *a.*

pla·no-con·cave, plā″nō·kon′kāv, *a.* Plane on one side and concave on the other, as a lens.

pla·no-con·vex, plā″nō·kon′veks, *a.* Plane or flat on one side and convex on the other, as a lens.

pla·no·graph, plā′no·graf″, plā′no·gräf″, plan′o·graf″, plan′o·gräf″, *v.t.* To reproduce or print by planography.—*n.* Material produced by this process.

pla·nog·ra·phy, pla·nog′ra·fē, *n.* A method of printing whereby the non-printing and printing areas are on the same surface.—**pla·no·graph·ic,** plā″no·-graf′ik, *a.*

plan po·si·tion in·di·ca·tor, *n.* A cathode ray indicator with a circular screen on which the range of a target or signal is represented by its radial distance from a point representing the location of the transmitter, and on which azimuth is determined by the angle between a fixed reference line and a radial line passing through the target or signal. Abbr. *PPI.*

plant, plant, plänt, *n.* [Fr. *plante,* a plant, < L. *planta,* a plant, a twig, the sole of the foot, < root of *planus,* plain.] *Bot.* One of the organisms of the vegetable kingdom, as distinct from the animal kingdom, having cellulose cell walls, often containing chlorophyll, lacking a nervous system and the power of locomotion and in green plants able to manufacture food from inorganic materials; a seedling ready for transplanting; a slip or cutting. The fixtures, machinery, tools, and sometimes the buildings, necessary to carry on any trade or business; the buildings and other equipment of any

institution; a person who is put into an audience to take an apparently spontaneous part in proceedings; in a play, a seemingly unimportant incident, statement, or character introducing a theme which is fully developed later. *Slang,* a scheme to trick or swindle; a person or thing placed to trap or mislead.—*v.t.* To put in the ground for growth; to sow with seeds or furnish with plants, as a plot of land; to establish in the mind, as a belief; to introduce into an area, as a strain of animals; to place in a lake or river, as spawn; to bed, as oysters; to stock or furnish with animals; to fix or set in position; to establish, as a colony; to settle, as persons. *Slang,* to place forcefully, as a punch; to station or place for purposes of observation or discovery; as, to *plant* a spy in a smuggling ring, to *plant* evidence; to conceal, as stolen articles.—**plant·a·ble,** *a.* —**plant·like,** *a.*

Plan·tag·e·net, plan·taj′e·nit, *a.* [Ult. < L. *planta,* sprout, spring, and *genesta, genista* (Fr. *genêt*), broom plant.] Of or pertaining to the line of English sovereigns that reigned from Henry II in 1154, to the accession of the House of Tudors in 1485: being a personal patronymic nickname of Geoffrey, the father of Henry II, who is said to have been in the habit of wearing a sprig of broom in his cap.

plan·tain, plan′tin, plan′tin, *n.* [O.Fr. Fr. *plantain,* < L. *plantago* (*plantagin-*), plantain.] Any plant of the widespread genus *Plantago,* esp. *P. major,* a common dooryard weed with broad, strongly ribbed, basal leaves and long tight flower heads.

plan·tain, plan′tin, plan′tin, *n.* [Sp. *plántano, plátano,* plantain, also plane tree, < L. *platanus.*] A tropical plant, *Musa paradisiaca,* in the banana family, whose cooked fruit is an important food in the tropics.

plan·tain lil·y, *n.* Any of several herbaceous ornamental species of the genus *Hosta,* in the lily family, having attractive clumps of foliage and spikes of white, lavender, or blue flowers. Also *funkia.* **hos·ta lil·y.**

plan·tar, plan′tẽr, *a.* [L. *planta,* the sole of the foot.] *Anat.* relating or belonging to the sole of the foot.

plan·ta·tion, plan·tā′shan, *n.* [L. *plantatio.*] A large estate, esp. in warm climates, planted in various crops and cultivated

chiefly by resident workers; the act of planting for growth; the area planted; a grove; *hist.* a colony or company of early settlers.

plant·er, plan′tẽr, plän′tẽr, *n.* One who plants; the owner or occupant of a plantation; an implement or machine for planting seeds; formerly, an early settler in a region, a colonist; an ornamental container, of various shapes and materials, in which plants can be grown.

plant·er's punch, *n.* An alcoholic beverage containing rum, sugar, lime or lemon juice, and either soda or water.

plant food, *n.* Nutriment for plants, as fertilizer or chemicals.

plan·ti·grade, plan′ti·grād″, *a.* [L. *planta,* the sole of the foot, and *gradior,* to walk.] Walking on the entire sole of the foot, that is with the heel touching the ground, as man, bears, and raccoon: distinguished from *digitigrade.*—*n.* A plantigrade animal.

plant louse, *n.* An aphid, or any of several related insects which infest plants.

plan·u·la, plan′ū·la, *n.* pl. **plan·u·lae,** plan′ū·lē″. [L. dim. of *planus,* a wanderer.] *Zool.* an oval, ciliated, free-swimming larva of coelenterates.—**plan·u·lar,** *a.*—**plan·u·late,** plan′ū·lāt″, *a.*

plaque, plak, *n.* [Fr.] A thin flat plate or tablet of metal or porcelain, intended for ornament, as on a wall or set in a piece of furniture; a platelike brooch or ornament, esp. one worn as the badge of an honorary order; *anat., zool.* a small, flat, rounded, abnormal formation or area, as on the skin.

plash, plash, *n.* [D. *plasch, plas,* a puddle, perh. from sound of splashing; cf. D. *plassen,* G. *platschen, platschern,* to paddle in water; L.G. *plasken,* E. to *splash.*] A puddle; a pond; a splash.—*v.i., v.t.* To splash.

plash, plash, *v.t.* [O.Fr. *plassier, plessier,* < L. *plexus,* pp. of *plecto,* to weave, to twist (as in *complex*). *Pleach* is a collateral form.] To bend down and interweave the branches or twigs of; as, to *plash* a hedge.—**plash·er,** *n.*

plasm, plaz′um, *n.* Plasma.

plas·ma, plaz′ma, *n.* [Gr. *plasma,* something formed or molded, < *plasso,* to form, whence *plastic.*] *Anat.* a nearly colorless fluid in which the corpuscles of the blood

a- fat, fāte, fär, fâre, f̧all;   **e-** met, mē, mēre, hẽr;   **i-** pin, pīne;   **o-** not, nōte, mõve;   **u-** tub, cūbe, b̧ull;   **oi-** oil;   **ou-** pound.

are suspended; *med.* a human blood product used for transfusions and prepared by removing all red cells, white cells, and platelets from whole blood; *biol.* protoplasm. *Phys.* an electrically charged gas occupying most of outer space beyond the earth's atmosphere; a gas compressed and confined magnetically to produce nuclear fusion in experiments on jet propulsion and jet power. A slightly translucent variety of quartz, either green, gray, or blue, popular as a gem in ancient Rome.—**plas·mic**, **plas·mat·ik**, plaz·mat'ik, *a.*

plas·ma·gel, plaz'ma·jel", *n.* An outer, gelatinous thickness of cytoplasm found in an amoeba, just beneath the membrane of the cell. Compare *plasmasol.*

plas·ma mem·brane, *n.* Cell membrane.

plas·ma·sol, plaz'ma·sŏl", plaz'ma·sạl", plaz'ma·sol", *n.* The fluid cytoplasm in the interior of an amoeba cell, as contrasted with *plasmagel.*

plas·min, plaz'min, *n.* *Biochem.* a proteolytic enzyme in the bloodstream causing fibrin breakdown and the dissolving of clots. Also **fi·bri·nol·y·sin**.

plas·mol·y·sis, plaz·mol'i·sis, *n.* *Bot.* shrinkage and dissolution of the protoplasm in a living cell when excessive water loss occurs by exosmosis.—**plas·mo·lyt·ic**, plaz"mo·lit'ik, *a.*—**plas·mo·lyt·i·cal·ly**, *adv.*

plas·ter, plas'tẽr, plä'stẽr, *n.* [In first sense, O.E. *plaster,* < L. *emplastrum,* < Gr. *emplastron,* a plaster, < *emplássein,* daub on or over; in later senses, O.Fr. *plastre* (Fr. *plâtre*), < L. *emplastrum.*] A pasty composition, as of lime, sand, water, and often hair, used for covering walls and ceilings, where it hardens in drying; a solid or semisolid preparation for spreading upon cloth and applying to the body for some remedial or other purpose. See *plaster of Paris.*—**plas·ter·work**, plas'tẽr·wụrk", plä'stẽr·wụrk", *n.*—**plas·ter·y**, *a.*

plas·ter, plas'tẽr, plä'stẽr, *v.t.* To apply a plaster to; to cover with plaster; daub or fill with plaster or something similar; to overspread with anything, esp. thickly or to excess; as, to *plaster* a wall with photographs; lay flat like a layer of plaster.—**plas·ter·er**, *n.*

plas·ter·board, plas'tẽr·bōrd", plas'tẽr·bạrd", plä'stẽr·bōrd", plä'stẽr·bạrd", *n.* Large boardlike sheets having an inner core of hardened gypsum bonded to outer layers of paper, felt, or other fiber, used for insulating or forming walls.

plas·ter cast, *n.* A piece of sculpture or other object molded from plaster of Paris; *med.* a rigid bandage made of overlapped layers of gauze saturated with plaster of Paris, used for immobilizing a fractured or diseased part. Also **cast**.

plas·tered, plas'tẽrd, plä'stẽrd, *a. Slang,* intoxicated, drunk.

plas·ter·ing, plas'tẽr·ing, plä'stẽr·ing, *n.* The application of plaster; a plaster coating.

plas·ter of Par·is, **plas·ter of par·is**, *n.* Calcined gypsum, a white powdery material which sets rapidly when mixed with water, used for making casts and molds. See *plaster.*

plas·tic, plas'tik, *a.* [L. *plasticus,* < Gr. *plastikós,* < *plássein,* form, mold.] Having the power of molding or shaping formless or yielding material; as, the *plastic* force which molds society; pertaining to molding or modeling, as in sculpture and ceramics; produced by molding; as, *plastic* figures; capable of being brought to a definite condition or character; pliable; impressionable; *surg.* concerned with the remedying or restoring of malformed, injured, or lost parts; as, *plastic* surgery; *biol.* pertaining to the formation of new tissue in the living body.—*n.* Any of various natural or synthetic, usu. resinous, organic substances, which, when subjected to heat and pressure, can be cast, pressed, extruded, or molded into a variety of shapes; anything that can be molded.—**plas·ti·cal·ly**, *adv.*

plas·tic·i·ty, pla·stis'i·tẽ, *n.* The quality of being plastic; capability of being molded or being brought into definite form.

plas·ti·cize, plas'ti·sīz", *v.t., v.i.—plasticized, plasticizing.* To render or be made plastic.

plas·ti·ciz·er, plas'ti·sī"zẽr, *n.* Any material which makes a substance plastic, giving it flexibility, stretchability, and softness.

plas·tic sur·ger·y, *n.* Surgery undertaken to restore or repair lost, malformed, or injured bones, other tissues, or organs of the body. Also *anaplasty.*—**plas·tic sur·geon**, *n.*

plas·tid, plas'tid, *n.* [G., < Gr. *plastis* (*plastid-*), fem., one who forms, < *plássein,* form, mold.] *Biol.* any of certain small specialized masses of protoplasm, as chloroplasts or chromoplasts, occurring in the cytoplasm of cells.

plas·tron, plas'tron, *n.* [Fr. *plastron,* a breastplate, same origin as *plaster.*] A metal, leather, or quilted shield worn in fencing to protect the upper part of the body; a starched shirt front; an ornamental bib front on a woman's dress; *zool.* the lower or ventral portion of the bony case of tortoises and turtles.—**plas·tral**, plas'tral, *a.*

plat, plat, *n.* [Same word as *plot*; but prob. affected by Fr. *plat, plate,* flat.] A small piece of ground; a map or chart. See *plot.*—*v.t.—platted, platting.* To make a chart or plan of.

plat, plat, *v.t.—platted, platting.* [Same as *plait.*] To interweave; to plait.—*n.* Braid. See *plait.*

plate, plāt, *n.* [O.Fr. *plate,* flat piece, plate, prop. fem. of O.Fr. *plat,* akin to It. *piatto* and G. *platt,* flat; < L.L. and perh. ult. < Gr. *platús,* broad, flat.] A shallow, usu. circular vessel, from which food is eaten; the contents of such a vessel; a service of food for one person at table; a course served on one plate; a vessel, as of metal or wood, resembling a plate for food, used for collecting offerings, as in a church. A thin, flat sheet or piece of metal or other material, esp. of uniform thickness; metal in such sheets; a flat piece of metal used in making armor, armor composed of such pieces; a flat, polished piece of metal on which something may be or is engraved; such a piece engraved to print from; a printed impression from such a piece, as a woodcut; a full-page inserted illustration forming part of a book; a sheet of metal for printing from, formed by stereotyping or electrotyping a page of type. *Chiefly Brit.* a flat strip of metal with a projecting flange, forming part of the track of a railway, or, sometimes, a rail of an ordinary railroad. A kind of light horseshoe worn by race horses; a thin piece or cut of beef at the lower end of the ribs; domestic vessels or utensils of gold or silver; plated metallic ware; a gold or silver cup or the like awarded as a prize in some contests; a contest for such a prize; *anat., zool.* a platelike part, structure, or organ; *dentistry,* a piece of metal or other firm substance, with artificial teeth attached, worn in the mouth after the loss of natural teeth; *photog.* a sensitized sheet of glass or metal, on which to take a photograph; *teleg., teleph.* one of the interior elements of a vacuum tube. *Arch.* a timber laid horizontally, as in a wall, to receive the ends of other timbers; also *wall plate.* Baseball, the home base. *Mining,* shale.

plate, plāt, *v.t.—plated, plating.* To cover or overlay with metal plates for protection; to coat with a thin film of gold, silver, or nickel by mechanical means; *papermaking,* to give a high gloss to, as paper, by super-calendering; *printing,* to make a stereotype or electrotype plate from; as, to *plate* type.

pla·teau, pla·tō', *esp. Brit.* plat'ō, *n. pl.* **pla·teaus**, pla·tōz', **pla·teaux**, pla·tō', pla·tōz'. [Fr., < *plat,* flat; akin to *plate.*] *Geog.* a broad, flat area of somewhat elevated land; a tableland. *Fig.* a time or area in the development of something evidenced by neither progress nor decline; *psychol.* a period in a person's learning process shown by a level line in a graph of achievement.—*v.i.* To make stable; to reach a plateau.

plate·ful, plāt'fụl, *n. pl.* **plate·fuls**. As much as a plate will hold.

plate glass, *n.* A fine kind of glass, cast in thick plates, used for mirrors and large windowpanes.

plate·let, plāt'lit, *n.* A minute plate or platelike body. A blood platelet; see *thrombocyte.*

plat·en, plat'en, *n.* [Fr. *platine,* < *plat,* flat.] *Mach.* a flat metal plate or rotating cylinder of a printing press, or the cylinder of a typewriter against which the paper rests while receiving an impression.

plate proof, *n.* A fine imprint made on paper of the inked surface of a letterpress plate or engraving. Also **en·grav·er's proof**.

plat·er, plā'tẽr, *n.* One who coats articles with a layer of gold, silver, or other metal; one engaged in the application or manufacture of metal plates; an inferior racehorse.

plate rail, *n.* A rail or narrow shelf placed along a wall to hold plates or other ornaments for display.

plat·form, plat'fạrm, *n.* [Fr. *plateforme—plate,* flat, and *forme,* a form.] Any flat or horizontal structure raised above an adjoining level; the raised walk at a railroad station for landing passengers and goods; the passage area between two railroad passenger cars; a place raised above the floor of a hall set apart for the speakers at public meetings; the aggregate of principles adopted or avowed by any body of people, such as a political party; a declared system of policy; as, a political *platform*; *milit.* the place where guns are mounted on a fortress or battery.

plat·form car, *n.* Flatcar.

plat·i·na, plat'i·na, pla·tē'na, *n.* [N.L. or Sp.] An alloy of zinc and copper; *archaic,* platinum, esp. native platinum.

plat·ing, plā'ting, *n.* The action of one who or that which plates; a thin coating of gold, silver, or nickel; an external layer of metal plates.

pla·tin·ic, pla·tin'ik, *a.* Pertaining to platinum, esp. to tetravalent platinum.

plat·i·nize, plat'i·nīz", *v.t.—platinized, platinizing.* To combine or cover with platinum.

plat·i·no·cy·an·ic ac·id, plat"i·nō·sī·an'ik as'id, *n. Chem.* an acid, $H_2Pt(CN)_4$, containing platinum and the cyano group.

plat·i·no·cy·a·nide, plat"i·nō·sī'a·nīd", plat"i·nō·sī'a·nid, *n. Chem.* a salt of platinocyanic acid, combining platinous cyanide with another cyanide.

plat·i·noid, plat'i·noid", *n.* [< *platinum.*] Any one of a series of metals allied to platinum; an alloy of zinc, copper, and nickel, with a very small amount of tungsten or aluminum, used to make electrical resistance coils.—*a.* Similar to platinum.

plat·i·no·type, plat'i·nō·tīp", *n.* [*Platinum* and *type.*] *Photog.* a permanent photographic print produced by a process in which platinum salt is used; the print produced according to this process.

plat·i·nous, plat'i·nus, *a.* Containing platinum, esp. in the bivalent state.

plat·i·num, plat′*i*·num, *n.* [< *platina*.] *Chem.* a heavy, grayish-white metallic element, ductile and resistant to most chemicals, used for jewelry and in chemistry, dentistry, electronics, and industry. Sym. Pt, at. no. 78, at. wt. 195.09. See Periodic Table of Elements.

plat·i·num black, *n. Chem.* a black powder of very finely divided metallic platinum, used as an oxidizing agent and a catalyst.

plat·i·num blonde, *n.* An extremely light hair color, nearing white, but having a slightly metallic tinge or sheen, usu. artificial; one whose hair is such a color.

plat·i·tude, plat′*i*·tūd″, plat′i·tūd″, *n.* [Fr., < *plat*, flat.] A trite or dull remark; dullness; repetition of the obvious.—**plat·i·tu·di·nal, plat·i·tu·di·nous,** plat″i·tōd′i·nus, plat″i·tūd′i·nus, *a.*

plat·i·tu·di·nize, plat″i·tōd′i·nīz″, plat″i·tūd′i·nīz, *v.i.—platitudinized, platitudinizing.* To utter platitudes.

Pla·ton·ic, pla·ton′ik, plā·ton′ik, *a.* Of or pertaining to the Greek philosopher Plato or his doctrines. (*l.c.*) purely spiritual or free from sensual desire, as applied to love or friendship between persons of the opposite sex; of persons, feeling or professing such love.—**pla·ton·i·cal·ly,** *adv.*

Pla·ton·ic love, *n.* Love evolving from passionate love, ascending to the spiritual and to an appreciation of ideal beauty; (usu. l.c.) pure spiritual affection existing between two persons of the opposite sex.

Pla·to·nism, plāt′o·niz″um, *n.* The philosophy or doctrines of Plato or his followers; the doctrine that physical objects are representations of unchanging ideas that alone are the objects of true knowledge; (*usu. l.c.*) the doctrine or the practice of platonic love.—**Pla·to·nist,** *n.*—**Pla·to·nis·tic,** *a.*

Pla·to·nize, plāt′o·nīz″, *v.i.—Platonized, Platonizing.* To follow the opinions or doctrines of Plato; reason like Plato.—*v.t.* To render Platonic; give a Platonic character to; explain in accordance with Platonic principles.

pla·toon, pla·tön′, *n.* [Fr. *peloton*, a ball of thread, a platoon, < *pelote*, a ball of thread, < L.L. *pelota, pilota,* < L. *pila,* a ball.] *Milit.* a unit of a company, troop, or battery, comprised of a headquarters and two or more squads or sections and commanded by a commissioned officer, usu. a second lieutenant; *football,* either the defensive or offensive team which plays in the game as a unit. A group, body, or unit of people, usu. with something in common; as, a *platoon* of firemen.

pla·toon ser·geant, *n. Army,* the senior noncommissioned officer in a platoon, usu. second in command, as a 'sergeant first class.'

plat·ter, plat′ér, *n.* [< O.Fr. *platel,* dim. of *plat,* a plate.] A plate; a large, shallow, serving dish, esp. one that is oval-shaped; *slang,* a phonographic record.

plat·y, plā′tē, *a.—platier, platiest.* Consisting of platelike layers, specif. of soil or rocks.

plat·y, plā′tē, *n. pl.* **plat·y, plat·ys, plat·ies.** A topminnow, originating in southern Mexico, favored for tropical aquariums, sometimes showing brilliant coloring, and considered one species, *Platypoecilus maculatus.*

plat·y·hel·minth, plat″i·hel′minth, *n.* [N.L. *Platyhelminthes,* n. pl., < Gr. *platys,* broad, flat, and *hélmins* (helminth-), worm.] *Zool.* any of the *Platyhelminthes,* a phylum or group of worms having bilateral symmetry and a soft, usu. flattened body, including tapeworms, planarians, and flukes. Also *flatworm.*

plat·y·pus, plat′i·pus, *n. pl.* **plat·y·pus·es, plat·y·pi,** plat′i·pī″. [Gr. *platys,* broad, *pous,* foot.] One of the most primitive mammals in the order *Monotremata,* having such birdlike characteristics as webbed feet, a bill similar to a duck's, and the ability to lay eggs. Also *duckbill.*

plat·yr·rhine, plat′i·rīn″, plat′i·rin, *a.* [Gr. *platyrris (platyrrin-),* broad-nosed, < *platys,* broad, flat, and *ris* (rin-), nose.] *Zool.* Having a short, broad nose; pertaining to the suborder *Platyrrhini,* monkeys of Central and South America, characterized by widely spaced nostrils and a long, prehensile tail.—*n.* Also **plat·yr·rhin·i·an,** plat″i·rin′ē·an.

plau·dit, plạ′dit, *n.* [L. *plaudite,* do you applaud, impv. of *plaudo, plausum,* to applaud.] *Usu. pl.* Applause; praise bestowed.

plau·si·ble, plạ′zi·bl, *a.* [L. *plausibilis,* from *plaudo.*] Apparently right; sometimes specious; using arguments that may be open to question; convincingly spoken.—**plau·si·bil·i·ty, plau·si·ble·ness,** plạ″zi·bil′i·tē, *n.*—**plau·si·bly,** *adv.*

plau·sive, plạ′ziv, plạ′siv, *a.* Applauding; indicating praise.

play, plā, *n.* [O.E. *plega.*] A dramatic performance, as on the stage; a dramatic composition or piece; a drama; exercise or action by way of amusement or recreation; diversion; sport; fun; jest or trifling, as opposed to *earnestness;* a playful use of a word or words, as to bring out differences of meaning, occurring with likeness of sound, as a pun; the playing or carrying on, of a game; manner or style of playing; an act or performance in playing; as, a stupid *play;* turn to play, as: It's your *play.* The state, as of a ball, of being played with or in use, in the active playing of a game; as, in *play;* a playing for stakes; as, to lose money at *play;* gambling; amusement, game, or sport of children; action, conduct, or dealing of a specific kind; as, fair *play,* foul *play.* Brisk movement or action; as, sword*play;* light and quick, alternating or irregular, motion; as, the *play* of lights on a fountain; elusive change, as of light or colors; action, activity, or operation; as, the *play* of fancy; freedom of movement within a space, as of a part of a mechanism; a space in which a thing, as such a part, can move; freedom for action, or scope for activity.—*v.t.* To perform, as a drama, on or as on the stage; act or sustain the part of in a dramatic performance or in real life; as, to *play* the tyrant; to give performances in, as a theatrical company does; as, to *play* the larger cities; to do, perform, or execute; as, to *play* tricks; to engage in a game or pastime; represent or imitate in sport; as, to *play* school; to stake or wager, as in playing; lay a wager or wagers on; as, to *play* the horses; to contend against in a game; to employ, as a player, in a game; to put forward, move, strike, or drive, in playing a game; to use as if in playing a game, as for one's own advantage; as, to *play* one person or thing against another; to perform, as music, on an instrument; perform on, as a musical instrument; to cause to move or change lightly or quickly; as, to *play* colored lights on a fountain; to allow, as a hooked fish, to exhaust itself by pulling on the line; to operate or cause to operate, esp. continuously or with repeated action: as, to *play* a hose on a fire, or guns on the enemy's position.—*v.i.* To exercise or employ oneself in diversion, amusement, or recreation; sport; frolic; to do something only in sport, which is not to be taken seriously; to amuse oneself or toy, often followed by *with;* as, to *play* with the ball; trifle; to take part or engage in a game; to take part in a game for stakes; gamble; to act or conduct oneself in a specified way; as, to *play* fair; to perform on a musical instrument; of the instrument or the music, to sound in performance; to act on or as on the stage; perform; to move freely within a space, as a part of a

mechanism; to operate continuously or with repeated action, often on something; as, cannons that *play* on the enemy lines; to move about lightly or quickly; move lightly or quickly with alternating or irregular motion, as flames, waves, or wind; present the effect of such motion, as light or the changing colors of an iridescent substance. —**make a play for,** *slang.* To try to enter into a sexual relationship; to try to profit by making a favorable impression.—**play in·to a per·son's hands,** to act in such a way as to give him an advantage.—**play on** or **up·on,** to work on the feelings or weaknesses of another for one's own purposes.— **play the game,** to play or behave fairly.— **play·a·ble,** *a.*

pla·ya, plī′a, *Sp.* plä′yä, *n. pl.* **pla·yas,** plī′az, *Sp.* plä′yäs. [Sp., shore, beach, < L. *plaga,* region, tract.] A plain of silt or mud, covered with water during the wet season.

play·act, plā′akt″, *v.i.* To pretend; to behave in an insincere or theatrical manner. —*v.t.* To act out or dramatize.—**play·act·ing,** plā′ak″ting, *n.*

play·back, plā′bak″, *n.* The act of translating back into sound, as a tape recording; an apparatus used for the reproduction of sound recordings; the recording so reproduced.

play back, *v.t.* To replay, as a tape, in order to hear the sounds recorded.

play·bill, plā′bil″, *n.* A placard or other notice exhibited as an advertisement of a play.

play·boy, plā′boi″, *n.* A man whose time is spent in the type of pleasure-producing activities found at parties, nightclubs, and similar places of entertainment.

play-by-play, plā′bi·plā′, *a.* Pertaining to a description or account of each incident in an event as it occurs, as in sports.

play·down, plā′doun″, *n. Canadian sports,* a play-off to determine a championship. Also **play-down.**

play down, *v.t.* To minimize.

played out, *a.* Exhausted; finished.

play·er, plā′ér, *n.* [O.E. *plegere.*] One who or that which plays; one who takes part or is skilled in some game; *Brit.* a person engaged in playing a game professionally. One who plays for stakes, as a gambler; a performer on a musical instrument; a mechanical device by which a musical instrument, esp. a piano, is played automatically; one who plays parts on the stage, as an actor.

play·er pi·an·o, *n.* A type of piano which plays automatically by means of a mechanical device contained within the instrument.

play·fel·low, plā′fel″ō, *n.* A playmate.

play·ful, plā′ful, *a.* Sportive; frolicsome; full of sprightly humor; pleasantly jocular or amusing.—**play·ful·ly,** *adv.*—**play·ful·ness,** *n.*

play·go·er, plā′gō″ér, *n.* One who frequents the theater.

play·ground, plā′ground″, *n.* A piece of ground set apart for open-air recreation, esp. one connected with a school; a resort area attractive to vacationers or tourists. Also *playland.*

play·house, plā′hous″, *n. pl.* **play·hous·es,** plā′hou″ziz. [O.E. *pleghūs.*] A theater; a house to play in; as, a child's *playhouse;* a toy house.

play·ing card, *n.* One of a set or pack of cards for use in playing games; one of the well-known set of 52 cards in four suits, diamonds, hearts, spades, and clubs, marked with a numeral, or a figure, as king, queen, or jack, used in playing games of chance and skill.

play·ing field, *n.* A piece of land or a field set aside for games and athletic contests.

play·land, plā′land″, *n.* Playground.

play·let, plā′lit, *n.* A short dramatic play, usu. in one act.

play·mate, plā'māt", *n.* A playfellow; a companion in diversions or play.

play-off, plā'af", plā'of", *n. Sports.* An additional game or part of a game played in a contest in the event of a tie; a succession of games to determine a championship.

play off, *v.t.* To play an additional game to decide on the winner in the event of a tie.

play out, *v.t.* To exhaust; to finish; to unwind, as a fishing reel.—*v.i.* To be spent.

play·pen, plā'pen", *n.* A small, movable enclosure where a very young child can be put to play by himself.

play·room, plā'rŏm", plā'rụm", *n.* A place set apart for children's play activities or for adult diversion.

play·suit, plā'sōt", *n.* An outfit, usu. a shirt and shorts, worn for sports or recreation by women or children.

play·thing, plā'thing", *n.* A toy; anything or anyone that serves to amuse.

play·time, plā'tīm", *n.* Time for play or recreation, as for children during their school day.

play up, *v.t.* To emphasize.—**play up to,** *colloq.* to attempt to curry favor by flattery and the like.

play·wright, plā'rīt", *n.* An author of plays; a dramatist.

pla·za, plä'za, plaz'a, *n.* [Sp., < L. *platea.*] A public square or open space in a city or town.

plea, plē, *n.* [O.Fr. *plai, plaid, plait,* a suit, a plea; < L. *placitum,* an opinion, a determination, < *placeo,* to please.] A pleading or appeal; that which is alleged in support, justification, or defense; an excuse. *Law,* a suit or action; that which is alleged by a party to a legal action in support of his demand; the answer of a defendant to the plaintiff's declaration; an answer admitting the truth of the charges, but expressing special reasons or evidence for having the case dismissed or delayed.

plead, plēd, *v.i.*—*pleaded* or *pled, pleading.* [Fr. *plaider,* to plead, < L.L. *placitare,* < L. *placitum.*] To argue in support of a claim, or in defense against the claim of another; to urge reasons for or against; to attempt to persuade one by argument or supplication. *Law,* to present a plea in a legal action; to present an answer to the declaration of a plaintiff; to present a plea of an indicated kind; as, to *plead* guilty; to deny the plaintiff's declaration and demand. —*v.t.* To discuss, defend, and attempt to maintain by arguments or reasons; as, to *plead* one's cause; to allege or cite in proof, support, or vindication; offer in excuse; as, to *plead* ignorance. *Law,* to continue or maintain by discourse or argument; to allege or claim in a legal plea; to present or allege in defense.—**plead·a·ble**, plē'da·bl, *a.*—**plead·er,** plē'dẽr, *n.*

plead·ing, plē'ding, *n.* The act of advocating any cause; an entreaty. *Law,* the act or practice of advocating a client's cause in a court of law; one of the usu. written, formal statements containing the subject matter of a litigant's demand or claim, or of his defense or answer; the act or process of introducing such statements.

pleas·ant, plez'ant, *a.* [Fr. *plaisant,* ppr. of *plaire.*] Pleasing; agreeable; enjoyable; giving pleasure to the mind or to the senses; amiable.—**pleas·ant·ly,** *adv.*—**pleas·ant·ness,** *n.*

pleas·ant·ry, plez'an·trē, *n. pl.* **pleas·ant·ries.** [Fr. *plaisanterie.*] A humorous remark or action; a jest; an amiable, good-humored spirit in conversation; banter.

please, plēz, *v.t.*—*pleased, pleasing.* [O.Fr. *plaisir, pleisir,* etc., Mod.Fr. *plaire,* < L. *placere,* to please; of similar origin are *placid, placable, plea, plead.*] To gratify, satisfy, or content; to be the will or desire of, as: May it *please* the court. To be so obliging or kind as to: used in the imperative with a request, as: *Please* pass the salt. —*v.i.* To give pleasure; to like or prefer, as: Do it whenever you *please.*

pleas·ing, plē'zing, *a.* Giving pleasure or satisfaction; agreeable; gratifying.—**pleas·ing·ly,** *adv.*—**pleas·ing·ness,** *n.*

pleas·ur·a·ble, plezh'ẽr·a·bl, *a.* Pleasing; gratifying; giving pleasure.—**pleas·ur·a·bil·i·ty, pleas·ur·a·ble·ness,** *n.*—**pleas·ur·a·bly,** *adv.*

pleas·ure, plezh'ẽr, *n.* [O.Fr. *plaisir, pleisir,* Mod.Fr. *plaisir,* < L. *placere,* to please; prop. an inf. but as in *leisure* the final syllable has been assimilated to that of nouns in -*ure,* L. -*ura.*] The feeling produced by the enjoyment or expectation of good; delight; a state of agreeable sensations or emotions; a source of gratification or happiness; amusement or entertainment; sensual gratification; will or choice; as, to go or stay at *pleasure.*—*v.t.*—*pleasured, pleasuring.* To give or afford pleasure to; to gratify.—*v.i.* To take satisfaction; delight; *colloq.* to look for pleasure.—**pleas·ure·ful,** *a.*—**pleas·ure·less,** *a.*

pleat, plēt, *n.* [Var. of *plait.*] A fold of definite, even width made by doubling cloth upon itself, and pressing, stitching, or otherwise fastening in place.—*v.t.* To fold or arrange in pleats. Also *plait.*—**pleat·ed,** *a.*—**pleat·er,** *n.*

pleb, pleb, *n.* A plebeian; a plebe.

plebe, plēb, *n.* A member of the lowest class at the U.S. Military Academy and the U.S. Naval Academy.

ple·be·ian, ple·bē'an, *a.* [L. *plebeius,* < *plebes, plebs,* the common people; same root as in *plenty.*] Pertaining to the common people, esp. of ancient Rome; vulgar; common.—*n.* One of the common people; one of the plebs of ancient Rome.—**ple·be·ian·ism,** *n.*—**ple·be·ian·ly,** *adv.*

pleb·i·scite, pleb'i·sīt", pleb'i·sit, *n.* [Fr. < L. *plebiscitum—plebis,* the people, and *scitum,* a decree.] An expression of will by direct vote of a whole people or community on a public issue, esp. one concerning change of government or constitution.

plebs, plebz, *n. pl.* **ple·bes,** plē'bēz. [L.] The lower class of the people of ancient Rome; the common people; the populace.

plec·tog·nath, plek'tog·nath", *n.* [N.L. *Plectognathi,* pl., < Gr. *plectós,* plaited, twisted, and *gnáthos,* jaw.] Any of the *Plectognathi,* an order of teleostean fishes having powerful jaws, including the filefishes, globefishes, and triggerfishes.—*a.*

plec·trum, plek'trum, *n. pl.* **plec·tra, plec·trums,** plek'tra. [L. *plectrum,* < Gr. *plēktron,* < *plēssō,* to strike.] The small instrument of ivory, horn, or metal used for striking the strings of the lyre, mandolin, zither, or other stringed instrument; a pick.

pledge, plej, *n.* [Fr. *pleige,* L.L. *plegius, plegium, plivium, pluvium,* pledge; origin uncertain.] A promise; a formal agreement to perform or refrain from performing some act; anything given as security for the payment of a debt or for performance of some agreement or obligation; the state of being held as such security; as, property being held in *pledge;* the drinking to another's health; one who has promised to join a fraternity or other social group, but has not been formally accepted.—*v.t.*—*pledged, pledging.* To give, as one's word of honor; to promise; to give as a pledge or pawn; to deposit in possession of a person as a security; to bind or engage solemnly; to drink a toast to; to promise to become a member of; to admit, as a pledge in an organization.—**pledg·ee,** plej·ē', *n.* The person to whom anything is pledged or a pawn or promise is given.—**pledg·er,** plej'ẽr, *n.*—**pledg·or,** plej·ạr', *n. Law,* one who deposits something as security.

pledg·et, plej'it, *n.* A compress or small flat mass of lint, cotton, or the like, laid over a wound to absorb the matter discharged or to apply medicine.

Ple·iad, *Fr.* **Plé·ia·de,** plē'ad, pli'ad, *Fr.* plä·yäd', *n.* [= Fr. *Pléiade,* < L. *Pleais (Pleiad-).*] Any of the Pleiades; a famous group of 16th century French poets. (*l.c.*) a group of brilliant persons or things, usu. of seven.

Ple·ia·des, plē'a·dēz", pli'a·dēz", *n. pl.* [L. (sing. *Pleias*), < Gr. *Pleiádes,* (sing. *Pleiás*).] *Class. mythol.* the seven daughters of Atlas, transformed by Zeus into the group of stars bearing their name; *astron.* a conspicuous group or cluster of stars in the constellation Taurus, commonly spoken of as seven, though only six can be seen by the average eye.

plein-air, plān'âr', *Fr.* ple·neʀ', *a.* [Fr. *plein air,* 'full air,' open air.] *Paint.* Pertaining to, working, or done in the open air; characterizing a school or style of painting that originated in France about 1870, concerned with rendering the effects of atmosphere and light in nature, as seen out of doors, rather than the artificial effects of the studio.—**plein-air·ism,** *n.*—**plein-air·ist,** *n.*

Plei·o·cene, pli'o·sēn", *a., n.* Pliocene.

plei·o·tax·y, pli'o·tak"sē, *n. Bot.* growth exceeding the normal number of parts in one or a cluster of flowers.

Pleis·to·cene, pli'sto·sēn", *n.* [Gr. *pleistos,* most, and *kainos,* recent.] *Geol.* The earlier of the two epochs constituting the Quaternary period, characterized by sedimentary and glacial deposits and fossil remains which include present-day as well as much older species; the system of rocks of this epoch.—*a.* See Table of Geologic Time.

ple·na·ry, plē'na·rē, plen'a·rē, *a.* [L.L. *plenarius,* < L. *plenus,* full.] Full; entire; complete; attended by the entire body of qualified members, as a meeting.

ple·na·ry in·dul·gence, *n. Rom Cath. Ch.* complete remission of the temporal punishment for sins that have been absolved.

plen·i·po·ten·ti·ar·y, plen"ē·po·ten'shē·er"ē, plen"ē·po·ten'she·rē, *n. pl.* **plen·i·po·ten·ti·ar·ies.** A person invested with full power to transact any business, as an ambassador or envoy.—*a.* Invested with full power; conferring full power.—**ple·nip·o·tent,** ple·nip'o·tent, *a.*

plen·ish, plen'ish, *v.t.* [O.Fr. *plenir (pleniss-),* fill, < L. *plenus,* full: cf. *replenish.*] *Provinc. E.* To fill up; stock; furnish.

plen·i·tude, plen'i·tŏd", plen'i·tūd", *n.* [L. *plenitudo,* < *plenus,* full.] The state of being full or complete; plenty; abundance; repletion.

plen·te·ous, plen'tē·us, *a.* Abundant; copious; yielding an abundance.—**plen·te·ous·ly,** *adv.*—**plen·te·ous·ness,** *n.*

plen·ti·ful, plen'ti·ful, *a.* Existing in great plenty; copious; abundant; ample; yielding an abundance; fruitful.—**plen·ti·ful·ly,** *adv.*—**plen·ti·ful·ness,** *n.*

plen·ty, plen'tē, *n. pl.* **plen·ties.** [O.Fr. *plente,* < L.L. *plenitas,* fullness, abundance, < L. *plenus,* full, < root of *pleo,* to fill, which is seen also in Gr. *plērēs, pleos,* full, and also in E. *full, fill.*] An abundance or copiousness; a full or adequate supply; an abundance of the necessities and luxuries of life; as, a time of *plenty.*—*a. Colloq.* Plentiful; being in abundance; ample.—*adv. Colloq.* sufficiently.

ple·num, plē'num, plen'um, *n. pl.* **ple·nums, ple·na,** plē'na, plen'a. [L. *plenus,* full.] Space conceived as being full of some form of matter, as opposed to a *vacuum;* an enclosed volume of gas or air under pressure that is greater than that outside; an assembly with all members present, esp. of a corporation or legislature; a state of fullness.

ple·o·mor·phism, plē"o·mặr'fiz·um, *n.* [Gr. *pleōn*, more, *mōrphē*, form.] *Biol.* The occurrence of more than one independent form in the life history, esp. of plants, as rusts; polymorphism. Also **ple·o·mor·phy.** —**ple·o·mor·phic,** plē"o·mặr'fik, *a.*

ple·o·nasm, plē'o·naz"um, *n.* [Gr. *pleonasmos*, < *pleon*, *pleion*, more.] The use of more words than necessary in expressing an idea; redundancy; a word or phrase that is redundant.—**ple·o·nas·tic,** *a.*—**ple·o·nas·ti·cal·ly,** *adv.*

ple·o·pod, plē'o·pod", *n. Zool.* a swimmeret.

ple·si·o·saur, plē'sē·o·sặr", *n.* [N.L. *plesiosaurus*, < Gr. *plēsios*, near, and *sauros*, lizard.] Any member of the extinct genus *Plesiosaurus*, comprising marine reptiles of the early Mesozoic era, having a small head, very long neck, and four limbs like large paddles.

pleth·o·ra, pleth'ẽr·a, *n.* [Gr. *plēthōra*, < *pletho*, to be full, < *pleos*, full.] Overfullness; superfluity; superabundance. *Med.* congestion; excess volume of blood.

ple·thor·ic, ple·thặr'ik, ple·thor'ik, pleth'o·rik, *a.* Extremely full; inflated; turgid; characterized by plethora; pertaining to plethora.—**ple·thor·i·cal·ly,** *adv.*

pleu·ra, plụr'a, *n.* pl. **pleu·rae,** plụr'ē. [Gr. *pleuron*, a rib, pl. *pleura*, the side.] *Anat.* a thin membrane which covers the inside of the thorax and also invests the lungs.—**pleu·ral,** plụr'al, *a.*

pleu·ri·sy, plụr'i·sē, *n. Pathol.* an inflammation of the pleura, often accompanied by fever and respiratory difficulty.—**pleu·rit·ic,** plụ·rit'ik, *a.*

pleu·ro·dont, plụr'o·dont", *a. Zool.* Ankylosed or attached to the inner edge of the jaw, as a tooth; having teeth so ankylosed, as certain lizards.—*n.* A pleurodont animal.

pleu·ro·pneu·mo·ni·a, plụr"o·nō·-mōn'ya, plụr"o·nö·mō'nē·a, plụr"o·nū·mōn'ya, plụr"o·nū·mō'nē·a, *n.* [Gr. *pleura*, and *pneumōn*, the lungs.] An inflammation of the pleura and of the lungs; a combination of pleurisy and pneumonia; a respiratory ailment of cattle and similar animals, often fatal.

plex·i·form, plek'si·fặrm", *a.* [L. *plexus*, a fold, and *forma*, form.] In the form of a network; complicated; having the characteristics of a plexus.

plex·us, plek'sus, *n.* pl. **plex·us·es, plex·us.** [L.] *Anat.* a network of vessels, nerves, or fibers. Any complicated structure forming a network of interlacing parts.

pli·a·ble, plī'a·bl, *a.* [Fr. *pliable*, < *plier*, to bend, to fold, < L. *plico*, to fold, to bend.] Bent easily; flexible; pliant; flexible in disposition; easily persuaded; adaptable. —**pli·a·bil·i·ty,** pli·a·ble·ness, plī'a·-bil'i·tē, *n.*—**pli·a·bly,** *adv.*

pli·ant, plī'ant, *a.* [Fr. ppr. of *plier*, to bend.] Easily bent; readily yielding to force or pressure without breaking; flexible; lithe; limber; plastic; easily yielding to moral influence; easily persuaded.—**pli·an·cy, pli·ant·ness,** *n.*—**pli·ant·ly,** *adv.*

pli·ca, plī'ka, *n.* pl. **pli·cae,** plī'sē. [M.L., a fold < L. *plicare*, fold.] *Zool., anat.* a fold or folding, as of skin; *pathol.* a matted, filthy condition of the hair caused by disease.—**pli·cal,** *a.*

pli·cate, plī'kāt, plī'kit, *a.* [L. *plicatus*, < *plico*, to fold, *plica*, a fold.] Pleated; folded like a fan. Also **pli·cat·ed.**—**pli·cate·ly,** *adv.*—**pli·cate·ness,** *n.*

pli·ca·tion, pli·kā'shan, pli·kā'shan, *n.* A folding or fold; the folded state; *geol.* a bending back of strata on themselves. Also **plic·a·ture,** plik'a·chẽr.

pli·ers, plī'ẽrz, *n. pl., sing. or pl. in constr.* [Fr. *plier*, to bend.] A small pair of pincers

with long jaws adapted to hold small articles and to bending and shaping wire.

plight, plīt, *n.* [A.Fr. *plit*, for O.Fr. *pleit, ploit*, fold, manner of folding, condition.] Condition, state, or situation, usu. a bad one; as, to be in a sorry *plight*.

plight, plīt, *v.t.* [O.E. *pliht*, danger, risk, akin to D. *plicht*, G. *pflicht*, duty, obligation.] To pledge in engagement to marry; as, to *plight* one's troth; to bind by a pledge or engagement, esp. of marriage; to give in pledge, as one's word of honor.—*n. Archaic*, a pledge.

plim·soll, plim'sol, plim'sặl, plim'sol, *n. Brit.* a rubber-soled shoe with a canvas top.

Plim·soll mark, *n.* [From Samuel *Plimsoll*, 1824–1898, member of Parliament, who urged shipping reforms.] A line or mark on the hull of merchant vessels, showing the depth to which they may be submerged by loading. Also **Plim·soll line.**

plink, plingk, *v.i.* To shoot at targets chosen capriciously, as in informal rifle practice; to make a light, sharp, jingling sound.— *v.t.* To shoot at informally or casually; as, to *plink* old tin cans; to cause to make a light, sharp, jingling sound.—*n.* The sound of plinking.

plinth, plinth, *n.* [Gr. *plinthos*, a brick or tile; L. *plinthus*.] *Arch.* a flat square member, in the form of a slab, which serves as the foundation of a column; the square molding or table at the base of any architectural part or trim. A usu. protruding course of rocks or stones at the bottom of a wall; also **plinth course.**

Pli·o·cene, Plei·o·cene, plī'o·sēn", *n.* [Gr. *pleiōn*, more, and *kainos*, recent.] *Geol.* The latest epoch of the Tertiary period; the strata deposited during that epoch.—*a.* See Table of Geologic Time.

Pli·o·film, plī'o·film", *n.* A clear, flexible plastic, made of rubber hydrochloride, that is water-resistant and is used for raincoats and as a packaging material. (Trademark.)

plis·sé, plis·se, plē·sā', pli·sā', *n.* A crinkled surface on a cloth, formed by chemical treatment; a fabric so treated.

plod, plod, *v.i.—plodded, plodding.* [Perh. imit.] To walk heavily, move laboriously, or trudge; to work with dull perseverance; to drudge.—*v.t.* To walk heavily over or along.—*n.* The act of plodding; a sound of or as of a heavy tread.—**plod·der,** *n.*—**plod·ding·ly,** *adv.*

plop, plop, *v.i.—plopped, plopping.* [Imit.] To make a sound like that of a flat object striking water without a splash; to fall plump, as: She *plopped* into bed.—*v.t.* To let loose or throw with a heavy drop.—*n.* A plopping sound or fall; the act of plopping. —*adv.* With a plop.

plo·sion, plō'zhan, *n. Phon.* the expelling of breath after the closing of the oral passages in the production of a stop consonant, as after the *b* in *bat.* Also *explosion.*—**plo·sive,** plō'siv, *a., n.*

plot, plot, *n.* [O.E. *plot*, a spot of ground, a spot; Goth. *plats*, a patch. *Plat* is another form. *Plot* in sense of scheme is related to *plot*, piece of ground, as *plan*, a scheme, to *plan*, a design on a flat surface, but *plot* has generally the sense of ill design.] A small piece of land, esp. one devoted to a special purpose; also *plat.* A plan or chart, as of an estate or building; a secret scheme, esp. one with an evil or illegal purpose; the main story or scheme of a play, poem, or novel.—*v.t.—plotted, plotting.* To make a plan or chart of; to mark on a map or plan, as a course or position; to secretly contrive and plan for; to create or draft the plot of, as a novel. *Math.* to locate and mark, as a point, on graph paper by means of the coordinates; to draw, as a curve, by joining plotted points; to represent, as an equation, by a curve constructed this way.

—*v.i.* To form plots; conspire.—**plot·ter, plot'ẽr,** *n.* One who plots; an instrument used in plotting.

plot·tage, plot'ij, *n.* The area constituting a plot of land.

plot·ting board, *n. Milit.* a device for representing the position of a fixed target or the course of a moving target, utilized in artillery firing.

plov·er, pluv'ẽr, plō'vẽr, *n.* pl. **plov·er, plov·ers.** [O.Fr. *plovier*, Fr. *pluvier*, lit. 'the rain bird,' < L. *pluvia*, rain, < *pluo*, to rain.] Any of several wading birds of the family *Charadriidae*, differing from sandpipers in being more compactly built and having bolder color patterns and shorter, stouter bills. Compare *dotterel.*

plow, *Brit.* **plough,** plou, *n.* [Late O.E. *plōh*, a plowland, = Icel. *plōgr* = D. *ploeg* = G. *pflug*, plow.] An agricultural implement for cutting furrows in and turning up the soil, as for sowing or planting; any of various implements resembling or suggesting this, as a kind of tool for cutting grooves or a contrivance for clearing away snow from a road or track. (*Cap.*), *astron.* the constellation Ursa Major.—*v.t.* To make furrows in or turn up, as the soil, with a plow; to make, as a furrow, ridge, or groove, with, or as if with a plow; to proceed through or cleave the surface of, as water.— *v.i.* To work with a plow; to admit of plowing in a specified way; as, soil that *plows* easily; to move through anything in the manner of a plow; to advance in a steady, laborious manner; plod.—**plow back,** to put back, as profits, into a business. —**plow un·der,** to obliterate or cause to disappear.—**plow·a·ble,** *a.*—**plow·er,** *a.*

plow·boy, *Brit.* **plough·boy,** plou'boi", *n.* A boy who handles a team pulling a plow; a country boy.

plow·head, *Brit.* **plough·head,** plou'hed", *n.* A U-shaped metal bar, with bolt or pin holes at the ends, for hitching a plow to a tractor or team.

plow·man, *Brit.* **plough·man,** plou'man, *n.* pl. **plow·men,** *Brit.* **plough·men.** A man who plows; formerly a farmer, farm laborer, or rustic.

plow·share, *Brit.* **plough·share,** plou'-shặr", *n.* The cutting edge of a plow.

plow·staff, *Brit.* **plough·staff,** plou'staf", plou'stäf", *n.* A paddle or small spade or shovel used to scrape and clean a plow blade.

ploy, ploi, *n.* A stratagem designed to disorient or defeat an enemy or rival; a maneuver; a tactic.

ploy, ploi, *n.* [Origin uncertain.] *Brit., Sc.* A frolic; a trick; a pastime.

pluck, pluk, *v.t.* [O.E. *pluccian*, to pluck = D. and L.G. *plukken*, Dan. *plukke*, Icel. *plokka, plukka*, G. *pflücken*.] To pick or pull; as, to *pluck* a blossom; to vibrate the strings of (a musical instrument) by a similar action; to jerk out or remove the feathers of; as, to *pluck* a chicken; to snatch or drag, with *off*, *away*; *slang*, to rob, defraud; *Brit. slang*, to reject for advancement because of failure to pass an examination.—*v.i.* To twitch; pull sharply.—**pluck·er,** *n.*

pluck, pluk, *n.* [Cf. Gael. and Ir. *pluc*, a lump, a knot, a bunch.] The act of picking or plucking; the heart, liver, and lungs of an animal used for food; courage and tenacity, esp. under unfavorable circumstances.

pluck·y, pluk'ē, *a.—pluckier, pluckiest.* Spirited; courageous.—**pluck·i·ly,** *adv.* In a plucky manner; spiritedly.—**pluck·i·ness,** *n.*

plug, plug, *n.* [Same as D. *plug*, L.G. *pluck*, a block.] Any piece of wood or other material used to stop a hole; an electrical device fitting like a plug into an opening or openings of an outlet to establish a connected circuit; a spark plug; a fireplug; a cake of tobacco, usu. for chewing. *Slang*, something worn-out or inferior, esp. a worn-out horse; favorable publicity; a top hat; a punch or blow; a shot or bullet. *Angling*, a lure for fish.

plug, plug, *v.t.*—*plugged, plugging.* To insert, as a plug; to make tight by stopping with a plug. *Slang*, to publicize a product favorably; to punch; to shoot.—*v.i. Slang.* To work steadily; to shoot at; to back a cause or individual.—**plug·ger**, *n.*

plug hat, *n. Slang*, a hat having a stiff body, usu. worn by men. See *plug.*

plug in, *v.i.* To complete an electrical circuit by putting a plug in an outlet.—*v.t.* To connect, as an electrical appliance, by inserting the plug into an outlet.

plug·ug·ly, plug'ug"lē, *n. pl.* **plug·ug·lies.** *Slang.* A city ruffian; a gangster; a rowdy; a tough.

plum, plum, *n.* [O.E. *plume*, L.G. *plumme*, G. *pflaume*, < L.L. *pruna* (Fr. *prune*), < L. *prunum*, a plum, < *prunus* = Gr. *prounos*, the plum tree.] The edible drupaceous fruit of a small tree, *Prunus domestica*, in the rose family, smooth-skinned, and containing an oblong stone; the tree itself; any of various other species of the genus *Prunus*, grown for ornament, as the flowering plum; a raisin when used in a pudding; a color varying in shade from light to dark reddish-purple; *slang*, some desirable thing; as, the *plums* given out by the party in power.—**plum·like**, *a.*

plum, plum, *a., adv.* See **plumb.**

plum·age, plō'mij, *n.* [Ō.Fr. Fr. *plumage*, < *plume*, feather, E. *plume.*] Feathers collectively; the entire feathery covering of a bird.

plu·mate, plō'māt, plō'mit, *a.* [L. *plumatus*, pp. of *plumare*, cover with feathers, < *pluma*, feather, E. *plume.*] *Zool.* resembling a feather, as a hair or bristle which bears smaller hairs.

plumb, plum, *n.* [O.Fr. Fr. *plomb*, < L. *plumbum*, lead.] A small weight of lead or another heavy material, esp. one attached to a line and used in testing the perpendicularity of walls or in sounding; a plummet.—*a.* True according to a plumb line; perpendicular; vertical. *Colloq.* downright or absolute; also *plum.*—*adv.* In a perpendicular or vertical direction; exactly, precisely, or directly. *Colloq.* completely or absolutely, as: He is *plumb* crazy; also *plum.*—*v.t.* To test or adjust by a plumb line; make vertical; to sound with or as with a plumb line, as the ocean; measure by sounding, as depth; to penetrate to the bottom of; as, to *plumb* motives; to seal with lead.—**out of plumb, off plumb**, not vertical; out of alignment.

plum·ba·go, plum·bā'gō, *n. pl.* **plum·ba·gos.** [L. *plumbago* (*plumbagin-*), lead ore, leadwort, < *plumbum*, lead.] *Mineral.* graphite. *Bot.* any of several herbaceous and shrubby species of the genus *Plumbago*, cultivated for their spikes of blue flowers; also *leadwort.*—**plum·bag·i·nous**, plum·baj'i·nus, *a.* Containing graphite.—**plum·bag·i·na·ceous**, plum·baj'i·nā'shus, *a.* Pertaining to flowers of the genus *Plumbago.*

plumb bob, *n.* The bob or weight of a plumb line.

plum·be·ous, plum'bē·us, *a.* [L. *plumbum*, lead.] Consisting of lead; leaden in appearance.

plumb·er, plum'ẽr, *n.* One who fits and repairs water and drainage pipes; orig. a worker in lead.—**plumb·er·y**, plum'e·rē, *n. pl.* **plumb·er·ies.**

plumb·er's snake, *n.* A long metal cable or tape maneuvered into drainage pipes to dislodge clogged material.

plum·bic, plum'bik, *a.* Pertaining to lead, esp. tetravalent lead; derived from lead.

plum·bif·er·ous, plum·bif'ẽr·us, *a.* [L. *plumbum*, lead, and *ferre*, bear.] Yielding or containing lead.

plumb·ing, plum'ing, *n.* Plumber's trade or work; the assemblage of pipes and fixtures used to convey water and waste; the act of using a plumb.

plum·bism, plum'biz·um, *n. Pathol.* poisoning by lead taken into the system.

plumb line, *n.* A cord having a metal weight attached to one end, used to determine the true vertical or perpendicular, and for sounding; a line of exact vertical direction.

plum·bous, plum'bus, *a. Chem.* consisting of, or related to bivalent lead compounds.

plumb rule, *n.* A narrow board with a plumb line attached to the upper edge, used by masons and builders for determining a perpendicular.

plume, plōm, *n.* [Fr. < L. *pluma*, the downy part of a feather, a small soft feather; cogn. W. *pluf*, plumage; Skt. *plu*, to swim, to fly.] The feather of a bird, particularly a large or conspicuous feather; a feather or collection of feathers worn as an ornament, token of honor, or prize; plumage.—*v.t.*—*plumed, pluming.* To preen; to adorn with feathers or plumes; to pride (oneself), as: She *plumed* herself on her beauty.—**plume·like**, *a.*

plume·let, plōm'lit, *n.* A small plume.

plum·met, plum'it, *n.* [Fr. *plumbet*, < *plumb*; O.Fr. *plummet*, Fr. *plomet.*] A piece of lead or other metal attached to a line, used in sounding the depth of water or testing perpendicularity; also **plumb bob.**—*v.i.* To drop or plunge straight down.

plu·mose, plō'mōs, *a.* [L. *plumosus.*] Having feathers or feathery appendages; resembling feathers; *bot.* consisting of long hairs which are subdivided into finer hairs; as, a *plumose* bristle.—**plu·mose·ly**, *adv.*—**plu·mos·i·ty**, plō·mos'i·tē, *n.*

plump, plump, *v.i.* [M.E. *plumpen* = D. *plompen*; prob. imit.] To fall heavily or suddenly; drop abruptly or with direct impact; to give one's wholehearted support used with *for*; as, to *plump* for a reform; *chiefly Brit.* to vote exclusively for one candidate at an election, instead of distributing or splitting one's votes among a number.—*v.t.* To drop or throw heavily or suddenly, often with *down*, as: She *plumped* herself *down* in the chair. To utter or say bluntly, often with *out*; to praise or publicize favorably.—*n.* A heavy or sudden fall; the sound caused by this fall.—*adv.* With a heavy or sudden fall or drop; with sudden encounter; directly or bluntly, as in speaking; straight down.—*a.* Direct; downright; blunt.—**plump·ly**, *adv.*

plump, plump, *a.* [M.E. *plompe*, dull, rude, = M.L.G. *plump* = D. *plomp*, blunt, thick, rude.] Well filled out or rounded in form; somewhat fleshy or fat; chubby.—*v.t.* To make plump; fatten, often with *up* or *out.*—*v.i.* To become plump, often with *up* or *out.*—**plump·ly**, *adv.*—**plump·ness**, *n.*

plump·ish, plum'pish, *a.* Moderately plump; somewhat overweight.

plum pud·ding, *n.* A rich boiled pudding containing raisins, currants, citron, and spices: a traditional Christmas dessert.

plu·mule, plōm'ūl, *n.* [L. *plumula*, dim. of *pluma*, a feather.] *Bot.* the growing point of the embryo of a plant; the rudiment of the future stem of a plant; also *epicotyl. Ornith.* a down feather.—**plu·mu·late**, *a.*—**plu·mu·lose**, plōm'ū·lōs", *a.*

plum·y, plō'mē, *a.*—*plumier, plumiest.* Having plumes or feathers; feathery.

plun·der, plun'dẽr, *v.t.* [G. *plündern* (< *plunder*, baggage) = D. *plunderen*, Sw. *plondra*, Dan. *plyndre*, to plunder. The word entered English and other tongues about the time of the Thirty Years' War.] To

rob of goods or valuables forcibly; pillage; to despoil; to take by pillage or open force.—*v.i.* To commit looting.—*n.* The act of plundering; robbing; that which is taken by theft; robbery or fraud.—**plun·der·a·ble**, *a.*—**plun·der·er**, *n.*—**plun·der·ous**, *a.*

plun·der·age, plun'dẽr·ij, *n.* The act of plundering; pillage; spoliation. *Maritime law*, the embezzlement of goods on board a ship; the goods embezzled.

plunge, plunj, *v.t.*—*plunged, plunging.* [< Fr. *plonger*, < hypothetical L. *plumbicare*, *plumbum*, lead; lit. 'to fall like lead' or 'to fall plumb.'] To thrust into water or other fluid substance, or into any easily penetrable substance; to immerse; to thrust; to drive into any state or condition; to place, as a potted plant, into sand or soil.—*v.i.* To thrust or drive oneself into water or a declivity; to drive or to rush in; to fall or rush impulsively into some situation; to descend suddenly, as on a hill or road; to throw the body forward and the hind legs up, as an unruly horse; to bet heavily and recklessly.—*n.* A dive, rush, or leap into something; the act of pitching or throwing the body forward and the hind legs up, as an unruly horse; a place for diving, as a swimming tank or deep pool; a reckless speculation.

plung·er, plun'jẽr, *n.* One who plunges; a wild, reckless gambler who risks heavy bets; *mach.* a pistonlike cylinder sometimes used in force pumps. A device consisting of a suction cup at one end of a stick, used in unclogging drains.

plung·ing fire, *n. Milit.* fire from a high elevation, or from a weapon angled in such a manner, that hits the target at a steep angle.

plunk, plungk, *v.t.* [Imit.] *Colloq.* To strum or pluck, as the strings of a stringed instrument; to throw or push heavily or suddenly, usu. followed by *down.*—*v.i. Colloq.* To give forth a twanging sound; to drop down heavily or suddenly.—*n. Colloq.* the act or sound of plunking.—*adv. Colloq.* with a plunking sound.—**plunk·er**, *n.*

plu·per·fect, plō·pur'fikt, *a.* [L. *plus quam perfectum*, more than perfect.] *Gram.* Applied to that tense of a verb which denotes that an action was finished at a certain period in the past; denoting the pluperfect or a form in the pluperfect. Also *past perfect.*—*n.*

plu·ral, plur'al, *a.* [L. *pluralis*, < *plus*, *pluris*, more.] Containing more than one; consisting of, involving, or designating two or more; concerning or being one among a plurality of persons or objects; *gram.* of a word, noting the linguistic form that designates more than one.—*n.* The plural number; a form of a word expressing more than one. Abbr. *pl.*, *plu.*, *plur.*—**plu·ral·ly**, plur'a·lē, *adv.*

plu·ral·ism, plur'a·liz"um, *n.* The quality of being plural; the nature of a society within which diverse ethnic, social, and cultural interests exist and develop together; the holding by one person of two or more offices, esp. ecclesiastical benefices, at the same time; *philos.* a theory or system that recognizes more than one ultimate substance or principle.—**plu·ral·ist**, *n.* One who holds two or more offices, esp. ecclesiastical benefices, at the same time; *philos.* an adherent of pluralism.—**plu·ral·is·tic**, *a.*

plu·ral·i·ty, plu·ral'i·tē, *n. pl.* **plu·ral·i·ties.** The state of being plural; the greater number; a multitude; the majority; in an election, the number of votes one candidate receives over those of his closest competitor for the same office; *eccles.* pluralism, or the benefices held by pluralism.

plu·ral·ize, plur'a·liz", *v.t.*—*pluralized, pluralizing.* To make plural; to express in the plural form.—*v.i.* To be made plural; to take the plural.—**plu·ral·i·za·tion**, *n.*

plur·i·ax·i·al, plur″ē·ak′sē·al, *a.* Having at least two axes; *bot.* pertaining to a plant that bears flowers on its secondary stems or shoots.

plus, plus, *a.* [L., more (used as compar. of *multus*, much, many), akin to Gr. *polús*, much, many, compar. *pleiōn*, and ult. to E. *full*.] More, by a certain amount; involving or denoting addition; as, a *plus* quantity, or having *plus* values; positive; *colloq.* with something in addition, as: The new car has power *plus*.—*n.* The plus sign; a plus quantity; something additional; a surplus or gain.—*prep.* More by the addition of, or increased by; as, 10 *plus* 3; with the addition of; with.

plus fours, *n. pl. but sing. in constr.* [*plus four*, the handicap of a first-rate Brit. golfer.] Men's baggy knickerbockers.

plush, plush, *n.* [Fr. *pluche*, *peluche*, It. *peluzzo*, < L. *pilus*, hair.] A fabric with a nap longer than that of velvet.—*a.* Made of plush; luxurious.—**plush·y**, *a.*—*plushier*, *plushiest.*—**plush·ly**, *adv.*

plus sign, *n.* Math. a symbol, +, signifying either addition or a positive quantity.

Plu·to, plö′tō, *n.* The Roman name in classical mythology for the god of the dead and the underworld; a planet of the solar system, which is the most remote from the sun, and visible only by the telescope.

plu·toc·ra·cy, plö·tok′ra·sē, *n. pl.* **plu·toc·ra·cies.** [Gr. *Ploutos*, god of wealth, and *krateia*, rule, *archē*, power.] The power or rule of wealth; a group possessing power or influence because of its riches.—**plu·to·crat**, plö′tō·krat″, *n.*—**plu·to·crat·ic**, plö″tō·krat′ik, *a.*—**plu·to·crat·i·cal·ly**, *adv.*

Plu·to·ni·an, plö·tō′nē·an, *a.* Of or pertaining to Pluto, the god of the lower world; infernal; (*often l.c.*), geol. plutonic.

plu·ton·ic, plö·ton′ik, *a.* Geol. Noting or pertaining to a class of igneous rocks which have solidified far below the earth's surface; (*sometimes cap.*) referring to the belief that the rocks of the earth evolved through the action of heat: contrasted with *Neptunian.* Also *plutonian.*

plu·to·ni·um, plö·tō′nē·um, *n.* [From the planet *Pluto.*] *Chem.* a synthetic radioactive element produced by bombarding neptunium from uranium 235 indirectly with neutrons. Sym. Pu, at. no. 94. at. wt. 239. See Periodic Table of Elements. —**plu·to·ni·um 239**, a fissionable isotope of plutonium, made by bombarding uranium 238 with slow neutrons in a reactor.

plu·vi·al, plö′vē·al, *a.* [L. *pluvialis*, < *pluvia*, rain, < *pluo*, to rain.] Rainy; relating to rain; *geol.* pertaining to conditions which depend on or arise from the action of rain.—**plu·vi·an**, *a.*

plu·vi·om·e·ter, plö′vē·om′i·tėr, *n.* [L. *pluvia*, rain, and Gr. *metron*, measure.] A rain gauge; an instrument for measuring rainfall.—**plu·vi·o·met·ric**, plö″vē·o·me′trik, *a.*—**plu·vi·o·met·ri·cal**, *a.*—**plu·vi·om·e·try**, *n.*

plu·vi·ous, plö′vē·us, *a.* [L. *pluviosus*, < *pluvia*, rain.] Abounding in rain; rainy; pertaining to rain. Also **plu·vi·ose.**—**plu·vi·os·i·ty**, plö″vē·os′i·tē, *n.*

ply, pli, *n. pl.* **plies.** An individual layer or thickness, as in fabric or plywood; one twist or strand of thread, rope, or yarn. A tendency; a prejudice.—*v.t.*—**plied**, **plying.** To twist, mold, or bend.

ply, pli, *v.t.*—**plied**, **plying.** [Fr. *plier* (also *ployer*), to fold, to bend, < L. *plicare*, to fold, coil, plait; same root as Gr. *pleko*, to plait.] To employ with diligence; as, to *ply* a needle; to practice or work at; as, to *ply* the trade of mason; to furnish with or offer insistently; as, to *ply* a guest with food; to repeatedly assault or assail; to question

constantly; to run or travel, as on a schedule.—*v.i.* To work steadily; to offer service; to run regularly between any two places, as a vessel or vehicle.

Plym·outh Rock, *n.* The rock in Plymouth Harbor, Mass., where the Pilgrims landed, Dec. 21, 1620; any of a N. American breed of chicken.

ply·wood, pli′wud″, *n.* A building material consisting of two or more thin sheets, strips, or layers of wood glued together.

p.m., P.M., pē′em′. Post meridiem; afternoon.

pneu·ma, nö′ma, nū′ma, *n.* [Gr. breath.] The vital soul or spirit; the breath of life.

pneu·mat·ic, nu·mat′ik, nū·mat′ik, *a.* [Gr. *pneumatikos*, < *pneuma*, *pneumatos*, breath, spirit, < *pneō*, to breathe or blow.] Consisting of, resembling, or pertaining to air, gas, or wind; moved or played by means of air, as an organ; filled with or fitted to contain air, as a tire; operated by means of the compression or exhaustion of air, as an air hammer. *Theol.* relating to the soul or spirit; *zool.* having air spaces, as in the bones of birds.—**pneu·mat·i·cal·ly**, *adv.*

pneu·mat·ics, nu·mat′iks, nū·mat′iks, *n. pl. but sing. in constr.* That branch of physics treating of the mechanical properties of air and other gases. Also **pneu·mo·dy·nam·ics.**

pneu·ma·tol·o·gy, nö″ma·tol′o·jē, nū″ma·tol′o·jē, *n. Theol.* the principles or creed of a religion, esp. the doctrines of the Holy Ghost. The teaching or study of the nature and operations of mind and spirit.

pneu·ma·tol·y·sis, nö″ma·tol′i·sis, nū″ma·tol′i·sis, *n. Geol.* the process by which minerals and ores are formed by the action of vapors given off from igneous magmas.

pneu·ma·to·lyt·ic, nö″ma·to·lit′ik, nū″ma·to·lit′ik, *a. Geol.* pertaining to or formed by pneumatolysis.

pneu·ma·tom·e·ter, nö″ma·tom′i·tėr, nū″ma·tom′i·tėr, *n.* An instrument for measuring the force or the quantity of air inhaled into the lungs at each inhalation and given out at each exhalation.

pneu·ma·to·phore, nö′ma·to·fōr″, nū″ma·to·fōr″, nö″ma·to·far″, nū″ma·to·far″, nö·mat′o·fōr″, nū·mat′o·fōr″, nö·mat′o·far″, nū·mat′o·far″, *n. Bot.* a specialized respiratory organ, an extension from the root of certain plants growing in marshy areas; *zool.* the bladderlike polyp which buoys up such hydrozoans as the Portuguese man-of-war.—**pneu·ma·toph·or·ous**, nö″ma·tof′ėr·us, nū″ma·tof′ėr·us, *a.*

pneu·mec·to·my, nö·mek′to·mē, nū·mek′to·mē, *n.* Pneumonectomy.

pneu·mo·ba·cil·lus, nö″mō·ba·sil′us, nū″mō·ba·sil′us, *n. pl.* **pneu·mo·ba·cil·li**, nö″mō·ba·sil′ī, nū″mō·ba·sil′ī. The bacillus, *Klebsiella pneumoniae*, associated with a type of pneumonia and other respiratory infections.

pneu·mo·coc·cus, nö″mo·kok′us, nū″mo·kok′us, *n. pl.* **pneu·mo·coc·ci**, nö″mo·kok′sī, nū″mo·kok′sī. [N.L.] A bacterium, *Diplococcus pneumoniae*, causing lobar pneumonia and other infectious diseases.—**pneu·mo·coc·cal**, **pneu·mo·coc·cic**, **pneu·mo·coc·cous**, nö″mo·kok′al, nū″mo·kok′al, nö″mo·kok′sik, nū″mo·kok′sik, nö″mo·kok′us, nū″mo·kok′us, *a.*

pneu·mo·gas·tric, nö″mo·gas′trik, nū″mo·gas′trik, *a. Anat.* pertaining to the lungs and the stomach.—*n.* Pneumogastric nerve. Also *vagus nerve.*

pneu·mo·nec·to·my, nö″mo·nek′to·mē, nū″mo·nek′to·mē, *n. pl.* **pneu·mo·nec·to·mies.** *Surg.* the removal of all or part of a lung. Also *pneumectomy.*

pneu·mo·nia, nu·mōn′ya, nū·mōn′ya, *n.* [N.L., < Gr. *pneumonia*, *pneúmōn*, lung.] *Pathol.* Inflammation of the lungs; an

acute infectious disease of the lungs, either viral or bacteriological in origin.

pneu·mon·ic, nu·mon′ik, nū·mon′ik, *a.* Pertaining to the lungs; pulmonary; relating to or having pneumonia.

pneu·mo·tho·rax, nö″mo·thōr′aks, nö″mo·thar′aks, nū″mo·thōr′aks, nū″mo·thar′aks, *n.* [N.L., < Gr. *pneuma*, wind, air, and *thorax*, chest.] *Pathol.* the presence of air or gas in the pleural cavity, sometimes used therapeutically in collapsing a lung.

poach, pōch, *v.t.* [< Fr. *pocher*, to poach eggs, < *poche*, a pouch or pocket, the white of the egg forming a sort of pocket for the yolk.] To cook in simmering water or other liquid, as eggs.—**poach·er**, pō′chėr, *n.*

poach, pōch, *v.i.* [Orig. to pouch or pocket thievishly, or a softened form of *poke*, to push, to intrude.] To intrude or trespass on the property of another in order to catch game or fish; to steal game or fish; to become soft and slushy by trampling, as ground.—*v.t.* To intrude or trespass on; to catch or take illegally; to convert into a soft, smooth consistency by blending with water.—**poach·er**, pō′chėr, *n.*

po·chard, pō′chėrd, pō′kėrd, *n. pl.* **po·chards**, **po·chard.** [Origin uncertain.] An Old World, marine duck, *Aythya ferina*, with a chestnut-red head.

pock, pok, *n.* [O.E. *poc* or *pocc*, D. *pok*, G. *pok*, a vesicle or pustule; perh. akin to *poke*, a bag. *Pox* = *pocks.*] A pustule raised on the surface of the body in an eruptive disease, as smallpox; a pit or scar left on the skin by such a disease.

pock·et, pok′it, *n.* [O.Fr. *pokete*, *pouquette*, dim. of *poke*, *pouque*, var. of *poche*, bag.] A small fabric pouch inserted in a garment, for carrying money or small articles; a bag or pouch; money or financial means; any pouchlike receptacle, hollow, or cavity; a cavity in the earth, esp. one containing gold or other ore; a small mass of ore; one of the small, open bags at the corners and each side of a billiard table; *sports*, in a race, a position in which a contestant is so hemmed in by others that his progress is impeded. A small, isolated group or region; as, a *pocket* of infection; *aeron.* an air pocket.—*a.* Suitable for carrying in the pocket; small enough to go in the pocket; diminutive.—*v.t.* To put into one's pocket; to take possession of as one's own, often dishonestly; to submit to or endure without protest or open resentment; as, to *pocket* an affront; conceal or suppress; as, to *pocket* one's pride; to enclose or confine as in a pocket; in billiards and pool, to drive, as a ball, into a pocket; in a race, to hem in, as a contestant, so as to impede progress; of the President or a legislative executive, to retain, as a bill, without acting on it, thus preventing it from becoming a law.— **in one's pock·et**, under one's control.

pock·et bat·tle·ship, *n.* A warship, heavily armed but of moderate tonnage as limited by treaty.

pock·et bil·liards, *n. pl. but sing. in constr.* See **pool.**

pock·et·book, pok′it·buk″, *n.* A small case or receptacle, as of leather, for papers or money, intended to be carried in the pocket; a women's handbag; pecuniary resources. A book, usu. paperback, small enough for the pocket; also **pock·et book.**

pock·et bor·ough, *n.* In England prior to the Reform Bill of 1832, a borough whose parliamentary representation was in the hands of some individual or family; a political district controlled by a limited group.

pock·et e·di·tion, *n.* A book published in a size small enough to be fitted in the pocket. See *pocketbook.*

pock·et·ful, pok′it·ful″, *n. pl.* **pock·et·fuls.** As much as can be carried in a pocket.

pock·et·knife, pok'it·nif", *n. pl.* **pock·et·knives.** A knife with one or more blades which fold into the handle, suitable for carrying in the pocket.

pock·et mon·ey, *n.* Money used for minor current expenses; spending money.

pock·et mouse, *n. pl.* **pock·et mice.** Any of various small, mouselike N. American rodents with external cheek pouches, as *Perognathus fasciatus,* of the western U.S.

pock·et ve·to, *n.* An oblique veto of a bill, done by an executive holding the bill unsigned past the adjournment of the legislative body in which the bill originated.

pock·mark, pok'märk", *n.* A mark or scar on the skin made by smallpox or some other disease.—*v.t.*—**pock·marked,** *a.*

po·co, pō'kō, *It.* pạ'kạ, *adv. Mus.* a little, somewhat; as, *poco* piano.

po·co a po·co, pō'kō ä pō'kō, *It.* pạ'kạ ä pạ'kạ, *adv. Mus.* Little by little; by degrees or stages; as, *poco a poco* diminuendo.

po·co·sin, po·kō'sin, pō'ko·sin, *n.* [N. Amer. Ind.] *Southeastern U.S.* A tract of swampy land in the coastal regions; a dismal.

pod, pod, *n.* [Origin uncertain.] *Bot.* a more or less elongated, two-valved fruit, as that of the pea or bean; a dehiscent fruit with two sutures and usu. containing several seeds; a general term for many dry fruits. *Aeron.* a streamlined housing for something carried externally on an airplane, as one beneath the wing holding a jet engine.—*v.i.*—**podded, podding.** To produce pods; to swell out like a pod.—**pod·like,** *a.*

pod, pod, *n.* The straight groove or channel in the body of certain augers or bits.

pod, pod, *n.* [Origin unknown.] A small herd or school, esp. of seals or whales; a small flock of birds.

po·dag·ra, pō·dag'ra, pod'a·gra, *n.* [Gr., < *pous, podos,* the foot, and *agra,* a seizure.] Gout in the foot.—**po·dag·ral,** *a.*

po·des·ta, pō·des'ta, *It.* pạ'de·stä', *n.* [It. *podesta,* a governor, < L. *potestas,* power.] A chief magistrate of the Italian republics of the Middle Ages; an Italian mayor or city magistrate during the Fascist rule.

podg·y, poj'ē, *a.* Pudgy.

po·di·a·trist, pō·dī'a·trist, po·dī'a·trist, *n.* [Gr. *poús* (*pod-*), foot, and *iatrós,* physician.] One who diagnoses and treats disorders of the human foot. Also *chiropodist.*—**po·di·a·try,** *n.*

pod·ite, pod'īt, *n.* A part of the limb of an arthropod.—**po·dit·ic,** po·dit'ik, *a.*

po·di·um, pō'dē·um, *n. pl.* **po·di·ums, po·di·a,** pō'dē·a. [L., elevated place, balcony, < Gr. *pódion,* dim. of *poús* (*pod-*), foot: cf. *pew.*] A small raised platform or stand used by conductors and public speakers; a dais. *Arch.* a continuous projecting base or pedestal; a raised platform surrounding the arena of an ancient amphitheater. *Zool., anat.* a foot or footlike structure; *bot.* a footstalk or stipe of certain algae.

pod·o·phyl·lin, pod"o·fil'in, *n.* [Gr. *poús, podos,* a foot, and *phyllon,* a leaf.] A resin obtained from the rhizome of the Mayapple, genus *Podophyllum,* used in medicine as a purgative.

Po·dunk, pō'dungk, *n.* Any small town or village considered as backward, dull, and insignificant.

pod·zol, pod'zol, *n.* An infertile, zonal soil type found in moist temperate and cold climates, as northern parts of Canada and the U.S.S.R., under mixed or coniferous forest, characterized by a strongly acidic, grayish upper layer whose mineral compounds and colloids have accumulated in a brown lower layer. Also **pod·sol.**—**pod·zol·ic, pod·sol·ic,** *a.*

pod·zol·i·za·tion, pod"zo·li·zā'shạn, *n.* The formation of podzolic soils by leaching of minerals from upper layers and accumulation in lower layers. Also **pod·sol·i·za·tion.**—**pod·zol·ize,** pod'zo·līz", *v.t., v.i.*—*podzolized, podzolizing.* Also **pod·sol·ize.**

po·em, pō'im, *n.* [Fr. *poème,* < L. *poema,* < Gr. *poiēma,* lit. 'the thing made,' < *poieō,* to make.] A verse composition, esp. one characterized by economy of linguistic expression, vivid imagery, and intense emotional tone; composition not in verse but characterized by beauty of form and emotional intensity; as, a symphonic *poem;* anything having qualities or effects reminiscent of poetry.

po·e·sy, pō'i·sē, pō'i·zē, *n. pl.* **po·e·sies.** [Fr. *poésie,* L. *poesis,* < Gr. *poiēsis,* the art of writing poems.] The art of or skill in composing poems; poetry; metrical composition. *Obs.* a short conceit or motto engraved on a ring or other thing; also *posy.*

po·et, pō'it, *n.* [Fr. *poète,* < L. *poeta,* Gr. *poiētēs,* lit. 'a maker,' < *poieō,* to make. So in Eng. poets were formerly often called 'makers.'] A person who writes poetry; one endowed with great imaginative and creative power.—**po·et·ess,** pō'i·tis, *n.* Feminine of poet.

po·et·as·ter, pō'it·as"tẽr, *n.* [< *poet,* and the pejorative *-aster.*] A poet of little merit; an inadequate writer of verses; a would-be poet.

po·et·ic, pō·et'ik, *a.* [L. *poeticus,* Gr. *poiētikos.*] Pertaining to poetry or poets; suitable for poetry or poets; showing the feelings or sensibility of a poet; possessing the peculiar beauties of poetry; expressed in poetry; commemorated in poetry. Also **po·et·i·cal.**—*n.* Poetics.—**po·et·i·cal·ly,** *adv.*

po·et·i·cize, pō·et'i·sīz", *v.t.*—*poeticized, poeticizing.* To give the quality of poetry to; as, to *poeticize* one's life; to write a poem about.—*v.i.* To write or speak poetically.

po·et·ic jus·tice, *n.* A distribution of rewards for virtue and punishments for vice such as is common in some literature; a similarly appropriate, sometimes ironic outcome in life.

po·et·ic li·cense, *n.* License or liberty taken by a poet, other writer, or artist in deviating from rule, conventional form, or fact, in order to produce a desired effect.

po·et·ics, pō·et'iks, *n. pl. but sing. in constr.* That part of literary criticism which treats of the nature and laws of poetry; a treatise on poetry.

po·et·ize, pō'i·tīz, *v.i.*—*poetized, poetizing.* [Fr. *poétiser.*] To write poetry.—*v.t.* To express poetically; to treat poetically; poeticize.—**po·et·iz·er,** *n.*

po·et lau·re·ate, *n. pl.* **po·ets lau·re·ate.** The poet who is appointed a salaried lifetime honorary member of the British royal household and was formerly expected to write odes in celebration of court and national events; a poet considered the most renowned or most representative of a country or area.

po·et·ry, pō'i·trē, *n.* [O.Fr. *poeterie,* < *poete,* a poet.] The art or craft of rhythmic composition; spoken or written expressions, intended to evoke an emotional response and to illuminate aspects of the emotional and perceptual worlds inexpressible in factual writing; poems collectively; any expression of the spirit or feeling reminiscent of such rhythmical composition; any manifestation of poetic qualities.

po·gey, pō'gē, *n. Canadian slang.* Any form of relief given by the government; dole; unemployment insurance.—*a.*

po·go·ni·a, po·gō'nē·a, po·gōn'ya, *n.* [N.L., < Gr. *pōgōn,* beard (with reference to the frequently fringed lip).] A N. American orchid, *Pogonia ophioglossoides,* of bogs and wet meadows, having a solitary pink flower with a crested, fringed lip; also **rose po·go·ni·a,** *snakemouth.* Any other plant of the genus *Pogonia,* comprising N. American terrestrial orchids.

pog·o·nip, pog'o·nip, *n.* [< Shoshonean.] A heavy fog, containing ice crystals, that forms in the valleys of the Sierra Nevada Mountains and other parts of western U.S.

po·go stick, pō'gō stik, *n.* A kind of pole containing a strong spring, with handles at the top and footrests near the bottom, propelled by jumping in a series of hops, and used esp. by children. Also **po·go·stick.**

po·grom, po·grum', po·grom', pō·grum', pō·grom', *n.* [Russ.] Any organized massacre or attack on a minority people, esp. one directed against the Jews.

po·gy, pō'gē, pog'ē, *n. pl.* **po·gy, po·gies.** [< N. Amer. Ind. name.] The menhaden.

poi, poi, pō'ē, *n.* [Hawaiian.] A Hawaiian dish made of the root of the taro baked, pounded, moistened, and fermented.

poign·ant, poin'yant, poin'ant, *a.* [Fr. *poignant,* ppr. of *poindre,* < L. *pungere, pungo,* to prick.] Very painful or acute to the feelings; strong, piercing, or keen; pointed or precise; apt; moving or arousing the emotions; pungent.—**poign·ant·ly,** *adv.*—**poign·an·cy,** *n.*

poi·ki·lo·ther·mal, poi"ki·lō·thur'mal, poi·kil'o·thur'mal, *a. Zool.* Having a body temperature that varies according to the temperature of the surrounding environment; cold-blooded: opposed to, *homoiothermal.* Also **poi·ki·lo·ther·mic.**—**poi·ki·lo·ther·mism,** *n.*

poi·lu, pwä'lö, *Fr.* pwä·lᵞ', *n.* [Fr. 'hairy.'] *Slang,* a term applied to French soldiers, esp. during World War I, deriving from their custom of letting a beard grow when on active service.

poin·ci·an·a, poin"sē·an'a, poin"sē·ä'na, *n.* [N.L.; from M. de *Poinci,* governor of the French West Indies in the 17th century.] Any of several species of ornamental tropical trees of the genus *Poinciana,* esp. *P. pulcherrima,* the flower fence, in the legume family, grown for its attractive, finely divided foliage and showy orange to yellow flowers. A closely related tree, *Delonix regia,* native to Madagascar, and now widely cultivated in tropical and subtropical countries, having large scarlet flowers; also **roy·al poin·ci·an·a, pea·cock flow·er.**

poin·set·ti·a, poin·set'ē·a, poin·set'a, *n.* [N.L.; from J. R. *Poinsett,* U.S. minister to Mexico, who discovered the plant there in 1828.] A greenhouse winter-flowering small shrub, *Euphorbia pulcherrima,* in the spurge family, having upper leaves which are red, pink, or white and surround the true, inconspicuous greenish-yellow flowers: grown esp. for the Christmas trade.

point, point, *n.* [Fr. *point,* a point, a spot, a matter, moment, etc., *pointe,* something sharp or pointed, wit or pungency, etc., the former < L. *punctum,* a puncture, < *pungo, punctum,* to puncture, the latter fem. part of Fr. *poindre,* to prick, from same; akin *pounce, punch,* etc.] The end of, or the mark made by the end of, a sharp piercing instrument, as a pin or needle; a protruding part of something; the tip of an extremity, as a fingertip; a tapering or sharp end, as of a pin; a tool or instrument which pricks or pierces; a mark of punctuation, as a period; a dot placed before a decimal fraction to show that it is a decimal; *phon.* a diacritical mark denoting a vowel sound; *geom.* that which has neither length, breadth, nor thickness, but has position; as, the *point* at which two lines intersect. A locality or place; a fixed or exactly indicated position, as in a course; *navig.* one of the 32 equal divisions of the card of the mariner's compass. A limit or degree reached; a precise instant or moment; a time or period when something is expected; eve or verge; as, at the *point* of death; the essential or critical idea or thing; as, the *point* of the speech; a salient trait of character; a particular purpose; as, to gain one's *point*; a suggestion; a single element or fact of something; as, some good *points* in the book; a single thing or subject; a quality or characteristic of an animal; *pl.* the extremities of an animal, as of a dog. A unit of scoring or counting, as: A field goal in football equals three *points*. A unit of measurement or counting; as, the number of *points* in a game; *craps*, the required number to be thrown to win; *cricket*, a fielder or a position situated a little to the off side of the batter's wicket; *hunting*, the action or position of a dog to denote the location and presence of game by standing and turning the nose in its direction. A branch or spike on a deer's antler; *sports*, a cross-country run. One of the spaces marked off on a backgammon board; *educ.* a credit unit which equals a defined hourly amount of academic work; *elect.* a contact which causes a break in a circuit, as in a relay or distributor; *Brit.* an electric socket or outlet; *com.* a unit employed in stating prices of shares or stocks; *milit.* a person or group preceding an advance guard or following a rear guard; *print.* a unit equal to one-seventy-second of an inch in type size. Lace worked by a needle; point lace; the vertex of the angle formed by two rails at a railroad frog; *archaic*, a lace or string with a tag, formerly used for fastening clothing. The act of pointing.

point, point, *v.t.* To direct, as the finger, toward an object or place; to aim; to indicate the position of or give attention to, often followed by *out*; to give a point to; to separate or mark with dots; to punctuate; to add to the point or force of, usu. followed by *up*; *hunting*, of a dog, to indicate the presence of, as game, by standing and turning the nose in its direction; *masonry*, to fill the joints of with mortar and smooth with the point of a trowel.—*v.i.* To designate an object or direction by use of the finger, usu. followed by *to* or *at*; to direct the thought, attention, or mind; to indicate a tendency toward or probability of something; to face, lie in, or have an indicated direction; *hunting*, to indicate the presence of game.

point-blank, point′blangk′, *a.* [From the directness with which an arrow is aimed at the white mark or blank in the center of a butt.] Aimed or fired directly at the mark; being so close as to have a projectile move in a straight line to a target; as, at *point-blank* range. Direct; plain; explicit; blunt. —*adv.*

point count, *n. Bridge.* A system for estimating the effectiveness of a hand by allotting points for high cards and distribution of cards according to usefulness in the game; the total number of points so counted.

point d'ap·pui, *Fr.* pwaɴ dä pwē′, *n. pl.* **points d'ap·pui,** *Fr.* pwaɴ dä pwē′. [Fr.] A base for military operations; a fulcrum.

point-de·vice, point″di·vīs′, *a.* [< *point*, condition, and *devise*, to imagine; lit. 'in as fine a condition as could be imagined.'] *Archaic*, precise, neat, or finical.—*adv.*

pointe, *Fr.* pwaɴt, *n. pl.* **pointes,** *Fr.* pwaɴt. A position in ballet executed on the tips of the toes.

point·ed, poin′tid, *a.* Having a sharp point; aimed, as a gun; aimed at or expressly referring to some particular person; marked;

pertinent; barbed, as wit or criticism; *arch.* relating to a Gothic style of architecture, distinguished by a pointed arch or crown.— **point·ed·ly,** *adv.*—**point·ed·ness,** *n.*

point·er, poin′tèr, *n.* One who or that which points; a variety of dog trained to hunt by scenting and pointing at game; a slender, conical rod used as an aid in pointing out specific items on charts, blackboards, and maps; an indicator, as the needle on a gauge. *Colloq.* a piece of beneficial advice or information; tip. *Nav.* the individual in a gun crew responsible for the gun's elevation. (*Cap.*), *pl.* the two outermost stars in the constellation Ursa Major, or Big Dipper, whose imaginary connecting line points to the North Star.

poin·til·lism, pwan′ti·liz″um, *n.* [Fr. *pointillisme*, < *pointiller*, cover with little points or dots, < *point*, E. *point*.] A method of painting, introduced by French impressionists, in which luminosity is produced by laying on the colors in points or dots of unmixed color, which are blended by the eye.—**poin·til·list,** *n.*—**poin·til·lis·tic,** *a.*

point lace, *n.* Needlepoint.

point·less, point′lis, *a.* Having no point; blunt; having no meaning, sense, or effectiveness, as a comment or act; devoid of score, as in an athletic competition.— **point·less·ly,** *adv.*—**point·less·ness,** *n.*

point of hon·or, *n.* A matter which may affect or reflect upon one's reputation or honor.

point of view, *n.* The position from which something is observed or appraised; personal standpoint; attitude; judgment.

point sys·tem, *n.* A system of ranking printing type sizes with the point, approximately one-seventy-second of an inch, as the base unit of measurement; any system of printing or writing for the blind which uses raised points as symbols; any system of evaluating work by assigning points, as used in schools to indicate the merit of a student's work or in industry to pay strictly on the basis of the amount and quality of work done.

point·y, poin′tē, *a.*—*pointier*, *pointiest*. Characterized by a relatively sharp point or points.

poise, poiz, *n.* [O.Fr. *poiser*, *peiser*, Fr. *peser*, < L. *penso*, to weigh out, < *pensus*, weighed, pp. of *pendo*, to weigh.] A balancing; equilibrium; self-possession during stress; composure; dignified bearing or movements; a suspension or wavering between two states, as between rest and motion.—*v.t.*—*poised*, *poising*. To set or maintain an equilibrium; to hold in suspension between two states; as, *poised* himself to throw a ball; to remain in place precariously; as, to *poise* a golf ball at the cup. —*v.i.* To sustain equilibrium; to hover; to be prepared for a change of state; as, a bird *poised* for flight.

poi·son, poi′zon, *n.* [Fr. *poison*, < L. *potio*, *potionis*, a drink, a draught, < *poto*, to drink.] Any agent that chemically destroys life or health upon contact with or absorption by an organism; something that taints, corrupts, or destroys. *Nuclear technology*, any atoms which may stop fission or change the speed of a reaction.—*v.t.* To give poison to; to kill or harm with poison; to put poison in or on; to impair, vitiate, corrupt.—*a.* Poisonous.—**poi·son·er,** *n.*

poi·son bean, *n.* A shrub, *Daubentonia drummondii*, producing poisonous seeds, and found in southern U.S.; the seed of the plant.

poi·son gas, *n.* Any toxic gas, such as chlorine or phosgene, especially when used against troops in warfare.

poi·son hem·lock, *n. Bot.* a large herbaceous plant, *Conium maculatum*, in the carrot family, having finely divided leaves,

stems spotted with purple, and a poisonous juice. See *hemlock*.

poi·son i·vy, *n.* A woody N. American climber or vine, *Rhus radicans*, with aerial rootlets variously toothed, trifoliate leaves, and white berries and possessing a volatile resinous oil which is poisonous to the touch, causing a severe skin rash.

poi·son oak, *n.* An erect, either herbaceous or vinelike sumac, *Rhus toxicodendron*, having no aerial rootlets, poisonous to the touch, and native to southeastern U.S.

poi·son·ous, poi′zo·nus, *a.* Having the qualities or effects of poison; venomous; malicious; corrupting.—**poi·son·ous·ly,** *adv.*

poi·son-pen, poi′zon·pen′, *a.* Pertaining to malicious writings intended to threaten or destroy another's reputation, esp. when sent anonymously.

poi·son su·mac, *n.* A highly poisonous shrub or small tree, *Rhus vernix*, a species of sumac with milky juice, smooth branches speckled with dark dots, pinnate leaves, and whitish berries, growing in swamps.

poke, pōk, *n.* [O.D. a *poke*, a sack or bag; Icel. *poki*, a sack, a bag; *pouch* is a softened form of this, and *pocket* a diminutive.] A pouch; a small bag; a sack.

poke, pōk, *v.t.*—*poked*, *poking*. [D. and L.G. *poken*, Sw. *pak*, a stick; cf. Ir. *poc*, a blow; Gael. *puc*, to push.] To push or thrust something long or pointed against, as the hand, finger, or a stick; to cause by pushing, thrusting, or jabbing; as, to *poke* an opening; to hit; to push out, in, from, or through; as, to *poke* out of the snow; to force or rouse, often with *up*; as, to *poke* a fire *up*.— *v.i.* To push, jab, or thrust with the finger or a stick; to grope, as in the dark; to hit out at something; to search, followed by *about*; to intrude; as, to *poke* into a neighbor's business; to busy oneself without a definite object, followed by *about*; to push out obtrusively.—*n.* One who dawdles; a sudden push; a punch with the fist; as, to take a *poke* at.—**poke one's nose in·to,** to meddle. —**poke fun at,** to ridicule.

poke·ber·ry, pōk′ber″ē, pōk′be·rē, *n. pl.* **poke·ber·ries.** The pokeweed plant or its berry.

poke bon·net, *n.* A woman's bonnet that has a brim which projects at the front and frames the face. Also **poke.**

poke check, *n. Ice hockey,* a maneuver to take the puck away from an opponent by slapping or hitting it with the stick.

pok·er, pō′kèr, *n.* One who pokes; something which pokes; an iron or steel bar or rod used in poking or stirring a fire.

pok·er, pō′kèr, *n.* A gambling game played with cards in which a bet is made by each player on the value of the cards dealt to him.

pok·er face, *n. Colloq.* An impassive face, appropriate for concealing the value of a poker hand; one who deliberately or habitually shows such a face.—**pok·er-faced,** *a.*

poke·weed, pōk′wēd″, *n.* [Of Amer. Ind. origin.] A N. American herb, *Phytolacca americana*, having drooping clusters of purple-black berries, and whose roots and seeds are sometimes used medicinally for emetic and purgative purposes. Also *pokeberry*, **poke·root**, **scoke**, pōk′rōt″, pōk′rut″, skōk.

pok·y, pok·ey, pō′kē, *a.*—*pokier*, *pokiest*. *Colloq.* Very slow; dull; narrow, cramped, or confined, as a space; shabby, as dress.— **pok·i·ly,** *adv.*—**pok·i·ness,** *n.*

pok·y, pok·ey, pō′kē, *n. pl.* **pok·ies**, **pok·eys.** *Slang*, jail.

po·lar, pō′lèr, *a.* [L.L. *polaris*, < L. *polus*, a pole.] Pertaining to a pole or the poles of a sphere; pertaining to one of the poles of the earth; proceeding from the poles of the earth; pertaining to a magnetic pole or poles; having direct opposites; being central; pivotal.

po·lar bear, *n.* A large white bear, *Thalarctos maritimus*, of the arctic regions.

po·lar bod·y, *n. Biol.* one of the minute cells arising by meiotic division of the ovum at or near the time of fertilization.

po·lar cir·cle, *n. Geog.* the Arctic or the Antarctic circle, 23 degrees 27 minutes from the respective poles.

po·lar co·or·di·nate, *n. Math.* a system of curvilinear coordinates in which a point in a plane is located by its distance from the origin or pole, and by the angle which a line joining the given point and the origin makes with a fixed reference line, called the polar axis.

po·lar front, *n. Meteor.* the zone or frontal surface acting as a boundary between a mass of cold polar air and warmer air from a temperate climate.

po·lar·im·e·ter, pō″la·rim′i·tėr, *n.* [M.L. *polaris*, polar.] An instrument for measuring the amount of polarized light in the light received from a given source; an instrument for measuring the angular rotation of the plane of polarization.—**po·lar·i·met·ric,** *a.*—**po·lar·im·e·try,** *n.*

Po·lar·is, pō·lâr′is, *n. Astron.* a star of the second magnitude, or among the 20 brightest, which is located at the tip of the handle of the Little Dipper, the northernmost star in the constellation Ursa Minor; also *polestar*, **po·lar star,** *North Star. Nav.* a two-stage guided missile capable of being fired from a submarine while submerged.

po·lar·i·scope, pō·lar′i·skōp″, po·lar′i·skōp″, *n.* [M.L. *polaris*, polar.] An instrument for exhibiting the polarization of light, or examining substances in polarized light. —**po·lar·i·scop·ic,** po·lar″i·skop′ik, *a.*

po·lar·i·ty, pō·lar′i·tē, po·lar′i·tē, *n. pl.* **po·lar·i·ties.** The power or tendency of a magnetized bar to point with its ends toward the magnetic poles of the earth; the quality of possessing magnetic poles; the possession of an axis with reference to which certain physical properties are determined; the possession of two poles or parts having opposite properties; positive or negative polar condition, as in electricity. *Fig.* the tendency, as of thought or feeling, in a particular direction; the possession or exhibition of two opposite or contrasted principles or tendencies.

po·lar·i·za·tion, pō″lėr·i·zā′shan, *n.* [Fr. *polarisation.*] The production or acquisition of polarity; *elect.* the process by which gases produced during electrolysis are deposited on the electrodes of a cell, giving rise to a reverse electromotive force; *optics,* a state, or the production of a state, in which rays of light exhibit different properties in different directions, as when they are passed through a crystal of tourmaline, which supposedly transmits rays in which the light or ether vibrations are confined to a single plane; *fig.* the existence of two opposing or contrasting tendencies or principles.—**plane of po·lar·i·za·tion,** *optics,* in light which has undergone polarization, the plane in which the light vibrations are confined, or, according to some authorities, to which they are at right angles.

po·lar·ize, pō′la·rīz″, *v.t., v.i.—polarized, polarizing.* To develop polarity or polarization in.—**po·lar·iz·a·ble,** *a.*—**po·lar·iz·er,** pō′la·rī″zėr, *n.*

Po·lar·oid, pō′la·roid″, *n.* A lens or other optical, photographic, or lighting device that has been plastic-treated to polarize light passing through it in order to reduce glare. (Trademark.)

pol·der, pōl′dėr, *n.* [D.] A tract of land below the level of the sea or other body of water which has been reclaimed for agricultural use and is protected by dikes.

pole, pōl, *n.* [O.E. *pal,* a pole, a stake; collateral form of *pale,* L.G. and D. *paal,* < L. *palus,* a stake.] A long slender piece of wood, metal, or other material; a long piece of wood or metal extending between the animals of a horse-drawn wagon; a perch or square rod equal to 30¼ square yards; a measure of length containing 16½ ft.; the inner lane of a race track.—*v.t.—poled, poling.* To support with poles; to bear or convey on poles; to push forward by the use of poles.—*v.i.* To move a raft or boat with a pole.—**pole·less,** *a.*

pole, pōl, *n.* [L. *polus,* < Gr. *pólos,* pivot, axis, pole, < *pélein,* move.] Each of the two points at which the axis of the earth cuts the celestial sphere, and about which the stars seem to revolve; each of the extremities of the axis of the earth or of any spherical body; either of two directly opposite opinions, principles, or tendencies; a focal point of interest or attention; *phys.* each of the two segments or parts of a magnet, electric battery, or dynamo at which certain opposite forces appear to be concentrated; *anat.* the point in a nerve cell where a process begins; *biol.* either end of an ideal axis in a nucleus, cell, or ovum about which parts are more or less symmetrically arranged; either end of a spindle-shaped figure formed in a cell previous to division into two new cells during mitosis; *math.* the singular point of origin of all radii in a polar coordinate system.

pole·ax, pole·axe, pōl′aks″, *n. p.* **pole·ax·es.** [Earlier *pollax.*] A medieval battle-ax; a halberd; a kind of ax used in felling or stunning animals; a hatchetlike weapon formerly used in the navy.—*v.t.—poleaxed, poleaxing.* To fell with a poleax.

pole bean, *n.* A climbing variety of bean, having the vine usu. supported by poles or a trellis.

pole·cat, pōl′kat″, *n. pl.* **pole·cats, pole·cat.** [Cf. Fr. *poule,* hen.] A European carnivore of the weasel family, *Mustela putorius,* a small, dark brown animal with a fetid odor, of which the ferret is a variety; the N. American skunk.

pole horse, *n.* A horse hitched to the pole, or tongue, of a wagon. Also *poler, wheeler.*

po·lem·ic, po·lem′ik, pō·lem′ik, *n.* [Gr. *polemikós,* of or for war, < *pólemos,* war.] Any controversial argument, particularly one attacking a strongly-held belief, principle, or doctrine; one who disputes another over a controversial issue; a controversialist, esp. in theology.—*a.*—**po·lem·i·cal,** *a.*—**po·lem·i·cal·ly,** *adv.* —**po·lem·i·cist,** *n.*

po·lem·ics, po·lem′iks, pō·lem′iks, *n. pl., sing. or pl. in constr.* The practice of arguing or debating subjects that are controversial in nature; the verbal or written attack or disputation of strongly-held doctrines or ideologies, esp. religious or theologic beliefs; a branch of theologic study which deals with areas of dispute and controversy, both historic and presently active.

pol·e·mist, pol′e·mist, *n.* [Gr. *polemistēs,* warrior, < *polemizein.*] One engaged in or adept in polemics. Also *polemicist.*

po·len·ta, pō·len′ta, *n.* [It., < L. *polenta,* peeled barley.] Corn meal, chestnut meal, or farina and water boiled to a thick consistency.

pol·er, pō′lėr, *n.* One who or that which poles; a pole horse or wheeler.

pole·star, pōl′stär″, *n.* Polaris or the North Star; that which serves as a guide; a lodestar; a guiding principle. A center of attraction; a cynosure.

pole vault, *n. Athletics,* a field event featuring a vault or leap, generally over a horizontal bar, performed with the aid of a long pole. Also **pole jump.—pole-vault,** pōl′vȧlt″, *v.i.—pole-vault·er,** *n.*

po·lice, po·lēs′, *n.* [M.Fr. *police,* government, civil administration, police, < L. *politia,* cf. *policy.*] An organized civil force for maintaining order, preventing and detecting crime, and enforcing the laws; *pl. in constr.* the members of such a force. The regulation and control of a community, esp. with reference to the maintenance of public order, safety, health, morals, and the like; any body of men officially maintained or employed to keep order and enforce regulations. *Milit.* in the U.S. army, the cleaning and keeping clean of a camp or garrison; the soldiers detailed to this task; the condition of a camp or garrison, with reference to cleanliness.—*v.t.—policed, policing.* To regulate, control, or keep in order, by or as by use of the police; *milit.* to clean and keep clean, as a camp.

po·lice ac·tion, *n.* A localized military operation involving regular forces, directed without a declaration of war against groups held to be endangering international peace and security.

po·lice court, *n.* An inferior court with summary jurisdiction for the trial of persons accused of any of certain minor offenses, and with power to hold those charged with more serious offenses for trial in a superior court or for the action of the grand jury.

po·lice dog, *n.* A dog of any kind used or trained to assist the police; *colloq.* any dog of the German Shepherd breed.

po·lice·man, po·lēs′man, *n. pl.* **po·lice·men.** A member of a force of police.

po·lice pow·er, *n.* The power of a government, within its constitutional limits, to exercise control over the conduct of citizens in order to promote general welfare.

po·lice state, *n.* A country in which the lives of citizens are rigidly controlled and supervised by an arbitrary use of police power, esp. through a secret police force.

po·lice sta·tion, *n.* The headquarters of the police in a particular area, to which arrested persons are taken.

pol·i·clin·ic, pol″ē·klin′ik, *n.* [G. *poliklinik,* < Gr. *pólis,* city and G. *klinik,* clinic.] A hospital department for the treatment of outpatients: distinguished from *polyclinic.*

pol·i·cy, pol′i·sē, *n. pl.* **pol·i·cies.** [L. *politia,* Gr. *politeia,* polity.] The principles on which any measure or course of action is based; the line of conduct which the rulers of a nation adopt on particular questions, especially with regard to foreign countries; prudence or wisdom of governments or individuals in the management of their affairs, public or private; general prudence or dexterity of management; sagacity.

pol·i·cy, pol′i·sē, *n. pl.* **pol·i·cies.** [Fr. *police,* < L.L. *poleticum,* a register, < L. *polyptychum,* Gr. *polyptychon,* an account book.] A written insurance contract; a lottery for gambling purposes.

pol·i·cy·hold·er, pol′i·sē·hōl′dėr, *n.* One who holds an insurance policy or contract.

po·li·o, pō′lē·ō″, *n.* Poliomyelitis.

po·li·o·my·e·li·tis, pō″lē·ō·mī″e·lī′tis, *n.* [N.L., < Gr. *poliós,* gray, and *myelós,* marrow.] *Pathol.* inflammation of the gray matter of the spinal cord, esp. an infectious form causing motor paralysis followed by atrophy of the muscles, and sometimes with lasting disability. Also *polio, infantile paralysis.*

po·lis, pō′lis, *n. pl.* **po·leis,** pō′līs. A city-state of ancient Greece.

pol·ish, pol′ish, *v.t.* [Fr. *polir, polissant,* < L. *polio,* to smooth.] To make smooth and glossy, usually by friction; to make elegant or refined; to bring to a finished state; perfect.—*v.i.* To take on a smooth and glossy surface, through being polished.—*n.* A substance used to impart a gloss; a gloss and smoothness of surface produced by friction; the process or act of polishing; elegance of manners; refinement of style.— **pol·ish off,** *slang.* To finish rapidly; dispose of completely.—**pol·ish up,** *colloq.* to improve.—**pol·ish·er,** *n.*

Pol·ish, pō'lish, *a.* Pertaining to Poland, a country in central Europe, its inhabitants, or its language.—*n.* The principal language of Poland, which is Slavic in origin.

Po·lit·bu·ro, pol'it·būr″ō, po·lit'būr″ō, *n.* [Russ. *politbyuro,* political bureau.] The powerful, policy-forming executive body of the Communist Party of the Soviet Union, prior to 1953.

po·lite, po·līt', *a.* [L. *politus,* < *polio,* to polish.] Showing by speech and behavior a considerate regard for others; polished, cultured; as, *polite* society; refined, well-bred.—**po·lite·ly,** *adv.*—**po·lite·ness,** *n.*

pol·i·tic, pol'i·tik, *a.* [L. *politicus,* Gr. *politikos,* < *polis,* a city.] Prudent and sagacious; cunning; artful; sagacious in adapting means to an end; expedient; political; as, body *politic.*

po·lit·i·cal, po·lit'i·kal, *a.* Having a fixed or regular system or administration of government; relating to civil government and its administration; concerned in state affairs or national measures; pertaining to a nation or state, or to nations or states, as distinguished from *civil* or *municipal*; treating of politics or government; as, *political* parties.—**po·lit·i·cal·ly,** *adv.*

po·lit·i·cal a·sy·lum, *n.* Sanctuary or protection extended by a country to citizens being sought by their native country for trial or punishment for political acts.

po·lit·i·cal e·con·o·my, *n.* The social science of the interrelations of economic processes and political and social organizations; a 19th century social science precedent to modern economics; economics.— **po·lit·i·cal e·con·o·mist,** *n.*

po·lit·i·cal sci·ence, *n.* That science which deals with the structure, organization, and principles of government.—**po·lit·i·cal sci·en·tist,** *n.*

pol·i·ti·cian, pol'i·tish'an, *n.* One versed in the science of government and the art of governing; one skilled in politics; one who occupies himself with politics as a profession; one involved in politics for personal gain, political appointment, or partisan objectives.

po·lit·i·cize, po·lit'i·sīz″, *v.i.*—*politicized, politicizing.* To engage in or discuss politics.—*v.t.* To lend a political character to; to make political in nature.

pol·i·tick, pol'i·tik, *v.i.* To enter into or become involved in political activity.— **pol·i·tick·er,** *n.*

po·lit·i·co, po·lit'i·kō′, *n. pl.* **po·lit·i·cos.** [< Sp., It.] A politician.

pol·i·tics, pol'i·tiks, *n. pl., sing. or pl. in constr.* [Fr. *politique,* Gr. *politikē.*] The science of government; political science; the policies and aims of a government of a nation or state; the conduct and contests of political parties; political affairs; political connections or beliefs of a person; the plotting or scheming of those seeking personal power, glory, position, or the like.

pol·i·ty, pol'i·tē, *n. pl.* **pol·i·ties.** [Gr. *politeia.*] The form or manner of government of a nation, state, or other institution; administrative control; the state of being organized under a particular form of government, or the community so organized.

pol·ka, pōl'ka, pō'ka, *n.* [Cf. Pol. *Polka,* fem. of *Polak,* a Polack or Pole.] A lively round dance of Bohemian origin, with music in duple time; a piece of music for such a dance or in its rhythm.—*v.i.*

pol·ka dot, *n.* A dot or round spot repeated to form a pattern on a textile fabric; a pattern of or a fabric with such dots.

poll, pōl, *n.* [M.E. *polle* = M.D. and L.G. *polle.*] The head, esp. the part of it on which the hair grows; the nape of the neck; a person or individual in a number or list; an enumeration or a list of individuals, as for purposes of taxing or voting; the registering of votes, as at an election; the voting at an election; the number of votes cast, or the numerical results of the voting; as, a heavy *poll*; *usu. pl.* the place where votes are cast.—*v.t.* To cut off or cut short the hair of; crop; shear; to cut off the top, as of a tree; to pollard; to cut off or cut short the horns of; to enroll in a list or register, as for purposes of taxing; to take or register the votes of; to bring to the polls, as voters; to receive at the polls, as votes; to deposit or cast at the polls, as a vote.—*v.i.* To vote at the polls; give one's vote.— **poll·ee,** pō·lē′, *n.*—**poll·er,** *n.*

poll, pol, *n.* [Cf. Gr. *hoi polloi,* 'the many.'] At Cambridge University, England, a student who reads for or obtains a 'pass' degree, that is, a degree without honors.

pol·lack, pol'ak, *n. pl.* **pol·lacks, pol·lack.** A food fish, found in the northern Atlantic, *Pollachius virens,* belonging to the cod family, although darker in color. Also **pol·lock,** *pl.* **pol·locks, pol·lock.**

pol·lard, pol'ėrd, *n.* [< *poll,* the head, and affix *-ard.*] A tree with the top cut off to induce a dense new growth of foliage; any usu. horned animal, as a stag or sheep, in a hornless state; a coarse product of wheat, finer than bran.—*v.t.* To convert into a pollard.

polled, pōld, *a.* Without horns, as some breeds of cattle; having the horns removed.

pol·len, pol'en, *n.* [L. *pollen* and *pollis,* fine flour or dust.] *Bot.* the male element in flowering plants made up of masses of fine, usu. yellow, powdery grains or microspores and produced in the anther of the stamen.— **pol·lin·ic,** po·lin'ik, *a.*

pol·len count, *n.* The average number of pollen grains of specified plants, usu. ragweed, in a cubic yard of air, taken over a 24 hour period at a stated place, and which is obtained by using an exposure meter located on the roof of a high, unobstructed building.

pol·lex, pol'leks, *n. pl.* **pol·li·ces,** pol'i·sēz. [L.] The thumb in man; a corresponding digit of other animals.—**pol·li·cal,** *a.*

pol·li·nate, pol'i·nāt′, *v.t.*—*pollinated, pollinating. Bot.* to transfer pollen from the anther of a flower to the stigma of (the same or another flower), by wind, water, insect, or man.—**pol·li·na·tion,** pol″i·nā′-shan, *n.*—**pol·li·na·tor,** *n.*

pol·li·nif·er·ous, pol″i·nif'ėr·us, *a.* Producing pollen.

pol·lin·i·um, po·lin'ē·um, *n. pl.* **pol·lin·i·a,** po·lin'ē·a. A coherent body of pollen particles, as found in milkweeds and orchids.

pol·li·nize, pol'i·nīz″, *v.t.*—*pollinized, pollinizing. Bot.* to pollinate.—**pol·li·niz·er,** *n.*

pol·li·no·sis, pol″i·nō′sis, *n. Pathol.* hay fever.

pol·li·wog, pol'ē·wog″, *n.* [Earlier *polliwig, polwigge,* M.E. *polwygle,* = E. *poll* and *wiggle.*] A tadpole. Also **pol·ly·wog.**

poll·ster, pōl'stėr, *n.* A poll taker.

poll tax, *n.* A tax levied on a person, usu. as a prerequisite for voting, and now declared unconstitutional by the Supreme Court.

pol·lu·tant, po·lōt'ant, *n.* Something that pollutes, esp. chemicals or refuse material released into the atmosphere or water.

pol·lute, po·lōt', *v.t.*—*polluted, polluting.* [L. *pulluo, pollutum,* < prep. *pol, por,* used in comp. and *luō,* to wash.] To make foul or unclean; soil, taint; to corrupt or

defile; make morally unclean; to profane, desecrate, or make ceremonially impure.— **pol·lut·er,** *n.*—**pol·lu·tion,** *n.*

Pol·lux, pol'uks, *n. Astron.* a star of the first magnitude in the Gemini constellation; *Gr. mythol.* the twin brother of Castor, son of Leda and Zeus.

Pol·ly·an·na, pol'ē·an'a, *n.* A blindly or overly optimistic person who tends to discover something good in everything: a name originating in Eleanor Porter's novel, *Pollyanna.*

po·lo, pō'lō, *n.* [Native Tibetan name in northern India.] A game resembling hockey, played on horseback with long-handled mallets and a wooden ball; any game resembling this, as water polo.— **po·lo·ist,** *n.*

po·lo coat, *n.* A tailored overcoat for informal wear often of a camel's hair fabric.

pol·o·naise, pol″o·nāz′, pō″lo·nāz′, *n.* [Fr.] *Mus.* a slow marchlike dance of Polish origin; music in three-four time, for or in the manner of this dance. An 18th century over-dress for women, made with a fitted bodice and a draped cutaway skirt.

po·lo·ni·um, po·lō′nē·um, *n. Chem.* a radioactive element discovered in pitch-blende by M. and Mme. Curie. Sym. Po, at. no. 84, at. wt. 209. Also *radium F.* See Periodic Table of Elements.

pol·ter·geist, pōl'tér·gīst″, *n.* [G.] A ghost or spirit which is said to manifest its presence by noises, knockings, and other disturbances.

pol·troon, pol·trön′, *n.* [Fr. and Sp. *poltron,* < It. *poltrone,* < *poltro,* lazy, dastardly, < O.H.G. *polstar,* a pillow.] An arrant coward; a dastard; a wretch without spirit or courage.—*a.* Base; vile; contemptible.—**pol·troon·er·y,** pol·trö′ne·rē, *n.* Cowardice.

po·ly, pol'ē, *n. pl.* **poly·ys.** A leukocyte having a varied-lobed nucleus.

pol·y·am·ide, pol″ē·am′īd, pol″ē·am′id, *n.* A polymeric compound in which the amide group links the monomer units together: sometimes used to make synthetic fibers, as nylon; synthetic analog to peptide or protein fibers.

pol·y·an·drous, pol″ē·an′drus, *a.* [Gr. *polys,* many, *anēr, andros,* a male.] *Bot.* having many stamens, that is, any number above twenty, inserted in the receptacle. Pertaining to or practicing polyandry.

pol·y·an·dry, pol'ē·an″drē, pol″ē·an′drē, *n.* [Gr. *polys,* many, *anēr, andros,* a man.] The practice of having more than one husband at the same time; bot. state of being polyandrous.—**pol·y·an·dric,** *a.*

pol·y·an·thus, pol″ē·an′thus, *n. pl.* **pol·y·an·thus·es.** [Gr. *polys,* many, *anthos,* a flower.] *Bot.* A garden variety of the primrose, *Primula polyantha*; a commonly cultivated narcissus, *Narcissus tazetta,* with many flowers in a cluster.

pol·y·ba·sic, pol″ē·bā′sik, *a. Chem.* relating to acids with more than one replaceable hydrogen atom.—**pol·y·ba·sic·i·ty,** pol″ē·ba·sis'i·tē, *n.*

pol·y·ba·site, pol″ē·bā′sīt, po·lib′a·sīt″, *n.* [G. *polybasit.*] A blackish mineral with a metallic luster, Ag_9SbS_6, a valuable silver ore.

pol·y·car·pel·lar·y, pol″ē·kär′pe·ler″ē, *a. Bot.* consisting of many carpels.

pol·y·car·pic, pol″ē·kär′pik, *a. Bot.* Pertaining to a plant which produces a fruit with two or more distinct carpels; pertaining to a plant which fruits more than once in a season. Also **pol·y·car·pous.**— **pol·y·car·py,** *n.*

pol·y·chaete, pol'i·kēt″, *n.* [N.L. *Polychaeta,* pl., < Gr. *polychaitēs,* having much hair.] *Zool.* any of the *Polychaeta,* a class of annelids having unsegmented rudimentary limbs with many chaetae or bristles, and including most of the common marine worms.—*a.* Pertaining or belonging to the *Polychaeta.*—**pol·y·chae·tous**, *a.*

pol·y·chro·mat·ic, pol″ē·krō·mat′ik, pol″ē·kro·mat′ik, *a.* Exhibiting many colors.

pol·y·chrome, pol′ē·krōm″, *a.* Having several or many colors; executed in the manner of polychromy.

pol·y·chro·my, pol′ē·krō″mē, *n.* [Gr.] The use of several colors in statuary, painting, or architecture.

pol·y·clin·ic, pol″ē·klin′ik, *n.* A general, nonspecialized clinic or hospital dealing with various diseases.

pol·y·con·den·sa·tion, pol″ē·kon″den·-sā′shan, pol″ē·kon″den·sā′shan, *n.* Chemical condensation producing a compound with great molecular weight.

pol·y·con·ic pro·jec·tion, pol″ē·kon′ik pro·jek′shan, *n. Cartography*, a map projection in which the parallels are arcs of circles of diminishing radii and are equidistant along a central straight meridian, while the other meridians are curved and equidistant along the curved parallels.

pol·y·cy·the·mi·a, pol″ē·sī·thē′mē·a, *n. Pathol.* a condition in which red blood cells are abnormally increased in number.—**pol·y·cy·the·mic**, *a.*

pol·y·dac·tyl, pol″ē·dak′til, pol″ē·dak′til, *a.* [Gr. *polydáctylos.*] Having many fingers or toes, esp. more than the normal number. —*n.* A polydactyl animal.—**pol·y·dac·tyl·ism**, —*n.*—**pol·y·dac·ty·lous**, *a.*— **pol·y·dac·ty·ly**, *n.*

pol·y·dip·si·a, pol″ē·dip′sē·a, *n. Med.* abnormal thirst.—**pol·y·dip·sic**, *a.*

pol·y·em·bry·o·ny, pol″ē·em′brē·o·nē, pol″ē·em′brē·ō″nē, pol″ē·em·bri′o·nē, *n. Biol.* the production of two or more embryos from a single fertilized ovule or egg.— **pol·y·em·bry·on·ic**, *a.*

pol·y·es·ter, pol′ē·es″tėr, pol″ē·es′tėr, *n. Chem.* a long-chain ester of high molecular weight produced by polymerization and used chiefly in making fibers, resins, and plastics.—**pol·y·es·ter·i·fi·ca·tion**, *n.*

pol·y·eth·yl·ene, pol″ē·eth′i·lēn″, *n.* A polymer of ethylene, $(C_2H_4)n$, which is a plastic film widely used in packaging and electrical insulation.

po·lyg·a·la, po·lig′a·la, *n.* [L., < Gr. *polygalon*, milkwort, < *polys*, much, and *gála*, milk.] *Bot.* any of several herbs of the genus *Polygala*, having a milky juice and rose-purple flowers often with fringed petals, esp. *P. paucifolia*, of N. America, the fringed polygala or gaywings. Also *milkwort.*—**pol·y·ga·la·ceous**, pol″ē·ga·-lā′shus, po·lig″a·lā′shus, *a.*

po·lyg·a·mist, po·lig′a·mist, *n.* A person who practices polygamy.

po·lyg·a·mous, po·lig′a·mus, *a.* Relating to or characterized by polygamy; having a plurality of mates. *Bot.* pertaining to a plant bearing bisexual and unisexual flowers.—**po·lyg·a·mous·ly**, *adv.*

po·lyg·a·my, po·lig′a·mē, *n.* [Gr. *polys*, many, and *gamos*, marriage.] The custom or practice of plural marriage; the state of having more than one wife or husband at the same time. *Zool.* the practice of simultaneously having more than one mate.

pol·y·gen·e·sis, pol″ē·jen′i·sis, *n.* [Gr.] The doctrine that beings have their origin in many cells or embryos of different kinds: opposed to *monogenesis.*—**pol·y·gen·e·sist**, *n.*—**pol·y·ge·net·ic**, pol″ē·je·-net′ik, *a.*—**pol·y·ge·net·i·cal·ly**, *adv.*

pol·y·glot, pol′ē·glot″, *n.* [Gr.] A book containing many languages, particularly a Bible that presents the Scriptures in several languages; a text made up of several languages; an individual who can speak or write a number of languages; a mixture of languages.—*a.* Versed in

several languages; multilingual; composed of several languages.—**pol·y·glot·ism**, *n.*

pol·y·gon, pol′ē·gon″, *n.* [Gr.] A closed plane figure with three or more straight sides. A figure on a sphere formed by arcs of great circles; also *spherical polygon.*— **po·lyg·o·nal**, po·lig′o·nal, *a.*—**po·lyg·o·nal·ly**, *adv.*

po·lyg·o·num, po·lig′o·num, *n.* [N.L., < Gr.] *Bot.* any plant of the herbaceous genus *Polygonum*, in the buckwheat family, having jointed stems with sheathed nodes, including many weeds, as the knotweed and smartweed, and a few ornamentals, as the prince's feather and silver-lace vine. Also **po·lyg·o·ny.**

pol·y·graph, pol′ē·graf″, pol′ē·gräf″, *n.* [< Gr.] An instrument for multiplying copies of a writing; a prolific or many-sided author. An instrument which records such bodily changes as fluctuations in blood pressure or heartbeat, and may be employed in lie detection: compare *pathometer.*— **pol·y·graph·ic**, pol″ē·graf′ik, *a.*

po·lyg·y·nous, po·lij′i·nus, *a.* [Gr. *polys*, much, many, and *gyné*, woman.] Having more than one wife or female mate at one time; characterized by plurality of wives for one husband.

po·lyg·y·ny, po·lij′i·nē, *n.* The custom, practice, or condition of having more than one wife or female mate at one time; marriage with several wives.

pol·y·he·dron, pol″ē·hē′dron, *n.* pl. **pol·y·he·drons**, **pol·y·he·dra**, pol″ē·hē′dra. [Gr. *polys*, many, *hedra*, a side.] A solid bounded by many plane faces.—**pol·y·he·dral**, pol″ē·hē′dral, *a.*

pol·y·his·tor, pol″ē·his′tėr, *n.* [L., < Gr.] A person of great or varied learning. Also **pol·y·math.**—**pol·y·his·tor·ic**, pol″ē·hi·star′ik, *a.*—**pol·y·his·tor·y**, *n.*

pol·y·hy·drox·y, pol″ē·hī·drok′sē, *a. Chem.* containing at least two hydroxyl groups.

pol·y·mer, pol′i·mėr, *n.* [Gr. *polymerés*, many parts.] *Chem.* any of two or more polymeric compounds, esp. a compound polymeric with and regarded as derived from another of lower molecular weight.— **pol·y·mer·ic**, pol″i·mer′ik, *a. Chem.* of compounds, or of one compound in relation to another, having the same elements combined in the same proportions by weight, but differing in molecular weight.— **po·lym·er·ism**, po·lim′e·riz″um, pol′i·-me·riz″um, *n. Chem.* polymeric state; *biol.* polymerous state.

po·lym·er·i·za·tion, po·lim″ėr·i·zā′shan, pol″i·mėr·i·zā′shan, *n. Chem.* The act or process of forming a polymer or polymeric compound; the union of two or more molecules of a compound to form a more complex compound with a higher molecular weight; the conversion of one compound into another by such a process; as, the *polymerization* of acetylene to benzene.— **po·lym·er·ize**, po·lim′e·rīz″, pol′i·me·-rīz″, *v.t., v.i.*—*polymerized, polymerizing.* To combine so as to form a polymer; subject to or undergo polymerization.

po·lym·er·ous, po·lim′ėr·us, *a. Zool.* composed of many parts; *bot.* of flowers, having numerous members in each whorl.

pol·y·morph, pol′ē·marf″, *n.* [Gr. *polymorphos*, multiform.] *Biol.* a polymorphous organism or substance, or one of its various forms; *crystal.* any form a polymorphous substance assumes.—**pol·y·mor·phic**, pol″ē·mar′fik, *a. Biol.* occurring in or assuming various forms or colors. Also **pol·y·mor·phous**, pol″ē·mar′fus.—**pol·y·mor·phi·cal·ly**, **pol·y·mor·phous·ly**, *adv.*—**pol·y·mor·phism**, pol″ē·mar′fiz″um, *n.*

pol·y·mor·pho·nu·cle·ar, pol″ē·mar″-fo·nō″klē·ėr, pol″ē·mar″fo·nū″klē·ėr, *a.*

Of a leukocyte, having a multilobed nucleus.—*n.*

Pol·y·ne·sian, pol″i·nē′zhan, pol″i·nē′shan, *a.* [< *Polynesia*, < Gr. *polys*, much, many, and *nesos*, island.] Of or pertaining to Polynesia, a geographical division comprising the numerous small islands in the Pacific Ocean east of Australia and the Malay Archepelago, or, more strictly, east of Melanesia and Micronesia, its inhabitants, or their languages.—*n.* A member of any of the brown races inhabiting Polynesia; any of the languages or dialects spoken in Polynesia.

pol·y·no·mi·al, pol″ē·nō′mē·al, *a.* Consisting of or pertaining to several names or terms.—*n. Math.* an algebraic expression made up of two or more terms; *biol.* a scientific name, as of a plant or animal, consisting of more than two terms.

pol·yp, pol′ip, *n.* [L. *polypus*, a polyp, a growth or tumor, < Gr. *polypous.*] A sedentary coelenterate animal, either single, as hydras, or part of a colony, as coral, usu. having a hollow cylindrical body with a fixed base at one end and a mouth surrounded by tentacles at the other; *pathol.* a bulging or projecting mass of tissue that may be new growth, a center of infection, a malformation, or degenerative tissue.— **pol·yp·ous**, *a.*

pol·y·par·y, pol′i·per″ē, *n.* pl. **pol·y·par·ies.** The common supporting structure of a colony of polyps, as corals.

pol·y·pep·tide, pol″ē·pep′tid, *n. Biochem.* a class of compounds formed from the linkage of four or more amino acids in a ring or chainlike structure.

pol·y·pet·al·ous, pol″ē·pet′a·lus, *a.* [< Gr.] *Bot.* having or consisting of many distinct petals.

po·lyph·a·gous, po·lif′a·gus, *a.* [< Gr.] Eating or subsisting on many kinds of food. —**pol·y·pha·gi·a**, pol″ē·fā′jē·a, pol″ē·-fā′ja, *n.* Excessive or extreme desire to eat.

pol·y·phase, pol′ē·fāz″, *a.* [< Gr.] *Elect.* having a combination of electric currents differing in their phases by constant amounts.

pol·y·phone, pol′ē·fōn″, *n.* [Gr. *polyphōnos*, having many tones.] *Phon.* a letter or other symbol having more than one phonetic value, as the letter *s*, voiced in *ease* and unvoiced in *case.*

pol·y·phon·ic, pol″ē·fon′ik, *a.* Consisting of or having many voices or sounds. *Mus.* having two or more voices or parts, each with an independent melody, but all harmonizing: opposed to *homophonic; contrapuntal;* pertaining to music of this kind; of a musical instrument, capable of producing more than one tone at a time, as an organ or a harp. *Phonetics,* having more than one phonetic value, as a letter. Also **po·lyph·o·nous**, po·lif′o·nus.—**pol·y·phon·i·cal·ly**, **po·lyph·o·nous·ly**, *adv.*

pol·y·phon·ic prose, *n.* Prose which makes use of such poetic devices as alliteration, rhyme, or assonance but does not keep a strictly measured rhythm.

po·lyph·o·ny, po·lif′o·nē, *n.* pl. **po·lyph·o·nies.** [Gr. *polyphōnia.*] The quality of being polyphonic. *Mus.* polyphonic composition; counterpoint. *Phon.* representation of different sounds by the same letter or symbol.

pol·y·phy·let·ic, pol″ē·fī·let′ik, *a.* [< Gr.] Developed from more than one ancestral type, as a group of animals. —**pol·y·phy·let·i·cal·ly**, *adv.*—**pol·y·phy·let·i·cism**, *n.*

pol·y·ploid, pol′ē·ploid″, *a. Biol.* having more than double the basic, or haploid, complement of chromosomes.—*n.* An organism or cell that is polyploid.—**pol·y·ploi·dic**, *a.*—**pol·y·ploi·dy**, *n.*

pol·yp·ne·a, pol″ip·nē′a, n. Med. extremely rapid panting or breathing.—**pol·yp·ne·ic**, a.

pol·y·po·dy, pol′ē·pō″dē, n. pl. **pol·y·po·dies**. [L. polypodium, < Gr. polypódion.] Any fern of the genus Polypodium, as P. vulgare, a common species with creeping rootstocks, deeply pinnatifid evergreen fronds, and round, naked sori.

pol·yp·tych, pol′ip·tik, n. [Gr. polyptychos, of many folds.] A combination of more than three panels or frames bearing pictures or carvings. Compare diptych and triptych.

pol·y·sac·cha·ride, pol″ē·sak′a·rīd″, pol″ē·sak′a·rid, n. Chem. a carbohydrate containing three or more monosaccharides linked together and including starch, glycogen, and cellulose.

pol·y·se·my, pol′ē·sē″mē, n. A variety of meanings of a single word.—**pol·y·se·man·tic, pol·y·se·mous**, a.

pol·y·sep·al·ous, pol″ē·sep′a·lus, a. [< Gr.] Bot. pertaining to a calyx which has its sepals separate from each other.

pol·y·sty·rene, pol″ē·stī′rēn, n. Chem. a colorless transparent plastic, $(C_6H_5CHCH_2)_n$, a polymer of styrene, used esp. as an insulator, and in packaging and making molded products.

pol·y·sul·fide, pol″ē·sul′fīd, pol″ē·sul′fid, n. Chem. a sulfide having two or more atoms of sulfur per molecule.

pol·y·syl·lab·ic, pol″ē·si·lab′ik, a. [Gr. polysyllabos, of many syllables.] Consisting of many, or more than three, syllables, as a word; characterized by such words, as a language.—**pol·y·syl·lab·i·cal·ly**, adv.—**pol·y·syl·la·ble**, pol′ē·sil″a·bl, pol″ē·sil′a·bl, n. A polysyllabic word.

pol·y·syn·de·ton, pol″ē·sin′di·ton″, n. [N.L., < Gr.] Rhet. the use of a number of conjunctions in close succession. Compare asyndeton.

pol·y·syn·the·sism, pol″i·sin′thi·siz″um, n. The combination of a number of elements into one; ling. the combining of the word elements of a sentence into a single word, as in American Indian languages.—**pol·y·syn·thet·ic**, pol″ē·sin·thet′ik, a. Also holophrastic.

pol·y·tech·nic, pol″ē·tek′nik, a. [< Gr.] Of or designating an educational institution in which instruction is given in many technical arts and applied sciences.—n. A school of instruction in applied sciences and technical arts.

pol·y·the·ism, pol′ē·thē·iz″um, pol″ē·thē′iz·um, n. [< Gr.] The doctrine or worship of a plurality of gods.—**pol·y·the·ist**, n.—**pol·y·the·is·tic, pol·y·the·is·ti·cal**, a.

pol·y·thene, pol′i·thēn″, n. Polyethylene.

pol·y·ton·al, pol″ē·tōn′al, a. Mus. pertaining to the use of two or more key signatures simultaneously, as in different voices of a harmonic structure.—**pol·y·to·nal·i·ty**, pol″ē·tō·nal′i·tē, n.

pol·y·troph·ic, pol″ē·trof′ik, a. Of bacteria, nourished from multiple organic sources.

pol·y·typ·ic, pol″ē·tip′ik, a. Biol. having or involving many or several types. Also **pol·y·typ·i·cal**.

pol·y·un·sat·u·rat·ed, pol″ē·un·sach′a·rā″tid, a. Of or pertaining to animal or vegetable fats having two or more double bonds per molecule: when consumed by humans, they help lower the cholesterol content in the blood.

pol·y·u·re·thane, pol″ē·ūr′e·thān″, n. A polymer with a light, foamy texture resulting from the entrapment of carbon dioxide in pores during production: used in the manufacture of padding and various resins.

pol·y·va·lent, pol″ē·vā′lent, po·liv′a·lent, a. Chem. multivalent; bact. pertaining to a vaccine having several strains of antibodies.—**pol·y·va·lence**, n.

pol·y·vi·nyl, pol″ē·vī′nil, pol″ē·vin′il, pol″ē·vin′il, pol″ē·vin′il, n. Chem. a vinyl polymer derivative, as plastic or resin.

pol·y·vi·nyl res·in, n. Chem. any of the many polymers and resins obtained from vinyl compounds by polymerization or copolymerization.

pol·y·zo·an, pol″ē·zō′an, n. [N.L., < Gr.] Zool. any member of the Polyzoa, a phylum of small aquatic animals forming colonies or compound masses, often moss-like in appearance, and found attached to objects under water. Also bryozoan.—a.

pol·y·zo·ar·i·um, pol″ē·zō·âr′ē·um, n. pl. **pol·y·zo·ar·i·a**, pol″ē·zō·âr′ē·a. [N.L., < polyzoön.] Zool. a colony of polyzoans, or its supporting skeleton.—**pol·y·zo·ar·i·al**, a.

pol·y·zo·ic, pol″ē·zō′ik, a. Of a polyzoan colony, composed of a number of zooids; denoting or relating to a spore which produces many sporozoites.

pom·ace, pom′is, n. [< L. pomum, an apple.] The substance of apples or of similar fruit crushed by grinding; the pulpy matter or substance resulting from crushing or grinding.

po·ma·ceous, pō·mā′shus, a. Pertaining to apples; like or pertaining to pears, apples, or other pomes.

po·made, po·mād′, po·mäd′, pō·mäd′, pō·mäd′, n. [Fr. pommade. It pomada, pomata, < L. pomum, an apple. Orig. it was prepared from apples.] A perfumed ointment used as a grooming aid for the hair and scalp.—v.t.—pomaded, pomading. To groom with pomade.

po·man·der, pō′man·dėr, pō·man′dėr, n. [O.Fr. pome (< M.L. pomum), apple, and ambre, ambergris, E. amber.] A mixture of aromatic substances, often in the form of a ball, formerly carried on the person as a guard against infection; the case or ball in which this was carried.

po·ma·tum, pō·mā′tum, pō·mä′tum, po·mä′tum, po·mä′tum, n. [< L. pomum, an apple.] Pomade.

pome, pōm, n. [L. pomum, an apple.] Bot. a juicy, plump fruit, having an inedible, compartmented core with seeds, as the pear, apple, and quince.

pome·gran·ate, pom′gran″it, pom′e·gran″it, pum′gran″it, pum′e·gran″it, pom″e·gran′it, pom·gran″it, n. [L. pomum, an apple, and granatum, grained, having many grains or seeds.] A globe-shaped edible fruit as large as an orange, having a reddish, hard rind filled with a tasty, red, many-seeded pulp; the small tree, Punica granatum, cultivated in warm climates, which produces this fruit.

pom·e·lo, pom′e·lō″, n. pl. **pom·e·los**. The shaddock; the grapefruit.

Pom·er·a·ni·an, pom″e·rā′nē·an, pom″e·rān′yan, a. Of or pertaining to Pomerania, a region on the south coast of the Baltic Sea.—n. One of a breed of small dogs of the spitz variety, with sharp nose, pointed ears, and long, thick, silky hair; a native or inhabitant of Pomerania.

po·mif·er·ous, pō·mif′ėr·us, a. [L. pomifer, fruit-producing.] Having pomes.

pom·mée, po·mā′, po·mā′, pō·mā′, Fr. pạ·mā′, a. Her. pertaining to the arms of a cross that end in a ball or knob.

pom·mel, pum′el, pom′el, n. [O.Fr. pomel (Fr. pommeau), dim. < M.L. pomum, apple, E. pome.] A knob or ball as on the hilt of a sword or dagger; the protuberant part at the front and top of a saddle.—v.t.—pommeled, pommeling, esp. Brit. pommelled, pommelling. To strike or beat with or as with the pommel of a sword; beat with the fists. Also pummel.

po·mol·o·gy, pō·mol′o·jē, n. [L. pomum, an apple, Gr. logos, discourse.] The branch of knowledge that deals with fruits and their cultivation.—**po·mo·log·i·cal**, pō″mo·loj′i·kal, a.—**po·mo·log·i·cal·ly**, adv.—**po·mol·o·gist**, n.

pomp, pomp, n. [Fr. pompe, L. pompa, < Gr. pompē, a procession, < pempō, to send.] A display distinguished by splendor or magnificence; a pageant; magnificence; splendor, pretentious display or show.

pom·pa·dour, pom′pa·dōr″, pom′pa·dạr″, pom′pa·dụr″, n. An arrangement of a woman's hair in which it is raised above the forehead usu. over a pad; a man's hair style in which the hair is brushed up from the forehead.

pom·pa·no, pom′pa·nō″, n. pl. **pom·pa·no, pom·pa·nos**. [Sp. pámpano.] A food fish of the carangoid genus Trachinotus, esp. T. carolinus, of the West Indies and the neighboring coasts of North America; any of certain other food fishes, as Palometa simillima, of the coast of California.

pom·pom, pom-pom, pom′pom, n. [Imit.] An automatic antiaircraft cannon.

pom·pon, pom′pon, Fr. pạN′pạN′, n. [Fr.] An ornament, as of wool or feathers, shaped into a ball or tuft, for a hat, slippers, or costumes; a type of chrysanthemum or dahlia having a small flower head resembling a pompon.

pom·pos·i·ty, pom·pos′i·tē, n. pl. **pom·pos·i·ties**. The state or quality of being pompous; also pompousness. A pompous act, habit, or characteristic.

pomp·ous, pom′pus, a. [Fr. pompeux.] Exhibiting an exaggerated sense of dignity; high-flown and ornate, as speech; ostentatious; displaying pomp; splendid; showing self-importance.—**pomp·ous·ly**, adv.—**pomp·ous·ness**, n.

Pon·ceau, pon·sō′, n. A bright reddish color; a coal-tar dye yielding a red color.

pon·cho, pon′chō, n. pl. **pon·chos**. [Sp.] A garment, orig. from South America, like a blanket with a slit in the middle for the head to pass through; a raincoat constructed like a poncho.

pond, pond, n. [= pound.] A body of still water smaller than a lake, often formed artificially, as by damming a stream.

pon·der, pon′dėr, v.t. [Fr. ponderer, < L. pondero, to weigh, < pondus, ponderis, weight.] To weigh carefully in the mind; to reflect upon; to examine carefully.—v.i. To think; to reflect seriously; to deliberate, often with on or over.—**pon·der·a·ble**, pon′dėr·a·bl, a.—**pon·der·er**, n.

pon·der·ous, pon′dėr·us, a. [L. ponderosus.] Very heavy; massive; unmanageable due to weight or size; stolid or dull.—**pon·der·ous·ly**, adv.—**pon·der·ous·ness**, n.

pond scum, n. A green scum formed on a body of fresh water by the presence of algae of the genus Spirogyra; any of these or related algae.

pond·weed, pond′wēd″, n. Any of the aquatic plants constituting the genus Potamogeton, most of which grow in ponds and quiet streams.

pone, pōn, n. [N. Amer. Ind.] Southern U.S. Bread, oval in shape, made of corn meal, and baked or fried; a loaf or cake of it. Also corn pone.

pon·gee, pon·jē′, pon′jē, n. [Chin.] A soft, unbleached, light tan Chinese silk of an uneven weave; a fabric of cotton or synthetic yarns resembling this.

pon·iard, pon′yėrd, n. [Fr. poignard, < poing, L. pugnus, the fist.] A dagger.—v.t. To pierce or stab with a poniard.

pons, ponz, n. pl. **pon·tes**, pon′tēz. [L.] Anat. a band of nerve fibers in the brain connecting the lobes of the cerebellum, medulla, and cerebrum; also **pons Va·ro·li·i**, ponz′ va·rō′lē·ī″. A connecting part.

pons as·i·no·rum, ponz′ as″i·nŏr′um, ponz′ as″i·na̲r′um, *n.* [L., 'bridge of asses.'] The geometrical proposition that if a triangle has two of its sides equal, the angles opposite these sides are also equal; any problem that is baffling to a beginner.

Pon·tic, pon′tik, *a.* [L. *Ponticus,* < Gr. *Pontikós,* < *Póntos,* the Black Sea, also Pontus, particular use of *póntos,* sea.] Pertaining to the Pontus, or Black Sea, or to Pontus, an ancient country south of it.

pon·ti·fex, pon′ti·feks″, *n.* pl. **pon·tif·i·ces,** pon·tif′i·sēz″. [L., usu. explained as *pons* (*pont*-) bridge, and *facere,* make.] A member of the principal college of priests in ancient Rome whose head was the *Pontifex Maximus,* or chief priest.

pon·tiff, pon′tif, *n.* Pontifex; chief priest. *Eccles.* the Pope; a bishop.

pon·tif·i·cal, pon·tif′i·kal, *a.* [L. *pontificalis,* < *pontifex.*] Of, pertaining to, or characteristic of a pontiff or pontifex; papal; ostentatiously dogmatic.—**pon·tif·i·cal·ly,** *adv.*

pon·tif·i·cal, pon·tif′i·kal, *n.* In the Western Church, a book containing the forms for the sacraments and rites to be performed by bishops; *pl.* the vestments and other insignia of a pontiff, esp. a bishop.

pon·tif·i·cate, pon·tif′i·kit″, pon·tif′i·kāt″, *n.* [L. *pontificatus.*] The office or term of office of a pontiff.—pon·tif′i·kāt″, *v.i.*—*pontificated, pontificating.* [M.L. *pontificatus,* pp. of *pontificare,* < L. *pontifex.*] To perform the function of a pontiff; to speak or behave dogmatically; officiate at pontifical mass.—**pon·tif·i·ca·tor,** *n.*

Pont l'É·vêque, pont le·vek′, *Fr.* pa̲N·lā·vek′, *n.* A pale yellow, soft-centered cheese.

pon·to·nier, pon″to·nēr′, *n.* [Fr.] A soldier having charge of pontoons; one who constructs pontoon bridges.

pon·toon, pon·tön′, *n.* [Fr. *ponton* < L. *pons, pontis,* a bridge.] A flat-bottomed boat or other float, as an airtight drum, used to support a temporary bridge spanning a river; *naut.* an inflatable device used to raise a submerged vessel. A float on a seaplane. Also **pon·ton,** pon′ton.

pon·toon bridge, *n.* A temporary bridge supported on pontoons.

po·ny, pō′nē, *n.* pl. **po·nies.** [Prob. < O.Fr. *poulenet,* dim. of *poulain,* colt, < L. *pullus,* young animal.] A horse of a small breed, specif. one not over 14 hands high; a small horse, esp. in western U.S.; something small of its kind; a small glass for liquor, or the amount of liquor it will hold; *slang,* a crib, translation, or other illicit aid. *Brit. slang,* the sum of £25.—*v.t., v.i.—ponied, ponying. Slang.* To prepare lessons, by means of a pony or crib; to pay, as in settling an account, used with *up.*

po·ny ex·press, *n.* A postal system operated through western U.S. during 1860–61, in which mail was carried by mounted relay riders.

po·ny·tail, pō′nē·tāl″, *n.* A long hair style in which the hair is pulled to the back of the crown, gathered with a rubber band or clip, and left to fall free, thus resembling a pony's tail.

pooch, pöch, *n. Slang,* a dog.

pood, pöd, *n.* A Russian weight, equal to 36.113 lbs.

poo·dle, pöd′l, *n.* [G. *pudel.*] One of three sizes of solid-colored house dogs having thick curly hair which is usu. trimmed in a stylized manner.

pooh, pö, pu̲, *interj.* An expression of scorn or contempt.

pooh bah, pö′ bä′, pö′ bä″, *n.* [From the character in Gilbert and Sullivan's *The Mikado.*] An inefficient person who holds many bureaucratic posts; any self-important individual.

pooh-pooh, pö″pö′, *v.t.* To express scorn or contempt for; to sneer at.

pool, pöl, *n.* [O.E. *pol* = M.L.G. *pōl* = D. *pool.*] A small body of standing, usu. fresh water; a small pond; a puddle; any small collection of liquid standing on a surface; as, a *pool* of blood; a still, deep place in a stream; a swimming pool; an underground pocket of oil or gas contained in porous rock.—*v.t., v.i.* To form or cause to form a pool; to collect, as blood in an organ.

pool, pöl, *n.* [Fr. *poule,* lit. 'hen.'] A federation of competing parties to reconcile interests, control prices, or the like; *finance,* a combination of individuals or organizations formed for the purpose of speculation, as for manipulating the prices of stocks. A combination of interests or funds for common advantage; a service or facility shared by a number of people; as, a car *pool;* the stakes in certain games; the total amount staked by a combination of bettors, as on a race, to be awarded to the successful bettor or bettors. A game played by two or more persons on a billiard table with six pockets, the object of the game being to pocket balls numbered 1–15 by means of cues; also *pocket billiards. Brit.* a game of billiards with a stake to which all players contribute; *fencing,* a competition in which each member of one team plays in succession each member of the other team.—*v.t.* To put, as interests or money, into a pool, or common stock or fund, as for distribution according to agreement; form a pool of; make a common interest of.—*v.i.* To enter into or form a pool.

pool·room, pöl′röm″, pöl′ru̲m″, *n.* A place, usu. public, where pool or billiards is played; also **pool hall, pool·hall.** *Slang,* a bookmaker's place of business.

poop, pöp, *n.* [Fr. *poupe,* < L. *puppis,* the poop.] Formerly, a ship's stern. A weather deck or superstructure at the stern of a ship; also **poop deck.** An enclosure under the poop deck; also **poop cab·in.**—*v.t. Naut.* To break over the stern of; to drive over the stern, as a wave.

poop, pöp, *v.t. Slang,* to exhaust or tire.—*v.i. Slang.* To become fatigued, usu. with *out;* to withdraw, usu. with *out.*

poop, pöp, *n. Slang,* information, possibly but not necessarily official.

poor, pu̲r, *a.* [O.Fr. *pouvre* (Fr. *pauvre*) < L. *pauper,* poor: cf. *pauper.*] Having little or nothing in the way of wealth, goods, or means of subsistence; lacking means to procure the comforts or the necessaries of life; *law,* dependent upon charity. Meagerly supplied or endowed with resources or funds; characterized by or showing poverty; deficient or lacking in something specified; as, a region *poor* in mineral deposits; deficient in desirable ingredients or qualities; as, *poor* soil; lean or emaciated, as cattle; of an inferior, inadequate, or unsatisfactory kind; as, *poor* health or eyesight; deficient in aptitude or ability; as, a *poor* head for figures; deficient in moral excellence; spiritless, cowardly, abject, or mean; scanty, meager, or paltry in amount or number; trifling or unimportant; humble or insignificant; unfortunate.—*n.* A poor person; poor persons collectively.—**poor·ish,** *a.*—**poor·ly,** *adv.* **poor·ness,** *n.*

poor box, *n.* A box, esp. in a church, for receiving contributions for the poor.

poor farm, *n.* A farm which houses and cares for needy persons at public expense.

poor·house, pu̲r′hous″, *n.* A residence for poor people which is maintained publicly.

poor law, *n.* A law providing for the use of public funds for the maintenance of the poor.

poor·ly, pu̲r′lē, *a.* Somewhat ill; indisposed;

not in good health.—*adv.* In a poor way; badly.

poor-spir·it·ed, pu̲r′spir′i·tid, *a.* Of little spirit; cowardly.—**poor-spir·it·ed·ness,** *n.* —**poor-spir·it·ed·ly,** *adv.*

poor white, *n.* A poverty-stricken white laborer or farmer of the southern U.S.: used pejoratively. Also **poor white trash.**

pop, pop, *n.* A popping; a short, quick, explosive sound; a shot with a firearm; an effervescent beverage, esp. one that is nonalcoholic.—*v.i.—popped, popping.* [Imit.] To make a short, quick, explosive sound or report; to burst open with such a sound, as popcorn; to shoot with a firearm; to come or go quickly, suddenly, or unexpectedly, used with *in, into, out, off, down,* or *up; protrude; baseball,* to hit a ball in a short high trajectory.—*v.t.* To cause to make a sudden, explosive sound; cause to burst open with such a sound; fire, as a gun; shoot; to put or thrust quickly, suddenly, or unexpectedly, with *in, into, out, up* or *down.*—*adv.* With a pop or explosive sound; quickly, suddenly, or unexpectedly; as: The engine went *pop.*—**pop the ques·tion,** *colloq.* to propose marriage.

pop, pop, *a. Colloq.* popular.

pop art, *n.* A style of painting and sculpture which employs examples of the popular communications media, as advertisements or comic strips, by either exaggerating them or faithfully reproducing them.—**pop art·ist,** *n.*

pop·corn, pop′ka̲rn″, *n.* A variety of Indian corn whose kernels on being heated burst into puffs of starchy material; popped corn.

pope, pōp, *n.* [O.E. *pāpa,* < L.L. *papa,* the pope, lit. 'father,' same word as *papa,* the childish name for father.] (*Often cap.*) the Bishop of Rome, the head of the Roman Catholic Church. One who assumes or is considered to have complete authority, as a pope; a priest or chaplain of the Eastern Orthodox Church.

pop·er·y, pō′pe·rē, *n.* The religion of the Church of Rome, including its doctrines and practices: used pejoratively.

pop·eyed, pop′īd″, *a.* Having wide, bulging eyes.

pop fly, *n. Baseball,* a short fly ball that can be caught by infield players. Also **pop·up.**

pop foul, *n. Baseball,* a pop fly into foul territory.

pop·gun, pop′gun″, *n.* A toy pellet gun which pops when fired.

pop·in·jay, pop′in·jā″, *n.* [O.E. *popingay,* Fr. *papegai,* Sp. and Pg. *papagayo,* L.Gr. *papagas,* < Ar. *babghā,* a parrakeet.] A fop or coxcomb. *Archaic,* a parrot; a bird-shaped target for archers.

pop·ish, pō′pish, *a.* Pertaining to the pope or the Roman Catholic Church: used pejoratively.—**pop·ish·ly,** *adv.*—**pop·ish·ness,** *n.*

pop·lar, pop′le̲r, *n.* [O.Fr. *poplier* (Fr. *pouplier*), < L. *populus,* poplar.] Any of various rapidly growing trees constituting the salicaceous genus *Populus,* yielding a light, soft wood, as the Lombardy and the white poplar; the wood itself; any of various trees resembling these, as the tulip tree.

pop·lin, pop′lin, *n.* [Fr. *popeline.*] Corded fabric of cotton, rayon, silk, or wool, used for clothing and household goods.

pop·lit·e·al, pop·lit′ē·al, pop″li·tē′al, *a.* [N.L. *popliteus,* < L. *poples* (*poplit*-), the ham.] *Anat.* of or pertaining to the ham, or part of the leg in back of the knee.

pop off, *v.i.* To go abruptly; to die suddenly; to talk volubly, often with anger.

pop·o·ver, pop′ō″ve̲r, *n.* A muffin made with a high proportion of eggs to flour and milk thus causing a hollow center and puffed top.

pop·per, pop′ẻr, n. One who or that which pops; a utensil for popping corn.

pop·pet, pop′it, n. Earlier form of puppet; a poppethead. *Mach.* a valve which in opening is lifted vertically from its seat instead of being hinged at one side; also **pop·pet valve**. *Chiefly Brit.* a term of endearment for a girl or child. *Naut.* a small wooden structure which carries the oarlock and is attached to the gunwale of a boat.

pop·pet·head, pop′it·hed″, n. The tailstock of a lathe.

pop·pied, pop′ēd, a. Covered or adorned with poppies; affected by or as by poppy juice or opium; listless.

pop·ple, pop′l, v.i.—poppled, poppling. [Dim. and freq. of *pop*.] To move quickly up and down in a bubbling manner, as boiling water.—n. This movement or its sound; choppy or heaving water.

pop·py, pop′ē, n. pl. **pop·pies**. [O.E. *popig, popaeg*, ult. < L. *papaver*, poppy.] Any plant of the genus *Papaver*, comprising herbs with showy flowers of various colors, including *P. somniferum*, which is the source of opium, and which yields a valuable oil; an extract, as opium, from such a plant. A bright orange-red color; also **pop·py red**.

pop·py·cock, pop′ē·kok″, n. *Colloq.* Idle talk; nonsense.

pop·py·head, pop′ē·hed″, n. A carved rosette or finial used to ornament the end post of a pew.

pop·py seed, n. The flavorful gray-black seed obtained from the poppy plant and used in baking.

pop·u·lace, pop′ū·las, n. [Fr. *populace*, It. *popolazzo*, < L. *populus*, the people (whence *popular, people*); the root is doubtful.] The common people; the multitude; population.

pop·u·lar, pop′ū·lẻr, a. [L. *popularis*.] Pleasing to or liked by the people in general; well-liked; pertaining to or of the common people; easy to comprehend; plain; familiar; constituted by or depending on the people; suitable to the majority of people; as, *popular* prices, *popular* music.—**pop·u·lar·ly**, adv.

pop·u·lar front, n. A temporary political coalition of leftist, liberal, and sometimes middle-of-the-road parties formed in opposition to a common political enemy, as fascism, and promoting liberal social reform. Also **peo·ple's front**.

pop·u·lar·i·ty, pop″ū·lar′i·tē, n. The state or quality of being popular, or esteemed by the people at large; good will or favor proceeding from the people.

pop·u·lar·ize, pop′ū·la·rīz″, v.t.—popularized, popularizing. To make popular; to make understandable to or spread among the people.—**pop·u·lar·i·za·tion**, n.—**pop·u·lar·iz·er**, n.

pop·u·lar sov·er·eign·ty, n. The doctrine that government is the trustee of the sovereign power of the populace, and must therefore conform to the general will in its actions; *hist.* the pre-Civil War ideology in America that the people of a new territory should decide domestic policy, esp. regarding slavery, through their own legislature, without federal interference.

pop·u·late, pop′ū·lāt″, v.t.—populated, populating. To inhabit; to furnish with inhabitants; to people.

pop·u·la·tion, pop″ū·lā′shan, n. The total number of persons inhabiting a country, city, or any district or area; the body of inhabitants of a place; the number or body of inhabitants of a particular race or class in a place; the act or process of populating; the state of a locality with reference to the number of its inhabitants.

pop·u·la·tion den·si·ty, n. The relation of population to the space it occupies,

expressed as a ratio, as people per square mile.

pop·u·la·tion ex·plo·sion, n. An extremely rapid rate of population increase.

Pop·u·list, pop′ū·list, n. A member of the Populist or People's Party.—a. Of or denoting the Populist Party or its doctrines. —**Pop·u·lis·tic**, a.

pop·u·lous, pop′ū·lus, a. [L. *populosus*.] Full of inhabitants; thickly settled with people; crowded.—**pop·u·lous·ly**, adv.—**pop·u·lous·ness**, n.

por·bea·gle, pẻr′bē′gl, n. [Cornish name; origin uncertain.] A shark of the genus *Lamna*, esp. *L. nasus*, a voracious species of the northern Atlantic and Pacific which attains a length of about ten feet.

por·ce·lain, pōr′se·lin, pẻr′se·lin, pōrs′lin, pẻrs′lin, n. [Fr. *porcelaine*, < It. *porcellana*, porcelain, orig. a kind of shell, appar. ult. < L. *porcus*, hog, pig.] A fine, strong, translucent ceramic material, usu. glazed; china; a vessel or object made of this material.—**por·ce·la·ne·ous**, **por·cel·la·ne·ous**, pōr″se·lā′nē·us, pẻr″se·lā′nē·us, a.

por·ce·lain e·nam·el, n. An opaque, glassy coating fused to a metal or to another enamel. Also *vitreous enamel*.

por·ce·lain·ize, pōr′se·la·nīz″, pẻr′se·la·nīz″, pōrs′la·nīz″, pẻrs′la·nīz″, v.t.—porcelainized, porcelainizing. To fire, as a metal, with a porcelain coating.

porch, pōrch, pärch, n. [Fr. *porche*, It. *portico*, < L. *porticus*, a porch, < *porta*, a gate, entrance.] An exterior appendage to a building forming a covered approach or vestibule to a doorway; a covered walk or portico; a veranda.—**the Porch**, a public portico in Athens, where Zeno, the Stoic philosopher, taught his disciples.

por·cine, pẻr′sin, pẻr′sīn, a. [L. *porcinus*, < *porcus*, a hog.] Pertaining to swine; like a swine; hoglike.

por·cu·pine, pẻr′kū·pīn″, n. [O.Fr. *porcespin*, lit. 'spine-hog'; < L. *porcus*, a pig, and *spina*, a spine or thorn.] Any of several rodents of the families *Hystricidae* and *Erethizontidae*, covered with sharp spines, or quills, which the animal can erect at will for his defense.

pore, pōr, pär, v.i.—pored, poring. [O.E. *poure*; origin uncertain; possibly same as *pour*.] To look with steady continued attention or application; to ponder; to read or examine anything with steady perseverance, usu. followed by *on, upon*, or *over*.

pore, pōr, pär, n. [Fr. *pore*, < L. *porus*, Gr. *poros*, a passage, a pore.] A minute opening, as in the skin or in plant leaves, through which fluids and other substances are excreted or absorbed; any small interstice of this nature, as in a stone or other solid.—**pored**, a. Possessing pores.

por·gy, pẻr′gē, n. pl. **por·gy**, **por·gies**. [Origin uncertain; prob. from several sources.] Any of numerous food fishes of the family *Sparidae*, esp. the red porgy, *Pagrus pagrus*, of Mediterranean and Atlantic waters, or a related fish, the scup, of the eastern U.S. coast.

po·rif·er·an, pō·rif′ẻr·an, pạ·rif′ẻr·an, po·rif′ẻr·an, n. Any of the invertebrates, as the sponges, that comprise the phylum *Porifera*.—a. Pertaining to or being in this phylum. Also **po·rif·er·al**.

po·rism, pōr′iz·um, pär′iz·um, n. [Gr. *porisma*, a corollary, < *porizō*, I gain.] One of a group of propositions of ancient mathematics, esp. one affirming the possibility of finding such conditions as will render a certain problem indeterminate or capable of innumerable solutions.

pork, pōrk, pärk, n. [O.Fr. Fr. *porc*, < L. *porcus*, hog, pig.] The flesh of swine used as food; *slang*, appropriations or favors

granted by governments for political reasons rather than because of public necessity.

pork bar·rel, n. *Slang*, a government bill, appropriation, or project undertaken or passed with the intent of placing legislators in the favor of their constituency.

pork·er, pōr′kẻr, pär′kẻr, n. A hog or pig, esp. one fattened for pork.

pork·pie hat, pōrk′pī″ hat, pärk′pī″, n. A man's hat, usu. of cloth or felt, with a low, flat crown and snap brim.

por·nog·ra·phy, pẻr·nog′ra·fē, n. [Gr. *pornē*, prostitute, *graphō*, I write.] Literature or art calculated solely to supply sexual excitement; obscene literature or art.—**por·nog·ra·pher**, pẻr·nog′ra·fẻr, n.—**por·no·graph·ic**, pẻr″no·graf′ik, a.—**por·no·graph·i·cal·ly**, adv.

po·ros·i·ty, pō·ros′i·tē, pạ·ros′i·tē, po·ros′i·tē, n. pl. **po·ros·i·ties**. State or property of being porous; porousness; the ratio of the volume of the pores of a material, as rock or soil, to the total volume of its mass; a pore.

po·rous, pōr′us, pär′us, a. Having many pores or interstices; permeable by liquids, light, or air.—**po·rous·ly**, adv.—**po·rous·ness**, n.

por·phy·rin, pẻr′fi·rin, n. Any of a group of metal-free pyrrole derivatives, formed in protoplasm by the decomposition of hemoglobin and chlorophyll.

por·phy·roid, pẻr′fi·roid″, n. A rock resembling porphyry; a sedimentary rock which has been metamorphosed so as to take on a porphyritic structure.

por·phy·ry, pẻr′fi·rē, n. pl. **por·phy·ries**. [Fr. *porphyre*, Pr. *porfiri*, < Gr. *porphyritēs*, lit. 'a purple-colored rock,' < *porphyra*, purple.] Orig. a very hard Egyptian rock containing crystals of rose-colored feldspar in a purplish base, susceptible of a fine polish and much used for sculpture; generally, any igneous rock in which crystals of feldspar or some other mineral are diffused through a compact, fine-grained base.—**por·phy·rit·ic**, pẻr″fi·rit′ik, a.

por·poise, pẻr′pos, n. pl. **por·poise**, **por·pois·es**. [O.Fr. *porpois, porpeis*, < L. *porcus*, hog, and *piscis*, fish.] Any of the gregarious cetaceans constituting the genus *Phocaena*, five to eight feet long, usu. blackish above and paler beneath, and having a blunt, rounded snout, esp. *P. phocaena*, the common porpoise; any of several other small cetaceans, as the common dolphin, *Delphinus delphis*.

por·rect, po·rekt′, pạ·rekt′, a. Extending forward; projecting.

por·ridge, pạr′ij, por′ij, n. [Perh. < L. *porrum, porrus*, a leek, and meaning orig. leek soup or broth; perh. a corruption of *pottage*.] *Brit.* a food made by slowly stirring oatmeal, or other meal, into boiling water or milk and cooking until thick.

por·rin·ger, pạr′in·jẻr, por′in·jẻr, n. [< *porridge*. The *n* has intruded as in *messenger*.] A small earthenware or metal bowl with one handle, for porridge, soup, or the like, used primarily by children.

port, pōrt, pärt, n. [O.E. *port*, < L. *portus*, harbor, haven.] A city or town at which ships load or unload; a recess, as of the sea or a lake, where vessels may take refuge from storms; a harbor; *colloq.* an airport. *Law*, any place where persons and merchandise are allowed to pass, by water or land, into and out of a country and where customs officers are stationed to inspect or appraise imported goods; also *port of entry*.

port, pōrt, pärt, n. [O.Fr. Fr. *porte*, < L. *porta*, gate, door, akin to *portus*, harbor, haven.] *Naut.* an opening in the side of a ship for loading cargo or for the admission of light and air; *mach.* an aperture for the passage of steam, air, or water. A small opening in an armored vehicle, airplane, or fortification for a gun or camera; *chiefly Sc.* a gate or portal, as of a town or fortress.

port, pōrt, part, *v.t.* [O.Fr. Fr. *porter*, < L. *portare*, carry.] *Milit.* to carry, as a rifle, with both hands, in a slanting direction across the front of the body, with the barrel or like part near the left shoulder.—*n.* [O.Fr. Fr. *port.*] *Milit.* the position of a rifle or other weapon when ported. Manner of bearing oneself; carriage.

port, pōrt, part, *n.* [Origin uncertain.] The left side of a ship or aircraft as one faces forward; also *larboard.*—*a.* Relating to port; on the left.—*v.t., v.i.* To turn or put to the left side.

port, pōrt, part, *n.* [< *Oporto,* whence it is shipped; *Oporto* means the *port.*] A type of sweet wine, usu. of a dark red color, orig. made in Portugal.

port·a·ble, pōr′ta·bl, par′ta·bl, *a.* [L. *portabilis.*] Capable of being carried or transported from place to place; easily carried.—*n.* An object which is portable.—**port·a·bil·i·ty,** *n.*—**port·a·bly,** *adv.*

por·tage, pōr′tij, par′tij, *n.* [O.Fr. Fr. *portage,* < *porter,* carry, E. *port.*] The act of carrying; carriage; the carrying of boats or goods overland from one navigable water to another; a place or course over which this must be done; cost of carriage or transporting.—*v.t., v.i.*—**portaged, portaging.**

por·tal, pōr′tal, par′tal, *n.* [O.Fr. *portal,* L.L. *portale,* < L. *porta,* a gate.] A door or gate, esp. a large and impressive one; the entrance to a mine, tunnel, or bridge.

por·tal, pōr′tal, par′tal, *a.* [N.L. *porta,* the transverse fissure of the liver, L. gate, door, E. *port.*] *Anat.* noting or pertaining to the transverse fissure of the liver.—*n.* The porta vein.

por·tal-to-por·tal pay, pōr′tal·to·pōr′tal pā′, par′tal·to·par′tal, *n.* A workman's pay computed from the time he enters his employer's property until he leaves it.

por·tal vein, *n. Anat.* a large vein carrying blood from the stomach, intestine, pancreas, and spleen to the liver.

por·ta·men·to, pōr″ta·men′tō, par″ta·men′tō, *It.* par″tä·men′ta, *n. pl.* **por·ta·men·ti, por·ta·men·tos,** pōr″ta·men′tē, par″ta·men′tē. [It.] *Mus.* the gliding from one note to another without a break.

por·ta·tive, pōr′ta·tiv, par′ta·tiv, *a.* [O.Fr. Fr. *portatif,* < L. *portare* (pp. *portatus*), carry, E. *port.*] Easily carried; portable; having or pertaining to the power or function of carrying.

port·cul·lis, pōrt·kul′is, part·kul′is, *n.* [Fr. *porte,* a gate, and *coulisse,* groove, < *couler,* to slip or slide.] A strong grating of timber or iron, made to slide in vertical grooves in the side posts of the entrance gate of a fortified place, and which can be lowered to cover the gate in case of assault.

Porte, pōrt, part, *n.* [The chief office of the Ottoman Empire is styled *Babi Ali,* lit. 'the High Gate,' from the gate (*bab*) of the palace at which justice was administered, the French translation of this term being *Sublime Porte,* hence the use of this word.] The Ottoman court; the government of the Ottoman Empire. Also **Sub·lime Porte.**

porte-co·chere, pōrt″kō·shâr′, pōrt″ko·shâr′, part″kō·shâr′, part″ko·shâr′, *n.* [Fr., 'gate for coaches.'] A carriage entrance leading into a courtyard; a porch at the door of a building for sheltering persons entering and leaving vehicles.

porte-mon·naie, pōrt′mun″ē, part′mun″ē, *Fr.* part·ma·ne′, *n. pl.* **porte-mon·naies,** pōrt′mun″ēz, part′mun″ēz, *Fr.* part·ma·ne′.

[Fr., 'carry-money.'] A purse or small pocketbook.

por·tend, pōr·tend′, par·tend′, *v.t.* [L. *portendere* (pp. *portentus*), point out, indicate, portend, < *por-* (= *pro*), before, and *tendere,* stretch, E. *tend.*] To indicate beforehand, or presage, as an omen does; to foreshadow.

por·tent, pōr′tent, par′tent, *n.* [L. *portentum,* prop. neut. of *portentus,* pp. of *portendere,* E. *portend.*] An indication or omen of something about to happen, esp. something momentous or calamitous; prophetic significance; a prodigy or marvel.

por·ten·tous, pōr·ten′tus, par·ten′tus, *a.* [L. *portentosus.*] Of the nature of a portent; of ominous significance; momentous; causing awe or amazement; prodigious.—**por·ten·tous·ly,** *adv.*—**por·ten·tous·ness,** *n.*

por·ter, pōr′tèr, par′tèr, *n.* [Fr. *portier.*] One who has charge of a door or gate; a doorkeeper.

por·ter, pōr′tèr, par′tèr, *n.* [Fr. *porteur,* < *porter,* to carry.] A carrier; a person who carries or conveys burdens or luggage for hire, as at a railroad terminal; an attendant in a railroad sleeping car or parlor car.

por·ter, pōr′tèr, par′tèr, *n.* A dark-colored malt liquor made wholly or partially with malt dried at a very high temperature.

por·ter·age, pōr′tèr·ij, par′tèr·ij, *n.* The carrying of burdens or parcels by a porter; money charged for this work.

por·ter·house, pōr′tèr·hous″, par′tèr·hous″, *n.* A choice cut of beefsteak from between the prime ribs and the sirloin; *archaic,* a house at which porter and other liquors are retailed.

port·fo·li·o, pōrt·fō′lē·ō″, part·fō′lē·ō″, *n. pl.* **port·fo·li·os.** [In imitation of Fr. *porte-feuille,* a portfolio, the office of a minister—*porter,* to carry (L. *portare*), and *feuille,* a leaf, L. *folium.*] A portable case in the form of a large book, for holding loose drawings or papers; a case of this type for transporting documents of state; the office and functions of a minister of state or cabinet member; the itemized securities and investments held by an investor or bank.

port·hole, pōrt′hōl″, part′hōl″, *n.* An opening like a window in a ship's side, for admitting light and air; an opening in a wall or door through which to shoot.

por·ti·co, pōr′ti·kō″, par′ti·kō″, *n. pl.* **por·ti·coes, por·ti·cos.** [It. and Sp. *portico,* < L. *porticus.*] *Arch.* a kind of porch fronted with columns, often at the entrance of a building.

por·tiere, por·tière, pōr·tyâr′, par·tyâr′, pōr″tē·âr′, par″tē·âr′, *Fr.* par·tyer′, *n.* [Fr., < *porte,* door.] A curtain hung at a doorway, either to replace the door or for decoration.

por·tion, pōr′shan, par′shan, *n.* [L. *portio, portionis,* a portion; akin to *pars, partis,* a part.] That which is divided off, as a part from a whole; a part considered by itself though not actually divided; an allotment; share; a person's lot or fate; the amount of food usu. served one person; the share of an estate to be inherited; a dowry.—*v.t.* To divide or distribute into portions or shares, often followed by *out*; to allot in shares; to endow with a portion, as a dowry or inheritance.—**por·tion·less,** *a.*

Port·land ce·ment, pōrt′land si·ment′, part′land, *n.* (*Sometimes l.c.*) a kind of hydraulic cement usu. made by burning a mixture of limestone and clay in a kiln.

port·ly, pōrt′lē, part′lē, *a.*—**portlier, portliest.** [< *port,* carriage, mien, demeanor.] Rather heavy or corpulent; stout. *Archaic, dial.* grand or dignified in appearance; stately.—**port·li·ness,** *n.*

port·man·teau, pōrt′man′tō, part′man′tō,

port″man·tō′, part″man·tō′, *n. pl.* **port·man·teaus, port·man·teaux,** pōrt·man′tōz, part·man′tōz, pōrt″man·tōz′, part″man·tōz′, pōrt″man·tō′, part·man·tō′, pōrt″man·tō′, part″man·tō′. [Fr. *portemanteau,* < *porter,* to carry, and *manteau,* a cloak or mantle.] A case or trunk, usu. leather and often divided into two compartments, for carrying clothing while traveling; formerly, a leather case attached to a saddle behind the rider.

port·man·teau word, *n. Ling.* a blend: a word created by combining parts of existing words.

port of call, *n.* A port where a ship makes a brief stop, for repairs, to pick up or discharge cargo or passengers, or as one of a scheduled series of such stops.

port of en·try, *n. Law,* a port.

por·trait, pōr′trit, pōr′trāt, par′trit, par′trāt, *n.* [Fr. *portrait,* pp. of *portraire,* to portray.] A painted picture or representation of a person, esp. of a face, generally drawn from life; a vivid description or delineation in words.—**por·trait·ist,** pōr′tri·tist, pōr′trā·tist, par′tri·tist, par′trā·tist, *n.*

por·trai·ture, pōr′tri·chèr, par′tri·chèr, *n.* [Fr.] A portrait; the art of drawing portraits, or of vividly describing in words.

por·tray, pōr·trā′, par·trā′, *v.t.* [Fr. *portraire,* to portray, to depict; < L. *portraho,* to draw forth.] To paint or draw the likeness of; to depict; enact the part of, as in a play; to describe in words.—**por·tray·er,** *n.*

por·tray·al, pōr·trā′al, par·trā′al, *n.* The act of portraying; representation; a portrait.

Por·tu·guese, pōr″cha·gēz′, pōr″cha·gēs′, par″cha·gēz′, par″cha·gēs′, pōr″cha·gēs′, par″cha·gēz′, par″cha·gēs′, *a.* Of or pertaining to Portugal, its people, or their language.—*n. pl.* **Por·tu·guese.** One born or residing in Portugal; the language spoken in Portugal and Brazil.

Por·tu·guese man-of-war, *n.* Any of several large oceanic coelenterates of the genus *Physalia,* having a large, crested, bladderlike structure by which they are buoyed up and from which hang numerous tentacles.

por·tu·lac·a, pōr″cha·lak′a, par″cha·lak′a, *n.* [L., purslane.] Any of several widely distributed herbs of the purslane family in the genus *Portulaca,* esp. *P. grandiflora,* a trailing flower garden annual.

po·sa·da, pa·sä′THä, *n. pl.* **po·sa·das,** pä·sa′THäs. [Sp.] An inn.

pose, pōz, *v.i.*—**posed, posing.** [O.Fr. Fr. *poser,* put, < M.L. *pausare,* lay down (a sense due to confusion with L. *ponere,* place, put: see *position.*), L. halt, cease < L. *pausa,* E. *pause.* Compounds of O.Fr. Fr. *poser,* E. *pose* are regularly associated with derivatives actually belonging to L. *ponere* (*composite, composition, disposition,* etc.).] To assume or hold a physical position or attitude for some artistic purpose; to affect a particular character, as with a view to the impression made on others; represent oneself, esp. falsely, as: He *posed* as an expert on French literature.—*v.t.* To place in a suitable position or attitude for a picture, tableau, or the like; to state, assert, or propound.—*n.* An attitude or posture of body, esp. one assumed in posing, or exhibited by a figure in a picture, sculpture, tableau, or the like; a mental attitude, esp. one assumed for mere effect; affectation.—**pos·er,** pō′zèr, *n.* One who poses.

pose, pōz, *v.t.*—**posed, posing.** [For obs. *appose,* for *oppose,* in an obs. sense.] To embarrass or puzzle by a difficult question or problem.—**pos·er,** pō′zèr, *n.* A question that puzzles or baffles.

po·seur, pō·zŭr′, *Fr.* pa·zOER′, *n. pl.* **po·seurs,** pa·zOERZ′. [Fr.] One who affects a particular manner or attitude with a view to the impression made on others.

posh, posh, *a.* Elegant or high-class.

pos·it, poz′it, *v.t.* [L. *pono, positum,* to place.] To set firmly; fix. To lay down as a position or principle; assume a fact; postulate; affirm as existent.

po·si·tion, po·zish′an, *n.* [Fr. *position,* L. *positio,* < *pono, positum,* to place, set, which appears as *-pound* in *compound,* etc., as *-pone* in post*pone,* and is seen also in *deposit, opposite, posture,* etc.] Situation, place, or location, esp. with reference to other objects; customary or appropriate place; a condition or situation which is advantageous or prestigious; rank or standing in society; status; situation of employment; a post or job; manner of standing or of being placed; attitude or posture of the body; as, in a prone *position;* mental attitude; that on which one takes a stand; point of view; the act of positing; a principle or thesis laid down.— *v.t.* To place; to put into correct position; to locate.—**po·si·tion·al**, *a.*—**po·si·tion·er**, *n.*

pos·i·tive, poz′i·tiv, *a.* [O.Fr. Fr. *positif,* < L. *positivus,* < *ponere.*] Explicitly laid down or expressed; as, a *positive* declaration; determined by enactment or convention; as, *positive* law; admitting of no question; as, *positive* proof; stated; definite; emphatic; confident in opinion or assertion, as a person; fully assured; overconfident or dogmatic; without relation to or comparison with other things: opposed to *relative* and *comparative;* absolute; having, or considered to have, actual existence; real; concerned with or based on matters of experience; as, *positive* philosophy; practical; not speculative or theoretical; concentrating on what is good or hopeful; constructive; consisting in or characterized by the presence or possession of distinguishing or marked qualities or features: opposed to *negative;* measured or proceeding in a direction assumed as that of increase, progress, or onward motion; of a government, assuming a control of activities beyond that needed merely to maintain law and order. *Elect.* noting or pertaining to the kind of electricity developed on glass when rubbed with silk; of a point or part in an electrical circuit, having a higher electric potential than that of another point or part, and away from which the current flows. *Chem.* of an element or radical, having a tendency to lose electrons; basic. *Photog.* showing the lights and shades as seen in the original print, not reversed; *gram.* denoting the primary, uncompared form of an adverb or adjective; *math.* denoting a quantity greater than zero; *biol.* of an organism, moving toward a stimulus, as light; *bact.* indicating the presence of bacteria that cause disease; *mach.* noting or relating to a motion or part which has a fixed, definite, or constant operation.—*n.* Something positive; a positive quality or characteristic; a positive quantity or symbol; *photog.* a positive picture; *gram.* the positive degree, or that form of an adjective or adverb expressing it.—**pos·i·tive·ly**, *adv.*—**pos·i·tive·ness**, *n.*

pos·i·tiv·ism, poz′i·ti·viz″um, *n.* [Fr. *positivisme.*] The state or quality of being positive; definiteness; assurance; a philosophical system founded by Auguste Comte, which concerns itself only with positive facts and phenomena, excluding speculation upon ultimate causes or origins.—**pos·i·tiv·ist**, *n.*—**pos·i·tiv·is·tic**, *a.*

pos·i·tron, poz′i·tron″, *n. Phys.* a positively charged particle with a mass and ionizing power equal to that of an electron.

pos·se, pos′ē, *n.* [M.L., power, force, noun use of L. *posse,* inf., be able, have

power.] A posse comitatus; a body or force armed with legal authority.

pos·se co·mi·ta·tus, pos′ē kom″i·tā′tus, pos′ē kom″i·tā′tus, *n.* [M.L., 'power of the county.'] The body of men that a sheriff is empowered to call into service, usu. in case of emergency; a body of men so called into service.

pos·sess, po·zes′, *v.t.* [O.Fr. *possesser,* L. *possidere* (pp. *possessus*), possess, own.] To have as property; have belonging to one; own; to have as a faculty, quality, or attribute; as, to *possess* patience; to have knowledge of or be conversant with, as a language; maintain control over, as oneself or one's mind; of a spirit, esp. an evil one, to occupy and control, or dominate from within, as a person; of a feeling or idea, to dominate or actuate after the manner of such a spirit, as: She was *possessed* by hatred. To make, as a person, the owner, holder, or master of property or information; to cause to be dominated or influenced, as by a feeling or idea; of a man, to have sexual relations with, as one of the opposite sex.—**pos·ses·sor**, *n.*

pos·sessed, po·zest′, *a.* Dominated or moved by a passion, madness, or an evil spirit; demented. Self-possessed; calm. Possessing or having, as: She is *possessed* of considerable talent.—**pos·sess·ed·ly**, po·zes′id·lē, po·zest′lē, *adv.*—**pos·sess·ed·ness**, *n.*

pos·ses·sion, po·zesh′an, *n.* [O.Fr. Fr. *possession,* < L. *possessio(n-).*] The act or fact of possessing; the state of being possessed; ownership; actual holding or occupancy, as distinct from ownership; a thing possessed; *pl.* property or wealth. A foreign dominion of a country; control over oneself or one's mind; domination or actuation by a feeling or idea.—**pos·ses·sion·al**, *a.*

pos·ses·sive, po·zes′iv, *a.* [L. *possessivus.*] Of or pertaining to possession or ownership; having a desire to possess; wishing to have complete emotional control over another person. *Gram.* denoting or relating to possession or ownership; as, a *possessive* pronoun or adjective; noting the case that expresses possession or ownership.—**pos·ses·sive·ly**, *adv.*—**pos·ses·sive·ness**, *n.*

pos·ses·sive, po·zes′iv, *n. Gram.* The possessive case; a form or a construction in the possessive.

pos·ses·sive ad·jec·tive, *n. Gram.* a pronominal adjective indicating possession; as, *his* coat.

pos·ses·sive pro·noun, *n. Gram.* a pronoun deriving from one of the personal pronouns and denoting possession, as: That glove is *mine.*

pos·ses·so·ry, po·zes′o·rē, *a.* Of or pertaining to possession; having possession; arising out of possession.

pos·set, pos′it, *n.* [Cf. W. *posel,* curdled milk, a posset, < *posiaw,* to gather.] A drink composed of hot milk curdled by wine or ale, and usu. sweetened and spiced.

pos·si·bil·i·ty, pos″i·bil′i·tē, *n. pl.* **pos·si·bil·i·ties**. The state or condition of being possible; something that is possible.

pos·si·ble, pos′i·bl, *a.* [L. *possibilis,* < *posse,* to be able, < *potis,* able, and *esse,* to be.] That may be or may exist; that may be now, or may happen or come to pass; that may be true; capable of coming to pass.

pos·si·bly, pos′i·blē, *adv.* Perhaps; in a possible manner; perchance.

pos·sum, pos′um, *n.* Opossum.

post, pōst, *n.* [O.E. *post,* < L. *postis,* post.] A stout piece of timber, metal, or the like, set upright as a support or a point of attachment; as, the *posts* of a door, a sign *post;* a pole marking the starting and winning positions on a racetrack.—*v.t.*

To affix, as a notice, to a post or wall; to bring to public notice by or as by a placard; as, to *post* a person for nomination; to *post* a reward; denounce by public notice or declaration; as, to *post* a person as a criminal; enter the name of in a published list; publish the name of, as a ship, as missing or lost; to placard, as a wall, with notices or bills.

post, pōst, *n.* [Fr. *poste,* < It. *posto,* < L. *positum,* pp. neut. of *ponere,* place, put: cf. *position* and *post.*] A position of duty, employment, or trust, to which one is assigned or appointed; the station, or the round or beat, of a soldier, sentry, or other person on guard or watch; a military position or station; a local branch of an ex-servicemen's organization; a trading post. —*v.t.* To station at a post or place as a sentry; *milit., naval,* to appoint to a post of command.—**first post** and **last post,** *Brit. milit.* either of two bugle calls giving notice of the hour for retiring for the night, comparable to *taps.*

post, pōst, *n.* [Fr. *poste,* < It. *posta,* < L. *posita,* pp. fem. of *ponere,* place, put: cf. *post.*] A single dispatch or delivery of mail, or the mail itself; the letters coming to a single person or recipient; an established service or system for the conveyance of letters, esp. under governmental authority; a post office or a postal letter box. *Archaic,* one of a series of fixed stations along a route, for furnishing relays of men and horses for carrying letters; one who travels express, esp. over a fixed route, with letters. —*v.t.* To place in a post office or a letter box for transmission; mail. *Bookkeeping,* to transfer, as an entry or item, as from the journal to the ledger; enter, as an item, in due place and form; make all the requisite entries in the ledger. To supply with information or inform.—*v.i.* To travel with post horses; to travel with speed; go or pass rapidly; *horsemanship,* to rise up from the saddle and fall back in rhythm with the horse's gait.—*adv.* By post horses; by post or courier; with speed or haste.

post·age, pō′stij, *n.* The charge for the conveyance of a letter or other matter sent by post or mail, ordinarily prepaid by means of a stamp or stamps.

post·age me·ter, *n.* A machine for printing markings as a substitute for stamps on letters sent in bulk, and for tabulating the postage cost.

post·age stamp, *n.* An official stamp in the form of a design on an envelope, or a printed adhesive label to be affixed to a letter or other mail, as evidence of prepayment of the required postage.

post·al, pōs′tal, *a.* Relating to the post office or the carrying of mails.

post·al card, *n.* See *post card.*

post·ax·i·al, pōst·ak′sē·al, *a.* Pertaining to or situated behind a body axis; of vertebrates, pertaining to the posterior side of a limb.—**post·ax·i·al·ly**, *adv.*

post bel·lum, pōst″bel′um, *a.* [L.] Concerning the period following a war, esp. the Civil War.

post·box, pōst′boks″, *n.* A mailbox, usu. one for public use.

post card, *n.* Any card, often with a picture on it, to which a stamp may be affixed for transmittal through the mail. A similar card, on which a stamp has been printed, issued by the government; also *postal card.*

post chaise, *n.* A horse-drawn carriage formerly used to transport passengers and mail.

post·com·mun·ion, pōst″ko·mūn′yan, *n. Eccles.* a prayer of thanksgiving and petition said or sung after communion has been received.

post·date, pōst·dāt′, *v.t.*—**postdated,** *post-dating.* To date, as a check, letter, or other document, later than the actual date of execution; to come later in time.

post·di·lu·vi·an, pōst″di·lŏ′vē·an, a. [L.] *Bib.* being or happening after the Flood in Noah's time. Also **post·di·lu·vi·al.**—n. A person who lived following the Flood.

post·doc·tor·al, pōst·dok′tẽr·al, a. Of or relating to advanced study or professional work after completion of one's doctorate.

post·er, pō′stẽr, n. A large printed bill or placard posted for advertising or public information; one who posts placards.

poste res·tante, pōst″ re·stänt′, *Brit.* pōst″ res′tänt, *Fr.* pạst res·täɴt′, n. [Fr., 'post remaining.'] A direction written on mail which is to remain at the post office until called for; *Brit.* general delivery department in a post office.

pos·te·ri·or, po·stēr′ē·ẽr, a. [L., compar. of *posterus*, coming after, < *post*, behind, after.] Situated behind, or hinder, as opposed to *anterior*; coming after in order, as in a series; coming after in time, as opposed to *prior*; later; subsequent, sometimes followed by *to*.—n. The hinder part of the body; the buttocks.—**pos·te·ri·or·i·ty**, po·stēr″ē·ạr′i·tē, po·stēr′·ē·or′i·tē, n. Posterior position or date. —**pos·te·ri·or·ly**, adv.

pos·ter·i·ty, po·ster′i·tē, n. [L. *posteritas*, < *posterus*, later.] All future or succeeding generations; the descendants that proceed from one progenitor.

pos·tern, pō′stẽrn, pos′tẽrn, n. [O.Fr. *posterne*, < L.L. *posterna*, *posterula*, a secret means of exit, < L. *posterus*, behind, posterior, < *post*, behind.] A back door or gate; a private entrance; any small door or gate that is not the main entrance.—a.

post ex·change, n. *U.S. Army*, a retail establishment operated by the Army on a military base where miscellaneous goods may be purchased by military personnel and other authorized persons. Abbr. *PX*.

post·ex·il·ic, pōst″eg·zil′ik, pōst″ek·zil′ik, a. Subsequent to the Babylonian exile or captivity of the Jews, 597–538 B.C.

post·gla·cial, pōst·glā′shal, a. *Geol.* existing or occurring subsequent to a glacial period.

post·grad·u·ate, pōst·graj′ŏ·it, pōst·graj′·ŏ·āt″, n. One who engages in advanced academic studies after graduation, usu. from high school or college.—a. Pertaining to such a student or to such studies.

post·haste, pōst·hāst′, n. *Archaic*, haste or speed.—adv. With great speed; promptly.

post horse, n. Formerly, a horse for the use of one riding post, kept at a post station along a fixed route.

post·hu·mous, pos′chạ·mus, pos′chụ·mus, a. [L. *postumus*, last, superl. of *posterus*, coming after, < *post*, behind.] Born after the death of the father; published after the death of the author; being or continuing after one's decease.—**post·hu·mous·ly**, adv.—**post·hu·mous·ness**, n.

post·hyp·not·ic, pōst″hip·not′ik, a. Of or pertaining to the period of time following hypnosis.

pos·tiche, pạ·stēsh′, po·stēsh′, a. [Fr., < It. *posticcio*, for *apposticcio*, *appositizio*, put on, superadded, factitious, false, < L. *appositus*.] Superadded, esp. inappropriately, as a sculptural or achitectural ornament; artificial, counterfeit, or false.— n. An imitation or substitute; pretense; a false hairpiece, switch.

pos·til·ion, *Brit.* **pos·til·lion**, pō·stil′yon, po·stil′yon, n. [Fr. *postillon*, < It. *postiglione*, < *posta*, E. *post*.] One who rides the near horse of the leaders when four or more horses are used to draw a carriage, or one who rides the near horse when only one pair is used with no driver on the box.

Post-Im·pres·sion·ism, pōst″im·presh′·a·niz″um, n. (*Often l.c.*) the doctrines and

methods of certain artists at the close of the 19th century, who opposed the objective realism and scientific methods of the later impressionists and maintained the theory that art must be expressive of the artist's subjective point of view, emphasizing form and color relationships.—**Post-Im·pres·sion·ist**, n.—**Post-Im·pres·sion·is·tic**, a.

post·lude, pōst′lŏd, n. *Mus.* A concluding piece or movement; a voluntary of organ music at the end of a church service.

post·man, pōst′man, n. pl. **post·men.** A letter carrier; mailman.

post·mark, pōst′märk″, n. An official mark stamped on a letter or other mail, to cancel the postage stamp and indicate the place and date of sending or of receipt.— v.t. To stamp with a postmark.

post·mas·ter, pōst′mas″tẽr, pōst′mä″stẽr, n. The official in charge of a post office.

post·mas·ter gen·er·al, n. pl. **post·-mas·ters gen·er·al.** The chief executive of a country's postal system.

post me·rid·i·em, pōst″ me·rid′ē·em, a. [L.] After noon. Abbr. *p.m.*, *P.M.*

post·mil·len·ni·al, pōst″mi·len′ē·al, a. Of or pertaining to the period following the millennium.—**post·mil·len·ni·al·ly**, adv.

post·mil·len·ni·al·ism, pōst″mi·len′ē·a·liz″um, n. The doctrine or belief that the second coming of Christ will follow the millennium.—**post·mil·len·ni·al·ist**, n.

post·mis·tress, pōst′mis″tris, n. A woman who has charge of a post office.

post·mor·tem, pōst″·mạr′tem, a. [L. *post mortem*, after death.] Subsequent to death, as an examination of the body.—n. A post-mortem examination; an autopsy.

post·mor·tem ex·am·i·na·tion, n. An examination of a body made after death; an autopsy.

post·na·sal, pōst″nā′zal, a. Pertaining to the posterior cavities of the nose; occurring behind the nose; as, *postnasal* drip.—n.

post·na·tal, pōst″nāt′al, a. Subsequent to birth.—**post·na·tal·ly**, adv.

post·nup·tial, pōst″nup′shal, pōst″nup′·chal, a. Being or happening after marriage. —**post·nup·tial·ly**, adv.

post·o·bit, pōst″·ō′bit, pōst″·ob′it, a. Effective after a particular person's death.

post·o·bit bond, n. A bond given by a borrower to repay a sum of money upon the death of some specified person from whom the borrower expects an inheritance.

post of·fice, n. The governmental department charged with the conveyance of letters; an office or station of a governmental postal system, for receiving, distributing, and transmitting mail, selling postage stamps, and other services.

post·paid, pōst′pād′, a., adv. Having the postage prepaid, as a letter or other mailing.

post·par·tum, pōst″pär′tum, a. *Med.* after childbirth.

post·pone, pōst″·pōn′, v.t.—postponed, post-poning. [L. *postpono—post*, after, and *pono*, to put.] To put off; to defer to a future or later time; to subordinate.—**post·pon·a·ble**, a. —**post·pone·ment**, n.—**post·pon·er**, n.

post·po·si·tion, pōst″po·zish′an, pōst″po·zish″an, n. The act of placing after; *gram.* a word or particle following the word to which it is related, esp. a suffixed particle functioning as a preposition, as *ward* in *skyward*.—**post·po·si·tion·al**, a.—**post·po·si·tion·al·ly**, adv.

post po·si·tion, n. *Horse racing.* The assigned position of each horse at the start of a race, positions being in numerical order from the inside rail; the favored starting position, number one, from which the horse runs the shortest distance.

post·pos·i·tive, pōst″poz′i·tiv, a. *Gram.* placed after something.—n. *Gram.* a postposition.—**post·pos·i·tive·ly**, adv.

post·pran·di·al, pōst·pran′dē·al, a. [L.] Happening after a meal, esp. dinner.

pos·trorse, pos′trạrs, po·strạrs′, a. Retrorse.

post·script, pōst′skript″, pōs′skript″, n. [L. *post*, after, and *scriptum*, written.] An addition to a letter after it is concluded and signed by the writer; any addition appended to a book or composition; something appended. Abbr. *p.s.*, *P.S.*

pos·tu·lan·cy, pos′chạ·lan·sē, n. pl. **pos·tu·lan·cies.** The condition or period of time of being a postulant, esp. in a religious order.

pos·tu·lant, pos′chạ·lant, n. [Fr. *postulant*, < L. *postulans*.] A petitioner or applicant for something; a candidate for admission into a religious order; a person aspiring to ordination in the Episcopal Church who is being considered for acceptance as a candidate for the ministry.

pos·tu·late, pos′chạ·lāt″, v.t.—postulated, postulating. [L. *postulatus*, pp. of *postulare*, ask, demand, prob. < *poscere*, to ask.] To ask, demand, or claim; to claim or assume the existence or truth of, esp. as a basis for reasoning; assume without proof, or as self-evident.—**pos·tu·la·tion**, n.

pos·tu·late, pos′chạ·lit, pos′chạ·lāt″, n. [L. *postulatum*, prop. pp. neut.] Something postulated or assumed without proof as a basis for reasoning or as self-evident; a fundamental principle; an axiom; a prerequisite.

pos·tu·la·tor, pos′chạ·lā″tẽr, n. *Rom. Cath. Ch.* an official who petitions that a deceased person be beatified or canonized.

pos·ture, pos′chẽr, n. [Fr. *posture* = It. *postura*, < L. *positura*, < *ponere*, place, put.] The relative disposition of the various parts of anything; the position or carriage of the body and limbs as a whole; as, a change of *posture*; an unnatural attitude, pose, or contortion of the body; a mental or spiritual attitude; a position, condition, or state, esp. of affairs.—v.t.— postured, posturing. To place in a particular posture or attitude, or dispose in postures. —v.i. To assume a particular posture or mental attitude, esp. one that is affected or unnatural.—**pos·tur·er**, n.— **pos·tur·al**, a.

post·war, pōst′wạr′, a. Belonging to the period after a war.

po·sy, pō′zē, n. pl. **po·sies.** [Corrupted from *poesy*, being orig. a piece of poetry.] A single flower; a nosegay; a bunch of flowers.

pot, pot, n. [O.E. *pott* = D. and L.G. *pot* = O.Fr. Fr. *pot*, pot.] An earthen, metallic, or other vessel, usu. rounded and deep, used for domestic or other purposes; a container holding a growing plant; a vessel with its contents; the quantity it will hold; a potful; a vessel to hold liquor or to drink liquor from; a potful of liquor; liquor or drink; a wicker vessel for trapping fish or crustaceans; a state of gradual ruination. *Brit.* a chimney pot. *Slang*, a large sum of money; marijuana. *Cards*, the aggregate of bets at stake at one time.— v.t.—potted, potting. To put into a pot; put up and preserve in a pot; cook or stew in a pot; plant in a flower pot; to shoot or kill; to bring down or shoot for food without regard for the rules of sport.—v.i. *Slang*, to take a pot shot; shoot.

po·ta·ble, pō′tạ·bl, a. [L.L. *potabilis*, < L. *poto*, to drink.] Suitable for drinking.—n. (*Often pl.*) something that may be drunk.— **po·ta·bil·i·ty**, **po·ta·ble·ness**, n.

po·tage, pō·täzh′, *Fr.* pạ·täzh′, n. [Fr.] Soup.

pot·ash, pot′ash″, n. [Orig. in *pot-ashes*, pl., = D. *potaschen*.] Potassium carbonate, esp. the crude impure form obtained from wood ashes; potassium hydroxide.

po·tas·si·um, po·tas′ē·um, *n.* [M.L.] *Chem.* a soft, whitish metallic element found combined in nature. Sym. K, at. no. 19, at. wt. 39.102. See Periodic Table of Elements.—**po·tas·sic,** po·tas′ik, *a.*

po·tas·si·um bro·mide, *n. Chem.* a water-soluble, crystalline powder, KBr, used in photographic and engraving processes, and in certain medicinal preparations.

po·tas·si·um car·bon·ate, *n. Chem.* a white solid, K_2CO_3, used in the manufacture of glass, soap, and other products.

po·tas·si·um chlo·rate, *n. Chem.* a poisonous solid salt, $KClO_3$, frequently used as the oxidizing agent by manufacturers of disinfectants and bleaches, as well as explosives, matches, and fireworks.

po·tas·si·um chlo·ride, *n. Chem.* a solid water-soluble salt, KCl, used as a source in the commercial preparation of various potassium compounds, and in mineral water and fertilizers.

po·tas·si·um cy·a·nide, *n. Chem.* a water-soluble, poisonous white powder, KCN, with a slight almondlike odor: used principally in photography and metallurgy.

po·tas·si·um di·chro·mate, *n. Chem.* a poisonous orange-red crystalline compound, $K_2Cr_2O_7$, used in dyeing and photography.

po·tas·si·um hy·drox·ide, *n. Chem.* a white caustic solid, KOH, used in making soft soap. Also *potash.*

po·tas·si·um ni·trate, *n. Chem.* a compound, KNO_3, used in preservatives, fertilizers, and gunpowders; niter; saltpeter.

po·tas·si·um per·man·ga·nate, *n. Chem.* a nearly black crystalline compound, $KMnO_4$, used as an oxidizing agent, an astringent, and a disinfectant.

po·tas·si·um sul·fate, *n. Chem.* a water-soluble salt, K_2SO_4, chiefly important in the manufacture of alums, fertilizers, and mineral water.

po·ta·tion, pō·tā′shan, *n.* The act of drinking; a drinking bout; a draft; a drink, esp. alcoholic.

po·ta·to, po·tā′tō, *n. pl.* **po·ta·toes.** [Sp. *patata,* white potato, *batata,* sweet potato; < Haitian.] The edible tuber of a cultivated plant, *Solanum tuberosum;* the plant itself. Also *Irish potato, white potato.* See *sweet potato*

po·ta·to bee·tle, *n.* A beetle, *Leptinotarsa decemlineata,* bearing yellow and black stripes, and causing great damage to potato plants by feeding on the leaves. Also **po·ta·to bug, Col·o·rad·o bee·tle.**

po·ta·to chip, *n.* A paper-thin potato slice, fried to a crispy state, and salted.

po·ta·to·ry, pō′ta·tōr″ē, pō′ta·tạr″ē, *a.* [L. *potatorius,* < *potare,* drink.] Of, pertaining to, or given to drinking.

pot-au-feu, pạ·tō·fœ′, *n. Fr. cookery,* a stew of meat and vegetables.

pot·bel·ly, pot′bel′ē, *n. pl.* **pot·bel·lies.** A protuberant belly.—**pot·bel·lied,** pot′bel′-ēd, *a.*

pot·boil·er, pot′boi′lẽr, *n. Colloq.* a work of literature or art, usu. inferior in content and structure, produced merely to provide monetary gain.—**pot·boil,** *v.i.* To author potboilers.

pot cheese, *n.* Cottage cheese.

po·teen, pō·tēn′, *n.* [< Ir. *potir,* little pot.] In Ireland, whiskey illicitly distilled. Also **po·theen,** pō·thēn′.

po·ten·cy, pōt′en·sē, *n. pl.* **po·ten·cies.** The state or quality of being potent; authority; strength; potentiality; an influential person or thing. Also **po·tence,** pōt′ens.

po·tent, pōt′ent, *a.* [L. *potens* (*potent-*), able, powerful, ppr. of *posse,* be able, have power, < *potis,* able, and *esse,* be: cf. Skt.

pati, master, lord, husband, Gr. *posis,* husband, *despotes,* master, lord, E. *despot.*] Possessed of great power or authority; powerful; mighty; exercising great moral influence; cogent or effective, as reasons or motives; producing powerful physical or chemical effects, as a drug; possessing sexual power, usu. said of a male.—**po·tent·ly,** *adv.*

po·ten·tate, pōt′en·tāt″, *n.* [Fr. *potentat.*] A person who possesses great power or sway; a prince; a sovereign; an emperor, king, or monarch.

po·ten·tial, po·ten′shal, *a.* [L. *potentia,* power.] Being a possibility, not an actuality; latent; that may be manifested; *gram.* being that form of the verb used to express the power, possibility, liberty, or necessity of an action or of being, as: I *may go,* he *can write.*—*n.* Anything that may be possible; a possibility; latent capability; *elect.* at a given point, the work required to bring a unit of positive electricity from an infinite distance to that point under given conditions of electrification.—**po·ten·tial·ly,** po·ten′-sha·lē, *adv.*

po·ten·tial en·er·gy, *n. Phys.* the energy of a body resulting from or depending on relative position rather than motion, as that of a coiled spring or a rock at the top of a hill. Compare *kinetic energy.*

po·ten·ti·al·i·ty, po·ten″shē·al′i·tē, *n. pl.* **po·ten·ti·al·i·ties.** State of being potential; possibility, but not actuality; inherent power or quality not actually exhibited.

po·ten·ti·ate, po·ten′shē·āt″, *v.t.*—*potentiated, potentiating.* To cause to be potent; to augment or intensify the effect of, as a drug.—**po·ten·ti·a·tion,** *n.*—**po·ten·ti·a·tor,** *n.*

po·ten·til·la, pōt″en·til′a, *n.* [N.L., dim. < L. *potens.*] Any plant of the rosaceous genus *Potentilla,* comprising herbs and shrubs with alternate pinnate or palmate leaves, as the European cinquefoil, *P. reptans,* or a N. American species, *P. canadensis.*

po·ten·ti·om·e·ter, po·ten″shē·om′i·tẽr, *n.* [< *potential,* and *meter.*] *Elect.* an electrical instrument which can be used to measure pressure, current, or resistance.—**po·ten·ti·o·met·ric,** po·ten″shē·o·me′-trik, *a.*

pot·ful, pot′fụl, *n. pl.* **pot·fuls.** As much as a pot will hold.

poth·e·car·y, poth′e·ker″ē, *n. pl.* **poth·e·car·ies.** *Dial.* apothecary.

poth·er, poTH′ẽr, *n.* [A different form of *bother* or of *potter.*] Bustle; confusion; tumult; a smothering cloud, as of smoke.—*v.t., v.i.* To bother; worry.

pot·herb, pot′ụrb″, pot′hụrb″, *n.* An herb having edible leaves or stems used in cooking, as beet greens; an herb used to flavor or season food.

pot·hole, pot′hōl″, *n.* A circular cavity in the rocky bed of a river, formed by the whirling action of stones in the current; a hole or deep pit in the surface of a highway, street, or sidewalk.

pot·hook, pot′hụk″, *n.* A hook on which pots and kettles are hung over a fire; a curved iron rod used to carry hot utensils; a stroke or character in elementary writing resembling an S.

pot·house, pot′hous″, *n. Brit.* An alehouse; a tavern.

pot·hunt·er, pot′hun″tẽr, *n.* A hunter who has more regard for winning prizes than for enjoying the sport; one who kills game for food.

po·tiche, pō·tēsh′, *Fr.* pạ·tēsh′, *n.* [Fr., < *pot,* pot.] A vase or jar, as of porcelain, with rounded or polygonal body narrowing at the top.

po·tion, pō′shan, *n.* [L. *potio,* a drinking, a

draught, < *poto,* to drink. *Poison* is the same word.] A draft or drink; a liquid supposedly having magical or poisonous powers.

pot·latch, pot′lach, *n.* [N. Amer. Ind.] Among some American Indians of the northern Pacific coast, a gift or present, or ceremonial festival at which gifts are exchanged, in a competitive display of wealth; *colloq.* a social event or party.

pot liq·uor, *n.* The broth remaining in a vessel after cooking and removing the meat or vegetables.

pot·luck, pot′luk″, pot′luk′, *n.* Whatever may be in a pot or provided for a family meal and given to guests; an informal meal where each guest brings a dish to be shared.—*a.*

pot mar·i·gold, *n.* A calendula cultivated mainly for its large orange or yellow flowers; a marigold, *Calendula officinalis,* the flower heads of which are sometimes used in cookery for seasoning.

pot·pie, pot′pī″, *n.* A combination of meat and vegetables, topped with a pastry crust, and baked in a deep dish; a stew of meat with dumplings.

pot·pour·ri, pō″pụ·rē′, pō′pụ·rē″, pot-pụr′ē, *Fr.* pạ·pō·Rē′, *n. pl.* **pot·pour·ris.** [Fr. *pot pourri,* 'rotten pot,' transl. Sp. *olla podrida.*] Dried flower petals and spices kept in a jar for the fragrance; a musical medley; a collection of miscellaneous literary extracts; any collection of mixed or unrelated parts.

pot roast, *n.* Meat, often chuck or round steak, cooked in a small amount of water in a covered pot, usu. with vegetables and seasoning.

pot·sherd, pot′shụrd″, *n.* [*Pot,* and *sherd* = *shard, shred,* a fragment.] A fragment of earthenware, esp. of archaeological interest.

pot shot, *n.* A shot fired at game merely to fill the pot, with little regard to the rules of sport; a shot at an animal or person within easy range, as from ambush; a haphazard shot; a casual attempt at something; a censorious remark.—*v.t.*

pot still, *n.* A large pot used in distilling whiskey, in which the heat of a fire is applied directly to its bottom surface.

pot·stone, pot′stōn″, *n.* A coarsely granular variety of steatite or soapstone, formerly used in making cooking vessels.

pot·tage, pot′ij, *n.* [Fr. *potage,* lit. 'what one puts in the *pot.*'] A vegetable stew or thick soup usu. with meat in it.

pot·ter, pot′ẽr, *n.* [< *pot.*] One who makes earthenware vessels or crockery of any kind.

pot·ter, pot′ẽr, *v.i.* [Appar. freq. of obs. or provinc. *pote,* push, *poke,* O.E. *potian,* push, thrust.] *Chiefly Brit.* To engage oneself ineffectively; dawdle; putter.—**pot·ter·er,** *n.*—**pot·ter·ing·ly,** *adv.*

pot·ter's clay, *n.* A variety of clay of a reddish color or gray which becomes red when heated, and which is used for making pottery.

pot·ter's field, *n.* [Matt. xxvii.7.] A piece of ground reserved as a burial place for strangers and the poor.

pot·ter's wheel, *n.* A horizontal revolving disk used to hold ceramic clay as it is shaped by the potter.

pot·ter·y, pot′e·rē, *n. pl.* **pot·ter·ies.** Ware made by shaping moist clay and then hardening it with intense heat; the business or art of a potter; a place where earthen vessels are manufactured.

pot·tle, pot′l, *n.* [Fr. *potel,* a dim. of *pot.*] Orig. a liquid measure of two quarts; any large drinking vessel or tankard that holds half a gallon; alcoholic drink. *Brit.* a vessel or small basket for holding fruit.

Pott's dis·ease, pots′ di·zēz″, *n.* [From Percival Pott, 1714-1788, Eng. surgeon, who described it.] *Pathol.* caries of the vertebrae usu. caused by a tubercular infection, often resulting in marked curvature of the spine.

pot·ty, pot′ē, *a.*—*pottier, pottiest. Brit.* of little import, petty. *Brit. slang,* slightly demented; silly.

pot·ty, pot′ē, *n. pl.* **pot·ties.** A pot for toilet use by small children.

pot·ty-chair, pot′ē-châr″, *n.* A small, open-seated chair placed over a pot for a child's use in toilet training.

pouch, pouch, *n.* [O.Fr. *pouche,* var. of *poche,* also *poque, poke,* bag: cf. *poke.*] A bag, sack, or similar receptacle, esp. one for small articles; a small moneybag; *chiefly Sc.* a pocket in a garment. A bag or case for ammunition; a cartridge box; a bag for carrying mail; something shaped like or resembling a bag or pocket; a baggy fold of flesh under the eyes. *Anat., zool.* a baglike or pocketlike part; a sac or cyst; the gular sac beneath the bill of pelicans; the saclike dilatation of the cheek of gophers; a marsupium. *Bot.* a baglike cavity; a silicle.—*v.t.* To put into or enclose in a pouch, bag, or pocket; to pocket; sometimes, of a fish or bird, to swallow; to arrange in pouchlike form.—*v.i.* To form a pouch or a pouchlike cavity.—**pouched,** poucht, *a.*—**pouch·y,** pou′chē, *a.*—*pouchier, pouchiest.*

pouf, pōf, *n.* [Fr.: cf. *puff.*] A kind of headdress worn by women in the latter part of the 18th century; an arrangement of the hair over a pad; a puff of material as an ornament on a dress or millinery; a cushioned ottoman.

pou·lard, pou·larde, pō·lärd′, *n.* [Fr. *poularde,* < *poule,* hen.] A hen spayed to improve the flesh for use as food.

poult, pōlt, *n.* [Fr. *poulet,* a dim. of *poule,* a hen.] A young fowl.

poul·ter·er, pōl′tėr·ėr, *n.* [Extended form of *poulter.*] A dealer in poultry.

poul·ter's mea·sure, *n. Poet.* a meter characterized by alternating lines of 12 and 14 syllables.

poul·tice, pōl′tis, *n.* [< L. *puls, pultis,* pottage, gruel, pap.] A soft dressing composed of meal, bread, or other mollifying substance, to be applied to sore or inflamed parts of the body; a cataplasm.—*v.t.*—*poulticed, poulticing.* To cover with a poultice; to apply a poultice to.

poul·try, pōl′trē, *n.* [A collective < *poult, pullet,* < Fr. *poulet,* a chicken, < *poule,* a hen, L. *pullus,* a young animal, a chicken; akin to Gr. *pŏlŏs,* E. *foal.*] Domestic fowls, as cocks and hens, turkeys, ducks, and geese.

poul·try·man, pōl′trē·man, *n. pl.* **poul·try·men.** A breeder of domestic fowl, esp. for commercial purposes; one who deals in poultry.

pounce, pouns, *n.* [M.E. *pownce;* prob. akin to *punch, puncheon.*] The claw or talon of a bird of prey; a pouncing or sudden swoop, as on prey.—*v.t.*—*pounced, pouncing.* To seize with the pounces or talons, or swoop down upon and seize suddenly, as does a bird of prey.—*v.i.* To swoop down suddenly and lay hold, as a bird on its prey; to spring, dash, or come suddenly; as, to *pounce* into a room.

pounce, pouns, *n.* [Fr. *ponce,* < L. *pumex (pumic-),* E. *pumice.*] A fine powder, as of cuttlebone, formerly used to prevent ink from spreading in writing, as over an erasure or on unsized paper, or to prepare parchment for writing; a fine powder used for transferring a design through a perforated pattern.—*v.t.*—*pounced, pouncing.* To sprinkle, smooth, or prepare with pounce; to trace with pounce rubbed through perforations; to finish the surface, as of hats, by rubbing with sandpaper.

poun·cet box, poun′sit boks″, *n.* [Perh. for *pounced box.*] A small box with a perforated lid, used for holding perfume.

pound, pound, *n.* [O.E. *pund,* < L. *pondo,*

a pound, prop. adv., 'in weight' (*libra pondo,* 'a pound in weight'), connected with *pondus,* weight.] A unit of weight, varying greatly in different periods and countries; in the British Empire and the U.S., either of two legally fixed units, the 'pound avoirdupois' of 7,000 grains, divided into 16 ounces, used for ordinary commodities, or the 'pound troy' of 5,760 grains, divided into 12 ounces, used for gold, silver, etc., and in the U.S. also serving as the basis of apothecaries' weight; abbr. *lb;* see Measures and Weights table. *Brit.* a 'pound sterling,' formerly equivalent to 20 shillings or 240 pence, now equivalent to 100 pennies, and denoted by the symbol £ before the numeral; a former Scottish money of account, 'pound Scots,' orig. the equivalent of the pound sterling, but at the union of the crowns of England and Scotland in 1603 worth only one twelfth of the pound sterling; the monetary unit of Australia, Egypt, Ireland, Israel, Lebanon, New Zealand, South Africa, South Rhodesia, Syria, and Turkey; see Moneys of the World table.

pound, pound, *v.t.* [O.E. *pūnian,* akin to D. *puin,* rubbish.] To crush by beating, as with an instrument; as, to *pound* drugs with a pestle in a mortar; to bray, pulverize, or triturate; to strike repeatedly with great force, as with an instrument, the fist, heavy missiles, or the like; to pummel or batter, often with *out;* to produce, as sound, by striking or thumping, or with an effect of thumping; as, to *pound* out a tune on the piano; to force, as a way through an obstacle, by battering; to make solid or firm by beating.—*v.i.* To strike heavy blows repeatedly or batter; to strike heavily against waves, as a boat; to beat or throb violently, as the heart; to give forth a thumping sound, as drums; to ride heavily; to move along with force or vigor.—*n.* The act of pounding; a heavy blow or its sound.

pound, pound, *n.* [O.E., recorded in *pundfald;* origin unknown.] An enclosure maintained by authority for confining trespassing or stray cattle, dogs, etc., or for keeping goods until redeemed; in general, an enclosure for sheltering, keeping, confining, or trapping animals; an enclosure or trap for fish; *fig.* a place of confinement or imprisonment.—*v.t.* To shut up in or as in a pound; impound; confine within limits.

pound·age, poun′dij, *n.* A tax, commission, or rate of so much per pound sterling or per pound weight; weight in pounds.

pound·age, poun′dij, *n.* Confinement of animals, usu. cattle, in a pound; the fee charged to free an impounded animal.

pound·al, poun′dal, *n. Physics,* a unit of force equivalent to the force which, acting for one second on a mass of one pound, gives it a velocity of one foot per second per second.

pound cake, *n.* A rich, sweet cake in which the butter, sugar, and flour are used pound for pound.

pound·er, poun′dėr, *n.* One who or that which pounds, pulverizes, or beats.

pound·er, poun′dėr, *n.* A person or thing having or associated with a weight or value of a pound or a specified number of pounds; a gun that discharges a missile of a specified weight in pounds.

pound-fool·ish, pound′fö′lish, *a.* Foolish or careless in regard to large sums: opposed to *penny-wise.*

pound mile, *n.* The conveyance of one pound of mail for one mile.

pound net, *n.* A kind of weir or fish trap of netting having a pound or enclosure with a contracted opening.

pour, pōr, par, *v.t.* [M.E. *pouren;* origin uncertain.] To send, as a liquid, fluid, or anything in loose particles, flowing or falling, as from a container, or into, over, or on

something; as, to *pour* water on fire, to *pour* sugar on cereal; to send forth or discharge continuously and rapidly, or in profusion; to express freely or without reserve; as, to *pour* forth one's ideas.—*v.i.* To flow continuously, as a stream; to rain hard; as, to *pour* all day; to move or proceed in great quantity or number, as: The crowd *poured* into the streets. To serve at a tea or reception.—*n.* A pouring; an abundant or continuous flow or stream; a hard rain; downpour.—**pour·a·ble,** *a.*—**pour·er,** *n.*—**pour·ing·ly,** *adv.*

pour·point, pụr′point″, pụr′pwant″, *n.* [O.Fr. Fr. *pourpoint,* orig. pp. of *pourpoindre,* quilt, < *pour-,* for *par-* (< L, *per*), through, and *poindre,* < L. *pungere.* prick, pierce.] A stuffed and quilted doublet worn by men in the 14th and 15th centuries.

pour point, *n. Chem.* the lowest degree of heat at which any given matter will flow under specified conditions.

pousse-ca·fé, pōs″kȧ·fā′, *Fr.* pōs·kȧ·fā′, *n. pl.* **pousse-ca·fés,** pōs″kȧ·fāz′, *Fr.* pōs·kȧ·fā′. [Fr., lit. 'push-coffee.'] *Fr.* A small glass of liqueur served after coffee; a glass of various liqueurs arranged in layers.

pous·sette, pōˈset′, *n.* [Fr., dim. < *pousser,* E. *push.*] A dancing round and round with hands joined, as of a couple or couples in a country dance.—*v.i.*—*poussetted, poussetting.* To perform a pousette.

pout, pout, *v.i.* [< W. *pwtiaw,* to push, or from dial. Fr. *pout, potte,* Pr. *pot,* the lip.] To thrust out the lips, as in sullenness, contempt, or displeasure; to look sullen; to swell out, as the lips; to express in a pouting manner.—*v.t.* To push out sulkily, as the lips.—*n.* A protrusion of the lips as in sullenness; a fit of sullenness.

pout, pout, *n. pl.* **pout, pouts.** [O.E. *pūta,* recorded in *ælepūta,* eelpout.] A marine food fish, *Gadus luscus,* of northern waters; any of certain large-headed fresh-water catfishes, as the *Amiurus nebulosus,* the horned pout.

pout·er, pou′tėr, *n.* One who pouts; a variety of pigeon, so called from its distensible crop.

pov·er·ty, pov′ėr·tē, *n.* [O.Fr. *poverté* (Fr. *pauvrete*), < L. *paupertas,* < *pauper,* poor: cf. *poor* and *pauper.*] The condition of being poor with respect to money, goods, or means of subsistence; indigence; deficiency or lack of something specified; as, *poverty* of ideas; deficiency of desirable ingredients or qualities; as, *poverty* of soil.

pov·er·ty-strick·en, pov′ėr·tē·strik″en, *a.* Suffering from poverty; very poor.

POW, pē′ō′dub′l·ū″, *n.* Prisoner of war. Also **P.O.W.**

pow·der, pou′dėr, *n.* [O.Fr. Fr. *poudre,* < L. *pulvis (pulver-),* dust, powder.] Any solid substance in the state of fine, loose particles, produced by crushing, grinding, or disintegration; dust; a preparation in this form for some special purpose, as for medicinal use; a cosmetic; as, face *powder;* gunpowder, or any similar explosive.—*v.t.* [O.Fr. Fr. *poudrer.*] To sprinkle or cover with powder; to reduce to powder; pulverize.—*v.i.* To use powder as a cosmetic; to become pulverized.—**pow·der·er,** *n.*

pow·der blue, *n.* Pale blue blended with gray.—**pow·der-blue,** *a.*

pow·der horn, *n.* A flask for gunpowder, made from the horn of an ox or cow.

pow·der keg, *n.* A small cask of metal or wood, containing gunpowder or blasting powder; a potentially violent situation or condition.

pow·der met·al·lur·gy, *n.* The process of pressure-molding metal and alloy powders into solid objects.

pow·der mon·key, *n.* A boy formerly employed on warships to carry powder;

a man in charge of explosives in any operation requiring their use.

pow·der puff, *n.* A soft, fluffy ball or pad, for applying cosmetic powder to the skin.

pow·der room, *n.* A ladies' rest room having washing and toilet facilities.

pow·der·y, pou′de·rĕ, *a.* Consisting of powder; easily reduced to powder; sprinkled or covered with powder.

pow·der·y mil·dew, *n.* A fungus which produces powdery conidia on the host surface; a disease caused by such a fungus.

pow·er, pou′ĕr, *n.* [O.Fr. *poeir* (Fr. *pouvoir*), power, prop. inf., be able, < M.L. *potere*, for L. *posse*, be able.] Ability to do or act; capability of doing or effecting something; *often pl.* a particular faculty of body or mind. Great or marked ability to do or act; strength, might, or force; political or national strength; as, the balance of *power* in Europe; the possession of control or command over others; dominion, authority, ascendancy, or influence; legal ability, capacity, or delegated authority; one who or that which possesses or exercises authority or influence; a state or nation having international authority or influence; as, the great *powers* of the world; *colloq.* a large number or amount. Any mechanical energy or force available for application to work; *phys.* the time rate at which energy or force is exerted or converted into work; *math.* the product obtained by multiplying a quantity by itself one or more times, as: Four is the second *power* of two. *Theol.* an order of angels; *opt.* the magnifying capacity of a microscope or telescope.—*v.t.* To supply with a means or source of power or energy.

pow·er·boat, pou′ĕr·bōt″, *n.* A motorboat.

pow·er dive, *n. Aeron.* a steep dive by an airplane, usu. at or near maximum engine power.—**pow·er-dive,** *v.t., v.i.* To do or cause to do a power dive.

pow·er·ful, pou′ĕr·ful, *a.* Having or exerting great power or force; strong physically, as a person; producing great physical effects, as a machine or a blow; potent, as a drug; having or showing great intellectual force, as the mind; having great moral influence, as a speech or speaker; having great power, authority, or influence, as a nation; mighty; *dial.* great in amount or number.—**pow·er·ful·ly,** *adv.*—**pow·er·ful·ness,** *n.*

pow·er·house, pou′ĕr·hous″, *n. Elect.* a station for generating electricity; *slang,* a person of dynamic energy and power.

pow·er·less, pou′ĕr·lis, *a.* Lacking power, ability, or authorization; unable to produce any ieffect; helpless.—**pow·er·less·ly,** *adv.* —**pow·er·less·ness,** *n.*

pow·er of at·tor·ney, *n. Law,* the authority a legally responsible adult may grant to another to speak for or act in behalf of the former in matters of legal consequence; the written instrument conferring such authority.

pow·er pack, *n.* A converter to adapt the voltage of one source of electric power to the needs of another circuit or electrical device.

pow·er plant, *n.* The apparatus for supplying power for a particular mechanical process or operation; as, the *power plant* of an automobile; the building and equipment involved in generating power.

pow·er play, *n. Sports,* a maneuver or tactic in which players of one team are concentrated at one place to force the opposition to yield ground, as in football or ice hockey. In business or warfare, a concentration of power to force cooperation or compliance from the opposition.

pow·er pol·i·tics, *n.* International politics when associated with coercion, esp. the use of military force.

pow·er se·ries, *n. Math.* a series whose terms consist of ascending integral powers of a known variable that is multiplied by constants.

pow·er steer·ing, *n.* A system of automotive steering in which engine power is used to augment the torque applied manually to the steering wheel by the driver.

pow·er take-off, *n.* A device for transmitting power from a tractor or truck engine to operate a mechanical apparatus or machine that does not generate its own power, as a winch, posthole digger, or certain agricultural implements.

pow·wow, pou′wou″, *n.* [Algonquian.] Among the N. American Indians, a priest or medicine man, or a ceremony, esp. one accompanied by magic, feasting, and dancing, performed for the cure of disease or for success in a hunt; a council or conference of or with Indians; *colloq.* any conference or meeting.—*v.i.* To hold a powwow; *colloq.* to confer.

pox, poks, *n.* [A peculiar spelling of *pocks,* pl. of *pock*—used as a sing.] *Pathol.* an eruptive disease characterized by pustules, as chicken pox; a vulgarism for syphilis.

poz·zo·la·na, pot″so·lä′na, *It.* pạt″tzạ·-lä′nä, *n.* A volcanic ash or powdered rock employed in the manufacturing of Roman or hydraulic cement. Also **poz·zuo·la·na, poz·zo·lan,** pot″swo·lä′na, *It.* pạt″tzwạ-lä′nä, pot′so·lan.—**poz·zo·la·nic,** pot″so·-lä′nik, *a.*

PPI, pē′pē′ī, *n.* Plan position indicator.

prac·ti·ca·ble, prak′ti·ka·bl, *a.* [< L.L. *practicare,* to transact, < L. *practicus,* active; Gr. *praktikos,* active, practical, < *prassō,* to do, to work.] Capable of being effected or performed; feasible; capable of serving a use or purpose; usable, useful.— **prac·ti·ca·bil·i·ty, prac·ti·ca·ble·ness,** *n.*—**prac·ti·ca·bly,** *adv.*

prac·ti·cal, prak′ti·kal, *a.* [Fr. (obs.) *practique,* now *pratique,* < L.L. *practicus,* < Gr. *praktikos,* active, practical, < *prassein,* do.] Pertaining or relating to practice or action; as, *practical* agriculture; consisting of, involving, or resulting from practice or action; as, a *practical* demonstration of one's power; pertaining to or connected with the ordinary activities, business, or work of the world; as, *practical* affairs; suitable or adapted for actual use; as, a *practical* method or device; engaged or experienced in actual practice or work; inclined toward or fitted for actual practice or work or useful activities; as, a *practical* man; interested in actualities; mindful of the results, usefulness, advantages, or disadvantages of action or procedure; matter-of-fact or prosaic; being such in practice or effect; virtual.—**prac·ti·cal·i·ty,** *n.*—**prac·ti·cal·ly,** prak′tik·lē, *adv.* —**prac·ti·cal·ness,** *n.*

prac·ti·cal joke, *n.* A joke or jest carried out in action instead of words; a trick which puts the victim in an unfavorable position.—**prac·ti·cal jok·er,** *n.*

prac·ti·cal nurse, *n.* A nurse, lacking a degree as a registered nurse, but with sufficient training and nursing skills to care for the sick professionally.

prac·tice, *Brit.* **prac·tise,** prak′tis, *v.t.*—*practiced, practicing, Brit. practised, practising.* To carry out in action, esp. to carry out or perform habitually or usually, as: *Practice* what you preach. To follow, observe, or use habitually or in customary practice; as, to *practice* moderation; to exercise or pursue, as a profession, art, or occupation; as, to *practice* medicine; to perform or do repeatedly in order to acquire skill or proficiency; to exercise or train, as a person, in order to achieve proficiency.—*v.i.* To do something habit-

ually or as a practice; to pursue a profession, esp. law or medicine; to exercise repeatedly in order to gain proficiency; as, to *practice* the piano.—**prac·ticed,** *Brit.* **prac·tised,** prak′tist, *a.* Experienced; skilled; expert; acquired or perfected through practice.—**prac·tic·er,** *n.*

prac·tice, prak′tis, *n.* [< *practice, practise, v.*] Habitual or customary performance; a habit or custom; the action or process of performing or doing something: opposed to *theory;* the exercise of a profession or occupation, esp. law or medicine; the business of a professional man; as, a lawyer with a large *practice;* repeated performance or systematic exercise for the purpose of acquiring skill or proficiency; a condition of proficiency resulting from frequent exercise; as, to be in *practice; law,* the established method of conducting legal proceedings.

prac·tice teach·er, *n.* Student teacher.

prac·ti·tion·er, prak·tish′a·nĕr, *n.* One who is engaged in the exercise of any art or profession, esp. in law or medicine; a Christian Science healer.

prae·di·al, pre·di·al, prē′dē·al, *a.* Consisting of or relating to land or its products.

prae·mu·ni·re, prē″mū·nī′rē, *n.* [M.L. *præmunire* (a word used in the writ), for L. *præmonere,* forewarn, admonish.] *Eng. law.* A writ of summons on the charge of resorting to a foreign court or authority, as that of the Pope, and disregarding the supremacy of the sovereign; the offense; the penalty of forfeiture, imprisonment, or outlawry incurred.

prae·no·men, prē·nō′men, *n. pl.* **prae·nom·i·na, prae·no·mens,** prē·nom′e·na. [L., < *præ,* before, and *nomen,* name.] The first or personal name of a Roman citizen, as 'Gaius' in '*Gaius* Julius Cæsar.' Also *prenomen.*

prae·tor, prē′tĕr, *n.* [L., < *prae,* before, and *eo,* I go.] In ancient Rome, a title originally of the consuls, but later belonging to the magistrates who administered justice in the city.—**prae·to·ri·al,** *a.*—**prae·tor·ship,** prē′tĕr·ship″, *n.*

prae·to·ri·an, prē·tōr′ē·an, prē·tạr′ē·an, *a.* Belonging or pertaining to a praetor; (*cap.*) of or belonging to the Praetorian Guard.—*n.*

Prae·to·ri·an Guard, *n.* Troops originally formed by the Roman Emperor Augustus to protect himself, later maintained as the Imperial Roman Guard; any of the household troops or bodyguards of emperors.

prag·mat·ic, prag·mat′ik, *a.* [L. *pragmaticus,* < Gr. *pragmatikós,* active, businesslike, versed in state affairs, *pragma,* a thing done, deed, affair, < *prassein,* do.] Treating historical phenomena with special reference to their causes, antecedent conditions, and results; of or pertaining to the philosophy of pragmatism; concerned with practical consequences or values; pertaining to the affairs of a state or community; busy or active; officiously busy; meddlesome; dogmatic.—*n.* A pragmatic sanction; a busybody; a conceited person.— **prag·mat·i·cal,** *a.*—**prag·mat·i·cal·ly,** *adv.*—**prag·mat·i·cal·ness,** *n.*

prag·mat·i·cism, prag·mat′i·siz″um, *n.* The specific pragmatist philosophy of C. S. Pierce, as opposed to the pragmatism of William James.—**prag·mat·i·cist,** *n.*

prag·mat·ics, prag·mat′iks, *n. pl. but sing. in constr.* A part of semiotics concerned with relationships between verbal or symbolic expressions of thought and the expressors of such thought.

prag·mat·ic sanc·tion, *n.* An imperial decree whose force is that of fundamental law.

prag·ma·tism, prag′ma·tiz″um, *n.* A concern for and emphasis on practical matters; a nonspeculative system of philosophy which regards the practical consequences and useful results of ideas as the test of their truthfulness and which considers truth itself to be a process; officiousness; dogmatism.—**prag·ma·tist,** *n., a.*—**prag·ma·tis·tic,** prag″ma·tis′tik, *a.*

prai·rie, prâr′ē, *n.* [Fr., < L.L. *prataria,* < L. *pratum,* a meadow.] An extensive, mostly level tract of grassland, usu. treeless, with fertile soil and flowering plants, esp. the one extending from the Mississippi River to the Rocky Mountains.

prai·rie chick·en, *n.* A gallinaceous bird native to the western plains, *Tympanuchus cupido,* or a smaller similar fowl, *Tympanuchus pallidicinctus.* Also **prai·rie fowl, prai·rie hen, prai·rie grouse.**

prai·rie dog, *n.* A small burrowing rodent, genus *Cynomys,* allied to the marmot and squirrel, found on the N. American prairies.

prai·rie schoon·er, *n.* A large covered wagon used by travelers to the West before the construction of railroads.

praise, prāz, *n.* [Formerly *preis, preys, praise, price, value,* < O.Fr. *pris, preis, price, honor* (Mod.Fr. *prix*), < L. *pretium, price, value, reward;* the same as *price* and to *prize.*] Commendation bestowed on someone or something; approbation; eulogy; homage offered as an act of worship and expressed in words or song.—*v.t.*—*praised, praising.* To commend; to applaud; to express approbation of; to extol in words or song.—**prais·er,** *n.*

praise·wor·thy, prāz′wur″THē, *a.* Worthy or deserving of praise; commendable.—**praise·wor·thi·ly,** *adv.*—**praise·wor·thi·ness,** *n.*

pra·line, prä′lēn, prä′lĕn, prä·lĕn′, *n.* [Fr.; from Marshal du Plessis-*Praslin,* 1598–1675, whose cook invented the sweetmeat.] Any of various confections of almonds or other nuts cooked in a boiling syrup.

prall·tril·ler, präl′tril″ĕr, *n.* [G.] *Mus.* a melodic embellishment consisting of a rapid alternation of a principal tone with a supplementary tone one degree above it. Also **in·vert·ed mor·dent.**

pram, pram, *n. Brit. colloq.* Baby carriage; perambulator.

pra·na, prä′na, *n. Hindu philos.* The vital breath; the life principle of the living body; force; energy.—**pra·nic,** *a.*

prance, prans, *v.i.*—*pranced, prancing.* [M.E. *prauncen.*] To spring or bound from the hind legs, as a horse in high mettle; to ride on a horse moving in this manner; to ride ostentatiously; to strut about in a showy or spirited manner; to caper.—*v.t.* To cause to prance.—*n.* A prancing act or movement.—**pranc·er,** *n.*

prank, prangk, *n.* [Cf. *prance,* also *prank.*] A trick of a frolicsome or malicious nature. —**prank·ish,** *a.*—**prank·ster,** *n.*

prank, prangk, *v.t.* [Allied to D. *pronk,* finery, *pronken,* to strut; Dan. *prange,* G. *prangen, prunken,* to make a show; comp. also G. *pracht,* D. and Dan. *pragt,* pomp.] To adorn in a showy manner.—*v.i.* To make a showy or gaudy appearance or display.

prase, prāz, *n.* [Fr., < Gr. *prason,* a leek.] A species of quartz which is transparent and of a leek-green color.

pra·se·o·dym·i·um, prä″zē·ō·dim′ē·um, prä″sē·ō·dim′ē·um, *n.* [Gr. *prasios,* leekgreen, and *didymium.*] *Chem.* a yellowishwhite metallic element of the rare earth series having green salts and tarnishing easily. *Sym.* Pr, at. no. 59, at. wt. 140.907. See Periodic Table of Elements.

prate, prāt, *v.i.*—*prated, prating.* [Same as L.G. *praten,* Dan. *prate,* D. *praaten,* Icel.

prata, to prate; prob. of imit. origin.] To talk much and without weight; to chatter; to babble.—*v.t.* To utter foolishly.—*n.* Continued talk to little purpose; unmeaning loquacity.—**prat·er,** *n.*—**prat·ing·ly,** *adv.*

prat·fall, prat′fạl″, *n. Slang.* A fall on the backside or buttocks; an embarrassing mistake or blunder.

prat·in·cole, prat′ing·kōl″, prā′tin·kōl″, *n.* [N.L. *pratincola,* < L. *pratum,* meadow, and *incola,* inhabitant.] Any of the limicoline birds of the Old World which constitute the genus *Glareola,* esp. *G. pratincola.*

pra·tique, pra·tēk′, prat′ik, Fr. prä·tēk′, *n.* [Fr.] *Naut.* a clearance given to a ship, esp. in the European ports of the Mediterranean, to enter a port and trade after passing quarantine.

prat·tle, prat′l, *v.i.*—*prattled, prattling.* [Freq. and dim. of *prate.*] To talk much and idly on trifling subjects; to talk like a child.—*v.t.* To speak in a childish or babbling manner.—*n.* Puerile or trifling talk; babble.—**prat·tler,** *n.*—**prat·tling·ly,** *adv.*

prau, prou, *n.* Proa.

prawn, prạn, *n.* [M.E. *prane;* origin uncertain.] Any of various shrimplike decapod crustaceans, as of the genera *Palaemon* and *Peneus,* certain of which are used as food.—*v.i.* To fish for prawns.— **prawn·er,** *n.*

prax·is, prak′sis, *n. pl.* **prax·is·es, prax·es,** prak′sēz. [Gr., < *prassō,* I do.] Practice, as opposed to theory; habitual practice, conduct, or custom.

pray, prā, *v.i.* [O.Fr. *preier* (Fr. *prier*), It. *pregare,* to pray, < L. *precari,* to pray, < *prex,* a prayer; same root as Skt. *prach,* to demand, O.E. *frignan,* G. *fragen,* to inquire.] To ask for something with earnestness or zeal; to supplicate; to beg; to address confession, supplication, or thanks to an object of worship.—*v.t.* To make earnest request to; to entreat; to ask earnestly for; to beseech by means of prayer.

prayer, prâr, *n.* [Not directly from *pray,* but < O.Fr. *proiere,* Fr. *prière,* a prayer, < L.L. *precaria,* a prayer, < L. *precarius,* obtained by begging.] The act of asking for a favor with earnestness; a petition, supplication, entreaty; that which is asked; a solemn petition addressed to an object of worship; the words of a supplication; a formula of church service or of worship, public or private; that part of a petition to a public body which specifies the thing desired to be done or granted.—**pray·er,** prā′ẽr, *n.* One who prays.

prayer book, prâr bụk, *n.* A book containing prayers used in worship; (*usu. cap.*) the Book of Common Prayer.

prayer·ful, prâr′fụl, *a.* Devotional; given to or expressive of prayer.—**prayer·ful·ly,** *adv.*—**prayer·ful·ness,** *n.*

prayer meet·ing, *n.* A meeting for prayer; in various Protestant churches, a midweek devotional service.

prayer wheel, *n.* An apparatus used mainly by Buddhists in Tibet, consisting of a wheel to which a written prayer is attached, each revolution of the wheel counting as an utterance of the prayer.

preach, prēch, *v.i.* [O.Fr. *precher* (Fr. *prêcher*), < L. *praedicare,* to declare in public—*prae,* before, and *dico, dicatum,* I proclaim; closely akin to *dico, dictum,* I say.] To deliver a sermon; to give earnest advice; to discourse in a tedious manner.— *v.t.* To endorse or inculcate in writing or public discourse; to expound or explain, as something, in a sermon; to deliver, as a sermon.—**preach·er,** prē′chẽr, *n.*—**preach·ing·ly,** *adv.*

preach·i·fy, prē′chi·fī″, *v.i.*—*preachified, preachifying.* To give tedious, long-winded moral advice: used disparagingly.

preach·ment, prēch′ment, *n.* The act of giving a sermon; a tedious discourse or sermon.

preach·y, prē′chē, *a.*—*preachier, preachiest. Colloq.* Inclined to preach or suggestive of preaching; tedious; sanctimonious.

pre·ad·o·les·cence, prē″ad·o·les′ens, *n.* The years which immediately precede adolescence, usu. from the age of 9 to 12.— **pre·ad·o·les·cent,** prē″ad·o·les′ent, *a., n.*

pre·am·ble, prē′am″bl, *n.* [= Fr. *préambule,* < M.L. *praeambulum,* prop. neut. of L.L. *praeambulus,* walking before, < L. *prae,* before, and *ambulare,* walk.] A preliminary statement; a preface; an introduction, esp. the introductory part of a statute or deed stating the reasons and intent of what follows; a preliminary or introductory fact or circumstance; a presage.

pre·ar·range, prē″a·rānj′, *v.t.*—*prearranged, prearranging.* To arrange beforehand.—**pre·ar·range·ment,** *n.*

pre·as·signed, prē″a·sīnd′, *a.* Assigned in advance.

pre·a·tom·ic, prē·a·tom′ik, *a.* Pertaining to the period of time prior to the use of atomic power and atomic energy.

pre·ax·i·al, prē·ak′sē·al, *a. Anat., zool.* situated in front of a body axis.—**pre·ax·i·al·ly,** *adv.*

preb·end, preb′end, *n.* [Fr. *prébende,* < L.L. *praebenda,* things to be supplied, < L. *praebeo,* to give, grant, furnish—*prae,* and *habeo,* to have.] That portion of the estate of a cathedral or collegiate church reserved as a stipend for an ecclesiastic; the stipend paid from this fund; a prebendary.—**preb·en·dal,** pri·ben′dal, *a.*

preb·en·dar·y, preb′en·der″ē, *n. pl.* **preb·en·dar·ies.** An ecclesiastic who enjoys a prebend; *Ch. of Eng.* an honorary canon without a stipend.

Pre·cam·bri·an, Pre-Cam·bri·an, prē″·kam′brē·an, *n.* [L. *pre,* before, *Cambrian.*] See Table of Geologic Time.—*a.*

pre·can·cel, prē·kan′sel, *v.t.*—*precanceled, precanceling, esp. Brit. precancelled, precancelling.* To cancel, as a postage stamp, before using in the mail.—**pre·can·cel·la·tion,** *n.*

pre·can·cer·ous, prē·kan′sẽr·us, *a.* Of or pertaining to a condition of the tissues which, while not now cancerous, may develop into cancer, as certain skin growths.

pre·car·i·ous, pri·kâr′ē·us, *a.* [L. *precarius,* primarily, depending on request, or on the will of another, < *precor,* I pray.] Depending on unknown or unforeseen causes or events; risky; having little base or foundation; depending on or held at the will or pleasure of another, and therefore dubious, insecure.—**pre·car·i·ous·ly,** *adv.* —**pre·car·i·ous·ness,** *n.*

pre·cau·tion, pri·kạ′shan, *n.* [L. *praecautio,* < *praecautus*—*prae,* before, and *caveo, cautum,* I take care.] Previous caution or care; a measure taken beforehand to ward off evil or secure good.—*v.t.* To warn or advise beforehand.—**pre·cau·tion·ar·y, pre·cau·tious,** pri·kạ′sha·nẽr″ē, pri·kạ′shus, *a.*

pre·cede, pri·sēd′, *v.t.*—*preceded, preceding.* [L. *praecedo*—*prae,* before, and *cedo,* I move.] To go before in the order of time, place, rank, or importance; to begin with introductory material; to preface.— *v.i.* To be or go before or ahead of.

prec·e·dence, pres′i·dens, pri·sēd′ens, *n.* The act or state of preceding or going before; the state of being before in rank or dignity; antecedence in time; the right to a more honorable place in social formalities;

order or adjustment of place according to rank. Also **prec·e·den·cy**, pres′i·den·sē, pri·sēd′en·sē.

prec·e·dent, pres′i·dent, *n.* Something done or said that may serve or be adduced as an example or rule to be followed in a subsequent act of a like kind; *law,* a judicial decision which serves as a rule for future decisions in similar or analogous cases.

pre·ced·ent, pri·sēd′ent, pres′i·dent, *a.* Going before in time; anterior; antecedent.

pre·ced·ing, prē·sē′ding, *a.* That precedes; going or coming before; previous.

pre·cen·sor, prē·sen′sėr, *v.t.* To censor, as a play, motion picture, or book, before it is available to the public.

pre·cen·tor, pri·sen′tẽr, *n.* [L.L. *prae-centor*—L. *prae,* before, and *cantor,* a singer, < *cano, cantum,* I sing.] An individual who leads choir or congregational singing.—**pre·cen·to·ri·al**, prē″sen·tōr′ē·al, prē′sen·tặr′ē·al, *a.*—**pre·cen·tor·ship**, *n.*

pre·cept, prē′sept, *n.* [Fr. *précepte,* L. *praeceptum,* < *praecipio,* I teach, instruct —*prae,* before, and *capio,* to take.] A commandment intended as an authoritative rule of action; a maxim or guide respecting moral conduct; an injunction; *law,* a writ or judicial order.

pre·cep·tive, pri·sep′tiv, *a.* [L. *praeceptivus.*] Giving or containing precepts for the regulation of conduct; admonitive; instructive.—**pre·cep·tive·ly**, *adv.*

pre·cep·tor, pri·sep′tẽr, prē′sep·tẽr, *n.* [L. *praeceptor.*] A teacher; an instructor; the head of a preceptory.—**pre·cep·to·ri·al**, prē″sep·tōr′ē·al, prē″sep·tặr′ē·al, *a.*—**pre·cep·tor·ship**, *n.*—**pre·cep·tress**, *n.* A female preceptor.

pre·cep·to·ry, pri·sep′to·rē, *n.* pl. **pre·cep·to·ries.** A subordinate religious house or establishment of the Knights Templars, an order of Freemasons.

pre·cess, prē·ses′, *v.i.* To move forward by means of precession.

pre·ces·sion, prē·sesh′an, *n.* [L.L. *praecessio(n-),* < L. *praecedere,* E. *precede.*] The act or fact of preceding; precedence; *astron.* the precession of the equinoxes. *Phys.* any motion analogous to that of the axis of the earth in the precession of the equinoxes; the slow, steady motion in which the axis of a rapidly spinning top or the like describes a right circular cone about the vertical.—**pre·ces·sion·al**, prē′sesh′a·nal, *a.*

pre·ces·sion of the e·qui·nox·es, *n.* *Astron.* the earlier occurrence of the equinoxes in each successive sidereal year because of a slow retrograde motion of the equinoctial points along the ecliptic, due to a gradual change in the direction of the earth's axis caused by the gravitational pull of the sun and moon on the mass of matter accumulated about the earth's equator.

pré·cieuse, prā″sē·ụz′, *Fr.* prā·syœz′, *n.* pl. **pré·cieus·es**, prā″sē·ụz′iz, *Fr.* prā·syœz′. An affected woman, esp. when pretentious in speech or manner; orig. a female personage of 17th century French literature who affected excessive refinement of language or taste.—*a.*

pré·cieux, prā″sē·ụ′, *Fr.* prā·syœ′, *n.* pl. **pré·cieux**, prā″sē·ụz′, *Fr.* prā·syœ′. A man whose behavior is marked by fastidious refinement of language or manner.—*a.*

pre·cinct, prē′singkt, *n.* [< L. *praecingo, praecinctum,* surrounded by—*prae,* before, and *cingo,* to gird.] Divisions within a city, town, or county for voting purposes; a district of a city under police control; the police station within such a district; the boundary line encompassing a place; a limit; a part near a border; a district within certain boundaries; a minor territorial division; *pl.* environs.

pre·ci·os·i·ty, presh″ē·os′i·tē, *n.* pl. **pre·ci·os·i·ties.** [O.Fr. *preciosite* (Fr. *préciosité*), < L. *pretiositas.*] The quality of being precious; fastidious or carefully affected refinement, as in language, style, or taste.

pre·cious, presh′us, *a.* [Fr. *précieux,* < L. *pretiosus,* < *pretium,* price.] Of high price; much esteemed; highly cherished; affectedly refined; flagrant; as, a *precious* ninny; *slang,* great, as: A *precious* amount of good her frankness did her!—*adv.* Extremely; very.—*n.* A beloved individual.—**pre·cious·ly**, *adv.*—**pre·cious·ness**, *n.*

prec·i·pice, pres′i·pis, *n.* [Fr. *précipice,* < L. *praecipitium,* a falling headlong, a precipice, < *praeceps,* headlong—*prae,* forward, and *caput,* head.] A headlong declivity; a steep bank, cliff, or extremely steep overhang; a dangerous situation.

pre·cip·i·ta·ble, pri·sip′i·ta·bl, *a.* Capable of being precipitated.

pre·cip·i·tance, pri·sip′i·tans, *n.* The quality of being precipitate; rash haste; haste in resolving, forming an opinion, or executing a purpose. Also **pre·cip·i·tan·cy.**

pre·cip·i·tant, pri·sip′i·tant, *a.* [L. *praecipitans, praecipitantis,* ppr. of *praecipito.*] Falling or rushing headlong; precipitate.—*n.* *Chem.* a substance which, when added to a solution, induces precipitation.—**pre·cip·i·tant·ly**, *adv.*—**pre·cip·i·tant·ness**, *n.*

pre·cip·i·tate, pri·sip′i·tāt″, *v.t.*—**precipitated,** *precipitating.* [L. *praecipitatus,* pp. of *praecipitare,* cast or fall headlong, lit. 'head first,' *prae,* before, and *caput,* head.] To hasten the occurrence of; bring about in haste or suddenly; *chem.* to separate out, as a substance, in solid form from a solution, as by means of a reagent; *phys.* to condense, as moisture, from a state of vapor into the form of rain or dew. To cast, plunge, or send violently or abruptly.—*v.i.* *Chem.* to separate from a solution as a precipitate; *phys.* to be condensed as rain or dew. To fall headlong.—pri·sip′i·tit, pri·sip′i·tāt″, *a.* Headlong; rushing headlong or rapidly onward; proceeding rapidly or with great haste; exceedingly sudden or abrupt; done or made without due deliberation; overhasty; rash.—pri·sip′i·tit, pri·sip′i·tāt″, *n.* *Chem.* a substance precipitated from a solution; *phys.* moisture condensed in the form of rain, dew, or snow.—**pre·cip·i·tate·ly**, *adv.*—**pre·cip·i·tate·ness**, *n.*—**pre·cip·i·ta·tive**, *a.*—**pre·cip·i·ta·tor**, *n.*

pre·cip·i·ta·tion, pri·sip″i·tā′shan, *n.* The act of precipitating, or state of being precipitated; a falling or rushing down with violence and rapidity; rash, tumultuous haste; *chem.* the process by which any substance is made to separate from another or others in a solution, and fall to the bottom. *Meteor.* the results of atmospheric condensation, i.e., snow, sleet, hail, dew, fog, or rainfall; the amount of such precipitation in a certain period at a certain place, usu. stated in inches.

pre·cip·i·tin, pri·sip′i·tin, *n.* [< *precipitate.*] An antibody formed in the blood that precipitates certain proteins when it unites with its antigen.

pre·cip·i·tous, pri·sip′i·tus, *a.* [L. *praeceps, praecipitis,* headlong.] Very steep; like or forming a precipice; headlong in descent.—**pre·cip·i·tous·ly**, *adv.*—**pre·cip·i·tous·ness**, *n.*

pré·cis, prā′sē, prā′sē, *n.* pl. **pré·cis**, prā·sēz′, prā′sēz. [Fr. *précis,* precise, also an abstract.] A concise summary or abstract of a book, manuscript, or document.

pre·cise, pri·sīs′, *a.* [L. *praecisus,* < *praecido,* to cut off—*prae,* before, and *caedo,* to cut (as in *concise, excision*).]

Sharply or exactly limited or defined as to meaning; exact; definite, not loose, vague, or equivocal; exact in conduct; strict; formal; punctilious.—**pre·cise·ly**, *adv.*—**pre·cise·ness**, *n.*

pre·ci·sian, pri·sizh′an, *n.* An overprecise person, esp. in religious matters; one ceremoniously exact in the observance of religious rules.—**pre·ci·sian·ism**, *n.*

pre·ci·sion, pri·sizh′an, *n.* The state of being precise as to meaning; exactness; accuracy.—*a.* Characterized by extremely exacting measurement.—**pre·ci·sion·ist**, *n.*

pre·clin·i·cal, prē·klin′i·kal, *a.* *Med.* of or during the time of an illness or disease before the symptoms appear.

pre·clude, pri·klōd′, *v.t.*—**precluded,** *precluding.* [L. *praecludo*—*prae,* before, and *cludo, claudo,* to shut.] To shut out; to impede; to hinder; to hinder or render inoperative by anticipative action.—**pre·clu·sion**, pri·klō′zhan, *n.*—**pre·clu·sive**, pri·klō′siv, *a.*—**pre·clu·sive·ly**, *adv.*

pre·co·cial, pri·kō′shal, *a.* *Ornith.* pertaining to certain birds which are downcovered and have the ability to run freely when hatched: contrasted with *altricial.*

pre·co·cious, pri·kō′shus, *a.* [L. *praecox* (*praecoc-*), early ripe, precocious, < *praecoquere,* cook beforehand, ripen early, < *prae,* before, and *coquere,* cook: cf. *apricot.*] Forward in development, esp. mental development, as a child or young person; prematurely developed, as the mind or faculties; pertaining to or showing premature development. *Bot.* bearing blossoms before leaves, as plants; flowering, fruiting, or ripening early, as plants, fruit.—**pre·co·cious·ly**, *adv.*—**pre·co·cious·ness**, *n.*—**pre·coc·i·ty**, pri·kos′i·tē, *n.*

pre·cog·ni·tion, prē″kog·nish′an, *n.* [L.L. *praecognitio(n-),* < L. *praecognoscere,* foreknow, < *prae,* before, and *cognoscere,* come to know.] Foreknowledge of a situation or of an event; *parapsychology,* extrasensory awareness of a future situation or event.—**pre·cog·ni·tive**, prē·kog′ni·tiv, *a.*

pre·con·ceive, prē″kon·sēv′, *v.t.*—**preconceived,** *preconceiving.* To form a conception or opinion of beforehand; to form a notion or idea of in advance.

pre·con·cep·tion, prē″kon·sep′shan, *n.* The act of preconceiving; conception or opinion previously formed; prejudice.

pre·con·cert, prē″kon·sụrt′, *v.t.* To arrange beforehand; to settle by previous arrangement.

pre·con·di·tion, prē″kon·dish′an, *n.* A condition that must exist before a certain end is achieved; a prerequisite.—*v.t.* To prepare, as a person or thing, beforehand for a particular event, situation, or use.

pre·con·scious, prē·kon′shus, *a.* *Psychoanal.* Pertaining to material absent from consciousness but readily recalled.—*n.* A portion of the mind on the borderline between consciousness and the unconscious.—**pre·con·scious·ly**, *adv.*

pre·cook, prē·kụk′, *v.t.* To partially or completely cook for quick heating and serving at a later time.

pre·crit·i·cal, prē·krit′i·kal, *a.* *Med.* pertaining to the period which precedes the crucial stage of a disease.

pre·cur·sor, pri·kụr′sėr, prē′kụr·sėr, *n.* [L. *praecursor*—*prae,* before, and *cursor,* a runner, < *curro, cursum,* I run.] A forerunner; a harbinger; one who or that which precedes an event and indicates its approach; a predecessor.

pre·cur·so·ry, pri·kụr′so·rē, *a.* Preceding as the harbinger; preliminary; going before. Also **pre·cur·sive.**

pre·da·cious, pri·dā′shus, *a.* [< L. *praeda,* prey, spoil, plunder, etc.] Predatory; given to prey on other animals.

—**pre·da·cious·ness**, *n.*—**pre·dac·i·ty**, pri·das′i·tē, *n.*

pre·date, prē·dāt′, *v.t.*—*predated, predating.* To date by anticipation; to antedate; to come before in time.

pre·da·tion, pri·dā′shan, *n.* The act of preying or pillaging; despoiling; the act of one animal killing another for food.

pre·da·tion pres·sure, *n.* The consequences of predation upon a community, esp. of wildlife, as it affects the continuance of the species that is preyed upon.

pred·a·tor, pred′a·tėr, *n.* Someone or something that is predatory.

pred·a·to·ry, pred′a·tōr″ē, pred′a·tạr″ē, *a.* [L. *praedatorius.*] Plundering; pillaging; practicing rapine.—**pred·a·to·ri·al**, *a.*—**pred·a·to·ri·ly**, *adv.*

pre·dawn, prē·dạn′, prē′dạn′, *a.* Pertaining to the time immediately preceding sunrise; the end of night.—*n.*

pre·de·cease, prē″di·sēs′, *v.t.*—*predeceased, predeceasing.* To die before.—*v.i.*—*n.*

pred·e·ces·sor, pred′i·ses″ėr, pred′i·ses·ėr, *Brit.* also prē′di·ses″ėr, *n.* [L. *praedecessor—prae,* before, and *decessor,* one who retires, < *decedo, decessum,* I depart—*de,* from, and *cedo,* to go.] One who precedes or goes before another in some position; a thing which is succeeded by another thing; *archaic,* an ancestor.

pre·des·ig·nate, prē·dez′ig·nāt″, prē·des′ig·nāt″, *v.t.*—*predesignated, predesignating.* To designate beforehand.—**pre·des·ig·na·tion**, *n.*

pre·des·ti·nar·i·an, pri·des″ti·nâr′ē·an, *a.* Of or pertaining to predestination.—*n.* One who believes in the doctrine of predestination.—**pre·des·ti·nar·i·an·ism**, *n.*

pre·des·ti·nate, pri·des′ti·nāt″, *v.t.*—*predestinated, predestinating.* [L. *praedestino, praedestinatum—prae,* before, and *destino,* I determine.] To predetermine or foreordain; *theol.* to appoint or ordain beforehand by divine decree.—pri·des′ti·nit, pri·des′ti·nāt″, *a.* Predestinated; foreordained.—**pre·des·ti·na·tor**, *n.*

pre·des·ti·na·tion, pri·des″ti·nā′shan, prē″des·ti·nā′shan, *n.* The act of decreeing or foreordaining events; fate; destiny. *Theol.* the doctrine that God has from eternity determined whatever comes to pass; the decree that God has preordained men to everlasting happiness or damnation.

pre·des·tine, pri·des′tiń, *v.t.*—*predestined, predestining.* To decree beforehand; to foreordain.

pre·de·ter·mine, prē″di·tụr′min, *v.t.*—*predetermined, predetermining.* To determine or decide beforehand; foreordain; to prejudice beforehand; influence.—**pre·de·ter·mi·na·tion**, *n.*

pre·di·al, prē′dē·al, *a.* Praedial.

pred·i·ca·ble, pred′i·ka·bl, *a.* [L *praedicabilis,* < *praedico.*] Capable of being affirmed.—*n.* Anything that may be predicated or affirmed; *logic,* one of the five things which can be predicated of something or someone, as genus, species, difference, property, and accident.—**pred·i·ca·bil·i·ty**, **pred·i·ca·ble·ness**, *n.*

pre·dic·a·ment, pri·dik′a·ment, *n.* [L.L. *praedicamentum.*] An unpleasant, trying, or dangerous situation; one of the classes or categories of logical predications.—**pre·dic·a·men·tal**, pri·dik″a·men′tal, *a.*

pred·i·cant, pred′i·kant, *a.* [L.L. *praedicans* (-*ant*-), ppr. of *praedicare,* preach.] Preaching.—*n.* A preacher.

pred·i·cate, pred′i·kāt″, *v.t.*—*predicated, predicating.* [L. *praedicatus,* pp. of *praedicare,* declare publicly, proclaim, assert, L.L. preach, < L. *prae,* before, and *dicare,* declare: cf. *preach.*] To proclaim or declare; affirm or assert. *Logic.* To affirm or assert concerning the subject of a proposition; make, as a term, the predicate of such a proposition. To connote or imply; to found or base, as a statement or action, on something.—*v.i.* To make an affirmation or assertion.—*pred″i·kit, a. Gram.* Belonging to the predicate; made, through the instrumentality of a verb, as a copula or linking verb, to qualify its subject.—*pred″i·kit, n. Logic,* that which is said of the subject in a proposition; *gram.* the word or words expressing what is affirmed or denied of a subject, being a finite verb alone or a finite verb with object or complement.—**pred·i·ca·tive**, *a.*—**pred·i·ca·tive·ly**, *adv.*

pred·i·cate nom·i·na·tive, *n.* A noun, pronoun, or adjective, in certain languages, in the nominative case, identifying or modifying the subject of a linking verb.

pred·i·ca·tion, pred″i·kā′shan, *n.* [L. *praedicatio*(n-).] The act of predicating; affirmation; assertion; *logic,* the assertion of something about a subject.—**pred·i·ca·tion·al**, *a.*

pred·i·ca·to·ry, pred′i·ka·tōr″ē, pred′i·ka·tạr″ē, *a.* Pertaining to preaching.

pre·dict, pri·dikt′, *v.t.* [L. *praedico, praedictum—prae,* before, and *dicere,* to tell.] To foretell; to prophesy.—*v.i.* To make a prediction.—**pre·dict·a·ble**, *a.*—**pre·dict·a·bly**, *adv.*—**pre·dict·a·bil·i·ty**, *n.*

pre·dic·tion, pri·dik′shan, *n.* The act of predicting; a foretelling; a prophecy.—**pre·dic·tive**, pri·dik′tiv, *a.*—**pre·dic·tive·ly**, *adv.*

pre·dic·tor, pri·dik′tėr, *n.* A person who predicts; *milit.* a mechanical device on antiaircraft guns for automatically determining flight characteristics of oncoming planes, as speed, altitude, and course.

pre·di·gest, prē″di·jest′, prē″dī·jest′, *v.t.* To treat, as food, by an artificial process, to make it more easily digestible.—**pre·di·ges·tion**, *n.*

pre·di·lec·tion, pred″i·lek′shan, prēd″i·lek′shan, *n.* [Fr. *prédilection*—L. *prae,* before, and *dilectio,* a choice, < *diligere,* to love.] A preconceived liking; a prepossession of mind in favor of something; partiality or preference.

pre·dis·pose, prē″di·spōz′, *v.t.*—*predisposed, predisposing.* To incline beforehand; to give a disposition or tendency to; to fit or adapt previously; to dispose of or bequeath in advance.

pre·dis·po·si·tion, prē·dis″po·zish′an, prē″dis·po·zish′an, *n.* The state of being previously disposed toward something; previous inclination or tendency.

pre·doc·tor·ate, prē·dok′tėr·it, *a.* Pertaining to scholastic study or accomplishments before receiving a doctorate.

pre·dom·i·nant, pri·dom′i·nant, *a.* Prevalent over others; superior in strength, influence, or authority; ruling; controlling.—**pre·dom·i·nant·ly**, *adv.*—**pre·dom·i·nance**, **pre·dom·i·nan·cy**, *n.*

pre·dom·i·nate, pri·dom′i·nāt″, *v.i.*—*predominated, predominating.* [Fr. *prédominer*—L. *prae,* before, and *dominari,* to rule, < *dominus,* lord.] To have surpassing power, influence, or authority; to have controlling influence among others; to surpass in number, size, or power.—*v.t.* To rule over; to dominate.—*a.*—**pre·dom·i·nate·ly**, pri·dom′i·nit·lē, *adv.*—**pre·dom·i·na·tion**, *n.*

pre·em·i·nent, prē·em′i·nent, *a.* [L. *praeminens* (-*ent*-), ppr. of *praeminere.*] Eminent before or above others; superior to or surpassing others; distinguished beyond others.—**pre·em·i·nence**, *n.*—**pre·em·i·nent·ly**, *adv.*

pre·empt, prē·empt′, *v.t.* To occupy, as public land, in order to establish a right to buy; to acquire or seize upon before others. —*v.i. Bridge,* to make a preemptive bid.— **pre·emp·tor**, *n.*

pre·emp·tion, prē·emp′shan, *n.* The act or the right of purchasing before others; a settler's right, granted by the government, to have first chance at purchasing public land on which he has settled; a prior assertion of ownership.

pre·emp·tive, prē·emp′tiv, *a.* Of that which preempts or is capable of preemption; *bridge,* relating to an unnecessarily high bid or overcall made with the intention of blocking the opponents' bidding.—**pre·emp·tive·ly**, *adv.*

preen, prēn, *v.t.* [O.E. *proine, proigne,* to prune, to preen.] To trim or clean with the beak, as birds dressing their feathers; to make, as oneself, attractive by careful grooming; to show vanity or pride, as in some personal achievement.—*v.i.* To primp; to gloat.—**preen·er**, *n.*

pre·en·gage, prē″en·gāj′, *v.t.*—*preengaged, preengaging.* To engage or contract for ahead of time, as for employment or for some special service; to put under obligation, as for marriage, by prior engagement.—**pre·en·gage·ment**, *n.*

pre·ex·il·i·an, prē″eg·zil′ē·an, prē″eg·zil′yan, prē″ek·sil′ē·an, prē″ek·sil′yan, *a.* Previous to the Babylonian exile or captivity of the Jews at the end of the 6th century B.C.

pre·ex·ist, prē·ex·ist, prē″ig·zist′, *v.t., v.i.* To exist beforehand or in a previous state; to exist before something or someone.—**pre·ex·ist·ence**, *n.*—**pre·ex·ist·ent**, *a.*

pre·fab, prē′fab″, *n.* Something that is prefabricated, as a house.

pre·fab·ri·cate, prē·fab′ri·kāt″, *v.t.*—*prefabricated, prefabricating.* To fabricate or construct beforehand; to manufacture in standardized parts or sections ready for rapid assembling and erection, as a house to be assembled on the site.—**pre·fab·ri·ca·tion**, prē″fab·ri·kā′shan, *n.*

pref·ace, pref′is, *n.* [Fr. *préface,* < L. *praefatio.*] Something spoken as introductory to a discourse, or written as introductory to a book or other composition.—*v.t.*—*prefaced, prefacing.* To introduce by preliminary remarks; to be a preface or preliminary for.

pref·a·to·ry, pref′a·tōr″ē, pref′a·tạr″ē, *a.* Having the character of a preface; pertaining to a preface. Also **pref·a·to·ri·al**.—**pref·a·to·ri·ly**, *adv.*

pre·fect, **prae·fect**, prē′fekt, *n.* [L. *praefectus,* < *praeficio.*] A name common to several officers, military and civil, in ancient Rome; an important functionary or magistrate in France; *Brit.* a senior student serving as a monitor in public schools; *Rom. Cath. Ch.* the dean of some religious or private schools.

pre·fect ap·os·tol·ic, *n. Rom. Cath. Ch.* a clergy member who ranks below but serves as a bishop in a division of a missionary region.

pre·fec·ture, prē′fek·chėr, *n.* The office or jurisdiction of a prefect; the official residence of a prefect.—**pre·fec·tur·al**, pri·fek′chėr·al, *a.*

pre·fer, pri·fụr′, *v.t.*—*preferred, preferring.* [L. *praefero,* to carry before, to present, to esteem more highly.] To set above something else in estimation; to hold in greater favor or esteem; to choose rather than; as, to *prefer* one to another; to offer for one's consideration or decision; to present, esp. petitions or prayers; to bring forward, as charges; to advance, as to an office or dignity; to raise; to exalt.—**pre·fer·rer**, *n.*

pref·er·a·ble, pref′ėr·a·bl, pref′ra·bl, *a.* Worthy to be preferred; more eligible; more desirable.—**pref·er·a·ble·ness**, **pref·er·a·bil·i·ty**, *n.*—**pref·er·a·bly**, *adv.*

pref·er·ence, pref′ėr·ens, pref′rens, *n.* The preferring of one thing before another;

the right or condition of having a choice or of being chosen; the thing or person preferred; a special advantage made available to one over another, as in trade between countries; a right of certain creditors to priority of payment; a prior claim on the distribution of dividends or other profit.

pref·er·en·tial, pref″*e*·ren′shal, *a*. Of or relating to preference; showing preference or partiality to, as in hiring union workers; designating preference received, as: He enjoyed *preferential* treatment. Permitting a statement of preference, as the ballot in voting.—**pref·er·en·tial·ly**, *adv*.

pre·fer·ment, pri·fur′ment, *n*. Advancement to a higher office, dignity, or station; promotion; a superior or valuable place or office. The bringing forward, as of charges.

pre·ferred stock, *n*. A form of capital stock given preference in payment of dividends, or other rights, over common stock.

pre·fig·u·ra·tion, prē·fig″ū·rā′shan, prē″fig·ū·rā′shan, *n*. The act of prefiguring; that which prefigures.—**pre·fig·ur·a·tive**, prē·fig′ūr·*a*·tiv, *a*.—**pre·fig·ur·a·tive·ly**, *adv*.—**pre·fig·ur·a·tive·ness**, *n*.

pre·fig·ure, prē·fig′ūr, *v.t.*—*prefigured, prefiguring.* To represent beforehand, as by types and similitudes; to envision in advance.—**pre·fig·ure·ment**, *n*.

pre·fix, prē·fiks′, prē′fiks, *v.t.* [Fr. *préfixer*, L. *praefigo, praefixus.*] To put or fix before or at the beginning of another thing, as a title preceding a name; to settle, fix, or appoint beforehand; as, to *prefix* the hour of meeting.—prē′fiks, *n. Gram.* a letter, syllable, or word put to the beginning of a stem, root, or base, usu. varying its signification.—**pre·fix·al**, prē′fik·sal, prē·fik′sal, *a*.—**pre·fix·al·ly**, *adv*.

pre·flight, prē·flīt′, *a*. Happening before or preparing for an airplane flight.

pre·form, prē·farm′, *v.t.* [L. *præformare.*] To form beforehand; to decide beforehand; determine beforehand the form or shape of.—prē·farm″, *n*. Something formed beforehand; something only partly formed.

pre·for·ma·tion, prē″far·mā′shan, *n*. Previous formation; the obsolete theory that development of an organism simply consists of increase in size because all parts are present in miniature in the germ cell.

preg·na·ble, preg′na·bl, *a*. [Fr. *prenable*, < *prendre*, to take, L. *prehendo, prehensum.*] Capable of being taken or won by force; vulnerable.—**preg·na·bil·i·ty**, *n*.

preg·nan·cy, preg′nan·sē, *n*. pl. **preg·nan·cies**. The state, period, or quality of being pregnant.

preg·nant, preg′nant, *a*. [L. *praegnans, praegnantis.*] Carrying a fetus in the body; being with young; full or replete, usu. followed by *with*; as, *pregnant with* significance; showing fertility; full of consequence or significance; rich in imagination or wit.—**preg·nant·ly**, *adv*.

pre·heat, prē·hēt′, *v.t.* To heat beforehand or before starting a subsequent process.

pre·hen·sile, pri·hen′sil, pri·hen′sīl, *a*. [L. *prehendere, prehensus*, to lay hold of.] Capable of or adapted to seize or grasp, esp. by wrapping around something; as, a *prehensile* tail of a monkey.—**pre·hen·sil·i·ty**, prē″hen·sil′i·tē, *n*.

pre·hen·sion, pri·hen′shan, *n*. A taking hold of or seizing; apprehension.

pre·his·tor·ic, prē″hi·star′ik, prē″hi·stor′ik, *a*. Relating to a period antecedent to that at which written history begins. Also **pre·his·tor·i·cal**.—**pre·his·tor·i·cal·ly**, *adv*.

pre·his·to·ry, prē·his′to·rē, prē·his′trē, *n*. The study of man in the time which precedes written events, based mainly on ethnological and archaeological discoveries; a history of the events prior to a situation or crisis.

pre·hom·i·nid, prē·hom′i·nid, *n*. Any of the extinct primitive men, as the Java, Peking, and Eyassi.—*a*.

pre·ig·ni·tion, prē″ig·nish′an, *n*. An ignition of the combustible charge in an internal-combustion engine before the piston is in a position to commence its working stroke.

pre·judge, prē·juj′, *v.t.*—*prejudged, prejudging.* [Fr. *préjuger*.] To judge before hearing, or before the arguments and facts are fully known; to condemn beforehand or prematurely—**pre·judg·er**, *n*.—**pre·judg·ment, pre·judge·ment**, *n*.

prej·u·dice, prej′a·dis, *n*. [Fr. *préjudice*, < L. *praejudicium*.] An opinion, judgment, or evaluation, favorable or more often unfavorable, conceived without proof or competent evidence, but based on what seems valid to one's own mind; a bias against a race, creed, group, or the like; the holding of such feelings; harm or damage done to one by unreasonable action or judgment of another or others.—*v.t.*—*prejudiced, prejudicing.* To implant a prejudice in the mind of; to bias by hasty and incorrect notions; to injure by an act or judgment; to hurt, damage, impair, or injure in general; as, to *prejudice* one's cause.—**with·out prej·u·dice**, *law*, without jeopardizing one's legal rights or claims.

prej·u·di·cial, prej″*a*·dish′al, *a*. Disposed to prejudice or hurt; injurious; detrimental.—**prej·u·di·cial·ly**, prej″·ū·dish′al·lē, *adv*.—**prej·u·di·cial·ness**, *n*.

pre·kin·der·gar·ten, prē·kin′der·gär″ten, prē·kin′der·gär″den, *a*. Of or denoting four-year-olds or the year before kindergarten.—*n*. Also **jun·ior kin·der·gar·ten**.

prel·a·cy, prel′a·sē, *n*. pl. **prel·a·cies**. The office or function of a prelate; the system of church government by prelates, sometimes used derogatorily; prelates collectively.

prel·ate, prel′it, *n*. [Fr. *prélat*, < L.L. *praelatus*, < L. *praelatus*, pp. of *praefero, praelatum*—*prae*, before and *latus*, borne.] An ecclesiastic of a high order, as an archbishop, bishop, or patriarch; a dignitary of the church.—**prel·ate·ship**, *n*.

prel·a·ture, prel′a·chér, *n*. The position of a prelate; prelates collectively; a prelate's jurisdiction.

pre·lect, pri·lekt′, *v.i.* [L. *praelego, praelectus*—*prae*, before, and *lego*, I read.] To give a lecture or discourse in public.—**pre·lec·tion**, pri·lek′shan, *n*.—**pre·lec·tor**, *n*.

pre·li·ba·tion, prē″li·bā′shan, *n*. [L. *prae*, before, and *libo*, to taste.] Foretaste; a tasting beforehand.

pre·lim, prē′lim, pre·lim′, *n. Slang*, preliminary.

pre·lim·i·nar·y, pri·lim′i·ner″ē, *a*. [Fr. *préliminaires*—L. *prae*, before, and *limen*, threshold.] Introductory; preceding the main discourse or business; prefatory.—*n.* pl. **pre·lim·i·nar·ies**. Something introductory or preparatory; a preliminary examination, as for a college degree; *sports*, an event occurring before the major scheduled event; *pl., print.* front matter.—**pre·lim·i·nar·i·ly**, *adv*.

prel·ude, prel′ūd, prāl′ūd, prē′lŏd, prā′lŏd, *n*. [Fr. *prélude*, < L. *prae*, before, and *ludus*, play.] Something preparatory or leading up to what follows; an introductory happening or performance; also *prelusion. Mus.* a short introductory strain preceding the principal movement; a separate, relatively short, instrumental piece; a piece of music introducing an opera, shorter than a formal overture; music played at the beginning of a church service; a voluntary.—*v.t.*—*preluded, preluding.* To introduce with a prelude; to serve as prelude to; play as a prelude.—*v.i.* To serve as a prelude; to give or play a prelude.—**pre·lud·er**, pri·lŏ′dér, prel′ū·dér, *n*.

pre·lu·sion, pri·lŏ′zhan, *n*. Prelude.

pre·lu·sive, pri·lŏ′siv, *a*. Having the character of a prelude; introductory. Also **pre·lu·so·ry**, pri·lŏ′so·rē.—**pre·lu·sive·ly**, *adv*.

pre·ma·ture, prē″ma·tur′, prē″ma·tūr′, prē″ma·chur′, prē″ma·chur″, *a*. [L. *praematurus*—*prae*, before, and *maturus*, ripe.] Happening, arriving, existing, or done before the proper time; untimely.—*n*. **pre·ma·ture·ly**, *adv*.—**pre·ma·ture·ness, pre·ma·tu·ri·ty**, *n*.

pre·max·il·la, prē″mak·sil′a, *n*. pl. **pre·max·il·lae**. *Anat., zool.* one of a pair of bones in front of the upper jaw of vertebrates, situated between the maxillary bones.—**pre·max·il·lar·y**, prē·mak′si·ler″ē, *a*.

pre·med, prē·med′, *a. Colloq.* premedical.

pre·med·i·cal, prē·med′i·kal, *a*. Pertaining to or engaged in studies preparatory to the professional study of medicine. Also **premed**.

pre·med·i·tate, pri·med′i·tāt″, *v.t.*—*premeditated, premeditating.* [Fr. *préméditer*, L. *praemeditor*—*prae*, before, and *meditor*, I meditate.] To plan, consider, or think on beforehand.—*v.i.* To deliberate or think beforehand.—**pre·med·i·ta·tor**, *n*.—**pre·med·i·tat·ed**, *a*.—**pre·med·i·tat·ed·ly**, *adv*.

pre·med·i·ta·tion, pri·med″i·tā′shan, *n*. The act of premeditating; *law*, planning or deliberation prior to an act which shows intent to commit this act.—**pre·med·i·ta·tive**, *a*.

pre·men·stru·al, prē·men′strŏ·al, prē·men′stral, *a*. Pertaining to the period just prior to menstruation.—**pre·men·stru·al·ly**, *adv*.

pre·mier, pri·mēr′, prim·yēr′, *a*. [Fr. *premier*, < L. *primarius*, of the first rank, < *primus*, first.] First; chief; principal; senior.—*n*. The first or chief minister of state; prime minister.—**pre·mier·ship**, *n*.

pre·miere, pri·mēr′, pri·myâr′, *Fr.* pRe·myeR′, *n*. The initial public performance of a drama, opera, etc.; the leading lady, as of a drama.—*v.i.* To be performed or shown publicly for the first time; to perform a particular role for the first time.—*v.t.* To present publicly for the first time.—*a*. First; principal; initial. Also *premier*.

pre·mil·le·nar·i·an, prē″mil·*e*·nâr′ē·an, *n*. A believer in premillennialism; a premillennialist.—*a*.—**pre·mil·le·nar·i·an·ism**, *n*.

pre·mil·len·ni·al, prē″mi·len′ē·al, *a*. Of or pertaining to the period preceding the millennium.—**pre·mil·len·ni·al·ly**, *adv*.

pre·mil·len·ni·al·ism, prē″mi·len′ē·a·liz″um, *n*. The doctrine or belief that the second coming of Christ will precede the millennium.—**pre·mil·len·ni·al·ist**, *n*.

prem·ise, prem′is, *v.t.*—*premised, premising.* [< L. *praemitto, praemissum prae*, before, and *mitto*, I send.] To set forth or make known beforehand, as introductory to the main subject; to lay down as an antecedent proposition.—*v.i.* To make or assume a premise.—*n.* [Fr. *premisse*, a premise (in logic). L. *praemissum*, what is sent or put before.] A proposition laid down as a base of argument; *logic*, the name applied to each of the two first propositions of a syllogism, from which the inference or conclusion is drawn. *Pl.* land including houses or tenements; a house and its appurtenances; *pl., law*, the matter already stated, specif. the beginning or early portion of a legal deed or document where the subject matter is stated or described in full. Also **prem·iss**.

pre·mi·um, prē″mē·um, *n*. [L. *praemium*, profit, reward, < *prae*, before, and *emere*, take, buy.] A reward given for a particular action or as an incentive; a bonus offered as an inducement to purchase a product, contract for a service, or the like; a bonus, or sum additional to price, wages, or interest; the amount paid or agreed to be paid as the consideration for a contract of insurance; the excess value of one form of money over another of the same nominal value; a sum above the nominal or par value of a thing; a sum, in addition to the interest, which is paid for the loan of money; a fee paid for instruction in a trade or profession.—**at a pre·mi·um**, above the usual price; valuable; in demand.

pre·mo·lar, prē·mō′lẽr, a. Noting or pertaining to those teeth situated in front of the molars.—n. A premolar tooth. Also *bicuspid*.

pre·mon·ish, pri·mon′ish, v.t. [Prefix *pre*, and *-monish*, as in *admonish*.] *Rare*. To forewarn; to admonish beforehand.

pre·mo·ni·tion, prē″mo·nish′an, prem″o·nish′an, n. A sense of foreboding concerning the future without factual substantiation; previous warning, notice, or information.

pre·mon·i·to·ry, pri·mon′i·tōr″ē, pri·mon′i·tąr″ē, a. Giving previous warning or notice.—**pre·mon·i·to·ri·ly**, adv.

pre·morse, pri·mạrs′, a. [L. *praemorsus*.] *Bot.* of a root or leaf, terminating abruptly and irregularly as if bitten off.

pre·na·tal, prē·nāt′al, a. Previous to birth. —**pre·na·tal·ly**, adv.

pre·no·men, prē·nō′men, n. pl. **pre·nom·i·na**, **pre·no·mens**, prē·nom′i·na, prē·nō′mi·na. Praenomen.

pre·no·tion, prē·nō′shan, n. [L. *praenotio-* (n-), < *praenoscere*, foreknow.] An anticipatory knowledge or perception; a preconception.

pre·oc·cu·pa·tion, prē·ok″ū·pā′shan, prē″ok·ū·pā′shan, n. The act of occupying or taking possession before another; the state of being mentally occupied with a subject other than the concern before one.

pre·oc·cu·pied, prē·ok′ū·pīd″, a. Having the attention taken up previously; totally absorbed in thought. *Biol.* of a Latin name in binomial nomenclature, being already in use.

pre·oc·cu·py, prē·ok′ū·pī″, v.t.—*preoccupied, preoccupying*. To occupy or take possession of before another; to engage or occupy the attention of.

pre·op·er·a·tive, prē·op′e·rā″tiv, prē·op′ẽr·a·tiv, prē·op′ra·tiv, a. *Med.* prior to an operation.—**pre·op·er·a·tive·ly**, adv.

pre·or·dain, prē″ạr·dān′, v.t. To ordain or appoint beforehand; predetermine.— **pre·or·dain·ment**, n.—**pre·or·di·na·tion**, prē″ạr·di·nā′shan, n.

prep, prep, n. *Colloq.* a preparatory school; *Brit. slang*, homework preparation.—v.i. To attend preparatory school.—v.t. To prepare or study, as for a school course.

prep·a·ra·tion, prep′a·rā′shan, n. [O.Fr. *preparacion* (Fr. *préparation*), < L. *praeparatio*(n-).] The act of preparing; the state of being prepared; a proceeding, measure, or provision by which one prepares for something; something prepared, manufactured, or compounded; as, a medicinal *preparation*. *Mus.* the preparing of a discord, as by introducing the dissonant tone as a consonant tone in the preceding chord; the tone so introduced.

pre·par·a·tive, pri·par′a·tiv, a. [Fr. *préparatif*.] Preparatory.—n. That which prepares; a preparation.—**pre·par·a·tive·ly**, adv.

pre·par·a·tor, pri·par′a·tẽr, n. [= Fr. *préparateur*, < L.L. *praeparator*.] One who prepares specimens for scientific purposes.

pre·par·a·to·ry, pri·par′a·tōr″ē, pri·par′a·tōr″ē, prep′ẽr·a·tōr″ē, a. Serving to prepare the way for something; introductory.—adv.—**pre·par·a·to·ri·ly**, adv.

pre·par·a·to·ry school, n. A private school providing an education which is designed primarily to prepare students for college; *Brit.* a private elementary school which prepares students for a public school.

pre·pare, pri·pâr′, v.t.—*prepared, preparing*. [O.Fr. *preparer* (Fr. *préparer*), < L. *praeparare*, make ready beforehand.] To make ready, or put in due condition; as, to *prepare* a manuscript for printing; fit out or equip; to get ready for eating, as a meal, by assembling, dressing, or cooking; manufacture, compound, or compose, as a medicine; *mus.* to lead up to, as a discord, by means of some preliminary tone or tones.—v.i. To put things or oneself in readiness; make preparations.—**pre·par·er**, n.

pre·par·ed·ness, pri·pâr′id·nis, pri·pârd′nis, n. The state of being prepared; readiness; specif. of a nation, the state of being prepared to meet threats or outbreaks of war.

pre·pay, prē·pā′, v.t.—*prepaid, prepaying*. To pay before obtaining possession of; to pay in advance.—**pre·pay·ment**, n.

pre·plan, prē·plan′, v.t.—*preplanned, preplanning*. To anticipate an accomplishment by setting forth the steps necessary to a successful conclusion.

pre·pon·der·ance, pri·pon′dẽr·ans, n. The quality or fact of being preponderant; superiority in weight, power, influence, or number. Also **pre·pon·der·an·cy**.

pre·pon·der·ant, pri·pon′dẽr·ant, a. Preponderating; superior in weight, force, influence, or number; predominant.—**pre·pon·der·ant·ly**, adv.

pre·pon·der·ate, pri·pon′de·rāt″, v.i.—*preponderated, preponderating*. [L. *praeponderatus*, pp. of *praeponderare*.] To exceed something else in weight; to incline downward or descend, as one scale or end of a balance, because of greater weight; to be superior in power, influence, or amount; predominate.—**pre·pon·der·at·ing·ly**, adv. —**pre·pon·der·a·tion**, n.

prep·o·si·tion, prep′o·zish′an, n. [L. *praepositio*(n-), < *praeponere*, place before.] *Gram.* an indeclinable part of speech, as *by, in, to, for, from*, usu. placed before a noun or its equivalent forming a prepositional phrase, and showing the relation to a substantive, verb, or adjective; as, a man *from* the city.—**prep·o·si·tion·al**, a.—**prep·o·si·tion·al·ly**, adv.

pre·pos·i·tive, prē·poz′i·tiv, a. [L.L. *praepositivus*, < L. *praeponere*.] *Gram.* Put before; prefixed.—n.—**pre·pos·i·tive·ly**, adv.

pre·pos·sess, prē″po·zes′, v.t. To possess or dominate mentally beforehand, as a prejudice does; imbue with a feeling or opinion, favorable or unfavorable, in advance; prejudice or bias, esp. favorably; impress favorably beforehand.

pre·pos·sess·ing, prē″po·zes′ing, a. That prepossesses, esp. favorably; making a favorable first impression; pleasing.— **pre·pos·sess·ing·ly**, adv.—**pre·pos·sess·ing·ness**, n.

pre·pos·ses·sion, prē″po·zesh′an, n. The state of being mentally preoccupied with a subject; a prejudice, esp. in favor of a person or thing; a favorable feeling or opinion conceived in advance.

pre·pos·ter·ous, pri·pos′tẽr·us, pri·pos′trus, a. [L. *praeposterus*.] Contrary to nature, reason, or common sense; utterly foolish; absurd.—**pre·pos·ter·ous·ly**, adv. —**pre·pos·ter·ous·ness**, n.

pre·po·ten·cy, prē·pōt′en·sē, n. The state of being prepotent; *biol.* the ability of one parent to impress his hereditary characteristics on the offspring due to having the greater number of dominant genes or greater homozygosity.

pre·po·tent, pri·pōt′ent, a. [L. *praepotens*.] Preeminent in power, authority, or influence; predominant. *Biol.* noting or pertaining to a preponderating tendency or power of one germ cell, one parent, or one ancestor to fix the character of descendants, as in dominant genes.—**pre·po·tent·ly**, adv.

pre·puce, prē′pūs, n. [L. *praeputium*.] A fold of skin covering the head of the penis or the clitoris; foreskin.—**pre·pu·tial**, pri·pū′shal, a.

Pre-Raph·a·el·ite, prē·raf′ē·a·līt″, prē·rā′fē·a·līt″, n. One of a group of English artists, the 'Pre-Raphaelite Brotherhood,' formed in 1848, and including Holman Hunt, John Everett Millais, and Dante Gabriel Rossetti, who endeavored to revive the style and spirit of the Italian artists before the time of Raphael; any modern artist of like aims or methods; one of the Italian painters who preceded Raphael.—a. Of, pertaining to, or characteristic of the Pre-Raphaelites; existing before the time of Raphael.—**Pre-Raph·a·el·it·ism**, n.

pre·re·cord, prē′ri·kạrd′, v.t. To record, as a television program, before the actual presentation to the public.

pre·req·ui·site, pri·rek′wi·zit, a. Necessary to something subsequent.—n. Something that is prerequisite, as a course required to qualify for advanced study.

pre·rog·a·tive, pri·rog′a·tiv, n. [L. *praerogativa*, < *praerogo*, to ask before.] An official or hereditary right which may be asserted without question; a special right or privilege of a sovereign or other executive of a government; a privilege belonging to one specific class or person.—a. Having or pertaining to a prerogative.

pre·sa, prä′sa, *It.* prᴇ′sä, n. pl. **pre·se**, prä′sā, *It.* prᴇ′se. [It., a taking, < *prendere*, < L. *prendere, prehendere*, take.] *Mus.* a mark, as :S:, +, or ✳, used in a canon or fugue, to indicate where the successive voice parts are to take up the theme.

pres·age, pres′ij, n. [Fr. *présage*, L., *praesagium*.] Something which portends or foreshadows a future event; a prognostic; an omen; a foreboding or presentiment; a feeling that something is to happen; a prophecy.—pres′ij, pri·sāj′, v.t.—*presaged, presaging*. To have a premonition of; to foreshadow; to foretell, predict, prophesy.— v.i. To form or utter a prediction.— **pres·age·ful**, a.—**pres·ag·er**, n.

pre·sanc·ti·fied, prē′sangk′ti·fīd″, a. *Rom. Cath. Ch.* consecrated at an earlier Mass: used in reference to the Eucharist elements.

pres·by·o·pi·a, prez″bē·ō′pē·a, pres″bē·ō′pē·a, n. [Gr. *presbys*, old, and *ōps*, the eye.] *Ophthalm.* an imperfection of vision in which near objects are seen less distinctly than those at a distance, common in old age.—**pres·by·ope**, prez″bē·ōp″, pres′bē·ōp″, n.—**pres·by·op·ic**, prez″bē·op′ik, pres″bē·op′ik, a.

pres·by·ter, prez′bi·tẽr, pres′bi·tẽr, n. [L.L. *presbyter*, < Gr. *presbyteros*, an elder, prop. adj., older, compar. < *présbys*, old man.] In the early Christian church, an elder; in hierarchical churches, a priest; in Presbyterian churches, a member of a presbytery.—**pres·byt·er·ate**, prez·bit′ẽr·it, prez·bit′e·rāt″, pres·bit′ẽr·it, pres·bit′e·rāt″, n.

pres·by·te·ri·an, prez″bi·tẽr′ē·an, pres″bi·tẽr′ē·an, a. Pertaining to or based on the principle of ecclesiastical government by presbyters or presbyteries; *(cap.)* designating or pertaining to various churches having this form of government and holding more or less modified forms of Calvinism.—n. *(Cap.)* a member or adherent of a Presbyterian church.— **Pres·by·te·ri·an·ism**, prez″bi·tẽr′ē·a·niz″um, pres″bi·tẽr′ē·a·niz″um, n.

pres·by·ter·y, prez′bi·ter″ē, pres′bi·ter″ē, *n. pl.* **pres·by·ter·ies**. [L. *presbyterium*, < Gr. *presbytérion*.] A body of presbyters or elders; specif. in Presbyterian churches, a judicatory consisting of all the ministers and certain of the lay or ruling elders within a district; the district under the jurisdiction of a presbytery; (*cap.*) Presbyterianism. (*l.c.*) the part of a church appropriated to the clergy; a clergyman′s or priest′s house, now only in Roman Catholic use.—**pres·by·te·ri·al**, prez″bi·-tēr′ē·al, pres″bi·tēr′ē·al, *a.*

pre·school, prē′skōl′, *a.* Pertaining to the period or to a child in the period from infancy to school age.—prē′skōl″, *n.* A nursery school.

pre·sci·ence, prē′shē·ens, prē′shens, presh′ē·ens, presh′ens, *n.* [L. *prescientia*.] Foreknowledge; knowledge of events before they take place; foresight.—**pre·sci·ent**, *a.*—**pre·sci·ent·ly**, *adv.*

pre·scind, pri·sind′, *v.t.* [L. *praescindere*, cut off in front.] To separate in thought; abstract; to cut off or away; remove.—*v.i.* To withdraw the attention, followed by *from*; turn aside in thought.

pre·score, prē′skōr′, prē·skar′, *v.t.*—*prescored, prescoring.* To record background music, as for motion pictures, prior to filming a movie.

pre·scribe, pri·skrīb′, *v.t.*—*prescribed, prescribing.* [L. *praescribere* (pp. *praescriptus*).] To lay down, in writing or otherwise, as a rule or a course to be followed; appoint, ordain, or enjoin, as duties or actions; *med.* to designate or order for use, as a remedy or treatment; *law*, to render invalid by negative prescription.—*v.i.* To lay down rules, direct, or dictate; *med.* to designate remedies or treatment to be used. *Law*, to claim a right or title by prescription, or by virtue of long use and enjoyment, usu. with *for* or *to*; to become invalid by negative prescription, or through lapse of time, as a claim or action.—**pre·scrib·er**, *n.*

pre·script, pri·skript′, prē′skript, *a.* Set down as a rule; prescribed.—prē′skript, *n.* That which is set down or prescribed, as a regulation or precept.

pre·scrip·ti·ble, pri·skrip′ti·bl, *a.* Suitable for or subject to being prescribed; depending upon or derived from prescription.

pre·scrip·tion, pri·skrip′shan, *n.* [L. *praescriptio(n-)*.] *Med.* a physician′s direction, usually written, for the preparation and use of a medicine or remedy; the medicine prescribed. The act of prescribing; that which is prescribed; ancient and continued custom; a claim which is founded on long use. *Law*, the operation of long or immemorial possession or use of a thing to give a right or title to it; right or title acquired by virtue of long and uninterrupted use and enjoyment; limitation of the time within which a claim may be made or an action brought.

pre·scrip·tive, pri·skrip′tiv, *a.* That prescribes; giving directions or injunctions; depending on or arising from legal prescription, as a right or title; established or sanctioned by long use or custom.—**pre·scrip·tive·ly**, *adv.*—**pre·scrip·tive·-ness**, *n.*—**pre·scrip·tiv·ism**, *n.*

pre·sea·son, prē·sē′zon, *a.* Of or pertaining to a time prior to a specified season of the year; *sports*, prior to the first games or other events of a regularly scheduled season, as exhibition professional baseball games.

pres·ence, prez′ens, *n.* [O.Fr. *presence* (Fr. *présence*), < L. *praesentia*.] The state of being present, as with others or in a place; attendance or company; as, to request one′s *presence* at a gathering; immediate vicinity or close proximity;

---

as, an act done in the *presence* of witnesses; the immediate personal vicinity of a great personage giving audience or reception or permitting attendance; as, admitted to the royal *presence*; a confident bearing which helps a performer to establish rapport with an audience; personal appearance or bearing,. esp. of a dignified or imposing kind; as, a man of fine *presence*; a person, esp. of dignified or fine appearance, or an imposing personage; something incorporeal felt as present.

pres·ence cham·ber, *n.* The room in which a man or woman of exalted rank receives visitors.

pres·ence of mind, *n.* Coolness and self-possession permitting prompt and effective action on difficult occasions.

pres·ent, prez′ent, *n.* [O.Fr. *present* (Fr. *présent*).] A thing presented as a gift; a gift.

pre·sent, pri·zent′, *v.t.* [O.Fr. *presenter* (Fr. *présenter*), < L. *præsentare* (pp. *præsentatus*), place before, show, present, < *præsens*.] To bring, as a person, before or into the presence of another, esp. a superior; introduce ceremoniously or formally; as, to be *presented* at court; bring before or introduce to the public; as, a theatrical manager *presents* an actor or a company in a play; come to show, as oneself, before a person, in or at a place, etc.; to show or exhibit; as, to *present* a fine appearance; bring before the mind, or offer for consideration; set forth in words; as, to *present* facts, reasons, or arguments; to represent, personate, or act, as on the stage; to direct, point, or turn to something or in a particular way; as, to *present* one′s face to the foe; to level or aim, as a weapon; to hold out or offer for taking, hand over, or deliver, esp. with formality; as, to *present* one′s card to a person; hand or send in, as a bill or a check, for payment; tender, render, or convey; give, esp. in a formal or ceremonious way; *fig.* to afford or furnish, as an opportunity, possibility, etc. To approach or furnish, as a person, with something offered; to furnish or endow with a gift or the like, esp. by formal act; as, to *present* a man with a gold watch; *eccles.* to offer or recommend, as a clergyman, to the bishop for institution to a benefice. *Law*, to bring formally to the notice of the proper authority, as an offense; bring a formal charge against, as a person.—**pre·sent·er**, *n.*

pres·ent, prez′ent, *a.* [O.Fr. *present* (Fr. *présent*), < L. *præsens* (*præsent-*), lit. ′being before (one),′ ppr. of *præesse*.] Being before or with one or others, or in a company or place specified or understood: opposed to *absent*; being here or there, rather than elsewhere; existing in a place, thing, combination, or the like, as: Copper is *present* in many minerals. Being actually or here under consideration; being at hand; as, a very *present* danger; being, existing, or occurring at this time or now: opposed to *past* and *future*; for the time being; as, articles for *present* use; *gram.* denoting action now going on or a state now existing; as, the *present* tense.—**pres·ent·ness**, *n.*

pres·ent, prez′ent, *n.* The present time; *pl., law*, the present writings, or this document: used in a deed of conveyance, a lease, or other document, to denote the document itself, as: Know all men by these *presents*. *Gram.* the present tense, or a verb form in the present tense.

pre·sent·a·ble, pri·zen′ta·bl, *a.* Capable of being presented; in such dress or appearance as to be able to present oneself without embarrassment; suitable to be exhibited or offered.—**pre·sent·a·bil·i·ty**, *n.*—**pre·sent·a·ble·ness**, *n.*—**pre·-sent·a·bly**, *adv.*

---

pre·sent arms, pri·zent′ ärmz″, *n. Milit.* The position in which a rifle is held perpendicularly in front of the body, in the manual of arms; the order to take this position.

pres·en·ta·tion, prez″en·tā′shan, prē″-zen·tā′shan, *n.* [O.Fr. *presentacion* (Fr. *présentation*), < L.L. *præsentatio(n-)*.] The act of presenting, or the state of being presented; introduction, as of a person at court; exhibition or representation, as of a play; offering or delivering, as of something to be taken; bestowal, as of a gift; that which is presented, as a gift; *eccles.* the act or the right of presenting a clergyman to the bishop for institution to a benefice; *com.* the presenting of a bill, note, or the like. *Psychol.* a cognitive modification of consciousness; an idea; a perceptual cognition.—**pres·en·ta·tion·al**, prez″en·tā′sha·nal, prē″zen·tā′sha·nal, *a.*

pre·sent·a·tive, pri·zen′ta·tiv, *a.* Serving to present; presenting; *philos.* applied to what may be apprehended directly, or to the faculty capable of apprehending directly or without cogitation or reflection; *eccles.* of or open to presentation.

pres·ent-day, prez′ent·dā′, *a.* Of this day; of the present or recent times; current; as, *present-day* styles.

pres·en·tee, prez″en·tē′, *n. Eccles.* one presented to a benefice. One who receives something; one who is presented, as at court.

pre·sen·tient, prē·sen′shent, *a.* [L. *præsentiens* (*-ent-*), ppr. of *præsentire*, feel beforehand.] Feeling or perceiving beforehand; having a presentiment.

pre·sen·ti·ment, pri·zen′ti·ment, *n.* [Pre, before, and *sentiment*; O.Fr. *presentiment*, foreboding.] Apprehension of something future; anticipation of impending evil; foreboding.—**pre·sen·ti·men·tal**, *a.*

pres·ent·ly, prez′ent·lē, *adv.* In a little time; soon; forthwith; now.

pre·sent·ment, pri·zent′ment, *n.* [O.Fr. *presentement*, < *presenter*, E. *present*.] The act or mode of presenting; the state of being presented; presentation; exhibition; a representation, picture, or likeness. *Com.* the presenting of a bill, note, or the like, as for acceptance or payment; *law*, the statement by a grand jury of an offense from their own knowledge or observation, without any indictment laid before them.

pres·ent par·ti·ci·ple, *n.* A participle having present meaning, formed by adding the suffix *-ing* to a verb.

pres·ent per·fect, *n.* A verb tense, formed from a past participle preceded by the present tense of *have*, and denoting a completed action completed at the present time, as: The boy *has eaten*.

pres·ent tense, *n.* The tense form used to express state or action in the present time.

pres·er·va·tion, prez″ėr·vā′shan, *n.* The act of preserving; the state of being preserved.

pre·serv·a·tive, pri·zur′va·tiv, *a.* Having the power to or tending to preserve.—*n.* That which preserves or has the power of preserving; something that is preventive, as a vaccine to prevent a disease.

pre·serve, pri·zurv′, *v.t.*—*preserved, preserving.* [Fr. *préserver*, L.L. *praeservo*.] To keep or save from harm or destruction; to defend from evil; to save; to keep in the same state; to uphold, sustain, protect; to save from deteriorating; to cause to remain good and wholesome, as food, by canning, smoking, pickling, or otherwise; to prevent being hunted and killed, except at certain seasons or by certain persons, as game, fish, etc.—*v.i.* To preserve foods; to protect game for purposes of sport.—*n.* That which preserves or is preserved; *usu. pl.* fruit which has been cooked and canned, as in the form of jam. A place set apart from the shelter and protection of game or other natural resources.—**pre·serv·a·ble,** *a.*—**pre·serv·er,** *n.*

pre-shrunk, prē·shrungk′, *a.* Pertaining to cloth shrunk during manufacturing to prevent or lessen later shrinking.

pre·side, pri·zīd′, *v.i.*—*presided, presiding.* [Fr. *présider,* < L. *praesideo.*] To hold a place of authority over others, as a president, director, chairman of a legislative body, judge of a court, or chairman of a meeting; to direct; to control; to be featured, as an instrumentalist, on a program.—**pre·sid·er,** *n.*

pres·i·den·cy, prez′i·den·sē, *n.* pl. **pres·i·den·cies.** The office of a president; (*often cap.*) the office of the president of the United States. The term during which a president holds office; superintendence. *Mormon Ch.* the governing body of the church or of a local stake, consisting of the president and his two councilors.

pres·i·dent, prez′i·dent, *n.* (*Often cap.*) the chief executive of a republic. The chief officer of a corporation, company, board of trade, governmental unit, or similar organization; the chief officer of a college or university.—**pres·i·den·tial,** prez″i·den′shal, *a.*

pres·i·den·tial gov·ern·ment, *n.* A form of government in which the chief executive, who holds office for a fixed term, is neither chosen by the legislature nor constitutionally responsible to it.

pres·i·dent·ship, prez′i·dent·ship″, *n. Brit.* the office, function, or term of president.

pre·sid·i·al, pri·sid′ē·al, *a.* Pertaining to or forming a garrison; presidential; pertaining to a province. Also **pre·sid·i·ar·y,** pri·sid′ē·er″ē.

pre·sid·i·o, pri·sid′ē·ō″, *Sp.* pre·sē′THya, *n.* pl. **pre·sid·i·os.** [Sp.] A fort or fortified station; a garrison town.

pre·sid·i·um, pri·sid′ē·um, *n.* An executive committee in Communist countries acting for a larger governmental unit; (*cap.*) the permanent, administrative, 14-member committee of the Union of Soviet Socialist Republics.

pre·sig·ni·fy, prē·sig′ni·fī″, *v.t.*—*presignified, presignifying.* To intimate or signify beforehand.

press, pres, *n.* [Fr. *presse,* a press, a crowd, a throng.] An instrument or machine by which any body is squeezed, crushed, or forced into a more compact form; a machine for printing; a printing press; printed literature in general, esp. newspapers, with *the*; newspaper reporters; a printing, publishing, or broadcasting establishment, and its personnel; a crowd; a throng; a multitude of individuals crowded together; the act of pressing; the state of being pressed or pressured; a wine vat or cistern; an upright cupboard in which clothes or other articles are kept; urgency; urgent demands of affairs; a wooden or metal frame to prevent warping, as of a tennis racket; the state of smoothness of a pressed garment. *Weight lifting,* a raising of the weight to shoulder height, and then vertically to arm's length.—**go to press,** to start being printed.

press, pres, *v.t.* [Fr. *presser,* < L. *presso,* a freq. of *premere, pressum,* to press.] To act on with force or weight; to squeeze; to crush; to extract the juice of by squeezing; to squeeze for the purpose of making smooth; to iron, as clothing; to embrace closely; to constrain or compel; to urge by authority or necessity; to impose importunately; as, to *press* a gift on one; to straiten or distress; as, to be *pressed* for money; to urge or solicit with earnestness; to importune; to enforce; to bear hard

upon.—*v.i.* To exert pressure; to act with compulsive force; to bear heavily; to strain or strive eagerly; to go forward with impulsive eagerness or energetic efforts; to crowd; to throng; to force one's way; to urge; to iron clothes.—**press·er,** pres′ẽr, *n.*

press, pres, *v.t.* [Orig. to *impress* or *imprest.*] To force into service, esp. military or naval service; to impress; to use in a manner other than that originally intended, as: Buses were *pressed* into service by the army.—*n.* Impressment.

press a·gent, *n.* A person employed to promote the interests of a person, product, or organization, through advertisements and other notices in the press.—**press·a·gent·ry,** *n.*

press·board, pres′bōrd″, pres′bärd″, *n.* A kind of millboard or pasteboard; an ironing board, usu. small.

press box, *n.* An area reserved for reporters at a sporting event.

press con·fer·ence, *n.* An interview granted by a celebrity or dignitary to many reporters at the same time.

press gang, *n.* A body of men under the command of an officer, employed to impress other men for service, esp. in the navy or army.—**press-gang,** *v.t.*

press·ing, pres′ing, *a.* Urgent; importunate; insistent.—**press·ing·ly,** *adv.*

press·man, pres′man, *n.* pl. **press·men.** A man who operates or has charge of a printing press; *Brit.* a writer or reporter for the press.

press·mark, pres′märk″, *n.* A mark put upon a volume to indicate its location in the library.

press mon·ey, *n.* [Earlier *prest-money.*] *Brit. hist.* money formerly paid to a soldier or sailor on enlistment.

press of sail, *n. Naut.* as much sail as wind conditions will permit. Also **press of can·vas.**

pres·sor, pres′ẽr, *a.* [N.L.] *Physiol.* increasing pressure; stimulating; as, a *pressor* nerve, a nerve whose stimulation causes an increase of blood pressure.

press re·lease, *n.* A prepared statement or bulletin given to a newspaper for publication. Also **news re·lease.**

press·room, pres′rōm″, pres′rum″, *n.* In a printing establishment, the room that contains the printing presses.

press·run, pres′run″, *n.* The press operation required to print a certain job or number of copies; the total of copies printed.

pres·sure, presh′ẽr, *n.* [O.Fr. *pressure,* L. *pressura.*] The act of pressing; the state of being squeezed or crushed; the force of one body acting on another by weight or the continued application of power; a constraining force acting on the mind; as: He brought moral *pressure* to bear. Severity of grievousness, as of personal circumstances; stress, strait, or difficulty; urgency; demand on one's time or energies; as, the *pressure* of business; *phys.* force exerted per unit area of surface; *meteor.* atmospheric pressure; *elect.* electromotive force.—*v.t.*—*pressured, pressuring.* To persuade forcefully, apply pressure to, or compel, as: He *pressured* them into doing it his way. To pressurize.

pres·sure cab·in, *n. Aeron.* an airplane cabin with artificially maintained air pressure.

pres·sure cook·er, *n.* An autoclave; an apparatus which may be sealed for rapid cooking or sterilizing under high-pressure steam at various temperatures above the boiling point of water, 212°F.—**pres·sure·cook,** *v.t.*

pres·sure gauge, *n.* A gauge used to measure the pressure of a gas or fluid, as

in a boiler; a device for determining explosive pressure.

pres·sure group, *n.* Any special interest group that attempts to influence legislative or public opinion through lobbying and propaganda.

pres·sure suit, *n.* A garment designed to provide pressure upon the body and permit near-normal respiratory and circulatory functions under low pressure conditions, such as occur at high altitudes or in space, without benefit of a pressurized cabin: distinguished from a *pressurized* suit, which simply inflates.

pres·su·rize, presh′a·rīz″, *v.t.*—*pressurized, pressurizing.* To fill with air under pressure in order to maintain near-normal levels when outside pressure is low, as in aircraft flying at high altitudes; to fill (a container) with compressed air, gas, or liquid; to cook with steam pressure.—**pres·su·riz·er,** *n.*—**pres·sur·i·za·tion,** presh′ẽr·i·zā′shan, *n.*

press·work, pres′wurk″, *n.* The operation of taking impressions from type and engravings by means of a printing press; the work done in this manner.

pres·ti·dig·i·ta·tion, pres″ti·dij″i·tā′shan, *n.* [L. *praesto,* at hand, ready, and *digitus,* a finger.] Sleight of hand; legerdemain; juggling.—**pres·ti·dig·i·ta·tor,** *n.*

pres·tige, pre·stēzh′, pre·stēj′, pres′tij, *n.* [Fr., < L. *praestigium,* an illusion, a juggler's trick; hence an impression made on spectators.] Renown or influence derived from previously established personal attributes, achievements, or associations, esp. that derived from past success; distinction or positive reputation which is attached to a thing, institution, or individual, and is dominant in the opinion of others.—*a.* Showing or having the attributes of quality, rank, or distinction.

pres·tig·ious, pre·stij′us, pre·stij′ē·us, pre·stē′jus, pre·stē′jē·us, *a.* [L. *praestigiosus,* < *praestigiae.*] Having an excellent reputation; highly esteemed or respected.—**pres·tig·ious·ly,** *adv.*—**pres·tig·ious·ness,** *n.*

pres·tis·si·mo, pre·stis′i·mō″, *It.* pre·stēs′sē·ma″, *a., adv.* [It., superl. of *presto.*] *Mus.* in the most rapid tempo.

pres·to, pres′tō, *n.* [It. *presto,* quick, quickly, < L. *praesto,* at hand, ready.] *Mus.* a quick, lively movement or passage.—*adv.* Quickly, immediately, in haste; *mus.* rapidly.—*a.*

pre·stress, prē·stres′, *v.t.* To apply stress to beforehand to increase resistance to later stresses; as, to *prestress* stretched wire embedded in concrete to brace it to hold great weight.

pre·sum·a·ble, pri·zō′ma·bl, *a.* Capable of being presumed; probable.—**pre·sum·a·bly,** pri·zō′ma·blē, *adv.*

pre·sume, pri·zōm′, *v.t.*—*presumed, presuming.* [Fr. *présumer,* < L. *praesumo,* to presume.] To take for granted; to assume beforehand; to suppose (something); to dare, used with an infinitive, as: I do not *presume* to know all.—*v.i.* To suppose or believe without examination; to take the liberty; to act overconfidently; to go beyond the boundaries laid down by reverence, respect, or politeness.—**pre·sum·er,** *n.*

pre·sum·ing, pri·zōm′ing, *a.* Presumptuous.—**pre·sum·ing·ly,** *adv.*

pre·sump·tion, pri·zump′shan, *n.* [L. *praesumptio.*] A supposition; a ground for presuming; a strong probability; that which is supposed to be true without direct proof; presumptuousness; arrogance; bold, disrespectful behavior or speech; *law,* the conclusion or inference that a fact exists, derived from other proved, existing facts.

---

pre·sump·tive, pri·zump'tiv, *a.* Based on presumption or probability; providing reasonable basis for belief.—**pre·sump·-tive·ly**, *adv.*

pre·sump·tu·ous, pri·zump'chö·us, *a.* Imbued with or characterized by presumption; taking undue liberties; given to presume or act in a forward manner; arrogant; overconfident.—**pre·sump·tu·-ous·ly**, *adv.*—**pre·sump·tu·ous·ness**, *n.*

pre·sup·pose, prē"sa·pōz', *v.t.*—*presupposed*, *presupposing.* To suppose or assume in advance; to take for granted; to imply as antecedent; to require as a previously existing condition.—**pre·sup·po·si·tion**, prē"sup·o·zish'an, *n.*

pre·tend, pri·tend', *v.t.* [L. *praetendo*, to hold out, pretend.] To allege falsely; to make false appearance or representation of; to feign or affect; as, to *pretend* zeal; to claim or put in a claim for.—*v.i.* To feign or make believe; to put in a claim, usu. with *to.*—**pre·tend·ed**, *a.*—**pre·-tend·ed·ly**, *adv.*

pre·tend·er, pri·ten'dèr, *n.* One who pretends; (*sometimes cap.*) one who lays claim to something, esp. one claiming the rights to a throne.

pre·tense, *Brit.* **pre·tence**, pri·tens', prē'tens, *n.* [< L. *praetentum*, later *praetensum*, pp. of *praetendo.*] The act of pretending; make-believe; false show or statement intended to mislead; affectation; a pretext; an excuse; a claim.

pre·ten·sion, pri·ten'shan, *n.* [Fr. *pré-tention.*] A demand or claim to privilege, honor, title, or rank; pretentiousness; an assertion or allegation of uncertain truth or value.—**pre·ten·sion·less**, *a.*

pre·ten·tious, pri·ten'shus, *a.* Full of pretension; pretending to or falsely claiming talents, skills, or qualities; showy; ostentatious.—**pre·ten·tious·ly**, *adv.*—**pre·ten·tious·ness**, *n.*

pret·er·it, **pret·er·ite**, pret'èr·it, *a.* [L. *praeteritus*, gone by, pp. of *praetereo*—*praeter*, beyond, and *ire*, *itum*, to go.] *Gram.* expressing past time: applied to the verb tense expressing action or existence past or finished.—*n. Gram.* the tense that expresses past time; a verb in this tense.

pre·ter·mit, prē"tèr·mit', *v.t.*—*preter-mitted*, *pretermitting.* [L. *praetermitto.*] To pass by; to omit; to interrupt or suspend.—**pre·ter·mis·sion**, prē"tèr·-mish'an, *n.*

pre·ter·nat·u·ral, prē"tèr·nach'èr·al, *a.* [L. *praeter*, beyond, and E. *natural.*] Beyond what is natural, or different from what is natural, as distinguished from *super-natural* and *unnatural.*—**pre·ter·nat·u·-ral·ly**, *adv.*—**pre·ter·nat·u·ral·ism**, *n.*—**pre·ter·nat·u·ral·ness**, *n.*

pre·test, prē'test, *n.* A preliminary trial or test for exploratory purposes; a trial test for practice, as in schools, or to determine a student's aptitude for a course.—prē·test', *v.t.* To administer a pretest to.

pre·text, prē'tekst, *n.* [Fr. *prétexte*, < L. *praetextum*, < *praetexe.*] An ostensible reason or motive assigned or assumed as a cover for the real reason or motive; a pretense.

pre·tor, prē'tèr, *n.* Praetor.

pret·ti·fy, prit'i·fī", *v.t.*—*prettified*, *pret-tifying.* To make pretty: often used with a disparaging intent; as, to *prettify* a work of art.—**pret·ti·fi·ca·tion**, *n.*

pret·ty, prit'ē, *a.*—*prettier*, *prettiest.* [O.E. *pratic*, *prety*, comely, clever; < *praet*, a trick; Icel. *prettugr*, tricky, *prettr*, a trick.] Having a pleasing and attractive appearance, without great beauty; pleasing, as to personal taste; neatly arranged; affected; nice; foppish. *Colloq.* good or fine: used ironically; as, a *pretty* state of affairs; a great deal; as, the car cost a *pretty* penny.

—*adv.* In some degree; moderately; as, *pretty* often.—*n.* pl. **pret·ties.** Someone or something that is pretty.—*v.t.*—*prettied*, *prettying.*—**pret·ti·ly**, *adv.*—**pret·ti·ness**, *n.*—**pret·ty·ish**, *a.*

pret·zel, pret'sel, *n.* [G. *bretzel.*] A crisp, glazed, salted, knot-shaped cracker.

pre·vail, pri·vāl', *v.i.* [Fr. *prévaloir*, < L. *praevaleo.*] To overcome; to gain victory or superiority, used with *over* or *against*; to be in force; to have extensive power or influence; to have predominant influence; to succeed; to overcome or gain mastery over by persuasion, with *on* or *upon*, as: They *prevailed on* him to go.

pre·vail·ing, pri·vā'ling, *a.* Predominant; having superior influence; prevalent; current; most common or general; as, the *prevailing* winds from the west.—**pre·-vail·ing·ly**, *adv.*

prev·a·lent, prev'a·lent, *a.* Prevailing; predominant; most generally accepted or current; widely existing.—**prev·a·lent·ly**, *adv.*—**prev·a·lence**, *n.*

pre·var·i·cate, pri·var'i·kāt", *v.i.*—*pre-varicated*, *prevaricating.* [L. *praevaricor*, *praevaricatus*, to straddle, to shuffle.] To act or speak evasively; to evade or swerve from the truth; to quibble; to lie.—**pre·-var·i·ca·tion**, *n.* The act of prevaricating; a deviation to evade the truth or dis-closure of truth.—**pre·var·i·ca·tor**, pri·-var'i·kā"tèr, *n.*

pré·ve·nance, prāv·e·näns', *n.* [Fr.] Con-sideration of or attention to others' needs. Also *prevenience.*

pre·ven·ient, pri·vēn'yent, *a.* [L. *prae-veniens.*] Going before; preceding; antici-patory.—**pre·ven·ient grace**, *theol.* the grace that precedes or anticipates re-pentance, but which disposes the heart of man to seek God.—**pre·ven·ience**, pri·-vēn'yens, *n.*—**pre·ven·ient·ly**, *adv.*

pre·vent, pri·vent', *v.t.* [L. *praeventus*, pp. of *praevenire*, come before, anticipate, prevent.] To keep from occurring; thwart; to hinder, as from an action.—*v.i.* To interpose a hindrance.—**pre·vent·a·bil·i·-ty**, *n.*—**pre·vent·a·ble**, **pre·vent·i·ble**, *a.*—**pre·vent·er**, pri·ven'tèr, *n.*

pre·ven·tion, pri·ven'shan, *n.* [L.L. *prae-ventio(n-).*] The act of preventing; effectual hindrance; that which prevents; a pre-ventive.

pre·ven·tive, pri·ven'tiv, *a.* Serving to prevent or hinder; *med.* pertaining to a vaccine or medication for preventing disease.—*n.* A precautionary agent or measure; *med.* a drug or other substance for preventing disease. Also **pre·vent·a·-tive**, pri·ven'ta·tiv.—**pre·ven·tive·ly**, *adv.*—**pre·ven·tive·ness**, *n.*

pre·view, prē'vū, *n.* A previous view or showing; a view in advance, as of a motion picture.—*v.t.* To view or exhibit before-hand or in advance. Also **pre·vue.**

pre·vi·ous, prē'vē·us, *a.* [L. *praevius.*] Going before in time; being or happening before something else; antecedent; prior; premature.—*adv.*—**pre·vi·ous·ly**, *adv.*—**pre·vi·ous·ness**, *n.*

pre·vi·ous ques·tion, *n.* In parliamentary procedure, the question whether a vote shall be taken on a main question, moved before the main question is put: in the U.S., resorted to in order to cut off debate and bring the main question to an immediate vote.

pre·vise, pri·vīz', *v.t.*—*prevised*, *prevising.* [L. *praevisus*, pp. of *praevideo.*] To foresee; to forewarn.

pre·vi·sion, pri·vizh'an, *n.* Foresight; foreknowledge; prescience.—**pre·vi·-sion·al**, **pre·vi·sion·ar·y**, *a.*

pre·vo·ca·tion·al, prē"vō·kā'sha·nal, *a.* Consisting of or pertaining to a preliminary type of vocational training.

pre·war, prē'wár', *a.* Before the war; as, *prewar* conditions. Compare *postwar.*

prex·y, prek'sē, *n.* pl. **prex·ies.** [For *president.*] *Slang*, a president, as of a college. Also **prex.**

prey, prā, *n.* [O.E. *preie*, *praie*, O.Fr. *preie*, *praie* (Fr. *proie*), < L. *praeda*, plunder, whence *predatory*, *depredation.*] An animal seized or hunted as food by a carnivorous animal; a person or thing that becomes the victim of an attacker, a fraud, or the like; the act or the habit of preying; as, a beast of *prey.*—*v.i.* To take and devour prey; to victimize, as by fraud; to have a harmful or wasting influence or effect; as, to *prey* on one's mind; to attack or plunder: usu. followed by *on* or *upon.*—**prey·er**, *n.*

pri·ap·ic, prī·ap'ik, *a.* Phallic; *class. mythol.* relating to Priapus, god of male procreative power. Also **pri·a·pe·an**, prī"a·pē'an.

price, prīs, *n.* [O.Fr. *pris* (Fr. *prix*), < L. *pretium*, price, value, worth.] The sum or amount of money or its equivalent for which anything is bought, sold, or offered for sale; a sum offered for the capture of a person alive or dead; the sum of money or other consideration for which a person's support or consent may be obtained; that which must be given, done, or undergone in order to obtain a thing; as, to gain a victory at a heavy *price*; value or worth.—*v.t.*—*priced*, *pricing.* To fix the price of; to ask the price of.—**pric·er**, prī'sèr, *n.*

price con·trol, *n.* Regulation of prices by the government in which a maximum price for a service or commodity is set.

price cut·ting, *n.* The reducing of the price of goods beneath the advertised or customary price.

price-earn·ings ra·tio, prīs'ụr'ningz rā'-shō, *n.* Of a share of common stock, the ratio of market price to earnings: used as a measure of the stock's value.

price in·dex, *n.* A number expressing the relation of the actual price of a commodity to its price during a base period: used to chart price level changes.

price·less, prīs'lis, *a.* Having a value beyond all price; invaluable. *Colloq.* very amusing; absurd.

price sup·port, *n.* The maintenance of prices at a given level, usu. by means of financial assistance or purchase of the material or product by the government.

price tag, *n.* A tag or label on goods giving the price at which they may be sold.

price war, *n.* A time of competition, usu. between retailers, during which each tries to undersell the other by repeatedly cutting prices.

prick, prik, *n.* [O.E. *prica*, puncture, point, dot, = M.L.G. *pricke*, sharp point or implement, = D. *prik*, puncture, point, = Icel. *prik*, dot, little stick.] A puncture made by a needle, thorn, or the like; the act or an act of pricking; the state or sensation of being pricked; any pointed instrument or weapon; *archaic*, a goad for oxen.—*v.t.* [O.E. *prician* = M.L.G. *pricken* = D. *prikken* = Icel. *prika*, prick.] To pierce with a sharp point; puncture; to cause sharp mental pain to; sting, as with remorse or sorrow; to urge on or incite with or as with a spur or goad; to mark, as a surface, with pricks or dots in tracing some-thing; mark or trace, as a design, on a surface by pricks or dots; to cause to stand erect or point upward, as the ears of an animal; to lame, as a horse, by piercing the quick of its hoof with a nail while shoeing; *hort.* to transplant, as a young seedling, into a larger container.—*v.i.* To perform the action of piercing or puncturing some-thing; to have a sensation of being pricked; to rise erect or point upward, as the ears of an animal, followed by *up*; *archaic*, to spur on or urge a horse on, or ride rapidly. —**prick up one's ears,** to listen carefully; become attentive.—**prick·er,** *n.*

prick·et, prik'it, *n.* [< *prick, n.*] A sharp metal point on which to stick a candle; a candlestick with one or more such points; a buck in his second year, having straight, unbranched horns.

prick·le, prik'l, *n.* [O.E. *pricel, pricels,* < the stem of *prician, E. prick, v.*] A sharp point or pointed projection, esp. a small, pointed process growing from the bark of a plant; a pricking or tingling sensation.— *v.t.—prickled, prickling.* To prick; to cause a pricking sensation in.—*v.i.* To be affected with a pricking sensation, or tingle as if pricked.

prick·ly, prik'lē, *a.—pricklier, prickliest.* Full of or armed with prickles; full of troublesome points, or difficult to deal with; as, a *prickly* question; having the sensation of being pricked; smarting; tingling.— **prick·li·ness,** *n.*

prick·ly ash, *n.* An aromatic shrub or small tree, *Zanthoxylum americanum,* having prickly branches and belonging to the rue family.

prick·ly heat, *n. Pathol.* a cutaneous eruption accompanied by a prickling and itching sensation, due to an inflammation of the sweat glands. Also *heat rash.*

prick·ly pear, *n.* The pear-shaped or ovoid, often prickly and sometimes edible, fruit of certain species of the cactus genus *Opuntia*; the plant itself.

prick·ly pop·py, *n.* pl. **prick·ly pop·pies.** Any of several plant species belonging to the genus *Argemone* in the poppy family, with prickly leaves and stem, and large, white or yellow flowers, esp. the Mexican annual, *A. mexicana.*

pride, prīd, *n.* [O.E. *prȳte,* pride, < *prūd,* proud.] The quality or state of being proud; an unreasonable opinion of one's own superiority over others; inordinate self-esteem; the reflection of this quality in disdainful or arrogant behavior; a reasonable self-respect based on a consciousness of worth; that which causes one to be proud; elation or satisfaction arising from one's achievements, possessions, or the like; the best part of some group or class; as, the *pride* of the army; the finest or most flourishing time or state; as, in the *pride* of life; *liter.* splendid or ostentatious show. A group of lions.—*v.t.—prided, priding.* To indulge in pride: used reflexively, with *on* or *upon*; as, to *pride* oneself *on* one's accomplishments.

pride·ful, prīd'ful, *a.* Full of pride; haughty; arrogant; insolent.—**pride·ful·ly,** *adv.—* **pride·ful·ness,** *n.*

prie-dieu, prē'dū, *Fr.* prᴇ·dyōᴇ', *n.* pl. **prie-dieus, prie-dieux, prie-dieu,** prē'dūz. [Fr., 'pray God.'] A piece of furniture for kneeling on during prayer, having a rest above, as for a book.

pri·er, prī'ėr, *n.* One who looks or searches curiously or inquisitively into something. Also *pryer.*

priest, prēst, *n.* [O.E. *prēost,* contr. < L. *presbyter.*] A clergyman ranking below bishop in the Roman Catholic, Eastern Orthodox, or Episcopalian church; a person consecrated to the ministry of the gospel; a man who officiates in sacred offices, acts of public worship, sacrifice, or other mediatorial offices between man and a divinity; among many non-Christian sects, the title of men selected and trained to perform sacred functions.—**priest·ess,** prē'stis, *n.*

priest·craft, prēst'kraft", prēst'kräft, *n.* Priestly policy or system of management based on temporal or material interest: used disparagingly; knowledge and skills of a priest.

priest·hood, prēst'hụd, *n.* The office or character of a priest; priests collectively.

priest·ly, prēst'lē, *a.—priestlier, priestliest.* Pertaining to a priest or to priests; sacerdotal; becoming to a priest.—**priest·li·ness,** *n.*

priest-rid·den, prēst'rid"en, *a.* Governed or entirely swayed by priests.

prig, prig, *n.* [Origin obscure.] One who affects great superiority in principles, views, or standards, esp. in a self-righteous way; a puritanical person; one who is precise to an extreme in attention to principle or duty; *archaic,* a coxcomb.—**prig·ger·y,** prig'e·rē, *n.*

prig, prig, *n.* [O.Fr. *briguer,* to steal, to act the highwayman; akin *brigand.*] *Brit. slang,* a thief.—*v.t.—prigged, prigging. Brit. slang.* To filch; to steal.

prig·gish, prig'ish, *a.* Having the character of a prig; excessively precise; affectedly superior or high-minded; self-righteous.— **prig·gish·ly,** *adv.—***prig·gish·ness,** *n.*

prig·gism, prig'iz·um, *n.* Priggish character or ideas.

prim, prim, *a.—primmer, primmest.* [Origin uncertain; perh. intended to suggest the drawing up of the lips or mouth in pronouncing *prim.*] Affectedly or formally precise or proper, as persons, demeanor, or behavior; stiffly formal, neat, or regular.— *v.i.—primmed, primming.* To draw up the mouth in an affectedly nice or precise way. —*v.t.* To make prim, as in appearance; to form, as the mouth or face, into a prim expression.—**prim·ly,** *adv.—***prim·ness,** *n.*

pri·ma bal·le·ri·na, prē'ma bal"e·rē'na, *n.* The chief ballerina in a ballet company.

pri·ma·cy, prī'ma·sē, *n.* pl. **pri·ma·cies.** [O.Fr. *primacie* (Fr. *primatie*), < M.L. *primatia,* < L. *primas.*] The state of being first in order, rank, or importance; *eccles.* the office, rank, or dignity of a primate.

pri·ma don·na, prē"ma don'a, prim"a don'a, *It.* prē'mä dạn'nä, *n.* pl. **pri·ma don·nas.** [It., first lady.] The first or chief female singer in an opera or operatic company; a vain, temperamental person.

pri·ma fa·ci·e, prī'ma fā'shē·ē", prī'ma fā'shē, prī'ma fā'she, *adv.* [L. *primus,* first, and *facies,* face.] At first view or appearance.—*a.* True or obvious at first glance; *law,* adequate to establish as true unless directly contradicted, as of evidence or a case.

pri·mage, prī'mij, *n.* [< verb to *prime.*] A charge other than wages formerly paid by a shipper to the master and sailors of a ship for loading goods; now, a percentage added to freight costs and paid to the shipowner.

pri·mal, prī'mal, *a.* [< L. *primus,* first.] Primary; original; primitive; first in importance; of fundamental importance.

pri·ma·ri·ly, prī·mâr'i·lē, prī'mer·i·lē, prī'mėr·i·lē, *adv.* Chiefly; principally; essentially; at first; originally.

pri·ma·ry, prī'mer·ē, prī'ma·rē, *a.* [L. *primarius,* < *primus,* first, E. *prime*: cf. *premier.*] First in time; earliest; primitive; first in order in any series or sequence; constituting, or belonging to, the first state in any process; preparatory, or lowest in order; as, *primary* schools; first or highest in rank or importance; chief; principal; of the nature of the ultimate or simpler constituents of which something complex is made up; original, not derived or subordinate; fundamental; basic; immediate or direct, or not involving intermediate agency; *ornith.* noting or pertaining to any of a set of flight feathers situated on the distal segment of a bird's wing; *elect.* noting or pertaining to the inducing circuit, coil, or current in an induction coil or the like. *Chem.* relating to the first or simplest stage in a reaction, as the replacement of one

atom or radical; indicating or having one carbon atom joined to no more than one other carbon atom in a molecule.—*n.* pl. **pri·ma·ries.** That which is first in order, rank, or importance; a meeting or gathering of the voters of a political party in an election district, as for nominating candidates for office or choosing convention delegates; caucus; an election in which voters of a political party nominate candidates, choose delegates for a convention, or select party officials; *ornith.* a primary feather; *elect.* a primary circuit or coil; *astron.* a body in relation to a smaller body or smaller bodies revolving around it, as a planet in relation to its satellites.

pri·ma·ry a·typ·i·cal pneu·mo·nia, *n.* A typically mild form of pneumonia, probably of viral origin.

pri·ma·ry cell, *n. Elect.* a cell which produces electric current by converting chemical energy to electrical energy by nonreversible reactions, consisting of two electrodes immersed in an electrolyte and connected by a conducting wire.

pri·ma·ry coil, *n. Elect.* in an induction coil or transformer, the coil which receives the inducing current and stimulates the secondary coil.

pri·ma·ry road, *n.* A principal artery in a highway system.

pri·mate, prī'māt, prī'mit, *n.* [O.Fr. Fr. *primat,* < L.L. *primas* (*primat-*), chief, head, M.L. eccles. *primate,* noun use of L. *primas, a.,* of the first rank, < *primus,* first, E. *prime.*] *Eccles.* an archbishop or bishop ranking first among the bishops of a province or country, prī'mit. *Zool.* any of the *Primates,* the highest order of mammals, including man, monkeys, apes, and lemurs, prī'māt.—**pri·mate·ship,** *n.—***pri·ma·tial,** prī·mā'shal, *a.*

prime, prīm, *a.* [O.Fr. Fr. *prime,* < L. *primus, a.,* first, superl. of *prior,* former; as *n.,* in part through O.Fr. < Fr., fem. of *primus,* in *prima hora,* first hour.] First in importance or significance; as, a *prime* consideration; principal; highest in rank, dignity, or authority; as, the *prime* minister; chief; first in excellence or value; of the first grade or best quality; as, *prime* ribs of beef; first in order of time or development; earliest; primitive; not derived from another; fundamental. *Math.* not divisible without remainder by any number except itself and unity; as, five is a *prime* number; having no common divisor except unity; as, two is *prime* to nine.—*n.* The most flourishing stage or state; the period or state of greatest perfection or vigor of human life, before strength begins to decline; the choicest or best part of anything; the beginning or earliest stage of any period; the spring of the year; the first hour or period of the day, after the sunrise; *eccles.* the second of the seven canonical hours, or the service for it, orig. fixed for the first hour of the day. *Math.* a prime number; one of the equal parts into which a unit is primarily divided, as one of the 60 minutes in a degree; the mark (′) indicating such a division. *Mus.* unison; in a scale, the tonic or keynote. *Fencing,* the first in a series of eight parries.—**prime·ly,** *adv.—* **prime·ness,** *n.*

prime, prīm, *v.t.—primed, priming.* [Origin uncertain; commonly associated with *prime,* as if expressing a first or preliminary action.] To prepare or make ready for a particular purpose or operation; to make ready for firing, as a gun or charge, by providing with a primer; to pour liquid into, as a pump, so as to exclude air and establish suction, thus preparing it for operation; to cover, as a surface, with a preparatory coat or color, as in painting; to supply or equip beforehand with information, words, or the like.—*v.i.* Of a boiler or steam engine, to operate so that water is carried over into the cylinder with the steam; to become prime.

prime cost, *n.* First or original cost; the cost of materials and labor necessary to make or produce an article.

prime me·rid·i·an, *n.* A meridian from which longitude east and west is reckoned, as that of Greenwich, England.

prime min·is·ter, *n.* The principal minister of a government; the chief of the cabinet or ministry; as, the British *prime minister.*—**prime min·is·ter·ship**, *n.*—**prime min·is·try**, *n.*

prime mov·er, *n. Mech.* the initial agent which puts a machine in motion, as wind or electricity; a machine, as a water wheel or steam engine, which receives and modifies energy as supplied by some natural source. *Aristotelianism,* the primary being which causes all motion, but is motionless itself. The primary or original force in a work.

prim·er, prim′ėr, *Brit.* also prī′mėr, *n.* [Fr. *primaire,* elementary, L. *primarius, primus,* first.] A small elementary book for teaching children to read; a book of elementary principles; *print.* a type size; as, *long primer* (10-point) and *great primer* (18-point).

prim·er, prī′mėr, *n.* One who or that which primes; a cap, cylinder, or other device, containing a compound which may be exploded by percussion or other means, used for firing a charge of powder.

prime rate, *n.* The minimum bank loan interest, usu. offered exclusively to large commercial borrowers.

pri·me·ro, pri·mâr′ō, *n.* [Sp. *primero,* first.] A game of cards in vogue in 16th century England.

prime time, *n. TV,* the major hours for watching television, between 8 p.m. and 11 p.m., the time most competed for among television performers and advertisers.

pri·me·val, prī·mē′val, *a.* [L. *primaevus—primus,* first, and *aevum,* age.] Original; primitive; belonging to the first ages.—**pri·me·val·ly**, *adv.*

prim·ing, prī′ming, *n.* The powder used to ignite a charge; the action or means with which something is primed; the first layer of paint or size laid on a surface which is to be painted.

pri·mip·a·ra, prī·mip′ėr·a, *n. pl.* **pri·mip·a·rae**, prī·mip′a·rē. [L., < *primus,* first, and *parere,* bring forth.] *Obstet.* a woman who has borne but one child, or who is parturient for the first time. —**pri·mip·ar·ous**, *a.*—**pri·mi·par·i·ty**, prī′mi·par′i·tē, *n.*

prim·i·tive, prim′i·tiv, *a.* [O.Fr. Fr. *primitif,* < L. *primitivus,* first of its kind, < *primus,* first, E. *prime.*] Being the first or earliest of the kind or in existence, esp. in an early age of the world; early in the history of the world or of mankind; characteristic of early ages or of an early stage of human development; as, *primitive* art; unaffected or little affected by civilizing influences; rude, or rudely simple; old-fashioned; being in its or the earliest period; early; original or radical, as opposed to *derivative;* primary, as opposed to *secondary. Biol.* rudimentary, as an organ; of early formation and temporary, as a part that subsequently disappears; primordial.—*n.* Something primitive; a word from which another is derived; *math.* a geometrical or algebraic form or expression from which another is derived. *Art,* an artist, esp. a painter belonging to an early period; a work of art by such an artist. A primitive person.—**prim·i·tive·ly**, *adv.*—**prim·i·tive·ness**, *n.*

prim·i·tiv·ism, prim′i·ti·viz″um, *n.* A philosophic and aesthetic theory that the

natural and simple style of living of the earliest or primitive cultures is superior to that of modern civilization.—**prim·i·tiv·ist**, *n., a.*—**prim·i·tiv·is·tic**, prim″i·tiv·iz′tic, *a.*

pri·mo, prē′mō, *It.* prē′ma, *n. pl.* **pri·mos**, *It.* **pri·mi**, prē′mē. [It., first, < L. *primus,* E. *prime.*] *Mus.* The first or principal part, as in a duet; its performer.—*adv.*

pri·mo·gen·i·tor, prī″mo·jen′i·tėr, *n.* [L. *primus,* and *genitor,* father.] The first father or earliest forefather; an ancestor.

pri·mo·gen·i·ture, prī″mo·jen′i·chėr, *n.* [Fr. *primogéniture,* < L. *primus,* first, and *genitūra,* a begetting, < *gigno, genitum,* to beget.] The state of being the first-born of the same parents; *law,* the right of the first-born son to succeed to his father's estate to the exclusion of the younger sons and any daughters.

pri·mor·di·al, prī·mạr′dē·al, *a.* [L. *primordialis,* < *primordium,* beginning, origin —*primus,* first, and *ordior,* to commence.] First in order of development; original; existing from the beginning; *biol.* earliest formed.—**pri·mor·di·al·ly**, *adv.*

pri·mor·di·um, prī·mạr′dē·ụm, *n. pl.* **pri·mor·di·a**, prī·mạr′dē·a. *Embryol.* the rudiments of an organ in the embryo.

primp, primp, *v.t.* [< *prim,* or perh. a form of *prink.*] To adorn, dispose, or dress in a fussy, exacting manner.—*v.i.* To groom oneself in a finicky, overly careful manner.

prim·rose, prim′rōz, *n.* [M.E. *primerose,* appar. an altered form of *primerole,* < O.Fr. *primerole,* primrose, dim. < *prime,* first: cf. *primula.*] *Bot.* any plant of the genus *Primula,* comprising perennial herbs, esp. *P. veris,* the yellow-flowered English primrose or cowslip commonly cultivated in gardens, and *P. sinensis,* the Chinese primrose of greenhouses; the plant family *Primulaceae.* Compare *evening primrose.* A pale yellow color; also **prim·rose yel·low.** —*a.* Pertaining to the primrose; of a pale yellow color.

prim·rose path, *n.* The leading of a gay or merry life; indulgence in the sensual pleasures of life; the tempting, easy way.

prim·u·la, prim′ū·la, *n.* [M.L., prop. fem. of L. *primulus,* dim. of *primus,* first, E. *prime.*] Any plant of the genus *Primula;* a primrose.—**prim·u·la·ceous**, prim″ū·lā′shus, *a.* Of the primrose family.

pri·mum mo·bi·le, prī′mum mob′i·lē″, *L.* prē′mụm mō′bi·le″, *n. pl.* **pri·mum mo·bi·les.** [M.L. 'first movable.'] In the Ptolemaic system of astronomy, the outermost of the concentric spheres of the universe, regarded as making a daily revolution around the earth and causing the others to move with it; *fig.* any prime source of movement.

pri·mus in·ter pa·res, prī′mụs in′tėr pā′rēz, *L.* prē′mụs in′tėr pä′res, *n.* [L.] First among equals.

prince, prins, *n.* [Fr., < L. *princeps, principis,* a prince, a chief—*primus,* first, and *capio,* take.] A male, nonreigning member of a royal family; *hist.* a king, monarch. In Great Britain, the son or grandson (if the child of a son) of a sovereign. The actual or nominal ruler of a small state or territory; a man at the head of any class or profession; as, a merchant *prince;* a man of admirable, likable personal qualities.—**prince·dom**, prins′dom, *n.*—**prince·ship**, *n.*

Prince Al·bert, prins al′bėrt, *n.* A long, double-breasted frock coat.

prince con·sort, *n. pl.* **princ·es con·sort.** A prince who is the husband of a reigning female sovereign.

prince·kin, prins′kin, *n.* A minor or small prince.

prince·ling, prins′ling, *n.* A young or petty prince. Also **prince·let**, prins′lit.

prince·ly, prins′lē, *a.*—**princelier**, **princeliest.** Pertaining to a prince; resembling a prince; noble; magnificent; generous; lavish.—**prince·li·ness**, *n.*

Prince of Wales, *n.* A title conferred on the eldest son, or heir apparent, of the British sovereign.

prince's-feath·er, prins′siz·feTH′ėr, *n.* A tall annual plant, *Polygonum orientale,* of the buckwheat family, with spikes of red or pink flowers; an annual plant of the amaranth family.

prin·cess, prin′sis, prin′ses, *n.* [O.Fr. Fr. *princesse,* fem. of *prince,* E. *prince.*] A nonregnant female member of a royal family; the consort of a prince; in Great Britain, a daughter, or a granddaughter (if the child of a son) of a king or queen; *hist.* a female sovereign.

prin·cess, prin·cesse, prin′sis, prin′ses, *a.* Of a woman's dress or other garment, cut in continuous length from top to bottom, with a close-fitting bodice and flared, often gored, skirt.

prin·cess roy·al, *n. pl.* **prin·cess·es roy·al.** The eldest daughter of a king or queen.

prin·ci·pal, prin′si·pal, *a.* [L. *principalis,* < *princeps,* first in time or order, a chief.] Chief; highest or first in rank, character, authority, or importance; constituting or relating to principal.—*n.* A chief or head; one who takes a leading part, as in a play; the chief executive of an educational institution, esp. of an elementary or secondary public school; the head or director of a college in Great Britain; something of main or principal importance. *Law,* the actor or absolute perpetrator of a crime, or an abettor; one who engages another person to act as his representative or agent; an individual mainly liable for a contract or other obligation; the body or capital of an estate, as differentiated from income. *Com.* a capital sum lent on interest, due as a debt, or used as a fund, as distinguished from *interest. Mus.* one of the main organ stops; see *diapason. Carp.* a main timber in an assemblage of pieces.—**prin·ci·pal·ly**, prin′si·pa·lē, prin′sip·lē, *adv.*—**prin·ci·pal·ship**, *n.*

prin·ci·pal·i·ty, prin″si·pal′i·tē, *n. pl.* **prin·ci·pal·i·ties.** [Fr. *principalité.*] The territory of a prince, or the country which gives title to a prince; the position or office of a prince; sovereignty; supreme power; *pl., theol.* one of the orders of angels.

prin·ci·pal parts, *n. pl. Gram.* inflected verb forms from which the other inflected forms can be derived: in English, the infinitive, past tense, and past participle, as *go, went, gone.*

prin·cip·i·um, prin·sip′ē·ụm, *n. pl.* **prin·cip·i·a**, prin·sip′ē·a. [L., pl. of *principium.*] First or fundamental principle; element.

prin·ci·ple, prin′si·pl, *n.* [Fr. *principe,* < L. *principium,* a beginning, origin, element, < *princeps, principis.* As to the insertion of the *l,* compare *participle, syllable.*] A general truth; a law comprehending many subordinate truths; a method or rule adopted as the basis for action or conduct; uprightness; as, a man of *principle;* the primary source from which anything proceeds; a basic doctrine or tenet; an underlying cause; a law on which others are founded or from which others are derived. A precept or conception manifested in natural phenomena or underlying the operation of a machine; as, the *principle* of gravity; *chem.* a main ingredient or component that gives something its distinctive character.—

prin·ci·pled, prin′si·peld, *a.* Characterized by, or founded on, ethical principles: usu. used in compounds; as, high-*principled.*

prink, pringk, *v.t.* [A slightly modified form of *prank.*] To dress for show; primp.—*v.i.*

To adorn or dress oneself fussily; fuss over one's appearance; primp.—**prink·er,** n.

print, print, n. [O.Fr. *preinte,* impression, print, < *preindre,* press, stamp, < L. *premere,* press.] An indentation or mark made by the pressure of one body or thing on another; something with which an impression is made; a stamp or die; something that has been subjected to impression, as a pat of butter or patterned cotton cloth; the state of being printed; printed lettering, esp. with reference to character, style, or size; printed matter; a printed publication, as a newspaper; a picture or design printed from an engraved or otherwise prepared block or plate; newsprint; *photog.* a picture made from a negative.—*v.t.* To indent or mark, as a surface, by pressing something into or on it; to produce or fix as by pressure, as an indentation or mark; to impress on the mind or memory; to apply with pressure so as to leave an indentation or mark; to produce, as a book or picture, by applying inked types, plates, or blocks with direct pressure to paper; cause to be reproduced in print; to write in letters like those commonly used in print; to mark, as cloth, with a pattern or design in color, transferred by pressure. *Photog.* to make a positive picture from, as from a negative, by the transmission of light.—*v.i.* To take impressions from type, as in a press; produce by means of a press or other printing process; to follow the vocation of a printer; to give an impression on paper, as type or plates; to write in characters such as are used in print.—**in print,** in printed form; published; of a book, still available for purchase from the publisher.—**out of print,** of a book, no longer available for purchase from the publisher.

print·a·ble, prin′ta·bl, a. Capable of being printed; fit to print; capable of being printed from.—**print·a·bil·i·ty,** print″a·-bil′i·tē n.

print·ed cir·cuit, n. A circuit for electronic equipment which utilizes paths of conductive material printed on an insulating sheet or panel to conduct the current.

print·er, prin′tėr, n. One who or that which prints, esp. one engaged in the business of printing; *computer,* the part or element that yields information in printed form.

print·er's dev·il, n. One who is an apprentice in a printing office.

print·er's mark, n. The name of a publisher printed at the bottom of a title page, usu. with the place and date of publication. Also *imprint.*

print·er·y, prin′te·rē, n. pl. **print·er·ies.** An establishment for the printing of calico or other cotton goods; an establishment for typographic printing.

print·ing, prin′ting, n. The act of one who or that which prints; the art, process, or business of producing books, newspapers, or periodicals by impression from movable type or plates; typography; words or other matter in printed form; printed matter; the whole number of copies of a book printed at one time; writing in which the letters are like those commonly used in print.

print·ing press, n. A machine for printing on paper or the like from type or plates.

print·less, print′lis, a. Making, retaining, or showing no print or impression.

print-out, print′out″, n. *Computer,* the processed data issued in printed form by a computer or similar apparatus, usu. on continuous strips of paper.

pri·or, prī′ėr, a. [L. *prior,* former, superior, a compar. form associated with *primus,* first, as superl.] Preceding in time or in order; earlier or former; anterior or antecedent.—**pri·or to,** in advance of; before.—**pri·or·ly,** adv.

pri·or, prī′ėr, n. [O.Fr. *prior* (Fr. *prieur),* < M.L. *prior,* < L. *prior.*] A superior officer in a monastic order or religious house next in rank below an abbot; a chief magistrate, as in the medieval republic of Florence.—**pri·or·ship,** n.

pri·or·ate, prī′ėr·it, n. [M.L. *prioratus.*] The office, rank, or term of office of a prior; a priory.

pri·or·ess, prī′ėr·is, n. [O.Fr. *prioresse.*] A woman holding a position corresponding to that of a prior, sometimes ranking next below an abbess.

pri·or·i·ty, prī·or′i·tē, pri·ar′i·tē, n. pl. **pri·or·i·ties.** The state of being earlier in time, or of preceding something else; precedence in order, importance, or rank; the having of certain rights and privileges before another; that which needs or merits attention before others.

pri·o·ry, prī′o·rē, n. pl. **pri·o·ries.** [O.Fr. *priorie.*] A religious house governed by a prior or prioress, often dependent upon an abbey.

prism, priz′um, n. [L.L. *prisma,* < Gr. *prisma,* lit. 'something sawed,' < *prizein,* saw.] A polyhedron whose bases or ends are similar, equivalent, and parallel polygons, and whose sides are parallelograms; *optics,* a body of this form, esp. with triangular bases, made of glass or other transparent substance, used esp. for polarizing or decomposing light into its spectrum; *crystal.* a form consisting of faces which are parallel to the vertical axis, and which intersect the horizontal axes. A glass ornament shaped like a prism.

pris·mat·ic, priz·mat′ik, a. Of, pertaining to, or like a prism; formed by or as if by a transparent prism; varied in color; brilliant; *crystal.* orthorhombic.—**pris·mat·-i·cal·ly,** adv.

pris·moid, priz′moid, n. A body whose form approaches that of a prism, with similar, parallel, but not congruent ends or bases and trapezoid faces.—**pris·moi·dal,** priz·moi′dal, a.

pris·on, priz′on, n. [Fr. *prison,* < L. *prehensio, prehensionis,* a capture, < *prehendo,* to seize, whence *prehensile.*] A place of confinement or involuntary restraint; a public building for the confinement or safe custody of criminals and others committed by process of law; a jail.—*v.t.* To shut up in a prison; to confine; to imprison.

pris·on·er, priz′o·nėr, priz′nėr, n. One who is confined in a prison; a person under arrest, whether in prison or not; a prisoner of war; in general, one whose liberty is restrained.

pris·on·er of war, n. A prisoner, captured in warfare, whose treatment is often subject to international rules.

pris·on·er's base, n. A children's game in which members of one team chase members of the other team to imprison them at goals or bases.

pris·on fev·er, n. Typhus fever.

pris·sy, pris′ē, a.—*prissier, prissiest.* [Cf. *precise.*] *Colloq.* Precise; prim; affectedly nice.—**pris·si·ly,** adv.—**pris·si·ness,** n.

pris·tine, pris′tēn, pris′tin, pris′tīn, a. [L. *pristinus.*] Belonging to a primitive or early state or period; original; primitive. Pure; uncontaminated.

prith·ee, priTH′ē, *interj. Archaic,* I pray thee; please.

pri·va·cy, prī′va·sē, *Brit.* also priv′a·sē, n. A state of being private or in retirement; seclusion; secrecy; solitude.

pri·vat·do·cent, pri·vat·do·zent, prē·-vät′dō·tsent′, n. [G., 'private instructor.'] In German and certain other universities, a private teacher or lecturer recognized by the university but receiving no compensation from it, being remunerated by students' fees.

pri·vate, prī′vit, a. [L. *privatus,* private, not public, pp. of *privare,* separate, deprive, < *privus,* single, individual, private, deprived.] Belonging to some particular person or persons; as, *private* property; pertaining to or affecting a particular person or a small group of persons; as, a *private* wrong; individual; personal; confined to or intended only for the person or persons immediately concerned; confidential; not holding public office or employment; not of an official or public character; removed from or out of public view or knowledge; secluded; intimate; not open or accessible to people in general; as, a *private* party; of, pertaining to, or receiving special privileges and services in a hospital; of the rank of private. —*n.* In the U.S. Army and Marine Corps, any enlisted man below the rank of corporal. *Pl.* the external organs of sex; also **pri·-vate parts.—in pri·vate,** in secret; not publicly.—**pri·vate·ly,** adv.—**pri·vate·ness,** n.

pri·va·teer, prī″va·tėr′, n. [Earlier called *private man-of-war;* < *private,* a.] An armed vessel owned by private persons, holding a government commission to act against an enemy's shipping or warships; the commander, or one of the crew, of such a vessel.—*v.i.* To cruise as a privateer.—**pri·va·teers·man,** prī″va·tėrz′man, n. pl. **pri·va·teers·men.** An officer or seaman of a privateer.

pri·vate first class, n. An enlisted man with a rank above private and immediately below that of corporal.

pri·vate law, n. That branch of the law which deals with the rights and duties of persons in their relations with one another as private individuals. Compare *public law.*

pri·vate school, n. A school which is founded, managed, and supported by a private group or corporation instead of the government.

pri·va·tion, prī·vā′shan, n. [L. *privatio,* < *privo,* to bereave.] The state of being deprived; deprivation of what is necessary for comfort or existence; destitution; want.

priv·a·tive, priv′a·tiv, a. [L. *privativus,* < *privare,* deprive.] Having the quality of depriving; serving to take away; consisting in or characterized by the taking away, loss, or want of something properly present; negative; *gram.* of or expressing privation or negation; as, a *privative* prefix.—*n.* That which is privative; *gram.* a negative element, as a prefix or suffix.—**priv·a·tive·ly,** adv.

priv·et, priv′it, n. [Origin uncertain.] A deciduous shrub of the olive family, *Ligustrum vulgare,* with small white flowers, much used for hedges; any of various other species of the genus *Ligustrum.*

priv·i·lege, priv′i·lij, priv′lij, n. [O.Fr. *privilege* (Fr. *privilège),* < L. *privilegium,* privilege, orig. a law in favor of or against an individual, < *privus,* private, and *lex (leg-),* law.] A right or immunity enjoyed by a person or persons beyond the common advantages of others; a special right or immunity granted to persons in authority or office; a grant to an individual or a corporation, of a special right or immunity, sometimes in derogation of the common right; the principle or condition of enjoying special rights or immunities; any of the more sacred and vital rights common to all citizens under a modern constitutional government; *stock exchange,* a speculative contract covering a call, put, spread, or straddle.—*v.t.*—*privileged, privileging.* To grant a privilege to; invest with some special right or immunity; to give, as a person, immunity; to exempt, usu. followed by *from;* to authorize or license, as something otherwise forbidden.

priv·i·leged, priv′i·lijd, priv′lijd, a. Relating to a favored person or group; exercising or possessing privileges; limited to a chosen individual or group; as, *privileged* documents.

priv·i·ty, priv'i·tē, *n. pl.* **priv·i·ties.** [O.Fr. *privite, privete,* < L. *privus,* private.] Private knowledge; participation in the knowledge of something private or secret, esp. as implying concurrence or consent; *law,* the relation between privies.

priv·y, priv'ē, *a.—privier, priviest.* [O.Fr. *prive* (Fr. *privé*), adj. and n., < L. *privatus.*] Participating in the knowledge of something private or secret, usu. followed by *to,* as: Many persons were *privy to* the plot. Private, as belonging or pertaining to some particular person or persons, esp. with reference to a sovereign.—*n. pl.* **priv·ies.** An outdoor toilet; *law,* one who has a legally recognized interest or responsibility in an estate or transaction.—**priv·i·ly,** priv'i·lē, *adv.*

priv·y coun·cil, *n.* A board or select body of personal advisers, as of a sovereign; (*cap.*), *Great Britain,* a body of advisers, some selected by the sovereign and others serving by usage, whose function of advising the crown in matters of state is now for the most part discharged by the Cabinet; (*sometimes cap.*) any similar body, as one appointed to assist the governor of a British dominion.—**priv·y coun·cil·or,** *n.*

priv·y purse, *n.* An allowance for the private expenses of the British sovereign.

prix fixe, prē' fiks', *Fr.* prē fēks', *n. pl.* **prix fixes,** prē' fiks', *Fr.* prē fēks'. [Fr., fixed price.] A fixed price for any meal listed under the heading 'table d'hôte' or 'prix fixe' at a restaurant; the price of such a meal.

prize, prīz, *n.* [O.Fr. Fr. *prise,* a taking, < *prendre,* < L. *prendere, prehendere,* seize, take; some uses being due to M.E. *pris, prise,* price, reward, prize, E. *price.*] A reward for victory or superiority, as in a contest or competition; that which is won in a lottery or the like; anything striven for, worth striving for, or much valued; something seized or captured, esp. an enemy's ship and its cargo taken at sea under the laws of war; the act of seizing or capturing, esp. the capture at sea of a ship and cargo. —*a.* That has gained a prize; worthy of a prize; outstanding; given or awarded as a prize.—*v.t.—prized, prizing.* To seize as a prize, as a ship.—**prize·win·ner,** prīz'win"ėr, *n.*—**prize·win·ning,** *a.*

prize, prīz, *v.t.—prized, prizing.* [O.Fr. *prisier* (Fr. *priser*), var. of *preisier,* value, prize.] To value or esteem highly; to estimate the value of.

prize, *Brit.* **prise,** prīz, *v.t.—prized, prizing, Brit.* also *prised, prising.* [O.Fr. Fr. *prise,* a taking, grasp, hold.] To raise, move, or force with a lever; pry.

prize fight, *n.* An exhibition contest between boxers for a prize, usu. money. Also **prize·fight.—prize fight·er, prize·fight·er,** *n.*—**prize fight·ing, prize·fight·ing,** *n.*

prize mon·ey, *n.* Money given as a prize; a portion of the money realized by the sale of a prize, esp. an enemy's vessel, distributed among the captors.

prize ring, *n.* A ring or enclosed square area for prize fighting.

pro, prō, *adv.* [L. *pro,* prep., before, for.] In favor of a proposition or opinion: opposed to *con.—n. pl.* **pros.** A consideration, argument, or vote for something; a person arguing or voting for a proposal.

pro, prō, *a.* [Short for *professional.*] *Colloq.* professional; as, a *pro* golfer.—*n. pl.* **pros.**

pro·a, prō'a, *n.* A swift Malaysian sailboat with a flat lee side and a single outrigger. Also **prao, prau, pra·hu,** prou, prä'hö.

prob·a·bi·lism, prob'a·bi·liz"um, *n.* [L. *probabilis.*] *Rom. Cath. theol.* the doctrine that in cases of doubt as to the lawfulness

or unlawfulness of an action, it is permissible to follow a soundly probable opinion favoring its lawfulness; *philos.* the doctrine that certainty is impossible, and that probability suffices to govern faith and practice.—**prob·a·bi·list,** *n., a.*—**prob·a·bi·lis·tic,** prob"a·bi·lis'tik, *a.*

prob·a·bil·i·ty, prob"a·bil'i·tē, *n. pl.* **prob·a·bil·i·ties.** [Fr. *probabilité,* L. *probabilitas.*] The state or quality of being probable; likelihood; a probable occurrence or condition; *statistics,* the ratio of the number of chances by which an event may happen to the number by which it may both happen and fail.

prob·a·ble, prob'a·bl, *a.* [Fr. *probable,* < L. *probabilis,* that may be proved, probable, < *probo,* to prove.] Supported by or based on evidence which inclines the mind to belief, but leaves some room for doubt; likely; rendering something believable or possible.—**prob·a·bly,** prob'a·blē, *adv.*

prob·a·ble cause, *n. Law,* reasonable grounds for believing in the guilt of one charged with an offense.

pro·bang, prō'bang, *n.* [Earlier *provang;* origin unknown.] *Med.* a long, slender, elastic rod with a sponge, ball, or the like at the end, used for removing foreign bodies from the esophagus or the larynx, or for applying medicine in those areas.

pro·bate, prō'bāt, *n.* [L. *probatus,* pp. of *probare,* E. *prove.*] *Law,* the official proving of a will as authentic or genuine; an officially certified copy of a will so proved.— *a.* Of or pertaining to probate or a court of probate.—*v.t.—probated, probating.* To establish the authenticity of, as a will.

pro·bate court, *n.* A court concerned with the probate of wills and the settlement of estates; also **court of pro·bate.**

pro·ba·tion, prō·bā'shan, *n.* [L. *probatio, probationis,* an approving.] The act of proving; proof; any proceeding designed to ascertain character, qualifications, or the like; a preliminary or preparatory trial or examination; a period of suspension of penalty, as of imprisonment for a crime or of dismissal because of scholastic failure: usu. preceded by *on;* a period of time during which a delinquent must report at regular intervals to a probation officer.—**pro·ba·tion·al, pro·ba·tion·ar·y,** prō·bā'sha·ner"ē, *a.*—**pro·ba·tion·al·ly,** *adv.*

pro·ba·tion·er, prō·bā'sha·nėr, *n.* One who is on probation or trial; a student nurse during her first year of training.

pro·ba·tion of·fic·er, *n.* One who supervises and reports on the behavior of an offender who is on probation.

pro·ba·tive, prō'ba·tiv, prob'a·tiv, *a.* [L. *probativus,* < *probare,* E. *prove.*] Serving or designed for testing or trial; affording proof or evidence. Also **pro·ba·to·ry,** prō'ba·tōr"ē, prō'ba·tạr"ē.

probe, prōb, *n.* [L. *probo,* to test, to try, to prove.] *Surg.* an instrument for examining the depth or other circumstances of a wound, ulcer, or cavity; an investigation, esp. of an alleged illegal activity. A device employed to explore outer space and send back data; a projecting pipe on an airplane used for refueling in the air.—*v.t.—probed, probing.* To apply a probe to; to examine by means of a probe; to inquire thoroughly into.—*v.i.—prob·er,* *n.*

prob·it, prob'it, *n. Statistics,* a measurement of probability which is based on deviation from the average.

pro·bi·ty, prō'bi·tē, prob'i·tē, *n.* [L. *probitas,* < *probus,* worthy, honest, good.] Demonstrated virtue or integrity; strict honesty; rectitude; uprightness.

prob·lem, prob'lem, *n.* [Fr. *problème,* L. *problema,* < Gr. *problēma.*] A question proposed for solution, decision, or determination; a knotty point requiring clarifica-

tion; *geom.* a proposition requiring some operation to be performed.—*a.* Not well adjusted in behavior; as, a *problem* child; dealing with matters arising out of conflicting social values and relationships; as, a *problem* drama.

prob·lem·at·ic, prob"le·mat'ik, *a.* Constituting a problem; doubtful.—**prob·lem·at·i·cal,** *a.*—**prob·lem·at·i·cal·ly,** *adv.*

pro·bos·cid·e·an, pro·bos·cid·i·an, prō"bo·sid'ē·an, prō"bo·sid'ē·an, prō·bos"i·dē'an, *a.* Pertaining to or belonging to the *Proboscidea,* an order of large mammals which have the nose prolonged into a prehensile trunk, as the elephant; pertaining to a proboscis.—*n.* Any animal belonging to this order.

pro·bos·cis, prō·bos'is, *n. pl.* **pro·bos·cis·es, pro·bos·ci·des,** prō·bos'i·dēz. [L. *proboscis,* < Gr. *proboskis—pro,* before, and *boskō,* to feed.] The snout or trunk projecting from the head of an elephant or other animal; *entom.* the horny tube formed by the modified jaws of insects, used for sucking or piercing; *humorous,* the human nose, esp. when extremely prominent.

pro·caine, prō·kān', prō'kān, *n. Pharm.* a compound, $C_{13}H_{20}O_2N_2$, used in the form procaine hydrochloride as a local anesthetic.

pro·ca·the·dral, prō"ka·thē'dral, *n.* A church that serves temporarily as a cathedral.

pro·ce·dure, pro·sē'jėr, *n.* [Fr. *procédure,* < *procéder,* E. *proceed.*] The act or manner of proceeding in any action or process; a particular course or mode of action, esp. a mode of conducting legal, parliamentary, or other business; conduct of litigation and judicial proceedings.—**pro·ce·dur·al,** *a.*—**pro·ce·dur·al·ly,** *adv.*

pro·ceed, pro·sēd', *v.i.* [Fr. *procéder;* L. *procedo.*] To go onward; to continue or renew motion or progress; to advance; to pass from one point, stage, or topic to another; to issue or come from an origin or source, used with *from;* to set to work and go on in a certain way; *law,* to begin and carry on a legal action.

pro·ceed·ing, pro·sē'ding, *n.* The act of one who or that which proceeds; action, course of action, or conduct; a particular action or course of action; *pl.* records of the doings of a society. *Law,* the instituting or carrying on of an action at law; a legal step or measure; as, to institute *proceedings* against a person.

pro·ceeds, prō'sēdz, *n. pl.* The financial return or total profit from a business undertaking or investment.

pro·ce·phal·ic, prō"se·fal'ik, *a.* [Gr.] *Zool.* pertaining to or forming the fore part of the head.

proc·ess, pros'es, *Brit.* prō'ses, *n.* [L. *processus,* < *procedo, processum,* to proceed.] A succession of actions undertaken to bring about some desired result; as, a *process* for refining metal; a series of gradual changes moving toward some particular end; as, the aging *process.* *Law,* a summons, writ, or judicial order to compel a defendant to appear in court; the proceedings of a court or legal action. *Biol., anat.* a bony prominence, or other projecting outgrowth or protuberance, as of tissue, in an organism. *Photog.* a method of reproducing pictures or prints by photoengraving or photomechanical means; a method of combining or superimposing motion picture film shots and backgrounds to create various effects. A forward movement; progression; a passing or elapsing; as, the *process* of time.

proc·ess, pros'es, *Brit.* prō'ses, *v.t.* To treat or prepare by some particular process;

to convert, as an agricultural commodity, into marketable form by some special treatment; to institute a legal action against; to serve a summons on; to organize, as mail, records, and other paperwork, and act upon them in a certain way; to put, as personnel, through a routine of filling out questionnaires, undergoing tests, and the like prior to entering service or employment.—*v.i.* To undergo processing.—**proc·es·sor, proc·ess·er,** *n.*

proc·ess, pros'es, *Brit.* prō'ses, *a.* Produced or treated by some artificial means; as, *process* sugar; of or pertaining to photographic reproduction that involves photoengraving or photomechanical means; relating to special effects obtained in motion pictures through the use of special filming techniques; as, a *process* shot.

pro·ces·sion, pro·sesh'an, *n.* [O.Fr. Fr. *procession,* < L. *processio(n-),* < *procedere,* E. *proceed.*] The proceeding or moving along in orderly succession, in a formal or ceremonious manner, of a line of persons, animals, vehicles, or other things; the line of persons or things moving along; *eccles.* an office or a litany said or sung in a religious procession. A continuous succession.—*v.i.* To move in procession.

pro·ces·sion·al, pro·sesh'a·nal, *a.* Of, pertaining to, or characteristic of a procession; sung or recited in procession, as a hymn.—*n.* A book containing hymns or litanies for use in religious processions; a processional hymn.—**pro·ces·sion·al·ly,** *adv.*

proc·ess print·ing, *n.* A method of printing in full color by using the primary colors on separate plates, printed one over the other.

pro·claim, prō·klām', pro·klām', *v.t.* [L. *prōclamo.*] To make known by public announcement; to announce officially; to outlaw by public denunciation; to promulgate.—**pro·claim·er,** *n.*

proc·la·ma·tion, prok"la·mā'shan, *n.* [L. *proclamatio.*] The act of proclaiming; an official public announcement or declaration; that which is announced or proclaimed.

pro·clit·ic, prō·klit'ik, *n.* [< Gr.] *Gram.* a word so closely attached to a following word as to have no phonological status and no accent, as *it* in *'tis,* or the French *je* in *j'ai.*—*a.*

pro·cliv·i·ty, prō·kliv'i·tē, *n.* pl. **pro·cliv·i·ties.** [L. *proclivitas.*]Inclination or propensity; proneness; tendency.

pro·con·sul, prō·kon'sul, *n.* [L.] In ancient Rome, an officer, generally an exconsul, who discharged the duties of a consul over a province or an army; an administrator of a colony, as a British viceroy.—**pro·con·su·lar,** *a.*—**pro·con·su·late, pro·con·sul·ship,** prō·kon'sa·lit, *n.*

pro·cras·ti·nate, prō·kras'ti·nāt", pro·kras'ti·nāt", *v.t.*—*procrastinated, procrastinating.* [L. *procrastino, procrastinatus.*] To put off from day to day; to delay; to defer to a future time.—*v.i.* To delay action; to be dilatory.—**pro·cras·ti·na·tion,** *n.*—**pro·cras·ti·na·tor,** *n.*

pro·cre·ant, prō'krē·ant, *a.* Procreating or generating; pertaining to procreation.

pro·cre·ate, prō'krē·āt", *v.t.*—*procreated, procreating.* [L. *procreo—pro,* before, and *creo,* to create.] To beget; to generate and produce; to reproduce.—**pro·cre·a·tion,** *n.* —**pro·cre·a·tive,** *a.*—**pro·cre·a·tor,** *n.*

Pro·crus·te·an, prō·krus'tē·an, *a.* [From *Procrustes,* a giant robber and torturer, of Greek mythology.] (*Sometimes l.c.*) producing uniformity ruthlessly.

pro·cryp·tic, prō·krip'tik, *a. Zool.* pertaining to coloring, as in insects, which serves as a protective disguise or for concealment.

proc·tol·o·gy, prok·tol'o·jē, *n.* That branch of medical science dealing with the anal region and rectum.—**proc·to·log·ic, proc·to·log·i·cal,** prok"to·loj'ik, *a.*—**proc·tol·o·gist,** *n.*

proc·tor, prok'tėr, *n.* [Contr. < *procurator;* cf. *proxy.*] A person employed to manage another's cause in civil, admiralty, or ecclesiastical courts; an individual in a university whose function is to see that order is kept and to supervise examinations.—*v.t., v.i.* To supervise.—**proc·to·ri·al,** prok·tōr'ē·al, prok·tȧr'ē·al, *a.*—**proc·tor·ship,** *n.*

proc·to·scope, prok'to·skōp", *n.* A surgeon's instrument for interior examination of the rectum.—**proc·tos·co·py,** prok·tos'ko·pē, *n.*

pro·cum·bent, prō·kum'bent, *a.* [L. *procumbens.*] Lying down; prone. *Bot.* trailing; prostrate; lying on the ground, but without putting forth roots, as a vine.

proc·u·ra·tion, prok"ū·rā'shan, *n.* Management of another's affairs; the document by which a person is empowered to transact the affairs of another; act of procuring.

proc·u·ra·tor, prok'ū·rā"tėr, *n.* [L., one who manages, an agent, < *procuro.*] The manager of another's affairs; one who undertakes the care of legal proceedings for another; *hist.* a governor of a province under the Roman emperors.—**proc·u·ra·to·ri·al,** prok"yėr·a·tōr'ē·al, prok"yėr·a·tȧr'ē·al, *a.* **proc·u·ra·tor·ship,** *n.*

pro·cure, prō·kūr', *v.t.*—*procured, procuring.* [Fr. *procurer,* < L. *procurare,* to take care of, to attend to.] To obtain, as by effort, labor, or purchase; to get, gain, come into possession of; to cause, bring about, effect, contrive; to obtain for prostitution.—*v.i.* To pimp.—**pro·cur·a·ble,** *a.*—**pro·cur·ance,** *n.*—**pro·cure·ment,** *n.*—**pro·cur·er,** prō·kūr'ėr, *n.* —**pro·cur·ess,** prō·kūr'is, *n.*

prod, prod, *v.t.*—*prodded, prodding.* [Origin uncertain.] To poke or jab with something pointed; as, to *prod* a person with the finger; to rouse or incite as if by poking; to urge or goad into action.—*n.* An act of prodding; a poke or jab; any of various pointed instruments, as a goad.—**prod·der,** *n.*

prod·i·gal, prod'i·gal, *a.* [L.L. *prodigalis,* < L. *prodigus,* prodigal.] Given to extravagant expenditure; expending wastefully; profuse; wasteful; lavishly bountiful.—*n.* One who spends money extravagantly; a waster; a spendthrift; one who is profuse or lavish.—**prod·i·gal·i·ty,** prod'i·gal'i·tē, *n.*—**prod·i·gal·ly,** *adv.*

pro·di·gious, pro·dij'us, *a.* [Fr. *prodigieux;* L. *prodigiosus,* strange, wonderful, < *prodigium,* a prodigy.] Extraordinary; huge; enormous; marvelous.—**pro·di·gious·ly,** *adv.*—**pro·di·gious·ness,** *n.*

prod·i·gy, prod'i·jē, *n.* pl. **prod·i·gies.** [L. *prodigium.*] A person, esp. a child or youth, of extraordinary talent or ability; a marvel or wonder, as a remarkable deed, occurrence, or accomplishment; something unnatural or inexplicable.

pro·drome, prō'drōm, *n.* [Fr. *prodrome,* < Gr. *pródromos,* running before.] *Pathol.* a premonitory symptom.—**prod·ro·mal, pro·dro·mic,** prod'ro·mal, *a.*

pro·duce, pro·dōs', pro·dūs', *v.t.*—*produced, producing.* [L. *produco.*] To bring forth into existence; to bring about; to cause or effect, esp. intellectually or creatively; to give birth to; to bear, furnish, yield; to make accrue; to bring about the performance of, as a movie or play; to extend, as a line.—*v.i.* To bring forth or yield appropriate offspring, products, or consequences.—**pro·duced,** *a.*—**pro·duc·i·ble, pro·duce·a·ble, pro·duct·i·ble,** *a.* **pro·duce,** prod'ōs, prod'ūs, prō'dōs, prō'dūs, *n.* That which is produced; yield;

product, specif. agricultural products collectively, as: Fruits and vegetables are displayed in the supermarket's *produce* department.

pro·duc·er, pro·dō'sėr, pro·dū'sėr, *n.* One who or that which produces; *econ.* one who produces goods or services for marketing. One who finances or supervises the making of motion pictures or plays; *Brit.* director. An apparatus that makes producer gas.

pro·duc·er gas, *n.* A combustible compound of hydrogen, nitrogen, and carbon monoxide, produced by passing steam and air over incandescent coke, and used in the production of ammonia and as a fuel.

pro·duc·er goods, *n. pl.* Instruments of production, as tools and raw materials, that benefit the consumer only indirectly.

prod·uct, prod'ukt, prod'ukt, *n.* [L. *productum.*] A thing which is produced by nature, as fruit, grain, or vegetables; that which is produced by labor or mental application; a production; something resulting as a consequence; result; *math.* the result of, or quantity produced by, the multiplication of two numbers or quantities together. *Chem.* a substance created by chemical change.

pro·duc·tion, pro·duk'shan, *n.* [L. *productio, productionis.*] The act or process of producing; that which is produced or made; as, the *productions* of the earth, of art, of intellect; the total amount of something produced, as: *Production* is low this year. *Econ.* the producing of articles having an exchange value. *Colloq.* an exaggerated process, as: He makes a *production* out of combing his hair.—**pro·duc·tion·al,** *a.*

pro·duc·tion con·trol, *n.* Systematized supervision of the manufacture of goods to ensure quality.

pro·duc·tive, pro·duk'tiv, *a.* Having the power of producing; fertile; producing good crops; bringing into being; causing to exist; as, an age *productive* of great men. *Econ.* producing commodities of great value; adding to the wealth of the world. —**pro·duc·tive·ly,** *adv.*—**pro·duc·tive·ness,** *n.*—**pro·duc·tiv·i·ty,** prō"duk·tiv'i·tē, prod"uk·tiv'i·tē, *n.*

pro·em, prō'em, *n.* [Fr. *proème,* < L. *procemium,* Gr. *prooimion.*] Preface; introduction; preliminary statement.—**pro·e·mi·al,** prō·ē'mē·al, *a.*

pro·en·zyme, prō·en'zīm, *n. Biochem., biol.* zymogen.

prof, prof, *n. Colloq.* professor.

prof·a·na·tion, prof"a·nā'shan, *n.* The act of profaning; the violation or maltreatment of sacred things; contempt; irreverence; desecration.

pro·fane, pro·fān', prō·fān', *a.* [Fr. *profane,* < L. *profanus,* profane, unholy.] Irreverent toward God or holy things; not sacred or devoted to sacred purposes; secular; implying contempt of religious things through speech or action; blasphemous; polluted or vulgar.—*v.t.*—*profaned, profaning.* To treat, as something sacred, with irreverence, impiety, or sacrilege; to desecrate; to misuse; to employ basely or unworthily.—**pro·fane·ly,** *adv.*—**pro·fane·ness,** *n.*—**pro·fan·a·to·ry,** pro·fan'a·tōr·ē, pro·fan'a·tȧr·ē, *a.*—**pro·fan·er,** *n.*

pro·fan·i·ty, pro·fan'i·tē, pro·fan'i·tē, *n.* pl. **pro·fan·i·ties.** The quality of being profane; that which is profane; profane language or conduct.

pro·fess, pro·fes', *v.t.* [L. *profiteri, professus,* to declare, acknowledge, profess.] To acknowledge or own publicly to be; to make protestations or a pretense of; to declare one's allegiance to; to declare oneself versed in; to accept into a religious community.—*v.i.* To make a declaration; to become a member of a religious order.

pro·fessed, pro·fest', *a.* Avowed; acknowledged; sometimes, alleged or pretended; professional rather than amateur; having taken the vows of, or been received into, a religious order.

pro·fess·ed·ly, pro·fes'id·lē, *adv.* Avowedly; allegedly.

pro·fes·sion, pro·fesh'an, *n.* [L. *professio.*] A vocation requiring specialized training in a field of learning, art, or science; a leading vocation or business; the body of persons engaged in a calling or vocation; an avowal or public acknowledgment of one's beliefs or loyalties; act of committing oneself to a religious community.

pro·fes·sion·al, pro·fesh'a·nal, *a.* Pertaining to a profession; engaged in a profession, esp. law, medicine, or the ministry.—*n.* A member of any profession, but more often applied, in opposition to *amateur*, to persons who make their living by arts or sports in which others engage as a pastime.—**pro·fes·sion·al·ly,** *adv.*

pro·fes·sion·al·ism, pro·fesh'a·na·liz"um, *n.* Character, spirit, and methods that distinguish a professional from an amateur; the earning of a livelihood from a sport or other activity that others enjoy as a pastime.

pro·fes·sion·al·ize, pro·fesh'a·na·liz", *v.t., v.i.—professionalized, professionalizing.* To make or become professional.

pro·fes·sor, pro·fes'ėr, *n.* [L.] The highest ranking teacher of any art, science, or other branch of learning, esp. in a university or college; any teacher with the title associate professor or assistant professor; one who teaches in a skilled sport or art; one who professes his religious faith or other beliefs.—**pro·fes·so·ri·al,** prof"e·sōr'ē·al, prof"e·sąr'ē·al, *a.*—**pro·fes·so·ri·al·ly,** *adv.*

pro·fes·sor·ate, pro·fes'ėr·it, *n.* The office, position, or period of service of a professor.

pro·fes·so·ri·ate, prō"fi·sōr'ē·it, prō"fi·sąr'ē·it, prof"i·sōr'ē·it, prof"i·sąr'ē·it, *n.* A body of professors; a teaching staff of professors; a professorship.

pro·fes·sor·ship, pro·fes'ėr·ship", *n.* The office of a professor.

prof·fer, prof'ėr, *v.t.* [Fr. *proférer*, < L. *proferre*, to bring forward—*pro*, before, and *ferre*, to bring.] To offer for acceptance.—*n.* An offer made; something proposed for acceptance by another; the act of so proposing.—**prof·fer·er,** *n.*

pro·fi·cien·cy, pro·fish'en·sē, *n.* The state of being proficient; skill, knowledge.

pro·fi·cient, pro·fish'ent, *a.* [L. *proficiens*, < *proficio*, I advance, make progress, improve—*pro*, forward, and *facio*, to make.] Well-versed in any business, art, or branch of learning; skilled, competent.—*n.* An expert.—**pro·fi·cient·ly,** *adv.*

pro·file, prō'fil, *n.* [Fr. *profil*, < It. *profilo*; < L. *pro*, before, and *filum*, a thread, line.] An outline or contour; esp. an outline of the human face seen sideways; the side view of the face; the outline or contour of anything, as a building or portion of country; a numerical or graphic analysis, as of the abilities disclosed by intelligence tests; a short biographical outline; *arch.* an outline of a vertical section or a drawing of this.—*v.t.—profiled, profiling.* To draw in profile; to give a profile of.

prof·it, prof'it, *n.* [Fr. *profit*, < L. *profectus*, progress, increase, < *proficio*, to advance, to improve.] Any advantage, benefit, or return; pecuniary gain; the advantage or gain resulting to the owner of capital from its employment in any undertaking; the excess of income over expenditure, specif. the difference, when an excess, between the original cost and selling price of anything; the ratio in any year of this gain to the sum invested; revenue from investments or property. See *gross profit, net profit.—v.i.* To derive profit or benefit; to be of use or advantage.—*v.t.* To benefit; to be of service to; to advance.—**prof·it·less,** *a.*

prof·it·a·ble, prof'i·ta·bl, *a.* Yielding or bringing profit or gain; gainful; lucrative; useful; advantageous.—**prof·it·a·bil·i·ty, prof·it·a·ble·ness,** *n.*—**prof·it·a·bly,** *adv.*

prof·it and loss, *n.* A summary of the gain and loss arising from commercial or other transactions, applied esp. to an account in bookkeeping showing gains and losses in business.—**prof·it-and-loss,** *a.*

prof·it·eer, prof"i·tēr', *n.* An individual who takes advantage of abnormal conditions, such as those of wartime, to make excessive profit.—*v.i.* To make or try to make excess profits.

prof·it shar·ing, *n.* The sharing of profits, as between employer and employee, esp. according to a method by which the employee receives, in addition to his wages, a share in the profits of the business.—**prof·it-shar·ing,** *a.*

prof·li·gate, prof'li·git, prof'li·gāt", *a.* [L. *profligatus,* pp. of *profligo*, to rout, to ruin.] Ruined in morals; lost to virtue or decency; rashly extravagant.—*n.* One who has lost all regard for principles, virtue, or decency; a spendthrift.—**prof·li·gate·ly,** *adv.*—**prof·li·ga·cy, prof·li·gate·ness,** prof'li·ga·sē, *n.*

prof·lu·ent, prof'lö·ent, *a.* [L. *profluens* (*-ent-*).] Flowing forth gently or abundantly.

pro for·ma, prō fär'ma, L. PRŌ FŌR'mä, *a.* [L., 'for form.'] For the sake of form; complying with some legal requirement; as, a *pro forma* invoice.

pro·found, pro·found', *a.* [Fr. *profond*, L. *profundus.*] Intellectually deep; deep in knowledge or skill; characterized by intensity; far beneath the superficial or overt; of deep, greatly significant, or inclusive meaning; far below the surface; low; deep.—*n.* The deep sea; the ocean; an abyss.—**pro·found·ly,** *adv.*—**pro·found·ness,** *n.*

pro·fun·di·ty, pro·fun'di·tē, *n.* pl. **pro·fun·di·ties.** The quality or condition of being profound; depth of place; something deep or abstruse.

pro·fuse, pro·fūs', *a.* [L. *profusus*, < *profundo.*] Extravagant; prodigal; poured forth abundantly; exuberant; copious.—**pro·fuse·ly,** *adv.*—**pro·fuse·ness,** *n.*

pro·fu·sion, pro·fū'zhan, *n.* [L. *profusio.*] Rich abundance; great amount, usu. followed by *of*; prodigality; lavish expenditure.

pro·gen·i·tor, prō·jen'i·tėr, *n.* An ancestor in the direct line; a forefather; an originator.

prog·e·ny, proj'e·nē, *n.* pl. **prog·e·nies.** [Fr. *progénie,* L. *progenies,* < *pro*, forth, and root *gen*, to bring forth; seen also in *gender, generation, genus.*] Offspring collectively; children; descendants.

pro·ges·ta·tion·al, prō"jes·tā'sha·nal, *a.* *Med.* Relating to certain alterations, esp. of the uterus in female mammals, requisite for the fertilization and growth of the ovum; receptive to pregnancy.

pro·ges·ter·one, prō·jes'te·rōn", *n.* *Biochem.* a female sex hormone, $C_{21}H_{30}O_2$, produced in the ovaries, which prepares the uterus for reception and development of the fertilized ovum. *Pharm.* a form of this hormone obtained from pregnant cows or by synthesis. Also **pro·ges·tin,** prō·jes'tin.

prog·na·thous, prog'na·thus, prog·nā'thus, *a.* [Gr. *pro*, before, and *gnathos,* the cheek or jawbone.] Characterized by forward-projecting jaws; contrasted with *opisthognathous.* Also **prog·nath·ic,** prog·nath'ik.—**prog·na·thism,** prog'na·thiz"um, *n.*

prog·no·sis, prog·nō'sis, *n.* pl. **prog·no·ses,** prog·nō'sēs. [Gr. *prognōsis,* a foreknowing.] *Med.* a forecast of the probable course of a disease and the possibility of recovery. Any forecast.

prog·nos·tic, prog·nos'tic, *a.* [Gr. *prognōstikos—pro,* before, and *gignōsko,* to know.] Foretelling; indicating something in the future by signs or symptoms; relating to a prognosis.—*n.* A sign by which a future event may be known or foretold; an omen; prediction. *Med.* a symptom or symptoms used as the basis for prognosis.

prog·nos·ti·cate, prog·nos'ti·kāt", *v.t.—prognosticated, prognosticating.* To foretell by means of present signs; to predict; to foreshow.—**prog·nos·ti·ca·tive,** *a.*—**prog·nos·ti·ca·tor,** *n.*

prog·nos·ti·ca·tion, prog·nos"ti·kā'shan, *n.* The act of prognosticating; a prediction.

pro·gram, *Brit.* **pro·gramme,** prō'gram, prō'gram, *n.* [= Fr. *programme,* < L.L. *programma,* < Gr. *programma,* public notice in writing, < *prographein,* write publicly.] A schedule or plan to be followed; a list of items, pieces, or performers in a musical, theatrical, or other entertainment; an entertainment with reference to its pieces or numbers; a performance on radio or television; a prospectus or syllabus.—*v.t.—programmed, programming, programed, programing.* To arrange or enter in a program; to draw up, as a program for.—*v.i.* To draw up a program.—**pro·gram·mer,** prō'gram·ėr, *n.*

pro·gram, *Brit.* **pro·gramme,** prō'gram, prō'gram, *n.* A logically related order of actions to be performed by a computer either to solve a problem or to process data; the instructions and data, reduced to computer code, for such a series of actions.—*v.t.—programmed, programming, programed, programing.* To enter or arrange in a program; to make up a program for; to give, as a computer, a program.—**pro·gram·mer,** prō'gram·ėr, *n.*

pro·gram·mat·ic, prō"gra·mat'ik, *a.* Pertaining to or of the nature of a program; of the nature of program music.—**pro·gram·mat·i·cal·ly,** *adv.*

pro·grammed in·struc·tion, *n.* Instruction which requires a student to respond to a prepared set of items or questions and to reply to each correctly before advancing to the next item.

pro·gram mu·sic, *n.* Music intended to convey an impression of a definite series of images, scenes, or events.

prog·ress, prog'rės, *Brit. also* prō'gres, *n.* [L. *progressus,* < *progredi,* go forward.] A going or traveling forward or onward, or a march or journey; a journey of state, as of a sovereign; onward movement in space; a forward course of action, of events, or of time; *fig.* a proceeding to a further or higher stage, or through such stages successively; as, the *progress* of a scholar in his studies; advance or advancement in general; growth or development; continuous improvement.—**pro·gres,** *v.i.* To go forward or onward; proceed; to make progress; advance; improve.

pro·gres·sion, pro·gresh'an, *n.* [L. *progressio(n-),* < *progredi.*] The act of progressing; forward or onward movement; a passing successively from one member of a series to the next; succession; advance; development; *math.* a succession of quantities in which there is a constant relation between each member and the one succeeding it; as, an arithmetical *progression,* in which the members increase or decrease by a constant difference, or a geometrical *progression,* in which each member is derived from the preceding one by multiplication by a constant factor. *Mus.* motion from one note or chord to another; a sequence.—**pro·gres·sion·al,** *a.*

pro·gres·sion·ist, pro·gresh′a·nist, *n.* One who believes in or advocates progress, as of society; one who holds that organic existence is characterized by progression from simpler to more complex forms.

prog·ress·ist, prog′res·ist, prō′gres·ist, *n.* One favoring progress, as in politics; a progressive.

pro·gres·sive, pro·gres′iv, *a.* [Fr. *progressif,* < L. *progressus,* pp. of *progredi.*] Characterized by progressing or going forward or onward; passing on successively from one member of a series to the next; proceeding step by step; marked by succession; *gram.* noting a verb form describing action continuing from a reference point in time, as: She 'is brushing' her hair. Noting a form of certain card games, as bridge, played simultaneously by several sets of players at a number of tables, under rules providing for the advancement, after each game or round, of certain players from one table to the next; noting or pertaining to a form of taxation in which the rate increases with certain increases in the amount taxed; making progress toward higher or better conditions, more enlightened or liberal ideas, or the use of new and advantageous methods; as, a *progressive* nation or community; characterized by such progress, or by continuous improvement; of a disease, continuously increasing in extent or severity; favoring or advocating progress, improvement, or reform, esp. in political matters; (*cap.*), *U.S. politics,* noting or pertaining to a party formed in 1912 under the leadership of Theodore Roosevelt, advocating popular control of government, direct primaries, the initiative, etc., or to parties formed in 1924 and 1948.—*n.* One who is progressive, or who favors progress or reform, esp. in political matters; (*cap.*) a member of the Progressive party.—**pro·gres·sive·ly,** *adv.*—**pro·gres·sive·ness,** *n.*

Pro·gres·sive Con·ser·va·tive, *a.* Relating to the Progressive Conservative party of Canada, formerly the Conservative party.—*n.* A member of that party.

pro·gres·sive jazz, *n.* A modern jazz style characterized by the mixture of jazz and non-jazz elements in disharmonious big-band arrangements; a jazz style which evolved in the 1940's, characterized by the influence of classical motifs, harmonic and rhythmic experimentation and complexity, and frequent use of written-out arrangements.

pro·gres·siv·ism, pro·gres′i·viz″um, *n.* The principles and practices of progressives.—**pro·gres·siv·ist,** *n., a.*

pro·hib·it, prō·hib′it, *v.t.* [L. *prohibitus,* pp. of *prohibere,* hold back, restrain, forbid.] To forbid, as an action, by authority or interdict; forbid, as a person, from doing something; to prevent or debar.

pro·hi·bi·tion, prō″i·bish′an, *n.* [L. *prohibitio(n-).*] The act of prohibiting; an order or decree forbidding or debarring; the interdiction by law of the manufacture and sale of alcoholic drinks.

pro·hi·bi·tion·ist, prō″i·bish′a·nist, *n.* One who favors or advocates prohibition of the manufacture and sale of alcoholic beverages.

pro·hib·i·tive, prō·hib′i·tiv, *a.* That prohibits or forbids something; serving to prevent the use or purchase of something; as, *prohibitive* costs. Also **pro·hib·i·to·ry,** prō·hib′i·tōr″ē, prō·hib′i·tar″ē.—**pro·hib·i·tive·ly,** *adv.*

pro·ject, pro·jekt′, *v.t.* [L. *projectus,* pp. of *projicere, proicere.*] To propose, contemplate, or plan, as something to be carried out; to throw, cast, or impel forward or onward; to throw or cause to fall upon a surface or into space, as an image or ray of light; to visualize and regard, as an idea or feeling, as an objective reality; to cause to jut out or protrude; to present or set forth for consideration, as a scheme; *geom.* to throw forward, as a figure, by straight lines or rays, either parallel or from a center, which pass through all points of it and reproduce it on a surface; *theatr.* to use, as one's voice or movements, so as to communicate clearly to the entire audience.—*v.i.* To extend or protrude beyond something else; jut out; to make oneself clearly understood by an audience, through proper use of one's voice or movements.—**pro·ject·a·ble,** *a.*

pro·ject, proj′ekt, *n.* [= Fr. *projet,* < L. *projectum,* neut. of *projectus,* pp.] Something contemplated or planned; a plan; scheme; a large undertaking; as, a housing *project;* a specific piece of research; *educ.* an assignment or task given to students, esp. one calling for individual initiative.

pro·jec·tile, pro·jek′til, pro·jek′til, *n.* [N.L. *projectilis,* < L. *projectus,* pp.] A body projected or impelled forward, as through the air; a missile for a gun, cannon, or other weapon.—*a.* Impelling or driving forward, as a force; capable of being projected or impelled forward, as a missile; *zool.* protrusile, as the jaws of a fish.

pro·jec·tion, pro·jek′shan, *n.* [L. *projectio(n-),* < *projicere.*] The act of projecting or the state of being projected; the state or fact of jutting out or protruding; a projecting or protruding part; *cartography,* a systematic representation on a flat surface of all or part of the earth's surface, or that of the celestial sphere. *Photog.* the act of projecting an image from a slide or motion picture onto a screen; the image produced. The calculation of a future possibility; the act of planning or scheming; the act of visualizing and regarding an idea or the like as an objective reality; that which is so visualized and regarded; *psychol.* the process of unwittingly ascribing one's own attitudes, feelings, or the like to others, esp. as an unconscious defense against a sense of inadequacy or guilt.—**pro·jec·tion·al,** pro·jek′sha·nal, *a.*

pro·jec·tion·ist, pro·jek′sha·nist, *n.* One who operates a motion-picture projector.

pro·jec·tive, pro·jek′tiv, *a.* Of or pertaining to projection; produced, or capable of being produced, by projection; *psychol.* relating or pertaining to standard tests used in the study of personality.—**pro·jec·tive·ly,** *adv.*—**pro·jec·tiv·i·ty,** prō″jek·tiv′i·tē, *n.*

pro·jec·tive ge·om·e·try, *n.* The study of geometric properties which are unchanged when projected.

pro·jec·tor, pro·jek′tĕr, *n.* An apparatus for throwing an image on a screen; as, a slide *projector;* a device for projecting a beam of light, as a lens; one who forms projects or plans; a schemer.

pro·jet, prō·zhā′, *Fr.* *n.* pl. **pro·jets,** prō·zhāz′, *Fr.* prꝒ·zhe′. [Fr.] A project; a plan; a draft of a proposed treaty.

pro·lac·tin, prō·lak′tin, *n. Biochem.* a hormone of the pituitary gland that stimulates production of milk in mammals and certain gland secretions in birds.

pro·lam·in, **pro·lam·ine,** prō·lam′in, prō′la·min, *n. Biochem.* one of a group of simple proteins obtained from the gluten of grain, as wheat, oats, and the like, and insoluble in pure water, absolute alcohol, and neutral solvents.

pro·lan, prō′lan, *n. Biochem.* a hormone similar to the pituitary sex hormones and present in the urine of pregnant women, permitting early diagnosis of pregnancy.

pro·lapse, prō·laps′, *v.i.*—*prolapsed, prolapsing.* [L. *prolapsus,* pp. of *prolabi.*] To fall or slip down or out of place.—**pro′laps,** prō·laps′, *n.* [L.L. *prolapsus,* n.] *Pathol.* a falling down of an organ or part, as the uterus, from its normal position.

pro·late, prō′lāt, *a.* [L. *prolatus,* pp. of *proferre,* bring forward, extend.] Elongated in the direction of the polar diameter, as a spheroid generated by the revolution of an ellipse about its longer axis: opposed to *oblate.*

pro·le·gom·e·non, prō″le·gom′e·non″, prō″le·gom′e·non, *n.* pl. **pro·le·gom·e·na,** prō″le·gom′e·na. [Gr.] A preliminary observation; *often pl.* an introductory discussion or discourse prefixed to a book or treatise.—**pro·le·gom·e·nous,** prō″le·gom′e·nus, *a.*

pro·lep·sis, prō·lep′sis, *n.* pl. **pro·lep·ses,** prō·lep′sēz. [Gr., preconception.] Something of the nature of an anticipation. *Rhet.* an expression by which a thing is represented as already done, though in reality it is to follow as a consequence of the action which is described; the use of an objective complement which anticipates the verbal outcome. A prochronism.—**pro·lep·tic,** prō·lep′tik, *a.*

pro·le·tar·i·an, prō″li·târ′ē·an, *a.* [L. *proletarius,* a citizen of the lowest class, one useful to the state only by producing children.] Pertaining to the proletarians.—*n.* A member of the wage-earning class.

pro·le·tar·i·at, prō″li·târ′ē·at, *n.* [Fr. *prolétariat.*] That class of the community which is dependent for support on daily or casual employment; the laboring class, or wage earners in general.

pro·lif·er·ate, prō·lif′e·rāt″, *v.t., v.i.*—*proliferated, proliferating.* To grow or produce by multiplication of parts, as in budding or cell division.—**pro·lif·er·a·tion,** *n.*—**pro·lif·er·a·tive,** *a.*

pro·lif·er·ous, prō·lif′ĕr·us, *a.* [L. *proles,* offspring, and *ferre,* bear.] Proliferating. *Bot.* producing new individuals by budding or the like; producing an organ or shoot from an organ which is itself normally ultimate, as a shoot or a new flower from the midst of a flower.

pro·lif·ic, prō·lif′ik, *a.* [Fr. *prolifique,* < L. *proles,* offspring, and *facere,* make.] Producing offspring or young; bearing or yielding fruit abundantly; fruitful; producing much; as, a *prolific* writer; abundantly productive of or fruitful in something specified; as, an age *prolific* of great men; characterized by abundant production; as, a *prolific* season for fruit.—**pro·lif·i·ca·cy,** **pro·lif·ic·ness,** prō·lif′i·ka·sē, *n.*—**pro·lif·i·cal·ly,** *adv.*

pro·line, prō′lēn, prō′lin, *n. Biochem.* the amino acid, $C_5H_9NO_2$, found in proteins.

pro·lix, prō·liks′, prō′liks, *a.* [L. *prolixus,* extended, prolix.] Long and wordy; extending to a great length; diffuse; indulging in lengthy discourse; tedious.—**pro·lix·i·ty,** prō·lik′si·tē, *n.*—**pro·lix·ly,** *adv.*

pro·loc·u·tor, prō·lok′ū·tĕr, *n.* [L., < *proloquor.*] One who speaks for another; the speaker or chairman of a convocation; *Ch. of Eng.* the chairman in the lower house of convocation.

pro·logue, prō′lôg, prō′log, *n.* [O.Fr. Fr. *prologue,* < L. *prologus,* < Gr. *prólogos,* < *prolégein,* say beforehand.] A preliminary discourse; a preface or introductory part of a discourse, poem, or novel; a speech, usually in verse, addressed to the audience by an actor at the beginning of a play; the actor who delivers the speech; an introductory act of a dramatic performance; any introductory proceeding or event.—*v.t.*—*prologued, prologuing.* To introduce with or as with a prologue.

pro·logu·ize, prō′la·gīz″, prō′lo·gīz″, *v.t.*—*prologuized, prologuizing.* To compose or deliver a prologue. Also **pro·log·ize,** prō′la·gīz, prō′lo·gīz″, prō′lo·jīz″.—**pro·logu·iz·er,** *n.*

pro·long, pro·l**a**ng′, pro·long′, *v.t.* [Fr. *prolonger*.] To lengthen in time; to extend the duration of; to lengthen; to extend in space. Also **pro·lon·gate**, pro·l**a**ng′gāt, pro·long′gāt.—**pro·lon·ga·tion**, prō″l**a**ng·gā′shan, prō″long·gā′shan, *n.*—**pro·long·er**, *n.*

pro·lo·ther·a·py, prō″lo·ther′a·pē, *n. Med.* the strengthening of a deficient or incompetent structure, such as a tendon or ligament, by inducing the growth of new cells.

pro·lu·sion, prō·lō′zhan, *n.* [L. *prolusio*, a prelude.] A prelude; a prologue; a preliminary article, esp. one introducing a more profound treatise.—**pro·lu·so·ry**, prō·lō′so·rē, *a.*

prom, prom, *n.* [< *promenade*.] A college or high school formal dance.

prom·e·nade, prom″e·nād′, prom″e·n**a**d′, *n.* [Fr. < *promener*, lead out, take for a walk or airing, < L. *prominare*, drive forward.] A walk, esp. in a public place, as for pleasure or display; a place for walking or promenading; the grand march of all guests at the opening of a formal ball; a prom or dance; one of the figures performed in a square dance.—*v.i.—promenaded, promenading.* To take a promenade.—*v.t.* To take a promenade through or about; to conduct others on, or as on, a promenade; parade.—**prom·e·nad·er**, *n.*

prom·e·nade deck, *n.* An upper deck of a passenger ship, where passengers promenade.

pro·me·thi·um, pro·mē′thē·um, *n.* A metallic element of the rare earth series, a fission product of uranium. Sym. Pm, at. no. 61, at. wt. 145. See Periodic Table of Elements.

prom·i·nence, prom′i·nens, *n.* [L. *prominentia*, *promineo*.] The state of being prominent; that which juts out; protuberance; conspicuousness; distinction; *astron.* a cloudlike formation of gas erupting from the sun's chromosphere, visible during an eclipse. Also **prom·i·nen·cy.**

prom·i·nent, prom′i·nent, *a.* [L. *prominens* (-*ent*-), ppr. of *prominere*, jut out.] Standing out beyond the adjacent surface or line; projecting; standing out so as to be easily seen; conspicuous; noticeable; famous, important, or leading; as, a *prominent* citizen.—**prom·i·nent·ly**, *adv.*

pro·mis·cu·i·ty, prom″i·skū′i·tē, prō″mi·skū′i·tē, *n. pl.* **pro·mis·cu·i·ties.** The state of being promiscuous; promiscuous mixture; indiscriminate mingling, or an instance of it; promiscuous sexual union.

pro·mis·cu·ous, pro·mis′kū·us, *a.* [L. *promiscuus*, < *promisceo*.] Mingled indiscriminately; forming part of a confused crowd or mass; indiscriminate, esp. in sexual relations; random; haphazard.—**pro·mis·cu·ous·ly**, *adv.*—**pro·mis·cu·ous·ness**, *n.*

prom·ise, prom′is, *n.* [L. *promissum*, a promise, prop. neut. of *promissus*, pp. of *promittere*, send forth, say beforehand, promise.] A declaration made, as to another person, with respect to the future, giving assurance that one will do or will not do something, or that something shall or shall not happen; a pledge; vow; something that has the effect of an assurance; an indication of what may be expected, as: The clouds give *promise* of rain. An indication of fulfillment or future excellence; as, a writer or a book that shows *promise*; basis for hope; apparent capacity for future achievement or distinction; as, a young man of talent and *promise*; that which is promised.—*v.t.—promised, promising.* To make a promise of; as, to *promise* help; to engage or undertake by promise, usu. followed by an infinitive or clause; to engage to give in marriage; to betroth, as: She *promised* herself to him. To provide grounds for expecting, as: The clouds *promise* rain. *Colloq.* to assure emphatically, as: It won't happen again, I *promise* you!—*v.i.* To make a promise; to afford ground for expectation, usu. followed by *well* or *fair.*—**prom·is·a·ble**, *a.*—**prom·is·er**, *n.*—**prom·ise·ful**, *a.*

Prom·ised Land, *n.* Heaven; Canaan, promised by God to Abraham and his descendants, Genesis xii. 7; in general, a place where hopes are realized and troubles cease.

prom·is·ee, prom″i·sē′, *n. Law*, one to whom a promise is given.

prom·is·ing, prom′i·sing, *a.* Giving favorable promise of future success; having qualities that suggest one is likely to turn out well.—**prom·is·ing·ly**, *adv.*

prom·i·sor, prom′i·s**a**r, prom′i·s**a**r″, *n. Law*, one who promises.

prom·is·so·ry, prom′i·sōr″ē, prom′i·s**a**r″ē, *a.* Containing a promise; pertaining to a binding declaration of something to be done in the future, as after agreement on an insurance policy.

prom·is·so·ry note, *n.* A written agreement which contains a promise of the payment of money to a certain person by a specified date or on demand.

prom·on·to·ry, prom′on·tōr″ē, prom′on·t**a**r″ē, *n. pl.* **prom·on·to·ries.** [L. *promontorium*—*pro*, forward, and *mons, montis*, a mountain.] A high point of land or rock projecting into the sea; a headland; *anat.* a bodily protuberance.

pro·mote, pro·mōt′, *v.t.—promoted, promoting.* [L. *promotus*, pp. of *promovere*, to move forward.] To contribute to the growth, enlargement, or power of; to forward; to advance to a higher rank; to raise to a higher grade at school; to help to organize, as a commercial undertaking; to attempt to increase the sale of by advertising; *slang*, to wangle.—**pro·mot·a·ble**, *a.*

pro·mot·er, pro·mō′tèr, *n.* One who or that which promotes; an encourager; one who aids in promoting some financial undertaking; one engaged in setting up a business venture; *chem.* a substance which, if used in small amounts, can increase catalysis.

pro·mo·tion, pro·mō′shan, *n.* Advancement; elevation in rank; preferment; the act of promoting; the state of being raised in status; active encouragement of sales by means of advertising.—**pro·mo·tion·al**, *a.*

pro·mo·tive, pro·mō′tiv, *a.* Tending to advance or promote.—**pro·mo·tive·ness**, *n.*

prompt, prompt, *a.* [Fr. *prompt*, < L. *promptus*, brought out, ready, quick, < *promo, promptum*, to bring forth.] Ready and quick to act as occasion demands; punctual; performed or rendered readily; as, a *prompt* answer; without delay.—*v.t.* To move or incite to action or exertion; to suggest to the mind; inspire; to assist, as a speaker at a loss, by pronouncing the words forgotten or next in order; as, to *prompt* an actor.—*v.i. Theatr.* to give cues to actors from a position off-stage.—*n. Com.* a time limit set for payment for goods purchased, stated in a note of reminder; the contract or agreement which sets this limit; also **prompt note.** An instance of prompting; something serving as a reminder.—**prompt·ly**, *adv.*—**prompt·ness**, *n.*

prompt·book, prompt′b**u**k″, *n. Theatr.* an annotated copy of a play for the use of the prompter or director.

prompt·er, promp′tèr, *n.* A person or thing that prompts; *theatr.* one placed behind the scenes who follows the play from a promptbook and prompts the actors in their lines.

promp·ti·tude, promp′ti·töd″, promp′ti·tūd″, *n.* Promptness.

prom·ul·gate, prom′ul·gāt″, prō·mul′gāt, *v.t.—promulgated, promulgating.* [L. *pro-*

mulgo, promulgatus; origin unknown.] To make known by open declaration, as laws, decrees, tidings; to make known publicly; to announce; to proclaim.—**prom·ul·ga·tion**, prom″ul·gā′shan, prō·mul·gā′shan, *n.*—**prom·ul·ga·tor**, *n.*

pro·na·tion, prō·nā′shan, *n.* [L. *pronus*, prone, having the face downward.] That motion of the arm whereby the palm of the hand is turned downward; position of the hand with the thumb toward the body and the palm downward.—**pro·na·tor**, *n.* A muscle of the forearm which turns the palm downward.—**pro·nate**, prō′nāt, *v.t.—pronated, pronating.*

prone, prōn, *a.* [L. *pronus*, hanging or leaning forward, prone, < *pro*, before, forward; cogn. Gr. *prēnēs*, Skt. *pravana*, prone.] Lying with the face downward; sloping downward; inclined; inclined by disposition or natural tendency.—**prone·ly**, *adv.*—**prone·ness**, *n.*

prong, pr**a**ng, prong, *n.* [A nasalized form of provinc. E. *prog*, to prod; W. *procio*, to thrust, to poke.] A sharp-pointed instrument; the tine of a fork or of a similar instrument; a pointed projection, as the tips of a deer's antlers.—*v.t.* To stab, as with a fork or prong.

prong·horn, pr**a**ng′harn″, prong′harn″, *n. pl.* **prong·horns, prong·horn.** A ruminant antelope, *Antilocapra americana*, having deciduous, hollow horns, found in western N. America.

pro·nom·i·nal, prō·nom′i·nal, *a.* [L. *pronomen*, a pronoun.] Belonging to or of the nature of a pronoun.—**pro·nom·i·nal·ly**, *adv.*

pro·noun, prō′noun″, *n.* [< *pro*, for, and *noun*; L. *pronomen*, a pronoun.] *Gram.* one of a certain class of words often used instead of a noun or noun phrase mentioned, asked for, or known in the context, so that the noun need not be repeated.

pro·nounce, pro·nouns′, *v.t.—pronounced, pronouncing.* [Fr. *prononcer*, < L. *pronuntio, pronuntiatus*.] To articulate, as phrases or words; to utter, as letters or words, in a specified manner; to utter formally, officially, or solemnly, as: The court *pronounced* sentence. To declare or affirm; as, to *pronounce* it a forgery.—*v.i.* To speak with confidence or authority; to utter an opinion; to articulate using a certain pronunciation.—**pro·nounce·a·ble**, *a.*—**pro·nounc·er**, *n.*

pro·nounced, pro·nounst′, *a.* [Fr. *prononcé*, pronounced.] Strongly marked or defined; decided; as, a man of *pronounced* views.—**pro·nounc·ed·ly**, pro·noun′sid·lē, *adv.*

pro·nounce·ment, pro·nouns′ment, *n.* The act of pronouncing; a formal announcement; a decision.

pron·to, pron′tō, *adv.* [Sp., a. and adv., < L. *promptus*, E. *prompt*.] *Colloq.* Promptly.

pro·nu·cle·us, prō·nö′klē·us, prō·nū′klē·us, *n. pl.* **pro·nu·cle·i**, prō·nö′klē·ī″, prō·nū′klē·ī″. [L.] One of the two nuclei seen in the course of fertilization of an ovum, the *female pronucleus* belonging to the ovum itself, and the *male pronucleus* to the sperm.—**pro·nu·cle·ar**, *a.*

pro·nun·ci·a·men·to, pro·nun″sē·a·men′tō, pro·nun″shē·a·men′tō, *n.* [Sp.] A manifesto or proclamation; a formal announcement or declaration.

pro·nun·ci·a·tion, pro·nun″sē·ā′shan, *n.* [L. *pronunciatio*.] The act of pronouncing or uttering; articulation; the mode of uttering words or letters.—**pro·nun·ci·a·tion·al**, *a.*

proof, pröf, *n.* [O.E. *profe*, Fr. *preuve*, L.L. *proba*.] Any effort, process, or operation that ascertains truth or fact; a test; a trial; what serves as evidence; what proves or establishes; a test applied to certain manufactured or other articles; the condition of having been successfully tested and proved; the act of testing the strength of alcoholic spirits; the degree of strength of liquor; as, 80 *proof*; *law,* that which convinces the mind and produces belief; *print.* a rough impression of type, in which errors may be detected and marked for correction. An early impression taken from an engraving, etching, or the like; a perfect, finished impression. *Photog.* a test print taken from a negative. *Math.* a means of verifying an equation by working back from the result; a series of steps that demonstrate the validity of a conclusion or theorem.

proof, pröf, *a.* Impenetrable; able to resist physically or morally, often used with *against* or in combination; as, *proof against* heat or temptation, water*proof,* shock*proof*; of proved quality or strength; of standard strength; as, 90 *proof* liquor; used for testing.

proof, pröf, *v.t.* To examine for and correct errors or flaws in; to proofread; to make resistant or impervious to; as, to *proof* a fabric against moths, soil, or water.

proof·read, pröf'rēd', *v.t., v.i.—proofread, proofreading.* To read, as printers' proofs, in order to detect and mark errors to be corrected.—**proof·read·er,** *n.*

proof·read·ers' marks, *n. pl.* A system of symbols marked on type proofs by proofreaders or editors to indicate corrections to be made by the typesetter. See page 765.

proof spir·it, *n.* An alcoholic liquor, or mixture of alcohol and water, containing a standard amount of alcohol; liquor having a specific gravity of .93353, and containing one half of its volume of alcohol of a specific gravity of .7939 at 60°; *Brit.* liquor with a specific gravity of .91984.

prop, prop, *n.* [Same as Ir. *propa,* Gael. *prop,* a prop.] That which sustains an incumbent weight; a support; a stay.—*v.t.* —*propped, propping.* To support by placing something under or against; to support by standing under or against; to help support or sustain.

prop, prop, *n. Theatr.* property.

prop, prop, *n. Avi. slang,* an airplane propeller.

pro·pae·deu·tics, prō"pi·dö'tiks, prō"-pi·dū'tiks, *n. pl. but sing. in constr.* [Gr. *propaideuō,* to instruct beforehand, < *pro,* before, and *paideuō,* to educate, < *pais, paidos,* a child.] The body of knowledge, principles, or rules presupposed by or preliminary to an art or science.—**pro·pae·-deu·tic, pro·pae·deu·ti·cal,** *a.*

prop·a·ga·ble, prop'a·ga·bl, *a.* Capable of being propagated.

prop·a·gan·da, prop"a·gan'da, *n.* [From the *congregatio de propaganda fide,* at Rome.] Allegations, facts, opinions, and the like, systematically spread with the intention of helping or harming some individual, group, institution, or movement; the dissemination of such information, now often used disparagingly to denote half-truths, distortions, and biased information, utilized mainly by political factions; (*often cap.*) *Rom. Cath. Ch.* a body of cardinals established in the 17th century by Pope Gregory XV to supervise the operation of foreign missions.

prop·a·gan·dist, prop"a·gan'dist, *n.* One who devotes himself to the spread of any system of principles or set of actions by the use of propaganda; publicity agent.—*a.*—**prop·a·gan·dis·tic,** prop"a·gan·dis'tik, *a.* —**prop·a·gan·dis·ti·cal·ly,** *adv.*—**prop·a·gan·dism,** *n.*—**prop·a·gan·dize,** prop"-a·gan'dīz, *v.t.—propagandized, propagandizing.* To subject, as a person or group, to propaganda.—*v.i.* To engage in the spreading of propaganda.

prop·a·gate, prop'a·gāt', *v.t.—propagated, propagating.* [L. *propagare, propagatus,* to peg down, to propagate.] To breed; continue or multiply by asexual or sexual reproduction; to cause to reproduce (itself), as applied to animals and plants; to pass on

by heredity, as certain traits or features; to spread from person to person or from place to place; to diffuse; to generate, or produce; to originate, as an effect that grows or spreads.—*v.i.* To have young or issue; to be reproduced or multiplied by generation, or by new shoots or plants; to spread.— **prop·a·ga·tive,** *a.*—**prop·a·ga·tor,** *n.*

prop·a·ga·tion, prop"a·gā'shan, *n.* The act of propagating; the multiplication of the kind or species by generation or reproduction; the spreading or extension of anything; diffusion.—**prop·a·ga·tion·al,** *a.*

pro·pane, prō'pān, *n.* [< *propyl.*] *Chem.* a gaseous hydrocarbon, C_3H_8, of the methane series, found in petroleum and used in organic synthesis, for household fuel, and numerous industrial purposes.

pro·pel, pro·pel', *v.t.—propelled, propelling.* [L. *propello.*] To drive forward; to urge or press onward.

pro·pel·lant, pro·pel'ant, *n.* Something or someone that propels; an explosive for projectile propulsion; rocket-engine fuel.— **pro·pel·lent,** *a., n.*

pro·pel·ler, pro·pel'ér, *n.* One who or that which propels; a device consisting of a rotating shaft fitted with blades angled in such a way as to provide thrust in air or water and thus propel a ship or aircraft. Also **pro·pel·lor.**

pro·pen·si·ty, pro·pen'si·tē, *n. pl.* **pro·pen·si·ties.** Natural inclination, tendency, or disposition.

prop·er, prop'ér, *a.* [O.Fr. Fr. *propre,* < L. *proprius,* one's own.] Strictly belonging or applicable; as, the *proper* use of a word; strict; accurate; strictly so called, or in the strict sense of; as, belonging to the fishes *proper*; normal or regular; adapted or appropriate to circumstances; as, the *proper* tool for the job; fit; suitable; fitting; right; in conformity with established standards of behavior or manners; decorous or decent; as, a *proper* young lady; *rare,* honest, respectable, or of good character. *Chiefly Brit., colloq.* complete or thorough; excellent, capital, or fine; good-looking or handsome. *Gram.* of a name, noun, or adjective, designating a particular person or thing, and written with an initial capital letter, as John, Chicago, Monday, English; *her.* of an object, represented in its natural color; as, an eagle *proper*; *eccles.* appointed for use on a particular day or festival.—**prop·er·ness,** *n.*

prop·er, prop'ér, *n. Eccles.* An office designated for a particular day or time; a part of the Mass or missal which varies with the day or feast.

prop·er ad·jec·tive, *n.* An adjective, usu. capitalized, whose form is derived from that of a proper noun.

prop·er frac·tion, *n. Math.* a fraction that has a larger denominator than numerator.

prop·er·ly, prop'ér·lē, *adv.* In a proper manner; suitably; fitly; rightly; correctly; strictly.

prop·er noun, *n.* A noun which denotes a specific place, person, or thing and is capitalized, as Mary, England, or Eiffel Tower. Also **prop·er name.**

prop·er·ty, prop'ér·tē, *n. pl.* **prop·er·ties.** [O.Fr. *proprete, propriete* (Fr. *propriété*), < L. *proprietas,* < *proprius,* one's own, E. *proper.*] That which one owns; the possession or possessions of a particular owner; goods or lands owned; a piece of land or real estate; ownership or right of possession, enjoyment, or disposal of anything, esp. of something tangible; something at the disposal of a person, a group of persons, or the community; as, advantages that are the *property* of every citizen; an essential or distinctive attribute or quality of a thing; *theatr.* any portable object, as a chair or rug, used in a play; also *prop.*—**prop·er·tied,** prop'ér·tēd, *a.*—**prop·er·ty·less,** *a.*

prop·er·ty man, *n. pl.* **prop·er·ty men.** A man employed in a theater to look after the stage properties. Also **prop man,** *propman.*

pro·phage, prō'fāj", *n.* An intracellular bacterial virus which protects its host from active viruses.

pro·phase, prō'fāz, *n. Biol.* the initial stage of cell division in which the chromosomes become distinct in the nucleus and divide longitudinally.—**pro·pha·sic,** *a.*

proph·e·cy, prof'i·sē, *n. pl.* **proph·e·cies.** [O.Fr. *prophecie, prophetie,* L. *prophetia,* < Gr. *prophēteia,* < *prophētēs,* a prophet— *pro,* before, and *phemi,* to tell; same root as *fame.*] A foretelling or declaration of something to come, esp. a prophet's foretelling inspired by God; a book of prophecies.

proph·e·sy, prof'i·sī", *v.t.—prophesied, prophesying.* To foretell; to predict; to speak as with divine guidance.—*v.i.* To utter predictions; to make declaration of events to come; to interpret or explain religious subjects.—**proph·e·si·er,** *n.*

proph·et, prof'it, *n.* [L. *propheta,* < Gr. *prophētēs.*] A person inspired or instructed by God to announce future events; an interpreter of divine will; one who foretells future events; a predictor; one who speaks for a group or cause; *Christian Science,* a seer.—**the Proph·et,** *Islam,* Mohammed.— **the Proph·ets,** the men who wrote the Old Testament predictive books; these books, consisting of those not included in the Hagiographa and the Pentateuch.—**proph·-et·ess,** prof'i·tis, *n.*—**proph·et·hood,** *n.*

pro·phet·ic, pro·fet'ik, *a.* Pertaining to a prophet or prophecy; having the character of prophecy; containing prophecy; predictive. Also **pro·phet·i·cal.**—**pro·phet·i·cal·ly,** *adv.*—**pro·phet·i·cal·ness,** *n.*

pro·phy·lac·tic, prō"fi·lak'tik, prof"i·lak'tik, *a.* [Gr. *prophylaktikos—pro,* before, and *phylassō,* to guard.] Preventive; defending from or warding off disease.—*n.* A medicine which protects or defends against disease; a preventive device, as a contraceptive.—**pro·phy·lac·ti·cal·ly,** *adv.*

pro·phy·lax·is, prō"fi·lak'sis, prof"i·lak'sis, *n. pl.* **pro·phy·lax·es,** prō"fi·lak'-sēz, prof"i·lak'sēz. [Gr.] Preventive or protective treatment against disease.

pro·pin·qui·ty, prō·ping'kwi·tē, *n.* [L. *propinquitas,* < *propinquus,* near, < *prope,* near; whence also (ap)-*proach.*] Nearness in place; neighborhood; nearness in time; nearness of blood; kinship.

pro·pi·o·nate, prō"pē·o·nāt", *n. Chem.* a salt or ester of propionic acid.

pro·pi·on·ic ac·id, prō"pē·on'ik as'id, prō"pē·ō'nik, *n. Chem., pharm.* a liquid, $CH_3CH_2CO_2H$, soluble in water, chloroform, ether, or alcohol, and used in perfumes, pharmaceuticals, and in mold inhibitors.

pro·pi·ti·ate, pro·pish'ē·āt", *v.t.—propitiated, propitiating.* [L. *propitio, propitiatum,* to propitiate, < *propitius,* propitious, < *pro-,* before, and *peto,* seek, primarily referring to a bird whose flight is of happy augury.] To appease and render favorable; to conciliate.—**pro·pi·ti·a·ble, pro·pi·-ti·a·tive,** *a.*—**pro·pi·ti·a·tor,** *n.*—**pro·-pi·ti·at·ing·ly,** *adv.*

pro·pi·ti·a·tion, pro·pish"ē·ā'shan, *n.* The act of propitiating; an atoning sacrifice or anything which propitiates.

pro·pi·ti·a·to·ry, pro·pish'ē·a·tōr"ē, pro·pish'ē·a·tər"ē, *a.* Having the power to make propitious; serving to propitiate.—*n. Jewish antiq.* the mercy seat.

pro·pi·tious, pro·pish'us, *a.* Favorably disposed toward a person; disposed to be gracious or merciful; affording favorable conditions or circumstances.—**pro·pi·-tious·ly,** *adv.*—**pro·pi·tious·ness,** *n.*

prop·jet en·gine, *n. Aeron.* turbo-propeller engine.

PROOFREADERS' MARKS

OPERATIONAL

Mark	Meaning	Example
ℐ	delete	He ~~proof~~ proofread that page.
⌒	close up	He proof read that page.
ℐ	delete and close up	He proofｏread that page.
#	insert space	He proofread thatpage.
eq #	equalize spacing	He✓proofread✓that✓page.
¶	begin new paragraph	the printer. He proofread that page. Unfortunately, he
no ¶	run paragraphs together	the printer. He proofread that page. Unfortunately, he
hr #	insert hair space	He proofread that page. Un-
□	indent one em	He proofread that page.
▱	indent two ems	He proofread that page.
⌐	move right	He proofread that page.
⌐	move left	[He proofread that page.
⌐⌐	center	]He proofread that page.[
⌐	move up	He proofread that page.
⌐	move down	He proofread that page.
‖	straighten type	He proofread that page.
‖	align vertically	He proofread that page.
⁀	transpose	He proofread page|that
SP	spell out circled words	He proofread the (1st) page.
Stet	let it stand	He proofread that page.
↓	push down type	He proofread that page.
ld	lead between lines	Unfortunately, he didn't as far ld
copy out	something omitted—check copy	He proofread page. copy out

TYPOGRAPHICAL

Mark	Meaning	Example
lc	make lower-case	He proofread that page.
caps	capitalize	he proofread that page.
sc	set in small caps	HE PROOFREAD THAT PAGE.
C+sc	set in caps and small caps	he PROOFREAD THAT PAGE, UN- FORTUNATELY
ital	set in italics	He proofread that page.
rom	set in roman type	He proofread that page.
bf	set in boldface	He proofread that page.
wf	wrong font; set in correct type	He proofread that page.
✕	reset broken letter	He proofread that page.
℗	reverse (type appears upside down)	He proofread that page.

PUNCTUATION

Mark	Meaning	Example
⌃	insert comma	He, James proofread that page.
∨	insert apostrophe or single quote	Its James' turn to proofread.
∨∨	insert quotation marks	I proofread that page, said James.
⊙	insert period	He proofread that page
?/	insert question mark	Who proofread that page
o/	insert missing letter	Who proofread that page?
;⌃	insert semicolon	He proofread those I'll do these.
:⌃	insert colon	He proofread the following page A. one, page two, page three.
=/	insert hyphen	He was a proofreader on the 9to5 shift.
—/	insert em dash	His work proofreading was his life.
–/	insert en dash	He was a proofreader all of his working life (1919 1964).
(/)	insert parentheses	He was a proofreader for all of his working life 1919–1964 the
[/]	insert brackets	He said, "I think all of us the proofreaders should go to lunch."

prop·man, prop′man″, *n.* pl. **prop·men.** *Theatr.* property man.

prop·o·lis, prop′o·lis, *n.* [Gr. *pro*, before, and *polis*, city.] A resinous substance resembling wax, collected from tree buds by bees and used to seal the holes and crevices in their hives.

pro·po·nent, pro·pō′nent, *n.* One who makes a proposal, or lays down a proposition; one in favor of a doctrine or cause; *law*, one who proposes probate for a will.

pro·por·tion, pro·pōr′shan, pro·par′shan, *n.* [O.Fr. Fr. *proportion*, < L. *proportio(n-)*.] Comparative relation between things or magnitudes as to size, quantity, number, etc.; as, the *proportion* of births to deaths in a community during a given period; ratio; in general, relation, comparison, or analogy; as, a large or a small *proportion* of a total amount or number; a portion or part; *pl.* dimensions; as, a rock of gigantic *proportions*. *Math.* the equality of ratios; a relation of four quantities such that the first divided by the second is equal to the third divided by the fourth; the method of finding one of these quantities when the other three are known: also **rule of three.** —*v.t.* [O.Fr. Fr. *proportioner*, < M.L. *proportionare*, < L. *proportio(n-)*.] To adjust in proper proportion or relation, as to size, quantity, or number; as, to *proportion* the thickness of a thing to its length; to adjust the proportions of; to bear a due proportion to; to divide into or distribute in proportionate parts.

pro·por·tion·a·ble, pro·pōr′sha·na·bl, pro·par′sha·na·bl, *a.* Being in proportion; having a due comparative relation.— **pro·por·tion·a·bly,** *adv.*

pro·por·tion·al, pro·pōr′sha·nal, pro·par′sha·nal, *a.* [L. *proportionalis*.] Being in or characterized by proportion; having due proportion; corresponding; of or pertaining to proportion; relative; *math.* having the same or a constant ratio or relation.—*n.* *Math.* one of the quantities of a proportion. —**pro·por·tion·al·i·ty,** pro·pōr″sha··nal′i·tē, pro·par″sha·nal′i·tē, *n.*—**pro··por·tion·al·ly,** *adv.*

pro·por·tion·al rep·re·sen·ta·tion, *n.* An electoral system whereby the legislative representation of political parties is based on their proportion of the popular vote cast.

pro·por·tion·ate, pro·pōr′sha·nit, pro··par′sha·nit, *a.* [L.L. *proportionatus*.] Proportioned; being in due proportion; proportional.—pro·pōr′sha·nāt″, pro·par′-sha·nāt″, *v.t.*—*proportionated, proportionating.* To make proportionate.—**pro·por·-tion·ate·ly,** *adv.*—**pro·por·tion·ate·ness,** *n.*

pro·pos·al, pro·pō′zal, *n.* The act of proposing, or suggesting something for acceptance, adoption, or performance; a plan or scheme proposed; an offer of marriage.

pro·pose, pro·pōz′, *v.t.*—*proposed, proposing.* [O.Fr. Fr. *proposer*, < pro- (< L. *pro*), before, and *poser*, put, but associated with derivatives of L. *proponere*.] To put forward, as a matter, subject, or case, for consideration, discussion, or disposal; to propound for solution, as a question or riddle; to present to the mind or attention; to state; to put forward for acceptance, adoption, or favorable action; to present, as a person, for acceptance for some position, office, membership, or candidacy; to offer or suggest, as a toast; to put before oneself as something to be done; to design; intend. —*v.i.* To make a proposal, esp. one of marriage; to formulate or entertain a purpose or design.—**pro·pos·er,** *n.*

prop·o·si·tion, prop″o·zish′an, *n.* [O.Fr. Fr. *proposition*, < L. *propositio(n-)*, a setting forth, < *proponere*, set forth, propose.] The act of putting forward or propounding something for consideration or discussion;

a statement wherein something is propounded; an assertion; the act of proposing, or a proposal of, something to be accepted, adopted, or done; an offer of terms for a transaction, as in business; a plan or scheme proposed; a thing presented for purchase, or considered with reference to its value to the purchaser or owner. *Colloq.* a thing, matter, or person considered as something to be dealt with, handled, or encountered; an immoral or indecent proposal. *Logic,* a statement in which something is affirmed or denied of a subject. *Math.* a formal statement of either a truth to be demonstrated or an operation to be performed; a theorem or a problem.—**prop·o·si·tion·al,** *a.*— **prop·o·si·tion·al·ly,** *adv.*

prop·o·si·tion, prop″o·zish′an, *v.t. Colloq.* To propose a project or deal to; to make an immoral suggestion to.

prop·o·si·tion·al func·tion, *n.* A sentential function.

pro·pos·i·tus, pro·poz′i·tus, *n.* pl. **pro·-pos·i·ti,** pro·poz′i·tī″. [L.] *Law,* the person from whom lineage is traced.

pro·pound, pro·pound′, *v.t.* [O.E. *propoune*, < L. *propono*, to put forth.] To offer for consideration; to propose; to put or set, as a question.—**pro·pound·er,** *n.*

pro·prae·tor, prō·prē′tér, *n.* [L.] A Roman magistrate who, having discharged the office of praetor at Rome, was sent into a province to perform praetorial duties. Also **pro·pre·tor.**

pro·pri·e·tar·y, pro·prī′i·ter″ē, *a.* [L.L. *proprietarius*, < L. *proprietas*, E. *property*.] Pertaining or belonging to a proprietor; denoting exclusive control over property; of manufacture and sale of a product, restricted by patent or copyright; as, a *proprietary* medicine; pertaining to property or ownership.—*n.* pl. **pro·pri·e·tar·ies.** An owner or proprietor; a body of proprietors; the grantee or owner of a proprietary colony; something owned or held as property; a proprietary medicine.

pro·pri·e·tar·y col·o·ny, *n. Amer. hist.* one of the colonies, as Delaware, Maryland, or Pennsylvania, whose government was granted by the British crown to an individual or group.

pro·pri·e·tor, pro·prī′i·tér, *n.* An owner; the person who has the legal right or exclusive title to anything.—**pro·pri·e·-tor·ship,** *n.*—**pro·pri·e·tress,** pro·prī′i-tris, *n.*

pro·pri·e·ty, pro·prī′i·tē, *n.* pl. **pro·pri·-e·ties.** [L. *proprietas*, < *proprius*, one's own.] Conformity to an acknowledged or correct standard of behavior; conformity with established principles, rules, or customs; decorum; suitability; justness.— **the pro·pri·e·ties,** the established customs of social life.

pro·pri·o·cep·tive, prō″prē·o·sep′tiv, *a. Physiol.* having the ability to receive stimuli originating within such body tissues as muscles and tendons.

pro·pri·o·cep·tor, prō″prē·o·sep′tér, *n. Physiol.* the peripheral end organ of nerves in organs that are responsive to internal stimuli.

prop root, *n. Bot.* a root of certain plants, as corn, that grows into the soil from above the surface and provides the main support of the stalk.

prop·to·sis, prop·tō′sis, *n. Pathol.* an outward displacement or protuberance of any organ, specif. bulging of the eyeballs.

pro·pul·sion, pro·pul′shan, *n.* [Fr. *propulsion*, < L. *propellere*, E. *propel*.] The act of propelling or driving forward or onward; the state of being propelled; a propulsive force.—**pro·pul·sive,** pro·pul′siv, *a.*

pro·pyl, prō′pil, *n.* [< *prop*(ionic) and -*yl*.] *Chem.* the univalent radical, C_3H_7, of propane.—**pro·pyl·ic,** prō·pil′ik, *a.*

prop·y·lae·um, prop″i·lē′um, *n.* pl. **prop·y·lae·a,** prop″i·lē′a. [L., < Gr. *propylaion*, neut. of *propylaios*, before the gate.] *Arch.* a vestibule or entrance to an ancient temple, esp. when elaborate or of architectural importance.

pro·pyl·ene, prō′pi·lēn″, *n. Chem.* a gaseous hydrocarbon, $CH_3CH{=}CH_2$, obtained as a by-product of petroleum refining, and used in organic synthesis. Also **pro·pene.**

pro·pyl·ene gly·col, *n. Chem.* a colorless hygroscopic organic compound, CH_3-$CHOHCH_2OH$, used as a solvent and antifreeze.

pro ra·ta, prō rā′ta, prō rä′ta, *adv.* Proportionately; in accordance with some determined standard.—*a.*

pro·rate, prō·rāt′, prō′rāt″, *v.t., v.i.*—*prorated, prorating.* To assess or distribute proportionately.—**pro·ra·tion,** *n.*

pro·ro·ga·tion, prō′ro·gā′shan, *n.* [L. *prorogatio(n-)*.] Discontinuance of the meetings of a parliament, as of the British Parliament, by command of the sovereign, without dissolution.

pro·rogue, prō·rōg′, *v.t.*—*prorogued, proroguing.* [O.Fr. *proroguer* (Fr. *proroger*), < L. *prorogare*, prolong, protract, defer.] To discontinue the meetings of, as a government body, esp. the British Parliament, for a definite or indefinite time, without dissolving it. Also **pro·ro·gate,** prōr′ō·gāt.

pro·sa·ic, prō·zā′ik, *a.* [L.L. *prosaicus*, < L. *prosa*, E. *prose*.] Commonplace or dull; as, to lead a *prosaic* life; matter-of-fact or unimaginative; of writing, having the character or spirit of prose as opposed to poetry.—**pro·sa·i·cal·ly,** *adv.*—**pro·sa·-ic·ness,** *n.*

pro·sa·ism, prō·zā′iz·um, *n.* [= Fr. *prosaïsme*, < L. *prosa*, E. *prose*.] Prosaic character; a prosaic expression.—**pro·sa·ist,** prō·zā′ist, *n.* A writer of prose; a prosaic, uninteresting person.

pro·sce·ni·um, prō·sē′nē·um, *n.* pl. **pro·sce·ni·a,** prō·sē′nē·a. [L. *proscenium*, < Gr. *proskēnion*.] *Arch.* The part in a theater from the curtain to the orchestra, sometimes including the curtain and its ornamental framework; in the ancient theater, the whole stage.

pro·scribe, prō·skrib′, *v.t.*—*proscribed, proscribing.* [L. *proscribo*.] To prohibit; to exclude from the protection of the law; to outlaw; to publish the name of as sentenced to death and seizure of property, as: In ancient Rome, a ruler could *proscribe* his enemy.—**pro·scrib·er,** *n.*

pro·scrip·tion, prō·skrip′shan, *n.* [L. *proscriptio*.] The act of proscribing; outlawry; exclusion.—**pro·scrip·tive,** *a.*— **pro·scrip·tive·ly,** *adv.*

prose, prōz, *n.* [Fr. *prose*, < L. *prosa* for *prorsa* (*oratio*, speech, understood), < *prorsus* (*oratio*, speech, understood), < *prorsus*, forward, straight on.] The ordinary written or spoken language of man; language without poetical measure: opposed to *verse*; dull and commonplace language or discourse. *Eccles.* a hymn having irregular meter, often sung after the gradual in the Christian Eucharist.—*a.*—*v.t., v.i.*—*prosed, prosing.* To write in prose; to write or speak tediously.

pro·sec·tor, prō·sek′tér, *n.* [L.L., < L. *prosecare*.] One who dissects cadavers for the illustration of anatomical lectures or the like.—**pro·sec·to·ri·al,** prō″sek·tōr′ē·al, prō″sek·tär′ē·al, *a.*—**pro·sect,** *v.t.*

pros·e·cute, pros′e·kūt″, *v.t.*—*prosecuted, prosecuting.* [L. *prosecutus*, pp. of *prosequi*, follow, pursue, continue.] To follow up or out, go on with, or pursue something undertaken or begun, usu. to its final determination; as, to *prosecute* one's studies; to carry on or practice. *Law,* to seek to enforce or obtain by legal process, as a claim or right; to institute legal proceedings against.—*v.i.*

Law. To institute and carry on a legal prosecution; act as prosecutor.—**pros·e·cut·a·ble,** *a.*

pros·e·cut·ing at·tor·ney, *n.* The attorney acting for the government as prosecutor of violators of criminal law.

pros·e·cu·tion, pros″e·kū′shan, *n.* [L.L. *prosecutio(n-).*] The act or process of prosecuting. *Law,* the institution and carrying on of legal proceedings; the party by whom such proceedings are instituted and carried on.

pros·e·cu·tor, pros′e·kū″tẽr, *n.* [L.L.] One who prosecutes. *Law,* one who institutes and carries on legal proceedings in a court of justice, esp. in a criminal court; a prosecuting attorney.

pros·e·lyte, pros′e·lit″, *n.* [L.L. *proselytus,* < Gr. *proselytos,* new-comer, proselyte.] One who has changed from one opinion, religious belief, sect, or the like to another; a convert.—*v.t., v.i.—proselyted, proselyting.* To make a proselyte of; to convert. Also **pros·e·lyt·ize,** pros′e·li·tīz″, pros′e·li·tīz″.—*proselytized, proselytizing.*—**pros·e·lyt·ism,** pros′e·li·tiz″um, *n.*

pros·en·ceph·a·lon, pros″en·sef′a·lon″, *n.* pl. **pros·en·ceph·a·las, pros·en·ceph·a·la,** pros″en·sef′a·la. [Prefix *pros,* toward, and Gr. *encephalon.*] *Anat.* The forebrain; the anterior part of the brain.—**pros·en·ce·phal·ic,** pros″en·se·fal′ik, *a.*

pros·en·chy·ma, pros·eng′ki·ma, *n.* [N.L., < Gr.] *Bot.* the tissue characteristic of the woody and bast portions of plants, consisting typically of long, narrow cells with pointed ends.—**pros·en·chym·a·tous,** pros″eng·kim′a·tus, *a.*

prose po·em, *n.* A prose composition resembling poetry in emotional tone, use of rhythm, or metaphorical language.—**prose po·et,** *n.*

pros·er, prō′zẽr, *n.* One who writes prose; one who writes or discourses in a dull, unimaginative manner.

pro·sit, prō′sit, L. prō′sit, *interj.* [L., 'May it do good!'] An expression of good wishes used esp. among Germans in drinking a toast. Also **prost.**

pros·o·dy, pros′o·dē, *n.* [L. *prosodia,* < Gr. *prosōidia,* tone or accent, modulation of voice, song sung to music.] The science of poetic meters and versification.—**pros·o·dist,** pros′o·dist, *n.*—**pro·sod·ic, pro·sod·i·cal,** pro·sod′ik, *a.*—**pro·sod·i·cal·ly,** *adv.*

pro·so·po·poe·ia, prō·sō″po·pē′a, *n.* [L. *prosopopœia,* < Gr. *prosōpopoiia,* < *prosōpon,* face, person, and *poieō,* to make.] *Rhet.* Personification, as of inanimate things; representation of an imaginary or absent person as speaking or acting. Also **pro·so·po·pe·ia.**—**pro·so·po·poe·ial, pro·so·po·pe·ial,** *a.*

pros·pect, pros′pekt, *n.* [L. *prospectus,* outlook, view, prospect, < *prospicere,* look forward.] The outlook for the future, or that which appears as an indication of what may be expected; *pl.* apparent probabilities of advancement, success, or profit. A looking forward, or contemplation of something future or expected; something in view as a source of profit; a prospective customer; a likely or potential candidate; a view or scene, esp. an expanse of natural scenery; outlook or view, as over a region or in a particular direction; a mental view or survey, as of a subject or situation. *Mining,* an apparent indication of minerals or metal; a spot giving such indications; the yield of minerals from a sample of gravel or ore.—*v.t., v.i.* To explore, as a region, as for gold.—**pros·pec·tor,** pros′pek·tẽr, pro·spek′tẽr, *n.*

pro·spec·tive, pro·spek′tiv, *a.* Being in the future; looking forward in time; expected or potential.—**pro·spec·tive·ly,** *adv.*

pro·spec·tus, pro·spek′tus, *n.* pl. **pro·spec·tus·es.** [L., prospect, sight, view.] A brief sketch describing the main features of some proposed enterprise, as the plan of a literary work, or the proposals of a new business; a descriptive outline of an established organization, as a college.

pros·per, pros′pẽr, *v.i.* [Fr. *prospérer,* L. *prosperare,* < *prosperus,* favorable, fortunate.] To be successful, esp. to gain in wealth; to turn out successfully, as affairs; to thrive.—*v.t.* To make prosperous; to render successful.

pros·per·i·ty, pro·sper′i·tē, *n.* pl. **pros·per·i·ties.** [L. *prosperitas.*] The state of being prosperous; success in any enterprise; good fortune.

pros·per·ous, pros′pẽr·us, *a.* [O.Fr. *prospereus,* for *prospere* (Fr. *prospère*), < L. *prosper, prosperus,* favorable, fortunate.] Characterized by good fortune; successful; flourishing or thriving; well-to-do; propitious.—**pros·per·ous·ly,** *adv.*—**pros·per·ous·ness,** *n.*

pros·tate, pros′tāt, *a. Anat.* designating or pertaining to the prostate gland. Also **pro·stat·ic,** prō·stat′ik.—*n. Anat.* the prostate gland.

pros·ta·tec·to·my, pros″ta·tek′to·mē, *n.* pl. **pros·ta·tec·to·mies.** *Surg.* complete or partial excision of the prostate gland.

pros·tate gland, *n.* [M.L. *prostata,* the prostate, < Gr. *prostatēs,* one standing before, < *proïstanai,* < *pro,* before, and *histanai,* cause to stand.] *Anat.* an organ, part muscle and part gland, which surrounds the male urethra at the bladder's base and secretes a milky fluid ejected with the sperm.

pros·ta·tism, pros′ta·tiz″um, *n. Pathol.* a condition resulting from a chronically diseased or enlarged prostate gland.

pros·the·sis, pros′thi·sis, *n.* pl. **pros·the·ses,** pros′thi·sēz″. [L.L., < Gr. *prósthesis,* a putting to, addition, < *prostithénai,* < *pros,* to, and *tithenai,* set, put.] *Surg.* the addition of an artificial part to supply a defect of the body; the part thus added; *ling.* prothesis.—**pros·thet·ic,** pros·thet′ik, *a.*—**pros·thet·i·cal·ly,** *adv.*

pros·thet·ics, pros·thet′iks, *n. pl., sing. or pl. in constr. Surg., dentistry,* the branch specializing in artificial replacements, as of limbs or teeth.—**pros·the·tist,** pros′thi·tist, *n.*

pros·tho·don·tics, pros″tho·don′tiks, *n. pl., sing. or pl. in constr.* That branch of dentistry dealing with the making of artificial teeth and other oral structures needed to replace missing or injured parts of the chewing apparatus; prosthetic dentistry. Also **pros·tho·don·tia,** pros″tho·don′sha, pros″tho·don′shē·a.—**pros·tho·don·tist,** pros″tho·don′tist, *n.*

pros·ti·tute, pros′ti·tōt″, pros′ti·tūt″, *n.* [L. *prostitutus,* pp. of *prostituere,* place before, expose publicly, prostitute, < *pro,* before, and *statuere,* set.] A woman given to sexual intercourse for gain or hire; a harlot. Any person who puts his abilities to a base or unworthy use for money or other gain.—*v.t.*—*prostituted, prostituting.* To offer, as oneself, for sexual intercourse for gain or hire; to surrender to any unworthy purpose for gain; to put, as oneself or one's talents, to any base or unworthy use.—**pros·ti·tu·tor,** *n.*

pros·ti·tu·tion, pros″ti·tō′shan, pros″ti·tū′shan, *n.* [L.L. *prostitutio(n-).*] The act or practice of prostituting; the business of a prostitute; any infamous or base use, as of resources or talents.

pro·sto·mi·um, prō·stō′mē·um, *n.* pl. **pro·sto·mi·a,** prō·stō′mē·a. The part of the head, usu. unsegmented, which is in front of the mouth in various worms and other lower invertebrates.—**pro·sto·mi·al,** *a.*

pros·trate, pros′trāt, *v.t.*—*prostrated, prostrating.* [L. *prostratus,* pp. of *prosternere,* < *pro,* before, and *sternere,* spread out.] To lay flat, as on the ground; to throw down level with the ground; to cast down, as oneself, in humility or adoration; to overthrow, overcome, or reduce to helplessness, as: In *prostrating* one enemy, he demoralized a hundred. To reduce to physical weakness or exhaustion; as, to be *prostrated* by disease, fatigue, or grief.—*a.* Lying flat or at full length, as on the ground; lying with the face to the ground, as in token of submission or humility; overthrown, overcome, or helpless; as, a *prostrate* country; in a state of physical weakness or exhaustion; *bot.* of a plant or stem, lying along the ground.—**pros·tra·tive,** pros′tra·tiv, *a.*—**pros·tra·tor,** *n.*

pros·tra·tion, pro·strā′shan, *n.* [L.L. *prostratio(n-).*] The act of prostrating, or the state of being prostrated; a laying or lying flat or prostrate; humiliation or abasement; reduction to a powerless or helpless condition; extreme mental depression or dejection; extreme physical weakness or exhaustion; as, nervous *prostration.*

pros·y, prō′zē, *a.*—*prosier, prosiest.* Like prose; prosaic; dull, tiresome, tedious.—**pros·i·ly,** *adv.*—**pros·i·ness,** *n.*

pro·tac·tin·i·um, prō″tak·tin′ē·um, *n. Chem.* a radioactive, metallic element yielding actinium upon disintegration. Sym. Pa., at. no. 91. Also **protoactinium.**

pro·tag·o·nist, prō·tag′o·nist, *n.* [Gr. *prōtagōnistēs—prōtos,* first, and *agōnistēs,* an actor.] The leading character or actor in a literary work; a leading character generally; a champion, leader, or principal advocate of a cause.

pro·ta·mine, prō′ta·mēn″, prō′ta·min, *n. Biochem.* any of a class of simple, basic proteins, soluble in ammonia, uncoagulable by heat, and forming amino acids upon hydrolysis.

prot·a·sis, prot′a·sis, *n.* pl. **prot·a·ses,** prot′a·sēz″. [L. < Gr. *prótasis,* < *proteinein,* stretch before, < *pró,* before, and *teinein,* stretch.] *Gram.* the clause expressing the condition in a conditional sentence; *anc. drama,* the first part of the play, in which the characters are introduced and the subject is proposed and entered upon.

pro·te·a, prō′tē·a, *n.* Any member of the genus *Protea,* family *Proteaceae,* composed of evergreen shrubs.

pro·te·an, prō′tē·an, prō·tē′an, *a.* Readily assuming different shapes, characters, or roles; exceedingly variable; (*cap.*) of or like Proteus, a marine deity of the ancient Greeks who had the faculty of assuming different shapes.

pro·te·ase, prō′tē·ās″, *n. Biochem.* any enzyme that exerts a digestive action on proteins.

pro·tect, pro·tekt′, *v.t.* [< L. *protectus,* pp. of *protego,* to protect—*pro,* before, and *tego,* to cover, from root seen also in E. *thatch.*] To cover or shield from danger or injury; to defend; to guard; *econ.* to shield or defend, as a nation's products or a particular industry, by import duties or tariffs; *com.* to supply funds to assure payment of, as a loan or note.—**pro·tect·ing,** pro·tek′ting, *a.*—**pro·tect·ing·ly,** *adv.*

pro·tec·tion, pro·tek′shan, *n.* The act of protecting or state of being protected; one who or that which protects; *econ.* a protective measure conferred by a government on articles of home production, usu. by duties imposed on the same articles introduced from abroad. *Slang,* money exacted by racketeers for exemption from injury or violence; bribery of a minor official for exemption from legal action. A passport or document of safe conduct; the coverage afforded by an insurance policy.—

pro·tec·tive, prō·tek′tiv, *a.*—**pro·tec·- tive·ly,** *adv.*

pro·tec·tion·ism, pro·tek′sha·niz″um, *n.* The economic system of protection for commodities of home production.

pro·tec·tion·ist, pro·tek′sha·nist, *n.* One who favors the economic protection of some branch of industry by legal enactments, as tariffs or any devices serving to restrict foreign competition; one opposed to free trade.—*a.*

pro·tec·tive tar·iff, *n.* A tariff serving as protection for domestic industries from foreign competition rather than as a source of revenue.

pro·tec·tor, pro·tek′ter, *n.* One who or that which protects; a defender; a guardian; a device which affords protection against injury; guard. *Eng. hist.* one who had the care of the kingdom during the king's minority; a regent.—**pro·tec·tor·ship,** *n.*— **pro·tec·tress,** pro·tek′tris, *n.* A female protector.

pro·tec·tor·al, pro·tek′ter·al, *a.* Pertaining to a protector; pertaining to a protectorate.

pro·tec·tor·ate, pro·tek′ter·it, *n.* The relationship in which a weaker territory or political unit has protection and some control by a stronger one; the dependent state or territory in this relationship; government by a protector; the rank, period of authority, or office of a protector; (*cap.*) the period in English history, 1653–1659, during which the Cromwells were protectors.

pro·tec·to·ry, pro·tek′to·rē, *n.* pl. **pro·tec·to·ries.** An institution for the shelter and training of destitute or delinquent children.

pro·té·gé, prō′te·zhā″, prō″te·zhā′, *n.* [Fr., one protected.] One under the care and protection of another who is interested in his career or future.—**pro·té·gée,** *n.* A female protégé.

pro·tein, prō′tēn, prō′tē·in, *n.* [< Gr. *prōtos,* first.] *Biochem.* one of a class of complex chemical compounds which contain carbon, hydrogen, nitrogen, oxygen, and sulfur, are essential constituents of living matter, and on decomposition yield various amino acids. Also **pro·teid,** prō′tēd, prō′- tē·id.—**pro·tein·a·ceous, pro·tein·ic, pro·tei·nous,** prō″tē·nā′shus, prō″tē·i·- nā′shus, *a.*

pro·tein·ase, prō′tē·nās″, prō′tē·i·nās″, *n.* *Biochem.* any of several enzymes, as pepsin and rennin, which hydrolyze proteins.

pro tem·po·re, prō tem′po·rē″, *L.* prō tem′pō·Re″, *adv. L.* For the time being; temporarily. Also **pro tem,** prō tem′.

pro·te·ol·y·sis, prō″tē·ol′i·sis, *n.* [< *proteid* and *-lysis.*] *Biochem.* the hydrolysis or breaking down of proteins into simpler compounds, as in digestion.—**pro·te·o·- lyt·ic,** prō″tē·o·lit′ik, *a.*

pro·te·ose, prō′tē·ōs″, *n.* [Gr. *prōtos,* first.] *Biochem.* any of a class of compounds produced in digestion and derived from proteins by hydrolysis.

Prot·er·o·zo·ic, prot″ĕr·o·zō′ik, prō″- tĕr·o·zō′ik, *a.* [Gr. *prōteros,* being before, and *zōē,* life.] Noting or pertaining to a geological era or a group of rocks preceding the Paleozoic.—*n.* The Proterozoic era or group. See Table of Geologic Time.

pro·test, pro·test′, *v.i.* [L. *protestor*—*pro,* before, and *testor,* to affirm, < *testis,* a witness.] To make a formal declaration of opposition to something; to object; to affirm with solemnity.—*v.t.* To object to; make or enter a protest against; to make a solemn declaration or affirmation of; to assert; to make a written protest of, under a notary's seal of office.—prō′test, *n.* A solemn declaration of opinion against some act; an expression of objection or dissent; a formal statement, usu. in writing, by which a

person declares that he dissents from something, as by a member of a legislature to an act or resolution; a declaration made by one paying a sum of money, as a tax, that he considers the claim for such money illegal; a formal, sworn declaration that acceptance or payment of a bill or promissory note has been refused; *sports,* an objection presented before the chief executive or executive body of an organized sport. The act of protesting.

Prot·es·tant, prot′i·stant, *n.* A Christian not belonging to a Roman Catholic or an Eastern Orthodox church; an adherent of any western Christian denomination that sprang from the Reformation; an adherent, as one of the German princes, of the party led by Martin Luther, which protested in 1529 against a decree of the Diet of Spires designed to put down the Reformation. (*l.c.*) one who protests.—*a.* Belonging or pertaining to the religion of the Protestants; (*l.c.*) protesting.—**Prot·es·tant·ism,** *n.*

prot·es·ta·tion, prot′i·stā′shan, prō″ti·- stā′shan, *n.* [L. *protestatio.*] A solemn declaration; an act of protesting; a declaration of dissent; a protest; an avowal.

pro·tha·la·mi·on, prō″tha·lā′mē·on″, prō″tha·lā′mē·on″, *n.* pl. **pro·tha·la·mi·a,** prō″tha·lā′mē·a. [N.L., < Gr. *pró,* before, and *thálamos,* bridal chamber.] A song or poem written to celebrate a marriage. Also **pro·tha·la·mi·um,** prō″tha·lā′mē·um.

pro·thal·li·um, prō·thal′ē·um, *n.* pl. **pro·thal·li·a,** prō·thal′ē·a. [N.L., < Gr. *prō,* before, and *thallion,* dim. of *thallós,* young shoot.] *Bot.* The gametophyte of ferns; the analogous rudimentary gametophyte of seed-bearing plants. Also **pro·- thal·lus,** prō·thal′us, pl. **pro·thal·li,** prō·- thal′ī.—**pro·thal·li·al, pro·thal·line,** prō·thal′ēn, prō·thal′īn, *a.*

proth·e·sis, proth′i·sis, *n.* pl. **proth·e·ses,** proth′i·sēz″. [L.L., < Gr. *próthesis,* a putting before, < *protithénai,* < *pró,* before, and *tithénai,* set, put.] *Ling.* the addition of a letter or syllable at the beginning of a word. *Gr. Orthodox Ch.* the preparation or preliminary oblation of the eucharistic elements; the table on which this is done; the part of the bema or sanctuary where this table stands.—**pro·thet·ic,** pro·thet′ik, *a.*

pro·thon·o·tar·y, prō·thon′o·ter″ē, prō″- tho·nō′ta·rē, *n.* pl. **pro·thon·o·tar·ies.** [L.L. *protonotarius*—Gr. *prōtos,* first, and L. *notarius,* a scribe. The insertion of *h* is a mistake.] A chief clerk of certain courts in the U.S. *Rom. Cath. Ch.* one of seven priests constituting a college, who records certain papal proceedings; also **pro·thon·- o·tar·y ap·os·tol·ic.** *Gr. Orthodox Ch.* the chief secretary of the patriarch of Constantinople. Also **pro·ton·o·tar·y,** prō″- ton′o·ter″ē, prōt″o·nō′ta·rē.—**pro·thon·- o·tar·i·al,** prō″thon′o·târ′ē·al, *a.*

pro·tho·rax, prō·thōr′aks, prō·thar′aks, *n.* pl. **pro·tho·rax·es, pro·tho·ra·ces,** prō·thōr′a·sēz″, prō·thar′a·sēz″. [Gr. *prō,* before, and *thórax.*] *Entom.* the first or anterior segment of the thorax of insects, which bears the first pair of legs.—**pro·- tho·rac·ic,** prō″thō·ras′ik, prō″tha·ras′ik, *a.*

pro·throm·bin, prō·throm′bin, *n.* *Biochem.* a proenzyme in the blood which, when activated, becomes thrombin, a substance which then changes fibrogen into fibrin and brings about blood coagulation. Also *thrombogen.*

pro·tist, prō′tist, *n.* [N.L. *Protista,* pl., < Gr. *prōtistos,* the very first.] *Biol.* any of a group of organisms, *Protista,* including all the unicellular animals and plants.— **pro·tis·tan,** prō·tis′tan, *a., n.*

pro·ti·um, prō′tē·um, prō′shē·um, *n.* *Chem.* the normal hydrogen isotope of atomic mass 1. Sym. H^1.

pro·to·ac·tin·i·um, prō″tō·ak·tin′ē·um, *n. Chem.* protactinium.

pro·to·col, prō′to·kạl″, prō′to·kol″, prō′- to·kōl″, *n.* [Fr. *protocole,* L.L. *protocollum,* the first leaf, the first sheet of a legal instrument glued to the cylinder around which the document was rolled—Gr. *prōtos,* first, *kolla,* glue.] Rules of etiquette and order in diplomatic or military ceremonies; the minutes or rough draft of some diplomatic document; a document relating the proceedings of a diplomatic meeting and, after ratification, having the force of a treaty.—*v.i.*—*protocoled, protocoling, protocolled, protocolling.* To draft a protocol.

pro·to·hu·man, prō′tō·hū′man, prō″tō·- ū′man, *a.* Of, or pertaining to, the earliest stages of prehistoric man, esp. to any manlike primate.—*n.* A protohuman creature.

pro·to·lan·guage, prō′tō·lang′gwij, prō′- tō·lang′gwij, *n. Ling.* a postulated parent language.

pro·to·lith·ic, prōt″o·lith′ik, *a.* [Gr. *prōtos,* first, and *lithos,* stone.] *Anthropol.* noting or pertaining to the beginning of the Stone Age.

pro·to·mar·tyr, prō″tō·mär′ter, *n.* [Gr. *prōtos,* first, and *martyr,* martyr.] The first martyr in any cause; Stephen, the first Christian martyr.

pro·ton, prō′ton, *n. Phys.* a nuclear particle with a positive charge equal and opposite to that of an electron, the number of nuclear protons being the atomic number of an atom.—**pro·ton·ic,** prō·ton′ik, *a.*

pro·ton-syn·chro·tron, prō′ton·sing′- kro·tron″, *n. Atomic phys.* a machine which accelerates protons to energy levels of billions of electron volts by means of radiofrequency voltages.

pro·to·path·ic, prō″to·path′ik, *a. Physiol.* responding solely and undiscriminatingly to gross stimuli, as extreme pain: opposed to *epicritic.*

pro·to·plasm, prō′to·plaz″um, *n.* [N.L. *protoplasma,* < Gr. *prōtos,* first, and *plásma,* something formed, E. *plasma.*] *Biol.* A complex substance, typically colorless and of viscid semifluid consistency, regarded as the physical basis of life, having the powers of spontaneous motion and reproduction; the living matter of all vegetable and animal cells and tissues.— **pro·to·plas·mic,** prō″to·plaz′mik, *a.*

pro·to·plast, prō′to·plast″, *n. Biol.* the primordial cell. An original; a thing first formed.—**pro·to·plas·tic,** prō″to·plas′tik, *a.*

pro·to·troph·ic, prō″to·trof′ik, *a.* Of some plants and bacteria, assimilating inorganic matter for nutrition.

pro·to·type, prō′to·tīp″, *n.* [Fr. *prototype,* < Gr. *prōtotypon,* prototype, prop. neut. of *prōtotypos,* original, primitive, < *prōtos,* first, and *typos,* E. *type.*] The original or model on which something is formed; an example displaying typical characteristics of a class; something exhibiting features of another that developed in a later age. *Biol.* an archetype; a form on which a group is based.—**pro·to·ty·pal, pro·to·typ·ic,** prō″to·tip′ik, *a.*

pro·tox·ide, prō·tok′sīd, prō·tok′sid, *n.* [Gr. *prōtos,* first, and E. *oxide.*] *Chem.* that member of a series of oxides having the lowest proportion of oxygen. Also **pro·- tox·id,** prō·tok′sid.

pro·to·zo·an, prō″to·zō′an, *n.* [N.L., < Gr. *prōtos,* first, and *zōon,* animal.] Any of the animals in the first or lowest zoological division or phylum, *Protozoa,* comprised of single-celled, microscopic organisms.—*a.* Like a protozoan or belonging to the Protozoa. Also **pro·to·zo·al, pro·to·- zo·ic.**

pro·to·zo·ol·o·gy, prō″tō·zō·ol′o·jē, *n.* The science or study of the protozoans: a division of zoology.—**pro·to·zo·o·log·i·-**

cal, prō"to·zō'o·loj'i·kal, *a.*—**pro·to··zo·ol·o·gist,** *n.*

pro·to·zo·on, prō"to·zō'on, prō"to·zō'ōn, *n.* pl. **pro·to·zo·a,** prō"to·zō'a. Protozoan.

pro·tract, prō·trakt', *v.t.* [< L. *protractus,* < *protraho.*] To draw out or lengthen in time; to prolong; to lengthen out in space; *surv., math.* to draw, using a protractor and scale; *anat.* to extend.—**pro·trac·tion,** *n.* —**pro·trac·tive,** *a.*

pro·tract·ed meet·ing, *n.* A series of revival meetings held over an extended period of time.

pro·trac·tile, prō·trak'til, *a.* Capable of being protracted or thrust forward.

pro·trac·tor, prō·trak'tẽr, *n.* One who or an object which protracts or delays; *surv.* an instrument for laying down and measuring angles on paper; *anat.* a muscle which draws a part forward.

pro·trude, prō·trōd', *v.t.*—*protruded, protruding.* [L. *protrudo.*] To thrust forward; to cause to project.—*v.i.* To stand out prominently.—**pro·trud·ent,** *a.*—**pro··tru·si·ble,** prō·trō'si·bl, *a.*

pro·tru·sile, prō·trō'sil, *a.* Capable of being protruded or extended.—**pro·tru··sil·i·ty,** prō·trō·sil'i·tē, *n.*

pro·tru·sion, prō·trō'zhan, *n.* The act of protruding; something which protrudes; the state of being thrust forward.

pro·tru·sive, prō·trō'siv, *a.* Projecting; protuberant; obtrusive.—**pro·tru·sive·ly,** *adv.*—**pro·tru·sive·ness,** *n.*

pro·tu·ber·ance, prō·tō'bẽr·ans, prō··tū'bẽr·ans, *n.* Protuberant state or form; a protuberant part; a rounded projection. Also **pro·tu·ber·an·cy,** pl. **pro·tu·ber··an·cies.**

pro·tu·ber·ant, prō·tō'bẽr·ant, prō·tū'bẽr·ant, *a.* Projecting beyond the surrounding surface.—**pro·tu·ber·ant·ly,** *adv.*

pro·tyle, prō'til, prō'til, *n.* [Gr.] The hypothetical undifferentiated matter or parent substance from which, according to some, all the chemical elements may have been derived.

proud, proud, *a.* [O.E. *prūd,* proud, whence *prýte,* pride; cogn. Dan. *prud,* stately, magnificent.] Having a proper self-esteem; self-respecting; feeling satisfaction or elation at some honor; taking pride in something; as, *proud* of one's country; actuating a feeling of pride; as, a *proud* history; high-spirited or vigorous, as a horse; *liter.* grand or magnificent. Possessing or displaying a high and unreasonable opinion of one's own excellence; arrogant.—**proud·ly,** *adv.* —**proud·ness,** *n.*

proud flesh, *n.* An excessive development of granulations in wounds and ulcers.

Proust·i·an, prōst'ē·an, *a.* Of or related to the 20th century French novelist Marcel Proust (1871–1922), or to his work.

prove, prōv, *v.t.*—*past proved,* pp. *proved* or *proven,* ppr. *proving.* [O.Fr. *prover, pruver,* Fr. *prouver,* < L. *probare,* to try, test, prove, lit. to test the good quality of, < *probus,* good (whence *probity*). *Proof* is a derivative.] To try or ascertain by an experiment; to test or make a trial of; to establish the truth or reality of by reasoning, induction, or evidence; to demonstrate; to establish the authenticity or validity of; as, to *prove* a will; to probate; *math.* to show or ascertain the correctness of by a further calculation.—*v.i.* To be found or ascertained by experience or trial; to turn out to be, as: The report *proved* to be false. —**prov·a·ble,** *a.*—**prov·a·bly,** *adv.*— **prov·er,** *n.*

prov·e·nance, prov'e·nans, *n.* [Fr.] Source or place of origin. Also **pro·ve·ni·ence,** prō·vē'nē·ens, prō·vēn'yens.

Pro·ven·çal, prō"ven·säl', prov"en·säl', *Fr.* prạ·vän·säl', *a.* [Fr., < *Provence,* < L. *provincia,* E. *province.*] Of or pertaining to

Provence, an area in southeastern France, or its people, or their language.—*n.* A native or inhabitant of Provence; the Romance tongue spoken in southeastern France.

prov·en·der, prov'en·dẽr, *n.* [< Fr. *provende* (with *r* somewhat unaccountably added), < L. *praebenda,* things to be supplied.] Dry food for livestock, as hay, straw, or corn; provisions; food.

pro·ven·tric·u·lus, prō"ven·trik'ū·lus, *n.* pl. **pro·ven·tric·u·li,** prō"ven·trik'ū·lī. [Gr. *pro,* in front of, L. *ventriculus,* a stomach.] In birds, the glandular portion of the stomach used for preliminary digestion.

prov·erb, prov'ẽrb, *n.* [O.Fr. Fr. *proverbe,* < L. *proverbium.*] A short, pithy, popular saying, long in use, embodying some familiar truth, practical precept, or useful thought in expressive and often picturesque language; an adage; a saw; hence, a person or thing that has become proverbial, an object of common mention or reference, or a byword; a wise saying or precept, or a didactic sentence. *Bib.* an oracular utterance requiring interpretation; (*cap.*), *pl. but sing in constr.* a book of the Old Testament consisting of wise sayings ascribed to Solomon and others.—*v.t.* To utter in the form of a proverb; to make (something) the subject of a proverb; to make a byword of.

pro·ver·bi·al, pro·vụr'bē·al, *a.* [L. *proverbialis.*] Of, pertaining to, or characteristic of a proverb; as, a *proverbial* mode of expression; expressed in a proverb or proverbs; of the nature of or resembling a proverb; as, *proverbial* sayings; having been made the subject of a proverb; as, the *proverbial* rolling stone; notorious.—**pro·ver··bi·al·ly,** *adv.*

pro·vide, pro·vid', *v.t.*—*provided, providing.* [L. *providēre* (pp. *provisus*), foresee, look after, provide for.] To bring about or ensure by foresight; arrange for or stipulate beforehand, as by a provision or proviso, as: The contract *provides* that specified materials shall be used. To get ready, prepare, or procure beforehand; as, to *provide* income for one's old age; to furnish or supply for a purpose; as, to *provide* food for the needy; to afford or yield; as, wealth the forests *provide*; to furnish or supply something; as, to *provide* a building with fire escapes.—*v.i.* To take measures with due foresight; as, to *provide* against accident; to make arrangements for supplying means of support, with *for*; as, to *provide for* a person in one's will; supply means of support, often with *for*, as: The Lord will *provide.*—**pro·vid·a·ble,** *a.*—**pro·vid·er,** *n.*

pro·vid·ed, pro·vī'did, *conj.* [Orig. pp.] It being stipulated or understood; on the condition or supposition; as, to consent *provided* or *provided that* all the others agree.

prov·i·dence, prov'i·dens, *n.* [L. *providentia.*] The care and supervision of God over His creatures; (*cap.*) God. Something due to an act of providential intervention; prudence.

prov·i·dent, prov'i·dent, *a.* [L. *providens,* ppr. of *provideo,* I provide.] Foreseeing wants and making provision to supply them; prudent in preparing for future exigencies; frugal; economical.—**prov·i··dent·ly,** *adv.*

prov·i·den·tial, prov"i·den'shal, *a.* Pertaining to or effected by the providence of God; fortunate.—**prov·i·den·tial·ly,** *adv.*

pro·vid·ing, pro·vī'ding, *conj.* [Orig. ppr. of *provide.*] Making the stipulation that; provided.

prov·ince, prov'ins, *n.* [Fr., < L. *provincia,* a province—*pro,* before, and *vinco,* I conquer.] Orig. a region controlled by the government of ancient Rome; an administrative unit of a country; *pl.* territory at some distance from the metropolis. *Eccles.* a division of a country under the jurisdiction of an archbishop; a geographic unit

belonging to a religious order. The proper duty, office, or business of a person; a sphere of action or speculation; a department of knowledge; *ecology,* a biogeographic area less extensive than a region.

pro·vin·cial, pro·vin'shal, *a.* Pertaining to a province; forming a province; characteristic of the inhabitants of a province; rustic; simple; of narrow interests or thought; descriptive of certain styles of architecture, furniture, or decor derived from the provinces; pertaining to an ecclesiastical province or to the jurisdiction of an archbishop.—*n.* A person belonging to a province as distinguished from the metropolis; one who displays narrowness of interests or thoughts; in some religious orders, a superior in a given district.—**pro·vin··cial·ly,** *adv.*—**pro·vin·ci·al·i·ty,** pro·vin"shē·al'i·tē, *n.* pl. **pro·vin·ci·al·i·ties.** —**pro·vin·cial·ist,** *n.*—**pro·vin·cial·ize,** *v.t.*—*provincialized, provincializing.*

pro·vin·cial·ism, pro·vin'sha·liz"um, *n.* Narrow-mindedness, ignorance, or naiveté which is the result of a provincial life isolated from intellectual or cultural activity; a habit, custom, trait, or peculiarity, particularly of speech, characteristic of a province or provincial.

Pro·vin·cial Stand·ard Time, *n.* (*Sometimes l.c.*) a Canadian time zone based on the standard of the 60th meridian. Also **At·lan·tic Stand·ard Time.** See *Standard Time.*

prov·ing ground, *n.* A site for testing the efficacy of an experimental product or system.

pro·vi·sion, pro·vizh'an, *n.* [L. *provisio, provisionis,* a foreseeing, foresight, purveying, < *providere, provisum,* to foresee.] The act of providing; a measure taken beforehand; accumulation of stores or materials beforehand. *Pl.* a stock of food provided; victuals. A stipulation or proviso.—*v.t.* To provide with victuals or food.—**pro·vi··sion·er,** *n.*

pro·vi·sion·al, pro·vizh'a·nal, *a.* Provided for present need or for the occasion; temporarily established; temporary. Also **pro·vi·sion·ar·y,** pro·vizh'a·ner"ē.—*n. Philately,* a stamp issued temporarily until the regular issue becomes available.—**pro··vi·sion·al·ly,** *adv.*

pro·vi·so, pro·vī'zō, *n.* pl. **pro·vi·sos, pro·vi·soes.** [L. *provisus,* pp. of *provideo,* ablative *proviso,* it being provided.] An article or clause in any statute, agreement, contract, grant, or other writing, by which a condition is introduced.—**pro·vi·so·ry,** pro·vī'zo·rē, *a.*

pro·vi·ta·min, prō·vī'ta·min, *n.* That which can become a vitamin when acted upon by certain substances in the body, as carotene, which is changed by liver action into vitamin A.

prov·o·ca·tion, prov"o·kā'shan, *n.* The act of provoking; anything that arouses or provokes; incitement; stimulus.

pro·voc·a·tive, pro·vok'a·tiv, *a.* Serving or apt to provoke; exciting; stimulating; vexing.—*n.* Anything that tends to provoke. —**pro·voc·a·tive·ly,** *adv.*—**pro·voc·a··tive·ness,** *n.*

pro·voke, pro·vōk', *v.t.*—*provoked, provoking.* [Fr. *provoquer,* < L. *provoco,* I call forth, challenge, excite.] To excite to anger; enrage; irritate; to excite or arouse, as hunger; to call forth; to stimulate to action; to bring about or instigate, as a fight.— **pro·vok·ing·ly,** *adv.*

pro·vo·lo·ne, prō"vo·lō'nē, *n.* A sharp Italian cheese with a distinct tangy flavor.

prov·ost, prov'ost, prō'vōst, *milit.* prō'vō, *n.* [O.Fr. *provost* (Fr. *prévôt*), < L. *praepositus,* one who is placed over others, < *praeponere.*] A superintendent; a university official directing educational activities; the head of certain colleges; the chief dignitary of a cathedral or collegiate church; the chief magistrate of a Scotch burgh, corresponding to a mayor.—**prov·ost·ship**, *n.*

pro·vost court, prō′vō kōrt″, *n.* A military court for the trial of minor offenses committed by soldiers or civilians within an occupied area.

pro·vost guard, prō′vō gärd″, *n.*, *pl. in constr.* Soldiers detailed for police duty under command of a provost marshal.

pro·vost mar·shal, prō′vō mär′shal, *n. Milit.* a staff officer at command or subordinate level who advises on, and exercises supervision and inspection over, the maintenance of discipline, enforcement of security, and the confinement of prisoners; *navy*, an officer who has the custody of prisoners being held for court-martial.

prow, prou, *n.* [Fr. *proue*, Sp. and Pg. *proa*, < L. *prora*, < Gr. *prōira*, a prow; akin to *pro*, before.] The forepart of a ship; the bow; a projecting forward part, esp. of an airplane; *poet.* a ship.

prow·ess, prou′is, *n.* [Fr. *prouesse*, prowess, < O.Fr. *prou* (Fr. *preux*), brave; origin doubtful.] Bravery; valor; military bravery combined with skill; exceptional ability.

prowl, proul, *v.i.*, *v.t.* [Origin doubtful; older forms were *proule*, *prolle*.] To rove or wander stealthily, as a beast in search of prey.—*n.* The act of prowling.—**prowl·er**, *n.*

prowl car, *n.* A police patrol or squad car.

prox·i·mal, prok′si·mal, *a.* [L. *proximus*, nearest.] Nearest the point of attachment or insertion, as the extremity of a bone or limb: opposed to *distal*.—**prox·i·mal·ly**, *adv.*

prox·i·mate, prok′si·mit, *a.* [L. *proximatus*, pp. of *proximare*, come near, < *proximus*.] Next; nearest; closely adjacent; imminent; coming next or very near in time; coming next in a chain of relation; as, a *proximate* cause; nearly or fairly accurate; approximate.—**prox·i·mate·ly**, *adv.*—**prox·i·mate·ness**, *n.*

prox·im·i·ty, prok·sim′i·tē, *n.* [L. *proximitas*.] The state of being proximate.

prox·im·i·ty fuze, *n. Milit.* a miniature radio receiving and sending set, fitted inside the nose of a missile, which sends out a radio signal, and on receiving a radio wave reflected back from a target, explodes the missile's charge. Also **var·i·a·ble-time fuze, VT fuze.**

prox·i·mo, prok′si·mō″, *a.* [L., on the next.] In or of the next month; as, the 5th *proximo*. Abbr. **prox.**

prox·y, prok′sē, *n. pl.* **prox·ies.** [Contr. < *procuracy* = L.L. *procuratia*.] The agency of a person who acts as a substitute for another person; authority to act for another; the person deputed to act for another; a deputy; a document by which one person authorizes another to vote in his place.

prox·y mar·riage, *n.* A marriage ceremony at which the role of an absent bride or groom is taken by a proxy.

prude, prōd, *n.* [Fr. *prude*; prob. < L. *prudens*, prudent.] A person who shows excessive propriety and modesty in conduct or speech.

pru·dence, prōd′ens, *n.* [O.Fr. Fr. *prudence*, < L. *prudentia*, < *prudens*, E. *prudent*.] The quality or fact of being prudent; cautious; practical wisdom; good judgment; discretion; provident care in management; economy or frugality.

pru·dent, prōd′ent, *a.* [Fr. *prudent*, < L. *prudens*, *prudentis*, prudent, < *providens*, *providentis*, ppr. of *providere*, to foresee.] Judicious and cautious in managing practical affairs; circumspect; sagacious; shrewd in planning for the future; provident; characterized or directed by prudence, as an action.—**pru·dent·ly**, *adv.*

pru·den·tial, prō·den′shal, *a.* Of, proceeding from, or characterized by prudence; exercising prudence; having discretionary powers, esp. in business dealings.—**pru·den·tial·ly**, *adv.*

prud·er·y, prō′de·rē, *n. pl.* **prud·er·ies.** [Fr. *pruderie*.] Extreme modesty or propriety; a prudish action or speech.

prud·ish, prō′dish, *a.* Characteristic of or like a prude; excessively modest; priggish. —**prud·ish·ness**, *n.*

pru·i·nose, prō′i·nōs″, *a.* [< L. *pruina*, hoarfrost.] Hoary; appearing as if frosted with a covering of minute dust, as a plant surface.

prune, prōn, *n.* [Fr. *prune*, < L. *prunum*, a plum.] A plum; specifically, a dried plum; *slang*, a tiresome person.

prune, prōn, *v.t.*—*pruned*, *pruning*. [Formerly *proine*, *proyne*, < Fr. *provigner*, dial. Fr. *preugner*, *progner*, < L. *propago*, *propaginis*, a slip or sucker.] To lop or cut off, as the superfluous branches or twigs of trees and shrubs; to trim with a knife; to clear, as of anything superfluous.—*v.i.*—**prun·er**, *n.*

pru·nel·la, prō·nel′a, *n.* [Fr. *prunelle*, *prunella*, from its prunelike color.] A twilled worsted used for dresses; formerly, a fabric used for academic and ecclesiastical gowns. Also **pru·nelle**, prō·nel′.

prun·ing hook, *n.* An instrument with a hooked blade for pruning trees, shrubs, or vines.

pru·ri·ent, prur′ē·ent, *a.* [L. *pruriens*, < *prurire*, to itch or long for a thing, to be lecherous.] Inclined or inclining to lascivious thoughts; bringing about lasciviousness or lust; eagerly desirous.—**pru·ri·ent·ly**, *adv.*—**pru·ri·ence, pru·ri·en·cy**, *n.*

Prus·sian, prush′an, *a.* Pertaining to Prussia, a former state in Europe which became the major state in the formation of the German Empire after 1871, its language or its inhabitants; militaristic.—*n.* The Prussian language; an inhabitant of Prussia.

Prus·sian blue, *n.* A deep blue pigment, essentially a cyanogen compound of iron.

Prus·sian·ism, prush′a·niz″um, *n.* The policies, attitudes, and practices advocated by the Prussian aristocracy after 1750, esp. their foreign policy of militarism and their admiration of military discipline.—**prus·sian·ize**, prush′a·nīz″, *v.t.*—*prussianized*, *prussianizing*. (*Often cap.*) to cause to have Prussian attitudes or practices.

prus·si·ate, prush′ē·āt″, prush′ē·it, prus′ē·āt″, prus′ē·it, *n.* A salt of hydrocyanic acid; a cyanide.

prus·sic ac·id, prus′ik as′id, *n.* [Orig. obtained from *Prussian* blue.] *Chem.* hydrocyanic acid.

pry, prī, *v.i.*—*pried*, *prying*. [M.E. *pryen*, *prien*; origin uncertain.] To look closely or curiously; peer; peep; to search or inquire inquisitively or impertinently into something; as, to *pry* into the affairs of others.— *n. pl.* **pries.** The act or an act of prying; an inquisitive person.—**pry·er, pri·er**, *n.*— **pry·ing**, *a.*—**pry·ing·ly**, *adv.*

pry, prī, *n. pl.* **pries.** [Reduced form of *prize*.] Any instrument for raising or moving a thing by force of leverage; leverage.— *v.t.*—*pried*, *prying*. To raise, move, or force with a pry, or by force of leverage; to extract, open, or obtain with difficulty.

psalm, säm, *n.* [L. *psalmus*, a psalm, < Gr. *psalmos*, a twitching or twanging with the fingers, < *psallein*, to play a stringed instrument, to sing to the harp.] A sacred song or hymn; (*usu. cap.*) any of the 150 religious poems forming the biblical Book of Psalms. A versification of a psalm.—*v.t.* To praise in psalms.

psalm·book, säm ′buk″, *n.* Psalter; a book containing the psalms or other songs for use in church services.

psalm·ist, sä′mist, *n.* A writer or composer of psalms.—**the Psalm·ist**, King David, another of many psalms of the Bible.

psal·mo·dy, sä′mo·dē, sal′mo·dē, *n. pl.* **psal·mo·dies.** The singing or writing of psalms; psalms collectively.

Psal·ter, sal′tēr, *n.* [L. *psalterium*, Gr. *psaltērion*, a kind of harp, < *psallō*.] The Book of Psalms of the Bible; a book containing the Psalms alone; a version of the Psalms used in religious services.

psal·te·ri·um, sal·tēr′ē·um, sal·tēr′ē·um, *n. pl.* **psal·te·ri·a**, sal·tēr′e·a, sal·tēr′ē·a. Omasum.

psal·ter·y, sal′te·rē, *n. pl.* **psal·ter·ies.** An early musical instrument, a form of dulcimer, resembling the zither. Also **psal·try**, *pl.* **psal·tries.**

pseud·e·pig·ra·pha, sōō″de·pig′ra·fa, *n. pl.* [N.L., < Gr. *pseudepigropha*, neut. pl. or *pseudepigraphos*, falsely inscribed, bearing a false title, < *pseudēs*, false, and *epigraphein*, inscribe.] Writings or books inscribed with a false title, or falsely ascribed to someone other than the true author; specif., certain writings (other than the canonical books and the Apocrypha) professing to be Biblical in character, but not considered canonical or inspired or worthy of a place in religious use.—**pseud·e·pig·ra·phal, pseud·e·pig·ra·phous**, *a.* Of or pertaining to pseudepigrapha. Also **pseud·ep·i·graph·ic**, sōō″dep·i·graf′ik.

pseud·e·pig·ra·phy, sōō″de·pig′ra·fē, *n.* The ascription of a literary work to someone other than its author.

pseu·do, sōō′dō, *a.* [Gr. *pseudos*, falsehood.] False; counterfeit; spurious.

pseu·do·carp, sōō′do·kärp″, *n. Bot.* a fruit which includes other parts in addition to the mature ovary and its contents, as the apple or pineapple.—**pseu·do·car·pous**, *a.*

pseu·do·clas·sic, sōō″dō·klas′ik, *a. Art, liter.* in imitation of or pretending to be classic.—*n.*—**pseu·do·clas·si·cism**, *n.* False or spurious classicism.

pseu·do·morph, sōō′do·mˈarf″, *n.* [Gr. *morphē*, shape.] A deceptive or irregular form; a mineral having a form belonging, not to the substance of which it consists, but to some other substance which it has wholly or partially replaced.—**pseu·do·mor·phic**, sōō″do·mˈar′fik, *a.*—**pseu·do·mor·phism**, *n.*—**pseu·do·mor·phous**, *a.*

pseu·do·nym, sōō′do·nim, *n.* [Gr. *onoma*, a name.] A false or feigned name, esp. one assumed by a writer; a pen name.

pseu·don·y·mous, sōō·don′i·mus, *a.* [Gr. *pseudonymos*—*pseudos*, and *onoma*, name.] Bearing a false name; written under a false name.—**pseu·don·y·mous·ly**, *adv.* **pseu·don·y·mous·ness**, *n.*

pseu·do·po·di·um, sōō″do·pō′dē·um, *n. pl.* **pseu·do·po·di·a**, sōō″do·pō′dē·a. *Zool.* a retractable extension from the body of a protozoan, used in moving and feeding.— **pseu·do·pod**, sōō′do·pod″, *n.* A protozoan having pseudopodia, as an amoeba; a pseudopodium.—**pseu·dop·o·dal**, sōō·dop′-o·dal, *a.*

pseu·do·preg·nan·cy, sōō″dō·preg′nan·sē, *n.* A condition of certain mammals which is similar to, but is not, pregnancy.—**pseu·do·preg·nant**, *a.*

pseu·do·sci·ence, sōō″dō·sī′ens, *n.* A body of related information, theories, and methods, inaccurately considered to be scientific.—**pseu·do·sci·en·tif·ic**, sōō″dō·sī″en·tif′ik, *a.*

pshaw, shạ, *interj.* An exclamation expressing impatience or contempt.

psi, sī, psē, *n. pl.* **psis.** [Gr. *psi*.] The twenty-third letter, Ψ, ψ, of the Greek alphabet.

psil·o·cy·bin, sil″o·sī′bin, sī″lo·sī′bin, *n.* An alkaloid of the fungus, *Psilocybe mexicana*, used as a hallucinogen.

psit·ta·cine, sit′a·sīn″, sit′a·sin, *a.* [L.

---

ch- chain, G. na*ch*t; **th-** THen, thin; **w-** wig, hw as sound in whig; **z-** zh as in azure, zeal. *Italicized vowel* indicates schwa sound.

psittacinus, < *psittacus,* < Gr. *psittakós,* parrot.] Parrotlike; of the parrot kind. Also **psit·ta·ceous,** si·tā′shus.—*n.*

psit·ta·co·sis, sit″a·kō′sis, *n. Pathol.* a serious, rickettsial, infectious disease which involves the lungs and is accompanied by high fever, found to be transmissible to man from parrots, and now known to occur in other birds. Also *parrot fever, ornithosis,* **par·rot dis·ease.**—**psit·ta·co·tic,** sit·a·· cot′ik, *a.*

pso·ri·a·sis, so·rī′a·sis, *n.* [N.L., < Gr. *psōriasis,* < *psōrian,* have the itch, < *psōra,* the itch.] *Pathol.* a chronic skin disease characterized by red scaly patches.—**pso·ri·at·ic,** sōr″ē·at′ik, sạr″ē·at′ik, *a.*

psy·chas·the·ni·a, sī″kas·thē′nē·a, sī″· kas·the·nī′a, *n.* [N.L., Gr. *psychē,* soul, mind and *asthéneia,* weakness.] *Psychiatry,* an emotional disorder manifested by morbid anxieties, fears, and phobias.—**psy·chas·· then·ic,** sī″kas·then′ik, *a., n.*

Psy·che, sī′kē, *n.* [L., < Gr. *Psychē,* personification of *psyche,* breath, spirit, soul, mind]. *Class. mythol.* the soul or spirit personified, usu. represented in art as a fair maiden, often with the wings of a butterfly; (*l.c.*), *psychoanal.* a person's mental components, both conscious and unconscious.

psych·e·del·ic, sī″ki·del′ik, *a.* Of, pertaining to, or causing extraordinary changes in consciousness, as the intensification of sense perception and awareness, hallucination, and delusion; of or pertaining to any of a group of drugs which produce this effect, as LSD, psilocybin, and mescaline; consciousness-expanding. Also **psy·cho·· del·ic,** sī″kō·del′ik.

Psy·che knot, *n.* A knot or coiled arrangement of a woman's hair at the back of the head.

psy·chi·a·trist, si·kī′a·trist, sī·kī′a·trist, *n.* A physician specializing in psychiatry.

psy·chi·a·try, si·kī′a·trē, sī·kī′a·trē, *n.* That field in medicine which deals with the diagnosis and treatment of emotional and mental disorders.—**psy·chi·at·ric,** sī″· kē·a′trik, *a.*—**psy·chi·at·ri·cal·ly,** *adv.*

psy·chic, sī′kik, *a.* [Gr. *psychikos,* < *psychē,* soul, mind.] Of or pertaining to the human soul or mind; mental, as opposed to *physical;* of or pertaining to, exerted by, or proceeding from a supposed nonphysical force or power assumed to operate in various obscure phenomena, as those of telepathy, clairvoyance, spiritualism; specially susceptible to supposedly supernatural influences.—*n.* A person unusually sensitive to some nonphysical or spiritual influence; a medium.—**psy·chi·cal,** *a.*—**psy·chi·cal·ly,** *adv.*

psy·cho, sī′kō, *n. Slang,* a mentally sick or neurotic individual.—*a.*

psy·cho·a·nal·y·sis, sī″kō·a·nal′i·sis, *n.* A method of studying and analyzing the subconscious thoughts of an individual, as disclosed by free association or dreams, in order to detect hidden mental conflicts which may produce disorders of mind and body.—**psy·cho·an·a·lyt·ic,** **psy·cho·· an·a·lyt·i·cal,** sī″kō·an·a·lit′ik, *a.*— **psy·cho·an·a·lyt·i·cal·ly,** *adv.*

psy·cho·an·a·lyst, sī″kō·an′a·list, *n.* One who is qualified to practice psychoanalysis.

psy·cho·an·a·lyze, sī″kō·an′a·līz″, *v.t.*— *psychoanalyzed, psychoanalyzing.* To examine and treat by psychoanalysis, as a patient.

psy·cho·bi·ol·o·gy, sī″kō·bī·ol′o·jē, *n.* The study of the interaction or relationship between mind and body, esp. as shown in the nervous system; the biological aspects of psychology.—**psy·cho·bi·o·log·ic,** **psy·· cho·bi·o·log·i·cal,** sī″kō·bī″o·loj′ik, *a.*— **psy·cho·bi·ol·o·gist,** *n.*

psy·cho·dra·ma, sī″kō·drä′ma, sī″kō·· dram′a, *n.* A type of group psychotherapy which seeks to aid in the rehabilitation of patients by enabling them to dramatize roles likely to shed light on their problems. —**psy·cho·dra·mat·ic,** sī″kō·dra·mat′ik, *a.*

psy·cho·dy·nam·ic, sī″kō·dī·nam′ik, *a.* Pertaining to the study of behavior in relation to motivation; pertaining to the development and effect of mental processes. —**psy·cho·dy·nam·i·cal·ly,** *adv.*—**psy·· cho·dy·nam·ics,** *n. pl., sing.* or *pl.* in constr.

psy·cho·gen·e·sis, sī″kō·jen′i·sis, *n.* The genesis or origin and development of the soul or mind; origin or development due to psychic or mental, as opposed to bodily, activity.—**psy·cho·ge·net·ic,** sī″kō·je·· net′ik, *a.*—**psy·cho·ge·net·i·cal·ly,** *adv.*

psy·cho·gen·ic, sī″kō·jen′ik, *a.* Of psychic or mental origin, or dependent on mental conditions or processes, as a disorder.— **psy·cho·gen·i·cal·ly,** *adv.*

psy·chog·no·sis, sī·kog′no·sis, sī″kog·· nō′sis, *n.* The study of the mind, esp. in relation to character.—**psy·chog·nos·tic,** sī″kog·nos′tik, *a.*

psy·cho·graph, sī′ko·graf″, sī′ko·gräf″, *n.* A graph setting out the personality traits of a particular individual; a biographical account of an individual's traits or abilities.

psy·cho·ki·ne·sis, sī″kō·ki·nē′sis, *n.* The hypothesized power of the will to control physical objects, as dice, without the use of physical force.

psy·cho·log·i·cal, sī″ko·loj′i·kal, *a.* Of or pertaining to psychology; pertaining to the mind or to mental phenomena as the subject matter of psychology; mental or subjective; as, a condition of affairs that is purely *psychological.*—Also **psy·cho·log·ic.**— **psy·cho·log·i·cal·ly,** *adv.*

psy·cho·log·i·cal he·don·ism, *n.* The theory that behavior is primarily motivated by the desire to avoid pain or to experience pleasure.

psy·cho·log·i·cal mo·ment, *n.* The most appropriate moment for acting or achieving an end; the critical moment.

psy·chol·o·gism, si·kol′o·jiz″um, *n.* A view that places a value on psychological insight in the interpretation of history and philosophy.

psy·chol·o·gist, si·kol′o·jist, *n.* One versed in psychology.

psy·chol·o·gize, si·kol′o·jīz″, *v.i.*—*psy-chologized, psychologizing.* To make psychological investigations or speculations.

psy·chol·o·gy, si·kol′o·jē, *n.* [Gr. *psychē* and *logos.*] That branch of knowledge which deals with the human mind; that knowledge of the mind which we derive from a careful examination of the facts of consciousness and of behavior; the aggregate of mental and behavioral qualities typical of a group or one of its members; a written exposition on psychology.

psy·cho·met·rics, sī″kō·me′triks, *n. pl.* but *sing.* in constr. See psychometry.— **psy·cho·met·ric,** *a.*—**psy·cho·met·ri·· cal·ly,** *adv.*

psy·chom·e·try, si·kom′i·trē, *n.* [Gr. *psychē,* soul, *metron,* measure.] *Psychol.* the measurement of the relative strength of mental faculties; also *psychometrics.* The supposed ability to discover facts about an object or an individual connected with it, by being close to, or in contact with, the object.—**psy·chom·e·trist,** *n.*

psy·cho·mo·tor, sī″kō·mō′tėr, *a.* Pertaining to movement induced by mental action.

psy·cho·neu·ro·sis, sī″kō·nụ·rō′sis, sī″· kō·nū·rō′sis, *n. pl.* **psy·cho·neu·ro·ses.** [N.L.] *Psychiatry,* a neurosis in which the patient's anxieties, fears, and various physical complaints are emotional, and without physical cause.—**psy·cho·neu·rot·ic,** sī″kō·nụ·rot′ik, sī″kō·nū·rot′ik, *a., n.*

psy·cho·path, sī′ko·path″, *n.* An individual with a psychopathic personality; a mentally unstable person.

psy·cho·path·ic per·son·al·i·ty, *n. Psychiatry,* a personality disorder evidenced by antisocial, nonconforming, amoral, and sometimes criminal behavior, by the inability to form deep attachments for others or to learn from experience, and by extreme personal indulgence; one having this type of personality.

psy·cho·pa·thol·o·gy, sī″kō·pa·thol′o·jē, *n.* Mental pathology.—**psy·cho·pa·thol·· o·gist,** *n.*—**psy·cho·path·o·log·ic,** **psy·· cho·path·o·log·i·cal,** sī″kō·path″o·loj′ik, *a.*

psy·chop·a·thy, sī·kop′a·thē, *n.* [Gr. *pathos,* suffering.] Abnormal mental condition.—**psy·cho·path·ic,** sī″ko·path′ik, *a., n.*—**psy·cho·path·i·cal·ly,** *adv.*

psy·cho·phys·i·cal par·al·lel·ism, *n.* The theory that there is a strict correspondence between physical and mental processes but no interaction.

psy·cho·phys·ics, sī″kō·fiz′iks, *n. pl.* but *sing.* in constr. *Psychol.* the experimental study of the connection between stimuli and sensation in its functional and quantitative aspects.—**psy·cho·phys·i·cal,** sī″kō·fiz′· i·kal, *a.*—**psy·cho·phys·i·cal·ly,** *adv.*— **psy·cho·phys·i·cist,** sī″kō·fiz′i·sist, *n.*

psy·cho·sis, sī·kō′sis, *n. pl.* **psy·cho·ses,** sī·kō′sēz. A major mental disorder, characterized by a disintegration of personality and an inability to relate to others.—**psy·· chot·ic,** sī·kot′ik, *a., n.*—**psy·chot·i·cal·· ly,** *adv.*

psy·cho·so·mat·ic, sī″kō·sō·mat′ik, sī″· kō·so·mat′ik, *a.* Having bodily symptoms of mental or emotional origin.—*n.*—**psy·· cho·so·mat·i·cal·ly,** *adv.*

psy·cho·so·mat·ics, sī″kō·sō·mat′iks, sī″kō·so·mat′iks, *n. pl.* but *sing.* in constr. A branch of medicine dealing with the interrelationship of physical disease and mental and emotional causes.

psy·cho·sur·ger·y, sī″kō·sur′je·rē, *n.* Surgery of the brain to relieve the symptoms of certain mental diseases.

psy·cho·ther·a·py, sī″kō·ther′a·pē, *n.* [Gr. *therapeuō,* I attend medically.] Psychological methods of treatment to correct maladjustments and mental disorders. Also **psy·cho·ther·a·peu·tics,** sī″kō·ther″a·· pū′tiks,—**psy·cho·ther·a·peu·tic,** *a.*— **psy·cho·ther·a·peu·ti·cal·ly,** *adv.*— **psy·cho·ther·a·pist,** *n.*

psy·chrom·e·ter, sī·krom′i·tėr, *n.* [Gr. *psychros,* cool, and *metron,* measure.] An instrument consisting of two thermometers, one having a wet bulb and one having a dry bulb, with the difference between their readings being the measurement of humidity in the atmosphere.

psy·chro·phil·ic, sī″kro·fil′ik, *a.* Able to thrive at or near freezing temperatures, as certain bacteria.—**psy·chro·phile,** sī′kro·· fīl″, sī′kro·fil, *n.*

ptar·mi·gan, tär′mi·gan, *n. pl.* **ptar·mi·· gans, ptar·mi·gan.** [Appar. < Gael. *tär-machan.*] Any of various species of grouse of the genus *Lagopus,* characterized by feathered feet, and found in mountainous and cold regions.

PT boat, pē′tē′ bōt, *n.* [(P)atrol (T)orpedo boat.] *U.S. Navy,* a small naval vessel, highly maneuverable and fast, which carries torpedoes and usu. depth charges for attacking enemy surface ships and submarines. Also **mos·qui·to boat, mo·tor tor·pe·do boat.**

pter·i·dol·o·gy, ter″i·dol′o·jē, *n.* [Gr. *pteris, pteridos,* a fern, *logos,* discourse.] The division of botany concerned with ferns.— **pter·i·do·log·i·cal,** ter″i·do·loj′i·kal, *a.* —**pter·i·dol·o·gist,** *n.*

pte·rid·o·phyte, te·rid′o·fīt″, ter′i·dō·· fīt″, *n.* [Gr. *pteris,* fern; *phyton,* plant.] One of the *Pteridophyta*, the phylum of plants without flowers or seeds which includes the ferns, club mosses, and allied forms.—**pte·rid·o·phyt·ic, pter·i·doph·y·tous,** te″rid″o·fit′ik, ter″i·dō·fit′ik, ter″i·dof′a·-tus, *a.*

pter·o·dac·tyl, ter″o·dak′til, *n.* [N.L. *Pterodactylus,* < Gr. *pterón,* wing, and *daktylos,* finger or toe.] Any member of the *Pterosauria,* an order of extinct flying reptiles of the Jurassic and Cretaceous periods, having one digit of the forelimb greatly elongated and supporting a wing membrane.—**pter·o·dac·tyl·oid, pter·o·-dac·tyl·ous,** *a.*

pter·o·pod, ter′o·pod″, *n.* [N.L. *Ptero-poda,* pl., < Gr. *pterópous(-pod-),* wing-footed, < *pterón,* wing, and *pous(pod-),* foot.] Any of the *Pteropoda,* a group of mollusks which have the lateral portions of the foot expanded into winglike lobes.—*a.*—**pte·-rop·o·dan,** te·rop′o·dan, *a., n.*—**pte·rop·-o·dous,** *a.*

pter·o·saur, ter′o·sạr″, *n.* [Gr. *pteron,* a wing, *sauros,* a lizard.] An extinct flying reptile, as the Mesozoic pterodactyl.

pter·y·goid, ter′i·goid″, *a.* [Gr. *pteryx, pterygos,* a wing.] Wing-shaped; *anat.* of or pertaining to anatomical features located near the sphenoid bone at the base of the skull.—*n.*

pter·y·goid proc·ess, *n. Anat.* either of two processes, one on each side of the sphenoid bone, each process consisting of two plates separated by a notch; either of these two plates.

ptis·an, tiz′an, ti·zan′, *n.* [L. *ptisana,* < Gr. *ptisanē,* peeled barley, barley water, < *ptissō,* to peel.] A type of tea or similar decoction of barley and other herbs; also *tisane.* A grape juice drained from the fruit without pressing.

Ptol·e·ma·ic, tol″e·mā′ik, *a.* Of the Greek philosopher Ptolemy or the Ptolemies, kings of ancient Egypt.

Ptol·e·ma·ic sys·tem, *n.* An astronomical system maintained by Ptolemy, a Greek philosopher of the 2nd century A.D., who supposed the earth to be fixed in the center of the universe with the sun and stars revolving around it.—**Ptol·e·ma·ist,** *n.* A believer in the Ptolemaic system.

pto·maine, pto·main, tō′mān, tō′mān′, *n.* [It. *ptomaina,* < Gr. *ptôma,* dead body, < *piptō,* fall.] *Biochem.* any of a class of basic organic compounds, some of them very poisonous, produced in animal and vegetable matter during putrefaction.

pto·maine poi·son·ing, *n. Pathol.* poisoning caused by ptomaine: applied in error to any other type of food poisoning.

pto·sis, tō′sis, *n.* [N.L., < Gr. *ptōsis,* a falling, < *piptein,* fall.] *Pathol.* a falling or drooping of the upper eyelid, due to paralysis of its levator muscle; the drooping or prolapsed state in any organ.—**pto·tic,** tō′tik, *a.*

pty·a·lin, tī′a·lin, *n.* [Gr. *ptyalon,* spittle, saliva, < *ptyein,* spit.] *Biochem.* an enzyme in the saliva of man and certain of the lower animals, possessing the property of converting starch into dextrin and maltose.

pty·a·lism, tī′a·liz″um, *n.* [Gr. *ptyalismós,* < *ptyalizein,* expectorate, < *ptyalon.*] Excessive secretion of saliva; salivation.

pub, pub, *n.* [Abbr. of *public.*] *Brit. colloq.* A public house; a tavern.

pu·ber·ty, pū′bẽr·tē, *n.* [L. *pubertas,* < *puber* or *pubes, puberis,* of ripe age, adult, same root as *puer,* a boy, *pullus,* a chicken.] The period in both male and female marked by the functional development of the generative system; the age at which persons become capable of reproduction.

pu·ber·u·lent, pū·ber′ū·lent, pū·ber′a·-lent, *a. Biol.* covered with down. Also **pu·-ber·u·lous,** pū·ber′ū·lus, pū·ber′a·lus.

pu·bes, pū′bēz, *n.* pl. **pu·bes.** [L., the hair which appears on the body at puberty.] *Anat.* the middle part of the lower abdominal region, covered with hair at puberty; the hair growing in this region. *Biol.* the down or downy substance on plants; pubescence.

pu·bes·cence, pū·bes′ens, *n.* The state of one who is arriving or has arrived at puberty; puberty; *biol.* short soft hairs, as those covering plants. Also **pu·bes·cen·cy.**

pu·bes·cent, pū·bes′ent, *a.* Arriving at puberty; *biol.* covered with fine short soft hairs, as the leaves of some plants or the bodies of some insects.

pu·bic, pū′bik, *a.* Pertaining to the pubes.

pu·bis, pū′bis, *n.* pl. **pu·bes,** pū′bēz. [For N.L. *os pubis,* bone of the pubes.] *Anat.* that part of either innominate bone which, with the corresponding part of the other, forms the front of the pelvis.

pub·lic, pub′lik, *a.* [Fr. *public* (masc.), *publique* (fem.), < L. *publicus,* for *populicus,* < *populus,* people.] Not private; pertaining to the whole people; relating to, regarding, or affecting a state, nation, or community; as, the *public* service; proceeding from many or the many; belonging to people in general; as, a *public* subscription; open to the knowledge of all; general; common; widely known; as, a *public* hero; notorious; as, a *public* disgrace; regarding not private interest but the good of the community; as, *public* spirit; open to common use; as, a *public* road.—*n.* The general body of mankind or of a nation, state, or community; the people, indefinitely: with *the*; the audience, as those who favor an author or celebrity.—**pub·lic·ness,** *n.*

pub·lic-ad·dress sys·tem, pub′lik·a·dres′ sis″tem, *n.* An electronic system of amplifying sound through a series of microphones and loudspeakers, used esp. for reaching large groups of people. Also *PA system.*

pub·li·can, pub′li·kan, *n.* [L. *publicanus.*] Among the ancient Romans, a collector of public revenues; any collector of public taxes or revenues. *Brit.* the keeper or owner of a tavern or a similar establishment.

pub·li·ca·tion, pub″li·kā′shan, *n.* [L. *publicatio,* < *publico,* to make public.] The act of publishing or offering for public notice; notification to people at large; promulgation; that which is offered, as a book, magazine, newspaper, map, or the like, to the public by sale or gratuitous distribution; the state of being printed and published.

pub·lic de·fend·er, *n.* An elected or court-appointed attorney who defends, at public expense, persons charged with criminal offenses who are without means to retain legal counsel.

pub·lic do·main, *n.* The state of being available for general use, usu. with *in the,* as any material or publication not subject to patent or copyright laws; land under the ownership of the government.

pub·lic en·e·my, *n.* A criminal or other person who is considered a menace or threat to the public; a government or state regarded as an enemy.

pub·lic house, *n.* An inn or hostelry; *Brit.* a tavern.

pub·li·cist, pub′li·sist, *n.* A publicity or press agent; a specialist in public relations; a writer on current political topics; a specialist or expert in international law.

pub·lic·i·ty, pu·blis′i·tē, *n.* [Fr. *publicité.*] Public awareness resulting from the spreading of information in the various communications media; the actions involved in bringing information to public notice; the information, advertisements, articles, and the like put forth to gain public attention; the state of being public or open to the knowledge of a community.

pub·li·cize, pub′li·sīz″, *v.t.—publicized, publicizing.* To give publicity to; bring to public notice; advertise.

pub·lic law, *n.* Any law or statute adopted or enacted by a state or nation that applies to the people as a whole; the constitutional and administrative laws of a government. Compare *private law.*

pub·lic·ly, pub′lik·lē, *adv.* In a public manner; openly; without concealment; by or in the name of the public.

pub·lic prop·er·ty, *n.* Anything considered as owned by the public, the state, or community, with control usu. vested in a government agency, as the national parks under jurisdiction of the U.S. Department of the Interior.

pub·lic re·la·tions, *n. pl. but sing. in constr.* Actions taken by an individual, group, or institution to promote favorable public opinion; the art or technique used to promote such favorable opinion.

pub·lic sale, *n.* An auction; a sale made following a public notice.

pub·lic school, *n.* An elementary or secondary school established by state law in a district, county, or town, and maintained by taxes as part of a free education system for the children of the community. *Brit.* any of certain large, endowed, private boarding schools for boys, as Eton, usu. patronized by the wealthy, which prepare pupils for college or for public service.

pub·lic serv·ant, *n.* An employee of the government.

pub·lic serv·ice, *n.* A business which supplies services and commodities, as electricity or transportation, to the public; a service furnished free to the public; government service, as civil service.

pub·lic-serv·ice cor·po·ra·tion, *n.* A corporation which furnishes essential services, as telephone or electric power, to the public.

pub·lic speak·ing, *n.* The action or art of effective oral expression in public.

pub·lic-spir·it·ed, pub′lik·spir′i·tid, *a.* Having or showing unselfish desire for the public good.—**pub·lic-spir·it·ed·ness,** *n.*

pub·lic u·til·i·ty, *n.* A business, industry, or agency engaged in providing or making available to the public a commodity or service of general importance or need, and subject to certain government regulations.

pub·lic works, *n. pl.* Anything built or constructed by the government with public funds for the use or pleasure of the general public, as libraries, roads, parks, airports, public housing, or other similar projects.

pub·lish, pub lish, *v.t.* [Fr. *puplier.*] To cause to be printed and offered for sale to the public, as a newspaper, book, magazine, or the like; to make public; to make known to people in general; to promulgate.—*v.i.—***pub·lish·a·ble,** *a.*

pub·lish·er, pub′li·shẽr, *n.* One who publishes, esp. one who publishes books and other literary productions, newspapers, magazines, maps, engravings, or the like.

puc·coon, pa·kön′, *n.* [N. Amer. Ind.] *Bot.* any of several species of N. American herbs of the genus *Lithospermum,* in the borage family, esp. *L. canescens,* having curled-over clusters of yellow or orange flowers and rough hairy leaves, and flourishing in dry sandy soils.

puce, pūs, *a.* [Fr. *puce,* < L. *pulex, pulicis,* a flea.] Dark brown; reddish brown.—*n.*

puck, puk, *n. Sports.* a rubber disk used in ice hockey.

puck, puk, *n.* [O.E. *pūca* (also *pūcel*) = Icel. *pūki,* a mischievous demon.] A malicious or mischievous demon or spirit; a goblin. (*Cap.*) the mischievous sprite or fairy in Shakespeare's *A Midsummer Night's Dream;* also *Hobgoblin, Robin Goodfellow.*

puck·a, puk′a, *a.* Pukka.

puck·er, puk'ẽr, v.t. [< *poke*, a bag or pocket; cf. to *purse* the lips.] To gather into small folds or wrinkles.—v.i. To become wrinkled; to gather into folds.—n. A fold or wrinkle, or a collection of folds.—**puck·er·y**, puk'e·rē, a.

puck·ish, puk'ish, a. Mischievous; elfish; impish.—**puck·ish·ly**, adv.—**puck·ish·ness**, n.

pud·ding, pụd'ing, n. [< M.E. *poding*, sausage.] A usu. baked or boiled dish made of flour, rice, or other starchy substance, with milk and eggs, sometimes enriched with fruit or other flavor, and sweetened. A type of sausage stuffed with seasoned meat; also **black pud·ding**.

pud·ding stone, n. Geol. a conglomerate, esp. a mass of flint pebbles cemented by a siliceous paste.

pud·dle, pụd'l, n. [Akin to L.G. *pudel*, pool; D. *poedelen*, to puddle; cf. Ir. and Gael. *plod*, a pool.] A small pool of water or other liquid; clay or earth tempered with water and thoroughly compacted so as to be impervious to water.—v.t.—*puddled, puddling*. To make turbid or muddy; to stir up the mud or sediment in; to render watertight by means of puddle; to mix, as earth or clay, into a compact paste; to convert, as pig iron, into wrought iron by the process of puddling.—**pud·dler**, n.

pud·dling, pụd'ling, n. The operation of working plastic clay behind piling in a cofferdam or in other situations, to resist the penetration of water; the clay thus used; the process by which cast iron is converted into malleable iron, consisting in working it in a special furnace, hammering, and rolling.—**pud·dling fur·nace**, a kind of reverberatory furnace for puddling iron; also **hearth**.

pu·den·cy, pūd'en·sē, n. [L. *pudens, pudentis*; ppr. of *pudere*, to be ashamed (seen also in *impudent*).] Modesty; shamefacedness.

pu·den·dum, pū·den'dum, n. pl. **pu·den·da**, pū·den'da. [L., neut. of *pudendus*, 'that one should be ashamed of,' gerundive of *pudere*, feel shame.] Usu. pl., anat. the external genital organs, esp. those of the female.—**pu·den·dal**, a.

pudg·y, puj'ē, a.—*pudgier, pudgiest.* [Also *podgy*, prob. akin to *pod*, *pad*.] Fat and short; thick; fleshy. Also *podgy*.—**pudg·i·ness**, n.

pueb·lo, pweb'lō, Sp. pwe'bla, n. pl. **pueb·los**. [Sp., people, town, village, < L. *populus*, E. *people*.] A village of certain Indians, built of adobe or stone in the form of a communal house or group of houses, esp. in New Mexico and Arizona; (cap.) a member of one of various tribes in Arizona, New Mexico, and Mexico, pweb'lō. In Spanish America, a town or village; in the Philippine Islands, a town or a township, pweb'lō, Sp. pwe'bla.

pu·er·ile, pū'ẽr·il, pū'e·rīl", pūr'il, pūr'il, a. [L. *puerilis*, < *puer*, child, boy.] Of or pertaining to a child; childish or juvenile; childishly foolish or trivial.—**pu·er·ile·ly**, adv.—**pu·er·il·i·ty**, pū'e·ril'i·tē, n.

pu·er·il·ism, pū'ẽr·i·liz"um, pūr'i·liz"·um, n. Psychiatry, immature, childish behavior by an adult, indicating an abnormal mental condition.

pu·er·per·al, pū·ụr'pẽr·al, a. [L. *puerpera*, a lying-in-woman—*puer*, a boy, and *pario*, to bear.] Pertaining to childbirth.

pu·er·pe·ri·um, pū"ẽr·pẽr'ē·um, n. [L.] Obstet. the state of a woman at and immediately following childbirth.

puff, puf, v.i. [M.E. *puffen*, puff, blow; of imit. origin.] To blow with short, quick blasts, as the wind; breathe quick and hard, as after violent exertion; to go or move with puffing; as, to *puff* up the stairs; to emit puffs or whiffs of vapor or smoke; to smoke a cigarette, cigar, or pipe with puffs; to become inflated or distended, usu. followed by *up*.—v.t. To send forth, as air or vapor, in short, quick blasts; to drive or impel with a short, quick blast; to smoke, as a cigarette; to inflate or distend with breath or air; to inflate with pride or vanity, often followed by *up*; elate; to give exaggerated praise to; to advertise with undue commendation; to arrange in puffs, as the hair.

puff, puf, n. A short, quick blast, as of wind or breath; an abrupt emission of air, vapor, or the like; the sound of an emission of air; a small quantity of vapor or smoke emitted at one blast; an inflated or distended part of a thing; a swelling; a protuberance; a form of light pastry with a filling of cream, jam, or the like; a loose cylindrical roll of hair; a portion of material gathered and held down at the edges but left full in the middle, as in a garment; a quilted bed cover, filled with wool, cotton, or down; a commendation, esp. an exaggerated one, as of a book or actor's performance; powder puff; puffball.—**puff·i·ness**, n.—**puff·y**, puf'ē, a.—**puffier, puffiest**.

puff ad·der, n. A large, venomous African viper, *Bitis arietans*, which puffs up its body when irritated.

puff·ball, puf'bạl", n. A usu. spherical fungus, esp. of the genus *Lycoperdon*, which bears spores inside a tough outer coat and when ripe discharges these brown spores in smokelike masses. Also **puff**.

puff·er, puf'ẽr, n. One who or that which puffs; any of various fishes capable of inflating their bodies, as a globefish.

puff·er·y, puf'e·rē, n. pl. **puff·er·ies**. Exaggerated or excessive praise; publicity characterized by such exaggerated praise.

puf·fin, puf'in, n. [In allusion to its puffed-out beak.] Any of several ducklike sea birds of the genera *Lunda* and *Fratercula*, esp. *F. arctica*, of the N. Atlantic, being stubby, short-necked, and with a conspicuous triangular red bill. Also **sea par·rot**.

puff paste, n. A dough which is used to make rich, light, flaky pastry, as for tarts or pies.

pug, pug, n. [Var. of *puck*.] One of a breed of dogs resembling a small bulldog, with short smooth hair, a wrinkled face, and a curled tail; a pug nose.

pug, pug, v.t.—*pugged, pugging*. [Origin uncertain: cf. *poke*.] To knead, as clay, with water to make it plastic, as in brickmaking; to stop or fill in with clay or the like; to pack or cover with mortar, esp. to deaden sound.—n. Pugged or plastic clay or the like.

pug, pug, n. Slang, pugilist.

pug, pug, n. [Hind. *pag*.] Anglo-Ind. a footprint of an animal.—v.t.—*pugged, pugging*. To track, as game, by footprints.

pu·gil·ism, pū'ji·liz"um, n. [< L. *pugil*, a pugilist; same stem as *pugnus*, a fist, *pugna*, a fight.] The practice of boxing or fighting with the fists.—**pu·gil·ist**, pū'ji·list, n.—**pu·gil·is·tic**, pū"ji·lis'tik, a.

pug·na·cious, pug·nā'shus, a. [L. *pugnax, pugnacis*, < *pugna*, a fight, < stem of *pugnus*, a fist; akin *impugn, oppugn, repugnant*, etc.] Disposed or inclined to fighting; belligerent; quarrelsome.—**pug·na·cious·ly**, adv.—**pug·na·cious·ness**, **pug·nac·i·ty**, pug·nas'i·tē, n.

pug nose, n. A short, somewhat wide nose turning up at the tip.—**pug-nosed**, pug'nōzd", a.

pug·ree, **pug·gree**, pug'rē, n. [Hind. *pagri*, a turban.] Ind. A piece of muslin cloth wound round a hat or helmet to ward off the rays of the sun; a turban. Also **pug·a·ree**, **pug·ga·ree**, pug'a·rē.

puis·ne, pū'nē, a. [O.Fr. *puisné*, < *puis*, L. *post*, after, and *né*, L. *natus*, born. Puny is the same word.] Law, younger or inferior in rank; as, a *puisne* judge.—n.

pu·is·sance, pū'i·sans, pū·is'ans, pwis'ans, n. Power; strength; might.—**pu·is·sant**, pū'i·sant, pū·is'ant, pwis'ant, a.—**pu·is·sant·ly**, adv.

puke, pūk, v.i., v.t.—*puked, puking*. [Akin G. *spucken*, to spit, E. *spew*.] To vomit; to retch.

puk·ka, puk'a, a. [Hind. *pakkā*, ripe.] Anglo-Ind. Substantial; genuine; good or superior. Also *pucka*.

pul·chri·tude, pul'kri·tōd", pul'kri·tūd", n. [L. *pulchritudo*, < *pulcher*, beautiful.] Beauty; grace; comeliness.—**pul·chri·tu·di·nous**, pul"kri·tōd'i·nus, pul"kri·tūd'i·nus, a.

pule, pūl, v.i.—*puled, puling*. [Fr. *piauler*, to make the cry represented by the syllable *piau*, to pule; an imit. word; cf. Fr. *miauler*, to mewl, to mew.] To cry, as a complaining child; to whimper or whine.—**pul·er**, n.—**pul·ing**, pū'ling, a.

pull, pụl, v.t. [O.E. *pullian*, pull, pluck: cf. M.L.G. *pulen*, strip of husks, pick.] To draw or tug at with force; as, to *pull* a person's hair; draw or haul toward oneself or itself, or in a particular direction, or into a particular position; as, to *pull* a trigger, to *pull* a sled up a hill, to *pull* one's hat down over one's eyes; draw, rend, or tear; as, *pull* it to pieces; to draw or pluck away from a place of growth or attachment; as, to *pull* a tooth; to strain, as a muscle or ligament; *colloq.* to draw out for use, as a knife or a pistol. To propel by rowing, as a boat; to receive or attract, as votes; *print.* to take, as an impression or proof, from type or a plate; *horse racing*, to hold in or check, as a horse, esp. so as to keep it from winning; *boxing*, to hold back or check, as a punch; *cricket*, to hit, as the ball pitched on the wicket or on the off side, to the on side; *golf*, to play, as the ball, with a curve to the left or, if a left-handed player, to the right.—v.i. To give a pull; to tug; to exert strength in drawing; to inhale; to row.—**pull a face**, to grimace.—**pull a·part**, to separate forcefully; to break into pieces; to examine critically.—**pull down**, to destroy; *slang*, to be paid or to receive, as wages.—**pull for**, to actively support; encourage.—**pull off**, *slang*, to put through successfully.—**pull one·self to·geth·er**, to quiet down; to recover from a momentary emotional disturbance.—**pull one's leg**, to take advantage of someone; to tease, esp. by humorous and repeated deceit; to kid someone.—**pull out**, to withdraw; to depart; *aeron.* to recover from a dive and resume horizontal flight; to break off or discontinue a landing approach.—**pull out**, n.—**pull strings**, to seek out and accept the advantage of another's power or influence in order to advance oneself.—**pull through**, to get through a difficult or dangerous situation or condition; to recover from surgery or a serious illness.—**pull to·geth·er**, to cooperate; to work together in harmony.—**pull up**, to halt; to move by pulling toward one.—**pull·er**, n.

pull, pụl, n. An act of pulling or drawing; a tug; the action of pulling or drawing; force expended in pulling; pulling power; specif. a pulling at an oar, or a spell at rowing; a pulling of the ball in baseball or golf; a drawing of cigar smoke or a draft of liquid into the mouth; *slang*, influence, as with persons able to grant favors; *print.* an impression or proof pulled from type or an engraving; a part or thing to be pulled, as a handle or the like; an instrument or device for pulling something.

pull·back, pụl'bak", n. The process of pulling back or withdrawing; something used for holding or drawing back such an object as an article of clothing or window draperies.

pul·let, pụl'it, n. [Fr. *poulette*, dim. of *poule*,

a hen, L.L. *pulla*, < L. *pullus*, a young animal.] A young hen or chicken.

pul·ley, pu̇l′ē, *n.* pl. **pul·leys**, pu̇l′ēz. [O.E. *poleyne*, a pulley, < Fr. *poulain*, a foal or colt, a slide for letting down casks into a cellar, a pulley rope, < L.L. *pullanus*, < L. *pullus*, the young of an animal. The names of the horse, ass, goat, and other animals are given in different languages to various mechanical contrivances.] *Mech.* one of the simple machines or mechanical powers used for raising weights and consisting of a small wheel which moves around an axle, and has a groove cut in its circumference in which a cord runs; a wheel placed upon a shaft which either transmits power to or from the different parts of machinery or changes the direction of motion by means of a belt or band which runs over it.

Pull·man, pu̇l′man, *n. Rail.* a luxury chair car or sleeping car with accommodations: orig. designed by G. M. *Pullman*, 1831–1897.

pul·lo·rum dis·ease, pa·lōr′um di·zēz′, pa·lar′um, *n. Veter. pathol.* a contagious, often fatal disease of fowl and other bird types, usu. transmitted by bacteria in the egg.

pull·o·ver, pu̇l′ō″vėr, *n.* Clothing, as a shirt or sweater, which is put on by pulling it over the head.—*a.* Pertaining to clothing which is so constructed.

pul·lu·late, pul′ya·lāt″, *v.i.—pullulated, pullulating.* [L. *pullulatus*, pp. of *pullulare*, < *pullulus*, sprout, orig. young animal, dim. of *pullus*.] To send forth sprouts or buds; germinate; to breed or multiply rapidly; to be produced as offspring; to spring up abundantly; teem or swarm.—**pul·lu·la·tion**, *n.*

pul·mo·nar·y, pul′mo·ner″ē, pu̇l′mo·ner″ē, *a.* [L. *pulmonarius*, < *pulmo*(n-), lung, akin to Gr. *pleúmōn*, later *pneúmōn*, lung.] Of or pertaining to the lungs; of the nature of a lung, or lunglike; affecting the lungs; having lungs or lunglike organs.

pul·mo·nar·y ar·ter·y, *n.* An artery conveying venous blood directly from the heart to the lungs.

pul·mo·nar·y vein, *n.* Any of four veins conveying arterial blood directly from the lungs to the heart.

pul·mo·nate, pul′mo·nāt″, pul′mo·nit, *a.* [N.L. *pulmonatus*, < L. *pulmo*(n-), lung.] Having lungs or lunglike organs; belonging to the *Pulmonata*, an order or group of gastropod mollusks usually breathing by means of a lunglike sac, and including most of the terrestrial snails, and the slugs and certain aquatic snails.—*n.* A pulmonate gastropod.

pul·mon·ic, pul·mon′ik, *a.* Pulmonary; pneumonic.

Pul·mo·tor, pul′mō″tėr, pu̇l′mō″tėr, *n.* [L. *pulmo*, lung, and *motor*, motor.] A mechanical device for inducing artificial respiration where respiration has ceased entirely or in part through asphyxiation or drowning. (Trademark.)

pulp, pulp, *n.* [Fr. *pulpe*, < L. *pulpa*, fleshy substance, pulp.] Soft undissolved animal or vegetable matter; the soft, succulent part of fruit; spongy condition of the pith of some plant stems; material reduced to a soft uniform mass for making paper; *dentistry*, the soft vascular substance in the interior of a tooth. A magazine or other publication, often containing lurid, sensational material, and printed on coarse, cheap paper; *min.* ground or pulverized ore combined with water.—*v.t.* To make into pulp; to deprive of the pulp.—*v.i.* To become pulp.—**pulp·i·ness**, *n.*—**pulp·y**, pul′pē, *a.*—**pulp·i·er**, **pulpiest**.

pul·pit, pu̇l′pit, pul′pit, *n.* [L. *pulpitum*, stage, platform, M.L. pulpit in a church.] A platform or raised structure in a church, from which the clergyman delivers the sermon or conducts the service.—**the pul·pit**, preachers collectively; the work performed by preachers.

pulp·wood, pulp′wu̇d″, *n.* The soft wood of spruce, pine, and various other trees, used to make paper.

pul·que, pu̇l′kē, *Sp.* pōl′ke, *n.* [Sp.] A winelike beverage made by fermenting the juice of the maguey and other species of the agave.

pul·sant, pul′sant, *a.* Pulsating.

pul·sate, pul′sāt, *v.i.—pulsated, pulsating.* [L. *pulsare, pulsatum*, to beat, < *pellere, pulsum*, to drive.] To beat or throb rhythmically; to vibrate.

pul·sa·tile, pul′sa·til, pul′sa·tīl″, *a.* [L. *pulsatilis*.] Throbbing, as the heart; vibrating or sounding, as a percussion instrument.

pul·sa·tion, pul·sā′shan, *n.* The process of beating or throbbing; a beat of the pulse; a throb.

pul·sa·tor, pul′sā·tėr, pul·sā′tėr, *n.* That which pulsates, beats, or throbs. *Mach.* a device that operates by pulsation, as a pump; a machine that separates mined diamonds from adhering earth particles.—**pul·sa·to·ry**, pul′sa·tōr″ē, pul′sa·tar″ē, *a.*

pulse, puls, *n.* [Fr. *pouls*, L. *pulsus*, a beating, < *pello, pulsum*.] The beating or throbbing of the arteries caused by contractions of the heart; the pulsation of the radial artery at the wrist; a pulsation; any rhythmic, regular throbbing or beat; vibration; public opinion; a poll or other indication of the sentiments of the citizenry or of a group.—*v.i.—pulsed, pulsing.* To beat; vibrate; throb.

pulse, puls, *n.* [< L. *puls*, pottage.] *Agric.* leguminous plants or their seeds.

pulse·jet en·gine, *n. Aeron.* A type of compressorless jet aircraft engine in which combustion takes place intermittently, producing thrust by a series of explosions commonly occurring at the approximate resonance frequency of the engine; also **pulse-jet**, puls′jet″.

pul·sim·e·ter, pul·sim′i·tėr, *n.* [L. *pulsus*, and Gr. *metron*, a measure.] *Med.* an instrument for measuring the strength and rate of the pulse.

pul·sive, pul′siv, *a.* Propulsive.

pul·som·e·ter, pul·som′i·tėr, *n.* A type of pump which acts by the condensation of steam sent into a reservoir, the water rushing up into the vacuum formed by the condensation; also *vacuum pump.* A pulsimeter.

pul·ver·a·ble, pul′vėr·a·bl, *a.* [L. *pulverare*, reduce to dust, < *pulvis* (*pulver-*), dust.] Capable of being reduced to dust or powder; pulverizable.

pul·ver·ize, pul′ve·rīz″, *v.t.—pulverized, pulverizing.* [Fr. *pulvériser*, < L. *pulvis, pulveris*, powder.] To reduce to fine powder, as by beating, grinding, or the like; to crush or demolish.—*v.i.* To become reduced to fine powder.—**pul·ver·iz·a·ble**, *a.*—**pul·ver·i·za·tion**, *n.*—**pul·ver·iz·er**, *n.*

pul·ver·u·lent, pul·ver′ya·lent, pul·ver′a·lent, *a.* Consisting of fine powder; reducible to powder; powdery; dusty.

pul·vil·lus, pul·vil′us, *n.* pl. **pul·vil·li**, pul·vil′ī. [L., little cushions, < *pulvinus*, a cushion.] A cushionlike mass on the feet of certain insects.

pul·vi·nar, pul·vī′nėr, *n.* pl. **pul·vi·nar·i·a**, pul″vi·när′ē·a. A special couch in ancient Rome held in readiness for the gods; a comfortable seat at the circus. *Arch.* a convex form ending in a volute on an Ionic building; also *pulvinus.*—*a.* Like a cushion; pertaining to a pulvinus.

pul·vi·nate, pul′vi·nāt″, *a. Bot.* Cushionshaped; possessing a pulvinus. Also *pulvinar, pulvinated.*—**pul·vi·nate·ly**, *adv.*

pul·vi·nus, pul·vī′nus, *n.* pl. **pul·vi·ni**, pul·vī′nī. *Bot.* a minute gland at the base of the petiole of a leaf or leaflet, responsive to vibrations and heat and causing changes in movements, as in the sensitive plant, *Mimosa; arch.* pulvinar.

pu·ma, pū′ma, *n.* pl. **pu·mas**, **pu·ma**. [Peruvian.] A large slender tawny cat, *Felis concolor*, native to N. and S. America, having a small head, a long tail tipped with black, and spotted young. Also *cougar, mountain lion, panther, catamount.*

pum·ice, pum′is, *n.* [L. *pumex, pumicis*, orig. *spumex*, < *spuma*, foam, < *spuo*, to spit.] A porous, stony substance from volcanoes, lighter than water, used for polishing and smoothing ivory, wood, marble, metals, or glass.—*v.t.—pumiced, pumicing.* To smooth or polish with pumice. Also **pum·ice·stone**, **pum·ic·ite**.—**pu·mi·ceous**, pū·mish′us, *a.*

pum·mel, pum′el, *v.t.—pummeled, pummeling, pummelled, pummelling.* To pommel.—*n.* A pommel.

pump, pump, *n.* [Fr. *pompe*, a pump, < D. and L.G. *pomp*, G. *pumpe*, a pump; origin unknown.] An instrument or machine, consisting of an arrangement of a piston, cylinder, and valves, employed for raising water or other liquid to a higher level, for moving liquids or gases through a pipe or pipeline, or for exhausting or compressing air or other gases.—*v.i.* To work a pump; to raise water with a pump, as from a well; to move up and down like a pump handle.—*v.t.* To raise with a pump; to free from water or other fluid by a pump, often with *out*; as, to *pump out* a ship; to inflate with a pump, usu. with *up*; to put artful questions to for the purpose of extracting information; to discharge, eject, drive, or force by means of a pump or as though by a pump.—**pump·a·ble**, *a.*—**pump·er**, *n.*—**pump·less**, *a.*—**pump·like**, *a.*

pump, pump, *n.* [Prob. from being worn for *pomp* or ornament by persons in full dress.] A woman's shoe, low-cut and without fastenings, holding to the foot chiefly at toe and heel; a similarly cut type of dress shoe for men.

pum·per·nick·el, pum′pėr·nik″el, *n.* [G.] A dark, coarse bread made from unsifted rye.

pump·kin, pump′kin, pung′kin, *n.* [Altered form of *pumpion*.] A long, trailing vine, *Cucurbita pepo*, in the gourd family, widely cultivated in temperate regions; the large orange furrowed fruit of this plant with a wide rind, used in pies and for cattle food; loosely, any of several related plants.

pump·kin·seed, pump′kin·sēd″, pung′-kin·sēd″, *n.* The seed of the pumpkin; any of various fresh-water sunfishes, esp. *Lepomis gibbosus* of eastern North America.

pump prim·ing, *n.* A device for, or the act of, priming a pump; *econ.* any action involving government expenditures to encourage business activity.

pun, pun, *n.* [Origin obscure.] The use of a word in such a manner as to bring out different meanings or applications, or the use of words alike or nearly alike in sound but different in meaning, often with humorous intent; a play on a word or words.—*v.i.—punned, punning.* To make puns; to play on words.

pu·na, pö′nä, *n.* [Peruvian.] A high, arid plateau, as in the Peruvian Andes.

punch, punch, *v.t.* [Appar. < *puncheon*.] To pierce or perforate with a pointed or sharp instrument; to cut or stamp with a punch; to force or drive with a punch; make, as a hole, with a pointed or other instrument; to give a sharp thrust or blow to, esp. with the fist; to drive, as cattle; to poke or prod, as with a stick.—*v.i.—n.* A tool or apparatus for piercing, perforating, or stamping materials, impressing a design, forcing nails beneath a surface, driving bolts out of holes, and the like; a thrusting blow, esp. with the fist; *colloq.* a vigorous, telling effect or force; as, an editorial with a *punch*; vigorous effectiveness; vitality; as, a story or a play that lacks *punch*.—**punch·a·ble**, *a.*—**punch·er**, *n.*

punch, punch, *n.* [< Hind. *păc*, Skt. *pañca*, five.] A beverage of India, originally composed of five ingredients: arrack, tea, sugar, water, and lemon juice; in the U.S., a cold beverage made from spirits and water, and sweetened and flavored with sugar and fruit juice, or a similar beverage of combined juices and without spirits.

Punch-and-Ju·dy show, punch'an·jō'dē·shō', *n.* A puppet show characterized by stylized plots and ludicrous fighting involving the humpbacked Punch and his wife, Judy.

punch·board, punch'bōrd", punch'bặrd", *n.* A gambling device, consisting of a small board filled with holes, each of which contains a tightly rolled, printed slip of paper that the player punches out in the hope of obtaining a winning name or number and prize.

punch bowl, *n.* A large bowl in which punch is served.

punch card, *n.* A card containing data which is recorded and retrievable by electronic calculators or computers according to the position of holes punched in the cards.

punch-drunk, punch'drungk", *a.* Having cerebral injury resulting from repeated head blows, as received while boxing, and showing grogginess and slowness in speech and muscular movement. *Colloq.* confused; groggy.

pun·cheon, pun'chon, *n.* [Fr. *poinçon*, a bodkin, a punch (the tool).] A perforating or stamping tool; a punch; *carp.* a short upright piece of timber in framing.

pun·cheon, pun'chon, *n.* A varying measure of liquids, or a cask containing from 84 to 120 gallons.

punch in, *v.i.* To punch the time of arrival, as of an employee, on a time clock.—**punch out**, *v.i.*

pun·chi·nel·lo, pun"chi·nel'ō, *n.* pl. **pun·chi·nel·los**, **pun·chi·nel·loes**. [It. *Pulcinella*, prob. orig. dim., < *pulcino*, chicken, < L. *pullus*.] The chief character in a puppet show of Italian origin, being the prototype of Punch of the Punch-and-Judy show; a grotesque or absurd person or thing.

punch·ing bag, *n.* An inflated or stuffed leather bag, which is usu. suspended, punched with the fists as an exercise.

punch line, *n.* The last part, phrase, or sentence of an anecdote that produces the humor or contains the major point.

punch press, *n.* A machine for forming metal by pressure cutting or shaping with dies.

punch·y, pun'chē, *a.*—*punchier, punchiest. Colloq.* punch-drunk.

punc·tate, pungk'tāt, *a.* [< L. *punctum*, a point.] Ending in a point; pointed; *bot.* marked with dots variously scattered over the surface, as leaves and seeds. Also **punc·tat·ed.**—**punc·ta·tion**, pungk·tā'shan, *n.*

punc·til·i·o, pungk·til'ē·ō", *n.* pl. **punc·til·i·os.** [< Sp. *puntillo* or It. *puntiglio*, a small point, a punctilio, < L. *punctum*, a point.] A nice point in conduct, ceremony, or proceeding; particularity or exactness in forms, as in etiquette.

punc·til·i·ous, pungk·til'ē·us, *a.* Attentive to punctilios; very formal or exact in behavior.—**punc·til·i·ous·ly**, *adv.*—**punc·til·i·ous·ness**, *n.*

punc·tu·al, pungk'chö·al, *a.* [Fr. *ponctuel*, < L. *punctum*, a point, < *pungo, punctum*, to prick.] Exact to the time agreed on; made at the exact time; as,

punctual payment.—**punc·tu·al·i·ty**, pungk"chö·al'i·tē, *n.*—**punc·tu·al·ly**, *adv.*—**punc·tu·al·ness**, *n.*

punc·tu·ate, pungk'chö·āt", *v.t.*—*punctuated, punctuating.* [M.L. *punctuatus*, pp. of *punctuare*, < L. *punctus*, a point.] To mark or divide with punctuation marks, as a sentence, in order to make the meaning clear; to interrupt at intervals; as, to *punctuate* a speech by cheers; to give point or emphasis to, as: He *punctuated* his remarks with gestures.—*v.i.* To insert or use marks of punctuation.

punc·tu·a·tion, pungk"chö·ā'shan, *n.* [M.L. *punctuatio(n-).*] The act of punctuating; esp., the practice, art, or system of inserting marks or points in writing or printing in order to make the meaning clear; the punctuating of written or printed matter with punctuation marks, as commas, semicolons, colons, periods, etc.—**punc·tu·a·tive**, *a.*—**punc·tu·a·tor**, *n.*

punc·tu·a·tion mark, *n.* Any of the conventional symbols which organize written language and clarify relations between words.

punc·tu·late, pungk'chö·lāt', *a.* [N.L. *punctulatus*, < L. *punctulum*, dim. of *punctum*, E. *point.*] Marked or studded with minute points, dots, or depressions; minutely punctate. Also **punc·tu·lat·ed.**—**punc·tu·la·tion**, *n.*

punc·ture, pungk'chẽr, *n.* [L. *punctura*, < *pungere*, prick, pierce.] The action or an act of pricking or perforating, as with a pointed instrument or object; a mark or hole so made; *zool.* a small pointlike depression.—*v.t.*—*punctured, puncturing.* To prick, pierce, or perforate; as, to *puncture* the skin with a pin; to make, as a hole, by pricking or perforating; to deflate, as a reputation.—*v.i.* To be pricked or punctured.—**punc·tur·a·ble**, *a.*

pun·dit, pun'dit, *n.* [Skt. *pandita*, a learned man.] A learned Brahmin, esp. one versed in the Sanskrit language and in the science, laws, and religion of India; one of great authority and learning; one who speaks or writes in an authoritative manner.

pung, pung, *n.* [Of N. Amer. Ind. origin, and related to *toboggan.*] *New Eng.* a rude, one-horse sleigh consisting of an oblong box on runners; any sleigh with a boxlike body.

pun·gent, pun'jent, *a.* [L. *pungens*, ppr. of *pungo, punctum*, to prick.] Sharply affecting the sense of smell and taste; biting; affecting the mind in a sharp or piercing manner; caustic; poignant; having a sharp, stiff point, as a pine needle.—**pun·gen·cy**, *n.*—**pun·gent·ly**, *a.*

Pu·nic, pū'nik, *a.* [L. *punicus*, Carthaginian, < *Puni, Pœni*, the Carthaginians.] Pertaining to the Carthaginians; faithless, deceitful.—*n.* The language of the Carthaginians, a form of Phoenician.

pun·ish, pun'ish, *v.t.* [O.Fr. Fr. *punir* (*puniss-*), < L. *punire* (pp. *punitus*), earlier *pœnire*, < *pœna*, penalty, punishment.] To inflict a penalty on, as for an offense, real or imputed; as, to *punish* mutineers, to *punish* a disobedient child; subject to pain, loss, confinement, death, or other penalty for some transgression or fault; to inflict a penalty for an offense or fault; as, to *punish* theft; to handle severely or roughly, as in a fight or struggle; put to painful exertion, as a horse in racing or hard driving.—*v.i.* To inflict punishment.—**pun·ish·a·bil·i·ty**, *n.*—**pun·ish·a·ble**, pun'i·sha·bl, *a.* Liable to or deserving of punishment.—**pun·ish·er**, *n.*

pun·ish·ment, pun'ish·ment, *n.* The act of punishing; pain or penalty inflicted on a person for a crime or offense; a penalty imposed in the enforcement of law; general ill-treatment.

pu·ni·tive, pū'ni·tiv, *a.* Pertaining to, involving, or inflicting punishment.—**pun·i·tive·ly**, *adv.*—**pun·i·tive·ness**, *n.*

pu·ni·tive dam·ag·es, *n. Law*, damages beyond normally appropriate compensation, awarded a plaintiff as a punishment to the defendant.

punk, pungk, *n.* [Origin unknown.] *Slang.* A person or thing of no importance; a hoodlum of limited experience or power; a young, naive boy; a homosexual's boy partner.—*a. Slang.* Poor or bad in quality; wretched; characterized by poor health.

punk, pungk, *n.* [Cf. *spunk.*] A preparation, usu. in stick shape, that will smolder: used for lighting fireworks or repelling insects; decayed wood used as tinder.

pun·kah, pun·ka, pung'ka, *n.* [Hindi.] A large fan of canvas or palmyra leaf slung from the ceilings of rooms and operated by a servant or a machine.

punk·ie, punk·y, pung'kē, *n.* pl. **punk·ies.** [< N. Amer. Ind.] Any of certain minute blood-sucking midges, common in wooded regions and on sandy beaches of the northeastern U.S.

pun·ster, pun'stẽr, *n.* One skilled in or fond of making puns.

punt, punt, *v.i.* [Fr. *punter*, It. *puntare*, < L. *punctum*, a point.] *Football*, to drop and kick the ball before it touches the ground.—*v.t.*—*n. Football*, a kick made in this way.—**punt·er**, *n.*

punt, punt, *n.* [A punt, a pontoon, < *pons, pontis*, a bridge.] A square flat-bottomed boat without masts, having a pole for propelling, and used for fishing and conveying goods.—*v.t.* To propel, as a boat, by pushing with a pole against the bed of the water; to convey in a punt.—*v.i.* To travel in a punt.—**punt·er**, *n.*

punt, punt, *v.i. Brit.* to gamble for big stakes, as against a bank at roulette.

pun·ty, pun'tē, *n.* pl. **pun·ties.** [Fr. *pontis, pontil.*] An iron rod used in glassmaking for handling the hot glass. Also **pon·til**, pon'til.

pu·ny, pū'nē, *a.*—*punier, puniest.* [< Fr. *puisné.*] Small and weak; underdeveloped in size and strength; petty or insignificant.—**pu·ni·ness**, *n.*

pup, pup, *n.* [Abbr. of *puppy.*] A puppy; a young seal.—*v.i.*—*pupped, pupping.* To give birth to pups.

pu·pa, pū'pa, *n.* pl. **pu·pae**, pū'pē. [N.L. use of L. *pupa*, girl, doll, puppet.] *Entom.* The intermediate and usu. quiescent form of an insect occurring between the larva and adult stages; an insect in this form.—**pu·pal**, *a.*

pu·pate, pū'pāt, *v.i.*—*pupated, pupating.* To become a pupa.—**pu·pa·tion**, *n.*

pu·pil, pū'pil, *n.* [Fr. *pupille*, L. *pupilla*, a little girl, the apple of the eye, dim. of *pupa*, a girl; also *pupillus*, an orphan boy, dim. of *pupus*, a boy.] A young person under the care of an instructor or tutor; a student; a disciple. *Civil law*, a young person under the care of a guardian; a ward.

pu·pil, pū'pil, *n. Anat.* the round, contractile aperture in the middle of the eye's iris through which the rays of light pass to the retina.—**pu·pil·ar**, *a.*—**pu·pil·lar·y**, pū'pi·ler"ē, *a.*

pu·pil·age, pu·pil·lage, pū'pil·lij, *n.* The period or state of being a pupil.

pu·pip·a·rous, pū·pip'ẽr·us, *a.* [N.L. *pupa*, pupa, and L. *parere*, bring forth.] Bringing forth larvae which are ready to become pupae, as horse ticks, sheep ticks.

pup·pet, pup'it, *n.* [O.E. *popet*, O.Fr. *poupette*, dim. < L. *pupa*, a doll, a puppet.] A small figure in a human or animal form, moved by hand or by cords or rods in a dramatic presentation; a marionette; *fig.* a person who is a mere tool of another.—**pup·pet·eer**, pup"i·tēr', *n.* One who operates puppets.

pup·pet·ry, pup′i·trē, *n. pl.* **pup·pet·ries.** The art of presenting puppet shows; artificial action, like that of puppets; mummery; mere show; puppets collectively; a set of puppets.

pup·py, pup′ē, *n. pl.* **pup·pies.** [Fr. *poupée,* a doll, a puppet, L. *pupa.*] A young animal, esp. a young dog; a conceited and insignificant young man.—**pup·py·ish,** *a.*

pup·py love, *n.* Adolescent love. Also *calf love.*

pup tent, *n.* Shelter tent.

pur·blind, pur′blīnd″, *a.* [From *pure* in sense of altogether, quite, and *blind.*] Dim-sighted; almost blind; deficient or lacking in understanding or insight.—**pur·blind·ly,** *adv.*—**pur·blind·ness,** *n.*

pur·chas·a·ble, pur′cha·sa·bl, *a.* Capable of being purchased or bought; that may be won over by money or other consideration; bribable; venal.—**pur·chas·a·bil·i·ty,** *n.*

pur·chase, pur′chas, *v.t.*—*purchased, purchasing.* [Fr. *pourchasser,* O.Fr. *purchacer,* to pursue, to get—*pour, pur,* for, and *chasser,* to chase.] To gain or acquire; to obtain by payment of money or its equivalent; to buy; to obtain by labor, danger, or other means.—*n.* Acquisition in general; the acquisition of anything by rendering an equivalent in money; buying; that which is purchased; any mechanical advantage, as is gained by a lever, used in the raising or removing of heavy bodies.—**pur·chas·er,** *n.*

pur·dah, pur′da, *n.* [Hind. and Pers. *parda.*] *India,* a curtain, esp. one serving to screen women secluded from the sight of men or strangers; the system of such seclusion for women. Also **pur·da, par·dah.**

pure, pūr, *a.*—*purer, purest.* [Fr. *pur,* < L. *purus,* pure, whence *purgo,* E. to *purge;* from root seen also in Skt. *pû,* to purify; and in *fire.*] Free from all extraneous matter, esp. from anything that impairs or pollutes; free from anything that defiles or contaminates; innocent; spotless; chaste; stainless; genuine; ceremonially clean; unpolluted; mere; sheer; absolute; as, *pure* agony; theoretical or abstract.—**pure·ness,** *n.*

pure·bred, pūr′bred′, *a.* Relating or pertaining to animals bred from a strain of generations of pure, unmixed ancestry.—pūr′bred″, *n.* An animal of such breeding.

pu·rée, pū·rā′, pū·rē′, pūr′ā, Fr. pY·RĀ′, *n.* Meat, fish, or vegetables boiled into a pulp and passed through a sieve; a soup having a purée'd base.—*v.t.*—*puréed, puréeing.*

pure·ly, pūr′lē, *adv.* In a pure manner; without adulteration or admixture; simply; merely; entirely; completely; exclusively; cleanly; innocently; chastely.

pur·fle, pur′fl, *v.t.*—*purfled, purfling.* [O.Fr. *pourfiler*—*pour,* L. *pro,* for, before, and *fil,* L. *filum,* a thread.] To decorate with a wrought or flowered border.—*n.* An inlaid decorative border, as on a guitar. Also **pur·fling.**

pur·ga·tion, pur·gā′shan, *n.* [L. *purgatio.*] The act of purging; purification.

pur·ga·tive, pur′ga·tiv, *a.* [Fr. *purgatif.*] Cathartic; purging; cleansing; bringing about a bowel movement.—*n.* A medicine that evacuates the bowels; a cathartic.

pur·ga·to·ry, pur′ga·tōr″ē, pur′ga·tar″ē, *n. pl.* **pur·ga·to·ries.** [L. *purgatorius.*] *Rom. Cath. Ch.* a place in which souls after death are purified from venial sins and suffer punishment for all sins not atoned for; *colloq.* any place or state of temporary suffering.—**pur·ga·to·ri·al,** pur″ga·tōr′ē·al, pur″ga·tar′ē·al, *a.*

purge, purj, *v.t.*—*purged, purging.* [L. *purgare,* to cleanse, < *purus,* clean, and *agere,* to do.] To cleanse or purify by carrying off whatever is impure, foreign, or superfluous; to remove or eliminate by cleansing, usu. followed by *out, away,* or *off;* to clear of moral defilement; to clear of accusation or the charge of a crime; to remove from a position of influence in a political party or nation, as persons considered harmful or disloyal; to evacuate the bowels by means of a cathartic.—*v.i.* To produce evacuations by a cathartic; to become purified or clean.—*n.* The act of purging; anything that purges; a cathartic medicine; the act of removing from a position of influence, often by assassination or execution, persons considered harmful or disloyal to the government in power.—**purg·er,** *n.*

pu·ri·fi·ca·tor, pūr′i·fi·kā″tēr, *n. Eccles.* the small rectangular piece of linen used by the priest at mass to cleanse the chalice, the paten, and his fingers.

pu·ri·fy, pūr′i·fī″, *v.t.*—*purified, purifying.* [Fr. *purifier,* < L. *purificare.*] To make pure or clear; to free from extraneous elements; to free from pollution ceremonially; to cleanse from whatever renders unclean and unfit for sacred services; to free from guilt or the defilement of sin.—*v.i.* To grow or become pure or clear.—**pu·ri·fi·ca·tion,** *n.*—**pu·rif·i·ca·to·ry,** pū·rif′i·ka·tōr″ē, pū·rif′i·ka·tar″ē, *a.*—**pu·ri·fi·er,** *n.*

Pu·rim, pūr′im, *Heb.* pö·Rēm′, *n.* [Heb. *pūrīm,* lots.] An annual spring festival among the Jews instituted to commemorate their preservation from the massacre with which they were threatened by the machinations of Haman.

pu·rine, pūr′ēn, pūr′in, *n.* [G. *purin,* < L. *purus,* pure, and N.L. *uricus,* uric.] *Chem.* a white crystalline compound, $C_5H_4N_4$, regarded as the parent substance of a group of compounds which includes uric acid, xanthine, caffeine, and theobromine; any of these compounds. Also **pu·rin,** pūr′in.

pur·ism, pūr′iz·um, *n.* Insistence on, and observance of, rigid purity in language; excessive nicety as to the use of words; *art,* a 20th century style of painting converting the natural appearance of objects to uncomplicated geometric forms.—**pur·ist,** *n.*—**pu·ris·tic,** pūr·is′tik, *a.*

pu·ri·tan, pūr′i·tan, *n.* [L.L. *puritas,* E. *purity.*] One who affects great purity or strictness of life and religious principles; (*cap.*) one of a class of Protestants that arose in the 16th century within the Church of England, demanding further reforms in doctrine and worship, with greater strictness in religious discipline.—*a.* Puritanical; (*cap.*) of or pertaining to the Puritans.

pu·ri·tan·i·cal, pūr″i·tan′i·kal, *a.* Of, pertaining to, or characteristic of puritans or the Puritans; having the character of a puritan; excessively strict, rigid, or austere. Also **pu·ri·tan·ic.**—**pu·ri·tan·i·cal·ly,** *adv.*

Pu·ri·tan·ism, pūr′i·ta·niz″um, *n.* The principles and practices of the Puritans. (*Sometimes l.c.*) strictness in matters of conduct or religion; puritanical austerity.

pu·ri·ty, pūr′i·tē, *n.* [L. *puritas.*] The condition of being pure; freedom from foreign matter; cleanness; freedom from anything underhanded or improper; innocence; chastity; freedom from improper use of words or phrases; degree of saturation or intensity, as of a color.

purl, purl, *v.t., v.i.* To invert, as a stitch, in knitting; to embroider, as a border of fabric.—*n.* An embroidered border; an inversion of the stitches in knitting; a thread of silver or gold wire for embroidering.

purl, purl, *v.i.* [Akin to Sw. *porla,* to purl; prob. from the sound; cf. *purr.*] To murmur, as a shallow stream flowing among stones; to flow with a gentle murmur; to ripple.—*n.* A ripple; an eddy; a murmuring sound, as of a shallow stream among stones.

pur·lieu, pur′lö, purl′ū, *n.* [< Norm. *purlieu, puraille,* O.Fr. *puralée,* perambulation—*< pur,* L. *per,* through, *alée,* a going. Both form and sense have been influenced by Fr. *lieu,* place.] A piece of land set apart from an ancient royal forest and returned to private ownership; a part lying adjacent; a haunt; a place where one may wander freely. *Pl.* the outer portion of any area; the environs.

pur·lin, pur′lin, *n.* [M.E. *purlyn, purlyon;* origin obscure.] A timber or piece laid horizontally on the principal rafters of a roof to support the common rafters. Also **pur·line,** pur′lin.

pur·loin, pēr·loin′, pur′loin, *v.t.* [O.Fr. *porloignier, purloignier,* < L. *prolongare,* to prolong.] To steal; to filch.—*v.i.* To practice theft.—**pur·loin·er,** *n.*

purl stitch, *n.* A reversal of the basic knitting stitch, producing a horizontal ribbing.

pur·ple, pur′pl, *n.* [Old form *purpre,* < L. *purpura,* purple, < Gr. *porphyra,* a kind of shellfish that yielded a purple dye. Akin *porphyry.*] A color that is a blend of red and blue in about equal proportions; raiment of this color formerly worn only by royalty and others of exalted rank; a position or rank that is exalted or regal; as, born to the *purple;* the office of a cardinal, or of a bishop.—*a.* Of a purple color; regal or imperial; of speech or writing that is highly ornate or overblown; as, *purple* prose; colored with profanity.—*v.t., v.i.*—*purpled, purpling.* To turn or to make purple.—**pur·plish,** pur′plish, *a.*

Pur·ple Heart, *n.* The badge of the Order of the Purple Heart, a decoration established by George Washington in 1782 and revived by the War Department in 1932, conferred on soldiers wounded in action.

pur·ple pas·sage, *n.* In poetry or prose, a highly stylized passage, generally florid in expression or feeling, that stands out from the ordinary or more commonplace work in which it appears. Also **pur·ple patch.**

pur·port, pur′pōrt, pur′part, *n.* [O.Fr. *purport,* < *pur,* Fr. *pour,* for, and *porter,* to bear.] Meaning; tenor; import, often as implied or professed rather than directly stated.—pēr·pōrt′, pēr·part′, pur′pōrt, pur′part, *v.t.* To convey, as a certain meaning; to signify; imply; to claim, esp. falsely.—**pur·port·ed,** *a.*—**pur·port·ed·ly,** *adv.*

pur·pose, pur′pos, *n.* [O.Fr. *pourpos,* Fr. *propos,* < L. *propositum,* < *propono*—*pro,* before, and *ponere, positum,* to place.] That which is set up as an objective to be reached or accomplished; the use for which something is intended, its reason for being; an end or aim; resolution; firm intention; a matter or subject being discussed.—*v.t.*—*purposed, purposing.* To intend; to resolve; to set as a goal or aim.—**on pur·pose,** with previous design; intentionally.—**to the pur·pose,** to the matter in question; to the point; as, to speak *to the purpose.*—**pur·pose·ful,** pur′pos·ful, *a.*—**pur·pose·ful·ly,** *adv.*—**pur·pose·ful·ness,** *n.*—**pur·pose·less,** *a.*

pur·pose·ly, pur′pos·lē, *adv.* By purpose or design; intentionally.

pur·pos·ive, pur′po·siv, *a.* Pertaining to, showing, or having purpose; adapted to or serving some useful function or end; firm; resolute.—**pur·pos·ive·ly,** *adv.*—**pur·pos·ive·ness,** *n.*

pur·pu·ra, pur′pū·ra, *n.* [N.L. use of L. *purpura,* E. *purple.*] *Pathol.* a disease characterized by purple or livid spots on the skin or mucous membrane, caused by the extravasation of blood.—**pur·pu·ric,** pu·pūr′ik, *a.*

purr, pur, *n.* [Imit. of sound.] The soft murmuring sound uttered by a cat when pleased.—*v.i.* To utter a soft murmuring sound.—*v.t.* To signify by or as by purring.

purse, purs, *n.* [O.E. *purs,* < M.L. *bursa,* bag, purse.] A small bag, pouch, or case for carrying money on the person; a woman's handbag for money and personal articles; a sum of money collected as a present or the like; a sum of money offered as a prize; any baglike receptacle resembling a purse or pocket; money, resources, or wealth.—*v.t.*—*pursed, pursing.* To pucker; to contract into folds or wrinkles as if drawing together the mouth of a purse or bag, as: She *pursed* her lips.

purse-proud, pɐrs′proud″, *a.* Proud of one's wealth; given to ostentatious display.

purs·er, pɐr′sĕr, *n.* An officer on board a ship, charged with the keeping of accounts and documents, and with the service and care of passengers on a passenger ship.

purse seine, *n.* A large seine maneuvered by a boat at each end to enclose a school of fish, the net being drawn together at the bottom to secure the catch.

purs·lane, pɐrs′lān, pɐrs′lin, *n.* [O.Fr. *porcelaine,* It. *porcellana,* < L. *porcilaca,* purslane.] A prostrate succulent herb, *Portulaca oleracea,* with rosettes of fleshy paddle-shaped leaves, each with a tiny flower, grown sometimes as a potherb and often found as a troublesome weed. Also *pussley.*

pur·su·ance, pɐr·sō′ans, *n.* A pursuing or carrying out, esp. of a plan, objective, or demand; prosecution.—**in pur·su·ance of,** in fulfillment or execution of.

pur·su·ant, pɐr·sō′ant, *a.* [O.Fr. *porsuiant, poursuiant.*] Done in consequence of anything; agreeable with, conformable to, or according to, used with *to.* Pursuing; following.—*adv.* Conformably, used with *to.*—**pur·su·ant·ly,** *adv.*

pur·sue, pɐr·sō′, *v.t.*—*pursued, pursuing.* [O.Fr. *poursuir, porsuir* (Fr. *poursuivre*)—*pour* = L. *pro,* forward, and *suir, suivre,* to follow, L. *sequor.*] To follow for the purpose of overtaking or capturing; to chase; to haunt, as: Misfortune *pursues* him. To seek to attain; to use measures to obtain; to continue or proceed in; to carry on; to continue to trouble or irritate; to proceed along, with a view to some end or object; to follow; as, to *pursue* a course.—*v.i.* To go in pursuit; to proceed.—**pur·su·er,** pɐr·sō′ĕr, *n.*

pur·suit, pɐr·sōt′, *n.* [Fr. *poursuite.*] The act of pursuing or following in order to overtake; a following with a view to reaching or attaining; a regular pastime or occupation.

pur·suit plane, *n.* A fighter plane designed primarily for pursuit of and attack on enemy aircraft.

pur·sui·vant, pɐr′swi·vant, *n.* [Fr. *poursuivant,* < *poursuivre.*] A member of the lowest order of heraldic officers, with a rank below a herald; an attendant; a follower.

pur·sy, pɐr′sē, *a.*—*pursier, pursiest.* [O.Fr. *pourcif,* also *poulsif,* < *pourcer, poulser* (Mod.Fr. *pousser*), to push, also to breathe or pant, < L. *pulsare,* to beat.] Short-winded; fat.—**pur·si·ness,** *n.*

pur·te·nance, pɐr′te·nans, *n.* [Cf. *appurtenance.*] *Archaic,* the entrails or pluck of an animal.

pu·ru·lent, pūr′a·lent, pūr′ū·lent, *a.* [L. *purulentus,* < *pus, puris,* matter.] Consisting of pus or matter; full of or resembling pus; discharging pus.—**pu·ru·lent·ly,** *adv.*—**pu·ru·lence, pu·ru·len·cy,** pūr′a·lens, pūr′ū·lens, *n.*

pur·vey, pĕr·vā′, *v.t.* [Fr. *pourvoir,* O.Fr. *proveoir, porveoir,* L. *providere,* to foresee; to provide.] To provide or furnish, as provisions or other necessities.—**pur·vey·or,** pĕr·vā′ĕr, *n.*

pur·vey·ance, pĕr·vā′ans, *n.* Act or business of purveying; provisions; *Eng.* the royal prerogative, prior to 1660, of procuring goods or exacting services at low costs.

pur·view, pɐr′vū, *n.* [O.Fr. *pourveu, purvieu,* Fr. *pourvu,* provided, < *pourvoir,* to provide.] *Law,* the body of a statute, as distinguished from the *preamble*; the limit or scope of a statute. Limit of the sphere of authority; the scope of concern or study, as of a paper or discussion; one's outlook or scope of vision.

pus, pus, *n.* [L., akin to Gr. *pyon,* pus.] A yellowish-white, more or less viscid substance produced by suppuration and found in abscesses and healing sores, consisting of a liquid plasma in which leucocytes are suspended.

push, push, *v.t.* [O.E. *pusse,* < Fr. *pousser,* O.Fr. *poulser,* < L. *pulsare,* to beat, < *pello, pulsum,* to drive.] To press against with force; to impel by pressure; to drive or move by steady pressure, without striking: opposed to *pull*; to press or urge forward; shove; thrust; to enforce; to press or ply hard, as an opponent in argument; to urge; to advocate; to importune; to press for or promote energetically; as, to *push* a trade or sale.—*v.i.* To make a thrust against something; to press oneself onward, as against obstacles; to project.—*n.* The act of pushing; a short pressure or force applied; impetus; a thrust; a vigorous effort; an emergency; persevering energy; enterprise; *slang,* a crowd or set of friends.—**push but·ton,** a button or knob which, when pushed, starts or stops a machine, rings a bell, controls an electric light, or otherwise actuates an electric circuit.—**push-but·ton,** push′but″on, *a.*—**pushed for,** in straits; having acute need of; being short of, as time or funds.—**push off,** to depart from shore, as in a boat, canoe, or raft.—**push on,** to resume one's journey after an interruption; to press on against difficulty or opposition.—**push·o·ver,** push′ō″vĕr, *n. Slang.* Anyone easily overcome or deceived; anything done without effort; an easy target; a woman of easy morals.—**push-pull,** push′pul′, *a.* Pertaining to an electronic system in which an alternate current causes two components to function alternately in opposite phase.—**push-up,** push′up″, *n. Usu. pl.* an exercise performed face down, the arms being used to raise and lower the torso while the body is held rigid from the toes to shoulders.—**push·er,** *n.*—**push·y,** *a.*—*pushier, pushiest.* Enterprising; annoyingly aggressive.—**push·i·ly,** *adv.*—**push·i·ness,** *n.*

push·ball, push′bal″, *n.* A game played with a large heavy ball, usu. six feet in diameter, which two sides of players endeavor to push across opposite goals; the ball used in this game.

push·cart, push′kärt″, *n.* A light cart to be pushed by hand, used by street venders.

push·pin, push′pin″, *n.* A children's game played with pins; child's play; triviality. A pin with an extra large round head, used esp. for mounting paper objects.

pu·sil·lan·i·mous, pū″si·lan′i·mus, *a.* [L. *pusillanimis,* < *pusillus,* very little, < *pusus,* little (same root as in *puerile*), and *animus,* the mind.] Without strength or firmness of mind; cowardly; characterized by a cowardly attitude.—**pu·sil·la·nim·i·ty,** pū″si·la·nim′i·tē, *n.*—**pu·sil·lan·i·mous·ly,** *adv.*

puss, pus, *n.* [Same as D. *poes,* L.G. *puus,* Gael. and Ir. *pus,* a cat; perh. imit. of the spitting of a cat.] A cat; an affectionate name for a child or young woman; *Brit. dial.* a hare.

puss, pus, *n. Slang.* The face; mouth.

puss·ley, puss·ly, pus·ley, pus′lē, *n.* Purslane.

puss·y, pus′ē, *n. pl.* **puss·ies.** A cat; kitten; a silky catkin, as of a willow.

pus·sy, pus′ē, *a.*—*pussier, pussiest. Med.* Full of pus; like pus.

puss·y·foot, pus′ē·fut″, *v.i.* To go with a soft, stealthy tread like that of a cat; proceed or act cautiously or timidly, as if afraid to commit oneself on a point at issue.

puss·y·foot, pus′ē·fut″, *n. Bot.* any of certain plants having cat's-paw-shaped flower heads or clusters of leaves.

puss·y wil·low, pus′ē wil′ō, *n.* A small American tree or shrub, *Salix discolor,* having conspicuous silky flower clusters or catkins opening before the leaves; loosely, any of various other willows similar to this.

pus·tu·lant, pus′cha·lant, *a.* [L.L. *pustulans (-ant-),* ppr. of *pustulare.*] Causing the formation of pustules.—*n.* A pustulant medicine or agent.

pus·tu·lar, pus′cha·lĕr, *a.* Having the character of or proceeding from a pustule or pustules; covered with pustules.

pus·tu·late, pus′cha·lāt″, *v.t., v.i.*—*pustulated, pustulating.* To form or cause to form pustules or blisters.—pus′cha·lit, pus′cha·lāt″, *a.* Covered with glandular excrescences such as pustules.—**pus·tu·la·tion,** pus″cha·lā′shan, *n.* The act of forming pustules; a pustule.

pus·tule, pus′chul, *n.* [Fr. *pustule,* L. *pustula,* a form of *pusula,* a blister or pimple.] *Pathol.* an elevation of the skin, having an inflamed base and containing pus; any small protuberance similar to a pimple or blister.

put, put, *v.t.*—*put, putting.* [M.E. *putten, puten,* push, thrust, put: cf. O.E. *putung,* an impelling, inciting, *potian,* push, thrust, also Dan. *putte,* put, put in.] To move, as a thing or person, so as to get it into or out of some place or position; place; lay; to place in or bring into some condition, state, or relation; as, to *put* his doubts at rest; to subject to the endurance or suffering of something; as, to *put* a person to expense; to set to a duty, task, or action; to force or drive to some course or action; as, to *put* someone to flight; to incite or urge; to render or translate into another language; to set or adapt, as words, to music; to express or state; to assign or attribute; as, to *put* a certain construction upon an action; to set at a particular place, point, or amount in a scale of estimation; as, to *put* the distance at three miles; to wager or bet; as, to *put* a sum on a horse; to apply, as to a use or purpose; to propose or submit for answer, consideration, or deliberation; as, to *put* a question; to impose as a burden, charge, or the like; as, to *put* a tax on an article; to invest; to lay the blame of, usu. followed by *on* or *to*; as, to *put* the blame *on* carelessness; to throw or cast, esp. with a forward motion of the hand when raised close to the shoulder; as, to *put* the shot.—*v.i.* To go, move, or proceed, as: The ship *put* back to port.—**put a·bout,** *naut.* to change direction, as on a course.—**put a·cross,** *slang.* To make understandable or acceptable, as a point of view; to carry out successfully, esp. through trickery or deception.—**put a·side, a·way,** or **by,** to place in safekeeping or reserve, as money; save; to discard or thrust aside.—**put down,** to write down; to repress or crush; to attribute; to depose or demote; *slang,* to humiliate or deflate.—**put forth,** to send out, as buds or leaves; to grow; to publish or issue; to propose or offer; to put into operation; exert; to set out, or start, esp. to sea.—**put for·ward,** to advance for consideration; propose.—**put in,** to interpose, as a remark; to make a request or application; *naut.* to enter a port or harbor; *colloq.* to pass or spend, as time, in a manner specified.—**put off,** to defer or postpone; to rebuff; to discard or take off, as one's clothes.—**put o·ver,** *colloq.* To carry out successfully; put across; to succeed in carrying out through trickery.—**put through,** to carry to successful completion; to cause to go through.—

put up, to erect or construct; to can or preserve, as fruit or vegetables; to provide, as capital; to show or offer; to nominate as a candidate. *Colloq.* to accommodate; to wager or stake, as a sum of money.—**put up to**, to incite or prompt.—**put up with**, to bear with patience; tolerate.

put, pụt, *n.* A throw or cast, esp. from the hand raised close to the shoulder; *finance*, the privilege of delivering a certain amount of stock or produce at a specified price, within a specified time.

put, pụt, *a. Colloq.* Fixed; in place; as, to stay *put.*

pu·ta·tive, pū′ta·tiv, *a.* [Fr. *putatif*, L. *putativus*, < L. *puto*, to suppose.] Supposed; reputed; as, the *putative* father of a child.—**pu·ta·tive·ly**, *adv.*

put·log, pụt′lag″, put′log″, put′lag″, put′log″, *n.* [< *put* and *log.*] *Carp.* one of the short pieces of timber used to carry the floor of a scaffold, having one end inserted into holes in the wall.

put on, *v.t.* To assume, as a manner, esp. insincerely or falsely; to don, as clothes; to apply or impose; to stage or produce, as a play; *slang*, to bait or tease by deception or exaggeration.

put-on, pụt′on′, pụt′an′, *a.* Assumed; affected; pretended.—pụt″on″, pụt′an″, *n.* An affectation, as of manner; *slang*, a deception or hoax.

put out, *v.t.* To extinguish, as a fire; to confuse or embarrass; to annoy or irritate; to inconvenience; to publish; to produce or manufacture for sale; *baseball, cricket*, to cause to be out.—*v.i. Naut.* to set out to sea.—**put-out**, pụt′out″, *n. Baseball*, the act of putting out a player who is batting or running between bases.

pu·tre·fac·tion, pū″tre·fak′shan, *n.* The act or process of putrefying; the decomposition of animal and vegetable substances, producing a malodorous compound; that which is putrefied.—**pu·tre·fac·tive**, *a.*

pu·tre·fy, pū′tre·fī″, *v.t.*—*putrefied, putrefying.* [Fr. *putrefier*, L. *putrefacio.*] To render putrid; to cause to rot with an offensive smell; to make gangrenous—*v.i.* To become putrid; to rot.

pu·tres·cent, pū·tres′ent, *a.* [L. *putrescens*, ppr. of *putresco*, to rot.] Becoming putrid; growing rotten; pertaining to the process of putrefaction.—**pu·tres·cence**, *n.*

pu·tres·ci·ble, pū·tres′i·bl, *a.* Capable of being putrefied; liable to become putrid.—*n.* Matter that putrefies.

pu·tres·cine, pū·tres′ēn, pū·tres′in, *n. Biochem.* a crystalline ptomaine, $NH_2 \cdot (CH_2)_4NH_2$, produced by putrid animal tissue.

pu·trid, pū′trid, *a.* [Fr. *putride*, L. *putridus*, < *putris*, rotten, *putreo*, to rot, < *puteo*, to stink, from a root seen also in L. *pus*, Gr. *pyon*, matter.] In a state of decay or putrefaction; corrupt; rotten; proceeding from putrefaction or pertaining to it; most offensive or vile.—**pu·trid·i·ty, pu·trid·ness**, pū·trid′i·tē, *n.*—**pu·trid·ly**, *adv.*

putsch, pụch, *n.* [G.] A sudden and secret uprising or insurrection.—**putsch·ist**, *n.*

putt, put, *n. Golf*, a gentle stroke made on a green, the object being to roll the ball into the cup.—*v.t., v.i.*—*putted, putting.* To tap, as a golf ball, in the direction of the cup.

put·tee, put·ty, put′ē, *n. pl.* **put·tees, put·ties.** [Hind. *patti.*] A long roll of cloth wound around a soldier's or sportsman's leg from ankle to knee as support and protection; a legging or gaiter of leather fastened around one's leg.

put·ter, put′ėr, *n. Golf.* A short-shaft golf club with an almost perpendicular face, used to roll the ball on the green to the cup; one who putts.

put·ter, put′ėr, *v.i.* To occupy oneself with frivolous or useless matters: often followed by *around.* To waste time idly; to dawdle.—**put·ter·er**, *n.*

put·ti·er, put′ē·ėr, *n.* One who putties, as a glazier.

put·ting green, *n. Golf*, smooth turf surrounding the hole.

put·ty, put′ē, *n. pl.* **put·ties.** [Fr. *potée*, calcined tin, brass, etc., putty powder, < *pot*, a pot, orig. perh. applied to a solder for pots.] A kind of paste or cement compounded of whiting or soft carbonate of lime and linseed oil, used by glaziers for fixing the panes of glass in window frames or filling in crevices in wooden surfaces; any of various compounds similar to this in use or in doughlike consistency; a fine cement made of lime and stone dust. A person who is easily influenced, as: She was *putty* in his hands.—*v.t.*—*puttied, puttying.* To cement with putty; to fill up with putty.

put·ty·root, put′ē·röt″, put′ē·rụt″, *n. Bot.* an American orchid, *Aplectrum hyemale*, having a slender naked rootstock which produces each year a single large leaf that lasts through the winter, and in the succeeding spring produces a scape with a loose raceme of brownish flowers.

put-up, pụt′up″, *a. Colloq.* planned beforehand in a secret or crafty manner; as, a *put-up* job.

put-up·on, pụt′a·pon″, *a.* Imposed upon; ill-used.

puz·zle, puz′l, *v.t.*—*puzzled, puzzling.* [Freq. < *pose*, to perplex with a question; or a form of *puddle*; cf. *muddle*, to make stupid.] To perplex or confuse; to discover or resolve by long cogitation, used with *out*; *archaic*, to make intricate or entangle.—*v.i.* To be bewildered, uncertain, or perplexed; to ponder over a problem.—*n.* A toy or contrivance which tries the ingenuity; something which is puzzling; state of being puzzled; perplexity.—**puz·zler**, *n.*

puz·zle·ment, puz′l·ment, *n.* The state of being puzzled; bewilderment or perplexity; that which puzzles.

pyc·nom·e·ter, pic·nom·e·ter, pik·nom′i·tėr, *n.* [Gr. *pyknós*, dense.] A flask or the like used in determining relative density of a liquid or solid.

py·e·li·tis, pī″e·lī′tis, *n.* [N.L., < Gr. *pyelos*, trough: cf. L. *pelvis*, basin.] *Pathol.* inflammation of the pelvis or the kidney.

py·e·log·ra·phy, pī″e·log′ra·fē, *n.* The art of making photographs of the kidneys and other internal organs by means of x-rays, after the injection of a dye.—**py·e·lo·graph**, pī′e·lo·graf″, pī′e·lo·gräf″, *n.* A photograph produced by pyelography. Also **py·e·lo·gram**, pī′e·lo·gram″.

py·e·lo·ne·phri·tis, pī″e·lō·ne·frī′tis, *n. Pathol.* an inflammation of the kidney and the pelvis of the kidney.

py·e·mi·a, py·ae·mi·a, pī·ē′mē·a, *n.* [N.L., < Gr. *pyon*, pus, and *aima*, blood.] *Pathol.* A form of blood poisoning caused by pyogenic bacteria; general septicemia marked by the development of abscesses.—**py·e·mic, py·ae·mic**, *a.*

py·gid·i·um, pī·jid′ē·um, *n. pl.* **py·gid·i·a**, pī·jid′ē·a. [Gr. *pygē* the posteriors.] *Zool.* The terminal division of the body of a flea or other invertebrate; a caudal structure in certain invertebrates.—**py·gid·i·al**, *a.*

pyg·mae·an, pyg·me·an, pig·mē′an, *a.* Pygmy.

Pyg·my, Pig·my, pig′mē, *n. pl.* **Pyg·mies, Pig·mies.** [L. *Pygmaei*, pl., < Gr. *Pygmaioi*, the Pygmies, prop. pl. of *pygmaios*, dwarfish, < *pygmē*, a measure of length, being the distance from the elbow to knuckles, orig. the fist.] A member of any of various Negroid peoples of small stature, esp. of Africa; one of a race of dwarfs in ancient Greek legend or literature. (*l.c.*)

a small or dwarfish person; anything very small of its kind; one who is of small importance, or who has some quality in very small measure.—*a.* (Often *l.c.*) of or pertaining to the Pygmies. (*l.c.*) of very small stature or size; diminutive or tiny; of very small capacity or power.—**pyg·moid**, *a.*—**pyg·my·ish**, *a.*—**pyg·my·ism**, *n.*

py·jam·as, pi·jä′maz, pi·jam′az, *n. pl. Brit.* pajamas.

pyk·nic, pik′nik, *a.* Characteristically short, broad, and rounded in body type; endomorphic.—*n.*

py·lon, pī′lon, *n.* [Gr. *pylōn*, < *pylē*, a gate.] The lofty massive doorway giving entrance to an Egyptian temple; a turning-point marker in airplane races; a large structure indicating the entrance to a bridge or street; a metal tower supporting electric power lines.

py·lo·rus, pī·lōr′us, pī·lar′us, pi·lōr′us, pi·lar′us, *n. pl.* **py·lo·ri**, pī·lōr′ī, pī·lar′ī, pi·lōr′ī, pi·lar′ī. [Gr. *pylōros*, < *pylē*, a gate, and *ouros*, a guard.] *Anat.* the outlet between the stomach and the duodenum through which the food passes to the intestines.—**py·lor·ic**, pī·lōr′ik, pī·lar′ik, pi·lōr′ik, pi·lar′ik, *a.*

py·o·der·ma, pī″ō·dur′ma, *n.* A bacterial infection and inflammation of the skin characterized by the presence of pus.—**py·o·der·mic**, *a.*

py·o·gen·ic, pī″o·jen′ik, *a. Pathol.* Producing or generating pus; attended with or pertaining to the formation of pus.—**py·o·gen·e·sis**, pī″o·jen′e·sis, *n.*

py·or·rhe·a, pī″o·rē′a, *n. Pathol.* discharge of pus.—**py·or·rhe·a al·ve·o·la·ris**, pī″o·rē′a al′vē″o·lar′is, *pathol.* a bacterial infection of the gums in and about the sockets of the teeth, with discharge of pus and loosening of the teeth; also *pyorrhea.*—**py·or·rhe·al**, *a.*

py·ra·can·tha, pī″ra·kan′tha, pir″a·kan′tha, *n.* Any of several hardwooded thorny evergreen shrubs of the genus *Pyracantha*, in the rose family, esp. *P. coccinea*, grown as an ornamental and bearing large flat-topped clusters of white flowers and orange to scarlet, small pome fruits. Also **fire thorn, ev·er·last·ing thorn.**

py·ral·i·did, pī·ral′i·did, *n.* [N.L. *Pyralididae*, pl., < L. *pyralis*, < Gr. *pyralis*, winged insect supposed to live in fire, < *pyr*, fire.] Any of the *Pyralidae*, a family of moths comprising numerous small or medium-sized, plain-colored species with a slender body. Also **pyr·a·lid**, pir′a·lid.—*a.* Belonging to the *Pyralididae*.

pyr·a·mid, pir′a·mid, *n.* [Fr. *pyramide*; L. *pyramis*, < Gr. *pyramis, pyramidos*, a pyramid.] A solid structure whose base is square and whose sides are triangular and meet at a point; one of the ancient structures of this form erected in different parts of the world, often used as tombs, the most noted being those of Egypt; anything pyramidal in form; *geom.* a solid with a polygonal base and sides which are triangular and meet at a common vertex.—**py·ram·i·dal**, pyr·a·mid·ic, pyr·a·mid·i·cal, pi·ram′i·dal, pir″a·mid′ik, *a.*

pyr·a·mid, pir′a·mid, *v.i.* To be disposed in the form or shape of a pyramid; to raise or increase something, as costs, by gradual additions; in speculating on margin, to enlarge one's operations in a series of transactions, as on a continued rise or decline in price, by using profits in transactions not yet closed, and consequently not yet in hand, as margin for additional buying.—*v.t.* To arrange in the form of a pyramid; to raise or increase, as costs or wages, by gradual additions; in speculating on margin, to operate in or employ, as a stock, in a pyramiding series of transactions.

py·rar·gy·rite, pī·rär′ji·rīt″, *n.* [Gr.

pyr, fire, and *argyros*, silver.] An important ore of silver, Ag_3SbS_3, chiefly sulfide or silver and antimony, with hexagonal crystallization.

pyre, pī′er, *n.* [L. *pyra*, < Gr. *pyra*, a pyre, < *pyr*, fire.] A heap of combustible materials, specif. such a heap on which a dead body is laid to be burned; a funeral pile.

py·rene, pī′rēn, *n.* [Gr. *pyrēn*.] *Bot.* the stone found in the interior of fruits.

py·re·thrum, pī·rē′thrum, *n. Bot.* any of several species of the genus *Chrysanthemum*, esp. *C. coccineum*, having lobed aromatic leaves and showy variously colored flowers, popular as a garden and florist plant; any of several species, esp. *C. cinerariaefolium*, the Dalmatian pyrethrum, widely cultivated as a source of an insecticide. *Pharm.* the dried and powdered flower heads used as an insecticide and for certain skin ailments; also **in·sect flow·ers.**

py·ret·ic, pī·ret′ik, *a.* [Gr. *pyretós*, fever, < *pyr*, fire.] Of, pertaining to, or producing fever; febrile.

Py·rex, pī′reks, *n.* A heat-resistant, siliceous glass used for cookware and in various industrial applications. (Trademark.)

py·rex·i·a, pī·rek′sē·a, *n.* [Fr. *pyrexie*, < Gr. *puressō*, to be feverish.] Fever.— **py·rex·i·al, py·rex·ic,** *a.*

pyr·he·li·om·e·ter, pī″er·hē·lē·om′i·tėr, pir″hē·lē·om′i·tėr, *n.* [Gr. *pyr*, fire, *hēlios*, the sun, *metron*, a measure.] An instrument for measuring the intensity of the radiant energy of the sun.

py·ric, pī′rik, *a.* Relating to or caused by burning.

pyr·i·dine, pir′i·dēn″, pir′i·din, *n.* [Gr. *pyr*, fire.] *Chem.* a liquid organic base, C_5H_5N, with a pungent odor, occurring in coal tar and serving as the parent substance of many compounds: used as a solvent and in pharmaceuticals and waterproofing substances.—**py·rid·ic,** pī·rid′ik, *a.*

pyr·i·dox·ine, pir′i·dok′sēn, pir″i·dok′-sin, *n. Biochem.* vitamin B_6, a phenolic alcohol, $C_8H_{11}NO_3$.

pyr·i·form, pir′i·fạrm″, *a.* [L. *pyrum*, a pear, and *forma*, shape.] Having the shape of a pear.

py·rite, pī′rīt, *n.* [L. *pyrites*.] *Mineral.* an iron disulfide, FeS_2, with a brass-yellow color and metallic luster, crystallizing in the isometric system. Also *fool's gold, iron pyrites.*

py·ri·tes, pī·rī′tēz, pi·rī′tēz, pī′rīts, *n. pl., sing. or pl. in contr.* [L., < Gr. *pyrītēs*, flint, *pyrites*, orig. < *pyr*, fire.] Pyrite; marcasite; any of various other metal sulfides, as of copper or nickel.—**py·rit·ic,** pī·rit′ik, pī·rit′ik, *a.*

py·ro·cat·e·chol, pī″ro·kat′e·kōl, pī″ro·-kat′e·chōl, pī″ro·kat′e·kol, pir″o·kat′e·kōl, pir″o·kat′e·chōl, pir″o·kat′e·kol, *n. Chem.* a white crystalline benzene derivative, $C_6H_6O_2$, occurring in plants and prepared from phenol by the distillation of catechin and synthetically: used as a photographic developing agent. Also **py·ro·cat·e·chin.**

py·ro·cel·lu·lose, pī″ro·sel′ū·lōs″, *n. Chem.* nitrocellulose containing less nitrogen than does guncotton: used in making smokeless powder.

py·ro·chem·i·cal, pī″ro·kem′i·kal, *a.* Pertaining to or producing chemical change at high temperatures.—**py·ro·chem·i·cal·ly,** *adv.*

py·ro·clas·tic, pī″ro·klas′tik, *a. Geol.* composed chiefly of fragments of volcanic origin, as agglomerate, tuff, and certain other rocks.

py·ro·crys·tal·line, pī″ro·kris′ta·lin, pī″ro·kris′ta·līn″, pī″ro·kris′ta·lēn″, *a. Petrog.* crystallized from a molten magma or highly heated solution.

py·ro·e·lec·tric·i·ty, pī″rō·i·lek·tris′i·tē, pī″rō·ē″lek·tris′i·tē, *n.* The electrified

state, or electric polarity, produced in certain crystals by a change in temperature.— **py·ro·e·lec·tric,** pī″rō·i·lek′trik, *a., n.*

py·ro·gal·late, pī″ro·gal′āt, *n. Chem.* a salt or ether of pyrogallol.

py·ro·gal·lic ac·id, *n.* Pyrogallol.

py·ro·gal·lol, pī″ro·gal′ōl, pī″ro·gal′ol, pī″ro·ga·lōl′, pī″ro·ga·lol′, *n. Chem.* a white crystalline compound, $C_6H_3(OH)_3$, obtained by heating gallic acid, and used as a photographic developing agent: classed as a phenol, but often regarded as a weak acid. —**py·ro·gal·lic,** *a.*

py·ro·gen, pī″ro·jen″, *n. Biochem.* a toxin that causes fever. Also **py·ro·tox·in,** pī·ro·-tok′sin.

py·ro·gen·ic, pī″ro·jen′ik, *a.* Producing heat or fever; produced by fire; as igneous rocks. Also **py·rog·e·nous,** pī·roj′e·nus, *a.*

py·ro·lig·ne·ous, pī″ro·lig′nē·us, *a.* [Gr. *pyr*, fire, and L. *lignum*, wood.] Generated or procured by the distillation of wood.

py·ro·lig·ne·ous ac·id, *n.* Impure acetic acid obtained by the distillation of wood. Also **wood vin·e·gar.**

py·ro·lu·site, pī″ro·lö′sīt, pī·rol′ū·sīt″, *n.* [Gr. *pyr*, fire, and *louō*, I wash.] A black ore of manganese, MnO_2, much used in such chemical processes as the depolarization of dry-cell batteries and glassmaking.

py·rol·y·sis, pī·rol′i·sis, *n. Chem.* chemical decomposition produced by exposure to a high temperature.—**py·ro·lyt·ic,** pī″ro·lit′ik, *a.*

py·ro·lyze, pī′ro·līz″, *v.t.*—*pyrolyzed, pyrolyzing. Chem.* to effect chemical change in, by the application of heat.—**py·rol·y·zate,** pī·rol′i·zāt, *n. Chem.* a product of pyrolysis.

py·ro·man·cy, pī′ro·man″sē, *n.* [Gr. *pyr, pyros*, fire, and *manteia*, divination.] Divination by fire.

py·ro·ma·ni·a, pī″ro·mā′nē·a, *n.* A mania or uncontrollable impulse to set things on fire.—**py·ro·ma·ni·ac,** *n.*— **py·ro·ma·ni·a·cal,** pī″rō·ma·nī′a·kal, *a.*

py·ro·met·al·lur·gy, pī″ro·met′a·lụr″jē, *n.* In metallurgy, the application and results of heat.

py·rom·e·ter, pī·rom′i·tėr, *n.* An instrument which measures extremely high temperatures above the range of the mercurial thermometer, as well as those in the thermometer range.—**py·ro·met·ric, py·ro·met·ri·cal,** pī″ro·me′trik, *a.*—**py·ro·met·ri·cal·ly,** *adv.*—**py·rom·e·try,** *n.*

py·ro·mor·phite, pī″ro·mạr′fīt, *n.* [G. *pyromorphit*, < Gr. *pyr*, fire, and *morphē*, form.] A mineral, $Pb_5(PO_4)_3Cl$, consisting of a chloride and phosphate of lead, occurring in crystals and masses, and of a green, yellow, or brown color.

py·rone, pī′rōn, pī·rōn′, *n. Chem.* either of two isomeric organic compounds, $C_5H_4O_2$, having important derivatives, as certain yellow dyes.

py·rope, pī′rōp, *n.* [G. *pyrop*, < Gr. *pyrōpós*, fiery, < *pyr*, fire, and *ōps*, eye, face.] A deep-red variety of garnet, frequently used as a gem.

py·ro·pho·bi·a, pī″ro·fō′bē·a, *n.* Abnormal fear of fire.

py·ro·phor·ic, pī″ro·fạr′ik, pī″ro·for′ik, *a.* Capable of spontaneous combustion; highly flammable.

py·ro·phos·phor·ic ac·id, pī′rō·fos′-fạr′ik as′id, pī′rō·fos·for′ik, pī′rō·fos-fạr′ik, pī″rō·fos·for′ik, *n. Chem.* a crystalline acid, $H_4P_2O_7$, formed by the pyrolysis of orthophosphoric acid.

py·ro·phyl·lite, pī″ro·fil′īt, *n.* [G. *pyrophyllit*, so called from its exfoliating when heated.] A mineral consisting of a hydrous silicate of aluminum, usu. having a white or greenish color, and occurring in foliated masses and compact masses, the latter variety being used for making slate pencils.

py·ro·sis, pī·rō′sis, *n. Pathol.* heartburn.

py·ro·tech·nics, pī″ro·tek′niks, *n. pl., sing. or pl. in constr.* The art of making fireworks; the making and use of fireworks for display or military purposes; a display of fireworks; a display of something resembling fireworks, as lightning; *fig.* a brilliant or sensational display, as of rhetoric.—**py·ro·tech·nist,** pī″ro·tek′nist, *n.*—**py·ro·tech·nic, py·ro·tech·ni·cal,** pī″ro·tek′nik, *a.*—**py·ro·tech·ni·cal·ly,** *adv.*

py·rox·ene, pī′rok·sēn″, *n.* [Gr. *pyr, pyros*, fire, and *xenos*, a stranger.] *Geol.* A silicate mineral corresponding to the gem augite, and found in colors ranging from white through green-black; any of various similar minerals.—**py·rox·en·ic,** pī″rok·sen′ik, *a.*

py·rox·e·nite, pī·rok′se·nīt″, *n.* Any rock composed essentially, or in large part, of pyroxene of any kind.

py·rox·y·lin, pī·rok′si·lin, *n.* [Fr. *pyroxyline*, < Gr. *pyr*, fire, and *xylon*, wood.] Any of various cellulose nitrates with fewer nitrate groups than guncotton, used in making plastics and lacquers. Also **py·rox·y·line,** pī·rok′si·lin, pī·rok′si·lēn″.

pyr·rhic, pir′ik, *n.* [Gr. *pyrrhiche*, a warlike dance.] An ancient Grecian war dance which imitated the actions of battle.—*a.*

pyr·rhic, pir′ik, *n.* A metrical foot consisting of two short syllables. Also **di·brach,** dī′brak. —*a.* Consisting of two short syllables, or of feet of two short syllables.

Pyr·rhic vic·to·ry, *n.* A victory, as that gained by King Pyrrhus of Epirus over the Romans in 279 B.C., costing more to the victor than to the vanquished.

Pyr·rho·nism, pir′o·niz″um, *n.* [From *Pyrrho*, Greek philosopher and founder of the Skeptics.] Skepticism; universal doubt. —**Pyr·rho·nist,** *n.*—**Pyr·rho·nis·tic,** pir·o·nis′tik, *a.*

pyr·rho·tite, pir′o·tīt″, *n.* [For earlier *pyrrhotine*, < Gr. *pyrrótēs*, redness, < *pyrrós*, red, < *pyr*, fire.] A native sulfide of iron, FeS, occurring in crystals and masses, of a bronze color and metallic luster, often containing nickel, and generally slightly magnetic.

pyr·rhu·lox·i·a, pir″a·lok′sē·a, *n.* [< N.L.] A colorful gray grosbeak, *Pyrrhuloxia sinuata*, of southwestern U.S. and Mexico, the male having a rose-colored breast and crest.

pyr·role, pi·rōl′, pir′ōl, *n.* [Gr. *pyrrós*, red, and L. *oleum*, oil.] *Chem.* an oily, liquid, organic compound, C_4H_5N, with an odor like chloroform, found naturally in chlorophyll and bile pigments, and derived commerically from coal tar.

py·ru·vic ac·id, pī·rū′vik as′id, pi·rō′vik, *n. Biochem.* a pale yellow or colorless ketone, $C_3H_4O_3$, formed in metabolism or synthetically: used in biochemical research.

Py·thag·o·re·an, pi·thag″o·rē′an, *a.* Pertaining to the Greek, Pythagoras, or his system of philosophy, which taught the doctrine of the transmigration of souls, and resolved all philosophy into the relations of numbers.—*n.* A follower of Pythagoras.— **Py·thag·o·re·an·ism,** pi·thag″o·rē′a·niz″um, *n.*

py·thon, pī′thon, pī′thon, *n.* [L. *Python*, the serpent, in L.L. *pytho(n)-*, a soothsaying spirit, < Gr. *Pythōn* (in both senses).] Any of various large, nonvenomous, old-world tropical snakes of the genus *Python*, which kill by constriction; any of various related or similar snakes, as a boa. (*Cap.*) in Greek legend, a huge serpent or monster fabled to have been slain by Apollo near Delphi. A possessing spirit or demon, or one who is possessed by a spirit and prophesies by its aid.

py·tho·ness, pī′tho·nis, pith′o·nis, *n.* [L.L. *pythonissa*.] A woman supposed to be possessed by a soothsaying spirit, esp. the

---

a- fat, fāte, fär, fâre, fạll; **e-** met, mē, mēre, hėr; **i-** pin, pīne; **o-** not, nōte, mōve; **u-** tub, cūbe, bụll; **oi-** oil; **ou-** pound.

priestess of Apollo at Delphi; a woman with power of divination; a witch.—**py·thon·ic**, pī·thon′ik, pi·thon′ik, a. Prophetic.

py·u·ri·a, pī·ūr′ē·a, n. [Gr. *puon*, pus, *ouron*, urine.] *Pathol.* the presence of pus in the urine.

pyx, piks, n. [Gr. *pyxis*, a box, esp. of boxwood, < *pyxos*, the box tree.] *Eccles.* a covered vessel or box used for holding the consecrated Host, esp. a watch-shaped container for carrying the Host to the sick. A box or chest in which specimen coins are deposited at the British mint.

pyx·id·i·um, pik·sid′ē·um, n. pl. **pyx·-id·i·a**, pik·sid′ē·a. [Gr. *pyxis*, a box, and *eidos*, resemblance.] *Bot.* a seed case that splits open so that the top forms a lid or cap.

pyx·ie, pik′sē, n. [Appar. < *Pyxidanthera*.] A trailing, shrubby, evergreen plant, *Pyxidanthera barbulata*, of the eastern U.S., bearing numerous small, starlike blossoms.

pyx·is, pik′sis, n. pl. **pyx·i·des**, pik′si·dēz. [L.] A small box or boxlike vase, used in Greek and Roman times to hold jewelry or ancient toilet articles; pyxidium.

Q

Q, q, kū, n. [L., < Gr. *koppa*, < Phoenician *qoph*.] A consonant and the seventeenth letter of the English alphabet, usu. followed by *u* and sounded 'kw' in such English words as *equal*, or 'k' in such French-derived words as *conquer*; a graphic representation, written or printed, of Q or q; anything in the shape of Q; the sound represented by Q or q; a printing type which reproduces Q or q.

Q-Celt·ic, kū′sel′tik, *esp. Brit.* kū′kel′tik, n., a. Goidelic.

Q.E.D. [L. (*Q*)uod (*E*)rat (*D*)emonstrandum.] Which was to be demonstrated: used at the end of mathematical proofs.

Q-fe·ver, kū′fē′vėr, n. *Pathol.* a fever accompanied by muscular pains and chills, caused by a rickettsia, *Coxiella burnetii*, and transmitted through contact with cattle and sheep or by drinking raw milk.

qua, kwā, kwä, adv. [L.] In the capacity or character of; as being; as.

quack, kwak, v.i. [Formed < the sound, like D. *kwaaken*, *kwakken*, G. *quaken*, Dan. *qvakke*, to croak, to quack; cf. Gr. *koax*, the croak of a frog.] To cry like the duck.—*n.* The cry of a duck or a similar sound.

quack, kwak, n. One who pretends to skill or knowledge which he does not possess; a charlatan; a pretender, esp. a pretender to medical skill.—*a.* Pertaining to or characterized by quackery; as, *quack* medicines, a *quack* doctor.—*v.i.* To make pretensions; to play the quack.—*v.t.*—**quack·ish**, a.—**quack·ish·ly**, adv.

quack·er·y, kwak′e·rē, n. pl. **quack·er·ies**. The boastful pretensions or fraudulent practice of a quack, particularly in medicine; humbug; imposture.

quack grass, n. A noxious weed, *Agropyron repens*. Also *quitch*. See *couch grass*.

quack·sal·ver, kwak′sal″vėr, n. [D. *kwakzalver*, L.G. *kuaksalver*, G. *quacksalber*, lit. 'a quack that deals in salves.'] A quack doctor.

quad, kwod, n. [Contr. for *quadrangle*.] *Colloq.* a quadrangle or court, as of a college.

quad, kwod, n. *Print.* a quadrat.—*v.t.*—**quadded**, **quadding**. *Print.* to space out with quads, as a line of type.

quad, kwod, n. *Colloq.* quadruplet.

quad, kwod, n. *Brit. slang*, quod.

quad·ran·gle, kwod′rang″gl, n. [L. *quadrus*—*quatuor*, four, and *angulus*, an angle.] A plane figure having four sides and four angles; a square or quadrangular court surrounded by buildings; the buildings surrounding such a court; the land area charted on one standard atlas sheet of the U.S. Geological Survey.—**quad·ran·gu·lar**, kwo·drang′gū·lėr, a. In the shape of a quadrangle; having four sides and four angles.

quad·rant, kwod′rant, n. [L. *quadrans*, *quadrantis*, a fourth.] The quarter of a circle; the arc of a circle containing 90°; the space included between this arc and two radii drawn from the center to each extremity; something having the shape of a quarter circle, as a machine part; any of four areas of a plane formed by dividing it with two axes; an instrument with a graduated arc of 90°, for measuring angular altitudes.—**quad·ran·tal**, kwo·dran′tal, a.

quad·rat, kwod′rat, n. [L. *quadratum*, a square, < *quadrus*, square.] *Print.* a piece of type metal cast lower than a type, used for filling out spaces between letters, words, or lines, so as to leave a blank on the paper at the place; also *quad*. *Ecology*, a plot of land marked off to examine and study plants and animals.

quad·rate, kwod′rit, kwod′rāt, a. [L. *quadratus*, pp. of *quadrare*, make or be square, < *quadra*, a square.] Square; rectangular. *Zool.* pertaining to a quadrate.—*n.* A square; something square or rectangular. *Zool.* in birds, fishes, reptiles, and certain other lower vertebrates, a bone or cartilage to which the lower jaw is hinged.—*v.t.* *quadrated*, *quadrating*. To bring into accord with; to adapt.—*v.i.* To agree; conform.

quad·rat·ic, kwo·drat′ik, a. [Fr. *quadratique*.] Pertaining to, denoting, or containing a square; *alg.* involving the square or second power of an unknown quantity; as, a *quadratic* equation.—*n.* A quadratic equation or polynomial.—**quad·rat·i·cal·ly**, adv.

quad·rat·ics, kwo·drat′iks, n. pl. but sing. in constr. That branch of algebra which treats of quadratic equations.

quad·ra·ture, kwod′ra·chėr, n. [L. *quadratura*.] The act of squaring; *math.* the finding of a square which contains just as much area as a certain given surface, esp. such a surface bounded by a curve; *astron.* the position of one heavenly body in respect to another when distant from it 90°.

quad·ren·ni·al, kwo·dren′ē·al, a. [< L. *quadriennium*, a space of four years—*quadrus* = *quatuor*, four, and *annus*, year.] Comprising four years; occurring once in four years.—*n.*—**quad·ren·ni·al·ly**, adv.

quad·ren·ni·um, kwo·dren′ē·um, n. pl. **quad·ren·ni·a**, **quad·ren·ni·ums**, kwo·dren′ē·a. A period of four years.

quad·ric, kwod′rik, a. [L. *quadra*, a square: cf. *quadrate*.] *Math.* of the second degree: said esp. of functions with more than two variables.—*n.* A quantic of the second degree.

quad·ri·ceps, kwod′ri·seps″, n. [L. *quadrus*, *quatuor*, four, *caput*, the head.] *Anat.* a large muscle in the front of the thigh which controls the extension of the leg.—**quad·ri·cip·i·tal**, kwod″ri·sip′i·tal, a.

quad·ri·fid, kwod′ri·fid, a. [L. *quadrus* = *quatuor*, four, and *findo*, *fidi*, to cleave.] Divided or cleft into four segments or lobes, as the petals of a flower.

quad·ri·ga, kwo·drī′ga, n. pl. **quad·ri·gae**, kwo·drī′jē. [L., contr. *quadrijuga*—prefix *quadrus*, fourfold, and *jugum*, a yoke.] A two-wheeled Roman chariot drawn by four horses harnessed abreast.

quad·ri·lat·er·al, kwod″ri·lat′ér·al, a. [L. *quadrus*—*quatuor*, four, and *latus*, *lateris*, side.] Having four sides.—*n.* A plane figure having four sides and four angles; something so formed. *Geom.* a four-sided polygon; a plane figure made with four straight lines having six points of inter-

section. The space enclosed between and defended by four fortresses.—**quad·ri·lat·er·al·ly**, adv.

qua·drille, kwa·dril′, ka·dril′, n. A dance consisting generally of five figures or movements executed by four couples each forming the side of a square; the music for such a dance.

qua·drille, kwa·dril′, ka·dril′, n. [Fr. *quadrille*, Sp. *cuadrilla*, a group of four persons, *cuadrillo*, a small square, < L. *quadra*, *quadrum*, a square, < *quatuor*, four.] An 18th century card game played by four persons, and employing a deck of forty cards.

quad·ril·lion, kwo·dril′yon, n. [L. *quadrus* = *quatuor*, four, and E. *million*.] In the U.S. and France, one thousand trillions, represented by a 1 followed by 15 zeros; in Great Britain and Germany, one million trillions, represented by a 1 followed by 24 zeros.—*a.*—**quad·ril·lionth**, a., n.

quad·ri·par·tite, kwod″ri·pär′tīt, a. [L. *quadrus* = *quatuor*, four, and *partitus*, divided.] Divided into four parts; having four participants.

quad·ri·va·lent, kwod″ri·vā′lent, kwo·driv′a·lent, a. [< L. *quadrus*—*quatuor*, four, and *valens*, *valentis*, ppr. of *valeo*, to be worth.] *Chem.* Having a valence of four; having four possible valences. Also *tetravalent*.—*n.*—**quad·ri·va·lence**, **quad·ri·va·len·cy**, n.—**quad·ri·va·lent·ly**, adv.

quad·riv·i·al, kwo·driv′ē·al, a. [L. *quadrivium*—prefix *quadrus* = *quatuor*, four, and *via*, a way.] Having four roads meeting in a point; going in or leading to four directions, as roads or walks.

quad·riv·i·um, kwo·driv′ē·um, n. pl. **quad·riv·i·a**, kwo·driv′ē·a. [L.L.] In the Middle Ages, a collective term for arithmetic, music, geometry, and astronomy, which formed the advanced group of the seven liberal arts.

quad·roon, kwo·drön′, n. [Sp. *cuarteron*, < L. *quartus*, fourth.] The offspring of a mulatto and a white person; a person having one Negro grandparent.

quad·ru·ma·nous, kwo·drö′ma·nus, a. Having four feet adapted to function as hands, as monkeys; four-handed; of a former order of mammals, *Quadrumana*, now grouped with man in the *Primates*.—**quad·ru·mane**, kwod′ru·mān″, n., a.—**qua·dru·ma·nal**, kwo·drö′ma·nal, a.

quad·rum·vi·rate, kwo·drum′vi·rit, kwo·drum′vi·rāt″, n. A group or coalition of four men, often exercising equal authority as managers or governors.—**quad·rum·vir**, n. A member of a quadrumvirate.

quad·ru·ped, kwod′ru·ped″, n. [L. *quadrupes*, *quadrupedis* = *quadrus* = *quatuor*, four, and *pes*, *pedis*, a foot.] A four-footed animal: a term applied to mammals, amphibians, and some reptiles.—*a.* Having four feet.—**quad·ru·pe·dal**, kwo·drö′pi·dal, kwod″ru·ped′al, a.

quad·ru·ple, kwo·drö′pl, kwod′ru·pl, a. [Fr. *quadruple*, < L. *quadruplus*, < *quadru-*, four, and *-plus*.] Fourfold; consisting of four parts; four times as great; *mus.* characterized by four beats to each measure.—*n.* A number or amount four times as great as another.—*v.t.*—*quadrupled*, *quadrupling*. To make four times as great.—*v.i.* To become four times as great.

quad·ru·plet, kwo·drup′lit, kwo·drö′plit, kwod′ru·plit, n. Any group or combination of four; one of four children born at one birth.

quad·ru·pli·cate, kwo·drö′pli·kit, kwo·drö′pli·kāt″, a. [L. *quadruplico*, *quadruplicatum*—*quadrus* = *quatuor*, four, and *plico*, to fold.] Four times repeated; fourfold.—*n.* One of four things that are identical.—kwo·drö′pli·kāt″, v.t.—*quadruplicated*, *quadruplicating*. To make fourfold.

quae·re, kwēr′ē, _v. impv._ [L., impv. of _quaerere,_ seek, ask.] Ask: used to introduce or suggest a question, as: _Quaere,_ is this point fully proved?—_n._ A query or question.

quaes·tor, kwes′tẽr, kwē′stẽr, _n._ An ancient Roman magistrate in charge of the prosecution of criminal cases; later, a magistrate in charge of public funds. Also _questor._

quaff, kwäf, kwaf, kwạf, _v.t., v.i._ [< Ir. and Gael. _cuach,_ Sc. _quaich, queff,_ a drinking cup.] To drink copiously and with great pleasure.—_n._ The act of drinking in this manner; the beverage consumed.—**quaff·-er,** _n._

quag, kwag, kwog, _n._ A piece of soft, boggy ground; a quagmire.

quag·ga, kwag′a, _n._ [Hottentot; name derived from its cry.] _Zool._ an extinct S. African mammal, _Equus burchellii quagga,_ closely related to the zebra, but having stripes on head, neck, and shoulders only.

quag·gy, kwag′ē, kwog′ē, _a._—_quaggier, quaggiest._ Yielding under foot, as soft wet earth; boggy; spongy; soft or flaccid, as flesh.

quag·mire, kwag′mīẽr″, kwog′mīẽr″, _n._ [_Quag_ for _quake,_ and _mire;_ lit. 'a mire or bog that quakes or shakes.'] A piece of soft boggy land that yields under foot; a bog; _fig._ a problem or situation not easily resolved.—**quag·mired, quag·mir·y,** _a._

qua·hog, kwạ′hog, kwạ′hạg, kwa·hog′, kwa·hạg′, _n._ [N. Amer. Ind.] A roundish, edible American clam, _Venus mercenaria,_ of the Atlantic coast. Also **qua·haug,** _hardshell clam, round clam._

quail, kwāl, _n. pl._ **quail, quails.** [O.Fr. _quaille_ (Fr. _caille_); from Teut.: cf. D. _kawkkel,_ quail, of imit. origin.] _Ornith._ A small American ruddy chickenlike bird, _Colinus virginianus,_ the bobwhite, with a white throat, stubby tail, and clearly enunciated whistle, now a restricted game bird; a small old-world brown partridge-like bird, _Coturnix coturnix,_ a game bird, often identified by its ventriloquial voice.—**quail·like,** _a._

quail, kwāl, _v.i._ [O.E. _cwelan,_ to die = D. _quelen,_ to pine away; O.H.G. _quelan,_ to suffer torment.] To cower or lose heart, as before danger or difficulty.

quaint, kwānt, _a._ [O.E. _queint, coint,_ < O.Fr. _coint,_ neat, fine, dainty; < L. _cognitus,_ known, the meaning prob. having been influenced by L. _comptus,_ trimmed, adorned.] Antique in appearance; attractive or pleasing in an unusual, old-fashioned, or picturesque way; whimsical; fanciful.—**quaint·ly,** _adv._—**quaint·ness,** _n._

quake, kwāk, _v.i._—_quaked, quaking._ [O.E. _cwacian,_ same root as _quick;_ cf. Provinc. G. _quacken,_ to waggle, to shake.] To shake, tremble, or shudder, as from fear; of objects, to vibrate, shake, or tremble from internal convulsions or shock.—_n._ An act of shaking or trembling; an earthquake; a tremulous agitation.

Quak·er, kwā′kẽr, _n._ One of the religious sect called the Society of Friends.—**Quak·er·ish,** _a._—**Quak·er·ism,** kwā′ke·riz″um, _n._—**Quak·er·ly,** kwā′kẽr·lē, _a._

Quak·er gun, _n._ [An allusion to the _Quaker_ opposition to war.] A dummy gun, as on a ship or fort.

quak·er-la·dies, kwā′kẽr·lā′dēz, _n., pl. in constr._ A flower, _Houstonia caerulea._ See _bluet._

Quak·er meet·ing, _n._ A Quaker religious meeting where silence is broken only when members are stirred to speak or pray; any gathering with long periods of silence.

qual·i·fi·ca·tion, kwol′i·fi·kā′shan, _n._ The act of qualifying, or the state of being qualified; that which qualifies or fits a person or thing for any use or purpose, as for a place, an office, or employment; modification, restriction, or limitation.

qual·i·fied, kwol′i·fīd″, _a._ Having the qualifications; competent; modified or limited; as, a _qualified_ statement.—**qual·i·fied·ly,** _adv._

qual·i·fi·er, kwol′i·fī″ẽr, _n._ One who or that which qualifies; _gram._ a word, phrase, or clause which modifies or qualifies another word's meaning.

qual·i·fy, kwol′i·fī″, _v.t._—_qualified, qualifying._ [Fr. _qualifier,_ < L.L. _qualificare,_ < L. _qualis,_ such, of such sort, and _facio,_ to make.] To furnish with the knowledge, skill, or other prerequisites necessary for a purpose; to make fit for any place, office, or occupation; to furnish with legal power or capacity; as, to _qualify_ persons for the franchise; to ascribe qualities to; name or characterize; to limit or modify; to restrict; to limit by exceptions; as, to _qualify_ a statement; _gram._ to modify. To moderate, abate, or soften; to modify the quality or strength of; to dilute or otherwise make fit for taste.—_v.i._ To make oneself capable of holding any office or enjoying any privilege; to establish a right to exercise any function; _sports,_ to exhibit the required skill in a preliminary race or contest; _riflery,_ to fire a rifle or other gun so as to receive a rating for marksmanship.—**qual·i·fi·a·ble,** _a._

qual·i·ta·tive, kwol′i·tā″tiv, _a._ Pertaining to quality; estimable according to quality.—**qual·i·ta·tive·ly,** _adv._

qual·i·ta·tive a·nal·y·sis, _n. Chem._ the process of analyzing a compound substance to determine what elements it contains.

qual·i·ty, kwol′i·tē, _n. pl._ **qual·i·ties.** [Fr. _qualité,_ < L. _qualitas,_ a quality or property, < _qualis,_ such.] That which makes or helps to make anything such as it is; a distinguishing property, characteristic, or attribute; the level of excellence of something; as, a product of high _quality;_ superiority; moral characteristic, good or bad; social position in relation to others; as, a man of _quality;_ _logic,_ the negative or affirmative character of a proposition; _phon._ the resonance or timbre of a voiced sound, esp. of a vowel; _mus._ timbre.

qual·i·ty con·trol, _n. Bus._ a continuous managerial system to ensure the quality of a product by a critical study of processes, materials, and finished items.

qualm, kwäm, kwạm, _n._ [O.E. _cwealm,_ pestilence, death; D. _kwalm,_ Dan. _qvalm,_ qualm, vapor; O.H.G. _qualm,_ death; < root of _quell, quail._] A sudden feeling of sickness or nausea; a scruple or twinge of conscience; compunction; a sudden sensation of uneasiness.

qualm·ish, kwä′mish, kwạ′mish, _a._ Affected with nausea; of or causing qualms.—**qualm·ish·ly,** —**qualm·ish·ness,** _n._

quam·ash, kwom′ash, kwa·mash′, _n._ An American bulbous plant which was eaten by the Indians. Also _camass._

quan·da·ry, kwon′da·rē, kwon′drē, _n. pl._ **quan·da·ries.** [Prob. < Fr. _Qu'en dirai-je ?_ what shall I say of it ?] A state of difficulty, perplexity, uncertainty, or hesitation; a predicament.

quant, kwant, kwont, _n. Brit._ a pole with a flat disk at the end to prevent it from sinking into the mud, used to propel punts and other small boats in shallow water.—_v.t., v.i._ To propel or be propelled by a quant.

quan·tal, kwon′tal, _a._ Of or pertaining to experimental data grouped in only two categories, as, all or none, asleep or awake.

quan·tic, kwon′tik, _n. Math._ a homogeneous polynomial in more than one variable, usu. rational and integral.

quan·ti·fi·er, kwon′ti·fī″ẽr, _n._ A word specifying quantity; _logic,_ an expression showing the quantity of a logical proposition.

quan·ti·fy, kwon′ti·fī″, _v.t._—_quantified, quantifying._ [M.L. _quantificare,_ < L. _quan-_

tus, how great, and _facere,_ make.] To determine the quantity of; measure; _logic,_ to make explicit the quantity of.—**quan·ti·fi·a·ble,** _a._—**quan·ti·fi·ca·tion,** _n._

quan·ti·ta·tive, kwon′ti·tā″tiv, _a._ Estimable according to quantity; relating or having regard to quantity; _class. pros._ denoting or relating to syllables grouped as long and short and not as accented and unaccented.—**quan·ti·ta·tive·ly,** _adv._—**quan·ti·ta·tive·ness,** _n._

quan·ti·ta·tive a·nal·y·sis, _n. Chem._ the process of analyzing a compound substance to determine the percentage or amount of each element it contains.

quan·ti·ty, kwon′ti·tē, _n. pl._ **quan·ti·ties.** [Fr. _quantité,_ L. _quantitas,_ quantity, extent, < _quantus,_ how great, < _quam,_ to what a degree.] That property by virtue of which a thing is measurable; extent; measure; size; any amount, bulk, or aggregate; as, a _quantity_ of earth; a large or considerable amount; as, wheat shipped in _quantity._ _Math._ anything which can be multiplied, divided, or measured; anything to which mathematical processes are applicable. _Pros., phon._ the measure of a sound or sequence of sounds, or the time taken to pronounce them; _logic,_ the extent of a term or proposition; _mus._ the continuance or duration of a note.

quan·tize, kwon′tīz, _v.t._—_quantized, quantizing. Phys._ to select a discrete set of values from a continuous range of possibilities.—**quan·ti·za·tion,** _n._

quan·tum, kwon′tum, _n. pl._ **quan·ta,** kwon′ta. [L., neut. of _quantus,_ how great, how much, akin to _quam,_ how, _qui, quis,_ who: cf. _quality._] Quantity or amount; a particular amount; a share or portion. _Phys._ in the quantum theory, a particle or cell composed of the smallest amount of energy capable of existing independently, or this amount of energy regarded as a unit.

quan·tum me·chan·ics, _n. pl., sing or pl. in constr. Phys._ a system of mathematics which defines the energy relationships of atomic and subatomic particles in terms of discrete levels.

quan·tum num·ber, _n. Phys._ in an atomic system, one of a set of integers or odd half-integers indicating any of the various energy levels in the system.

quan·tum the·o·ry, _n. Phys._ the theory that the emission or absorption of energy by atoms or molecules is not continuous but occurs in discrete amounts, each amount being called a quantum.

quar·an·tine, kwạr′an·tēn″, kwor′an·tēn″, _n._ [It. _quarantana,_ a space of forty days, < _quaranta,_ < L. _quadraginta,_ forty.] A detention or isolation to prevent the spread of disease; a period of detention or isolation imposed upon ships, persons, or cargo on arrival at a port or place, when exposed to or suspected of bearing an infectious or contagious disease; a place of confinement or isolation; a system of measures, as for observation or disinfection, maintained by governmental or public authority at ports or frontiers thus preventing the spread of disease; the branch of public service concerned with such measures; a politically or socially enforced isolation; a period of forty days.—_v.t._—_quarantined, quarantining._ To detain, isolate, or ostracize by quarantine; to put in or subject to quarantine.—**quar·an·tin·a·ble,** _a._

quar·rel, kwạr′el, kwor′el, _n._ [O.Fr. _querele,_ Fr. _querelle,_ a quarrel, < L. _querela,_ a complaint, < _queror,_ to complain; akin _querulous._] An angry dispute; a wrangle; an altercation; a breach of friendship; the basis or ground of variance, complaint, or objection.—_v.i._—_quarreled, quarreling, esp. Brit. quarrelled, quarelling._ To dispute violently; to wrangle; to squabble; to fall

QRS

out; to find fault; to cavil.—**quar·rel·er**, *esp. Brit.* **quar·rel·ler**, *n.*

quar·rel, kwạr′el, kwor′el, *n.* [O.Fr. *quarrel* (Fr. *carreau*), dim. of L. *quadrum*, something square, < *quatuor*, four.] A lozenge-shaped pane of glass in a window; also *quarry*. A tool with a pyramidlike point, used for cutting or chiseling; formerly, a bolt or arrow having a square-shaped head and intended to be shot from a crossbow.

quar·rel·some, kwạr′el·som, kwor′el·-som, *a.* Inclined or apt to quarrel; irascible. —**quar·rel·some·ly**, *adv.*—**quar·rel·-some·ness**, *n.*

quar·ri·er, kwạr′ē·ėr, kwor′ē·ėr, *n.* One who works in a quarry. Also **quar·ry·man**, pl. **quar·ry·men**.

quar·ry, kwạr′ē, kwor′ē, *n.* pl. **quar·ries.** [Fr. *curée*, the portion given to the dogs, wrapped in the skin of the beast killed, < L. *corium*, a hide, leather.] Any animal pursued for prey; game, esp. game pursued with hawks or hounds; any object of pursuit.

quar·ry, kwạr′ē, kwor′ē, *n.* pl. **quar·ries.** [O.Fr. *quarriere* (Fr. *carrière*), lit. 'a place where stones are squared,' < L. *quadro*, to square.] An open pit where stones are dug, cut, or blasted from the earth.—*v.t.*—*quar-ried, quarrying.* To dig or take from a quarry; to form a quarry in.—**quar·ry·ing**, *n.*

quar·ry, kwạr′ē, kwor′ē, *n.* pl. **quar·ries.** [For *quarrel.*] A quarrel, or small square- or diamond-shaped pane of glass; a square stone or tile.

quart, kwạrt, *n.* [Fr. *quarte*; lit. 'a fourth part,' < L. *quartus*, fourth, < *quatuor*, four.] Two liquid pints; one-quarter gallon. See Measures and Weights table.

quar·tan, kwạr′tan, *a.* [L. *quartanus*, fourth.] Intermitting so as to occur every fourth day; as, a *quartan* fever; referring to the fourth in a group or series.—*n. Pathol.* a form of malarial fever marked by paroxysms that occur every fourth day, counting inclusively.

quarte, kärt, *Fr.* kärt, *n.* pl. **quartes**, kärts, *Fr.* kärt. [Fr.] *Fencing*, the fourth parrying position in a series of eight.

quar·ter, kwạr′tėr, *n.* [O.Fr. *quarter, quartier* (Fr. *quartier*), a quarter, < L. *quartarius*, a fourth part, < *quartus*, fourth, < *quatuor*, four.] One of four parts into which anything is divided or divisible; a fourth part or portion, as of a pound, yard, mile, or calendar year; a fourth part of an hour, or the point marking the beginning or end of this period of time; one-fourth of a dollar, or 25 cents; a U.S. or Canadian coin having this value; a fourth part of a hundredweight, equal to 25 pounds in the U.S. and 28 pounds in Britain; a measure, esp. of grain, equal to a fourth of a ton or eight bushels; in schools and universities, one-fourth of the teaching period of the year; one of the four cardinal points of the compass or one of the corresponding regions of the horizon; any region or point of the compass; a district or locality, specif. a particular region of a town, city, or country; as, the Latin *quarter* of Paris; an unspecified individual, group, locality, or the like; as, orders from a higher *quarter*; a fourth part of the carcass of a mammal, including a limb; *pl.* residence, shelter, or lodging; *sports*, one-fourth of the playing time of a game, as football or basketball; *shoemaking*, the piece of leather in a shoe which forms the side from the heel to the vamp. *Astron.* a fourth part of the moon's period or monthly revolution around the earth; one of two phases of the moon when a quarter of its sphere is visible. *Milit.* mercy, esp. the sparing of the life of a vanquished enemy; a station or encampment occupied by troops; as, winter *quarters*. *Naut.* the part of a vessel's side which lies toward the stern;

one of the posts allotted to men or officers, as for an engagement or drill. *Her.* one of the four divisions of a shield formed by horizontal and perpendicular lines meeting in the center; the charge or figure borne on such a division.—*a.* Equal to or being a quarter of anything.—**at close quar·ters**, nearby; in a confined space.

quar·ter, kwạr′tėr, *v.t.* To divide into four equal parts; to separate or cut into parts; to furnish, as soldiers, with lodgings or shelter; to pass over, as a region, by crossing back and forth. *Her.* to divide, as a shield, into four compartments; to place, as a coat of arms, with others on a shield.—*v.i.* To be stationed; to lodge; to pass back and forth over an area, as hounds while hunting.

quar·ter·age, kwạr′tėr·ij, *n.* The quartering of troops; the expenses of quartering; quarters or lodging; a quarterly payment, charge, or allowance.

quar·ter·back, kwạr′tėr·bak″, *n. Football.* A player who calls signals and directs the offensive plays of his team from a position behind the center from whom he may receive the ball, either carrying it or passing it to another member of the team; the position of such a player.—*v.t.* To direct, as the offensive plays of a football team.—*v.i.* To play or execute the position or duties of a quarterback.

quar·ter crack, *n.* A split or sand crack on the side of a horse's hoof.

quar·ter day, *n. Chiefly Brit.* one of the four days regarded as marking off the quarters of the year, on which tenancies begin and end and quarterly payments fall due.

quar·ter-deck, kwạr′tėr·dek″, *n. Naut.* the stern or rear part of the upper deck, usu. reserved for the exclusive use of the ship's officers.

quar·ter·fi·nal, kwạr″tėr·fīn′al, *n. Sports*, a match or round of matches that precedes the semifinal in tournament competition.—*a.*—**quar·ter·fi·nal·ist**, kwạr″tėr·fīn′a·-list, *n.*

quar·ter horse, *n.* A sturdy, short-legged horse bred for racing short distances, usu. one quarter mile, and in herding cattle.

quar·ter-hour, kwạr′tėr·our′, kwạr″tėr·-ou′ėr, *n.* An interval of 15 minutes; a point on a timepiece indicating 15 minutes before or after the hour.

quar·ter·ing, kwạr′tėr·ing, *n.* The act of one who or that which divides into quarters; the providing of lodging or the quarters themselves. *Her.* the division of a shield into quarters; the placing or marshaling of various coats of arms upon one shield, as to indicate family alliances; *usu. pl.* one of the coats so marshaled.—*a.* That quarters; set at right angles; *naut.* of a wind, blowing on a ship's quarter.

quar·ter·ly, kwạr′tėr·lē, *a.* Pertaining to or consisting of a quarter, esp. a quarter of a year; occurring or done at the end of every quarter of a year.—*n.* pl. **quar·ter·lies.** A periodical issued once every quarter of a year.—*adv.* In or by quarters; once in a quarter of a year. *Her.* with division into quarters; in the quarters of a shield.

quar·ter·mas·ter, kwạr′tėr·mas″tėr, kwạr′tėr·mä″stėr, *n. Milit.* an officer who has charge of quarters, clothing, food, supplies, and other necessities; *naut.* a petty officer who attends a ship's compass, signals, and navigational apparatus.

quar·tern, kwạr′tėrn, *n.* [O.Fr. Fr. *quarteron*, < *quart*, fourth.] *Chiefly Brit.* A quarter or fourth part, esp. of certain weights and measures, as of a pound, ounce, peck, or pint; a loaf of bread weighing about four pounds.

quar·ter note, *n. Mus.* a note held one quarter as long as a whole note. Also *crotchet.*

quar·ter-phase, kwạr′tėr·fāz″, *a. Elect.* noting or pertaining to a phase differential of one quarter of a cycle.

quar·ter·saw, kwạr′tėr·sạ″, *v.t.*—past *quartersawed*, pp. *quartersawed* or *quarter-sawn*, ppr. *quartersawing.* To saw, as a log, into lengthwise quarters that are then cut into boards, the faces of which cross the annual rings nearly at right angles.

quar·ter sec·tion, *n.* In Canadian and U.S. government land surveying, a square area of land comprising one quarter of a square mile or 160 acres.

quar·ter ses·sions, *n. pl. but sing. in constr. Law*, an English court of limited criminal jurisdiction combined with certain other powers, held quarterly; in some states of the U.S., a court with limited criminal jurisdiction and sometimes administrative power, held quarterly.

quar·ter·staff, kwạr′tėr·staf″, kwạr′tėr·-stäf″, *n.* pl. **quar·ter·staves**, kwạr′tėr·stāvz″, kwạr′tėr·stavz″, kwạr′tėr·stävz″. Formerly, an English weapon formed of a stout, iron-tipped pole from six to eight feet in length; the use of a quarterstaff.

quar·ter tone, *n. Mus.* an interval equal to half a semitone.

quar·tet, kwạr·tet′, *n.* [It. *quartetto*, < L. *quartus*, fourth.] A piece of music arranged for four voices or four instruments; the persons who execute a quartet; any set of four. Also **quar·tette.**

quar·tic, kwạr′tik, *a. Math.* pertaining to or belonging to the fourth degree.—*n. Math.* a quartic equation.

quar·tile, kwạr′tīl, kwạr′til, *n.* [L. *quartus*, fourth.] *Statistics*, a point on a distribution curve indicating the division of that distribution into quarters or sections equivalent to one-quarter of the total number of units.—*a.*

quar·to, kwạr′tō, *n.* pl. **quar·tos.** [L. *quartus*, fourth.] A book or pamphlet size, usu. about nine by twelve inches, made by twice folding a printed sheet to make four leaves or eight pages; a book or pamphlet this size. Abbr. *4to, 4°, qto.*—*a.* Denoting a book or pamphlet so bound.

quartz, kwạrts, *n.* [< G. *quarz*, quartz, quartz, a word of unknown origin.] *Mineral.* an abundant and important mineral, silicon dioxide, SiO_2, appearing in many forms and colors, and occurring in amorphous masses such as chalcedony and jasper, or in hexagonal crystals as amethyst and rock crystal.—**quartz·ose**, **quartz·-ous**, kwạrt′sōs, kwạrt′sus, *a.*

quartz bat·ter·y, *n.* Stamp mill.

quartz·if·er·ous, kwạrt·sif′ėr·us, *a.* [*Quartz*, and L. *fero*, to bear.] Consisting of quartz or chiefly of quartz.

quartz·ite, kwạrt′sīt, *n. Mineral.* a hard metamorphic rock formed essentially from hardened sandstone.—**quartz·it·ic**, kwạrt·-sit′ik, *a.*

qua·sar, kwä′sär, kwä′sėr, kwä′zėr, *n. Astron.* a very distant heavenly object which emits immense amounts of radio waves.

quash, kwosh, *v.t.* [O.Fr. *quasser*, Fr. *casser*, < L. *quassare*, to shake, shatter, shiver; intens. < *quatio*, *quassum*, to shake.] To subdue, put down, or quell; to put an end to; as, to *quash* a rebellion.

quash, kwosh, *v.t. Law*, to make void or annul.

qua·si, kwä′zī, kwä′sī, kwä′sē, kwä′zē, *a.* Resembling or alike in certain characteristics or features.—*adv.* As if; seemingly but not absolutely; as, a *quasi*-historical account.

qua·si-con·tract, kwä′zī·kon′trakt, kwä′-sī·kon′trakt, kwä′sē·kon′trakt, kwä′zē·-kon′trakt, *n. Law*, a legal obligation imposed in the absence of a promise or contract, to ensure the payment or service which a just contract would specify.

---

qua·si-ju·di·cial, kwä″zĭ·jö·dish′al, kwä″-sĭ·jö·dish′al, kwä′sē·jö·dish′al, kwä′zē·-jö·dish′al, *a.* Having some judicial characteristics, as that of conducting investigations.—**qua·si·ju·di·cial·ly,** *adv.*

qua·si-stel·lar, kwä′sĭ·stel′ĕr, *a. Astron.* indicating a body situated beyond the galaxy, appearing greater in size than a star but smaller than a nebula, and constituting the origin of forceful electromagnetic wave emissions.

quas·sia, kwosh′a, kwosh′ē·a, *n.* [From *Quassy,* a Negro who first made known the medicinal virtues of one species.] A tree of the genera *Quassia* or *Picrasma* of tropical S. America containing an extremely bitter principle which is useful as an insecticide and medicinally as a tonic; the principle itself.

qua·ter·nar·y, kwä′tĕr·ner″ē, kwa·tur′na·rē, *a.* [L. *quaternarius,* < *quaterni,* four each, distributive of *quattuor,* four.] Consisting of four; arranged in fours.—*n. pl.* **qua·ter·nar·ies.** A group of four; the number four.

Qua·ter·nar·y, kwä′tĕr·ner″ē, kwa·tur′na·rē, *n.* The present geological time period in the Cenozoic era comprising the two epochs Pleistocene and Recent. See Table of Geologic Time.—*a.*

qua·ter·ni·on, kwa·tur′nē·on, *n.* [L.L. *quaternio(n-),* the number four, a group of four, < L. *quaterni.*] A group or set of four persons or things. *Math.* the quotient of two vectors considered as depending on four elements, three complex numbers and one real number, and expressible by an algebraic quadrinomial; *pl.* the calculus of such quantities.

quat·rain, kwo′trān, *n.* [Fr., < *quatre,* L. *quatuor,* four.] A stanza of four lines, usu. rhyming alternately.

quat·re·foil, kat′ĕr·foil″, ka′tre·foil″, *n.* [O.Fr. *quatre,* four, and *foil,* leaf.] A leaf composed of four leaflets, as some clover; *arch.* an ornament or decorative feature having four foils or lobes.

quat·tro·cen·to, kwo″trŏ·chen′tŏ, *It.* kwät″trạ·chen′ṭạ, *n.* [It., four hundred, short for *mille quattrocento,* one thousand four hundred.] The 15th century with reference to Italy, esp. to the Italian art or literature of that period.—*a.*

qua·ver, kwā′vĕr, *v.i.* [< older *quave,* to shake, akin to *quiver;* and to L.G. *quabbeln,* to quiver; perh. also to *quake.*] To shake or tremble; to speak or sing with a tremulous voice; to produce trills on a musical instrument or in singing.—*v.t.* To utter or sing with a tremulous sound.—*n.* A shake or tremble, esp. of the voice; a trill; *chiefly Brit., mus.* an eighth note.—**quav·er·-ing·ly,** *adv.*—**qua·ver·y,** *a.*

quay, kē, *n.* [< Fr. *quai,* a quay, a Celtic word = Bret. *cae,* W. *cae,* an enclosure.] A landing place built along a line of coast or a river bank, or forming the side of a harbor, at which vessels are loaded and unloaded; a wharf.—**quay·like,** *a.*

quay·age, kē′ij, *n.* Quay dues; space on or for a quay; quays considered collectively.

quean, kwēn, *n.* [O.E. *cwene,* a woman, a base woman.] *Archaic.* A woman who is brazen and impudent; a slut; a prostitute.

quea·sy, kwē′zē, *a.*—**queasier, queasiest.** [Allied to Icel. *kveisa,* pain in the stomach; N. *kveis,* sickness after a debauch.] Sick at the stomach; affected with nausea; apt to cause nausea; uneasy or qualmish, as the conscience.—**quea·si·ly,** *adv.*—**quea·si·ness,** *n.*

Que·bec, kwi·bek′, *n.* A communications code word to designate the letter *Q.*

que·bra·cho, kā·brä′chŏ, *Sp.* ke·vrä′chạ, *n.* [Sp., < *quebrar,* break, and *hacha,* ax.] The heartwood of a S. American tree, *Schinopsis lorentzii,* in the cashew family, the

world's most important source of tannin; the tree itself; also **red que·bra·cho.** The bark of a S. American tree, *Aspidosperma quebrachoblanco,* in the dogbane family, used for medicinal purposes; the tree itself; also **white que·bra·cho.**

queen, kwēn, *n.* [O.E. *cwén,* a queen, a wife (akin *quean*) = Goth. *qvens, qveins;* a woman; Icel. *kván,* a wife, *kona,* a woman; Dan. *qvinde,* a woman, *kone,* a wife; O.H.G. *quena,* a woman; Ir. and Gael. *coinne,* Gr. *gyne,* Skt. *jani,* a woman. < root *gan,* Gr. and L. (*gen*), to produce.] The spouse, consort, or widow of a king; a woman who is the sovereign of a kingdom; a woman preeminent among others; a playing card on which a queen is depicted; *chess,* the most powerful of all the pieces in a set; *entom.* the fertile female in a colony, as of ants or bees. *Slang,* an extraordinarily attractive girl or young woman; a male homosexual.—**queen·dom,** kwēn′dom, *n.*—**queen·like,** *a.*—**queen·li·ness,** *n.*—**queen·ly,** kwēn′lē, *adv.*—*a.*—*queenlier, queenliest.*

queen, kwēn, *v.i.* To reign or act as a queen.—*v.t. Chess,* to gain the power of a queen for(a pawn).—**queen it,** to behave in an overbearing manner.

Queen Anne's lace, *n. Bot.* an attractive, sometimes weedy herb, *Daucus carota,* in the carrot family, having finely divided leaves and umbels of delicate white flowers forming a lacelike pattern; also *wild carrot, bird's nest.* The plant from which the cultivated carrot was developed.

Queen Anne style, *n.* A style of English architecture and furniture design of the 18th century reign of Queen Anne, the buildings displaying red brickwork of simple, unpretentious form and ornamentation of modified classic design, and the furniture emphasizing comfort, marked by soft curved lines and upholstery of simple damask. A type of furniture design showing medieval, Japanese, and 18th century English influences, characterized esp. by marquetry and oriental fabric.

queen con·sort, *n. pl.* **queens con·sort.** A ruling king's wife who has no share in his exercise of sovereignty.

queen dow·a·ger, *n.* The widow of a king.

queen moth·er, *n.* A queen dowager who is also the mother of the reigning sovereign.

queen ol·ive, *n.* One of a variety of large olives grown in Spain.

queen post, *n.* One of a pair of vertical posts set in the truss of a roof equidistant from the apex, supporting the sloping upper structure.

queen re·gent, *n. pl.* **queens re·gent.** A queen who reigns as a proxy or regent for another; a queen regnant.

queen reg·nant, *n. pl.* **queens reg·nant.** A queen reigning in her own right and not in behalf of another.

Queen's Coun·sel, *n. Brit.* a group of barristers or one of the group appointed counsel to the reigning sovereign and so called when that sovereign is a queen. See *King's Counsel.*

queen truss, *n. Arch.* a truss having a pair of queen posts rather than a king post.

queer, kwēr, *a.* [Origin obscure: cf. G. *quer,* oblique, cross, adverse.] Strange or odd from a conventional point of view; singular; of questionable character; suspicious; giddy, faint, or queasy; mentally unbalanced or deranged. *Slang,* homosexual; bad, worthless, or counterfeit.—*v.t.* To ruin or spoil; jeopardize; to put, as a person, in a hopeless or unfavorable position as to success, favor, or the like.—*n. Slang.* A homosexual; counterfeit money.—**queer·ly,** *adv.*—**queer·ness,** *n.*

quell, kwel, *v.t.* [O.E. *cwellan,* to kill = Dan. *quaele,* to stifle, torment; Icel. *kvelja,* Sw.

qvalja, G. *quälen,* to torment; same root as to *quail.*] To subdue; to cause to cease by using force; to crush, as an insurrection; to quiet; to allay, as anxieties or fears.—**quell·er,** *n.*

quench, kwench, *v.t.* [O.E. *cwencan,* to quench, to extinguish; akin to *cwinan,* to dwindle; O.Fris. *kwinka,* to vanish.] To extinguish; to put out, as a fire; to allay; to slake or satisfy, as thirst; to suppress, stifle, or check; to cool abruptly, as heated steel in the tempering process, by sudden immersion into water.—*v.i.* To be extinguished; to go out; to lose zeal.—**quench·a·ble,** *a.*—**quench·er,** *n.*—**quench·less,** kwench′lis, *a.*

quer·ce·tin, kwur′si·tin, *n. Chem.* a yellow crystalline powder, $C_{15}H_{10}O_7$, obtained from the bark of the quercitron oak and from other vegetable substances, and used as a yellow dye.—**quer·cet·ic,** kwĕr·set′ik, kwĕr·sē′tik, *a.*

quer·ci·tron, kwur′si″tron, *n.* [L. *quercus,* an oak, and *citrus,* the citron tree.] The black oak, *Quercus velutina,* a large forest tree of N. America; the bark of this tree yielding a yellow dye; the dyestuff itself.

que·rist, kwēr′ist, *n.* One who puts a query; one who asks questions.

quern, kwurn, *n.* [O.E. *cwyrn, cweorn* = D. *kweern,* Icel. *kvern,* Dan. *qvaern,* Goth. *qvairnus,* a millstone, a quern; < root meaning to grind, same as in *corn.*] A stone hand mill formerly used for grinding grain; a small hand-operated spice mill.

quer·u·lous, kwer′a·lus, kwer′ya·lus, *a.* [L. *querulus,* < *queror,* to complain.] Complaining or of a habitually complaining disposition; fretful; peevish.—**quer·u·lous·ly,** *adv.*—**quer·u·lous·ness,** *n.*

que·ry, kwēr′ē, *n. pl.* **que·ries.** [A modified form of L. *quaere,* impv. of *quaero,* to ask, to inquire, to seek.] A question; an inquiry to be answered or resolved; *print.* the mark or sign of interrogation(?), esp. when used to indicate a questioning of the text.—*v.i.* queried, querying. To ask a question or questions.—*v.t.* To seek by questioning; to examine by questions; to express doubt of; to mark with a query.

quest, kwest, *n.* [O.Fr. *queste,* Fr. *quête,* L. *quaesitus,* pp. of *quaero,* to seek.] The act of seeking; search; pursuit; an expedition or adventurous journey taken to achieve or to find something; the members of such an expedition.—*v.i.* To make search or inquiry; to pursue game.—*v.t.* To search or seek for.—**quest·er,** *n.*—**quest·ing·ly,** *adv.*

ques·tion, kwes′chan, kwesh′chan, *n.* [Fr. *question,* L. *quaestio,* an inquiry, an investigation.] An interrogative sentence soliciting an answer; a query; an inquiry; a subject or matter of investigation or discussion, esp. by an official body; a subject of debate; a point of doubt or difficulty; a controversy; the act of inquiring.—*v.i.* To ask a question or questions; to debate; to doubt.—*v.t.* To interrogate; to inquire of by asking questions; to express doubt of; to challenge.—**ques·tion·er,** *n.*

ques·tion·a·ble, kwes′cha·na·bl, *a.* Open to being questioned or inquired into; liable to question; disputable; suspicious; doubtful as to honesty or morality; uncertain.—**ques·tion·a·ble·ness, ques·tion·a·bil·i·ty,** *n.*—**ques·tion·a·bly,** *adv.*

ques·tion·ar·y, kwes′cha·ner″ē, *n. pl.* **ques·tion·ar·ies.** A questionnaire.—*a.* Of a questioning nature.

ques·tion·less, kwes′chan·lis, *a.* Unquestionable; indubitable; unquestioning.—*adv.* Without question; beyond doubt.

ques·tion mark, *n.* A symbol (?) used in writing and printing to indicate a question, and usu., as in English, placed at the end of the question; also *interrogation point. Fig.*

---

a- fat, fāte, fär, fâre, fặll;   **e-** met, mē, mêre, hẽr;   **i-** pin, pīne;   **o-** not, nŏte, mōve;   **u-** tub, cūbe, bụll;   **oi-** oil;   **ou-** pound.

something unknown, a mystery, as: The enemy's strategy is still a *question mark*.

ques·tion·naire, kwes˝chȧ·nâr′, *n.* A systematic series of questions prepared for distribution in order to gather detailed information for analytical purposes.

ques·tion time, *n. Brit.* a period of time within a parliamentary session in which members may ask a minister questions pertaining to his department.

ques·tor, kwes′tẽr, kwē′stẽr, *n.* [L. *quaestor*.] Quaestor.

quet·zal, ket·säl′, *n.* pl. **quet·zals**, **quet·zal·es**, ket·säl′ās. [Sp.] *Ornith.* an iridescent red and bronze-green bird, *Pharomarchus mocino*, native to the mountain forests of Central and South America, and noted for its compressed regal crest and elongated upper tail coverts: the national symbol or emblem of Guatemala. The monetary unit of Guatemala; see Moneys of the World table. Also **que·zal**, kā·säl′.

queue, kū, *n.* [Fr., tail, < L. *cauda*, a tail.] Braided hair hanging behind the head; a line of people or vehicles, esp. those awaiting their turn.—*v.t.*, *v.i.*—queued, queuing. To line up; to form a queue.

quib·ble, kwib′l, *n.* [A freq. of *quib*, *quip*.] A turn of language to evade the point in question; an evasion; a trivial point of disagreement.—*v.i.*—quibbled, quibbling. To evade the point in question by means of trivial objections or misleading questions, to bicker.—**quib·bler**, *n.*

quick, kwik, *a.* [O.E. *cwic*, living, lively = D. *kwik*, Icel. *kvikr*, Dan. *qvik*, Sw. *qvick*, L.G. *quick*, Goth. *qvius*; same root as L. *vivus*, living, Gr. *bios*, life, Skt. *jiv*, to live.] Taking place rapidly; immediate, prompt, as an action or procedure occurring or finishing in a short time; mentally agile; alert; perceptive; receptive to learning; as, a *quick* mind; physically adept; nimble; acting or able to act with rapidity; emotionally sensitive or volatile; easily offended or hurt; impatient; as, a *quick* temper; twisting or reversing direction abruptly; as, a *quick* turn in the road.—*adv.* In a quick manner.—*n.* The living; as, the *quick* and the dead; living flesh, esp. sensitive areas beneath fingernails or toenails; as, nails trimmed down to the *quick*; the center of sensibility, as: The insult stung her to the *quick*. *Bot.* a shrublike plant, usu. hawthorn, used in hedges; a hedge consisting of such plants.—**quick·ly**, *adv.*—**quick·ness**, *n.*

quick as·sets, *n. pl.* Cash and assets that can readily be converted to cash.

quick bread, *n.* Any bread, biscuit, or the like made with a quick-acting leavening agent, thus allowing immediate baking.

quick·en, kwik′en, *v.t.* To make quicker; to accelerate; to make alive; to revive or resuscitate; to refresh; to stimulate.—*v.i.* To come alive; to become quicker or more rapid; to arrive at that state of pregnancy in which the fetus gives indications of life; of the fetus, to begin to give signs of life in the womb.—**quick·en·er**, *n.*

quick-freeze, kwik′frēz″, *v.t.*—past *quick-froze*, pp. *quick-frozen*, ppr. *quick-freezing*. To preserve, as foods, by rapid freezing that permits lengthy storage and prevents damage to taste and appearance on thawing.

quick·hatch, kwik′hach″, *n.* Wolverine.

quick·ie, kwik′ē, *n. Slang.* Something produced or accomplished in an extremely short period of time, often trivial in subject or makeshift in execution; an alcoholic beverage quickly drunk or meant to be quickly drunk.

quick kick, *n. Football*, a punt made on any but the fourth down from a non-kicking formation, and intended to prevent a punt return by the opposing team.

quick·lime, kwik′līm″, *n.* [So called because of its active, burning properties.] Lime

in the dry state, before it is slaked with water.

quick·sand, kwik′sȧnd″, *n.* An area of soft or loose, wet sand of considerable depth, yielding under weight and hence apt to engulf persons, animals, and objects coming upon it.

quick·set, kwik′set″, *n. Chiefly Brit.* A living plant, cutting, or slip, esp. some variety of hawthorn, set to grow, particularly for a hedge; the hedge so formed.—*a.* Made of quickset.

quick·sil·ver, kwik′sil″vẽr, *n.* [Living silver, so called from its fluidity.] Mercury, liquid at ordinary temperatures.—*v.t.* To cover with an amalgam of mercury.

quick·step, kwik′step″, *n.* A lively, spirited style of ballroom dancing; music in a lively march tempo; formerly, a marching step.

quick-tem·pered, kwik′tem′pẽrd, *a.* Easily moved to anger.

quick time, *n. Milit.* a marching rate or time of 120 steps per minute, each step being 30 inches long.

quick turn, *n. Stock market*, the purchase and resale of stock as a speculation, usu. within hours or days.

quick-wit·ted, kwik′wit″id, *a.* Having a ready wit; mentally quick and alert.—**quick-wit·ted·ly**, *adv.*—**quick-wit·ted·ness**, *n.*

quid, kwid, *n.* pl. **quid**, **quids**. *Brit. slang.* One pound sterling; formerly, a sovereign.

quid, kwid, *n.* [A form of *cud*.] A piece of tobacco or other substance chewed and rolled about in the mouth.

quid·di·ty, kwid′i·tē, *n.* pl. **quid·di·ties**. [Fr. *quiddité*, < L.L. *quidditas*, < L. *quid*, what.] The essence of something, taking in both the substance and qualities; a trifling nicety.

quid·nunc, kwid′nungk″, *n.* [L., 'what now?'] One curious to know everything that happens; a busybody.

quid pro quo, kwid″ prō kwō′, *n.* Something in exchange for something; a direct even exchange; what is given or received in an exchange; a substitute.

qui·es·cent, kwē·es′ent, *a.* [L. *quiescens*, *quiescentis*, ppr. of *quiesco*, to keep quiet.] Being in a state of repose; still; quiet; inactive; tranquil; *gram.* silent, not sounded.—**qui·es·cence**, *n.*—**qui·es·cent·ly**, *adv.*

qui·et, kwī′it, *a.* [Fr. *quiet*, L. *quietus*, < *quiesco*, to keep quiet, < *quies*, *quietus*, rest.] Marked by silence or relative silence; as, a *quiet* road; secluded; making no objectionable or disturbing noise; as, *quiet* people for neighbors; silent, as: Keep *quiet*. Not in action or motion; still; in a state of rest; free from alarm or disturbance; tranquil; peaceable; not turbulent; free from emotion; calm; mild; unobtrusive; as, a *quiet* warning; subdued, as a sense of humor; not glaring or showy, as colors.—*n.* Stillness; rest; tranquillity; calmness; peace or repose.—*v.t.* To make or cause to be quiet; to calm; to pacify.—*v.i.* To become quiet or still.—*adv.* In a silent or calm manner.—**qui·et·er**, *n.*—**qui·et·ly**, *adv.*—**qui·et·ness**, *n.*

qui·et·ism, kwī′i·tiz″um, *n.* [It. *quietismo*, < *quiete*, < L. *quies*, E. *quiet*, *n.*] A form of religious mysticism taught by Molinos, a Spanish priest, in the latter part of the 17th century, requiring extinction of the will, withdrawal from worldly interests, and passive meditation on God and divine things; some similar form of religious mysticism; quietness of mind or life; inactivity.—**qui·et·ist**, *n.*, *a.*—**qui·et·is·tic**, *a.*

qui·e·tude, kwī′i·tōd″, kwī′i·tūd″, *n.* [L. *quietudo*.] A state of rest; quiet; tranquillity.

qui·e·tus, kwi·ē′tus, *n.* pl. **qui·e·tus·es**. [L. *quietus*, quiet. *Quietus* or *quietus est* was a formula used in discharging accounts, equiv. to quit, discharged.] A final settle-

ment, as of an account; a quittance; that which conclusively ends; a final stroke; a release from or a cessation of activity; death.

quiff, kwif, *n. Brit.* a curl or small strand of hair brought low on the forehead.

quill, kwil, *n.* [M.E. *quil*: cf. L.G. *quiele*, G. *kiel*, quill.] One of the large feathers of the wing or tail of a bird; the hard tubelike part of a feather nearest the body; a feather, as of a goose, formed into a pen for writing; a piece of reed or a bobbin on which yarn is wound; a musical pipe, as of reed; a roll of bark, as one formed of dried cinnamon; a plectrum made from the quill of a feather; a toothpick made of the quill of a feather; one of the hollow spines of a porcupine or hedgehog; a narrow fold or a pleated ruffle; *mach.* a hollow shaft through which another shaft or cylinder passes.—*v.t.* To flute or pleat, as cloth, in small, regular folds; to wind, as thread, on a quill; to pierce with a quill; to remove quills from.

quill·back, kwil′bak″, *n.* pl. **quill·back**, **quill·backs**. *Ichth.* a carpsucker, *Carpiodes cyprinus*, common in the streams of central U.S.

quilt, kwilt, *n.* [O.Fr. *cuilte*, *coutre*, *coultre*, < L. *culcitra*, *culcita*, a mattress, a pillow, a quilt.] A cover or coverlet made by stitching one cloth over another, with some soft substance between; any thick or warm coverlet; any quilted article.—*v.t.* To stitch together, as two pieces of cloth, with some soft substance between; to stitch in the ornamental pattern of a quilt; to line in the manner of a quilt.—*v.i.* To make a quilt; to do quilted work.—**quilt·er**, *n.*

quilt·ing, kwil′ting, *n.* The act or operation of forming a quilt; the material used for making quilts; quilted work.

quin·a·crine, kwin′a·krēn″, *n.* A crystalline compound, $C_{23}H_{30}ClN_3O \cdot 2HCl$, of a bright yellow color, used in treating malaria.

qui·na·ry, kwī′na·rē, *a.* Having or consisting of five; grouped in fives; pertaining to a quinary system.—*n.* pl. **qui·na·ries**. A number in a system based on five.

quince, kwins, *n.* [< Fr. *coignasse*, a kind of quince, < L. *cotonium*, *cydonium*, Gr. *kydōnion* (*mēlon*), a quince, lit. 'Cydonian fruit,' from *Cydonia*, a town in Crete.] The acid, yellow, fuzzy pome fruit of the small tree *Cydonia oblonga*, in the rose family, used in making jellies and marmalade; the tree itself, native to western Asia.—**flow·er·ing quince**, any of several cultivated shrubs of the genus *Chaenomeles*, esp. *C. lagenaria*, grown for its brilliant orange flowers appearing in advance of the leaves; also *Japanese quince*.

quin·cun·cial, kwin·kun′shal, *a.* [L. *quincuncialis*.] Of, pertaining to, or consisting of a quincunx; *bot.* noting a five-ranked arrangement of leaves. Also **quin·cunx·ial**, kwin·kungk′shal.—**quin·cun·cial·ly**, *adv.*

quin·cunx, kwing′kungks, kwin′kungks, *n.* [L., *quincunx*, orig. five-twelfths (a Roman coin worth five-twelfths of the as and marked with a quincunx of spots), < *quinque*, five, and *uncia*, twelfth part, E. *ounce*.] An arrangement of five objects, as trees, in a square or rectangle, one at each corner and one in the middle; *bot.* an imbricated arrangement of five petals or leaves, in which two are interior, two are exterior, and one is partly interior and partly exterior.

quin·i·dine, kwin′i·dēn″, kwin′i·din, *n.* [< *quinine*.] *Chem.*, *pharm.* a clear crystalline alkaloid isomeric with quinine, found in the bark of certain cinchona trees, and used in its sulfate form in the regulation of the heart rhythm and the treatment of malaria.

qui·nine, kwī′nīn, *also Brit.* kwi·nēn′, *n.* [< *quina*.] A bitter crystalline alkaloid, $C_{20} \cdot H_{24}N_2O_2$, obtained from the bark of several species of cinchona trees, and used,

---

ch- chain, G. na*ch*t; **th-** THen, thin; **w-** wig, hw as sound in whig; **z-** zh as in azure, zeal. *Italicized vowel* indicates schwa sound.

esp. in the form of a salt, as a remedy for malaria; a salt of this alkaloid, esp. the sulfate. Also **qui·ni·na, quin·in**, kē·nē′na, kwi′nin.

qui·nine wa·ter, n. Carbonated water to which a little quinine is added along with lemon and lime flavoring.

qui·no·a, kē·nō′a, n. An herb, *Chenopodium quinoa*, cultivated in the Andes for its edible seeds.

qui·noi·dine, kwi·noi′dēn, kwi·noi′din, n. *Chem.* a brownish-black, resinous substance consisting of a mixture of alkaloids, obtained as a by-product in the manufacture of quinine and used as a cheap substitute for it.

quin·o·line, kwin′o·lēn′, kwin′o·lin, n. [Gr. *chinolin*, < *china* (= E. *china, quina*) and L. *oleum*, oil.] *Chem.* a colorless liquid with a pungent odor, occurring in coal tar, obtained by oxidation of aniline and glycerol, and used in the making of dyes and as a solvent and a preservative.

qui·none, kwi·nōn′, kwin′ōn, n. [G. *chinon*, < *china*.] *Chem.* A yellowish crystalline compound, $C_6H_4O_2$, formed by the oxidation of aniline, used primarily in photography and in the tanning industry; any of a class of similar compounds.

quin·o·noid, kwin′o·noid″, kwi·nō′noid, a. *Chem.* Similar to quinone; relating to quinone. Also **quin·oid**, kwin′oid.

Quin·qua·ges·i·ma, kwing″kwa·jes′i·ma, kwin′kwa·jes′i·ma, n. [L.] The Sunday directly preceding the beginning of Lent, being approximately 50 days before Easter. Also **Quin·qua·ges·i·ma Sun·day, Shrove Sun·day.**

quin·que·fo·li·ate, kwin″kwe·fō′lē·it, kwin″kwe·fō′lē·āt, a. [L. *quinque*, five, and *folium*, leaf.] *Bot.* having five leaflets. Also **quin·que·fo·li·o·late.**

quin·quen·ni·al, kwin·kwen′ē·al, kwing··kwen′ē·al, a. [L. *quinquennium*, a period of five years—*quinque*, five, and *annus*, year.] Occurring once in five years, or lasting five years.—n. Something that happens at five-year intervals; a fifth-year anniversary; a quinquennium.—**quin·quen·ni·al·ly**, adv.

quin·quen·ni·um, kwin·kwen′ē·um, kwing·kwen′ē·um, n. pl. **quin·quen·ni·ums, quin·quen·ni·a**, kwin·kwen′ē·a, kwing·kwen′ē·a. A space of five years. Also **quin·quen·ni·ad**, kwin·kwen′ē·ad″, kwing·kwen′ē·ad″.

quin·que·va·lent, kwing″kwe·vā′lent, kwin″kwe·vā′lent, kwin·kwev′a·lent, kwing·kwev′a·lent, a. [L. *quinque*, five, and *valens, valentis*, ppr. of *valeo*, to be worth.] *Chem.* Having a valence of five; having five possible valences.—**quin·que·va·lence**, kwing″kwe·vā′lens, kwin″kwe·vā′lens, kwin·kwev′a·lens, kwing·kwev′a·lens, n.

quin·sy, kwin′zē, n. [< Fr. *esquinancie, squinancie*, < L. *cynanche*, Gr. *kynangchē*, a kind of sore throat, < *kyōn*, a dog, and *angchō*, to throttle—'dog' having a pejorative effect.] *Pathol.* an inflammation of the tonsils, esp. a suppurating inflammation.

quint, kwint, kint, n. [L. *quintus*, fifth.] *Cards*, a set or sequence of five, as in piquet; *mus.* an organ stop sounding notes a fifth higher than those being played on the keys, kwint, kint. *Colloq.* a quintuplet, kwint.

quin·tain, kwin′tan, n. [Fr. *quintaine*, L.L. *quintana*, a quintain, < L. *quintana*, a street or broad way in a camp (< *quintus*, fifth), hence a public place and the exercise practiced in such a place.] In the medieval game of tilting, a figure or other target to be tilted at, as one attached to a free-swinging crossbar fixed to an upright post; the game itself of tilting at such an object.

quin·tal, kwin′tal, n. [Fr. *quintal*, < L. *centum*, a hundred, through the Sp. *quintal*, Ar. *kintār*, a weight of 100 lb.] In the metric system, 100 kilograms of weight; a hundredweight.

quinte, kaNt, n. [Fr., fem. of *quint*, < L. *quintus*, fifth, < *quinque*, five.] *Fencing*, the fifth in a series of eight parries.

quin·tes·sence, kwin·tes′ens, n. [L. *quinta essentia*, fifth essence.] An extract from anything, containing the most essential part of it; the perfect embodiment of a thing; according to ancient and medieval philosophy, the fifth or highest essence, the element of which the heavenly bodies are formed.—**quin·tes·sen·tial**, kwin″ti·sen′shal, a.—**quin·tes·sen·tial·ly**, adv.

quin·tet, quin·tette, kwin·tet′, n. [Fr. *quintette*, < It. *quintetto*, < *quinto*, L. *quintus*, fifth.] *Mus.* a vocal or instrumental composition in five parts; the five people or instruments performing it. A group of five persons or things.

quin·tile, kwin′til, a. [= Fr. *quintil*, < L. *quintus*, fifth.] *Astrol.* noting the aspect of two heavenly bodies when they are the fifth part of the zodiac or 72° distant from each other.—n. *Astrol.* a quintile aspect. *Statistics*, a distribution of observed cases or samples into five equal groups; one fifth of the sample.

quin·til·lion, kwin·til′yon, n. [L. *quintus*, fifth, and term. of E. *million*.] In U.S. and France, a thousand quadrillions, signified by 1 followed by 18 zeros; in Great Britain and Germany, a million quadrillions, signified by 1 followed by 30 zeros.—a.—**quin·til·lionth**, a., n.

quin·tu·ple, kwin·tö′pl, kwin·tū′pl, kwin··tup′l, kwin′tu̇·pl, kwin′tū·pl, a. [L. *quintuplus*, fivefold—*quintus*, fifth, and term. *-plus*, Gr. *pleon*.] Arranged or divided in five or in fives; five times as large or as many.—n. A number that is five times another in amount.—v.t., v.i.—*quintupled, quintupling*. To make or be made five times as great.

quin·tu·plet, kwin·tup′lit, kwin·tö′plit, kwin·tū′plit, kwin′tu̇·plit, kwin′tū·plit, n. A collection of five of a kind; any one of five offspring born at the same birth. Also *quint.*

quin·tu·pli·cate, kwin·tö′pli·kit, kwin··tū′pli·kit, a. Reproduced five times.—n. Any of five identical things.—kwin·tö′pli·kāt′, kwin·tū′pli·kāt′, v.t.—*quintuplicated, quintuplicating*. To reproduce or repeat five times; to quintuple.

quip, kwip, n. [< L. *quippe*, indeed.] A smart sarcastic comment or observation; a clever impromptu remark; a quibble.—v.i. —*quipped, quipping*. To make or utter a quip.—**quip·pish**, a.—**quip·ster**, kwip′stėr, n.

qui·pu, kē′pö, kwip′ö, n. [Peruvian, lit. 'knot.'] Among the ancient Peruvians, a device consisting of a cord with knotted strings of various colors attached, used for recording events, keeping accounts, and the like.

quire, kwī′ėr, n. [O.Fr. *quayer*; Fr. *cahier*, < L.L. *quaternum*, a book of four leaves, < L. *quatuor*, four.] A collection of paper, one-twentieth of a ream, consisting of 24 or 25 sheets of equal size and weight; a collection of all the printed sheets for a book, folded, and in right sequence.

quirk, kwu̇rk, n. [Provinc. E. *quirk*, to turn sharply; cf. W. *chwired*, a sudden start, craft, deceit.] A peculiar characteristic or mannerism; a subterfuge; a shift; a quibble; a sudden or sharp turn; a sweeping or flourish, as in writing; *arch.* a recess or groove in or between moldings.—**quirk·i·ly**, adv.—**quirk·i·ness**, n.—**quirk·y**, kwu̇r′kē, a.—*quirkier, quirkiest.*

quirt, kwu̇rt, n. [Cf. *cuarta*.] A riding whip consisting of a short, stout stock and a lash of braided leather.—v.t. To strike with a quirt.

quis·ling, kwiz′ling, n. [After Vidkun Quisling, a pro-Nazi Norwegian politician. A

person who undermines his own country from within; a fifth columnist.—**quis··ling·ism**, n.

quit, kwit, v.t.—*quit or quitted, quitting*. [< O.Fr. *quite*, Mod.Fr. *quittée*, discharged, freed, quit, < L. *quietus*, quiet. *Quiet* is thus the same word, as is also *quite*.] To discontinue or cease; to depart from; to leave; to give up or abandon; to let go of, as something grasped.—v.i. To stop doing something; to resign from employment; to go away; to give up a struggle; accept defeat.—a. Released or absolved from a debt, penalty, or obligation; free; rid, sometimes followed by *of*.—n. Act of quitting.

quitch, kwich, n. [A. form of *quick grass*—named after its vitality and vigorous growth.] Couch grass, *Agropyron repens*, a species of worthless grass. Also **quitch grass**, *quack grass.*

quit·claim, kwit′klām″, n. *Law*, the giving up of a claim.—v.t. *Law*, to give up or release one's claim, as to a right or possession.

quite, kwīt, adv. [Old form of *quit*, that is, primarily, free or clear by complete performance.] Completely, wholly, entirely, or totally; as, not *quite* done; really, actually; to a great extent or degree; very; as, *quite* warm.

quit·rent, kwit′rent″, n. Rent of a fixed amount once paid by freeholders and copyholders of a manor in place of other services.

quits, kwits, a. [Cf. *quit*, a.] Even, or on equal terms, by repayment or retaliation.—**call it quits**, to stop an activity.

quit·tance, kwit′ans, n. Discharge from a debt or obligation; a written acknowledgment verifying release from an obligation; recompense; repayment.

quit·ter, kwit′ėr, n. One who quits or gives up; one who withdraws under adverse circumstances.

quit·tor, kwit′ėr, n. *Veter. pathol.* an ulcer on the hoof of a horse or other animal having solid hoofs.

quiv·er, kwiv′ėr, n. [O.Fr. *quivre, cuivre*, < O.H.G. *kohhar, kochar*, G. *köcher*, a quiver; cogn. Dan. *koger*, D. *koker*, O.E. *cocer*—a case, a quiver.] A case for arrows; the arrows carried in this case.

quiv·er, kwiv′ėr, v.i. [Same as D. *quiveren*, to tremble, closely connected with *quaver*, and with old *quiver*, active, nimble, O.E. *cwifer*, perh. also with *quick*.] To shake or tremble; to show a slight tremulous motion.—n. The act or state of quivering; a tremor.

quix·ot·ic, kwik·sot′ik, a. [After Don Quixote, the hero of Cervantes' celebrated romance, who is painted as a half-crazy reformer and champion, and is a caricature of the ancient knights of chivalry.] Resembling Don Quixote; in the manner of Don Quixote; romantic to extravagance; visionary; high-flown and impractical. Also **quix·ot·i·cal**.—**quix·ot·i·cal·ly**, adv.—**quix·ot·ism**, kwik′so·tiz″um, n.

quiz, kwiz, n. pl. **quiz·zes**. [Said to have been originated simply to puzzle people by Daly, the manager of a Dublin playhouse, who had the letters *q u i z* put on all the walls of Dublin.] A questioning or examining; a brief, informal examination.—v.t.—*quizzed, quizzing*. To test, as a student, by questioning; to question intensively; as, to *quiz* the vagrant; *Brit.* to ridicule.—**quiz·zer**, n.

quiz·zi·cal, kwiz′i·kal, a. Comical or odd; confused or questioning; teasing; ridiculing. —**quiz·zi·cal·i·ty**, kwiz·i·kal′i·tē, n.—**quiz·zi·cal·ly**, adv.

quod, kwod, n. [A form of *quad*, a contr. of *quadrangle*.] *Brit. slang*, a jail. Also *quad.*

quod·li·bet, kwod′li·bet″, n. [L. *quod libet*, 'what it pleases,' what you please.] *Mus.* a fanciful polyphonic combination of two or more well-known melodies; *hist.* a theological or scholastic question proposed for exercise in argument, or the subtle debate on such a question.

quoin, koin, kwoin, *n.* [Variant spelling of *coin.*] An external solid angle of a wall or the like; one of the stones forming it; a cornerstone; a wedge-shaped piece of wood, stone, or other material; *print.* a wedge of wood or metal for securing types in a chase. —*v.t.* To provide with quoins, as a corner of a wall; to secure or raise with a quoin or wedge. Also **coign, coigne.**

quoit, kwoit, *n.* [Origin doubtful; cf. provinc. E. and Sc. *coit; quoit,* to throw; also O.D. *koot,* a die.] A flattened iron ring, or a circle of heavy rope, used in a game in which it is thrown at a fixed peg in the ground; *pl.* but *sing. in constr.* the game played with such rings.—*v.t.* To throw like quoits.

quon·dam, kwon'dam, *a.* [L., formerly.] Having been formerly; former; sometime; as, one's *quondam* friend.

Quon·set hut, kwon'sit hut, *n.* [From *Quonset,* Rhode Island.] A compact, serviceable, prefabricated metal shelter or hut resembling a semicircular arch in cross section. (Trademark.)

quo·rum, kwōr'um, kwạr'um, *n.* [Lit. 'of whom,' being the genit. pl. of L. *qui,* who—from the phraseology of commissions, etc., written in Latin, certain persons being therein named generally, 'of whom' certain were specially designated as in all cases necessary and therefore constituting a quorum.] The number of members of any body that must be present to legally transact business, usu. a majority; a selected group.

quo·ta, kwō'ta, *n.* [< L. *quotus,* which number in the series ?] A proportional part or share of a fixed quantity; the share or proportion assigned to each or which each person or group has to contribute; the quantity or number representing such a share.

quot·a·ble, kwō'ta·bl, *a.* Capable of or suitable for being quoted or cited.— **quot·a·bil·i·ty,** *n.*

quo·ta·tion, kwō·tā'shan, *n.* The act of quoting; the passage quoted or cited. *Com.* the stated current price of a commodity or stock, or the statement or publishing of this.

quo·ta·tion mark, *n.* One of the pair of marks used to indicate the beginning and end of a quotation, in English usu. consisting of two inverted commas (") at the beginning and two apostrophes (") at the end, or, for a quotation within a quotation, of single marks of this kind, as in "He said, 'I will go,'" though frequently, esp. in Great Britain, single marks are used instead of double, the latter being then used for a quotation within a quotation.

quote, kwōt, *v.t.*—*quoted, quoting.* [O.Fr. *quoter,* Fr. *coter,* < L.L. *quotare,* to give chapter and verse for, < L. *quotus,* which number in the series ? < *quot,* how many ?] To repeat from some author or speaker; to repeat by way of authority or illustration; to cite or cite the words of; as, to *quote* a passage or an author; to surround with quotation marks. *Com.* to name, as the price of an article or service; to state the current price of, as of stocks or bonds.—*v.i.* To make quotations.—*n. Colloq.* Quotation; quotation mark.

quoth, kwōth, *v.t.* [Pret. of *quethe* (otherwise obs.), < O.E. *cwethan,* say: cf. *bequeath.*] *Archaic,* said: used with nouns and with pronouns of the first and third persons, and always placed before the subject.

quoth·a, kwō'tha, *interj.* [For *quoth a,* 'quoth he.'] *Archaic,* forsooth or indeed: generally used disparagingly.

quo·tid·i·an, kwō·tid'ē·an, *a.* [L. *quotidianus,* < *quotidie,* daily—*quot,* how many,

every, and *dies,* a day.] Daily; occurring or returning daily; ordinary, common.—*n.* Anything that returns every day; a fever whose paroxysms return every day.

quo·tient, kwō'shent, *n.* [Fr., < L. *quoties,* how often ?] *Math.* the number resulting from the division of one number by another, and showing how often the lesser quantity is contained in the greater.

quo war·ran·to, kwō wạ·ran'tō, kwō-wo·ran'tō, *n.* [M.L. 'by what warrant.'] *Law.* Formerly, in England, a writ calling upon a person to show by what warrant or authority he exercises an office, privilege, franchise, or liberty; now, in England and the U.S., a legal proceeding used for a similar purpose.

R

R, r, är, *n.* The eighteenth letter of the English alphabet and fourteenth consonant; the sound of the letter R, as represented in speech; the delineation of the letter R or r in writing or printing; something designated by or having the shape of the letter R or r; a graphic device used for printing the letter R or r.

R, är. *Chem.* gas constant; an alkyd radical. *Math.* ratio; radius. *Phys.* roentgen. *Chess,* rook.

r, är. *Phys.* roentgen unit; specific gas constant. *Elect.* resistance; *statistics,* correlation coefficient. Ruble; rupee; see Moneys of the World table.

Ra, rä, *n.* [Egypt.] The sovereign god of the Egyptians, the sun god, typically represented as a hawk-headed man bearing on his head the solar disk and the royal uraeus. Also **Re,** rā.

ra·ba·to, ra·bā'tō, ra·bä'tō, *n.* pl. **ra·ba·- tos.** A stiff, wide, flaring collar, often of linen or lace, that extended over the shoulders or was arranged to stand up at the back, worn in the 16th and 17th centuries. Also *rebato.*

rab·bet, rab'it, *n.* [Prob. < O.Fr. *rabat,* a beating down (Fr. a rabat), < *rabattre,* beat or put down.] A cut, groove, or recess made on the edge or surface of a board so as to receive the end or edge of another board similarly or otherwise appropriately shaped; a joint so made. Also *rebate.*—*v.t.* To cut or form a rabbet in; to join by a rabbet or rabbets.—*v.i.* To be joined by means of a rabbet. Also *rebate.*—**rab·bet joint,** a joint formed by a rabbet or rabbets.

rab·bi, rab'ī, *n.* pl. **rab·bis.** *Judaism.* The ordained leader of a synagogue empowered to perform religious and legal ceremonies; a teacher or master, used as a title; a learned Jew qualified to interpret Jewish law; (*often cap.*) a Jewish scholar of the early Christian era engaged in the formulation of the Talmud.

rab·bin·ate, rab'i·nit, *n.* The office or dignity of a rabbi; rabbis collectively.

Rab·bin·ic, ra·bin'ik, *n.* The Hebrew language as used by the rabbis in their writings in early medieval times.

rab·bin·i·cal, ra·bin'i·kal, *a.* Of or pertaining to the rabbis or their learning, opinions, or writings. Also **rab·bin·ic.— rab·bin·i·cal·ly,** *adv.*

rab·bin·ism, rab'i·niz"um, *n.* A rabbinical expression or phrase; the teachings or traditions of the rabbis.

rab·bit, rab'it, *n.* pl. **rab·bits, rab·bit.** [M.E. *rabet:* cf. Walloon *robett,* rabbit.] A small long-eared burrowing rodent, *Lepus cuniculus,* of the hare family; any of various other long-eared mammals, genus *Sylvilagus,* as the cottontail; the pelt of a hare or

rabbit.—*v.i.* To hunt or catch rabbits. —**rab·bit·er,** *n.*—**rab·bit·y,** *a.*

rab·bit fe·ver, *n.* Tularemia.

rab·bit punch, *n.* A blow with the back of the hand or fist to the nape of the neck or base of the skull.

rab·bit·ry, rab'i·trē, *n.* pl. **rab·bit·ries.** A place in which rabbits are kept; a collection of rabbits.

rab·ble, rab'l, *n.* [M.E. *rabel,* pack (of hounds).] A disorderly crowd or assemblage of persons, esp. of a low, rough, or turbulent kind; a mob.—*v.t.*—*rabbled, rabbling.* To beset as a rabble does; to mob. —**the rab·ble,** contemptuously, the lower classes as a whole; the masses.

rab·ble, rab'l, *n.* [Fr. *râble,* earlier *rouable,* < L. *rutabulum,* instrument for raking or stirring, < *ruere,* turn up, rake up.] *Metal.* An iron bar sharply bent at one end, used for stirring, skimming, or gathering molten iron in puddling; any device used for the same purpose. Also **rab·bler.**—*v.t.*—*rabbled, rabbling.* To stir, skim, or gather with a rabble.

rab·ble·ment, rab'l·ment, *n.* Disorder or tumult; rabble.

rab·ble-rous·er, rab'l·rou"zér, *n.* One who attempts to arouse the prejudices and passions of people, usu. for personal gain; demagogue.

Rab·e·lai·si·an, rab"e·lā'zē·an, rab"- e·lā'zhan, *a.* [Fr. *Rabelais.*] Denoting, pertaining to, or marked by the style of François Rabelais, French writer; characterized by bawdy humor and perceptive satire.—*n.* One who studies Rabelais or imitates him.—**Rab·e·lai·si·an·ism,** *n.*

rab·id, rab'id, *a.* [L. *rabidus,* < *rabies,* madness, < *rabo,* to rave.] Furious; raging; mad; affected with rabies; excessively or unreasonably enthusiastic; as, a *rabid* boxing fan.—**rab·id·i·ty,** *n.*—**rab·id·ly,** *adv.* —**rab·id·ness,** *n.*

ra·bies, rā'bēz, rā'bē·ēz", *n.* [L.] Hydrophobia; an infectious disease of small animals, particularly dogs, believed to be caused by a virus, transmitted to man by the bite of an infected animal, and usu. proving fatal unless treatment is instituted early in the incubation period.

rac·coon, ra·coon, ra·kön', *n.* pl. **rac·coons, rac·coon.** [Corruption of the Amer. Ind. name, *arrathkune, arathcone,* formerly in use.] A N. American plantigrade carnivorous mammal, *Procyon lotor,* identified by its bushy tail ringed with black and white, pointed snout, and black masklike patch extending through the eyes; the fur of this animal.

race, rās, *n.* [M.E. *rase, ras* < Scand.: cf. Icel. *rás,* a running, race, rush or flow of liquid, course, channel, = O.E. *raes,* a running, rush.] A contest of speed, as in running, riding, driving, or the like; *pl.* a series of races, as of horses, which are run at a set time over a regular course. Any competition; as, a *race* for election; onward movement, or an onward or regular course; the course of time; the course of life or a part of life; a strong or rapid current of water, as in the sea or a river; the channel or bed of such a current or of any stream; a channel leading water to or from a place where its energy is utilized; the current of water in such a channel. *Mach.* a channel, groove, or the like, for a sliding or rolling part, as for balls in a ball bearing; also *raceway.*—*v.i.*—*raced, racing.* To engage in a contest of speed; run a race; to run, move or go swiftly; to run with undue or uncontrolled speed when the load or resistance is diminished without corresponding diminution of power, as of an engine, wheel, or the like.—*v.t.* To run a race with; tr· to beat in a contest of speed; to cause to ⟨un in a race or races; to cause to run, move, or go swiftly; as, to *race* an engine.

race, rās, *n.* [Fr. *race,* < It. *razza,* race, breed, lineage; origin uncertain.] A group of persons connected by common descent or origin; a family, tribe, or people; *ethnol.* a major division of mankind characterized by a combination of certain physical traits which are genetically transmitted; as, the Mongoloid *race.* The human race or family; mankind; a group of tribes or peoples forming an ethnic stock; the condition of belonging to a particular people or stock; the qualities or characteristics due to this; a breed, stock, or strain of animals; *biol.* a subspecies or a variety. Any group, class, or kind, esp. a class of persons; as, the *race* of politicians; the characteristic taste or flavor of wine; a characteristic quality, esp. a lively or piquant quality, as of speech or writing.

race·course, rās′kōrs″, rās′kạrs″, *n.* Race-track.

race horse, *n.* A horse bred or kept for racing. Also **race·horse.**

ra·ceme, rā·sēm′, ra·sēm′, *n.* [L. *racemus,* a cluster of grapes.] *Bot.* an inflorescence composed of a primary axis which bears, at intervals along its length, flowers with equal stalks.—**ra·cemed,** *a.*—**ra·ce·mi·form,** rā·sē′mi·fạrm″, *a.*

ra·ce·mic, rā·sē′mik, rā·sem′ik, ra·sē′mik, ra·sem′ik, *a.* [L. *racemus.*] *Chem.* Noting or pertaining to an isomeric modification of tartaric acid, which is sometimes found in the juice of grapes in conjunction with the common dextrorotatory form, and which is optically inactive, but can be separated into the two usual isomeric forms, dextrorotatory and levorotatory; noting or pertaining to any of various organic compounds with analogous optical properties.

ra·ce·mic ac·id, *n. Chem.* the optically inactive mixture of the dextrorotatory and the levorotatory isomers of tartaric acid, found in the juice of grapes and used in medicine.

rac·e·mi·za·tion, ras″e·mi·zā′shan, *n. Chem.* the production of an optically inactive substance by combining the optically active dextrorotatory isomer in equal quantity with the optically active levorotatory isomer of a compound.

rac·e·mose, ras′e·mōs″, *a.* [L. *racemosus,* clustering, < *racemus,* E. *raceme.*] *Bot.* having the form of a raceme; racemelike. *Anat.* arranged as in racemes, as a gland.

rac·er, rā′sẽr, *n.* One who or that which races or takes part in a race, as a race horse, a bicycle, a yacht; anything having great speed; an American blacksnake, *Coluber constrictor.*

race ri·ot, *n.* A conflict or riot arising from racial animosity.

race·track, rās′trak″, *n.* A course, usu. oval, where races of horses, dogs, automobiles, or the like, are held. Also *racecourse,* **race track, race-track.**

race·way, rās′wā″, *n.* A passage or channel for water, as a millrace; a channel or tube for shielding electric wires; a track for harness racing.

ra·chis, rā′kis, *n.* pl. **ra·chis·es, rach·i·des,** rak′i·dēz″, rā′ki·dēz″. [N.L. for *rhachis,* < Gr. *ráchis,* spine, ridge.] Any of various axial structures, esp. the axis of an inflorescence when somewhat elongated, as in a raceme; *anat.* the spinal column; *ornith.* the shaft of a feather, esp. the part bearing the web, as distinguished from the quill portion. Also **rha·chis.**

ra·chi·tis, ra·kī′tis, *n.* [N.L., for *rhachitis,* < Gr. *rachitis,* disease of the spine, < *ráchis,* spine.] *Pathol.* rickets.—**ra·chit·ic,** ra·kit′ik, *a.*

ra·cial, rā′shal, *a.* Pertaining to or characteristic of race or extraction, a race, or races; stemming from differences between races.—**ra·cial·ly,** *adv.*

ra·cial·ism, rā′sha·liz″um, *n.* Racial discrimination; racism.—**ra·cial·ist,** *n.*—**ra·cial·is·tic,** *a.*

rac·ing form, *n.* A sheet providing data relevant to horse races, as information on jockeys, horses, and barrier positions.

rac·ism, rā′siz·um, *n.* The belief, not substantiated scientifically, that each human race is characterized by distinctive attributes which determine behaviors and capacities, and that a particular race is inherently superior; a social or political policy based upon this notion.—**rac·ist,** *n.*

rack, rak, *n.* [M.E. *rakke, racke.*] A framework, grating, or stand on or in which articles may be placed or displayed; such a framework, as in a stable or elsewhere, for holding fodder for horses or cattle; a spreading framework set on a wagon for carrying hay or straw in large loads; a triangle-shaped frame in which billiard balls are arranged for a game of pool. *Mach.* a bar with teeth on one of its sides, adapted to engage with teeth of a pinion or the like, as for converting circular into rectilinear motion or vice versa. An apparatus or instrument used for torturing persons by stretching the body; a cause, situation, or state of intense suffering of body or mind; torment; anguish.—*v.t.* To torture, as with a rack; to distress acutely; torment; to strain in mental effort; as, to *rack* one's brains; to strain beyond what is normal or usual; to raise to an exorbitant degree, as rent; to oppress with high rents or by extorting money; to put in or on a rack.—**on the rack,** in a mental or emotional state of pain or distress induced by conflicting pressures or stresses.—**rack·er,** *n.*

rack, rak, *n.* [Form of *wreck.*] *Obs.* wreck, ruin, destruction.—**go to rack and ru·in,** to decline or decay.—**rack up,** *slang,* to wreck.

rack, rak, *v.i.* [Origin obscure.] Of a horse, to go with a gait, similar to a pace, in which the legs move in lateral pairs but not quite simultaneously; to pace.—*n.* The gait of a horse in which the legs move in lateral pairs but not quite simultaneously; single-foot.

rack, rak, *n.* [M.E. *rak, rakke;* prob. < Scand.] Drifting broken clouds; a mass of clouds driven by the wind.—*v.i.* To drive or move, as clouds before the wind. Also *wrack.*

rack, rak, *v.t.* [< Fr. *raque,* mud, dregs.] To draw off from the lees, as pure liquor, cider, or wine.

rack, rak, *n.* [O.E. *hracca,* and Sc. *crag,* the neck.] The neck section of veal or mutton.

rack·et, rac·quet, rak′it, *n.* [Fr. *raquette,* perhaps < Ar. *rāhat,* palm of the hand.] A light bat having a network of nylon or catgut stretched in a more or less elliptical frame, used in tennis, badminton, and the like; the paddle used in playing table tennis; a snowshoe made in the form of a tennis or squash racket. *Pl. but sing. in constr.* a game of ball, played in a walled court, in which such bats or rackets are used.

rack·et, rak′it, *n.* [Prob. imit.] Loud noise, or a loud noise, esp. of a disturbing or confusing kind; din; uproar; clamor or noisy fuss; a noisy disturbance or affair; social excitement, gaiety, or dissipation. *Slang,* any scheme, trick, dodge, or special way of proceeding; an organized illegal activity, such as bootlegging or the extortion of money by threat or violence from those engaged in some legitimate business.—*v.i.* To make a din or noise; to indulge in social gaiety or dissipation.

rack·et·eer, rak″i·tẽr′, *n. Slang,* one engaged in some dishonest or illegal racket.—*v.i. Slang.* To act as a racketeer; to engage in some racket.

rack·e·ty, rak′i·tē, *a.* Making a din or clamor; noisy. *Colloq.* rowdy; seeking excitement.

rack rail·way, *n.* An inclined-plane railway, having a between-the-rails rack with cogs or teeth with which a cogwheel on the locomotive engages. Also *cog railway.*

rack-rent, rak′rent″, *n.* Excessively or unreasonably high rent; a rent for land equal or nearly equal to the full annual value of the land. Also **rack rent.**—*v.t.* To exact rack-rent from, as a tenant; to exact rackrent for, as a farm.—**rack-rent·er,** *n.*

ra·con, rā′kon, *n.* A radar beacon.

rac·on·teur, rak″on·tûr′, *n.* [Fr.] A skilled teller of anecdotes; one who tells a good story.

ra·coon, ra·kōn′, *n.* Raccoon.

rac·y, rā′sē, *a.*—*racier, raciest.* Having or showing a native vigor or liveliness; spirited; sprightly; pungent or piquant; as, a *racy* style; having a strong, characteristic taste or flavor, as wine, fruits, or the like; slightly indecent or risqué; suggestive; as, a *racy* anecdote.—**rac·i·ly,** *adv.*—**rac·i·ness,** *n.*

ra·dar, rā′där, *n.* [Short for *(ra)*dio *(d)*etecting *(a)*nd *(r)*anging.] An electronic system or device for determining the presence and location of an object by transmitting radio signals, which are reflected by the object and picked up by a receiving system.—**ac·qui·si·tion and track·ing ra·dar,** a radar installation used to search for, locate, and track a spacecraft in flight.—**ra·dar·man,** rā′där·man, rā′där·man″, *n.* pl. **ra·dar·men.**

ra·dar bea·con, *n.* A radar device of fixed location which, in response to incoming signals transmits a coded radar signal enabling aircraft and ships to determine their position in relation to it. Also *racon.*

ra·dar·scope, rā′där·skōp″, *n.* The device for visual indication of signals received by radar equipment.

rad·dle, rad′l, *v.t.*—*raddled, raddling.* [Perh. a corruption < *hurdle* or *riddle.*] To interweave; to twist or wind together.

rad·dle, rad′l, *n.* A red pigment used for marking sheep.—*v.t.*—*raddled, raddling.* To paint with raddle. Also *reddle, ruddle.*

ra·di·al, rā′dē·al, *a.* [< L. *radius,* a ray, a spoke.] Pertaining to a ray or radius; grouped or appearing like radii or rays; shooting out from a center, as the petals of a daisy or the pistons of an engine; *anat.* pertaining to the radius; *zool.* pertaining to structures resembling rays, as the appendages of a starfish.—*n.*—**ra·di·al·ly,** *adv.*

ra·di·al en·gine, *n.* An engine having radially situated cylinders.

ra·di·al sym·me·try, *n.* A symmetrical arrangement of parts around a center axis, as in a starfish or buttercup; a condition of being actinomorphic.

ra·di·an, rā′dē·an, *n.* [< *radius.*] *Math.* an angle at the center of a circle, equal to 57.2958 degrees, which subtends the arc of the circle equal in length to the radius.

ra·di·ance, rā′dē·ans, *n.* [< *radiant.*] Brightness; brilliant or sparkling luster; quality of being radiant or shining. Also **ra·di·an·cy,** *n.,* pl. **ra·di·an·cies.**

ra·di·ant, rā′dē·ant, *a.* [L. *radians (radiant-),* ppr. of *radiare.*] Emitting rays of light; bright; shining; as, the *radiant* sun; bright with joy, hope, or the like; as, a *radiant* face; emitting heat in rays; *phys.* emitted or transmitted in rays.—*n.* A point or object from which rays proceed; *astron.* the point in the heavens from which a shower of meteors appears to radiate.—**ra·di·ant·ly,** *adv.*

ra·di·ant en·er·gy, *n. Phys.* energy transmitted through space by the propagation of an electromagnetic wave through any form of matter, by the interaction of the electromagnetic wave with matter.

ra·di·ant flux, *n. Phys.* the time rate of flow of radiant energy.

ra·di·ant heat·ing, *n.* Panel heating.

ra·di·ate, rā′dē·āt″, *v.i.—radiated, radiating.* [L. *radio, radiatum.*] To issue or proceed in rays or straight lines from a point or surface, as heat or light; to emit rays. Also *eradiate.—v.t.* To emit or send out in direct lines or rays from a point or surface; also *eradiate.* To give forth an aura of, as: She *radiates* joy.—rā′dē·it, rā′dē·āt″, *a.* Having rays; having lines proceeding as from a center like radii; having radial structures or parts.—**ra·di·ate·ly,** *adv.*

ra·di·a·tion, rā″dē·ā′shan, *n.* [L. *radiatio, radiationis.*] The act of radiating or state of being radiated; that which is radiated; radiant energy. *Phys.* the emission of energy as waves or as nuclear particles; the process by which such energy is emitted, then transmitted through space or matter, and absorbed.—**ra·di·a·tion·al,** *a.*—**ra·di·a·tive,** rā′dē·ā′tiv, *a.*

ra·di·a·tor, rā′dē·ā″tėr, *n.* That which radiates; an appliance for heating a room by means of water or steam; a mechanism for cooling circulating water in engines; *radio,* a transmitter for broadcasting; *phys.* a source of electromagnetic radiation.

rad·i·cal, rad′i·kal, *a.* [L.L. *radicalis,* < L. *radix,* root.] Of or pertaining to a root or roots; existing inherently in a thing or person; as, *radical* defects of character; forming the basis or foundation; going to the root or origin, or touching what is fundamental; as, a *radical* change; thorough; extreme, esp. in the way of reform; as, *radical* opinions or principles; (*often cap.*) belonging or pertaining to extremists in politics; (*l.c.*), *bot.* of or arising from the root or the base of the stem. *Math.* pertaining to or forming a root; noting or pertaining to the radical sign.—*n.* One who holds or follows extreme principles. (*Often cap.*) an extremist in politics; one who advocates fundamental political reforms or changes by direct and uncompromising methods. (*l.c.*), *math.* a quantity expressed as a root of another quantity; radical sign. *Chem.* an atom or group of atoms which is regarded as an important constituent of the molecule of a given compound, and which remains unchanged during certain reactions; *gram.* the ultimate root form or basis of a word, as *lucid* from which *lucidity* is formed.—**rad·i·cal·ness,** *n.*

rad·i·cal·ism, rad′i·ka·liz″um, *n.* The holding or following of radical or extreme views or principles; the principles or practices of radicals.

rad·i·cal·ly, rad′ik·lē, *adv.* Referring to root or origin; fundamentally; completely; in a radical manner.

rad·i·cal sign, *n.* The mathematical symbol, $\sqrt{\ }$, put in front of a term to indicate the extraction of its root.

rad·i·cand, rad′i·kand″, *n. Math.* the term within a radical sign.

rad·i·cle, rad′i·kl, *n.* [L. *radicula,* dim. of *radix,* root.] *Bot.* the lower part of the axis of an embryo; a rudimentary root. *Anat.* a small rootlike part, as the beginning of a nerve fiber. *Chem.* a radical.—**ra·dic·u·lar,** ra·dik′ya·lėr, rā·dik′ya·lėr, *a.*

ra·di·o, rā′dē·ō″, *n.* pl. **ra·di·os.** [Short for *radiotelegraph,* etc., *radiotelephone,* etc.] Wireless telegraphy or telephony; a wireless telegraph, telephone, or other apparatus for transmitting or receiving messages by means of modulated electromagnetic waves; a wireless message or broadcast; the radio communications industry.—*a.* Of, pertaining to, used in, or sent by radiotelegraphy or radiotelephony; wireless; relating to or involved in the radio communications industry; pertaining to electromagnetic waves with frequencies exceeding 15,000

cycles per second.—*v.t., v.i.—radioed, radioing.* To transmit, as a message or a program, or transmit a message to by radio.

ra·di·o·ac·tive, rā″dē·ō·ak′tiv, *a.* Pertaining to or caused by radioactivity.—**ra·di·o·ac·tive·ly,** *adv.*

ra·di·o·ac·tive de·cay, *n. Phys.* decrease with time of the number of radioactive atoms in a radioactive substance, due to spontaneous emission of particles and corresponding transformation of the atoms into a nonradioactive substance.

ra·di·o·ac·tiv·i·ty, rā″dē·ō·ak·tiv′i·tē, *n. Phys.* the emission of alpha rays, beta rays, or gamma rays in elements, as uranium, which undergo spontaneous atomic disintegration.

ra·di·o a·stron·o·my, *n.* A branch of astronomy which utilizes electromagnetic radio waves to study celestial bodies.

ra·di·o·au·to·graph, rā″dē·ō·ạ′to·graf″, rā″dē·ō·ạ′to·gräf″, *n.* Autoradiograph.—**ra·di·o·au·tog·ra·phy,** rā″dē·ō·ạ·tog′ra·fē, *n.*

ra·di·o bea·con, *n.* A radio station which sends a characteristic signal out to enable ships or aircraft to determine their position or bearing.

ra·di·o·bi·ol·o·gy, rā″dē·ō·bī·ol′o·jē, *n.* The division of biology that is concerned with the effects of radiant energy or radioactive materials on living matter.—**ra·di·o·bi·o·log·i·cal, ra·di·o·bi·o·log·ic,** rā″dē·ō·bī″o·loj′i·kal, *a.*—**ra·di·o·bi·ol·o·gist,** *n.*

ra·di·o·broad·cast, rā″dē·ō·brạd′kast″, rā″dē·ō·brạd′käst″, *v.t., v.i.—radiobroadcast* or *radiobroadcasted, radiobroadcasting.* To transmit by radio.—rā″dē·ō·brạd″kast, rā′dē·ō·brạd″käst, *n.* The transmission of messages, music, or speeches by radio.—**ra·di·o·broad·cast·er,** *n.*

ra·di·o car, *n.* An automobile having a radio for receiving and sending information.

ra·di·o·car·bon, rā″dē·ō·kär′bon, *n.* Carbon 14.

ra·di·o·chem·is·try, rā″dē·ō·kem′i·strē, *n.* That branch of chemistry which deals with radioactive bodies, their reactions, and radioactivity.—**ra·di·o·chem·i·cal,** rā″dē·ō·kem′i·kal, *a.*

ra·di·o com·pass, *n.* A radio receiver that ascertains the direction from which received signals are transmitted.

ra·di·o·el·e·ment, rā″dē·ō·el′e·ment, *n.* An element displaying radioactivity.

ra·di·o·fre·quen·cy, rā″dē·ō·frē′kwen·sē, *n.* pl. **ra·di·o·fre·quen·cies.** A wave frequency above 15,000 cycles per second, used in radio transmission; the frequency of a particular radio transmission. Also **ra·di·o fre·quen·cy.**

ra·di·o·gen·ic, rā″dē·ō·jen′ik, *a. Phys.* resulting from radioactive disintegration; as, *radiogenic* helium.

ra·di·o·gram, rā′dē·ō·gram″, *n.* A message sent by radiotelegraphy; a radiograph.

ra·di·o·graph, rā′dē·ō·graf″, rā′dē·ō·gräf″, *n.* An image or picture produced by the action of x-rays or other rays from radioactive substances.—*v.t.* To make a radiograph of.—**ra·di·o·graph·ic,** rā″dē·ō·graf′ik, *a.*—**ra·di·o·graph·i·cal·ly,** *adv.*

ra·di·og·ra·phy, rā″dē·ō·og′ra·fē, *n.* The production of radiographs.—**ra·di·og·ra·pher,** *n.*

ra·di·o·i·so·tope, rā″dē·ō·ī′so·tōp″, *n. Phys., chem.* an isotope exhibiting radioactivity, usu. one created artificially from a nonradioactive element, used in research and in the diagnosis and treatment of disease. Also **ra·di·o·ac·tive i·so·tope.**

ra·di·o·lar·i·an, rā″dē·ō·lâr′ē·an, *n.* [N.L. *Radiolaria,* pl. < L. *radiolus,* dim. of *radius,* ray.] *Zool.* any of the *Radiolaria,* an extensive order of minute marine proto-

zoans, having an amoeboid body with radiating pseudopodia and a siliceous skeleton.

ra·di·o·lo·ca·tion, rā″dē·ō·lō·kā′shan, *n.* The determination of the location of an object by radar.

ra·di·ol·o·gy, rā″dē·ol′o·jē, *n.* The science dealing with Roentgen rays or rays from radioactive substances, esp. for medical uses; examining or photographing organs or bones with such rays; the reading of medical x-rays.—**ra·di·o·log·ic, ra·di·o·log·i·cal,** rā″dē·ō·loj′i·kal, *a.*—**ra·di·ol·o·gist,** *n.*

ra·di·o·lu·cen·cy, rā″dē·ō·lö′sen·sē, *n.* The quality of being permeable to x-rays and other kinds of radiation.—**ra·di·o·lu·cent,** rā′dē·ō·lö′sent, *a.*

ra·di·o·man, rā′dē·ō·man″, *n.* pl. **ra·di·o·men.** An operator of radio apparatus, esp. one who sends and receives messages; a technician in a radio station.

ra·di·o·me·te·or·o·graph, rā″dē·ō·mē′tē·ėr·o·graf″, rā″dē·ō·mē′tē·ėr·o·gräf″, *n.* Radiosonde.

ra·di·om·e·ter, rā″dē·om′i·tėr, *n.* An instrument consisting of vanes in a partial vacuum, which, under the influence of sunlight, revolve and demonstrate the energy of solar rays; any of various instruments which detect and usu. measure radiant energy; an instrument for measuring the intensity of sounds.—**ra·di·o·met·ric,** rā″dē·ō·me′trik, *a.*—**ra·di·om·e·try,** *n.*

ra·di·o·phone, rā′dē·ō·fōn′, *n.* A radiotelephone; any of various devices for producing sound by the action of radiant energy.—**ra·di·o·phon·ic,** rā″dē·ō·fon′ik, *a.*—**ra·di·oph·o·ny,** rā″dē·of′o·nē, *n.*

ra·di·o·pho·to·graph, rā″dē·ō·fō′to·graf″, rā″dē·ō·fō′to·gräf″, *n.* A photograph or other picture transmitted by a radio process. Also **ra·di·o·pho·to, ra·di·o·pho·to·gram,** rā″dē·ō·fō′to·gram″.—**ra·di·o·pho·tog·ra·phy,** rā″dē·ō·fo·tog′ra·fē, *n.*

ra·di·o pill, *n.* A small radio transmitter in a capsule which, when swallowed, sends out information on physiological, esp. gastrointestinal, conditions.

ra·di·o range, *n.* The reach and scope of radio beams emitted by a given station for use as directional signals for aircraft; the station or installation which sends such beams out.

ra·di·os·co·py, rā″dē·os′ko·pē, *n.* A study of an object opaque to light, such as an Egyptian mummy, with the aid of x-rays or some kind of radiation.—**ra·di·o·scop·ic, ra·di·o·scop·i·cal,** rā″dē·ō·skop′ik, *a.*

ra·di·o·sen·si·tive, rā″dē·ō·sen′si·tiv, *a.* Capable of being reduced or destroyed by certain forms of radiant energy; as, a *radiosensitive* tumor.

ra·di·o·sonde, rā′dē·ō·sond″, *n. Meteor.* a device for broadcasting atmospheric pressure, temperature, and humidity at high altitudes by means of an automatic radio transmitter and a meteorograph attached to a balloon. Also *radiometeorograph.*

ra·di·o spec·trum, *n.* That part of the electromagnetic spectrum lying above the spectrum of audible frequencies but below that of infrared frequencies; the range of useful radio frequencies in this spectrum.

ra·di·o·stron·ti·um, rā″dē·ō·stron′shē·um, rā″dē·ō·stron′tē·um, *n.* Strontium 90.

ra·di·o·te·leg·ra·phy, rā″dē·ō·te·leg′ra·fē, *n.* Wireless telegraphy; the art of sending messages through the air by means of coded electromagnetic waves.—**ra·di·o·tel·e·graph,** rā″dē·ō·tel′e·graf″, rā″dē·ō·tel′e·gräf″, *n.*—**ra·di·o·tel·e·graph·ic,** *a.*

ra·di·o te·lem·e·ter, *n.* A type of telemeter that transmits data from a remote point, as from outer space, to a receiver by means of radio signals.—**ra·di·o te·lem·-e·try,** *n.*

ra·di·o·tel·e·phone, rā″dē·ō·tel′e·fōn″, *n.* A telephonic system using radio waves instead of wires; a wireless telephone.—**ra·di·o·tel·e·phon·ic,** rā″dē·ō·tel″·e·fon′ik, *a.*—**ra·di·o·te·leph·o·ny,** rā″dē·ō·te·lef′o·nē, *n.*

ra·di·o tel·e·scope, *n.* An astronomical instrument that receives, amplifies, and measures radio waves coming from sources in outer space.

ra·di·o·ther·a·py, rā″dē·ō·ther′a·pē, *n.* Treatment of diseases by radioactivity, as by x-rays or by a radioactive element such as radium or thorium. Also *radium therapy.*

ra·di·o tube, *n.* A vacuum tube used in radio receivers for the amplification and rectification of electromagnetic waves. See *vacuum tube.*

ra·di·o·ul·na, rā″dē·ō·ul′na, *n. Zool.* a bone in the skeleton of certain lower vertebrates, as the frog, equivalent to the two bones of radius and ulna in higher vertebrates.

ra·di·o wave, *n.* An electromagnetic wave having a frequency useful for radio communication.

rad·ish, rad′ish, *n.* [Fr. *radis,* < It. *radice,* < L. *radix* (*radic-*), root, radish.] The crisp, pungent, edible root of a garden plant, *Raphanus sativus,* in the mustard family; the plant itself.

ra·di·um, rā′dē·um, *n. Chem.* a radioactive metallic element found in certain minerals, as pitchblende, in the uranium series, and discovered by M. and Mme Curie in 1898: used in radiography, in medicine for treating cancer, and in luminous materials, as paints. Sym. Ra, at. no. 88, at. wt. 226. See Periodic Table of Elements.

ra·di·um F, *n. Chem.* polonium.

ra·di·um ther·a·py, *n.* Radiotherapy.

ra·di·us, rā′dē·us, *n.* pl. **ra·di·i, ra·di·us·es,** rā′dē·ī″. [L., staff, rod, spoke of a wheel, radius of a circle, radius of the arm, also ray or beam of light: cf. *ray.*] A straight line extending from the center of a circle or sphere to the circumference or surface; any radial line, as of a curve; any radial or radiating part; a circular area of an extent indicated by the length of a given radius; as, every house within a *radius* of 40 miles; field or range of operation or influence; extent of possible operation, travel, or the like under certain conditions; as, the flying *radius* of an airplane; *anat.* that one of the two bones of the forearm which is on the thumb side; *zool.* a corresponding bone in the forelimb of other vertebrates.

ra·di·us vec·tor, *n.* pl. **ra·di·i vec·to·res, ra·di·us vec·tors,** rā′dē·ī″ vek·tōr′ēz. [N.L.] *Math.* a straight line or its length joining a fixed point or origin and a variable point; *astron.* such a line or distance from the sun or other central body to a body, as a planet, orbiting around it.

ra·dix, rā′diks, *n.* pl. **rad·i·ces, ra·dix·es,** rad′i·sēz″, rā′di·sēz″. [L. *radix* (*radic-*), root.] The source or origin. *Math.* a number taken as the base of a system of numbers, logarithms, or the like. *Anat.* a root, esp. of a spinal or cranial nerve. *Bot.* a plant root; radicle.

ra·dome, rā′dōm, *n.* A dome-shaped housing used esp. on aircraft to protect a radar antenna.

ra·don, rā′don, *n.* A radioactive, heavy, gaseous element, chemically inert, formed as a disintegration product of radium. Sym. Rn, at. no. 86, at. wt. 222. See Periodic Table of the Elements.

rad·u·la, raj′u·la, *n.* pl. **rad·u·lae,** raj′u·lē″. [L., a scraper, < *radere,* scrape.] *Zool.* a chitinous band in the mouth of most mollusks, set with numerous minute horny teeth, and functioning in the process of breaking up food.—**rad·u·lar,** *a.*

raff, raf, *n.* [O.E. *raff,* to sweep; Fr. *raffer,* < G. *raffen,* to sweep, to snatch; akin *raffle.*] The lower classes or rabble; riffraff. *Brit. dial.* refuse.

raf·fi·a, raf′ē·a, *n.* [Name in Madagascar.] A fibrous substance obtained from the palm, *Raphia pedunculata,* of Madagascar, used for plant tie bands, hats, mats, baskets, and similar products; the tree itself.

raf·fi·nose, raf′i·nōs″, *n.* [Fr. *raffiner,* refine.] *Chem.* a colorless crystalline sugar, $C_{18}H_{32}O_{16}\cdot 5H_2O$, with little or no sweetness, occurring in various plants, as in the sugar beet and cottonseed.

raff·ish, raf′ish, *a.* Having a tawdry, cheap, or flashy quality or appearance; rakish; unconventional; disreputable.—**raff·ish·ly,** *adv.*—**raff·ish·ness,** *n.*

raf·fle, raf′l, *n.* [Fr. *rafle,* O.Fr. *raffle,* a kind of game at dice, < G. *raffen, raffeln,* to sweep or snatch.] A lottery in which persons participate by buying chances for a specific prize.—*v.i.*—**raffled, raffling.** To engage in a raffle.—*v.t.* To dispose of by means of a raffle, usu. followed by *off.*

raf·fle, raf′l, *n.* [Cf. *raff.*] Rubbish; *naut.* a tangle, as of ropes, canvas, or other material.

raf·fle·sia, ra·flē′zha, ra·flē′zhē·a, ra·flē′zē·a, ra·flē′zha, ra·flē′zhē·a, ra·flē′zē·a, *n.* [After Sir Stamford *Raffles,* the discoverer of the first known species.] *Bot.* any of the parasitic, almost stemless plants, genus *Rafflesia,* native to Malaya, Sumatra, and Java, esp. *R. arnoldi,* remarkable for foul-smelling, gigantic flowers almost three feet in diameter.

raft, raft, räft, *n.* [Prop. a float made of beams or rafters; Icel. *raptr* (pron. *raftr*), Dan. *raft,* a rafter.] A float of logs, planks, or other pieces of timber fastened together, for the convenience of transporting them by water; a flat, floating structure; a rescue craft or life raft.—*v.t.* To transport on a raft; to fashion into a raft.—*v.i.* To work or travel on a raft.

raft, raft, räft, *n.* [Var. of *raff.*] *Slang.* A great quantity or number; a lot; as, a whole *raft* of children.

raft·er, raf′tèr, räf′tèr, *n.* [O.E. *raefter* = Icel. *raptr,* Dan. *raft,* a rafter, a beam.] One of the sloping timbers of a roof, which support the outer covering.

rafts·man, rafts′man, räfts′man, *n.* pl. **rafts·men.** A man who performs the labor on or manages a raft.

rag, rag, *n.* [Orig. a tuft of rough hair; cf. Sw. and Dan. dial. *ragg,* rough hair; Icel. *rögg,* shagginess, a tuft; allied to *rug.*] Any piece of useless or discarded cloth; a tattered cloth, torn or worn; a fragment; a shred; *pl.* tattered or threadbare garments. *Slang,* wearing apparel considered as having little value or appeal; a contemptuously regarded publication or newspaper.—**glad rags,** *slang,* one's dressy or fancy clothes.—**chew the rag,** *slang.* To engage in conversation; chat.

rag, rag, *n.* [M.E. *ragghe, ragge;* origin obscure.] Any of various kinds of hard rocks having a grainy texture; a type of slate used in roofing, having one rough, untrimmed side.

rag, rag, *v.t.*—**ragged, ragging.** [Origin doubtful.] *Slang,* to torment, scold, tease, or subject to annoyance; *Brit.* to perpetrate a practical joke or prank on.—*n. Brit.* a practical joke.

rag, rag, *n.* [< *ragtime.*] *Slang,* music written in ragtime tempo.—*v.t.*—**ragged, ragging.** *Slang,* to play, as music, in ragtime.

ra·ga, rä′ga, *n.* [Hind. < Skt. *rāga,* tone.] *Mus.* A melodic piece based on an ancient traditional Hindu mode or pattern; the melodic mode, pattern, or formula on which such a piece is based, resembling a key or scale, but also including tone

quality and mood, as determined by the needs of season, time, and occasion.

rag·a·muf·fin, rag′a·muf″in, *n.* [*Ragamofin* was the name of a demon in some old mystery plays, perh. < *rag,* and old *mof, muff,* a long sleeve, or < *tag,* and D. *muf,* musty.] A child in very ragged clothing; any unkempt, raggedly dressed person.

rag bag, *n.* A bag for holding rags or small pieces of fabric.

rag doll, *n.* A doll fashioned from cloth, orig. stuffed with rags, and often having a painted face.

rage, rāj, *n.* [Fr. *rage,* < L. *rabies,* rage, madness (by a change similar to that seen in *abridge*); < *rabo,* to rave, to be mad; cogn. Skt. *rabh,* to desire eagerly.] Violent anger; fury; violent force or intense activity, as of a storm; intense or violent desire or feeling; passion; that which is extremely popular or in style; a fad.—*v.i.*—**raged, raging.** To be furious with anger; to act or move furiously; as, the sea that *rages;* to prevail unchecked, as disease.—**rag·ing,** *a.* —**rag·ing·ly,** *adv.*

rag·ged, rag′id, *a.* Torn, worn to rags, or tattered; as, *ragged* clothing; clothed in rags or tattered garments; having or characterized by loose or hanging shreds or fragmentary bits; as, a *ragged* wound; shaggy, as an animal's coat; full of rough or sharp projections, as rocks; in a rough, wild, neglected state; as, a *ragged* garden; rough, imperfect, or faulty; as, a *ragged* piece of work; harsh, as sound.—**rag·ged·-ly,** *adv.*—**rag·ged·ness,** *n.*—**rag·ged·y,** rag′i·dē, *a.*

rag·ged rob·in, *n.* A perennial herb, *Lychnis flos-cuculi,* of the pink family, naturalized in N. America, having deeply four-cleft, pink to white flowers which give the plant a ragged aspect.

rag·gle, rag′l, *n.* An indentation or groove cut in stonework to accommodate the flashing set above a roof.

rag·gle-tag·gle, rag′l-tag′l, *a.* Composed of odds and ends; made up of greatly diverse elements.

rag·i, rag·gee, rag·gy, rag′ē, *n.* [Ind. word.] A grain plant, *Eleusine coracana,* of the East Indies, cultivated as a staple food.

rag·lan, rag′lan, *n.* A type of coat or overcoat with sleeves that extend to the neckline, giving a slanting line to the shoulders.— *a.*

rag·man, rag′man″, rag′man, *n.* pl. **rag·-men,** rag′men″, rag′men. A man who gathers or deals in rags and discarded objects.

ra·gout, ra·gö′, *n.* [Fr. *ragout,* < L. *re,* again, *ad,* to, and *gustus,* a tasting.] A dish of stewed and highly seasoned meat and various vegetables.—*v.t.*—**ragouted, ragouting.** To cook or make into a ragout.

rag·pick·er, rag′pik″ėr, *n.* One who goes about picking up rags and other junk material from the streets or refuse heaps for a livelihood.

rag·tag 'and bob·tail, rag′tag″ and bob′-tāl″, *n.* Ragged commoners; the riffraff; rabble. Also **rag·tag; rag, tag, and bob·-tail.**

rag·time, rag′tīm″, *n.* Syncopated music with a regularly accented accompaniment, one of the earliest forms of jazz; the rhythm characteristic of this music.

rag·weed, rag′wēd″, *n.* One of two herbs of the composite family in the genus *Ambrosia,* the common ragweed, *A. artemisiifolia,* and the giant ragweed, *A. trifida,* plants whose pollen is a major cause of hay fever.

rag·wort, rag′wurt″, *n.* Any of various cosmopolitan herbaceous plants of the genus *Senecio,* in the composite family, having flat-topped clusters of small yellow-rayed flowers, esp. *S. aureus,* the golden ragwort, and *S. jacobaea,* the tansy ragwort.

---

a- fat, fāte, fär, fâre, fạll; **e-** met, mē, mēre, hėr; **i-** pin, pīne; **o-** not, nōte, mōve; **u-** tub, cūbe, bụll; **oi-** oil; **ou-** pound.

rah, rä, *interj*. Hurrah: a shout of encouragement, esp. for a team or player, often used in school and college yells.—**rah-rah**, rä′rä′, *a*.

raid, rād, *n*. [< stem of *ride*; same as Icel. *reith*, a riding, a raid; same as to *road*.] *Milit*. a sudden assault or incursion on an enemy, whether by air, sea, or land. Any sudden attack or foray; an unannounced entry or sudden attack by officers of the law in order to make seizures and arrests; an effort to attract the key employees of a competitor; *finance*, concerted selling of stocks by holders to effect a lowering of stock prices.—*v.t*. To make a raid on.—*v.i*. To take part in a raid.—**raid·er**, *n*.

rail, rāl, *n*. [Same as L.G. and Sw. *regel*, G. *riegel*, a bar, a rail; akin G. *reihe*, a row.] A bar of wood or metal extending from one upright post to another, as in a fence; one of the parallel steel bars forming a track for the wheels of a locomotive, railroad car, streetcar, elevated, or subway; a horizontal timber in any piece of framing or paneling; a series of posts or balusters connected by crossbeams, bars, or rods, for enclosure; a railing, as on the deck of a ship; railroad.—*v.t*. To enclose or provide with rails.—**ride out on a rail**, to punish, usu. extralegally, by banishing from the community.

rail, rāl, *n*. [O.Fr. *rasle*, *raale*, a rail; same origin as *rattle*, being so called from its noisy cry.] Any of several species of marsh birds of secretive habits in the family *Rallidae*, having short wings and long toes adapted for running over boggy areas, esp. the Virginia and Clapper rails. An old-world rail, *Crex crex*, common in grain fields; also **corn crake**.

rail, rāl, *v.i*. [Fr. *railler*, to banter; < L.L. *radiculare*, < L. *radere*, to scrape.] To utter reproaches; to use insolent and reproachful language; to scold: followed by *at* or *against*.—*v.t*. To force or cause as a result of railing.—**rail·er**, rā′lėr, *n*.

rail·head, rāl′hed″, *n*. The most advanced point of a railroad under construction; the terminating point of a railroad; *milit*. the point at which goods are transferred from a railroad to some other means of transport.

rail·ing, rā′ling, *n*. A fence or barrier of wood or iron, constructed of posts and rails; balustrade; rails in general; the materials for rails.

rail·ler·y, rā′le·rē, *n*. pl. **rail·ler·ies**. [Fr. *raillerie*.] Good-humored teasing; jesting language; banter.

rail·road, rāl′rōd″, *n*. A permanent roadway consisting of one or more pairs of steel rails laid parallel to each other and several feet apart, making a track over which locomotives, freight cars, or passenger cars may run; the tracks and all the land, trains, works, buildings, machinery, franchises, and other assets required for the support and use of the road; the company or owners operating and managing such an organization. Abbr. *RR*, *R.R.*, *R.*—*v.t*. to transport or ship by railroad; *colloq*. to rush through forcefully and without careful consideration, esp. a bill through a legislature; *slang*, to send a person to prison on a false charge.—*v.i*. To work for a railroad.—**rail·road·er**, rāl′rō″dėr, *n*. A person who works for a railroad.

rail·road flat, *n*. A long, narrow apartment with rooms connected by a long, straight hall.

rail·road·ing, rāl′rō″ding, *n*. Construction or operation of railroads; employment on a railroad.

rail·road worm, *n*. The larva of a fruit fly, *Rhagoletis pomonella*, that tunnels in the fruit of apple and certain other orchard trees. Also **ap·ple mag·got**.

rail-split·ter, rāl′split″ėr, *n*. A person who splits logs into fence posts and rails. (*Cap*.) a nickname for Abraham Lincoln.

rail·way, rāl′wā″, *n*. A railroad, esp. one operating with lightweight equipment and tracks; as, a street *railway*. *Brit*. any railroad. A line or lines of rails forming a runway, as for a wheeled apparatus. Abbr. *Ry.*, *Rwy.*

rai·ment, rā′ment, *n*. [Contr. < obs. *arrayment*.] Clothing in general; garments.

rain, rān, *n*. [O.E. *regn*, *ren*, = D. and G. *regen* = Icel., Sw., and Dan. *regn* = Goth. *rign*, rain.] The moisture of the atmosphere condensed and deposited in drops of water; the descent of such watery drops; a rainfall, rainstorm, or shower; *fig*. a heavy continuous quantity of anything falling in the manner of rain; as, a *rain* of tears; *pl*. the seasonal rainfalls, or the rainy season, in some regions, as India.—*v.i*. [O.E. *regnian*.] To fall, as rain, usu. preceded by *it*, as: It *rained* all night. To fall like rain; to send down rain.—*v.t*. To send down or shower, as rain; to cause to fall or send down like rain; as, to *rain* abuse.—**rain or shine**, under any weather conditions.

rain·bird, rān′bụrd″, *n*. One of the common names for the slender long-tailed American cuckoos of the genus *Coccyzus*, derived from their voice, a series of rapid calls on one pitch, and said to portend rain. Also **rain crow**.

rain·bow, rān′bō″, *n*. A bow or arc of prismatic colors, formed by the refraction and reflection of rays of light through drops of rain, appearing in the part of the heavens opposite to the sun; a similar natural display of prismatic colors, as in the spray of a waterfall; a display with many bright colors.

rain·bow trout, *n*. A trout, *Salmo gairdnerii*, native to the mountain streams of western N. America and named from its coloring.

rain check, *n*. A check or ticket given for future use to spectators at a baseball game or other outdoor performance which is stopped by rain; an invitation or offer made or requested for a later time.

rain·coat, rān′kōt″, *n*. A coat of waterproof material for wearing as a protection from rain.

rain crow, *n*. A name applied loosely to various American cuckoos or rain birds.

rain·drop, rān′drop″, *n*. A drop of rain.

rain·fall, rān′fal″, *n*. A fall or shower of rain; the amount of water or other form of moisture falling within a given time and area.

rain for·est, *n*. A dense tropical forest containing many varieties of trees which grow to great heights, often topped with flowering vines and epiphytes: found where the yearly rainfall exceeds 100 inches. Also **trop·i·cal rain forest**.

rain gauge, *n*. An instrument for measuring the quantity of rain which falls at a given place.

rain·mak·er, rān′mā″kėr, *n*. One who claims he can make rain fall, esp. in certain American Indian tribes, one who attempts to cause rain by means of incantations and rituals; one who induces rain by scientific means, as seeding clouds with silver iodide crystals.—**rain·mak·ing**, *n*.

rain·out, rān′out″, *n*. A performance or contest that has been interrupted or cancelled because of rain; atomic fallout disseminated by precipitation.—**rain out**, *v.t*. To cause to be cancelled or postponed.

rain·proof, rān′prōf″, *a*. Preventing the entrance of rain; impervious to rain.

rain·storm, rān′stȧrm″, *n*. A storm of rain.

rain wa·ter, *n*. Water that has fallen as rain.

rain·wear, rān′wâr″, *n*. Water-repellent or waterproof apparel.

rain·y, rā′nē, *a*.—*rainier*, *rainiest*. Characterized by rain; wet with rain; bringing or threatening rain.—**rain·i·ly**, *adv*.—**rain·i·ness**, *n*.

rain·y day, *n*. A time of want which may develop in the future.

raise, rāz, *v.t*.—*raised*, *raising*. [M.E. *raisen*, *reisen*, < Scand.: cf. Icel. *reisa* = Sw. *resa* = Dan. *reise* = Goth. *-raisjan* = O.E. *raeran*, raise, causative of the Teut. verb (O.E. *risan*, etc.) represented by E. *rise*: cf. *rear*.] To set upright, as an overturned table; set erect; to cause to rise or move upward; elevate; to cause to come to a standing posture, as a person; to restore to life; as, to *raise* the dead; reanimate or revivify; to rouse from cover, as a pheasant; to rouse for common action, as in attack or defense; to stir up, as to do something; excite or agitate; give vigor to; as, to *raise* his spirits; to build, erect, or construct, as a skyscraper; to set up the framework of, as a house; to cause to rise or form, as a blister; to breed, as animals; to rear, as a young person; to cause or promote growth of, as flowers; *Bib*. to cause to appear, as a person. To bring into existence or action; as, to *raise* a commotion; to begin or institute, as a lawsuit; put forward, as an objection; bring up; as, to *raise* a question; to cause, give rise to, or bring about, as a controversy; to lift to a higher position; as, to *raise* one's hand; turn upward, as the eyes; to advance in rank, dignity, or position; as, to *raise* to the peerage; promote; to make higher or nobler, as one's philosophy of life; to get together or gather together; as, to *raise* money for charity; to *raise* an army; to bring to an end; as, *raise* the siege; to increase in height; as, to *raise* a roadbed; to cause to become light, as dough or bread; to increase in amount, as rent or prices; to increase the specified amount by fraud, as a check; to increase the value of, as a commodity; to bet more than another player, as in poker; to increase in degree, intensity, or force, as temperature or noise; to utter in a loud voice, as a cry; to cause to be heard; as, voices *raised* in opposition. *Naut*. to cause to appear by approaching closer; to come into sight of.—*v.i. Dial*. To rise.—*n*. A raising; a raised place; a rising place, passage, or road; a getting together or procuring by special effort, as money; an increase, as of prices or wages; the amount of such an increase.—**rais·er**, *n*.

raised, rāzd, *a*. Elevated in relief, as a surface pattern or design. *Cooking*, leavened; made with yeast, instead of baking soda or powder.

rai·sin, rā′zin, *n*. [O.Fr. *raizin* (Fr. *raisin*), grapes, a grape, a raisin, < L. *racemus*, cluster of grapes: cf. *raceme*.] A grape of some sweet variety dried in the sun or artificially, and used in cooking or eaten raw; a dark shade of purplish blue.

raj, räj, *n*. [Hind. *rāj*, < Skt. *rāj-*, rule: cf. *raja*.] *India*. Rule; dominion; sovereignty; as, the British *raj*.

ra·jah, **ra·ja**, rä′ja, *n*. [Skt. and Hind. *râjâ*, a rajah; root in Skt. *râj*, to rule; cogn. L. *rex* (for *regs*), a king, *rego*, to rule; Gael. and Ir. *righ*, a king; O.E. *rice*, dominion.] A title, often conferred as an honor or courtesy, given to Hindus of rank; a Hindu prince or chief; a Malay chief.

Raj·put, räj′pŏt, *n*. [Hind. *rājpūt*, < Skt. *rājaputra*, king's son, prince: cf. *rajah*.] A member of a Hindu race claiming descent from the ancient Kshatriya or warrior caste and noted for their military spirit.

rake, rāk, *n*. [O.E. *raca*, *racu*, a rake (implement); later senses being from *rake*, *v*.] An agricultural implement with teeth or tines for gathering together hay or leaves, or breaking and smoothing the surface of ground; any of various implements of a similar form but having a blade, notched or plain, instead of teeth, as a croupier's implement for gathering in money on a gaming table.—*v.t.*—*raked, raking.* To gather together, draw, or remove with a rake; to clear, smooth, or prepare with a rake; to clear, as a fire, by stirring with a poker or the like; to search through industriously or thoroughly; to scrape, scratch, or graze; *milit.* to sweep with shot lengthwise, as a place, a troops. To sweep with the eye or glance.—*v.i.* To use a rake; to search with or as with a rake; to scrape or sweep, with *over*.—**rake in**, *slang,* to gather or take in, as winnings or large gains.—**rake up,** *slang,* to bring up out of oblivion or obscurity, as something forgotten or unknown.—**rak·er,** *n.*

rake, rāk, *v.i.*—*raked, raking.* [Same as Sw. *raka,* Dan. *rage,* to project, a Scand. verb = E. *reach.*] To incline or to slope.—*v.t.* To cause to incline or slope.—*n.* A slope or inclination; the angle between the edge of a cutting tool and a plane perpendicular to the area being cut.

rake, rāk, *n.* [Shortened < M.E. *rakehell,* prop. vagabond, wandering; Sw. *raka,* Icel. *reika,* to wander; Dan. *raekel,* a lout.] One who is lewd; a libertine; a roué.

rake·hell, rāk′hel″, *n.* [< *rake,* and *hell;* meaning lit. 'one such as to be found only by raking hell.'] A profligate or licentious person; a dissolute man; a rake.—*a.*

rake-off, rāk′af″, rāk′of″, *n.* A share or amount taken or received illicitly; a share or portion, as of profits; a discount.

ra·ki, rä·kē′, rak′ē, *n.* [Turk. *raqi.*] A spirituous liquor distilled from grain, grapes, or plums, in southeastern Europe and the Levant. Also **ra·kee.**

rak·ish, rā′kish, *a.* Stylish, dashing, jaunty; *naut.* having an inclination which suggests or implies speed; as, *rakish* masts.—**rak·ish·ly,** *adv.*—**rak·ish·ness,** *n.*

rak·ish, rā′kish, *a.* Given to the practices of a rake; dissolute; debauched.—**rak·ish·ly,** *adv.*—**rak·ish·ness,** *n.*

râle, ral, räl, *n.* [Fr., < *râler,* make a rattling sound in breathing.] *Pathol.* an abnormal sound accompanying the normal respiratory murmur, as in a pulmonary disease.

ral·len·tan·do, rä″len·tän′dō, *It.* Räl″len·tän′dạ, *a.* [It.] *Mus.* pertaining to a tempo that is to be gradually slowed down.—*adv.*

ral·li·form, ral′i·fạrm″, *a.* [N.L. *Rallus* and L. *forma,* form.] *Ornith.* pertaining to the rails or to birds closely resembling the rails.

ral·ly, ral′ē, *v.t.*—*rallied, rallying.* [Fr. *rallier,* < *re-* (< L. *re-*), back, again, and *allier,* unite, E. *ally.*] To bring together or into order again, as an army or company which has been scattered; to draw or call together, as persons, to give assistance or for common action; to concentrate or revive, as one's strength or spirits.—*v.i.* To come together or into order again, as to renew a conflict; to come together in a body for common action; to come to the assistance or support of a person, party, or cause; to acquire fresh strength or vigor; revive or recover; recover partially from illness; *tennis,* to engage in a rally; *stock market,* to make a sharp rise in price after a decline, as stocks.—*n.* pl. **ral·lies.** An act of rallying; a recovery from dispersion or disorder, as of troops; a drawing or coming together of persons for common action; a renewal of recovery of strength or activity; a partial recovery of strength during illness; *stock market,* a sharp price rise or increase in trading following a decline; *tennis,* the return of the ball by both sides a number of times consecutively. An automobile race in which sports cars compete on public roads.

ral·ly, ral′ē, *v.t., v.i.*—*rallied, rallying.* [Fr. *railler,* to banter.] To attack with raillery; to tease.

ram, ram, *n.* [O.E. *ramm* = D. and L.G. *ram* = G. *ramm,* ram, male sheep.] A male sheep; any of various devices for battering, crushing, driving, or forcing something; a battering ram; the heavy weight which strikes the blow in a pile driver or the like; a piston, as on a hydraulic press; a hydraulic ram; the beak or spur projecting from the bow of a warship for penetrating an enemy's ship; a ship so equipped. (*Cap.*) the zodiacal constellation or sign Aries.—*v.t.*—*rammed, ramming.* To drive or force by heavy blows; as, to *ram* piles into the earth; to compact by pounding or blows; to strike against with great force; dash violently against; to cram or forcibly stuff with something.—**ram·mer,** ram′ėr, *n.*

Ram·a·dan, ram″a·dän′, *n.* [Ar., the hot month, < *ramida, ramiza,* to be hot.] The ninth month of the Mohammedan year; the great annual Mohammedan fast, kept throughout this entire month from sunrise to sunset.

ram·ble, ram′bl, *v.i.*—*rambled, rambling.* [Appar. related to *roam.*] To wander about in a leisurely manner, without definite aim or direction; to take an irregular course with turns or windings, as a stream or a path; to grow in an irregular, haphazard way, as certain plants; to talk or write discursively or without sequence of ideas.—*v.t.* To wander about or over.—*n.* A walk or excursion without definite aim or direction, taken simply for recreation or pleasure.

ram·bler, ram′blėr, *n.* One who or that which rambles; any of various climbing roses, having small flowers in clusters.

ram·bling, ram′bling, *a.* That rambles; wandering aimlessly; meandering; spreading out irregularly; as, a *rambling* house; straying from one subject to another, as thoughts.—**ram·bling·ly,** *adv.*

Ram·bouil·let, ram′bu̇·lā″, *Fr.* RÄN·bö·ye′, *n.* A large hardy merino sheep, bred orig. in France, and noted for good mutton and fine wool.

ram·bunc·tious, ram·bungk′shus, *a.* [Var. of *rumbustious* for *robustious.*] Boisterous, turbulent, or noisy; unruly.—**ram·bunc·tious·ly,** *adv.*—**ram·bunc·tious·ness,** *n.*

ram·bu·tan, ram·böt′an, *n.* [Malay *rambūtan.*] *Bot.* The bright red oval fruit of a Malayan tree, *Nephelium lappaceum,* in the soapberry family, covered with soft spines or hairs, and containing a pulp of pleasant subacid taste; the tree itself.

ram·e·kin, ram·e·quin, ram′e·kin, *n.* [Fr. *ramequin;* < Teut.] A small, separately cooked portion of some cheese preparation, esp. one made of grated cheese, breadcrumbs, and eggs baked and served in a small dish; a dish suitable for such use.

ra·men·tum, ra·men′tum, *n.* pl. **ra·men·ta,** ra·men′ta. *Bot.* a thin, scaly, chafflike substance adhering to the stems or leaves of some ferns.—**ram·en·ta·ceous,** ram″en·tā′shus, *a.*

ram·ie, ram′ē, *n.* [Malay *rāmī.*] *Bot.* An Asiatic shrub, *Boehmeria nivea,* in the nettle family, yielding a fiber used in making textiles, upholstery, thread, and paper; the fiber itself. Also *rhea,* **ram·ee, Chi·nese grass.**

ram·i·fi·ca·tion, ram″i·fi·kā′shan, *n.* [Fr. *ramification.*] A result or outgrowth; as, to pursue a subject in all its *ramifications;* the act, process, or manner of ramifying; a branch. *Bot.* a division or subdivision springing or derived from a main stem or source; the arrangement of such divisions.

ram·i·form, ram′i·fạrm″, *a.* [L. *ramus,* branch, and *forma,* form.] Having the form of a branch; branchlike; branched. Also **ra·mal,** rā′mal.

ram·i·fy, ram′i·fī″, *v.t., v.i.*—*ramified, ramifying.* [Fr. *ramifier*—L. *ramus,* a branch, and *facio,* to make.] To divide into branches or parts; to develop new extensions or form new constituent categories.

ram·jet, ram′jet″, *n. Aeron.* a kind of jet engine consisting essentially of a tube open at both ends in which fuel is burned continuously to create a jet thrust, and having neither a compressor nor turbine, the air for oxidizing the fuel being injected into the engine as the engine moves forward. Also **ram·jet en·gine.**

ra·mose, rā′mōs, ra·mōs′, *a.* [L. *ramosus,* *ramus,* branch.] *Bot.* Having many branches; branching. Also **ra·mous,** *ramiform.*

ramp, ramp, *n.* [Fr. *rampe,* < O.Fr. *ramper,* climb.] A sloping passage or surface connecting two different levels, as of a road, stadium, building, or the like; a short concave slope or bend, as one connecting the higher and lower parts of a staircase railing at a landing; a movable flight of stairs for boarding or debarking an aircraft; any sloping or inclined plane or surface.—*v.t.* To furnish with a ramp or ramps.

ramp, ramp, *v.i.* [O.Fr. *ramper,* climb (Fr. *creep*); origin uncertain: cf. *romp.*] To rise or stand on the hind legs, as a mammal, esp. a lion, as represented in heraldry or sculpture; to rear as if to spring; to leap or dash with fury; act violently, rage, or storm, as a person; rampage.—*n.* The act of ramping; *her.* a ramping posture or movement.

ram·page, ram·pāj′, *v.i.*—*rampaged, rampaging.* [< *ramp.*] To rush, rage, or storm about violently.—ram′pāj, *n.* A state of boisterous passion or excitement; violent conduct.—**ram·pa·geous,** ram·pā′jus, *a.*—**ram·pa·geous·ly,** *adv.*—**ram·pa·geous·ness,** *n.*—**ram·pag·er,** *n.*

ram·pant, ram′pant, *a.* [Fr. *rampant,* ppr. of *ramper,* to clamber.] Violent, wild; unchecked; bursting usual limits; standing upon hind legs, as an animal; *her.* of a beast, represented in profile, standing upright on the left hind leg with the forelegs elevated; *arch.* springing from a point on one level to a point on another, as an arch.—**ramp·an·cy,** ram′pan·sē, *n.*—**ramp·ant·ly,** *adv.*

ram·part, ram′pärt, ram′pėrt, *n.* [Fr. *rempart,* a rampart, < *remparer,* to fortify a place—*re,* again, *em* for L. *in,* and *parer,* to defend, < L. *parare,* to prepare.] *Fort.* an elevation or mound of earth around a place, on which the parapet is raised; such a structure including the parapet. A bulwark; a defense.—*v.t.* To fortify with or as with ramparts.

ram·pike, ram′pīk″, *n. Canadian,* the skeleton of a burned-out tree. Also **ram·pole.**

ram·pi·on, ram′pē·on, *n.* [Cf. Fr. *raiponce,* It. *ramponzolo, raperonzolo.*] A European bellflower, *Campanula rapunculus,* having an edible white tuberous root used in salads; any of the similar plants of the genus *Phyteuma,* in the bellflower family.

ram·rod, ram′rod″, *n.* A rod for ramming down the charge of a muzzle-loading firearm; in general, a rod used to clean the barrels of firearms; a martinet.—*v.t.* To force upon, esp. by means of authority.

ram·shack·le, ram′shak″l, *a.* [Perh. pp. of *ransackle, ransack.*] Tumble-down; tumble-down through careless construction; rickety.

ram's horn, *n.* Shofar.

rams·horn, ramz′harn″, *n.* A scavenger snail, genus *Planorbis,* frequently used in aquariums.

ram·son, ram′zon, ram′son, *n.* [O.E. *hramsa, hramse,* ramsons, (pl. *hramsan,* so that *ramsons* is a double pl.); G. *rams, ramsel, ramsen,* Sw. *rams,* ramsons; allied to

Gr. *kromyon*, an onion.] A species of garlic, *Allium ursinum*, having broad leaves and a bulbous root, eaten as a relish and used in salads.

ram·til, ram'til, *n*. [Bengali *rāmtil*.] A plant of African origin, *Guizotia abyssinica*, in the composite family, cultivated in many parts of India for its seeds, which yield an oil used as food and in making soap.

ram·u·lose, ram'ya·lōs", *a*. *Biol*. having many small branches. Also **ram·u·lous**, ram'ya·lus.

ra·mus, rā'mus, *n*. pl. **ra·mi**, rā'mī. [L.] *Biol., anat.* a branch, as of a plant, a vein, or a bone.

ranch, ranch, *n*. [Sp. *rancho*, a mess, a set of persons who eat and drink together, a messroom.] An establishment and tract of land for raising and grazing livestock, esp. in western U.S.; the buildings and personnel of such an establishment; an extensive farm, as for fruit growing.—*v.i*. To manage, own, or work on a ranch.

ranch·er, ran'chėr, *n*. One who owns or is employed on a ranch. Also **ranch·man**, ranch'man, pl. **ranch·men**.

ran·che·ro, ran·châr'ō, *Sp*. Rän·che'Rạ, *n*. pl. **ran·che·ros**, ran·châr'ōz, *Sp*. Rän·che'Rạs. In southwestern U.S. and Spanish America, a person who owns, manages, or works on a ranch.

ranch house, *n*. The owner's house or principal building on a ranch; a one-story, low-pitched house often designed for informal living, usu. found in suburban areas.

ran·cho, ran'chō, rän'chō, *Sp*. Rän'chạ, *n*. pl. **ran·chos**, ran'chōz, rän'chōz, *Sp*. Rän'chạs. [Sp. Amer.] A hut or cluster of huts for ranch or farm workers; a ranch.

ran·cid, ran'sid, *a*. [L. *rancidus*, < *ranceo*, to be rank (whence also *rancor*.)] Having a rank smell or taste; rank or sour-smelling from spoilage, as oils, fats, or butter.— **ran·cid·i·ty**, **ran·cid·ness**, ran·sid'i·tē, *n*.—**ran·cid·ly**, *adv*.

ran·cor, *Brit*. **ran·cour**, rang'kėr, *n*. [L. *rancor*, an ill smell, rancor, < *ranceo*, to be rank or rancid (whence *rancid*.)] Bitterness, deep resentment, or spite; malice. —**ran·cor·ous**, rang'kėr·us, *a*.—**ran·cor·ous·ly**, *adv*.—**ran·cor·ous·ness**, *n*.

ran·dom, ran'dom, *n*. [O.Fr. *randon*, an impetuous course or efflux, vivacity, violence; *à randon*, at random; *randoner*, *randir*, to run rapidly; < G. *rand*, edge, brim, the word orig. having reference to the violence of a stream flowing full to the brim.] A lack of direction, rule, or method. —*a*. Done without aim or purpose; left to chance; fortuitous.—**at ran·dom**, in a haphazard or fortuitous manner; by chance. —**ran·dom·ly**, *adv*.—**ran·dom·ness**, *n*.

R and R, *n*. *Milit*. abbreviation for 'rest and recuperation,' as: He was flown to Hawaii for a period of *R and R*.

ran·dy, ran'dē, *a*. Lustful; lecherous. *Brit., Sc*. rude, vulgar.

range, rānj, *v.t*.—*ranged, ranging*. [< Fr. *ranger*, to range, < *rang*, O.Fr. *reng*, a rank; < the German.] To set in a row or rows; to arrange systematically; to classify; to rank; to rove through or over; to roam; to place, as livestock, on grazing land.—*v.i*. To have a certain position or rank in a line or sequence; to rove or wander without restraint; to have or go in a particular direction; to extend; to have a certain scope of action; to pass from one point to another, as conversation; to fluctuate, as prices; of a weapon, to have a certain range; of plants and animals, to be located or found.

range, rānj, *n*. A series of things in a line; a row; a rank; as, a *range* of mountains; the extent of variations of quantity, degree, or quality; as, the *range* of sizes; extent or scope; as, a wide *range* of thought, the whole *range* of religion; an expanse of open country used for livestock grazing; the distance from a weapon to its designated target; a specified area for shooting practice; an area for bombing practice; the capacity of an aircraft, ship, car, or other vehicle, that indicates how far it can travel before its fuel is exhausted, as: The helicopter's *range* is 1,000 miles. The act of wandering around; a stove for cooking and baking; a single row of townships lying between meridian lines, numbered east and west of a base meridian and north and south of a base survey line, each containing 36 square miles of land; *statistics*, the difference between the high and low values in a series of inconstant quantities; *mus.* the gamut of tones of an instrument or a voice; *biol.* the region or area in which a certain plant or animal is commonly found.

range find·er, *n*. Any of various instruments for determining the range or distance of an object, as for accurately sighting a rifle.

range pa·ral·y·sis, *n*. A leukosis occurring in birds and characterized by paralysis of the wings and legs.

rang·er, rān'jėr, *n*. One who ranges; a member of a mounted, roving troop or police force; a warden patrolling forest areas; a commando or guerrilla soldier.

rang·y, rān'jē, *a*.—*rangier, rangiest*. Slender and long-limbed; adapted for ranging or moving about; having a long, slender body, as certain animals or persons; permitting ranging, as a place; spacious; mountainous. —**rang·i·ness**, *n*.

ra·ni, **ra·nee**, rä'nē, *n*. pl. **ra·nis**, **ra·nees**. [Hind. *rānī*, < Skt. *rājñī*, fem. of *rājan*, king.] In India, the wife of a rajah; a reigning queen or princess.

rank, rank, *n*. [O.E. *ranc, renk*, < Fr. *rang*, O.Fr. *reng, renc*, a rank, row, range (whence also *range*), orig. a circular row, < O.H.G. *hring, hrinc*, a ring, a circle.] A row or line of persons or things. *Milit.* a line of soldiers; a line of men, esp. soldiers, standing abreast or side by side, as distinguished from *file*; *pl.* the order of common soldiers; as, to reduce an officer to the *ranks*. Official class, place, or standing in a social or business order; as, *ranks* of management; degree of dignity, eminence, or excellence; comparative station, relative place; as, a writer of the first *rank*; high social position; distinction or eminence; as, a man of *rank*; *chess*, the horizontal row of squares which extends across the chessboard.—*v.t*. To place abreast in a rank or line; to place in a particular class, order, or division; to outrank.—*v.i*. To be ranged, classed, or included, as in a particular class, order, or division; to have a certain rank; to be highest in rank.—**pull rank on**, *slang*, to make use of one's superior position in demanding obedience and respect from subordinates.

rank, rank, *a*. [O.E. *ranc*, fruitful, rank, proud = Icel. *rakkr*, straight, bold; Dan. *rank*, erect; D. *rank*, slender; Provinc. G. *rank*, slender, upright—all nasalized forms < same root as *rack, right, reach*.] Luxuriant in growth; causing vigorous growth; strong and offensive to the smell or taste; total; utter; as, *rank* nonsense; gross or coarse; disgusting.—**rank·ly**, *adv*.—**rank·ness**, *n*.

rank and file, *n*. The general body of any party, society, or organization, apart from officers or leaders; the lines of soldiers from side to side and from front to rear.

rank·er, rang'kėr, *n*. One who ranks. *Brit.* a soldier in the ranks; a commissioned officer promoted from the ranks.

Ran·kine, rang'kin, *a*. *Phys.* Referring to a scale of absolute temperature where the intervals of degree are equivalent to intervals of the Fahrenheit scale; equivalent to Fahrenheit temperature plus 460°. See *Kelvin*.

rank·ing, rang'king, *a*. Outranking others of the same classification; holding the foremost rank or standing; as, the *ranking* officer in a military force.

ran·kle, rang'kl, *v.i*.—*rankled, rankling*. To produce bitterness or rancor in the mind; to continue to irritate; to fester.—*v.t*. To irritate; to inflame; to make bitter.

ran·sack, ran'sak, *v.t*. [A Scand. word: Icel. *rannsaka*, Sw. *ransaka*, to search, as for stolen goods—Icel. *rann* (Goth. *razns*), a house, and *saekja*, to seek.] To search thoroughly; to plunder; to strip by plundering.—**ran·sack·er**, *n*.

ran·som, ran'som, *n*. [Fr. *rancon*, O.Fr. *raenson, raanson*, etc., < L. *redemptio, redemptionis*, redemption; < *redimo—re-*, back, and *emo*, I buy. The word is therefore *redemption* in another form.] The payment for the release of an individual from captivity, bondage, or possession by an enemy; the price paid for such release or for goods captured by an enemy; price paid for the pardon of sins.—*v.t*. To pay a ransom for; to redeem from captivity, bondage, or punishment; to deliver or release after ransom payment; to redeem, as from sin.—**ran·som·er**, *n*.

rant, rant, *v.i*. [Same as O.D. *ranten*, to be enraged, G. *ranten, ranzen*, to move noisily, Provinc. G. *rant*, noisy mirth.] To talk or declaim in a loud, agitated, or extravagant manner; rave.—*v.t*. To utter in a wild or immoderate way.—*n*. Vehement or exaggerated declamation; a ranting speech; *Brit. and Sc. dial.* a boisterous spree.— **rant·er**, *n*.—**rant·ing·ly**, *adv*.

ran·u·la, ran'ū·la, *n*. A cyst occurring beneath the tongue, caused by obstruction and subsequent swelling of a glandular duct.

ra·nun·cu·lus, ra·nung'kya·lus, *n*. pl. **ra·nun·cu·lus·es**, **ra·nun·cu·li**, ra·nung'kya·li. [L., kind of medicinal plant, perh. crowfoot, orig. little frog, tadpole, dim. of *rana*, frog.] Any plant of the large and widely distributed genus *Ranunculus*, comprising herbs with alternate or compound leaves and flowers, commonly yellow, with five petals; a buttercup. Also **crow·foot**, pl. **crow·foots**.

rap, rap, *v.t*.—*rapped, rapping*. [Same as Sw. *rapp*, a blow, a stroke; Dan. *rap*, a rap; imit. of sound made by a blow; cf. *pat, tap*.] To strike with a sharp quick blow; to utter curtly or abruptly, usu. followed by *out*; as, to *rap out* a command.—*v.i*. To strike a quick blow; knock; *slang*, to converse, chat, or discuss; as, to have a cup of coffee and *rap* awhile.—*n*. A quick smart blow; a knock; the sound resulting from such a blow. *Slang*, blame, responsibility, or punishment for an action, esp. a crime; a criminal charge.—**beat the rap**, *slang*. To escape punishment for a crime; to be freed of a criminal charge.—**bum rap**, *slang*, conviction or blame for a crime or misdeed of which one is not guilty.—**rap ses·sion**, *slang*, a friendly chat or discussion.—**take the rap**, *slang*, to take the punishment or blame for a crime, esp. when not guilty.

rap, rap, *n*. [Possibly < G. *rappe*, a coin of slight value.] The least bit, as: It isn't worth a *rap*. A counterfeit halfpenny in circulation in 18th century Ireland.

ra·pa·cious, ra·pā'shus, *a*. [L. *rapax, rapacis*, < *rapio*, I seize (whence also *rapine, rapture*); same root as *rapid*.] Given to plunder; accustomed to seizing or taking possession of property by violence; subsisting on living animals seized in predation; avaricious; grasping.—**ra·pa·cious·ly**, *adv*.—**ra·pa·cious·ness**, **ra·pac·i·ty**, ra·pas'i·tē, *n*.

rape, rāp, *n.* [< *rap*, to seize, to snatch, the meaning being influenced by L. *rapere, raptum*, to seize.] The offense of sexual intercourse with a woman forcibly and against her will; *archaic*, the act of seizing and carrying away by force or violence.— *v.t.* To ravish or forcibly have sexual intercourse with; to pillage, as in war; *archaic*, to seize forcibly and carry away.—*v.i.* To ravish or commit rape.—**rap·ist,** *n.*

rape, rāp, *n.* [< L. *rapa, rapum*, a turnip (whence also rampion).] An annual herb of the genus *Brassica*, a member of the mustard family, widely cultivated as forage for sheep, hogs, and cattle, and for its oil-yielding seeds.

rape, rāp, *n.* [Fr. *râpe.*] The pulpy residue of grapes, remaining after the extraction of the juice for wine, and used for filters by vinegar makers.

rape oil, *n.* A brownish-yellow oil extracted by pressure from rapeseed and used as an illuminating agent, lubricant, and in the production of rubber substitutes. Also **rape·seed oil, col·za oil.**

rape·seed, rāp'sēd", *n.* The seed of the rape; the plant itself.

ra·phe, rā'fē, *n. pl.* **ra·phae,** rā'fē. [N.L. for *rhaphe,* < Gr. *rhaphē,* seam, suture, < *rháptein,* sew.] *Anat.* a seamlike union between two parts or halves of an organ or the like. *Bot.* in certain seeds, a ridge along the surface of the seed coat; a median line or rib on a valve of a diatom. Also *rhaphe.*

ra·phi·a, raf'ē·a, *n.* Raffia.

ra·phide, rā'fid, *n. pl.* **raph·i·des,** raf'i·dēz". [Gr. *raphis,* a needle.] *Bot.* a crystal of an acicular or needlelike form occurring in plant cells, usu. consisting of calcium oxalate.

rap·id, rap'id, *a.* [Fr. *rapide,* < L. *rapidus,* rapid, < *rapio,* to seize; same root as Gr. *harpazō,* to seize.] Very swift or quick; moving or advancing with speed; showing speed in progression; as, *rapid* growth; marked by speed or swiftness; as, a *rapid* knitter.—*n. Usu. pl.* a swift current in a river, where the channel is descending.— **rap·id·ly,** *adv.*—**rap·id·ness,** *n.*

rap·id-fire, rap'id·fī"ẽr', *a. Milit.* firing shots in rapid succession; noting or pertaining to any of various mounted guns of moderate caliber which can be fired rapidly. Characterized by or occurring in rapid procedure, esp. in speech; as, *rapid-fire* questions and replies.

rap·id fire, *n.* An intermediate firing rate for small arms.

ra·pid·i·ty, ra·pid'i·tē, *n.* [L. *rapiditas.*] The state or quality of being rapid; swiftness; celerity. Also *rapidness.*

rap·id trans·it, *n.* An elevated or subway train system which serves a city and its suburbs.

ra·pi·er, rā'pē·ẽr, *n.* [Fr. *rapière,* lit. 'a rasper,' < Sp. *raspar,* to rasp.] A sword used in the 16th and 17th centuries mainly for thrusting, and having a straight, two-edged, long blade.

rap·ine, rap'in, *n.* [Fr., < L. *rapina,* < *rapio,* to seize.] The act of plundering; the seizing and carrying away of things by force.

rap·pee, ra·pē', *n.* [Fr. *râpé,* ppr. of *râper,* to rasp, lit. 'rasped or powdered tobacco.'] A strong, pungent snuff made from the darker and ranker kinds of tobacco.

rap·pel, ra·pel', ra·pel', *n.* [Fr. a recall.] The descent of a steep incline by use of a secured rope passing under a thigh, across the body, and over the opposite shoulder.— *v.i.*—*rappelled, rappelling.* To descend using a rappel.

rap·per, rap'ẽr, *n.* A door knocker; anyone or anything that raps.

rap·port, ra·pōr', ra·pōr', *Fr.* Rä·pôR', *n.* [Fr., < L. *re-,* again, *ad,* to, and *portare,* to carry.] Harmony; affinity.

rap·proche·ment, *Fr.* Rä·pRᾳsh·mäN', *n.* [Fr., < *re-* (< L. *re-*), back, and *approcher,* E. *approach.*] A coming or bringing together or into accord; a reconciling; an establishment or restoration of harmonious relations.

rap·scal·lion, rap·skal'yon, *n.* A good-for-nothing fellow; a rascal.

rapt, rapt, *a.* [< *rap,* to snatch, but influenced by L. *raptus,* seized, < *rapio.*] Entirely absorbed; transported emotionally; enraptured; ecstatic.—**rapt·ly,** *adv.*— **rapt·ness,** *n.*

rap·to·ri·al, rap·tōr'ē·al, rap·tạr'ē·al, *a.* [N.L. *Raptores,* pl. of L. *raptor,* robber, plunderer, < *rapere,* seize, carry off: cf. *rape.*] Belonging or pertaining to the *Raptores,* an order consisting of the birds of prey, as the eagles, hawks, or vultures; preying upon other animals; predatory; adapted for seizing prey, as the beak or claws of a bird.

rap·ture, rap'chẽr, *n.* [< L. *rapere, raptum,* to seize and carry away; whence also *rapine.*] A state of great delight or ecstasy; *often pl.* a showing of extreme joy or pleasure.—*v.t.* raptured, rapturing. *Poet.* to enthrall.—**rap·tur·ous,** rap'chẽr·us, *a.*—**rap·tur·ous·ly,** *adv.*—**rap·tur·ous·ness,** *n.*

ra·ra a·vis, rãr'a ã'vis, *L.* Rä'Rä ä'wis, *n. pl.* **ra·rae a·ves,** rãr'ē ã'vēz, *L.* Rä'Rī ä'wes. [L., lit. 'a rare bird.'] An unusual or uncommon person or thing.

rare, rãr, *a.*—*rarer, rarest.* [L. *rarus,* thin, not dense, scattered, infrequent.] Coming or occurring far apart in time; seldom seen or occurring; unusual; uncommon; unusually excellent or fine; thinly distributed over an area, or few and widely separated; having the component parts not closely compacted together, as air or gases.— **rare·ness,** *n.*

rare, rãr, *a.*—*rarer, rarest.* [Var. of *rear.*] Not thoroughly cooked; underdone.

rare·bit, rãr'bit, *n.* [A word made to account for the expression 'Welsh rabbit.'] Welsh rabbit.

rare earth, *n. Chem.* An oxide of any of the rare-earth metals; a rare-earth metal.

rare-earth met·al, rãr"urth' met'al, *n. Chem.* any one of the lanthanide series of 15 relatively rare metallic elements that are very similar in chemical properties, extremely difficult to isolate, and used chiefly in alloys. Also **rare-earth el·e·ment.** See Periodic Table of the Elements.

rar·ee show, rãr'ē shō", *n.* A peep show; a show carried about in a box; a carnivallike street production or show.

rar·e·fac·tion, rãr"e·fak'shan, *n.* The act of rarefying or state of being rarefied; expansion or distension by separation of constituent particles.—**rar·e·fac·tion·al,** *a.*—**rar·e·fac·tive,** rãr"e·fak'tiv, *a.*

rar·e·fied, rãr'e·fīd", *a.* Elevated; lofty; esoteric; pertaining to or interesting to a small or select group.

rar·e·fy, rãr'e·fī", *v.t.*—*rarefied, rarefying.* [Fr. *raréfier;* L. *rarefacio—rarus,* rare, and *facio,* I make.] To make rare, thin, porous, or less dense; to expand by separation of constituent atoms or particles; *fig.* to refine.—*v.i.* To become thin or less dense.

rare·ly, rãr'lē, *adv.* Seldom; extremely; with uncommon excellence.

rare·ripe, rãr'rīp", *a.* [For *rathripe.*] Early ripe.—*n.* A fruit or vegetable that is ripe early.

rar·i·ty, rãr'i·tē, *n. pl.* **rar·i·ties.** [L. *raritas.*] The state or quality of being rare or uncommon; someone or something that is rare or uncommon; someone or something valued for scarcity or excellence; the state of being thin or less dense.

ras·bo·ra, raz·bōr'a, raz·bạr'a, raz'bẽr·a, *n.* Any of various tropical minnows of the

genus *Rasbora,* some species of which are kept in aquariums.

ras·cal, ras'kal, *n.* [O.Fr. *rascaille* (Fr. *racaille*), rabble; origin uncertain.] A base or dishonest person; a playful designation for a knavish, roguish person or mischievous animal. *Archaic,* the rabble; a person belonging to the rabble.—*a.* Rascally; knavish; dishonest. *Archaic,* belonging to or being the rabble.

ras·cal·i·ty, ra·skal'i·tē, *n. pl.* **ras·cal·i·ties.** Rascally or knavish conduct; a rascally act or practice.

ras·cal·ly, ras'ka·lē, *a.* Being, characteristic of, or befitting a rascal; knavish; dishonest. —*adv.*

rase, rāz, *v.t.*—*rased, rasing.* [Fr. *raser,* < L.L. *rasere,* freq. of L. *rado, rasum,* to scrape.] Raze.

rash, rash, *a.* [Same as L.G., Dan., and Sw. *rask,* Icel. *röskr,* D. and G. *rasch,* rash; perh. < same root as G. *rad,* a wheel. Skt. *ratha,* a chariot.] Acting or speaking without due deliberation and caution; precipitate; uttered, formed, or undertaken hastily or recklessly.—**rash·ly,** *adv.*— **rash·ness,** *n.*

rash, rash, *n.* [O.Fr. *rasche,* rash, scurf, itch; same origin as *rascal.*] An eruption on the skin, usu. in the form of red spots or patches; an unusually large number of occurrences within a certain length of time.

rash·er, rash'ẽr, *n.* [Prob. a piece hastily cooked, < *rash,* a.] A slice of bacon or ham for frying or broiling, or several cooked slices served as a portion.

rash·er, rash'ẽr, *n.* The vermilion rockfish, *Sebastodes miniatus,* of N. Pacific coastal waters.

ra·so·ri·al, ra·sōr'ē·al, ra·sạr'ē·al, *a.* Pertaining to the gallinaceous birds having the characteristic of scratching the ground for food.

rasp, rasp, räsp, *v.t.* [O.Fr. *rasper* (Fr. *râper*), scrape, grate; prob. < Teut.] To scrape or abrade with a rough instrument; scrape or rub roughly; to grate upon or irritate; to remove by scraping; to utter with a grating sound.—*v.i.* To scrape or grate; to make a grating sound.—*n.* A coarse form of file, having separate pointlike teeth; the act of rasping; a rasping or grating sound.—**rasp·er,** *n.* A person or thing that rasps.—**rasp·ing·ly,** *adv.*

rasp·ber·ry, raz'ber"ē, raz'be·rē, räz'ber"ē, räz'be·rē, *n. pl.* **rasp·ber·ries.** [< archaic or provinc. *rasp,* raspberry (fruit or plant), earlier *raspis;* origin uncertain.] The fruit of several shrubs of the rosaceous genus *Rubus,* consisting of small juicy drupelets, red, black, or pale yellow, forming a detachable cap about a convex receptacle; a plant bearing such fruit; a pinkish or purplish-red color. *Slang,* a sound of derision or contempt made by vibrating the lips and tongue; a Bronx cheer; also **razz·ber·ry,** *razz.*

rasp·y, ras'pē, räs'pē, *a.*—*raspier, raspiest.* Grating; harsh; rough; irritable.

ras·ter, ras'tẽr, *n. TV.* the definite pattern of scanning lines traced by the electron beam and covering the picture area in the cathode ray tube.

ra·sure, rā'zhẽr, *n.* The act of scraping or erasing; an erasure.

rat, rat, *n.* [O.E. *raet* = D. *rat* = G. *ratz, ratte,* rat: cf. Fr. *rat,* Sp. and Pg. *rato,* It. *ratto,* M.L. *ratus, rattus,* rat.] Any of certain long-tailed rodents of the genus *Rattus* and allied genera, distinguished from the mouse by larger size and by certain dental features; any of various similar animals. *Slang,* one who abandons his party or associates, esp. in time of trouble; a scab; a stool pigeon or informer. A pad of hair or other material used by women to give a hair style a certain fullness.—*v.i.*—*ratted,* *ratting*. To hunt or catch rats. *Slang*, to desert one's party or associates, esp. in time of trouble; to perform as a scab; to act as an informer.—**smell a rat**, to be suspicious that something is amiss.—**rat·like**, *a*.

rat·a·ble, rate·a·ble, rā′ta·bl, *a*. Capable of being rated or appraised; proportional; *Brit*. liable to rates or local taxes.—**rat·a·bil·i·ty, rat·a·ble·ness**, rā″ta·bil′i·tē, *n*.—**rat·a·bly**, *adv*.

rat·a·fi·a, rat″a·fē′a, *n*. [Sp., < Malay *arak*, arrack, and *tafia*, a spirit distilled from molasses.] A liqueur flavored with the kernels of cherries, apricots, peaches, and almonds; an almond-flavored, sweet biscuit. Also **rat·a·fee, rat″a·fē′**.

rat·a·ny, rat′a·nē, *n*. Rhatany.

rat·a·plan, rat″a·plan′, *n*. [Fr.; imit.] A sound of or as of the beating of a drum.—*v.i., v.t.—rataplanned, rataplanning*. To make this sound on; play a rataplan.

rat·a·tat, rat′a·tat′, *n*. [Imit.] A knocking or rapping sound. Also **rat-a-tat, rat-a-tat-tat**.

rat·bite fe·ver, rat′bīt″ fē′vėr, *n*. *Pathol*. a disease transmitted through the bite of a rat carrying the bacterium, *Spirillum minus*, and marked by recurring fever, skin sores, and muscular aches.

ratch, rach, *n*. Ratchet.

ratch·et, rach′it, *n*. [Fr. *rochet*, ratchet, bobbin; < Teut.] A toothed bar with which a pawl engages; the pawl used with such a device; a mechanism consisting of such a toothed bar or wheel together with the pawl.—**ratch·et wheel**, a wheel with sloping teeth on the edge, into which a pawl drops or catches to prevent reversal of motion or to convert reciprocating motion into rotatory motion.

rate, rāt, *v.t., v.i.—rated, rating*. [Same word as Sw. *rata*, to blame; N. *rata*, to reject.] To chide with vehemence; to scold.

rate, rāt, *n*. [O.Fr. *rate*, < L. *rata* (*pars*, part, understood), < *ratus*, reckoned, ppr. of *reor*, to reckon, to calculate; akin *ratio*, *reason*, *ratify*.] A given quantity or value measured with relation to a specific unit value or to a standard; as, typing at the rate of 60 words per minute; a proportion or ratio; comparative value or amount; the price or amount fixed on anything with relation to a standard; as, long distance telephone *rates*; degree as regards speed, performance, or the like; grade, rank, or rating; a ratio for determining tax assessed on property; gain or loss of time by a timepiece within a given period; *Brit*. the property assessment for local taxes.—*v.t.—rated, rating*. To settle or fix the value, rank, or degree of; to estimate; to fix the relative scale, rank, or position of; to deem or consider; *colloq*. to be entitled to.—*v.i.* To have a certain value, rank, or position.—**at an·y rate**, at least; under any conditions.

ra·tel, rāt′el, rät′el, *n*. [S. Afr. D.] Either of two carnivorous, badgerlike mammals, genus *Mellivora*, of Africa and India.

rate·pay·er, rāt′pā″ėr, *n*. *Brit., Canadian*, a payer of local taxes.

rat·er, rā′tėr, *n*. One who determines rates, values, or ratings; a person or thing that is of a stated rating: used in compounds; as, first-*rater*.

rathe, rath, rāTH, *a*. [O.E. *hraeth*, *hraed*, quick, hasty, *hrathe*, quickly; Icel. *hrathr*, O.H.G. *hrad*, quick.] *Archaic*. Early; coming before others, or before the usual time.—**rathe·ness**, *n*.

rath·er, raTH′ėr, rä′THėr, raTH′u̇r, rä′THu̇r, *adv*. [Compar. of *rath*, quickly; O.E. *hrathor*: we use *sooner* in an equiv. sense.] More readily or willingly; with preference or choice; with better reason; more properly; more correctly speaking; to the

contrary of what has been stated; somewhat; as, *rather* pretty, raTH′ėr, rä′THėr. *Brit. colloq*. definitely; decidedly: used interjectionally as a strong affirmative in answer to a question, raTH′u̇r, rä′THu̇r.

raths·kel·ler, rät′skel″ėr, rat′skel″ėr, rath′-skel″ėr, *n*. [G., also *ratskeller*.] In Germany, the cellar of a town hall, often used as a beer hall or restaurant; any saloon or restaurant of the German type in a cellar or basement.

rat·i·cide, rat′i·sīd″, *n*. Any material for exterminating rats.

rat·i·fy, rat′i·fī″, *v.t.—ratified, ratifying*. [Fr. *ratifier—ratus*, fixed by calculation, valid, firm (rate), and *facio*, I make.] To confirm; to approve and sanction by formal action.—**rat·i·fi·ca·tion**, rat″i·fi·kā′shan, *n*.—**rat·i·fi·er**, *n*.

rat·i·né, rat″i·nā′, *Fr*. Rä·tē·nā′, *n*. [Fr.; origin unknown.] Any of various coarsely woven fabrics with a tufted nap or a rough surface. Also **ra·tine**, rat″i·nā′, ra·tēn′.

rat·ing, rā′ting, *n*. A grading, as of rank or class, esp. of military or naval personnel; status; the act of estimating or evaluating; a personal or business credit evaluation; the stated limit of a machine's operating capacity, as expressed in horsepower, load, or kilowatts; *Brit*. an enlisted man in the navy.

rat·ing bu·reau, *n*. *Insurance*, a firm which collects data concerning risks within an area and sets coverage rates accordingly.

ra·tio, rā′shō, rā′shē·ō′, *n*. *pl*. **ra·tios**. [L., reckoning, account, relation, reason, < *reri* (pp. *ratus*), reckon, calculate, think, judge: rate and *ration*.] The relation between two similar magnitudes in respect to the number of times the first contains the second, integrally or fractionally; as, the *ratio* of 5 to 2, which may be written 5:2 or $\frac{5}{2}$; the relative value of gold and silver as established by the currency laws in a country.

ra·ti·oc·i·nate, rash″ē·os′i·nāt″, *v.i.—ratiocinated, ratiocinating*. [L. *ratiocinor*, *ratiocinatus*, < *ratio*, reason.] To reason.—**ra·ti·oc·i·na·tion**, rash″ē·os″i·nā′shan, *n*. The process of reasoning; an instance or example of this.—**ra·ti·oc·i·na·tive**, *a*.—**ra·ti·oc·i·na·tor**, *n*.

ra·tion, rash′an, rā′shan, *n*. [Fr., < L. *ratio*, *rationis*, proportion.] A daily allowance of provisions to soldiers and sailors; any fixed amount or quantity allotted; a share or portion; *pl*. provisions.—*v.t.* To supply with rations; to allot in a fixed amount; to issue provisions to; to limit or restrict the use of.

ra·tion·al, rash′a·nal, *a*. [Fr. *rationnel*, L. *rationalis*, < *ratio*, *rationis*, proportion.] Having reason or the faculty of reasoning; endowed with reason; agreeable to reason; pertaining to or acting in conformity to reason; sane; judicious; *math*. pertaining to an expression in finite terms: opposed to *irrational*; *class. pros*. measurable in metrical units.—*n*. A rational number.—**ra·tion·al·ly**, *adv*.—**ra·tion·al·ness**, *n*.

ra·tion·ale, rash″a·nal′, *n*. [< L. *rationalis*, < *ratio*, *rationis*, in sense of reason, account, plan.] A statement of reasons; an account or exposition of the principles of some process, phenomenon, or belief; the basis or reason for something.

ra·tion·al·ism, rash′a·na·liz″um, *n*. The development of opinions deduced from reason as distinct from inspiration or revelation; *philos*. the theory that reason rather than sense perception is the criterion of truth and the source of knowledge; *theol*. acceptance of reason as the source of religious truths to the disregard of revelation or anything supernatural.—**ra·tion·al·ist**, *n*.—**ra·tion·al·is·tic**, rash″a·na·lis′tik, *a*.—**ra·tion·al·is·ti·cal·ly**, *adv*.

ra·tion·al·i·ty, rash″a·nal′i·tē, *n*. *pl*. **ra·tion·al·i·ties**. The quality of being rational; possession of reason; reasonableness; *usu*. *pl*. a rational act or belief.

ra·tion·al·ize, rash′a·na·līz″, rash′na·-līz″, *v.t.—rationalized, rationalizing*. To explain or justify; to cause to conform to reason; *psychol*. to attribute logical or creditable motives for actions actually resulting from other, often unrecognized, motives; *math*. to remove irrational expressions, as from an equation; *Brit*. to modernize, as an industry.—*v.i.* To find motives for conduct which are plausible but false.—**ra·tion·al·i·za·tion**, *n*.—**ra·tion·al·iz·er**, *n*.

ra·tion·al num·ber, *n*. A number expressible in the form of a ratio of two integers.

rat·ite, rat′īt, *a*. [L. *ratis*, raft.] Having a flat breastbone with no keel, as an ostrich; of or pertaining to the superorder *Ratite*, which includes flightless birds as the ostrich, emu, cassowary, and rhea.—*n*. Any bird of this superorder.

rat·line, rat·lin, rat′lin, *n*. [Prob. < *raddling*, an E. dial. weaving term.] *Naut*. one of the small ropes which horizontally traverse the shrouds, forming a rope ladder. Also **rat·tling**.

ra·toon, rat·toon, ra·tön′, *n*. [Sp. *retoño*.] A sprout or shoot springing up from the root of a plant, esp. a sugar cane after it has been cropped.—*v.i.* To sprout from a root. —*v.t.* To produce from ratoons, as a crop.

rat race, *n*. *Slang*. Any hectic, usu. futile, activity or mode of existence, esp. one of a competitive nature; a place or scene of chaotic activity.

rats·bane, rats′bān″, *n*. A substance poisonous to rats, esp. arsenic trioxide, As_2O_3.

rat snake, *n*. Chicken snake.

rat·tail, rat-tail, rat′tāl″, *n*. A fish. See grenadier.

rat-tail cac·tus, *n*. A vinelike plant, *Aporocactus flagelliformis*, with long slender branches and crimson flowers, often cultivated in window boxes.

rat·tan, ra·tan, ra·tan′, *n*. [Malay *rōtan*.] The commercial name for the long trailing stems of several Asiatic species of palm of the genera *Calamus* and *Rhapis*, used for making light furniture, wickerwork, and walking sticks.

rat·ter, rat′ėr, *n*. One who or that which catches rats; *slang*, one who deserts his party or his associates.

rat·tle, rat′l, *v.i.—rattled, rattling*. [From an O.E. verb seen in *hraetele*, rattlewort = L.G. *ratteln*, D. *ratelen*, G. *rasseln*, Dan. *rasle*, to rattle; all from a root prob. onomatopoeic.] To make quick, sharp, rapidly repeated noises, as from the collision of hard objects; to clatter; to go or act with clattering noises; to speak eagerly and rapidly; to chatter.—*v.t.* To cause to make a rapid succession of sharp, clattering sounds; to speak, execute, or render rapidly; *colloq*. to upset or confuse.—*n*. A rapid succession of sharp, clattering sounds; an instrument, as an infant's toy, constructed to produce a clattering sound; loud, rapid talk; one who talks rapidly and without constraint; the horny organ at the extremity of the tail of the rattlesnake; the death rattle.

rat·tle·brain, rat′l·brān″, *n*. A flighty, harebrained, talkative person.—**rat·tle·brained**, rat′l·brānd′, *a*.

rat·tler, rat′lėr, *n*. One who rattles; a rattlesnake; *slang*, a freight train.

rat·tle·snake, rat′l·snāk″, *n*. Any of various venomous American serpents of the genera *Crotalus* and *Sistrurus*, having several loosely joined horny pieces or rings at the end of the tail, which produce a rattling or whirring sound when shaken.

rat·tle·snake plan·tain, *n*. Any small terrestrial orchid of the genus *Goodyera*, of northern temperate regions, as *G. pubescens* or *G. repens*, having a checkered leaf pattern.

rat·tle·snake root, *n.* Any of certain plants of the composite family, genus *Prenanthes*, whose roots or tubers were once regarded as a remedy for snake bites, as *P. serpentaria* or *P. alba*; the Seneca snakeroot, *Polygala senega.*

rat·tle·snake weed, *n.* A hawkweed, *Hieracium venosum*, of eastern N. America, whose leaves and root were formerly thought to be a remedy for rattlesnake bites; the button snakeroot, an herb of the genus *Eryngium*, in the carrot family.

rat·tle·trap, rat′l·trap″, *n.* A shaky, rickety object, esp. a dilapidated car.

rat·tling, rat′ling, *a.* Making a quick succession of sharp sounds. *Colloq.* lively; fast; very good.—**rat·tling·ly**, *adv.*

rat·tly, rat′lē, *a.* Apt to rattle; making or having a rattling sound.

rat·trap, rat′trap″, *n.* Any device for trapping rats; *fig.* a very difficult or hopeless position; *colloq.* a neglected building.

rat·ty, rat′ē, *a.—rattier, rattiest.* Pertaining to or characteristic of a rat; full of rats; *slang*, mean, wretched, or shabby.

rat u·nit, *n. Biol.* the minimum quantity of food, drugs, or the like, that will cause a response in a group of laboratory rats.

rau·cous, rạ′kus, *a.* [L. *raucus*, hoarse.] Hoarse; harsh, as the voice; boisterous and unruly.—**rau·cous·ly**, *adv.*—**rau·cous·ness, rau·ci·ty**, rạ′si·tē, *n.*

raun·chy, rạn′chē, roun′chē, rän′chē, *a.* —*raunchier, raunchiest. Slang.* Sloppy; careless; awkward; inept; old or worn-out; smutty; indecent; lewd.

rau·wol·fi·a, rạ·wụl′fē·a, *n.* Any shrub or tree of the genus *Rauwolfia*, of the dogbane family, esp. *R. serpentina*, a source of the drug reserpine.

rav·age, rav′ij, *n.* [Fr. *ravage*, < *ravir*, to carry off, to ravish.] Desolation or destruction by violence; devastation; ruin.—*v.t. ravaged, ravaging.* [Fr. *ravager.*] To lay waste; to devastate; to pillage.—*v.i.* To do damage; to be destructive.—**rav·ag·er**, *n.*

rave, rāv, *v.i.—raved, raving.* [O.Fr. *raver*, to be delirious, < L. *rabies*, madness.] To speak irrationally; to be delirious; to be wild, furious, or raging; to talk with excessive enthusiasm.—*v.t.* To utter wildly and excitedly.—*n.* Frenzy; an extravagantly enthusiastic review.—**rav·er**, *n.*

rav·el, rav′el, *v.t.—raveled, raveling, Brit. ravelled, ravelling.* [Same as O.D. *ravelen*, D. *rafelen*, to disentangle; connections uncertain.] To untwist; to unwind, as the threads of a knitted fabric; to entangle; to make intricate; to involve; to disentangle; to make clear, often followed by *out.—v.i.* To become frayed.—*n.* A tangle; a faulty thread.—**rav·el·er**, *Brit.* **rav·el·ler**, *n.*

rav·el·ment, rav′el·ment, *n.* Entanglement; confusion.

ra·ven, rā′ven, *n.* [O.E. *hraefn* = Icel. *hrafn*, D. *raaf*, Dan. *ravn*, O.H.G. *hraban*, G. *rabe*. Like *crow*, ult. from its cry.] *Ornith.* a large bird of the crow family, *Corvus corax*, having glossy black iridescent plumage, shaggy throat feathers, and a croaking voice, and inhabiting wild regions of the northern hemisphere.—*a.* Of a shiny black color.

rav·en, rav′en, *n.* [O.Fr. *ravine*, < L. *rapina*, rapine.] Prey; plunder.—*v.i.* To prey with rapacity; to eat greedily.—*v.t.* To devour; to seize as prey. Also **rav·in**, rav′in.—**rav·en·er**, *n.*

rav·en·ing, rav′e·ning, *a.* Hunting savagely for prey; devouring.—*n.* A tendency to prey.—**rav·en·ing·ly**, *adv.*

rav·en·ous, rav′e·nus, *a.* Rapacious; voracious; starved; eager for gratification.—**rav·en·ous·ly**, *adv.*—**rav·en·ous·ness**, *n.*

ra·vine, ra·vēn′, *n.* [Fr. *ravine*, a ravine, < L. *rapina*, rapine, violence, < *rapio*, to seize, or carry away.] A long deep hollow or gorge worn by a flowing stream.

ra·vi·o·li, rav″ē·ō′lē, rä″vē·ō′lē, *It.* Rä··vyạ′lē, *n. pl., sing. or pl. in constr.* [It. *ravioli, raviuoli.*] Small squares of dough enclosing meat or cheese, cooked and served in sauce or otherwise.

rav·ish, rav′ish, *v.t.* [Fr. *ravir, ravissant*, < L. *rapio, rapere*, to seize, to snatch.] To seize and carry away, as a woman, by violence; to commit a rape upon; to violate; to plunder, as a city. To transport with joy or ecstasy.—**rav·ish·er**, *n.*

rav·ish·ing, rav′i·shing, *a.* Delightful; entrancing.—**rav·ish·ing·ly**, *adv.*

rav·ish·ment, rav′ish·ment, *n.* An act of ravishing; the condition of being ravished; ecstasy.

raw, rạ, *a.* [O.E. *hreáw, hraew* = D. *raauw*, Dan. *raa*, Icel. *hrár*, O.H.G. *râo*, G. *roh*, raw; same root as L. *crudus*, raw, *cruor*, blood: Gr. *kreas*, flesh.] Not altered from its natural state by cooking; not subjected to some industrial or manufacturing process; not manufactured; as, *raw* silk, *raw* hides; not mixed or diluted; as, *raw* spirits; not covered with the natural covering; having the flesh exposed; sore; harsh; coarse; lacking refinement; just finished; as, *raw* work; immature; inexperienced; as, *raw* soldiers; bleak; chilly; cold and damp; as, a *raw* day.—*n.* A raw, galled, or sore place, as on a horse.—**in the raw**, uncultivated, unrefined; *slang*, naked.—**raw·ly**, *adv.*—**raw·ness**, *n.*

raw·boned, rạ′bōnd′, *a.* Having little flesh on the bones; gaunt; lean.

raw deal, *n. Slang*, an instance of very unjust or very harsh treatment.

raw·hide, rạ′hīd″, *n.* The untanned skin of cattle; a rope or whip made of this.—*v.t.—rawhided, rawhiding.* To whip with a rawhide.

ra·win·sonde, rā′win·sond″, *n.* The procedure of obtaining weather and wind information by means of a radiosonde and receiving and tracking equipment; a radiosonde or radiosonde balloon used in this procedure.

raw ma·te·ri·al, *n.* Any material in its natural form suitable for being manufactured or processed into a finished form.

ray, rā, *n.* [O.Fr. *rai* (Fr. *rais*), < L. *radius*, rod, spoke, ray, beam: cf. *radius*.] Any of the lines or streams in which light appears to issue from a luminous object; a narrow beam of light; radiance; a raylike line or stretch of something, as of color; any of a system of parts radially arranged; *fig.* a gleam, trace, or slight manifestation; as, a *ray* of hope; *math.* one of a system of straight lines passing through a point. *Phys.* the straight line perpendicular to the wave front in the propagation of radiant energy; a stream of material particles as produced by a radioactive element. *Zool.* one of the branches or arms of a starfish; one of the soft, jointed, sometimes branched rods which support and extend the fin of a fish: distinguished from *spine. Bot.* a ray flower; one of the branches of an umbel.—*v.i.* To emit rays; to issue in rays; to spread like rays or radii; radiate.—*v.t.* To send forth in rays; to furnish with rays or radiating lines; to throw rays upon; irradiate; to subject to the action of rays; to treat with rays, as in radiotherapy.

ray, rā, *n.* [Fr. *raie*, < L. *raia*, a ray.] One of a class of cartilaginous fishes, of which the skate is a well-known example, having a flattened body and broadened pectoral fins.

ray flow·er, *n. Bot.* one of the marginal florets surrounding the disk of tubular florets in the flower heads of many composite plants, as in the sunflower. Also **ray flo·ret**.

ray·less, rā′lis, *a.* Without rays or ray flowers; sending out no rays; dark or gloomy.—**ray·less·ness**, *n.*

ray·on, rā′on, *n.* [Fr., ray, beam, gleam, < O.Fr. *rai*, E. *ray*.] A synthetic fiber made by forcing semiliquid cellulose material through a finely perforated metal plate; fabric or yarn made from these fibers.

raze, rase, rāz, *v.t.—razed, razing, rased, rasing.* [= *rase.*] To tear down, demolish, or level to the ground.—**raz·er**, *n.*

ra·zee, ra·zē′, *n.* [Fr. *rasé*, pp. of *raser, rase, raze.*] A wooden ship, esp. a war vessel, reduced in height by the removal of the upper deck.—*v.t.—razeed, razeeing.* To cut down, as a ship, by removing the upper deck.

ra·zor, rā′zėr, *n.* [O.Fr. *rasor*, < *raser*, scrape, shave.] A sharp-edged instrument used esp. for shaving or cutting hair.

ra·zor·back, rā′zėr·bak″, *n.* A half-wild hog with a ridgelike back, found in the southeastern U.S.; the finback whale; a hill that is sharp and narrow along the top.—**ra·zor·backed**, *a.* Having a sharp, ridgelike back.

ra·zor·billed auk, rā′zėr·bild″ ạk′, *n. Ornith.* a black-and-white auk, *Alca torda*, of the N. Atlantic coast, ducklike but having a heavy head, thick neck, and a compressed bill which is crossed midway by a white mark. Also **ra·zor·bill**.

ra·zor clam, *n.* Any of various bivalve mollusks of the family *Solenidae*, with a long, narrow shell. Also **jack·knife clam**.

razz, raz, *n. Slang*, bronx cheer. See *raspberry.—v.t. Slang.* To tease; to deride.

raz·zle-daz·zle, raz′l·daz′l, *n.* [Varied redupl. of *dazzle.*] *Slang*, a state of confusion, bewilderment, or hilarity; *football*, a deceptive play. Exciting, colorful, often flashy activity; also *razzmatazz*.

razz·ma·tazz, raz′ma·taz′, *n. Slang*, colorful but flashy activity. Also *razzle-dazzle*.

r-col·or, är′kul″ėr, *n. Phon.* a quality imparted to certain vowels as a result of a retroflex articulation.—**r-col·ored**, är′kul″ėrd, *a.*

re, rā, *n. Mus.* The syllable used for the second tone of the diatonic scale, sometimes specif. for the tone D.

re, rē, *prep.* [< L. abl. of *res*, thing.] In the matter of; with reference to, often with *in*; as, *in re.*

reach, rēch, *v.t.* [O.E. *rǽcan* = D. *reiken* = G. *reichen*, reach.] To succeed in touching or seizing with the outstretched hand or anything extended or cast; as, to *reach* a book on a high shelf; to take or bring by a stretching effort with the hand or the like; to succeed in striking or hitting, as with a weapon or missile; to get at effectively in attack or retribution; as, to seek to *reach* the instigators of a crime; to succeed in influencing, impressing, interesting, or convincing; as, to *reach* a person through his vanity, to *reach* a desired class of customers; to penetrate to and affect; as, to *reach* one's audience; to stretch or extend so as to touch or meet; as, the bookcase which *reaches* the ceiling; to get to, or get as far as, in moving, going, or traveling, as: The boat *reached* the shore. In general, to come to, as: Sound *reaches* the ear. To come to or arrive at in some course of progress or procedure; as, to *reach* a conclusion by reasoning; to attain; as, to *reach* an age, rank, or condition; to amount to, as in the sum or total, as: The cost will *reach* millions. *Obs.* to succeed in understanding. *Colloq.* to hold out to be taken, or give or pass by extending or handling, as: Please *reach* me the salt.—*v.i.* To make a stretch, as with the hand or arm, or become outstretched, as the hand or arm; to make a movement or effort as if to touch or seize something; as, to *reach* for a weapon;

---

a- fat, fāte, fär, fâre, fạll;   **e-** met, mē, mēre, hėr;   **i-** pin, pīne;   **o-** not, nōte, mōve;   **u-** tub, cūbe, bụll;   **oi-** oil;   **ou-** pound.

to make a stretch of a certain length with the hand, arm, or something else; to extend in operation or effect; as, news *reaching* to the homefront; to stretch in space, or extend in direction, length, or distance; sometimes, to extend or continue in time, as: Elizabeth's reign *reached* into the 17th century. To get or come to a specified place, person, or point, often followed by *to*; to amount, with *to*; as, sums *reaching to* a considerable total. *Naut.* to sail on a leg or reach; to sail close-hauled; to sail on a course with the wind forward of the beam.— *n.* The act or an act of reaching; as, to make a *reach* for a weapon; the extent or distance of reaching; as, the *reach* of the arm, grapes above one's *reach*, out of *reach*; range of effective action, power, or capacity; mental range or capacity of thought or understanding; a continuous stretch or extent of something; as, a *reach* of woodland; a portion of a river between bends; a portion of a canal, of uniform level, between locks; the pole connecting the hind gear of a vehicle with the forward gear. *Naut.* a leg; a course with the wind forward of the beam.—**reach·a·ble,** *a.*—**reach·er,** *n.*—**reach·less,** *a.*

reach-me-down, rĕch′mē·doun″, *n. Brit.* A secondhand garment; a hand-me-down.—*a.*

re·act, rē·akt′, *v.i.* To act or perform in response to an influence; to reciprocate; to be moved to action by a particular stimulus; to act against or in opposition to an influence or force; to move in a reverse manner or way; *chem.* to undergo a reaction.

re·act, rē·akt′, *v.t.* To act or perform anew.

re·ac·tance, rē·ak′tans, *n.* [*Re*, back, and *act*.] *Elect.* that part of the impedance in an alternating current of an electric circuit which is due to induction and capacity.

re·ac·tant, rē·ak′tant, *n.* A person or substance that reacts; *chem.* any substance in a given chemical reaction that is capable of undergoing a chemical change.

re·ac·tion, rē·ak′shan, *n.* Action in return or in response; reciprocal action; reversed action or action tending toward a previous condition; a countermovement or counteraction, esp. a movement toward a previous social or political order; a trend toward political conservatism; *physiol.* reflex action, as in a muscle or nerve. *Med.* the specific effect in a organism or its systems by introduction of a foreign′element; depression or exhaustion as a consequence of excessive excitement or stimulation; increase of activity succeeding depression. *Psychol.* abnormal behavior resulting from a personal experience or situation. *Phys.* the response of a body or system to an action by another agent, manifested as an action opposite in direction and equal in magnitude to the applied force.

re·ac·tion·ar·y, rē·ak′sha·ner″ē, *a.* Pertaining to, proceeding from, or favoring reaction.—*n. pl.* **re·ac·tion·ar·ies.** A person opposed to progress or change in politics or society. Also **re·ac·tion·ist.**

re·ac·tion en·gine, *n.* Any engine producing power or thrust by the reaction to the ejection of a stream of substances, as a jet or rocket engine.

re·ac·ti·vate, rē·ak′ti·vāt″, *v.i., v.t.—reactivated, reactivating.* To become or cause to become effective or operative again.—**re·ac·ti·va·tion,** *n.*

re·ac·tive, rē·ak′tiv, *a.* Tending to react; caused by a reaction; able to respond to a stimulus.—**re·ac·tive·ly,** *adv.*—**re·ac·tive·ness, re·ac·tiv·i·ty,** rē″ak·tiv′i·tē, *n.*

re·ac·tor, rē·ak′tėr, *n.* A person or substance that reacts; *elect.* a device for the introduction of opposition into a circuit of alternating current; *biol.* a person or animal reacting positively to a foreign substance; *chem.* a vat for a chemical reaction, usu. in

industry. *Phys.* an apparatus that initiates and controls spontaneous disintegration of fissionable material; also *atomic pile,* **nu·cle·ar re·ac·tor,** *pile.*

read, rēd, *v.t.—read, reading,* red, rē′ding. [M.E. *reden* < O.E. *rædan,* counsel, advise, deliberate, consider, interpret, read, = *rādan* = O.H.G. *rātan* (G. *raten*) = Icel. *rādha* = Goth. *-rēdan,* all used orig. of taking or giving counsel: cf. *rede.*] To apprehend the meaning of, as something written or printed; to peruse, as a letter or book; to peruse and utter aloud; render in speech, as something written or printed; to have such knowledge of, as a particular language, as to be able to understand things written in it; to make out the significance of, by scrutiny or observation; as, to *read* the sky; to foresee, foretell, or predict, as a person's future; to discover or explain the meaning of, as a dream or riddle; to make out the character of, as a person, by the interpretation of outward signs; to attribute, as something not expressed or directly indicated, to what is read or considered; as, to *read* hostility into a person's remarks; to understand or take, as something read or observed, in a particular way; to adopt or give as a reading in a particular passage, as: For 'fail,' a misprint, *read* 'fall.' To make a study of, as by perusing books; as, to *read* philosophy; to learn or discern by or as by perusal; as, to *read* another's thoughts; to bring or put by reading; as, to *read* a child to sleep; of a thermometer or other instrument, to register or indicate. To determine the meaning of, as information in code form; to acquire, as information, from storage, as on a punched card or on a tape: of an electronic computer.—*v.i.* To inspect and apprehend the meaning of written or other signs or characters; to read or peruse writing or printing; to utter aloud or render in speech, written or printed words that one is perusing; to give a public reading or recital; to occupy oneself seriously with reading or study; to obtain knowledge or learn of something by reading; to admit of being read, esp. properly or well, as: This paragraph *reads* well. To have a certain wording; to admit of being taken or interpreted; as, a sentence that *reads* two different ways.—red, *a.* Having knowledge gained by reading; well-informed through reading, usu. used in compounds; as, well-*read.*—rēd, *n. Colloq.* An act of reading; time passed in reading.—**read be·tween the lines,** to discover a meaning, implication, or purpose not explicitly expressed.—**read in,** to feed data into a computer.—**read out,** to expel, as a member, from a party or organization by public declaration; to recover data from a computer.

read·a·ble, rē′da·bl, *a.* Capable of being read; legible; easy or interesting to read.— **read·a·bil·i·ty, read·a·ble·ness,** rē″da·bil′i·tē, *n.*—**read·a·bly,** *adv.*

read·er, rē′dėr, *n.* One who reads; a schoolbook for instruction and practice in reading; one employed to read manuscripts offered for publication in order to report on their merits; one employed to read printers' proofs for correction; one authorized to read the lessons in a church service; a professor's assistant who grades tests and papers. *Brit.* one who reads or recites before an audience.

read·er·ship, rē′dėr·ship″, *n.* The condition or profession of a reader; people, collectively, who read a published work, as: The magazine has a wide *readership.*

read·i·ly, red′i·lē, *adv.* In a ready manner; quickly; promptly; willingly.

read·i·ness, red′ē·nis, *n.* The state or quality of being ready; aptitude; quickness; cheerfulness; willingness; alacrity.

read·ing, rē′ding, *n.* The action or practice of one who reads; the extent to which one has read; literary knowledge; the utterance or recital of recorded words; a given passage in a particular text; the indication of a dial or a graduated instrument; an interpretation given to anything; as, her *reading* of the situation; a rendering of a dramatic part or musical composition.

read·ing desk, *n.* A desk adapted for use in reading, esp. by a person standing; a church lectern.

read·ing rate, *n. Educ.* a measure of reading speed, usu. expressed in words per minute; *computer,* the rate of speed, expressed in characters, cards, or words per time unit, at which a sensing device can operate.

re·ad·just, rē″a·just′, *v.t.* To adjust or settle again; to put in order again.—**re·ad·just·ment,** *n.*

read·out, rēd′out″, *n. Computer.* A machine that sets forth computed or stored information, esp. in digit form; information provided by such a machine.

read·y, red′ē, *a.—readier, readiest.* [O.E. *redi, readi, raede,* ready = Dan. *rede,* Sw. *reda,* Icel. *reithr,* G. *(be)reit,* ready; perh. from root of *ride.*] Fit for immediate use; prompt in perception; prompt in performance or action; willing; inclined; apt; offering itself at once; at hand; convenient; on the point or brink, followed by *to*; as, *ready to* begin.—*v.t.—readied, readying.* To prepare, make ready.—*n.* The condition of being ready; the position of a rifle before aiming; *colloq.* ready money.

read·y-made, red′ē·mād′, *a.* Made or prepared beforehand and kept in stock ready for use or sale; as, *ready-made* clothes; conventional; commonplace.—*n.*

read·y room, *n.* A place where air crews receive their orders and briefings just prior to flight.

read·y-to-wear, red′ē·to·wâr′, *a.* Ready-made, as clothes.—*n.*

read·y-wit·ted, red′ē·wit′id, *a.* Having quick wit.

re·a·gent, rē·ā′jent, *n. Chem.* any substance which, by the reactions it produces, can be used in chemical analysis.

re·al, rē′al, rēl, *a.* [O.Fr. *real, reel* (Fr. *reel*), < M.L. *realis,* < L. *res,* thing, object, matter, fact.] True rather than merely nominal or apparent, as the reason for an act; existing or occurring as fact; actual rather than imaginary, ideal, or fictitious, as conditions; being an actual thing with objective existence rather than merely imaginary; being actually such, rather than merely so called, as a victory; genuine or not counterfeit, as an antique; not artificial; not imitation; unfeigned or sincere. *Philos.* existent, actual or essential, rather than potential or possible; existing independently of the mind or thought. *Law,* noting or pertaining to immovable property, as lands and tenements: opposed to *personal. Opt.* noting an image formed by the actual convergence of rays, as the image produced in a camera. *Math.* either rational or irrational, not imaginary, as a quantity or a number.— *adv. Colloq.* Really; very.—*n.* Something that is real or has a real existence, usu. preceded by *the*; a real number.—**for re·al,** *slang.* In reality; existing.—**re·al·ness,** *n.*

re·al es·tate, *n.* Land and whatever by nature or artificial annexation is a part of it, as trees or buildings; ownership of or property in lands.

re·al·gar, rē·al′gėr, *n.* [M.E. *realgar,* through O.Fr. or M.L. < Ar. *rahj al-ghār,* 'powder of the mine.'] Arsenic sulfide, As_2S_2, found native as an orange-red mineral and prepared artificially: used in pyrotechnics.

---

re·a·li·a, rē·ä′lē·a, rä·ä′lē·a, n. pl. Activities or objects used in teaching to relate the classroom situation to real life.

re·al·ism, rē′a·liz″um, n. Attention to or concern with what is real; the tendency to view or represent things as they really are, as opposed to *idealism* or *romanticism*; close resemblance in literature or art to what is real; a style of writing that emphasizes fidelity to the details, often unpleasant, of nature or everyday life; *philos.* the doctrine that universals have a real, objective existence outside the mind.—**re·al·ist,** rē′a·list, n.—**re·al·is·tic,** rē″a·lis′tik, a.—**re·al·is·ti·cal·ly,** adv.

re·al·i·ty, rē·al′i·tē, n. pl. **re·al·i·ties.** [M.L. *realitas.*] The state or fact of being real, having actual existence, or having actually occurred; a real thing or fact; that which is real as opposed to that which is imagined or merely apparent; *philos.* an independent absolute from which all else derives.—**in re·al·i·ty,** actually; in fact or truth.

re·al·i·za·tion, rē″a·li·zā′shan, n. The act of realizing, or the state of being realized; the making or being made real of something imagined or planned; the result of such a process; the act of forming a clear conception of the reality of something, or the conception formed.

re·al·ize, rē′a·līz″, v.t.—*realized, realizing.* [Fr. *réalizer.*] To grasp or understand clearly; to make real, or give reality to, as dreams or fears; to make realistic or lifelike, as a description or a picture; to conceive or comprehend as real; to convert into cash or money; to obtain or gain for oneself by trade or effort; of property, to bring as a return, as from sale or investment.—v.i. To convert property or anything of value into cash or money.—**re·al·iz·a·ble,** a.—**re·al·iz·er,** n.—**re·al·iz·ing,** a. That realizes; clear in apprehending or understanding.—**re·al·iz·ing·ly,** adv.

re·al·ly, rē′a·lē, rē′lē, adv. In reality; actually or truly; indeed.

realm, relm, n. [O.Fr. *realme* (Fr. *royaume*), < L. *regalis,* < *rex, regis,* a king.] A kingdom; a region, sphere, domain, or scope of influence or power.

re·al num·ber, n. *Math.* A number that is not imaginary; an irrational or rational number.

Re·al·po·li·tik, rē·äl′pō″li·tēk′, n. [G.] (*Sometimes l.c.*) Realistic or practical politics: contrasted with idealistic or theoretical politics; a policy advocating strength or power.

re·al pres·ence, n. (*Often cap.*), *theol.* the belief in the presence of the body and blood of Christ in the Eucharist. See *consubstantiation, transubstantiation.*

re·al time, n. *Computer,* the relative time between the availability of a computer computation and the physical process requiring this computation for its operation.

Re·al·tor, rē′al·tẽr, rē′al·tar″, n. [< *realty;* coined by C. N. Chadbourn, of Minneapolis, a member of the National Association of Real Estate Boards, and formally adopted by the Association in 1916.] A broker or other individual in the real estate business who is an active member of the National Association of Real Estate Boards, subject to its rules and regulations. (Trademark.)

re·al·ty, rē′al·tē, n. [A contr. of *reality.*] *Law.* That kind of property termed real; real estate.

re·al wag·es, n. pl. The amount of commodities and services which can be purchased by a worker's wages; wages judged by buying power rather than money paid. Compare *nominal wages.*

ream, rēm, n. [O.Fr. *raime,* < Sp. *resma,* a ream, < Ar. *rizmah,* a bale, a packet, a ream.] A bundle or package of paper of 480 sheets; also **short ream.** A bundle of paper consisting of 500 sheets; also **long ream.** A package of paper consisting of 516 sheets; also **print·er's ream, per·fect ream.** *Pl., colloq.* a voluminous amount; as, *reams* of information.

ream, rēm, v.t. [Increase, to enlarge, < O.E. *rúm,* space.] To enlarge with a reamer, as a hole or cannon bore; to conically shape or bevel, as a hole, with a reamer; to remove, as a defect, by reaming; to squeeze juice from with a reamer.

ream·er, rē′mẽr, n. A rotating tool for enlarging, finishing, or conically shaping a hole; a utensil for squeezing juice from fruit; someone or something that reams.

re·a·nal·y·sis, rē′a·nal′i·sis, n. A repeated analysis.—**re·an·a·lyze,** rē·an′a·līz″, v.t.—*reanalyzed, reanalyzing.*

re·an·i·mate, rē·an′i·māt″, v.t.—*reanimated, reanimating.* To revive, resuscitate, or restore to life or animation; to infuse new vigor or courage into.—**re·an·i·ma·tion,** rē·an″i·mā′shan, n.

re·an·nex, rē″a·neks′, v.t. To annex again, as territory that has been disjoined.—**re·an·nex·a·tion,** rē·an″ek·sā′shan, rē·an″ek·sā′shan, n.

reap, rēp, v.t. [O.E. *ripan,* to reap; closely allied to Goth. *raupjan,* to pluck; D. *rapen,* to gather; L.G. *rapen,* to pluck. *Ripe* is from same stem.] To cut with a sickle, scythe, or machine, as a grain crop; to gather or harvest; to receive as a recompense or return; as, to *reap* the benefits, or other results, of an act or deed.—v.i. To perform the act of reaping; to receive the results of one's labor or actions.

reap·er, rē′pẽr, n. One who reaps; a reaping machine.

reap·ing ma·chine, n. A machine drawn by horse or tractor which harvests grain, often including a device which presses, bundles, and binds the grain.

re·ap·pear, rē″a·pẽr′, v.i. To appear again or anew.—**re·ap·pear·ance,** rē″a·pẽr′ans, n.

re·ap·ply, rē″a·plī′, v.t., v.i.—*reapplied, reapplying.* To apply again.—**re·ap·pli·ca·tion,** rē·ap″li·kā′shan, n.

re·ap·point, rē″a·point′, v.t. To appoint again.—**re·ap·point·ment,** rē″a·point′ment, n.

re·ap·por·tion·ment, rē″a·pōr′shan·ment, rē″a·par′shan·ment, n. The act of changing the allotment of something; a redistribution of representatives in a legislature.—**re·ap·por·tion,** v.t. To apportion again or anew.

re·ap·praise, rē″a·prāz′, v.t.—*reappraised, reappraising.* To estimate or evaluate again.—**re·ap·prais·al,** rē″a·prā′zal, n.

rear, rēr, v.t. [O.E. *raeran,* raise.] To support, bring up, or care for to maturity; as, to *rear* children; to nurture or educate; to breed or raise, as animals; to grow, as plants; to raise or erect by building; to raise to an upright position; to lift or hold up; to elevate.—v.i. To rise on the hind legs, as a horse or other animal; to rise high or tower aloft, as a building; to rise to an upright position; to start up in angry excitement or hot resentment, usu. followed by *up,* as: The crew *reared up* against the captain.

rear, rēr, n. [For *arrear, n.*] The back or the side opposite the front; backside; the space or position behind, or at the back of, anything; background; the posterior or rump; *milit.* the area and that part of an army or fleet farthest from a battle or a front.—a. Situated at or pertaining to the rear of anything.

rear ad·mi·ral, n. A commissioned naval officer ranking higher than captain and lower than vice-admiral.

rear ech·e·lon, n. *Milit.* a supply and administrative headquarters situated in an area to the rear of the front.

rear guard, n. *Milit.* a part of an army detached from the main body to bring up and guard the rear, or to protect its retreat.

rear-guard ac·tion, rēr′gärd″ak′shan, n. A delaying or defensive fight involving the rear guard of an army; a delaying or preventive effort defending the existing order, usu. in opposition to great odds.

re·arm, rē·ärm′, v.t. To arm again; to furnish with new or better weapons.—**re·ar·ma·ment,** rē·är′ma·ment, n.

rear·most, rēr′mōst″, a. Farthest in the rear; last of all.

rear·mouse, rēr′mous″, n. Reremouse.

re·a·rouse, rē″a·rouz′, v.t.—*rearoused, rearousing.* To reawaken or reanimate; to provoke or stimulate to new action.—**re·a·rous·al,** rē″a·rou′zal, n.

re·ar·range, rē″a·rānj′, v.t.—*rearranged, rearranging.* To arrange again; to put in proper order again.—**re·ar·range·ment,** rē″a·rānj′ment, n.

re·ar·rest, rē″a·rest′, v.t. To apprehend, without a warrant, a person who previously escaped from arrest.

rear·ward, rēr′wẽrd, a. Last; backward.—adv. Toward or in the rear. Also **rear·ward·ly, rear·wards.**—n. A last or rear position.—**rear·ward·ness,** n.

rea·son, rē′zon, n. [O.Fr. Fr. *raison,* < L. *ratio(n-),* reckoning, account, relation, respect, ground or motive, reason, reasonableness, < *reri* (pp. *ratus*), reckon, calculate, think, judge: cf. *rate* and *ratio.*] A ground or motive for a belief or a course of action; a statement in justification or explanation of belief or action; the intellectual faculty; normal or sound powers of mind; sanity; sound judgment or good sense; sensible speech or advice; *logic,* a premise of an argument, esp. the minor premise when placed after the conclusion.—v.i. [O.Fr. *raisoner* (Fr. *raisonner*), < M.L. *rationare,* reason, argue, discourse, < L. *ratio(n-).*] To exercise the faculty or powers of reason; draw conclusions or inferences from facts or premises; to discuss or argue in a logical manner.—v.t. To argue about or discuss; to think out logically, often used with *out;* as, to *reason out* a problem; to conclude or infer; to persuade by reasoning or argument.—**bring to rea·son,** to direct, as someone, to a reasonable course of thought.—**by rea·son of,** by virtue of.—**in rea·son,** in accordance with reason; justly or properly; within limits prescribed by reason.—**stand to rea·son,** to be obvious or reasonable.—**with rea·son,** with justifiable cause.—**rea·son·er,** n.

rea·son·a·bil·i·ty, rē″zo·na·bil′i·tē, rēz″na·bil′i·tē, n. The condition or quality of being reasonable.

rea·son·a·ble, rē′zo·na·bl, rēz′na·bl, a. [O.Fr. Fr. *raisonnable.*] Agreeable to reason or sound judgment; as, a *reasonable* supposition; rational; having or exercising sound judgment; not exceeding the limit prescribed by reason, or not excessive; moderate, as charges or prices.—**rea·son·a·ble·ness,** n.—**rea·son·a·bly,** adv.

rea·son·ing, rē′zo·ning, n. The act or process of one who reasons; the process of drawing conclusions or inferences from facts or premises.

rea·son·less, rē′zon·lis, a. Not endowed with reason; not based on reason or good sense.—**rea·son·less·ly,** adv.

re·as·sem·ble, rē″a·sem′bl, v.t.—*reassembled, reassembling.* To collect or assemble again.—v.i. To come or meet together again.—**re·as·sem·bly,** rē″a·sem′blē, n.

re·as·sert, rē″a·surt′, v.t. To assert again.—**re·as·ser·tion,** n.

re·as·sess, rē″a·ses′, v.t. To assess anew; reconsider.—**re·as·sess·ment**, n.

re·as·so·ci·ate, rē″a·sō′shē·āt″, rē″a·sō′sē·āt″, v.t., v.i.—reassociated, reassociating. To associate once more.—**re·as·so·ci·a·tion**, rē″a·sō″shē·ā′shan, rē″a·sō″sē·ā′shan, n.

re·as·sort, rē″a·sạrt′, v.t., v.i. To assort again.—**re·as·sort·ment**, n.

re·as·sume, rē″a·sŏm′, v.t. To resume; to take up again.—**re·as·sump·tion**, rē″a·sump′shan, n.

re·as·sure, rē″a·shụr′, v.t.—reassured, reassuring. To restore courage and self-confidence to; to hearten; to assure anew.—**re·as·sur·ance**, n.—**re·as·sur·ing·ly**, adv.

re·a·ta, ri·a·ta, rē·ä′ta, n. [< Sp. reata, rope.] A lariat.

re·at·tack, rē″a·tak′, v.t. To attack anew.—v.i. To begin another attack.

re·at·tain, rē″a·tān′, v.t. To attain anew.—**re·at·tain·ment**, rē″a·tān′ment, n.

re·at·tempt, rē″a·tempt′, v.t. To attempt anew.—v.i. To make another attempt.

Ré·au·mur, rā′a·mūr″, Fr. Rā·ō·MYR′, a. Designating, or in accordance with, the thermometric scale introduced by René Antoine Ferchault de Réaumur, a French physicist of the early 18th century, in which, under a pressure of 1 atmosphere, the freezing point of water is at 0°, and the boiling point at 80°. Abbr. R.

re·au·thor·ize, rē·a′tho·rīz″, v.t.—reauthorized, reauthorizing. To authorize anew.

reb, reb, n. Colloq. a rebel, esp. a soldier of the Confederate army.

re·bap·tize, rē″bap·tīz′, rē·bap′tīz, v.t.—rebaptized, rebaptizing. To baptize a second time.—**re·bap·tism**, rē·bap′tiz·um, n. A second baptism.

re·bar·ba·tive, rē·bär′ba·tiv, a. Arousing aversion or irritation; repellent.

re·bate, rē′bāt, ri·bāt′, v.t.—rebated, rebating. [O.Fr. rebatre—re-, back, and battre, L. batuere, to beat.] To diminish, reduce; to return; to deduct or make a discount from, as an invoice.—rē′bāt, n. A refund; abatement in price; deduction.—**re·bat·er**, rē′bā·tèr, ri·bā′tèr, n.

re·bate, rē·bāt′, rab′it, n. Rabbet.—v.t., v.i.—rebated, rebating.

re·ba·to, re·bä′tō, n. Rabato.

re·bec, re·beck, rē′bek, n. [Fr. rebec, rebebe, < Ar. rabâb, a kind of musical instrument.] A medieval stringed instrument somewhat similar to the violin, having a pear-shaped body, and played with a bow.

reb·el, reb′el, n. [Fr. rebelle, < L. rebellis, making war again.] One who revolts from the government to which he owes allegiance; one who defies and seeks to overthrow any authority or control.—reb′el, a. Rebellious; relating to rebels; defiant.—ri·bel′, v.i.—rebelled, rebelling. To reject or take up arms against one's government; to refuse to obey an authority, tradition, or control; to feel or show disgust or revulsion.

re·bel·lion, ri·bel′yon, n. [L. rebellio, rebellionis.] The act of rebelling; an armed rising against an established government; open resistance to, or refusal to obey, lawful authority.

re·bel·lious, ri·bel′yus, a. Engaged in, or characterized by, rebellion; mutinous; resisting control.—**re·bel·lious·ly**, adv.—**re·bel·lious·ness**, n.

re·birth, rē·bụrth′, rē′bụrth″, n. Birth anew; renascence; revival.

reb·o·ant, reb′ō·ant, a. [L. reboans (-ant-), ppr. of reboare, < re-, back, and boare, bellow, roar.] Bellowing in return; resounding loudly.

re·born, rē·bạrn′, a. Born anew; regenerated.

re·bound, ri·bound′, v.i. [Prefix re-, and bound; Fr. rebondir, to rebound.] To spring or bound back; to fly back by force after impact with another body.—v.t. To cause to bound or spring back.—rē′bound″, ri·bound′, n. The act of rebounding on collision with another body; resilience; an emotional reaction following frustration, preceded by on the, as: He married on the rebound after his divorce.

re·bo·zo, ri·bō′zō, Sp. Re·bạ′thạ, Re·bạ′sạ, n. pl. **re·bo·zos**. [Sp.] A shawl or long scarf worn by Spanish-American and Spanish women as a covering for the head and shoulders.

re·broad·cast, rē·brạd′kast″, rē·brạd′käst″, v.t., v.i.—rebroadcast or rebroadcasted, rebroadcasting. To broadcast again; to relay by broadcasting a program received from another radio or TV station.—n. The program broadcast again.

re·buff, ri·buf′, rē′buf, n. [Prefix re-, back, and old buff, a blow, < O.Fr. buffe, bufe, a blow.] A forcing or driving back; a sudden check; a repulse; a refusal; a rejection of solicitation.—ri·buf′, v.t. To beat back; to offer sudden resistance to; to repel the advances of; to snub.

re·build, rē·bild′, v.t.—rebuilt or archaic rebuilded, rebuilding. To build again; to build after having been demolished; to reconstruct.

re·buke, ri·būk′, v.t.—rebuked, rebuking. [A.Fr. rebuker, O.Fr. rebuchier, to beat or strike back.] To reprehend sharply; to reprimand; to reprove.—n. A direct and severe reprimand; reproof; reprehension.—**re·buk·er**, n.

re·bus, rē′bus, n. pl. **re·bus·es**. [L., ablative pl. of res, a thing—lit. 'by things,' because the meaning is indicated by things.] A set of words represented by figures or pictures of objects whose names resemble in sound those words or the syllables of which they are composed; a kind of puzzle made up of such figures or pictures.

re·but, ri·but′, v.t.—rebutted, rebutting. [Fr. rebuter, rebouter, to put or thrust back—re-, back, and bouter, to put, to thrust.] To refute, as by counter evidence; oppose; law, to oppose by argument, plea, or countervailing proof.—**re·but·ta·ble**, a.

re·but·tal, ri·but′al, n. The act of rebutting; refutation; confutation.

re·but·ter, ri·but′ér, n. Something or someone that rebuts; law, the answer of a defendant to a plaintiff's surrejoinder.

re·cal·ci·trant, ri·kal′si·trant, a. Exhibiting resistance or opposition to regulation or authority; refractory; difficult to handle or manage.—n.—**re·cal·ci·trance, re·cal·ci·tran·cy**, n.

re·cal·cu·late, rē·kal′kū·lāt″, v.t.—recalculated, recalculating. To calculate or compute again, esp. to locate an error.—**re·cal·cu·la·tion**, rē·kal′kū·la′shan, n.

re·ca·lesce, rē″ka·les′, v.i.—recalesced, recalescing. [L. recalescere, to grow warm again.] To become hot again, said esp. of cooling iron, which glows with increased brilliancy upon passing certain temperatures.—**re·ca·les·cence**, n.

re·call, ri·kạl′, v.t. To call or bring back; to order to return; to take back or revoke; to revive in memory.—ri·kạl′, rē′kạl, n. A calling back; revocation; the power of calling back or revoking; the removal of an official from office by a popular vote.—**re·call·a·ble**, a.

re·cant, ri·kant′, v.t., v.i. [L. recantare, to recant, to recall.] To retract; to unsay; to make formal contradiction of something which one had previously asserted.—**re·can·ta·tion**, rē″kan·tā′shan, n.

re·cap, rē′kap″, rē·kap′, v.t.—recapped, recapping. To recondition, as an automobile tire, by cementing a strip of prepared rubber to the worn tread and vulcanizing by heat and pressure in a mold.—rē′kap″, n. A recapped tire.—**re·cap·pa·ble**, a.

re·cap, rē′kap″, v.t.—recapped, recapping. Colloq. recapitulate.—n. Colloq. recapitulation.

re·cap·i·tal·i·za·tion, rē·kap″i·ta·li·zā′shan, n. A revised form of the capital organization of a corporation.—**re·cap·i·tal·ize**, rē·kap′i·ta·līz″, v.t.—recapitalized, recapitalizing. To revise or renew the capital organization of.

re·ca·pit·u·late, rē″ka·pich′a·lāt″, v.t.—recapitulated, recapitulating. [Fr. recapituler, L.L. recapitulo, recapitulatum.] To repeat or summarize, as the principal facts or points mentioned in a preceding discourse; biol. to repeat ancestral evolutionary stages in the embryo; mus. to restate main themes in a composition, esp. in the sonata form.—v.i. To repeat in brief what has been said before.

re·ca·pit·u·la·tion, rē″ka·pich″a·lā′shan, n. [L.L. recapitulatio(n-).] The act of recapitulating; a summary or brief review; biol. the repetition of ancestral evolutionary stages in the embryonic development of an organism. Mus. a restatement of main themes in a composition, esp. in the sonata form; reprise. Also recap.

re·cap·ture, rē·kap′chér, v.t.—recaptured, recapturing. To capture again; recover by capture; of the government, to take by recapture.—n. Recovery or retaking by capture; the taking by the government of a fixed part of all earnings in excess of a certain percentage of property value, as in the case of a railroad; the act of taking, or the fact of being taken, a second time; international law, the lawful retaking of a possession.

re·cast, rē·kast′, rē·käst′, v.t.—recast, recasting. To cast or found again; to mold again or reconstruct, as a speech; to put into a new form.—rē′kast″, rē′käst″, n.

re·cede, ri·sēd′, v.i.—receded, receding. [L. recedo—re-, back, and cedere, to walk.] To move back; to retreat; to withdraw; to become more distant; to slope or slant backward; to take back an assertion or promise.

re·cede, rē·sēd′, v.t.—receded, receding. To cede back; to grant or yield to a former possessor.

re·ceipt, ri·sēt′, n. [O.Fr. recete, recepte (Fr. recette), < L. receptus-, pp. of recipere, to receive.] The act of receiving. Usu. pl. that which is received. A written acknowledgment of something received, as money or goods. A recipe.—v.t. To give a receipt for.—v.i. To make out a receipt.

re·ceiv·a·ble, ri·sē′va·bl, a. Such as may be received; as, accounts receivable; capable of being received, as payment due.—**re·ceiv·a·bles**, n. pl. Assets listed as outstanding accounts.

re·ceive, ri·sēv′, v.t.—received, receiving. [O.Fr. recever, receveir, Fr. recevoir, < L. recipio.] To get or obtain; to take, as a thing given, paid, or communicated; to accept; to believe; to allow to enter in an official capacity; to welcome as a guest; to hold, admit, contain, have capacity for; as, a box to receive contributions; to be the object of; to suffer; to experience; to take from a thief, knowing the thing to be stolen.

re·ceiv·er, ri·sē′vèr, n. One who receives; a person appointed to manage the affairs of an enterprise in reorganization or liquidation; one who purchases goods from a thief, knowing them to be stolen. Chem. a vessel for receiving and containing the product of distillation; a vessel to receive gases. An electronic device which converts signs or waves into observable sensory forms.

re·ceiv·er·ship, ri·sē′vẽr·ship″, n. The legal status of an enterprise under jurisdiction of the court for the purpose of a trust, reorganization, or liquidation; the position of being in the hands of a receiver.

re·cen·sion, ri·sen′shan, n. A critical revision of a text by an editor; an edited version established from such a revision.

re·cent, rē′sent, a. [Fr. *récent*, < L. *recens, recentis*, recent.] Of late origin, occurrence, or existence; new; not of remote date, antiquated style, or the like; fresh. (*Cap.*), *geol.* pertaining to the present epoch, which follows the Pleistocene or glacial epoch; occurring or formed since the glacial epoch. See Table of Geologic Time.—**re·cent·ly**, *adv.*—**re·cen·cy, re·cent·ness,** *n.*

re·cep·ta·cle, ri·sep′ta·kl, n. [L. *receptaculum*, < *recipio, receptum*, to receive.] A place or vessel in which something is received and contained; a repository; *bot.* the end of a stalk which bears the flower, seeds, or fruit or a plant; *elect.* a socket, connected to a source of electricity, and which receives the plug of an appliance.

re·cep·tion, ri·sep′shan, n. [L. *receptio*, < *recipio*, to receive.] A receiving; a manner of receiving a person or thing; as, a favorable *reception*; a formal occasion or ceremony of receiving guests or official personages; admission or credence, as of an opinion or doctrine; *radio, TV*, the act or process of receiving programs or signals.

re·cep·tion·ist, ri·sep′sha·nist, n. A person employed to greet callers, esp. at a business office.

re·cep·tive, ri·sep′tiv, a. Able to receive readily, as impressions, suggestions, or teachings; able to take in, hold, or contain; pertaining to a receptor.—**re·cep·tive·ly**, *adv.*—**re·cep·tive·ness,** *n.*—**re·cep·tiv·i·ty,** rē″sep·tiv′i·tē, *n.*

re·cep·tor, ri·sep′tẽr, n. A receiver; *physiol.* the ending of an afferent neuron which receives stimuli and transmits them to other parts of the nervous system.

re·cess, ri·ses′, rē′ses, n. [L. *resessus, recedo, recessum.*] The time or period during which normal activity is suspended; *usu. pl.* place of seclusion or secrecy. A cavity or indentation in an otherwise smooth surface, as a niche, alcove, or sunken space formed in a wall.—*v.t.* To make a recess in; to put in a recess.—*v.i.* To take a recess.

re·ces·sion, ri·sesh′an, n. [L. *recessio(n-)*, < *recedere*.] The act of receding; a going back; a withdrawal; departure or retirement, as the procession of clergy at the conclusion of a religious service; *econ.* a business slump during a generally rising economy.—**re·ces·sion·ar·y,** *a.*

re·ces·sion, ri·sesh′an, n. Cession or a ceding back, as to a former possessor.

re·ces·sion·al, ri·sesh′a·nal, a. Of or pertaining to recession; as, a *recessional* hymn; of or pertaining to a recess, as of a legislative body.—*n.* A musical composition played or sung at the end of a religious service or program.

re·ces·sive, ri·ses′iv, a. [L. *recedere* (pp. *recessus*).] Tending to recede; receding; *phon.* of accent, showing a tendency to recede from the end toward the beginning of a word; *genetics*, pertaining to or exhibiting a hidden or recessive character, as opposed to a *dominant* character.—*n.* A recessive character, or an organism exhibiting it.—**re·ces·sive·ly,** *adv.*—**re·ces·sive·ness,** *n.*

re·charge, rē·chärj′, v.t., v.i.—*recharged, recharging.* To charge again or anew, as a battery; reload.—*n.* A second or additional charge.

ré·chauf·fé, rā·shō·fā′, *Fr.* Rā·shō·fā′, *n. pl.* **ré·chauf·fés,** *Fr.* Rā·shō·fā′. [Fr., prop. pp. of *réchauffer*, warm again.] A

warmed-up dish of food; anything old brought out anew, as a rehash of a literary work.

re·cher·ché, re·shâr′sha, *Fr.* Re·sheR·-shā′, *a.* [Fr.] Overrefined or pretentious; choice; rare; exquisite; far-fetched.

re·cid·i·vism, ri·sid′i·viz″um, n. Repeated or habitual relapse into crime or antisocial behavior.—**re·cid·i·vist,** *n.*—**re·cid·i·vis·tic, re·cid·i·vous,** *a.*

rec·i·pe, res′i·pē″, n. [L. *recipe*, take, receive, impv. of *recipio*, to take or receive.] A list of instructions for preparing, mixing, and cooking food to produce a particular dish. *Med.* a physician's prescription: so named from its first word: abbr. ℞.

re·cip·i·ent, ri·sip′ē·ent, n. [L. *recipiens, recipientis*, ppr. of *recipio*.] A person or thing that receives; a receiver.—*a.* Receptive or receiving.—**re·cip·i·ence, re·cip·i·en·cy,** ri·sip′ē·ens, *n.*

re·cip·ro·cal, ri·sip′ro·kal, a. [L. *reciprocus*, returning, reciprocal.] Moving alternately backward and forward; given, performed, or felt in return; given or felt by each to or toward the other; mutual; as, *reciprocal* affection; mutually responsive, answering, or corresponding; inversely corresponding; inverse; *gram.* expressing mutual relation, as the pronouns, 'each other,' 'one another.'—*n.* A thing that is reciprocal to something else; a return; an equivalent; a counterpart; a complement; *math.* that by which a given quantity is multiplied to produce unity.—**re·cip·ro·cal·i·ty,** ri·sip″ro·kal′i·tē, *n.*—**re·cip·ro·cal·ly,** *adv.*

re·cip·ro·cate, ri·sip′ro·kāt″, v.t.—*reciprocated, reciprocating.* [L. *reciprocatus*, pp. of *reciprocare*, < *reciprocus*.] To cause to move alternately backward and forward; to give or feel in return; to give and receive reciprocally; as, to *reciprocate* favors; to interchange; to make correspondent.—*v.i.* To move alternately backward and forward; to make return, as for something given; to make interchange; to be correspondent.

re·cip·ro·cat·ing en·gine, n. That form of engine in which the piston moves back and forth in a straight line within the cylinder.

re·cip·ro·ca·tion, ri·sip″ro·kā′shan, n. [L. *reciprocatio(n-)*.] The act or fact of reciprocating; motion backward and forward; a making return for something; a mutual giving and receiving.—**re·cip·ro·ca·tive,** *a.*

rec·i·proc·i·ty, res″i·pros′i·tē, n. The state or character of being reciprocal; reciprocal obligation or right; equal rights or benefits mutually yielded or enjoyed, as equal commercial or trade rights or privileges enjoyed mutually by two countries.

re·ci·sion, ri·sizh′an, n. [L. *recisio*.] The act of voiding or rescinding.

re·cit·al, ri·sīt′al, n. The act of reciting; a narrative or description; a detailed statement; an entertainment usu. given by a single performer or by several soloists; as, an organ *recital*.

rec·i·ta·tion, res″i·tā′shan, n. The act of reciting, as a composition committed to memory; public performance of a literary reading; classroom response to a teacher after studied preparation; anything recited.

rec·i·ta·tive, res″i·ta·tēv′, n. [It. *recitativo*.] *Mus.* A vocal form having no definite rhythmic pattern or strictly constructed melody; a musical recitation or declamation. Also **rec·i·ta·ti·vo,** res″i·ta·tē′vō, *It.* Re″chē·ta·tē′va.—*a.*

re·cite, ri·sīt′, v.t.—*recited, reciting.* [L. *recitare* (pp. *recitatus*), < *re-*, again, and *citare*, call, E. *cite*.] To say over or repeat the words of, as from memory, esp. in a formal manner; to repeat, as a piece of poetry or prose, before an audience; to relate the facts, or give an account of; to

enumerate.—*v.i.* To recite or repeat something from memory; to recite a lesson or some part of a lesson before a teacher.—**re·cit·er,** *n.*

reck·less, rek′lis, a. Heedless, rash, careless, usu. with *of* before an object; as, *reckless of* consequences.—**reck·less·ly,** *adv.*—**reck·less·ness,** *n.*

reck·on, rek′on, v.t. [O.E. *(ge)recenian* = D. *rekenen* = G. *rechnen*, reckon.] To count, compute, or calculate as to number or amount; to esteem, regard as, or consider; as, to be *reckoned* a fool; *colloq., dial.* to think or suppose.—*v.i.* To count; make a computation or calculation; to settle accounts, as with a person; to count, depend, or rely, as in expectation, usu. followed by *on*.—**reck·on with,** to deal with, as something to be taken into account.

reck·on·ing, rek′o·ning, n. The act of reckoning; count, computation, or calculation; the settlement of accounts, as between parties; a statement of an amount due, or a bill; an accounting, as for things received or done; as, a day of *reckoning*; *naut.* dead reckoning.

re·claim, rē·klām′, v.t. To claim once more.

re·claim, ri·klām′, v.t. [O.Fr. *reclaimer, reclamer* (Fr. *réclamer*), < L. *reclamare*, < *clamare*, cry out.] To bring, as wild, waste, or marshy land, into a condition for cultivation or other use; to recover, as substances, in a pure or usable form from waste matter or used articles; as, to *reclaim* rubber; to bring back from wrongdoing or error; reform.—**re·claim·a·ble,** *a.*—**re·claim·er,** *n.*

rec·la·ma·tion, rek″la·mā′shan, n. [L. *reclamatio(n-)*.] The act or process of reclaiming; the state of being reclaimed; the reclaiming of waste, desert, marshy, or submerged land for cultivation or other use; the process or the industry of recovering usable substances from waste matter or the like.

ré·clame, *Fr.* Rā·kläm′, n. [Fr., < *réclamer*, E. *reclaim*.] Public attention; advertisement of oneself; notoriety.

rec·li·nate, rek′li·nāt″, rek′li·nit, a. [L. *reclinatus*, pp. of *reclinare*, E. *recline*.] *Bot.* bending downward.

re·cline, ri·klīn′, v.i.—*reclined, reclining.* [L. *reclinare*, < *-clinare*, bend, incline.] To lean or lie back; to rest in a recumbent position.—*v.t.* To cause to lean back on something; to place in a recumbent position.—**re·clin·er,** *n.*

rec·luse, rek′lōs, ri·klōs′, n. [Fr. *reclus*, fem. *recluse*, < L. *reclusus*, pp. of *recludo, reclusum*, to lay open, but in L.L. signifying to shut.] A person who lives in retirement or seclusion; a religious devotee who lives in an isolated cell.—ri·klōs′, *a.* Living shut up or apart from the world; sequestered.—**re·clu·sion,** ri·klō′zhan, *n.* A state of seclusion.

rec·og·ni·tion, rek″og·nish′an, n. [L. *recognitio(n-)*, < *recognoscere*.] The act of recognizing or the state of being recognized; formal acknowledgment, conveying approval or sanction; the acknowledgment by one government of the existence or independence of another government; the acknowledgment of something as valid or as entitled to consideration; friendly cognizance or attention; the acknowledgment or token appreciation of kindness, service, or merit; the perception of something as identical with something previously known or in the mind; the perception of something as existing or true.—**re·cog·ni·tive, re·cog·ni·to·ry,** ri·kog′ni·tiv, ri·kog′ni·tōr″·ē, ri·kog′ni·ṭar″ē, *a.*

re·cog·ni·zance, ri·kog′ni·zans, ri·kon′i·zans, n. [Fr. *reconnaissance*, O.Fr. *recognoissance*.] *Law*, an obligation agreed upon before a magistrate or court, wherein a particular act must be performed; the sum of money liable to forfeiture for nonperformance of such an obligation. Recognition.

rec·og·nize, *Brit. also* **rec·og·nise,** rek′og·nīz″, *v.t.*—recognized, recognizing. [O.Fr. *reconoistre (recognoiss-, reconuiss-)* (Fr. *reconnaitre*), < L. *recognoscere* (pp. *recognitus*), know again, recognize, inspect; come to know: cf. *reconnoiter*.] To know again, or perceive to be identical with something previously known; to identify from knowledge of appearance or character; to perceive as existing or true; realize; to acknowledge or treat as valid; to acknowledge formally as existing or as entitled to consideration, as: One government *recognizes* another. To acknowledge as the person entitled to speak at the particular time; to give the floor to, as in a legislative assembly; to acknowledge acquaintance with, as by a salute; to show appreciation of, as by some reward or tribute. *Law,* to examine to discover the truth; to obligate by a recognizance.—**rec·og·niz·a·bil·i·ty,** *n.*—**rec·og·niz·a·ble,** rek′og·nī″za·bl, rek″og·nī′za·bl, *a.* —**rec·og·niz·a·bly,** *adv.*—**rec·og·niz·er,** *n.*

re·coil, ri·koil′, *v.i.* [Fr. *reculer,* < L. *re-,* back, and *culus,* the posteriors; same root as in Gael. *cul,* W. *cil,* the back.] To rebound; to fall back; to take a sudden backward motion after an advance; to return after a certain driving force or impetus, as a gun; to start or draw back, as from anything repulsive or alarming; to shrink back.—rē′koil″, *n.* A starting or falling back; rebound; the backward movement of a gun when discharged; a shrinking back.—**re·coil·less,** ri·koil′lis, rē′koil″lis, *a.*

re·coin, rē·koin′, *v.t.* To coin again.— **re·coin·age,** rē·koi′nij, *n.*

re·col·lect, rē″ko·lekt′, *v.t.* To collect or gather again, as something scattered; to compose or rally; as, to *re-collect* oneself.—**re·col·lec·tion,** rē″kŏ·lek′shan, *n.*

rec·ol·lect, rek″o·lekt′, *v.t.* [L. *recollectus,* to collect or gather again.] To recover or recall; to bring back to the mind or memory; to remember.—*v.i.* To remember or recall something.—**rec·ol·lec·tion,** rek″o·lek′shan, *n.*

rec·ol·lect·ed, rek″o·lek′tid, *a.* Cool, calm, and composed; recalled to mind.

re·com·bi·na·tion, rē″kom·bi·nā′shan, *n. Genetics,* the act or process of forming new gene combinations by crossing over at meiosis or combining again in fertilization.

rec·om·mend, rek″o·mend′, *v.t.* [Fr. *recommander,* to recommend, to commend, to entrust.] To commend to another; to entrust; to commend or give favorable representations of; to make acceptable; to attract favor to; to advise, as an action, practice, measure, or remedy; to set forward as advisable.—**rec·om·mend·a·ble,** *a.*—**rec·om·mend·a·to·ry,** rek″o·men′da·tōr″ē, rek″o·men′da·tạr″ē, *a.* —**rec·om·mend·er,** *n.*

rec·om·men·da·tion, rek″o·men·dā′shan, *n.* The act of recommending; a favorable representation; that which recommends; that which recommends, procures favor, or obtains a favorable reception; a letter commending another.

re·com·mit, rē″ko·mit′, *v.t.*—recommitted, recommitting. To commit again; to refer again to a committee.—**re·com·mit·ment, re·com·mit·tal,** *n.*

rec·om·pense, rek′om·pens″, *v.t.*—recompensed, recompensing. [Fr. *récompenser,* L.L. *recompenso*—L. *re-,* again, and *compenso, compensatum,* to compensate.] To give or render an equivalent to, as for services, loss, or the like; to reward; to

compensate; to return an equivalent for; repay; to make compensation for.—*n.* An equivalent returned for anything given, done, or suffered; compensation; reward.

re·com·pose, rē″kom·pōz′, *v.t.*—recomposed, recomposing. To compose again; reconstitute; rearrange; restore to composure or calm.—**re·com·po·si·tion,** rē″kom·po·zish′an, *n.*

rec·on·cil·a·ble, rek′on·sī″la·bl, rek″on·sī′la·bl, *a.* Capable of being again brought to friendly feelings; capable of being made to agree or to be consistent; capable of being harmonized.—**rec·on·cil·a·bil·i·ty, rec·on·cil·a·ble·ness,** *n.*—**rec·on·cil·a·bly,** *adv.*

rec·on·cile, rek′on·sīl″, *v.t.*—reconciled, reconciling. [Fr. *réconcilier,* < L. *reconcilio.*] To conciliate anew; to restore to union and friendship after estrangement; to adjust or settle, as differences or quarrels; to bring to acquiescence or quiet submission; as, to *reconcile* oneself to afflictions; to make consistent or congruous, followed by *with* or *to*; to remove apparent discrepancies from; to harmonize, followed by *to* or *with*.—*v.i.* To become reconciled. —**rec·on·cile·ment,** *n.*

rec·on·cil·i·a·tion, rek″on·sil″ē·ā′shan, *n.* [L. *reconciliatio.*] The act of reconciling estranged parties; renewal of friendship after disagreement or enmity; the act of harmonizing or making consistent; agreement of things seemingly opposite or inconsistent.—**rec·on·cil·i·a·to·ry,** rek″on·sil′ē·a·tōr″ē, rek″on·sil′ē·a·tạr″ē, *a.*

rec·on·dite, rek′on·dīt″, ri·kon′dīt, *a.* [L. *reconditus,* pp. of *recondo.*] Hidden from perception or understanding; obscure; abstruse; dealing with things abstruse.— **rec·on·dite·ly,** *adv.*—**rec·on·dite·ness,** *n.*

re·con·di·tion, rē″kon·dish′an, *v.t.* To restore to a good or satisfactory condition; put in operating condition again, as a used car or appliance, by repairing, making over, or another process; reform.

re·con·firm, rē″kon·fụrm′, *v.t.* To confirm again; to give more strength to; as, to *reconfirm* one's opinions with additional evidence.—**re·con·fir·ma·tion,** rē″kon··fẽr·mā′shan, *n.*

re·con·nais·sance, ri·kon′i·sans, *n.* [Fr.] The act of reconnoitering; preliminary examination or survey of the potentialities of a territory; *milit.* an examination or observation of territory, esp. enemy territory, by ground troops or aircraft.

re·con·noi·ter, *Brit.* **re·con·noi·tre,** rē″ko·noi′tẽr, rek″o·noi′tẽr, *v.t.*—reconnoitered, reconnoitering, *Brit.* reconnoitred, reconnoitring. [O.Fr. *reconnoitre,* Fr. *reconnaitre,* < L. *recognosco.*] To examine or survey, as a tract or region, for military, geologic, or engineering purposes; to make a preliminary survey of.—*v.i.* To carry out a reconnaissance.—**re·con·noi·ter·er,** *n.*

re·con·quer, rē·kong′kẽr, *v.t.* To conquer again; to regain by conquest.

re·con·sid·er, rē″kon·sid′ẽr, *v.t.* To consider again; to turn over in the mind again; to take into consideration a second time, generally with the view to rescinding a previous action or decision.—*v.i.* To again take up a settled matter.—**re·con·sid·er·a·tion,** rē″kon·sid″ẽr·ā′shan, *n.*

re·con·sti·tute, rē·kon′sti·tōt″, rē·kon′sti·tūt″, *v.t.*—reconstituted, reconstituting. To constitute anew, as whole milk from dried powdered milk; to reconstruct.— **re·con·sti·tu·tion,** *n.*

re·con·struct, rē″kon·strukt′, *v.t.* To construct again; to rebuild.

re·con·struc·tion, rē″kon·struk′shan, *n.* The act of constructing again; something reconstructed; (*often cap.*), *U.S. hist.* the governmental reorganization of the seceded states after the Civil War.

re·con·struc·tion·ism, rē″kon·struk′sha·niz″um, *n.* (*Often cap.*) support of the reconstruction of the Confederate states following the Civil War; (*usu. cap.*) the 20th century movement of American Judaism that stresses adjustment to contemporary life by the cultivation of the Jewish heritage and traditions.—**re·con·struc·tion·ist,** rē″kon·struk′sha·nist, *n.* (*Usu. cap.*)

re·con·vene, rē″kon·vēn′, *v.t.*—reconvened, reconvening. To convene or call together again.—*v.i.* To reassemble.

re·con·vert, rē″kon·vụrt′, *v.t.* To convert back to a previous state; to convert to a previously held religious faith; *law,* to convert back to an original equity or its equivalent.—**re·con·ver·sion,** rē″kon·vụr′zhan, rē″kon·vụr′shan, *n.*

re·con·vey, rē″kon·vā′, *v.t.* To convey to its former place; to transfer back to a former owner.—**re·con·vey·ance,** *n.*

re·cord, ri·kạrd′, *v.t.* [O.Fr. Fr. *recorder,* < L. *recordari,* call to mind, remember, *re-,* back, again, and *cor (cord-),* heart, mind.] To note, chart, or inscribe, manually or mechanically, as for the purpose of preserving evidence; to set down in writing or register in some permanent form; to indicate; to set down, register, or fix by characteristic marks, incisions, or magnetic pulses, often for the purpose of reproduction by a phonograph or tape player.—*v.i.* To record something; to make a record.— **rec·ord,** rek′ẽrd, *n.* The state or fact of being recorded, as in writing; an account in writing or mechanical form preserving the memory or knowledge of facts or events; *specif.,* an official writing recording facts or events; an authentic or official written report of proceedings of a court of justice; an authentic or official copy of a writing; a disc having characteristic grooves for reproducing sound on a phonograph; a report, list, or aggregate of actions or achievements, as in the case of a person, an organization, a horse, or a ship; a notable degree of achievement or attainment, esp. the highest or furthest attested degree attained.—**rec·ord,** rek′ẽrd, *a.* Making or affording a record; being foremost in degree of attainment; as, a *record* year for sales.— **off the rec·ord,** unofficial; not intended for quotation publicly.—**on rec·ord,** intended for public knowledge.

rec·ord chang·er, *n.* A device on a phonograph by which records are automatically positioned one by one onto a turntable.

re·cord·er, ri·kạr′dẽr, *n.* One who records official transactions; a registering apparatus; a magistrate with limited jurisdiction in court proceedings. *Mus.* an old simple flute with eight finger holes; a reproduction device for recording music, voice, or other sound on tape or wire.

re·cord·ing, ri·kạr′ding, *n.* The process of making a record; that which is recorded; a phonograph record or tape; *specif.,* the making of a phonograph record or tape recording, with regard to the quality of the sound reproduction.

rec·ord play·er, *n.* A machine consisting of a turntable, loudspeaker, and other equipment which plays phonograph records; a phonograph.

re·count, rē·kount′, *v.t.* [Fr. *reconter.*] To count again.—rē′kount″, rē·kount′, *n.* An additional or second count, as of ballots in an election.

re·count, ri·kount′, *v.t.* To relate in detail; to narrate or tell in order; to enumerate.

re·coup, ri·köp′, *v.t.* [Fr. *recoupe,* cloth remaining after cutting out clothes.] To obtain or regain an equivalent for, as something lost or relinquished; to repay, indemnify; *law,* lawfully to hold back, as part

---

ch- chain, G. na*ch*t; **th-** THen, thin; **w-** wig, hw as sound in whig; **z-** zh as in azure, zeal. *Italicized vowel* indicates schwa sound.

of money legally due, in order to discharge a counterclaim.—*v.i.* To regain or obtain an equivalent of something lost or relinquished; *law*, to propose that part of money legally due be held back to discharge a counterclaim.—*n.* The act of recouping.— **re·coup·a·ble,** *a.*—**re·coup·ment,** *n.*

re·course, rē'kōrs, rē'kạrs, ri·kōrs', ri·kạrs', *n.* [Fr. *recours,* < L. *recursus,* a running back, a return, < *recurro,* to run back.] A going to, as for help or protection; the person or thing that helps, protects, or supplies; the right to payment demanded by the producer or endorser of an instrument that is negotiable.

re·cov·er, ri·kuv'ẽr, *v.t.* [O.Fr. *recover* (Fr. *recouvrer*), < L. *recuperare,* to recover; of doubtful origin.] To regain after losing; to restore, as oneself, from sickness, faintness, or the like; to retrieve; to make up for; to reclaim for use, as resources or materials; to rescue; in some sports, to reclaim, as a position or advantage. *Law,* to gain as a compensation; to obtain in return for injury or debt; to obtain title to by judgment in a court of law.—*v.i.* To regain health after sickness; to regain a former state or condition, as after misfortune or disturbance of mind; in some sports, to reclaim an advantage or position; *law,* to succeed in a lawsuit.—**re·cov·er·a·ble,** ri·kuv'ẽr·a·bl, *a.*

re·cov·er, rē·kuv'ẽr, *v.t.* To cover again.

re·cov·er·y, ri·kuv'e·rē, *n.* pl. **re·cov·er·ies.** The act or power of regaining; restoration from sickness, faintness, or misfortune; *law,* obtaining the right to something by a verdict or judgment of a court.

re·cov·er·y room, *n.* A hospital room equipped for observation and emergency care of postoperative patients.

rec·re·ant, rek're·ant, *a.* [O.Fr. *recreant,* ppr. of *recoire,* L.L. *recredere,* to give in, to confess defeat.] Treacherous; yielding to an enemy; cowardly; unfaithful; false.—*n.* One who yields; one who begs for mercy; a deserter.—**rec·re·an·cy,** *n.*—**rec·re·ant·ly,** *adv.*

re-cre·ate, rē'krē·āt', *v.t.*—**re-created,** **re-creating.** To create anew, as in one's imagination.—**re-cre·a·tion,** rē'krē·ā'shan, *n.*

rec·re·ate, rek're·āt', *v.t.*—**recreated,** **recreating.** [L. *recreo, recreatum.*] To revive or refresh, as after toil or exertion, by some amusement or diversion; to reanimate the spirits or strength of.—**rec·re·a·tive,** *a.*

rec·re·a·tion, rek're·ā'shan, *n.* Amusement or diversion which gives enjoyment; refreshment of the strength and spirits, as after toil; anything providing entertainment or relaxation.—**rec·re·a·tion·al,** *a.*

re·crim·i·nate, ri·krim'i·nāt', *v.i.*—**recriminated,** **recriminating.** [L. *re-,* again, and *criminor,* I accuse.] To answer one accusation with another; to charge an accuser with the like.—*v.t.* To accuse in return.— **re·crim·i·na·tion,** *n.* The act of recriminating; the response to one accusation with another; a counter-accusation; *law,* an accusation brought by the accused against the accuser upon the same fact.—**re·crim·i·na·tive,** **re·crim·i·na·to·ry,** ri·krim'i·na·tōr'ē, ri·krim'i·na·tạr'ē, *a.*

re·cru·desce, rē'krō·des', *v.i.*—**recrudesced,** **recrudescing.** [L. *recrudescere,* < *re-,* again, and *crudescere,* lit. 'grow raw,' < *crudus,* raw, E. *crude.*] To break out afresh, as a sore or a disease that has been quiescent; to return to activity; reappear.— **re·cru·des·cence,** **re·cru·des·cen·cy,** rē''krō·des'ens, *n.*—**re·cru·des·cent,** *a.*

re·cruit, ri·krōt', *n.* [Fr. *recruter,* < *recrute,* a participial noun < O.Fr. *recroistre,* pp. *recru,* < L. *recresco.*] A newly enlisted soldier; a new member of an organization or group.—*v.t.* To make up by enlistment;

to supply with new men; to refresh; to renew, as the health, spirits, or strength.— *v.i.* To enlist new soldiers; to gain health, spirits, or the like; to gain new supplies of anything wasted or needed.—**re·cruit·er,** *n.*—**re·cruit·ment,** ri·krōt'ment, *n.*

re·crys·tal·lize, rē·kris'ta·līz'', *v.t.*—*recrystallized,* recrystallizing.* To crystallize a second time; *metal.* to change the structure of crystals by various processes.—**re·crys·tal·li·za·tion,** rē·kris''ta·li·zā'shan, *n.*

rec·tal, rek'tal, *a. Anat.* proximal to, involving, or pertaining to the rectum.— **rec·tal·ly,** *adv.*

rec·tan·gle, rek'tang''gl, *n.* [L. *rectangulus*— *rectus,* right, and *angulus,* an angle.] A right-angled parallelogram; a quadrilateral figure with all its angles being right angles.

rec·tan·gu·lar, rek·tang'gū·lẽr, *a.* Right-angled; having an angle or angles of ninety degrees; having the shape of a rectangle.— **rec·tan·gu·lar·i·ty,** rek·tang''gū·lar'i·tē, *n.*—**rec·tan·gu·lar·ly,** *adv.*

rec·tan·gu·lar co·or·di·nate, *n. Math.* The shortest distance from a point on a plane to each of two perpendicular lines; the shortest distance from a point in space to each of three mutually perpendicular planes. See *Cartesian coordinate system.*

rec·ti·fi·er, rek'ti·fī''ẽr, *n.* One who or that which rectifies; one who or that which refines by repeated distillations; a device for obtaining direct electric current from alternating current.

rec·ti·fy, rek'ti·fī'',*v.t.*—*rectified,rectifying.* [Fr. *rectifier,* < L. *rectus,* right, and *facio,* to make.] To make or put right; to correct when wrong, erroneous, or false; to amend; to refine by repeated distillation; to make a direct current from an alternating current; make an adjustment for possible error in an observation or calculation.—**rec·ti·fi·a·ble,** rek'ti·fī''a·bl, *a.*—**rec·ti·fi·ca·tion,** rek''ti·fi·kā'shan, *n.*

rec·ti·lin·e·ar, rek''ti·lin'ē·ẽr, *a.* [L. *rectus,* right, and *linea,* a line.] Bounded by straight lines; consisting of a straight line or lines; straight.—**rec·ti·lin·e·ar·ly,** *adv.*

rec·ti·tude, rek'ti·tōd'', rek'ti·tūd'', *n.* [L. *rectitudo,* < *rectus,* pp. of *rego, rectum,* to keep or lead straight.] Rightness of principle or practice; uprightness; integrity; honesty; correct judgment; correctness.

rec·to, rek'tō,*n.* pl. **rec·tos.** [L.*rectus,*right.] The right-hand page, as of an open book: opposed to *verso.*

rec·tor, rek'tẽr, *n.* [L. *rector,* a ruler, < *rego, rectum,* to rule, to keep right.] A clergyman of the Protestant Episcopal Church who has charge of a parish. *Rom. Cath. Ch.* a priest who is responsible for a congregation or directs a religious establishment, as a school or religious house. *Anglican Ch.* a clergyman who has charge of a parish, and to whom belong the rights and tithes. A headmaster or chief administrator of a school, university, or college.— **rec·tor·ate,** rek'tẽr·it, *n.*—**rec·to·ri·al,** rek·tōr'ē·al, rek·tạr'ē·al, *a.*

rec·to·ry, rek'to·rē, *n.* pl. **rec·to·ries.** A parish church; a parish held by a rector; a rector's habitat; parsonage.

rec·trix, rek'triks, *n.* pl. **rec·tri·ces,** rek·trī'sēz. [L. *rectrix,* a female governor.] One of the long quill feathers in the tail of a bird, which directs its flight.—**rec·tri·cial,** rek·trish'al, *a.*

rec·tum, rek'tum, *n.* pl. **rec·tums,** **rec·ta,** rek'ta. [L. *rectum,* straight, because once thought to be straight.] *Anat.* the lower six to eight inches of the large intestine, terminating in the anus.

rec·tus, rek'tus, *n.* pl. **rec·ti,** rek'tī. [N.L., 'straight (muscle),' < L. *rectus,* straight.] *Anat.* any of several muscles that are straight, as of the abdomen, thigh, or eye.

re·cum·bent, ri·kum'bent, *a.* [L. *recumbens, recumbentis,* ppr. of *recumbo.*] Leaning; reclining; lying down; reposing; inactive; *biol.* denoting a part that leans or reposes upon anything.—**re·cum·ben·cy,** *n.*—**re·cum·bent·ly,** *adv.*

re·cu·per·ate, ri·kö'pe·rāt'', *v.i.*—*recuperated, recuperating.* [L. *recupero, recuperatum.*] To recover from illness or fatigue; to regain financial solvency.—*v.t.* To regain what was lost, as health or finances; to recover.—**re·cu·per·a·tion,** *n.*—**re·cu·per·a·tive, re·cu·per·a·to·ry,** ri·kö'pe·rā''tiv, ri·kö'pẽr·a·tiv, ri·kū'pe·rā''tiv, ri·kū'pẽr·a·tiv, ri·kö'pẽr·a·tōr''ē, ri·kū'pẽr·a·tōr''ē, *a.*

re·cur, ri·kụr', *v.i.*—*recurred, recurring.* [L. *recurro*—*re-,* back, and *curro,* to run.] To occur again or be repeated at a stated interval; to return to one's thoughts.—**re·cur·rence,** ri·kụr'ens, ri·kur'ens, *n.*

re·cur·rent, ri·kụr'ent, ri·kur'ent, *a.* Returning from time to time; recurring; *anat.* turning back in its course, as a nerve or blood vessel.—**re·cur·rent·ly,** *adv.*

re·cur·ring dec·i·mal, *n.* Repeating decimal.

re·cur·vate, ri·kụr'vit, ri·kụr'vāt, *a.* [L. *re-,* back, and *curvus,* bent.] Bent, bowed, or curved backward.—**re·curve,** ri·kụrv', *v.t., v.i.*—*recurved, recurving.* To bend or curve back.

rec·u·sant, rek'ya·zant, ri·kū'zant, *a.* [Fr. *recusant,* L. *recusans, recusantis,* ppr. of *recuso,* to refuse, to reject—*re-,* back, and *causa,* cause.] Persistent in refusal; refusing to acknowledge established authority.—*n.* One persistent in refusing; one who will not conform to general opinion or practice; in English history, an individual, esp. a Roman Catholic, who would not join the Church of England during the 17th and 18th centuries, when religious conformity was required by law.—**rec·u·san·cy,** rek'ya·zan·sē, ri·kū'zan·sē, *n.*

red, red, *a.*—*redder, reddest.* [O.E. *reád,* red; cogn. Dan. and Sw. *rod,* Icel. *rauthr (raudr),* D. *rood,* G. *roth,* Goth. *rauds;* same root as in L. *rufus, ruber,* W. *rhudd,* Ir. and Gael. *ruadh,* red; Skt. *rudhira,* blood.] Of a red hue; resembling the color of blood; being ruddy or florid; having a shade of red as a predominant or distinguishing color; *(often cap.)* communistic, or endorsing revolutionary political or social change.—*n.* A primary color at the lower extreme of the visible spectrum; a color like that of blood; a dye or pigment that imparts a red shade; a red signal light meaning 'stop' or 'danger'; *(often cap.)* a Communist, or a far left radical or revolutionary. The debit side of account keeping, with entries made in red.—**in the red,** *colloq.* in debt. —**paint the town red,** *slang,* carouse or celebrate riotously.—**see red,** *colloq.* to be very angry.—**red·ness,** red'nis, *n.*

re·dact, ri·dakt', *v.t.* [L. *redactus,* pp. of *redigere,* bring back, reduce.] To prepare, as written matter, for publication; revise; edit; to draw up or frame, as a statement or announcement.—**re·dac·tion,** *n.* The act or process of revising or editing; a work thus prepared.—**re·dac·tion·al,** *a.* —**re·dac·tor,** *n.*

red a·lert, *n. Milit.* the final, most urgent classification of alert, given when enemy attack seems imminent.

red al·ga, *n.* Any of the reddish, reddish-brown, or purplish seaweeds in the phylum *Rhodophyta.*

re·dan, ri·dan', *n.* [Fr. *redan,* O.Fr. *redent.*] *Fort.* an earthwork consisting of two parapets constructed so as to form a salient angle, with the apex toward the enemy.

red ant, *n. Entom.* any of several ants of

reddish color, as the sanguinary and Pharaoh ants.

red birch, *n.* A N. American tree, *Betula nigra*, growing naturally in river valleys and having reddish-brown bark which peels into papery strips; also **riv·er birch.** Loosely applied, the lumber of the yellow birch, *B. lutea*, and the sweet birch, *B. lenta*.

red·bird, red′bụrd″, *n.* The N. American bird, *Richmondena cardinalis*, all red except for a small black area around the bill, with a conspicuous red crest and a distinct whistling voice. Also *cardinal*.

red blood cell, *n.* A cell that gives the red color to the blood of vertebrates; an erythrocyte. Also **red blood cor·pus·cle.**

red-blood·ed, red′blud′id, *a.* Having red blood; of healthy strength or vigor; vigorous; virile.—**red-blood·ed·ness,** *n.*

red·bone, red′bōn″, *n.* A medium-sized American hunting dog with a red or red and brown coat.

red·breast, red′brest″, *n. Ornith.* the American robin, *Turdus migratorius*; the European robin, *Erithacus rebucula*; a name loosely applied to the knot and the dowitcher, both of which are red-breasted. *Ichth.* a fresh-water sunfish, *Lepomis auritis*, of the eastern U.S.; also **red-breast·ed bream.**

red·bud, red′bud″, *n.* A small tree, *Cercis canadensis*, in the legume family, which bears abundant pink flowers close to the wood before the leaves appear in the spring. Also *Judas tree.*

red·cap, red′kap″, *n.* A baggage porter, esp. in a railway station; *Brit. colloq.* a military policeman; *colloq.* the European goldfinch, *Carduelis carduelis.*

red car·pet, *n.* A long, narrow piece of carpet put down for dignitaries and distinguished persons to walk upon when entering or leaving a vehicle or building; any exceptional or ceremonial courtesy, as usu. shown to distinguished persons.—**red-car·pet,** *a.*—**red-car·pet treat·ment,** *n. Fig.* effusive greetings or lavish hospitality.

red ce·dar, *n.* An eastern N. American coniferous tree, *Juniperus virginiana*, of the cypress family, whose wood is used in the making of lead pencils, chests, and panels for interior finishings; a related species, *J. scopulorum*, of western U.S.; the wood of these trees, being soft, even-grained, fragrant and resistant to decay. See *cedar.*

red cent, *n.* A U.S. one-cent piece; *fig.* a trifle: used in negative expressions; as, not worth a *red cent.*

Red Cham·ber, *n.* [From the color of its furnishings.] *Canada*, a familiar name for the Canadian Senate chamber.

red clo·ver, *n.* The common round-headed purple-red clover, *Trifolium pratense*, of fields and roadsides; the State flower of Vermont, widely cultivated as a forage crop.

red·coat, red′kōt″, *n.* A British soldier of the 18th century; a Canadian policeman.

red cor·al, *n.* A coral of the genus *Corallium*, having a pink or red skeleton, esp. *C. nobile*, used in jewelry making.

Red Cross, *n.* The Red Cross Society, an international humanitarian organization, the emblem of which is a Greek cross in red on a white field; an affiliate of this society, the American Red Cross. (*l.c.*) the red cross of St. George, an English national emblem; the Geneva cross.

redd, red, *n.* A spawning nest or area of various fishes.

redd, red, *v.t.*—*redd* or *redded, redding. Dial.* To make tidy, usually followed by *up*; arrange in order; to clear.

red deer, *n.* A species of deer, *Cervus elaphus*, native to Europe and Asia, and formerly very abundant in England; the

American whitetail, *Odocoileus virginianus*, in its summer coat.

red·den, red′en, *v.t.* To make red.—*v.i.* To become red; to flush or blush.

red·dish, red′ish, *a.* Somewhat red; tending to redness.—**red·dish·ness,** *n.*

red·dle, red′l, *n.* [< *red*; cf. G. *rothel*, < *roth*, red.] Red chalk; a species of ironstone ore used as a pigment and for marking sheep.—*v.t.*—*reddled, reddling.* To mark with reddle. Also *raddle, ruddle.*—**red·dle·-man,** red′l·man, *n.* pl. **red·dle·men.**

rede, rēd, *v.t.*—*reded, reding.* [An older spelling of *read.*] To counsel or advise; to relate or tell.—*n.* Counsel or advice; a plan, design, or scheme; a narrative, story, etc.

re·dec·o·rate, rē·dek′o·rāt′, *v.t., v.i.*—*redecorated, redecorating.* To decorate again or anew.—**re·dec·o·ra·tion,** rē·dek″o·rā′shan, *n.*

re·ded·i·cate, rē·ded′i·kāt″, *v.t.* To dedicate again.—**re·ded·i·ca·tion,** rē″ded·i·kā′shan, *n.*

re·deem, ri·dēm′, *v.t.* [O.Fr. *redimer* (Fr. *rédimer*), < L. *redimere* (pp. *redemptus*), buy back, redeem.] To buy or pay off, or clear by payment; as, to *redeem* a mortgage; to buy back; to recover, as something pledged or mortgaged, by payment or other satisfaction; to convert into coin, as paper money; to discharge or fulfill, as a pledge or promise; to make atonement or amends for; to offset; to obtain the release or restoration of, as from captivity or bondage, by paying a price or ransom; to deliver or rescue; *theol.* to deliver from sin and its consequences by means of a sacrifice offered for the sinner.

re·deem·a·ble, ri·dē′ma·bl, *a.* Capable of being redeemed; that is to be redeemed; as, bonds *redeemable* in 1998. Also **re·demp·ti·ble,** ri·demp′ti·bl.

re·deem·er, ri·dē′mer, *n.* One who redeems; (*cap.*) Jesus Christ.

re·de·fine, rē″di·fīn′, *v.t.*—*redefined, redefining.* To define once more; to alter the definition of.—**re·def·i·ni·tion,** rē″def·i·-nish′an, *n.*

re·de·liv·er, rē″di·liv′ẽr, *v.t.* To deliver again or anew; to deliver back; return; to liberate a second time.—**re·de·liv·er·y,** *n.*

re·de·mand, rē″di·mand′, rē″di·mänd′, *v.t.* To demand back; to demand again.—**re·de·mand·a·ble,** *a.*

re·demp·tion, ri·demp′shan, *n.* [O.Fr. *redemption* (Fr. *redemption*), < L. *redemptio(n-)*, < *redimere*, E. *redeem.*] The act of redeeming, or the state of being redeemed; repurchase, as of something sold; recovery by payment, as of something pledged or mortgaged; a paying off, as of a mortgage, bond, or note; the conversion into coin of paper money. *Theol.* deliverance from sin and its consequences through the atonement of Jesus; salvation.—**re·demp·tion·al,** *a.*

re·demp·tion·er, ri·demp′sha·nẽr, *n.* In the 18th and 19th centuries, an emigrant from Europe who obtained passage to America by turning over to the master or owner of the vessel the right to sell his services or claim his earnings for a term sufficient to repay all expenses.

re·demp·tive, ri·demp′tiv, *a.* Serving to redeem; of or relating to redemption. Also **re·demp·to·ry,** ri·demp′to·rē.

Re·demp·tor·ist, ri·demp′tẽr·ist, *n.* [Fr. *rédemptoriste*, < L. *redemptor*, E. *redemptor.*] A member of the Congregation of the Most Holy Redeemer, a Roman Catholic order founded by St. Alfonso Liguori of Naples in 1732 for missionary work among the poor.

re·de·ploy, rē″di·ploi′, *v.t., v.i. Milit.* to transfer, as troops or supplies, to another location or a different theater of war.—**re·de·ploy·ment,** *n.*

re·de·pos·it, rē″di·poz′it, *v.t.* To deposit again or subsequent to withdrawal.—*n.*

re·de·sign, rē″di·zīn′, *v.t.* To change in function, content, or appearance.

re·de·ter·mine, rē″di·tụr′min, *v.t., v.i.*—*redetermined, redetermining.* To come again to a decision; to ascertain after reinvestigation.—**re·de·ter·mi·na·tion,** rē″di·tụr″mi·nā′shan, *n.*

re·de·vel·op, rē″di·vel′op, *v.t.* To develop again; *photog.* to intensify by a second developing process.—*v.i.* To develop again.—**re·de·vel·op·er,** *n.*—**re·de·vel·op·-ment,** *n.*

red·eye, red′ī″, *n.* A fish with red eyes, as a rudd or rock bass; *slang*, a cheap inferior grade of strong whiskey; *rail.* a signal of danger in semaphore code.

red·fin, red′fin″, *n.* Any of various small, chiefly cyprinoid, fresh-water fish with reddish fins, as *Notropis cornutus*, of eastern and central N. America.

red fire, *n.* Any of various combustible preparations, as one containing strontium nitrate, which burn with a vivid red light: used in pyrotechnic displays and signaling.

red·fish, red′fish″, *n.* pl. **red·fish, red·-fish·es.** Any of several N. Atlantic food fish having some reddish color, as the rosefish, ocean perch, or blueback salmon.

red fox, *n.* A species of fox distinguished by its reddish coat; the fur of this animal.

Red Guard, *n.* A youth corps of Communist China.

red gum, *n.* Any of several trees of the genus *Eucalyptus*, esp. *E. camaldulensis*, so named from the reddish gum which they exude; the sweet gum or liquidambar tree, *Liquidambar straciflua.*

red-hand·ed, red′han′did, *a.* In the very act: said of a person caught committing a crime; self-incriminating.—**red-hand·ed·-ly,** *adv.*—**red-hand·ed·ness,** *n.*

red·head, red′hed″, *n.* A person having red hair; *ornith.* a N. American diving duck, *Aythya americana*, grayish with a black crest and a round red-brown head, often confused with the canvasback; the Old World, red-crested pochard duck, *Netta rufina.*—**red-head·ed, red·head·ed, '** red′hed″id, *a.*

red heat, *n.* The temperature of a substance when it is red-hot; a red-hot condition.

red her·ring, *n.* A smoked and salted herring. A subterfuge whose object is to distract or divert notice from the relevant problem. *Finance*, an announcement of an issue of corporate stocks or bonds whose prospectus must carry a notice printed in red ink that approval of the offering is pending before the Securities and Exchange Commission.

red-hot, red′hot′, *a.* Red with heat; very hot; greatly excited; very enthusiastic; violent or furious; as, a *red-hot* debate; very new or fresh, as news.

red·in·gote, red′ing·gōt″, *n.* [Fr. < E. *riding coat.*] A man's outer coat with long skirts that overlap in front, popular in the 18th century; a garment for women consisting of a coat that opens in front to show the dress worn beneath.

red·in·te·grate, red·in′te·grāt″, *v.t.*—*redintegrated, redintegrating.* [L.] To make whole again; renew; revive. *Psychol.* to repeat the response made to a former complex stimulus when any part of the stimulus recurs.—**red·in·te·gra·tion,** red·in″te·grā′shan, *n.*

re·di·rect, rē″di·rekt′, rē″di·rekt′, *v.t.* To direct again or anew.—*a. Law*, pertaining to the examination of a witness by the party calling him, after cross-examination.—**re·di·rec·tion,** *n.*

re·dis·count, rē·dis′kount, *n. Bus.* A second discount applied to commercial paper; *usu. pl.* the paper so discounted.—*v.t.* To discount again.—**re·dis·count·a·ble,** *a.*

---

ch- chain, G. na*ch*t; **th-** THen, thin; **w-** wig, hw as sound in whig; **z-** zh as in azure, zeal. *Italicized vowel* indicates schwa sound.

re·dis·till, rē″di·stil′, v.t. To distill again. —**re·dis·til·la·tion**, rē″dis·ti·lā′shan, n.

re·dis·trib·ute, rē″di·strib′ūt, v.t.—redistributed, redistributing. To distribute again or anew; reallocate.—**re·dis·tri·bu·tion**, rē″dis·tri·bū′shan, n.—**re·dis·trib·u·tive**, rē″di·strib′ū·tiv, a.

re·dis·trict, rē·dis′trikt, v.t. To divide anew into districts for administrative or electoral purposes.

red·i·vi·vus, red″i·vī′vus, a. [L.] Alive again; returned to life; revived; reborn.

red jas·mine, n. An American tropical ornamental shrub, Plumeria rubra, of the dogbane family, having pink to purplish-red, very fragrant flowers borne in large terminal clusters. Also frangipani.

red lead, n. An oxide of lead, Pb_3O_4, of orange-red color, used in making glass and glazes, storage battery parts, and most paint pigments. Also minium.

red-let·ter, red′let′ẽr, a. Memorable or especially happy; as, a red-letter day in one's life; indicated by red letters, as festival days in the church calendar.

red light, n. A red light signaling 'stop' or 'danger,' used esp. to regulate traffic.—**red-light**, red′lit′, a.

red-light dis·trict, n. That part of a city having many brothels, named from the custom of identifying such establishments with a red light.

red mul·ber·ry, n. See mulberry.

red·neck, red′nek″, n. Slang, a poor white rural laborer of southern U.S.

re·do, rē′dö′, v.t.—pres. sing. redo, redo, redoes; pres pl. redo; past redid; pp. redone; ppr. redoing. To do over; do again; to redecorate.

red oak, n. Either of two N. American trees, Quercus borealis or Quercus rubra, valuable for their hard reddish lumber; any member of the red oak group, a number of oak species classified together because of certain common characteristics, esp. their bristle-tipped leaves.

red o·cher, n. A red, earthy mixture, containing iron oxide, used as a coloring agent.

red·o·lent, red′o·lent, a. [L. redolens, redolentis, ppr. of redoleo, to emit a scent.] Having or diffusing a sweet scent; odorous; reminiscent, often with of.—**red·o·lence**, **red·o·len·cy**, n.—**red·o·lent·ly**, adv.

re·dou·ble, rē·dub′l, v.t.—redoubled, redoubling. To increase; to double; to fold again. Bridge, to double again, as a double made by an opponent.—v.i. To become twice as much; to become intensified.— Bridge, the doubling of the double made by an opponent.

re·doubt, ri·dout′, n. [Fr. redoute, reduit, < L.L. reductus, a retired spot, < L. reductus, retired.] Fort. A small enclosed temporary fieldwork; an earthwork placed within a fortification as a reinforcement.

re·doubt·a·ble, ri·dout′a·bl, a. [O.Fr. redoutable, < redoubter, to fear.] Formidable; to be dreaded; deserving respect. Also **re·doubt·ed**, ri·dou′tid.—**re·doubt·a·bly**, adv.—**re·doubt·a·ble·ness**, n.

re·dound, ri·dound′, v.i. [O.Fr. Fr. redonder, < L. redundare, overflow, redound, < red- for re-, back, and undare, rise in waves, < unda, a wave.] To come back in effect, or have an effect or result, as to the advantage or disadvantage, or the credit or discredit, of a person or thing, followed by to; to result or accrue, as to a person; to come back or recoil, as upon a person, as: Disgrace redounds upon one caught stealing.

re·dox, rē′doks, n. Chem. abbr. for the oxidation-reduction process.

red-pen·cil, red′pen′sil, v.t.—red-penciled, red-penciling, red-pencilled, red-pencilling. To revise, delete, or otherwise correct; to censor.

red pep·per, n. One of many cultivated varieties of Capsicum frutescens, a pepper plant having red pods, used as a pungent condiment; cayenne pepper.

red·poll, red′pōl″, n. [From the red color of the poll or head.] Ornith. any of several small, streaked gray-brown finches, esp. Acanthis flammea, with a bright red forehead and black chin, breeding in subarctic regions and wintering in northern U.S.

Red Poll, n. An English breed of reddish, hornless dairy cattle, often raised for beef. Also **Red Polled**.

re·draft, rē′draft″, rē′dräft″, n. A second draft or drawing; com. a draft on the drawer or endorsers of a protested bill of exchange for the amount of the bill plus the costs and charges.

re·dress, ri·dres′, v.t. [Fr. redresser, to straighten again, to put right.] To remedy or put right, as a wrong; to repair, as an injury; to relieve, as suffering; to compensate; to adjust; to make reparation or amends to.—**rē′dres**, ri·dres′, n. Relief from wrong, injury, or oppression; undoing of wrong; reparation; indemnification; correction.—**re·dress·er**, **re·dres·sor**, n.

red rib·bon, n. A ribbon, usu. suitably marked, given to the winner of the second prize in a competition.

red·root, red′röt″, red′rut″, n. A N. American plant, Lachnanthes tinctoria, having sword-shaped leaves, woolly yellow flowers, and a red root formerly used in dyeing; any of various other plants with red roots, as the alkanet, Alkanna tinctoria, and a pigweed, Amarantus retroflexus.

red sal·mon, n. Sockeye.

red·shank, red′shangk″, n. Ornith. an Old World, long-legged wader of the sandpiper family, having red bills, legs, and feet, esp. Totanus totanus and T. erythropus.

red shift, n. Astron. the physical effect which causes light emitted by a distant galaxy or other receding object to appear redder the farther it moves away from earth.

red sis·kin, n. A scarlet and black finch, Carduelis cucullata, native to northern S. America, popular as a cage bird.

red·skin, red′skin″, n. A N. American Indian.

red snap·per, n. A reddish, edible, salt water fish of the genus Lutjanus, found along the Florida coast and in the Gulf of Mexico.

red spi·der, n. Any of various small mites, parasitic on certain crops. Also **red spi·der mite**.

red squill, n. An onionlike European plant, Urginea maritima, used in making rat poison.

red·start, red′stärt″, n. A brightly colored American warbler, Setophaga ruticilla, the male largely black with orange patches on wing and tail, and constantly spreading its tail like a fan. A small European thrush, Phoenicurus phoenicurus, with red on tail and breast; also **bran·tail**.

red tape, n. Rigid or excessive routines and procedures causing delay or inaction, as in a bureaucracy.—**red·tap·ism**, n.

red tide, n. A reddish tinge on sea water caused by aggregations of tiny marine plants, esp. dinoflagellates.

red·top, red′top″, n. A pasture and lawn grass, Agrostis alba, having a reddish panicle. Also **fi·o·rin**.

re·duce, ri·dös′, ri·dūs′, v.t.—reduced, reducing. [L. reduco—re-, back, and duco, to lead.] To diminish in size, quantity, or value; to make less or lower, as in strength or degree; to bring to an inferior condition; to subdue or subjugate; to bring to an indicated state or condition, with to; as, reduce someone to despair; to bring into orderly arrangement; to weaken or dilute, as alcohol; math. to bring to the simplest form or to a lower denomination without altering the value; metal. to separate, as pure metal, from a metallic ore; surg. to restore to its proper place or state, as a dislocated or fractured bone. Chem. to lower the oxygen content of; to lower the positive valence of, as an atom, by the addition of electrons.—v.i. To become smaller, less, or lower; to lower one's weight; biol. to divide by meiosis.—**re·duc·er**, n.—**re·duc·i·bil·i·ty**, ri·dö″si·bil′i·tē, ri·dū″si·bil′i·tē, n.—**re·duc·i·ble**, a.—**re·duc·i·bly**, adv.

re·duc·ing a·gent, n. Chem. a substance capable of causing the reduction of another substance by supplying it with electrons.

re·duc·tase, ri·duk′tās, ri·duk′tāz, n. Biochem. an enzyme causing reduction through catalytic action.

re·duc·ti·o ad ab·sur·dum, ri·duk′-shē·ō″ ad ab·sur′dum, L. Re·duk′ti·ō äd äb·sör′dum, n. [L.] The refuting of a proposition by disclosure of the absurdity of its conclusion if carried to its logical end.

re·duc·tion, ri·duk′shan, n. [L. reductio.] The act of reducing; the state of being converted into a reduced form; diminution; subjugation; the act of making a copy, as of a map, on a smaller scale; math. the act of bringing to the simplest form or to a lower denomination without altering the value; metal. the operation of obtaining pure metals from metallic ores; surg. the operation of restoring a dislocated or fractured bone to its former place. Chem. the lowering of the oxygen content; the lowering of the positive valence of, as an atom, by the addition of electrons. Biol. division by meiosis.—**re·duc·tion·al**, a.—**re·duc·tive**, ri·duk′tiv, a.

re·dun·dan·cy, ri·dun′dan·sē, n. pl. **re·dun·dan·cies**. The state or quality of being redundant; superfluity; superabundance; unnecessary repetition, esp. of words, or an instance of this; that which is redundant or superfluous.

re·dun·dant, ri·dun′dant, a. [L. redundans, redundantis, ppr. of redundo.] Superfluous; exceeding what is natural or necessary; superabundant; verbose.—**re·dun·dant·ly**, adv.

re·du·pli·cate, ri·dö″pli·kāt″, ri·dū″pli·kāt″, v.t.—reduplicated, reduplicating. [L. reduplico, reduplicatum.] To double again; to multiply; to repeat; gram. to repeat, as the initial syllable or the root of a word, sometimes for the purpose of marking past time.—v.i. Gram. to be doubled or repeated. To undergo reduplication.—ri·dö″pli·kit, ri·dö″pli·kāt″, ri·dū″pli·kit, ri·dū″pli·kāt″, a. Redoubled; repeated; bot. denoting a bud in which the edges of the sepals or petals are turned outward and do not overlap.

re·du·pli·ca·tion, ri·dö″pli·kā′shan, ri·dū″pli·kā′shan, n. The act or end product of doubling or reduplicating; gram. the repetition of a root or of the initial syllable, more or less modified, as in Gr. pheugo, to flee, perfect pepheuga: the new form resulting from reduplication. Rhet. anadiplosis.—**re·du·pli·ca·tive**, ri·dö″pli·kā″tiv, ri·dū″pli·kā′tiv, a.—**re·du·pli·ca·tive·ly**, adv.

red·wing, red′wing″, n. A European thrush, Turdus musicus, having a reddish-brown and white body, with reddish feathers on the inner surfaces of the wings; the red-winged blackbird.

red-winged black·bird, red′wingd″ blak′-burd″, n. A N. American blackbird, Agelaius phoeniceus, the male having scarlet patches on the bend of the wings. Also redwing, **red·wing black·bird**.

red·wood, red'wŭd", *n.* A pinaceous tree, *Sequoia sempervirens,* of northern California, remarkable for its great girth, and its height which ranges from 200 to more than 300 feet; also **Cal·i·for·ni·a red-- wood.** The valuable brownish-red lumber of the redwood; any red-colored wood; any of various trees having reddish wood.

red worm, *n.* Bloodworm.

re·ech·o, rē·ek'ō, *v.t.*—reechoed, reechoing. To echo back; to reverberate again.—*v.i.* To resound.—*n.* pl. **re·ech·oes.** The echo of an echo; a repeated echo.

reed, rēd, *n.* [O.E. *hrēod* = D. *riet* = G. *ried,* reed.] The straight stalk of any of various tall grasses, esp. of the genera *Trichoön* and *Arundo,* growing in marshy places; the plant itself; such stalks or plants collectively; any of various things made from such a stalk or from something similar, as a dart or an arrow; an ancient measure of length equal to six cubits. *Mus.* a pastoral or rustic musical pipe made from a reed or the hollow stalk of some other plant; a thin, pliant plate or tongue of wood or metal partially covering the mouthpiece of wind instruments, producing sound when vibrated by a current of air; an instrument with such a device. *Weaving,* the series of parallel strips or wires which force the weft up to the web and separate the threads of the warp. *Arch.* a small convex molding; a reeding.

reed·bird, rēd'bŭrd", *n.* In southern U.S., another name for the bobolink, esp. those in autumnal plumage which frequent southern marshes in the autumn, being largely yellow-buff with dark stripes on crown and back.

reed·buck, rēd'buk", *n.* pl. **reed·bucks, reed·buck.** A yellowish-brown African antelope of the genus *Redunca,* frequenting marshy areas, the male having forward-curving, ringed horns.

reed·ing, rē'ding, *n.* A small convex or semicylindrical molding resembling a reed; a set of such moldings, as on a column; ornamentation consisting of such moldings; a series of narrow ridges on a coin's edge.

reed or·gan, *n. Mus.* a keyboard instrument in which air currents vibrate a set of metal reeds to produce the tone.

reed pipe, *n.* A pipe in an organ producing sound by means of a reed that is vibrated by a flow of air.

reed stop, *n.* A knob or stop in a pipe organ controlling the tone of a set of reed pipes.

re·ed·u·cate, rē·ej'u·kāt", rē·ed'ū·kāt", *v.t.*—reeducated, reeducating. To educate again or anew; rehabilitate by educating.— **re·ed·u·ca·tion,** *n.*—**re·ed·u·ca·tive,** *a.*

reed·y, rē'dē, *a.*—reedier, reediest. Abounding with reeds; resembling a reed; having the thin, high tone of a reed instrument.— **reed·i·ness,** *n.*

reef, rēf, *n.* [Same as D. *rif,* a roof; Icel. *rif,* Dan. *rev, riv,* Sw. *rev,* G. *riff,* reef; < root of *rive.*] A ledge of rocks or coal in the ocean lying at or near the surface of the water; *min.* a vein or lode.

reef, rēf, *n.* [M.E. *riff* = D. *reef* = Icel. *rif,* reef in a sail.] *Naut.* the part of a sail which may be or is rolled or folded up, in order to diminish the extent of canvas exposed to the wind; the act of reefing.—*v.t. Naut.* to reduce the size of, as a sail, by rolling or folding up a part.

reef·er, rē'fẽr, *n. Naut.* one who reefs. A close-fitting jacket of strong cloth.

reef·er, rē'fẽr, *n. Slang.* a cigarette of marijuana. Also *joint.*

ree·fer, rē'fẽr, *n.* [Shortened form of refrigerator.] *Slang.* A refrigerator, esp. a walk-in type used commercially; a refrigerator freight car, ship, or truck.

reef knot, *n.* A square knot used by sailors for reefing a sail.

reek, rēk, *v.i.* [O.E. *rēc* = D. *rieken* = G. *riechen* = Icel. *rjūka,* reek.] To emit a strong and unpleasant odor; to be strongly pervaded with something unpleasant or offensive; to emit vapor, smoke, or steam; to sweat, or be wet with sweat, as from heat or exertion; to be wet with blood, or be wet as blood, as: The altars *reek* of gore.— *v.t.* To emit, as smoke or fumes; to lay open to the action of smoke.—*n.* A strong unpleasant smell; vapor or steam.— **reek·er,** *n.*—**reek·ing·ly,** *adv.*—**reek·y,** *a.*—reekier, reekiest.

reel, rēl, *n.* [O.E. *hrēol,* a reel; Icel. *hraell,* a weaver's rod or sley.] A machine on which yarn is wound to form it into hanks or skeins; a revolving frame for winding a flexible substance; a revolving appliance attached to the butt of a fishing rod, on which the line is wound; the photographic film of a motion picture.—*v.t.* To wind upon a reel; to pull by winding around a reel, with *in.*—**reel off,** to produce without effort.—**reel·a·ble,** *a.*—**reel·er,** *n.*

reel, rēl, *v.i.* [M.E. *relen;* origin uncertain; cf. *reel.*] To turn round and round, or whirl; to sway, swing, or rock under a blow, shock, or any great stress; sway about unsteadily in standing or walking from dizziness, intoxication, or faintness; stagger; totter.—*v.t.* To cause to reel; to reel along.—*n.* The act of reeling; a reeling or staggering movement.

reel, rēl, *n.* A lively group dance; the music for this dance, written in four-four or six-eight rhythm.

re·e·lect, rē"i·lekt', *v.t.* To elect again.— **re·e·lec·tion,** rē"i·lek'shan, *n.* Election for a second term in office; a repeated election.

re·em·pha·size, rē·em'fa·siz", *v.t.*—reemphasized, reemphasizing. To stress again; to reiterate; to pronounce again with strong accent; to render emphatic again.—**re-- em·pha·sis,** rē·em'fa·sis, *n.* pl. **re·em-- pha·ses,** rē·em'fa·sēz.

re·em·ploy, rē"em·ploi', *v.t.* To hire again; to make use of a person's services on another occasion; to again provide with a paying job or position.—**re·em·ploy-- ment,** rē"em·ploi'ment, *n.*

re·en·act, rē"en·akt', *v.t.* To enact again, as a law; perform once more, as a role. —**re·en·act·ment,** rē"en·akt'ment, *n.*

re·en·force, rē"en·fôrs', rē"en·fars', *v.t.* —reenforced, reenforcing. Reinforce.—**re-- en·force·ment,** *n.*

re·en·list, rē"en·list', *v.t., v.i.* To enlist a second time.—**re·en·list·ment,** rē"en-- list'ment, *n.* The act of reenlisting; the duration of the reenlistment; one who enlists a second time.

re·en·ter, rē·en'tẽr, *v.t.* To enter again or anew; *bus.* to enter again in an account; *engraving,* to cut deeper, as the incisions of a plate.—**re·en·trance,** rē·en'trans, *n.*

re·en·trant, rē·en'trant, *a.* Reentering, as an angle; extended inward.—*n.* That which or one who reenters, as a part or angle, or a political candidate.

re·en·try, rē·en'trē, *n.* pl. **re·en·tries.** A new or second entry; the return of a space vehicle, rocket, or the like from outer space into the earth's atmosphere; *law,* resuming or retaking possession of lands under the right reserved in a former property transfer; *bridge,* a card of higher rank than the lowest card of the same suit in the partner's hand, as that used by the declarer to overtake a lead from or to the dummy.

re·es·tab·lish, rē"e·stab'lish, *v.t.* To establish anew.—**re·es·tab·lish·ment,** *n.*

re·e·val·u·ate, rē"i·val'ū·āt", *v.t.*—reevaluated, reevaluating. To evaluate again; to reconsider.—**re·e·val·u·a·tion,** rē"i-- val"ū·ā'shan, *n.*

re·e·vap·o·ra·tion, rē"i·vap"o·rā'shan, *n.* A second evaporation.

reeve, rēv, *n.* [O.E. *gerēfa.*] An Old English official of a town or district who represented the crown; a bailiff, steward, or overseer in medieval England. The elected head of a town council in some parts of Canada.

reeve, rēv, *v.t.*—past *rove* or *reeved,* pp. *reeved* or *roven,* ppr. *reeving.* [Origin uncertain: cf. D. *reven,* to reef (sails).] *Naut.* To pass, as a rope, through a hole, ring, or the like; fasten by placing through or around something; to pass a rope through, as a block.

reeve, rēv, *n.* A sandpiper, the female of the ruff.

re·e·voke, rē"i·vōk', *v.t.*—reevoked, reevoking. To evoke anew.

re·ex·am·ine, rē"ig·zam'in, *v.t.*—reexamined, reexamining. To examine anew; *law,* to exact testimony from, as from a witness, after a cross-examination and usu. on matters stemming from it.—**re·ex-- am·i·na·tion,** rē"ig·zam'i·nā'shan, *n.*

re·ex·change, rē"iks·chānj', *n.* A second or new exchange.

re·ex·port, rē"ik·spôrt', rē"ik·spart', rē-- eks·pôrt, rē·eks·part, *v.t.* To export again; to export after having been imported.— rē·eks'pôrt, rē·eks'part, *n.* Any commodity reexported; the act of reexporting.— **re·ex·por·ta·tion,** rē"iks·pôr·tā'shan, *n.*— **re·ex·port·er,** *n.*

re·face, rē·fās', *v.t.*—refaced, refacing. To renew, restore, or repair the face or surface of, as of buildings; to provide, as a garment, with a new facing.

re·fash·ion, rē·fash'an, *v.t.* To revamp; remodel; reconstruct; modify.

re·fect, ri·fekt', *v.t.* [L. *refectus,* pp. of *reficere,* < *re-,* again, and *facere,* make.] *Archaic.* To restore after hunger or fatigue; refresh, esp. with food or drink.

re·fec·tion, ri·fek'shan, *n.* [L. *refectio, refectionis,* < *reficio,* to restore, to refresh— *re-,* again, and *facio,* to make.] Refreshment after hunger or fatigue; a repast.

re·fec·to·ry, ri·fek'to·rē, *n.* pl. **re·fec-- to·ries.** A room, esp. in convents and colleges, where meals are taken; dining hall.

re·fec·to·ry ta·ble, *n.* A long, narrow table with a large trestlelike leg at either end.

re·fer, ri·fur', *v.t.*—referred, referring. [L. *refero, referre,* to bring back, to refer, etc.— *re-,* back, and *fero,* to carry.] To send or direct for assistance, information, or decision; to hand over, as to another person, for treatment or decision; as, to *refer* a matter to a third party; to assign, as to an order, kind, period, or class; to attribute to a cause, source, or motive.—*v.i.* To have relation; to have recourse; to consult; as, to *refer* to one's notes; to allude; to direct the attention.—**ref·er·a·ble, re·fer·ra-- ble, re·fer·ri·ble,** ref'ẽr·a·bl, ri·fur'i·bl, *a.*—**re·fer·rer,** *n.*

ref·er·ee, ref"e·rē', *n.* One to whom a matter in dispute has been referred for settlement or decision; the authoritative official in football or other sports; *law,* a court-appointed arbitrator whose function is to hear disputes and render recommendations to the court.—*v.t., v.i.*—refereed, refereeing.

ref·er·ence, ref'ẽr·ens, *n.* The act of referring; the act of alluding; direct allusion; respect or regard; as, with *reference* to his letter; a person or thing referred to; a passage or note in a work by which a person is referred to another passage or book; one of whom inquiries may be made in regard to a person's character and ability; a written statement or letter as to one's ability and character.—*v.t.*—referenced, referencing. To supply or furnish with references.

ref·er·en·dum, ref″e·ren′dum, *n.* pl. **ref·er·en·dums, ref·er·en·da.** [L., a thing to be referred.] The referral to public vote, for final approval or rejection, of measures proposed or passed by a representative body having legislative powers; the vote so taken. See *initiative.*

ref·er·ent, ref′ér·ent, *n.* Something referred to, as a word, person, or concept. *Logic,* the initial term in a proposition, to which following terms refer.

ref·er·en·tial, ref″e·ren′shal, *a.* Having reference; for use as a reference; containing one or more references.—**ref·er·en·tial·ly,** *adv.*

re·fer·ral, ri·fur′al, *n.* An instance or act of referring; a person or thing referred.

re·fight, rē·fīt′, *v.t.*—*refought, refighting.* To wage battle or combat again, esp. in the mind or imagination.

re·fig·ure, rē·fig′yèr, *v.t.*—*refigured, refiguring.* To figure once more.

re·fill, rē·fil′, *v.t.* To fill again.—rē′fil″, *n.* A second filling, as of a medical prescription; a second serving, as of a beverage; any product packaged to replace the original contents of a refillable container. —**re·fill·a·ble,** *a.*

re·film, rē·film′, *v.t.* To film anew.

re·fil·ter, rē·fil′tèr, *v.t.* To filter anew.

re·fi·nance, rē·fī′nans, rē″fī·nans′, *v.t.*—*refinanced, refinancing.* To provide another loan for on new terms; to renew a loan for or restructure the financing arrangements of.

re·fine, ri·fīn′, *v.t.*—*refined, refining.* [Fr. *raffiner,* to refine—*re-,* and *affiner—af* (for L. *ad*), to, and *fin,* fine.] To make fine or pure; to free from impurities; to separate from other metals or from dross or alloy; to purify from what is coarse, inelegant, or rude; make elegant, cultured, or cultivated, as tastes or manners; to make precise or more subtle.—*v.i.* To become fine or pure; to become more elegant or polished; to use fine distinctions or subtlety in thought or language.—**re·fin·a·ble,** *a.*—**re·fin·er,** *n.*

re·fined, ri·fīnd′, *a.* Having no impurities; polished or elegant in character; characterized by precision or exactness.

re·fine·ment, ri·fīn′ment, *n.* Elegance of manners or language; fineness of feeling or taste; polish; culture; an instance of refined feeling, taste, or manners; subtle reasoning; a fine point or subtle distinction; an improved, higher, or extreme form of something; the act of refining or state of being refined; process of refining.

re·fin·er·y, ri·fī′ne·rē, *n.* pl. **re·fin·er·ies.** A place and apparatus for refining sugar, metals, or oil.

re·fin·ish, rē·fin′ish, *v.t.* To put a new surface on, as wood or metal.—**re·fin·ish·er,** *n.*

re·fit, rē·fit′, *v.t.*—*refitted, refitting.* To restore, repair, or fit out anew, as ships.—*v.i.* To be repaired, supplied, or made ready again.—*n.* The act of so repairing or supplying.

re·fix, rē·fiks′, *v.t.*—*refixed, refixing.* To fix or fasten again; to repair again.

re·flect, ri·flekt′, *v.t.* [L. *reflecto*—*re-,* back, and *flecto, flexum,* to bend, seen in *flexure, deflect, inflect, inflection,* etc.] To cast or direct back from a surface, as light, heat, or sound; to give back an image of; to mirror or imitate; as, to *reflect* another's attitude or opinion; to cast or direct back as a result, as: His courtesy *reflects* credit on his upbringing. To make evident or reveal, as: His act *reflects* his true feelings on the matter.—*v.i.* To throw back rays, beams, or the like; to turn back one's thoughts upon anything; to think at length or consider seriously; to revolve matters in the mind; to bring reproach; to cast censure or blame; to give a certain impression.

re·flect·ance, ri·flek′tans, *n. Phys.* the intensity of radiance reflected from a surface in proportion to the total illumination received by that surface.

re·flect·ing tel·e·scope, *n.* A telescope using a concave mirror as the focusing lens: opposed to *refracting telescope.*

re·flec·tion, *Brit.* also **re·flex·ion,** ri·flek′shan, *n.* The act of reflecting, or the state of being reflected; an image given back from a reflecting surface; a counterpart; attentive or continued consideration, contemplation, or meditation; the conclusion or thought resulting from such meditating; a discrediting remark; reproach. *Phys.* the return or directing back of light, heat, or sound from a reflecting surface; that which is returned or reflected. *Anat.* a folding or flexing back upon itself, as by a membrane.—**re·flec·tion·al,** *a.*

re·flec·tive, ri·flek′tiv, *a.* Having the capability of throwing back rays, beams, or the like; reflecting; resulting from reflection; given to extended contemplation.—**re·flec·tive·ly,** *adv.*—**re·flec·tive·ness, re·flec·tiv·i·ty,** rē″flek·tiv′i·tē, *n.*

re·flec·tom·e·ter, rē″flek·tom′i·tèr, *n.* An instrument for measuring the power of reflection of bodies or surfaces.

re·flec·tor, ri·flek′tèr, *n.* One who reflects; that which reflects; a polished surface of metal or other suitable material for reflecting light, heat, or sound in any required direction; a reflecting telescope; *phys.* an inhibiting substance used to control the reaction level in a nuclear reactor.—**re·flec·tor·ize,** ri·flek′to·rīz″, *v.t.*—*reflectorized, reflectorizing.* To construct so as to reflect light.

re·flex, rē′fleks, *n.* [L. *reflexus,* n., < *reflectere,* to reflect.] Reflection, as of light; reflected light or color resulting from reflection; the light reflected or cast from an illuminated surface to one in shade; the reflection or image of an object, as exhibited by a mirror or the like; a reproduction as if in a mirror; a copy or adaptation; *physiol.* a reflex action or movement; *wireless teleph.* a reflex radio receiving apparatus or set.

re·flex, rē′fleks, *a.* [L. *reflexus,* pp.] Bent or turned back; cast back or reflected, as light; directed back upon the mind itself or its operations, as a mental act; pertaining to or derived from such mental acts; occurring in reaction, or responsive; *physiol.* noting or pertaining to an action or movement of an involuntary nature, in which a stimulus is transmitted along an afferent nerve to a nerve center, and from there reflected along an efferent nerve to call into play muscular or other activity. *Wireless teleph.* designating a radio receiving apparatus or set in which a single part performs two functions; pertaining to such an apparatus or set.—**re·flex·ly,** *adv.*

re·flex arc, *n.* The path followed by an impulse from afferent neurons through intermediate neurons to efferent neurons, in the production of a reflex response: the basic unit of function of the nervous system.

re·flex cam·er·a, *n.* A camera in which the image is reflected by a mirror or prism onto a ground-glass screen for focusing, and recorded on film by the same or a separate lens.

re·flex·ive, ri·flek′siv, *a. Gram.* of a verb, having a pronoun object which is the same as its subject, as *cut* in *He cut himself.* Of a pronoun, used as an object and identical with the subject, as *himself* in *He cut himself.* Bending or turning back upon; having the ability to reflect; reflective; responsive.—*n.* A reflexive verb or pronoun.—**re·flex·ive·ly,** *adv.*—**re·flex·ive·ness, re·flex·iv·i·ty,** rē″flek·siv′i·tē, *n.*

re·float, rē·flōt′, *v.t., v.i.* To float again; to raise back to the surface, as a boat.

re·flo·res·cence, rē″flo·res′ens, rē″fla·- res′ens, rē″flo·res′ens, *n.* A renewed flowering; the act of blossoming again.

ref·lu·ent, ref′lö·ent, *a.* [L. *refluens, refluentis,* flowing, surging, or rushing back; ebbing.—**ref·lu·ence,** *n.*

re·flux, rē′fluks″, *n.* A flowing back; as, the flux and *reflux* of the tides; ebb.

re·fo·cus, rē·fō′kus, *v.t., v.i.*—*refocused, refocusing, refocussed, refocussing.* To focus again.

re·for·est, rē·far′ist, rē·for′ist, *v.t.* To replant with forest trees.—**re·for·est·a·tion,** *n.*

re·forge, rē·fōrj′, rē·farj′, *v.t.*—*reforged, reforging.* To forge again; to make over.

re·form, ri·farm′, *v.t.* [Fr. *réformer,* to reform or amend, < L. *reformare < forma,* form.] To change from worse to better; to introduce improvement in; to bring from a bad to a good state, as a person; to remove or abolish for something better.—*v.i.* To abandon evil and return to good; to amend one's behavior.—*n.* A rearrangement or reconstruction which brings a better order of things; an instance of such; reformation, as an improvement in behavior; amendment of what is defective, vicious, corrupt, or depraved.—**re·form·a·ble,** *a.*

re·form, rē·farm′, *v.t., v.i.* To form again or anew; to give the same or another disposition or arrangement to; as, to *re-form* troops that have been scattered.—**re·for·ma·tion,** *n.* The act of forming anew.

Ref·or·ma·tion, ref″èr·mā′shan, *n.* The religious revolution of the 16th century which divided the Roman Catholic Church, with the dissidents establishing the Protestant churches. (*l.c.*) the act of reforming or the condition of being reformed.

re·form·a·to·ry, ri·far′ma·tōr″ē, ri·far′ma·tor″ē, *n.* pl. **re·form·a·tor·ies.** An institution for the reformation of juveniles who have been convicted of lesser criminal offences. Also *reform school.*—*a.* Tending to reform; also **re·form·a·tive.**

re·formed, ri·farmd′, *a.* Corrected; amended; restored to a good state; having turned from evil ways; as, a *reformed* profligate; (*cap.*) of or pertaining to Protestant churches, esp. those accepting the tenets of Calvin on various doctrines as opposed to those of Martin Luther.

re·formed spell·ing, *n.* A spelling method designed to give English words increased phonetic uniformity by eliminating silent letters.

re·form·er, ri·far′mèr, *n.* One who promotes, urges, or effects political or social reform; (*sometimes cap.*) any leader of the Reformation.

re·form·ist, ri·far′mist, *n.* An advocate of reform.—**re·form·ism,** *n.*

Re·form Ju·da·ism, *n.* A form of Judaism having the rites, manners, and ceremonies revised to adhere more closely to rationalism and contemporary conditions, and putting greater emphasis on the religious character and morals of Judaism than on ritual orthodoxy.

re·form school, *n.* A reformatory.

re·fract, ri·frakt′, *v.t.* [Fr. *refracter,* < L. *refringo, refractum,* to break up.] *Optics.* To deflect, as a ray of light, at a certain angle on passing from one medium into another of a different density; to determine the refraction power of.

re·fract·ing tel·e·scope, *n.* A telescope in which the rays are refracted by an object glass, at the focus of which they are viewed by a magnifying eyepiece: opposed to *reflecting telescope.*

re·frac·tion, ri·frak′shan, *n.* The act of refracting or state of being refracted; *phys.* a deflection or change of direction impressed upon rays of light or heat passing from one transparent medium into another of different density, as from air into water, or upon rays traversing a medium the density of which is not uniform, as the atmosphere; *opt.* the refracting of light rays entering the eye, creating an image on the retina; *astron.* the bending of light waves from a celestial body caused by the atmosphere.

re·frac·tive, ri·frak′tiv, *a.* Pertaining to refraction; serving or having power to refract.—**re·frac·tive·ly,** *adv.*—**re·frac·tive·ness, re·frac·tiv·i·ty,** rē″frak·tiv′i·tē, *n.*

re·frac·tive in·dex, *n. Opt.* index of refraction.

re·frac·tom·e·ter, rē″frak·tom′i·tēr, *n. Opt.* an instrument for exhibiting and measuring the refraction of light.—**re·frac·to·met·ric,** rē·frak″tō·me′trik, *a.*—**re·frac·tom·e·try,** *n.*

re·frac·tor, ri·frak′tēr, *n.* Something which refracts; a refracting telescope.

re·frac·to·ry, ri·frak′tō·rē, *a.* [Fr. *réfractaire;* < L. *refractarius,* stubborn, < *refringo, refractum.*] Perverse or disobedient; stubborn; unmanageable; resisting ordinary treatment, as certain diseases, or as metals that are difficult to fuse.—*n.* pl. **re·frac·to·ries.** A noncompliant person; brick or ceramic material that is resistant to high temperatures or corrosion.—**re·frac·to·ri·ly,** *adv.*—**re·frac·to·ri·ness,** *n.*

re·frain, ri·frān′, *v.i.* [Fr. *refréner,* to bridle in, to repress, < L. *refringere.*] To keep oneself from saying, doing, or feeling something; forbear; abstain, often followed by *from.*—**re·frain·ment,** *n.*

re·frain, ri·frān′, *n.* [Fr. *refrain,* < O.Fr. *refraindre,* L. *refringo*—*re*-, again, and *frango,* to break. The *refrain,* therefore, is literally the break or interruption to the course of the piece.] A verse or phrase repeated at intervals in a poem or song, esp. at the end of every stanza; the musical setting for this verse or phrase.

re·fran·gi·ble, ri·fran′ji·bl, *a.* Capable of being refracted; subject to refraction, as rays of light.—**re·fran·gi·bil·i·ty, re·fran·gi·ble·ness,** ri·fran″ji·bil′i·tē, *n.*

re·fresh, ri·fresh′, *v.t.* [O.Fr. *refreschir, refraischir,* to refresh.] To make fresh or vigorous again; to give new strength or energy to; to reinvigorate; to recreate or revive after fatigue, want, pain, or the like; to reanimate; to freshen in looks.—*v.i.* To have refreshment; to become fresh anew; revive. Also **re·fresh·en.**

re·fresh·er, ri·fresh′ēr, *n.* One who or that which refreshes; *Brit.* among lawyers, an additional fee paid to counsel when the case is adjourned from one court term or sitting to another.—**re·fresh·er course,** a review of a scholastic, business, or technical subject at any time subsequent to one's first successful study of it.

re·fresh·ment, ri·fresh′ment, *n.* The act of refreshing, or the condition of being refreshed; that which refreshes; that which gives fresh strength or vigor, as food, drink, or rest; *pl.* food or drink, as a light meal or snack.

re·frig·er·ant, ri·frij′ēr·ant, *a.* Cooling; allaying heat or a fever.—*n.* A cooling agency; ice; a gas used in mechanical refrigerators, as ammonia; a medicine which abates fever.

re·frig·er·ate, ri·frij′e·rāt′, *v.t.*—*refrigerated, refrigerating.* [L. *refrigero, refrigeratum,* to refrigerate.] To cool; keep cool; to chill or freeze, as foods, in order to preserve.—**re·frig·er·a·tion,** ri·frij″e·rā′shan, *n.*

re·frig·er·a·tor, ri·frij′e·rā″tēr, *n.* That which refrigerates, cools, or keeps cool; a box or room in which materials, as foods, are kept cool, either by the action of ice or

by evaporation of various liquid gases, as sulfur dioxide or ammonia; an apparatus that cools hot liquids or vapors rapidly in the distilling process.

re·frin·gent, ri·frin′jent, *a.* Possessing the quality of refracting; refractive.—**re·frin·gence, re·frin·gen·cy,** *n.*

re·fu·el, rē·fū′el, *v.t.*—*refueled, refueling, refuelled, refuelling.* To supply afresh with fuel; as, to *refuel* an airplane.—*v.i.* To take on a fresh supply of fuel.

ref·uge, ref′ūj, *n.* [Fr., < L. *refugium,* < *refugio.*] Shelter or protection from danger or distress; that which shelters or protects from danger, distress, or calamity; any place where one is out of the way of any evil or danger; a wildlife preserve.

ref·u·gee, ref″ū·jē′, *n.* [Fr. *réfugié.*] One who flees for refuge; one who in times of persecution, political commotion, or the like, flees to a foreign country for safety.

re·ful·gent, ri·ful′jent, *a.* [L. *refulgens, refulgentis,* ppr. of *refulgeo.*] Casting a bright light; shining; radiant.—**re·ful·gent·ly,** *adv.*—**re·ful·gence, re·ful·gen·cy,** *n.*

re·fund, ri·fund′, *v.t.* [L. *refundo,* to pour back, to restore.] To return in payment or compensation for what has been taken; to pay back; to restore; to reimburse.—*v.i.* To make compensation.—rē′fund, *n.* A repayment; the sum repaid.—**re·fund·a·ble,** *a.*

re·fund, rē·fund′, *v.t.* To fund anew. Also **re-fund.**

re·fur·bish, rē·fur′bish, *v.t.* To furbish a second time or anew; to renovate; to clean.—**re·fur·bish·ment,** *n.*

re·fur·nish, rē·fur′nish, *v.t.* To furnish anew; to redecorate, as with new or different furniture.

re·fus·al, ri·fū′zal, *n.* The act of refusing; denial of anything demanded, solicited, or offered for acceptance; option of taking or buying.

re·fuse, ri·fūz′, *v.t.*—*refused, refusing.* [Fr. *réfuser,* to refuse.] To deny, as a request, demand, invitation, or command; to decline to do or grant, often with an infinitive as object, as: He *refused* to give me the book. To decline to accept; to reject; as, to *refuse* an office; to deny the request of; to say no to, as: I could not *refuse* him.—*v.i.* To decline a request; not to comply.—**re·fus·er,** *n.*

ref·use, ref′ūs, *n.* [Appar. < O.Fr. *refus,* refusal, rejection, or *refusé,* pp. refused, < *refuser,* E. *refuse.*] That which is discarded as worthless or useless; garbage; trash; rubbish.—*a.* Rejected as worthless; discarded; as, *refuse* matter.

ref·u·ta·tion, ref″ū·tā′shan, *n.* The act of refuting or proving to be false or erroneous; the act of overthrowing by argument. Also **re·fut·al,** ri·fūt′al.

re·fute, ri·fūt′, *v.t.*—*refuted, refuting.* [Fr. *réfuter,* L. *refutare*—*re*-, back, and *futare,* to beat.] To disprove and overthrow by argument, evidence, or countervailing proof; to prove to be false or erroneous; to confute; to prove to be in error.—**re·fut·er,** *n.*—**re·fu·ta·ble,** ri·fū′ta·bl, ref′ū·ta·bl, *a.* Capable of being refuted.—**ref·u·ta·bly,** ref′ū·ta·blē, *adv.*

re·gain, ri·gān′, *v.t.* To gain anew; to recover what has been lost; to reach again, as: He *regained* the shore.

re·gal, rē′gal, *a.* [L. *regalis,* < *rex, regis,* a king, < stem of *rego,* to rule.] Of, pertaining to, or befitting a king; royal; stately; magnificent.—**re·gal·ly,** *adv.*

re·gale, ri·gāl′, *v.t.*—*regaled, regaling.* [Fr. *régaler,* < *régale.*] To entertain in a lavish or agreeable manner; to provide a feast for; to delight with something pleasing.—*v.i.* To feast.—*n. Archaic.* A splendid repast; a treat.

re·ga·li·a, ri·gā′lē·a, ri·gāl′ya, *n. pl.* [L. *regalia,* royal or regal things, nom. pl. neut. of *regalis,* regal.] Royal privileges or rights; the ensigns or symbols of royalty, as the scepter, crown, or the like; the insignia or decorations of some society or office; fancy clothes.

re·gal·i·ty, ri·gal′i·tē, *n. pl.* **re·gal·i·ties.** [O.Fr. *regalite,* < M.L. *regalitas,* < L. *regalis,* E. *regal.*] Royalty, sovereignty, or kingship; a right or privilege pertaining to a king; a kingdom. In Scotland, territorial jurisdiction of a royal nature formerly conferred by the king; a territory subject to such jurisdiction.

re·gard, ri·gärd′, *v.t.* [O.Fr. Fr. *regarder,* < *re*- (< L. *re*-), back, again, and *garder,* E. *guard:* cf. *reward.*] To look upon or think of in a particular way; view or consider; as, to *regard* a person as a friend; to have or show consideration, respect, or concern for; to heed; to esteem or think highly of; to take into consideration or account; to look at, contemplate, or observe; to relate to or concern, as: This scheme *regards* your child's education.—*v.i.* To pay attention; heed; to look or gaze.—*n.* [O.Fr. Fr. *regard.*] Reference or relation; as, to err with *regard* to facts; an aspect or particular; as, quite pleasing in this *regard;* notice, attention, or heed; consideration; look or gaze; respect or deference; esteem; kindly feeling, liking, or affection; as, a token of my *regard; pl.* sentiments of esteem or affection, as expressed in greetings, as: Give her my *regards.*

re·gard·ful, ri·gärd′ful, *a.* Observant, attentive, or mindful, often followed by *of;* as, *regardful of* appearances; feeling or showing regard; respectful.—**re·gard·ful·ly,** *adv.*—**re·gard·ful·ness,** *n.*

re·gard·ing, ri·gär′ding, *prep.* [Like *concerning, during,* a participle, now established as a prep.] Respecting; concerning; in reference to; as, to be at a loss *regarding* something.

re·gard·less, ri·gärd′lis, *a.* Having or showing no regard; heedless, unmindful, or careless; unregarded or unheeded; not esteemed; despised, paltry.—*adv.* Without regard to advice, expense, or consequence; despite.—**re·gard·less of,** in spite of; notwithstanding.—**re·gard·less·ly,** *adv.*—**re·gard·less·ness,** *n.*

re·gat·ta, ri·gat′a, ri·gä′ta, *n.* [It.] Originally a gondola race in Venice; now any boat race or a program of such races.

re·ge·la·tion, rē″je·lā′shan, *n.* [L. *re*-, again, and *gelatio, gelationis,* a freezing.] The phenomenon of ice refreezing after being partially melted, caused by a change in air pressure, even in a warm atmosphere. —**re·ge·late,** rē′je·lāt″, rē″je·lāt′, *v.i.—regelated, regelating.*

re·gen·cy, rē′jen·sē, *n. pl.* **re·gen·cies.** [M.L. *regenita.*] The office or function of a regent; the office, jurisdiction, or control of a regent or body of regents exercising the ruling power during the minority, absence, or disability of a sovereign; a body of regents, or a government consisting of regents; a territory under the control of a regent or regents; the term of office of a regent; (usu. cap.) *Fr. hist.* the period, 1715–23, during which Philip, Duke of Orleans, was regent in the minority of Louis XV. *E. hist.* the period, 1811–20, during which George, Prince of Wales, afterwards George IV, was regent, owing to the mental incapacity of George III.—*a.* Pertaining to a regency; (usu. cap.) denoting the architecture in France, 1715–23, or in England, 1811–20; as, in the *Regency* style.

re·gen·er·a·cy, ri·jen′ēr·a·sē, *n.* The state of being regenerated.

re·gen·er·ate, ri·jen'e·rāt', v.t.—regenerated, regenerating. [L. regeneratus, pp. of regenerare.] To generate or produce anew; to bring into existence again, as cells, tissues, or chemical compounds; to re-create, reconstitute, or make over, esp. in a better form or condition; electronics, to cause regeneration in; theol. to cause to be born again spiritually.—v.i. To come into existence or be formed again; to reform; to become regenerate.—ri·jen'ér·it, a. Formed again or anew; reconstituted or made over in a better form; reformed; theol. born again spiritually.—re·gen·er·ate·ly, adv. —re·gen·er·ate·ness, n.

re·gen·er·a·tion, ri·jen'e·rā'shan, n. [L.L. regeneratio(n-).] The act of regenerating, or the state of being regenerated; production or new formation; reconstitution, esp. in a better form or condition; reformation; theol. spiritual rebirth; electronics, a process by which some of the energy of the plate circuit of a vacuum tube is transferred back to the grid circuit by means of induction or the like, thus reinforcing the current of the grid and causing larger variations in the current of the plates with a corresponding increase in the volume of the signals; biol. the replacement of lost tissues in some plants and animals; mech. the regenerative use of heat.

re·gen·er·a·tive, ri·jen'e·rā"tiv, ri·jen'-ér·a·tiv, a. Tending to regenerate; pertaining to regeneration; electronics, of or pertaining to regeneration.—re·gen·er·a·tive·ly, adv.

re·gen·er·a·tor, ri·jen'e·rā"tér, n. One who or that which regenerates; mech. the device for heating the incoming air or fuel gas in a furnace or gas burner.

re·gent, rē'jent, n. One who exercises the ruling power in a kingdom during the minority, absence, or disability of the sovereign; a member of the governing board of certain universities and other institutions; an officer who exercises a general supervision over the conduct and welfare of the students of a university; in old universities, a member of certain governing and teaching bodies.—a. Exercising ruling authority in behalf of a young, absent, or disabled sovereign.

reg·i·cide, rej'i·sīd", n. [Fr. régicide, < L. rex, regis, a king, and caedo, to slay.] One who murders a king or aids in his killing; the killing or murder of a king.—reg·i·cid·al, a.

re·gime, re·zhēm', rā·zhēm', n. [Fr. regime, < L. regimen, guidance, < rego, to govern.] Mode or system of management or rule; government, esp. as connected with certain social features; administration. Also ré·gime, rā·zhēm'.

reg·i·men, rej'i·men", rej'i·men, n. [L. regimen (regimin-), guidance, direction, rule, < regere.] Rule or government; a particular form or system of government; med. a regulated course of diet, exercise, or manner of living, intended to preserve or restore health or to attain some result; gram. government of the form of a word by another word related to it, as a verb by its subject or subjects.

reg·i·ment, rej'i·ment, n. [O.Fr. regiment, rule, Fr. régiment, regiment of troops, < L.L. regimentum, rule, government, < L. regere.] Milit. a unit of organization in an army, being next below a brigade and usu. commanded by a colonel. A large body or number, as of persons.—rej'i·ment", v.t. To form into a regiment or regiments; to form into an organized body or group for control; organize or systematize; to assign to a regiment or group; to make uniform.—reg·i·men·tal, rej'i·men'tal, a.—reg·i·men·tal·ly, adv.—reg·i·men·ta·tion, n.

reg·i·men·tals, rej"i·men'talz, n. pl. The uniform worn by a regiment; military dress.

re·gion, rē'jan, n. [O.Fr. regiun (Fr. region), < L. regio(n-), direction, quarter, region, < regere, to direct.] Any more or less extensive, continuous part of a surface or space; a part of the earth's surface, as land or sea, of considerable and usu. indefinite extent; a tract or district without respect to boundaries or extent; a locality; an administrative division of a city or territory; a part or division of the universe, the heavens, or the interior of the earth; any of the successive divisions into which the atmosphere is considered as divided according to height, or the sea according to depth; a part of a space or a body; a domain, realm, or sphere; a large faunal area of the earth's surface; anat. a place in, or a division of, the body or a part of the body.

re·gion·al, rē'ja·nal, a. Of or pertaining to a particular region, district, area, or part; sectional; local; of or pertaining to a region of considerable extent; not merely local; anat. pertaining to particular regions or parts of the body.—re·gion·al·ly, adv.

re·gion·al·ism, rē'ja·na·liz"um, n. Govt. a system of political administration based on regional, self-governing divisions; liter. the emphasis of local characteristics, as topographical features, social mores, and dialects.—re·gion·al·ist, n., a.—re·gion·al·is·tic, a.

reg·is·ter, rej'i·stér, n. [O.Fr. Fr. registre, < M.L. registrum, regestrum, regestum, a register, < L. regerere (pp. regestus), carry back, transcribe, record, < re-, back, and gerere, bear.] A book in which entries of occurrences, names, or the like are recorded; an entry in such a book, record, or list; any list of such entries; a roll; a roster; registration or registry; a mechanical contrivance by which certain data are recorded; as, a cash register; a contrivance for regulating the passage of heat, air, or the like, usu. placed where a duct opens into a room; com. an official document issued to a ship as evidence of its nationality. Mus. the range, placement, or tone quality of a voice or instrument; in a pipe organ, the set of pipes, or in an electric or electronic organ, the tonal units, that are controlled by a single stop or tab. Print. the precise adjustment or correspondence, as of lines or columns, esp. on the two sides of a leaf; the correct relation, or exact superimposition, as of colors in color printing.—v.t. [O.Fr. Fr. registrer, < M.L. registrare, < registrum.] To enter formally, or cause to be so entered, in a register; to enroll, as voters or students; to cause to be recorded for security in transmission, as mail at a post office, by payment of a special fee; to indicate or show, as on a scale; to show, as one's emotions, by facial expression or by actions. Print. to adjust so as to secure exact correspondence; to cause to be in register.—v.i. To enter one's name, or cause it to be entered, in a register; to indicate something, as by a record or on a scale; to register surprise, joy, or the like; to be registered or indicated; to create an impression; print. to be in register. Mus. in playing the organ, to program, as for a piece of music, the stops or tabs to be employed throughout the composition; also reg·is·trate, rej'i·strāt.—reg·is·trant, n. One who registers something, as a copyright or patent; one who is registered, as a student or voter.—reg·is·tra·ble, reg·is·ter·a·ble, a.

reg·is·ter, rej'i·stér, n. [For registrer, registrar.] A registrar.

reg·is·tered, rej'i·stérd, a. Recorded in a register, as human births and deaths, pure-blooded animals, or security owners. Legally or officially qualified; as, a registered appraiser.

reg·is·tered mail, n. Mail recorded at the post office of origin and at each successive transmission point, with special care in delivery guaranteed.

reg·is·tered nurse, n. A nurse licensed by state authority to practice nursing, having completed her training and passed a state examination. Abbr. R.N.

reg·is·trar, rej'i·strär, rej"i·strär', n. [L.L. registrarius.] One whose business is to write or keep a register; a keeper of records, esp. at a university or college. Also register.

reg·is·tra·tion, rej'i·strā'shan, n. [M.L. registratio(n-).] The act or an instance of registering or recording; a document indicating this; an entry in a register; the number of those registered; enrollment. Mus. the selection of stops in a pipe organ, or tabs in an electric organ, to be used in the performance of a musical composition; the arrangement of stops or tabs so selected.—reg·is·tra·tion·al, a.

reg·is·try, rej'i·strē, n. pl. reg·is·tries. The act of entering in a register; the place where a register is kept; a fact recorded in an official book; the book; a ship's nationality as displayed on the register.

re·gi·us, rē'jē·us, rē'jis, a. [L., < rex (reg-), king.] Royal: applied to professors in British universities who hold chairs founded by the sovereign.—re·gi·us pro·fes·sor, n.

reg·let, reg'lit, n. [Fr. réglet, < régle, rule, L. regula.] Arch. a flat narrow molding, as between panels. Print. a strip of wood or metal used for separating lines of type; these strips collectively or the material for them.

reg·nal, reg'nal, a. [M.L. regnalis, < L. regnum, E. reign, n.] Of or pertaining to a reigning sovereign, sovereignty, or a reign; as, a regnal year.

reg·nant, reg'nant, a. [L. regnans (regnant-), ppr. of regnare, E. reign, v.] Reigning or ruling; as, a queen regnant; exercising sway or influence; predominant; prevalent or widespread.—reg·nan·cy, reg'nan·sē, n.

reg·o·lith, reg'o·lith, n. Mantle rock.

re·grate, ri·grāt', v.t.—regrated, regrating. [O.Fr. regrater, Fr. regratter; origin uncertain.] To buy up, as grain, provisions, or the like, in order to sell again at a profit in or near the same market; to sell at retail, as the commodities so bought.—re·grat·er, re·gra·tor, n.

re·gress, ri·gres', v.i. [L. regressus, pp. of regredi, < re-, back, and gradi, walk, go.] To go back; move in a backward direction; return; statistics, to tend to return to a mean value.—rē'gres, n. [L. regressus, n.] The act of going back; return; the right or liberty of returning; backward movement or course; retrogression.—re·gres·sor, n.

re·gres·sion, ri·gresh'an, n. [L. regressio(n-).] The act of going back or returning; retrogradation or retrogression; biol. reversion to an earlier or less advanced state or form, or to the common or general type; statistics, tendency to return to the mean; psychoanal. a reversion to earlier or less mature patterns of behavior; med. progressive subsidence of an ailment or disease.

re·gres·sive, ri·gres'iv, a. Characterized by regression or going back or backward; backward in course, tendency, or action; of a tax rate, proportionately decreasing as the tax base increases.—re·gres·sive·ly, adv.—re·gres·sive·ness, n.

re·gret, ri·gret', v.t.—regretted, regretting. [O.Fr. regreter, Fr. regretter; < Teut., and akin to O.E. graetan, weep, E. greet.] To think of with a sense of loss, as a person or thing that is gone; to feel sorrow or be sorry for the loss of; to feel sorry about; as, to *regret* an unfortunate mistake; to feel sorry for, as some fault or error of one's haste, harshness, or folly.—*n.* [Fr. *regret.*] The feeling of one who regrets; sorrow or sense of loss over a person or thing that is gone; sorrowful feeling, disappointment, or dissatisfaction over anything that one wishes might have been otherwise; *pl.* a polite expression of regretful feeling, as due to an inability to accept an invitation.—**re·gret·ta·ble,** *a.*—**re·gret·ta·bly,** *adv.*—**re·gret·ter,** *n.*—**re·gret·ful,** *a.*—**re·gret·ful·ly,** *adv.*—**re·gret·ful·ness,** *n.*

re·group, rē·grōp', *v.t., v.i.* To group anew.—**re·group·ment,** *n.*

re·grow, rē·grō', *v.t.*—past *regrew*, pp. *regrown*, ppr. *regrowing.* To grow again, as a missing member or part.—*v.i.* To resume growth after an interruption.—**re·growth,** rē·grōth', *n.*

reg·u·lar, reg'yȧ·lėr, *a.* [L. *regularis,* < *regula,* a rule, < *rego,* to rule.] Conforming to what is common custom, usual, or normal; as, a *regular* practice; of uniform or even construction, degree, or arrangement; as, *regular* temperature, *regular* features; of an ordered or habitual character; as, a *regular* patron, a *regular* meeting of the board; periodic, or methodically recurring; as, a *regular* heartbeat. *Colloq.* free from affection or pretense; as, a *regular* gal or fellow; utter, unqualified; as, a *regular* scoundrel. *Bot.* usu. of a flower, having certain parts of uniform size or shape; *gram.* having the most common form of inflectional ending, often called 'weak'; *math.* obeying one law or procedure throughout; *geom.* having equal sides and equal angles; *milit.* pertaining or attached to the permanently maintained armed forces of a country; as, the *regular* army. *Politics,* of a person, loyal to a political party; of a candidate or ticket, authorized by party officials. *Eccles.* obedient to a religious rule or belonging to a religious or monastic order.—*n.* One who is habitually steady or loyal, as a customer, political party member, or the like; *milit.* a soldier belonging to a permanent army. A clothing size for men of intermediate or average build; a suit or other garment in this size; an athletic team member scheduled to play in each game or event; *eccles.* one who is bound to a religious rule or order.—**reg·u·lar·i·ty, reg·u·lar·ness,** reg'yȧ·lar'i·tē, *n.*—**reg·u·lar·ly,** reg'yȧ·lėr·lē, *adv.*

reg·u·lar ar·my, *n.* The standing or permanent army of a nation.

reg·u·lar·ize, reg'yȧ·lȧ·rīz", *v.t.*—*regularized, regularizing.* To make regular.—**reg·u·lar·iz·er,** *n.*

reg·u·lar sol·id, *n.* One of the five regular polyhedra: the tetrahedron (4 faces), hexahedron (6), octahedron (8), dodecahedron (12), and icosahedron (20).

reg·u·late, reg'yȧ·lāt", *v.t.*—*regulated, regulating.* [L. *regulo, regulatum,* < *regula,* a rule.] To adjust by rule or established mode; to govern by or subject to certain rules or restrictions; to direct; to put or keep in good order; to control and cause to act properly.—**reg·u·la·tive,** reg'yȧ·lā"tiv, reg'yȧ·lȧ·tiv, *a.*—**reg·u·la·tor,** reg'yȧ·lā"tėr, *n.*—**reg·u·la·to·ry,** reg'yȧ·lȧ·tōr"ē, reg'yȧ·lȧ·tȧr"ē, *a.*

reg·u·la·tion, reg"yȧ·lā'shȧn, *n.* The act of regulating; a rule prescribed by a superior as to the actions of those under his control; a governing direction; a precept; a law. *Elect.* percentage of speed or voltage capacity differential of machines, transformers, or motors.

reg·u·lus, reg'yȧ·lus, *n.* pl. **reg·u·lus·es, reg·u·li,** reg'yȧ·lī". [L., a petty king or sovereign, a dim. of *rex, regis,* a king.] A metallic residue accumulating beneath the slag in furnaces treating ore; an inter-mediate metallic product in the smelting of ore; *(cap.)* a star of the first magnitude in the constellation Leo.

re·gur·gi·tate, ri·gur'ji·tāt", *v.i.*—*regurgitated, regurgitating.* [L.L. *regurgito, regurgitatum.*—L. *re-,* back, and *gurges, gurgitis,* a whirlpool.] To rush or surge back; to pour forth.—*v.t.* To cause to rush or surge back; to pour forth.

re·gur·gi·ta·tion, ri·gur"ji·tā'shȧn, *n.* The act of regurgitating; *physiol.* the backward circulation of blood through a faulty heart valve.

re·ha·bil·i·tate, rē"hȧ·bil'i·tāt", *v.t.*—*rehabilitated, rehabilitating.* [Fr. *réhabiliter.*] To restore to a former capacity or position; to reinstate; to reestablish in the esteem of others; to restore to a healthy condition or useful capacity.—**re·ha·bil·i·ta·tion,** *n.*—**re·ha·bil·i·ta·tive,** *a.*

re·hash, rē·hash', *v.t.* To hash anew; to repeat; discuss again; to work up in a new form, as old writings.—rē'hash", *n.* Something made up of materials formerly used.

re·hear·ing, rē·hēr'ing, *n.* *Law,* a second hearing or trial before the court of first instance.

re·hears·al, ri·hur'sȧl, *n.* A trial performance or drill for preparing the finished public performance; a telling or recounting.

re·hearse, ri·hurs', *v.t.*—*rehearsed, rehearsing.* [O.E. *reherce, reherse,* < O.Fr. *rehercer, reherser,* to repeat over again—*re-,* again, and *hercer, herser,* to harrow, < *herce, herse,* a harrow.] To practice repeatedly prior to public performance; to repeat; recite; narrate or recount; to improve by practice.—*v.i.* To take part in a rehearsal.—**re·hears·er,** *n.*

re·hy·drate, rē·hī'drāt, *v.t.*—*rehydrated, rehydrating.* To replace water removed in dehydration.—**re·hy·dra·tion,** *n.*

re·i·fy, rē'i·fī", *v.t.*—*reified, reifying.* [L. *res,* thing.] To convert into or regard as material; as, to *reify* an abstract concept.—**re·i·fi·ca·tion,** *n.*

reign, rān, *n.* [O.Fr. *reigne,* Fr. *regne,* L. *regnum,* a kingdom.] Royal authority; sovereignty; the time during which a monarch reigns; power, sway, or influence.—*v.i.* [O.Fr. *reigner,* Fr. *regner,* < L. *regnare,* to rule, < *regnum,* a kingdom.] To possess or exercise sovereign power or authority; to rule; to be predominant; to prevail; to have controlling authority or influence.

Reign of Ter·ror, *n.* *Fr. hist.* a period of the Revolution, from about March, 1793, to July, 1794, during which persons who were politically suspect by the ruling faction were guillotined.

re·im·burse, rē"im·burs', *v.t.*—*reimbursed, reimbursing.* [Fr. *rembourser*—*re-,* again, *en, in,* and *bourse,* a purse.] To pay back; to refund; to pay back to; to recompense; to pay an equivalent to for expenditure or loss.—**re·im·burs·a·ble,** *a.*—**re·im·burse·ment,** *n.*—**re·im·burs·er,** *n.*

re·im·port, rē"im·pōrt', rē"im·pȧrt', *v.t.* To import again into the original country of exportation.—rē·im'pōrt, rē·im'pȧrt, *n.* Something reimported.—**re·im·por·ta·tion,** *n.*

re·im·pres·sion, rē"im·presh'ȧn, *n.* A second impression; a reprint.

rein, rān, *n.* [Fr. *rêne,* O.Fr. *resne,* It. *redina;* < L. *retineo,* to retain.] Usu. *pl.* the thin strap on each side of a bit, by which the rider or driver restrains and governs a horse or other animal. A means of curbing, restraining, or guiding.—*v.t.* To govern, guide, or restrain, as by reins.—*v.i.* To restrain a horse by use of reins, followed by *up* or *in*; *archaic,* to respond to control by reins.—**draw rein,** slow one's speed; to curtail.—**give rein to,** to allow complete freedom.—**rein·less,** *a.* Uncontrolled.

re·in·car·na·tion, rē"in·kär·nā'shȧn, *n.* Belief that the soul returns after death to live in a new body; rebirth of the soul in a new living form; a new embodiment.—**re·in·car·na·tion·ist,** *n.*

re·in·cor·po·rate, rē"in·kȧr'po·rāt", *v.t., v.i.*—*reincorporated, reincorporating.* To incorporate anew.—rē"in·kȧr'po·rit, rē"in··kȧr'prit, *a.*

rein·deer, rān'dēr", *n.* pl. **rein·deer,** *occasionally* **rein·deers.** [M.E. *reindere;* cf. Icel. *hreinn,* reindeer.] Any of various species of deer of the genus *Rangifer,* with branched antlers in both male and female, found in northern or arctic regions of Asia, Europe, and N. America and often domesticated.

rein·deer moss, *n.* A lichen, *Cladonia rangiferina,* gray, erect, and branched, growing in arctic regions and furnishing winter food for reindeer and caribou.

re·in·fec·tion, rē"in·fek'shȧn, *n.* A second infection of the same type as one from which an individual is suffering or from which he has recovered.—**re·in·fect,** *v.t.*

re·in·force, rē"in·fōrs', rē"in·fȧrs', *v.t.*—*reinforced, reinforcing.* To strengthen; to strengthen with more troops, ships, or equipment; to increase; *psychol.* to strengthen the likelihood of, as a response, in a given situation, by a reward. Also **re·en·force.**—**re·in·forc·er,** *n.*

re·in·forced con·crete, *n.* Concrete in which steel bars are embedded so as to increase the resistance of the structure to tension.

re·in·force·ment, rē"in·fōrs'ment, rē"in·fȧrs'ment, *n.* The act of reinforcing; something that strengthens; *often pl.* additional troops or forces to augment an army or fleet. Also **re·en·force·ment.**

reins, rānz, *n. pl.* [O.Fr. Fr. *reins,* < L. *renes,* pl. of *ren,* kidney.] *Archaic.* The kidneys; the region of the kidneys or the lower part of the back; the seat of feelings or affections, formerly identified with the kidneys.

re·in·state, rē"in·stāt', *v.t.*—*reinstated, reinstating.* To place again in possession; to restore to a former state.—**re·in·state·ment.**

re·in·sur·ance, rē"in·shur'ans, *n.* Insurance again or anew; insurance by which a first insurer relieves himself from the risk and devolves it upon another insurer; the amount covered by such insurance.—**re·in·sure,** rē"in·shur', *v.t.*—*reinsured, reinsuring.* To insure again; to insure under a contract by which a first insurer relieves himself from all or part of a risk and devolves it upon another insurer.—**re·in·sur·er,** *n.*

re·in·te·grate, rē·in'te·grāt", *v.t., v.i.*—*reintegrated, reintegrating.* To integrate again.—**re·in·te·gra·tion,** rē"in·te·grā'shȧn, *n.*—**re·in·te·gra·tive,** *a.*

re·in·ter·pret, rē"in·tur'prit, *v.t., v.i.* To give an additional or new interpretation to.—**re·in·ter·pre·ta·tion,** *n.*

re·in·vest, rē"in·vest', *v.t.* To invest anew, as income from earlier investments.—**re·in·vest·ment,** rē"in·vest'ment, *n.*

re·in·vig·or·ate, rē"in·vig'o·rāt", *v.t.*—*reinvigorated, reinvigorating.* To fill with renewed vigor.—**re·in·vig·o·ra·tion,** *n.*

re·is·sue, rē·ish'ō, *v.t., v.i.*—*reissued, reissuing.* To issue, send out, or put forth a second time; as, to *reissue* bank notes.—*n.*

re·it·er·ate, rē·it'e·rāt", *v.t.*—*reiterated, reiterating.* [L. *re-,* again, and *itero, iteratum,* to repeat, < *iterum,* again.] To repeat again and again; to do or say repeatedly.—**re·it·er·a·tion,** *n.*—**re·it·er·a·tive,** rē·it'er·a·tiv, rē·it'er·ā"tiv, *a.*—**re·it·er·a·tive·ly,** *adv.*—**re·it·er·a·tive·ness,** *n.*

re·ject, ri·jekt', *v.t.* [L. *rejicio, rejectum,* to

reject—*re-*, again, and *jacio*, to throw (whence also *eject, inject, project*, etc.).] To refuse to receive, recognize, or acknowledge; to rebuff; to refuse to grant or consider; to decline haughtily or harshly; to throw away as useless or vile; to cast off; to discard; to disgorge or vomit.—rē′jekt, *n.* One who or that which is rejected.—**re·jec·tion**, ri·jek′shan, *n.* The act of rejecting; the result of being rebuffed or refused; something that is rejected.—**re·ject·ee**, ri·jek·tē′, ri·jek′tē, rē″jek·tē′, *n.*—**re·ject·er**, **re·jec·tor**, *n.*—**re·jec·tive**, *a.*

re·joice, ri·jois′, *v.i.*—*rejoiced, rejoicing.* [O.E. *rejoisse, rejoyse,* < O.Fr. *rejoir, rejoissant,* Fr. *réjouir, réjouissant;* prefix *re-,* and *éjour,* older *esjoir*—L. *ex-,* intens., and *gaudeo,* to rejoice.] To experience joy and gladness in a high degree; to be joyful; to exult, usu. followed by *in.*—*v.t.* To make joyful; to gladden.—**re·joic·er**, *n.*—**re·joic·ing**, ri·joi′sing, *n.*—**re·joic·ing·ly**, *adv.*

re·join, rē·join′, ri·join′, *v.t.* To join again; to unite after separation; to join, as a party, again, rē·join′. To answer; to say in answer; to reply, ri·join′.—*v.i.* To become united again, rē·join′. To answer to a reply, *law,* to reply to the replication of a plaintiff, ri·join′.

re·join·der, ri·join′dèr, *n.* [An inf. form; Fr. *rejoindre,* to rejoin. *Attainder, remainder* are similar forms.] An answer to a reply; a retort; *law,* the defendant's answer to the plaintiff's replication.

re·ju·ve·nate, ri·jö′ve·nāt″, *v.t.*—*rejuvenated, rejuvenating.* [L. *re-,* again, and *juvenis,* young.] To make young again; to restore to youthful vigor or freshness; to restore to the vigorous or flourishing condition of the early period, as an institution. *Phys. geog.* to renew the activity or erosive power, as of a stream, by the uplifting of the region it drains; to impress again the characters of youthful topography on, as a region, by the action of rejuvenated streams. Also **re·ju·ve·nize**.—**re·ju·ve·na·tion**, *n.*—**re·ju·ve·na·tor**, *n.*

re·ju·ve·nes·cence, ri·jö″ve·nes′ens, *n.* A renewal of youth or youthful vigor. *Biol.* the renewal of vitality by the conjugation or fusion of two distinct cells; a process by which the contents of a cell escape and form a new cell with a new wall.—**re·ju·ve·nes·cent**, *a.*

re·kin·dle, rē·kin′dl, *v.t., v.i.*—*rekindled, rekindling.* To kindle again, to inflame again; to rouse anew.

re·lapse, ri·laps′, *v.i.*—*relapsed, relapsing.* [L. *relabor, relapsus,* to slide back—*re-,* back and *labor, lapsus,* to slide.] To slip or slide back, esp. from recovery or convalescence to illness; to return to a former bad state or practice; to backslide.—ri·laps′, rē′laps, *n.* A recurrence of illness; a falling back.—**re·laps·er**, *n.*

re·laps·ing fe·ver, *n.* Any of several chiefly tropical diseases resulting from spirochetal infections spread by ticks and lice, and marked by recurrent attacks of chills and high fever. Also **re·cur·rent fe·ver**.

re·late, ri·lāt′, *v.t.*—*related, relating.* [Fr. *relater,* to state, to mention; L. *refero, relatum,* to refer, to bring back—*re-,* back, and *latus,* brought (as in *elate, oblate, translate*).] To tell; to narrate the particulars of; to form or show a connection or relationship.—*v.i.* To have reference to; to stand in some relation with, followed by *to.*—**re·lat·ed**, ri·lā′tid, *a.* Allied; connected by blood, alliance, or marriage; narrated; as, a *related* experience.—**re·lat·er**, *n.*—**re·lat·a·ble**, *a.*—**re·lat·ed·ness**, *n.*

re·la·tion, ri·lā′shan, *n.* [L. *relatio, relationis.*] Connection perceived or imagined between things; a certain position or connection of one thing with regard to another;

pl. the state or conditions of being related, as individual to individual, or nation to nation. Relationship by blood or marriage; kinship; a kinsman or kinswoman; the act of recounting that which is related or told; narrative; *law,* application of an act retroactively.—**in re·la·tion to,** with reference, respect, or regard to.

re·la·tion·al, ri·lā′sha·nal, *a.* Pertaining to kinship; showing relation; indicating or specifying syntactic relation, as the pronoun, preposition, and conjunction.

re·la·tion·ship, ri·lā′shan·ship″, *n.* The state of being related by blood, marriage, or other alliance; kinship; connection.

rel·a·tive, rel′a·tiv, *a.* [L. *relativus.*] Having relation to or bearing on something, close in connection; pertinent; relevant; not absolute or existing by itself; depending on or incident to something else; *gram.* applied to a word which relates to another word or words, called the antecedent.—*n.* Something considered in its relation to something else; a person connected by blood or affinity, esp. one allied by blood; a kinsman or kinswoman; *gram.* a word which relates to or represents another word, called its antecedent, esp. the pronouns *who, which,* and *that.*—**rel·a·tive·ly**, rel′a·tiv·lē, *adv.*—**rel·a·tive·ness**, *n.*

rel·a·tive hu·mid·i·ty, *n.* Humidity.

rel·a·tiv·ism, rel′a·ti·viz″um, *n. Philos.* the doctrine that knowledge or truth is relative and dependent upon time, place, and individual experience.—**rel·a·tiv·ist**, rel′a·ti·vist, *n.*—**rel·a·tiv·is·tic**, rel″a·ti·vis′tik, *a.*

rel·a·tiv·i·ty, rel″a·tiv′i·tē, *n.* The state or fact of being relative; relativeness; *philos.* existence only in relation to a thinking mind; *phys.* the theory, formulated mathematically by Albert Einstein, asserting the equivalence of mass and energy and the interdependence of space and time.

rel·a·tiv·i·ty of knowl·edge, *n. Philos.* the doctrine that all human knowledge is relative to the human mind, or that the mind can know only the effects which things produce upon it and not what the things themselves are; *psychol.* the doctrine that we can become conscious of objects only in their relations to one another.

re·la·tor, ri·lā′tèr, *n.* One who relates; narrator; *law,* an individual who furnishes information of an accusatory nature, and in whose behalf, or at whose instance, a writ is issued, as in the case of a quo warranto writ.

re·lax, ri·laks′, *v.t.* [L. *relaxo,* to relax—*re-,* back, and *laxo,* to loosen, < *laxus,* loose.] To slacken, make lax; to make less tense or rigid; to make less severe or rigorous; to lessen in strictness; to slacken or abate in respect to attention, effort, or labor; to relieve from strain, restraint, or worries.—*v.i.* To become loose, lax, or languid; to abate in severity; to become less tense or worried; to slacken in attention or effort; to unbend; to rest or seek recreation.—**re·laxed**, *a.*—**re·lax·ed·ly**, *adv.*—**re·lax·ed·ness**, *n.*—**re·lax·er**, *n.*

re·lax·ant, ri·lak′sant, *n. Med.* a drug that relaxes tension, esp. of muscles.—*a.*

re·lax·a·tion, rē″lak·sā′shan, *n.* [L. *relaxatio.*] The act of relaxing or state of being relaxed; a lessening of tension, effort, or severity; recreation; entertainment.

re·lay, rē·lā′, *v.t.*—*re-laid, re-laying.* To lay again, as paving blocks; to lay anew. Also **re·lay**.

re·lay, rē′lā, *n.* [O.Fr. *relais,* orig. reserves of dogs posted along the line of a hunt: cf. O.Fr. *relais,* what is left or remains (< *relaissier*), also *relaier,* put (a dog) in a relay.] A set of persons relieving each other or taking turns in any service or performance; a shift of workers; a relay race;

a fresh supply of anything, as food, horses, other animals, or men; *elect.* any device by which telephonic or telegraphic messages are sent to a greater distance or strengthened; *mach.* a servomotor.—*v.t.*—*relayed, relaying.* To station in relays, as along a route; to provide with or to replace by fresh relays; to carry forward by or as by relays; *elect.* to transmit by means of telephonic or telegraphic relay, or in the manner of such a relay.—*v.i. Elect.* to relay a message.

re·lay race, *n. Sports,* a race involving two or more teams or contestants, each contestant going a part of the distance, then being relieved by a teammate. Also *relay.*

re·lease, ri·lēs′, *v.t.*—*released, releasing.* [< O.Fr. *relesser, relaisser,* to release, to relinquish—prefix *re-,* and *laisser,* to leave, < L. *laxare,* to loosen, < *laxus,* loose, lax.] To set free from restraint or confinement; to liberate; to free from pain, grief, or worry; to free from obligation or penalty; to allow to be published, shown, or sold; *law,* to give up or let go, as a claim.—*n.* Liberation from restraint of any kind; liberation from confinement or oppression; relief from grief, pain, or burden; discharge from obligation or responsibility; the act of introducing to the public, as news, plays, films, or books; the material released, esp. to the press. *Law,* the waiving of a claim or right; a quitclaim or other document comprising the waiver. The escape of steam or other working fluid from an engine cylinder during the return stroke; that point in the return stroke at which such escape occurs; a mechanical device to start or stop a motor or machine; a device to fasten or unfasten an object or mechanism.—**re·leas·a·ble**, *a.*—**re·leas·er**, *n.*

re·lease, rē·lēs′, *v.t.*—*re-leased, re-leasing.* [Prefix *re-,* and *lease.*] To lease again or anew.

rel·e·gate, rel′e·gāt″, *v.t.*—*relegated, relegating.* [L. *relego, relegatum,* to banish—*re-,* back, and *lego,* to send.] To send away; to consign to some obscure destination or position; to assign, as to a class or order; to refer for performance or decision; to banish.—**rel·e·ga·tion**, *n.*

re·lent, ri·lent′, *v.i.* [Fr. *ralentir,* to slacken, to abate—prefix *re-,* back, and *lent,* L. *lentus,* pliant, slow.] To become less harsh, cruel, or obdurate; to soften in temper; to become more mild and sympathetic; to yield.

re·lent·less, ri·lent′lis, *a.* Unrelenting; harsh; merciless; implacable; pitiless; unremitting.—**re·lent·less·ly**, *adv.*—**re·lent·less·ness**, *n.*

rel·e·vant, rel′e·vant, *a.* [Fr. *relevant,* ppr. of *relever,* to relieve, to help or aid.] To the purpose; pertinent; applicable; bearing on the issue in question.—**rel·e·vance**, **rel·e·van·cy**, *n.*—**rel·e·vant·ly**, *adv.*

re·li·a·ble, ri·lī′a·bl, *a.* Such as may be relied on; worthy of being relied on; to be depended on for support; trustworthy; dependable.—**re·li·a·bil·i·ty**, **re·li·a·ble·ness**, *n.*—**re·li·a·bly**, *adv.*

re·li·ance, ri·lī′ans, *n.* The act of relying; the state of mind of one who relies; dependence; confidence; trust; a person or thing depended upon; basis for trust.

re·li·ant, ri·lī′ant, *a.* Having reliance; confident; self-reliant.—**re·li·ant·ly**, *adv.*

rel·ic, rel′ik, *n.* [Fr. *relique,* < L. *reliquiae,* remains.] That which is left after the loss, decay, or destruction of the rest; something preserved in remembrance, as a memento, souvenir, or keepsake. *Pl.* a remaining fragment; the body of a deceased person. *Eccles.* a bone or other part of saints or martyrs, some part of their garments, or the like, preserved and regarded with veneration. Any outmoded custom, practice, institution, or the like. Also *relique.*

rel·ict, rel'ikt, n. [O.Fr. relicte, a widow, L. relicta, fem. of relictus, pp. of relinquo, to leave.] Ecol. a species of a plant or animal existing anomalously in an area after the period in which it flourished. Archaic, a widow.—ri·likt', a. Geol. remaining after erosion.

re·lic·tion, ri·lik'shan, n. The permanent uncovering of land by recession of water; the land so uncovered.

re·lief, ri·lēf', n. [< Fr. relief, artistic raised work, < L. relever.] The removal of anything painful or burdensome by which some ease is obtained; ease from pain; alleviation; succor; that which mitigates or removes pain, grief, or other evil; help given to the poor in the form of food or money; release from duty by a substitute or substitutes; such a substitute. Sculp., arch. the projection or prominence of a figure above or beyond the ground or plane on which it is formed, being of three kinds: high relief, low relief, and middle or half relief, according to the degree of projection; a piece of artistic work in one or other of these styles; also relievo. Painting, the appearance of projection and solidity in represented objects; prominence or distinctness given to anything by something presenting a contrast to it. Phys. geog. the undulations or surface elevations of a country; feudal law, a payment which the heir of a tenant made to his lord for the privilege of succeeding to an estate.

re·lief map, n. A map portraying by means of contour lines the elevations of a land area.

re·lief pitch·er, n. Baseball. A pitcher who replaces another during a game; a pitcher whose regular function is relief duty. Also **re·lief·er, re·liev·er.**

re·li·er, ri·lī'ér, n. One who or something that relies or has reliance on another.

re·lieve, ri·lēv', v.t.—relieved, relieving. [O.E. releve, < Fr. relever, to set up again, to release, to assist, < L. relevare, to lift up again.] To remove or lessen, as anything that pains or distresses; to mitigate; alleviate, as pain, misery, or want; to free, wholly or partially, from pain, grief, anxiety, or anything considered to be an evil; to help, aid, or succor, as the poor or the sick; to release from a post or duty by substituting another person or party, or serving as the substitute; to free, as from a debt; to pass urine or excrement; as, to relieve oneself; to reduce monotony by the introduction of some variety; to make conspicuous; to set off by contrast; to give the appearance of projection to.—re·lieve of, to rob; as, to relieve one of his wallet.—re·liev·a·ble, a. —re·liev·er, ri·lē'vèr, n.

re·lie·vo, ri·lē'vō, ri·lyev'ō, n. pl. re·lie·vos. Sculp., arch. relief.

re·li·gion, ri·lij'an, n. [O.Fr. Fr. religion, < L. religio(n-); origin uncertain.] Recognition on the part of man of a controlling superhuman power entitled to obedience, reverence, and worship; the feeling or the spiritual attitude of those recognizing such a controlling power, with the manifestation of such feeling in conduct or life; the practice of sacred rites or observances; a particular system of faith in and worship of a Supreme Being or a god or gods; the state of life of the members of a religious order; a practice of devotion or conscientiousness, as: He has made a religion out of making money.

re·li·gion·ism, ri·lij'a·niz"um, n. Excessive inclination toward or exaggerated zeal in religion.—re·li·gion·ist, n.

re·li·gi·ose, ri·lij"ē·ōs', a. Sentimentally or artificially religious; extremely religious. —re·lig·i·os·i·ty, ri·lij"ē·os'i·tē, n.

re·li·gious, ri·lij'us, a. [O.Fr. Fr. religieur, < L. religiosus, < religio(n-), E. religion.] Of, pertaining to, concerned or connected with religion; imbued with or exhibiting religion; pious, devout, or godly; appropriate to religion or to sacred rites or observances; scrupulously faithful or conscientious.—n. pl. **re·li·gious.** A member of a religious order or congregation, as a monk, friar, or nun; anyone devoutly religious.—**re·li·gious·ly**, adv.—**re·li·gious·ness**, n.

re·line, rē·lin', v.t.—relined, relining. To line again; to put in a new lining.

re·lin·quish, ri·ling'kwish, v.t. [O.Fr. relinquir, relinquissant, < L. relinquo, to leave.] To give up, as the possession or occupancy of; to withdraw from; to abandon; to give up the pursuit or practice of; to renounce, as a right; release.—**re·lin·quish·er**, n.—**re·lin·quish·ment**, n.

rel·i·quar·y, rel'i·kwer"ē, n. pl. **rel·i·quar·ies.** [Fr. reliquaire, < L. reliquiae, relics.] A repository or container for relics, as a shrine or casket.

rel·ique, rel'ik, Fr. Re·lēk', n. pl. **rel·iques**, rel'iks, Fr. Re·lēk'. Archaic, relic.

re·liq·ui·ae, ri·lik'wē·ē", n. pl. [L., remnants, remains.] Relics; remains; fossil remains.

rel·ish, rel'ish, v.t. [O.Fr. relecher, lit. 'to lick again' < O.H.G. lecchon, to lick.] To like the taste or flavor of; to be pleased with or gratified by; to have a liking for; to give an agreeable taste or flavor to.—v.i. To have a pleasing taste; to have a flavor.—n. The sensation produced by anything pleasing to the palate; savor; taste; commonly a pleasing taste; inclination; liking; delight given by anything; characteristic quality, esp. that giving zest; a touch or trace; a pickled, spiced, or glazed seasoning served with the meat or fish course; an appetizer.—**rel·ish·a·ble**, a.

re·live, rē·liv', v.t.—relived, reliving. To live or experience over again.—v.i. To live again.

re·lo·cate, rē·lō'kāt, v.t., v.i.—relocated, relocating. To locate again; to move to a different place to live.—**re·lo·ca·tion**, rē"lō·kā'shan, n.

re·lu·cent, ri·lō'sent, a. [L. re-, back, and luceo, to shine.] Reflecting light; luminous; shining.

re·luct, ri·lukt', v.i. [L. reluctari (pp., reluctatus), < re-, back, and luctari, wrestle, struggle.] Archaic. To struggle against something; offer resistance or opposition; show reluctance.

re·luc·tance, ri·luk'tans, n. The state or quality of being reluctant; unwillingness; elect. the resistance of a magnetic circuit to magnetic flux, as shown in a ratio of the magnetic force to the magnetic flux in the circuit. Also **re·luc·tan·cy.**

re·luc·tant, ri·luk'tant, a. [L. relutans, reluctantis, ppr. of reluctor, to struggle—re-, back, and luctor, to struggle, lucta, a struggle.] Striving against doing something; unwilling; averse; granted unwillingly; as, reluctant obedience.—**re·luc·tant·ly**, adv.

rel·uc·tiv·i·ty, rel"uk·tiv'i·tē, n. Elect. specific reluctance, or the magnetic reluctance of a material compared with that of air, and equal to the circuit's reciprocal of permeability.

re·lume, ri·lōm', v.t.—relumed, reluming. [L. re-, again, and lumen, light.] To light anew; to illuminate again; rekindle. Also **re·lu·mine**, ri·lō'min.

re·ly, ri·lī', v.i.—relied, relying. [< Fr. relier, to bind, to attach—L. re-, back, and ligare, to bind (hence ligament): formerly often used with refl. pron. (to rely one's self upon).] To have confidence or trust; depend, with on or upon.

rem, rem, n. pl. **rem, rems.** [(r)oentgen (e)quivalent in (m)an.] A measure of absorbed radiation having an effect on human tissue equal to one roentgen of x-rays.

REM, rem, n. [(R)apid (E)ye (M)ovement.] A manifestation of dreaming during sleep.

re·main, ri·mān', v.i. [O.Fr. remaindre, L. remanere—re-, back, and manere, stay.] To continue in a place; to continue in an unchanged form or condition; to endure; to last; to stay behind after others have gone; to be left; to be left as not included, destroyed, or consumed; to be left as something still to be dealt with or done.—**re·mains**, n. pl. That which is left; that which is left of a human being after life is gone; a dead body; the unpublished literary works of a writer after his death; that which is left from previous ages or civilizations.

re·main·der, ri·mān'dèr, n. [An infinitive form; cf. rejoinder.] That which remains; anything left after the removal of the rest; arith. the quantity that is left after subtraction or division; law, the part of an estate which is left after the provisions of a will have been fulfilled; philately, an issue of demonetized stamps sold in quantities at a discount. A book in a publisher's stock sold at a reduction when sales have stopped or slowed.—a. Remaining; leftover.—v.t. To sell or get rid of as remainders.

re·man, rē·man', v.t.—remanned, remanning. To man again; to furnish with a fresh supply of men; to restore the manliness or courage of.

re·mand, ri·mand', ri·mänd', v.t. [Fr. remander, < L. re-, and mando, to commit to one's charge.] To send, call, or order back. Law, to return, as a case, to a lower court with instructions as to further disposition; to send back to jail, as after a preliminary or partial hearing, to await trial or resumption of the hearing.—n. The state of being remanded; the act of remanding; one who is remanded.

rem·a·nence, rem'a·nens, n. Elect. the magnetic induction left in a substance or circuit after the magnetomotive force present has become zero.

rem·a·nent, rem'a·nent, a. [L. remanens, remanentis, ppr. of remaneo.] Remaining or leftover.

re·mark, ri·märk', n. [Fr. remarque—re-, and marque.] A brief statement taking notice of something; an observation; a comment; the act of observing or taking notice.—v.t. To express or utter by way of comment or observation; to observe or to note in the mind.—v.i. To make a remark, comment, or observation, with on or upon.

re·mark·a·ble, ri·mär'ka·bl, a. Worthy of notice; extraordinary; unusual; noteworthy; conspicuous.—**re·mark·a·ble·ness**, n.—**re·mark·a·bly**, adv.

re·marque, ri·märk', n. [Fr.] Engraving. A distinguishing mark or peculiarity indicating a particular stage of a plate; a small sketch engraved on the margin of a plate, and usu. removed after a fixed number of early proofs have been taken; a proof or print having such a distinguishing feature.

re·mar·ry, rē·mar'ē, v.t., v.i.—remarried, remarrying. To marry again or a second time.—**re·mar·riage**, rē·mar'ij, n.

re·match, rē'mach, n. A match between opponents who competed against each other in a previous contest.

re·me·di·a·ble, ri·mē'dē·a·bl, a. Capable of being remedied.—**re·me·di·a·ble·ness**, n.—**re·me·di·a·bly**, adv.

re·me·di·al, ri·mē'dē·al, a. [L. remedialis.] Affording a remedy; intended to remedy; as, remedial measures; intended to correct deficiencies or improve skills in certain areas of learning; as, a remedial reading class.—**re·me·di·al·ly**, adv.

rem·e·di·less, rem'i·dē·lis, a. Not admitting a remedy; incurable; irreparable.—**rem·e·di·less·ly**, adv.

rem·e·dy, rem'i·dē, n. pl. **rem·e·dies.** [L. remedium, < re-, again, and mederi, heal: cf. *medic.*] Something that cures or relieves a disease or bodily disorder; a healing medicine, application, or treatment; something that corrects or removes an evil of any kind; a corrective. *Law*, legal redress; the legal means of enforcing a right, or preventing or redressing a wrong. *Coinage*, tolerance.—*v.t.*—*remedied, remedying.* To cure, heal, or relieve; to put right, or restore to the natural or proper condition; as, to *remedy* a matter; to counteract or remove; as, to *remedy* an evil.

re·mem·ber, ri·mem'bėr, *v.t.* [O.Fr. *remembrer, se remembrer,* < L.L. *rememorare*—L. *re-*, again, and *memorare,* to bring to mind, < *memor,* mindful.] To bring back to the mind or recall from memory; recollect; to hold in the mind purposefully; to maintain awareness of; as, to *remember* to keep an important appointment; to have in mind, as a person, for rewarding with a gift, tip, or bequest; as, to *remember* the doorman or mailman at Christmas; to mention in the sending of greetings; as: *Remember* me to your sister.—*v.i.* To have or make use of one's memory; to recollect.—**re·mem·ber·er**, *n.*

re·mem·brance, ri·mem'brans, *n.* [O.Fr. *remembrance.*] That which is remembered; a retained memory; something kept in mind; the condition of being remembered; the power or faculty of remembering; the limit of time over which the memory extends; a memorial; a keepsake; a gift given as a token of regard; *often pl.* warm greetings. **Re·mem·brance Day**, *n.* Brit., *Canadian,* a day corresponding to U.S. Veterans' Day and honoring those who served in World Wars I and II.

re·mem·branc·er, ri·mem'bran·sėr, *n.* One who reminds; something which serves as a reminder; a memento. (*Usu. cap.*) a judiciary officer in England who collects debts due the sovereign; formerly, a recording officer of the Exchequer in England.

re·mex, rē'meks, *n.* pl. **rem·i·ges**, rem'i·jēz". [N.L. use of L. *remex* (*remig-*), oarsman, < *remus,* oar.] *Ornith.* a flight feather.—**re·mig·i·al**, ri·mij'ē·al, *a.*

re·mil·i·ta·rize, rē·mil'i·ta·rīz", *v.t.*—*remilitarized, remilitarizing.* To reequip with armed forces.

re·mind, ri·mīnd', *v.t.* To put in mind; to cause to recollect or remember; as, to *remind* a person of his promise.—**re·mind·er**, *n.*

re·mind·ful, ri·mīnd'ful, *a.* Serving to remind; reminiscent; remembering or mindful.

rem·i·nisce, rem"i·nis', *v.i.*—*reminisced, reminiscing.* [Back-formation < *reminiscence.*] To indulge in reminiscence; recall past experiences.

rem·i·nis·cence, rem"i·nis'ens, *n.* [Fr. *réminiscence,* L. *reminiscentia,* < *reminiscor,* to recall to mind—*re-*, again, and *miniscor,* < root *men,* whence *mens,* the mind.] Recollection; that which is recollected or recalled to mind; something very similar to and suggestive of something else; *often pl.* a narration of past incidents within one's personal experience; *Platonic philos.* a recollection of the Ideas which were known by the soul in an earlier existence.

rem·i·nis·cent, rem"i·nis'ent, *a.* Calling to mind; suggestive, usu. followed by *of*; pertaining to reminiscence; given to reminiscing.—**rem·i·nis·cent·ly**, *adv.*

re·mise, ri·mīz', *v.t.*—*remised, remising.* [Fr., < *remettre,* L. *remitio.*] *Law.* To grant; surrender; release, as a claim.

re·miss, ri·mis', *a.* [L. *remissus,* relaxed, languid, not strict, pp. of *remitto*—*re-*, back, and *mitto,* to send.] Careless or negligent in performing duty or business; showing carelessness or negligence; lacking energy; languid.—**re·miss·ly**, *adv.*—**re·miss·ness**. *n.*

re·mis·si·ble, ri·mis'i·bl, *a.* Capable of being remitted or forgiven.—**re·mis·si·bly**, *adv.*

re·mis·sion, ri·mish'an, *n.* The act of remitting; diminution or cessation of intensity; abatement; forgiveness or pardon; a temporary subsidence of the force, violence, or symptoms of a disease or of pain. Also **re·mit·tal**, ri·mit'al.

re·mit, ri·mit', *v.t.*—*remitted, remitting.* [L. *remitto,* to send back, slacken, relax.] To transmit or send, as money, in payment; to refrain from exacting, as a payment or punishment; to pardon; to forgive, as sins; to relax; to abate; to allow to slacken; as, to *remit* vigilance; to send or give back; to put off; to reestablish; *law,* to send back, as a case, from one tribunal to another for further review; *rare,* to again put into custody.—*v.i.* To transmit money; to slacken; to become less intense for a time, as: The fever *remits* at a certain time every day.—*n. Law,* the transmission of a case from one tribunal to another for further judgment.—**re·mit·ment**, *n.*—**re·mit·ta·ble**, *a.*—**re·mit·ter**, *n.*

re·mit·tance, ri·mit'ans, *n.* The act of transmitting money, vouchers, or the like, in return or payment for goods purchased or services rendered; the amount remitted.

re·mit·tance man, *n.* One who lives abroad on remittances from home.

re·mit·tent, ri·mit'ent, *a.* [L. *remittens, remittentis,* ppr. of *remitto.*] Temporarily ceasing or abating; having remissions from time to time.—*n.* A remittent fever.—**re·mit·tent·ly**, *adv.*

rem·nant, rem'nant, *n.* [Contr. < *remanent.*] That which remains after the removal of the rest of a thing; the remaining piece of cloth after the rest is sold or used; a remaining trace or sign, as of a former time or condition; a scrap or fragment.—*a.*

re·mod·el, rē·mod'el, *v.t.*—*remodeled, remodeling, Brit. remodelled, remodelling.* To model or fashion anew; to reconstruct, as a home or other building.

re·mon·e·tize, rē·mon'i·tīz", rē·mun'i·tīz", *v.t.*—*remonetized, remonetizing.* [L. *re-*, again, and *moneta,* money.] To restore to circulation as money; as, to *remonetize* silver.—**re·mon·e·ti·za·tion**, rē·mon"e·ti·zā'shan, *n.*

re·mon·strance, ri·mon'strans, *n.* [O.Fr. *remonstrance.*] The act of remonstrating or expostulating; a strong statement of reasons against something.

re·mon·strant, ri·mon'strant, *a.* Expostulatory; remonstrating.—*n.*—**re·mon·strant·ly**, *adv.*

re·mon·strate, ri·mon'strāt, *v.i.*—*remonstrated, remonstrating.* [O.Fr. *remonstrer* (Fr. *remontrer*); L.L. *remonstro*—L. *re-*, again, and *monstro,* to show.] To exhibit or present strong reasons against an act, measure, or any course of proceedings; to expostulate.—*v.t.* To plead or say in opposition or protest.—**re·mon·stra·tion**, rē"mon·strā'shan, rem"on·strā'shan, *n.*—**re·mon·stra·tive**, ri·mon'stra·tiv, *a.*—**re·mon·stra·tive·ly**, *adv.*—**re·mon·stra·tor**, ri·mon'strā·tėr, *n.*

rem·o·ra, rem'ėr·a, *n.* [L., < *re-*, back, and *mora,* delay.] The suckfish, family *Echeneididae,* having a flattened, adhesive disk on the top of the head, by which it attaches itself firmly to other fishes or to the bottoms of vessels; any hindrance or delay.—**rem·or·id**, *a.*

re·morse, ri·mars', *n.* [L.L. *remorsus,* a biting again, < L. *remordeo, remorsum*—*re-*, again, and *mordeo,* to bite.] The keen pain or anguish excited by a sense of guilt; painful memory of wrongdoing.—**re·morse·ful**, ri·mars'ful, *a.*—**re·morse·ful·ly**, *adv.*—**re·morse·ful·ness**, *n.*

re·morse·less, ri·mars'lis, *a.* Without

remorse; cruel; pitiless.—**re·morse·less·ly**, *adv.*—**re·morse·less·ness**, *n.*

re·mote, ri·mōt', *a.*—*remoter, remotest.* [L. *remotus,* < *removeo,* to remove—*re-*, and *moveo, motum,* to move.] Distant in place; far off; distant in time, past or future; not directly producing an effect; not proximate; slight; inconsiderable; as, a *remote* resemblance; of a person, aloof or abstracted.—**re·mote·ly**, *adv.*—**re·mote·ness**, *n.*

re·mote con·trol, *n.* Control of a mechanical or other operation from a distance, esp. electronically, as the remote guiding of missiles.

re·mo·tion, ri·mō'shan, *n.* [L. *remotio(n-)*, < *removere,* E. *remove.*] The act of removing; removal.

re·mount, rē·mount', *v.t., v.i.* To mount again.—rē'mount", rē·mount', *n.* A fresh horse or horses to mount.

re·mov·a·ble, ri·mö'va·bl, *a.* Capable of being removed or obliterated.—**re·mov·a·bil·i·ty**, re·mov·a·ble·ness, ri·möv"a·bil'i·tē, *n.*—**re·mov·a·bly**, *adv.*

re·mov·al, ri·mö'val, *n.* A moving from one place to another; change of place or site; the act of displacing from an office or post; the act of removing; a dismissal.

re·move, ri·möv', *v.t.*—*removed, removing.* [O.Fr. *remouvoir,* < L. *removeo,* to remove —*re-*, and *moveo,* to move.] To shift from the position occupied; to put in another place in any manner; to take off, as clothing; to displace from an office, post, or position; to cause to leave, as a person or thing; to put an end to; to banish; to kill or assassinate; to make away with; to cut off.—*v.i.* To change place in any manner; to move from one place to another.—*n.* The act of removing; a removal; change of place; the distance or space by which anything is removed; an interval; stage; a step in any scale of gradation.—**re·mov·er**, ri·mö'vėr, *n.*

re·moved, ri·mövd', *a.* Changed in place; displaced from office; remote; separate from others in time, place, or relationship; as, a cousin twice *removed.*

re·mu·da, ri·mö'da, *Sp.* Re·mö'THä, *n.* A herd of horses out of which ranchhands chose their mounts or saddlehorses for the day.

re·mu·ner·ate, ri·mū'ne·rāt', *v.t.*—*remunerated, remunerating.* [L. *remunero, remuneratum*—*re-*, back, and *munus, muneris,* a present, gift.] To reward; to recompense; to pay an equivalent to for any service, loss, or sacrifice.—**re·mu·ner·a·bil·i·ty**, ri·mū"nėr·a·bil'i·tē, *n.*—**re·mu·ner·a·ble**, *a.*—**re·mu·ner·a·tor**, *n.*

re·mu·ner·a·tion, ri·mū"ne·rā'shan, *n.* The act of remunerating; what is given to remunerate; reward; compensation.

re·mu·ner·a·tive, ri·mū'ne·rā"tiv, ri·mū'nėr·a·tiv, *a.* Affording remuneration; yielding a sufficient return; profitable.—**re·mu·ner·a·tive·ly**, ri·mū'ne·rā"tiv·lē, ri·mū'nėr·a·tiv·lē, *adv.*—**re·mu·ner·a·tive·ness**, *n.*

ren·ais·sance, ren"i·säns', ren"i·zäns', ren'i·säns", ren'i·zäns", ri·nä'sans, *Fr.* Re·ne·säns', *n.* [Fr. regeneration or new birth—*re-*, again, and *naissance,* birth, L. *nascentia,* < *nascor, natus,* to be born.] The revival of anything which has long been in decay or extinct. (*Cap.*) the transitional movement in Europe from the Middle Ages to the modern world; the European revival of letters and arts in the 14th to 17th centuries; the time of that revival.—*a.* (*Cap.*) pertaining to the European Renaissance; of or pertaining to the styles of art and literature prevalent at that time.

re·nal, rēn'al, *a.* [L. *renalis,* < *ren,* pl. *renes,* the kidneys.] Pertaining to or located near the kidneys or reins.

Ren·ard, ren'ėrd, *n.* Reynard.

---

re·nas·cence, ri·nas'ens, *n*. The state of being renascent; (*cap*.) Renaissance.

re·nas·cent, ri·nas'ent, *a*. [L. *renascens*.] Rejuvenated; reborn.

ren·con·tre, ren·kon'tėr, *Fr*. RäN·kạN'tRe, *n*. [Fr.] A rencounter; an encounter.

ren·coun·ter, ren·koun'tėr, *n*. [Fr. *rencontre* = *re-encounter*.] A casual or chance meeting of persons; a meeting in opposition or contest; a debate; a duel; slight combat. Also *rencontre*.—*v.t*. To meet unexpectedly. —*v.i*. To have an unexpected meeting.

rend, rend, *v.t*.—*rent* or *rended*, *rending*. [O.E. *rendan*, *hrendan*, to tear, to rend = O.Fris. *renda*.] To separate into parts with force or sudden violence; to tear asunder; to split; to take away with violence; to tear away, used with *from*, *away*, or *off*; to affect, as the heart, with deep anguish or sorrow; to pierce with noise, as the air.— *v.i*. To be or to become rent or torn; to split something.

ren·der, ren'dėr, *v.t*. [Fr. *rendre*, to restore.] To give in return; to give or pay back; to give, often officially or in compliance with a request or duty; to submit or present for action or consideration; to furnish; to report; as, to *render* an account; to afford; to perform; to give for use or benefit; as, to *render* services; to make or cause to be; to convert; to invest with qualities; as, to *render* a fortress more secure; to translate from one language into another; to interpret or bring into full expression to others; to reproduce; as, to *render* a piece of music; to depict; to yield or surrender; to boil down and clarify; as, to *render* tallow; to apply, as a layer of plaster, to.—*v.i*. To yield or give way to force applied; to give one his due; *naut*. to pass freely through a block: said of a rope.—*n*. A return; a payment, esp. to a feudal lord; a coat of plaster applied directly to a surface.— **ren·der·a·ble**, *a*.—**ren·der·er**, *n*.

ren·dez·vous, rän'de·vö", rän'dā·vö", *Fr*. RäN·de·vö', *n. pl.* **ren·dez·vous**, rän'de·vöz", rän'dā·vöz", *Fr*. RäN·de·vö'. [Fr. *rendez-vous*, lit. 'render (or present) yourselves' (as at a place appointed).] An appointment or engagement made between two or more persons to meet at a fixed place and time; a meeting arranged by special appointment or engagement; a place appointed for meeting or assembling, esp. for the assembling of troops or ships; a meeting place, gathering place, or place of common resort.—*v.i*., *v.t*.—*rendezvoused*, *rendezvousing*, rän'de·vöd", rän'dā·vöd", rän'de·vö"ing, rän'dā·vö"ing. To assemble at a time or place previously appointed.

ren·di·tion, ren·dish'an, *n*. [L. *reddition*.] A rendering or giving the meaning of a word or passage; interpretation; translation; the act of reproducing or exhibiting artistically; *archaic*, surrender.

ren·dzi·na, ren·jē'na, *n*. [Pol.] An intrazonal soil type formed from chalk or marl in humid, grassy regions.

ren·e·gade, ren'e·gād", *n*. [Sp. *renegado*, Fr. *renégat*, L.L. *renegatus*, one who denies his religion—L. *re-*, back, and *nego*, *negatum*, to deny.] An apostate from a religious faith; one who deserts to an enemy or opposing party; a deserter. Also **ren·e·ga·do**, ren"e·gä'dō.—*a*. Traitorous; of or similar to a renegade.

re·nege, ri·nig', ri·neg', ri·nēg', *v.i*.— *reneged*, *reneging*. [L.L. *renego*.] To play a card of another suit when able and required by the game rules to follow suit; *colloq*. to fail to keep one's word or a promise.—*v.t. Archaic*. To deny; to renounce. —**re·neg·er**, *n*.

re·ne·go·ti·ate, rē"ni·gō'shē·āt", *v.t*., *v.i*. —*renegotiated*, *renegotiating*. To negotiate anew, esp. with a view to preventing the loss of profits, as a contract.—**re·ne·go··**

ti·a·ble, rē"ni·gō'shē·a·bl, *a*.—**re·ne··go·ti·a·tion**, *n*.

re·new, ri·nö', ri·nū', *v.t*. To make new again; to restore to former soundness, completeness, or perfection; to revive; to restore to a former state, or to a good state, after decay or impairment; to make again; as, to *renew* a treaty; to resume; to recommence; to continue by repeating; as, to *renew* a subscription; to begin again; to grant or furnish again, as a new loan; to replenish, as supplies.—*v.i*. To become new; to grow afresh; to begin again.— **re·new·a·bil·i·ty**, *n*.—**re·new·a·ble**, *a*. —**re·new·a·bly**, *adv*.—**re·new·er**, *n*.

re·new·al, ri·nö'al, ri·nū'al, *n*. An act or instance of renewing, the state of being renewed.

ren·i·form, ren'i·farm", rē'ni·farm", *a*. [L. *ren*, a kidney.] Having the form or shape of the kidney.

re·nig, ri·nig', *v.i*.—*renigged*, *renigging*. Renege.

re·nin, rē'nin, *n. Biochem*. a proteolytic enzyme of ischemic kidneys.

re·ni·tent, ri·nit'ent, ren'i·tent, *a*. [L. *renitens*, *renitentis*, ppr. of *renitor*—*re-*, back, and *nitor*, to struggle.] Resisting pressure; persistently opposed.—**re·ni··ten·cy**, **re·ni·tence**, *n*.

ren·net, ren'it, *n*. [Also written *runnet*, and formed < the verb to *run*, O.E. *renne*; *rinnan*, to run, *gerinnan*, to curdle or coagulate; cf. G. *rennen*, to run, to curdle, *rennse*, rennet; D. *rinnen*, to curdle.] The inner membrane of the calf's fourth stomach; the rennin-producing substance of the stomach; a derivation from this membrane, used to coagulate milk.

ren·nin, ren'in, *n*. A milk-curdling enzyme contained in the gastric juice of the calf, the active ingredient of prepared rennet.

re·nom·i·nate, rē·nom'i·nāt", *v.t*.—*renominated*, *renominating*. To nominate again or anew; to nominate for another term of office.—**re·nom·i·na·tion**, rē"nom·i·nā'shan, *n*.

re·nounce, ri·nouns', *v.t*.—*renounced*, *renouncing*. [Fr. *renoncer*, < L. *renuncio*.] To disown, disclaim, abjure, forswear; to repudiate; to cast off or reject.—*v.i. Cards*, to fail to follow the suit led.—*n. Cards*, an instance of renouncing.—**re·nounce·a·ble**, *a*.—**re·nounce·ment**, *n*.—**re·nounc·er**, *n*.

ren·o·vate, ren'o·vāt", *v.t*.—*renovated*, *renovating*. [L. *renovo*, *renovatum*.] To renew; to repair and render as good as new; to restore to freshness or to a good condition.—**ren·o·va·tion**, *n*.—**ren·o·va·tor**, *n*.

re·nown, ri·noun', *n*. [O.E. *renowne*, < Fr. *renom*, < L. *re-*, and *nomen*, a name.] Exalted reputation accruing from widespread knowledge of one's great achievements.—*v.t. Obs*. to make famous.

re·nowned, ri·nound', *a*. Famous; celebrated; eminent.

rens·se·laer·ite, ren'se·la·rīt", ren"se·lär'īt", *n*. [After Stephen Van *Rensselaer*, U.S. army officer.] A type of talc with a fine compact texture, worked into inkstands and other articles.

rent, rent, *n*. [Fr. *rente*, It. *rendita*, that which is rendered or given up, < L.L. *rendo*, for L. *reddo*, to give up.] Compensation paid at intervals to the owner of a property by the tenant or user; the amount paid. *Econ*. the return from cultivated land in excess of production costs; the yield from land as a production factor.—*v.t*. To grant the possession and enjoyment of for a certain rent; to let on lease; to take and hold on the payment of rent.—*v.i*. To be leased or let for rent.—**rent·a·ble**, rent'-a·bl, *a*. Capable of being rented.

rent, rent, *n*. [< pp. of *rend*.] An opening made by rending or tearing; a break or breach of relations, as between individuals.

rent·al, ren'tal, *n*. A schedule or account of rents; a sum paid or received as rent; the act or an instance of renting; the thing rented.—*a*.

rent·al li·brar·y, *n*. A library which lends books for a small fee. Also **lend·ing li·brar·y**.

rent·er, ren'tėr, *n*. The lessee or tenant who pays rent; the owner who lets his property.

ren·tier, RäN·tyā', *n. pl.* **ren·tiers**, RäN·tyä'. [Fr., < *rente*.] *Fr*. one who has a fixed income, as from lands or stocks.

re·num·ber, rē·num'bėr, *v.t*. To number anew; to change the numeration or pagination of.

re·nun·ci·a·tion, ri·nun"sē·ā'shan, ri·nun"shē·ā'shan, *n*. The act of renouncing or repudiating; an instance of this.— **re·nun·ci·a·tive**, **re·nun·ci·a·to·ry**, ri·nun'sē·a·tŏr"ē, ri·nun'shē·a·tŏr"ē, *a*.

re·oc·cu·py, rē·ok'ū·pī", *v.t*.—*reoccupied*, *reoccupying*. To occupy anew.—**re·oc·cu·pa·tion**, rē"ok·ū·pā'shan, *n*.

re·o·pen, rē·ō'pen, *v.t*., *v.i*. To open again; to resume, as a discussion; to begin anew, as a session or a trial.

re·or·der, rē·ar'dėr, *v.t*. To order again or anew; *com*. to give a reorder for.—*n. Com*. an order for additional goods of the same kind as previously ordered, given to the same person or dealer.

re·or·gan·i·za·tion, rē"ar·ga·ni·zā'shan, *n*. The act or process of reorganizing, or the state of being reorganized; the thorough reconstruction or rehabilitation of a corporation either after it has failed and gone into receivership or before such, failure occurs.

re·or·gan·ize, rē·ar'ga·nīz", *v.t*., *v.i*.— *reorganized*, *reorganizing*. To organize anew.

re·or·i·ent, rē·ōr'ē·ent", rē·ar'ē·ent", *v.i*., *v.t*. To orient anew.

rep, **repp**, rep, *n*. [Perh. < *rib*.] A dress fabric having a ribbed or corded appearance, the ribs being transverse.

re·pair, ri·pâr', *v.t*. [Fr. *réparer*, < L. *reparo*—*re-*, again, and *paro*, to get or make ready.] To restore to a sound or good state after decay, injury, dilapidation, or partial destruction; to make amends for, as for an injury, by an equivalent; to give indemnity for.—*n. Often pl*. restoration to a sound or good state; the part that is repaired, or added while repairing. Reparation; condition as regards repairing; as, a building in good or bad *repair*.—**re·pair·a·ble**, *a*.—**re·pair·er**, ri·pâr'ėr, *n*.

re·pair, ri·pâr', *v.i*. [O.Fr. *repairer*, < L.L. *repatriare*.] To go; to betake oneself; to resort.—*n*. The act of betaking oneself to any place; a haunt; a resort.

re·pair·man, ri·pâr'man", ri·pâr'mạn, *n. pl.* **re·pair·men**, ri·pâr'men", ri·pâr'men. A man whose trade is making repairs.

re·pand, ri·pand', *a*. [L. *repandus*, bent backward, turned up.] *Bot*. having an uneven, slightly sinuous margin, as a leaf.

rep·a·ra·ble, rep'ėr·a·bl, *a*. [L. *reparabilis*.] Capable of being repaired or corrected.

rep·a·ra·tion, rep"a·rā'shan, *n*. The act of repairing; repair; what is done to repair a wrong; *pl*. indemnification for loss or damage, as demanded of a country defeated in war.

re·par·a·tive, ri·par'a·tiv, *a*. Capable of effecting repair; pertaining to reparation.

rep·ar·tee, rep"ėr·tē', rep"ėr·tā', *n*. [Fr. *repartie*—*re-*, back, and *partir*, < L. *partire*, to share, part, < *pars*, *partis*, a part.] A smart, ready, and witty reply; conversation distinguished by witty responses.

re·par·ti·tion, rē"pär·tish'an, rē"pėr·tish'an, *n*. Distribution; allotment; a fresh partition or division.

---

ch- chain, G. na*ch*t;   **th-** T*H*en, thin;   **w-** wig, hw as sound in whig;   **z-** zh as in azure, zeal.   *Italicized vowel* indicates schwa sound.

re·pass, rē·pas', rē·päs', *v.t., v.i.* To pass again; to pass back.—**re·pas·sage**, rē·-pas'ij, *n.*

re·past, ri·past', ri·päst', *n.* [O.Fr. *repast*, Fr. *repas*, < L. *re-*, again, and *pasco*, *pastum*, to feed.] A meal; food comprising a meal; food.

re·pa·tri·ate, rē·pā'trē·āt', *v.t.*—*repatriated, repatriating.* [L. *repatrio, repatriatum*—*re-*, again, and *patria*, one's country.] To return, as a war prisoner or refugee, to his own country.—rē·pā'trē·it, *n.* A person who has been repatriated.—**re·pa·tri·a·tion**, *n.*

re·pay, ri·pā', *v.t.*—*repaid, repaying.* To pay back, as money; to make some return to; to make return or requital for; as, to *repay* kindness with surliness; to return, as a visit.—*v.i.* To make return or repayment.—**re·pay·a·ble**, *a.*—**re·pay·ment**, *n.*

re·peal, ri·pēl', *v.t.* [Fr. *rappeler*—*re-*, back, and *appeler*, L. *appello*, to call upon, speak to.] To rescind, as a law or statute; to revoke; to abrogate by an authoritative act.—*n.* The act of repealing; revocation.—**re·peal·a·ble**, *a.*—**re·peal·er**, *n.*

re·peat, ri·pēt', *v.t.* [O.Fr. *repeter*, (Fr. *répéter*), < L. *repetere*, (pp. *repetitus*), attack again, seek again, return to, repeat, < *re-*, and *petere*, fall on, seek.] To say or utter again, or iterate; as, to *repeat* a word for emphasis; to say or utter in reproducing the words of another; as, to *repeat* a sentence after the teacher; to reproduce, as utterances or sounds; to do, make, perform, or execute again; as, to *repeat* an action; to tell, as a secret, to another or others; to go through or undergo again; to produce or present again, or reproduce; to say over again from memory.—*v.i.* To do or say something again; to recur; to strike the hour or division of an hour, as a watch or clock; to cause indigestion, as: The garlic bread may *repeat* on him. To illegally vote more than once at an election.—*n.* The act or an act of repeating; repetition; something repeated; a duplicate or reproduction of something; a decorative figure or pattern repeated uniformly over the surface of cloth or paper. *Mus.* a passage to be repeated; a sign, as a vertical arrangement of dots, calling for the repetition of a passage. *TV, radio*, a program previously broadcast.—**re·peat·a·bil·i·ty**, ri·pēt″a·bil′i·tē, *n.*—**re·peat·a·ble**, *a.*

re·peat·ed, ri·pē'tid, *a.* Done, made, or uttered again and again.—**re·peat·ed·ly**, *adv.*

re·peat·er, ri·pē'tėr, *n.* One who or that which repeats. *Horol.* a watch or clock which may be made to strike the hour and sometimes a part of an hour. A repeating firearm; a repeating decimal; a student who repeats a previously failed course; a person repeatedly or previously imprisoned; one who violates election laws by voting two or more times in a single election; a device which automatically amplifies, repeats, forwards, or reshapes electromagnetic signals or telegraphic messages.

re·peat·ing dec·i·mal, *n.* A decimal number in which a certain figure or series of figures repeats itself ad infinitum, as 6.4131313 . . . .

re·peat·ing fire·arm, *n.* A gun having the capability of discharging successive bullets without reloading.

re·pe·chage, re·pe″shäzh', *n. Sports*, an additional trial heat, esp. in Olympic rowing races, in which losers of the first round of races can attempt to enter the semifinals by winning first or second place.

re·pel, ri·pel', *v.t.*—*repelled, repelling.* [L. *repello*—*re-*, back, and *pello*, to drive, as in *expel, compel, explusion*, etc.] To drive back; to force away; discourage; to reject; to check the advance of; to repulse; to

create aversion or distaste in, as: That smell *repels* me. To encounter with effectual resistance; to resist absorption of or mixture with; to resist or oppose successfully, as an argument.—*v.i.* To cause repugnance or aversion; to act with force in opposition.—**re·pel·ler**, *n.*—**re·pel·len·cy**, *n.*

re·pel·lent, ri·pel'ent, *a.* Having the effect of repelling; able or tending to repel or drive off; repulsive; deterring.—*n.* That which repels; a substance, as a waterproofing agent, used on fabric; a substance that wards off insects; a medicine which reduces swelling.—**re·pel·lent·ly**, *adv.*

re·pent, ri·pent', *v.i.* [Fr. *repentir*—*se repentir*, to repent—L. *re-*, and *paenitēre*, to repent, < *paena*, pain.] To feel sorrow, remorse, or regret for one's past conduct; to be penitent; to have a change of mind about a past action, usu. with *of*; as, to *repent of* a rash decision; to experience such contrition as to amend one's way of life.—*v.t.* To remember with compunction or self-reproach; to feel remorse on account of; as, to *repent* cruel words.—**re·pent·ance**, ri·pen'tans, *n.*—**re·pent·er**, *n.*—**re·pent·ing·ly**, *adv.*

re·pent, ri·pent', *a.* [L. *repens, repentis*, ppr. of *repo*, to creep.] *Bot.* having a stem that grows along the ground and sends out roots at the nodes. *Zool.* creeping; reptant.

re·pent·ant, ri·pen'tant, *a.* Experiencing or showing repentance; penitent.—**re·pent·ant·ly**, *adv.*

re·peo·ple, rē·pē'pl, *v.t.*—*repeopled, repeopling.* To people anew; to restock with settlers.

re·per·cus·sion, rē″pėr·kush'an, *n.* [L. *repercussio(n-).*] The act of driving back; the state of being driven back by a resisting body; rebounding or recoil; reverberation or echo; a reaction; an indirect or unexpected consequence or result; *mus.* in a fugue, the reetrance of subject and answer following an episode or development.—**re·per·cus·sive**, rē″pėr·kus'iv, *a.*

rep·er·toire, rep'ėr·twär', rep'ér·twar″, *n.* [Fr. *répertoire*.] A list of dramas, operas, or other works which can be performed by a dramatic, operatic, or other company or person; those pieces, parts, or songs that are usu. performed by an actor, vocalist, or other artist.

rep·er·to·ry, rep'ėr·tōr″ē, rep'ér·tạr″ē, *n.* pl. **rep·er·to·ries**. [L. *repertorium*, < *reperio*, to find again—*re-*, again, and *pario*, to produce.] A repertoire; a repository, store, or collection of things; the presentation of plays alternately or in succession in one season.

rep·e·tend, rep'i·tend", rep″i·tend', *n.* [L. *repetendum*, a thing to be repeated.] That which is repeated, as a word, phrase, or musical note; *math.* that part of a repeating decimal which recurs continually.

rep·e·ti·tion, rep″i·tish'an, *n.* The act of repeating or saying over; a reciting or rehearsing; something said, done, or experienced a second time; that which is repeated; a copy or replica.—**rep·e·ti·tious**, rep″i·tish'us, *a.* Containing repetitions, esp. to the point of tedium.—**re·pet·i·tive**, ri·-pet'i·tiv, *a.* Of or marked by repetition.—**rep·e·ti·tious·ness, re·pet·i·tive·ness**, *n.*—**rep·e·ti·tious·ly, re·pet·i·tive·ly**, *adv.*

re·pine, ri·pin', *v.i.*—*repined, repining.* [O.E. *repoyne*, Fr. *repoindre*, to prick again—L. *re-*, again, and *pungo*, to prick, influenced by verb, to *pine*.] To fret; to feel a dispiriting discontent; to complain, followed by *at* or *against*.—**re·pin·er**, *n.*

re·place, ri·plās', *v.t.*—*replaced, replacing.* To put again in the former place; to repay or refund; to restore or return; to fill the place of; to be a substitute for.—**re·place·a·ble**, *a.*—**re·plac·er**, *n.*

re·place·ment, ri·plās'ment, *n.* The act of replacing; that which replaces; a substitute; a person assigned to a vacant position in the military. *Mineral.* the replacing of an edge or an angle by a new crystal surface; the process by which a new mineral, having a different chemical composition, forms in an old one.

re·play, rē·plā', *v.t.* To play over or again.—rē'plā, *n.* That which is replayed.

re·plead·er, rē·plē'dėr, *n. Law.* A second pleading; the right or privilege of pleading again.

re·plen·ish, ri·plen'ish, *v.t.* [O.Fr. *replenir, replenissant*, < L. *re-*, again, and *plenus*, full, < *pleo*, to fill.] To fill again after having been emptied or diminished; to fill completely; to restock.—**re·plen·ish·er**, *n.*—**re·plen·ish·ment**, *n.*

re·plete, ri·plēt', *a.* [L. *repletus*, pp. of *repleo*, to fill again.] Completely filled; abounding; sated, as with food or drink; thoroughly imbued or supplied, usu. followed by *with*; as, a scene *replete with* pathos.—**re·plete·ness**, *n.*—**re·ple·tive**, *a.*—**re·plete·ly, re·ple·tive·ly**, *adv.*

re·ple·tion, ri·plē'shan, *n.* The state of being replete or completely filled; surfeit; the fulfillment of a desire; satisfaction.

re·plev·in, ri·plev'in, *n.* [A.Fr. *replevine*, < O.Fr. *replevir*.] *Law.* The recovery of goods or chattels taken or detained, on security given that the case shall be tried at law and the goods returned in case of an adverse decision; the writ by which goods are so recovered, or the action arising therefrom.—*v.t.* To replevy.

re·plev·y, ri·plev'ē, *v.t.*—*replevied, replevying.* [O.Fr. *replevir*.] *Law.* To recover possession of, as goods, upon giving surety to try the right to them in court; to take back by writ of replevin.—*n.*—**re·plev·i·a·ble, re·plev·i·sa·ble**, ri·plev'ē·a·bl, ri·plev'i·sa·bl, *a.*

rep·li·ca, rep'li·ka, *n.* [It. *replica*, a reply, a repetition—L. *re-*, back, and *plica*, a fold.] A copy of a picture or piece of sculpture made by the original artist; any reproduction or copy.

rep·li·cate, rep'li·kit, *a.* Folded back on itself, as a leaf. Also **rep·li·cat·ed**, rep'li·kā″tid.—rep'li·kāt, *v.t.*—*replicated, replicating.* To fold or bend back; to reproduce or copy; to say in reply.

rep·li·ca·tion, rep″li·kā'shan, *n.* A reply or rejoinder, esp. a reply to an answer. *Law*, the reply of the plaintiff or complainant to the defendant's plea or answer. Reverberation or echo; a copy; a reproduction or copy; the repetition of an experiment to reduce the probability of error.

re·ply, ri·pli', *v.i.*—*replied, replying.* [O.Fr. *replier* (Mod.Fr. *répliquer*), to reply, < L. *replico*, to fold back, to reply—*re-*, back, and *plico*, to fold.] To make answer in words or writing, as to something said or written by another; to respond; to answer by deeds, as to meet an attack by fitting action; *law*, to give an answer to the defendant.—*v.t.* To say or return in answer, often followed by a noun clause, as: He *replied* that he would go.—*n.* pl. **re·plies**. That which is said, written, or performed in answer.—**re·pli·er**, *n.*

re·port, ri·pōrt', ri·part', *v.t.* [Fr. *reporter*, to carry back; < L. *reportare*, to carry back.] To bear or bring back, as an answer; to relate, as facts or discoveries; to give an account of; to tell, esp. publicly; to give an official or formal account or statement of; to lay a charge or make a disclosure against, as: I will *report* you.—*v.i.* To make a statement of facts; to discharge the office of a reporter; to go or present oneself, as: *Report* to the office in ten minutes.—*n.* An account brought back; a statement of facts given in reply to inquiry; a news account; a story circulated; rumor; fame; repute; public character; as, a man of good *report*; an account of a judicial decision or of a case argued and determined in a court of law; an official statement of facts; an account of the proceedings of a legislative assembly or other meeting, intended for publication; the sound of an explosion; a loud noise; as, the *report* of a gun.—**re·port·- a·ble**, *a*.

re·port·age, ri·pôr'tij, ri·par'tij, re·pôr'- täzh', re·par·täzh', *n*. The procedure or act of news reporting; a written report of directly observed or carefully researched events.

re·port card, *n*. A report or written evaluation of a student's scholastic achievement, issued periodically by a school to a student's parents or legal guardian.

re·port·ed·ly, ri·pôr'tid·lē, *adv*. According to rumor or report.

re·port·er, ri·pôr'tėr, ri·par'tėr, *n*. One who reports; a member of a newspaper staff whose duty is to give an account of public events; one who prepares reports of court proceedings for publication.—**rep·- or·to·ri·al**, rep"ėr·tōr'ē·al, rep"ėr·tar'- ē·al, rē"pôr·tōr'ē·al, rē"pôr·tar'ē·al, re"par·tōr'ē·al, rē"par·tar'ē·al, *a*.—**rep·- or·to·ri·al·ly**, *adv*.

re·pose, ri·pōz', *v.t.*—*reposed, reposing*. [M.E. *reposen*.] To put, as confidence or trust, in a person or thing; to place under the management or control of another; *archaic*, to deposit.

re·pose, ri·pōz', *v.i.*—*reposed, reposing*. [O.Fr. Fr. *reposer*, < M.L. *repausare*, < L. *re-*, again, and *pausare*, halt, cease, L.L. rest: cf. *pose*.] To lie at rest; to rest from exertion or toil; to lie, as in state or in death; to be at peace or tranquil; to lie or rest on something; to depend or rely on a person or thing.—*v.t.* To lay to rest; rest; refresh by rest: often used reflexively.—*n*. [O.Fr. Fr. *repos*.] The state of reposing or resting; rest; sleep; peace or tranquillity; dignified calmness, as of manner; composure; poise; absence of movement or animation.—**re·pos·al**, ri·pō'zal, *n*.

re·pose·ful, ri·pōz'ful, *a*. Full of repose; calm; quiet.—**re·pose·ful·ly**, *adv*.—**re·- pose·ful·ness**, *n*.

re·pos·it, ri·poz'it, *v.t.* [L. *repono, repositum*—*re-*, back, and *pono*, to place.] To store or put away; to lodge, as for safety; deposit; to replace.

re·po·si·tion, rē'po·zish'an, rep"o·zish'- an, *n*. The act of repositing or putting away; a surgical replacement.

re·pos·i·tor·y, ri·poz'i·tōr'ē, ri·poz'i·- tar"ē, *n*. pl. **re·pos·i·tor·ies**. [L. *repositorium*.] A place where things are, or may be, deposited for safety, preservation, or sale; a depository; a storehouse or warehouse; a place of burial or entombment; sepulcher; a person entrusted with confidences.

re·pos·sess, rē"po·zes', *v.t.* To possess again, esp. for default of payment; to restore ownership or possession to.— **re·pos·ses·sion**, rē"po·zesh'an, *n*.

re·pous·sé, re·pö·sā', *a*. [Fr., pp. of *repousser*, push back, < *re-* (< L. *re-*), back, and *pousser*, E. *push*.] Raised in relief, as a design on thin metal, by hammering on the reverse side; ornamented or made in this manner.—*n*. The technique of forming repoussé patterns; the work produced in this manner.

rep·re·hend, rep"ri·hend', *v.t.* [L. *reprehendo*.] To charge with a fault; to chide sharply; to reprove; to blame; to censure.

rep·re·hen·si·ble, rep"ri·hen'si·bl, *a*. Deserving to be reprehended or censured;

deserving reproof.—**rep·re·hen·si·ble·- ness**, *n*.—**rep·re·hen·si·bly**, *adv*.

rep·re·hen·sion, rep"ri·hen'shan, *n*. [L. *reprehensio*.] The act of reprehending; reproof; censure; blame.—**rep·re·hen·- sive**, *a*.—**rep·re·hen·sive·ly**, *adv*.

rep·re·sent, rep"ri·zent', *v.t.* [Fr. *représenter*, < L. *repraesento*.] To exhibit the image or counterpart of; to typify; to portray by pictorial or sculptured art; to act the part of, as in a play; to personate; to construct mentally; to bring before the mind; to give an account of; to describe; to speak and act with authority on behalf of, as a foreign diplomat or member of a legislative body; to be a substitute or agent for; as, to *represent* the owners; to serve as a sign or symbol of, as: Words *represent* ideas or things.—**rep·re·sent·- a·ble**, *a*.—**rep·re·sent·er**, *n*.

rep·re·sen·ta·tion, rep"ri·zen·tā'shan, *n*. The act of representing; the state or condition of being represented; the acting or speaking for an individual or a group, such as a company or a constituency, by an authorized person or persons; the fact or system of being represented by such agents or spokesmen; such representatives collectively; that which represents or portrays, as a picture or statue; a dramatic performance; a mental construct; a statement of arguments or facts for the purpose of remonstrance or protest.—**rep·re·sen·- ta·tion·al**, *a*.

rep·re·sen·ta·tion·al·ism, rep"ri·zen·- tā'sha·na·liz"um, *n*. *Philos*. the epistemological doctrine that ideas, rather than the real objects they represent, are the bases of knowledge. *Paint*. the practice of representing objects as they appear to the eye.— **rep·re·sen·ta·tion·al·ist**, *n*.

rep·re·sent·a·tive, rep"ri·zen'ta·tiv, *a*. Fitted to represent, portray, or typify; acting as a substitute for another or others; pertaining to or characterized by representationalism; performing a function for another; representing a citizenry or constituency; as, a *representative* congress; pertaining to or based on the principle of government by representation; typical of a kind, class, or group.—*n*. One who or that which represents; someone or something that exemplifies a class, kind, or quality; that by which anything is represented; something standing for something else; an agent, deputy, or substitute who takes the place of another or others, being invested with his or their authority; a member of the U.S. House of Representatives or the lower house of a state in the U.S.; *law*, one that stands in the place of another as heir. —**rep·re·sent·a·tive·ly**, *adv*.—**rep·re·- sent·a·tive·ness**, *n*.

re·press, ri·pres', *v.t.* [Prefix *re-*, and *press*, L. *reprimo, repressum*.] To press back or down effectually; to crush, quell, or subdue, as rebellion; to check or control, as desires; to restrain; *psychoanal*. to reject from consciousness, as fearful ideas or impulses.—**re·press·i·ble**, *a*.—**re·pres·- sive**, *a*.—**re·pres·sor, re·press·er**, *n*.

re-press, rē'pres', *v.t.* To press again.

re·pressed, ri·prest', *a*. Characterized by repression; affected by restraint.

re·pres·sion, ri·presh'an, *n*. The act of repressing, restraining, or subduing; repressed state or condition; check; restraint. *Psychoanal*. the process of repressing; that which is repressed.

re·prieve, ri·prēv', *n*. [< O.Fr. *reprover, repruver*, to blame, condemn, < L. *reprovare*, to reject, condemn, meaning orig. the rejection of a sentence already passed.] The suspension of the execution of a sentence; a warrant or authorization for this; respite; temporary ease or relief.—*v.t.*— *reprieved, reprieving*. To grant a reprieve or

respite to; to suspend or delay the execution of; to provide temporary relief to.

rep·ri·mand, rep'ri·mand", rep'ri·mand", *n*. [Fr. *réprimande*, < L. *reprimenda*, a thing to be checked or repressed, < *reprimo, repressum*, to repress.] A severe reproof; a sharp or formal rebuke; reprehension.— *v.t.* To reprove severely; to reprehend publicly or officially.

re·print, rē·print', *v.t.* To print again; to print a second or new edition of.—rē'- print", *n*. A verbatim reproduction of a printed work.—**re·print·er**, *n*.

re·pris·al, ri·prī'zal, *n*. [Fr. *représaille*, < It. *rappresaglia*, < L.L. *reprisaliae*, < L. *reprehendo*, to take again; cf. *prize*, a capture, which is also < L. *prehendo*.] The seizure of anything from an enemy as retaliation or indemnification; that which is so taken; any taking by way of retaliation; an act of force done in retaliation.

re·prise, ri·prīz', re·prēz', *n*. [O.Fr. Fr. *reprise*, < *reprendre*, take back.] Usu. pl., *law*, an annual deduction, duty, or payment out of a manor or estate, as an annuity, ri·prīz'. *Mus*. a repetition, esp. a return to the first theme or subject, ri·prīz', re·prēz'. —*v.t.*—*reprised, reprising*. *Mus*. To repeat; to return to.

re·pro, rē'prō, *n*. pl. **re·pros**. *Colloq*. reproduction proof.

re·proach, ri·prōch', *v.t.* [Fr. *reprocher*, O.Fr. *reprochier*, Pr. *repropchar*, to reproach, < L.L. *repropiare*, < L. *re-*, back, and *prope*, near; lit. to bring near or set before.] To charge with a fault; to rebuke; to censure; to upbraid; to bring disgrace to. —*n*. An expression of censure or blame; rebuke; blame for something considered reprehensible; source of discredit; disgrace, as: He was a *reproach* to his family. Object of contempt, scorn, or derision.— **re·proach·a·ble**, *a*.—**re·proach·er**, *n*.— **re·proach·ing·ly**, *adv*.

re·proach·ful, ri·prōch'ful, *a*. Containing or expressing reproach or censure; as, a *reproachful* glance.—**re·proach·ful·ly**, *adv*.—**re·proach·ful·ness**, *n*.

rep·ro·bate, rep'ro·bāt", *a*. [L. *reprobatus*, disapproved, rejected, pp. of *reprobo*—*re-*, denoting reverse, and *probo*, to approve.] Unprincipled; morally depraved; profligate; *theol*. excluded by God from salvation.—*n*. One who is profligate, depraved, or wicked; *theol*. a person excluded by God from salvation.—*v.t.*—*reprobated, reprobating*. [L. *reprobo, reprobatum*.] To disapprove or condemn; to reject; *theol*. of God, to abandon or condemn.—**rep·ro·ba·tion**, rep"ro·bā'shan, *n*.—**rep·ro·ba·tive**, rep'- ro·bā"tiv, *a*.

re·proc·essed, rē·pros'est, *a*. Treated and remade after manufacture but before consumer use, as wool or iron scraps.

re·pro·duce, rē"pro·dōs', rē"pro·dūs', *v.t.* —*reproduced, reproducing*. To produce again or anew, as music on wire or tape. *Biol*. to produce, as offspring, sexually or asexually; to produce again, as an organ, by regeneration; to foster the reproduction of, as plants or animals. To portray or represent again; to bring again to the memory or imagination.—*v.i.* To bear or produce offspring.—**re·pro·duc·er**, *n*.—**re·pro·- duc·i·bil·i·ty**, *n*.—**re·pro·duc·i·ble**, *a*.

re·pro·duc·tion, rē"pro·duk'shan, *n*. The act or process of reproducing. That which is produced or presented anew; a copy. *Biol*. the process by which a plant or animal gives rise to another of its kind, perpetuating the species.

re·pro·duc·tion proof, *n*. *Print*. a proof of special fineness and accuracy, usu. on enamel paper, suitable for making a printing plate photographically. Also **re·- pro proof, re·pro.**

re·pro·duc·tive, rē"pro·duk'tiv, *a*. Pertaining to reproduction; tending to reproduce.—**re·pro·duc·tive·ly**, *adv.*—**re·pro·duc·tive·ness, re·pro·duc·tiv·i·ty,** *n.*

re·proof, ri·prööf′, *n.* The expression of blame or censure; a reproving; blame; censure for a fault; reprimand; rebuke.

re·prove, ri·prööv′, *v.t.*—*reproved, reproving.* [Fr. *réprouver,* to blame, to censure; O.Fr. *reprover,* < L. *reprobare.*] To charge with a fault; censure; rebuke; to express disapproval of; as, to *reprove* someone for his sins.—**re·prov·er,** *n.*—**re·prov·ing·ly,** *adv.*

rep·tant, rep′tant, *a.* [L. *reptans (reptant-),* ppr. of *reptare,* freq. of *repere,* creep.] Creeping or crawling, as animals; repent, as plants.

rep·tile, rep′til, rep′til, *n.* [Fr. *reptile,* < L. *reptilis,* creeping, < *repo, reptum,* to creep; akin to *serpo,* to creep.] Any of the air-breathing, cold-blooded vertebrates belonging to the class *Reptilia,* as snakes, lizards, and alligators; an animal that moves on its belly, or by means of short legs; a crawling creature; a groveling, vile, or mean person.—*a.* Of or like a reptile; groveling; low; mean; vile.—**rep·til·i·an,** rep·til′e·an, rep·til′yan, *a.* Reptile.—*n.* A reptile.

re·pub·lic, ri·pub′lik, *n.* [Fr. *république,* L. *respublica—res,* an affair, interest, and *publica,* fem. of *publicus,* public.] A state or other political unit in which the supreme power is vested in the whole voting community which elects, indirectly or directly, representatives to exercise the power; any group of persons with a common cause.

re·pub·li·can, ri·pub′li·kan, *a.* Pertaining to or having the character of a republic; consonant with the principles of a republic; (*cap.*), *politics,* pertaining or relating to the Republican party.—*n.* One who favors or prefers a republican form of government; (*cap.*), *politics,* a member of the Republican party.

re·pub·li·can·ism, ri·pub′li·ka·niz″um, *n.* Republican system of government; republican principles; (*cap.*), *politics,* principles and policies of the Republican party.—**re·pub·li·can·ize,** ri·pub′li·ka·nīz″, *v.t.*—*republicanized, republicanizing.*

re·pub·li·ca·tion, rē″pub·li·kā′shan, *n.* The act of publishing again; something published again, as a book.—**re·pub·lish,** *v.t.*—**re·pub·lish·er,** *n.*

re·pu·di·ate, ri·pū′dē·āt″, *v.t.*—*repudiated, repudiating.* [L. *repudio, repudiatum,* to divorce, to cast off, < *repudium,* a casting off, a divorce.] To reject as not valid or not binding; to cast away or disown; to disavow; to refuse to acknowledge or pay, as a debt.—**re·pu·di·a·tive,** *a.*—**re·pu·di·a·tor,** *n.*

re·pu·di·a·tion, ri·pū″dē·ā′shan, *n.* [L. *repudiatio.*] The act of repudiating; state or condition of being repudiated; rejection; refusal on the part of a government to pay debts.

re·pugn, ri·pūn′, *v.t., v.i. Archaic,* to oppose.

re·pug·nance, ri·pug′nans, *n.* [Fr. *répugnance;* L. *repugnantia,* < *repugno,* to resist —*re-,* against, and *pugno,* to fight.] The state of being opposed or of feeling aversion; a feeling of strong dislike or objection; inconsistency or incongruity. Also **re·pug·nan·cy.**

re·pug·nant, ri·pug′nant, *a.* [L. *repugnans, repugnantis,* ppr. of *repugno.*] Highly distasteful; offensive; objectionable; contrary, as in character; standing or being in opposition.—**re·pug·nant·ly,** *adv.*

re·pulse, ri·puls′, *v.t.*—*repulsed, repulsing.* [L. *repello, repulsum—re-,* back, and *pello,* to drive.] To repel; to drive back; to refuse, reject, or rebuff by discourtesy or coldness. —*n.* The condition of being repelled or

driven back by force; the act of driving back; a rejection; refusal; denial.

re·pul·sion, ri·pul′shan, *n.* [L. *repulsio.*] The act of repulsing or repelling; the condition of being repelled; a feeling of repugnance or aversion; *phys.* the action which two bodies exert upon one another which tends to increase their distance from one another.

re·pul·sive, ri·pul′siv, *a.* Causing aversion, distaste, or disgust; acting so as to repel; tending to deter or forbid approach or familiarity; repellent; forbidding.—**re·pul·sive·ly,** *adv.*—**re·pul·sive·ness,** *n.*

re·pur·chase, rē·pur′chas, *v.t.*—*repurchased, repurchasing.* To buy back; to regain by purchase.—*n.* The act of buying again; a repurchasing.

rep·u·ta·ble, rep′ū·ta·bl, *a.* Being in good repute; held in esteem; honorable; of words, considered to be proper usage, standard.—**rep·u·ta·bly,** *adv.*—**rep·u·ta·bil·i·ty,** *n.*

rep·u·ta·tion, rep″ū·tā′shan, *n.* [L. *reputatio.*] Character by report; opinion of character generally held; repute in a good or bad sense; good name; distinction; a specific credit or character attributed to someone or something; as, a *reputation* for integrity.

re·pute, ri·pūt′, *v.t.*—*reputed, reputing.* [Fr. *réputer,* < L. *reputo,* to count over—*re,* and *puto,* to reckon, to estimate (as in *compute, impute,* etc.).] To hold in thought; to regard, account, or consider as indicated, usu. used in the passive, as: It is *reputed* to be the best.—*n.* Reputation; character attributed by public report; honorable name.—**re·put·ed,** *a.*—**re·put·ed·ly,** *adv.*

re·quest, ri·kwest′, *n.* [O.Fr. *requeste* (Fr. *requête*), < L. *requisita,* a thing required, a want, < *requiro, requisitum—re-,* again, and *quaero, quaesitum,* to seek.] The expression of desire to some person for something to be granted or done; a petition; the thing asked for or requested; a state of being esteemed and sought after, or asked for; as, an article in much *request.*—*v.t.* To make a request for; to solicit or express desire for; to express a request to; as, to *request* the class to leave; to ask for.—**re·quest·er,** *n.*

req·ui·em, rek′wē·em, rē′kwē·em, *n.* [Acc. case of L. *requies,* rest, respite, relaxation—*re-,* again, and *quies,* rest, repose.] A dirge, service, or hymn for the repose of souls of the dead. (*Usu. cap.*), *Rom. Cath. Ch.* a funeral mass for the dead; the musical setting of this mass.

req·ui·em shark, *n.* A ravenous shark of the family *Carcharhinidae.* Also **re·quin.**

req·ui·es·cat, rek″wē·es′kat, *n.* [< L. *requiescat in pace,* 'may he (or she) rest in peace.'] A wish or prayer for the repose of the dead.

re·quire, ri·kwī′ẽr, *v.t.*—*required, requiring.* [O.Fr. *requerre, requierre, requirre* (Fr. *requerir*), < L. *requiro, requirere,* to ask for.] To demand; to order; to insist on having; to have need or necessity for; as, to *require* a blood transfusion; to need or want.—*v.i.* To demand or force; compel.

re·quire·ment, ri·kwī′ẽr·ment, *n.* The act of requiring; demand; that which requires the doing of something; an essential condition; as, the *requirements* for a job; something required or necessary.

req·ui·site, rek′wi·zit, *a.* [L. *requisitus,* < *requiro.*] Required by the nature of things or by circumstances; necessary.—*n.* That which is necessary; something indispensable.—**req·ui·site·ly,** *adv.*—**req·ui·site·ness,** *n.*

req·ui·si·tion, rek″wi·zish′an, *n.* [L. *requisitio.*] An authoritative request; a demand; a written application or request, as for supplies; a demand for or a levying of necessaries by soldiers occupying a country,

as quarters and rations; state of being required or much sought after; a requirement; request; *law,* a formal request by one government to another for the return of a fugitive criminal.—*v.t.* To make a requisition or demand upon.

re·quit·al, ri·kwīt′al, *n.* The action or act of requiting; something done or given in return; compensation; reward; retaliation.

re·quite, ri·kwīt′, *v.t.*—*requited, requiting.* [< *re-,* back, and *quit.*] To repay; to recompense or reward; to retaliate for or on; to do or give in return.—**re·quit·a·ble,** *a.*—**re·quit·er,** *n.*

re·read, rē·rēd′, *v.t.*—*reread, rereading,* rē·red′, rē·rē′ding. To read again or anew.

rere·dos, rēr′dos, rēr′i·dos, râr′i·dos, *n.* The decorated screen or portion of the wall behind and rising above the altar in a church; the back of an open hearth or fireplace.

rere·mouse, rear·mouse, rēr′mous″, *n.* pl. **rere·mice, rear·mice.** [O.E. *hrēremūs,* < *hrēnan,* to raise, to move, and *mūs,* a mouse.] *Brit. dial.* a bat.

re·run, rē′run″, *n.* An added running, as a later showing of a motion picture or television show after its first run; that which is being reshown; the action of rerunning.— rē·run′, *v.t.*—past *reran,* pp. *rerun,* ppr. *rerunning.* To run again.

res, rēz, räz, *n.* pl. **res.** *Law.* A thing or object; matter.

res ad·ju·di·ca·ta, rēz′ *a*·jö″di·kā′ta, räs *a*·jö″di·kā′ta, *n.* Res judicata.

re·sale, rē′sāl″, rē·sāl′, *n.* A sale of second-hand merchandise; a second sale; the action of selling once again.—**re·sal·a·ble,** rē·sā′la·bl, *a.*

re·scind, ri·sind′, *v.t.* [Fr. *rescinder,* < L. *rescindo, rescissum—re-,* again, and *scindo,* to cut (as in *concise, precise,* etc.).] To abrogate; to repeal; to revoke or annul. As a law or judgment.—**re·scis·sion,** ri·sizh′an, *n.*—**re·scis·so·ry,** ri·sis′o·rē, ri·siz′o·rē, *a.*—**re·scind·a·ble,** *a.*—**re·scind·er,** *n.*

re·script, rē′skript″, *n.* [L. *rescriptum,* < *rescribo, rescriptum,* to write back—*re-,* and *scribo,* to write.] The answer or decision of a Roman emperor to some matter set before him; the decision by a pope of a question officially propounded; an edict or decree; a rewriting.

res·cue, res′kū, *v.t.*—*rescued, rescuing.* [O.Fr. *rescoure, rescourre,* to rescue, < L. *re-,* again, and *excutere,* to shake off—*ex,* away, and *quiato, quassum,* to shake.] To free from confinement, danger, or evil; save; *law,* to take by forcible or illegal means from lawful custody.—*n.* The act or an instance of rescuing.—**res·cu·er,** *n.*

res·cue mis·sion, *n.* An urban religious establishment for the rehabilitation of derelicts.

re·search, ri·surch′, rē′surch, *n.* [Fr. *recherche.*] Diligent inquiry or examination in seeking facts or principles; an experimental investigation.—*v.i., v.t.* To investigate.—**re·search·er,** **re·search·ist,** *n.*

re·search, rē·surch′, *v.t., v.i.* To search or investigate again.

re·seat, rē·sēt′, *v.t.* To seat again; to furnish with a new seat or seats.

ré·seau, rā·zō′, *n.* pl. **ré·seaux,** rā·zō′. [Fr. dim. < L. *rete,* net.] A network; a netted or meshed ground in lace; *astron.* a network of fine lines on a glass plate, used in a photographic telescope to produce a corresponding network on photographs of the stars; *meteor.* a network of weather stations operated as a unified system; *photog.* a filter for color photography, having tiny colored filaments in a geometric arrangement. Also **re·seau,** ra·zō′, pl. **re·seaus.**

re·sect, ri·sekt′, *v.t.* [L. *reseco, resectum,* to cut off—*re-,* back, and *seco,* to cut.] *Surg.*

To cut or trim off; to cut out, as a segment of an organ.—**re·sect·a·bil·i·ty**, *n.*—**re·sect·a·ble**, *a.*

re·sec·tion, ri·sek'shan, *n.* [L. *resectio.*] *Surg.* the removal of a section of a bone or of a piece of an organ or tissue; *surv.* a method of establishing the location of a position from the bearings of two or more known points.—**re·sec·tion·al**, *a.*

re·se·da, ri·sē'da, *n.* [N.L. < L. *reseda,* kind of plant.] Any plant of the genus *Reseda,* esp. *R. odorata,* the garden mignonette; a grayish-green color.—**res·e·da·ceous**, res'i·dā'shus, *a.*

re·seed, rē·sēd', *v.t.* To scatter or plant, as with seed, again; to keep in existence by self-sown seed: used reflexively.—*v.i.* To keep itself in existence by self-sown seed.

re·sem·blance, ri·zem'blans, *n.* The state or quality of resembling; likeness; similarity either of external form or of qualities; something similar; a similitude.

re·sem·blant, ri·zem'blant, *a.* Resembling; similar; having or dealing with resemblance.

re·sem·ble, ri·zem'bl, *v.t.*—*resembled, resembling.* [Fr. *ressembler,* < L. *similare,* < *similis,* like.] To be or look like; to have similarity to in form, figure, or qualities.

re·sent, ri·zent', *v.t.* [Fr. *ressentir,* < L. *re-,* and *sentio,* to feel.] To consider as an injury or affront; to be angry, indignant, or provoked at; to show ill or injured feeling by words or acts for.

re·sent·ful, ri·zent'ful, *a.* Inclined or apt to resent; full of resentment.—**re·sent·ful·ly**, *adv.*—**re·sent·ful·ness**, *n.*

re·sent·ment, ri·zent'ment, *n.* The act of resenting; a deep sense of injury; anger arising from a sense of wrong; strong displeasure.

res·er·pine, res'ér·pin, res'ér·pēn', re·sur'pin, re·sur'pēn, *n.* A white crystalline alkaloid, $C_{33}H_{40}N_2O_9$, derived from the root of *Rauwolfia serpentina,* an East Indian plant, and used in medicine to alleviate extreme anxiety and hypertension.

res·er·va·tion, rez"ér·vā'shan, *n.* The act of reserving or keeping back; concealment or withholding from disclosure; a condition, limitation, or qualification, as in a contract; a tract of public land set aside for some special purpose, esp. for the protection of wild life, or for the use of a tribe of Indians; the reserving in advance of accommodations in a hotel, airplane, or the like.

re·serve, ri·zurv', *v.t.*—*reserved, reserving.* [Fr. *réserver,* < L. *reservo*—*re-,* back, and *servo,* to keep.] To keep in store for future use; to withhold from present use for another purpose; to keep back for a time; to retain; as, to *reserve* a right; to settle or arrange ahead; as, to *reserve* a room.—*n.* The act of reserving or keeping back; that which is reserved or retained from present use or disposal; a piece of land set aside; a reservation; something in the mind withheld from disclosure; the habit of keeping back or restraining the feelings; a certain formality or coldness toward others; caution in personal behavior; banking capital retained in order to meet liabilities. *Milit.* a body of troops kept back from action to be ready to provide support where needed; that part of a nation's available military strength not in the field; a branch of the military forces, not included in the regular services but trained and kept for active service in exigencies.

re·serve bank, *n.* A central bank which keeps certain reserve funds on deposit for other banks, as one of the Federal Reserve Banks.

re·served, ri·zurvd', *a.* Kept for another or future use; showing reserve in behavior;

distant; cold.—**re·serv·ed·ly**, *adv.*—**re·serv·ed·ness**, *n.*

re·serv·ist, ri·zur'vist, *n.* A member of the reserve forces of an army, navy, or other military organization.

res·er·voir, rez'ér·vwär, rez'ér·vär, rez'e·vwär, rez'e·vär, *n.* [Fr. *réservoir,* < *réserver.*] A pond or similar place where water is collected and stored for use, esp. for supplying a community, irrigating land, or furnishing electric power; a receptacle or chamber for holding a liquid or fluid, as oil or gas; *biol.* a cavity or other part in an animal or plant which holds some fluid or secretion. A great supply, store, or reserve of anything.

re·set, rē·set', *v.t.*—*reset, resetting.* To set again; as, to *reset* a diamond.—rē'set", *n.* The act of resetting; something set over again.—**re·set·ter**, *n.*

res ges·tae, rēz jes'tē, räs jes'tē, *n.* [L.] Things done; deeds; facts; *law,* certain facts or circumstances related to a case that may be admitted in evidence.

re·shape, rē·shāp', *v.t.*—*reshaped, reshaping.* To shape again; to shape differently.

re·ship, rē·ship', *v.t.*—*reshipped, reshipping.* To ship again; to move or transfer to another ship.—*v.i.* To embark again; to sign on for another tour of service as a crew member.—**re·ship·ment**, *n.*

re·side, ri·zīd', *v.i.*—*resided, residing.* [Fr. *résider,* < L. *resideo*—*re-,* and *sedeo,* to sit, to settle down.] To dwell permanently or for a length of time; to abide continuously; to abide or be inherent, as a quality, usu. followed by *in*; to be vested, as a privilege, usu. followed by *in.*—**re·sid·er**, *n.*

res·i·dence, rez'i·dens, *n.* The act of residing; period of abode; the place where a person resides; a dwelling; the act of living in a particular place in connection with an official duty, with study, or with the establishment of a legal home; the location at which a corporation is legally registered.

res·i·den·cy, rez'i·den·sē, *n.* pl. **res·i·den·cies.** Residence, usu. an official abode; a territory in a protected state governed by a resident agent; *med.* a period of training in a specialized field of medical practice.

res·i·dent, rez'i·dent, *a.* [L. *residens, residentis.*] Dwelling in a place to carry out one's duties; residing; inherent; *ornith.* not migratory.—*n.* One who resides in a place for some time; an agent who resides at a foreign court, esp. one having authority in a protectorate; *med.* a doctor during a period of training in a specialized field. Also **res·i·den·ti·ar·y**, rez"i·den'shē·er"·ē, rez"i·den'sha·rē, pl. **res·i·den·ti·ar·ies.**

res·i·dent com·mis·sion·er, *n.* One who represents a dependency in the U.S. House of Representatives and has the right to speak but not to vote.

res·i·den·tial, rez"i·den'shal, *a.* Relating or pertaining to residence or to residents; suitable or used for a residence.—**res·i·den·tial·ly**, *adv.*

re·sid·u·al, ri·zij'ö·al, *a.* Pertaining to or constituting a residuum; remaining or left over; remaining unexplained; left uncorrected; *math.* formed by the subtraction of one quantity from another; as, a *residual* amount.—*n.* A residuum; a remainder; a residual quantity; usu. *pl., math.* the difference noted between a result based on observation and one derived from a theory, or the deviation between the value of one item and the mean of the set in which it is included; *usu. pl.* an extra payment made, as to a TV actor, for any filmed or taped rerun in which he appears.—**re·sid·u·al·ly**, ri·zij'ö·a·lē, *adv.*

re·sid·u·ar·y, ri·zij'ö·er"ē, *a.* Pertaining to a residue or part remaining; forming a residue or portion not dealt with.

res·i·due, rez'i·dö", rez'i·dū", *n.* [Fr. *résidu,* < L. *residuum,* what is left behind, < *residuus,* remaining, < *resideo.*] That which remains after a part is taken, separated, or dealt with in some way; remainder; the rest. *Chem.* the product remaining after a liquid has been filtered; one or more atoms isolated from a molecule; residuum. *Law,* the remainder of a testator's estate after payment of debts and legacies; *math.* a difference obtained mathematically.

re·sid·u·um, ri·zij'ö·um, *n.* pl. **re·sid·u·a**, ri·zij'ö·a. [L.] That which is left after any process of separation or purification; a residue; *chem.* the product remaining after distillation, as of coal tar; *law,* the part of an estate remaining after the payment of debts and legacies.

re·sign, ri·zīn', *v.t.* [Fr. *résigner,* L. *resigno,* to resign—*re-,* and *signo,* to mark, < *signum,* to sign.] To assign or give back; to give up, as an office or post, to the person or authority that conferred it; to surrender or relinquish; to give over or consign; to withdraw, as a claim.—*v.i.* To submit; to relinquish one's position, often with *from.*—**re·signed**, ri·zīnd', *a.*—**re·sign·ed·ly**, *adv.*—**re·sign·ed·ness**, *n.*—**re·sign·er**, *n.*

res·ig·na·tion, rez"ig·nā'shan, *n.* The act of resigning or giving up, as a claim; a document stating that one is giving up something, esp. an office; the state of being resigned or submissive; patience.

re·sile, ri·zīl', *v.i.*—*resiled, resiling.* [L. *resilire,* < *re-,* back, and *salire,* leap.] To spring back, recoil, or rebound; return to the original form or position, as an elastic body; to draw back or recede, as from an agreement or purpose; to shrink back or recoil, as with aversion.

re·sil·ience, ri·zil'yens, ri·zil'ē·ens, *n.* The capacity to spring back to the original shape or form after being bent, stretched, or compressed; flexibility; elasticity; *fig.* the capacity to rebound quickly from misfortune or illness. Also **re·sil·ien·cy.**

re·sil·ient, ri·zil'yent, ri·zil'ē·ent, *a.* Rebounding; springing back to original shape; quickly regaining spirits or health after misfortune or illness; flexible.—**re·sil·ient·ly**, *adv.*

res·in, rez'in, *n.* [O.Fr. *resine,* also *rasine, rosine,* < L. *resina:* cf. *rosin.*] Any of a class of solid or semisolid substances as rosin, copal, and mastic, obtained from the exudations of many plants or by chemical processing of inorganic materials, and used in making plastics, varnishes, medicines, and printing inks.—*v.t.* To treat or rub with resin.—**res·in·ous**, rez'i·nus, *a.*

res·in·ate, rez'i·nāt", *v.t.*—*resinated, resinating.* To fill, treat, cover, or impregnate with resin.

res·in·oid, rez'i·noid", *a.* Resinlike.—*n.* A resinoid substance, esp. one of the synthetic resins; a gum resin.

re·sist, ri·zist', *v.t.* [Fr. *résister,* < L. *resisto,* to withstand—*re-,* and *sisto,* to place, to stand, < *sto,* to stand.] To withstand; to form an impediment to; to oppose or act in opposition to; to strive against; defeat.—*v.i.* To offer opposition.—*n.* Any material that hinders or prevents an action; an application preventing corrosion.—**re·sist·er**, *n.*—**re·sist·i·ble**, ri·zis'ti·bl, *a.*—**re·sist·i·bil·i·ty**, *n.*—**re·sist·i·bly**, *adv.*

re·sist·ance, ri·zis'tans, *n.* The act of resisting, whether actively or passively; the quality or property in matter of not yielding to force or external impression; a force acting in opposition to another force so as to destroy it or to diminish its effect; *elect.* the property of a conductor that limits the strength of a current by causing part of the electrical energy to be dissipated in the

---

ch- chain, G. na*ch*t;   **th-** THen, thin;   **w-** wig, hw as sound in whig;   **z-** zh as in azure, zeal.   *Italicized vowel* indicates schwa sound.

form of heat or light; (often cap.) a guerrilla or underground force.

re·sist·ant, ri·zis′tant, a. Offering resistance; resisting.—n. One who or that which resists.

re·sis·tive, ri·zis′tiv, a. Resisting; capable of or inclined to resistance.—re·sis·tive·ly, adv.—re·sis·tive·ness, n.

re·sis·tiv·i·ty, rē″zis·tiv′i·tē, n. The ability to resist. Elect. a characteristic proportionality factor equal to the resistance of a centimeter cube of a substance to the passage of an electric current perpendicular to two parallel faces; also spe·cif·ic re·sist·ance.

re·sist·less, ri·zist′lis, a. Incapable of being resisted or withstood; irresistible; powerless to resist.—re·sist·less·ly, adv.—re·sist·less·ness, n.

re·sis·tor, ri·zis′tẽr, n. Elect. a conducting body or device put into a circuit to offer resistance for such purposes as the production of light or heat, or the control of current.

res ju·di·ca·ta, rēz′ jŏ″di·kā′ta, rās′ jŏ″di·kä′ta, n. [L.] Law, a case that has been decided, cited as a precedent in a similar case. Also res adjudicata.

res·o·jet en·gine, rez′ō·jet″ en′jin, n. Pulse jet engine.

re·sole, rē·sōl′, v.t.—resoled, resoling. To put a new sole on; as, to resole a shoe.

re·sol·u·ble, ri·zol′ū·bl, rez′ol·ū·bl, a. [Fr. résoluble.] Capable of being resolved.

res·o·lute, rez′o·lŏt″, a. [Fr. résolu, pp. of résoudre, L. resolvere, to resolve.] Having a fixed purpose; determined; steadfast; bold; firm.—res·o·lute·ly, adv.—res·o·lute·ness, n.

res·o·lu·tion, rez″o·lŏ′shan, n. [Fr. résolution, L. resolutio.] The state of being resolute; a resolve made; a fixed purpose or determination; the state of acting with fixed purpose; firmness; a formal decision or opinion of a legislative body or other group, usu. arrived at by voting; the act of resolving or separating into component parts; the answer or solution to a problem. Mus. the resolving of a tone or chord, in a progressive fashion, from a discord to a concord; the resulting tone or chord. Med. the diminution or disappearance of a tumor or inflammation.

re·solve, ri·zolv′, v.t.—resolved, resolving. [L. resolvo, to unloose, break up, dissolve, to do away with (hence, to determine; that is, to do away with doubts or disputes)— re-, back or again, and solvo, to loose.] To reduce to constituent elements or simple parts; to analyze; to separate or change by or through a process; to clear of difficulties; as, to resolve doubts; to explain; to solve; to fix in determination or purpose; to determine; to form, constitute, or express by resolution and vote, as a legislative body; mus. to cause to resolve from discord to concord; med. to cause to diminish or disappear, as an inflammation, without pus formation; chem. to divide or separate into its optically active components, as a racemic substance; opt. to make visible the separate parts of.—v.i. To form an opinion or decision; to determine; to become separated into component parts or principles; mus. to go through resolution.—n. That which has been resolved; fixed purpose of mind; a settled determination; a resolution.—re·solv·a·ble, ri·zol′va·bl, a.—re·solv·er, n.

re·sol·vent, ri·zol′vent, a. Having the power to resolve; causing solution.—n. That which has the power of causing solution; med. a substance which diminishes or dispels inflammation.

re·solv·ing pow·er, n. Opt. the ability of a microscope or other optical instrument to separate the images of two or more clustered objects so that each can be seen distinctly.

res·o·nance, rez′o·nans, n. The state or quality of being resonant. Phys. the property of a mechanical system enabling it to vibrate sympathetically in response to vibrations of a particular frequency from another body; the prolongation or increase of sound by the sympathetic vibration of other bodies. Elect. that condition of a circuit with respect to a given frequency in which the total reactance is zero and the current flow a maximum. Phon. an increase in the audibility of spoken sounds; the combination of resonances from various cavities, as the mouth or sinuses, which are characteristic of a phoneme. Med. the sound resulting from tapping on the chest or other part of the body.

res·o·nant, rez′o·nant, a. [L. resonans, resonantis, ppr. of resono—re-, again, and sono, to sound.] Capable of returning sound; resounding; full of resonance; intensified by resonance; echoing back.—n. A vowel.—res·o·nant·ly, adv.

res·o·nate, rez′o·nāt″, v.i.—resonated, resonating. [L. resonatus, pp. of resonare.] To resound; exhibit resonance; act as a resonator.—res·o·na·tion, n.

res·o·na·tor, rez′o·nā″tẽr, n. [N.L.] Something that produces resonance. Acoustics, any apparatus for increasing sound by resonance; an instrument for detecting a particular tone by means of resonance. Electron. any device for utilizing, detecting, or showing the effects of electromagnetic resonance.

re·sorb, ri·sȧrb′, ri·zȧrb′, v.t. [L. resorbēre (pp. resorptus), < re-, back, and sorbēre, suck in.] To absorb again, as an exudation.

re·sorb·ent, a. Absorbing again.—re·sorb·ence, n.

res·or·cin·ol, rez·ȧr′si·nōl, rez·ȧr′si·nol″, n. [(res)in and orcinol.] Chem. a colorless crystalline benzene derivative, $C_6H_4(OH)_2$, orig. obtained from certain resins, used in medicine, tanning, and making dyes. Also res·or·cin.

re·sorp·tion, ri·sȧrp′shan, n. [= Fr. résorption, < L. resorbēre, E. resorb.] Petrog. in the formation of igneous rocks, the process by which a crystal becomes partially or wholly remelted and reabsorbed by the molten magma from which it crystallized.—re·sorp·tive, a.

re·sort, ri·zȧrt′, v.i. [O.Fr. resortir, Fr. ressortir, to go out again, to resort, < L. sortiri, to obtain, to acquire by lot, < sors, sortis, lot.] To go; as, to resort to a place; to have recourse; as, to resort to force; to betake oneself; to repair, esp. frequently.—n. Recourse; the act of visiting or frequenting; a place frequented; a vacation or recreation place; a haunt; a refuge.—re·sort·er, n.

re·sound, ri·zound′, v.i. [O.E. resounen, < L. resono, to resound.] To be filled with sound; to echo; to reverberate; to sound loudly; to be echoed; to be celebrated or extolled.—v.t. To sound loudly; to echo; to extol.—re·sound·ing, a.—re·sound·ing·ly, adv.

re·source, rē′sōrs, rē′sȧrs, ri·sȯrs′, ri·sȧrs′, n. [Fr. ressource, < O.Fr. resourdre, to arise anew.] Any source of aid or support, esp. one kept in reserve; an expedient action or measure; means yet untried; resort. Pl. funds; available property, natural sources, means, or capabilities of any kind; the ability to deal with any problem or situation.—re·source·ful, ri·sȯrs′ful, ri·sȧrs′ful, a.—re·source·ful·ly, adv.—re·source·ful·ness, n.

re·spect, ri·spekt′, n. [Fr. respecter, < L. respicio, respectum—re-, back, and obs. specio, to look.] Regard; a holding in high estimation or honor; the state of being held in high esteem, regard, or reverence; pl. an expression of regard, esteem, or deference;

as, to pay one's respects. Consideration or courtesy; as, respect for his privacy; a point or particular; as, wrong in this respect; relation; reference; as, with respect to delivery.—v.t. To hold in high estimation or honor; to treat with consideration; to avoid interfering with or intruding upon; to have reference or regard to.—re·spect·er, ri·spek′tẽr, n.—re·spect·ful, ri·spekt′ful, a.—re·spect·ful·ly, adv.—re·spect·ful·ness, n.

re·spect·a·bil·i·ty, ri·spek″ta·bil′i·tē, n. pl. re·spect·a·bil·i·ties. The condition or quality of being respectable; estimable repute, social status, or character; a respectable person or people; pl. conventions considered respectable.

re·spect·a·ble, ri·spek′ta·bl, a. Worthy of respect; having a good reputation or character; decent; presentable; moderately excellent; average; moderately large in number or size.—re·spect·a·ble·ness, n.—re·spect·a·bly, adv.

re·spect·ing, ri·spek′ting, prep. Regarding; in regard to; concerning.

re·spec·tive, ri·spek′tiv, a. Relating or pertaining severally to each of a number of persons or things.—re·spec·tive·ness, n.

re·spec·tive·ly, ri·spek′tiv·lē, adv. In their respective relations; individually in their given order.

re·spell, rē·spel′, v.t. To spell again; to spell in a new way, esp. in systems in which pronunciation is the guide.

re·spir·a·ble, res′pẽr·a·bl, ri·spiẽr′a·bl, a. Capable of respiring or fit for being respired or breathed.

res·pi·ra·tion, res″pi·rā′shan, n. [L. respiratio(n-).] The act of respiring; the inhalation and exhalation of air; breathing; in animals and plants, the sum total of the chemical and physical processes involved in oxidation by which oxygen is absorbed into the system and the oxidation products, esp. carbon dioxide, are released.—res·pi·ra·tion·al, a.—res·pi·ra·to·ry, res′pẽr·a·tõr″ē, res′pẽr·a·tȧr″ē, ri·spiẽr′a·tõr″ē, ri·spiẽr′a·tȧr″ē, a.

res·pi·ra·tor, res′pi·rā″tẽr, n. A masklike contrivance covering the mouth, or nose and mouth, which serves as protection against the inhalation of cold air or harmful matter; a machine used for providing artificial respiration, as an iron lung; Brit. a gas mask.

res·pi·ra·to·ry quo·tient, n. The ratio of the amount of carbon dioxide exhaled in respiration to the oxygen taken in.

re·spire, ri·spiẽr′, v.i.—respired, respiring. [Fr. respirer, < L. respiro—re-, and spiro, to breathe.] To breathe; to inhale air into the lungs and exhale it, for the purpose of maintaining life; to breathe easily; to recover after labor, worry, or suffering.—v.t. To breathe in and out, as air; to exhale.

res·pite, res′pit, n. [O.Fr. respit, < L. respectus, respect.] A temporary intermission of labor or suffering; a time of relief or rest; delay; postponement. Law, a reprieve; temporary suspension of the execution of a condemned person.—v.t. respited, respiting. To give or grant temporary relief to; law, to reprieve.

re·splend·ent, ri·splen′dent, a. [L. resplendens, resplendentis, ppr. of resplendeo—re-, and splendeo, to shine.] Very bright; shining with brilliant luster; handsomely accoutered; magnificent.—re·splend·ent·ly, adv.—re·splend·ence, re·splend·en·cy, ri·splen′dens, n.

re·spond, ri·spond′, v.i. [O.Fr. respondre (Fr. répondre), L. respondeo—re-, back, and spondeo, to promise solemnly.] To make answer; to give a reply in words; to answer or reply in any way; to answer by action; to react; correspond; law, to be responsible.—v.t. To reply.—n. Arch. a half pier or column extending out from a wall to support an arch whose opposite side rests on a free-standing column; *eccles.* responsory.

re·spond·ent, ri·spon'dent, *a.* [L. *respondens, respondentis.*] Answering; responding, as to a lawsuit.—*n.* One who responds; one who maintains a thesis in reply; *law,* one who answers in a suit; a defendant, esp. in equity or divorce cases.

re·spond·er, ri·spon'dẽr, *n.* One who or that which responds; *elect.* the part of a transponder that sends the reply.

re·sponse, ri·spons', *n.* [L. *responsum.*] The act of responding or replying; a reply; an answer. *Eccles.* the answer of the choir or congregation to the priest during a church service; responsory. *Biol.* the activity or behavior of an animal or a plant as a result of stimulation; reaction. *Bridge,* the answer to the bid of one's partner.

re·spon·si·bil·i·ty, ri·spon″si·bil'i·tẽ, *n. pl.* **re·spon·si·bil·i·ties.** The state of being responsible; that for which one is responsible; a trust, obligation, or duty; ability to meet payments or obligations; trustworthiness.

re·spon·si·ble, ri·spon'si·bl, *a.* Accountable for performance or discharge of duty or trust; involving responsibility; capable of making ethical and moral decisions; able to answer for one's behavior; politically accountable; able to discharge or meet any claim, debt, or obligation; reliable; trustworthy.—**re·spon·si·ble·ness**, *n.*—**re·spon·si·bly**, *adv.*

re·spon·sions, ri·spon'shanz, *n. pl.* [L. *responsio,* an answering.] The first examination for the B.A. degree which the students at Oxford University, in England, are obliged to pass.

re·spon·sive, ri·spon'siv, *a.* Answering; responding; sensitive to influences; typically employing responses.—**re·spon·sive·ly**, *adv.*—**re·spon·sive·ness**, ri·spon'siv·nis, *n.*

re·spon·so·ry, ri·spon'so·rẽ, *n. pl.* **re·spon·so·ries.** *Eccles.* a response, esp. a response recited or sung during or following a lection. Also *respond, response.*

res pu·bli·ca, rēz pub'li·ka, räs pub'li·ka, L. Rẽs pö'bli·kä″, *n.* [L.] The commonwealth; the state; the republic.

rest, rest, *n.* [O.E. *rest, raest,* rest, resting-place, = O.H.G. *rasta* (G. *rast*), rest, also stage of a journey, = Icel. *röst* and Goth. *rasta,* stage of a journey, mile.] The refreshing quiet or repose of sleep; refreshing ease or inactivity after exertion or labor; relief or freedom from anything that wearies, troubles, or disturbs; mental or spiritual ease or tranquillity; the repose of death; cessation or absence of motion; as, a body at *rest,* to bring a machine to *rest;* an establishment for providing shelter or lodging; a piece or thing for something to rest on; a support or supporting device. *Mus.* an interval or silence between tones; a mark or sign indicating it. *Pros.* a short pause in reading; a caesura. *Billiards, pool,* a support for a cue, as the hand, or a notched wooden piece; a bridge.—*v.i.* [O.E. *restan, raestan.*] To take rest or refresh oneself with rest, as by sleeping, lying down, or relaxing the body or mind; relieve weariness by cessation of exertion or labor; to be at ease, or have tranquillity or peace; to repose or lie in death; to cease from motion, come to rest, or stop; to be discontinued, or go without further action or notice; as, to let a matter *rest;* to recline, sit, or lean for rest or ease; lie or be set for support; as, a ladder *resting* against a wall; to be fixed or directed, as the gaze or the eyes, on something; to be imposed as a burden or responsibility, followed by *on* or *upon;* to rely, followed by *on* or *upon;* be based or founded, followed by *on* or *upon;* to lie, be found, or be as indicated, as: The

blame *rests* with them. *Law,* to terminate voluntarily the introduction of evidence in a case; *agric.* to lie idle or unworked, as farmland.—*v.t.* To give rest to, or refresh with rest; to bring to rest, or to a halt or stop; to lay or place for rest, ease, or support; to base, or let depend; as, to *rest* one's hopes on assurances; to direct or fix, as the eyes; *law,* to terminate voluntarily the introduction of evidence on; as, to *rest* one's case.—**at rest,** in a motionless state, as in death or sleep; still; immobile; tranquil. —**rest·er**, *n.*

rest, rest, *n.* [Fr. *reste,* < *rester,* to rest, to remain, < L. *resto*—*re*-, back, and *sto,* to stand.] That which is left after the separation of a part; the remainder; the others, as: The *rest* of the boys have gone. *Brit.* a surplus fund held in reserve, as by a bank. —*v.i.* [Fr. *rester.*] To remain; to continue to be.

rest, rest, *n.* A contrivance fixed to the side of the breastplate in medieval armor for receiving and supporting the butt of a lance when couched for charging.

re·start, rē·stärt', *v.t., v.i.* To start anew or again; to resume.—*n.*

re·state, rē·stāt', *v.t.*—**restated, restating.** To state again or in a different way.— **re·state·ment**, *n.*

res·tau·rant, res'tẽr·ant, res'ta·ränt″, *n.* [Fr.] A commercial establishment serving meals or refreshments.

res·tau·ra·teur, res″tẽr·a·tur', *Fr.* Rẽs·tȧ·Rä·tœr', *n.* [Fr.] The owner or operator of a restaurant.

rest·ful, rest'ful, *a.* Full of rest; giving rest; quiet; being at rest; peaceful.—**rest·ful·ly**, *adv.*—**rest·ful·ness**, *n.*

rest home, *n.* An institution offering an environment and treatment suited to the needs of persons who are elderly, in ill health, or convalescent.

rest house, *n.* A house or building providing shelter for travelers; a house for paying guests at a resort, affording facilities and an environment that encourages leisure and relaxation.

res·ti·form, res'ti·fạrm″, *a.* [N.L. *restiformis,* < L. *restis,* rope, cord, and *forma,* form.] Cordlike; twisted into ropelike strands.

res·ti·form bod·ies, *n. pl. Anat.* a pair of cordlike bundles of nerve fibers lying one on each side of the medulla oblongata and connecting it with the cerebellum.

rest·ing, res'ting, *a.* That rests; reposing; *bot.* dormant: applied esp. to spores which germinate after a period of dormancy.

res·ti·tu·tion, res″ti·tö'shan, res″ti·tū'shan, *n.* [L. *restitutio(n-).*] Restoration to the former or original state or position; the restoration of property or rights previously taken away; reparation made by giving an equivalent or compensation for loss, damage, or injury caused; indemnification; *phys.* the return of an elastic body to its original form or position when released from strain.

res·tive, res'tiv, *a.* [O.Fr. *restif,* drawing backward, refusing to go forward, < *rester,* L. *restare,* to stay back, to remain.] Restless; resisting control; balky; unruly; constantly fidgeting or moving about; impatient under restraint or opposition.— **res·tive·ly**, *adv.*—**res·tive·ness**, *n.*

rest·less, rest'lis, *a.* Unquiet; continually moving; being without rest; unable to rest or sleep; not satisfied to be at rest; unsettled; discontented.—**rest·less·ly**, *adv.* —**rest·less·ness**, *n.*

rest mass, *n. Phys.* according to relativistic theory, the mass of a body when it is at absolute rest, excluding that which it acquires when in motion.

res·to·ra·tion, res″to·rā'shan, *n.* The act of restoring; state or condition of being

restored; replacement; renewal; reestablishment; the repairing of injuries suffered, as by works of art; that which has been restored, repaired, or reconstructed, as an ancient building or a fossil.—**the Res·to·ra·tion**, the return of King Charles II to the English throne in 1660, and the reestablishment of the English monarchy; the period during which Charles II reigned; sometimes, the period covering the reign of Charles II and James II.

re·stor·a·tive, ri·stōr'a·tiv, ri·stạr'a·tiv, *a.* Capable of restoring; pertaining to restoration.—*n.* That which restores; that which is efficacious in restoring consciousness or health.—**re·stor·a·tive·ly**, *adv.*—**re·stor·a·tive·ness**, *n.*

re·store, ri·stōr', ri·stạr', *v.t.*—**restored, restoring.** [O.Fr. *restorer, restaurer* (Fr. *restaurẽr*), < L. *restaurare,* restore, repair, rebuild, < *re*-, back, and *-staurare,* occurring also in *instaurare,* renew, restore.] To bring back into existence, use, or the like; reestablish; as, to *restore* peace; to bring back to a former, original, or normal condition; renew; as, to *restore* a building; to bring back to a state of health, soundness, or vigor; to put back to a former place, or to a former position, rank, or the like; as, to *restore* a king to the throne; to give back, or make return or restitution of, as anything taken away or lost.—**re·stor·a·ble**, *a.* —**re·stor·er**, *n.*

re·strain, ri·strān', *v.t.* [O.Fr. *restraindre* (Fr. *restreindre*), < L. *restringo.*] To hold back; to check; to hold from action; to repress; to restrict; to deprive of liberty, as one who is arrested.—**re·strain·a·ble**, *a.*— **re·strain·ed·ly**, *adv.*—**re·strain·er**, *n.*

re·straint, ri·strānt', *n.* The act of restraining; a holding back or hindering from motion in any manner; hindrance of the will; abridgment of liberty; confinement; that which restrains or hinders; a limitation; constraint.

re·strict, ri·strikt', *v.t.* [L. *restringo, restrictum.*] To limit; to confine; to restrain within bounds.—**re·strict·ed**, ri·strik'tid, *a.*—**re·strict·ed·ly**, *adv.*

re·stric·tion, ri·strik'shan, *n.* The act of restricting, or state of being restricted; that which restricts; a restraint; limitation.

re·stric·tion·ism, ri·strik'sha·niz″um, *n.* A national policy advocating restriction, as of commerce or foreign trade.—**re·stric·tion·ist**, *a., n.*

re·stric·tive, ri·strik'tiv, *a.* Having the quality of limiting or expressing limitation; imposing restraint; *gram.* limiting the meaning or identity of a word or phrase that is modified.—**re·stric·tive·ly**, *adv.*— **re·stric·tive·ness**, *n.*

rest room, *n.* A public toilet or lavatory. Also *powder room, toilet, Brit. water closet.*

re·sult, ri·zult', *v.i.* [Fr. *résulter,* to result, orig. to rebound, < L. *resulto,* to rebound, < *resilio*—*re*-, back, and *salio,* to leap.] To proceed, spring, or rise, as a consequence, from facts, arguments, premises, a combination of circumstances, or the like; to ensue; to accrue; to have an issue; to terminate, followed by *in,* as: This measure will *result in* good or evil.—*n.* Consequence; conclusion; outcome; issue; effect; product; that which proceeds naturally or logically from facts, premises, or the state of things.—**re·sult·ful**, *a.*—**re·sult·less**, *a.*

re·sult·ant, ri·zul'tant, *a.* Following as a result or consequence; resulting from the combination of two or more agents.—*n.* Result; outcome; *math., phys.* the single force, such as velocity or acceleration, to which several forces are together equivalent; *math.* a determinant of a set of polynomial equations.—**re·sul·tant·ly**, *adv.*

re·sume, ri·zöm', *v.t.*—**resumed, resuming.** [Fr. *résumer,* < L. *resumo.*] To take up again after interruption; to take again; as, to *resume* your positions; to take back; as, to *resume* the car's title.—*v.i.* To begin again.

ré·su·mé, re·su·me, rez′u̯·mā″, rez″u̯·mā′, *n.* [Fr.] A summing up; a summary; a condensed statement, as a short history of a job applicant's qualifications and experience.

re·sump·tion, ri·zump′shan, *n.* The act of resuming, taking back, or taking again.

re·su·pi·nate, ri·sö′pi·nāt″, *a.* [L. *resupinatus—re-,* and *supinus,* lying on the back, supine.] Inverted; bent over backward; reversed; appearing as if turned upside down.—**re·su·pi·na·tion,** ri·sö″pi·nā′shan, *n.*

re·su·pine, rē″sö·pīn′, *a.* Lying on the back; supine.

re·sur·face, rē·sur̯′fis, *v.t.—resurfaced, resurfacing.* To put on a different or new surface.—*v.i.* To bring back to the water's surface, as applied to a submarine.

re·sur·gent, ri·sur̯′jent, *a.* Rising again; reviving; tending to surge back.—**re·sur·gence,** *n.*

res·ur·rect, rez″a·rekt′, *v.t.* To raise from the dead; to restore to life; to bring back into practice or use.—*v.i.* To be restored from death.

res·ur·rec·tion, rez″a·rek′shan, *n.* [L. *resurrectio, < resurgo, resurrectum—re-,* again, and *surgo,* to arise.] A rising again to life; the state of those who have returned to life; a revival or restoration.—**the Res·ur·rec·tion,** the rising of Christ after the Crucifixion; the rising of the dead on the day of judgment.—**res·ur·rec·tion·al,** *a.*

res·ur·rec·tion·ist, rez″a·rek′sha·nist, *n.* One who steals bodies from the grave for dissection; one who revives or restores something to use; one who believes that the dead will rise.—**res·ur·rec·tion·ism,** rez″a·rek′sha·niz″um, *n.*

res·ur·rec·tion plant, *n.* Any of several plants having strong revival properties, esp. the club moss, *Selaginella lepidophylla,* native to southwestern N. America, whose foliage curls inward upon drying and loses its green color, but revives when placed in water. See *rose of Jericho, selaginella.*

re·sur·vey, rē″sĕr·vā′, *v.t.* To survey again or anew.—rē·sur̯′vā, rē″sĕr·vā′, *n.* A new survey.

re·sus·ci·tate, ri·sus′i·tāt, *v.t.—resuscitated, resuscitating.* [L. *resuscito, resuscitatum—re-,* again, and *suscito,* to rouse up.] To revive; to recover, esp. from apparent death or unconsciousness.—*v.i.* To revive; to come to life again.—**re·sus·ci·ta·tion,** *n.*—**re·sus·ci·ta·tive,** *a.*

re·sus·ci·ta·tor, ri·sus′i·tā″tĕr, *n.* One who resuscitates; a device used to initiate respiration and relieve asphyxiation.

ret, ret, *v.t.—retted, retting.* [D. *reten,* to ret flax; allied to *rot.*] To steep or macerate in water, as flax, in order to separate the fiber by incipient rotting.

re·ta·ble, ri·tā′bl, *n.* [Fr., prob. < O.Fr. *rere,* at the back (cf. *reredos*), and *table,* E. *table.*] A decorative structure raised above an altar at the back, often forming a frame for a picture or bas-relief, and sometimes including a shelf or shelves, as for ornaments.

re·tail, rē′tāl, *n.* [Fr. *retail,* a piece cut off—*re-,* again, and *tailler,* to cut; < L.L. *talea, talia,* a tally, L. *talea,* a stick (hence also *tailor, tally*). *Retail* is thus to sell by pieces cut off.] The sale of goods in small quantities directly to a consumer.—*a.* Engaged in, pertaining to, or relating to the sale of merchandise at retail.—rē′tāl, ri·tāl′, *v.t.* To sell in small quantities or by the piece; to sell, as goods, directly to a consumer, rē′tāl. To repeat in detail, as a story or gossip, ri·tāl′.—rē′tāl, *v.i.* To cost at retail.—*adv.*—**re·tail·er,** *n.*

re·tain, ri·tān′, *v.t.* [O.Fr. Fr. *retenir,* < L. *retinēre* (pp. *retentus*), hold back, keep, < *re-,* back, and *tenēre,* hold.] To keep possession of; to continue to use or practice; as, to *retain* a system; to continue to hold or have; as, to *retain* heat or moisture; to keep in mind; remember; to hold in place or position; to engage, esp. by the payment of a preliminary fee, as a lawyer.

re·tained ob·ject, *n. Gram.* in a passive construction, that which corresponds to the direct or indirect object in the active construction, as *ticket* in *He was given a ticket,* the object retained from the active construction: *They give the ticket to him.*

re·tain·er, ri·tā′nĕr, *n.* The act of retaining in one's service; the fact of being so retained; a fee paid to secure services, as of a lawyer.

re·tain·er, ri·tā′nĕr, *n.* One who or that which retains; *hist.* a person attached to a noble house and owing it service; *mach.* a device for holding in place the rollers or balls in a bearing.

re·take, rē·tāk′, *v.t.—past retook,* pp. *retaken,* ppr. *retaking.* To take again; to recapture; to photograph, film, or record again.—rē′tāk″, *n.* The act of retaking; a retaking, as: A *retake* was ordered of both the film and sound tracks.

re·tal·i·ate, ri·tal′ē·āt″, *v.t.—retaliated, retaliating.* [L. *retalio, retaliatum,* to retaliate.] To repay, as a wrong or injury, with the like.—*v.i.* To return like for like, esp. to do evil in return for evil.—**re·tal·i·a·tion,** ri·tal″ē·ā′shan, *n.*—**re·tal·i·a·tive,** ri·tal′ē·a·tiv, *a.*—**re·tal·i·a·to·ry,** ri·tal′ē·a·tōr″ē, ri·tal′ē·a·tar″ē, *a.*

re·tard, ri·tärd′, *v.t.* [Fr. *retarder,* < L. *retardo—re-,* and *tardo,* to delay, < *tardus,* slow.] To cause to slow; delay or hinder, as the course, progress, or advance of; to impede.—*v.i.* To be delayed.—*n.* Retardation; delay.—**re·tard·ant,** ri·tär′dant, *a.,* *n.*—**re·tard·er,** *n.*

re·tar·da·tion, rē″tär·dā′shan, *n.* The act of retarding; the condition of being delayed or retarded; that which retards; hindrance; abnormally slow physical, intellectual, and emotional development. *Mus.* a form of discord resolved by raising a tone by a degree; a slowing of tempo.—**re·tard·a·tive,** ri·tär′da·tiv, *a.*

re·tard·ed, ri·tär′did, *a.* Showing or exhibiting retardation; abnormally slow in mental and emotional development; abnormally slow in action, awareness, or progress.—**re·tard·ate,** ri·tär′dāt, *n.*

retch, rech, *v.i.* [O.E. *hrǣcan,* to retch, to hawk; allied to *hrāca,* the throat, a cough; Icel. *hraekja,* to spit, *hráki,* spittle.] To make an effort to vomit; to strain, as in vomiting.

re·te, rē′tē, *n.* pl. **re·ti·a,** rē′shē·a, rē′sha, rē′tē·a. [L., net.] A network, as of fibers, nerves, or blood vessels.

re·tem, rē′tem, *n.* A white-flowered shrub, *Retama raetam,* of the deserts of Arabia and Syria, that belongs to the legume family and is thought to be the juniper of the Old Testament.

re·tene, rē′tēn, ret′ēn, *n.* [Gr. *rhētinē,* resin.] *Chem.* a crystalline hydrocarbon, $C_{18}H_{18}$, obtained from the tar of resinous woods and certain fossil resins.

re·ten·tion, ri·ten′shan, *n.* [L. *retentio, retentionis, < retineo, retentum.*] The act of retaining; the state of being retained; the capacity for retaining; the power of memory; *med.* the retaining in the body of matter, such as urine, which is normally discharged.

re·ten·tive, ri·ten′tiv, *a.* Characterized by retention; having strong powers of recollection, esp. of learned material.—**re·ten·tive·ly,** *adv.*—**re·ten·tive·ness,** *n.*

re·ten·tiv·i·ty, rē″ten·tiv′i·tē, *n.* pl. **re·**

ten·tiv·i·ties. The capacity for retaining; retentiveness; *phys.* the ability of a substance to retain its magnetic quality after the magnetizing force has been withdrawn.

re·ti·ar·i·us, rē″shē·âr′ē·us, *n.* pl. **re·ti·ar·i·i,** rē″shē·âr′ē·ī″. [L.] In ancient Rome, a gladiator equipped with a net for casting over his opponent.

re·ti·ar·y, rē′shē·er″ē, *a.* [M.L. *retiarius,* < L. *rete,* net.] Using a net or any entangling device; making a net or web, as a spider; netlike.

ret·i·cent, ret′i·sent, *a.* [L. *reticens (-ent-),* ppr. of *reticēre,* remain silent, < *re-,* back, and *tacēre,* be silent.] Disposed to be silent; not inclined to speak freely; reserved.—**ret·i·cence,** ret·i·cen·cy, *n.*—**ret·i·cent·ly,** *adv.*

ret·i·cle, ret′i·kl, *n.* [= reticule, reticulum.] *Opt.* a network of fine lines, wires, or the like, placed in the focus of the objective of a telescope.

re·tic·u·lar, ri·tik′ya·lĕr, *a.* Having the form of a net; netlike; intricate or entangled—**re·tic·u·lar·ly,** *adv.*

re·tic·u·late, ri·tik′ya·lit, ri·tik′ya·lāt″, *a.* [L. *reticulatus, < reticulum.*] Netted; netlike; covered with a network; *bot.* having the veins disposed like the threads of a net; also **re·tic·u·lat·ed.**—*v.t.* *reticulated, reticulating.* To form into a network; cover or mark with a network.—*v.i.* To form a network.

re·tic·u·la·tion, ri·tik″ū·lā′shan, *n.* Reticulated formation, arrangement, or appearance; a network.

ret·i·cule, ret′i·kūl″, *n.* [Fr. *réticule,* L. *reticulum,* dim. of *rete,* net.] A kind of ladies bag or purse, formerly of network, but now of every description of materials, carried in the hand; *opt.* a micrometer attached to a telescope, having a network of fine fibers crossing at right angles.

re·tic·u·lum, ri·tik′ya·lum, *n.* pl. **re·tic·u·la.** [L., dim. of *rete,* net.] A network; any reticulated system or structure; *anat.* a network of protoplasmic structures, as cells or tissues; *zool.* the second stomach of ruminating animals, between the rumen and the omasum.

re·ti·form, rē′ti·farm″, ret′i·farm″, *a.* [L. *retiformis—rete,* a net, and *forma,* form.] Having the form of a net in texture; composed of crossing lines and interstices; reticulate.

ret·i·na, ret′i·na, ret′na, *n.* pl. **ret·i·nas, ret·i·nae,** ret′i·nē″. [M.L., < L. *rete,* net.] *Anat.* the innermost coat of the posterior part of the eyeball, consisting of light-sensitive cells connected to the brain by the optic nerve, and serving to receive the image transmitted by the lens.—**ret·i·nal,** *a.*

ret·i·nene, ret′i·nēn″, *n.* Either the orange or yellow carotenoid pigment of the vertebrate retina.

ret·i·nite, ret′i·nīt″, *n.* [Fr. *rétinite,* < Gr. *rhētinē,* resin.] A translucent fossil resin derived from lignite.

ret·i·ni·tis, ret″i·nī′tis, *n. Pathol.* inflammation of the retina.

ret·i·nos·co·py, ret″i·nos′ko·pē, ret′i·no·skō″pē, *n. Ophthal.* examination of the retina to determine the degree of any faulty refraction of the eye.

ret·i·nue, ret′i·nö″, ret′i·nū″, *n.* [O.Fr. *retenue, < retenir,* to retain.] The attendants of a distinguished personage; a suite; a cortege.

re·tire, ri·tīer′, *v.i.—retired, retiring.* [Fr. *retirer—re-,* back, and *tirer,* to draw.] To withdraw; to go back; to draw back; to go from a company or from a public place into privacy; to retreat from action or danger; to withdraw from business or active life; to recede; to go to bed.—*v.t.* To designate as no longer being qualified for active service;

as, to *retire* a military officer; to withdraw from circulation by taking up and paying; as, to *retire* a bill; *baseball*, to put out, as a player.

re·tired, ri·tīerd', *a.* Secluded from society or from public notice; apart from public view; as, a *retired* life, a *retired* locality; private; secret; withdrawn from business or active life; given to seclusion; inclining to retirement; due to or pertaining to one in retirement.

re·tire·ment, ri·tīer'ment, *n.* The act of retiring; state of living a retired life; seclusion; privacy; retired or private abode.

re·tir·ing, ri·tīer'ing, *a.* Withdrawing; retreating; reserved; pertaining to retirement.—**re·tir·ing·ly**, *adv.*—**re·tir·ing·ness**, *n.*

re·tool, rē·tōl', *v.t.*, *v.i.* To equip with new tools or machinery, esp. for the manufacture of new or redesigned products; to reorganize, as for the purpose of modernizing.

re·tort, ri·tạrt', *v.t.* [L. *retortus*, pp. of *retorquēre*, twist back, cast back.] To answer, as an argument or the like, by another to the contrary. To make return of or retaliate, as an injury, upon the originator; return, as an accusation, epithet, or the like, upon the person uttering it; to reply in kind to, as to a sarcasm.—*v.i.* To reply in retaliation, esp. sharply; to make a retort or retorts.—*n.* The act of retorting; a retaliatory act or remark; a severe, incisive, or witty reply, esp. one that counters a first speaker's statement or argument.

re·tort, ri·tạrt', *n.* [Fr. *retorte*, < L. *retorta*, fem. of *retortus*, pp.] *Chem.* a vessel, commonly a glass bulb with a long neck bent downward, used for distilling or decomposing substances by heat; *metal.* a vessel in which an ore can be heated for removal of the metal content.

re·tor·tion, ri·tạr'shan, *n.* [M.L. *retortio* (n-), < L. *retorquēre*.] The act of turning or bending back; retaliation. *International law*, the infliction, by one nation on another, of the same ill-treatment imposed on its own citizens by that other nation; also **re·tor·sion**.

re·touch, rē·tuch', *v.t.* [Fr. *retoucher*.] To improve by new touches or the like, as a painting; *photog.* to correct or improve, as a photographic negative or print, by the use of a pencil, scraping knife, or the like.—*n.* An added touch, as to a painting, by way of improvement.—**re·touch·er**, *n.*

re·trace, ri·trās', *v.t.*—*retraced, retracing.* To trace or track back; to go over again, as with the sight, attention, or memory.—**re·trace·a·ble**, *a.*

re-trace, rē·trās', *v.t.*—*re-traced, re-tracing.* To trace over or another time, as lines in a drawing or in writing.

re·tract, ri·trakt', *v.t.* [Partly < L. *retractus*, pp. of *retrahere*, draw back, < *re-*, back, and *trahere*, draw; partly < L. *retractare*, (pp. *retractatus*), withdraw, freq. of *retrahere*: cf. *retreat.*] To draw back or in, as claws; to withdraw as unjustified, as a statement or opinion; to withdraw or revoke, as a decree or promise.—*v.i.* To draw or shrink back; to withdraw a vow, promise, or the like; to make disavowal of a statement or an opinion; recant.—**re·tract·a·ble**, *a.*—**re·tract·a·bil·i·ty**, *n.*

re·trac·tile, ri·trak'til, *a.* Capable of being drawn back or in, as the head of a tortoise; exhibiting the power of retraction.—**re·trac·til·i·ty**, ri″trak·til'i·tē, *n.*

re·trac·tion, ri·trak'shan, *n.* [L. *retractio*(n-), < *retrahere.*] The act of retracting; the state of being retracted; the withdrawal of a promise, statement, charge, or the like; the power of retracting.

re·trac·tor, ri·trak'tẽr, *n.* One who or that which retracts; *anat.* a muscle that retracts an organ or a protruded part; *surg.* an

instrument or appliance for drawing back an impeding part, as the edge of a wound or incision.

re·tral, rē'tral, *a.* At the back or posterior; backwards; retrograde.—**re·tral·ly**, *adv.*

re·tread, rē·tred', *v.t.* To put a new tread on, as a pneumatic tire.—rē'tred″, *n.* A tire whose tread has been replaced; anything used again after repairs.

re-tread, rē·tred', *v.t.*, *v.i.*—past *re-trod*, pp. *re-trodden* or *re-trod*, ppr. *re-treading.* To tread again.

re·treat, ri·trēt', *n.* [Fr. *retraite*, < *retraire*, to withdraw, < L. *retrahere.*] The act of retiring or withdrawing from any place; state or place of retirement, privacy, or refuge. *Milit.* a military operation, either forced or strategical, by which troops retire in advance of an enemy; the signal for a retreat; on a military post, the ceremony at sunset of the lowering of the flag; the signal given by a bugle or drum to lower the flag at this ceremony. A period of retirement with a view to self-examination, meditation, and special prayer.—*v.i.* To make a retreat; to retire from any position or place; to withdraw; to take shelter; to slope backward or recede.—*v.t.* In the game of chess, to move or draw back, as a piece.—**beat a re·treat**, to give the signal to retreat, as by beating a drum or drums; to retreat quickly or ignominiously.

re·trench, ri·trench', *v.t.* [Fr. (obs.) *retrencher* (now *retrancher*), O.Fr. *trenchier*, cut, E. *trench*, v.] To cut down, reduce, or diminish; curtail, as expenses; to cut off or remove; omit.—*v.i.* To economize; reduce expenses.

re·trench·ment, ri·trench'ment, *n.* The act of retrenching; a cutting down or off; a reduction of expenses; *fort.* an interior work which cuts off one part of a fortification from the rest, and to which a garrison may retreat.

re·tri·al, rē·trī'al, rē·trīl', *n.* A second or new trial, as in a judicial court; a second test or experiment.

ret·ri·bu·tion, re″tri·bū'shan, *n.* The act of requiting; a reward, recompense, or requital, esp. a requital or punishment for wrong or evil done; the dispensing of rewards and punishments in a future life.—**re·trib·u·tive**, **re·trib·u·to·ry**, re·trib'ya·tiv, ri·trib'ya·tōr″ē, *a.*—**re·trib·u·tive·ly**, *adv.*

re·trieve, ri·trēv', *v.t.*—*retrieved, retrieving.* [O.Fr. *retrover* (retruev-), < *re-* (< L. *re-*), again, and *trouver*, find.] To recover or regain; to rescue or save; to restore or bring back to a former and better state; to make amends for; to make good or repair; to remember or recall to mind; to correct, as the consequences; to return, as a ball in tennis; *hunting*, of dogs, to find and fetch, as killed or wounded game.—*v.i. Hunting*, to retrieve game.—*n.* The act of retrieving; recovery; possibility of recovery.—**re·triev·a·ble**, *a.*—**re·triev·al**, ri·trē'val, *n.*

re·triev·er, ri·trē'vẽr, *n.* One who or that which retrieves; a dog trained to retrieve game; any of various breeds of dog developed and used for this purpose.

re·tro·ac·tion, re″trō·ak'shan, *n.* Reverse or opposed action; operation on something past or preceding.

ret·ro·ac·tive, re″trō·ak'tiv, *a.* Designed to retroact; referring to a prior time and effective as of that time; as, a *retroactive* pay raise; retrospective.—**ret·ro·ac·tive·ly**, *adv.*—**ret·ro·ac·tiv·i·ty**, *n.*

ret·ro·cede, re″trō·sēd', *v.i.*—*retroceded, retroceding.* [L. *retro*, back, and *cedo*, to go.] To go back; to recede; to retire.—*v.t.* To yield or cede back.—**ret·ro·ces·sion**, re″tro·sesh'an, *n.*

ret·ro·flex, re′tro·fleks', *a.* [L. *retroflexus*,

pp. of *retroflectere* < *retro*, back, and *flectere*, bend.] Bent backward; exhibiting retroflexion; also **ret·ro·flexed**, re′trō·flekst″. *Phon.* involving or articulated with the tongue tip curled up and back near or against the place where the hard and soft palates join.

ret·ro·flex·ion, **ret·ro·flec·tion**, re″trō·flek'shan, *n.* A bending backward; *pathol.* a bending backward of the body of the uterus. *Phon.* retroflex articulation.

ret·ro·gra·da·tion, re″trō·grä·dā′shan, *n.* [L.L. *retrogradatio*(n-).] The act of retrograding; backward movement; withdrawal or retreat; decline or deterioration.

ret·ro·grade, re′trō·grād″, *a.* [L. *retrogradus.*] Moving backward; having a backward motion or direction; withdrawing or retreating; inverse or reversed, as order; tending to fall back toward a worse condition; deteriorating. *Astron.* denoting an apparent or actual motion in a direction contrary to the order of the signs of the zodiac or from east to west; having such a motion, as a planet.—*v.i.*—*retrograded, retrograding.* [L. *retrogradi* (L.L. *retrogradare*), < *retro*, back, and *gradi*, walk, go.] To move or go backward; withdraw or retreat; to fall back toward a worse condition; decline or deteriorate; *astron.* to have a retrograde motion.

ret·ro·gress, re′trō·gres″, re″trō·gres′, *v.i.* [L. *retrogressus.*] To move backward; go back; revert.—**ret·ro·gres·sion**, re″trō·gresh′an, *n.* The act of retrogressing or retrograding; backward movement; decline or deterioration; *biol.* a returning to a simpler form a more complex or more perfect structure.—**ret·ro·gres·sive**, re″trō·gres′iv, *a.* Moving or going backward; retrograde; degenerating.—**ret·ro·gres·sive·ly**, *adv.*

ret·ro·len·tal, re″trō·len'tal, *a.* Situated posterior to a lens, as of the eye.

ret·ro·lin·gual, re″trō·ling′gwal, *a.* Situated at or behind the base of the tongue.

ret·ro·per·i·to·ne·al, re″trō·per″i·to·nē′al, *a.* Located posterior to the peritoneum.—**ret·ro·per·i·to·ne·al·ly**, *adv.*

ret·ro·rock·et, re′trō·rok″it, *n.* A decelerating rocket attached to a space vehicle to supply braking action under certain conditions.

re·trorse, ri·trạrs′, *a.* [L. *retrorsus*, < *retro*, backward, and *versus*, turned.] *Bot.* turned backward.—**re·trorse·ly**, *adv.*

ret·ro·ser·rate, re″trō·ser′it, re″trō·ser′āt, *a. Biol.* characterized by retrorse barbs; as, a *retroserrate* leaf.

ret·ro·spect, re′trō·spekt″, *n.* Contemplation of the past; a survey of past time, events, or experiences.—*v.i.* [L. *retrospectus*, pp. of *retrospicere*, < *retro*, back, and *specere*, look at.] To look back in thought; reflect; to refer back, often followed by *to.*—*v.t.* To look back upon; to contemplate, as something past.—**in ret·ro·spect**, in considering what is past.

ret·ro·spec·tion, re″trō·spek′shan, *n.* The action or faculty of looking back on things past; a survey of past events or experiences.

ret·ro·spec·tive, re″trō·spek′tiv, *a.* Directed to the past; contemplative of past events; looking or directed backward; retroactive, as a statute.—*n.* A comprehensive exhibit of an artist's work produced over a period of years.—**ret·ro·spec·tive·ly**, *adv.*

ret·rous·sé, re″trö·sā′, Fr. Rᴇ·tʀö·sā′, *a.* [Fr.] Turned up, as the nose.

ret·ro·ver·sion, re″tro·vụr′zhan, re″tro·vụr′shan, *n.* [L. *retro*, backward, and *verto, versum*, to turn.] A turning or looking backward; *pathol.* a turning or bending backward, as of a part or an organ, esp. the uterus.

re·try, rē·trī′, v.t.—retried, retrying. To try again or anew, as before a court.

re·turn, ri·tụrn′, v.t. [O.Fr. retorner (Fr. retourner), < re- (< L. re-), back, and torner, turn.] To give back; to turn back or in the reverse direction; to reflect, as light or sound; to put, bring, take, or send back; as, to return a book to its shelf or to a library; to restore; to report or announce officially; to render, as a verdict; to elect, as to a legislative body; to send or give back in reciprocation, recompense, or requital; as, to return an answer to a question; to reciprocate, repay, or requite with something similar; as, to return a compliment, a salute, or a visit; to repay or requite with anything specified; as, to return kindness with ingratitude; cards, to respond to by a similar lead; arch. to turn away from, or at an angle to, the previous line of direction.—v.i. To turn back or away; to go or come back, as to a former place, position, state, or practice; to go back or revert to a former owner; to revert or recur in thought or discourse, as to a subject; to make reply, or retort.

re·turn, ri·tụrn′, n. The act or fact of returning; a bringing, sending, or giving back; a going or coming back; a recurrence; reciprocation, repayment, or requital; response or reply; as, to speak or write in return; that which is returned; a response. Often pl. a report, esp. a formal or official report; as, election returns; a yield or profit, as from labor, land, business, or investment. Arch. the continuation of a molding or projection in a different direction; a side or part which falls away from the front of any straight work. Mech. a bend or turn, or a part between two bends. Law, the bringing or sending back of a writ or process, with a brief report usually endorsed upon it, as by a sheriff, to the court from which it issued; the report or certificate endorsed on the document.—a. Of or pertaining to return or returning; as, the return trip, the return fare, the return stroke of a piston; sent, given, or done in return; as, a return shot or thrust; recurring or taking place a second time; as, a return match in sports; reversing direction; as, a return bend in the road.—**re·turn·er**, n.

re·turn·a·ble, ri·tụr′na·bl, a. Able to be returned, as merchandise; law, legally required to be returned or delivered, as a writ.

re·turn·ee, ri·tụr·nē′, ri·tụr′nē, n. One who has come back, as from a journey; a veteran who has returned from overseas military service.

re·turn tick·et, n. A ticket issued by a common carrier for passage to a given point and return within a specified time; a round-trip ticket.

re·tuse, ri·tōs′, ri·tūs′, a. [L. retusus, blunted, pp. of retundere, < re-, back, and tundere, beat.] Bot. having an obtuse or rounded apex with a shallow notch, as petals or leaves.

re·u·ni·fi·ca·tion, rē″ū·ni·fi·kā′shan, n. The act or method of reconsolidating.

re·u·ni·fy, rē·ū′ni·fī″, v.t.—reunified, reunifying. To bring back into a unit.

re·un·ion, rē·ūn′yan, n. The act of coming together again; a renewed union; a gathering of relatives, friends, or associates meeting after separation; the annual meeting of a school or college class.—**re·un·ion·ism**, n. Advocacy of reunion; the principles of reunionists.—**re·un·ion·ist**, rē·ūn′ya·nist, n. An advocate of reunion; one who advocates the reunion of the Anglican Church with the Roman Catholic Church.—**re·un·ion·is·tic**, rē·ūn″ya·nis′tik, a.

re·u·nite, rē″ū·nīt′, v.t., v.i.—reunited, reuniting. To unite or cohere again; to join

after separation; to bring together again; to reconcile after variance.

re-up, rē·up′, v.i.—re-upped, re-upping. Milit. slang; to reenlist.

re·use, rē·ūz′, v.t.—reused, reusing. To use again.—rē·ūs′, n. Repeated use; a using again.—**re·us·a·ble**, rē·ū′za·bl, a. Capable of repeated use or of being used again.

rev, rev, n. Colloq. a revolution, as of a motor, propeller, wheel, or the like.—v.t.—revved, revving. To increase the speed of, usu. used with up.—v.i. To be accelerated.

re·val·u·ate, rē·val′ū·āt″, v.t.—revaluated, revaluating. Revalue.—**re·val·u·a·tion**, rē″val·ū·ā′shan, n.

re·val·ue, rē·val′ū, v.t.—revalued, revaluing. To value again, as currency; to reappraise.

re·vamp, rē·vamp′, v.t. To patch up again; to reconstruct or renovate; revise; to vamp again, as a shoe.

re·vanche, rē·vänch′, n. A political policy of revenge or violent recovery of territory lost in war. Also **re·vanch·ism**, rē·vänch′-iz·um.—**re·vanch·ist**, a., n.

re·veal, ri·vēl′, v.t. [O.Fr. reveler (Fr. révéler), < L. revelare (pp. revelatus), < re-, back, and velum, veil.] To make known, disclose, or divulge; to lay open to view, display, or exhibit.—n. Arch. That part of a jamb or vertical face of an opening for a window or door, included between the face of the wall and that of the frame containing the window or door; the whole jamb or vertical face of an opening.—**re·veal·a·ble**, a.—**re·veal·er**, n.

re·veal·ment, ri·vēl′ment, n. The act of revealing; revelation.

rev·eil·le, rev′e·lē, n. [< Fr. réveiller, to awake—L. re-, and vigilo, to watch.] Milit. the beat of a drum, a bugle call, or some other signal given about daybreak to awaken soldiers.

rev·el, rev′el, v.i.—reveled, reveling, Brit. revelled, revelling. [O.Fr. reveler, revel, orig. rebel, < L. rebellare, E. rebel, v.] To take great pleasure or delight, usu. followed by in, as: He reveled in their astonishment. To make merry; indulge in boisterous festivities.—n. [O.Fr. revel.] Boisterous merrymaking or festivity; revelry; often pl. an occasion of noisy festivity with dancing, masking, and other forms of entertainment.—**rev·el·er**, Brit. **rev·el·ler**, n.—**rev·el·ous**, a.

rev·e·la·tion, rev″e·lā′shan, n. [O.Fr. revelation (Fr. révélation), < L.L. revela-tio(n-).] The act or an act of revealing or disclosing; disclosure; something revealed or disclosed; a striking disclosure, as of something not before realized. Theol. God's disclosure of himself and of his will to his creatures; an instance of such communication or disclosure; something thus communicated or disclosed; that which contains such disclosure, as the Bible.—**re·ve·la·tion·ist**, rev″e·lā′sha·nist, n. One who believes in revelation of the Divine.

Rev·e·la·tion, rev″e·lā′shan, n. Often pl. The last book of the New Testament; the Apocalypse. Also **the Rev·e·la·tion of St. John the Di·vine**.

rev·e·la·tor, rev′e·lā″tẽr, n. [L.L.] One who makes a revelation.

rev·e·la·to·ry, ri·vel′a·tōr″ē, ri·vel′a·-tãr″ē, rev′e·la·tōr″ē, rev′e·la·tãr″ē, a. Of or pertaining to revelation; affording a revelation.

rev·el·ry, rev′el·rē, n. pl. **rev·el·ries**. An act of reveling; boisterous or noisy festivity.

rev·e·nant, rev′e·nant, n. [Fr. prop. ppr. of revenir, return.] One who returns; one who returns as a spirit after death; a ghost.

re·venge, ri·venj′, v.t.—revenged, revenging. [O.Fr. revenger, revengier (Fr. revancher)—re-, in return, and vengier, venger, to avenge, < L. vindicare, to vindicate.] To

take vengeance for; to avenge; to inflict injury for or on account of, in a spiteful or malignant spirit.—n. The act of revenging; the executing of vengeance; retaliation; the deliberate infliction of pain or injury in return for an injury received; the desire to inflict pain on one who has done an injury.—**re·veng·er**, n.

re·venge·ful, ri·venj′ful, a. Full of revenge; harboring revenge.—**re·venge·ful·ly**, adv.—**re·venge·ful·ness**, n.

rev·e·nue, rev′en·ū″, rev′e·nö″, n. [Fr. revenu, lit. 'what comes back', < revenir, to return.] Receipts of a government from excise taxes, imposts, and duties; the department of the government which collects this income; income in general; an income source, as that derived from an investment.

rev·e·nu·er, rev′e·nö″ẽr, rev′e·nū″ẽr, n. Colloq. A U.S. Treasury Department agent; the boat or cutter used by revenue agents.

rev·e·nue stamp, n. A stamp on an item indicating that tax payment has been made.

re·ver·ber·ant, ri·vụr′bẽr·ant, a. Reverberating; returning sound; resounding; reechoing.—**re·ver·ber·ant·ly**, adv.

re·ver·ber·ate, ri·vụr′be·rāt″, v.t.—reverberated, reverberating. [L.L. reverbero, reverberatum—L. re-, back, and verbero, to beat, < verber, a lash, a whip.] To return, as sound; to send back; to reecho; to reflect, as heat or light; to repel from side to side; as, flame reverberated in a furnace.—v.i. To rebound; to be reflected, as rays of light; to reecho; to resound.—a. Reverberant.

re·ver·ber·a·tion, ri·vụr″be·rā′shan, n. The act of reverberating; an object which is reverberated; heat, light, or sound reverberated or echoed; the state or fact of being reflected or reechoed.—**re·ver·ber·a·tive**, ri·vụr′bẽr·a·tiv, a.

re·ver·ber·a·to·ry, ri·vụr′bẽr·a·tōr″ē, ri·vụr′bẽr·a·tãr″ē, a. Producing reverberation; reverberating; acting by reverberation; deflected, as heat.—n. pl. **re·ver·ber·a·to·ries**.

re·ver·ber·a·to·ry fur·nace, n. A furnace with a low roof that reflects the flame and heat down onto the hearth where the material, as ores and metal to be treated, can be heated without coming in direct contact with the fuel. Also reverberatory.

re·vere, ri·vēr′, v.t.—revered, revering. [Fr. révérer, L. revereor—re-, and vereor, to feel awe of, to fear; same root as E. wary.] To regard with respect and affection mingled with awe; to venerate.

re·vers, ri·vēr′, n. Revers.

rev·er·ence, rev′ẽr·ens, rev′rens, n. An attitude of deep respect and esteem mingled with affection; veneration; an obeisance or respectful act, as a bow; the state of being honored; (cap.) a common title of the clergy, used with his and your.—v.t.—reverenced, reverencing. To regard with reverence.

rev·er·end, rev′ẽr·end, rev′rend, a. [L. reverendus, to be revered.] Worthy of reverence; (often cap.) a title of respect given to clergymen; characteristic of or referring to the clergy.—n. A clergyman. Abbr. Rev.

rev·er·ent, rev′ẽr·ent, rev′rent, a. Expressing reverence or veneration; humble or deeply respectful; impressed with reverence.—**rev·er·ent·ly**, adv.

rev·er·en·tial, rev″e·ren′shal, a. Proceeding from reverence, or expressing it.—**rev·er·en·tial·ly**, adv.

rev·er·ie, rev·er·y, rev′e·rē, n. pl. **rev·er·ies**. [Fr. rêverie, < rêver, to dream; akin to rave.] A waking dream; a loose or irregular train of thought occurring in musing or meditation; a musical composition expressing such thought.

re·vers, ri·vēr′, ri·vâr′, n. pl. **re·vers**, ri·vērz′, ri·vârz′. [Fr.] A part of a garment turned back to show the lining or facing, as a lapel; a trimming simulating such a part; the facing used. Also *revere*.

re·ver·sal, ri·vụr′sal, *n*. The act of reversing or the condition of being reversed; *law*, the setting aside of a court decision by a higher court.

re·verse, ri·vụrs′, *v.t.—reversed, reversing*. [L. *revertor, reversus—re-*, back, and *verto*, to turn.] To turn or put in an opposite or contrary direction or position; to turn upside down or inside out; to turn about in an opposite order or sequence; as, to *reverse* the steps of a procedure; to alter to the opposite; as, to *reverse* one's political beliefs; to make void, overturn, set aside, or annul; as, to *reverse* a judgment or decree; to cause to operate or revolve in a contrary direction, as a mechanism; *print.* to reproduce in the reverse, as white lettering on a black ground, or inverted photographic plates.—*v.i.* To move or change to a contrary direction, as when dancing; to shift a mechanism into reverse direction—*a.* Of an opposite or contrary condition, arrangement, character, or the like; as, in *reverse* direction; having the back or opposite side presented to view; as, the *reverse* side of the question; of a motion or manner of operation opposite to the usual; as, a mechanism running in *reverse* gear. *Print.* printed in such a way that what is normally dark is light, and vice versa; of a photoengraving or reproduction, turned backward or inverted.—*n.* That which is turned about or contrary; the back or opposite side or surface of something; that side of a medal or coin not having the main design: opposed to *obverse*; an unfavorable change or turn of affairs; as, a business *reverse*; a setback; defeat; a gear or mechanism that reverses something; the state of moving in reverse; an offensive football play featuring a back running with the ball in one direction and then handing the ball to a second back moving the opposite way.—**re·vers·ed·ly**, **re·verse′ly**, ri·vụr′sid·lẽ, ri·vụrs′lẽ, *adv.*—**re·vers·er**, *n.*

re·vers·i·ble, ri·vụr′si·bl, *a*. Capable of being reversed; capable of being turned outside in, as a jacket; having the ability to change and then revert to the original state; having two usable sides.—*n.* A coat or jacket worn either side out.—**re·vers·i·bil·i·ty**, *n.*—**re·vers·i·bly**, *adv.*

re·ver·sion, ri·vụr′zhan, ri·vụr′shan, *n.* [L. *reversio*.] A reverting or returning, as to original form or condition; the act of turning about; a reversal. *Biol.* a return toward some ancestral type or character; atavism. *Law*, the returning of an estate to the grantor or his heirs.

re·ver·sion·ar·y, ri·vụr′zha·ner″ẽ, ri·vụr′sha·ner″ẽ, *a.* Involving or pertaining to a reversion. Also **re·ver·sion·al**.

re·ver·sion·er, ri·vụr′zha·nẽr, ri·vụr′sha·nẽr, *n. Law*, one who has an estate in reversion.

re·vert, ri·vụrt′, *v.i.* [L. *reverto*.] To return or come back; to turn back; to turn to something thought or spoken of before. *Biol.* to go back to a former state or condition; to exhibit characteristics inherited from a primitive generation. *Law*, to return to the possession of the donor, or of the former owner or heirs.—*n.*—**re·vert·er**, *n.*—**re·vert·i·ble**, **re·vert·ed**, *a*.

re·vest, rẽ·vest′, *v.t.* To reinvest; to vest again, as a person, with possession or office; reinstate.—*v.i.* To revert or return, as to a former owner.

re·vet, ri·vet′, *v.t.—revetted, revetting.* [Fr. *revêtir*, to reclothe; L.L. *revestio*.] To construct or face with masonry or other material; as, to *revet* an embankment.

re·vet·ment, ri·vet′ment, *n*. A facing to a wall or bank, as of a scarp or parapet; a

retaining wall, as for the protection of an embankment.

re·vict·ual, rẽ·vit′al, *v.t.—revictualed, revictualing*, Brit. *revictualled, revictualling*. To victual again; to furnish again with provisions.

re·view, ri·vū′, *v.t.* To view or examine again; to notice or study critically; to write a critical notice of or discuss critically after an examination to discover merits or defects, as a newly published book; to inspect, esp. to make a formal or official examination of the state of; as, to *review* troops; to look back on; *law*, to reexamine judicially.—*v.i.* To make or write reviews.—*n.* A second or repeated view; a reexamination or revision; renewed study, as for a test; a general survey; a critical examination of a new publication, with remarks; a criticism; a critique; the name given to certain periodical publications, consisting of essays which contain critical examinations of new publications and happenings; an official inspection of military or naval forces; *theatr.* revue; *law*, a judicial reexamination for the purpose of correction, as in a higher court.

re·view·er, ri·vū′ẽr, *n.* One who reviews; a writer of a review; one who critically examines a new publication, movie, play, or the like, and reports his opinion.

re·vile, ri·vil′, *v.t.—reviled, reviling*. To assail with opprobrious and contemptuous language; to vilify; to speak evil of.—*v.i.* To use contemptuous language.—**re·vile·ment**, *n.*—**re·vil·er**, *n.*

re·vis·al, ri·vi′zal, *n.* The act of revising; a revision.

re·vise, ri·viz′, *v.t.—revised, revising*. [Fr. *reviser*; L. *reviso—re-*, again, and *viso*, to look at attentively, intens. of *video, visum*, to see.] To examine or reexamine and make corrections on; to look over with care for corrections; to change and amend.—*n.* A revision; a reexamination and correction; *print.* a proof examined after incorporating corrections of an earlier proof.—**re·vis·a·ble**, *a.*—**re·vis·er**, **re·vis·or**, *n.*

Re·vised Stand·ard Ver·sion, *n.* A revision and correction of the King James Bible, based in part on the American Standard Version and published complete in 1952.

Re·vised Ver·sion, *n.* A modernized form of the Authorized Version of the Bible, first published complete in 1885.

re·vi·sion, ri·vizh′an, *n.* The act of revising; a reexamination for correction; that which is revised.—**re·vi·sion·ar·y**, *a.*—**re·vi·sion·al**, *a*.

re·vi·sion·ism, ri·vizh′a·niz″um, *n.* A preference for change or revision; among Marxists, a preference for and encouragement of pragmatic deviation from the theories of Karl Marx.—**re·vi·sion·ist**, ri·vizh′a·nist, *a., n.*

re·vis·it, rẽ·viz′it, *v.t.* To visit again.—*n.* A second visit.—**re·vis·it·a·tion**, rẽ″viz·i·tā′shan, *n*.

re·vi·so·ry, ri·vi′zo·rẽ, *a.* Having power to revise; effecting revision.

re·vi·tal·ize, rẽ·vit′a·liz″, *v.t.—revitalized, revitalizing*. To restore vitality or vigor to; to bring back to life.—**re·vi·tal·i·za·tion**, *n.*

re·viv·al, ri·vi′val, *n.* The act of reviving, or the state of being revived; restoration to life or consciousness, or to vigor, strength, or the like; restoration to use, acceptance, or currency; as, the *revival* of old customs; a new presentation of an old play or film; an awakening, in a church or a community, of interest in and care for matters relating to personal religion; a service or a series of services for the purpose of effecting a religious awakening; *law*, the renewal of the legal force of a judgment, contract, or obligation.

re·viv·al·ism, ri·vi′va·liz″um, *n.* The tendency to revive what belongs to the past; that form of religious activity which manifests itself in revivals.—**re·viv·al·ist**, *n.*—**re·viv·al·is·tic**, ri·vĩv″a·lis′tik, *a.*

Re·viv·al of Learn·ing, *n.* The Renaissance in its relation to learning.

re·vive, ri·vĩv′, *v.t.—revived, reviving*. [O.Fr. Fr. *revivre*, < L. *revivere*.] To set going or activate again; as, to *revive* old feuds; to make operative or valid again; to bring back into notice, use, or currency; to present again, as an old play or film; to restore to life or to consciousness; to resuscitate; to reanimate or cheer; to quicken or renew in the mind; to bring back to the mind.—*v.i.* To return to life or consciousness; to gain fresh strength or vigor; to be quickened, restored, or renewed, as hope, suspicions, or the like; to return to notice, use, or currency, as a subject, practice, or doctrine; to become operative or valid again.—**re·viv·er**, *n.*

re·viv·i·fy, ri·viv′i·fĩ″, *v.t.—revivified, revivifying*. [Fr. *revivifier*—L. *re-*, again, *vivus*, living, *facio*, to make.] To give new life or vigor to; revive.—**re·viv·i·fi·ca·tion**, ri·viv″i·fi·kā′shan, *n.*

rev·i·vis·cence, rev″i·vis′ens, *n.* The act of reviving; the condition of being revived; renewal of life; revival.—**rev·i·vis·cent**, *a.*

rev·o·ca·ble, rev′o·ka·bl, *a.* [L. *revocabilis*.] Capable of being revoked. Also **re·vok·a·ble**, ri·vō′ka·bl.

rev·o·ca·tion, rev″o·kā′shan, *n.* [L. *revocatio*.] The act of recalling, revoking, or annulling; *law*, a repeal, recall, or annulment of some power, deed, or grant previously given.

re·voke, ri·vōk′, *v.t.—revoked, revoking*. [Fr. *révoquer*, < L. *revocare—re-*, back, and *voco*, to call.] To annul by recalling or taking back; to make void; to cancel, repeal, or reverse.—*v.i. Cards.* To neglect to follow suit when possible; renege.—*n. Cards*, the act of reneging or failing to follow suit.—**re·vok·er**, *n.*

re·volt, ri·vōlt′, *v.i.* [Fr. *révolter*, < It. *rivoltare, revoltare*, to revolt—*re-*, and *volte, volta*, a volt, bounding, turn, < L. *volvo, volutum*, to roll.] To rebel against established authority by an overt act, as an uprising against a government; to renounce allegiance or submission to organizations or persons in authority; to rebel in thought or feeling, followed by *against*; to be grossly offended or disgusted, followed by *at*.—*v.t.* To repel; to disgust.—*n.* The act of revolting; rebellion; a renunciation of allegiance or subjection to institutions or persons in authority; the mental condition of one who revolts, preceded by *in*.—**re·volt·er**, *n.*

rev·o·lute, rev′o·löt″, *a.* [L. *revolutus*, < *revolvo*.] Rolled or curled backward or downward; *bot.* rolled back or toward the lower surface.

rev·o·lu·tion, rev″o·lö′shan, *n.* [L. *revolutio, revolutionis*, a revolving, < *revolvo, revolutum*, to revolve.] The act of revolving or rotating; a sudden and violent change of the government or the political constitution of a country, usu. by internal instigation; a radical change of circumstances in a scientific, social, or industrial system; a cycle of time or a succession of events that recurs periodically. *Mech.* a circular motion around an axis; the completed turn so made. *Astron.* one complete orbit made by a heavenly body around another; one full rotation of a planet or body on its axis.

rev·o·lu·tion·ar·y, rev″o·lö′sha·ner″ẽ, *a.* Pertaining to a political revolution; tending to produce a revolution; suggesting drastic change; revolving.—*n.* A revolutionist. pl. **rev·o·lu·tion·ar·ies**.

rev·o·lu·tion·ist, rev″o·lö′sha·nist, *n.*

One who advocates or participates in a revolution; a revolutionary.

rev·o·lu·tion·ize, rev″o·lö′sha·nīz″, v.t. —*revolutionized, revolutionizing.* To bring about a revolution in; to effect a complete or fundamental change in.—**rev·o·lu·-tion·iz·er**, n.

re·volve, ri·volv′, v.i.—*revolved, revolving.* [L. *revolvo*—*re-*, again, and *volvo*, to roll.] To move along a curving path around a center; to travel in an orbit; to rotate on an axis; to recur cyclically, as: The years *revolve.*—v.t. To cause to circle round or rotate; to turn over in the mind; to ponder. —**re·volv·a·ble**, a.

re·volv·er, ri·vol′vèr, n. A pistol having a revolving breech cylinder so constructed as to discharge several shots in quick succession without being reloaded; one who or that which revolves.

re·volv·ing, ri·vol′ving, a. Turning; moving; moving around; recurring.

re·volv·ing fund, n. A fund set up for a particular purpose, as the financing of scholarships, continuously maintained through repayments.

re·vue, ri·vū′, n. [Fr.] A loosely constructed and often satirical theatrical exhibition of a topical character, consisting of dances, skits, and songs; review.

re·vul·sion, ri·vul′shan, n. [L. *revulsio*, < *revello, revulsum*—*re-*, again, and *vello*, to pull.] A sudden and strong emotional reaction or change of feeling, usu. in the direction of extreme displeasure; repulsion; repugnance or loathing; an abrupt withdrawal or drawing away from; the fact of being so drawn; *med.* a counterirritant.— **re·vul·sive**, ri·vul′siv, a.—**re·vul·sion·-ar·y**, a.

re·ward, ri·wŏrd′, v.t. [O.Fr. *rewarder*, < *re-* and the Teut. word *ward* = guard, so that *reward* = *regard.*] To give something to in return; to requite; to bestow a recompense, remuneration, or token of favor upon.—n. That which is given in return for good or evil done or received, esp. that which is in return for achievement or service; recompense; the fruit of men's labor or work; a sum of money offered for capturing or detecting a criminal, or for the recovery of anything lost.—**re·ward·a·ble**, a.—**re·ward·er**, n.

re·wind, rē·wīnd′, v.t.—*rewound, rewinding.* To wind again.—n.

re·wire, rē·wīèr′, v.t.—*rewired, rewiring.* To wire anew, as the electrical circuit of a building.

re·word, rē·wŭrd′, v.t. To word again; repeat; put into other words.

re·work, rē·wŭrk′, v.t. To work again; to revise; to reprocess, as something used before.

re·write, rē·rīt′, v.t.—past *rewrote*, pp. *rewritten*, ppr. *rewriting.* To write over again, esp. in altered form; to revise; to write a second time; *journ.* to write or put into form ready for publication, as a news item originally prepared by a reporter.— rē′rīt″, n. A revision; a news story or other article that has been rewritten.—**re·writ·-er**, n.

rex, reks, L. Reks, n. pl. **re·ges**, rē′jēz, L. Re′ges. [L., < *regere*, rule.] (*Often cap.*) king. Abbr. R.

Reyn·ard, ren′èrd, rā′närd, n. [O.Fr. *renart* (Fr. *renard*); < Teut.] The fox, orig. in the medieval beast epic, *Reynard the Fox*, personifying craftiness; (*l.c.*) a fox. Also **Ren·ard**, ren′èrd.

rhab·do·man·cy, rab′do·man″sē, n. [Gr. *rhabdos*, a rod, and *manteia*, divination.] Divination by a rod or wand; the supposed discovery of things concealed in the earth, as ores of metals and springs of water, by a divining rod.—**rhab·do·-man·tist**, n.

rhad·a·man·thine, rad″a·man′thin, a. Of or pertaining to Rhadamanthus, a Greek mythological figure, who was so noted on earth for his exemplary justice that he was made a judge in the lower world; scrupulously just; strict; as, a *rhadamanthine* decision.

rham·na·ceous, ram·nā′shus, a. [N.L. *Rhamnus*, the typical genus, < Gr. *rhamnos*, kind of prickly shrub.] *Bot.* belonging or pertaining to the *Rhamnaceae*, or buckthorn family of plants.

rha·phe, rā′fē, n. Raphe.

rhap·sod·ic, rap·sod′ik, a. Having the characteristics of a rhapsody in form or feeling; excessively enthusiastic. Also **rhap·sod·i·cal.**—**rhap·sod·i·cal·ly**, adv.

rhap·so·dist, rap′so·dist, n. One who speaks or writes in a rhapsodical manner; among the ancient Greeks, one who recited epic poetry, esp. that of Homer.

rhap·so·dize, rap′so·dīz″, v.i.—*rhapsodized, rhapsodizing.* To compose or recite rhapsodies; to talk or write in an ecstatic manner.—v.t. To recite rapturously.

rhap·so·dy, rap′so·dē, n. pl. **rhap·so·dies.** [Gr. *rhapsōdia*,—*rhaptō, rhapso*, to sew, and *odē*, a song.] A spoken or written work of an ecstatic sort, depending less on logical structure than on emotional appeal; originally, a short epic poem or portion of a longer epic such as would be recited by a rhapsodist; a similar work in modern literature; a musical composition of irregular form, resembling an improvisation, usu. instrumental.

rhat·a·ny, rat′a·nē, n. pl. **rhat·a·nies.** [Pg. *ratânhia*, or Sp. *ratania*; < Peruvian.] Either of the S. American shrubs, *Krameria triandra* or *K. argentea*, the roots of which are used as an astringent and in medicine. Also *ratany.*

rhe·a, rē′a, n. [N.L. use of L. *Rhea*, < Gr. *Réa*, the goddess Rhea, mother of Zeus and other deities.] *Ornith.* any of the large, flightless S. American birds of the genus *Rhea*, resembling the African ostrich but smaller and having three toes instead of two, and a completely feathered neck and head; *bot.* ramie.

rhe·ni·um, rē′nē·um, n. *Chem.* a rare metallic element resembling manganese, with a high melting point. Sym. Re, at. no. 75, at. wt. 186.2. See Periodic Table of Elements.

rhe·ol·o·gy, rē·ol′o·jē, n. The study of the action or behavior of liquid matter and semisolids in the fluid state.—**rhe·o·log·-i·cal**, a.

rhe·om·e·ter, rē·om′i·tèr, n. [Gr. *rheō*, to flow, and *metron*, measure.] An instrument used to measure the flow of liquids, esp. the force or velocity of the blood stream.

rhe·o·stat, rē′o·stat″, n. [Gr. *rheō*, and *statos*, standing.] An instrument for regulating the strength of an electric current by means of adjustable resistances.—**rhe·o·-stat·ic**, rē″o·stat′ik, a.

rhe·sus, rē′sus, n. A short-tailed, light brown monkey, *Macaca mulatta*, native to India, used for research in medicine and biology.

rhe·tor, rē′tèr, n. [L., rhetorician, < Gr. *rhētōr*, speaker, orator, from the root of *eirein*, say, speak: cf. *irony.*] A master or teacher of rhetoric; an orator.

rhet·o·ric, ret′èr·ik, n. [Fr. *rhétorique*, L. *rhetorica*, < Gr. *rhētorikē* (*technē*, art, understood), < *rhētōr*, a public speaker, < *rheo*, to speak.] The art or branch of knowledge which treats the rules or principles underlying all effective composition whether in prose or verse; the art which teaches oratory; persuasive oratory; eloquence, esp. artificial eloquence; bombast. **rhe·tor·i·cal**, ri·tar′i·kal, ri·tor′i·kal, a.

Pertaining to, exhibiting, or involving rhetoric; used for pompous effect.—**rhe·-tor·i·cal·ly**, adv.—**rhe·tor·i·cal·ness**, n.

rhe·tor·i·cal ques·tion, n. A question which is put forward to create an effect, not to receive an answer.

rhet·o·ri·cian, ret″o·rish′an, n. One who teaches the art of rhetoric; one well versed in the rules and principles of rhetoric; a speaker or writer of elaborate prose.

rheum, rōm, n. [Gr. *rheuma*, a flowing, rheum, < *rheō*, to flow.] A thin watery fluid discharged by the mucous glands, as in catarrh; a cold; any watery matter which collects in the eyes, nose, or mouth.— **rheum·ic**, a.—**rheu·my**, a.—*rheumier, rheumiest.*

rheu·mat·ic, rö·mat′ik, a. [L. *rheumaticus.*] Pertaining to or characteristic of rheumatism; affected with rheumatism.— n. One subject to or afflicted with rheumatism.—**rheu·mat·i·cal·ly**, adv.

rheu·mat·ic fe·ver, n. *Pathol.* a severe infectious disease, usu. occurring in young adults or children, characterized by painful swollen joints, fever, and often by inflamed heart lining and valves. See *rheumatism.*

rheu·ma·tism, rö′ma·tiz″um, n. [Gr. *rheumatismos*, < *rheuma*—the ancients supposing the disease to proceed from a defluxion of humors.] *Pathol.* A painful inflammation affecting muscles and joints, attended by swelling and stiffness.

rheu·ma·toid, rö′ma·toid″, a. Resembling rheumatism; rheumatic. Also **rheu·ma·-toi·dal.**—**rheu·ma·toi·dal·ly**, adv.

rheu·ma·toid ar·thri·tis, n. *Pathol.* a progressive disease of the joints causing painful swelling and shortening of fibrous tissues, frequently resulting in deformities.

Rh fac·tor, n. *Biochem.* any of several inherited antigens in red blood cells of most humans, who are Rh positive, which, under certain conditions such as blood transfusions and pregnancies, are capable of destroying red corpuscles in persons whose blood is Rh negative, or deficient in these substances. Also **Rhe·sus fac·tor.**

rhi·nal, rin′al, a. [Gr. *rhis, rhinos*, the nose.] Pertaining to the nose; nasal.

rhi·nen·ceph·a·lon, rī″nen·sef′a·lon″, n. pl. **rhi·nen·ceph·a·lons**, L. **rhi·nen·-ceph·a·la**, rī″nen·sef′a·la. [N.L.] *Anat.* the olfactory portion of the brain.— **rhi·nen·ce·phal·ic**, rī″nen·se·fal′ik, a.

rhine·stone, rīn′stōn″, n. [< Fr. *caillou du Rhin*, 'pebble of the Rhine.'] An artificial gem made of paste or glass, often cut to imitate the diamond.

Rhine wine, rīn′ wīn″, n. Wine of many varieties produced in the valley of the Rhine in Germany; any of a class of white wines, mostly light, still, and dry.

rhi·ni·tis, ri·nī′tis, n. [N.L., < Gr. *ris* (*rin-*), nose.] *Pathol.* inflammation of the nose or its mucous membrane.

rhi·no, rī′nō, n. pl. **rhi·nos, rhi·no.** A rhinoceros.

rhi·no, rī′nō, n. *Brit. slang.* Money; cash.

rhi·noc·er·os, ri·nos′èr·os, n. pl. **rhi·-noc·er·os·es, rhi·noc·er·os.** [L., < Gr. *rhinokerōs*, < *ris* (*rin-*), nose, and *keras*, horn.] Any of various large, thick-skinned, perissodactyl mammals of the family *Rhinocerotidae*, found in Asia and Africa, and having one or two upright horns on the snout.— **rhi·noc·er·ot·ic**, ri·nos″e·rot′ik, a.

rhi·noc·er·os bee·tle, n. A large beetle belonging to the genus *Dynastes*, or other related genera and having a projecting horn on the head.

rhi·nos·co·py, ri·nos′ko·pē, n. pl. **rhi·-nos·co·pies.** *Med.* examination of the nasal cavity.

rhi·zan·thous, ri·zan′thus, a. *Bot.* bearing flowers so short-stemmed that they appear to grow from the root.

rhi·zo·bi·um, rĭ·zō′bē·um, *n.* pl. **rhi·-zo·bi·a**, rĭ·zō′bē·a. *Bact.* any of the symbiotic, nitrogen-fixing bacteria of the genus *Rhizobium*, in root nodules on legumes, responsible for the nitrogen fixation in maintaining soil fertility.

rhi·zo·car·pous, rī′zō·kär′pus, *a. Bot.* having the root perennial but the stem annual, as the perennial herbs. Also **rhi·zo·car·pic**, rī′zō·kär′pik.

rhi·zo·ceph·a·lan, rī′zō·sef′a·lan, *n. Zool.* one of an order of degenerate crustaceans, *Rhizocephala*, that live as parasites on crabs, causing the host to lose its reproductive capability.

rhi·zo·gen·ic, rī′zō·jen′ik, *a. Bot.* producing roots, as certain cells or tissues. Also **rhi·zog·e·nous**, rī·zoj′e·nus, **rhi·zo·ge·net·ic**, rī′zō·je·net′ik.

rhi·zoid, rī′zoid, *n.* [Gr. *rhiza*, a root, *eidos*, form.] In mosses, liverworts, and ferns, one of the hairlike structures that functions as a root.—**rhi·zoi·dal**, *a.*

rhi·zome, rī′zōm, *n.* [Gr. *rizōma*, mass of roots, < *rizoun*, cause to take root, < *rhiza*, root.] *Bot.* a rootlike stem, commonly horizontal or oblique in position, either lying on the ground or subterranean, which usually produces roots below ground and sends up shoots progressively from the upper surface.—**rhi·zom·a·tous**, rī·zom′a·tus, rī·zō′ma·tus, *a.*

rhi·zo·mor·phous, rī″zō·mạr′fus, *a.* [Gr. *rhiza*, a root, *morphē*, shape.] Rootlike in shape or form.

rhi·zo·plane, rī′zo·plān″, *n.* The surface area of the roots of a plant, including attached soil or other particles.

rhi·zo·pod, rī′zo·pod″, *n.* [N.L. *Rhizopoda*, pl., < Gr. *rhiza*, root, and *pous* (*pod-*), foot.] Any of the *Rhizopoda*, a class of protozoans having pseudopodia.—**rhi·zop·-o·dan**, rī·zop′o·dan, *a., n.*—**rhi·zop·o·-dous**, *a.*

rhi·zo·pus, rī′zō·pus, rī′zo·pus, *n.* Any of the mold fungi of the genus *Rhizopus*, including *R. nigricans*, a bread mold.

rhi·zo·sphere, rī′zo·sfēr″, *n.* The soil zone which surrounds a plant's roots and is modified by their presence and activity.

rhi·zot·o·my, rī·zot′o·mē, *n.* pl. **rhi·-zot·o·mies.** The surgical section of the posterior roots of the spinal nerves, performed as treatment for pain or spastic paralysis.

rho, rō, *n.* [Gr. *rhō.*] The seventeenth letter of the Greek alphabet, P, ρ.

rho·da·mine, rō′da·mēn″, rō′da·min, *n.* [Gr. *ródon*, rose, and E. *amine.*] A red dye obtained by heating an amino derivative of phenol with phthalic anhydride; any of various related dyes.

Rhode Is·land bent, rōd ī′land bent′, *n.* A European grass grown in eastern N. America as a lawn grass.

Rhode Is·land Red, rōd″ ī′land red′, *n.* One of a breed of domestic N. American chickens having reddish-brown feathers and yellow legs.

Rhode Is·land White, rōd″ ī′land hwīt, *n.* Any of a breed of domestic N. American chickens resembling the Rhode Island Reds but having white feathers.

Rhodes grass, rōdz′ gras″, *n.* A tall African grass, *Chloris gayana*, cultivated for forage.

Rho·de·sian man, rō·dē′zhan man′, *n. Anthropol.* a type of primitive man, *Homo rhodesiensis*, whose remains were uncovered in Northern Rhodesia in 1921 and similar in many respects to the Neanderthal man.

Rho·de·sian Ridge·back, rō·dē′zhan rij′-bak″, *n.* Any of a breed of large, domesticated African hunting dogs characterized by a ridge of hair on the spine.

Rhodes schol·ar, rōdz′ skol·ẽr, *n.* A holder of one of a number of scholarships for study at Oxford University in England provided for by the will of Cecil J. Rhodes and granted for a period of two or three years to selected candidates from the U.S. and the British Commonwealth.

rho·di·um, rō′dē·um, *n.* [< Gr. *rhodon*, a rose, due to the red color of some of its salts when dissolved in water.] *Chem.* a silver-white metallic element found in platinum ores, used in the electroplating of silverware, microscopes, jewelry, pen tips, and instrument components to inhibit corrosion. Sym. Rh, at. no. 45, at. wt. 102.905. See Periodic Table of Elements.

rho·do·chro·site, rō″do·krō′sīt, *n.* [G. *rhodochrosit*, < Gr. *rhodochrōs*, rose-colored, < *rhod*, rose, and *chrōs*, color.] A mineral, MnCO₃, consisting of manganese carbonate, usu. pinkish or rose-red in color.

rho·do·den·dron, rō″do·den′dron, *n.* [N.L., < Gr. *rhododendron*, oleander, < *rhod-*, and *dendron*, tree.] *Bot.* any plant of the ericaceous genus *Rhododendron*, comprising evergreen shrubs and trees with showy pink, purple, or white flowers and oval or oblong leaves; *R. maximum*, or the great rhododendrum, the state flower of West Virginia. Also *rosebay.*

rho·do·lite, rōd′o·līt″, *n.* [Gr. *rhod-*, rose, and *lithos*, stone.] A rose-red or reddish-violet variety of garnet, used as a gem.

rhod·o·mon·tade, rod″o·mon·tād′, rod″-o·mon·tād′, rō″do·mon·tād′, rō″do·mon·tād′, *n., a., v.i.*—**rhodomontaded**, *rhodomontading.* Rodomontade.

rho·do·nite, rōd′o·nīt″, *n.* [G. *rhodonit*, < Gr. *rhod-*, rose.] A mineral usu. rose-red, consisting of manganese, iron, and calcium silicates, sometimes used as an ornamental stone. Also *manganese spar.*

rho·dop·sin, rō·dop′sin, *n. Biochem.* a photosensitive red pigment in the rodlike retinal cells of the eye that is considered important for night vision, and that in light breaks down to protein components allied to vitamin A. Also *visual purple.*

rho·do·ra, rō·dōr′a, rō·dạr′a, ro·dōr′a, ro·dạr′a, *n.* [N.L., with form < L. *rhodora*, kind of plant.] *Bot.* a showy shrub, *Rhodora canadense*, in the heath family, native to northeastern U.S. and Canada, having magenta flowers that bloom before the leaves unfold.

rhomb, rom, romb, *n.* Rhombus.

rhom·ben·ceph·a·lon, rom″ben·sef′a·-lon″, *n. Anat.* the rearmost part of the brain.

rhom·bic, rom′bik, *a.* Being of the form of a rhombus; of solid figures, having rhombuses as bases. *Crystal.* orthorhombic; having three unequal axes crossing at right angles.

rhom·bo·he·dron, rom″bo·hē′dron, *n.* [Gr. *rhombos*, and *hedra*, a side.] A solid bounded by six rhombic planes.—**rhom·-bo·he·dral**, *a.*

rhom·boid, rom′boid, *n.* A quadrilateral figure whose opposite sides and angles are equal, but which is neither equilateral nor equiangular; a solid having a rhomboidal form.—*a.* In the form of a rhomboid; rhomboidal; diamond shaped.—**rhom·-boi·dal**, *a.*

rhom·bus, rom′bus, *n.* pl. **rhom·bus·es**, **rhom·bi**, rom′bī. [Fr. *rhombe*, L. *rhombus*, < Gr. *rhombos.*] A quadrilateral figure whose sides are equal and the opposite sides parallel, and whose angles are usually oblique rather than right; a figure of a diamond or lozenge. Also *rhomb.*

rhon·chus, rong′kus, *n.* pl. **rhon·chi**, rong′kī. [L., a snoring, akin to Gr. *rhenchein*, to snore.] A râle, esp. when produced in bronchial tubes that are partially obstructed.—**rhon·chal**, **rhon·chi·al**, rong′-kal, rong′kē·al, *a.*

rhu·barb, rō′bärb, *n.* [Fr. *rhubarbe*; L.L. *rheubarbarum*; Gr. *rhēon barbaron*, < *Rha*, a name of the river Volga (where the plant is native), and *bárbaron*, barbarian.] A large garden plant, *Rheum rhaponticum*, having thick leaf stalks used for making dessert sauces, pies, and tarts; a similar species, *R. officinale*, the roots of which are used in medicine for making laxatives, tonics, and astringents. *Slang*, a noisy dispute, esp. in baseball.

rhumb, rum, rumb, *n.* [< *rhomb.*] One of the 32 points of a mariner's compass; a rhumb line.—**rhumb line**, a navigational line along the earth's surface which crosses consecutive meridians at identical oblique angles and enables an aircraft or ship to hold a fixed compass direction; a loxodromic curve.

rhum·ba, rum′ba, rụm′ba, *Sp.* rŏm′vä, *n., v.i.*—**rhumbaed**, *rhumbaing.* Rumba.

rhyme, rīm, *n.* [O.E. *ryme*, *rime*, < *rīm*, number, rhyme = Icel, *rím*, D. *rijm*, Dan. *riim*, G. *reim*, rhyme. The proper spelling is *rime*; the *h* has been inserted by influence of L. *rhythmus*. Gr. *rhythmos*, rhythm.] A correspondence of sound in the final portions of two or more syllables; a word having a sound similar to another, as, *sound* and *round*; the correspondence in sound of the terminating word or syllable of one line of poetry with that of another line; poetry; meter; a verse or poem with corresponding sounds at the ends of the lines.—*v.i.*—*rhymed*, *rhyming.* To accord in the terminational sounds; to form a rhyme; to make verses.—*v.t.* To put into rhyme; to use, as sounds or as rhymes. Also *rime.*—**rhym·er**, **rhyme·ster**, rī′mẽr, rīm′-stẽr, *n.*

rhyme roy·al, *n.* A stanza of seven iambic pentameter lines in the rhyme formation *ababbcc*, possibly named from its use by James I of Scotland in *The King's Quair.*

rhyme scheme, *n.* The systematic ordering of rhymes in a poem, generally described by letters denoting recurring rhyme sounds, as the *ababbcc* of rhyme royal.

rhy·o·lite, rī′o·līt″, *n.* [G. *rhyolith*, < Gr. *rhyax*, stream, and *lithos*, stone.] A kind of rock that is a volcanic form of granite —**rhy·o·lit·ic**, rī″o·lit′ik, *a.*

rhythm, rĭTH′um, *n.* [Fr. *rhythme*, < L. *rhythmus*, < Gr. *rythmos*, < *rhein*, flow.] Measured movement, as in dancing, music, verse, or the like; movement or procedure with uniform recurrence of a beat, accent, or the like; in general, procedure marked by the regular recurrence of particular elements, phases, or the like; *mus.* the structure of a composition with reference to the distribution of its successive beats or accents; a particular form of this; as, duple *rhythm. Pros.* metrical movement; metrical or rhythmical form. *Art*, a proper relation and interdependence of parts with reference to one another and to an artistic whole; *physiol.* a regular recurrence of a function or action, as the heart beat.—**rhyth·mic**, rĭTH′mik, *a.*—**rhyth·mi·cal**, rĭTH′mi·kal, *a.*—**rhyth·mi·cal·ly**, *adv.*

rhyth·mics, rĭTH′miks, *n. pl. but sing. in constr.* The system or science of rhythmic forms and rhythm.—**rhyth·mist**, rĭTH′-mist, *n.*

rhythm meth·od, *n.* A system of birth control through abstinence from sexual intercourse during the estimated monthly interval of female ovulation and fertility.

rhythm stick, *n.* One of a pair of wooden sticks used as part of a rhythm band by young children learning simple musical rhythm.

Ri·al·to, rē·al′tō, *n.* [From the *Rialto* district in Venice, from which the famous bridge of the same name crosses the Grand Canal to the island of San Marco.] A part of or a region along Broadway, in New York City, frequented by theatrical people and the center of many theatrical enterprises; (*l.c.*) an exchange or mart.

ri·ant, rī'ant, *a.* [Fr. ppr. of *rire*, to laugh.] Laughing; gay; smiling.—**ri·ant·ly**, *adv.*

ri·a·ta, rē·ä'ta, *n.* A rope or lariat.

rib, rib, *n.* [*rib, ribb* = D. *rib, ribbe*, L.G. *ribbe*, Dan. *rib*, G. *rippe*, Icel. *rif*, a rib.] *Anat.* one of the slender curved bones that attach from each side of the vertebral column in man and most other vertebrates enclosing the thoracic cavity and protecting certain important organs. A cut of beef or other meat that includes one or several ribs; something resembling a rib in form, use, or position, as a spoke of an umbrella. *Arch.* a piece of timber or metal that supports or decorates an arched ceiling or vaulted dome; a reinforcing beam or rod in a concrete casting, or a like structural support. *Naut.* one of the transverse timbers or metal bars that curve outward and upward from the keel to form and strengthen the sides of a ship; *aeron.* one of the structural crosspieces spaced at intervals along the length of an airplane wing to distribute the load from the wing covering to the wing spars; *bot.* a principal vein in a leaf. A prominent ridge or wale on cloth, such as corduroy or rep, or in knitted work; *slang*, a joke directed toward a person. A wife, in humorous reference to the Biblical account of the creation of the first woman from Adam's rib. Gen. ii. 21–22.—*v.t.*—*ribbed, ribbing.* To form or equip with ribs; to enclose or protect with ribs. *Slang*, to make, as a person, the butt of a joke; to tease.—**rib·ber**, *n.*

rib·ald, rib'ald, *a.* [O.Fr. *ribalt, ribaut* (Fr. *ribaud*), = M.L. *ribaldus*; prob. < Teut.] Offensive or vulgar in speech; coarsely joking or mocking; abusive or irreverent.—*n.* A ribald person.—**rib·ald·ry**, rib'al·drē, *n. pl.* **rib·ald·ries.** Ribald language, in speech or writing; ribald nature.

rib·band, rib'band", rib'and, rib'an, *n.* [Appar. < *rib* and *band*.] *Shipbuilding,* a lengthwise metal or wood support used to secure a ship's ribs in position while the outside planking or plating is being put on.

rib·bing, rib'ing, *n.* An assemblage or arrangement of ribs, as on cloth; ribs collectively.

rib·bon, rib'on, *n.* [O.E. *ribane, riban, ribant* < O.Fr. *ruban.* Mod.Fr. *ruban,* perh. < Celtic; cf. Gael. *ribean,* a ribbon, a fillet for the hair; *rib, ribe,* a hair; Ir. *ribin,* a ribbon.] A narrow band of silk, satin, or other material generally used as an ornament or a fastener; a narrow band of inked cloth, as used in a typewriter; a narrow, thin strip of anything suggestive of a ribbon, as a metal spring; *carpentry,* a horizontal strip inserted into the studs to support joists. A strip of silk or satin worn as evidence of a decoration, esp. a military one, or to signify a prize winner in a competition; *usu. pl.* shreds; as, sails torn to *ribbons*; *pl., colloq.* driving reins.—*v.t.* To adorn or furnish with ribbons; to make into ribbons or shreds.—**rib·bon·like,** *a.*

rib·bon de·vel·op·ment, *n.* Buildings erected along a highway, usu. without previous planning of the area.

rib·bon·fish, rib'on·fish", *n. pl.* **rib·bon·fish, rib·bon·fish·es.** Any of a number of marine fishes belonging to the family *Trachipteridae,* with lengthened bodies much flattened on the sides, as a dealfish.

rib cage, *n.* Zool., anat. The bone structure comprised of the ribs of most vertebrates; in man, the chest.

rib·grass, rib'gras", *n.* Ribwort.

ri·bo·fla·vin, rī"bō·flā'vin, rī'bō·flā"vin, *n.* [< *ribo(se)* and *flavin*.] A growth-produc-

ing crystalline compound, $C_{17}H_{20}N_4O_6$, orange-yellow in color, belonging to the vitamin B complex, occurring naturally in milk, liver, egg yolk, leafy vegetables, and prepared synthetically. Also **lac·to·fla·vin,** *vitamin G, vitamin B₂.*

ri·bo·nu·cle·ic ac·id, rī'bō·nö·klē'ik as'id, rī'bō·nū·klē'ik, rī'bō·nō·klē'ik, rī"·bō·nū·klē'ik, *n.* A nucleic acid containing ribose, occurring chiefly in cytoplasm. Abbr. *RNA.*

ri·bose, rī'bōs, *n. Chem.* a pentose sugar, $HOCH_2$—CH—CHOH—CHOH—CH₂,

obtained from some nucleic acids.

ri·bo·some, rī'bo·sōm", *n.* One of a number of minute particles containing ribonucleic acid and protein, found in the cytoplasm of cells.

rib·wort, rib'wûrt", *n. Bot.* an old-world plantain, *Plantago lanceolata,* now a familiar dooryard weed with slender three-ribbed leaves and a short bushy flower head. Also *rib grass,* **Eng·lish plan·tain.**

rice, rīs, *n.* [O.Fr. *ris* (Fr. *riz*), < It. *riso,* < L. *oryza,* < Gr. *oryza,* rice; of Eastern origin.] The starchy fruit or grain of a species of grass, *Oryza sativa,* cultivated in warm climates and constituting an important food; the plant itself.—*v.t.*—*riced, ricing.* To reduce to a form resembling that of rice; as, to *rice* potatoes.

rice·bird, rīs'bûrd", *n.* Any of various small birds, esp. the bobolink or reedbird, found frequently in rice fields of southern U.S.; the Javanese sparrow.

rice Chris·tian, *n.* Originally, a native who embraced Christianity only to obtain the food dispensed by missionaries; now, anyone who converts to Christianity mainly for material advantages.

rice pa·per, *n.* Paper made from rice straw; a thin, fragile paper produced in China by slicing and pressing the pith of certain shrubs and plants into flat sheets.

rice-pa·per tree, rīs'pā"pèr trē", *n.* The shrub or small tree, *Tetrapanax papyriferum,* grown chiefly in China for its pith which is used in making rice paper, and in warm areas of the U.S. as a decorative plant.

ric·er, rī'sèr, *n.* A perforated implement which rices potatoes and other soft foods, by pressing them through small holes.

ri·cer·car, rē"chèr·kär', *n. Mus.* a composition written in the contrapuntal form, which contains two or more independent but harmonizing melodies heard concurrently, prevalent in the 16th and 17th centuries.

rich, rich, *a.* [Partly < O.E. *rice,* rich, powerful, partly < Fr. *riche,* rich, the latter being < O.H.G. *riche,* rich, which again is cogn. with O.E. *rice,* Icel. *rikr,* Goth. *reiks,* the root being that of E. *right.*] Having abundant material possessions; wealthy; well supplied; abounding; producing abundantly; productive; fertile; composed of valuable or costly materials or ingredients; sumptuous; highly valued; costly; abounding in nutritive or agreeable qualities; as, *rich* soil; excessively sweet, luscious, or highly flavored, as food; gratifying to the senses; vivid; bright; sweet, mellow, or full in tone; highly fragrant; containing a high ratio of gasoline to air. *Colloq.* very amusing; laughable; absurd.—**rich·ness,** *n.*

Rich·ard Roe, rich'èrd rō', *n.* A fictitious personage in legal proceedings, used esp. when persons are involved whose real names are not known. Compare *John Doe.*

rich·es, rich'iz, *n. pl.* [Formerly *richesse* < Fr. *richesse* (sing. n.), < *riche,* rich.] That which makes rich; abundant possessions; wealth.

rich·ly, rich'lē, *adv.* In a rich manner; opulently; abundantly; amply.

ri·cin, rī'sin, ris'in, *n. Chem.* a poisonous white powder derived from the castor bean, used in medicine to cause agglutination of red blood corpuscles.

ric·in·o·le·ic ac·id, ris"i·nō·lē'ik as'id, ris"i·nō'lē·ik, *n.* [N.L. *Ricinus,* the castor-oil plant genus, and L. *oleum,* oil.] *Chem.* an organic acid, $C_{18}H_{34}O_3$, occurring in castor oil in the form of a glyceride.—**ric·in·o·le·in,** ris"i·nō'lē·in, *n. Chem.* a glyceride of ricinoleic acid, the chief constituent of castor oil.

ric·in·us, ris'i·nus, *n.* Castor oil plant.

rick, rik, *n.* [O.E. *hrēac,* a rick; cogn. Icel. *hraukr,* a pile, W. *crug,* Ir. *cruach,* a heap, rick.] A stack or pile of corn or hay, the top part rounded and often thatched to protect the pile from rain.—*v.t.* To pile up in ricks.

rick, rik, *v.t. Brit.* to sprain or wrench, as the back. Also **wrick.**—*n.*

rick·ets, rik'its, *n.* [< old *wrick, wrikken* to twist; allied to *wring, wriggle*.] *Pathol.* a disease of children in which there is usually some softening and distortion of the bones due to faulty deposition of calcium or a vitamin D deficiency, or both.

rick·ett·si·a, ri·ket'sē·a, *n. pl.* **rick·ett·si·ae, rick·ett·si·as,** ri·ket'sē·ē", ri·ket'sē·az. [From H. T. *Ricketts* (1871–1910), Amer. pathologist.] Any of the microorganisms of the genus *Rickettsia,* parasitic in arthropods and transmitted by them to man, causing such diseases as typhus.—**rick·ett·si·al,** *a.*

rick·et·y, rik'i·tē, *a.*—**ricketier, ricketiest.** Shaky; ready to collapse; affected with rickets; feeble or imperfect in general; irregular, as in movement.—**rick·et·i·ness,** *n.*

rick·ey, rik'ē, *n. pl.* **rick·eys.** [From a Colonel *Rickey.*] A drink in which lime juice, carbonated water, and liquor, esp. gin, are the principal ingredients.

rick·rack, ric·rac, rik'rak", *n.* [Cf. *rack.*] A kind of openwork trimming, used esp. for clothing, made out of a narrow zigzag braid; a braid in zigzag shape.

rick·shaw, rik'shạ", *n.* Jinrikisha. Also **rick·sha.**

ric·o·chet, rik"o·shā', *Brit.* rik"o·shet', *n.* [Fr.; etym. unknown.] A rebounding from a flat surface, as of a stone from water; an object or projectile that rebounds.—*v.i.*— *ricocheted, ricocheting, Brit. ricochetted, ricochetting,* rik"o·shād', rik"o·shā'ing, *Brit.* rik"o·shet'id, rik"o·shet'ing. To skip, as a stone, along the surface of water.

ric·tus, rik'tus, *n. pl.* **ric·tus, ric·tus·es.** [L. < *ringi,* open the mouth wide.] The orifice of the open mouth; the gape; the wide open position of a bird's beak; any opening, fissure, or cleft.—**ric·tal,** *a.*

rid, rid, *v.t.*—*rid* or *ridded, ridding.* [O.E. *hreddan,* to take or snatch; akin to Icel. *rydja* (*rythja*), Dan. *rydde,* to clear, to remove; D. *redden,* G. *retten,* to rescue.] To free; to deliver; to clear; to disencumber; as, to *rid* a person of a burden.

rid·a·ble, rī'da·bl, *a.* Capable of being ridden, as a horse; capable of being ridden over or through, as a road or a stream.

rid·dance, rid'ans, *n.* The act of ridding; a clearing away; a getting rid of something. —**good rid·dance,** fortunate relief from something disagreeable.

rid·dle, rid'l, *n.* [O.E. *rǣdelse,* a riddle, < *rǣdan,* to read, discern, guess = D. *raadsel,* G. *rätsel,* a riddle.] A proposition put in obscure or ambiguous terms to puzzle or exercise the ingenuity in discovering its meaning; a puzzling question; an enigma; a conundrum; anything or anyone puzzling.—*v.t.*—*riddled, riddling.* To solve; to explain; to unriddle.—*v.i.* To speak ambiguously, enigmatically, or in riddles.

rid·dle, rid'l, *n.* [O.E. *hriddel,* a fan for winnowing.] A large sieve with coarse meshes, employed for separating coarser materials from finer, as in a foundry.—*v.t.* —*riddled, riddling.* To pass through or separate with a riddle; screen; to perforate with holes, so as to make like a riddle; as, to *riddle* the target with shot; to weaken, as if by perforation.

ride, rīd, *v.i.*—past *rode* or archaic *rid,* pp. *ridden* or archaic *rid,* ppr. *riding.* [O.E. *rīdan* = D. *rijden* = G. *reiten* = Icel. *rīdha,* ride.] To be carried on the back of an animal; sit on and manage a horse or other animal in motion; to be borne along on or in a vehicle or any kind of conveyance; to be carried on something as if on horseback; to move or float on the water; to move along, be carried, or supported in any way; appear to float in space, as a heavenly body; turn or rest on something; extend or project over something, as the edge of one thing over the edge of another thing; to work or move up from the proper position, as an article of clothing; to depend upon; as, the future *rides* on this election; *naut.* lie at anchor, as a vessel; *slang,* to continue without change or interruption, as: Let the matter *ride.*—*v.t.* To sit on and manage; to sit or be mounted on, as if on horseback; be carried or borne along on; to rest on, esp. by overlapping; to control, dominate, or tyrannize over; *slang,* to harass or torment. To traverse over, along, or through, as a road or region; to execute by riding; as, to *ride* a race; to cause to ride; carry astraddle, as a person, on something; *naut.* to keep at anchor or moored.—*n.* A journey or excursion on a horse or in a vehicle; a way or road made esp. for riding; a device or conveyance for riding on, as in an amusement park.—**ride out,** to sustain or endure successfully.—**ride for a fall,** to invite trouble or injury by one's conduct.— **ride herd on,** to have charge of; to maintain discipline over.—**take for a ride,** *slang.* To abduct and murder; to deceive.

rid·er, rī′dẽr, *n.* One who or that which rides; a passenger on a conveyance; one who rides a horse, motorcycle, or the like; *legislative usage,* a clause added to a bill up for passage, often having nothing to do with the subject of the bill itself; *mech.* any part which overlies others or moves along with them.—**rid·er·less,** *a.*

ridge, rij, *n.* [O.E. *hrycg* = D. *rug* = G. *rücken* = Icel. *hryggr,* the back.] The long and narrow upper part or crest of something, as a hill or a wave; a long, narrow elevation of land, or a chain of hills or mountains; the back or spine of an animal; the horizontal line in which the tops of the rafters of a roof meet; any raised narrow strip, as in plowed ground or on cloth; *meteor.* a narrow strip of high pressure.— *v.t.*—*ridged, ridging.* To provide with or form into a ridge or ridges; mark with or as with ridges.—*v.i.* To form ridges.— **ridg·y,** rij′ē, *a.*—*ridgier, ridgiest.* Rising to a ridge or ridges.

ridge·pole, rij′pōl″, *n.* The horizontal timber or member at the top of a roof, to which the upper ends of the rafters are fastened; the horizontal pole at the top of a tent.

rid·i·cule, rid′i·kūl″, *n.* [Fr. *ridicule,* a. and n., < L. *ridiculus,* laughable, ridiculous (as n., *ridiculum,* something laughable, a jest), < *ridere,* laugh.] Words or actions intended to excite contemptuous laughter at a person or thing; derision.—*v.t.*—*ridiculed, ridiculing.* To deride; make fun of.— **rid·i·cul·er,** *n.*

ri·dic·u·lous, ri·dik′ū·lus, ri·dik′ya·lus, *a.* [L. *ridiculosus* or *ridiculus.*] Deserving or causing ridicule or derision; absurd, preposterous, or laughable.—**ri·dic·u·lous·-ly,** *adv.*—**ri·dic·u·lous·ness,** *n.*

rid·ing, rī′ding, *n.* The act of one who or

that which rides; a way or road intended esp. for persons riding.—*a.* Used when riding; as, *riding* boots.

rid·ing, rī′ding, *n.* [For *thriding,* < Scand.: cf. Icel. *thrithjungr,* third part.] Each of the three administrative divisions into which Yorkshire, England, is divided: the North Riding, East Riding, and West Riding; each of similar groups of divisions elsewhere.

rid·ing hab·it, *n.* A costume or dress worn while horseback riding, esp. one worn by women.

rid·ley, rid′lē, *n. pl.* **rid·leys.** Any small marine turtle of the genus *Lepidochelys,* esp. *L. kempii,* found along the S. Atlantic coast.

Rie·mann·i·an ge·om·e·try, rē·män′ē·an jē·om′i·trē, rē·man′ē·an, *G.* Rē-män′e·an, *n.* A system of non-Euclidean geometry developed by Georg Friedrich Riemann, 1826–1866, in which he substituted for Euclid's parallel postulate the statement that for a straight line there is no other line parallel to it passing through a point outside the line.

rife, rīf, *a.* [O.E. *rȳf,* rife, prevalent = Icel. *rīfr* (allied to *reifa,* to enrich), O.D. *ryf, rijf,* plenteous.] Prevailing; prevalent; abundant; of large numbers or great quantity; abounding, followed by *with.*

riff, rif, *n. Jazz,* a continually repeated passage or phrase played as background for a soloist.—*v.i.* To execute a riff.

rif·fle, rif′l, *n.* A ridge, shallow, or other obstruction in a river or stream, causing ripples or waves; an expanse of wavy, ripply water; a method of shuffling cards.— *v.t.*—*riffled, riffling.* To create in ripples; to leaf through quickly, as pages of a book. —*v.i.* To intermix or shuffle cards by separating and holding the two parts of the deck so that the raised edges alternately slip together as they are released by each hand.

rif·fle, rif′l, *n. Min.* The lining at the bottom of a sluice or the like, made of blocks or slats of wood or stones, arranged in such a manner that grooves or openings are left between them for catching and collecting particles of gold; one of the slats of wood or the like so used; one of the grooves or openings formed.

riff·raff, rif′raf″, *n.* [M.E. *rif(and)raf,* < O.Fr. *rif (et) raf,* every bit.] Worthless or low persons; the disreputable element of society; the rabble. Also *raff.*—*a.* Belonging to the rabble; worthless or trashy.

ri·fle, rī′fl, *n.* A shoulder gun having spiral grooves cut in the inner surface of the gun barrel to impart a rotatory motion to the bullet so as to increase its range and accuracy; one of the spiral grooves in a gun barrel; a piece of artillery with such grooves; *pl.* a company or regiment of soldiers armed with rifles.—*v.t.*—*rifled, rifling.* To groove, as the inside of a gun barrel; to shoot with a rifle; *sports,* to throw or hit, as a baseball, with speed and accuracy.—**ri·fle·man,** rī′fl·man, *n.* A soldier or other person armed with a rifle; one skilled in shooting a rifle.

ri·fle, rī′fl, *v.t.*—*rifled rifling.* [O.Fr. *rifler,* scrape, graze, strip, plunder (Fr. scrape, file).] To ransack and rob, as a house; to search and rob, as a person; to plunder, pillage, or strip, as a conquered city; to carry off, as booty; *fig.* to take away or steal, as youth or beauty.—**ri·fler,** *n.*

ri·fle bird, *n.* Any of several Australian birds of the genus *Ptilorhis,* esp. *Paradisea,* the male of which has velvety-black plumage with purple, blue, and green iridescence: said to have been so named by the early colonists because the coloration suggested the uniform of a British rifle brigade.

ri·fle·ry, rī′fl·rē, *n.* The military exercise or sporting activity of shooting at a target with a rifle.

ri·fling, rī′fling, *n.* The act or process of cutting rifles or spiral grooves in a barrel; the system of spiral grooves in a rifle.

rift, rift, *n.* [< *rive;* so Dan. *rift,* a rift, a rent.] A cleft; a fissure; an opening made by riving or splitting; a geological fault; a disagreement or estrangement.—*v.t., v.i.* To burst open; to split.

rift, rift, *n.* A shoal, or shallow area in a body of water.

rig, rig, *v.t.*—*rigged, rigging.* [Cf. Norw. *rigga,* bind up, wrap round, rig, Sw. *rigga,* rig.] *Naut.* to fit, as a vessel or a mast, with the necessary shrouds, stays, and other equipment; to fit, as shrouds, stays, or braces, to the proper mast, yard, or the like. To furnish or provide with equipment; to fit, usu. with *out* or *up;* to prepare, put together, or get up, esp. in a makeshift fashion, often with *up;* to fit or deck with clothes or personal adornment, often with *out* or *up. Colloq.* to control by fraud; to set prices for goods without reference to their value in order to make a profit.

rig, rig, *n. Naut.* the arrangement of the masts, spars, and sails on a boat or ship. Equipment; apparatus for some purpose; as, the *rig* of an oil well. *Colloq.* a vehicle with a horse or horses, as for driving; costumes or dress, esp. when odd or conspicuous.

rig·a·doon, rig″a·dön′ *n.* [Fr. *rigaudon, rigodon:* said to be named after *Rigaud,* the originator of the dance.] A lively 17th and 18th century dance for one couple, characterized by a peculiar jumping step, and usu. in quick duple rhythm; a piece of music for this dance or in its rhythm. Also **ri·gau·don,** *Fr.* Rē·gō̇·daṇ′.

rig·a·ma·role, rig′a·ma·rōl″, *n.* Rigmarole.

rig·a·to·ni, rig″a·tō′nē, *n.* Short, ribbed pieces of macaroni.

Ri·gel, rī′jel, rī′gel, *n. Astron.* a first-magnitude star belonging to the constellation Orion.

rig·ger, rig′ẽr, *n.* One who rigs; one whose occupation is the fitting of the rigging of ships; one who works with hoisting tackle and similar gear; a mechanic engaged in assembling and aligning aircraft parts.

rig·ging, rig′ing, *n. Naut.* the ropes and other equipment used to support and work the sails of a ship. Tackle used for lifting or moving, as in logging; *colloq.* clothing or dress.

right, rīt, *a.* [O.E. *riht* = D. and G. *recht* = Icel. *rēttr* = Goth. *raihts,* straight, right; akin to L. *rectus,* straight, right, *regere,* keep straight, direct, rule, Skt. *rju,* straight, right, Gr. *orégein,* reach out.] In accordance with what is just or good, as conduct; in conformity with fact, reason, or some standard or principle; correct; as, the *right* answer; correct in judgment, opinion, or action; sound or normal, as the mind; mentally sound or sane; in good health or spirits, as persons; in a satisfactory state or in good order; as, the *right* set up; principal, front, or upper; as, the *right* side of cloth; most advantageous or desirable; fitting or appropriate; as, to say the *right* thing; real or genuine; belonging, pertaining to, or near the side of a person or thing which is turned toward the east when the face is turned toward the north: opposed to *left.* (*Often cap.*) noting or relating to the conservative faction in politics. Straight; as, a *right* line; formed by or with reference to a line or plane that is perpendicular to a base; as, a *right* angle; *geom.* having the axis perpendicular to the base; as, a *right* cone.

right, rīt, *n.* A just claim or title, whether legal, prescriptive, or moral; *often pl.* that which is due to anyone by just claim. That which is in accordance with morality or justice; as, a choice between *right* and wrong; *often pl.* the interest that a person or group has in property. *Finance*, the privilege given to stockholders to purchase additional shares in a corporation at a favorable price; the negotiable document which certifies this privilege. That which accords with fact, reason, or propriety; the condition or quality of being correct; the right hand; the right side or direction; as, to turn toward the *right*; in a pair, as of shoes, gloves, or the like, that member which is intended for the right side. (*Usu. cap.*) in continental Europe, that part of a legislative assembly which is on the right side of the chamber as viewed by the presiding officer, a position customarily assigned to those members holding more conservative views than the other members; the members who are situated on the Right. (*Cap.*) those individuals who favor traditional practices and attitudes, and who advocate maintenance of the established social order, sometimes by authoritarian methods; the position which is held by these individuals, usu. preceded by *the*. *Boxing*, a blow given by the right hand.

right, rīt, *adv.* [O.E. *rihte.*] In a straight line; straight or directly; quite or completely; as, *right* to the ceiling; immediately; as, *right* after dinner; exactly, precisely, or just; as, *right* there; uprightly or righteously; correctly or accurately; as, to hear *right*; properly or fittingly; as, to serve one *right*; advantageously, favorably, or well; toward or on the right; as, to turn *right*; very: used in titles; as, the *Right* Reverend; *dial.* very or extremely, as: I was *right* glad.

right, rīt, *v.t.* [O.E. *rihtan.*] To bring or restore to an upright position; to put in a proper state or order; to bring into conformity with fact; correct; as, to *right* errors; to do justice to; to relieve from wrong; to redress, as a wrong.—*v.i.* To resume an upright or the proper position. —**by rights,** in justice or fairness.—**right a·way** or **off,** immediately; without condition or order.—**right·er,** *n.*—**right·ness,** *n.*

right an·gle, *n. Geom.* The angle formed by two straight lines drawn perpendicular to each other; an angle of 90 degrees.—**right-an·gled,** *a.*

right as·cen·sion, *n. Astron.* one of the two coordinates of the equatorial system of stellar coordinates, indicating angular distances from the vernal equinox on the celestial equator, measured in sideral time. Abbr. *R.A.* See *declination.*

right·eous, rī′chus, *a.* [O.E. *rihtwīs,* righteous—*riht,* right, and *wīs,* wise, prudent; similarly Icel. *rétt-viss,* righteous.] Upright; virtuous; acting in accordance with the dictates of morality; agreeing with right; just; equitable.—**right·eous·ly,** *adv.* —**right·eous·ness,** rī′chus·nis, *n.*

right field, *n. Baseball,* the section on the right-hand side of the outfield as viewed by the batter, back of the line between first and second base.—**right·field·er,** *n.* The person who plays the right field position.

right·ful, rīt′ful, *a.* [O.E. *rihtfull.*] Having a right or just claim, as to some possession or position; legitimate; equitable or just, as actions; belonging by right or just claim; legal; correct or proper.—**right·ful·ly,** *adv.*—**right·ful·ness,** *n.*

right-hand, rīt′hand′, *a.* Of, for, or with the right hand; on or to the right; most efficient or useful as a helper; plain-laid.— **right hand,** *n.* The hand on the right side of an individual; the side or position of courtesy or honor.—**right-hand·ed,** rīt′- hand′did, *a.* Having the right hand or arm more serviceable than the left; preferring to use the right hand; adapted to or performed by the right hand; situated on the

side of the right hand; moving or rotating from left to right, or clockwise; as, a *right-handed* screw.—*adv.*—**right-hand·ed·ly,** *adv.*—**right-hand·ed·ness,** *n.*—**right-hand·er,** rīt′han′dėr, *n.* A right-handed person; *baseball,* a pitcher whose delivery is made with his right arm and hand. *Colloq.* a blow dealt by the right hand.

right·ism, rī′tiz·um, *n.* (*Sometimes cap.*) The principles, views, or behavior of the Right, esp. in politics; advocacy of conservatism or reactionary actions or ideas, as in politics.—**right·ist,** rī′tist, *n., a.* (*Sometimes cap.*)

right·ly, rīt′lē, *adv.* According to right or justice; properly; suitably; according to truth or fact; correctly.

right of a·sy·lum, *n. International law,* the right to avoid seizure or arrest by seeking sanctuary in a place acknowledged by custom or treaty, as in an embassy.

right of search, *n. International law,* the prerogative of a ship's captain to stop a vessel of another nationality on the high seas to examine her papers and cargo; specif. in wartime, the right of belligerents to search neutral ships at sea for contraband cargo.

right of way, *n.* A right of passage, as over another's land; a path that may lawfully be used; the strip of land traversed by a railroad; public land over which power wires pass; statutory or common law allowing one particular vehicle to proceed before another. Also **right-of-way.**

Right Rev·er·end, *n.* A title conferred on various high officials of the Protestant and Roman Catholic church, as Anglican bishops and Roman Catholic prelates.

right tri·an·gle, *n.* A triangle which has a right angle.

right whale, *n.* A large-headed whale of the genus *Balaena,* inhabiting the polar seas.

right wing, *n.* Persons belonging to a reactionary or conservative political group; a faction of a party opposing departure from past political policies; the party itself. —**right-wing,** *a.*—**right-wing·er,** *n.*

rig·id, rij′id, *a.* [Fr. *rigide,* L. *rigidus,* < *rigēo,* to be stiff or numb.] Stiff; not pliant; not easily bent; as, a *rigid* pole; set; fixed; strict in opinion, practice, or discipline; severe or inflexible in disposition; severely just or stringent; as, *rigid* standards. *Aeron.* of a dirigible or airship, having an inflexible framework that encases the containers of gas; pertaining to the firmly fixed rotor of a helicopter.—**ri·gid·i·ty,** **rig·id·ness,** ri·jid′i·tē, *n.* **rig·id·ly,** *adv.*

ri·gid·i·fy, ri·jid′i·fī″, *v.t.*—*rigidified, rigidifying.* To make firm or rigid.—*v.i.* To become inflexible or rigid.—**ri·gid·i·fi·ca·tion,** ri·jid″i·fi·kā′shan, *n.*

rig·ma·role, rig′ma·rōl″, *n.* [A corruption of *ragman-roll,* a lengthy list.] A succession of confused, disjointed, or incoherent statements; an unnecessarily complicated process. Also *rigamarole.*

rig·or, *Brit.* **rig·our,** rig′ėr, *n.* [L. *rigor,* < *rigeo,* to be stiff.] Rigidity; severity of life; austerity; strictness; exactness without allowance, flexibility, or indulgence; sternness; harshness; intensity of atmospheric cold or inclemency; *med.* a sudden coldness, accompanied by shivering which precedes certain fevers; *physiol.* rigidity of the body tissues or organs causing lack of response to stimuli.

rig·or·ism, *Brit.* **rig·our·ism,** rig′o·riz″um, *n.* Rigidity or strictness in principles or practice, as in life style or religion.— **rig·or·ist,** rig′or·ist, *n.*—**rig·or·is·tic,** *a.*

rig·or mor·tis, rig′ėr mạr′tis, rī′gạr mạr′tis, *n.* The stiffening of the muscles of the body after death.

rig·or·ous, rig′ėr·us, *a.* Characterized by rigor; severe; stringent; scrupulously accurate or precise; very harsh or inclement, as

weather.—**rig·or·ous·ly,** *adv.*—**rig·or·ous·ness,** *n.*

rile, rīl, *v.t.*—*riled, riling.* [A form of *roil.*] *Colloq.* To stir or unsettle, as water; to anger; to irritate.—**ri·ley,** rī′lē, *a. Colloq.* Turbid; vexed or irritated.

rill, ril, *n.* [Same as L.G. *rille,* a brook, a furrow.] A small brook; a rivulet.

rill, ril, *n.* [G.] *Astron.* any of certain long, narrow trenches or valleys observed on the surface of the moon. Also **rille.**

rill·et, ril′it, *n.* [Dim. of *rill.*] A small stream or brook.

rim, rim, *n.* [O.E. *rima,* rim, edge, lip; perh. a Celtic word; cf. W. *rhim,* Armor. *rim,* a rim, a border.] The border, edge, or margin of a thing, esp. of an object that is circular; a brim; the outer circular portion of the wheel connected by spokes to the hub; the circular metal strip, often removable, on the automobile wheel connecting the tire to the wheel; a frame, as of glasses for the eyes.—*v.t.*—*rimmed, rimming.* To provide or form with a rim; *sports,* to move around the edge of, as of a basket or a golf cup, without going in.—**rim·less,** *a.*

rime, rim, *n.* [O.E. *hrīm,* rime = Icel. *hrīm,* D. *rijm,* Dan. *riim,* Sw. *rim,* hoarfrost.] A white coating of ice that is formed, as on grass, by supercooled moisture; hoarfrost. —*v.t., v.i.*—*rimed, riming.* To coat with or congeal into hoarfrost.—**rim·y,** rī′mē, *a.*— *rimier, rimiest.*

rime, rīm, *n.* Rhyme.—*v.t., v.i.*—*rimed, riming.* Rhyme.—**rim·er,** *n.*

rime·ster, rīm′stėr, *n.* Rhymester.

ri·mose, rī′mōs, rī·mōs′, *a.* [L. *rimosus,* < *rima,* a fissure or crack.] Full of chinks, fissures, or cracks. Also **ri·mous,** rī′mus.— **ri·mose·ly,** *adv.*—**ri·mos·i·ty,** rī·mos′i·- tē, *n.*

rim·rock, rim′rok″, *n. Geol.* Rock forming the rim of a land elevation; the raised rim of bedrock which forms the natural limits of a gold-bearing deposit or of gravel deposits.

rind, rīnd, *n.* [O.E. *rind, hrind,* bark, crust = G. *rinde,* rind; same root as *rim.*] The outward coat or covering, usu. firm or hard, as of trees, fruits, or cheese; peel, husk, or skin.

rin·der·pest, rin′dėr·pest″, *n.* [Gr. *rinder,* pl. of *rind,* a horned beast, and *pest,* a plague.] *Veter. pathol.* an acute, contagious virus disease affecting ruminant animals, esp. cattle, and characterized by inflamed mucous membranes, fever, and diarrhea.

ring, ring, *n.* [O.E. *hring* = O.Fries. *hring* = O.H.G. *hring* (G. *ring*) = Icel. *hringr,* ring.] A circular band of metal or other material; as, a key *ring*; a small circular band, as of gold or other precious metal, often set with gems, for wearing on the finger as an ornament or as a token of betrothal or marriage; anything having the form of a circular band; one of the concentric layers of wood produced yearly in the trunks of exogenous trees; a circular line or mark; a circular course; as, to dance in a *ring*; a single turn in a spiral or helix, or in a spiral course; a number of persons or things disposed in a circle; a group of persons cooperating for selfish, sometimes illicit, purposes, as for control of a business or market, politics, or the like; an enclosed circle-shaped or other type of area, as one in which some sport or exhibition takes place; an enclosure in which prize fights take place, now usually a square area marked off by stakes and ropes; a space devoted to betting at a racecourse; *geom.* the area or space between two concentric circles; *chem.* a number of atoms so united that they may be graphically represented in circular form.—*v.i.* To form a ring or rings; move in a ring or in a constantly curving course.—*v.t.* To surround with a ring; to hem in, as animals, by circling around them; to draw a ring around; to form into a ring; to provide with a ring or rings; to mark with rings; to cut away the bark in a ring, as from a tree branch, usu. to check too luxuriant growth and induce a state of fruitfulness, or to cause death, depending on the depth of the ring. —**ring·like,** *a.*

ring, ring, *v.i.*—past *rang,* pp. *rung,* ppr. *rang.* [O.E. *hringan,* to ring = Dan. *ringe,* Sw. *ringa,* Icel. *hringja,* O.D. *ringhen,* to ring.] To produce a resonant sound, as a bell which is struck; to resound or reverberate; to cause to sound, as a bell; to express or exhibit a specified quality; as, his offer *rings* hollow; to experience tinnitus or buzzing.—*v.t.* To cause to sound; to sound by striking or ringing; to celebrate or proclaim by ringing; as: The chimes *rang* the news. To summon, usher, or signal by a bell ring, followed by *in* or *out;* as, to *ring in* the New Year; to test metal objects, as a coin, by the sound produced when struck against another object; *chiefly Brit.* to telephone, followed by *up.*—*n.* The sound of a bell or other sonorous body; any loud sound continued, repeated, or reverberated; characteristic sound; as, the *ring* of falsehood; a telephone call; a chime of bells; the act of ringing a bell.

ring·bolt, ring′bŏlt″, *n.* A bolt with a ring fitted in an eye at its head.

ring·bone, ring′bōn″, *n.* A callus growth on the pastern bones of a horse, frequently causing lameness.—**ring·boned,** *a.*

ring·dove, ring′duv″, *n.* The largest European pigeon, *Columba palumba,* with two whitish patches on the neck and a purplish-red breast; also **cu·shat, wood pi·geon.** A pigeon of southern Europe and western Asia, *Streptopelia risoria,* with a black half-ring around its neck.

rin·gent, rin′jent, *a.* [L. *ringens, ringentis,* < *ringor,* to make a wry face, to gape.] Gaping. *Bot.* of certain corollas, having a space between the lips resembling an open mouth.

ring·er, ring′ĕr, *n.* One who or something which rings, as a chime or bell. *Slang,* an athlete, race horse, or other competitor whose qualifications are misrepresented; one who or that which is remarkably like another person or thing, as: He is a *ringer* for my brother. *Pl.* ring taw, a variation of the game of marbles. *Aust.* a sheepshearer of great skill.

ring·er, ring′ĕr, *n.* One who or that which surrounds with a ring or encircles; a quoit, horseshoe, or the like so thrown as to encircle the peg aimed at; the throw itself.

ring fin·ger, *n.* [O.E. *hring fingre.*] The third finger of the left hand, on which the wedding ring is worn.

ring·lead·er, ring′lē″dĕr, *n.* One who leads a group, esp. in violation of law or in an illegal enterprise.

ring·let, ring′lit, *n.* [Dim. of *ring.*] A curl, esp. a curl of hair; a small circle or ring.

ring·mas·ter, ring′mas″tĕr, ring′mä″stĕr, *n.* One who has charge of the performances in a circus ring.

ring·necked, ring′nekt″, *a.* Having the neck marked by a ring or rings of color, as a bird.—**ring·neck,** ring′nek″, *n.* A bird so marked; the ring snake.

ring-necked pheas·ant, *n.* A large chicken-like bird, *Phasianus colchicus torquatus,* native to Asia, having a long pointed tail, the male being highly colored with a white neck-ring: now established in northern farming regions of the U.S. as a game bird. See *pheasant.*

ring·side, ring′sīd″, *n.* The area directly around a ring, as the first row around a boxing ring; a place which offers a very close view.—*a., adv.*

ring spot, *n. Bot.* a localized area of diseased plant tissue characterized by yellowish or purplish, usu. circular, spots.

ring-streaked, ring′strēkt″, *a.* Having streaks or bands of color around the body.

ring-tailed, ring′tāld″, *a.* Having the tail or the tail feathers ringed transversely with alternating colors; having the tail curled into a ring at the end.

ring-tailed cat, *n.* Cacomistle.

ring taw, *n.* A game of marbles in which the contestants each place a predetermined number of marbles in a circle on the ground and then take turns attempting to win possession of these marbles by knocking them out of the circle with other marbles shot with the thumb. Also *ringers.*

ring·toss, ring′tas″, ring′tos″, *n.* A game played with rings which are tossed so as to drop over a short upright stick.

ring·worm, ring′wụrm″, *n. Pathol.* a disease caused by fungi, appearing in the form of rings or patches on different parts of the body, esp. on the scalp.

rink, ringk, *n.* [A form of *ring,* an area, or of *rank,* a row.] A smooth, usu. artificial expanse of ice, often inside a building, used for ice skating, curling, or hockey; a smooth, usu. wooden flooring for roller skating; the building used for ice or roller skating; the area of a bowling green used by one side; in a game of bowling, quoits, or curling, the participants on one side.

rinse, rins, *v.t.*—*rinsed, rinsing.* [O.Fr. *rinser, reinser,* Fr. *rincer,* to rinse, to wash.] To wash lightly, as by running water over or into or by plunging momentarily into water; as, to *rinse* a dish; to cleanse by the introduction of water or other liquid; as, to *rinse* one's mouth; to immerse in clear water as the final step in the washing process; to remove, as dirt or soap, in this way.—*n.* The act or process of rinsing; any product used for rinsing; a preparation for tinting the hair.

rins·ing, rin′sing, *n.* The act of one who rinses; a rinse. *Usu. pl.* the liquid with which anything has been rinsed; residue or dregs.

ri·ot, rī′ot, *n.* [O.Fr. *riote,* disturbance, combat, Fr. *rioter,* to make a disturbance; origin doubtful.] Any public disturbance of a boisterous and violent nature, usu. caused by a large crowd. *Law,* a tumultuous public disturbance by at least three persons who act in a disruptive or unlawful manner while carrying out certain private objectives. A vivid or brilliant display, as of colors; boisterous festivity; revelry; wild or loose activity; *slang,* an amusing or hilarious person or thing.—*v.i.* To participate in a public disorder; to act in an unrestrained or wanton manner.—*v.t.* To spend in riotous activity, as time or money. —**run ri·ot,** to act without restraint; to grow abundantly, as vines.—**ri·ot·er,** *n.*

Ri·ot Act, A law passed in England in 1715 for the prevention of unlawful assembly and unruly disturbance holding that if 12 or more persons do not disperse after being so ordered by legal authority, they shall be treated as felons.—**read the ri·ot act to,** to direct or order cessation of an activity or wrongdoing, with warning of appropriate consequences.

ri·ot gun, *n.* A shotgun, usu. having a short barrel, that scatters shot over a wide area, used chiefly for riot control and guard duty.

ri·ot·ous, rī′o·tus, *a.* Characterized by or of the nature of rioting or disturbance of the peace; inciting to or taking part in a riot; marked by or indulging in unrestrained revelry; loose; profligate; boisterous or uproarious; as, *riotous* mirth.—**ri·ot·ous·ly,** *adv.*—**ri·ot·ous·ness,** *n.*

rip, rip, *v.t.*—*ripped, ripping.* [Same as Dan. *rippe,* to rip, to tear; allied prob. to *rive.*]

To separate or divide by cutting or tearing, as fabric; to tear or cut open, as a package; to take out by cutting or tearing, as a page; to cut or split wood with the grain.—*v.i.* To be torn apart; *colloq.* to move recklessly, as: He *ripped* into the fracas.—*n.* A rent caused by tearing; a tear.—**rip·per,** rip′ĕr, *n.*

rip, rip, *n.* [Cf. *rip, v.,* also *ripple.*] A stretch of choppy water at sea or in a river.

rip, rip, *n.* [Cf. D. *rap,* scab; Dan. *ripsraps, riffraff.*] *Colloq.* A base or worthless person; a useless, worn-out horse; anything worthless.

ri·par·i·an, ri·pâr′ē·an, rī·pâr′ē·an, *a.* [L. *ripa,* a bank.] Pertaining to or situated on the bank of a body of water.

ri·par·i·an right, *n. Law,* a right, as for water, access, or fishing, possessed by an owner of riparian land.

rip cord, *n. Aeron.* The cord or cable which, when pulled, opens the parachute pack in a free fall and causes the pilot chute to open; a cord or rope attached to a rip panel in a free or dirigible balloon, which when torn loose or opened causes immediate deflation.

rip cur·rent, *n.* A current of water beneath and flowing in a different direction than the surface water, esp. when flowing outward from shore.

ripe, rip, *a.* [O.E. *ripe,* ripe = L.G. *ripe,* D. *rijp,* G. *reif,* ripe, allied to reap.] Ready for reaping and use; resembling a ripe or mature fruit; rosy; brought to perfection in growth or to the best state; advanced to the state of being fit for use, as cheese; fully developed; matured; advanced; as, of a *ripe* age; consummate; as, a *ripe* scholar; ready for action or effect; as, *ripe* for a war; ready for removal; as, a *ripe* appendix.—**ripe·ly,** *adv.*—**ripe·ness,** *n.*

rip·en, rī′pen, *v.t., v.i.* To grow or cause to grow ripe; to mature.—**rip·en·er,** *n.*

ri·pie·no, ri·pyä′nō, *It.* Rē·pye′na, *a.* [It., < L. *re-,* again, and *plenus,* full.] *Mus.* additional or reinforcing.—*n.* pl. **ri·pie·nos,** *It.* **ri·pie·ni,** *It.* Rē·pye′nē. *Mus.* A section or movement to be played by the full group of performers; a tutti passage.

ri·poste, ri·post, ri·pōst′, *n.* [Fr., < It. *risposta.*] *Fencing,* the quick return thrust which follows a successful parry. A clever retaliatory response; a retort.—*v.i.*—*riposted riposting. Fencing,* to make a riposte. To reply or answer back quickly; to retaliate.

rip·ping, rip′ing, *a.* Of or relating to rending or tearing; *chiefly Brit. slang,* wonderful, great, or excellent.

rip·ple, rip′l, *v.i.*—*rippled, rippling.* [Origin uncertain: cf. *rip* and *rimple.*] To form small waves or undulations on the surface, as water when agitated by a gentle breeze; to flow with a light ruffling of the surface; to form or have small undulations, as of a surface that is solid; of sound, to have alternate rising and falling of tone or volume, giving an effect like that of water flowing in ripples.—*v.t.* To form small waves or undulations on; to agitate lightly; to mark, as with ripples; to cause to undulate slightly, or give a wavy form to.—*n.* A small wave or undulation, as on water or in hair; any similar movement or appearance; a sound, as of water flowing in ripples; a stretch of rough water, as over a rocky bottom, or a small rapid.—**rip·pler,** rip′lĕr, *n.*

rip·ple, rip′l, *v.t.*—*rippled, rippling.* [Dim. from *rip;* like L.G. *repeln,* G. *riffeln,* to ripple.] To clean or remove the seeds or capsules from, esp. from the stalks of flax.—*n.* A large comblike or toothed device for separating the seeds or capsules from flax or the like.

rip·ple mark, *n.* One of the wavy lines or ridges produced, as on sand or mud, by the action of waves, wind, or the like.

rip·rap, rip′rap″, *n.* [Same as *riffraff,*

Dan. *ripsraps*.] A wall or foundation of stones thrown together without order, as in deep water or on a soft bottom; the stones used in this way.—*v.t.*—*riprapped, riprapping*. To construct or strengthen with riprap.

rip·roar·ing, *a. Slang.* Lively and unrestrained; noisy; boisterous; riotous.

rip·saw, rip′sạ″, *n.* A saw that is coarse-toothed, used for cutting wood along the grain.

rip·snort·er, rip′snạr′tẽr, *n. Colloq.* Something or some person of extraordinary violence or power; someone or something of exceptional merit or quality.—**rip·snort·-ing,** *a.*

rip·tide, rip′tīd″, *n.* The clash of opposing tides or currents causing a violent agitation in the water.

rise, rīz, *v.i.*—past *rose*, pp. *risen*, ppr. *rising*. [O.E. *rīsan* = D. *rijzen* = O.H.G. *rīsan* = Icel. *rīsa* = Goth. *-reisan*, rise: cf. *raise*.] To get up from a lying, sitting, or kneeling posture; to assume a standing position; to get up from sleep or rest; to come back from the dead, as: Christ *rose* on the third day. To become active in opposition or resistance; revolt or rebel; to come into being; appear, as: Worries *rose* in his mind. To take place; occur; to originate, issue, or be derived; to have a source, as a river; to move from a lower to a higher position; move upward; ascend; to come above the horizon, as a heavenly body; to extend directly upward, as: The tower *rises* to a height of 60 feet. To have an upward slant or curve, as: The ground *rises* at the back of the house. To attain higher rank, importance, or social standing, or to advance in wealth; to prove oneself equal to a demand, emergency, or the like, followed by *to*; to become animated or cheerful, as the spirits; of a fish, to come up to the surface of the water to take bait or food; to increase in height, as water level; to increase in degree, intensity, or force, as fever, color, or the like; to increase in amount, as prices; to increase in price or value, as commodities; to become louder or of higher pitch, as the voice; to swell or puff up, as dough from the action of yeast; to adjourn or close a session, as a deliberative body or a court.—*v.t.* To cause to rise. *Naut.* to cause, as a ship, to rise above the visible horizon by approaching nearer to it; raise.—*n.* The act or an act of rising; appearance above the horizon, as of the sun or moon; elevation or advance in position, fortune, power, prosperity, or the like; as, the *rise* and fall of a movement; an increase in amount, price, or value; an increase in loudness or in pitch, as of the voice; origin, source, or beginning, as of a stream; a coming into existence or notice; extension upward; the amount of this extension; upward slope, as of ground or a road; a piece of rising or high ground; the coming of a fish to the surface of the water to seize bait or food. *Arch.* vertical height, as of a step, flight of stairs, or a roof; the height of an arch, measured from springing line to highest point. *Brit.* an increase in wages; the amount of such an increase.—**get a rise out of,** *colloq.* to draw an angry or emotional response from, by deliberate provocation.—**give rise to,** to originate or produce, as: Her secretive conduct *gave rise to* suspicions.

ris·er, rī′zẽr, *n.* One who rises, as from bed; as, an early *riser*; the vertical face of a stair step; a vertical pipe, as for conveying steam or gas.

ris·i·bil·i·ty, riz″i·bil′i·tē, *n.* pl. **ris·i·bil·i·ties.** *Often pl.* the quality of being risible; proneness or ability to laugh; an appreciation of the amusing or ridiculous. Laughter.

ris·i·ble, riz′i·bl, *a.* [Fr. *risible*, < L. *risibilis*, < *rideo*, *risum*, to laugh.] Able to

laugh; inclined or disposed to laugh; capable of exciting laughter; pertaining to or associated with laughter.

ris·ing, rī′zing, *a.* Moving upward or ascending; growing in height; sloping upward; becoming more active or vigorous; as, the *rising* rebellion; increasing in wealth, power, or distinction; as, a *rising* young executive; advancing to adulthood; as, the *rising* generation—*n.* The act of one who or that which rises; something that rises, is prominent, or is elevated; a resurrection; an insurrection or rebellion; the process of causing dough to rise by yeast or leaven.

risk, risk, *n.* [Fr. *risque* < It. *risco*, *risico*, risk; origin uncertain.] Exposure to the chance of injury or loss; a hazard or dangerous chance. *Insurance*, the hazard or chance of loss; the degree of probability of such loss; the amount which the insurance company may lose; a person or thing with reference to the risk involved in insuring him or it; the category of insured loss, as fire, and the insurance policy covering it.—*v.t.* [Fr. *risquer*.] To expose to the chance of injury or loss; hazard; to take or run the risk of; as, to *risk* defeat or loss; to venture upon.—**take a risk,** to endanger oneself.—**risk·er,** *n.*

risk cap·i·tal, *n.* Venture capital.

risk·y, ris′kē, *a.*—**riskier, riskiest.** Dangerous; hazardous; full of or involving risk.—**risk·i·ness,** *n.*

ri·sor·gi·men·to, It. Rē̇·sạR′jē·men′tō, *n.* [It.] A resurrection; a revival; (*cap.*) the liberation movement or period of unification of Italy during the 18th century.

ri·sot·to, ri·sạt′tō, ri·sot′ō, It. Rē̇·zạt′tō, *n.* [It., < *riso*, < L. *oryza*, E. *rice*.] *Cooking*, rice cooked in broth and served with grated cheese and other seasoning.

ris·qué, ri·skā′, *Fr.* Rēs·kā′, *a.* [Fr. pp. of *risquer*.] Tending toward or verging on impropriety; off-color.

ris·sole, ri·sōl′, ris′ōl, *Fr.* Rē·sạl′, *n.* [Fr., perh. < L.L. *russeolus*, reddish, < L. *russes*, red.] A small fried ball, roll, or cake of minced meat or fish mixed with bread crumbs, egg, and seasonings enclosed in pasta.

ri·tar·dan·do, rē̇″tär·dän′dō, It. Rē̇″tär·-dän′dō, *a.* [It.] *Mus.* retarding: a direction to slow down the tempo gradually.—*n.* pl. **ri·tar·dan·dos.**

rite, rīt, *n.* [Fr. *rite*, < L. *ritus*, a rite.] A prescribed or formal procedure used in religious or other solemn ceremonies; as, the baptismal *rite*; a particular system of religious or ceremonial practice; as, the Orthodox *rite*; any customary practice or observance; as, the *rite* of the cocktail before dinner.

ri·tor·nel·lo, rit″ẽr·nel′ō, It. Rē̇″tạR·nel′ō, *n.* pl. **ri·tor·nel·los,** It. **ri·tor·nel·li,** Rē̇″tạR·nel′lē. [It., dim. of *ritorno*, a return.] *Mus.* An instrumental refrain in a vocal work; an orchestral interlude in 17th century opera; a tutti passage or repeated rondo theme in an instrumental concerto.

rit·u·al, rich′ō·al, *a.* [L. *ritualis*.] Pertaining to, consisting of, or prescribing rites.—*n.* The rites or ceremonies, collectively, of a church or other religious body; the order of any solemn ceremony; a book describing or prescribing such rites.—**rit·u·al·ly,** *adv.*

rit·u·al·ism, rich′ō·a·liz″um, *n.* Strict observance of prescribed forms of ritual; the study of rituals; an excessive use of rituals. —**rit·u·al·ist,** *n.*—**rit·u·al·is·tic,** rich′ō-a·lis′tik, *a.*—**rit·u·al·is·ti·cal·ly,** *adv.*

rit·u·al·ize, rich′ō·a·līz″, *v.i.*—**ritualized, ritualizing.** To engage in ritualism.—*v.t.* To give ritual form to; to bring to a belief in ritualism; to impose such a belief on.—**rit·u·al·i·za·tion,** rich′ō·al·i·zā′shan, *n.*

ritz·y, rit′sē, *a.*—**ritzier, ritziest.** *Slang.* Having an air of swanky elegance; ostentatiously fashionable; snobbish.

ri·val, rī′val, *n.* [Fr. *rival*, < L. *rivalis*, pertaining to a brook, *rivales* those who use the same brook, hence competitors, rivals; < *rivus*, a brook, whence *rivulet*.] One who is in pursuit of the same object as another; a competitor; one who emulates or strives to equal or exceed another in excellence.— *a.* Having the same pretensions or claims; standing in competition for superiority.— *v.t.*—*rivaled, rivaling, esp. Brit. rivalled, rivalling.* To stand in competition with; to strive to equal or excel.

ri·val·ry, rī′val·rē, *n.* pl. **ri·val·ries.** The act of rivaling; competition; strife or an effort to obtain an object which another is pursuing; emulation.

rive, rīv, *v.t.*—past *rived*, pp. *rived* or *riven*, ppr. *riving.* [A Scand. word = Icel. *rifa*, Dan. *rive*, to rive, to tear; akin perh. to *rip*.] To split; to cleave; to rend asunder by force; to affect by painful or harrowing thoughts; to give or cause emotional distress.—*v.i.* To be split or rent asunder.— **riv·er,** rī′vẽr, *n.*

riv·er, riv′ẽr, *n.* [O.Fr. *rivere, riviere* (Fr. *rivière*), bank, shore, later river, < M.L. *riparia*, prop. fem. of L. *riparius*, belonging to a riverbank or shore, < *ripa*, bank, shore.] A natural stream of water of considerable size flowing in a definite course or channel; a similar stream of something other than water; any abundant stream or copious flow; (*cap.*), *astron.* the southern constellation Eridanus.—**sell down the riv·er,** to betray or deceive.—**send up the riv·er,** *slang,* to send or sentence to prison.

riv·er·bed, riv′ẽr·bed″, *n.* The channel or bottom of a river or what was formerly a river.

riv·er horse, *n.* The hippopotamus.

riv·er·ine, riv′e·rīn″, riv′ẽr·in, *a.* Concerning, similar to, or formed by a river; situated on a river.

riv·er·side, riv′ẽr·sīd″, *n.* The bank of a river.—*a.*

riv·er·weed, riv′ẽr·wēd″, *n.* Any of the small submerged fresh-water plants of the genus *Podostemon*, as the N. American species *P. ceratophyllum.*

riv·et, riv′it, *n.* [Fr. *rivet*, a clinch, a rivet; *river*, to rivet; origin doubtful, prob. < the Teut.; cf. Icel. *rifa*, to tack together, to sew together.] A short metallic pin or bolt with a head, used to join pieces, as sheets of metal, by inserting the shaft through aligned holes in the pieces and then hammering the plain end to form a second head; in garment manufacture, a modification of this, used for reinforcing seams at points of strain, as in heavy work clothes.— *v.t.*—*riveted, riveting, Brit. rivetted, riveting.* To fasten with a rivet or in the manner of rivets; to clinch; to fasten firmly; to make firm or immovable; to hold or engross, as the eyes or attention.—*v.i.* To be firmly attached.—**riv·et·er,** *n.*—**riv·-et·less,** *a.*

riv·i·er·a, riv″ē·âr′a, It. Rē·vye′Rä, *n.* A coastal resort area usu. characterized by a temperate climate; (*cap.*) a Mediterranean resort area extending eastward from Marseilles, France, to La Spezia, Italy.

ri·vière, riv″ē·âr′, ri·vyâr′, *Fr.* Rē·vyeR′, *n.* pl. **ri·vières,** riv″ē·ârz′, ri·vyârz′, *Fr.* Rē·vyeR′. [Fr. lit. 'river.'] A necklace of diamonds or other gems, esp. in more than one string.

riv·u·let, riv′ū·lit, *n.* [L. *rivulus*, dim. of *rivus*, a river (seen also in *derive, rival*).] A small stream or brook; a streamlet.

RNA, är″en·ā′. *Biochem.* ribonucleic acid.

roach, rōch, *n.* pl. **roach, roach·es.** [O.Fr. *roche, roque;* origin uncertain.] A European freshwater fish, *Rutilus rutilus*, of the carp family; any of various similar American fishes, as certain fresh-water sunfishes.

a- fat, fāte, fär, fâre, fạll; **e-** met, mē, mẽre, hẽr; **i-** pin, pīne; **o-** not, nōte, mŏve; **u-** tub, cūbe, bụll; **oi-** oil; **ou-** pound.

roach, rōch, *n. Naut.* a curve cut into the edges of a sail, esp. the bottom edge, to obtain a good fit. A section of front hair rolled off the forehead to stand like a pompadour.—*v.t.* To effect an arch in; to roll or brush, as hair, into a roach; to crop or cut, as a horse's mane, so the remainder stands erect.

roach, rōch, *n.* Cockroach; *slang,* the butt of a cigarette, esp. a marijuana cigarette.

roach back, *n.* A curved or arched back.

road, rōd, *n.* [O.E. *rad,* a riding, a journey on horseback, a road, < *ridan,* to ride. *Raid* is a collateral form.] An open way or public passage; a piece of ground between one city, town, or place and another appropriated for travel by foot passengers or vehicles; a highway or the like; *fig.* any action or experience that leads to a change in one's fortune; as, the *road* to happiness. *Colloq.* a railroad; a means or way of approach or access. *Often pl., naut.* a partly protected place where ships may ride at anchor at some distance from the shore; also *roadstead.* Abbr. *R., Rd., rd.*—**on the road,** *colloq.* Traveling, as a salesman; on tour, as a circus or a theatrical company.

road·a·bil·i·ty, rō″da·bil′i·tē, *n.* Of an automobile, the ability to travel over roads of all kinds easily and smoothly.

road a·gent, *n. Colloq.* a highwayman, esp. those who preyed on stagecoach routes.

road al·low·ance, *n. Canada.* A strip of public land set aside by the government for road building; the land bordering a road.

road·bed, rōd′bed″, *n.* The foundation on which the rails, ties, and ballast of a railroad lie; the material or surface of which a road is made.

road·block, rōd′blok″, *n.* An obstacle on a road; a barricade across a road as set up by the police for the purpose of intercepting law violators; an obstruction, as barbed wire, for blocking passage of an enemy.

road hog, *n.* A driver who blocks traffic by driving down the center of a road.

road·house, rōd′hous″, *n.* An eating place, bar, nightclub, or the like, usu. situated on a highway outside the city limits to take advantage of more liberal liquor laws.

road met·al, *n.* Broken stones, cinders, or the like used for repairing or building roads.

road·run·ner, rōd′run″ẽr, *n. Ornith.* a long slender bird, largely terrestrial, *Geococcyx californianus,* in the cuckoo family, having a shaggy crest and strong legs enabling rapid running, inhabiting the arid regions of southwestern N. America, and feeding largely on lizards and snakes. Also *chaparral cock.*

road·side, rōd′sīd″, *n.* The edge of a road. —*a.* On or close to the edge of a road.

road·stead, rōd′sted″, *n.* A sheltered place where ships may ride at anchor off the shore.

road·ster, rōd′stẽr, *n.* An early type of open automobile having a single seat for two people, and a compartment for luggage or a rumble seat in the rear; a horse well fitted for driving on roads.

road test, *n.* An examination of an automobile's performance, made under natural conditions on a highway or other road.

road·way, rōd′wā″, *n.* A road; the land through which a road runs; specif. the part of a road on which vehicles or people travel.

road·work, rōd′wẽrk″, *n.* Long-distance running, esp. such running as training for an athletic event.

roam, rōm, *v.i.* [O.E. *rome,* also *rame,* to roam or rove; of doubtful connections; cf. O.H.G. *ramen,* to aim, to strive. *Ramble* is from this verb.] To wander; to ramble; to rove; to walk or move about from place to place without any certain purpose or direction.—*v.t.* To range; to wander over.—

n. The act of wandering; a ramble.—**roam·er,** *n.*

roan, rōn, *a.* [O.Fr. *roan,* Mod.Fr. *rouan,* It. *roano, rovano,* Sp. *ruano, roano;* origin unknown.] Having a bay, sorrel, or dark color, with numerous spots of gray or white: said of horses; made from a leather of roan color.—*n.* A roan color; a horse or animal of a roan color; a leather prepared from sheepskin, used in bookbinding to imitate morocco.

roar, rōr, rạr, *v.i.* [O.E. *rarian,* L.G. *raren,* D. *reeren,* Prov. G. *reren, roren,* to roar; akin perh. to Dan. *rost,* Icel. *raust,* the voice.] To cry out with a full, loud, continued sound, as in distress or anger; to howl, as a beast; to make a loud, continued, confused sound, as wind, waves, or a multitude of people shouting together; to laugh loudly, exuberantly, or boisterously; to function or act with a loud sound, as an airplane; to breathe with a loud sound, as a horse.—*v.t.* To indicate or express with a roar; to put or make by roaring.—*n.* A full loud sound of some continuance, as of wind, waves, a motor, or the like; the strong deep cry of a beast; the loud cry of a person in distress, pain, or anger; an outcry of joy or mirth.—**roar·er,** *n.*

roar·ing, rōr′ing, rạr′ing, *n.* A loud cry or a continuous roar, as of a beast or a person; loud continued sound, as of the billows of the sea; a disease in horses causing loud, noisy, rasping breathing.—*a.* Characterized by or causing roars or noise; disorderly; riotous; brisk, thriving, or prosperous, as a business.

roast, rōst, *v.t.* [O.Fr. *rostir* (Fr. *rôtir*), to roast.] To cook or prepare for the table by exposure to the direct action of heat, on a spit, in an oven, or the like; to heat to excess; to dry and parch by exposure to heat, as coffee or chestnuts; *metal.* to burn in a heap, as broken ore, in order to free it from foreign matter; *colloq.* to criticize or banter severely.—*v.i.* To become roasted or fit for eating by exposure to heat; to cook food by roasting.—*n.* That which is roasted or intended for roasting, as a piece of beef; a social gathering where meat or other food is roasted; an act of roasting; *colloq.* extreme criticism.—*a.* Roasted; as, *roast* beef.

roast·er, rō′stẽr, *n.* One who or that which roasts; a pan or other contrivance for roasting; something, as a pig or chicken, suitable for roasting.

rob, rob, *v.t.*—*robbed, robbing.* [O.Fr. *rober,* rob; from Teut. (cf. G. *rauben*).] To deprive of something by unlawful force, violence, or threat of violence; as, to *rob* a traveler; to commit robbery upon; as, to *rob* a home; to deprive of something legally belonging or due; as, to *rob* one of an inheritance; to divest unjustly or injuriously, as: The sun *robbed* him of sight.—*v.i.* To commit robbery.

rob·a·lo, rob′a·lō″, rō′ba·lō″, *n. pl.* **rob·a·los, rob·a·lo.** [Sp.] Any of the marine fishes constituting the family *Centropomidae,* esp. a snook, *Centropomus undecimalis,* a large and valuable food fish of West Indian and adjacent waters.

rob·ber, rob′ẽr, *n.* One who robs; bandit; thief.

rob·ber fly, *n.* Any of the swift, often large, predatory flies constituting the family *Asilidae,* which resemble bumblebees.

rob·ber·y, rob′e·rē, *n. pl.* **rob·ber·ies.** The act or practice of robbing; *law,* the forcible and felonious taking of property from the person of or in the presence of another by fear or violence.

robe, rōb, *n.* [O.Fr. Fr. *robe,* robe, orig. spoil, booty, < *rober,* E. *rob.*] A long, loose or flowing gown or outer garment worn by men or women, esp. for formal or state

occasions; a bathrobe or dressing gown; an official vestment, as of a judge; a woman's gown, esp. of the more elaborate kind; a piece of fur, cloth, or knitted work, used as a covering or wrap; *fig.* any vesture or covering; as, a *robe* of silence.—*v.t.*—*robed, robing.* To clothe or invest in a robe or robes; dress; array.—*v.i.* To put on a robe.

robe-de-cham·bre, *Fr.* Rạb·de·shän′bRe, *n. pl.* **robes-de-cham·bre,** *Fr.* Rạb·de-shän′bRe. [Fr., 'chamber robe.'] A dressing gown.

rob·in, rob′in, *n.* [O.Fr. *Robin,* for *Robert,* Robert, man's name.] *Ornith.* One of the most familiar of N. American. birds, *Turdus migratorius,* a large thrush recognized by its gray back and brick-red breast; a smaller thrush of Europe, *Erithacus rubecula,* having a yellowish-red face and breast. Also *redbreast,* **rob·in red·breast.**

ro·ble, rō′blä, *n.* [Sp., oak, < L. *robur.*] A white oak tree, *Quercus lobata,* found chiefly in California; any of several oak or beech trees of southwestern U.S. and Mexico.

ro·bot, rō′bot, rob′ot, *n.* [Czech *robotiti,* to work.] A mechanical, manlike device capable of performing certain mechanical motions and tasks; an automaton; a person who works mechanically.—**ro·bot·ism,** *n.*—**ro·bot·is·tic,** rō″bo·tis′tik, rob″o·tis′tik, *a.*—**ro·bot·like,** *a.*

ro·bot bomb, *n.* An explosive-carrying winged missile or rocket normally launched from the surface and directed toward its target by an automatic pilot and other automatic devices.

ro·bot·ize, rō′bo·tīz″, rob′o·tīz″, *v.t.*—*robotized, robotizing.* To automate, as a plant or factory; to make automatic.—**ro·bot·i·za·tion,** rō″bo·ti·zā′shan, *n.*

ro·bust, rō·bust′, rō′bust, *a.* [L. *robustus,* < *robus, robur,* strength.] Possessed of or indicating great strength or health; strong or enduring; muscular; vigorous; requiring vigor or strength; rude, rough, or boisterous; strong or full-flavored, as coffee.—**ro·bust·ly,** *adv.*—**ro·bust·ness,** *n.*

ro·bus·tious, rō·bus′chus, *a.* Robust or sturdy; rough, boisterous, or rude.—**ro·bus·tious·ly,** *adv.*—**ro·bus·tious·ness,** *n.*

roc, rok, *n.* [Ar. *rukh.*] A legendary enormous bird that figured in Arabian mythology and is thought to have been the fossil elephant bird, *Aepyornis maximus,* whose remains have been found in Madagascar.

roc·am·bole, rok′am·bōl″, *n.* [Fr., < G. *rockenbolle—rocken,* rye, and *bolle,* a bulb, because it grows among rye.] A kind of cultivated garlic, *Allium scorodoprasum.*

Ro·chelle pow·ders, rō·shel′ pou′dẽrz, *ro·shel′, n. pl.* Seidlitz powders.

Ro·chelle salt, rō·shel′ sạlt, *ro·shel′, n.* [From being first prepared at La *Rochelle* in France.] The double tartrate of soda and potash, $KNaC_4H_4O_6 \cdot 4H_2O$, used for manufacturing Seidlitz powders and for other commercial purposes.

roche mou·ton·née, rôsh′ möt″o·nā′, *Fr.* Rạsh mö·tạ·nä′, *n. pl.* **roches mou·ton·nées,** rôsh′ möt″o·näz′, *Fr.* Rạsh mö·tä·nä′. [Fr., 'rock shaped like a sheep.'] A knob of rock rounded and smoothed by glacial action.

roch·et, roch′it, *n.* [O.Fr. Fr. *rochet,* dim. < O.H.G. *roc* (G. *rock*) = O.E. *rocc,* outer garment.] *Eccles.* a vestment of linen or lawn, resembling a surplice, worn esp. by bishops and abbots.

rock, rok, *n.* [O.Fr. *roke, roque,* also *roche* (Fr. *roche*) = M.L. *rocca;* origin unknown.] A large mass of stone forming a cliff or the like; a large detached mass of stone, as a boulder; a stone of any size; stone in the mass; something resembling or suggesting a rock; a firm foundation or support, or a means of safety; a kind of hard sweetmeat or candy, variously flavored; the striped bass. *Geol.* mineral matter of various composition, consolidated or unconsolidated, assembled in masses or considerable quantities in nature, as by volcanic action or the action of water; a particular kind of such matter. *Slang, often pl.* a piece of money. *Slang,* any gem; a diamond.—**on the rocks,** into or in a state of disaster or ruin; destitute of funds or bankrupt; served with or over ice cubes only, as a beverage.

rock, rok, *v.t.* [Late O.E. *roccian,* rock: cf. Dan. *rokke,* move, shake, Icel. *rykkja,* G. *rücken,* pull.] To move or sway to and fro or from side to side, as on a support; move to and fro in a cradle, a chair, the arms, or the like, esp. gently and soothingly; to shake or cause to vibrate strongly; to lull in security, hope, or the like; to move or sway powerfully, as with emotion; *engraving,* to abrade the surface of, as a copperplate, with a cradle or rocker; *min.* to wash, as ores, in a rocker or cradle.—*v.i.* To move or sway to and fro or from side to side; to be moved or swayed powerfully with emotion or the like; to be washed, as ores, in a rocker or cradle.—*n.* A rocking movement; an act of rocking.

rock-and-roll, rok'an·rōl', *n.* Rock 'n' roll.

rock and rye, *n.* A bottled beverage, with rye whiskey as the principal ingredient, to which rock candy and fruit have been added.

rock·a·way, rok'a·wā", *n.* [Appar. from *Rockaway,* New Jersey.] A light, four-wheeled carriage with two or three seats and a standing top.

rock bass, rok' bas", *n.* An American food fish, *Ambloplites rupestris,* common in northern lakes and rivers; the striped bass; a sea bass, *Paralabrax clathratus,* found off the coasts of California and Mexico.

rock bot·tom, *n.* The lowest point possible. —**rock-bot·tom,** *a.*

rock-bound, rok'bound", *a.* Hemmed in, covered, or surrounded by rocks; rocky.

rock brake, *n.* Any of several ferns that grow in rocky places, esp. members of the genus *Pellaea;* the parsley fern, *Cryptogramma crispa.*

rock can·dy, *n.* Sugar in hard cohering crystals of considerable size.

Rock Corn·ish, *n.* A small roasting chicken, bred by crossing Plymouth Rock and Cornish chickens.

rock crys·tal, *n.* Transparent quartz, esp. of the colorless kind.

rock dove, *n.* The bluish-grey fan-tailed wild pigeon, *Columba livia,* from which many domesticated varieties have developed, native to the rocky coasts of the Old World and now fully established in N. America. Also **rock pi·geon, do·mes·ti·cat·ed pi·geon.**

rock·er, rok'ẽr, *n.* One who or that which rocks; one of the curved pieces on which a cradle or a rocking chair rocks; a rocking chair; any of various devices that operate with a rocking motion; *pl.* ice skates with curved runners; *graphic arts,* a device used by engravers to prepare a copper plate for a mezzotint engraving; *min.* a miner's cradle used for washing gold out of gold-bearing sand.—**off his rock·er,** *slang,* crazy.

rock·er arm, *n. Mach.* an armlike piece attached to a rockshaft.

rock·et, rok'it, *n.* [It. *rocchetta,* < *rocca,* a distaff, a rock; < the German.] A firework, signal, weapon, missile, propelling unit for a space vehicle, or other self-propelled and usu. cylindrical device, which is pushed upward through the air by a vigorous thrust of escaping gases released by the explosive reaction of combustible substances carried within it; the space vehicle itself.— *v.t.* To transport or convey with rocket

propulsion.—*v.i.* To move with speed, direction, or other aspects similar to those of a rocket.

rock·et, rok'it, *n.* [Fr. *roquette,* < It. *rochetta,* dim of *ruca,* < L. *eruca,* kind of colewort.] A plant, *Eruca sativa,* that grows in Europe and is eaten as a salad; any plant of the genus *Hesperis,* with fragrant white, pinkish, or purple flowers.

rock·et bomb, *n.* An aerial bomb which uses rocket propulsion for added speed after release from the aircraft; a guided ballistic or other missile which uses rocket propulsion and is usually launched from the ground or the sea.

rock·e·teer, rok"i·tẽr', *n.* One whose specialty is rocketry; a person who uses or operates rockets.

rock·et plane, *n. Aeron.* An airplane powered wholly or mainly by rockets; an airplane equipped with rocket ammunition. Also **rock·et air·plane.**

rock·et pro·pul·sion, *n.* Propulsion by means of a rocket.

rock·et·ry, rok'i·trē, *n. Aerospace,* the science or study of rocket flight, development, and design.

rock·fish, rok'fish", *n.* pl. **rock·fish, rock·-fish·es.** Any of various fishes found about rocks; the striped bass, *Roccus saxatilis.* Any fish of the marine family *Scorpænidae,* certain of which are common food fishes of the Pacific coast of N. America; any of several groupers of the Atlantic coast of the U.S.; also **rock cod.**

rock gar·den, *n.* A garden on rocky ground or among rocks on which are grown alpine or other suitable plants.

rock·ing chair, *n.* A chair mounted on rockers.

rock·ing horse, *n.* A toy horse upon which a child may ride, made of wood or the like and mounted on rockers; a hobbyhorse.

rock·ling, rok'ling, *n.* A type of small codfish of the family *Gadidae.*

rock lob·ster, *n.* Spiny lobster, a popular seafood.

rock ma·ple, *n.* Sugar maple.

rock 'n' roll, rok'an·rōl', *n.* A style of popular music characterized by strong, regularly accented beat and formal elements of blues, originating in the U.S. in the 1950's, later an increasingly eclectic and abstract musical form using electronically amplified instruments. Also **rock-and-roll, rock-'n'-roll, rock.**

rock oil, *n. Chiefly Brit.* petroleum.

rock·oon, rok'ŏn, *n.* [(*rock*)et ball(*oon*).] A small rocket furnished with a variety of meteorological recording instruments carried aloft by a balloon for release at specified altitudes.

rock rab·bit, *n.* A hyrax; pika.

rock-ribbed, rok'ribd", *a.* Having ribs or ridges of rock; exceedingly strong, firm, or unyielding.

rock·rose, rok'rōz", *n.* Any plant of the family *Cistaceae,* esp. those of the genus *Cistus,* most of which are flowering shrubs.

rock salt, *n.* Mineral salt; common salt found in masses or beds.

rock·shaft, rok'shaft", rok'shäft", *n. Mech.* a shaft that oscillates or rocks on its journals instead of revolving.

rock tripe, *n.* Either of the edible lichens, genera *Gyrophora* or *Umbilicaria,* found on rocks in arctic and subarctic areas.

rock·weed, rok'wēd", *n.* Any of various seaweeds common on rocks exposed at low tides, esp. brown algae of the genus *Fuscus.*

rock wool, *n.* A material of woollike fibers, made by passing steam through molten rock or slag, and used for insulation.

rock·y, rok'ē, *a.*—*rockier, rockiest.* Inclined to rock; tottering or shaky; unsteady; uncertain. *Slang,* out of sorts physically, as

from excessive drinking or sickness; unstable; woozy; weak.

rock·y, rok'ē, *a.*—*rockier, rockiest.* Containing, consisting of, or full of rocks; resembling a rock or rocks; having hazards or difficulties; firm; resolute; insensitive.— **rock·i·ness,** *n.*

Rock·y Moun·tain sheep, *n.* A bighorn.

Rock·y Moun·tain spot·ted fe·ver, *n.* An infectious disease caused by the microorganism, *Rickettsia rickettsii,* transmitted by the bite of certain wood ticks, and marked by pains in muscles and joints, fever, prostration, skin eruptions, and chills.

ro·co·co, ro·kō'kō, *Fr.* Ṛạ·ḳạ·ḳạ', *n.* [Fr., < *roc,* rock, < rockwork being a characteristic of the style.] A flamboyant style of French decoration and architecture, influenced by the baroque period, which flourished in the early part of the 18th century, distinguished by exceptionally elaborate and dainty ornamentation and by curved rather than straight lines; *mus.* a musical style of the same period characterized by more than one melodic part and gay ornamentation; *liter.* literary works considered ornate or florid.—*a.* Like or in the manner of the rococo; gaudy or overdone, esp. in reference to art or decoration; tasteless; antiquated.

rod, rod, *n.* [O.E. *rodd,* a rod or beam, a rood or cross = D. *roede,* L.G. *rood, rode,* G. *ruthe,* rod; akin to L. *rudis,* a wand, < same root as Skt. *ruh,* to grow. *Rood* is a form of this word.] A stick, staff, bar, or the like, of various materials, as wood or metal; a shoot or slender stem of any woody plant. *Bib.* a branch or offshoot of a family or tribe; a scion. A stick or switch used to punish; chastisement or punishment. A staff used for measuring. A linear measurement equal to $5\frac{1}{2}$ yards or $16\frac{1}{2}$ feet; a square measure of $30\frac{1}{4}$ square yards; also *perch, pole.* A scepter or staff carried to symbolize office or authority; one of the rod-shaped cells of the retina that are sensitive to dim light; a type of bacteria that is rod-shaped; a long slender pole strung with a line and used for angling; as, a fishing *rod;* a machine part; as, a piston *rod* in an engine or a connecting *rod* on a railroad car; *slang,* a pistol.—*v.t.*—*rodded, rodding.* To equip or fit with a rod, usu. a lightning rod.—**ride the rods,** *slang,* to obtain a free ride on a train by riding on the connecting rods of the cars.—**rod·less, rod·like,** *a.*

ro·dent, rōd'ent, *a.* [L. *rodens, rodentis,* ppr. of *rodo,* to gnaw (see also in *erode, corrode*). Same root as *rado,* to shave or scrape.] Gnawing; belonging or pertaining to the order of gnawing animals called *Rodentia.*— *n.* A mammal, as the squirrel, rat, mouse, or the like, of the large order *Rodentia,* characterized by continually growing incisors adapted for nibbling or gnawing.

ro·den·ti·cide, rō·den'ti·sīd", *n.* A substance used to kill rodents; that which is used to repel rodents.

ro·de·o, rō'dē·ō", rō·dā'ō, *n.* pl. **ro·de·os.** [Sp.] A public performance of cowboy skills, including bronco riding, steer wrestling, and calf roping; a cattle roundup.

rod·man, rod'man, *n.* pl. **rod·men.** A surveyor's assistant; the man whose duty is to carry the leveling rod in surveying.

rod·o·mon·tade, rō"do·mon·tād', rō"do·mon·täd', *n.* [Fr.] Vain boasting; pretentious bluster or vaunting; rant.—*v.i.*— *rodomontaded, rodomontading.* To brag; to rant in a boastful way.—*a.* Also *rhodomontade.*

roe, rō, *n.* [Akin to Dan. *rogn,* Icel. *hrogn,* G. *rogen,* roe, spawn; Sc. *ran, rawn,* the female roe.] The sperm or eggs of fishes, the roe of the male being called *soft roe* or *milt,* that of the female *hard roe* or *spawn;* the eggs of some crustaceans.

roe, rō, *n.* pl. **roes,** *coll.* **roe.** [O.E. *rā, rāha,* = D. *ree* = G. *rēh* = Icel. *rā*, roe.] The roe deer.—**roe·buck,** rō′buk″, *n.* A male roe deer; less properly, any roe deer.—**roe deer,** *n.* [O.E. *rāhdēor.*] A small, agile old-world deer, *Capreolus capræa.*

roent·gen, rent′gen, rent′jen, *n.* The unit used internationally as a measure of radiation, named for Wilhelm Konrad *Röntgen*, the discoverer of x-rays. *Abbr.* R or r—*a.* Pertaining most commonly to x-rays, but also to the roentgen unit or to Röntgen, the physicist.—**roent·gen·ize,** rent′ge·nīz″, rent′je·nīz″, *v.t.*—*roentgenized, roentgenizing.* To subject to the action of x-rays.

roent·gen·o·gram, rent′ge·no·gram″, rent′je·no·gram″, *n.* A photograph made by means of x-rays. Also **roent·gen·o·graph.—roent·gen·og·ra·phy,** rent″ge·nog′ra·fē, rent″je·nog′ra·fē, *n.* X-ray photography.—**roent·gen·o·graph·ic,** rent″ge·no·graf′ik, rent″je·no·graf′ik, *a.*—**roent·gen·o·graph·i·cal·ly,** *adv.*

roent·gen·ol·o·gy, rent″ge·nol′o·jē, rent″je·nol′o·jē, *n.* The study of all applications of x-rays, esp. those relating to medical diagnosis and therapy.—**roent·gen·o·log·ic,** **roent·gen·o·log·i·cal,** rent″ge·no·loj′ik, rent″je·no·loj′ik, *a.*—**roent·gen·o·log·i·cal·ly,** *adv.*—**roent·gen·ol·o·gist,** *n.*

roent·gen·o·scope, rent′ge·no·skōp″, rent′je·no·skōp″, *n.* An apparatus having a fluorescent viewing screen on which a shadow picture of an opaque object is projected by means of x-rays.—**roent·gen·o·scop·ic,** rent″ge·no·skop′ik, rent″je·no·skop′ik, *a.*—**roent·gen·os·co·py,** rent″ge·nos′ko·pē, rent″je·nos′ko·pē, *n.*

roent·gen·o·ther·a·py, rent″ge·nō·ther′a·pē, rent″je·nō·ther′a·pē, *n.* Remedial medical treatment through the use of x-rays.

roent·gen ray, *n.* (*Often cap.*) x-ray.

ro·ga·tion, rō·gā′shan, *n.* [L. *rogatio*(n-), < *rogare*, ask.] *Usu. pl., eccles.* solemn supplication. *Rom. law*, sponsorship by the consuls or tribunes of a law to be passed by the people; a law so proposed.—**Ro·ga·tion Days,** *eccles.* the three days before Ascension Day, on which rogations are chanted during processions.

rog·er, roj′ẽr, *interj.* Radio communication code meaning, 'message received and understood.'

rogue, rōg, *n.* [Prob. a Celtic word; cf. Ir. *roguire*, a rogue; Fr. *rogue*, arrogant, Armor, *rog*, arrogant, proud.] A dishonest person; a rascal; a vagrant; a vagabond. *Biol.* a specimen showing traits at variance with the species' norm, esp. inferior traits. A lone animal, as an elephant, displaying a fierce disposition.—**ro·guish,** rō′gish, *a.*—**ro·guish·ly,** *adv.*—**ro·guish·ness,** *n.*

rogue, rōg, *v.i.*—*rogued, roguing.* To assume the manner of a rogue.—*v.t.* To swindle; *bot.* to extirpate, as plants deviating from biological norms.

rogue el·e·phant, *n.* A savage elephant which has been excluded from the herd.

ro·guer·y, rō′ge·rē, *n.* pl. **ro·guer·ies.** An act or conduct characteristic of one who is a rogue; trickery; dishonest practice; mischief in a playful manner.

rogue's gal·ler·y, *n.* A collection of portraits of criminals, used by police as a means of identification.

roil, roil, *v.t.* [Origin unknown.] To make turbid by stirring; to annoy or anger.—**roil·y,** roi′lē, *a.*—*roilier, roiliest.* Turbid; muddy.

roist·er, roi′stẽr, *v.i.* [< Fr. *rustre*, a boor, < L. *rusticus*, rustic; or connected with Sc. *roust*, to roar, Icel. *rosta*, a riot.] To bluster; to swagger; to be noisy, vaunting, or turbulent.—**roist·er·er,** *n.*

role, rōl, *n.* [Fr., a roll, scroll, character in a play.] A character portrayed by an actor; a customary function.

roll, rōl, *v.i.* [O.Fr. *roeler, roler* (Fr. *rouler*), to roll; Pr. *rolar*, rotlar; < L.L. *rotulare* < L. *rotulus, rotula*, a little wheel, < *rota*, a wheel (whence also *rotary*, or *rotate*).] To move smoothly along a surface while maintaining a constantly changing portion of the circumference in contact with the surface by turning from top to bottom, as a ball or wheel; to move or to be moved on wheels, rollers, or the like; to flow or appear to move or to be moved on wheels, rollers, or the like; to flow or appear to move or flow with the undulations and continuity of waves or a stream; as, hills *rolling* to the sea; *slang*, to wallow or luxuriate in the abundance of some commodity; as, to be *rolling* in money. To take the shape of a ball or cylinder by curling or turning over on itself one or many times; to pass or elapse as if by the progression of a cycle, as: Time *rolls* by. To make a low, deep rumbling sound, as thunder or drums; to trill, as a canary; to move in a circular or semicircular path; as, eyes *rolling* in fright; to move from side to side in a swaying, rocking motion, as a ship; to swagger or walk with a swinging, swaying gait; to roam or travel about; to become flat or spread out by the use of a roller; to carry out a revolution or cycle, as a planet; to get started or progress, as: Let's get *rolling*. *Aeron.* to rotate on a longitudinal axis, as an airplane.—*v.t.* To set in motion by causing to turn over and over, or revolve across a surface, as a ball; to convey or move using wheels or rollers; to form into a ball or cylinder by turning over upon itself, or wrapping around itself; to cause to undulate, surge, or flow steadily onward; to spread out, flatten, or make level by using pressure from a type of roller; to give a swaying, rocking, or circular motion to, as: Waves *roll* a ship. To wrap, enfold, encircle, or contain with a substance or covering; to turn from top to bottom, or side to side in a circular motion; as, to *roll* one's eyes; to voice or sound with a trill, as r's; to give forth in a full, reverberating manner, as a laugh; to beat, as a drum, with such rapidity that the successive beats seem to blend; *slang*, to rob by searching through the pockets of a victim, esp. of a drunk or sleeping person.—*n.* A piece of parchment or paper which is or may be rolled up, esp. one inscribed with some formal or official record; a scroll; a list, register, or catalog containing the names of the persons belonging to any company, class, society, or the like; a muster roll; anything rolled up in a cylindrical form; a quantity of cloth, wallpaper, or the like rolled up in cylindrical form, often forming a definite measure; a case made of leather or other material which is rolled up about its contents; some foods which are prepared and served rolled up; as, jelly *roll*; a small lump of bread dough rolled or doubled on itself and baked; a cylindrical or rounded form or mass of something; as, *rolls* of fat; a roller with which something is spread out, leveled, crushed, or compacted; a roller around which materials are wrapped for storing; an act of rolling; an undulation of surface; as, the *roll* of a prairie; a rolling motion, as of a ship; a sonorous or rhythmical flow of words; a deep, prolonged sound or rumble; the sound of a drum rapidly beaten; the trill of certain birds. *Slang*, a wad of folded paper money, usu. carried on the person; money or funds one has saved. *Aeron.* any rotational movement of an aircraft about its longitudinal axis; a maneuver in which an aircraft executes a complete revolution around its axis. *Aerospace*, a spinning motion about the long dimension of a spacecraft; one of the three axes, with pitch and yaw, on which the altitude of the

vehicle may be controlled.—**roll out,** *slang*, to get out of bed.—**roll up,** *colloq.* to increase or accumulate, as profits.—**roll·a·ble,** *a.*—**roll·ing,** rō′ling, *a., n.*

roll·back, rōl′bak″, *n.* A rolling back, as of prices and wages, to a former and lower level, esp. by governmental action.—*v.t.*

roll call, *n.* The calling of a roll or list of names, as of soldiers or students, to find out who is present; a time or signal for this, as one given by a drum in the military.

roll·er, rō′lẽr, *n.* One who or that which rolls; a cylinder, wheel, or caster upon which something is rolled along; a cylindrical body, revolving on a fixed axis, employed to facilitate the movement of something passed over or around it; a cylindrical body upon which cloth or other material is rolled up; a cylindrical body for rolling over something to be spread out, leveled, crushed, compacted, impressed, or inked; a similar body revolving on a fixed axis, or one of a set of such bodies, forming part of some machine or apparatus, and operating on something to be similarly acted upon; a hollow cylinder of plastic or wire mesh or the like, on which strands of hair are wrapped to form a wave or curl; a long, swelling wave advancing steadily.

roll·er, rō′lẽr, *n. Ornith.* Any of several species of colorful old-world birds allied to the kingfisher, esp. *Coracias garrulus*, largely blue with a red back, and distinguished by a rolling or undulating flight; a variety of the canary, having a rolling, trilling voice.

roll·er bear·ing, *n. Mach.* a bearing in which the shaft or journal turns on a number of steel rollers running in an annular track.

roll·er coast·er, *n.* A railroad, found esp. in amusement parks, which has open cars and operates on a course marked by steep ascents and descents and sharp curves.

roll·er skate, *n.* A form of skate with small wheels or rollers instead of a runner.—**roll·er-skate,** rō′lẽr-skāt″, *v.i.*—*roller-skated, roller-skating.* To move around on roller skates.—**roll·er skat·er,** *n.*

roll·er tow·el, *n.* A long towel sewed together at the ends and hung on a roller.

roll film, *n.* A narrow strip of film on a spool, used in still cameras for taking a series of pictures.

rol·lick, rol′ik, *v.i.* To move in a jolly, swaggering manner; to be jovial in behavior; to frolic.—**rol·lick·ing,** rol′i·king, *a.*; lively; light-hearted. Also **rol·lick·some,** rol′ik·som.

roll·ing hitch, *n.* A kind of hitch which is made around a spar or the like with the end of a rope, and which jams when the rope is pulled.

roll·ing mill, *n.* A mill or establishment where iron or other metal is rolled into sheets, bars, or the like; a machine or set of rollers for rolling out or shaping metal.

roll·ing pin, *n.* A cylinder of wood or other material for rolling out dough.

roll·ing stock, *n.* The wheeled vehicles of a railroad, including locomotives and cars.

roll man, *n.* The operator of a machine in a rolling mill.

roll out, *v.t.* To flatten and spread by rolling, as dough.—*v.i. Slang*, to arise from bed. *Football*, to execute a roll-out play.—**roll-out,** rōl′out″, *n. Football*, a play in which the quarterback circles to either left or right before electing to run with the ball, hand it off to another back, or pass.—*a.*

roll top, *n.* A sliding, flexible cover which rolls down over the surface of a desk.—**roll-top, roll·top,** rōl′top″, *a.*

roll up, *v.t.* To gather together; to collect.—*v.i.* To arrive; to grow by accumulation, as a fund.

ro·ly-po·ly, rō′lē·po′lē, rō′lē·pō″lē, *a.* Rotund; plump.—*n.* pl. **ro·ly·po·lies.** A short, plump person or animal; *chiefly Brit.* a sheet of pastry spread with jam, rolled, and baked.

ro·maine, rō·mān', ro·mān', *n.* [Fr. *romaine,* fem. of *romain,* E. *Roman.*] A variety of cos lettuce, *Lactuca sativa longifolia,* with long, comparatively narrow, crisp leaves.

Ro·man, rō'man, *a.* [L. *Romanus,* < *Roma,* Rome, the principal city of the Romans.] Pertaining to or resembling Rome or the Roman people; pertaining to or professing the Roman Catholic religion; (*usu. l.c.*) applied to the common upright letter in printing, as distinguished from *italic,* and to numerals expressed by letters, and not in the Arabic characters.—*n.* A native or citizen of Rome; the Italian dialect of Rome; (*usu. l.c.*) Roman lettering in printing.

ro·man, ra·mäN', *n.* [Fr.] A metrical epic narrative, common in France in the Middle Ages; a romantic novel.

Ro·man ar·chi·tec·ture, *n.* The architecture of the ancient Romans, characterized by the round arch and vault, stone, brick, and concrete masonry, and the adoption of Greek orders as exterior ornaments.

Ro·man cal·en·dar, *n.* The lunar calendar of ancient Rome, used prior to the Julian calendar which was introduced in 46 B.C.

Ro·man can·dle, *n.* A kind of firework, consisting of a tube which discharges upward a stream of white or colored balls of fire.

Ro·man Cath·o·lic, *a.* Of or pertaining to the Roman Catholic Church of which the pope, or bishop of Rome, is the visible head; referring to a member of the Roman Catholic Church.—*n.*—**Ro·man Ca·thol·i·cism,** the dogmas, practice, and organization of the Roman Catholic Church.

ro·mance, rō·mans', rō'mans, *n.* [O.Fr. *romans,* a romance or tale, orig. one in the vulgar tongue (French, as opposed to Latin), also the vulgar tongue (Fr. *roman,* a novel), M.L. *Romanice, adv.,* in the vulgar tongue of France (derived from the Romans), < L. *Romanicus,* E. *Romanic.*] A medieval tale, orig. one in verse in some Romance dialect, treating of heroic personages or events; as, the Arthurian *romances*; in general, a tale depicting heroic or marvelous achievements, colorful events or scenes, chivalrous devotion, unusual experiences, or other matters of a kind to appeal to the imagination; a tale or novel dealing less with real or familiar life than with extraordinary adventures, fortunes, or occurrences or with imaginary or ideal conditions; the world, life, or conditions depicted in such literature; romantic character or quality; romantic spirit or sentiment; a romantic affair or experience, as a love affair; a made-up story, or a statement proceeding wholly or chiefly from the imagination; fanciful or extravagant invention or exaggeration.—rō·mans', *v.i.*—*romanced, romancing.* To invent or relate romances; to indulge in fanciful or extravagant stories; to think or talk romantically; to seek or indulge in love affairs.

ro·mance, rō·mans', *n.* [Fr. *romance,* < Sp. *romance,* kind of poem, ballad, = O.Fr. *romans,* E. *romance.*] *Sp. liter.* a short, epic, narrative poem or historical ballad, later, a short lyric poem. *Mus.* a short, simple melody, vocal or instrumental, of tender character.

Ro·mance, rō'mans, *a.* Belonging or pertaining to the group of languages called Romance; composed in or using some language of this group.—rō·mans', rō'·mans, *n.* The group of dialects or languages of southern Europe which descended from Latin, including the French,

Provençal, Spanish, Portuguese, Italian, Rhaeto-Romantic, Catalan, and Rumanian.

ro·manc·er, rō·man'ser, *n.* One who romances; a writer of romance.

Ro·man col·lar, *n.* A clerical collar.

Ro·man·esque, rō"ma·nesk', *a. Arch.* noting or pertaining to the style which, developing from that of the later Roman Empire, prevailed in western Europe until the middle of the 12th century, characterized esp. by the round arch and vault and by massive, weighty decorative effects; *art,* noting or pertaining to the early medieval style. (*Usu. l.c.*), *liter.* unrestrained; lavish; characteristic of romance. Of Romance languages, esp. that of southern France.—*n.* The Romanesque style of art or architecture; the Romance languages.

ro·man-fleuve, *Fr.* ra·män'flœv', *n.* pl. **ro·mans-fleuves** [Fr., 'river novel.'] A form of French novel distinguished by a rambling, sagalike chronicling of the history of a family, community, or the like, usu. in several volumes. Also *saga novel.*

Ro·man·ic, rō·man'ik, *a.* [L. *Romanicus,* < *Romanus,* E. *Roman.*] Derived from the Romans or from Latin; pertaining to Romance languages.—*n.*

Ro·man·ism, rō'ma·niz"um, *n.* The tenets of Roman Catholicism: often used derogatorily.

Ro·man·ist, rō'ma·nist, *n.* A Roman Catholic: often used derogatorily. One learned in the language, customs, or law of Rome; one versed in any of the Romance languages.—*a.*—**Ro·man·is·tic,** rō"ma·nis'tik, *a.*

Ro·man·ize, rō'ma·nīz", *v.t.*—*Romanized, Romanizing.* To latinize; to convert to the Roman Catholic religion.—*v.i.* To conform to Roman Catholic opinions, customs, or modes of speech; to become a Roman Catholic; to write in Roman characters.

Ro·man nu·mer·als, *n.* The letters of ancient Rome which were used as numerals through the 9th century A.D. and which remain in limited use today. The basic Roman letters and their numeric equivalents are: I = 1, V = 5, X = 10, L = 50, C = 100, D = 500, and M = 1000, with other numbers being formed by the positioning of these letters to indicate the adding to, or subtracting from their value: the symbol that precedes one of equal or greater value is subtracted from the latter, so that IV becomes 4 and XL becomes 40; the symbol that follows one of equal or greater value is added to it, with II becoming 2, and XV becoming 15; this applies as well to a symbol standing between two others: if it is of greater value than the one following on the right, it is added to that numeral, while if it is of lesser value it is subtracted and, in either case, the result is added to the preceding, or first symbol; thus XIX is 19 and LIV is 54, while LVII is 57 and XXI is 21. Roman numerals are sometimes written in lower case, but more commonly appear in capitals.

Ro·ma·no, rō·mä'nō, *n.* A sharp Italian cheese, commonly made from ewe's milk, and often used on spaghetti in grated form.

ro·man·tic, rō·man'tik, *a.* [Fr. *romantique.*] Pertaining to romance or romances; partaking of romance; fanciful, imaginative, or ideal; extravagantly amorous; ardent; chimerical; not belonging to real life; of or pertaining to romanticism; wildly picturesque; having striking natural features; full of wild or fantastic scenery.—*n.* A romantic individual; romanticist; *pl.* romantic concepts or manners.—**ro·man·ti·cal·ly,** *adv.*

ro·man·ti·cism, rō·man'ti·siz"um, *n.* A literary and artistic movement marked by lyricism and emphasis on the feelings and imagination, with philosophical sources in 18th century German idealism, and con-

stituting a reaction against the social and aesthetic principles associated with neoclassicism by insisting upon greater creative freedom and a wider range of subjects open to artistic or literary treatment.—**ro·man·ti·cist,** rō·man'ti·sist, *n.*

ro·man·ti·cize, rō·man'ti·sīz, *v.t.*—*romanticized, romanticizing.* To make romantic; invest with a romantic character.—*v.i.* To be romantic; act, talk, or write in a romantic manner.—**ro·man·ti·ci·za·tion,** rō·man"ti·si·zā'shan, *n.*

Ro·me·o, rō'mē·ō", *n.* A communications code word to designate the letter *R.*

Rom·ney, rom'nē, rum'nē, *n.* One of a breed of sheep with long wool, bred in England and found in low, wet, and swampy regions. Also **Rom·ney Marsh, Rom·ney marsh.**

romp, romp, *v.i.* [A slightly different form of *ramp.*] To play boisterously; to frolic; to run or proceed rapidly and effortlessly, as in a race.—*n.* Spirited play or frolic; a romping girl or other person; a rapid, seemingly effortless pace; *slang,* a quick easy victory.

romp·er, rom'per, *n.* One who romps; *usu. pl.* a child's one-piece garment.

ron·deau, ron'dō, ron·dō', *n.* pl. **ron·deaux.** [Fr. *rondeau,* < *rond,* round.] A poem of 13 lines and two refrain phrases, with a fragment of the first line as the refrain. *Mus.* a song of the 13th and 14th centuries, esp. in France, in which a soloist alternates with a choral refrain; a 17th century instrumental form of a refrain and contrasting passages, derived from the 13th century rondeau.

ron·del, ron'del, *n.* [O.Fr. *rondel* (Fr. *rondeau*), dim. < *rond,* round.] A short poem of fixed form, consisting usu. of 14 lines on two rhymes, of which four are made up of the initial couplet repeated in the middle and at the end, the second line of the couplet sometimes being omitted at the end.

ron·de·let, ron'de·let", ron"de·let', *n.* [O.Fr., dim. of *rondel.*] A short poem of fixed form, consisting of five lines on two rhymes, and having the opening words or word used after the second and fifth lines as an unrhymed refrain.

ron·do, ron'dō, ron·dō', *n.* pl. **ron·dos.** [It., < Fr. *rondeau.*] *Mus.* a work or movement having one principal subject or theme to which return is made in the identical key after the introduction of each subordinate theme.

ron·dure, ron'jer, *n.* [Fr. *rondeur,* < *rond,* E. *round.*] *Poet.* A sphere, circle, or round space; a gracefully curved or rounded form.

rönt·gen, rent'gen, rent'jen, *n.* Roentgen.

rood, rōd, *n.* [The same word as *rod,* O.E. *rōd,* a cross, a rod or pole; akin to D. *roede,* G. *ruthe,* a rod or switch and a measure of length.] A large crucifix in a medieval church placed at the entrance to the chancel; a cross or crucifix; a measure varying in length from 5½ to 8 yards; a square rod; a square measure equal to a quarter of an acre or 40 square rods.

roof, rōf, ruf, *n.* [O.E. *hrōf,* a roof; cogn. Icel. *hrōf,* a shed under which ships are built; *raf,* a roof; D. *roef,* a cover, a cabin.] The cover of any house or building irrespective of the materials of which it is composed; the top or highest part of something; that which corresponds with or resembles the covering of a house, as the top of a carriage or car; a house.—*v.t.* To cover with a roof; to enclose in a house; to shelter.—**roof·er,** rō'fer, ruf'er, *n.*—**roof·less,** rōf'lis, ruf'lis, *a.*—**roof·like,** *a.*

roof gar·den, *n.* A garden on the flat roof of a house or other building; the top or top story of a building, ornamented with plants, utilized as a recreational space or as a restaurant.

roof·ing, rŏŏ′fing, rŭf′ing, n. The act of covering with a roof; material used or suitable for roofs; a roof.

roof·top, rŏŏf′top″, rŭf′top″, n. The roof on any building, esp. the surface on the outside.

roof·tree, rŏŏf′trē″, rŭf′trē″, n. The ridge pole of a roof; the roof; a shelter or dwelling.

rook, rŏŏk, n. [Fr. roc, It. rocco, Sp. roque, < Pers. and Ar. rukh, the rook or castle at chess.] Chess, one of the four turret-shaped pieces placed on the corner squares of the board and moved lengthwise or crosswise an unlimited number of unfilled squares. Also castle.

rook, rŏŏk, n. [O.E. hrōc, D. roek, L.G. rók, Icel. hrōkr, Sw. roka, O.H.G. hruoh, prob. from the cry which the bird utters; akin to Gael. roc, to croak, L. raucus, hoarse.] Ornith. a metallic-black European crow, Corvus frugilegus, having a naked area surrounding the bill appearing as a light gray patch, nesting in colonies and feeding on insects and seeds. A cheat; a trickster.— v.t., v.i. To cheat; to defraud.—**rook·y,** rŏŏk′ē, a.—rookier, rookiest. Relating to rooks; having many rooks.

rook·er·y, rŏŏk′e·rē, n. pl. **rook·er·ies.** A place used by rooks for breeding and nesting; a colony of rooks; an area used for breeding by flocks of sea birds and seals; an old, neglected building, crowded with tenants.

rook·ie, rŏŏk′ē, n. Slang. An inexperienced newcomer, as in professional sports; a beginner; a novice; a new recruit, as on the police force, in the army, or the like.

room, rŏŏm, rŭm, n. [O.E. rūm = Icel. rúm, D. ruim, O.E., O. Fris., L.G., Sw., and Dan. rum, G. raum, room, space; Goth. rums, place, space; same root as L. rus. country.] One of the partitioned areas inside a building or structure, usu. for occupancy or a specific purpose; a chamber; a place of lodging that is rented; an amount of space available for use, or occupied in a particular way; as, plenty of room in the backyard; latitude, possibility, opportunity; as, room for improvement; fig. the group of people inside a room; as, a room becoming hushed.—v.i. To have lodgings; to inhabit a rented room.

room·er, rŏŏm′ėr, rŭm′ėr n. One who rents a room or group of rooms, esp. without board; a lodger.

room·ette, rŏŏ·met′, rŭ·met′, n. Rail. a private and small compartment in a sleeping car on a train, containing a folding bed and a washroom, and occupied usu. by a single person.

room·ful, rŏŏm′fŏŏl, rŭm′fŏŏl, n. As much or as many as a room will hold; the objects or people collectively in a room.

room·ing house, n. A house where rooms are rented, usu. furnished; lodging house.

room·mate, rŏŏm′māt″, rŭm′māt″, n. One who shares a room or several rooms with another person or persons.

room·y, rŏŏm′ē, rŭm′ē, a.—roomier, roomiest. Having ample room; spacious.—**room·i·ly,** adv.—**room·i·ness,** n.

roor·back, roor·bach, rŏŏr′bak″, n. Colloq. a false and malicious report circulated for purposes that are political.

roost, rŏŏst, n. [O.E. hrōst, D. roost, roost.] The pole or support on which fowls rest at night; a place in which birds may roost; any place for resting or the like.—v.i. To occupy a roost; to lodge; to settle down or rest.—**rule the roost,** to dominate or be master; to control.

roost·er, rŏŏs′tėr, n. The male of the domestic chicken; a cock; colloq. a person who is cocky or vain.

root, rŏŏt, rŭt, n, [< Icel. rót, Sw. rot, Dan. rod; connected with L. radix (whence radical), Gr. rhiza, root, E. wort.] That part of a plant which fixes itself in the earth, and by means of its radicals absorbs nutriment; a bulb, tuber, or similar part of a plant; that which resembles a root in position or function; as, the root of a tooth or hair; the foundation or base; the essence or heart of; the origin or cause of something; a progenitor or ancestor. Gram. that part of a word which conveys its essential meaning, as distinguished from the formative or inflectional parts by which this meaning is modified; an ultimate form or element from which words are derived or thought to be derived. Math. a number a so related to a larger number b that, when multiplied by itself a given number of times, it yields exactly number b; as, two is the square root of four and the cube root of eight; that which satisfies a polynomial equation with one unknown. Mus. the note that is the lowest of a chord in basic position; the tone whose harmonics or overtones form a chord; a fundamental.—v.i. To send forth roots; to begin to develop; to be firmly fixed or established; to have a beginning, source, or cause.—v.t. To establish by or as if by roots; to plant or impress deeply; as, principles rooted in the mind; to extirpate, with out or up.—**root·like,** a.

root, rŏŏt, rŭt, v.t. [< O.E. wrōtan, to root up, < wrōt, a snout.] To turn up with the snout, as a swine; to unearth or find, as if by rooting.—v.i. To turn up the earth with the snout, as swine; to hunt, poke about, or rummage for something.

root, rŏŏt, rŭt, v.i. To show active interest in a team or in a participant in a contest by cheering, shouting, or applauding; to favor and support a particular person or thing, usu. with for.—**root·er,** rŏŏt′ėr, n.

root·age, rŏŏt′ij, rŭt′ij, n. The act of taking root; firm fixture by means of roots; a root system.

root beer, n. A carbonated beverage made from various root and herb extracts, which are fermented in solution with yeast and sugar.

root bor·er, n. An adult insect or its larva which destroys plants by tunneling into the roots.

root cel·lar, n. A cool pit or cave used to store vegetables, esp. root crops, as potatoes, beets, turnips, and the like.

root climb·er, n. A plant with climbing qualities due to adventitious roots.

root crop, n. A crop cultivated chiefly for its enlarged, edible roots, as carrots, beets, sweet potatoes, parsnips, and turnips, which are widely used for human consumption and as feed for livestock.

root hair, n. Bot. a delicate tubular filament growing from the tip region of a root, increasing the plant's absorption area of water and of nutrients from the soil.

root·less, rŏŏt′lis, rŭt′lis, a. Having no roots; having no strong attachment to any particular place.—**root·less·ness,** n.

root·let, rŏŏt′lit, rŭt′lit, n. A radicle; a little root, or branch of a root.

root out, v.t. To dig up or discover; to eradicate or destroy completely, as a weed.

root rot, n. Plant pathol. A symptom or aspect of various plant diseases causing root decay; a disease of this type.

root·stalk, rŏŏt′stak″, rŭt′stak″, n. Bot. A rhizome; rootstock.

root·stock, rŏŏt′stok″, rŭt′stok″, n. Origin or source. Bot. a rhizome; a root or part of a root used as a source of plant reproduction; also rootstalk.

root·y, rŏŏt′ē, rŭt′ē, a.—rootier, rootiest. Full of roots; resembling roots.

rope, rōp, n. [O.E. rāp, a rope = Icel. reip, D. reep, roop, G. reif, Goth. raips.] A thick, long cord of twisted or braided fibers, as hemp, wire, nylon, or other material; a series of things or quantity of material linked together in a braided or twisted fashion; as, a rope of onions; a hangman's noose or halter; the death sentence of hanging; a lasso; one of the viscid, glutinous strands that form in liquids or food substances, often due to contamination by bacteria; usu. pl. lines used to demarcate or enclose a boxing ring or other area.— v.t.—roped, roping. To tie, fasten, or bind with a rope; to demarcate or enclose with a rope, ropes, or the like, usu. followed by off; to lasso; to draw, involve, lure, esp. through deception, usu. followed by in.— v.i. To be drawn or twisted into a form resembling a rope; to become ropy.—**end of one's rope,** colloq. The extremity of one's resources; the lack of further resorts or alternatives.—**give one e·nough rope,** colloq. to allow a person the freedom to pursue a mistaken course or deed.—**know the ropes,** colloq. to be well-acquainted with the methods and details of any business or operation.—**on the ropes,** slang, to be in a defenseless or hopeless position.—**rop·er,** n.—**rop·i·ness,** n.

rope·danc·er, rōp′dan″sėr, rōp′dän″sėr, n. One who dances or performs acrobatic feats on a rope or wire strung above the floor or ground; tightrope walker; rope walker. —**rope·danc·ing,** n.

rope·walk, rōp′wak″, n. A long covered walk or a long building where ropes are manufactured.

rope·walk·er, rōp′wa″kėr, n. Ropedancer.

rope yarn, n. The single strands of hemp or the like, from which rope is spun.

rop·y, rō′pē, a.—ropier, ropiest. Drawing into viscous filaments or threads; stringy; glutinous; resembling or similar to one rope or ropes.—**rop·i·ly,** adv.—**rop·i·ness,** n.

roque, rōk, n. [Arbitrary reduction of croquet.] A form of croquet played on a specially prepared court and modified so as to demand greater skill.

Roque·fort, rōk′fėrt, n. [After a town in southern France where made.] A cheese made from the milk of sheep and goats, strongly flavored, and marked by a blue mold.

ror·qual, rar′kwal, n. Any of the large whalebone whales belonging to the genus Balenoptera; a finback.

Ror·schach test, rōr′shäk test″, rar′shäk, n. [From Hermann Rorschach, 1884–1922, Swiss psychiatrist.] Psychol. a technique for appraising personality by an analysis of the subject's interpretation of a standard series of ten ink blots of varied design.

ro·sa·ceous, rō·zā′shus, a. [L. rosaceus.] Roselike; having five petals in a circular form; as, a rosaceous corolla; pertaining to the rose family of plants.

ros·an·i·line, rō·zan′i·lin, rō·zan′i·lēn″, n. Chem. a crystalline base, $C_{20}H_{21}N_3O$, derived from aniline, and forming salts which yield red and other dyes.

ro·sar·i·an, rō·zâr′ē·an, n. A cultivator of roses.—**ro·sar·i·um,** n. A rose garden.

ro·sa·ry, rō′za·rē, n. pl. **ro·sa·ries.** [L. rosarium, rose garden, M.L. rosary, prop. neut. of L. rosarius, of roses, < rosa, E. rose.] Rom. Cath. Ch. a sequence or series of prayers and devotions divided into 15 decades or groups of ten each; a string of beads, joined to a crucifix, used to count and separate the sequence of such prayers; such a string of beads with five decades; prayer beads. Among other religious bodies, a string of beads similarly used in praying. A rose garden; a bed of roses.

rose, rōz, n. [O.E. rose, Fr. rose, < L. rosa, a rose; allied to Gr. rhodon, a rose, prob. < an Eastern source.] Any plant of the genus Rosa, in the family Rosaceae, many species of which are cultivated for their attractive flowers; the flower of such a plant; any of numerous plants that resemble roses; a deep pinkish color; a perfume made from roses; a knot of ribbon in the form of a rose, used as an ornament; a design, ornament, or gem in the shape of a rose, made of various materials; a perforated nozzle to distribute water in fine showerlike jets; a compass card.—*a*. Like the rose flower in color or scent; abounding in roses, as a garden.—**bed of ros·es**, a condition of ease or contentment.—**through rose-col·ored glass·es**, optimistically; with confident expectation of good—**un·der the rose**, confidentially; in private.—**rose·like**, *a*.

ro·sé, rō·zā′, *n*. [Fr.] A wine, usu. served at dinner, whose pink color is created by removing the red grape skins early in the fermentation process.

ro·se·ate, rō′zē·it, rō′zē·āt″, *a*. Rose-colored; deep pink; rosy; blooming; full of roses; happy; favorable; promising. —**ro·se·ate·ly**, *adv*.

rose·bay, rōz′bā″, *n*. A common name for any plant of the genus *Rhododendron*, which consists chiefly of flowering shrubs.

rose·bud, rōz′bud″, *n*. The bud of a rose; the flower of the rose just appearing and before opening; *fig*. a debutante.

rose chaf·er, *n*. A beetle, *Macrodactylus subspinosus*, highly destructive to the flowers and leaves of roses, grapes, and peach trees. Also **rose bug**, **rose bee·tle**.

rose-col·ored, rōz′kul″ĕrd, *a*. Of rose color; pink or rosy; bright or promising; as, *rose-colored* prospects; cheerful or optimistic.

rose comb, *n*. A flat, red-colored, serrated protuberance on the head of domestic fowl, as chickens, usu. more prominent on the male.

rose fe·ver, *n*. *Pathol*. an allergy similar to hay fever, associated with rose pollen and usu. occurring in early summer. Also **rose cold**.

rose·fish, rōz′fish″, *n*. A marine food fish, *Sebastes marinus*, mostly red in color, common on both coasts of the North Atlantic.

rose ge·ra·ni·um, *n*. A geranium of the genus *Pelargonium*, esp. *P. graveolens*, cultivated for its fragrant lobed or narrowly subdivided leaves rather than for its small pink or purplish flowers.

rose mal·low, *n*. Any of numerous plants of the genus *Hibiscus*, in the mallow family, all characterized by white or pinkish flowers with red or purple centers, esp. *H. moscheutos*.

rose·mar·y, rōz′mâr″ē, *n*. pl. **rose·mar·ies**. [O.E. *rosmarine*, < L. *rosmarinus*, rosemary—*ros*, dew, and *marinus*, marine, < *mare*, the sea.] A species of green shrub, *Rosmarinus officinalis*, native to the Mediterranean regions and well known as a garden plant, its aromatic leaves being used as a seasoning and as the source of a volatile oil used in medicines and perfumes.

rose of Jericho, *n*. An Asiatic desert plant, *Anastatica hierochuntica*, which has the property, after drying and curling up, of expanding when moistened and appearing to revive. See *resurrection plant*.

rose of Shar·on, *n*. The shrubby althea, *Hibiscus syriacus*, a tall plant bearing rose or purple bell-shaped flowers; also *Aaron's beard*. A flowering plant mentioned in the Bible, Cant. ii. 1, thought to be the autumn crocus, *Colchium autumnale*, or a narcissus; St.-John's-wort, *Hypericum calycinum*.

ro·se·o·la, rō·zē′o·la, *n*. [N.L., dim. < L. *roseus*, rosy, < *rosa*, E. *rose*.] *Pathol*. A kind of rose-colored rash; rubella, or German measles.—**ro·se·o·lar**, *a*.

rose-pink, rōz′pingk″, *n*. A soft, medium pink color.—*a*.

rose slug, *n*. The larval form of a sawfly, esp.

Claudius isomerus or *Endelomyia aethiops*, which feeds on rose leaves.

Ro·set·ta stone, rō·zet′a stōn″, *n*. A black basalt slab with three parallel inscriptions in Egyptian demotic and hieratic symbols and in Greek, found in 1799 near Rosetta, Egypt, and important for having given Champollion a key for deciphering Egyptian hieroglyphics: now in the British Museum.

ro·sette, rō·zet′, *n*. [Fr., a dim. of *rose*.] Any formation, object, part, or arrangement which resembles a rose; a badge or an ornament, as of ribbon or the like, which is rose-shaped or arranged to resemble a rose; *arch*. a sculptured or painted ornament having its parts arranged circularly or resembling a rose; *bot*. a cluster of organs, petals, leaves, or the like in a circular arrangement. Markings arranged in a circle, as the grouped spots of the leopard.

rose wa·ter, *n*. Water tinctured with the essential oil of roses.—**rose-wa·ter**, rōz′wa″tĕr, rōz′wo″tĕr, *a*. Having the odor of, being made with, or resembling rose water; *fig*. affectedly delicate, nice, or fine; sentimental.

rose win·dow, *n*. *Arch*. a circular window divided by mullions or tracery radiating from the center.

rose·wood, rōz′wụd″, *n*. Any of several species of tropical S. American trees of the genus *Dalbergia*, esp. *D. nigra*, which yields one of the finest of cabinet woods, having coarse, dense, even grain streaked with red or purple; the tree itself.

Rosh Ha·sha·nah, rōsh″ ha·shä′na, rōsh hä·shạ′na, *Heb*. Rōsh hä·shä·nä′, *n*. The Jewish New Year commemorated by Orthodox and Conservative Jews on the 1st and 2nd of the month of Tishri, and by Reform Jews only on the 1st of Tishri.

Ro·si·cru·cian, rō″zi·krō′shan, roz″i·krō′shan, *n*. [L. *rosa*, rose, and *crux* (*cruc-*), cross; prob. referring to the 'rose cross' (G. *rosenkreuz*) used as a Rosicrucian emblem, but also alleged to represent the name of a mythical 15th century founder, Christian *Rosenkreuz*.] A member of a society prominent in the 17th and 18th centuries, laying claim to various forms of occult knowledge and power, and professing esoteric principles of religion; a member of any of several later or modern bodies or societies professing principles attributed to the earlier Rosicrucians, esp. of an organization known as the Rosicrucian Order or the Ancient Mystic Order Rosae Crucis, AMORC, which is active in America.—*a*. Of, pertaining to, or characteristic of the Rosicrucians.—**Ro·si·cru·cian·ism**, *n*.

ros·i·ly, rō′zi·lē, *adv*. With a rosy color; in a rosy or cheerful manner.

ros·in, roz′in, *n*. [Corrupt. of *resin*.] The hard, translucent, yellowish-to-amber-colored resin formed when oil of turpentine is distilled from crude turpentine: used in making varnish and printing inks, and for rubbing on violin bows.—*v.t.* To rub or cover over with rosin.—**ros·in·y**, *a*.

ros·in·weed, roz′in·wēd″, *n*. Any of several sunflowerlike N. American plants of the genus *Silphium*, in the composite family, having large, coarse, rough leaves, and named for their resinous juices, esp. *S. laciniatum*, and *S. perfoliatum*. See *compass plant*, *cup plant*.

ross, rạs, ros, *n*. The exterior of bark which is rough and often scaly.—*v.t*. To remove the outermost portion of bark from; as, to *ross* a log.

ros·tel·lum, ro·stel′um, *n*. pl. **ros·tel·la**, ro·stel′a. [L., dim. of *rostrum*, beak.] *Bot*. any small, beaklike process, esp. a modification of the stigma in many orchids.—**ros·tel·late**, ros′te·lāt″, ros′te·lit, *a*.

ros·ter, ros′tĕr, *n*. [D. *rooster*.] A list of persons or groups, such as military personnel with their order of duty; any itemized series of names or events.

ros·trum, ros′trum, *n*. pl. **ros·tra**, ros′trums, ros′tra. [L., the beak of a bird or other animal, the beak of a ship, < *rodo*, to gnaw.] A platform from which a speaker addresses his audience; a pulpit; the beak of a ship, esp. that on an ancient war galley, used for ramming purposes; an elevated place in the Roman forum adorned with the beaks of captured ships, where orations were delivered in ancient times; *biol*. the beaklike process of a bird or other animal.—**ros·tral**, **ros·trate**, ros′tral, ros′trāt, *a*.

ros·y, rō′zē, *a*.—*rosier, rosiest*. Pink or pinkish-red, like the color of many roses; of persons, the cheeks, lips, or the like, having a fresh, healthy redness of complexion or color; blushing, as with emotion or confusion; bright or promising; cheerful or optimistic; made or consisting of roses.—**ros·i·ly**, *adv*.—**ros·i·ness**, *n*.

rot, rot, *v.i.*—*rotted, rotting*. [O.E. *rotian*, to rot; D. *rotten*, Icel. *rotna*, to rot, *rotinn*, rotten.] To decompose; to become putrid; to decay; to become corrupt morally; to become unsound or weak; to fall off due to decay.—*v.t.* To make putrid; to cause to decompose; to bring to corruption; to ret, as flax or other fiber.—*n*. The process of decaying; the condition of being rotten; decay; putrefaction; something that is rotted or rotting; certain wasting or parasitic diseases, esp. in sheep; certain bacterial or fungus infections in plants that cause rotting. *Colloq*. an absurdity; drivel, as: That's a lot of *rot*.

ro·ta, rō′ta, *n*. [L. *rota*, a wheel.] *Chiefly Brit*. a rotating order of individuals or tasks; a regular course of procedure; a roll or agenda. A roster. (*Usu. cap.*) an ecclesiastical court of Rome, composed of ten prelates, acting as a court of appeal; also **Sa·cra Ro·man·a Ro·ta**.

Ro·tar·i·an, rō·târ′ē·an, *n*. One who belongs to a Rotary Club.—*a*. Of or relating to a Rotary Club or its members.—**Ro·tar·i·an·ism**, *n*.

ro·ta·ry, rō′ta·rē, *a*. [< L. *rota*, a wheel; allied to G. *rad*, a wheel; W. *rhod*, a wheel, *rhedu*, to turn; Skt. *rathas*, a chariot.] Turning, as a wheel on its axis; pertaining to or characterized by a rotating motion; rotatory; having one or more parts that turn around an axis; as, a *rotary* printing press.—*n*. pl. **ro·ta·ries**. A rotary part or machine. A circular routing of traffic in one direction at the junction of three or more roads, to permit vehicles to reach their desired route without intersecting; also *traffic circle*.

Ro·ta·ry Club, *n*. A club of local professional and business men, allied to an international organization called Rotary International, and devoted to improving civic service and advancing good will among nations.

ro·ta·ry cul·ti·va·tor, *n*. A tool with claws or rotating blades for tilling soil.

ro·ta·ry en·gine, *n*. An engine in which torque is produced directly by impulsion of fuel, as a turbine; a radial internal-combustion engine whose cylinders revolve around a fixed crankshaft.

ro·ta·ry plow, *n*. A plow consisting of blades attached to a rotating, power-driven shaft.

ro·ta·ry-wing air·craft, *n*. An aircraft, as a helicopter, whose flight is supported by airfoils rotating on a vertical axis.

ro·tate, rō′tāt, rō·tāt′, *v.i.*, *v.t.*—*rotated, rotating*. [L. *roto*, *rotatum*, to turn round, < *rota*, a wheel.] To revolve or cause to move around a center or on an axis; to succeed or cause to succeed in a regular order.—

rō′tāt, *a. Bot.* Wheel-shaped; radiating parts in a circular pattern, as the corolla of various flowers.—**ro·tat·a·ble,** *a.*—**ro·tat·a·bly,** *adv.*

ro·ta·tion, rō·tā′shan, *n.* [L. *rotatio, rotationis.*] The act of rotating or turning on an axis; one complete turn on an axis; *astron.* the motion of the earth or of other heavenly bodies on an axis. A return or succession in a series; established succession; *agric.* a recurring series of different crops grown on the same ground.—**ro·ta·tion·al,** *a.*—**ro·ta·to·ry,** rō′ta·tōr″ē, rō′ta·tar″ē, *a.*

ro·ta·tive, rō′tā·tiv, *a.* Pertaining to, occurring in, or producing rotation; turning or rotating, as a wheel.—**ro·ta·tive·ly,** *adv.*

ro·ta·tor, rō′tā·tėr, rō·tā′tėr, *n.* pl. **ro·ta·tors, ro·ta·tor·es.** That which or one who rotates or causes rotation; pl. **ro·ta·tors.** *Anat.* a muscle that rolls a body part around its axis; pl. **ro·ta·tor·es,** rō″ta·tōr′ēz, rō″ta·tar′ēz.

rote, rōt, *n.* [O.Fr. *rote,* a way, a *route.*] Repetition or routine; repetition of words or sounds without attending to the signification.—**by rote,** merely by memory with little intelligence or understanding.

rote, rōt, *n.* [O.Fr. Fr. *rote*; of Celtic origin, and akin to *crowd.*] *Mus.* an ancient distinctively British stringed instrument orig. having three strings, later having six, that was played by bowing. Also **crowd, crwth,** kroud, krōth.

rote, rōt, *n.* [Origin uncertain.] The sound of the sea or surf.

ro·te·none, rōt′e·nōn″, *n. Chem.* a crystalline compound, $C_{23}H_{22}O_6$, obtained from roots of plants of the genus *Derris,* and *Lonchocarpus,* and used as an insecticide.

ro·ti·fer, rō′ti·fėr, *n.* [N.L., < L. *rota,* wheel, and *ferre,* bear.] Any of the microscopic, many-celled aquatic animals constituting the class *Rotifera,* found in fresh and salt water, and characterized by rings of cilia which often resemble rotating wheels. Also *wheel animalcule, wheel animal.*—**ro·tif·er·al, ro·tif·er·ous,** rō·tif′ėr·al—**ro·tif·er·an,** *n., a.*

ro·ti·form, rō′ti·farm″, *a.* Wheel-shaped; rotate.

ro·tis·ser·ie, rō·tis′e·rē, *n.* [Fr.] A restaurant or shop at which meats, poultry, or the like are roasted; a device with a rotating spit for roasting food, esp. meat.

ro·tis·ser·ie roll, *n. Aerospace slang,* the slow rolling of a spacecraft in flight, to avoid continuous exposure of any part of the craft to the 280-degree F. heat from the sun, or the 280-degree below zero in the dark. Also **bar·be·que mode.**

ro·to·gra·vure, rō′to·gra·vūr′, rō′to·grā′vūr, *n.* Gravure; a newspaper section including pictures reproduced by gravure. Also **ro·to,** rō′tō.

ro·tor, rō′tėr, *n.* [For *rotator.*] The rotating part of a machine or apparatus, esp. the rotating element, armature, or field of a motor or dynamo: opposed to *stator.* A kind of high, tower like, cylindrical metal structure rising above the deck of a vessel and rotated by a small electric motor, which operates with the wind to propel the vessel; *aeron.* an assemblage of revolving airfoils which supports jet planes and helicopters during flight.

ro·tor·craft, rō′tėr·kraft″, rō′tėr·kräft″, *n.* An airplane which utilizes a system of revolving airfoils or wings. Also *rotor plane.*

ro·tor plane, *n.* Rotorcraft.

ro·tor ship, *n.* A wind-propelled vessel employing rotors instead of sails, and having auxiliary means of propulsion by propeller.

Ro·to·till·er, rō′tō·til′ėr, *n.* A mechanical device used for overturning soil. (Trademark.)—**ro·to·till,** *v.t.* To overturn, as soil, for cultivation.

rot·ten, rot′en, *a.* [A Scand. word = Icel.

---

rotinn, Sw. *rutten,* rotten, a participle of an old verb akin to *rot.*] Putrid, decaying, or decomposed by the natural process of decay; foul-smelling; corrupt; unsound or weak; *colloq.* unsatisfactory or worthless.—**rot·ten·ly,** *adv.*—**rot·ten·ness,** *a.*

rot·ten bor·ough, *n.* Any of certain boroughs in England before the reform of 1832 which had a greater number of voters in Parliament than its small population warranted; now any such district.

rot·ten·stone, rot′en·stōn″, *n.* A soft stone much used for polishing articles of brass or other metal, derived from the decomposition of siliceous limestones. Also *tripoli.*

rot·ter, rot′ėr, *n.* [< *rot.*] *Chiefly Brit. slang.* One who is thoroughly bad; a good-for-nothing or worthless person.

ro·tund, rō·tund′, *a.* [L. *rotundus,* formed < *rota,* a wheel. *Round* is a form of the same word.] Round or rounded; spherical; plump; full-toned, resonant, or sonorous, as a voice.—**ro·tun·di·ty, ro·tun′di·tē,** *n.* pl. **ro·tun·di·ties.**—**ro·tund·ly,** *adv.*—**ro·tund·ness,** *n.*

ro·tun·da, rō·tun′da, *n.* [L., fem. of *rotundus,* round, F. *rotund.*] A round building, esp. one with a dome; a large and high circular hall or room in a building, esp. one surmounted by a dome.

ro·tu·rier, *Fr.* Ra·tУ·Ryā′, *n.* [Fr.] A person of low rank; a plebeian.

rou·é, rö·ā′, rö′ā, *n.* [Fr. ppr. of *rouer,* to break on the wheel, < *roue,* L. *rota,* a wheel; lit. 'one worthy of suffering on the wheel.'] A person devoted to a life of pleasure and sensuality; a rake or debauchee.

rouge, Rōzh, *n.* [Fr. *rouge,* < L. *rubeus,* red.] A cosmetic used to give an artificial red color to the cheeks or lips; a ferrous oxide powder used for polishing glass, gold, silver, or the like.—*v.i.* —rouged, rouging. To paint the cheeks or lips with rouge.—*v.t.*

rouge et noir, rōzh′ ā nwär′, *Fr.* Rōzh ā nwär′, *n.* [Fr., red and black.] A game of cards played between a 'banker' and an unlimited number of persons, at a table marked with four spots of a diamond shape, two colored black and two red.

rough, ruf, *a.* [O.E. *rūh,* rough, shaggy; cogn. D. *ruig, ruw,* L.G. *rug,* Dan. *ru,* G. *rauh, rauch,* rough; Lith. *raukas,* wrinkle.] Having many irregularities of surface; not smooth; as, *rough* skin; shaggy or fuzzy; as, the *rough* coat of an animal; uneven or uncultivated; as, *rough* terrain. Tending toward violence or characterized by purposeful disregard for rules; as, *rough* play; agitated or turbulent, as water or air; stormy or made uncomfortable by unusual phenomena, as weather; harsh or rude; as, a *rough* reply; out of control or rebellious; as, a *rough* mob; exhausting or unpleasant; as, a *rough* day; dissonant or harsh, as a sound; sour or astringent to the taste; as, a *rough* vintage; of coarse texture, as material or food; unrefined or discourteous; as, a *rough* individual; requiring physical exertion rather than intelligence; as, a *rough* job; not perfected or polished; as, a *rough* outline; approximate; not fully thought out; as, a *rough* idea; crude or unpolished, as a grain; *phon.* aspirated.—*n.* That which is coarse or rough; the state of being in a preliminary or unrefined form or shape; any rough terrain, as on a golf course; *chiefly Brit.* a rowdy or bully.—*v.t.* To give a rough appearance to; to make rough; to subject to physical violence, usu. followed by *up*; as, to *rough up* an opponent; to make a first draft of, as in sketching or writing, followed by *in*; as, to *rough in* the characters.—*v.i.* To roughen or become rough; to behave in a rough manner.—*adv.* Roughly.—**rough·er,** ruf′ėr, *n.*—**rough·ly,** *adv.*—**rough·ness,** *n.*

---

rough·age, ruf′ij, *n.* Rough or coarse material; the coarser kinds of fodder or food, as certain fruits, bran, or straw, which are proportionately high in indigestible constituents stimulating peristalsis, as cellulose.

rough-and-read·y, ruf′an·red′ē, *a.* Of a hasty and unfinished sort, but sufficient for the intent; characterized by crude manners, but reliable and prepared for action; as, a *rough-and-ready* individual.

rough-and-tum·ble, ruf′an·tum′bl, *a.* Characterized by rough struggling without regard to self-defense or rules; as, a *rough-and-tumble* fight; given to such action, as a fighter.—*n.*

rough blue·grass, *n.* A European grass, *Poa trivialis,* having rough bluish-green stems, now naturalized in the U.S. and sown as a pasture grass.

rough breath·ing, *n.* A symbol used in Classical Greek to denote an h-sound before the first vowel of a word; the written mark (ʽ) for this sound.

rough·cast, ruf′kast″, ruf′käst″, *v.t.* —roughcast, roughcasting. To form in its first rudiments; to mold without nicety or elegance; to cover with a coarse sort of plaster composed of lime and gravel, as a building.—*n.* The form of a thing in its first rudiments; a coarse kind of plastering for an external wall.—**rough·cast·er,** *n.*

rough-dry, ruf′drī′, *v.t.* —rough-dried, rough-drying. To dry after washing, as laundry, without smoothing or ironing.—*a.* Dry after being washed, but not smoothed or ironed.

rough-hew, ruf′hū″, *v.t.* —past *rough-hewed,* pp. *rough-hewed* or *rough-hewn,* ppr. *rough-hewing.* To hew coarsely without smoothing; to form or shape crudely.—**rough-hewn,** *a.*

rough·house, ruf′hous″, *n. Slang.* Rough or disorderly behavior; a general fight; rough play; rowdy conduct.—*v.i.* —roughhoused, roughhousing. *Slang,* to engage or take part in a roughhouse.—*v.t. Slang,* to treat or handle roughly without intent to injure.

rough·ish, ruf′ish, *a.* Rather rough; as, a *roughish* sea.

rough-leg·ged hawk, ruf′leg″id hak, ruf′-legd″, *n.* A large American hawk, *Buteo lagopus,* of the open country, identified by its whitish tail with a broad black band and by its habit of hovering with beating wings. Also **rough·leg.**

rough·neck, ruf′nek″, *n. Slang,* a rough, coarse fellow; *colloq.* a laborer on an oil-drilling crew.

rough·rid·er, ruf′rī″dėr, *n.* One who breaks horses; one accustomed to strenuous riding; *(cap.)* in the Spanish-American War, a soldier of the 1st U.S. Volunteer Cavalry organized and later led by Theodore Roosevelt.

rough·shod, ruf′shod′, *a.* Shod, as a horse, with shoes having calks or points.—**ride rough·shod o·ver,** to pursue a violent or selfish course, regardless of the effect on others.

rou·lade, rö·läd′, *n.* [Fr., < *rouler,* to roll.] *Mus.* a run or flourish of short notes; a vocal embellishment, consisting of a series of rapid notes sung on one syllable. A slice of meat rolled around a minced filling and cooked.

rou·leau, rö·lō′, *n.* pl. **rou·leaus,** *Fr.* **rou·leaux,** rö·lōz′. [Fr., lit. 'a little roll.'] A roll of coin made up in paper; a narrow folded or rolled trim for hats; piping.

rou·lette, rö·let′, *n.* [Fr. prop. 'a little wheel,' < *rouler,* to roll.] A game of chance in which a moving ball drops into a numbered compartment of a spinning disk, with bets placed on which compartment the ball will settle in; a tool furnished with a small toothed wheel, used by en-

---

gravers for producing dotted work. *Philately*, a series of small cuts in paper to facilitate tearing: opposed to *perforation.—v.t. rouletted, rouletting*. To make a series of printed spots or small cuts on with a roulette.

round, round, *a.* [O.Fr. *roont*, round, Mod.Fr. *rond*, round, < L. *rotundus*, round, rotund, < *rota*, a wheel.] Having every part of the surface at an equal distance from the center; spherical; globular; circular; cylindrical; having a curved form; hemispherical; semicircular; swelling; plump; moving in circles; as, a *round* dance; returning; as, a *round* trip; given in the closest multiple of ten; as, in *round* numbers; large; considerable; as, a good *round* sum; unqualified, as, a *round* assertion.— **round·ly**, *adv.*—**round·ness**, *n.*

round, round, *adv.* In a circle, ring, or the like, or so as to surround something; as, to gather *round* a speaker; on all sides, or about, whether circularly or otherwise; in all directions from a center; in the region about a place; as, the country *round*; in circumference; as, a tree 40 inches *round*; in a circular or rounded course; through a round, circuit, or series, as of places or persons; as, enough to go *round*; through a round, or recurring period, of time, esp. to the present or particular time; as, time rolls *round*; throughout, or from beginning to end of, a recurring period of time; as, the year *round*; by a circuitous or roundabout course.—*prep.* On every side of; around; about; in a circular course.

round, round, *n.* That which is round, as a circle, sphere, or globe; a series coming back to where it began; as, a *round* of toasts; a series of events or duties which come back to the point of commencement; the step of a ladder; a recurring circuit of events, duties, or the like; a short musical canon in which three or more voices, starting at the beginning of stated successive phrases, sing the same music in unison or octave, the combination of all the parts producing correct harmony; *sports*, an interval of play or of a match. A cut of beef from the thigh between the knee and the rump; a dance in a ring; a general discharge of firearms by a body of troops, in which each soldier fires once; ammunition for firing once.—*v.t.* To make round; to make full or complete; to make full, smooth, and flowing; to go in a circular course about.—*v.i.* To grow or become round; to become complete or full; to travel around.—**make the rounds**, to make a series of stops or visits.—**in the round**, surrounded on all sides, as a theatre stage surrounded by audience seats.

round·a·bout, round′a·bout″, *n. Brit.* a merry-go-round. A short close-fitting jacket; a circuitous road, line of thought, or the like.—*a.* Indirect; going round; not straightforward; encompassing.

round an·gle, *n. Math.* The angle created by one complete rotation of a straight line; 360° angle; a perigon.

round clam, *n.* Quahog.

round dance, *n.* A dance, as a polka or waltz, in which the couples move in a circular pattern; a dance in which all participants form a circle.

round·ed, roun′did, *a.* Made round; spherical; with smooth edges; *phon.* produced by rounding the lips, as a kind of vowel sound. Fully developed, polished; as, a *rounded* education.

roun·del, roun′del, *n.* [O.Fr. *rondel*, dim. < *rond*, round.] Something round or circular; a small disk or rounded piece; a small round shield; a small round pane or window; a decorative plate, panel, tablet, or the like, round in form. A dance in a circle or ring; a rondel or rondeau; modification

of the rondeau consisting of nine lines with two refrains.

roun·de·lay, roun′de·lā″, *n.* [O.Fr. *rondelet*, < Fr. *rond*, round. The spelling has been influenced by *lay*, a song.] A song or tune with a simple melody and a recurrent refrain; a dance enacted in a circle.

round·er, roun′dèr, *n.* Someone or something that rounds, esp. a tool or machine for rounding surfaces or edges; a drunkard or dissolute wastrel; *pl. but sing. in constr.* a game, played chiefly in England, somewhat resembling baseball.

Round·head, round′hed″, *n. Brit. hist.* a name given by the Cavaliers or adherents of Charles I to members of the Puritan or parliamentary party, from the latter having their hair closely cut, while the Cavaliers wore theirs long.

round·head·ed, round′hed′id, *a.* Having an extremely round head; brachycephalic. Shaped like a sphere, as the head of a screw. —**round·head·ed·ness**, *n.*

round·house, round′hous″, *n.* A circular building in which locomotives are repaired; a cabin on the after part of the quarterdeck of a ship, having the poop for its roof. *Pinochle*, a meld of four queens and four kings; also *round trip. Slang*, a punch delivered with a circular flourish of the fist.

round·ish, roun′dish, *a.* Somewhat round.

round·let, round′lit, *n.* [O.Fr. *rondelet*.] A small circle or circular object.

round rob·in, *n.* A written petition, memorial, or remonstrance signed by names in a ring or circle so that it may be impossible to ascertain who headed the list; a letter sent to group members which is signed and usu. commented on by each member; a sports tournament arranged so that each contestant plays all the other contestants, resulting in the eventual elimination of the losers.

round-shoul·dered, round′shol′dèrd, round′shol″dèrd, *a.* Having a rounded back or stooping shoulders.

rounds·man, roundz′man, *n.* pl. **rounds·-men.** One who makes rounds, as of inspection; a police officer who inspects the policemen on duty in a particular district.

round steak, *n.* A cut of meat from below the rump section and above the shank of beef.

Round Ta·ble, *n.* The legendary table, purposely circular in shape in order to avoid arguments about precedence, where King Arthur and his knights assembled; King Arthur and his knights as a group.

round trip, *n.* A trip to a destination and back. A train, plane, or bus ticket for such a trip; also *return ticket. Pinochle*, a roundhouse.—**round-trip**, *a.*

round·up, round′up″, *n.* The driving together of cattle or other animals for inspection, branding, or the like, as in the western U.S.; the men and horses who do this, or the herd so collected; any similar driving or bringing together; as, a police *roundup* of known hoodlums; a résumé, summary, or outline of related events or facts; as, a sports *roundup* in a newscast.— **round up**, *v.t.*

round·worm, round′wurm″, *n.* A nematode, esp. *Ascaris lumbricoides*, a parasite infesting the intestines of vertebrates.

roup, röp, *n. Veter. pathol.* a virus affecting the respiratory system of poultry.

rouse, rouz, *v.t.—roused, rousing.* [Connected with O.H.G. *ruozjan*, to rouse.] To wake from sleep; to excite to thought or action from a state of idleness, languor, or inattention; to agitate; to startle; to surprise; *hunting*, to drive from a lurking place or cover.—*v.i.* To wake from sleep or repose; to be excited to thought or action; to be driven from cover, as game.—*n.* The act of rousing.—**rous·er**, *n.*

rous·ing, rou′zing, *a.* Able to awaken or excite; stirring; lively or brisk; vigorous; *colloq.* extraordinary, astonishing, or outrageous, as an untrue statement.

roust, roust, *v.t., v.i. Colloq.* to arouse, often followed by *up*; to expel, followed by *out*.

roust·a·bout, rous′ta·bout″, *n.* An unskilled laborer, esp. a dockworker or deckhand, oil field or refinery worker, or circus laborer; any unskilled laborer who lives by odd jobs. Also **roust·er**.

rout, rout, *n.* [O.Fr. *route*, troop, band, < M.L. *rupta*, lit. 'a division,' prop. pp. fem. of L. *rumpere*, to break.] A riot, disturbance, or uproar; the breaking or defeat of troops; the disorder and confusion of troops thus defeated. A large evening party or social gathering. *Law*, an assemblage of three or more persons, gathered to commit an unlawful act. A tumultuous or disorderly crowd of persons; a rabble or mob.

rout, rout, *v.i.* [Var. of *root*.] To root, as swine; turn over or dig up with the snout, as swine; poke, search, or rummage.—*v.t.* To bring or get out by poking about or searching, usu. followed by *out*; to break the ranks of and put to flight in disorder; force or drive out, usu. with *out*; cause to get up or out of bed, usu. with *out* or *up*, as: He'll have you *routed up* by four o'clock in the morning. To hollow out or furrow, as with a scoop, gouge, or machine.

rout, rout, röt, *v.i. Brit.* To roar; bellow; make a loud noise.

route, röt, rout, *n.* [O.Fr. Fr. *route*, < M.L. *rupta*, lit. 'a way broken,' another use of *rupta*. E. *rout*.] A way or road for passage or travel; a way or course taken, or to be taken; as, to fix a *route* for a procession; a customary or regular line of passage or travel; the line or direction of a road, railroad, canal, or the like, existing or proposed; *milit.* an order to move from one station or place to another.—*v.t.—routed, routing.* To fix the route of; send or forward by a particular route.

route·man, röt′man, rout′man, *n.* pl. **route·men.** A person who works in a particular locale, usu. delivering or selling a product from a car or light truck; one who arranges such routes; one who assigns work to employees, as in a factory.

route march, *n. Milit.* A practice march in which the men must maintain ranks but are not required to keep step or to be silent.

rout·er, rou′tèr, *n.* Any of various tools or machines for routing, hollowing out, or furrowing; a tool or machine for routing out parts of an etched plate or die; *carp.* a plane used for burrowing interior angles around a sash.

rou·tine, rö·tēn′, *n.* [Fr., < *route*, a way: prop. the way which one invariably takes through custom.] A procedure, daily or frequently pursued, as in business; duties or actions done regularly or at regular intervals; as, the *routine* of dentist's visits; a practice adhered to by force of habit; an unvarying and repeated speech or formula; all or part of a performer's regular act; *computer technology*, the set of systematized instructions that directs an electronic computer to execute desired operations.—*a.* Commonplace; habitual; of, by, or relating to an established procedure.—**rou·tine·ly**, *adv.*

rou·tin·ize, rö·tē′nīz, *v.t.—routinized, routinizing.* To develop into or reduce to an established procedure or routine.

roux, rö, *n.* [Fr., red, reddish, russet.] *Cookery*, a paste of flour and fat used to thicken sauces and the like.

rove, röv, *v.i.—roved, roving.* [Orig. to wander for plunder, a collateral form of *reave*, directly from the L.G. or D.; L.G. *roven*, D. *rooven*, Dan. *rove*, Sw. *rofva*, to rob; Icel. *rafa*, *rapa*, to wander.] To wander; to ramble; to go, move, or pass without specific direction or destination.—*v.t.* To wander over or about.—*n.* An act of wandering or roving.

rove, rōv, *v.t.*—*roved, roving.* To draw through an eye or aperture, as fibers; to bring, as fibers of wool or cotton, into a form that prepares it for being spun into thread; to card into twisted, compressed fibers, as wool, cotton, or silk.

rove bee·tle, *n.* [Cf. *rove.*] Any beetle of the large family *Staphylinidae,* typically having a long, slender body and very short wing covers, and capable of running swiftly.

rov·er, rō′vèr, *n.* One who roves; a wanderer; *archery,* a mark selected at random; *croquet,* a ball that needs only to strike the winning peg to be out of the game; *archaic,* a pirate or a pirate ship. A machine for twisting fibers.

rov·ing, rō′ving, *n.* A roll of wool, cotton, or other fibers drawn out and slightly twisted before being made into yarn.

row, rō, *v.i.* [O.E. *rōwan,* to row = Icel. *rōa.*] To move a boat by means of oars.—*v.t.* To impel along the surface of water by oars, as a boat; to transport by rowing; to use or be provided with, as a number of oars; to take part in by rowing, as a race; to employ for rowing, as oars or oarsmen; to row against in a competition.—*n.* An excursion taken in a boat having oars; an act of rowing.—**row·er,** *n.*

row, rō, *n.* [O.E. *rāew,* a row; perh. from same root as *room,* and meaning orig. the space or interval between rows.] A series of persons or things arranged in a continuous line; a line; a rank; a file; a street having a continuous line of buildings on both sides; a single line of seats, as in an auditorium.—*v.t.* To place or form in a row.—**long row to hoe,** a difficult undertaking.

row, rou, *n.* A noisy disturbance, dispute, or commotion.—*v.i.* To take part in a quarrel.

row·an tree, rō′an trē, rou′an, *n.* [< Scand.] An ornamental round-headed, smooth-barked tree, *Sorbus aucuparia,* in the rose family, having pinnate leaves and clusters of bright red berries, native to Eurasia′, now widely cultivated. Also **Eu·ro·pe·an moun·tain ash, row·an.**

row·boat, rō′bōt″, *n.* A small boat propelled by rowing.

row·dy, rou′dē, *n.* pl. **row·dies.** [Origin obscure.] A rough, disorderly person; one given to quarreling or fighting.—*a.*—*rowdier, rowdiest.* Of the nature of or characteristic of a rowdy; rough and disorderly.—**row·di·ly,** *adv.*—**row·di·ness,** *n.*—**row·dy·ish,** rou′dē·ish, *a.*—**row·dy·ism,** rou′dē·iz″um, *n.*

row·el, rou′el, *n.* [O.Fr. *rouele, roele,* little wheel (Fr. *rouelle,* round slice), < M.L. *rotella,* dim. of L. *rota,* wheel.] A small disk with radiating points, forming the end of a horseman′s spur; *veter. surg.* a number of hairs or silk threads inserted beneath the skin of a horse or other animal to aid in the drainage of pus.—*v.t.*—*roweled, roweling, esp. Brit. rowelled, rowelling.* To spur or urge on with a rowel; *veter. surg.* to place or insert a rowel in.

row·en, rou′en, *n.* [M.E. *roweyn, raweyne, rewayn,* akin to O.Fr. Fr. *regain.*] The second crop of grass or hay in a season; the aftermath; a field of stubble left for fall grazing.

row house, rō, *n.* One of a group of houses built in a row, usu. alike in design, and joined by a common sidewalk to its neighbor.

row·lock, rō′lok″, *n.* Oarlock.

roy·al, roi′al, *a.* [O.Fr. *roial, reial,* < L. *regalis,* E. *regal.*] Of or pertaining to a king, queen, or sovereign; originating from or connected with a king or a line of kings;

as, the *royal* family; having the rank of a king or queen; established or chartered by, or existing under the patronage of, a sovereign; as, a *royal* society or academy; (*usu. cap.*), *Brit.* serving the sovereign as head of the state; as, *Royal* Air Force. Befitting or appropriate to a sovereign; magnificent; majestic, noble; *colloq.* fine, very good; as, in *royal* spirits. Beyond the common or ordinary in size or quality; *naut.* pertaining to a part, as a sail or mast, above the topgallant.—*n.* A size of writing paper, 19 × 24 inches, and of printing paper, 20 × 25 inches; *naut.* a sail set on the royal mast.—**roy·al·ly,** *adv.*

roy·al blue, *n.* A deep, vivid blue often tinged with red.

roy·al com·mis·sion, *n. Brit., Canada,* an individual or individuals authorized by the Crown to conduct an investigation and report its findings.

roy·al·ism, roi′a·liz·um, *n.* Monarchism.

roy·al·ist, roi′a·list, *n.* A supporter or adherent of a king or a royal government, esp. in times of rebellion or civil war. (*Cap.*) a Cavalier or follower of King Charles I of England; an adherent of the House of Bourbon of France; a follower of the king in the American Revolution.—*a.*

roy·al jel·ly, *n.* A concentrated nutriment produced from the pharyngeal glands of the worker honeybee, fed for three days to all larvae and to queen bees during the period of their development.

roy·al palm, *n.* Any of several tall, striking, feather palms with a columnar single trunk, genus *Roystonea,* esp. *R. regia,* a native of Florida and the W. Indies.

roy·al poin·ci·an·a, *n. Bot.* a striking, widely-branched, leguminous tree, *Delonix regia,* having large racemes of bright scarlet flowers striped with orange, dark brown pods two feet in length, native to Madagascar, and now planted in the southern parts of Florida and California. Also **flam·boy·ant, pea·cock flow·er.**

roy·al pur·ple, *n.* A deep purple tinged with red.

roy·al·ty, *n.* pl. **roy·al·ties.** [M.E. *roialte* < M.L. *regalitas:* cf. *regality.*] Royal status, dignity, or power; sovereignty; character or quality proper to or befitting a sovereign; kingliness; nobility; generosity; a royal person; royal persons collectively; a prerogative or right belonging to a king or sovereign; a royal domain; a kingdom; a realm; a compensation or portion of proceeds paid to the owner of a right, as an oil right or a patent, for the use of it; a fixed portion of the proceeds from his work, paid to an author or composer; a royal right, as over minerals, granted by a sovereign to a person or corporation; the payment made for such a right.

rub, rub, *v.t.*—*rubbed, rubbing.* [Same word as Dan. *rubbe,* to rub, to scrub.] To move along the surface of, backwards, forwards, or in a circular motion, with friction or stress; to apply friction to; to wipe; to clean; to scour or scrub; to smear all over; to chafe; to gall; to gibe; to efface or obliterate, often followed by *on* or *out.*—*v.i.* To move along the surface of a body with pressure; to grate; to chafe; to fret; to have the capacity to be rubbed in some way, as: Newsprint *rubs* off easily. To get on or along with difficulty, usually followed by *on, along,* or *through;* as, to *rub through* the world.—*n.* An act of rubbing; as, a back *rub;* a difficulty or obstruction, as: I′d like to buy a dress, but the *rub* is that I have no money. A sarcasm; a gibe; something grating to the feelings, as: I resent that *rub* concerning my cooking. An area that is irregular or rough from being rubbed.—**rub it in,** *colloq.* to repeatedly stress something dis-

agreeable in order to irritate.—**rub the wrong way,** *colloq.* To aggravate; vex.

Ru·bai·yat stan·za, rō″bī·yät″ stan′za, rō′bi·yät″, *n. Poet.* a four-line stanza, in iambic pentameter, rhyming *abab, abba,* or *aaba.*

ru·basse, rö·bas′, rö·bäs′, *n.* [Fr., < L. *rubeus,* red; akin *ruby.*] A variety of rock crystal speckled with minute bits of specular iron which reflect a ruby-red color.

ru·ba·to, rö·bä′tō, *It.* Rö·bä′ta, *a.* [It., ′robbed.′] *Mus.* having certain notes of a measure arbitrarily lengthened while others are correspondingly shortened.

rub·ber, rub′ér, *n.* An elastic, resilient, cohesive solid made from the juice of certain tropical trees and shrubs; also *caoutchouc, India rubber.* This substance chemically treated for manufacture into tires and various industrial items; a similar synthetic material; something made of these materials, as an eraser or overshoe; a person who rubs to polish or smooth; a massager; something used to rub with; *slang,* a condom; *baseball,* the pitcher′s field position.—*a.*—**rub·ber·y,** rub′ér·ē, *a.*

rub·ber, rub′ér, *n.* A series of games, usu. an odd number, of which winning the majority determines the winning side, as in whist, two out of three, or in bridge, two games out of either two or three; the decisive game of such a series.

rub·ber-base paint, rub′ér·bās′ pänt′, *n.* A paint whose vehicle is either a rubber derivative or a resinous synthetic, rather than oil or water.

rub·ber ce·ment, *n.* A liquid adhesive composed of rubber dispersed in an organic solvent, usu. benzene.

rub·ber·ize, rub′e·rīz″, *v.t.*—*rubberized, rubberizing.* To coat or impregnate with rubber or rubber preparation, as a fabric.

rub·ber·neck, rub′ér·nek″, *n. Slang.* One who stretches or cranes his neck to look at something; a sightseer.—*v.i. Slang,* to look or gape at something by stretching the neck. —*a.*

rub·ber plant, *n.* Any of several East Indian plants yielding caoutchouc or India rubber of commerce, esp. of the genera *Hevea* and *Ficus;* an ornamental, *F. elastica,* in the mulberry family, a familiar greenhouse plant with thick glossy green oblong leaves.

rub·ber stamp, *n.* A small, inked rubber printing plate to which hand pressure is applied to imprint documents, packages, or the like. One who tenders his approval without question or careful personal judgment.—**rub·ber-stamp,** rub′ér·stamp′, *v.t.*

rub·bing, rub′ing, *n.* The act of one who or that which rubs; a reproduction of an incised or sculptured surface made by laying paper or the like upon it and rubbing with some marking substance.

rub·bish, rub′ish, *n.* Debris, waste, or rejected matter; trash. Nonsense.—**rub·bish·y,** rub′i·shē, *a.*

rub·ble, rub′l, *n.* [Akin to *rubbish.*] Pieces of solid material irregularly broken, as debris; the upper fragmentary and weathered portion of a mass of stone in quarrying; stones of irregular shapes and dimensions or broken bricks used in coarse masonry; rubblework. —**rub·bly,** rub′lē, *a.*—*rubblier rubbliest.*

rub·ble·work, rub′l·wurk″, *n.* Walls or masonry built of broken stones or rubble.

rub·down, rub′doun″, *n.* A brisk massage.

rube, röb, *n. Slang,* an unsophisticated, provincial fellow; a yokel.

ru·be·fa·cient, rö″be·fä′shent, *a.* [L. *rubefaciens, rubefacientis—rubeo,* to be red, and *facio,* to make.] Making red; producing redness on the skin.—*n. Med.* a substance for external application which produces redness of the skin, not followed by a blister.—**ru·be·fac·tion,** rö″be·fak′shan, *n.*

ru·bel·la, rŏ·bel′a, *n.* [L. *rubellus*, reddish, < *ruber*, red.] German measles.

ru·bel·lite, rŏ·bel′ĭt, rō′be·lit″, *n.* [L. *rubellus*, dim. of *ruber*, red.] Red tourmaline, a siliceous mineral of a red color, used as a gem.

ru·be·o·la, rŏ·bē′o·la, rō″bē·ō′la, *n.* [< L. *ruber*, red.] *Pathol.* Measles; German measles.—**ru·be·o·lar**, rŏ·bē·o·loid, *a.*

Ru·bi·con, rō′bĭ·kon″, *n.* The river forming the southern boundary of Caesar's province of Cisalpine Gaul in northern Italy, the crossing of which was considered a declaration of war. *Fig.* any difficulty or crisis faced in a resolute manner; any irreversible decision.

ru·bi·cund, rō′bĭ·kund″, *a.* [L. *rubicundus*, < *rubeo*, to be red.] Inclining to redness; reddish; ruddy, as a complexion.—**ru·bi··cun·di·ty**, *n.*

ru·bid·i·um, rŏ·bĭd′ē·um, *n.* [< L. *rubidus*, red—from the nature of its spectrum.] A silver-white metallic element resembling, but more active than, potassium. Sym. Rb, at. no. 37, at. wt. 85.47.

ru·big·i·nous, rŏ·bij′i·nus, *a.* [L. *rubiginosus*, < *rubigo, robigo*, rust.] *Biol.* Rusty; rust-colored. Also **ru·big·i·nose**, rŏ·bij′i·nōs″.

ru·bi·ous, rō′bē·us, *a.* Ruby-colored; red.

ru·bric, rō′brik, *n.* [Fr. *rubrique*, < L. *rubrica* (*terra*), red earth, < *ruber*, red.] Some part of a manuscript or printed matter that is, or in former times usu. was, colored red, to distinguish it from other portions; the color red; *law*, the title of a statute, formerly printed in red letters. *Eccles.* the directions and rules for the conduct of a service, often printed in red; an ecclesiastical or episcopal rule or injunction. A distinctive mark placed after a signature or the like; any formulated, fixed, or authoritative injunction of duty.—*a.*—**ru·bri·cal**, *a.*—**ru·bri·cal·ly**, *adv.*

ru·bri·cate, rō′brĭ·kāt″, *v.t.*—*rubricated, rubricating.* [L. *rubricatus*, pp. of *rubricare*, < *rubrica.*] To mark or color with red; to furnish with or regulate by rubrics.—**ru··bri·ca·tion**, rō″brĭ·kā′shan, *n.*—**ru·bri··ca·tor**, *n.*

ru·by, rō′bē, *n.* pl. **ru·bies.** [Fr. *rubis*, Sp. *rubi*, Pruss. *rubin*, < L.L. *rubinus*, a carbuncle, < L. *rubeus*, red, reddish, *ruber*, red.] A gem of various shades of red corundum; a deep red color, as in a wine; something resembling or made of this gem; a carbuncle; *Brit. print.* a type size of 5½ points comparable to the American agate.—*a.* Deep red in color; resembling or having a ruby.—**ru·by·like**, *a.*

ru·by glass, *n.* Deep red glass colored by a copper oxide or gold chloride.

ru·by spi·nel, *n.* A spinel of a deep red color, popular as a gem.

ru·by-throat·ed hum·ming·bird, *n.* One of the smallest of birds, *Archilochus colubris,* native to eastern N. America, having iridescent metallic green plumage and, in the male, a red throat. See *hummingbird.*

ruche, rōsh, *n.* [Fr. *ruche*, a beehive < the quillings resembling honeycomb cells.] A piece of quilled, fluted, crimped, or frilled fabric used to trim women's clothing. Also **ruch·ing**, rō′shing.

ruck, ruk, *n.* [Akin to *rick*, O.Sw. *ruka*, a heap.] An undistinguished crowd of people or quantity of things; trash.

ruck, ruk, *v.t., v.i.* [Icel. *hrukka*, a wrinkle, a fold, *rykkja*, to draw into folds; cf. Gael. *roc*, a wrinkle, to become wrinkled.] To wrinkle; to crease.—*n.* A wrinkle; a crease.

ruck·sack, ruk′sak″, ru̇k′sak″, *n.* [G., lit. 'back sack.'] A kind of knapsack carried by tourists, hikers, or other travelers.

ruc·tion, ruk′shan, *n.* [Perh. a corruption of *eruption.*] *Colloq.* a disturbance, quarrel, or row.

rud·beck·i·a, rud·bek′ē·a, *n.* [N.L., from O. *Rudbeck,* a Swedish botanist.] *Bot.* any of several coarse summer-blooming N. American herbs of the genus *Rudbeckia,* in the composite family, having large blossoms with long daisylike rays and chocolate-colored center disks, esp. *R. hirta,* the brown-eyed susan, and *R. triloba,* the thin-leaved coneflower. See *coneflower.*

rud·der, rud′ėr, *n.* [O.E. *rōther,* lit. 'rowing implement,' orig. a kind of oar, < *rōwan,* to row; D. *roeder,* Sw. *roder,* G. *ruder,* rudder.] *Naut.* a movable, vertical instrument attached in a submerged position at the helm and used in steering a ship; *fig.* that which guides or governs a course; *avi.* the subsidiary airfoil, more or less perpendicular to the main supporting surfaces, by means of which an aircraft is turned to left or right.

rud·der·post, rud′ėr·pōst″, *n. Naut.* an additional sternpost to which the rudder is hinged. Also **rud·der·stock**, rud′ėr·stok″.

rud·dle, rud′l, *n.* [Akin to *ruddy,* red.] A red ocher sometimes used for marking sheep.—*v.t.*—*ruddled, ruddling.* To mark with ruddle. Also *raddle.*—**rud·dle·man**, *n.*

rud·dock, rud′ok, *n.* [O.E. *rudduc,* a dim. akin to *ruddy.*] *Brit.* the European robin redbreast, *Erithacus rubecola,* a small thrush, brown above with a bright red breast and throat, abundant near human habitations. Also **Eu·ro·pe·an rob·in.**

rud·dy, rud′ē, *a.*—*ruddier, ruddiest.* [< O.E. *rud,* red, *rudu,* redness.] Having a red color; of a lively fresh rosy color; as, a ruddy complexion; *Brit. slang,* an understatement for the more distasteful word 'bloody.'—**rud·di·ly**, *adv.*—**rud·di·ness**, *n.*

rude, rōd, *a.*—*ruder, rudest.* [Fr. *rude,* < L. *rudis,* in a natural state, rough, wild.] Unformed by art, taste, or skill; having coarse manners; discourteous; roughly or crudely done; as, a *rude* building; untaught or uncivil; violent or boisterous, as the weather; strong or robust; as, a *rude* spirit.—**rude·ly**, *adv.*—**rude·ness**, *n.*

ru·di·ment, rō′di·ment, *n.* [L. *rudimentum,* < *rudis,* rude.] That which is in an undeveloped state; an unformed or unfinished beginning; *anat.* an organ or part rendered not functional because of its stunted capacity or size. *Usu. pl.* elements or first principles of any art or science; the introduction to any branch of knowledge; the elements or elementary notions.—**ru·di·men·tal**, *a.*—**ru·di·men·ta·ri·ly**, *adv.*—**ru·di·men··ta·ri·ness**, *n.*—**ru·di·men·ta·ry**, rō′di··men′ta·rē, rō″di·men′trē, *a.*

rue, rō, *v.t.*—*rued, ruing.* [O.E. *hrēowan,* to rue = D. *rouwen,* G. *reuen,* to repent; same root as *crude,* L. *crudus,* raw, *cruel,* L. *crudelis.* Hence *ruth.*] To regret; to repent; to repent of and wish undone.—*v.i.* To have compassion; to become sorrowful, grieved, or repentant.—*n.*

rue, rō, *n.* [O.Fr. Fr. *rue,* < L. *ruta,* < Gr. *rhytē,* rue.] *Bot.* a perennial herb, *Ruta graveolens,* having clusters of tiny yellow flowers and strongly scented leaves containing aromatic oils used in medicine and for flavoring.

rue a·nem·o·ne, *n.* A delicate N. American woodland flower, *Anemonella thalictroides,* in the buttercup family, with two or three pinkish-white flowers on stalks that rise above a whorl of three-lobed leaves.

rue·ful, rō′ful, *a.* Causing lamentation or sorrow; as, a *rueful* situation; sorrowful or remorseful; as, a *rueful* expression on one's face.—**rue·ful·ly**, *adv.*—**rue·ful·ness**, *n.*

ru·fes·cent, rŏ·fes′ent, *a.* [L. *rufescens,* < *rufus,* red.] Reddish; tinged with red.—**ru·fes·cence**, *n.*

ruff, ruf, *n.* [Connected with Provinc. Fr. *rufo,* a crease or wrinkle, Armor. *roufen,* a wrinkle, a fold; Sp. *rufo,* frizzled, curled; cf. also D. *ruif,* a fold.] A large, stiff, pleated collar formerly a popular ornament of dress among both sexes; a frill of feathers or hair standing out around the neck of an animal; a bird, *Philomachus pugnax,* of the Eurasian sandpiper family, the male having an erectile ruff of feathers on the neck. A low vibrating beat of a drum; a ruffle.—**ruffed**, *a.*

ruff, ruf, *n.* [Pg. *rufa,* a game with dice.] An old game at cards, the predecessor of whist; the act of trumping when you have no cards of the suit led.—*v.t., v.i.* To trump instead of following suit.

ruffed grouse, *n.* A N. American ground-dwelling chickenlike bird, *Bonasa umbellus,* with a pair of tufted feathers at the neck and a fan-shaped tail with a broad black band, the male of which makes a distinctive drumming sound.

ruf·fi·an, ruf′ē·an, ruf′yan, *n.* [O.Fr. *rufien, ruffien,* a ruffian; Sp. *rufian,* a ruffian, a pimp; It. *ruffiano,* a pimp; prob. of G. origin.] A boisterous brutal fellow.—*a.* Like or belonging to a ruffian; brutal.—**ruf·fi··an·ism**, ruf′ē·a·niz″um, ruf′ya·niz″um, *n.*—**ruf·fi·an·ly**, *a.*

ruf·fle, ruf′l, *v.t.*—*ruffled, ruffling.* [A freq. of *ruff* = D. *ruyffeln,* to wrinkle.] To disturb the surface of; to disorder; to rumple; to disarrange; to furnish or adorn with ruffles; to contract into plaits or folds; to erect, as the feathers of a bird; to agitate; to disturb, as the mind; to turn hastily, as the pages of a book; *cards,* to shuffle.—*v.i.* To become disordered or rumpled; to flutter, as: The banners *ruffled* in the wind. To become agitated or disturbed; to grow rough or noisy; to put on airs; to swagger. —*n.* A surface disturbance; a ripple; a state of agitation or disturbance; discomposure. —**ruf·fly**, *n.*—**ruf·flier, ruffliest.**

ruf·fle, ruf′l, *n.* A strip of plaited fabric attached to some border of a garment, as to the wristband or bosom; a frill.

ruf·fle, ruf′l, *n.* [Also earlier *ruff*: cf. Pg. *rufla, rufo,* roll of a drum, *rufar,* beat a roll.] A low, continuous beating of a drum, less loud than the roll.—*v.t.*—*ruffled, ruffling.* To beat a ruffle on, as a drum.

ru·fous, rō′fus, *a.* [L. *rufus,* red; allied to *ruber,* red (whence *rubric*).] Reddish; of a yellowish or brownish red.

rug, rug, *n.* [Akin to Icel. *röggr,* a tuft, shagginess; Sw. *rugg, ragg,* rough hair.] A floor covering of thick, heavy fabric, often wool, with a nap or pile, generally woven in a simple rectangular shape. A piece of thick woolen material used to cover the legs when driving, traveling, or sitting outdoors; also *lap robe.*

ru·ga, rō′ga, *n.* pl. **ru·gae,** rō′jē. *Usu. pl., biol.* a crease, fold, or wrinkle.—**ru·gate,** rō′gāt, rō′git, *a.*

Rug·by, rug′bē, *n.* [From a city and school in Warwickshire, England.] *Brit.* one of the two principal varieties of football, played by fifteen men to a side with an oval ball. Also **rug·by foot·ball,** *rugger.*

rug·ged, rug′id, *a.* [M.E. *rugged, roggyd*; prob. from Scand.] Rough with projections or irregularities of surface; as, *rugged* rocks, *rugged* bark; of ground, etc., roughly broken, rocky, hilly, or otherwise difficult of passage; of the brow or face, wrinkled or furrowed; of the features or face, roughly irregular, heavy, or hard in outline or form, rather than smoothly rounded or delicately shaped; rough or tempestuous, as weather; severe, hard, or trying, as times or life; rough, harsh, or stern, as persons; ungentle, or roughly rude, as actions; harsh to the ear, as sounds; rude, unpolished, or unrefined as, *rugged* manners; often, homely or plain, but with a rough force or effectiveness; as, *rugged* maxims hewn from life; stalwart, sturdy, or strong, rather than elegant; *colloq.* robust or vigorous.—**rug·-ged·ly**, *adv.*—**rug·ged·ness**, *n.*

rug·ger, rug′ẽr, *n.* Rugby.

ru·gose, rõ′gōs, rõ·gōs′, *a.* [L. *rugosus*, < *ruga*, a wrinkle.] Wrinkled; full of wrinkles; ridged; *bot.* being wrinkled or rough, as the surface of various prominently veined leaves. Also **ru·gous**, rõ′gus.—**ru·gose·ly**, *adv.*—**ru·gos·i·ty**, rõ·gos′i·tē, *n.*

ru·gu·lose, rõ′gū·lōs″, *a.* Finely corrugated; closely wrinkled.

ru·in, rõ′in, *n.* [Fr. *ruine*, < L. *ruina*, a falling down, downfall, ruin, < *ruo*, *rutum*, to fall, to rush down.] That change of anything which destroys it or entirely unfits it for use; destruction; overthrow; downfall; that which promotes injury, decay or destruction; bane; perdition; the act of occasioning downfall or destruction; a building or anything in a state of decay or dilapidation; the state of being destroyed or rendered worthless; as, to go to *ruin*; *often pl.* the remains of a decayed city, house, or fortress.—*v.t.* To bring to destruction; to damage essentially; to destroy, defeat, or demolish; to create a state of insolvency; to seduce (a woman).—*v.i.* To fall into ruins; to run to ruin.—**ru·in·a·ble**, *a.*—**ru·in·er**, *n.*

ru·in·ate, rõ′i·nāt″, *v.t.*—*ruinated, ruinating.* To ruin.—*a.* Ruined; in ruins.

ru·in·a·tion, rõ″i·nā′shan, *n.* The act of ruinating; ruin; demolition or destruction.

ru·in·ous, rõ′i·nus, *a.* [L. *ruinosus*.] Fallen to ruin; dilapidated; composed of ruins; bringing or tending to bring ruin; as, a *ruinous* tornado.—**ru·in·ous·ly**, *adv.*—**ru·in·ous·ness**, *n.*

rule, rõl, *n.* [O.E. *reule*, *rewle*, < O.Fr. *reule*, *riule* (Fr. *règle*), < L. *regula*, a straight piece of wood, a ruler, a rule or pattern (whence *regular*), < *rego*, to keep straight, to govern.] Government; sway; control; supreme command or authority; an established principle, standard, or guide for action; something settled by authority or custom for guidance and direction; a maxim, canon, or precept to be observed; the body of laws or regulations observed by a religious society and its members; as, the *rule* of St. Benèdict; a point of law settled by authority; custom or habitual practice, as: As a *rule* I rise late. An instrument by which straight lines are drawn; an instrument for measuring short lengths, and performing various operations in measurement; *arith.* a determinate mode prescribed for performing any operation and producing a certain result; *gram.* an established form of construction in a particular class of words, or the expressions of that form in words; *print.* a strip of metal for printing decorative or solid lines.

rule, rõl, *v.t.*—*ruled, ruling.* To govern; to exercise authority or dominion over; to control, conduct, guide; to mark with lines, using a ruler; *law*, to establish by rule; to determine; to decide.—*v.i.* To have power or command; to exercise supreme authority, often followed by *over*; *com.* to maintain a level, as: Prices *rule* lower than formerly.

rule of thumb, *n.* A rule suggested by practical rather than scientific knowledge; a rough calculation.

rule out, *v.t.* To refuse to consider; eliminate; omit; reject; exclude; prevent.

rul·er, rõ′lẽr, *n.* One that rules or governs; an instrument, made of wood, plastic, or metal, with straight edges or sides which by guiding a pen or pencil along the edge draws straight lines: also used for measuring length; a person or an instrument that rules or marks straight, usu. parallel lines on something, as paper.

rul·ing, rõ′ling, *a.* Governing; reigning; prevalent; predominant.—*n.* A rule, point, or decision settled by a judge, a court of law, or another authority; the act of controlling.

trolling or governing; the process of drawing lines or measuring by using a ruler.

ru·ly Eng·lish, rõ′lē ing′glish, *n. Computers*, a special form of the English language in which each word denotes only one concept, and vice versa: used in computer programming.

rum, rum, *n.* [Perh. of West Indian origin.] Liquor distilled from sugar cane juice or molasses; any alcoholic liquor.—**rum·my**, rum′ē, *a.*—*rummier, rummiest.* Pertaining to or flavored like rum.

rum, rum, *a.* [From an old cant word *rum*, *rome*, great, good, used in a contemptuous sense, from *Rom*, applied by gypsies to themselves.] *Slang.* Peculiar; odd; queer. Also *Brit.* **rum·my**, rum′ē.

rum·ba, rum′ba, rụm′ba, *Sp.* Rõm′bä, *n.* A flamboyant dance of complex rhythm having a Cuban Negro origin; a modified American ballroom version of this dance; music for the rumba or in a characteristic rumba rhythm.—*v.i.*—*rumbaed, rumbaing.* To perform the rumba. Also *rhumba.*

rum·ble, rum′bl, *v.i.*—*rumbled, rumbling.* [Same as D. *rommelen*, Dan. *rumle*, G. *rummelen*, *rumpeln*, prob. imit. of sound.] To make a low, heavy, muffled, continued sound; to proceed with or travel as with such a sound.—*v.t.* To cause to emit or to utter with a deep rolling sound; to subject to processing in a tumbling barrel.—*n.* A low, heavy, continuous sound; a seat or a baggage compartment at the rear portion of a carriage or a roadster; tumbling barrel; *slang*, a street fight, usu. among rival gangs of youths.—**rum·bler**, *n.*—**rum·bling**, *adv.*

rum·ble seat, *n.* An unroofed seat which folded into the rear of an early roadster or coupé when not in use.

rum·bly, rum′blē, *a.*—*rumblier, rumbliest.* Producing or characterized by a rumbling noise.

ru·men, rõ′min, *n. pl.* **ru·mi·na**, rõ′mi·na. [L.] The upper or first stomach characteristic of ruminants; the cud chewed by such animals.—**ru·mi·nal**, *a.*

ru·mi·nant, rõ′mi·nant, *a.* [L. *ruminans*, *ruminantis*, ppr. of *rumino*.] Chewing the cud; characterized by chewing again what has been swallowed, as *ruminant* animals. Given to deep thought; contemplative.—*n.* A member of an order of herbivorous hoofed mammals that chew the cud, as the camel, cow, deer, goat, and the like; having a stomach composed of four separate cavities or compartments.—**ru·mi·nant·ly**, *adv.*

ru·mi·nate, rõ′mi·nāt″, *v.i.*—*ruminated, ruminating.* [L. *rumino*, *ruminatum*, < *rumen*, the throat, the gullet.] To chew the cud; to chew again what has been slightly chewed and regurgitated. To muse; to meditate; to think again and again; to ponder.—*v.t.* To chew over again; to muse or meditate on.—**ru·mi·na·tion**, rõ″mi·nā′shan, *n.*—**ru·mi·na·tive**, *a.*—**ru·mi·na·tive·ly**, *adv.*—**ru·mi·na·tor**, *n.*

rum·mage, rum′ij, *v.t.*—*rummaged, rummaging.* [Obs. Fr. *arrumage* (now *arrimage*), < *arrumer*.] To search thoroughly or actively through, as a place, turning over or looking through contents; to ransack; to hunt through; to bring, find, or fetch by searching, usu. followed by *out* or *up*.—*v.i.* To search actively, as in a place or receptacle. —*n.* Miscellaneous articles; odds and ends, as items in a rummage sale; a rummaging search.—**rum·mag·er**, *n.*

rum·mage sale, *n.* The sale of miscellaneous articles, old or new, contributed to raise money for charity; a sale of unclaimed goods at a wharf or warehouse, or of odds and ends of merchandise at a shop.

rum·mer, rum′ẽr, *n.* [D. *roomer*, Sw. *remmer*, G. *römer*, a large drinking glass; perh. lit. a *Roman* glass.] A large glass or drinking cup.

rum·my, rum′ē, *n.* A popular card game with numerous variations, all of which involve the combining of three or more cards in specified patterns, as by rank or suit.

rum·my, rum′ē, *n. pl.* **rum·mies**. *Slang.* An habitual drunk; an intoxicated person.

ru·mor, *Brit.* **ru·mour**, rõ′mẽr, *n.* [Fr. *rumeur*, < L. *rumor*, common talk.] A current story, report, or statement passing from one person to another, without any known authority for the truth of it; hearsay; gossip.—*v.t.* To tell or circulate by an unverified report.

ru·mor·mon·ger, *Brit.* **ru·mour·mon·-ger**, rõ′mẽr·mung″gẽr, rõ′mẽr·mong″gẽr, *n.* One who begins and encourages the spread of rumors, esp. malicious ones.

rump, rump, *n.* [A Scand. word = Icel. *rumpr*, Sw. *rumpa*, D. *rompe*, G. *rumpf*, the trunk.] The end of the backbone of an animal, with the parts adjacent; the buttocks; the section of beef from this area; *fig.* the tag end of something usu. of inferior quality, which lasts longer than the original organization or territory.

rum·ple, rum′pl, *v.t.*—*rumpled, rumpling.* [Same as D. *rompelen*, to rumple; akin to O.L.G. *rumpele*, a wrinkle; G. *rumpfen*, D. *rompelen*, to crimp, to wrinkle.] To wrinkle or crumple; to ruffle; to dishevel.—*v.i.* To become creased, crumpled, or wrinkled.—*n.* An irregular fold or crease; a wrinkle, esp. untidy.

Rump Par·lia·ment, *n. Eng. hist.* the remaining end of the Long Parliament, after the expulsion of the majority of its members by Cromwell in 1648.

rum·pus, rum′pus, *n. pl.* **rum·pus·es**. [Perh. imit. of a noise, like *rumble*; or allied to *romp*.] A riot; a great noise; disturbance.

rum·pus room, *n.* A room, usu. on the lower level of a home, furnished and used for parties and other recreation.

rum·run·ner, rum′run″ẽr, *n.* A person or a vessel engaged in smuggling rum or liquors, as for illicit sale.—**rum·run·ning**, *n.*

run, run, *v.i.* past *ran*, pp. *run*, ppr. *running*. [O.E. *rinnan* (pret. *ran*, pl. *runnon*, pp. *runnen*); O.E., Goth., and O.H.G. *rinnan*, D. *rennen*, *rinnen*, Icel. *renna*, G. *rennen*, to run; same root as in Skt. *ri*, to go.] To move more quickly than in walking, using the legs to lift the feet from the ground for a fraction of time in each step; to move quickly; to flee; to retreat hurriedly; resort; to make a short, hasty trip or visit; to go freely; to move or be propelled, as: The ball *ran* along the ground. To contend in a race; to enter into a contest; to campaign for public office; to finish a contest in a designated position; as, to *run* second; to migrate or ascend a river to spawn, as a fish; to move on wheels or runners, as a locomotive or sledge; to move or be moved; as, the ship *ran* aground; to pass or go back and forth from place to place; to ply, as ships or railway trains between different places; to revolve on an axis or pivot; to turn as a wheel; to move freely; to creep or climb, as a vine; to unravel; to move or pass, as a fluid; to flow; to leak; to become fluid; to fuse; to melt; to discharge pus or other matter, as: An ulcer *runs*. To spread on a surface; to spread and blend, as: Colors *run* in washing. To continue going or in operation, as: The mills are *running*. To pass from one state or condition to another; as, to *run* into error or into debt; to pass or proceed in thought or speech; as, to *run* from one topic to another; to proceed or pass, as time; to have a certain course, track, or direction; to extend, stretch, lie, as: The street *runs* east and west. To have a certain written form, as: The story *runs* as follows. To have a tendency; recur; as: Artistic ability *runs* in the family. To be spread, published, or circulated; to continue or be repeated for a certain time, as: The play *ran* for a hundred nights. To be carried to a pitch; to rise, as: Feeling *runs* high. To grow exuberantly; to vary in growth, as: Apples *run* large this season. To make withdrawals, as from a bank, in quick succession; to continue in time before it becomes due and payable, as: A bill has ninety days to *run*. *Naut.* to sail with a following wind.— *v.t.* To cause to run or go quickly, as: He *ran* his eyes over the page. To go over, as a distance, quickly; to accomplish by running; to contend against, as in a race; to cause, as a horse, to go fast; to enter as a contestant in a race; to bring about a certain condition, as: She *ran* herself into a state of collapse. To pursue; to force to go, as: The hounds *ran* the fox to cover. To leave; to cause to ply; to transport; as, he *ran* her there in his car. To break through or evade; as, to *run* a blockade; smuggle; to maintain in running; as, to *run* a machine; to print; to publish; to analyze, treat, or refine; to cause to be carried in a certain course; as, to *run* a ship aground; to stand for office; as, to *run* for mayor; to carry on or conduct, as a hotel or other enterprise; to make a number of strokes without a miss, as in games; to play a series of winning cards from one suit; to encounter; to incur; as, to *run* the risk of being killed; to cause, as water, to flow; to pour forth in a stream; to accumulate, as charges, for payment at a later date; to make slide freely, as a rope; *golf*, to cause, as a ball, to roll onward when it lands. To sew by passing the needle through and through in a continuous line; to push; to thrust; to pierce; to stab; as, to *run* a person through with a rapier; to graze; to melt; to melt and clarify; to form in a mold by melting; to mark, trace, or draw, as a line.—**run a·cross**, to discover or meet accidentally.—**run af·ter**, to chase.—**run foul of**, to come into collision with; to clash with.—**run in**, to visit informally *slang*, to arrest. *Print.* to insert without indenting, as typeset matter; to arrange, as typeset matter, without a break.—**run in·to**, collide with; meet; to total; to follow; to blend.—**run off**, to depart hurriedly; to repeat or create quickly; to decide the winner of a dead heat by a subsequent contest; to send away; to produce on a machine such as a printing press or typewriter.—**run on**, to continue; to talk incessantly. *Print.* to continue without a break or new paragraph; to add, as a sentence, at the conclusion of a text.—**run out**, to stop after running to the end of its time, as an hourglass; to come to an end; to become expended or exhausted; to expire, as: The lease *runs out* in October. Expel.—**run out of**, to use up a quantity of.—**run o·ver**, to ride or drive over; as, to *run over* a chicken; to overflow; to go over, examine, or recount cursorily; rehearse.—**run through**, to stab or pierce; to consume or spend rapidly or recklessly; to rehearse or practice rapidly, as a play or speech.—**run up**, to sew, make, or build hastily; to increase, as prices or expenses; to accumulate, as wealth or debts.

run, run, *n*. The act of running; a running gait; a period of rapid movement; a distance traversed; as, a ten-mile *run*; a passage from one place to another; a trip; the distance traveled by a golf ball after it lands; an interval during which a factory or machine operates continuously; that which is produced in a period of continuous operation; a defect in knitted fabric, where stitches have come undone; direction or arrangement; grain; particular or distinctive course, progress, or tenor; general tendency; privilege or use; as, the *run* of the building; *theatr.* an unbroken period of performances; a continued course; as, a

run of ill luck; an unbroken length of something; a series of playing cards, usu. in a given suit, in rank order; a general or uncommon pressure or demand, as on a bank or treasury for payment of its notes; a sustained sale or demand as for some commodity; the flow, as of a liquid, during a particular period; a stream; a swift current; the typical or average; as, the normal *run* of students; a sloping course, as for skiing; a path where animals, as deer, run; a large extent of ground for livestock; a trough or similar support, as for water; the movement of fish migrating to spawn; the fish thus migrating; *mus.* a succession of notes, either ascending or descending, played or sung rapidly. The horizontal measurement of a flight of stairs; the distance from wall face to building center; *baseball*, the score made when a player circles all the bases. Successful shots or strokes made successively in a game; *naut.* the stern of the immersed body of a ship where it commences to narrow off.—*a.* Liquefied or melted; made from material molten and cast in a mold.—**a run for one's mon·ey**, a satisfactory return for one's effort or expenditure, often in competition.—**in the long run**, in the final result; in the conclusion or end.—**on the run**, hastily; fleeing from, as: He is *on the run* from prison.

run·a·bout, run'a·bout", *n.* One who runs about from place to place; a light open wagon; a small, usu. open automobile; a small motorboat.

run·a·round, run'a·round", *n. Slang*, evasive action, esp. in answer to a question or request; *print.* a way of arranging type by narrowing the lines to fit around something, as an illustration. Also **run·a-round**, **run·round.**

run·a·way, run'a·wā", *n.* One who runs away; a fugitive; a deserter; that which cannot be controlled or halted; an act of running away, as an elopement; an overwhelming or easily won victory or race.— *a.* Having run away; escaped; fugitive; of a machine, horse, car, or the like, having escaped from the control of the rider or operator; pertaining to or accomplished by running away or eloping; decisive or easily won, as a race; characterized by a rise in price which is usu. rapid.—**run a·way**, to flee; to leave home or another confining place; to bolt.—**run a·way with**, to take or go away with, esp. hurriedly or secretly; to elope with; steal; to outdo others, as in a performance.

run·ci·ble spoon, run'si·bl spōn', *n.* A fork with one curved, sharp-edged tine and two broad tines.

run·ci·nate, run'si·nit, run'si·nāt", *a.* [L. *runcina*, a plane.] *Bot.* having sharp, triangular lobes curving backward, as leaves.

run·dle, run'dl, *n.* [Var. of *roundel*.] A rung of a ladder; a wheel or similarly rotating object; one of the bars of a lantern wheel.

rund·let, rund'lit, *n.* [M.E. *rondelet*, dim. < O.Fr. *rondelle*, small cask, < *rond*, E. *round*.] A small cask or barrel; an old liquid measure of capacity equaling approximately 18 gallons. Also **run·let**, run'lit.

run down, *v.t.* To run against, strike, and overturn; to pursue or give chase to, leading to capture, as a quarry; to read through, as a column of figures; to speak about in a disparaging way; to seek out and find, as facts.—*v.i.* To stop, through exhaustion of power, as a watch; to depreciate in value or condition, as: That neighborhood has *run down*.—**run·down**, run'doun", *n.* A summing-up of important points of information; a concise review; as, a *rundown* of expenses; *baseball*, a play in which a base runner is tagged out between bases;

as, to be caught in a *rundown*.—**run-down**, run'doun', *a.* In a state of fatigue or exhaustion; in poor health as a result of physical or emotional pressures; no longer running because unwound, as in a timepiece.

rune, rōn, *n.* One of the figures or characters of the runic alphabet, which is characterized by the arrangement of straight lines, and was used by Germanic peoples during the years 200 to 1200 A.D., esp. in Scandinavia and Britain; a poem, song, or short writing expressed in runes, or in the style and mood of the same period; a mystical or magical poem, song, or saying.—**rune·like**, *a.*

rung, rung, *n.* [O.E. *hrung* = D. *rong* = G. *runge*.] One of the horizontal crosspieces forming the steps of a ladder; a rounded or shaped piece fixed for strengthening purposes, as between the legs of a chair; a stout stick, rod, or bar, esp. a rounded one, forming a piece in something framed or constructed, as one of the spokes of a wheel.

ru·nic, rō'nik, *a.* Composed of or characterized by runes; having mystical or secret meaning or significance.

run-in, run'in", *n.* An altercation; *print.* additional copy added to a typeset text without starting a new paragraph.—*a.*

run·nel, run'el, *n.* A rivulet or small brook. Also **run·let**, run'lit.

run·ner, run'ér, *n.* One who runs; a racer; a messenger; *baseball*, a base runner. One who solicits business; a device which enables an object to move or slide; that on which something runs or slides; as, the *runner* of a sleigh or skate; narrow carpeting, as for a staircase or hallway; a narrow piece of cloth, usu. decorative, suitable for a dresser or table; smuggler; any of a number of carangid fishes, *Caranx crysos*, found in the Atlantic from Massachusetts to Brazil. *Bot.* a slender prostrate stem sending out leaves and roots, as in the strawberry; a plant sending out such stems; any of a number of twining plants.

run·ner bean, *n.* A plant of tropical American origin, *Phaseolus coccineus*, grown for both its bright red flowers and its edible seeds. Also **mul·ti·flo·ra bean**, *scarlet runner*, **scar·let run·ner bean.**

run·ner-up, run'ér·up', *n.* A term applied to the player who finishes second to the winner in a competition.

run·ning, run'ing, *a.* Moving rapidly; kept for racing; as, a *running* horse; climbing or creeping, as a plant; moving freely; functioning; linear; as, ten miles *running*; flowing; fluid; current; sustained; repeated; accomplished or initiated while running; in sucession; without any intervening day or year; as, to visit two days *running*; discharging pus or matter.—*n.* The act of one who runs; a quantity run; as, the first *running* of a still.—*adv.*—**out of the run·-ning**, out of the race.

run·ning board, *n.* A narrow platform or step just above the ground, as along the side of some automobiles, open streetcars, and other vehicles.

run·ning gear, *n.* The wheels and axles of a vehicle and their attachments, as distinguished from the body; the working parts, as of a locomotive.

run·ning hand, *n.* The style of handwriting in which the letters usu. slant forward and are formed without the pen being lifted from the paper.

run·ning head, *n. Print.* a word or words appearing as a heading at the top of consecutive pages, as of a periodical or book.

run·ning knot, *n.* A knot made round and so as to slide along a part of the same rope, thus forming a noose which tightens as the rope is pulled; slipknot.

run·ning light, *n.* Any of the colored

lights which a ship or aircraft must display at night.

run·ning mate, *n.* A horse admitted to a race to act as a pacesetter for another horse; a candidate for the subordinate of two related offices, as the vice-president; a close associate.

run·ning stitch, *n.* Small sewing stitches of even length, made by running a needle in and out of cloth.

run·ning ti·tle, *n. Print.* a descriptive headline placed continuously at the top of pages of type, esp. a general title of a volume placed at the top of the left-hand pages or all the pages of the volume.

run·ny, run'ē, *a.*—**runnier, runniest.** Tending to drip or run; as, a *runny* nose.

run·off, run'af″, run'of″, *n.* Something which runs off, as rain which flows off from the land in streams; a deciding final race or contest held after a dead heat, or after an earlier contest which left the final decision undecided.

run-of-the-mill, run'ov·THe·mil′, *a.* Average; ordinary. See *run-of-the-mine.*

run-of-the-mine, run'ov·THe·mīn′, *a.* Ungraded. Average; also *run-of-the-mill.*

run-on, run'on″, run'an″, *a.* Of something added; continuing, as a thought, from a line of poetry to the following line.—*n.* Added material.

run-on sen·tence, *n.* A sentence in which a comma is used in a position where a period would be customary.

run·o·ver, run'ō'vėr, *n.* Material for publication requiring space in excess of the amount allotted to it; material carried over to additional space, as on subsequent pages of a periodical.

run·o·ver, run'ō'vėr, *a.* Extended beyond the designated space, as a news story or other editorial material.

runt, runt, *n.* [Origin doubtful.] Any animal below the usual size of the breed; the smallest in a litter, esp. puppies or pigs; an undersized person, often used contemptuously.—**runt·y,** run'tē, *a.*—**runtier, runtiest.**—**runt·i·ness,** *n.*

run-through, run'thrō″, *n.* A rapid rehearsal of a part, play, or speech before public performance; a cursory review.

run·way, run'wā″, *n.* A way along which something runs; a hard-surfaced, clear pathway used by planes for taking off and landing; the beaten track of animals; a way, track, or groove along which something moves or slides; the bed of a stream; a narrow ramp leading from the stage into the audience area of a theater.

rup·ture, rup'chėr, *n.* [Fr. *rupture,* < L.L. *ruptura,* a breaking, < L. *rumpo, ruptum,* to break.] The act of breaking or bursting; the state of being broken or violently parted; *pathol.* a hernia. A breach of concord between either individuals or nations.—*v.t.*—**ruptured, rupturing.** To make a rupture in; to burst; to part by violence; to affect with or cause to suffer from rupture.—*v.i.* To suffer a breach or rupture.—**rup·tur·a·ble,** *a.*

ru·ral, rụr'al, *a.* [L. *ruralis,* < *rus, ruris,* the country (whence also *rustic*); same root as *room.*] Pertaining to the country, as distinguished from a city or town; pertaining to country life and country people; pertaining to agriculture or farming.—**ru··ral·ism, ru·ral·i·ty,** rụ·ral'i·tē, *n.*—**ru··ral·ist,** *n.*—**ru·ral·ly,** *adv.*

ru·ral dean, *n. Chiefly Brit., eccles.* a priest appointed by the bishop to supervise a section of the diocese containing several parishes.

ru·ral free de·liv·er·y, *n.* The service of free mail delivery to country districts by government carriers. Abbr. *RFD, R.F.D.*

ru·ral·ize, rụr'a·līz″, *v.i.*—*ruralized, ruralizing.* To go into or dwell in the country;

to rusticate.—*v.t.* To render rural; to give a rural character to.—**ru·ral·i·za·tion,** rụr″a·li·zā'shan, *n.*

ru·ral route, *n.* A country mail route serviced by U.S. post office carriers.

ruse, rōz, *n.* [Fr. *ruse,* < *ruser,* to dodge.] An artifice, trick, or stratagem; a wile.

rush, rush, *v.i.* [M.E. *ruschen,* rush, dash: cf. D. *ruischen,* M.L.G. *rüschen,* G. *rauschen,* rush, move with noise, roar.] To move, act, or go with speed, impetuosity, or violence; to dash forward for an attack or onslaught; as, to *rush* upon the enemy; to go, come, or pass rapidly, as: Tears *rush* to the eyes.—*v.t.* To act, move, or drive with speed or violence; to carry or convey with haste; as, to *rush* the injured to the hospital; to cause to act or move quickly, hurry; to send, push, or force with unusual speed; as, to *rush* a bill through Congress; to attack suddenly and swiftly; to take or overcome by sudden attack, as a place or person. *Slang,* to heap attention on; as, to *rush* a girl; to entertain or seek the favor of, as a student desired for membership in a fraternity or sorority. *Football,* to carry forward, as the ball, toward the opposition's goal line.—*n.* The act of rushing; a rapid, impetuous, or headlong onward movement; a hostile charge or onslaught; an eager rushing of numbers of persons to some region to be occupied or exploited; as, the *rush* to the gold fields; an unexpected sudden surge or appearance; as, a *rush* of blood to his face; hurried activity or busy haste; as, the *rush* of city life; a hurried state, as from pressure of affairs; press of work, business, or traffic requiring extraordinary effort or haste. *Slang,* lavish attention paid a woman by a suitor; entertainment and attention given by a fraternity or sorority to prospective members. *Football,* an attempt to carry the ball across the opposition's goal line; *pl., films,* a first print of the shooting of one or more scenes of a movie.—*a.* Requiring haste; as, a *rush* order for goods; characterized by rush, press of work, or traffic; as, the *rush* hours on the subway.—**rush·er,** *n.*

rush, rush, *n.* [O.E. *rysc, risc,* akin to D. and G. *rusch,* rush.] Any plant of the genus *Juncus,* in the family *Juncaceae,* which comprises grasslike herbs with pithy or hollow stems, found in wet or marshy places; any of various similar plants; a stem of such a plant, used for making chair bottoms, mats, and baskets; something of little or no value; as, not worth a *rush.*—**rush·y,** *a.*—**rushier, rushiest.**

rush can·dle, *n.* A small taper made by dipping a dried and peeled rush in tallow. Also **rush light.**

rush·ee, ru·shē', *n. Slang,* a college student who is being entertained by a fraternity or sorority as a prospective member.

rusk, rusk, *n.* [Perh. akin to L.G. *rusken,* to crackle.] Slices of sweet, light bread that are rebaked or toasted; zwieback.

rus·set, rus'it, *n.* [O.Fr. *rousset,* dim. of *rous* (Fr. *roux*), red, reddish, russet, < L. *russes,* red.] A yellowish-brown, light-brown, or reddish-brown color; a kind of winter apple with a rough brownish skin; a coarse reddish-brown or brownish homespun cloth formerly used for clothing; leather finished but not polished or colored except as by the tanning liquid.—*a.* Yellowish-brown or reddish-brown in color.

Rus·sia leath·er, *n.* A fine, smooth leather produced by careful tanning and dyeing, esp. in dark red: orig. prepared in Russia, but imitated elsewhere.

Rus·sian, rush'an, *a.* Of or relating to the country, inhabitants, or language of Russia. —*n.* A native or inhabitant of Russia, esp. a Great Russian; the principal Slavic

language of Russia; Great Russian, Ukrainian, or Belorussian.

Rus·sian dress·ing, *n.* A salad dressing of which the basic ingredients are mayonnaise, chili sauce, pimientos, and chopped pickles, to which caviar is often added.

Rus·sian ol·ive, *n.* Oleaster. Also **Treb·-i·zond date.**

Rus·sian rou·lette, *n.* A suicidal game or stunt in which the participants take turns spinning the cylinder of a revolver loaded with one bullet, placing the muzzle against the head, and pulling the trigger.

Rus·sian this·tle, *n.* A prickly Eurasian weed, *Salsola pestifer,* in the goosefoot family, now common in N. America, the entire plant dying in the late summer, breaking from the ground, and blowing about scattering its seeds. Also *tumbleweed.*

Rus·sian wolf·hound, *n.* One of a breed of large dogs having a slender body, narrow head, silky coat, and long legs, originally raised by the Russians for wolf hunting. Also *borzoi.*

Rus·so-Byz·an·tine, rus'ō·biz'an·tēn″, rus'ō·biz'an·tīn″, rus'ō·bi·zan'tin, *a.* Both Russian and Byzantine; Russian, as developed from the Byzantine style; as, *Russo-Byzantine* architecture.

Rus·so-Jap·a·nese, rus'ō·jap'a·nēz″, rus'-ō·jap'a·nēs″, *a.* Pertaining to Russia and Japan; as, the *Russo-Japanese* War of 1904–1905 in which the Russians were defeated.

Rus·so·phile, rus'o·fīl″, rus'o·fil, *n.* One who admires or favors Russia or anything Russian.

Rus·so·phobe, rus'o·fōb″, *n.* One who fears or hates Russia or anything Russian.—**Rus·so·pho·bi·a,** *n.*

rust, rust, *n.* [O.E. *rust* = D. *roest* = G. *rost,* rust.] The red or orange coating which forms on the surface of iron when exposed to air and moisture, consisting chiefly of ferris hydroxide and ferric oxide; any accretion resembling rust; a reddish or yellowish-brown color; any of various plant diseases caused by fungi, in which the leaves and stems become spotted or discolored; a fungus producing such a disease; *fig.* any growth, habit, influence, or agency tending to injure the mind, character, abilities, or usefulness.—*v.i.* To contract rust, or grow rusty, as iron; to become rust-colored; *fig.* to deteriorate or become impaired, as through inaction or disuse.—*v.t.* To affect with rust; to make rust-colored; to affect, as plants, with the disease of rust; *fig.* to impair as if with rust.

rus·tic, rus'tik, *a.* [L. *rusticus,* < *rus,* country.] Of, pertaining to, or living in the country as distinguished from towns or cities; rural; simple, artless, or unsophisticated, after the manner of the country; uncouth, rude, or boorish; made or built in country fashion or of simple materials, esp. made of roughly dressed limbs or roots of trees, as garden seats.—*n.* A country person; an unsophisticated countryman.—**rus·ti·cal,** *a.*—**rus·ti·cal·ly,** *adv.*

rus·ti·cate, rus'ti·kāt″, *v.i.*—*rusticated, rusticating.* [L. *rusticatus,* pp. of *rusticari,* < *rusticus,* E. *rustic.*] To go to the country; stay or sojourn in the country.—*v.t.* To send to or domicile in the country; *Brit.* to send, as a student, away from a university or college for a time by way of punishment; to render rustic or countrified, as persons or manners; to construct or finish, as masonry, in the rustic manner.—**rus·ti·ca·tion,** rus″ti·kā'shan, *n.*—**rus·ti·ca·tor,** *n.*

rus·tic·i·ty, ru·stis'i·tē, *n. pl.* **rus·tic·i·ties.** The state or quality of being rustic; rural character or life; a rustic characteristic or peculiarity.

rus·tle, rus'l, *v.i.*—*rustled, rustling.* [M.E. *rustel,* prob. imit.] To make a succession of slight, soft sounds, as of parts rubbing gently one on another, as leaves or bushes, silks, or papers; to cause such sounds to be made by moving or stirring something; to move, go, or pass with such sounds, as: The wind *rustles* through the woods. *Colloq.* to move, proceed, or work energetically or vigorously.—*v.t.* To move or stir something so as to cause a rustling sound, as: The wind *rustles* the leaves. *Colloq.* to move, bring, or get by energetic action; *slang,* to steal, esp. cattle.—*n.* The sound made by anything that rustles; as, the *rustle* of leaves.—**rus·tler,** rus′lêr, *n.* One who or that which rustles. *Colloq.* an active, energetic person; *slang,* a cattle thief.

rust·proof, rust′prŏf″, *a.* Not subject to rusting.

rust·y, rus′tē, *a.—rustier, rustiest.* [O.E. *rustig.*] Affected by or covered with rust; consisting of or produced by rust; having the color of rust or rust-colored; faded or shabby, or impaired by time or wear, as clothes or a person's appearance; impaired through disuse or neglect; having lost agility or alertness, or out of practice, as persons; affected with rust disease, as a plant.—**rust·i·ly,** *adv.*—**rust·i·ness,** *n.*

rus·ty, rus′tē, *a.—rustier, rustiest.* [= *restive.*] Restive, as of horses; refractory or stubborn, as people; *chiefly dial.* in an unpleasant temper, ill-tempered, or cross.

rut, rut, *n.* [Fr. *rut,* O.Fr. *ruit,* the noise which male deer make when they desire to mate, < L. to bellow.] The periodical sexual excitement of deer and some other animals; the time during which this occurs.—*v.i. rutted, rutting.* To be in rut.—*v.t.* To copulate.

rut, rut, *n.* [Same word as *route, rote.*] A furrow or track worn into a surface, as by the passage of wheels; a habitual or stereotyped pattern of behavior.—*v.t.—rutted, rutting.* To make ruts in or on.

ru·ta·ba·ga, rŏ″ta·bā′ga, *n.* [Origin doubtful.] *Bot.* A garden vegetable, *Brassica napobrassica,* in the mustard family, producing a solid underground tuber with white or yellow flesh; the edible tuber itself. Also *Swedish turnip.*

ru·ta·ceous, rŏ·tā′shus, *a.* [L. *rutaceus,* < *ruta,* E. *rue.*] *Bot.* belonging to the *Rutaceae* or rue family, a group of plants which includes the genus *Citrus,* the rue, and the gas-plant, and characterized by strongly scented essential oils.

ruth, rŏth, *n.* [< *rue,* cf. *truth,* < *true.*] *Archaic.* Pity; compassion, or sorrow for the misery of another; sorrowful or tender regret; grief.

ru·the·ni·um, rŏ·thē′nē·um, *n.* [From *Ruthenia,* a Latin name for Russia the element having been first obtained in ore from the Ural.] A rare steel-gray metallic element of the platinum group. Sym. Ru, at. no. 44, at. wt. 101.07.—**ru·then·ic,** rŏ·then′ik, rŏ·thē′nik, *a.*—**ru·the·ni·ous,** rŏ·thē′nē·us, *a.* See Periodic Table of Elements.

ruth·er·ford, ruTH′êr·fêrd, *n.* [After Sir Ernest *Rutherford,* 1871–1937, Brit. physicist.] A unit of measurement of radioactivity.

ruth·ful, rŏth′ful, *a.* Sorrowful or mournful; pitiful or compassionate; exciting sorrow or pity.—**ruth·ful·ly,** *adv.*—**ruth·ful·ness,** *n.*

ruth·less, rŏth′lis, *a.* Having no mercy or pity; cruel.—**ruth·less·ly,** *adv.*—**ruth·less·ness,** *n.*

ru·ti·lant, rŏt′i·lant, *a.* [L. *rutilans* (-*ant-*), ppr. of *rutilare,* have a reddish glow, < *rutilus.*] Glowing with a golden or reddish color; shining; glittering.

ru·tile, rŏ′tēl, rŏ′til, *n.* [G. *rutil,* < L. *rutilus,* red, golden-red, shining.] A mineral consisting of titanium dioxide, TiO_2, having a brilliant adamantine or metallic luster, usu. of a reddish-brown color.

rut·tish, rut′ish, *a.* Lustful; lascivious; dis-

posed or tending to rut.—**rut·tish·ly,** *adv.* —**rut·tish·ness,** *n.*

rut·ty, rut′ē, *a.—ruttier, ruttiest.* Full of ruts, as a highway or road.—**rut·ti·ness,** *n.*

rye, rī, *n.* [O.E. *ryge,* Icel. *rugr,* Dan. *rug,* Sw. *rog,* D. *rogge,* G. *roggen, rocken.*] A cereal plant, *Secale cereale,* which bears grain fruits furnished with awns like barley, cultivated as food for livestock and for making flour, whiskey, and grain alcohol.

rye·grass, rī′gras″, rī′gräs″, *n.* [Earlier *ray-grass;* origin obscure.] Any of several cultivated grasses grown for forage or other purposes, esp. *Lolium perenne,* perennial ryegrass.

rye whis·key, *n.* Straight or blended whiskey distilled partly from rye.

S

S, s, es, *n.* The nineteenth letter and fifteenth consonant of the English alphabet; the sound of the letter *S* as represented in speech; the delineation of the letter *S* or *s* in writing or printing; something designated by or having the shape of the letter *S* or *s;* a device for printing the letter *S* or *s;* an early Roman numeral representing 7 or 70.

S, es. South; satisfactory; Saxon; *chem.* sulfur.

's. A written ending representing the possessive of most singular nouns, plural nouns that do not end in *s* or *es,* pronouns, and noun phrases, and adding the sound of *s* or *z;* as, child's, men's, someone's, the man in the street's opinion. With most nouns ending in *s* or *es,* the possessive is formed by adding only the apostrophe, as James' book or the babies' toys, but where pronunciation of the possessive requires an additional syllable, *'s* is used; as, the witness's testimony or someone else's idea.

's. A contraction of *has,* as: He's arrived. A contraction of *is,* as: He's here. A contraction of *us,* as: Let's go. *Colloq.* a contraction of *does,* as: What's he need? *Colloq.* a contraction of *as;* as, so's to let him know.

sab·a·dil·la, sab″a·dil′a, *n.* [Sp. *cebadilla,* dim. of *cebada,* barley.] A liliaceous plant, *Schoenocaulon officinale,* of Mexico and Central America, with long grasslike leaves and bitter seeds; the seeds, which are used as a source of veratrine and veratridine.

sab·bat, sab′at, *n.* (Sometimes *cap.*), *demonology.* A midnight orgy or festival of sorcerers and witches, presided over by Satan, supposedly held annually as an orgy or festival. Also *Sabbath.*

Sab·ba·tar·i·an, sab″a·târ′ē·an, *a.* [L. *sabbatarius.*] Pertaining to the Sabbath, or to the tenets of the Sabbatarians.—*n.* One who observes the seventh day of the week, Saturday, as the Sabbath; one who adheres to or favors a strict religious observance of the Sabbath.—**Sab·ba·tar·i·an·ism,** *n.*

Sab·bath, sab′ath, *n.* [Fr. *sabbat,* < L. *sabbatum,* < Gr. *sábbaton,* < Heb. *shabbāth,* < *shābath* to rest from labor.] The seventh day of the week, Saturday, as the day of rest and religious observances among the Jews and certain Christian sects, Ex. xx. 8–11; the first day of the week, Sunday, similarly observed by most Christians and in commemoration of the resurrection of Christ; the sabbatical year of the ancient Jews, Lev. xxv. 4; a time or period of rest or quiet; (*usu. l.c.*) sabbat.—*a.* Pertaining to or characteristic of the Sabbath; as, *Sabbath*

morning, a *Sabbath* stillness.—**Sab·bat·ic, Sab·bat·i·cal,** sa·bat′ik, *a.* Relating to or characteristic of the Sabbath; (*l.c.*) providing time for rest and regeneration; sabbatical year.—**Sab·bat·i·cal·ly,** *adv.*

sab·bat·i·cal year, *n.* A year's leave, with remuneration, granted by some educational institutions every seven years to teachers and professors for study, travel, or research. *Chiefly Bib.* in ancient Judea, the period, occurring every seven years, during which, as decreed by Mosaic law, the fields were to lie fallow and all agricultural toil to cease; Lev. xxv.

sa·ber, *Brit.* **sa·bre,** sā′bêr, *n.* [Fr. *sabre,* < D., Dan., and Sw. *sabel,* G. *sabel,* a saber; ultimate origin unknown.] A heavy cavalry sword having a broad, thick-backed, and slightly curved blade; *fencing,* a type of light sword, used for slashing with either edge or thrusting with the blunt point.—*v.t.—sabered, sabering, Brit. sabred, sabring.* To strike, cut, or kill with a saber.

sa·ber rat·tling, *n.* A verbal threat of war or an aggressive show of military power intended to impress a nation's adversaries.

sa·ber-toothed, sā′bêr·tŏtht″, *a.* Having greatly elongated canine teeth extending from the upper jaw, sometimes to below the margin of the lower jaw.

sa·ber-toothed ti·ger, *n.* Any of the extinct large, catlike carnivores, ranging throughout the western hemisphere from the Oligocene through the Pleistocene epochs, that had excessively long upper canine teeth of curved, saberlike appearance.

sa·bin, sā′bin, *n. Phys.* a measurement of sound absorption, one unit of which is equal to one square foot of perfect absorption, as that afforded by an open window which is one square foot.

Sa·bine, sā′bīn, *a.* [L. *Sabinus.*] Pertaining or belonging to an ancient people of central Italy who lived chiefly in the Apennines to the northeast of Rome and who were subjugated by the Romans about 290 B.C.; pertaining to the language of the Sabines.—*n.* One of the Sabine people; the language they spoke.

sa·ble, sā′bl, *n.* [O.Fr. *sable,* < Pol. *sabol,* Russ. *sobol,* a Slavonic word.] A carnivorous mammal, *Martes zibellina,* allied to the marten, found chiefly in the northern regions of Asia, and hunted for its dark, lustrous fur; the fur of the sable. *Pl.* garments, esp. a coat, made of this fur. The color black or dark brown; the color of mourning.—*a.* Extremely dark; black; consisting of the fur from the sable.

sa·ble·fish, sā′bl·fish″, *n. pl.* **sa·ble·fish, sa·ble·fish·es.** A large, edible, blackish fish, *Anoplopoma fimbria,* of the N. Pacific. Also *beshow,* **black·cod.**

sab·ot, sab′ō, *Fr.* sa·bō′, *n. pl.* **sab·ots,** sab′ōz, *Fr.* sa·bō′. [Fr. Origin unknown.] A wooden shoe worn by the peasantry in France and Belgium; a shoe with a wooden sole and leather upper. *Artillery,* a support or container in which a projectile is centered to permit firing the projectile in a gun of larger caliber than the projectile; an aluminum case fitting around the steel core of certain armor-piercing ammunition.

sab·o·tage, sab′o·täzh″, sab″o·täzh′, *n.* [Fr., the making of sabots, the doing of work quickly and badly, the intentional garbling of work by a printer, sabotage, < *sabot.*] Malicious injury or destruction to work, tools, or machinery, or any underhanded interference with production or business, as caused by discontented employees or by agents of the enemy during a time of war; any malicious attacking or undermining.—*v.t.—sabotaged, sabotaging.* To injure, destroy, or attack by sabotage.

sab·o·teur, sab″o·tûr′, *n.* [Fr.] One who commits or practices sabotage.

sa·bra, sä′bra, sä′brä, *n.* A native of Israel.

sa·bre·tache, sä′bêr·tash″, sab′êr·tash″, *n.* [Fr. *sabretache*, < G. *säbeltasche*, 'saber pocket.'] A leather case suspended by long straps from the sword belt of a cavalryman.

sab·u·lous, sab′ū·lus, *a.* [L. *sabulosus*, < *sabulum*, sand.] Sandy; gritty.

sac, sak, *n.* [L. *saccus*, a bag.] A bag or cyst in an animal or plant, often a receptacle for a liquid; as, the lachrymal *sac*.—**sac·like**, *a.*

sac·a·ton, sak′a·tŏn′, *n.* A perennial grass, *Sporobolus wrightii*, used in southwestern U.S. and Mexico for hay.

sac·cate, sak′it, sak′āt, *a. Biol.* furnished with or having the form of a sac or pouch.

sac·cha·rate, sak′a·rāt″, *n.* [< *saccharic*.] *Chem.* A salt of any saccharic acid; a compound of sucrose and metallic acid.

sac·char·ic, sa·kar′ik, *a.* [L. *saccharum*, sugar, < Gr. *sakchar, sakcharon*, sugar, a word of oriental origin.] Pertaining to or obtained from saccharin or compounds containing saccharin; relating to or from saccharic acid.

sac·char·ic ac·id, *n. Chem.* a white, crystalline, water-soluble acid, $C_6H_{10}O_8$, made by oxidizing glucose with nitric acid.

sac·cha·ride, sak′a·rīd″, sak′a·rid, *n.* [M.L. *saccharum*, sugar.] *Chem.* A carbohydrate compound containing sugar; a simple sugar or a combination of sugars.

sac·char·i·fy, sa·kar′i·fī″, sak′êr·i·fī″, *v.t.*—saccharified, saccharifying. [Fr. *saccharifier*.] To convert into sugar.—**sac·char·i·fi·ca·tion**, sak″i·fi·kā′shan, *n.*

sac·cha·rim·e·ter, sak″a·rim′i·têr, *n.* [M.L. *saccharum*, sugar.] An optical instrument for determining the strength of sugar solutions by measuring the amount of rotation of a plane of polarized light after it passes through a sugar solution.

sac·cha·rin, sak′a·rin, *n. Chem.* a white crystalline substance, $C_6H_4COSO_2NH$, synthetically produced, which in dilute form is 300 to 500 times as sweet as cane sugar and is used primarily as a calorie-free sugar substitute.

sac·cha·rine, sak′a·rin, sak′a·rīn″, *a.* [M.L. *sacchrum*, L. *saccharon*, or Gr. *sácchar, sáccharon*, sugar, from the same ult. source as E. sugar.] Pertaining to, of the nature of, containing, or resembling sugar; sugary; *fig.* of a sugary sweetness; as, his *saccharine* flattery.—*n.* Saccharine matter; saccharin.—**sac·cha·rine·ly**, *adv.*—**sac·cha·rin·i·ty**, sak″a·rin′i·tē, *n.*

sac·cha·roid, sak′a·roid″, *a. Geol.* having a texture resembling that of loaf sugar. Also **sac·cha·roi·dal**.

sac·cha·rom·e·ter, sak″a·rom′i·têr, *n Chem.* an instrument for determining the quantity of sugar in any solution.

sac·cha·ro·my·cete, sak″a·rō·mī′sēt, *n.* Any fungus of the genus *Saccharomyces*, of the yeast family, and used in the fermentation of sugar.—**sac·cha·ro·my·ce·tic**, sak″a·rō·mī·sē′tik, *a.*

sac·cha·rose, sak′a·rōs″, *n. Chem.* sucrose.

sac·cu·late, sak′ū·lāt″, *a.* Having saccules or saclike expansions. Also **sac·cu·lat·ed**.—**sac·cu·la·tion**, sak″ū·lā′shan, *n.*

sac·cule, sak′ūl, *n.* [L. *sacculus*, dim. of *saccus*, bag, E. *sac, sack*.] A little sac; *anat.* the smaller of two sacs in the membranous labyrinth of the inner ear.

sac·er·do·tal, sas″êr·dōt′al, *a.* [L. *sacerdotalis*, < *sacerdos* (*sacerdot-*), priest, < *sacer*, sacred, and *-dos*, connected with *dare*, give.] Of or pertaining to priests or the priesthood; priestly.—**sac·er·do·tal·ism**, *n.* The sacerdotal system; the spirit or methods of the priesthood.—**sac·er·do·tal·ist**, *n.*—**sac·er·do·tal·ly**, *adv.*

sac fun·gus, *n.* pl. **sac fun·gi, sac fun·gus·es**. *Bot.* the common name of a class of fungi, *Ascomycetes*, characterized by a sac, the ascus, in which the spores are produced.

sa·chem, sä′chem, *n.* [Algonquian: cf. *sagamore*.] Among some tribes of American Indians, the chief; *politics*, one of a body of high officials in the Tammany Society of New York City.—**sa·chem·ic**, sä·chem′ik, sä′che·mik, *a.*—**sa·chem·ship**, *n.*

sa·chet, sa·shā′, *Brit.* sash′ā, *n.* [Fr.] A small bag or case which contains a perfumed powder; the sachet powder itself.

sack, sak, *n.* [O.E. *sacc* = O.Fr. Fr. *sac* = It. *sacco*, < L. *saccus*, < Gr. *sáckos*, bag, sack, sackcloth; of Semitic origin.] A large bag of some strong, woven material, as for grain, flour, potatoes, or coal; the amount which a sack will hold, constituting a varying unit of measure; any bag; as, a *sack* of candy. A kind of loose gown worn by women in the 17th and 18th centuries; a loose-fitting coat or jacket, esp. for women and children; also *sacque*. *Slang*, a bed; dismissal or discharge, as from employment; as, to get the *sack* or to give someone the *sack*. *Baseball*, a base.—*v.t.* To put into a sack or sacks; *slang*, to dismiss or discharge, as from employment.—**hit the sack**, *slang*, to go to sleep or to bed.—**sack out**, *slang*. To fall asleep; to go to bed.

sack, sak, *v.t.* [Fr. *sac*, < It. *sacco*, sack, pillage; origin uncertain.] To pillage or loot after capture, as a city; plunder.—*n.* The pillaging of a captured place.—**sack·er**, *n.*

sack, sak, *n.* [Fr. *sec*, < L. *siccus*, dry.] Any of several different types of dry, light-colored wines which were formerly imported into England in great quantities from Spain and southern Europe, esp. in the 16th and 17th centuries.

sack·but, sak′but″, *n.* [Fr. *saquebute*, < Sp. *sacabuche*, a kind of trumpet, < *sacar*, to draw, and *buche*, the stomach.] A musical instrument, medieval precursor of the trombone. *Bib.* a musical stringed instrument. Dan. iii.5.

sack·cloth, sak′klạth″, sak′kloth″, *n.* Coarse cloth of which sacks are made; coarse cloth worn in mourning or for penance.—**in sack·cloth and ash·es**, in a condition of remorse, sorrow, or repentance; *Bib.* the wearing of sackcloth garments and the scattering of ashes upon a person's head to express penitence, sorrow, or humility.

sack coat, *n.* A man's loose-fitting jacket or short coat having no waist seam and a straight back.

sack·ful, sak′fụl, *n.* pl. **sack·fuls**. The amount or quantity a sack will hold.

sack·ing, sak′ing, *n.* A coarse woven fabric, as of hemp or flax, used to make sacks.

sack race, *n.* A race in which the legs of each contestant are enclosed in a sack, so that the racers can progress only by jumping.—**sack rac·er**, *n.*—**sack rac·ing**, *n.*

sacque, sak, *n.* [A form of *sack*, Fr. *sac*, a bag.] A loose-fitting dress or coat. See *sack*.

sa·cral, sä′kral, *a.* [L. *sacra*, sacred things or rites, pl. of *sacrum*, prop. neut. of *sacer*, sacred.] Pertaining to sacred rites or observances.

sac·ra·ment, sak′ra·ment, *n.* [O.Fr. Fr. *sacrement*, < L. *sacramentum*, oath, solemn engagement, L.L. *sacrament*, mystery, < L. *sacrare*, make sacred.] Any of certain solemn religious ceremonies of the Christian church instituted by Christ and regarded as outward and visible signs of inward and spiritual grace: in the Roman Catholic and Orthodox churches, these are baptism, Eucharist, confirmation, matrimony, holy orders, penance, and extreme unction, and, in most Protestant churches, the Lord's Supper and baptism. (*Often cap.*) the consecrated elements of the Eucharist, esp. the bread; also *Blessed Sacrament*; the Eucharist, or Lord's Supper. Something regarded as possessing a sacred character or a mysterious significance; a sign, token, or symbol.

sac·ra·men·tal, sak″ra·men′tal, *a.* Of, pertaining to, or of the nature of a sacrament, esp. the sacrament of the Eucharist; peculiarly sacred, as an obligation; pertaining to or of the nature of an outward sign or symbol.—*n.* A rite or observance similar to but not included among the recognized sacraments of the church, as the sign of the cross or the use of holy water.—**sac·ra·men·tal·ly**, *adv.*

sac·ra·men·tal·ism, sak″ra·men′ta·liz·um, *n.* Any doctrine or belief which stresses the importance of sacramental ceremonies; belief in the effectiveness of the sacraments for the soul's salvation.—**sac·ra·men·tal·ist**, sak″ra·men′ta·list, *n.*

Sac·ra·men·tar·i·an, sak″ra·men·târ′ē·an, *n.* One who maintains that the bread and wine of the Eucharist can be said to be the body and blood of Christ only in a symbolical or metaphorical sense; (*l.c.*) a sacramentalist.—*a.* Pertaining to the sacraments or to Sacramentarians.—**sac·ra·men·tar·i·an·ism**, *n.*

sa·cred, sä′krid, *a.* [Orig. pp. of *sacre*.] Appropriated or dedicated to a deity or to some religious purpose; consecrated; entitled to veneration or religious respect by association with divinity or divine things; hallowed; holy; pertaining to or connected with religion; as, *sacred* music: opposed to *profane* and *secular*; reverently dedicated to some person or object; as, a monument *sacred* to the memory of a person; regarded with reverence similar to that due to holy things; as, the *sacred* memory of a dead hero; secured against violation or infringement, by reverence, sense of right, or the like; as, a *sacred* oath; properly immune from violence or interference, as a person or his office.—**sa·cred·ly**, *adv.*—**sa·cred·ness**, *n.*

sa·cred cow, *n. Colloq.* any person, group, or organization considered to be above criticism or censure.

sac·ri·fice, sak′ri·fīs″, *n.* [O.Fr. Fr. *sacrifice*, < L. *sacrificium*, < *sacer*, (*sacr-*), sacred, and *facere*, make.] The offering of an animal or a possession to a deity in propitiation or homage; that which is so offered; the surrender or destruction of something prized or desirable for the sake of something considered as having a higher or more pressing claim; the thing so surrendered or devoted; a loss of profit incurred in selling something below its value.—*v.t.*—sacrificed, sacrificing. To make a sacrifice or offering of; to surrender or give up, or permit injury or disadvantage to, for the sake of something else; to dispose of regardless of profit.—*v.i.* To offer or make a sacrifice.—**sac·ri·fic·er**, *n.*

sac·ri·fice fly, *n. Baseball*, a deep fly ball enabling a runner already on base to advance or score after the ball is caught by an outfielder.

sac·ri·fice hit, *n. Baseball*, an intentional bunt or ground ball which advances a runner one base while the batter is retired at first base. Also **sac·ri·fice bunt**.

sac·ri·fi·cial, sak″ri·fish′al, *a.* Pertaining to sacrifice; consisting in sacrifice.—**sac·ri·fi·cial·ly**, *adv.*

sac·ri·lege, sac′ri·lij, *n.* [O.Fr. *sacrilege* (Fr. *sacrilège*), < L. *sacrilegium*, < *sacrilegus*, stealing sacred things, sacrilegious, < *sacer* (*sacr-*), sacred, and *legere*, gather.] The violation or profanation of anything sacred or held sacred; an instance of this; the stealing of anything consecrated to the service of God.

sac·ri·le·gious, sak″ri·lij′us, sak″ri·lē′jus, *a.* Guilty of or involving sacrilege; impious.—**sac·ri·le·gious·ly**, *adv.*—**sac·ri·le·gious·ness**, *n.*

sac·ris·tan, sak′ri·stan, n. [L.L. *sacristanus*. *Sexton* is a contr. of this word.] One who has charge of the sacristy and its contents. Also **sac·rist.**

sac·ris·ty, sak′ri·stē, n. pl. **sac·ris·ties.** [Fr. *sacristie*.] A room in a church where sacred vessels and clerical vestments are stored; the vestry.

sac·ro·il·i·ac, sak″rō·il′ē·ak, sā″krō·il′ē·ak″, a. Anat. Pertaining to the sacrum and the ilium; of or relating to the joint between these two bones and the joining ligaments.—n.

sac·ro·sanct, sak′rō·sangkt″, a. [L. *sacrosanctus—sacer,* sacred, *sanctus,* holy.] Exceptionally sacred and inviolable; holy and venerable.—**sac·ro·sanc·ti·ty, sac·ro·sanct·ness,** n.

sac·ro·sci·at·ic, sak″rō·sī·at′ik, sā″krō·sī·at′ik, a. [< *sacrum* and *sciatic*.] Anat. pertaining jointly to the sacrum and ischium.

sac·rum, sak′rum, sā′krum, n. pl. **sac·ra,** sak′ra, sā′kra. [N.L., for L.L. *os sacrum,* 'sacred bone': *sacrum,* neut. of L. *sacer,* sacred; the name being said to refer to the offering of this part in sacrifice.] Anat. a bone resulting from the fusion of two or more vertebrae between the lumbar and the coccygeal regions: in man forming the posterior wall of the pelvis.—**sa·cral,** sā′kral, a.

sad, sad, a.—**sadder, saddest.** [O.E. *saed,* satisfied, sated, weary, sick; Icel. *saddr,* sated, full; Goth. *saths,* satiated, full; cogn. with L. *satur,* full, *satis,* enough.] Sorrowful; mournful; affected with grief; gloomy; causing sorrow; expressing sorrow; bad or sorry; as, a *sad* attempt at success.—**sad·ly,** adv.—**sad·ness,** sad′nis, n.

sad·den, sad′en, v.t. To make sad or sorrowful.—v.i. To become sad or sorrowful.

sad·dle, sad′l, n. [O.E. *sadol* = D. *zadel* = G. *sattel* = Icel. *sodhull,* saddle; perh. from the root of E. *sit*.] A contrivance secured on the back of a horse or other animal to serve as a seat for a rider; a similar seat, as on a bicycle; a part of a harness which is laid across the back of the animal and girded under the belly, and to which the terrets are attached and the checkrein is secured; something resembling a saddle in shape or position; a ridge connecting two higher elevations; the bearing resting on the journal of the axle of a railroad car wheel; a block with a hollowed top to sustain a round object which is being worked upon; of mutton, venison, or the like, a cut including part of the backbone and both loins; of poultry, the posterior part of the back.—v.t.—**saddled, saddling.** To put a saddle upon, as a horse; to load or charge as with a burden, as: They *saddled* him with responsibilities. To impose as a burden.—v.i. To saddle a horse or get into the saddle, often followed by *up.*

sad·dle-backed, sad′l·bakt″, a. Having the back or upper surface concavely curved like a saddle, as a sway-backed horse; having a saddlelike marking on the back, as certain birds.

sad·dle·bag, sad′l·bag″, n. One of a pair of bags hanging from a saddle or laid over the back of an animal, bicycle, or motorcycle.

sad·dle·bow, sad′l·bō″, n. The upper front part of a saddle, formed of two curved pieces united in an arch; a pommel.

sad·dle·cloth, sad′l·klạth″, sad′l·kloth″, n. A cloth placed between a horse's back and the saddle.

sad·dle horse, n. A horse used or trained esp. for riding with a saddle; American saddle horse.

sad·dle leath·er, n. Vegetable-tanned cattle hide used in making saddlery; skins from other animals that are treated to resemble vegetable-tanned cattle leather.

sad·dler, sad′lėr, n. One whose occupation is to make, repair, or sell saddles and other equipment for horses.

sad·dle roof, n. A simple pitched roof having a gable on both ends and a ridge between them.

sad·dler·y, sad′le·rē, n. pl. **sad·dler·ies.** A saddle and its parts; the shop and manufactured products of a saddler; the trade or craft of a saddler.

sad·dle shoe, n. An oxford shoe, usu. white, which has a broad, dark band over the instep.

sad·dle soap, n. A mild castile soap mixed with neat's-foot oil, used to clean and condition leather.

sad·dle sore, n. A sore which develops on a horse's back from the rubbing of an improperly fitted saddle; an irritation on the rider caused by the chafing of a saddle.—**sad·dle·sore,** sad′l·sōr″, sad′l·sạr″, a. Stiff or sore from, or as if from, riding in a saddle.

sad·dle·tree, sad′l·trē″, n. The wooden frame of a saddle.

Sad·du·cee, saj′a·sē″, sad′ya·sē, n. [Gr. *saddoukaios,* Heb. *tsadûkim,* 'the righteous ones,' 'the just.'] A member of the Jewish sect that flourished from I B.C. through I A.D., composed primarily of priests and aristocracy who held to a literal interpretation of the Mosaic Law, rejecting such oral traditions as resurrection, retribution in a life after death, and angels.—**Sad·du·ce·an,** a.—**Sad·du·cee·ism,** n.

sa·dhu, sä′dö, n. Hinduism. A religious ascetic; a monk.

sad·i·ron, sad′ī″ėrn, n. A solid flatiron, pointed at each end, with a handle that can be removed.

sad·ism, sad′iz·um, sā′diz·um, n. [From Comte D. A. F. de *Sade,* 1740–1814, Fr. writer, infamous for the licentiousness of his life and writings.] Psychoanal. The pathological derivation of sexual pleasure from inflicting physical or mental pain upon another; the tendency to take pleasure in cruelty. Compare *masochism.*—**sad·ist,** n., a.—**sa·dis·tic,** sa·dis′tik, sa·dis′tik, sā·dis′tik, a.—**sa·dis·ti·cal·ly,** adv.

sad·o·mas·o·chism, sad″ō·mas′o·kiz″um, sad″ō·maz′o·kiz″um, sā″dō·mas′o·kiz″um, sā″dō·maz′o·kiz″um, n. A derivation of pleasure from inflicting pain upon oneself and another.—**sad·o·mas·o·chist,** n.—**sad·o·mas·o·chis·tic,** a.

sad sack, n. Slang. a bumbling, ineffectual person.

sa·fa·ri, sa·fär′ē, n. pl. **sa·fa·ris.** [Ar. *safarī.*] A journey or expedition, esp. in eastern Africa, as for hunting; a body of persons and provisions employed on such an expedition.

safe, sāf, a.—**safer, safest.** [O.E. *sauf,* < Fr. *sauf,* safe, < L. *salvus,* safe (whence also *salvation*).] Free from or not liable to danger; having escaped hurt, injury, or damage; not exposing to harm; trustworthy; dependable; placed beyond the power of doing harm; involving no danger, risk, or error; without danger of controversy; as, a *safe* judgment; *baseball,* having reached base successfully.—**safe·ly,** adv.—**safe·ness,** n.

safe, sāf, n. A receptacle, usu. a metal box or vault, for keeping valuables secure from damage or theft; any storage area used for protecting perishable items, as meats.

safe-con·duct, sāf′kon′dukt, n. A document serving as a pass or warrant of security used when traveling in a foreign or hostile country, esp. during war; such a privilege; a convoy or guard providing protection for safe passage.—**safe·con·duct,** v.t.

safe-crack·er, sāf′krak″ėr, n. A person who forces open safes with the intent of theft. Also **safe·break·er.**—**safe·crack·ing,** n.

safe-de·pos·it, sāf′di·poz″it, a. Providing safekeeping for valuables; as, *safe-deposit* vaults.—n. A room or vault where valuables may be stored in safety. Also **safe·ty-de·pos·it.**

safe-de·pos·it box, n. A box, drawer, or similar fireproof container in which to store valuables, usu. found in banks and safe-deposit companies. Also **safe·ty-de·pos·it box.**

safe·guard, n. One who or that which defends or protects; a defense; protection; a convoy or guard; a protective contrivance; a warrant of protection to a traveler.—v.t. To guard; to protect; to defend.

safe·keep·ing, sāf′kē′ping, n. The act of keeping in safety; a state of safety; protection.

safe·light, sāf′līt″, n. Photog. a filtered light or a red lamp used in darkrooms that allows some vision while screening out rays harmful to film.

safe·ty, sāf′tē, n. pl. **safe·ties.** The state or quality of being safe; freedom from danger or injury; the state or quality of not causing danger; a device for the prevention of accidents; as, a *safety* on a gun; *football,* a play that results in two points for the defensive team when an offensive team player downs the ball in back of his own goal line: distinguished from *touchback*; *baseball,* any base hit.—a.

safe·ty belt, n. A life belt. A strap for fastening a person to a seat or other fixed object to prevent injury; seat belt.

safe·ty glass, n. Glass panes fused with a middle protective agent such as plastic or wire to prevent its shattering on impact.

safe·ty lamp, n. A lamp for lighting coal mines, having the flame enveloped in a cylinder of wire gauze to prevent ignition of any inflammable gas.

safe·ty match, n. A match which will light only when rubbed on a specially prepared friction substance.

safe·ty pin, n. A pin bent back on itself to form a spring and having a guard to cover the point.

safe·ty ra·zor, n. A razor provided with one or more guards to prevent its cutting the skin.

safe·ty valve, n. A valve, as in a steam boiler, which opens automatically under abnormal pressure and allows excess steam or fluid to escape; any outlet for the release of excess emotion, energy, or anxiety.

safe·ty zone, n. A marked section usu. in the middle of a thoroughfare, reserved for the use of pedestrians to ensure their safety from motorized vehicles. Also **safe·ty is·land.**

saf·flow·er, saf′lou″ėr, n. [D. *saffloer,* < O.Fr. *safleur, safour,* appar. ult. < Ar. *'uçfur,* safflower: cf. *saffron.*] A thistlelike composite herb, *Carthamus tinctorius,* a native of the Old World, bearing large orange-red flower heads and seeds abundant with oil; the dried florets, used medicinally or as a red dyestuff.

saf·fron, saf′ron, n. [O.Fr. *safran,* ult. < Ar. *za'farān,* saffron.] A crocus, *Crocus sativus,* with handsome purple flowers; an orange-colored product consisting of the dried ştigmas of this crocus, used to color and flavor confectionery and other foods. A color similar to that of plant stigmas, an orange-yellow; also **saf·fron yel·low.**—a. Orange-yellow; as, a *saffron* moon.

saf·ra·nine, saf′ra·nēn″, saf′ra·nin, n. Chem. any of the synthetic, usu. red to violet dyes formed from phenazine, used in dying textiles and in microscopy. Also **saf·ra·nin,** saf′ra·nin.

saf·role, saf·rol, saf′rōl, n. Chem. a poisonous, faintly yellow to clear liquid, $C_3H_5C_6H_3O_2CH_2$, found in the oils of sassafras, camphorwood, and similar oils, used in perfume, soap, flavoring, medicine, and insecticides.

sag, *v.i.*—**sagged, sagging.** [Allied to L.G. *sacken,* D. *zakken,* to sink; also perh. to *sink.*] To incline or hang away owing to insufficiently supported weight; to sink or curve in the middle; to hang unevenly; to droop; to yield under the pressure of difficulties; to lose vigor or firmness; to fall in value. *Naut.* to incline to the leeward; to drift.—*v.t.* To cause to bend or give way.—*n.* The state or act of sagging; a depressed or sagging area; the degree to which something sags; a price drop or financial decline; *naut.* a drift or leeward inclination.

sa·ga, sä´ga, *n.* [Icel. *saga,* story, tale, legend, or history.] A medieval Icelandic or Norse prose narrative of achievements and events in the history of a personage or family; any narrative or legend of heroic exploits.

sa·ga·cious, sa·gā´shus, *a.* [L. *sagax, sagacis,* < *sagio,* to perceive keenly, < a root signifying to be sharp, Gr. *sagaris,* a battle-ax, Skt. *saghnomi,* to kill.] Wise; quick in apprehension; acute in discernment; shrewd; showing intelligence resembling that of man; as, a *sagacious* animal.—**sa·ga·cious·ly,** *adv.*—**sa·ga·cious·ness,** *n.*

sa·gac·i·ty, sa·gas´i·tē, *n.* [L. *sagacitas.*] The quality of being sagacious; quickness of discernment; soundness of judgment.

sag·a·more, sag´a·mōr″, sag´a·mąr″, *n.* A secondary chief among Algonquin Indian tribes of the New England area.

sa·ga nov·el, *n.* Roman-fleuve.

sage, sāj, *a.*—**sager, sagest.** [Fr. *sage,* < L. *sapius,* wise, < *sapio,* to be wise (whence *sapient*).] Wise; sagacious; judicious; proceeding from wisdom.—*n.* An extremely wise man; a man esteemed for his years, sound judgment, and prudence.—**sage·ly,** *adv.* In a sage manner; wisely.—**sage·ness,** *n.* Sagacity.

sage, sāj, *n.* [O.Fr. Fr. *sauge,* < L. *salvia,* sage, < *salvus,* safe, well: cf. *salvia.*] A shrubby menthaceous perennial, *Salvia officinalis,* whose grayish-green leaves are used in medicine and for seasoning; the leaves themselves; any species of the genus *Salvia,* as *S. splendens;* sagebrush.

sage·brush, sāj´brush″, *n.* Any sagelike bushy plants of the genus *Artemisia,* in the composite family common on the dry plains of the western U.S. Also *sage.*

sag·ger, sag´ẽr, *n.* [Prov. E. *saggara, saggar,* contr. for *safeguard.*] The box or case of fire clay in which fine stoneware is enclosed while being baked in the kiln; the clay used in making this case.—*v.t.* To place in a sagger. Also **sag·gar, seg·gar.**

sag·it·tal, saj´i·tal, *a.* [L. *sagittalis,* < *sagitta,* an arrow.] Pertaining to or resembling an arrow; *anat.* applied to the suture which unites the parietal bones of the skull; a plane which divides an animal body into right and left halves.—**sag·it·tal·ly,** *adv.*

Sag·it·ta·ri·us, saj″i·târ´ē·us, *n.* [L., an archer.] *Astron.* The ninth zodiacal sign which the sun enters November 22nd; the constellation represented by the figure of a centaur in the act of shooting an arrow.

sag·it·tate, saj´i·tāt″, *a. Bot.* shaped like the head of an arrow; as, a *sagittate* leaf. Also **sa·git·ti·form.**

sa·go, sā´gō, *n. pl.* **sa·gos.** [Malay *sāgū.*] A starchy foodstuff derived from the soft interior of the trunk of various palms, used in making puddings; a sago palm.

sa·go palm, *n.* A tree usu. grown in the Far East yielding sago, as certain large palms of the genus *Metroxylon.*

sa·gua·ro, sa·gwä´rō, sa·wä´rō, *n. pl.* **sa·gua·ros.** [Mex. Sp.] A giant southwestern N. American cactus, *Carnegia*

gigantea, with columnar trunk and white flowers, yielding a useful wood, and having a palatable fluid and edible fruit. Also **gi··ant cac·tus, sa·hua·ro,** sa·wä´rō.

sa·hib, sä´ib, sä´ēb, *n.* [Hind., < Ar. *sahib,* lord, master.] Sir; mister, formerly a term of respect used by the natives of India in addressing or speaking of non-Indians.

said, sed, *a.* [Past tense and past participle of *say.*] *Chiefly law,* previously referred to or mentioned; as, the *said* testimony.

sail, sāl, *n. pl.* **sails, sail.** [O.E. *segel, segl,* a sail = Icel. *segl,* G. and Sw. *segel,* Dan. *seil,* D. *zeil;* prob. from an Indo-Eur. root (*sagh*) meaning to check, to resist (the wind).] A piece of cloth, usu. canvas, spread to the wind to cause a boat to move through the water; something similar to that in form and function, as that portion of the arm of a windmill which catches the wind; sails collectively; pl. **sails.** A ship or other vessel; pl. **sail.** A passage in a vessel, esp. in a sailing vessel; pl. **sails.**—*v.i.* To be conveyed in a vessel on water; to travel across the water by the action of wind or motor; to begin a voyage; to operate a sailboat; to glide through the air; to pass smoothly along in an easy, dignified manner. *Colloq.* to pass quickly; to hurry into action, used with *in.*—*v.t.* To pass over, as water, by means of sails; to navigate, as a ship.—**make sail,** to put up a sail or sails; to begin a journey on water.—**sail in·to,** to hurry into action; to attack; to criticize.—**set sail,** to embark upon a voyage.—**un·der sail,** having the sails spread; sailing.—**sail·a·ble,** *a.*

sail·boat, sāl´bōt″, *n.* A boat propelled by or fitted for a sail or sails.

sail·cloth, sāl´kląth″, sāl´kloth″, *n.* Canvas, cotton, or synthetic materials of strong weave used in making sails, tents, and clothing.

sail·er, sä´lẽr, *n.* A ship or vessel, esp. in reference to its speed or manner of sailing; as, a fast *sailer;* a vessel propelled by sails.

sail·fish, sāl´fish″, *n. pl.* **sail·fish, sail··fish·es.** Any of the large marine fishes constituting the genus *Istiophorus,* characterized by a very large dorsal fin likened to a sail, and related to the swordfish.

sail·ing, sā´ling, *n.* The act of one who or that which sails; the methods and art of navigation, as the determination of distance traveled, direction, and the like; the departure or time of departure of a ship.

sail·or, sä´lẽr, *n.* A seaman; a mariner; a member of a ship's crew; a rigid straw hat with a flat, low crown and a circular brim.

sail·or's-choice, sä´lẽrz-chois, *n. pl.* **sail··or's-choice.** Any of several fishes common off the U.S. Atlantic coast, esp. the pigfish, *Orthopristis chrysopterus,* and the pinfish, *Lagodon rhomboides;* a grunt, *Haemulon parra,* of the S. Atlantic.

sail·plane, sāl´plān″, *n.* A glider which is light enough to rise on an upward air movement or current.—*v.i.*—**sailplaned, sailplaning.**

sain, sān, *v.t.* [O.E. *segnian,* < L. *signare,* mark, E. *sign, v.*] *Brit. dial., archaic.* To make the sign of the cross on, as to protect against evil influences; to protect by prayer; to bless.

sain·foin, saint·foin, sān´foin, *n.* [Fr. *sainfoin,* also formerly *saintfoin,* appar. < *saint,* holy, or perh. *sain,* wholesome (< L. *sanus,* E. *sane*), and *foin,* < L. *faenum,* hay.] A European leguminous herb, *Onobrychis viciaefolia,* cultivated as a forage plant.

saint, sānt, *n.* [O.Fr., < L. *sanctus,* sacred, holy, pp. of *sancio,* to render sacred.] A person of exceptional virtue who has died and, in certain Christian Churches, been officially recognized as having reached a glorified state in heaven; one of the blessed in heaven; an angel; the self-assigned name

of members of certain religions; *N.T.* any adherent of Christ. An uncommonly patient, benevolent, unselfish person; a predecessor, founder, or patron of a movement of some type.—*v.t.* To enroll among the saints; to canonize.—*a.* Holy.—**saint··less,** *a.*

Saint An·drew's Cross, *n.* A cross shaped like the letter X.

Saint An·tho·ny's Cross, *n.* A cross shaped like the letter T.

Saint An·tho·ny's fire, *n. Pathol.* a gangrenous or inflamed skin condition, as erysipelas or ergotism.

Saint Ber·nard, *n.* [Named from the hospice on the pass of the Great St. Bernard in the Swiss Alps.] One of a breed of large dogs with a massive head and long hair, used in the Swiss Alps for rescuing travelers from the snow.

saint·dom, sānt´dom, *n.* The state of being sainted, or of possessing sainthood.

saint·ed, sān´tid, *a.* Canonized; holy; pious; no longer living: often a euphemism for 'dead.'

Saint El·mo's fire, sānt el´mōz fiẽr′, *n.* A flamelike discharge of atmospheric electricity, esp. as observed on masts and spars of ships.

saint·hood, sānt´hụd, *n.* The character, rank, or position of a saint; the collective body of all saints.

Saint-John's-wort, sānt″jonz´wụrt″, *n.* Any of various herbs or shrubs of the genus *Hypericum,* having yellow flowers and translucent dots on the leaves.

saint·ly, sānt´lē, *a.*—**saintlier, saintliest.** Resembling a saint; appropriate to a saint. —**saint·li·ness,** *n.*

Saint Pat·rick's Day, *n.* March 17th, observed by the Irish in honor of St. Patrick, the patron saint of Ireland, who converted the country to Christianity.

saint·ship, sānt´ship, *n.* The character, qualities, or rank of a saint.

Saint Val·en·tine's Day, *n.* February 14th, a day for exchanging valentines and gifts as tokens of affection in commemoration of St. Valentine.

Saint Vi·tus's dance, sānt vītu″siz dans, *n. Pathol.* the disease chorea. Also **Saint Vi·tus' dance, Saint Vi·tus dance.**

sake, sāk, *n.* [O.E. *sacu,* contention, case or suit at law; Icel. *sök,* L.G. *sake,* G. *sache,* suit, affair, thing; akin to O.E. *sacan,* Icel. *saka,* to contend, accuse, etc.] Purpose; benefit; interest; account, used with *for;* as, *for* his *sake, for* the *sake* of the community.

sa·ke, sa·ki, sä´kē, *n.* An alcoholic beverage made in Japan from fermented rice, usu. served hot.

sa·ker, sā´kẽr, *n.* [O.Fr. Fr. *sacre,* prob. < Ar. *çaqr,* hawk.] A large old-world falcon, *Falco sacer,* used in falconry; an old form of cannon.

sal, sal, *n.* Salt: used in combination; as, *sal* soda.

sa·laam, sa·läm′, *n.* [Ar. *salam,* peace.] In the Near East, a salutation or formal greeting of 'good health,' 'happiness,' or 'peace'; a very low bow or obeisance.—*v.t., v.i.* To salute with or perform a salaam.

sal·a·ble, sale·a·ble, sā´la·bl, *a.* Capable of being sold; in demand.—**sal·a·bil·i·ty,** *n.*—**sal·a·bly,** *adv.*

sa·la·cious, sa·lā´shus, *a.* [L. *salax, salacis,* salacious, < *salio,* to leap.] Lustful; lecherous; obscene, as writings or paintings. —**sa·la·cious·ly,** *adv.*—**sa·la·cious·ness,** *n.*

sal·ad, sal´ad, *n.* [Fr. *salade,* It. *salata,* a salted dish, < *salare,* to salt, < L. *sal,* salt.] A combination of vegetables or fruits, usu. fresh, that are cut up, dressed with oil and vinegar, mayonnaise, or other dressing and usu. served chilled as a side dish or entree; a similar dish prepared with fruit, meat, seafood, or cheese, usu. served as a main course.

sal·ad days, *n. pl.* The period of youthful inexperience and imprudence.

sal·ad dress·ing, *n.* A seasoned sauce for a salad, usu. containing a base of mayonnaise or vinegar and oil.

sal·a·man·der, sal′*a*·man″dẽr, *n.* [O.Fr. Fr. *salamandre,* < L. *salamandra,* < Gr. *salamandra.*] Any of various lizardlike, scaleless amphibians with a long tail and short limbs, certain of which are aquatic; a lizard or similar creature formerly supposed to be able to live in fire; an imaginary being inhabiting fire; any of various articles that are used in connection with fire or that withstand fire or great heat without damage, as cooking utensils; a mass of slag or metal left at the bottom of a smelt furnace after the fire is banked.— **sal·a·man·drine,** sal′*a*·man′drin, *a.* Pertaining to, characteristic of, or resembling a salamander; that which is capable of living in or enduring fire or great heat.

sa·la·mi, sa·lä′mē, *n.* A spicy beef, or beef and pork sausage, orig. Italian, usu. seasoned with garlic and pepper.

sal am·mo·ni·ac, *n.* Ammonium chloride.

sal·a·ry, sal′*a*·rē, *n. pl.* **sal·a·ries.** [L. *salarium,* < *sal,* salt orig. 'salt money,' money given to buy salt, as part of the pay of Roman soldiers; hence, stipend, pay.] The recompense or consideration stipulated to be paid periodically to a person for regular work, esp. other than manual labor. —**sal·a·ried,** sal′*a*·rēd, *a.*

sale, sāl, *n.* [Icel. *sal, sala,* sale; bargain; this word stands in same relation to *sell* as *tale* to *tell.*] The act of selling; the amount sold; the exchange or transfer of a commodity for an agreed upon price; an offering of goods at reduced prices; public transfer to the highest bidder; auction; opportunity of selling; demand, as: There is a large *sale* for this item. *Pl.* the collective operation of promoting, selling, and distributing goods or services.—**for sale,** available to purchasers.—**on sale,** offered at a reduced price.—**sales,** *a.*

sal·ep, sal′ep, *n.* [Turk. *sālep,* prob. < Ar. *tha'lab,* fox, in a name meaning 'fox's testicles,' for the orchis.] A starchy drug or foodstuff consisting of the dried tubers of certain orchids.

sal·e·ra·tus, sal″*e*·rā′tus, *n.* [For *salaeratus,* lit. 'aerated salt.'] *Cooking,* sodium bicarbonate that is combined with flour for leavening.

sales·clerk, sālz′klũrk″, *n.* One who sells merchandise in a retail store.

sales·man, sālz′man, *n. pl.* **sales·men.** A man whose occupation is to sell goods or merchandise.—**sales·girl,** sālz′gũrl.—**sales·per·son,** sālz′pũr″son.—**sales·wom·an,** sales·la·dy, sālz′wum″an, sālz′lā″dē, *n.*

sales·man·ship, sālz′man·ship″, *n.* The occupation of a salesman; adeptness at selling; sales technique.

sales pro·mo·tion, *n.* The activities and methods used to sell or create acceptance of a product.

sales re·sis·tance, *n.* The power or ability to resist persuasion and pressure to buy a product or accept an idea.

sales·room, sālz′rōm″, sālz′rum″, *n.* A place in which merchandise is displayed and sold.

sales talk, *n.* An argument designed to persuade others to purchase, to believe, or to do something.

sales tax, *n.* A tax placed upon merchandise, levied by state or federal governments and collected by the seller, usu. calculated as a direct percentage of the sale price.

Sa·li·an, sā′lē·*a*n, sāl′yan, Pertaining to a tribe of the Frankish people who lived in the lower Rhine valley during the 4th century A.D.

Sal·ic, sal′ik, sā′lik, *a.* [O.Fr. Fr. *salique,* < M.L. *Salicus,* < L.L. *Salii.*] Of or pertaining to the Salian Franks; also *Salique.*— **Sal·ic** or **Sa·lique law,** a code of laws of the Salian Franks and other Germanic tribes; a provision in this code excluding females from the inheritance of land; the alleged law of the French monarchy which excluded females from succession to the crown.

sal·i·ca·ceous, sal″i·kā′shus, *a.* [L. *salix* (*salic-*), willow.] Belonging to the *Salicaceae,* a family of trees and shrubs including the willows and poplars.

sal·i·cin, sal′i·sin, *n.* [Fr. *salicine,* < L. *salix* (*salic-*), willow.] *Chem.* a bitter crystalline glucoside, $C_{13}H_{18}O_7$, obtained from the bark of various species of willow and poplar or produced synthetically, used medicinally in the treatment of rheumatism.

sa·lic·y·late, sa·lis′i·lāt″, sa·lis′i·lit, sal″i·sil′āt, sal′i·sil″āt, *n. Chem.* a salt of salicylic acid.

sal·i·cyl·ic ac·id, sal′i·sil″ik as′id, *n. Chem.* a white powder, soluble in water, $C_6H_4OHCOOH$, used as a food preservative and in the preparation of aspirin.

sa·li·ence, sā′lē·*e*ns, sāl′yens, *n.* The quality of being salient; projection; protrusion. Also **sa·li·en·cy.**

sa·li·ent, sā′lē·ent, sāl′yent, *a.* [L. *saliens, salientis,* ppr. of *salio,* to leap.] Conspicuous; prominent; springing; shooting up or out, as a jet of water; projecting outward; as, a *salient* angle.—*n.* A protruding part or angle, esp. a part of a military defense system which projects outward.— **sa·li·ent·ly,** *adv.*—**sa·li·ent·ness,** *n.*

sa·li·en·ti·an, sā″lē·en′shē·*a*n, *a.* Of the amphibian suborder *Salientia,* which includes frogs and toads, tailless and possessing large hind legs for leaping and for swimming.—*n.*

sa·lif·er·ous, sa·lif′ẽr·us, *a.* [L. *sal,* salt, and *fero,* to produce.] Producing or bearing salt in rock strata.

sal·i·fy, sal′i·fī″, *v.t.*—*salified, salifying.* [L. *sal,* salt, and *facio,* to make.] *Chem.* To form into a salt by combining an acid with a base; to infuse with a salt.—**sal·i·fi·ca·tion,** sal″i·fi·kā′shan, *n.*—**sal·i·fi·a·ble,** *a.*

sa·lim·e·ter, sa·lim′i·tẽr, *n.* [L. *sal, salis,* salt, and Gr. *metron,* a measure.] Salinometer.

sa·li·na, sa·lī′na, *n.* [Sp., < L. *sal,* salt.] A salt marsh; a salt pond enclosed from the sea; a saltworks.

sa·line, sā′līn, sā′lēn, *a.* [Fr. *salin,* < L. *sal,* salt.] Consisting of salt; partaking of the qualities of salt; *chem.* relating to or containing chemical salt, as the alkali metals. —*n.* A salt spring, or any place where salt water is collected in the earth. *Chem.* one of the metallic salts; a medicinal solution of salt.—**sa·lin·i·ty,** sa·lin′i·tē, *n.*

sal·i·nom·e·ter, sal″i·nom′i·tẽr, *n.* An instrument for measuring the amount of salt present in any given solution. Also **salimeter.**

Sa·lique, sa·lēk′, sal′ik, sā′lik, *a.* Salic.

Sal·is·bur·y steak, salz′ber″ē stāk″, salz′ba·rē, *n.* [Named for J. H. *Salisbury,* Eng. physician of the 19th century.] Ground beef mixed with other ingredients and formed into patties, served broiled or fried.

sa·li·va, sa·lī′va, *n.* [L., akin to Gr. *sialon,* saliva; and to Gael. and Ir. *seile,* saliva, E. *slime.*] The watery, viscid, slightly acid fluid which is secreted by glands of the mouth, serving to moisten the mouth and food, and containing the enzyme, ptyalin, which starts the digesting of starches. See *spittle.*— **sal·i·var·y,** sal′i·ver″ē, *a.*

sal·i·vate, sal′i·vāt″, *v.i.*—*salivated, salivating.* [L. *salivare.*] To secrete saliva.—*v.t.*

To cause to have an abnormal secretion and discharge of saliva in, as by using mercury.

sal·i·va·tion, sal″i·vā′shan, *n.* The process or action of salivating; an excessive flow of saliva, as caused by mercury.

Salk vac·cine, salk′ vak·sēn″, sȧk, *n.* [From Jonas *Salk,* U.S. physician, born 1914–.] An injected vaccine against poliomyelitis, made from inactivated poliomyelitis virus.

sal·let, sal′it, *n.* A light, rounded, medieval helmet with an extension in back to protect the neck.

sal·low, sal′ō, *n.* A willow, esp. a broadleafed European willow, *Salix caprea,* often used to make charcoal.—**sal·low·y,** *a.*

sal·low, sal′ō, *a.* [O.E. *salu, sealwe,* sallow, dark—Icel. *sōlr,* D. *saluwe,* O.H.G. *salo,* pale.] Of a pale, sickly, grayish-yellow color; as, a *sallow* complexion.—*v.t.* To make sallow.—**sal·low·ish,** *a.*—**sal·low·ness,** *n.*

sal·ly, sal′ē, *n. pl.* **sal·lies.** [Fr. *saillie,* < *saillir,* to leap, < L. *salire,* to leap.] An offensive sortie by besieged troops; a sudden leaping or rushing forth; a brief outburst; an excursion or side trip; a clever remark or flight of wit or fancy.—*v.t.*— *sallied, sallying.* To make a sally; to go forth energetically or vigorously.—*v.i.* To go forth, as besieged troops.—**sal·li·er,** *n.*

sal·ly lunn, Sal·ly Lunn, sal′ē lun′, *n.* A lightly sweetened, hot, buttered tea cake, named for *Sally Lunn,* 18th century English baker.

sal·ly port, *n. Fort.* a gateway affording the passage of troops making a sally.

sal·ma·gun·di, sal″ma·gun′dē, *n.* [Fr. *salmigondis.*] A dish of chopped meat, eggs, anchovies, vegetables, and oil, often used as a salad.

sal·mi, sal′mē, *n.* [Fr. *salmis,* appar. short for *salmigondis,* E. *salmagundi.*] A spiced dish of roasted or partly roasted game or fowl cut up and stewed with wine and other ingredients; a ragout. Also **sal·mis,** sal′mē, *Fr.* säl·mē′.

salm·on, sam′on, *n. pl.* **salm·ons, salm·on.** [O.Fr. Fr. *saumon,* < L. *salmo*(*n-*), perh. < *salire,* leap: cf. *sally.*] A marine and freshwater food fish, *Salmo salar,* of the family *Salmonidae,* with yellowish-pink flesh, common in the northern Atlantic Ocean near the mouths of large rivers, which it ascends in order to spawn; a variety of this species confined to lakes, and called 'landlocked salmon'; any of various other fishes of the same family, esp. any of these fishes belonging to the genus *Oncorhynchus,* which is common in the northern Pacific Ocean and the rivers flowing into it. A pinkish-orange color.—**salm·on·like,** *a.*

salm·on·ber·ry, sam′on·ber″ē, *n. pl.* **salm·on·ber·ries.** The salmon-colored edible fruit, *Rubus spectabilis,* a raspberry with large red or purple flowers, of the Pacific coast of N. America; the plant itself.

sal·mo·nel·la, sal″mo·nel′a, *n. pl.* **sal·mo·nel·lae,** sal″mo·nel′ē. Any of a number of rod-shaped bacteria, genus *Salmonella,* associated with food poisoning, intestinal inflammations, or genital-tract diseases in man and other warm-blooded animals.— **sal·mo·nel·lo·sis,** *n.*

sal·mo·noid, sal′mo·noid, *a.* [L. *salmo*(*n-*).] Resembling a salmon; belonging or pertaining to the suborder *Salmonoidea,* which includes the salmon family.—*n.*

salm·on pink, *n.* A pinkish-orange color, resembling the flesh of salmon.

sal·mon trout, *n.* An anadromous European trout, *Salmo trutta,* belonging to the salmon family and resembling the common salmon; any of various N. American lake trout resembling the common salmon.

sal·ol, sal′ōl, sal′al, sal′ol, *n.* [< *sal*(icyl) and *-ol.*] *Chem.* a white crystalline substance,

$C_{13}H_{10}O_3$, prepared by the interaction of salicyclic acid and phenol: used as an antipyretic and antiseptic. Also **phen·ylsa·lic·y·late.**

sa·lon, sa·lon′, *n.* [Fr., < It. *salone,* aug. of *sala* (= Fr. *salle*), hall; Teut.: cf. *saloon* and *salle.*] A drawing room or reception room for guests, as in a large, elegant apartment or house; an assembly of guests in such a room; a hall or place used for the exhibition of works of art; a stylish shop or place of business; as, a Parisian dress *salon,* a beauty *salon.*

sa·loon, sa·lōn′, *n.* [Fr. *salon,* It. *salone,* < O.H.G. *sal,* a house—O.E. *sael,* a hall.] A bar, taproom, or tavern; a large public room or place used for one particular purpose; as, an exhibiting *saloon,* a dining *saloon;* a large cabin commonly used by all passengers of a ship. *Brit.* a railway car used specifically as a sleeping or dining car; also **sa·loon car.** *Brit.* a secluded area of a bar which is lavishly furnished and reserved for those of high social status.

sa·loop, sa·lōp′, *n. Brit.* a hot drink made from salep or sassafras, milk, and sugar.

sal·pa, sal′pa, *n.* pl. **sal·pas, sal·pae,** sal′pē. [N.L.: cf. L. *salpa,* Gr. *salpē,* kind of seafish.] Any of the free-swimming oceanic tunicates constituting the genus *Salpa,* common in warm regions, and having a transparent, spindle-shaped body.—**sal·pi·form,** *a.*

sal·pin·gec·to·my, sal′′pin·jek′to·mē, *n.* pl. **sal·pin·gec·to·mies.** [See *salpinx,* and *-ectomy.*] *Surg.* The removal of a Fallopian tube.

sal·pinx, sal′pingks, *n.* pl. **sal·pin·ges,** sal·pin′jēz. [N.L., < Gr. *sálpigx (salpigg-),* trumpet.] *Anat.* A Eustachian tube; a Fallopian tube.—**sal·pin·gi·an,** sal·pin′jē·an,—**sal·pin·gi·tis,** sal′′pin·ji′tis, *n. Pathol.* inflammation of a Fallopian tube or Eustachian tube.

sal·si·fy, sal′si·fē, sal′si·fī, *n.* pl. **sal·si·fies.** [Also *salsafy;* Fr. *salsafis,* earlier *sercifi:* cf. It. *sassefrica,* goatsbeard.] A purple-flowered plant, *Tragopogon porrifolius,* whose edible root has an oysterlike flavor and is used as a culinary vegetable. Also *goatsbeard, oyster plant.*

sal so·da, *n.* [M.L. *sal sodae,* salt of soda.] Crystalline sodium carbonate, $Na_2CO_3 \cdot 10 - H_2O,$ used as a cleansing agent.

salt, salt, *n.* [O.E. *sealt* (prop. an a.) = Fris., Dan., Sw., Icel., and Goth. *salt,* D. *zout,* G. *salz;* cogn. W. *halen,* Gael. and Ir. *salann,* L. *sal* (Fr. *sel*), Gr. *hals* (= *sals*), salt.] Sodium chloride, NaCl, a crystalline compound used as a seasoning and preservative; *chem.* a compound produced by the combination of a base, commonly a metallic oxide, with an acid; *pl.* any of several salts used as purgatives. *Colloq.* wit or sarcasm; piquancy; pungency; an old sailor.—*a.* Preserved with salt; abounding in or containing salt; prepared with or tasting of salt; *obs.* lascivious. *Colloq.* sharp; pungent.—*v.t.* To season with or as with salt; to preserve with salt; to supply with salt, as an animal; to add, as a mineral, to a mine to give a false impression of value; to give zest to.—**take with a grain of salt,** with an attitude of doubt or disbelief.— **worth one's salt,** worthy of one's reward or wages.—**salt a·way,** to preserve in salt; *colloq.* to save, as money.—**salt·ness,** *n.*

salt-and-pep·per, salt′an·pep′ér, *a.* Pepper-and-salt.

sal·ta·rel·lo, sal′′ta·rel′ō, sal′′ta·rel′ō, *It.* säl′′tä·Rel′la, *n.* pl. **sal·ta·rel·li,** sal′′ta·rel′ē, sal′′ta·rel′ē, It. säl′′tä·Rel′lē. [It., < L. *saltare.*] A lively Italian dance, including jumps and skips, for one person or a couple; the music for such a dance.

sal·ta·tion, sal·tā′shan, *n.* [L. *saltatio.*] A leaping or jumping; dancing; a sudden movement or change; beating or palpi-

tation; *biol.* a mutation in macroevolution.

sal·ta·to·ri·al, sal′′ta·tōr′ē·al, sal′′ta·tar′-ē·al, *a.* Pertaining to saltation; *zool.* characterized by or adapted for leaping.

sal·ta·to·ry, sal′ta·tōr′′ē, sal′ta·tar′′ē, *a.* [L. *saltatorius.*] Pertaining to saltation; proceeding by abrupt movements.

salt·box, salt′boks′′, *n.* A house commonly found in New England with two stories in front and one story in back, and having a double sloping roof, the longer slope being in the rear.

salt·cel·lar, salt′sel′ér, *n.* [A tautological term, lit. 'a salt dish,' *cellar* being = Fr. *salière,* a saltcellar, < L. *sal,* salt.] A small dish used for holding salt.

salt·ed, salt′id, *a.* Seasoned, cured, or otherwise treated with salt; preserved; *colloq.* experienced, as in some occupation.

salt·er, salt′ér, *n.* One who salts something, as fish or meat; one who sells or manufactures salt; *Brit.* a drysalter.

salt·ern, salt′tèrn, *n.* A saltworks; a building in which salt is made by boiling or evaporation.

salt grass, *n.* Any of various grasses growing in salt meadows or marshes or in alkaline regions.

sal·ti·grade, sal′ti·grād′′, *a.* [L. *saltus,* a leap, *gradi,* walk.] *Zool.* Moving by leaping; belonging to the *Salticidae,* a family of saltatorial spiders.—*n.* A saltatorial spider.

sal·tine, sal·tēn′, *n.* A crisp, thin, salted cracker.

salt·ish, salt′tish, *a.* Somewhat salty.

salt lick, *n.* A place where animals lick an exposed natural salt deposit; a salt spring.

salt marsh, *n.* Coastal land covered with coarse grasses, subject to being overflowed by sea water.

salt mine, *n.* An area where salt is mined. *Fig.* one's place of work when considered as drudgery.

salt out, *v.t. Chem.* to precipitate from solution by adding salt.

salt·pe·ter, *Brit.* **salt·pe·tre,** salt′′pē′tèr, *n.* [For M.E. *salpetre,* < O.Fr. *salpetre,* Fr. *salpêtre* < M.L. *salpetra,* for *sal petræ,* 'salt of rock' (because found as an incrustation on rocks).] Potassium nitrate, $KNO_3.$ Sodium nitrate, $NaNO_3,$ a crystalline compound used as a fertilizer; also *Chile saltpeter.*

salt shak·er, *n.* A salt container with a perforated top through which the salt is sprinkled.

salt-wa·ter, salt′wa′tèr, salt′wot′ér, *a.* Of or pertaining to water impregnated with salt, as that of the ocean and of certain lakes; living in or frequenting salt water, as animals.—**salt wa·ter,** *n.*

salt·works, salt′wurks′′, *n.* pl. **salt·works.** A place where salt is made, esp. commercially.

salt·wort, salt′wurt, *n.* Any of various plants of sea beaches, salt marshes, and alkaline regions, esp. of the genus *Salsola,* as *S. kali,* a bushy plant with prickly leaves used in the production of soda ash; glasswort.

salt·y, salt′tē, *a.*—*saltier, saltiest.* Impregnated with, containing, or tasting of salt; *fig.* pungent or risqué, as literature; *colloq.* an ocean-going vessel on the Great Lakes. —**salt·i·ness,** *n.*

sa·lu·bri·ous, sa·lō′brē·us, *a.* [L. *salubris,* < *salus, salutis,* health, safety, akin to *salvus,* safe.] Conducive to health; as, *salubrious* food; healthful.—**sa·lu·bri·ous·ly,** *adv.*—**sa·lu·bri·ous·ness, sa·lu·bri·ty,** sa·lō′bri·tē, *n.*

sa·lu·ki, sa·lō′kē, *n.* (*Sometimes cap.*) one of an old breed of swift, sharp-eyed, often tricolor hunting dogs having fringed ears, legs, and tail, and bred orig. in the Near East and Egypt.

sal·u·tar·y, sal′ū·ter′′ē, *a.* [Fr. *salutaire,* L.

salutaris, < *salus, salutis,* health.] Promoting health; contributing to some beneficial purpose; wholesome.—**sal·u·tar·i·ly,** *adv.* —**sal·u·tar·i·ness,** *n.*

sal·u·ta·tion, sal′′ū·tā′shan, *n.* [L. *salutatio.*] The act of greeting; any manner of greeting; the direct address of a letter following the heading, as 'Dear Sir.'— **sal·u·ta·tion·al,** *a.*

sa·lu·ta·to·ri·an, sa·lö′′ta·tōr′ē·an, sa·lö′′ta·tar′ē·an, *n.* In some colleges and high schools in the U.S., the second highest-ranking student in the graduating class who delivers the salutatory oration at commencement.

sa·lu·ta·to·ry, sa·lö′ta·tōr′′ē, sa·lö′ta·tar′′ē, *a.* [L. *salutatorius.*] Pertaining to or of the nature of a salutation; as, a *salutatory* oration.—*n.* pl. **sa·lu·ta·to·ries.** An address of welcome usu. delivered at the beginning of commencement ceremonies.

sa·lute, sa·lōt′, *v.t.*—*saluted, saluting.* [L. *saluto,* < L. *salus, salutis,* health.] To address with expressions of kind wishes; to bow or otherwise show homage or courtesy; to greet or hail. *Milit.* to show respect by touching the cap with the right hand; to honor by presenting arms, dipping colors, firing a volley of shots, or the like.—*v.i.* To perform a salute; to greet.—*n.* The act or attitude of saluting; a greeting or salutation. —**sa·lut·er,** *n.*

sal·u·tif·er·ous, sal′′yū·tif′ér·us, *a.* [L. *salutifer,* < *salus (salut-),* well-being, health, and *ferre,* bear.] Referring to that which is beneficial or healthful.

salv·a·ble, sal′va·bl, *a.* That which may be salved or salvaged; savable.—**sal·va·bil·i·ty,** *n.*—**sal·va·bly,** *adv.*

sal·vage, sal′vij, *n.* [Fr. *salvage,* < O.Fr. *salver, sauver,* < L.L. *salvare,* E. *save.*] The act of saving a ship or its cargo from wreck or capture by an enemy; the saving of anything from fire or danger; property so saved; an allowance or compensation given those who voluntarily saved a ship or its cargo.—*v.t.*—*salvaged, salvaging.* To save from shipwreck or fire; make salvage of.— **sal·vage·a·ble,** *a.*—**sal·vag·er,** *n.*

Sal·var·san, sal′vér·san′′, *n.* [G., < L.L. *salvare,* save, and L. *arsenicum,* E. *arsenic.*] *Pharm.* an organic arsenical compound used in the treatment of syphilis and other spirochetal diseases, orig. introduced under the name '606,' the number of the substance in a series of experiments. (Trademark.) Also **ars·phen·a·mine.**

sal·va·tion, sal·vā′shan, *n.* [O.Fr. *salvation,* < L. *salvo, salvatum,* to save, < *salvus,* safe, same root as *salus, salutis,* safety (whence *salute*).] The act of saving; preservation from destruction, danger, or great calamity; the means or cause of saving, as: His agility was his *salvation. Theol.* the redemption of man from the bondage and penalty of sin; redemption.—**sal·va·tion·al,** *a.*—**sal·va·tion·ism,** *n.*

Sal·va·tion Ar·my, *n.* A religious society founded in 1865 by William Booth, organized along quasi-military lines for purposes of evangelism and care of the poor and degraded.—**Sal·va·tion·ist,** sal′′vä′sha·nist, *n.* One who belongs to the Salvation Army; (*often l.c.*) a revivalist or evangelist preacher.—*a.*

salve, sav, säv, *n.* [O.E. *sealf,* a salve, an ointment = D. *zalve,* Dan. *salve,* G. *salbe,* O.H.G. *salba,* salve, allied to Skt. *sarpis,* ghee or clarified butter.] A soothing ointment applied to wounds or sores; a balm; anything that heals, relieves, or placates.— *v.t.*—*salved, salving.* To ease or soothe by, or as if by, applying salve; assuage.

salve, salv, *v.t.*—*salved, salving.* [< L. *salvo salvatum,* to salve, < *salvus,* safe.] To salvage, as a ship or goods.—**sal·vor,** sal′vèr, *n.*

sal·ve, sal′vē, L. säl′wā, *interj.* Hail!

sal·ver, sal′vẽr, *n.* [Sp. *sálva*, a salver, also the previous tasting of a great man's food by a servant to see that it is wholesome, < L. *salvus*, safe.] A tray for the presentation of food, beverage, visiting cards, or letters.

sal·vi·a, sal′vē·a, *n.* [L., sage.] Any of the herbs or small shrubs, genus *Salvia*, of the mint family, as the scarlet sage and common sage.

sal·vo, sal′vō, *n.* pl. **sal·vos, sal·voes.** [It. *salva*, < L. *salve*, hail.] A simultaneous discharge of artillery, firearms, or other weapons, often as a salute; a volley; a round of cheers or applause.

sal·vo, sal′vō, *n.* pl. **sal·vos.** [< L. *salvo jure*, 'the right being intact,' an expression used in reserving rights.] A mental reservation, evasion, or excuse that serves as an appeasement for conscience, honor, or pride; *law*, a saving clause.

sal vo·la·ti·le, sal vō·lat′i·lē″, *n.* An aromatic smelling salt composed of ammonium carbonate in ammonia water or alcohol.

sam·a·ra, sam′ẽr·a, sa·mâr′a, *n.* [L. *samara*, the seed of the elm.] *Bot.* an indehiscent, one-seeded fruit with winglike expansions, as of the ash, elm, or maple. See *key*.

Sa·mar·i·tan, sa·mar′i·tan, *a.* Pertaining to Samaria, formerly a section of Palestine, or to its people, the Samaritans.—*n.* A native or inhabitant of Samaria; the language of Samaria. (Often *l.c.*) A benevolent person; also **good Sa·mar·i·tan.**

sa·mar·i·um, sa·mâr′ē·um, *n. Chem.* a metallic element of the rare-earth series, discovered in samarskite. Sym. Sm, at no. 62, at. wt. 150.35. See Periodic Table of Elements.

sa·mar·skite, sa·mär′skĭt, *n.* [G. *samarskit*; named from *Samarski*, a 19th century Russian.] A black orthorhombic mineral and minor source of uranium, thorium, and rare-earth oxides.

sam·ba, sam′ba, säm′ba, *n.* pl. **sam·bas.** A popular Brazilian dance which originated in Africa; music for a samba.—*v.i.*—*sambaed, sambaing.* To dance the samba.

sam·bar, sam·bur, sam′bẽr, säm′bẽr, *n.* [Hind. *sāmbar.*] A large Asian deer, *Cervus unicolor*, with coarse hair on the throat and three-pointed antlers.

Sam Browne belt, *n.* A sword belt with a shoulder strap, worn by military officers.

same, sām, *a.* [O.E. *same*, Icel. *samr*, Dan. and Sw. *samme*, O.E. and Goth. *sama*; allied to L. *similis* (whence *similar, simulate*), like *simul*, together; Gr. *hama*, together, *homos*, same; Skt. *sama*, like.] Identical; not different or another; as, the *same* man; of the identical kind, species, or degree; exactly similar, though not the specific thing; just mentioned or denoted; monotonous.—*pron.* The same thing or person; the thing just denoted.—*adv.* Similarly; in the same way or manner.—**all the same,** nevertheless; immaterial, as: It's *all the same* to me. —**just the same,** nevertheless; in like manner.

same·ness, sām′nis, *n.* The state of being the same; identity; similarity; want of variety.

sam·iel, sam·yel′, *n.* [Turk.] Simoom.

sam·i·sen, sam′i·sen, *n.* [Jap.; < Chin.] A guitarlike Japanese musical instrument with three strings, played with a plectrum.

sam·ite, sam′ĭt, sā′mĭt, *n.* [O.Fr. *samit*, < L.L. *samitum*, < Fr. *hexamiton—hex*, six, and *mitos*, a thread.] A rich silk fabric, often woven with gold or silver, used in the Middle Ages.

sam·let, sam′lit, *n.* Parr.

Sa·mo·an, sa·mō′an, *a.* Pertaining to Samoa, a group of islands in the Pacific, or to its Polynesian people.—*n.* A native or inhabitant of Samoa; the Polynesian language spoken by Samoans.

sam·o·var, sam′o·vär″, sam″o·vär′, *n.* [Russ.] A tea urn used in Russia in which the water is heated by a tube containing live coals.

Sam·o·yed, Sam·o·yede, sam″o·yed′, *n.* [Russ.] A member of a Ural-Altaic people dwelling in northwestern Siberia and along the northeastern coast of the Soviet Union; the group of Uralic languages of this people; one of a breed of Russian dogs.—*a.* Pertaining to the Ural-Altic people or their language.—**Sam·o·yed·ic,** sam″o·yed′ik, *a.*

samp, samp, *n.* [Algonquian.] Coarsely ground American Indian corn; a porridge made of it.

sam·pan, sam′pan, *n.* [Malay and Javanese.] A small boat, usu. open and propelled by a single oar, used for river traffic in Japan and China.

sam·phire, sam′fī·ẽr″, *n.* [Earlier *sampire, sampere*, < Fr. (*herbe de*) *saint Pierre*, (herb of) St. Peter.] A succulent herb, *Crithmum maritimum*, of Europe, growing in clefts of rocks near the sea; the glasswort, genus *Salicornia*.

sam·ple, sam′pl, säm′pl, *n.* [O.Fr. *essampre, example*, an example.] A small part or quantity of anything intended to be representative of the whole.—*v.t.*—*sampled, sampling.* To take a sample of; to examine or judge by a specimen or sample.—*a.*

sam·pler, sam′plẽr, säm′plẽr, *n.* [L *exemplar*, a pattern, < *exemplum*, an example.] A piece of embroidered work done by beginners for practice.

sam·pler, sam′plẽr, säm′plẽr, *n.* One who samples; a collection of samples.

sam·ple room, *n.* A room where samples are kept or shown.

sam·pling, sam′pling, säm′pling, *n.* The act of selecting a sample, as for analyzing; a sample.

sam·sa·ra, sam·sär′a, *n.* In Eastern philosophy, the cycle of birth, death, and rebirth through which the soul passes; metempsychosis.

sam·shu, sam′shō, sam′sū, *n.* [Chin.] A Chinese liquor distilled from rice or millet.

Sam·son, [From *Samson* in the Bible.] One of the Israelite judges possessed of great strength; any extraordinarily strong man.—**Sam·so·ni·an,** sam·sō′nē·an, *a.*

sam·u·rai, sam′u̯·rī″, *n.* pl. **sam·u·rai.** [Jap.] A member of the military class in feudal Japan, esp. a retainer of a daimyo.

san·a·tive, san′a·tiv, *a.* [M.L. *sanativus*, < L. *sanare*.] Having healing power; curing.

san·a·to·ri·um, san″a·tōr′ē·um, san″a·tạr′ē·um, *n.* pl. **san·a·to·ri·ums,** san″a·to·ri·a, san″a·tōr′ē·a, san″a·tạr′ē·a. [N.L., prop. neut. of L.L. *sanatorius*, healthgiving; cf. *sanitarium* (a different word, < L. *sanitas*, health).] An establishment for the treatment of diseases, as tuberculosis, or for invalids or convalescents, esp. in a locality where climatic and other conditions are favorable; a health resort. Also *sanitarium*.

san·a·to·ry, san′a·tōr″ē, san′a·tạr″ē, *a.* [L.L. *sanatorius*, < L. *sano*, to heal.] Conducive to health; healing; curing.

san·be·ni·to, san″be·nē′tō, *n.* pl. **san·be·ni·tos.** [Sp. *sambenito*, < *San Benito*, St. Benedict; from its resemblance to the scapular introduced by St. Benedict.] Under the Spanish Inquisition, a yellow penitential garment worn by a confessed heretic; a black garment ornamented with flames, devils, and the like, worn by a condemned heretic.

sanc·ti·fy, sangk′ti·fī″, *v.t.*—*sanctified, sanctifying.* [Fr. *sanctifier*, L. *sanctifico*, < *sanctus*, holy (whence *saint*), and *facio*, to make.] To make holy or sacred; to set apart for holy or religious use; to hallow; to purify from sin; to make the means of holiness.—**sanc·ti·fi·ca·tion,** *n.*—**sanc·ti·fi·er,** *n.*—**sanc·ti·fied,** sangk′ti·fīd″, *a.*

sanc·ti·mo·ny, sangk′ti·mō″nē, *n.* [L. *sanctimonia*, < *sanctus*, holy.] The external appearance of sanctity; affected or hypocritical devoutness.—**sanc·ti·mo·ni·ous,** sangk″ti·mo′nē·us, *a.* Making a show of sanctity; affecting the appearance of piety.—**sanc·ti·mo·ni·ous·ly,** *adv.*—**sanc·ti·mo·ni·ous·ness,** *n.*

sanc·tion, sangk′shan, *n.* [L. *sanctio (n-)*, < *sancire*, make sacred, establish as inviolable, ordain, ratify (pp. *sanctus*, often as adj., sacred, holy: cf. *saint, sanctity*, and *sanctum*), akin to L. *sacer*, sacred, holy: cf. *sacre*.] Authoritative permission; countenance or support given to an action; an official confirmation or ratification of some specific action. *Law*, a provision of a law which enacts a penalty for disobedience of that law or provides a reward for obedience to it; the penalty or reward. Binding force given, or something which gives binding force, as to an oath; *usu. pl.* a method often adopted by a group of nations to force another nation to desist in its violation of some particular international law; as, *sanctions* of boycotting.—*v.t.* To ratify or confirm; as, to *sanction* a law or a covenant; to authorize, countenance, or approve.—**sanc·tion·er,** *n.*—**sanc·tion·a·ble,** *a.*

sanc·ti·ty, sangk′ti·tē, *n.* pl. **sanc·ti·ties.** [L. *sanctitas*, < *sanctus*, holy.] The state or quality of being sacred or holy; holiness; solemnity; inviolability. Also **sanc·ti·tude,** sangk′ti·tŏd″, sangk′ti·tūd″.

sanc·tu·ar·y, sangk′chŏ·er″ē, *n.* pl. **sanc·tu·ar·ies.** [O.Fr. *sanctuarie*, Fr. *sanctuaire*, < L.L. *sanctuarium*, < L. *sanctus*, sacred, holy.] A sacred or holy place, as a church, a temple, or a sacred grove; an esp. holy place in a temple or church, as the part of a church about the altar; the chancel; a place in which fugitives were formerly entitled to immunity from arrest; an asylum; immunity from arrest afforded by refuge in such a place; an area where wildlife is protected by the prohibition of hunting.

sanc·tum, sangk′tum, *n.* pl. **sanc·tums,** **sanc·ta,** sangk′ta. A sacred place; a private retreat or room.

sanc·tum sanc·to·rum, sangk′tum sangk·-tōr′um, sangk′tum sangk·tạr′um, *n.* The holy of holies; the innermost or holiest place of the Jewish temple; a private retreat.

Sanc·tus, sangk′tus, *n. Eccles.* A prayer which ends the preface of many eucharistic services and which begins with the Latin word *sanctus* 'holy'; a musical setting used for this prayer.

Sanc·tus bell, *n. Rom. Cath. Ch.* a small bell rung during the Mass to focus attention upon solemn passages.

sand, sand, *n.* [O.E. *sand* = D. *zand* = G. *sand* = Icel. *sandr*, sand: cf. Gr. *ámathos*, sand.] The more or less fine debris of rocks, consisting of small, loose grains, usu. of quartz; *usu. pl.* a tract or region, as a desert, a beach, or a shoal, composed principally of sand; the sand in an hourglass or sandglass; *usu. pl.*, *fig.* moments of life or time, as: The *sands* of time are flowing. *Slang*, courage; grit. A reddish-yellow color.—*v.t.* To sprinkle with or as with sand; overlay with or bury under sand; fill up with sand, as a harbor; to add sand to; as, to *sand* sugar; to abrade or polish with sand or sandpaper.

san·dal, san′dal, *n.* [Fr. *sandale*, L. *sandalium*, < Gr. *sandalion*.] A kind of shoe, usu. leather, consisting of a sole fastened to the foot, generally by means of straps; any of several kinds of low slippers or shoes; a tie or strap for a low shoe; a low-cut rubber overshoe.—*v.t.*—*sandaled, sandaling,* Brit. *sandalled, sandalling.*

san·dal·wood, san'dal·wụd″, *n.* The fragrant heartwood of any of certain Asiatic trees of the genus *Santalum*, used for ornamental carving and burned as incense; any of these trees, esp. *S. album*, the white sandalwood, an evergreen of India; any of various other trees or their woods, esp. an E. Indian leguminous tree, *Pterocarpus santalinus*, the red sandalwood, or its heavy dark red wood which is used as a dyestuff.

san·da·rac, san'da·rak″, *n.* [L. *sandaracha*, < Gr. *sandarachē*, a word of Oriental origin.] A pale yellow aromatic resin which exudes from the bark of the sandarac tree of Morocco, used as incense and for making varnish.—**san·da·rac tree**, a pinaceous tree, *Tetraclinis articulata*, native in northwestern Africa, yielding the resin sandarac, and having a fragrant, hard, dark-colored wood much used in building.

sand·bag, sand'bag″, *n.* A bag filled with sand, used in flood control or fortification, or as ballast; a weapon consisting of a narrow cylindrical bag or the like, filled with sand by which a heavy blow may be struck which leaves little or no mark.—*v.t.* —*sandbagged, sandbagging.* To furnish with sandbags; hit or stun with a sandbag; *slang*, coerce violently.—**sand·bag·ger**, *n.*

sand·bank, sand'bangk″, *n.* A bank of sand, esp. one formed by tides or currents, as a shoal.

sand bar, *n.* A ridge of sand formed in a river or the sea by the action of tides or currents.

sand·blast, sand'blast″, sand'bläst″, *n.* A blast of air or steam laden with sand, used to clean, grind, cut, or decorate hard surfaces, as of glass, stone, or metal; the apparatus used to apply such a blast.—*v.t., v.i.* To cleanse or engrave with a sandblast. —**sand·blast·er**, *n.*

sand-blind, sand'blīnd″, *a.* [Corrupted < *samblind*, < O.E. *sám* (akin to L. *semi*), half.] Having imperfect eyesight.

sand·box, sand'boks″, *n.* A box of sand for children's play; a box of sand for any purpose, as that carried on a locomotive for drying rail treads.

sand·bur, sand·burr, sand'bụr″, *n.* Any o several bur-bearing weeds growing in sandy places, as *Solanum rostratum*, a species of nightshade of the western U.S., or *Cenchrus tribuloides*, a species of grass of the U.S. and Mexico.

sand-cast, sand'kast″, sand'käst″, *v.t. sandcast, sand-casting.* To prepare, as a casting, by pouring metal into molds made of sand. —**sand cast·ing**, *n.*

sand cher·ry, *n.* One of several N. American cherry shrubs growing in sandy soil, esp. *Prunus pumila*, native to the Great Lakes region of the U.S. and Canada; the fruit of a sand cherry.

sand crack, *n.* *Veter. pathol.* a crack or fissure in the hoof of a horse, extending from the coronet downward toward the sole, and occurring mostly on the inner quarters of the forefeet and on the toes of the hind feet, due to a diseased condition, and liable to cause lameness. Also **quar·ter crack.**

sand dol·lar, *n.* Any of various flat, disklike sea urchins, esp. *Echinarachnius parma*, which live on sandy bottoms off the eastern coast of the U.S.

sand·er, san'dẹr, *n.* One who or that which sands; one who sandpapers; an apparatus for sandpapering.

sand·er·ling, san'dẹr·ling, *n.* [So called because it feeds among the moist sands of the shore.] A small gray and white sandpiper, *Crocethia alba*, which breeds in the Arctic and frequents shores.

sand flea, *n.* A chigoe or other flea which lives in sandy places; a beach flea.

sand·fly, sand'flī″, *n. pl.* **sand·flies.** A small biting fly of the family *Psychodidae*, inhabiting the seashore; a bloodsucking fly of the genus *Phlebotomus*, whose bite transmits certain diseases of man.

sand·glass, sand'glas″, sand'gläs″, *n.* A glass that measures time by the running of sand from one division of it to the other. Also *hourglass.*

sand grouse, *n.* Any bird of the family *Pteroclidae*, inhabiting arid sandy plains of Europe, Asia, and Africa.

san·dhi, san'dē, sän'dē, *n. pl.* **san·dhis.** A phonetic change in words or word groups as a result of their phonemic environment, as the assimilation of *d* and *y* to *j* in 'did you.'

sand·hog, sand'hog″, sand'hạg″, *n.* A laborer who digs or works in sand, esp. one who works in a caisson in tunneling under water.

sand launce, *n.* Any of a family, *Ammodytidae*, of slender marine fish which swim in schools and burrow into sandy beaches at ebb tide. Also *launce*, **sand lance, sand eel.**

sand lil·y, *n. pl.* **sand lil·ies.** An herb, *Leucocrinum montanum*, of the western U.S., bearing stalks of lily-shaped flowers.

sand·lot, sand'lot″, *n.* A vacant urban lot used for playing games.—*a.* Pertaining to or played in a sandlot; as, *sandlot* baseball. —**sand·lot·ter**, sand'lot″ẹr, *n.*

sand·man, sand'man″, *n. pl.* **sand·men.** An imaginary person, in fairy tales, who puts sand into children's eyes to make them sleepy.

sand paint·ing, *n.* An art form practiced by the Indians of the southwestern U.S., particularly the Navaho, in which designs are traced in multi-colored sand on a flat surface of sand of a neutral color.

sand·pa·per, sand'pā″pẹr, *n.* Strong paper upon which a layer of sand has been fixed with glue, used for smoothing or polishing. —*v.t.* To smooth or polish with or as with sandpaper.

sand pile, *n.* Sand for children to play in; *constr.* a fill of sand compressed in a deep hole to provide a solid foundation, as in soft soil.

sand·pi·per, sand'pī″pẹr, *n.* Any of the various small, shore-inhabiting birds, family *Scolopacidae*, of N. America and Europe, breeding in the Arctic and having a piping call.

sand·soap, sand'sōp″, *n.* Soap with tiny granules of sand in it, used for cleaning deep dirt from the hands.

sand·stone, sand'stōn″, *n.* Stone composed of agglutinated grains of sand, cemented together by calcareous, siliceous, or of any other mineral nature. See *freestone.*

sand·storm, sand'stạrm″, *n.* A windstorm which blows along great clouds of sand.

sand ta·ble, *n.* A table used to hold sand for children to play in; *milit.* a table with a scale model of the terrain of an area, used to study the topography when planning maneuvers.

sand trap, *n. Golf*, a shallow sand-filled pit placed as a hazard on a golf course, usu. on the approach to a green.

sand ver·be·na, *n.* Any plant of the genus *Abronia*, in the four o'clock family, and growing in the dry, sandy soil of the western U.S.

sand·wich, sand'wich, san'wich, *n.* [After an Earl of *Sandwich*.] Two thin slices of bread between which is placed meat, fish, cheese, or the like; anything similar to or resembling a sandwich.—*v.t.* To form into a sandwich; to place in between two other things; as, to *sandwich* a vacation between two jobs.

sand·wich board, *n.* Two advertising signs, joined by straps and hanging from

a man's shoulders, one board in front and one behind.—**sand·wich man**, *n.*

sand·worm, sand'wụrm″, *n.* Any of several marine annelids, class *Polychaeta*, that live in the sand along the seashore and are used by fishermen as bait. Also *lugworm.*

sand·wort, sand'wụrt″, *n.* Any of the tufted herbaceous plants constituting genus *Arenaria*, many of which grow in sandy soil.

sand·y, san'dē, *a.*—**sandier, sandiest.** Consisting of or abounding with sand; resembling sand; of the color of sand; of a yellowish-red color.—**sand·i·ness**, *n.*

sane, sān, *a.*—**saner, sanest.** [L. *sanus*, sound, whole, healthy (whence *sanitary*); same root as Gr. *sōs*, safe.] Mentally sound; not deranged; having reason and the other mental faculties.—**sane·ly**, *adv.*— **sane·ness**, *n.*

San·for·ize, san'fo·rīz″, *v.t.*—*Sanforized, Sanforizing.* To treat, as cloth, by mechanically shrinking, thereby lessening the amount of shrinkage when washed. (Trademark.)

san·ga·ree, sang″ga·rē′, *n.* A refreshing iced drink of wine and water sweetened and spiced. Also **san·gri·a**, sang·grē′a, *Sp.* säng·grē′ä.

sang-froid, *Fr.* sän·frwä′, *n.* [Fr., 'cold blood.'] Coolness of mind; calmness; composure.

San·graal, sang·grāl′, *n.* [O.Fr. *saint graal*, also later *sangreal*, 'holy vessel.'] The Holy Grail. Also **San·gre·al**, sang'grē·al.

san·guic·o·lous, sang·gwik'o·lus, *a.* [L. *sanguis*, blood]. Living in the blood, as a parasite.

san·guif·er·ous, sang·gwif'ẹr·us, *a.* [L. *sanguis*, blood, and *fero*, to carry.] Conveying blood, as the arteries and veins.

san·gui·nar·i·a, sang″gwi·nâr′ē·a, *n.* [N.L., prop. fem. of L. *sanguinarius*, pertaining to blood, E. *sanguinary*.] A plant, *Sanguinaria canadensis*, of the poppy family, having a white flower, lobed leaf, and a red juice; the rhizome of this plant, used as an emetic or expectorant. Also **blood·root.**

san·gui·nar·y, sang'gwi·ner″ē, *a.* [L. *sanguinarius*, < *sanguis*, blood; same root as *sucus* or *succus*, juice, *sugo*, to suck.] Consisting of blood; bloody; characterized by much bloodshed; murderous; bloodthirsty.—**san·gui·nar·i·ly**, *adv.*—**san·gui·nar·i·ness**, *n.*

san·guine, sang'gwin, *a.* [Fr. *sanguin*, < L. *sanguineus*, < *sanguis*, blood.] Having the color of blood; ruddy, as a complexion; characterized by vigor and confidence.—*n.* —**san·guine·ly**, *adv.*—**san·guine·ness**, *n.* —**san·guin·e·ous**, sang·gwin′ē·us, *a.*

san·guin·o·lent, sang·gwin'o·lent, *a.* [L. *sanguinolentus*.] Tinged or mingled with blood; bloody.

San·hed·rin, san·hed′rin, san·hē′drin, san'hi·drin, san'i·drin, *n.* [Late Heb. *sanhedrīn*, < Gr. *synédrion*, council, < *syn*, with, and *édra*, seat.] The supreme council and highest ecclesiastical and judicial tribunal of the ancient Jewish nation; a similar lower tribunal. Also **San·he·drim**, san'hi·drim, san'i·drim.

san·i·cle, san'i·kl, *n.* [Fr. *sanicle*, < L. *sano*, to heal—from its supposed healing virtues.] An herb of the genus *Sanicula*, in the parsley family, with certain medicinal properties. Also **black snake·root.**

sa·ni·es, sā'nē·ēz″, *n.* [L.] *Pathol.* a thin serous fluid, often greenish, discharged from ulcers or wounds.—**sa·ni·ous**, *a.*

san·i·tar·i·an, san″i·târ′ē·an, *n.* An authority or a promoter of sanitary measures, public health, or the like.—*a.* Clean; healthful.

san·i·tar·i·um, san″i·târ′ē·um, *n.* Sanatorium.

san·i·tar·y, san'i·ter"ē, *a*. [Fr. *sanitaire*, < L. *sanitas*, health, < *sanus*, sound.] Pertaining to or designed to promote health; relating to the preservation of health; hygienic.—*n*. pl. **san·i·tar·ies**. A public toilet.—**san·i·tar·i·ly**, *adv*.—**san·i·tar·i·ness**, *n*.

san·i·tar·y nap·kin, *n*. A pad of absorbent material, usu. cotton, used by women during the menstrual period.

san·i·tate, san'i·tāt", *v.t.*—*sanitated*, *sanitating*. [Back formation < *sanitation*.] To subject to sanitation; make sanitary by supplying sanitary equipment.

san·i·ta·tion, san"i·tā'shan, *n*. The adoption of sanitary measures to eliminate unhealthy elements; hygiene.

san·i·tize, san'i·tīz", *v.t.*—*sanitized*, *sanitizing*. [< (*sanit*)*ary* and -*ize*.] To render sanitary; disinfect.

san·i·ty, san'i·tē, *n*. pl. **san·i·ties**. The state of being sane or of sound mind; rationality; reasonableness.

San Jo·se scale, san'hō·zā"skāl', *n*. A scale insect, *Aspidiotus perniciosus*, injurious esp. to fruit trees, first appearing in the United States at San Jose, California.

San·khya, säng'kya, *n*. A philosophy which is among the six oldest major Hindu systems and which teaches the dualism of matter and spirit.

san·nup, san'up, *n*. [Algonquian.] A married man among N. American Indians.

sann·ya·si, sun·yä'sē, *n*. A Hindu religious mendicant. Also **sann·ya·sin**, sun·yä'sin.

sans, sanz, *Fr.* säN, *prep*. [Fr., < L. *sine*, without.] Without.

sans-cu·lotte, sanz"kū·lot', *Fr.* säN·ky·lät', *n*. pl. **sans-cu·lottes**, *Fr.* säN·ky·lat'. [Fr., without breeches.] A revolutionary, orig. a derisive term used by aristocrats at the time of the French Revolution of 1789, later, a popular designation for a revolutionary; any radical or revolutionary.—**sans-cu·lot·tic**, sanz"kū·lot'ik, *a*.—**sans-cu·lot·tish**, *a*.—**sans-cu·lot·tism**, *n*.—**sans-cu·lot·tist**, *n*.

san·sei, sän'sā', *n*. pl. **san·sei**, **san·seis**. (*Often cap*.) a native American whose grandparents immigrated from Japan. Compare *Nisei*.

san·se·vi·e·ri·a, san"se·vē·ēr'ē·a, san"se·vēr'ē·a, *n*. Any tropical herb of the genus *Sansevieria*, belonging to the lily family, with mottled, rigid, sword-shaped leaves, often cultivated as an ornamental.

San·skrit, **San·scrit**, san'skrit, *n*. [Skt. *sanskrita*, perfectly formed—*sam* (= Gr. *syn*), with, and *krita*, made, perfected, < *kri*, to make.] The ancient Indic language of the Hindus, which is the language of religion and classical literature in India.—*a*.—**San·skrit·ic**, **San·scrit·ic**, *a*. Pertaining to any of the languages of India derived from Sanskrit, such as Bengali, Pali, Punjabi, or Eastern and Western Hindi related, similar to, or written in Sanskrit.—**San·skrit·ist**, *n*.

sans ser·if, sanz"ser'if, *n. Print*. a type style without serifs.

San·ta Claus, san'ta klạz", *n*. The symbolic figure of Christmas; a stout, white-bearded, jovial old gentleman in red clothing, who supposedly distributes presents at Christmas. Also **Saint Nich·o·las**, *Brit. Father Christmas*.

San·ta Ger·tru·dis, san'ta gėr·trö'dis, *n*. A type of beef cattle in the western U.S., which is a Brahman-Shorthorn crossbreed, valued for its resistance to hot climates.

san·ta·la·ceous, san"ta·lā'shus, *a*. [M.L. *santalum*.] Belonging to the *Santalaceae*, or sandalwood family of plants.

san·ton·i·ca, san·ton'i·ka, *n*. [N.L., prop. fem. of L. *Santonicus*, pertaining to the *Santoni*, a people of Aquitania, in south-

western Gaul.] A species of wormwood, *Artemisia maritima*, of the Old World; a drug consisting of the dried flower heads of this plant used to expel parasitic intestinal worms.

san·to·nin, san'to·nin, *n*. [< *santonica*.] *Chem*. a crystalline compound, $C_{15}H_{18}O_3$, the active principle of santonica.

sap, sap, *n*. [O.E. *saep* = D. *sap* = G. *saft*, sap.] The juice or vital circulating fluid of a plant; any vital fluid, as blood; vigor or vitality; sapwood. *Slang*, someone foolish or gullible; a saphead.—*v.t.*—*sapped*, *sapping*. To drain the sap from.

sap, sap, *n*. [Fr. *sappe*, now *sape*, = It. *zappa*.] *Fort*. a narrow trench dug for the purpose of approaching a besieged place or an enemy's position.—*v.t.*—*sapped*, *sapping*. [Fr. *sapper*, now *saper* (= It. *zappare*), < O.Fr. *sappe* (Fr. *sape*) = It. *zappa*, < M.L. *sappa*, *sapa*, hoe, mattock.] *Fort*. to approach, as an enemy position, with narrow trenches protected by parapets. To weaken or destroy insidiously; to enervate; to undermine.—*v.i. Fort*. to dig or prepare saps.

sap green, *n*. A green coloring matter derived from the juice of buckthorn berries, used in dyes; a yellow-green color.

sap·head, sap'hed", *n*. [< *sap* (cf. *sappy*) and *head*.] *Slang*. A simpleton; a fool.—**sap·head·ed**, sap'hed"id, *a*.—**sap·head·ed·ness**, *n*.

sa·phe·nous, sa·fē'nus, *a*. [M.L., < Ar. *çâfin*.] Pertaining to the large superficial veins of the leg, the 'long' or 'internal' saphena on the inner side of the leg, and the 'short,' 'external,' or 'posterior' saphena on the outer and posterior sides.—**sa·phe·na**, sa·fē'na, *n*. pl. **sa·phe·nae**, sa·fē'nē.

sap·id, sap'id, *a*. [L. *sapidus*, < *sapio*, to taste.] Having an agreeable flavor; savory; pleasing to one's mind.—**sa·pid·i·ty**, *n*.

sa·pi·ence, sā'pē·ens, *n*. [L. *sapientia*, wisdom.] Wisdom; sagacity: often used with irony. Also **sa·pi·en·cy**.

sa·pi·ens, sā'pē·enz, *a*. The specific name of modern man, *Homo sapiens*.

sa·pi·ent, sā'pē·ent, *a*. [L. *sapiens*, *sapientis*, wise, discreet, pp. of *sapio*, to taste, to know, to be wise; *sapid*, *insipid*, *savor*, *sage*, are of similar origin.] Wise; sage; knowing; discerning, often used ironically. Pertaining to affected wisdom.—**sa·pi·ent·ly**, *adv*.

sap·less, sap'lis, *a*. Destitute of sap; dry; withered; lacking vigor or vitality; dull.

sap·ling, sap'ling, *n*. A young tree; a youth.

sap·o·dil·la, sap"o·dil'a, *n*. [Sp. *zapotillo*, dim. of *zapote*.] A large, tropical evergreen tree, *Achras zapota*, bearing an edible fruit and yielding chicle. The fruit of this tree; also **sap·o·dil·la plum**. Also *sapota*.

sap·o·na·ceous, sap"o·nā'shus, *a*. [< L. *sapo*, *saponis*, soap.] Soapy; resembling soap.—**sap·o·na·ceous·ness**, *n*.

sa·pon·i·fi·ca·tion, sa·pon"i·fi·kā'shan, *n*. The process by which fatty substances, through combination with an alkali, form soap; the decomposition of an ester, using heat, water, and an alkali, into acid and alcohol.—**sa·pon·i·fi·a·ble**, *a*.—**sa·pon·i·fi·er**, *n*.—**sa·pon·i·fy**, sa·pon'i·fī", *v.t.. v.i.*—*saponified*, *saponifying*.

sap·o·nin, sap'o·nin, *n*. Any of several glucosides found in the root of soapwort and other plants, which causes water to froth like soap when agitated and which acts as an emulsifier.

sap·o·nite, sap'o·nīt", *n. Mineral*. a magnesium aluminum silicate which occurs as a soft, amorphous mass in veins and rock cavities.

sa·por, *Brit.* **sa·pour**, sā'pėr, sā'par, *n*. [L., *sapid*.] That which affects the taste sense; taste; savor; flavor.—**sap·o·rif·ic**, sap"o·rif'ik, *a*.—**sap·o·rous**, sap'ėr·us, *a*.

sa·po·ta, sa·pō'ta, *n*. [N.L., < Sp. *zapote*; < Mex.] *Bot*. sapodilla.—**sap·o·ta·ceous**,

sap"o·tā'shus, *a. Bot*. belonging to the *Sapotaceae*, or sapodilla family of plants.

sap·pan·wood, **sa·pan·wood**, sa·pan'wụd", *n*. A dyewood which yields a red color, produced by an East Indian tree; the tree itself, *Caesalpinia sappan*.

sap·per, sap'ėr, *n*. That which or one who saps; a soldier of an engineer corps, who is trained in fortification.

Sap·phic, saf'ik, *a*. Of or pertaining to the Greek poetess *Sappho*; *pros*. applied to a kind of verse said to have been invented by Sappho.—*n*. Sapphic verse, consisting of trochaic pentameter lines with a dactylic third foot.

sap·phire, saf'i·ėr, *n*. [L. *sapphirus*, Gr. *sappheiros*, of Eastern origin = Heb. *sappir*, Ar. *safir*.] *Mineral*. any of the various kinds of corundum, with the exception of the ruby, used for gems, esp. those of various shades of blue; such a precious gem. A rich blue color.—*a*.

sap·phir·ine, saf'ėr·in, saf'i·rēn", saf'i·rin", *n. Mineral*. A green or blue silicate composed of magnesium and aluminum; a blue variety of spinel.—*a*. Composed of sapphire; resembling a sapphire, esp. as to color.

sap·phism, saf'iz·um, *n*. Lesbianism.

sap·py, sap'ē, *a*.—*sappier*, *sappiest*. Abounding with sap; juicy; succulent; energetic; young. *Slang*, stupid; sentimental.—**sap·pi·ness**, *n*.

sa·pre·mi·a, sa·prē'mē·a, *n*. [N.L., < Gr. *sapros*, rotten, and *aima*, blood.] *Pathol*. a form of blood poisoning, esp. that due to the absorption of the toxins produced by certain microorganisms.—**sa·pre·mic**, *a*.

sap·ro·gen·ic, sap"rō·jen'ik, *a*. [Gr. *sapros*, rotten.] Producing putrefaction or decay, as certain bacteria; formed by putrefaction. Also **sa·prog·e·nous**, sa·proj'e·nus.

sap·ro·lite, sap'ro·līt", *n*. [Gr. *saprós*, rotten, decayed, and *lithos*, stone.] *Petrog*. soft, disintegrated, usu. decomposed rock, remaining in its orig. place.—**sap·ro·lit·ic**, sap"ro·lit'ik, *a*.

sa·proph·a·gous, sa·prof'a·gus, *a*. [Gr. *sapros*, putrid, and *phago*, to eat.] *Biol*. feeding on organic substances in a state of decomposition.

sap·ro·phyte, sap'ro·fīt", *n*. [Gr. *sapros*, and *phyton*, a plant.] A plant, as one of various bacteria or fungi, that grows on decaying vegetable matter.—**sap·ro·phyt·ic**, sap"ro·fit'ik, *a*.—**sap·ro·phyt·i·cal·ly**, *adv*.

sap·sa·go, sap'sa·gō", *n*. [Corruption of G. *schabzieger*.] A kind of green, hard cheese made in Switzerland.

sap·suck·er, sap'suk"ėr, *n*. Any of several small woodpeckers, genus *Sphyrapicus*, that damage trees by exposing the sapwood to drink the sap.

sap·wood, sap'wụd", *n*. The new, outer, physiologically active wood of a tree, usu. light-colored.

sar·a·band, sar'a·band", *n*. [Fr. *sarabande*, < Sp. *zarabanda*; origin uncertain.] A slow, stately Spanish dance in triple rhythm; a piece of music for, or in the rhythm of, this dance, usu. forming one of the movements in the classical music suite following the courante.

Sar·a·cen, sar'a·sen, *a*. [L.L. *Saraceni*, pl.] Pertaining or relating to a member of the nomadic tribes on the Syrian borders of the Roman Empire; designating an Arab; pertaining to a Moslem, esp. with reference to the Crusades.—*n*.—**Sar·a·cen·ic**, **Sar·a·cen·i·cal**, sar"a·sen'ik, *a*.

sa·ran, sa·ran', *n*. A polymerized vinyl chloride, a thermoplastic which is durable, flexible, and waterproof, used for packaging, for making chemically resistant pipes, and other products.

sa·ra·pe, se·rä'pe, *Sp.* sä·Rä'pe, *n*. Serape.

Sar·a·to·ga trunk, sar″a·tō′ga trungk, *n.* [From *Saratoga* Springs, New York.] A large trunk having a rounded top that was used principally by women in the 19th century.

sar·casm, sär′kaz·um, *n.* [L. *sarcasmus*, < Gr. *sarkasmos*, a bitter laugh, < *sarkazo*, to tear flesh like dogs, to speak bitterly, < *sarx*, *sarkos*, flesh.] A bitter, cutting expression; a caustic remark; a gibe; a taunt; the employment of ironical or satirical language.—**sar·cas·tic,** sär·kas′tik, *a.*—**sar·cas·tic·ness, sar·cas·ti·cal·ness,** *n.*—**sar·cas·ti·cal·ly,** *adv.*

sarce·net, sarse·net, särs′nit, *n.* [O.Fr. *sarcenet*; L.L. *saracenicum*, lit. 'cloth made by *Saracens*.'] A fine, thin woven silk, esp. used for linings.

sar·co·carp, sär′kō·kärp″, *n.* [Gr. *sarx*, *sarkos*, flesh, and *karpos*, fruit.] The fleshy part of certain fruits, as the plum; a fleshy fruit.

sar·coid, sär′koid, *a.* Fleshy.—*n.* *Pathol.* a sarcomalike tumor.

sar·co·ma, sär·kō′ma, *n.* pl. **sar·co·mas, sar·co·ma·ta,** sär·kō′ma·ta. [N.L., < Gr. *sárcōma*, < *sarcoun*, make fleshy, < *sárx*(*sarc*-), flesh.] *Pathol.* any of various malignant tumors originating in the connective tissue.—**sar·co·ma·toid, sar·co·ma·tous,** sär·kō′ma·toid″, sär·kō′ma·tus, sär·kom′a·tus, *a.*

sar·coph·a·gous, sär·kof′a·gus, *a.* [L. *sarcophagus*, < Gr. *sarcophágos*, < *sárx* (*sarc*-), flesh, and *phagein*, eat.] Flesh-eating; carnivorous. Also **sar·co·phag·ic,** sär″ko·faj′ik.

sar·coph·a·gus, sär·kof′a·gus, *n.* pl. **sar·coph·a·gi, sar·coph·a·gus·es,** sär·kof′a·jī″. [Gr. *sarkophagos*; it was orig. the name of a type of stone used for making coffins, and believed to have the property of consuming the dead bodies.] A stone tomb or coffin usu. ornamented and open to view, as a monument.

sar·cous, sär′kus, *a.* [Gr. *sarx*, *sarkos*, flesh.] Belonging to or consisting of flesh or muscle.

sard, särd, *n.* [Fr. *sarde*, < *Saraes*, the ancient capital of Lydia.] *Mineral.* a compact variety of chalcedony having a translucent, brownish-red color. Also *sardine*, *sardius*.

sar·dine, sär·dēn′, *n.* pl. **sar·dines, sar·dine.** [Fr. *sardine*, < L. *sardina*, so called because caught near *Sardinia*.] One of several small edible clupeid fish, related to the herring and pilchard, and preserved in tins with oil.

sar·dine, sär′dīn, *n.* Sard.

Sar·din·i·an, sär·din′ē·an, sär·din′yan, *a.* Of or pertaining to Sardinia, a large island in the Mediterranean west of Italy, its inhabitants, or their language.—*n.* A native or inhabitant of the island or of the former kingdom of Sardinia; a language spoken by Sardinians.

sar·di·us, sär′dē·us, *n.* A variety of chalcedony; sard. *Bib.* one of the stones in Aaron's breastplate; Ex. xxviii. 17.

sar·don·ic, sär·don′ik, *a.* [Fr., *sardonique*, < L. *Sardonica herba*, the Sardinian herb, an herb said to cause a peculiar twitching of the 'face when eaten.] Bitterly ironical; sarcastic; derisive and mocking.—**sar·don·i·cal·ly,** *adv.*

sar·don·yx, sär·don′iks, sär′do·niks, *n.* [Gr. *sardonyx*.] A variety of onyx, consisting of alternate layers of sard and white chalcedony.

sar·gas·so, sar·gas′ō, *n.* Gulfweed; sargassum.

sar·gas·sum, sär·gas′um, *n.* [N.L., < Pg. *sargaço*.] Any seaweed of the genus *Sargassum*, the species of which are widely distributed in the warmer waters of the globe, as *S. bacciferum*, the common gulfweed. Also *sargasso*.

sa·ri, sa·ree, sär′ē, *n.* pl. **sa·ris, sa·rees.** [Hind.] The chief garment of a Hindu woman, consisting of a long piece of cloth wound round the waist, with one edge hanging down in front, and the other taken up and thrown over the head and shoulders.

sar·men·tose, sär·men′tōs, *a.* *Bot.* Having runners; having the character of a runner. Also **sar·men·tous, sar·men·ta·ceous,** sär·men′tus, sär″men·tā′shus.

sar·men·tum, sär·men′tum, *n.* pl. **sar·men·ta,** sär·men′ta. The running stem of a plant. Also **sar·ment.**

sa·rong, sa·rang′, sa·rong′, *n.* [Malay *sārung*.] The principal garment for both sexes in the Malay Archipelago, consisting of a piece of cloth enveloping the lower part of the body like a skirt; a kind of cloth for such garments.

sar·ra·ce·ni·a, sar″a·sē′nē·a, *n.* [N.L. from Dr. *Sarrazin* of Quebec, who first sent specimens of the plant to Europe.] Any of the genus *Sarracenia*, comprising N. American marsh plants with hollow leaves of a pitcherlike form in which insects are trapped and digested, esp. *Sarrecenia purpurea*, a common pitcher plant.—**sar·ra·ce·ni·a·ceous,** sar″a·sē″nē·ā′shus, *a.*

sar·sa·pa·ril·la, sas″pa·ril′a, sär″sa·pa·ril′a, *n.* [Sp. *zarzaparrilla*.] The dried root of certain trailing or climbing, tropical American plants of the genus *Smilax*; an extract made from these roots and used in the making of soft drinks, such as root beer, and in medicine.—**sar·sa·pa·ril·lin,** *n.*

sar·to·ri·al, sär·tōr′ē·al, sär·tạr′ē·al, *a.* Of or pertaining to a tailor or to his work; pertaining to dress, esp. of men; *anat.* pertaining to the sartorius.—**sar·to·ri·al·ly,** *adv.*

sar·to·ri·us, sär·tōr′ē·us, sär·tạr′ē·us, *n.* pl. **sar·to·ri·i,** sär·tōr′ē·ī″, sär·tạr′ē·ī″. [N.L. < L. *sartor*.] *Anat.* a flat, narrow muscle, the longest in man, running from the ilium to the top of the tibia and crossing the thigh obliquely in front, the chief muscle involved in rotating the leg to the cross-legged position.

Sar·um use, sär′um ūs″, *n.* The rite used in the churches of Salisbury, before the Reformation.

sash, sash, *n.* [Pers. *shash*, a sash, scarf, or shawl.] A band or scarf worn over the shoulder or around the waist for ornament or as an emblem of distinction.

sash, sash, *n.* pl. **sash·es, sash.** [Fr. *châsse*, a frame, a sash, < L. *capsa*, a box, < *capio*, to take.] The framed part of a window in which the glass is fixed.—*v.t.* To furnish with window sashes.

sa·shay, sa·shā′, *n.* *Colloq.* to move in a strutting or conspicuous way, as in dancing.

sas·ka·toon, sas″ka·tön, *n.* [N. Amer. Ind.] The serviceberry, *Amelanchier canadensis*, or its fruit. Also *Juneberry*, *serviceberry*, *shadberry*, *shadbush*.

sass, sas, *n.* *Colloq.* A pert, discourteous retort; back talk.—*v.t.* *Colloq.* To respond or speak to in an impertinent manner; to talk back.

sas·sa·fras, sas′a·fras″, *n.* [Sp. *sasafrás*; origin uncertain: cf. *saxifrage*.] A N. American lauraceous tree, *Sassafras albidum*; the aromatic bark of its root, used medicinally and esp. for flavoring beverages or confectionery.

Sas·se·nach, sas′e·nach, sas′e·nak, *n.* *Brit.* An Englishman; a Saxon: often used disparagingly by Celts of the British Isles.

sas·sy, sas′ē, *a.*—*sassier*, *sassiest*. *Colloq.* Saucy; pert; impudent.

sas·sy bark, *n.* [Appar. < W. Afr. name.] The bark of a large African leguminous tree, *Erythrophleum guineense*, used by the natives as a poison in ordeals; the tree

itself. Also **sass·wood, sas·sy, sas·sy·wood,** sas′ē, sas′ē·wụd″.

Sa·tan, sāt′an, *n.* [L.L. *Satan*, *Satanas*, < Gr. *Satan*, *Satanas*, < Heb. *sātān*, adversary, < *sātan*, oppose.] *Bib.* The chief evil spirit; the great adversary of man; the devil.

sa·tan·ic, sā·tan′ik, sa·tan′ik, *a.* Of, characteristic of, or befitting Satan; extremely wicked; diabolical. Also **sa·tan·i·cal.**—**sa·tan·i·cal·ly,** *adv.*

sa·tan·ism, sāt′a·niz″um, *n.* Satanic disposition or practice; (*cap.*) the worship of Satan, esp. in mockery of Christian ritual.—**sa·tan·ist,** *n.*

satch·el, sach′el, *n.* [Also written *sachel*, a dim. of *sack*, the *k* sound having undergone the common softening to *ch*.] A small suitcase or bag which may be carried either by the hand or slung from the shoulder.

sate, sāt, *v.t.*—*sated*, *sating*. [Perh. < O.E. *saed*, *satisfied*, satiated, the form having been influenced by *satisfy*, *satiate*.] To satisfy completely, as the appetite or desire; to glut or satiate.

sa·teen, sa·tēn′, *n.* [< *satin*.] Cotton cloth woven and treated to resemble satin.

sat·el·lite, sat′e·līt″, *n.* [Fr. *satellite*, < L. *satelles*, *satellitis*, one who guards the person of a prince.] *Astron.* a small planet revolving around a larger one; a secondary planet or moon. Anything dependent on another thing; a subservient follower; a small city or nation which is under the economic, military, or political domination of a larger state; any man-made object orbiting the earth or a celestial body.—*a.* Also **sat·el·lit·ic,** sat″e·lit′ik.

sa·tem, sä′tem, *a.* Pertaining to a group of Indo-European languages, the Albanian, Indo-Iranian, Slavic, Baltic, and Armenian, having the first or prehistoric palatal stops developing into fricatives.

sa·ti·a·ble, sä′shē·a·bl, *a.* Capable of being satiated or satisfied.—**sa·ti·a·bly,** *adv.*—**sa·ti·a·bil·i·ty, sa·ti·a·ble·ness,** *n.*

sa·ti·ate, sä′shē·āt″, *v.t.*—*satiated*, *satiating*. [L. *satio*, *satiatum*, to satisfy, to satiate, < *satis*, enough; akin to *satur*, full; akin to *satisfy*, *saturate*, *satire*.] To satisfy, as the appetite or desire; to fill or gratify to excess; to surfeit.—sä′shē·it, sä′shē·āt″, *a.* Filled to satiety.—**sa·ti·at·ed,** *a.*—**sa·ti·a·tion,** *n.*

sa·ti·e·ty, sa·tī′i·tē, *n.* pl. **sa·ti·e·ties.** [L. *satietas*.] The state of being satiated; surfeit.

sat·in, sat′in, *n.* [O.Fr. Fr. *satin*, < It. *setino*, < *seta*, silk, < L. *seta*, *sæta*, bristle: cf. *seta*.] A silk fabric so woven and finished as to have a characteristic smoothness and gloss on one surface.—*a.* Of or like satin; smooth or glossy as satin; satiny.

sat·i·net, sat·i·nette, sat″i·net′, *n.* [Cf. Fr. *satinette*.] A thin, light satin or an inferior kind of satin; a fabric woven to resemble satin.

sat·in stitch, *n.* A method of embroidery in which stitches made in close parallel lines resemble satin.

sat·in weave, *n.* A type of weave in which the interlacing of the warp and woof threads fabricate a cloth with a smooth, unbroken finish.

sat·in·wood, sat′in·wụd, *n.* The satiny wood of an East Indian tree, *Chloroxylon swietenia*, belonging to the mahogany family, used for cabinetwork and fine furniture; the tree itself; a tree of the rue family, *Zanthoxylum flavum*, a native of the West Indies and Florida.

sat·in·y, sat′i·nē, *a.* Satinlike, as in smoothness or gloss; lustrous.

sat·ire, sat′ī·èr, *n.* [Fr. *satire*, < L. *satira*, earlier *satura*, orig. a dish filled with various fruits, a medley, prop. fem. of *satur*, full, sated.] The use of irony, sarcasm, or ridicule in exposing, denouncing, or deriding vice, folly, or the like; a literary composition, in verse or prose, in which vices, abuses, or follies are held up to scorn, derision, or ridicule; the literary type constituted by such compositions.

sa·tir·i·cal, sa·tir′i·kal, *a*. Of, relating to, or marked by satire; of the nature of satire; indulging in or given to satire, as a person. Also **sa·tir·ic.—sa·tir·i·cal·ly**, *adv*.—**sa·tir·i·cal·ness**, *n*.

sat·i·rist, sat′ér·ist″, *n*. A writer of satires; one who indulges in satire.

sat·i·rize, sat′i·rīz″, *v.t.—satirized, satirizing*. To assail with satire; make the object of satire.—**sat·i·riz·er**, *n*.

sat·is·fac·tion, sat″is·fak′shan, *n*. [O.Fr. Fr. *satisfaction*, < L. *satisfactio(n-)*.] The act of satisfying, or the state of being satisfied; fulfillment of desires, demands, or needs. Gratification or pleasure occasioned by some fact or circumstance; the cause of such gratification; payment, as for debt; discharge, as of obligations; reparation, as of a wrong or injury; the opportunity of repairing a supposed wrong, as by a duel; release from doubt or conviction; *eccles.* the performance by a penitent of the penal acts enjoined by ecclesiastical authority.—**sat·is·fac·tion·al**, *a*.

sat·is·fac·to·ry, sat″is·fak′to·rē, *a*. Affording satisfaction; fulfilling all demands or requirements; adequate; *theol.* making atonement.—**sat·is·fac·to·ri·ly**, *adv*.—**sat·is·fac·to·ri·ness**, *n*.

sat·is·fy, sat′is·fī″, *v.t.—satisfied, satisfying*. [O.Fr. *satisfier*, < L. *satisfacere* (passive *satisfieri*), < *satis*, enough, and *facere*, do, make.] To fulfill the desires, expectations, or demands of, as a person; to supply fully the needs of; to put an end to, as a want; to supplying fully; to pay, as a creditor; to discharge fully, as a debt; to make reparation to or for; to give assurance to or convince; to answer sufficiently, as an objection; *math.* to fulfill the requirements or conditions of; as, to *satisfy* an algebraic equation.—*v.i.* To give contentment or satisfaction; to make reparation or to atone.—**sat·is·fi·a·ble**, *a*.—**sat·is·fi·er**, *n*.—**sat·is·fy·ing·ly**, *adv*.

sa·to·ri, sa·tōr′ē, sa·tᵤr′ē, *n. Zen Buddhism*, spiritual enlightenment.

sa·trap, sā′trap, sa′trap, *n*. [Gr. *satrapēs*; borrowed from the Persian.] A governor of a province under the ancient Persian monarchy; a petty official or ruler, who is often despotic.—**sa·trap·y**, sā′tra·pē, sa′tra·pē, *n. pl.* **sa·trap·ies**. The principality or jurisdiction of a satrap.

sat·u·ra·ble, sach′ér·a·bl, *a*. Able to be saturated.

sat·u·rant, sach′ér·ant, *a*. Saturating.—*n*. A substance which neutralizes or saturates.

sat·u·rate, sach′a·rāt″, *v.t.—saturated, saturating*. [L. *saturo, saturatum*, < *satur*, filled (whence *satire*); < root of *satis*, enough.] To cause to become completely penetrated, impregnated, or soaked; to charge fully, as a solution; to imbue thoroughly; to impregnate or unite with a substance until no more can be absorbed or added; *milit.* to demolish completely by massive use of missiles.—**sach′ér·it**, sach′a·rāt″, *a*. Saturated.—**sat·u·ra·tor**, *n*.

sat·u·rat·ed, sach′a·rā″tid, *a*. Soaked, impregnated, or imbued thoroughly; charged thoroughly or completely; brought to a state of saturation; free from the admixture of white, as colors; *chem.* lacking the capacity to absorb or combine with additional substances.

sat·u·ra·tion, sach″a·rā′shan, *n*. The act of saturating; the state of being saturated; the degree of color intensity, which is determined by the absence of white; the impregnating of a solution until the solvent can contain no more; the state of

maximum magnetization; *meteor.* the atmospheric condition in which relative humidity reaches its highest percentage.

Sat·ur·day, sat′ér·dē, sat′ér·dā″, *n*. [O.E. *Saeterdaeg, Saeterndaeg*, lit. 'Saturn's day.'] The seventh or last day of the week; the day following Friday.—**Sat·ur·days**, sat′ér·dēz, sat′ér·dāz″, *adv*. On Saturdays; every Saturday.

Sat·urn, sat′érn, *n*. [L. *Saturnus*, connected with *sero, satum*, to sow.] *Astron.* the planet, located between Jupiter and Uranus and second in size to Jupiter, encircled by rings thought to be composed of icy particles; *Rom. mythol.* the agricultural deity supposed to have been dominant during a period of abundance called the Golden Age; *alchem.* the name for lead. See Table of the Planets.—**Sa·tur·ni·an**, sa·tᵤr′nē·an, *a*. Pertaining to or of Saturn, the planet; pertaining to the god Saturn or to his reign known as the Golden Age; simple, virtuous, and happy.

sa·tur·ni·id, sa·tᵤr′nē·id, *n*. Any member of the moth family, *Saturniidae*, large, hairy, and usu. brightly colored. Also **gi·ant silk·worm moth.—***a*.

sat·ur·nine, sat′ér·nīn″, *a*. Under the influence of the planet Saturn. Morose; of a gloomy temper; sluggish; heavy; pertaining to lead or the absorbing of lead, as a person with lead poisoning.—**sat·ur·nine·ly**, *adv*.—**sat·ur·nine·ness**, **sat·ur·nin·i·ty**, *n*.

sat·ur·nism, sat′ér·niz″um, *n. Pathol.* lead poisoning.

Sat·ya·gra·ha, sat·ya·gra·ha, sut′ya-·gru″ha, sat·yä′gra·ha, *n*. [Hind. < Skt. *satya*, truth, and *graha*, hold or grasping = the hold or power of truth.] A movement for civil reform through passive, nonviolent resistance, started by Mohandas Gandhi in India during the British rule.

sa·tyr, sā′tér, sat′ér, *n*. [L. *satyrus*, < Gr. *satyros*.] A sylvan deity or demigod of the Greeks and Romans, half man and half goat; a lecher; *zool.* a butterfly of the family *Satyridae*, marked with small eyelike spots on the wings. A man with satyriasis.—**sa·tyr·ic**, sa·tir′ik, *a*.

sa·ty·ri·a·sis, sā″ti·rī′a·sis, sat″i·rī′a·sis, *n. Pathol.* an uncontrollable sexual appetite in males.

sa·tyr play, *n*. An ancient Greek burlesque with a chorus portraying satyrs, usu. presented as an afterpiece to a tragic trilogy.

sauce, sᴀs, *n*. [O.Fr. *sausse, salse* (Fr. *sauce*), < M.L. *salsa*, sauce, lit. 'something salted,' prop. fem. of L. *salsus*, pp. of *salire*, to salt; < *sal*, salt.] Any preparation, usu. liquid or soft, eaten as a relish, dressing, or gravy accompaniment to food; something that adds piquancy; stewed fruit; as, apple *sauce*. *Colloq.* sauciness or impertinence; *dial.* garden vegetables such as are eaten with meat.—*v.t.—sauced, saucing*. To dress or prepare with sauce; to season; to give zest to; *colloq.* to speak impertinently to.

sauce·box, sᴀs′boks″, *n. Colloq.* a saucy, impudent fellow.

sauce·pan, sᴀs′pan″, *n*. A small pot, deeper than a frying pan, for boiling or stewing.

sau·cer, sᴀ′sér, *n*. [Orig. a small pan or other vessel for sauce.] A shallow piece of china or other ware, small and round in shape, in which a cup is set; any dish, plate, or vessel shaped like a saucer.

sau·cy, sᴀ′sē, *a.—saucier, sauciest*. [< *sauce*, in the sense of pertness or impudence.] Flippant or impudent; treating superiors with impertinence; pert; sprightly.—**sau·ci·ly**, *adv*.—**sau·ci·ness**, *n*.

sau·er·bra·ten, sour′brät″en, sou′ér·brät″-en, *G*. zou′ér·brät″en, *n*. A marinated beef pot roast.

sauer·kraut, sour′krout″, sou′ér·krout″, *n*. [G. *sauer*, sour, and *kraut*, herb, cabbage.]

A traditionally German cabbage cut fine, pressed into a cask between layers of salt, and allowed to ferment.

sau·ger, sᴀ′gér, *n*. [Origin uncertain.] A N. American pikeperch, *Stizostedion canadense*.

sau·na, sou′nä, sou′na, sᴀ′nä, sᴀ′na, *n*. A steam bath taken in the Finnish manner, the steam coming from water being poured over heated stones; a bathhouse or room for taking a sauna.

saun·ter, sᴀn′tér, sän′tér, *v.i.* [Origin obscure.] To walk along leisurely; to stroll.—*n*. A leisurely, aimless walk; a stroll.—**saun·ter·er**, *n*.

sau·rel, sᴀr′el, *n*. [Fr.] Any of the small marine fishes constituting the genus *Trachurus*, as the scad, a common species of the northern Atlantic.

sau·ri·an, sᴀr′ē·an, *a*. [N.L. *Sauria*, pl., < Gr. *sauros, saura*, lizard.] Belonging or pertaining to the *Sauria*, a suborder of reptiles orig. including the lizards, crocodiles, and certain extinct forms, as dinosaurs, but now commonly restricted to the lizards; lizardlike.—*n*. A saurian animal.

sau·ro·pod, sᴀr′o·pod″, *n*. [N.L. *Sauropoda*, pl., < Gr. *sauros*, lizard, and *pous(pod-)*, foot.] Any of the *Sauropoda*, a suborder of herbivorous dinosaur with small head, long neck and tail, and five-toed limbs, the largest of all known land animals.—*a*. Belonging or pertaining to the *Sauropoda*. —**sau·rop·o·dous**, sᴀ·rop′o·dus, *a*.

sau·ry, sᴀr′ē, *n. pl.* **sau·ries**. [Origin uncertain.] An edible, long-snouted fish, *Scomberesox saurus*, of the Atlantic; any of various related fishes. Also **skip·per**.

sau·sage, sᴀ′sij, *n*. [O.Fr. *saussiche, saussice* (Fr. *saucisse*), < M.L. *salsicia*, sausage, < L. *salsus*, pp., salted.] Minced pork, beef, or other meats, often combined with various added ingredients and seasonings, either stuffed into a casing, usu. of a prepared intestine, or formed into patties; also *wurst. Aeron.* a sausage-shaped barrage or captive balloon.—**sau·sage·like**, *a*.

sau·té, sō·tā′, sa·tā′, *a*. [Fr., pp. of *sauter*, leap, cause to leap, toss, < L. *saltare*.] Cooked or browned quickly in a pan containing a little fat.—*n*. A dish of food sautéed.—*v.t.—sautéed, sautéing*. To cook or pan-fry quickly using little fat.

sau·terne, sau·ternes, sō·tᵤrn′, sa·tᵤrn′, Fr. sō·tᴇrn′, *n*. [Fr. *Sauternes*, district in southwestern France, near Bordeaux.] A French white wine, sweet or dry.

sav·age, sav′ij, *a*. [O.E. and O.Fr. *salvage* (Mod.Fr. *sauvage*), L.L. *salvaticus*, L. *silvaticus*, wild, < *silva*, a wood.] Untamed, ferocious, or fierce; as, *savage* beasts; barbarous or uncivilized; furious or violent; as, a *savage* temper; untaught or rude; as, *savage* manners; uncultivated or wild, as the forest or wilderness.—*n*. A human being in his native, uncivilized state; a cruel or brutal person; a barbarian; one who is rude or uncultivated.—**sav·age·ly**, *adv*.—**sav·age·ness**, *n*.—**sav·age·ry**, sav′-ij·rē, *n. pl.* **sav·age·ries**.—**sav·ag·ism**, sav′a·jiz″um, *n*.

sa·van·na, sa·van·nah, sa·van′a, *n*. [Sp. *sabana*, prop. a sheet for a bed, a plain, < L. *sabanum*, Gr. *sabanon*, a linen cloth.] An extensive open grassy plain or meadow with scattered shrubs and trees, found in tropical or subtropical regions.

sa·vant, sa·vänt′, sav′ant, Fr. sä·vän′, *n*. [Fr., ppr. of *savoir*, L. *sapere*, to know.] A man of learning; scholar.

sav·a·rin, sav′a·rin, *n*. A spongy, leavened cake, made in a mold, and often in rum syrup.

save, sāv, *v.t.—saved, saving*. [O.Fr. *sauver, salver* (Fr. *sauver*), < L.L. *salvare*, save, < L. *salvus*, safe, unharmed.] To rescue from danger; preserve from harm, injury, loss, or destruction; to keep intact or unhurt; maintain; safeguard; to keep from being lost, as a game or match; to set apart, reserve, or lay by, as for future use; to avoid the spending, consumption, or waste of, as money, goods, or time; to treat carefully in order to reduce wear or fatigue; to prevent the occurrence of; to obviate the necessity of, as: A stitch in time *saves* nine. *Theol.* to deliver from the power and consequences of sin; *sports*, to prevent, as a ball or a puck, from passing through one's goal.—*v.i.* To lay up money as the result of economy; to be economical in expenditure; to keep someone or something from injury or danger; to keep without spoiling, esp. food, as: Ham *saves* well. *Sports*, to prevent a ball or a puck from passing through one's goal.—*n.* An act of saving, esp. in certain sports.—**sav·a·ble**, **save·a·ble**, *a.*—**sav'er**, *n.*

save, sāv, *prep.* Except or but, as: All the children *save* two went to the picnic.

save, sāv, *conj.* Except; but.

save-all, sāv'al", *n.* [*Save* and *all.*] A contrivance intended to save anything from being wasted; a secondary sail to catch wind spillage; a net hung beneath the site of cargo transfer; overalls; pinafore.

sav·e·loy, sav'e·loi", *n.* [Fr. *cervelas*, < *cervelle*, the brains, < L. *cerebellum.*] A highly seasoned dried sausage, orig. made of pigs' brains, now made of young salted pork.

sav·in, sav·ine, sav'in, *n.* [O.Fr. *savine* (Fr. *sabine*), < L. *Sabina (herba)*, 'Sabine (herb).'] A small juniper of Asia and Europe, *Juniperus sabina*, whose dried tops are used as a drug; the drug itself.

sav·ing, sā'ving, *a.* That saves; rescuing; preserving; redeeming or compensating; as, a *saving* feature; accustomed to save; economical; making a reservation; as, a *saving* clause.—*n.* Economy; a reduction in expenditure; as, a *saving* of 20 percent; that which is saved; *pl.* sums of money saved by the exercise of economy and put aside; *law*, a reservation or exception.—*prep.* Except or save; as, none *saving* imperfect ones; with all due respect to or for; as, *saving* your presence.—*conj.* Save.—**sav·ing·ly**, *adv.*

sav·ings and loan as·so·ci·a·tion, *n.* A cooperative organization that exchanges share capital for the deposits and savings of its members, and invests for profit in home mortgages. Also **build·ing and loan as·so·ci·a·tion.**

sav·ings bank, *n.* An institution which receives and invests savings, and returns interest on deposits.

sav·ings bond, *n.* A bond sold by the U.S. Government in principal amounts of up to $10,000, with a maturity time of ten years.

sav·ior, *Brit.* **sav·iour**, sāv'yèr, *n.* [O.Fr. *sauveour* (Fr. *sauveur*), < L.L. *salvator*, < *salvare*, E. *save.*] One who saves, rescues, or delivers; (*cap.*) a title of God and esp. of Christ, often preceded by 'the.'

sa·voir-faire, sav'wär·fâr', *Fr.* sä·vwaR·-feR', *n.* [Fr., lit. 'to know how to do.'] The knowledge of just what to do or say under any circumstances; tact.

sa·vor, *Brit.* **sa·vour**, sā'vèr, *n.* [O.Fr. *savor*, Mod.Fr. *saveur*, L. *sapor*, *sapio*, to taste.] The power or quality of something that affects the palate, esp. in a favorable way; a specific flavor or smell; a distinctive quality; the ability to stimulate or excite.—*v.i.* To have a particular taste or flavor; to have the distinctive quality, nature, or appearance, followed by *of*, as: His conduct *savors* of pride.—*v.t.* To season; to taste or smell with relish; to enjoy or take delight in.—**sa·vor·er**, *n.*

sa·vor·y, *Brit.* **sa·vour·y**, sā'vo·rē, *a.*—*savorier*, *savoriest.* Having a pleasant

flavor and smell; pleasantly piquant to the taste; respectable.—*n.* pl. **sa·vor·ies.** *Brit.* a spicy dish eaten either before a meal to stimulate the appetite or afterward as a dessert.—**sa·vor·i·ly**, *adv.*—**sa·vor·i·ness**, *n.*

sa·vor·y, sā'vo·rē, *n.* [M.E. *saverey*, ult. < L. *satureia*, savory.] *Bot.* any of the aromatic, menthaceous plants of the genus *Satureia*, esp. *S. hortensis*, an herb native in southern Europe and much cultivated as a seasoning. Also **sum·mer sa·vor·y.**

sa·voy, sa·voi', *n.* [Because brought from *Savoy.*] A variety of cabbage with a closely packed head of wrinkled leaves. Also **sa·voy cab·bage.**

sav·vy, sav'ē, *v.t.*, *v.i.*—*savvied*, *savvying.* [Sp. *sabe* (*sabe usted*, 'do you know,' *no sabe*, 'he does not know,' etc.), < *saber*, know, < L. *sapere*, be wise: see *sapient.*] *Slang.* To know; understand.—*n.* *Slang.* Understanding; intelligence; common sense.—*a.*—*savvier*, *savviest.* Characterized by shrewdness or understanding.

saw, sạ, *n.* [O.E. *saga*, *sage*, a saw = Dan. *sav*, Icel. *sög*, D. *zaag*, O. *sage*; same root as L. *seco*, to cut.] A hand tool or powered cutting instrument consisting of a blade, band, or disk of thin metal with a dentated or toothed edge.—*v.t.*—past *sawed*, pp. *sawed* or *sawn*, ppr. *sawing.* To cut with a saw; to form by cutting with a saw; to move through, slash, or slice as if operating a saw; as, to *saw* the air.—*v.i.* To use a saw; to cut with a saw; to be cut with a saw, as wood.—**saw·er**, *n.*—**saw·like**, *a.*

saw, sạ, *n.* [O.E. *sagu*, a saying, a saw, from stem of to *say.*] A saying; proverb; maxim.

saw·buck, sạ'buk", *n.* [= D. *zaagbok*.] A sawhorse with X-shaped end supports; *slang*, a ten-dollar bill.

saw·dust, sạ'dust", *n.* The small bits and particles of wood or another material produced by the operation of a saw.

sawed-off, sạd'af", sạd'of", *a.* Cut off with a saw at one end; *slang*, short or of unusually small stature, as a man.

saw·fish, sạ'fish", *n.* pl. **saw·fish, saw·-fishes.** A large, elongate elasmobranch fish of the genus *Pristis*, common in tropical seas, and having teethlike spines on both edges of its long bony snout.

saw·fly, sạ'flī", *n.* pl. **saw·flies.** Any of the hymenopterous insects constituting the family *Tenthredinidae*, the females of which are characterized by a sawlike ovipositor for cutting slits in plants for the depositing of eggs.

saw grass, *n.* Any of various sedge plants, esp. of the genus *Cladium*, with the edges of the leaves toothed like a saw.

saw·horse, sạ'hars", *n.* A frame for holding wood that is being sawed.

saw log, *n.* A log that is big enough to be cut into lumber.

saw·mill, sạ'mil", *n.* An establishment where timber is sawed into planks or boards by machinery; a machine for sawing timber.

saw pal·met·to, *n.* A shrublike palmetto, *Serenoa repens*, of the southern U.S. and West Indies, having leafstalks edged with spiny teeth.

saw set, *n.* An instrument used to set a saw and bend the teeth outward.

saw·tim·ber, sạ'tim"bèr, *n.* Suitable trees of appropriate size to be sawed into boards.

saw-toothed, sạ'tötht", *a.* Having teeth like a saw; serrated. Also **saw·tooth, sạ'töth".**

saw-whet owl, sạ'hwet" oul', sạ'wet", *n.* An extremely small, brown-streaked, N. American owl, *Aegolius acadicus.* Also **saw-whet.**

saw·yer, sạ'yèr, soi'èr, *n.* One who saws wood, usu. as an occupation; any of the various longicorn beetles having larvae that bore holes into the wood of dead trees, esp. conifers; a tree caught in a riverbed with branches visible above the water.

sax, saks, *n. Colloq.* a saxophone.

sax·a·tile, sak'sa·til, *a.* [L. *saxatilis*, < *saxum*, a rock.] Living upon or among rocks. Also *saxicolous.*

sax·horn, saks'harn", *n.* [After *A. F. Sax*, of Paris, the inventor.] *Mus.* any of a brass-wind family of instruments with a wide mouthpiece, valves, and a large range of tones.

sax·ic·o·lous, sak·sik'o·lus, *a.* [L. *saxum*, a rock, and *colo*, to inhabit.] Growing on or amidst rocks. Also *saxatile*, **sax·ic·o·line**, sak·sik'o·lin, sak·sik'o·lin".

sax·i·frage, sak'si·frij, *n.* [L. *saxifraga*—*saxum*, a stone, and *frango*, to break.] Any of the mostly perennial herbs belonging to the genus *Saxifraga*, usu. having clustered basal leaves and pentamerous flowers, and found growing among rocks in temperate and subarctic regions.—**sax·i·fra·ga·-ceous**, *a.*

Sax·on, sak'son, *n.* [L. *Saxo*, pl. *Saxones*, O.E. *Seaxa*, pl. *Seaxe*, *Seaxan*, usu. derived < *seax*, O.H.G. *sahs*, a short sword; G. *Sachse*, a Saxon.] An Anglo-Saxon; an Englishman; the language of the Saxons; a native or inhabitant of modern Saxony; one of the people formerly dwelling in the northern part of Germany who invaded and conquered England in the 5th and 6th centuries.—*a.* English; pertaining to the ancient Saxons, their country, or their language; pertaining to modern Saxony.—**Sax·on·ism**, sak'so·niz"um, *n.* An idiom, phrase, or word of English, esp. early Anglo-Saxon origin.

sax·o·ny, sak'so·nē, *n.* pl. **sax·o·nies.** A fine wool orig. from Saxony, Germany; the soft, compactly woven cloth made of this or similar wool; a fine-textured woolen yarn.

sax·o·phone, sak'so·fōn", *n. Mus.* a tubular brass or silver wind instrument, with a reed mouthpiece and tonal finger keys.—**sax·o·phon·ic**, sak"so·fon'ik, *a.*—**sax·o·phon·ist**, *n.*

sax·tu·ba, saks'tö"ba, saks'tū"ba, *n.* [Cf. *saxhorn* and *tuba.*] A large, bass form of saxhorn.

say, sā, *v.t.*—*said*, *saying.* [O.E. *secgan*, to say = Icel. *segja*, D. *zeggen*, Dan. *sige*, G. *sagen*, to say.] To utter or speak; to state or express in words; to give as a belief or opinion; to repeat or recite; as, to *say* a pledge; to communicate; to allege or report, as: They *say* he will be promoted.—*v.i.* To speak; to declare; to state an opinion.—*n.* What one has to say or says; something said; opportunity or turn to speak; authority, as: He has the final *say.*—*adv.* About; approximately, as: That will cost, *say*, ten dollars.—**that is to say**, in other words; otherwise.—**say·a·ble**, sā'a·bl, *a.*—**say·er**, *n.*

say·ing, sā'ing, *n.* That which is said; a proverb; a maxim; an adage.

say-so, sā'sō", *n.* pl. **say-sos.** *Colloq.* One's personal statement or assertion; the right to decide; dictum.

say·yid, say·id, sā'yid, sä'id, *n.* [Ar., 'lord': cf. *Cid.*] *Mohammedan*, a title of respect given to a person supposed to be descended from Mohammed through his daughter Fatima. Also **sa·id**, sä'id.

scab, skab, *n.* [O.E. *scaeb*, < L. *scabies*, scab, itch, < *scabo*, to scratch. Hence *shabby.*] A sort of crust formed over a sore in healing; *veter. pathol.* scabies or mange in animals, esp. in sheep. A fungous or bacterial plant disease causing crustlike spots in the affected areas. *Slang*, a non-union workman, esp. one who works in the place of a striker; a union worker who does not participate in a strike; a scoundrel or villainous fellow. *Metal.* a roughness or scale on the surface of a piece of iron or steel.—*v.i.*—*scabbed, scabbing.* To form or to have scabs; to work as a scab.—**scab·like**, *a.*

scab·bard, skab'ẽrd, *n.* [Formerly *scaubert*, *scaberke*, *scaberge*, etc.; perh. < O.E. *sceatha*, scathe, and *beorgan*, O.H.G. *bergan*, to protect (cf. *hauberk*), the scabbard being what prevents the weapon from doing harm when not in use.] The sheath of a sword or other similar weapon.—*v.t.* To put in a scabbard or sheath.

scab·ble, skab'l, *v.t.*—*scabbled, scabbling.* *Masonry,* to dress, as stone, with a rough, slightly furrowed surface.

scab·by, skab'ē, *a.*—*scabbier, scabbiest.* Covered or coated with scabs; affected with scabies, as an animal or plant. *Slang,* low or mean; vile.—**scab·bi·ness**, *n.*

sca·bies, skā'bēz, skā'bē·ēz”, *n. pl. but sing. in constr.* [L., < *scabere*, scratch, scrape; prob. akin to E. *shave.*] *Pathol.* an easily transmitted skin disease, the itch, due to the itch mite, afflicting cattle and sheep as well as man.—**sca·bi·et·ic**, skā”bē·et'ik, *a.*

sca·bi·ous, skā'bē·us, *a.* [L. *scabiosus*, < *scabies.*] Pertaining to or of the nature of scabies; scabby.

sca·bi·ous, skā'bē·us, *n.* [O.Fr. Fr. *scabieuse*, < M.L. *scabiosa* (so called from its repute as a cure for skin diseases), prop. fem. of L. *scabiosus*, E. *scabious.*] Any plant of the genus *Scabiosa*, which comprises a large number of teasellike herbs with showy, dense flower heads of various colors. Also **sca·bi·o·sa**, skā”bē·ō'sa.

scab·rous, skab'rus, *a.* [L.L. *scabrosus*, for L. *scaber* (*scabr-*), rough, scurfy, < *scabere.*] Rough with minute points or projections; harsh; full of difficulties; indelicate or risqué.—**scab·rous·ly**, *adv.*—**scab·rous·ness**, *n.*

scad, skad, *n. pl.* **scad, scads.** [Origin unknown.] The saurel, *Trachurus symmetricus*, a popular salt-water food fish, as the pompano, cavalla, jacks, and the like, of America and Europe; any of various other carangid fishes.

scad, skad, *n. Usu. pl., slang,* large amounts or quantities of; as, *scads* of money.

scaf·fold, skaf'old, skaf'ōld, *n.* [< a var. of O.Fr. *eschafaut* (Fr. *échafaud*), < *es-* (< L. *ex-*, out) and *chafaut*, platform, stage, ult. the same word as *catafalque*, appar. < Gr. *katá*, down, and L. *fala, phala*, scaffold, high wooden structure.] A temporary structure for holding workmen and materials during the erection, repair, or decoration of a building; an elevated platform on which a criminal is executed; a raised platform, stage, or stand for exhibiting spectacles, seating spectators, or the like; any raised framework.—*v.t.* To furnish with a scaffold or scaffolding; to support by or place on a scaffold.—**scaf·fold·ing**, skaf'ol·ding, skaf'ōl·ding, *n.* A scaffold or system of scaffolds, as for use in building; materials for scaffolds.

scagl·io·la, skal·yō'la, *n.* [It.] A composition of glue and gypsum, imitative of marble, and used for columns and internal walls of buildings.

scal·a·ble, skā'la·bl, *a.* That may be scaled, as a mountain or wall.

sca·lade, ska·lād', *n.* Escalade. Also **sca·la·do**.

scal·age, skā'lij, *n.* The proportionate reduction allowed in dealings with merchandise liable to shrinkage, leakage, or similar decrease, to allow for the amount of loss expected; the amount of good lumber contained or estimated to be contained in a log, logs, or standing timber.

sca·lar, skā'lẽr, *a.* [L. *scalaris*, < *scala*, flight of steps, ladder, E. *scale.*] Resembling a ladder, as numbers and lines on a thermometer; *math.* of a quantity, having magnitude but not direction, as temperature.

—*n. Math.* an entity representing that which has a magnitude without direction. Compare *vector.*

sca·lar·e, ska·lâr'ē, ska·lär'ē, *n.* A S. American silver and black, fresh-water fish, *Pterophyllum scalare*, often kept in aquariums.

sca·lar·i·form, ska·lar'i·fạrm”, *a.* [L. *scalaria*, a ladder, and *forma*, form.] *Bot.* shaped like or resembling a ladder, as vessel cells in plants.

sca·lar prod·uct, *n. Math.* a scalar equal to the product of the magnitudes of any two vectors and the cosine of an angle between their positive directions.

scal·a·wag, *Brit.* **scal·la·wag**, skal'a·-wag”, *n.* [Origin obscure.] *Slang,* a scamp, rascal, or good-for-nothing fellow; *U.S. hist.* a native white Southerner of the Reconstruction period after the Civil War, who acted with the Republican party. Also *scallywag.*

scald, skạld, *v.t.* [O.Fr. *excalder, eschalder* (Fr. *échauder*), scald, < L.L. *excaldare*, wash in hot water, < L. *ex-*, out, and *caldus, calidus*, hot: cf. *caldron.*] To burn or affect painfully with or as with hot liquid or steam; to subject to the action of boiling or hot liquid, as for cleansing purposes; to heat to a temperature just short of the boiling point; as, to *scald* milk.—*v.i.* To be or become scalded.—*n.* A burn caused by hot liquid or steam; *plant pathol.* tissue discoloration due to unsuitable conditions during storage or growth, or to fungus or other parasitic infections.—**scalding**, *a.* Imparting a burning sensation; boiling hot; *fig.* searing or scathing; as, a *scalding* reprimand.

scald, scalled, skạld, *a.* [Earlier *scalled*, < *scall.*] Affected with scall or scurf; scabby.

scald, skạld, skäld, *n.* Skald.—**scald·ic**, *a.*

scale, skāl, *n.* [M.E. *scale, scole*, < Scand.: cf. Icel. *skāl*, bowl, scale for weighing, akin to O.H.G. *scāla*, bowl, *scala*, shell (G. *schale*), O.E. *scealu*, dish, shell, also to E. *scale* and *shell.*] A balance or any other device for weighing; either of the dishes or pans of a balance.—*v.t.*—*scaled, scaling.* To weigh in or as in scales; to have a weight of.—**tip the scale**, to weigh, usu. with *at.*—**turn the scales**, to change an expected outcome.

scale, skāl, *n.* [O.Fr. *escale, eschale*, scale, shell (Fr. *écale*, shell, *écaille*, scale); < Teut., and akin to E. *scale.*] One of the thin, flat, horny plates that form the covering of certain animals, as fishes; any thin, plate-like piece, lamina, layer, or flake such as peels from a surface. *Bot.* a thin scarious or membranous part of a plant, as a bract of a catkin; a specialized leaf which protects a plant bud; a bud scale. A scale insect; coating or incrustation, as on the inside of a boiler; an oxidized coating that forms on the surface of heated metals, esp. iron. —*v.t. scaled, scaling.* To remove the scales from; to remove in scales or thin layers; to cover with an incrustation or scale; to skip over water, as a flat stone.—*v.i.* To come off in scales; to become coated with scale.—**scaled**, *a.*—**scale·less**, *a.*—**scale·like**, *a.*—**scal·i·ness**, *n.*

scale, skāl, *n.* [L. *scala*, usu. pl. *scalae*, flight of steps, ladder, < *scandere*, climb.] A succession or progression of steps or degrees; a graduated series or table, as of prices; a series of marks separated by distances for measurement; an instrument with graduated spaces for measuring; the proportion which the representation of an object bears to the object; as, a model on a *scale* of one inch to a foot; a certain relative or proportionate size or extent; *arith.* a system of numerical notation; as, the decimal *scale*; *mus.* a definite series or succession of tones ascending or descending

according to fixed intervals, esp. such a series beginning on a particular note; as, the major *scale* of C; *psychol., educ.* an arranged and graded series of results of tests, tasks, or questions given a large group of people, and used to measure the relative performance of an individual.—*v.t.* —*scaled, scaling.* To climb by or as by a ladder; to climb up or over; to ascend or mount; to measure by or as if by a scale; *lumbering,* to measure or estimate, as the amount of lumber yielded by standing timber. To make according to scale; to reduce in amount according to a fixed scale or proportion, usu. with *down.*—*v.i.* To climb, ascend, or mount.—*a.*

scale in·sect, *n.* Any of various small, plant-destroying insects of the homopterous family *Coccidae*, the females of which have the body and eggs covered by a large scalelike or waxy secretion.

scale leaf, *n.* A modified scalelike leaf, as a bract or leaf covering a leaf bud.

scale moss, *n.* Any of certain liverworts of the class *Hepaticae*, with small, imbricated, scalelike leaves.

sca·lene, skā·lēn', *a.* [Gr. *skalēnos*, limping, uneven.] Of a triangle, having three unequal sides; of a cone, having an inclined axis; *anat.* relating to the scalenus. Also **sca·le·nous**.

sca·le·nus, skā·lē'nus, *n. pl.* **sca·le·ni**, skā·lē'nī. *Anat.* any of a group of three muscles on either side of the cervical vertebrae which aid in respiration and in bending the neck.

scal·er, skā'lẽr, *n.* A person who or something which scales; an electronic instrument which gives one pulse for every group of a specified number of pulses that it receives.

Scales, skālz, *n. Astron.* the constellation or zodiacal sign of Libra.

scall, skạl, *n.* [M.E. *scall*: cf. Icel. *skalli*, bald head.] A scaly or scabby skin eruption, esp. on the scalp; a scurf.

scal·lion, skal'yan, *n.* [O.Fr. *escalogne*, It. *scalogno*, < L. (*caepa*) *Ascalonia*, the onion of *Ascalon.*] A kind of onion with a long stalk and small, narrow bulb; a shallot; a leek. Also *green onion.*

scal·lop, skol'op, skal'op, *n.* [O.Fr. *escalope*, shell, < Teut.: cf. D. *schelp*, shell, and E. *scalp.*] Any of the bivalve mollusks of the genus *Pecten*, and related genera; the adductor muscle of certain species of mollusks, valued as seafood; one of the shells or valves of a mollusk, usually having radial ribs and a wavy outer edge; a scallop shell or a dish in which seafood is baked or served; one of a series of semi-circular shapes along an edge for ornamentation. Also *scollup.*—*v.t.* To mark, cut, or ornament with scallops, as the edge of a garment; to bake, usu. with a milky sauce topped with crumbs. Also *escallop, scollop.* —*v.i.* To gather or collect scallops.— **scal·lop·er**, *n.*

scal·ly·wag, skal'ē·wag”, *n.* Scalawag.

sca·lop·pi·ne, sca·lo·pi·ni, skä”lo·pē'-nē, skal'o·pē·nē, *n.* A meat dish of thin slices of veal or other meat floured or breaded and usu. cooked in wine sauce.

scalp, skalp, *n.* [M.E. *scalp*, < Scand. cf. Icel. *skālpr*, sheath, D. *schelp*, shell, and E. *scallop.*] The integument of the upper part of the head, usu. including the associated subcutaneous structures; a part of this integument with the accompanying hair, cut from a person's head by the N. American Indians as a trophy of victory; any souvenir of victory; *colloq.* a small profit made in quick buying and selling.— *v.t.* To cut or tear the scalp from; to remove the top or covering of. *Colloq.* to buy cheap and sell at less than official rates, as theater tickets; to buy and sell so as to make small, quick profits, as stocks.—*v.i.*

Colloq. To scalp tickets; to buy and sell stocks so as to make small, quick profits.—**scalp·er**, *n.*

scal·pel, skal′pel, *n.* [L. *scalpellum*, dim. of *scalprum*, a knife, < *scalpo*, to cut, to scrape.] A small, sharp-bladed knife used in anatomical dissections and surgical operations.

scalp lock, *n.* A long lock or tuft of hair left on an otherwise clean-shaven scalp, and worn by various N. American Indians as an implied challenge to their enemies.

scal·y, skā′lē, *a.*—*scalier, scaliest.* Covered with or abounding in scales or scale; characterized by scales; consisting of scales or scale; of the nature of scales. *Slang,* shabby; despicable; mean.—**scal·i·ness**, *n.*

scal·y ant·eat·er, *n.* Pangolin.

scam·mo·ny, skam′o·nē, *n.* pl. **scam·mo·nies.** [O.Fr. *escamonie* < Fr. *scammonée*, < L. *scammonia*, < Gr. *scammonia*, scammony.] A twining Asiatic species of convolvulus, *Convolvulus scammonia,* of the morning-glory family; the cathartic gum resin obtained from it.

scamp, skamp, *n.* [Orig. one who decamps or runs off without paying debts.] A worthless fellow; a knave; a rogue; a rascal.—*v.t.* To act or function in a careless or perfunctory manner.—**scamp·er**, *n.*

scamp·er, skam′pẽr, *v.i.* [< O.Fr. *escamper,* Pr. *escampar,* It. *scampare,* to save one's life, to escape; lit. 'to decamp,' < L. *ex,* out of, and *campus,* a field. Hence *scamp.*] To run hastily or in a frolicking manner; to hurry away.—*n.* A hurried or quick run.

scan, skan, *v.t.*—*scanned, scanning.* [Formerly *scand,* < Fr. *scander,* to scan verse, < L. *scando,* to climb, to scan (seen in *ascend, descend*); Skt. *skand,* to climb.] To examine minutely; to scrutinize; to pass over quickly with the eyes; as, to *scan* a newspaper; to examine, as verse, by counting the metrical feet or syllables; to read so as to indicate the metrical structure; *TV,* to pass over(an object)with an electronic beam so as to pick up and transmit the image; *radar,* to sweep or traverse(an airspace) with beams emanating from a radar station.—*v.i.* To examine the metrical content of verse; to comply with metrical rules; *TV,* to pass an electronic beam over a surface or object.—*n.*

scan·dal, skan′dal, *n.* [Fr. *scandale,* < L. *scandalum,* Gr. *skandalon,* a snare, a scandal. *Slander* is a different form of this word.] A discreditable or disgraceful event, action, or circumstance; an offense resulting from fault or misdeed; public reproach or disgrace; malicious, defamatory talk; one who disgraces or offends, as: She was a *scandal* to her family.

scan·dal·ize, skan′da·līz″, *v.t.*—*scandalized, scandalizing.* To offend by some action considered improper or outrageous; to shock; to give offense to; to disgrace; to malign.—**scan·dal·iz·er**, *n.*—**scan·dal·i·za·tion**, skan″da·liz·ā′shan, *n.*

scan·dal·mon·ger, skan′dal·mung″gẽr, skan′dal·mong″gẽr, *n.* One who repeats gossip or scandal.

scan·dal·ous, skan′da·lus, *a.* Causing scandal or offense; shameful; harmful to reputation; liking and spreading scandal; as, a *scandalous* conduct.—**scan·dal·ous·ly**, *adv.*—**scan·dal·ous·ness**, *n.*

scan·dal sheet, *n.* A publication, as a magazine or newspaper, based on gossip and scandal.

scan·dent, skan′dent, *a.* [L. *scandens, scandentis,* ppr. of *scando,* to climb.] *Bot.* climbing, as a vine.

Scan·di·na·vi·an, skan″di·nā′vē·an, *a.* [L. *Scandinavia:* cf. Icel. *Skāni, Skāney,* southernmost district of the Scandinavian peninsula.] Of or pertaining to Scandinavia, the region comprising Norway,

Sweden, and Denmark, and sometimes Iceland, Finland, and the Faroe Islands, or to the inhabitants or languages of Scandinavia. Also **Scan·di·an**, skan′dē·an.—*n.* A native or inhabitant of Scandinavia; the Scandinavian languages.

scan·di·um, skan′dē·um, *n.* A rare trivalent metallic element. Sym. Sc, at. no. 21, at. wt. 44.956. See Periodic Table of Elements.

scan·ner, skan′er, *n.* One who scans; an instrument that inspects, as for accuracy or performance, a certain operation or condition.

scan·sion, skan′shan, *n.* The act of scanning; an analysis of the metrical structure of verse.

scan·so·ri·al, skan·sōr′ē·al, skan·sạr′ē·al, *a.* [L. *scansorius,* < *scandere,* climb.] *Zool.* Pertaining to or adapted for climbing, as the feet of some birds; habitually climbing, as a bird.

scant, skant, *a.* [Same as Icel. *skamt,* short, brief, akin to Norse *skanta,* exactly measured. Cf. Provinc. E. and Sc. *skimp, skemp,* to give short measure.] Scarcely sufficient; less than is wanted for the purpose; having a limited supply, usu. followed by *of;* as, *scant* of resources; meager; not quite amounting to a specified quantity; as, a *scant* cup of flour.—*v.t.* To limit; to stint; to give out sparingly; to grudge; to treat slightingly or in a cursory manner.—*adv. Dial.* Scarcely; hardly; not quite.—**scant·ly**, *adv.*—**scant·ness**, *n.*

scan·ties, skan′tēz, *n. pl.* Women's brief panties.

scant·ling, skant′ling, *n.* [O.Fr. *escantillon,* a gauge.] A relatively small building timber, such as a rafter or a stud; this timber collectively; the thickness and breadth of a timber or the length, breadth, and thickness of a building stone; a small quantity.

scant·y, skan′tē, *a.*—*scantier, scantiest.* Barely adequate; meager; lacking in amplitude or extent.—**scant·i·ly**, *adv.*—**scant·i·ness**, *n.*

scape, skāp, *n.* [L. *scapus,* shaft, stem.] *Bot.* a leafless stalk rising from the ground; *zool.* a stemlike part of an animal, as the shaft of a feather; *arch.* the shaft of a column.—**sca·pi·form**, skā′pi·fạrm″, skap′-i·fạrm″, *a.*

scape, 'scape, skāp, *v.t.*—*scaped, scaping,* '*scaped,* '*scaping. Archaic,* to escape.—*n. Archaic.* A means of escape; a small mistake of forgetfulness.

scape·goat, skāp′gōt″, *n.* One made to bear the blame for the misdeeds of others. *Bib.* among the ancient Jews, a goat sent into the wilderness on Yom Kippur, the Day of Atonement, bearing the iniquities of the people, which were symbolically laid on its head by the high priest; Lev. xvi: 8.

scape·grace, skāp′grās″, *n.* An unprincipled or mischievous fellow; a rascal; a rogue.

scaph·oid, skaf′oid, *a.* [Gr. *skaphoeidēs,* < *skaphē,* boat, and *eidos,* form.] Boat-shaped; *anat.* noting a bone of the radial side of the carpus, or a bone on the inner side of the tarsus.—*n. Anat.* a scaphoid bone.

scap·o·lite, skap′o·līt″, *n.* [Fr. *scapolite,* < Gr. *skapos,* rod, and *lithos,* stone.] Any of a group of minerals of variable composition, essentially silicates of aluminum, calcium, and sodium, occurring in tetragonal crystals and in masses, and usu. of a white or grayish-white color. Also **wer·ner·ite.**

sca·pose, skā′pōs, *a. Bot.* Having scapes; consisting of or resembling a scape.

scap·u·la, skap′ū·la, skap′ya·la, *n.* pl. **scap·u·lae, scap·u·las**, skap′ū·lē″, skap′-ya·lē″. [L.] *Anat.* shoulder blade.

scap·u·lar, skap′ū·lẽr, skap′ya·lẽr, *n.* The outer garment, usu. sleeveless and without side seams, that is a part of some monastic habits; two small squares of cloth joined by cord and worn over the chest and back as a

symbol of religious devotion; *ornith.* a short feather found on the shoulder structure of birds; *surg.* a supportive bandage used to hold the shoulder or another surgical dressing in position.—*a.* Of or pertaining to the scapula or shoulder. Also **scap·u·lary**, skap′ū·ler″ē, skap′ya·ler″ē.—**scap·u·lar med·al**, the medal counterpart of the cloth squares worn in token of religious devotion.

scar, skär, *n.* [Fr. *escarre, escharre,* L. *eschara,* < Gr. *eschara,* a scar or scab on a wound caused by burning.] The mark of a wound remaining on the skin after healing; *med.* a cicatrix; *bot.* a mark left on a branch or stem, as by a fallen seed, leaf, or severed branch. Any lasting effect caused by past action, emotional stress, or mental injury.—*v.t.*—*scarred, scarring.* To mark with a scar; to cause lasting injury to.—*v.i.* To be marked with a scar; to form a scar.

scar, skär, *n.* [Same as Icel. *skor,* a rift in a precipice, *sker,* a rocky islet; Dan. *skjaer,* a cliff; root seen in *shear, short.*] A cliff; an isolated detached rock; a bare and rocky area on the side of a hill or mountain. Also *Sc. scaur.*

scar·ab, skar′ab, *n.* [L. *scarabaeus,* a beetle.] Any of the group of scarabaeid beetles, esp. *Scarabaeus sacer,* which the ancient Egyptians considered sacred; the figure or representation of a beetle, as cut in a gem.

scar·a·bae·id, skar″a·bē′id, *n.* A beetle of the family *Scarabaeidae,* including dung beetles, June bugs, scarabs, and the like.—*a.*—**scar·a·bae·oid**, skar″a·bē′oid, *a.* Of or pertaining to a scarabaeid; having a stout body and plated antennae.

scar·a·bae·us, skar″a·bē′us, *n.* pl. **scar·a·bae·us·es, scar·a·bae·i**, skar″a·bē′ī. A scarab.

scar·a·boid, skar′a·boid″, *a.* Like a scarab; resembling a scarabaeid.—*n.* A scarab; a scarabaeid.

Scar·a·mouch, Scar·a·mouche, skar′a·mouch″, skar′a·mösh″, *n.* [Fr. *Scaramouche,* < It. *Scaramuccio,* lit. 'skirmish.'] A stock character in Italian comedy and farce, being a cowardly braggart who is constantly beaten by Harlequin. (*l.c.*) a masquerader or buffoon representing or resembling this character; a rascal or scamp.

scarce, skârs, *a.* [< O.Fr. *escars, eschars,* It. *scarso,* D. *schaars,* < L.L. *excarpsus, scarpsus,* for *excerptus,* pp. of L. *excerpo,* to pluck or cull out.] Small in quantity in proportion to the demand; not plentiful or abundant; deficient; rare; uncommon.—*adv.* Scarcely.—**scarce·ness**, *n.*—**scar·ci·ty**, skâr′si·tē, *n.*

scarce·ment, skârs′ment, *n.* The distinct setoff or change in thickness of a wall, bank of earth, or face of other surfaces, along a horizontal line, leaving a wide base or footing, and a′ ledge below the narrowed upper part of the wall or surface.

scare, skâr, *v.t.*—*scared, scaring.* [Akin to Icel. *skjarr,* apt to flee, shy, *skirra,* to drive away.] To frighten; to terrify suddenly.—*v.i.* To become fearful or alarmed.—*n.* A sudden fright or panic, usu. inspired by a trifling cause; a state or time of dread or fear.—*a.*—**scare off** or **scare a·way,** to drive away or force to flee by inducing fear.—**scare up,** to obtain or collect with some difficulty, or on short notice.—**scar·er**, *n.*

scare·crow, skâr′krō″, *n.* An object, usu. a crude figure of a man dressed in old and ragged clothes, set up in a field to frighten away birds, esp. crows, from growing crops; anything of terrifying, but not really dangerous, aspect; *fig.* one who resembles a scarecrow, as in dress.

scare·head, skâr′hed″, *n. Slang,* an unusually large newspaper headline. Also *screamer.*

scare·mon·ger, skâr′mung″gẽr, skâr′- mong″gẽr, *n.* One who instigates or per- petuates a state of alarm by circulating rumors or frightening news.—**scare·mon·- ger·ing,** *n.*

scarf, skärf, *n.* pl. **scarfs, scarves,** skärvz. [Same as L.G. *sherf,* Dan. *skjaerf, skierf,* G. *scharpe,* O.H.G. *scherbe,* orig. a pocket, hence the band suspending the pocket, a scarf.] A square or long piece of material usu. worn around a woman's head, neck, or shoulders, decoratively or for protection or warmth; a sash indicating official rank; a necktie, kerchief, muffler, or tippet; a runner or cloth for a piece of furniture; as, a dresser *scarf.*—*v.t.* To tie, decorate, wrap, or cover using, or as if using, a scarf; to use in the loose, wrapping fashion of a scarf.— **scarf·less,** *a.*—**scarf·like,** *a.*

scarf, skärf, *n.* [Same as Sw. *skarf,* a joint.] *Carp.* the type of joint formed by notching or cutting the ends of two pieces so they interlock and can be bolted to form one continuous piece; the end of a piece so cut. *Whaling,* a long strip of blubber and skin on a whale.—*v.t.* To unite by means of a scarf; to cut a scarf into.—**scarf joint,** a joint formed by scarfing.—**scarf·er,** *n.*

scarf·skin, skärf′skin″, *n.* [< *scarf* (as an outer covering).] The outermost layer of the skin; the epidermis.

scar·i·fy, skar′i·fī″, *v.t.*—*scarified, scari- fying.* [Fr. *scarifier,* L. *scarifico,* < Gr. *skariphasthai,* to scratch open, < *skariphos,* a sharp-pointed instrument.] To super- ficially pierce the skin, as in vaccinating; to criticize harshly; to stir up or break the soil, as with a disc harrow; to scratch or soften seed skins to shorten the germination period.—**scar·i·fi·ca·tion,** skar″i·fi·kā′- shan, *n.*—**scar·i·fi·er,** *n.*

scar·i·ous, skâr′ē·us, *a.* [N.L. *scariosus.*] *Bot.* thin, dry, and membranous, as certain bracts; *zool.* scaly.

scar·la·ti·na, skär″la·tē′na, *n.* [N.L., < It. *scarlattina,* < *scarlatto,* scarlet.] *Pathol.* Scarlet fever; a mild form of scarlet fever.— **scar·la·ti·nal, scar·la·ti·nous,** skär″la- tē′nus, skär·lat′i·nus, *a.* Pertaining to or of the nature of scarlatina.

scar·less, skär′lis, *a.* Bearing no scar; un- scarred; producing or leaving no scar.

scar·let, skär′lit, *n.* [O.Fr. *escarlate, saqalāt,* a word of Persian origin.] A red color brighter than crimson; cloth or apparel of such a color.—*a.* Of the color scarlet; *fig.* lewd, dissolute.

scar·let fe·ver, *n. Pathol.* a contagious streptococcal disease, usu. of children, characterized by fever, inflammation of the throat, and an extensive scarlet rash. Also *scarlatina.*

scar·let let·ter, *n.* [From the novel by Nathaniel Hawthorne.] A scarlet "A," a mark of shame worn by an adulterous woman during Puritan times.

scar·let run·ner, *n.* A high-twining bean, *Phaseolus coccineus,* of tropical America, commonly having scarlet flowers.

scar·let sage, *n.* A red-flowered shrub, *Salvia splendens.*

scarp, skärp, *n.* [< Fr. *escarpe,* < It. *scarpa,* a scarp, a slope, < O.H.G. *scarp,* Mod.G. *scharf,* E. *sharp*—the scarp being cut sharp or steep.] *Fort.* the inner sloping wall of the surrounding ditch of a rampart; an escarp. Any steep slope.—*v.t.* To cut into or furnish with a scarp; to form into a steep slope.

scar tis·sue, *n. Pathol.* connective tissue which has contracted and replaced normal tissue destroyed by disease, surgery, or injury.

scar·y, skâr′ē, *a.*—*scarier, scariest. Colloq.* Causing fright or alarm; easily frightened; timorous.

scat, skat, *v.i.*—*scatted, scatting. Colloq.* to go or drive away in haste.—*interj.* [Appar. < *cat,* preceded by a hissing sound.] An exclamation used to drive away animals, as a cat.

scat, skat, *n. Slang,* singing consisting of improvised nonsense or meaningless syl- lables, esp. in jazz.—*v.i. Slang,* to sing or improvise in such a manner.

scat·back, skat′bak″, *n. Football,* a running back who is unusually fast and deceptive.

scathe, skāᴛʜ, *v.t.*—*scathed, scathing.* [< Scand.: cf. Icel. *skathi,* Sw. *skada,* Dan. *skade,* G. *schade,* harm, damage.] To assail with harsh criticism; hurt, harm, or injure, esp. by scorching or searing.—*n.* Hurt, harm, or injury.—**scathe·less,** *a.*

scath·ing, skā′ᴛʜing, *a.* Bitterly severe, as a remark or reprimand; harmful or searing.— **scath·ing·ly,** *adv.*

sca·tol·o·gy, ska·tol′o·jē, *n.* [Gr. *skor, skatos,* dung.] *Paleon.* the study of dung, or of savage practices in which excrement or filth is used. Obscenity, esp. in literature.— **scat·o·log·i·cal,** skat″o·loj′i·kal, *a.*—**sca·- toph·a·gous,** ska·tof′a·gus, *a.*

scat·ter, skat′ẽr, *v.t.* [O.E. *scaterian,* to scatter; same word as *shatter.*] To throw loosely about; to distribute in various directions at irregular intervals; to sprinkle; to separate in various directions; to dis- perse, as a mob; *phys.* to refract, reflect, or deflect, as light or other radiant energy, irregularly in order to diffuse it.—*v.i.* To disperse and separate; to continue in dif- ferent directions.—*n.* The act of scattering. —**scat·ter·a·ble,** *a.*—**scat·ter·er,** *n.*

scat·ter·brain, skat′ẽr·brān″, *n.* One in- capable of serious, logical thought, a thoughtless, giddy person.—**scat·ter·- brained,** *a.*

scat·ter·good, skat′ẽr·gud″, *n.* A spend- thrift.

scat·ter·ing, skat′ẽr·ing, *n.* The act of one who or that which scatters; that which is scattered, esp. a small amount or number scattered or interspersed; *phys,* the change in direction of particles, as of beams or waves, owing to collision with other particles or systems.—*a.* Dispersing in different directions; distributed here and there at irregular intervals or occurring sparsely or irregularly; straggling, as an assemblage of parts; cast in small numbers for various candidates, as votes.—**scat·- ter·ing·ly,** *adv.*

scat·ter rug, *n.* A rug suitable in size for placing over a small area on a floor rather than for carpeting a room. Also *throw rug.*

scaup, skäp, *n.* [Origin uncertain.] Any of certain diving ducks of the genus *Aythya,* esp. *A. marila,* the male of which has a black head and neck, and a white body and belly. Also **scaup duck, blue·bill.**

scaur, skär, skạr, *n.* Scar.

scav·enge, skav′inj, *v.t.*—*scavenged, scav- enging.* [Back formation < scavenger.] To cleanse from dirt or filth, as a street; to search out, as useful material, from amid refuse; to expel burnt gases from, as the cylinder of an internal-combustion engine; *metal.* to rid, as molten metal, of impurities by introducing a substance that chemically joins with and separates the impurities.— *v.i.* To act as a scavenger; to become cleared of burnt gases; to seek or ransack, as for food.

scav·en·ger, skav′in·jẽr, *n.* [< *scavage,* L.L. *scavagium,* an old law term equiv. to *showage,* a duty on goods *shown,* < O.E. *sceawian,* to show. The scavenger was orig. one who looked after the scavage. As to the insertion of *n,* cf. *messenger, passenger.*] One who searches in refuse for valuable, usable, or redeemable items; an animal that feeds on dead matter; a person or firm employed to clean streets.

sce·nar·i·o, si·när′ē·ō″, si·när′ē·ō″, *n.* pl. **sce·nar·i·os.** [It., < L.L. *scenarius,* per- taining to stage scenes, < L. *scena,* E. *scene.*] An outline of the plot of a dramatic work, giving particulars as to the scenes, characters, and situations; the outline or manuscript of a motion picture, giving the action in the order in which it takes place, the description of scenes and characters, and the printed matter to be shown on the screen.

sce·nar·ist, si·nâr′ist, si·när′ist, *n.* A writer of the scenario for a motion picture.

scend, send, *v.i. Naut.* to heave or rise up- ward, as a ship on a wave: opposed to *pitch.*—*n. Naut.* the heaving movement of a ship. Also *send.*

scene, sēn, *n.* [Fr. *scène;* L. *scena,* < Gr. *skēnē,* a covered place, a tent, a stage, < root of Skt. *sku,* to cover. E. *shade.*] The surroundings amid which anything hap- pens; location or locale; a landscape or view; a unified series of actions and events connected and exhibited. *Theatr.* a part of a play, the division of an act; the imaginary place in which the action of a play is sup- posed to occur; one of the painted slides, hangings, or other devices serving as back- ground or scenery for a play; a stage, esp. in the ancient theaters of Greece and Rome. A display of strong emotion, esp. in the presence of others, as: She made quite a *scene* in the restaurant.

scen·er·y, sē′nẽ·rē, *n.* pl. **scen·er·ies.** The general appearance or natural features of a place, as a landscape; the backdrops, hangings, screens, and accessories repre- senting the setting of a play or other stage production.

scene steal·er, *n.* An actor who ostenta- tiously or skillfully makes himself the focus of audience attention.

sce·nic, sē′nik, sen′ik, *a.* [Fr. *scénique,* < L. *scenicus, scaenicus,* < Gr. *skēnikós,* < *scēnē,* E. *scene.*] Of or pertaining to natural scenery; affording a beautiful view; repre- senting a scene, action, incident, or the like, as a painting. Also **sce·ni·cal.**

sce·nic rail·way, *n.* Any miniature railroad as one which operates at an amusement park.

sce·nog·ra·phy, sē·nog′ra·fē, *n.* Repre- sentation or drawing according to the rules of perspective; this art applied to stage scene painting.—**sce·no·graph·ic,** sē″no·- graf′ik, sen″o·graf′ik, *a.*—**sce·no·graph·- i·cal·ly,** *adv.*

scent, sent, *n.* [For *sent,* < Fr. *sentir,* to perceive, to smell, *sentire,* < L. *sentire,* to perceive by the senses.] A specific smell, esp. when pleasing; an odor left on the ground by an animal enabling it to be followed; a track left by an animal; small scraps of paper scattered during the game of hare and hounds; perfume; the sense of smell.—*v.t.* To recognize by smelling; to be suspicious of, as trouble; to perfume.— *v.i.* To track by the sense of smell.— **scent·ed,** *a.*—**scent·less,** *a.*—**scent·less·- ness,** *n.*

scep·ter, *Brit.* **scep·tre,** sep′tẽr, *n.* [O.Fr. *ceptre,* Fr. *ceptre,* Fr. *sceptre,* < L. *sceptrum,* < Gr. *skēptron,* staff, scepter, < *skeptein,* to prop.] A rod or wand, borne in the hand as an emblem of regal or imperial power; royal or imperial power or authority; sovereignty; supremacy.—*v.t.*—*sceptered, sceptering, Brit. sceptred, sceptring.* To invest with regal authority.

scep·tic, skep′tik, *n., a.* Skeptic.

sched·ule, skej′ŏl, skej′ạl, skej′ō·al, *Brit.* shed′ūl, shej′ŏl, *n.* [< L.L. *schedula,* M.L. *scedula,* dim. of L. *scheda, scida,* leaf of paper, strip of papyrus, prob. < *scindere,* cut, split.] A written procedure for a par- ticular objective, usu. specifying the sequence and time appropriated for each item in the procedure; a list, catalog, or table, esp. a timetable; a written or printed statement of details, often in classified or tabular form, forming an appendix or explanatory addition to another document. —*v.t.*—*scheduled, scheduling.* To make a schedule of; to enter in a schedule; to fix by a schedule.—**sched·u·lar,** *a.*

scheel·ite, shā′līt, shē′līt, *n.* [G. *scheelit;* named from K. W. *Scheele,* 1742–1786, Swedish chemist.] A mineral consisting of calcium tungstate, $CaWO_4$, occurring in tetragonal crystals.

sche·ma, skē′ma, *n.* pl. **sche·ma·ta,** skē′ma·ta. [L. *schema* or Gr. *schēma (schēmat-).*] A diagram, plan, or scheme; an abstract or conceptual outline or plan, as of doctrines or a process.—**sche·mat·ic,** skē·mat′ik, *a., n.*—**sche·mat·i·cal·ly,** *adv.*

sche·ma·tism, skē′ma·tiz″um, *n.* [Gr. *schēmatismós, < schēmatizein,* E. *schematize.*] The particular form or disposition of a thing; a schematic arrangement or presentation, as of the principles of a philosophic system.—**sche·ma·tist,** *n.*

sche·ma·tize, skē′ma·tīz″, *v.t.*—*schematized, schematizing.* [Gr. *schēmatizein,* form, arrange, < *schēma,* E. *scheme.*] To reduce to or arrange according to a scheme.—**sche·ma·ti·za·tion,** *n.*—**sche·ma·tiz·er,** *n.*

scheme, skēm, *n.* [Fr. *schème,* L. *schema,* < Gr. *schēma,* < *schein,* to hold, to keep.] A plan of something to be done; a project; a plot, esp. one that is underhanded or crafty; a system or framework of related theories or precepts; the manner or form of such an arrangement; an impractical project; a tabulated account or statement; a sketch or diagrammatic representation; as, an astrological *scheme* of the heavens.—*v.t.* —*schemed, scheming.* To make a plan for; to contrive or design; to plot.—*v.i.* To lay plans; to connive; to intrigue.—**schem·er,** *n.*—**schem·ing,** skē′ming, *a.*

scher·zan·do, sker·tsän′dō, sker·tsan′dō, *adv.* [It.] *Mus.* in a playful or sportive manner: a direction to the performer.—*a.* —*n.*

scher·zo, sker′tsō, *n.* pl. **scher·zos, scher·zi,** sker′tsē. [It.] *Mus.* a passage of a sprightly or sportive character in musical pieces of some length, as in symphonies or sonatas.

Schick test, shik′ test″, *n.* [From Bela *Schick,* b. 1877, U.S. pediatrician.] An injection of small amounts of dilute diphtheria toxin, just below the skin's surface: used to test immunity to diphtheria, nonimmunity being indicated by a reddening of the skin.

schil·ler, shil′ĕr, *n.* [G., play of colors.] A metallic, bronzelike luster, sometimes with iridescence, occurring on certain minerals. —**schil·ler·ize,** shil′e·rīz″,*v.t.*—*schillerized, schillerizing.* To give schiller to, as a crystal, by developing microscopic inclusions.—**schil·ler·i·za·tion,** *n.*

schip·per·ke, skip′ĕr·kē, skip′ĕr·ke, *n.* [D., 'little boatman.'] One of a breed of small, black, short-haired, tailless dogs, first used as watchdogs on boats in Holland and Belgium.

schism, siz′um, *n.* [O.Fr. *scisme, cisme* (Fr. *schisme*), < L.L. *schisma,* < Gr. *schisma,* cleft, division, later *schism,* < *schizein,* to split, cleave.] Division, separation, or disunion, esp. a division into mutually opposed or hostile parties; a formal division within or separation from a church or religious body, on account of some difference of opinion with regard to matters of faith or discipline; the offense of causing or seeking to cause such a division; a sect or body formed by division within a church or other organization.

schis·mat·ic, siz·mat′ik, *a.* [O.Fr. *scismatique* (Fr. *schismatique*) < L.L. *schismaticus,* < Gr. *schismatikós,* < Gr. *schisma.*] Of or per-

taining to schism; of the nature of schism; guilty of schism. Also **schis·mat·i·cal.**—*n.* One who promotes schism; an adherent of a schismatic body.—**schis·ma·tize,** siz′ma·tīz″, *v.i.*—*schismatized, schismatizing.* To act as a schismatic; to advocate a schism; to belong to a schismatic body.—**schis·mat·i·cal·ly,** *adv.*—**schis·ma·tist,** *n.*

schist, shist, shist, *n.* [Fr. *schiste,* < L. *schistos,* splitting readily, < Gr. *schistós, a. < schizein,* split.] Any of certain crystalline rocks whose constituent minerals have a parallel or foliated arrangement, due mainly to metamorphic action.—**schis·tose, schis·tous,** shis′tōs, shis′tus, *a.*

schis·to·some, shis′to·sōm″, *n.* Any trematode worm of the genus *Schistosoma,* including some flukes which parasitize blood vessels of man and other mammals and cause schistosomiasis in man.—*a.*

schis·to·so·mi·a·sis, shis″to·sō·mī′a·sis, *n.* Infestation with schistosomes; a disease caused by schistosomes. Also **bil·har·zi·a·sis,** bil″här·zī′a·sis.

schiz·o, skit′sō, *n.* pl. **schiz·os.** *Slang,* a person who is schizophrenic.

schiz·o·carp, skiz′o·kärp″, *n.* [Gr. *schizo-,* to split, < *schizein, karpos,* fruit.] *Bot.* a dry fruit which splits at maturity into distinct one-seeded, indehiscent carpels.— **schiz·o·car·pous, schiz·o·car·pic,** *a.*

schiz·o·gen·e·sis, skiz″o·jen′i·sis, *n. Biol.* reproduction by fission.—**schiz·o·gen·ic, schiz·o·ge·net·ic, schi·zog·e·nous,** skiz″o·jen′ik, skiz″ō·je·net′ik, ski·zoj′e·nus, *a.* —**schiz·o·ge·net·i·cal·ly, schi·zog·e·nous·ly,** *adv.*

schi·zog·o·ny, ski·zog′o·nē, *n. Biol.* the asexual reproductive process of protozoans by multiple fission, as of many of the sporozoans.—**schi·zog·o·nous, schiz·o·gon·ic,** skiz″o·gon′ik, *a.*

schiz·oid, skit′soid, skiz′oid, *a. Psychiatry,* pertaining to, resembling, or predisposed to schizophrenia.—*n. Psychiatry,* one whose behavior suggests a tendency toward the abnormalities characteristic of schizophrenia.

schiz·o·my·cete, skiz″ō·mī·sēt′, *n.* [N.L. *Schizomycetes,* pl. < Gr. *schizein,* to split, and *mykēs (mykēt-),* fungus.] Any of the *Schizomycetes,* a class or group of plant organisms allied to the fungi.—**schiz·o·my·ce·tous,** *a.*—**schiz·o·my·co·sis,** skiz″ō·mī·kō′sis, *n.* [N.L.] *Pathol.* any disease due to schizomycetes.

schi·zont, ski′zont, skiz′ont, *n.* A cell found in certain sporozoans which reproduces itself by repeated asexual fission to form many small cells.

schiz·o·phre·ni·a, skit″so·frē′nē·a, skit″so·frēn′ya, skiz″o·frē′nē·a, skiz″o·frēn′ya, *n. Psychiatry,* psychosis characterized by emotional, intellectual, and behavioral disturbances, such as withdrawal from reality, delusions, and progressive deterioration; dementia praecox—**schiz·o·phren·ic,** skit″so·fren′ik,skiz″o·fren′ik,*n.*One afflicted with schizophrenia. Also **schiz·o·phrene,** skit′so·frēn″, skiz′o·frēn″.—*a.*

schiz·o·phyte, skiz′o·fīt″, *n.* [N.L. *Schizophyta,* pl., < Gr. *schizein,* to split, and *phytón,* plant.] *Bot.* any of the *Schizophyta,* a group of plants comprising the schizomycetes and the blue-green algae, having a simple structure and reproducing by simple fission or by spores.—**schiz·o·phyt·ic,** skiz″o·fit′ik, *a.*

schiz·o·pod, skiz′o·pod″, *n.* [N.L. *Schizopoda,* pl., < Gr. *schizein,* to split, and *poús(pod-),* foot.] Any of the former order now placed in the subclasses *Malacostraca* and *Euphausiacea,* of crustaceans with a soft carapace and with branched and apparently double thoracic appendages, which comprises the opossum shrimps and their allies.—*a.*—**schi·zop·o·dous,** ski·zop′o·dus, ski′zop·o·dus, *a.*

schiz·o·thy·mi·a, skit″so·thī′mē·a, skiz″o·thī′mē·a, *n. Psychiatry,* a schizoid tendency characterized by introversion and withdrawal which remains within the range of normality.—**schiz·o·thy·mic,** *a.*

schle·miel, shle·mēl′, *n.* [Yiddish.] *Slang.* An unlucky person prone to clumsiness; an inept, bungling clod. Also **schle·mihl.**

schlie·ren, shlēr′en, *n.* [G.] *Petrog.* streaks or irregularly shaped masses in an igneous rock, which differ in texture or composition from the main mass; *phys.* detectable streaks in a transparent liquid caused by variations in temperature or pressure and visible in photographs of light beams passing through the liquid.—**schlier·ic,** *a.*

schmaltz, shmälts, shmalts, *n.* [Yiddish < G.] *Slang,* anything expressing exaggerated emotions, as certain literature or music. Chicken fat. Also **schmalz.**— **schmaltz·y,** shmält′sē, shmalt′sē, *a.*— *schmaltzier, schmaltziest.*

Schmidt sys·tem, shmit′ sis′tem, *n.* An optical system used for reflecting telescopes and cameras which utilizes a spherical mirror objective and a transparent corrector plate near the focus to reduce spherical aberration.

schmo, shmō, *n.* [< Yiddish.] *Slang.* A naive, foolish, or boring person; a jerk. Also **schmoe.**

schnapps, shnäps, shnaps, *n.* [G. *schnapps,* D. *snaps,* a dram.] A dram of Hollands gin or other ardent spirits; liquor generally.

schnau·zer, shnou′zĕr, *n.* A breed of German terrier with a wiry coat of pepper-and-salt or black and tan color.

schnit·zel, shnit′sel, *n.* [G., akin to *schneiden,* cut.] A cutlet, esp. of veal.

schnook, shnŭk, *n.* [< Yiddish.] *Slang.* An insignificant or stupid person; a dope.

schnor·kel, shnar′kel, *n., v.i.* Snorkel.

schnor·rer, shnôr′ĕr, shnar′ĕr, *n.* [Yiddish, < G. *schnurrer,* < *schnurren,* hum, go begging.] *Slang.* A beggar; one who solicits unjustified help from others; a sponger.

schnoz·zle, shnoz′l, *n.* [< Yiddish.] *Slang,* the nose.

scho·la can·to·rum, skō′la kan·tōr′um, skō′la kan·tar′um, *n.* pl. **scho·lae can·to·rum,** skō′lē kan·tōr′um, skō′lē kan·tar′um. An ecclesiastical choir; a choir school; the section of an ecclesiastical building used by the choir.

schol·ar, skol′ĕr, *n.* [O.Fr. *escolier* (Fr. *écolier*), < L.L. *scholaris,* < L. *schola,* a school.] A person of great learning or academic accomplishment, usu. in the humanities; such a savant who does research, study, writing, and is often a published authority in one particular field; as, a Shakespeare *scholar;* the holder of an honor or monetary award to facilitate his study; one who attends school or learns from a teacher.—**schol·ar·ism,** *n.*—**schol·ar·less,** *a.*

schol·ar·ly, skol′ĕr·lē, *a.* Characteristic of a scholar; showing good scholarship.— **schol·ar·li·ness,** *n.*

schol·ar·ship, skol′ĕr·ship″, *n.* The body of learning and knowledge attained through scholarly procedures and study; the quality of scholarly work; the aid or award given to a student by a fund, school, or institution, usu. financial assistance on the basis of his merit or need, sometimes strictly an honor.

scho·las·tic, sko·las′tik, *a.* [L. *scholasticus,* < Gr. *scholastikós,* < *scholázein,* have leisure, devote one's time to learning, < *scholē.*] Of or pertaining to schools, scholars, or education; of, pertaining to, or characteristic of medieval schoolmen; pedantic. Also **scho·las·ti·cal.**—*n.* (*Sometimes cap.*) a schoolman, a disciple of the schoolmen, or an adherent of scholasticism. A pedant;

ch- chain, G. na*ch*t; **th-** THen, thin; **w-** wig, hw as sound in whig; **z-** zh as in azure, zeal. *Italicized vowel* indicates schwa sound.

Rom. Cath. Ch. one who is studying in a scholasticate.—**scho·las·ti·cal·ly,** *adv.*

scho·las·ti·cate, sko·las'ti·kāt″, sko·las'-ti·kit, *n. Rom. Cath. Ch.* a school or place of higher learning attended before undertaking theological courses of study.

scho·las·ti·cism, sko·las'ti·siz″um, *n.* (*Cap.*) the system of theological and philosophical teaching predominant in the middle ages, based chiefly on the authority of the church fathers and of Aristotle and his commentators, and characterized by marked formality in methods; (*l.c.*) narrow adherence to the teachings of the schools or to traditional doctrines and methods.

scho·li·ast, skō'lē·ast″, *n.* [Gr. *scholiastēs.*] An ancient annotator or commentator of classical texts; one who makes scholiums; an annotator.—**scho·li·as·tic,** *a.*

scho·li·um, skō'lē·um, *n.* pl. **scho·li·ums, scho·li·a,** skō'lē·a. [Gr. *scholion,* < *scholē,* lecture.] A marginal note, annotation, or remark, as in a mathematical proof; an explanatory comment, such as those annexed to the Latin and Greek authors by early grammarians.

school, skōl, *n.* [O.E. *scol* = O.Fr. *escole* (Fr. *école*), < L. *schola,* < Gr. *scholē,* leisure time given to learning.] A place or establishment where instruction is given; a regular course of meetings of a teacher or teachers and students for instruction; as, a business *school*; a session of an establishment for instruction; as no *school* today; the body of students or pupils attending a school; any place, situation, or experience constituting a source of instruction or training; the body of pupils or followers of a particular master; a body of persons who accept the same teachings or principles, as in philosophy or economics; persons who follow the same general method, as in painting or music; a set or body of persons who agree in certain principles, opinions, or methods, as those prevalent at a particular time; as, a politician of the old *school*; one of the various organized bodies of teachers and students which constituted a medieval university; a particular faculty or department of a modern university; as, the graduate *school*; a building or room in a university, set apart for the use of one of the faculties or for some particular purpose; *milit., naval,* special drill regulations or drill applying to the individual; as, *school* of the soldier.—*v.t.* To teach or educate, as at an institution or school.

school, skōl, *n.* [M.E. *scole, sculle,* prob. < M.D. *schole* (D. *school*), school or shoal of fish, = O.E. *scolu,* troop, multitude: cf. *shoal.*] A large number of fish, porpoises, or whales feeding or migrating together.—*v.i.* To form into or move in a school, as fish.

school age, *n.* Childhood years during which school attendance is customary or required.

school·bag, skōl'bag″, *n.* A bag used by students to carry school materials.

school board, *n.* A local board or committee, often elected, in charge of public education.

school·boy, skōl'boi″, *n.* A boy attending school.—**school·boy·ish,** *a.*

school bus, *n.* A means of transportation for students in travelling between school and home or between school and activities related to school.

school·child, skōl'chīld″, *n.* pl. **school·chil·dren.** A child attending school.

school·fel·low, skōl'fel″ō, *n.* A schoolmate.

school·girl, skōl'gurl″, *n.* A girl attending school.—**school·girl·ish,** *a.*

school·house, skōl'hous″, *n.* A building in which school, esp. the elementary grades, is conducted.

school·ing, skō'ling, *n.* Education or instruction received in a school; the act of teaching or the process of being taught in school.

school·man, skōl'man, *n.* pl. **school·men.** One versed in scholastic learning or engaged in scholastic pursuits. (*Sometimes cap.*) a master in one of the schools or universities of the Middle Ages; one of the medieval writers who dealt with theology and philosophy after the methods of scholasticism.

school·marm, skōl'märm″, *n. Colloq.* a woman teacher, usu. one thought to be old-fashioned, spinsterish, and prudish. Also **school·ma'am,** skōl'mam″, skōl'-mäm″.—**school·marm·ish,** *a.*

school·mas·ter, skōl'mas″tėr, skōl'mä″stėr, *n.* A man who presides over or teaches in a school; any person or thing that directs. *Ichth.* an edible snapper found in tropical waters.

school·mate, skōl'māt″, *n.* A companion or associate at school.

school·mis·tress, skōl'mis″tris, *n.* A woman who presides over or teaches in a school.

school·room, skōl'rōm″, skōl'rum″, *n.* A room in which school is conducted or pupils are taught.

school·teach·er, skōl'tē″chėr, *n.* One who instructs in a grammar school or high school.—**school·teach·ing,** skōl'tē″ching, *n.*

school·work, skōl'wurk″, *n.* All of the work done for studies at a school, including classwork and homework.

schoon·er, skō'nėr, *n. Naut.* a sailing vessel having at least two masts, fore and aft. A tall beer glass holding approximately one pint; *archaic,* a covered wagon.—**schoon·er-rigged,** skō'nėr·rigd″, *a.*

schorl, shärl, *n.* [G. *schörl.*] Tourmaline, esp. a black variety.—**schor·la·ceous,** shär·lā'-shus, *a.*

schot·tische, shot'ish, *n.* [G. *schottische,* Scottish, lit. 'a Scottish dance.'] One of the round dances, resembling but slower than the polka; the music suited for such a dance.

schuit, schuyt, skoit, skīt, *D. schoEit, n.* A Dutch boat with a flat bottom and blunt bow, used mainly on canals and rivers.

schuss, shus, shös, *n. Skiing.* A high-speed, straight, downhill run on skis; the skiing course itself.—*v.t., v.i.*

schwa, shwä, *G.* shvä, *n.* [G. < Heb.] *Phon.* the indeterminate vowel sound of most syllables that are not stressed in English, as the *a* in *scholar,* the *u* in *tetanus,* the *i* and *e* in *prominent,* and the *o* in *piston;* the phonic symbol denoting that sound (ə).

sci·ae·noid, sī·ē'noid, *n.* [N.L. *Sciænidæ,* pl., < *Sciæna,* the typical genus, < L. *sciæna,* < Gr. *sciaina,* kind of sea fish.] Any of the *Sciaenidae,* a family of carnivorous acanthopterygian fishes including the drumfishes and certain kingfishes. Also **sci·ae·nid.**—*a.* Belonging or pertaining to the sciaenoids. Also **sci·ae·nid,** sī·ē'nid.

sci·at·ic, sī·at'ik, *a.* [Fr. *sciatique,* < M.L. *sciaticus, ischiaticus,* for L. *ischiadicus.*] Affecting or pertaining to the hip or the sciatic nerves, either of two nerves distributed along the back part of each thigh and leg.—*n.* A nerve or part that is sciatic.

sci·at·i·ca, sī·at'i·ka, *n.* [M.L.] *Pathol.* Pain and tenderness in a sciatic nerve and its branches; sciatic neuritis; sciatic neuralgia.—**sci·at·i·cal·ly,** *adv.*

sci·ence, sī'ens, *n.* [O.Fr. Fr. *science,* < L. *scientia,* knowledge, < *sciens* (scient-), ppr. of *scire,* to know.] Knowledge, esp. of facts or principles, gained by systematic study; a particular branch of knowledge, esp. one dealing with a body of facts or truths systematically arranged and showing the operation of general laws; as, the *science* of mathematics; systematized knowledge, esp. of the laws and facts of the physical or material world; skill resulting from training; (*cap.*) Christian Science.—**sci·en·tial,** sī·en'shal, *a.*

sci·ence fic·tion, *n.* Fiction that imaginatively uses scientific fact and speculation to create a fantastic situation.

sci·en·tif·ic, sī″en·tif'ik, *a.* [L. *scientia,* knowledge, and *facio,* to make.] Pertaining to science; as, *scientific* experiments; evincing or endowed with a knowledge of science; as, a *scientific* mind; according to the rules or principles of science.—**sci·en·tif·i·cal·ly,** *adv.*

sci·en·tif·ic meth·od, *n.* A research method characterized by the definition of a problem, the gathering of data, and the drafting and empirical testing of the hypotheses.

sci·en·tism, sī'en·tiz″um, *n.* The mental attitude or the practices of scientists; the application of scientific methods in other realms of investigation whether suitable or not.

sci·en·tist, sī'en·tist, *n.* A person versed in or devoted to science; a scientific person. (*Cap.*) a believer in the teachings of Christian Science.

scil·la, sil'a, *n.* Any of the bulbous plants, genus *Scilla,* of the lily family, with bell-shaped blooms of blue, purple, or white.

scim·i·tar, sim·i·tar, sim'i·tėr, *n.* [It. *scimitarra.*] An oriental sword, the blade of which is single-edged, short, and curved. Also **scim·i·ter.**

scin·coid, sing'koid, *a.* Pertaining to the skink and allied reptiles.—*n.* A scincoid lizard.

scin·til·la, sin·til'a, *n.* [L.] A spark; the least particle; a trace.

scin·til·lant, sin'ti·lant, *a.* Sparkling; twinkling.—**scin·til·lant·ly,** *adv.*

scin·til·late, sin'ti·lāt″, *v.i.*—*scintillated, scintillating.* [L. *scintilla, scintillatum.*] To emit sparks; to sparkle or twinkle, as the stars; to flash.—*v.t.* To send forth, as sparks or flashes.—**scin·til·la·tor,** sin'ti·lā″tėr, *n.*—**scin·til·lat·ing·ly,** *adv.*

scin·til·la·tion, sin″ti·lā'shan, *n.* The act of scintillating or sparkling; a flash or spark; *astron.* the twinkling of the stars; *phys.* the flashing of light resulting from ionizing a phosphor.

scin·til·la·tion count·er, *n.* *Phys.* a detecting and measuring device for radioactivity by use of a phosphor.

sci·o·lism, sī'o·liz″um, *n.* Superficial knowledge.—**sci·o·list,** *n.*—**sci·o·lis·tic,** *a.*

sci·o·man·cy, sī'o·man″sē, *n.* [Gr. *skia,* a shadow, and *manteia,* divination.] Divination by contact with the shadows of the dead, or ghosts.—**sci·o·man·tic,** sī″o·man'tik, *a.*

sci·on, sī'on, *n.* [Fr. *scion,* < L. *sectio, sectionis,* a cutting, < *seco,* to cut.] A descendant; an heir. *Hort.* a shoot or cutting from plant material, esp. one used for grafting; also *cion.*

sci·re fa·ci·as, sī'rē fā'shē·as″, L. skē'rε fä'kē·äs″, *n.* [L., 'that you cause to know.'] *Law.* A writ requiring the party against whom it is brought to show cause why a judgment, letters patent, or the like, should not be executed, vacated, or annulled; this type of legal proceeding.

scir·rhus, skir'us, sir'us, *n.* pl. **scir·rhi.** [L. *scirrus,* < Gr. *skirrhos,* a hardened swelling or tumor.] *Pathol.* a relatively hard tumor, frequently indurated in fibrous tissue, often cancerous, or terminating in a cancer.—**scir·rhoid,** skir'oid, sir'oid, *a.*—**scir·rhous,** skir'us, sir'us, *a.* Indurated; knotty.

scis·sile, sis'il, *a.* Capable of being split or cut evenly and without much effort.

scis·sion, sizh'an, sish'an, *n.* [L. *scissio,* < *scindo,* to cut.] The act of cutting or dividing; the state of being cut or split; a division; a separation.

scis·sor, siz'ėr, *v.t.* To cut, clip, or slash with scissors.

scis·sors, siz'ĕrz, *n. pl.* [< O.Fr. *cisoires, ciseaux,* < L. *caedo,* to cut; but influenced by *scissor,* one who cuts, < *scindo, scissum,* to cut.] A cutting instrument consisting of two blades with handles movable on a pivot in the center, and which cut from opposite sides against an object placed between them: often spoken of as a *pair of scissors. Pl. but sing. in constr.* a wrestling hold applied by locking the legs around an opponent's neck or midsection; scissorlike leg movements in gymnastics.

scis·sors kick, *n. Sports,* a kick used while swimming in a side position, as in the trudgen and side strokes, in which the legs are virtually rigid at the knee, spread apart laterally, extended, and moved fast and forcefully with scissorlike action.

scis·sor·tail, siz'ĕr·tāl″, *n.* A bird, *Muscivora forficata,* a type of flycatcher in the southern U.S. and Mexico, having a deeply cleft tail resembling a pair of scissors. Also **scis·sor·tailed fly·catch·er.**

sci·u·roid, sī·ūr'oid, *a.* Squirrellike; *zool.* belonging to the squirrel family, *Sciuridae,* of rodents, which includes the woodchuck, chipmunk, and others; *bot.* resembling a squirrel's tail, as the spikes of certain grasses. Also **sci·u·rine**, sī'ū·rīn″, sī'ū·rin.

sclaff, sklaf, *v.t.* [Orig. Sc., and prob. imit.] *Golf,* to scrape, as the ground, with the head of the golf club before striking the ball. —*v.i.*—*n.* A sclaffing golf stroke; *Sc.* a light blow or slap.

scle·ra, sklĕr'a, *n. Anat.* the fibrous white outer coating of the eyeball which is contiguous with the cornea. Also **scle·rot·i·ca.**

scle·ren·chy·ma, skli·reng'ki·ma, *n.* [N.L., < Gr. *sclēros,* hard, and *-enchyma* as in *parenchyma.*] *Bot.* plant tissue composed of thick-walled, fibrous cells which serve as protection and support.—**scle·ren·chym·a·tous**, sklĕr″eng·kim'a·tus, sklĕr″eng·kim'a·tus, *a.*

scle·rite, sklĕr'īt, sklĕr'īt, *n.* [Gr. *sclēros,* hard.] *Zool.* any chitinous, calcareous, or similar hard plate, spicule, or part.—**scle·rit·ic**, skli·rit'ik, *a.*

scle·ro·der·ma, sklĕr″o·dur'ma, sklĕr″o·dur'ma, *n.* [N.L., < Gr. *sclēros,* hard, and *derma,* skin.] *Pathol.* a disease in which the skin becomes hard and rigid.

scle·ro·der·ma·tous, sklĕr″o·dur'ma·tus, sklĕr″o·dur'ma·tus, *a. Zool.* being covered by a hard, horny, or bony substance, as a snake or armadillo.

scle·roid, sklĕr'oid, sklĕr'oid, *a. Biol.* having a hard texture; indurated; hardened.

scle·rom·e·ter, skli·rom'i·tĕr, *n.* An instrument for determining with precision the degree of hardness of a substance, esp. of a mineral.

scle·ro·pro·tein, sklĕr″ō·prō'tēn, sklĕr″ō·prō'tē·in, *n.* A fibrous protein functioning in a protective, supportive, connective, as well as elastic manner in the animal body. See *albuminoid.*

scle·rose, skli·rōs', sklĕr'ōz, sklĕr'ōz, *v.t., v.i.*—*sclerosed, sclerosing. Pathol.* To affect or become affected with sclerosis; harden.

scle·ro·sis, skli·rō'sis, *n. pl.* **scle·ro·ses,** skli·rō'sēz. [Gr. *sclēros,* hard.] *Pathol.* a hardening and thickening of a tissue or a part, usu. from excessive growth of fibrous or connective tissue; a disease exhibiting such hardening. *Bot.* a hardening of a plant tissue, as a cell wall, by lignification.

scle·rot·ic, skli·rot'ik, *a.* [Gr. *sclērotēs,* hardness.] *Anat.* pertaining to the sclera; as, the *sclerotic* coat of the eye; hard, firm, as the sclera. *Pathol., bot.* affected with or pertaining to sclerosis.

scle·ro·ti·um, skli·rō'shē·um, *n. pl.* **scle·ro·ti·a**, skli·rō'shē·a. [Gr. *sclērotēs,* hardness.] In fungi, a hard compact mass of food-storing mycelia which germinates after a dormant period.

scle·rous, sklĕr'us, sklēr'us, *a. Anat., biol.* Hard; bony.

scoff, skạf, skof, *n.* [Same as O.Fris. *skof,* sport; Icel. *skop, skaup,* mockery, ridicule; O.H.G. *scoph,* sport.] An expression of derision, mockery, scorn, or contempt; a gibe; a jeer; an object of derision.—*v.i.* To show insolent ridicule or mockery; to utter derisive language; to mock, often followed by *at.*—*v.t.* To mock; to ridicule.—**scoff·er**, *n.*—**scoff·ing·ly**, *adv.*

scoff·law, skạf'lạ, skof'lạ, *n. Colloq.* one who flouts or constantly violates the law.

scold, skōld, *v.t.* [Akin to Sc. *scald,* L.G. and D. *schelden,* Dan. *skielde,* G. *schelten,* to scold; Icel. *skjalla,* to clash; *skellr,* a crash; G. *schelle,* a bell.] To find fault with in an ill-tempered manner, as a result of impatience, irritation, or anger; to chide or rebuke.—*v.i.* To find fault; to be censorious; to use nagging or abusive language. —*n.* One who scolds, esp. a woman addicted to constant fault-finding.—**scold·er**, *n.*—**scold·ing**, *n.*

scol·e·cite, skol'i·sīt″, skō'li·sīt″, *n.* [G. *scolezit,* < Gr. *scōlēx (scōlēk-),* worm; from its curling up sometimes before the blowpipe.] A mineral, a hydrous silicate of calcium and aluminum, occurring in needle-shaped crystals and in masses.

sco·lex, skō'leks, *n. pl.* **sco·le·ces, scol·i·ces**, skō·lē'sēz, skol'i·sēz″, skō'li·sēz. [N.L., < Gr. *scōlēx* (pl. *scōlēces*), worm.] The round, headlike segment at one extremity of a tapeworm, serving as an organ of attachment; the larva of a tapeworm.

sco·li·o·sis, skō″lē·ō'sis, skol″ē·ō'sis, *n.* [Gr. *skolios,* crooked.] *Pathol.* a curvature of the spine, a lateral one in particular.—**sco·li·ot·ic**, skō″lē·ot'ik, *a.*

scol·lop, skol'op, *n., v.t.* Scallop.

scol·o·pen·drid, skol'o·pen'drid, *n.* [N.L. < L. *scolopendra,* < Gr. *Skolopendra,* kind of multipede.] Any of the *Scolopendridae,* an order of myriapods which comprises many large and poisonous centipedes. Also **scol·o·pen·dra.**—**scol·o·pen·dri·form**, *a.*—**scol·o·pen·drine**, skol″o·pen'drin, skol″o·pen'drīn, *a.*

scom·broid, skom'broid, *a.* [Gr. *skombros,* mackerel.] Resembling the mackerel; belonging or pertaining to the mackerel family, *Scombridae,* or the suborder *Scombroidea* containing the mackerel family.—*n.* A mackerel or other scombroid fish.

sconce, skons, *n.* [O.Fr. *esconse,* < M.L. *absconsa,* dark lantern, prop. fem. of L. *absconsus,* pp. of *abscondere,* hide.] An ornamental bracket, as attached to a wall, for holding one or more candles or other lights.

sconce, skons, *n.* [D. *schans* = M.L.G. *schantze* = G. *schanze,* sconce; origin uncertain: cf. *schanz.*] *Fort.* a small detached fort or earthwork for defense of a pass or ford.—*v.t.*—*sconced, sconcing.* To defend with a sconce.

sconce, skons, *n.* [Origin uncertain.] A fine, as among undergraduates at Oxford University, for breach of etiquette. *Archaic,* the head or skull, esp. the top of the head; sense or wit.—*v.t.*—*sconced, sconcing.* To fine, as for breach of etiquette.

scone, skōn, skon, *n.* [Cf. M.D. *schoonbrot,* fine bread.] A flat, round cake of wheat flour, barley meal, or the like, cooked on a griddle; one of the four quadrant-shaped pieces into which it is often cut.

scoop, skọp, *n.* [M.E. *scope:* cf. M.L.G. and M.D. *schōpe,* scoop, also M.D. *schoppe,* D. *schop,* shovel.] A ladle or ladlelike utensil, esp. one resembling a small deep-sided shovel with a short handle, for taking up and carrying loose materials, as flour or sugar; a spoon-shaped or gougelike instrument for removing or dishing up soft food; as, an ice-cream *scoop;* the quantity taken up at one time by any such instrument; as, a double

scoop of ice cream; the shovellike bucket attached to heavy construction equipment used to dig, hollow out, and remove such materials as earth in road building; a place scooped or hollowed out thereby; the amount of material taken up; the act of scooping; a movement as of scooping; *surg.* a spoonlike instrument used in extracting the contents of cysts or cavities. *Slang,* an item or story released by one newspaper or newscast ahead of the competition; a news beat; information or explanatory details, usu. of recent origin, as: What's the *scoop* on that deal? *Colloq.* a big haul, as of money made in speculation.— *v.t.* To take up or out with or as with a scoop; to gather or collect with a scoop; to gather or appropriate as if with a scoop, usu. followed by *in* or *up;* to form a hollow in, with or as with a scoop; to form with or as with a scoop; *slang,* to get the better of by a scoop or beat, as a rival newspaper.— **scoop·er**, *n.*—**scoop·ful**, *n.*

scoot, skōt, *v.t.* [Appar. orig. Sc.; perh. from Scand. and akin to E. *shoot.*] *Colloq.* to send or impel at high speed.—*v.i. Colloq.* to dart, go, or make off swiftly or hastily.—*n. Colloq.* The act or an act of scooting; a swift, darting movement or course.

scoot·er, skō'tĕr, *n.* A child's vehicle with a board set between tandem wheels guided by a vertical handlebar and driven by standing with one foot on the board and pushing against the ground with the other foot; a motor scooter; a flat-bottomed sailboat with steel runners for sailing on ice or water.

scop, skop, *n.* A bard or poet of Old English literature.

scope, skōp, *n.* [It. *scopo,* < L. *scopos,* < Gr. *skopos,* mark, aim.] Extent or range of view, outlook, application, operation, or effectiveness; as, a mind of limited *scope;* space for movement or activity; opportunity for operation; as, to give one's fancy full *scope;* extent in space; a tract or area; length or a length.

sco·pol·a·mine, sko·pol'a·mēn″, sko·pol'a·min, skō″po·lam'in, *n.* [G. *scopolamin,* < N.L. *Scopolia* or *Scopola,* genus of plants, and G. *amin,* amine.] *Chem., phar.* a crystalline alkaloid, $C_{17}H_{21}NO_4$, obtained from the rhizome of a plant, *Scopolia carniolica,* or from other solanaceous plants: used as a sedative, truth serum, and mydriatic. Also *hyoscine.*

scop·u·la, skop'ū·la, skop'ya·la, *n. pl.* **scop·u·las, scop·u·lae.** *Zool.* a clump or cluster of hairs on the feet of some arachnids, as certain spiders.—**scop·u·late**, *a. Zool.* Broom-shaped; brushlike.

scor·bu·tic, skạr·bū'tik, *a.* [Fr. *scorbutique,* < *scorbut,* the scurvy.] Pertaining to or affected with scurvy. Also **scor·bu·ti·cal.**—**scor·bu·ti·cal·ly**, *adv.*

scorch, skạrch, *v.t.* [M.E. *scorchen;* perh. < Scand.] To burn superficially or slightly; affect in color, taste, etc., by burning slightly; parch or shrivel with heat; to assault verbally.—*v.i.* To be or become scorched; *colloq.* to ride at high speed, as in an automobile.—*n.* A superficial burn; scorching effect.—**scorched**, *a.*

scorched-earth pol·i·cy, a military policy of destroying, usu. by burning, everything of value, as crops or buildings, in the path of an advancing enemy.

scorch·er, skạr'chĕr, *n.* One who or that which scorches. *Colloq.* a very hot day; a cutting, stinging rebuke.

scorch·ing, skạr'ching, *a.* That scorches; burning; withering; very hot; caustic or scathing; as, *scorching* criticism.—**scorch·ing·ly**, *adv.*

score, skōr, skạr, *n. pl.* **scores, score.** [< Scand.: cf. Icel. *skor,* notch, incision, tally (notched for each twenty), hence twenty, akin to E. *shear.*] A notch, groove, cut, or scratch; a stroke, mark, or line, as the mark at which competitors stand in beginning a race; a notch cut or a mark made in keeping an account or record; a reckoning or account, as of charges, kept by means of notches or marks; any account showing indebtedness. A grievance or grudge; account, reason, ground, or motive. The record of points made by the competitors in a game or match; the aggregate of points made by a side or individual; the scoring of a point or points; a grade or rating, as in a test or an examination. A group or set of twenty; *pl.* an indeterminately large number. *Mus.* a written or printed piece of music with all the vocal and instrumental parts arranged on staves, one under another; the written or printed piece of music for a particular voice or instrument in a concerted composition.—*v.t.*—*scored, scoring.* To make notches or cuts in; to mark with strokes or lines; to draw a line through in order to cancel, used with *out*; to censure severely; to produce by cutting or marking, as marks or figures; to record, as by notches or marks; to write down as a debt; record, as a debtor; to gain for addition to one's score in a game; make a score of; to gain or win, as a success; to grade or evaluate, as on an examination or in a test; *cookery*, to cut shallow slashes in, as meat or fish. *Mus.* to write out in score; to orchestrate.—*v.i.* To make notches, cuts, marks, or lines on something; to keep score, as of a game; to make a point or points in a game or contest; to win an advantage; achieve a success.—**know the score,** *slang,* to have complete awareness of the realities or essential facts of one's circumstance or situation.—**score·less,** *a.*—**scor·er,** *n.*

score·board, skōr′bōrd″, skar′bȧrd″, *n.* A large display board in a stadium or other sports arena which shows the score and other facts of the game or event.

score·card, skōr′kärd″, skar′kärd″, *n.* A card on which to record the progress of a contest or game; a card for a sports event with the players' numbers, names, and positions printed on it.

score·keep·er, skōr′kē″pȧr, skar′kē″pȧr, *n.* An official who keeps score at a sports contest or game.

sco·ri·a, skōr′ē·a, skar′ē·a, *n. pl.* **sco·ri·ae.** [L., < Gr. *skōria*, dross, < *skōr*, dung.] The refuse, dross, or slag left after smelting or melting metals; a clinkerlike piece of lava.— **sco·ri·a·ceous,** skōr′ē·ā′shus, skar′ē·ā′shus, *a.*

sco·ri·fi·ca·tion, skōr″i·fi·kā′shan, skar″i·fi·kā′shan, *n.* The act or process by which gold or silver ore is fused with lead and borax in order to form scoria or slag and a lead button containing the silver and gold; the fusion of a lead button thus obtained in order to purify it.—**sco·ri·fy,** skōr′i·fī″, skar′i·fī″, *v.t.*—*scorified, scorifying.*

scorn, skȧrn, *n.* [O.Fr. *escorne,* affront, disgrace; *escorner,* It. *scornare,* to break off the horns, to affront, < L. *ex,* and *cornu,* a horn.] Extreme and open contempt due to one's opinion of the meanness or unworthiness of an object or person; the expression of this feeling; the object or focus of scornful feeling.—*v.t.* To act or feel toward with disdain; to reject with derision or contempt.—**laugh to scorn,** to deride; to make a mockery of.—**scorn·er,** *n.* —**scorn·ing·ly,** *adv.*—**scorn·ful,** skȧrn′ful, *a.* — **scorn·ful·ly,** *adv.* — **scorn·ful·ness,** *n.*

scor·pae·nid, skȧr·pē′nid, *n.* Any fish of the marine family *Scorpaenidae,* as rockfish or scorpionfish, having large mouths, sharp teeth, and usu. a growth of loose, wavy skin which provides camouflage against the rocks and seaweed.—*a.*—**scor·pae·noid,** skȧr·pē′noid, *a., n.*

Scor·pi·o, skȧr′pē·ō″, *n.* [L.] The eighth sign of the zodiac; *astron.* Scorpius.

scor·pi·oid, skȧr′pē·oid″, *a.* Scorpionlike; having to do with the order *Scorpionida,* of arachnids; curved or circinate at the end in the manner of a scorpion's tail.

scor·pi·on, skȧr′pē·on, *n.* [L. *scorpio, scorpionis,* < Gr. *skorpion,* a scorpion.] An arachnid, order *Scorpionida,* having a pair of large, clawlike pinchers and a long, jointed, curled tail terminating in a venomous sting; *Bib.* a kind of painful scourge or whip; *astron.* Scorpius or Scorpio.—**scor·pi·on·ic,** skȧr″pē·on′ik, *a.*

scor·pi·on·fish, skȧr′pē·on·fish″, *n. pl.* **scor·pi·on·fish,** **scor·pi·on·fish·es.** A marine fish, esp. of the genus *Scorpaena,* having poisonous spines on the dorsal fin.

scor·pi·on·fly, skȧr′pē·on·flī″, *n. pl.* **scor·pi·on·flies.** An insect of the order *Mecoptera,* the male exhibiting a scorpioid curved tail.

Scor·pi·us, skȧr′pē·us, *n. pl.* **Scor·pi·i,** skȧr′pē·ī″. *Astron.* a constellation suggesting a scorpion, and containing Antares as its brightest star. Also *Scorpio.*

scot, skot, *n.* [O.E. *scot,* Icel. *skot,* D. and L.G. *schot,* H. *schoss.*] A payment of money or a charge; a tax, assessment, or contribution.

Scot, skot, *n.* A native of Scotland; an ancient Gaelic Highlander.

scot and lot, *n.* *Brit.* formerly, a municipal tax assessed proportionately upon the members of a community.—**pay scot and lot,** to make full payment.

Scotch, skoch, *a.* Of or pertaining to the Scots, Scotland, or the dialect of English spoken in Scotland; *colloq.* frugal or miserly.—*n.* Scotch whisky; collectively, the people of Scotland; loosely, the language of the Scots.

scotch, skoch, *v.t.* [M.E. *scocchen;* origin uncertain.] To cut, gash, or score; to wound, injure, or harm so as to cripple or make harmless; to suppress, crush, or stamp out, as something dangerous.—*n.* A cut or gash.

scotch, skoch, *n.* [Origin uncertain.] A block or wedge used to prevent moving or slipping, as when put under a wheel or barrel.—*v.t.* To block or prop with a scotch, as a wheel.

Scotch broth, *n.* A soup of mutton, vegetables, and barley.

Scotch-I·rish, skoch′ī′rish, *a.* Designating or relating to the Scottish settlers in Northern Ireland, those settlers who later emigrated to the U.S. before the Irish potato blight of 1846, or their descendants.—*n.* One whose ancestors are Scottish and Irish.

Scotch·man, skoch′man, *n. pl.* **Scotch·men.** A Scotsman; a Scot.

Scotch tape, *n.* A thin, rolled transparent or translucent adhesive tape, usu. made of cellulose or cellophane. (Trademark.)

Scotch ter·ri·er, *n.* Scottish terrier.

Scotch whis·ky, *n.* A whiskey made from malted barley, distilled in Scotland.

Scotch wood·cock, *n.* A dish composed of scrambled eggs served on toast and seasoned with anchovy paste.

sco·ter, skō′tȧr, *n.* [Origin uncertain.] Any of the large ducks constituting the genera *Oidemia* and *Melanitta,* common in northern regions and seas. Also **coot scoot·er.**

scot-free, skot′frē, *a.* Unhurt or unpunished; free from payment of scot.

sco·tia, skō′sha, *n.* [Gr. *skotia,* lit. 'darkness.'] A hollow molding in the base of a column in classical architecture.

Sco·tism, skō′tiz·um, *n.* The doctrines of Joannes Duns Scotus, 1265–1308, the scholastic theologian.—**Sco·tist,** *n.*—**Sco·tis·tic,** *a.*

Scot·land Yard, *n.* Metropolitan police headquarters in London, England, the name deriving from the street which was the site of these headquarters until 1890; the street

itself; the London police force, esp. its department of crime investigation.

sco·to·ma, skō·tō′ma, *n. pl.* **sco·to·mas,** **sco·to·ma·ta,** skō·tō′ma·ta. [L.L., < Gr. *scotōma,* < *scotos,* darkness.] *Pathol.* a blind spot in the field of vision.—**sco·tom·a·tous,** skō·tom′a·tus, *a.*

Scots, skots, *a.* Scotch or Scottish.—*n.* The dialect of English which is spoken in Scotland.

Scots·man, skots′man, *n. pl.* **Scots·men.** A Scot. Also *Scotchman.*

Scot·ti·cism, skot′i·siz″um, *n.* An idiom or peculiar expression of the Scottish language, esp. in comparison with Standard English; loyalty for Scotland or the Scots.

scot·tie, skot′ē, *n.* (Often cap.) A Scottish terrier; (cap.) a Scotsman.

Scot·tish, skot′ish, *a.* Characteristic of or pertaining to Scotland, the people of Scotland, or their language. Also *Scots.*—*n.* The inhabitants of Scotland; the dialect of English which is spoken in Scotland. Also *Scots.*

Scot·tish Gael·ic, *n.* The Gaelic language spoken in the Scottish Highlands.

Scot·tish rite, *n.* A system of higher degrees in Masonry by which a member may advance beyond the basic three degrees to the 33rd or honorary degree; the ritual observed by this system.

Scot·tish ter·ri·er, *n.* A small, wiry-haired terrier with erect ears and short legs, originally raised in Scotland. Also *Scotch terrier,* **Scottie,** **Scot·ty.**

scoun·drel, skoun′drel, *n.* A base, mean, worthless person; a rascal; a man without honor or virtue.—*a.* Characteristic of a scoundrel; base; unprincipled.—**scoun·drel·ly,** *a.*

scour, skour, skou′ȧr, *v.t.* [M.E. *scouren,* prob. through Scand. < O.Fr. *escurer* (Fr. *ecurer*), cleanse, scour, < L. *ex-,* out, and *curare,* care for.] To cleanse or polish by hard rubbing as with some suitable implement or substance; as, to scour pots and pans; remove dirt and grease from by rubbing or by any cleansing process; as, to scour soiled clothing; clear out, as a channel or drain, by removing dirt or by flushing with water; to purge thoroughly, as the bowels of an animal; to remove by or as by cleansing; get rid of.—*v.i.* To rub a surface in order to cleanse or polish it; remove dirt or grease by rubbing or by any cleansing process; to become shiny and bright, as by rubbing.—*n.* A scouring; the action of a current or flow of water in clearing away deposits; the place scoured; an apparatus or a material used in scouring; *pl., sing.* or *pl. in constr.* a kind of diarrhea in cattle.— **scour·er,** skour′ȧr, skou′ȧr·ȧr, *n.*

scour, skour, skou′ȧr, *v.i.* [M.E. *scouren, scuren;* origin uncertain.] To move rapidly or energetically; range about, as in search of something.—*v.t.* To run or pass quickly over or along; range over, as in quest of something.—**scour·er,** skour′ȧr, skou′ȧr, *n.*

scourge, skurj, *n.* [Fr. *escourgée,* a scourge; L.L. *excorrigiata,* < L. *ex-,* intens., and *corrigia,* a rein, a shoe tie.] A lash, whip, or similar instrument for the infliction of pain or punishment; a punishment or vindictive affliction; one who or that which causes universal affliction or disaster, as: Disease is a *scourge* of humanity.—*v.t.*—*scourged, scourging.* To lash or whip with a scourge; to chastise for correction; to afflict greatly; to satirize.—**scourg·er,** *n.*

scour·ing rush, *n. Bot.* any of certain species of the genus *Equisetem,* esp. *E. hyemale,* a horsetail used for scouring and polishing.

scour·ings, skour′ingz, skou′ȧr·ingz, *n. pl.* Dirt or refuse material removed by scouring; refuse removed from grain before milling.

scouse, skouz, *n.* Lobscouse.

scout, skout, *n.* [O.Fr. *escoute*, a scout, < *escouter, escolter*, to hear, < L. *auscultare*, to listen.] One sent out to gain and bring in information; the act of reconnoitering; boy scout; girl scout; *Sports*, a person sent to locate and obtain new talent for the team; *slang*, a friend or guy.—*v.i.* To act as a scout.—*v.t.* To observe or watch closely.

scout, skout, *v.t., v.i.* [Icel. *skūta*, a taunt; perh. from root of *shoot*.] To treat with disdain and contempt; to reject with scorn.

scout car, *n.* An armored motor vehicle used for reconnaissance.

scout·craft, skout′kraft″, skout′kräft″, *n.* Scouting; the skill involved in scouting, as in the Girl Scouts or Boy Scouts.

scout·er, skou′tẽr, *n.* A person who scouts; a boy scout at least 18 years old.

scout·ing, skou′ting, *n.* The activities of those who scout, esp. of Girl Scouts and Boy Scouts of America.

scout·mas·ter, skout′mas″tẽr, skout′mä″stẽr, *n.* The leader or officer in charge of a band of scouts; the adult leader of a troop of Boy Scouts.

scow, skou, *n.* [D. *schouw*, a ferryboat.] A kind of large flat-bottomed boat used chiefly as a barge or a ferryboat.—*v.t.* to carry by scow.—**scow·man**, *n.*

scowl, skoul, *v.i.* [Same as Dan. *skule*, to scowl; cf. Icel *skaela*, to make a wry face.] To wrinkle the brows, as in frowning or displeasure; to look sullen, angry, or threatening.—*v.t.* To express or affect by scowling.—*n.* A deep angry frown.—**scowl·er**, *n.*

scrab·ble, skrab′l, *v.i.*—*scrabbled, scrabbling*. [A dim. of *scrape*; allied to *scribble* and *scramble*.] To scratch about or scrape with the hands, claws, or paws; to struggle; to scramble; to make irregular marks; to scrawl; to scribble.—*v.t.* To gather or scrape together hurriedly; to scramble; to scrawl or scribble.—*n.* A scratching, scraping, or clawing; a scrawling mark; a scribble; a scramble or struggle.—**scrab·bler**, *n.*

scrag, skrag, *n.* [Perh. < *crag*.] Something skinny, scrawny, or stunted, as a person, animal, or plant; of mutton or veal, the lean part of the neck; *slang*, the neck of a person.—*v.t.*—*scragged, scragging. Slang*, to wring, twist, strangle, or hang by the neck.

scrag·gly, skrag′lē, *a.*—*scragglier, scraggliest*. Jagged, craggy, splintered, or shattered; hanging in strings or scrags; disheveled or shaggy.

scrag·gy, skrag′ē, *a.*—*scraggier, scraggiest*. Lean or scrawny; rough; irregular; bony or angular.—**scrag·gi·ly**, *adv.*—**scrag·gi·ness**, *n.*

scram, skram, *v.i.*—*scrammed, scramming. Slang*. To leave immediately; go away quickly.

scram·ble, skram′bl, *v.i.*—*scrambled, scrambling*. [Akin to D. *scrammen*, to scratch; Dan. *skramle*, to ramble; Sw. *skramla*, to clatter.] To move or climb quickly by the aid of the hands, or on all fours; to snatch eagerly at or struggle to get, before others; to move hastily and somewhat clumsily; *milit.* to rush to become airborne for interception of enemy aircraft.—*v.t.* To throw or mix together; to disorder or confuse; as, to *scramble* the letters in a word; to assemble or collect in a disorganized rush; to stir and mix together, usu. with milk, before and during cooking; as, to *scramble* eggs; to systematically alter in order to prevent interception; as, to *scramble* a radio message; *milit.* to instigate a hurried takeoff; as, to *scramble* an interceptor aircraft squadron.—*n.*—**scram·bler**, skram′blẽr, *n.*—**scram·bling**, *n.*

scran·nel, skran′el, *a.* [Origin obscure, possibly < Norw. *skran*, thin, lean.] Thin or slight; squeaky or unmelodious.

scrap, skrap, *n.* [Lit. 'what is *scraped*'; same as Icel. *skrap*, scraps, trifles.] A small piece or fragment; a portion or particle of leftover food, usu. to be thrown away; crisp bits of rendered fat; a detached or extracted bit of written or printed matter, as a newspaper clipping; material which has been manufactured, used, and discarded as being fit only for reworking; as, *scraps* of iron; the fragmental excess left after the making or processing of something.—*v.t.*—*scrapped, scrapping*. To cause to become scrap; to give up or discard as no longer sufficiently workable.—*a.* Having the discarded status of scrap; composed of fragments.

scrap, skrap, *n.* [Cf. *scrape.*] *Colloq.* a fight, scrimmage, or quarrel.—*v.i.*—*scrapped, scrapping. Colloq.* to fight or get into a quarrel.—**scrap·per**, skrap′ẽr, *n.*

scrap·book, skrap′buk″, *n.* A book for the preservation of such mementos as prints, engravings, invitations, or other extracts from other books; an album.

scrape, skrāp, *v.t.*—*scraped, scraping*. [Same as Icel. *skrapa*, to scrape, to scratch; L.G. and D. *schrapen*, Dan. *skrabe*, to scrape; akin *scrape, scramble*, perh. *sharp*.] To pull or push a sharp or straight edge or an abrasive along (a surface), thereby smoothing, roughing, or removing an outer layer or an adherent substance; to remove from (a surface) in this way; to grate, rasp, or scratch against or across; to move or pull with pressure or roughness across a surface; to mar, scar, or damage in this way; to form in this way; to collect, gather, or organize as if by scraping, as with difficulty or on the spur of the moment, usu. with *together.*—*v.i.* To rub or scrape something; to produce a harsh, discordant sound; to drag back a foot in executing a low bow; to barely succeed with great effort; to be excessively frugal.—*n.* The action, act, or result of scraping; the rasping, grating, or screeching sound of scraping; the dragging back of the foot while bowing; an uncomfortable, difficult situation; a quarrel.—**scrap·able**, *a.*—**scrape·age**, *n.*—**scrap·er**, skrā′pẽr, *n.*

scrap heap, *n.* A heap of scraps, esp. of discarded or broken ironwork for remelting or reworking.—*v.t.* To consign to the scrap heap; to discard as useless or worthless.

scrap·per, skrap′ẽr, *n. Colloq.* One who scraps or fights; one given to and enthusiastic about fighting.

scrap·ple, skrap′l, *n.* [Dim. of *scrap.*] A sausagelike preparation of minced pork, herbs, and rye or other meal, fried in slices.

scrap·py, skrap″ē, *a.*—*scrappier, scrappiest*. Consisting of scraps; disconnected.—**scrap·pi·ly**, *adv.*—**scrap·pi·ness**, *n.*

scrap·py, skrap′ē, *a.*—*scrappier, scrappiest. Colloq.* Tending toward argument or scrapping; pugnacious; competitive.—**scrap·pi·ly**, *adv.*—**scrap·pi·ness**, *n.*

scratch, skrach, *v.t.* [O.E. *cratch*, to scratch; same as O.D. *kratsen*, Sw. *kratsa*, Dan *kradse*, G. *kratzen*, to scratch, the *s* having been prefixed through the influence of *scrape*, etc.] To rub, tear, or mark the surface of with something sharp or abrasive; to gouge, dig, or peel off with scraping or clawing action; to scrape gently with fingernails, claws, or the like, to ease an itch; to pull or rub along a rough, abrasive surface; to strike out or discard by or as if by crossing off with a line; to withdraw from entry in a horserace or other competition; to reject, as one candidate, while retaining or endorsing the rest of a political ticket; to scribble, draw, or sketchily write; as, to *scratch* a note.—*v.i.* To claw, tear, scrape, or the like by using fingernails or claws; to soothe an itch by gently scraping or stroking with fingernails or claws; to make a gritty, screeching sound; to withdraw from competition; to work and expend effort and just get by; *games*, to make no score; *billiards*, to incur a penalty. —*n.* A slight wound, break, furrow, or mark on a surface, made by scratching; an instance of scratching; the sound of scratching; *sports*, the normal starting place, time, or conditions of one without a handicap. *Billiards*, a turn which incurs a penalty; an accidentally good shot; a fluke. *Games*, no score; zero.—*a.* Used for doodling, sketching, jotting, or practice; as, a *scratch* pad of paper; unplanned, accidental, relying on chance; assembled or gathered indeterminately or haphazardly, as a committee; *sports*, without handicap.—**start from scratch**, to begin with nothing; to start from the beginning.—**scratch·a·ble**, *a.*—**scratch·er**, *n.*—**scratch·less**, *a.*—**scratch·like**, *a.*

scratch hit, *n. Baseball*, a ball that is not hit squarely, yet which results in a safe hit for the batter.

scratch line, *n. Sports*, a line drawn for various sporting events, such as a race, broad jump, or javelin throw, which marks the starting point or the farthest limit of take off.

scratch pa·per, *n.* Paper which is used for writing down reminders, ideas, or other casual notes.

scratch sheet, *n.* A race track publication which lists eliminated entries as well as the odds on the horses which will compete in each race.

scratch test, *n. Pathol.* a test which determines allergic susceptibility by the application of allergens into scratches made in the skin, an allergic condition being indicated by subsequent inflammation of the area.

scratch·y, skrach′ē, *a.*—*scratchier, scratchiest*. Causing a harsh, grating noise; consisting of or marked with scratches; as, a *scratchy* desk; causing itching or other skin irritation; as, a *scratchy* woolen shirt; rough or ragged; likely to scratch; as, *scratchy* rose thorns.—**scratch·i·ly**, *adv.*—**scratch·i·ness**, *n.*

scrawl, skral, *v.t.* [A contr. form of *scrabble*; cf. D. *schravelen*, to scratch.] To draw or mark awkwardly and irregularly; to write illegibly; to scribble.—*v.i.* To write unskillfully and hastily.—*n.* A sample of hasty or illegible writing.—**scrawl·er**, *n.*—**scrawl·y**, *a.*—*scrawlier, scrawliest*. Written awkwardly or carelessly.

scrawn·y, skra′nē, *a.*—*scrawnier, scrawniest*. Thin; rawboned.—**scrawn·i·ness**, *n.*

screak, skrēk, *v.i.* [A form of *screech, shriek* = Sw. *shrika*, Icel. *skraekja*, to screak.] To scream or screech; to creak.—*n.*—**screak·y**, *a.*—*screakier, screakiest*.

scream, skrēm, *v.i.* [Cf. Icel. *skramsa*, to scream; prob. imit. like *screech, shriek*, etc.] To cry out with a loud, shrill voice; as, to *scream* at a person; to laugh with uncontrolled hysteria; to utter a sudden, sharp outcry, as in a fright or in extreme pain; to shriek; to shock, as does a piercing noise or brilliant color; to give out a shrill sound, as: The jets *screamed* overhead.—*v.t.* To say in a loud, shrill voice.—*n.* A shriek or sharp, shrill cry; a sharp, harsh sound.

scream·er, skrē′mẽr, *n.* One who screams; any of several S. American birds, of the family *Anhimidae*, characterized by a harsh, discordant voice; *slang*, one who or that which creates laughter; *journ.* a startling headline.

scream·ing·ly, skrē′ming·lē, *adv.* To a great degree; extraordinarily; as, *screamingly* funny.—**scream·ing**, *a., n.*

scree, skrē, *n.* [Cf. Icel. *skritha*, landslide]. *Geol.* talus.

screech, skrēch, *v.i.* [A softened form of *screak*, Icel. *skraekja*, Sw. *skrika*, Dan.

skrige, to screech; an imit. word.] To cry out with a sharp, shrill voice; to shriek.—*v.i.* To emit with a screech.—*n.* A sharp, shrill cry; a harsh scream; a sharp, shrill noise.—**screech·er**, *n.*

screed, skrēd, *n.* A discursive statement; a harangue or tirade; a strip, as of plaster, placed on a surface being constructed as a guide to the thickness desired; *Sc.* a shred.

screen, skrēn, *n.* [O.Fr. *escren, escrein, escran*, Fr. *écran*, a screen, perh. < O.H.G. *skranna*, a table.] A framework or curtain used to shut out the sun, rain, or cold, or to conceal something from sight; anything which shelters, protects, or conceals; as, a *screen* of mist; a surface on which a stereopticon picture or motion picture is projected; motion pictures collectively; a frame containing mesh, usu. of metal, inserted in a window or doorway to shut out insects; a wire sieve used for sifting grain, sand, or lime; *arch.* an ornamental partition of wood, stone, or metal, usu. in a church; *photoengraving*, a clear piece of glass crossed with fine lines which is placed between the camera and the object to be photographed in the halftone process; *milit.* a protective unit of troops or ships positioned ahead of or surrounding the main body of men or ships; *phys.* an apparatus which prevents interference among various agencies; as, a magnetic *screen*; *psychoanal.* in dreams, a person or object which symbolizes another, concealing the real object of the emotions of the dreamer.—*v.t.* To shelter or protect from inconvenience, injury, or danger; to conceal; to sift by passing through a screen; to supply with a screen to shut out insects; to project, as a picture, on a screen; to select by a process of elimination, as: The company *screens* all applicants carefully.—*v.i.* To appear on a motion picture screen.—**screen·a·ble**, *a.*—**screen·er**, *n.*

screen·ing, skrē'ning, *n.* The exhibiting of a motion picture; the plastic or metal material used as a mesh in screens. *Phys.* the process or procedure of that which screens.

screen·ings, skrē'ningz, *n. pl.* The residual material that has been separated from more desirable material through the use of a sieve.

screen pass, *n. Football*, a pass to a receiver who is surrounded by his teammates for deception and protection.

screen·play, skrēn'plā″, *n.* The scenario for a motion picture.

screen test, *n.* A brief film audition for determining the qualifications of a person for acting in movies.—**screen-test**, skrēn'test″, *v.t.*

screen writ·er, *n.* One who writes screen plays.

screw, skrö, *n.* [Same as Dan. *skrue*, Sw. *skruf*, Icel. *skrúfa*, D. *schroef*, O.D. *schroeve*, L.G. *schruwe*, G. *shraube*, a screw.] A helical pointed metal cylinder having a slotted head, driven into a surface by turning with a screwdriver. A similar headed metal cylinder for fitting into a specific socket; also **ex·ter·nal screw, male screw.** A helical socket for fitting a spirally threaded cylinder; also **in·ter·nal screw, fe·male screw.** Anything spirally formed; a screw propeller; one complete turn of a screw; a twisting or rotating movement; force or pressure. *Slang*, sexual intercourse; a prison guard. *Brit.* a small quantity, as of tobacco, twisted up in a piece of paper; one who makes a sharp bargain; an old or worthless horse. *Brit. slang*, salary or pay.—*v.t.* To press, operate, or make firm by means of a screw; to apply or adjust by turning; to twist; to contort, as features; to extort. *Slang*, to have sexual intercourse with; to

cheat.—*v.i.* To operate or to be adjusted by turning; to be made firm by or as by a screw; to engage in extortion.—**get screwed**, *slang*, to be cheated or punished.—**have a screw loose**, *slang*, to be peculiar, eccentric, or mentally unbalanced.—**put the screws on**, to use force.—**screw a·round**, *slang*. To loaf; to engage in frivolous activity.— **screw up**, *slang*, to ruin, confuse, or bungle. —**screw·er**, *n.*

screw·ball, skrö'bạl″, *n. Slang*, a person characterized by capricious or unconventional behavior; an eccentric character. *Baseball*, a ball pitched to curve in the same direction as the side from which it is thrown: opposed to *curve ball.*—*a.*

screw bean, *n.* A leguminous tree, *Prosopis pubescens*, of the southwestern U.S., bearing twisted pods which are used as fodder; the pod itself. Also *tornillo*, **screw-pod mes·quite**, skrö'pod″ me·skēt′.

screw·driv·er, skrö'drī″vẽr, *n.* A tool for setting or adjusting screws, consisting of a handle and a metal shaft that is flat and blunt at the end so as to fit into a slot in a screw head; a vodka and orange juice cocktail.

screw eye, *n.* A screw with a ring-shaped head.

screw jack, *n.* Jackscrew.

screw pine, *n.* The common name for useful trees, genus *Pandanus*, native to the East Indies, New Guinea, and the tropics, supported above the ground by aerial roots and having palmlike branches with pointed leaves.

screw pro·pel·ler, *n.* A rotating core with radiating blades twisted at an angle, used to propel an aircraft or a ship.

screw thread, *n.* The helical ridge which forms the essential part of an external screw, or a corresponding ridge of an internal screw; one full rotation of this ridge.

screw·worm, skrö'wụrm″, *n.* The larva of a fly, genus *Callitroga*, a dipterous insect which deposits its eggs in sores or in the nose of living animals and after development lives upon the tissue of the animal attacked, often with fatal results.

screw·y, skrö'ē, *a.*—*screwier, screwiest.* Winding or twisting about like the thread of a screw. *Slang*, unsound or upsetting, as a story; crazy; ridiculous or irrational.

scrib·ble, skrib'l, *v.t.*—*scribbled, scribbling.* [Based partly on *scrabble*, partly on L. *scribo*, to write.] To write with haste, or without care; to fill with careless or illegible writing.—*v.i.* To scrawl; to write without care or beauty.—*n.* Hasty or careless writing; a scrawl.

scrib·bler, skrib'lẽr, *n.* One who scribbles or writes carelessly; a writer of no reputation.

scribe, skrīb, *n.* [Fr. *scribe*, < L. *scriba*, a clerk, a secretary, < *scribo, scriptum*, to write; seen also in *ascribe, describe, inscribe*.] One who writes; a penman or copyist, esp. one who copied manuscripts in ancient times; a public secretary or amanuensis; among the ancient Jews, a teacher, interpreter, or copyist of Jewish scripture and law; in humorous reference, a journalist or author.—*v.t.*—*scribed, scribing. Carp.* To mark wood with a pointed tool; to score or mark for accurate fitting. —**scrib·al**, *a.*

scrib·er, skrī'bẽr, *n. Carp.* a sharp tool for marking wood or other material as a guide for cutting.

scrim, skrim, *n.* [Origin obscure.] A cotton or linen fabric of open, canvaslike weave, used for curtains and clothing; *theatr.* a fabric of this type used to give the image of a backdrop or wall, or forming a transparent curtain under various lighting conditions.

scrim·mage, skrim'ij, *n.* [Var. of *skirmish*.] A skirmish; a rough or vigorous fight or

struggle, esp. between a number of persons. *Football, rugby*, the action between contesting players when the ball is put into play and until it is declared dead; game practice or informal play. Also *Brit.* **scrum·mage**, *colloq.* **scrum.**—*v.i.*, *v.t.* —*scrimmaged, scrimmaging.*—**scrim·mage line**, line of scrimmage.—**scrim·mag·er**, *n.*

scrimp, skrimp, *v.t.* [Cf. M.L.G. *schrimpen*, *schrempen*, wrinkle, contract, G. *schrumpfen*, shrink, also E. *shrimp* and *skimp*.] To be sparing of or in; to stint on the amount of, as food; to make too scanty or small; to keep on short allowance.—*v.i.* To use severe economy; to be parsimonious or niggardly.—*a.* Scanty; meager; deficient.— **scrimp·y**, skrim'pē, *a.*—*scrimpier, scrimpiest.* Scanty; meager.

scrim·shaw, skrim'shạ″, *n.* [Origin obscure.] Carving or other work on articles of ivory, whalebone, shell, wood, or the like executed by whalers in their leisure time. Also **scrim·shaw work.**—*v.t., v.i.* To make into, or make, scrimshaw work.

scrip, skrip, *n.* [Appar. for *script*.] A printed or written paper, as a receipt or certificate; a written schedule or other list; a provisional certificate, as for shares of stock, issued on payment of an installment of the amount due; a certificate of a right to a fractional part of a share of stock; certificates of any such kind collectively; paper currency in denominations of less than $1, formerly issued in the U.S.; money issued for temporary emergency use.

script, skript, *n.* [L. *scriptum*, something written, prop. neut. of *scriptus*, pp. of *scribere*, write.] Handwriting; the characters used in handwriting; a mode of writing; *print.* a style of type imitating handwriting; *law*, an original document or writing; *theatr.* the manuscript of a play or movie, or of a player's role.

scrip·to·ri·um, skrip·tōr′ē·um, skrip-tạr′ē·um, *n. pl.* **scrip·to·ri·ums**, scrip-to·ri·a**, skrip·tōr′ē·a, skrip·tạr′ē·a. [M.L., a place for writing, prop. neut. of L. *scriptorius*, of or for writing, < *scribere*, to write.] A room in a monastery set apart for the writing or copying of manuscripts.

scrip·tur·al, skrip'chẽr·al, *a.* Contained in any religious or sacred writing; *(cap.)* contained in or according to the Scriptures. —**scrip·tur·al·ly**, *adv.*—**scrip·tur·al·ness**, *n.*

scrip·ture, skrip'chẽr, *n.* [L. *scriptura*, a writing, < *scribo, scriptum*, to write.] *(Cap.)* the Bible; the books of the Old or New Testament; a passage or quotation from the Bible; also **Ho·ly Scrip·tures.**(*l.c.*)anything written, esp. religious or sacred writings; the writings considered sacred by any religious group.

script·writ·er, skript'rī″tẽr, *n.* An author of scripts for radio, television, or motion pictures.

scrive·ner, skriv'nẽr, *n.* [M.E. *scriveyner*, for *scriveyn*, < O.Fr. *escrivain* (Fr. *écrivain*), < M.L. *scribanus*, < L. *scriba*, E. *scribe*, *n.*] Formerly, a professional or public writer, as of letters or documents for others; a clerk or scribe; a notary.

scro·bic·u·late, skrō·bik'ū·lit, skrō·bik′ū·lāt″, *a.* [L. *scrobiculus*, dim. of *scrobis*, ditch, trench.] *Biol.* furrowed or pitted.

scrod, skrod, *n. pl.* **scrods, scrod.** [Origin uncertain; perh. < D.] A young codfish, esp. one that is split for cooking.

scrof·u·la, skrof'ū·la, skrof'ya·la, *n.* [M.L., < L.L. *scrofulæ*, pl., scrofulous swellings, scrofula, dim. < L. *scrofa*, a breeding sow.] *Pathol.* a constitutional disorder of a tuberculous nature, characterized chiefly by swelling and degeneration of the lymphatic glands, esp. of the neck, and by inflammation of the joints.—**scrof·u·lous**

skrof′ū·lus, skrof′ya·lus, *a.* Pertaining to or of the nature of scrofula; affected with scrofula; morally degenerate.

scroll, skrōl, *n.* [O.Fr. *eskrol, escrou* (Fr. *écrou*), a scroll, a register; prob. Teut.; cf. Icel. *skra,* a scroll, Sw. *skra,* a short writing.] A roll of paper, parchment, or the like; a writing formed into a roll; an ornament of a coiled or spiral form, as the volute of the Ionic and Corinthian capitals; a list or schedule; the curved head of instruments of the violin family; a flourish added to a person's name in signing.—**scroll·head,** skrōl′hed″, *n.* An ornament at the bow of a ship.

scroll saw, *n.* A narrow saw with a long, ribbonlike blade used for sawing out curved shapes.

scroll·work, skrōl′wųrk″, *n.* Ornamental work prominently decorated with scrolls; decorative work cut with a scroll saw.

scrooge, skrȫj, *n.* [From the character in *A Christmas Carol,* by Charles Dickens.] *Often cap.* a stingy, miserly person.

scro·tum, skrō′tum, *n.* pl. **scro·ta, scro·tums,** skrō′ta. [L.] In mammals, the external pouch which contains the testicles.—**scro·tal,** *a.*

scrounge, skrounj, *v.t., v.i.* To search or look around for; to forage; pilfer; to borrow without intent to repay.—**scrounge a·round,** to search at random or haphazardly. —**scroung·er,** *n.* A moocher; borrower.— **scroung·ing,** skroun′jing, *n.* Borrowing without intent to repay.

scrub, skrub, *v.t.*—**scrubbed, scrubbing.** [Cf. M.L.G. *schrubben, schrobben,* scratch, rub, scrub, D. *schrobben,* scrub: cf. *scribble.*] To clean by rubbing, as a part of the body, as: He *scrubbed* his hands. To rub hard with a brush, sponge, cloth, or the like, or against a rough surface, as in washing or cleansing; as, to *scrub* a floor; to wash or cleanse. *Slang,* to eliminate, cancel; to delay; to postpone, as: The airline *scrubbed* the flight.—*v.i.* To cleanse things by hard rubbing, as with a brush, soap, and water.—*n.* A scrubbing.

scrub, skrub, *n.* [= *shrub.*] A low or stunted tree; low trees or shrubs collectively, or an extended growth of them; as, a small glen grown over with a low oak *scrub*; anything undersized or inferior; as, *scrubs* among domestic animals; a mean, insignificant person; *sports,* a player not carried on the varsity or first team.

scrub·bed, skrub′id, *a. Archaic,* scrubby.

scrub·ber, skrub′ẽr, *n.* One who or that which scrubs; an instrument for scrubbing, as a brush; an apparatus for washing a gas or gaseous mixture.

scrub·by, skrub′ē, *a.*—**scrubbier, scrubbiest.** Low or stunted, as trees and shrubs; consisting of or covered with stunted trees; as, a *scrubby* wood on the hillside, a *scrubby* region; undersized, inferior, or poor; as, a *scrubby* cow; sorry, wretched, or shabby; mean, paltry, or insignificant.

scrub ty·phus, *n. Pathol.* tsutsugamushi disease.

scrub·wom·an, skrub′wųm″an, *n.* pl. **scrub·wom·en.** A woman who is hired to do heavy cleaning work.

scruff, skruf, *n.* The back or nape of the neck.

scruff·y, skruf′ē, *a.*—**scruffier, scruffiest.** Slovenly; unkempt; threadbare.

scrum·mage, skrum′ij, *n. Brit.* scrimmage. Also **scrum.**—*v.i.*—**scrummaged, scrummaging.**—**scrum·mag·er,** *n.*

scrump·tious, skrump′shus, *a. Slang.* Superlatively fine or nice; splendid.— **scrump·tious·ly,** *adv.*

scrunch, skrunch, skrųnch, *v.t., v.i.* [Imit.: cf. *crunch.*] To chew or crunch, as food; to crush or crumple.—*n.* An act or sound of scrunching.

scru·ple, skrȫ′pl, *n.* [L. *scrupulus,* cause or feeling of uneasiness, scruple, lit. 'small, sharp stone,' dim. of *scrupus,* sharp or rough stone, *fig.* uneasiness, anxiety.] A feeling of uneasiness affecting the conscience or the sense of propriety, which tends to restrain one's action.—*v.i.*— *scrupled, scrupling.* To have scruples; to hesitate or be reluctant on conscientious or similar grounds.—*v.t.* To have scruples about; to hesitate at.

scru·ple, skrȫ′pl, *n.* [L. *scrupulus, scrupulum, scripulum,* unit of weight or measure, identified by some with *scrupulus,* small stone.] An ancient Roman unit of weight equivalent to $\frac{1}{24}$ of an ounce. A modern unit of weight equivalent to 20 grains or one-third of a dram, apothecaries' weight; see Measures and Weights table. A very small portion or amount of anything; an iota.

scru·pu·lous, skrȫ′pū·lus, skrȫ′pya·lus, *a.* [L. *scrupulosus.*] Having scruples; restrained by scruples; having or showing a strict regard for what is right; minutely careful, precise, or exact.—**scru·pu·los·i·ty,** skru·pu·lous·ness, skrȫ′pū·los′i·tē, skrȫ′pya·los′i·tē, *n.*—**scru·pu·lous·ly,** *adv.*

scru·ta·ble, skrȫ′ta·bl, *a.* [L. *scrutari:* cf. *inscrutable.*] Capable of being penetrated or understood by investigation.

scru·ta·tor, skrȫ·tā′tẽr, *n.* [L., < *scrutari.*] One who examines or investigates.

scru·ti·neer, skrȫt″i·nēr′, *n.* One who scrutinizes; *chiefly Brit.* one who acts as an examiner of votes, as at an election.

scru·ti·nize, skrȫt′i·nīz″, *v.t.*—**scrutinized, scrutinizing.** To subject to scrutiny; to investigate closely; to examine or inquire into critically.—*v.i.* To conduct a careful investigation.—**scru·ti·ni·za·tion,** *n.*—**scru·ti·niz·er,** *n.*—**scru·ti·niz·ing·ly,** *adv.*

scru·ti·ny, skrȫt′i·nē, *n.* pl. **scru·ti·nies.** [L. *scrutinium,* < *scrutor,* to search carefully, to rummage, < *scruta,* trash, frippery.] Close investigation or examination; a minute inquiry; a searching look; *chiefly Brit.* an examination of votes by a competent authority for the purpose of enforcing election laws.

scu·ba, skȫ′ba, *n.* [(s)elf-(c)ontained (u)nderwater (b)reathing (a)pparatus.] A compact underwater breathing device worn on the back by free divers, consisting of one or two compressed air tanks and a connecting hose with a mouthpiece.

scud, skud, *v.i.*—**scudded, scudding.** [Origin obscure.] To run or move along quickly or hurriedly; dart or fly hastily off or away; *naut.* to run before a gale with little or no sail set.—*n.* The act of scudding; clouds, spray, or the like, driven by the wind; a driving shower; a gust of wind.

scu·do, skȫ′dō, *n.* pl. **scu·di,** skȫ′dē. [It., < L. *scutum,* shield.] A coin of gold or silver and money of account issued in various Italian states from the 16th into the 19th century.

scuff, skuf, *v.i.* [Origin uncertain: cf. *scuffle.*] To walk without raising the feet; shuffle; to become roughened by rubbing or wear.—*v.t.* To scrape with the feet; to mar the surface of by scraping or hard usage, as shoes or furniture; to graze in passing.—*n.* The act or sound of scuffing; a flat house slipper that covers only the front portion of the foot; a rough or worn place caused by scuffing.

scuf·fle, skuf′l, *v.i.*—**scuffed, scuffling.** [Freq. akin to O.E. *scufan,* Sw. *skuffa,* to shove; same word as *shuffle.*] To struggle or grapple closely; to fight confusedly; to walk in a shuffling manner.—*n.* A confused, tumultuous fight.

scuf·fle hoe, *n.* [D. *schoffel,* hoe, = E. *shovel.*] A form of garden hoe which is pushed instead of pulled.

scull, skul, *n.* [M.E. *sculle, skulle;* origin uncertain.] An oar worked from side to side over the stern of a boat as a means of propulsion; one of a pair of short, laterally placed oars operated by one person; a boat propelled by sculls, esp. a light racing boat propelled by one or more rowers, each with a pair of oars.—*v.t.* To propel or convey by means of a scull or sculls.—*v.i.* To propel a boat with a scull or sculls.—**scull·er,** *n.*

scul·ler·y, skul′e·rē, *n.* pl. **scul·ler·ies.** [Perh. < O.Fr. *escuelle, escuele,* a bowl, < L. *scutella,* dim. of *scutera,* a dish.] A place where culinary utensils are cleaned and kept; a back kitchen.

scul·lion, skul′yon, *n.* [Perh. (with form modified by association with *scullery*) < Fr. *souillon,* scullion, < *souiller,* E. *soil.*] A domestic servant who does menial work in a kitchen.

scul·pin, skul′pin, *n.* pl. **scul·pins, scul·pin.** [Cf. *scorpene.*] Any of various marine fishes of the family *Cottidae,* esp. of the genus *Myoxocephalus,* with large spiny head, wide mouth, and repulsive appearance; a scorpaenoid fish, *Scorpaena guttata,* of the coast of southern California; a scorpene.

sculpt, skulpt, *v.t., v.i. Informal,* to sculpture.

sculp·tor, skulp′tẽr, *n.* One who creates artwork that is three-dimensional, usu. by processes such as hewing, chiseling, and carving.—**sculp·tress,** skulp′tris, *n.* Feminine of sculptor.

sculp·ture, skulp′chẽr, *n.* [Fr. *sculpture,* < L. *sculptura,* < *sculpo, sculptum* (also *scalpo*), to carve.] The art form of a three-dimensional work, either realistic or abstract, created by a sculptor; a statue or other example of such art; such objects of art collectively; the process of chiseling, cutting, carving, or otherwise preparing such art; the patterned appearance of the surfaces of some shells and leaves that is a result of a contrast in texture and depth.—*v.t.*— *sculptured, sculpturing.* To fashion and produce, as a work of art that is three-dimensional; to depict or portray by means of this form of art.—*v.i.* To mold or model in the manner of a sculptor. *Physical geog.* to change the surface of the earth by processes of erosion and redistribution of mass. —**sculp·tur·al,** *a.*—**sculp·tur·al·ly,** *adv.*

sculp·tur·esque, skulp″che·resk′, *a.* Possessing the quality of sculpture; in the manner of sculpture; statuesque; majestic; dignified.—**sculp·tur·esque·ly,** *adv.*— **sculp·tur·esque·ness,** *n.*

scum, skum, *n.* [Same as Sw. and Dan. *skum,* G. *schaum,* D. *schuim,* O.H.G. *scūm,* from a root meaning to cover (seen in *sky,* etc.). *Skim* is a derivative verb.] The extraneous matter which rises to the surface of liquids in boiling or fermentation; the scoria of molten metals; refuse; a group of worthless, vile, or despicable persons; one who is despicable; rabble.— *v.t.*—*scummed, scumming.* To clear from the surface, as impure matter.—*v.i.* To form scum; to be covered with scum.—**scum·my,** skum′ē, *a.*—*scummier, scummiest.*

scum·ble, skum′bl, *v.t.*—**scumbled, scumbling.** [Freq. of *scum.*] To cover thinly, as in painting, with opaque or semiopaque colors to modify the effect; to soften by blending with the fingers, as the outlines in drawings.—*n.* The effect created by scumbling; the substances used for scumbling.

scun·ner, skun′ẽr, *n.* A feeling of disgust or loathing; abomination.

scup, skup, *n.* pl. **scup, scups.** [N. Amer. Ind.] A marine food fish allied to the grunts, *Stenotomus chrysops,* of the eastern coast of the U.S., having a compressed body and a high back.

scup·per, skup′ẽr, *n.* [Akin to *scoop,* or < O.Fr. and Sp. *escupir,* to spit.] *Naut.* a channel or gutter at the outer edge of the deck of a ship for carrying off water.—*v.t. Brit. milit. slang*, to overwhelm and massacre in a surprise attack.

scup·per·nong, skup′ẽr·nang″, skup′ẽr--nong″, *n.* [From the *Scuppernong* River in eastern North Carolina; N. Amer. Ind. name.] A cultivated variety of the fox grape of the southern U.S.; a sweet, white wine made from this grape.

scurf, skurf, *n.* [O.E. *scurf,* scurf; Icel. *skurfur* (pl.), Dan. *skurv,* Sw. *skorf,* G. *schorf,* scurf; allied to *scrape.*] Matter composed of minute scales of dry skin which is continually flaking from the body, as dandruff; a crusty or scaly layer of matter adhering to a surface; *bot.* the loose scaly matter that is found on some plants.—**scurf·y,** skur′fē, *a.*—*scurfier, scurfiest.*—**scurf·i·ness,** *n.*—**scurf·like,** *a.*

scur·rile, scur·ril, skur′il, *a.* [L. *scurrilis,* < *scurra,* a buffoon, a jester.] Scurrilous.

scur·ril·i·ty, ska·ril′i·tē, *n.* pl. **scur·ril·i·ties.** The quality of being scurrilous; that which is scurrilous.

scur·ril·ous, skur′i·lus, *a.* Characterized by base, off-color, derogatory, or offensive language or humor; coarsely or vulgarly abusive.—**scur·ril·ous·ly,** *adv.*—**scur·ril·ous·ness,** *n.*

scur·ry, skur′ē, skur′ē, *v.i.*—*scurried, scurrying.* [Cf. *scour.*] To run or move rapidly; to scamper; to hurry.—*n.* pl. **scur·ries.** A scurrying; the sound of scurrying; a short, quick run or horse race.

scur·vy, skur′vē, *n.* [< *scurf.*] *Pathol.* a disease characterized in part by swollen and readily bleeding gums, livid skin patches, and generalized exhaustion, affecting persons who are deprived of vitamin C.—*a.*—*scurvier, scurviest.* Vile; mean; low; malicious.—**scur·vi·ly,** *adv.*—**scur·vi·ness,** *n.*

scur·vy grass, *n.* A cress, *Cochlearia officinalis,* formerly used as a remedy for scurvy.

scut, skut, *n.* [< W. *cwt,* a tail.] A short tail, as that of a hare or deer.

scu·tage, skū′tij, *n.* [L.L. *scutagium,* < L. *scutum,* a shield.] A tax on feudal tenants, payment of which excused them from military service.

scu·tate, skū′tāt, *a. Bot.* formed like an ancient round buckler or shield; *zool.* protected or covered by large scales or plates. Also **scu·tat·ed.**

scutch, skuch, *v.t.* [Perh. same as *scotch,* to cut, to strike.] To prepare, as textile fibers, by beating, as to separate woody parts from the cellulose fibers of flax or hemp. *Constr.* to shape for laying, as bricks; also **scotch.**—*n.* A beater for preparing textile fibers; also *scutcher.* A hammerlike implement for dressing bricks; also **scotch.**

scutch·eon, skuch′on, *n.* [A contr. of *escutcheon.*] Escutcheon; *zool.* scute.

scutch·er, skuch′ẽr, *n.* One who or that which scutches. A device for scutching fiber or brick; also *scutch.*

scute, skūt, *n.* [L. *scutum,* a buckler.] *Zool.* a bony or horny scale, shield, or plate found on the protective covering of various animals; a large scale or plate. Also *scutcheon, scutum.*

scu·tel·late, skū′tel·it, skū·tel′āt, skūt′e--lāt′, *a. Zool.* of, pertaining to, shaped like, or covered with scales. Also **scu·tel·lat·ed.**

scu·tel·la·tion, skūt′e·lā′shan, *n. Zool.* the occurrence or arrangement of scute.

scu·tel·lum, skū·tel′um, *n.* pl. **scu·tel·la,** skū·tel′a. [L. dim of *scutum,* a shield.] *Bot.* any small plates or scales having the shape or function of a shield; *zool.* a shield-like part, esp. on the thorax of certain insects.

scu·ti·form, skū′ti·farm″, *a.* Shaped like a shield.

scut·ter, skut′ẽr, *v.i. Brit. colloq.* to run or scamper quickly. Also *scuttle.*

scut·tle, skut′l, *n.* [O.E. *scutel,* < L. *scutella,* dim. of *scutra,* a dish or platter.] A broad shallow basket; a metal pail for carrying coal, usu. with a wide-mouthed spout.

scut·tle, skut′l, *n.* A square hole with a lid in the wall or roof of a house; the lid itself; *naut.* a small hatchway, with a lid or cover, in the deck, side, or bottom of a ship.—*v.t.*—*scuttled, scuttling. Naut.* to sink (a ship) by making holes through the bottom or by opening the scuttles. To abandon, destroy, or discard, as an idea.

scut·tle, skut′l, *v.i.*—*scuttled, scuttling.* [For *scuddle,* a freq. of *scud.*] To run hastily; to scurry or hurry.—*n.* A quick pace; a short run.

scut·tle·butt, skut′l·but″, *n.* A drinking fountain installed on a ship; formerly, a cask holding fresh water for daily use; *slang,* rumor, gossip.

scu·tum, skū′tum, *n.* pl. **scu·ta,** skū′ta. [L., a shield.] *Zool.* a shield-shaped plate on an animal, as the back of a turtle; a scute. The shield of the Ancient Roman legionaries. (*Cap.*), *astron.* a constellation whose shape resembles a shield, found in the Milky Way.

Scyl·la, sil′a, *n.* Gr. *mythol.* a female monster named from 'Scilla', a rock off the south coast of Italy, who preyed on the crews of passing ships.—**be·tween Scyl·la and Cha·ryb·dis,** having a choice between equally dangerous alternatives.

scy·pho·zo·an, si″fo·zō′an, *a.* [N.L. *Scyphozoa,* pl., < Gr. *skyphos,* cup, and *zōon,* animal.] Belonging or pertaining to the Scyphozoa, a group or class of coelenterates comprising many of the large jellyfish.—*n.* A scyphozoan animal.

scy·phus, si′fus, *n.* pl. **scy·phi,** si′fī. [Gr. *skyphos,* a cup or goblet.] A deep, footed drinking cup used in ancient Rome and Greece, having two horizontal handles level with the rim; also *skyphos. Bot.* the cup-shaped part of flowers, as of the narcissus.

scythe, sīth, *n.* [M.E. *sithe;* O.E. *sīthe* for *sigthe,* the older form = Icel. *sigth;* from root of *sickle.*] An instrument used in mowing or reaping, consisting of a long curving blade fixed to a handle at an angle. —*v.t.*—*scythed, scything.* To mow or cut with a scythe.

sea, sē, *n.* [O.E. *sǣ,* sea or lake = D. *see, zee,* Dan. *sö,* Icel. *saer,* G. *see,* Goth. *saivs.*] The continuous mass of salt water which covers the greater portion of the earth; the ocean; a segment of this that is enclosed to some degree by land; as, the North Sea; a name given to some large landlocked lakes; as, the Caspian Sea; a large wave or surge, as: A *sea* put the deck awash. Large swells or series of waves, as: A heavy *sea* was running that night. Any large quantity; as, a *sea* of difficulties; a flood; the vocation of a sailor, as: The *sea* is a hard life.—*at sea,* aboard ship on the ocean; bewildered or perplexed; as, to be all *at sea* about the matter.—**fol·low the sea,** to make a career of seafaring.—**go to sea,** to voyage on the sea, esp. as an occupation.—**put to sea,** to set out, as a ship, onto the ocean.—**sea·most,** *a.* Located closest to the sea.

sea an·chor, *n.* A floating anchor used at sea to prevent a ship from drifting or to keep its head to the wind, usu. consisting of a framed cone of canvas dragged along with its large open base toward the ship.

sea a·nem·o·ne, *n.* Any of several marine polyps of the class *Anthozoa,* found in rocky crevices and easily observable in tide pools, resembling flowers because of their cylindrical body form and one or more circles of bright colored tentacles.

sea bag, *n.* A large canvas bag, cylindrical in shape, with a drawstring at the top, in which a sailor stows his clothing and other effects.

sea bass, *n.* A common serranoid marine food fish, *Centropristes striatus,* of the Atlantic Ocean; any of various allied fish.

sea·bed, sē′bed″, *n.* The sea or ocean floor.

Sea·bee, sē′bē″, *n.* [(C)onstruction (B)attalion.] One who serves with any of the construction battalions established by the U.S. Navy to build air bases, harbor facilities, and the like and to defend them.

sea bird, *n.* A bird frequenting the sea or seacoast.

sea bis·cuit, *n.* A dry, hard ship's bread or biscuit; hardtack.

sea·board, sē′bōrd″, sē′bärd″, *n.* [*Sea* and *board,* Fr. *bord,* side.] The seacoast; the country bordering on the sea.—*a.*

sea·borne, sē′bōrn″, sē′bärn″, *a.* Conveyed by sea; carried on the sea.

sea bread, *n.* Sea biscuit; hardtack.

sea bream, *n.* Any of certain sparoid fishes, esp. *Pagellus centrodontus,* a European marine food fish; a sparoid or percoid fish, as the pinfish or porgy, found along the Atlantic coast.

sea breeze, *n.* A cool breeze blowing from the sea toward land.

sea cap·tain, *n.* The captain or commanding officer of a ship.

sea change, *n.* A change in weather, usu. favorable, brought about by the sea; *fig.* a striking transformation.

sea chest, *n. Naut.* A chest for the storage of a sailor's personal belongings; a fitting connected to the hull under the water line, which admits and discharges sea water.

sea·coast, sē′kōst″, *n.* The land immediately adjacent to the sea; the coast.

sea cow, *n.* Any aquatic mammal of the order *Sirenia,* as the dugong and the manatee.

sea cray·fish, *n.* A small spiny lobster. Also **sea craw·fish.**

sea cu·cum·ber, *n.* Any of the various marine echinoderms, class *Holothuroidea,* which are shaped like cucumbers and have long anterior tentacles.

sea dev·il, *n.* The devilfish; stonefish.

sea dog, *n.* The dogfish; the common seal; a sailor, esp. one with much experience; a pirate.

sea·dog, sē′dag″, sē′dog″, *n.* A fogbow.

sea·drome, sē′drōm″, *n. Aeron.* a floating airport which serves as an emergency servicing and landing area for aircraft during overseas flights.

sea duck, *n.* Any of the various diving ducks that frequent the sea, as the eider, scoter, and goldeneye.

sea ea·gle, *n.* A fish-eating eagle, esp. *Haliaetus albicilla.* Also **gray sea ea·gle.**

sea ear, *n.* Abalone.

sea fan, *n.* Any of certain anthozoans, esp. *Gorgonia flabellum* of the West Indies, in which the colony assumes a fanlike form.

sea·far·ing, sē′fâr″ing, *a.* Following the occupation of a seaman; traveling by sea.—*n.* Travel by sea; a sailor's calling.—**sea·far·er,** *n.* A seaman or sea traveler.

sea feath·er, *n.* Any of certain anthozoans that grow in colonies, as the corals of the order *Gorgonacea,* having a skeleton that resembles a feather in appearance. Also **sea fan.**

sea fight, *n.* An engagement between ships at sea.

sea fire, *n.* A weak, fluorescentlike glow emitted by certain deep-sea fishes at night.

sea·folk, sē′fōk″, *n.* People whose work is aboard ship at sea; seamen.

sea·food, sē′fōd″, *n.* Any edible fish, shellfish, or other aquatic animal.

sea·fowl, se′foul″, *n.* Any bird that lives by the sea and procures its food from it. Also *seabird.*

sea front, *n.* Buildings or land fronting or bordering on the sea.

sea gate, *n.* A channel giving access to the sea.

sea·girt, sē′gurt″, *a.* Surrounded by the sea.

sea·go·ing, sē′gō″ing, *a.* Made for ocean-going; as, a *seagoing* vessel; seafaring.—**sea·go·er,** *n.*

sea-green, sē′grēn′, *a.* Having the color of sea water; of a bluish-green color.—**sea green,** *n.*

sea gull, *n.* A gull of the genus *Larus,* inhabiting the sea; loosely, any gull.

sea hol·ly, *n.* A spiny-leaved, herbaceous plant, *Eryngium maritimum,* having blue flowers, found in European coastal areas.

sea horse, *n.* Any marine fish of the genus *Hippocampus;* the walrus; a small, plated, lophobranch fish, related to the pipefish, with head and neck likened to a horse; a fabled animal, half horse and half fish.

sea-is·land cot·ton, sē′ī″land, *n.* A long-staple variety of cotton grown on the islands off the coast of South Carolina and Georgia and elsewhere, or the plant producing it. Also **Sea Is·land Cot·ton.**

sea kale, *n.* A cabbagelike plant of the mustard family, *Crambe maritima,* found along the European coast.

sea king, *n.* One of the piratical Norsemen who harassed the coasts of western Europe during the Middle Ages.

seal, sēl, *n.* pl. **seals, seal.** [O.E. *seol, seolh,* Sc. *selch, silch,* Icel. *selr,* Dan. *sael;* O.H.G. *selah;* origin doubtful.] A large, carnivorous marine mammal, suborder *Pinnipedia,* having limbs adapted into webbed flippers for propulsion through the cold waters it inhabits, including the hair seal, family *Phocidae,* having no external ears, and hind fins which extend straight back, and the sea lion, family *Otariidae,* having external ears, dense soft fur, and hind fins bent forward under the body; any seal pelt products, as fur or leather; a very dark, rich gray-brown color.—*v.i.* To hunt seals. —**seal·like,** *a.*

seal, sēl, *n.* [O. Fr. *seel,* < L. *sigillum,* a seal, dim. of *signum,* a sign.] A ring, stone, piece of metal, or other hard object engraved with a figure, sign, or inscription for the purpose of making an impression on a soft substance, as wax, plastic, or paper; the impression or mark made; the wax, wafer, stamp, or other fastening of a letter, envelope, or other piece; that which shuts, fastens, or secures; that which insures secrecy, usu. by preventing opening without breakage of the seal; a mark or sign which authenticates, confirms, ratifies, or pledges; the symbol of a high office; an ornamental piece of gummed paper sold to raise funds for a cause; as, an Easter *seal; mech.* an amount of liquid in the upward opening of a pipe or tube which prevents the escape of gases through it.—*v.t.* To affix, as a seal, as a mark of authenticity; to make final or binding by or as by fastening a seal to; to place, as a mark or sign, upon to confirm fulfillment of standard specifications; to fasten securely to prevent undetected opening; to close with or as with a seal; to close hermetically; to fix, determine, or finalize; as, to *seal* one's fate; to authorize or give under the power of a seal; *mech.* to close tightly, caulk, or fill to prevent escape from or flow into; *Mormon Ch.* to finalize or make binding for eternity, as a marriage or adoption.—**un·der seal,** affixed with or as with the authority and assurance of a seal.

sea lad·der, *n.* A simple rope ladder or any series of steps which can be lowered from the main deck to the water and used to board a large vessel, esp. at sea.

sea lam·prey, *n.* A large lamprey, *Petromyzon marinus,* which ascends rivers to spawn, and which in this way entered the Great Lakes.

sea-lane, sē′lān″, *n.* See *lane.*

sea lav·en·der, *n.* An Old World plumbago plant of the family *Limonium vulgare,* a seashore perennial bearing one-sided spikes of small lavender-colored flowers; a similar plant of the same genus, as *L. carolinianum* of the eastern coast of North America.

sea law·yer, *n. Colloq.* an argumentative, querulous, or captious sailor who criticizes the orders of his superiors and complains about his work.

sealed bid, *n.* One of the proposals submitted in sealed packets by several contractors in competition for a particular contract, the contract being awarded to the most reasonable bidder.

sea legs, *n. pl.* The ability to walk on a ship's deck while it is pitching or rolling without losing one's balance; resistance to seasickness.

seal·er, sē′lėr, *n.* A person who or something which seals; an officer appointed to examine and test weights and measures, and to set a stamp upon such as are true to the standard.

seal·er, sē′lėr, *n.* A seaman or a ship engaged in seal hunting.

seal·er·y, sē′le·rē, *n.* pl. **seal·er·ies.** The occupation of hunting or taking seals; a place where seals are frequently caught.

sea let·tuce, *n.* Any seaweed of the genus *Ulva,* whose green fronds are sometimes eaten like lettuce.

sea lev·el, *n.* The surface of the sea; the horizontal plane or level corresponding to the surface of the sea when halfway between high and low water or tide.

sea lil·y, *n.* One of a class, *Crinoidea,* of echinoderms having a lily-shaped body attached to the ocean floor by a jointed stem. Also **cri·noid.**

seal·ing wax, *n.* A composition of resinous materials which softens when heated and solidifies when cooled, used for fastening folded papers, envelopes, and the like.

sea li·on, *n.* Any of various eared seals of large size, as Steller's sea lion, *Eumetopias jubata,* of the northern Pacific, or *Zalophus californianus* of the Pacific coast of N. America.

seal ring, *n.* A finger ring bearing a seal which can be impressed in sealing wax; a signet ring.

seal·skin, sēl′skin″, *n.* The skin of the fur seal; this fur or skin when processed for fur or leather articles; a coat or other garment made of sealskin.—*a.*

Seal·y·ham ter·ri·er, sē′lē·ham″ ter′ē·-ėr, sē′lē·am, *n.* [From *Sealyham,* name of an estate in Pembrokeshire, Wales, where the breed originated.] A breed of terriers having short legs and a rough or shaggy white coat.

seam, sēm, *n.* [O.E. *sēam,* a seam; Icel. *saumr,* Dan. and Sw. *söm,* D. *zoom,* G. *saum,* all from verb, to *sew.*] A joining line formed by sewing together two pieces of material; the stitches in this joining line; a suture; a scar or cicatrix; the line formed by the joining of any two edges; a wrinkle; the line or space between planks joined together; *knitting,* a line of purled stitches. *Geol.* the line of separation between two strata; a thin layer or stratum, as of ore or coal, between two thicker strata.—*v.t.* To unite with a seam; to mark with a cicatrix or scar; to wrinkle; *knitting,* to purl.—*v.i.* To become cracked or clefted; *knitting,* to form a seam by purling.—**seam·er,** *n.*—**seam·less,** *a.*—**seam·less·ly,** *adv.*—**seam·less·ness,** *n.*—**seam·like,** *a.*

sea-maid, sē′mād″, *n.* A mermaid; a goddess or nymph of the sea. Also **sea-maid·en,** sē′mād″en.

sea·man, sē′man, *n.* pl. **sea·men.** One whose occupation is to assist in the navigation of a ship; a sailor, esp. one below the rank of officer; *nav.* an enlisted man whose rank is below that of petty officer.

sea·man·like, sē′man·lik″, *a.* Like or befitting a seaman. Also **sea·man·ly.**

sea·man·ship, sē′man·ship″, *n.* The art of operating, navigating, and maintaining a ship; skill in this art.

sea·mark, sē′märk″, *n.* Any elevated object on land which serves as a direction or guide to mariners; a beacon.

sea mew, *n.* A sea gull, esp. a common European species, *Larus canus.*

sea mile, *n.* Nautical mile. See Measures and Weights table.

sea·mount, sē′mount″, *n. Geol.* a mountain found beneath the surface of the sea reaching a height of at least 500 fathoms from its base on the ocean floor.

sea mouse, *n.* Any of various large marine annelids of the genus *Aphrodite* and allied genera, so called from their mouselike appearance, due to a covering of long, fine hairlike setae.

seam·stress, sēm′stris, *Brit.* sem′stris, *n.* [O.E. *sēamestre,* with term. -*ess* added.] A woman whose occupation is sewing; a woman proficient in sewing. Also *sempstress.*—**seam·ster,** *n.* Masculine of seamstress.

seam·y, sē′mē, *a.*—*seamier, seamiest.* Lowly; sordid; showing the least pleasant or attractive aspect; having seams or showing them, as the underside of a garment.—**seam·i·ness,** *n.*

sé·ance, sā′äns, *n.* [Fr. *séance,* < *séant,* sitting, L. *sedens, sedentis,* ppr. of *sedeo,* to sit.] A session of some public body; a meeting conducted by a spiritualist with the view of evoking communication with spirits of the dead.

sea net·tle, *n.* A jellyfish having stinging organs known as nematocysts in its tentacles.

sea on·ion, *n.* A liliaceous plant, *Urginea maritima,* a native of the Mediterranean region, yielding the medicinal bulb squill. Also **sea squill.**

sea ot·ter, *n.* A rare marine otter, *Enhydra lutris,* of the shores of the northern Pacific, with a very valuable brown fur.

sea pen, *n.* Any of various coelenterates of the family *Pennatulidae,* which form featherlike colonies.

sea·plane, sē′plān″, *n.* A hydroplane for use over the sea, esp. one provided with floats rather than a boatlike under part.

sea·port, sē′pōrt″, sē′part″, *n.* A port, or a town with a port, on or near the sea.

sea pow·er, *n.* A nation having an important navy or great influence on the sea; naval strength.

sea purse, *n.* The corneous egg case of certain rays and sharks; a swirl of the undertow making a small whirlpool on the surface of the water, dangerous to bathers.

sea·quake, sē′kwāk″, *n.* A submarine eruption or earthquake.

sear, sēr, *v.t.* [O.E. *sēarian,* to parch, < *sēar,* dry; akin to L.G. *soor,* O.D. *sore, soore,* D. *zoor,* dry.] To wither; to burn the surface of; to cauterize; to scorch; to make callous or insensible; to brand.—*v.i.* To wither or dry up.—*a.* [O.E. *sēar.*] Dry; withered; no longer green and fresh; as, a *sear* leaf.—*n.* A scar caused by searing.

sear, sēr, *n.* [Fr. *serre,* a lock, a bar, < L. *sera,* a bolt or bar.] The pivoted piece in a gunlock which holds the hammer at full or half cock.

sea ra·ven, *n.* A marine fish, *Hemitripterus americanus,* common on the northern Atlantic coast of America, of large size and having a long spinous dorsal fin.

search, surch, *v.t.* [O.Fr. *cerchier* (Fr. *chercher*), < L.L. *circare,* go about,

traverse, < L. *circus*, circle: cf. *circus*.] To go through or look through carefully in seeking to find something; to examine, as a person, by going through his pockets or removing his garments, in order to ascertain whether he has some article concealed on his person; to read attentively or examine, as a record, register, or collection, for information; to examine carefully or with earnest effort in order to discover intention, real nature, or the like; as, to *search* one's own heart; to probe, as a wound; of wind or cold; to pierce or penetrate; to uncover or learn by a search, usu. followed by *out.*—*v.i.* To make a search; to seek; to make an examination or investigation.—*n.* [O.Fr. *cerche* (Fr. *cherche*).] The act or an act of searching; careful examination or investigation; the boarding and examination of a neutral vessel at sea by officers of a belligerent state, in order to verify its nationality and ascertain whether it carries contraband; as, the right of *search.*—**search·a·ble,** *a.*—**search·er,** *n.*

search·ing, sur'ching, *a.* Examining carefully or thoroughly; thorough or rigorous, as an examination; keenly observant or penetrating, as the eyes or gaze; piercing or sharp, as the wind.—**search·ing·ly,** *adv.*—**search·ing·ness,** *n.*

search·light, surch'lit", *n.* An apparatus pivoted so as to project a strong beam of light in any desired direction; the beam of light.

search war·rant, *n.* A warrant granted by a judge or magistrate legalizing a police search of private premises.

sea rob·in, *n.* A gurnard, family *Triglidae*, esp. any of the reddish American fish, genus *Priontus*, having extended pectoral fins with three long, sensitive rays.

sea room, *n.* Adequate open sea to allow a ship full movement and maneuverability.

sea rov·er, *n.* A pirate; a ship engaged in cruising for plunder.

sea·scape, se'skap", *n.* [Formed on the model of *landscape*.] An expanse of sea or seashore within view; a vista or scene of the sea; a painting or other artistic representation of the sea.

sea scout, *n.* A boy scout given training in the marine branch of scouting which specializes in the areas of seamanship and water safety.—**sea·scout·ing,** se'skou"ting, *n.*

sea ser·pent, *n.* A huge, legendary, serpentine, sea-dwelling monster discussed and speculated upon by seamen and some scientists, but as yet unverified; a venomous marine snake in the Indian Ocean.

sea·shell, se'shel, *n.* The shell of any marine mollusk.

sea·shore, se'shor", se'shar", *n.* The rocky or sandy place where the land meets the edge of the sea; *law*, the ground between the normal high-water mark and low-water mark.

sea·sick·ness, se'sik"nis, *n.* Nausea and vomiting produced by the rolling or pitching of a vessel at sea.—**sea·sick,** se'sik", *a.*

sea·side, se'sid", *n.* The land by the sea; the seacoast; the beach.—*a.* Belonging to, situated at, or pertaining to the seaside.—**sea·sid·er,** *n.*

sea slug, *n.* A marine gastropod which lacks a shell at maturity, breathes through projecting tubelike branches, and is found in a variety of delicate colors and unusual shapes. Also **nu·di·branch, hol·o·thu·ri·an.**

sea snake, *n.* A venomous snake belonging to the family *Hydrophidae*, and inhabiting tropical seas; a serpent that inhabits the sea.

sea·son, se'zon, *n.* [O.E. *seson, sesoun,* O.Fr. *seson, seison,* Mod.Fr. *saison,* lit. 'time

of sowing,' < L. *satio, sationis,* a sowing, < *sero, satum,* to sow.] One of the four divisions of the year (spring, summer, autumn, winter) characterized by distinctive temperature, rainfall, vegetation, and the like, which occurs at different times in different regions and is determined by the position of the earth in relation to the sun; that period of the year in which something is most obtainable; as, the peach *season*; that part of the year when a particular activity, profession, or the like is greatest; as, the hockey *season*; that period of time immediately preceding and following an important holiday; as, the Christmas *season*; any particular time; a convenient, right, or suitable time.—**in sea·son,** available for use; at the right or most suitable time; within the period prescribed by law; as, the hunting *season*; of an animal, ready for mating.

sea·son, se'zon, *v.t.* To enhance or heighten the flavor of, by adding spices, salt, herbs, or the like; to give relish or zest to; to bring to the best state for use; as, to *season* timber by drying or hardening; to inure or accustom; as, to *season* by experience.—*v.i.* To become seasoned.—**sea·son·er,** *n.*

sea·son·a·ble, se'zo·na·bl, *a.* Suitable to the time or season; happening in proper time; opportune.—**sea·son·a·ble·ness,** *n.*—**sea·son·a·bly,** *adv.*

sea·son·al, se'zo·nal, *a.* Pertaining to or accompanying the seasons, or a certain season only.—**sea·son·al·ly,** *adv.*

sea·son·ing, se'zo·ning, *n.* An ingredient, esp. a spice, salt, or herb, added to food to heighten or enhance the flavor.

sea·son tick·et, *n.* A ticket which entitles its holder to certain privileges during a specified period of time, as a pass for traveling by railroad issued at a lower rate than that charged for single trips.

sea squirt, *n.* An ascidian which ejects water when touched or otherwise disturbed.

sea·strand, se'strand", *n.* Seashore.

seat, set, *n.* [M.E. *sete,* < Scand.: cf. Icel. *saeti,* Sw. *säte,* Dan. *saede,* seat, also O.E. *sæt,* ambush; cf. E. *sit*.] Something made or used for sitting on, as a chair or bench; the particular part of a chair or the like on which one sits; that part of the body on which one sits; the buttocks, or that part of a garment which covers them; that on which the base of anything rests; the base itself; a place in which something is situated or established; site or location; as, a *seat* of learning; the established center, as of government; a place to seat one person, as in a theater; the right to use such a place; a right to sit as a member in a legislative or similar body; a right to the privileges of membership in a stock exchange.—*v.t.* To place on a seat or seats; cause to sit down; to find seats for; to accommodate with seats, as: This theater *seats* four hundred people. To put a seat on, as a chair; to renew the seat of, as a garment; to install or settle in a position of authority, a legislative body, or the like; to set firmly or securely on a base.—**seat·er,** *n.*

sea tan·gle, *n.* Any of several sea weeds of the genus *Laminaria,* a brown alga. See *kelp.*

seat belt, *n.* See *safety belt.*

seat·ing, se'ting, *n.* The act of furnishing with a seat or seats; the arrangement of the seats, as in a theater or room; material used to cover seats.

seat·mate, set'mat", *n.* A person one sits next to or shares a double seat with, as in an automobile or an airplane.

sea·train, se'tran", *n.* A ship which is equipped to transport railroad cars.

sea trout, *n.* Any of various species of trout found in salt water, as the salmon trout, *Salmo trutta*; any of the various weakfish.

sea ur·chin, *n.* Any marine animal, order *Echinodermata,* having a roundish or disklike body with many projecting spines or prickles. See *echinus.*

sea wall, *n.* A strong embankment or wall on the shore to prevent encroachment of the sea.

sea·ward, se'werd, *a.* Directed toward the sea; coming from the sea.—*adv.* Toward the sea; also **sea·wards.**—*n.* A course or position away from the shore.

sea·ware, se'war", *n.* The algae thrown up on shore, sometimes used as a fertilizer.

sea·way, se'wa", *n.* The sea as a route for travel; an ocean traffic lane; a rough or rugged sea; an inland waterway deep enough to admit ocean shipping; progress made by a vessel through the waves.

sea·weed, se'wed", *n.* Any plant or plants growing in the sea, esp. a marine alga.

sea·worn, se'worn", se'warn", *a.* Eroded by the sea; as, a *seaworn* coast; exhausted or destroyed by many sea voyages; as, a *seaworn* ship.

sea·wor·thy, se'wur"THe, *a.* Of a ship, in good condition and fit for a voyage.—**sea·wor·thi·ness,** *n.*

sea wrack, *n.* Seaweed, esp. in masses rolled upon the shore.

se·ba·ceous, si·ba'shus, *a.* [L.L. *sebaceus,* < L. *sebum,* tallow.] *Physiol.* Pertaining to or containing fat; made of or secreting fatty matter; fatty.

se·bac·ic ac·id, si·bas'ik as'id, si·ba'sik, *n.* An acid, $HOOC(CH_2)_8COOH$, distilled in white crystalline form from castor oil, and used in the manufacture of many synthetic polymers, as resins, nylon, and plastic.

seb·or·rhe·a, seb"o·re'a, *n.* [L. *sebum,* tallow, Gr. *rheo,* to flow.] *Pathol.* an unnatural and excessive increase in the sebum secreted by the sebaceous glands.—**seb·or·rhe·al, seb·or·rhe·ic,** *a.*

se·bum, se'bum, *n.* [L. tallow, suet, grease; cf. *suet*.] *Physiol.* the fatty secretion of the sebaceous glands.

sec, sek, *a.* [Fr., < L. *siccus,* dry.] Of wines, dry, not sweet.

se·cant, se'kant, se'kant, *a.* [L. *secans, secantis,* ppr. of *seco,* to cut.] Cutting; dividing into two parts.—*n.* *Geom.* a straight line that cuts a curve at two or more points; a straight line from the center of a circle cutting the circumference and proceeding till it meets a tangent to the same circle. *Trig.* the ratio of the hypotenuse to the side adjacent to an acute angle in a right triangle: multiplied by the cosine it equals one.

sec·a·teurs, sek'a·terz, sek'a·turz, *n. pl., sing. or pl. in constr. Brit.* a type of pruning shears.

sec·co, sek'o, *It.* sek'ka, *n.* *Fine arts,* the technique of applying tempera paint to dry plaster. Also **dry fres·co, fres·co sec·co.**

se·cede, si·sed', *v.i.*—*seceded, seceding.* [L. *secedo*—*se-,* apart, and *cedo,* to go.] To withdraw formally from an association, esp. a political or religious organization, as: South Carolina was the first state to *secede* from the Union.—**se·ced·er,** *n.*

se·cern, si·surn', *v.t.* [L. *secerno, secretum* (whence *secret*)—*se-,* apart, and *cerno,* to separate.] To differentiate mentally; to make a distinction between.—*v.i.* To become separate.—**se·cern·ment,** *n.*

se·ces·sion, si·sesh'an, *n.* [L. *secessio*.] The act or event of seceding; (*usu. cap.*), *U.S. hist.* the withdrawal of Southern States from the Union which touched off the Civil War in 1861.—**se·ces·sion·al,** *a.*—**se·ces·sion·ism,** si·sesh'a·niz·um, *n.*—**se·ces·sion·ist,** si·sesh'a·nist, *n.*

se·clude, si·klod', *v.t.*—*secluded, secluding.* [L. *secludo*—*se-,* apart, and *claudo,* to shut.]

To isolate, keep apart, or retire from natural contact or intercourse with society; to sequester, separate, or shelter from public observation or influence.

se·clud·ed, si·klöō′did, *a.* Shut off or separated from others; withdrawn from public observation; retired or sequestered; private.—**se·clud·ed·ly,** *adv.*—**se·clud·- ed·ness,** *n.*

se·clu·sion, si·klö′zhan, *n.* The act of secluding; the state of being secluded; retirement; solitude; an isolated, private place.—**se·clu·sive,** si·klö′siv, *a.*—**se·clu·- sive·ly,** *adv.*—**se·clu·sive·ness,** *n.*

sec·ond, sek′ond, *a.* [O.Fr. Fr. *second,* < L. *secundus,* following, next, second, secondary, favorable, < *sequi,* follow: cf. *sequent.*] Next after the first; following the first in serial order, as in order of place, time, or rank; next after the first in degree, as of value, quality, importance, responsibility, or authority; being the ordinal of two; subordinate or inferior to a first; alternate to a first; as, every *second* month; other or another; as, a *second* family car; bearing likeness to a prototype; as, a *second* home; acquired, but deeply ingrained, as a characteristic; as, *second* nature; *mach.* pertaining to the second gear in an auto- mobile or truck transmission. *Mus.* being next to the highest in pitch, as a part in concerted music; rendering such a part by voice or instrument; as, *second* soprano, *second* violin.—*n.* One who or that which follows the first; one who acts as the aide and representative of a principal in a duel; one who acts as the aide of a pugilist; *pl.* an additional helping of food; *usu. pl.* merchandise that is flawed or otherwise substandard in quality. In parliamentary procedure, the expression signifying formal support of another's proposal, such support being considered a prerequisite to further discussion of the proposal; *mach.* the second gear in an automobile or truck transmission. *Mus.* the lower of two parts scored for the same instrument or voice; such a part in concerted music; the interval between two consecutive tones on the scale.—*adv.*— **sec·ond·ly,** *adv.*

sec·on·da, sek′ond, *n.* [Fr. *seconde,* < M.L. *secunda* (for *secunda minuta,* 'second minute,' that is, a division of the second order), prop. fem. of L. *secundus,* E. *second,* adj.] The sixtieth part of a minute of time; *fig.* a moment or instant; *math.* the sixtieth part of a minute of a degree, often represented by the sign ″. Abbr. *s.,* *sec.*

sec·ond, sek′ond, *v.t.* [Fr. *seconder,* < L. *secundare,* < *secundus.*] To support, back up, or assist, as a person or his efforts; to further or advance; to act as an assistant to, as a debater, a duelist, or a pugilist; to express approval or support of, as a motion or proposal.—**sec·ond·er,** *n.*

sec·ond·ar·y, sek′on·der″ē, *a.* [L. *secun- darius.*] Of less than first rating, place, rank, or importance; being other than primary; subordinate; derivative, rather than original; of or pertaining to a school or an education between the elementary and collegiate levels, as a high school; *ornith.* of or pertaining to a feather found on the second segment of a bird's wing; *elect.* of or pertaining to induced current or its cir- cuit, esp. that of an induction coil; *chem.* of or pertaining to a compound formed by cer- tain basic atomic changes in another. *Geol.* of later origin; of or pertaining to a mineral derived from structural changes in another. —*n.* A person or object that is second in order or position; a subordinate agent such as a deputy, aide, or assistant; *ornith.* a flight feather, as found on the second joint of a bird's wing.—**sec·ond·ar·i·ly,** sek′- on·der″i·lē, sek″on·dâr′i·lē, *adv.*—**sec·- ond·ar·i·ness,** *n.*

sec·ond·ar·y cell, *n. Elect.* storage cell.

sec·ond·ar·y col·or, *n.* A color produced by the mixture of any two primary colors in approximately equal proportions.

sec·ond·ar·y e·mis·sion, *n. Phys.* the ejection of electrons from a substance as a result of its bombardment by charged particles.

sec·ond·ar·y ra·di·a·tion, *n. Phys.* nuclear particles or photons emitted by matter as a result of incident primary radiation.

sec·ond·ar·y road, *n.* A tributary road which leads to or from a main highway.

sec·ond·ar·y sex char·ac·ter·is·tic, *n.* Any manifest characteristic specific to either sex but not necessary to reproduction, and due to the effect of gonadal secretions of hormones, as the development of beards or breasts in humans at puberty, differences in color and plumage between the sexes of many birds, and the horns or antlers of most male deer.

sec·ond base, *n. Baseball.* The base to which a runner from first base proceeds; the position of the player defending the area around that base.

sec·ond-best, sek′and·best′, *a.* Next to or nearly the best.

sec·ond child·hood, *n.* Dotage; senility.

sec·ond-class, sek′ond·klas′, sek′ond·- kläs′, *a.* Of or relating to the class next after the first; pertaining to the second grade of conveyances or accommodations for travel; designating a class of mail including newspapers and periodicals; a secondary or inferior grade or quality; second-rate.—**sec·ond class,** *n.*

Sec·ond Com·ing, *n.* The return to earth of Jesus on the Judgment Day.

sec·ond-de·gree burn, *n. Pathol.* a burn characterized by blistering and redness of the affected area, without destruction of the epidermis.

se·conde, si·kond′, *Fr.* se·gaNd′, *n.* [Fr. fem. of *second.*] *Fencing,* the second in a series of eight parties or positions of defense.

Sec·ond Em·pire, *a.* Pertaining to or characteristic of furniture and other interior decorations in the heavy, much gilded, and ornate style developed and popularized in France during the reign of Napoleon III.

sec·ond fid·dle, *n. Colloq.* One who plays a role subsidiary to another; one who is overshadowed by another.

sec·ond growth, *n.* A natural reforestation that follows the destruction or removal of the trees in a virgin forest.

sec·ond-guess, sek′ond·ges′, *v.t.* To specu- late or reflect on alternatives after a choice has been made or can no longer be made; to use hindsight as a basis for criticism; to attempt to foretell; to attempt to outguess or outsmart.—**sec·ond-guess·er,** *n.*

sec·ond hand, sek′ond hand″, *n.* The hand of a watch or clock that indicates seconds.

sec·ond·hand, sek′ond·hand′, *a.* Not original or primary; received from another; not new; having been used or worn; dealing in used goods; as, a *secondhand* bookstore.—*adv.*—**at sec·ond hand,** from an intermediary means.

sec·ond lieu·ten·ant, *n. Milit.* the lowest rank accorded to commissioned U.S. Army, Air Force, or Marine Corps officers.

sec·ond mort·gage, *n.* A mortgage secured by property that also secures a first mort- gage; a mortgage usu. considered to be next entitled to satisfaction after a first mortgage, out of the proceeds of property that secures them both.

se·con·do, si·kon′dō, si·kōn′dō, *It.* se·- kan′dō, *n. pl.* **se·con·di,** si·kon′dē, si·- kōn′dē, *It.* se·kan′dē. [It., < L. *secundus,* E. *second,* adj.] *Mus.* The second or sub-

ordinate part in a duet; the performer of such a part.

sec·ond per·son, *n. Gram.* the form of many languages used to signify the one or ones that a speaker or writer is addressing.

sec·ond-rate, sek′ond·rāt′, *a.* Of the second rank or class; inferior; mediocre.—**sec·ond- rate·ness,** *n.*—**sec·ond-rat·er,** *n.*

sec·ond read·ing, *n.* In legislative pro- cedure, a stage through which a proposed statute usually passes before coming to eventual enactment or defeat, and affording the opportunity for its debate and possible amendment from the floor: occurring in Great Britain before the bill's submission to committee, and in the U.S. after its return.

sec·ond sight, *n.* The power of seeing things future or distant; prophetic vision.

sec·ond-sto·ry man, *n. Slang,* one who burglarizes, using an aperture above the ground floor as his means of entry.

se·cre·cy, sē′kri·sē, *n. pl.* **se·cre·cies.** The state or quality of being secret or hidden; retirement or concealment from the obser- vation of others; fidelity to a secret; the act or habit of keeping secrets.

se·cret, sē′krit, *a.* [Fr. *secret,* < L. *secretus,* pp. of *secerno, secretum,* to set apart; *se-,* apart, and *cerno,* to sift, distinguish.] Apart from the knowledge of others; known only to one or to few; as, *secret* password; not made public; as, *secret* negotiations between Russia and France; secluded; as, a *secret* hideout; not inclined to betray confidence; occult; as, *secret* rites; hidden; as, a *secret* compartment; *milit.* of a document, placed in the second highest category of military classification.—*n.* Something studi- ously concealed; a thing kept from general knowledge; a thing not discovered or explained; a mystery; *milit.* the second highest classification for information or documents.—**se·cret·ly,** *adv.*

sec·re·tar·i·al, sek″ri·târ′ē·al, *a.* Per- taining to a secretary or to a secretary's work.

sec·re·tar·i·at, sek″ri·târ′ē·at, *n.* The office or group of officials assigned to the administration, supervision, and perform- ance of secretarial duties for a governmental organization; a staff or corps of secretaries; the place where a secretary maintains records and transacts business. Also **sec·re·tar·i·ate.**

sec·re·tar·y, sek′ri·ter″ē, *n. pl.* **sec·re·- tar·ies.** [L.L. *secretarius,* < L. *secretus,* secret; orig. a confidant, one entrusted with secrets.] One who carries on another's correspondence and performs other routine tasks; an officer of an organization or business who keeps records and assists in major decisions; (*cap.*) a government officer whose business is to superintend and manage the affairs of a particular depart- ment of government; as, *Secretary* of Defense. A piece of furniture with facilities for writing; also *escritoire.*—**sec·re·tar·y·- ship,** *n.*

sec·re·tar·y bird, *n.* An African bird of prey, *Sagittarius serpentarius,* which feeds primarily on reptiles and derives its name from its plumed crest which resembles a quill pen placed behind the ear.

sec·re·tar·y-gen·er·al, sek′ri·ter″ē·jen′- ér·al, *n. pl.* **sec·re·tar·ies-gen·er·al.** The head or principal officer of a secretariat, as of the United Nations.

se·crete, si·krēt′, *v.t.*—*secreted, secreting.* *Physiol.* to produce, release, or discharge by secretion.—**se·cre·tive,** si·krē′tiv, *a.* *Physiol.* causing or promoting secretion.

se·crete, si·krēt′, *v.t.*—*secreted, secreting.* [L. *secerno, secretum,* to set apart.] To hide; to deposit in some secret place.

se·cre·tin, si·krē′tin, *n.* [< *secretion.*] *Biochem.* a hormone, produced in the lining of the small intestine, which stimulates the secretive activity of the pancreas.

se·cre·tion, si·krē′shan, *n.* The process by which functionally specialized and excretory substances are separated from the blood, elaborated into different materials, such as bile, saliva, mucus, or urine, and released into or from the body; a secreted substance.—**se·cre·tion·ar·y,** si·krē′sha-·ner″ē, *a.*

se·cre·tive, sē′kri·tiv, si·krē′tiv, *a.* Given to secrecy or to keeping secrets.—**se·cre·tive·ly,** *adv.*—**se·cre·tive·ness,** *n.*

se·cre·to·ry, si·krē′to·rē, *a.* Pertaining to secretion; performing the act of secretion.—*n. pl.* **se·cre·to·ries.** A secretory organ, gland, or the like.

se·cret po·lice, *n.* A police group operating in a covert manner, usu. to protect political interests of the government.

se·cret serv·ice, *n.* Intelligence or espionage, as conducted by a government; an agency or group organized for espionage purposes. (*Cap.*) a division of the U.S. Treasury Department, charged with detecting violations of laws relating to this department, as counterfeit currency or fraudulent bank checks, and assigned to protect the president and vice-president and their families, former presidents, their wives or unmarried widows and their children under 16, and certain presidential and vice-presidential candidates as approved by congressional committee.

se·cret so·ci·e·ty, *n.* A social organization whose oaths, rites, and practices are kept secret.

sect, sekt, *n.* [Fr. *secte,* < L. *secta,* < *seco, sectum,* to cut; or < *sequor, secuntus,* to follow.] A body of persons who follow a teacher or leader, or are united by philosophical or religious tenets; a school; a denomination, esp. one regarded as heretical; *hort.* a cutting or segment.

sec·tar·i·an, sek·târ′ē·an, *a.* Pertaining to a sect or sects; strongly or bigotedly attached to a sect or religious denomination. —*n.* One of a sect; a member or adherent of a special denomination or party; a bigot. —**sec·tar·i·an·ism,** sek·târ′ē·a·niz″um, *n.*

sec·tar·i·an·ize, sek·târ′ē·a·nīz″, *v.t.*—*sectarianized, sectarianizing.* To imbue with sectarian principles or feelings.

sec·ta·ry, sek′ta·rē, *n. pl.* **sec·ta·ries.** One who belongs to a sect; a schismatic or dissenter from any established church; a nonconformist.

sec·tile, sek′til, *a.* [L. *sectilis,* < *seco, sectum,* to cut (see in *bisect, dissect, intersect,* etc.); same root as *scythe, saw.*] Capable of being cut evenly or smoothly, as with a knife.—**sec·til·i·ty,** *n.*

sec·tion, sek′shan, *n.* [L. *sectio,* < *seco, sectum,* to cut.] A part cut or separated from the rest; a portion or division; a distinct part of a country or people, community or class; as, the Italian *section* of the city; the act of cutting or separation by cutting, as in surgery or biology; a distinct part or portion of a book or writing; as, a *section* of a newspaper; the subdivision of a chapter, denoted by the character §; the representation of the internal structure of an object as if the object were cut through by an intersecting plane; one of the 36 subdivisions of a township in the U.S.; the space in a railroad sleeping car containing two berths, upper and lower; the portion of an orchestra made up of one class of instruments; *biol.* a thin slice of anything for microscopic examination; *milit.* a small division or tactical unit of a military body.—*v.t.* To separate or divide into sections; *drawing,* to depict or denote a section or sections of by shading.

sec·tion·al, sek′sha·nal, *a.* Pertaining to a section or sections; regional, local, or insular; of a particular zone or sphere of activity; comprised of sections or parts.—*n.* A couch or sofa consisting of several sections, often curved, which may be arranged in a variety of ways.—**sec·tion·al·ly,** *adv.*

sec·tion·al·ism, sek′sha·na·liz″um, *n.* Excessive regard for sectional or local interests; regional spirit or prejudice.—**sec·tion·al·ist,** *n.*

sec·tion gang, *n. Rail.* a crew of workers responsible for upkeep on a section of track.

sec·tion hand, *n. Rail.* one of the workmen in a section gang.

sec·tor, sek′tēr, *n.* [L., a cutter.] A separate part; a distinguishable subdivision; as, the government *sector* of an economy; *geom.* a nearly triangular figure formed by two radii cutting the arc of a circle. A mathematical instrument consisting of two legs hinged at one end and marked to fit various radii and scales, used in making diagrams; *milit.* an area of varying extent in war, over which operations are conducted.—*v.t.* To separate into sectors.

sec·to·ri·al, sek·tōr′ē·al, sek·tar′ē·al, *a.* Relating to or characteristic of a sector. *Zool.* adapted or intended for cutting, as the cutting teeth of certain carnivores; carnassial.

sec·u·lar, sek′ya·lêr, *a.* [L. *saecularis,* < *saeculum,* an age or generation, a century, the times, the world.] Pertaining to this present world or to things not spiritual or sacred; temporal; worldly; not devoted to sacred or religious use; as, *secular* music; of the clergy, not bound by monastic vows or rules, as opposed to *regular*; happening or observed at long intervals, as once a century; extending over a very long period of time.—*n.* A layman; an ecclesiastic who is not bound by monastic rules.—**sec·u·lar·ly,** *adv.*

sec·u·lar·ism, sek′ya·la·riz″um, *n.* Secular spirit or tendencies, esp. a system of beliefs which rejects all forms of religious faith and worship; the view that public education and other matters of civil policy should be conducted without the introduction of a religious element.—**sec·u·lar·ist,** *n.*—**sec·u·lar·is·tic,** *a.*

sec·u·lar·i·ty, sek″ya·lar′i·tē, *n. pl.* **sec·u·lar·i·ties.** Secular quality; secularism; worldliness; a secular matter.

sec·u·lar·ize, sek′ya·la·rīz″, *v.t.*—*secularized, secularizing.* To make secular; to separate from religious or spiritual connections or influences; to make worldly or unspiritual; to imbue with secularism; to transfer, as property, from ecclesiastical to civil possession or use; to change, as clergy, from regular to secular.—**sec·u·lar·i·za·tion,** *n*—**sec·u·lar·iz·er,** *n.*

se·cund, sē′kund, sek′und, *a.* [L. *secundus,* second.] *Bot.* Growing on only one side of the stem, as the inflorescence of certain flowers; unilateral.—**se·cund·ly,** *adv.*

sec·un·dine, sek′un·dīn″, sek′un·din, *n. Bot.* the inner first-formed integument or coat of an ovule; usu. *pl. zool.* the afterbirth.

se·cure, si·kūr′, *a.* [L. *securus,* without care, unconcerned, free from danger, safe—*se-,* apart, and *cura,* care, cure. *Sure* is this word in a more modified form.] Free from fear or apprehension; confident of safety; free from or not exposed to danger; not likely to give way or fail; fixed in place; safe; such as to be depended on; capable of resisting assault or attack; stable; certain, sure, or confident; in safe custody.—*v.t.*—*secured, securing.* To make secure; to guard effectually from danger; to protect; to make certain; to assure; to enclose or confine effectually; to guard effectually against escape; to make certain of payment, as a creditor; to warrant against loss; to make fast or firm; as, to *secure* a door; to get possession of.—*v.i.* To become safe; *naut.* to fasten loose objects and cover all openings, as on a ship.—**se·cure·ly,** *adv.*—**se·cure·ness,** *n.*—**se·cure·ment,** *n.*—**se·cur·er,** *n.*

se·cu·ri·ty, si·kūr′i·tē, *n. pl.* **se·cu·ri·ties.** [Fr. *sécurité,* L. *securitas.*] The state of being secure; freedom from apprehension; confidence of safety; freedom from danger or risk; that which secures or makes safe; something that secures against financial want or loss; surety; a person who guarantees another's obligations; pledge or deposit of property, as a bond, a certificate of stock, or the like, as surety; *milit.* measures taken to guard against sabotage or theft of classified information; *pl.* certificates of stocks, bonds, or notes.

Se·cu·ri·ty Coun·cil, *n.* The organ of the United Nations which has as its primary function the maintenance of international peace and security, composed of the United States, United Kingdom, France, Republic of China, and the U.S.S.R. as permanent members along with six members elected by the General Assembly for two-year terms.

se·dan, si·dan′, *n.* A type of automobile that is enclosed, has two or four doors; a sedan chair.

se·dan chair, *n.* A covered chair or ornamental box for carrying one person, borne on poles by two men.

se·date, si·dāt′, *a.* [L. *sedatus,* < *sedo,* to calm or appease, to cause to subside, < *sedeo,* to sit (see also in *sedentary, sediment, session, preside, reside, supersede, assiduous,* etc.); same root as *sit.*] Calm or tranquil in feelings and manner; serene; unruffled; staid; dignified.—*v.t.*—*sedated, sedating.* To place under sedation, as a person.—**se·date·ly,** *adv.*—**se·date·ness,** *n.*

se·da·tion, si·dā′shan, *n. Med.* the practice or act of alleviating pain, distress, or tension through the use of sedatives.

sed·a·tive, sed′a·tiv, *a.* Tending to calm or tranquilize. *Med.* allaying irritability and irritation; assuaging pain.—*n. Med.* a medicine which allays irritability and irritation, and which assuages pain.

sed·en·tar·y, sed′en·ter″ē, *a.* [L. *sedentarius,* < *sedens, sedentis,* ppr. of *sedeo,* to sit.] Accustomed to sit; requiring much sitting; inactive; indolent. *Zool.* staying in one locale, as contrasted with *migratory*; permanently affixed to something.—**sed·en·tar·i·ly,** sed″en·târ′i·lē, sed′en·ter″i·lē, *a.*—**sed·en·tar·i·ness,** *n.*

Se·der, sā′dēr, *n. pl.* **Se·ders, Se·dar·im.** *Judaism,* the ritual dinner which commemorates the Israelites' exodus from Egypt, celebrated the evening before the first day of the Passover holidays by people of the Jewish faith and again the evening before the second day by Orthodox and Conservative observers.

sedge, sej, *n.* [O.E. *secg* = Sc. *segg,* L.G. *segge,* a reed, sedge; same root as in L. *seco,* to cut, being a plant with swordlike leaves.] Any member of the family *Cyperaceae,* an extensive group of grasslike plants growing mostly in swamps and marshes and on river banks, distinguished from the grasses by having solid, usu. three-sided stems without joints.—**sedg·y,** sej′ē, *a.*—*sedgier, sedgiest.*

se·dil·i·a, se·dil′ē·a, *n. pl.* [L. *sedile,* a seat.] The seats or bench on the south wall of the chancel of many churches and cathedrals for the use of the celebrant and his assistants.

sed·i·ment, sed′i·ment, *n.* [L. *sedimentum,* < *sedeo,* to settle.] The matter which subsides to the bottom of water or any other liquid; settlings; lees; dregs; *geol.* the matter or particles deposited by wind and water.

sed·i·men·ta·ry, sed"*i*·men'ta·rĕ, *a.* Pertaining to, of, or consisting of sediment; formed by sediment or matter that has subsided; *geol.* pertaining to rocks which have been formed by sediment deposited by water, wind, or ice. Also **sed·i·men·tal.**

sed·i·men·ta·tion, sed"*i*·men·tā'shan, *n.* The depositing or accumulation of sediment.

se·di·tion, si·dish'an, *n.* [L. *seditio, seditionis,* discord, sedition—*sed,* apart, and *itio, itionis,* a going, < *eo, itum,* to go.] The stirring up of unrest in a state; an offense tending toward but stopping short of an open act of treason.

se·di·tion·ar·y, si·dish'a·ner"ĕ, *n.* pl. **se·di·tion·ar·ies.** An inciter or promoter of sedition.—*a.* Seditious.

se·di·tious, si·dish'us, *a.* [L. *seditiosus.*] Pertaining to sedition; exciting or aiding in sedition; guilty of sedition; seditionary.—**se·di·tious·ly**, *adv.*—**se·di·tious·ness**, *n.*

se·duce, si·dōs', si·dūs', *v.t.*—*seduced, seducing.* [L. *seduco.*] To persuade or entice from the path of rectitude or duty; to lead astray; to corrupt; to tempt; to entice to a surrender of chastity.—**se·duc·er**, *n.*—**se·duc·i·ble, se·duce·a·ble**, *a.*

se·duc·tion, si·duk'shan, *n.* [L. *seductio, seductionis.*] The act of seducing; the means employed to seduce; anything which seduces. Also **se·duce·ment**, si·dōs'ment, si·dūs'ment.

se·duc·tive, si·duk'tiv, *a.* Tending to seduce; tempting; alluring; enticing.—**se·duc·tive·ly**, *adv.*—**se·duc·tive·ness**, *n.*

se·duc·tress, si·duk'tris, *n.* A female who seduces.

se·du·li·ty, si·dŏ'li·tē, si·dū'li·tē, *n.* The state or quality of being sedulous; assiduity.

sed·u·lous, sej'a·lus, *a.* [L. *sedulus,* < *sedeo,* to sit.] Assiduous; diligent in application; steady and persevering in endeavors; steadily industrious.—**sed·u·lous·ly**, *adv.*—**sed·u·lous·ness**, *n.*

se·dum, sē'dum, *n.* [N.L. use of L. *sedum,* houseleek.] Any plant of the genus *Sedum,* of the stonecrop family, which comprises fleshy, chiefly perennial herbs with cymes of yellow, white, or pink flowers, as the houseleek and live-forever.

see, sē, *v.t.*—past *saw,* pp. *seen,* ppr. *seeing.* [O.E. *seŏn,* to see = Icel. *sáj,* Dan. *see,* D. *zien,* Goth. *saihwan,* G. *sehen*—to see; same root as L. *sequor,* to follow.] To perceive by the eye; to look at or behold; to perceive mentally; to form a conception or idea of; to understand; to comprehend; to view, as a play; to visualize; to recognize; to ascertain; to discover; to examine; to experience; to know by personal experience; to ensure; to meet or associate with; to consult; as, to *see* an expert; to have communication with; to receive; to visit; as, to go to *see* a friend; to provide for; to help; as, to *see* her through this difficult period; to attend or escort; as, to *see* a lady home; to find fitting, appropriate, or acceptable; to choose to have, as: I would *see* him in prison before I gave him money. *Poker,* to equal a bet.—*v.i.* To have the power or sense of sight; to perceive mentally; to discern; to examine or inquire; to be attentive; to take heed; to take care; to observe.—**see a·bout**, to investigate; to give attention to.—**see off**, to escort to a place of departure.—**see out**, to stay with, as an undertaking, until it is finished.—**see through**, to penetrate; to comprehend the actual character of; to detect; to persevere.—**see·a·ble**, *a.*—**see·a·ble·ness**, *n.*

see, sē, *n.* [< O.Fr. *se, sed,* < L. *sedes,* a seat, < stem of *sedeo,* to sit.] The authority, office, or seat of a bishop; the diocese or jurisdiction of a bishop, archbishop, or, in Rome, of the pope.

seed, sēd, *n.* pl. **seeds, seed.** [O.E. *sǣd,* < *sawan,* to sow; Icel. *saethi,* Dan. *saed,* D. *zaat,* G. *saat.*] The impregnated and matured ovule of a plant, containing an embryo which may develop into a new plant; loosely, one of the grains of wheat and other grasses; any plant part capable of reproduction, as a bulb or tuber; the fecundating fluid of male animals; semen; that from which anything springs; offspring; progeny; descendants.—*v.t.* To scatter or sow, as seeds; to plant seeds in, as a field; to take the seeds out of, as fruit; *meteor.* to sprinkle or scatter chemicals into, as clouds, to cause rainfall. *Sports,* to arrange or schedule, as competitive teams or players, so that the most skilled are matched in the later rounds of play; to handle in this manner, as a team or player.—*v.i.* To bear and drop seeds; to plant or sow seed.—**go to seed**, to bear and shed seed, as a flower; to become shabby or weak; to deteriorate, as a person.—**seed·less**, *a.*—**seed·like**, *a.*—**seed·ful**, *a.*

seed·bed, sēd'bed", *n.* Any plot of soil which has been prepared for planting; a patch of fine soil in which plants are raised until mature enough for transplanting.

seed·cake, sēd'kāk", *n.* A sweet cake containing caraway or other aromatic seeds; oil cake.

seed·case, sēd'kās", *n. Bot.* a seed vessel or pericarp. See *pod.*

seed coat, *n. Bot.* the testa or outer integument of a seed. Also *tunic.*

seed·eat·er, sēd'ē"tèr, *n.* A bird living chiefly on seeds, and usu. having a short, stout bill, as the sparrow.

seed·er, sē'dèr, *n.* One who or that which seeds; an apparatus for sowing or planting seeds; a device for removing seeds.

seed fern, *n.* Any plant of the extinct order *Cycadofilicales,* having some characteristics of both ferns and trees, and thought to be the ancestor of the conifers.

seed leaf, *n. Bot.* cotyledon.

seed·ling, sēd'ling, *n.* A plant produced from seed rather than from a graft; a young tree under three feet in height; any very small or young plant, sometimes nursery grown for future transplantation.

seed oy·ster, *n.* An oyster that is very young but has developed to the proper size for transplanting.

seed pearl, *n.* A small, often flawed, pearl used for ornamentation.

seed plant, *n.* Any plant bearing seeds; a spermatophyte.

seed·pod, sēd'pod", *n. Bot.* The capsule or container which holds the seeds of such plants as the lima bean and milkweed, and which usu. splits open on ripening; pod.

seeds·man, sēdz'man, *n.* pl. **seeds·men.** A person who deals in seeds; one who scatters or sows seeds. Also **seed·man**, sēd'man.

seed stock, *n.* A reserve supply of seed or tubers reserved for planting; a source of propagation.

seed·time, sēd'tīm", *n.* The proper season for sowing.

seed ves·sel, *n. Bot.* pericarp.

seed·y, sē'dē, *a.*—*seedier, seediest.* Abounding with seeds; producing seeds; gone to seed. Wornout; shabby; poor and miserable looking; feeling or appearing wretched or unwell; slightly disreputable.—**seed·i·ly**, *adv.*—**seed·i·ness**, *n.*

see·ing, sē'ing, *conj.* Inasmuch as; since; considering; taking into account that.

See·ing Eye dog, *n.* A dog trained by the Seeing Eye organization to guide a blind person.

seek, sēk, *v.t.*—*sought, seeking.* [M.E. *seke,* O.E. *sēcan,* to seek, Icel. *saekja,* G. *suchen,* Goth. *sokjan;* akin to *sake.* Beseech is < *seek,* with prefix *be-*.] To go in search or

quest of; to look or search for; to take pains to find, often followed by *out;* to ask for or request; as, to *seek* advice; to try to gain; to go to; as, to *seek* a shady spot; to aim at; to attempt; to try, usu. followed by an infinitive; to strive after.—*v.i.* To make search or inquiry.—**seek·er**, *n.*

seel, sēl, *v.t.* [Fr. *ciller, siller,* < *cil,* L. *cilium,* an eyelash.] *Falconry,* to close with a thread, as the eyes of a hawk.

seem, sēm, *v.i.* [M.E. *semen,* to conciliate, to adjust, to seem, < root of *same.*] To appear; to present the appearance of being, as: The boys *seem* happy. To feel as if; to imagine; to appear to one's senses, judgment, or observation, as: I still *seem* to hear his voice. To give an indication of being present, as: There *seems* good reason to fear him. To be apparent; to assume an air; to present the appearance of being; to pretend.—**seem·er**, sē'mèr, *n.*

seem·ing, sē'ming, *a.* Appearing; having the appearance or semblance, whether real or not.—*n.* Appearance, esp. a false appearance; show; semblance.—**seem·ing·ly**, *adv.*—**seem·ing·ness**, *n.*

seem·ly, sēm'lē, *a.*—*seemlier, seemliest.* [Same as Icel. *saemiligr,* < *saemr,* fit, seemly.] Becoming; fitting; proper; decorous; handsome or pleasing in appearance.—*adv.* Becomingly; fittingly.—**seem·li·ness**, *n.*

seep, sēp, *v.i.* [Var. of *sipe.*] To pass gradually, as liquid, through a porous substance; percolate; ooze.—*n.* Moisture that seeps out; seepage; a small spring formed by the oozing of liquid from the ground.—**seep·y**, sē'pē, *a.*—*seepier, seepiest.*

seep·age, sē'pij, *n.* The act or process of seeping; leakage; that which seeps or leaks out; the amount of leakage.

se·er, sē'èr, sēr, *n.* One who sees, sē'èr. A prophet; one with deep spiritual insight; a person said to be gifted with second sight; a crystal gazer, sēr.—**seer·ess**, sēr'is, *n.* A female seer.

seer, sēr, sâr, *n.* Any of various units of weight in India, the most common being equivalent to almost two pounds one ounce. Also *ser.*

seer·suck·er, sēr'suk"èr, *n.* [Pers. *shīr o shakkar,* lit. 'milk and sugar,' with allusion to the stripes.] A fabric of linen, rayon, or cotton, usu. striped, with alternate stripes being crinkled in the weaving.

see·saw, sē'są", *n.* [Varied redupl. of *saw.*] An amusement in which children move alternately up and down when seated one or more at each end of a plank balanced on some support; a plank adjusted for this sport; an up-and-down or a back-and-forth movement or procedure. Also *teeterboard, teeter-totter. Whist,* the playing of two partners so that each alternately trumps a nontrump card led by the other; a cross ruff.—*a.* Moving up and down or back and forth.—*v.i., v.t.* To move or cause to move in a seesaw manner.

seethe, sēTH, *v.t.*—*seethed, seething.* [O.E. *seŏthan* (pp. *soden*) = D. *zieden* = G. *sieden,* boil.] To boil; to cook by boiling; to soak or steep.—*v.i.* To boil; to surge or foam as if boiling; to be in a state of agitation or excitement.—*n.* The act or the fact of seething; ebullition; a state of agitation or excitement.—**seeth·ing**, *a.*—**seeth·ing·ly**, *adv.*

seg·ment, seg'ment, *n.* [L. *segmentum,* < *secare,* to cut.] A piece or part cut or marked off; one of the parts into which anything naturally separates or is naturally divided; a division or section; *geom.* a part cut off from a figure, esp. a circular or spherical one, by a line or plane. *Zool.* a metamere; any section of a leg or the like between joints.—**seg·ment'**, *v.t., v.i.* To separate or divide into segments.—**seg·men·tar·y**, seg'men·ter"ē, *a.*

seg·men·tal, seg·men′tal, _a._ Pertaining to a segment or segments; composed of segments; of the nature of a segment; having the form of a segment of a circle; as, a _segmental_ arch.—**seg·men·tal·ly**, _adv._

seg·men·ta·tion, seg″men·tā′shan, _n._ A division into segments. _Biol._ the division of the adult body into successive segments or metameres, as in the earthworm; cell division.

seg·men·ta·tion cav·i·ty, _n. Embryol._ the central cavity of a blastula. Also **blas·to·- coel, blas·to·coele.**

se·gno, sān′yō, sen′yō, _It._ se′nya, _n._ pl. **se·gni**, sān′yē, sen′yē, _It._ se′nyē. [It., < L. _signum_, E. _sign_, n.] _Mus._ a sign, esp. a sign or mark placed at the beginning or end of a passage indicating it is to be repeated.

se·go, sē′gō, _n._ Sego lily.

se·go lil·y, _n._ A perennial plant of western N. America, _Calochortus nuttallii_, bearing flowers shaped like bells: the state flower of Utah; the edible root of this plant. Also _sego_.

seg·re·gate, seg′re·gāt″, _v.t._—segregated, segregating. [L. _segregatus_, pp. of _segregare_, lit. 'separate from the flock,' < _se-_, without, apart, and _grex_ (_greg-_), flock.] To separate or set apart from the others or from the rest; isolate; to subject to separation from the main body of society, as for racial reasons.—_v.i._ To separate or go apart; separate from the main body and collect in one place; to enforce racial segregation; _genetics_, to separate, as allelic genes, during meiosis.—**seg′re·git, seg′re·gāt″**, _n._ A segregated object, person, or class of persons.—**seg·re·ga·tive**, _a._

seg·re·gat·ed, seg′re·gā″tid, _a._ Characterized by racial segregation; as, _segregated_ schools; having separate facilities for those of a different racial or ethnic group; as, _segregated_ transportation; working against the interests of a particular group; as, _segregated_ housing ordinances.

seg·re·ga·tion, seg″re·gā′shan, _n._ [L.L. _segregatio(n-)._] The act of segregating, or the state of being segregated; isolation; something segregated; the practice of separating from the main body an ethnic or other group, as in education, housing, or employment; _genetics_, the separation of paired or allelic genes into different gametes in the process of meiosis.

seg·re·ga·tion·ist, seg″re·gā′sha·nist, _n._ One who advocates or enforces segregation, esp. the segregation of races.

se·gue, sā′gwa, seg′wā, _v.i._—segued, segueing. _Mus._ to proceed to the following section or composition without interruption.—_n.—a.,_ _adv._ Performed without interruption.

se·gui·dil·la, sā″gi·dēl′ya, sā″gi·dē′ya, seg″i·dēl′ya, seg″i·dē′ya, _Sp._ se″gē·dē′lyä, _n._ pl. **se·gui·dil·las**, sā″gi·dēl′yaz, sā″gi·- dē′yaz, seg″i·dēl′yaz, seg″i·dē′yaz, _Sp._ se″gē·dē′lyäs. [Sp.] A Spanish dance in triple rhythm for two persons, often accompanied by castanets; the music for it.

sei·cen·to, sā·chen′tō, _It._ se·chen′ṭa, _n._ [It., six hundred, short for _mille seicento_, one thousand six hundred.] The 17th century, with reference to Italy, esp. to the Italian art or literature of that period.

seiche, sāsh, _n._ [Swiss Fr.] A sudden rhythmical movement from side to side of the water of a lake or other landlocked body, occasioning fluctuation of the water level from inches to several feet, and due to sudden variations in atmospheric pressure, wind, or small earthquakes.

sei·del, sīd′el, zīd′el, _n._ A large mug for beer, often with a hinged cover.

Seid·litz pow·ders, sed′lits pou′dėrz, _n._ [After _Seidlitz_, village in Bohemia, with mineral springs.] An aperient consisting of two powders, one tartaric acid and the other a mixture of sodium bicarbonate and

Rochelle salt, which are dissolved separately and the solutions mixed and drunk while effervescing. Also **Seid·litz pow·ders.**

sei·gneur, sēn·yụr′, _Fr._ se·nyOER′, _n._ [Fr.] _Fr. hist._ a feudal lord. _Canada_, formerly one who held a landed estate by feudal tenure; one of the landed gentry.—**sei·gneu·ri·al,** _a._

seign·ior, sēn′yėr, _n._ [Fr. _seigneur_, It. _signore_, Sp. _señor_, Pg. _senhor_, titles or words of respectful address, equiv. to Sir, Mr., gentleman; < L. _senior_, elder.] A lord; sir: used as a title of respect; in feudal times, the lord of a fee or manor.—**seign·- ior·al,** sēn′yėr·al, _a._—**sei·gno·ri·al,** sēn·- yōr′ē·al, sēn·yạr′ē·al, _a._

seign·ior·age, sēn′yėr·ij, _n._ Something claimed by the sovereign or by a superior as a prerogative; the profit derived by the government from issuing coins at a rate above their intrinsic value, or by giving back rather less in coin than is received in bullion; a royalty or share of profit. Also **seign·or·age.**

seign·ior·y, sēn′yo·rē, _n._ pl. **seign·ior·ies.** Power or authority of a lord; _hist._ domain of a lord. _Canada_, the manor house belonging to a seigneur; the estate formerly held by feudal tenure. Also _signory_, **sei·gneur·y**, sēn′yụr·e.

seine, sān, _n._ [O.E. _segne_, < L. _sagena_, < Gr. _sagēnē_, large net, seine.] A fishing net which hangs vertically in the water, having floats at the upper edge and sinkers at the lower, the fish being enclosed and taken by drawing the ends of the net together.—_v.i._—seined, seining. To fish with a seine.—_v.t._ To catch with a seine; to use a seine in.—**sein·er,** _n._

sei·sin, sē′zin, _n. Law._ The possession of chattels or land; the possession or right to possession of a freehold estate. Also **sei·zin.**

seism, sī′zum, sī′sum, _n._ [Gr. _seismós_, < _seiein_, shake.] An earthquake.

seis·mic, sīz′mik, sīs′mik, _a._ Characteristic of, resulting from, or subject to earthquakes. Also **seis·mal, seis·mi·cal.** —**seis·mi·cal·ly,** _adv._

seis·mic·i·ty, sīz·mis′i·tē, sīs·mis′i·tē, _n._ pl. **seis·mic·i·ties.** The relative frequency, strength, and range of earthquakes in a given area.

seis·mism, sīz′miz·um, sīs′miz·um, _n._ The phenomena, collectively, of earthquakes.

seis·mo·gram, sīz′mo·gram″, sīs′mo·- gram″, _n._ A record of earth vibrations made by a seismograph.

seis·mo·graph, sīz′mo·graf″, sīz′mo·gräf″, sīs′mo·graf″, sīs′mo·gräf″, _n._ An instrument that detects and records the phenomena of earthquakes. Also _seismometer._ —**seis·mo·graph·ic,** sīz″mo·graf′ik, sīs″- mo·gräf′ik, _a._

seis·mog·ra·phy, sīz·mog′ra·fē, sīs·- mog′ra·fē, _n._ The scientific recording of earthquake phenomena; the use of the seismograph; seismology.—**seis·mog·ra·- pher,** _n._

seis·mol·o·gy, sīz·mol′o·jē, sīs·mol′o·jē, _n._ The science of the origin, development, and characteristics of vibrations in the earth, primarily those generated by earthquakes but also including vibrations produced by man-made explosions and weather conditions. Also _seismography._— **seis·mo·log·ic, seis·mo·log·i·cal,** sīz″- mo·loj′ik, sīs″mo·loj′ik, _a._—**seis·mo·log·- i·cal·ly,** _adv._—**seis·mol·o·gist,** _n._

seis·mom·e·ter, sīz·mom′i·tėr, sīs·- mom′i·tėr, _n._ An instrument which measures the direction, intensity, and duration of earthquakes. Also _seismograph._ —**seis·mo·met·ric, seis·mo·met·ri·cal,** sīz″mo·me′trik, sīs″mo·me′trik, _a._—**seis·- mom·et·ry,** _n._

seis·mo·scope, sīz′mo·skōp″, sīs′mo·- skōp″, _n._ An instrument for indicating the

time and occurrence of an earthquake.— **seis·mo·scop·ic,** sīz″mo·skop′ik, sīs″mo·- skop′ik, _a._

seize, sēz, _v.t._—seized, seizing. [O.Fr. _seisir, saisir_ (Fr. _saisir_), < M.L. _sacire_, take, seize; prob. < Teut.] To lay hold of suddenly or forcibly; clutch or grasp; as, to _seize_ a weapon; catch or take hold suddenly or forcibly; grasp with the mind; as, to _seize_ an idea; to take possession of by force or at will; as, to _seize_ enemy ships; to take possession or control of as if by suddenly laying hold, as: A fever _seized_ him. To arrest, as the attention, or impress, as the mind, suddenly and forcibly; to take possession of by legal authority, or confiscate; as, to _seize_ smuggled goods. _Law_, to put in legal possession of something; also **seise.** To capture; to take prisoner or take into custody; take advantage of promptly; as, to _seize_ an opportunity. _Naut._ to bind, lash, or fasten together with several turns of small rope, cord, or similar material.—_v.i._ To take possession by force or at will, usu. followed by _on_ or _upon_; to have recourse to some expedient, usu. followed by _on_ or _upon_; as, to _seize_ on a pretext or excuse.—**seiz·er,** _n._

seiz·ing, sē′zing, _n._ The act of one who or that which seizes. _Naut._ the act of binding, lashing, or fastening together with several turns of small rope, cord, or similar material; the fastening so made; the cordage used.

seiz·er, sē′zėr, sē′zạr, _n._ One who seizes. _Law_, one who seizes or takes possession; also **sei·sor, sei·zor.**

sei·zure, sē′zhėr, _n._ The act of seizing or taking sudden hold; a taking into possession of an individual or property; a sudden attack, as of some disease; a fit.

se·jant, se·jeant, sē′jant, _a._ [O.Fr., < L. _sedēre_, to sit.] _Her._ represented sitting, with erect forepaws.

se·la·chi·an, si·lā′kē·an, _n._ [Gr. _selachos_, a shark.] A loosely delimited group of elasmobranchs, _Selachii_, comprising the sharks, dogfishes, skates, and rays.—_a._

sel·a·gi·nel·la, sel″a·ji·nel′a, _n._ Any low-growing plant, genus _Selaginella_, resembling mosses but more closely allied to ferns, and popular in terrariums and greenhouses.

se·lah, sē′la, sel′a, _n._ A Hebrew word in the Psalms, thought to be a direction for the musician or reader.

sel·dom, sel′dom, _adv._ [O.E. _seldum_, for _seldan_ = D. _zelden_ = G. _selten_.] Rarely; infrequently; not often.—_a._ Rare; infrequent.—**sel·dom·ness,** _n._

se·lect, si·lekt′, _v.t._ [L. _selectus_, pp. of _seligere_, < _se-_, without, apart, and _legere_, gather, choose.] To choose in preference to another or others; pick out from a number. —_v.i._ To make a choice or selection.—_a._ Selected; chosen in preference to others; choice; of special value or excellence; superior; careful or fastidious in selection; exclusive.—**se·lect·ed,** _a._—**se·lect·ness,** _n._ —**se·lec·tor,** _n._

se·lect·ee, si·lek·tē′, _n._ One selected, as a recruit by the selective draft.

se·lec·tion, si·lek′shan, _n._ [L. _selectio(n-)._] The act of selecting or the fact of being selected; choice; a thing or a number of things selected; as, a volume of prose _selections_; man's agency in singling out certain forms of animal and plant life for reproduction and perpetuation. Compare _natural selection, survival of the fittest._

se·lec·tive, si·lek′tiv, _a._ Having the function or power of selecting; making selection; characterized by selection or choice. _Mach._ noting or pertaining to a system of transmission, as in automobiles, in which the speeds may be changed in any order, without the necessity of passing progressively through the different changes of gear; also **se·lec·tive trans·mis·sion.** *Elect.* having selectivity, as a radio receiving set.—**se·lec·tive·ly,**   *adv.*—**se·lec·tive·ness,** *n.*

se·lec·tive serv·ice, *n.* Compulsory service in one of the armed forces.

se·lec·tiv·i·ty, si·lek·tiv′i·tē, *n.* The state or quality of being selective. *Elect.* the property of a circuit, instrument, or the like, by virtue of which it responds to electric oscillations of a particular frequency; of a radio receiving set, the ability to receive any one of a band of frequencies or waves to the exclusion of others.

se·lect·man, si·lekt′man, *n.* pl. **se·lect·men.** One of a board of town officers, as in New England, chosen annually to manage certain public affairs.

sel·e·nate, sel′e·nāt″, *n. Chem.* a salt of selenic acid.

se·le·nic, si·lē′nik, si·len′ik, *a. Chem.* of or containing selenium, esp. in a high valence state.—**se·le·ni·ous,** si·lē′nē·us, *a.* Of or containing silenium, esp. in a low valence state.

se·le·nic ac·id, *n.* A strong corrosive dibasic acid, H_2SeO_4, capable of dissolving gold and platinum.

sel·e·nite, sel′e·nīt″, si·lē′nīt, *n.* [L. *selenites,* < Gr. *selēnítēs (lithos),* 'stone of the moon,' < *selēnē,* moon.] A variety of gypsum, found in transparent crystals and foliated masses.

se·le·ni·um, si·lē′nē·um, *n.* [< Gr. *selēnē,* the moon; so named from its being associated with *tellurium,* < L. *tellus,* the earth.] A nonmetallic element chemically resembling sulfur and tellurium, and having an electrical resistance that changes under the action of light: used in photoelectric cells. Sym. Se, at. no. 34, at. wt. 78.96. See Periodic Table of Elements.—**se·le·nif·er·ous,** *a.*

se·le·ni·um cell, *n.* A photoelectric cell having a plate of light-sensitive selenium as its chief component.

sel·e·nog·ra·phy, sel″e·nog′ra·fē, *n..* The science dealing with the moon, esp. with its physical features.—**sel·e·nog·ra·pher,** *n.*—**se·le·no·graph·ic,** si·lē″no′graf′ik, *a.*

sel·e·nol·o·gy, sel″e·nol′o·jē, *n.* The branch of astronomy dealing with the moon, esp. the surface features.—**sel·e·nol·o·gist,** *n.*

self, self, *n.* pl. **selves.** [O.E. *self* = D. *zelf* = G. *selb* = Icel. *sjalfr* = Sw. *sjelf* = Dan. *selv* = Goth. *silba,* self.] A person or thing, with respect to his, her, or its own person, individuality, or identity; as, his very *self,* religion's *self;* the individual consciousness, as the seat of subjective thought and action; personal advantage; the nature or character of a person or thing at a particular time or in a particular aspect, usu. in contrast to previous or other facets of the whole identity; as, her better *self.*—*pron.* Myself, himself, herself. —*a.* Being the same throughout, as a flower of a single color; uniform; unmixed; being of the same material or kind as the rest; as, a *self* belt. Of, by, to, for, or from oneself or itself: used in combination.

self, self, *v.t. Bot.* To inbreed; to cause to fertilize itself, as certain plants.—*v.i. Bot.* to inbreed.

self-a·ban·doned, self′a·ban′dond, *a.* Having been abandoned by one's own self; no longer guiding oneself; uninhibited. —**self-a·ban·don·ment,** *n.*

self-a·base·ment, self′a·bās′ment, self″a·bās′ment, *n.* Degradation of oneself, esp. because of feelings of guilt, inferiority, or shame.

self-ab·ne·ga·tion, self′ab″ne·gā′shan, *n.*

Self-sacrifice; self-denial.—**self-ab·ne·gat·ing,** *a.*

self-ab·sorbed, self′ab·sarbd′, self′ab·zarbd′, self″ab·sarbd′, self″ab·zarbd′, *a.* Absorbed in oneself or one's own thoughts, affairs, or the like.—**self-ab·sorp·tion,** self′ab·sarp′shan, self′ab·zarp′shan, self″ab·sarp′shan, self″ab·zarp′shan, *n.*

self-a·buse, self′a·būs′, self″a·būs′, *n.* The act of belittling oneself; self-reproach; disregard for one's own health; masturbation.

self-ac·cu·sa·tion, self′ak″ū·zā′shan, *n.* A charging of oneself with blame or error.— **self-ac·cu·sa·tive, self-ac·cu·sa·to·ry,** *a.* —**self-ac·cus·ing,** *a.*

self-act·ing, self′ak′ting, *a.* Acting of or by itself; automatic.—**self-ac·tion,** *n.*—**self-ac·tive,** *a.*—**self-ac·tiv·i·ty,** *n.*

self-ad·dressed, self′a·drest′, *a.* Addressed to oneself, as: In writing for information, enclose a *self-addressed* envelope.

self-ad·just·ing, self′a·jus′ting, *a.* Adjusting itself; requiring no external adjustment.—**self-ad·just·ment,** *n.*

self-ad·min·is·tered, self′ad·min′i·stérd, *a.* Under the direction of or applied by oneself.

self-ad·mi·ra·tion, self′ad″mi·rā′shan, *n.* Conceited approval of oneself.—**self-ad·mir·ing,** *a.*

self-ag·gran·dize·ment, self′a·gran′diz·ment, self″a·gran′diz·ment, *n.* The increase of one's position, power, or wealth with little or no regard for the rights of others.—**self-ag·gran·diz·ing,** self′a·gran′dī·zing, *a.*

self-a·nal·y·sis, self′a·nal′i·sis, self″a·nal′i·sis, *n.* The search for understanding of oneself, usu. by methods similar to those of professionals but without the services of such trained persons.—**self-an·a·lyt·i·cal,** self′an″a·lit′i·kal, self″an″a·lit′i·kal, *a.*— **self-an·a·lyzed,** self″an′a·līzd′, *a.*

self-an·ni·hi·la·tion, self′a·nī″i·lā′shan, self″a·nī″i·lā′shan, *n.* Destruction of oneself; renunciation, surrender, or sacrifice of the self during mystical contemplation of God.

self-ap·plause, self′a·plaz′, *n.* An expression of approval or appreciation for oneself. —**self-ap·plaud·ing,** *a.*

self-ap·point·ed, self′a·poin′tid, *a.* Self-righteously appointed, or selected by oneself.

self-as·ser·tion, self′a·sur′shan, self″a·sur′shan, *n.* The asserting of or insistence on one's own importance, claims, wishes, or opinions.—**self-as·sert·ing,** *a.*—**self-as·sert·ing·ly,** *adv.*—**self-as·ser·tive,** *a.*— **self-as·ser·tive·ly,** *adv.*—**self-as·ser·tive·ness,** *n.*

self-as·sur·ance, self′a·shur′ans, self″a·shur′ans, *n.* A feeling of confidence as to oneself or one's own powers or abilities; self-confidence.—**self-as·sured,** self′a·shurd′, *a.* Self-confident.—**self-as·sur·ed·ness,** self′a·shur′id·nis, *n.*

self-cen·tered, *Brit.* **self-cen·tred,** self′sen′térd, *a.* Centered in oneself; engrossed in self, selfish; being itself fixed as a center. —**self-cen·ter·ed·ly,** *Brit.* **self-cen·tred·ly,** *adv.*—**self-cen·tered·ness,** *Brit.* **self-cen·tred·ness,** *n.*

self-clos·ing, self″klō′zing, *a.* Closing automatically.

self-col·lect·ed, self′ko·lek′tid, self″ko·lek′tid, *a.* Self-possessed; exhibiting self-control.

self-col·ored, self′kul′érd, self″kul′érd, *a.* All of one color, as a blossom or piece of cloth; of the natural color.

self-com·mand, self′ko·mand′, self′ko·mänd′, self″ko·mand′, self″ko·mänd′, *n.* Command of feelings; self-control; coolness; poise.

self-com·pla·cen·cy, self′kom·plā′sen·sē,

self″kom·plā′sen·sē, *n.* Satisfaction with oneself or one's own doings; self-satisfaction.—**self-com·pla·cent,** *a.*—**self-com·pla·cent·ly,** *adv.*

self-com·posed, self′kom·pōzd′, self″kom·pōzd′, *a.* In control of one's emotions; calm.—**self-com·pos·ed·ly,** self′kom·pō′zid·lē, self″kom·pō′zid·lē, *adv.*—**self-com·pos·ed·ness,** *n.*

self-con·ceit, self′kon·sēt, self″kon·sēt′, *n.* An exceedingly high opinion of oneself; vanity.—**self-con·ceit·ed,** *a.*

self-con·cern, self′kon·surn′, *n.* Undue anxiety or solicitude about oneself.— **self-con·cerned,** *a.*

self-con·fessed, self′kon·fest′, self″kon·fest′, *a.* Openly avowed or admitted.— **self-con·fes·sion,** self′kon·fesh′an, *n.*

self-con·fi·dence, self′kon·fi·dens, self″kon″fi·dens, *n.* The state or quality or being confident or certain of oneself of one's abilities.—**self-con·fi·dent,** *a.*— **self-con·fi·dent·ly,** *adv.*

self-con·grat·u·la·tion, self′kon·grach″u·lā′shan, *n.* Uncritical acceptance of or contentment with one's own achievements, good fortune, or the like.—**self-con·grat·u·la·to·ry,** self′kon·grach′u·la·tōr″ē, self′kon·grach′u·la·tar″ē, self″kon·grach′u·la·tōr″ē, *a.*

self-con·scious, self′kon′shus, self″kon′shus, *a.* Conscious of oneself or one's own thoughts or actions; excessively conscious of oneself; given to thinking excessively of oneself as an object of observation to others; exhibiting shyness or embarrassment; *philos., psychol.* aware of the existence, actions, or thinking of oneself.— **self-con·scious·ly,** *adv.*—**self-con·scious·ness,** *n.*

self-con·se·quence, self′kon″se·kwens, self″kon′se·kwens, *n.* The sense of one's own consequence; self-importance.

self-con·sti·tut·ed, self″kon′sti·tö″tid, self″kon′sti·tū″tid, *a.* Constituted by oneself or itself; as, a *self-constituted* board of inquiry.

self-con·tained, self′kon·tānd′, self″kon·tānd′, *a.* Containing in oneself or itself all that is necessary; reserved or uncommunicative; self-controlled; of a machine, complete in itself.—**self-con·tain·ed·ly,** self′kon·tā′nid·lē, self″kon·tā′nid·lē, *adv.* —**self-con·tain·ed·ness,** *n.*—**self-con·tain·ment,** *n.*

self-con·tempt, self′kon·tempt′, *n.* Disapproval of or disgust with oneself.

self-con·tent, self′kon·tent′, self″kon·tent′, *n.* Contentment or satisfaction with oneself; self-complacency. Also **self con·tent·ment.**—*a.* Self-satisfied. Also **self-con·tent·ed.**—**self-con·tent·ed·ly,** *adv.*—**self-con·tent·ed·ness,** *n.*

self-con·tra·dic·tion, self′kon″tra·dik′shan, self″kon″tra·dik′shan, *n.* The act or fact of contradicting oneself or itself; a statement or the like containing mutually contradictory elements.—**self-con·tra·dict·ing,** self-con·tra·dic·to·ry, *a.*

self-con·trol, self′kon·trōl′, self″kon·trōl′, *n.* Control of oneself or one's actions and feelings; self-command which prevents the exhibition of emotion.—**self-con·trolled,** *a.*

self-cor·rect·ing, self′ko·rek′ting, self″ko·rek′ting, *a.* Geared to the automatic correction of errors in operation, as mechanisms.

self-cre·at·ed, self″krē·ā′tid, *a.* Brought into existence or arranged by oneself.

self-crit·i·cism, self′krit′i·siz″um, self′krit″i·siz″um, *n.* The act or capability of viewing one's acts or motives in an objective manner; the tendency to underrate one's capabilities or find fault with one's own actions.—**self-crit·i·cal,** self′krit′i·kal, self′krit′i·kal, *a.*

---

ch- chain, G. na*ch*t;   **th-** THen, thin;   **w-** wig, hw as sound in whig;   **z-** zh as in azure, zeal.   *Italicized vowel* indicates schwa sound.

self-de·ceit, self'di·sēt', self"di·sēt', *n.* Self-deception.—**self-de·ceived,** self'di·-sēvd', self"di·sēvd', *a.*—**self-de·ceiv·er,** *n.* —**self-de·ceiv·ing,** self'di·sē'ving, self"-di·sē'ving, *a.*

self-de·cep·tion, self'di·sep'shan, self"-di·sep'shan, *n.* The act or fact of fooling or deceiving oneself. Also *self-deceit.*—**self-de·cep·tive,** *a.*

self-ded·i·ca·tion, self'ded"i·kā'shan, *n.* The committing of oneself to something, as to a cause or goal.—**self-ded·i·cat·ed,** self'ded"i·kā'tid, *a.*

self-de·feat·ing, self'di·fē'ting, self"di·-fē'ting, *a.* Acting to thwart, hinder, or frustrate one's own end.

self-de·fense, self'di·fens', self"di·fens', *n.* The defense of one's own person, property, or reputation; the physical art of self-defense, as in boxing or judo; *law,* a plea claiming that violence committed against another was needed in defending oneself from actual or potential harm. Also *chiefly* Brit. **self-de·fence.**—**self-de·fen·sive,** *a.*

self-de·lu·sion, self'di·lö'zhan, self"di·-lö'zhan, *n.* The action of deluding oneself; self-deception.—**self-de·lud·ed,** *a.*

self-de·ni·al, self'di·ni'al, self"di·ni'al, *n.* The denial of oneself; the sacrifice of one's own desires; an instance of such self-sacrifice.—**self-de·ny·ing,** *a.*—**self-de·-ny·ing·ly,** *adv.*

self-de·pend·ence, self'di·pen'dens, *n.* Reliance on one's own efforts, resources, and the like.—**self-de·pend·ent,** *a.*

self-dep·re·cat·ing, self"dep're·kā'ting, self'dep're·kā'ting, *a.* Undervaluating or belittling oneself; overly modest.—**self-dep·re·ca·tion,** *n.*

self-de·struc·tion, self'di·struk'shan, self"di·struk'shan, *n.* The destruction of oneself or itself; suicide.—**self-de·struc·tive,** self'di·struk'tiv, self"di·struk'tiv, *a.*

self-de·ter·mi·na·tion, self'di·tur"mi·-nā'shan, self"di·tur"mi·nā'shan, *n.* Determination by oneself or itself, without constraint or influence from without; free will; the determining by a people of the form of government they shall have, without reference to the wishes of any other nation.—**self-de·ter·mined,** *a.*—**self-de·-ter·min·ing,** *a., n.*

self-de·ter·min·ism, self'di·tur"mi·-niz"um, self"di·tur"mi·niz"um, *n.* Philos. the doctrine that each condition or action of a self is determined by previous conditions or actions of the self.

self-de·vel·op·ment, self'di·vel'op·ment, *n.* The growth, maturation, or unfolding of one's own capabilities or potentialities.

self-de·vo·tion, self'di·vō'shan, self"di·-vō'shan, *n.* Devotion of oneself to a chosen cause, activity, profession, or the like; sacrifice of one's own interests or happiness for the sake of another or others.—**self-de·vot·ed,** *a.*—**self-de·vot·ed·ly,** *adv.*—**self-de·vot·ed·ness,** *n.*

self-di·rec·tion, self"di·rek'shan, self"-di'rek·shan, *n.* The guidance, instruction, or regulation of oneself.—**self-di·rect·ed,** *a.*—**self-di·rect·ing,** *a.*

self-dis·ci·pline, self"dis'i·plin, self'dis'-i·plin, *n.* Self-imposed regulation or ordering of one's own thoughts or actions, often with a view toward improvement.—**self-dis·ci·plined,** *a.*

self-dis·cov·er·y, self'di·skuv'e·rē, *n.* The realization of self through self-knowledge.

self-dis·trust, self'dis·trust', self"dis·-trust', *n.* Distrust of or want of confidence in oneself or one's abilities or judgment.—**self-dis·trust·ful,** *a.*

self-doubt, self'dout', *n.* A lack of confidence or assurance in oneself.—**self-doubt·ing,** *a.*

self-dram·a·ti·za·tion, self"dram"a·-ti·zā'shan, self'dram"a·ti·zā'shan, *n.* Over-

statement of one's own attitudes, physical characteristics, or conditions, for effect or attention.—**self-dram·a·tiz·ing,** *a.*

self-driv·en, self"driv'en, self'driv'en, *a.* Moved by its own source of power; automotive.

self-ed·u·cat·ed, self"ej'u̇·kā'tid, self'-ej'u̇·kā'tid, *a.* Educated by one's own efforts, without formal instruction.—**self-ed·u·ca·tion,** *n.*

self-ef·face·ment, self'i·fās'ment, self"i·-fās'ment, *n.* The act or fact of keeping oneself in the background, as in modesty or humility.—**self-ef·fac·ing,** *a.*—**self-ef·-fac·ing·ly,** *adv.*

self-em·ployed, self'em·ploid', self"em·-ploid', *a.* Deriving one's income directly from one's profession, skills, or services, without dependence upon employment by others.—**self-em·ploy·ment,** self'em·-ploi'ment, self"em·ploi'ment, *n.*

self-en·rich·ment, self"en·rich'ment, *n.* The act or process by which a person seeks to improve, esp. his intellectual or aesthetic capabilities.

self-es·teem, self'e·stēm', self"e·stēm', *n.* Esteem or respect for oneself; an excessively favorable opinion of oneself.

self-ev·i·dent, self"ev'i·dent, self'ev'i·-dent, *a.* Evident without proof or reasoning; axiomatic.—**self-ev·i·dence,** *n.*—**self-ev·-i·dent·ly,** *adv.*

self-ex·am·i·na·tion, self'ig·zam"i·nā'-shan, self"ig·zam"i·nā'shan, *n.* Examination into one's own state, conduct, motives, or the like.

self-ex·cit·ed, self'ik·sī'tid, *a.* Elect. pertaining to a dynamo having a magnetic field developed by the electric current the dynamo itself produces.

self-ex·e·cut·ing, self"ek'se·kū"ting, self'ek'se·kū"ting, *a.* Providing for its own execution, and needing no enforcing legislation; as, a *self-executing* treaty.

self-ex·ist·ent, self'ig·zis'tent, self"ig·-zis'tent, *a.* Existing by its own nature or essence, independent of any other cause.—**self-ex·ist·ence,** *n.*

self-ex·plan·a·to·ry, self'ik·splan'a·-tōr"ē, self"ik·splan'a·tōr"ē, self"ik·-splan'a·tər"ē, self"ik·splan'a·tər"ē, *a.* Explaining itself; needing no explanation; obvious. Also **self-ex·plain·ing,** self'ik·-splā'ning, self"ik·splā'ning.

self-ex·pres·sion, self'ik·spresh'an, self"-ik·spresh'an, *n.* The act of giving expression to one's personality, esp. through creative means as painting or writing.—**self-ex·press·ive,** *a.*

self-feed, self"fēd', self'fēd', *v.t.*—**self-fed,** *self-feeding.* To supply food to, as animals, in a manner that leaves the quantity and frequency of ingestion up to those fed.

self-fer·ti·li·za·tion, self'fur"ti·li·zā'-shan, self"fur"ti·li·zā'shan, *n.* Biol. The fertilization of a flower by its own pollen; the fertilization of an animal by its own sperm as in some hermaphrodites.—**self-fer·ti·lized,** self'fur"ti·līzd", *a.*

self-flat·ter·y, self"flat'e·rē, self'flat'e·rē, *n.* Excessive praise of one's own attributes, accomplishments, and the like, accompanied by the ignoring of one's own short-comings or faults.—**self-flat·ter·ing,** *a.*

self-for·get·ful, self'fėr·get'fu̇l, self"fėr·-get'fu̇l, *a.* Forgetful of or showing no thought for one's own advantage or interest. Also **self-for·get·ting,** self"fėr·get'ing, self"fėr·get'ing.—**self-for·get·ful·ly,** *adv.* —**self-for·get·ful·ness,** *n.*—**self-for·get·-ting·ly,** *adv.*

self-ful·fill·ment, self'fu̇l·fil'ment, self"-fu̇l·fil'ment, *n.* The realization of one's ambitions or the full development of one's potentialities through one's own efforts or endeavors.—**self-ful·fill·ing,** *a.*

self-giv·en, self"giv'en, *a.* Self-originated;

given by and to oneself; as, *self-given* power.

self-giv·ing, self'giv'ing, *a.* Generous with one's own time and efforts; unselfish.

self-gov·erned, self"guv'ėrnd, self'guv'-ėrnd, *a.* Governed by itself or having self-government, as a state or community; governing one's own actions or affairs, or independent, as a person; exercising self-control. Also **self-gov·ern·ing.**

self-gov·ern·ment, self"guv'ėrn·ment, self"guv'ėr·ment, self'guv'ėrn·ment, self'-guv'ėr·ment, *n.* Government of a state, community, or other body of persons by its members jointly; autonomy; the state or condition of being governed in this way; self-control.

self-grat·i·fi·ca·tion, self'grat"i·fi·kā'-shan, self"grat"i·fi·kā'shan, *n.* The gratification of oneself or one's own desires or needs.

self-hard·en·ing, self"här'de·ning, self'-här'de·ning, *a.* Noting or pertaining to any of certain steels which will harden without the special treatments, as quenching, necessary for ordinary steel.

self-heal, self'hēl', *n.* Bot. A menthaceous plant, *Prunella vulgaris,* once credited with great medicinal properties; any of various other plants supposed to possess healing properties, as the sanicle, *Sanicula europaea.*

self-help, self"help', self'help', *n.* The act or the faculty of helping oneself, or getting along without assistance from others.

self-hood, self'hu̇d, *n.* The character of being oneself; the mode of being of an individual person; personality; selfishness.

self-hyp·no·sis, self'hip·nō'sis, self"-hip·nō'sis, *n.* Self-induced hypnosis.—**self-hyp·no·tized,** self'hip'no·tīzd", self"-hip'no·tīzd", *a.*

self-i·den·ti·cal, self'ī·den"ti·kal, self"-ī·den'ti·kal, *a.* Identical with itself.—**self-i·den·ti·ty,** self'ī·den'ti·tē, self"ī·-den'ti·tē, *n.*

self-i·den·ti·fi·ca·tion, self'ī·den"ti·-fi·kā'shan, self"ī·den"ti·fi·kā'shan, *n.* The identifying of oneself with something or someone else.

self-ig·nite, self'ig·nīt', self"ig·nīt', *v.i.*—*self-ignited, self-igniting.* To ignite by internal action, without application of spark or flame.—**self-ig·ni·tion,** *n.*

self-im·age, self'im'ij, *n.* One's conception or idea of oneself.

self-im·mo·la·tion, self'im"o·lā'shan, *n.* Sacrifice of oneself, undertaken freely, as for a person, cause, or the like.

self-im·por·tance, self'im·pȯr'tans, self"-im·pȯr'tans, *n.* High opinion of oneself; conceit; pretentiousness.—**self-im·por·-tant,** *a.*—**self-im·por·tant·ly,** *adv.*

self-im·posed, self'im·pōzd', self"im·-pōzd', *a.* Set or thrust upon one by oneself.

self-im·prove·ment, self'im·prȯv'ment, self"im·prȯv'ment, *n.* Improvement of oneself, one's mind, abilities, or the like, by one's own efforts.—**self-im·prov·ing,** *a.*

self-in·crim·i·na·tion, self'in·krim"i·-nā'shan, self"in·krim"i·nā'shan, *n.* Implication or involvement of oneself, esp. by providing testimony or evidence which subjects oneself to criminal prosecution.—**self-in·crim·i·nat·ing,** *a.*

self-in·duced, self'in·dōst', self'in·dūst', self"in·dōst', self"in·dūst', *a.* Induced by oneself or itself; *elect.* produced by self-induction.

self-in·duc·tion, self"in·duk'shan, *n.* Elect. the production of an induced voltage in an electrical circuit by the variation, as in amount or direction, of the current in that circuit.—**self-in·duct·ance,** self"in·-duk'tans, *n.*

self-in·dul·gence, self'in·dul'jens, self"-in·dul'jens, *n.* Free indulgence or gratification of one's passions, appetites, or desires.—**self·in·dul·gent,** *a.*—**self-in·-dul·gent·ly,** *adv.*

self-in·flict·ed, self'in·flik'tid, self"in·-flik'tid, *a.* Inflicted on one by oneself, as a wound.

self-in·sur·ance, self'in·shạr'ans, self"-in·shụr'ans, *n.* The insuring of oneself or one's property by setting aside a fund for the purpose, rather than by obtaining coverage with an insurance company.—**self-in·sured,** *a.*—**self-in·sur·er,** *n.*

self-in·ter·est, self'in'tėr·ist, self"in'trist, self'in"tėr·ist, self'in"trist, *n.* Interest or concern for oneself or one's own advantage; selfishness.—**self-in·ter·est·ed,** *a.*—**self-in·ter·est·ed·ness,** *n.*

self·ish, self'fish, *a.* Caring only or chiefly for oneself; regarding one's own interest or advantage chiefly or solely; proceeding from love of self.—**self·ish·ly,** *adv.*—**self·ish·ness,** *n.*

self-know·ledge, self"nol'ij, self'nol'ij, *n.* The knowledge of one's own real character, abilities, or worth.

self·less, self'lis, *a.* Having no regard for or thought for oneself; unselfish.—**self·less·-ly,** *adv.*—**self·less·ness,** *n.*

self-lim·it·ed, self"lim'i·tid, self'lim'i·tid, *a.* Limited by the nature of oneself or itself; running a defined, limited course, as a disease.—**self-lim·i·ta·tion,** *n.*—**self-lim·it·ing,** *a.*

self-liq·ui·dat·ing, self"lik'wi·dā"ting, self'lik'wi·dā"ting, *a.* Pertaining to a commercial enterprise in which commodities can be converted into cash within a brief period of time; providing, through the normal course of business, funds sufficient to pay back the original investment.

self-load·ing, self"lō'ding, self'lō'ding, *a.* Of or pertaining to a firearm that is semi-automatic or automatic.—**self-load·er,** *n.*

self-love, self'luv', *n.* Love of one's own person which serves to direct one's actions; regard for one's own well-being, welfare, advantage, or happiness.—**self-lov·ing,** *a.*

self-lu·mi·nous, self"lö'mi·nus, *a.* Possessing in itself the property of emitting light.—**self-lu·mi·nos·i·ty,** self"lö"mi·-nos'i·tē, *n.*

self-made, self'mād', *a.* Having achieved success by one's personal efforts; as, a *self-made* man; created by oneself.

self-op·er·at·ing, self"op'e·rā"ting, self'-op'e·rā"ting, *a.* Automatic. Also **self-op·er·a·tive,** self"op'e·rā"tiv, self"op'ėr·-a·tiv, self'op'e·rā"tiv, self'op'ėr·a·tiv.

self-o·pin·ion, self'o·pin'yon, self"o·pin'-yon, *n.* Opinion of oneself, esp. an unduly exalted one; self-conceit.—**self-o·pin·-ion·at·ed,** self"o·pin'yo·nā"tid, self'o·-pin'yo·nā"tid, *a.*—**self-o·pin·ioned,** *a.*

self-per·cep·tion, self'pėr·sep'shan, *n.* Perception of the inner self as an immediate, unreflective experience.

self-per·pet·u·at·ing, self'pėr·pech'ö·-ā"ting, self'pėr·pech'ö·ā"ting, *a.* Denoting a situation in which one manages to remain in a certain position indeterminately; regeneration of oneself.—**self-per·pet·u·-a·tion,** self'pėr·pech"ö·ā'shan, self"pėr·-pech"ö·ā'shan, *n.*

self-pit·y, self"pit'ē, self'pit'ē, *n.* Pity for oneself.—**self-pit·y·ing,** *a.*—**self-pit·y·-ing·ly,** *adv.*

self-poised, self'poizd", *a.* Poised or balanced of itself or without external aid; having or showing mental poise, steadiness, or self-possession, regardless of external circumstances.—**self-poise,** *n.*

self-pol·li·na·tion, self"pol'i·nā'shan, self"pol"i·nā'shan, *n.* [< *pollen.*] *Bot.* pollination of a flower by its own pollen or by pollen from another flower on the same plant.—**self-pol·li·nate,** *v.i.*, *v.t.*—*self-pollinated,* *self-pollinating.*—**self-pol·li·nat·ed,**self"pol'i·nā"tid,slef'pol'i·nā"tid,*a.*

self-por·trait, self"pōr'trit, self"pōr'trāt, *n.* A portrait of a person executed by himself.

self-pos·sessed, self'po·zest', self"po·zest', *a.* Composed; not excited or flustered; cool; not disturbed.—**self-pos·sess·ed·ly,** *adv.*—**self-pos·ses·sion,** self'po·zesh'an, self"po·zesh'an, *n.*

self-praise, self'prāz', self"prāz', *n.* Praise of oneself.

self-pres·er·va·tion, self'prez"ėr·vā'shan, self"prez"ėr·vā'shan, *n.* The preservation of oneself from destruction or injury; an instinct to protect oneself from injury.—**self-pre·serv·ing,** *a.*

self-pro·pelled, self'pro·peld', self"pro·-peld', *a.* Propelled by itself; of a vehicle, containing an engine, motor, or the like, by which it is propelled, as distinguished from a vehicle which is drawn or pushed; mounted on a vehicle, as a gun. Also **self-pro·pel·ling.**—**self-pro·pul·sion,** self'-pro·pul'shan, self"pro·pul'shan, *n.*

self-re·al·i·za·tion, self'rē"a·li·zā'shan, self"rē"a·li·zā'shan, *n.* The development or fulfillment of one's potentialities.—**self-re·al·i·za·tion·ism,** *n.*—**self-re·al·i·za·tion·ist,** *n.*

self-re·cord·ing, self'ri·kạr'ding, self"ri·-kạr'ding, *a.* Recording automatically, as an instrument.

self-re·flec·tion, self'ri·flek'shan, *n.* Observation of one's emotional and mental self; introspection.—**self-re·flec·tive,** self'-ri·flek'tiv, *a.*

self-re·gard, self'ri·gärd', self"ri·gärd', *n.* Consideration of or respect for oneself or one's own concerns.—**self-re·gard·ing,** *a.*

self-reg·is·ter·ing, self"rej'i·stėr·ing, self"rej'i·string, self'rej"i·stėr·ing, self'-rej"i·string, *a.* Registering or recording automatically, as a thermometer.—**self-reg·is·tra·tion,** *n.*

self-re·li·ance, self'ri·li'ans, self"ri·li'ans, *n.* Dependence on one's own powers or abilities.—**self-re·li·ant,** *a.*

self-re·nun·ci·a·tion, self'ri·nun"sē·ā'-shan, self"ri·nun"sē·ā'shan, *n.* The act of renouncing one's own rights or desires; self-abnegation.—**self-re·nounc·ing,** *a.*

self-re·proach, self'ri·prōch', *n.* Reproach or censure dictated by one's own conscience.—**self-re·proach·ful,** *a.*—**self-re·-proach·ing,** *a.*—**self-re·proach·ing·ly,** *adv.*—**self-re·proach·ing·ness,** *n.*

self-re·spect, self'ri·spekt', self"ri·spekt', *n.* Respect for oneself or one's own character.—**self-re·spect·ing,** *a.* Having self-respect.

self-re·straint, self'ri·strānt', self"ri·-strānt', *n.* Restraint or control imposed on oneself; self-command; self-control.—**self-re·strain·ing,** *a.*

self-rev·e·la·tion, self'rev"e·lā'shan,self"-rev"e·lā'shan, *n.* The revealing of one's true character, feelings, or thoughts, esp. when involuntary.—**self-re·veal·ing,** self'-ri·vē'ling, self"ri·vē'ling, *a.*

self-right·eous, self"rī'chus, self'rī'chus, *a.* Assured of one's own uprightness, morality, and virtue, esp. when intolerant of the beliefs and actions of others.—**self-right·-eous·ly,** *adv.*—**self-right·eous·ness,** *n.*

self-rule, self'rōl', *n.* Control or authority over oneself; self-government.—**self-rul·-ing,** *a.*

self-sac·ri·fice, self"sak'ri·fīs", self'-sak'ri·fīs", *n.* The denial of oneself or of self-interest for the benefit of another.—**self-sac·ri·fic·er,** *n.*—**self-sac·ri·fi·cial,** **self-sac·ri·fic·ing,** *a.*—**self-sac·ri·fic·-ing·ly,** *adv.*

self·same, self'sām", *a.* The very same; identical.—**self·same·ness,** *n.*

self-sat·is·fied, self'sat'is·fīd", self"sat'-is·fīd", *a.* Content with oneself.—**self-sat·-is·fac·tion,** self'sat"is·fak'shan, *n.*—**self-sat·is·fy·ing,** self"sat'is·fī"ing, self'sat'is·-fī"ing, *a.*

self-seek·er, self'sē'kėr, *n.* One who seeks only his own interest or pleasure.—**self-seek·ing,** *a.*, *n.*

self-serv·ice, self'sụr'vis, *n.* Service by oneself; the serving of oneself in a restaurant, shop, or the like, rather than being served by attendants.—*a.*—**self-serv·ing,** self'sụr'ving, *a.* Putting one's own interest first; selfish.

self-sown, self'sōn', *a.* Sown by itself, or without human or animal agency; sown by any agency other than man, as by birds, the wind, or the like.—**self-sow,** *v.i.*

self-start·er, self'stär'tėr, *n.* A device which starts an internal-combustion engine without the necessity of cranking it by hand, as by the action of an electric motor, a spring, gas pressure, or the like; *fig.* one who applies his efforts without instruction, urging, or directions from others.—**self-start·ing,** *a.*

self-styled, self'stīld', *a.* Called or styled by oneself; as, a *self-styled* expert.

self-suf·fi·cient, self'sa·fish'ent, self"sa·-fish'ent, *a.* Independent of the aid of others; strongly confident of one's own resources, ability, or endowments; somewhat conceited. Also **self-suf·fic·ing,** self"sa·fī'sing.—**self-suf·fi·cien·cy,** *n.*—**self-suf·fic·ing·ly,** *adv.*—**self-suf·fic·-ing·ness,** *n.*

self-sup·port, self'sa·pōrt', self'sa·pärt' self"sa·pōrt', self"sa·pärt', *n.* The act or fact of supporting or maintaining oneself or itself without outside aid.—**self-sup·-port·ed,** *a.*—**self-sup·port·ing,** *a.*

self-sus·tained, self'sa·stānd', self"sa·-stānd', *a.* Supported or maintained by oneself or itself without outside aid.—**self-sus·tain·ing,** *a.*—**self-sus·tain·ing·-ly,** *adv.*

self-taught, self'tạt', *a.* Taught by oneself without formal instruction; learned by oneself.

self-will, self'wil', self'wil', *n.* Determination to have one's own way; willfulness; obstinacy.—**self-willed,** *a.*—**self-willed·ly,** *adv.*—**self-willed·ness,** *n.*

self-wind·ing, self'wīn'ding, *a.* Winding itself: applied to a timepiece or other mechanism which is wound automatically.

sell, sel, *v.t.*—**sold,** *selling.* [O.E. *sellan* (pret. *sealde*) = *sellian* = M.H.G. *sellen* = Icel. *selja,* give, sell, = Goth. *saljan,* offer, sacrifice; from a noun represented by E. *sale.*] To give possession of, control over, title to, or the services of, to a purchaser for money or other payment; to invite purchase of; to deal in or stock for sale, as a certain commodity; to accept a price or reward for, or make profit or gain on, usu. on an object improper for such use, as a friend or one's soul; to betray for a price or in order to gain some advantage; as, to *sell* a cause; to give up or sacrifice at some cost to an adversary, as one's life or honor. *Colloq.* to cause, though salesmanship, to be accepted, approved, desired, adopted, or purchased by a person or group, used with *to*; as, to *sell* an idea, yourself, or a song *to* the public; to cause through salesmanship to accept, approve, desire, adopt, or purchase something; as, to *sell* the public on a new trend. *Slang,* to cheat, trick, or hoax.—*v.i.* To sell something; to engage in selling commodities; to be on sale at a particular price; as, wool that *sells* for three dollars a yard; to be in demand as an item for purchase, as: Bathing suits *sell* in hot weather. To win acceptance, approval, or adoption when presented by, or as if by salesmanship; as, a look that will *sell*; to accomplish a sale.—*n.* An instance of cheating; a ruse or hoax.—**sell short,** to underrate or undervalue; to sell without having full possession of, while expecting to both profit by the sale and eventually fulfill the terms of sale.

sell·er, sel′ėr, *n.* One who sells; an item for sale, usu. with regard to the speed or volume in which it is sold; as, a car which is a poor *seller.*

sell·ing-plat·er, sel′ing·plā″tėr, *n.* A horse that competes in a selling race.

sell·ing race, *n.* A horse race in which horses are offered for sale after the race at prices stated before the race, and in which the winning horse is sold at auction.

sell off, *v.t., v.i.* To sell at lowered prices for the purpose of disposing of the whole quantity.

sell-off, sel′af″, sel′of″, *n.* A decrease in the value of securities.

sell out, *v.t.* To exhaust or completely dispose of by selling; to sell the goods of, in order to pay creditors; *colloq.* to betray by secret bargain.—*v.i.* To have sold all of one's stock of something. *Colloq.* to quit an agreement or cause; to become a betrayer or traitor.—**sell·out,** sel′out″, *n.* An event, usu. theatrical, musical, or athletic in nature, to which every seat or place has been sold; the operation of selling out.

sel·syn, sel′sin, *n.* An electronic self-synchronizing device which uses a generator to transmit and a motor to receive and duplicate any angular movement. (Trademark.) Also *synchro.*

Selt·zer, selt′sėr, *n.* [From (*Nieder-*)*Selters,* village in Hesse-Nassau, Prussia, with mineral springs.] A natural, effervescent mineral water containing salt and small amounts of sodium, calcium, and magnesium carbonates; (*often l.c.*) a commercial product of similar composition. Also **Selt·zer wa·ter.**

sel·vage, sel·vedge, sel′vij, *n.* [< *self* and *edge*; lit. 'an edge formed of the stuff itself'; cf. D. *zelfkant, zelfegge,* G. *selbende,* lit. 'self-edge, self-end'.] A woven border on a fabric, made of the threads of the fabric, and designed to prevent fraying; that portion of a lock which accommodates the bolt; a border of excess material, as on wallpaper.—**sel·vaged, sel·vedged,** *a.*

se·man·tics, si·man′tiks, *n. pl. but sing. in constr. Ling.* the study of word meanings, esp. as they develop and change. The study of the relationship between signs or symbols and that which they represent; also *significs.* See *general semantics.*—**se·man·tic, se·man·ti·cal,** *a.*—**se·man·ti·cal·ly,** *adv.*—**se·man·ti·cist,** si·man′ti·sist, *n.*

sem·a·phore, sem′a·fōr″, sem′a·fạr″, *n.* [Gr. *sēma,* a sign, and *pherō,* to bear.] An apparatus for conveying visual signals at a distance by moving flags, lights, blades, arms, or the like, into the various positions of a code.—*v.t.*—*semaphored, semaphoring.* To signal by means of a semaphore.—*v.i.*—**sem·a·phor·ic,** sem′a·fạr′ik, sem′a·fōr′ik, *a.*—**sem·a·phor·i·cal,** *a.*—**sem·a·phor·i·cal·ly,** *adv.*

se·ma·si·ol·o·gy, si·mā″sē·ol′o·jē, *n.* [Gr. *sēmasia,* signification (< *sēmainein*).] The branch of philology that deals with semantics, esp. semantic change and development. — **se·ma·si·o·log·i·cal,** si·mā″sē·o·loj′i·kal, si·mā″zē·o·loj′i·kal, *a.*—**se·ma·si·o·log·i·cal·ly,** *adv.*—**se·ma·si·o·lo·gist,** *n.*

se·mat·ic, si·mat′ik, *a.* [Gr. *sēma* (*sēmat-*), sign.] *Zool.* serving as a sign of danger or recognition, as the conspicuous coloring or markings of certain animals.

sem·blance, sem′blans, *n.* [Fr. *semblance,* < *sembler,* to seem, to appear, < L. *similare, simulare,* to make like, < *similis,* like.] Similarity or resemblance; mere external show or appearance; form, figure, image, or likeness; the smallest or flimsiest resemblance. Also **sem·bla·tive.**—**sem·bla·ble,** sem′bla·bl, *a., n.*—**sem·bla·bly,** *adv.*

se·mé, se·mā′, *a.* Sprinkled at regular intervals with the same small design, as fleurs-de-lis on an heraldic coat of arms.

se·men, sē′men, *n.* [L., < root of *sero,* to sow.] The whitish, viscous substance which carries spermatozoa, and is secreted by the male reproductive organs.

se·mes·ter, si·mes′tėr, *n.* [L. *semestris,* half-yearly—*sex,* six, and *mensis,* month.] A period or term of six months; half an academic year, usu. lasting 15 to 18 weeks. —**se·mes·tral, se·mes·tri·al,** si·mes′trē·al, *a.*

sem·i·an·nu·al, sem″ē·an′ū·al, sem″i·an′ū·al, *a.* Occurring or appearing every half-year or twice in a year; lasting for half a year.—**sem·i·an·nu·al·ly,** *adv*

sem·i·a·quat·ic, sem″ē·a·kwat′ik, sem″ē·a·kwot′ik, sem″i·a·kwat′ik, sem″i·a·kwot′ik, *a. Biol.* Partly aquatic; growing or living close to water and sometimes found in or frequenting water.

sem·i·ar·id, sem″ē·ar′id, sem″i·ar′id, *a.* Characterized by scant annual rainfall, usu. between 10 and 20 inches.

sem·i·au·to·mat·ic, sem″ē·a′to·mat″ik, sem″i·a′to·mat″ik, *a.* Partly self-operating; of a firearm, self-loading but requiring a pull on the trigger to fire each shot.—*n.*—**sem·i·au·to·mat·i·cal·ly,** *adv.*

sem·i·au·ton·o·mous, sem″ē·a·ton′o·mus, sem″i·a·ton′o·mus, *a.* Not completely self-governing.

sem·i·base·ment, sem″ē·bās′ment, sem″i·bās′ment, *n.* A basement that extends under only part of the superstructure.

sem·i·breve, sem″ē·brēv′, sem″i·brēv′, *n.* [< *semi* and *breve.*] *Chiefly Brit., mus.* A note of half the duration of the breve; a whole note.

sem·i·cen·te·nar·y, sem″ē·sen′te·ner″ē, sem″i·sen′te·ner″ē, *a.* Semicentennial.—*n.* pl. **sem·i·cen·te·nar·ies.**

sem·i·cen·ten·ni·al, sem″ē·sen·ten′ē·al, sem″i·sen·ten′ē·al, *a.* Occurring at the end of, or celebrating the completion of, fifty years. Also *semicentenary.*—*n.* A semicentennial anniversary or celebration.

sem·i·cir·cle, sem′i·sur″kl, *n.* [L. *semicirculus.*] The half of a circle; the part of a circle comprehended between its diameter and half of its circumference; anything in the form of a half circle.—**sem·i·cir·cu·lar,** sem″i·sur′kya·lėr, *a.*

sem·i·cir·cu·lar ca·nals, *n. pl. Anat.* three curved tubular canals in the labyrinth of the ear, responsible for maintaining equilibrium.

sem·i·civ·i·lized, sem″ē·siv′i·līzd″, sem″i·siv′i·līzd″, *a.* Half or partly civilized.—**sem·i·civ·i·li·za·tion,** sem″ē·siv″i·li·zā′shan, sem″i·siv″i·li·zā′shan, *n.*

sem·i·clas·si·cal, sem″ē·klas′i·kal, sem″i·klas′i·kal, *a.* Being less in quality and importance than the classical. *Mus.* pertaining to or being a classical composition that has become popular through public appeal; pertaining to or being a composition that has characteristics of both classical and popular music.—**sem·i·clas·sic,** *n.*

sem·i·co·lon, sem′i·kō″lon, *n.* [*Semi* and *colon.*] The punctuation sign (;) indicating a separation less definite than a period and more definite than the comma.

sem·i·com·mer·cial, sem″ē·ko·mur′shal, sem″i·ko·mur′shal, *a.* Of or pertaining to limited commercial marketing.

sem·i·con·duc·tor, sem″ē·kon·duk′tėr, sem″i·kon·duk′tėr, *n.* A material having an electrical conductivity intermediate between that of a metal and an insulator, esp. germanium and silicon, and used in making electronic components, as transistors or rectifiers.—**sem·i·con·duct·ing,** *a.*

sem·i·con·scious, sem″ē·kon′shus, sem″i·kon′shus, *a.* Not completely conscious; half conscious.—**sem·i·con·scious·ly,** *adv.* —**sem·i·con·scious·ness,** *n.*

sem·i·des·ert, sem″ē·dez′ėrt, sem″i·dez′ėrt, *n.* A very dry area having many characteristics of a desert, frequently found adjacent a desert.

sem·i·de·tached, sem″ē·di·tacht′, sem″i·di·tacht′, *a.* Partly detached; designating either of two houses joined by one common wall.

sem·i·di·am·e·ter, sem″ē·di·am′i·tėr, sem″i·di·am′i·tėr, *n.* Half a diameter; a radius.

sem·i·di·ur·nal, sem″ē·di·ur′nal, sem″i·di·ur′nal, *a.* Pertaining to, made up of, or accomplished in half a day; continuing half a day; occurring each half day or twice in a day.

sem·i·di·vine, sem″ē·di·vīn′, sem″i·di·vīn′, *a.* Not quite divine, but more godlike than mortal.

sem·i·doc·u·men·ta·ry, sem″ē·dok″ū·men′ta·rē, sem″i·dok″ū·men′ta·rē, *a.* Combining fact with fiction, as a motion picture that presents a true story outline against a fictional background, or vice versa.—*n.*

sem·i·dome, sem′ē·dōm″, sem′i·dōm″, *n. Arch.* half a dome, esp. as formed by a vertical section over a semicircular enclosure or room.—**sem·i·domed,** *a.*

sem·i·do·mes·ti·ca·tion, sem″ē·do·mes″ti·kā′shan, sem″i·do·mes″ti·kā′shan, *n.* A condition of partial domestication, as of wild animals in a zoo whose living habits and surroundings are modified by man.—**sem·i·do·mes·ti·cat·ed,** *a.*

sem·i·dry, sem″ē·drī′, sem″i·drī′, *a.* Partially or not completely dry; somewhat damp.—**sem·i·dry·ing,** *a.*

sem·i·el·lip·ti·cal, sem″ē·i·lip′ti·kal, sem″i·i·lip′ti·kal, *a.* Shaped like the half of an ellipse, esp. like one which is cut transversely.—**sem·i·el·lipse,** sem″ē·i·lips′, sem″i·i·lips′, *n.*—**sem·i·el·lip·tic,** *a.*

sem·i·e·rect, sem″ē·i·rekt′, sem″i·i·rekt′, *a.* Not fully erect; slouchy; drooping.

sem·i·fi·nal, sem″ē·fīn′al, sem″i·fīn′al, *a. Sports,* designating or pertaining to a round, contest, or match which immediately precedes the final and decisive one, as in a tournament.—*n. Often pl.* a semifinal round, contest, match, or the like.—**sem·i·fi·nal·ist,** sem″ē·fīn′a·list, sem″i·fīn′a·list, *n.*

sem·i·fin·ished, sem″ē·fin′isht, sem″i·fin′isht, *a.* Incomplete or partially finished; existing in a state suitable for working to completion, as some manufactured products.

sem·i·fit·ted, sem″ē·fit′id, sem″i·fit′id, *a.* Designed to follow the shape of the body without fitting tightly, as a dress, jacket, or coat.

sem·i·flex·i·ble, sem″ē·flek′si·bl, sem″i·flek′si·bl, *a.* Partially flexible.

sem·i·flu·id, sem″ē·flō′id, sem″i·flō′id, *a.* Imperfectly fluid; able to flow, but heavy and viscous.—*n.* Semiliquid.

sem·i·for·mal, sem″ē·fạr′mal, sem″i·fạr′mal, *a.* Partially or moderately formal.

sem·i·fos·sil, sem″ē·fos′il, sem″i·fos′il, *a.* Partially fossilized.—**sem·i·fos·sil·ized,** *a.*

sem·i·glob·u·lar, sem″ē·glob′ya·lėr, sem″ē·glob′ū·lėr, sem″i·glob′ya·lėr, sem″i·glob′ū·lėr, *a.* Hemispherical in shape.

sem·i·gloss, sem″ē·glos′, sem″ē·glạs′, sem″i·glos′, sem″i·glạs′, *a.* Having a low gloss or luster.

sem·i·gov·ern·men·tal, sem″ē·guv″ėrn·men′tal, sem″i·guv″ėrn·men′tal, *a.*

Possessing some governmental powers or functions.

sem·i·in·de·pend·ent, sem″ē·in″di·-pen′dent, sem″ī·in″di·pen′dent, a. Partially autonomous.

sem·i·in·di·rect, sem″ē·in″di·rekt′, sem″-ē·in″di·rekt′, sem″ī·in″di·rekt′, sem″ī·-in″di·rekt′, a. Lighting. Permitting the passage of some direct light but reflecting a large share of it; translucent.

sem·i·leg·end·ar·y, sem″ē·lej′en·der″ē, sem″ī·lej′en·der″ē, a. Partially legendary in character or reputation.

sem·i·liq·uid, sem″ē·lik′wid, sem″ī·lik′-wid, a. Imperfectly liquid; semifluid.—n. A semiliquid substance.

sem·i·lit·er·ate, sem″ē·lit′ẽr·it, sem″ī·-lit′ẽr·it, a. Having minimal reading and writing skills; having the ability to read but not to write.

sem·i·lu·nar, sem″ē·lö′nẽr, sem″ī·lö′nẽr, a. [L. semi, half, and luna, the moon.] Resembling in form a half moon; crescent.

sem·i·lu·nar valve, n. Anat. one of two valves located at the entrance to the aorta and to the pulmonary artery, having three crescentic cusps which prevent regurgitation of blood into the ventricles of the heart.

sem·i·man·u·fac·tures, sem″ē·man″-ū·fak′chẽrz, sem″ī·man″ū fak′chẽrz, n. pl. but sing. in constr. Products such as leather, steel, or synthetic fabrics, which are manufactured from raw materials and then used in the making of other finished products.—**sem·i·man·u·fac·tured,** a.

sem·i·mat, sem″ē·mat′, sem″ī·mat′, a. Having a light gloss or luster, as paint. Also **sem·i·matt,** **sem·i·matte.**

sem·i·mo·nas·tic, sem″ē·mo·nas′tik, sem″ī·mo·nas′tik, a. Having certain features of monastic orders.

sem·i·month·ly, sem″ē·munth′lē, sem″-ī·munth′lē, a. Occurring or appearing every half month.—n. pl. **sem·i·month·-lies.** A semi-monthly publication; anything happening every half month or two times a month.—adv. Every half month.

sem·i·mys·ti·cal, sem″ē·mis′ti·kal, sem″-ī·mis′ti·kal, a. Having certain of the qualities of mystics or mysticism.

sem·i·nal, sem′i·nal, a. [L. seminalis, < semen, seed, < stem of sero, to sow.] Pertaining to or consisting of seed or semen; having the power of future development; germinal; acting as a source; influencing later developments; as, a seminal writer.—**sem·i·nal·ly,** adv.

sem·i·nar, sem′i·när′, n. [G., < L. seminarium, E. seminary.] A group of students, as in a university, engaged in advanced study and original research under an instructor; a course of study so arranged; a room where such a course is taught.

sem·i·nar·i·an, sem″ī·nâr′ē·an, n. A member of or a student in a religious seminary.

sem·i·nar·y, sem′i·ner″ē, n. pl. **sem·i·-nar·ies.** [L. seminarium, < semen, seminis, seed.] A school, college, or university in which men are instructed in preparation to be rabbis, priests, or ministers; a place of education, esp. for girls; an area where something originates or grows.

sem·i·nif·er·ous, sem″ī·nif′ẽr·us, a. [L. semen, and fero, to produce.] Seed-bearing; producing or bearing semen.

sem·i·niv·or·ous, sem″ī·niv′ẽr·us, a. Seed-eating.

Sem·i·nole, sem′i·nōl″, n. pl. **Sem·i·nole, Sem·i·noles.** Any of a tribe of the Muskhogean family, closely related to Choctaws, Chickasaws, and Creeks, belonging to the Hokan-Siouan language group of American Indians, and now residing in Florida and Oklahoma; the language spoken by the tribe.—a. Of or relating to the tribe or their language.

sem·i·no·mad, sem″ē·nō′mad, sem″ē·-nom′ad, sem″ī·nō′mad, sem″ī·nom′ad, n. One of a people that migrates to a limited degree, as seasonally, but returns to a base camp where some crops or livestock are raised.—**sem·i·no·mad·ic,** sem″ē·nō·-mad′ik, sem″ī·nō·mad′ik, a.

sem·i·of·fi·cial, sem″ē·o·fish′al, sem″ī·-o·fish′al, a. Partly official; having some degree of official authority.—**sem·i·of·-fi·cial·ly,** adv.

sem·i·o·paque, sem″ē·ō·pāk′, sem″ī·ō·-pāk′, a. Almost opaque; partly opaque; barely translucent.

se·mi·ot·ic, se·mei·ot·ic, sē″mē·ot′ik, sē″mi·ot′ik, sem″ē·ot′ik, sem″ī·ot′ik, a. [Gr. sēmeiōtikós, < sēmeion, sign, < sēma, sign: cf. sematic.] Pertaining to signs or symptoms; symptomatic.—**se·mi·ot·-ics, se·mei·ot·ics,** n. pl. but sing. in constr. A general theory of signs and their use in languages, and including pragmatics, syntactics, and semantics.—**se·mi·ot·i·cal,** a.—**se·mi·o·ti·cian,** n.

sem·i·pal·mate, sem″ē·pal′māt, sem″ē·-pal′mit, sem″ī·pal′māt, sem″ī·pal′mit, a. Partially or imperfectly palmate, as a bird's foot; half-webbed. Also **sem·i·pal·mat·ed.** —**sem·i·pal·ma·tion,** n.

sem·i·par·a·sit·ic, sem″ē·par″a·sit′ik, sem″ī·par″a·sit′ik, a. Biol. commonly functioning as a parasite but also capable of deriving nourishment from dead organic matter.—**sem·i·par·a·site,** sem″ē·par′a·-sīt′, sem″ī·par′a·sīt′, n.—**sem·i·par·a·-sit·ism,** sem″ē·par′a·sī″tiz·um, sem″ī·-par′a·sī″tiz·um, n.

sem·i·per·ma·nent, sem″ē·pur′ma·-nent, sem″ī·pur′ma·nent, a. Permanent in certain ways; lasting indefinitely.

sem·i·per·me·a·ble, sem″ē·pur′mē·a·-bl, sem″ī·pur′mē·a·bl, a. Permeable only to certain substances, as a membrane that permits the passage of a solvent but not the solute.

sem·i·po·lit·i·cal, sem″ē·po·lit′i·kal, sem″ī·po·lit′i·kal, a. Having or relating to features or activities partially political in nature.

sem·i·por·ce·lain, sem″ē·pôr′se·lin, sem″ē·par′se·lin, sem″ē·pôrs′lin, sem″ē·-pars′lin, sem″ī·pôr′se·lin, sem″ī·par′se·lin, sem″ī·pôrs′lin, sem″ī·pars′lin, n. An inferior grade of porcelain, being less translucent than true porcelain and often having an uneven surface; earthenware made to resemble porcelain.

sem·i·post·al, sem″ē·pōs′tal, sem″ī·pōs′-tal, n. A type of postage stamp issued and sold by a government for a premium price over face value, the excess proceeds going usu. to a charity.—a.

sem·i·pre·cious, sem″ē·presh′us, sem″ī·-presh′us, a. Of or belonging to a class of gems, as the amethyst and garnet, ranked below such precious gems as the diamond and ruby.

sem·i·pri·vate, sem″ē·prī′vit, sem″ī·prī′-vit, a. Somewhat but not completely private, as a hospital room containing two or three beds.

sem·i·pro·fes·sion·al, sem″ē·pro·fesh′-a·nal, sem″ī·pro·fesh′a·nal, a. Engaged in some sport or other activity for pay but only as a part-time occupation; engaged in by part-time paid players or members; resembling professional work but demanding less skill, knowledge, and the like.—n.—**sem·i·pro,** sem″ē·prō″, sem″ī·prō″, a., n. Colloq. semiprofessional.—**sem·i·pro·fes·-sion·al·ly,** adv.

sem·i·pub·lic, sem″ē·pub′lik, sem″ī·pub′-lik, a. Partly or to some degree available to the public; as, a semipublic golf course.

sem·i·qua·ver, sem″ē·kwā″vẽr, n. Brit., mus. A note of half the duration of a quaver; a sixteenth note.

sem·i·re·li·gious, sem″ē·ri·lij′us, sem″-i·ri·lij′us, a. Having somewhat religious characteristics.

sem·i·rig·id, sem″ē·rij′id, sem″ī·rij′id, a. Partly rigid; aeron. designating or pertaining to a type of airship whose shape is maintained by means of a rigid keellike structure, as a dirigible balloon.

sem·i·sa·cred, sem″ē·sā′krid, sem″ī·sā′-krid, a. Somewhat religious in character.

sem·i·sed·en·tar·y, sem″ē·sed′en·ter″ē, sem″ī·sed′en·ter″ē, a. Partially settled in one position or place as by requirement or habit; zool. pertaining to animals which live attached to a substratum most of the time but are also capable of moving around, as a sea anemone.

sem·i·skilled, sem″ē·skild′, sem″ī·skild′, a. Having or requiring some degree of skill but not as much as skilled labor.

sem·i·soft, sem″ē·saft′, sem″ē·soft′, sem″-i·saft′, sem″ī·soft′, a. Of a moderately soft consistency.

sem·i·sol·id, sem″ē·sol′id, sem″ī·sol′id, a. Partially solid; of a somewhat firm consistency; extremely viscous.—n. A semisolid substance.

Sem·ite, sem′īt, Brit. sē′mīt, n. [N.L. Semita, < L.L. Sem, < Gr. Sēm, Shem.] A member of a group of Caucasian peoples said to be descended from Shem, son of Noah, now comprising chiefly the Hebrews and Arabians, but formerly also including the Babylonians, Canaanites, Assyrians, Phoenicians, and others of southwestern Asia.

sem·i·ter·res·tri·al, sem″ē·te·res′trē·-al, sem″ī·te·res′trē·al, a. Biol. Living part of the time on land; growing in marshy areas.

Se·mit·ic, se·mit′ik, a. Of or pertaining to the Semites or their languages.—n. The Semitic branch of the Afro-Asian family of languages, including Hebrew, Phoenician, Aramaic, Akkadian, Arabic, and Ambaric.

Se·mit·ics, se·mit′iks, n. pl. but sing. in constr. The study of the Semitic languages, literature, and culture.—**Sem·i·tist, Sem·-it·i·cist,** sem′i·tist, Brit. sē′mi·tist, n.

Sem·i·tism, sem′i·tiz″um, Brit. sē′mi·-tiz″um, n. Semitic character or characteristics, esp. the ways, ideas, or influence of the Jewish people; a Semitic word or idiom, esp. in Hebrew.

sem·i·tone, sem″ē·tōn″, n. Mus. An interval one half the distance of a whole step; the interval of a minor second. Also half step, half tone.—**sem·i·ton·al, sem·i·ton·ic,** sem″ī·tōn′al, sem″ī·ton′ik, a.

sem·i·trail·er, sem′i·trā′lẽr, n. A freight carrier having only rear wheels and supported in front by its connection to a truck tractor; the entire apparatus, including tractor and trailer. Also **sem·i,** sem′ī.

sem·i·trans·lu·cent, sem″ē·trans·lö′-sent, sem″ē·tranz·lö′sent, sem″ī·trans·lö′-sent, sem″ī·tranz·lö′sent, a. Imperfectly translucent.

sem·i·trans·par·ent, sem″ē·trans·pâr′-ent, sem″ē·trans·par′ent, sem″ī·trans·pâr′-ent, sem″ī·trans·par′ent, a. Half or imperfectly transparent or clear; translucent.

sem·i·trop·ics, sem″ē·trop′iks, sem″ī·-trop′iks, n. pl. but sing. in constr. Subtropics.—**sem·i·trop·ic, sem·i·trop·i·-cal,** sem″ē·trop′ik, sem″ī·trop′i·kal, a.

sem·i·vow·el, sem″ē·vou″el, n. Phon. a sound having the sonorous quality of a vowel, but lacking the duration, distinction, and central position of a vowel, as w in wish, r in red, and y in yellow; a letter signifying a semivowel.

sem·i·week·ly, sem″ē·wēk′lē, sem″ī·-wēk′lē, a. Occurring or appearing every half week.—n. pl. **sem·i·week·lies.** A semiweekly publication.—adv. Every half week.

sem·i·year·ly, sem″ē·yēr′lē, sem″i·yēr′lē, *a.* Occurring half-yearly or twice yearly.— *adv.* Twice yearly; half-yearly.

sem·o·li·na, sem″o·lē′na, *n.* [It. *semolino.*] The milled grains of durum wheat, used for making macaroni.

sem·pi·ter·nal, sem″pi·tŭr′nal, *a.* [Fr. *sempiternel,* L. *sempiternus—semper,* always, and *eternus,* eternal.] Eternal; everlasting; having beginning but no end.—**sem·pi·ter·nal·ly,** *adv.*—**sem·pi·ter·ni·ty,** *n.*

sem·pli·ce, sem′pli·chā, *It.* sem′plē·che, *a. Mus.* Simple; played with as little elaboration or sentiment as possible.—*adv.*

sem·pre, sem′prā, *It.* sem′pRe, *adv.* [It., 'always.'] *Mus.* throughout.

semp·stress, semp′stris, sem′tris, *n.* Seamstress.

sen·a·ry, sen′a·rē, *a.* [L. *senarius,* < *seni,* six each, < *sex,* six.] Of, pertaining to, or containing six.

sen·ate, sen′it, *n.* [O.Fr. *senat* (Fr. *sénat*), < L. *senatus,* council of elders, senate, < *senex,* old.] An assembly or council having the highest deliberative and legislative powers in a government; (*cap.*) the upper of the two houses in various legislatures, as in France, Canada, the U.S., or individual states of the U.S.; a governing, advisory, or disciplinary body composed of representative students and faculty members in certain colleges and universities; the supreme council of state in ancient Rome.

sen·a·tor, sen′a·tĕr, *n.* (*Often cap.*) a member of a senate. Abbr. *sen.,* Sen.

sen·a·to·ri·al, sen″a·tōr′ē·al, sen″a·tąr′ē·al, *a.* Composed of, pertaining to, or worthy of a senator or senate; entitled to elect a senator.—**sen·a·to·ri·al·ly,** *adv.*

sen·a·to·ri·al cour·te·sy, *n.* A tradition by which the U.S. Senate will not confirm an appointee of the President if the appointee is from a state in which both senators, or one senator of the President's party is opposed to the appointment.

sen·a·to·ri·al dis·trict, *n.* One of a definite number of divisions in a state, each of which is entitled to election of and representation by one senator in the state legislature.

sen·a·tor·ship, sen′a·tĕr·ship″, *n.* The office, status, or term of a senator.

send, send, *v.t.*—*sent, sending.* [O.E. *sendan* = D. *zenden* = G. *senden* = Icel. *senda* = Goth. *sandjan,* send, causative from a root meaning 'go': cf. O.E. *sīth,* a going, journey.] To cause, as a person, to go; to enable to go, as: They *sent* him to college. To cause to be conveyed or transmitted; to direct, order, or compel to go; to drive, impel, throw, or deliver, as a ball, blow, or the like; to drive or bring, as a person, into a certain condition; as, to send one mad; to emit or discharge, as light, odor, or sound, usu. followed by *forth* or *out;* *slang,* to thrill, exhilarate, or excite.—*v.i.* To dispatch a messenger, agent, or message.—**send down,** to compel to leave a university; expel or suspend.—**send for,** to request by message to come or to be brought.—**send in,** to dispatch to a central destination, as entries in a competition.—**send out,** to put into circulation; distribute; to dispatch from a central place.—**send pack·ing,** to dismiss in an abrupt way; to send off in disgrace.—**send up,** *colloq.* to sentence to a term of imprisonment.—**send·er,** *n.*

send, send, *n. Naut.* the driving impulse of a wave or waves upon a ship.—*v.i.*—*sent, sending. Naut.* scend.

sen·dal, sen′dal, *n.* [O.Fr. *cendal;* L.L. *cendalum,* < Gr. *sindon,* a fine Indian cloth, < *Sindhu,* the river Indus.] A light, thin fabric of silk, used for church vestments and other fine clothing in the Middle Ages.

send-off, send′ạf″, send′of″, *n. Colloq.* A friendly demonstration in honor of a person setting out on a journey, course, career, or the like; a start given to a person or thing.

Sen·e·ca, sen′e·ka, *n.* pl. **Sen·e·cas, Sen·e·ca.** An Iroquois Indian tribe which formerly inhabited western New York and was the largest and most warlike of the Five Nations confederation; the language spoken by this and other Iroquois tribes.

sen·e·ga snake·root, *n.* [N.L., for *seneca,* so called from the *Seneca* Indians.] A milkwort, *Polygala senega,* of the northeastern U.S.; also **Sen·e·ca snake·root.** The root of this plant, which is used medicinally as an expectorant and diuretic; also **sen·e·ga.**

se·nes·cence, se·nes′ens, *n.* [L. *senesco,* < *senex,* old.] The state of growing old.— —**se·nes·cent,** *a.*

se·nhor, sin·yōr′, sin·yąr′, *Pg.* si·nyąr′, *n.* pl. **se·nhors,** *Pg.* **se·nho·res,** *Pg.* si·nyą′Rish. [Pg., < L. *senior.*] *Pg.* A gentleman; a term of address meaning *sir* or *mister;* (*cap.*) a title of respect; as, *Senhor* Soares de Oliveira. Abbr. *Sr.*

se·nho·ra, sin·yōr′a, sin·yąr′a, *Pg.* si·nyą′Ra, *n.* pl. **se·nho·ras,** sin·yōr′az, sin·yąr′az, *Pg.* si·nyą′Rash. [Pg.] *Pg.* A married lady; a term of address for a married lady meaning madam or mistress; (*cap.*) a title of respect.

se·nho·ri·ta, sēn″yo·rē′ta, sän″yo·rē′ta, *Pg.* se″nyą·Rē′ta, *n.* pl. **se·nho·ri·tas,** sēn″yo·rē′taz, sän″yo·rē′taz, *Pg.* se″nyą·Rē′tash. [Pg., dim. of *senhora.*] *Pg.* A young lady; a term of address for an unmarried lady; a title of respect.

se·nile, sē′nīl, sē′nil, sen′īl, *a.* [L. *senilis,* < *senex,* old.] Pertaining to old age; proceeding from age; characterized by the weakness of old age, esp. to a decline in mental faculties; *phys. geog.* nearing the close of a particular erosion cycle.—**se·nile·ly,** *adv.*

se·nil·i·ty, si·nil′i·tē, *n.* The state of being senile; old age, esp. the infirmity of age; dotage.

sen·ior, sēn′yĕr, *a.* [L., older, elder (as n., an elder, elderly person), compar. of *senex* (gen. *senis*), old, akin to Gr. *enos,* Skt. *sana,* Goth. *sineigs,* old: cf. *seignior, senhor, senor, signor,* and *sire.*] Older or elder, often abbreviated and used following the name of a person who is the older of two persons bearing the name; as, John Smith, *Sr.;* of earlier date; ranking before others by virtue of tenure in office, position, or service; of higher rank or standing; noting or pertaining to the highest class or the final year of the course, as in universities, colleges, and high schools.—*n.* A person who is older than another; an aged person; one ranking before others by virtue of tenure; one of higher rank or standing; a member of the highest class in a university, college, or high school. Abbr. *Sr., sr.*

sen·ior chief pet·ty of·fi·cer, *n. Navy,* a noncommissioned officer next highest in rank to a master chief petty officer.

sen·ior cit·i·zen, *n.* An elderly person, esp. one sixty-five years or older whose income is derived, in whole or in part, from a pension.

sen·ior high school, *n.* A high school comprised of grades 10 through 12 or grades 9 through 12.

sen·ior·i·ty, sēn·yąr′i·tē, sēn·yor′i·tē, *n.* State of being senior; superior age; priority of birth; priority due to length of service or superiority in rank or office.

sen·na, sen′a, *n.* [Ar. *senā,* senna.] Any of various leguminous herbs, shrubs, or trees of the genus *Cassia;* the dried leaflets of various species of these plants, esp. *C. acutifolia* and *C. angustifolia,* used as a laxative medicine.

sen·net, sen′it, *n.* [Appar. a var. of *signet,* in old sense of 'signal.'] A particular set of tones on a trumpet or cornet: ordered in stage directions of Elizabethan plays, as upon a ceremonial entrance or exit.

sen·night, sen′it, sen′it, *n.* [M.E. *sennygt, sevenygt,* < O.E. *seofon niht,* seven nights: cf. *fortnight.*] *Archaic,* a week. Also **se′n·night.**

sen·nit, sen′it, *n.* [< *seven* and *knit.*] A sort of flat braided cordage formed by plaiting rope yarns, used on ships; a grass or straw plait for making hats.

se·ñor, sān·yōr′, sän·yąr′, sēn·yōr′, sēn·-yąr′, *Sp.* se·nyąr′, *n.* pl. **se·ñors,** *Sp.* **se·ño·res,** *Sp.* se·nyą′Res. [Sp., < L. *senior.*] *Sp.* A gentleman; as a term of address, sir; (*cap.*) as a title, Mr. Abbr. *Sr.*

se·ño·ra, sān·yōr′a, sän·yąr′a, sēn·yōr′a, sēn·yąr′a, *Sp.* se·nyą′Rä, *n.* pl. **se·no·ras,** sän·yōr′az, sän·yąr′az, sēn·yōr′az, sēn·-yąr′az, *Sp.* se·nyą′Räs. [Sp.] *Sp.* A lady, usu. married or elderly; as a term of address, madam; (*cap.*) as a title, Mrs. Abbr. *Sra.*

se·ño·ri·ta, sān″yo·rē′ta, sēn″yo·rē′ta, *Sp.* se·nyą·Rē′tä, *n.* pl. **se·no·ri·tas,** sān″yo·rē′taz, sēn″yo·rē′taz, *Sp.* se·nyą·Rē′täs. [Sp., dim. of señora.] *Sp.* A young lady, esp. unmarried; as a term of address, miss; (*cap.*) as a title, Miss. Abbr. *Srta.*

sen·sate, sen′sāt, *a.* [Back formation < *sensation.*] Perceived by a sense or the senses.

sen·sa·tion, sen·sā′shan, *n.* [Fr. *sensation,* L.L. *sensatio,* < L. *sentio, sensum,* to feel, to perceive.] An impression made upon the mind through the medium of one of the organs of sense; a conscious experience resulting from sensory stimulation, as seeing, hearing, or kinesthesis; *physiol.* the power of feeling or receiving impressions. A nonlocalized feeling arising from intrapsychic sources and not dependent upon bodily stimulation; as, a *sensation* of awe; a state of excitement or heightened interest, esp. in a group or among a number of people; something that produces excited interest or feeling.

sen·sa·tion·al, sen·sā′sha·nal, *a.* Relating to sensation or the senses; producing excited interest or emotion, esp. when superficial; startling or exciting; exceedingly good or excellent.—**sen·sa·tion·al·ly,** *adv.*

sen·sa·tion·al·ism, sen·sā′sha·na·liz″-um, *n.* Something, as language, subject matter, or style, able to cause striking or shocking impressions or to excite interest; *philos.* the theory or doctrine that all our ideas are solely derived through our senses; *ethics,* the theory of judging good only by the satisfaction of the senses.—**sen·sa·tion·al·ist,** *n.*—**sen·sa·tion·al·is·tic,** *a.*

sense, sens, *n.* [= Fr. *sens,* < L. *sensus,* < *sentire* (pp. *sensus*), perceive, feel: cf. *scent, sentence, sentiment, resent.*] Any of the special faculties connected with bodily organs by which man and other animals perceive external objects and their own bodily changes, as sight, hearing, smell, taste, and touch; these faculties collectively; their operation or function; sensation;' a feeling or perception produced through the organs of touch, taste, and the like, or resulting from a particular condition of some part of the body; as, a *sense* of cold; any special capacity for perception, estimation, or appreciation; as, an esthetic *sense; usu. pl.* clear or sound mental faculties, as: He has lost his *senses.* Any more or less vague perception or impression of something; sound practical intelligence; what is sensible or reasonable; meaning, substance, or signification; the meaning or one of the meanings of a word or phrase;

an opinion or judgment formed or held by an assemblage or body of persons; as, the *sense* of a meeting; *math.* either of two directly opposite ways in which a line, surface, or the like, may be generated, described, or conceived.—*v.t.*—*sensed, sensing.* To perceive through the senses; become aware of; to comprehend or understand.

sense da·tum, *n.* pl. **sense da·ta.** *Psychol.* What is experienced as a direct result of the stimulation of a sense receptor; an object of sensation.

sense·less, sens′lis, *a.* Destitute or deprived of sensation; in a state of unconsciousness; destitute of mental perception or appreciation; stupid or foolish, as persons or their actions; nonsensical or meaningless, as words.—**sense·less·ly,** *adv.*—**sense··less·ness,** *n.*

sense or·gan, *n.* A specialized organ, such as the nose, ear, or eye, that is sensitive to or registers external stimuli; a receptor.

sen·si·bil·i·ty, sen″si·bil′i·tē, *n.* pl. **sen··si·bil·i·ties,** The state or quality of being sensible or capable of sensation; the capacity to experience emotion or feeling; delicacy or keenness of feeling; as, an artistic *sensibility*; quick emotion, esp. for the pathetic; that quality of an instrument which makes it indicate very slight changes of condition; as, the *sensibility* of a thermometer.

sen·si·ble, sen′si·bl, *a.* [Fr. *sensible,* L. *sensibilis,* < *sensus.*] Possessing or containing sense, judgment, or reason; as, a *sensible* remark; having good or sound sense; reasonable; judicious; capable of perceiving or having perception either by the senses or intellect; cognizant of; aware; persuaded, usu. followed by *of*; as, *sensible of* his problem; of sufficient magnitude or quantity to excite sensation; perceptible; felt; as, *sensible* cold; capable of sensation or impression, as: The eye is *sensible* to light. Capable of emotional influences; liable to impression or emotion; conscious.—**sen··si·ble·ness,** *n.*—**sen·si·bly,** *adv.*

sen·si·tive, sen′si·tiv, *a.* [Fr. *sensitif,* L.L. *sensitivus.*] Having the capacity to receive impressions from external influences; having feelings easily excited; readily and acutely affected; of keen sensibility; pertaining to work or operations of a highly delicate, secretive, or precarious nature, as: He was in a *sensitive* position. Readily affected by or responsive to the action of appropriate agents; as, photographic paper that is *sensitive* to light; easily affected, moved, or liable to change; as, a *sensitive* balance.—**sen·si·tive·ly,** *adv.*—**sen·si··tive·ness,** *n.*

sen·si·tive plant, *n.* A tropical American plant, *Mimosa pudica,* cultivated in greenhouses, with bipinnate leaves whose leaflets fold together when touched; any of various other plants showing sensitiveness to touch.

sen·si·tiv·i·ty, sen″si·tiv′i·tē, *n.* pl. **sen··si·tiv·i·ties.** The state of being sensitive; *physiol.* the state of being readily affected by the action of appropriate chemical or other agents; readiness of muscles or nerves to respond to stimuli; *elect.* the extent to which a radio device responds to incoming signals.

sen·si·tize, sen′si·tīz, *v.t.*—*sensitized, sensitizing.* [< (*sensit*)*ive* and *-ize.*] To render sensitive; *photog.* to render, as a plate or film, sensitive to the influence of light.—*v.i.* To be rendered sensitive.—**sen·si·ti·za··tion,** *n.*—**sen·si·tiz·er,** *n.*

sen·si·tom·e·ter, sen″si·tom′i·tèr, *n.* [< (*sensit*)*ive* and *-meter.*] *Photog.* an apparatus or device for determining the degree of sensitiveness of plates or film to light through a series of increasing exposure tests.—**sen·si·to·met·ric,** sen″si·tō·me′-trik, *a.*—**sen·si·tom·e·try,** *n.*

sen·sor, sen′sèr, *n. Electron.* that which is capable of receiving and responding to a stimulus, esp. a mechanism, as an electric eye.

sen·so·ri·mo·tor, sen″so·rē·mō′tèr, *a. Psychol.* pertaining to an act whose nature depends primarily upon the motor reaction to sensory stimuli; *physiol.* having both sensory and motor attributes, as a mixed nerve. Also **sen·so·mo·tor,** sen″so·mō′tèr.

sen·so·ri·um, sen·sōr′ē·um, sen·sȯr′ē-um, *n.* pl. **sen·so·ri·ums, sen·so·ri·a,** sen·sōr′ē·a, sen·sȯr′ē·a. [L.L., < L. *sentire,* perceive, feel.] *Anat.* The supposed seat of sensation in the brain; the whole sensory apparatus of the body.

sen·so·ry, sen′so·rē, *a.* Relating to the sensorium or to sensation; conveying sense impulses; as, *sensory* nerves. Also **sen··so·ri·al,** sen·sōr′ē·al, sen·sȯr′ē·al.

sen·su·al, sen′shö·al, *a.* [L. *sensualis,* < *sensus,* sense.] Pertaining to the body and the physical senses as distinguished from those of the spirit; carnal; pertaining to excessive gratification of physical appetites; voluptuous; indulging in lust; grossly luxurious; lacking moral or spiritual inhibitions; pertaining to sensualism as a philosophical doctrine.—**sen·su·al·i·ty,** sen′shö·al′i·tē, *n.*—**sen·su·al·ly,** *adv.*

sen·su·al·ism, sen′shö·a·liz″um, *n.* A state of subjection to the sensual appetites; sensuality; a kind of sensationalism.—**sen·su·al·ist,** sen′shö·a·list, *n.*—**sen·su··al·is·tic,** *a.*

sen·su·al·ize, sen′shö·a·līz″, *v.t.*—*sensualized, sensualizing.* To make sensual; to debase by carnal gratifications.—**sen·su··al·i·za·tion,** *n.*

sen·su·ous, sen′shö·us, *a.* Pertaining to the senses; appealing to the senses, esthetically as well as physically; readily affected through the senses; alive to the pleasure to be received through the senses; as, a *sensuous* nature.—**sen·su·ous·ly,** *adv.*—**sen·su·ous·ness,** *n.*

sen·tence, sen′tens, *n.* [L. *sententia,* an opinion, a judgment, a maxim, a sentence, < *sentio,* to perceive.] *Gram.* a group of interrelated words consisting of a subject and predicate, expressed or implied, with or without modifiers, which conveys or implies a complete thought or emotion and which may be declarative, exclamatory, interrogative, or imperative in construction or mood. *Law,* a judgment or decision arrived at by a judge or court in a criminal proceeding, formally pronounced upon the defendant following his conviction and designating the punishment imposed; the punishment so inflicted.—*v.t.*—*sentenced, sentencing.* To pronounce sentence or judgment on; to condemn or doom to punishment.—**sen·ten·tial,** sen·ten′shal, *a.*—**sen·ten·tial·ly,** *adv.*

sen·tence frag·ment, *n.* A group of words usu. having the pitch pattern of a sentence, but lacking one or both necessary parts of speech.

sen·tence stress, *n. Phon.* the arrangement of stresses in a sentence. Also **sen·tence ac·cent.**

sen·ten·tial func·tion, *n. Logic,* an expression containing one or more variables that becomes a meaningful sentence if constants supplant the variables.

sen·ten·tious, sen·ten′shus, *a.* [L. *sententiosus,* Fr. *sentencieux.*] Abounding in axioms, maxims, or epigrams; employing pious, often pretentious language; pithy; terse.—**sen·ten·tious·ly,** *adv.*—**sen·ten··tious·ness,** *n.*

sen·tience, sen′shens, *n.* The state of being sentient; the capability for perceiving or feeling; consciousness without involving thought. Also **sen·tien·cy.**

sen·tient, sen′shent, *a.* [L. *sentiens, sen-*

tientis, ppr. of *sentio,* to perceive.] Capable of perceiving or feeling; having the faculty of perception; conscious.—*n.* Something or someone who is sentient; the perceptive or conscious mind.—**sen·tient·ly,** *adv.*

sen·ti·ment, sen′ti·ment, *n.* [Fr. *sentiment,* L.L. *sentimentum,* < L. *sentio,* to perceive.] A thought prompted by feeling; a feeling or attitude respecting some person or thing; *often pl.* a particular disposition of mind in view of some subject, as: Those are my *sentiments* on the matter. A tendency to be swayed by feeling; emotion; sensibility, esp. that which is refined or artistic; the thought or opinion contained in words, but considered as distinct from them.

sen·ti·men·tal, sen″ti·men′tal, *a.* Having or pertaining to emotion or sentiment; apt to be swayed by sentiment; manifesting an excess of sentiment; artificially or mawkishly tender; appealing to sentiment rather than to reason.—**sen·ti·men·tal·ly,** *adv.*

sen·ti·men·tal·i·ty, sen″ti·men·tal′i·tē, *n.* pl. **sen·ti·men·tal·i·ties.** A sentimental condition or quality, often to excess; the affectation of fine feeling or exquisite sensibility; any sentimental expression.—**sen·ti·men·tal·ism,** sen″ti·men′ta·liz″-um, *n.*—**sen·ti·men·tal·ist,** sen″ti·men′-ta·list, *n.*

sen·ti·men·tal·ize, sen″ti·men′ta·līz″, *v.i.*—*sentimentalized, sentimentalizing.* To indulge in or act with sentiment.—*v.t.* To regard sentimentally, as a thing or person; to form into that which is sentimental.—**sen·ti·men·ta·li·za·tion,** *n.*

sen·ti·nel, sen′ti·nel, *n.* [Fr. *sentinelle;* It. *sentinella;* origin doubtful.] One who watches or keeps guard; a sentry.—*v.t.*—*sentineled, sentineling,* esp. *Brit. sentinelled, sentinelling.* To watch over as a sentinel; to furnish with a sentinel or sentinels; to appoint as sentinel.

sen·try, sen′trē, *n.* pl. **sen·tries.** [Corruption of *sentinel.*] One placed on guard, as at a gate or other entrance, to prevent unauthorized persons from passing, or to warn of any danger; a guard or watch.

sen·try box, *n.* A small shed to cover and shelter a sentry at his post.

se·pal, sē′pal, *n.* [< Fr. *sépale,* < N.L. *sepalum,* irreg. < Gr. *scépē,* a covering.] One of the divisions or parts of the calyx of a flower.—**se·paled, se·palled,** *a.*—**sep··a·lous,** *a.*

se·pal·oid, sē′pa·loid″, sep′a·loid, *a.* Resembling or acting like a sepal.

sep·a·ra·ble, sep′èr·a·bl, sep′ra·bl, *a.* [L. *separabilis.*] Capable of being separated or disjoined.—**sep·a·ra·bil·i·ty,** *n.*—**sep·a·ra·ble·ness,** *n.*—**sep·a·ra·bly,** *adv.*

sep·a·rate, sep′a·rāt″, *v.t.*—*separated, separating.* [L. *separo, separatum*—*se-,* apart, and *paro,* to cut or place.] To divide, disconnect, or keep apart, as by a barrier; as, to *separate* two houses by a wall; to part or put apart; as, to *separate* a group of fighting dogs; to disunite or sever; to sever relations with, as by legal separation; to disperse, divide, or scatter into individual parts; as, to *separate* members of a group; to isolate or extract from a mixture or compound.—*v.i.* To withdraw from association; as, a husband *separated* from his wife; to cleave, split, or come apart; to become isolated or extracted from a compound or mixture; as, oil *separates* from water; to go apart or in different directions.—*sep′èr·it, a.* [L. *separatus,* pp. of *separo.*] Disjoined or disconnected; distinct or individual; as, many *separate* reasons; considered or existing distinct from others; as, *separate* committees; private and apart from others; as, *separate* quarters; (*often cap.*) severed from a parent organization; as, a *Separate* church.—sep′èr·it, *n.* An excerpt from a printed work, often issued

separately; *usu. pl.* the matching or contrasting articles of women's clothes which may be worn in various combinations.—**sep·a·rate·ly,** *adv.*—**sep·a·rate·ness,** *n.*

sep·a·ra·tion, sep″a·rā′shan, *n.* [L. *separatio.*] The act of separating; the state of being separate or disconnected; a means, line, point, or place of division; a gap, space, or the like; *law,* the cessation of conjugal cohabitation of husband and wife.

sep·a·ra·tion en·er·gy, *n. Phys.* binding energy.

sep·a·ra·tist, sep′a·rā″tist, sep′ér·a·tist, *n.* One who withdraws or separates; one who advocates separation, esp. political or ecclesiastical separation.—*a.*—**sep·a·ra·tism,** *n.*—**sep·a·ra·tis·tic,** *a.*

sep·a·ra·tive, sep′a·rā″tiv, sep′ér·a·tiv, *a.* Tending or inclined to separate; causing or used in separation.

sep·a·ra·tor, sep′a·rā″tèr, *n.* One who or that which separates; any of various devices used for separating things, as butterfat from milk.

se·pi·a, sē′pē·a, *n.* [Gr. *sēpia,* the cuttlefish or squid.] The brown pigment prepared from the inky secretion of various cuttlefish and used in drawing; a picture or photograph tinted with this pigment or in this color; the dark brown color of the pigment; a cuttlefish, genus *Sepia.*—*a.*

se·pi·o·lite, sē′pē·o·līt″, *n.* See *meerschaum.*

se·poy, sē′poi, *n.* [Pers. *sipahi,* a soldier.] Formerly, a name given to native Hindustan soldiers trained and employed by the British Army.

sep·pu·ku, se·pö′kö, *n.* A method of suicide practiced by the Japanese; hara-kiri.

sep·sis, sep′sis, *n.* pl. **sep·ses,** sep′sēz. [Gr. *sēpsis,* putrefaction, < *sēpō,* to rot.] *Pathol.* a poisoned state of the system due to a spread of infection through the blood.

sept, sept, *n.* [Perh. a var. of *sect.*] A clan, orig. with reference to tribes or families in Ireland; *anthropol.* a social group, usu. localized and whose association is derived from common descent.

sep·tal, sep′tal, *a. Biol.* of or pertaining to a septum or septa.

sep·tar·i·um, sep·târ′ē·um, *n.* pl. **sep·tar·i·a,** sep·târ′ē·a. [< L. *septum,* an enclosure, a wall, a partition.] *Geol.* a concretion, generally of limestone or ironstone, whose interior presents numerous fissures containing calcite or other minerals which divide the mass.

sep·tate, sep′tāt, *a.* [N.L. *septatus.*] *Biol.* divided by a septum or septa.

Sep·tem·ber, sep·tem′bèr, *n.* [L. *September,* the seventh month of the Roman year, < *septem,* seven.] The ninth month of the year, containing 30 days.

sep·ten·de·cil·lion, sep″ten·di·sil′yan, *n.* In Great Britain and Germany, the cardinal number equal to a million sexdecillions, represented by 1 followed by 102 zeros; in France and the U.S., a thousand sexdecillions, represented by 1 followed by 54 zeros.—*a.*

sep·ten·ni·al, sep·ten′ē·al, *a.* [L. *septennis—septem,* seven, and *annus,* a year.] Lasting or continuing seven years; happening once every seven years.—**sep·ten·ni·al·ly,** *adv.*

sep·ten·tri·on, sep·ten′trē·on, *n.* [L. *septentrio* (n-), sing. of *septentriones,* lit. 'seven plow-oxen' (seven stars of the Great Bear), < *septem,* seven and *triones,* pl. of *trio* (n-), plow-ox.] *Obs.* the north. (*Cap.*) the constellation of the Great Bear, Ursa Major.—**sep·ten·tri·o·nal,** *a.* Northern; boreal.

sep·tet, sep·tette, sep·tet′, *n.* [G. *septett,* < *septem,* seven.] A company of seven singers or players; any group of seven persons or things; a musical composition for seven voices or seven instruments.

sep·tic, sep′tik, *a.* [L. *septicus,* < Gr. *sēptikos,* putrefactive, < *sēpein,* make rotten: cf. *sepsis.*] *Pathol.* Putrefactive; infective; pus-forming; pertaining to or of the nature of sepsis.—*n.* A substance which causes putrefaction or sepsis.—**sep·ti·cal·ly,** *adv.*—**sep·tic·i·ty,** sep·tis′i·tē, *n.*

sep·ti·ce·mi·a, sep·ti·cae·mi·a, sep″ti·sē′mē·a, *n.* [Gr. *sēptikos, sēptos,* putrefying, < *sēpō,* to putrefy, and *haima,* blood.] *Pathol.* The presence in the bloodstream of infectious microorganisms or their toxins; blood poisoning.—**sep·ti·ce·mic, sep·ti·cae·mic,** *a.*

sep·ti·cid·al, sep″ti·sīd′al, *a.* [L. *septum* and *caedere,* cut.] *Bot.* characterized by splitting lengthwise along the septa or dissepiments, as a mode of dehiscence.—**sep·ti·ci·dal·ly,** *adv.*

sep·tic sore throat, *n. Pathol.* an acute infection of the throat caused by streptococcus bacteria and characterized by inflammation of the throat and tonsils, fever, toxemia, and often prostration.

sep·tic tank, *n.* A tank into which sewage is conveyed and where organic solids remain until decomposed by the action of anaerobic bacteria.

sep·tif·ra·gal, sep·tif′ra·gal, *a.* [L. *septum* and *frangere,* break.] *Bot.* characterized by the breaking away of the valves from the septa or dissepiments, as a mode of dehiscence.—**sep·tif·ra·gal·ly,** *adv.*

sep·til·lion, sep·til′yan, *n.* [Fr. *septillion,* < L. *septem,* seven, and Fr. (m)*illion,* million.] In Great Britain and Germany, the cardinal number equal to a million sextillions, represented by 1 followed by 42 zeros; in France and the U.S., a thousand sextillions, represented by 1 followed by 24 zeros.—*a.*

sep·time, sep′tēm, *n.* [L. *septimus,* seventh, < *septem,* seven.] *Fencing,* the seventh in a series of eight parries.

sep·tu·a·ge·nar·i·an, sep″chō·a·je·när′ē·an, *n.* [L. *septuagenarius,* consisting of seventy, *septuageni,* seventy each, < *septem,* seven.] A person seventy years of age, or anywhere in his seventies.—*a.*

Sep·tu·a·ges·i·ma, sep″tö·a·jes′i·ma, sep″tū·a·jes′i·ma, sep″chō·a·jes′i·ma, *n.* [L. *septuagesimus,* seventieth.] The third Sunday before Lent, so called because it is about seventy days before Easter. Also **Sep·tu·a·ges·i·ma Sun·day.**

Sep·tu·a·gint, sep′tö·a·jint″, sep′tū·a·jint″, sep′chō·a·jint″, *n.* [L. *septuaginta,* seventy, < *septem,* seven.] The oldest; a Greek version of the Old Testament, usu. denoted by the symbol LXX, executed for the Greek-speaking Jews of Alexandria and said to have been the work of 70 translators employed by Ptolemy Philadelphus, king of Egypt, about 280 B.C.—**Sep·tu·a·gint·al,** *a.*

sep·tum, sep′tum, *n.* pl. **sep·ta,** sep′ta. [L. *septum, saeptum,* inclosure, fence, wall, < *saepire,* hedge in, inclose, < *saepes,* a hedge, fence.] *Biol.* A dividing wall, membrane, or the like in a plant or animal structure; a dissepiment or partition of tissue.

sep·tu·ple, sep′tụ·pl, sep′tū·pl, sep·tö′pl, sep·tū′pl, *a.* [L. *septulus,* < *septem,* seven.] Composed of seven; sevenfold; repeated seven times.—*v.t.*—**septupled, septupling.** To multiply seven times.—*v.i.* To be multiplied seven times.—*n.* A sevenfold quantity or number.

se·pul·cher, sē′pul·kèr, *n.* [L. *sepulchrum,* < *sepelio, sepultum,* to bury.] A burial place; a tomb; a small cavity in an altarstone in which the relics of saints are placed.—*v.t.*—**sepulchered, sepulchering,** *Brit.* **sepulchred, sepulchring.** To bury or inter in a sepulcher. Also *Brit.* **sep·ul·chre.**

se·pul·chral, se·pul′kral, *a.* [L. *sepulchralis.*] Pertaining to burial, to the grave, or to tombs; suggestive of a sepulcher; gloomy; deep and hollow in tone; as, a *sepulchral* voice.—**se·pul·chral·ly,** *adv.*

sep·ul·ture, sep′ul·chèr, *n.* [L. *sepultura,* < *sepelio, sepultum,* to bury.] Burial; act of interment.

se·qua·cious, si·kwā′shus, *a.* [L. *sequax, sequacis,* < *sequor,* to follow.] Following; disposed to follow a leader; servile; consecutive in development or transition of thought.—**se·qua·cious·ly,** *adv.*—**se·quac·i·ty,** si·kwas′i·tē, *n.*

se·quel, sē′kwel, *n.* [L. *sequela,* sequel, result, consequence, < *sequor,* to follow.] That which follows and forms a continuation; a succeeding part; consequence; result; a literary piece that is in itself complete but further develops a story line previously narrated.

se·que·la, si·kwē′la, *n.* pl. **se·que·lae,** si·kwē′lē. [L., < *sequor.*] *Pathol.* the consequent of a disease; a morbid affection which results from and follows another. Something that follows; a consequence or result.

se·quence, sē′kwens, *n.* [Fr. *séquence,* L.L. *sequentia,* < L. *sequens, sequentis,* ppr. of *sequor, secutus,* to follow (see also in *prosecute, consequent, ensue,* etc.).] The process of following; a particular order or arrangement of succession; a series of things; a consequence or following development; *mus.* the recurrence of a melodic or harmonic figure at different levels of pitch; *Rom. Cath. Ch.* a hymn or prayer in the Proper of special Masses, following the Gradual and coming before the Gospel; *motion pictures,* a story episode that takes place without interruptions; *cards,* a group of playing cards immediately following each other in rank, esp. when of the same suit. Also **se·quen·cy.**—**se·quenc·er,** *n.* That which determines an order or arrangement.

se·quent, sē′kwent, *a.* [L. *sequens, sequentis.*] Following; succeeding; resultant; following by logical consequence.—*n.* That which comes after or follows; a result; a consequence.

se·quen·tial, si·kwen′shal, *a.* [L.L. *sequentia.*] Following in sequence; succeeding; subsequent; resultant or consequent; forming a sequence or connected series; characterized by regular sequence of parts.—**se·quen·tial·ly,** *adv.*

se·ques·ter, si·kwes′tèr, *v.t.* [L. *sequestro,* to put into the hands of an indifferent person, < *sequester,* a depositary or trustee.] To set apart or separate. *Often refl.* to seclude or withdraw; *law,* to seize, as the property of a debtor, until claims against him have been settled. Also **se·ques·trate,** si·kwes′trāt.—**se·ques·tered,** *a.*—**se·ques·tra·ble,** *a.*

se·ques·tra·tion, sē″kwes·trā′shan, si·kwes·trā′shan, *n.* A retirement, withdrawal, or removal into seclusion; *law,* the act of confiscating or sequestering property.

se·ques·trum, si·kwes′trum, *n.* [< L. *sequestro,* to sever.] *Pathol.* a detached dead bone fragment that adjoins sound bone.

se·quin, sē′kwin, *n.* [Fr. *sequin,* < It. *zecchino,* < *zecca,* mint, < Ar. *sikkah,* die for coining.] A small glittering disk or spangle used to ornament a dress, sweater, or the like; a former Italian gold coin, first minted in Venice about 1280 and subsequently introduced into Turkey.—**se·quined, se·quinned,** *a.*

se·quoi·a, si·kwoi′a, *n.* [N.L.; named from *Sequoia,* an Indian (part white) of the Cherokee tribe, who invented an alphabet.] Either of two gigantic coniferous trees of California, the redwood, *Sequoia sempervirens,* and the big tree, *Sequoiadendron giganteum.*

sé·rac, si·rak′, *Fr.* sā·Räk′, *n.* [Fr. (Swiss) *sérac*.] *Geol.* a large block or pinnaclelike mass of ice formed by the breaking of a glacier.

se·ragl·io, si·ral′yō, si·räl′yō, *n.* pl. **se·ragl·ios**. [It. *serraglio*, partly < Turk. *serai*, Pers. *sarai*, a palace, partly < It. *serrare*, to shut up, < L. *sera*, a bar.] A harem for secluding wives or concubines; a palace of the former Sultans of Turkey. Also **se·rail**, se·rī′, se·rīl′, se·räl′.

se·ra·i, se·rä′ē, se·rī′, *n.* [Pers. *serai*, palace.] In Eastern countries, a caravansary; in Turkey, a palace.

ser·al, sēr′al, *a. Ecology*, of, pertaining to, or constituting a sere.

se·ra·pe, sa·ra·pe, se·rä′pē, *Sp.* se·Rä′pe, *n.* pl. **se·ra·pes**, se·rä′pēz, *Sp.* se·Rä′pes. [A Mex. word.] A blanket or shawl made of colorful wool or other heavy material, worn as an outer garment in Mexico and other Latin American countries; poncho.

ser·aph, ser′af, *n.* pl. **ser·aphs**, **ser·a·phim**, ser′a·fim. [< Heb. *seraph*, to burn; to be eminent or noble.] An angel of the highest order, esp. one of those said to be around the throne of God. Isa. vi. 2.— **se·raph·ic**, se·raph·i·cal, si·raf′ik, *a.*— **se·raph·i·cal·ly**, *adv.*

Ser·bi·an, sur′bē·an, *a.* Of or relating to Serbia, one of the federated republics of Yugoslavia, or to its inhabitants or their language. Also **Serb.**—*n.* A native or resident of Serbia; the language spoken there. Also **Serb.**

sere, sēr, *a.* Sear.

sere, sēr, *n. Ecology*, the series of stages in the growth of a plant formation.

ser·e·nade, ser″e·nād′, *n.* [Fr. *sérénade*, < It. *serenata*, a serenade, clear fine weather at night, < L. *serenus*, serene.] A presentation of vocal or instrumental music traditionally performed at night in the open air, esp. by a gentleman as a complimentary gesture to a lady; any such entertainment performed as a mark of esteem and good will toward distinguished persons; a piece of music appropriate to such an occasion; a musical form for instruments consisting of several movements. —*v.t.*—*serenaded, serenading.* To entertain with a serenade.—*v.i.* To perform a serenade.—**ser·e·nad·er**, *n.*

ser·e·na·ta, ser″e·nä′ta, *n.* pl. **ser·e·na·tas**, ser·e·nä′te, or ser″e·nä′tä. [It., *serenade*, appar. < *sereno*, open air (< L. *serenus*, E. *serene*), perh. with sense affected by *sera*, evening, < L. *serus*, late: cf. *serein*.] *Mus.* An 18th century dramatic cantata of a secular nature, often written as a birthday present for a royal personage; an instrumental composition in several movements forming an intermediate link with the suite and the symphony.

ser·en·dip·i·ty, ser″en·dip′i·tē, *n.* [Coined (1754) by Horace Walpole from *Serendip*, old name for Ceylon, in a fairy tale called "The Three Princes of Serendip," in which the princes are described as making such discoveries.] The faculty of making happy or interesting discoveries unexpectedly or by accident.—**ser·en·dip·i·tous**, *a.*

se·rene, se·rēn′, *a.* [L. *serenus*, serene; allied to L. *sol*, the sun, Gr. *seirinos*, hot, scorching, *Seirios*, Sirius, Skt. *surya*, the sun.] Clear or fair, as the sky; calm; placid; unruffled; undisturbed; (*usu. cap.*) exalted or august: used in titles of the members of some royal families; as, His *Serene* Highness.—*n. Poet.* Calmness; serenity; a tranquil or clear expanse or condition, as of the sky or sea.—**se·rene·ly**, *adv.*—**se·rene·ness**, *n.*

se·ren·i·ty, se·ren′i·tē, *n.* pl. **se·ren·i·ties**. [L. *serenitas*.] The quality or condition of being serene; tranquility; calmness;

quietness; peace; (*usu. cap.*) a title showing respect and used in addressing or speaking of members of some royal families, usu. preceded by *Your, His*, or *Her*.

serf, surf, *n.* [Fr. *serf*, < L. *servus*, a slave.] In the Middle Ages, a person bound in the service of a landowner and attached to the land and transferred with it.—**serf·age**, **serf·dom, serf·hood, serf·ism**, sur′fij, surf′dom, *n.*—**serf·ish**, *a.*

serge, surj, *n.* [Fr. *serge*; origin doubtful, perh. < L. *serica*, a silken fabric.] A kind of twilled fabric woven of wool, used esp. for men's suits; a twilled fabric of cotton, silk, or rayon, used esp. for linings.

ser·geant, sär′jent, *n.* [< Fr. *sergent*, O.Fr. *serjent*, orig. a servant, < L. *serviens, servientis*, ppr. of *servio*, to serve.] A non-commissioned officer in the army and marine corps of any rank above corporal and in the air force above airman first class; a police officer next in rank below a captain or lieutenant; a sergeant at arms; the sergeant fish. *Brit.* a police officer in rank next below that of inspector; one of the servants or officials of the royal household. A lawyer of the highest rank; also *Brit.* **ser·jeant.** Abbr. *Sgt.*—**ser·gean·cy**, sär′jen·sē, *n.*

Ser·geant, sär′jent, *n. Aerospace*, a single-stage, ground-to-ground ballistic missile.

ser·geant at arms, *n.* An officer of a court, legislature, or other formal body, whose duty is to preserve order.

ser·geant first class, *n.* An enlisted army officer superior in rank to a staff sergeant and subordinate to a first sergeant.

ser·geant fish, *n.* A large fusiform fish with a long black stripe along its side, found in warm seas, esp. on the southeastern coast of the U.S. and in the East Indies. Also *cobia, snook.*

ser·geant ma·jor, *n.* The highest noncommissioned officer in the U.S. Army and Marine Corps; the noncommissioned officer who assists the commanding officers of a battalion or regiment in clerical and personnel work. A small fish of the genus *Abudefduf*, found in warm waters of the Atlantic.

se·ri·al, sēr′ē·al, *a.* Pertaining to a series; consisting of or constituted by a series; successive; published or appearing in installments at consecutive intervals; *mus.* pertaining to or of a composing technique of using tone rows.—*n.* A story or composition running through a successive number of periodicals or broadcasts; a publication issued in successive numbers; *Brit.* a periodical.—**se·ri·al·ly**, *adv.*— **se·ri·al·ist**, *n.*—**se·ri·al·i·za·tion**, *n.*— **se·ri·al·ize**, sēr′ē·a·līz″, *v.t.*—*serialized, serializing.*

se·ri·ate, sēr′ē·it, sēr′ē·āt″, *a.* Arranged in a series; pertaining to a series.—**se·ri·ate·ly**, *adv.*—**se·ri·a·tion**, *n.*

se·ri·a·tim, sēr′ē·ā′tim, ser″ē·ā′tim, *adv.* [L.] One after the other; serially.

se·ri·ceous, si·rish′us, *a.* [L. *sericeus*, < *sericum*, silk.] Pertaining to or consisting of silk; silky; *bot.* covered with very soft, silky hairs pressed close to the surface, as in certain leaves.

ser·i·cin, ser′i·sin, *n.* [L.L. *sericum*, silk.] *Chem.* a gelatinous organic compound obtained from raw silk.

ser·i·cul·ture, ser′i·kul″chēr, *n.* [L. *sericum*, silk, and *cultura*, cultivation.] The breeding and treatment of silkworms for producing raw silk.—**ser·i·cul·tur·al**, *a.*— **ser·i·cul·tur·ist**, *n.*

se·ries, sēr′ēz, *n.* pl. **se·ries**. [L. *series*, same root as *sero*, to join, to weave together (seen also in *assert, insert, exert, desert*); Gr. *seira*, a cord; Skt. *sarat*, a thread.] A succession of like, correlated, or corresponding items, occurrences, or

events; a sequence of things having a progressive order, arrangement, or relation; a number of games, volumes, stamps, or the like, considered to form a whole. *Math.* a usu. infinite succession of terms, each determined by a particular law; the predicted sum of such a series. *Electron.* an arrangement of electric components end-to-end without forking or branching off, so that full current flows through every part; *geol.* a set of strata, of shorter duration than a system, possessing some common mineral or fossil characteristic; *gram.* a succession of grammatically equivalent words or groups of words in a sentence.—*a.* —**in se·ries**, having a series arrangement.

se·ries-wound, sēr′ēz·wound″, *a. Electron.* arranged so that the windings of the armature and the field circuits are connected in series with the outside circuit, as an electric motor.—**se·ries wind·ing**, *n.*

ser·if, ser′if, *n.* [Origin uncertain.] *Typog.* a smaller line used to finish off a main stroke of a letter, as at the top and bottom of 'M.'

ser·i·graph, ser′i·graf″, ser′i·gräf″, *n.* [L.L. *sericum*, silk.] An original print, often of several colors, produced from a series of specially prepared silkscreens.—**se·rig·ra·pher**, si·rig′ra·fēr, *n.*—**se·rig·ra·phic**, *a.*—**se·rig·ra·phy**, *n.*

ser·in, ser′in, *n.* A yellow-bodied, European finch, *Serinus serinus*, related to and resembling the canary.

ser·ine, ser′ēn, ser′in, sēr′ēn, sēr′in, *n.* [L.L. *sericum*, silk.] *Biochem.* an amino acid, $HOCH_2CH(NH_2)COOH$, which is white, crystalline, and essential to the body, and which can be hydrolyzed from the protein of silk gum, sericin.

se·ri·o·com·ic, sēr″ē·ō·kom′ik, *a.* Having a mixture of seriousness and comicalness.— **se·ri·o·com·i·cal**, *a.*—**se·ri·o·com·i·cal·ly**, *adv.*

se·ri·ous, sēr′ē·us, *a.* [Fr. *sérieux*, < L. *serius*, serious, earnest.] Grave in manner or disposition; solemn; deliberative or thoughtful; really intending what is said; being in earnest; not jesting; important; weighty; not trifling; involving or requiring diligence; as, *serious* research; attended with danger; giving rise to apprehension.— **se·ri·ous·ly**, *adv.* In a serious manner; earnestly; gravely; solemnly.—**se·ri·ous·ness**, *n.*

se·ri·ous-mind·ed, sēr′ē·us·mīn′did, *a.* Being in earnest; tending toward issues of importance rather than frivolity.—**se·ri·ous-mind·ed·ly**, *adv.*—**se·ri·ous-mind·ed·ness**, *n.*

ser·jeant, sär′jent, *n. Brit.* sergeant.

ser·jeant·y, **ser·geant·y**, sär′jan·tē, *n.* [O.Fr. *serjantie*.] *Hist.* a kind of land tenure in medieval England, requiring some specified personal service to the king.

ser·mon, sur′mon, *n.* [L. *sermo, sermonis*, a speech or connected discourse, < *sero*, to join together.] A discourse delivered in public, esp. by a clergyman during a church service, for religious instruction or the inculcation of morality, and often grounded on a text or passage of Scripture; any other type of discourse which is similar in intent; any lengthy, tedious harangue; a homily.—**Ser·mon on the Mount**, a sermon delivered by Jesus to his disciples. Matt. v-vii.—**ser·mon·ic**, sèr·mon′ik, *a.*—**ser·mon·ize**, sur′mo·nīz″, *v.i.*—*sermonized, sermonizing.* To preach; to discourse.—*v.t.* To deliver a sermon to.—**ser·mon·iz·er**, *n.*

se·rol·o·gy, si·rol′o·jē, *n.* The scientific study of the nature and actions of blood serum.—**se·ro·log·ic, se·ro·log·i·cal**, sēr″o·loj′ik, *a.*—**se·rol·o·gist**, *n.*—**se·ro·log·i·cal·ly**, *adv.*

se·ro·sa, si·rō′sa, si·rō′za, *n.* pl. **se·ro·sas, se·ro·sae**, si·rō′sē, si·rō′zē. *Anat.* serous membrane, esp. the peritoneal membrane that coats most of the viscera of the intestines.—**se·ro·sal**, *a.*

ser·o·tine, ser'o·tin, ser'o·tīn", *n.* A European bat, small and brown, *Eptesicus serotinus.*

se·rot·i·nous, si·rot'i·nus, *a.* [L. *serotinus*, < *serus*, late.] *Bot.* developing or blooming late in a season. Also **ser·o·tine**, ser'o·tin, ser'o·tīn".—**se·rot·i·nal**, si·rot'i·nal, ser"o·tīn'al, *a.* Of, or occurring late in the summer.

ser·o·to·nin, ser"o·tō'nin, *n. Biochem.* a crystalline substance, normally found in certain blood, brain, and intestinal cells of mammals, that causes muscle contractions and vasoconstriction.

se·rous, sēr'us, *a.* [Fr. *séreux*, < L. *serum*, E. *serum.*] Resembling serum; of a thin, liquid nature; containing or secreting serum; pertaining to serum.

se·rous mem·brane, *n. Anat.* any of various thin membranes, as the peritoneum, which line certain cavities of the body and secrete serous fluid.

ser·ow, ser'ō, *n.* [Native name.] Any of the Asiatic goat antelopes constituting the genus *Capricornis.*

ser·pent, sur'pent, *n.* [L. *serpens, serpentis*, < *serpo*, to creep; cogn. Gr. *herpō*, to creep; Skt. *saepa*, a serpent, < *srip*, to creep.] A reptile without limbs that is of an extremely elongated form and moves by muscular contractions of the body; a snake; a treacherously subtle, malicious person; *Bib.* Satan or the devil.

ser·pen·tine, sur'pen·tēn, sur'pen·tīn", *a.* [L. *serpentinus.*] Pertaining to, resembling, or having the qualities of a serpent; treacherously subtle; cunning; curving, winding, or turning like a moving serpent; sinuous; crooked.—*n.* A rock or mineral, often used as a decorative material, consisting principally of hydrous magnesium silicate and usu. colored green with shades and spots resembling a serpent's skin.

ser·pi·go, ser·pī'gō, *n.* A skin disease that spreads from one area to another, as ringworm.—**ser·pig·i·nous**, ser·pij'i·nus, *a.* —**ser·pig·i·nous·ly**, *adv.*

ser·ra·nid, se·rā'nid, se·rä'nid, se·ran'id *a.* [N.L. *Serranus*, genus of fishes, < L. *serra*, saw, saw-fish.] *Zool.* belonging to the family *Serranidae*, of percoid marine fishes, and including the sea bass, groupers, and jew-fishes.—*n.* A serranid fish.—**ser·ra·noid**, ser'a·noid", *a., n.*

ser·rate, ser'it, ser'āt, *a.* [L. *serratus*, < *serra*, saw: cf. *sierra.*] Notched like the edge of a saw; toothed; *bot.* having small, sharp marginal teeth, as a leaf. Also **ser·rat·ed**.—ser'āt, *v.t.*—**serrated, serrating.** To render serrate.

ser·ra·tion, se·rā'shan, *n.* Serrated condition or form; a serrated edge or formation; one of the series of notches or teeth of such an edge or formation.

ser·ried, ser'ēd, *a.* [For earlier *serr*, < Fr. *serrer*, close up, press close, < L.L. *serare*, to bar, bolt, < L. *sera*, bar for fastening a door: cf. *sear, seraglio*, and *serrefile.*] Crowded closely together or in close order, as ranks or files of armed men.—**ser·ried·ly**, *adv.*—**ser·ried·ness**, *n.*

ser·ru·late, ser'ū·lit, ser'ū·lāt", ser'a·lit, ser'a·lāt", *a.* [N.L. *serrulatus*, < L. *serrula*, dim. of *serra*, saw.] Finely or minutely serrate, as a leaf. Also **ser·ru·lat·ed**.

ser·ru·la·tion, ser"ū·lā'shan, ser"a·lā'shan, *n.* Serrulate condition or form; a fine or minute serration.

ser·tu·lar·i·an, sur"chu·lâr'ē·an, *a.* [N.L. *Sertularia*, < L. *sertula*, dim. of *serta*, garland, prop. pp. fem of *serere*, join: cf. *serics.*] *Zool.* belonging or relating to the genus *Sertularia*, family *Sertulariidae*, comprising arborescent colonies of hydroids.—*n.*

se·rum, sēr'um, *n.* pl. **se·rums**, **se·ra**,

sēr'a. [L., whey, watery fluid, serum.] *Anat.* a clear, pale-yellow liquid which separates from the clot in the coagulation of blood; *pathol.* a fluid, obtained from the blood of an animal which has been rendered immune to some disease by inoculation, used as an antitoxic or therapeutic agent. The whey or fluid remaining after milk sours; that which remains after the extraction of butterfat, cassein, and albumin.

se·rum al·bu·min, *n. Biochem.* A simple protein that is the principal one found in plasma and the body's serous fluids; such a substance precipitated from animal blood and prepared for commercial uses.

se·rum glo·bu·lin, *n. Biochem.* a plasma protein which may be separated by electrophoresis into three blood fractions which have been shown to serve related functions and are identified as alpha, beta, and gamma globulin, the latter being responsible for the body's ability to resist certain infections.

ser·val, sur'val, *n.* [Fr. *serval*, for Pg. *lobo cerval*, lynx, < L. *lupus*, wolf, and *cervus*, deer.] An African wildcat, *Felis serval*, with a shoulder height of approximately two feet at maturity, having long legs, untufted ears, and a tawny coat spotted with black.—**ser·va·line**, *a.*

serv·ant, sur'vant, *n.* [Fr. *servant*, < *servir*, L. *servire*, to serve; *servant* is a doublet of *sergeant*.] One who serves or does services for another; a person who is employed by another for domestic duties; a slave; public or civil servant

serve, surv, *v.i.*—*served, serving*. [O.Fr. Fr. *servir*, < L. *servire*, be a slave or servant, serve, < *servus*, slave, servant: cf. *serf, sergeant, servant, service, deserve*, and *subverse.*] To act as a servant; to wait at table; to offer or hand food or drink to guests; to perform duties for others; to go through a term of service, as a soldier or sailor; to perform official duty, as on a jury; to have a definite use or function; to answer the purpose, or suffice, as: This apartment will *serve* for the moment. To be favorable, suitable, or convenient, as weather or time; in tennis, handball, and certain other games, to put the ball in play; *eccles.* to act as a server.—*v.t.* To be a servant to, to render assistance or service to; to go through, as a term of service or imprisonment; to render active service to, as a king or commander, in the army or navy; to render obedience or homage to, as God; to perform the duties of, as an office; to answer the requirements of; as, to *serve* one's needs; to contribute to; promote; to wait upon at table; to set, as food or drink, on a table or before a person; to provide with a regular or continuous supply of something; to treat in a specified manner; of a male animal, to mate or copulate with; in tennis and the like, to put, as the ball, in play. *Law*, to make legal delivery of, as a process or writ; to present, as a person, with a writ. To operate, as a gun; *naut.* to bind or wind, as a rope or a stay, with small cord or the like, so as to strengthen or protect it.—*n.* The act, manner, or right of serving, as in tennis or handball.

serv·er, sur'vér, *n.* One who serves; that which serves or is used in serving food or drink; the player who puts the ball in play, as in tennis; *eccles.* an attendant on the priest at Mass, who arranges the altar and makes the responses.

serv·ice, sur'vis, *n.* [O.Fr. *servise* (Fr. *service*), < L. *servitium*, < *servus*, slave, servant.] An act of helpful activity; the rendering of assistance or aid; the performance of duties as a servant; the act or manner of waiting at table; employment in any duties or work for another or others, or for a government, institution, or the like;

a department of public employment; the duty or work of public servants; the armed forces; as, to be in the *service*; one of the branches of these forces; *usu. pl.* work done for others which does not result in tangible commodities; as, medical *services.* The supplying of some commodity, as water or gas, accommodation or transport, required by the public; the organized system of apparatus, appliances, and employees for supplying a commodity or accommodation; repair, maintenance, or installation provided for the buyer of an article by the seller; public religious worship according to prescribed form and order; a ritual or form prescribed for public worship or for some particular occasion; as, the marriage *service*; the serving of God by obedience or piety; a musical setting of those portions of a liturgy which are sung; a set of dishes or other tableware required for a particular use; as, a tea *service*; *law*, the serving of a process or writ upon a person; *naut.* small cord or yarn wound about a rope as for strengthening or protection. In tennis, handball, and certain other games, the act or manner of putting the ball in play; the ball as put into play. The copulation of a female animal with a male.—*a.* Pertaining to or for use by servants or tradesmen; supplying services; as, a *service* industry; providing repair and maintenance; of or relating to armed services.—*v.t.*—*serviced, servicing.* To make fit for service, or restore to condition for service, as an automobile; to supply a service to.—**at one's serv·ice**, ready to serve one; at one's disposal.

serv·ice·a·ble, sur'vi·sa·bl, *a.* [O.Fr. *servisable.*] Being of service; useful; capable of doing good service; capable of standing long or hard use; durable, as materials or clothing.—**serv·ice·a·bil·i·ty**, **serv·ice·a·ble·ness**, *n.*—**serv·ice·a·bly**, *adv.*

serv·ice·ber·ry, sur'vis·ber"ē, *n.* pl. **serv·ice·ber·ries**. Juneberry.

serv·ice book, *n.* A book containing the various forms for religious services.

serv·ice ceil·ing, *n. Avi.* the height above sea level at which a given airplane is unable to climb faster than at a specific rate per minute under normal conditions (100 feet per minute in the U.S. and England).

serv·ice charge, *n.* A sum charged for a service, often as an addition to an original or basic fee.

serv·ice club, *n.* An organization formed for the purpose of providing service to the community; a social and recreational facility for members of the armed forces.

serv·ice door, *n.* A door primarily for the use of servants and to deliver goods.

serv·ice·man, sur'vis·man", sur'vis·man, *n.* pl. **serv·ice·men**. A man who is a member of any nation's armed forces; a man whose income is derived from maintenance and repair work.

serv·ice med·al, *n.* A medal presented to a member of the armed forces in recognition of honorable participation and performance in a specified campaign or theater of war.

serv·ice sta·tion, *n.* Gas station; an establishment providing a service, esp. repairs and parts for mechanical or electronic appliances.

serv·ice stripe, *n.* A diagonal stripe worn by an enlisted man on the left sleeve of his uniform to indicate completion of three years of duty in the Air Force or Army, or four years in the Navy. Also *hash mark.*

serv·ice tree, *n.* A European tree, *Sorbus domestica*, which bears a small, acid, edible fruit; also **serv·ice**. The Juneberry or shadbush, *Amelanchier canadensis.*

ser·vi·ette, sur"vē·et', *n.* [Fr.] *Brit., Canadian*, a table napkin.

ser·vile, sur'vil, sur'vil, *a.* [L. *servilis.*] Pertaining to or characteristic of a slave or servant; submissive; fawning; yielding or slavishly obedient, usu. followed by *to*; held in subjection; oppressed.—**ser·vile·-ly**, *adv.*—**ser·vil·i·ty**, **ser·vile·ness**, *n.*

serv·ing, sur'ving, *n.* The act of one who or that which serves; an amount of food or drink sufficient for one person; a helping.

ser·vi·tor, sur'vi·tẽr, *n.* [L.L., < L. *servio*, to serve.] A male servant; an attendant.

ser·vi·tude, sur'vi·tŏd″, sur'vi·tūd″, *n.* [O.Fr. Fr. *servitude*, < L. *servitudo*, < *servus*, slave, servant.] The condition of being a slave; slavery, bondage, or serfdom; any condition of subjection; as, intellectual *servitude*; compulsory service or labor as a punishment for criminals; as, penal *servitude*. *Law*, the condition of property subject to some right of enjoyment possessed by another than its owner or attaching to some other property; such a right of enjoyment.

ser·vo·mech·an·ism, sur'vō·mek″a·-niz″um, sur'vō·mek′a·niz″um, *n.* A low-power device or control system used to actuate and control a more complex or more powerful mechanism. Also **ser·vo.**

ser·vo·mo·tor, sur'vō·mō″tẽr, *n.* A motor serving as part of and supplying power to a servomechanism. Also **ser·vo.**

ses·a·me, ses'a·mē, *n.* [L. *sesamum*, *sesama*, < Gr. *sēsamon*, *sēsámē*.] A tropical herbaceous plant, *Sesamum indicum*, whose small, oval seeds are edible and yield an oil; the seeds themselves. See *open sesame*.

ses·a·moid, ses'a·moid″, *a.* Anat. resembling a sesame seed in form, as some nodular cartilages and bones.

ses·qui·cen·ten·ni·al, ses″kwi·sen·ten′-ē·al, *a.* Pertaining to or marking the completion of a period of 150 years.—*n.* A 150th anniversary or its celebration.

ses·qui·pe·da·li·an, ses″kwi·pi·dā'lē·an, ses″kwi·pi·dāl'yan, *a.* [L. *sesquipedalis* (in neut. pl., *sesquipedalia verba*, words a foot and a half long: Horace's "Ars Poetica," 97), < *sesqui-* and *pes* (*ped-*), foot.] Of words or expressions, very long, containing many syllables; of persons, given to using long words. Also **ses·quip·e·dal**, ses·-kwip'i·dal.—*n.* A lengthy word.

ses·sile, ses'il, ses'īl, *a.* [L. *sessilis*, sitting, low, < *sedere*, sit.] Bot. attached by the base, or without any distinct projecting support, as a leaf issuing directly from the stem without a petiole or a flower without a peduncle. *Zool.* permanently or firmly attached; sedentary.—**ses·sil·i·ty**, se·sil'i·-tē, *n.*

ses·sion, sesh'an, *n.* [O.Fr. Fr. *session*, < L. *sessio(n-)*, a sitting, session, < *sedere*, sit.] The sitting together of a court, council, legislature, or the like, for conference or the transaction of business, as: Congress is now in *session*. A single continuous sitting, or period of sitting, of persons assembled for conference, business, or the like; a continuous series of sittings or meetings of a court, legislature, or the like; the period or term during which such a series is held; a single continuous course or period of lessons or study in the work of a day at school; as, a morning or afternoon *session*; a portion of the year during which instruction is given at a college or the like; as, a summer *session*; the lowest court in Presbyterian churches, composed of the pastor and the lay or ruling elders of the local church; *pl.* local courts dealing, esp. with lesser criminal offenses; as, the Court of *Sessions*.—**ses·sion·al**, *a.*

ses·terce, ses'tŭrs, *n.* [L. *sestertius*, prop. a., 'two and a half,' < *semis*, half, and *tertius*, third.] An ancient Roman coin orig. of silver and later bronze.

ses·ter·ti·um, se·stur'shē·um, se·stur'-shum, *n.* pl. **ses·ter·ti·a**, se·stur'shē·a, se·stur'sha. [L.] An ancient Roman money of account equal to a thousand sesterces.

ses·tet, se·stet', ses'tet, *n.* [It. *sestetto*, < L. *sextus*, sixth, < *sex*, six.] *Pros.* a six-line stanza, esp. the last six lines of an Italian sonnet; *mus.* a sextet.

ses·ti·na, se·stē'na, *n.* pl. **ses·ti·nas**, ses·ti·ne, se·stē'nä. [It., < *sesto*, sixth.] A poem of six six-line stanzas and a three-line envoy, orig. without rhyme, in which each stanza repeats the end words of the lines in the first stanza, but in different order, the envoy using the six words again, three in the middle of the lines and three at the end. Also **ses·tine.**

set, set, *v.t.*—*set*, *setting.* [O.E. *settan* = D. *zetten* = G. *setzen* = Icel. *setja* = Goth. *satjan*, set, lit. 'cause to sit'; causative of the verb (O.E. *sittan*, etc.) represented by E. *sit*.] To put in a particular or proper position; to put into a specific condition; put, as a price or value, on something; to post, station, or appoint for the purpose of performing some duty; to fix, appoint, or ordain, as a boundary; to present, as an example; to prescribe or assign, as a task; to put in proper position or order for use, as a table or a trap; spread, as sails, so as to catch the wind; to fix or mount in a frame or setting, as a gem; to adorn, as with precious stones; to place under a fowl or in an incubator, as eggs; to shape or curl, as moist hair; to adjust according to a standard, as a clock; to place in thought or estimation; as, to *set* great store by a thing; put in a fixed, rigid state, as the muscles or the mind; to cause to become firm or hard, as mortar; to give a fine edge to, as a razor; to incline the teeth, as of a saw, alternately to the right and left; *theatr.* to arrange, as a stage, for performance. *Mus.* to fit, as words to music; arrange for musical performance; arrange, as music, for certain voices or instruments. *Surg.* to put in a position suitable for restoration to the normal condition, as a broken or dislocated bone; *dial.* to cause to sit. *Print.* to arrange in the order required for printing, as type; to put into words for printing, as type.—*v.i.* To decline toward or pass below the horizon, as the sun; to sink, decline, or wane; to sit on eggs, as a hen; to hang or fit in a particular manner, as clothes; to assume a fixed or rigid state, as muscles; to become firm or solid, as mortar; to develop or grow as the result of fertilization, as a blossom or fruit; to begin to move or start, usu. followed by *forth*, *off*, or *out*; to begin to apply oneself to something; of a hunting dog, to indicate the position of game.—*n.* The act or an act of setting or the state of being set; a number of things customarily used together or forming a collection, as golf clubs; a number or group of things having in common their nature or function; a collection of books by one author or on one subject; a number or group of persons associating or classed together; the way in which clothing hangs or fits; fixed direction or bent, as of the wind; bearing or carriage; the assumption of a fixed, rigid, or hard state, as by cement; a radio or television receiver; *tennis*, a group of at least six games in which the winner defeats his opponent by at least two games, as 8–6. A construction representing a place in which action occurs in a motion picture, stage, or television production; *mech.* the alternating deflection of saw teeth to left and right. A young plant, slip, or tuber ready for planting; the direction of the wind or current; *psychol.* the temporary or permanent state of giving a

specific response to a specific stimulus; *math.* a number of elements grouped together.—*a.* Fixed or appointed beforehand; prescribed beforehand; deliberately composed, rather than spontaneous or original; fixed, rigid, or unvarying; resolved or determined; habitually or stubbornly fixed; ready or prepared; formed, built, or made; as, thick-*set*.—**set a·bout**, to start work upon; begin upon.—**set a·gainst**, to instigate hostility against; to balance or correlate.—**set a·part**, to place separately; to lend distinction.—**set a·side**, to put to one side; dismiss from the mind; to annul or quash.—**set back**, to hold up or hinder; to adjust backward to the correct time, as a watch or clock.—**set down**, to put down in writing or printing; to consider; ascribe or attribute; to place at rest on a flat surface; to make a landing, as with an airplane.—**set forth**, declare or offer an account of.—**set for·ward**, to adjust forward to the correct time, as a watch or clock—**set in**, to begin; to blow or flow toward the shore, as a wind or current.—**set off**, to cause ignition or explosion; to offer a contrast to.—**set on**, to attack; to encourage.—**set out**, to begin a trip; to attempt or try; to design or lay out, as a plan; to plant; to place on display.—**set to**, to make a beginning or start work.—**set up**, to place in an erect position, to raise to an elevated or exalted position; to erect or construct; to establish or set in active existence; to establish in business; to propose or suggest; to arrange or bring about. *Colloq.* to pay for or treat; to exhilarate or elate.

se·ta, sē'ta, *n.* pl. **se·tae**, sē'tē. [L. *seta*, *saeta*, bristle: cf. *satin* and *seton*.] *Biol.* a stiff hair; a bristle; a bristlelike part of an animal or plant. *Bot.* the stalk that supports the spore case of mosses.—**se·tal**, *a.*

se·ta·ceous, si·tā'shus, *a.* [N.L. *setaceus.*] Bristlelike; bristle-shaped; bristly.—**se·-ta·ceous·ly**, *adv.*

set·back, set'bak″, *n.* A halt or interruption of progress; *arch.* a receding of the upper wall of a building in building from the plane of the building's base line.

set-in, set'in″, *a.* Formed or constructed separately and attached to another part or unit; as, a *set-in* sleeve, *set-in* bookcase.

set·off, set'af″, set'of″, *n.* Something that counterbalances or makes up for something else; a compensative circumstance; *accounting*, a counterbalancing debt or claim. *Arch.* a reduction in the thickness of a wall; a flat or sloping projection on a wall, buttress, or the like, below a part of less thickness. *Print.* an offset.

se·tose, sē'tōs, si·tōs', *a.* [L. *setosus*, < *seta*, bristle.] Covered with setae or bristles; bristly.

set piece, *n. Theatr.* a free-standing part of a stage set, as a profile of a building or rocky cliff. A composition in literature, art, or music having a formal or stylized theme or structure; as, the *set pieces* of pastoral romances; a framework or structural design of fireworks which when lighted forms a composition or pattern; a military maneuver of fixed and rigid plan and execution.

set point, *n.* In tennis, the point which if scored would enable the scoring side to win that set.

set·screw, set'skrö″, *n.* A screw that is screwed through one part tightly into or upon another to bring the pieces into close contact.

set·tee, set·ē', *n.* [< *set*.] A long seat with a back to it; a sofa large enough for several persons to sit on at one time.

set·ter, set'ẽr, *n.* One who or that which sets. Any of three breeds of long-haired hunting dogs which originally had the habit of crouching when game was scented, but which are now trained to stand stiffly and point the muzzle toward the scented game; see *English setter, Gordon setter, Irish setter.*

set the·o·ry, *n.* A division of mathematics which deals with sets and the relations between sets.

set·ting, set′ing, *n.* The act of one who or that which sets; the manner or position in which anything is set; that in which something, as a jewel, is set or mounted; the surroundings or environment of anything; the scenery, costumes, and the like of a play; a piece of music composed for certain words, as poetry; eggs put together in a certain place for hatching; the items, as silver, china, or glass, needed to set one place at a table or an entire table.

set·tle, set′l, *v.t.—settled, settling.* [< *set*; a freq. in form = O.E. *setlan,* to seat, to place.] To resolve, determine, or fix conclusively; as, to *settle* on a selling price; to place in order or a proper state; to pay, satisfy, or close, as an account or claim; to colonize or establish residence in; to furnish with settlers or inhabitants; to establish or fix in any way of life, occupation, dwelling, or the like; to quiet or free of agitation; to place in a fixed or permanent position; to clear, as liquid, of dregs or sediment by causing them to sink; to cause to sink to the bottom; to make compact or firm by causing to sink gradually; to bring to a conclusion, finish. *Law,* to secure or assign by legal act; as, to *settle* property; to terminate by mutual agreement of the litigants; as, to *settle* a lawsuit.—*v.i.* To come to an agreement, decision, or resolution, often followed by *on* or *upon*; to pay or adjust an account, bill, or debt; to establish residence in a different country or place; to cease moving and come to rest; to become fixed in a certain area or position; to become calm or free from agitation, often followed by *down*; to sink or fall gradually or subside; to become transparent or clear by the sinking of particles or sediment; to become compact or firm; said of an animal, to conceive.—**set·tle down,** to begin living an orderly, routine life after being independent or irresponsible; as, to *settle down* after marriage; to become composed or calm; to become absorbed in or apply oneself to one's assignment, work, or the like.

set·tle, set′l, *n.* [O.E. *setl,* seat; from the root of E. *sit.*] A long seat or bench, with arms and a high back, usu. made of wood, and sometimes enclosed from the bottom of the seat to the floor to form a storage chest; a ledge or platform.

set·tle·ment, set′l·ment, *n.* The act of settling or state of being settled; establishment in life or business; the act of colonizing or peopling; colonization; a tract of land which has been colonized, esp. a colony in the early stages of development; the adjustment or liquidation of a claim or account; the sinking or settling of a building. *Law,* a deed by which property is settled; the property settled in such a way. *Relig.* a community inhabited by members of one ideological group; *Brit.* the right of a pauper to maintenance in a particular parish or town. An establishment providing educational and social services to the people of a particular slum area; also **set·tle·ment house.**

set·tler, set′lėr, *n.* One who settles, esp. one who fixes his residence in a new region or country; a colonist; that which or one who decides anything definitely.

set·tling, set′ling, *n.* The act of one who settles or that which sinks. *Pl.* dregs; sediment.

set·tlor, set′lėr, *n. Law,* one who makes a settlement of property.

set-to, set′tö″, *n.* pl. **set-tos.** A brief but intense argument or fight.

set up, *v.t.* To elevate to a high station or position; to place, as a statue, upright; erect; to establish; as, to *set up* a government; to organize to commence, as a new business; to utter loudly; as, to *set up* a loud cry; to put in superior position; to propose; as, to *set up* a doctrine; to make upright in posture, as by exercise; to raise from depression; to restore to health and vigor.—*v.i.* To begin a new business; to come into use; to lay claim to; as, to *set up* to be better than others.

set·up, set′up″, *n.* The way in which something is arranged or organized; makeup; the plan, preparation, or arrangement for performing or accomplishing a specific task or undertaking; a plan of action; the manner of carrying the body; poise. *Colloq.* the glassware and ingredients, except liquor, provided to one mixing his own drink; a match, contest, game, task, or undertaking made easy to win or accomplish; a table setting, esp. in a restaurant. *Sports,* the position of a ball, puck, or the like, as in pool or hockey, affording an easy score or point; the play resulting in a score or victory.

sev·en, sev′en, *n.* [O.E. *seofon* = D. *zeven,* Goth. and O.H.G. *sibun,* Icel. *sjau,* Dan. *syv,* W. *saith,* Ir. *seacht,* Russ. *semj,* L. *septem,* Gr. *hepta* (for *septa*), Pers. *haft,* Skt. *saptan.*] The cardinal number between six and eight; a symbol representing it; a set of seven persons or things.—*a.*

sev·en seas, *n.* pl. (*Sometimes cap.*) the oceans of the world.

sev·en·teen, sev′en·tēn′, *n.* The cardinal number between sixteen and eighteen; a symbol representing it; a set of seventeen persons or things.—*a.*

sev·en·teenth, sev′en·tēnth′, *a.* Following the sixteenth; being the ordinal of 17; being one of 17 equal parts into which anything is divided.—*n.* One of 17 equal parts; that which follows the sixteenth in a series.

sev·en·teen-year lo·cust, sev′en·tēn′ yēr″ lō′kust, *n.* The periodical cicada, *Magicicada septendecim,* the nymph of which grows from 13 to 17 years in the ground before emerging as an adult locust to shed the nymphal covering, mate, lay eggs, and then die.

sev·enth, sev′enth, *a.* Following the sixth; being the ordinal of seven; being one of seven equal parts into which anything is divided.—*n.* One of seven equal parts; that which follows the sixth in a series; *mus.* the interval between the first and the seventh note of the diatonic scale.—*adv.*

sev·enth chord, *n. Mus.* a chord consisting of a root tone plus its third, fifth, and seventh.

sev·enth-day, sev′enth·dā″, *a.* (*Often cap.*) designating any of certain Christian religious bodies who make Saturday their chief day of rest and religious observance; as, *Seventh-Day* Adventists.

sev·enth heav·en, *n.* A state of great joy or happiness; in certain religious faiths, as Islam, the heaven of God and the archangels.

sev·en·ti·eth, sev′en·tē·ith, *a.* Following the sixty-ninth; being the ordinal of 70; being one of 70 equal parts into which anything is divided.—*n.* One of 70 equal parts; that which follows the sixty-ninth in a series.

sev·en·ty, sev′en·tē, *n.* The cardinal number between 69 and 71; a symbol representing it; a set of 70 persons or things.—*a.*

sev·en·ty-eight, *n.* The cardinal number between 77 and 79; a symbol representing it; a set of 78 persons or things. A phonograph record meant to be played at 78 revolutions per minute.—*a.*

sev·en-up, sev′en·up′, *n.* A card game played by two or more persons, in which there are four special chances of scoring a point, seven points constituting a game. Also **all-fours, high-low-jack, old sledge,** and **pitch.**

sev·er, sev′ėr, *v.t.* [O.Fr. *sevrer, severer,* < L. *separare,* to separate.] To part or divide, esp. by force; to separate into parts by cutting or rending; cleave; to disjoin or break off, as a relationship or family tie; disunite.—*v.i.* To undergo separation; to be divided.—**sev·er·a·bil·i·ty,** *n.*—**sev·er·a·ble,** sev′ėr·a·bl, sev′ra·bl, *a.*

sev·er·al, sev′ėr·al, sev′ral, *a.* [O.Fr. *several,* < *severer.*] More than two but not very many; divers; separate or respective; as, experts in their *several* areas; individual, distinct; as, *several* attempts; *law,* relating separately to each participant in a joint contractual obligation.—*n.* A small number of persons or things; some; a few considered individually.—**sev·er·al·ly,** sev′ėr·a·lē, sev′ra·lē, *adv.*

sev·er·al·fold, sev′ėr·al·fōld″, sev′ral·fōld″, *a.* Several times as great as or much; consisting of several parts, ways, or aspects.—*adv.*

sev·er·al·ty, sev′ėr·al·tē, sev′ral·tē, *n.* pl. **sev·er·al·ties.** The state or quality of being distinct or separate. *Law,* the condition of being the exclusive owner of property, of holding land by individual right; the property or land so held.

sev·er·ance, sev′ėr·ans, sev′rans, *n.* The act of severing or state of being severed; separation; partition.

se·vere, si·vēr′, *a.—severer, severest.* [Fr. *sévère,* < L. *severus,* serious, severe; seen also in *persevere, asseverate.*] Very strict or unnecessarily harsh in discipline, government, or judgment; as, *severe* punishment; serious, austere, or stern in disposition, appearance, or manner; critical or serious; as, a *severe* disease; plain, simple, or restrained in manner, decoration, or style; causing physical discomfort or pain, hardship, or distress; as, *severe* weather; rigorous, arduous, or difficult to undergo or perform; as, a *severe* test or examination; rigidly or scrupulously methodical or exact.—**se·vere·ly,** *adv.*—**se·vere·ness,** *n.*

se·ver·i·ty, si·ver′i·tē, *n.* pl. **se·ver·i·ties.** [L. *severitas.*] The quality or state of being severe; harshness or sternness of treatment, condition, or disposition; extreme simplicity or plainness; sharpness or keenness, as of weather or injury; seriousness or gravity; exactness or methodicalness; strict conformity to rules, standards, laws, and the like.

Sè·vres, sev′re, sev, *Fr.* se′vRe, *n.* A kind of porcelain ware of high quality, manufactured at Sèvres, France. Also **Sè·vres ware.**

sew, sō, *v.t.—past sewed, pp. sewn or sewed, ppr. sewing.* [O.E. *siwian, seowian,* to sew = O.H.G. *siuwan,* Goth. *siujan,* Dan. *sye,* Icel. *sȳja;* cogn. L. *suo,* Skt. *siv,* to sew. *Seam* is from this stem.] To unite or fasten together with stitches; to make or mend with needle and thread; to enclose with stitches.—*v.i.* To practice sewing; to join things together with stitches.

sew·age, sō′ij, *n.* [< old verb *sew,* to drain, < O.Fr. *essuier,* to drain, < L. *ex,* out, and *aqua,* water.] The waste matter carried away by sewers. Also *sewerage.*

sew·er, sō′ėr, *n.* [O.Fr. *essuier, essuyer,* a drain, a conduit.] An artificial channel or canal, usu. underground, which carries off drainage water and other waste materials.

sew·er, sō′ėr, *n.* One who sews or that which sews.

sew·er, sō′ėr, *n.* [< O.Fr. *assegier,* to seat guests.] In medieval Europe, a household officer in charge of seating the guests and serving the meals.

sew·er·age, sō′ĕr·ij, *n.* The removal of water and other waste materials by sewers; the system of sewers; sewage.

sew·ing, sō′ing, *n.* The act or task of one who sews; something that is to be or has been sewn.

sew·ing ma·chine, *n.* Any of various machines used for making stitches or for sewing.

sew up, *v.t. Colloq.* To gain exclusive control of; to conclude or finish with success, as business negotiations; to gather or be sure of, as votes in an election.

sex, seks, *n.* [Fr. *sexe*, < L. *sexus*, a sex, < *seco*, to cut.] The total physical and behavioral differences, properties, and characteristics by which the male and female are distinguished; either of the two groups, male and female, into which organisms are divided, esp. according to their distinct functions in the reproductive process; activities relating to or based on sexual attraction, sexual relations, or sexual reproduction; sexual intercourse.—*v.t.* To find out the sex of, as of chicks.—**sex up**, to stir or excite sexually; to make more sexually interesting, appealing, or enticing, as a novel.

sex·a·ges·i·mal, seks″sa·jes′i·mal, *a.* Sixtieth; pertaining to the number 60.—*n.* A fraction based on a denominator of 60.

sex ap·peal, *n.* Physical appeal or attractiveness to those belonging to the opposite sex.

sex chro·mo·some, *n.* A chromosome which carries sex-linked traits and acts as a determinant of the sex of the offspring.

sex·de·cil·lion, seks″di·sil′yan, *n.* A cardinal number represented by a 1 followed in America and France, by 51 zeros and in Great Britain and Germany, by 96 zeros.—*a.*—**sex·de·cil·lionth**, *a.*, *n.*

sexed, sekst, *a.* Belonging to a sex or possessing sexual traits; being sexually attractive or appealing.

sex hor·mone, *n.* A hormone affecting the growth or function of the sexual organs or the development of secondary sex characteristics.

sex hy·giene, *n.* That part of hygiene concerned with sexual activity as it affects personal and community well-being.

sex·less, seks′lis, *a.* Having or seeming to have no sex; exciting or evidencing no sexual desires.—**sex·less·ly**, *adv.*—**sex·less·ness**, *n.*

sex-linked, seks′lingkt″, *a. Genetics*, designating a gene contained in a sex chromosome, or a character controlled by such a gene.—**sex-link·age**, seks′ling″kij, *n.*

sex·ol·o·gy, sek·sol′o·jē, *n.* The science that deals with sexual behavior, esp. of humans.—**sex·o·log·i·cal**, sek″so·loj′i·kal, *a.*—**sex·ol·o·gist**, *n.*

sext, sekst, *n.* [Fr. *sexte*, L. *sixtus*.] (*Often cap.*), *Rom. Cath. Ch.* that part of the Divine Office, the fourth canonical hour, to be said at the sixth hour or noon.

Sex·tans, seks′tanz, *n. Astron.* a small constellation between Leo and Hydra in the equatorial area of the sky. Also **Sex·tant**.

sex·tant, seks′tant, *n.* [L. *sextans, sextantis*, a sixth part, < *sex*, six.] An instrument for determining angular distances, chiefly employed by navigators for measuring the altitudes of celestial objects in determining position; the sixth part of a circle contained by two radii and an arc.

sex·tet, seks·tet′, *n.* Any collection of six items or any group of six. *Mus.* a group of six performers; a piece for six voices or instruments. Also **sex·tette**.

sex·tile, seks′til, *n. Astron.* the aspect of two planets distant from each other sixty degrees; *statistics*, one of the dividing

points or groups of values of a frequency distribution when the total number of cases is divided into six equal parts.—*a.*

sex·til·lion, seks·til′yan, *n.* [L. *sextus*, sixth, *sex*, six, and E. *million*.] A cardinal number represented by a 1 followed in America and France, by 21 zeros and in Gr. Brit. and Germany, by 36 zeros.—*a.*—**sex·til·lionth**, *a.*, *n.*

sex·to·dec·i·mo, seks″tō·des′i·mō″, *n. pl.* **sex·to·dec·i·mos**. Sixteenmo.

sex·ton, seks′ton, *n.* [O.Fr. *secrestain, segrestein*, < M.L. *sacristanus*, E. *sacristan*.] An official of a church charged with taking care of the edifice and its contents, ringing the bell, and formerly with digging graves.—**sex·ton·ship**, *n.*

sex·tu·ple, seks·tö′pl, seks·tū′pl, seks·tu·pl, seks′tū·pl, *a.* [< L. *sex*, six, after *quintuple, septuple*, etc.] Sixfold; consisting of six parts; six times as much or as great.—*n.* An amount or number six times greater than another.—*v.t.*, *v.i.*—**sextupled**, **sextupling**. To make or become six times as great.

sex·tu·plet, seks·tup′lit, seks·tō′plit, seks·tū′plit, seks′tu·plit, seks′tū·plit, *n.* Six of a kind; one of six offspring born at the same birth to a single mother. *Mus.* six equal notes performed in the time usu. taken by four such notes; also **sex·to·let**, seks′to·let″.

sex·tu·pli·cate, seks·tō′pli·kit, seks·tū′pli·kit, *a.* Having six identical parts or elements; sixth in such a group of parts.—*n.* One of six identical things.—seks·tu′pli·kāt″, seks·tū′pli·kāt″, *v.t.*—*sextuplicated*, *sextuplicating*. To sextuple.—**sex·tu·pli·cate·ly**, *adv.*—**sex·tu·pli·ca·tion**, *n.*

sex·u·al, sek′shö·al, *a.* [L. *sexualis*.] Pertaining to sex or the sexes; motivated by or exhibiting sex; *biol.* denoting reproduction by processes involving both a male and a female.—**sex·u·al·ly**, *adv.*—**sex·u·al·i·ty**, sek″shö·al′i·tē, *n.*

sex·u·al in·ter·course, *n.* Coitus or copulation usu. by the insertion of the male penis into the female vagina, esp. between humans.

sex·y, sek′sē, *a.*—*sexier*, *sexiest*. Involving excessive sex; as, a *sexy* story; sexually provocative or exciting.—**sex·i·ness**, *n.*

sfer·ics, **spher·ics**, sfer′iks, sfer′iks, *n. pl. but sing. in constr.* An electronic instrument sensitive to the electrical phenomena of the atmosphere and used in tracking storms; atmospherics.

sfor·zan·do, sfart·sän′dō, *It.* sfaʀ·tsän′da, *a.*, *adv. Mus.* forcefully or with emphasis: a direction to the performer.—*n.* A chord or tone of this type or played in this way. Also *forzando*, **sfor·za·to**, sfart·sä′tō, *It.* sfaʀ·tsä′ta.

sgraf·fi·to, skrä·fē′tō, *It.* zgʀäf·fē′ta, *n. pl.* **sgraf·fi·ti**, skrä·fē′tē. The art of incising a design through the top layer of a substance to reveal a contrasting color beneath, as with plaster or pottery; a piece, esp. of pottery, so decorated.

sh, sh, *interj.* A shortened form of *hush*, used in commanding silence.

shab·by, shab′ē, *a.*—*shabbier*, *shabbiest*. [A softened form of *scabby*; Prov. E. *shabby*, itchy, mangy, < *shab*, itch.] Threadbare or much worn; wearing threadbare or worn clothes; mean; despicable; inferior or slovenly.—**shab·bi·ly**, *adv.*—**shab·bi·ness**, *n.*

shack, shak, *n.* [Origin uncertain.] A roughly built hut, cabin, or shanty; *rail. slang*, a brakeman.—**shack up**, *slang*, to cohabit or have illicit sexual relations.

shack·le, shak′l, *n.* [O.E. *scacul, sceacul*, a shackle, prob. orig. a loose, dangling fastening, < *scacan, sceacan*, to shake.] A fetter, handcuff, or the like that restricts

the use of either set of limbs; usu. pl. that which obstructs or restrains free action or thought. The inverted metal U of a lock which pulls out and pivots at one end to enable the other, shorter end to release from the lock, hook through an object, and lock back into place; a fastener, clasp, or clevis.—*v.t.*—*shackled*, *shackling*. To fetter; to tie or confine the limbs of, so as to prevent free motion; to bind or confine so as to inhibit or prevent independent action or thought.—**shack·ler**, *n.*

shad, shad, *n. pl.* **shad**, **shads**. [O.E. *sceadd*.] Any fish of the genus *Alosa*, esp. *A. sapidissima*, of the northern Atlantic coast, related to the herring but with a comparatively deep body, and highly esteemed as food.

shad·ber·ry, shad′ber″ē, shad′be·rē, *n. pl.* **shad·ber·ries**. The fruit of the shadbush.

shad·bush, shad′bush″, *n.* [So called from the appearance of profuse white blossoms on the shrubs when the shad appear in the river each spring.] A N. American shrub, *Amelanchier canadensis*, of the rose family; any similar species of this genus, as *A. laevis*, cultivated as an ornamental. Also *Juneberry, saskatoon, service tree, service-berry*, **shad·blow**, shad′blō″.

shad·dock, shad′ok, *n.* [After Captain *Shaddock* who brought the seed from the East Indies to the West Indies in the 17th century.] A large, round, pale pinkish-yellow edible fruit of the citrus family, closely related to the grapefruit, and grown in tropical and semitropical regions of the Far East; the tree, *Citrus grandis*, which bears this fruit. Also *pomelo*.

shade, shād, *n.* [O.E. *scadu, sceadu*, shade.] Comparative darkness; a place of such comparative darkness; a state or place of relative obscurity; a place or state of dimness or gloom caused by interception of the sun's rays or other source of light; anything used to intercept light; as, a window *shade*; a cover used to soften the light cast by a lamp; a visor worn to protect the eyes; the dark or darker part of a picture; degree or gradation of light or brightness of color; a small or scarcely perceptible degree or amount; as, a *shade* of difference; a spirit or ghost. *Pl.* the abode of spirits; Hades; twilight, the gathering darkness. *Pl.*, *slang*, sunglasses.—*v.t.*—*shaded*, *shading*. To produce a darkening or a shadowing effect on or in; to protect, shelter, or screen from light by intercepting its rays; to shelter or hide from view; to dim or darken; to obscure; in artwork and other color work, to darken or to mark with gradations of color.—*v.i.* To vary or change by slight degrees, as one color into another.—**shade·less**, *a.*

shad·ing, shā′ding, *n.* The representation of light and shade in a picture; a subtle distinction or variation; shade.

shad·ow, shad′ō, *n.* [O.E. *sceadu*, a shadow, *scadu*, a shade; *scado*, a shadow, Goth. *skadus*, D. *schaduw*, G. *schatten*; a root *skad*, Skt. *chhad*, to cover; cf. Gr. *skotos*, darkness.] A figure projected in silhouette on the ground or other surface by means of interception of light; a space from which light has been intercepted; semidarkness; semiobscurity; shelter, protection, or security afforded by someone; the merest hint, trace, or implication; as, a *shadow* of doubt; a dark part of a picture; any actuality that seems insubstantial or unreal; a spirit or ghost; a shade; an imperfect and faint representation; an inseparable companion or follower; a remnant; as, a *shadow* of his former self; a period of unpleasantness; a dire promise or threat; an evil that impends; *pl.* the semidarkness.—*v.t.* To shade; to intercept light from; to cloud; to darken; to throw a gloom over; to obscure;

to protect; to screen from danger; to mark with slight gradations of color or decreasing light; to represent faintly or imperfectly; to follow closely, as a detective; to attend closely.—**shad·ow·er,** *n.*—**shad·ow·less,** *a.* —**shad·ow·like,** *a.*

shad·ow box, *n.* A decorative case or cabinet, often of wood, usu. glass-fronted and sometimes shelved, for the enclosure and display of art objects or personal treasures, esp. those that are small, three-dimensional, and fragile.

shad·ow·box, shad′ō·boks″, *v.i.* To practice boxing, as for exercise, by pretending an imaginary opponent.—**shad·ow·box·er,** *n.*—**shad·ow·box·ing,** *n.*

shad·ow cab·i·net, *n.* Brit. influential parliament members of the party not in power who are expected to become cabinet members when their party attains leadership.

shad·ow·graph, shad′ō·graf″, shad′ō·-gräf″, *n.* A picture produced by throwing a shadow, as of the hands, on a lighted screen or surface; a radiograph. A drama composed of such images in a series; also **shad·ow play.**—**shad·ow·graph·ic,** *a.*—**shad·ow·graph·ist,** *n.*—**shad·ow·graph·y,** *n.*

shad·ow·y, shad′ō·ē, *a.* Full of shade or shadow; causing shade; unsubstantial; unreal; dimly seen; dim; obscure.

shad·y, shā′dē, *a.*—*shadier, shadiest.* Abounding with shade or shades; casting or causing shade; sheltered from light or heat; *slang,* disreputable.—**shad·i·ly,** *adv.* —**shad·i·ness,** *n.*

shaft, shaft, shäft, *n.* [O.E. *sceaft,* a dart, arrow, spear, pole = Icel. *skaft, skapt,* Dan. *skaft,* D. and G. *schaft;* lit. 'the thing shaped or smoothed by shaving,' < O.E. *scafan,* to shave; cf. L. *scapus,* a shaft; Gr. *skaptron, skēptron,* a staff.] The long and narrow body of a spear or arrow; the spear or arrow itself; a pointed remark; a ray of light; the long handle of certain tools or instruments; one of a pair of bars by which a horse is harnessed to a vehicle; the columnar part of anything; a tree trunk; the supporting upright part of a candelabrum; a flagpole; the stem or main rib of a feather; the vertical mainstay of a cross; *anat.* the long middle portion of a bone; *mech.* a rotating, cylindrical bar used to transmit motive power. *Arch.* a small column; the body of a column between the base and the capital; a pillar, obelisk, or columnar monument. *Textiles,* a long lath at each end of the heddles of a loom.—*v.t.* To fit or push with a shaft.—**get the shaft,** *slang,* to be cheated or treated unfairly.

shaft, shaft, shäft, *n.* [< G. *schacht,* the shaft of a mine.] A narrow, deep passage in the earth for mining; a passageway for light or ventilation; an opening passing between floors in a building.

shaft·ing, shaf′ting, shäf′ting, *n. Mach.* A system of shafts through which motion is communicated; the material used to make shafts.

shag, shag, *n.* [O.E. *sceacga,* shag of hair, akin to Icel. *skegg,* Sw. *skägg,* Dan. *skjæg,* beard: cf. *shaw.*] Rough, matted hair, wool, or the like, or a mass of this; the long or rough nap of cloth; a cloth with a heavy nap; a rough mass or growth of vegetation; a coarse tobacco cut in fine shreds; *ornith.* a cormorant.—*v.t.*—*shagged, shagging.* To make rough or shaggy, esp. with vegetation; to roughen or make sharply broken, as a surface.—*v.i.* To become or appear shaggy.—*a.* Shaggy; also **shag·ged.**— **shag·like,** *a.*

shag, shag, *v.t.*—*shagged, shagging.* To pursue; to retrieve; *baseball,* to catch, as fly balls, during batting practice.

shag, shag, *n.* A dance step which involves hopping energetically on alternate feet.— *v.i.*—*shagged, shagging.* To dance the shag.

shag·bark, shag′bärk″, *n.* A species of hickory, *Carya ovata,* with rough gray bark, yielding high-grade hickory nuts; the nut of this tree; the wood. Also **shell-bark, shag·bark hick·o·ry,** shel′bärk″.

shag·gy, shag′ē, *a.*—*shaggier, shaggiest.* Long, rough, matted, or tangled; forming a thick, bushy, irregular mass; covered with or having long, rough growth; having a long or rough nap; untrimmed or unkempt; crass.—**shag·gi·ly,** *adv.*—**shag·gi·ness,** *n.*

shag·gy dog sto·ry, *n.* A rambling joke whose punch line is absurdly irrelevant.

shag·gy-mane, shag′ē·mān″, *n.* A common, edible mushroom, *Coprinus comatus,* having an elongated, white, shaggy cap or pileus.

sha·green, sha·grēn′, *n.* [Fr. *chagrin,* Venetian, *sagrin,* < Turk. *sagri,* Pers. *saghri,* shagreen. *Chagrin* is the same word.] Rough, untanned, granulated leather; the abrasive skin of some sharks and rays, used as a polisher.—*a.*

Shah, shä, *n.* [Pers. a king, a prince (hence *chess, check.*)] (*Sometimes l.c.*) a title of the monarch of Iran, formerly called Persia.

Shai·tan, shī·tän′, *n.* [Ar., = E. *Satan.*] In Mohammedan lore, Satan or the devil. (*l.c.*) a person of evil disposition; a vicious animal.

shake, shāk, *v.i.*—past *shook,* pp. *shaken,* ppr. *shaking.* [O.E. *scacan, sceacan,* pret. *scóc,* pp. *scacen;* Icel. and Sw. *skaka,* to shake; allied to D. *schokken,* to shake; G. *schaukeln,* to swing.] To move with jerky vibrations to and fro, up and down, or in different directions; to quiver, tremble, shiver, or vibrate by or as if by a physical or mental cause, condition, or blow; to react in a certain way to vigorous joggling, followed by *off, out, from,* or *down;* as, wrinkles that *shake out;* to be unstable or to totter; to clasp each other's hand in making an agreement, greeting, or the like; *mus.* to trill a note.—*v.t.* To cause to move with jerky vibrations; to brandish or wave toward, usu. as if in threat or reprimand; to grab and jostle vigorously in order to bring about certain action or reaction; to unsettle, disturb, mix, or make turbulent; to cause to wobble, vascillate, or totter; to cause to shiver or tremble; to unfix, dislodge, or remove by joggling; as, to *shake* salt; to throw off or make oneself free from; as, to *shake* a fear; *mus.* to trill.—*n.* The act or occurrence of shaking, vibrating, jerking, or rocking; a rapid wavering motion from side to side, as a tremor or shiver; a handshake; an unsettling blow, disturbance, or jolt; an earthquake; that which results from shaking, as a crack or fissure; a milk shake; *pl.* a period of shuddering shivers, as from a chill, usu. preceded by *the; mus.* a trill; *carp.* a thick, rough wooden shingle; *nuclear phys.* .000000001 of a second; *games,* a mixing and casting of the dice. *Slang,* a very short amount of time; as, to be done in a *shake;* a chance, opportunity, or deal; as, a fair *shake.*—**no great shakes,** *slang,* not exceptionally talented, exciting, or interesting.— **shake a leg,** *slang,* to move faster or hurry. —**shak·a·ble, shake·a·ble,** *n.*

shake down, *v.t.* To bring down by shaking; as, to *shake down* nuts from a tree; to cause to settle by shaking; bring into optimum condition or working order; as, to *shake down* a naval cruiser by a first voyage. *Slang,* to exact money from by compulsion, esp. dishonestly or illicitly; to search, as for contraband.

shake·down, shāk′doun″, *n. Slang,* an exaction of money by compulsion, esp. dishonestly or illicitly; an exhaustive search. A bed made of straw, blankets, or other bedding spread on the floor; any makeshift bed for temporary use; a process of shaking down; a bringing into optimum condition or working order by practice; as, to give a naval vessel a *shakedown* by a voyage which permits a trial of the engines and armaments in use.—*a.* Also **shake-down.**

shake·out, shāk′out″, *n.* The removal of companies or their products in a competitive market as a result of a decline in sales or the introduction of products of a higher standard; a rapid decline in the value of certain securities on the stock market resulting from a surge of activity in their sale.

shak·er, shā′kẽr, *n.* One who or that which shakes; a container, as for a condiment, designed with perforations through which its contents may be shaken out; any container in which ingredients, usu. liquid, may be mixed by a shaking motion; (*cap.*) one belonging to a religious sect, officially the United Society of Believers in Christ's Second Appearing, advocating celibacy and communal and simple living, so called, popularly, from the agitations or movements of the body which at one time formed part of their ceremonial.—**Shak·er·ism,** shā′ke·riz″um, *n.*

Shake·spear·e·an, Shake·spear·i·an, shāk·spēr′ē·an, *a.* [From William *Shakespeare,* 1564–1616, English playwright and poet.] Relating to Shakespeare.—*n.* A scholar making Shakespeare's works his special field of study.

Shake·spear·e·an son·net, *n.* English sonnet.

shake up, *v.t.* To stir, mix, or loosen by shaking vigorously, as ingredients; to upset by drastic or unexpected changes, dismissals, or reorganization, as a business, institution, or department; to jar bodily or emotionally; as, to be *shaken up* in football. —**shake-up,** shāk′up″, *n.* An upsetting change or reorganization, as in a business or institution.

shak·ing pal·sy, *n.* Paralysis agitans. Also *Parkinson's disease.*

shak·o, shak′ō, shā′kō, *n.* [Fr. *schako,* < Hung., *csákó,* a shako.] A kind of military cap somewhat resembling a truncated cone, with a peak in front.

shak·y, shā′kē, *a.*—*shakier, shakiest.* Given to shaking; shaking; trembling; tremulous, as the voice; liable to break down or give way, as a structure; weak or feeble, or not strong in health; insecure or unreliable; wavering or unsettled, as in allegiance or belief; uncertain or not to be depended on, as one's knowledge of a subject.—**shak·i·ly,** *adv.*—**shak·i·ness,** *n.*

shale, shāl, *n.* [Appar. another use of *shale,* with reference to the fissile structure.] A rock of laminated structure formed by the consolidation of claylike, fine-grained sediments, which may metamorphose into slate.

shale oil, *n.* A crude mineral oil distilled from shale that is bituminous.

shall, shal, *unstressed* shal, *aux. v.*—past *should.* [O.E. *sceal,* I shall, I have to, I ought to; pl. *sculon,* pret. *sceolde, scolde,* inf. *sculon;* Icel. and Dan. *skal,* D. *zal,* G. *soll,* literal meaning seen in Goth. *skulan,* 'to owe, to have to pay.'] Used in first person to indicate simple futurity, as: We *shall* ask the waiter. Used in the second and third persons to denote determination or resolve; as, then you *shall* succeed; to denote pledge or promise; as, for we *shall* not fail you; to denote obligation or command; as, then said proprietor *shall* obtain a license; to denote inescapability or inevitability; as, since each *shall* meet his destiny. Used interrogatively in all persons to ask direction or propriety, as: *Shall* I pick him up?

shal·loon, sha·lön′, *n.* [Appar. named from *Châlons*-sur-Marne, city in northeastern

France.] A light, twilled woolen fabric used chiefly for linings.

shal·lop, shal′op, *n.* [Fr. *chaloupe* = Sp. *chalupa;* origin uncertain: cf. *sloop.*] A vessel with one or more masts, esp. a type of vessel with two masts and lug sails prevalent during the 17th and 18th centuries; a small, light boat with or without a mast for use in shallow waters, as for fishing.

shal·lot, sha·lot′, *n.* [O.Fr. *eschalote,* < *Ascalon.*] A plant of the lily family, *Allium ascalonicum,* having mild-flavored, clustered bulbs used in cooking and pickling.

shal·low, shal′ō, *a.* [M.E. *schalowe;* prob. related to *shoal.*] Of little depth, or not deep, as water or a dish; lacking depth or superficial, as thought, knowledge, or feeling; wanting depth of thought, observation, knowledge, or feeling, as persons.—*n.* Often *pl.* A shallow part of a body of water; a shoal.—*v.t., v.i.* To make or become shallow.—**shal·low·ly,** *adv.*—**shal·low·ness,** *n.*

sha·lom, sha·lōm′, Heb. shä·lōm′, *interj.* *Heb.* peace: a word used in either greeting or farewell.—**sha·lom a·lei·chem,** sha·lōm′ a·lā′chem, sha′lom a·lā′chem, *Heb.* shä·lōm′ ä·lā′chem, shä·lōm′ ä;lä·chem′, *interj.* *Heb.* peace to you: commonly expressed as a greeting.

shalt, shalt, *aux. v.* *Archaic, poet.* present tense, second person singular of 'shall.'

sham, sham, *n.* [Said to be a var. of *shame.*] Something that is not what it purports to be; a spurious imitation; a cover for giving a thing a different outward appearance; as, a pillow *sham;* a pretender; *archaic,* a trick or hoax.—*a.* Pretended; imitation; counterfeit.—*v.t.*—**shammed, shamming.** To produce a deceptive imitation of, or pretend falsely to be; assume the appearance of; as, to *sham* illness.—*v.i.* To make a false pretense; pretend to be or do what one is not or does not.

sha·man, shä′man, shā′man, sham′an, *n.* [Tungusic.] A priest or sorcerer among various tribes of northern Asia and northwestern North America, supposed to have the power to deal with and protect against spirits; a medicine man.

sha·man·ism, shä′ma·niz″um, shā′ma·niz″um, sham′a·niz″um, *n.* The primitive religion of northern Asia embracing a belief in controlling spirits who can be influenced only by shamans; any similar religion, including some N. American Indian religions.—**sha·man·ist,** *n., a.*—**sha·man·is·tic,** *a.*

sham·ble, sham′bl, *v.i.*—**shambled, shambling.** [Origin obscure.] To walk or go awkwardly or unsteadily; shuffle.—*n.* A shambling gait.

sham·bles, sham′blz, *n. pl., sing. or pl. in constr.* A slaughterhouse; a place or scene of carnage or execution; a place, state, or scene of disorder or destruction. *Brit. dial.* a market for meat; in the singular, a stall or shop for meat.

shame, shām, *n.* [O.E. *sceamu, scamu,* = O.H.G. *scama* (G. *scham*) = Icel. *skömm* = Sw. Dan. *skam,* shame: cf. *shend* and *sham.*] The painful feeling arising from the consciousness of something dishonorable, improper, ridiculous, or the like done by oneself or another, or of being in a situation offensive to decency, self-respect, or pride; as, to blush with *shame;* susceptibility to this feeling; as, to be without *shame;* ignominy, disgrace, or dishonor; as, to bring *shame* upon one's family; a fact or circumstance bringing disgrace or discredit, or much to be regretted or lamented, as: It's a *shame* that you can't come.—*v.t.*—**shamed, shaming.** [O.E. *sceamian, scamian.*] To cause to feel shame; to make ashamed,

as: His actions, under the circumstances, *shamed* us all. To drive or force through shame, as: He *shamed* the child into silence. To cover with ignominy or reproach; disgrace; dishonor.—**for shame!** you ought to feel shame.—**put to shame,** to bring shame upon; to eclipse or outshine, as: Her cooking skills *put* mine *to shame.*

shame·faced, shām′fāst″, *a.* [For *shamefast,* by association with *face.*] Modest or bashful; characterized by or showing shame; as, *shamefaced* apologies.—**shame·fac·ed·ly,** shām″fā′sid·lē, shām′fāst″lē, *adv.*—**shame·fac·ed·ness,** *n.*

shame·ful, shām′ful, *a.* Bringing shame or disgrace; scandalous; indecent.—**shame·ful·ly,** *adv.*—**shame·ful·ness,** *n.*

shame·less, shām′lis, *a.* Having no shame or modesty; insensible to disgrace; done without shame.—**shame·less·ly,** *adv.*—**shame·less·ness,** *n.*

sham·mer, sham′ėr, *n.* One who shams.

sham·mes, shä′mes, *n. pl.* **sham·mo·sim,** shä·mos′im. *Judaism.* A particular menorah candle with which the others are lit; an individual whose duties in a synagogue are similar to those of a sexton in a church. Also **sha·mes, sham·mas, sham·mash, sham·mos.**

sham·my, sham′ē, *n.* [A corruption of *chamois,* the animal and its prepared skin.] A kind of soft leather. See *chamois.*

sham·poo, sham·pö′, *v.t.*—**shampooed, shampooing.** [Prob. < Hind. *chāmpo,* impv. of *chāmpnā,* press.] To wash, as the hair and scalp, esp. with a special solution; to clean, as a carpet, with a special substance; orig. to massage.—*n. pl.* **sham·poos.** A cleansing compound used for shampooing; the act or an act of shampooing.—**sham·poo·er,** *n.*

sham·rock, sham′rok, *n.* [Ir. *seamrog,* dim. of *seamar,* trefoil.] A plant with trifoliate leaves, usu. a yellow-flowered species of trefoil, *Trifolium dubium:* the national emblem of Ireland; loosely, wood sorrel, white clover, and black medic.

sha·mus, shä′mus, shā′mus, *n. pl.* **sha·mus·es.** *Slang.* A policeman; a private investigator.

shan·dry·dan, shan′drē·dan″, *n.* [Origin obscure.] A light two-wheeled cart or gig; any old-fashioned rickety conveyance.

shan·dy·gaff, shan′dē·gaf″, *n.* [Origin obscure.] A mixed drink, usu. beer with ginger beer.

shang·hai, shang′hī, shang·hī′, *v.t.*—**shanghaied, shanghaiing.** [Appar. meaning 'to ship to Shanghai': cf. *shanghai.*] To render insensible, as by drugs, and ship on a vessel wanting hands; to bring about the performance of an action by deception or force.

Shan·gri-la, shang′grí·lä″, shang″gri·lä′, *n.* [From the locale of the novel and movie, *Lost Horizon,* by James Hilton.] An earthly paradise; any secluded, idyllic hideaway.

shank, shangk, *n.* [O.E. *sceanca, seanca,* shank, akin to G. *schenkel,* thigh, *schinken,* ham.] *Anat.* in man, that part of the leg between the knee and the ankle; the corresponding part in certain animals. A cut of meat from this part of an animal; the leglike, stemlike, or shaftlike part of many objects, as a golf club or a smoker's pipe; the main stem of an anchor, fishhook, pin, or nail; that portion of an instrument or tool connecting the acting part with the handle or any like part; the body of a printing type; the part of a shoe beneath the instep that connects the broad part of the sole with the heel; a loop at the back of a button, serving for attachment; *colloq.* the latter end or best part of anything; as, the *shank* of the evening.

shank·piece, shangk′pēs″, *n.* A firm

material, often metal, shaped to provide support for the arch in a shoe.

shan't, shant, shänt. *Colloq.* contraction of shall not.

shan·tey, shan′tē, *n. pl.* **shan·teys.** Chantey.

shan·tung, shan′tung, *n.* [For *Shantung pongee;* from *Shantung,* province of eastern China.] A silk fabric, a heavy grade of pongee; a similar fabric made of cotton or rayon.

shan·ty, shan′tē, *n. pl.* **shan·ties.** [Canadian Fr. *chantier,* log hut, in Fr. supporting framework, open or roofed enclosure, shed, shop, < L. *cantherius,* gelding, framework.] A roughly built hut, cabin, or house, as in lumbering regions or frontier districts; any building of flimsy or rough construction.—*a.* Of or relating to a shanty; referring, in a disparaging way, to a disadvantaged socioeconomic class; as, *shanty* Irish.

shan·ty·town, shan′tē·toun″, *n.* That part of a town or city, or a town itself, in which most of the dwellings are shanties.

shape, shāp, *n.* [M.E. *shape, shap,* < O.E. *gesceap,* creation, created thing, form, shape.] The external form, outline, or contour of a thing; the form of a particular thing. The form, structure, or characteristics of a thing; as, a present in the *shape* of money, the *shape* danger takes; an orderly, neat, or proper arrangement or form; as, to put one's room into *shape;* the condition or state of existence, esp. good condition; as, a man out of *shape;* the form of the human body, esp. the female figure; a figure or form seen dimly or as a silhouette; as, *shapes* romping in the mist; a phantom or ethereal form; an embodiment or disguise; something used to give form, as a shaped mold; *constr.* a piece of rolled or hammered iron or steel or any of various special shapes or cross-sections, as an I-beam.—*v.t.*—**shaped, shaping.** To create, fashion, or give a definite form to; as, to *shape* a government; to adjust, modify, or adapt in outline, contour, or form to obtain fit or appropriateness; as, to *shape* a head of hair; to give definite form, character, or direction to; as, to *shape* the future; to express or put into words; as, to *shape* a question; fashion or develop into something specified; as, to *shape* men into leaders.—*v.i.* To develop or assume a definite shape, form, or character; to happen or turn out.—**shap·a·ble, shape·a·ble,** *a.*—**shaped,** shāpt, *a.*—**shap·er,** shā′pėr, *n.*

shape·less, shāp′lis, *a.* Without shape; having no definite or regular shape or form; wanting beauty or elegance of form.—**shape·less·ly,** *adv.*—**shape·less·ness,** *n.*

shape·ly, shāp′lē, *a.*—**shapelier, shapeliest.** Having a pleasing shape; well-formed.—**shape·li·ness,** *n.*

shape-up, shāp′up″, *n.* A method of hiring longshoremen for a shift or for the day, by which the workers assemble and a crew is selected by a union agent.

shard, shärd, *n.* [O.E. *sceard,* noun use of *sceard,* cut, notched, a pp. formation from the root of E. *shear.*] A fragment, esp. of broken earthenware; *zool.* a scale or shell; *entom.* the shell-like wing cover or elytron of a beetle. Also *sherd.*

share, shâr, *n.* [O.E. *scearu,* cutting, division; < the root of E. *shear.*] The portion or part allotted or belonging to, or contributed or owed by, an individual among a number, all of whom receive or contribute; one's just or full portion; each of the equal parts into which the capital stock of a joint-stock company or a corporation is divided.—*v.t.*—**shared, sharing.** To divide and distribute in shares; apportion; to use or occupy jointly; to participate in, enjoy, or suffer with others.—*v.i.* To have a share or part; participate, often with *in;* to apportion something.—**shar·er,** *n.*

share, shâr, *n.* Plowshare.

share·crop·per, shâr′krop″ẽr, *n.* A tenant farmer who pays as rent a share of the crop.—**share·crop,** shâr′krop″, *v.i.,* *v.t.*—sharecropped, sharecropping.

share·hold·er, shâr′hōl″dẽr, *n.* One who holds or owns a share or shares, as in a corporation; a stockholder.

sha·rif, sha·rēf′, *n.* [Ar.] A descendant of Muhammad through his daughter Fatima; an Islamic prince; the chief magistrate of Mecca. Also **she·rif, she·reef.—sha·ri·fi·an,** sha·rē′fē·an, *a.*

shark, shärk, *n.* [Origin uncertain.] Any of a group of elongate, cartilaginous, mostly marine fishes, order *Selachii,* certain species of which are large and ferocious, destructive to other fish and to man.—**shark·like,** *a.*

shark, shärk, *n.* [Origin uncertain; commonly associated with *shark* (recorded earlier), but perh. from a different source: cf. G. *schurke,* rascal, also E. *shirk.*] One who preys greedily on others by usury, swindling, or other trickery; *slang,* one who has unusual ability or proficiency in a particular field.—*v.t.* To obtain by trickery or fraud; steal.—*v.i.* To live by shifts and stratagems.

shark·skin, shärk′skin″, *n.* Shark hide made into leather; a fabric made of any of various yarns, characterized by an even, compact, basket-type weave with a smooth, durable finish.

sharp, shärp, *a.* [O.E. *scearp;* D. *scherp;* G. *scharf;* Icel. *skarpr;* Sw. and Dan. *skarp,* sharp: cf. *scarp* and *scrape.*] Having a thin cutting edge or a fine point; well-adapted for cutting or piercing; keen; acute; terminating in an edge or point; not blunt or rounded; characterized by sudden change of direction, as a turn; abrupt, as a descent; angular, as the features; composed of hard, angular grains, as sand; clear or distinct in outline; strongly marked, as a contrast; keenly affecting the senses; pungent in taste; sour, biting, or acrid; piercing or shrill in sound; keenly cold, as weather; intensely painful or distressing; as, a *sharp* pain; severe, harsh, or caustic; as, *sharp* words; fierce or violent; as, a *sharp* struggle; keen or eager; as, *sharp* desire; quick or brisk; as, a *sharp* walk or run; of keen perception; as, *sharp* ears; vigilant or attentive; as, a *sharp* watch; mentally acute or quick; as, a *sharp* lad; shrewd or astute; as, *sharp* at making a bargain; shrewd to the point of dishonesty; as, *sharp* practice. *Mus.* above an intended pitch, as a note; too high; raised a half step in pitch; as, F *sharp;* either major or augmented, as an interval; having sharps in the signature, as keys or tonalities. *Slang,* stylish; as, a *sharp* dresser. *Phon.* of a consonant, pronounced with breath and not with voice; surd.—*v.t. Mus.* to raise in pitch, esp. a half step.—*v.i. Mus.* to sound above the true pitch.—*adv.* [O.E. *scearpe.*] In a sharp manner; keenly or acutely; abruptly or suddenly; as, to pull a horse up *sharp;* punctually; as, at one o'clock *sharp;* quickly or briskly; vigilantly or attentively, as: Look *sharp! Mus.* above the true pitch; as, to sing *sharp.*—*n.* Something sharp; a needle with a very sharp point; a sharper or swindler; *colloq.* an expert. *Mus.* a tone one half step above a given tone; the character, ♯, which indicates this on the musical staff.—**sharp·ly,** *adv.*—**sharp·ness,** *n.*

sharp·en, shär′pen, *v.t.* To make sharp or sharper; to whet; to make more eager, intense, or keen.—*v.i.* To grow or become sharp.—**sharp·en·er,** *n.*

sharp·er, shär′pẽr, *n.* A tricky fellow or swindler; a cheat; one who lives by cheating, esp. in gambling games. Also *sharpie.*

sharp·eyed, shärp′īd″, *a.* Having acute vision; observant.

sharp-fanged, shärp′fangd′, *a.* Possessing sharp teeth. *Fig.* caustic; sarcastic.

sharp-freeze, shärp′frēz″, *v.t.*—past *sharp-froze,* pp. *sharp-frozen,* ppr. *sharp-freezing.* Quick-freeze.

sharp·ie, sharp·y, shär′pē, *n.* [Appar. a dim. of *sharp.*] A kind of long, flat-bottomed boat with one or two masts, each rigged with a triangular sail, used originally as a fishing boat in New England; a sharper. *Slang,* an extremely alert or keenly intelligent person; a person who dresses in a showy or flashy manner.

sharp-nosed, shärp′nōzd′, *a.* Having a slender, pointed nose; possessing an acute sense of smell; having a pointed or projecting front; as, a *sharp-nosed* racing car.

sharp-set, shärp′set″, *a.* Keen or eager for food; very hungry; keen, eager, or extremely desirous; set so as to be at a sharp angle or form a sharp edge.—**sharp-set·ness,** *n.*

sharp·shoot·er, shärp′shoo″tẽr, *n.* A person skilled in shooting with exactness; an excellent marksman. *Milit.* the rating of skill with a rifle that is ranked above marksman or below expert; a soldier achieving this particular rating.—**sharp·shoot·ing,** *n.*

sharp-sight·ed, shärp′sī′tid, *a.* Having acute vision; having acute discernment; mentally quick or alert.—**sharp-sight·ed·ly,** *adv.*—**sharp-sight·ed·ness,** *n.*

sharp-tongued, shärp′tungd′, *a.* Vitriolic in speech; using or characterized by caustic, harsh language.

sharp-wit·ted, shärp′wit′id, *a.* Having acute mental faculties.—**sharp-wit·ted·ly,** *adv.*—**sharp-wit·ted·ness,** *n.*

shash·lik, shäsh·lik′, shäsh′lik, *n.* Shish kebab. Also **shash·lick, shas·lik.**

shat·ter, shat′ẽr, *v.t.* [M.E. *schateren;* assibilated form of *scatter.*] To reduce to scattered or loose fragments, or break in pieces, as by a sudden blow; damage or injure severely by some breaking or crushing action; to wreck or ruin, as fortunes, happiness, or lives; to impair, as health or nerves, seriously or completely; to crush in spirit.—*v.i.* To break suddenly into fragments, or fly in pieces, as glass; to break up or smash, as a wave dashing against rocks.—*n.* A shattered state, as of the nerves; *usu. pl.* fragments due to shattering.

shat·ter·proof, shat′ẽr·prōf″, *a.* Not subject to shattering; designed so as to be proof against shattering; as, *shatterproof* glass.

shave, shāv, *v.i.*—past *shaved,* pp. *shaved* or *shaven,* ppr. *shaving.* [O.E. *sceafan, scafan,* shave, scrape, = D. *schaven* = G. *schaben* = Icel. *skafa* = Goth. *skaban,* prob. akin to L. *scabere,* scratch, scrape.] To remove hair or a beard by means of a razor.—*v.t.* To remove hair from, as from the chin, upper lip, or legs, by cutting close to the skin with a razor; to cut off, as hair, esp. the beard, close to the skin with a razor; to cut or trim closely, or reduce to a smooth or bare surface; to cut or scrape away the surface of, with a sharp-edged tool; to reduce to the form of shavings or thin slices; to take off, as a surface layer or a thin slice, by cutting or scraping; to scrape, graze, or pass so close as almost to graze; *colloq.* to purchase, as a note, at a rate of discount greater than is legal or customary.—*n.* An act or process of shaving; a shaving of a person by removing a growth of beard; a thin piece or slice shaved off; a shaving; an approach so close as almost to graze; a narrow miss or escape; as, a close *shave;* a tool, as for scraping or shaving wood.

shave·ling, shāv′ling, *n.* A tonsured ecclesiastic: used disparagingly. A young fellow.

shav·er, shā′vẽr, *n.* One who shaves; a tool used for shaving; an electric razor. *Colloq.* a youngster; a boy.

shave·tail, shāv′tāl″, *n. Slang.* A newly commissioned second lieutenant; an untrained, young mule; a person who is inexperienced.

Sha·vi·an, shā′vē·an, *a.* [As if < a N.L. *Shavius,* for *Shaw;* with *v* for *w,* there being no *w* in (classical) Latin.] Of, pertaining to, or characteristic of George Bernard Shaw, the Irish dramatist; as, *Shavian* humor.—*n.* A devoted admirer of or specialist on George Bernard Shaw or his works.

shav·ie, shā′vē, *n. Sc.* A practical joke; trick.

shav·ing, shā′ving, *n.* The act of that which or one who shaves; a thin slice, esp. of metal or wood pared off.

shaw, shâ, *n.* [O.E. *sceaga,* akin to *sceacga,* E. *shag.*] *Dial.* a thicket, coppice, or small wood.

shaw, shâ, *n.* [Origin uncertain: cf. *shaw.*] *Brit.* the top, or stalk and leaves, as of potatoes or turnips.

shawl, shâl, *n.* [Fr. *châle,* < Ar. and Pers. *shâl,* a shawl.] An article of dress of various textures, usu. of a square or oblong shape, worn chiefly by females as a loose covering for the shoulders or head.—*v.t.* To cover with a shawl.

shawm, shâm, *n.* [M.E. *schalme,* through O.Fr. < L. *calamus,* reed.] A medieval musical wind instrument, forerunner of the oboe, having a double reed enclosed in a globular mouthpiece.

Shaw·nee, shâ·nē′, *n. pl.* **Shaw·nee, Shaw·nees.** A nomadic tribe of N. American Indians of Algonquian stock, orig. living in Tennessee and many central and southern states, now in Oklahoma.

shay, chay, shā, *n. Dial.* a chaise.

she, shē, *pron.*—sing. nom. *she,* poss. *her* or *hers,* obj. *her;* pl. nom. *they,* poss. *their* or *theirs,* obj. *them.* [M.E. *she, sche, scheo, se,* < O.E. *sēo,* fem. of *se,* demonstrative pronoun, later *the.*] A personal pronoun of the third person, referring to the female in question or last mentioned; the woman or female, as: *She* who listens learns. Anything traditionally considered feminine, as: *She* was a good ship.—*n. pl.* **shes.** Any female person; any female animal: often used in combination; as, a *she*-goat.

shea but·ter, shē′ but″ẽr, *n.* A solid fat obtained from the seeds of the shea tree and used in western Africa as food and in making soap and candles.

sheaf, shēf, *n. pl.* **sheaves.** [O.E. *scēaf;* L.G. *skof, schof,* D. *schoof,* Icel. *skauf,* G. *schaub;* < stem of *shove.*] A quantity of the stalks of wheat, rye, oats, or other plants, bound together; a bundle of papers or the like tied together; a quiver full of arrows; anything comparable in appearance to a sheaf of grain.—*v.t.* To collect and bind; to make sheaves of.—**sheaf·like,** *a.*

shear, shēr, *v.t.*—past *sheared,* pp. *sheared* or *shorn,* ppr. *shearing.* [O.E. *sceran* (pp. *scoren*) = D. *scheren* = G. *scheren* = Icel. *skera,* shear, cut; prob. akin to Gr. *keirein,* cut short, shear: cf. *corm.*] To cut off or remove by or as by cutting with a sharp instrument; to cut the wool, fleece, or hair from, as sheep; to strip or deprive, as by cutting, usu. followed by *of; chiefly Sc.* to reap, as grass or grain, with a sickle. To pass through as by cutting or cleaving; to cut with a sharp instrument, usu. with some form of shears.—*v.i.* To cut with a sharp instrument; to move by or as if by cutting; *mech.* to become fractured beneath a load because of sliding action; *chiefly Sc.* to cut grain or other crops with a sickle. —*n.* The act or process of shearing; a shearing of sheep, used in stating age; as, a sheep of one *shear*; the quantity, esp. of wool or fleece, cut off at one shearing. *Phys.* a deformation in a solid produced by stress and consisting of a relative displacement of two contacting laminar layers in opposite directions parallel to their common plane of contact; the stress involved in such a strain.—**shears**, shērz, *n. pl.* Any of several cutting tools or machines with two blades resembling those of scissors but generally larger. An apparatus for hoisting heavy weights, consisting of two or more spars fastened together near the top with their lower ends separated to form a base, the tackle being suspended from the top and the whole structure being steadied by guys; also **sheers, shear legs.**—**shear·er**, *n.*

sheared, shērd, *a.* Formed, shaped, or completed by shearing; trimmed to a uniform length; as, a *sheared* hedge.

shear·ling, shēr′ling, *n.* A yearling sheep having been once shorn; skin from such a sheep or from a sheep recently shorn, tanned and with its wool still on it.

shear·water, shēr′wạ″tẽr, shēr′wot″ẽr, *n.* Any of various long-billed sea birds, esp. of the genus *Puffinus*, allied to the petrels, that appear to shear or cleave the water with their long wings when flying low.

sheat·fish, shēt′fish″, *n. pl.* **sheat·fish·es, sheat·fish.** [Earlier *sheath-fish* < G. *scheid, schaid*, the fish, *scheide*, sheath.] A large fresh-water fish, *Silurus glanis*, the great catfish of central and eastern Europe, sometimes weighing about 400 pounds; any of various allied fishes.

sheath, shēth, *n. pl.* **sheaths**, shēTHZ. [O.E. *scēath, scæth,* = D. *scheede* = G. *scheide* = Icel. *skeidhir*, pl., sheath; from the root of E. *shed.*] A case or covering for the blade of a sword, dagger, or the like; any similar encasing cover; *biol.* a closely enveloping part or structure, as in an animal or plant organism; *bot.* a tubular structure encasing certain leaves at their base. A dress that is unbelted and usu. close-fitted; the covering or coating on a wire, cord, or cable.—**sheath·less**, *a.*—**sheath·like**, *a.*

sheath·bill, shēth′bil″, *n.* Either of two birds, *Chionis alba* and *C. minor,* inhabiting Antarctica, both having a horny case which partly sheathes the bill.

sheathe, shēTH, *v.t.*—**sheathed, sheathing.** To put into or supply with a sheath or scabbard; to thrust into, as into a sheath; as, to *sheathe* a dagger into his side; to protect by encasing or covering with sheathing. —**sheath·er**, *n.*

sheath·ing, shē′THing, *n.* The act of one who sheathes; that which sheathes; any material used for such a purpose.

sheath knife, *n.* A knife carried in a sheath.

shea tree, shē′ trē″, *n.* A large African tree, *Butyrospermum parkii,* with fruit whose seeds yield shea butter.

sheave, shiv, shēv, *n.* [Same as O.D. *schijve,* D. *schijf,* Icel. *skifa,* Dan. *skive,* G. *scheibe,* a slice, a disc; akin to *schift.*] A grooved pulley wheel on which a rope works; the grooved wheel of a device converting circular motion into straight motion.

sheave, shēv, *v.t.*—**sheaved, sheaving.** [< *sheaf.*] To gather or collect into a sheaf or sheaves.

sheaves, shēvz, *n. pl.* Plural form of *sheaf* and *sheave.*

she·bang, she·bang′, *n. Slang,* a thing, a matter, or an affair in its entirety, usu. preceded by *whole,* as: The *whole shebang* collapsed.

she·been, she·bēn′, *n.* [Ir.] An illegally operated, unlicensed shop where liquors are sold. Also **she·bean, shib·been.**

shed, shed, *v.t.*—**shed, shedding.** [O.E. *scēadan,* to separate, to disperse; G. *scheiden,* Goth. *skaidan,* to part, to separate;

allied to L. *scindo,* to cut.] To let flow or fall, as tears; to lose, as blood; to emit, throw off, or give out, as a light, an odor, or an aura; to drop or cast off, separate, or detach from, seasonally or in a life process, as a seed, leaf, feather, hair, or fur; to disperse, repel, or by other means prevent penetration; as, a roof or a coat that *sheds* water.—*v.i.* To drop off, as a leaf; to lose, as hair; to cast off in a life process, as feathers or fur.—*n. Textiles,* in weaving, a triangular space running the length of the loom formed when part of the warp threads are raised for the passage of the shuttle across the loom between them. Anything that sheds or has been shed.

she'd, shēd. Contraction of she had or she would.

shed, shed, *n.* [Perh. orig. a sloping roof or penthouse to *shed* off the rain.] A crude structure intended only for storage or shelter; a structure that is roofed, but open on one or more sides.—**shed·like**, *a.*

shed·der, shed′ẽr, *n.* Something or someone that sheds; a crab or lobster in the mating process.

sheen, shēn, *n.* [O.E. *scēne, scīene, scȳne* = D. *schoon* = G. *schön* = Goth. *skauns,* beautiful; < the root of O.E. *scēawian,* look at, E. *show,* though in later English use associated with *shine.*] Brightness, radiance, or light; luster; a gleam or luster resulting from the reflection of light; as, the *sheen* of satin or of pearls.—*v.i.* Shine.—*a.* —**sheen·y**, shē′nē, *a.*—**sheenier, sheeniest.**

sheep, shēp, *n. pl.* **sheep.** [O.E. *scēap, scēp;* D. *schaap;* G. *schaf,* sheep.] Any of the ruminant mammals constituting the genus *Ovis,* of the family *Bovidae,* closely allied to the goats, esp. *Ovis aries,* which has many domesticated varieties or breeds, valuable for their flesh, wool, and other products; leather made from the skin of these animals; *fig.* a meek, timid, or stupid person.

sheep·ber·ry, shēp′ber″ē, shēp′be·rē, *n. pl.* **sheep·ber·ries.** A shrub or small tree, *Viburnum lentago,* of N. America, bearing cymes of small white flowers and berrylike black drupes; the edible fruit. Also **nan··ny·ber·ry.**

sheep·cote, shēp′kōt″, *n.* A small yard or enclosure for sheep. Also **sheep·cot,** *sheepfold,* shēp′kot″.

sheep-dip, shēp′dip″, *n.* A liquid disinfectant, usu. in vats, into which sheep are immersed to rid them of parasitic vermin.

sheep·dog, sheep dog, shēp′dạg″, shēp′dog″, *n.* A dog trained to tend sheep, often a collie; also *shepherd dog.* An Old English sheepdog.

sheep·fold, shēp′fōld″, *n.* A pen where sheep are kept or sheltered.

sheep·herd·er, shēp′hụr″dẽr, *n.* One who herds or tends sheep grazing over large, open areas.—**sheep·herd·ing**, *n.*

sheep·ish, shē′pish, *a.* Foolishly bashful; overmodest; diffident; like a sheep in meekness or obedience; abashed.—**sheep··ish·ly**, *adv.*—**sheep·ish·ness**, *n.*

sheep ked, *n.* Sheep tick.

sheep's eyes, *n. pl.* Wishful, amorous glances.

sheep·shank, shēp′shangk″, *n.* A kind of knot, hitch, or bend made on a rope to shorten it temporarily.

sheeps·head, shēps′hed″, *n.* [< G. *schafs-kop,* sheep's head.] A deep-bodied, black striped, marine food fish, *Archosargus pro-batocephalus,* abundant on the Atlantic coast of the U.S. and so called from the resemblance of its head to that of a sheep. *Fig.* a dull, stupid person.

sheep·shear·ing, shēp′shēr″ing, *n.* The act of shearing sheep; the season when sheep are sheared; a festival held for the occasion of shearing sheep.—**sheep·shear·er**, *n.*

sheep·skin, shēp′skin″, *n.* The skin of a

sheep, esp. such a skin dressed with the wool on, as for a garment; that which is made from the skin of sheep, as parchment or leather; *colloq.* a diploma, sometimes made of parchment.

sheep sor·rel, *n. Bot.* a small, triangular-leaved, acid weed, *Rumex acetosella,* of the buckwheat family, *Polygonaceae,* found in dry, barren soil.

sheep tick, *n.* A bloodsucking, wingless insect, *Melophagus ovinus,* in the order *Diptera,* which lives as a parasite on sheep. Also *sheep ked.*

sheep·walk, shēp′wạk″, *n.* A tract or area of land where sheep are pastured.

sheer, shēr, *a.* [O.E. *scir,* pure, clear, bright; Icel. *skirr, skaer,* bright, clear; Goth. *skeirs,* clear, evident; G. *schier,* free from knots; prob. from root of *shine.*] Being transparent or nearly so, with little body or substance; as, a *sheer* fabric; total or complete in the sense of being unrelieved by any other element; as, streets of *sheer* ice; total or complete, without reservation or qualification; as, *sheer* foolishness; of or pertaining to steepness that is extreme; as, a *sheer* cliff.—*adv.* Totally, completely, or nearly so; as, a quarrel that split them *sheer* apart; vertically, or extremely steeply; as, to climb *sheer* up the wall.—*n.* A fabric that is lightweight and diaphanous; any of certain garments for females.—**sheer·ly**, *adv.* —**sheer·ness**, *n.*

sheer, shēr, *v.i.* [A form of *shear;* so D. and G. *scheren,* to shear and to sheer.] To deviate or swerve from an intended or proper course, said esp. of a ship.—*v.t.* To cause to swerve.—*n.* The curving line of a ship from fore to aft, as seen from the side; one of the positions taken by a moving ship, esp. as a maneuver to avoid its own lowered anchor; swerve.

sheet, shēt, *n.* [O.E. *scēte,* a sheet, a flap, also *scēat,* a nook, a projecting corner, part, region, < *scēotan,* to shoot, the root-meaning being something shot out or extended.] A large, oblong piece of cotton, linen, or other cloth used as bedding; a piece of paper, usu. rectangular in shape; a newspaper, a periodical, or an infrequent publication; *print.* any rectangular piece of paper used for printing, esp. a printed signature which has not yet been cut, folded, or bound; a large, flat, and usu. thin layer, surface, or the like; a large, rectangular, and relatively thin slab or piece of glass, metal, cloth, or other material; the sail of a boat; a single rectangular section of undivided postage stamps, printed on paper by one impression of a plate; a broad expanse, surface, or stretch of something; as, a *sheet* of ice; a flat, thin, metal utensil used for baking; as, a cookie *sheet; geol.* a horizontal mass of igneous or sedimentary rock.—*v.t.* To provide with sheets or a sheet; to cover or wrap with a sheet.—*v.i.* To spread or fall in a sheet.—*a.*—**sheet·like**, *a.*

sheet, shēt, *n. Naut.* a chain or rope fastened to the lower corner of a sail to extend or regulate the angle; *pl., naut.* the spaces unoccupied by thwarts at the ends of any open boat; as, the fore *sheets,* the stern *sheets.*—*v.t. Naut.* to fasten or extend with sheets or a sheet.—**three sheets to the wind,** *slang,* intoxicated.

sheet an·chor, *n.* [That is, the anchor *shot,* or thrown out for preservation.] *Naut.* the largest anchor of a ship, which is shot out only in an emergency. *Fig.* the chief support; the last refuge or resource for safety.

sheet bend, *n. Naut.* a knot or hitch used to fasten one rope to another or to an eye, by threading one end through the loop or bight of the other, then continuing it around and passing it under itself. Also **mesh knot, net·ting knot,** *weaver's hitch.*

sheet glass, *n.* Glass cut into large flat sheets from a wide ribbon of glass drawn through rollers directly from the furnace.

sheet·ing, shē′ting, *n.* Cloth or other material used for or formed into sheets; the process or act of making into or covering with sheets.

sheet light·ning, *n.* Lightning appearing in sheet form or as wide, expanded, diffused flashes: caused by a distant flash of lightning being reflected, as by clouds.

sheet met·al, *n.* Metal in sheets or thin plates.

sheet mu·sic, *n.* Musical compositions usu. printed separately on unbound sheets.

Sheet·rock, shēt′rok″, *n.* A kind of plasterboard. (Trademark.)

sheik, sheikh, shēk, *n.* [Ar. an old man, an elder.] A title of dignity belonging to the chiefs of the Arabic tribes or clans, or to Moslem priests, now widely used among Moslems as a title of respect or reverence. *Slang,* a rake or Lothario.—**sheik·dom, sheikh·dom,** shēk′dom, *n.* The territory ruled over by a sheik.

shek·el, shek′el, *n.* [Heb., < *shakal,* to weigh.] An ancient Babylonian weight and coin; later the principal silver coin among the early Hebrews, with a weight probably equaling 250 grains Troy. *Pl., slang,* money; wealth.

shel·drake, shel′drāk″, *n.* pl. **shel·drakes, shel·drake.** [M.E. *sheldedrake, schelledrake:* cf. obs. or prov. *sheld,* party-colored, piebald.] Any of the Old World ducks constituting the genera *Tadorna* and *Casarca,* certain species of which are characterized by variegated coloring; any of various other large ducks, as a merganser.

shelf, shelf, *n.* pl. **shelves,** shelvz. [O.E. *scelfe, scylfe,* a shelf; Icel. *skjalf,* a bench; cf. Sc. *skelb, skelve,* a splinter, a thin slice; akin to *shell, shale, scale.*] A board of wood or a thin narrow slab of another material fixed horizontally to a wall or other frame, for holding articles; that which the shelf contains; any projection similar to this, as a ledge of rock; a ledge of rocks, a reef, or a sandbar in the sea or a river; a shoal; bedrock, as found under soil or gravel deposits.—**on the shelf,** put aside or out of use; laid aside temporarily.—**shelf·like,** *a.*

shelf ice, *n.* Ice that forms along a coast and projects into the water like a shelf.

she'll, shēl. Contraction of she will or she shall.

shell, shel, *n.* [O.E. *scel, scell* = Icel. *skel,* D. *schel,* G. *schale,* husk, shell, peel; same root as *shale, scale.*] A hard outside covering, esp. that of a mollusk; the material of which such a covering is composed; the hard outside casing of a nut; the outside and calcareous layer of an egg; an object that is concave or hollow like a shell; any protective, usu. hard outside case or covering; any outside framework, as of a house, with an unfinished or destroyed interior; a hollow projectile containing a bursting charge, as for heavy artillery; a small paper or metal cartridge holding the powder or shot used in small arms or in shotguns; a casing containing explosives for fireworks displays; a long, slender, very light boat manned by multiple oarsmen for racing; a withdrawn, reserved attitude or façade behind which one's emotions or thoughts are concealed, as: Her gay charm drew him out of his *shell.* *Cooking,* pastry in pie crust or cuplike form baked prior to filling. An arena or stage covered with a half dome or vaulted roof; as, a band *shell* in the park; *fig.* that which is a hollow form or merely an outline of what was or is real; as, a *shell* of one's former self. *Phys.* any of the various energy levels at which electrons theoretically orbit around the center of an atom; a similar grouping of nucleons around a nucleus.—*v.t.* To remove or separate from a natural casing, husk, pod, or the like; to strip, as kernels of corn, from a cob; to bombard with explosives.—*v.i.* To shed, emerge from, or cast off a casing or shell; to fall away or off, as in thin layers or strips.—**shell out,** *slang.* To hand over or give out, as money; contribute.—**shelled, shell-like, shel·ly,** *a.*—**shel·ler,** *n.*

shel·lac, shel·lack, she·lak′, *n.* [For *shell lac.*] Lac which has been purified and formed into thin plates, used for making varnish; a varnish made by dissolving this material in alcohol or some other solution; a substance containing shellac used to make phonograph records; any record so made. —*v.t.*—**shellacked, shellacking.** To coat or treat with shellac; *slang,* to vanquish, defeat, or throttle.

shel·lack·ing, she·lak′ing, *n. Slang.* A definite defeat; a whipping or beating.

shell·back, shel′bak″, *n.* An experienced sailor, often an elderly man; a person who has sailed across the equator.

shell bean, *n.* Any of various kinds of bean whose seeds are used for food; the seed itself.

shell·fire, shel′fī·ėr″, *n. Milit.* the firing of explosive shells or projectiles.

shell·fish, shel′fish″, *n.* pl. **shell·fish, shell·fish·es.** An animal that is aquatic and whose external covering consists of a shell, as a crustacean or a mollusk.

shell game, *n.* A swindling game resembling thimblerig but employing walnut shells instead of thimblelike cups; any other game or scheme intended to swindle unexpecting persons.

shell jack·et, *n.* A tightly fitted jacket, short in the back, which is semiformal, worn as a substitute for the tuxedo, esp in countries that are tropical; a short close-fitting military jacket; a mess jacket.

shell·pink, shel′pingk, *n.* A soft, delicate pink with a tinge of yellow.

shell·proof, shel′proof″, *a.* Protected against bombs or shells and their destructive effects.

shell shock, *n.* Combat fatigue.—**shell-shocked,** *a.*

shel·ter, shel′tėr, *n.* [Related to O.E. *scild,* a shield.] That which provides a cover or protection against injury, danger, or discomfort, as from the weather, bombs, or the like; a refuge; the protection so provided, as: The cyclist took *shelter* under an overpass. Protection from condemnation or blame; temporary quarters or refuge; as, an animal *shelter.*—*v.t.* To provide shelter for; to protect from violence, injury, or attack; to place under cover.—*v.i.* To take shelter.—**shel·ter·er,** *n.*—**shel·ter·less,** *a.*

shel·ter half, *n.* Either of the two halves of a shelter tent.

shel·ter tent, *n.* A small tent designed for military use, as on field maneuvers, and having two interchangeable parts which can be fastened together to accommodate two men. Also *pup tent.*

shel·ty, shel′tē, *n.* pl. **shel·ties.** *Colloq.* Shetland pony; Shetland sheepdog. Also **shel·tie.**

shelve, shelv, *v.t.*—**shelved, shelving.** To place on a shelf; to put aside from active employment, use, or consideration; to dismiss; to furnish with shelves.—*v.i.* To slope or incline gradually.—**shelv·er,** *n.*

shelv·ing, shel′ving, *n.* The shelves, as of a room or shop, collectively; the material used for making shelves; the degree or condition of sloping; the action of placing something on a shelf; a putting away or aside.

shelv·y, shel′vē, *a.*—**shelvier, shelviest.** Inclining or sloping gradually.

she·nan·i·gan, she·nan′i·gan, *n.* Usu. *pl., colloq.* Mischief, nonsense, or trickery; a deceitful or treacherous act or action.

She·ol, shē′ōl, *n.* [Heb.] *Heb. theol.* The abode of the dead or of departed spirits; *(l.c.)* hell.

shep·herd, shep′ėrd, *n.* [O.E. *sceaphyrde* = *sheep-herd.*] A person employed in tending sheep; one who exercises spiritual care over a community; a pastor or minister.—*v.t.* To guard, herd, or watch like a shepherd.—**shep·herd·ess,** shep′ėr·dis, *n.* A female shepherd.

shep·herd dog, *n.* A sheepdog.

shep·herd's check, *n.* A small evenly checked pattern; a fabric with such a pattern. Also **shep·herd's plaid.**

shep·herd's pie, *n.* A baked pie of diced or ground meat and a mashed potato topping or crust.

shep·herd's-purse, shep′erdz·pųrs′, *n.* A common weed, *Capsella bursa-pastoris,* having small white flowers and triangular, somewhat heart-shaped pods.

Sher·a·ton, sher′a·ton, *a.* [From Thomas *Sheraton,* 1751–1803.] Designating a style of English furniture characterized by straight lines, gracefulness, and simplicity.

sher·bet, shur′bit, *n.* [Ar. *sharbat,* < *sharaba,* to drink; akin *sirup.*] A fruit-flavored water ice containing milk, gelatin, and egg white; *Brit.* an Eastern drink of sweetened, diluted fruit juices.

sherd, shųrd, *n.* Shard.

she·rif, she·rēf′, *n.* Sharif.

sher·iff, sher′if, *n.* [O.E. *scire-geréfa,* a shire-reeve.] The chief law enforcement officer of a county, usually elected for a term of years, who, with his appointed staff of deputy sheriffs, maintains law and order, executes mandates of the county court, maintains the jail, has custody of prisoners, and summons jurors to court sessions.—**sher·iff·dom,** sher′if·dom, *n.*

sher·lock, shųr′lok, *n. Slang,* a person skilled in the solution of crimes and other mysteries through intuition and logic.

sher·ry, sher′ē, *n.* pl. **sher·ries.** A fortified Spanish wine of amber color; any of a number of similar wines that are made elsewhere. Also *archaic* **sher·ris.**

she's, shēz. Contraction of she is or she has.

Shet·land po·ny, shet′land pō′nē, *n.* A very small, hardy, shaggy breed of pony originally bred in the Shetland Islands.

Shet·land sheep·dog, shet′land shēp′-dag″, shēp′dog″, *n.* One of a breed of small sheepdogs, resembling the collie, and originating in the Shetland Islands.

Shet·land wool, shet′land wųl′, *n.* A thin, loosely twisted, woolen yarn made from the wool of sheep from the Shetland Islands; the wool itself.

shew, shō, *v.t., v.i.*—past *shewed,* pp. *shewn,* ppr. *shewing. Archaic,* show.—*n.*

shew·bread, show·bread, shō′bred″, *n.* Unleavened bread which the Jewish priest placed before the Lord.

Shi·ah, Shi·a, shē′a, *n.* [Ar.] *Islam,* one of the two great divisions in Mohammedanism which holds Ali, Mohammed's son-in-law, to be the chief Imam and proper successor to Mohammed.—**Shi·ism,** *n.*—**Shi·ite,** shē′it, *n.* A member of the Shiah sect: opposed to *Sunnite.*

shib·bo·leth, shib′o·lith, shib′o·leth″, *n.* [Heb.] *Bib.* a word, the pronunciation of which distinguished the Ephraimites from the Gileadites. Judg. xii. 4–6. A peculiarity of speech or custom that distinguishes a particular group or class of people; the watch-word of a party; a pet phrase of a party.

shield, shēld, *n.* [O.E. *scild, scyld,* a shield, protection; Goth. *skildus,* Icel. *skjöldr,* G. *schild;* akin to *shelter.*] A broad piece of defensive armor carried on the arm; a buckler, used in war for the protection of the body; any defense or protection; a small piece of fabric worn inside a garment at the underarms to protect the garment from perspiration; anything shaped like a shield, as a badge or emblem; *her.* the escutcheon or field on which are placed the bearings in coats or arms; *milit.* a metal screen permanently fixed to a gun, designed to protect the gunner; *min.* a structure which shelters miners from cave-ins; *zool.* a hard outer covering, as a carapace; *elect.* a case or binding surrounding an electric circuit or element to minimize the effect of electric current.—*v.t.* To cover, as with a shield; to cover or protect from danger or anything harmful or disagreeable, as a rubberized apron worn to shield the clothing; to defend; to protect.—**shield·er,** *n.*

shiel·ing, sheal·ing, shē'ling, *n.* [< Icel. *skjol,* a shelter.] *Brit. dial.* a temporary cottage, hut, or another similar building; a hut for shepherds, fishermen, or other sportsmen. *Sc.* a shed for sheltering sheep during the night; ground for grazing or a pasture. Also **shiel.**

shift, shift, *v.t.* [O.E. *scyftan,* to divide, to drive away = Dan. *skifte,* Icel. *skipta,* to divide, change, shift; akin to *shive, sheave,* or perh. to *shove.*] To transfer or change from one place, arrangement, person, direction, or position to another; to remove and exchange for another; *mech.* to change the arrangement of, as gears while driving an automobile; *ling.* to alter systematically, as vowel sounds.—*v.i.* To change place, position, or direction; to undergo a change, often a systematic change; to live, get along, or succeed; to adopt some course of action in case of difficulty; to contrive or resort to expedients; to change the arrangement of gears in an automobile while driving.—*n.* An instance of shifting; a movement, change, or switch among things, people, places, or from one thing to another; as, a *shift* of responsibility to the next man; the period of time which comprises a person's working hours, esp. at a concern operating all or most of a twenty-four hour day; as, an 11 P.M. to 7 A.M. *shift;* the group of people who work during a particular one of such specified periods; as, an energetic night *shift;* an expedient tried in difficulty; a contrivance or resource, usu. deceptive; *mech.* gearshift; *mus.* a change in the placement of the hand on the fingerboard of a string instrument; *ling.* a series of parallel or similar alterations occurring about the same time in a language and evidencing an overall pattern or system. —**shift for one·self,** to be independent or to make one's own way.—**shift·er,** *n.*—**shift·ing·ly,** *adv.*—**shift·ing·ness,** *n.*

shift·less, shift'lis, *a.* Lazy; inefficient; wanting in incentive; wanting in resourcefulness.—**shift·less·ly,** *adv.*—**shift·less·ness,** *n.*

shift·y, shif'tē, *a.*—*shiftier, shiftiest.* Full of shifts; changing; fertile in expedients; given to tricks, evasions, or deceptions; suggesting a nature that is tricky.—**shift·i·ly,** *adv.*—**shift·i·ness,** *n.*

shi·kar, shi·kär', *n.* [Hind. and Pers. *shikār.*] *India,* hunting game.—*v.t., v.i.*—*shikarred, shikarring.* To hunt.

shi·ka·ri, shi·ka·ree, shi·kär'ē, *n.* [Hind. *shikārī.*] *India,* a hunter or sportsman, esp. a professional or native hunter or a native serving as guide.

shill, shil, *n. Slang,* a person posing as a purchaser or gambler to decoy onlookers into participating.

shil·le·lagh, shil·la·lah, shi·lā'lē, shi·lā'la, *n.* [From *Shillelagh,* a barony in Wicklow famous for its oaks.] An Irish name for an oaken sapling or other stick used as a cudgel.

shil·ly-shal·ly, shil'ē·shal"ē, *v.i.*—*shilly-shallied, shilly-shallying.* [A reduplication of

shall I? and equal to *shall I or shall I not?*] To act in an irresolute or undecided manner; to hesitate; to be concerned with trifles.—*n. pl.* **shil·ly-shal·lies.** Vacillation; irresolution.—*a.*—*adv.*

shim, shim, *n.* [Origin uncertain.] A thin strip of metal, wood, or the like, for filling in, as for bringing one part in line with another.—*v.t.*—*shimmed, shimming.* To fill out or bring to a level by inserting a shim or shims.

shim·mer, shim'ẽr, *v.i.* [O.E. *scimrain,* freq. of *scimian,* to gleam; Dan. *skimre,* G. *schimmern,* to gleam.] To emit or shine with a tremulous light; to gleam in a subdued manner; to seem to waver or quiver, as in poor light; to glimmer.—*n.* A tremulous subdued gleam or glistening; a quivering image reflected from heat waves or in poor light.—**shim·mer·y,** shim'e·rē, *a.*

shim·my, shim'ē, *n. pl.* **shim·mies.** An American jazz dance first popularized during the 1920's, characterized by rapid shaking of the hips and shoulders; unusual vibration or wobbling, as of an automobile wheel; *colloq.* a chemise.—*v.i.*—*shimmied, shimmying.* To dance the shimmy, or shake and quiver as if doing it; to vibrate or wobble, as a defective wheel of an auto.

shin, shin, *n.* [O.E. *scin, scina,* the shin; D. *scheen,* the shin; Da. *skinne,* the shin, a splint; G. *schiene,* a splint of wood, *schienbein,* the shinbone.] *Anat.* the forepart of the leg between the ankle and the knee; in humans, the sharp-edged front of the tibia, or shinbone; in four-footed animals, the lower part of the foreleg.—*v.i., v.t.*—*shinned, shinning.* To climb, as a polelike structure, by means of the hands and legs alone, using them alternately to clutch and then ascend.

Shin, shin, *n. Buddhism,* a Japanese sect whose followers deviate from other Buddhists in their belief that salvation can be achieved simply by faith in Amida, the ruler of paradise.

shin·bone, shin'bōn", *n.* The bone of the shin; the tibia.

shin·dig, shin'dig", *n. Colloq.* a large or often elaborate party, dance, or another social gathering, esp. one that is noisy.

shin·dy, shin'dē, *n. pl.* **shin·dies.** *Slang.* A row; a quarrel; a shindig.

shine, shīn, *v.i.*—*shone* or *shined, shining.* [O.E. *scinan* = D. *schijnen,* Icel. *skina,* Dan. *skinne,* Goth. *skeinan,* G. *scheinen,* to shine; same root as in *shimmer, sheer.*] To emit rays of light; to be radiant by reflected light; to exhibit brightness or splendor; to be eminently splendid or beautiful; as, to *shine* in society; to be noticeably bright or clear.—*v.t.* To cause or make to shine; to project the light of, as a flashlight; to polish.—*n.* Brightness due to the emission or reflection of light; luster; brilliancy; fair weather; sunshine; a polish given to shoes. *Slang,* a prank or caper; a fancy or liking, as: He's taken a *shine* to you.—**shine up to,** *slang,* to try to impress or please, esp. in order to win favor for oneself.

shin·er, shī'nẽr, *n.* One who or that which shines; a coin of gold or silver; any of various small American fresh-water fish with glistening scales, esp. the genus *Notropis;* a minnow. *Slang,* a black eye resulting from a blow.

shin·gle, shing'gl, *n.* [Corrupted < *shindle,* which, like G. *schindel,* was borrowed < L. *scindula,* a shingle, < L. *scindo,* to split.] A thin piece of wood or other building material, usu. having parallel sides and thicker at one end than the other, used in overlapping rows as a roof covering; a ladies' short haircut; *colloq.* a small signboard, as displayed outside the office of a

doctor or lawyer.—*v.t.*—*shingled, shingling.* To cover with shingles; to cut, as hair, short and shaped to the head.—**shin·gler,** *n.*

shin·gle, shing'gl, *n.* [Cf. Norw. *singl,* M.L.G. *singele,* shingle.] A loose sheet or bed of small, water-worn stones or pebbles such as lies on the seashore; rounded detritus; an extent of small, loose stones or pebbles, as a beach.—**shin·gly,** *a.*

shin·gle, shing'gl, *v.t.*—*shingled, shingling.* [Cf. Fr. *cingler,* G. *zangeln,* shingle (metal).] *Metal.* to hammer or squeeze, as a mass of iron taken from a puddling furnace, in order to press out the slag and impurities.

shin·gles, shing'glz, *n. pl., sing.* or *pl.* in *constr.* [< L. *cingulum,* a belt, < *cingo,* to gird.] *Pathol.* a painful viral infection involving the central nervous system and characterized by the eruption of groups of blisters on the skin along the affected nerves. Also *herpes zoster.*

shin·ing, shī'ning, *a.* Luminous; radiant; gleaming; bright; resplendent; brilliant; conspicuously fine; as, a man of *shining* talents.—**shin·ing·ly,** *adv.*

shin·leaf, shin'lēf", *n. pl.* **shin·leaves.** [Cf. *shinplaster.*] A N. American herb, *Pyrola elliptica,* of the wintergreen family, having broad oval leaves; any plant of the same genus.

shin·ner·y, shin'e·rē, *n.* A thick growth of dwarf trees, esp. of scrub oaks.

shin·ny, shin·ney, shin'ē, *n.* Schoolboys' hockey; the curved stick used in playing the game.

shin·ny, shin'ē, *v.i.*—*shinnied, shinnying.* *Colloq.* to climb, as a pole, using shins and arms.

shin·plas·ter, shin'plas"tẽr, shin'plä"stẽr, *n.* A plaster for the shin or leg. Fractional currency; a piece of paper money of low denomination or little value, as one issued on insufficient security or greatly depreciated in value.

Shin·to, shin'tō, *n.* [Chin. *shin,* god or spirit, and *to,* way or law.] The ancient religion of Japan, combining nature worship, reverence of ancestors, and worship of the spirits of departed heroes, with intense loyalty to the god-emperor, who is believed to be descended from the sun goddess. Also **Shin·to·ism.**—*a.* Pertaining to Shinto. Also **Shin·to·is·tic.**—**Shin·to·ist,** *n., a.*

shin·y, shī'nē, *a.*—*shinier, shiniest.* Characterized by sunshine; bright; luminous; glossy; brilliant.—**shin·i·ness,** *n.*

ship, ship, *n.* [O.E. *scip* = D. *schip* = G. *schiff* = Icel. and Goth. *skip,* ship: cf. *skiff.*] A seagoing vessel of considerable size; a sailing vessel with a bowsprit and three or more masts, all having square-rigged sails; the personnel or crew of a vessel; an airship or airplane.—*v.t.*—*shipped, shipping.* To put or take on board a ship for transportation, as persons or goods; to send or transport by ship, rail, or other means of conveyance; *naut.* to take in, as water, over the side, as a vessel does in rough seas. To draw, as an object, into a ship or boat; as, to *ship* the oars; to fix in a ship or boat in the proper place for use; to engage for service on a ship, as a seaman; to set, as oars, in place for rowing; *colloq.* to send away or get rid of; as, to *ship* the kids to camp.—*v.i.* To go on board a ship; embark; to engage to serve on a ship.— **when one's ship comes in,** when one attains financial success.

ship bis·cuit, *n.* Hardtack.

ship·board, ship'bōrd", ship'bärd", *n. Archaic,* the deck or the side of a ship.—*a.* Happening aboard a ship; as, a *shipboard* romance.—**on ship·board,** on a ship.

ship·build·er, ship'bil"dẽr, *n.* One whose business or work is the designing and building of ships.—**ship·build·ing,** *n.*

ship ca·nal, *n.* A canal through which seagoing or other vessels of large size can pass.

ship chan·dler, *n.* One who deals in equipment, parts, and supplies for ships.

ship·fit·ter, ship′fit″ẽr, *n.* One whose work is shaping and fitting together the steel and other metal parts of a ship; *naval*, an enlisted man who works as a plumber aboard a ship, and is also capable of doing sheet metalwork.

ship·lap, ship′lap″, *n. Constr.* sheathing with overlapping joints made by cutting a groove or recess in each board and then joining the boards edge to edge.

ship·man, ship′man, *n. pl.* **ship·men.** [O.E. *scipmann.*] *Archaic.* A seaman or sailor; the master of a ship.

ship·mas·ter, ship′mas″tẽr, ship′mä″stẽr, *n.* The master or captain of a ship carrying cargo or passengers.

ship·mate, ship′māt″, *n.* One who serves on the same ship with another; a fellow sailor.

ship·ment, ship′ment, *n.* The act of transporting goods or cargo; the goods shipped.

ship mon·ey, *n. Old English law,* a tax levied on ports and maritime towns to provide ships for national defense.

ship of the line, *n.* An armed ship large enough to be in the line of battle, used before the advent of steam propulsion.

ship·pa·ble, ship′a·bl, *a.* In condition or adaptable for transporting.

ship·per, ship′ẽr, *n.* One who sends goods by any means of transportation, as by railroad, truck, airplane, or ship.

ship·ping, ship′ing, *n.* The collective fleet of ships serving a country or port; tonnage; the business of transporting merchandise.

ship·ping clerk, *n.* A clerk who attends to the details of sending or receiving shipments.

ship-rigged, ship′rigd″, *a.* Rigged like a ship, with square sails on all the masts.

ship·shape, ship′shāp″, *a.* Having a seamanlike order; neat and trim; well-arranged.

ship·side, ship′sīd″, *n.* The dock or other open area along the side of a ship, used for the boarding of passengers and the loading of cargo and supplies.

ship's pa·pers, *n. pl.* Papers or documents required by law to be carried by ships, showing certificate of registry, bills of lading, and designation.

ship·way, ship′wā″, *n.* The track or framework supporting a ship during its construction and launching; a ship canal.

ship·worm, ship′wẽrm″, *n.* Any of various marine bivalve mollusks of the family *Teredinidae,* with a long wormlike body, which burrow into underwater wooden structures, as the timbers of ships and pilings.

ship·wreck, ship′rek″, *n.* The wreck of a ship; the destruction or loss at sea of a ship. *Fig.* destruction; failure; ruin.—*v.t.* To make to suffer shipwreck; to wreck, as a ship; to ruin.

ship·wright, ship′rīt″, *n.* One whose occupation is the building or repairing of ships.

ship·yard, ship′yärd″, *n.* A place in which ships are constructed or repaired.

shire, shī′ẽr, *n.* [O.E. *scīr,* official charge, office, district, shire, = O.H.G. *scīra,* care, official charge.] An administrative district, as one of the counties into which Great Britain is divided, esp. one of those having names with the suffix *shire.*

shire town, *n.* The town where the business of a shire is transacted; county seat.

shirk, shẽrk, *v.t.* [Possibly a form of *shark.*] To avoid or get out of unfairly.—*v.i.* To avoid an obligation or the performance of duty.—*n.* One who seeks to avoid duty.—**shirk·er,** shẽrk′ẽr, *n.*

Shir·ley pop·py, *n.* A cultivated variety of the corn poppy, *Papaver rhoeas,* usu. having red, pink, or purple petals.

shirr, shẽr, *v.t.* [Origin obscure.] To draw up or gather, as cloth, on several parallel threads; to bake, as eggs removed from the shell, in a shallow dish or in individual dishes.

shirr·ing, shẽr′ing, *n.* The gathering of fabric resulting from drawing together the material on several parallel lines of thread.

shirt, shẽrt, *n.* [O.E. *scyrte* = Icel. *skyrta,* shirt = D. *schort,* G. *schürze,* apron; prob. orig. meaning 'short garment,' from the Teut. a. represented by E. *short:* cf. *skirt.*] A loose, usu. lightweight garment worn by men or women on the upper part of the body and usu. having a collar, sleeves, and a button-front closing; an undershirt; a woman's shirtwaist.—**keep one's shirt on,** *slang.* To be patient; to keep calm.—**lose one's shirt,** *slang,* to suffer a severe financial loss.—**shirt·less,** *a.*

shirt·ing, shẽrt′ing, *n.* Material or fabric used for making shirts.

shirt·tail, shẽrt′tāl″, *n.* The extended part of a shirt, below the waist, which is tucked into the trousers.

shirt·waist, shẽrt′wāst″, *n.* A woman's loosely fitting tailored blouse worn tucked into a skirt. A dress with the front opening and bodice details of a man's shirt; also **shirt·waist dress.**

shish ke·bab, shish′ke·bob″, *n.* Kabob roasted or broiled on a skewer. Also *shashlik.*

shit·tah, shit′a, *n. pl.* **shit·tim, shit·tahs,** shit′im. [Heb. *shittāh* (pl. *shittīm*).] A tree mentioned in the Bible, probably some species of acacia, as *Acacia seyal,* with a hard, durable wood. Isa. xli. 19.

shit·tim wood, *n.* [Heb. *shittīm,* pl. of *shittāh.*] The wood of the shittah, of which the ark of the covenant and various parts of the Jewish tabernacle were made. Ex. xxv. 10. Also **shit·tim.**

shiv, shiv, *n. Slang.* A knife, esp. one having a switchblade; a razor.

shiv·a·ree, shiv″a·rē′, *n.* Charivari.—*v.t.*—*shivareed, shivareeing.*

shiv·er, shiv′ẽr, *v.i.* [M.E. *chiveren;* origin uncertain.] To shake involuntarily or tremble, as with cold, fear, or excitement; to shake tremulously, tremble, or quiver, as leaves in the breeze; *naut.* to flutter in the wind, as a sail—*v.t. Naut.* to make, as a sail, to shake.—*n.* A shivering motion or state; an involuntary trembling, or a sensation of trembling as from cold or fear; a tremulous motion.—**shiv·er·y,** shiv′e·rē, *a.*

shiv·er, shiv′ẽr, *n.* [M.E. *schivere, scifre,* = O.H.G. *scivero,* splinter, G. *schiefer,* splinter, flake, slate.] A fragment; a splinter; as, to shatter a spear to *shivers.*—*v.t., v.i.* To break or split into fragments or splinters; shatter.—**shiv·er·y,** shiv′e·rē, *a.* Brittle.

shoal, shōl, *n.* [Allied to *shallow.*] A place where the water of a river, lake, or sea is shallow; a sandbank or bar, esp. one seen above the water's surface at low tide.—*a.* Shallow; of little depth; as, *shoal* water.—*v.i.* To become shallow.—*v.t.* To cause or allow to become shallow; to sail into a shallower part of.

shoal, shōl, *n.* [= *school.*] A school of fish, porpoises, or the like; a large number of persons or things gathered together.—*v.i.* To collect or swim in a shoal; to crowd together; to throng.

shoat, shote, shōt, *n.* A weanling pig, esp. one less than a year old.

shock, shok, *n.* A sudden, violent blow or impact; a violent collision or encounter; a sudden disturbance or commotion; a sudden and startling effect on the mind or emotions; a startled sense of outraged propriety or decency; the reason for such disturbances. *Pathol.* a sudden debilitating effect on the bodily functions due to some violent impression on the nervous system, as from a severe injury, a surgical operation, a violent emotional disturbance, or the like; the resulting condition of nervous depression or prostration. The effect produced on the body by the sudden passage of a current of electricity through it.—*v.t.* To strike with intense and painful surprise; to strike against suddenly and violently; to give an electric shock to; to subject to bodily or nervous shock; to startle by outraging the sense of propriety or decency.—*v.i.* To experience a shock.

shock, shok, *n.* [O.E. *scoc,* threescore, D. *schok,* G. *schock,* Dan. *skok,* a heap, threescore.] A group or pile of stalks or sheaves, usu. of grain, placed upright in a field to dry before removal.—*v.t.* To arrange or stack in shocks; as, to *shock* corn.

shock, shok, *n.* [Modified < *shag.*] A matted, bushy mass, esp. of hair.—*a.* Shaggy.

shock ab·sorb·er, *n. Mech.* a device for deadening the shock or concussion of sudden impact or rapid motion; as, the *shock absorbers* of an automobile.

shock·er, shok′ẽr, *n.* One who or that which shocks; *colloq., chiefly Brit.* a highly sensational work of fiction.

shock·ing, shok′ing, *a.* Causing horror, disgust, pain, or intense surprise; causing to recoil with horror or disgust, as extremely offensive or improper habits. *Slang,* dreadful; awful.—**shock·ing·ly,** *adv.*

shock ther·a·py, *n. Psychiatry,* a treatment for mental disorders, based on the coma or other shock effects induced by injections of drugs, such as insulin, or by the application of electrical currents to the brain. Also **shock treat·ment.**

shock troops, *n. pl. Milit.* troops specif. selected for assault duty.

shock wave, *n. Phys.* a wave formed by compression in a medium when an object moves violently through the medium at a speed in excess of that sound.

shod, shod, *a.* Equipped with a shoe or shoes.

shod·dy, shod′ē, *n. pl.* **shod·dies.** [Origin uncertain; perh. related to *shed.*] A fibrous material obtained by shredding woolen rags or waste; a cloth made of any inferior material; anything inferior made to resemble what is of superior quality.—*a.*—*shoddier, shoddiest.* Made of or containing shoddy; inferior but pretentious.—**shod·di·ly,** *adv.*—**shod·di·ness,** *n.*

shoe, shö, *n. pl.* **shoes.** [O.E. *sceōh, scōh,* = D. *schoen* = G. *schuh* = Icel. *skōr* = Sw. and Dan. *sko* = Goth. *skōhs,* shoe.] An external covering, usu. of leather, for the human foot, consisting of a heavy sole and a lighter upper part, esp. such a covering ending a short distance above, at, or below the ankle, as distinguished from a boot; a horseshoe, or a plate for similar use on the hoof of some other animal; a thing or part resembling a shoe in form, position, or use; a drag or skid for the wheel of a vehicle; the part of a brake which acts upon the wheel; a ferrule or the like for protecting the sharp end of a staff or pole; a band of iron on the bottom of a sleigh runner; the outer casing of a pneumatic tire; the sliding plate or contact by which an electric car or locomotive takes its current from the third rail.—*v.t.*—past *shod,* pp. *shod* or *shodden,* ppr. *shoeing.* To provide or fit with a shoe, ferrule, metal plate, or the like.—**be in some·one's shoes,** to be in someone else's position or situation.—**fill some·one's shoes,** to equal someone's ability, achievement, or success, or to face the responsibility of some particular person.—**the**

shoe is on the oth·er foot, the situation has been reversed and positions have been switched.—**shoe·less,** a.

shoe·bill, shō'bil", n. A large African wading bird, *Balaeniceps rex,* having a broad bill shaped somewhat like a shoe, related to the stork.

shoe·black, shō'blak", n. Bootblack.

shoe·horn, shō'hȧrn", n. A curved piece of polished horn, metal, or similar material used to aid in putting on shoes.

shoe·lace, shō'lās", n. A shoestring.

shoe·mak·er, shō'māˇkȧr, n. One who makes or repairs shoes.

sho·er, shō'ȧr, n. One who puts shoes on horses.

shoe·string, shō'string", n. A string or lace for fastening a shoe.—**on a shoe·string,** slang, with a very small amount of money or capital used to start or carry on an enterprise or business.

shoe·tree, shō'trē", n. A foot-shaped form of wood or other material for fitting inside a shoe to maintain its shape.

sho·far, shō'fȧr, Heb. shō·fär', n. pl. **sho·fars,** Heb. **sho·froth,** Heb. shō·frȧt'. *Judaism,* the horn of a ram finished as a simple wind instrument and blown in present-day synagogues to herald certain solemn occasions, esp. the celebration of the Jewish New Year.

sho·gun, shō'gun", shō'gȯn", n. [Jap.] The hereditary commander-in-chief of the Japanese army, virtual ruler of Japan until 1868, when power was returned to the throne. Also *tycoon.*—**sho·gun·ate,** shō'gun"it, shō'gun"āt, shō'gȯ"nit, shō'gȯ"nāt, n. The office of a shogun.

sho·ji, shō'zhē, shō'jē, n. pl. **sho·ji, sho·jis.** A translucent and often sliding or movable screen, usu. of paper in a wooden framework, used to partition or wall off one area from another in Japanese homes and other buildings.

sho·lom, shȧ'lom, shō'lom, n. Shalom.

shoo, shō, interj. [M.E. *schowe, ssou*: cf. Fr. *chou,* G. *schu,* It. *scio,* Gr. *sou,* interj.] An exclamation used to scare or drive away poultry, animals, and the like.—v.t. To scare or drive away by calling out 'shoo.'—v.i. To call out 'shoo.'

shoo·fly, shō'flī", n. pl. **shoo·flies.** A child's rocker having a seat surrounded by sides, usu. decorated with animals; *print.* an arm which removes a printed sheet from the press; *rail.* an alternate track used to avoid an obstruction.

shoo-in, shō'in", n. Slang. A contestant who is favored to be a sure winner; a candidate expected to win easily.

shook, shụk, n. [< *shook,* archaic pp. of *shake,* as applied to casks taken to pieces.] A set of staves and headings sufficient for one hogshead, barrel, or the like; a set of the parts of a box, piece of furniture, or the like, ready to be put together; a shock, as of sheaves or stalks.

shook up, a. Slang. Emotionally shaken by wrong, fear, or other circumstance; upset; agitated, sometimes preceded by *all,* as: It left me *all shook up.*

shoot, shōt, v.t.—*shot, shooting.* [O.E. *scēotan* (pret. *sceat*) = D. *schieten* = G. *schiessen* = Icel. *skjōta* = Sw. *skjuta* = Dan. *skyde,* shoot: cf. *shot, shut, shuttle,* and *sheet.*] To fire or discharge; as, to *shoot* a rifle; to hit, wound, or kill with a missile discharged from a weapon; to discharge or send forth rapidly and with force; as, to *shoot* a silver bullet; to propel, emit, thrust, or send forth forcefully, suddenly, or rapidly; as, to *shoot* a question, to *shoot* a ray of light from behind a cloud; to put forth or extend; as, a plant *shooting* up stems and leaves; to hunt or engage in the killing or shooting of for sport; as, to *shoot* pheasant; to hunt upon, as a piece of

land; to break or destroy by discharging a shot into; to discard or dump; to send down a chute; to pass rapidly through, over, or down; as, to *shoot* the rapids; to slide into or out of its fastenings, as a door bolt; to take a snapshot or picture of; to photograph with a movie camera; to variegate by interspersing threads or streaks of a different color, usu. past tense; as, hair *shot* with silver; to wear out, exhaust, or squander; as, to *shoot* a wad of money. *Sports,* to aim and send toward a goal, as a ball or puck; to score in such a manner; as, to *shoot* a goal. *Golf,* to play; *surv.* to take or determine the altitude of.—v.i. To take a shot, or to thrust forth missiles from a weapon; to eject or propel missiles, or to be discharged, as a firearm; to move, dart, or spurt swiftly or suddenly; as, sparks which *shoot* upward; to come forth from the ground, grow, germinate, or put forth buds or shoots, as a plant; to grow rapidly, often with *up*; to project, extend, or jut; as, a cape which *shoots* into the sea; to hunt and kill game with a gun; to take a snapshot with a camera; to take movies with a camera; to slide, as a bolt into its fastenings; *games, sports,* to propel a ball, puck, marble, dice, or the like in a particular direction, as toward the goal or another player. To start to talk or give information, used imperatively.—n. Any growing or sprouting from a main stock; an offshoot; the amount of such growth; a new or young growth which shoots off from some portion of a stem, root, tuber, or germinating seed, as a young branch, stem, twig, or sprout; *forestry,* a sprout which is less than three feet high. The act of shooting with a weapon; an expedition for shooting game; the right to hunt game within a certain area; the area itself; a match or contest for shooting; a swift or sudden movement; spurt; twinge; a cast or throw; a heavy rush, as of water down a steep and narrow channel; a rapid; a sloping trough, upright shaft, or the like, for conveying coal, ore, or grain to a receptacle below; a chute; *rowing,* the glide between strokes.—**shoot at,** **shoot for,** to aim at or aspire to.—**shoot down,** to fell or destroy with or as with a gun; as, to *shoot down* a dove; slang, to thwart or betray; as, to *shoot down* an idea.—**shoot off one's mouth,** to talk too much and indiscreetly.—**shoot the breeze,** to chat or talk aimlessly, casually.—**shoot the bull,** to exaggerate or brag.—**shoot the works,** to expend all of one's effort or resources.—**shoot up,** to grow rapidly. *Colloq.* to maim or damage by shooting; as, to *shoot up* a bar. —**shoot·er,** n.

shoot·ing gal·ler·y, n. A place for practice in shooting, furnished with targets which may be permanent, as in an amusement arcade, or temporary, as at a carnival.

shoot·ing i·ron, n. Slang, a firearm.

shoot·ing script, n. A detailed motion picture script in which the scenes are ordered the way they will be photographed.

shoot·ing star, n. A meteor; *bot.* a perennial herb, *Dodecatheon meadia,* in the primrose family, native to N. American prairies.

shoot·ing stick, n. A stick with a folding seat on one end and a point on the other, used by spectators at outdoor events; *print.* an implement of hard wood or metal used by striking with a mallet to tighten or loosen the quoins in a chase.

shoot-the-chutes, shōt'THe·shōtz", n. pl., sing. or pl. in constr. A ride, usu. found in an amusement park, in which the passengers seated in boatlike conveyances are propelled down a steep incline ending in a slide across an expanse of water. Also **chute-the-chutes.**

shop, shop, n. [M.E. *shoppe,* shop, < O.E.

sceoppa (used of the 'treasury' in Luke xxi. 1), akin to *scypen,* cattle shed, O.H.G. *scopf,* porch, M.L.G. *schoppe,* G. *schoppen, schuppen,* shed, barn.] A building or room in which articles are made or prepared and sold; a building or room appropriated to the selling of goods. A store or department of a store that sells a particular type of merchandise; also **shoppe.** A building or room set apart for the carrying on of some handiwork or mechanical industry; a workshop; one's place of business or occupation; matters pertaining to one's trade, occupation, or profession, as a subject of conversation; as, to talk *shop;* the instruction in working with machinery, tools, or in a specific trade; the place in which this instruction is given.—v.i. *shopped, shopping.* To visit shops or stores for the purpose of purchasing or examining goods; to examine that which is presented for sale; to hunt for a bargain.—v.t. To seek out or inspect something presented for sale by or in. *Brit. dial.* to shut up as in a building; to imprison; to send to jail; to place under arrest; to betray or inform on.

shop·keep·er, shop'kē"pȧr, n. One who sells goods in a shop; a tradesman.

shop·lift·er, shop'lif"tȧr, n. One who steals goods from a shop, as while seemingly making purchases.—**shop·lift·ing,** n.

shop·per, shop'ȧr, n. One who shops; one who visits shops for the purpose of buying or comparing the value of goods for others or for an employer.

shop·ping bag, n. A sturdy, large-size bag made of paper or net and equipped with handles, used by shoppers to carry home the merchandise they purchase; *Brit.* carrier bag.

shop stew·ard, n. A union member chosen to represent his fellow workers in dealing with the management. Also **shop chair·man.**

shop·talk, shop'tȧk", n. Specialized terminology having to do with a particular occupation or profession; a conversation in these terms and concerning one's job, esp. outside working hours.

shop·worn, shop'wȯrn", shop'wȧrn", a. Worn, marred, or damaged from exposure or handling in a shop; *fig.* hackneyed or trite; as, a *shopworn* expression.

shor·an, shȯr'an, shȧr'an, n. [(*Sho*)rt (*ra*)nge (*n*)avigation.] A radar system for precision position finding, used in aerial navigation and missile guidance.

shore, shȯr, shȧr, n. [O.E. *score,* the shore, < *sceran, sciran,* to shear; to divide; O.D. *schoore, schoor.*] The land immediately adjacent to an ocean, sea, lake, or river; the land along the edge of any sizeable body of water; land, as differentiated from water; as, the sailor served on *shore;* land, in the sense of homeland; as, native *shores.*—a. Of or pertaining to land, as differentiated from water, as: The sailor had *shore* duty. —**shore·line,** shȯr'lin", shȧr'lin", n.

shore, shȯr, shȧr, n. [Lit. 'a piece shorn or cut to a certain length'; same as D. and L.G. *schore, schoor,* Icel. *skortha,* a prop, a shore.] A prop; a strut; an apparatus designed for the temporary support of something, often resting obliquely against it.—v.t.—*shored, shoring.* To support by a shore or shores; to prop, usu. followed by *up;* as, to *shore up* a building.

shore bird, n. Any of the shore-dwelling birds of the families *Charadridae* and *Scolopacidae;* any bird such as the plover or sandpiper whose preferred habitat is the seashore.

shore din·ner, n. A full meal which consists principally of seafood, often of various kinds.

shore leave, n. A limited period of free time which may be spent ashore, granted to navy personnel stationed aboard ship.

shore pa·trol, *n.* A police detail of the U.S. Navy, Marine Corps, and Coast Guard that is maintained for the purpose of surveillance ashore.

shor·ing, shōr'ing, shär'ing, *n.* A support made of shores; a set of shores collectively; the act of supporting with shores.

short, shärt, *a.* [O.E. *sceort, scort,* short, < stem of *shear;* O.H.G. *scure,* short, cut off; Icel. *skort,* scantily supplied.] Not having great length or linear extension; not long; not tall; not of long duration; not extended in time; not containing many words; curt; brief; abrupt; sharp; severe; uncivil; as, a *short* answer; not tenacious or retentive; as, a *short* memory; not reaching a certain point; limited in quantity; insufficient; inadequate; scanty; deficient; as, in *short* supply, *short* weight; scantily supplied or furnished, followed by *on;* as, *short on* equipment; not possessed of a reasonable or usual quantity or amount; as, to be *short* of money; containing shortening; breaking or crumbling readily in the mouth; crisp. *Metal.* brittle; friable. *Finance,* not being in possession of commodities one is selling; relating to commodities or stocks not possessed when sold. *Phon.* not prolonged in sound, as: The vowel sound in 'din' is *short* in contrast to the vowel sound in 'dine.' *Pros.* not prolonged in sound; as, a *short* syllable; unstressed.—**short of,** inferior to; less than, as: His escape was nothing *short of* a miracle.—**short·ish,** *a.*

short, shärt, *adv.* Abruptly; curtly; at a point before some specified standard or condition; as, to fall *short,* to cut *short;* without actually possessing the commodities sold; as, to sell *short.*

short, shärt, *n.* Anything short; deficiency; upshot. *Pl.* trousers worn to the knee or above; short pants worn as underwear by men; remnants, clippings, or refuse from manufacturing processes. *Phon.* a short sound; *pros.* a short syllable. *Motion pictures,* a film, as a brief documentary, shown on a program in addition to the feature film; also **short sub·ject.** *Finance,* one who sells bonds or commodities without being in possession thereof; bonds thus sold.—**for short,** for the purpose of brevity.—**in short,** in summary.—**short·ness,** *n.*

short, shärt, *v.t. v.i.* To cheat, as by delivering less than the agreed amount or quantity; to short circuit.

short ac·count, *n. Finance.* The account of one who sells short; the total short sales in a specified commodity or stock, or in the market.

short·age, shär'tij, *n.* Any deficiency; an amount short or deficient; an amount by which a sum of money is deficient.

short bal·lot, *n.* A ballot which restricts elective office to important posts and leaves other positions open to appointment.

short·bread, shärt'bred", *n.* A kind of rich cookie, commonly in thick pieces, made with butter or other shortening.

short·cake, shärt'kāk", *n.* A cake made with butter or other shortening; a biscuit, sometimes unsweetened, spread with fruit.

short-change, shärt'chānj', *v.t.—short-changed, short-changing. Colloq.* To give less change for money than is properly due; to cheat.—**short-chang·er,** *n.*

short cir·cuit, *n. Elect.* a side circuit or shunt of relatively low resistance connecting two points of an electric circuit of greater resistance, sometimes resulting in an excessive current flow.—**short-cir·cuit,** shärt"sur'kit, *v.t.* To establish a short circuit in; to carry, as a current, by acting as a short circuit, as a conducting body does; to cut off by the establishment of a short circuit. *Colloq.* to by-pass; hinder.—*v.i. Elect.* to form a short circuit.

short·com·ing, shärt'kum"ing, *n.* A failure

to reach a quantity or amount; deficiency; a failure to perform fully, as one's duty; a defect.

short cov·er·ing, *n. Bus., finance,* a purchase of enough shares of stock, or enough of some commodity, to meet the obligations of a short sales contract.

short·cut, shärt'kut", *n.* A route shorter than one usu. used; a timesaving method of accomplishing any work or undertaking.—*a.*—**short-cut,** *v.t., v.i.—short-cut, short-cutting.* To use a shorter way or method.

short di·vi·sion, *n. Math.* a method of division in which all computations are made mentally without being written down.

short·en, shär'ten, *v.t.* To make short or shorter; to abridge; to curtail; to lessen; to diminish in extent or amount; to furl, as a sail; to make, as pastry, crisp with the addition of fat or other shortening.—*v.i.* To become short or shorter.—**short·en·er,** *n.*

short·en·ing, shär'te·ning, shärt'ning, *n.* The act of abbreviating or becoming abbreviated; *ling.* the dropping of the initial or final part of a word to form a shorter word. Butter, lard, or other edible fat used to make pastry crisp.

short·hand, shärt'hand", *n.* Any system of quick writing, substituting contractions and symbols for letters and words; stenography; any system of contracted communication.—*a.*

short-hand·ed, shärt'han'did, *a.* Not having the full or necessary number of workmen or helpers.—**short-hand·ed·ness,** *n.*

Short·horn, shärt'härn", *n.* One of a dual-purpose breed of beef and dairy cattle originating in northern England, having very short horns. Also *Durham.*

short-horned grass·hop·per, shärt'-härnd" gras'hop"ĕr, *n.* Any of a large group of orthopterous insects having antennae shorter than the length of the body. See *locust.*

short in·ter·est, *n. Finance,* the total short sales of securities or commodities. See *short account.*

short line, *n.* Any comparatively short route operated by a bus company, airline, or the like; *rail.* the shortest distance by rail between the two stations at the beginning and end of a route; *stock market,* the number of shares in a trader's account that have been sold short.

short-lived, shärt'līvd', shärt'livd', *a.* Not living or lasting long; being of short continuance.—**short-lived·ness,** *n.*

short·ly, shärt'lē, *adv.* In a short or brief time; soon; in a few words; curtly.—**short·ness,** *n.*

short or·der, *n.* Food that can be cooked and served quickly when ordered in a restaurant.—**in short or·der,** quickly; without delay.—**short-or·der,** shärt'ar"dĕr, *a.*

short ribs, *n.pl.* A section of beef between the rib roast and plate, composed of rib ends covered with meat.

short shrift, *n.* A short period granted a condemned prisoner to make confession and receive absolution before death; slight consideration, mercy, or attention as given people or situations.

short-sight·ed, shärt'sī'tid, *a.* Unable to see far; near-sighted; myopic. Lacking in foresight, as persons; characterized by or showing lack of foresight; as, a *short-sighted* policy.—**short sight,** *n.*—**short-sight·ed·-ly,** *adv.*—**short-sight·ed·ness,** *n.*

short snort·er, *n. Aeron.* An individual belonging to an informal club open to those who have flown across the ocean; paper money endorsed by club members, which serves as a certificate of membership.

short-spo·ken, shärt'spō'ken, *a.* Speaking in a short, brief, or curt manner; curt in speech.

short·stop, shärt'stop", *n. Baseball,* a defensive player stationed in the infield between second and third base; the position he covers. *Photog.* stop bath.

short sto·ry, *n.* A short prose narrative, usu. less than 10,000 words.

short-tem·pered, shärt'tem'pĕrd, *a.* Having a short or hasty temper; quick-tempered.

short-term, shärt'turm', *a.* Involving or applying to a comparatively short time; payable or maturing within a brief period, usu. a year, as a note or loan.

short·wave, shärt'wāv', *n. Radio,* an electromagnetic wave, shorter than those in the standard broadcast band, 60 meters or less in length.—**short·wave,** *a.*

short-wind·ed, shärt'win'did, *a.* Affected with shortness of breath after brief physical effort.

Sho·sho·ni, Sho·sho·ne, shō·shō'nē, *n. pl.* **Sho·sho·ni, Sho·sho·nis, Sho·sho·ne, Sho·sho·nes.** A large Indian tribe which was once spread over California, Idaho, Nevada, Utah, Colorado, and Wyoming; any member of the Shoshoni people; their language.

shot, shot, *n. pl.* **shots.** [< *shoot;* O.E. *gescot,* an arrow.] A discharge of a firearm or other missile weapon; the act of shooting; a missile, esp. a ball or bullet for firing from ordnance. Any of the small globular pieces of lead for use in shotguns or the like; pl. **shot.** The flight of a missile, or its range or distance; one who shoots; a marksman; a heavy, usu. metal ball put or cast for distance by contestants in an athletic event; an aimed throw or stroke, often for scoring, as in certain games; a try, attempt, or guess; as, taking a *shot* at finding the error; a remark with telling effect directed at a person. *Colloq.* an injection of a drug given hypodermically; as, a rabies *shot;* a small quantity of liquor, specif. an ounce or jigger, to be drunk in one swallow. *Photog.* a camera exposure or snapshot; a scene or single unit photographed as for moving pictures or television. A chance relating to gambling odds; as, to bet on a horse that is a 10 to 1 *shot;* naut. a 15 fathom, or 90 foot, length of chain or cable; *metal.* small globules of hardened metal in a casting. In blasting, a charge of powder or other explosive ready for detonating.—*v.t.—shotted, shotting.* To load with shot; to use shot for weighting.—*v.i.* To manufacture or form shot.—**call one's shots,** to specify in advance what know one will make or attempt to make.—**call the shots,** *slang,* to direct or control what will happen; as, being in a position where he can *call the shots.*—**like a shot,** quickly; at once.—**not by a long shot,** *slang,* decidedly not, never.—**shot in the arm,** *slang,* something having a revitalizing or stimulating effect, as: Receiving the promotion was a *shot in the arm* for him.—**shot in the dark,** *slang,* a random guess or conjecture.

shot, shot, *a.* Having a changeable color, like that produced in weaving, by all the warp threads being of one color and all the weft of another; variegated; interspersed; as, brown hair *shot* with silver; permeated, usu. followed by *through with;* as, a sermon *shot through with* humor; *colloq.* completely worn out; ruined; *slang,* intoxicated, as: He was half *shot.*

shot·gun, shot'gun", *n.* A light, smooth-bored, often double-barreled gun for firing shot at short range.—*a.* Pertaining to or as with a shotgun; involving the use of force; covering a wide range in an indiscriminate or hit-or-miss fashion; as, to prescribe a *shotgun* remedy.—*v.t.—shotgunned, shotgunning.* To shoot at with a shotgun; to coerce.

shot·gun wed·ding, *n. Slang.* A marriage necessitated by the bride's pregnancy; a merger, agreement, or compromise compelled by circumstances, as: The joining of the two political factions was more or less a *shotgun wedding.* Also **shot·gun mar·riage.**

shot hole, *n.* A hole drilled for the insertion of a stick of dynamite; a hole bored in wood by an insect; *bot.* a plant condition in which the leaves become riddled with small round holes, as by shot, due to a parasite or disease.

shot put, *n.* An athletic event in which a heavy shot or ball is cast as far as possible; a single put or throw in such a contest.—**shot-put·ter,** shot′pu̇t″ȇr, *n.*—**shot-put·ting,** *n.*

shot·ten, shot′en, *a.* [An old pp. of *shoot.*] Having ejected the spawn, said esp. of a herring.

should, shu̇d, *aux. v.* The past form of *shall,* used as such only in indirect discourse, as: He told me I *should* never fail. Used to indicate condition in conjunction with or instead of *if,* as: She will laugh, *should* I fall, she will laugh *if* I *should* fall. Used to show obligation or duty, often with doubtful fulfillment, as: I *should* go home now. Used in the present perfect tense of the obligatory sense to indicate failure to do something, as: I *should* have gone home an hour ago. Used to denote a surprise happening, as: Who *should* appear, but my father! Used to express probability or expectancy, as: She *should* arrive tomorrow. Used to soften or temper a command, suggestion, or opinion, as: I *should* think you had had enough to eat. *Colloq.* used ironically to mean the opposite, as: With grades like mine, I *should* talk. Used interrogatively to ask direction or inquire as to propriety, used similarly to *shall* but often with more emphasis on duty or obligation, as: *Should* I apologize?

shoul·der, shōl′dȇr, *n.* [O.E. *shulder,* Sc. *shouther,* O.E. *sculdor* = Dan. *skulder,* Sw. *skuldra,* D. *schouder,* G. *schulter,* the shoulder, the shoulder blade.] The joint by which the arm of a human or the foreleg of other mammals is connected with the body; the bones and muscles of this part conjointly; *pl.* both shoulders and the area below or behind the neck lying between them. The upper joint of the foreleg of an animal dressed for market, as of a steer; a prominent or projecting part; as, the *shoulder* of a hill; that part of wearing apparel which covers the shoulders; the forepart of an animal hide; the flat open space bordering either side of a roadway; *print.* the upper surface of a type block which extends beyond the bottom of the letter or character.—*v.t.* To push or thrust with the shoulder; shove; bump; to take upon the shoulder or shoulders, as an obligation.—*v.i.* To force one's way, as through a crowd.—**cry on one's shoul·der,** to tell another person one's woes or troubles; to seek solace.—**put one's shoul·der to the wheel,** to work earnestly; work hard.—**rub shoul·ders with,** to join or mix with; associate in close relationship with.—**shoul·der arms,** *milit.* to position a rifle against a shoulder, gripping the heel of the butt by the hand on the same side and with the forearm parallel to the ground.—**shoul·der to shoul·der,** with combined effort; pulling together; cooperating; as, working *shoulder to shoulder.*—**straight from the shoul·der,** in a straightforward manner; directly; openly; frankly.

shoul·der blade, *n. Anat., zool.* Either of the two large, flat, triangle-shaped bones in the upper back on either side and forming the dorsal part of the shoulders in humans and other mammals; an analogous structure in other vertebrates. Also *scapula.*

shoul·der board, *n. Milit.* Either of two stiff, oblong pieces of cloth on the shoulders

of certain uniforms worn by U.S. Navy and Coast Guard officers on which are insignia of rank and branch of duty or service; a similar device worn on some formal dress uniforms of Army and Air Force officers. Also *shoulder mark.*

shoul·der gir·dle, *n. Anat., zool.* the bony or cartilaginous semicircular band or arch that serves for the attachment and support of the forelimbs of a vertebrate. Also *pectoral girdle.*

shoul·der knot, *n.* An ornamental knot of ribbon or lace worn on the shoulder, esp. by men in the 17th and 18th centuries; an ornament of braided cord, signifying duty assignment, worn on the left or right shoulder of military personnel on various occasions.

shoul·der mark, *n.* Shoulder board.

shoul·der patch, *n. Milit.* A cloth insignia designating a unit, worn on the upper left sleeve, one-half inch below the shoulder seam of a uniform coat or shirt; a similar emblem denoting an overseas unit in a theater of operation, esp. during World War II, usu. worn on the right sleeve. Also **shoul·der em·blem.**

should·n't, shu̇d′ant. Contraction of should not.

shout, shout, *n.* A loud cry, as one expressing joy, triumph, fear, or the like; a loud and sudden outcry or uproar.—*v.i.* To utter a sudden and loud cry.—*v.t.* To utter with a shout.—**shout·er,** *n.*

shout·ing dis·tance, *n.* Easy or comfortable reach of the voice, usu. preceded by *within.*

shove, shuv, *v.t.*—**shoved, shoving.** [O.E. *scūfan;* Icel. *skūfa,* D. *schuiven,* to shove; akin to *shovel.*] To force or push along; to cause to slide by pushing; to press against; to jostle.—*v.i.* To push or drive forward; to urge a course.—*n.* An act of shoving; a push.—**shove off,** to push a boat from the shore; *slang,* to leave.—**shov·er,** *n.*

shov·el, shuv′el, *n.* [O.E. *scofl,* to shove = D. *schoffel,* G. *schaufel,* a shovel.] An implement consisting of a broad and slightly hollow blade, or shallow scoop, with a long handle, used for gathering up, throwing, or removing loose matter such as coal, sand, earth, or the like.—*v.t.*—**shoveled, shoveling,** *Brit.* **shovelled, shovelling.** To take up and throw with a shovel; to clear, as a path, with a shovel; to scoop up hastily or in masses using or as if using a shovel.—*v.i.* To work with or as with a shovel.

shov·el·bill, shuv′el·bil″, *n. Ornith.* a shoveler.

shov·el·er, shov·el·ler, shuv′e·lȇr, shuv′lȇr, *n.* One who or that which shovels. *Ornith.* a widely distributed fresh-water duck, *Spatula clypeata,* of the northern hemisphere, with a broad shovellike bill used for sifting the water for food. Also *shovelbill.*

shov·el·ful, shuv′el·fu̇l″, *n.* A quantity sufficient to fill a shovel.

shov·el hat, *n.* A hat with a broad brim turned up at the sides and projecting in front: worn by some clergymen, esp. in England.

shov·el·head, shuv′el·hed″, *n.* A species of shark; a subspecies of sturgeon.

shov·el·nose, shuv′el·nōz″, *n.* Any of various animals with a shovellike snout or head, as a shark, *Hexanchus corinus,* of the Pacific, and an American sturgeon, *Scaphirhynchus platyrhynchus.*—**shov·el·nosed,** shuv′el·nōzd″, *a.*

show, shō, *v.t.*—past *showed,* pp. *shown* or *showed,* ppr. *showing.* [M.E. *showen,* look at, let see, show, < O.E. *scēawian,* look at = D. *schouwen* = G. *schauen,* look at, view; akin to L. *cavēre,* take heed.] To cause or allow to be seen or manifested to the sight; expose to view; to present or exhibit, as for amusement; to display, as for sale; to guide,

escort, or conduct; to point out or indicate in order to inform; to illustrate, demonstrate, prove, explain, or otherwise make clear, evident, or understandable in order to instruct; to make evident by appearance, behavior, or by other action; to accord or grant; as, to *show* favor. *Law,* to allege, as in a legal document; to plead, as a reason or cause.—*v.i.* To be seen; be or become visible; to appear or arrange to appear in a certain manner; as, to *show* to advantage; to finish in third place in certain kinds of races; to give an exhibition, display, or performance; *colloq.* to make an appearance, usu. followed by *up,* as: I waited but he didn't *show up.*—*n.* An exhibition, display, or performance; the act or an act of exhibiting, displaying, or performing; as, a *show* of hands; a radio or television production or program, a motion picture, or a theatrical production; the theater or company providing these entertainments; an appearance or performance that intentionally or inadvertently conveys a specific impression, as one that is striking or imposing, or one that is ostentatious, foolish, or inappropriate; an indication or trace; as, a *show* of blood; a minimal or token, empty, or half-hearted display or performance made in gesture only, or born of weakness, irresolution, or a deliberate intention to deceive; a racer who finishes in third place; *colloq.* a chance or opportunity, as: He was given a fair *show.*—**show·er,** *n.*

show bill, *n.* A poster or a placard advertising a show or another matter for public attention.

show·boat, shō′bōt″, *n.* A river steamboat with stage and a troupe of actors, used as a floating theater.

show·bread, shō′bred″, *n.* Shewbread.

show·case, shō′kās″, *n.* A glass cabinet or case within which articles are placed for sale or exhibition; a setting or program for exhibiting or displaying something, as a model or idea.—*v.t.*—**showcased, showcasing.**

show·down, shō′doun″, *n.* The laying down of one's cards, face upward, in a card game; a disclosure of actual resources or power as required by an opponent or as forced by some decisive test; confrontation.

show·er, shou′ȇr, *n.* [O.E. *scūr* = D. *schoer* = G. *schauer* = Icel. *skūr,* shower = Goth. *skūra,* storm (of wind).] A brief fall of rain, hail, sleet, or snow; a similar fall, as of tears, sparks, bullets, or other objects which are small; a copious supply or quantity bestowed; a bestowal of presents, usu. of a particular kind, as on a prospective bride. A bath in which water is showered upon the body from above; the room or apparatus for such a bath; also *shower bath.*—*v.t.* To pour down in a shower; send down abundantly and rapidly; bestow liberally or lavishly; to wet or sprinkle with or as with a shower; to clean by means of a shower bath.—*v.i.* To rain in a shower or showers; fall or come in a shower or a copious supply of quantity; to take or have a shower.—**show·er·y,** shou′e·rē, *a.*

show·er bath, *n.* See *shower.*

show·ing, shō′ing, *n.* The act of one who or that which shows; exhibition; display; show; a record or performance; a setting forth or presentation, as of facts or conditions; evidence.

show·man, shō′man, *n. pl.* **show·men.** One who produces or exhibits a show; a person who has skill in doing this or in presenting anything dramatically.—**show·man·ship,** shō′man·ship″, *n.* The ability or skill to present something dramatically.

show-off, shō′af″, shō′of″, *n.* Pretentious display; a person who shows off.—**show off,** *v.t.* To display arrogantly.—*v.i.* To seek attention by showy behavior.

show·piece, shō'pēs", n. That which is exhibited or displayed; that which is an outstanding example of its type or sort and worthy of being exhibited.

show·place, shō'plās", n. A place recognized as an example of fine taste, as in architecture, furnishings, or overall beauty; a home or public place renowned for its esthetic beauty or historical significance.

show·room, shō'room", shō'rụm", n. A room in which goods are exhibited for the purpose of advertising or sale.

show up, v.t. To disclose or reveal, as defects; colloq. to outshine, as: Are you trying to show me up?—v.i. To be easily distinguishable or evident, as: The sailboats show up well against the setting sun. Colloq. to reach a destination or put in an appearance, as: He'll show up.

show·y, shō'ē, a.—showier, showiest. Making a show or imposing display; as, showy flowers; given to show or ostentatious display; gaudy.—show·i·ly, adv.—show·-i·ness, n.

shrap·nel, shrap'nel, n. pl. shrap·nel. [From the inventor, H. Shrapnel, 1761–1842, officer in the Brit. army.] A hollow projectile containing a collection of bullets or the like and a bursting charge, arranged to explode before reaching the object in order to set free a shower of missiles; such projectiles collectively; shell fragments.

shred, shred, n. [O.E. scrēade, Sc. screed, a piece torn off; O. Fris. skreda, D. schrooden, O.H.G. scrōtan, to tear. Shroud is akin.] An irregular piece torn or cut off; a tatter; a fragment—v.t.—shredded or shred, shredding. To tear or cut into small pieces, esp. narrow strips, as paper.—v.i. To be torn into shreds, as: Cabbage shreds easily.—shred·der, n.

shrew, shrō, n. [M.E. shrewe, schrewe; commonly supposed to be another use of shrew, from an old belief that the animal was venomous or exercised a malignant influence.] One of several small insect-eating mammals of the family Soricidae, distinguished by a pointed nose and small eyes; see shrewmouse. A woman of violent temper and speech; a termagant or an ill-tempered scold.—shrew·like, a.

shrewd, shrōd, a. [M.E. shrewed, schrewed, appar. < shrewe, schrewe, E. shrew, n.] Astute or sagacious; sharp in discernment or grasp of practical considerations.—shrewd·ly, adv.—shrewd·ness, n.

shrew·ish, shrō'ish, a. Having the disposition or ways of a shrew; nagging; ill-tempered.—shrew·ish·ly, adv.—shrew·ish·ness, n.

shrew·mouse, shrō'mous", n. pl. shrew·-mice, shrō'mīs. A shrew, esp. Sorex vulgaris, the common shrew of Europe.

shriek, shrēk, n. [= screak and screech.] A loud, sharp, shrill cry or other sound.—v.i. To utter a loud, sharp, shrill cry or sound; to cry out sharply at a high pitch of voice.—v.t. To utter or cry in a shriek.

shriev·al·ty, shrē'val·tē, n. pl. shriev·al·-ties. [< obs. shrieve, a sheriff.] The office, jurisdiction, or term of a sheriff.—shriev·al, shrē'val, a.

shrift, shrift, n. [O.E. scrift, < scrīfan, E. shrive.] Archaic. The imposition of penance by a priest on a penitent after confession; absolution or remission of sins granted after confession and penance; confession to a priest; act of shriving. See short shrift.

shrike, shrīk, n. [O.E. scrīc, kind of bird.] Any of numerous predaceous birds of the family Laniidae, as the butcherbirds, with a strong hooked and toothed bill, which feed on insects and sometimes small birds and other animals.

shrill, shril, a. [M.E. shrille = G. schrill, schrill.] High-pitched and piercing, as the voice; uttering or producing such sound;

characterized by or resounding with such sound; intemperate; lacking in moderation; poet. sharp, keen, piercing, or poignant.—adv. With or in a shrill sound.—v.i. To sound shrilly, as the voice; to utter or produce shrill sounds, as a thing.—v.t. To utter or give forth shrilly.—n. A shrill sound.—shril·ly, adv.—shrill·ness, n.

shrimp, shrimp, n. pl. shrimps, shrimp. [M.E. shrimpe: cf. M.L.G. schrimpen, to wrinkle, contract.] Any of various small, long-tailed, chiefly marine, ten-footed crustaceans of the genus Crangon, and allied genera, several of which are esteemed as a table delicacy; slang, a diminutive or insignificant person.—a. Of or pertaining to the catching and handling of shrimp; as, a shrimp fisherman; cooking, of or pertaining to a dish made of shrimp.—v.i. To try to catch shrimp.

shrine, shrīn, n. [O.E. scrin, < scrinium, a box.] A reliquary; a container for holding the remains or fragments of something held sacred; a tomb, mausoleum or other structure, often large, that houses such articles of veneration; a place hallowed because of its history or other significant associations; as, a shrine of art.—v.t.—shrined, shrining. To place in a shrine; to enshrine.

shrink, shringk, v.i.—past shrank or shrunk, pp. shrunk or shrunken, ppr. shrinking. [O.E. scrincan, O.D. schrincken, to shrink; from root of shrimp, shrug.] To draw back, as from danger; to recoil; to contract or become reduced in size as a result of subjection to conditions of moisture or temperature or both, as woolen cloth in hot water; to be drawn into less compass or extent, as: Distances have shrunk since the introduction of air travel. To diminish in amount or value, as a legacy.—v.t. To cause to contract.—n. The act of shrinking; shrinkage.—shrink·a·ble, a.—shrink·er, n.

shrink·age, shring'kij, n. The process or condition of shrinking; the amount or extent of shrinking; depreciation in value or quantity, as of business assets; contraction of cloth, as by washing or processing; loss in weight of livestock from the time of shipping through the final step of its processing as meat.

shrink·ing vi·o·let, n. One who tends to make himself as inconspicuous as possible, esp. when confronted by public appreciation of his worth.

shrive, shrīv, v.t.—past shrove or shrived, pp. shriven or shrived, ppr. shriving. [O.E. scrifan (pret. scrāf, pp. scrifen), prescribe, impose, shrive; < L. scribere, write.] Eccles. To impose penance on for sin; to grant absolution to, as a penitent; to hear the confession of; to receive forgiveness for through confession and penance.—v.i. Eccles. To hear confessions; to go to or make confession.

shriv·el, shriv'el, v.t., v.i.—shriveled, shriveling, Brit. shrivelled, shrivelling. [Prob. based on rivel, to shrivel, partly on shrink.] To contract or shrink; to draw or be drawn into wrinkles; to wither; to become or make inefficient, useless, or helpless.

shroff, shrof, n. In India, a banker or moneychanger; in the Orient, a native expert employed to test coins and separate the base from the genuine.—v.t. To test, as coins, in order to separate the counterfeit from the genuine.

Shrop·shire, shrop'shēr, shrop'shėr, n. Any of a breed of hornless, black-faced sheep, orig. from Shropshire, England, noted for mutton and heavy wool.

shroud, shroud, n. [O.E. scrūd, a garment, a shroud; Icel. skrūth, shrouds, tackle; Dan. skrud, dress; from root of shred.] The garment of the dead; that which cloaks,

covers, or conceals in the manner of a long, loose wrap or garment; naut. any one of the rope supports extending from the right and left sides of a ship to the head of its mast.—v.t. To enshroud for burial; to envelop, cover, hide, or veil, as: Mystery shrouded the incident.—v.i. Archaic, to take shelter.

shroud-laid, shroud'lād", a. Of a rope, made with four strands and laid right-handed, usu. with a central core or heart.

Shrove·tide, shrōv'tīd", n. The period of three days preceding Ash Wednesday.

Shrove Tues·day, n. The day before Ash Wednesday.

shrub, shrub, n. [O.E. scrybb, a bush.] Any of various low, woody perennial plants, usu. with several permanent woody stems dividing from the base.

shrub, shrub, n. [Ar. shurb, a drink; allied to syrup, sherbet.] A beverage composed of fruit juice, sugar, and often rum or other spirits.

shrub·ber·y, shrub'e·rē, n. pl. shrub·-ber·ies. Shrubs collectively.

shrub·by, shrub'ē, a.—shrubbier, shrubbiest. Full of or consisting of shrubs; being or resembling a shrub.

shrug, shrug, v.t., v.i.—shrugged, shrugging. To raise or draw up the shoulders, as in expressing dissatisfaction, aversion, or uncertainty.—n. A drawing up of the shoulders; a woman's short jacket, usu. without a front fastener.—shrug off, to ignore or take little notice of, as something occurring to or directed toward one; to become free from the effects of.

shuck, shuk, n. [Origin obscure.] A husk or pod, as the outer covering of maize, hickory nuts, or chestnuts; the shell of an oyster or clam; usu. pl., colloq. something worthless or of little use; as, not worth shucks.—interj. Usu. pl. an exclamation showing contempt or disgust.—v.t. To remove the shucks from; to remove as or like shucks; slang, to undress or take off, as one's clothes.—shuck·er, n.

shud·der, shud'ėr, v.i. [Same as L.G. schuddern, O.D. schudderen, G. schüttern, to shake, to shiver, freq. forms < L.G. and D. schudden, G. schütten, O.H.G. scuitan, to shake; allied to E. shed, to cast.] To tremble as with fear or horror.—n. An agitation or convulsive shaking of the body; tremor.—shud·der·y, a.

shuf·fle, shuf'l, v.t.—shuffled, shuffling. [A freq. form related to shove: cf. scuffle.] To move, as the feet, along the ground or floor without lifting them; to perform, as a dance, with such movements; to move this way and that; to mix, as cards in a pack, so as to change their relative position; to jumble together or mingle indiscriminately. To put, thrust, or bring trickily, surreptitiously, or carelessly, usu. followed by into, in, or out; as, to shuffle oneself into a position of power.—v.i. To move the feet without lifting them; to walk with clumsy steps or a shambling gait; to scrape the feet over the floor in dancing; to move in a clumsy manner, usu. with into; as, to shuffle into one's clothes; to act in a shifting or evasive manner; equivocate; to mix cards in a pack so as to change their relative position.—n. A scraping movement of the feet; a dragging gait; an evasive trick; artifice; a shuffling of cards in a pack; the right or turn to shuffle in card playing; a dance in which the feet are shuffled along the floor.—shuf·fle off, to thrust aside or get rid off.—shuf·fler, n.

shuf·fle·board, shuf'l·bōrd", shuf'l·bȧrd", n. A game played by propelling disks forcefully with a cue so that they will slide the length of the playing area, officially 45 feet, and come to rest in one of five scoring positions marked off.

a- fat, fāte, fär, fåre, fạll; e- met, mē, mēre, hėr; i- pin, pīne; o- not, nōte, mōve; u- tub, cūbe, bụll; oi- oil; ou- pound.

shul, shụl, shöl, *n*. pl. **shuln**. [< Yiddish.] Synagogue.

shun, shun, *v.t.*—**shunned, shunning**. [O.E. *scunian*, to shun.] To keep clear of; to avoid consistently.—**shun·ner**, *n*.

shunt, shunt, *v.t.* [M.E. *schunten*; perh. related to *shun*.] To shove or turn aside or out of the way; to shift, as a train or part of it, from one line of rails to another or from the main track to a siding; to switch; to sidetrack; to put aside; to get rid of; *med.* to divert the blood by using a shunt. *Elect.* to divert, as a part of a current, by means of a shunt; place on or furnish with a shunt.— *v.i.* To move or turn aside or out of the way; to shift one's way or views; of a train, to move from one line of rails to another; *med.* of the blood, to be diverted by a shunt; *elect.* to be or to become diverted by means of a shunt.—*n*. An act of shunting; a turning aside; a shift; a railroad switch; *med.* a channel, other than the usual one, through which the blood is diverted, as one formed surgically; *elect.* a conductor joining two points in a circuit and forming a path through which a part of the current will pass.—**shunt·er**, *n*.

shunt-wound, shunt′wound′, *a. Elect.* arranged so that the windings of the armature and the field circuits are connected in parallel, thus dividing the current between them, as in an electric motor.— **shunt wind·ing**, *n*.

shush, shush, *interj*. Be quiet; hush: an expression demanding silence.—*v.t.* To hush; to tell, as a person, to be silent or quiet.

shut, shut, *v.t.*—**shut, shutting**. [O.E. *scyttan* = D. *schutten*, shut; from the root of E. *shoot*.] To put in position to close an entrance, passage, or aperture, as a door, gate, cover, or lid; to close by folding or bringing together the outward covering parts of, as the eyes, a book, or a knife; to obstruct, block, or prevent ingress to or egress from, by or as if by a door, gate, or other barrier; to confine or enclose, usu. followed by *in* or *up*; to bar, exclude, or cut off, usu. followed by *out* or *off*.—*v.i.* To become shut or closed; to close.—*n*. The act, time, or place of shutting or closing; the line where two pieces of welded metal are joined.—*a*. Closed; *phon.* stopped, as a consonantal sound.—**shut down**, to close for a time; as, to *shut down* a factory; to settle down or descend upon so as to cover or envelop, as: Night *shut down* on us swiftly. To cease temporarily; to put a stop or check to something, usu. followed by *on* or *upon*.— **shut in**, to enclose or confine.—**shut off**, to exclude; to prevent the passage of; to close. —**shut out**, to bar or exclude; *sports,* to prevent from scoring, as a baseball team.— **shut up**, to close tightly, as a house; to enclose, confine, or imprison; *colloq.* to stop talking or cause to stop talking.

shut·down, shut′doun″, *n*. A shutting down or stopping for a time, as a factory or other place of business.

shut-eye, shut′ī″, *n. Slang*, sleep.

shut-in, shut′in″, *n*. A person who is confined to a place by infirmity or disease.— *a.* Confined by infirmity; *psychol.* designating a personality seriously lacking in openness, expressiveness, and sociability.

shut·off, shut′af″, shut′of″, *n*. The mechanism or device for shutting off something.

shut·out, shut′out″, *n*. The act of shutting out, or the state of being shut out. *Sports,* a preventing of the opposite side from scoring, as in baseball; a game in which shutting out is accomplished.

shut·ter, shut′ér, *n*. One who or that which shuts; a hinged or sliding cover for a window; a movable cover, slide, or the like, for closing an aperture; *photog.* a mechanical device for opening and closing the

aperture of a camera lens in order to expose the film.—*v.t.* To close with or as with a shutter; provide with shutters.

shut·ter·bug, shut′ér·bug″, *n. Slang,* an avid amateur photographer.

shut·tle, shut′l, *n*. [M.E. *schutylle, schetylle,* weaver's shuttle, < O.E. *scytel,* dart, missile; from the root of E. *shoot*.] A device in a loom, for passing or shooting the weft thread through the shed from one side of the web to the other, usu. a boat-shaped piece of wood containing a bobbin of weft thread; an implement on which thread is wound, used in tatting or netting; the rotating container that carries the lower thread or bobbin in a sewing machine; a means of transportation which makes short and frequent trips between two points.—*v.t., v.i.*—**shuttled, shuttling**. To move or cause to move to and fro like a shuttle.—**shut·tle·like**, *a*.

shut·tle·cock, shut′l·kok″, *n*. A piece of cork or light material, with feathers on one end, intended to be struck in the air with a battledore or badminton racket; the game battledore or shuttlecock.—*v.t.* To send or bandy to and fro like a shuttlecock.

shy, shī, *a*.—**shier, shiest, shyer, shyest**. [Same as Dan. *sky*, shy, skittish, G. *scheu*, shy, timid; akin to O.E. *schiech, sceoh,* Sc. *skiech,* Sw. *skygg,* shy. *Eschew* is akin to *shy*.] Reserved, retiring, modest, and coy rather than gregarious or social; diffident, self-conscious, timid, and readily frightened; cautious, wary, and careful; hesitant, indecisive, and noncommittal; wanting, lacking, or short of, usu. used with *on*; not fecund, as certain animals and plants.—*v.i.*—**shied, shying**. To start away, recoil, or rear in fright or revulsion, as a horse; to avoid or show an aversion to something, usu. used with *from*; as, to *shy* away *from* political discussions.—*n*. pl. **shies**. An instance of shying; a starting or recoiling from.—**shy·er**, *n*.—**shy·ly**, *adv*.— **shy·ness**, *n*.

shy, shī, *v.i., v.t.*—**shied, shying**. [Origin uncertain.] To throw with a swift, sudden movement; fling.—*n*. pl. **shies**. A quick, sudden throw; a fling. *Fig.* a gibe or sneer; a try at something.—**shy·er**, *n*.

Shy·lock, shī′lok, *n*. A relentless money-lender in Shakespeare's *Merchant of Venice*; any usurer.

shy·ster, shī′stér, *n. Slang*. A dishonest or unscrupulous lawyer; anyone similarly unethical.

si, sē, *n. Mus.* the syllable given in some systems to the seventh note of the eight-tone diatonic scale, or B in the major scale of C.

si·al·a·gogue, sī·al′a·gag″, sī·al′a·gog″, *n*. [Gr. *sialon,* saliva, and *agōgos,* leading.] A medicine that promotes the salivary flow. Also **si·al·o·gogue**.—**si·al·a·gog·ic, si··al·o·gog·ic**, sī″a·la·goj′ik, *a*.

si·a·mang, sē′a·mang″, *n*. [Malay.] A black anthropoid ape, *Symphalangus syndactylus,* of Sumatra and the Malay Peninsula, the largest of the gibbons, with very long arms and the second and third digits partially webbed.

Si·a·mese, sī″a·mēz′, sī″a·mēs′, *a*. Of or pertaining to Thailand, formerly Siam, to its people, the Thais, or to their language; being joined, as twins; of close connection. *n*. pl. **Si·a·mese**. A native of Thailand; a Thai; the Thai language.

Si·a·mese cat, *n*. A short-haired breed of cat, thought to have originated in Siam, typically of slender build and fawn colored, with dark ears, face, feet, and tail, and blue eyes.

Si·a·mese twins, *n*. Orig. Eng and Chang, 1811–74, Siamese male twins born joined at the chest by a cartilaginous band; any twins congenitally united.

sib, sib, *n*. A relative, esp. a sister or brother; kinsmen or relatives collectively; *anthropol.* a unilateral kin group which controls the institutions of marriage and religion among its members.—*a*. Related by blood; akin.

Si·be·ri·an husk·y, sī·bē′rē·an hus′kē, *n*. One of a breed of sled dogs of medium size, resembling the Alaskan malamute.

sib·i·lant, sib′i·lant, *a*. [L. *sibilans, sibilant-is,* ppr. of *sibilo,* to hiss.] Hissing; *phon.* making a hissing sound, as when pronouncing *s, sh, z, zh, ch,* or *j*.—*n. Phon.* the hissing sound made when pronouncing *s, sh, z, zh, ch,* or *j*.—**sib·i·lance, sib·i·lan-·cy**, *n*.—**sib·i·lant·ly**, *adv*.

sib·i·late, sib′i·lāt″, *v.t.*—**sibilated, sibilating**. [L. *sibilo, sibilatum,* to hiss.] To pronounce with a hissing sound.—*v.i.* To hiss.—**sib·i·la·tion**, *n*.

sib·ling, sib′ling, *n*. A brother or a sib.—*a. anthropol.* a member of a sib.—*a*. Having to do with a brother or a sister.

sib·yl, sib′il, *n*. [Gr. *sibylla*.] One of certain women mentioned by Greek and Roman writers, said to have been endowed with a prophetic spirit; a prophetess.—**si·byl·ic, si·byl·lic, sib·yl·line**, si·bil′ik, sib′i′lēn″, sib′i·lin, sib′i·lin, *a*.

sic, sik, *v.t.*—**sicked, sicking**. To pursue; attack, as in a command given to a dog; to rouse to an attack, as: He *sicked* his dog on the intruder. Also **sick**.

sic, sik, L. sēk, *adv*. [L.] So; thus: usu. inserted within brackets in a text to vouch for a word, spelling, date, or the like being exactly as in the original.

sic·ca·tive, sik′a·tiv, *a*. Drying; causing to dry by the slow elimination of moisture.— *n*. A substance which hastens the drying process, as an additive in oil-based paint.

sick, sik, *a*. [O.E. *sēoc* = Goth. *siuks,* D. *ziek,* Icel. *sjūkr,* G. *siech,* sick.] Affected with disease of any kind; not healthy; ill; affected with nausea; inclined to vomit; as, being *sick* to the stomach; languishing; longing; depressed; as, being heart*sick* or home*sick;* feeling tedium; satiated; wearied, usu. with *of;* as, *sick of* rainy weather; mentally unsound; deranged; morally corrupt; as, the *sick* fancies of a *sick* mind; obsessed or preoccupied with that which is morbid, gruesome, or sadistic; as, *sick* humor; used by or set apart for the ill; as, a *sick*bed, or on the *sick* list; accompanying or suggesting illness; as, a *sick* smell or a *sick* look; disgusted; repelled; as, an attitude that makes one *sick;* menstruating; decidedly outclassed, as: His form and speed made the other contestants look *sick.* Declining, impaired, or weakened; as, a *sick* corporation in need of new capital. *Agric.* of soil, incapable of producing a normal yield due to depletion by certain crops; as, cotton-*sick* soil; infected with disease-producing organisms; as, a *sick* field.—*n., pl. in constr.* Those who are sick collectively, usu. preceded by *the.*

sick bay, *n. Naut.* the portion of a ship used as a hospital.

sick·bed, sik′bed″, *n*. A bed on which a sick person lies, often specially built for the purpose.

sick call, *n. Milit.* the time of day when sick personnel may report for treatment.

sick·en, sik′en, *v.t.* To make sick; to make squeamish; to disgust.—*v.i.* To become sick; to feel wearied or satiated; to languish.—**sick·en·er,** sik′e·nér, *n*.—**sick·en-·ing,** sik′e·ning, *a*.—**sick·en·ing·ly,** *adv*.

sick head·ache, *n*. Headache accompanied by nausea; migraine.

sick·ish, sik′ish, *a*. Nauseating or sickening; indisposed or somewhat sick.—**sick·ish·ly,** *adv*.—**sick·ish·ness,** *n*.

sick·le, sik′l, *n*. [O.E. *sicel, sicol* = D. *sikkel,* G. *sichel,* Dan. *segel,* a sickle; a dim.

form from root of *scythe*.] A curved blade or hook of steel with a handle, for use in cutting grain or grass; (*cap.*) a sickle-shaped formation of stars forming the constellation Leo.

sick leave, *n.* Time away from work or duty, usu. with pay, accorded to employees when ill.

sick·le·bill, sik'l·bil″, *n.* Any of various birds with a curved bill suggestive of the blade of a sickle, as a curlew or hummingbird.

sick·le cell, *n. Pathol.* a crescent-shaped red blood cell with abnormal hemoglobin, often causing a fatal anemic disease.

sick·le feath·er, *n.* Any of the long, curving tail feathers of a rooster.

sick·ly, sik'lē, *a.*—sicklier, sickliest. Habitually ailing or indisposed; not robust; pertaining to, connected with, or arising from ill health; as, a *sickly* complexion; marked by the prevalence of ill health, as a region or a period; causing sickness; nauseating; weak or mawkish; as, *sickly* sentimentality; faint or feeble, as light or color.—*adv.*—*v.t.*—sicklied, sicklying. To make sickly; cover with a sickly hue.— **sick·li·ness**, *n.*

sick·ness, sik'nis, *n.* The state of being sick; disease; ill health; a particular disease or malady; nausea; stomach distress; any disordered state.

sick·room, sik'rōm″, sik'rųm″, *n.* A room occupied by a sick person.

sic pas·sim, sik pas'im, *L.* sēk päs'sim, *adv.* [L.] Thus throughout: used freq. as a footnote to denote an idea found throughout a book.

sid·dur, sid'ėr, *Heb.* sē·dōr', *n. pl.* sid·dur, *Heb.* sid·du·rim, sē·dö·rēm'. A Hebrew book of daily prayers.

side, sīd, *n.* [O.E. *sīde* = D. *zijde* = G. *seite* = Icel. *sīdha* = Sw. *sida* = Dan. *side*, side: cf. O.E. *sīd*, long, large, spacious.] One of the surfaces or lines bounding a thing; either of the two surfaces of paper, cloth, or other thin objects; one of the two surfaces of an object other than the front, back, top, and bottom; either of the two lateral parts of a thing, usu. specified as right or left; either lateral half of the body of a person or an animal, esp. of the trunk; direction, position, or area with reference to a central line, space, or point; a slope, as of a bank or hill; an aspect or phase; as, to study all *sides* of a question; one of the two or more parties concerned in a case, controversy, contest, or the like; the position, course, or part of one person or party as opposed to that of another or others; as, the losing *side* in a dispute; either part, or line of descent, of a family, with reference to the father or the mother; the space adjacent to one; usu. *pl.*, *theatr.* sheets containing the lines and the cues for a single role; *Brit. slang*, pretentious airs or haughtiness; as, to put on *side*; *naut.* the portion of the hull from the stem to the stern which is normally above water, either to starboard or to port; *billiards*, a spinning motion imparted to a ball by a quick stroke on one side of its center.—*a.* Being at or on one side; coming from or directed toward one side; subsidiary or incidental; seen or taken from the side.—*v.t.*—sided, siding. To furnish, as a building, with sides; to put aside or away.—**on side**, *sports*, on one's own or the proper side, as of the ball, in football: opposed to *off side*.—**on the side**, as a secondary occupation, interest, or concern; in addition to the main issue.— **side by side**, being one beside the other; together.—**side with**, to support or sympathize with in a dispute.—**take sides**, to support or favor one side or party in a controversy.

side·arm, sīd'ärm″, *a. Baseball*, pertaining to a pitching style in which the throwing arm swings horizontally while extended away from the body.—*adv.*

side arms, *n. pl.* Weapons carried at the side of the body, as revolvers, swords, or bayonets.

side band, *n. Radio*, the frequency band, resulting from modulation, on each side of the carrier frequency. Also **side·band**.

side·board, sīd'bōrd″, sīd'bǎrd″, *n.* A piece of dining room furniture consisting of a kind of table with drawers or compartments in which articles for use on the dining table, esp. silver and linens, may be kept; one of the boards used to form a side, as of a farm wagon.

side·burns, sīd'bürnz″, *n. pl.* Whiskers extending down from the hairline on the sides of the face and worn with the chin shaved.

side·car, sīd'kär″, *n.* A small car, usu. for a passenger, attached to the side of a motorcycle, with one wheel supporting the off side; a mixed drink consisting of orange liqueur, brandy, and lemon juice.

sid·ed, sī'did, *a.* Characterized by or having sides, usu. preceded by a number; as, a one-*sided* conversation.

side dish, *n.* A food served in addition to the principal part of a course; the dish in which such food is served.

side ef·fect, *n.* An unintended, esp. harmful, secondary reaction to a drug or chemical.

side·kick, sīd'kik″, *n. Slang.* A constant companion or close associate; a pal.

side·light, sīd'līt″, *n.* Light coming from the side; incidental light or information on a subject; either of two lights carried by a vessel under way at night, a red one on the port side and a green one on the starboard side; a window or other aperture for light in the side of a building, ship, or the like; a window at the side of a door or another window.

side·line, sīd'līn″, *n.* A line at the side of something; a secondary business or activity followed in addition to a primary occupation; an additional or auxiliary line of goods; as, a *sideline* of groceries in a drug store. *Sports*, one of the marks or lines which defines the limit of play on the side of the field or court in football, tennis, basketball, or the like; usu. *pl.* the area outside these boundary lines.—*v.t.*—sidelined, sidelining. To remove or prevent from participation, esp. in any such physical activity as a sporting event.

side·long, sīd'lǎng″, sīd'long″, *a.* Inclined, slanting, or in the direction of the side; lateral; oblique; not directly in front; indirect or subtle; as, a *side-long* remark.— *adv.* Laterally; obliquely.

side·man, sīd'man″, sīd'mạn, *n. pl.* side·men, sīd'men″. *Mus.* an instrumentalist other than the leader or a solo performer, esp. in a jazz band.

side·piece, sīd'pēs″, *n.* A piece forming a side or a part of a side, or fixed by the side, of something.

si·de·re·al, sī·dēr'ē·al, *a.* [L. *sidereus*, < *sidus* (*sider-*), constellation, star.] Of or pertaining to the constellations or fixed stars; determined by the stars.—**si·de·re·al·ly**, *adv.*

si·de·re·al day, *n.* The fundamental unit of sidereal time, being the interval between two successive passages of the vernal equinoctial point over the meridian, about four minutes shorter than a mean solar day.

si·de·re·al hour, *n.* One twenty-fourth of a sidereal day.

si·de·re·al min·ute, *n.* One-sixtieth of a sidereal hour.

si·de·re·al month, *n.* The period of revolution of the moon around the earth measured with reference to the fixed stars, being about two days and five hours shorter than the period between successive new moons.

si·de·re·al sec·ond, *n.* One-sixtieth of a sidereal minute.

si·de·re·al time, *n.* Time measured with reference to the sidereal day.

si·de·re·al year, *n.* The period of revolution of the earth around the sun measured with reference to the fixed stars, equal to about 365.25 days.

sid·er·ite, sid'e·rīt″, *n.* [L. *siderites*, lodestone, < Gr. *siderités*, of iron, < *sideros*, iron.] A native carbonate of iron, FeCO$_3$, usually of a brownish color, valued as an ore of iron; also **chal·y·bite**. A meteorite consisting mainly of metallic iron.—**sid·er·it·ic**, sid″e·rit'ik, *a.*

sid·er·o·lite, sid'ėr·o·līt″, *n.* [Gr. *sideros*, and *lithos*, a stone.] A stony meteorite containing large quantities of iron.

side·sad·dle, sīd'sad″l, *n.* A woman's saddle having only one stirrup and made so that the rider sits with both legs on the same side of the horse.—*adv.*

side show, *n.* A small or minor show or exhibition in connection with a principal one, as with a circus; any minor proceeding or affair connected with a more important one; a subordinate matter or event.

side·slip, sīd'slip″, *v.i.*—sideslipped, sideslipping. To slip to one side; *aeron.* of an airplane when banked excessively, to slide sideways in a downward direction, toward the center of the curve executed in turning.—*n.* A slip or slipping to one side; *aeron.* the act or an act of sideslipping.

side·spin, sīd'spin″, *n.* A revolving motion in which a ball rotates around its own vertical axis.

side·split·ting, sīd'split″ing, *a.* Extremely hearty or uproarious, as laughter; of humor, causing hearty laughter.

side step, *n.* A step or stepping to one side, as to avoid or evade something; a step at the side of something, as a building or ship.—**side·step**, sīd'step″, *v.i.*—side-stepped, side-stepping. To step to one side; to avoid a problem or decision.—*v.t.* To dodge or avoid by stepping to one side, as an obstacle, problem, or decision.

side·stroke, sīd'strōk″, *n.* A stroke in swimming executed on one's side by moving the arms forward and pulling them back alternately while performing a scissors kick with the legs.

side·swipe, sīd'swīp″, *n.* [Cf. *swipe*.] A sweeping stroke or blow with or along the side of something.—*v.t.*—sideswiped, sideswiping. To give a sideswipe to; collide with in a sideswipe.

side·track, sīd'trak″, *v.t.*, *v.i.* To shift to a side track, as a train; to divert, as from a subject.—*n.* A railroad siding.

side·walk, sīd'wạk″, *n.* A walk, usu. paved, by the side of a street or road, for use by pedestrians. Also *Brit. pavement*.

side·walk su·per·in·tend·ent, *n. Colloq.* a bystander watching work in progress at a construction or demolition site.

side·wall, sīd'wạl″, *n.* Any wall forming a side of something, esp. the side surface of a pneumatic tire.

side·ward, sīd'wėrd, *adv.*, *a.* Toward one side.—**side·wards**, *adv.*

side·way, sīd'wā″, *n.* A byway.—*adv.*, *a.* Sideways.

side·ways, sīd'wāz″, *adv.* Toward or from one side; obliquely; laterally; indirectly; with the side foremost; facing to the side. —*a.* Facing, moving, or projected toward or away from one side; oblique or evasive. Also *sideway*, **side·wise**.

side·wheel, sīd'hwēl″, sīd'wēl″, *a.* Having a paddle wheel on each side, as some types of steamboats.—**side·wheel·er**, *n.* A side-wheel steamer.

side whisk·ers, *n.* The hair growing long on each side of a man's face, worn with the chin clean-shaven. See *muttonchops, sideburns.*—**side-whisk·ered,** *a.*

side·wind·er, sīd'wīn″dėr, *n.* A heavy blow swung from the side, usu. with the fist; a small horned rattle snake, *Crotalus cerastes,* of the desert regions of southwestern U.S. that moves by extending its body laterally in a series of loops which gives the effect of a sidewise or diagonal movement; (*cap.*), *aeron.* a supersonic missile used in air combat that utilizes an infrared guidance system to zero in on enemy aircraft.

sid·ing, sī'ding, *n.* Any material, as overlapping boards or metal strips, that covers the outer wall surface of frame buildings; a short additional line of rails laid at the side of a main line for the purpose of switching.

si·dle, sī'd'l, *v.i.*—*sidled, sidling.* [< *side.*] To approach by moving laterally or side foremost, as in a cautious or shy manner.—*n.* A sideways movement.

siege, sēj, *n.* [O.Fr. *siege, sege* (Fr. *siège*), through L.L. < L. *sedes,* seat.] The encampment of an army about a fortified place to reduce and capture it by cutting off supplies, undermining, bringing guns to bear, and other offensive operations; any prolonged or persistent endeavor to overcome resistance; a long period of distress, illness, or trouble.—*v.t.*—*sieged, sieging.* To besiege.—**lay siege to,** to besiege.

Sieg·fried Line, sēg'frēd līn″, *G.* zēch'frēt, *n.* [Named for *Siegfried,* a legendary German hero.] A World War II German fortification system constructed facing the French Maginot Line.

si·en·na, sē·en′a, *n.* [For It. *terra di Siena,* 'earth of Siena.'] A ferruginous earth used as a yellowish-brown pigment called 'raw sienna' before roasting in a furnace, and a reddish-brown pigment called 'burnt sienna' after roasting; the color of such a pigment.

si·er·ra, sē·er′a, *n.* [Sp., lit. 'saw,' < L. *serra,* saw: cf. *serrate.*] A chain of hills or mountains, the peaks of which suggest the teeth of a saw; any of a number of large fishes of the genus *Scomberomorus,* which resemble the mackerel, as a Spanish mackerel or a cero.

Si·er·ra, sē·er′a, *n.* A communications code word to designate the letter S.

si·es·ta, sē·es′ta, *n.* [Sp.] Orig. in Spain, a nap or rest taken in the heat of midday or early afternoon.

sieve, siv, *n.* [O.E. *sife* = D. *zeef* = G. *sieb,* sieve: cf. *sift.*] An instrument with a meshed or perforated bottom, used for separating the coarser from the finer parts of loose matter, or for straining liquids and the like, esp. one with a circular frame and fine mesh or perforations; *fig.* a person who tells all that he knows and cannot keep a secret.—*v.t., v.i.*—*sieved, sieving.* To sift.

sieve cell, *n. Bot.* an elongated cell whose walls contain perforations or sieve pores, which are arranged in circumscribed areas, called sieve plates, and which afford passageway of food materials to abutting or adjacent cells of a similar nature.

sieve plate, *n.* See *sieve cell.*

sieve pore, *n.* See *sieve cell.*

sieve tube, *n. Bot.* an end to end, columnar arrangement of sieve cells in the phloem, functioning in the transmission of food materials.

sift, sift, *v.t.* [O.E. *siftan* = D. *ziften,* sift; related to E. *sieve.*] To separate the coarser from the finer parts of, as meal or ashes, by shaking in a sieve; to let fall through or scatter by means of a sieve; as, to *sift* sugar; to separate by or as by a sieve; to examine with close scrutiny, as evidence.—*v.i.* To use a sieve; to pass or fall through or as through a sieve.—**sift·er,** *n.*

sift·ings, sif'tingz, *n. pl.* Parts of matter sifted out.

sigh, sī, *v.i.* [M.E. *sichen, siken,* < O.E. *sīcan,* sigh.] To emit a prolonged and audible breath, as from sorrow, weariness, relief, or yearning; to yearn or long for; to make a sound resembling or suggesting a sigh, as wind.—*v.t.* To utter or express with a sigh; to lament with sighing.—*n.* An act or sound of sighing.—**sigh·er,** *n.*

sight, sīt, *n.* [O.E. *sihth* (also *gesihth*) = D. *zicht* = G. *sicht,* sight; from the Teut. verb represented by E. *see.*] The power or faculty of seeing; the sense whereby objects are perceived with the eye; vision; the act or fact of seeing; the range or field of vision; as, land being in *sight*; a view or glimpse; mental view, regard, or estimation; *pl.* something seen or that merits seeing; as, the *sights* of the city. Something extraordinary or shocking; a spectacle, as: She looked a *sight* in that hat. An observation taken with a surveying instrument, sextant, or the like to determine exact direction or position; an aim with a gun; a device on a firearm, optical instrument, or the like to guide the eye in aiming or viewing; *chiefly dial.* a great number or quantity; as, to cost a *sight* of money.—*v.t.* To get sight of; to see; as, to *sight* land; to take a sighting or observation of, esp. with an instrument; to aim or direct by means of a sight or sights, as a firearm; to provide with sights or adjust the sights of, as a gun.—*v.i.* To take a sight or aim, as in shooting; to make a careful observation; as, to *sight* along the hedgerow while trimming it in a straight line.—*a.* Based upon unprepared or unstudied comprehension or recognition; as, a *sight* translation.—**at first sight,** as soon as glimpsed; as, knowing *at first sight* that he liked her.—**at sight,** immediately upon sight of; without preliminary notice or study; as, to play a musical composition *at sight*; *com.* immediately upon presentation; as, a note payable *at sight*.—**catch sight of,** to get a brief look at; glimpse; as, to *catch sight* of the deer through the trees.—**know by sight,** to recognize by appearance only; not to be well acquainted with, as: He's someone I *know* only *by sight*.—**not by a long sight,** *colloq.* decidedly not, as: I would not take such a risk, *not by a long sight*.—**on sight,** as soon as seen; as, orders to shoot the escaped killer *on sight*.—**out of sight,** too far away to see; unreasonable; excessively high, as a price.—**sight un·seen,** without preliminary viewing; as, property purchased *sight unseen*.—**sight·a·ble,** *a.*—**sight·ed,** *a.*—**sight·er,** *n.*

sight draft, *n. Com.* an unconditional draft payable on demand. Also **sight bill.**

sight·ed, sī'tid, *a.* Having sight or vision: often used in compounds; as, dim-*sighted.* Having a sight or sights, as a firearm.

sight·less, sīt'lis, *a.* Without sight; blind; invisible.—**sight·less·ly,** *adv.*—**sight·less·ness,** *n.*

sight·ly, sīt'lē, *a.* Pleasing to the eye; attractive; offering a fine view.—*adv.*—**sight·li·ness,** *n.*

sight-read, sīt'rēd″, *v.t.*—*sight-read, sight-reading.* To read or perform without previous acquaintance with the subject matter, as a musical composition.—*v.i.* To perform at first sight, esp. music.—**sight-read·er,** *n.*

sight·see·ing, sīt'sē″ing, *n.* The act of seeing sights or visiting points or places of general interest, as in a foreign city.—*a.* Pertaining to seeing sights or providing such services, as a bus company.—**sight·se·er,** *n.*

sig·il, sij'il, *n.* [L. *sigillum* (usu. pl., *sigilla*) small figure, seal, dim. of *signum,* E. *sign,* *n.*: cf. *seal.*] A seal or signet; an occult sign or mark, as in astrology or magic.

sig·ma, sig'ma, *n.* [L., < Gr. *sigma.*] The eighteenth letter of the Greek alphabet, written Σ, σ, or s, analogous to the English letter *S*; something shaped like a sigma; *math.* the symbol Σ, indicating the summation of terms in a defined series.—**sig·mate,** sig'mit, sig'māt.—*a.* Having the form of the Greek sigma or of the letter S.

sig·moid, sig'moid, *a.* [Gr. *sigmoeidēs.*] Shaped like the uncial sigma or the letter *C*; shaped like the letter *S.* Of or pertaining to a flexure of the colon, specif. its last curve before terminating in the rectum. Also **sig·moi·dal.**—**sig·moi·dal·ly,** *adv.*

sig·moid flex·ure, *n.* An S-shaped or C-shaped bend or curve; *anat.* a sharply curving final segment of the large intestine's descending colon, beginning at a point opposite the crest of the ileum and ending in juncture with the rectum.

sign, sīn, *v.t.* [O.Fr. Fr. *signer,* < L. *signare,* < *signum.*] To affix a signature, as to a document; to write as a signature; as, to *sign* one's name; dispose of by affixing one's signature to a document, followed by *away*; engage by written agreement; as, a baseball club *signs* a new player; to indicate or betoken; to mark or impress with a sign; make the sign of the cross; communicate by a sign; direct by a sign.—*v.i.* To write one's signature, as in token of agreement or obligation or of the receipt of something; to make a sign or signal; to enlist, followed by *up.*—**sign off,** to announce the end of a radio or TV program or a cessation of broadcasting until some future time.—**sign·er,** *n.*

sign, sīn, *n.* [O.Fr. Fr. *signe,* < L. *signum,* mark, token.] A token or indication; a symbol, esp. a conventional mark, figure, or symbol used instead of the word or words which it represents; as in math or music; a motion or gesture intended to express or convey an idea; a signal; a characteristic figure or representation attached to or placed before an inn or shop as a means of distinguishing it or attracting attention to it; an inscribed board, plate, space, or the like providing information, guidance, or advertisement, as on or in front of a building or place of business or along a street or road; any objective indication of animal or plant disease; a trace or vestige; the trace or trail of wild animals; an indication of a coming event; an omen or portent; a miraculous act or occurrence; *astron.* any of the twelve divisions of the zodiac, each denoted by the name of a constellation, and each, because of the precession of the equinoxes, now containing the constellation west of the one from which it took its name.

sig·nal, sig'nal, *n.* [O.Fr. Fr. *signal,* < M.L. *signale,* < L. *signum,* E. *sign,* *n.*] Something used or serving to give warning, information, direction, or the like, as a gesture, action, light, sound, or object; anything agreed upon or understood as the occasion for concerted action; anything that causes, arouses, or incites to action; a token or indication; the electrical impulse, wave, sound, or image transmitted or received in telegraphy, telephony, television, radio, or radar; a play in certain card games which conveys information between partners.—*a.* Used for signaling or as a signal; conspicuous, notable, or outstanding; as, a *signal* success.—*v.t.*—*signaled, signaling,* *Brit. signalled, signalling.* To make a signal or signals to; to communicate, direct, or make known by a signal or signals.—*v.i.* To make communication by a signal or signals. —**sig·nal·er,** *Brit.* **sig·nal·ler,** *n.*

Sig·nal Corps, *n.* A branch of the U.S. Army, charged with the development, maintenance, and operation of communications systems within the army. Abbr. *Sig C.*

sig·nal·ize, sig′na·līz″, *v.t.*—signalized, signalizing. To make conspicuous or notable; to distinguish; to point out or indicate particularly.

sig·nal·ly, sig′na·lē, *adv.* In a striking or outstanding manner; notably.

sig·nal·man, sig′nal·man, *n. pl.* **sig·nal·men.** A man employed in signaling, as in the army, navy, or on a railroad.

sig·nal·ment, sig′nal·ment, *n.* [Fr. *signalement.*] A description of a person, including distinguishing marks or features, as for police purposes.

sig·na·to·ry, sig′na·tōr″ē, sig′na·ṭạr″ē, *a.* [L. *signatorius,* pertaining to signing, < *signator,* a signer, < *signum,* a mark.] Setting a signature to a document, esp. a public document, as a treaty.—*n. pl.* **sig·na·to·ries.** One who signs; the representative, as of a state, who signs a public document.

sig·na·ture, sig′na·chẽr, *n.* [Fr. *signature,* < M.L. *signatura,* < L. *signare,* E. *sign, v.*] A person's name, or a mark representing it, as signed or written by himself or by a deputy, as in subscribing a letter or other document; the act of signing a document; *mus.* a sign or set of signs, called sharps and flats, indicating the key, or the numbers indicating the time of a piece of music. A theme song or other sight or sound effect used regularly, usu. at the opening and closing of a program, by an orchestra or a radio or television series. *Pharm.* that part of a prescription giving directions for the use of the medicine. A characteristic of a plant or other natural material that was formerly thought to indicate its medical usefulness. *Print.* one of a series of letters or numbers placed on printed sheets of pages for books or magazines to serve as a key for their folding and gathering so that when the pages are cut apart, and bound or stapled together, they will be in consecutive order; any sheet of printed pages so keyed.

sign·board, sīn′bōrd″, sīn′bạrd″, *n.* A board displaying information, guiding, or advertising.

sig·net, sig′nit, *n.* [O.Fr. *signet,* signet (Fr. bookmark), < M.L. *signetum,* dim. of L. *signum,* seal, E. *sign, n.*] A small seal, as in a finger ring; a small official seal used for certain official documents; the impression made by a signet or as by a signet.—*v.t.* To mark or stamp with a signet.

sig·net ring, *n.* A finger ring containing a signet, seal, or the wearer's initials; a seal ring.

sig·nif·i·cance, sig·nif′i·kans, *n.* The quality of being significant; meaning; import; that which is intended to be expressed; impressiveness; importance; moment. Also **sig·nif·i·can·cy,** sig·nif′i·kan·sē, *pl.* **sig·nif·i·can·cies.**

sig·nif·i·cant, sig·nif′i·kant, *a.* [L. *significans, significantis,* ppr. of *significo.*] Having meaning; expressive; expressive or suggestive of a concealed meaning; as, a *significant* look; important; momentous.— **sig·nif·i·cant·ly,** *adv.*

sig·nif·i·cant fig·ures, *n. pl. Math.* the digits of a number, excluding any zeros to the left of its integral part and any final digits to the right of the decimal point not considered to be accurate.

sig·ni·fi·ca·tion, sig′ni·fi·kā′shan, *n.* [L. *significatio.*] The act of signifying; that which is signified or expressed by signs or words; meaning; import; sense.

sig·nif·i·ca·tive, sig·nif′i·kā″tiv, *a.* [Fr. *significatif.*] Signifying; serving to signify; expressive or suggestive of a meaning.— **sig·nif·i·ca·tive·ly,** *adv.*—**sig·nif·i·ca·tive·ness,** *n.*

sig·nif·ics, sig·nif′iks, *n. pl. but sing. in constr.* Semantics.

sig·ni·fy, sig′ni·fī″, *v.t.*—signified, signifying. [O.Fr. Fr. *signifier,* < L. *significare,* < *signum,* sign, indication, and *facere,* to make.] To make known by signs, speech, or action; to be a sign or indication of; represent; to betoken or portend.—*v.i.* To be of importance or consequence.—**sig·ni·fi·a·ble,** *a.*—**sig·ni·fi·er,** *n.*

si·gnior, sēn′yŏr, sēn′yạr, sin·yŏr′, sin·yạr′, *It.* sē·nyạR′, *n. pl.* **si·gniors,** *It.* **si·gnio·ri,** sē·nyạ′Rē. Signor.

sign lan·guage, *n.* A system of manual signs or gestures used as a substitute for speech by the deaf or between people who do not speak the same language. Also **hand lan·guage.**

sign man·u·al, *n. pl.* **signs man·u·al.** An individual signature, esp. that of a sovereign or magistrate on an official document.

si·gnor, sēn′yŏr, sēn′yạr, sin·yŏr′, sin·yạr′, *It.* sē·nyạR′, *n. pl.* **si·gnors, si·gno·ri,** *It.* sē·nyạ′Rē. [It., reduced form of *signore,* < L. *senior.*] *It.* a title of respect used separately or before a man's name, equivalent to *Mister* in English. Also *signior.*

si·gno·ra, sin·yŏr′a, sin·yạr′a, *It.* sē·nyạ′Rä, *n. pl.* **si·gno·ras, si·gno·re,** *It.* sē·nyạ′Rē. [It.] *It.* a title of respect used separately or before a married woman's name as the equivalent to *Mrs.* or *Madam* in English.

si·gno·ri·na, sēn″yạ·rē′na, *It.* sē″nyạ·Rē′nä, *n. pl.* **si·gno·ri·nas, si·gno·ri·ne,** *It.* sē″nyạ·Rē′ne. [It., dim. of *signora.*] *It.* a title of respect used separately or before an unmarried woman's name, equivalent to *Miss* in English.

si·gno·ri·no, sēn″yạ·rē′nō, *It.* sē″nyạ·Rē′nō, *n. pl.* **si·gno·ri·nos, si·gno·ri·ni,** *It.* sē″nyạ·Rē′nē. [It., dim of *signore.*] *It.* a title or term of address for a young man, equivalent to *Master* in English.

si·gno·ry, sē′nyō·rē, *n. pl.* **si·gno·ries.** Seigniory.

sign·post, sīn′pōst″, *n.* A post on which a sign hangs, giving guidance or information; an immediately evident indication or obvious clue.

sike, sīk, sik, *n. Sc. and Brit. dial.* A streamlet or rivulet; a gully that becomes a small stream after a rainstorm. Also **syke.**

Sikh, sēk, *a.* [Hind. *Sikh,* lit. 'disciple.'] Of or pertaining to a religious sect of northern India, founded about 1500, professing the principles of monotheism and human brotherhood.—*n.* A member of this religious sect.—**Sikh·ism,** sē′kiz·um, *n.*

si·lage, sī′lij, *n.* Fodder preserved in a silo; ensilage.

si·lence, sī′lens, *n.* [O.Fr. Fr. *silence,* < L. *silentium,* < *silens.*] Absence of any sound or noise; stillness; the state or fact of being silent; forbearance of speech or utterance; muteness; omission of mention; as, to pass over a matter in *silence;* a state or period of being silent or still; obscurity or oblivion; concealment or secrecy.—*v.t.*—silenced, silencing. To put or bring to silence; restrain from making noise of any kind; to still; to put to rest, as doubts or scruples; to quiet; *milit.* to still, as enemy guns, by a more effective fire.—*interj.* Be quiet: an exclamation to still noisy chatter.

si·lenc·er, sī′len·sẽr, *n.* One who or that which silences; a device for deadening the report of a firearm; *Brit.* the muffler on an internal-combustion engine.

si·lent, sī′lent, *a.* [L. *silens* (silent-), ppr. of *silere,* be silent.] Refraining from speech or utterance; speechless or mute; taciturn or reticent; omitting mention of something, as in a narrative; making no sound of any kind; noiseless, quiet, or still; characterized by absence of speech or sound; tacit or unspoken; not sounded or pronounced; taking no open or active part in something; inactive or quiescent, as a volcano; *motion pictures,* having no spoken dialogue or sound track to accompany the film.—**si·lent·ly,** *adv.*—**si·lent·ness,** *n.*

si·lent but·ler, *n.* A small, handled container with a hinged cover, to collect table crumbs and the trash in ashtrays.

si·lent part·ner, *n.* One sharing finance but not management of a business.

si·le·nus, sī·lē′nus, *n. pl.* **si·le·ni,** sī′lē′nī. *Gr. mythol.* One of a band of minor woodland deities resembling satyrs but depicted, like their leader Silenus, as older, drunken, and with the legs and the ears of a horse.

si·le·sia, si·lē′zha, si·lē′sha, *n.* [< *Silesia.*] A linen fabric, originated in Silesia; a lightweight, smooth-finished, twilled cotton fabric, used esp. for linings.

si·lex, sī′leks, *n.* [L., stone, flint.] Silica; glass which is heat-resistant. (*Cap.*) a coffee maker made of this glass; (Trademark.)

sil·hou·ette, sil″ŏ·et′, *n.* [From Etienne de *Silhouette,* Fr. controller of finances in 1759.] A flat representation of the profile, external outline, or shape of a person or thing, usu. cut out of black paper and mounted on a light background; the dark solid shape or outline of a thing against a light background; as, the *silhouette* of a tree.—*v.t.*—silhouetted, silhouetting. To represent or show in or as in a silhouette.

sil·i·ca, sil′i·ka, *n.* [N.L., < L. *silex* (silic-), stone, flint.] Silicon dioxide, SiO_2, a hard, white or colorless substance occurring in nature as quartz, sand, flint, opal, agate, and other forms: used in glass manufacture. Also *silex.*

sil·i·ca gel, *n. Chem.* silica in a highly adsorbent, colloidal form, used as an agent for dehumidifying, dehydrating, and deodorizing air and gases.

sil·i·cate, sil′i·kit, sil′i·kāt″, *n. Chem.* a salt of silicic acid.

si·li·ceous, si·li·cious, si·lish′us, *a.* [L. *siliceus,* < *silex.*] Containing, consisting of, or resembling silica; found in silica-rich soil, as a growing plant.

si·lic·ic, si·lis′ik, *a. Chem.* Of or pertaining to silica; denoting any of certain acids regarded as derivatives of silica.

si·lic·ic ac·id, *n. Chem.* any of the gelatinous precipitates, resulting from the acidification of silicates and drying gradually into pure silica.

sil·i·cide, sil′i·sīd″, sil′i·sid, *n. Chem.* a compound of silicon with another, usu. metallic, element or a radical.

sil·i·cif·er·ous, sil″i·sif′ẽr·us, *a.* Yielding, containing, or united with silica.

si·lic·i·fied wood, si·lis′i·fīd″ wụd′, *n.* Wood petrified by siliceous water.

si·lic·i·fy, si·lis′i·fī″, *v.t., v.i.*—silicified, silicifying. To convert or be converted into silica; to make or become siliceous.— **si·lic·i·fi·ca·tion,** si·lis″i·fi·kā′shan, *n.*

sil·i·cle, sil′i·kl, *n.* [L. *silicula,* dim. of *siliqua,* pod.] *Bot.* a short silique.

sil·i·con, sil′i·kon, sil′i·kon″, *n.* [N.L., < *silica.*] *Chem.* a nonmetallic element having both crystalline and amorphous forms, occurring in a combined state in rocks and minerals, and constituting more than one-fourth of the earth's crust. Sym. Si, at. no. 14, at wt. 28.086. See Periodic Table of Elements.

sil·i·cone, sil′i·kōn″, *n. Chem.* a compound made by substituting silicon for carbon in substances such as oils, greases, synthetic rubber, and resins, to provide greater stability and resistance to water and to temperature extremes.

sil·i·co·sis, sil″i·kō′sis, *n.* [N.L., < *silica.*] *Pathol.* a disease of the lungs due to the inhaling of siliceous particles, as by stonecutters.—**sil·i·cot·ic,** sil″i·kot′ik, *a.*

a- fat, fāte, fär, fâre, fạll; **e-** met, mē, mẽre, hėr; **i-** pin, pīne; **o-** not, nōte, mŏve; **u-** tub, cūbe, bụll; **oi-** oil; **ou-** pound.

si·lic·u·lose, si·lik'ya·lōs", *a*. [N.L. *siliculosus*, < L. *silicula*, E. *silicle*.] *Bot*. Bearing silicles; having the form or appearance of a silicle.

si·lique, si·lēk', sil'ik, *n*. [L. *siliqua*, pod; hence Fr. *silique*.] *Bot*. the fruit of the mustard family, *Cruciferae*, in which the two fused carpels separate leaving a persistent partition. Also **sil·i·qua**, sil'i·kwa. —**sil·i·quose, sil·i·quous**, sil'i·kwōs", sil'i·kwus, *a*.

silk, silk, *n*. The fine, soft, lustrous fiber obtained from the cocoon of the silkworm; thread, cloth, or any material made of this fiber; a garment of such material; *Brit. colloq.* the gown worn distinctively by a King's or Queen's Counsel at the English bar; a King's or Queen's Counsel. Similar fibers or filamentous material produced by some other animal, plant, or process, as the hairlike styles on an ear of corn; a parachute; *pl*. the cap and shirt made of a particular color of silk or silklike fabric, and worn by a jockey to represent his stable. —*v.i.* To be in the course of developing silk, as corn.—**hit the silk**, *slang*, to parachute. —**take silk**, *Brit*. to assume the post of King's or Queen's Counsel at the English bar.—**silk·like**, *a*.

silk·a·line, sil"ka·lēn', *n*. [Arbitrary formation based on *silk*.] A soft, thin cotton fabric with a smooth finish resembling silk, as that used for curtains or quilt coverings. Also **silk·o·lene, silk·o·line**.

silk cot·ton, *n*. A silky fiber surrounding the seeds of several species of tropical trees, family *Bombacaceae*, used as stuffing, esp. kapok.

silk-cot·ton tree, silk'kot"on trē", *n*. A tropical tree of the family *Bombacaceae*, whose seeds are enfolded by silk cotton, esp. the kapok tree, *Ceiba pentandra*.

silk·en, sil'ken, *a*. Made of silk; having certain qualities of silk, as softness, smoothness to the touch, delicateness, gloss, sheen, or luster; smooth-tongued, ingratiating, or unctuous; luxurious; clothed in silk.

silk hat, *n*. A man's tall, cylindrical, dress hat, usu. covered with shiny, black silk plush. See *top hat*.

silk oak, *n*. A tree, *Grevillea robusta*, with soft, fernlike leaves and long, bright inflorescences in orange, red, or white, which grows to a height of one hundred and fifty feet in Australia.

silk·screen proc·ess, silk'skrēn" pros'es, *n*. A technique of printing in which silk, stretched tightly over a frame, is painted with a resist or is partially covered with a waxy stencil to block out areas of a design, so that when the screen is lowered onto the paper or textile to be printed, paint may be forced by squeegee through the unobstructed areas. Also **silk·screen**.

silk-stock·ing, silk'stok'ing, *a*. Wearing silk stockings; elegant in dress; luxurious; aristocratic; wealthy.—*n*. One who wears silk stockings; a richly-dressed person; a person of the elegant or luxurious class; an aristocrat; a Whig or Federalist during the 19th century.

silk·weed, silk'wēd", *n*. Any milkweed of the family *Asclepiadaceae*, having silky down in the seed pod.

silk·worm, silk'wurm", *n*. A hairless, yellow caterpillar which produces a cocoon of valuable silk and emerges as a moth, *Bombyx mori*, of Asia; any larva which spins a silken cocoon.

silk·y, sil'kē, *a*.—*silkier, silkiest*. Similar to or made of silk; soft and smooth to the touch; glossy; delicate; tender.—**silk·i·ly**, *adv*.—**silk·i·ness**, *n*.

sill, sil, *n*. [O.E. *syl, syll*, base, sill; Icel. *syll, svill*, Sw. *syll, swill*, G. *schwelle*.] A horizontal stone or timber on which a structure rests; the horizontal piece at the bottom of

the door, window, or similar opening; *geol*. a horizontal intrusion of igneous rock between flat layers of other rock.

sil·la·bub, sil'a·bub", *n*. [Origin doubtful.] A dish, drink, or desert of wine or cider with cream or milk added to form a soft curd or whip to a froth, sometimes sweetened or flavored. Also *syllabub*.

sil·li·man·ite, sil'i·ma·nīt", *n*. [From Benjamin *Silliman*, 1779–1864, U.S. scientist.] A mineral consisting of a silicate of aluminum, and occurring in either long slender, crystalline needles or compact, fibrous masses.

sil·ly, sil'ē, *a*.—*sillier, silliest*. [Var. of earlier *seely*, M.E. *seli*, happy, blessed, good, innocent, helpless, < O.E. (*ge*)*sælig* (= D. *zalig* = G. *selig*), happy, blessed, < *sæl*, happiness.] Deficient in strength of intellect or in common sense, or showing such deficiency, as persons, the mind, actions, or speech; weakly foolish or stupid; opposed to or remote from sober or good sense; absurdly foolish or senseless; absurd or ridiculous; feeble-minded or imbecilic; *colloq.* stunned or dazed.—*n. pl.* **sil·lies**. *Colloq.* a silly person.—**sil·li·ly**, *adv*.—**sil·li·ness**, *n*.

sil·ly sea·son, *n*. A period, often in midsummer, when frivolity and exaggeration pervade newspaper stories, publicity stunts, and public entertainments.

si·lo, sī'lō, *n. pl.* **si·los**. [Sp.] A pit or chamber, usu. an airproof towerlike structure, in which green fodder and grain are preserved for future use as ensilage; a pit or underground chamber for storing grain; *milit.* an underground structure for housing and launching ballistic missiles or rockets. —*v.t.*—*siloed, siloing*. To put into or preserve in a silo.

silt, silt, *n*. [< Prov. E. *sile*, Sw. *sila*, to strain or filter.] A deposit of mud or fine soil from running water; fine earthy sediment.—*v.i.* To become filled or choked up with silt; to ooze.—*v.t.* To choke or fill up with silt or mud.—**silt·a·tion**, *n*.—**silt·y**, sil'tē, *a*.—*siltier, siltiest*.

Si·lu·ri·an, si·lur'ē·an, sī·lur'ē·an, *a*. Of or pertaining to the Silures, an ancient people of South Wales, or the land they inhabited; *geol.* of or designating the time period or rock system which fell between the Ordovician and the Devonian periods in the Paleozoic era.—*n. Geol.* the Silurian time period or rock system. See Table of Geologic Time.

si·lu·roid, si·lur'oid, sī·lur'oid, *a*. Catfishlike; of the catfish family, *Siluridae*.—*n*. A siluroid fish.

sil·va, syl·va, sil'va, *n*. The forest cover of a particular region; a treatise or other written work describing the forest trees of an area.

sil·van, sil'van, *a*. Sylvan.

sil·ver, sil'ver, *n*. [O.E. *seolfer* = Icel. *silfr*, D. *zilver*, Dan. *solv*, G. *silber*, Goth. *silubr*.] A white metallic element, ductile and malleable, having the highest electrical and thermal conductivity of any substance. Sym. Ag, at. no. 47, at. wt. 107.87. See Periodic Table of Elements. Money, esp. coin; a standard of government currency; dining utensils, such as hollow-ware made of or plated with this metal; flatware, whether made of this metal or another; a color, specif. a shade of gray.—*a*. Of or pertaining to this metal; made of, covered by, or plated with this metal or an imitation thereof; having the sheen or brightness of this metal; of or pertaining to the twenty-fifth anniversary, esp. of a marriage; *colloq.* having a certain glibness of speech; as, a *silver* tongue.—*v.t.* To cover, as flatware, with silver or a similar coating; to apply an amalgam to; as, to *silver* a mirror; to give a silvery sheen or luster to; to make hoary; to tinge with gray.—*v.i.*—

To become lustered, silvery, or tinged with grey.—**sil·ver·er**, *n*.

sil·ver age, *n. Mythol.* the second period in the history of the world following the golden age; (*usu. cap.*) a period in Latin literature subsequent to the Augustan Age, from about A.D. 14 to A.D. 180.

sil·ver bell, *n*. Any of the handsome N. American and Chinese shrubs or small trees, with white bell-shaped flowers, of the genus *Halesia*. Also **sil·ver·bell tree**.

sil·ver·ber·ry, sil'ver·ber"ē, *n. pl.* **sil·ver·ber·ries**. A shrub, *Elaeagnus commutata*, of the north-central part of North America, having silvery leaves and flowers and silvery berries.

sil·ver bro·mide, *n. Chem.* the pale yellow compound, AgBr, precipitated by the addition of an alkali bromide to silver nitrate, used in coatings for photographic plates and films because of its sensitivity to light.

sil·ver cer·tif·i·cate, *n*. A unit of paper currency formerly issued by the U.S. government which could be redeemed for a stated value of silver and was valid as legal tender for all debts and public charges.

sil·ver chlo·ride, *n. Chem.* the white compound, AgCl, produced by the addition of chloride solutions to that of silver nitrate, used esp. in photography and silver plating because of its sensitivity to light.

sil·ver·fish, sil'ver·fish", *n. pl.* **sil·ver·fish, sil·ver·fish·es**. A white or silvery variety of the goldfish, *Carassius auratus*; any of various other silvery fishes, as tarpon, silversides, or shiner; *entom.* any of certain small, silvery, wingless insects, order *Thysanura*, esp. *Lepisma saccharina*, which damages paper, cloth, and books by feeding on the starch in them.

sil·ver fox, *n*. A genetic variation of the common red fox having black, silver-tipped fur, a color phase which may be bred reliably.

sil·ver i·o·dide, *n. Chem.* the pale yellow compound, AgI, which darkens when subjected to light, produced by the addition of an iodide solution to that of silver nitrate, and used in photography, medicine, and rain-making.

sil·ver-lace vine, sil'ver·lās" vīn", *n*. An ornamental twining perennial, *Polygonum aubertii*, native of western China and bearing clusters of fragrant flowers. Also *fleece-vine*.

sil·ver lin·ing, *n. Fig.* a reason or prospect for hope in an unfavorable situation.

sil·ver·ly, sil'ver·lē, *adv*. With the appearance or sound of silver.

sil·vern, sil'vern, *a*. [O.E. *seolfren*.] *Poet., archaic*, of or like silver.

sil·ver ni·trate, *n*. A white, crystalline salt of silver, AgNO₃, obtained from the dissolution of silver in dilute nitric acid and widely used in photography and industry and as an antiseptic.

sil·ver perch, *n. Ichth.* a drum, *Bairdiella chrysura*, habitat southern U.S.; also **mad·e·moi·selle**. Any of several silvery fishes resembling perch, as the white crappie.

sil·ver plate, *n*. Flatware made of silver or of a base metal coated with silver; the coating itself.

sil·ver pro·tein, *n. Med.* any of several colloidal preparations of protein and silver used in solutions as external antiseptics.

sil·ver screen, *n*. The screen upon which moving pictures are shown; collectively, motion pictures, often preceded by *the*.

sil·ver·sides, sil'ver·sīdz", *n. pl.* **sil·ver·sides**. Any of the small fishes, characterized by a silvery stripe along the sides, which constitute the family *Atherinidae*. Also **sil·ver·side**.

---

ch- chain, G. na*ch*t;   th- THen, thin;   w- wig, hw as sound in whig;   z- zh as in azure, zeal.   *Italicized vowel* indicates schwa sound.

sil·ver·smith, sil'vēr·smith", *n.* A person whose occupation is repairing or making silver articles.

sil·ver spoon, *n. Fig.* riches, esp. wealth which has been inherited; as, to be born with a *silver spoon* in one's mouth.

sil·ver stand·ard, *n.* A monetary system or standard in which the basic unit is equivalent to a specified amount and quality of silver.

Sil·ver Star Med·al, *n. Milit.* a decoration consisting of a small silver star in the center of a bronze star, awarded by the U.S. Army for valor in action. Also **Sil·ver Star.**

sil·ver-tongued, sil'vēr·tungd', *a.* Convincing and fluent; eloquent.

sil·ver·ware, sil'vēr·wâr", *n.* A collective name for various articles, esp. eating utensils, made of silver, silverplate, or other metals.

sil·ver·weed, sil'vēr·wēd", *n.* A rosaceous plant, *Potentilla anserina*, having pinnate leaves with a silvery pubescence on the underside.

sil·ver·y, sil've·rē, *a.* Like silver in appearance or sound; containing or coated with silver.—**sil·ver·i·ness,** *n.*

sil·vic·o·lous, sil·vik'o·lus, *a.* Living in a woodland area.

sil·vi·cul·ture, syl·vi·cul·ture, sil'vi-·kul"chēr, *n.* Forestry; the cultivation and care of trees in a forest.—**sil·vi·cul·tur·al, syl·vi·cul·tur·al,** *a.*—**sil·vi·cul·tur·al·ly, syl·vi·cul·tur·al·ly,** *adv.*—**sil·vi·cul·tur·ist, syl·vi·cul·tur·ist,** *n.*—**sil·vics,** *n. pl. but sing. in constr.* The study of silviculture.—**sil·vi·cal,** *a.*

si·mar, si·mär', *n.* [Fr. *simarre,* < It. *cimarra, zimarra,* robe, cassock; = Sp. *chamarra, zamarra,* sheepskin coat.] A loose, light garment or robe worn by women in former times; also **cy·mar.** *Rom. Cath. Ch.* a garment resembling a cassock and worn by the prelates; also **zi·mar·ra,** zi·mär'a.

sim·i·an, sim'ē·an, *a.* [L. *simia,* an ape, < *simus,* flat-nosed.] Pertaining to, characteristic of, or like apes and monkeys.—*n.* An ape or monkey.

sim·i·lar, sim'i·lēr, *a.* [Fr. *similaire,* < L. *similis,* like; akin to *simul,* together, from root of E. *same.*] Like; resembling but not identical; having a like form or appearance; *geom.* having like parts and relations or shape, but not the same position or size, as figures.—**sim·i·lar·ly,** *adv.*

sim·i·lar·i·ty, sim'i·lar'i·tē, *n. pl.* **sim·i·lar·i·ties.** The state of being similar; close likeness; resemblance; an instance or point similar to another.

sim·i·le, sim'i·lē, *n.* [L., a like thing, < *similis,* like.] A figure of speech likening or comparing two dissimilar things by the use of *like* or *as,* as: *Her lips are like roses.* A poetic or imaginative comparison.

si·mil·i·tude, si·mil'i·tōd", si·mil'i·tūd", *n.* [L. *similitudo.*] Likeness; a person or thing resembling another in nature, qualities, or appearance; a counterpart or double; an image or visible resemblance; an imaginative likening, as an allegory or parable.

sim·mer, sim'ēr, *v.i.* [Var. of earlier *simper;* perh. imit.] To make a gentle murmuring sound under the action of continued heat, as liquids just below the boiling point; to continue in a state approaching boiling or just at the point of boiling, as liquids; to continue in a state of subdued activity or suppressed excitement; to develop slowly toward the point of breaking forth, as in revolt.—*v.t.* To keep in a state or cook in a liquid approaching boiling or just at the point of boiling.—*n.* A process or condition of simmering.—**sim·mer down,** to reduce in amount or

quantity by simmering; *slang,* to become quiet or to calm down.

sim·nel, sim'nel, *n.* [O.Fr. *simenel,* < L. *simila,* fine wheat flour.] A kind of bread or biscuit made of fine wheat flour; *Brit.* a kind of rich cake containing currants and other fruit, eaten at mid-Lent, Easter, and Christmas.

si·mo·le·on, si·mō'lē·an, *n.* [Origin obscure.] *Slang,* a dollar.

si·mo·ni·ac, si·mō'nē·ak", *n.* [Fr. *simoniaque.*] One who practices simony.—*a.*—**si·mo·ni·a·cal,** si"mo·ni'a·kal, sim"o·ni'·a·kal, *a.*—**si·mo·ni·a·cal·ly,** *adv.*

si·mon·ize, si'mo·nīz", *v.t.*—*simonized, simonizing.* [From *Simonize,* trademark.] To polish or make glossy and smooth, esp. with or as with wax.

Si·mon Le·gree, si'mon li·grē', *n.* The brutal slave overseer in *Uncle Tom's Cabin* by Harriet Beecher Stowe; any brutal, relentless master.

si·mon-pure, sim'on·pūr', *a.* [From *Simon Pure,* a Quaker in Susanna Centlivre's 1718 comedy, *A Bold Stroke for a Wife,* who is impersonated by an imposter.] Real; genuine; authentic; as, the *simon-pure* heir.

si·mo·ny, sī'mo·nē, sim'o·nē, *n.* [Fr. *simonie,* L.L. *simonia,* from *Simon Magus,* who wished to purchase the power of conferring the Holy Spirit.] The buying or selling of ecclesiastical preferment; the presentation of anyone to an ecclesiastical benefice for money or reward.

si·moom, si·mōm', *n.* [Ar. *samūm,* < *samma,* to poison.] An intensely hot suffocating wind, laden with dust and sand, of the deserts of Africa and Arabia. Also **si·moon.**

sim·pa·ti·co, sim·pä'ti·kō", sim·pat'i·kō", *a.* [It.] *Slang.* Congenial; sympathetic.

sim·per, sim'pēr, *v.i.* [Akin to Prov. G. *simpern,* to be affectedly coy; Dan. *semper, simper,* coy.] To smile in a self-conscious, silly, or affected manner; to smirk.—*v.t.* To tell or state with a simper.—*n.* A smile which is silly or shows self-consciousness; an affected smile or smirk.—**sim·per·er,** *n.*—**sim·per·ing·ly,** *adv.*

sim·ple, sim'pl, *a.*—*simpler, simplest.* [Fr. *simple,* < L. *simplex,* simple, < a root meaning one or unity (also in E. *same*), and that of *plica,* a fold.] Easily intelligible; not complicated; not difficult to use or deal with; unadorned; plain; not elaborate or ornate; as, a *simple* pattern or design; unaffected and artless in manner; fundamental; elementary; as, the *simple* truth; single; not complex or compound; as, a *simple* fracture; free from duplicity or deceit; sincere; as, a *simple,* open reply; mere; unpretentious; common; humble; as, just *simple* folk; not wise or knowledgeable; as, a foolishly *simple* brand of logic; naive; gullible; weak in intellect; mentally retarded. *Chem.* not compound; unmixed; composed of a single element or substance. *Bot.* not exhibiting divisions: said of a leaf when not divided into leaflets. *Zool.* not subdivided or compound.—*n.* Something not mixed or compounded; formerly, a medicinal herb or a medicine obtained from a single herb; an ingenuous or a foolish person; simpleton. —**sim·ple·ness,** *n.*

sim·ple frac·tion, *n. Math.* a fraction which has whole numbers for both denominator and numerator.

sim·ple hon·ors, *n. pl. Auction Bridge,* three honors held by one side in the trump suit, or three aces if the contract is at notrump.

sim·ple in·ter·est, *n.* Interest calculated only on the original principal.

sim·ple ma·chine, *n.* Any of a number of elementary mechanical devices, as the lever, wedge, wheel and axle, pulley, screw, and inclined plane. See *machine.*

sim·ple-mind·ed, sim'pl·mīn'did, *a.* Artless or without sophistication; lacking in keen mental perception; deficient mentally; foolish.—**sim·ple-mind·ed·ly,** *adv.*—**sim·ple-mind·ed·ness,** *n.*

sim·ple sen·tence, *n.* A sentence having one main and no subordinate clause.

sim·ple·ton, sim'pl·ton, *n.* [< *simple,* with Fr. term. *-ton.*] A silly or foolish person; a person showing ignorance or lacking in sound judgment or common sense.

sim·ple vow, *n. Rom. Cath. Ch.* a temporary, public vow taken by a religious and subject to renewal, permitting retention of property and, while regarding marriage as illicit, recognizing its validity under canon law.

sim·plex, sim'pleks, *a.* [L.] Simple; consisting of or characterized by a single element or action; as, *simplex* telegraphy in which one message at a time is sent over a single wire.—*n. pl.* **sim·plex·es.** An uncompounded word.

sim·plic·i·ty, sim·plis'i·tē, *n. pl.* **sim·plic·i·ties.** [Fr. *simplicité,* L. *simplicitas.*] The state or quality of being simple, uncompounded, or uncomplex; plainness or freedom from ornament, luxury, ostentation, or the like; artlessness, candor, or absence of deceit, cunning, or guile; sincerity or unaffectedness; deficiency of mental acuteness, subtlety, or good sense.

sim·pli·fy, sim'pli·fī", *v.t.*—*simplified, simplifying.* [Fr. *simplifier,* L.L. *simplificare,* L. *simplex,* and *facio,* to make.] To make simple, less complicated, or easier.—**sim·pli·fi·ca·tion,** *n.*—**sim·pli·fi·er,** *n.*

sim·plism, sim'pliz·um, *n.* Oversimplification; the process or act of reducing a situation or problem to a single factor while disregarding the other complicating factors.—**sim·plis·tic,** sim·plis'tik, *a.*—**sim·plis·ti·cal·ly,** *adv.*

sim·ply, sim'plē, *adv.* In a simple manner; clearly; without art or subtlety; plainly; sincerely; merely or solely; foolishly; absolutely; as, *simply* beautiful.

sim·ply or·dered set, *n. Math.* a set said to be ordered by a relation between members denoted by '*x* precedes *y*' if for any two members *x* and *y* not equal, either '*x* precedes *y*' or '*y* precedes *x*' holds and if given that *x* precedes *y* and *y* precedes *z,* then *x* precedes *z.* The set of positive integers in their natural order is a simply ordered set ordered by the relation '*x* is less than *y.*' Also **or·dered set, lin·e·ar·ly or·dered set, to·tal·ly or·dered set.**

sim·u·la·crum, sim"ya·lā'kram, *n. pl.* **sim·u·la·cra,** sim"ya·lā'kra. [L.] An image or likeness. Also **sim·u·la·cre,** sim"ya·lā"kēr.

sim·u·lar, sim'ū·lēr, sim'ya·lēr, *n.* [Irreg. < L. *simulare.*] *Archaic.* One who or that which simulates; a pretender.—*a. Archaic.* Simulated; counterfeit; imitative.

sim·u·late, sim'ū·lāt", sim'ya·lāt", *v.t.*—*simulated, simulating.* [L. *simulo, simulatum,* < *similis,* like.] To feign; to assume the appearance or character of.—**sim·u·la·tive,** *a.*

sim·u·la·tion, sim"ū·lā'shan, sim"ya·lā'shan, *n.* The act of simulating or of feigning; a copy, imitation, or fake.

sim·u·la·tor, sim'ū·lā"tēr, sim'ya·lā"tēr, *n.* One who simulates; a machine or other device capable of reproducing certain states or environments for controlled experimentation or training purposes.

si·mul·cast, sī'mul·kast", sī'mul·käst", sim'ul·kast", sim'ul·käst", *v.t.*—*simulcast, simulcasting.* [(*simul*)taneous and broad(*cast*).] To broadcast by radio and television at the same time.—*n.* A program that is broadcast in such manner.

si·mul·ta·ne·ous, sī″mul·tā′nē·us, sim″- ul·tā′nē·us, *a.* [L.L. *simultaneus,* < L. *simul,* at the same time, akin to *similis,* like, E. *same.*] Taking place or happening at the same time; done at the same time; coincident in time.—**si·mul·ta·ne·ous·ly,** *adv.*—**si·mul·ta·ne·ous·ness,** si·mul·ta·ne·i·ty, sī″mul·ta·nē′i·tē, sim″ul·ta·nē′i-- tē, *n.*

sin, sin, *n.* [O.E. *synn, sinn,* sin; Icel. and Dan. *synd,* O.D. *sunde,* G. *sunde,* sin; connected with L. *sons, sontis,* guilty.] The voluntary or willful departure of an individual from a custom prescribed by divine law, divine command, or society in general; moral depravity; wickedness; iniquity; a transgression; an offense against any standard; as, a *sin* against community standards.—*v.i.*—*sinned, sinning.* To commit a sin; to violate any known rule of duty; to transgress.

Sin·an·thro·pus, sin·an′thro·pus, sī′nan-- thrō′pus, *n. Anthropol.* Peking man.

sin·a·pism, sin′a·piz″um, *n.* [Fr. *sina- pisme,* L. *sinapismus,* < *sinapis,* Gr. *sinapi,* mustard.] *Med.* a mustard plaster.

since, sins, *adv.* [O.E. *sins, sinnes, sithens, sithence,* all genitive forms < O.E. *siththan,* lit. 'since that.'] From then till now; in the interval; before this; before now; ago; after that time.—*prep.* Continuously from the time of; as, *since* yesterday; subsequent to; after.—*conj.* In the interval after the time when, as: I have been ill twice *since* I saw you last. Without interruption; from the time when; as, *since* we saw you last; because; seeing that; inasmuch as.

sin·cere, sin·sēr′, *a.* [L. *sincerus,* sincere, pure, unmixed.] Being in inward reality or intent the same as in outward appearance; undissembling, unfeigned, and without guile; honest; hiding or withholding nothing; real, genuine, or true.—**sin·- cere·ly,** *adv.*

sin·cer·i·ty, sin·ser′i·tē, *n.* The quality, condition, or state of being sincere; freedom from hypocrisy; truthfulness; genuineness; earnestness. Also **sin·cere·ness.**

sin·ci·put, sin′si·put″, *n.* pl. **sin·ci·puts,** **sin·cip·i·ta,** sin·sip′i·ta. [L.] *Anat.* The upper part of the head, esp. the front; forehead.—**sin·cip·i·tal,** sin·sip′i·tal, *a.*

sine, sīn, *n.* [L. *sinus,* a bending, a curve.] *Trig.* A function of an acute angle in a right triangle, equal to the ratio of the opposite leg to the hypotenuse; a function of any angle, equal to the ordinate of a point on a line divided by its distance from the origin, when the angle is shown in Cartesian coordinates as the angle the line makes with the positive x-axis at the origin.

si·ne·cure, sī′ne·kūr″, sin′e·kūr″, *n.* [L. *sine,* without, and *cura,* cure, care.] Any office which provides revenue without requiring work; *eccles.* a benefice without cure of souls.

sine curve, *n. Math.* the graph of the equation, $y = \sin x$, in rectangular coordinates. Also *sinusoid.*

si·ne di·e, sī′nē dī′ē, *L.* sī′ne dē′e, *adv.* [L., lit. 'without day.'] Without a day fixed for future meeting or action; as, to adjourn *sine die.*

si·ne qua non, sī′nē kwä non′, *L.* sī′ne kwä nōn′, *n.* [L., lit. 'without which not.'] Something indispensable.

sin·ew, sin′ū, *n.* [O.E. *sinewe, sinu;* D. *zenuw;* G. *sehne,* Icel. *sin,* Dan. *sene,* a sinew.] A tendon; that which gives strength or vigor; that in which strength or support lies.—*v.t.* To knit or strengthen, as by sinews.

sine wave, *n. Phys.* a periodic oscillation which can be described as a linear function of a sine, represented geometrically by a sinusoidal curve.

sin·ew·y, sin′ū·ē, *a.* Consisting of or resembling a sinew or sinews; well braced with sinews; strong; having prominent sinews; vigorous or firm, as language.

sin·fo·ni·a, sin″fō·nē′a, *It.* sēn″fa·nē′ä, *n.* pl. **sin·fo·ni·e,** sin″fō·nē′ā, *It.* sēn″- fa·nē′e. *Mus.* A symphony; a baroque orchestral composition used as the introduction to an opera.

sin·fo·niet·ta, sin″fon·yet′a, sin″fōn·yet′- a, *n. Mus.* A symphony for fewer instruments or of shorter duration than a standard symphony; a symphony orchestra that is smaller than usual, often consisting entirely of strings.

sin·ful, sin′ful, *a.* Tainted with or full of sin; wicked.—**sin·ful·ly,** *adv.*—**sin·ful·- ness,** *n.*

sing, sing, *v.i.*—past *sang* or *sung,* pp. *sung,* ppr. *singing.* [O.E. *singan,* pret. *sang,* pp. *sungen;* = Icel. *singja,* Dan. *synge,* D. *zingen,* G. *singen;* cf. Gael. *seinn,* to ring as a bell, to sing.] To utter words or sounds with musical inflections of the voice; to perform a vocal composition; to utter sweet sounds, as birds; to make musical sounds, as a violin; to give out a small shrill or humming sound; as, the kettle *sings;* to buzz, hum, or ring; to tell or relate something in verse; to compose poetry; *slang,* to disclose information or confess to a crime.—*v.t.* To utter with musical modulations of the voice; to chant or utter in monotone; to relate, celebrate, or give praise to in verse; to accompany with songs; to act or produce an effect on by singing; as, to *sing* one to sleep.—*n.* The performance of a vocal composition; a public gathering for singing; a buzzing, humming, or ringing sound.—**sing out,** to shout loudly.—**sing·a·ble,** *a.*

singe, sinj, *v.t.*—*singed, singeing.* [O.E. *sengan,* to singe, lit. 'to cause to sing,' a caus. of *singan,* to sing; so also G. *sengen,* to singe.] To burn slightly or superficially; to scorch; to burn the surface, ends, or outside of; to remove feathers, hair, down, or the like from, as from a chicken, by passing the carcass through a flame.—*n.* A superficial burning of the surface; a slight burn.

sing·er, sing′ér, *n.* One who sings, esp. a skilled or professional vocalist; a poet; a songbird.

sing·ing bird, *n.* A bird that sings; a songbird; any oscine bird.

sin·gle, sing′gl, *a.* [O.Fr. *single, sengle,* < L. *singulus,* single, separate, individual: see *simple.*] Alone, solitary; unmarried, or pertaining to the unmarried state; consisting of one part, element, or member; singular; unique; sole; one only; separate; individual; suitable for one person; as, a *single* bed; of one against one, as combat or a fight; sincere, honest, dedicated; as, *single* devotion; *bot.* having but one set of petals, as a flower; *Brit.* of only moderate strength, as beer or ale.—*n.* One individual person or thing; a hotel, restaurant, or other accommodation suitable for just one person; *baseball,* a hit which allows the batter to reach first base only; *cricket,* a hit for which one run is scored; *pl.* a game or match, as tennis, played with only one person on each side; *golf,* a match between only two players.—*v.t.*—*singled, singling.* To pick or choose out from others; as, to *single* out a rose. *Baseball,* to advance, as a base runner, by a one-base hit; to cause, as a run, to be scored by a one-base hit.—*v.i. Baseball,* to make a one-base hit.

sin·gle-breast·ed, sing′gl·bres′tid, *a.* Having a front center fastening with only one row of loops, buttons, or the like; as, a *single-breasted* coat.

sin·gle com·bat, *n.* A fight restricted to two persons.

sin·gle en·try, *n.* The simplest of bookkeeping methods in which the accounting is limited to a register of money due to and owed by a business.

sin·gle file, *n.* A file or line of persons or things arranged or moving along one behind another.—*adv.*

sin·gle-foot, sing′gl·fut″, *n.* A gait of a horse, in which each foot falls singly, those of one side followed by those of the other. Also *rack.*—*v.i.* Of a horse, to go at such a gait.—**sin·gle-foot·er,** *n.*

sin·gle-hand·ed, sing′gl·han′did, *a.* Accomplished by one person; unassisted; possessing or using only one hand; requiring one hand or one person.—*adv.*— **sin·gle-hand·ed·ly,** sing′gl·han′did·lē, *adv.*—**sin·gle-hand·ed·ness,** *n.*

sin·gle-heart·ed, sing′gl·här′tid, *a.* Sincere in feeling or spirit; undivided in feeling or purpose; dedicated; loyal.— **sin·gle-heart·ed·ly,** *adv.*—**sin·gle-heart·- ed·ness,** *n.*

sin·gle knot, *n.* An overhand knot.

sin·gle-mind·ed, sing′gl·mīn′did, *a.* Having or showing a single purpose; having or showing a mind undivided in feeling or purpose; steadfast.—**sin·gle-mind·ed·ly,** *adv.*—**sin·gle-mind·ed·ness,** *n.*

sin·gle-name pa·per, sing′gl·nām″ pā′- pér, *n. Com.* an unendorsed promissory note which bears the maker's signature only.

sin·gle·ness, sing′gl·nis, *n.* The state or quality of being single; oneness; sincerity; freedom from duplicity.

sin·gle-phase, sing′gl·fāz″, *a. Elect.* of or pertaining to an apparatus or system energized by an alternating current with one phase.

sin·gle-space, sing′gl·spās′, *v.t., v.i.*— *single-spaced, single-spacing.* To type or print on every successive blank line.

sin·gle·stick, sing′gl·stik″, *n.* A stout stick; a slender stick held in one hand, employed in fencing; fencing with such a stick.

sin·gle·stick·er, sing′gl·stik″ér, *n. Naut.* A sailing ship with one mast; a sloop.

sin·glet, sing′glit, *n.* [< *single,* after *doublet.*] *Chiefly Brit.* a kind of undershirt or jersey worn by men.

sin·gle tax, *n.* The theory of taxing a single object, as land, as the only source of revenue; a tax of this particular type.

sin·gle·ton, sing′gl·ton, *n. Cards,* an only card of a suit in a hand. A single person or thing distinct from others in a group.

sin·gle-track, sing′gl·trak″, *a.* Having only a single track, as a railroad; *fig.* able to go or act but one way at a time, as the mind. Also **one-track,** wun′trak″.

sin·gle·tree, sing′gl·trē″, *n.* Whiffletree.

sin·gly, sing′glē, *adv.* Individually; separately; each alone; without partners or aid; one at a time.

sing·song, sing′sang″, sing′song″, *n.* Regular, rhythmical sounds; verse having regular, monotonous rhyme and rhythm.— *a.*

sing·spiel, sing′spēl″, *G.* zing′shpēl″, *n.* [G., < *singen,* to sing, and *spiel,* to play.] A kind of semidramatic musical work or performance, formerly common in Germany, in which singing and spoken dialogue alternate.

sin·gu·lar, sing′gū·lér, sing′gya·lér, *a.* [O.Fr. *singuler* (Fr. *singulier*), < L. *singularis,* < *singulus,* E. *single.*] Extraordinary or remarkable, as in character or extent; as, a *singular* success; unusual or strange; as, a *singular* occurrence; peculiar, odd, eccentric, or bizarre; as, a *singular* person, *singular* behavior, taste, or dress; being the only one of the kind; unparalleled or unique; separate; individual; *gram.* noting a word form which signifies or implies but one person or thing; as, a *singular* noun or a *singular* verb form: opposed to *plural* or *dual*; *logic*, pertaining or relating to but one being or thing, or not general.—*n. Gram.* The singular number; a word form in this number.—**sin·gu·lar·ly,** *adv.*—**sin·gu·lar·ness,** *n.*—**sin·gu·lar·ize,** *v.t.*—*singularized, singularizing.* To make singular.

sin·gu·lar·i·ty, sing″gu·lar′i·tē, sing″-gya·lar′i·tē, *n. pl.* **sin·gu·lar·i·ties.** The state, fact, or quality of being singular; something singular; an individual or unusual feature or characteristic; peculiarity.

sin·gu·lar point, *n. Math.* any point of a function of a complex variable where the derivative does not exist but every neighborhood of which contains points of the function having derivatives.

sin·gu·lar prop·o·si·tion, *n. Logic,* a proposition which has no quantifiers.

sin·is·ter, sin′i·stėr, *a.* [L., left, unlucky, bad; origin doubtful.] Foreboding, ominous; threatening evil, disaster, or ill fortune; malevolent, wicked, or evil; disastrous or unfortunate; on the left hand or the left side; also **sin·is·trous,** sin′i-·strus. *Her.* denoting one side of the escutcheon which is to the bearer's left.—**sin·is·ter·ly,** *adv.*—**sin·is·ter·ness,** *n.*

sin·is·tral, sin′i·stral, *a.* Of, pertaining to, or inclining to the left side; left-handed; coiled from left to right when viewed from the apex, said of various gastropod shells.—**sin·is·tral·ly,** *adv.*

sin·is·trorse, sin′i·strȯrs″, si·nis′trȯrs, sin″-i·strȯrs′, *a.* [L. *sinistrorsus, < sinister,* left, and *vorsus, versus,* turned.] *Bot.* turning or twining upward to the left, usu. said of the stems of plants. Also **sin·is·tror·sal.**—**sin·is·trorse·ly,** sin′i·strȯrs″lē, sin″i·strȯrs′-lē, *adv.*

Si·nit·ic, si·nit′ik, *n.* A constituent of the Sino-Tibetan family of languages, comprising Chinese and other dialects which use Chinese as their standard written language.—*a.* Referring to the Chinese language, culture, or people.

sink, singk, *v.i.*—past *sank* or *sunk,* pp. *sunk,* ppr. *sinking.* [O.E. *sincan* (pret. *sanc,* pp. *suncen*) = D. *zinken* = G. *sinken.*] To go under or to the bottom, as in water; to go down until completely or partly covered, as in quicksand; become submerged; to settle or fall gradually or gently downward, as a leaf; to fall slowly from weakness or fatigue; settle down into a reclining, sitting, or kneeling posture; as, *sink* into a chair; to descend gradually to a lower level, as water; to go down toward or below the horizon, as the sun; settle down, as darkness upon the earth; to have a downward slope, as ground; to assume a hollow appearance, as the cheeks; to enter, usu. with *in* or *into,* as ideas or truth penetrating into the mind; to pass gradually into some state, as silence; pass or fall into some lower state, as of fortune or estimation; fail markedly in physical strength or vital power, esp. in approaching death; fall into depression, as one's spirits; to decrease in amount, extent, or degree, as value, prices, or rates; become lower in tone or pitch, as the voice; to sink a shaft, well, or the like, by excavating or drilling.—*v.t.* To cause to sink or become submerged; as, to *sink* the enemy's ships; to cause to fall, descend, or go down; to put down, as a post or pipe, into the ground; to depress, as an area, below the general level, as by excavating; to make, as a hole, by digging; bring to some lower or worse state; to reduce, lower, or degrade; to bring to ruin; to reduce in amount or extent, as value or prices; to lower, as the voice; to suppress, as facts; omit, ignore, or avoid; to invest, as money; to lose, as money in an unfortunate invest-

ment.—*n.* A basin or receptacle, as in a kitchen, equipped with a water supply and drain and used for washing; a place of vice or corruption; a low-lying area where waters collect, or where they disappear by sinking downward or by evaporating; a sinkhole.—**sink·a·ble,** *a.*

sink·age, sing′kij, *n.* The amount, process, or act of sinking; depression; *print.* the distance the top line of the body of the text is lowered from its normal position on the page, as at the start of a chapter.

sink·er, sing′kėr, *n.* One who or that which sinks; a weight, as on a fish line or net, to sink it; *slang,* a doughnut.

sink·hole, singk′hōl″, *n.* A hole or funnel-like cavity formed in rock by the action of water, and serving to conduct surface water to an underground passage; a depression or hollow where waste or drainage collects. Also **swal·low, swal·low hole.**

sink·ing fund, *n.* A fund formed to pay off an indebtedness by a government, a corporation, or the like, by periodically setting aside certain amounts of money to accumulate an interest.

sin·less, sin′lis, *a.* [O.E. *synlēas.*] Free from or without sin.—**sin·less·ly,** *adv.*—**sin·less·ness,** *n.*

sin·ner, sin′ėr, *n.* One who sins; a transgressor; an offender.

Si·nol·o·gy, si·nol′o·jē, si·nol′o·jē, *n.* The branch of knowledge or study that deals with the language, literature, history, institutions, and customs of China.—**Si·no·log·i·cal,** sīn″o·loj′i·kal, sin″o·log′-i·kal, *a.*—**Si·nol·o·gist, Si·no·logue,** si·nol′o·jist, si·nol′o·jist, sin′o·lạg″, sīn′-o·log″, sin′o·lạg″, sīn′o·log″, *n.*

Si·no-Ti·bet·an, sī″nō·ti·bet′an, sin″ō-·ti·bet′an, *n. Ling.* a language family which comprises the subfamilies Sino-Thai and Tibeto-Burman, and contains Chinese as well as many lesser known languages and dialects of Asia.—*a.*

sin·syne, sin′sin, *adv. Sc.* Since then; ago.

sin·ter, sin′tėr, *n.* [G., = E. *cinder.*] Siliceous or calcareous matter deposited by springs, as that formed around the vent of a geyser; *metal.* the product resulting from sintering.—*v.t. Metal.* to heat, as particles of powdered and pressed metal, to a temperature at which the individual particles cohere to each other.

sin·u·ate, sin′ū·it, sin′ū·āt″, *a.* [L. *sinuatus,* pp. of *sinuare,* to bend, to wind, < *sinus.*] Bent in and out; winding; sinuous; *bot.* having the margin strongly or distinctly wavy, as a leaf. Also **sin·u·at·ed.**—sin′ū-·āt″, *v.i.*—*sinuated, sinuating.* To curve or bend in and out; to wind.—**sin·u·ate·ly,** *adv.*

sin·u·os·i·ty, sin″ū·os′i·tē, *n. pl.* **sin·u·-os·i·ties.** Sinuous form or character; a curve, bend, or turn, as of a winding road or river.

sin·u·ous, sin′ū·us, *a.* [L. *sinuosus, < sinus.*] Abounding in curves, bends, or turns; winding; indirect; devious; *bot.* sinuate.—**sin·u·ous·ly,** *adv.*—**sin·u·ous·ness,** *n.*

si·nus, sī′nus, *n. pl.* **si·nus·es.** [L., a bend, fold, inner place, hollow, bay or gulf: cf. *sine.*] A curve, bend, or fold; a curving part or recess. *Anat.* any of various cavities, recesses, or passages, as a hollow in a bone, or a reservoir or channel for venous blood; a cranial hollow, containing air, which connects with the nasal cavities; a dilated part in a canal or vessel. *Pathol.* a narrow, elongated abscess with a small orifice; a narrow passage leading to an abscess or the like. *Bot.* a small, rounded depression between two projecting lobes, as of a leaf.

si·nus·i·tis, sī″na·sī′tis, *n. Pathol.* inflammation of any sinus, as of those in the bones of the face.

si·nus·oid, sī′na·soid″, *n. Math.* The graph in rectangular coordinates of a function that varies with the sine of some variable, *i.e.,* the graph of $y = a \sin x$; a sine curve.—**si·nus·oi·dal,** sī″na·soid′al, *a.*

si·nus·oi·dal pro·jec·tion, *n. Cartography,* an equal-area projection with the parallels appearing as equidistant horizontal lines, the central meridian as a vertical line half the length of the equator, and the other meridians as sinusoidal curves with amplitudes proportional to their east or west longitude.

Si·on, sī′on, *n.* Zion.

Siou·an, sō′an, *a.* Belonging to or constituting a linguistic stock of N. American Indians formerly widespread through the central U.S. and Canada, as the Dakota Blackfeet, the Missouri Crow and Osage, and the Virginia Catawba.—*n.*

Sioux, sō, *n. pl.* **Sioux.** A linguistic stock of N. American Indians; a tribe belonging to the Siouan confederation; any member of this tribe; Dakota.

sip, sip, *v.t.*—*sipped, sipping.* [A lighter form of *sup* = D. and L.G. *sippen,* to sip.] To drink by drawing through the lips in small quantities; to drink in or absorb, esp. in small quantities.—*v.i.* To drink by drawing through the lips small quantities of a fluid.—*n.* A small draft taken with the lips; the act of sipping.—**sip·per,** sip′ėr, *n.*—**sip·ping·ly,** *adv.*

si·phon, sy·phon, sī′fon, *n.* [Gr. *siphōn,* a hollow tube, a reed.] A curved tube used to convey a liquid up over a side or elevation to a lower level by resting the short end of the tube in the higher container where, after suction has been used to create a partial vacuum, atmospheric pressure pushes the liquid up the curve of the tube where it is pulled down the longer, lower end by gravity. A bottle which dispenses aerated water when a lever is depressed, releasing accumulated gas which drives the liquid through a siphon tube extending out through the bottle lid; also **si·phon bot·tle, sy·phon bot·tle.** *Zool.* a tube in various animals, as the squid and clam, for taking in or forcing out liquids.—*v.t.* To convey, remove, or empty by means of a siphon.—*v.i.* To pass or be conveyed through or as if through any siphon.—**si·phon·al, si·phon·ic,** sī·fon′ik, *a.*—**siphon·less,** *a.*—**si·phon·like,** *a.*

si·pho·no·phore, sī′fo·no·fōr″, sī′fo·no-·far″, sī·fon′o·fōr″, sī·fon′o·far″, *n.* [N.L. *Siphonophora,* pl., < Gr. *siphōn,* tube and *phóros,* bearing.] *Zool.* any of the order *Siphonophora,* of oceanic hydrozoans of diverse forms, but usu. consisting of a hollow stem or stock budding into a number of appendages, as a jellyfish.

si·phon·o·stele, sī·fon′o·stēl″, sī′fo·nō-·stēl″, *n. Bot.* the vascular stele in higher plants which encloses the pithy center of the stem.—**si·pho·no·ste·lic,** sī″fo·no·stē′-lik, *a.*—**si·pho·no·ste·ly,** *n.*

sip·pet, sip′it, *n.* [Appar. dim. < *sop:* cf. *sip.*] A small bit or fragment; a small piece of bread, usu. toasted or fried, served in soup or used for sopping gravy, sauces, or the like; a crouton.

sir, sụr, *n.* [Shortened form of *sire.*] A respectful or formal term of address used to a man; (*cap.*) the distinctive title of a knight or a baronet, used before the given name; as, *Sir* Walter Scott. A gentleman or lord.

sir·dar, sėr·dar′, *n.* [Hind. *sardār,* < Pers. *sardār, < sar,* head, and *dār,* holder.] In Pakistan, India, and Afghanistan, a military chief or leader; formerly, the British commander of the Egyptian army.

sire, sī′ėr, *n.* [O.Fr. Fr. *sire,* lord, < L. *senior,* elder.] The male parent of a mammal; a respectful term of address used to a man, formerly to any superior or elder, but now only to a king or other sovereign; *poet.* a father or forefather.—*v.t.—sired, siring.* To beget; become the sire of, now used esp. of stallions and other domestic animals.

si·ren, si'ren, *n.* [Gr. *seirēn,* a siren.] *Greek myth.* any of several sea nymphs, being part bird and part charming, alluring, enticing woman, who by their singing brought sailors to rocky destruction; a dangerously enticing woman. Any of the eellike salamanders, family *Sirenidae,* having only two small limbs in the front, and both external gills and lungs; any aquatic mammal of the order *Sirenia,* as the sea cow. An instrument which produces musical tones from air or gas passing forcefully through holes in a rapidly rotating disk; an instrument which produces a loud, piercing sound by this same technique, usu. used to sound an emergency alert or warning.—*a.—si·ren·ic,* si'ren'ik, *a.*

si·re·ni·an, si·rē'nē·an, *n.* [N.L. *Sirenia,* pl., < L. *siren,* E. *siren.*] *Zool.* any of the aquatic herbivorous mammals, order *Sirenia,* as the manatee and sea cow.

Sir·i·us, sir'ē·us, *n. Astron.* the most brilliant star observed, a member of the constellation Canis Major. Also *Dog Star.*

sir·loin, sur'loin, *n.* [Formerly *surloin*—Fr. *surlonge, surlogne,* a sirloin—*sur,* over, upon, and *longe, logne,* a loin.] The upper part of a loin cut of beef that is closest to the rump.

si·roc·co, si·rok'ō, *n.* [It. *sirocco, scirocco,* < Ar. *sharq,* east.] A hot, dry, dust-laden wind blowing from northern Africa across the Mediterranean, and affecting certain parts of southern Europe; a warm, sultry south or southeast wind accompanied by rain, occurring in the same regions; any hot, oppressive wind.

sir·rah, sir'a, *n.* [Extended form of *sir.*] *Archaic,* a term of address used to men and boys in impatience, contempt, or anger.

sir·ree, si·rē', *n.* (Sometimes *cap.*) Sir, used with *yes* or *no* for emphasis. Also **sir·ee.**

sir·vente, sĕr·vänt', *Fr.* sĕr·väNt', *n.* pl. **sir·ventes,** sĕr·vents', *Fr.* sĕr·väNt'. [Fr., < Pr. *sirventes,* appar. orig. a poem by a *sirvent,* lit. 'one serving,' < L. *serviens,* ppr., E. *servient.*] A type of poem of the medieval troubadours, often satirical, and usually devoted to political or moral subjects. Also **sir·ventes,** sĕr·vent'es.

si·sal, sī'sal, sis'al, *n.* A fiber prepared from a plant, *Agave sisalana,* of the West Indies and Mexico and used for rope; also **si·sal hemp.** The fiber-yielding plant.

sis·kin, sis'kin, *n.* Any of several finches of the genus *Spinus,* as *Spinus spinus* of Europe and Asia, with greenish and yellowish plumage; *S. pinus,* the pine siskin.

sis·sy, sis'ē, *n.* pl. **sis·sies.** [Dim. of *sis.*] An effeminate boy or man; a coward; a little girl.—*a.—sis·si·fied, a.—sis·si·ness, sis·sy·ness, n.—sis·sy·ish, a.*

sis·ter, sis'tĕr, *n.* [< Icel. *systir,* Sw. *syster,* a sister = D. *zuster,* O.E. *sweoster,* Goth. *swistar,* G. *schwester,* sister; cogn. Russ. *sestra,* L. *soror,* Skt. *swasri.*] A female born of the same parents with respect to any other offspring of this same family; any female enjoying the intimacy and affection of a sister; a female fellow Christian; a female belonging to a community of nuns; an object thought of as female in relationship to other similar objects, as: This ship is the *sister* of the other. *Brit.* a nurse having charge of a hospital ward.

sis·ter·hood, sis'tĕr·hud", *n.* The state of being a sister; a society of females united in one faith or one community, as nuns; a group of women bound by common interests.

sis·ter-in-law, sis'tĕr·in·lä", *n.* pl. **sis-ters-in-law.** A husband's or wife's sister; a brother's wife.

sis·ter·ly, sis'tĕr·lē, *a.* Like or pertaining to a sister; becoming a sister.—*adv.—sis·ter·li·ness, n.*

Sis·tine, sis'tēn, sis'tin, sis'tīn, *a.* [It. *Sistino,* < *Sisto,* Sixtus.] Of or pertaining to any of various popes named Sixtus. Also *Sixtine.*

sis·trum, sis'trum, *n.* pl. **sis·trums, sis·tra.** [L., < Gr. *seistron,* < *seiō,* to shake.] A percussion instrument used by the ancient Egyptians in their religious ceremonies, consisting of a small metal frame with metal rods loosely inserted in it.

sit, sit, *v.i.—sat, sitting.* [O.E. *sittan* = Icel. *sitja,* D. *zitten,* G. *sitzen,* Goth. *sitan,* to sit; from root seen also in L. *sedeo,* to sit.] To rest upon the haunches or buttocks; to repose on a seat; to remain or rest; be situated or located; to lie or weigh on, as: Grief *sits* heavily on his heart. To have a position theoretically involving sitting; as, to baby-*sit*; to perch or to roost; to incubate, as a bird covers and warms eggs for hatching; to suit, or be found personally suitable, often followed by *well*; to fit or suit when put on; to undergo portraiture, either by a photographer, painter, or sculptor; *meteor.* to derive from, as: The wind *sits* in, or comes from, the East. To have title to the occupancy of a place in a public assemblage or governing body, as: The senator *sits* for Ohio. To convene, as: An assembly *sits* when in session. To be officially engaged, as: A student *sits* for examinations. To hold or pass a pseudo-authoritarian opinion; as, to *sit* in judgment. —*v.t.* To usher to, or place in a seat, as a waiter; to contain seats for; as, a theater that *sits* 500 people; to exercise a certain style or skill in the matter of seating; as, to *sit* a horse.—*n.* The act of one who is sitting; a session of sitting; the hang or fit of a garment.—**sit on one's hands,** to do nothing.—**sit on,** to squelch or quash.—**sit pret·ty,** to be in a favorable position.—**sit tight,** to be patient.—**sit loose,** *slang,* to relax.—**sit un·der,** to study, teach, or serve under.—**sit out,** to outwait.—**sit up,** to extend one's bedtime; *colloq.* to become alert, often followed by *and take notice.*—**sit in on,** to join or be party to.

si·tar, si·tär', *n.* [Hindi.] *Mus.* a stringed instrument of India having a pear-shaped body, a long neck, and a varied number of strings.

sit-down strike, *n.* A strike in which the employees stop work but remain in their place of employment, refusing to quit the premises until their demands are met. Also **sit-down,** *stay-in strike.*

site, sīt, *n.* [L. *situs,* site, situation.] A place where anything is constructed or planned; as, the *site* of the new bank; the scene of an event; as, the *site* of the explosion.

sit-in, sit'in", *n.* The organized, usu. passive, occupying of premises customarily denied to members of a group; as, a *sit-in* held in a hotel dining room by Negroes protesting racial discrimination, or in college buildings by students opposing administrative policies.

si·tol·o·gy, si·tol'o·jē, *n.* [Gr. *sitos, sition,* food, and *logos,* discourse.] That branch of medicine which relates to diet and nutrition; dietetics.

si·tos·ter·ol, sī·tos'te·rōl", sī·tos'te·ral", sī·tos'te·rol", *n. Chem.* any one of several sterols or groups of sterols which occur widely in plants, esp. soybeans, and are used in varying forms and combinations for the synthetic production of steroid hormones.

sit·ter, sit'ĕr, *n.* One who sits; one who poses, as for his portrait; a hen that is brooding; a baby-sitter; *slang,* buttocks.

sit·ter-in, sit'ĕr·in", *n.* pl. **sit·ters-in.** *Brit.* a baby-sitter.

sit·ting, sit'ing, *a.* Holding a seated position; for the purpose of sitting; incubating; occupying a place in an official capacity; presiding in a court.—*n.* The act of a person who sits or of a thing which sits; a period of time spent seated for a specific purpose, as for a studio photograph; the incubation and hatching, as by a bird on eggs; an authorized meeting of a group, as a legislative session; space or time given to meal service, as on shipboard.

sit·ting duck, *n. Slang.* One who or that which is very vulnerable; an easy target.

sit·ting room, *n.* A living room, usu. of a residence; parlor.

sit·u·ate, sich'ö·āt", *v.t.—situated, situating.* [Fr. *situé,* situated, < L. *situs,* a site.] To give a place to; to locate; to position; to fix permanently; to put or place in a certain situation.—*sich'ö·it, sich'ö·āt", a. Archaic,* situated.

sit·u·at·ed, sich'ö·ā"tid, *a.* [A later form of *situate,* but now more common.] Having a site; located; placed or permanently fixed with respect to any other object or place; being in any state or condition with regard to men or things; circumstanced.

sit·u·a·tion, sich"ö·ā'shan, *n.* [Fr. *situation.*] Position or location in respect to physical surroundings; locality; state, condition, or position with respect to society or circumstances; temporary state or position; place, post, or permanent employment; job.—*sit·u·a·tion·al, a.—sit·u·a·tion·al·ly, adv.*

si·tus, sī'tus, *n.* pl. **si·tus.** [L.] Position, situation, or location; the proper or original position, as of a part or organ.

sitz bath, sits bath, zits, *n.* [G. *sitzbad*—*sitz,* a seat, and *bad,* a bath.] A form of bath, usu. taken for therapeutic purposes, in which only the hips and thighs are covered with water.

sitz·krieg, sits'krēg", zits'krēg", *n.* Stalemated warfare.

sitz·mark, sits'märk", *n.* An impression made in the snow by a skier who has fallen backward.

six, siks, *n.* [O.E. *six* = Icel., Dan., and Sw. *sex,* D. *zes,* G. *sechs,* Goth. *saihs,* L. *sex,* Gr. *hex.*] The cardinal number between five and seven; a symbol representing it; a set of six persons or things.—*a.* Being one more than five in number; twice three.—**at six·es and sev·ens,** in confusion; disordered; estranged; in disagreement.

six-pack, siks'pak", *n.* A package, usu. fitted with a handle, which contains six cans or six bottles of a beverage.

six·pence, siks'pens, *n.* A sum equivalent to six pennies; an English coin. See Moneys of the World table.—**six·pen·ny,** siks'pen'ē, siks'pe·nē, *a.* Valued at a sixpence; cheap or trashy; of a nail, two inches long.

six-shoot·er, siks'shö"tĕr, *n.* A revolver with six chambers. Also **six-gun.**

sixte, sikst, *n.* [Fr., < L. *sextus,* sixth, < *sex,* six.] *Fencing,* the sixth in a series of eight parries.

six·teen, siks'tēn', *n.* The cardinal number between 15 and 17; a symbol representing it; a set of 16 persons or things.—*a.*

six·teen·mo, siks'tēn'mō, *n.* pl. **six·teen·mos.** A page size formed by folding a printer's sheet into 16 leaves, each measuring about 4 × 6 inches; a book or page of this size.—*a.* Having pages of this size. Also *sextodecimo.*

six·teenth, siks'tēnth', *a.* Following the fifteenth; being the ordinal of 16; being one of the 16 equal parts into which anything is divided.—*n.* One of 16 equal parts; that which follows the fifteenth in a series.

---

ch- chain, G. na*ch*t; **th-** THen, thin; **w-** wig, hw as sound in whig; **z-** zh as in azure, zeal. *Italicized vowel* indicates schwa sound.

six·teenth note, *n. Mus.* A note having one sixteenth of the time value of a whole note; a semiquaver.

sixth, siksth, *a.* Following the fifth; being the ordinal of six; being one of six equal parts into which anything is divided.—*n.* A sixth part; the one following the fifth in a series. *Mus.* an interval between two tones, six degrees apart in the diatonic scale; a tone exactly six degrees from any given tone; submediant; the combination formed by two tones six degrees apart.—*adv.*—**sixth·ly,** *adv.*

sixth sense, *n.* Intuition; the ability to perceive without the support of overt sensual stimuli or clues; an instance of such perception; a strong suspicion that is not necessarily logically tenable.

six·ti·eth, siks′tē·ith, *a.* Following the fifty-ninth; being the ordinal of 60; being one of 60 equal parts into which anything is divided.—*n.* One of 60 equal parts; that which follows the fifty-ninth in a series.

Six·tine, siks′tēn, siks′tin, siks′tīn, *n.* Sistine.

six·ty, siks′tē, [O.E. *sixrig*.], *n.* The cardinal number between 59 and 61; a symbol representing it; a set of 60 persons or things.—*a.*

six·ty-fourth note, *n. Mus.* a note equivalent in time value to one sixty-fourth of a whole note. Also *hemidemisemiquaver.*

siz·a·ble, size·a·ble, sī′za·bl, *a.* Of considerable size; quite large.—**siz·a·ble·ness,** *n.*—**siz·a·bly,** *adv.*

siz·ar, siz·er, sī′zėr, *n.* [< *size.*] In the colleges of the University of Cambridge, England, and at Trinity College, Dublin, one of a class of undergraduates who receive from the college assistance toward maintenance.—**siz·ar·ship,** *n.*

size, sīz, *n.* [Contr. for *assize,* and meaning orig. quantity or dimensions assessed or settled.] The volume, bulk, or spatial surface dimensions of anything; comparative magnitude; a conventional relative measure of dimension, as of shoes, gloves, or the like; the degree, range, extent, or amount; the total number or the count; as, the *size* of a class; a usu. succinct recapitulation, as: That's about the *size* of it.—*v.t.*—*sized, sizing.* To make, adjust, or arrange according to size.—**size up,** *colloq.* To form or make a judgment or estimate of, as: He *sized* the applicant *up* from his appearance. To meet certain specifications or be equivalent to.

size, sīz, *n.* [It. *sisa, assisa,* a kind of glue.] A filler for porous material, such as wood, paper, or cloth, that is compounded of glues and varnishes, or of starches, glutens, or gelatins.—*v.t.*—*sized, sizing.* To apply or prepare with sizing.—**siz·ing,** sī′zing, *n.* A coating of size.

sized, sīzd, *a.* Having a particular or specified size or magnitude, used in compounds; as, a middle-*sized* house; adjusted to or suitable for a certain size, used in compounds; as, a purse-*sized* mirror.

siz·zle, siz′l, *v.i.*—*sizzled, sizzling.* [Imit.] To make a hissing sound, as in frying or burning. *Colloq.* to be very hot; to be angry or resentful, as: She's *sizzling* over the offense.—*n.* A sizzling sound.—**siz·zler,** *n.*

skald, scald, skạld, skäld, *n.* [< Scand.: Icel. *skåld,* Norw. and Sw. *skald,* Dan. *skjald:* cf. *scold.*] A poet or bard in ancient Scandinavia.—**skald·ic,** *a.*

skat, skät, *n.* [G., the game, also cards put aside in playing, < It. *scarto,* a discard, < *scartare,* to discard.] A card game, with three players using 32 cards, sevens through aces, two cards being dealt to the table.

skate, skāt, *n.* [< D. *schaats,* a skate.] A steel runner or blade fixed to a metal frame that is fastened onto the sole of a shoe, and which enables the wearer to glide rapidly over ice. See *ice skate, roller skate.*—*v.i.*—*skated, skating.* To glide or move on or as if on skates.—**skat·er,** skā′tėr, *n.*

skate, skāt, *n.* pl. **skates, skate.** [Icel. *skata,* a skate; cf. L. *squatina,* the angelfish.] Any of several species of the ray fishes, genus *Raja,* which have a pointed snout and broad pectoral fins that give the flat body a rhomboidal form.

skate, skāt, *n. Slang.* An inferior or worn-out horse; a nag; a person or fellow; as, a good *skate,* a cheap*skate*; a contemptible individual.

skat·ole, skat′ōl, skat′ạl, *n.* [Gr. *skatos,* genit. of *skor,* dung.] *Chem.* a crystalline compound, C_9H_9N, with a strong fecal odor, produced in the decomposition of proteins in the intestine, in feces, and in some plants; produced synthetically for commercial use as a fixative in perfume.

skean, skene, shkēn, skēn, *n.* [Gael. *sgian.*] A short sword or dagger formerly used by the Irish and the Scottish Highlanders.

ske·dad·dle, ski·dad′l, *v.i.*—*skedaddled, skedaddling.* [Of obscure origin.] *Colloq.* To scamper off hastily; run away.—*n. Colloq.* a hurried departure.

Skee-Ball, skē′bạl″, *n.* An indoor game in which players score points by rolling balls up an inclined surface into holes of varying size and point value. (Trademark.)

skeet, skēt, *n.* A type of trapshooting in which the shooter fires at clay disks hurled at varying speeds and angles to simulate the flight of game birds. Also **skeet shoot·ing.**

skeg, skeg, *n.* [< D. *scheg.*] *Naut.* The after part of a ship's keel; a projection abaft a ship's keel for the support of a rudder.

skein, skān, *n.* [O.Fr. *escaigne,* skein; perh. from Celtic.] A quantity of thread or yarn formed in loose loops or rounds of uniform size by winding upon a reel; something that suggests the coils or twists of the skein; a flight of a flock of wildfowl.

skel·e·ton, skel′i·ton, *n.* [Gr. *skeleton,* a dried body, a mummy, *skeletos,* dried up, < *skellō,* to dry.] *Anat.* the total bony framework which sustains the softer body parts of vertebrates; these same bones when separated from the flesh and rejoined artificially in their natural position; the supporting framework of anything; an outline or rough draft; *colloq.* one who is very thin or lean.—*a.* Of or pertaining to the total bony structure; the barest minimum, as: Only a *skeleton* crew operates in the summer.—**skel·e·tal,** skel′i·tal, *a.*—**skel·e·tal·ly,** *adv.*—**skel·e·ton·ize,** skel′i·to·nīz″, *v.t.*—*skeletonized, skeletonizing.*—**skel·e·ton·iz·er,** *n.*

skel·e·ton key, *n.* A key, with most of the bit filed away, which can be used to open several different locks.

skelp, skelp, *v.t.* [M.E.; perh. imit.] *Sc., North. Eng.* To strike, beat, slap, or spank; to drive along, as animals, by slapping.—*v.i. Sc., North. Eng.* to go quickly.—*n. Sc., North. Eng.* A blow, esp. with the flat of the hand; a slap; a smack.

skep, skep, *n.* [O.E. *sceppe,* a basket, chest, box.] A wooden or wicker basket; *Sc.* a beehive, esp. one of straw.

skep·tic, scep·tic, skep′tik, *n.* [Fr. *sceptique,* < Gr. *skeptikos,* thoughtful, skeptic, *skepsis,* speculation, doubt, < *skeptesthai,* to examine critically.] One who doubts the truth of any principle or system of principles or doctrines; one who disbelieves or hesitates to believe; a disbeliever; a person who doubts the fundamental beliefs of Christianity or any religion. (*Cap.*), *philos.* a member of a school of philosophy in ancient Greece, esp. a follower of Pyrrho, who held the attainment of certain knowledge to be impossible; (*sometimes cap.*) a follower of a school of skepticism.

skep·ti·cal, scep·ti·cal, skep′ti·kal, *a.* Doubting. (*Sometimes cap.*) belonging to or characteristic of a skeptic or skepticism; holding the opinions of a skeptic.—**skep·ti·cal·ly,** *adv.*—**skep·ti·cal·ness,** *n.*

skep·ti·cism, scep·ti·cism, skep′ti·siz″-um, *n.* Disbelief or inability to believe; doubt; incredulity; a doubting of the truth of religious beliefs as revelation, esp. the Christian religion; (*sometimes cap.*), *philos.* the doctrines or opinions of a skeptic.

sker·ry, sker′ē, *Sc.* skeR′ē, *n.* pl. **sker·ries.** [Icel. *sker* = Sw. *skar.*] *Chiefly Sc.* an isolated rock, rocky island, or reef in the sea.

sketch, skech, *n.* [< It. *schizzo,* a sketch, < L. *schedius,* Gr. *schedios,* offhand, sudden.] A drawing rapidly executed and intended to give only general features or characteristic aspect; a first rough or incomplete draft, as of a play, painting, book, or the like; an outline or general delineation of anything; a short essay or story; a short dramatic piece, as a one-act play or between-acts presentation.—*v.t.* To draw a sketch of; to make a rough draft of; to give a brief accounting of one's actions; as, to *sketch* one's role in the incident; to give the principal points or ideas of; to delineate.—*v.i.* To do a sketch.—**sketch·er,** *n.*

sketch·book, skech′buk″, *n.* A drawing book for making sketches; a book of literary sketches. Also **sketch book.**

sketch·y, skech′ē, *a.*—*sketchier, sketchiest.* Possessing the character of a sketch; giving rough outlines; unfinished, imperfect, or superficial.—**sketch·i·ly,** *adv.*—**sketch·i·ness,** *n.*

skew, skū, *a.* Having an oblique position; turned or twisted to one side; slanting; sloping.—*adv.*—*v.i.* To move in an oblique course; turn aside; swerve; to squint; gaze obliquely or look askance.—*v.t.* To put askew; to shape or form in an oblique way; to distort; to change the meaning of.—*n.* A sideward or oblique movement; a slant.

skew arch, *n.* An arch which is not at right angles to its abutments or face.

skew·back, skū′bak″, *n. Arch.* A sloping surface against which the end of an arch rests; a stone, course of masonry, or the like, presenting such a surface.

skew·bald, skū′bạld″, *a.* [Cf. obs. or prov. *skewed,* skewbald (of uncertain origin), and *piebald.*] Of horses, having patches of different colors, esp. of white and brown.

skew dis·tri·bu·tion, *n. Statistics,* an asymmetrical frequency distribution in which the most frequent value is above or below the mean.

skew·er, skū′ėr, *n.* [Prov. E. *skiver,* a skewer = *shiver,* a splinter.] A pin of wood or metal for fastening and holding meat in place or for keeping it in form while cooking; anything similar in appearance or use.—*v.t.* To fasten with skewers; to pierce or transfix.

skew·ness, skū′nis, *n.* The state of being skew or asymmetric; *statistics,* asymmetry in the curve of a frequency distribution or the measure of such distortion.

skew pol·y·gon, *n. Math.* a figure of four or more sides formed by joining points, not all of which are in the same plane.

ski, skē, *Brit.* shē, *n.* pl. **skis, ski.** [O.N. *skith,* snowshoe.] One of a pair of long, narrow runners curving up in front, made of metal, wood, or plastic, and fastened to the feet for use in gliding and traveling over snow.—*v.i.*—*skied, skiing.* To travel on skis; to glide on skis, as for sports. Also **skee.**

ski·a·gram, skī′a·gram″, *n.* Skiagraph.

ski·a·graph, skī′a·graf″, skī′a·gräf″, *n.* An object shown by shadowed outline, as by X-rays; a radiograph. Also *skiagram.*—**ski·ag·ra·pher,** skī′ag′ra·fėr, *n.*—**ski·a·**

graph·ic, ski·a·graph·i·cal, skī″a·graf′-ik, *a.*—**ski·a·graph·i·cal·ly,** *adv.*

ski·ag·ra·phy, ski·ag′ra·fē, *n.* [Gr. *skiagraphia—skia*, a shadow, and *grapho*, to describe.] The act or art of delineating shadows; the making of skiagraphs.

ski·a·scope, skī′a·skōp″, *n. Ophthalm.* An instrument for detecting errors of refraction in the eye by observing the movement of light and shadow from the retina as it is illuminated from various angles; a retinoscope.—**ski·as·co·py,** ski·as′ko·pē, *n.*

ski boot, *n.* An ankle-high, padded boot of heavy leather, used in skiing, designed to fit tightly and comfortably to the ski.

skid, skid, *n.* [Origin uncertain: cf. O.E. *scīd*, Icel. *skīth*, piece of wood.] An act of skidding; a sideslip; a plank, bar, log, or the like, esp. one of a pair, on which something heavy may be slid or rolled along; one of a number of such logs forming a skidway; a low, small, sometimes wheeled platform upon which materials are piled to facilitate handling; a plank, framework, or the like on which something rests for storage or is held in position, as stacks of newsprint; *usu. pl., naut.* a wooden plank or fender hung over the side of a ship to protect it from injury when docking, handling cargo, and the like; *aeron.* part of the landing gear of an aircraft, designed to slide along the ground; as, a tail *skid.* A shoe or some other device for preventing the wheel of a vehicle from rotating, as when descending a hill.—*v.t.*—*skidded, skidding.* To place on, equip, or check with skids; to send into a skid.—*v.i.* To slide onward without rotating, as the wheels of a speeding car after sudden braking; to slip sidewards while in motion, as the wheels of a vehicle on an icy surface; to sideslip in the air, as an airplane that is insufficiently banked while making a turn.—**on the skids,** *slang,* on a downward route to ruin or defeat.—**put the skids un·der,** *slang,* to cause the failure or downfall of.—**skid·der,** *n.*—**skid·ding·ly,** *adv.*

skid·doo, ski·dö′, *v.i.*—*skiddooed, skiddooing. Colloq.* To go away; to get out. Also **ski·doo.**

skid fin, *n. Aeron.* on some of the early biplanes, an upright surface used to increase lateral stability, usu. placed above the upper wing, and lying within the plane of symmetry.

skid road, *n. Lumbering,* a trail or log road on which the freshly cut logs are carried or hauled; (*sometimes cap.*), *colloq.* skid row.

skid row, (*Sometimes cap.*), *colloq.* an area of any town which contains cheap hotels, barrooms, and luncheonettes frequented by such people as vagrants and alcoholics.

ski·er, skē′ẽr, *n.* One who skis.

skiff, skif, *n.* [Fr. *esquif*, < O.G. *scif*, Mod. G. *schiff*, a ship.] Any small, light boat that can be rowed or sailed easily by one person. A lightweight boat, equipped with a centerboard and spritsail, that can be propelled by oars as well as by sail; also **St. Law·rence skiff.**

ski·ing, skē′ing, *n.* The act, art, or sport of racing, gliding, or jumping on skis.

ski·jor·ing, skē·jōr′ing, skē·jar′ing, skē′-jōr·ing, skē′jar·ing, *n.* The sport in which a skier is drawn by a horse or some motor vehicle over snow or ice.

ski jump, *n.* A specially prepared track or course, usu. constructed on a hill, from which a skier may get added speed to jump and land at a greater distance down the slope; a jump by a person on skis from such a takeoff course.—*v.i.*

ski lift, *n.* A motor-driven device, usu. consisting of numerous chairs or bars attached to an endless cable, which conveys skiers up a slope or mountain.

skill, skil, *n.* [< Icel. *skil*, Dan. *skiel*, discrimination, discernment, O.E. *scylian*, to divide, to separate, to distinguish. *Scale, shell, scalp, scull, shale* are akin.] A developed proficiency or dexterity in some art, craft, or the like; deftness in execution or performance; a trade or craft requiring special training for competence or expertness in its practice.

skilled, skild, *a.* Having skill, as a person trained in a craft, art, or trade; requiring or involving skill or a special technique.

skil·let, skil′it, *n.* A frying pan. *Brit.* a saucepan or pot with a long handle and three or four legs, used in cooking on an open hearth.

skill·ful, *Brit.* **skil·ful,** skil′ful, *a.* Having skill; dexterous; expert; displaying or involving skill.—**skill·ful·ly,** *Brit.* **skil·ful·ly,** *adv.*—**skill·ful·ness,** *Brit.* **skil·ful·ness,** *n.*

skil·ling, skil′ing, *n.* A former coin of the Scandinavian countries, variously issued in silver and copper.

skill·less, skil·less, skil′lis, *a.* Lacking skill; unskilled.—**skill·less·ness,** *n.*

skim, skim, *v.t.*—*skimmed, skimming.* [< M.E.] To clear, as liquid, from any substance floating on the top; to lift or remove, as floating substance, from liquid; as, to *skim* cream from milk; to pass or move lightly and rapidly over; to cause to move or pass lightly and rapidly over; as, to *skim* a pebble across water; to glance over in a superficial manner; as, to *skim* a newspaper article; to coat or cover with or as with a thin film or layer, as: Water *skimmed* the field.—*v.i.* To move or pass lightly and rapidly over or along a surface; to glance over or examine hastily; to become coated or covered with a film.—*n.* An instance of skimming; something skimmed off, as cream; a thin coating or film.—*a.* Skimmed.

skim·ble-scam·ble, skim·ble-skam·ble, skim′bl·skam″bl, skim′l·skam″l, *a.* Rambling; worthless, nonsensical.

skim·mer, skim′ẽr, *n.* One who or that which skims; a flat spoon or ladle for skimming liquids; a wide-brimmed, flat-crowned hat, usu. made of hard straw; *ornith.* a marine bird of N. America, *Rhynchops nigra,* having a lower mandible longer than the upper, which it dips in the water as it skims along in search of food.

skim milk, *n.* Milk from which the cream has been removed. Also **skimmed milk.**

skim·ming, skim′ing, *n.* The act of one who or that which skims; *usu. pl.* that which is removed by skimming.

skimp, skimp, *v.t.* [Cf. *scrimp* and *scamp.*] To scrimp; to keep, as a person, on short allowance of something; to stint the amount of; to scamp; to do carelessly.—*v.i.* To use severe or stingy economy; to scamp work.—*a.* Meager; scanty.—**skimp·i·ly,** *adv.*—**skimp·i·ness,** *n.*—**skimp·ing·ly,** *adv.*—**skimp·y,** skim′pē, *a.*—*skimpier, skimpiest.*

skin, skin, *n.* [M.E. *skin,* < Scand.: cf. Icel. and Sw. *skinn,* Dan. *skind,* skin, akin to O.H.G. *scindan,* G. *schinden,* to skin, flay.] The external covering or integument of an animal body, esp. when soft and flexible; such an integument stripped from the body of a small animal, as distinguished from the *hide* of a large animal; a hide or pelt; a vessel made of the skin of an animal, used for holding liquids; any integumentary covering, outer coating, or surface layer, as an investing membrane, the rind or peel of fruit, or a film on liquid; the outer covering of a ship or airplane. *Slang,* a skinflint; a swindler or cheat; a fleecing or swindling proceeding.—*v.t.*—*skinned, skinning.* To furnish or cover with or as with skin; to strip or deprive of skin; flay; peel; to strip or pull off, as a covering; to abrade or scrape skin from; as, to *skin* an elbow. *Slang,* to strip of money or belongings; to fleece, as in gambling, swindling, or any sharp practice; to defeat; to reprimand.—*v.i.* To become covered with skin, as a wound; *slang,* to slip away or make off hastily.—**by the skin of one's teeth,** *colloq.* by a very narrow margin, barely.—**get un·der one's skin,** *colloq.* To irritate, annoy; impress deeply.—**save one's skin,** *colloq.* to escape or avoid bodily or personal harm.—**skinned,** *a.*

skin-deep, skin′dēp′, *a.* Not penetrating beyond the skin; superficial; slight.—*adv.* Superficially.

skin div·ing, *n.* A water sport in which a swimmer wearing a light mask or goggles, fins, a device for breathing, and, depending upon water temperature, a tight-fitting rubber garment, is able to move about freely and explore underwater.—**skin-dive,** skin′dīv″, *v.i.*—**skin-dived** or **skin-dove,** *skin-diving.*—**skin div·er,** *n.*

skin ef·fect, *n. Elect.* the propensity of an alternating current to concentrate its flow at or near the surface of the conductor in proportion to the increase in its frequency.

skin·flint, skin′flint″, *n.* A very stingy or miserly person.

skin·ful, skin′ful″, *n. pl.* **skin·fuls.** The liquid capacity or contents of a container made of skin; *slang,* a person's fill of something or all he can stand, esp. of liquor.

skin game, *n.* A fraudulent gambling game; any similar swindle.

skin graft, *n. Surg.* the viable skin transplanted in skin grafting.—**skin graft·ing,** *surg.* the process whereby pieces of healthy skin are transplanted from a donor's or the patient's body to replace skin which has been destroyed, as by burns.

skink, skingk, *v.t. Brit. dial.* to draw or dispense, as liquor.

skink, skingk, *n.* [Gr. *skinkos,* a kind of lizard.] Any of various lizards of the family *Scincidae,* found in several regions of the U.S. and extensively in other parts of the world, typically small with small, flat scales.

skink·er, sking′kẽr, *n. Brit. dial.* one who draws or dispenses liquor; a barkeeper.

skin·less, skin′lis, *a.* Having no skin or casing, as a sausage.

skin·ner, skin′ẽr, *n.* One who skins; one who prepares skins, as for the market; a dealer in skins; *U.S. slang,* a driver of mules, oxen, or other draft animals.—**skin·ner·y,** skin′e·rē, *n.* Any area where skins are prepared, as for sale.

skin·ny, skin′ē, *a.* Very thin; undesirably slender; emaciated; consisting of skin or like skin.

skin test, *n. Med.* A test in which a particular substance, as pollen, is applied to or injected into the skin in order to determine the extent of the patient's allergic sensitivity to it; a similarly administered test, as the Schick test for diphtheria.

skin·tight, skin′tīt′, *a.* Fitting nearly as tightly as the skin, as an item of clothing.

skip, skip, *v.i.*—*skipped, skipping.* [M.E. *skippen;* prob. < Scand.] To spring, jump, or leap lightly from the ground; to move along with light, springing movements; to ricochet, as a missile passing with rebounds along a surface; to pass from one point, thing, or subject to another, disregarding or omitting whatever intervenes; *educ.* to be advanced more than one grade at a time; *colloq.* to leave hastily or secretly.—*v.t.* To spring or jump lightly over; to pass over without reading, notice, mention, or action; to omit, miss, or disregard, as one step in a series; to send, as a missile, ricocheting along a surface; *colloq.* to leave hastily, or flee from, as a place.—*n.* A skipping movement; a light spring, jump, or leap; a gait marked by such springs; a passing from one point or thing to another, with disregard for whatever intervenes.

skip, skip, *n.* [Cf. *skipper.*] The captain of a team or side at curling or bowling.—*v.t.* To act as the skip of.

ski pants, *n. pl.* Tapered pants worn for outdoor winter sports, esp. skiing, often having an elastic strap fitting under the feet.

skip-bomb, skip′bom″, *v.t.* To attack by releasing bombs from a plane flying at a low altitude so that they glance off water or a ground surface before striking the target.

skip·jack, skip′jak″, *n. pl.* **skip·jacks, skip·jack.** One of a variety of fish that leap above or skim along the water's surface, as bluefish or alewives.

ski pole, *n.* A pointed metal pole used in pairs as a skiing aid, having a hand strap at the top and a horizontal disk near the bottom to limit its penetration of the snow.

skip·per, skip′ėr, *n.* [D. *schipper.*] The captain of a ship, esp. a small trading or merchant vessel; any captain or leader.—*v.t.* To act as captain of, as a ship.

skip·per, skip′ėr, *n.* One who or that which skips; any insect whose motion is jerky or resembles skipping; any of the quick-flying lepidopterous insects constituting the family *Hesperidae*; the saury.

skirl, skųrl, *v.i.* [Prob. from Scand., and related to *shrill.*] To sound loudly and shrilly, as a bagpipe.—*v.t.* To play, as a bagpipe; play, as a tune, on a bagpipe.—*n.* The sound of the bagpipe.

skir·mish, skųr′mish, *n.* [O.Fr. *eskermir,* to fence; < O.H.G. *skirmen,* to fight, to defend oneself, < *skirm,* a shield.] A brief fight in war between small parties; a short, minor contest of any kind.—*v.i.* To take part in a skirmish.—**skir·mish·er,** *n.*

skirr, skųr, *v.i.* [Cf. *scour.*] To go rapidly; rush; fly; scurry.—*v.t.* To go rapidly over; scour.—*n.* A whirring sound.

skirt, skųrt, *n.* [The older form of *shirt.*] The lower and loose part of a coat or other garment from the waist downward; a woman's garment resembling a petticoat; something that resembles a skirt; a border, margin, or extreme part; a free hanging piece of leather on a saddle; the diaphragm or midriff in animals; *slang,* a woman; *usu. pl.* the outer borders of a city; as, the *skirts* of town.—*v.t.* To border; to form the border or edge of; to run along the edge of; to evade, as: The speaker *skirted* any controversial issues.—*v.i.* To be on or pass along the border of.—**skirt·er,** *n.*

skirt·ing, skųr′ting, *n.* Cloth for making skirts; an edging or border; a bordering finish of wood or other material placed along the base of an interior wall of a building; *Brit.* a baseboard.

ski run, *n.* A snow-covered incline, slope, or marked path used for skiing.

ski suit, *n.* A warm one-piece or two-piece outfit consisting of a short jacket and fitted pants, worn for outdoor winter sports, such as skiing.

skit, skit, *n.* A brief literary piece with humorous or satiric intent; a short comic theatrical scene.

ski tow, *n.* One of the various types of ski lifts consisting of an endless, motor-driven rope which skiers grasp to be pulled up a slope.

skit·ter, skit′ėr, *v.i.* [Freq. of *skit.*] To go, run, or glide lightly or rapidly; skim or skip along a surface; *angling,* to draw a spoon or a baited hook over the surface of the water with a skipping motion.—*v.t.* To cause to skitter.

skit·tish, skit′ish, *a.* [Cf. Prov. E. *skit,* hasty.] Easily frightened, as a horse; shy or timid; restlessly playful or lively; changeable or fickle.—**skit·tish·ly,** *adv.*—**skit·tish·ness,** *n.*

skit·tles, skit′lz, *n. pl. but sing. in constr.* An English game of ninepins in which the player uses a wooden ball or wooden disk

to upset the pins; one of the pins used in this game.

skive, skīv, *v.t.*—*skived, skiving.* [< Scand.] To split or cut, as rubber or leather, into layers or slices; to shave, as hides; to pare off.

skiv·er, skī′vėr, *n.* One who or that which skives; a knife or tool for skiving. A thin leather or sheepskin, used for bookbinding.

skiv·vy, skiv′ē, *n. pl.* **skiv·vies.** *Slang.* A man's, usu. a sailor's, undershirt; *pl.* such a shirt and shorts.

skiv·vy, skiv′ē, *n. pl.* **skiv·vies.** *Brit.* A disparaging term for a female servant; a slave.

skoal, skōl, *interj.* [Dan. and Norw. *skaal,* Icel. *skål,* bowl.] A toast wishing good health to someone in drinking.

sku·a, skū′a, *n.* [< Scand.] A large, dark-colored sea bird, *Catharacta skua,* closely related to the jaegers, and known for its practice of robbing weaker birds of their food.

skul·dug·ger·y, skull·dug·ger·y, skul′-dug′e·rē, *n.* [Var. of Scot. *skulduddery.*] Dishonorable proceedings; mean dishonesty or trickery.

skulk, skulk, *v.i.* [Dan. *skulke,* to sneak.] To lie or wait in a place of concealment, as for a sinister purpose; to lurk or move around in a sneaky manner. *Chiefly Brit.* to shun doing one's duty or work; malinger.—*n.* One who skulks; a group or pack of foxes.—**skulk·er,** *n.*

skull, skul, *n.* [Same as Sw. *skull, skoll,* a bowl or drinking cup; Dan. *skal,* a shell, *hjerneskal,* the skull, lit. 'brain-shell'; the skull being so called from forming a kind of vessel.] The cranium or bony case that forms the framework of the head and encloses the brain; the brain as the seat of intelligence, as: Can't you get it through your thick *skull?* A human skull symbolizing death.

skull and cross·bones, *n.* A representation of the face of a human skull, with two bones crossed beneath it, formerly the design on a pirate flag, now a generalized warning of danger to life.

skull·cap, skul′kap″, *n.* A brimless cap of silk, velvet, or the like, fitting closely to the head, as sometimes worn by Jewish men; the upper, domed part of the skull, covering the brain; *bot.* any of various menthaceous herbs, genus *Scutellaria,* in which the calyx of the flower suggests a helmet.

skunk, skungk, *n. pl.* **skunks, skunk.** Any of various small, black-and-white, omnivorous mammals of N. America, esp. of the genus *Mephitis,* related to the weasels and provided with glands that eject a fetid fluid when the animal is disturbed or attacked; *informal,* a despicable, obnoxious person.—*v.t. Slang,* to defeat overwhelmingly in a game or contest, esp. so as to keep an opponent scoreless.

skunk cab·bage, *n.* A wide-leaved, fetid, N. American perennial, *Symplocarpus foetidus,* of the arum family; a similar plant, *Lysichitum americanum,* of the same family, found in the Pacific coast regions.

sky, skī, *n. pl.* **skies.** [Same as Icel. *skȳ,* Dan. and Sw. *sky,* a cloud; allied to O.E. *scēo,* a shade; also to E. *shade.*] The apparent arch or vault of heaven; the firmament. *Pl.* the region of clouds; weather; climate.—*v.t.*—*skied, skying. Colloq.* To hit or throw, as a ball, high into the air; to hang or place in an obscure or overly high position, as a painting.

sky blue, *n.* A color of blue, as of the sky on a day that is clear.—**sky-blue,** *a.*

sky·borne, skī′bōrn″, skī′bạrn″, *a.* Airborne.

sky·cap, skī′kap″, *n.* A person employed to carry passenger luggage at an airline terminal or airport.

sky·div·ing, skī′dī″ving, *n.* The sport of jumping from an airplane and performing various acrobatic maneuvers before opening the parachute.—**sky·dive,** *v.i.*—*past sky-dived* or *skydove,* pp. *skydived,* ppr. *sky-diving.*

sky·ey, skī′ē, *a.* Pertaining to, resembling, or of the sky; ethereal.

sky-high, skī′hī′, *a., adv.* As high as the sky; very high.

sky·lark, skī′lärk″, *n.* A lark, *Alauda arvensis,* common in Europe and celebrated for the song it sings as it rises in flight.

sky·lark, skī′lärk″, *v.i.* [Appar. orig. a sailor's word for frolicking in the rigging or elsewhere aboard ship: cf. *lark.*] *Colloq.* To frolic; play pranks; indulge in boisterous or rough play.—**sky·lark·er,** *n.*

sky·light, skī′līt″, *n.* A window admitting daylight through the roof of a house or a ship's deck; the indirect refracted illumination from the sky, as opposed to direct sun rays not passing through the diffusing medium of the earth's atmosphere.

sky·line, sky line, skī′līn″, *n.* The horizon that is visible; a silhouette, as of trees or buildings, observed against the sky.

sky·phos, skī′fos, *n. pl.* **sky·phoi,** skī′foi. See *scyphus.*

sky pi·lot, *n. Slang.* Any clergyman, esp. a chaplain connected with the armed forces; one who is an aviator.

sky·rock·et, skī′rok″it, *n.* A rocket that ascends high in the air, exploding with brilliant sparks and color.—*v.i.* To rise or shoot up rapidly, as prices.—*v.t.* To cause to rise or shoot up rapidly.

sky·sail, skī′sāl″, *Naut.* skī′sal, *n. Naut.* a sail in a square-rigged vessel next above the royal.

sky·scrap·er, skī′skrā″pėr, *n.* A high building, esp. an office building, characteristically American, which owes its origin to the lack of available land for building purposes.

sky·ward, skī′wėrd, *a., adv.* Directed toward the sky; on upward flight.—**sky·wards,** *adv.*

sky wave, *n.* That portion of a radio wave traveling outwards from the earth and, in some cases, reflected back by the ionosphere.

sky·way, skī′wā″, *n.* A highway which is elevated, usu. in order to facilitate traffic flow over a densely populated section of a city; *colloq.* an air lane.

sky·writ·ing, skī′rī″ting, *n.* The writing in the air, as for advertising purposes, done by means of vapor discharged from an airplane.—**sky·write,** skī′rīt″, *v.i., v.t.*—*past skywrote,* pp. *skywritten,* ppr. *skywriting.*—**sky·writ·er,** *n.*

slab, slab, *n.* [M.E. *slabbe, sclabbe*; origin uncertain.] A broad, flat, somewhat thick piece of stone, wood, or other solid material; a thick slice of anything; as, a *slab* of meat; a rough outside piece cut from a log, as in sawing it into boards; *baseball slang,* the pitcher's mound. A section or piece of concrete pavement.—*v.t.*—*slabbed, slabbing.* To make into a slab or slabs; to cover or lay with slabs; to cut the slabs or outside pieces from, as a log.

slab, slab, *a.* [Prob. < Scand.] *Archaic.* Thick in consistency; viscous.

slab·ber, slab′ėr, *v.i., v.t.* [Same as D. and L.G. *slabberen,* G. *schlabbern,* to slabber, freqs. of *slabben, schlabben,* to lap; *slaver* is akin.] To drivel; to slobber.—*n.* Slobber.

slab-sid·ed, slab′sī″did, *a. Colloq.* Having the sides long and flat, like slabs; tall and lank.

slack, slak, *a.* [O.E. *slaec, sleac,* = O.H.G. *slach* (G. dial. *schlack*) = Icel. *slakr* = Sw. *slak,* slack.] Not drawn as a rope; not tense or taut; loose; lacking in diligence; negligent or remiss; lacking in vigor or strength; slow or sluggish, as the water, tide, or wind; not brisk or active, as business or work; dull; not firm or compact; soft or limp, as a handclasp.—*adv.* In a slack manner.—*n.* A slack condition, interval, or part; a part of a rope, sail, or the like, that hangs loose, without strain upon it; a decrease in activity, as in business or work; a period of decreased activity; *geog.* cessation in flow of a current, as at a turn; *pl.* men's or women's trousers, usu. for casual wear.—*v.t.* To be slack or remiss in respect to, as some matter or duty; to neglect or shirk; to cause or allow to become slack or less active, vigorous, or intense; relax or abate, as efforts; moderate; to make loose, or less tense or taut, as a rope; to slake, as lime.—*v.i.* To be slack or remiss; shirk one's duty or part; to become less vigorous, active, or rapid; to become less tense or taut.—**slack·ly,** *adv.*—**slack·-ness,** *n.*

slack, slak, *n.* [M.E. *slak;* < Scand.] *Scot. and Brit. dial.* A depression between hills in a hillside or in the surface of ground; a boggy or wet hollow; a morass.

slack, slak, *n.* [Cf. G. *schlacke,* dross, slag, slack, also E. *slag.*] The finer screenings of coal; small or refuse coal.

slack-baked, slak′bākt′, *a.* Insufficiently baked or underdone, as bread; not well made or imperfect.

slack·en, slak′en, *v.t.* To make less active, vigorous, rapid, or intense, as efforts, action, pace, or speed; abate; moderate; to make looser or less taut, as a rein, rope, or sail.—*v.i.* To become less active, vigorous, or brisk; to become less tense or taut, as a rope.

slack·er, slak′ẽr, *n.* A person who shirks duties or work, esp. one who seeks to evade military service during war.

slack-jawed, slak′jạd′, *a.* Having one's mouth hanging open, as in surprise.

slack suit, *n.* Pants suit.

slack wa·ter, *n.* The period of time between tides, when a body of water has little or no tidal motion; water that has very little or practically no current.

slag, slag, *n.* [Same as Sw. *slagg,* G. *schlacke,* slag.] Vitrified mineral waste removed in the reduction of metals from their ores; the scoria from a volcano; cinder.

slake, slāk, *v.t.—slaked, slaking.* To quench, as thirst; to satisfy; to extinguish, as a fire; to abate; to lessen; to cause crumbling of, as quicklime, by mixing with water.—*v.i.* To become slaked.

sla·lom, slä′lom, slä′lōm, *n. Skiing,* a descent or race which requires the skier to make a series of sharp turns in alternate directions over a course marked by upright poles.—*v.i.* To ski over such a course.

slam, slam, *v.t.—slammed, slamming.* [Prob. < Scand.] To shut with force and noise, as a door; thrust or cast violently and noisily, as: He *slammed* the window. Dash or throw with a bang, as: He *slammed* the ball against the wall. *Slang,* to strike or hit violently; to criticize severely.—*v.i.* To close with a bang, as a door; dash or strike with violent and noisy impact; as, shutters *slamming* in the wind.—*n.* A slamming, as of a door; a violent and noisy closing, dashing, or impact, or the noise made; a bang. *Slang,* a violent blow; severe or captious criticism.

slam, slam′, *n.* [Origin obscure.] *Bridge.* The winning of all the tricks in ·one deal, called a grand *slam;* the winning of all the tricks but one, called a little *slam;* the bid to do so.

slam-bang, slam′bang′, *adv. Colloq.* With noisy or headlong violence; recklessly and swiftly.—*a. Colloq.* Violent and noisy; careless and quick.

slan·der, slan′dẽr, *n.* [O.E. *sclaunder, esclaundre,* < Fr. *esclandre,* < L. *scandalum,*

this word is simply *scandal* in another form.] A false tale or report maliciously uttered, and tending to injure the reputation of another; the uttering of such reports; *law,* defamation by means of an oral statement: opposed to *libel.*—*v.t.* To defame by slander; to calumniate.—*v.i.* To speak slander.—**slan·der·er,** *n.*—**slan·-der·ous,** *a.*—**slan·der·ous·ly,** *adv.*—**slan·der·ous·ness,** *n.*

slang, slang, *n.* [Connected with *sling,* being orig. abusive language hurled at a person.] Colloquial words and phrases typically more colorful, metaphorical, facetious, inelegant, vulgar, or short-lived than those in standard usage; vocabulary peculiar to a profession or group; jargon; argot.—*v.i.* To use slang; to engage in vulgar, abusive language.—*v.t.* To address with slang or ribaldry; to abuse with vulgar language.—*a.*—**slang·i·ly,** *adv.*—**slang·-i·ness,** *n.*—**slang·y,** slang′ē, *a.—slangier, slangiest.*

slant, slant, slänt, *v.i.* [Var. of earlier *slent,* M.E. *slenten,* Sw. *slinta,* to slip, glance, *slänt, n.,* slope, slant.] To have or take an oblique direction or position; to slope; to have a mental leaning or bias.—*v.t.* To give an oblique direction or position to; to write or present, as information, so as to reflect a certain attitude or bias.—*n.* A slanting or oblique direction or position; slope; a slanting line, side, or surface; a virgule; a mental leaning or tendency; a bias; a way of looking at or regarding something; viewpoint; *colloq.* a glance or look.—*a.* Slanting; oblique.—**slant·ways,** slant′wāz″, slänt′-wāz″, *adv.*—**slant·wise,** slant′wīz″, slänt′-wīz″, *a., adv.*

slap, slap, *n.* [Imit: cf. L.G. *slapp,* G. *schlapp,* used interjectionally to express the sound of a blow.] A smart blow, esp. with the open hand or with something flat; a smack; a sound like that made by a slap; a sarcastic or censuring hit; a direct rebuke, rebuff, or affront.—*v.t.—slapped, slapping.* To strike smartly, esp. with the open hand or with something flat; to bring, as the hand, upon or against something with a smart blow; to dash or cast forcibly; slam; to insult or rebuff.—*v.i.—slapped, slapping.* To strike or beat with a sharp, resounding impact, as waves.—*adv. Colloq.* with or as with a slap; smartly; suddenly; directly or straight.—**slap·per,** *n.*

slap·dash, slap′dash″, *adv.* In a careless, hasty manner.—*a.* Careless; haphazard.

slap·hap·py, slap′hap″ē, *a.—slaphappier, slaphappiest. Slang.* Punch-drunk; giddy; irresponsible.

slap·jack, slap′jak″, *n.* A simple card game in which the object of each player is to be the first to slap a jack when played; a flapjack or griddlecake.

slap·stick, slap′stik″, *n.* A type of broad comedy in which rough play and knockabout methods prevail; a stick or lath used by harlequins or clowns, as in pantomime, for striking other performers, often a combination of laths, so arranged as to make a loud, clapping noise without hurting the person struck.—*a.* Using or marked by the use of broad rough comedy.

slash, slash, *v.t.* [M.E. *slaschen,* cut, hew.] To cut or wound with a sweeping stroke, as of an edged instrument; gash; to make slits in, as a garment, in order to show an underlying fabric of different color or kind; to lash, as with a whip; to crack or snap, as a whip; to assail sharply, as with criticism; to cut, reduce, abridge, or alter unsparingly as in editing a manuscript or text or in preparing a play for the stage.—*v.i.* To deliver a sweeping, cutting stroke, as at something; to fight one with sharp strokes, as with a sword in battle; to make one's way by or as by cutting, as through the

waves.—*n.* A sweeping stroke, as with an edged instrument or a whip; a cut or wound made with such a stroke; a gash; an ornamental slit in a garment serving to show an underlying fabric, often of different color; virgule. *Forestry,* an open area strewn with debris of trees from falling or from wind or fire; the debris itself.—**slash·er,** *n.*

slash, slash, *n. Often pl., dial.* a tract of wet or swampy ground overgrown with bushes or trees.

slash·ing, slash′ing, *a.* Dealing sweeping, cutting strokes; sharp and violent, as a stroke or blow; unsparingly severe, as criticism or epithets; dashing, impetuous, or recklessly rapid; *colloq.* very large, great, or fine.—*n.* The act of one who or that which slashes, cuts, or lashes; a slash.—**slash·ing·ly,** *adv.*

slash pine, *n.* A pine, *Pinus caribaea,* with a hard, durable wood, common in slashes and swamps of the southeastern U.S.; the wood of these trees; the loblolly pine.

slash pock·et, *n.* A pocket which is set in either diagonally or vertically on a garment, accessible by an exterior, finished slit.

slat, slat, *n.* [M.E. *slat, sclat,* < O.Fr. *esclat* (Fr. *éclat*), fragment, piece, also bursting, burst, < *esclater,* to shiver, burst.] A long, thin, narrow strip of wood or metal; a lath; a support for a bed; one of the horizontal laths of a Venetian blind. *Pl., slang,* the buttocks; the ribs.—*v.t.—slatted, slatting.* To furnish or make with slats.—**slat·ted,** *a.*

slat, slat, *v.t.—slatted, slatting.* [Origin uncertain: cf. Icel. *sletta,* to slap.] *Brit. colloq.* to throw, dash, or knock with force or violence.—*v.i.* To flap violently, as sails.—*n. Brit. colloq.* A slap; a sharp blow or stroke.

slate, slāt, *n.* [O.Fr. *esclate,* fem. corresponding to masc. *esclat.*] A fine-grained rock formed by the compression of clay, shale, or sometimes coal, that tends to split along parallel cleavage planes which are usu. at an angle to the planes of stratification; a thin piece or plate of this rock or a similar material, used esp. for roofing or for writing on; a tentative list of candidates, officers, or the like to be considered for acceptance by a nominating committee or convention; a dark, dull bluish or purplish-gray color like that of slate; a record of behavior or deeds; as, a clean *slate.*—*v.t.—slated, slating.* To cover or roof with slates; to set down, designate, or schedule for nomination, appointment, or action.—*a.*—**slate·like,** *a.*

slate, slāt, *v.t.—slated, slating.* [Origin uncertain.] To criticize severely; to berate; to thrash or punish severely.

slate black, *n.* A dull black color tinged slightly with purple.

slate blue, *n.* A dull grayish blue color.

slat·er, slāt′ẽr, *n.* One who lays slates; *zool.* any of various small isopods, esp. a wood louse or sow bug.

slath·er, slaTH′ẽr, *v.t. Colloq.* to spread thickly or in a lavish manner, as jam on bread.—*n. Usu. pl.* lavish or wasteful amounts.

slat·tern, slat′ẽrn, *n.* [Prov. E. *slatter,* to spill carelessly, to waste; akin to Icel. *sletta,* to squirt; or akin to G. *schlotterig,* negligent; D. *slodderen,* to hang and flap.] A slovenly, untidy woman; a slut.—**slat·-tern·li·ness,** *n.*—**slat·tern·ly,** slat′ẽrn·lē, *a., adv.*

slat·y, slā′tē, *a.—slatier, slatiest.* Consisting of, resembling, or pertaining to slate; slate-colored.

slaugh·ter, slạ′tẽr, *n.* [M.E. *slaghter,* < Scand., from the root seen in E. *slay.*] The killing or butchering of cattle, sheep, or pigs, for food or for the market; the brutal or violent killing or slaying of a person; the killing, by violence, of great numbers of persons or animals, as in a battle or a massacre.—*v.t.* To kill or butcher, as animals, for food or for the market; to slay in a brutal or violent manner; to slay in great numbers; to massacre.—**slaugh·-ter·er,** *n.*—**slaugh·ter·ous,** slạ'tėr·us, *a.* —**slaugh·ter·ous·ly,** *adv.*

slaugh·ter·house, slạ'tėr·hous″, *n.* A place or establishment in which animals are butchered for the market; an abattoir.

Slav, släv, slav, *a.* Of, pertaining to, or characteristic of the Slavs; Slavic.—*n.* One of a race of peoples widely spread over eastern, southeastern, and central Europe, including the Russians and Ruthenians (eastern Slavs), the Bulgars, Serbs, Croats, Slavonians, Slovenes (southern Slavs), and the Poles, Czechs, Moravians, Slovaks (western Slavs).

slave, släv, *n.* [O.Fr. Fr. *esclave,* < M.L. *sclavus,* a slave, orig. (M.L. *Sclavus*) a Slav; many Slavs having been reduced to slavery by Germanic conquerors.] One who is the property of and wholly subject to another; a bond servant; one entirely under the domination of some influence; as, a *slave* to the use of a drug; one who labors like a slave; a drudge; a device operated directly by a machine or a mechanism that is under the control of another.—*v.i.*—**slaved, slaving.** To work like a slave, or to toil or drudge; to traffic in or hold slaves.

slave ant, *n.* Any ant seized by and forced to toil for ants of a different species.

slave driv·er, *n.* An overseer of slaves at their work; a harsh or exacting taskmaster.

slave·hold·er, släv'hōl″dėr, *n.* One who owns slaves.—**slave·hold·ing,** *n., a.*

slave-mak·ing ant, *n.* An ant that invades colonies of other species of ants and abducts the larvae and the pupae to be raised in its colony as slaves.

slav·er, slav'ėr, slä'vėr, slä'vėr, *v.i.* [M.E. *slaveren.*] To allow saliva to issue from the mouth; slobber.—*v.t.* To smear with saliva —*n.* Saliva driveling from the mouth; drivel or nonsense.

slav·er, slä'vėr, *n.* A dealer in or an owner of slaves; a vessel engaged in the traffic in slaves; a white slaver.

slav·er·y, slä've·rē, släv'rē, *n.* The state or condition of a slave; bondage; complete subjection; the system of keeping or holding slaves; a condition of subjection resembling that of slaves, as to a habit, influence, or the like; exhausting and mean labor; drudgery.

slave state, *n.* (*Often cap.*) any one of the fifteen states of the U.S. in which Negro slavery was legal during the pre-Civil War period. A nation or country under the domination of totalitarian rule.

slave trade, *n.* The buying and selling of slaves, esp. of Negroes prior to the Civil War.

slav·ey, slä'vē, *n. pl.* **slav·eys.** *Brit. colloq.* A female domestic servant; a maid of all work.

Slav·ic, slav'ik, slä'vik, *a.* Pertaining to the Slavs or to their language.—*n.* A branch of the Aryan or Indo-European family or class of languages, which includes East Slavic or Russian, Ukranian, Byelorussian, and West Slavic or Czech, Polish, Slovak, Wendish, and South Slavic or Bulgarian, Slavonic, Serbo-Croatian, Macedonian, and Slovene. Also **Sla·von·ic,** sla·von'ik.—**Slav·i·cist,** slä'vi·sist, slav'i·sist, *n.* One who specializes in Slavic literature or languages. Also **Sla·vist.**

slav·ish, slä'vish, *a.* Pertaining to, characteristic of, or befitting a slave; as, *slavish* submission; being or resembling a slave or slaves; servilely imitative, or lacking originality.—**slav·ish·ly,** *adv.*—**slav·ish·ness,** *n.*

slav·oc·ra·cy, slä·vok'ra·sē, *n. pl.* **slav·-oc·ra·cies.** The rule or domination of slaveholders; a dominating body of slave-holders, as in the southern U.S. before 1865.

Sla·vo·ni·an, sla·vō'nē·an, *a.* Of or pertaining to Slavonia, a region of Croatia, northern Yugoslavia, or its inhabitants.—*n.* A native or inhabitant of Slavonia.

Slav·o·phile, Slav·o·phil, slä'vo·fīl″, slä'vo·fil, *a.* Friendly to or admiring the Slavs; favoring Slavic interests or aims.—*n.* A friend or admirer of the Slavs.— **Sla·voph·i·lism,** slä'vo·fil·iz″um, *n.*

slaw, slạ, *n.* [D. *sla,* for *salade,* salad.] Sliced or chopped cabbage served uncooked or cooked, cold or hot, with seasoning or dressing; coleslaw.

slay, slā, *v.t.*—past *slew,* pp. *slain,* ppr. *slaying.* [O.E. *slahan,* or contr. *slēan,* to beat, to slay; D. *slaan,* Icel. *slā,* Goth. *slahan,* G. *schlagen;* akin slaughter, sledge (-hammer).] To put to death in a violent manner. *Colloq.* to affect powerfully; overwhelm, as: He *slays* the women everywhere he goes.— **slay·er,** *n.*

sleave, slēv, *v.t.*—*sleaved, sleaving.* [Related to *sliver.*] To divide or separate into filaments, as silk; disentangle.—*n.* A filament of silk obtained by separating a thicker thread; silk in the form of such filaments; something that is tangled or matted.

slea·zy, slē'zē, slā'zē, *a.*—*sleazier, sleaziest.* Lacking firmness of texture; flimsy, as fabric; cheap in character or in quality; as, a *sleazy,* middle-aged actor.—**slea·zi·ly,** *adv.*—**slea·zi·ness,** *n.*

sled, sled, *n.* [M.E. *sledde* = M.L.G. *sledde,* sled; akin to E. *slide.*] A vehicle mounted on runners for conveying loads or people over snow, ice, or rough ground; a sledge; a small vehicle of this kind, as used in coasting; a sleigh.—*v.t.*—*sledded, sledding.* To convey on a sled.—*v.i.* To ride or be carried on a sled.—**sled·der,** sled'ėr, *n.* One who conveys loads on or rides on a sled; a horse or other animal that draws a sled.

sled·ding, sled'ing, *n.* The act of conveying or riding on a sled; the going, or kind of travel, for sleds, as determined by the condition of the ground or weather; the state or condition of any work or progress.

sledge, slej, *n.* [O.E. *slecge,* a hammer; < *slahan, slagan,* to strike, to slay.] Sledge hammer.—*v.t.,* *v.i.*—*sledged, sledging.* Sledge-hammer.

sledge, slej, *n.* [Formed < *sled,* or perh. directly < D. *sleedse,* dim. of *sleede,* a sled.] A vehicle mounted on low runners for the conveyance of loads or passengers over snow, ice, or rough ground; a sled; *Brit.* a sleigh.—*v.t.*—*sledged, sledging.* To convey in a sledge or sledges.—*v.i.* To travel in or with a sledge; *Brit.* to sleigh.

sledge ham·mer, *n.* A large heavy hammer usu. wielded with both hands. —**sledge-ham·mer,** *v.t.,* *v.i.* To strike or beat with or as with a sledge hammer. —*a.* Crushing, as blows; extremely heavy-handed or unsubtle.

sleek, slēk, *a.* [Var. of *slick.*] Smooth or glossy to the touch or in appearance, as hair, fur, an animal, or the like; having a well-fed or well-groomed appearance; smooth or suave in speech, manners, conduct, or the like; artful or sly.—*v.t.* To make smooth or glossy; to calm or soothe. Also **sleek·en.**—**sleek·er,** *n.*—**sleek·ly,** *adv.*—**sleek·ness,** *n.*

sleek·it, slē'kit, *a. Sc.* Sleek; deceitful.

sleep, slēp, *v.i.*—*slept, sleeping.* [O.E. *slǣpan* = D. *slapen* = G. *schlafen* = Goth. *slēpan,* sleep.] To take the repose or rest afforded by a suspension of the voluntary exercise of the bodily functions and the natural suspension, complete or partial, of consciousness; to be in a state of sleep; slumber; to lie in death, or rest in the grave; to rest or lie quietly; to be quiet or still, as the sea; to be dormant, quiescent, or inactive, as faculties; to be slothful, negligent, or remiss; to spin with a smooth, scarcely perceptible motion, as a top. *Bot.* of plants, to assume, esp. at night, a state similar to the sleep of animals, as marked by the closing of petals.—*v.t.* To take rest in, as a particular type of sleep; as, to *sleep* the sleep of the righteous; to spend or pass, as the time, in sleep, usu. used with *away* or *out;* to get rid of, as a headache, by sleeping, usu. used with *off* or *away;* to provide the sleeping quarters for.—*n.* The state of a person or an animal that sleeps; a period of sleeping or slumber; the repose of death, or rest in the grave; reposeful quiet or stillness, dormancy or inactivity; the globule formed at the eye's inner corner, esp. while sleeping; *bot.* the condition of a plant when sleeping.—**sleep on,** to postpone or defer a particular decision upon.—**sleep with,** to engage in sexual intercourse with.—**sleep·like,** *a.*

sleep·er, slē'pėr, *n.* One who or that which sleeps; a slumberer; something in a dormant or inactive state, as a hibernating animal; a railroad sleeping car; a horizontal beam or plank serving as a foundation or support; *often pl.* a sleeping garment with feet, usu. worn by children. *Carp.* a piece of wood, metal, or stone serving as a sill or footing; any of the long wooden strips that underlie floorboards. *Colloq.* something which at first is not successful or promising, as a book, play, racehorse, line of merchandise, or the like, but which after a period wins acclaim and popularity.

sleep in, *v.i.* To sleep on the premises where employed, as a domestic servant; *colloq.* to sleep later than usual in the morning.

sleep·ing bag, *n.* A large, front-zippered bag made of warmly lined nylon or canvas, used for sleeping outdoors.

sleep·ing car, *n.* A railroad car fitted with berths or compartments for sleeping.

sleep·ing part·ner, *n. Chiefly Brit.* a partner whose connection with a business is not generally known and who is not active in its operation. Also **si·lent part·-ner.**

sleep·ing porch, *n.* A glass-enclosed, screened, or open porch, veranda, or other similar part of a house used for sleeping.

sleep·ing sick·ness, *n. Pathol.* a disease, generally fatal, which is common in certain parts of Africa, characterized usu. by fever, weight loss, and progressive lethargy, and caused by a parasitic protozoan, *Trypanosoma gambiense,* transmitted through the bite of a tsetse fly, *Glossina palpalis.* Also **en·ceph·a·li·tis le·thar·gi·ca.**

sleep·less, slēp'lis, *a.* Without sleep; wakeful; unable to sleep; watchful.— **sleep·less·ly,** *adv.*—**sleep·less·ness,** *n.*

sleep out, *v.i.* To sleep away from the premises on which one is employed, as a domestic servant who returns daily to her own home; *colloq.* to sleep in the open.

sleep·walk, slēp'wạk″, *v.i.* To walk while asleep; somnambulate.—**sleep·walk·er,** *n.* —**sleep·walk·ing,** *n.*

sleep·y, slē'pē, *a.*—*sleepier, sleepiest.* Drowsy or inclined to sleep; characterized by or showing drowsiness; as, *sleepy* eyes; languid or languorous, as if from drowsiness; lethargic or sluggish; quiet; as, the *sleepy* streets of the village; inducing sleep. —**sleep·i·ly,** *adv.*—**sleep·i·ness,** *n.*

sleep·y·head, slē'pē·hed″, *n.* A sleepy or drowsy person.

sleet, slēt, *n.* [M.E. *slete,* akin to M.L.G. *slote,* G. *schlosse,* hail.] Snow or rain in a half-frozen state; a covering of ice that forms, as on roads or trees, when rain freezes; the combination of rain with either hail or snow.—*v.i.* To send down sleet; to fall as sleet.—**sleet·y**, slē′tē, *a.*—**sleetier**, *sleetiest.*—**sleet·i·ness**, *n.*

sleeve, slēv, *n.* [O.E. *slēfe*, a sleeve; O.H.G. *slauf*, clothing; < root of *slip*.] The part of a garment, usu. of tubular form, that is fitted to cover the arm; a paper or plastic envelope in which a phonograph record is stored; *mach.* a tubular part that fits around a cylindrical shaft.—*v.t.*—*sleeved, sleeving.* To furnish with sleeves; to put in sleeves.—**laugh in** or **up one's sleeve**, to be inwardly amused, often with disdain.—**up one's sleeve**, hidden but readily available, as: He had several plans *up his sleeve.*—**sleeved**, *a.*—**sleeve·less**, slēv′lis, *a.*—**sleeve·like**, *a.*

sleeve·let, slēv′lit, *n.* A fitted covering of cloth, paper, plastic, or the like worn on the forearm, usu. to protect the underlying sleeve or cuff from dirt or wear.

sleeve tar·get, *n.* A cylindrical or cone-shaped cloth form trailed by an aircraft for use in antiaircraft target practice.

sleigh, slā, *n.* [D. *slee*; akin to E. *sled*.] A light, usu. open vehicle on runners generally drawn by a horse or horses, used for pleasure or for carrying passengers or goods over snow and ice.—*v.i.* To travel or ride in a sleigh.—**sleigh·er**, *n.*

sleigh bed, *n.* A bed of the early 19th century having outward scrolls on the ends of both the high headboard and footboard.

sleigh bell, *n.* A small bell, commonly attached to the harness of a horse drawing a sleigh or to the sleigh.

sleight, slīt, *n.* Skill, dexterity, or cleverness; adroitness or nimbleness, as of mind or body.

sleight of hand, *n.* Skill or dexterity in using the hands; skill in feats of jugglery or legerdemain; the performance of such feats; jugglery or legerdemain.

slen·der, slen′dėr, *a.* [M.E. *slendre, sclendre*; origin uncertain.] Small in girth or circumference in proportion to height or length, as persons, animals, or things; slim or slight of form; thin, as a book; small in size, amount, or extent; inconsiderable, meager, or scanty; thin or weak, as sound; having little value, force, or justification.—**slen·der·ly**, *adv.*—**slen·der·ness**, *n.*

slen·der·ize, slen′de·rīz″, *v.t., v.i.*—*slenderized, slenderizing.* To make or to become slender or more slender.

sleuth, slōth, *n.* [M.E. *sleuth, slōth*, < Scand.: cf. Icel. *slōth*, track, trail; also E. *slot.*] *Colloq.* a detective. A bloodhound. Also **sleuth·hound.**—*v.t., v.i.* To track or trail as a detective.—**sleuth·like**, *a.*

slew, slō, *n.* A swamp or backwater. Also *slough.*

slew, slō, *v.t., v.i.* To slue.—*n.*

slew, slō, *n. Slang*, a large amount or number.

slice, slīs, *n.* [O.Fr. *esclice* (Fr. *éclisse*), < *esclicier*, split, reduce to pieces; < Teut., and akin to E. *slit.*] A relatively thin, broad, flat piece cut from something; as, a *slice* of bread; a part, portion, or share of something; a spatula; a cut or movement as in slicing. *Golf,* a slicing stroke of the club; the flight of the ball to the right, resulting from such a stroke.—*v.t.*—*sliced, slicing.* To cut into slices; divide into parts, portions, or shares; cut through or cleave like a knife; to cut as or like a slice, often used with *off, away, from*; to remove by means of a spatula, slice bar, or similar implement; *golf,* to hit, as the ball, with a glancing stroke that causes it to curve off to the right or in the case of a left-handed player, the left.—*v.i.* To cut a slice or slices; to cut through something, as with a knife; *golf,* to slice the ball.—**slic·er**, *n.*

slice bar, *n.* A long-handled instrument with a blade at the end, for clearing away or breaking up clinkers of coal in a furnace.

slick, slik, *a.* [M.E. *slike, slyk*: cf. Icel. *slīkr*, sleek, smooth, also E. *sleek.*] Sleek, smooth, or glossy; craftily smooth of manners, speech, or behavior; artful or sly; shrewdly adroit, clever, ingenious; cleverly devised; slippery, esp. as a roadway or walkway; facile, glib, superficial, as the output of certain authors, or the magazine or book that features such writing; *slang,* excellent or first rate, used as an expression of enthusiastic approval.—*n.* A slippery or greasily smooth place or spot, as an oil-covered area on water; a wide-bladed chisel or tool used for slicking a surface. *Colloq.* a magazine printed on glossy paper; a magazine featuring facile, glib, or superficial writing.—*adv.* In a slick manner; smoothly; cleverly; quickly; glibly.—*v.t.* To make sleek or smooth; to make smart or fine, often followed by *up.*—**slick·ly**, *adv.*—**slick·ness**, *n.*

slick·en·side, slik′en·sīd″, *n. Usu. pl.*, *geol.* a rock surface which has become more or less polished and striated from the sliding or grinding motion of an adjacent mass of rock.

slick·er, slik′ėr, *n.* A long, loose oilskin or waterproof outer coat; a raincoat; *colloq.* a tricky or cleverly sly person. A sophisticated city dweller.

slide, slīd, *v.i.*—past *slid*, pp. *slid* or *slidden*, ppr. *sliding.* [O.E. *slīdan*, M.H.G. *slīten*, slide: cf. G. *schlitten*, a sledge, sled, and E. *sled.*] To move along in continuous contact with a smooth or slippery surface under the impetus of a thrust or initial effort; as, to *slide* on ice; slip, followed by *down, off*; to slip, as one losing his foothold or as a vehicle skidding; to glide or pass smoothly onward, as over ground or water or through the air; slip easily, quietly, imperceptibly, or unobtrusively, followed by *in, out, away*; go unregarded, or take its own course; as, to let matters *slide*; pass or fall gradually into a specified state, character, practice; *baseball,* to fling one-self along the ground toward a base, usu., to lessen the risk of being tagged out.—*v.t.* To cause to slip or slide, as over a surface or with a smooth, gliding motion; slip, as some article, easily or quietly, followed by *in, into.*—*n.* The act or an act of sliding; a smooth surface, esp. of ice, for sliding on; a chute for children's play. *Geol.* a landslide; an avalanche; the mass of matter sliding down. A plate of glass or film on which a picture is prepared for projection on a screen; a plate of glass or other material on which objects are placed for microscopic examination. *Mus.* an embellishment or grace consisting of an upward or downward series of three or more tones, the last of which is the principal tone; a portamento; in instruments of the trumpet class, a U-shaped section of the tube, which can be pushed in or out so as to alter the length of the air column and thus the pitch of the tone. A sledge or sled; an inclined plane for goods to slide on; a chute. *Mech.* a sliding piece or part; a rail or groove on or in which something slides.—**slid·er**, *n.*

slide fas·ten·er, *n.* A contrivance for fastening together or unfastening two edges of flexible material, as on the placket of a skirt or the sides of a briefcase.

slide rule, *n.* A device used for rapid mathematical calculation, as in engineering, consisting essentially of a rule having a sliding piece moving along it, both parts being marked with graduated logarithmic scales.

slide valve, *n. Mech.*, a valve that slides without lifting to open or close an aperture,

as the valves that control the ports in the cylinders of certain steam engines.

slide·way, slīd′wā″, *n.* An inclined plane along the surface of which things can slide.

slid·ing scale, *n. Econ.* A scale of prices for goods regulated by the variation in the price of the materials used in their manufacture; a scale of wages adjusted to the rise and fall of the market price of goods produced, the cost-of-living index, or other variables.

slight, slīt, *a.* [M.E. *slight, sleght*, < Scand.: cf. Icel. *slēttr*, Sw. *slät*, also Goth. *slaihts*, smooth, flat, G. *schlicht*, smooth, plain, *schlecht*, plain, low, base, bad.] Small in amount, degree, or the like; as, a *slight* increase; of little importance or consequence; trifling or petty; slender or slim; frail or flimsy; lacking in solid or substantial qualities, as a literary production or a person.—*v.t.* To treat as of slight importance; to treat with indifference or disrespect; disregard or ignore, as in contempt; to do negligently; to scamp, as work.—*n.* Slighting indifference or treatment; an instance of slighting treatment; a pointed and contemptuous ignoring.—**slight·er**, *n.*—**slight·ing**, slī′ting, *a.*—**slight·ing·ly**, *adv.*—**slight·ly**, *adv.*—**slight·ness**, *n.*

slim, slim, *a.*—*slimmer, slimmest.* [Same as D. *slim*, L.G. *slimm.*] Slender; of small diameter or thickness in proportion to height; slight; unsubstantial; flimsy; inferior; small or scanty.—*v.t., v.i.*—*slimmed, slimming.* To make or become slender.—**slim·ly**, *adv.*—**slim·ness**, *n.*

slime, slim, *n.* [O.E. *slim* = D. *slijm* = G. *schleim* = Icel. *slīm*, slime: cf. L. *limus*, slime, mud.] Thin, glutinous mud; any ropy or viscous liquid matter, esp. of a foul or unpleasant kind; a viscous secretion of animal or vegetable origin; as, the trail of *slime* left by a snail; *min.* a muddy substance consisting of ore reduced to a very fine powder.—*v.t.*—*slimed, sliming.* To cover or smear with or as with slime; to remove slime from, as fish for canning.

slime mold, *n.* Any of the funguslike organisms of the group *Myxomycetes*, occurring in slimy masses on decaying logs, in soil, and sometimes in living plants.

slim-jim, slim′jim″, *n. Colloq.* an unusually slender person or thing.

slim·sy, slim′zē, *a.*—*slimsier, slimsiest.* [Appar. a mixture of *slim* and *flimsy.*] *Colloq.* Flimsy; frail. Also **slimp·sy**, slimp′sē.

slim·y, slī′mē, *a.*—*slimier, slimiest.* Like or consisting of slime; covered with slime; revolting; vile.—**slim·i·ly**, *adv.*—**slim·i·ness**, *n.*

sling, sling, *n.* [Cf. Icel. *slanga*, Dan *slynge*, O.Fr. *eslingue* (< Teut.), O.H.G. *slinga* (G. *schlinge*), a sling.] An instrument for hurling stones and other missiles, consisting of a strap with two strings attached, the impetus being supplied by whirling the whole rapidly before releasing one string, thus discharging the missile; a slingshot; a bandage for holding an injured limb suspended; a shoulder strap by which something is suspended or carried, as a rifle; the act or an instance of slinging; a device fashioned by looping a rope, band, or chain so that it can hold heavy articles while being raised or lowered. *Usu. pl.*, *naut.* any of several ropes or chains supporting the midsection of a yard; that part of the yard itself which is thus supported, namely, the middle portion. A drink consisting of spirits and water, sweetened and flavored with lime or lemon.—*v.t.*—*slung, slinging.* To throw, cast, hurl, or fling, as from the hand; to throw or cast, as stones or other missiles, by means of a slingshot or other slinging device; to place in or secure with a sling in order to raise or lower; to raise, lower, or otherwise move by such means; to hang in a sling or situate so as to swing loosely; to suspend.—**sling·er,** *n.*

sling·er ring, *n. Aeron.* a tube encircling the propeller hub of an airplane and containing an antifreeze solution to be delivered to the blades under icing conditions.

sling·shot, sling'shot″, *n.* A forked piece of wood which has an elastic band fastened to the prongs for shooting small stones and pebbles; *Brit.* a catapult.

slink, slingk, *v.i.*—*slunk, slinking.* [O.E. *slincan,* to creep, crawl, = Sw. *slinka,* slink, = M.L.G. and D. *slinken,* shrink.] To go in a furtive, abject manner, as from fear, cowardice, or shame; to creep stealthily.—*v.t.* Of cows or other animals, to bring forth, as young, prematurely.—*n.* A prematurely born calf or other animal; its flesh.—*a.* Born prematurely.

slink·y, sling'kē, *a.*—*slinkier, slinkiest.* Characterized by slow, furtive, slinking movements; *slang,* delineating the figure and its movements; as, a *slinky* dress.

slip, slip, *v.i.*—*slipped, slipping.* [M.E. *slippen* = M.L.G. and D. *slippen,* slip.] To pass or go smoothly or easily; to glide or slide, followed by *along, away, down, off, over, through;* as, a scarf that *slips* off; to slide suddenly and involuntarily, as on a smooth surface; to lose one's foothold; to move, slide, or start from place, position, or fastening, as: An ax *slips* from the handle. To get away, escape, or be lost; as, to let an opportunity *slip;* to pass insensibly, as from the mind or memory; to pass quickly or imperceptibly, as time, followed by *away, by;* to get easily or quickly into or out of; as, to *slip* into or out of a garment; to go quietly or steal, as: She *slipped* in the back door. Pass superficially, carelessly, or without attention, as over a matter; to make an error or mistake; *aeron.* sideslip. —*v.t.* To pass, put, or draw with a smooth, easy, or sliding motion; as, to *slip* one's hand into a drawer; put or draw quietly or stealthily; as, to *slip* a thing out of sight; put on or take off easily or quickly, as a garment, followed by *on* or *off;* release from a leash or the like, as a hound or hawk; escape from or elude, as a pursuer; get loose or free from, as a halter or collar. *Naut.* to let go entirely, as an anchor cable or an anchor. To let pass unheeded; to neglect or miss; to pass over or omit, as in speaking or writing; to escape, as one's memory, notice, or knowledge; to shed, as the skin. *Boxing,* to evade, as a blow, by turning to one side. To bring forth, as animal offspring, prematurely.—*n.* The act of slipping; a landslide; a slipping of the feet, as on slippery ground; an error in judgment or conduct; an indiscretion; a mistake, often inadvertently made, as in speaking or writing; as, a *slip* of the tongue or of the pen; something easily slipped on or off; a kind of leash for a dog; a decline, as in amount or standard; a woman's undergarment of dress or skirt length and sleeveless. A pillowcase; also *pillow slip.* An artificial slope beside navigable water, serving as a landing place; an inclined plane sloping to the water, on which vessels are built or repaired. *Naut.* the difference between the speed at which a screw propeller or paddle wheel would move forward if it were working against a solid, and the actual speed at which it advances through water; a space between two wharves or in a dock, for vessels to lie in. *Mech.* the moving on each other of two surfaces or parts which are intended to be immovable with respect to each other; as, the *slip* of plates in a riveted joint; slippage. *Cricket,* the position of a fielder who stands behind and to the off side

of the wicket keeper; the fielder himself. *Geol.* a small fault due to sinking of one section of strata.—*a.*—**give some·one the slip,** to slip quietly or stealthily away from someone.—**let slip,** to reveal unintentionally.—**slip some·thing ov·er on,** *colloq.* to deceive.

slip, slip, *n. Bot.* a piece cut from a plant and suitable for propagation; a scion or cutting. Any long, narrow piece or strip, as of wood, paper, or land; a young person of either sex, esp. one of slender form; a paper form used as a record; as, a sales *slip;* a long seat or narrow pew in a church.—*v.t. slipped, slipping. Bot.* to take a cutting or cuttings; as, to *slip* a philodendron.

slip, slip, *n.* [O.E. *slype,* paste, slime.] *Ceram.* potters' clay reduced to a semifluid state with water, used either for coating or for decorating pottery, or for cementing handles or other parts.

slip·case, slip'kās″, *n.* A box for books, having one open side which exposes the spines.

slip·cov·er, slip'kuv″ĕr, *n.* A fitted, removable covering made of cloth or plastic used on upholstered furniture.—*v.t.*

slip·knot, slip'not″, *n.* A knot which may easily be slipped or undone; a knot which slips easily along the cord or line around which it is made. Also **slip knot,** *running knot.*

slip·noose, slip'nōs″, *n.* A noose having a slipknot which tightens when the rope is drawn. Also **slip noose.**

slip-on, slip'on″, slip'ạn″, *a.* Designed to be put on or slipped on easily, as a glove loose at the wrist; designed for slipping on over the head, as a blouse or a sweater.—*n.* A slip-on garment or article of dress.

slip·o·ver, slip'ō″vĕr, *a.* Designed for easily slipping over the head, as a blouse or a sweater; pullover.—*n.* A slipover garment.

slip·page, slip'ij, *n.* The act of slipping, as of gears; the amount or extent of slipping.

slipped disk, *n.* An inflamed or displaced intervertebral disk resulting in pressure on the spinal nerves.

slip·per, slip'ĕr, *n.* A low-cut, lightweight shoe, easily slipped on and off, worn mainly indoors for leisure or casual wear; as, bedroom *slippers;* a fancy shoe, often of colored fabric, designed for formal wear; as, evening *slippers.*

slip·per·y, slip'e·rē, slip'rē, *a.*—*slipperier, slipperiest.* [O.E. *sliper,* slippery.] Allowing or causing anything to slip or slide readily; so smooth as to cause slipping; inclined to slip away or from the grasp; not to be trusted; deceitful; tricky; unstable; changeable.—**slip·per·i·ness,** *n.*

slip·py, slip'ē, *a.*—*slippier, slippiest. Colloq.* slippery; *chiefly Brit.* adroit, nimble, quick, or quick-witted, often preceded by *to look, to be.*—**slip·pi·ness,** *n.*

slip ring, *n. Elect.* in an electric motor, a revolving metal ring which allows electricity to flow through the motor when it comes into contact with stationary brushes.

slip·sheet, slip'shēt″, *n. Print.* a blank interleaf inserted between two freshly printed sheets to avoid offset.—*v.t. Print.* to insert blank sheets between.

slip·shod, slip'shod″, *a.* Wearing slippers or loose shoes, esp. those worn down at the heel; untidy, careless, or slovenly.

slip·slop, slip'slop″, *n.* [Varied redupl. of *slop.*] *Colloq.* A sloppy food or drink; loose or trifling talk or writing; a blunder in the use of words.

slip·sole, slip'sōl″, *n.* A loose, thin sole put inside a shoe for size adjustment or warmth; a half sole between the inner and outer soles of a shoe to provide extra thickness.

slip·stick, slip'stik″, *n. Slang,* slide rule.

slip stitch, *n. Sewing,* a hemming stitch

that is not visible on right side of a garment or article. Also **blind stitch.**—**slip-stitch,** slip'stitch″, *v.t.,v.i.*

slip·stream, slip'strēm″, *n. Aeron.* the turbulent flow of air driven backward by the propeller of an aircraft.

slip-up, slip'up″, *n. Colloq.* A slip, mishap, or failure, as in a course of proceedings; a mistake, error, or oversight.—**slip up,** *v.i.*

slit, slit, *v.t.*—*slit, slitting.* [O.E. *slite,* a slit, Sw. *slita,* G. *schleissen,* to slit, to split.] To cut lengthwise; to cut into long pieces or strips; to cut a long fissure or opening in.—*n.* A long, narrow opening; a slash.—**slit·ter,** *n.*

slith·er, sliTH'ĕr, *v.i.* [M.E. *slitheren,* var. of *slideren,* < O.E. *slidrian,* freq. of *slidan,* E. *slide.*] To slide down or along a surface, esp. unsteadily or with more or less friction or noise; to go or walk with a sliding motion, as a snake; slip along.—*v.t.* To cause to slither or slide.—*n.* A slithering movement or passage; a slide.—**slith·er·y,** *a.*

slit trench, *n.* A narrow, shallow trench used by a soldier in combat as shelter from artillery attack.

sliv·er, sliv'ĕr, *n.* [M.E. *slivere,* < *sliven,* < O.E. *slifan,* split: cf. *sleave.*] A small piece, as of wood, split, broken, or cut off, usually lengthwise or with the grain; a slender fragment or piece; a splinter; a continuous strand or band of wool, cotton, or other fiber in a loose, untwisted condition, ready for roving or slubbing.—*v.t.* To split or cut off, as a sliver; split or cut into slivers; to form into slivers, as wool or cotton.—*v.i.* To split.—**sliv·er·er,** *n.*—**sliv·er·like,** *a.*

sliv·o·vitz, sliv'o·vits, shliv'o·vits, *n.* A usu. colorless, dry plum brandy, much favored in the Slavic countries.

slob, slob, *n.* A person who is untidy, stupid, or boorish; *Irish,* mud, slime.

slob·ber, slob'ĕr, *v.i.* To let saliva or other liquid run from the mouth; to slaver or drool; to gush with excessive sentimentality. —*v.t.* To wet or make foul by slobbering; to utter with slobbering.—*n.* Saliva or liquid dribbling from the mouth; gushing, excessively sentimental talk or actions. Also *slabber.*—**slob·ber·er,** *n.*—**slob·ber·ing·ly,** *adv.*—**slob·ber·y,** slob'e·rē, *a.*

sloe, slō, *n.* [O.E. *slah.*] The shrub, *Prunus spinosa;* the fruit of this shrub. See *blackthorn.*

sloe-eyed, slō'īd″, *a.* Having soft, dark, slanted eyes.

sloe gin, *n.* An alcoholic beverage or cordial, flavored with sloe.

slog, slog, *v.t.*—*slogged, slogging.* To hit hard, as in boxing or cricket; to drive with blows.—*v.i.* To deal heavy blows; to walk or plod heavily; to work hard; to toil.—*n.* A hard hit or blow.—**slog·ger,** *n.*

slo·gan, slō'gan, *n.* [< Gael. *sluagh-ghairm,* lit. 'an army cry.'] The war cry or gathering word or phrase of a highland clan; a catchword or phrase, as of a political party or in advertising.—**slo·gan·eer,** slō″ga·nēr′, *n.* One who coins or uses slogans.

sloop, slōp, *n.* [< D. *sloep.*] *Naut.* a vessel with one mast, fore-and-aft sails, and usu. one jib.

sloop of war, *n. Naut.* Formerly, a sailing vessel rigged in one of several ways and armed with 10 to 32 guns; later, any warship of greater draft than a gunboat, mounting guns on only one deck.

slop, slop, *n.* [M.E. *sloppe:* cf. O.E. *oferslop,* overgarment, Icel. *sloppr,* gown.] A loose outer garment, as a jacket, tunic, or smock. *Pl.* clothing, bedding, etc., supplied to seamen from the ship's stores; cheap ready-made clothing in general.

slop, slop, *n.* [M.E. *sloppe,* a muddy place, O.E. *slyppe,* slime, E. *slip.*] Liquid mud; a quantity of liquid carelessly spilled or splashed about; liquid refuse; *slang,* weak or unappetizing liquid or food. *Pl.* swill; the refuse of the kitchen, used as food for pigs and livestock; the remains left after distilling grain.—*v.t.*—*slopped, slopping.* To spill or splash, as liquid; spill liquid upon; to drink or eat messily and noisily; to feed with slops, as livestock.—*v.i.* To walk or go through mud, slush, or water; to spill or splash liquid; to run over in spilling, as liquid. *Colloq.* to be unduly effusive; to gush.

slop ba·sin, *n. Brit.* a deep dish or bowl into which the leavings of coffee or tea cups are poured at table. Also **slop bowl.**

slop chest, *n.* A store of seamen's clothing and personal supplies kept on board a ship for sale to the crew during a voyage.

slope, slōp, *n.* Inclination or slant; deviation from the vertical or horizontal; an inclined surface; an extent of ground marked by gradual descent or ascent. *Math.* the tangent of the angle that a given line makes with the positive x-axis when the line is drawn in Cartesian coordinates; the slope of the line tangent to the curve of a given function at a given point when the curve is plotted in Cartesian coordinates; the derivative of the particular function at this point.—*v.i.*—*sloped, sloping.* To take or have an inclined or slanting direction downward or upward from the horizontal; to slant; to descend or ascend at a slant; *colloq.* to depart or decamp.—*v.t.* To direct at a slope or inclination; to incline from the vertical or horizontal; to form with a slope or slant.—*a. Archaic.* Slanting; sloping.—**slop·er,** *n.*—**slop·ing·ly,** *adv.*—**slop·ing·ness,** *n.*

slop pail, *n.* A pail used for collecting garbage or slops.

slop·py, slop'ē, *a.*—*sloppier, sloppiest.* Muddy, slushy, or very wet, as: The ground is *sloppy* after a heavy rain. Splashed or soiled with liquid; watery and unappetizing; excessively sentimental or maudlin; loose, careless, or slovenly; untidy, as in dress.—**slop·pi·ly,** *adv.*—**slop·pi·ness,** *n.*

slop·work, slop'wurk", *n.* The manufacture of cheap clothing; clothing of this kind; any work done cheaply or poorly.—**slop·work·er,** *n.*—**slop·work·ing,** *n.*

slosh, slosh, *n.* [Cf. *slush.*] Slush or watery snow; the splash of any liquid; *colloq.* a watery or weak drink.—*v.i.* To splash in slush, mud, or water; to move about with an active splashing motion, as a liquid.—*v.t.* To splash around in a liquid; to splash with a liquid.—**slosh·y,** *a.*—*sloshier, sloshiest.* Slushy.

slot, slot, *n.* [M.E. *slot*; origin uncertain.] A narrow, elongated depression, aperture, slit, or groove, esp. one to receive or admit something; as, a coin *slot*; a position or place in a succession, series, or sequence; *aeron.* the gap in an airplane wing providing space for airflow or room for the auxiliary airfoil to be depressed in such a manner as to make for smooth air passage on the upper surface.—*v.t.*—*slotted, slotting.* To provide with a slot or slots; to make a slot in.

slot, slot, *n.* [O.Fr. *esclot*; prob. akin to E. *sleuth.*] The track or trail of a deer or other animal; the track, trace, or trail of anything.

sloth, slạth, slōth, *n.* [< *slow,* and equiv. to *slowth* (like *growth* < *grow*); O.E. *slǣwth,* slowness, < *slāw,* slow.] Disinclination to action, slạth. Indolence, laziness; any of several edentate American mammals of the family *Bradypodidae* which live in trees and are characterized by sluggish movements, slōth, slạth.—**sloth·ful,** *a.*—**sloth·ful·ly,** *adv.*—**sloth·ful·ness,** *n.*

slot ma·chine, *n.* A machine for vending small articles, gambling, or weighing, operated by dropping a coin in a slot.

slouch, slouch, *v.i.* [Origin obscure.] To sit or stand in an awkward, drooping posture; to fail to maintain an erect posture; to move or walk with loosely drooping body and careless gait; to have a droop or downward bend, as a hat.—*v.t.* To cause to droop or bend down, as the shoulders or a hat.—*n.* A drooping or bending forward of the head and shoulders; an awkward, drooping posture or carriage; an awkward, ungainly, or slovenly person; slouch hat; *colloq.* an inefficient or inferior person, esp. used negatively, as: He's no *slouch* at this game.—**slouch·er,** *n.*—**slouch·i·ly,** *adv.*—**slouch·i·ness,** *n.*—**slouch·y,** *a.*—*slouchier, slouchiest.* Not erect.

slouch hat, *n.* [Earlier *souched hat.*] A soft hat, esp. one of felt with a broad, flexible brim.

slough, slou, slō, *n.* [O.E. *slōh.*] A section of soft, muddy ground or bog; a hole full of mud or mire, as in a road, slou. A marsh or swamp; a marshy or reedy pool, stagnant pond, inlet, or the like; a boggy depression in an otherwise dry area such as a prairie, slō; also *slew, slue. Fig.* a condition of degradation, embarrassment, or helplessness; as, being mired in a *slough* of ignorance, slou.—**slough·y,** *a.*

slough, sluff, sluf, *n.* [M.E. *slughe, sloghe, slouh:* cf. M.H.G. *slūch,* snake, G. *schlauch,* skin, bag.] The outer skin of a snake which is shed periodically; any part of an animal that is naturally shed or molted; anything that is shed or cast off; *pathol.,* a mass of dead tissue which separates from the surrounding or underlying living tissue; *cards,* a discard.—*v.i.* To be shed or cast off, as the slough or skin of a snake; to cast off a slough; *pathol.* to separate from the sound flesh, as a slough; *cards,* to throw off or discard one or more cards.—*v.t.* To shed as or like a slough; to cast, throw off, or rid oneself of, usu. followed by *off*; as, to *slough off* responsibility.—**slough·i·ness,** *n.*—**slough·y,** *a.*

slough of de·spond, *n.* [< John Bunyan's allegory *Pilgrim's Progress,* the "Slough of Despond" into which Christian falls and from which he is rescued by Help.] A state of profound despondency or dejection.

Slo·vak, slō'vak, slō'väk, slō·vak', slō·väk', *a.* [Slovák and Bohem. *Slovak:* cf. *Slovene.*] Of or pertaining to the Slovaks, a Slavic people dwelling in Slovakia, a region of eastern Czechoslovakia or to the Slavic language of this people, closely connected with Czech or Bohemian.—*n.* The language or the people.—**Slo·va·ki·an,** slō·vä'kē·an, slō·vak'ē·an, *a., n.*

slov·en, sluv'en, *n.* [M.E. *sloveyn:* cf. D. *slof,* careless, negligent.] One who is habitually negligent of neatness or cleanliness in dress, personal appearance, habits, or the like; one who works or acts in a negligent, slipshod manner.

Slo·vene, slō·vēn', slō'vēn, *a.* Of or pertaining to the Slovenes, a Slavic people dwelling in the Slovenia region in N.W. Yugoslavia, and closely related to the Croats, Serbians, and other southern Slavs; of or relating to their language.—*n.* The language or the people.—**Slo·ve·ni·an,** slō·vē'nē·an, slō·vēn'yan, *a., n.*

slov·en·ly, sluv'en·lē, *a.*—*slovenlier, slovenliest.* Having the habits of a sloven; untidy in dress or appearance; careless or slipshod.—*adv.*—**slov·en·li·ness,** *n.*

slow, slō, *a.* [M.E. *slow, slaw,* < O.E. *slāw,* sluggish, dull, = D. *sleeuw* = O.H.G. *slēo* = Icel. *sljōr* = Sw. *slö* = Dan. *slōv,* blunt: cf. *sloth.*] Sluggish in nature, disposition, or function; naturally inactive or lacking in energy; dull of perception or understanding; tardy or dilatory; as, *slow* in arriving; not prompt or readily disposed, used with *to*; as, *slow to* wrath; taking or requiring a comparatively long time for

moving, going, acting, or occurring; as, a *slow* walker; not fast, rapid, or swift; leisurely; gradual, as change or growth; burning or heating with little speed or intensity, as a fire or oven; slack, as trade; causing a low or lower rate of speed; as, a *slow* track; running at less than the proper rate of speed; indicating a time earlier than the correct time, as a clock or watch; passing heavily or dragging, as time; unprogressive, or behind the times; as, a *slow* old town; dull, humdrum, uninteresting, or tedious; as, *slow* company.—*adv.*—*v.t.* To make slow or slower; retard; reduce the speed of.—*v.i.* To become slow or slower; move or go more slowly; slacken in speed.—**slow·ish,** *a.*—**slow·ly,** *adv.*—**slow·ness,** *n.*

slow·down, slō'doun", *n.* A slowing or retarding of motion or effort, esp. the deliberate reduction of effort by laborers to force concessions from employers.

slow match, *n.* A match or fuse, used for firing explosives, that burns very slowly and often consists of a rope or cord that has been soaked in a solution of saltpeter.

slow-mo·tion, slō'mō'shan, *a.* Referring to or describing motion pictures or videotapes in which the action shown appears much slower than it actually was.

slow·poke, slō'pōk", *n.* A person whose temperament or pace is slow.

slow-wit·ted, slō'wit'id, *a.* Slow of wit, of intelligence, or in understanding; dull.

slow·worm, slō'wurm", *n.* [Not < *slow,* but < O.E. *slāwyrm,* lit. 'slayworm' (< *slahan,* to slay), because it feeds on worms.] A small European lizard, *Anguis fragilis,* having a long, dark, limbless body, a small head, and tiny eyes. Also **blind·worm.**

sloyd, sloid, *n.* [Sw. *slöjd,* akin to E. *sleight.*] A system of manual training in woodworking, originated in Sweden. Also **sloid, slojd.**

slub, slub, *v.t.*—*slubbed, slubbing.* [Origin obscure.] To draw out and twist slightly after carding or slivering, as wool or cotton.—*n.* The partially twisted wool or cotton produced by slubbing; a lump, as of cotton or wool, which becomes attached to or twisted into the yarn during the process of spinning.

slub·ber, slub'er, *v.t.* To daub; to stain or soil; to perform or deal with in a hasty or careless manner.

sludge, sluj, *n.* [Also (provinc.) *slutch*; origin uncertain.] Mud, mire, or ooze; slush; sediment; swarf; broken ice, as on the surface of the sea; any of various more or less mudlike deposits or mixtures; sediment deposited, as on the sea bottom or in any container holding water; sediment resulting from treating waste or sewage; a mixture of any finely powdered substance and water.—**sludg·y,** sluj'ē, *a.*—*sludgier, sludgiest.*

slue, slō, *n.* See slough.

slue, slō, *v.t.*—*slued, sluing.* [Origin uncertain.] To turn or swing round, as the boom of a ship. Also **slew.**—*v.i.* To swing around; rotate; pivot. Also *slew.*—*n.* The position attained from sluing; the act of sluing.

slue, slō, *n.* Slew.

slug, slug, *n.* Any of various slimy, elongated terrestrial gastropods related to the terrestrial snails, but having no shell or only a rudimentary one; any of several insect larva that resemble gastropods; a slow-moving animal, vehicle, or the like; sluggard.

slug, slug, *n.* A piece of lead or other metal for firing from a gun; bullet; any heavy piece of crude metal; a piece of metal formed like a coin and used illegally as currency, esp. in parking meters and pay telephones. *Print.* a thick strip of type metal less than type-high; such a strip containing a type-high number or other mark or sign, for temporary use; a line of type in one piece, as produced by a linotype machine. *Phys.* a unit of mass: the mass of a free body which if acted upon by a force of one pound would experience an acceleration of one foot per second per second, thus approximating 32.17 pounds.

slug, slug, *v.t.*—*slugged, slugging.* [Origin uncertain.] To strike heavily; hit hard, esp. with the fist or with a bat, as: He *slugged* the baseball out of the park.—*n. Slang.* A heavy blow, esp. with the fist; a single drink of straight liquor usu. without a chaser; a shot.

slug·a·bed, slug′a·bed″, *n.* One given to lying in bed late, as from laziness.

slug·fest, slug′fest″, *n. Slang.* Any occasion characterized by brawling and aggressive behavior and in which blows are exchanged; a baseball game marked by many hits and runs by both teams.

slug·gard, slug′ẽrd, *n.* One who is habitually inactive or slothful.—*a.* Slothful; lazy.— **slug·gard·ly,** *a.*—**slug·gard·li·ness,** *n.*

slug·ger, slug′ẽr, *n.* One who slugs or strikes hard, esp. with the fists, as a boxer; in baseball, a strong-hitting batter.

slug·gish, slug′ish, *a.* Habitually indolent; inactive; lazy; not disposed to exertion; slow, as business or trade; having little motion; as, a *sluggish* stream; inert.— **slug·gish·ly,** *adv.*—**slug·gish·ness,** *n.*

sluice, slös, *n.* [O.Fr. *escluse* (Fr. *écluse*), < M.L. *exclusa,* prop. fem. of L. *exclusus,* pp. of *excludere,* shut out, shut off, E. *exclude.*] A canal or other artificial channel through which water is conducted; the flow regulated by means of a valve or gate; the body of water so controlled; a sluice-gate; floodgate; any contrivance for regulating a flow from or into a receptacle; a channel, esp. one carrying off surplus water; a drain; a stream of surplus water. *Min.* a long, sloping trough or the like, with grooves in its bottom into which water is directed to separate gold from gravel or sand; any such trough for washing ore.— *v.t.*—*sluiced, sluicing.* To let out, as water; to draw off the contents of, as by opening a sluice; to open a sluice upon; to flush or cleanse with a rush of water; *min.* to wash in a sluice.—*v.i.* To flow or pour through or as through a sluice.—**sluice·like,** *a.*

sluice·way, slös′wā″, *n.* A channel controlled or fed by a sluice; any small artificial channel for running water.

slum, slum, *n.* [Origin obscure.] *Often pl.* a thickly populated, squalid part of a city, inhabited by the poorest or lowest class of the people.—*v.i.*—*slummed, slumming.* To visit, esp. out of curiosity, slums or other areas regarded inferior to one's ordinary surroundings.—**slum·mer,** *n.*

slum·ber, slum′bẽr, *v.i.* [O.E. *slumerian,* < *slūma,* slumber; G. *schlummern,* to slumber. As to insertion of *b,* cf. *number, humble.*] To sleep, usu. lightly; to drowse or doze; to be inert or in a state of inactivity.—*v.t.* To spend sleeping, as: He *slumbered* the day away.—*n.* Sleep, usu. light sleep; repose or quiescence.—**slum·ber·er,** *n.*—**slum·ber·less,** *a.*

slum·ber·ous, slum′bẽr·us, *a.* Inviting or causing sleep; soporific. Also **slum·brous, slum·ber·y.**—**slum·ber·ous·ly,** *adv.*— **slum·ber·ous·ness,** *n.*

slum·ber par·ty, *n.* A party usu. of teen-age girls who dress in their nightclothes and stay overnight at one of the girls' homes. Also **pa·ja·ma par·ty.**

slum·gul·lion, slum·gul′yan, slum′gul″-yan, *n.* [Appar. a made word < *slum,* and *gullion,* cesspool.] A stew of meat and vegetables; a thin or watered beverage; the watery refuse from fish or whale processing; a muddy, reddish deposit in a mining sluice.

slump, slump, *v.i.* [Appar. imit.] To drop heavily; to sink into a bog, muddy place, or the like, or through ice or snow; to decline or fall suddenly and markedly, as prices, the market, or the like; to decline or fall suddenly in quality, value, efficiency, or the like; to assume a bent, slouching posture; to sink heavily, as the spirits.—*n.* The act or an act of slumping; a drop, fall, or decline; a sudden, marked decline in prices or the like; a period of decline in interest, efficiency, or the like, esp. in sports; any sustained period of unusually inferior scoring or playing; a bent, slouching posture.

slung shot, *n.* A shot, a piece of metal, or a stone fastened to a short strap, chain, or thong, used as a weapon.

slur, slur, *v.t.*—*slurred, slurring.* [Appar. from obs. or provinc. *slur,* M.E. *sloor, slore,* mud.] To pass over lightly, or without due mention or consideration, often followed by *over;* to go through hurriedly or inattentively; to pronounce indistinctly, as a syllable or word, as in hurried or careless utterance; to slander; calumniate; disparage; belittle. *Mus.* to sing to a single syllable or play without a break, as two or more tones of different pitch; to mark with a slur. To smear; smudge; blur.—*v.i.* To go through hurriedly and carelessly, as in speaking or singing.—*n.* A slurred utterance or sound; a disparaging or slighting remark; a slight; a smear; *fig.* a blot or stain, as upon a reputation. *Mus.* the combination of two or more tones of different pitch sung to a single syllable or played without a break; a curved mark indicating this. *Print.* a blur or smudge.

slurp, slurp, *v.t., v.i. Slang,* to eat or drink with audible sucking sounds.—*n.*

slur·ry, slur′ē, *n. pl.* **slur·ries.** A liquid containing solids in suspension, as water mixed with a small amount of clay, cement, plaster of Paris, or the like; *ceram.* a slip of thin consistency.—*v.t.*—*slurried, slurrying.* To prepare a slurry of.

slush, slush, *n.* [Appar. a var. of *sludge,* in part imit.] Partly melted, watery snow; liquid mud or watery mire; refuse fat, grease, or other waste materials from a ship's galley; a lubricating mixture of grease and other materials; a mixture of white lead and lime for covering bright parts of machinery to prevent rusting; overly sentimental, silly, or weakly emotional talk or writing.—*v.t.* To splash with slush or mud; to grease, polish, or cover with slush; to fill or cover with mortar or cement; to wash with much water, as by dashing it on.—*v.i.* To go through slush or mud with a splashing sound; to wash or dash with splashes.—**slush·i·ness,** *n.*— **slush·y,** slush′ē, *a.*—*slushier, slushiest.*

slush fund, *n.* A fund available for use, as in a political campaign or for propaganda, esp. secretly or illicitly, as for bribery; a fund derived from the sale of slush or refuse fat aboard ship, to be spent on luxuries for the crew.

slut, slut, *n.* [M.E. *slutte, slotte;* origin uncertain.] A dirty, slovenly woman; a slattern; a woman of loose character; a bold or impudent girl; a female dog.— **slut·tish,** *a.*—**slut·tish·ly,** *adv.*—**slut·-tish·ness,** *n.*

sly, sli, *a.*—*slyer* or *slier, slyest* or *sliest.* [M.E. *sly, sley,* < Scand.: cf. Icel. *slægr,* sly, cunning, Sw. *slög,* dexterous; prob. related to Icel. *slā,* strike, and to E. *slay.*] Cunning, artful, crafty, or wily in actions or ways, as persons or animals; stealthy, insidious, underhand, or secret; playfully artful, mischievous, or roguish.—**on the sly,** in a stealthy or secret manner.— **sly·ly, sli·ly,** *adv.*—**sly·ness,** *n.*

slype, slip, *n. Arch.* a covered passage, esp. one from the transept of a cathedral to the chapterhouse.

smack, smak, *v.i.* [O.E. *smæccan,* to taste, < *smæc,* smack, taste = G. *schmecken,* to taste.] To have a taste or flavor, as: It *smacks* of onions.—*v.t.* To have or impart a suggestion or trace.—*n.* A slight taste or flavor; savor; tincture; a small amount; a smattering.

smack, smak, *v.t.* [Cf. D. *smakken,* M.L.G. *smacken,* G. *schmatzen,* smack; prob. imit.] To separate forcefully, as the lips, so as to produce a sharp sound, often as a sign of relish, as in eating; to bring, throw, or send with a sharp, resounding blow or stroke; to strike smartly, esp. with the open hand or anything flat; *colloq.* to kiss loudly.—*v.i.* To smack the lips; to strike or come together smartly or forcibly, as against something; to make a sharp sound, as of striking against something.—*n.* A smacking of the lips, as in relish; a smart, resounding blow, esp. with something flat; *colloq.* a loud kiss.—*adv.* Suddenly and sharply; directly; straight.

smack, smak, *n.* [D. *smak.*] A sailing vessel, usu. one rigged as a sloop or a cutter, used chiefly in coasting and fishing; a fishing vessel with a well in which to keep fish alive.

smack-dab, smak′dab′, *adv. Colloq.* Precisely; adjusted exactly; directly; as, to walk *smack-dab* into a closed door.

smack·er, smak′ẽr, *n.* One who or that which smacks; *slang,* a dollar.

smack·ing, smak′ing, *a.* Resounding sharply, as a kiss or a smart blow; smart, brisk, or strong, as a breeze.

small, smạl, *a.* [O.E. *smæl* = L.G. and D. *smal,* G. *schmal.*] Little in size; not great or large; of relatively limited dimensions, as: One mountain might be *small* compared to another. Little in degree, quantity, amount, duration, or number; trivial; petty; trifling; of little talent or ability; insignificant; of little strength or force; weak; gentle; soft; not loud; characterized by littleness of mind or character; narrow-minded; ungenerous; mean.—*adv.*—*n.*—**small·ness,** *n.*

small·age, smạ′lij, *n.* [M.E. *smalege, smalache,* < *smal,* small, and *ache,* < O.Fr. *ache,* < L. *apium,* parsley.] A celery, *Apium graveolens,* esp. in its wild state.

small arms, *n. pl.* Rifles, carbines, pistols, and other firearms of small caliber designed to be held in the hands when firing.

small beer, *n.* Weak or inferior beer. *Brit. colloq.* an unimportant person; a trivial affair.

small cap·i·tal, *n.* A letter of the form of an ordinary capital of a font of specified text-type, but smaller, as in '70 B.C.' Also **small cap.**

small change, *n.* Coins of low denomination; *fig.* a person or thing of little significance or value.

small·clothes, smạl′klōz″, smạl′klōᴛʜz″, *n. pl.* Breeches or trousers, esp. the close-fitting kind worn in the 17th to the 19th century; also **smalls.** Small personal articles of clothing, as hose, underwear, and the like.

small fry, *n. pl.* Small creatures collectively, esp. young fish; young children; persons or things considered of little importance.

small game, *n. Hunting,* game animals smaller than big game, as rabbits or squirrels.

small hours, *n. pl.* The early hours of the morning; the hours immediately following midnight.

small in·tes·tine, *n.* The long, narrow, upper section of the intestines which extends from the pyloric valve of the stomach to the cecum of the large intestine, and which serves, through its secretion of enzymes, to digest and assimilate the nutritive substances.

small·ish, smạ'lish, *a.* Somewhat small.

small-mind·ed, smạl'mīn'did, *a.* Selfish, petty, mean, or vindictive; narrow-minded. **—small-mind·ed·ly,** *adv.***—small-mind·-ed·ness,** *n.*

small po·ta·toes, *n. pl., sing. or pl. in constr. Colloq.* Insignificant things or persons; something insignificant or of little consequence.

small·pox, smạl'poks", *n. Pathol.* an acute virus disease, highly contagious, and marked by fever and pustular eruptions which leave permanent scarring of the skin. Also *variola.*

small-scale, smạl'skāl', *a.* Small in size; limited in extent or output; reproducing or representing something in so small a size that relatively few details are clear.

small slam, *n. Bridge,* a little slam.

small stores, *n. pl.* Miscellaneous articles, as soap or tobacco, sold to naval personnel by the supply officer or the ship's store.

small·sword, smạl'sōrd", smạl'sạrd", *n.* A light sword for thrusting, tapering from the hilt to the point, used esp. in fencing and dueling.

small talk, *n.* Light, trivial social conversation.

small-time, smạl'tīm', *a.* Unimportant; of little or no value or influence.**—small-tim·er,** *n.*

smalt, smạlt, *n.* [It. *smalto,* kind of glass, enamel; < Teut., and akin to E. *smelt.*] A deep blue pigment prepared by powdering glass or fused silica and potash with cobalt.

smalt·ite, smạl'tīt, *n.* A tin-white to steel-gray mineral, $CoAs_2$, consisting usu. of cobalt arsenide and usu. nickel, occurring in crystals or in granular masses.

smal·to, smäl'tō, *It.* zmäl'tạ, *n. pl.* **smal·-tos,** *It.* **smal·ti.** A variety of colored glass, enamel, or the like, utilized in mosaics; a piece of such material.

smar·agd, smar'agd, *n.* An emerald.**—sma·rag·dine,** sma·rag'din, *a.*

sma·rag·dite, sma·rag'dīt, *n. Mineral.* an emerald green, foliated type of amphibole.

smart, smärt, *v.i.* [O.E. *smeortan* = D. *smarten* = G. *schmerzen,* smart; prob. akin to L. *mordēre,* to⁻ bite.] To be a source of sharp, local, and usu. superficial pain, as a wound; to cause a sharp pain, as an irritating application or a blow; to wound the feelings, as with sharp words; to feel stinging pain, as from a wound; to suffer keenly from wounded feelings; as, to *smart* under unjust criticism; to suffer in punishment, as: He shall *smart* for this.**—*v.t.** To cause a sharp pain to or in.**—*a.** [O.E. *smeart.*] Keen or stinging, as pain; sharply severe, as blows or taps; brisk or vigorous; as, to set a *smart* pace; prompt or quick in action, as persons; having or showing quick intelligence or ready capability; shrewd or sharp, as a person in dealing with others; clever, as in business dealings or in bargaining; advantageous; as, a *smart* deal or transaction; cleverly ready or effective, as a remark or rejoinder; witty, esp. in a superficial way; dashing, chic, or trim in appearance, as persons, dress, or the like; socially established or fashionable; as, a *smart* restaurant; impertinent or saucy, as remarks; *dial.* considerable or fairly large; as, a *smart* sum or a *smart* distance.**—*adv.—n.** A sharp localized pain; acute mental anguish.**—smart·ly,** *adv.***—smart·ness,** *n.*

smart al·eck, smärt' al"ik, *n.* [*aleck,* for *Alexander,* man's name.] *Colloq.* a self-assertive, conceited, irritating person.**—smart-al·eck·y, smart-al·ick,** *a.*

smart·en, smär'ten, *v.t.* To make smart or trim; improve one's appearance, followed by *up*; as, to *smarten up* your hair; to render

brisk or lively; to educate, followed by *up*; as, to *smarten up* his sales approach.

smart mon·ey, *n.* Legal damages in excess of the injury done, as for gross misconduct on the part of the defendant; money risked, as an investment or a bet, by men reputed to have sophistication or inside information; the men who risk such money.

smart set, *n.* Fashionable society people regarded as a group.

smart·weed, smärt'wēd", *n.* The marsh plant, *Polygonum hydropiper,* or some allied species, as a nettle, which upon contact causes smarting or inflammation of the skin; water pepper.

smart·y, smär'tē, *n. pl.* **smart·ies.** *Colloq.* A person who is showoffish or cocky; smart aleck; smarty-pants. Also **smart·ie.**

smart·y-pants, smär'tē·pants", *n. pl. but sing. in constr.* Smarty.

smash, smash, *v.t.* [Perh. formed from *mash* through the influence of *smite*; cf. G. *schmiss,* Sw. *smisk,* a dash, a blow.] To break in pieces by violence; to dash to pieces; to crush by a sudden blow; flatten; to wreck financially, as to bankrupt; to demolish, as a theory; to strike violently, usu. followed by *into* or *against*; to hit, as in tennis, with driving, downward force.**—*v.i.** To be broken into pieces; to be reduced to utter wrack and ruin, often followed by *up*; to become bankrupt or to fail financially; to administer a smashing stroke, as in tennis.**—*n.** A violent, shattering blow; the sound of such a blow; a destructive, smashing collision; defeat or total financial ruin; an iced drink usu. consisting of brandy mixed with water, sugar, and mint; a tennis stroke in which the ball is hit with driving, downward force; *colloq.* a resounding success, as: The party was a real *smash.***—*a.** *Colloq.* Outstanding; overwhelmingly acclaimed, as: The play was a *smash* hit.**—smash·er,** *n.*

smash·ing, smash'ing, *a.* Violent or crushing; as, a *smashing* blow. *Colloq.* outstandingly good or successful, as: They had a simply *smashing* vacation.**—smash·ing·ly,** *adv.*

smash-up, smash'up", *n. Colloq.* A smashing to pieces; a complete smash or collision, esp. one involving motor vehicles; a collapse, defeat, or catastrophe.

smat·ter, smat'ẽr, *v.t.* To have a slight superficial knowledge of; to talk or to dabble in superficially.**—*n.** Superficial knowledge; a smattering.**—smat·ter·er,** *n.*

smat·ter·ing, smat'ẽr·ing, *n.* A superficial or slight knowledge, usu. followed by *of.*

smaze, smāz, *n.* A mixture or blend of smoke and haze, less damp than smog.

smear, smēr, *v.t.* [O.E. *smerian,* < *smerõu,* grease; G. *schmer,* grease.] To overspread with anything unctuous, viscous, or adhesive; to daub; to soil or stain, as by smearing; to soil or defame, as a reputation; *slang,* to defeat overwhelmingly.**—*v.i.** To become or be overspread or smeared.**—*n.** An unctuous, viscous, or adhesive substance; a stain; material daubed on a slide for microscopic analysis; a substance to be daubed or spread on a surface, as lacquer on furniture; defamation; slander.**—smear·er,** *n.*

smear·case, smier·case, smẽr'kās", *n. Dial.* cottage cheese.

smear word, *n.* A defaming or slanderous name or epithet.

smear·y, smẽr'ē, *a.***—smearier, smeariest.** Showing smears; smeared; bedaubed; tending to smear or soil.**—smear·i·ness,** *n.*

smell, smel, *v.t.***—smelled** or **smelt, smelling.** [< M.E. *smellen,* to smoulder.] To perceive through the function of the olfactory nerves in the nose; to perceive or detect the scent or odor of; to test by the smell of; to detect by sagacity, often with *out*; as, to *smell out*

the truth.**—*v.i.** To exercise the sense of smell; to have or emit a scent or odor; to search or inquire, usu. followed by *about*; to suggest or indicate something; as, a deal that *smells* of duplicity; to be unacceptable or suspect, as: In my opinion, the entire scheme *smells.***—*n.** The sense or faculty of perceiving by smelling with the nose; that which affects the olfactory organs; an odor; scent; an instance of smelling; a faint trace or vestige, as: There wasn't a *smell* of cake left.**—smell·er,** smel'ẽr, *n.***—smell·y,** smel'ē, *a.***—smellier, smelliest.**

smel·ling salts, *n. pl.* Ammonium carbonate, often fragrantly scented, used for resuscitation and stimulation.

smelt, smelt, *n. pl.* **smelts, smelt.** [O.E. *smelt.*] Any of various food fishes of the genus *Osmerus,* having a salmonlike structure but small in size, esp. *O. eperlanus,* a European smelt, and *O. mordax,* the common American smelt; any of various similar fishes.

smelt, smelt, *v.t.* [Same as D. *smelten,* G. *schmelzen,* to melt.] To melt or fuse, as ore, for the purpose of separating the metal from extraneous substances; to obtain, as a metal, by this process.

smelt·er, smel'tẽr, *n.* One who smelts ore; a worker in or owner of an establishment where smelting is done. A place for smelting ores; also **smelt·er·y,** smel'te·rē.

smew, smū, *n.* A swimming bird, *Mergus albellus,* of the merganser family, found in the northern part of Europe and Asia, the male being black and white with a white crest.

smid·gen, smij'en, *n. Colloq.* A small bit or amount; a trifle. Also **smid·geon, smid·gin.**

smi·lax, smī'laks, *n.* [L. *smilax,* < Gr. *smilax,* bindweed.] Any plant of the genus *Smilax,* consisting mostly of woody vines often with prickly stems, and widely distributed through most temperate and tropical regions, as *S. rotundifolia,* a common species of eastern U.S.; also greenbrier. A different plant, *Asparagus asparagoides,* the smilax of florists.

smile, smil, *v.i.***—smiled, smiling.** [Same as Dan. *smile,* to smile; same root as Skt. *smi,* to smile.] To express pleasure or slight amusement by a change of the features, esp. the mouth; to express slight contempt, sarcasm, or pity by look; to look gay and joyous; to appear propitious or favorable.**—*v.t.** To express by a smile; as, to *smile* contentment; to put an end to or dispel by smiling, followed by *away.***—*n.** A contraction of the features, esp. an upward movement of the lips, expressing pleasure, approbation, or kindness; gay or joyous appearance; favor.**—smil·er,** *n.***—smil·ing·ly,** *adv.***—smil·ing·ness,** *n.*

smirch, smụrch, *v.t.* [From stem of *smear.*] To stain or discolor; to smear; to smudge or spot; to disgrace or dishonor, as one's reputation or character. Also *besmirch.***—*n.**

smirk, smụrk, *v.i.* [O.E. *smearcian.*] To smile in an affected, artificial, or offensively familiar way.**—*v.t.** To utter or say with a smirk.**—*n.** The smile or the facial expression of one who smirks.**—smirk·er,** *n.***—smirk·ing·ly,** *adv.*

smite, smīt, *v.t.***—past smote, pp. smitten** or *smit,* ppr. *smiting.* [O.E. *smītan,* to smite = D. *smijten,* G. *schmeissen,* to strike, to cast or fling; orig. to smear or defile; cf. Sc. *smit,* to communicate a disease to.] To strike forcibly; to hit with the hand, something in the hand, or something thrown; to slay; to kill; to assail or visit with something disastrous; to afflict, chasten, punish; to strike or affect with love or other sudden and powerful feeling.**—*v.i.** To strike; to administer a blow.**—smit·er,** *n.*

smith, smith, *n.* [O.E. *smith,* a craftsman, a smith; Icel. *smithr,* Goth. *smitha,* D. *smid,*

G. *schmidt*, a smith.] One who works in metals, often used in compounds; as, silver*smith*. A blacksmith; also *smithy*.

smith·er·eens, smiTH"*e*·rēnz', *n. pl.* [Perh. < Ir. *smidirīn*, dim. of *smiodar*, fragment.] *Colloq.* Small pieces or fragments; bits. Also **smith·ers**, smiTH'ẽrz.

smith·er·y, smith'*e*·rẽ, *n. pl.* **smith·er·ies**. The trade, work, or art of a smith; the workshop of a smith.

smith·son·ite, smith'so·nīt", *n.* [From J. *Smithson*, Brit. chemist.] *Mineral.* A native carbonate of zinc, $ZnCO_3$ occurring in crystals but more commonly massive or earthy, and forming an important ore of zinc; native hydrous silicate of zinc. Compare *calamine, hemimorphite*.

smith·y, smith'ē, smiTH'ē, *n. pl.* **smith·ies**. [O.E. *smiththe*, a smithy.] The workshop of a smith, esp. that of a blacksmith; a blacksmith.

smit·ten, smit'en, *a.* Struck forcibly; seriously or grievously affected; enamored or captivated.

smock, smok, *n.* [O.E. *smocc.*] A loose outer garment, usu. knee length, worn to protect other garments while working.—*v.t.* To gather by stitching through material, following a desired honeycomb pattern; to dress in a smock.

smock frock, *n.* A loose overgarment of linen or cotton, esp. of a type worn by European field laborers; blouse.

smock·ing, smok'ing, *n.* Smocked needlework; decorative stitches of embroidery used to gather cloth into even folds.

smog, smog, smạg, *n.* A mixture or blend of smoke and fog, as seen esp. in highly populated manufacturing and industrial areas.—**smog·gy**, *a.*—*smoggier, smoggiest.*

smoke, smōk, *n.* [O.E. *smoca*, smoke, akin to *smēocan*, to smoke, also to D. *smook*, G. *schmauch*, smoke.] The visible, cloudlike, gray, brown, or blackish mixture of gases and suspended carbon particles resulting from combustion, esp. of wood, peat, coal, or other organic matter; anything resembling this, as vapor or mist; something unsubstantial, evanescent, or without result; something obscuring; as, the *smoke* of controversy; an instance or the act of smoking tobacco or other smokable material; that which is smoked, as a cigar or cigarette.—*v.i.*—*smoked, smoking.* [O.E. *smocian.*] To give off or emit smoke, as in burning; to give out smoke offensively or improperly, as a stove; to send forth steam or vapor, dust, or the like; to draw into the mouth and puff out the smoke from a pipe, cigar, or cigarette; to ride or travel with great speed; *slang,* to be intensely angry.—*v.t.* To suck in and exhale the smoke of, as a cigar, cigarette, or the like; to use in this manner, as smokable materials; to expose to the action of smoke; fumigate; to cure, as meat, by exposure to smoke; to color or darken by the action of smoke; to drive from cover, as an animal, with annoying or stifling smoke, usu. followed by *out*; to bring into public view or knowledge, usu. followed by *out.*—**smok·a·ble, smoke·a·ble**, smō'ka·bl, *a.*—**smoke·less**, smōk'lis, *a.*—**smoke·like**, *a.*

smoke·chas·er, smōk'chā"sẽr, *n.* A fighter of forest fires, esp. one whose light equipment enables him to reach fires quickly.

smoke-eat·er, smōk'ē"tẽr, *n. Slang,* a fireman.

smoke-filled room, smōk'fild" rōm', smōk'-fild', *n.* A room in which private strategies and negotiations are carried on, as by politicians during party conventions.

smoke·house, smōk'hous", *n.* A building or room used for curing meat or fish by means of smoke.

smoke·jack, smōk'jak", *n.* A machine for

turning a roasting spit by means of a fly-wheel or wheels set in motion by the current of ascending gases in a chimney.

smoke·jump·er, smōk'jum"pẽr, *n.* A firefighter who parachutes to otherwise inaccessible forest fire sites.

smoke·less pow·der, *n.* Any of various substitutes for ordinary gunpowder which give off little or no smoke on exploding, esp. one composed wholly or mostly of guncotton.

smoke·proof, smōk'pröf", *a.* Impervious to smoke; intended to prevent smoke from spreading; as, a *smokeproof* door.

smok·er, smō'kẽr, *n.* One who or that which smokes. A railroad car, or a compartment in one, for travelers who wish to smoke; also **smok·ing car.** An informal gathering of men for smoking and entertainment.

smoke screen, *n.* A screen of smoke used to hide a maneuver, force, place, or activity from an enemy; *fig.* anything used, done, or said as a means of concealing the truth or facts of a case.

smoke·stack, smōk'stak", *n.* A vertical pipe or chimney through which the smoke and gases of combustion are discharged, as on a steamboat, locomotive, or building.

smoke tree, *n.* A treelike shrub, *Cotinus coggygria*, of the cashew family, native in southern Europe and Asia Minor, bearing small flowers in large panicles that give a light, feathery appearance suggestive of smoke; a related N. American species, *C. americanus.*

smok·ing jack·et, *n.* A man's lounging jacket worn in the home.

smok·ing room, *n.* A room set apart for smoking, as in a hotel, clubhouse, or the like.

smok·ing-room, smōk'ing·röm", smōk'-ing·rum", *a.* Characterized by obscenity or indecency; smutty.

smok·y, smō'kē, *a.*—*smokier, smokiest.* Emitting smoke or much smoke, as a fire or a torch; apt to emit smoke offensively or in the wrong way, as a stove or a chimney; filled with or abounding in smoke; hazy; darkened or begrimed with smoke; having the character or appearance of smoke; pertaining to or suggestive of smoke; as, a *smoky* appearance or flavor; smokelike in color, as dull or brownish gray; cloudy.—**smok·i·ly**, *adv.*—**smok·i·ness**, *n.*

smok·y quartz, *n.* Cairngorm.

smol·der, smoul·der, smōl'dẽr, *v.i.* [M.E. *smolder:* cf. D. *smeulen*, to smolder.] To burn and smoke without flame; to burn by suppressed or slow combustion; to exist or continue in a suppressed state or without outward demonstration; to display signs of suppressed feelings, as of hate or anger.—*n.* Dense smoke resulting from slow or suppressed combustion; smoldering matter; *fig.* an inward burning or continued heat of feeling.

smolt, smōlt, *n.* A silvery salmon, a year or two old, in the period of its migration from fresh water to the sea.

smooch, smōch, *v.t., n.* Smutch.

smooch, smōch, *v.i. Slang.* To kiss; caress; to neck.—*n. Slang,* a kiss.

smooth, smōōTH, *a.* [O.E. *smōth*, also *smoethe, smēthe*; origin uncertain.] Free from projections or irregularities of surface as perceived by touching; free from hairs or a hairy growth; as, a *smooth* face; free from inequalities of surface, as ridges, hollows, or obstructions; as, a *smooth* road; even; flat; generally flat or unruffled, as a calm sea; free from unevenness or roughness; as, a *smooth* voyage; having uniform consistency or being free from lumps, as batter; free from or proceeding without breaks or abrupt bends; as, *smooth* curves; easy and uniform, as motion or the working

of a machine; free from interference or difficulties; as, *smooth* progress; easy, elegant, or polished, as a speaker or writer; undisturbed, tranquil, or equable, as the feelings or temper; serene; pleasant, agreeable, or ingratiatingly polite, as speech, manner, or persons; suave; free from harshness or sharpness of taste, as wine; not harsh to the ear, as sound; *phon.* without aspiration.—*v.t.* To make smooth, as a surface, by scraping, planing, or sanding; make even, flat, or easy, as a way; as, to *smooth* one's path; remove projections or obstructions in making something smooth, usu. with *away* or *out*; as, to *smooth away* difficulties; to make more smooth or elegant, as wording; polish; refine, as manners; to tranquilize, calm, or soothe, as the feeling or temper; to make smooth, agreeable, or plausible, as speech; soothe, compliment, or flatter with soft words, as a person; to gloss over, as something unpleasant or wrong.—*v.i.* To become smooth.—*n.* An act of smoothing; that which is smooth; a smooth part of anything; a smooth place.—*adv.* Evenly.—**smooth·er**, *n.*—**smooth·ly**, *adv.*—**smooth·ness**, *n.*

smooth·bore, smōōTH'bōr", smōōTH'bạr", *a.* Of firearms, having a smooth bore; not rifled.—*n.*

smooth breath·ing, *n.* A symbol used in Classical Greek to denote the absence of an h-sound before the first vowel of a word; the written mark (') for this sound.

smooth·en, smōō'THen, *v.t., v.i.* To make or become smooth.

smooth·hound, smōōTH'hound", *n.* A type of dogfish found in European waters, esp. *Mustelus mustelus*, that lacks a spine in front of the dorsal fin.

smooth·ie, smooth·y, smōō'THē, *n. Colloq.* One who has polished manners, performs with assurance and competence, and is persuasive, esp. a man having this manner toward women; a person who is glib, or smooth-tongued.

smooth mus·cle, *n. Anat.* Any nonstriated muscle, such muscles being mainly those not controlled by the will but operant in such involuntary movements as breathing or digestion, the principal exception being the heart, which consists of involuntary but striated muscle; involuntary muscle.

smooth-tongued, smōōTH'tungd', *a.* Smooth of tongue or fluent in speech, as a person; convincing, glib, suave, plausible, or flattering, as a speaker or his utterances.

smor·gas·bord, smạr'gas·bōrd", smạr'-ga·bạrd", *n.* [Sw.] A buffet consisting of a variety of hot and cold foods, such as hors d'oeuvres, salads, cheeses, fish, and meats; a restaurant serving such a buffet; *fig.* any hodgepodge or conglomeration. Also *Sw.* **smör·gås·bord**, smœr'gõs·bõrd".

smoth·er, smuTH'ẽr, *v.t.* [M.E. *smorther* < O.E. *smorian*, to smother = D. and M.L.G. *smoren*, G. *schmoren*, to smother, stifle, to cook in a close vessel: cf. *smoor.*] To stifle, as smoke does; to stifle or suffocate with smoke or by any means of impeding respiration; to kill by depriving of the air necessary for life, often by closely covering the mouth and nose; to extinguish or deaden, as a fire, by covering so as to exclude air; to cover closely or thickly; envelop, often followed by *in*; as, a house *smothered in* vines; *fig.* to suppress as by covering up; to repress, as feelings or impulses; to check or quell, as attempts or outbreaks; to deaden or muffle, as sound. *Cooking,* to cook in a closed vessel; to cover thickly with something; as, beefsteak *smothered* with onions.—*v.i.* To become stifled or suffocated; to be prevented from breathing freely, as by smoke; to be suppressed or hidden; *dial.* to smolder, as a fire.—*n.* Dense, stifling smoke; a smoking or smoldering state, as of burning matter; a smoldering fire; dust, fog, spray, or the like in a dense or enveloping cloud; an overspreading profusion of anything; a welter.—**smoth·er·y,** *a.* Tending to smother; stifling.

smudge, smuj, *n.* [A form of *smutch.*] A spot; a stain; a smear; a blur; a smoldering fire to repel insects or protect fruit from frost; the smoke from such a fire.—*v.t.*—*smudged, smudging.* To smear or stain; to blur; to protect by a smoldering fire, as against insects or frost.—*v.i.* To cause or make a smudge; to become smudged.—**smudg·i·ly,** *adv.*—**smudg·i·ness,** *n.*—**smudg·y,** smuj´ē, *a.*—*smudgier, smudgiest.*

smug, smug, *a.*—*smugger, smuggest.* [Same as L.G. *smuck,* Dan. *smuk,* G. *schmuck,* handsome, fine, neat; akin to *smock.*] Self-important or self-satisfied; neat; trim; spruce; tidy; affectedly nice in dress.—**smug·ly,** *adv.*—**smug·ness,** *n.*

smug·gle, smug´l, *v.t.*—*smuggled, smuggling.* [Same as L.G. *smuggeln,* Dan. *smugle,* G. *schmuggeln,* to smuggle, < stem of O.E. *smūgan,* Icel. *smjúga,* to creep.] To import or export secretly and contrary to law, without payment of legally required duties; to manage, convey, or introduce clandestinely.—*v.i.* To practice smuggling.—**smug·gler,** *n.*

smut, smut, *n.* [Cf. earlier (M.E.) *smot,* besmirch, also G. *schmutzen,* soil.] A particle of soot or sooty matter; a black or dirty mark; a smudge; *fig.* obscenity, as indecent talk or writing. *Plant pathol.* a fungus disease of plants, esp. cereals, in which the affected parts are converted into a black powdery mass of spores; any of the various fungi of the order *Ustilaginales* which cause this disease.—*v.t.*—*smutted, smutting.* To smudge or soil with some black or dirty substance; *plant pathol.* to affect with smut.—*v.i.* To become smutty; *plant pathol.* to become affected with smut.

smutch, smuch, *v.t.* [Closely allied to *smut;* same as Sw. *smuds,* Dan. *smuts,* G. *schmutz,* filth, dirt. *Smudge* is another form.] To soil, make dirty, or smudge.—*n.* A smudge or dark stain; smut, soot, or grime. Also *smooch.*—**smutch·y,** *a.*—*smutchier, smutchiest.*

smut·ty, smut´ē, *a.*—*smuttier, smuttiest.* Soiled with smut, soot, or the like; grimy; dirty. *Fig.* indecent or obscene, as talk or writing; given to such talk or writing, as a person. Affected with the disease smut, as a plant.—**smut·ti·ly,** *adv.*—**smut·ti·ness,** *n.*

snack, snak, *n.* [Lit. a 'snatch' or morsel hastily taken.] A light portion of food, usu. eaten between meals, that can be prepared and eaten hastily; a portion, share, or bit of something.—*v.i.* To eat a light portion of food, esp. between meals.

snack bar, *n.* A restaurant or similar establishment which serves snacks or light meals.

snack ta·ble, *n.* A small folding table designed for informal service of food or beverages to one person. Also **TV ta·ble.**

snaf·fle, snaf´l, *n.* [Cf. D. *snavel,* a snout or animal's muzzle.] A plain lightweight bit having a joint in the middle and no curb. Also **snaf·fle bit.**—*v.t.*—*snaffled, snaffling.* To put on or control with a snaffle.

sna·fu, sna·fö´, snaf´ö, *a.* [(s)ituation (n)ormal: (a)ll (f)ouled (u)p.] *Slang.* Confused; snarled; chaotic.—*v.t.*—*snafued, snafuing. Slang,* to render confused, chaotic, or disordered.—*n. Slang,* anything in a state of confusion or chaos.

snag, snag, *n.* [Prob. < Scand.: cf. Norw. *snag, snage,* sharp point, projection, Icel. *snagi,* peg.] A short, projecting stump, as of a branch broken or cut off; any sharp or rough projection; a stump of a tooth or any projecting tooth; a branch or tine of a deer's antler; a tree or part of a tree held fast in the bottom of a river or other water and forming an impediment or danger to navigation; a jagged hole or tear made from or as if from catching and tearing on a projection; any obstacle or impediment; as, to strike a *snag* in carrying out plans.—*v.t.*—*snagged, snagging.* To run, catch upon, or damage by a snag; to obstruct or impede, as a snag does; to clear of snags.—*v.i.* To become caught in or entangled with an impediment or obstacle.—**snag·gy,** snag´ē, *a.*—*snaggier, snaggiest.*

snag·gle·tooth, snag´l·töth″, *n.* pl. **snag·gle·teeth.** [With *snaggle* appar. as a dim. of *snag.*] A tooth growing out beyond or apart from others.—**snag·gle-toothed,** *a.*

snail, snāl, *n.* [O.E. *snaegl, snegl* = G. dial. *schnegel* (cf. G. *schnecke*) = Icel. *snigill* = Dan. *snegl,* snail.] Any of various aquatic and terrestrial gastropod mollusks, esp. those of the family *Helicidae,* having a spiral shell, as *Helix pomatia,* an edible European species, and including the shell-less slug, *Limax maximus;* a slow or lazy person; a sluggard.—**snail·like,** *a.*—**snail-paced,** snāl´-pāst″, *a.*

snake, snāk, *n.* [O.E. *snaca* = M.L.G. *snake* = G. dial, *schnake,* snake.] Any of the scaly, limbless, long-bodied reptiles constituting the order *Ophidia;* a serpent; a treacherous person; an insidious enemy; *plumbing,* a flexible metal device to be fed through a curving pipe to clear it of obstruction; *elect.* a flexible, wirelike device to be fed through a conduit, pulling wires through with it.—*v.i.*—*snaked, snaking.* To progress or move in a tortuous manner, as a snake.—*v.t.* To move, twist, or wind in the manner of a snake; to make, as one's way, in a creeping or sinuous manner; to drag or haul, as a log, esp. by means of a chain or rope; to pull forcibly, or jerk.—**snake·like,** *a.*—**snak·i·ly,** *adv.*

snake·bird, snāk´bụrd″, *n. Ornith.* a fish-eating bird, *Anhinga anhinga,* having a slender head and a long, snakelike neck, inhabiting swamplands of the southern U.S. Also *water turkey,* **an·hin·ga.**

snake·bite, snāk´bit″, *n.* The bite of a snake, esp. that of a poisonous species; illness resulting from venom introduced into the body of the victim of a snakebite.

snake charm·er, *n.* An entertainer who mesmerizes venomous snakes by music or by rhythmically moving to and fro, prompting the snake to rise and follow his swaying movements.

snake dance, *n.* An American Indian ceremonial dance in which live snakes or the images of snakes are carried or imitated by the celebrants, esp. the dance of the Hopi Indians in which live rattlesnakes are held in the dancers' mouths; a parade or procession in single file that moves in serpentine fashion.

snake doc·tor, *n.* Dragonfly; hellgrammite.

snake fence, *n.* A fence of zigzag outline, made of rails laid horizontally with the ends resting one across another at an angle, and often held in place by slanting posts at the point of meeting. Also *worm fence, Virginia fence.*

snake in the grass, *n.* A hidden danger; a treacherous, yet seemingly innocent or harmless person.

snake·mouth, snāk´mouth″, *n.* An orchid, *Pogonia ophioglossoides,* of eastern North America, with rose or pink nodding flowers.

snake oil, *n.* A valueless mixture or concoction formerly sold as medicine by hucksters in traveling shows.

snake pit, *n. Slang.* A mental hospital, esp. one having inadequate facilities and offering inhumane or cursory treatment; any place where there is disorder or maltreatment.

snake·root, snāk´röt″, snāk´rụt″, *n.* The popular name of various American plants whose roots were formerly thought to be a remedy for snakebite, as the black snake-root, *Sanicula marilandica,* and the white snakeroot, *Eupatorium rugosum.*

snake·skin, snāk´skin″, *n.* The skin of a snake; leather made from such a skin.

snake·weed, snāk´wēd″, *n.* Bistort.

snak·y, snā´kē, *a.*—*snakier, snakiest.* Of or pertaining to snakes; consisting of, entwined with, or bearing snakes or serpents; abounding in snakes, as a place; snakelike; twisting, winding, or sinuous; venomous; treacherous or insidious.—**snak·i·ly,** *adv.* —**snak·i·ness,** *n.*

snap, snap, *v.i.*—*snapped, snapping.* [M.D. D. *snappen* = M.L.G. and M.H.G. *snappen* (G. *schnappen*), snap; prob. related to D. *snavel,* G. *schnabel,* beak, snout, but in part of imit. origin.] To make a sudden, sharp sound; to crack, as a whip; crackle; click, as a mechanism; move, strike, or catch, as a door, lid, or lock; to break suddenly, esp. with a sharp, cracking sound, as something slender and brittle; to break apart suddenly from tension; to flash, as the eyes; to act with a sudden movement, as: He *snapped* into action. *Photog.* to take instantaneous photographs. To make a quick or sudden bite or snatch, often with *at;* to utter a quick, sharp reproof or retort, often with *at.*—*v.t.* To seize with or as with a quick bite or snatch, usu. followed by *up,* as: He'll *snap* up their offer. To take with or as with one bite or snatch, usu. followed by *off;* as, to *snap off* his head; to crack, as a whip; to bring, strike, shut, open, or operate with a sharp sound or movement; as, to *snap* the jaws together; to address or interrupt quickly and sharply, usu. followed by *up;* to utter or say in a quick, sharp manner, sometimes followed by *out;* to break suddenly, esp. with a cracking sound; as, to *snap* a pipe stem; to cause, as a rope, to part suddenly; *photog.* to take, as an instantaneous photograph of; *football,* to put, as the ball, in play by the center handing it to the quarterback. To fire, as a gun, without first taking deliberate aim.—*n.* A sharp cracking or clicking sound, or a movement or action causing such a sound; as, a *snap* of a whip; a catch or fastener operating with such a sound; a sudden breaking, as of something brittle or tense, or a sharp, cracking sound caused by it; briskness, vigor, or energy, as of persons or actions; a quick, sharp speech or manner of speaking; a quick or sudden bite or snatch, as at something; something obtained by or as by biting or snatching; a short spell, as of cold weather; *photog.* a snapshot; *colloq.* an easy and profitable or agreeable position or piece of work. A small, thin, brittle, or crisp cake; as, a ginger*snap;* a bit or morsel. —*a.* Shutting with a snap; without thought; *colloq.* easy.—*adv.* Briskly.—**snap** one's **fin·gers at,** to be indifferent to.—**snap out of it,** *colloq.* to recover.—**snap·per,** *n.*

snap·back, snap´bak″, *n.* A sudden or abrupt recovery or rebound. *Football,* the snapping or passing back of the ball by the center which puts it in play; an instance of snapping.

snap bean, *n.* Any of various kinds of beans whose unripe pods, which break with a snap, are used as food; the pod itself. Also **string bean.**

snap brim, *n.* A man's hat, usu. of felt, with a flexible brim turned down in front and up in back.—**snap-brim, snap-brimmed,** snap´brim″, *a.*

snap·drag·on, snap´drag″on, *n.* A plant of the genus *Antirrhinum,* esp. *A. majus,* an herb long cultivated for its spikes of showy flowers of various colors, with corollas suggesting the mouth of a dragon.

snap fas·ten·er, *n.* A small disk-shaped fastener consisting of two interlocking parts which may be snapped together, as for closing a placket on a skirt.

snap·per, snap'ẽr, *n. pl.* **snap·per, snap·-pers.** Any of various large, edible, marine fishes of the family *Lutjanidae*, abundant off the coast of Florida, as *Lutjanus black-fordii*, the red snapper; any of various other fishes, as *Pagrosomus auratus* of Australia and New Zealand, and *Pomatomus saltratix*, the bluefish.

snap·per, snap'ẽr, *n.* One who or that which snaps; a snappish person; a snapping turtle; a snapping beetle.

snap·per·back, snap'ẽr·bak″, *n. Football,* the center who snaps or passes back the ball, thus putting it in play.

snap·ping bee·tle, *n.* Any of several beetles of the family *Elateridae*, able to right themselves with a clicking noise when on their backs. Also **click bee·tle.**

snap·ping tur·tle, *n.* A large edible turtle, *Chelydra serpentina*, of N. American rivers, having powerful jaws; any other member of the freshwater turtle family, *Chelydridae*.

snap·pish, snap'ish, *a.* Apt to snap or bite; apt to use sharp words; sharp, irritable, or impatient in reply or speech; cross.— **snap·pish·ly,** *adv.*—**snap·pish·ness,** *n.*

snap·py, snap'ē, *a.*—*snappier, snappiest.* Snappish, as a dog or a person; snapping or crackling in sound, as a fire; quick or sudden in action or performance. *Colloq.* lively; brisk; stylish or smart.—**make it snap·py,** *slang,* hurry up; be quick.— **snap·pi·ly,** *adv.*—**snap·pi·ness,** *n.*

snap roll, *n. Aeron.* an aerial maneuver in which an airplane is made to effect a quick, complete roll about its longitudinal axis while keeping an almost level flight.

snap·shoot, snap'shōt″, *v.t.*—*snapshot, snap-shooting.* To photograph in a quick, informal way.—**snap·shoot·er,** *n.*

snap·shot, snap'shot″, *n.* A photograph, usu. small and informal, taken with a hand-held camera; *hunting,* a quick shot fired without aiming.

snare, snâr، *n.* [O.E. *snear*, a snare, a noose; Icel. *snara*, Dan. *snare*, a snare, D. *snaar*, a string; < a root meaning to twist, seen also in L. *nervus*.] A contrivance, as a noose or set of nooses, by which a bird or other small animal may be entangled; a trap; anything that serves to entangle or entrap one; a lure; *surg.* a looped wire instrument for excising tumors or other such growths; *mus.* one of the spiraled metal or catgut strings stretched across a head of a snare drum.—*v.t.*—*snared, snaring.* To catch with a snare; to trap; to catch or take by guile or trickery.— **snar·er,** *n.*

snare drum, *n.* A small, double-headed drum carried at the side, having snares stretched across the lower head which produce a rattling or reverberating effect.

snarl, snärl, *v.t.* [A freq. < *snare*.] To entangle; to form knots in, as string; to create confusion; to complicate; to emboss, as thin metal.—*v.i.* To become complicated or entangled.—*n.* A knot; a complication; a confused state.—**snarl·er,** *n.*—**snarl·y,** *a.*

snarl, snärl, *v.i.* [A freq. corresponding to old *snar* = L.G. and O.D. *snarren*, G. *schnarren*, to snarl; akin to *snore, snort*.] To growl exposing the teeth, as an angry dog; to speak in belligerent and surly tones.—*v.t.* To express in an angry and threatening manner; as, to *snarl* a reply.—*n.* A menacing growl.—**snarl·er,** *n.*—**snarl·-ing·ly,** *adv.*—**snarl·y,** *a.*

snatch, snach, *v.i.* [M.E. *snacchen, snecchen*; origin uncertain: cf. *snack.*] To make a sudden motion or effort to seize something, as with the hand, usu. followed by *at*; to

catch or grasp, followed by *at.*—*v.t.* To seize or take by a sudden or hasty grasp, often used with *up, from, out of,* or *away*; to take, get, or secure suddenly or hastily; as, to *snatch* a kiss; to remove suddenly, often used with *away* or *from*; to rescue or save by prompt action; as, to *snatch* from danger or death; *slang,* to kidnap.—*n. pl.* **snatch·es.** An act of snatching; a sudden motion to seize something; a hasty catch, grasp, or grab; something snatched or taken hastily; a bit, scrap, or fragment of something; a brief spell of effort, activity, or any experience; as, to work in *snatches*; a brief period or space of time; *slang,* a kidnaping.—**snatch·er,** *n.*

snatch block, *n. Naut.* a block with an opening in one side to receive the bight of a rope.

snatch·y, snach'ē, *a.*—*snatchier, snatchiest.* Consisting of, occurring in, or characterized by snatches; spasmodic; irregular; as, *snatchy* reading.—**snatch·i·ly,** *adv.*

snath, snath, *n.* [Var. of *snead*.] The shaft or handle of a scythe. Also **snathe,** snāᴛʜ.

snaz·zy, snaz'ē, *a.*—*snazzier, snazziest. Slang.* Stylish; fancy; flashy.

sneak, snēk, *v.i.*—*sneaked* or dial. *snuck, sneaking.* [Origin uncertain: cf. O.E. *snican*, creep, crawl, as a reptile.] To go in a stealthy or furtive manner, as if afraid or ashamed to be seen, usu. followed by *about, along, in, off,* or *out*; slink; skulk; to go away quickly and quietly; to act in a furtive, underhand, or mean way; *Brit. slang,* to inform or tell tales.—*v.t.* To move, put, or pass in a stealthy or furtive manner; as, to *sneak* a thing out of the house. *Colloq.* to take surreptitiously; to steal.—*n.* One who sneaks; a sneaking, underhanded, or contemptible person; an act of sneaking; *colloq.* a going away quietly or a stealthy departure; *pl., colloq.* sneakers.—*a.* Stealthy; happening without warning or as a surprise.

sneak·er, snē'kẽr, *n.* One who sneaks; a sneak; *colloq.* tennis shoe.

sneak·ing, snē'king, *a.* Acting in a furtive or underhanded way; deceitfully underhanded, as actions; contemptible; secret or not generally avowed, as a feeling, notion, or suspicion.—**sneak·ing·ly,** *adv.*

sneak pre·view, *n.* The showing of a motion picture prior to its release in order to determine audience reactions.

sneak thief, *n.* One who steals without using force or violence, as by sneaking into houses through unlocked doors or windows.

sneak·y, snē'kē, *a.*—*sneakier, sneakiest.* Pertaining to or acting like a sneak; deceitful; sneaking.—**sneak·i·ly,** *adv.*— **sneak·i·ness,** *n.*

sneer, snēr, *v.i.* [Same as Dan. *snaerre*, to snarl; allied to *snarl.*] To show contempt by a particular facial expression; to insinuate contempt in words; to speak or write derisively.—*v.t.* To utter with a sneer.—*n.* A look of contempt or disdain; an oral expression of contemptuous scorn; indirect expression of contempt.—**sneer·er,** *n.*—**sneer·ing·ly,** *adv.*

sneeze, snēz, *v.i.*—*sneezed, sneezing.* [M.E. *snesen,* for *fnesen,* < O.E. *fnēosan* = D. *fniezen,* sneeze, = Icel. *fnȳsa,* Sw. *fnysa,* Dan. *fnyse,* snort.] To emit air or breath suddenly, forcibly, and audibly through the nose and mouth by involuntary, spasmodic action.—*n.* An act or sound of sneezing.— **sneeze at,** *colloq.* To show contempt for or treat with contempt; to consider lightly.— **sneez·er,** *n.*—**sneez·y,** *a.*

sneeze·weed, snēz'wēd″, *n.* The herb *Helenium autumnale,* a North American composite plant, the powdered leaves and flowers of which produce violent sneezing when snuffed; any of various other plants of the genus *Helenium.*

sneeze·wort, snēz'wụrt″, *n.* A perennial,

white-flowered plant, *Achillea ptarmica,* of Europe and Asia, whose powdered leaves cause sneezing.

snell, snel, *n.* [Origin obscure.] A short piece of gut, nylon, or horsehair by which a fishhook is attached to a fishing line.

snell, snel, *a.* Severe; piercing; quick.

snick, snik, *n.* [Icel. *snikka,* to cut or work with a knife; D. *snik* a chisel.] A small cut or mark; nick; *cricket,* a quick hit to a ball. —*v.t.* To cut, esp. slightly; to clip or snip; to hit with a sharp blow; *cricket,* to give, as the ball, a quick or glancing hit.

snick, snik, *v.t.* [Imit.] To cause to make a clicking sound; to snap, as a gun.—*v.i.* To make a slight, sharp sound; to click.— *n.* A snicking sound; a click.

snick·er, snik'ẽr, *v.i.* [Imit. of the sound.] To laugh in a partially smothered way, usu. indicating derision; to titter.—*v.t.* To express audibly with a snicker.—*n.* A half-smothered, usu. derisive laugh. Also **snig·ger.**

snick·er·snee, snik'ẽr·snē″, *n.* [From an old phrase, *snick or snee* (also *snick and snee*), by corruption < D. *steken,* stick, stab, and *snijden,* cut.] A large knife for use as a weapon. Also **snick-a-snee, snick-or-snee.**

snide, snīd, *a.*—*snider, snidest.* Malicious; insinuating; slyly derogatory.

sniff, snif, *v.i.* [A lighter form of snuff.] To draw air audibly through the nose, usu. in a series of quick inhalations; to convey scorn or disdain by or as by short, quick breaths, followed by *at.*—*v.t.* To draw in through the nose, as odors or air; to sense as by sniffing; as, to *sniff* impending danger.—*n.* The act of sniffing; the sound so produced; that which is sniffed; as, a *sniff* of fresh air.

snif·fle, snif'l, *v.i.*—*sniffled, sniffling.* [Freq. of *sniff:* cf. *snivel.*] To sniff repeatedly, as from a cold in the head or from repressing tearful emotion.—*n.* An act or sound of sniffling; *pl.* a condition, as nasal congestion, marked by sniffling, usu. preceded by *the.*— **snif·fler,** *n.*

snif·fy, snif'ē, *a.*—*sniffier, sniffiest. Colloq.* Inclined to sniff, as in disdain; disdainful; supercilious.—**sniff·i·ly,** *adv.*—**sniff·i·-ness,** *n.*—**sniff·ish,** *a.*—**sniff·ish·ly,** *adv.* —**sniff·ish·ness,** *n.*

snif·ter, snif'tẽr, *n.* A large bowl-shaped glass, usu. with a short stem, which permits the user to warm the contents, as brandy, with both hands and inhale or sniff the aroma through the narrower top; *slang,* a drink of liquor, usu. a small one.

snig·gle, snig'l, *v.i.*—*sniggled, sniggling.* [< *snig.*] To fish for eels by thrusting a baited hook into their holes or lurking places.—*v.t.* To take or catch, as an eel, by sniggling.—**snig·gler,** snig'lẽr, *n.*

snip, snip, *v.t.*—*snipped, snipping.* [D. *snippen,* snip, clip = G. *schnippen,* snip, snap.] To cut with a small, quick stroke, or a succession of such strokes, as with scissors; to take off by or as by cutting in this way.—*v.i.* To cut with small, quick strokes.—*n.* An act of snipping, as with scissors; a small cut made by snipping; a small piece snipped off; a small piece, bit, or amount of anything; *colloq.* a young, small, or insignificant person; *pl.* small, sturdy shears used in cutting sheet metal.— **snip·per,** *n.*

snipe, snip, *n. pl.* **snipes, snipe.** [M.E. *snype:* cf. Icel. *snipa,* M.D. and M.L.G. *snippe,* G. *schnepfe,* snipe.] *Ornith.* any of a group of long-billed game birds frequenting marshy places, as the jacksnipe or Wilson's snipe of N. America, *Capella gallinago,* and a common European species, *C. media;* any of various birds related to or resembling snipes. A shot fired from a concealed position; a despicable person.—*v.i.*—*sniped, sniping.* To shoot or hunt snipe; to shoot at soldiers or civilians at will from under-cover, as a hunter picking off game.—*v.t.* To shoot at or shoot by sniping.—**snip·er,** *n.*

snip·er·scope, snī′pêr·skōp″, *n.* A snooperscope devised for attachment to a rifle.

snip·pet, snip′it, *n.* [Dim. of *snip,* a part.] A small fragment snipped off; a bit or scrap; a small part or share. *Colloq.* a person who is small; anyone regarded as insignificant; a snip.

snip·py, snip′ē, *a.*—*snippier, snippiest.* [< *snip, v.* and *n.*] *Colloq.* sharp or curt in speech or manner, esp. in a supercilious way. Scrappy or fragmentary. Also **snip·-pe·ty.**—**snip·pi·ness, snip·pet·i·ness,** *n.*—**snip·pi·ly,** *adv.*

snips, snips, *n. pl., sing. or pl. in constr.* [Pl. of *snip, n.*] Small, stout hand shears, esp. for the use of workers in sheet metal.

snit, snit, *n.* A state of agitation or vexation.

snitch, snich, *v.t.* [Origin obscure.] *Colloq.* To steal or swipe; pilfer.—*v.i. Colloq.* To turn informer; to tattle; to inform or tell, usu. followed by *on.*—**snitch·er,** *n.*

sniv·el, sniv′l, *v.i.*—*sniveled, sniveling,* Brit. *snivelled, snivelling.* [M.E. *snyvelen, snevelen*: cf. O.E. *snyflung,* sniveling, < *snofl,* mucus of the nose.] To weep or cry with sniffling; to affect a tearful state; whine; to run at the nose; to sniffle; to draw up mucous audibly through the nose.—*v.t.* To utter with sniveling or sniffing.—*n.* Weak, forced, or pretended weeping; a light sniff, as in weeping; a hypocritical show of feeling; mucous running from the nose; *pl.* a mild head cold, usu. preceded by *the.*—**sniv·el·-er,** Brit. **sniv·el·ler,** *n.*

snob, snob, *n.* [Origin unknown.] One who snubs people whom he considers his social or intellectual inferiors, and who cultivates and imitates persons of wealth, social status, and intelligence; an individual having a smug, superior attitude; a person who apes gentility or pretends to intellectual superiority.—**snob·ber·y,** snob′e·rē, *n. pl.* **snob·ber·ies.**

snob·bish, snob′ish, *a.* Characteristic of or resembling a snob.—**snob·bish·ly,** *adv.*—**snob·bish·ness,** *n.*

snob·by, snob′ē, *a.*—*snobbier, snobbiest.* Exclusive; snobbish.

snood, snōd, *n.* [O.E. *snōd.*] A band or fillet for confining the hair; a meshlike cap for holding a woman's hair in place; the distinctive hairband formerly worn by young unmarried women in Scotland and northern England; *fishing,* a snell.—*v.t.* To bind or confine with a snood, as hair; to attach to another line with a snood, as a fishhook.

snook, snŏk, snụk, *n. pl.* **snook, snooks.** Any of several spiny-finned fishes, genus *Centropomus,* esp. *C. undecimalis,* a large pikelike food and game fish found in the warm Atlantic waters from Florida to Brazil; any of a variety of similar fishes.

snook, snụk, snŏk, *n.* A defiant or disrespectful gesture made by thumbing one's nose.

snook·er, snụk′êr, *n. Billiards,* a kind of pool game in which any one of 15 red balls, having a point value of one each, must be pocketed before playing the remaining 6 balls of other colors and higher values.

snoop, snōp, *v.i.* [D. *snoepen.*] *Colloq.* to prowl or pry.—*n.* An act or instance of snooping; one who snoops.—**snoop·y,** *a.*—*snoopier, snoopiest.*—**snoop·er,** *n.*

snoop·er·scope, snō′pêr·skōp″, *n.* A device which, by means of reflected infrared radiations, provides visual access to objects in the dark.

snoot, snōt, *n. Slang,* the nose. *Colloq.* a contemptuous grimace; a snob.

snoot·y, snō′tē, *a.*—*snootier, snootiest. Colloq.* Snobbish; contemptuous; haughty.—**snoot·i·ly,** *adv.*—**snoot·i·ness,** *n.*

snooze, snōz, *v.i.*—*snoozed, snoozing.* [Origin obscure.] *Colloq.* To sleep; slumber; doze; nap.—*n. Colloq.* A short sleep; a doze; a nap.—**snooz·er,** *n.*

snore, snōr, snár, *v.i.*—*snored, snoring.* [M.E. *snoren,* snort, snore; prob. imit.: cf. *snort.*] To breathe during sleep through the open mouth, or the mouth and nose, making hoarse or harsh sounds.—*v.t.* To spend or pass, as time, in snoring, usu. followed by *away* or *out.*—*n.* An act of snoring, or the sound made; a loud, harsh respiration during sleep.—**snor·er,** *n.*

snor·kel, snár′kel, *n.* [G. *schnörkel,* spiral.] A device enabling a submarine to stay submerged for long periods, made up of tubes projecting above the water's surface for intake and exhaust of air; a mouth-held tube enabling a swimmer or skin diver to breathe with his face in the water.—*v.i.* To swim underwater, breathing by means of a snorkel. Also *schnorkel.*

snort, snárt, *v.i.* [M.E. *snorten,* snort, snore; prob. imit.: cf. *snore.*] To force the breath violently through the nostrils with a loud, harsh sound, as a horse; to make some sound resembling this; to express contempt, indignation, or the like by such a sound; *colloq.* to laugh outright or boisterously.—*v.t.* To utter with a snort; to force out by or as by snorting.—*n.* An act or sound of snorting; *colloq.* a small quick drink, usu. of straight liquor.—**snort·er,** snár′tèr, *n.* That which or one who snorts; *colloq.* anything that is exceptional or extraordinary.

snot, snot, *n.* [M.E. *snotte* = D. *snot.*] *Vulgar,* nasal mucus; *slang,* a low person.—**snot·ty,** *a.*—*snottier, snottiest. Slang.* Impudent; contemptible.

snout, snout, *n.* [M.E. *snoute, snute,* = D. *snuit* = M.L.G. *snūte* = G. *schnauze,* snout.] A part of an animal's head projecting forward and containing the nose or the nose and jaws; the muzzle; the proboscis of any animal; *entom.* a rostrum, as of an insect, esp. the snout beetle. Anything that resembles or suggests an animal's snout in shape or function; a nozzle or spout; *colloq.* a person's nose, esp. when large or prominent.—**snout·ed,** *a.*—**snout·ish,** *a.*—**snout·y,** *a.*

snout bee·tle, *n.* Any of a large group of beetles constituting the suborder *Rhynchophora,* having the head prolonged into a snout or beak, often injurious to cultivated plants; a weevil; a curculio.

snow, snō, *n.* [O.E. *snaw* = D. *sneeuw* = G. *schnee* = Icel. *snær* = Goth. *snaiws,* snow; akin to L. *niv* = (nom. *nix*), Gr. *nipha* (acc.) snow.] The aqueous vapor of the atmosphere precipitated in partially frozen, usu. hexagonal, white, crystalline flakes; these flakes as forming a layer on the ground or elsewhere; the fall of these flakes when the temperature falls below 32° F.; a snowfall or snowstorm; something resembling snow, as in color or texture; any of various congealed or chemical substances of snowlike appearance; as, carbon dioxide *snow; slang,* cocaine or heroin. *Poet.* the white hair of age; white blossoms; the white color of snow.—*v.i.* To send down snow; to fall or descend like snow.—*v.t.* To let fall, as or like snow; to cover, bury, or obstruct with or as with snow, usu. followed by *over, under,* or *up; slang,* to overwhelm or impress with glib charm or persuasiveness.

snow·ball, snō′bál″, *n.* A round mass of snow pressed or rolled together; any of various shrubs, genus *Viburnum,* with white, sterile flowers in large globular clusters; any of various desserts or confections having the appearance of a ball of snow.—*v.t.* To throw or pelt snowballs at; to cause to increase, become larger,

multiply, or accumulate at a quickly accelerating speed.—*v.i.* To throw snowballs; to increase, become larger, multiply, or accumulate at a quickly accelerating speed.

snow·bell, snō′bel″, *n.* Any of several small trees or shrubs of the genus *Styrax,* bearing clusters of white flowers, esp. *S. americana* of the southeastern U.S.

snow·ber·ry, snō′ber″ē, snō′be·rē, *n. pl.* **snow·ber·ries.** A honeysuckle shrub, *Symphoricarpos albus,* native in North America, cultivated for its ornamental white berries; the berry itself.

snow·bird, snō′bûrd″, *n.* The junco; the snow bunting; *slang,* a person addicted to cocaine or heroin.

snow blind·ness, *n.* Temporarily reduced sight caused by the glare of sunlight reflected by snow.—**snow-blind,** snō′-blind″, *a.*

snow·blink, snō′blingk″, *n.* The peculiar white, glary reflection that arises from fields of snow.

snow·blow·er, snō′blō″êr, *n.* A snowplow that operates by drawing the snow through the machine and blowing it aside.

snow·boots, snō′bōts″, *n. pl.* Galoshes.

snow·bound, snō′bound″, *a.* Shut in, confined, or brought to a halt by snow.

snow·broth, snō′bráth″, snō′broth″, *n.* Melting or melted snow; a snow and water mixture; any extremely cold liquid.

snow bunt·ing, *n.* A bunting, *Plectrophenax nivalis,* inhabiting cold regions, commonly of a white color varied with black or brown. Also *snowbird, snowflake.*

snow·bush, snō′bush″, *n.* Any of several ornamental shrubs bearing a profusion of white flowers, as *Ceanothus velutinus,* a tall shrub belonging to the buckthorn family, of western N. America.

snow·cap, snō′kap″, *n.* A covering of snow that forms a cap on the top of anything, as on the peak of a mountain.—**snow-capped,** snō′kapt″, *a.*

snow·drift, snō′drift″, *n.* A bank or mass of snow driven together by the wind.

snow·drop, snō′drop″, *n.* A low, bulbous, European plant, *Galanthus nivalis,* bearing solitary, drooping, white flowers which appear very early in the year.

snow·fall, snō′fál″, *n.* A fall of snow; the amount of snow falling at a particular place, or in a given time.

snow fence, *n.* A lightweight, wood lath fence woven with wire, placed in winter along the windward side of a highway, railroad, and the like to impede drifting snow.

snow·field, snō′fēld″, *n. Geol.* a broad, flat expanse of snow which continues to exist perennially.

snow·flake, snō′flāk″, *n.* One of the small feathery masses or flakes in which snow falls; *ornith.* the snow bunting; *bot.* any of certain European plants of the amaryllis family, genus *Leucojum,* resembling the snowdrop.

snow job, *n. Slang,* an effort to persuade or influence by means of misleading, exaggerated, or insincere talk.

snow leop·ard, *n.* A large cat, *Panthera uncia,* of mountainous regions of central Asia, having long, light-colored fur spotted with black. Also *ounce.*

snow lil·y, *n.* A dogtooth lily, *Erythronium grandiflorum,* of the Rocky Mountain region, with bright white or yellow flowers.

snow line, *n.* The line above which mountains are covered with perpetual snow; the line of latitude which marks the limit of snowfall area at sea level. Also **snow lim·it.**

snow·man, snō′man″, *n. pl.* **snow·men.** A figure made of snow that is packed to suggest a man's form.

snow·mo·bile, snō′mo·bēl″, *n.* An automotive vehicle designed for traveling on snow.

snow-on-the-moun·tain, snō′on·THe·-moun′tan, snō′an·THe·moun′tan, *n.* A plant, *Euphorbia marginata*, native to the western U.S. but now commonly cultivated in eastern U.S., and named for the broad white margins on its prominent greenish bracts.

snow·pack, snō′pak″, *n.* An upland area of hard-packed snow which melts gradually during the summer and provides water for the irrigation of fields below.

snow plant, *n.* A bright red herb, *Sarcodes sanguinea*, native to the forested areas of the high Sierras of California, often found blooming while the snow is still on the ground; algae of the genus *Spherella*, which, in abundance, give a reddish cast to the surface of the snow on which they are found.

snow·plow, snō′plou″, *n.* An automotive implement for clearing away the snow from roads, railroads, and other surfaces; *skiing*, a maneuver made by forcing the heels of the skis apart in order to turn, slow down, or stop.

snow pud·ding, *n.* A fluffy pudding made with flavored gelatin, sugar, and stiffly beaten egg whites.

snow·shed, snō′shed″, *n.* A structure, as over a portion of railroad tracks on a mountainside, for protection against snow.

snow·shoe, snō′shō″, *n.* A contrivance, esp. a light racket-shaped frame across which is stretched a network of rawhide, attached to the foot to enable the wearer to walk on deep snow without sinking in. —*v.i.*—*snowshoed, snowshoeing.* To walk or travel on snowshoes.—**snow·sho·er,** *n.*

snow·slide, snō′slid″, *n.* The sliding down of a mass of snow on a steep slope; the mass of snow.

snow·suit, snō′sōt″, *n.* An outer garment consisting of a jacket and long trousers either in one or two pieces, and worn by children in winter weather.

snow tire, *n.* A tire, as of an automobile, which has a deep tread for added traction on icy and snowy surfaces.

snow train, *n.* A train carrying passengers to winter sports areas.

snow-white, snō′hwīt′, snō′wīt′, *a.* White as snow.

snow·y, snō′ē, *a.*—*snowier, snowiest.* Abounding with snow; covered with snow; relating to snow; like snow in color; pure; spotless; unblemished.—**snow·i·ly,** *adv.*—**snow·i·ness,** *n.*

snow·y owl, *n.* A large diurnal owl, *Nyctea nyctea*, of arctic and subpolar regions, with white plumage sparsely flecked with gray or brown, and migrating to middle latitudes during the winter.

snub, snub, *v.t.*—*snubbed, snubbing.* [Same as older E. *snib*; Icel. *snubba*, to snub, to chide, Dan. *snubbe*, to snap or snip off; akin to *snap, snip*.] To treat with contempt or neglect; to slight designedly; to check, stop, or rebuke with a sarcastic remark; to abruptly halt or arrest movement of, as of a cord, rope, or the like; to halt a boat or the like by securing it with a line or cord to some fixed object.—*n.* A checking; a rebuke; a rebuff; the abrupt halting of the movement of a line, rope, or the like.—*a.* Turned up, as the nose.—**snubbed,** *a.*—**snub·ber,** *n.*—**snub·ness,** *n.*

snub·by, snub′ē, *a.*—*snubbier, snubbiest.* Short, wide, and turned up, as a nose; inclined to snub; snubbing.—**snub·bi·ness,** *n.*

snub-nosed, snub′nōzd″, *a.* Having a short, upturned nose.

snuff, snuf, *n.* [M.E. *snoffe*: cf. G. *schnuppe*, snuff of a candle.] The charred or partly consumed portion of a candlewick.—*v.t.*

To cut off or remove the snuff of, as a candle; to extinguish, followed by *out.*—**snuff out,** *colloq.* put an end to, suddenly and completely, as to kill.

snuff, snuf, *v.t.* [Same as D. *snuffen*, to snuff; *snuf*, a sniffing; akin Dan. *snöfte*, G. *schnupfen*, to snuff; akin *sniff, snivel, snuffle.*] To draw in through the nose, as air; to inhale; to scent; to smell; to sniff or smell in examination, as animals.—*v.i.* To inhale air through the nose with noise; to snort or sniff.—*n.* An inhalation through the nose; a sniff.

snuff, snuf, *n.* A powdered preparation of tobacco inhaled through the nose; a small pinch of this used at a time.—**up to snuff,** *colloq.* meeting the standard or satisfactory; *Brit. colloq.* shrewd or sharp-witted.

snuff·box, snuf′boks″, *n.* A box for snuff small enough for carrying in one's pocket.

snuf·fer, snuf′ẽr, *n. Usu. pl.* an instrument for snuffing or snuffing out candles. That which or one who snuffs candles.

snuf·fer, snuf′ẽr, *n.* One who snuffs or sniffs; one who takes snuff.

snuf·fle, snuf′l, *v.i.*—*snuffled, snuffling.* [Freq. of *snuff* = L.G. *snuffeln*, D. *snuffelen*, Sw. *snufla*, to snuffle.] To breathe noisily through the nose; to sniffle; to speak through the nose or with a nasal twang; to snivel or whine.—*v.t.* To speak or utter nasally.—*n.* An act of snuffling; the sound produced by snuffling; an affected nasal twang; *pl.* nasal congestion or the sniffles.—**snuf·fler,** *n.*—**snuf·fly,** *a.*

snuff·y, snuf′ē, *a.*—*snuffier, snuffiest.* Resembling snuff; soiled with snuff, or smelling of it; given to taking snuff; unpleasant or disagreeable; dingy.—**snuff·i·ness,** *n.*

snug, snug, *a.*—*snugger, snuggest.* [Origin uncertain.] Comfortable or cozy, as a place; more or less compact or limited in size, and sheltered or warm; trim, neat, or compactly arranged, as a ship or its parts; adequately protected from the weather; fitting closely, but not too closely, as a garment; comfortably placed or circumstanced, as persons; pleasant or agreeable, esp. in a small, exclusive way; enabling one to live in comfort; as, a *snug* fortune; well-concealed; secret.—*adv.*—*v.i.*—*snugged, snugging.* To lie closely or comfortably; snuggle; nestle.—*v.t.* To make snug; to put in a secure position; *naut.* to put, as a vessel, in readiness for a storm, as by lashing down movable gear or reducing sail, followed by *down.*—**snug·ly,** *adv.*—**snug·ness,** *n.*

snug·ger·y, snug·ger·ie, snug′e·rē, *n. pl.* **snug·ger·ies.** *Chiefly Brit.* A snug place or position; a comfortable or cozy room, esp. a small one into which a person retires for seclusion; a den; a comfortable or cozy house or dwelling.

snug·gle, snug′l, *v.i.*—*snuggled, snuggling.* [Freq. of *snug.*] To lie or press closely, as for warmth or comfort or from affection; assume a snug position; nestle; cuddle.—*v.t.* To draw or press closely to, as for comfort or from affection.—*n.* The act of snuggling.

so, sō, *adv.* [O.E. *swá*, so, as; Icel. *svá, svo, so,* Goth. *sva, sve,* L.G. and G. *so,* D. *zoo.* It appears in *as, also, whosoever,* etc.] To an unspecified but understood degree or quantity, as: Do only *so* much and no more. In a corresponding manner; likewise, as: He left and *so* did she. In this manner; as demonstrated, as: It should be done *so.* As was mentioned or stated, as: I think *so.* Very much; greatly, as: The cruel remark hurt him *so.* Extremely or very, as: You are *so* pretty. The case being such, as: *So* you came back, did you? Definitely affirmative; most certainly, as: I did *so* lock the door! In such a manner,

as: *So* conduct yourself that you won't be noticed. As a consequence; accordingly, as: He is ill and *so* cannot attend. Having the aim or purpose of; as, a gift *so* honoring the occasion; in a way which follows or results from, as: As you sow, *so* shall you reap. Indeed; assuredly: to emphasize or confirm something stated before, as: He said he would stay, and *so* he will. Thereupon; as, and *so* they set out on their journey.—*a.* Understood or accepted; very well, as: *So* be it. True as previously described or predicted, as: She said it would be hot and *so* it turned out.—*conj.* For which reason; therefore, as: It was late, *so* she went home.—*interj. Colloq.* Indeed! Well! Steady! What about it? as: *So* what?—*pron.* Such as previously stated or suggested, as: He was the only tenant and remained *so.* That which is approximate to something in amount or number, as: He bought ten or *so* items.—**so as,** in order to; for the purpose of, usu. followed by an infinitive, as: He came along *so as* to provide an escort. Used as an antecedent, in a comparative or qualitative sense; as, *so far as* I know, *so* new *as* to be questionable.—**so that,** in order that; with the result, as: She started early *so that* she would arrive on time.—**so to speak,** figuratively; in a manner of speaking, as: We were all at sea, *so to speak,* until the situation was finally explained to us.

so, sō, *n. Mus.* sol.

soak, sōk, *v.i.* [O.E. *socian,* soak, related to *súcan,* E. *suck.*] To lie in and become saturated or permeated with water or some other liquid; to be thoroughly wet; to pass, as a liquid, through pores or openings, usu. with *in, through,* or *out*; to permeate; to penetrate the consciousness or mind, used with *in* or *into*; *colloq.* to drink immoderately.—*v.t.* To place and keep in liquid in order to saturate thoroughly; to wet thoroughly or drench; to steep; absorb; to permeate thoroughly, as liquid or moisture does; to draw, remove, or extract by or as by soaking; to take in or up by absorption, often with *up,* as: Blotting paper *soaks up* ink. *Slang,* to intoxicate with liquor; to drink, esp. to excess; to put in pawn; to beat hard or punish severely; to charge or tax exorbitantly.—*n.* The act of soaking or the state of being soaked; the liquid in which anything is soaked; *slang,* a heavy drinker.—**soak·age,** *n.* The act of soaking; liquid which has oozed out; liquid absorbed by soaking.—**soak·er,** *n.*—**soak·ing·ly,** *adv.*

so-and-so, sō′an·sō″, *n. pl.* **so-and-sos.** *Colloq.* An indefinite or unnamed person or thing; an irritating, annoying, or offensive person: used as a euphemism.

soap, sōp, *n.* [O.E. *sápe* = Sw. *sopa,* L.G. *sepe,* O.H.G. *seifa,* < same root as L. *sebum,* tallow.] A chemical compound of an alkali and fat, soluble in water, and used for detergent or cleansing purposes; *slang,* flattery.—*v.t.* To rub or wash over with soap; *slang,* to flatter.—**no soap,** rejected, as a proposal or idea.—**soap·less,** *a.*—**soap·like,** *a.*

soap·bark, sōp′bärk″, *n.* The inner bark of a tree, *Quillaja saponaria,* of Chile, used as a substitute for soap; any of various other saponaceous barks, as of several tropical American shrubs of the leguminous genus *Pithecellobium*; a plant yielding such bark.

soap·ber·ry, sōp′ber″ē, sōp′be·rē, *n. pl.* **soap·ber·ries.** The fruit of any of certain tropical and subtropical trees of the genus *Sapindus,* used as a substitute for soap; any of the trees bearing such fruit, as *S. saponaria.*

soap·box, sōp′boks″, *n.* A box, esp. a wooden box, in which soap is packed; an empty wooden box of this kind used as a temporary platform by speakers addressing gatherings of persons on public streets. Also **soap box.**—*v.i.* To address or harangue an audience from a soapbox or other informal platform.—*a.* Of or characteristic of impassioned orators or oratories.

soap·box der·by, *n.* A children's race over a downhill course in motorless, orig. wooden, vehicles constructed by the drivers themselves.

soap bub·ble, *n.* A thin film of soap forming a hollow globule; *fig.* something pleasant but ephemeral.

soap op·er·a, *n.* A daytime, serialized broadcast program dramatizing personal or domestic situations in a highly melodramatic, emotional, or sentimental manner: so-called because many were sponsored by soap manufacturers.

soap plant, *n.* Any of various plants of which some portion can be used as a substitute for soap, esp. a plant of the lily family, *Chlorogalum pomeridianum,* of California, whose bulbs were so used.

soap·stone, *n.* A massive variety of talc in soft stone form with a soapy or greasy feel, used for hearths, foot warmers, and griddles. Also *steatite.*

soap·suds, sōp′sudz″, *n. pl.* Foamy, soapy water; the bubbles on such water.

soap·wort, sōp′wųrt″, *n.* A widespread perennial plant, *Saponaria officinalis,* the leaves of which, upon being crushed in water, form a soaplike lather. Also **bounc·· ing Bet.**

soap·y, sō′pē, *a.*—*soapier, soapiest.* Containing or resembling soap; having the qualities of soap; smeared with soap. *Slang,* flattering; unctuous; oily.—**soap··i·ly,** *adv.*—**soap·i·ness,** *n.*

soar, sōr, sąr, *v.i.* [Fr. *essorer,* < L.L. *exaurare,* to take to the air—L. *ex,* out, and *aura,* the air.] To fly aloft, as a bird or airplane; to glide upward or at a height, as a bird on motionless wings or an airplane without engine power; to rise to a height; as, a mountain that *soars* above a plain; to rise above what is usual; as, costs that *soar;* to be transported upward; as, hopes *soaring* high.—*n.* An act of upward flight or ascent; the range or height of a soaring flight.—**soar·er,** *n.*

sob, sob, *v.i.*—*sobbed, sobbing.* [Akin to O.E. *seófian,* to sigh; G. *seufzen,* to sigh; E. *sough.*] To weep with convulsive catching of the breath; to produce such a sound, as: Wind *sobs* through the trees.—*v.t.* To cause or put as by weeping; as, to *sob* herself to sleep; to express with sobs, as: She *sobbed* out the answer.—*n.* A convulsive catching of the breath; a sound like a sob.

so·ber, sō′bėr, *a.* [O.Fr. Fr. *sobre,* < L. *sobrius,* sober, not drunk, temperate, moderate, prudent, appar. < *so-,* for *se-,* without, apart, and *ebrius,* drunk: cf. *solve* and *ebriety.*] Not intoxicated or drunk; habitually temperate, notably in the use of liquor; quiet or sedate in demeanor, as persons; serious, grave, or solemn; marked, as by seriousness, gravity, or solemnity, as in demeanor or speech; showing self control; free from excess, extravagance, or exaggeration; subdued in tone, as color; not gay or showy, as clothes; sane or rational.—*v.t., v.i.* To make or become sober.—**so·ber·ing·ly,** *adv.*—**so·ber·ize,** *v.t.*—*soberized, soberizing.*—**so·ber·ly,** *adv.* —**so·ber·ness,** *n.*

so·ber·sid·ed, sō′bėr·sīd″did, *a.* Of a solemn or serious disposition or character; earnest; grave.—**so·ber·sides,** sō′bėr·sīdz″, *n. pl. but sing. in constr. Slang,* a habitually solemn or humorless person.

so·bri·e·ty, so·brī′i·tē, sō·brī′i·tē, *n.* [L. *sobrietas.*] The condition of being sober; temperance, esp. in the use of intoxicating liquors; seriousness or gravity. **so·bri·quet, sou·bri·quet,** sō′bri·kā″,

sō″bri·ket″, sō″bri·kā′, so″bri·ket′, Fr. sǎ·brē·ke′, *n.* [Fr.] A nickname.

sob sis·ter, *n. Slang,* a journalist specializing in human-interest stories of the very sentimental type; an extremely sentimental person who persistently engages in good deeds or works.

sob sto·ry, *n. Slang,* a sentimental tale intended to evoke compassion or sympathy, often used as an alibi.

soc·age, sok′ij, *n.* [L.L. *socagium,* socage; lit. 'the tenure of one over whom the feudal lord had a certain jurisdiction,' < O.E. *soc,* the privilege of holding a court in a district.] A tenure of land in medieval England by the performance of certain determined but nonmilitary services, or by the payment of rent. Also **soc·cage.**—**soc·ag·er,** sok′a·- jėr, *n.*

so-called, sō′kạld′, *a.* Commonly called or designated thus; as, the *so-called* birthplace of football; improperly, incorrectly, or falsely called thus; as, robbed by his *so-called* honest employee.

soc·cer, sok′ėr, *n.* A variation of football played by two opposing teams of eleven members in which a ball is moved toward the opposing team's goal by striking or kicking it, using any part of the body but the hands and arms. Also *association football.*

so·cia·bil·i·ty, sō″sha·bil′i·tē, *n.* The quality of being sociable; the inclination to be gregarious; an act of being friendly, sociable, or convivial.

so·cia·ble, sō′sha·bl, *a.* [Fr. *sociable,* L. *sociabilis,* < *socio,* to associate or unite, < *socius,* a companion.] Inclined to associate with or seek friends; companionable; social; conducive to or affording opportunity for congenial relations.—*n.* An informal party or social gathering, esp. of members of the same church.—**so·cia·· ble·ness,** *n.*—**so·cia·bly,** *adv.*

so·cial, sō′shal, *a.* [Fr. *social,* < L. *socialis,* < *socius.*] Pertaining to society; relating to man living in society or to the public as an aggregate body. Ready to mix in friendly relationships; sociable; promoting sociability. Relating to fashionable society; as, a *social* occasion; desirous of living in society; gregarious; relating to status; as, a comparable *social* group; pertaining to the welfare, relationships, and living conditions of people collectively in communities. *Bot.* growing naturally in large groups or masses; *zool.* living in communities, as wolves, ants, or bees; *hist.* occurring between allies or confederates, as Roman wars.—*n.* A social gathering.

so·cial climb·er, *n.* An individual who endeavors to ingratiate himself with affluent or eminent people in order to attain a higher social position for himself.— **so·cial climb·ing,** *n.*

so·cial con·tract, *n.* An agreement entered into voluntarily by individuals for their mutual protection; a theory of Hobbes, Locke, Rousseau, and other philosophers that organized society and government evolve from such loose agreements among early associations of individuals.

so·cial de·moc·ra·cy, *n.* A political doctrine based on a Marxist politico-economic ideology that advocates a gradual transition from a capitalistic to a socialistic society by democratic means and processes. —**so·cial dem·o·crat,** *n.*—**so·cial-dem·· o·crat·ic,** *a.*

so·cial dis·ease, *n.* A venereal disease; any disease usu. related to social and economic conditions, as tuberculosis.

So·cial Gos·pel, *n. Relig.* a Protestant movement in N. America, esp. during the first part of the 20th century, advocating the application of the teachings of Jesus to contemporary life.

so·cial in·sur·ance, *n.* A government-subsidized plan for protecting individual citizens from the full impact of certain risks, such as unemployment, disability, and old age.

so·cial·ism, sō′sha·liz″um, *n.* A theory or method of social organization and government whereby the citizenry jointly owns the means of production and distribution, and the power of administrative control is vested in the state; in Marxism, an intermediate state which must necessarily follow capitalism before the goal of a totally classless society can become a functional reality.

so·cial·ist, sō′sha·list, *n.* One who advocates socialism; (*cap.*) a person who belongs to the political party so named, as: He is a dues-paying *Socialist.*—*a.*— **so·cial·is·tic,** sō′sha·lis′tik, *a.*—**so·· cial·is·ti·cal·ly,** *adv.*

so·cial·ite, sō′sha·līt″, *n.* A man or woman who is well known and accepted as a peer in socially elite circles.

so·ci·al·i·ty, sō″shē·al′i·tē, *n.* The quality of being social; the tendency of individuals to organize in groups.

so·cial·ize, sō′sha·līz″, *v.t.*—*socialized, socializing.* To render social, as to suit something to the uses or needs of society; to render sociable, as to make fit for life in companionship with others; to render socialistic, as to establish or regulate according to the theories of socialism.—*v.i.* To participate in friendly interchange with other people.—**so·cial·i·za·tion,** *n.*—**so·· cial·iz·er,** *n.*

so·cial·ized med·i·cine, *n.* The concept of governmental subsidy of physicians and certain health care facilities in order to provide for the medical care of an entire population, avoiding some of the inequities arising from a system based on individual ability to pay for such services. Also *state medicine.*

so·cial·ly, sō′sha·lē, *adv.* In a social manner or way; as, *socially* agreeable; in relation to social standards; as, *socially* unacceptable; by or in society; as, *socially* active.

so·cial-mind·ed, sō′shal·mīn′did, *a.* Actively concerned with conditions in society, esp. with the institutions and services contributing to social welfare.

so·cial sci·ence, *n.* The branch of knowledge dealing with all that relates to the social condition, or to the relations and institutions involved in man's existence and his well-being as a member of an organized community; any study dealing with a single aspect of man in relation to society and its institutions, as economics or sociology.— **so·cial sci·en·tist,** *n.*

so·cial sec·re·tar·y, *n.* A secretary responsible for handling matters of a personal nature for a socially active employer, esp. personal correspondence and social appointments.

so·cial se·cu·ri·ty, *n.* (*Usu. cap.*) a plan for old-age pensions, survivors' benefits, and health or disability insurance administered by the U.S. government and maintained by federal funds and payments required of certain groups of employers and their employees. Any system providing public economic assistance and services for the welfare of the individual.

so·cial serv·ice, *n.* Any organized activity for the betterment of the individual in relation to the community, usu. done under professional guidance by volunteer or trained workers.

so·cial stud·ies, *n. pl.* Those courses in an elementary, secondary, or college curriculum which are concerned with man in his relation to society and its functioning, as history or sociology.

so·cial wel·fare, *n.* Any or all services organized and sponsored by an agency, as a municipality or a private group, for the benefit of the disadvantaged and the overall betterment of society.

so·cial work, *n.* Any activity, service, or other professional approach directed toward the betterment of social conditions in the community, as by organizations or individuals seeking to improve the condition of the poor, promote the welfare of children, or carry on other philanthropic activities.— **so·cial work·er,** *n.*

so·ci·e·ty, so·sī′i·tē, *n.* pl. **so·ci·e·ties.** [Fr. *société,* L. *societas.*] A group of persons united for the promotion of a common aim, typically literary, scientific, political, religious, benevolent, or convivial; an association of individuals, as a nation, organized for mutual profit and protection; persons from any region or any period of time viewed in regard to manners, customs, or standards of living; human beings collectively, seen as having characteristics in common; those who recognize each other as associates, friends, and acquaintances; the leisured, wealthy, or fashionable section of any community, its manner of living, and its influence; the relationship of men to one another when in association; companionship; fellowship; company; *ecology,* a group of animals or plants kept together by interdependence.—*a.*—**so·ci·e·tal,** so·sī′i·tal, *a.*—**so·ci·e·tal·ly,** *adv.*

so·ci·e·ty verse, *n.* Poetry of a light, entertaining, polished character, considered appealing to polite society.

So·cin·i·an, sō·sin′ē·an, *n.* A follower of Laelius Socinus, 1525–1562, and his nephew Faustus Socinus, 1539–1604, Italian Protestant theologians, who denied certain traditional Christian tenets, as the divinity of Christ, original sin, the Trinity, and eternal punishment.—*a.* Of or pertaining to the Socinians or their doctrines.— **So·cin·i·an·ism,** *n.*

so·ci·o·ec·o·nom·ic, sō″sē·ō·ek″o·nom′ik, sō″shē·ō·ek″o·nom′ik, *a.* Of or pertaining to a concept of social and economic factors as intertwined in their effect, with each factor tending to reinforce and enhance the influence of the other.

so·ci·o·log·i·cal, sō″sē·o·loj′i·kal, sō″shē·o·loj′i·kal, *a.* Of or pertaining to sociology or its methodology; pertaining to human society or to subjects or questions relating to it. Also **so·ci·o·log·ic.**— **so·ci·o·log·i·cal·ly,** *adv.*

so·ci·ol·o·gy, sō″sē·ol′o·jē, sō″shē·ol′o·jē, *n.* [L. *socius,* a companion, and Gr. *logos,* discourse.] The science of the evolution, structure, and functioning of human society; the systematic study of human institutions and social relationships and the principles underlying their functioning.—**so·ci·ol·o·gist,** *n.*

so·ci·om·e·try, sō″sē·om′i·trē, sō″shē·om′i·trē, *n.* The study of relationships between people in a social group, esp. the quantitative measurement of expressed attitudes of acceptance or rejection within a group.—**so·ci·o·met·ric,** sō″sē·o·me′trik, sō″shē·o·me′trik, *a.*—**so·ci·om·e·trist,** *n.*

so·ci·o·po·lit·i·cal, sō″sē·ō·po·lit′i·kal, *a.* Pertaining to or involving factors that are both social and political.

sock, sok, *n.* pl. **socks, sox.** [O.E. *socc,* < L. *soccus,* kind of light, low-heeled shoe, slipper.] A short stocking reaching just above the ankle or about halfway to the knee; a light shoe worn by ancient Greek and Roman comic actors, sometimes taken as a symbol of comedy; a windsock.— **socked in,** prohibited from flying a plane because of adverse weather conditions.

sock, sok, *v.t.* [Origin obscure.] *Slang,* to strike or hit hard.—*n. Slang,* a hard blow.

sock·dol·a·ger, sock·dol·o·ger, sok-·dol′a·jėr, *n.* [Origin obscure.] *Slang.* Something unusually large, heavy, or remarkable; a heavy knockdown or finishing blow; a reply, argument, or the like that decisively settles a discussion.

sock·et, sok′it, *n.* [M.E. *soket, sokette;* origin uncertain.] A hollow part or piece for receiving and holding some part or thing; as, an electric light bulb *socket. Anat.* a hollow in one part, which receives another part; as, the *socket* of the eye; the concavity of a joint; as, the *socket* of the hip.—*v.t.* To place in or fit with a socket.

sock·eye, sok′ī″, *n.* A commercially important game fish, *Oncorhynchus nerka,* found along the coasts of the Pacific from California to the Bering Strait, chiefly in rivers whose upper reaches have lakes in which this species spawns, and which the young may continue to inhabit. Also **sock·-eye salm·on,** *red salmon.*

so·cle, sok′l, sō′kl, *n.* [Fr. *socle,* L. *socculus,* dim. of *soccus.*] *Arch.* A plain or low pedestal that supports a column or statue; a plain face or plinth at the lower part of a wall.

So·crat·ic, so·krat′ik, sō·krat′ik, *a.* Pertaining to Socrates, the Athenian philosopher, or to his philosophy, manner of teaching, or followers.—*n.* One influenced or guided by Socrates or his teachings.— **So·crat·i·cal·ly,** *adv.*

sod, sod, *n.* [Same as L.G. and O.D. *sode,* D. *zode.*] The surface layer of the ground with the grass growing on it; a piece lifted from that surface; turf; sward.—*v.t.*— *sodded, sodding.* To cover with sod.

sod, sod, *n. Brit. slang,* a bugger or sodomite.

so·da, sō′da, *n.* [Sp., Pg., and It. *soda,* glasswort, barilla.] A common name for various compounds of sodium, esp. sodium carbonate or washing soda, bicarbonate of soda or baking soda, and sodium hydroxide or caustic soda; a soft drink consisting of soda water, flavoring, and ice cream.

so·da ash, *n.* Partially purified sodium carbonate, Na_2CO_3, as that formerly obtained from the ashes of various plants growing by the seashore; the commercial name for anhydrous sodium carbonate.

so·da bis·cuit, *n.* A biscuit containing baking soda and buttermilk or sour milk as leavening; a soda cracker.

so·da crack·er, *n.* A crisp, light cracker made from a yeast dough to which baking soda has been added as a neutralizing agent; a soda biscuit.

so·da foun·tain, *n.* A serving table or counter equipped to prepare and serve ice cream, soft drinks, and the like; a vessel or apparatus for holding soda water, provided with faucets for drawing the water off as required.

so·da jerk, *n. Slang,* the waiter who makes and serves sodas, ice cream, or the like at a soda fountain.

so·da lime, *n.* A mixture of sodium hydroxide or caustic soda, and calcium hydroxide or slaked lime, used in the production of ammonia and for the absorption of moisture, esp. from certain gases.

so·da·lite, sō′da·līt″, *n.* [< *soda* and *lite.*] A mineral, a silicate of sodium and aluminum with sodium chloride, blue, gray, or white in color, used in ornamental stonework.

so·dal·i·ty, sō·dal′i·tē, so·dal′i·tē, *n.* pl. **so·dal·i·ties.** [L. *sodalitas,* < *sodalis,* mate, fellow, comrade.] Fellowship, brotherhood, or association; an association, society, or fraternity; *Rom. Cath. Ch.* a society for religious and charitable purposes.

so·da pop, *n.* A bottled, carbonated soft drink, usu. flavored artificially.

so·da wa·ter, *n.* An effervescent beverage consisting of water charged with carbon dioxide; soda pop; a mixture of sodium bicarbonate, water, and often an acid, used as a gastric aid.

sod·den, sod′en, *a.* [Old pp. of *seethe.*] Soaked with liquid or moisture; heavy, doughy, or soggy, as food; having the appearance of having been soaked; bloated, as the face; expressionless, dull, or stupid. —*v.t., v.i.* To make or become sodden.— **sod·den·ly,** *adv.*—**sod·den·ness,** *n.*

sod·dy, sod′ē, *a.* Of or like sod; made of sod.—*n.* pl. **sod·dies.** A house made of sod or turf. Also **sod house.**

so·di·um, sō′dē·um, *n.* [Named from its oxide *soda.*] *Chem.* a soft, silver-white metallic element abundant in nature but always in a combined state, and chemically very active, forming many useful compounds. Sym. Na, at. no. 11, at. wt. 22.9898. See Periodic Table of Elements.

so·di·um ben·zo·ate, *n.* Benzoate of sodium.

so·di·um bi·car·bo·nate, *n. Chem., pharm.* a white crystalline compound, $NaHCO_3$, used in making baking powder, medical preparations, and fire extinguisher liquid. Also *baking soda, bicarbonate of soda, saleratus.*

so·di·um car·bon·ate, *n. Chem.* an alkaline compound of sodium, Na_2CO_3, used as an ingredient in many manufacturing processes, as a bleaching agent, and as a water softener. Also *sal soda, soda ash, washing soda.*

so·di·um chlo·rate, *n. Chem.* a colorless crystalline salt, $NaClO_3$, used as an oxidizing and bleaching agent, and as an ingredient in matches, explosives, dyes, and weed-killing compounds.

so·di·um chlo·ride, *n. Chem.* common salt, NaCl.

so·di·um cy·a·nide, *n. Chem.* a white, poisonous salt, NaCN, used in electroplating, metal-treating, fumigating, gold and silver refining, and the making of dyes, pigments, insecticides, and nylon products.

so·di·um cyc·la·mate, sō′dē·um sik′la·-māt″, sī′kla·māt″, *n. Chem.* a white powder, $C_6H_{11}NHSO_3Na$, extremely sweet but nonnutritive, and used as a substitute for sugar by people on certain diets.

so·di·um di·chro·mate, *n. Chem.* a reddish crystalline compound, $Na_2Cr_2O_7 \cdot 2H_2O$, a strong oxidizing agent, used in the making of inks, dyes, and leather.

so·di·um hy·drox·ide, *n. Chem.* a white compound, NaOH, used in manufacturing chemicals, textiles, soap, leather, paper, and petroleum products. Also *caustic soda, lye, soda.*

so·di·um hy·po·sul·fite, *n. Chem.* sodium thiosulfate.

so·di·um ni·trate, *n. Chem.* a colorless salt, $NaNO_3$, used in the making of fertilizer, nitric acid, and other chemicals, explosives, matches, and glass, and for curing meats.

so·di·um ste·a·rate, *n. Chem.* a white powder, $NaC_{18}H_{35}O_2$, used as a waterproofing and jelling agent, and as an ingredient in medicines, cosmetics, and plastics.

so·di·um thi·o·sul·fate, *n. Chem.* a white powder, $Na_2S_2O_3 \cdot 5H_2O$, used in photography, dyeing, leather and paper manufacturing, and as a germicide. Also *hypo, sodium hyposulfite.*

so·di·um-va·por lamp, sō′dē·um·vā″pėr lamp″, *n.* A lamp containing sodium vapor which becomes luminous when an electric current is passed between two electrodes, thus producing a glareless light often used for street and highway lighting.

Sod·om, sod′om, *n.* [From *Sodom,* ancient biblical city which was destroyed by fire by God because of the wickedness of its people.] A sinful wicked place.—

Sod·om·ite, sod′o·mīt″, n. An inhabitant of Sodom; (l.c.) one who practices sodomy.

sod·om·y, sod′o·mē, n. [Fr. sodomie.] Unnatural sexual intercourse, esp. of one man with another or of a human being with an animal.

so·ev·er, sō·ev′ẽr, adv. [< so and ever.] At all; in any case; of any kind; in any way: used with generalizing force, as after who, what, when, where, how, any, or all, as: Choose whatsoever person you please. Sometimes separated by intervening words, as: Choose what person soever you please.

so·fa, sō′fa, n. [Ar. çuffah.] A long, upholstered seat or couch, usu. with a back and raised ends or arms.

so·fa bed, n. A sofa which can be opened to form a full-sized bed by lowering the back to a horizontal position.

so·far, sō′fär, n. [(so)und (f)ixing (a)nd (r)anging.] A system to determine by triangulation the position at sea, as of a downed spacecraft, by shore listening stations which receive sound signals produced by depth charges dropped by the craft in distress.

sof·fit, sof′it, n. [Fr. soffite, It. soffitta, < L. sub, under, and figo, to fasten.] Arch. the under surface of an arch, architrave, overhanging cornice, projecting balcony, or staircase.

soft, sȧft, soft, a. [O.E. sōfte, var. of sēfte, akin to O.H.G. semfti, G. sanft, D. zacht, soft.] Yielding readily to touch or pressure; easily penetrated, divided, or altered in shape; not hard or stiff; relatively deficient in hardness, as metal; smooth and agreeable to the touch, as skin or hair; not rough or coarse; producing agreeable sensations; pleasant, easeful, or comfortable; low or subdued in sound; gentle and melodious; not harsh or unpleasant to the eye; not glaring, as light or color; not hard or sharp, as outlines; gentle or mild, as wind or rain; genial or balmy, as climate or air; not rough or turbulent, as a stream; leisurely or easy, as pace or movement; gradual, as a slope or ascent; colloq. not hard, trying, or severe; as, a soft job. Gentle, mild, lenient, or compassionate, as persons; characterized by gentleness or tenderness, as the disposition, look, feelings, or actions; smooth, smoothing, or ingratiating, as words; not harsh or severe, as terms; yielding readily to tender emotions; impressionable; sentimental, as language; easily influenced or swayed, as a person or the mind; colloq. easily imposed upon. Effeminate or unmanly; of delicate constitution; not strong or robust, or incapable of great endurance or exertion; foolish or silly; of money, in paper currency rather than coin; of water, relatively free from mineral salts that interfere with the action of soap; not alcoholic or intoxicating, as beverages. Phon. having a more or less sibilant sound, as the c and g in cite and gin; sonant or voiced, as g, b, and d, in contrast to k, p, and t, which are hard, surd, or breathed. Rocketry, of a landing or falling, done gently, with minimal damage.—adv.—n. That which is soft or yielding; the soft part of anything; softness.—**soft·ly**, adv.—**soft·ness**, n.

soft·ball, sȧft′bȧl″, soft′bȧl″, n. A game similar to baseball but requiring a larger, softer ball that is pitched underhand, fewer innings, and a smaller diamond; the ball so employed.

soft-boiled, sȧft′boild′, soft′boild′, a. Cooking, of eggs, boiled only until the yolk and white are semicongealed, usu. three to four minutes. Fig. sentimental; mild-mannered.

soft coal, n. Bituminous coal.

sof·ten, sȧ′fen, sof′en, v.t. To make soft or more soft; mitigate; alleviate.—v.i. To become soft or less hard.—**sof·ten·er**, sȧ′fe·nẽr, sof′e·nẽr, n.

soft-finned, sȧft′find′, soft′find′, a. Ichth. having fins with the membrane supported by soft, flexible, or jointed rays rather than by hard, stiff, unbranched spines.

soft-head·ed, sȧft′hed′id, soft′hed′id, a. Foolish or silly; weak in intellect.—**soft-head**, n.—**soft-head·ed·ly**, adv.—**soft-head·ed·ness**, n.

soft-heart·ed, sȧft′här′tid, soft′här′tid, a. Fig. Having tenderness of heart; sympathetic; merciful.—**soft-heart·ed·ly**, adv.—**soft-heart·ed·ness**, n.

soft land·ing, n. Aerospace, the act of landing on the surface of a planet without damage to any portion of the space vehicle or payload except possibly the landing gear.

soft pal·ate, n. See palate.

soft ped·al, n. A pedal on a piano or other musical instrument used to dampen or reduce the volume of its tone; colloq. something that dampens, reduces, or restrains effect.

soft-ped·al, sȧft″ped′al, soft″ped′al, v.i.— soft-pedaled, soft-pedaling, Brit. soft-pedalled, soft-pedalling. To use the soft pedal, as in playing the piano.—v.t. To soften the sound of by means of the soft pedal; colloq. to tone down, make less emphatic or less noticeable; as, to soft-pedal an issue in a political campaign.

soft rot, n. Plant pathol. a plant disease in which the affected parts show a pulpy, watery decay due to the action of bacteria or fungi.

soft sell, n. A method of using indirect and subtle persuasion or suggestion in advertising or selling.

soft-shell, sȧft′shel″, soft′shell″, a. Having a fragile or soft shell, as an animal after shedding its shell. Also **soft-shelled.**—n. An animal with a soft shell, as the crab.

soft-shelled tur·tle, n. Any of various aquatic turtles belonging to the family Trionychidae, and having leathery skin rather than horny protective plates.

soft-shoe, sȧft′shō″, soft′shō″, a. Of or pertaining to a type of tap dancing in which the dancer wears shoes that are soft-soled rather than those with the conventional metal taps.

soft soap, n. A soap in a semifluid or liquid form; colloq. flattery.—**soft-soap**, sȧft′sōp′, soft′sōp′, v.t. To apply this form of soap to. Colloq. to ply with smooth words; cajole; flatter.—**soft-soap·er**, n.

soft-spo·ken, sȧft′spō′ken, soft′spō′ken, a. Speaking softly; having a mild or gentle voice; mild; affable.

soft·ware, sȧft′wâr″, soft′wâr″, n. Computer, the programs and programming support necessary to put a computer through its assigned tasks, as distinguished from hardware or the actual machine and its parts. Any aspect of an apparatus not specifically connected with its hardware.

soft wa·ter, n. Water containing little or no salts of calcium or magnesium, as rain water.

soft wheat, n. Any variety of wheat having relatively soft kernels with a high starch content and usu. a low gluten content, used for making pastry flour and breakfast foods.

soft·wood, sȧft′wụd″, soft′wụd″, n. Any wood which is relatively soft or easily cut; a tree yielding such wood. Forestry, the wood of any coniferous tree; a coniferous tree.—a.—**soft-wood·ed**, a.

soft·y, soft·ie, sȧf′tē, sof′tē, n. pl. soft·ies. Colloq. One who is easily imposed upon or is extremely sentimental; an effeminate or unmanly male; a soft, silly, or weak-minded person.

sog·gy, sog′ē, a.—soggier, soggiest. Soaked; soppy; thoroughly wet; humid or sultry, as weather; damp and heavy, as ill-baked bread; sodden; fig. spiritless, dull, or stupid.—**sog·gi·ly**, adv.—**sog·gi·ness**, n.

soi-di·sant, swä·dē·zän′, a. [Fr. < soi (< L. se), oneself, and disant, ppr. of dire (< L. dicere), say.] Calling oneself thus or self-styled; as, a soi-disant teacher; so-called or pretended; as, a soi-disant expert in all matters.

soi·gné, soi·gnée, swän·yā′, Fr. swä·nyä′, a. Stylish or elegant; sleekly groomed; well-dressed; exceptionally neat or fastidious.

soil, soil, n. [M.E. soyle, < A.Fr. soil, appar. with sense < L. solum, ground, earth, but with form due to O.Fr. soil, mire or other words.] That portion of the earth's surface in which plants grow, usu. consisting of a mixture of disintegrated rock and decayed organic matter; earth; a particular kind of earth; as, a light, loose, or sandy soil; the ground, as producing vegetation or cultivated for its crops; as, to till the soil; a country or region; as, to set foot on foreign soil; an environment which permits growth and development.—**soil·less**, a.

soil, soil, v.t. [O.Fr. saouler, to satiate, < saoul, L. satullus, sated, dim. of satur, sated, full.] To feed and fatten, as cattle or horses, with fresh grass or green fodder instead of putting out to pasture; to purge with soilage.

soil, soil, v.t. [O.Fr. soillier (Fr. souiller), soil, O.Fr. also roll in mire, as swine, perh. < L. suculus, dim. of sus. swine.] To make dirty or foul, esp. on the surface; as, to soil a book by handling; smirch, smudge, or stain. Fig. to sully or tarnish, as with disgrace; as, to soil one's name or reputation; defile morally, as with sin.—v.i. To become soiled or smirched.—n. A soiling or being soiled; as, to protect clothes from soil; a spot, mark, or stain due to soiling; corruption; dirty or foul matter; filth; sewage; ordure; manure or compost.

soil·age, soil′lij, n. Grass or other herbage used for fodder.

soil con·ser·va·tion, n. Any of various practices, as crop rotation or prevention of erosion, designed to maintain or improve the resources of the soil and obtain optimum yields.

soil pipe, n. A pipe for conveying from a dwelling the liquid waste containing human excrement.

soil·ure, soil′yẽr, n. The act of soiling, smirching, or staining, or the state of being soiled.

soi·ree, soi·rée, swä·rā′, Fr. swä·Rā′, n. [Fr. soirée, evening, an evening party, < soir, evening, < L. serus, late.] An evening party, reception, or social gathering.

so·journ, sō′jụrn, sō·jụrn′, v.i. [O.Fr. sojorner (Fr. séjourner), < L. sub, under, and diurnus, of the day, daily.] To dwell for a time in a place; to make a temporary stay.—sō′jụrn, n. A temporary stay at a place; a place of temporary stay.—**sojourn·er**, n.

soke, sōk, n. [M.L. soca, < sōcn, seeking, inquiry, jurisdiction, related to sēcan.] Early E. law. The right of local jurisdiction of causes; a district over which such a right was exercised.

soke·man, sōk′man, n. Early E. law, a tenant residing on a soke. Also **soc·man.**

sol, sōl, sol, n. Mus. The fifth tone of the diatonic scale; the tone G in the key of C; the syllable used to represent the fifth tone in a scale of solmization. Also so.

sol, sol, sōl, n. [< solution.] Chem. a colloidal dispersion composed of a liquid solvent and a solid solute.

Sol, sol, n. [L.] The Roman god of the sun; the sun.

sol·ace, sol'is, n. [O.Fr. *solas*, Fr. *soulas*, < L. *solacium*, *solatium*, < *solari*, comfort, soothe: cf. *solatium*, *console*.] Comfort in sorrow or trouble; alleviation of distress or discomfort; something that gives comfort, consolation, or relief.—*v.t.*—*solaced*, *solacing*. To comfort, console, or cheer, as a person, oneself, or the heart; alleviate or relieve, as sorrow or distress; amuse or cheer.—**sol·ace·ment**, n.—**sol·ac·er**, n.

so·lan, sō'lan, n. [Icel. *súlan*, the gannet.] The gannet. Also **so·lan goose**.

sol·a·na·ceous, sol″a·nā′shus, a. *Bot.* belonging or pertaining to the nightshade family, *Solanaceae*.

so·la·num, sō·lā′num, n. [L., nightshade.] Any plant of the genus *Solanum*, of the nightshade family, which comprises herbs, shrubs, and small trees, and includes the white potato, the tomato, the eggplant, and the bittersweet.

so·lar, sō′lėr, a. [L. *solaris*, < *sol*, sun.] Of or pertaining to the sun; as, *solar* phenomena, the *solar* system; determined by the sun; as, *solar* day; proceeding from the sun, as light or heat; operating by the light or heat of the sun, as a mechanism; indicating time by means of or with reference to the sun; as, a *solar* chronometer; sacred to the sun or connected with the worship of the sun; as, a *solar* deity; *astrol.* subject to the influence of the sun.

so·lar bat·ter·y, n. *Elect.* a device using photovoltaic cells for converting the sun's energy into electricity.

so·lar cell, n. A unit that converts radiant energy, as sunlight, into electrical energy.

so·lar con·stant, n. The amount of radiant solar energy received normally by the earth at the outer layer of its atmosphere when at its mean distance from the sun, equal to 1.94 gram calories per square centimeter per minute.

so·lar flare, n. A temporary but violent eruption of energy from some spot on the sun's surface.

so·lar house, n. A house planned and equipped to store and utilize heat from the rays of the sun.

so·lar·i·um, sō·lâr′ē·um, so·lâr′ē·um, n. pl. **so·lar·i·a**, **so·lar·i·ums**, sō·lâr′ē·a, so·lâr′ē·a. [L.] Any glass-enclosed porch, room, or similar area exposed to the rays of the sun, as for the benefit of hospital patients; any enclosed area having overhead sun lamps, as in a resort or health club.

so·lar·ize, sō′la·rīz″, v.t.—*solarized*, *solarizing*. [< *solar*.] To affect or harm by sunlight; *photog.* to injure or alter by excessive exposure to light.—*v.i. Photog.* to become injured by overexposure.—**so·lar·i·za·tion**, n.

so·lar plex·us, n. *Anat.* a network of nerves situated at the upper part of the abdomen, behind the stomach and in front of the aorta; *colloq.* the middle part of the abdomen.

so·lar sys·tem, n. The sun together with all the planets and other bodies directly or indirectly revolving round it.

so·lar wind, n. The continuous emanation of charged particles in all directions from the sun, which affects the magnetic fields of planets in the solar system.

so·la·ti·um, sō·lā′shē·um, n. pl. **so·la·ti·a**. [L.] A solace or compensation, as for suffering or loss; *law*, compensation, beyond actual damages, paid as a solace for injured feelings.

sol·dan, sol′dan, sōl′dan, sōd′an, n. [O.Fr.] (*Sometimes cap.*), *archaic*. The sovereign of a Mohammedan country; a sultan, esp. of Egypt.

sol·der, sod′ėr, n. [O.Fr. *soldure*, *soudure* (Fr. *soudure*), < *solder*, *souder* (Fr. *souder*) to solder, < L. *solidare*, make solid, < *solidus*, E. *solid*.] Any of various fusible alloys applied in a melted state to metal surfaces to unite them.—*v.t.* To unite with solder; to join with or unite by means of some other substance or device; *fig.* to join closely and intimately.—*v.i.* To unite things with solder; to become soldered; to grow together.—**sol·der·er**, n.

sol·dier, sōl′jėr, n. [O.Fr. *soldier*, *soldeier*, < *solde*, *soldee*, pay (as of soldiers), < M.L. *solidus*, a coin, piece of money.] One who serves in an army for pay; one engaged in military service, esp. an enlisted man as contrasted with a commissioned officer; a man of military skill or experience; one who contends or serves in any cause; *entom.* any of the worker ants or sterile termites with large heads and powerful jaws for defense purposes.—*v.i.* To act or serve as a soldier.—**sol·dier·ly**, sōl′jėr·lē, a.—**sol·dier·ship**, n.

sol·dier of for·tune, n. A military adventurer ready to serve wherever there is promise of profit, adventure, or other advantage.

sol·diers' home, n. An institution providing care, relief, and shelter for military veterans.

Sol·dier's Med·al, n. A military decoration bestowed upon any member of the U.S. Army or a connected military organization for heroism not involving combat with an enemy.

sol·dier·y, sōl′je·rē, n. pl. **sol·dier·ies**. Soldiers collectively; a body of soldiers; military training, skill, or technique.

sole, sōl, n. [O.Fr. Fr. *sole*, < M.L. *sola*, for L. *solea*, sole, sandal, < *solum*, ground, earth, foundation, sole of foot or shoe.] The bottom or undersurface of the foot; the corresponding underpart of a shoe, boot, or the like, exclusive of the heel; the bottom, undersurface, or lower part of anything; *golf*, the undersurface of the head of a golf club, which rests on the ground.—*v.t.*—*soled*, *soling*. To furnish with a sole, as a shoe; *golf*, to place, as the sole of a club, on the ground.—**soled**, a.

sole, sōl, n. pl. **soles**, **sole**. [O.Fr. Fr. *sole*, < M.L. *sola*, for L. *solea*, sole (fish), another use (from the flat shape) of *solea*, sandal.] Any of various flatfishes with a small mouth, family *Soleidae*, as *Solea solea*, a food fish common along European coasts; any of various flatfishes, as *Psettichthys melanostictus*, of the Pacific coast of N. America.

sole, sōl, a. [O.Fr. *sol*, fem. *sole* (Fr. *seul*, fem. *seule*), < L. *solus*, fem. *sola*, alone, single: cf. *solus*, *solo*, and *sullen*.] Being the only one or ones; as, the *sole* reason for his conduct; being unique or the only one of a kind; belonging or pertaining to one individual or group to the exclusion of all others; as, having the *sole* right to something; functioning with independent power and without assistance; as, the *sole* decision maker; unaccompanied by others; lonely or solitary; *law*, unmarried, usu. said of women.

sol·e·cism, sol′i·siz″um, n. [Fr. *solecisme*, < L. *soloecismus*, < Gr. *soloicismós*, < *soloicizein*, violate the rules of grammar; said to have referred orig. to the bad Greek spoken at Soli, Gr. Soloi, town in Cilicia.] An ungrammatical construction or expression at variance with approved usage, as 'We was cold' for 'We were cold'; a breach of good manners or etiquette; any error, impropriety, or inconsistency.—**sol·e·cist**, n.—**sol·e·cis·tic**, **sol·e·cis·ti·cal**, a.

sole·ly, sōl′lē, adv. As the only one or ones; as, the employers are *solely* responsible; exclusively or only; as, plants found *solely* in the tropics; wholly; merely.

sol·emn, sol′em, a. [O.Fr. *solemne*, *solempne*, < L. *solemnis*, *sollemnis*, also *sollennis*, established, appointed, solemn.] Grave, sober, or mirthless, as a person, the face, speech, tone, or mood; such as to cause serious thoughts or a grave mood; as, a *solemn* sight; gravely or somberly impressive; serious or earnest, as assurances, feelings, or purposes; characterized by dignified or serious formality, as proceedings of a formal ceremonious character; made in due legal or other express form, as a declaration or agreement; marked by or observed with religious rites, as feasts or feast days; having a religious character, as rites or ceremonies; made according to religious forms, as a vow or oath.—**sol·emn·ly**, adv.—**sol·emn·ness**, n.

so·lem·ni·ty, so·lem′ni·tē, n. pl. **so·lem·ni·ties**. The state or character of being solemn, serious, or earnest; observance of rites or ceremonies; solemn celebration of an occasion or event; *usu. pl.* a solemn observance, ceremonial proceeding, or special formality; as, to commemorate an event with all due *solemnities*; *law*, a formality requisite to render an act or document valid.

sol·em·nize, Brit. **sol·em·nise**, sol′em·nīz″, v.t.—*solemnized*, *solemnizing*, Brit. *solemnised*, *solemnising*. To commemorate with rites or ceremonies, as an event or occasion; to hold or perform in due manner, as ceremonies or services; to perform the ceremony of, esp. marriage; to go through with, as a ceremony or formality; to render solemn, serious, or grave.—**sol·em·ni·za·tion**, Brit. **sol·em·ni·sa·tion**. n.

sol·emn Mass, n. (*Often cap.*), Rom. Cath. Ch. a Mass in which the celebrant is assisted by a deacon and a subdeacon.

sol·emn vow, n. Rom. Cath. Ch. a very grave public vow taken by a religious, renouncing marriage and ownership of property for life.

sole·ness, sōl′nis, n. The state or condition of being sole, alone, or without others.

so·le·noid, sō′le·noid″, n. [Gr. *sōlen*, channel.] *Elect.* a coil of wire wound in the form of a helix, within which a magnetic field is established when the coil conducts an electric current.—**so·le·noi·dal**, sō″le·noid′al, a.

sole·plate, sōl′plāt″, n. The ironing surface of a flat iron. *Carp.* a piece or plate forming the base upon which studs are erected; also **sole**, **sole·piece**.

sole·print, sōl′print″, n. A print of the sole of the foot, esp. as used in hospitals to identify infants.

sol-fa, sōl″fä′, sol′fä″, sol″fä′, sol′fä″, n. *Mus.* The set of syllables, *do, re, mi, fa, sol, la*, and *ti* sung to the respective tones of the scale; the system of singing tones to these syllables; a scale or exercise sung in this way.—*v.i.—sol-faed*, *sol-faing*. To use the sol-fa syllables in singing.—*v.t.* To sing to the sol-fa syllables, as tones. See *tonic sol-fa*.—**sol-fa·ist**, n.

sol·fa·ta·ra, sōl″fa·tär′a, sol″fa·tär′a, n. [It., < *solfo*, < L. *sulfur*, E. *sulphur*.] A volcanic vent or area which gives off only sulfurous gases, steam, and the like.—**sol·fa·ta·ric**, a.

sol·feg·gio, sol·fej′ō, sol·fej′ē·ō″, n. pl. **sol·feg·gi**, **sol·feg·gios**, sol·fej′ē. [It.] *Mus.* A type of ear and sight training in which one sings notes and names them with the solmization syllables; an exercise adapted to this technique. Also **sol·fège**, sol′fezh′.

so·lic·it, so·lis′it, v.t. [O.Fr. *soliciter* (Fr. *solliciter*), < L. *sollicitare*, disturb, rouse, incite, urge, < *sollicitus*, thoroughly moved, disturbed.] To seek for by entreaty, earnest or respectful request, or formal application; to entreat or petition, as a person, for something, or to do something; urge or importune; to seek to influence or incite to action, esp. unlawful or wrong action; to importune or accost with immoral intention.—*v.i.* To make petition or request, as for something desired; solicit orders or trade, as for a business house; to importune a person with immoral intention.

so·lic·i·ta·tion, so·lis″i·tā′shan, *n.* [O.Fr. *solicitation* (Fr. *sollicitation*), < L. *sollici-tatio(n-).*] The act of soliciting; entreaty, urging, or importunity; a petition or request; enticement or allurement; an importuning with immoral intention.

so·lic·i·tor, so·lis′i·tēr, *n.* [O.Fr. *soliciteur* (Fr. *solliciteur*), < *soliciter*, E. *solicit.*] One who solicits, esp. one who seeks funds for charity; one whose business it is to solicit orders or trade; an officer having charge of the legal business of a city or town; *Brit. law*, one qualified to advise clients, to plead cases in the lower courts only and to prepare cases for barristers to plead in the higher courts.—**so·lic·i·tor-ship**, *n.*

so·lic·i·tor gen·er·al, *n.* pl. **so·lic·i·tors gen·er·al.** The second officer of the U.S. Department of Justice, next in rank to the attorney general; the chief law officer in some states; *Brit.* a law officer serving the Crown, next in rank to the attorney general.

so·lic·i·tous, so·lis′i·tus, *a.* [L. *sollicitus*, thoroughly moved, disturbed, anxious, careful, < *sollus*, whole, and *citus*, pp. of *ciere*, move: cf. *excite.*] Anxious or concerned over something, used with *about* or *for*; anxiously desirous, with *of*; eager, used with infinitive; careful or particular.—**so·lic·i·tous·ly**, *adv.*—**so·lic·i·tous·ness**, *n.*

so·lic·i·tude, so·lis′i·tŏd″, so·lis′i·tūd″, *n.* The state of being solicitous; concern; anxiety; *usu. pl.* causes of concern, care, or anxiety.

sol·id, sol′id, *a.* [O.Fr. Fr. *solide*, < L. *solidus*, solid: cf. L. *sollus*, whole, entire, unbroken.] Having the interior completely filled up; compact, not hollow; having relative firmness or coherence of particles, as matter neither liquid nor gaseous; pertaining to or having the dimensions of length, breadth, and thickness, as a geometrical body or figure; substantial or not flimsy; united, firm, or unanimous, as in opinion or policy; sound or valid, as reasons or arguments; consolidated; reliable or sensible; financially sound or strong; undivided or continuous; entire or uninterrupted; forming the whole or being the only substance; uniform in tone or shade; real or genuine; as, *solid* comfort; written without a hyphen, as a compound word; *print.* having the lines uninterrupted by leads or having few open spaces: opposed to *open.*—*n.* A spatial figure having the three dimensions of length, breadth, and thickness, as a cube; matter exhibiting relative firmness and volume.—**sol·id·ly**, *adv.*—**sol·id·ness**, *n.*

sol·i·da·go, sol″i·dā′gō, *n.* pl. **sol·i·da·gos.** [N.L. use of M.L. *solidago*, plant of reputed healing virtue, < L. *solidus*, E. *solid.*] *Bot.* any plant of the genus *Solidago*, in the composite family, having small yellow flowers massed in clusters. Also *goldenrod.*

sol·id an·gle, *n. Geom.* an angle formed at a point of intersection of three or more planes or at the vertex of a cone, measured by the area intercepted on a sphere of unit radius with the point as center.

sol·i·dar·i·ty, sol″i·dar′i·tē, *n.* pl. **sol·i·dar·i·ties.** [Fr. *solidarité*, < *solidaire.*] Union or fellowship arising from common responsibilities and interests, as between members of a class or body of persons, or between classes, peoples, or groups; community of interests, feelings, purposes, or action; *sociol.* social cohesion.

sol·id ge·om·e·try, *n.* The geometry that deals with three-dimensional figures. Compare *plane geometry.*

so·lid·i·fy, so·lid′i·fī″, *v.t.*—*solidified, solidifying.* [Fr. *solidifier.*] To make solid or into a hard or compact mass; to change from a liquid or gaseous form to a solid; to unite firmly or consolidate.—*v.i.* To become solid or compact.—**so·lid·i·fi·a·ble**, *a.*—**so·lid·i·fi·ca·tion**, *n.*

so·lid·i·ty, so·lid′i·tē, *n.* pl. **so·lid·i·ties.** The state, property, or quality of being solid; firmness, hardness, or strength of substance; substantialness; soundness of character, mind, finances, or the like. *Geom.* the amount of space occupied by a solid body; volume.

sol·id-look·ing, sol′id·lŏk″ing, *a.* Giving the appearance of stability or worth.

sol·id pro·pel·lant, *n. Milit.* a rocket or guided missile propellant in solid form, usu. containing both fuel and oxidizer combined.

sol·id-state, sol′id·stāt′, *a. Electron.* of any electronic device, having solid material such as transistors substituted for gaseous elements, movable parts, filaments, or vacuum tubes.

sol·id·un·gu·late, sol″i·dung′ya·lit, sol″-i·dung′ya·lāt″, *a.* [L. *solidus*, solid, and *ungula*, a hoof.] Having hoofs that are whole and not cloven, as the horse or zebra.

so·lil·o·quy, so·lil′o·kwē, *n.* pl. **so·lil·o·quies.** [L. *soliloquium—solus*, alone, and *loquor*, to speak.] The act or an instance of talking to oneself; in drama, a monologue, usu. giving the illusion of unuttered reflections in which the character discloses his innermost thoughts only to the audience and not to the other performers.—**so·lil·o·quize**, so·lil′o·kwīz″, *v.i.—soliloquized, soliloquizing.* To utter a soliloquy; to talk to oneself.—**so·lil·o·quist**, so·lil′o·quiz·er, so·lil′o·kwist, *n.*

sol·ip·sism, sol′ip·siz″um, *n.* [L. *solus*, alone, and *ipse*, self.] *Philos.* the theory that nothing but the self exists, and therefore that the self is the only object of real knowledge.—**sol·ip·sist**, *n.*—**sol·ip·sis·tic**, sol″-ip·sis′tik, *a.*

sol·i·taire, sol′i·târ″, *n.* [Fr. *solitaire*, < L. *solitarius.*] Any of numerous card games played by a single individual; also *patience.* A gem, esp. a diamond, set alone, as in a ring; *Brit.* a game for one person in which marbles or pegs are arranged in cupped depressions or holes on a board.

sol·i·tar·y, sol′i·ter″ē, *a.* [L. *solitarius*, < *solus*, alone.] Alone; without companions, or unattended; living alone or avoiding the society of others; being the only one or ones; as, a *solitary* instance; characterized by solitude, as a place; unfrequented, secluded, or lonely. *Zool.* not social, as certain wasps; simple, or not compound, as certain ascidians. *Bot.* occurring or growing singly, as a flower.—*n.* pl. **sol·i·tar·ies.** One who lives alone or in solitude, or avoids the society of others, esp. from religious motives; a hermit; *colloq.* solitary confinement in prison.—**sol·i·tar·i·ly**, *adv.*—**sol·i·tar·i·ness**, *n.*

sol·i·tude, sol′i·tŏd″, sol′i·tūd″, *n.* [Fr. *solitude*, < L. *solitudo*, < *solus*, alone.] The state of being alone; remoteness from society; absence of human inhabitants; a lonely, deserted place.

sol·ler·et, sol″er·et′, sol′er·et″, sol″e·ret′, sol′e·ret′, *n.* That part of a suit of medieval armor serving as a foot covering or shoe, made of overlapping plates of steel.

sol·mi·za·tion, sol″mi·zā′shan, *n.* [Fr. *solmisation*, < *solmiser*, use the syllables *sol, mi*, etc., in singing.] *Mus.* the act, process, or system of using certain syllables, esp. the sol-fa syllables, to represent the tones of the scale in singing.

so·lo, sō′lō, *n.* pl. **so·los, so·li.** [It., < L. *solus*, alone, E. *sole.*] A musical composition or passage intended for performance by one voice or one instrument, with or without accompaniment; any performance, as a dance, by one person; an airplane pilot's first unaccompanied flight; *cards*, any of certain games in which one person plays alone against others.—*a. Mus.* performing alone, as an instrument or its player; performed alone; not combined with other parts of equal importance; not concerted. Alone; without a companion or partner.—*adv.* Alone; unaccompanied.—*v.i.—soloed, soloing.* To perform a solo.—**so·lo·ist**, sō′lō·ist, *n.*

Sol·o·mon, sol′o·mon, *n.* [From *Solomon*, Son of David and king of Israel in the 10th century B.C., renowned for his great wisdom.] An extraordinarily wise man; a sage. —**Sol·o·mo·ni·an, Sol·o·mon·ic**, sol″-o·mō′nē·an, sol″o·mōn′ya, sol″o·mon′ik, *a.* Of or pertaining to Solomon or his wisdom.

Sol·o·mon's seal, *n.* Star of David.

Sol·o·mon's-seal, sol′o·monz-sēl″, *n.* Any of various plants of the genus *Polygonatum*, in the lily family, with a thick rootstock bearing circular, seallike scars.

So·lon, sō′lon, *n.* [From *Solon*, the Athenian lawgiver, about 638 to 558 B.C.] (*Often l.c.*) A wise lawgiver or legislator; a sage.— **So·lo·ni·an**, sō·lō′nē·an, *a.—*So·lon·ic, sō·lon′ik, *a.*

so long, *interj. Colloq.* good-by.

sol·stice, sol′stis, sōl′stis, *n.* [O.Fr. Fr. *solstice*, < L. *solstitium*, < *sol*, sun and *sistere*, stand.] *Astron.* either of the two times in the year when the sun is at its greatest distance from the celestial equator, reaching the northernmost point on June 21 and the southernmost point on Dec. 22, called respectively, in the northern hemisphere, *summer solstice* and *winter solstice*; either of the two points in the ecliptic reached by the sun at these times. *Fig.* a farthest or culminating point; a turning point.—**sol·sti·tial**, sol-stish′al, sōl-stish′-al, *a.—*sol·sti·tial·ly, *adv.*

sol·u·bil·i·ty, sol″ū-bil′i·tē, *n.* The quality of being soluble; capability of being dissolved or liquefied.

sol·u·ble, sol′ū-bl, *a.* [L. *solubilis*, < *solvo*, to melt.] Susceptible of being dissolved in a fluid; capable of being solved or resolved. —**sol·u·ble·ness**, *n.—*sol·u·bly, *adv.*

sol·u·ble glass, *n.* See *water glass.*

sol·ute, sol′ūt, sō′lōt, *n.* [L. *solutio*, < *solvo*, to melt, dissolve.] A dissolved substance.— *a.* Having passed into solution; *bot.* not adnate.

so·lu·tion, so·lö′shan, *n.* The act of solving, clearing up, or explaining; an explanation or answer; the method of resolving a problem; a coming to a conclusion; the act of dissolving or state of being dissolved. *Chem.* the homogeneous combination of a liquid, solid, or gas with another liquid or, more rarely, a gas or solid; the preparation formed by this combination. *Med.* the crises or termination of a disease; a rupture or separation such as a laceration or fracture. *Law*, settlement of a debt or claim.

So·lu·tre·an, So·lu·tri·an, so·lö′trē·an, *a.* Relating to or characteristic of an Upper Paleolithic culture distinguished by the skilled working of flint blades and implements.

solv·a·ble, sol′va·bl, *a.* Capable of being solved, as a problem.—**solv·a·bil·i·ty**, solv·a·ble·ness, *n.*

solv·ate, sol′vāt, *n.* The compound formed by combining a solute and its solvent.—*v.t., v.i.—solvated, solvating.*—**sol·va·tion**, *n.*

Sol·vay proc·ess, sol′vā pros′es, *Fr.* sạl·vä′, *n.* [From E. *Solvay*, Belgian chemist.] A process for the manufacture of sodium carbonate by the interaction of common salt, ammonia, carbon dioxide, and calcium carbonate.

solve, solv, v.t.—solved, solving. [L. solvo, solutum, to loosen, release, solve, for se-luo, < se, apart, and luo, to loosen; solvo is seen also in soluble, dissolute, resolute, etc.] To find an answer for; to explain; to make clear; to find or attain a solution to, as a problem.—**solv·er**, n.

sol·vent, sol'vent, a. [L. solvens, solventis, ppr. of solvo.] Able to pay all just debts; having the power of dissolving.—n. Any substance that dissolves other substances; that which explains or solves.—**sol·ven·cy**, sol'ven·sē, n.—**sol·vent·ly**, adv.

sol·vol·y·sis, sol·vol'i·sis, n. Chem. a protolytic reaction between a solute and solvent that forms a new compound. Also **ly·ol·y·sis**.

so·ma, sō'ma, n. [Skt., < su-, press out, extract.] A shrubby climber, Sarcostemma acidum, native to eastern India and having an aciduluous, milky juice; an intoxicating drink prepared from the juice of this plant, used in religious ceremonies in ancient India; (cap.) the drink or the plant personified and worshiped as a god.

so·ma, sō'ma, n. pl. **so·ma·ta**, **so·mas**. [N.L. < Gr. sōma, body.] Biol. all the body cells of an organism except the germ cells.

So·ma·li, sō·mä'lē, so·mä'lē, n. pl. **So·ma·li**, **So·ma·lis**. A member of a Hamitic race with an admixture of Arab, Negro, and other blood, and dwelling in eastern Africa, including Somaliland, and adjacent regions; their language.

so·mat·ic, sō·mat'ik, a. [Gr. sōmatikós, < sōma, body.] Of or pertaining to the body; bodily, corporeal, or physical; biol. of or pertaining to the soma; anat., zool. pertaining to the cavity of the body of an animal, or more esp. to its walls.—**so·mat·i·cal·ly**, adv.

so·mat·ic cell, n. Biol. any of the cells that compose the various organs, tissues, and other parts of the body, except the reproductive cells: opposed to germ cell.

so·ma·to·gen·ic, sō''ma·to·jen'ik, so·mat''o·jen'ik, a. Having origin in or affecting somatic cells. Also **so·ma·to·ge·net·ic**, sō''ma·to·je·net'ik.

so·ma·tol·o·gy, sō''ma·tol'o·jē, n. The science dealing with the body in all its physical aspects; a branch of anthropology in which the physical nature of evolving man is subjected to comparative study and evaluation.—**so·ma·to·log·ic**, **so·ma·to·log·i·cal**, sō''ma·to·loj'ik, so·mat''o·loj'ik, a.—**so·ma·to·log·ic·al·ly**, adv.—**so·ma·tol·o·gist**, n.

so·ma·to·plasm, sō''ma·to·plaz''um, so·mat''o·plaz'um, n. Biol. the protoplasm making up the composition of a body or soma cell of an organism: distinguished from germ plasm.—**so·ma·to·plas·tic**, a.

so·ma·to·pleure, sō'ma·ta·plụr', so·mat'a·plụr'', n. [Gr. pleura, side.] Embryol. the embryonic layer formed out of the association between the ectoderm and the parietal layer of the lateral mesoderm.—**so·ma·to·pleu·ral**, **so·ma·to·pleu·ric**, a.

so·ma·to·type, sō'ma·to·tīp'', so·mat'o·tip'', n. Physique; body type; one of the types of body build, ectomorph, endomorph, or mesomorph, differentiated by the relative prominence of structures developed from one of the three embryonic germ layers.—**so·ma·to·typ·ic**, sō''ma·to·tip'ik, so·mat''o·tip'ik, a.—**so·ma·to·typ·i·cal·ly**, adv.

som·ber, Brit. **som·bre**, som'bēr, a. [Fr. sombre; appar. < L. umbra, shade, with some prefix.] Dark; shadowy; dimly lighted; dark and dull, as color, or as things in respect to color; gloomy, dismal, or

depressing in mood or character; grave, serious, or melancholy in appearance.—**som·ber·ly**, Brit. **som·bre·ly**, adv.—**som·ber·ness**, Brit. **som·bre·ness**, n.

som·bre·ro, som·brâr'ō, Sp. sạm·bRe'Rạ, n. pl. **som·bre·ros**. [Sp. < sombra, shade: cf. somber.] A broad-brimmed hat with a high crown, made of felt or straw, worn in Spain, Mexico, and the southwestern U.S.

some, sum, unstressed som, a. [O.E. sum, some, one, a certain; Goth. sums, Icel. sumr, Dan. somme (pl.), some; perh. akin to same.] Expressing a certain indeterminate quantity or number, sometimes a considerable quantity; as, situated at some distance; indicating a person or thing not definitely known or not specific, often followed by or other; certain, as distinct from others, as: Some people don't think so. Colloq. considerable; important; unusual, as: That was some game!—pron. Unspecified persons or things, often followed by of; as, some of us, some of our provisions; a certain undetermined additional amount; as, a pound and then some.—adv. Approximately; as, some 20 people; colloq. considerably; as, to go some to win.

some·bod·y, sum'bod''ē, sum'bud''ē, sum'-bo·dē, pron. A person unknown or of uncertain identity.—n. pl. **some·bod·ies**. A person of distinction or consequence.

some·day, sum'dā'', adv. At some unspecified time in the future.

some·how, sum'hou'', adv. In some way not yet known or evident.

some·one, sum'wun'', sum'won', pron. Some person; somebody.

some·place, sum'plās'', adv. In some locality or other.

som·er·sault, sum'ēr·sạlt'', n. [Corrupted < O.Fr. soubresault, It. soprassalto, lit. 'an overleap'; < L. supra, over, and salio, to leap.] A head-over-heels revolution of the body performed either forward or backward, from a standing or a sitting position.—v.i. To execute a somersault. Also **som·er·set**, summersault, sum'ēr·set''.

some·thing, sum'thing, n. An indeterminate or unknown event or thing; an indefinite quantity or degree; a little; a person or thing of considerable importance; an additional amount that is inconsequential or not worth remembering.—adv. In some degree or measure, as: It was something like that.

some·time, sum'tīm'', adv. At some vaguely indefinite time in the future; at an unspecified time.—a. Having been formerly; former; late.

some·times, sum'tīmz'', adv. At times; now and then; on occasion.

some·way, sum'wā'', adv. In some way; somehow. Also **some·ways**.

some·what, sum'hwut'', sum'hwot'', sum'-hwạt, sum'wut'', sum'wot'', sum'wạt, adv. In some degree or measure; rather; slightly. —pron. Some indeterminate quantity, degree, portion, or the like; a person or thing having in some measure a nature and quality, as: She is somewhat of a bore.

some·where, sum'hwâr'', sum'wâr'', adv. In, at, or to some place unspecified or not known; in one place or another; at some location not definitely known or stated. Also dial. **some·wheres**.—n. A place not known or not specified.

some·whith·er, sum'hwiTH''ēr, sum'-wiTH''ēr, adv. To some indeterminate place; somewhere.

so·mite, sō'mīt, n. [Gr. sōma, body.] Biol. One of the successive parts or segments making up the body of certain animals; metamere.—**so·mi·tal**, sō'mi·tal, a.—**so·mit·ic**, sō·mit'ik, a.

som·me·lier, sum''el·yā', Fr. sä·me·lyä', n. pl. **som·me·liers**. [Fr.] A steward in

charge of the storage and dispensing of wines in a restaurant.

som·nam·bu·late, som·nam'bya·lāt'', som·nam'bya·lāt'', v.i.—somnambulated, somnambulating. [L. somnus, sleep, and ambulo, ambulatum, to walk.] To walk in one's sleep.—v.t. To walk through or across while sleeping.—**som·nam·bu·lant**, a.—**som·nam·bu·la·tion**, n.

som·nam·bu·lism, som·nam'bya·liz''um, som·nam'bya·liz''um, n. The state or practice of walking or performing other motor acts while asleep; sleepwalking.—**som·nam·bu·list**, n.—**som·nam·bu·lis·tic**, a.—**som·nam·bu·lis·ti·cal·ly**, adv.

som·ni·fa·cient, som''ni·fā'shent, a. Producing or inducing sleep or sleepiness.—n.

som·nif·er·ous, som·nif'ēr·us, som·nif'-ēr·us, a. [L. somnifer—somnus, sleep, and fero, to bring.] Causing or inducing sleep, as a narcotic; soporific. Also **som·nif·ic**, som·nif'ik, som·nif'ik.

som·no·lence, som'no·lens, n. [L. somnolentia < somnolentus, sleepy, < somnus, sleep.] Sleepiness; drowsiness; inclination to sleep Also **som·no·len·cy**.

som·no·lent, som'no·lent, a. Sleepy; drowsy; inducing sleep; inclined to sleep.—**som·no·lent·ly**, adv.

son, sun, n. [O.E. sunu = D. zoon = G. sohn = Icel. sunr = Goth. sunus, son; akin to Skt. sūnu and Gr. yiós, son.] A male child or person in relation to his parents; any male descendant; one related as if by ties of sonship; a male child or person considered as a son through marriage, adoption, or regard, as a foster son, stepson, or son-in-law; a familiar term of address to a man or boy, as from an older person or ecclesiastic; a person considered native to a particular place or country; as, a son of the plains. (Cap.) the second person of the Trinity, preceded by the; Jesus Christ; also **Son of God, Son of Man**.

so·nant, sō'nant, a. [L. sonans (sonant-), ppr. of sonare, sound.] Sounding; having sound; phon. uttered with voice or vocal sound, as the sounds b, z, v: opposed to surd.—n. Phon. A sonant speech sound; the sound of a syllable; in Indo-European, sonorant.—**so·nance**, sō'nans, n.

so·nar, sō'när, n. [(SO)und (NA)vigation (R)anging.] A device similar to radar for detecting a submerged submarine, mine, or school of fish, for measuring water depths, and for communicating, based on the outward projection of sound waves and the echoes which they send back when they strike a submerged object.—a.

son·ar·man, sō'när·man, n. pl. **son·ar·men**. Nav. a petty officer in charge of the operation and maintenance of sonar equipment.

so·na·ta, so·nä'ta, n. [It., < sonare, < L. sonare, sound.] Mus. a work for one or two instruments, or more in older music, typically of three or four movements, one or more having sonata form.

so·na·ta form, n. Mus. a form of composition in three main sections, an exposition, a development, and a recapitulation, and used commonly in movements, esp. the first, of sonatas, symphonies, and chamber works.

son·a·ti·na, son''a·tē'na, It. sạ''nä·tē'nä, n. pl. **son·a·ti·nas**, **son·a·ti·ne**. [It., dim. of sonata.] Mus. a short or simplified sonata.

sonde, sond, n. Radiosonde.

sone, sōn, n. A subjective unit of measurement of loudness equal to a tone of 1000 cycles per second at 40 decibels above the hearing threshold of the listener.

song, sạng, song, n. [O.E. sang, song = D. zang = G. sang = Icel. söngr = Goth. saggws, song; from the verb represented by E. sing.] The act or art of singing; vocal music; that which is sung; poetical composition or poetry; a short metrical composition intended or adapted for singing, esp. one in rhymed stanzas; a lyric; a ballad; a piece of music adapted for singing or simulating a piece to be sung; as, Mendelssohn's *Songs Without Words*; the musical or tuneful sounds produced by certain birds or insects.—**for a song**, for a low price.

song·and·dance, *n.* A theatrical act which consists of some song and dance, esp. as seen in vaudeville. *Colloq.* an alibi or explanation that is misleading or untrue; nonsense.

song·bird, sạng′bûrd″, song′bûrd″, *n. Ornith.* a bird that sings; an oscine bird. *Fig.* a woman who sings.

song·fest, sạng′fest″, song′fest″, *n. Colloq.* a festival at which group singing is the chief entertainment.

song·ful, sạng′fụl, song′fụl, *a.* Abounding in song; melodious.—**song·ful·ly,** *adv.*—**song·ful·ness,** *n.*

song·less, sạng′lis, song′lis, *a.* Devoid of song; lacking the power of song, as certain birds.—**song·less·ly,** *adv.*

song·ster, sạng′stẽr, song′stẽr, *n.* One who sings; a singer; a songbird; a writer of songs; a poet; a book of songs.—**song·stress,** *n.* A female singer.

song·writ·er, sạng′rī″tẽr, song′rī″tẽr, *n.* A composer or lyricist of popular songs.

son·ic, son′ik, *a.* [L. *sonus*, sound.] Of or pertaining to sound waves; *aeron.* referring to speeds approximating that of sound, about 740 miles per hour.—**son·i·cal·ly,** *adv.*

son·ic bar·ri·er, *n. Aeron.* the point at which an aircraft passing from subsonic to supersonic speed encounters sudden increased turbulence or drag caused by compression of the surrounding air. Also *sound barrier,* **tran·son·ic bar·ri·er.**

son·ic boom, *n.* A loud explosive report caused by the sudden dissipation of a pressure field built up around an airplane as it reaches the speed of sound.

son·ic depth find·er, *n.* Echo sounder.

son-in-law, sun′in·lạ″, *n.* pl. **sons-in-law.** A man married to one's daughter.

son·less, sun′lis, *a.* Having no son.

son·net, son′it, *n.* [Ff. *sonnet* < It. *sonetto,* dim. of *sono, suono,* sound, song, < L. *sonus,* E. *sound, n.*] A poem, properly expressive of a single complete thought, idea, or sentiment, of 14 lines usu. in five-foot iambic meter, with rhymes arranged according to one of two definite schemes.

son·net·eer, son′i·têr″, *n.* A composer of sonnets; an inferior poet.—*v.i.* To compose sonnets.

son·net·ize, son′i·tīz″, *v.i.*—**sonnetized,** *sonnetizing.* To create or write a sonnet.—*v.t.* To create a sonnet on or to, as a subject or a person.—**son·net·i·za·tion,** *n.*

son·net se·quence, *n.* A series of sonnets written by one author which has a single, basic theme and a discernible development.

son·ny, sun′ē, *n.* pl. **son·nies.** [Dim. of *son.*] Little son: often used as a familiar term of address to a boy.

son·o·buoy, son′o·boi″, son′bō″ē, *n. Navig.* an acoustic receiver and radio transmitter mounted in a buoy, used to detect and transmit underwater sounds.

so·no·rant, so·nôr′ant, so·nạr′ant, sō·-nôr′ant, sō·nạr′ant, *n. Phon.* a consonant which is voiced, but less sonorously than a vowel, as *l, m,* and *r* in unstressed final syllables of certain English words.

so·no·rous, so·nôr′us, so·nạr′us, son′ẽr·us, *a.* [L. *sonorus,* < *sonor,* sound, < *sonare.*] Giving out or capable of giving out a sound, esp. a deep or resonant sound, as a thing or a place; loud, deep, or resonant, as a sound; rich and full in sound, as language or verse; resounding, as in an

orator's delivery.—**so·nor·i·ty, so·no·-rous·ness,** so·nạr′i·tē, so·nor′i·tē, *n.*—**so·no·rous·ly,** *adv.*

so·no·vox, sō′no·voks″, son′o·voks″, *n.* An electronic device for transmitting recorded sounds to the laryngeal area to be emitted in turn as words through the mouth, as by a person whose larynx has been removed.

son·ship, sun′ship, *n.* The state of being a son; the kinship of son to father.

son·sy, son·sie, son′sē, *a.*—*sonsier, sonsiest.* [Gael. *sonas,* good fortune, prosperity.] *Sc., Ir., North E. dial.* Bringing luck or good fortune; thriving or plump; buxom or comely; comfortable-looking; cheerful; jolly.

soon, sön, *adv.* [O.E. *sóna* = O.E. *sāna,* immediately: cf. Goth. *suns,* immediately, soon.] Within a short period after this or that time, event, or the like, as: We shall *soon* know. Before long; in the near future; at an early date or preceding the normal or usual time; promptly or quickly; readily or willingly, as: I would as *soon* walk as ride. *Dial.* early in a period of time; as, *soon* in the morning.—**soon·er or lat·er,** eventually.

soon·er, sö′nẽr, *n. Slang.* One who settles on government land before it is legally opened to settlers in order to gain the choice of location, specif. one who staked out a claim in Indian territory in 1889; one who gains an unfair advantage by getting ahead of others; (*cap.*) a resident or native of Oklahoma.

soot, sụt, sõt, *n.* [O.E. *sót,* soot = Icel. *sót,* Dan. *sod,* L.G. *sott,* soot.] A black substance formed from fuel in combustion, rising in fine particles and adhering to the sides of the chimney conveying the smoke.—*v.t.* To smudge or cover with soot.—*v.i.* To use soot as a fertilizer or as a slug repellant.

sooth, söth, *a.* [O.E. *soth,* akin to Icel. *sannr,* Goth. *sunjis,* true, also Skt. *satya,* real, true, and *sant,* real, true, prop. ppr., 'being.'] *Archaic.* True or real; soothing, soft, or delicious.—*n.* [O.E. *sõth.*] *Archaic.* truth, reality, or fact.—**sooth·ly,** *adv.*

soothe, sõ͞TH, *v.t.*—*soothed, soothing.* [O.E. *sõthian,* < *sõth,* E. *sooth, a.*] To tranquilize or calm the feelings of, as a person; relieve, ease, comfort, or refresh; to mitigate, assuage, or allay, as pain, sorrow, or doubt. —*v.i.* To exert a soothing influence; bring tranquility, calm, ease, or comfort.—**sooth·er,** *n.*

sooth·fast, söth′fast″, söth′fäst″, *a.* [O.E. *sõthfæst,* < *sõth,* E. *sooth, n.* and *fæst,* E. *fast, a.*] *Archaic.* True, as statements; truthful or veracious, as persons; faithful or loyal.—**sooth·fast·ly,** *adv.*—**sooth·fast·-ness,** *n.*

sooth·ing, sö͞′THing, *a.* Assuaging; relieving; tending to calm or quiet, as a sedative.—**sooth·ing·ly,** *adv.*—**sooth·ing·-ness,** *n.*

sooth·say, söth′sā″, *v.i.*—*soothsaid, soothsaying.* To foretell; to predict.—**sooth·-say·er,** söth′sā″ẽr, *n.*

sooth·say·ing, söth′sā″ing, *n.* A foretelling; a prediction; the practice of foretelling events.

soot·y, sụt′ē, sõt′ē, *a.*—*sootier, sootiest.* Covered, blackened, or smudged with soot; consisting of or resembling soot; of a black, dark brown, or dusky color.—**soot·i·ly,** *adv.*—**soot·i·ness,** *n.*

sop, sop, *n.* [Same as Icel. *soppa,* a sop, a sup; Sw. *soppa,* broth, soup; D. *sop;* L.G. *soppe,* a sop. Closely connected with *sup, soup.*] Something dipped in broth or other liquid food, and intended to be eaten; something given to pacify or bribe; a weak-willed person; a wet mass.—*v.t.*—*sopped, sopping.* To soak or saturate in a liquid; to wet through; to absorb, as a liquid, usu. followed by *up.*—*v.i.* To be or become completely wet.—**sop·ping,** *a.*

soph·ism, sof′iz·um, *n.* [O.Fr. *sophisme,* *sophime* (Fr. *sophisme*), < L. *sophisma,* < Gr. *sóphisma,* clever device, trick, sophism, < *sophizesthai,* deal subtly, < *sophós,* skilled, clever, wise.] A specious or fallacious argument, used either to display ingenuity in reasoning or for the purpose of deception; any false argument; a fallacy; sophistry; *philos.* a specious syllogism, intended to deceive.

soph·ist, sof′ist, *n.* [= Fr. *sophiste,* < L. *sophista, sophistes,* < Gr. *sophistēs,* adept, wise man, sophist, < *sophizesthai.*] (Often *cap.*) any of a class of professional teachers in ancient Greece who gave instruction in various fields, as in general culture, rhetoric, politics, or disputation; any member of a portion of this class who, while professing to teach skill in reasoning, concerned themselves with ingenuity and specious effectiveness rather than soundness of argument. (*l.c.*) one who reasons speciously rather than soundly; a man of learning; a philosopher.

so·phis·tic, so·fis′tik, *a.* [L. *sophisticus,* < Gr. *sophistikós.*] Of the nature of sophistry; fallacious; characteristic or suggestive of sophistry; of or pertaining to sophists or sophistry; given to the use of sophistry. Also **so·phis·ti·cal.**—**so·phis·ti·cal·ly,** *adv.*—**so·phis·ti·cal·ness,** *n.*

so·phis·ti·cate, so·fis′ti·kāt″, *v.t.*—*sophisticated, sophisticating.* [M.L. *sophisticatus,* pp. of *sophisticare,* < L. *sophisticus,* E. *sophistic.*] To make less natural, simple, or ingenuous; to alter, as a person, by education or experience; disillusion; to increase the capability of, as a device, process, or system, by making it more complex or intricate.—*v.i.* To use sophistry; to quibble.—**so·fis′ti·kit,** so·fis′ti·kāt″, *n.* One who is sophisticated or worldly-wise.— **so·phis·ti·ca·tor,** *n.*

so·phis·ti·cat·ed, so·fis′ti·kā″tid, *a.* Changed from the natural character or original simplicity, as a person whose ideas, tastes, manners, or the like have been altered by education or experience; having a quality appreciated by or identified with intellectuals or sophisticates; intricate or complex, as certain techniques, devices, or systems; as, a *sophisticated* radar alarm system; altered by refining or adulteration, as an industrial oil.—**so·phis·ti·cat·ed·ly,** *adv.*

so·phis·ti·ca·tion, so·fis″ti·kā′shan, *n.* [M.L. *sophisticatio(n-).*] Sophisticated character, ideas, tastes, or ways as the result of education or worldly experience; change from the natural character or simplicity, or the resulting condition; impairment or debasement, as by altered purity or genuineness; as, the *sophistication* of religion; the use of sophistry; a sophism, quibble, or fallacious argument.

soph·ist·ry, sof′i·strē, *n.* pl. **soph·ist·ries.** [O.Fr. Fr. *sophisterie.*] Specious or fallacious reasoning; the doctrine of the ancient Greek Sophists.

soph·o·more, sof′o·mōr″, sof′o·mạr″, sof′-mōr, sof′mạr, *n.* [< Gr. *sophos,* wise, and *moros,* foolish.] In American high schools, colleges, and universities, a student in the second year of a four-year course; one in the second year of any endeavor.

soph·o·mor·ic, sof″o·mạr′ik, sof″o·mor′ik, *a.* Of, pertaining to, or characteristic of a sophomore or sophomores; suggestive of or resembling the traditional stereotyped sophomore, as in intellectual conceit, pretensions, or self-assurance. Also **soph·-o·mor·i·cal.**—**soph·o·mor·i·cal·ly,** *adv.*

so·por, sō′pẽr, *n.* [L., deep sleep, akin to *somnus,* also Gr. *hypnos,* Skt. *svapna,* O.E. *swefn,* sleep.] *Pathol.* A deep, unnatural sleep; lethargy.

so·po·rif·er·ous, sop″o·rif′ẽr·us, sō″po·rif′ẽr·us, a. [L. soporifer—sopor, soporis, sleep (cogn. with Skt. svapna, to sleep, Gr. hypnos, sleep), and fero, to bring.] Tending to bring sleep; soporific.—**so·po·rif·er·ous·ly,** adv.—**so·po·rif·er·ous·ness,** n.

sop·o·rif·ic, sop″o·rif′ik, sō″po·rif′ik, a. [L. sopor, and facio, to make.] Causing sleep; tending to cause sleep; marked by lethargy or drowsiness.—n. A drug or agent inducing sleep.

sop·py, sop′ē, a.—**soppier, soppiest.** Soaked, drenched, or very wet, as ground; rainy, as weather; Brit. slang, overly sentimental.

so·pran·o, so·prän′ō, so·prä′nō, n. pl. **so·pran·os,** It. **so·pra·ni.** [It., < sopra, L. supra, above.] Mus. The highest range of female voice; a singing voice, usu. of women and boys, having a range from middle C upward two octaves or higher; one who sings soprano; an instrument with a soprano range; the music or part for such an instrument or voice.—a. Mus. Having a soprano range; pertaining to a soprano voice, music, part, or instrument.

so·ra, sōr′a, sạr′a, n. [Origin uncertain.] A small, short-billed N. American rail, Porzana carolina. Also **Car·o·li·na rail, so·ra rail.**

sorb, sạrb, n. [L. sorbus, service tree, sorbum, its fruit: cf. service.] A European service tree, Sorbus domestica, or a rowan, S. aucuparia; the fruit of either. Also **sorb ap·ple.**

sor·bose, sạr′bōs, n. Biochem. a simple crystalline sugar, $C_6H_{12}O_6$, produced industrially from bacterial oxidation of sorbitol: a main agent in the chemical synthesis of vitamin C.

sor·cer·er, sạr′sẽr·ẽr, n. [Fr. sorcier, a sorcerer, < L.L. sortiarius, a caster of lots, < L. sors, sortis, a lot (whence also sort).] A conjuror; one practicing witchcraft or sorcery; a magician.—**sor·cer·ess,** sạr′sẽr·is, n. A female sorcerer.

sor·cer·y, sạr′sẽ·rē, n. pl. **sor·cer·ies.** [O.Fr. sorcerie.] Divination through the supposed assistance of evil spirits; black magic; enchantment; witchcraft.—**sor·cer·ous,** sạr′sẽr·us, a.

sor·did, sạr′did, a. [Fr. sordide, L. sordidus, < sordes, filth.] Filthy; neglected or squalid; base or mean in character; meanly avaricious; covetous; selfish.—**sor·did·ly,** adv.—**sor·did·ness,** n.

sor·di·no, sạr·dē′nō, It. sạr·dē′nạ, n. pl. **sor·di·ni,** sạr·dē′nē. [It., < sordo, deaf, dull, < L. surdus, E. surd.] Mus. A device for deadening the sound of various instruments; a mute.

sore, sōr, sạr, a.—**sorer, sorest.** [O.E. sār, Icel. sārr, Dan. saar, Goth. sair, a wound; G. sehr, very.] Painful or tender, as a bruise, wound, or inflammation on the body or skin; stiff and tender, as from physical exertion; suffering mental anguish or grief; as, sore in mind and heart; producing misery or suffering; colloq. angered, irritated, or resentful.—n. A place on the body where the skin or flesh is bruised, cut, infected, or painful; any cause of sorrow, pain, misery, or vexation.—adv. Archaic, sorely.—**sore·ly,** adv.—**sore·ness,** n.

sore·head, sōr′hed″, sạr′hed″, n. Slang, one easily offended or angered.—**sore·head·ed,** a.

sore throat, n. Inflammation of The pharynx, fauces, or tonsils, marked by pain, esp. in swallowing.

sor·ghum, sạr′gum, n. [< sorgo, its Italian name.] A cereal plant, Sorghum vulgare, cultivated for fodder, grain, and juice; a syrup or molasses boiled down from the juice.

sor·go, sạr′gō, n. pl. **sor·gos.** Any of a number of varieties of sorghum cultivated chiefly for its sweet juice that is used in the manufacture of syrup and sugar, and for silage or fodder. Also **sor·gho,** sweet sorghum.

so·ri, sōr′ī, sạr′ī, n. Plural of sorus.

sor·i·cine, sạr′i·sin″, sạr′i·sin, sor′i·sin″, sor′i·sin, a. [L. soricinus, < sorex, shrew.] Of, pertaining to, or resembling a shrew.

sor·i·tes, sō·rī′tēz, sạ·rī′tēz, n. pl. **sor·i·tes.** [Gr. sōreitēs, < sōros, a heap.] Logic, a series of syllogisms so linked together that the predicate of each that precedes forms the subject of each that follows, as $a=b$, $b=c$, $c=d$, therefore $a=d$.—**so·rit·ic, so·rit·i·cal,** a.

so·rop·ti·mist, so·rop′ti·mist, n. One belonging to an international organization of executive and professional business women associated principally for service projects.

so·ror·ate, sōr′o·rāt″, sạr′o·rāt″, n. Anthropol. a man's marriage with his wife's sister or sisters.

so·ror·i·ty, so·rạr′i·tē, so·ror′i·tē, n. pl. **so·ror·i·ties.** A group of girls or women belonging to a national or local organization, often designed to promote social life, as in colleges, or mutual interests, as in a profession.

sorp·tion, sạrp′shan, n. Phys., chem. the action by which the molecules of one substance are taken up and retained by another substance, as by the process of adsorption or absorption.

sor·rel, sạr′el, sor′el, n. [O.Fr. sorel, < sor, E. sore.] A reddish-brown color; a horse of this color.—a. Reddish-brown.

sor·rel, sạr′el, sor′el, n. [Fr. surelle, sorrel, < O.H.G. sūr, sour.] Any of certain perennial plants, esp. Rumex acetosa, a succulent acid herb used in salads; any of several plants of the genus Oxalis, as wood sorrel.

sor·rel tree, n. A N. American tree, Oxydendrum arboreum, of the heath family, having leaves with an acid flavor and racemes of white flowers.

sor·row, sor′ō, sạr′ō, n. [O.E. sorwe, sorg, sorh, care, sorrow; Icel., Dan., and Sw. sorg, G. sorge, Goth. saurga, sorrow.] Pain of mind from loss, disappointment, or calamity; grief; regret; sadness; an incident causing grief, distress, or regret; the manifestation of sadness or grief.—v.i. To be affected with sorrow; to grieve; to be sad.—**sor·row·er,** n.—**sor·row·ful,** sor′o·ful, sạr′o·ful, a.—**sor·row·ful·ly,** adv.—**sor·row·ful·ness,** n.

sor·ry, sor′ē, sạr′ē, a.—**sorrier, sorriest.** [O.E. sārig, < sār, E. sore, n.] Feeling regret, compunction, sympathy, pity, or the like, for some reason expressed or understood; as, to be sorry for a loss; of a deplorable, pitiable, or miserable kind; as, a sorry plight; sorrowful, grieved, or sad; fraught or associated with, or causing sorrow; wretched, poor, mean, or pitiful; as, a sorry horse.—interj. Pardon; an expression of apology.—**sor·ri·ly,** adv.—**sor·ri·ness,** n.

sort, sạrt, n. [O.Fr. Fr. sorte, fem. (beside sort, masc., E. sort), < L. sors (sort-), lot, condition, rank, L.L. class, order.] A particular kind, species, variety, or class; as, to have more of that sort in stock; a number of persons or things ranked together as being of the same general character or as having attributes in common, as: The cases fall into two sorts. A person or thing as being of a particular character, kind, or class; as, a good sort of man; a more or less adequate example of something, as: A unicorn is a sort of mythical horse. Usu. pl., print. one of the kinds of characters of a font of type.—v.t. To arrange according to sort, kind, or class; as, to sort the laundry; to separate into kinds; classify; to assign to a particular sort or class; to separate or take from others, followed by out; as, to sort out clothes needed for the trip; to class, group, or place, followed by with or together.—v.i. To consort or join with others.—**af·ter a sort,** in an imperfect manner; after a fashion.—**of sorts, of a sort,** of a mediocre or an undetermined kind; as, a writer of sorts.—**out of sorts,** not in the normal condition of good health, high spirits, or calm temper; print. lacking certain characters in a font.—**sort of,** colloq. to a certain extent; as, to feel sort of discouraged.—**sort·a·ble,** a.—**sort·er,** n.

sor·tie, sạr′tē, n. [Fr., < sortir, to issue.] Milit. A sudden or surprise incursion against the enemy by troops under siege; a flight of a single aircraft into enemy airspace; a sally.—v.i. To go on a sortie.

sor·ti·lege, sạr′ti·lij, n. [L. sortilegium—sors, lot, and lego, to select.] The act or practice of drawing lots; divination by lots; magic; sorcery.—**sor·ti·leg·ic,** sạr″ti·lej′ik, a.

sor·ti·tion, sạr·tish′an, n. [L. sortitio(n-), < sortiri, E. sort, v.] The casting or drawing of lots; determination or selection by lot; an instance of determining by lot.

so·rus, sōr′us, sạr′us, n. pl. **so·ri,** sōr′ī, sạr′ī. [Gr. sōros, a heap.] Bot. a cluster of spore cases on the back of the fronds of ferns.

S.O.S., es′ō′es′, n. The international radio code signal used by aircraft or ships at sea when in distress; any signal or request for aid.

so-so, sō′sō″, a. Indifferent or mediocre; neither very good nor very bad.—adv. In an indifferent, mediocre, or passable manner; indifferently; tolerably. Also **so·so.**

sos·te·nu·to, sos″te′nō·tō, sō″ste·nō′tō, It. sạs″te·nō′tạ, a. [It., pp. of sostenere, < L. sustinere, E. sustain.] Mus. sustained or prolonged in tone.—adv. Mus. in a sostenuto manner or style.—n. pl. **sos·te·nu·tos, sos·te·nu·ti,** It. sạs″te·nō′tä. Mus. a passage or movement whose notes are played sostenuto.

sot, sot, n. [Fr. sot, a fool, prob. < the Celtic; cf. Ir. suthan, ạ blockhead, sotaire, a fop.] A person stupefied by excessive consumption of alcohol; a habitual drunkard.—**sot·ted,** sot′id, a.—**sot·tish,** sot′ish, a.—**sot·tish·ly,** adv.—**sot·tish·ness,** n.

so·te·ri·ol·o·gy, so·tēr″ē·ol′o·jē, n. [Gr. sōterios, saving, salutary, and logos, discourse.] Theol. the doctrine of salvation, esp. through Jesus Christ.—**so·te·re·o·log·i·cal,** sō·tēr″ē·o′loj′i·kal, a.

So·thic, sō′thik, soth′ik, a. [Gr. Sōthis, an Egyptian name of the Dog Star.] Of or pertaining to Sothis or Sirius, the Dog Star. —**So·thic year,** the fixed year of the ancient Egyptians, determined by the heliacal rising of Sirius and equivalent to $365\frac{1}{4}$ days. —**So·thic cy·cle, So·thic period,** an interval of 1,460 Sothic years which is equal to 1,461 ordinary years of 365 days.

So·this, sō′this, n. Sirius.

so·tol, sō′tōl, sō·tōl′, n. [Mex.] Any plant of the liliaceous genus Dasylirion, of the southwestern U.S. and northern Mexico, resembling the yucca.

sot·to vo·ce, sot′ō vō′chē, It. sạt′tạ vạ′che, adv. [It., 'under voice.'] In an undertone; privately; softly.

sou·a·ri nut, sö·är′ē nut″, n. The large, edible, oily nut of a tall tree, Caryocar nuciferum, of tropical South America.

sou·bise, sö·bēz′, n. [From Prince Charles de Soubise, 1715–1787, marshal of France.] A strained onion sauce for meats, made with butter and either a brown or a white roux.

sou·brette, sö·bret′, n. [Fr.] Theatr. the role of a frivolous young maid engaged in flirtation and intrigue in comedy and light opera; an actress portraying such a role. Any pert young girl.

sou·bri·quet, sö′bri·kā″, sö′bri·ket″, sö″bri·kā′, sö″bri·ket′, n. Sobriquet.

sou·chong, sö′shong′, sö′chong′, n. [Chin., 'little sprouts.'] A kind of black tea grown in China, India, and Ceylon.

souf·flé, sö·flā′, sö′flä, a. [Fr. *soufflé* (fem. *soufflée*), pp. of *souffler*, blow, puff, < L. *sufflare*.] *Cooking*. Puffed up; made light, as by beating and baking. Also **souf·fléed**. —n. A light and puffy baked entrée, prepared with egg yolks, stiffly beaten egg whites, seasonings, and often with a white sauce and various other ingredients.

sough, sou, suf, v.i. [O.E. *swough*, *swōgan*, to sound.] To emit a rushing, murmuring, or whistling sound, like that of the wind; to sound like the roar of the sea; *Brit.* to speak in a whining voice.—n. A sound of this kind; a deep sigh. *Brit.* a rumor; a damp or swampy place; a sewer or ditch.

soul, sōl, n. [O.E. *sáwl*, *sāwol* = D. *ziel* = G. *seele* = Icel. *sála* = Goth. *saiwala*, soul.] The principle of life, feeling, thought, and action in man, regarded as a distinct entity separate from the body, and commonly held to be separable in existence from the body; the spiritual part of man as distinct from the physical; the spiritual part of man regarded in its moral aspect, or as believed to survive death and to be subject to happiness or misery in a life to come; *slang*, an umbrella term with many meanings including the heart and essence of being black, and the unadorned and true expression of what it is to be black. A disembodied spirit of a deceased person; the emotional part of man's nature, or the seat of the feelings or sentiments; the capacity for exalted or noble emotions or feelings; a human being or person; as, every *soul* aboard the ship; high-mindedness, noble warmth of feeling, spirit, or courage; the animating principle or essential element or part of something; the inspirer or moving spirit of some action, movement, or group; the embodiment of some quality, as: His brother was the *soul* of honor. *Christian Science*, God or the divine nature of God manifested in man.—a. Characteristic of or relating to blacks or black culture; as, a *soul* man.—**souled**, a. Usu. used in combination; as, whole-*souled* co-operation.

soul·force, sōl′färs″, sōl′fôrs″, n. [From a similar movement, Satyagraha, initiated by Mahatma Gandhi in India during the British rule.] The power, influence, feeling, or energy generated by the American Negro's struggle for social justice; the nonviolent movement characterized by protest marches and demonstrations aimed at establishing racial equality for black Americans.

soul·ful, sōl′ful, a. Full of soul; of a deeply emotional nature or character; expressive of deep feeling or emotion.—**soul·ful·ly**, adv.—**soul·ful·ness**, n.

soul·less, sōl′lis, a. Without a soul or spirit; lacking in feeling or sensitivity; heartless; without emotion.—**soul·less·ly**, adv.—**soul·less·ness**, n.

soul mate, n. One for whom a person feels a strong attraction, usu. someone of the opposite sex; an illicit sexual partner; a paramour.

soul·searching, sōl′sur″ching, n. A deep self-analysis of one's innermost motives and convictions.

sound, sound, n. [O.Fr. Fr. *son*, < L. *sonus*, sound: cf. Skt. *svan-*, to sound.] The sensation produced in the organs of hearing by certain vibrations or sound waves conveyed by the atmosphere, water, or other elastic medium; the sound wave producing this sensation; the particular auditory effect produced by a given source or medium; as, the *sound* of bells; any audibly perceptible vibrations or auditory effect; as, a variety of

sounds; a noise, vocal utterance, musical tone, or the like; as, the *sounds* from next door. *Phon.* any one of the simple elements that compose vocal utterance; the element or elements of this nature corresponding to a letter, word, or word part. The import or effect of a communication or event, as: The offer of peace had a glorious *sound*. Mere noise without meaning, as: His speech was all *sound* and no substance.—v.i. To make or emit a sound, as: The gong *sounds* for lunch. To be heard, as a sound; to impart a certain effect or impression; as, a story that *sounds* false; to resound; as: The hall *sounded* to the beat of the drums.—v.t. To cause to make or emit a sound; as, to *sound* a trumpet; to give forth, as a sound, as: The soprano *sounded* high C. To announce, order, or direct by a sound; as, to *sound* a retreat; to utter audibly, pronounce, or express; as, to *sound* each syllable; to examine by percussion or auscultation, as: A physician *sounds* the sick man's chest.— **sound off**, *slang*, To call out, as each member of a group giving in sequence his name, number, or the like; to speak out frankly, as in airing a grievance.—**with·in sound of**, not far from; within earshot.—**sound·a·ble**, a.

sound, sound, a. [M.E. *sund*, < O.E. *gesund* = D. *gezond* = G. *gesund*, sound: cf. L. *sanus*, sound, healthy.] In good condition; undamaged or unimpaired; solid; as, *sound* walls or floors; free from disease, injury, decay, or the like; as, a *sound* body or mind; financially strong, secure, or reliable; as, a *sound* investment; reliable, valid, or sensible; as, *sound* judgment, *sound* advice; of substantial or enduring character or worth; as, a *sound* value; well-founded, relevant, or without logical defect; as, *sound* reasoning; having no legal defect, as a property title; unbroken and deep; as, a *sound* sleep; vigorous, hearty, and thorough; as, a *sound* scolding; theologically correct or orthodox, as doctrines; free from moral defect or weakness; upright; good; loyal.—adv. Deeply; as, *sound* asleep.—**sound·ly**, adv.—**sound·ness**, n.

sound, sound, v.t. [O.Fr. Fr. *sonder*, < *sonde*, sounding pole; prob. < Scand.] To measure or try the depth of, as water, a deep hole, or the like, by letting down a lead plummet on the end of a line or by some equivalent means; to examine or test, as the bottom of the sea or a deep hole, with a weighted device that brings up adhering samples of matter; to investigate; to seek to fathom or ascertain; as, to *sound* the depth of a person's faith or character; to seek to elicit the views or sentiments of, as a person, through indirect inquiry, suggestive allusions, or the like, often followed by *out*; as, to *sound out* his feelings on the subject; *surg.* to explore, as a body cavity, or to dilate, as strictures in a canal, by means of a sound.—v.i. To use the lead and line or similar device for measuring depth, as at sea; to descend downward or dive to the bottom, as a whale; to make investigations, seek information, or explore, esp. by indirect inquiry.— *Surg.* a long, slender, usu. curved instrument for sounding or exploring cavities or canals of the body.—**sound·a·ble**, a.

sound, sound, n. [O.E. *sund*, a strait, a sound; Icel., Dan., Sw., and G. *sund*, a sound; from root of *sunder*, or akin to *swim*.] A passage or channel of water, as between the mainland and an isle or connecting two seas; a relatively large inlet or arm of the sea or ocean; *zool.* the air bladder of a fish.

sound bar·ri·er, n. Sonic barrier.

sound·board, sound′bôrd″, sound′bärd″, n. Sounding board.

sound bow, n. The part of a bell against which the clapper strikes.

sound·box, sound′boks″, n. The hollow chamber of a stringed musical instrument which increases sonority of tone; the mechanism in a record player which converts the undulations of record grooves into sound by means of a diaphragm and vibrating needle.

sound ef·fects, n. pl. Lifelike imitations of sounds, as of ocean waves, rain, creaking doors, hoofbeats, and the like, produced mechanically as called for during production of motion pictures, plays, or radio and television programs.

sound·er, soun′dėr, n. One who or that which sounds or measures the depth of water; a telegraphic device that sounds or clicks in response to electromagnetic impulses; a surgical sound or probe.

sound·ing, soun′ding, n. *Often pl.* the act or process of measuring depth or examining the bottom of water with or as with a lead and line. *Pl.* depths of water, usu. not more than 100 fathoms, ascertained by means of a lead and line, as at sea; parts of the water in which the ordinary deep-sea lead will reach bottom. *Meteor.* measurement of the conditions of the atmosphere at different heights.

sound·ing, soun′ding, a. Emitting or producing a sound or sounds, esp. of a loud kind; resounding; sonorous; having an imposing sound; high-sounding; pompous. —**sound·ing·ly**, adv.

sound·ing board, n. A thin, resonant plate of wood forming part of a musical instrument, and so placed as to enhance the strength and quality of the tones; a board or reflecting structure placed over or behind and above a speaker, orchestra, or the like, to direct the sound toward the audience; one or more persons toward whom ideas or opinions are directed in order to test their reactions; one who or that which serves to propagate ideas or sentiments; as, a novelist who is more a *sounding board* than a creator of fiction. Also *soundboard*.

sound·ing line, n. A lead-weighted line or cable with markings at various intervals for measuring water depth.

sound·ing rock·et, n. *Aerospace*, a rocket containing instruments used to measure and analyze meteorological conditions at high altitudes.

sound·less, sound′lis, a. Having no sound; noiseless; silent.—**sound·less·ly**, adv.— **sound·less·ness**, n.

sound·less, sound′lis, a. Unfathomable; too deep to sound.—**sound·less·ly**, adv.— **sound·less·ness**, n.

sound·proof, sound′prōf″, a. Impervious to sound.—v.t. To insulate against sound.

sound track, n. A sound record on a motion-picture film.

sound truck, n. A truck with a loudspeaker attached, used for amplifying public announcements and advertisements.

sound wave, n. *Phys.* a pressure wave, in the air or any other elastic medium, that constitutes audible or ultrasonic sound.

soup, söp, n. [Fr. *soupe*, sop (of bread, as in broth), soup, related to *souper*, take supper.] A liquid food in which meat, fish, or vegetables have been boiled with various added ingredients and seasonings. *Slang*, a heavy fog or overcast; nitroglycerin.—**in the soup**, *slang*, in difficulty or trouble.— **soup up**, *slang*, to improve or better the capacity for higher speed, as of an automobile engine.

soup·çon, söp′sän′, söp′sän, n. [Fr., < O.Fr. *souspecon*, a suspicion.] A very small quantity; a taste or slight trace.

soup kitch·en, n. A place, usu. operated by a charitable organization, which serves food to the poor either free or for a nominal charge.

soup·y, sō'pē, *a.—soupier, soupiest.* Like soup; having the consistency or appearance of soup; dense or thick, as a fog; *colloq.* sentimental.

sour, sour, sou'ēr, *a.* [O.E. *sūr* = D. *zuur* = G. *sauer* = Icel. *sūrr* = Sw. and Dan. *sur*, *sour.*] Having an acid taste, such as vinegar or lemon juice; tart; rendered acid by fermentation; affected or spoiled by fermentation; characteristic of what is so affected. *Fig.* distasteful or disagreeable; unpleasant; of persons, harsh in spirit or temper; austere; morose; peevish; of the temper, looks, words, or the like, marked by austerity, moroseness, or peevishness. Cold and wet, excessively acid, or retaining stagnant moisture, as soil; wet or inclement, as weather; rendered impure by compounds of sulfur, as gasoline.—*n.* That which is sour; something sour; a drink, as whiskey or the like, with lemon juice and sugar added; in bleaching, dyeing, or the like, a bath of an acid nature.—*v.i.* To become sour or acid; to turn sour; *fig.* to become harsh, morose, or peevish.—*v.t.* To make sour or acid; to render acid by fermentation; to spoil by fermentation. *Fig.* to make disagreeable or unpleasant; to render harsh, morose, or peevish; to embitter.—**sour·ish**, *a.*—**sour·ly**, *adv.*—**sour·ness**, *n.*

sour·ball, sour'bạl", sou'ēr·bạl", *n.* A tart, fruit-flavored, hard candy; *slang*, one who is constantly ill-tempered and grouchy.

source, sōrs, sạrs, *n.* [O.Fr. *sourse* (Fr. *source*), orig. pp. fem. of *sourdre*, < L. *surgere*, rise.] The place from which anything comes or is obtained; anything from which something proceeds or arises; the beginning or the place of origin of a stream or river; a spring or issue of water from the earth, or the place of issue; a fountain or fountainhead; an originating cause or ground; an origin; that from which news, information, or evidence, esp. of an original character, is obtained; a book or other publication supplying such information; the business or person making payments of interest, dividends, or the like.

source, book, *n.* A book or compilation of orig. material, as laboratory notes, letters, or official documents, presenting authoritative knowledge in a particular field or on a particular subject.

sour cher·ry, *n.* A small, red, tree-grown fruit, edible but extremely tart if eaten raw and unsweetened; the classic pie cherry, esp. in the United States; a tree, *Prunus cerasus*, bearing this fruit, prized also as an ornamental for its cloudlike beauty when in bloom.

sour·dine, sụr·dēn', *n. Mus.* A mute, esp. of a trumpet; an instrument of the reed family, akin to the oboe.

sour·dough, sour'dō", sou'ēr·dō", *n.* Leaven; *colloq.* a prospector, pioneer, or old settler, esp. in western Canada or Alaska.—*a.* Of or pertaining to baked goods leavened with sour dough.

sour grapes, *n.* [From Aesop's fable "The Fox and the Grapes," in which a fox, after vain efforts to reach some grapes on a high vine, gives up, saying, "The grapes are sour!"] False contempt or scorn displayed for something one does not or cannot have.

sour gum, *n.* The tupelo tree, *Nyssa sylvatica.* Also *black gum, cotton gum.*

sour or·ange, *n.* A flowering evergreen tree of the genus *Citrus*, found in warm countries and used for grafting citrus; the fruit of this tree.

sour salt, *n.* Citric acid in a crystallized form.

sour·sop, sour'sop", sou'ēr·sop", *n.* A small tree, *Annona muricata*, native to tropical America, bearing large, green, spiny fruit with a slightly acid pulp; the edible fruit of this tree.

sour·wood, sour'wụd", sou'ēr·wụd", *n.* The sorrel tree.

sou·sa·phone, sō'za·fōn", sō'sa·fōn", *n.* [Named after John Philip *Sousa*, the developer.] A large helical-shaped bass tuba which is used esp. in military bands.

souse, sous, *v.t.—soused, sousing.* [O.Fr. *sous*, < Teut.] To plunge into water or other liquid; to drench, immerse, or saturate, as with a liquid; to dash or pour, as water; to steep in pickle or brine; *slang*, to intoxicate.—*v.i.* To be plunged into water or a liquid; to fall with a splash; to be soaked or drenched; to be steeping or soaking in something; *slang*, to drink to intoxication.—*n.* An act of sousing; a plunging into or drenching with water; something kept or steeped in pickle, esp. the head, ears, and feet of a pig; a liquid used as a pickle; *slang*, a drunkard.

souse, sous, *v.i.*, *v.t.—soused, sousing. Archaic*, to pounce on, swoop, or fall suddenly.—*n. Archaic.* A pouncing down upon, as a bird on its prey; the rising or starting of the flight of a bird.

sou·tache, sō·tash', *Fr.* sō·täsh', *n.* [Fr., < Hung. *sujtas*, curl of hair.] A narrow braid, as of mohair or silk, used for trimming.

sou·tane, sō·tän', *n.* [Fr., < L.L. *subtana*, < L. *subtus*, beneath.] *Eccles.* a cassock, worn by Roman Catholic and other clergy.

sou·ter, sō'tēr, *n.* [O.E. *sūtere*, < L. *sutor*, < *suere*, sew.] *Sc., North. Eng.* A maker or mender of shoes; a shoemaker; a cobbler.

south, south, *n.* [O.E. *sūth*; Icel. *suthr*, *sunnē*, Dan. *syd*, *sönden*, O.H.G. *sund*, Mod. G. *süd*, south; allied to *sun*, being the region of the sun.] One of the four cardinal points of the compass, directly opposite to the north; the region or locality lying opposite to the north; the wind that blows from the south; (*cap.*) the section of the U.S. below the Mason-Dixon line and east of the Mississippi River.—*a.* Situated in the south or in a southern direction; pertaining to the south; proceeding from the south.—*adv.* Toward, from, or in the south.

South Af·ri·can, *a.* Of or pertaining to the southern part of Africa, esp. the Republic of South Africa.—*n.* A native of or one who resides in the Republic of South Africa, esp. one of European ancestry; Afrikaner.

south·bound, south'bound", *a.* Going or traveling south.

south by east, *n. Navig.* a point on the compass indicating a direction east of south by one point. Abbr. *SbE.*

south by west, *n. Navig.* a point on the compass indicating a direction west of south by one point. Abbr. *SbW.*

south·east, south"ēst', *Naut.* sou"ēst', *n.* [O.E. *sūthēast.*] The point or direction midway between south and east; a region in this direction; the point or direction on the compass halfway between the south and east points; a region situated in this direction; (*cap.*) the region in the southeast part of the U.S.—*a.* Lying or situated in the southeast; directed or proceeding toward the southeast; coming from the southeast, as a wind.—*adv.* In or toward the direction which is midway between south and east.

south·east by east, *n. Navig.* a point on the compass indicating a direction east of southeast by one point.

south·east by south, *n. Navig.* a point on a compass indicating a direction south of southeast by one point.

south·east·er, south"ē'stēr, *Naut.* sou"ē'-stēr, *n. Naut.* a strong wind, usu. of gale proportions, from the southeast.

south·east·er·ly, south"ē'stēr·lē, *Naut.* sou"ē'stēr·lē, *a., adv.* Toward or from the southeast.

south·east·ern, south"ē'stērn, *a.* Situated in, or going toward the southeast; coming from the southeast, as a wind; of or pertaining to the southeast.—**south·east·ern·most**, *a.*

south·east·ern·er, south"ē'stēr·nēr, *n.* A native or resident of a southeastern region; (*cap.*) one born or residing in the southeastern U.S.

south·east·ward, south"ēst'wērd, *Naut.* sou"ēst'wērd, *adv.* Toward the southeast. Also **south·east·wards.**—*a.* Toward, in, or from the southeast.—*n.* The southeast.—**south·east·ward·ly**, *a., adv.*

south·er, sou'THēr, *n.* A wind, gale, or storm from the south.

south·er·ly, suTH'ēr·lē, *a., adv.* Moving, directed, or situated toward the south; coming from the south, as a wind. Also *southernly.*—*n. pl.* **south·er·lies.** A wind that blows from the south.

south·ern, suTH'ērn, *a.* [O.E. *sūtherne*, < *sūther*, *sūth*, south.] (*Sometimes cap.*) Belonging to or of the south or South; *astron.* lying south of the celestial equator. Coming from the south, as a storm.—**south·ern·most**, *a.* Farthest south.

South·ern Cross, *n. Astron.* a bright constellation in the southern hemisphere, the four principal stars of which form a cross.

South·ern Crown, *n. Astron.* the southern constellation Corona Australis.

south·ern·er, suTH'ēr·nēr, *n.* A native or inhabitant of the south; (*usu. cap.*) a native or inhabitant of the southern U.S.—**south·ern·ism**, suTH'ēr·niz"um, *n.*

South·ern Hem·i·sphere, *n.* That half of the earth lying south of the equator.

South·ern Lights, *n. pl. Astron.* the aurora australis.

south·ern·ly, suTH'ērn·lē, *a., adv.* Toward, from, or in the south. Also *southerly.*—**south·ern·li·ness**, *n.*

south·ern·wood, suTH'ērn·wụd", *n.* [O.E. *sūtherne wudu.*] A woody-stemmed species of wormwood, *Artemisia abrotanum*, native in southern Europe and naturalized in N. America, cultivated for its aromatic, finely dissected leaves. Also **Old Man.**

south·ing, sou'THing, *n. Astron.* the time at which the moon or other heavenly body passes the meridian of a place. *Navig.* the difference in latitude southward from the last point of reckoning; movement toward the south.

south·land, south'land, south'land", *n.* [O.E. *sūthland.*] (*Sometimes cap.*) The land or region in the south; the southern part of a country.—**south·land·er**, *n.*

south·paw, south'pạ", *n. Baseball*, a left-handed pitcher; *slang*, a left-handed person.—*a.*

South Pole, *n.* The southern end of the earth's axis; (*l.c.*) the pole on a magnet pointing to the south.

south-south·east, south'south'ēst', *Naut.* sou'sou"ēst', *n. Navig.* a point on the compass halfway between southeast and due south.—*a., adv.*

south-south·west, south'south"west', *Naut.* sou'sou"west', *n. Navig.* a point on a compass halfway between southwest and due south.—*a., adv.*

south·ward, south'wērd, *Naut.* suTH'ērd, *adv.* [O.E. *sūthweard.*] Toward the south; south. Also **south·wards.**—*a.* Moving, bearing, facing, or situated toward the south.—*n.* The southward part, direction, or point.—**south·ward·ly**, *adv.*

south·west, south"west', *Naut.* sou"west', *n.* The point of the compass halfway between the south and west points; (*cap.*) the southwestern area of the U.S.—*a.* Lying in the direction of the southwest; coming from the southwest.—*adv.* From, toward, or in the southwest.

south·west by south, *n. Navig.* a point on the compass indicating a direction south of southwest by one point.

south·west by west, *n. Navig.* a point on the compass indicating a direction west of southwest by one point.

south·west·er, south″wes′tẽr, *Naut.* sou″-wes′tẽr, *n.* A strong wind or storm out of the southwest; a waterproof hat worn by seamen designed to protect them from wind and rain. Also *sou′wester.*

south·west·er·ly, south″wes′tẽr·lē, *Naut.* sou″wes′tẽr·lē, *a., adv.* Toward or from the southwest.

south·west·ern, south″wes′tẽrn, *a.* Of, pertaining to, or coming from the southwest; situated in the southwest.—**south·-west·ern·most,** *a.*

south·west·ern·er, south″wes′tẽr·nẽr, *n.* One born in or residing in a southwestern region; (*cap.*) one born or living in the southwestern part of the U.S.

south·west·ward, south″west′wẽrd, *Naut.* sou″west′wẽrd, *adv.* Toward the southwest. Also **south·west·wards.**—*a.* Toward or in the southwest.—*n.* The southwest.—**south·west·ward·ly,** *a., adv.*

sou·ve·nir, sō̄′ve·nẽr′, sō̄′ve·nẽr′, *n.* [Fr. < L. *subvenire*, to occur to mind.] That which calls to mind or revives the memory of anything; a memento; a keepsake.

sou′·west·er, sou″wes′tẽr, *n.* A waterproof coat or slicker worn by seamen to protect them in stormy weather; a hat of waterproof material with a brim broader in back to keep the neck dry; a southwester.

sov·er·eign, sov′rin, sov′ẽr·in, suv′rin, suv′ẽr·in, *a.* [O.Fr. *soverain,* Mod.Fr. *souverain;* < L.L. *superanus,* < L. *super,* above, over.] Supreme in power; possessing supreme dominion or jurisdiction; royal; free of outside influence or control; as, a *sovereign* nation; having power and importance; paramount; excellent; efficacious; producing or capable of producing the greatest effect; as, a *sovereign* medicine.—*n.* A supreme ruler; the person having the highest power or authority in a state, as a king, queen, or other ruler; a monarch; a British gold coin equal to one pound sterling. Also **sov·ran, sov′ran, suv′ran.**—**sov·er·eign·ly,** *adv.*

sov·er·eign·ty, sov′rin·tē, suv′rin·tē, *n. pl.* **sov·er·eign·ties.** The state of being sovereign; the supreme power in a state; a sovereign's status; dominion; sovereign authority; an independent government. Also **sov·ran·ty.**

so·vi·et, sō̄′vē·et″, sō̄′vē·it, sō̄′vē·et′, *n.* [Russ.] An elected legislative body or council, esp. in the Soviet Union; the form of government in the Soviet Union which provides for a hierarchy of local, provincial, and national councils composed of the people and the military, and culminating in the Supreme Soviet; similar councils in other socialist governments; (*cap.*), *pl.* the citizens and the leaders of the Soviet Union.—*a.* Pertaining to or of a soviet.—**so·vi·et·ism,** sō̄′vē·i·tiz″um, *n.*

so·vi·et·ize, sō̄′vē·i·tiz″, *v.t.*—**sovietized, sovietizing.** (*Sometimes cap.*) To impose the doctrines and practices of the Soviet Union on; to organize following a soviet concept of government.—**so·vi·et·i·za·-tion,** *n.*

sow, sō̄, *v.t.*—past **sowed,** pp. **sowed** or **sown, sowing.** [O.E. *sāwan* (pret. *seow;* pp. *sāwen*), to sow = Icel. *sā,* Dan. *saae,* G. *säen,* Goth. *saian;* same root as L. *sero, satum,* to sow (whence *season*). *Seed* is from this stem.] To scatter, as seed upon the earth, for the purpose of growth; to plant by strewing; to spread abroad; to disseminate; to implant; to propagate; as, to

sow discord.—*v.i.* To scatter seed for growth and the production of a crop.—**sow·er,** *n.*

sow, sou, *n.* [O.E. *sugu, sū,* a sow = L.G. *suge,* O.D. *sowe,* G. *sau,* Dan. and Sw. *so,* sow; cogn. L. *sus,* Gr. *hus,* sow; perh. from root *su,* to bring forth (whence *son*).] The female of the swine. *Metal.* the main channel leading to a pig bed into which metal is run for molding; the metal which has hardened in the mold.

sow·bel·ly, sou′bel″e, *n. Colloq.* fat meat or bacon taken from the lower sides of the hog. Also **salt pork.**

sow bug, *n.* Any of various small terrestrial crustaceans, esp. of the genus *Oniscus,* that live mostly in damp places, as beneath rocks and logs. Also *wood louse.*

sow this·tle, sou′ this″l, *n.* Any plant of the genus *Sonchus,* esp. *S. oleraceus,* a common weed having thistlelike leaves, yellow flowers, and a milky juice.

soy, soi, *n.* [Jap., < Chin.] A salty brown sauce, as for fish, made in the Orient from soybeans that were steeped and fermented in brine; a soybean. Also **soy sauce.**

soy·a, soi′a, *n.* Soybean.

soy·bean, soi′bēn″, *n.* A protein-rich leguminous plant, *Glycine max,* used for forage; its seeds, used as a source of oil, flour, and other foods, and in the production of commercial products such as paints, plastics, and chemicals.

spa, spä, *n.* A mineral spring; a place, as a resort, which people frequent for its mineral waters.

space, spās, *n.* [O.Fr. Fr. *espace,* < L. *spatium,* space.] The unlimited or indefinitely great general area or expanse of three dimensions in which, or in portions of which, all material objects are located; the portion or extent of this in a given instance; as, the *space* occupied by a body; a reserved seat or room, as on a train, ship, or airplane; extent or room in three dimensions; a particular extent of surface; as, forests covering acres of *space;* linear distance, or a particular distance; as, trees set at an equal *space* apart; extent or a particular extent of time; as, a *space* of two hours; an interval of time or a while. *Aero-space,* the territory outside the atmosphere of the earth; outer space. *Print.* one of the blank types used to separate sentences or words; *mus.* one of the degrees or intervals between the lines of the staff. Time or linage open for advertising.—*v.t.*—**spaced, spacing.** To fix the space or spaces of; divide into spaces; to set some distance apart. *Print.* to separate, as words, letters, or lines, by space or spaces; to extend by inserting more space or spaces, usu. followed by *out.*

Space Age, *n.* The period ushered in with the successful launching of the first space satellite, Sputnik, on October 4, 1957, and continuing with subsequent space probes and manned spaceships.

space charge, *n. Electron.* the positive or negative electrical charge which a stream of ions or electrons distributes in a three-dimensional area, as in a vacuum tube or space of low atmospheric pressure.

space·craft, spās′kraft″, spās′kräft″, *n.* Spaceship.

space flight, *n.* A journey by an unmanned or manned vehicle into outer space.

space heat·er, *n.* A small stove or a portable heating device for warming a space that is enclosed, esp. a room—**space heat·ing,** *n.*

space lat·tice, *n. Phys.* the geometric or spacial arrangement of the atomic or molecular units in the structure of a crystal.

space·less, spās′lis, *a.* Infinite; boundless or limitless; occupying no space.

space·man, spās′man″, spās′man, *n. pl.*

space·men, spās′men″, spās′men. A person who travels beyond the atmosphere of the earth; astronaut.

space mark, *n. Print.* the symbol # which denotes a space between letters or words.

space med·i·cine, *n.* That branch of medicine concerned with the effects of flight through the atmosphere and in space upon the human body and with the prevention or cure of physiological or psychological malfunctions arising from these effects. Also **aer·o·space med·i·-cine.**

space·port, spās′pōrt″, spās′part″, *n.* An installation or base for testing, maintaining, storing, and launching spacecraft.

space·ship, spās′ship″, *n.* Any unmanned or manned vehicle, as a rocket, for travel outside of the earth's atmosphere. Also *spacecraft.*

space sta·tion, *n.* An artificial satellite that is manned in an earth orbit and operates as a base for observation, space research, and the launching and servicing of spacecraft. Also **space plat·form.**

space suit, *n.* A pressurized suit supplied with oxygen and other necessities for human life, work, and movement in outer space or at great heights in the atmosphere.

space-time, spās′tīm′, *n.* A system of three spatial coordinates and one time coordinate comprising a four-dimensional continuum in which all physical realities of matter or events exist. Also **space-time con·tin·u·um.**—*a.*

space walk, spās′wạk″, *n.* Any movement made by a man outside of a vehicle orbiting in space.

space writ·er, *n.* A writer, usu. a copy writer or journalist, paid in proportion to the space filled by his printed copy.

spac·ing, spā′sing, *n.* The act of one who or that which spaces; the manner in which spaces are arranged; a space or the spaces collectively in printed matter or other work.

spa·cious, spā′shus, *a.* [L. *spatiosus,* < *spatium,* E. *space.*] Containing much space, as a house, room, or street; amply large or roomy; occupying much space or vast; as, this *spacious* world; of great extent or area, as land or grounds; broad in scope, range, or inclusiveness.—**spa·cious·ly,** *adv.*—**spa·cious·ness,** *n.*

spack·le, spak′l, *n.* (*Sometimes cap.*) a product with the pastelike consistency of plastering material, used to repair cracks in walls or ceilings before decorating. (Trademark.)—*v.t.*—**spackled, spackling.** To repair or spread with this product.

spade, spād, *n.* [It. *spada,* spade at cards, orig. sword, < L. *spatha,* < Gr. *spathē,* broad blade.] A black figure shaped like a heart placed with the point upward and supported beneath by a short stem at the cusp opposite the point, used on playing cards; a card of this suit bearing such figures; *pl.* the suit of playing cards bearing such markings.

spade, spād, *n.* [O.E. *spada* = D., Dan., and Sw. *spade,* Icel. *spathi,* G. *spaten;* cogn. Gr. *spathē,* any broad blade.] An instrument for digging, having a broad blade of iron and a stout handle, adapted for use with both hands and one foot; a tool or instrument which resembles a spade; the pointed protrusion of a gun trail that holds the carriage in place at the time of recoil.—*v.t.*—**spaded, spading.** To dig with a spade.—**call a spade a spade,** to call things by their proper names; to speak plainly and candidly.—**spade·ful,** *n.*—**spad·er,** *n.*

spade·fish, spād′fish″, *n. pl.* **spade·fish, spade·fish·es.** A deep-bodied food fish, *Chaetodipterus faber,* with spiny fins, found along the eastern coast of N. America; the paddlefish.

spade·work, spād′wụrk″, *n.* Preparatory work for a project; any labor in which a spade is used.

spa·dix, spā′diks, *n.* pl. **spa·di·ces**, **spa·-dix·es**. [N.L. use of L. *spadix*, < Gr. *spadix*, palm-branch: cf. *spadiceous*.] *Bot.* a floral spike with a fleshy or thickened axis, usu. enclosed in a spathe.

spa·ghet·ti, spa·get′ē, *n.* A kind of flour paste of Italian origin cut in long, slender, solid, cordlike pieces, to be boiled and then served with various sauces; *elect.* an insulating tubing of small diameter into which bare wire can be slipped, consisting typically of plastic or cotton coated with varnish.

spa·gir·ic, **spa·gyr·ic**, spa·jēr′ik, *a.* [N.L. *spagiricus*.] *a.* Pertaining to alchemy. Also **spa·gyr·i·cal.**—*n.* An alchemist.

spa·hi, spa·hee, spä′hē, *n.* [= Fr. *spahi*, < Turk. *sipahi*, < Pers.] Formerly, one of a body of Turkish cavalry; one of a body of native Algerian cavalry in the French service.

spall, spạl, *n.* [M.E. *spalle*, a chip: cf. M.E. *spalden*, M.L.G. *spalden*, to splinter, split, G. *spalten*, split.] A chip or splinter, as of stone or ore.—*v.t.* To break into smaller pieces, as ore; to chip.—*v.i.* To chip or split off.

spall·a·tion, spạ·lā′shan, *n.* [L. *spall*, to split.] *Phys.* the splitting of an atom's nucleus, releasing several nucleons.

span, span, *n.* [O.E. *spann*, a span (the measure), *spannan*, to bind; Icel. *sponn*, Dan. *spand*, D. *span*, G. *spanne*, a span.] The space between the point of a man's thumb to that of the little finger when his hand is spread, usu. taken as nine inches; a short space of time; the total stretch, extent, or reach of anything; the portion contained between limits of space or time; *aeron.* the maximum width of an aircraft measured from wing tip to wing tip.—*v.t.*—*spanned, spanning.* To measure by the hand with fingers encompassing the object; to measure or extend across; to construct with something that bridges across.

span, span, *n.* [D. *spannen*, akin to E. *span*. D. *span*.] A pair of horses or other animals, esp. a pair matched in size and looks, harnessed and driven together; *naut.* a chain or rope used for securing.—*v.t.*—*spanned, spanning.* To harness or attach; to bind.

span·drel, span′drel, *n. Arch.* the irregular triangular space between the outer curve of an arch and a straight-sided figure surrounding it. Any space of similar shape, as on a postage stamp; an ornament which fills a spandrel. Also **span·dril.**

span·gle, spang′gl, *n.* [Dim. of O.E. *spang, spange*, a buckle, a clasp; D. *spang*, Icel. *spöng*, a spangle, a stud.] A small circular ornament of metal stitched on an article of dress; any small sparkling object.—*v.t.*—*spangled, spangling.* To set, sprinkle, or adorn with spangles.—*v.i.* To glitter with or as with spangles; to glisten.

Span·iard, span′yẻrd, *n.* An inhabitant of Spain; a person of Spanish birth.

span·iel, span′yel, *n.* [O.Fr. *espaignol*, spaniel, orig. lit. 'Spanish dog,' < L. *Hispania*, Spain.] Any of various breeds of dogs of small or medium size, usu. with a long, silky coat and drooping ears; *fig.* a submissive, fawning, or cringing person.

Span·ish, span′ish, *a.* Of or relating to Spain, its people, or its language.—*n.* pl. **Span·ish.** The native language of Spain and its dialects spoken in the Philippines and Latin America; the natives or inhabitants of Spain, usu. preceded by *the*.

Span·ish A·mer·i·ca, *n.* The countries in the Western Hemisphere where the language is Spanish, including Mexico, Central America, South America, and most of the Caribbean islands with the exclusion of British Honduras, the Guianas, and Brazil.

Span·ish bay·o·net, *n.* Any of certain plants of the liliaceous genus *Yucca*, with narrow, rigid, spine-tipped leaves.

Span·ish fly, *n.* A blister beetle, esp. *Lytta vesicatoria*, used in medicine, after drying and powdering, as a counterirritant, a diuretic, and an aphrodisiac. See *cantharis*.

Span·ish heel, *n.* A curved, high, wooden shoe heel which is covered with leather and has a straight front part.

Span·ish in·flu·en·za, *n. Pathol.* A very contagious respiratory disease produced by a virus and resulting in fever, coughing, and general body pains; the world-wide epidemic of such respiratory infections in 1917–1918.

Span·ish mack·er·el, *n.* A large, edible American fish, *Scomberomorus maculatus*, which lives in the warm waters of the Atlantic; the jack mackerel of California.

Span·ish moss, *n.* A lichen–like epiphytic plant of the pineapple family, *Tillandsia usneoides*, of the southern U.S., forming long, pendulous gray tufts which drape the branches of trees. Also *Florida moss*, **long moss.**

Span·ish nee·dles, *n. pl., sing. or pl. in constr.* An American plant, *Bidens bipinnata*, in the composite family, having achenes with downwardly barbed awns; the fruit of this plant.

Span·ish om·e·let, *n.* An omelet topped with a Spanish sauce which is made of chopped onions, tomatoes, green peppers, seasonings, and sometimes mushrooms.

Span·ish pap·ri·ka, *n.* A variety of pimiento from Spain which is dried and ground for use as a condiment or spice.

Span·ish rice, *n.* A dish of rice mixed with chopped tomatoes, onions, green peppers, and cayenne pepper.

spank, spangk, *v.t.* To slap or smack with the open hand against the buttocks as a punishment.—*n.*

spank, spangk, *v.i.* [Same as Dan. *spanke*, to strut, to stalk; cf. Sc. *spang*, to leap.] To move with a quick lively step; to move or run along quickly.

spank·er, spang′kẻr, *n.* One who spanks; *naut.* a large fore-and-aft sail set upon the mizzenmast of a ship. *Colloq.* a speedy horse; anyone or anything large, handsome, or impressive.

spank·ing, spang′king, *a.* Moving with a quick lively pace; brisk. *Colloq.* distinctive or exceptional; extremely fine.—*adv. Colloq.* unusually or extremely; as, a *spanking* new car.—*n.* Several slaps against the buttocks for punishment.

span·ner, span′ẻr, *n. Chiefly Brit.* A tool with jaws or sockets at the end of a lever, used for tightening nuts; a wrench.

span-new, span′nŏ′, span′nū′, *a.* [Icel. *spānnȳr*, span-new, lit. chip-new, splinter-new, < *spánn*, G. *span*, a chip; in allusion to work fresh from the hands of the workman.] *Dial.* really new.

span·worm, span′wụrm″, *n.* Measuring worm.

spar, spär, *n.* [M.E. *sparre* = D. *spar* = G. *sparren* = Icel. *sparri* = Sw. and Dan. *sparre*, spar.] A piece of timber of considerable length in proportion to its thickness; *naut.* a stout pole or round stick of timber such as those used for masts, yards, and booms; *aeron.* a principal lateral member of a wing or other airfoil in an aircraft.—*v.t.*—*sparred, sparring.* To furnish or fit with spars.

spar, spär, *v.i.*—*sparred, sparring.* To move the arms in a way suitable for immediate attack or defense; to fight with boxing gloves; to box; to fight by striking with spurs, as cocks; to argue; to dispute.—*n.* A preliminary flourish of the fists; a boxing match; a dispute.

spar, spär, *n.* [O.E. *spærstān*, gypsum.] Any of various crystalline minerals which break easily into rhomboidal, cubical, or laminated fragments of vitreous luster; as, feld*spar*, fluor*spar*, and Iceland *spar*.

Spar, spär, *n.* A woman member of the U.S. Coast Guard Reserve. Also **SPAR.**

spar·a·ble, spar′a·bl, *n.* [Corruption of *sparrow bill*.] A headless, small nail driven into the soles of shoes and boots to prevent wear.

spare, spâr, *v.t.*—*spared, sparing.* [O.E. *sparian* = D. and G. *sparen* = Icel. and Sw. *spara* = Dan. *spare*, spare.] To refrain from harming or destroying, or leave uninjured; to forbear to punish; as, to *spare* an enemy; to save from strain, discomfort, or annoyance, or from the cause of it; to refrain from, forbear, omit, or withhold, as action or speech; to refrain from employing, as some instrument, means, or aid; as, to *spare* no pains, time, or expense; to set aside or allow for a particular use or purpose; as, to *spare* time or money for an undertaking; to give, lend, or part with, as from a supply, esp. without inconvenience or loss; to dispense with or do without; to use economically or frugally; to refrain from using, using up, or wasting; to have left in excess or as surplus.—*v.i.* To refrain from inflicting injury or punishment; to exercise leniency or mercy; to use economy, or be frugal or saving.—*a.*—*sparer, sparest.* Kept in reserve, as for possible future need or extra use; as, a *spare* tire; being in excess of present need, or free for other use; as, *spare* time; sparing, economical, or temperate, as persons; frugally restricted or meager, as living, diet, or fare; scanty or scant, as in amount or fullness; lean or thin, as a person.—*n.* A spare thing or part, as an extra tire carried for emergency use; sparing or economical use of; *bowling*, the knocking down of all the pins with two bowls in any single frame and the resulting score.—**spare·a·ble**, *a.*—**spare·ly**, *adv.*—**spare·ness**, *n.*—**spar·er**, *n.*

spare·rib, spâr′rib″, *n.* A cut of pork containing ribs from the upper or fore end of the row, where there is little meat adhering.

sparge, spärj, *v.t., v.i.*—*sparged, sparging.* [L. *spargere* (pp. *sparsus*), scatter, sprinkle: cf. *sparse*.] To scatter or sprinkle.—*n.* A sprinkling.—**sparg·er**, *n.*

spar·id, spar′id, *a., n.* Sparoid.

spar·ing, spâr′ing, *a.* Saving or frugal; chary, often followed by *of* or *in*; as, *sparing of* words; meager or limited; merciful or lenient.—**spar·ing·ly**, *adv.*—**spar·ing·ness**, *n.*

spark, spärk, *n.* [O.E. *spærca, spearca*, = M.L.G. *sparke* = D. *spark*, spark.] An ignited or fiery particle such as is thrown off by burning wood or produced by one hard body striking against another. *Elect.* the luminous effect produced by a sudden discontinuous discharge of electricity through air or other dielectric; a small arc at a point where the continuity of a circuit is interrupted. A small amount or trace of something; a trace of life or vitality, as in a person; a scintillation, gleam, or flash, as of light; *pl. but sing. in constr., colloq.* an operator of a radio on an aircraft or ship.—*v.i.* To emit sparks, as of fire; to send forth gleams or flashes; to issue as or like sparks; *elect.* to produce sparks.—*v.t.* To stimulate, as activity or interest; activate; incite.—**spark·er**, *n.*

spark, spärk, *n.* A gay, gallant, or showy young man; a beau, lover, or suitor.—*v.i. Colloq.* To engage in courtship; to play the beau or suitor.—*v.t. Colloq.* To pay attentions to, as a woman; to court.—**spark·er**, spär′kẻr, *n.*—**spark·ish**, *a.*

spark ar·rest·er, *n.* A device consisting of wire netting or other material used to stop or deflect sparks thrown from an open fireplace, a smokestack, or the like; *elect.* a device used to stop the occurrence of dangerous sparking in circuits.

spark coil, *n.* An induction coil for producing sparks.

spark gap, *n. Elect.* an open space in any electric circuit, across which a discharge in the form of a spark takes place.

spar·kle, spär′kl, *v.i.*—*sparkled, sparkling.* [Freq. < *spark.*] To issue in or as in little sparks, as fire or light; to emit little sparks, as burning matter; to send forth or shine with little gleams or flashes of light, as a brilliant gem or star, or dew or waves in the sunlight; to glisten brightly; to glitter; to move or flow with gleams or flashes of light, as a stream; be bright as with flashes, as the eyes; to effervesce with small, glistening bubbles, as wine; to be brilliant, showily clever, or smart, as wit or conversation; be lively or vivacious, as a person; to show by brightness; as, eyes that *sparkle* with joy.—*v.t.* To cause to sparkle or glisten.— *n.* A little spark or fiery particle; sparkling appearance, luster, or flashing play of light; as, the *sparkle* of a diamond; brilliance, animation, or vivacity.

spar·kler, spär′klėr, *n.* One who or that which sparkles; a firework that emits little sparks; a sparkling gem, esp. a diamond; *colloq.* a sparkling or bright eye.

spark plug, *n.* A device inserted in the cylinder of an internal-combustion engine, containing the two terminals between which passes the electric spark for igniting the explosive gases; also *Brit.* **spark·ing plug.** *Colloq.* one who serves as an animating force in an organization or undertaking.

spark·plug, spärk′plug″, *v.t.*—*sparkplugged, sparkplugging. Colloq.* to inspire, direct, or activate, as an undertaking, activity, or organization.

spark trans·mit·ter, *n. Radio,* a transmitter which sends out signals by using an oscillating discharge from a condenser across a spark gap.

spar·ling, spär′ling, *n.* pl. **spar·lings, spar·ling.** [O.Fr. *esperlenc* (Fr. *eperlan*); cf. G. *spierling,* smelt.] The European smelt, *Osmerus eperlanus;* a young herring.

spar·oid, spär′oid, spar′oid, *a.* [L. *sparus,* < Gr. *spáros,* kind of sparoid fish.] Belonging to or pertaining to the *Sparidae,* a family of spiny-rayed fishes including the porgy, sea bream, scup, and sheepshead.—*n.* A sparoid fish. Also *sparid.*

spar·ring part·ner, *n.* Anyone who acts as a boxing partner for a prize fighter in practice training.

spar·row, spar′ō, *n.* [O.E. *spearwa,* Goth. *sparwa,* Dan. *spurv, spörr,* G. *spar, sperling,* sparrow.] Any of several small, hardy European birds of the *Ploceidae* family, esp. the common *Passer domesticus,* introduced into N. America from Europe; also **Eng·lish spar·row, house spar·row.** Any of a number of small American finches, as the song sparrow or chipping sparrow, belonging to the family *Fringillidae.*

spar·row·grass, spar′ō·gras″, spar′ō·gräs″, *n. Colloq.* asparagus.

spar·row hawk, *n.* Any of several small hawks, esp. *Accipiter nisus* of Europe, or small falcons, as *Falco sparverius* of N. America, which feed on insects, small birds, and other small prey.

sparse, spärs, *a.*—*sparser, sparsest.* [L. *sparsus,* pp. of *spargere,* scatter: cf. *sparge.*] Thinly scattered, distributed, or diffused; as, a *sparse* population; not thick or dense; as, *sparse* hair; scanty or meager.— **sparse·ly,** *adv.*—**sparse·ness, spar·si·ty,** spär′si·tē, *n.*

Spar·ta·cist, spär′ta·sist, *n.* A member of the revolutionary socialist party of Germany which formed in 1918.

Spar·tan, spär′tan, *a.* Of or pertaining to Sparta, an ancient city of southern Greece; pertaining to its people; suggestive of the ancient Spartans in simplicity, austerity, discipline, fortitude, and courage; brave; stoical. Also **Spar·tan·ic.**—*n.* A native or inhabitant of Sparta; a person of Spartan characteristics.—**Spar·tan·ism,** *n.*

spar·te·ine, spär′tē·ēn″, spär′tē·in, *n.* [N.L. *Spartium,* genus of broom, < Gr. *spártos,* broom.] A bitter, poisonous liquid alkaloid obtained from the common broom, *Cytisus scoparius,* used in medicine.

spar var·nish, *n.* A varnish composed usu. of linseed oil, sulfur, and rosin, used on exterior, wooden surfaces to waterproof and prevent weather wear.

spasm, spaz′um, *n.* [O.Fr. Fr. *spasme,* < L. *spasmus,* < Gr. *spasmós,* < *span,* draw, convulse.] *Pathol.* a sudden, abnormal, involuntary muscular contraction; an affection consisting of continued muscular contraction (tonic *spasm*); a series of alternating muscular contractions and relaxations (clonic *spasm*). A convulsion; any sudden, brief fit or spell of unusual energy, feeling, or activity.

spas·mod·ic, spaz′mod′ik, *a.* [Gr. *spasmōdēs.*] Pertaining to or of the nature of a spasm; characterized by spasms; resembling a spasm or spasms; convulsive; sudden and violent, but brief; occurring or proceeding intermittently; given to or characterized by bursts of excitement. Also **spas·mod·i·-cal.**—**spas·mod·i·cal·ly,** *adv.*

spas·tic, spas′tik, *a.* [L. *spasticus,* < Gr. *spastikós,* < *span.*] *Pathol.* pertaining to, of the nature of, or characterized by spasm, esp. muscular spasm.—*n.* A person given to spasms or convulsions, esp. one suffering from cerebral palsy.—**spas·ti·cal·ly,** *adv.*

spas·tic pa·ral·y·sis, *n. Pathol.* a paralytic condition marked by prolonged muscular contractions and increased reflexes of the tendons.

spat, spat, *n.* [Prob. imit.] A petty quarrel or tiff; a light blow; a slap; a smack; a splash, esp. of large rain drops.—*v.i.*— *spatted, spatting.* To engage in a petty quarrel or dispute; to administer slaps; strike sharply; to spatter.—*v.t.* To strike lightly; to slap.

spat, spat, *n.* [Abbr. of *spatterdash.*] *Usu.* pl. a short gaiter worn over the instep, usu. fastened under the foot with a strap.

spat, spat, *n.* [Origin uncertain; perhaps related to *spit.*] The spawn of an oyster or similar shellfish; young oysters; a young oyster.—*v.i.*—*spatted, spatting.* To spawn.

spate, spāt, *n.* [M.E. *spate;* origin uncertain.] Any sudden, floodlike outburst, flow, or the like, as of feeling. *Chiefly Brit.* a flood or inundation; a freshet; a sudden, heavy downpour of rain.

spathe, spāTH, *n.* [L. *spatha,* < Gr. *spathē,* a broad blade, a spathe.] *Bot.* a large bract or bract pair situated at the base of a spadix, which it encloses as a sheath.— **spathed,** *a.*—**spa·tha·ceous, spa·those,** spā·thā′shus, spā′THōs, spā′thōs, *a. Bot.* formed like or having a spathe.

spath·ic, spath·ik, *a. Mineral.* similar to spar. Also **spa·those,** spā′thōs, spath′ōs.

spath·u·late, spath′ya·lit, spath′ya·lāt″, *a.* Spatulate.

spa·tial, spā′shal, *a.* [L. *spatium,* E. *space.*] Of or pertaining to space; existing or occurring in space; having extension in space. Also **spacial.**—**spa·ti·al·i·ty,** spā″-shē·al′i·tē, *n.*—**spa·tial·ly,** *adv.*

spa·ti·o·tem·po·ral, spā″shē·ō·tem′pėr·-al, *a.* Relating to both space and time; of or concerning space-time.—**spa·ti·o·tem·-po·ral·ly,** *adv.*

spat·ter, spat′ėr, *v.t.* [Cf. D. *spatten,* spatter, sprinkle.] To scatter or dash in small particles or drops; as, to *spatter* mud, water, or ink; to splash with something in small particles; as, to *spatter* the ground with water; to sprinkle or spot with something that soils or stains; to slander or defame.—*v.i.* To send out small particles or drops; to fly out or fall in small particles or drops; to strike as in a shower, as bullets.—*n.* The act or the sound of spattering; a splash or spot of something spattered.

spat·ter·dock, spat′ėr·dok″, *n.* A yellow pond lily, esp. *Nuphar advena,* a coarse plant common in stagnant waters.

spat·u·la, spach′a·la, *n.* [L., dim. of *spatha,* Gr. *spathē,* a broad flat instrument.] An implement with a thin, broad, flexible blade, used for spreading a variety of substances, as icing on a cake, for mixing drugs, and for turning and removing, as pancakes.

spat·u·late, spach′a·lit, spach′a·lāt″, *a.* Shaped like a spatula or a spoon; *bot.* having a broad, rounded end and a narrow, attenuate base, as various leaves. Also *spathulate.*

spav·in, spav′in, *n.* [O.Fr. *espavain, esparvain* (Fr. *éparvin*); origin uncertain.] *Veter. pathol.* Any of certain diseases of horses affecting the hock, esp. one in which a bony enlargement forms at the joint; a growth or enlargement so formed.—**spav·ined,** spav′-ind, *a.* Affected with spavin; lame. *Fig.* crippled; halting; broken-down.

spawn, spän, *n.* [Appar. < O.Fr. *espandre* (Fr. *épandre*), spread, pour out, shed, < L. *expandere,* E. *expand.*] *Zool.* the eggs of fishes, amphibians, mollusks, or crustaceans extruded in masses. A swarming brood or numerous progeny: often used disparagingly; persons regarded as the offspring of some stock; any product or result; *bot.* the mycelium of mushrooms.—*v.i.* To produce eggs or spawn; to be reproductive; to issue like spawn.—*v.t.* To produce, as spawn; to give birth to; to bring forth, esp. in great numbers; to give rise to, as rumors; *bot.* to plant with mycelium.

spay, spā, *v.t.* [Gael, *spoth,* to castrate.] To remove the ovaries, as from female animals, to incapacitate them for producing young.

speak, spēk, *v.i.*—past *spoke* or archaic *spake,* pp. *spoken* or archaic *spoke,* ppr. *speaking.* [O.E. *specan,* earlier *sprecan* = O.E. *sprekan* = D. *spreken* = G. *sprechen,* speak: cf. *speech.*] To utter words or articulate sounds with the ordinary voice; to talk or exercise the faculty of speech; to make oral communication or mention; as, to *speak* to someone of various matters; to converse, as: They *speak* for hours on the phone. To deliver an address or discourse; as, to *speak* at a rally; to make a statement in written or printed words; to make communication or disclosure by any means; convey significance; *phon.* to make or produce characteristic sounds of a language through any of the various speech processes. To emit a sound, as a musical instrument; make a report or noise; to bark, as dogs.— *v.t.* To utter orally and articulately; as, to *speak* words of praise; to express or make known with the voice; as, to *speak* the truth; to declare in writing, printing, or by any means of communication; to make known, indicate, or reveal; to use, or be able to use, in oral utterance, as a language; as, to *speak* French; *naut.* to communicate with, as a passing vessel at sea, by voice or signal.—**so to speak,** in a way of speaking.—**speak for,** to represent or speak in behalf of; to claim for oneself.—**speak out,** to verbalize one's ideas and opinions freely.—**speak·a·ble,** *a.*

speak-eas·y, spēk′ē″zē, *n.* pl. **speak-eas·ies.** A place where intoxicating liquors are sold illegally: used esp. when prohibition was in effect in the U.S., 1920–1933.

speak·er, spē′kẽr, *n.* One who speaks; one who speaks formally before an audience; one who engages in public speaking; an orator; (*usu. cap.*) the presiding officer of the House of Commons of Great Britain, the House of Representatives of the U.S., or some other similar assembly. A book of selections for practice in declamation; a loudspeaker.—**spea·ker·ship,** *n.*

speak·ing, spē′king, *n.* The act, utterance, or discourse of one who speaks.—*a.* That speaks; giving information as if by speech; expressive or eloquent; lifelike; suited to or involving speaking or talking; declaiming.—**on speak·ing terms,** having an association that allows speaking or conversing.—**speak·ing·ly,** *adv.*

speak·ing tube, *n.* A tube or device designed to carry the sound of a voice, as from one part of a building or ship to another.

spear, spēr, *n.* [O.E. *spere* = D. and G. *speer,* spear: cf. L. *sparus,* hunting-spear.] A weapon for thrusting or throwing, consisting of a long staff to which a sharp head, as of iron or steel, is fixed; a soldier or other person armed with such a weapon; spearman; some similar weapon or instrument, as one for spearing fish; the act of spearing. —*v.t.* To pierce with or as with a spear; to catch by the use of a spear, as fish.—*v.i.* To go or penetrate like a spear.—**spear·er,** *n.*

spear, spēr, *n.* [Var. of *spire.*] A sprout or shoot of a plant, as a blade of grass.—*v.i.* To sprout; to shoot up; to send up or rise in a spear or spears.

spear·fish, spēr′fish″, *n.* pl. **spear·fish, spear·fish·es.** Any of various large marine fish of the genus *Tetrapturus,* with a long, spearlike beak.—*v.i.* To catch fish by using a spear.

spear·head, spēr′hed″, *n.* The sharp-pointed head which forms the piercing end of a spear; a leader or a leading force.—*v.t.* To act as leader of.

spear·man, spēr′man, *n.* pl. **spear·men.** One who is armed with or uses a spear.

spear·mint, spēr′mint″, *n.* The common mint, *Mentha spicata,* an aromatic herb used for flavoring.

spear side, *n.* The male side or line of descent of a family.

spear·wort, spēr′wụrt″, *n.* Any of certain species of the buttercup family, with long, spear-shaped leaves, as the lesser spearwort, *Ranunculus flammula.*

spe·cial, spesh′al, *a.* [O.Fr. *special, especial* (Fr. *spécial*), < L. *specialis,* special, particular, not general, < *species:* cf. *especial.*] Of a distinct or particular kind or character; as, a *special* type of food; particular, individual, or unique; pertaining or peculiar to a particular person, thing, or instance; as, the *special* features of a plan; having a particular function, purpose, or application; as, a *special* messenger; specific or dealing with particulars; distinguished or different from what is ordinary or usual; as, a *special* occasion; additional; extra; extraordinary, exceptional, or especial, as in amount or degree; as, *special* care.—*n.* A special person or thing; a train scheduled for a particular occasion, time, or purpose; an extra or featured edition of a newspaper or issue of a magazine; a temporary reduction in the selling price of food, clothing, or other merchandise; a single television program of particular interest which replaces the regularly scheduled program.—**spe·cial·ly,** *adv.*

spe·cial de·liv·er·y, *n.* The delivering of pieces of mail outside the normal delivery schedule, for an extra fee and by a specially designated messenger.—**spe·cial-de·liv·er·y,** *a.*

spe·cial han·dling, *n.* The treating of fourth-class mail or parcel post mail like first class, when a special fee is paid.

spe·cial in·ter·est, *n.* Any group of persons, as a corporation, seeking special benefits or advantages, esp. from the government, often at a disadvantage to the public's welfare.

spe·cial·ism, spesh′a·liz″um, *n.* Restriction or devotion to a single branch of a general study or pursuit; the special field itself.

spe·cial·ist, spesh′a·list, *n.* One who devotes himself to one subject or to one particular branch of a subject or pursuit, esp. a medical practitioner who devotes his attention to a particular class of diseases; *army,* an enlisted man entitled by technical qualifications to a noncommissioned officer's salary but whose rank in command is below that of a corporal.—**spe·cial·is··tic,** spesh′a·lis′tik, *a.*

spe·cial·i·za·tion, spesh″a·li·zā′shan, *n.* The act of specializing or the process involved in becoming specialized; *biol.* the development of an organ or part of an animal or plant in its adaptation to a specific environment.

spe·cial·ize, spesh′a·līz″, *v.i.*—*specialized, specializing.* [Fr. *spécialiser.*] To pursue a particular line of study, work, or the like; *biol.* of an organism or part of an organism, to adapt to a particular habitat or function by modification.—*v.t.* To render special or specific; to invest with a special character, function, or the like; *biol.* to adapt to special conditions. To endorse to a certain payee; as, to *specialize* a check; to specify or particularize.

spe·cial ju·ry, *n.* A jury, with special qualifications and presumably more able, selected to try cases of an unusually complex, serious, or intricate nature. Also *blue-ribbon jury.*

spe·cial plead·ing, *n. Law,* pleading that alleges special or new matter in avoidance of the allegations made by the opposite side. Pleading or arguing that ignores unfavorable features of a case; one-sided or unfair presentation of one's case.

spe·cial priv·i·lege, *n.* A privilege, as power or immunity, accorded esp. by constitutional law to a person or group of persons over and above the common right of others.

spe·cial ses·sion, *n.* An extra, unscheduled session, as of a court or legislature, called under urgent circumstances.

spe·cial·ty, spesh′al·tē, *n.* pl. **spe·cial-ties.** [O.Fr. *especialte:* cf. *speciality.*] The state or condition of being particular or special; special or particular character; a special characteristic or peculiarity; a special subject of study, line of work, or the like; an article particularly dealt in, manufactured, or one to which the dealer or manufacturer professes to devote special care; an article of trade of special character; a novelty; a special or particular point, item, matter, or thing; *law,* a special agreement or contract expressed in an instrument under seal. Also *Brit.* **spe·ci·al·i·ty,** pl. **spe·ci·al·i·ties.**

spe·ci·a·tion, spē″shē·ā′shan, *n. Biol.* the evolutionary process whereby new plant and animal species become differentiated.—**spe·ci·ate,** *v.i.*—*speciated, speciating.*—**spe·ci·a·tion·al,** *a.*

spe·cie, spē′shē, spē′sē, *n.* [The ablative of L. *species.*] Coin, as opposed to paper money, usu. preceded by *in;* as, paid *in specie; law,* identical form.

spe·cies, spē′shēz, spē′sēz, *n.* pl. **spe·cies.** [L., sight, appearance, form, particular sort or kind, species < *specere,* look at.] A class of individuals having some common characteristics or qualities; a distinct sort or kind; *biol.* a classification next below a genus or subgenus, consisting of animals or plants having certain distinctive characteristics in common and able to interbreed; *logic,* a number of individuals having common characteristics or attributes indigenous to them, and forming a group which, with other similar groups, is included in a genus. *Eccles.* the visible form or appearance of the bread or the wine used in the Eucharist; either of the Eucharistic elements.—**the spe·cies,** the human race.

spec·i·fi·a·ble, spes′i·fī″a·bl, *a.* That may be specified.

spe·cif·ic, spi·sif′ik, *a.* [M.L. *specificus,* < L. *species,* kind, and *facere,* make.] Having a special application, bearing, or reference; specifying, explicit, or definite; as, to be *specific* in one's statements; specified, precise, or particular; as, a *specific* sum of money; peculiar or proper to something, as qualities, characteristics, or effects; specially belonging to and characteristic of a thing or group of things; of a special or particular kind; *biol.* of or pertaining to a species; as, *specific* characteristics. *Med.* produced by a special cause or infection, as a disease; having special effect in the cure of a certain disease.—*n.* Something specific, as a statement or quality; *med.* a specific remedy.—**spe·cif··i·cal·ly,** *adv.*—**spec·i·fic·i·ty,** *n.*

spec·i·fi·ca·tion, spes″i·fi·kā′shan, *n.* [Fr. *spécification,* < M.L. *specificatio(n-).*] The act of specifying; that which is specified; *usu. pl.* a detailed, itemized description of dimensions, plans, materials, and other requirements, as for something proposed for construction or manufacture. Something specified, as in a bill of particulars; the act of making specific or clarifying; the state of having a specific character.

spe·cif·ic grav·i·ty, *n. Phys.* the ratio of the weight of a given volume of any substance to that of the same volume of some other substance taken as a standard, water being the standard for solids and liquids, and hydrogen or air for gases. Also **rel·a·tive den·si·ty.**

spe·cif·ic heat, *n. Phys.* The quantity of heat, measured in calories, required to raise one gram of a given substance 1°C. of temperature; the ratio of the heat capacity of water to that of an equal amount of another substance.

spec·i·fy, spes′i·fī″, *v.t.*—*specified, specifying.* [Fr. *spécifier,* as if < L. *specifico—species,* and *facio,* to make.] To mention or state explicitly; to designate as one condition of a group of specifications; to designate in detail, so as to clearly distinguish or limit.—**spec·i·fi·er,** *n.*

spec·i·men, spes′i·men, *n.* [L., an indication, evidence, example, < *specere,* look at: cf. *species.*] A part or an individual taken as representative or typical of a whole or group; an animal, plant, mineral, or organism preserved as an example of its kind, as for scientific study; *med.* a sample of a body substance to be analyzed for diagnostic purposes. *Colloq.* a strange sort of person; one who is out of the ordinary.

spe·cious, spē′shus, *a.* [L. *speciosus,* good-looking, fair-seeming, plausible, specious, < *species.*] Apparently good or right but without real merit; as, *specious* promises; plausible; fair-seeming or superficially pleasing; pleasing to the eye, but deceptive; as, a *specious* appearance.—**spe·ci·os·i·ty,** spē″shē·os′i·tē, *n.* pl. **spe·ci·os·i·ties.** —**spe·cious·ly,** *adv.*—**spe·cious·ness,** *n.*

speck, spek, *n.* [O.E. *specca,* a speck; akin L.G. *spaak,* a speck; *speckle* is a derivative.] A tiny spot; a particle; a fleck; as, a *speck* of dirt; a small mark; a minute dot.—*v.t.* To spot; to mark, as with specks or spots.

speck·le, spek′l, *n.* [Dim. of *speck.*] A little spot in anything, of a different color from that of the thing itself; a speck.—*v.t.* *speckled*, *speckling*. To mark with small specks or spots.

specs, speks, *n. pl. Colloq.* spectacles, eyeglasses. Shortened form of *specifications*.

spec·ta·cle, spek'ta·kl, *n.* [O.Fr. Fr. *spectacle*, < L. *spectaculum*, sight, spectacle, < *spectare*, look at or to, freq. of *specere*, look at: cf. *species*.] Anything presented to the sight or view, esp. something of a striking kind; a public show or display, esp. on a large scale; as, a dramatic *spectacle*; a person or thing exhibited to public view as an object of wonder or of contempt. *Pl.* a device to aid defective vision or to protect the eyes from light, dust, or the like, consisting usu. of two glass lenses set in a frame which rests on the nose and is held in place by pieces passing over or around the ears, often preceded by *pair of*; something through which things are viewed, or by which one's views are colored or affected. *Often pl.* any of various devices resembling or suggesting a pair of spectacles, as one attached to a semaphore to display lights of different colors by means of colored glass.

spec·ta·cled, spek'ta·kld, *a.* Provided with or wearing spectacles; having a marking resembling a pair of spectacles, as an animal.

spec·tac·u·lar, spek·tak'ū·lẽr, *a.* [L. *spectaculum*.] Pertaining to or of the nature of a spectacle or show; marked by or given to a great, strikingly unusual display or show.—*n.* That which is spectacular, esp. a lavish television production.—**spec·tac·u·lar·i·ty**, spek·tak"ū·lar'i·tē, *n.*—**spec·tac·u·lar·ly**, *adv.*

spec·ta·tor, spek'tā·tẽr, spek·tā'tẽr, *n.* [L. < *specto*, freq. of *specio*, to behold.] One who observes, watches, or looks on; a beholder; one who is present at and watches a play or spectacle.—**spec·ta·to·ri·al**, *a.*—**spec·ta·tress**, **spec·ta·trix**, spek·tā'tris, spek'tā·tris, spek·tā'triks, spek'tā·triks, *n.* pl. **spec·ta·tri·ces**, **spec·ta·trix·es**, spek·tā'tri·sēz", spek'tā·tri·sēz". A woman spectator.

spec·ta·tor sport, *n.* Any sport which many individuals choose to enjoy as spectators rather than by actual participation, as baseball, hockey, or soccer.

spec·ter, *Brit.* **spec·tre**, spek'tẽr, *n.* [Fr. *spectre*, < L. *spectrum*, an appearance, an apparition, < *specto*, to behold.] A disembodied but visible spirit; a ghost, apparition, or phantom; anything that haunts or horrifies.

spec·tral, spek'tral, *a.* Pertaining to or characteristic of a specter; of the nature of a specter; ghostly; resembling or suggesting a specter; *phys.* of, pertaining to, or produced by a spectrum or spectra.—**spec·tral·i·ty**, **spec·tral·ness**, *n.*—**spec·tral·ly**, *adv.*

spec·tro·gram, spek'tro·gram", *n.* A drawing, diagram, or photograph of a spectrum.

spec·tro·graph, spek'tro·graf", spek'tro·gräf", *n.* An apparatus for making a representation or photograph of a spectrum; a spectrogram.—**spec·tro·graph·ic**, spek"tro·graf'ik, *a.*—**spec·tro·graph·i·cal·ly**, *adv.*

spec·tro·he·li·o·gram, spek"tro·hē'lē·o·gram", *n.* A photograph of the sun made with a spectroheliograph.

spec·tro·he·li·o·graph, spek"tro·hē'lē·o·graf", spek"tro·hē'lē·o·gräf", *n.* [Cf. *heliograph*.] An apparatus for monochromatically photographing the sun so as to show deatils of its surface, esp. prominences.—**spec·tro·he·li·o·graph·ic**, spek"tro·hē'lē·o·graf'ik, *a.*

spec·tro·he·li·o·scope, spek"tro·hē'lē·o·skōp", *n. Astron.* An instrument designed for direct visual observation of the sun; a spectroheliograph.—**spec·tro·he·li·o·scop·ic**, spek"tro·hē'lē·o·skop'ik, *a.*

spec·trom·e·ter, spek·trom'i·tẽr, *n.* An optical instrument for observing a spectrum and measuring the deviation of the refracted rays, and for determining wave lengths and angles between two faces of a prism; a spectroscope equipped with such a device.—**spec·tro·met·ric**, spek"tro·me'trik, *a.*—**spec·trom·e·try**, *n.*

spec·tro·pho·tom·e·ter, spek"trō·fō·tom'i·tẽr, *n.* An instrument for making comparisons of color intensity between corresponding parts of different spectra, or between parts of the same spectrum.—**spec·tro·pho·to·met·ric**, spek"trō·fō"to·me'trik, *a.*—**spec·tro·pho·tom·e·try**, *n.*

spec·tro·scope, spek'tro·skōp", *n.* [*Spectrum* and Gr. *skopeō*, to look at.] An optical instrument used to form and analyze spectra.—**spec·tro·scop·ic**, **spec·tro·scop·i·cal**, spek"tro·skop'ik, *a.*—**spec·tro·scop·i·cal·ly**, *adv.*

spec·tros·co·py, spek·tros'ko·pē, spek'tro·skō"pē, *n.* The branch of science concerned with the use of the spectroscope and with spectrum analysis.—**spec·tros·co·pist**, spek·tros'ko·pist, *n.*

spec·trum, spek'trum, *n.* pl. **spec·tra**, **spec·trums**, spek'tra. [L. *spectrum*, appearance, apparition, specter; N.L. *spectrum*.] A continuum; as, the ideological *spectrum*. *Chem., phys.* a visual expression, as a graph, screen display, or photographic record of the distribution of the phases of a radiated wave cycle or of the intensity of radiation when some property, as frequency, mass, or energy, is allowed to vary; a band or broad range of frequencies having a common characteristic, as audibility, visibility, or electromagnetism, esp. the colored lines or colored bands formed when a beam of light from a luminous body or incandescent gas undergoes dispersion by being passed through a prism or reflected from a diffraction grating; a series of colors, usu. described as passing by degrees through red, orange, yellow, green, blue, indigo, and violet, produced when white light is passed through a prism; the pattern, as recorded by some device, which results when particles of a given mass are physically isolated from particles of similar masses, as in the analysis of isotopes. *Math.* a property of a matrix, equal to the set of all roots of an equation obtained by introducing an arbitrary variable into the matrix—**spec·trum a·nal·y·sis**, the determination of the constitution or condition of bodies and substances by means of the spectra they produce.

spec·u·lar, spek'ū·lẽr, *a.* [L. *specularis*, of or like a mirror, < *speculum*.] Pertaining to or having the reflecting property of a mirror; having a smooth, reflecting surface or a lustrous metallic appearance; pertaining to a speculum.—**spec·u·lar·ly**, *adv.*

spec·u·late, spek'ū·lāt", *v.i.*—*speculated*, *speculating*. [L. *speculor*, *speculatus*, *specula*, a lookout, < *specio*, to see.] To meditate or reflect; to consider or ponder upon various aspects of a subject; to theorize; to purchase goods, stocks, or other commodities with the expectation of some profit by selling at an opportune time; to engage in speculation.

spec·u·la·tion, spek'ū·lā'shan, *n.* The act of speculating or forming conjectures about a subject; the process or act of conjectural contemplation; a conclusion related to or reached by such consideration; a theory or theoretical view. A financial investment which is hazardous but offers the possibility of large profits; the act of buying and selling stocks or commodities with the hope of profiting from favorable market prices.

spec·u·la·tive, spek'ū·lā"tiv, spek'ū·la·tiv, *a.* Given to or engaging in speculation; contemplative; pertaining to, involving, or formed by speculation; theoretical; not verified by fact, experiment, or practice; pertaining to or given to speculation in trade.—**spec·u·la·tive·ness**, *n.*

spec·u·la·tor, spek'ū·lā"tẽr, *n.* One who speculates; one who speculates in trade; one who incurs great risks in the hope of great gain.—**spec·u·la·to·ry**, spek'ū·la·tōr"ē, spek'ū·la·tạr"ē, *a.*

spec·u·lum, spek'ū·lum, *n.* pl. **spec·u·la**, **spec·u·lums**, spek'ū·la. [L. mirror, < *specere*, look at: cf. *species*.] A mirror or reflector, esp. one of polished metal, as on a reflecting telescope; *ornith.* a lustrous or distinctively colored area on the wing of certain birds; *surg.* an instrument for rendering a part accessible to observation, as by enlarging an orifice.

speech, spēch, *n.* [O.E. *spæc*, *spræc*, speech, < *specan*, *sprecan*, to speak.] The faculty or power of expressing thoughts and emotions by articulated sounds and words; the act of speaking; anything that is spoken, as an utterance, conversation, or remark; an oration, public discourse, address, or the like; a particular language or dialect; an individual style of speaking; the study of the theory and various practices of oral communication.

speech com·mu·ni·ty, *n. Ling.* the totality of persons who use a specific language or dialect in one particular area or in several different areas.

speech·i·fy, spē'chi·fī", *v.i.*—*speechified*, *speechifying. Colloq.* to make a speech or to harangue: used humorously or derisively.

speech·less, spēch'lis, *a.* Destitute or deprived of the faculty of speech; dumb; mute; not speaking for a time; silent; incapable of expression in words.—**speech·less·ly**, *adv.*—**speech·less·ness**, *n.*

speed, spēd, *n.* [O.E. *spēdan*, to hasten, to prosper, < *spēd*, haste, prosperity, < *spōwan*, to thrive, same as O.H.G. *spuōn*, to succeed.] Rapidity of movement; the rate or swiftness of motion or action; the act of moving swiftly. *Photog.* the sensitivity of a photographic medium to light; the rapidity with which a camera lens exposes film to light. *Automotive*, a gear or set of gears in the transmission of a motorized vehicle which provides different rates of movement.—*v.t.*—*sped* or *speeded*, *speeding*. To accelerate the rate of; to further the progress of; to expedite; to cause to move or go with haste; to dismiss with good wishes.—*v.i.* To make haste; to move with celerity; to accelerate the rate of motion, usu. followed by *up*; to drive a vehicle at an excessive rate or beyond the legal limit.—**speed·er**, **speed·ster**, spēd'stẽr, *n.*

speed·boat, spēd'bōt", *n.* A motorboat designed for speed.—**speed·boat·ing**, spēd'bō"ting, *n.*

speed light, *n.* A lamp whose light source is an electronic tube which produces an intense flash, used esp. in photography to catch motion and action. Also **strobe light**, *flash lamp.*

speed lim·it, *n.* The maximum or minimum limit of speed permitted by law, often under specified conditions, for a certain road, waterway, or other area.

speed·om·e·ter, spē·dom'i·tẽr, spi·dom'i·tẽr, *n.* An instrument for indicating the speed of a vehicle, usu. in miles per hour, often combined with an odometer.

speed read·ing, *n.* Any of several teaching or learning techniques for accelerating the reading rate, usu. to over 1,000 words a minute.

speed trap, *n.* A section of roadway, often with inadequately posted or hard to see speed limit signs, where hidden police or electronic devices trap unwary drivers exceeding the speed limit.

speed-up, spēd′up″, *n.* An increase in the rate of speed, as in some process or work; *labor,* a required increase in production without an increase in wages.

speed·way, spēd′wā″, *n.* A non-public road or course used for racing automobiles or motorcycles; a public highway where high-speed driving is permitted.

speed·well, spēd′wel″, *n.* The common name of several plants and herbs of the genus *Veronica,* having clusters of violet, white, or blue flowers.

speed·y, spē′dē, *a.*—*speedier, speediest.* Rapid in motion; swift; quick; fast; prompt.—**speed·i·ly,** *adv.*—**speed·i·ness,** *n.*

speiss, spīs, *n.* [G. *speise,* speiss, lit. 'food.'] A product consisting chiefly of one or more metallic arsenides, as of iron or nickel, obtained in smelting certain ores.

spe·le·ol·o·gy, spe·lae·ol·o·gy, spē″lē·ol′o·jē, *n.* [Fr. *spéléologie,* < Gr. *spēlaion,* cave, and *-logia,* < *legein,* speak.] The study and exploration of caves for scientific purposes.—**spe·le·o·log·i·cal,** spē″lē·o·loj′i·kal, *a.*—**spe·le·ol·o·gist,** *n.*

spell, spel, *v.t.*—*spelled* or *spelt, spelling.* [O.E. *spellian,* to say, speak, tell.] To repeat, point out, write, or print the proper letters of in their regular order; to form by letters; to mean, amount to, or signify, as: The job *spelled* success for her.—*v.i.* To form words with the proper letters, either in reading or writing; to read letter by letter.—**spell out,** to explain clearly; as, objectives that were *spelled out;* to discern or make out; to read with labor or difficulty.

spell, spel, *n.* [O.E. *spell,* a saying, tale, or a charm; Icel. *spjalla,* O.G. *spel,* Goth. *spill,* a tale. Hence the latter part of *gospel.*] A charm consisting of some words of occult power; an incantation; any magic charm.

spell, spel, *n.* [O.E. *spelian,* to supply the room of another; cf. D. and Sw. *spel,* G. *spiel,* play, game.] Any period of time; a particular period or type of weather; as a hot *spell;* a period of illness. A continuing work period; a turn of work done by one person in relief of another.—*v.t.* To relieve for a while.—*v.i.* To take a rest period.

spell·bind, spel′bīnd″, *v.t.*—*spellbound, spellbinding.* [Backformation < *spellbound.*] To hold spellbound, or as by a spell; to entrance.

spell·bind·er, spel′bīn″dėr, *n.* An eloquent political orator; any spellbinding person or thing.

spell·bound, spel′bound″, *a.* Bound as by a spell or charm; enchanted or fascinated.

spell·down, spel′doun″, *n.* A spelling contest, the winner being determined by the elimination of contestants who misspell certain words. Also **spell·ing bee.**—**spell down,** *v.t.*

spell·er, spel′ėr, *n.* One who spells. A manual or textbook of exercises used for spelling instruction; also **spell·ing book.**

spell·ing, spel′ing, *n.* The formation of words by using letters; orthography; a combination of letters representing a word; a particular way in which a word is spelled; the act of one who spells words.

spelt, spelt, *n.* [O.E. *spelt,* L.G. and D. *spelt,* G. *spelz,* from root of *split.*] A kind of wheat, *Triticum spelta,* grown as livestock feed in western Asia and southern Europe.

spel·ter, spel′tėr, *n.* Commercial zinc, usu. cast in ingots or slabs.

spe·lun·ker, spi·lung′kėr, *n.* A person who likes to explore caves; speleologist.—**spe·lun·king,** *n.*

spence, spens, *n.* [O.Fr. *despense* (Fr. *depense),* < M.L. *dispensa,* < L. *dispendere,* weigh out, E. *dispend.*] Brit. *dial.* A room or place where provisions are kept; a buttery or larder; a pantry; a cupboard.

spen·cer, spen′sėr, *n.* [From the second Earl *Spencer,* 1758–1834.] A short overcoat formerly worn by men; a man's short coat or jacket; a short jacket or outer bodicelike garment for women.

spen·cer, spen′sėr, *n. Naut.* A fore-and-aft sail with a gaff and boom set abaft the fore and main masts; trysail.

Spen·ce·ri·an, spen·sēr′ē·an, *a.* Having to do with Herbert Spencer, 1890–1903, or his philosophy.—*n.* An advocate of Herbert Spencer's philosophy.—**Spen·ce·ri·an·ism,** spen·sēr′ē·a·niz″um, *n.* Herbert Spencer's philosophy in which he sets forth the mechanical evolution of the world from a simple to a relatively complex state.

Spen·ce·ri·an, spen·sēr′ē·an, *a.* Of a style of handwriting having rounded letters which slant to the right, developed by a 19th century American, P. R. Spencer.

spend, spend, *v.t.*—*spent, spending.* [O.E. *spendan,* borrowed < L. *expendo* or *dispendo,* to expend, to dispense.] To expend or pay out, as funds or wealth; to consume or exhaust, as energy or strength; to waste, as efforts or resources; to pass or allow to elapse, as time; to employ, as time, effort, or thought on some project or activity; to sacrifice or give up, as for a reason or cause.—*v.i.* To make disbursements or expenditures; to be exhausted, consumed, or wasted.—**spend·a·ble,** spen′da·bl, *a.*—**spend·er,** spen′dėr, *n.*

spend·ing mon·ey, *n.* Money available or used for small personal expenses.

spend·thrift, spend′thrift″, *n.* One who spends his means lavishly or improvidently; a prodigal.—*a.*

Speng·le·ri·an, speng·glēr′ē·an, shpeng·glēr′ē·an, *a.* Having to do with the theories of Oswald Spengler, a German philosopher and historian, 1880–1936, setting forth the notion of a common cyclical pattern in the rise and fall of major cultures.—*n.* Anyone who adheres to the theories of Oswald Spengler.

Spen·se·ri·an, spen·sēr′ē·an, *a.* Having to do with the English poet Edmund Spenser, 1552?–1599, or with his literary works.—*n.* Anyone who follows, admires, or imitates the style of Spenser.

Spen·se·ri·an son·net, *n.* A sonnet first developed by Edmund Spenser, consisting of three quatrains and a final couplet: *abab, bcbc, cdcd, ee.*

Spen·se·ri·an stan·za, *n. Pros.* a stanza originally used by Edmund Spenser, consisting of eight lines of iambic pentameter plus an Alexandrine in the form of *ababbcbcc.*

spent, spent, *a.* Expended; passed or gone, as time; used up, consumed, or exhausted; exhausted of strength, as by exertion or hardship; as, a *spent* swimmer; exhausted of force, effective qualities, or usefulness; as, a *spent* bullet.

sperm, spurm, *n.* pl. **sperm, sperms.** [L. and Gr. *sperma, spermatos,* seed, < *speirō,* to sow.] The reproductive seminal fluid of males; semen; a microscopic male fertilizing cell, usu. motile; a spermatozoon. Shortened form of *spermaceti, sperm oil, sperm whale.*

sper·ma·cet·i, spur″ma·set′ē, spur″ma·sē′tē, *n.* [Lit. 'sperm of whale'; L. *sperma,* and *cetus,* a whale.] *Chem., pharm.* a white, waxy material obtained from the oil of the sperm whale and some other marine mammals and used in making ointments, cosmetics, and other commercial products. Also *sperm.*

sper·ma·ry, spur′ma·rē, *n.* pl. **sper·ma·ries.** The organ in males in which spermatozoa are produced; testis.

sper·mat·ic, spur·mat′ik, *a.* Pertaining to, resembling, or conveying sperm; seminal; relating to a spermary.

sper·mat·ic cord, *n. Anat.* the cord by which the testicle is suspended within the scrotum, and which contains, the vas deferens, the blood vessels, and nerves of the testicle.

sper·ma·tid, spur′ma·tid, *n.* A cell which has developed from a lower cell, called spermatocyte, and which will grow into a fully developed male reproductive cell.

sper·ma·ti·um, spur·mā′shē·um, *n.* pl. **sper·ma·ti·a,** spur·mā′shē·a. [Gr. *sperma, spermatos,* seed.] *Bot.* a nonmotile male reproductive cell in certain lower plant forms, as the red algae.

sper·mat·o·cyte, spur·mat′o·sīt″, spur′ma·to·sīt″, *n. Biol.* a primary male germ cell which develops from the division of a spermatogonium and then itself divides to produce a spermatid and subsequent spermatozoon.

sper·mat·o·gen·e·sis, spur·mat″o·jen′i·sis, spur″ma·to·jen′i·sis, *n. Biol.* the genesis or origin and development of spermatozoa.—**sper·ma·to·ge·net·ic,** spur″ma·tō·je·net′ik, spėr·mat″ō·je·net′ik, *a.*

sper·mat·o·go·ni·um, spur·mat″o·gō′nē·um, spur″ma·to·gō′nē·um, *n.* pl. **sper·mat·o·go·ni·a,** spur·mat″o·gō′nē·a, spur″ma·to·gō′nē·a. [N.L.] *Biol.* one of the primitive germ cells which give rise to the spermatocytes.—**sper·mat·o·go·ni·al,** *a.*

sper·mat·o·phore, spur·mat′o·fōr″, spur·mat′o·far″, spur″ma·to·fōr″, spur″ma·to·far″, *n. Zool.* a special case or capsule containing a number of spermatozoa, produced by the male of various lower animals, as certain insects, mollusks, and annelids.—**sper·ma·toph·or·al, sper·ma·toph·o·rous,** spur″ma·tof′ėr·al, spur″ma·tof′ėr·us, *a.*

sper·mat·o·phyte, spur·mat′o·fīt″, spur″ma·to·fīt″, *n.* [Gr. *sperma,* and *phyton,* plant.] *Bot.* any of a division or phylum, *Spermatophyta,* comprising the seed-bearing plants.—**sper·ma·to·phyt·ic,** spur″ma·to·fit′ik, spėr·mat″o·fit′ik, *a.*

sper·mat·o·zo·id, spur·mat″o·zō′id, spur·mat″o·zō′id, *n.* [= Fr. *spermatozoïde.*] *Bot.* a motile male reproductive cell produced in the antheridium of a plant. Also **sper·ma·to·zo·oid.**

sper·ma·to·zo·on, spur″ma·to·zō′on, spur″ma·to·zō′on, spur·mat″o·zō′on, spur·mat″o·zō′on, *n.* pl. **sper·ma·to·zo·a,** spur″ma·to·zō′a, spur·mat″o·zō′a. [N.L. < Gr. *sperma (spermat-),* seed, and *zōon,* animal.] *Biol.* One of the numerous minute, usu. actively motile bodies contained in semen or sperm, which serve to fertilize the ovum of the female; any mature male reproductive cell.—**sper·ma·to·zo·al, sper·ma·to·zo·ic,** *a.*

sperm·ine, spur′mēn, spur′min, *n.* [Fr., *sperme,* E. *sperm.*] *Chem.* a colorless, crystalline, basic compound, $C_{10}H_{26}N_4$, found in semen, yeasts, and pancreatic tissue and used in medicine as a tonic.

sper·mi·o·gen·e·sis, spur″mē·ō·jen′i·sis, *n. Biol.* the production of male reproductive cells.

sperm oil, *n.* The thin yellowish oil obtained from the sperm whale's cranial cavity and blubber, used esp. as a lubricant for delicate machinery. Also *sperm.*

sper·mo·phile, spur′mo·fīl″, spur′mo·fil, *n.* [N.L. *Spermophilus,* < Gr. *spérma,* seed, and *philos,* loving.] *Zool.* any of various burrowing rodents of the squirrel family, esp. of the genus *Citellus,* as the suslik and gopher.

sperm whale, *n.* An enormous, toothed whale, *Physeter catodon,* having spermaceti in the cranial basin of its blunt head. Also *cachalot, sperm.*

sper·ry·lite, sper′*i*·līt″, *n.* [From F. L. *Sperry*, of Sudbury, Ontario, Canada, where it was found.] A mineral, PtAs₂, an arsenide of platinum, occurring in minute isometric crystals of a tin-white color.

spes·sart·ite, spes′ẽr·tīt″, *n.* A semi-precious mineral, manganese garnet, having traces of iron, magnesium, and aluminum and colored red or yellow. Also **spes·sart·-ine**, spes′ẽr·tēn″, spes′ẽr·tin.

spew, spue, spū, *v.i.*—*spued, spuing.* [O.E. *spiwan,* also *spiowan,* = O.H.G. *spiwan* (G. *speien*) = Icel. *spyja* = Goth. *speiwan,* spew, spit; akin to L. *spuere,* Gr. *ptuein,* spit.] To discharge the contents of the stomach through the mouth; vomit; to flow or run in or like a stream.—*v.t.* To eject from the stomach through the mouth; vomit; to throw out or cast forth, as if vomiting, as: The encampment began to *spew* out men.—*n.* That which is spewed; vomit.—**spew·er,** *n.*

sphag·num, sfag′num, *n.* [Gr. *sphágnos,* a kind of moss.] Any of various mosses of the large genus *Sphagnum,* which grow in wet, acid areas and are much used in the potting and shipping of plants.—**sphag·nous,** sfag′nus, *a.*

sphal·er·ite, sfal′*e*·rīt″, sfā′le·rīt″, *n.* [Gr. *sphalerós,* slippery, uncertain.] A native zinc sulfide, ZnS, and zinc's principal ore. Also *blende, zinc blende.*

sphene, sfēn, *n.* [< Gr. *sphēn,* a wedge from the shape of its crystals.] A mineral silicate, CaTiSiO₅, composed of calcium titanium. Also *titanite.*

sphen·o·don, sfē′no·don, *n.* Tuatara.

sphe·noid, sfē′noid, *a.* [Gr. *sphēnoeidēs,* wedge-shaped, < *sphen,* wedge, and *eidos,* form.] Wedge-shaped; *anat.* noting or pertaining to a compound bone at the base of the skull. Also **sphe·noi·dal.**—*n. Anat.* the sphenoid bone.

spher·al, sfẽr′al, *a.* [L.L. *sphærālis.*] Of or pertaining to a sphere; having the form of a sphere, or spherical; symmetrical or perfect in form.

sphere, sfēr, *n.* [O.Fr. *espere* (Fr. *sphère*), < L. *sphæra,* later *sphera,* < Gr. *sphaira,* ball, globe, sphere.] A solid geometrical figure generated by the revolution of a semicircle about its diameter; a round body whose surface is at all points equidistant from the center; any rounded body of this form, as a globe or a ball; a heavenly body, as a planet or star; an orbit, as of a planet; the place, region, or environment within which a person or thing exists or has being; a particular social world, stratum of society, or walk of life; a field of activity or operation; the whole field or realm of something specified; as, the *sphere* of science or of law.—*v.t.*—*sphered, sphering.* To enclose in or as in a sphere; to form into a sphere; to place among the heavenly spheres.—**spher·ic,** *a.*—**sphe·ric·i·ty,** sfi·ris′i·tē, *n.*

sphere of in·flu·ence, *n.* Any territory over which the power, interests, and influence of another country or nation are predominant.

spher·i·cal, sfẽr′i·kal, *a.* [Fr. *sphérique;* L. *sphæricus.*] Having the form of a sphere; globular; pertaining or belonging to a sphere or spheres; relating to the celestial bodies, esp. to their astrological influence.—**spher·i·cal·ly,** *adv.*

spher·i·cal ab·er·ra·tion, *n.* The change or distortion in an image due to the spherical shape of a lens or mirror.

spher·i·cal an·gle, *n. Math.* an angle formed on the surface of a sphere by the intersection of two great circles.

spher·i·cal co·or·di·nate, *n. Math.* one of the three coordinates of a coordinate system in which a point in space is located by its radial distance from the intersection of two perpendicular reference axes, the

angle between the vertical or polar axis and the radius, and the angle between the plane of the axes and the plane containing the radius and polar axis.

spher·i·cal ge·om·e·try, *n. Math.* that branch of geometry which treats of figures on a sphere's surface.

spher·i·cal pol·y·gon, *n. Math.* a polygon on the surface of a sphere. See *polygon.*

spher·i·cal tri·an·gle, *n. Math.* a spherical polygon having three sides.

spher·i·cal trig·o·nom·e·try, *n.* That branch of trigonometry which deals with spherical triangles and polygons.

spher·ics, sfẽr′iks, *n. pl. but sing. in constr.* The study of geometric and trigonometric figures found on the surface of a sphere.

spher·ics, sfẽr′iks, *n. pl. but sing. in constr.* [atmo(*spherics*).] *Meteor.* the science of using electronic devices to study atmospheric conditions and weather forecasting. Atmospherics.

sphe·roid, sfẽr′oid, *n.* [L. *sphæroides,* < Gr. *sphairoeides,* spherelike, < *sphaira,* sphere, and *eidos,* form.] *Geom.* An ellipsoid formed by rotating an ellipse about one of its axes; a body resembling a sphere, but not perfectly spherical—*a.* Spheroidal.

sphe·roi·dal, sfi·roid′al, *a.* Pertaining to a spheroid or spheroids; shaped like a spheroid; approximately spherical. Also **sphe·roi·dic,** *spheroid.*—**sphe·roi·dal·ly,** *adv.*

sphe·rom·e·ter, sfi·rom′i·tẽr, *n.* [Fr. *sphéromètre,* < Gr. *sphaira,* sphere, and *metron,* measure.] An instrument for measuring the curvature of spheres and curved surfaces.

spher·ule, sfẽr′öl, sfẽr′ūl, sfẽr′öl, sfẽr′ūl, *n.* A little sphere or spherical body.—**spher·u·lar,** sfẽr′*u*·lẽr, sfẽr′*u*·lẽr, *a.*

spher·u·lite, sfẽr′*u*·līt″, sfẽr′ū·līt″, sfẽr′*u*·līt″, sfẽr′ū·līt″, *n.* [Gr. *sphaira,* and *lithos,* a stone.] A radiating spherical aggregation of crystal fibers found in various volcanic rocks.—**spher·u·lit·ic,** sfẽr″*u*·lit′ik, sfẽr″-ū·lit′ik, sfẽr″*u*·lit′ik, sfẽr″ū·lit′ik, *a.*

spher·y, sfẽr′ē, *a.* Resembling a sphere or orb, as a celestial body; starlike.

sphinc·ter, sfingk′tẽr, *n.* [L.L., < Gr. *sphinghter < sphingein,* bind tight.] *Anat., zool.* a contractile ringlike muscle surrounding and capable of closing a natural orifice or passage.—**sphinc·ter·al,** *a.*—**sphinc·te·ri·al,** sfingk·tẽr′ē·al, *a.*—**sphinc·ter·ate,** sfingk′tẽr·it, sfingk′te·rāt″, *a.*—**sphinc·ter·ic,** sfingk·tẽr′ik, *a.*

sphin·gid, sfin′jid, *n.* Hawk moth.

sphinx, sfingks, *n. pl.* **sphinx·es, sphin·ges,** sfin′jēz. [L., < Gr. *sphigx,* sphinx, commonly explained as meaning 'strangler,' 'throttler,' < *sphiggein,* bind tight: cf. *sphincter.*] (*Sometimes cap.*), Gr. *mythol.* a monster with the head of a woman on the winged body of a lion or a dog, which, near Thebes, proposed a riddle to passersby, killing those unable to guess it. A sphinx-like person or thing, as one presenting difficult questions or being of an inscrutable nature. *Egyptol.* a figure of an imaginary creature having the head of a man, a ram, or a hawk, and the body of a lion; (*usu. cap.*) the colossal recumbent stone figure of this kind near the pyramids of Gizeh. *Entom.* hawk moth.—**sphinx·i·an,** *a.*

sphinx moth, *n.* Hawk moth.

sphra·gis·tics, sfra·jis′tiks, *n. pl. but sing. in constr.* [Gr. *sphragis,* a seal.] The science of engraved seals or signets, their history, peculiarities, and distinctions.—**sphra·gis·tic,** *a.*

sphyg·mo·graph, sfig′mo·graf″, sfig′mo·gräf″, *n.* An instrument which, when applied over an artery, graphically records the uniformity, strength, and rapidity of the pulse.—**sphyg·mo·graph·ic,** *a.*—**sphyg·mog·ra·phy,** sfig·mog′ra·fē, *n.*

sphyg·mo·ma·nom·e·ter, sfig″mō·ma·-nom′i·tẽr, *n.* An instrument for measuring the pressure of the blood in an artery.—**sphyg·mo·man·o·met·ric,** sfig″mō·man″-o·me′trik, *a.*—**sphyg·mo·man·o·met·ri·cal·ly,** *adv.*—**sphyg·mo·ma·nom·e·try,** *n.*

sphyg·mom·e·ter, sfig·mom′i·tẽr, *n.* An instrument that measures the rate and force of the pulse.—**sphyg·mo·met·ric,** sfig″mo·me′trik, *a.*

spi·ca, spī′ka, *n. pl.* **spi·cae,** **spi·cas,** spī′sē. *Bot.* a spike or ear of grain, as on a flower; *surg.* a plaster or plain bandage having a spiraled and reversed form and looking like a spike of wheat.

spi·cate, spī′kāt, *a.* [L. *spicatus,* pp. of *spicare,* furnish with spikes, < *spica,* E. spike.] *Bot.* Having or bearing spikes, as a plant; arranged in spikes, as flowers; having the form of a spike, as an inflorescence.

spic·ca·to, spi·kä′tō, *It.* spēk·kä′tạ, *a.* [It., pp. of *spiccare,* detach, separate.] *Mus.* in violin playing, noting distinct tones produced by short, abrupt motions of the bow, which is allowed to rebound off the strings.—*n. Mus.* A spiccato method of bowing; a spiccato passage.

spice, spīs, *n.* [O.Fr. *espice, espece* (Fr. *épice*), spice, < L.L. *species,* spice, L. sort, kind.] Any of a class of pungent or aromatic substances of plant origin, as pepper, cinnamon, cloves, and the like, used as seasoning or preservatives; such substances as a material or collectively; a spicy or aromatic odor or fragrance; something that gives zest.—*v.t.*—*spiced, spicing.* To prepare or season with a spice or spices; *fig.* to give zest, piquancy, or interest to by something added.

spice·ber·ry, spīs′ber″ē, spīs′be·rē, *n. pl.* **spice·ber·ries.** A small, white-flowered, W. Indian tree, *Eugenia rhombea,* of the myrtle family, cultivated in Florida for its black or orange fruit; the fruit of this tree.

spice box, *n.* A receptacle for holding jars or other containers of spices.

spice·bush, spīs′bush″, *n.* A yellow-flowered, N. American shrub, *Lindera benzoin,* of the laurel family, whose bark and leaves have a spicy odor; also *benjamin-bush.* A tall, N. American strawberry shrub, *Calycanthus occidentalis,* with brownish, fragrant flowers; also **sweet shrub.**

spice·bush swal·low·tail, *n.* Troilus butterfly.

spic·er·y, spī′se·rē, *n. pl.* **spic·er·ies.** Spices collectively; spicy aroma or flavor.

spick-and-span, spic-and-span, spik′an·-span′, *a.* [< *spick-and-span-new.*] Perfectly new; fresh; spruce or smart; neat and clean.

spic·u·la, spik′ū·la, *n. pl.* **spic·u·lae,** spik′ū·lē″. [N.L., dim of L. *spica.*] A small, needlelike body or part; a spicule; a needle-shaped crystal, as of ice.—**spic·u·lar,** *a.*

spi·cule, spik′ūl, *n.* [N.L. *spicula* or L. *spiculum.*] A small or minute, slender, sharp-pointed body or part; a small needle-like crystal, process, or the like. *Zool.* one of the small, hard calcareous or siliceous bodies which serve as the skeletal elements of some invertebrate animals, as sponges; spiculum. *Bot.* a floral spikelet; *astron.* a long streamer of burning gas spurting from the surface of the sun.—**spic·u·late,** spic·u·lar,** *a.*—**spic·u·la·tion,** *n.*

spic·u·lum, spik′ū·lum, *n. pl.* **spic·u·la,** spik′ū·la. [L., dim. of *spica,* E. spike.] A small organ of certain invertebrates, such as starfishes or sea urchins, shaped like a needle or dart; a spicule.

spic·y, spī′sē, *a.*—*spicier, spiciest.* Seasoned with or containing spice; of the nature of or resembling spice; abounding in or yielding spices; characteristic or suggestive of spice; aromatic or fragrant. *Fig.* piquant or pungent; as, a *spicy* speech; of a somewhat improper or scandalous nature; as, a *spicy* story.—**spic·i·ly,** *adv.*—**spic·i·ness,** *n.*

spi·der, spī'dẽr, *n.* [M.E. *spithre*, appar. < O.E. *spinnan,* E. *spin.*] Any of the eight-legged, wingless, predaceous arachnids which constitute the order *Araneae,* notable for the spinning of webs which serve as nests and as traps for prey; any of various things resembling or suggesting a spider; a frying pan, orig. one with legs or feet; a trivet or tripod, as for supporting a pot or pan on a hearth; any of various mechanical structures or frames with radiating parts.

spi·der crab, *n.* Any of various crabs of the genus *Libinia,* with long, slender legs and a comparatively small body.

spi·der mite, *n.* Red spider.

spi·der mon·key, *n.* Any of various tropical American monkeys of the genus *Ateles,* with a slender body, long slender limbs, a long prehensile tail, and with the thumb either rudimentary or lacking.

spi·der pha·e·ton, *n.* A high, lightweight carriage with a covered driver's seat at the front, and uncovered footman's seat at the rear.

spi·der·wort, spī'dẽr·wụrt″, *n.* Any plant of the genus *Tradescantia,* comprising perennial herbs with blue, purple, or rose-colored flowers; any of various related plants.

spi·der·y, spī'de·rē, *a.* Like or suggesting a spider; long and thin, as the legs of a spider; delicate, suggesting a spider's web; full of or infested with spiders.

spie·gel·ei·sen, spē'gel·ī″zen, *n.* [G., 'mirror iron.'] A lustrous, crystalline pig iron containing 15 to 30 percent of manganese, used in making steel. Also **spie·gel, spie·gel·i·ron.**

spiel, spēl, shpēl, *n.* [G., < *spielen,* to play.] *n. Slang.* A talk or speech usu. voluble and used as a lure; a pitch.—*v.i. Slang,* to talk or speak with extravagance or volubly.—**spiel·er,** spē'lẽr, *n. Slang.* One who spiels; a talker or speaker; an announcer, crier, or barker.

spi·er, spī'ẽr, *n.* One who spies, watches, or discovers.

spiff·y, spif'ē, *a.*—*spiffier, spiffiest.* [Origin obscure.] *Slang.* Spruce; smart; fine.—**spiff·i·ness,** *n.*

spig·ot, spig'ot, *n.* [O.E. *spigotte, speget, spykette,* dim. forms < *spick = spike.*] A faucet; a plug or peg that is turned to open or stop a faucet, or that stops the bunghole in a cask of liquid.

spike, spīk, *n.* [M.E. *spike =* Sw. and Norw. *spik,* nail, spike, related to M.L.G. *spīker,* G. *spieker,* D. *spijker,* nail; all perh. < L. *spica.*] A large, strong nail or pin, esp. of iron, as for fastening rails to ties; that which resembles a spike; a stiff, sharp-pointed piece or part; a sharp-pointed piece, as of metal, fastened in something with the point outward, as for defense; a sharp metal projection on the sole or the heel of a shoe, as of a golfer, to prevent slipping. *Pl.* shoes, as a pair, with such projections; high heels, as on shoes for women, that are very narrow. The antler of a young deer, when straight and without branches; a mackerel that is young and usu. not longer than six inches.—*v.t.—spiked, spiking.* To fasten or secure with a spike or spikes; to provide or set with a spike or spikes, as for protection or to prevent slipping; to pierce with or impale on a spike; to set or stud with something suggesting spikes; to injure, as another player or a competitor, with the spikes of one's shoe, as in baseball; to render useless, as a gun, by driving a spike into the touch

hole; *fig.* to make ineffective, or frustrate the action or purpose of; as, to *spike* an attempt; *colloq.* to add liquor or alcohol to, as a drink.

spike, spīk, *n.* [L. *spica,* spike of grain, ear, top, or tuft of a plant, orig. something sharp or pointed.] *Bot.* An ear, as of wheat or other grain; an inflorescence in which the flowers are sessile, or apparently so, along an elongated, unbranched common axis.—**spiked,** *a.*

spike lav·en·der, *n.* A kind of lavender, *Lavandula latifolia,* having spikes of pale purple flowers, and yielding lavender oil, used in cosmetics and artists' paints.

spike·let, spīk'lit, *n. Bot.* a small spike making up a part of a larger spike which forms the compound inflorescence of grasses and sedges.

spike·nard, spīk'nẽrd, spīk'närd, *n.* [M.L. *spica nardi,* 'spike of the nard.'] An aromatic East Indian plant of the valerian family, *Nardostachys jatamansi,* supposedly the same as the ancient nard; an aromatic substance used by the ancients to make ointments, thought to be obtained from this plant; any of various other plants, esp. a N. American spikenard, *Aralia racemosa,* of the ginseng family, with an aromatic root used in medicine.

spik·y, spī'kē, *a.*—*spikier, spikiest.* In the shape of a spike; set with spikes.

spile, spīl, *n.* [Same as D. *spijl,* L.G. *spile,* a bar, a stake; G. *speil,* a skewer.] A small peg or wooden pin used to stop a hole in a cask or barrel; a spigot; a large, heavy, supporting pile or stake; a spout put in a sugar maple tree for drawing off the sap.—*v.t.—spiled, spiling.* To supply with a spigot; to support with piles or spiles.—**spil·ing,** *n.*

spill, spil, *v.t.—spilled* or *spilt, spilling.* [O.E. *spillan =* Icel. *spilla,* destroy, = M.L.G. and D. *spillen,* waste.] To cause or allow, as liquid, or any matter in grains or loose pieces, to run or fall from a vessel or container, esp. accidentally or wastefully; to shed, esp. blood, as in killing or wounding; to scatter; *naut.* to let the wind out of, as a sail; *colloq.* to cause to fall from a horse, vehicle, or the like; *slang,* to divulge, disclose, or tell, as secret or confidential information.—*v.i.* To run or escape from a vessel or container, esp. by accident or in careless handling, as liquid, loose particles, or the like.—*n.* A spilling, as of liquid, or a quantity spilled or the mark made. *Colloq.* a throw or fall from a horse, vehicle, or the like; spillway.—**spill the beans,** *colloq.* to reveal information inadvertently, as a secret.

spill, spil, *n.* [M.E. *spille,* splinter: cf. *spile.*] A sharp-pointed fragment of wood, as a splinter; a slender piece of wood or of folded or twisted paper, for lighting candles, lamps, or the like; a metallic peg or pin; a small peg for stopping or plugging a cask; a spile.

spil·lage, spil'ij, *n.* The action of spilling something; the amount of whatever is spilled.

spil·li·kin, spil'i·kin, *n.* A jackstraw, or strip of wood, bone, or the like used in the game of jackstraws; *pl. but sing. in constr.* the game itself. Also **spil·i·kin, spil·li·ken.**

spill·way, spil'wā″, *n.* A channel or passage for the overflow water of a lake, reservoir, dam, or river.

spi·lo·site, spī'lo·sīt″, *n.* [Gr. *spilos,* spot, speck.] *Geol.* a spotted rock resulting from local metamorphism of slate in contact with diabase or granite.

spilth, spilth, *n.* The act of spilling, or that which is spilled; effusion; refuse.

spin, spin, *v.t.—past spun* or archaic *span,* pp. *spun,* ppr. *spinning.* [O.E. *spinnan =* D.

and G. *spinnen =* Icel, and Sw. *spinna =* Goth. *spinnan,* spin.] To draw out and twist, as a fiber of wool, flax, cotton, etc., either by hand or by machinery, into thread or yarn; to form, as any material into thread; as, to *spin* glass; to make, as thread or yarn, by drawing out, twisting, or the like; to produce, as a thread, cobweb, gossamer, or silk, by extruding from the body a long, slender filament of a natural viscous matter that hardens in the air, as of spiders or silkworms; to cause to turn around rapidly, as on an axis; as, to *spin* a top; whirl; to produce, fabricate, or evolve in a manner suggestive of spinning thread; to tell, as a yarn or story; to draw out, protract, or prolong, often used with *out*; as, to *spin out* a story.—*v.i.* To turn round rapidly, as on an axis, as the earth or a top; to produce a thread from the body, as spiders, silkworms, or the like; to draw out and twist wool, flax, or the like into thread or yarn; to move, go, run, ride, or travel rapidly; to be affected with a sensation of whirling, as the head; to fish with a spinning or revolving bait.—*n.* The act of causing a spinning or whirling motion; a spinning motion given to a ball or the like when thrown; a spinning or whirling motion of anything; a rapid run, ride, drive, or the like, as for exercise; a moving or going rapidly along. *Aeron.* an aerial maneuver or performance, either controlled or uncontrolled, in which an airplane makes a vertical descent with its nose pointed sharply or slightly downward, while revolving about the line of descent in any of various attitudes; also *tailspin. Phys.* an intrinsic angular momentum, as of an electron or atom, as: In a stable molecule of hydrogen, the two electrons have opposite *spins.*

spin·ach, spin'ich, *n.* [O.Fr. *espinoche,* It. *spinace,* Sp. *espinaca,* < L. *spina,* a spine—being named from the prickles on its fruit.] An annual plant, *Spinacia oleracea,* with hollow stems and edible, fleshy leaves: its leaves used as a vegetable.

spi·nal, spīn'al, *a.* Pertaining to or resembling the spine or backbone.—*n.* An anesthetic injected into the spinal cord.—**spi·nal·ly,** *adv.*

spi·nal ca·nal, *n.* The tube or canal that holds the spinal cord as well as its membranes and which is formed by the vertebral arches.

spi·nal col·umn, *n.* In a vertebrate animal, the series of small bones or vertebrae forming the axis of the skeleton and protecting the spinal cord; the spine; the backbone. Also *vertebral column.*

spi·nal cord, *n.* The cord of nervous tissue extending through the spinal canal, and enclosed within the spinal column.

spin·dle, spin'dl, *n.* [O.E. *spinel,* < *spinnan,* E. *spin.*] A rounded, usu. wooden rod with tapered ends used in hand-spinning to twist into thread the fibers drawn from the mass on the distaff, and to wind the thread as it is spun; the rod or pin on a spinning wheel by which the thread is twisted and on which it is wound; one of the rods of a spinning machine or shuttle holding the bobbins on which the thread is wound as it is spun. *Mech.* any rod or pin which turns around or on which something turns, as an axle, axis, or shaft; a small axis, arbor, or mandrel. A needlelike spike secured on a wider and heavier base, used to hold bills, notes, and other papers; a measure of yarn, containing 15,120 yards for cotton and 14,400 yards for linen; *biol.* the fibrous strands of achromatic material which form in a cell during mitosis; *naut.* an iron rod or pipe surmounted by a ball, lantern, or similar perceptible object, fixed to a rock or sunken reef to serve as a guide and warning in navigation.—*v.i.—spindled,* *spindling*. To shoot up or grow into a long, slender stalk or stem, as a plant; to grow long and slender.—*v.t.* To form into the shape of a spindle; to furnish with a spindle; to impale, as papers, on the needlelike rod of a spindle.

spin·dle·legs, spin'dl·legz", *n. pl.* Long, slender legs; *sing. in constr., colloq.* a person having long, slender legs. Also **spin·dle·-shanks**, spin'dl·shangks".—**spin·dle·leg·-ged**, *a.*—**spin·dle-shanked**, *a.*

spin·dle tree, *n.* A small European tree, *Euonymus europaeus*, the wood of which is used for making spindles and other wooden articles. Any of several trees or shrubs, esp. a N. American species, *E. atropurpureus*, an ornamental which yields drugs used in medicine; also *burning bush, wahoo*.

spin·dling, spind'ling, *a.* Long, or tall and slender, often disproportionately so; *bot.* growing into a long, slender stalk or stem, often a too slender or weakly one.—*n.* That which is spindling.

spin·dly, spind'lē, *a.*—*spindlier, spindliest*. Of a slender weak form.

spin·drift, spin'drift", *n.* [A form of *spoon-drift*.] *Naut.* the fine spray from a choppy sea blown into the air by winds of gale force. Also *spoondrift*.

spine, spīn, *n.* [L. *spina*, a thorn, the spine, from a root seen also in *spike*.] The back-bone of a vertebrate animal which provides the main support for its body; any rigid, pointed outgrowth on the body of an animal, as the quills of a porcupine or the fin rays of a fish; a thornlike, slightly woody structure, as on a plant or tree; a long, narrow projection or outcropping, as of rock, or a crest or ridge of mountains or hills; *fig.* an inner quality of resolution, fortitude, strength of character; *book-binding*, the back part of a book cover which bears the title and author's name.

spi·nel, spi·nel', spin'el, *n.* [Fr. *spinelle*, < It. *spinella*, dim. < L. *spina*, thorn; prob. with reference to the sharp angles of the crystals.] A mineral consisting chiefly of the oxides of magnesium and aluminum, and having varieties used in jewelry as gem-stones, esp. ruby spinel. Also **spi·nelle**.

spine·less, spīn'lis, *a.* Without spines or sharp-pointed processes; having no spine or backbone; having a weak spine or back-bone; lacking the natural strength of spine; limp. *Fig.* without moral force, resolution, or courage; irresolute; feeble.—**spine·less·-ly**, *adv.*—**spine·less·ness**, *n.*

spi·nes·cent, spi·nes'ent, *a.* [L. *spinesco*, to grow thorny.] *Biol.* Having spines; becoming spiny; terminating in a spine.—**spi·-nes·cence**, *n.*

spin·et, spin'it, *n.* [O.Fr. *espinette*, < L. *spina*, a spine, because its strings were twitched by spinelike pieces of quill.] A small musical instrument of the harpsichord family; a small, compact, upright piano.

spin·i·fex, spin'i·feks", *n.* Any of several related grasses of the genera *Spinifex* and *Triodia*, with sharp-pointed leaves, found in large areas of Australia.

spin·na·ker, spin'a·kėr, *n.* [< *spin*, in sense of to go rapidly.] *Naut.* a triangular racing sail carried by yachts on the opposite side to the mainsail when running before the wind.

spin·ner, spin'ėr, *n.* One who or that which spins; a fishing lure consisting of a blade or spoon, used in trolling or casting; a cone-shaped structure fitted over an airplane propeller hub; *football*, a play in which the ball carrier twirls about in order to deceive the opposing team as to the direction in which he will go.

spin·ner·et, spin'e·ret", *n.* An organ, as of certain spiders, caterpillars, or other arthropods, which produces a silky filament used in spinning the web or cocoon. A metal device with tiny holes through which a chemical solution is forced in the making of synthetic fibers, such as rayon; also **spin·ner·ette**.

spin·ney, **spin·ny**, spin'ē, *n. pl.* **spin·-neys, spin·nies**. [O.Fr. *espinaye*, < *espine*, a brier, < L. *spina*, a thorn.] *Brit.* a small wooded area with undergrowth, as a grove or thicket.

spin·ning frame, *n.* A machine which can spin, wind, and twist yarn.

spin·ning jen·ny, *n.* A spinning machine invented in England about 1767 by James Hargreaves, which made possible the spinning of numerous threads simul-taneously. Also *jenny*.

spin·ning wheel, *n.* A small device operated by foot or hand for spinning wool, cotton, or flax into thread or yarn.

spin-off, spin'af", spin'of", *n. Finance*, a parent corporation's distribution to its own stockholders of the stock of a subsidiary corporation.

spi·nose, spī'nōs, spī·nōs', *a.* [L. *spinosus*.] Full of spines; spiny; spinous.—**spi·nose·-ly**, *adv.*—**spi·nos·i·ty**, spī·nos'i·tē, *n.*

spi·nous, spī'nus, *a.* [L. *spinosus*, < *spina*, thorn, E. *spine*.] *Biol.* Covered with or having spines; thorny, as a plant; armed with or bearing sharp-pointed processes, as an animal; spinelike or spiniform; slender and sharp-pointed, as a process of bone; spinose.

spi·nous proc·ess, *n. Anat.* the dorsal bony projection from the middle of the neural arch of a vertebra.

spin·ster, spin'stėr, *n.* An unmarried woman past the usual or conventional age for marrying; an old maid; a woman who spins as an occupation.—**spin·ster·hood**, *n.*—**spin·ster·ish**, *a.*

spin·thar·i·scope, spin·thar'i·skōp", *n.* [Gr. *spintharis*, spark, and *-scope*.] *Phys.* an apparatus for observing the scintillations produced by alpha rays striking a prepared screen.—**spin·thar·i·scop·ic**, spin·thar"i·skop'ik, *a.*

spin the bot·tle, *n.* A game played by boys and girls sitting in a circle with the boys spinning a bottle and receiving a kiss from the girl the bottle is pointing to when it stops.

spin the plate, *n.* A kind of parlor game in which a plate is spun on edge by one sex; a member of the opposite sex, whose name is called out, must catch the plate before it falls or pay with a kiss. Also **spin the plat·ter**.

spi·nule, spī'nūl, spin'ūl, *n.* [L. *spinula*, dim. of *spina*.] *Biol.* a minute spine.—**spin·u·lose**, spin'ū·lōs", spin'ū·lōs", *a. Biol.* covered with small spines.

spin·y, spī'nē, *a.*—*spinier, spiniest*. Full of spines, as a gooseberry shrub; having spines, as a porcupine; like a spine. *Fig.* perplexing; troublesome.—**spin·i·ness**, *n.*

spin·y ant·eat·er, *n. Zool.* an echidna.

spin·y-finned, spī'nē·find', *a. Ichth.* having fins supported by sharp, hard, unarticulated rays, as a bass, perch, or mackerel. Compare *soft-finned*.

spin·y lob·ster, *n.* An edible marine crustacean, genus *Palinurus*, similar to the common lobster but not having the large pincers. Also *rock lobster*.

spi·ra·cle, spī'ra·kl, spir'a·kl, *n.* [L. *spiraculum*, < *spirare*, to breathe.] A breathing hole. *Zool.* an external opening for the passage of air or water in the act of respiration; the blowhole of a whale; the inlet to the gills of sharks and tadpoles; one of the tracheal tube apertures along the sides of insects.—**spi·rac·u·lar**, spī·rak'-ū·lėr, spī·rak'ū·lėr, *a.*

spi·ral, spī'ral, *n. Geom.* a curve traced in a plane by a point moving around a fixed point while continually approaching it or continually receding from it. A helix; one of the turns or coils of a spiral or helix; an object or form in the shape of a spiral or helix; *football*, a type of pass or kick in which the ball rotates on its longitudinal axis; *econ.* a continuously accelerating increase or decrease, as of costs, wages, or prices; *aeron.* an airplane maneuver in which the plane descends or rises in a helical path.—*a.* Curving around a fixed point in the form of a spiral; winding about an axis in continually advancing planes; helical; of or resembling a spire or spiral.—*v.i.*—*spiraled, spiraling, Brit. spiralled, spiralling*. To take the form of a spiral; to move in a spiral path.—*v.t.* To make into the form of a spiral; to cause to spiral.—**spi·ral·ly**, *adv.*

spi·ral gal·ax·y, *n. Astron.* a distant star system having a spiral shape or structure. Also **spi·ral neb·u·la**.

spi·rant, spī'rant, *n.* [L. *spirare*, to breathe.] *Phon.* a continuant or fricative consonant, as the *sh* sound in shoes, as distinguished from a stop or affricative consonant, as the *ch* sound in choose.—*a.*

spire, spī'ėr, *n.* [O.E. *spir*, a spike or stalk; D. *spier*, a spire of grass; Dan. *spire*, a sprout, *spiir*, a spire; akin to *spear* and *spar*.] A slender, tapering formation directed upward to a point; a pyramidal or conical structure upon a tower or roof; the terminal upper part of a steeple; a blade, sprout, shoot, or stalk of a plant.—*v.i.*—*spired, spiring*. To taper upwards; to pyramid; to shoot up, as a blade of grass.—**spired**, *a.*

spire, spī'ėr, *n.* [L. *spira*, < Gr. *speira*, a spiral line, something twisted.] A spiral; a coil; a twist; *zool.* the convolutions of certain mollusks' shells.—**spired**, *a.*

spi·re·a, **spi·rae·a**, spī·rē'a, *n.* An ornamental shrub of the genus *Spiraea*, belonging to the rose family and having small pink or white flowers, as bridal wreath.

spi·reme, spī'rēm, *n.* [Gr. *speirēma, speirama*, a coil, < *speirasthai*, be coiled, < *speira*, E. *spire*.] *Biol.* the chromatin of a cell nucleus, when it assumes a continuous or segmented threadlike form, during the process of mitosis.

spi·rif·er·ous, spī·rif'ér·us, *a.* [L. *spira*, a coil.] *Zool.* Having a spire, or spiral upper part, as a univalve shell; having spiral appendages, as a brachiopod.

spi·ril·lum, spī·ril'um, *n. pl.* **spi·ril·la**, spī·ril'a. [From its *spiral* growth.] A microscopic, flagellate bacteria of the genus *Spirillum*.

spir·it, spir'it, *n.* [O.Fr. *espirit* (Fr. *esprit*), < L. *spiritus*, breathing, breath, air, life, soul, spirit, N.L. distilled or alcoholic spirit, < L. *spirare*, breathe, blow.] That which is believed to be the principle of con-scious life and the vital principle in man; the incorporeal part of man; as, to be present in *spirit* if not in body; the soul, regarded as separable from the body at death; conscious incorporeal being, as opposed to matter; as, the world of *spirit*; a supernatural, incorporeal being or presence inhabiting a place or thing, or having a particular character; as, *spirits* of the air or water; a fairy, sprite, or elf; an angel or demon; the soul or heart as the seat of feelings or sentiments, or of anima-tion of the body; as, to break a person's *spirit*; mettle or courage; as, a man of *spirit*; vigor or liveliness, as in action, words, or music; temper or attitude; as, something done in the right *spirit*; *pl.* feelings with respect to exaltation or depression; as, to be in high or low *spirits*. Character or disposition; as, meek in *spirit*; an inspiring or animating person or influence; as, the leading *spirit* in an undertaking. (*Cap.*) the divine influence as an agency working in man; the third person of the Trinity, the Holy Spirit. An inspiring or animating principle that pervades and tempers thought, feeling, or action; as, the *spirit* of love, or *spirit* of reform; the dominant tendency of anything; as, the *spirit* of the age; the general meaning or intent of a regulation, statement, or the like, as opposed to its literal interpretation; as, the *spirit*, not the letter, of the law; *chem.* the essence or active principle of a substance as extracted in liquid form, esp. by distillation. *Often pl.* a liquor obtained by distillation, esp. a strong distilled alcoholic liquor; alcohol; any of certain subtle fluids formerly supposed to permeate the body; as, natural or animal *spirits. Phar., chem.* a solution in alcohol of an essential or volatile principle; also *essence.* (*Cap.*), *Christian Science,* God.—*v.t.* To carry off mysteriously or secretly, usu. followed by *away,* as: The witnesses were *spirited away.* To animate with fresh ardor or courage; to inspirit; encourage; to urge on or stir up, as to action.—*a.* Pertaining to that which operates by burning a volatile liquid such as alcohol; as, a *spirit* lamp or *spirit* stove.

spir·it·ed, spir'i·tid, *a.* Animated; lively; full of spirit, courage, energy, or the like; having a spirit or disposition of a certain character, used in compounds; as, high-spirited.—**spir·it·ed·ly,** *adv.*—**spir·it·ed·ness,** *n.*

spir·it gum, *n.* A special kind of glue, arabic gum in ether, which is used to fix artificial hair to a person's skin.

spir·it·ism, spir'it·tiz"um, *n.* The doctrine or practices of spiritualism.—**spir·it·ist,** *n.*—**spir·it·is·tic,** *a.*

spir·it lamp, *n.* A lamp in which alcohol or other volatile fuel in liquid form is burned.

spir·it·less, spir'it·lis, *a.* Without spirit, ardor, vigor, animation, or enthusiasm; depressed or listless.—**spir·it·less·ly,** *adv.*—**spir·it·less·ness,** *n.*

spir·it lev·el, *n.* A glass tube nearly filled with alcohol, for determining a line or plane parallel to the horizon by the central position of an air bubble on its upper side.

spir·it of harts·horn, *n. Chem.* an aqueous solution of ammonia. Also **spir·its of harts·horn.** See *hartshorn.*

spi·ri·to·so, spir"i;tō'sō, *It.* spē"Rē·ta'sa̠, *a.* [It.] *Mus.* Spirited; lively.

spir·i·tous, spir'i·tus, *a.* Spirituous or alcoholic.

spir·it rap·ping, *n.* A spiritualistic manifestation allegedly indicating communication between the dead and the living, involving audible raps or knocks on boards or tables.

spir·its of tur·pen·tine, *n.* See *turpentine.* Also **spir·it of tur·pen·tine.**

spir·its of wine, *n.* Ethyl alcohol purified by redistillation. Also **spir·it of wine.**

spir·it·u·al, spir'i·chō·al, *a.* [O.Fr. Fr. *spirituel,* < L.L. *spiritualis,* < L. *spiritus,* E. *spirit.*] Of, pertaining to, or consisting of spirit or incorporeal being; pertaining to incorporeal or disembodied spirits, esp. the spirits of the dead; of or pertaining to the spirit or soul as distinguished from the physical nature; of or pertaining to the spirit, esp. as the seat of moral or religious nature; symbolic or mystical, with reference to the spirit or to things having acquired a religious nature; religious; devotional; sacred; of or pertaining to sacred things; pertaining or belonging to the church or things ecclesiastical.—*n.* A spiritual or religious song; as, Negro *spirituals; usu. pl.* spiritual things or matters, esp. of the church.—**spir·it·u·al·ly,** *adv.*—**spir·it·u·al·ness,** *n.*

spir·it·u·al bou·quet, *n.* The making of one of several pious or devotional acts by a Roman Catholic for a person, living or dead, on some special occasion, as a pilgrimage on the anniversary of someone's death.

spir·it·u·al·ism, spir'i·chō·a·liz"um, *n.* The belief or doctrine that the spirits of the dead survive after mortal life and communicate with the living, esp. through the intercession of a medium; the practices or phenomena associated with this belief; the doctrine that reality is spiritual rather than material; *philos.* a type of idealism which defines ultimate reality as spirit and the world as a realm of thoughts and ideas. Spiritual quality or tendency; insistence on the spiritual side of things, as in philosophy or religion.—**spir·it·u·al·ist,** spir'i·chō·a·list, *n.*—**spir·it·u·al·is·tic,** *a.*

spir·it·u·al·i·ty, spir"i·chō·al'i·tē, *n. pl.* **spir·it·u·al·i·ties.** [O.Fr. *spiritualite* (Fr. *spiritualité*), < L.L. *spiritualitas.*] The quality or fact of being spiritual; incorporeal or immaterial nature; predominantly spiritual character, as shown in thought, teachings, life, or appearance; *often pl.* property or revenue of the church or of an ecclesiastic in his official capacity.

spir·it·u·al·ize, spir'i·chō·a·liz", *v.t.* spiritualized, spiritualizing. To make spiritual, esp. to free from corrupting secular influences; to provide with a spiritual sense or meaning.—**spir·it·u·al·i·za·tion,** *n.*

spir·it·u·al·ty, spir'i·chō·al·tē, *n. pl.* **spir·it·u·al·ties.** [O.Fr. *spiritualte:* cf. *spirituality.*] *Often pl.* ecclesiastical property or revenue. The body of ecclesiastics; the clergy.

spi·ri·tu·el, spi·ri·tu·elle, spir"i·chō·el', *Fr.* spē·Rē·tʏel', *a.* [Fr.] Showing fineness of mind or wit; characterized by a refined and graceful intellectuality; witty; ethereal.

spir·it·u·ous, spir'i·chō·us, *a.* [Fr. *spiritueux.*] Containing alcohol as the characteristic ingredient; alcoholic; of beverages, distilled: contrasted with *fermented.*—**spir·it·u·os·i·ty,** *n.*

spir·it writ·ing, *n.* Involuntary writing declared to be implemented by some invisible, supernatural force.

spi·ro·chete, spi·ro·chaete, spī'rō·kēt", *n.* [N.L. *Spirochaeta* < Gr. *speira,* a coil, and *chaitē,* hair.] *Bact.* any of the slender, threadlike bacteria characterized by spiral or screwlike shapes, which constitute the genus *Spirochaeta,* some species of which cause diseases, as syphilis and yaws.—

spi·ro·che·to·sis, spī"rō·kē·tō'sis, *n.* [N.L.] Any disease, infection, or condition caused by spirochetes.

spi·ro·graph, spī'rō·graf", spī'rō·graf", *n.* [L. *spirare,* breathe.] An instrument for recording the frequency and extent of respiratory movements.—**spi·ro·graph·ic,** spī"rō·graf'ik, *a.*

spi·ro·gy·ra, spī"rō·jī'ra, *n. Bot.* a kind of green algae of the genus *Spirogyra,* which grows in fresh water and has spiral bands of chloroplasts.

spi·rom·e·ter, spī·rom'i·tėr, *n.* [L. *spirare,* breathe.] An instrument for determining the capacity of the lungs.—**spi·ro·met·ric,** spī"rō·me'trik, *a.*—**spi·rom·e·try,** *n.*

spirt, spùrt, *n.* Spurt.—*v.t., v.i.*

spir·u·la, spir'ū·la, spir'u̠·la, *n. pl.* **spir·u·lae,** spir'ū·lē, spir'u̠·lē. [N.L., dim. < L. *spira,* E. *spire.*] Any of the small marine mollusks of the genus *Spirula,* having a partially internal, multichambered shell in the form of a flat spiral.

spir·y, spī·ėr'ē, *a.* Having the form of a spire, slender shoot, or tapering, pointed body; tapering up to a point like a spire; abounding in spires or steeples.

spir·y, spī'rē, *a.*—*spirier, spiriest.* Spiral; coiled; curling.

spit, spit, *v.i.*—*spit* or *spat, spitting.* [O.E. *spittan, gespittan,* spit: cf. O.E. *spǽtan* and Icel. *spÿta,* spit.] To eject saliva from the mouth; expectorate; to do this at or on a person to express hatred, contempt, or the like; to sputter; to fall in scattered drops or flakes, as rain or snow; to produce a hissing noise.—*v.t.* To eject, as saliva, from the mouth; to throw out or emit like saliva; to utter angrily or spitefully, often used with *out;* to say or speak without hesitation or reserve, often used with *out;* to light or set; as, *spit* a fuse.—*n.* Saliva, esp. when ejected; spittle; the act or an act of spitting; a frothy or spitlike secretion exuded by various insects; spittle insect; a light fall of rain or snow.—**spit and im·age,** *colloq.* Perfect image or likeness; a copy or counterpart; also **spit·ting im·age.**—**spit·ter,** spit'ėr, *n.*

spit, spit, *n.* [O.E. *spitu* = D. *spit* = G. *spiess,* spit.] A sharply pointed, slender rod or bar for thrusting into or through and holding meat to be roasted over heat; any of various rods, pins, or the like used for particular purposes; a narrow point of land projecting into the water; a long, narrow shoal extending from the shore.—*v.t.*—*spitted, spitting.* To pierce, stab, or transfix, as with a spit; impale on something sharp; to thrust a spit into or through.

spit and pol·ish, *n.* Great attention, possibly to the extreme, given to neatness, smartness, orderliness, and appearance, esp. in military affairs.

spit·ball, spit'bȧl", *n.* A small ball or lump of chewed paper used as a missile; *baseball,* a variety of curve pitched by moistening one side of the ball with saliva or sweat, now illegal.

spit curl, *n.* A ringlet of hair, usu. moistened and flattened against the cheek or forehead.

spite, spīt, *n.* [An abbreviated form of *despite.*] Malicious ill will; a desire to frustrate, annoy, or thwart another; malevolent bitterness; an instance or act of spite or grudge.—*v.t.*—*spited, spiting.* To show malice toward; to thwart.—**in spite of,** despite; in opposition to all efforts of; notwithstanding.

spite·ful, spīt'fu̠l, *a.* Filled with spite; having a malicious disposition.—**spite·ful·ly,** *adv.*—**spite·ful·ness,** *n.*

spit·fire, spit'fī·ėr", *n.* A person, usu. feminine, of fiery disposition; (*cap.*) a single engine, World War II, R.A.F. fighter plane.

spit·tle, spit'l, *n.* The secretion of the salivary glands; spit; *entom.* the secretion of spittle insects in their nymph stage.

spit·tle·bug, spit'l·bug", *n.* Froghopper.

spit·tle in·sect, *n.* Any of various small, leaping homopterous insects of the family *Cercopidae,* whose nymphs exude and surround themselves with a frothy secretion called cuckoo-spit or spittle; a froghopper. Also *spittlebug.*

spit·toon, spi·tōn', *n.* A container for spit. Also *cuspidor.*

spitz, spits, *n.* [G. *spitz,* lit. 'pointed,' from its pointed muzzle and ears.] A small, solidly built dog, descendant of the Pomeranian breed, usu. white and having long thick hair, a tail curved forward, and pointed upright ears.

spiv, spiv, *n. Brit. slang.* A petty swindler; one who relies on his wits for a living, rather than honest work.

splanch·nic, splangk'nik, *a.* [N.L. *splanchniucus,* < Gr. *splanchnicós,* < *splanchnon,* pl. *splánchna,* inward parts, viscera.] *Anat.* Of or pertaining to the viscera or entrails; visceral.

splash, splash, *v.t.* [Altered form of *plash.*] To wet or soil by dashing masses or particles of water, mud, or other liquid or semiliquid substance; spatter; to fall upon in scattered masses or particles, as a liquid does; to cause to appear as if spattered; to mark as if with splashes; to dash, as water, about in scattered masses or particles; to make, as one's way, with splashing.—*v.i.* To dash a liquid or semiliquid substance about; fall, move, or go with a splash or splashes; to dash with force in scattered masses or particles.—*n.* An act of splashing; the sound of splashing; a quantity of some liquid or semiliquid substance splashed upon a thing; a spot caused by something splashed; a patch, as of color or light; *colloq.* a striking show, or an ostentatious display.—**splash·er,** *n.*—**splash·y,** *a.*—**splashier, splashiest.**—**splash·i·ly,** *adv.*—**splash·i·ness,** *n.*

splash·board, splash'bŏrd", splash'bạrd", *n.* A board, guard, or screen to protect from splashing; a guard placed over a wheel of a vehicle to intercept water or dirt; a screen to prevent water or spray from coming on the deck of a boat; a gate to control the flow of water in a sluice or spillway.

splash·down, splash'doun", *n.* The landing at sea of a spacecraft, manned or unmanned.—**splash down,** *v.i.*

splash guard, *n.* Heavy material, usu. rubber, hung from the back of a motorcycle or other motor vehicle to cover the rear wheels and keep water and mud from being thrown onto cars behind. Also *mud guard,* **mud flap.**

splat, splat, *n.* [Prob. related to *split.*] A thin, flat piece of wood, as that forming the central upright part of the back of a chair.

splat·ter, splat'ẽr, *v.t., v.i.* [Appar. a mixture of *splash* and *spatter.*] To splash; spatter; sputter.

splay, splā, *v.t.* [For *display.*] To spread out, expand, or extend; to form with an oblique angle; to make slanting; bevel; to make with a splay or splays; to dislocate, as a bone.—*v.i.* To have an oblique or slanting direction; to flare or spread out.—*n. Arch.* a surface which makes an oblique angle with another, as one where the opening through a wall for a window or door widens from the position of the window or door proper toward the face of the wall. A spread or flare.—*a.* Spread out; wide and flat; turned outward; clumsy or awkward; oblique or awry.

splay·foot, splā'fut", *n. pl.* **splay·feet,** splā'fēt". A broad, flat foot, esp. one turned more or less outward; the condition or deformity of having a splay foot.—*a.*—**splay·foot·ed,** *a.*

spleen, splēn, *n.* [L. *splen,* < Gr. *splēn,* the spleen.] A spongy glandular organ situated in the upper part of the abdomen, forming one of the ductless glands concerned with modification of the blood: in ancient times, believed to be the seat of melancholy, anger, ill temper, or spirit; any ill humor, latent spite, depression, or peevish outburst.—**spleen·ful,** *a.*

spleen·wort, splēn'wụrt", *n.* Any fern of the genus *Asplenium,* many varieties of which are grown for ornamental purposes, all being characterized by linear spore sacs along the veins.

spleen·y, splē'nē, *a.*—**spleenier, spleeniest.** Having an abundance of spleen; spleenful; having reference to a person who tends to be irritable or peevish and a hypochondriac.

splen·dent, splen'dent, *a.* [L. *splendens* (*splendent-*), ppr. of *splendere,* shine, be bright.] Shining or radiant, as the sun; gleaming or lustrous, as metal; brilliant in appearance or color; gorgeous; magnificent; splendid; celebrated; eminent.

splen·did, splen'did, *a.* [L. *splendidus,* < *splendere.*] Gorgeous; magnificent; sumptuous, or luxuriously elegant; grand; superb, as beauty; glorious, as a name,

reputation, or victory; strikingly admirable or fine; as, a *splendid* idea; excellent or very good; as, a *splendid* chance; shining or brilliant.—**splen·did·ly,** *adv.*—**splen·did·ness,** *n.*

splen·dif·er·ous, splen·dif'ẽr·us, *a.* [Cf. O.Fr. *splendifere,* also L.L. *splendorifer,* splendor-bringing.] *Colloq.* Splendid; magnificent; fine.—**splen·dif·er·ous·ly,** *adv.* —**splen·dif·er·ous·ness,** *n.*

splen·dor, *Brit.* **splen·dour,** splen'dẽr, *n.* [L. *splendor.*] Brilliancy; resplendence; magnificence; pomp; glory; grandeur; eminence.—**splen·dor·ous, splen·drous,** *a.*

sple·nec·to·my, spli·nek'to·mē, *n.* pl. **sple·nec·to·mies.** Surgical removal of the spleen.

sple·net·ic, spli·net'ik, *a.* [L.L. *spleneticus,* < L. *splen,* E. *spleen.*] Of or pertaining to the spleen; splenic; ill-humored, irritable, peevish, or spiteful, as a person; *liter.* affected with or marked by melancholy. Also **sple·net·i·cal.**—*n.*—**sple·net·i·cal·ly,** *adv.*

splen·ic, splen'ik, *a.* Pertaining to the spleen; situated in or near the spleen.

sple·ni·tis, spli·nī'tis, *n. Pathol.* inflammation of the spleen.

sple·ni·us, splē'nē·us, *n.* pl. **sple·ni·i,** splē'nē·ī". [N.L., < Gr. *splēnion,* bandage.] *Anat.* a broad, flat muscle of the upper dorsal region and the back and side of the neck, which divides into two sections in ascending the neck, and serves in rotating the head and neck, as well as in drawing the head backward.

sple·no·meg·a·ly, splē"no·meg'a·lē, *n.* Abnormal growth of the spleen resulting in its gross enlargement.

splice, splīs, *v.t.*—**spliced, splicing.** [Same as Dan. *splisse, splidse,* D. *splitsen,* Sw. *splissa,* G. *splissen,* to splice. Closely akin to *split,* the ends of the rope being *split* in splicing.] To unite, as two ropes, by interweaving the strands of the ends; to join, as wires, by twisting and soldering; to overlap and fasten, as rails or pieces of timber; to butt and bind, as film or recording tapes; to insert, as new sound track into film; to graft; to piece; *slang,* to marry.—*n.* The act or result of splicing; as, the *splice* in a rope; *slang,* a marriage or wedding.—**splic·er,** *n.*

spline, splīn, *n.* [Origin obscure.] *Mach.* a flat, rectangular piece of metal fitting into a groove or slot between parts, as a hub and axle; *mechanical drawing,* a long strip of flexible material used in drawing curves; *constr.* a long, narrow, thin strip of wood, metal, or the like, as a slat.—*v.t.*—**splined, splining.** To fit with a spline; to provide a groove in for a spline.

splint, splint, *n.* [M.E. *splynte, splente,* = M.D. and M.L.G. *splinte.*] *Surg.* a thin piece of wood or other stiff material used to hold a fractured or dislocated bone in position when set, or to maintain any part of the body in a fixed position. One of a number of thin strips of wood to be woven together to make a chair seat, basket, or the like; *vet. med.* a bony enlargement of the splint bone of a horse or allied animal—*v.t.* To secure, hold in position, or support by means of a splint or splints, as a fractured bone; to support as with splints.

splint bone, *n.* One of the two small bones extending from the knee to the fetlock of a horse, behind the shank bone.

splin·ter, splin'tẽr, *n.* [M.E. *splynter* = M.D. D. *splinter;* related to E. *splint.*] A rough piece of wood, bone, or the like, usu. long, thin, and sharp, split or broken off from a main body; a splint; a sliver; a shiver.—*v.t.* To split or break into splinters; to break off in splinters; to break or split into parts or factions; to shiver.—*v.i.* To be split or broken into splinters; to break off

in splinters.—*a.* Independent of or separated from a larger or main body or organization; as, a *splinter* group.—**splin·ter·y,** *a.*

split, split, *v.t.*—**split, splitting.** [D. *splitten,* akin to *splijten,* M.L.G. *splīten,* G. *spleissen,* split.] To separate or part from end to end or between layers, often forcibly or by cutting; to separate off by rending or cleaving lengthwise; as, to *split* a piece from a block; to break or tear apart; to divide into distinct parts or portions; to separate, as a part, by such division; to divide, as persons, into different groups, factions, or parties, as by discord; to divide between two or more persons; as, to *split* a bottle of wine with a friend; to separate into parts by interposing something; as, to *split* an infinitive; *stock market,* to distribute, as supplementary shares of stock, to stockholders at no extra cost, thereby increasing the total of company shares outstanding.— *v.i.* To break or part lengthwise; to become separated off by such division, as a piece or part from a whole; to break asunder, as a ship, by striking on a rock or by the violence of a storm; to part, divide, or separate in any way; to break up or separate through disagreement; to divide something, usu. in equal parts, with another or others.—**split hairs,** to make excessively fine distinctions, as in arguing.—**split the dif·fer·ence,** to divide equally the difference between two parties, in order to effect an agreement.—**split·ta·ble,** *a.*— **split·ter,** *n.*

split, split, *n.* The act or an act of splitting; a crack, rent, or fissure caused by splitting; a strip split from an osier, used in basket-making; a breach or rupture in a party, or between persons; a schism; a faction or party, formed by a rupture or schism; one of the thicknesses of leather into which a skin is sometimes split or cut. *Colloq.* a drink containing only half the usual quantity; a bottle, as of champagne or aerated water, half the usual size. A confection made from a sliced banana, ice cream, syrup, whipped cream and nuts; *often pl.* the feat of separating the legs, while sinking to the floor, until they extend at right angles to the body; *bowling,* the position of the pins standing after one bowl, making a spare extremely difficult.—*a.* That has undergone splitting; parted lengthwise; cleft; divided; as, a *split* vote; *stock market,* referring to a stock quotation given in sixteenths, not eighths, as: The stock quotation 20 1/16 is a *split* quotation.

split de·ci·sion, *n.* In boxing, a decision in which the judges and the referee do not agree unanimously.

split in·fin·i·tive, *n. Gram.* an infinitive with a modifier between the *to* and the verb, as *to* readily *understand:* a usage not now considered grammatically incorrect, but one commonly avoided by careful writers.

split-lev·el, split'lev'el, *a. Arch.* having reference to the layout of a house in which the distance between adjacent levels is about half a story.—*n.*

split pea, *n.* A dried garden pea, *Pisum sativum,* in which the two cotyledons, usu. separate, are used generally in making soup.

split rail, *n.* A section of fence rail made by splitting a log lengthwise.

split sec·ond, *n.* A portion of a second; a brief instant.—**split-sec·ond,** *a.* Accurate; as, *split-second* timing.

split shift, *n.* A division of working hours into several time segments which are separated by periods or hours during which the employee is not working.

split tick·et, *n.* An election ballot on which the votes cast are not all for the candidates of a single political party.

---

ch- chain, G. na*ch*t;   **th-** THen, thin;   **w-** wig, hw as sound in whig;   **z-** zh as in azure, zeal.   *Italicized vowel* indicates schwa sound.

splotch, sploch, *n.* [< *spot,* with inserted *l* (as in *spatter, splatter, sputter, splutter*), and term. borrowed from *botch.*] A spot or stain, esp. of large and irregular shape; a daub; a smear; a blot; a splash, as of paint.—*v.t.* To mark with a splotch or splotches.—**splotch·y,** *a.*—*splotchier,* *splotchiest.*

splurge, splurj, *n.* [Prob. a coined word, suggested by *splash, surge,* or the like.] *Colloq.* A showing off; great display or ostentation; an exorbitant expenditure.—*v.i., v.t.*—*splurged, splurging.*

splut·ter, splut'ẽr, *n.* [< *sputter,* with inserted *l.*] A stammering utterance; a confused sound; a bustle; a stir.—*v.i.* To speak hastily and confusedly, as when bewildered or frightened; to sputter, as fireworks, esp. a sparkler; sizzle, as frying fat.—*v.t.* To utter or emit in a hasty and confused manner; stammer.—**splut·ter·er,** *n.*

spod·u·mene, spoj'u·mēn", *n.* [Gr. *spodoumenos,* converted into *spodos* or ashes.] A mineral, LiAl(SiO$_3$)$_2$, a silicate of aluminum and lithium, which occurs in the form of prismatic crystals of various colors, and is used in ceramics and glassmaking and as a gemstone

spoil, spoil, *v.t.*—*spoiled* or *spoilt, spoiling.* [O.Fr. *espoillier* (Fr. *spolier*), < L. *spoliare* (pp. *spoliatus*), strip, plunder < *spolium,* booty, spoil.] To damage or impair irreparably as to excellence, value, or usefulness; as, to *spoil* a cake in the making; to impair in character or disposition by unwise treatment, esp. by excessive indulgence.—*v.i.* To plunder, pillage, or rob; to become spoiled, bad, or unfit for use, as food or other perishable substances.—*n.* [Partly < O.Fr. *espoille,* < *espoillier,* partly < L. *spolium.*] Often *pl.* booty, loot, or plunder taken in war or robbery; usu. *pl.* public offices with their emoluments and advantages viewed as won by a victorious political party; as, the *spoils* of office. Something spoiled, as in the process of manufacturing; waste material, as that cast up in mining, excavating, or quarrying.—**spoil·ing for,** *colloq.* to crave or be extremely eager for.

spoil·age, spoi'lij, *n.* The act of spoiling; that which is spoiled; decay; the loss due to spoilage.

spoil·er, spoi'lẽr, *n.* One who or that which spoils; a plunderer or despoiler; *aeron.* a projecting member, as on the wing of an airplane, used to break down the airflow around the body so as to slow down its movement or decrease its lift.

spoils·man, spoilz'man, *n.* pl. **spoils·men.** One who seeks or receives a share in political spoils; an advocate of the spoils system in politics.

spoil·sport, spoil'spōrt", spoil'spȧrt", *n.* One who, by his critical attitude and unsociable actions, spoils the sport or enjoyment of others.

spoils sys·tem, *n.* The practice of removing political incumbents from office to be replaced by supporters of the incoming administration as a reward for their services.

spoke, spōk, *n.* [O.E. *spāca* = D. *speek* = G. *speiche,* spoke.] One of the bars or rods radiating from the hub of a wheel and supporting the rim; one of a number of handles projecting from a ship's steering wheel; a rung of a ladder.—*v.t.*—*spoked, spoking.* To fit or furnish with or as with spokes.

spo·ken, spō'ken, *a.* Oral, as opposed to *written;* equivalent to *speaking,* used in compounds; as, civil-*spoken.*

spoke·shave, spōk'shāv", *n.* A cutting tool having a blade set between two handles, orig. for shaping spokes, but now in general use for dressing wood, esp. curved surfaces.

spokes·man, spōks'man, *n.* pl. **spokes·men.** One who speaks for another or others.—**spokes·wom·an,** spōks'wum"an, *n.* pl. **spokes·wom·en.** A female spokesman.

spo·li·ate, spō'lē·āt", *v.t., v.i.*—*spoliated, spoliating.* [L. *spolio, spoliatum,* to plunder.] To plunder; to pillage; to despoil.

spo·li·a·tion, spō"lē·ā'shan, *n.* The act of plundering; authorized plundering or capture of neutral ships in wartime; *law,* the mutilation or destruction of a will or bill of exchange.—**spo·li·a·tor,** *n.*

spon·dee, spon'dē, *n.* [L. *spondeus,* Gr. *spondeios,* < Gr. *spondē,* a solemn libation, such libations being accompanied by a slow and solemn melody.] *Pros.* a metric foot made up of two long syllables or of two stressed ones, as in English versification.—**spon·da·ic,** spon·dā'ik, *a.*

spon·dy·li·tis, spon"di·lī'tis, *n. Pathol.* a disorder of the spine or vertebrae which causes inflammation, rigidity, or deformity.

sponge, spunj, *n.* [O.Fr. *esponge* (Fr. *éponge*), < L. *spongia,* Gr. *spongia,* a sponge.] Any aquatic animals belonging to the phylum *Porifera,* having a porous calcareous skeleton and living in sessile colonies; the framework or skeleton of these animals, which is composed of horny elastic fibers, easily compressible, readily imbibing fluids, and as readily giving them out again upon compression, and used for bathing and general cleaning; a sterile dressing used in surgery; a kind of mop for cleaning cannon after a discharge; a sponge bath. *Colloq.* one intentionally dependent upon others; a sycophantic or cringing dependent; a parasite. *Baking,* dough before it is kneaded and formed, when full of globules of carbonic acid generated by the yeast; *metal.* iron in soft or pasty condition, as delivered from the puddling furnace.—*v.t.*—*sponged, sponging.* To cleanse or wipe with a sponge; to efface; to destroy all traces of; *colloq.* to gain by sycophantic or underhanded methods.—*v.i.* To imbibe, as a sponge; to dive for or gather sponges; *colloq.* to live parasitically.—**throw in the sponge,** *colloq.* To yield or admit defeat; to give up, as an effort or undertaking.—**spong·er,** *n.* A person who or a boat which gathers sponges; *colloq.* one who lives at the expense of others.

sponge cake, *n.* A light sweet cake, prepared with many eggs, but containing no shortening.

sponge cloth, *n.* A kind of woven cotton fabric, porous and soft, often woven in a honeycomb pattern and used in making summer clothes.

sponge rub·ber, *n.* A kind of rubber having the texture or structure of that of a sea sponge and used for padding and insulating purposes. Also *foam rubber.*

spon·gin, spun'jin, *n.* A scleroprotein which is the chief element in the pliable fibers of the skeletal structure of a sponge.

spon·gy, spun'jē, *a.*—*spongier, spongiest.* Resembling a sponge; soft and full of cavities; of an open, loose, easily compressible texture; highly absorbent.—**spon·gi·ness,** *n.*

spon·son, spon'son, *n.* [Origin obscure.] A protuberance on either side of the hull of a flying boat near the water line, used to give the plane stability in the water; a similar projection on a ship; an air chamber in the gunwale of a canoe; a gun turret or platform at the side of a naval vessel, warplane, or tank.

spon·sor, spon'sẽr, *n.* [L. *sponsor,* a surety.] One who binds himself to answer for another; one who is responsible for another's default; a firm which finances the broadcasting of a television or radio program and receives in return the advertisement of its service or product; one who is patron for an infant at baptism; a godfather or godmother.—*v.t.* To be or act as sponsor for.—**spon·so·ri·al,** spon·sōr'ē·al, spon·sȧr'ē·al, *a.*—**spon·sor·ship,** *n.*

spon·ta·ne·i·ty, spon"ta·nē'i·tē, spon"ta·nā'i·tē, *n.* pl. **spon·ta·ne·i·ties.** The fact, state, or quality of being spontaneous; activity or behavior that is spontaneous.

spon·ta·ne·ous, spon·tā'nē·us, *a.* [L. *spontaneus,* < *sponte,* of free will.] Arising from one's own tendencies or impulses, without forethought, constraint, or external effort; caused by inborn qualities; self-originating; created by inherent forces; *bot.* growing in a natural state without human cultivation, as weeds.—**spon·ta·ne·ous·ly,** *adv.*—**spon·ta·ne·ous·ness,** *n.*

spon·ta·ne·ous com·bus·tion, *n.* The ignition of a substance or body from the rapid oxidation of its own constituents, without the application of heat from an external source.

spon·ta·ne·ous gen·er·a·tion, *n. Biol.* A generally disproved doctrine that new organisms are generated from decaying matter; abiogenesis.

spon·toon, spon·tōn', *n.* [Fr. *sponton,* It. *spuntone,* spontoon.] A short spear borne by officers of the infantry in the 17th and 18th centuries. Also **half-pike.**

spoof, spöf, *n. Colloq.* A playful hoax; an act of good-natured teasing; deception.—*v.t., v.i. Colloq.* To hoax; deceive; tease.

spook, spök, *n.* [D. and L.G. *spook.*] *n. Colloq.* A ghost or apparition; a specter.—*v.t. Colloq.* To haunt; to startle, frighten, or cause to stampede, esp. as animals.—**spook·ish,** *a.*

spook·y, spö'kē, *a.*—*spookier, spookiest. Colloq.* Pertaining to or resembling spooks; ghostly; haunted; uncanny; uneasy or skittish, as animals, esp. horses.—**spook·i·ly,** *adv.*—**spook·i·ness,** *n.*

spool, spöl, *n.* [M.D. *spoele* (D. *spoel*) = M.L.G. *spōle* = G. *spule,* spool.] A small cylinder of wood or other material, typically expanded with a collar at each end and having a hole lengthwise through the center and on which wire, yarn, tape, or thread, is wound; any cylindrical piece or contrivance on which something is wound; the amount of material upon it.—*v.t.* To wind on a spool.

spoon, spön, *n.* [O.E. *spōn* = M.L.G. *spōn,* chip, shaving, = Icel. *spōnn,* spoon; akin to Icel. *spänn,* D. *spaan,* G. *span,* chip.] A utensil used for eating, measuring, taking up, or stirring, consisting of a small, usu. oval, shallow bowl with a handle; any of various implements, objects, or parts resembling or suggesting this. *Angling,* a bright, spoon-shaped lure used in casting or trolling for fish; also **spoon bait.** *Golf,* a club with a wooden head having a face more lofted than that of a brassie, and with a shorter shaft; also **num·ber three wood.** *Gun.* a curved projection at the top of a torpedo tube for guiding the missile on a horizontal path.—*v.t.* To take up or transfer in a spoon; to hollow out or shape like a spoon. *Games,* to push or shove, as the ball, with a lifting motion, as in golf or croquet; to hit, as the ball, up in the air, as in cricket. *Colloq.* to make love to, esp. in an openly sentimental manner.—*v.i. Colloq.* to make love, esp. in an openly sentimental manner; *games,* to spoon a ball; *angling,* to fish with a spoon.

spoon·bill, spön'bil", *n.* Any of various long-legged wading birds with spoonlike bills, esp. the roseate spoonbill, *Ajaia ajaja;* the paddlefish.—**spoon-billed,** *a.*

spoon·bill cat, *n.* Paddlefish.

spoon bread, *n.* A kind of bread made from corn meal, eggs, and milk, sometimes also with hominy or rice, and usu. served with a spoon.

spoon·drift, spön'drift", *n.* Spindrift.

spoon·er·ism, spö'ne·riz"um, *n.* [From Rev. W. A. *Spooner,* 1844–1930, of New College, Oxford, noted for such slips] A phrase in which the initial or other sounds are accidentally transposed, as in *dats and cogs* for *cats and dogs.*—**spoon·er·is·tic,** *a.*

spoon-fed, spön'fed", *a.* Fed with a spoon. *Fig.* treated with excessive care and concern; coddled; pampered; not allowed to develop self-reliance or independence.—**spoon-feed,** spön'fēd', spön'fēd", *v.t.*—**spoon-fed, spoon-feeding.** To feed as with a spoon; *fig.* to supply with facts or information, with the effect of inhibiting independent inquiry.

spoon·ful, spön'fül, *n. pl.* **spoon·fuls.** As much as a spoon can contain.

spoon·y, spoon·ey, spö'nē, *a.*—*spoonier, spooniest. Colloq.* foolishly or sentimentally amorous. *Brit.* foolish; silly.—*n. pl.* **spoon·ies, spoon·eys.** *Colloq.* one who is foolishly or sentimentally amorous; *Brit.* a simple or foolish person.

spoor, spür, spör, spär, *n.* [Borrowed < D. *spoor,* a track; the same word as O.E. and Icel. *spor,* G. *spur,* a track.] A track or trail of an animal, esp. of a wild animal when pursued by hunters as game.—*v.t., v.i.* To follow or track by a spoor.

spo·rad·ic, spö·rad'ik, spa·rad'ik, spo·-rad'ik, *a.* [Gr. *sporadikos,* < *sporas,* dispersed, < *speirō,* to sow, to scatter.] Occurring at irregular intervals; occasional; scattered; occurring singly or in isolated instances, as a disease. Also **spo·rad·i·cal.**—**spo·rad·i·cal·ly,** *adv.*

spo·ran·gi·um, spö·ran'jē·um, spa·ran'-jē·um, *n. pl.* **spo·ran·gi·a,** spö·ran'jē·a, spa·ran'jē·a. [Gr. *sporos,* and *angeion,* a vessel.] *Bot.* a case or covering in which the asexual spores of algae, mosses, and ferns are produced. Also *spore case.*—**spo·ran·gi·al,** *a.*

spore, spör, spar, *n.* [Gr. *sporos,* a seed, < *speiro,* to sow.] *Bot.* an asexual reproductive cell of algae, fungi, mosses, and ferns, as distinguished from a true seed; *bact.* a thick-walled bacterium in a dormant or resting stage.—*v.i.*—*spored, sporing.* To develop spores, as in plants.—**spo·ral, spo·roid,** *a.*

spore case, *n.* Sporangium.

spore fruit, *n. Bot.* a special structure where spores can be formed and grown, as an ascoscarp.

spo·ri·ci·dal, spör"i·sī'dal, spar"i·sī'dal, *a.* Having reference to the killing of spores.—**spo·ri·cide,** spör'i·sīd", spar'i·sīd", *n.* A substance which kills spores.

spo·rif·er·ous, spö·rif'er·us, spa·rif'er·us, *a.* Bearing spores.

spo·ro·carp, spör'o·kärp", spar'o·kärp", *n.* [Gr. *sporos,* and *karpos,* a fruit.] *Bot.* a spore-producing body in red algae and certain fungi.

spo·ro·cyst, spör'o·sist", spar'o·sist", *n. Zool.* an asexual structure in certain trematodes; a cystlike case produced by some sporozoans. *Bot.* a resting cell in certain algae capable of giving rise to several asexual spores.

spo·ro·gen·e·sis, spör"o·jen'i·sis, spar"-o·jen'i·sis, *n. Biol.* The production of spores; sporogony; reproduction by means of spores.—**spo·ro·gen·ic, spo·rog·e·nous,** spö·roj'e·nus, spa·roj'e·nus, *a. Biol.* Producing spores; reproducing by means of spores.

spo·rog·o·ny, spö·rog'o·nē, spa·rog'o·nē, *n. Biol.* reproduction by means of spores, as in certain sporozoans, where sporozoites are formed by the multiple division of an encysted mature zygote.

spo·ro·phore, spör'o·för", spar'o·far", *n. Bot.* A spore-bearing process or stalk; that part of the thallus of certain fungi which develops spores.—**spo·ro·phor·ic, spo·-roph·o·rous,** spör"o·far'ik, spör"o·for'ik, spar"o·far'ik, spar"o·for'ik, spö·rof'er·us, spa·rof'er·us, *a.*

spo·ro·phyll, spo·ro·phyl, spör'o·fil, spar'o·fil, *n. Bot.* a leaf, often modified, which bears sporangia containing spores, as a frond of a fern.—**spo·ro·phyl·la·ry,** spör"o·fil'a·rē, spar"o·fil'a·rē, *a.*

spo·ro·phyte, spör'o·fīt", spar'o·fīt", *n.* [Gr. *sporos,* and *phyton,* a plant.] *Bot.* the asexual, spore-producing generation, as opposed to the alternate *gametophyte* generation, in the life history of plants which reproduce through the alternation of these two generations.—**spo·ro·phyt·ic,** spör"o·fit'ik, spar"o·fit'ik, *a.*

spo·ro·zo·an, spör"o·zō'an, spar"o·zō'an, *a.* Belonging or pertaining to the *Sporozoa,* a class of parasitic protozoans that form spores as part of their reproductive cycle.—*n.*—**spo·ro·zo·al,** *a.*

spo·ro·zo·ite, spör"o·zō'it, spar"o·zō'īt, *n. Zool.* one of the minute, active bodies into which the spore of certain sporozoans divides, each finally developing into an adult individual.

spor·ran, spor'an, *n.* [Gael. *sporan.*] A large pouch for men, usu. of fur, which hangs from a belt in front of the kilt and is worn by Scottish Highlanders.

sport, spört, spart, *n.* [For *disport.*] Diversion, amusement, or recreation; a pleasant pastime; a pastime pursued in the open air or having an athletic character, as hunting, fishing, racing, baseball, bowling, or wrestling; playful trifling, jesting, or mirth; mere jest or pleasantry; as, to do or say a thing in *sport;* derisive jesting or ridicule; something sported with or tossed about like a plaything; an object of jesting, mirth, or derision; a laughingstock; one who is interested in sports; a sportsman. *Colloq.* a person of sportsmanlike or admirable qualities, or considered with reference to such qualities; as, a good *sport;* a sporting man; one who is interested in pursuits involving betting or gambling; a flashy or vulgarly showy person; one who affects fine clothes, smart manners, or expensive pastimes. *Biol.* an animal or a plant, or a part of a plant, that shows an unusual or singular deviation from the normal or parent type.—*a.* Of or pertaining to sport or sports, esp. of the outdoor or athletic kind; pertaining to clothes suitable for use in outdoor sports, or for outdoor or informal use generally; as, a *sport* shirt. Also **sports.**—*v.t.* To pass, as time, in amusement or sport; as, to *sport* the hours away; spend or squander lightly or recklessly, often followed by *away; colloq.* to display freely in public; as, to *sport* a roll of money.—*v.i.* To amuse oneself with some pleasant pastime or recreation; play, frolic, or gambol, as a child or an animal; engage in some outdoor or athletic pastime or sport; to deal lightly, or too lightly, or to trifle, as with something serious; jest, as in fun or ridicule. *Biol.* to develop as a sport, as an animal or a plant; produce sports.—**sport·er,** spör'ter, spar'ter, *n.*—**sport·ful,** *a.*—**sport·ful·ly,** *adv.*—**sport·ful·ness,** *n.*

sport fish, *n.* Any fish sought by fishermen, not primarily for food or profit but for adventure and the pleasure of the skill they apply to catching it. Also **game fish.**

sport·ing, spör'ting, spar'ting, *a.* Engaging in, given to, or interested in open-air or athletic sports; pertaining to, concerned with, or suitable for such sports; as, *sporting* goods; sportsmanlike, as qualities or conduct; interested in or connected with sports or pursuits involving betting or gambling; as, *sporting* men; *colloq.* involving or inducing the taking of risk; as, a *sporting* proposition;—**sport·ing·ly,** *adv.*

spor·tive, spör'tiv, spar'tiv, *a.* Inclined toward or characterized by sport; playful or frolicsome; jesting or merry; pertaining to or of the nature of sport or sports; done in sport, rather than in earnest; *biol.* tending to vary from the normal or parent type—**spor·tive·ly,** *adv.*—**spor·tive·ness,** *n.*

sports car, *n.* A small, high-powered, low-lined, two-seated automobile. Also **sport car.**

sports·cast, spörts'kast", spörts'käst", sparts'kast", sparts'käst", *n.* A program on radio or television in which a sporting event is broadcast or sports news is reported.—**sports·cast·er,** *n.*

sport shirt, *n.* A soft, short- or long-sleeved shirt for informal wear, usu. squared-off around the bottom so that it may be worn outside or inside slacks. Also **sports shirt.**

sports·man, spörts'man, sparts'man, *n. pl.* **sports·men.** A man who engages in sports, esp. in some open-air sport as hunting, fishing, racing, or yachting; one who exhibits qualities, esp. esteemed in those who engage in sports, such as fairness, self-control, and courtesy.—**sports·wom·an,** spörts'wum"an, sparts'wum"an, *n. pl.* **sports·wom·en.** Feminine of sportsman.—**sports·man·like, sports·man·ly,** *a.*

sports·man·ship, spörts'man·ship", sparts'man·ship", *n.* The character, practice, or skill of a sportsman; sportsmanlike conduct, as fairness, self-control, and uncomplaining acceptance of defeat.

sports·wear, spörts'wâr", sparts'wâr", *n.* Clothes worn for outdoor or informal activities.

sports·writ·er, spörts'rī"ter, sparts'rī"ter, *n.* One who writes news stories about sporting events or about athletes or other people involved in sports.

sport·y, spör'tē, spar'tē, *a.*—*sportier, sportiest. Colloq.* Flashy or vulgarly showy; gay or fast; smart in dress, appearance, manners, or the like; stylish; like or befitting a sport or sportsman; sportsmanlike or sporting.—**sport·i·ly,** *adv.*—**sport·i·ness,** *n.*

spor·u·late, spar'ū·lāt", spor'ū·lāt", *v.i.*—*sporulated, sporulating. Biol.* to convert into or form sporules or spores, esp. by multiple division of a cell.

spor·u·la·tion, spar"ū·lā'shan, spor"ū·lā'-shan, *n. Biol.* the production of new spores by the dividing of older spore mother cells after encystment.—**spor·u·la·tive,** *a.*

spor·ule, spar'ūl, spor'ūl, *n.* [N.L. *sporula,* dim. of *spora.*] *Biol.* A small spore; a spore.

spot, spot, *n.* [M.E. *spot* = M.D. *spotte,* spot: cf. Icel. *spotti,* small piece, bit.] A mark made by foreign matter, as mud, blood, paint, or ink; a stain, blot, splotch, blotch, or fleck; a blemish or flaw, as a small scar, eruption, or birthmark; a stigma, as on character or reputation; a part of a surface, as a patch of color or light; a place or locality, as where a house stood or a ship sank; a place of specific interest; as, a *spot* for sightseeing, skiing, or fishing, a night *spot;* a position in sequence or in order, as in a narrative or on a program; a pip, as on dice, dominoes, or playing cards; *slang,* reference to a card or currency note by its face value; as, a five *spot.* A domestic pigeon with a spot on the forehead; a food fish of the genus *Leiostomus* with a spot above each pectoral fin; *Brit. colloq.* a small amount; as, a *spot* of lunch.—*v.t.*—*spotted, spotting.* To mark, as with foreign matter such as mud, blood, paint, or ink; to stain, blot, splotch, blotch, speck, fleck, dot, or stud; to note, as an individual, for future consideration; to position; as, to *spot* a billiard ball on the table; to handicap, as among contestants by giving points to the weaker; *milit.* to observe; as, to *spot* and adjust the deviations of artillery, rocket, mortar, or machine gun fire in order to hit the target.—*v.i.* To cause a stain; to become marked; as, silk *spotted* by water.—*a.* Made, paid, or delivered at once; as, a *spot* sale; made at random; as, a *spot* check; broadcast locally; as, a *spot* news announcement, a *spot* commercial message.—**in spots,** at times or by snatches; as, sleeping *in spots.*—**in a spot,** *colloq.* in a difficult situation.—**on the spot,** *colloq.* At the very place; at once; where or when needed.—**high spot,** *colloq.* something memorable.—**hit the spot,** *slang,* to satisfy a craving or need.—**spot·ta·ble,** *a.*

spot check, *n.* The random investigation or inspection of typical items to determine and ensure the general quality of some product.—*v.i., v.t.*

spot·less, spot´lis, *a.* Free from spots, stains, or impurities; pure; immaculate.—**spot··less·ly,** *adv.*—**spot·less·ness,** *n.*

spot·light, spot´līt″, *n.* A strong light thrown upon a particular spot in order to render some object, person, or group esp. conspicuous, as on a stage; a supplementary light mounted on a vehicle and capable of casting a strong beam to illuminate objects not directly in the path of the headlights; *fig.* intense or unusual prominence resulting in wide public interest.—*v.t.* To cast a beam of light upon; *fig.* to focus attention on.

spot pass, *n. Football, basketball,* the deliberate throwing of a ball to a specific place on the field or court instead of to an individual player, though intending that the receiver will be there when the ball arrives.

spot·ted, spot´id, *a.* Marked with or characterized by a spot or spots; stained with a spot or spots; sullied; blemished.

spot·ted ad·der, *n.* Milk snake.

spot·ted fe·ver, *n.* Any of various fevers characterized by spots on the skin. Tick fever carried by the wood tick; also *Rocky Mountain spotted fever.*

spot·ter, spot´ẽr, *n.* One who volunteers to watch for enemy aircraft, as in time of war; *colloq.* an employee designated by his superiors to watch for and report any evidence of dishonesty among his fellow employees; *milit.* one who, by watching the fall of shells, helps to ascertain the range for which the guns should be set. *Aeron.* a person within an aircraft who spots or looks for other aircraft, troops, or artillery hits; the aircraft in which this is done. An employee in a dry cleaning plant whose specific job is the removal of spots; *sports,* one who assists a sportscaster during a broadcast of a game by identifying the players.

spot test, *n.* A random inquiry, poll, or sampling undertaken to obtain quick but tentative statistical information.

spot·ty, spot´ē, *a.*—**spottier, spottiest.** Full of or having spots; spotted; characterized by or occurring in spots; lacking in uniformity or harmony of parts; irregular or uneven in quality or character; as, a *spotty* market for wheat.—**spot·ti·ly,** *adv.*—**spot·ti·ness,** *n.*

spous·al, spou´zal, *n.* [O.Fr. *espousaille.*] Often *pl.* The ceremony of marriage; nuptials.—*a.* Of or pertaining to marriage; nuptial; matrimonial.

spouse, spous, spouz, *n.* [O.Fr. *espouse,* < L. *sponsus,* betrothed, pp. of *spondeo,* to promise solemnly, to engage oneself.] A married person; husband or wife.—*v.t.*—*spoused, spousing.*

spout, spout, *n.* [< stem of *spit, spew,* perh. directly < D. *spuit,* a spout, *spuiten,* to spout.] A nozzle or projecting mouth of a vessel, as a pitcher, used in directing the stream of liquid poured out; a pipe or conduit. A pipe for conducting water, as rain from a roof; also **down·spout.** *Brit.* a

pawnshop.—*v.t.* To pour out in a jet and with some force; to throw out through a spout or pipe; *colloq.* to utter in the pompous manner of an actor or orator; *Brit.* to pawn.—*v.i.* To issue in a strong jet; to run, as from a spout; to spurt; *colloq.* to make a speech, esp. in a pompous manner. —**spout·er,** *n.*

sprag, sprag, *n.* [Origin obscure.] A bar or metal rod attached to the rear end or axle of a vehicle which can be let down to dig into or catch in the ground should the vehicle start to roll backward or downhill; any piece of wood or the like used to check the revolution of a wheel; *min.* a prop used to shore up a wall, roof, or other structure in a mine.

sprain, sprān, *v.t.* [O.Fr. *espreindre* (Fr. *épreindre*), press out, wring, < L. *exprimere.*] To overstrain or wrench, as the ankle, wrist, or other part of the body at a joint, so as to injure without producing dislocation.—*n.* An act of spraining; the condition of being sprained.

sprat, sprat, *n.* [Formerly also *sprot,* < D. and L.G. *sprot,* G. *sprotte,* sprat; allied to *sprout.*] A small fish, *Clupea sprattus,* of the herring family, found in great abundance in European waters and excellent as food; a young herring, anchovy, or the like; *fig.* one who or that which is very young or inconsequential.

sprawl, sprȧl, *v.i.* [A contr. word allied to Sc. *sprattle, sprachle,* to scramble, Dan. *spraelle,* to sprawl; Sw. *sprattla,* to palpitate.] To spread and stretch the body carelessly in an ungraceful position; to lie or sit with the limbs stretched out or straggling; to spread irregularly or ungracefully, as flowers, vines, or handwriting.—*v.t.* To cause to extend, straggle, or spread out.—*n.* An awkward, sprawling position.

spray, sprā, *n.* [Origin uncertain: cf. M.D. *sprayen,* to sprinkle.] Water or other liquid broken up into small particles and blown or falling through the air; a jet of fine particles of liquid discharged from an atomizer or other appliance, as for medicinal treatment, disinfecting, killing insects, or the like; a liquid to be discharged in such a jet, or an appliance for discharging it; a quantity of particles of matter, or of small objects, flying or discharged through the air; as, a *spray* of sand.—*v.t.* To scatter in the form of spray or fine particles; to apply as a spray; as, to *spray* an insecticide on plants; to sprinkle or treat with a spray; as, to *spray* the throat; to direct a spray of particles, missiles, or the like, upon; as, to *spray* the enemy's lines with artillery fire.— *v.i.* To scatter spray; to discharge a spray; to take the form of spray; to issue forth as spray.—**spray·er,** *n.*

spray, sprā, *n.* [M.E. *spray, sprai*; origin uncertain.] A small branch, twig, or shoot of some plant with its leaves, flowers, or berries, either growing or detached; as, a *spray* of holly or roses; an arrangement of foliage or flowers in a decorative fashion; an artificial imitation of such a branch or piece, as in millinery or jewelry, or a decorative figure representing one, as on a fabric.

spray gun, *n.* A mechanical device using air pressure to squirt out a liquid, as a spray of pesticide or paint, and looking like a gun.

spread, spred, *v.t.*—*spread, spreading.* [O.E. *sprǣden* = D. *spreiden* = G. *spreiten,* spread.] To draw or stretch out to the full width or extent, as a cloth, a rolled or folded map, or wings; to extend over a greater or a relatively greater area, space, or period, often followed by *out*; as, to *spread out* a group of papers; to *spread* payments over a term of years; to display or set

forth in full, as on a record; to dispose or distribute in a sheet or layer; as, to *spread* hay to dry; to apply in a thin layer or coating on something; as, to *spread* plaster on walls; to overlay or cover with something; to set or prepare, as a dining table; to extend or distribute over a region or place; to send out in various directions, as light or sound; to scatter abroad or disseminate, as knowledge, terror, or disease; to force apart under pressure, as rails; to flatten out; as, to *spread* the end of a rivet by hammering.—*v.i.* To become stretched out or extended, as a flag in the wind; to extend over a greater or a considerable area or period; to be or lie outspread or fully extended or displayed, as a landscape or scene; to be able to be spread or applied in a thin layer, as a soft substance; to become extended or distributed over a region, as population, animals, or plants; to become shed abroad, diffused, or disseminated, as light, influences, rumors, ideas, or infections; to be forced apart or separate, as rails.—*n.* The act of spreading, or the state of being spread; expansion; extension, or diffusion; the extent of spreading; as, to measure the *spread* of the branches of a tree. *Finance,* the difference between the bid and asked price of a stock; the difference between the price of the same stock or security in two different markets; an option or put and call contract. Capacity for spreading; as, the *spread* of an elastic material; a stretch, expanse, or extent of something; a covering for a bed, table, or the like, esp. a bedspread; *colloq.* a repast set out, esp. a choice repast or feast. Any food preparation used for spreading on bread or crackers, as jam or peanut butter; *journ.* pictures or a major story across several columns or facing pages; as, a center *spread*; *colloq.* a ranch or farm, esp. in the west.—**spread one·self thin,** *fig.* to dissipate one's energies and interests at the expense of thoroughness in any one project or even of one's health.

spread ea·gle, *n.* A representation of an eagle with outspread wings, used as an emblem of the U.S.; a figure performed in skating.

spread-ea·gle, spred´ē″gl, *a.* Having or suggesting the form of a spread eagle; having the arms and legs stretched away from the body; *colloq.* boastful or bombastic, esp. in the display of patriotism or vanity.—*v.t.*—*spread-eagled, spread-eagling.* To stretch out in the manner of a spread eagle, as a person or thing.—*v.i.* To affect the position of a spread eagle; to perform a spread eagle, as in skating.

spread·er, spred´ẽr, *n.* One who or that which spreads; a blunt-edged knife for applying food preparations to crackers or bread; a mechanical implement which scatters or spreads seeds or fertilizer; a device used to space objects, or to hold them apart.

spree, sprē, *n.* [< Ir. *spre,* animation, spirit, vigor; cf. *spry.*] A merry frolic; a drinking frolic or carousal; excessive indulgence in a particular activity; as, a shopping *spree.*

sprig, sprig, *n.* [M.E. *sprigge*: cf. M.L.G. *sprik,* dry twig.] A shoot, twig, or small branch; a small spray of some plant with its leaves or flowers; an ornament or a decorative figure having the form of such a spray; *fig.* a person as a scion or offshoot of a family or class; as, a *sprig* of the nobility. A youth or young fellow; a brad or headless nail with a projection on one side at the top; a brad or small wedge-shaped piece of metal, for holding glass in a sash.—*v.t.*—*sprigged, sprigging.* To decorate, as fabrics or pottery, with a design of sprigs or small floral sprays; to fasten with sprigs or brads; to remove one or more sprigs from, as any plant or bush.

---

a- fat, fāte, fär, fâre, fạll;   **e-** met, mē, mēre, hẽr;   **i-** pin, pīne;   **o-** not, nōte, mŏve;   **u-** tub, cūbe, bụll;   **oi-** oil;   **ou-** pound.

spright·ful, sprīt′ful, *a.* Full of spirit or life; spirited; sprightly.—**spright·ful·ly,** *adv.*—**spright·ful·ness,** *n.*

spright·ly, sprīt′lē, *a.*—*sprightlier, sprightliest.* Animated, vivacious, or cheerfully gay; spirited.—*adv.* Lively; briskly; gaily.—**spright·li·ness,** *n.*

spring, spring, *v.i.* past *sprang* or *sprung,* pp. *sprung,* ppr. *springing.* [O.E. *springan* (pret. *sprang,* pp. *sprungen*) = D. and G. *springen* = Icel. and Sw. *springa* = Dan. *springe,* spring.] To rise or move suddenly and lightly; as, to *spring* into the air; leap, jump, or bound; go or come suddenly as if with a leap; to fly back or away in escaping from a forced position, as by resilient or elastic force or from the action of a spring; start or work out of place, as parts of a mechanism or structure; split or crack, as a baseball bat; become bent or warped, as boards; explode, as a mine; to issue suddenly, as water, blood, sparks, or fire, often with *forth, out,* or *up;* spout, gush, or burst forth; come into being, rise or arise, often with *up;* as, towns, sects, or industries *spring up;* to arise by growth, as from a seed or germ, bulb, or root; to grow, as plants; proceed or originate, as from a source or cause; have one's birth or be descended, as from a family, person, or stock; to rise or extend upward, as a spire; *arch.* to take an upward course or curve from a point of support, as an arch.—*v.t.* To cause to spring; to cause to fly back, move, or act by elastic force or a spring; as, to *spring* a trap or a lock; to cause to start out of place or work loose; split or crack; to bend by force, or to force in by bending, as a slat or bar; to bring out, disclose, produce, or make suddenly; as, to *spring* a surprise or a piece of news on a person; to spring or leap over.—*n.* [O.E. *spring, spryng.*] The act of springing; a leap, jump, or bound; a flying back from a forced position; an elastic or springy movement; elasticity or springiness; an elastic contrivance or body, as a strip or wire of steel coiled spirally, which, when compressed, bent, or otherwise forced from its normal shape, has the power of recovering this by virtue of its elasticity; a springing or starting from place; a split or crack, as in a mast; a bend or warp, as in a board; an issue of water from the earth, flowing away as a small stream or standing as a pool or small lake; the place of such an issue; as, hot *springs;* a source of something; the act or time of springing; the first season of the year, in N. America taken as comprising March, April, and May, following winter and preceding summer; the time beginning after the vernal equinox and lasting until the summer solstice; *arch.* the rise of an arch, or the point or line at which an arch springs from its support.—*a.* Of, pertaining to, characteristic of, or suitable for the season of spring.

spring beau·ty, *n. pl.* **spring beau·ties.** Any N. American spring flower of the genus *Claytonia,* in the purslane family, esp. *C. virginica,* a low, succulent herb with a raceme of white or pink flowers.

spring·board, spring′bōrd″, spring′bȧrd″, *n.* A flexible board used by gymnasts and acrobats in vaulting, tumbling, or leaping; a similar board, projected over water, used for diving; *fig.* a point of departure toward a new beginning or change.

spring·bok, spring′bok″, *n. pl.* **spring·bok, spring·boks.** [S.Afr. D., 'spring-buck.'] A S. African gazelle, *Antidorcas marsupialis,* noted for springing high into the air in play or when alarmed. Also *springer,* **spring·buck,** spring′buk″.

spring-clean·ing, spring′klē′ning, *n.* A thorough cleaning of a place, traditionally the complete, painstaking housecleaning done each spring.

springe, sprinj, *n.* [< *spring;* cf. *swinge* < *swing.*] A kind of small game trap having a noose attached to a bent branch or spring.—*v.t.*—*springed, springing.* To entrap in a springe.—*v.i.* To construct or set a springe.

spring·er, spring′ēr, *n.* One who or that which springs; *arch.* the impost of an arch, or the bottom stone of an arch resting upon the impost; *mus.* an extra note, conveyed in smaller type, that takes time away from the preceding note. Any of several animals, as the springer spaniel, springbok, or grampus.

spring·er span·iel, *n.* A hunting dog used for flushing or retrieving game birds; either of the English or Welsh breeds of large spaniels.

spring fe·ver, *n.* The lazy, restless, or listless feeling usu. accompanying the arrival of spring.

Spring·field ri·fle, spring′fēld″ rī′fl, *n.* [Named after the U.S. Armory at *Springfield,* Mass.] Any of several rifles used by the U.S. Army from 1867 until World War II, esp. a .30 caliber, bolt-controlled, magazine-loading rifle.

spring·halt, spring′hȧlt″, *n.* Stringhalt.

spring·head, spring′hed″, *n.* A fountain-head or spring; a source.

spring·house, spring′hous″, *n.* A small structure built over a brook or spring, used for the cool storing of dairy products and meat.

spring·ing line, spring′ing lin″, *n. Arch., constr.* the level at which an arch rises from its supports.

spring·let, spring′lit, *n.* A little spring, as of water; streamlet.

spring peep·er, *n.* A little brown tree frog, *Hyla crucifer,* which has an *X* mark on its back and a high, shrill call, found in the springtime in eastern N. America.

spring·tail, spring′tāl″, *n.* Any of numerous minute, wingless insects of the order *Collembola,* having a forked, taillike appendage which is ordinarily folded under the abdomen, but when suddenly extended enables the insect to spring into the air.

spring tide, *n.* The tide which occurs at or soon after the new and full moon, and which rises higher than normal tides; any large rush or flood, as of feeling; springtime.

spring·time, spring′tīm″, *n.* The spring; the vernal season; *fig.* the earliest stage; as, the *springtime* of life. See *spring tide.*

spring wag·on, *n.* A lightweight wagon having springs.

spring·wood, spring′wu̇d″, *n.* That section of the annual growth of wood on a tree which is produced early in the spring and is more porous and softer than the rest of the wood. Compare *summerwood.*

spring·y, spring′ē, *a.*—*springier, springiest.* Having springlike action or elasticity; light and lively; as, a *springy* step; containing many springs of water; spongy, as turf underfoot.—**spring·i·ly,** *adv.*—**spring·i·ness,** *n.*

sprin·kle, spring′kl, *v.t.*—*sprinkled, sprinkling.* [M.E. *sprenklen* = D. *sprenkelen* = G. *sprenkeln,* sprinkle.] To scatter, as a liquid or powder, in drops or particles; to let fall in minute quantities here and there; to strew thinly or lightly; to disperse or distribute here and there; to overspread, as with drops or particles of water or powder; to diversify or intersperse with objects scattered here and there.—*v.i.* To be sprinkled; to issue in drops or particles; to rain slightly.—*n.* The act or an act of sprinkling; that which is sprinkled; a light rain; a small quantity or number; usu. *pl.* bits of candy or other confection used as a topping.—**sprink·ler,** *n.*

sprink·ler sys·tem, *n.* An overhead arrangement of pipes and sprinklers which activate automatically at a specified temperature showering water or extinguishing chemicals in a room, area, or building on fire; an underground pipeline connected to sprinklers elevated slightly above ground, used to water lawns.

sprin·kling, spring′kling, *n.* A small quantity falling in drops or particles; a small number or quantity scattered as if sprinkled; the act of scattering in small drops or particles.

sprint, sprint, *v.i.* [Akin to *spurt.*] To race, move, or run at high speed, esp. at short intervals or over a short distance.—*n.* A short run or race at high speed; a spurt of speed; a short period of accelerated activity.—**sprint·er,** *n.*

sprit, sprit, *n.* [O.E. *spreōt,* a sprout, a shoot; D. *spriet,* a sprit, *boeysprit,* the bowsprit.] *Naut.* A spar extending diagonally outward and upward from a mast to the corner of a fore-and-aft sail which it serves to extend; a bowsprit.

sprite, sprīt, *n.* A kind of fairy, elf, or goblin.

sprit·sail, sprit′sāl″, *Naut.* sprit′sal, *n. Naut.* a sail extended by a sprit.

sprock·et, sprok′it, *n.* [Origin obscure.] *Mach.* A sprocket wheel; one of a set of projections on the rim of a wheel, arranged so as to engage the links of a chain.

sprock·et wheel, *n.* A wheel with cogs or sprockets to engage with the links of a power chain. Also *sprocket.*

sprout, sprout, *v.i.* [Same as L.G. *spruten,* D. *spruiten,* to sprout; akin to O.E. *sprūtan,* to sprout, whence *spreōt,* a sprout.] To begin growth; to germinate; to shoot forth, as a plant from a seed; to bud; to grow rapidly, as a beard.—*v.t.* To remove shoots, as from a potato.—*n.* [D. *spruit,* a sprout.] The shoot or bud of a plant; a fresh outgrowth from a plant or tree; anything similar to or like a sprout.

spruce, sprös, *n.* [M.E. *Spruce,* for *Pruce,* Prussia, used attributively to designate boards, coffers, leather, etc., from that country.] Any member of the genus *Picea,* of the pine family, consisting of coniferous evergreen trees, as the Norway spruce, *P. abies,* and the white spruce, *P. canadensis;* any of various allied trees; the wood of any such tree.

spruce, sprös, *a.*—*sprucer, sprucest.* [Lit. 'after the *Prussian* style,' < *Spruce, Pruce,* formerly used for *Prussia, Prussian.*] Neat or smart in dress; trim; smug; fastidious; dandified.—*v.t.*—*spruced, sprucing.* To trim or dress in a spruce manner.—*v.i.*—**spruce·ly,** *adv.*—**spruce·ness,** *n.*

spruce beer, *n.* A fermented liquor made from sugar or molasses, and flavored with spruce twigs and leaves.

sprue, sprö, *n.* [D. *spruw.*] *Pathol.* A tropical disease characterized by an inflamed condition of the mucous membranes of the digestive tract; thrush, a disease affecting the mouth and throat.

sprue, sprö, *n.* [Origin obscure.] *Foundry.* An opening or passage through which molten metal is poured or run into a mold; the waste piece of metal cast in this opening.

sprung rhythm, *n. Pros.* a rhythm having feet which are equal in time length but are different in the number of syllables in each foot, the first syllable being accented.

spry, sprī, *a.*—*spryer, spryest, sprier, spriest.* [Akin to *spree;* or to old *sprack,* N. *spræk,* Sw. *spräk,* lively.] *Colloq.* Nimble; active; vigorous; lively.—**spry·ly,** *adv.*—**spry·ness,** *n.*

spud, spud, *n.* [A form of *spade;* or akin to Dan. *spyd,* Icel. *spjot,* a spear.] A straight, narrow spade for digging up weeds or cutting roots; a heavy, long-handled tool with a chisel edge used to remove the bark of trees; *colloq.* a potato.—*v.t.*—*spudded,* *spudding.* To take out, as weeds or roots, with a spud.

spue, spū, *v.i.*, *v.t.*—*spued, spuing.* Spew.—*n.*

spume, spūm, *n.* [L. *spuma*, foam, < *spuo*, to spit out.] Froth; foam; scum; frothy matter on turbulent water or on liquors.—*v.i.*—*spumed, spuming.* To froth; to foam.—*v.t.* To spew forth, eject, or discharge.—**spum·ous, spum·y,** *a.* [L. *spumosus.*] Covered with or resembling spume.

spu·mo·ne, spu·mo·ni, spa·mō′nē, spa·-mō′nä, *It.* spö·mȧ′ne, *n.* [It. < *spuma*, froth, foam, < L. *spuma.*] A dessert of Italian origin, consisting of layers of different flavors of ice cream or water ice enclosing an inner mass of whipped cream containing bits of candied fruit or chopped nut kernels: often made in the form of a truncated cone, which is cut vertically in wedge-shaped pieces for serving.

spun glass, *n.* Fiber glass; blown glass consisting of fine threads of glass, often in a filigree pattern.

spunk, spungk, *n.* [Ir. *sponc*, Gael. *spong*, tinder, touchwood, sponge; < L. *spongia*, a sponge.] Touchwood; tinder; tinder made from a species of fungus. *Colloq.* a quick, ardent temper; mettle or pluck.—*v.i.* Kindle.

spunk·y, spung′kē, *a.*—*spunkier, spunkiest. Colloq.* Full of pluck or spirit; plucky; courageous; spirited.—**spunk·i·ly,** *adv.*—**spunk·i·ness,** *n.*

spun ray·on, *n.* Yarn made by spinning rayon fibers into a connected strand.

spun sug·ar, *n.* Melted sugar usu. colored and drawn into long fine threads for decorating cakes, candies, or desserts. See *cotton candy.*

spun yarn, *n. Naut.* cord formed of rope yarns loosely twisted together, used for serving ropes and bending sails on ships. Yarn made by fibers spun together into a strand.

spur, spur, *n.* [O.E. *spura, spora*, a spur; Icel. *spori*, Dan. *spore*, O.G. *spor*, Mod.G. *sporn*; from a root meaning to kick, seen also in *spurn, spurious.*] An instrument having a rowel or little wheel with sharp points or projections, worn on a horseman's heel for pricking the horse to hasten its pace; *fig.* an incitement or stimulus. The hard pointed projection on certain birds' or insects' legs which serves as an instrument of offense and defense; a gaff used in cockfighting; *geog.* a mountain or ridge that branches from another greater mountain mass and extends for some distance. Something that projects; a snag; a short branch or root of a tree that projects. *Arch.* a short wooden brace used to strengthen posts; an offset, as a buttress, from any wall. *Bot.* any projecting appendage of a flower resembling a spur. A small sidetrack of a railroad.—*v.t.* —*spurred, spurring.* To prick with or as with spurs. *Fig.* to urge or encourage to action; incite; stimulate. To gash or strike with one or more spurs; to put spurs on; to furnish with spurs.—*v.i.* To spur one's horse to make it go fast; to ride fast; to press forward; to hurry.—**on the spur of the mo·ment,** impulsively; without thought; hastily.—**win one's spurs,** to achieve honor or distinction, esp. the first time; to prove or show one's ability.

spurge, spurj, *n.* [O.Fr. *espurge*, spurge, < L. *expurgare*, to purge.] *Bot.* any of a number of shrubs and herbs of the family *Euphorbiaceae*, esp. of the genus *Euphorbia*, characterized by having a milky juice. See *euphorbia.*

spur gear, *n. Mach.* a gear having radial teeth cut parallel to the wheel axis. Also **spur wheel.**

spurge lau·rel, *n.* A Eurasian shrub, *Daphne laureola*, with oblong evergreen leaves and yellow flowers.

spu·ri·ous, spūr′ē·us, *a.* [L. *spurius*, bastard, from same root as *sperno*, to despise.] Not legitimate; bastard; not proceeding from the true source or from the source pretended; not genuine; counterfeit; adulterate; *bot.* in reference to two plants that have the appearance of similitude but which are structurally or functionally different.—**spu·ri·ous·ly,** *adv.*—**spu·ri·ous·ness,** *n.*

spurn, spurn, *v.t.* [O.E. *spurnan*, to spurn; Icel. *sporna, spyrna*, O.H.G. *spurnan, spornan*, to kick; same root as *spur*, and L. *sperno*, to despise.] To reject with disdain; to treat with contempt; to kick.—*v.i.* To reject anything with disdain or contempt.— *n.* Disdainful rejection; contemptuous treatment; a kick.—**spurn·er,** *n.*

spurred, spurd, *a.* Wearing spurs; having prolongations or shoots like spurs, as on the leg of a rooster.

spur·ri·er, spur′ē·ėr, spur′ē·ėr, *n.* One who makes spurs.

spur·ry, spur·rey, spur′ē, spur′ē, *n.* pl. **spur·ries, spur·reys.** [D. *spurrie*: cf. M.L. *spergula*, spurry.] Any of various herbs of the genus *Spergula*, in the pink family, esp. the common corn spurry, *S. arvensis*, with numerous whorled, linear leaves and white flowers.

spurt, spurt, *v.i.* [Also *spirt*; cf. M.E. *sprit* (rare), spring, dart, Icel. *spretta*, spring, dart, *spurt* (as water), Sw. *spritta*, spring, start, *sprätta*, spurt, G. *spritzen*, spurt.] To gush or issue suddenly in a stream or jet, as a liquid; to show marked, increased activity, energy, or effort for a short period. Also *spirt.*—*v.t.* To force out suddenly in a stream or jet, as a liquid; to squirt. Also *spirt.*—*n.* A sudden jet or gush of water or other liquid; a marked increase of effort for a short period or distance, as in running or rowing; a sudden outburst, as of feeling. Also *spirt.*—**spurt·er,** *n.*—**spur·tive,** *a.*

spur track, *n. Rail.* a short branch track leading from the main track, and connected with it at only one end. Also *spur.*

sput·nik, sput′nik, sput′nik, *Russ.* spöt′nik, *n.* [Russ.] Any of a series of artificial earth satellites placed into orbit by the Soviet Union, the first of which was launched in October of 1957.

sput·ter, sput′ėr, *v.i.* [Akin to *spout* or *spit*; same as L.G. *sputtern*, to sputter.] To speak excitedly, in a rapid, incoherent, or confused manner; to give off particles or drops of moisture explosively with snapping or popping sounds, as green wood or a candle does when burning; to involuntarily spit saliva or particles of food from the mouth when speaking.—*v.t.* To jabber; to utter rapidly, indistinctly, or with great excitement; to give out in particles explosively or forcibly.—*n.* The sound or act of sputtering; speaking in confused, excited bursts.— **sput·ter·er,** *n.*

spu·tum, spū′tum, *n.* pl. **spu·ta,** spū′ta. [L. *sputum*, spittle, *spuo*, to spit.] Spittle or any matter mixed with saliva which is expectorated.

spy, spī, *n.* pl. **spies.** [O.Fr. *espier* (Fr. *épier*), < O.H.G. *spehōn* (G. *spähen*), watch, spy; akin to L. *specere*, look at, Gr. *sképtesthai*, look, Skt. *spaç-, paç-*, see, look.] One who keeps a person or place under close or secret surveillance; one employed by a government to obtain secret information or intelligence by clandestine means, or on false pretenses, usu. pertaining to diplomatic, military, or naval affairs of other countries, esp. a belligerent in time of war; the act of spying or watching secretly.—*v.i.*—*spied, spying.* To make secret observations; to act as a spy; to examine or search for something closely or carefully; to be on the lookout, or keep watch.—*v.t.* To watch or make secret observations, as of a place, person, or actions, usu. with hostile intent; to discover or seek to discover by secret observation; to find out by observation or scrutiny; to inspect, look at, or examine closely or carefully; to catch sight of, or see.

spy·glass, spī′glas″, spī′gläs″, *n.* A telescope, esp. a small telescope.

squab, skwob, *n.* pl. **squabs, squab.** [Akin Sw. *sqvabba*, a fat woman; Dan. *kvabbet*, fat, squab.] A young unfledged pigeon; a short fat person; a kind of sofa or couch; a soft cushion.—*a.* Fat; short and stout; bulky; unfledged; unfeathered.

squab·ble, skwob′l, *v.i.*—*squabbled, squabbling.* [Same as Sw. *sqvabbel*, a dispute; cf. L.G. *kabbeln*, to quarrel.] To engage in a noisy quarrel; to have a petty dispute.— *v.t. Print.* to put awry, as types that have been set up.—*n.* A scuffle; a wrangle; a petty quarrel.—**squab·bler,** *n.*

squad, skwod, *n.* [Fr. *escouade*, earlier *esquade*, for *esquadre* (now *escadre*), < It. *squadra*.] A small unit of soldiers organized for drill, inspection, or duty; the smallest tactical unit of the U.S. Army, esp. of the infantry; any small group of persons engaged in a common enterprise; as, a police *squad.*—*v.t.*—*squadded, squadding.* To form into squads; assign to a squad.

squad car, *n.* An automobile used for patrol duty by police, equipped with a radio-telephone for two-way communicating with headquarters. Also *prowl car.*

squad·ron, skwod′ron, *n.* [O.Fr. *esquadron* (Fr. *escadron*), < It. *squadrone*, a squadron < *squadra*, a square.] *Air Force*, a flight formation of airplanes, usu. of the same type; a basic tactical unit, subordinate to a group, having two or more flights of aircraft. *Navy*, one or more divisions of vessels or aircraft; a group of vessels assigned to a special duty. *Army*, a unit composed of a headquarters and two or more troops of armored cavalry; any group of soldiers in formation. An organized group formed for a particular purpose.— *v.t.* To put into squadrons, or squadron formation.

squad·ron, lead·er, *n. Milit.* A pilot in command of a squadron of aircraft; a commissioned rank or person in the Royal Air Force or Royal Canadian Air Force, corresponding to major in the U.S. Air Force; the commanding officer of a detachment of warships or an armored cavalry unit.

squad room, *n. Milit.* a large room in a barracks used to house a number of troops, usu. a squad. A room in a police station used for roll call by the policemen reporting for duty.

squa·lene, skwā′lēn, *n. Biochem.* a colorless oil, $C_{30}H_{50}$, which is found in the fat secretions of humans, but esp. in the liver of sharks: used in manufacturing cosmetics and some pharmaceuticals, and as a precursor in synthesizing cholesterol.

squal·id, skwol′id, skwal′id, *a.* [L. *squalidus, squalid*, < *squaleo*, to be foul or filthy.] Foul or filthy due to neglect; miserable; wretched; morally debased or disgusting; sordid.—**squal·id·ly,** *adv.*—**squal·id·ness, squa·lid·i·ty,** skwo·lid′i·tē, *n.*

squall, skwal, *n.* [Cf. Sw. *sqval*, rush of water, *sqvalregn*, downpour.] A sudden, violent gust of wind, often accompanied by rain, snow, or sleet; *fig.* any disturbance or commotion.—*v.i.* To blow like a squall.

squall, skwal, *v.i.* [Imit.: cf. *squeal*.] To cry out or scream loudly, discordantly, and violently.—*v.t.* To utter in a harsh screaming tone.—*n.* The act or sound of squalling; a loud, discordant cry.—**squall·er,** *n.*

squal·ly, skwa′lē, *a.*—*squallier, squalliest.* Characterized by squalls; stormy; gusty; *colloq.* threatening.

---

a- fat, fāte, fär, fâre, fall;   **e-** met, mē, mēre, hėr;   **i-** pin, pīne;   **o-** not, nōte, möve;   **u-** tub, cūbe, bull;   **oi-** oil;   **ou-** pound.

squal·or, skwol′ẽr, skwā′lẽr, *n.* The state or condition of being squalid; wretchedness and filth.

squa·ma, skwā′ma, *n. pl.* **squa·mae**, skwā′mē. [L., scale.] *Biol.* a scale or scale-like part, as of epidermis or bone.—**squa·ma·ceous**, *a.* Scaly.—**squa·mate**, skwā′māt, *a.* Provided or covered with squamae or scales; scalelike.—**squa·ma·tion**, skwā·mā′shan, *n.*

squa·mo·sal, skwa·mō′sal, *a. Anat.* pertaining to a thin, scalelike element of the temporal bone in the skull of man, or a corresponding bone in other vertebrates.—*n.* A squamosal bone.

squa·mous, skwā′mus, *a.* [L. *squamosus*, < *squama*, scale.] *Zool.* Furnished or covered with, or formed of, squamae or scales, or parts resembling scales; characterized by the development of scales; scalelike; squamosal.—**squa·mous·ly**, *adv.*—**squa·mous·ness**, *n.* Also **squa·mose**, skwā′mōs, skwa·mōs′.

squam·u·lose, skwam′ū·lōs″, skwā′mū·lōs″, *a.* [L. *squamula*, dim. of *squama*, scale.] *Biol.* furnished or covered with small scales.

squan·der, skwon′dẽr, *v.t.* [Origin obscure.] To spend extravagantly or wastefully, as money or time; as, to *squander* an entire inheritance; *obs.* to scatter or disperse.—*n.* The act of squandering; extravagant or wasteful expenditure.—**squan·der·er**, *n.*

square, skwâr, *n.* [O.Fr. *esquarre*, *esquerre* (Fr. *équerre*) = It. *squadra*, ult. < L. *ex-*, out, and *quadra*, a square.] A four-sided plane figure having all its sides equal and all its angles right angles; any space or area, or any flat object or piece, having this form or a form approximating it; a rectangular area, object, or piece; a cubical or rectangular block; a square, rectangular, or quadrilateral area in a city or town, marked off by neighboring and intersecting streets; the distance along one side of such an area; as, a house two *squares* from here; an open area of this or other form, in a city or town, usually planted with grass and trees; an L-shaped or T-shaped instrument for determining or testing right angles; squared form or condition; *milit.* a body of troops drawn up in quadrilateral form; *arith., alg.* the second power of a number or quantity, that is the product of the number or quantity multiplied by itself, as: The *square* of 4, 4 × 4, is 16.—*a.* Having four equal sides and four right angles, as a figure or area; of a specified length on each side of a square; as, an area 2 feet *square*, which contains 4 *square* feet; designating a unit representing an area in the form of a square of the length of a specified linear unit along each edge, used in expressing surface measurement; as, a *square* inch, *square* foot, *square* mile, an area of 4 *square* feet, which is equivalent to an area 2 feet *square*; pertaining to such units, or to surface measurement; as, *square* measure; having four sides and four right angles, but not equilateral; cubical or approximately so, or rectangular and of three dimensions; as, a *square* box; having a square section, or one that is merely rectangular; as, a *square* file; having a solid, sturdy form with rectilinear and angular outlines; as, a man of *square* build; of the form of a right angle, or having some part or parts rectangular; as, a *square* corner; at right angles, or perpendicular; as, one line *square* to another; straight, level, or even, as one surface with another. *Fig.* leaving no balance of debt on either side, or having all accounts settled; as, to make accounts *square*, to get *square* with a person; just, fair, or equitable; as *square* dealing; honest, honorable, or upright; straightforward, direct, or unequivocal. *Colloq.*

substantial or satisfying; as, a *square* meal; *naut.* at right angles to the mast and the keel, as a yard; *golf*, having an even or equal score; *arith., alg.* being a square; pertaining to a square. *Slang*, disdainful or ignorant of the latest customs, fashions, or fads; conservative; old-fashioned.—*adv.* So as to be square; in square or rectangular form; at right angles; *colloq.* fairly, honestly, or uprightly.—*v.t.*—*squared*, *squaring*. To reduce to square or rectangular form; to make cubical, or approximately so; make square or rectangular in cross section; to mark out in one or more squares or rectangles; bring to the form of a right angle or right angles; set at right angles to something else; as, to *square* the yards of a vessel; to set so as to present a square or rectangular outline; make straight, level, or even; test the squareness of, as with a try square; to regulate, as by a standard; conform to or harmonize with; adjust harmoniously or satisfactorily; to balance, as accounts; settle, as a debt, often with *up*. *Math.* to find the equivalent of in square measure; to multiply, as a number or quantity, by itself.—*v.i.* To accord or agree, often with *with*; *boxing*, to assume a posture of defense, often with *off*.—**on the square**, at right angles; not obliquely. *Colloq.* in an honest or upright manner; honest or straightforward.—**out of square**, not at right angles; oblique; out of order; out of the proper condition; incorrect or incorrectly.—**square·ly**, *adv.*—**square·ness**, *n.*

square a·way, *v.i.* To straighten things up or to make something ready; to assume an offensive or defensive position or posture, as in prize fighting. *Naut.* to set a ship's yards at 90° angles so the ship can sail directly before the wind.

square dance, *n.* A group dance, as a quadrille, performed by several couples arranged in a square or other set pattern.—**square-dance**, *v.i.*—**square-danced**, **square-dancing**.—**square danc·ing**, *n.*

squared cir·cle, *n. Colloq.* a boxing ring.

square deal, *n. Colloq.* a trade or transaction which is honest and just.

square knot, *n.* A common knot in which the ends of the cord or rope come out alongside of the standing parts. Also *reef knot*.

square meal, *n. Colloq.* a meal which is satisfying and full.

square meas·ure, *n.* A unit for measuring surface area; a system of such units. See Measures and Weights table, Metric System table.

square num·ber, *n. Math.* a number, as 1, 4, 9, or 16, which is the square of some integer.

square-rigged, skwâr′rigd′, *a. Naut.* having the principal sails of a square shape, and extended by yards suspended by the middle.—**square-rig·ger**, *n.* A square-rigged ship. Also **square-rig**.

square root, *n. Math.* a quantity whose square equals a given quantity, as: 3 is the *square root* of 9.

square sail, *n. Naut.* a sail extended on a horizontal yard and suspended so as to hang athwart the ship.

square shoot·er, *n. Colloq.* any person who is considered to be just, honest, and fair in dealing with others.

square-shoul·dered, skwâr′shōl′dẽrd, *a.* Having shoulders which are held high, erect, and back so that the posture is straight.

square-toed, skwâr′tōd′, *a.* Having toes which are squared and broad, as some shoes; having to do with a formal, conservative, old-fashioned person.—**square-toed·ness**, *n.*

square-toes, skwâr′tōz″, *n. pl. but sing. in constr. Colloq.* a formal, conservative, old-fashioned person.

squar·ish, skwâr′ish, *a.* Approximately square.—**squar·ish·ly**, *adv.*

squar·rose, skwar′ōs, skwo·rōs′, *a.* [L. *squarrosus*, appar. erron. for *squamosus*, scaly.] *Bot.* rough with spreading processes, or thickly set with divergent or recurved bracts or leaves, as on the surface of a stem.—**squar·rose·ly**, *adv.*

squash, skwosh, *v.t.* [Cf. O.Fr. *esquachier*, *escachier* (Fr. *écacher*), crush, squash.] To press into a flat mass or pulp; to crush; to suppress or put down; to quash; *colloq.* to silence, as with a crushing retort.—*v.i.* To be pressed into a flat mass or pulp; to make a splashing sound; splash.—*n.* The act of squashing, or the fact or sound of being squashed; the impact of a soft, heavy body falling on a surface, or the sound produced by this; something squashed or crushed, or a squashed or crushed mass; something soft and easily crushed. A game resembling rackets, played in a walled court with rackets and a hollow rubber ball; also **squash rack·ets**. A game resembling tennis and squash rackets, but played with a larger ball; also **squash ten·nis**.—*a.*—*adv.*—**squash·er**, *n.*

squash, skwosh, *n. pl.* **squash·es**, **squash**. [From Amer. Indian name.] A plant of the genus *Cucurbita*, cultivated in the Americas as an article of food; the flesh of this fruit boiled and mashed, served as a vegetable or used as a filling for pies.

squash bug, *n.* An ill-smelling, dark-colored insect, *Anasa tristis*, injurious to the leaves of squash, pumpkin, and other plants of the gourd family.

squash·y, skwosh′ē, *a.*—*squashier*, *squashiest*. Soft or pulpy, as overripe food; soft and wet; miry; muddy.—**squash·i·ly**, *adv.*—**squash·i·ness**, *n.*

squat, skwot, *v.i.*—*squatted* or *squat*, *squatting*. [O.Fr. *esquatir*, < *es-* (< L. *ex-*, out) and *quatir*, press down, < L. *coactus*, pp. of *cogere*, drive together.] To sit down in a low or crouching position with the legs drawn up closely beneath or in front of the body; to crouch or cower down, as an animal; to settle on land, esp. public or new land, without any title or right; to settle on public land under government regulation, as for the purpose of acquiring title.—*v.t.* To cause, as a person, to squat; to put in a squatting attitude or posture. *Brit. dial.* to flatten, crush, or bruise; to knock, dash, or throw.—*a.*—*squatter*, *squattest.* [Orig. pp. of *squat*, *v.*] Short and thickset or thick, as persons or animals, the body or figure, or the like; low and thick or broad; seated or being in a squatting position; squatting; crouching.—*n.* The act or fact of squatting or crouching; a squatting attitude or posture. *Brit. dial.* a bump, jar, or jolt; a bruise.—**squat·ly**, *adv.*—**squat·ness**, *n.*

squat·ter, skwot′ẽr, *n.* One who or that which squats; one who settles on land, esp. public or new land, without any title or permission; one who settles on land under government regulation, for the purpose of acquiring title.

squat·ter sov·er·eign·ty, *n.* A derisive term applied by its opponents to the pre-Civil War political doctrine of popular sovereignty. See *popular sovereignty*.

squat·ty, skwot′ē, *a.*—*squattier*, *squattiest.* Squat; short and thick; low and broad; as, a *squatty* house.

squaw, skwa, *n.* [Algonquian.] A N. American Indian woman, esp. a wife; *slang*, any woman: used facetiously.

squaw·fish, skwa′fish″, *n. pl.* **squaw·fish**, **squaw·fish·es**. A large carplike food fish of the genus *Ptychocheilus*, common in rivers of the Pacific coast of the U.S. and Canada; a viviparous surf fish, *Taeniotoca lateralis*, found in the Pacific Ocean off N. America.

squawk, skwạk, *v.i.* [Imit.] To utter a loud, harsh cry, as a duck or other fowl when frightened; *slang*, to protest or complain, esp. vehemently or loudly.—*v.t.* To give forth with a squawk.—*n.* A loud, harsh cry or sound; *slang*, a complaint which is loud or vehement; *ornith.* the night heron.—**squawk·er**, *n.*

squawk box, *n. Electronics, slang*, the speaker element of a public-address system or of an intercommunication system.

squawk·y, skwạ́kē, *a.*—*squawkier, squawkiest.* Discordant; unpleasantly harsh or disagreeable in sound.

squaw man, *n.* pl. **squaw men.** A non-Indian man who takes an Indian woman as his wife, often having the rights of her tribe.

squaw·root, skwạ́rŏt″, skwạ́rut″, *n.* A fleshy, leafless plant, *Conopholis americana*, of eastern N. America, having yellowish flowers, and found growing as a parasite on the roots of trees, esp. oaks. The blue cohosh; see *cohosh.*

squeak, skwēk, *v.i.* [Imit.; cf. *squawk*, G. *quieken*, to squeak; Sw. *sqväka*, to cry like a frog.] To utter a sharp, shrill cry; to cry with an acute tone, as a pig or mouse; to to make a sharp noise, as an ungreased wheel or door; *slang*, to squeal or become an informer.—*v.t.*—*n.* A sharp, shrill cry or noise; *colloq.* a close escape, usu. preceded by *close* or *narrow.*—**squeak·er**, *n.*—**squeak·ing·ly**, *adv.*—**squeak·y**, skwḗkē, *a.* —*squeakier, squeakiest.*

squeal, skwēl, *n.* [M.E. *squelen*; imit.] A more or less prolonged, sharp, shrill cry or sound. *Slang*, an act of informing on a person; a complaint.—*v.i.* To utter a more or less prolonged, sharp, shrill cry, as in pain, fear, or the like, as persons or animals; to emit a shrill sound. *Slang*, to turn informer; to complain or protest.—*v.t.* To utter or produce with a squeal.—**squeal·er**, *n.*

squeam·ish, skwḗmish, *a.* [M.E. *squaymysch*, var. of *squaymus, squoymous*; origin uncertain.] Easily shocked or offended; prudish; easily disgusted; excessively particular or scrupulous as to the moral aspect of things; fastidious or dainty in taste or requirements; easily nauseated; qualmish.— **squeam·ish·ly**, *adv.*—**squeam·ish·ness**, *n.*

squee·gee, skwḗjē, skwē·jḗ, *n.* [Var. of *squilgee.*] An implement edged with rubber or leather, for sweeping water from wet decks, scraping water off windows after washing, or the like; any of various similar devices, as one for expressing water from photographic prints.—*v.t.*—**squeegeed**, *squeegeeing.* To sweep, scrape, or press with or as with a squeegee. Also *squilgee.*

squeeze, skwēz, *v.t.*—*squeezed, squeezing.* [Cf. O.E. *cwesan, cwȳsan*, squeeze, crush.] To press forcibly together; compress; to apply pressure upon in order to extract; as, to *squeeze* a lemon; to thrust forcibly or force by pressure; as, to *squeeze* one's hand into a tight glove; to hug; to press in one's hand, as: She *squeezed* his hand when she said good night. To oppress, as with abhorrent duties; to obtain a facsimile impression of; *bridge*, to force the discarding of a valuable card; *baseball*, to permit scoring on a squeeze play, as: With a bunt, the batter *squeezed* the run across the plate.—*v.i.* To exert a compressing force; to force a way through some narrow or crowded place; as, to *squeeze* between the two cars; to yield to pressure.—*n.* The act of squeezing; a tight pressure of another's hand within one's own, as in friendliness or affection; a hug; a small quantity or amount of anything obtained by squeezing; a facsimile impression of an inscription, coin, or the like, obtained by pressing some plastic substance over or around it; *bridge*, a play in which a player is forced by his opponents' maneuver to discard a valuable card; *colloq.* exertion of pressure to extort favors or money.—**squeez·er**, *n.*—**squeez·ing·ly**, *adv.*

squeeze bot·tle, *n.* A bottle made of flexible material, usu. plastic, which yields some of its contents when squeezed.

squeeze play, *n. Baseball*, a play executed when there is a runner on third base and usu. not more than one man out, in which the runner starts for home as soon as the pitcher makes a motion to pitch, the batter bunting the ball when pitched; *bridge*, a maneuver forcing an opponent to discard a card that is a potential winner; *colloq.* the application of pressure of any sort to gain some end.

squelch, skwelch, *v.t.* [Prob. imit.] To strike or press with crushing force; squash. *Colloq.* to put down or suppress completely; to silence, as with a crushing retort.—*v.i.* To make a splashing sound, as of something wet under impact; to tread heavily, as in water, mud, or wet shoes, with such a sound; to become squelched or squashed.—*n.* A squelched or crushed mass of anything; a squelching sound; *colloq.* a crushing argument or retort.—**squelch·er**, *n.*

sque·teague, skwē·tēg′, *n.* pl. **sque·-teague.** [Algonquian.] A common weakfish, *Cynoscion regalis*, found along the Atlantic coast of N. America; any of various related fishes.

squib, skwib, *n.* [Origin unknown.] A short witty or sarcastic saying or writing; a lampoon; *journ.* a news story which is short and sometimes used to fill space. A firework consisting of a tube or ball filled with powder, which burns with a hissing noise terminated usu. by a slight explosion; a firecracker broken in the middle so that when lighted it burns with a hissing noise.— *v.t., v.i.*—**squibbed**, *squibbing.* To assail in or put forth squibs or lampoons.

squid, skwid, *n.* pl. **squids, squid.** [Origin uncertain.] Any of various ten-armed cephalopods, esp. any of certain small species of the genera *Loligo* and *Ommastrephes*, having slender bodies and caudal fins and much used for bait; a kind of artificial bait made to resemble a squid, used in angling or trolling for fish. Also **cal·a·mar·y.**—*v.i.*—**squidded**, *squidding.* To fish, using a squid for bait.

squif·fy, skwif′ē, *a. Slang*, drunk or intoxicated. Also **squiffed.**

squig·gle, skwig′l, *v.i.*—*squiggled, squiggling.* To make hasty and illegible twisting marks, as in writing; to move restlessly.— *v.t.* To mark or write in squiggles.—*n.* A short twisting mark, usu. illegible.

squil·gee, skwil′jē, skwil·jē′, *n.* [Origin obscure.] A squeegee.—*v.t.*—**squilgeed**, *squilgeeing.* To squeegee. Also **squil·la·-gee**, skwil′a·jē″.

squill, skwil, *n.* [L. *squilla, scilla*, Gr. *skilla*, a squill.] *Bot.* a plant, *Urginea maritima*, found along the coastal regions of the Mediterranean, the bulb of which is processed for medical use as an expectorant and tonic; also *sea onion.* The bulb of a reddish variety of squill, *U. maritima*, used in high concentration as a poison for rats; also *red squill.* Any spring-blooming plant of the genus *Scilla*; also *scilla.*

squil·la, skwil′a, *n.* pl. **squil·las, squil·-lae.** [L.] *Zool.* any of the squills, or stomatopod crustaceans of the genus *Squilla*, in the family *Squillidae.*

squinch, skwinch, *n. Arch.* a small arch formed across an angle, as in a square tower, to support the side of a superimposed octagon.

squint, skwint, *v.i.* [Cf. Prov. E. *squinny, squiny*, to squint; D. *schuinte*, a slope, *schuin, schuinsch*, sloping, oblique.] To look with partially closed eyes, as toward a brilliant light; to suffer from cross-eye; to peer or look quickly sideways; to make an oblique allusion or have an indirect bearing; to incline.—*v.t.* To cause to look sideways or with partially closed eyes; to cause, as the eyes, to be half-shut.—*n. Ophthalm.* strabismus, or cross-eye; *colloq.* a cursory look, as: I took a *squint* at the report. A side glance; an oblique tendency.—*a.* Peering obliquely, as with distrust; suffering from cross-eye.—**squint·er**, *n.*—**squint·ing·ly**, *adv.*—**squint·y**, skwin′tē, *a.*

squint-eyed, skwint′īd″, *a.* Having eyes that squint; being half shut, as the eyes in glaring light; glancing sideways; displaying a malicious attitude.

squint·ing con·struc·tion, *n. Gram.* a clumsy sentence construction having a word or group of words that could modify either what goes before or follows it, as: Exercising *frequently* helps prevent obesity.

squire, skwī′ér, *n.* [O.Fr. *esquier.*] A young man of aristocratic birth who, as an aspirant to knighthood, waited or attended upon a knight; a title used by a justice of the peace, local judge, or other dignitary, esp. in country districts and small towns; a personal attendant, as of a person of rank; a man who escorts or accompanies a lady in public; *Brit.* a country gentleman, esp. the chief landed proprietor in a district.—*v.t.*—*squired, squiring.* To attend as or in the manner of a squire; to accompany or escort, as a girl or woman, to a social or dance.

squire·ar·chy, squir·ar·chy, skwī′ér·är·-kē, *n.* pl. **squire·ar·chies, squir·ar·-chies.** *Brit.* the class of squires collectively; the country gentry; rule or government by a squire or squires.

squirm, skwurm, *v.i.* [Origin obscure; perh. suggested by *worm.*] To move like a worm or eel, with writhing or similar contortions; wriggle; to display or feel suffering or distress, as from humiliation, embarrassment, or pain.—*n.* A wriggling motion; an act of wriggling.—**squirm·y**, skwur′mē, *a.*—*squirmier, squirmiest.*

squir·rel, skwur′el, skwur′el, *Brit.* skwėr′-el, *n.* [O.Fr. *esquireul* (Fr. *écureuil*), dim. < L. *sciurus*, < Gr. *skiouros*, squirrel, appar. < *skiá*, shadow, and *oura*, tail.] Any of the arboreal, bushy-tailed rodents constituting the genus *Sciurus*, as *S. vulgaris*, the common European squirrel, *S. hudsonius*, red squirrel, and *S. carolinensis*, gray squirrel of N. America; any of various other members of the family *Sciuridae*, as the chipmunks, flying squirrels, or prairie squirrels; any of certain African rodents, family *Anomaluridae*, resembling flying squirrels; the pelt of a squirrel.

squir·rel cage, *n.* A cage designed for a squirrel or other small rodent, containing a cylinder inside of which the animal may run, as on a treadmill; *fig.* any state of affairs which appears to be lacking in purpose or accomplishment.

squir·rel corn, *n.* A perennial N. American herb, *Dicentra canadensis*, in the family *Fumariaceae*, with finely dissected leaves, cream-colored heart-shaped flowers, and a rootstock bearing numerous small tubers which resemble grains of Indian corn. Also **tur·key corn.**

squir·rel·ly, squir·rel·y, skwur′e·lē, skwur′e·lē, *a. Slang.* Slightly crazy; unpredictable; eccentric.

squir·rel ri·fle, *n.* A small caliber rifle used for hunting small game. Also **squir·rel gun.**

squirt, skwurt, *v.i.* [Late M.E. *squyrt*: cf. earlier M.E. *swirting, n.*, squirting, also L.G. *swirtjen*, squirt.] To eject liquid in a jet or stream from a narrow orifice; to issue in a jetlike stream.—*v.t.* To cause, as a liquid, to issue in a jet from a narrow orifice; eject in a jetlike stream; to wet or bespatter with a liquid so ejected.—*n.* An act of squirting; a jet, as of water; a small quantity of liquid squirted; an instrument for squirting, as a syringe. *Colloq.* an insignificant, self-assertive fellow; a young or small person.—**squirt·er,** *n.*

squirt·ing cu·cum·ber, *n.* A plant of the gourd family, *Ecballium elaterium,* native in the Mediterranean region, whose ripened fruit forcibly ejects the seeds and juice.

squish, s̲kwish, *v.t., v.i.* To squash or squeeze.—*n.* A squashing sound.—**squish·y,** *a.*—*squishier, squishiest.*

sri, shrē, *n.* A title of respect used in India when speaking of or to a person of distinguished rank, equivalent to English sir or mister.

stab, stab, *v.t.*—*stabbed, stabbing.* [Allied to *staff;* cf. Gael. *stob,* Ir. *stobaim,* to stab; Gael. and Sc. *stob,* a stake, a prickle; also Goth. *stabs,* a rod; G. *stab,* a staff.] To pierce or wound with a pointed weapon; to kill by a pointed weapon; to drive in; to inflict keen or severe pain on; *fig.* to pierce. —*v.i.* To aim a blow with a pointed weapon; to be extremely cutting.—*n.* The thrust of a pointed weapon; keen, poignant pain; *colloq.* a brief effort or attempt, as: He took a *stab* at writing.—**stab·ber,** *n.*

sta·bile, stā′bil, stā′bīl, *Brit.* stā′bĭl, *a.* [L. *stabilis.*] Fixed in position; firmly established, or stable. *Med.* unaffected by moderate degrees of heat, as some serum components; noting or pertaining to a mode of application of electricity in which the active electrode is kept stationary over the part to be acted upon: opposed to *labile.*—stā′bĕl, *Brit.* stā′bĭl, *n. Art,* a fixed abstract sculpture, usu. of metal or wood, composed of nonmoving parts: contrasted with *mobile.*

sta·bil·i·ty, sta·bil′i·tē, *n.* pl. **sta·bil·i·ties.** [L. *stabilitas,* < *stabilis.*] The state or quality of being stable; fixedness or firmness in position; continuance in the same state or without change; *chem.* the property of a substance which retards the rate of reaction or maintains chemical equilibrium in a solution, suspension, or mixture. Endurance or permanence; steadfastness, as of character or purpose; *aeron.* a characteristic of an aircraft in flight that causes it, if disturbed from its condition of equilibrium or steady flight, to return to that condition; *Rom. Cath. Ch.* a vow binding a monk to lifelong residence in one monastery.

sta·bi·lize, stā′bi·līz″, *v.t.*—*stabilized, stabilizing.* [Fr. *stabiliser,* < L. *stabilis.*] To make or keep firm, stable, constant, steadfast, or unfluctuating; to put or keep in stable equilibrium, as an aircraft, ship, chemicals, prices, governments, or other things capable of changing.—*v.i.*—**sta·bi·li·za·tion,** *n.*

sta·bi·liz·er, stā′bi·lī″zėr, *n.* A person or thing which causes or produces stabilization; *aeron.* any airfoil, or any combination of airfoils as the horizontal stabilizer and vertical stabilizer considered as a single unit, the primary function of which is to give an aircraft stability: *naut.* a device, as a gyroscope, that prevents a ship from rolling; *chem.* some substance which is added to other substances to retard explosion, combustion, or chemical change.

sta·ble, stā′bl, *n.* [O.Fr. *estable* (Fr. *étable*), < L. *stabulum,* standing place, habitation, enclosure for animals, < *stare,* stand.] A building fitted for the lodging and feeding of horses and cattle, esp. of horses; a collection of animals belonging in such a building. *Horse racing,* an establishment where race horses are kept and trained; the horses belonging to, or the persons connected with, such an establishment.—*v.t.* *stabled, stabling.* To put or lodge in or as in a stable.—*v.i.*—**sta·ble·man,** stā′bl·man,

sta·ble·man″, *n.* pl. **sta·ble·men.**—**sta·bler,** *n.*

sta·ble, stā′bl, *a.* [O.Fr. *estable* (Fr. *stable*), < L. *stabilis,* standing firm, firm, steady, stable, < *stare,* stand.] Able to stand firm, or not likely to fall or give way, as a structure, support, or foundation; firmly fixed in position; firm; steady; stationary; able or likely to continue or last, or firmly established; as, a *stable* government; not liable to change, fail, or cease; enduring or permanent; firm, steadfast, or not wavering or changeable; reliable; level-headed. *Phys.* having or showing an ability or tendency to maintain, or resist change in, position or form; tending to keep the position, or to return to it after displacement, as a body; characterized by or showing such a tendency in a body, as position or equilibrium. *Chem.* not readily decomposing, as a compound; resisting molecular or chemical change.—**sta·bly,** *adv.*—**sta·ble·ness,** *n.*

sta·bling, stā′bling, *n.* The act of one who stables horses or other animals; accommodation for animals in a stable or building; stables collectively.

stac·ca·to, sta·kä′tō, *a.* [It., pp. of *staccare,* to separate.] *Mus.* characterized by performing the notes of a passage in a crisp, detached, or abrupt manner: opposed to *legato.* Consisting of short, sharp, or distinct sounds; as, a *staccato* burst of machine-gun fire.—*adv.*—*n.* pl. **stac·ca·toes, stac·ca·ti,** sta·kä′tē. *Mus.* a method of performance; a staccato style. Something that is short, sharp, or abrupt, as a sound.

stac·ca·to mark, *n. Mus.* a dot placed over a note indicating that the note is to be performed in a staccato manner.

stack, stak, *n.* [M.E. *stac, stak,* from Scand.: cf. Icel. *stakkr,* Sw. *stack,* Dan. *stak,* stack.] A large, usu. circular or rectangular pile of hay, straw, or the like; any more or less orderly pile or heap; a set of bookshelves ranged one above another, as in a library; *pl.* the section in any library where books are kept. A number of chimneys or flues grouped together; a single chimney or funnel for smoke; smokestack; a vertical exhaust or vent pipe; *colloq.* a great quantity or number. A number of rifles, usu. three, standing together in a conical group; a number of airplanes that circle an airport while awaiting landing turns; an English measure for coal and wood, equal to 108 cubic feet; *geol.* a high, detached rock rising out of the sea. The pile or amount of chips bought or held by one player, as in the game of poker.—*v.t.* To pile or arrange in the form of a stack; as, to *stack* hay; to cover or load with something in stacks or piles; to arrange, as aircraft, at various altitudes while awaiting landing instructions.—**blow one's stack,** *slang,* to blow one's top.—**stack the cards** or **deck,** to arrange the playing cards in the pack in a particular manner, so as to secure an unfair advantage; *fig.* to arrange circumstances to secure an advantage, usu. unfairly.—**stack·er,** *n.*

stac·te, stak′tē, *n.* [Gr. *staktē,* < *stazō,* to drop.] One of the sweet spices in the holy incense of the ancient Jews.

stad·dle, stad′l, *n.* [O.E. *stathol,* foundation, base; from the root of E. *stand.*] The lower part of a stack of hay or the like; a platform, as of timber, on which a stack or the like is placed; any supporting base or framework.

stad·hold·er, stad′hōl″dėr, *n.* [D. *stadhouder*—*stad,* a city, and *houder,* holder.] The chief magistrate of the United Provinces of Holland; formerly, the governor or viceroy of a province or town of the Netherlands. Also **stadt·hold·er.**—**stad·hold·er·ate,** *n.*—**stad·hold·er·ship,** *n.*

sta·di·a, stā′dē·a, *n.* [N.L. < L. *stadium.*]

Civil engin. Surveying with an instrument, a form of theodolite, which is fitted with two horizontal parallel cross hairs and used in connection with a vertical graduated rod to measure distances; the stadia rod itself.

sta·dim·e·ter, sta·dim′i·tėr, *n.* An optical instrument for determining the distance to an object of known dimension by measuring the angle subtended at the observer by the object, the instrument being graduated directly in distance.

sta·di·um, stā′dē·um, *n.* pl. **sta·di·ums, sta·di·a,** stā′dē·a. [L., < Gr. *stádion,* measure of length, race course, < *histánai,* cause to stand.] A structure for athletic games, usu. having an oval shape and tiers of seats for spectators; an ancient Greek linear measure, equal to about 607 English feet; an ancient Greek course for foot races.

sta·di·um, stā′dē·um, *n. Med.* a stage in the progress of a disease.

staff, staf, stäf, *n.* pl. **staves, staffs,** stāvz. [O.E. *staef,* a staff; D. and L.G. *staf,* Icel. *stafr,* Dan. *stav,* G. *stab,* a staff; same root as *stab, stem,* and Skt. *stabh, stambh,* to make firm.] A stick or club carried for support or combat; a rod used as a symbol of office, as a baton or mace; a supporting pole; as, a flag*staff*; a graduated stick used in surveying for leveling. *Mus.* the five parallel lines and four spaces between them on which notes and other musical characters are written; also *stave.*

staff, staf, stäf, *n.* A group of people assisting a supervisor in carrying out an undertaking; as, a hospital *staff*; a body of military officers who help the commander plan, administer, or coordinate operations; *fig.* that which provides support or sustenance; as, bread, the *staff* of life.—*v.t.* To provide with personnel; as, to *staff* an office with clerks.—*a.*

staff, staf, stäf, *n.* A composition of plaster combined with fibrous material, used for temporary buildings and ornamental structures.

staff·er, staf′ėr, stä′fėr, *n.* One of a staff of workers, esp. a newspaper writer or editor.

staff of·fi·cer, *n. Milit., nav.* a commissioned officer who serves on the advisory staff of a commanding officer.

staff of life, *n.* Bread, being considered man's fundamental food.

Staf·ford·shire ter·ri·er, staf′ėrd·shėr″ ter′ē·ėr, staf′ėrd·shėr, *n.* A stocky, English breed of dog of medium size with short hair of various colors; bullterrier.

staff ser·geant, *n. Air Force,* a noncommissioned officer who ranks above airman first class and below technical sergeant. *Army,* a noncommissioned officer who ranks above sergeant and below sergeant first class. *Marine Corps,* a noncommissioned officer who ranks above sergeant and below gunnery sergeant.

staff tree, *n.* The common name of the plant family *Celastraceae,* which includes the bittersweet and burning-bush.

stag, stag, *n.* [Same as O.E. *stag,* a young horse, a cock turkey; Sc. *staig,* a stallion; Icel. *steggr,* a male animal; stem of O.E. *stigan,* Icel. *stiga,* G. *steigen,* to mount; lit. 'the mounter.'] The male red deer; the male of other members of the deer family, as the caribou; a hart, sometimes applied particularly to a hart in its fifth year; a man at a dance unaccompanied by a lady; a social gathering of men only.—*v.i.*— *stagged, stagging.* To attend a social event without a companion of the opposite sex.— *v.t. Brit.* to spy on.—*a.* For men only.— *adv.*

stag bee·tle, *n.* A large-sized lamellicorn beetle, of the family *Lucanidae,* which is distinguished by the size of the horny and toothed mandibles in the males.

---

stage, stāj, *n.* [O.Fr. *estage,* (Fr. *étage,*) ult. < L. *stare,* stand.] A single step or degree in a process; a particular period in a course of progress, action, or development; a level in a series of levels; a raised platform or floor for any purpose, esp. a platform or raised floor for theatrical performances; the platform with all the parts of the theater and all the apparatus back of the proscenium. *Fig.* the theater; the drama; the dramatic profession; the scene of any action or career. A stopping point or station on a journey; the distance between such stations; any portion of a journey; a motorbus; a stagecoach; a landing place for boats; the height of a river's surface above an established level; *microscopy,* the small platform of a microscope on which the object to be viewed is placed; *biol.* any of several successive periods in the development of many animals and plants; *aerospace,* one of the propulsion elements of a rocket vehicle, usu. separated and dropped off when its fuel is exhausted. *Geol.* A time division in stratigraphy ranking immediately below a series; a subdivision of the Pleistocene epoch in N. American geologic tables.—*v.t.* —*staged, staging.* To present on the theatrical stage; to conduct, as any sort of exhibition, as a rodeo; to furnish with a stage or staging.—*v.i.* To go by stages; to travel by stagecoach.

stage·coach, stāj'kōch", *n.* A coach drawn by horses, formerly used on regular runs between scheduled places for the conveyance of passengers, freight, or mail.

stage·craft, stāj'kraft", stāj'kräft", *n.* Skill in or the art of writing, adapting, or directing plays for effective presentation on the state.

stage di·rec·tion, *n.* Any instruction or direction which indicates setting, actions of a character, or other requirements on stage.—**stage di·rec·tor,** *n.*

stage fright, *n.* Nervousness experienced on facing an audience.

stage·hand, stāj'hand", *n.* A worker in a theater who handles props and scenery.

stage man·a·ger, *n.* One who superintends the technical aspects of production and performance of a play, regulating all matters behind the scenes including lights, props, costumes, and other details.—**stage-man·age,** stāj'man"ij, *v.t.*—*stage-managed, stage-managing.*

stag·er, stā'jėr, *n.* A person of experience or one having skill derived from long experience; *archaic,* an actor.

stage-struck, stāj'struck", *a.* Having a great love for the theater; seized by a passionate desire to become an actor; referring to an immature or unrealistic idea or feeling about the theater.

stage whis·per, *n.* A loud whisper by an actor on stage, intended to be heard by the audience but not by the other actors; an aside.

stag·ger, stag'ėr, *v.i.* [< older *stacker,* to stagger, Sc. *stacher, stacker,* Icel. *stakra,* to stagger.] To sway from one side to the other while standing or walking; to reel; to walk or stand unsteadily; to hestitate; to become less confident or determined.—*v.t.* To cause to doubt and waver; to make to hesitate; to make less confident; to strike as incredible; to amaze.—*n.* A sudden swing or reel of the body, as if about to fall; divergence from straightness, as when spokes or rivets are arranged on the two sides of a median line; *pl.* a disease of horses and cattle attended with reeling or dizziness.—*a.*—**stag·ger·er,** *n.*—**stag·ger·-ing,** *a.*—**stag·ger·ing·ly,** *adv.*

stag·ger·bush, stag'ėr·bush", *n.* A N. American shrub, *Lyonia mariana,* of the heath family, having nodding white or pinkish flowers with foliage poisonous to animals.

stag·hound, stag'hound", *n.* One of a breed of hounds formerly used for hunting stags.

stag·ing, stā'jing, *n.* The act or process of putting a play on the stage; a temporary platform or structure of posts and boards for support, as in building; scaffolding; the business of running stagecoaches; the act of traveling by stages or by stagecoach; *aerospace,* the separation of a rocket stage following blast-off.

stag·ing ar·e·a, *n. Milit.* an area or general locality where troops, equipment, or the like are brought in preparation for further movement or before an operation.

stag·nant, stag'nant, *a.* [L. *stagnans, stagnantis,* ppr. of *stagno.*] Not flowing, as a stream; not running in a current or stream, as air or water; impure from lack of motion, as water; stale; inactive; dull; not brisk, as: Trade is *stagnant.*—**stag·nan·cy,** *n.*—**stag·nant·ly,** *adv.*

stag·nate, stag'nāt, *v.i.*—*stagnated, stagnating.* [L. *stagno, stagnatum,* to stagnate (whence *stanch*), < *stagnum,* standing water, a pool (whence *stank, tank*).] To cease to run or flow; to have no current, as water; to become impure from lack of current; to become dull, quiet, or inactive, as trade.—**stag·na·tion,** *n.*

stag·y, stage·y, stā'jē, *a.*—*stagier, stagiest.* Suggestive of the theater; theatrical in manner or other characteristics; displaying theatrical artificiality or pomposity.—**stag·i·ly,** *adv.*—**stag·i·ness,** *n.*

staid, stād, *a.* [< *stay,* to stop, to steady.] Sober; steady; sedate; not volatile, flighty, or fanciful; established or fixed.—**staid·ly,** *adv.*—**staid·ness,** *n.*

stain, stān, *v.t.* [For *distain.*] To discolor with spots or streaks of dirt, blood, or other foreign matter; to bring reproach upon; to blemish; to color in a particular way, esp. to color with something which penetrates the substance; to treat, as a microscopic specimen, with some reagent or dye in order to color the whole or certain parts and so give distinctness or contrast to tissues.—*v.i.* To produce a stain or to become stained; take a stain.—*n.* A discoloration produced by foreign matter; a spot, esp. one penetrating beneath the surface and not easily removable; a cause of reproach, or a blemish; coloration produced by staining anything; a dye or pigment used in staining; a reagent or dye used in staining microscopic specimens.—**stain·a·ble,** *a.*—**stained,** *a.*—**stain·er,** *n.*—**stain·less,** *a.*—**stain·less·ly,** *adv.*

stained glass, *n.* Any glass that is colored by having metallic oxides or other pigments fused, baked, or burned into its surface: used mostly in church windows.—**stained-glass,** *a.*

stain·less steel, *n.* An alloy of steel having a small percentage of chromium and other elements which make the steel highly resistant to rust or corrosion.

stair, stâr, *n.* [Lit. 'that by which a person mounts'; O.E. *staeger,* < *stigan,* Icel. *stiga,* G. *steigen,* to mount, to climb, whence also *stag, stile* (on a fence), and the first part of *stirrup.*] A succession of steps rising one above the other arranged as a way between two points at different heights in a building. *Pl.* a stairway; a flight or sequence of steps.

stair·case, stâr'kās", *n.* Any structure of stairs with the supporting devices needed for safety and support.

stair·way, stâr'wā", *n.* A passageway which allows movement from one level or floor of a building to another by a series of stairs; a staircase.

stair·well, stâr'wel", *n. Arch.* a vertical shaft, opening, or enclosed area within which are stairs or a stairway.

stake, stāk, *n.* [O.E. *staca,* a stake = L.G. *stake,* D. *staak,* Dan. *stage.*] A piece of wood sharpened at one end and set in the ground, or prepared for setting, as a support to something, or as part of a fence; the post to which one condemned to die by fire was fastened; that which is pledged or wagered; that which is risked on the issue of a contest, to be gained by victory or lost by defeat; something hazarded; the state of being pledged or put at hazard, preceded by *at,* as: His honor is *at* stake. A group of Mormon ecclesiastical wards under the jurisdiction of a president and two counselors.—*v.t.*—*staked, staking.* To set and plant like a stake; to fasten; to support or defend with stakes; to mark the limits of by stakes, followed by *out;* as, to *stake out* land; to pledge; to lay down as a stake; to hazard upon the issue of a competition, or upon a future contingency.

stake bod·y, *n.* A truck bed which is open, having no permanent sides or panels, but having holes along the sides of the bed where stakes may be inserted to prevent a load from sliding off.

stake driv·er, *n. Ornith.* the American bittern.

stake·hold·er, stāk'hōl"dėr, *n.* One who holds the money or other stakes when a wager is laid.

stake race, *n. Horse racing,* a race in which the purse is provided by the owners of the horses entered in the race.

sta·lac·tite, sta·lak'tīt, stal'ak·tīt", *n.* [< Gr. *stalaktos,* trickling or dropping, < *stalassō* or *stalazō,* to let fall drop by drop.] A mass of calcareous matter, usu. in a conical or cylindrical form, pendent from the roof of a cavern, and produced by the percolation through fissures and pores of rocks of water containing carbonate of lime: opposed to *stalagmite.*—**stal·ac·tit·-ic, stal·ac·tit·i·cal,** stal"ak·tit'ik, *a.*

sta·lag, stal'ag, G. shtä'läk, *n.* A prisoner-of-war camp in Germany, esp. during World War II, for captured noncommissioned officers and enlisted personnel.

sta·lag·mite, sta·lag'mīt, stal'ag·mīt", *n.* [Gr. *stalagmos,* a dropping, < *stalazō,* to drop.] A deposit of calcareous matter on the floor of a cavern, often rising into columns which meet and unite with the stalactites above.—**stal·ag·mit·ic, stal·-ag·mit·i·cal,** stal"ag·mit'ik, *a.*

stale, stāl, *a.*—*staler, stalest.* [Akin to *stall,* the meaning being from standing long; cf. O.D. *stel,* that remains standing, quiet, ancient.] Vapid or tasteless from age; having lost its life, spirit, or flavor from being long kept; being worn out or valueless from use or long familiarity; trite; *law,* having lost effectiveness through long neglect or lack of action, as a deed.—*v.t., v.i.*—*staled, staling.* To make or be vapid, useless, or stale.—**stale·ly,** *adv.*—**stale·-ness,** *n.*

stale, stāl, *v.i.*—*staled, staling.* [Same as D. and G. *stallen,* Dan. *stalle,* Sw. *stalla,* to make water, < G. *stall,* O.E. *stael,* a stable.] To discharge urine, as horses and cattle.—*n.* Urine of horses and cattle.

stale·mate, stāl'māt, *n. Chess,* a position of the pieces when no move can be made without putting the king in check. *Fig.* any position in which no action can be taken; a deadlock.—*v.t.*—*stalemated, stalemating.* To subject to a stalemate; bring to a standstill.

Sta·lin·ism, stä'li·niz"um, *n.* The principles by which Joseph Stalin controlled the political, economic, intellectual, and social life of the Soviet Union, esp. referring to his repressive and dictatorial methods.—**Sta·lin·ist,** *n., a.*

stalk, stąk, *n.* [Same as Dan. *stilk,* Icel. *stilker,* a stalk.] The stem or main axis of a plant; the connecting or supporting part of a flower, leaf, or plant; a similar supporting part in animals; a supporting part or stem of anything.—**stalked**, *a.*—**stalk·less**, *a.*—**stalk·y**, stạ́kē, *a.*—*stalkier, stalkiest.*

stalk, stạk, *v.i.* [O.E. *stealcian*, walk stealthily, akin to *stelan*, E. *steal*.] To pursue or approach game stealthily, as behind a cover; to walk with slow, stiff, or haughty strides; to proceed in a sinister or deliberate manner.—*v.t.* To pursue, as game, stealthily, as behind a cover.—*n.* An act or course of stalking game or the like; a slow, stiff stride or striding gait.—**stalk·er**, *n.*

stalk·ing-horse, stạ́king-hạrs″, *n.* A horse behind which a hunter conceals himself from the sight of the game; *fig.* anything thrust forward to conceal a more important object; *politics*, a candidate used to keep the candidacy of someone else secret or to divide the opposing party.

stall, stạl, *n.* [O.E. *steall*, stand, position, place, stall, = D. *stal* = O.H.G. *stal* (G. *stall*) = Icel. *stallr*, stall; < the same root as E. *stand*: cf. *forestall*, *install*, *stale*, and *stallion*.] A compartment in a stable or shed for the accommodation of one animal; a stable or shed for horses or cattle; a booth in which merchandise is displayed for sale or in which some business is carried on; as, a butcher's *stall*; a stand or table on which goods are displayed for sale; as, a book*stall*; one of a number of fixed enclosed seats, as in the choir or chancel of a cathedral or church, esp. for the use of the clergy; a compartment or chamber for any of various purposes; as, a shower *stall*; a space, as in a garage or parking lot, set aside for individual automobile parking; the condition of being stalled; a sheath or finger covering; *aeron.* the loss of altitude or control of an airplane resulting from insufficient forward speed or exorbitant angle of attack; *Brit.* a chairlike seat in a theater, separated from others by arms or rails, esp. one in the front division of the parquet.—*v.t.* To put or keep in a stall or stalls, as animals or automobiles; to confine in a stall for fattening, as cattle; to furnish with stalls; to bring to a standstill; to check the progress or motion of, esp. unintentionally; to cause, as an engine or motor driven vehicle, to stop, usu. unintentionally; to cause to stick fast, as in mire or snow; *aeron.* to cause a stall of, as an airplane.—*v.i.* To occupy a stall, as an animal; to come to a standstill; to be brought to a stop, esp. unintentionally; to stick fast, as in mire; *aeron.* to become stalled, as an airplane.—**stalled**, *a.*

stall, stạl, *n.* [Var. of *stale*.] *Colloq.* anything used as a pretext, pretense, or trick.—*v.t.* *Colloq.* to put off, evade, or deceive, often followed by *off*; to divert attention from, as a thief at work.—*v.i.* *Colloq.* to act evasively or deceptively.

stall-feed, stạl′fēd″, *v.t.*—*stall-fed*, *stall-feeding.* To feed and fatten in a stall or stable, as an ox.

stal·lion, stal′yan, *n.* [O.E. *stalon*, O.Fr. *estalon* (Fr. *étalon*), a stallion; < O.H.G. *stal*, E. *stall*; lit. 'the horse kept in the stall.'] An uncastrated male horse, esp. an adult used for breeding purposes.

stal·wart, stạl′wèrt, *a.* [O.E. *stalword*, *stallworth*, < *staelweorth*, lit. 'worthy of place,' < *staell*, stall, place.] Large and strong in frame; muscular; sturdy; brave; bold; valiant; steadfast or resolute.—*n.* A person having such qualities; a partisan who is uncompromising.—**stal·wart·ly**, *adv.*—**stal·wart·ness**, *n.*

sta·men, stā′men, *n.* pl. **sta·mens**, stam·i·na. [L. *stamen* (*stamin-*), thread, fiber, orig. the warp in the upright loom, < *stare*, stand.] *Bot.* the pollen-bearing organ, and the so-called male organ, of a flower,

consisting of the filament and the anther.—**stam·i·nate**, **stam·i·nif·er·ous**, stam′i-nit, stam′i·nāt″, stam″i·nif′ẻr·us, *a.*

stam·i·na, stam′i·na, *n.* [L., pl. of *stamen*.] Strength of physical constitution; power to endure conditions of difficulty or hardship, as disease, fatigue, or privation.

stam·i·nal, stam′i·nal, *a.* Of or pertaining to stamina; *bot.* of or pertaining to stamens.

stam·i·no·di·um, stam″i·nō′dē·um, *n.* pl. **stam·i·no·di·a**, stam″i·nō′dē·a. [N.L., < L. *stamen* (*stamin-*), thread, and Gr. *eidos*, form.] *Bot.* a sterile or abortive stamen, or a part resembling such a stamen. Also **stam·i·node**, stam′i·nōd″.

stam·i·no·dy, stam′i·nō″dē, *n.* [L. *stamen* (*stamin-*), thread, with termination as in E. *petalody*.] *Bot.* the metamorphosis of any of various flower organs, as a sepal or a petal, into a stamen.

stam·mer, stam′ẻr, *v.i.* [A freq. form from a root *stam*; O.E. *stamor*, *stamer*, Icel. *stamr*, *stammr*, *stammering*, speaking with difficulty; L.G. *stammern*, D. *stameren*, *stamelen*, G. *stammeln*, Icel. *stamma* to stammer.] To pause, hesitate, or falter involuntarily while speaking.—*v.t.* To utter with hesitations, repetitions, or stops. —*n.* A stammering manner of speaking; a defective utterance.—**stam·mer**, *n.*—**stam·mer·ing·ly**, *adv.*

stamp, stamp, *v.t.* [Same as Sw. *stampa*, Dan. *stampe*, D. *stampen*, G. *stampfen*, to stamp, nasalized forms corresponding to Icel. *stappa*, D. *stappen*, G. *stapfen*, to step.] To strike or press forcibly by thrusting the foot downward; to impress with some mark or figure; to mark with an impression; to imprint; to fix deeply; as, *stamp* in memory; to coin or mint; to affix a stamp to, as a postage or receipt stamp; to cut out with a stamp; to crush by the downward action of a kind of pestle, as ore in a stamp mill.—*v.i.* To strike the foot forcibly downward, or to walk in such a manner, esp. in rage.—*n.* The act of stamping; an instrument for making impressions on other bodies; a mark imprinted; an official mark set upon things chargeable with some duty or tax showing that the duty is paid: often used as a means of raising revenue; a small piece of stamped paper used by government; a postage stamp; an instrument for cutting materials into various forms by a downward pressure; general character fixed on anything; as, the *stamp* of genius; sort or character; as, a man of the same *stamp*; *metal.* a kind of hammer for crushing or beating ores to powder.—**to stamp out**; to extinguish, as fire, by stamping on with the foot; to extirpate; to eradicate; to suppress or quell by strong measures, as a revolution.

stam·pede, stam·pēd′, *n.* [Amer. Sp. *estampida*, stampede, Sp. crack, crash, connected with Sp. *estampar*, stamp, from Teut.] A sudden rush or headlong flight of a body of animals in fright, as cattle, horses, elephants; any headlong general flight, as of troops in panic; an unconcerted general rush or movement, as of persons actuated by a common impulse.—*v.i.*—*stampeded, stampeding.* To scatter or flee in a stampede, as cattle or persons; make an unconcerted general rush, as persons actuated by a common impulse.—*v.t.* To produce a stampede among; cause to stampede. —**stam·ped·er**, *n.*—**stam·ped·ing·ly**, *adv.*

stamp·er, stam′pèr, *n.* One who or that which stamps; an instrument, tool, or machine for stamping; a pestle, esp. in a stamp mill; one who applies the postmark and cancels the postage stamps on letters, in a post office.

stamp·ing ground, *n.* A person's or

animal's most familiar surroundings or usual place of activity.

stamp mill, *n.* *Metal.* a mill or machine in which ore is crushed to a powder by means of heavy stamps or pestles. Also *quartz battery.*

stance, stans, *n.* [Obs. Fr. *stance*, O.Fr. *estance*, stand, stay, station, position, = It. *stanza*, < L. *stare*, stand: cf. *stanza*.] A style of standing or positioning the body; a particular attitude, emotional or mental, toward something; *sports*, the way a player places his feet and/or body when he is playing at his sport.

stanch, stanch, stanch, stänch, *v.t.* [O.Fr. *estanchier* (Fr. *étancher*), ult. < L. *stagnum*, pool, pond: cf. L. *stagnare*, form a pool of standing water, also make stagnant, and E. *stagnate*.] To stop the flow of, as a liquid, esp. blood; stop the flow of blood from, as a wound. Also *staunch.*—**stanch·er**, *n.*

stanch, stanch, stänch, stanch, *a.* Staunch.

stan·chion, stan′shan, *n.* [O.Fr. *estanchon* (Fr. *étançon*), < *estance*, a prop, also stand, station.] An upright bar, beam, post, or support, as in a window, in a stall for cattle, in a building, structure, or framework, or in or on a ship.—*v.t.* To furnish with stanchions; to secure by or to a stanchion or stanchions.

stand, stand, *v.i.*—*stood, standing.* [O.E. *standan* (pret. *stōd*) = standan = O.H.G. *stantan* = Icel. *standa* = Goth. *standan*, stand; akin to L. *stare*, stand, *sistere*, cause to stand, stand, Gr. *histánai*, cause to stand, stand, Skt. *sthā*, stand.] To take or keep an upright position on the feet; to have a specified height when in this position, as: He *stands* six feet in his socks. To cease walking or moving; to halt; to stop; to take a position or stand as indicated; as, to *stand* aside or back; to remain firm or steadfast, as in a cause; to take up or maintain a position or attitude with respect to others or to some question; to adopt a certain course, as of adherence, support, opposition, or resistance; to be in an upright position, as things; to be set on end; to rest on or as on a support; to be set, placed, or fixed; to be located or situated; to be at a certain degree, as in a scale of measurement or valuation, as: The temperature *stands* at 80°. To show a specified position of the parties concerned, as: The score *stands* 14 to 12 at the quarter. To resist change, decay, or destruction; to continue in force or remain valid, as: That rule still *stands*. To remain motionless, still, or stationary; to be or become stagnant, as water; to be or remain in a specified state, condition, relation, or situation, as persons or things, as: He *stood* alone in that opinion. To point: said of a hunting dog; *Brit.* to become or be a candidate, as for political office. *Naut.* to move or tend steadily in a particular direction; to take or hold a particular course at sea.—*v.t.* To cause to stand; to set upright; set; to face or encounter; as, to *stand* an assault; to endure, undergo, or submit to; as, to *stand* trial; to endure or undergo without hurt or damage, or without giving way, as: Material that will *stand* wear. To put up with or tolerate; *colloq.* bear the expense for, as, to *stand* him to a dinner.—*n.* The act of standing; an assuming of, or a remaining in, an upright position; a coming to a position of rest, as a halt or a stop; a determined effort against or for something, as of retreating troops, for defense or resistance; a position taken or maintained with respect to others or to some question; the place where a person or thing stands, as a position or station. The place where a witness stands to testify in court; also *witness stand.* Usu. *pl.* a raised platform or other structure, as for spectators at a race course or an athletic field, or along the route of a parade, or for a speaker. A framework on or in which articles are placed for support or exhibition; a piece of furniture of various forms, on or in which to put articles; as, a wash*stand*; a small, light table; a stall, booth, table, or the like, where articles are exposed for sale or some business is carried on; as, a fruit *stand* or news*stand*; a site or location for business; a place or station occupied by vehicles which are available for hire; the growing trees or those of a particular species or grade, in a given area; a standing growth, as of grass or wheat; a halt of a theatrical company on tour; as, a one-night *stand*.—**stand a chance** or **a show,** to have a chance or possibility, esp. to have a chance of winning, surviving, or the like.—**stand for,** to be a symbol of; represent; to put up with or tolerate.—**stand on,** to base one's position on; to rest or depend on; to be based on; to be punctilious about; to assert or claim respect for, as one's rights; *naut.* to continue on the same course or tack.—**stand o·ver,** to postpone for consideration, treatment, or settlement.—**stand to rea·son,** to be in accordance with reason.—**stand·er,** *n.*

stand·ard, stan'dėrd, *n.* Anything taken by general consent as a basis of comparison, or established as a criterion; an authorized unit of weight or measure; the legal rate of intrinsic value in coins; the prescribed degree of fineness for gold or silver; a certain commodity, as gold or silver, treated as being of invariable value and serving as a measure of value for all other commodities; a grade or level of exellence or advancement generally regarded as right or fitting; as, the *standard* of living in a community; a grade of quality for a commodity; something which stands upright, as a tall candlestick, a timber, or a rod; *hort.* a tree, shrub, or other plant having a tall, erect stem, and not grown in bush form or trained on a support; *bot.* the broad upper petal of flowers in the legume family; *ornith.* a lengthened wing feather. A flag, emblematic figure, or other object raised on a pole to indicate a rallying point of an army or fleet; any of various flags, esp. a long, narrow pennant; a soldier who carries a standard; *Brit.* any of the grades or degrees of attainment by which school children are classified. —*a.* Serving as a standard of weight, measure, or value, or of comparison or judgment; conformed or conforming to any such standard; of recognized excellence or established authority; standing or set upright; *hort.* grown as a standard.

stand·ard-bear·er, stan'dėrd bâr"ėr, *n.* A conspicuous leader of a movement, as a head of a political party. *Milit.* an individual assigned to carry an organizational flag; a guidon. One who carries a banner in a procession; an African bird, *Macrodipteryx longipennis,* of the goatsucker family.

stand·ard·bred, stan'dėrd·bred", *n.* (Usu. cap.) a breed of speedy horses who are particularly good trotters and pacers, known for their endurance.—stan'dėrd·bred', *a.* Having reference to standardbred horses.

stand·ard can·dle, *n.* The international standard unit for measurement of the intensity of light; *phys.* the luminous intensity equal to 1/60 of the luminous intensity of a square centimeter of a black body heated to 1773.5°C., which is equal to the temperature at which platinum solidifies.

stand·ard de·vi·a·tion, *n. Statistics,* a measure of the degree of scattering of a frequency distribution about its arithmetic mean, equal to the square root of the mean of the squared deviations from the distribution mean. Also *mean square deviation.*

Stand·ard Eng·lish, *n.* The linguistic patterns of the English language, both oral and written, which are accepted and used by those considered to be educated and articulate in the use of English as a mother tongue.

stand·ard gauge, *n.* A width of railroad track being 4 ft. 8½ in., considered to be standard; any locomotive or car used on a standard gauge railroad; a gauge used in determining the standard size of tools.

stand·ard·ize, stan'dėr·dīz", *v.t.*—*standardized, standardizing.* To conform to or regulate by a standard; bring to or make of an established standard size, shape, weight, quality, or strength; as, to *standardize* manufactured articles or parts; to compare with or test by a standard.—**stand·ard·i·za·tion,** *n.*

stand·ard of liv·ing, *n.* The amount and quality of material goods and services which a person, group, class, or nation needs and uses to live in a particular way or style. Also **stand·ard of life.**

stand·ard time, *n.* The mean solar time based on the transit of the sun over a specific meridian, called the time meridian, and adopted for use over a considerable area or time zone; the local time of a zone which is established by an approximate multiple of 15° longitude from the base meridian of Greenwich, England, because each 15° of longitude makes a difference of exactly one hour. In the U.S., the mean local time of the seventy-fifth meridian, used approximately between 67.5° and 82.5° west longitude, is eastern *standard time,* abbr. *EST*; the mean local time of the ninetieth meridian, used approximately between 82.5° and 97.5° west longitude, is central *standard time,* abbr. *CST*; the mean local time of the one hundred and fifth meridian, used approximately between 97.5° and 112.5° west longitude, is mountain *standard time,* abbr. *MST*; the mean local time of the one hundred and twentieth meridian, used approximately between 112.5° and 127.5° west longitude, is Pacific *standard time,* abbr. *PST*.

stand by, *v.t.* To side with, aid, uphold, or sustain, as a person; to adhere to, as an agreement or promise; to affirm or maintain, as a conviction.—*v.i.* To stand near at hand; be present; to be ready; to stand aside; wait passively. *Radio, TV,* to be ready to perform when a signal is given, as an announcer; as a listener or viewer, to stay tuned during an interruption to a program.—**stand·by,** stand'bī", *n. pl.* **stand·bys.** One who stands by another to render assistance; a staunch supporter or adherent; someone or something to be relied upon; a situation in which a person or thing stands ready to fill a vacancy or need, as an airline passenger or a naval vessel, usu. preceded by *on*; *radio, TV,* a person or program held in readiness to be used in case of an interruption in the schedule.—*a.* Maintained as a resource in case of need.

stand down, *v.i. Law,* to leave the witness stand.

stand·ee, stan·dē', *n. Colloq.* one who stands when no seats are available, as in a public conveyance or the theater.

stand-in, stand'in", *n.* A person employed to substitute for a movie star during dangerous action or while cameras and lights are being adjusted; a substitute; *colloq.* a favorable or influential position.—**stand in,** *v.i.* To act as a substitute. *Colloq.* to enjoy the influence or favor of; to be on favorable terms with; to be in partnership, association, or conspiracy with; also **stand in with.**

stand·ing, stan'ding, *n.* Position or status as to social, professional, or personal reputation; as, his *standing* as a lawyer;

good reputation, position, or credit; length of existence, continuance, residence, membership, or experience; as, a friend of long *standing*; the act of one who or that which stands; *sports,* a ranking of teams or individual contestants according to their competitive performances during a given season.—*a.* Remaining in an upright or erect position; performed in or from an erect position; as, a *standing* jump; motionless, still, or stagnant, as water; lasting, permanent, or continuing for an unlimited period of time; continuing in operation, force, or use; as, a *standing* rule.

stand·ing ar·my, *n.* Troops organized and maintained on a permanent basis.

stand·ing com·mit·tee, *n.* A fixed committee, as of a society or legislature: opposed to *ad hoc committee.*

stand·ing crop, *n.* That crop which remains uncut or otherwise left on the field.

stand·ing or·der, *n. Milit.* an order of relative permanence establishing procedure; *parl. law,* the permanent rules pertaining to procedure during all sessions of an assembly.

stand·ing room, *n.* Room or space in which to stand; accommodation only for standing, as in a theater where all the seats have been taken.

stand·ing wave, *n. Phys.* A graphic representation of the oscillatory motion of some physical phenomenon, as a swinging pendulum; that physically observed effect of a driven oscillator on a compressible substance, as a siren. Also *stationary wave.*

stand·ish, stan'dish, *n.* [Appar. < *stand* and *dish.*] *Archaic,* a stand for ink, pens, and other writing materials.

stand off, *v.t.* To evade or put off; to deny or be unsuccessful in agreement or compliance with.—*v.i.* To remain at some distance; *naut.* to sail or maintain a certain course that is away from shore.—**stand-off,** stand'af", stand'of", *n.* A standing off or apart; a tie or draw, as in a game; something that counter-balances. Also **stand·off.**—*a.* Standing off or apart; reserved or distant. Also **stand·off.**

stand-off·ish, stand'ạ'fish, stand'of'ish, *a.* Somewhat reserved and unfriendly.—**stand-off·ish·ness,** *n.*

stand oil, *n.* A drying oil, made by thickening a mixture of linseed oil and wood oil: used in making printing inks, paints, and varnishes.

stand out, *v.i.* To protrude, project, or stick out; to be distinct or clear in relief; to excel; to continue in resistance or opposition; *slang,* to refuse to conform with the majority.—**stand·out, stand-out,** stand'out", *n.* One who is notable, conspicuous, or prominent, esp. due to excellence.

stand·pat, stand'pat", *a. Colloq.* characterized by refusing to consider or agree to change. — **stand·pat·ter,** stand'pat'ėr, stand'pat"ėr, *n.*

stand·pipe, stand'pīp", *n.* A vertical pipe or tower into which water is pumped in order to obtain a required level for adequate pressure.

stand·point, stand'point", *n.* [Tr. G. *standpunkt.*] The point at which one stands to view something; the mental position from which one views and judges things, or a mental point of view; view point.

stand·still, stand'stil", *n.* A standing still; a state of cessation of movement or action; a halt; a stop.

stand-up, stand'up", *a.* Standing erect; upright; performed, taken, or consumed while one stands, as a meal; stiffened to remain erect without folds, as a collar; pertaining to a comedian who delivers monologues on stage by himself.—**stand up,** *v.i.* To remain whole or intact; to hold up under pressure; to assume an upright position.—*v.t. Colloq.* to fail to keep an appointment or a date with.—**stand up for,** to side with against criticism; to support or defend; to serve as best man or maid of honor for in a wedding.—**stand up to,** to confront or deal with courageously.

Stan·ford-Bi·net test, stan′ferd·bi·nā′ test″, *n. Psychol.* An intelligence test consisting of a series of questions and performance tasks, originally developed at Stanford University in 1916 as an American revision of the French Binet-Simon scale for intelligence; the further revised versions of this intelligence test. Also **Stan·ford re·vi·sion.**

stan·hope, stan′hōp″, stan′op, *n.* A light two- or four-wheeled carriage without a top, with high seat and closed back.

sta·nine, stā′nīn″, *n. (sta)*ndard and *nine.*] A normalized standard aptitude score of single-digit units ranging from the lowest, or one, to the highest, or nine, and having a median of five: first developed for use by the U.S. Air Force during World War II.

stan·na·ry, stan′a·rē, *n.* pl. **stan·na·ries.** [M.L. *stannaria,* < L.L. *stannum,* tin.] A tin-mining region or district; a tin mine; a tin smelter.

stan·nic, stan′ik, *a.* [< L. *stannum,* tin.] Pertaining to or containing tin, esp. tin with a valence of four.

stan·nite, stan′īt, *n.* A granular mineral, Cu_2FeSnS_4, of an iron-black, steel-gray, or bronze-yellow color, with a metallic luster, consisting chiefly of the sulfides of tin, copper, and iron; an ore of tin. Also **tin py·ri·tes.**

stan·nous, stan′us, *a.* Pertaining to or containing tin, esp. tin with a valence of two.

stan·za, stan′za, *n.* [It., < L. *stare,* stand: cf. *stance.*] *Pros.* a group of lines of verse, usu. four or more in number, arranged in pattern as regards length, rhyme scheme, and meter, and forming a division of a poem.—**stan·zaed,** *a.*—**stan·za·ic, stan·za·i·cal,** stan·zā′ik, *a.*—**stan·za·i·cal·ly,** *adv.*

sta·pe·li·a, sta·pē′lē·a, *n.* [N.L., after J. B. van *Stapel,* died 1636, D. botanist.] Any of the plants of the milkweed family constituting the genus *Stapelia,* native in southern Africa and sometimes seen in cultivation, with short, fleshy, leafless stems, and flowers which are often oddly colored or mottled and in most species emit a fetid, carrionlike odor.

sta·pes, stā′pēz, *n.* pl. **sta·pes, sta·pe·dez.** [L., a stirrup.] *Anat.* the innermost of the three small bones in the middle ear of mammals.—**sta·pe·di·al,** sta·pē′dē·al, *a.*

staph, staf, *n.* Staphylococcus.

staph·y·lo·coc·cus, staf″i·lo·kok′us, *n.* pl. **staph·y·lo·coc·ci,** staf″i·lo·kok′sī. [N.L. < Gr. *staphylē,* a bunch of grapes, and N.L. *coccus,* seed.] *Bact.* any of certain species of the genus *Staphylococcus,* in which the individual organisms form irregular clusters, as *S. aureus,* a species which causes inflammation and the formation of pus. Also *staph.*—**staph·y·lo·coc·cal, staph·y·lo·coc·cic,** staf″i·lo·kok′al, staf″i·lo·kok′sik, *a.*

sta·ple, stā′pl, *n.* [M.E. *stapul, stapel,* appar. < O.E. *stapol,* post, prop, = M.L.G. *stapel,* post, platform, pile; prob. akin to E. *step.*] A loop of metal with pointed ends for driving into a surface to hold a hasp, hook, pin, bolt, or the like; some other device of similar shape or function; a bent piece of wire used to bind papers, magazines, or sections of a book together.—*v.t.*—**stapled, stapling.** To secure or fasten by a staple or staples.—**sta·pler,** stā′pler, *n.* A wire-stitching machine used in bookbinding; a hand-operated device for fastening paper together with staples.

sta·ple, stā′pl, *n.* [Same as D. and G. *stapel,* a post, prop; so also Sw. *stapel,* Dan. *stabel;* same root as that of *stamp* and *step.*] *Usu. pl.* a necessary or basic article, esp. a food, as sugar. The principal commodity grown or manufactured in a country, district, or town; the principal element or ingredient in anything; raw or unmanufactured material; *textiles,* the thread or pile of wool, cotton, or flax; as, wool of a long or coarse *staple. Archaic,* a town where certain commodities, esp. wool, were taken for sale; a settled marketplace; an emporium.—*a.* Established in commerce; as, a *staple* trade; chief; principal; regularly produced or made for market.—*v.t.*—**stapled, stapling.** To sort or adjust the different staples of, as wool.—**sta·pler,** stā′pler, *n.* A dealer in staple commodities; one employed in assorting wool according to its staple.

star, stär, *n.* [O.E. *steorra,* Sc. *starn,* Icel. *stjarna,* Goth. *stairno,* D. *ster,* O.D. *sterne,* G. *stern;* cogn. L. *stella* (or *sterula*), also *astrum,* Gr. *astēr,* Armor. *stēren,* Skt. *târâ* (for *stârâ*), *stri,* to straw, from scattering light.] Any luminous body seen in the heavens, at night appearing apparently as fixed points of light; any celestial body except the moon, the planets, comets, meteors, and nebulae; any of the celestial bodies that shine by their own light, as the sun; *astrol.* any of the celestial bodies which are said to influence man and his destiny. Anything which resembles a star; a figure with points radiating like the spokes of a wheel; an ornamental figure rayed like a star worn upon the breast to indicate rank or honor; a radiated mark in writing or printing; an asterisk (*) used as a reference to a note in the margin or to fill a blank in writing or printing where letters or words are omitted; a distinguished, celebrated, or prominent person; a person who has performed conspicuously in any given field; a brilliant theatrical or operatic performer; a movie star.—*v.t.*—**starred, starring.** To set or adorn with stars; to bespangle; to set apart for special attention with an asterisk; to feature as the leading performer.—*v.i.* To shine as a star; to be celebrated; to appear as a distinguished actor in a theater of inferior players.—*a.*—**star·less,** *a.*—**star·like,** *a.*

star ap·ple, *n.* A W. Indian tree, *Chrysophyllum cainito;* its edible fruit, of the size of an apple, which when cut across presents a star-shaped figure within.

star·board, stär′berd, stär′bōrd″, stär′bärd″, *n.* [O.E. *stēorbord,* that is, *steer-board,* < *stēoran,* to steer, the old rudder being a kind of large oar used on the right side of the ship.] *Naut.* the right-hand side of a ship looking toward the prow: opposed to *port.*—*a.* Pertaining to the right-hand side of a ship; being or lying on the right-hand side.—*adv.* In the direction of starboard.—*v.t., v.i.* To steer to the right.

starch, stärch, *n.* [M.E. *starche,* akin to O.E. *stearc,* stiff, rigid, E. *stark.*] A white tasteless carbohydrate, $(C_6H_{10}O_5)_n,$ occurring in the form of minute granules in the seeds, tubers, and other parts of plants, and forming an important constituent of rice, corn, wheat, beans, potatoes, and many other vegetable foods; a commercial preparation of the substance used to stiffen fabrics in laundering, and employed for many industrial purposes; *fig.* stiffness or formality, as of manner; *colloq.* stamina, vigor, or vitality.—*v.t.* To stiffen or treat with starch; *fig.* to make stiff or rigidly formal.—**starch·i·ness,** *n.*—**starch·y,** stär′chē, *a.*—**starchier, starchiest.**

Star Cham·ber, *n.* [Said to have been so called from a decoration of stars on its roof (ceiling).] A former English court of civil and criminal jurisdiction concerned with the interests of the crown, noted for its arbitrary procedure, and abolished in 1641; any tribunal, committee, or the like which proceeds by arbitrary or unfair methods.

star-crossed, stär′krạst″, stär′krost″, *a.* Without the benefit of favorable astrological influence; ill-fated; as, *star-crossed* lovers; unfortunate.

star·dom, stär′dom, *n.* The world or class of professional stars, as of the performing arts or sports; the status of a star.

star dust, *n.* Masses of stars so minute in appearance as to suggest particles of dust; *colloq.* a dreamy, romantic, enchanting mood.

stare, stâr, *v.i.*—**stared, staring.** [O.E. *starian,* to stare, to gaze; D. and L.G. *staren,* G. *starren,* Icel. *stara;* lit. 'to look fixedly,' the root being that of G. and Sw. *starr,* stiff, fixed, E. *stark,* stiff, strong.] To look with eyes fixed wide open; to be conspicuous or extremely apparent; to stand on end, as feathers or hair; to gaze intently, as in admiration, surprise, horror, or impudence.—*v.t.* To affect or abash by gazing at; to look earnestly or fixedly at.—*n.* The act or look of one who stares.—**star·er,** *n.*

sta·re de·ci·sis, stâr′ē di·sī′sis, *n. Law,* the doctrine of adhering to principles established in prior judicial decisions unless these decisions contradict the basic concepts of justice.

star fac·et, *n. Jewelry,* a facet, one of eight, of the crown of a brilliant-cut gem, as a diamond.

star·fish, stär′fish″, *n.* pl. **star·fish, star·fish·es.** Any echinoderm of the class *Asteroidea,* comprising marine animals having the body radially arranged, usu. in the form of a star, with five or more rays or arms radiating from a central disk. Also *asteroid.*

star·flow·er, stär′flou″ĕr, *n.* Any of various plants with starlike flowers, as the star-of-Bethlehem, genus *Ornithogalum;* a plant of the primulaceous genus *Trientalis.*

star·gaze, stär′gāz″, *v.i.*—**stargazed, stargazing.** To gaze at the stars; *fig.* to engage in daydreaming.—**star·gaz·ing,** *n.*

star·gaz·er, stär′gā″zĕr, *n.* One who gazes at the stars; an astrologer; any of various salt-water fishes of the family *Uranoscopidae,* with small eyes protruding from the top of the head; *fig.* one who daydreams or is absent-minded.

star grass, *n.* Any of various grasslike plants with star-shaped flowers or a stellate arrangement of leaves, as *Hypoxis hirsuta,* a N. American plant of the amaryllis family.

stark, stärk, *a.* [O.E. *stearc,* stiff, hard; G. and Sw. *stark,* D. *sterk,* Icel. *sterkr;* akin G. *starr,* stiff; E. *stare. Starch* is a softened form.] Mere, pure, or downright; as, *stark* nonsense; harsh or desolate, as a landscape; very severe or grim, as a furnished room; stiff; rigid, as in death.—*adv.* Wholly; entirely.—**stark·ly,** *adv.*—**stark·ness,** *n.*

star·let, stär′lit, *n.* Any young actress being groomed and given publicity leading to eventual stardom, esp. in the movies; *astron.* a diminutive star or similar heavenly body.

star·light, stär′līt″, *n.* The light proceeding from the stars.—*a.* Lighted by the stars; also **star·lit,** stär′lit.

star·ling, stär′ling, *n.* [O.E. *stærlinc,* < *stær* = O.H.G. G. *stara* = Icel. *stari,* starling; akin to L. *sturnus.*] Any of numerous passerine birds of the genus *Sturnus,* esp. the common, gregarious species, *S. vulgaris,* with a dark, iridescent plumage, native to Europe and introduced into N. America.

star·ling, stär′ling, *n.* [Origin uncertain.] A protecting enclosure of piles, as for resisting waves.

star-of-Beth·le·hem, stär′ov·beth′lē·em, stär′ov·beth′li·hem″, *n.* A liliaceous plant, *Ornithogalum umbellatum,* native in Europe and common in N. American gardens, with star-shaped flowers that are white within and greenish on the underside.

star of Beth·le·hem, *n.* The star which the New Testament says led the Wise Men to Bethlehem and to the stable where Jesus Christ was born. Matthew ii. 1–10.

Star of Da·vid, *n.* A geometric figure in the form of a six-pointed star, composed of two equilateral triangles interlaced or placed one upon the other, used chiefly as a Jewish religious symbol, but also as an amulet, and formerly as a magic charm. Also *Magen David, Mogen David, Solomon's seal.*

star route, *n.* [So called from asterisks used to mark such routes in official papers.] In the U.S. postal service, a route, other than the ordinary routes, over which mail is carried by private individuals on special contract, often from railroad station to post office or from post office to post office and, in rural areas, usu. requiring delivery to private mailboxes.

star·ry, stär′ē, *a.*—*starrier, starriest.* Abounding with or lighted by stars; as, a *starry* sky; of, pertaining to, or proceeding from the stars; as, *starry* light; of the nature of or consisting of stars; as, *starry* worlds; resembling a star; star-shaped or stellate; shining like stars; as, *starry* eyes; studded with starlike figures or markings.—**star··ri·ly,** *adv.*—**star·ri·ness,** *n.*

star·ry-eyed, stär′ē·īd″, *a.* Tending to be idealistic or fanciful.

Stars and Bars, *n.* An informal name for the flag adopted by the Confederate States of America, having three bars, red, white, and red, and a blue union with seven white stars.

Stars and Stripes, *n.* An informal name for the flag of the United States, consisting of thirteen horizontal stripes, alternately red and white, and a blue union with fifty white stars to represent the states.

star sap·phire, *n.* A convex-shaped sapphire which is cut in such a way that a six-pointed star is visible.

star shell, *n.* A shell designed to burst when fired into the air, releasing a shower of bright, starlike lights, used for illuminating the enemy's position and for signaling.

star-span·gled, stär′spang″gld, *a.* Decorated or spangled with stars.—**The Star-Span·gled Ban·ner,** a patriotic song written in 1814 by Francis Scott Key, and adopted as the national anthem of the U.S. by act of Congress in 1931; the flag of the U.S.

start, stärt, *v.i.* [O.E. *sterte, sturte, stirte,* not in Icel.; allied to D. *storten,* Dan. *styrte,* G. *stürzen,* to rush, to spring.] To move suddenly and spasmodically; to make a sudden and involuntary motion of the body, caused by surprise, pain, or any sudden feeling; to shrink or wince; to make a sudden or unexpected change of place; to spring up; to protrude, as eyes; to change condition at once; to set out; to commence a course, as a race or a journey; to be one of the original participants in a race; to shift or spring from a fixed position; to be dislocated.—*v.t.* To rouse suddenly from concealment; to cause to flee or fly from a place of concealment; as, to *start* a hare; to begin; to set going; to originate, establish, or introduce; to tap or withdraw, as the contents of a container; to displace; to aid or encourage.—*n.* A sudden involuntary twitch, spring, or motion, caused by surprise, fear, or pain; a sudden change of place; a quick movement; a bursting forth; a spasmodic effort; the beginning of a crack or opening

in a structure; a beginning of motion; the setting of something going; a first motion from a place or in a race; the outset.

start·er, stär′tẽr, *n.* One who starts; one who sets out; one who sets persons or things in motion, as a bus or train dispatcher, or one who signals the start of a race; in an automobile, the electric motor that starts the internal-combustion engine; in a horse race, an animal who starts as a competitor; a microorganism used to induce fermentation in the manufacture of some dairy products.

star this·tle, *n.* A low, spreading composite plant, *Centaurea calcitrapa,* introduced into N. America from Europe, with purple flower heads; a related plant, *C. solstitialis,* with yellow flowers.

star·tle, stär′tl, *v.t.*—*startled, startling.* [Dim. of *start.*] To excite by sudden alarm, surprise, or apprehension; to alarm.—*v.i.* To be moved with a start through surprise or alarm; to start involuntarily.—*n.* A sudden surprise or shock; an alarm.

star·tling, stärt′ling, *a.* Causing sudden alarm or surprise.—**star·tling·ly,** *adv.*

star·va·tion, stär·vā′shan, *n.* [One of those words which have a Latin termination tacked on to an Anglo-Saxon base; cf. *flirtation, talkative, readable.*] The state of starving or being starved; extreme suffering from want of food.—*a.* Liable to cause starvation; insufficient to maintain the ordinary level of subsistence; as, *starvation* wages.

starve, stärv, *v.i.*—*starved, starving.* [O.E. *steorfan,* to perish of hunger or cold.—L.G. *starven,* D. *sterven,* G. *sterben,* to die.] To perish or suffer extremely from hunger; to suffer from poverty or want; to be overwhelmed by a sense of deprivation, usu. followed by *for*; as, *starving for* attention; *Brit. dial.* to die or suffer severely from cold.—*v.t.* To kill or distress with hunger; to subdue by famine; to destroy by want; to deprive of some strongly felt need; *Brit. dial.* to cause to die or suffer severely from cold.

starve·ling, stärv′ling, *a.* Hungry; pining with want; lean; of poor quality or condition.—*n.* A person, animal, or plant that is thin and weak through want of nutriment.

stash, stash, *v.t. Slang,* to hide or store in a secret place for safekeeping or future use.—*n. Slang.* A place for hiding or its contents; a cache.

sta·sis, stā′sis, stas′is, *n.* pl. **sta·ses,** stā′sēz, stas′ēz. The state of inactivity or static balance caused by the opposition of equal forces; *pathol.* the retardation or stoppage of the regular flow of fluids in the body, as of the contents of the intestines or of blood in the circulatory system, due to a diseased condition.

state, stāt, *n.* [O.Fr. *estat,* state, condition, etc. (Fr. *état*); < L. *status,* state, position, < *sto,* to stand (seen also in *station, status, statue, stage, rest, arrest, constant*).] Condition of a person or thing; as, a *state* of repair; condition of circumstances; as, a *state* of bankruptcy; a condition of a specific kind; as, an anxiety *state*; a condition in form, structure, or nature; as, a liquid *state*; a condition of certain time, phase, or stage; as, an embryonic *state*; a condition connoting riches, rank, dignity, and pomp; as, traveling in *state,* lying in *state*; the body politic of a nation; the sovereign political entity of a fixed territory; the supreme civil authority recognized by a politically organized people of a given geographical area; the civil rule of government, as distinguished from *church* or *military*; (*sometimes cap.*) one of the commonwealths or bodies politic which together make up a federal union; as, a *state* of the U.S. The authority or domain of a regional government, as distinguished from the *federal*;

(*cap.*), *colloq.* the U.S. State Department; (*cap.*), *pl.* the continental U.S., preceded by *the*: usu. used overseas.—*a.* Of, for, or pertaining to a state or nation; of or denoting a government agency or authority; as, *state* police; involving or characterized by protocol or ceremony; as, a *state* dinner.

state, stāt, *v.t.*—*stated, stating.* To express, as the particulars of a thing, in writing or words; as, to *state* the problem; to set down in detail; to set forth in a formal manner; to narrate; to recite; to aver, allege, or declare; to settle.—**stat·a·ble, state·a·ble,** *a.*—**stat·ed,** *a.* Established, determined, fixed, or settled; as, *stated* rules; official, pronounced as fact, or recognized.—**stat·ed·ly,** *adv.*

state aid, *n.* Financing extended to a local public institution, as a library, school, or hospital, by the state government.

State bank, *n.* A bank chartered by the state in which it is located, and conducted according to that state's banking laws.

state cap·i·tal·ism, *n.* A type of capitalism in which most of the industry, natural resources, and capital are controlled by the state.

state church, *n.* Established church.

state·craft, stāt′kraft″, stāt′kräft″, *n.* The art of conducting state affairs; statesmanship.

State flow·er, *n.* A flower chosen by a state as its floral emblem.

State guard, *n.* A militia force activated usu. when the state's National Guard reverts to federal control in wartime or during a period of national emergency.

state·hood, stāt′hụd, *n.* The condition or status of a state, esp. a state of the U.S.

State·house, stāt′hous″, *n.* The building in which the legislature of a state holds its sittings; the capitol building.

state·less, stāt′lis, *a.* Being without a state or nationality.—**state·less·ness,** *n.*

state·ly, stāt′lē, *a.*—*statelier, stateliest.* Dignified; imposing; lofty; majestic; magnificent.—*adv.*—**state·li·ness,** *n.*

state med·i·cine, *n.* Socialized medicine.

state·ment, stāt′ment, *n.* The act or the manner of stating something; something stated; a communication in speech or writing setting forth facts or particulars; a declaration, esp. of a formal, explicit, or specific character; the appearance of a subject or theme in a musical piece; *com.* an abstract of an account, as one rendered periodically to show the balance due.

state of war, *n.* Open armed conflict between or among sovereign states or belligerent powers, esp. armed conflict recognized by formal declaration of the powers involved; any intense and hostile strife between sovereign states; the time a period of war exists.

State pris·on, *n.* (*Sometimes l.c.*) a prison run by a state.

sta·ter, stā′tẽr, *n.* [L. < Gr. *statér,* < *histánai,* cause to stand, weigh.] Any of various gold or silver coins of the ancient Greek states or cities.

state·room, stāt′rōm″, stāt′rụm″, *n.* A private room on a ship or train.

State's at·tor·ney, *n.* A lawyer in the U.S., usu. appointed, who represents the state in any judicial proceedings. Also **State at·tor·ney.**

state's ev·i·dence, *n. Law.* Testimony given by one against an accomplice in a felony, usu. under promise of immunity; evidence by the state in criminal cases.

States-Gen·er·al, stāts′jen′ẽr·al, *n.* The legislative assemblies of France before the revolution of 1789; the parliament of the Netherlands.

state·side, stāt′sīd″, *a.* Toward, leaving, or being in the U.S.—*adv.* In or in the direction of the U.S.

states·man, stāts′man, n. pl. **states·men.** A man who is versed in government and in the management of government affairs; one engaged in directing the affairs of a government; a political leader showing an unselfish interest in the common good. **states·man·like**, **states·man·ly**, a.— **states·man·ship**, stāts′man·ship″, n.

state so·cial·ism, n. Government control of the economy of a country by ownership of its industry and public utilities; one of various socioeconomic or political theories or movements advocating nationalization, as opposed to *capitalism.* See *socialism.* Compare *Nazism, communism, Marxism, Fabianism, social democracy.*

States' right·er, n. One who advocates States' rights; one who objects to Federal intervention in or usurpation of powers he deems the proper concern of the state.

States' rights, n. pl., sing. or pl. in constr. All powers that the Constitution neither gives the Federal government nor denies the state; an interpretation of the Constitution marked by an extremely broad conception of these state privileges and opposing Federal claims to these powers through liberal interpretation; belief in the right of the state to nullify an action of the Federal government that it deems unconstitutional. Also **State rights.**

State u·ni·ver·si·ty, n. A university administered and supported by a government of any state in the U.S. as the highest institution of learning in its system of public education.

stat·ic, stat′ik, a. [Gr. *statikós,* causing to stand, pertaining to weighing, < *histánai,* cause to stand, weigh.] Pertaining to or characterized by a fixed or stationary condition; exhibiting slight or no change, movement, or development; pertaining to bodies at rest or forces in equilibrium; *sociol.* pertaining to a mode of social life embedded in tradition. *Elect.* noting or pertaining to electricity at rest, as that produced by friction; noting or pertaining to atmospheric electricity that interferes with radar, radio reception, or television reception. *Phys.* acting by mere weight without producing motion; as, *static* pressure; *econ.* pertaining to stable or constant rather than fluctuating conditions. Also **stat·i·cal.**—n. A disturbance in radio or television reception due to atmospheric electrical interference; *elect.* atmospheric electricity at rest. *Slang,* difficulty; back talk.—**stat·i·cal·ly**, *adv.*

stat·i·ce, stat′i·sē, n. [N.L., in L. a kind of astringent herb, < Gr. *statikē,* prop. fem. of *statikós,* causing to stand.] Sea lavender; thrift.

stat·ic line, n. A flexible cord or webbing which is attached to both the parachute pack and the inside of an airplane, and serves to open the pack and withdraw the parachute, as in dropping supplies or paratroops.

stat·ics, stat′iks, n. pl. but sing. in constr. [Fr. *statique,* < Gr. *statikē,* statics, < *statikós,* causing to stop or stand; same root as *state,* stand.] That branch of mechanics which treats of the relations of forces in equilibrium, the body upon which they act being in a state of rest.

stat·ic tube, n. *Phys.* a tube that measures the static pressure, as distinguished from the impact pressure, in a stream of fluid.

sta·tion, stā′shan, n. [O.Fr. Fr. *station,* < L. *statio(n-),* a standing, position, post, station, < *stare,* stand; see *stand.*] The act or manner of standing; the place in which anything stands; position; a position assigned for standing or remaining in. *Milit.* a place where soldiers are garrisoned; a military post. The headquarters of the police force or other public service in a municipality or a district thereof; a place or building equipped for some particular kind of work, research, or the like; as, a postal *station;* a studio equipped for radio and television broadcasting; standing, as of persons or things, in a scale of estimation or dignity; relative position in the social scale; the place at which something stops; a regular stopping place, as on a railroad; the building or collection of buildings erected at such a place; *surv.* a point where an observation is taken.—v.t. To assign a station to; place or post in a station or position.

sta·tion·ar·y, stā′sha·ner″ē, a. [L. *stationarius.*] Remaining in the same station or place; not moving; fixed; remaining in the same condition.—n. pl. **sta·tion·ar·ies.**

sta·tion·ar·y en·gine, n. An engine in a fixed position, as in a building's foundation. —**sta·tion·ar·y en·gi·neer**, n.

sta·tion·ar·y front, n. *Meteor.* a front along which neither of two dissimilar air masses is replacing the other to any significant degree.

sta·tion·ar·y wave, n. Standing wave.

sta·tion break, n. *Radio, TV,* an interruption during or between programs to identify the station or network.

sta·tion·er, stā′sha·nėr, n. [From booksellers orig. having a station or stall (L.L. *statio*) at fairs or in market places.] One who sells paper, pens, pencils, ink, and various other materials connected with writing.

sta·tion·er·y, stā′sha·ner″ē, n. Paper and envelopes used in letter writing; various materials employed in writing, as pencils, pens, and paper.

sta·tion house, n. A place or building used as a station, esp. a police station.

sta·tion·mas·ter, stā′shan·mas″tėr, stā′shan·mä″stėr, n. The official in charge of a railroad station.

sta·tions of the cross, n. pl., sing. or pl. in constr. (*Often cap.*) A series of 14 crosses or pictures depicting the stages of the passion of Christ; a devotion involving appropriate meditation and prayers at each station of the cross.

sta·tion wag·on, n. An automobile without a trunk but with seating accommodations behind the front seat that may be folded down or removed to provide a large area for packages and suitcases loaded through a tailgate.

stat·ism, stā′tiz·um, n. A system in which the economy is regulated by the state; adherence to the sovereignty of a state.

stat·ist, stā′tist, stat′ist, n. An adherent of statism, stā′tist. A statistician, sta′tist.—a. Advocating or characteristic of statism.

sta·tis·tic, sta·tis′tik, n. [= Fr. *statistique,* < G. *statistik,* < L. *status,* E. *state.*] An element or datum of statistics; a statistical fact, as the mean, median, or standard deviation.—a. Statistical.

sta·tis·ti·cal, sta·tis′ti·kal, a. Of or relating to statistics; involving, consisting of, or originating in statistics. Also *statistic.*— **sta·tis·ti·cal·ly**, *adv.*

stat·is·ti·cian, stat″i·stish′an, n. A person knowledgeable in statistics; a person skilled in the use or practices of statistics. Also *statist.*

sta·tis·tics, sta·tis′tiks, n. pl. but sing. in constr. [Fr. *statistique,* < Gr. *statos,* fixed, settled, < stem *sto,* to stand.] The science of the systematic collection, organization, and mathematical analysis of quantifiable data so as to present descriptive information about the data, to induce characteristics of a larger population of which the data is construed as representative, or to infer the significance of underlying factors whose effects are reflected in the data; *pl. in constr.* the numerical data of statistics.

stat·o·blast, stat′o·blast″, n. [Gr. *statos,* standing, and *blastós,* sprout, germ.] *Zool.* a bud enclosed in a chitinous envelope, developed within the body cavity of many fresh-water bryozoans, and eventually set free in the water, where it usu. remains in a quiescent state through the winter, giving rise to a new individual in the spring.— **stat·o·blas·tic**, a.

sta·tor, stā′tėr, n. *Elect.* the stationary part of an electric generator or motor: opposed to *rotor.*

stat·o·scope, stat′o·skōp″, n. [Gr. *statos,* standing, and *skopein,* to view.] *Meteor.* a highly sensitive aneroid barometer for detecting slight changes in the pressure of the atmosphere; *aeron.* an instrument, usu. containing an aneroid barometer, for indicating slight variations in the altitude of an aircraft.

stat·u·ar·y, stach′ö·er″ē, n. pl. **stat·u·ar·ies.** [L. *statuaria,* the art of statuary, *statuarius,* a statuary, < *statua,* a statue.] Statues collectively; a group or assemblage of statues; the art of sculpting statues; an artist who makes statues; a sculptor.—a. Of or pertaining to a statue or statues; consisting of or suitable for statues.

stat·ue, stach′ö, n. [O.Fr. Fr. *statue,* < L. *statua,* related to *statuere,* set up.] A representation of a person or an animal carved in stone or wood, molded in some plastic material, or cast in bronze or the like, properly one of considerable size and in the round.—**stat·ued**, stach′öd, a. Adorned with statues; in the form of a statue or of statuary.—**stat·ue·less**, a.—**stat·ue·like**, a.

Stat·ue of Lib·er·ty, n. A colossal copper statue of a woman symbolizing hope and freedom, located in New York harbor on Liberty Island and presented in 1886 by France to the U.S.

stat·u·esque, stach″ö·esk′, a. Like or suggesting a statue, as in formal dignity, studied grace, or classic beauty.—**stat·u·esque·ly**, *adv.*—**stat·u·esque·ness**, n.

stat·u·ette, stach″ö·et′, n. [Fr. dim. of *statue.*] A small statue.

stat·ure, stach′ėr, n. [L. *statura,* < *sto, statum,* to stand.] The natural height of an animal body; bodily tallness; growth, maturity, development; as, professional *stature.*

sta·tus, stā′tus, stat′us, n. [L. *status,* state.] Standing or position in regard to rank or condition; as, his *status* as a minister; prestige; position or state of affairs.

sta·tus quo, stā′tus kwō′, stat′us kwō′, n. [L., 'state in which.'] The state in which anything was or is; the existing state of affairs. Also **sta·tus in quo.**

sta·tus sym·bol, n. A habit or object enabling judgment of the possessor's economic or social level; a habit or object developed or acquired to demonstrate high status whether or not the status has been attained.

stat·ute, stach′öt, stach′ut, n. [Fr. *statut,* L. *statutum,* < *statuo,* to set up, to fix, to determine.] *Law,* an enactment of the legislative body of a government that is formally expressed and documented as a law; written law, as opposed to *common law;* a legal instrument appended to an international agreement. A permanent rule or law enacted by the governing body of a corporation or institution.—**stat·u·ta·ble**, **stat·u·to·ry**, stach′u·tōr″ē, stach′u·tar″ē, a. Governed by statute law.

stat·ute book, n. A compilation of the laws enacted by a legislature.

stat·ute mile, n. A mile.

stat·ute of lim·i·ta·tions, n. *Law,* a statute imposing limits on the period during which certain rights, as the collection of debts, may be legally enforced.

stat·u·to·ry of·fense, n. *Law,* an offense as proclaimed by statute, rather than as recognized by common law. Also **stat·u·-to·ry crime.**

stat·u·to·ry rape, *n. Law,* sexual relations with a female under the legal age of consent.

staunch, stȧnch, stänch, *a.* [O.Fr. *estanche,* fem. of *estanc* (Fr. *étanche,* masc. and fem.), < *estanchier,* E. *stanch.*] Impervious to water or liquids; watertight; sound or firm in structure or substance; strong; substantial; firm or steadfast in principle, adherence, or loyalty, as a person; characterized by firmness or steadfastness. Also *stanch.*—**staunch·ly,** *adv.*—**staunch·ness,** *n.*

staunch, stȧnch, *v.t.* Stanch.

stau·ro·lite, stȧr'o·līt″, *n.* [Fr. *staurolite,* < Gr. *staurós,* cross, and *lithos,* stone.] A mineral consisting of a basic silicate of aluminum and iron, and occurring in brown to black prismatic crystals, which are often twinned in the form of a cross.—**stau·ro·lit·ic,** stȧr″o·lit'ik, *a.*

stave, stāv, *n.* [< *staves,* pl. of *staff.*] One of the thin, narrow, shaped pieces of wood which form the sides of a cask, tub, or similar vessel; a stick, rod, pole, or the like; a rung of a ladder or chair; *pros.* a verse or stanza of a poem or song; *mus.* the staff on which musical notes are written.—*v.t.*—*staved* or *stove, staving.* To break in a stave or staves of, as a barrel; to break or crush inward, followed by *in;* to break, as a hole, in a boat's hull; to break to pieces; splinter; to furnish with a stave or staves.—*v.i.* To become staved in, as a boat; break in or up, as a carton; to move or walk swiftly.—**stave off,** to put, ward, or keep off, as by force or evasion.

staves·a·cre, stāvz'ā″kėr, *n.* [A corruption of Gr. *staphisagria.*] *Bot.* a tall larkspur, *Delphinium staphisagria,* of southern Europe and Asia Minor, with purple flowers and poisonous seeds, the latter having emetic and purgative properties.

stay, stā, *v.i.*—*stayed* or *staid, staying.* [Prob. < O.Fr. *ester,* stand, stop, remain (cf. *estant, estaiant, esteaunt, steant,* ppr.), < L. *stare,* stand.] To remain, as in a place, situation, or company, instead of departing; to dwell or reside; to continue to be as specified, as to condition; as, to *stay* young; to keep up, as with a competitor in a race, often followed by *with;* to hold out or endure, as in a race or other contest, often followed by *with;* to stop or halt; to pause or wait, as for a moment, before proceeding or continuing; to linger or tarry; *poker,* to remain in a hand or game by matching the ante, bet, and any subsequent raise.—*v.t.* To bring to a stop or halt; to hold back, detain, or restrain, as from going or proceeding further; to suspend or delay, as proceedings; to suppress or quell, as violence, strife, or emotions; to temporarily appease or satisfy, as the cravings of the stomach or appetite; to check, arrest, or stop, as movement, action, or processes; to remain through or during, as a period of time; to remain to the end of, remain beyond, or outstay, usu. followed by *out.*—*n.* The act of staying or stopping; a stop, halt, or pause; a standstill; continuance in a place; a sojourn or temporary residence; *colloq.* staying power, or endurance. *Law,* a stoppage or arrest of action; a suspension of a judicial proceeding.—**stay put,** *colloq.* To remain where or as placed; remain fixed.—**stay·er,** *n.*

stay, stā, *n.* [O.E. *staeg* = D. and G. *stag* = Icel., Sw., and Dan. *stag,* stay (rope).] *Naut.* A strong rope or wire, used to support a funnel or mast; a guy.—*v.t.*—*stayed, staying. Naut.* To support or secure, as a mast, with a stay or stays; to put, as a ship, on another tack.—*v.i. Naut.* to change to another tack.—**in stays,** *naut.* in the act of going about from one tack to another.

stay, stā, *n.* [O.Fr. *estaie, estai* (Fr. *étai*),

stay, prop; prob. < Teut.] Something that supports or steadies; a prop; a brace; a flat piece of plastic, bone, or metal used to stiffen collars, corsets, and other clothing; pl., chiefly Brit. a corset.—*v.t.*—*stayed, staying* [Cf. O.Fr. *estaier* (Fr. *étayer*), < *estaie.*] To support, prop, or hold up; to sustain or strengthen mentally or spiritually; to fix or rest on for support.

stay-at-home, stā'at·hōm″, *a.* Staying at home; not given to or characterized by roaming, or traveling.—*n.* One who stays at home, esp. habitually.

stay·ing pow·er, *n.* Capacity or talent for remaining firm and functioning under adverse conditions.

stay-in strike, stā'in″ strīk″, *n. Brit.* sit-down strike. Also *sit-down,* **stay-in.**

stay·sail, stā'sāl″, *Naut.* stā'sal, *n. Naut.* any sail which hoists upon a stay.

stead, sted, *n.* [O.E. *stede* = D. and L.G. *stede,* Dan. *sted,* Icel. *stathr,* Goth. *staths,* G. *statt,* place, stead; from root of *stand;* hence, *steady, steadfast, bestead, bedstead, roadstead, homestead,* etc.] The place or position of a person or thing for which someone or something is substituted, preceded by *in,* as: David died, and Solomon reigned *in* his *stead.*—*v.t. Archaic,* to be of use, service, or advantage to.—**stand in good stead,** to be helpful or of use to, as: All that work should *stand* him *in good stead.*

stead·fast, sted'fast, sted'fast″, sted'fäst″, sted'fȧst, *a.* [*Stead,* place, and *fast;* lit. 'firm in place.'] Fixed; firm; constant or firm in resolution; resolute; not fickle or wavering; as, a *steadfast* person.—**stead·-fast·ly,** *adv.*—**stead·fast·ness,** *n.*

stead·ing, sted'ing, *n.* [< *stead, n.*] *Sc., N. Eng.* a farmhouse and outbuildings.

stead·y, sted'ē, *a.*—*steadier, steadiest.* [Appar. < *stead, n.*] Firmly placed or fixed; stable in position or equilibrium; even or regular in movement; free from change, variation, or interruption; uniform; continuous; as, a *steady* wind; constant, regular, or habitual; as, *steady* attendance; free from excitement or agitation; as, *steady* nerves; firm, unwavering, or steadfast; settled, staid, or sober, as a person; *naut.* keeping nearly upright, as a ship in a heavy sea.—*interj.* An exclamation ordering one to control his temper or emotions; *naut.* an order to the helmsman to keep the ship on its present course.—*n.* pl. **stead·ies.** *Colloq.* a person's regular date or sweetheart.—*v.t.* —*steadied, steadying.* To make steady.—*v.i.* To become steady.—*adv.* In a steady manner.—**stead·i·er,** *n.*—**stead·i·ly,** *adv.*—**stead·i·ness,** *n.*

steak, stāk, *n.* [A Scand. word; Icel. *steik,* Sw. *stek,* a steak; perh. akin to stick, as being *stuck* on a spit to roast.] A cut of beef, pork, fish, or the like, suitable for broiling or frying; sometimes, chopped meat cooked as a steak.

steak knife, *n.* A sharp table knife, usu. having a serrated edge, used to cut meat.

steal, stēl, *v.t.* past *stole,* pp. *stolen,* ppr. *stealing.* [O.E. *stelan* = D. *stelen* = G. *stehlen* = Icel. *stela* = Goth. *stilan,* steal: cf. *stalk.*] To take, or take away, dishonestly or wrongfully, esp. secretly; to appropriate, as ideas, credit, or words, without right or acknowledgment; to take, get, or win by insidious arts or subtle means; to take, get, or effect surreptitiously; to take by surprise or without permission; as, to *steal* a kiss; to move, bring, convey, or put secretly or quietly, usu. followed by *away, from, in, into,* or the like; to gain, as a point, by strategy, or by chance or luck, as in various games; *baseball,* of a runner, to reach, as a base, with no help from another player, as of an error or a hit.—*v.i.* To commit or practice theft; to move, go, or come secretly, quietly, or unobserved; to pass, come,

spread, or the like, imperceptibly, gently, or gradually; as, the years *steal* by; *baseball,* of a runner, to reach a base with no help from another player, as of an error or a hit.—*n. Colloq.* an act of stealing; a theft; the thing stolen; bargain. *Baseball,* the act or instance of stealing, as a base.—**steal·er,** *n.*

steal·ing, stē'ling, *n.* The act of one who steals; theft; *usu. pl.* items stolen.—*a.* Characterized by or pertaining to theft.

stealth, stelth, *n.* [Cf. *heal, health; till, tilth.*] A secret or clandestine method of procedure; a proceeding by secrecy.

stealth·y, stel'thē, *a.*—*stealthier, stealthiest.* Done by stealth; accompanied by efforts at concealment; furtive; sly.—**stealth·i·ly,** *adv.*—**stealth·i·ness,** *n.*

steam, stēm, *n.* [O.E. *stēam,* steam, smoke; D. *stoom,* Fris. *stoame,* steam; akin L.G. *stüm,* drift of snow or rain.] The vaporous or gaseous substance into which water is converted under certain circumstances of heat and pressure; the vapor generated by heating water to the boiling point, 212° F.; the visible moist vapor which rises from water, and from all moist and liquid bodies, when subjected to heat; an exhalation of vapor; *colloq.* energy.—*v.i.* To give out or be covered by steam or vapor; to rise in a vaporous form; to pass off in visible vapor; to sail by the agency of steam; *colloq.* to exhibit anger.—*v.t.* To expose to steam; to apply steam to; to exhale.—*a.* Producing or effected by steam; conducting steam; heated by steam.

steam·boat, stēm'bōt″, *n.* A ship powered by a steam engine.

steam·boat Goth·ic, *n.* An architectural style used in homes of the 19th century in the Mississippi and Ohio River region, characterized by elaborate ornamentation imitating river steamboats.

steam boil·er, *n.* A strong closed vessel in which water is converted into steam.

steam chest, *n.* A box or chamber above a steam boiler from which the steam passes to the engine. Also **steam box.**

steam en·gine, *n.* An engine in which steam pressure is directed against a piston or turbine to produce power.

steam·er, stē'mėr, *n.* A steamship; a vehicle powered by steam; a container in which articles are subjected to the action of steam; a steamed clam.

steam·er rug, *n.* A warm lap robe used by persons sitting on the deck of a ship.

steam·er trunk, *n.* A small trunk orig. designed to be stored under a ship's bunk.

steam fit·ter, *n.* One who installs and repairs steam pipes and their accessories for ventilating, heating, or refrigerating systems.—**steam fit·ting,** *n.*

steam heat·ing, *n.* A building's heating system which generates steam and circulates it through pipes to radiators.

steam i·ron, *n.* An iron designed with a water container for emitting steam onto the material being ironed.

steam·roll·er, stēm'rō″lėr, *n.* A heavy machine having one or more wide rollers for crushing, compacting, or leveling materials, as in road construction, and orig. steam-driven but later gasoline- or diesel-powered; *fig.* an agency for crushing opposition, esp. with ruthless disregard of rights. Also **steam roll·er.**—*a.*—*v.t.* Often *fig.* to go over or crush as with a steam-roller. Also **steam·roll,** stēm'rōl″.—*v.i.*

steam·ship, stēm'ship″, *n.* A ship propelled by steam. Also *steamer.*

steam shov·el, *n.* A machine for digging or excavating, operated by its own engine and boiler.

steam ta·ble, *n.* A long counter or table which has openings for holding receptacles of food and keeping them warm by circulating steam or hot water beneath them.

steam tur·bine, *n.* A turbine powered by steam discharged under high pressure.

steam·y, stē′mē, *a.*—**steamier, steamiest.** Consisting of or abounding in steam; vaporous; misty.—**steam·i·ly,** *adv.*—**steam·i·ness,** *n.*

ste·ap·sin, stē·ap′sin, *n.* [Formed, after *pepsin,* < Gr. *stéar,* fat, tallow.] *Biochem.* the lipase of the pancreatic juice.

ste·a·rate, stē′a·rāt″, stēr′āt, *n. Chem.* a salt or ester of stearic acid.

ste·ar·ic, stē·ar′ik, stēr′ik, *a.* [Fr. *stéarique,* < Gr. *stéar,* fat, tallow.] Pertaining to, resembling, or derived from stearin.

ste·ar·ic ac·id, *n. Chem.* a monobasic organic acid, $C_{18}H_{36}O_2$, used in making lubricants, soaps, cosmetics, and rubber.

ste·a·rin, stē′ēr·in, stēr′in, *n.* [Fr. *stéarine,* < Gr. *stéar,* fat, tallow.] *Chem.* any of the three glyceryl esters of stearic acid, esp. $C_3H_5(C_{18}H_{35}O_2)_3$, which is a soft, white, odorless solid found in many natural fats, used in making candles, soaps, polishes, and adhesive pastes; crude stearic acid as used commerically. Also **ste·a·rine,** stē′ēr·in, stē′a·rēn″, stēr′in.

ste·a·tite, stē′a·tīt″, *n.* [Fr. *steatite,* < Gr. *stéar, steatos,* fat, tallow.] Soapstone.—**ste·a·tit·ic,** stē″a·tit′ik, *a.*

ste·a·to·py·gi·a, stē″a·tō·pī′jē·a, stē″a·tō·pij′ē·a, *n.* [N.L. < Gr. *stéar* (*steatr-*), fat, tallow, and *pygē,* rump.] Abnormal accumulation of fat on and about the buttocks, esp. of females, as among the Hottentots, Bushmen, and some other African peoples. Also **ste·a·to·py·ga.**—**ste·a·to·pyg·ic, ste·a·to·py·gous,** stē″a·tō·pij′ik, stē″a·tō·pī′gus, stē″a·top′i·gus, *a.*

ste·a·tor·rhe·a, stē″a·tō·rē′a, *n. Pathol.* excess fat in the feces, due to a disease of the intestine or pancreas and usu. accompanied by diarrhea and weight loss.

sted·fast, sted′fast″, sted′fäst″, sted′fast, *a.* Steadfast.

steed, stēd, *n.* [O.E. *stēd, stēda,* a steed; akin to *stud;* < stem of *stand.*] *Chiefly liter.* A horse, esp. a spirited one; a horse for state or war.

steel, stēl, *n.* [O.E. *stél, stýle,* steel = Dan. *staal,* Icel. *stal,* G. *stahl,* O.G. *stahal.*] An alloy of iron and carbon with various other constituents which is categorized as hard, medium, or soft according to its carbon content, and which can be alloyed with other metals to produce variations in hardness, strength, elasticity, and malleability; a weapon, as a sword or spear; a kind of steel file for sharpening knives; a piece of steel for striking sparks from flint to ignite tinder or matches; *fig.* a condition of extreme hardness, sternness, or rigor; as, a heart of *steel.*—*a.*—*v.t.* To overlay, point, or edge with steel; to make hard or stubborn; to render insensible or obdurate; as, to *steel* one's heart against mercy.

steel band, *n. Mus.* a type of percussion band common in the West Indian islands, esp. Trinidad, using drums made from steel oil barrels whose sides have been cut to different heights to give certain tones.

steel blue, *n.* A lustrous blue-gray color, resembling steel-tempered blue.

steel en·grav·ing, *n.* The process of incising or etching the surface of a steel plate or block; the engraved steel; an impression or print from an engraved steel plate.

steel gui·tar, *n.* Hawaiian guitar.

steel·head, stēl′hed″, *n.* pl. **steel·heads, steel·head.** A rainbow trout, *Salmo gairdneri,* having a silver luster, much sought after by sportsmen on its fresh-water runs to and from the Pacific coast.

steel wool, *n.* A mass of fine steel filaments matted or woven together for use in polishing or scouring.

steel·work, stēl′wᵤrk″, *n.* Any article, part,

or structure made of steel.—**steel·works,** *n. pl., sing. or pl. in constr.* An establishment where steel is made and often manufactured into girders, rails, parts of machinery, and the like.—**steel·work·er,** stēl′wᵤr″kėr, *n.*

steel·y, stē′lē, *a.*—**steelier, steeliest.** Made of steel; resembling or suggestive of steel, as in color or hardness.—**steel·i·ness,** *n.*

steel·yard, stēl′yärd″, *n.* [Appar. < *steel* and *yard.*] A weighing instrument consisting of a balance with unequal arms, the longer being graduated and having a weight which is moved to counterbalance any object hung from a hook on the short arm.

steen·bok, stēn′bok″, stän′bok″, *n.* pl. **steen·bok, steen·boks.** [D. *steen,* stone, and *bok,* a buck.] A small, light-brown antelope, *Raphicerus campestris,* found in the plains of southern and eastern Africa. Also **stein·bok,** stīn′bok.

steep, stēp, *a.* [O.E. *stēap,* high, steep; Icel. *steypthr,* high; prob. allied to *stoop,* and signifying lit. sinking down abruptly. *Steeple* is a derivative.] Ascending or descending sharply, as a roof or slope; sloping sharply; precipitous, as a hill. *Colloq.* exorbitant, as prices; excessive or incredible, as statements.—*n.* A precipitous place; a steep slope.—**steep·ly,** *adv.*—**steep·ness,** *n.*

steep, stēp, *v.t.* [Same as D. and G. *stippen,* Fris. *stiepen,* to dip, to steep; perh. connected with *steep, a.*] To soak in a liquid; to immerse and saturate; to macerate; to extract the essence of by soaking; as, to *steep* tea; to imbue or saturate.—*v.i.* To be subjected to soaking in a liquid.—*n.* A liquid in which things are steeped; the process of steeping; the state of being steeped.—**steep·er,** *n.*

steep·en, stē′pen, *v.i., v.t.* To become or cause to become steeper.

stee·ple, stē′pl, *n.* [O.E. *stēpel, stýpel,* steeple, a tower; L.G. *stipel,* a pillar; Icel. *stöpull,* a steeple; allied to *steep.*] A tall, tapering structure, usu. culminating in a spire, surmounting the roof or tower of a building, esp. a church; a tower topped by such a structure; a spire.

stee·ple·bush, stē′pl·bush″, *n.* A N. American shrub, *Spiraea tomentosa,* of the rose family, with woolly, rust-colored leaves and dense clusters of pink flowers. Also **hard·hack.**

stee·ple·chase, stē′pl·chās″, *n.* A race in which horses jump over a prepared course of artificial obstacles; a foot race over such a course or across country; orig. a horse race over natural country jumping any obstacles in the way, using a church steeple as a goal.—**stee·ple·chas·er,** *n.*

stee·ple·jack, stē′pl·jak″, *n.* A person whose job is to climb steeples, smokestacks, and towers to inspect, paint, or make repairs.

steer, stēr, *v.t.* [O.E. *stēoran, stīeran* = D. *sturen* = G. *steuern* = Icel. *stýra,* steer: cf. O.E. *stēor,* guidance, prob. also rudder, also E. *starboard* and *stern.*] To guide the course of, as a vessel, by means of a rudder or helm; to guide the course of by any means; to guide, pilot, or lead; to direct the course of, as proceedings or affairs; to govern or rule; to restrain or control; to follow or pursue by means of a rudder or otherwise.—*v.i.* To direct the course of a vessel, vehicle, or airplane by the use of a rudder or other means; to direct or pursue a course; to direct one's course of action. To admit of being steered, as: The ship would not *steer* at all. To be steered or guided in a particular direction.—*n. Colloq.* Information, a suggestion, or advice intended for guidance; a tip.—**steer clear of,** to avoid; to purposely keep or stay away from.—**steer·a·ble,** *a.*—**steer·er,** *n.*

steer, stēr, *n.* [O.E. *stēor* = D. and G. *stier*

= Goth. *stiur,* steer.] A young castrated bovine, esp. one raised for beef; a male animal of any age of the beef cattle class.

steer·age, stēr′ij, *n.* A part or division of a ship, orig. that containing the steering apparatus; in a passenger ship, formerly, the part with minimal accommodations allotted to passengers traveling at the cheapest rate, as during the decades of peak immigration to the U.S.; the act or method of steering a vessel; the manner in which a vessel answers to the helm or steering apparatus.

steer·age·way, stēr′ij·wā″, *n. Naut.* the minimum degree of forward movement required to make a ship subject to the helm.

steer·ing com·mit·tee, *n.* A committee, usu. of a lawmaking body, responsible for drawing up and directing the order of business to be taken up at meetings.

steer·ing gear, *n.* The apparatus or mechanism for steering something, as a vessel, automobile, or airplane.

steer·ing wheel, *n.* A wheel which is turned by hand to operate the steering of a vehicle, as an automobile.

steers·man, stērz′man, *n.* pl. **steers·men.** One who steers a vessel; a helmsman.

steeve, stēv, *v.t.*—**steeved, steeving.** [Fr. *estiver* = Sp. *estibar* = It. *stivare,* < L. *stipare,* crowd, pack: cf. *stevedore* and *stive.*] To stow, as cotton or other cargo, compactly in a ship's hold.—*n.* A long derrick or spar, with a block at one end, used in stowing cargo.

steeve, stēv, *v.i., v.t.*—**steeved, steeving.** [Akin to *stiff;* cf. D. *stevig,* stiff, firm.] *Naut.* of a bowsprit, to project or be projected upward at an angle rather than horizontally. —*n. Naut.* the angle which the bowsprit makes with the horizon.

steg·o·saur·us, steg″o·sạr′us, *n.* pl. **steg·o·saur·i,** steg″o·sạr′ī. [N.L. < Gr. *stégos,* roof, and *sauros,* lizard.] Any of the huge, herbivorous dinosaurs constituting the genus *Stegosaurus,* of the Jurassic and Cretaceous periods, having a small head and large, erect, bony plates extending along the backbone.

stein, stīn, *n.* [G., lit. 'stone.'] An earthenware mug, esp. for beer; the quantity of beer this mug holds.

ste·le, stē′lē, *n.* pl. **ste·lai, ste·les,** stē′lī, stē′lēz, stēlz. [N.L. *stele* (L. *stela*) < Gr. *stélē,* upright block, post, akin to *histánai,* cause to stand.] An upright slab or pillar of stone bearing an inscription or sculptural design; a prepared surface on the face of a building or a rock, bearing an inscription or the like. Also **ste·la,** stē′la.

ste·le, stē′lē, *n. Bot.* the central cylinder of vascular tissue in the stem or root of a plant.—**ste·lar, ste·lic,** *a.*

stel·lar, stel′ēr, *a.* [L. *stellaris,* < *stella,* a star.] Pertaining to, consisting of, or resembling stars; starry; pertaining to a renowned film, stage, or sports personality.

stel·late, stel′it, stel′āt, *a.* [L. *stellatus.*] Resembling the form of a star; radiated. Also **stel·lat·ed.**—**stel·late·ly,** *adv.*

stel·li·form, stel′i·fạrm″, *a.* Having the shape or form of a star.

stel·lu·lar, stel′ū·lēr, *a.* [L. *stellula,* dim. of *stella,* a star.] Having the appearance of small stars; having marks resembling stars.

stem, stem, *n.* [O.E. *stemn, stefn,* stem of tree, also prow or stern of vessel, akin to D. *stam,* O.H.G. *stam,* G. *stamm,* stem of tree, also D. *steven,* Icel. *stamn, stafn,* prow or stern; prob. from the root of E. *stand.*] *Bot.* the main body of that portion of a tree, shrub, or other plant which is above ground; the firm part which supports the branches; a trunk; a stock; a stalk; the ascending axis of a plant, whether above or below ground, which ordinarily grows in an opposite direction to the root; the stalk which supports a leaf, flower, or fruit; a petiole; a peduncle; a pedicel. The stock or line of descent of a family; ancestry or pedigree; a race or ethnic stock; *arch.* something resembling or suggesting the stem of a plant, flower, or the like; *print.* the main or relatively thick stroke of a letter in printing. A long, slender part of an object in distinction from the head or from branches or projections, as the tube of a tobacco pipe; the slender, upright part of a goblet, wineglass, or other vessel, which unites the body to the foot or base; a knob for winding a watch; *mus.* the vertical line forming part of a note; *ling.* a part of a word, usu. a derivative of a root, which serves as the base of inflectional forms.— *v.t.*—**stemmed, stemming.** To remove the stem from, as a fruit, or the midrib from, as a tobacco leaf.—*v.i.* To be derived or descended; to originate.—**stem·less,** *a.* Having no stem; acaulous.—**stem·mer,** *n.* One who or that which removes stems from fruits.

stem, stem, *v.t.*—**stemmed, stemming.** [Icel. *stemma,* Sw. *stamma,* G. *stemmen,* to dam, to bank up.] To dam up; to stop; to check, as the flow of a stream or other force; to stanch.—*v.i. Skiing,* to use a particular technique to turn, slow down, or stop.—*n.*

stem, stem, *n. Naut.* The curved piece of timber or metal to which the two sides of a ship are united at the foremost end; the bow or forward part of a vessel.—*v.t.*—**stemmed, stemming.** To make progress or headway against, as any current or gale, or opposition.—**from stem to stern,** thoroughly; from one particular end of anything to the opposite end; throughout.

stemmed, stemd, *a.* Having a stem, usu. in reference to a certain kind; as, long-*stemmed;* with the stem taken off; as, *stemmed* stringbeans.

stem·son, stem′son, *n.* [< *stem,* with *-son* as in *keelson.*] *Naut.* a curved timber in a ship's bow, having its lower end scarfed into the keelson.

stem turn, *n. Skiing,* a turn in which a skier stems or faces the heel of the uphill ski outward from the line of descent, then points the other ski in the direction to be turned, bringing the stemming ski parallel when the desired angle is reached.

stem·ware, stem′wâr″, *n.* Vessels, as of glass, having a stem uniting the body to the foot or base, as goblets or wineglasses.

stem-wind·er, stem′wīn′dėr, *n.* A watch wound by turning a knob at the stem.— **stem-wind·ing,** *a.*

stench, stench, *n.* [A softened form of O.E. *stenc,* E. *stink.*] A foul smell; a stink.— **stench·ful,** *a.*

sten·cil, sten′sil, *n.* [Prob. < obs. *stencel,* adorn with bright colors, < O.Fr. *estenceler,* < *estencele* (Fr. *étincelle*), a spark, < L. *scintilla.*] A thin sheet of metal, paper, or other material, pierced with letters or designs, which, when brushed with ink or color, are reproduced on the surface beneath; the letters or designs so produced. —*v.t.*—**stenciled, stenciling,** *Brit.* **stencilled, stencilling.** To mark or paint by means of a stencil.—**sten·cil·er,** *Brit.* **sten·cil·ler,** *n.*

sten·o, sten′ō, *n. Colloq.* stenographer.

sten·o·graph, sten′o·graf″, sten′o·gräf″, *n.* Any of various keyboard instruments, somewhat resembling a typewriter, used for writing in shorthand, as by means of phonetic or arbitrary symbols; a writing, as a report or memorandum, in shorthand. —*v.t.* To write in shorthand.

ste·nog·ra·pher, ste·nog′ra·fėr, *n.* One who uses stenography to record letters, memoranda, or other spoken material and then transcribes and types the notes.

ste·nog·ra·phy, ste·nog′ra·fē, *n.* Any system of shorthand writing.—**sten·o·**-

graph·ic, sten·o·graph·i·cal, sten″o·graf′-ik, *a.*—**sten·o·graph·i·cal·ly,** *adv.*

ste·no·sis, sti·nō′sis, *n.* pl. **ste·no·ses,** sti·nō′sēz. [N.L. < Gr. *stenōsis* < *stenoun,* make narrow, < *stenos,* narrow.] *Pathol.* contraction of a passage or canal.—**ste-**-**nosed,** sti·nōst′, sti·nōzd′, *a.* Contracted or narrowed.—**ste·not·ic,** sti·not′ik, *a.*

sten·o·therm, sten″o·thurm′, *n. Biol.* an organism capable of existing only within narrow limits of temperature change.— **sten·o·ther·mal,** *a.*—**sten·o·ther·my,** *n.*

Sten·o·type, sten′o·tīp″, *n.* A keyboard stenograph resembling a typewriter but smaller and with fewer keys, which prints symbols representing sounds, words, or phrases. (Trademark.)—**sten·o·typ·ist,** *n.* A stenographer who operates a Stenotype.— **sten·o·typ·y,** sten′o·tī″pē, *n.*

sten·tor, sten′tạr, *n.* [From *Stentor,* a Greek herald in the Trojan War.] A person having a very loud or powerful voice.

sten·tor, sten′tạr, *n. Zool.* a ciliate protozoan belonging to the genus *Stentor,* having a trumpet-shaped body.

sten·to·ri·an, sten·tōr′ē·an, sten·tạr′ē·an *a.* Very loud or powerful in sound.— **sten·to·ri·an·ly,** *adv.*

step, step, *n.* [O.E. *staepe.*] A movement made by lifting the foot and setting it down again in a new position, as in walking, running, or dancing; the space passed over or measured by one movement of the foot in such stepping; the sound made by the foot in stepping; a mark or impression made by the foot on the ground; footprint; a manner of walking; gait; pace in marching; a pace uniform with that of others or in time with music; *pl.* movements or course in walking or running; as, to retrace one's *steps.* A move or proceeding, as toward some end or course of action; a measure; a stage in a process; degree, grade, or rank; a support for the foot in ascending or descending, as on a ladder or stair; a very short distance; a pattern of movement in a dance. *Mus.* a degree of the staff or of the scale; the interval between two successive degrees of the scale. An offset part of an object; *naut.* a socket, frame, or platform for supporting the lower end of a mast.—*v.i.*—**stepped, stepping.** [O.E. *steppan,* *stæppan,* = O.Fries. *steppa,* akin to D. *stappen,* G. *stapfen,* step.] To move by lifting the foot and setting it down again in a new position, or by using the feet alternately in this manner; as, to *step* forward; to walk or go on foot, esp. for a few steps or a short distance; as, to *step* to the corner store; to move with measured steps, as in a dance; to go briskly or fast, as a horse; to come or happen with ease, as if by just a step of the foot; as, to *step* into a fortune; to put the foot down; to tread by intention or accident; to press with the foot, in order to operate some mechanism.— *v.t.* To take, as a step, pace, or stride; to perform the steps of, as a dance; to move or set, as the foot, in taking a step; to measure, as ground or distance, by steps, followed by *off* or *out*; to make or arrange in the manner of a series of steps; *naut.* to fix, as a mast, in its step.—**in step,** moving in rhythm, as in dancing, or in cadence, as in marching; in harmony or agreement.—**take steps,** to begin action on a project or problem.—**watch one's step,** to exercise care or caution.—**step on it,** *slang,* to hurry or move faster.—**step·like,** *a.*

step·broth·er, step′bruTH″ėr, *n.* One's stepfather's or stepmother's son by a former marriage.

step-by-step, step′bī·step′, *a.* Taking place or accomplished by consecutive degrees; gradually.

step·child, step′chīld″, *n.* pl. **step·child·ren.** [O.E. *stēopcild.*] A child of one's husband or wife by a former marriage.

step·daugh·ter, step′dạ″tėr, *n.* [O.E. *stēop-dohtor.*] A daughter of one's husband or wife by a former marriage.

step down, *v.i.* To reduce slowly or by degrees; to give up one's position, office, or authority.—*v.t. Elect.* to reduce the voltage of.—**step-down,** step′doun″, *a.* Tending to lower or decrease; *elect.* decreasing voltage.

step·fa·ther, step′fä″THėr, *n.* The husband of one's mother in a second or subsequent marriage.

steph·a·no·tis, stef″a·nō′tis, *n.* [N.L. < Gr. *stephanōtis,* fit for a crown, < *stephanos,* a crown.] Any milkweed of the genus *Stephanotis,* with thick, glossy leaves and fragrant, waxy, white or cream-colored flowers.

step-in, step′in″, *n. Usu. pl.* any article of clothing which may be put on by stepping into it, esp. women's loose-fitting panties or open-backed slippers.—*a.* Easily donned by being stepped into.—**step in,** *v.i.* To come between quarreling individuals or factions, usu. without being asked to do so; to participate.

step·lad·der, step′lad″ėr, *n.* A portable ladder having four legs and flat steps, hinged at the top, and opening to form its own support.

step·moth·er, step′muTH″ėr, *n.* The wife of one's father in a second or subsequent marriage.

step out, *v.i.* To leave the premises, esp. for a brief time only; to walk in a vigorous manner, as with a quick march step. *Colloq.* to go out socially; to seek the company of one other than one's spouse, followed by *on.*

step·par·ent, step′pâr″ent, step′par″ent, *n.* A stepfather or stepmother.

steppe, step, *n.* [= Fr. and G. *steppe,* < Russ. *step.*] One of the vast, more or less level plains, devoid of trees, of southeastern Europe and of Asia; an extensive plain, esp. one without trees.

stepped-up, stept′up′, *a. Colloq.* Accelerated; expanded; increased.

step·per, step′ėr, *n.* One who steps; a horse that has a fast or showy gait; *colloq.* a dancer.

step·ping stone, *n.* A raised stone in a stream or in a swampy place used to step on in crossing; an aid by which an end may be accomplished or an object gained; an assistance to progress. Also **step·ping·stone.**

step rock·et, *n. Aerospace,* a rocket having two or more stages, each of which is fired successively and then discarded when its fuel is exhausted.

step·sis·ter, step′sis″tėr, *n.* A stepfather's or stepmother's daughter by a former spouse.

step·son, step′sun″, *n.* The son of a husband or wife by a former spouse.

step·stool, step′stöl″, *n.* A stool used for reaching high objects, usu. having two steps which fold underneath the seat when not in use.

step turn, *n. Skiing,* a turn variation in which a skier lifts one ski, steps in the direction to be turned, and then brings the other ski parallel to it.

step up, *v.t.* To accelerate, increase, or advance by stages; *elect.* to raise, as the voltage of an alternating-current circuit, by means of a transformer.—*v.i.* To be increased; to be given a promotion in one's employment; to come forward, as: *Step up and be counted.*—**step-up,** step′up″, *a.* Bringing about an increase; *elect.* increasing voltage.—*n.* An advance or rise in size or quantity.

step·wise, step′wīz″, *a.* Arranged by steps; *mus.* moving from one tone to the next by step.

ster·co·ra·ceous, stur″ko·rā′shus, *a.* [L. *stercus* (*stercor-*), dung.] *Zool.* Consisting of, resembling, or pertaining to dung or feces; frequenting or feeding on dung, as certain insects.

stere, stēr, *n*. [Fr. *stère*, < Gr. *stereos*, solid.] A French unit of solid measure, equal to a cubic meter, about 1.31 cubic yards or 35.3156 cubic feet.

ster·e·o, ster′ē·ō″, stēr′ē·ō″, *n*. **ster·e·os.** Shortened form of *stereophonic, stereotype,* and *stereoscope.*—*a.*

ster·e·o·bate, ster′ē·o·bāt″, stēr′ē·o·bāt″, *n*. [L. *stereobata,* < Gr. *stereós,* firm, solid, and *-bátēs,* E. *stylobate.*] *Arch.* the foundation or base upon which a building or the like is erected; the solid platform or structure, including the stylobate, upon which the columns of a classical building rest.

ster·e·o·chem·is·try, ster″ē·ō·kem′i·strē, stēr″ē·ō·kem′i·strē, *n*. [Gr. *stereos,* solid.] A branch of chemistry which deals with the geometrical arrangement of the atoms of a molecule, and the effect of this arrangement on its chemical properties.

ster·e·o·gram, ster′ē·o·gram″, stēr′ē·o·gram″, *n*. [Gr. *stereós,* and *grapho,* to write.] A diagram or picture which represents objects so as to give the impression of relief or solidity; a picture for a stereoscope; a stereograph.

ster·e·o·graph, ster′ē·o·graf″, stēr′ē·o·gräf″, stēr′ē·o·graf″, stēr′ē·o·gräf″, *n*. A single or double picture, usu. a photograph, for a stereoscope.—*v.t.* To make a stereograph of.

ster·e·og·ra·phy, ster″ē·og′ra·fē, stēr″ē·og′ra·fē, *n*. The art of delineating the forms of solid bodies on a plane; perspective; a branch of solid geometry dealing with the construction of regularly defined solids.—**ster·e·o·graph·ic,** ster″ē·o·graf′ik, stēr″ē·o·graf′ik, *a.*—**ster·e·o·graph·i·cal·ly,** *adv.*

ster·e·o·i·so·mer, ster″ē·ō·ī′so·mėr, stēr″ē·ō·ī′so·mer, *n*. [Gr. *stereós,* solid, *isos,* equal, *meros,* a part.] A chemical compound having the same composition as some other compound but with its atoms differently arranged.

ster·e·o·i·som·er·ism, ster″ē·ō·ī·som′e·riz″um, stēr″ē·ō·ī·som′e·riz″um, *n. Chem.* a kind of isomerism assumed to be due to the different relative positions in space of the atoms or groups of atoms in a molecule. —**ster·e·o·i·so·mer·ic,** ster″ē·ō·ī′so·mer′ik, stēr″ē·ō·ī′so·mer′ik, *a.*

ster·e·om·e·try, ster″ē·om′i·trē, stēr″ē·om′i·trē, *n*. [Gr.] The mensuration of solid figures; solid geometry.—**ster·e·o·met·ric,** ster″ē·o·me′trik, stēr″ē·o·me′trik, *a.*—**ster·e·o·met·ri·cal·ly,** *adv.*

ster·e·o·mi·cro·scope, ster′ē·ō·mī′kro·skōp″, stēr′ē·ō·mī′kro·skōp″, *n*. A kind of microscope having the lenses arranged so that the object in view is seen in three dimensions. Also **ster·e·o·scop·ic mi··cro·scope.**

ster·e·o·phon·ic, ster″ē·o·fon′ik, stēr″ē··o·fon′ik, *a*. Pertaining to a sound system in which a number of acoustical elements are arranged so as to reproduce the spatial distribution of the original sound for the listener.—**ster·e·oph·o·ny,** *n.*

ster·e·o·pho·tog·ra·phy, ster″ē·ō·fo··tog′ra·fē, stēr″ē·ō·fo·tog′ra·fē, *n*. Photography which produces three-dimensional images.

ster·e·op·sis, ster″ē·op′sis, stēr″ē·op′sis, *n*. Stereoscopic vision.

ster·e·op·ti·con, ster″ē·op′ti·kon, stēr″ē··op′ti·kon, stēr″ē·op′ti·kọn, stēr″ē·op′ti··kon, *n*. [N.L. < Gr. *stereós,* solid, and *optikón,* neut. of *optikós,* of or for sight.] An improved form of magic lantern, usu. designed with two lenses for projecting dissolving views.—**ster·e·op·ti·can,** *a.*

ster·e·o·scope, ster′ē·o·skōp″, stēr′ē·o··skōp″, *n*. [Gr. *stereós,* and *skopeo,* to view.] An optical instrument which enables the viewer to look upon two pictures taken with a small difference in angular view, each eye looking upon one picture only, so that two images are conveyed to the brain as one, and the objects thus appear solid and real as in nature.—**ster·e·o·scop·ic,** *a.*—**ster·e·o·scop·i·cal·ly,** *adv.*—**ster·e·os·co·py,** stēr″ē·os′ko·pē, *n.*

ster·e·o·scop·ic mi·cro·scope, *n*. Stereomicroscope.

ster·e·o·tax·is, ster″ē·o·tak′sis, stēr″ē·o··tak′sis, *n. Biol.* movement by a motile organism or cell in reaction to contact with a solid body or surface.

ster·e·ot·o·my, ster″ē·ot′o·mē, stēr″ē·ot′··o·mē, *n*. The process or art of cutting hard, solid materials, esp. stone; stonecutting.

ster·e·ot·ro·pism, ster″ē·o′tro·piz″um, stēr″ē·o′tro·piz″um, *n. Biol.* growth curvature of an organism, esp. of one of its parts, in response to contact with a solid body.

ster·e·o·type, ster′ē·o·tīp″, stēr′ē·o·tīp″, *n*. [Fr. *stéréotype,* < Gr. *stereós,* solid, and *typos,* E. *type.*] A process of making metal plates for printing by taking a mold of composed type or the like in plaster, papiermaché, or other material and then taking a cast from this mold in type metal; a printing plate of type metal made by this process. A set image; a standardized or typical image or conception held by or applied to members of a certain group.—*v.t.* *stereotyped, stereotyping.* To make a stereotype of; to give a fixed or settled form to.—**ster·e·o·typ·er,** **ster·e·o·typ·ist,** *n.*

ster·e·o·typed, ster′ē·o·tīpt″, stēr′ē·o··tīpt″, *a*. Reproduced in stereotype plates; fixed or settled in form; conventional.

ster·e·o·typ·y, ster′ē·o·tī″pē, stēr′ē·o··tī″pē, *n*. The art or business of making stereotype plates; printing from plates made by the stereotype process; *psychol.* maintenance of a posture or repetition of an action or a speech pattern with such frequency as to be considered abnormal, as in certain mental disorders.

ster·ic, ster′ik, stēr′ik, *a. Chem.* referring to the spatial arrangement or position of atoms in a molecule. Also **ster·i·cal.**—**ster·i··cal·ly,** *adv.*

ster·i·lant, ster′i·lant, *n*. A chemical or other agent that sterilizes, as a herbicide with a residual effect in the soil or an agent that destroys the fertility of insects.

ster·ile, ster′il, *Brit.* ster′īl, *a*. [L. *sterilis,* akin to Goth. *stairō,* Gr. *steira,* barren, Skt. *starī,* barren cow.] Free from living germs or microorganisms; as, *sterile* needles. Incapable of producing, or not producing, offspring, used chiefly of females; barren; unproductive of vegetation, as soil; infertile; unfruitful; *fig.* unproductive of results, or fruitless. *Bot.* lacking reproductive elements that are normally present; incapable of reproduction.—**ste·ril·i·ty,** ste·ril′i·tē, *n.*

ster·i·lize, ster·i·lise, ster′i·līz″, *v.t. sterilized, sterilizing, sterilised, sterilising.* To render sterile, esp. to free from living germs, as by heating; to inhibit or destroy by surgery the reproductive capabilities of the sex organs of; to make unproductive, as land areas.—**ster·i·li·za·tion,** ster″i·li·zā′shan, *n.*—**ster·i·liz·er,** *n.*

ster·let, stėr′lit, *n*. [= Fr. and G. *sterlet* < Russ. *sterlyadʹ.*] A small sturgeon, *Acipenser ruthenus,* of the Black Sea, Caspian Sea, and neighboring waters, highly esteemed for its flavor, and yielding roe from which a superior caviar is prepared.

ster·ling, stėr′ling, *a*. [M.E. *sterling,* the silver coin; of disputed origin; possibly < O.E. *steorra,* star, and *-ling,* with reference to some device on the coin.] Pertaining to English money; of silver, being of the same quality as the silver in English coin, 0.925 standard fineness; made of silver of this quality; conforming to the highest standard or thoroughly excellent.—*n.* The standard fineness, in the United Kingdom, of 0.91666 for gold and 0.500 for silver; silver of 0.925 fineness, as used in silverware or jewelry; articles made of sterling silver.—**ster·ling·ly,** *adv.*—**ster·ling·ness,** *n.*

stern, stụrn, *a*. [O.E. *sterne, styrne,* stern; same root as to *stare,* and *stark.*] Severe, as regards facial expression; austere of aspect; gloomy; severe of manner; harsh; rigidly steadfast; immovable.—**stern·ly,** *adv.*—**stern·ness,** *n.*

stern, stụrn, *n*. [M.E. *sterne* = O.Fries. *stiarne, stiorne,* rudder = Icel. *stjörn,* steering.] The hinder part of a ship or boat, often opposed to *stem;* the hinder part of anything.

ster·nal, stụr′nal, *a*. Of or pertaining to the sternum.

stern chase, *n. Naut.* a chase in which the pursuing vessel follows in the wake of the other.—**stern chas·er,** *naut.* a cannon in a ship's stern, pointing backward, for use against pursuers.

stern·fore·most, stụrn″fōr′mōst, stụrn″··far′mōst, *Brit.* stụrn″fōr′most, stụrn″far′··most, *adv*. With the stern or hind part foremost; clumsily or with difficulty.

stern·most, stụrn′mōst, *Brit.* stụrn′most, *a*. Farthest in the rear; farthest astern.

ster·no·cos·tal, stụr″nō·kos′tal, stụr″nō··ka′stal, *a. Anat., zool.* in the area between the sternum and the ribs or functionally related to that area.

stern·post, stụrn′pōst″, *n. Naut.* the principal piece of timber or iron in the stern of a vessel, fastened to the keel, and usu. serving as a support for the rudder.

stern·son, stụrn′son, *n*. [< *stern,* with *-son,* as in *keelson.*] *Naut.* the continuation of a vessel's keelson, to which the sternpost is bolted.

ster·num, stụr′num, *n*. pl. **ster·na, ster··nums,** stụr′na. [N.L. < Gr. *sternon,* breast, chest.] *Anat., zool.* A bone or series of bones extending along the middle line of the ventral portion of the body of most vertebrates, consisting in man of a flat, narrow bone connected with the clavicles and the true ribs; the breastbone; the ventral part of a somite in arthropods.

ster·nu·ta·tion, stụr″nū·tā′shan, *n*. [L. *sternutatio* < *sternuto,* freq. of *sternuo,* to sneeze.] The act of sneezing.

ster·nu·ta·tor, stụr′nū·tā″tėr, *n*. A substance used in chemical warfare that causes sneezing, coughing, and other nasal and respiratory irritations.

ster·nu·ta·to·ry, stėr·nö′ta·tōr″ē, stėr··nō′ta·tạr″ē, stėr·nū′ta·tōr″ē, stėr·nū′ta·tạr″ē, *a*. Causing sneezing. Also **ster·nu·ta·tive.**—*n.* pl. **ster·nu·ta·to·ries.** A substance that induces sneezing.

stern·ward, stụrn′wėrd, *adv., a.* Toward the stern; astern. Also **stern·wards.**

stern·way, stụrn′wā″, *n. Naut.* the movement of a ship backward or with the stern foremost.

stern·wheel, stụrn′hwēl′, stụrn′wēl″, *a*. Of a boat, having a paddle wheel at the stern. Compare *side-wheel.*

stern·wheel·er, stụrn′hwē″lėr, stụrn′wē″··lėr, *n. Naut.* a boat propelled at the stern by an engine-powered paddle wheel.

ster·oid, ster′oid, stēr′oid, *n. Chem.* a class of fat-soluble organic compounds including sterols, bile acids, sex hormones, and certain digitalis compounds.—*a.*—**ster·oi··dal,** ste·roid′al, sti·roid′al, *a.*

ster·ol, ster′ōl, ster′ol, stēr′ōl, stēr′ol, *n*. [Gr. *stereós,* solid.] *Chem.* any of a class of complex cyclic alcohol compounds found in many animals and plants.

ster·tor, stụr′tėr, *n*. [N.L. < L. *stertere,* snore.] Snoring; *pathol.* a heavy snoring sound accompanying respiration in certain diseases.—**ster·to·rous,** *a.*—**ster·to·rous··ly,** *adv.*—**ster·to·rous·ness,** *n.*

stet, stet, *v.t.*—*stetted, stetting.* [L., 'Let it stand.'] To mark with the word *stet* or with dots: used as a direction on a printer's proof, manuscript, or the like to retain cancelled material.—*impv.* Let it stand: a direction to the printer concerning cancelled material.

steth·o·scope, steth'o·skōp″, *n.* [Fr. *stéthoscope* < Gr. *stethos*, breast, chest, and *skopein*, view.] *Med.* an instrument used in auscultation, to convey sounds in the body, esp. those in the chest, to the ear of the examiner.—**steth·o·scop·ic, steth·o·scop·i·cal,** steth″o·skop′ik, *a.*—**steth·o·scop·i·cal·ly,** *adv.*—**ste·thos·co·py,** ste·thos′ko·pē, steth'o·skō″pē, *n.*

ste·ve·dore, stē′vi·dōr, stē′vi·dạr″, *n.* [Sp. *estivador*, a packer of wool, < *estivar*, to stow, < L. *stipare*, to cram, to stuff.] One whose occupation is to stow goods and packages in a ship's hold; one who loads or unloads vessels.—*v.t.*—*stevedored, stevedoring.* To load or unload the freight or lading of, as a ship.—*v.i.* To load or unload a cargo vessel.

ste·ve·dore's knot, *n.* A knot tied to prevent a line from unreeving or loosening. Also **ste·ve·dore knot.**

stew, stö, stū, *n.* A preparation of meat, fish, or other food cooked by stewing; *colloq.* a state of uneasiness, agitation, or perturbation.—*v.t.* To cook, as food, by simmering or slow boiling.—*v.i.* To be cooked by simmering or slow boiling. *Colloq.* to fret, worry, or fuss; to swelter, as in hot, humid weather.—**stew in one's own juice,** *fig.* to remain in discomfort or trouble occasioned by oneself.

ste·ward, stö′érd, stū′érd, *n.* [O.E. *styward, stiweard*, a steward, lit. 'a *styward*,' < *stige*, a sty, a pen, and *weard*, a keeper. Orig. one who took charge of the cattle, which constituted the chief wealth of a household.] A manager of a large estate or other establishment; an agent who takes care of financial or other affairs for another person; an executive of a club, hotel, passenger ship, or restaurant who buys food and liquor and superintends their preparation and serving; a man on a passenger ship who waits on table; a person in charge of any matter, as a race track official; a minor union official in a factory; a foreman; a person in charge of finances or similar affairs in certain churches; *Brit.* any of various elected municipal officials; *Brit. hist.* a high officer of state.—*v.t.* To serve or perform the tasks of a steward for.—*v.i.* To serve as a steward.—**stew·ard·ess,** stö′ér·dis, stū′ér·dis, *n.* A female who serves the passengers on an airplane, bus, or train.—**stew·ard·ship,** *n.* The office or functions of a steward.

stew·pan, stö′pan″, stū′pan″, *n.* A pan for stewing; a saucepan.

sthen·ic, sthen′ik, *a.* [Gr. *sthenos*, strength.] *Med.* attended with abnormal increase of activity in the heart and arteries. Extremely vigorous; strong.

stib·ine, stib′ēn, stib′in, *n. Chem.* a colorless, poisonous, malodorous gas, SbH₃, formed by the decomposition of an antimony compound in hydrochloric acid. Also **an·ti·mo·ny hy·dride.**

stib·nite, stib′nīt, *n.* A crystalline ore of antimony of a lead-gray color, yielding most of the antimony of commerce.

sti·cho·myth·i·a, stik″o·mith′ē·a, *n.* [N.L. < Gr. *stichomythia*, < *stichos*, row, line, and *mythos*, word, speech.] *Gr. liter.* dialogue in alternate lines, or pairs or groups of lines, of antithetical character. Also **sti·chom·y·thy,** sti·kom′i·thē.—**sti·cho·myth·ic,** *a.*

stick, stik, *n.* [O.E. *sticca* = O.H.G. *stecko* (G. *stecken*), stick.] A relatively long and slender piece of wood; a branch or shoot of a tree or shrub cut or broken off; an elon-

gated piece of wood for burning, carpentry, or other special purpose; a rod or wand; a club or cudgel; any of various elongated articles or pieces resembling sticks; as, a *stick* of candy; a stalk, as of celery. *Colloq.* an item of furniture; a stiff, dull person; a portion of liquor added to a nonalcoholic beverage. *Slang*, a golf club; baseball bat; hockey stick; baton; billiard cue; a marijuana cigarette. *Brit.* a walking stick or cane; *naut.* a mast or yard; *aeron.* the steering lever of an airplane; *milit.* a grouping of bombs released in succession so as to fall in a line over the target. *Print.* a composing stick; a stickful of type.—*v.t.*—*stuck, sticking.* To furnish, as a plant, with a stick or sticks in order to prop or support; *print.* to set, as type, in a composing stick.—**the sticks,** *colloq.* The backwoods; rural districts.

stick, stik, *v.t.*—*stuck, sticking.* [O.E. *stician*, to stab, pierce, adhere; Dan. *stikke*, D. *steken*, to pierce; G. *stecken*, to thrust, to stand fast; from a root *stig*, seen also in L. *stinguo*, to quench (as in *extinguish*), *stimulus* (for *stigmulus*), Gr. *stizō*, to prick, E. *sting*. *Stitch* is a softened form, and *stick*, n., *steak, stake, stock, ticket, etiquette*, etc., are akin.] To pierce or stab; to thrust so as to wound or penetrate; to kill in this manner; to fasten onto by piercing; as, to *stick* a pin on a dress; to secure with something inserted; as, to *stick* the sign on the wall with a thumbtack; to thrust into, out, or through, as a pin in a balloon or an arm out a window; to attach by causing to adhere to the surface. To fix or adorn with a quantity of something, usu. followed by *full of*; as, to *stick* the wall *full of* pictures; to put or set in a specified place; as, to *stick* the box behind the door; to fix into place; as, to *stick* the peg in the hole; to fix or impale on a pointed instrument; to obstruct or bring to a halt, usu. in the passive; as, to be *stuck* in a traffic jam; *colloq.* to baffle or confound, usu. in the passive; as, to be *stuck* for an answer. *Slang*, to cheat or swindle; to impose a task, responsibility, or expense upon; as, to *stick* him with the job or the bill.—*v.i.* To cleave or cling to the surface, as by tenacity or attraction; to adhere; to be fixed by a sharp point thrust in; to stay or remain in place; to hold firm or cling resolutely, as to an idea or promise, followed by *with* or *at*; to continue unremittingly or persevere, as in some work or task, followed by *with, at,* or *to*; stay close, as when shadowing or chasing someone, followed by *with* or *to*; to project, protrude, or be conspicuous, followed by *from, out, in, through,* or *up*; to be hindered from making progress; to be brought to a stop by some impediment; to have scruples about or hesitate, used with *at*.—*n.*—**stick a·round,** *slang*, to wait or remain nearby.—**stick by,** to remain loyal or faithful to.—**stick it out,** *colloq.* to endure or see something through to the end.—**stick up,** *slang*, to hold up and rob, esp. with a gun.—**stick up for,** *colloq.* to support or defend.—**stick·a·bil·i·ty,** *n.*—**stick·a·ble,** *a.*

stick·er, stik′ér, *n.* One who or that which sticks; an adhesive label; one who causes something to adhere, as by pasting; a weapon for sticking or stabbing; a burr, thorn, or the like; one who remains constant or attached; one who keeps steadily at a task or undertaking; one who kills swine by sticking or stabbing. *Colloq.* something that nonpluses one; a puzzle; a stickler.

stick·ful, stik′fụl, *n.* pl. **stick·fuls.** *Print.* as much set type as a composing stick will hold.

stick·i·ness, stik′ē·nis, *n.* The quality of being sticky; viscousness; glutinousness.—**stick·i·ly,** *adv.*

stick·ing plas·ter, *n.* An adhesive tape for closing minor wounds.

stick in·sect, *n.* Any of certain insects, as grasshoppers, locusts, or crickets, of the family *Phasmidae*, with a long, slender, twiglike body, esp. *Diapheromera femorata*, a wingless species of the U.S. Also *walking stick.*

stick-in-the-mud, stik′in·THe·mud″, *n. Colloq.* a slow, dull, or unprogressive person.

stick·le, stik′l, *v.i.*—*stickled, stickling.* [Modified by influence of *stick*, < O.E. *stihtle, stightle*, to rule, direct, < *stihtan*, to dispose, to govern.] To pertinaciously stick up for something, esp. some trifle; to demur.

stick·le·back, stik′l·bak″, *n.* [O.E. *stickle*, a prickle, and *back*, < the spines on its back.] Any of certain very small fishes found in ponds and streams, belonging to the family *Gasterosteidae*, having spines on their backs, and remarkable for building nests. Also **stick·le·back fish.**

stick·ler, stik′lér, *n.* One who insists on perfection, usu. followed by *for*; as, a *stickler for* manners; an obstinate contender about things of little consequence. *Colloq.* anything puzzling; a sticker.

stick·man, stik′man″, stik′man, *n.* pl. **stick·men.** The attendant at a craps table in a gambling establishment who uses a stick to reach the dice and handle the money. *Sports*, a player of any game, as hockey or lacrosse, in which a stick is used.

stick·pin, stik′pin″, *n.* A decorative pin, often bejeweled, to be worn on a man's tie.

stick·seed, stik′sēd″, *n.* Any of the weedy herbs constituting the genus *Lappula*, characterized by prickly seeds which adhere to clothing or animal fur.

stick·tight, stik′tīt″, *n.* A composite herb, *Bidens frondosa*, having flat, barbed achenes which adhere to animal fur or clothing. Also *bur marigold.*

stick-to-it-ive·ness, stik″tō′it·iv·nis, stik″tō′i·tiv·nis, *n. Colloq.* Dogged persistence; tenacity.

stick-up, stick·up, stik′up″, *n. Slang.* A sticking up; a holdup; a robbery.

stick·weed, stik′wēd″, *n.* Ragweed.

stick·work, stik′wụrk″, *n. Sports*, effective manipulation of the bat or stick by a player of baseball, hockey, or other games.

stick·y, stik′ē, *a.*—*stickier, stickiest.* Having the quality of adhering; viscous; coated with gluey matter; humid or damp, as the weather. *Colloq.* awkward; difficult; unpleasant; as, a *sticky* situation or problem.—**stick·i·ly,** *adv.*

stiff, stif, *a.* [O.E. *stif* = O. Fris. *stef*, D. *stijf*, L.G. *stief*, G. *steif*; root in *stand*, Skt. *stha*, to stand.] Rigid; not easily bent; not working or moving smoothly or easily, as a mechanism or machine; not supple, pliant, or free in movement; as, *stiff* joints and muscles; constrained; ungraceful; not natural or flowing; as, a *stiff* style of writing; thick or dense in consistency; not liquid or fluid; haughty, obstinate, or excessively formal in manner; tense, or drawn very tight; stable or firm against any tendency to decrease, as stock market prices; maintained in a stubborn, tenacious, or violent manner; as, a *stiff* fight; potent; as, a *stiff* remedy; having strength, power, or force of movement; as, a *stiff* current. *Slang*, unusually severe or harsh; exceedingly difficult or arduous; intoxicated or drunk; expensive or very high in price. *Naut.* carrying sails without rolling or turning over from the force of wind or waves, as a ship.—*adv.* Excessively, extremely, or totally; as, bored or scared *stiff*. —*n. Slang.* A corpse; a clumsy, rough, or boring person; a fellow, esp. a manual laborer; a vagrant.—**stiff·ish,** *a.*—**stiff·ly,** *adv.*—**stiff·ness,** *n.*

stiff-arm, stif´ärm″, *v.t. Football,* straight-arm.—*n.*

stiff·en, stif´en, *v.t.* To make stiff; to make less pliant or flexible.—*v.i.* To become stiff or stiffer; to become more rigid; to become taut; to grow more obstinate.—**stif·fen·er,** stif´e·nèr, stif´nèr, *n.*

stiff-necked, stif´nekt´, *a.* Stubborn; obstinate; haughty.

sti·fle, stī´fl, *v.t.*—**stifled, stifling.** [Icel. *stifla,* to dam up (akin to *stiff*), the sense being influenced by old *stive,* to stuff up, < Fr. *estiver,* L. *stipare,* to cram close.] To kill by impeding respiration; to suffocate or greatly oppress by foul or close air; to smother; to deaden, as flame or sound; to suppress or conceal; to repress; to restrain; to check or quell; to keep from being known.—*v.i.* To suffocate; to perish by suffocation; to breathe with difficulty, as from poor ventilation.—**sti·fler,** *n.*—**sti·fling,** *a.*—**sti·fling·ly,** *adv.*

sti·fle, stī´fl, *n.* [Perh. akin to *stiff.*] The joint of a horse or other mammal next to the buttock and corresponding to the knee in man. Also **sti·fle joint.**

stig·ma, stig´ma, *n.* pl. **stig·mas, stig·ma·ta,** stig´ma·ta, stig·mä´ta, stig·mat´a. [Gr. *stigma,* a prick with a pointed instrument, < *stizō,* to prick.] Any mark of infamy; a blemish or stain, as on one's character; a brand of disgrace attached to a person; a natural mark on the skin; *pathol.* petechia; *bot.* the upper extremity of the style, and the part which receives the pollen; *entom.* one of the apertures in the bodies of insects communicating with the air vessels.—**stig·mal,** *a.*—**stig·ma·ta,** *n.* pl. marks like the wounds on the crucified body of Christ, said to have been supernaturally impressed upon the bodies of certain persons, as St. Francis.—**stig·ma·tist,** *n.* A person marked with stigmata resembling the wounds of Christ.

stig·mas·ter·ol, stig·mas´te·rōl″, stig·mas´te·ral″, *n. Biochem.* a water-insoluble, plant sterol, $C_{29}H_{48}O$, obtained from soybeans and calabar beans, and used in manufacturing progesterone and other steroids.

stig·mat·ic, stig·mat´ik, *a.* Marked with a stigma; having the character of a stigma; *opt.* anastigmatic; *bot.* belonging to the stigma. Also **stig·mat·i·cal.**—*n.* Stigmatist.—**stig·mat·i·cal·ly,** *adv.*

stig·ma·tism, stig´ma·tiz″um, *n. Pathol.* the condition in which stigmata are present; *opt.* a condition in which there is no astigmatism.

stig·ma·tize, stig´ma·tīz″, *v.t.*—**stigmatized, stigmatizing.** [Fr. *stigmatiser,* Gr. *stigmatizō,* to brand.] To mark with a stigma or brand; to set a mark of disgrace on; to call or characterize by some opprobrious epithet; to produce marks or spots on; to mark with supernatural stigmata, as Christ's wounds at the crucifixion.—**stig·ma·ti·za·tion,** *n.*—**stig·ma·tiz·er,** *n.*

stil·bene, stil´bēn, *n.* [Gr. *stilbein,* glitter.] *Chem.* a crystalline hydrocarbon, C_6H_5CH-CHC_6H_5, used in preparation of dyes.

stil·bes·trol, stil·bes´trōl, stil·bes´tral, stil·bes´trol, *n. Chem.* a synthetic crystalline compound similar to but more powerful than estrogen. Also **di·eth·yl·stil·bes·trol.**

stil·bite, stil´bīt, *n.* [Gr. *stilbo,* to shine.] A zeolite mineral which is a hydrous silicate of aluminum, calcium, and sodium, and which frequently occurs in aggregates of crystals resembling wheat sheaves.

stile, stil, *n.* [O.E. *stigel,* a step, a ladder, < *stigan,* to mount, which appears also in *stair, stirrup,* being same as Icel. *stiga,* G. *steigen,* Goth. *steigan,* Skt. *stigh,* to ascend.] A series of steps or a frame of bars and steps in the form of an inverted 'v' for getting over a fence; a turnstile.

stile, stil, *n. Carp., furniture,* a perpendicular element in a paneling arrangement, door, window, or piece of furniture.

sti·let·to, sti·let´ō, *n.* pl. **sti·let·tos, sti·let·toes.** [It., dim. of *stilo,* a dagger, < L. *stilus,* a stile.] A small dagger having a slender blade; a pointed instrument for making eyelet holes.—*v.t.*—**stilettoed, stilettoing.** To stab or pierce with a stiletto.

still, stil, *a.* [O.E. *stille,* still, quiet, firm, fixed = D. *stil,* Dan. *stille,* G. *still.*] Motionless; silent; soft or low; as, a *still* small voice; without agitation; not sparkling or effervescing; *photog.* of or indicating a fixed or motionless picture.—*v.t.* [O.E. *stillan.*] To silence or quiet, as: Death *stilled* his powerful voice in the Senate. To appease or allay; to quiet or restrain.—*v.i.* To grow silent or calm.—*n. Poet.* noiselessness or quiet; *photog.* a motionless picture. —*adv.* Continuously, as: The boys are *still* here. Despite, nonetheless, however; motionlessly; to a greater extent; also **stil·ly.** —**still·ness,** *n.*

still, stil, *n.* [Shortened form of *distill.*] A distilling apparatus consisting essentially of a vessel or retort in which the substance is heated and vaporized, and a cooling device or coil for condensing the vapor; the vessel or retort alone; a distillery, esp. an illegal one.—*v.t., v.i.* To distill.

still a·larm, *n.* Any fire alert by other than the standard alarm signal system, esp. one by telephone.

still·birth, stil´bųrth″, *n.* The birth of any fetus or offspring which is dead; a fetus or offspring which is stillborn.

still·born, stil´bårn″, *a.* Dead at birth; abortive; produced unsuccessfully; *fig.* not attaining fruition.

still hunt, *n. Colloq.* A hunt for game carried on stealthily, as by stalking; a quiet or secret pursuit of any object.—**still-hunt,** stil´hunt″, *v.t.* To pursue by stealth.—*v.i.* To carry on a still hunt.—**still-hunt·er,** *n.*

still life, *n.* pl. **still lifes.** *Art,* the portrayal in painting or photography of such inanimate subjects as fruit, flowers, and decorative accessories; a painting or photograph of inanimate objects.—**still-life,** *a.*

still·man, stil´man″, *n.* pl. **still·men.** A distillery owner or operator; a distillation equipment operator.

still wa·ter, *n.* A section in a stream in which there is no apparent current, due to a very slight degree of inclination or a widening of the stream.

stil·ly, stil´ē, *a.* Still; quiet.—stil´lē, *adv.* Silently; without noise; calmly; quietly.

stilt, stilt, *n.* [Same as Dan. *stylte,* Sw. *stylta,* L.G. and D. *stelt,* G. *stelze,* a stilt.] A long piece of wood, metal, or like material with a rest for the foot, used in pairs for walking with the feet raised above the ground. One of several pillars used to support a structure above water or land, as: *Stilts* hold the boathouse above water.— *v.t.* To provide with or as with stilts.

stilt·ed, stil´tid, *a.* Elevated as if on stilts; pompous; stiff and bombastic; as, *stilted* language; *arch.* leaning on the uppermost section of a post treated partly as a descending extension of the arch, which appears to move upward vertically.— **stilt·ed·ly,** *adv.*—**stilt·ed·ness,** *n.*

stilt, stilt, *n.* pl. **stilt, stilts.** *Ornith.* any of various wading birds of the genus *Himantopus,* having long legs, three evident toes, and narrow bills, usu. found in low wet land.

Stil·ton, stil´ton, *n.* A well-known and highly esteemed solid, rich, white cheese, originally made at Stilton, Huntingdonshire, England, but now chiefly made in Leicestershire.—*a.*

stim·u·lant, stim´ū·lant, *n.* [L. *stimulans, stimulantis,* ppr. of *stimulo.*] That which stimulates; a stimulus; *med.* an agent, such as caffeine, which produces a quickly diffused and transient increase of vital energy, activity, and strength in an organism or some part of it.—*a.*

stim·u·late, stim´ū·lāt″, *v.t.*—**stimulated, stimulating.** [L. *stimulo, stimulatum,* to prick, to urge on, < *stimulus,* a goad; root *stig,* as in Gr. *stizo,* to prick; allied to *stick, sting.*] To excite or arouse to action by some strong motive or by persuasion; to spur on; to incite, instigate, or rouse; to excite greater vitality or keenness in; *med.* to produce a quickly diffused and transient increase of vital energy and strength of action in.—*v.i.* To act as a stimulus.— **stim·u·la·tion,** *n.*—**stim·u·la·tive,** *a.*— **stim·u·lat·er, stim·u·la·tor,** *n.*

stim·u·lus, stim´ū·lus, *n.* pl. **stim·u·li,** stim´ū·lī″. [L.] Something that incites to action or exertion; an incitement; a stimulant; *bot.* a sting, as of the nettle.

sting, sting, *v.t.*—**stung, stinging.** [O.E. *stingan* = Icel. and Sw. *stinga* = Dan. *stinge,* sting.] To prick or wound with some sharp-pointed often venom-bearing organ, as a sting or fang with which bees and certain other animals are furnished; to affect painfully or irritatingly as the result of contact, as certain plants do; as, to be *stung* by nettles; to pain sharply, hurt, or wound; to cause to smart; to affect with acute mental pain; as, to be *stung* with remorse; to goad or drive as by sharp irritation. *Slang,* to stick or impose upon; to charge exorbitantly.—*v.i.* To use or have a sting, as bees; to cause a sharp, smarting pain, as some acrid liquids; to cause acute mental pain or irritation, as by criticism; to feel a smarting pain, as from the sting of an insect or from a blow; to feel acute mental pain or irritation.—*n.* The act of stinging; a wound inflicted by stinging; the pain or smart caused by stinging; any sharp or smarting wound, hurt, or physical or mental pain; any of various sharp-pointed, often venom-bearing organs of insects and other animals capable of inflicting painful or dangerous wounds; a glandular hair on certain plants, as nettles, which emits an irritating fluid; anything or an element in anything that wounds, pains, or irritates; the capacity to wound or pain; something that goads to action by causing sharp irritation; a sharp stimulus or incitement; as, to be driven by the *sting* of jealousy.— **sting·ing·ly,** *adv.*—**sting·less,** *a.*

sting·a·ree, sting´a·rē″, sting″a·rē´, *n.* Stingray.

sting·er, sting´ẽr, *n.* One who or that which stings; an animal or plant that stings; the sting or stinging organ of an insect or other animal; *colloq.* a stinging blow, remark, or the like. A short mixed drink, made with white creme de menthe and brandy.

sting·ing hair, *n. Bot.* a protective hair, of nettles or certain other plants, whose stinging secretion is discharged when the plant is touched.

sting·ray, sting´rā″, *n.* Any of the ray family of marine fish, *Dasyatidae,* whose dorsal spines at the base of a whiplike tail are able to inflict severe, sometimes poisonous wounds. Also *stingaree, whipray.*

stin·gy, stin´jē, *a.*—**stingier, stingiest.** [Prob. < *sting*; cf. *spring, springe; swing, swinge.*] Extremely closefisted and miserly; lacking generosity; niggardly; scanty.—**stin·gi·ly,** *adv.*—**stin·gi·ness,** *n.*

stink, stingk, *v.i.*—past **stank** or **stunk,** pp. **stunk,** ppr. **stinking.** [O.E. *stincan* = D. and G. *stinken,* Dan. *stinke,* to stink; closely allied to *sting, stick.* Stench is a derivative form.] To emit a strong offensive smell; to be odious or loathsome; to have a bad reputation. *Slang,* to be of distastefully low quality; as, a movie that *stinks*; to possess an offensively large amount of something usu. followed by *of* or *with*; as, to *stink of* money, to *stink with* culture.—*v.t.* To cause to have an offensive smell, followed by *up*; as, to *stink up* the kitchen.—*n.* A strong offensive smell; a stench; *slang*, a disagreeable or scandalous commotion, as: They made a *stink* about the dismissal.—**stink out**, to repulse or force out with a repugnant odor.—**stink·ing**, sting′king, *a.*—**stink·ing·ly**, *adv.*—**stink·y**, sting′kē, *a.*—*stinkier*, *stinkiest*.

stink bug, *n.* Any of various malodorous bugs, esp. any of the broad, flat insects of the family *Pentatomidae*.

stink·er, sting′kėr, *n.* One who or that which stinks. *Slang*, an ill-smelling, disgusting, or objectionable person; something of poor quality; as, a *stinker* of a play; something considered unfairly difficult; as, a *stinker* of a math. problem. Any mechanism designed to give off an unpleasant odor. *Dial.* any of several large petrels.

stink·horn, stingk′harn″, *n.* Any of various ill-smelling fungi of the genus *Phallus*, esp. *P. impudicus*, having a very thick stalk and a cap scarcely wider than the stalk.

stink·ing smut, *n.* A disease caused by the parasitic fungus, *Tilletia foetens*, which attacks grains of wheat, replacing them with black powdery spores. Also *bunt*.

stink·pot, stingk′pot″, *n. Zool.* a type of musk turtle, *Sternotherus odoratus*, common in the southeastern U.S.

stink·stone, stingk′stōn″, *n.* Any of various stones which emit a fetid odor on being struck or rubbed, as from embedded organic matter which has become decomposed.

stink·weed, stingk′wēd″, *n.* Any one of several odious-smelling plants, as the jimson weed. See *ailanthus*.

stink·wood, stingk′wụd″, *n.* Any one of several trees whose wood has an offensive odor; the wood of a stinkwood tree.

stint, stint, *v.t.* [O.E. *styntan*, to blunt or dull, < *stunt*, dull, stupid; akin Sw. *stunta*, Icel. *stytta*, to shorten.] To limit to a particular amount or quantity, often unduly or unnecessarily; to restrict; as, to *stint* one's efforts.—*v.i.* To exert restraint; to set limits.—*n.* Limit or restraint exerted; as, to give money without *stint*; a specific amount of work assigned to be completed; as, one's *stint* for the day.—**stint·ed·ly**, *adv.*—**stint·er**, *n.*—**stint·ing·ly**, *adv.*

stint, stint, *n.* [M.E. *stynte*; origin obscure.] Any of various small sandpipers of the genus *Erolia*, abounding in N. America, esp. the least sandpiper, *Erolia minutilla*.

stipe, stīp, *n.* [L. *stipes*, a stock, a trunk.] *Bot.* the petiole of the fronds of ferns; the stem of tree ferns; the stem of certain fungi and algae. *Zool.* anything which resembles a stem in form or function.—**stiped**, *a.*

sti·pel, stī′pel, *n. Bot.* a secondary stipule at the base of a leaflet.—**sti·pel·late**, stī·pel′it, stī·pel′āt, stī″pe·lit, stī′pe·lāt″, *a.*

sti·pend, stī′pend, *n.* [L. *stipendium*—*stips*, a donation, and *pendo*, to weigh out.] Any periodical payment or compensation for services rendered; periodic payment for defraying expenses, esp. money granted to a student, as in connection with a scholarship.

sti·pen·di·ar·y, stī·pen′dē·er″ē, *a.* [L. *stipendiarius*.] Receiving wages; performing services for a stated compensation; paid or compensated for by a stipend.—*n. pl.* **sti·pen·di·ar·ies**. The recipient of a stipend.

sti·pes, stī′pēz, *n. pl.* **stip·i·tes**, stip′i·tēz″. [L. *stipes* (*stipit-*), stock, trunk, post; perh. akin to E. *stiff*.] *Bot.* a stipe. *Zool.* a stemlike part, as a footstalk; a stalk, esp. the second segment of an insect or a crustacean maxilla. —**stip·i·tate**, stip′i·tāt″, *a.*

---

stip·ple, stip′l, *v.t.*—*stippled, stippling*. [< D. *stippelen*, dim. of *stippen*, to make dots or points, < *stip*, a dot, a point; akin *stab*.] To paint, draw, or engrave by means of dots, as distinct from lines.—*n.* Painting, drawing, or engraving by means of dots; a painting done by stippling.—**stip·pler**, *n.*

stip·u·late, stip′ū·lāt″, *v.i.*—*stipulated, stipulating*. [L. *stipulor*, *stipulatus*, to stipulate, < *stipulus*, firm; akin *stipes*, a tree trunk; same root as *step, stand*.] To make an agreement or covenant to do or forbear anything, often followed by *for*.—*v.t.* To specify or arrange, as for an agreement; to require, as a condition for an agreement; to promise.—**stip·u·la·tor**, *n.*

stip·u·la·tion, stip″ū·lā′shan, *n.* [L. *stipulatio, stipulationis*.] The act of stipulating; a particular article or item in a contract; a condition.—**stip·u·la·to·ry**, stip′ū·la·tōr″ē, stip′ū·la·tạr″ē, *a.*

stip·ule, stip′ūl, *n.* [L. *stipula*, a stalk, a straw, dim. of *stipes*, a trunk.] *Bot.* a small leaflike appendage to a leaf at the base of the petiole in some species of plants.—**stip·u·lar**, *a.*—**stip·u·late**, **stip·uled**, *a.*

stir, stụr, *v.t.*—*stirred, stirring*. [O.E. *styrian, stirian*, to stir, to move; allied to D. *storen*, Sw. *stora*, G. *stören*, to disturb.] To move a utensil through, as a fluid or semisolid, in order to blend, dissolve, or agitate the ingredients; as, to *stir* paint with a paddle; to move or disturb the arrangement of, usu. to a slight degree only, as: The morning breeze *stirred* the curtains. To bestir or arouse, as from sleep; to excite or incite to action; to foment, usu. followed by *up*; as, to *stir up* dissension; to evoke, as an emotion; as, to *stir* one's anger.—*v.i.* To move slightly, as: No one *stirred* when the bell rang. To be in brisk motion; as, to be up and *stirring*; to be in progress or going on, as: What's *stirring* in that part of the world? To be deeply moved or aroused.—*n.* The action involved in stirring; bustle or brisk motion; agitation; tumult; general excitement or commotion.—**stir·rer**, *n.*

stir, stụr, *n. Slang*, a place of confinement, as a penitentiary.—**stir-cra·zy**, stụr′krā″zē, *a. Slang*, emotionally disturbed, as by long incarceration.

stir·a·bout, stụr′a·bout″, *n. Brit.* a porridge made of oatmeal or corn meal, boiled in milk or water and constantly stirred.

stirk, stụrk, *n.* [O.E. *styrc, styric*, a dim. < *steor*, a steer.] *Brit.* a bullock or heifer between one and two years old.

stirps, stụrps, *n. pl.* **stir·pes**, stụr′pēz. [L. *stock, stem, root, race, family*: cf. *extirpate*.] A stock; a family or a branch of a family; a line of descent; *law*, the person from whom a family is descended.

stir·ring, stụr′ing, *a.* Active or busy, as in business; bustling; animating; rousing; exciting.—**stir·ring·ly**, *adv.*

stir·rup, stụr′up, stir′up, stur′up, *n.* [O.E. *stigráp, stiráp*, a stirrup, < *stigan*, to mount, O.E. *steye, stye*, and *ráp*, a rope; Icel. *stigreip*.] A strap hanging from a saddle having at its lower end a suitable device for receiving the foot of the rider, used to assist one in mounting a horse, posting, and retaining one's seat; anything resembling in shape and function the stirrup of a saddle; *naut.* a rope with a thimble or an eye at the end used to support another rope that gives footing for men.

stir·rup cup, *n.* A cup of liquor presented to a rider after having mounted his horse and just before his departure; a parting drink.

stir·rup leath·er, *n.* The leather strap from which a stirrup hangs. Also **stir·rup strap**.

stir·rup pump, *n.* A small, portable pump, usu. used in putting out small fires, that is held upright by a foot bracket and pumped by hand.

stitch, stich, *v.t.* [Softened form of *stick*,

Sc. *steke*, O.E. *stician*, to pierce; cf. G. *sticken*, to embroider, to stitch.] To sew; to decorate by passing the needle repeatedly through (a material) in a continuous line; to unite together by sewing.—*v.i.* To practice needlework; to sew.—*n.* A single pass of the needle in sewing; a single turn of the thread around a needle in knitting, netting, tatting, or crocheting; a sharp pain in the side; *agric.* a furrow or ridge. *Colloq.* a small part; as, not willing to do a *stitch* of work; clothing; as, not a *stitch* to wear.—**a good stitch**, *Brit. dial.* a great distance, as in walking.—**in stitch·es**, in a state of violent laughter.—**stitch·er**, *n.*

stitch·work, stich′wụrk″, *n.* Needlework; embroidery.

stitch·wort, stich′wụrt″, *n.* Any of certain herbs of the genus *Stellaria*, as *S. holostea*, in the pink family, a white-flowered species of the Old World. One of the chickweeds, *S. graminea*, native to the U.S.; also **les·ser stitch·wort**.

stith·y, stiTH′ē, stith′ē, *n. pl.* **stith·ies**. [Also *stiddy*, Sc. *studdy*, < Icel. *stethi*, an anvil; same root as *steady, stead*.] An anvil; a forge; a smithy.

sto·a, stō′a, *n. pl.* **sto·as**, **sto·ai**, **sto·ae**, stō′ī, stō′ē. [Gr., a porch] *Gr. arch.* a long covered walk or portico with columns at the front and a wall at the back.

stoat, stōt, *n.* [Armor. *stot, staot*, urine of animals, from the fetid fluid secreted by the anal glands.] The ermine, esp. in summer when its coat is brown.

stob, stob, *n. Chiefly dial.* A stake or post; pole; a tree stump.

stoc·ca·do, sto·kä′dō, *n.* [Sp. *estocada*, It. *stoccata*, < Sp. *estoque*, It. *stocco*, a rapier, < G. *stock*, a stick.] *Archaic*, a stab or thrust with a rapier or similar weapon, as a bayonet. Also **stoc·ca·ta**, sto·kä′ta.

sto·chas·tic, sta·kas′tik, *a.* Pertaining to conjecture; random; *statistics*, pertaining to a method of approximating a correct result or achieving a certain degree of assurance of an outcome by using applicable observations that are random rather than determined or biased.

stock, stok, *n.* [O.E. *stocc* = O.Fries. and D. *stok* = O.H.G. *stoc* (G. *stock*) = Icel. *stokkr*, stock: cf. *stoccado*.] Money or property serving as capital; the subscribed capital of a company or corporation, divided into transferable shares of uniform amount; the shares of a particular company or corporation, esp. as a form of investment or as subject to fluctuation in market value; shares representing the capital of companies and corporations, as a form of property or investment, or as an article of purchase and sale. A quantity of something accumulated, as for future use, or a store which may be drawn upon as occasion demands; an aggregate of goods kept on hand by a merchant or a commercial house for sale to customers. Implements or animals used, kept, or employed in operating an establishment; the horses, cattle, sheep, and other useful animals kept or raised on a farm or ranch. A part of an object or instrument in which other parts are inserted or to which they are attached, as a body or handle supporting working parts; the wooden piece to which the barrel and lock of a rifle or other firearm are attached; the support upon which the bow of a crossbow is mounted; the beam of a plow to which the blades and handles are attached; the hub of a wheel; the block of wood from which a bell is hung; the block of wood or piece of metal which constitutes the body of a carpenter's plane; the shorter and thicker piece of a T-square; the handle or brace by which a boring bit is held and rotated; an adjustable handle for holding and turning the dies used in cutting screw

---

threads; the handle of a whip. The person from whom a given line of descent is derived; the original progenitor of a family, tribe, or race; the person with whose ownership a given succession of inheritance is considered as commencing; lineal descent or lineage; a line of descent; a family or body of descendants of a common ancestor; a tribe, race, or ethnic group; the orig. type from which a race or other group of animals or plants has been derived; a race or other related group of animals or plants; a related group of languages. The main upright part of anything, as the vertical beam of a cross; a supporting structure of various kinds; the support of the block on which an anvil is fitted, or of the anvil itself; the frame of a spinning wheel. *Pl.* the timbers or frame on which a ship or boat rests while in course of construction; a frame in which a horse or other animal is secured for shoeing or for a veterinary operation; an old instrument of punishment consisting of a framework between two posts with holes for confining the ankles and sometimes the wrists of an offender placed in a sitting position and exposed to public derision. The material from which anything is made; the broth, prepared by boiling meat with or without vegetables, used as a foundation for soups and sauces; a butt or object of unfavorable action or notice; as, a laughing*stock*; a box or trough in which hides are beaten in tanning; the part of a tally formerly given to a person making payment to the English Exchequer; *theatr.* the repertoire of a theatrical company or the company itself.—*v.t.* To furnish with a store of something; to furnish, as a shop, with goods; to lay up in store, as for future use; to lay in a stock of; to fasten or to provide with a stock, as a rifle, crossbow, plow, or anchor; to furnish with stock, as a farm with horses, cattle, and sometimes implements; to sow, as land with seed.—*v.i.* To accumulate a store of supplies; to sprout. —*a.* Of or pertaining to stock; kept regularly in stock or on hand, as for use or sale; staple; standard; of the common or ordinary type; in common use; commonplace. *Theatr.* forming part of a repertoire, as a play or piece; appearing together in repertoire, as a company; pertaining to stock plays or pieces, or to a stock company.— *adv.* Completely, used in compounds; as, *stock*-still.—**in stock,** in store or on hand as for use or sale; actually present in the stock of goods of a dealer.—**out of stock,** lacking, esp. temporarily, from the stock of goods of a dealer.—**stock up,** to lay up a stock or supply of something.—**take stock,** to make an appraisal or estimate of resources or prospects; to make an examination or inspection for the purpose of forming an opinion.—**take stock in,** take an interest in; attach importance to or put confidence in.

stock, *n. Bot.* the main stem or trunk of a tree or other plant; a rhizome or rootstock; a stem in which a graft is inserted and which is its support; a plant that furnishes slips or cuttings. A common garden plant, *Matthiola incana,* in the mustard family; also *gilly flower.*

stock·ade, sto·kād′, *n.* [= Fr. *estacade,* < Sp. *estacada,* < *estaca,* a stake; from Teut., and akin to E. *stake.*] A defensive barrier consisting of strong posts or timbers fixed upright in the ground; an enclosure or pen made with posts and stakes.—*v.t.*—*stock-aded, stockading.* To protect, fortify, or encompass with a stockade.

stock·brok·er, stok′brō″kėr, *n.* A broker who purchases and sells stocks or shares for his customers.—**stock·brok·er·age,** stok′-brō″kėr·ij, *n.*—**stock·brok·ing,** *n.*

stock car, *n.* A standard assembly line model car modified for racing; *rail.* a wooden-

slatted boxcar for transporting livestock.— **stock-car,** *a.*

stock cer·tif·i·cate, *n.* A document representing legal evidence of ownership of one or more shares of a corporation's capital stock.

stock clerk, *n.* A person who handles the goods in a stockroom.

stock com·pa·ny, *n. Finance,* a company or corporation whose capital is divided into stock shares; *theatr.* a company employed more or less permanently under the same management and appearing together in a repertoire, usu. at a single theater.

stock div·i·dend, *n. Finance.* A dividend payment to a corporation's stockholders consisting of additional shares of its own stock in lieu of a cash payment; the stock issued in such a dividend.

stock·er, stok′ėr, *n.* One who or that which stocks, esp. a maker or fitter of stocks of rifles; an animal, as a young steer, to be kept until matured or fattened before killing.

stock ex·change, *n.* The building, place, or mart where corporate stocks or securities are bought and sold; an association of brokers or dealers in stocks and bonds who buy and sell securities among themselves.

stock·fish, stok′fish″, *n.* pl. **stock·fish, stock·fish·es.** [Cf. D. and M.L.G. *stokvisch,* G. *stockfisch,* Sw. *stockfisk,* Dan. *stokfisk,* stockfish.] Any of various fishes, as cod or haddock, cured by splitting and drying in the air without salt.

stock·hold·er, stok′hōl″dėr, *n.* One who is the recorded owner of shares of stock in a corporation; also *shareholder. Aust.* a livestock owner or dealer, as a rancher.

stock·i·net, stock·i·nette, stok″i′net′, *n.* [Prob. for earlier *stocking-net.*] *Brit.* an elastic machine-knitted fabric used for making undergarments and the like. A stitch used in knitting, consisting of alternate rows of knit and purl.

stock·ing, stok′ing, *n.* A close-fitting covering, usu. knitted and of nylon, wool, cotton, or the like, for the foot and leg; something resembling such a covering, as an elastic surgical covering or wrapping for the leg, or a noticeably different ring of coloring on the lower part of an animal's leg.—**in one's stock·ing feet,** wearing stockings but not shoes.—**stock·inged,** *a.*—**stock·ing·less,** *a.*

stock·ing cap, *n.* A long cap, knitted and cone-shaped, having a pompon or tassel on the end.

stock in trade, *n.* The goods kept on hand for sale in a store; one's resources for any work, undertaking, or purpose; one's mental equipment.

stock·ish, stok′ish, *a.* Similar to a block of wood; stupid; blockish.

stock·job·ber, stok′job″ėr, *n.* One who is unscrupulous in his dealings with stocks; *Brit.* one who deals only between brokers.— **stock·job·ber·y, stock·job·bing,** *n.*

stock·man, stok′man, stok″man″, *n.* pl. **stock·men.** One having charge of stock, as on a large ranch; one who owns livestock, as a cattleman, stok′man. One who works with a stock of goods in a store or warehouse, stok′man″.

stock mar·ket, *n.* A market where stocks or shares are bought and sold; a stock exchange; the purchase and sale of stocks or shares, as: The *stock market* was dull today.

stock·pile, stok′pīl″, *n.* An accumulation of supplies or goods for future use; a stock or store, as of war materials.—*v.t., v.i.—stock-piled, stockpiling.* To amass and put away for future use; store or lay up, as critical war materials; hoard.

stock·pot, stok′pot″, *n.* A pot in which stock for soups is prepared and kept.

stock·proof, stok′prōf″, *a.* Impenetrable to livestock, as by an electrified fence.

stock·room, stok′rōm″, stok′rụm″, *n.* A

room in which a reserved stock of materials or goods for use or sale is stored.

stock split, *n.* The division of corporate stock in which additional shares are issued in specified amounts for each share already held.

stock-still, stok′stil′, *a.* Still as a fixed post; perfectly still; motionless.

stock·y, stok′ē, *a.—stockier, stockiest.* Of solid and sturdy form or build; thickset and often short, as a person; having a strong, stout stem, as a plant.—**stock·i·ly,** *adv.—* **stock·i·ness,** *n.*

stock·yard, stok′yärd″, *n.* A yard, esp. an enclosure with pens or sheds, connected with a slaughterhouse, railroad, or market, for temporarily keeping cattle, sheep, swine, or horses.

stodge, stoj, *v.t.—stodged, stodging.* [Origin obscure.] To fill to distention; cram or stuff, esp. with food; *fig.* to satiate or weary with something heavy, dull, or stodgy.—*v.i.* To move on or through with difficulty; tramp or trudge.—*n.* Any heavy, substantial food; *fig.* something heavy, tedious, or dull.

stodg·y, stoj′ē, *a.—stodgier, stodgiest.* Of a thick, semisolid consistency; heavy, as food; heavy, dull, or uninteresting; stupidly or tediously commonplace; heavy or bulky in appearance or figure; overly formal; old-fashioned; lacking style and interest; dowdy.—**stodg·i·ly,** *adv.—***stodg·i·ness,** *n.*

sto·gy, sto·gie, sto·gey, stō′gē, *n.* pl. **sto·gies.** [Earlier *stoga,* < *Conestoga,* town in southeastern Pennsylvania: cf. *Conestoga wagon.*] A long, slender, roughly made, inexpensive cigar; a rough, heavy boot or shoe; a brogan.

Sto·ic, stō′ik, *n.* [Gr. *Stoikos,* < *Stoa,* a porch in Athens where the philosopher Zeno taught.] A disciple of the Greek philosopher Zeno, who founded a sect about 308 B.C., regarding virtue as the highest good and teaching that men should strive to be free from passion, unmoved by joy or grief, and able to submit without complaint to the unavoidable necessity by which all things are governed; (*l.c.*) one who is indifferent to pleasure or pain.— *a.* Pertaining to the Stoics or their teaching; (*l.c.*) stoical.

sto·i·cal, stō′i·kal, *a.* Impassive; manifesting or maintaining indifference to pleasure or pain; (*cap.*) Stoic.—**sto·i·cal·ly,** *adv.—***sto·i·cal·ness,** *n.*

stoi·chi·om·e·try, stoe·chi·om·e·try, stoi·chei·om·e·try, stoi″kē·om′i·trē, *n.* [G. *stöchiometrie,* < Gr. *stoicheion,* element, and *-metria,* < *métron,* measure.] The science of calculating the quantities of chemical elements or compounds involved in chemical reactions.—**stoi·chi·o·met·ric, stoi·chi·o·met·ri·cal,** stoi″kē·o·me′-trik, *a.—***stoi·chi·o·met·ri·cal·ly,** *adv.*

Sto·i·cism, stō′i·siz″um, *n.* The set of opinions and maxims of the Stoics. (*l.c.*) indifference to pleasure or pain; uncomplaining endurance; impassiveness.

stoke, stōk, *v t.—stoked, stoking.* [D. *stoken,* make or tend a fire = M.L.G. *stoken,* poke and feed a fire.] To poke, stir up, and feed, as a fire; to tend the fire of, as a furnace.— *v.i.* To tend a fire or furnace; to act as a stoker.

stoke·hold, stōk′hōld″, *n. Naut.* the space or compartment containing the furnaces and boilers of a steamship. Also *stokehole.*

stoke·hole, stōk′hōl″, *n.* A hole or aperture through which a furnace is stoked; stokehold.

stok·er, stō′kėr, *n.* [D. *stoker.*] One who or that which stokes; one employed to tend a furnace used in generating steam, as on a locomotive or a steamship; a mechanical device for stoking.

Sto·ke·si·a, stō·kē′zhē·a, stō·kē′zē·a, stō-kē′zha, stōk′sē·a, *n.* An herb, *Stokesia laevis,* in the composite family, grown in the U.S. for its showy blue flowers. Also **Stokes as·ter.**

STOL, stōl, *n.* [(*S*)hort (*T*)ake-off (*O*)r (*L*)anding.] Aircraft which require only 1,500 feet of runway to safely take-off or land rather than the usual 5,000 feet.

stole, stōl, *n.* [O.E. *stole*, < L. *stola*, < Gr. *stole*, equipment, dress, garment, < *stellein*, set, place, equip, array.] An ecclesiastical vestment made of a narrow strip of ornamented silk or other material worn over the shoulders or, by deacons, over the left shoulder only, and hanging down in front to the knee or below; a scarf of fur, marabou, or fabric worn around the shoulders by women. See *tippet.*—**stoled,** *a.*

stol·id, stol'id, *a.* [L. *stolidus*, dull, *doltish*; akin to *stultus*, foolish; prob. < root of L. *sto*, E. *stand.*] Slow to feel or show emotion; dull; unexcitable.—**sto·lid·i·ty, stol·id·ness,** sto·lid'i·tē, *n.*—**stol·id·ly,** *adv.*

sto·lon, stō'lon, *n.* [L. *stolo(n-)*, shoot, sucker.] *Bot.* a slender branch or shoot which takes root at the tip and eventually develops into a new plant; *zool.* a prolongation in colonial organisms, as corals, from which arises new organisms.—**sto·lon·ate,** stō'lo·nit, stō'lo·nāt", *a.*—**sto·lo·nif·er·ous,** stō"lo·nif'ẽr·us, *a.*—**sto·lo·nif·er·ous·ly,** *adv.*

sto·ma, stō'ma, *n.* pl. **sto·ma·ta, sto·mas,** stō'ma·ta, stom'a·ta. [Gr. *stoma*, the mouth.] *Bot.* a minute pore in leaves through which gaseous exchange takes place; *zool.* a breathing pore or similar mouthlike orifice common in nematodes and insects.—**stom·a·tous,** stom'a·tus, stō'ma·tus, *a.*

stom·ach, stum'ak, *n.* [L. *stomachus*, the gullet, the stomach, < Gr. *stomachos*, the gullet, < *stoma*, a mouth.] *Anat., zool.* the pouchlike enlargement in the alimentary canal of a vertebrate body, being the principal organ of digestion where food is acted upon to yield nutrients to the body; an analogous sac or cavity for the digestion of food in an invertebrate body. The desire for food caused by hunger; appetite; inclination; liking.

stom·ach, stum'ak, *v.t.* To be able to eat, retain, or digest; to bear, as without open resentment or without opposition; to brook; as, to *stomach* an affront.

stom·ach ache, *n.* Pain in the stomach or abdomen; abdominal cramps; gastralgia; colic.

stom·ach·er, stum'a·kẽr, *n.* An ornamental covering for the chest and stomach, formerly worn by women and men, later worn only by women.

sto·mach·ic, stō·mak'ik, *a.* Pertaining to or strengthening the stomach; exciting the action of the stomach.—*n.* A medicine that strengthens the stomach and stimulates digestion.—**sto·mach·i·cal·ly,** *adv.*

stom·ach·y, stum'a·kē, *a.* Having a large, protruding stomach. *Brit. dial.* easily annoyed; irritable.

stom·a·tal, stom'a·tal, stō'ma·tal, *a.* Of, pertaining to, or of the nature of a stoma or stomata; having stomata. Also **sto·mal.**—**sto·mat·ic,** stō·mat'ik, *a.*

sto·ma·ti·tis, stō"ma·tī'tis, stom"a·tī'tis, *n. Pathol.* inflammation of the mouth.

sto·ma·tol·o·gy, stō"ma·tol'o·jē, stom"a·tol'o·jē, *n.* The medical science dealing with the mouth and its diseases.

sto·ma·to·pod, stō'ma·to·pod", stom'a·to·pod", *n.* [N.L. *Stomatopoda,* pl., < Gr. *stoma* (stomat-), mouth, and *pous* (*pod-*), foot.] Any of the *Stomatopoda,* an order of crustaceans, including the squills, having some of the legs close to the mouth, and the gills borne on the abdominal segments.—*a.* Belonging or pertaining to the *Stomatopoda.* Also **sto·ma·top·o·dous.**

sto·mo·de·um, sto·mo·dae·um, stō"mo·dē'um, stom"o·dē'um, *n.* pl. **sto·mo·de·a, sto·mo·dae·a.** [N.L. < Gr. *stoma,* mouth, and *odaios,* on the way, < *odos,* way.] *Embryol.* the oral or anterior part of the alimentary canal or digestive tract, beginning as an invagination of the ectoderm.—**sto·mo·de·al, sto·mo·dae·al,** *a.*

stomp, stomp, *v.t., v.i. Colloq.* stamp, esp. with intent to harm, often followed by *on.*—*n. Colloq.* stamp. A dance which is done to jazz music and is characterized by a step that is lively and heavy.

stone, stōn, *n.* [O.E. *stan,* a stone, a rock = D. *steen,* Dan. and Sw. *sten,* Icel. *steinn,* G. *stein,* Goth. *stains,* stone; cogn. Slav. *stjena,* Gr. *stia, stion,* a pebble. Prob. < root *sta* seen in *stand.*] A hard concretion of earth or mineral matter, as lime, silica, or clay; a generally movable mass of such material; material obtained from stones or rocks; products utilizing this material; as, paving *stone;* the nut of a drupe; a hard endocarp or seed; a backgammon piece. *Med.* a calculous concretion in the kidneys or bladder; the disease arising therefrom. *Print.* the imposing stone; the surface on which pages are composed by setting type from galleys into page forms. *Sports,* a heavy rock, sometimes polished, used in certain sports of strength, esp. curling; *Brit.* a common measure of weight, the English standard stone being 14 pounds avoirdupois, although other values are in use for certain commodities; *glass manuf.* an imperfection caused by crystallization of glass around unmelted raw material or of particles from the melting crucible.—*v.t. stoned, stoning.* To throw stones at; to drive by pelting with stones; to put to death by pelting with stones; to remove the seed from, as a drupe; to utilize stones in constructing; as, to *stone* a driveway; to use a stone to sharpen or polish.—*v.i.*—*a.*—**cast the first stone,** to be the first to accuse.—**leave no stone un·turned,** to pursue all possibilities.—**stoned,** *a. Slang,* intoxicated or drugged.—**ston·er,** *n.*

Stone Age, *n.* The age in the history of mankind, preceding the Bronze and Iron Ages and marked by the use of stone implements.

stone-blind, stōn'blīnd', *a.* Entirely blind. —**stone-blind·ness,** *n.*

stone-broke, stōn'brōk', *a. Colloq.* Completely destitute; without funds.

stone·chat, stōn'chat", *n.* Any of various thrushlike birds of Europe of the genus *Saxicola,* esp. *S. torquata,* which has a brown back and a red breast, and an alarm note resembling the striking together of pebbles.

stone·crop, stōn'krop", *n.* [O.E. *stan-crop, crop* meaning cluster.] A mosslike herb, *Sedum acre,* of the orpine family, *Crassulaceae,* having small fleshy leaves and yellow flowers, and found on rocks and walls.

stone·cut·ter, stōn'kut"ẽr, *n.* One who cuts or processes stone; a mechanical apparatus for cutting or processing stone.—**stone·cut·ting,** *n.*

stone-deaf, stōn'def', *a.* Totally deaf.

stone·fish, stōn'fish", *n.* pl. **stone·fish, stone·fish·es.** A tropical scorpion fish, *Synanceja verrucosa,* having venomous dorsal spines.

stone·fly, stōn'flī", *n.* pl. **stone·flies.** Any of the numerous insects constituting the order *Plecoptera,* whose larvae abound under stones in streams, and are used as bait by fishermen.

stone fruit, *n.* Fruit having a hard endocarp or stone, as peaches, cherries, or plums; a drupe.

stone·lil·y, *n.* An echinoderm; the fossil of a sea lily having jointed cylindrical stems with radial arms and anchored to the ocean floor by stalks.

stone·ma·son, stōn'mā"son, *n.* One who prepares stones for building, or builds with them.—**stone·ma·son·ry,** *n.*

stone pars·ley, *n.* A European plant, *Sison amomum,* yielding aromatic seeds, used as a spice in cooking.

stone·roll·er, stōn'rō"lẽr, *n.* A small fish of the carp family, *Campostoma anomalum,* of the U.S.; the hammerhead, *Hypentelium nigricans,* a fish of the sucker family.

stone·wall, stōn'wạl", *v.i.* Of a batsman in cricket, to play defensively by continually blocking the ball instead of batting it. *Brit.* to use delaying tactics in politics; to filibuster.—**stone·wall·er,** *n.*

stone·ware, stōn'wâr", *n.* A type of opaque, highly glazed pottery made from a composition of sand, clay, and flint.

stone·work, stōn'wụrk", *n.* Any work or construction made of stone, esp. masonry; the various processes involved in cutting, finishing, designing, or setting stone; *pl.* the building or place where stone is processed for use.—**stone·work·er,** *n.*

stone·wort, stōn'wụrt", *n.* Any green alga of the family *Characeae,* which grows in fresh water and is characterized by a jointed body encrusted with lime deposits.

ston·y, ston·ey, stō'nē, *a.*—**stonier, stoniest.** Pertaining to, abounding in, or resembling stone or rock; pitiless or insensitive; obdurate; rigid or without motion; expressionless; petrifying; *slang,* stonebroke.—**ston·i·ly,** *adv.*—**ston·i·ness,** *n.*

ston·y-heart·ed, ston·y·heart·ed, stō'nē·här'tid, *a.* Hard-hearted; unfeeling.—**ston·y-heart·ed·ly, ston·y·heart·ed·ly,** *adv.*—**ston·y-heart·ed·ness, ston·y·heart·ed·ness,** *n.*

stooge, stōj, *n.* [Origin unknown.] One who acts as a foil, as for a comedian; *slang,* an underling or stool pigeon.—*v.i.*—**stooged, stooging.** To act as a stooge.

stook, stụk, stōk, *n.* [L.G. *stuke,* G. *stauch,* a heap of turf, flax, etc.] *Brit.* a shock or grouping of sheaves of grain.—*v.t. Brit.* to set up in stooks.—**stook·er,** *n.*

stool, stōl, *n.* [O.E. *stól,* a seat = D. *stoel,* Sw. and Dan. *stol,* Icel. *stóll,* G. *stuhl,* Goth. *stolls;* cogn. Slav. *stul, stol.*] A seat with three or four legs but without arms or back, intended as a seat for one person; a low seat used as a footrest or support for the knees while kneeling; the seat used in evacuating the bowels; a discharge from the bowels. *Bot.* the stump of a timber tree which throws up shoots; the cluster of shoots thus produced; a plant which produces new shoots or plants.—*v.i.* To send out shoots, as a plant; *slang,* to be an informer or stool pigeon.

stool pi·geon, *n.* A pigeon used as a decoy. *Slang,* one who acts as a spy or informer for the police; a person employed as a decoy or secret confederate, as by gamblers; also **stool·ie.**

stoop, stōp, *v.i.* [O.E. *stupian* = M.D. *stuypen* = Icel. *stupa* = Sw. *stupa,* stoop, incline.] To bend, bow, lean, or collapse the head and shoulders or the body forward and downward from an erect position; as, to *stoop* down to pick a flower, to *stoop* for a low door; to carry the head and shoulders habitually bowed forward; as, to *stoop* from age; to condescend or deign; to demean, degrade, or lower oneself; as, to *stoop* to another's level, to *stoop* to flattery; to pounce or swoop, as: A hawk *stoops* on prey.—*v.t.* To bend, bow, lean, or collapse, as the top part of something; as, to *stoop* the head; to bring down from an accustomed or proper level of dignity; to let down or lower, as a sail or flag.—*n.* An act of stooping; a stooping movement; a stooping attitude or carriage of body, as a slouch; a descent from dignity or superiority; a condescension; the downward swoop of a bird of prey.—**stoop·er**, *n.*—**stoop·-ing·ly**, *adv.*—**stoop-shoul·dered**, *a.* Having a habitual stoop to the shoulders.

stoop, stŏp, *n.* [D. *stoep* (pron. *stoop*); the word was brought to America by the Dutch.] The steps rising into a platform at the entrance of a house; a small porch entranceway to a house.

stop, stop, *v.t.*—*stopped, stopping.* [O.E. *stoppian* (recorded in composition) = D. *stoppen* = G. *stopfen*, < M.L. *stuppare, stupare*, stop, orig. with tow, < L. *stuppa*, tow: cf. *stupe* and *estop*.] To halt, arrest, interrupt, check, bring to a standstill; to restrain, hinder, prevent, or hold back from proceeding, acting, operating, continuing, or completing; to cut off, intercept, or withhold; as, to *stop* payment on a check; to cease, desist, or to put an end to; as, to *stop* gambling; to discontinue; as, to *stop* manufacturing; to obstruct; to block shut or block open; to close, as a door; to stanch, as a flow of blood. *Sports*, to check, ward off, or parry, as a blow or stroke; to knock out, as in boxing; to keep, as an opponent, from making a score; to end, as an opponent's winning streak or run of tricks in a game of bridge; to defeat, as an opponent. *Mus.* to close, as one of the holes in a wind instrument, to produce a particular note; to press, as a string on a stringed instrument, to alter a note; to play, as to manipulate a stop on an organ. *Phon.* to occlude, as by halting then releasing the breath stream, to voice a plosive consonant; *gram.* to punctuate, as with marks or use of the word stop in a telegram; *naut.* to make fast or lash, as a sail.—*v.i.* To come to a halt, as in a journey; to cease moving, proceeding, speaking, acting, or operating; to pause or come to an end; to make a stay at a place; to stay, remain, or sojourn.—**stop down**, *photog.* to limit the size of the aperture of, as a lens, by utilizing a diaphragm.

stop, stop, *n.* The act of stopping or halting; a closing or filling up, as of a hole; a blockage or obstruction, as of a passage or way; the state of being at a standstill; an arrest of movement, action, or operation; a check; an end put to anything; a coming to a standstill or to an end of movement; a halt or pause; a cessation; a stay or sojourn made at a place, as in the course of a journey; something that stops; a plug or other stopper for an opening, as in a sink; an obstacle or hindrance; any device that serves to check or control movement or action in a mechanism; *sports*, a save or play that stops an opponent from scoring; *naut.* a binding or lash, as for a sail; *gram.* a punctuation mark, as a period. *Mus.* a hole in a wind instrument; the act of closing a hole in a wind instrument or pressing the string in a stringed instrument to produce a particular note; a row of pipes in an organ; a lever that puts a row of organ pipes into or out of operation. *Phon.* an occlusion or plosion; an explosive sound voiced by halting then releasing the breath stream, as in the consonants *p* and *b* formed by the lips, *k* and *g* formed by the tongue and soft palate, and *t* and *d* formed by the tongue and gums; see *glottal stop*, *suction stop*; compare *continuant.*—*a.*—**stop knob**, the knob of a lever that controls a row of pipes or some other part of an organ.

stop bath, *n. Photog.* an acid wash or bath used to stop the development of a photographic print or negative. Also *shortstop*, **short·stop bath**.

stop·cock, stop′kok″, *n.* A short pipe with a valve operated by a handle, used to regulate the flow of a liquid or gas from a receptacle or through a pipe; a cock; a faucet; a tap.

stope, stŏp, *n. Min.* an underground excavation from which ore is removed in a

series of horizontal steps, either from above or below a level.—*v.t.*, *v.i.*—*stoped, stoping. Min.* to work or excavate by stopes.

stop·gap, stop′gap″, *n.* That which fills up a gap; a temporary expedient or substitute; makeshift.—*a.*

stop·light, stop′lit″, *n.* A traffic signal which directs the pedestrian or motorist to stop; a red taillight on a vehicle which lights up to indicate when the driver is slowing down or stopping.

stop-loss or·der, *n. Stock market*, a standing order from a client to a broker to sell a stock if it goes down to a specified market price.

stop or·der, *n. Stock market*, a directive given by a client to a broker to buy or sell a stock at a specified market price.

stop·o·ver, stop′ŏ″vėr, *n.* A short stop at a point in a journey; a stop with the privilege of continuing the journey later without extra fare.

stop·page, stop′ij, *n.* The act of stopping or state of being stopped; arrest of progress or motion; a halt; as, work *stoppage*; a deduction made from pay or allowances.

stop pay·ment, *n.* An order by a customer to his bank to withhold payment on a certain check drawn by him.

stop·per, stop′ėr, *n.* One who or that which stops; a plug or piece for closing a bottle, tube, drain, or the like; a stopple. *Colloq.* a specific actor, scene, or number, esp. in an elaborate stage production, which attracts prolonged applause thereby temporarily stopping the action; any item which attracts unusual attention. *Cards*, any card in a suit which effectively blocks further taking of tricks in that suit by the opponents.—*v.t.* To close or fit with any stopper or plug.

stop·ple, stop′l, *n.* [Dim. of *stop*: same as L.G. *stöppel*, G. *stöpfel*, *stöpsel*, a stopple.] That which stops or closes the mouth of a bottle; a stopper, cork, or plug.—*v.t.*—*stoppled, stoppling.* To close with a stopple.

stop street, *n.* A secondary street on which vehicular traffic is required to stop before entering or crossing an intersecting through street.

stop·watch, stop′woch″, *n.* A watch, marked in fractions of seconds, which can be instantaneously stopped or started, used for timing races or test runs.

stor·age, stōr′ij, star′ij, *n.* The act of storing or being stored; the act of depositing in a warehouse; a certain place or space in which to keep something. *Computer*, the component in a computer that stores pertinent information for ready access; also *memory*. The act of charging a storage battery; a price for keeping goods in storage.

stor·age cell, *n. Elect.* a cell or connection of cells capable of being recharged by a reverse flow of current through the electrolyte. Also **stor·age bat·ter·y.**

sto·rax, stōr′aks, star′aks, *n.* [L. *storax*, *styrax*, < Gr. *stúrax*, storax (resin and tree).] A solid resin with a vanillalike odor obtained from a small styracaceous tree, *Styrax officinalis*, and formerly much used in medicine and perfumery; the tree itself; any plant of the genus *Styrax*, having groups of white flowers; a liquid balsam obtained from species of *Liquidambar*, esp. from the wood and inner bark of *L. orientalis*, a tree of Asia Minor. Also *styrax.*

store, stōr, star, *n.* [O.Fr. *estor*, supplies, stock, < *estorer*.] A place where goods are kept for sale; a shop; *pl.* supplies of food, clothing, or other requirements, as for a household or other establishment, a ship, naval or military forces, or the like; a supply or stock, as for future use; a stock of anything accumulated or possessed; as, a *store* of information.—*v.t.*—*stored, storing.* [O.Fr. *estorer*, build, establish, supply, stock, < L.

instaurare, renew, restore, erect, make: cf. *instauration* and *restore.*] To supply or stock with something, as for future use; to lay up or put away, as a supply for future use, often with *up* or *away*; deposit in a storehouse, warehouse, or other place, for keeping.—**in store**, the state of being stored up, on hand, or in reserve; as, to keep a thing *in store.*—**set store by**, to esteem or regard; as, to *set* much, great, or little *store by* a thing.—**stor·er**, *n.*

store·house, stōr′hous″, star′hous″, *n.* A house or building in which things are stored; any repository or source of abundant supplies; a treasury, as of facts or knowledge.

store·keep·er, stōr′kē″pėr, star′kē″pėr, *n.* An owner or manager of a retail shop; a shopkeeper; one in charge of a store or stores; an officer or official in charge of naval or military stores.

store·room, stōr′rōm″, stōr′rųm″, star′-rōm″, star′rųm″, *n.* A room in which supplies, household articles, or odds and ends may be stored.

sto·ried, stōr′ēd, star′ēd, *a.* Recorded or celebrated in history or story; as, the *storied* monarch; ornamented with designs representing historical, legendary, or similar subjects, by means of painting, sculpture, needlework, or other art; as, a *storied* urn.

sto·ried, **sto·reyed**, stōr′ēd, star′ēd, *a.* Having stories or floors, usu. used in compounds; as, two-*storied* houses.

stork, stark, *n.* pl. **storks**, **stork**. [O.E. *storc* = D., Dan., and Sw. *stork*, Icel. *storkr*, G. *storch*, stork; root meaning doubtful.] Any of several tall wading birds of the family *Ciconiidae*, mostly of the Old World, as the white stork, *Ciconia ciconia.*

stork's-bill, starks′bil″, *n.* Any plant of the genus *Pelargonium*, or the related genus *Erodium*, in the geranium family, so-called from the long-beaked pods.

storm, starm, *n.* [O.E. *storm* = D. *storm* = G. *sturm* = Icel. *stormr* = Sw. and Dan. *storm*, storm.] A disturbance of the normal condition of the atmosphere, manifesting itself by winds of unusual force or direction, often accompanied by rain, snow, hail, thunder and lightning, or flying sand or dust; a wind force of the 11th degree, 64–72 miles per hour, on the Beaufort scale; a tempest; a heavy fall of rain, snow, or hail, or a violent outbreak of thunder and lightning, unaccompanied by strong wind; a disturbance resembling a storm of wind or rain; as, a magnetic *storm. Fig.* a heavy descent or discharge of missiles or blows; a violent disturbance of affairs, as a civil, political, social, or domestic commotion; a violent outburst or outbreak, as of sounds, speech, or emotional expression; a fit of violent emotion or other disturbance within the mind.—*v.i.* To blow with unusual force, or to rain, snow, or hail, esp. with violence. *Fig.* to rage with violence or angry fury; to complain or scold violently; to rush with violence; as, to *storm* out of a room; to go or travel with furious speed. *Milit.* to deliver a violent attack or fire, as with artillery; to rush to an assault or attack.—*v.t.* To subject to or as to a storm; to utter or say with angry vehemence; *milit.* to make a violent assault on, as a fortified position, or take by assault or storm.

storm and stress, *n.* Sturm und Drang.

storm boat, *n. Milit.* assault boat.

storm·bound, starm′bound″, *a.* Confined or detained by storms.

storm cel·lar, *n.* A cellar or underground chamber for refuge during violent storms.

storm cen·ter, *n. Meteor.* the center of a cyclonic storm, the area of lowest pressure and of comparative calm; *fig.* a center of disturbance, tumult, trouble, or the like.

storm door, *n.* An outer or additional door for protection against stormy weather and winter cold.

storm pet·rel, *n. Ornith.* an oceanic bird, *Hydrobates pelagicus,* occurring more frequently near ships during stormy weather. Also *Mother Carey's chicken, stormy petrel.*

storm troop·er, *n.* A member of Germany's former Nazi party militia known as the 'Sturmabteilung.' Also *Brown Shirt.*

storm win·dow, *n.* An additional window used outside another window to provide insulation and protection from weather; *colloq.* storm.

storm·y, stȯr′mē, *a.*—stormier, stormiest. Characterized by storm or tempest; tempestuous; boisterous; characterized by violence of feeling; passionate; angry.—**storm·i·ly,** *adv.*—**storm·i·ness,** *n.*

storm·y pet·rel, *n. Ornith.* storm petrel; *fig.* a person whose coming is supposed to portend trouble.

sto·ry, stȯr′ē, stȯr′ē, *n.* pl. **sto·ries.** [A.Fr. *storie, estorie,* O.Fr. *estoire* (Fr. *histoire*), < L. *historia,* history, story.] A narrative, either true or fictitious, in prose or verse, designed to interest or amuse the hearer or reader; a tale; a fictitious tale, shorter and less elaborate than a novel; such narratives or tales as a branch of literature; as, a character famous in *story* and song; the plot, or succession of incidents, of a novel, poem, drama, or the like; a narration of a series of events, or a series of events that are or may be narrated; a real or fictitious incident related to interest, amuse, or illustrate some point; an anecdote; a narration of the events in the life of a person or the existence of a thing, or such events, as a subject for narration; a report, account, or rumor of a matter; a statement or allegation; *journ.* an account of something, as of some item of news, in a newspaper; *colloq.* a falsehood or lie. A history, legend, or romance.—*v.t.*—storied, storying. To ornament with pictured scenes as from history or legend.—**sto·ry·writ·er,** *n.*

sto·ry, stȯr′ē, stȯr′ē, *n.* pl. **sto·ries.** [M.E. *story,* < A.L. *historia,* story or stage of a building, appar. the same word as L. *historia,* history, story.] A complete horizontal section of a building, having one continuous or approximately continuous floor; the set of rooms on the same floor or level of a building; one of the structural architectural divisions in the height of a building; each of a series of divisions or stages of anything, placed horizontally one above another. Also *chiefly Brit.* **sto·rey.**

sto·ry·book, stȯr′ē·bŏŏk″, stȯr′ē·bŏŏk″, *n.* A book containing one or more stories, often illustrated in color, usu. for children.

sto·ry line, *n.* The plot or main series of happenings of a novel, play, film, or the like.

sto·ry·tell·er, stȯr′ē·tel″ėr, stȯr′ē·tel″ėr, *n.* One who tells stories, true or fictitious; a writer of stories; *colloq.* a liar or fibber.—**sto·ry·tell·ing,** *a., n.*

stoss, stȯs, *G.* shtȯs, *a. Geol.* having to do with the side of a hill, boss, or crag that meets the impact of a glacier or other moving body.

stound, stound, stȯnd, *n. Brit. dial.* sudden amazement; surprise. *Obs.* a moment; a short while.

stoup, stȯp, *n.* [Same as Icel. *staup,* G. *stauf,* a pot, vessel, cup.] A basin for holy water placed in a niche at the entrance of Roman Catholic churches. *Brit. dial.* a deep narrow vessel for holding liquids; a flagon or tankard; the measure of liquid content; as, a pint *stoup.*

stout, stout, *a.* [O.Fr. *estout, estult,* proud, bold, stout; < Teut., and akin to G. *stolz,* proud, and perh. also to E. *stilt.*] Bulky in

figure, solidly built, or thickset, as persons; corpulent or fat; bold, hardy, or dauntless; as, a *stout* heart; firm, determined, stubborn, or uncompromising; as, *stout* resistance; violent or forceful; as, a *stout* storm; strong of body, stalwart, or sturdy; possessed of endurance or staying power, as a horse; strong in substance or construction; as, *stout* walls; strong and thick or heavy; as, a *stout* club.—*n.* Strong dark ale, beer, or porter; a stout or corpulent person, or a garment for such a person.—**stout·ish,** stou′tish, *a.*—**stout·ly,** *adv.*—**stout·ness,** *n.*

stout-heart·ed, stout′här″tid, *a.* Brave and resolute; dauntless; courageous.—**stout-heart·ed·ly,** *adv.*—**stout-heart·ed·ness,** *n.*

stove, stȯv, *n.* [O.E. *stofe,* a stove; Icel. *stofa, stufa,* a bathing room with a stove; D. *stoof,* a stove; G. *stube,* a room; akin *stew.*] An apparatus which provides heat for cooking or for heating a room or house by means of electricity or by burning fuel; a house or room artificially heated to a high temperature, and used for drying, baking, and the like; *Brit. hort.* a hothouse in which artificial heat is maintained at a constantly high temperature.—*v.t.*—stoved, stoving. To heat in or as in a stove.

stove·pipe, stȯv′pīp″, *n.* A pipe, as of sheet metal, serving as the chimney of a stove or connecting a stove with a chimney flue. *Colloq.* a man's hat, which is very tall and made of silk; also **stove·pipe hat.**

sto·ver, stȯ′vėr, *n.* [O.Fr. *estover.*] Fodder or litter for cattle.

stow, stȯ, *v.t.* [M.E. *stowen,* < *stowe* < O.E. *stōw* = O.Fries. *stō,* a place; from the root of E. *stand.*] *Naut.* to place, as cargo, in proper order in the hold or some other part of a ship; to place, as guns or oars, in the proper receptacles. To put in a place or receptacle, as for storage or reserve; to place or arrange compactly, or pack; to fill, as a place or receptacle, by packing; of a place or receptacle, to afford room for or to hold; *slang,* to desist from, as: *Stow* it.

stow·age, stȯ′ij, *n.* The act or operation of stowing; the state or manner of being stowed; room or accommodation for stowing something; a place in which something is or may be stowed; that which is stowed or to be stowed; a charge for stowing something.

stow·a·way, stȯ′a·wā″, *n.* One who conceals himself aboard a ship or other conveyance in order to obtain free passage or to escape by stealth from a place.—**stow a·way,** to conceal, as oneself, aboard a ship or other conveyance; to put away, as in a safe or convenient place or so as to be out of the way; to put, as a person, in a place of concealment.

stra·bis·mus, stra·biz′mŭs, *n.* [N.L. < Gr. *strabismós,* < *strabizein,* to squint, < *strabós,* oblique, squinting.] *Pathol.* A disorder of vision due to the turning of one eye or both eyes from the normal position so that both cannot be directed at the same point or object at the same time; squint; cross-eye.—**stra·bis·mal,** **stra·bis·mic,** **stra·bis·mi·cal,** *a.*

strad·dle, strad′l, *v.t.*—straddled, straddling. [A freq. form connected with *stride.*] To spread wide apart, as the legs; to walk, stand, or sit with one leg on each side of; to stand or sit astride of; to take up or occupy an equivocal position in regard to, or appear to favor both sides of; as, to *straddle* a touchy question.—*v.i.* To walk, stand, or sit with the legs wide apart; as, a child *straddling* across a room; to stand or sit astride; to stand spread apart; as, legs *straddled* wide; *colloq.* to take up or occupy an equivocal position in regard to something, or appear to favor both sides.—*n.* The action or an act of straddling; the distance

straddled; *colloq.* a taking or holding of an equivocal or noncommittal position; *finance,* a privilege giving the holder the right, at his option, either of delivering or of buying a certain amount of stock, or the like, at a specified price, within a fixed time.—**strad·dler,** *n.*

Strad·i·var·i·us, strad″i·vâr′ē·ŭs, *n.* One of the stringed instruments, esp. a violin, famous for outstanding quality, made by Antonio Stradivari, c. 1644-1737, of Cremona, Italy.

strafe, sträf, sträf, *v.t.*—strafed, strafing. [G. *strafen,* punish, chastise: much used in 1914 and following years in German maledictions directed against England.] To bombard heavily; assail with machine guns fired from attack planes. *Slang,* to punish or chastise.—*n.* A strafing; *milit.* an air attack on enemy troops, esp. by machine-gun fire.—**straf·er,** *n.*

strag·gle, strag′l, *v.i.*—straggled, straggling. [Appar. a freq. form connected with M.E. *straken,* move, go, perh. related to E. *stretch.*] To wander about in a scattered fashion, as a number of persons or animals without a fixed common course; to scatter from a road or a line of march; to wander away, as individuals, from a group; to stray from the road, course, or line of march; to go, come, or travel in a scattered or rambling fashion; to wander, stray, or ramble; to move, pass, or come in an irregular, erratic, or random way; to extend irregularly in various directions, or without orderly and compact arrangement.—**strag·gler,** *n.*

strag·gly, strag′lē, *a.*—stragglier, straggliest. Straggling; disorganized; rambling; spreading or extending irregularly.

straight, strāt, *a.* [M.E. *streight, streiht,* orig. pp. of *strecchen,* E. *stretch.*] Without crooks, bends, or curvature; having the linear form or uniform direction of stretched string; evenly formed or set; as, *straight* shoulders; direct, or leading or going directly to some point; as, a *straight* path to ruin; *fig.* candid, plain, or without circumlocution; as, *straight* talk; straightforward, honest, honorable, or upright, as conduct or dealings; virtuous or chaste, as a woman; right or correct, as reasoning; in the proper order or condition; as, *straight* accounts; continuous or unbroken; as, a *straight* flush in poker; thoroughgoing or unreserved; as, a *straight* Republican; unmodified or unaltered; as, *straight* comedy; *colloq.* undiluted or unblended, as whiskey; reliable, as reports.—*n.* The condition of being straight; a straight form or position; a straight line; a straight section, as of an auto racing course; *poker,* a sequence of five cards of various suits.—*adv.* In a straight line; without crookedness, bends, or curves; as, to walk *straight;* in a straight or even form or position; as, to sit *straight;* in a straight or direct course to some point, or directly; as, to go *straight* to a place. *Fig.* without circumlocution; straightforwardly, honestly, honorably, or virtuously; as, to go *straight;* in a continuous course; as, to keep *straight* on; without delay; immediately, followed by *off;* without qualification of any kind; as, selling cigars at ten cents *straight.*—**straight·ly,** *adv.*—**straight·ness,** *n.*—**straight·ish,** *a.*

straight an·gle, *n. Geom.* an angle of 180°.

straight-arm, strāt′ärm″, *v.t. Football,* to ward off, as an opponent, using the arm held out straight and stiff.—*n.* Also *stiff-arm.*

straight·a·way, strāt′a·wā″, *a.* Straight onward, without turn or curve, as a course in horse racing or yacht racing.—*n.* A straightaway course for racing, or a race over such a course; a straight section of a race course.—*adv. Chiefly Brit.* immediately, or right away. Also *straightway.*

straight chain, *n. Chem.* an open chain of atoms, most often carbon, without branches or side chains.

straight·edge, strāt′ej″, *n.* A piece or bar of wood, plastic, or metal made perfectly straight on the edge, and used to test surfaces or to draw straight lines.

straight·en, strāt′en, *v.t., v.i.* To make straight; to become straight.—**straight·en·er**, *n.*

straight face, *n.* A face without expression, esp. when concealing merriment.—**straight-faced**, *a.*

straight·for·ward, strāt″fȧr′wėrd, *a.* Proceeding ahead in a straight course; not deviating; upright; honest; open; absent of deceit.—*adv.*—**straight·for·ward·ly**, **straight·for·wards**, *adv.*—**straight·for·ward·ness**, *n.*

straight-line, strāt′lin′, *a.* Having straight lines. *Mach.* denoting a machine or other mechanism whose principal parts lie or function in a straight line; denoting a linkage mechanism designed to produce or reproduce motion in a straight line. Changing by uniform increments or decrements over a period of time; as, a *straight-line* amortization.

straight man, *n.* A stooge; an entertainer who feeds lines to another comedian and acts as his foil.

straight off, *adv.* Immediately; right away.

straight-out, strāt′out′, *a. Colloq.* Thoroughgoing; out-and-out; forthright.

straight ra·zor, *n.* A straight steel razor, the blade of which folds into the handle.

straight tick·et, *n.* A vote cast for all nominees of the same political party; a party slate on which all candidates are regular party members.

straight·way, strāt′wā′, *adv.* Immediately; forthwith; without delay.—*a.*

strain, strān, *n.* [O.E. *strēon*, *gestrēon*, gain, acquisition, begetting, progeny.] Ancestry or descent; as, a man of noble *strain*; the group of descendants of a common ancestor, as a family, stock, or race; hereditary or natural character or disposition; a hereditary tendency or trait; an element in one's make-up; as, to have a *strain* of melancholy; a streak or trace; a kind or sort; a group of animals or plants equivalent to, or forming a part of a race, breed, or variety; an artificial variety, or a slight variation from a given breed or stock, of a domestic animal; a group of cultivated plants distinguished from other plants of the species or variety to which it belongs by some intrinsic quality, as a tendency to yield heavily.

strain, strān, *v.t.* [O.Fr. *estreindre* (Fr. *étreindre*), < L. *stringere* (pp. *strictus*), draw tight.] To draw tight or taut, as a line; stretch; bring to a state of tension; stretch to the upmost tension or exert to the utmost; as, to *strain* every nerve to accomplish something; to impair, injure, or weaken by stretching or overexertion, as a muscle or tendon; imperil the strength of by subjecting to too great stress; cause mechanical deformation in, as a body or structure, as the result of stress; *fig.* to stretch or force beyond the proper point or limit; as, to *strain* one's authority. Make excessive demands upon, or tax severely, as resources or credit; clasp tightly in the arms or the hand; to press or pass, as thick liquid, through a colander, cloth, or other filter, to separate the clear liquid from denser or solid constituents.—*v.i.* To exert a stretching force; pull forcibly against something; as, a dog *straining* at a leash; *fig.* to balk; as, to *strain* at doing an unpleasant chore. Make extraordinarily physical or mental effort; to be subjected to

tension or stress; suffer a strain, as to a muscle or tendon.—*n.* A forcible straining or stretching of something; stress; the condition of being strained or stretched; an injury to a muscle, tendon, or other ligament, due to excessive tension or use; a distortion of any body or structure resulting from stress; *mech.* the deformation of a body, resulting from mechanical stress. Strong muscular or physical effort; great effort of any kind; a severe demand or tax, or something that makes such a demand, on powers, resources, feelings, or character traits; as, a *strain* on one's pocketbook, credulity, or good nature. A melody, tune, or song; a passage or piece of poetry; a flow or burst of language; eloquence; tone, style, or spirit in expression.

strain·er, strā′nėr, *n.* One who or that which strains, esp. a filter, colander, or cloth, for straining liquids; a device for stretching or tightening.

strain·om·e·ter, strā·nom′i·tėr, *n.* Extensometer.

strait, strāt, *n.* [O.Fr. *estreit* (Fr. *étroit*), < L. *strictus*, pp. of *stringere*, draw tight.] *Often pl. but sing. in constr.* a narrow passage of water connecting two larger bodies of water; *often pl.* a position of difficulty, distress, or need; as, in desperate *straits*. —*a.* Strict, as in standards; limited in space.—**strait·ly**, *adv.*—**strait·ness**, *n.*

strait·en, strāt′en, *v.t.* To make strait; to contract, confine, hem in, narrow; to press with poverty or other necessity; to put in financial difficulties.

strait jack·et, *n.* A kind of jacket or coat of strong material for confining violent patients or other persons, the arms being made fast within the jacket or within very long sleeves whose ends are secured.—**strait-jack·et**, *v.t.* To bind or confine, as in a strait jacket.

strait-laced, strāt′lāst′, *a.* Constrained; strict in manners or morals; excessively and puritanically strict.—**strait-lac·ed·ly**, *adv.* —**strait-lac·ed·ness**, *n.*

strake, strāk, *n.* [A form of *streak*.] *Naut.* a continuous line of planking or plates on a ship's side, reaching from stem to stern.

stra·mo·ni·um, stra·mō′nē·um, *n.* The jimson weed; the thorn apple; a powerful alkaloid extracted from the dried leaves of a poisonous plant, *Datura stramonium*, used as a narcotic, and in medicine for the treatment of asthma.

strand, strand, *n.* [O.E. *strand* = D. and G. *strand* = Icel. *strönd* (*strand-*), strand, shore.] The land bordering a sea or other body of water; shore; that part of the shoreline between high and low tide marks. —*v.t.* To drive or leave, as a ship or fish, aground on a shoreline; to leave in a position of helplessness or isolation: usu. used in the passive.—*v.i.* To be driven or run ashore; to become halted in difficulties.

strand, strand, *n.* [M.E. *strond*; origin uncertain.] A number of yarns or threads constituting one of the parts which are twisted together to form a rope or cord; as, a rope of three *strands*; a similar part of a wire rope; a thread, hair, fiber, or filament; a string of pearls or beads.—*v.t.* To break one or more of the strands of; to form by the union or twisting of strands.

strand line, *n.* A dividing line between an ocean or lake and its shore, esp. one marking a higher water level from which the water has receded; shoreline.

strange, strānj, *a.*—*stranger*, *strangest*. [O. Fr. *estrange* (Fr. *étrange*), < L. *extraneus*, that is without, foreign.] Unfamiliar, unknown, or outside of one's previous experience; out of one's natural environment or locality; as, the move to a *strange* place; singular, extraordinary, or curious; as, a *strange* accident; queer, odd,

surprising, or unaccountable; unaccustomed to or inexperienced at.—**strange·ly**, *adv.* —**strangeness**, *n.*

strange par·ti·cle, *n. Phys.* any of the mesons and hyperons having certain properties, as their relatively long life span, that are not in accord with current atomic theories or have not been wholly substantiated.

stran·ger, strān′jėr, *n.* [O.Fr. *estrangier* (Fr. *étranger*), < *estrange*, E. *strange*.] A foreigner or alien; a newcomer in a place or locality, esp. one that is not yet known or well-known; a person whose face is unfamiliar to one, or whose name and character are unknown; a person with whom one has, or has hitherto had, no personal acquaintance; a person with whom one has no longer any personal acquaintance; an outsider, as with reference to a family, society, or other associated body; a visitor or guest who does not belong to a household; a person or thing that is new or unfamiliar, usu. followed by *to*; as, a *stranger to* hard work; *law*, one not privy or party to an act or proceeding.—**stran·ger·like**, *a.*

stran·gle, strang′gl, *v.t.*—*strangled*, *strangling*. [O.Fr. *estrangler*, L. *strangulare*, to strangle, < Gr. *stranggalaō*, *stranggaloō*, to knot, *stranggō*, to tie tight; same root as E. *string*.] To destroy the life of by compressing the windpipe; to choke; *fig* to suppress or stifle.—*v.i.* To die from strangulation; to be choked.—**stran·gler**, *n.*

stran·gle hold, *n. Wrestling*, an illegal hold by which the opponent's breathing is cut off; *fig.* any influence which limits or curbs development or freedom of action.

stran·gles, strang′glz, *n. pl.*, *sing. or pl. in constr. Veter. pathol.* a disease which attacks horses, characterized by inflammation, esp. of the nose and eyes.

stran·gu·la·tion, strang″gū·lā′shan, *n.* [L. *strangulatio*.] The act of strangling; the state of being strangled; *pathol.* the state of a part too closely constricted, as the intestine in hernia.—**stran·gu·late**, strang′gū·lāt″, *v.t., v.i.*—*strangulated*, *strangulating*.

stran·gu·ry, strang′gū·rē, *n.* [L. *stranguria*, Gr. *strangouria—stranx*, *strangos*, a drop, and *ouron*, urine.] *Pathol.* a condition in which the passing of urine occurs drop by drop and is accompanied by pain.

strap, strap, *n.* [A collateral form of *strop*, < root of *stripe*, *strip*; or < L. *struppus*, a thong.] A flexible, narrow strip of leather or other substance having various uses, as binding, fastening, or holding, and often provided with a buckle; a plate, band, or strip of metal to connect or hold other parts together; a loop which may be used to hold onto, as on a bus; a strop for sharpening a razor.—*v.t.*—*strapped*, *strapping*. To beat or chastise with a strap; to fasten or bind with a strap; to sharpen on a strop, as a razor; to cause to undergo a scarcity; as, *strapped* for cash.—**strap·less**, *a.*—**strap·per**, *n.*

strap·hang·er, strap′hang″ėr, *n. Colloq.* a passenger on a crowded bus or other vehicle who has to cling for support to an overhead strap.

strap·pa·do, stra·pā′dō, stra·pä′dō, *n. pl.* **strap·pa·does**. [O.Fr. *strapade*, It. *strappata*, < *strappare*, to pull.] An old form of punishment, consisting of having the hands of the victim tied behind his back, drawing him up by a rope tied to his hands, and then letting him drop almost to the ground; the machine so used.

strap·ping, strap′ing, *a. Colloq.* Of imposing stature; muscular; robust.

strass, stras, *n.* [From J. *Strasser*, 18th century G. jeweller and inventor.] A variety of flint glass used in the manufacture of artificial gems.

strat·a·gem, strat′a·jem, n. [Fr. stratagème, < L. stratagema, Gr. stratēgēma, < stratēgos, a general, < stratos, an army, agō, to lead.] A maneuver in war; a plan for deceiving an enemy; an instance of clever generalship. Fig. any ploy to gain an advantage; trick or scheme.

stra·te·gic, stra·tē′jik, a. [Fr. stratégique, < Gr. stratēgikós, pertaining to a general, < stratēgós, general.] Pertaining to, characterized by, or of the nature of strategy; as, strategic maneuvers; important in strategy. Also **stra·te·gi·cal.—stra·te·gi·cal·ly**, adv.

stra·te·gics, stra·tē′jiks, n. pl. but sing. in constr. Milit. strategy.

strat·e·gy, strat′i·jē, n. pl. **strat·e·gies**. Milit. the science of forming and carrying out military operations; generalship: distinguished from tactics. The use of artifice or finesse in carrying out any project; a method, plan, or stratagem to achieve some goal.—**strat·e·gist**, strat′i·jist, n.

strath, strath, Sc. sträth, n. [Gael. srath.] Sc. a valley of considerable size, usu. having a river running through it: often used in place names; as, Strathspey, Strathdon.

stra·tic·u·late, stra·tik′ū·lit, stra·tik′ū·lāt″, a. [Dim. < stratum.] Geol. arranged in thin strata or layers.—**stra·tic·u·la·tion**, n.

strat·i·fi·ca·tion, strat″i·fi·kā′shan, n. Geol. the process by which strata are formed; an arrangement in strata or layers. Sociol. any hierarchical division of society according to income, culture, or other characteristics. The act of stratifying or the state of being stratified.

strat·i·form, strat′i·farm″, a. In the form of strata; in the nature of uniform, parallel, concentric layers; geol. denoting a bed or beds of rocks occurring in strata or in a series of layers; anat., med. formed in layers or arranged in strata; as, stratiform cartilage or stratiform stab culture; meteor. resembling or having the character of stratus clouds.

strat·i·fy, strat′i·fī″, v.t.—stratified, stratifying. [Fr. stratifier—L. stratum, and facio, to make.] Geol. to form into strata or layers, as substances in the earth. To lay or arrange in strata, as seeds for preserving. Sociol. to divide, as society, according to hierarchies of social status.—v.i. To be or become arranged or divided into strata.

stra·tig·ra·phy, stra·tig′ra·fē, n. That division of geology which is concerned with the nature and arrangement of strata, and the order in which they succeed each other. —**stra·tig·ra·pher**, stra·tig′ra·fèr, n.— **strat·i·graph·ic, strat·i·graph·i·cal**, strat″i·graf′ik, a.—**strat·i·graph·i·cal·ly**, adv.

stra·toc·ra·cy, stra·tok′ra·sē, n. pl. **stra·toc·ra·cies**. [= Fr. stratocratie, < Gr. stratós, army, and -kratia, < kratein, rule.] A form of government in which the army exercises the ruling power.—**strat·o·crat·ic**, strat″o·krat′ik, a.

stra·to·cu·mu·lus, strā′tō·kū′mya·lus, strat″ō·kū′mya·lus, n. pl. **stra·to·cu·mu·li**, stra·to·cu·mu·lus. A cloud consisting of large, dark, rounded masses, usu. lower than 8,000 feet and often fully covering the sky.

strat·o·sphere, strat′o·sfēr″, n. A layer of the atmosphere about seven miles above the surface of the earth, between the troposphere and the thermosphere, within which the temperature remains approximately constant.—**strat·o·spher·ic**, a.

stra·tum, strā′tum, strat′um, strä′tum, n. pl. **stra·ta, stra·tums**, strā′ta, strat′a, strä′ta. [N.L. use of L. stratum, bed covering, prop. neut. of stratus, pp. of sternere, spread out.] A layer of material, formed either naturally or artificially, often one of a number of parallel layers placed one upon another; fig. one of a number of portions of some body, mass, or the like, likened to layers or levels; sociol. a level or grade of a people or population with reference to social position or education; geol. a bed of one kind of sedimentary rock or earth, usu. consisting of a series of layers representing continuous periods of deposition. Biol. a layer of tissue; a lamella.

stra·tus, strā′tus, strat′us, n. pl. **stra·ti**, **stra·tus**. [L., a strewing, a covering.] A low, dense, horizontal cloud.

straw, strą, n. [O.E. streáw, straw = Icel. strá, Dan. straa, D. stroo, G. stroh, straw, akin to strew; cogn. L. stramen, straw, < sterno, to strew.] The stalk or stem of certain species of grain; such stalks collectively when cut, and after being thrashed; a fiber from such stalks or made artificially, used in baskets, hats, and the like; fig. a bit or a trifle, as: I don't care a straw. A tube of any material, used to draw up a beverage to one's mouth.—a. Pertaining to, made of, or resembling straw; having the pale yellow color of straw; worthless.— **straw·y**, a.—strawier, strawiest.

straw·ber·ry, strą′ber″ē, strą′be·rē, n. pl. **straw·ber·ries**. [O.E. streáwberie, streówberie, from its habit of spreading or strewing itself along the ground.] A fruit and plant, genus Fragaria, the fruit being edible and succulent.

straw·ber·ry bush, n. A N. American shrub, Euonymus americanus, with crimson pod and seeds with a scarlet aril.

straw·ber·ry mark, n. A reddish, usu. raised, vascular birthmark.

straw·ber·ry roan, n. A horse having a reddish coat thickly spotted with white.

straw·ber·ry shrub, n. Any of various species of the genus Calycanthus, shrubs with dark brownish or purplish-red flowers of distinctive fragrance, common in cultivation.

straw·ber·ry to·ma·to, n. The small, edible tomatolike fruit of any of various herbs of the nightshade family, as Physalis pruinosa; the plant bearing it.

straw·ber·ry tree, n. An evergreen tree, Arbutus unedo, in the heath family, a native of southern Europe, bearing a scarlet, warty berry.

straw·board, strą′bōrd″, strą′bärd″, n. Thick paper board made solely from straw, used esp. for cartons and book covers.

straw boss, n. Colloq. an assistant foreman or overseer of a work gang who has no real status or authority, but who assists in supervision.

straw·flow·er, strą′flou″èr, n. Any one of several everlasting flowers, esp. the Australian annual herb, Helichrysum bracteatum, having long, tapering leaves and yellow, red, orange, or white flowers.

straw·hat·the·a·ter, n. Summer stock theater, usu. performed in makeshift theaters or tents in resort or nonmetropolitan areas.

straw man, n. A figure of a man shaped of straw; a puppet; a person, as a perjured witness, used to disguise another man's activities; a weak opponent or argument set up so as to be readily defeated.

straw vote, n. An unofficial vote or poll taken to obtain some indication of the general drift of opinion on an issue or a candidate's strength.

straw wine, n. A wine, usu. sweet and rich, made from grapes that have been dried or partly dried in the sun on a bed of straw.

straw·worm, strą′wųrm″, n. A caddisworm; any of several jointworms which infest the stalks of grain.

stray, strā, v.i. [O.Fr. estrayer, extraier, to wander, < O.Fr. estrée, It. strada, a road or street; < L.L. strata, a street.] To wander from a direct course; to roam, ramble, meander, straggle, or go astray; to deviate or to err, as to wander from the path of duty or rectitude; to digress while thoughts wander.—a. Having strayed; occasional; incidental.

stray, strā, n. Any domestic animal that wanders at large or is lost; any aimless, homeless, friendless person or animal; the act of straying; law, an estray; radio, random electromagnetic waves, which interfere with radio reception.—**stray·er**, n.

streak, strēk, n. [M.E. streke, strike, < O.E. strica, stroke, mark, line.] A relatively long, narrow, usu. irregular mark, smear, band, or stripe; a long, usu. irregularly shaped portion or layer of substance, distinguished by color or nature from the rest; as, a streak of fat in lean meat; a vein, strain, or admixture of anything; as, a streak of humor; colloq. a period or run; as, a streak of hard luck; mineral. the line of colored powder often differing in color from the mineral in the mass and forming an important distinguishing characteristic, obtained by scratching a mineral or rubbing it upon a hard, rough, white surface; bact. a narrow smear of bacterial or viral agent on a culture medium. v.t. To mark with a streak or streaks.—v.i. To become streaked or streaky; to flash or move as a streak, as lightning; to go rapidly.

streak·y, strē′kē, a.—streakier, streakiest. Occurring in streaks or a streak; marked with or characterized by streaks; varying or uneven in character or quality.—**streak·i·ly**, adv.—**streak·i·ness**, n.

stream, strēm, n. [O.E. streám, a stream, a river = D. stroom, Icel. straumr, Dan. and Sw. ström, G. strom; from root seen in Skt. sru, to flow (with t inserted).] Any river, brook, or course of running water; a flow or gush of any fluid substance; a flow of air or gas, or of light; a steady current in the sea or in a river; as, the Gulf Stream; anything issuing as if in a flow; as, a stream of words; a steady procession of many individuals moving uniformly forward without interval; the dominant opinion of a group; as, the stream of public opinion.— v.i. To flow in a stream; to issue or move continuously; to issue or shoot in streaks or beams; to stretch out in a long line; to float at full length in the air.—v.t. To send forth in a current or stream; to cause to stretch out or float at full length, as a flag.— **stream·ing**, n.

stream·er, strē′mèr, n. Anything which streams; a long narrow flag; a pennon; a banner; a stream of light shooting upward from the horizon, as in some forms of the aurora borealis.

stream·let, strēm′lit, n. A small stream; a rivulet; a rill.

stream·line, strēm′līn″, n. In a fast-moving body, a shape or contour that decreases air or liquid resistance, as the design of an airplane or boat to minimize drag; phys. the path followed by a particle of fluid flowing without eddies or turbulence about a solid object.—**stream·lined**, strēm′līnd″, a. Having characteristics of a streamline; possessing a smooth flow; as, a streamlined method of operation; being free of factors causing resistance or obstructions; as, a streamlined chassis.

stream·line, strēm′līn″, v.t.—streamlined, streamlining. To contour in a streamlined shape; to smooth out, as by removing protuberances that interfere with a flow; to reduce, simplify, or alter, as for faster or more efficient operation; to modernize.

stream·line flow, n. Phys. a steady flow of fluid past a body in which the fluid remains smooth and relatively unchanged. Compare turbulent flow.

stream·lin·er, strēm′lī′nèr, n. A streamlined train; any object that is streamlined.

---

a- fat, fāte, fär, fâre, fąll; e- met, mē, mēre, hèr; i- pin, pīne; o- not, nōte, mŏve; u- tub, cūbe, bųll; oi- oil; ou- pound.

stream-of-con·scious·ness, strĕm′ov·- kon′shus·nis, *a.* Pertaining to a literary technique in which plot and character are revealed through the presentation of a character's perceptions, sensations, and other thought processes without regard to conventional syntactic structure.

street, strēt, *n.* [O.E. *straet*, a street, < L. *strata* (*via*), a paved way, < *sterno, stratum*, to strew, to pave.] A way, road, or thoroughfare in a city having buildings on one or both sides, chiefly a main way, as distinguished from a lane or alley; this thoroughfare with the houses or other property as well as the open way; the people who live on the street, as: The whole *street* contributed. (*Cap.*) a district of a city, as Wall Street, associated with a particular activity or profession, usu. preceded by *the.*—*a.* Suitable for wear or use on the street.

street Ar·ab, *n.* A homeless, neglected child who wanders the city streets; a waif; a gamin.

street·car, strēt′kär″, *n.* A public passenger car powered by electric cable and running on rails set in the street.

street rail·way, *n.* A railway operating on the street in a city; the company that manages a streetcar or bus line.

street vi·rus, *n.* A virulent virus as found in nature, not attenuated in a laboratory.

street·walk·er, strēt′wạ″kẽr, *n.* A prostitute who solicits on the street.—**street·walk·ing,** *n.*

strength, strengkth, strength, *n.* [O.E. *strengthu*, strength, < *strang*, strong; cf. *length* and *long.*] The state or inherent capacity of being strong; the capacity to sustain the application of force without breaking or yielding; toughness; as, the *strength* of bone and muscle; power or vigor of any kind; capacity for exertion; as, *strength* of mind, memory, evidence, argument, or affection; power of resisting, as stress, strain, or attacks; that on which confidence or reliance is placed; as, on the *strength* of encouragement or logic; support; force or power in expressing meaning, as in vehemence of speech; vividness, as of light or color; intensity, as of sound or odor; potency; as, *strength* of wine, poison, or acid; legal or moral force or efficacy; force as measured or stated in figures; as, the organization is up to full *strength*; force proceeding from motion; as, on the *strength* of momentum; the firmness of a price level or tendency to rise, as in brokerage.— **strength·en,** strengk′then, streng′then, *v.t.* To make strong or stronger; to add strength to; to confirm; to establish; to encourage; to fix in resolution; to make greater; to add intensity to.—*v.i.* To grow strong or stronger.—**strength·en·er,** *n.*—**strength·- less,** *a.*—**strength·less·ness,** *n.*

stren·u·ous, stren′ū·us, *a.* [L. *strenuus*, vigorous, strenuous; allied to Gr. *strenes*, strong, hard.] Zealous, vigorous, or energetic; requiring great exertion.—**stren·u·- os·i·ty,** stren″ū·os′i·tē, *n.*—**stren·u·ous·- ly,** *adv.*—**stren·u·ous·ness,** *n.*

strep, strep, *a. Colloq.* streptococcal.

strep throat, *n.* A communicable streptococcal infection of the throat.

strep·to·ba·cil·lus, strep″tō·ba·sil′us, *n.* pl. **strep·to·ba·cil·li.** Any of the rod-shaped, anaerobic, pathogenic or parasitic bacteria of the genus *Streptobacillus*, found in chains.

strep·to·coc·cus, strep″tō·kok′us, *n.* pl. **strep·to·coc·ci.** [Gr. *streptos*, twisted, *kokkos*, a berry.] Any of several spherical or oval bacteria of the genus *Streptococcus*, which are usu. found in long chains or pairs and are usu. non-motile, Gram positive varieties which divide in only one plane, including strains pathogenic to man.

strep·to·coc·cal, strep·to·coc·cic, strep″- to·kok′al, strep″tō·kok′sik, *a.*

strep·to·ki·nase, strep″tō·ki′nās, strep″- tō·kin′ās, *n. Pharm.* an enzyme present in certain streptococcal cultures that is used clinically to break down blood clots and fibrinous material.

strep·to·my·ces, strep″tō·mī′sēz, *n.* pl. **strep·to·my·ces, strep·to·my·cetes.** *Bact.* any of a group of soil microorganisms, genus *Streptomyces*, some of which are cultured for the antibiotic substances they form.

strep·to·my·cin, strep″tō·mī′sin, *n. Pharm.* an antibiotic, $C_{21}H_{39}N_7O_{12}$, derived from a soil fungus, *Streptomyces griseus*, and esp. effective against tuberculosis.

strep·to·thri·cin, strep″tō·thrī′sin, *n.* An antibiotic which is produced by a soil fungus, *Actinomyces lavendulae.*

stress, stres, *n.* [O.Fr. *estrecer, estrecier* (Fr. *étrecir*), to straiten, to narrow, < L. *strictus*, pp. of *stringo, strictum*, to draw tight.] A constraining, urging, or impelling physical force; strain. *Mech.* a force tending to produce strain or tension and to change the form or dimensions of a solid; the degree of stress, as evidenced by the reaction of a solid against the straining forces. A factor causing mental or emotional strain or tension; the physical or mental state resulting from such strain; importance or weight ascribed to something; as, to lay *stress* on certain facts; *phon.* emphasis provided by the relative loudness of a word, syllable, or other speech sound; *pros.* the accent or emphasis on a word or word part to denote meter or rhythm.—*v.t.* To put accent or emphasis on, as a word, idea, musical note, or the like; to cause to undergo mechanical, physical, or emotional strain or stress.—**stress·ful,** stres′ful, *a.*—**stress·- ful·ly,** *adv.*—**stress·less,** *a.*—**stress·less·- ness,** *n.*

stretch, strech, *v.t.* [A softened form < O.E. *streccan*, to stretch = D. *strekken*, G. *strecken*, Dan. *sträkke*, to stretch. Straight is a derivative.] To extend or distend forcibly; to draw tight; to make tense; to spread out or extend to full dimensions, often followed by *out*; to extend beyond normal dimensions or bounds; as, to *stretch* one's patience; to reach or extend across, as a line from one pole to another; to reach out or hold forth, usu. followed by *out*; as, to *stretch out* a hand; to augment the quantity of through dilution; as, to *stretch* the soup by adding water; to strain or exert extra effort; as, to *stretch* oneself to win; to make a limited amount cover a larger need; as, to *stretch* one's income to meet an unexpected expense.—*v.i.* To attain greater length or width; to bear extension without breaking; to extend or reach across an area; to be continuous over a distance or period of time; to recline one's body at full length, usu. followed by *out*; to extend one's limbs and muscles to their limit, as for relief from a cramped position; to become sufficient for increased need; as, a budget *stretching* to cover expenses.—*n.* A stretching or the state of being stretched; elasticity; an extended portion or expanse, as of time, road, water, or the like; the utmost extent or reach of something; *horse racing*, a straight portion of the racetrack; *slang*, a period of confinement in prison; *colloq.* a period of limbering up or relaxing; as, the seventh inning *stretch* at a baseball game.—*a.*—**stretch·a·bil·i·ty,** *n.*— **stretch·a·ble,** *a.*

stretch·er, strech′ẽr, *n.* One who or that which stretches, esp. a device or mechanism for expanding something; a type of litter, as a frame of stretched canvas for carrying the disabled or dead; a frame on which canvas is stretched for painting; *carp.* a tie

timber in a frame; *masonry*, a brick laid so that its length is exposed on the surface of a wall: distinguished from *header.*

stretch·er-bear·er, strech′ẽr·bâr″ẽr, *n.* One who assists in carrying a stretcher or litter, esp. for the wounded in battle.

stretch-out, strech′out″, *n.* An arrangement in which employees are obliged to undertake an increased work load without a concomitant increase in wages; a deliberate slackening in work speed by employees in order to make work last longer.

stret·to, stret′ō, *n.* pl. **stret·ti, stret·tos,** stret′ē, *Mus.* In closing portions of a fugue or similar composition, an overlapping of the subject, each voice breaking in upon the preceding one ahead of its time; a direction that a terminating passage be played at a quicker pace. Also **stret·ta,** stret′a.

strew, strö, *v.t.*—past *strewed*, pp. *strewed* or *strewn*, ppr. *strewing.* [O.E. *streowian*, to scatter = Goth. *straujan*, G. *streuen*, Icel. *strá*, Dan. and Sw. *strö*; same root as *straw*, *star*, L. *sterno, stratum* (E. *stratum*), Skt. *stri*, to strew.] To scatter or sprinkle: always applied to dry substances separable into parts or particles; to cover by scattering or being scattered over; to throw loosely apart; to spread abroad; to disseminate.

stri·a, strī′a, *n.* pl. **stri·ae,** strī′ē. [L., a furrow, channel, flute.] A slight furrow or ridge; a narrow stripe or streak, as of color or texture, esp. one of a number in parallel arrangement; *geol.* one of many parallel scratches or intermittent gouges on the surface layer of a rock, resulting from abrasion by ice formations; *mineral.* one of many small, parallel grooves on the cleavage face or the entire surface of a crystal; *arch.* a fillet between the flutes of columns.

stri·ate, strī′āt, *v.t.*—*striated, striating.* [L. *striatus*, pp. of *striare*, to furrow, channel, < *stria.*] To mark with striae; to furrow, stripe, or streak.—strī′it, strī′āt, *a.*

stri·at·ed, strī′ā·tid, *a.* Marked with striae; furrowed; striped; streaked.

stri·a·tion, strī·ā′shun, *n.* A striated condition or appearance; a stria; one of a number of parallel striae.

strick, strik, *n.* [M.E. *stric, strik*; connected with E. *strike.*] A bunch of flax or other fiber in the process of dressing.

strick·en, strik′en, *a.* [pp. of *strike.*] Afflicted, as with disease, trouble, or sorrow; deeply affected, as with horror, fear, or other emotion; characterized by or showing the effects of affliction, trouble, misfortune, a mental blow, or the like; as, a *stricken* look; struck, as hit or wounded by a weapon, missile, or the like.

strick·le, strik′l, *n.* [O.E. *stricel*, connected with *strīcan*, E. *strike.*] A straightedge used to sweep off heaped grain or the like to a level with the rim of a measure; a piece of wood covered with grease and sand, emery, or the like, used to sharpen scythes; *foundry*, a templet or piece of wood with a special profile, drawn over the sand in a flask to impart to it a required contour. —*v.t.*—*strickled, strickling.* To sweep or remove, or shape or form, with a strickle.

strict, strikt, *a.* [L. *strictus*, pp. of *stringere*, draw tight: cf. *strait* and *stringent.*] Narrowly or carefully limited or restricted; as, a *strict* construction of the Constitution; exact or precise; as, the *strict* meaning of a word; close, careful, or minute; absolute, perfect, or complete; as, *strict* neutrality; characterized by or acting in close conformity to requirements or principles; as, *strict* observance; stringent or exacting in requirements or obligations; as, *strict* rules; severe in rule, discipline, or management; as, to be *strict* with a child; rigorously scrupulous, strait-laced, or austere, as persons or their views; closely or rigorously enforced or maintained, as discipline, guard, or imprisonment.—**strict·ly**, *adv.*—**strict·ness**, *n.*

stric·ture, strik'cher, *n.* [L. *strictura, stringo, strictum,* to draw tight.] A sharp criticism or censorious remark; censure; a restriction. *Pathol.* a morbid contraction of any canal or duct of the body; a stenosis.

stride, strid, *v.i.*—past **strode**, pp. **stridden**, ppr. **striding**. [O.E. *strīdan* = M.L.G. *strīden,* stride: cf. *straddle.*] To walk with long steps, as with vigor, haste, impatience, or arrogance; to take a long step; to pass, as over or across, by a long step; *fig.* to straddle; as, an arch *striding* over a temple entrance.—*v.t.* To walk with long steps along, on, through, over, or the like; as, to *stride* the deck of a ship; pass over or across by one stride; as, to *stride* a ditch; to straddle or bestride.—*n.* A progressing by long steps or a striding gait; as, his natural *stride;* a long step in walking; the measure of gain made by such a step, sometimes used as a unit of distance; a single movement or step in running. *Fig.* advancement or rapid progress; regular or steady course of procedure; as, to get into one's *stride.*— **take in stride**, to cope with or accept without undue stress.—**strid·er**, *n.*

stri·dent, strid'ent, *a.* [L. *stridens (strident-),* ppr. of *stridere,* make a harsh sound.] Making or having a harsh, shrill sound; grating; creaking.—**stri·dence, stri·den·cy**, *n.*—**stri·dent·ly**, *adv.*

stri·dor, strī'der, *n.* [L., < *stridere.*] A harsh, grating, or creaking sound; *pathol.* a harsh respiratory sound due to any of various forms of obstruction.

strid·u·late, strij'a·lāt", *v.i.*—**stridulated, stridulating**. [N.L. *stridulatus,* pp. of *stridulare,* < L. *stridulus.*] To produce a shrill, grating sound by rubbing together certain parts of the body, as a cricket or katydid does.—**strid·u·la·tion**, *n.*—**strid·u·la·to·ry**, strij'a·la·tōr"ē, strij'a·la·tar"ē, *a.*

strid·u·lous, strij'a·lus, *a.* [L. *stridulus,* < *stridere.*] Making or having a harsh or grating sound; strident; *pathol.* pertaining to or characterized by stridor.—**strid·u·lous·ly**, *adv.*—**strid·u·lous·ness**, *n.*

strife, strīf, *n.* [O.Fr. *estrif,* connected with *estriver,* E. *strive.*] The striving or contending of opposing parties; contention, quarreling, fighting, or conflict; discord, dissension, or variance, as: *Strife* existed between members of the family. A quarrel, struggle, clash, or dispute.—**strife·less**, *a.* —**strife·ful**, *a.*

strig·il, strij'il, *n.* [L. *strigilis,* < *stringere,* touch, graze.] An instrument with a curved blade used by the ancient Greeks and Romans for scraping the skin at the bath; *arch.* one of a series of S-shaped vertical flutings used as a decoration, esp. in Roman architecture.

stri·gose, strī'gōs, stri·gōs', *a.* [N.L. *strigosus,* < *striga,* row of bristles, bristle, L. swath, furrow.] *Bot.* set with stiff bristles or hairs; hispid. *Zool.* marked with fine, closely set ridges, grooves, or points.

strike, strīk, *v.i.*—past **struck**, pp. **struck** or **stricken**, ppr. **striking**. [O.E. *strīcan, v.i.,* move, go; *v.t.,* rub, wipe, = O.Fries. *strīka,* = O.H.G. *strīhan* (G. *streichen*).] To hit or dash on or against something, as a moving body does; impinge; come into forcible contact; to deal or aim a blow or stroke, as with the fist or a weapon; to deal blows; knock, rap, or tap; *milit.* to launch an attack. To quit work together, as a group of employees, to compel an employer to grant certain benefits; to sound a percussion, as: The clock *strikes.* To ignite or be ignited by friction, as a match; to make a vigorous movement as if dealing a blow; to pass suddenly and quickly, usu. followed by *through* or *in;* to enter suddenly, as into

conversation, used with *up;* to come suddenly or unexpectedly upon; to make an impression on the mind; to fall upon, as light; to take root, as a slip of a plant; to sink in, as dye; to lower a sail or flag, as a salute or signal of surrender; to proceed on a path or trail, esp. in a new direction, usu. followed by *into* or *out; army,* to act as an officer's servant.—*v.t.* To deal, as a blow, to a person or thing; to hit; to smite; to remove or separate with a cut, usu. followed by *off;* to produce, as fire, by percussion, esp. by using a match; to come into forcible contact with, as: The ship *struck* a rock. To attack with military forces; to bomb from airplanes; to stamp or impress, as a coin; to print from type or the like, usu. followed by *off;* to pierce or stab with a sharp weapon; to make level, smooth, or even by using a strickle or other tool; to mark with a line; to draw, as an arc; to cancel, as a name from a list; to hook, as a fish, by a jerking motion; to knock, rap, or tap; to play upon, as a harp or the like; to indicate, as the hour of the day, by ringing a chime; to blast with some natural agency, as lightning; to afflict suddenly, as with disease or misfortune; to affect deeply or overwhelm, as with terror; to render blind, dumb, or the like; to cause a feeling; to enter suddenly; to start suddenly into motion, usu. with *out;* to assume, as an attitude or posture; to cause to penetrate quickly, as a chill; to put forth or send down, as roots; to impinge upon; to fall upon, as light; to enter the mind of or occur to, as a person; to impress strongly, as a beautiful scene; to come upon or encounter suddenly; to find or discover, as an ore deposit; to make or conclude, as an agreement or bargain; to enter upon or form, as an acquaintance; to fix or establish, as a price; to balance, as ledger accounts; to estimate or determine, as a mean or average; to lower or take down, as a sail or flag; to take down or remove, as tents at a camp site, or stage settings; to quit in a body, as work.—*n.* An act of striking; concerted quitting of work by a body of employees to coerce their employer in some way, usu. to obtain higher wages; the part of a lock which holds a bolt; the striker in a clock; the rooting of certain plants; a strickle for leveling grain; *baseball,* an unsuccessful attempt on the part of the batter to hit a pitched ball, or anything ruled to be equivalent to this; *bowling,* the knocking down of all the pins with the first bowl; *fig.* sudden success or good fortune; *mining,* the discovery of petroleum or of a rich vein of ore; *milit.* a bombing or strafing attack by airplanes; *foundry,* a tool for leveling the surface of clay, sand, or other material; *Brit.* a dry measure usu. equivalent to a bushel; *geol.* the direction of the line of intersection between the plane of an inclined stratum and a horizontal plane; *coining,* the quantity or number struck off at any one time; *fishing,* the action of a fish as it rises to seize the bait.— **strike·less**, *a.*

strike·bound, strīk'bound", *a.* Closed or blocked by pickets due to a strike, as a factory, business, or construction site.

strike·break·er, strīk'brā"kėr, *n.* One who takes part in breaking up a strike of workers by working or by furnishing workers for the employer.—**strike·break·ing**, *n.*

strike off, *v.t.* To do or make easily and quickly; to print from type; to cross out or cancel from a list or the like; to cut off or knock off.

strike out, *v.i. Baseball,* to make three strikes while at bat and be declared 'out.'— *v.t.* To put out, as a batter, by pitching.— **strike-out**, strīk'out", *n.*

strike·o·ver, strīk'ō"vėr, *n. Typing.* An act or occasion of striking over a typing error

without erasing the original letter or word; the typed-over letter or letters.

strik·er, strī'kėr, *n.* One who or that which strikes; a worker who is on strike; *army,* a soldier who acts as an officer's servant; *navy,* a seaman in training for a technical rating. A clapper in a bell or clock; a firing pin in a gun or torpedo.

strike up, *v.i.* To begin playing or singing; to begin to sound, as music.—*v.t.* To begin to play or sing, as a tune; to enter upon, as an acquaintance, conversation, or friendship.

strike zone, *n. Baseball,* the area directly over home plate, between the batter's knees and shoulders when in batting stance, through which the pitched ball must pass to be considered a strike.

strik·ing, strī'king, *a.* Having an impact of surprise or admiration; remarkable; forcible; dramatic or impressive, esp. in appearance.—**strik·ing·ly**, *adv.*

string, string, *n.* [O.E. *streng* = D. *streng* = Icel. *strengr,* akin to G. *strang,* string, and prob. also to Gr. *straggálē,* halter, and L. *stringere,* draw tight.] A slender cord or thick thread; something resembling this, as tape, ribbon, a strip of fabric, leather, or the like used for binding, tying, lacing, or drawing together; as, a shoe *string,* a purse *string,* apron *strings;* a strand or necklace of beads or other objects threaded or strung on a cord; a number or series of objects, events, or utterances in a row; as, a *string* of islands, a *string* of bad luck, a *string* of oaths; the tightly stretched cord or wire of musical instruments which produces a tone when caused to vibrate; as, a guitar, piano, or violin *string;* a bowstring. *Pl.* stringed instruments; the players of stringed instruments in an orchestra; as, to call the *strings* to rehearsal. *Often pl., colloq.* a condition or counterproposal appended to an offer or proposition; as, a gift with *strings* attached. A set or number of; as, to own a *string* of race horses; a cord or fiber in a plant; *sports,* a group of players rated according to their skill; as, to make first *string* on the team. *Arch.* a stringcourse; one of the sloping sides of a stair supporting the treads and risers; also *stringer. Billiards,* the stroke made to determine who opens the game; the line from behind which the cue ball is played after having been out of play; the line of movable counters on which the score is kept.—*v.t.*—past **strung**, pp. **strung** or **stringed**, ppr. **stringing**. To thread on or as on a line; as, to *string* beads; to extend, as a cord, from one point to another; to furnish with or as with a string or strings; to arrange in a string or series; as, to *string* phrases; to provide or adorn with something suspended or slung; as, to *string* the tree with tinsel; to strip the strings from; as, to *string* the beans; to kill by hanging, usu. followed by *up.*—*v.i.* To form into a string or strings, as a glutinous substance does when pulled; to form or move in a string; as, thoughts that *string* together; *billiards,* to hit one's ball against the back of the table in determining who shall open the game. To be hanged or to die by hanging.—**on a string**, *slang,* under another's control or influence.—**pull strings**, to gain an objective, often surreptitiously, through the use of one's influence or power.—**string a·long**, *slang.* To keep someone available or waiting through promises or deceit; to falsely encourage.— **string a·long with**, *slang,* to go along with, esp. as in agreement or trust.—**string out**, to lengthen, extend, or prolong.—**string·less**, *a.*

string bass, *n. Mus.* double bass.

string bean, *n.* Any of several kinds of beans, esp. a variety of *Phaseolus vulgaris,* the unripe pod of which is used for food, usu. after the fibrous threads or strings along the sides are stripped off; the pod itself; *colloq.* a tall, slim person.

string·board, string′bōrd″, string′bȧrd″, *n. Arch.* a board or the like used to cover the ends of the steps in a staircase.

string·course, string′kōrs″, string′kȧrs″, *n. Arch.* a narrow molding or band, as of brick or stone, continued horizontally along the face of a building. Also *cordon.*

stringed, stringd, *a.* Having strings; produced by strings.

stringed in·stru·ment, *n.* A musical instrument which uses taut strings to produce its tones, as a guitar or violin.

strin·gen·do, strin·jen′dō, *It.* strēn·jen′dȧ, *adv. Mus.* with a hastening of the tempo, as in leading to a climax: used as a musical direction.

strin·gent, strin′jent, *a.* [L. *stringens* (*stringent-*), ppr. of *stringere* (pp. *strictus*), draw tight.] Compelling, constraining, or urgent; as, *stringent* necessity; convincing or forcible, as arguments; rigorously exacting, binding, strict, or severe; as, *stringent* regulations or obligations; *com.* pertaining to conditions of money scarcity or tight credit in loaning or investing.—**strin·gen·cy**, *n.* pl. **strin·gen·cies.**—**strin·gent·ly**, *adv.*

string·er, string′ẽr, *n.* One who or that which strings. *Constr.* a long horizontal timber for connecting upright posts or supporting a floor; a tie in a truss; a stringpiece; a stringcourse; the string of a stair. *Rail.* a longitudinal timber on which a rail is fastened. *Journ.* a newspaper correspondent who works on a part-time basis.

string·halt, string′hȧlt″, *n. Veter. pathol.* an excessive flexing of the hind legs of a horse, caused by a nerve disorder. Also *springhalt.* —**string·halt·ed**, *a.*

string·ing, string′ing, *n. Tennis*, that with which a racket is strung; as gut or nylon.

string line, *n. Billiards*, balkline.

string·piece, string′pēs″, *n. Constr.* a long, horizontal piece of timber or the like in a framework, pier, or other structure, for strengthening it or for connecting or supporting its parts.

string quar·tet, *n. Mus.* A composition written normally for the four stringed instrument parts of first and second violin, viola, and cello; four musicians constituting a group to perform string quartets and other chamber music.

string tie, *n.* A narrow bow tie with long, loose-hanging ends.

string·y, string′ē, *a.*—*stringier, stringiest.* Consisting of or resembling strings; fibrous; as, *stringy* meat; ropy; sinewy; wiry.—**string·i·ness**, *n.* The state of being stringy.

stri·o·late, strī′o·lāt′, *a.* Finely or minutely striated. Also **stri·o·lat·ed.**

strip, strip, *v.t.*—*stripped, stripping.* [O.E. *strȳpan* (recorded in *bestrȳpan*, strip clean) = D. *strooper* = G. *streifen*, strip.] To rob, plunder, or dispossess; as, to *strip* a man of his possessions; to remove, as a covering, from; to divest; as, to *strip* a tree of its fruit; to deprive of covering or clothing; to make bare or naked; undress; to deprive of insignia or honors; as, *strip* a soldier of his rank; to dismantle or divest of equipment; as, to *strip* a ship of rigging; to remove color from, as cloth or one's hair, as for redyeing; to draw the last milk from, as a cow; *fish culture*, to press or squeeze the ripe roe or milt from, as a fish; *tobacco manuf.* to separate the leaves from the stalks of, or to remove the midrib from, as tobacco leaves; *mach.* to tear off the thread of, as a screw or bolt, or the teeth of, as a gear, by applying too much force; *steel manuf.* to remove the mold from, as an ingot.—*v.i.* To become stripped; to divest oneself of clothes; to execute a striptease.

strip, strip, *n.* [Appar. a var. of *stripe.*] A

narrow piece, comparatively long and usu. of uniform width, as of cloth, paper, metal, or the like; a long, narrow tract of land or forest; a connected series of pictures or cartoons; as, a film or comic *strip*; *aeron.* a landing strip; *philately*, several stamps connected in a vertical or horizontal row, from either a coil or a sheet; (*usu. cap.*) a street or avenue constituting a main thoroughfare in a city; as, Los Angeles' Sunset *Strip*; *auto racing*, a straight course used for drag races.—*v.t.*—*stripped, stripping.* To cut into strips.

strip crop·ping, *n.* The contour planting of several feed crops in alternate strips to retain rain water and forestall soil erosion. Also **strip farm·ing.**

stripe, strīp, *n.* [Cf. M.D. *strijpe*, stripe, M.L.G. *strīpe*, G. *streif*, stripe, strip.] A relatively long, narrow band of a different color, appearance, weave, material, or nature from the rest of a surface or thing; as, the *stripes* of a zebra; a particular style or pattern of such bands, as in a striped fabric or a wallpaper; a long narrow piece of anything, as a strip of braid; a streak or layer of a different nature within a substance; *fig.* style, variety, or distinctive quality; as, a man of a different *stripe*. *Pl.* a number or combination of bands or strips, as a chevron, worn on a military or other uniform as a badge of rank, service, good conduct, wounds, or the like; a striped uniform; as, prison *stripes.*—*v.t.*—*striped, striping.* To mark or alter with a stripe or stripes.—**striped**, strīpt, strī′pid, *a.*—**stripe·less**, *a.*

stripe, strīp, *n.* [M.E. *strype*: cf. D. *strips*, a whipping, *strippen*, to whip, M.L.G. *strippe*, strap, whiplash.] A stroke with a whip, rod, or the like, as in punishment; a mark made by a stroke.

striped bass, *n.* An American fresh- and salt-water game fish, *Roccus saxatilis*, with blackish stripes along the sides, and weighing 25 to 30 pounds, common on the coasts of the U.S. Also *rockfish, striper.*

strip·er, strī′pẽr, *n. Slang*, any member of the armed forces who wears stripes on the sleeve of his uniform indicating rank or years of service. A striped bass.

strip film, *n.* Filmstrip.

strip·ing, strī′ping, *n.* The process of adding stripes to a design or surface; the stripes added or a striped pattern; as, the *striping* on a model plane.

strip·ling, strip′ling, *n.* [< *strip, stripe*, with dim. term. *-ling*; primarily, a tall slender youth, one that shoots up suddenly; cf. *slip, scion.*] A youth in adolescence, or passing from boyhood to manhood; a boy.

strip·per, strip′ẽr, *n.* One who strips; that which strips, as an appliance or machine for stripping; *slang*, a stripteaser.

strip·tease, strip′tēz″, *n.* An act, formerly associated with burlesque, in which a woman performer disrobes gradually, usu. accompanied by music, body gyrations, and the audience's vocal encouragement.— **strip·teas·er**, strip′tē″zẽr, *n.* One who performs a striptease; a stripper.

strip·y, strī′pē, *a.*—*stripier, stripiest.* Striped; having stripes; suggestive of stripes.

strive, strīv, *v.i.*—*past strove*, pp. *striven*, ppr. *striving.* [O.Fr. *estriver*, to strive, < O.H.G. *streban*, G. *streben*, Dan. *straebe*, D. *streven*, to strive.] To make efforts; to endeavor with earnestness; to try; to contend or vie.—**striv·er**, *n.*

strobe, strōb, *n.* A stroboscope; a strobe light.

strobe light, *n. Photog.* an electron tube which produces short-duration, high-intensity flashes of light.

stro·bi·la, strō·bī′la, *n.* pl. **stro·bi·lae**, strō·bī′lē. *Zool.* a long continuous chain of

similar structures produced by budding, as the chain of segments comprising the body of a tapeworm.—**stro·bi·lar**, *a.*—**stro·bi·la·tion**, **stro·bi·li·za·tion**, *n.*

strob·ile, strob′il, *n.* [L.L. *strobilus*, < Gr. *stróbilos*, pine cone, akin to *stréphein*, turn, twist.] *Bot.* A strobilus or cone; the cone-like female inflorescence of the hop plant, consisting of imbricated scales.

stro·bi·lus, strō·bī′lus, *n.* pl. **stro·bi·li**, strō·bī′lī. *Bot.* A cone-shaped aggregation of sporophylls bearing spores, as in horsetails and club mosses; the cone of a gymnosperm bearing exposed seeds, as a pine cone. Also *strobile.*

stro·bo·scope, strō′bo·skōp″, strob′o·skōp″, *n.* [Gr. *stróbos*, a whirling round.] An instrument used in studying the rapid revolution or vibration of a body by rendering it visible at frequent intervals, usu. by illuminating it intermittently with a flash of light or by viewing it through openings in a revolving disk.—**stro·bo·scop·ic**, strō″bo·skop′ik, strob″o·skop′ik, *a.*—**stro·bo·scop·ic·al·ly**, *adv.*

stro·bo·tron, strō′bo·tron″, strob′o·tron″, *n. Electron.* a gas-filled tetrode which can be regulated by voltage pulses and which produces brilliant flashes of light: used in a stroboscope.

stro·ga·noff, strä′ga·nȧf″, strō′ga·nȧf″, *a.* Cooked in a sauce containing sour cream, seasonings, onions, and mushrooms; as, beef *stroganoff.*

stroke, strōk, *n.* [M.E. *strok, strak*, O.E. *strīcan*, E. *strike.*] An act of striking, as with the fist, a weapon, or a hammer; a blow dealt or aimed; a hitting of or upon anything; a striking of a clapper or hammer, as on a bell, or the sound produced by this; a throb or pulsation, as of the heart; a beat or accent, as in music; something likened to a blow in its effect, as in causing pain or injury; an act of divine chastisement; an attack of apoplexy or of paralysis; a discharge of lightning; a piece of luck befalling one; as, a *stroke* of bad or good luck; a vigorous movement as if in dealing a blow; a single complete movement, esp. one continuously repeated in some process; each of the succession of movements of the arms and legs in swimming; a vigorous attempt to attain some object; as, a bold *stroke* for liberty; a measure adopted for a particular purpose; as, a *stroke* of policy; a feat or achievement; as, a *stroke* of genius; an act, piece, or amount of work; a movement of a pen, pencil, brush, or graver, as in writing, drawing, or painting; a mark traced by or as if by a pen, pencil, or brush; a distinctive or effective touch in a literary composition. *Rowing*, a single pull of the oar; a manner or style of moving the oars, as with reference to the length, speed, or frequency of the successive pulls; the oarsman nearest to the stern of the boat, to whose strokes those of the other oarsmen must conform; the position in the boat occupied by this oarsman. *Mech.* one of a series of alternating continuous movements of something back and forth over or through the same line; the complete movement of a moving part, esp. a reciprocating part, in one direction, or the distance traversed.—*v.t.*—*stroked, stroking.* To rub lightly or caress; to row as stroke or oarsman of, as a boat or crew; to mark with a stroke or strokes, as of a pen; to cancel, as by a mark of a pen.

stroke oar, *n. Rowing.* The oar nearest to the stern of a racing shell; the oarsman directly opposite the coxswain, who pulls this oar to set the speed for the others. Also *stroke.*

stroll, strōl, *v.i.* [Origin uncertain: cf. G. dial. *strollen*, stroll, ramble, G. *strolch*, a vagabond.] To walk leisurely as inclination directs; ramble; saunter; take an unhurried walk; to wander, rove, or roam from place

---

ch- chain, G. na*ch*t;   **th-** THen, thin;   **w-** wig, hw as sound in whig;   **z-** zh as in azure, zeal.   *Italicized vowel indicates schwa sound.*

to place, as a vagrant or an itinerant; as, Gypsies *strolling*, a player *strolling*.—*v.t.* To wander idly along or through; as, *stroll* the woodland paths.—*n.* A leisurely walk; a ramble, a saunter.

stroll·er, strō′lẽr, *n.* A saunterer; a wanderer; a vagrant; a strolling or itinerant player or performer; a light, often folding, carriage resembling a chair, designed for young children.

stro·ma, strō′ma, *n.* pl. **stro·ma·ta**, strō′ma·ta. [N.L. use of L.L. *stroma*, < Gr. *stroma*, bed covering, bed, < *stromynai*, spread out.] *Anat.* The sustentacular framework of an organ or part, usu. consisting of connective tissue; the colorless, spongelike framework of a red blood corpuscle or other cell.—**stro·mal, stro·mat·al, stro··mat·ic**, strō′mat′ik, *a.*

stro·mey·er·ite, strō′mī·e·rīt″, *n.* [From F. *Stromeyer*, died 1835, German chemist and mineralogist.] A steel-gray mineral, a sulfide of silver and copper with a metallic luster, occurring in compact masses or crystals.

strong, strạng, strong, *a.* [O.E. *strang*, *strong*, strong, robust = Icel. *strangr*, Dan. and D. *streng*, strong; G. *streng*, strict; same root as *string*, and L. *stringo*, to draw tight (whence *strict*).] Having physical power; having the power of exerting great bodily force; robust; muscular; able or powerful mentally or morally; of great power or capacity; as, a *strong* mind, memory, or imagination; naturally sound or healthy; hale; not easily broken; firm; solid; compact; well-fortified; not easily subdued or taken; as, a *strong* fortress or position; having great military power or force; having great wealth or resources; having force from moving with rapidity, as a wind; violent; impetuous; adapted to make a deep impression on the mind or imagination; cogent; ardent or zealous; as, a *strong* supporter; having a particular quality or qualities in a great degree; as, *strong* tea; intoxicating; affecting the senses forcibly; as, a *strong* light, scent, or flavor; substantial; well-established; firm; not easily overthrown or altered; vehement; earnest; as, a *strong* affection; having great resources; powerful; mighty; having great force or expressiveness; forcibly expressed; amounting to an indicated number; as, an army 10,000 *strong*. *Com.* tending upward in price; rising; as, a *strong* market. *Gram.* of a verb, forming inflected forms by internal vowel change and not by adding syllables, as *swim, swam, swum.*—*adv.* In a strong manner.—**strong·ish**, *a.*—**strong·ly**, *adv.* —**strong·ness**, *n.*

strong-arm, strạng′ärm″, strong′ärm″, *a. Colloq.* having, using, or involving the use of muscular or physical force; as, *strong-arm* methods.—*v.t. Colloq.* To use force against; to rob using violent methods.

strong·box, strạng′boks″, strong′boks″, *n.* A strong, lockable box or chest for the storage of valuables, as jewels or documents.

strong breeze, *n. Meteor.* a wind of from 25 to 31 miles per hour, on the Beaufort scale.

strong drink, *n.* Alcoholic beverage.

strong gale, *n. Meteor.* a wind of from 47 to 54 miles per hour, on the Beaufort scale.

strong·hold, strạng′hōld″, strong′hōld″, *n.* A fortified place; a place of security; a center or place where any particular group exerts a dominating influence.

strong-mind·ed, strạng′mīn′did, strong′-mīn′did, *a.* Having a strong, determined, or vigorous mind; showing independent thinking.—**strong-mind·ed·ly**, *adv.*— **strong-mind·ed·ness**, *n.*

strong·room, strạng′rōm″, strạng′rụm″, strong′rōm″, strong′rụm″, *n. Brit.* a strongly constructed room, burglarproof and fireproof, for the safekeeping of valuables.

strong suit, *n. Cards*, the suit in a hand of bridge which is either one's longest or most powerful; *fig.* any outstanding skill or talent.

stron·gyle, stron·gyl, stron′jil, *n.* [N.L. *Strongylus*, the typical genus, < Gr. *strongylos*, round.] Any of certain nematode worms constituting the family *Strongylidae*, parasitic in the organs and tissues of man and many animals, esp. horses, and often giving rise to serious pathological conditions.—**stron·gy·lo·sis**, stron″ji·lō′sis, *n.* Any disease caused by strongyles.

stron·ti·a, stron′shē·a, stron′sha, *n.* [N.L.] *Chem.* Strontium oxide, SrO, a white amorphous powder resembling lime; strontium hydroxide, $Sr(OH)_2$.

stron·ti·an, stron′shē·an, stron′shan, *n.* [Orig. in *Strontian mineral* or *spar*, strontium carbonate, first found in lead mines at *Strontian*, in Argyllshire, Scotland.] Native strontium carbonate, $SrCO_3$; strontianite; strontia; strontium.—**stron·ti·an·ite**, stron′shē·a·nīt″, stron′sha·nīt″, *n.* A mineral consisting of strontium carbonate, varying in color from white to yellow and pale green, an ore of strontium.

stron·ti·um, stron′shē·um, stron′shum, stron′tē·um, *n. Chem.* a pale yellow metallic element of the rare earth series, occurring only in combination, and having compounds used in making medicines, flares, fireworks, and electronic tubes, and in refining beet sugar. Sym. Sr; at. no. 38, at. wt. 87.62. See Periodic Table of Elements.—**stron··tic**, stron′tik, *a.*

stron·ti·um 90, *n. Chem., phys.* a radioactive isotope of strontium present in the fallout from certain nuclear reactions, constituting a hazard due to its assimilability by plants and animals.

strop, strop, *n.* [O.E. *stropp*, < L. *stroppus*, *struppus*, a thong.] A strip of leather, or a strip of wood covered with leather or other suitable material, used for sharpening straight razors; a razorstrop.—*v.t.*—*stropped, stropping*. To sharpen with a strop.

stro·phan·thin, strō·fan′thin, *n.* [< *Strophanthus*, the plant—Gr. *stropho*, to turn, twist, *anthos*, flower.] *Pharm.* a glycoside drug obtained from the seeds of an African plant of the dogbane family, used as a stimulant in the treatment of heart disease.

stro·phe, strō′fē, *n.* [Gr. *strophe*, < *strepho*, to turn.] The part of a Greek choral ode sung in turning from right to left; the stanza alternated with the antistrophe in the Pindaric ode.—**stroph·ic, stroph·i·cal**, *a.*

stroud, stroud, *n.* A garment or blanket of coarse woolen material, once used for bartering with N. American Indians.

struck, struk, *a.* Shut down by striking workers, as a factory or industry.

struc·tur·al, struk′chẽr·al, *a.* Of or pertaining to structure; essential to a structure. *Biol.* pertaining to organic structure; morphological. *Geol.* pertaining to the structure of rock; *chem.* pertaining to or showing the arrangement or mode of attachment of the atoms which constitute a molecule of a substance; as, a *structural* formula. Resulting from or due to structure, as an economy.—**struc·tur·al·ly**, *adv.*

struc·tur·al for·mu·la, *n. Chem.* the diagrammatic form for symbolizing the bonding relationships among atoms in a molecule.

struc·tur·al i·ron, *n.* Iron cast or forged in shapes suitable for construction.

struc·tur·al steel, *n.* Steel rolled and shaped for use in building construction.

struc·ture, struk′chẽr, *n.* [L. *structura*, < *struere* (pp. *structus*), pile up, build, make.] Mode of building, construction, or organization; arrangement of parts, elements, or constituents; make; constitution; a particular arrangement of parts or elements; something built or constructed; a building; an edifice; a bridge, dam, or framework; any

construction; anything composed of parts arranged together in some way; an organization; *sociol.* a relatively stable pattern of beliefs, rules, or principles and of intergroup, interpersonal, and institutional relationships which forms a framework for the corporate action of a social group. *Biol.* mode of organization; construction and arrangement of tissues and organs; a part or the whole of an organism. *Chem.* relative arrangement of atoms in molecules. *Phys.* a configuration of parts; the points of relation of such a configuration. *Geol.* the arrangement of the parts of which a mineral or rock is composed; various characteristic features of rocks, as stratification and cleavage, considered collectively; the character of a mass of rock with regard to one or more such features; the arrangement of beds or strata.—*v.t.*—*structured, structuring.* To provide with a structure; to construct.— **struc·tured**, struk′chẽrd, *a.*—**struc·ture·less**, *a.*—**struc·ture·less·ness**, *n.*

stru·del, strōd′el, *G.* shtRöd′el, *n.* A pastry made by rolling together a very thin sheet of dough with fruit or cheese and baking.

strug·gle, strug′l, *v.i.*—*struggled, struggling.* [M.E. *strugle, strogel*; origin uncertain.] To contend with an adversary, as in wrestling; put forth violent bodily effort against any opposing force; to offer obstinate opposition or resistance; to content resolutely with a task or problem; to make strenuous efforts toward an end, or strive; to do something difficult; as, to *struggle* for existence; to advance or progress with violent effort; as, to *struggle* through the snow.—*v.t.* To bring or put by struggling; as, to *struggle* oneself out of a tight place; to make, as one's way, with violent effort.—*n.* The act or process of struggling; a course of violently exerted bodily efforts, as between wrestlers or against an opposing force; a strong effort, or series of efforts, against any adverse agencies or conditions, as in order to maintain one's existence or to attain some end.—**strug·gler**, *n.*—**strug·gling**, *a.* That struggles; having a struggle to make a living; as, a *struggling* professional man.— **strug·gling·ly**, *adv.*

strum, strum, *v.i.* [An imit. word.] To play by brushing the fingers lightly across the strings of a musical instrument.—*v.t.* To brush the fingers across the strings of, as a musical instrument; as, *strum* a guitar.—*n.* A strainer, as in tubing.—**strum·mer**, *n.*

stru·ma, strō′ma, *n.* pl. **stru·mae**, strō′mē. [L., < *struo*, to build.] *Pathol.* a scrofulous swelling or tumor; scrofula; goiter. *Bot.* a swelling at one side of a capsule, as in mosses.—**stru·mat·ic, stru·mous, stru··mose**, *a.*

strum·pet, strum′pit, *n.* [Origin doubtful; perh. < O.Fr. *strupre, stupre*, L. *stuprum*, fornication, debauchery.] A prostitute; a harlot; a whore.

strut, strut, *v.i.*—*strutted, strutting.* [O.E. *strut, strout*, to swell or bulge, to strut; akin Dan. *strutte*, to strut, to stick out; L.G. *strutt*, sticking out; G. *strotzen*, to teem.] To walk with a lofty, proud gait and erect head; to walk with affected dignity or pompousness.—*v.t.* To exhibit or show off. —*n.* A proud, exaggerated step or walk.— **strut·ter**, *n.*

strut, strut, *n.* A supporting structural piece designed to relieve weight or stress lengthwise; a brace.—*v.t.*—*strutted, strutting.* To support or brace with a strut or struts.

stru·thi·ous, strō′thē·us, *a.* [L.L. *struthio*, < Gr. *stroythiōn*, ostrich, < *stroythós*, sparrow, bird.] Related to or resembling the ostrich; pertaining to any of the large, flightless birds of the family *Struthionidae*, as the ostrich.

strych·nine, strik′nin, strik′nēn, strik′nin, *n.* [Gr. *strychnos*, a name of several plants of the nightshade family.] *Pharm.* a colorless crystalline, poisonous alkaloid, $C_{21}H_{22}N_2O_2$, obtained from the seeds of an E. Indian tree, *Strychnos nux-vomica*, and used as an antidote for poisoning by depressant drugs. The tree itself; a rodenticide. Also **strych·-ni·a,** strik′nē·*a*.—**strych·nic,** strik′nik, *a.*

strych·nin·ism, strik′ni·niz″*u*m, *n. Pathol.* a morbid condition induced by an overdose, or by excessive use, of strychnine.

stub, stub, *n.* [O.E. *styb*, a stub = Icel. *stubbi, stubbr, stobbi,* a stump, Dan. *stub,* stump, stubble; L.G. *stubbe,* D. *stobbe,* a stump.] The stump of a tree; any remaining part after use or wear, as of a cigarette or pencil; a blunt-nibbed pen; the portion detached from a ticket or check; a stub nail.—*v.t.*—*stubbed, stubbing.* To strike, as one's foot, against a projecting obstruction; to crush, as a cigarette, to extinguish; to grub up by the roots; to clear of roots.—**stub·by,** stub′ē, *a.*

stub·ble, stub′l, *n.* [A dim. form < *stub;* Dan. and Sw. *stub,* stubble.] The stumps of corn or other grain left in the ground by the scythe or sickle; any rough growth, as bristly hair or a beard.—**stub·bled, stub·bly,** *a.*

stub·born, stub′ẽrn, *a.* [< *stub,* O.E. *styb,* lit. 'like a *stub*,' blockish, obstinate, with O.E. *a.* term. *-or* and *-n* added.] Unreasonably or perversely obstinate; not moved or persuaded by reason; maintained in an obstinate or inflexible manner; hard to control or manage; not easily worked, as soil or metal.—**stub·born·ly,** *adv.*—**stub·born·ness,** *n.*

stuc·co, stuk′ō, *n. pl.* **stuc·coes, stuc·cos.** [It. prob. < Teut.: cf. O.H.G. *stukki,* piece of crust, G. *stück,* piece.] A cement or concrete in imitation of stone, for coating exterior walls of houses; any of various plasters, cements, and finishes, esp. one made of slaked lime, chalk, and pulverized white marble, or of plaster of Paris and glue, used for cornices and moldings of rooms and other decorations; the final coat of plastering on a wall.—*a.*—*v.t.*—*stuccoed, stuccoing.* To cover or ornament with stucco. —**stuc·co·work,** stuk′ō·wụrk″, *n.*

stuck-up, stuk′up′, *a. Colloq.* conceited, snobbish, or arrogant.

stud, stud, *n.* [O.E. *stōd* = O.H.G. *stuot* = Icel. *stōdh* = Dan. *stod,* stud of horses (Sw. *sto,* G. *stute,* broodmare); < the root of E. *stand.*] A studhorse or stallion; an establishment in which horses are kept for breeding; the collection of horses kept there; a number of horses, esp. those for racing or hunting, belonging to one owner; a collection of animals of some other kind; a breeding male of certain other domestic animals, as a bull or ram.—*a.*—**at stud,** available or used for breeding: said of male animals.

stud, stud, *n.* [O.E. *studu, stuthu,* = Icel. *stodh* = Sw. *stöd,* post, prop, akin to G. *stütze,* prop, support.] A post or upright prop, as in the wall of a building, esp. one of the smaller vertical timbers to which laths or boards are nailed in forming partitions or walls in houses; a boss, knob, nail head, or other protuberance projecting from a surface or part, esp. as an ornament; an ornamental button or fastener, in the form of a small knob and a disk connected by a stem, for holding together parts of a dress or shirt; any of various projecting pins, lugs, or the like on machines.—*v.t.*—*studded, studding.* To furnish with or support by studs or upright props; to set with or as with studs, bosses, or the like; to scatter over with things set at intervals.—**stud·ding,** *n.*

stud·book, stud′bụk″, *n.* A register containing a genealogy of horses, cattle, or other domestic animals of particular breeds.

stud·ding·sail, stud′ing·sāl″, *Naut.* stun′-sal, *n.* [< *stud,* a support, or altered < steadying sail.] *Naut.* a sail set on the outer edge of any of the principal sails during a light wind. Also *stunsail,* **stun·s′l.**

stu·dent, stōd′ent, stūd′ent, *n.* [L. *studens, studentis,* ppr. of *studeo,* to study.] A person attending an educational institution, esp. a high school or college; one studying anything; one devoted to careful and systematic study.—**stu·dent·ship,** *n.*

stu·dent lamp, *n.* A desk lamp mounted on an upright standard on which it may be raised and lowered.

stu·dent teach·er, *n.* A person studying to become a teacher who engages in a training program of supervised trial teaching in a school classroom. Also *practice teacher.*

stud·horse, stud′hạrs″, *n.* A breeding horse; a stallion.

stud·ied, stud′ēd, *a.* Well-considered; designing; premeditated; deliberate; as, a *studied* insult.—**stud·ied·ly,** *adv.*—**stud·ied·ness,** *n.*

stu·di·o, stōd′ē·ō″, *n. pl.* **stu·di·os.** [It., < L. *studium,* study.] The working room of a painter or sculptor; any room used for the study or execution of an art; a place used for the filming of motion pictures; a place from which television or radio programs are broadcast.

stu·di·o couch, *n.* A couch, usu. backless, that can be converted into a double bed by pulling out a single bedframe from underneath it.

stu·di·ous, stōd′ē·us, stūd′ē·us, *a.* [Fr. *studieux,* L. *studiosus.*] Given to study; devoted to the acquisition of knowledge; pertaining to or used for study; intent and diligent in scholastic effort; planned with deliberation; studied.—**stu·di·ous·ly,** *adv.* —**stu·di·ous·ness,** *n.*

stud pok·er, *n.* A poker game in which five cards are dealt each player, the first card face down with betting taking place on the next four rounds; a variation of this using seven cards.

stud·work, stud′wụrk″, *n.* Construction or work containing, supported, or ornamented by studs.

stud·y, stud′ē, *n. pl.* **stud·ies.** [L. *studium,* zeal, study, < *studeo,* to study.] Application of the mind to books, to arts or science, or to any subject for the purpose of learning; earnest endeavor; diligence; a branch of learning studied; an object of study; a building, apartment, or room devoted to study; a period of deep thought; a reverie; a report written on specific research; one who studies, as an actor; *mus.* a composition which is primarily used to improve technique; *art,* an initial sketch.—*v.i.*—*studied, studying.* To apply one's mind to learning; to dwell in thought; to ponder; to be zealous.—*v.t.* To apply the mind to, as a subject, for the purpose of learning; to consider attentively; to examine closely; to commit to memory.

stud·y hall, *n.* A room, in some schools, used only for studying; a time period in a pupil's day designated for studying.

stuff, stuf, *n.* [O.Fr. *estoffe* (Fr. *étoffe*), stuff, material, < L. *stuppa,* tow.] Substance or matter indefinitely; the matter of which anything is formed; material; furniture; refuse or worthless matter; foolish or irrational language; trash; personal property or equipment; that which is consumed, as food, drink, or medicine; *Brit.* a general name for woven fabrics, as wool or silk. *Colloq.* particular talk or action; one's field or ability.—*v.t.* To fill by packing or crowding material into; to cram; to crowd in together; to fill or pack with material necessary to make complete; as, to *stuff* a cushion; to fill the skin of, as a dead animal, for presenting and preserving its form; to

fill mentally full; to put fraudulent ballots into; as to *stuff* the ballot box; to crowd with facts or idle tales or fancies; to fill with seasoning; as, to *stuff* a leg of veal.—*v.i.* To feed gluttonously.—**stuff·er,** *n.*—**stuff·less,** *a.*

stuffed shirt, *n. Colloq.* a pompous or pretentious person.

stuff·ing, stuf′ing, *n.* The act of one who or that which stuffs; that with which anything is or may be stuffed; seasoned bread crumbs or other filling used to stuff a fowl, roast, or other meat before cooking.

stuff·ing box, *n. Mach.* a contrivance for securing a steamtight, airtight, or watertight joint at the place or hole where a movable rod, as a piston rod, enters; the vessel, consisting typically of a cylindrical box or chamber through the middle of which the rod passes, the space between the rod and the walls of the box being filled with packing.

stuff·y, stuf′ē, *a.*—*stuffier, stuffiest.* [O.Fr. *estouffer,* to stifle, < *estoffe,* stuff.] Difficult to breathe in or close, as the air of a room; obstructing respiration; *colloq.* stodgy or old-fashioned.—**stuff·i·ly,** *adv.*—**stuff·i·ness,** *n.*

stull, stul, *n.* [Cf. G. *stollen,* prop, post.] *Min.* A log post to support walls or facings; a framework of timber covered with horizontal boards, built in an excavation or stope as a support or for protection.

stul·ti·fy, stul′ti·fī″, *v.t.*—*stultified, stultifying.* [L.L. *stultificare,* < L. *stultus,* foolish, and *facere,* make.] To make or cause to appear foolish or ridiculous; to reduce to foolishness or absurdity; to render wholly futile or ineffectual, as efforts; *law,* to allege or prove to be of unsound mind.—**stul·ti·fi·ca·tion,** *n.*— **stul·ti·fi·er,** *n.*

stum, stum, *n.* [< D. *stom,* unfermented wine, must, < *stom,* G. *stumm,* Dan. and Sw. *stum,* dumb, mute.] Unfermented grape juice; must or new wine; wine made from must by fermentation.—*v.t.*—*stummed, stumming.* To renew by mixing with must and fermenting.

stum·ble, stum′bl, *v.i.*—*stumbled, stumbling.* [O.E. *stomble, stomel;* allied to E. *stammer,* Prov. E. *stummer,* Icel. *stumra,* to stumble, N. *stumle,* to totter, L.G. *stumpeln,* to walk heavily.] To trip in walking; to make a false step; to stagger; to walk unsteadily; to speak falteringly; to discover by chance, usu. followed by *on* or *upon.*—*v.t.* To cause to stumble; to puzzle.—*n.* The act of stumbling; a trip in walking or running; a blunder.—**stum·bler,** *n.*—**stum·bling·ly,** *adv.*

stum·ble·bum, stum′bl·bum″, *n. Slang.* One who acts as though in a daze; a clumsy, blundering prize fighter.

stum·bling block, *n.* Any obstacle which causes stumbling; *fig.* any hindrance to progress or success.

stump, stump, *n.* [M.E. *stumpe, stompe,* = D. *stomp* = M.L.G. *stump* = G. *stumpf,* stump.] The lower end of a tree or plant left after the main part falls or is cut off; any basal portion remaining after the main part has been removed in some way, as after the amputation of a limb of the body; a rudimentary or undeveloped limb or member; a short remnant or stub, as of a pencil or cigar; a heavy step or gait, as of a wooden-legged or lame person; a short, thickset person; an imitation leg; a challenge; the platform or place of political speechmaking; *cricket,* each of the three upright sticks which, with the two bails laid on top of them, form a wicket. A rubbing instrument consisting of a short, thick roll of paper, leather, or other soft material, with a blunt point at each end, used for toning the shading in crayon, pencil, or charcoal drawings.—*v.t.* To reduce to a stump; truncate; lop; to clear of stumps, as land; *slang*, to nonplus, embarrass, or render completely at a loss. *Colloq.* to stub, as one's toe; to challenge or dare to do something; to make stump speeches in or to. To tone or modify, as the shading in drawings, by means of a stump.—*v.i.* To walk heavily or clumsily, as if with a wooden leg; to make stump speeches.—**stump·er,** *n.*

stump·age, stum′pij, *n.* Standing timber considered with reference to its value; the right to cut such timber on another's land; the price paid for such timber.

stump speak·ing, *n.* Speechmaking done while in a political campaign.

stump·y, stum′pē, *a.*—*stumpier, stumpiest.* Of the nature of or resembling a stump; short and thick; stubby; stocky; abounding in stumps.—**stump·i·ly,** *adv.*—**stump·i·ness,** *n.*

stun, stun, *v.t.*—*stunned, stunning.* [O.E. *stunian,* to stun, < *stun,* noise; same root as Skt. *stan,* to thunder.] To render insensible or dizzy by force or violence; to render senseless by a blow; to surprise completely; to confound by a loud or distracting noise. —*n.* The action of stunning or the state of being stunned.

stun·ner, stun′ẽr, *n.* Someone or something that stuns; *colloq.* a person or thing of striking beauty or appearance.

stun·ning, stun′ing, *a.* Of striking excellence, beauty, style, or attractiveness; rendering or able to render senseless; causing surprise or confusion.—**stun·ning·ly,** *adv.*

stun·sail, stun′sal, *n.* Studdingsail. Also **stun·s'l.**

stunt, stunt, *v.t.* [< O.E. *stunt,* blunt, stupid; Sw. *stunt,* docked, short; akin Icel. *stuttr,* short, stunted; G. *stutzen,* to dock.] To hinder from normal or free growth or progress; to check in development or growth; dwarf.—*n.* A hindrance or check in growth, development, or progress; that which is hindered from normal growth; *plant pathol.* a disease causing a dwarfing of the affected plant.—**stunt·ed,** *a.*—**stunt·ed·ness,** *n.*

stunt, stunt, *n.* [Cf. *stint, n.,* in sense of 'allotted piece of work.'] A performance serving as a display of strength, skill, or the like, as in athletics; an unusual or daring feat done, esp. to attract publicity or attention.—*v.i.* To do a stunt or stunts.—*v.t.* To employ or use in the performance of stunts, as an automobile.

stu·pa, stö′pa, *n.* [Skt. *stûpa.*] A dome-shaped structure dedicated as a shrine to Buddha or one of his saints. Also *tope.*

stupe, stöp, stūp, *n.* [L. *stupa,* tow.] *Med.* a heated wet compress, sometimes medicated, which is applied to a wound or sore.

stu·pe·fa·cient, stö″pe·fā′shent, stū″pe·-fā′shent, *a.* [L. *stupefaciens* (-*ent-*), ppr.] Stupefying; producing stupor. Also **stu·-pe·fac·tive,** stö″pe·fak′tiv, stū″pe·fak′tiv. —*n.* A drug or agent that produces stupor.

stu·pe·fac·tion, stö″pe·fak′shan, stū″pe·-fak′shan, *n.* The act of stupefying; the state of being stupefied or stunned; insensibility; amazement.

stu·pe·fy, stö′pe·fī″, stū′pe·fī″, *v.t.*—*stupe-fied, stupefying.* [Fr. *stupéfier,* < L. *stupe-facere* (passive *stupefieri*), < *stupere,* be struck senseless and *facere,* make.] To put into a state of stupor; deprive of sensibility; benumb or dull the faculties of; make stupid, as with a narcotic, shock, or strong emotion; stun; to overwhelm with amazement; astound.—**stu·pe·fied·ness,** stö′-pe·fīd″nis, stö′pe·fī″id·nis, stū′pe·fīd″nis, stū″-pe·fī″id·nis, *n.*—**stu·pe·fi·er,** *n.*—**stu·pe·fy·ing·ly,** stö′pe·fī″ing·lē, stū′pe·-fī″ing·lē, *adv.*

stu·pen·dous, stö·pen′dus, stū·pen′dus, *a.* [L. *stupendus,* amazing, < *stupeo,* to be astonished.] Great and wonderful; of astonishing magnitude or elevation; grand. —**stu·pen·dous·ly,** *adv.*—**stu·pen·dous·-ness,** *n.*

stu·pid, stö′pid, stū′pid, *a.* [L. *stupidus,* < *stupeo,* to be astonished or struck senseless (seen also in *stupefy, stupendous*); perh. same root as *stand.*] Extremely dull of perception or understanding; mentally slow; senseless; stupefied; boring or dull; as, a *stupid* movie; in a state of stupor.—*n.*— **stu·pid·ly,** *adv.*—**stu·pid·ness,** *n.*

stu·pid·i·ty, stö·pid′i·tē, stū·pid′i·tē, *n.* pl. **stu·pid·i·ties.** The state, quality, or fact of being stupid; stupid action, behavior, notion, or speech.

stu·por, stö′pẽr, stū′pẽr, *n.* [L., < *stupere.*] Suspension or great diminution of sensibility, as in disease or as caused by narcotics, intoxicants, or the like; a state of suspended or deadened sensibility; mental torpor or apathy; stupefaction.—**stu·por·ous,** *a.*

stur·dy, stẽr′dē, *a.*—*sturdier, sturdiest.* [O.Fr. *estordi, estourdi,* stunned, dizzy, giddy, reckless, violet, pp. of *estordir, estourdir* (Fr. *étourdir*), stun, daze, make dizzy; origin uncertain.] Strongly built, stalwart, robust, or lusty; strong, as in substance, construction, texture, or the like; as, *sturdy* walls; firm, stout, or indomitable; as, *sturdy* resistance; of strong or hardy growth, as a plant.—**stur·di·ly,** *adv.*—**stur·di·ness,** *n.*

stur·dy, stẽr′dē, *n.* [Gael. *stuird, stuirdean,* vertigo, sturdy.] *Veter. pathol.* a disease in sheep. Also *gid.*

stur·geon, stẽr′jen, *n.* pl. **stur·geon, stur·geons.** [O.Fr. *sturgun* (Fr. *esturgeon*), < M.L. *sturio*(*n*-); < Teut.] Any of various large ganoid fishes of the family *Acipenseridae,* found in fresh and salt waters of northern regions, valued for their flesh and as a source of caviar and isinglass.

Sturm und Drang, shtựrm″ ụnt dråäng′, *n.* [Tr. G. *sturm und drang*: with allusion to a drama of this title, 1776, by F. M. von Klinger, 1752–1831, taken as expressing the spirit of the movement.] A movement and a period in German literature from about 1770 to 1790, characterized by vehement passion and by reaction against the established formalities; any period of passionate or rebellious unrest; loosely, any turmoil or trouble, as in the life of a person. Also *Storm and Stress.*

stut·ter, stut′ẽr, *v.t., v.i.* [Freq. of *stut*: cf. D. *stotteren,* M.L.G. *stoteren,* G. *stottern,* stutter.] To utter with involuntary or spasmodic repetitions of syllables or sounds in the effort to speak, esp. habitually, from a defect in the powers of speech; stammer. —*n.* A stuttering mode of utterance; a habit of stuttering; a stuttered utterance.—**stut·ter·er,** *n.*—**stut·ter·ing·ly,** *adv.*

sty, stī, *n.* pl. **sties.** [O.E. *stige,* a sty or pen = Icel. *stia,* Dan. *sti,* Sw. *stia,* O.H.G. *stiga,* a sty.] A pen or enclosure for swine; any filthy hovel or place; a place of bestial debauchery.—*v.t.*—*stied, stying.* To shut up or keep as in or in a sty.—*v.i.* To live or stay in a sty.

sty, stī, *n.* pl. **sties.** [O.E. *stīgend,* a tumor on the eye, < *stīgan,* to rise; akin *stair.*] *Pathol.* a small inflammatory protuberance or enlargement of a sebaceous gland on the edge of the eyelid. Also **stye.**

Styg·i·an, stij′ē·an, *a.* [L. *Stygius,* < *Styx,* Gr. *Styx, Stygos,* the Styx, < *stygeō* to hate.] (*Sometimes l.c.*) Pertaining to the river Styx; hellish; infernal; gloomy or dismal; inviolable, binding, as an oath.

sty·lar, stī′lẽr, *a.* Of, pertaining to, or like a stylus; styliform.

style, stīl, *n.* [Fr. *style,* < L. *stilus, stylus,* a stake, pointed instrument, style for writing, hence mode of expression; < root of *stimulus, stick, sting.* Spelling influenced by Gr. *stylos,* a pillar.] Manner of writing or speaking with regard to language; that which has to do with form rather than content in a piece of literature; a distinctive manner of writing belonging to an author or body of authors; a characteristic mode of presentation in any of the fine arts; external manner, mode, or fashion; manner deemed elegant and appropriate; fashion; as, a person dressed in *style*; a formal or official designation; title; as, a company operating under the *style* of Brown and Smith; that which is appropriate for oneself; the form observed by a particular printer or publisher in typography; a pointed instrument for writing, drawing, or engraving; a stylus; the gnomon of a sundial. *Surg.* a slender blunt-pointed probe; also *stylet. Bot.* a slender structure which arises from the top of an ovary and through which pollen tubes grow; *zool.* a slender elongated part of the body, usu. part of another organ; *chronology,* a system of arranging the length of the calendar year so as to conform with a true solar year, specif. the New Style calendar which replaced the Old Style calendar in 1582.—*v.t.*—*styled, styling.* To name or call; to give a particular form to; as, to *style* a dress.—*v.i.* To do work with a stylus.—**style·less,** *a.*—**style·less·ness,** *n.* —**style·like,** *a.*—**styl·er,** *n.*

style·book, stīl′bụk″, *n.* A manual used by editors, writers, and printers comprising current standards of printing, spelling, and punctuation.

sty·let, stī′lit, *n.* [Fr. *stylet,* < It. *stiletto.*] A stiletto or dagger; some similar sharp-pointed instrument. *Surg.* the stiffening wire or rod in a flexible catheter; a probe; see *style.*

sty·li·form, stī′li·fạrm″, *a.* Having the shape of or resembling a stylus; stylar.

styl·ish, stī′lish, *a.* Pertaining to current fashion standards; chic; pertaining to a particular style.—**styl·ish·ly,** *adv.*—**styl·-ish·ness,** *n.*

styl·ist, stī′list, *n.* One who maintains, creates, or is master of a particular style, esp. a writer or speaker; a designer of fashions, as clothing.—**sty·lis·tic, sty·lis·-ti·cal,** stī·lis′tik, ... —**sty·lis·ti·cal·ly,** *adv.*

sty·lite, stī′lit, *n.* [Gr. *stylītēs,* < *stylos,* a pillar.] A pillar saint, an early ascetic who lived on the top of high columns or pillars. —**sty·lit·ic,** stī·lit′ik, *a.*

styl·ize, stī′līz, *v.t.*—*stylized, stylizing.* To conform or cause to conform to a particular style, as of representation or treatment in art; conventionalize.—**styl·i·za·tion,** *n.*— **styl·iz·er,** *n.*

sty·lo·bate, stī′lo·bāt″, *n.* [L. *stylobates, stylobata,* < Gr. *stylobatēs*—*stylos,* a pillar, and *bainō,* to go.] *Arch.* a continuous and unbroken pedestal or elevation upon which a range of columns stands.

sty·lo·graph, stī′lo·graf″, stī′lo·gräf″, *n.* A type of fountain pen with a conical hollow tube for its writing point.

sty·log·ra·phy, stī·log′ra·fē, *n.* A method of writing or engraving with a style.— **sty·lo·graph·ic, sty·lo·graph·i·cal,** stī″-lo·graf′ik, *a.* Pertaining to a stylograph; pertaining to or employed in stylography. —**sty·lo·graph·i·cal·ly,** *adv.*

sty·loid, stī′loid, *a.* Having some resemblance to a style or pen; *anat.* pertaining to certain stylus-shaped skeletal processes, as on the ulna, radius, or temporal bone.

sty·lo·lite, stī′lo·līt″, *n.* [Gr. *stylos,* pillar, column, and *lithos,* stone.] *Geol.* a longitudinally streaked, columnar structure occurring in various rocks, esp. limestone, and of the same material as the rock in which it occurs.—**sty·lo·lit·ic,** stī″lo·lit′ik, *a.*

sty·lo·po·di·um, stī″lo·pō′dē·um, *n.* pl. **sty·lo·po·di·a,** stī″lo·pō′dē·a. [N.L., <

L. *stylus* (used to mean a style in bot.) and Gr. *poús* (*pod*-), foot.] *Bot.* a glandular disk or expansion surmounting the ovary in umbelliferous plants, and supporting the styles.

sty·lus, stī′lus, *n.* pl. **sty·lus·es**, **sty·li**, stī′lī. [L., prop. *stilus*.] A style or pointed instrument for writing on wax; the pointed piece which produces the indentations or incisions in making a phonograph record; a similar device in a phonograph, for reproducing sounds from such a record; a pointed instrument used in art, drawing, or engraving, as on stencils or carbons.

sty·mie, stī′mē, *n.* pl. **sti·mies**. [Cf. Sc. *stymie*, a dim-sighted person, *stime*, *styme*, a glimpse, glimmer.] *Golf*, an opponent's ball on a putting green when it is directly between the player's ball and the hole for which he is playing, and when the distance between the balls is more than six inches; the occurrence of a ball in such a position, or the position of the ball. A difficult situation or problem with little possibility of solution.—*v.t.*—*stimied*, *stimieing*. To hinder with a stymie, or as a stymie does. Also **sty·my**, **sti·my**.

styp·tic, stip′tik, *a.* [L. *stypticus*, < Gr. *styptikos*, < *styphō*, to contract.] Having the quality of stopping the bleeding of a wound; astringent. Also **styp·ti·cal.**—*n.* —**styp·tic·i·ty**, stip·tis′i·tē, *n.*

styp·tic pen·cil, *n.* A stick, similar to a pencil in shape, containing a styptic material used to check bleeding, as from a razor nick.

sty·ra·ca·ceous, stī″ra·kā′shus, *a.* Belonging to the *Styraceæ*, or storax family of shrubs and trees, characterized by the presence of resins and often large attractive flowers.

sty·rax, stī′raks, *n.* Storax.

sty·rene, stī′rēn, stēr′ēn, *n.* [L. *styrax*, storax.] *Chem.* a colorless liquid hydrocarbon, $C_6H_5CH=CH_2$, with an aromatic odor, used in making synthetic rubber, plastics, and resins.

Sty·ro·foam, stī′ro·fōm″, *n.* The brand name of a lightweight polystyrene plastic, usu. used as insulating material or in decorations. (Trademark.) Also **sty·ro·foam.**

Styx, stiks, *n.* Gr. *mythol.* One of the five rivers of hell over which dead souls were ferried by the boatman Charon; the river by which the gods swore their oaths.

su·a·ble, sö′a·bl, *a.* Capable of being sued; liable to be sued.—**su·a·bil·i·ty**, *n.*— **su·a·bly**, *adv.*

sua·sion, swā′zhan, *n.* [L. *suasio*, *suasionis*, < *suadeo*, *suasum*, to advise (as in *dissuade*, *persuade*).] The act of persuading.—**sua·sive**, swā′siv, *a.*—**sua·sive·ly**, *adv.*—**sua·sive·ness**, *n.*

suave, swäv, *a.* [Fr. *suave*, sweet, pleasant, < L. *suavis*, sweet; same root as *suadeo*, to persuade, and as E. *sweet*.] Gracious or agreeable in manner; blandly polite; pleasant; polished or sophisticated.—**suave·ly**, *adv.*—**suave·ness**, *n.*—**suav·i·ty**, *n.*

sub, sub, *a.* Secondary in rank or importance, used in combination; as, a *subplot.*

sub, sub, *v.i.*—*subbed*, *subbing*. *Colloq.* to substitute, or act as substitute, for another. —*v.t. Photog., colloq.* to cover with an underlayer, as film.—*n. Colloq.* One who acts for another; a substitute; a substratum, as on film.

sub, sub, *n. Colloq.* submarine.

sub·ac·e·tate, sub·as′i·tāt″, *n. Chem.* a basic acetate.

sub·ac·id, sub·as′id, *a.* [L. *sub*, slightly.] Moderately acid or sour, as some fruits; *fig.* biting or sharp to some degree; as, a *subacid* reply.—**sub·a·cid·i·ty**, **sub·ac·id·ness**, sub″a·sid′i·tē, *n.*—**sub·ac·id·ly**, *adv.*

sub·a·cute, sub″a·kūt′, *a.* [L. *sub*, slightly.] Acute in a modified degree; *pathol.* between the stages or degrees of acute and chronic, as of some disease.—**sub·a·cute·ly**, *adv.*

sub·a·gent, sub·ā′jent, *n.* A person who is a subordinate to and works under an agent. —**sub·a·gen·cy**, *n.*

su·bah·dar, **su·ba·dar**, sö″ba·där′, *n.* A ruler of a province or district in India; formerly, the highest native officer of a native troop of the British Indian Army.

sub·al·pine, sub·al′pīn, sub·al′pin, *a.* [L. *sub*, under.] Relating to the lower slopes or foothills of the Alps; belonging to a region on mountains immediately below the timberline, but above the foothill slopes.

sub·al·tern, sub·al′tern, sub′al·turn″, *a.* [L. *subalternus*, subordinate—*sub*, under, *alter*, another.] Holding an inferior or subordinate position; *Brit. milit.* below the rank of a captain, sub·al′tern. *Logic*, referring to a particular proposition related to the same universal proposition, sub′al·turn″, sub·al′tern.—*n.* A subordinate; *Brit. milit.* a commissioned military officer below the rank of captain, sub·al′tern. *Logic*, a subaltern statement, sub′al·turn″, sub·al′tern.

sub·al·ter·nate, sub·al′ter·nit, sub·al′ter·nit, *a.* Subordinate or inferior; successive; *bot.* arranged in an alternate manner but tending to be opposite, as leaves.—*n. Logic*, a proposition which is particular, as opposed to a proposition which is universal. —**sub·al·ter·nate·ly**, *adv.*—**sub·al·ter·na·tion**, *n.*

sub·ap·i·cal, sub·ap′i·kal, sub·ā′pi·kal, *a.* Situated near or beneath an apex.—**sub·ap·i·cal·ly**, *adv.*

sub·a·quat·ic, sub″a·kwat′ik, sub″a·kwot′ik, *a.* [L. *sub*, under, and *aqua*, water.] Existing, functioning, or being partly under water; partially aquatic.

sub·a·que·ous, sub·ā′kwē·us, sub·ak′wē·us, *a.* Existing, functioning, or being under water; formed, deposited, or used under water.

sub·arc·tic, sub·ärk′tik, sub·är′tik, *a.* [L *sub*, slightly.] Applied to a region or climate next to the Arctic Circle; anything approximating conditions or life in areas near the Arctic.

sub·as·sem·bly, sub″a·sem′blē, *n.* pl. **sub·as·sem·blies.** Any assembled unit which forms part of a more extensive assembly.—**sub·as·sem·bler**, *n.*

sub·au·di·tion, sub″a·dish′an, *n.* [L. *subauditio*, < *subaudio*, to understand or supply a word omitted—*sub*, under, and *audio*, to hear.] The act of understanding or presenting something not expressed; an implied or understood meaning.

sub·av·er·age, sub·av′ėr·ij, sub·av′rij, *a.* Lower than the norm; below average.

sub·base, sub′bās″, *n.* The lowest part of an architectural base, as of a column, which consists of two or more horizontal members; *milit.* a base subordinate to another in some respect, as for logistic support.

sub·base·ment, sub′bās″ment, *n.* A basement, or one of a series of basements, below the main basement of a building.

sub·bass, sub′bās″, *n. Mus.* a pedal stop producing the lowest tones of an organ.

sub·bing, sub′ing, *n. Colloq.* doing work as a substitute, esp. in teaching. *Photog.* the application of a substrate; a substance used as a substrate. *Agric.* subirrigation.

sub·cal·i·ber, sub·kal′i·bėr, *a. Milit.* Of a projectile having a diameter less than the caliber of the gun from which it is fired, the projectile being fitted with a disk large enough to fill the bore, or fired from a small tube attached to the inside or the outside of the gun; pertaining to such a projectile or its firing.

sub·car·ti·lag·i·nous, sub″kär·ti·laj′i·-

nus, *a. Anat.* Situated beneath cartilage; less than completely cartilaginous.

sub·ce·les·tial, sub″si·les′chal, *a.* Being beneath the heavens; terrestrial; mundane; *astron.* being directly below the zenith.—*n.* A being which is subcelestial.

sub·cen·tral, sub·sen′tral, *a.* Situated below a center; nearly or almost central. —**sub·cen·tral·ly**, *adv.*

sub·chas·er, sub′chā″sėr, *n.* Submarine chaser.

sub·chlo·ride, sub·klōr′īd, sub·klōr′id, sub·klar′īd, sub·klar′id, *n. Chem.* a chloride that contains a relatively small proportion of chlorine.

sub·class, sub′klas″, sub′kläs″, *n.* A fundamental subgroup of a class; *biol.* a subdivision of a class, consisting of related orders.—*v.t.*

sub·cla·vi·an, sub·klā′vē·an, *a.* [L. *sub*, under, and *clavis*, a key, used in sense of Gr. *kleis*, the collarbone.] *Anat.* Situated under the clavicle or collarbone; referring to a vein, artery, or similar part under the clavicle.—*n. Anat.* a vein, artery, or similar part under the clavicle.

sub·cla·vi·an ar·te·ry, *n. Anat.* the main artery, beneath the clavicle, of the arm.

sub·cla·vi·an vein, *n. Anat.* the main vein beneath the clavicle leading to the arm.

sub·cli·max, sub·klī′maks, *n. Ecology*, a period in the development of a plant or animal population which fails to reach a stable climax stage due to interference by outside influences, as soil, floods, or fire.

sub·clin·i·cal, sub·klin′i·kal, *a. Med.* referring to a disorder virtually undetectable in general clinical tests because its symptoms are so moderate.—**sub·clin·i·cal·ly**, *adv.*

sub·com·mit·tee, sub′kȯ·mit″ē, *n.* [L. *sub*, under.] A part or division of a committee usu. doing a specific task.

sub·con·scious, sub·kon′shus, *a.* Existing or operating beneath or beyond consciousness; imperfectly or not wholly conscious. —*n.* That part of the mental processes which is not in the realm of consciousness. —**sub·con·scious·ly**, *adv.*—**sub·con·scious·ness**, *n.*

sub·con·ti·nent, sub·kon′ti·nent, sub′kon″ti·nent, *n.* A large, comparatively independent subdivision of a continent, as India; a large body of land smaller than a continent, as Greenland.—**sub·con·ti·nen·tal**, sub″kon·ti·nen′tal, *a.*

sub·con·tract, sub·kon′trakt, sub′kon″trakt, *n.* A contract under another contract for carrying out the previous contract or a part of it.—sub″kon·trakt′, *v.t.* To make a subcontract for.—*v.i.* To make a subcontract.—**sub·con·trac·tor**, sub·kon′trak·tėr, sub′kon″trak·tėr, sub′kon·trak″tėr, *n.*

sub·con·tra·ri·e·ty, sub″kon·tra·rī′i·tē, *n.* pl. **sub·con·tra·ri·e·ties.** The relationship between two subcontrary propositions.

sub·con·tra·ry, sub·kon′trer·ē, *n.* pl. **sub·con·tra·ries.** One of two propositions so related that both cannot be false but both may be true.—*a.*

sub·cool, sub·köl′, *v.t.* Supercool.

sub·cor·date, sub·kȯr′dāt, *a.* Approximately heart-shaped, as of leaves.

sub·cor·tex, sub·kȯr′teks, sub′kȯr″teks, *n.* pl. **sub·cor·ti·ces**, sub·kȯr′ti·sēz, sub′kȯr″ti·sēz. *Biol.* those parts of the brain which lie directly beneath the cerebral cortex.—**sub·cor·ti·cal**, sub·kȯr′ti·kal, *a. Biol.* directly beneath the cortex.

sub·crit·i·cal, sub·krit′i·kal, *a. Phys.* pertaining to a state or quantity of radioactive material which is less than that required to support a chain reaction at a continuous level, esp. in reference to mass.

sub·cul·ture, sub·kul′chėr, *v.t.*—*subcultured*, *subculturing*. To transfer a small portion of, as a bacterial culture, onto a new medium.—*n. Bact.* a bacterial culture derived from another culture; *sociol.* a portion of an ethnic group which has enough distinctive characteristics to be distinguished from the overall group.—**sub·-cul·tur·al**, *a.*

sub·cu·ta·ne·ous, sub″kū·tā′nē·us, *a.* [L. *sub*, under, *cutis*, skin.] Situated, used, lying, or made immediately under the skin; introduced beneath the skin, as an injection. —**sub·cu·ta·ne·ous·ly**, *adv.*

sub·cu·tis, sub·kū′tis, *n.* The lowest part of the dermis.

sub·dea·con, sub·dē′kon, sub′dē″kon, *n.* [L. *sub*, under.] Second to the deacon in an ecclesiastic hierarchy.

sub·deb·u·tante, sub·deb′ū·tänt″, sub·-deb′ū·tant″, *n.* A young girl in the years before her debut into society; a girl in her middle teens. Also **sub·deb**, sub′deb″.

sub·den·tate, sub·den′tāt, *a.* Imperfectly or partially toothed; as, a *subdentate* leaf.

sub·de·pot, sub·dē′pō, *Brit.*, *milit.* sub·-dep′ō, *n.* A depot operating under the control of another depot, usu. a military one, and performing a specialized function.

sub·di·ac·o·nal, sub″dī·ak′o·nal, *a.* Referring to a subdeacon.

sub·di·ac·o·nate, sub″dī·ak′o·nit, sub″-dī·ak′o·nāt″, *n.* The office or position of subdeacon; a group of subdeacons.

sub·di·vide, sub″dī·vīd′, sub′di·vīd″, *v.t.* —*subdivided*, *subdividing*. [L. *subdivido -sub*, under, and *divido*.] To divide parts into more parts; to part into subdivisions; to divide into lots, as in land.—*v.i.* To be subdivided.—**sub·di·vid·a·ble**, *a.*—**sub·-di·vid·er**, *n.*

sub·di·vi·sion, sub′di·vizh″an, *n.* The result of subdividing; a tract of land which has been subdivided for the purpose of a housing development.—**sub·di·vi·sion·al**, *a.*

sub·dom·i·nant, sub·dom′i·nant, *n.* [L. *sub*, under.] *Mus.* the fourth note of the diatonic scale lying a tone under the dominant or fifth of the scale.—*a.* Not quite dominant.

sub·duct, sub·dukt′, *v.t.* [L. *subduco, subductum—sub*, under, and *duco*, to draw, to lead.] *Archaic.* To withdraw; to take away; to subtract by arithmetical operation.—**sub·duc·tion**, *n.*

sub·due, sub·dō′, sub·dū′, *v.t.*—*subdued*, *subduing*. [O.Fr. *subduzer*, to subdue, < L. *sub*, under, and *duco*, to lead.] To conquer and bring into permanent subjection; to reduce under dominion; to overpower by superior force; to vanquish; to overcome by discipline; to tame; to prevail over by some mild or softening influence; to gain complete sway over; to melt or soften, as the heart; to tone down or make less intense. —**sub·du·a·ble**, *a.*—**sub·du·er**, *n.*—**sub·-du·al**, *n.*

sub·en·try, sub′en″trē, *n.* pl. **sub·en·tries**. An entry listed under a main entry.

su·ber, sō′bêr, *n.* [L., the cork tree, cork.] Cork; phellem.—**su·be·re·ous**, **su·ber·ic**, su̯·bĕr′ĕ·us, su̯·ber′ik, *a.*

sub·e·rect, sub″i·rekt′, *a.* Being in an almost erect position; as, a *suberect* tree.

su·ber·ic ac·id, *n. Chem.* a dibasic acid, COOH(CH₂)₆COOH, taking a white crystalline form, synthesized by the reaction of nitric acid on cork or other fatty substances.

su·ber·in, sō′bêr·in, *n.* A fatty waterproof substance resembling wax, contained in and characteristic of cork tissue in plants.

su·ber·ize, sō′be·rīz″, *v.t.*—*suberized*, *suberizing*. *Bot.* to convert into cork tissue. —**su·ber·i·za·tion**, sō″bĕr·i·zā′shan, *n.*

su·ber·ose, sō′be·rōs″, *a.* [L. *suber*, cork.] Of the nature of cork. Also **su·ber·ous**, sō′bêr·us.—**su·ber·ic**, su̯·ber′ik, *a.*

sub·fam·i·ly, sub·fam′i·lē, sub·fam′lē, sub′fam″i·lē, sub′fam′lē, *n.* pl. **sub·fam·i·lies**. *Biol.* a group or category ranking

below a family and above a genus; *ling.* a division above a branch in classifying related languages.

sub·fix, sub′fiks″, *n.* A subscript letter, sign, or character.

sub·fos·sil, sub·fos′il, *a.* In the process of becoming a fossil.—*n.*

sub·freez·ing, sub′frē′zing, *a.* Lower than the temperature needed to solidify a liquid.

sub·fusc, sub·fusk′, *a.* [L. *subfuscus, suffuscus*: cf. *fuscous*.] Somewhat dark or dusky in color.—**sub·fus·cous**, *a.*

sub·ge·nus, sub·jē′nus, *n.* pl. **sub·gen·-er·a**, **sub·gen·us·es**, sub·jen′êr·a. *Biol.* a subordinate genus, group, or category ranking below a genus and above a species.

sub·gla·cial, sub·glā′shal, *a.* Beneath a glacier; as, a *subglacial* stream.—**sub·-gla·cial·ly**, *adv.*

sub·grade, sub′grād″, *n.* A surface of rock or earth which has been prepared as a foundation for the pavement of a road.

sub·group, sub′grōp″, *n.* [L. *sub*, under.] One of the parts of a group; a secondary grouping or division; *chem.* a component group of elements within one of the larger vertical groupings in the periodic table; *math.* a group, all of whose elements are elements of another group.

sub·head, sub′hed″, *n.* A subordinate head or title, under which is treated one of the divisions of a subject treated under a larger heading; a subordinate division of a heading or title; a subordinate to the head of a school.

sub·hu·man, sub·hū′man, sub·ū′man, *a.* Below the human race or type; less than or not quite human; almost human.

sub·in·dex, sub·in′deks, *n.* pl. **sub·in·-di·ces**, sub·in′di·sēz″. *Math.* a subscript.

sub·in·feu·date, sub″in·fū′dāt, *v.t.*, *v.i.* —*subinfeudated*, *subinfeudating*. To sublet or grant by subinfeudation. Also **sub·in·feud**.

sub·in·feu·da·tion, sub″in·fū·dā′shan, *n. Feudal law.* Secondary infeudation; the granting of a portion of an estate by a feudal tenant to a subtenant, to be held by the tenant on terms similar to those of the grant to him; the tenure established by this; the estate or fief so created.—**sub·in·feu·da·-to·ry**, sub″in·fū′da·tōr″ē, sub″in·fū′da·-tar″ē, *n.*

sub·in·ter·val, sub·in′tẽr·val, *n.* An interval that is a part or a subdivision of another interval.

sub·ir·ri·gate, sub·ir′i·gāt″, *v.t.*—*subirrigated*, *subirrigating*. To irrigate beneath the surface of the ground, as with water passing through a system of underground pipes or transmitted through the subsoil from ditches.—**sub·ir·ri·ga·tion**, sub·-ir″i·gā′shan, *n.*

su·bi·to, sō′bi·tō″, *It.* sō′bē·tạ, *adv.* [It. < L. *subito*, abl. of *subitus*, sudden.] *Mus.* Suddenly; quickly.

sub·ja·cent, sub·jā′sent, *a.* [L. *subjacens* (-*ent*), ppr. of *subjacere*, lie under, < *sub*, under, and *jacere*, lie.] Situated or occurring underneath or below; underlying; forming a basis; being in a lower situation, though not directly beneath.—**sub·ja·cen·cy**, *n.*— **sub·ja·cent·ly**, *adv.*

sub·ject, sub′jikt, *n.* [O.Fr. *subjet, suget* (Fr. *sujet*), < L. *subjectus*, pp.; some senses being derived through L. *subjectum*, underlying matter, the foundation or subject of a proposition, prop. neut. of *subjectus*, pp.] One who is under the dominion or rule of a sovereign, esp. one who owes allegiance to a government and lives under its protection; one who or that which is under the control or influence of another; a person as an object of medical or surgical treatment, or a psychological experiment; a dead body as used for dissection and study; something that forms a matter of thought or discourse; as, a *subject* of conversation, the *subjects*

taught in a college course; the theme of a sermon, book, or story; an object, scene, or incident chosen by an artist for representation, or as represented in art; a motive or cause; as, to give one a *subject* for complaint; *mus.* a theme or melodic phrase on which a musical work or movement is based; *gram.* the word or words in a sentence, denoting that of which something is predicated; *logic*, that term of a proposition of which the other is affirmed or denied; *philos.* the self or ego to which all mental representations or operations are attributed.

sub·ject, sub′jikt, *a.* [O.Fr. *subject, subjet, suget* (Fr. *sujet*), < L. *subjectus*, pp. of *subjicere, subicere*, throw or place under, subject, < *sub*, under, and *jacere*, throw.] Being under dominion, rule, or authority, as of a monarch, state, or some governing power; owing allegiance or obedience to a supreme authority; being under domination, control, or influence, often used with *to*; as, *subject* to laws; being under the neccesity of undergoing something, usu. used with *to*, as: All men are *subject* to death. Liable, or having a tendency, usu. followed by *to*; as, *subject* to headaches; open or exposed, used with *to*; as, *subject* to attack or ridicule; being dependent or conditional upon something, usu. followed by *to*, as: His consent is *subject* to your approval.

sub·ject, sub·jekt′, *v.t.* [O.Fr. *subjecter, subgetter*, < L. *subjectare*, place under, freq. of *subjicere*.] To bring under dominion, rule, or authority, as of a governing power, usu. followed by *to*; bring under domination, control, or influence, usu. followed by *to*; cause to undergo or experience something, usu. followed by *to*; as, to *subject* metal *to* heat; make liable, lay open, or expose, usu. followed by *to*; as, to *subject* oneself *to* unpleasant comment.—**sub·-jec·tion**, sub·jek′shan, *n.*

sub·jec·tive, sub·jek′tiv, *a.* [L. *subjectivus*.] Existing in the mind; belonging to the thinking subject rather than to the object of thought: opposed to *objective*; pertaining to or characteristic of an individual thinking subject; personal; individual; habitually concerned with one's own mental states or processes; introspective; *philos.* relating to an object that is known in or by the mind rather than the thing itself, which is independent of the mind. Relating to conditions or properties of the mind rather than from experience either universal or general; pertaining to the subject or substance in which attributes inhere; essential. *Gram.* pertaining to or constituting the subject of a sentence; designating the case specifically for this use; nominative. *Liter.*, *art*, expressing or displaying the individuality and esp. the thoughts or emotions of the author or artist; as, *subjective* poetry, a *subjective* painter. Without foundation in reality; illusory; imaginary.—*n.* That which is subjective or nominative.—**sub·jec·-tive·ly**, *adv.*—**sub·jec·tive·ness**, **sub·-jec·tiv·i·ty**, sub″jek·tiv′i·tē, *n.*

sub·jec·tiv·ism, sub·jek′ti·viz″um, *n. Philos.* The theory that all knowledge is subjective, and that objective knowledge is impossible; any theory that lays stress on the subjective elements in experience; the doctrine which conceives the highest good to be the attainment of certain subjective experiences or states of feeling; the doctrine that the apprehension and feeling of the individual are the only criteria for judging the good and right.—**sub·jec·tiv·ist**, *n.*— **sub·jec·ti·vis·tic**, *a.*

sub·ject mat·ter, *n.* The substance of a discourse, book, writing, or the like, as distinguished from its form or style; the matter which is subjected to some operation, or out of which a thing is formed, esp. matter or material with which thought, discourse, investigation, study, or the like is occupied.

sub·join, sub·join', *v.t.* [O.Fr. *subjoindre*, < L. *subjungere* (pp. *subjunctus*), < *sub*, under, and *jungere*, E. *join*.] To add at the end, as of something said or written; to append; to place in immediate sequence or juxtaposition to something else.

sub ju·di·ce, sub jö'di·sē", L. sub ū'di·ke", *adv.* Pending judicial decision.

sub·ju·gate, sub'ju·gāt", *v.t.*—*subjugated*, *subjugating*. [L. *subjugo*, *subjugatum*—*sub*, under and *jugum*, a yoke.] To subdue and bring under dominion; to conquer; to compel to submit; to enslave.—**sub·ju·ga·tion**, *n.*—**sub·ju·ga·tor**, *n.*

sub·junc·tion, sub·jungk'shan, *n.* [L. *subjungere* (pp. *subjunctus*).] The act of subjoining; the state of being subjoined; something subjoined.

sub·junc·tive, sub·jungk'tiv, *a.* [L. *subjunctivus*, < *subjungo*, *subjunctum*—*sub*, under, near, and *jungo*, to join.] *Gram.* designating a mood or form of verbs expressing condition, hypothesis, or contingency, generally subordinate to another verb and preceded by a conjunction, as 'I suggest that he be consulted.'—*n.*

sub·king·dom, sub·king'dom, sub'king"dom, *n.* [L. *sub*, under.] One of the primary groups into which the animal and plant kingdoms are divided, higher than a phylum.

sub·lease, sub'lēs", *n.* A lease granted by one who is himself a lessee of the property.—sub·lēs', *v.t.*—*subleased*, *subleasing*. To grant a sublease of; sublet; to take or hold a sublease of.—**sub·les·see**, sub"le·sē' *n.* The receiver or holder of a sublease.—**sub·les·sor**, sub·les'ǝr, sub"le·sǝr', *n.* The grantor of a sublease.

sub·let, sub·let', *v.t.*—*sublet*, *subletting*. To sublease; of a contractor, to let under a subcontract.—sub'let", sub·let', *n.*

sub·li·mate, sub'li·māt", *v.t.*—*sublimated*, *sublimating*. [L. and M.L. *sublimatus*, pp. of *sublimare*.] *Psychol.* to transfer the energy of, as a basic drive, into a higher, nobler, or more ethical goal. *Chem.* to sublime, as a solid substance; to extract by this process; to refine or purify, as a substance.—*v.i.* To become sublimated; to undergo sublimation.—sub'li·mit, sub'li·māt", *n. Chem.* the crystals, deposit, or material obtained when a substance is sublimed.—**sub·li·ma·tion**, *n.*

sub·lime, su·blīm', *a.*—*sublimer*, *sublimest*. [L. *sublimis*, uplifted, lofty.] Elevated or lofty in thought, sentiment, language, or style; *poet.* of lofty bearing or aspect, or sometimes, haughty or proud. Striking the mind with a sense of grandeur or power, or awakening awe, veneration, or exalted feeling by reason of grandeur, beauty, or the like, as scenes in nature or works of art; supreme or perfect; as, a *sublime* moment. —*n.* That which is sublime, usu. used with *the*; the highest degree or example, or the supreme, usu. followed by *of*.—*v.t.* —*sublimed*, *subliming*. [L. *sublimare*, lift up on high, elevate, M.L. sublime chemically, < L. *sublimis*.] To elevate or exalt in character; make lofty or sublime. *Chem.* to convert, as a solid substance, by heat into a vapor, which on cooling condenses again to solid form without apparent liquefaction; to cause to be given off by this or some analogous process; extract by or as by sublimation.—*v.i.* To become sublimed. *Chem.* to undergo the process of subliming; to be given off or extracted by sublimation.—**sub·lime·ly**, *adv.*—**sub·lime·ness**, *n.*—**sub·lim·er**, *n.*

sub·lim·i·nal, sub·lim'i·nal, sub·li'mi·nal, *a.* [L.L. *sub*, under, *limen*, threshold.] *Psychol.* Below consciousness; noting stimuli which lack the intensity to produce a clear perception or sensation.—**sub·lim·i·nal·ly**, *adv.*

sub·lim·i·ty, su·blim'i·tē, *n. pl.* **sub·lim·i·ties.** [Fr. *sublimité*; L. *sublimitas*.] The state or quality of being sublime; the emotion produced by what is sublime.

sub·lin·gual, sub·ling'gwal, *a.* [L. *sub*, under, *lingua*, the tongue.] Situated under the tongue.

sub·lu·nar·y, sub'lu·ner"ē, sub·lö'na·rē, *a.* [L. *sub*, under, *luna*, the moon.] Situated under the moon; located between the moon and the earth; pertaining to the earth; mundane; earthly; worldly. Also **sub·lu·nar**, sub·lö'nẽr.

sub·ma·chine gun, sub"ma·shēn' gun", *n.* A lightweight, portable, automatic or semiautomatic gun which uses pistol ammunition, has a short stock and barrel, and is designed to be fired from the shoulder or hip.

sub·mar·gin·al, sub·mär'ji·nal, *a.* [L. *sub*, near.] Below the margin; unproductive, as land; *bot.* situated near the margin.— **sub·mar·gin·al·ly**, *adv.*

sub·ma·rine, sub"ma·rēn', *a.* [L. *sub*, under, and *mare*, sea.] Situated, occurring, or living under the surface of the sea, either at the bottom or elsewhere below the surface; as, a *submarine* volcano; constructed, carried on, operating, or intended for use below the surface of the sea; as, a *submarine* telegraph; of, pertaining to, or carried on by submarine boats; as, *submarine* warfare.—sub"ma·rēn", sub"ma·rēn', *n.* A vessel so designed that it can be submerged and navigated under water, esp. such a vessel used in warfare.—*v.t.*— *submarined*, *submarining*. To attack, torpedo, or sink through the agency of a submarine, or as a submarine does.—*v.i.* To operate a submarine.—**sub·ma·rin·er**, sub"ma·rē'nẽr, sub·mar'i·nẽr, *n.*

sub·ma·rine chas·er, *n.* A small, fast patrol boat designed to carry depth charges and light deck guns for offensive action against submarines. Also *subchaser*.

sub·max·il·lar·y, sub·mak'si·ler"ē, sub"· mak·sil'a·rē, *a. Anat.* Of, pertaining to, or just beneath the lower jaw; pertaining to or situated near the submaxillary gland.— *n. pl.* **sub·max·il·lar·ies.** *Anat.* The lower jawbone; the submaxillary gland.—**sub·· max·il·la**, sub"mak·sil'a, *n. pl.* **sub·· max·il·lae.**

sub·me·di·ant, sub·mē'dē·ant, *n.* [L. *sub*, under, *medius*, middle.] *Mus.* the sixth note of the diatonic scale, or middle note between the octave and subdominant.

sub·merge, sub·mûrj', *v.t.*—*submerged*, *submerging*. [L. *submergere* (pp. *submersus*), *summergere*, < *sub*, under, and *mergere*, dip, plunge, sink, E. *merge*.] To put or sink below the surface of water or any enveloping medium; to cover or flood with water; to conceal or suppress.—*v.i.* To sink or plunge under water, or beneath the surface of any enveloping medium. Also *submerse*. —**sub·mer·gence**, *n.*—**sub·mer·gi·ble**, sub·mûr'ji·bl, *a.*

sub·merged, sub·mûrjd', *a.* Under water or beneath the surface of something; living in profound poverty and misery; as, the *submerged* classes of society; concealed or unknown, as facts.

sub·merse, sub·mûrs', *v.t.*, *v.i.*—*submersed*, *submersing*. Submerge.

sub·mersed, sub·mûrst', *a.* Underwater; *bot.* being or growing under water.

sub·mers·i·ble, sub·mûr'si·bl, *a.* Adapted to submersion; operative under water.— *n.* A ship able to operate while submerged, as a submarine.

sub·mer·sion, sub·mûr'zhan, sub·mûr'shan, *n.* [L. *submersio*, *submersionis*.] The act of putting or state of being put under water or other fluid; a dipping or plunging.

sub·mi·cro·scop·ic, sub"mī·kro·skop'ik, *a.* Having a size smaller than is visible with an ordinary microscope.

sub·min·i·a·ture, sub·min'ē·a·chẽr, *a.* Denoting something very small, as electronic components and cameras.

sub·mis·sion, sub·mish'an, *n.* [O.Fr. *submission* (Fr. *soumission*), < L. *submissio(n-)*, < *submittere*.] The act of submitting; the condition of having submitted; submissive conduct or attitude; something submitted for consideration, criticism, or approval; *law*, an agreement to abide by the decision of an authority or arbitrator.

sub·mis·sive, sub·mis'iv, *a.* Inclined or ready to submit; unresistingly or humbly obedient; marked by or indicating submission; as, a *submissive* reply.—**sub·mis·sive·ly**, *adv.*—**sub·mis·sive·ness**, *n.*

sub·mit, sub·mit', *v.t.*—*submitted*, *submitting*. [L. *submittere* (pp. *submissus*), *summittere*, put under, lower, submit, < *sub*, under, and *mittere*, send.] To yield, as something, in surrender, compliance, or obedience; to subject to imposed conditions or treatment; to refer or present for the decision or approval of another or others; as, to *submit* a plan; to declare or suggest with deference, as one's opinion.— *v.i.* To yield in surrender, compliance, or obedience; to allow oneself to be subjected to something imposed or to be undergone; as, to *submit* to punishment; to yield to the decision or opinion of another.

sub·mon·tane, sub·mon'tān, *a.* [L. *sub*, under, and *mons* (*mont-*), mountain.] Under or beneath a mountain or mountains; at or near the foot of mountains; pertaining to the lower slopes of mountains.—**sub·mon·tane·ly**, *adv.*

sub·mul·ti·ple, sub·mul'ti·pl, *n.* [L. *sub*, under.] *Math.* a number or quantity which is contained in another a certain number of times, leaving no remainder, as: The number four is a *submultiple* of eight.

sub·nor·mal, sub·nar'mal, *a.* Below the normal; *psychol.* less than the normal intelligence.—*n.*—**sub·nor·mal·i·ty**, *n.*

sub·o·ce·an·ic, sub"ō·shē·an'ik, *a.* Beneath the floor of the ocean; referring to the ocean floor.

sub·oc·u·lar, sub·ok'ū·lẽr, *a.* Located below the eye.

sub·or·bic·u·lar, sub"ǝr·bik'ū·lẽr, *a.* Nearly circular.

sub·or·bit·al, sub·ǝr'bi·tal, *a.* Not in orbit; not completing a full orbit of the earth, as a rocket; *anat.* situated below the orbit of the eye.

sub·or·der, sub'ǝr"dẽr, *n.* [L. *sub*, under.] *Biol.* A subdivision of an order in classification; a group of animals or plants greater than a family and less than an order.

sub·or·di·nate, su·bar'di·nit, *a.* [M.L. *subordinatus*, pp. of *subordinare*, < L. *sub*, under, and *ordinare*, order, arrange, E. *ordain*.] Placed in or belonging to a lower order or rank; of inferior importance; secondary; subject to or under the authority of a superior; subservient, as to something of greater importance; dependent. *Gram.* dependent; modifying; as, a *subordinate* clause or *subordinate* conjunction.—*n.* subordinate person or thing.—su·bar'di·nāt", *v.t.*—*subordinated*, *subordinating*. To place in a lower order or rank; to make secondary, as in importance, usu. followed by *to*; to make subject, subservient, or dependent, usu. followed by *to*.—**sub·or·di·nate·ly**, *adv.*—**sub·or·di·nate·ness**, *n.*—**sub·or·di·na·tion**, *n.*—**sub·or·di·na·tive**, su·bar'di·nā"tiv, su·bar'di·na·tiv, *a.*

sub·orn, su·barn', *v.t.* [L. *subornare* (pp. *subornatus*), < *sub*, under, and *ornare*, equip.] To bribe or unlawfully procure, as a person, to commit some illegal act or crime; to bribe or induce, as a witness, to give false evidence.—**sub·or·na·tion,** sub″ar·nā'shan, n.—**sub·orn·er,** n.

sub·ox·ide, sub·ok'sīd, sub·ok'sĭd, n. Chem. an oxide having a smaller proportion of oxygen than its basic oxide, as Pb_2O compared to PbO.

sub·phy·lum, sub·fī'lum, n. pl. **sub·phy·la,** sub·fī'la. Biol. In classification, a subdivision of a phylum; a group of animals or plants that is greater than a class and less than a phylum.

sub·plot, sub'plot″, n. A subordinate plot in a literary work.

sub·poe·na, sub·pe·na, su·pē'na, sub·pē'na, n. [L. sub, and poena, pain, penalty.] Law, a judicial writ or process commanding, under threat of penalty, the attendance in court of the witness on whom it is served.—v.t.—subpoenaed, subpoenaing. To serve with a writ of subpoena.

sub·prin·ci·pal, sub·prin'si·pal, sub'prin″si·pal, n. An assistant or deputy principal; carp. an auxiliary rafter or the like; mus. in an organ, a subbass of the open diapason class.

sub·re·gion, sub'rē″jen, n. A division or subdivision of a region, esp. of a zoogeographical region.—**sub·re·gion·al,** a.

sub·rep·tion, sub·rep'shan, n. [L. subreptio(n-), surreptio(n-), < subripere, surripere, take secretly.] The act of obtaining something, as an ecclesiastical dispensation, by suppression or fraudulent concealment of facts; a fallacious representation or an inference derived from it.—**sub·rep·ti·tious,** sub″rep·tish'us, a. [L. subrepticius, surrepticius: cf. surreptitious.] Obtained by subreption; clandestine or surreptitious.—**sub·rep·ti·tious·ly,** adv.

sub·ro·gate, sub'rō·gāt, v.t.—subrogated, subrogating. [L. subrogatus, pp. of subrogare, surrogare, put in another's place.] To put into the place of another; substitute for another, esp. to put, as a person, into the position of another in respect to a legal right or claim.—**sub·ro·ga·tion,** n.

sub ro·sa, sub rō'za, adv. Secretly or confidentially.

sub·rou·tine, sub″rō·tēn', n. Computer, a routine or sequence of mathematical statements nested within a larger routine or sequence of statements.

sub·sat·u·rat·ed, sub·sach'a·rā″tid, a. Slightly less than fully saturated.—**sub·sat·u·ra·tion,** sub·sach'a·rā'shan, n.

sub·scap·u·lar, sub·skap'ū·lêr, a. [L. sub, under.] Beneath the scapula or shoulder blade.

sub·scribe, sub·skrīb', v.t.—subscribed, subscribing. [L. subscribere (pp. subscriptus), < sub, under, and scribere, write.] To promise, as by signing an agreement; to give or pay, as a sum of money, whether as a contribution toward some object or as in payment for something; to give or pay in fulfillment of such a promise; to write, inscribe, or sign, as one's name, to a document, letter, or other paper; to express assent to, as a contract, by signing one's name; to attest to by signing, as a statement.—v.i. To undertake, as by signing an agreement; to give or pay money for some special purpose; to give or pay money as a contribution or in payment; to agree to pay for the future delivery of a specified number of magazines, newspapers, or periodicals, usu. for a reduced rate; to sign one's name to something; to assent by or as by signing one's name; to give consent or sanction.—**sub·scrib·er,** n.

sub·script, sub'skript, a. [L. subscriptus, pp. of subscribere.] Written below another character.—n. A symbol, number, or letter written below another character.

sub·scrip·tion, sub·skrip'shan, n. [L. subscriptio(n-).] The act of subscribing; the

signing of one's name, as to a document; something subscribed, or written beneath or at the end of a thing; a signature attached to a paper; assent, agreement, or approval expressed by or as by signing one's name; the subscribing of money as a contribution toward some object or in payment for shares, a book, a periodical, or service; joint contribution as a means of carrying out some purpose; as, a public ball held by subscription; a sum subscribed; a right obtained for a sum subscribed; as, one's subscription to a magazine; a fund raised through sums of money subscribed by a number of persons; a method of ensuring the publication of a book by the promise of a sufficient number of persons in advance to purchase copies; the sale of books by canvassers; law, affixing one's signature to authenticate, attest, or bind oneself to the terms of a document; relig. signing one's name to indicate adherence to a dogma, as the 39 points of doctrine of the Church of England; med. the part of a prescription preceding the signature that gives directions for compounding.

sub·se·quent, sub'se·kwent, a. [L. subsequens, subsequentis, ppr. of subsequor, to follow close after—sub, under, near, and sequor, to follow.] Following, coming, or being after something else in time; following in the order of place or succession.—**sub·se·quence,** sub'se·kwens, n.—**sub·se·quent·ly,** adv.—**sub·se·quent·ness,** n.

sub·serve, sub·surv', v.t.—subserved, subserving. [L. subservio—sub, under, and servio, to serve.] To serve or be of advantage to; to be of service to; to assist or promote.

sub·ser·vi·ent, sub·sur'vē·ent, a. [L. subserviens, ppr. of subservio.] Useful as an instrument to promote a purpose; serving to promote some end; acting as a subordinate; servile, submissive, or obsequious.—**sub·ser·vi·ence,** **sub·ser·vi·en·cy,** n.—**sub·ser·vi·ent·ly,** adv.

sub·set, sub'set″, n. A set within a larger set; math. a set whose elements are members of a given set.

sub·shrub, sub'shrub″, n. A perennial plant with a woody base; a small shrub.—**sub·shrub·by,** a.

sub·side, sub·sīd', v.i.—subsided, subsiding. [L. subsido—sub, under, and sido, to settle, akin to sedeo, to sit.] To sink or fall to the bottom; to settle; to sink or settle to a lower level; to fall into a state of quiet; to become tranquil; to abate.—**sub·sid·ence,** sub·sīd'ens, sub'si·dens, n.

sub·sid·i·ar·y, sub·sid'ē·er″ē, a. [L. subsidiarius.] Lending some aid or assistance; furnishing help; aiding or assisting; subordinate; contributory; pertaining to a subsidy.—n. pl. **sub·sid·i·ar·ies.** One who or that which is subsidiary; an auxiliary; an assistant; mus. a secondary theme. A company controlled by another company by virtue of ownership of the controlling stock; also **sub·sid·i·ar·y com·pa·ny.**—**sub·sid·i·ar·i·ly,** sub·sid″ē·âr′i·lē, sub·sid′ē·er″i·lē, adv.—**sub·sid·i·ar·i·ness,** n.

sub·si·dize, sub'si·dīz″, v.t.—subsidized, subsidizing. To furnish with a subsidy; to purchase the assistance of by a subsidy; to obtain the services of, sometimes through bribery.—**sub·si·di·za·tion,** n.—**sub·si·diz·er,** n.

sub·si·dy, sub'si·dē, n. pl. **sub·si·dies.** [L. subsidium, < sub, under, sedeo, to sit; lit. 'that which is placed beneath as a support.'] A sum of money granted by a government to an organization, institution, or industry, esp. one benefiting the health and welfare of the country, as a charity, hospital, or public service; a gift of money; grant; Brit. an aid or tax formerly granted by parliament to the crown for special

occasions; a sum paid by one government to another, usu. providing in return certain commercial advantages or other services.

sub·sist, sub·sist', v.i. [Fr. subsister, < L. subsistere—sub, under, and sisto, sistere, to stand, to be fixed, < sto, to stand.] To exist; to have continued existence; to continue to retain the present state; to be maintained with food and clothing; to be supported; to live; to inhere in something.—v.t. To support, as a family, with provisions.

sub·sist·ence, sub·sis'tens, n. [Fr. subsistance.] Existence; that which furnishes support to life; means of support; support; livelihood; the state of maintaining one's existence.—**sub·sist·ent,** sub·sis'tent, a. Existing; having reality; inherent.

sub·soil, sub'soil″, n. [L. sub, under.] The bed or stratum of earth or earthy matter which lies immediately under the surface soil. Also undersoil.—**sub·soil·er,** sub'soi″lêr, n.

sub·so·lar, sub·sō'lêr, a. Located beneath the sun or between the sun and earth; equatorial; located between the tropics.

sub·son·ic, sub·son'ik, a. Aeron. Pertaining to or possessing a speed which is less than the speed of sound, as in air or some other medium; operable at such speeds. Pertaining to sound waves having a frequency lower than the auditory capacity of the human ear; also infrasonic.

sub·space, sub'spās″, n. Math. a subset of a space.

sub·spe·cies, sub·spē'shēz, sub'spē″shēz, n. pl. **sub·spe·cies.** [L. sub, under.] A subordinate species; a division of a species, esp. as distinguished by geographic location.—**sub·spe·cif·ic,** sub″spi·sif'ik, a.

sub·stance, sub'stans, n. [Fr. substance, < L. substantia, substance, essence; < substans, substantis, ppr. of substo—sub, under, and sto, to stand.] That of which a thing consists or is made up; matter; material; a distinct type of matter with regard to chemical composition; a body; that which is real; the characteristic constituents collectively; the essential or material part; the purport; solidity, as: Their suggestions have substance. Firmness; substantiality; material means and resources; goods; estate. Philos. the essence which underlies all phenomena; that which has qualities and characteristics. Theol. that in which the divine attributes inhere.

sub·stand·ard, sub·stan'dêrd, a. Less than or deviating from the norm or requirement; ling. pertaining to language deviating from socially accepted usage.

sub·stan·tial, sub·stan'shal, a. Of considerable size or amount; having considerable worth or value; actually existing; real; not seeming or imaginary; corporeal; material; firm in substance or material; strong; solid; possessed of considerable wealth; philos. denoting something of real rather than abstract existence.—**sub·stan·ti·al·i·ty,** n.—**sub·stan·tial·ly,** adv.—**sub·stan·tial·ness,** n.

sub·stan·ti·ate, sub·stan'shē·āt″, v.t.—substantiated, substantiating. To establish by proof or competent evidence; to verify; to prove; to give form or substance to; to make real or actual.—**sub·stan·ti·a·tion,** n.—**sub·stan·ti·a·tive,** a.

sub·stan·tive, sub'stan·tiv, n. [O.Fr. Fr. substantif, < L.L. substantivus, < L. substantia, E. substance.] Gram. A noun; a word or a phrase which is used like a noun.—a. Gram. denoting a substance; of the nature of, equivalent to, or employed as a substantive; as, a substantive adjective; expressing existence; as, the substantive verb, the verb 'to be.' Having independent existence; independent; belonging to the real nature or essential part of a thing;

essential; real or actual; enduring; permanent; of considerable amount or quantity; *law*, pertaining to the rules of right which courts are called on to administer, as distinguished from rules of procedure; as, *substantive* law; *dyeing*, attaching, as colors, directly to the material without the aid of a mordant or the like: opposed to *adjective*.—**sub·stan·ti·val**, *a.*—**sub·stan·ti·val·ly**, **sub·stan·tive·ly**, *adv.*—**sub·stan·tive·ness**, *n.*—**sub·stan·tiv·ize**, *v.t.*—*substantivized, substantivizing. Gram.* To make a substantive of; use as a substantive.

sub·sta·tion, sub'stā"shan, *n.* A subordinate station; a station subsidiary to a main station.

sub·stit·u·ent, sub·stich'ö·ent, *n.* [L. *substituens* (-*ent*), ppr. of *substituere.*] *Chem.* an atom or atomic group which takes the place of another atom or group present in the molecule of the original compound.—*a.*

sub·sti·tute, sub'sti·töt", sub'sti·tūt", *v.t.*—*substituted, substituting.* [L. *substituo, substitutum—sub*, under, and *statuo*, to place, to set (whence statute, etc.).] To put in the place of another; to put in exchange.—*v.i.* To act as one who or that which substitutes; *chem.* to serve as a substituent.—*n.* A person or thing acting for or serving the purpose of another; formerly, a person who for a consideration serves in the army in the place of a conscript; *gram.* a word, clause, or phrase replacing another word, clause, or phrase.—*a.* —**sub·sti·tut·a·ble**, *a.*—**sub·sti·tu·tion**, *n.*—**sub·sti·tu·tion·al**, *a.*—**sub·sti·tu·tion·al·ly**, *adv.*—**sub·sti·tu·tion·ar·y**, sub"sti·tö'sha·ner"ē, sub"sti·tu'sha·ner"ē, *a.*

sub·sti·tu·tive, sub'sti·tö"tiv, sub'sti·tū"tiv, *a.* Serving as or capable of serving as a substitute; pertaining to or involving substitution.—**sub·sti·tu·tive·ly**, *adv.*

sub·strate, sub'strāt, *n.* A substratum; *biochem.* a material acted upon by a ferment or an enzyme.

sub·strat·o·sphere, sub·strat'o·sfēr", *n.* The upper troposphere: not in technical usage.—**sub·strat·o·spher·ic**, sub"strat·o·sfer'ik, *a.*

sub·stra·tum, sub·strā'tum, sub·strat'um, sub'strä"tum, sub'strat"um, *n. pl.* **sub·stra·ta**, **sub·stra·tums**, sub·strā'ta, sub·strat'a, sub'strä"ta, sub'strat"a. [L. *sub*, under, and *stratum*, something spread.] That which is laid or spread under something; a foundation; *geol.* a layer of rock lying under another layer; *agric.* subsoil; *metaph.* matter or substance in which qualities inhere; *biol.* any material on which a plant or animal grows; *ling.* a submerged language that influences a dominant language.

sub·struc·tion, sub·struk'shan, *n.* [L. *sub*, under, and *struo*, to build.] A mass of building below another; a foundation.—**sub·struc·tion·al**, *a.*

sub·struc·ture, sub·struk'chèr, sub'struk"chèr, *n.* An understructure; groundwork or foundation.

sub·sume, sub·söm', *v.t.*—*subsumed, subsuming.* [L. *sub*, under, and *sumere* (pp. *sumptus*), take.] To include, as a specific idea, term, or proposition, under another more general one; bring under a rule, as a case or instance; include in a larger, higher, or more inclusive class.—**sub·sum·a·ble**, **sub·sump·tive**, *a.*—**sub·sump·tion**, sub·sump'shan, *n.*

sub·sur·face, sub·sur'fas, sub'sur"fas, *n.* The part lying immediately under the surface.—*a.* Lying, occurring, or operating under the surface, as of the earth or the water.

sub·teen, sub'tēn', *n.* A person near

adolescence; clothing sizes 8–14 designed for girls under 13 years of age.

sub·tem·per·ate, sub·tem'pėr·it, *a.* Pertaining to or occurring in the colder parts of the Temperate Zone.

sub·ten·ant, sub·ten'ant, *n.* [L. *sub*, under.] One who leases or rents land or houses from a tenant.—**sub·ten·an·cy**, *n.*

sub·tend, sub·tend', sub·tend', *v.t.* [L. *subtendo—sub*, under, and *tendo*, to stretch.] *Geom.* to extend under or be opposite to, as the side of a triangle opposite an angle; *bot.* to stand below and close to, as a bract beneath a flower.

sub·ter·fuge, sub'tėr·fūj", *n.* [Fr. *subterfuge*, L.L. *subterfugium*, < L. *subter*, under, and *fugio*, to flee (whence *fugitive*, etc.).] A shift or expedient; deception or other artifice to conceal something or to escape difficulty or unpleasantness.

sub·ter·ra·ne·an, sub"te·rā'nē·an, *a.* [L. *subterraneus—sub*, under, and *terra*, the earth (whence *terrace, terrestrial, terrier*, etc.).] Being or lying at some depth in the earth; situated within the earth; underground; being hidden or secret. Also **sub·ter·ra·ne·ous.—sub·ter·ra·ne·an·ly**, **sub·ter·ra·ne·ous·ly**, *adv.*

sub·te·tan·ic, sub"te·tan'ik, *a. Med.* Referring to muscle tension not yet tetonic; remittingly contracted.

sub·tile, sut'il, sub'til, *a.* Subtle.—**sub·tile·ly**, *adv.*—**sub·tile·ness**, **sub·til·i·ty**, *n.*

sub·til·ize, sut·i·liz", sub'ti·liz", *v.t.*—*subtilized, subtilizing.* To make subtle; to refine; to make sharp, as the mind; to argue or discuss in a subtle manner.—*v.i.* To refine in argument; to make nice or subtle distinctions.—**sub·til·i·za·tion**, *n.*

sub·ti·tle, sub'tīt"l, *n.* A secondary or subordinate title of a literary work, usually of explanatory character; repetition of the leading words of the full title of a book at the head of the first page of the text. *Motion pictures*, the written translation of the dialogue of a foreign film, usu. projected on the bottom of the screen; the captions and titles used between scenes of a silent film.—*v.t.*—*subtitled, subtitling.*

sub·tle, sut'l, *a.* [O.E. *sotel, sotil, subtil*, O.Fr. *sutil, soutil, subtil* (Fr. *subtil*), < L. *subtilis*, slender, delicate, subtle, < *sub*, under, and *tela*, for *textela*, a web, < *texo*, to weave (whence *texture*).] Sly in design; artful; cunning; cunningly devised; ingenious; thin or tenuous in substance; delicate in texture of workmanship; acute or penetrating in intellect; discerning; difficult to understand.—**sub·tle·ness**, *n.*—**sub·tle·ty**, sut'l·tē, *n.*—**sub·tly**, *adv.*

sub·ton·ic, sub·ton'ik, *n.* [L. *sub*, under.] *Mus.* The seventh degree of a major or minor scale; the semitone below the upper tonic; the leading note of the scale.

sub·tract, sub·trakt', *v.t.* [L. *subtractus*, pp. of *subtrahere*, draw from under, withdraw, < *sub*, under, and *trahere*, draw.] To withdraw or take away, as a part from a whole. *Math.* to take, as one number or quantity, from another; to deduct.—*v.i.* To take away something or a part, as from a whole.—**sub·tract·er**, *n.*

sub·trac·tion, sub·trak'shan, *n.* [L.L. *subtractio(n-).*] The act or operation of subtracting. *Math.* the taking of one number or quantity from another; the operation of finding the difference between two numbers or quantities.

sub·trac·tive, sub·trak'tiv, *a.* Tending to subtract; having power to subtract. *Math.* of a quantity, that is to be subtracted; having the minus sign.

sub·tra·hend, sub'tra·hend", *n.* [L. *subtrahendus*, that must be subtracted.] The sum or number to be subtracted from another, as opposed to *minuend*.

sub·trop·i·cal, sub·trop'i·kal, *a.* [L. *sub*, near, slightly.] Adjoining the tropics; indigenous to or characteristic of the regions lying near the tropics. Also **sub·trop·ic.—sub·trop·ics**, sub·trop'iks, *n. pl.*

su·bu·late, sö'bū·lit, sö'bū·lāt", *a.* [< L. *subula*, an awl, < *suo*, to sew.] Shaped like an awl; *biol.* slender and gradually tapering toward the end or point.

sub·urb, sub'urb, *n.* [O.Fr. *suburbe*, < L. *suburbium*, < *sub*, under, near, and *urbs*, city.] *Often pl.* A district lying immediately outside a city or town, esp. a residential section outside of the city boundaries but adjoining them; an outlying part.—**sub·ur·ban**, su·bur'ban, *a.*, *n.*—**sub·ur·ban·ite**, su·bur'ba·nīt", *n.*

sub·ur·bi·a, su·bur'bē·a, *n.* Suburbs as a group; suburbanites as a group; activities, standards, and outlooks considered as typical of suburbanites.

sub·ven·tion, sub·ven'shan, *n.* A financial grant, esp. by a government or institution, to aid or support some endeavor; subsidy; the granting of financial aid.—**sub·ven·tion·ar·y**, *a.*

sub·ver·sion, sub·vur'zhan, sub·vur'shan, *n.* [L. *subversio.*] The act of subverting or overthrowing; overthrow; ruin; a subverted or overthrown condition; something that subverts or destroys.—**sub·ver·sion·ar·y**, *a.*—**sub·ver·sive**, sub·vur'siv, *a.*, *n.*—**sub·ver·sive·ly**, *adv.*—**sub·ver·sive·ness**, *n.*

sub·vert, sub·vurt', *v.t.* [L. *subvertere* (pp. *subversus*), < *sub*, under, and *vertere*, turn.] To overturn; to demolish or destroy; to overthrow; as, to *subvert* a government; to cause the downfall, ruin, or destruction of; to undermine the principles of; corrupt.—**sub·vert·er**, *n.*

sub·way, sub'wā", *n.* An electric railway beneath the surface of the streets in a large city; also *Brit. underground.* A subterranean passage for traffic, watermains, electric wires, and the like; a pedestrian tunnel under streets or railroads.

suc·ce·da·ne·um, suk"si·dā'nē·um, *n. pl.* **suc·ce·da·ne·a**, suk"si·dā'nē·a. [N.L. prop. neut. of L. *succedaneus*, taking the place of something, < *succedere*, E. *succeed.*] A substitute.—**suc·ce·da·ne·ous**, *a.*

suc·ceed, suk·sēd', *v.i.* [L. *succedere* (pp. *successus*), go under, go up, come next, follow, be successful.] To occur or terminate according to desire; turn out successfully; to accomplish what is attempted or intended; to be successful in an undertaking; to come after or take the place of another by descent, election, appointment, or the like, often followed by *to*; to come next after something else in an order or series.—*v.t.* To come after and take the place of, as in an office or estate; to come next after in an order or series, or in the course of events; follow.—**suc·ceed·er**, *n.*

suc·cès d'es·time, syk·se des·tēm', *n. Fr.* success achieved on the basis of critical esteem rather than by the approval of the general public.

suc·cess, suk·ses', *n.* [L. *successus*, < *succedere*, E. *succeed.*] The favorable or prosperous termination of attempts or endeavors; the satisfactory accomplishment of something attempted; the attainment of wealth, position, or the like; a successful performance or achievement, as: The program was a *success.* A thing or a person that is successful.

suc·cess·ful, suk·ses'ful, *a.* Resulting in or attended with success; achieving or having achieved success; having succeeded in obtaining wealth, position, recognition, or the like.—**suc·cess·ful·ly**, *adv.*—**suc·cess·ful·ness**, *n.*

suc·ces·sion, suk·sesh'an, *n.* [L. *successio(n-)*, < *succedere*, E. *succeed.*] The coming of one thing or person after another in order, sequence, or the course of events; as, five sunny days in *succession*; a number of persons or things following one another in order or sequence; a series or line of things coming one after the other; the process, right, or act by which one person succeeds to the office, rank, estate, or the like of another; the order or line of those entitled to succeed; the descent or transmission of a throne, dignity, estate, or the like; the act or fact of succeeding under established custom or law to the dignity and rights of a sovereign.—**suc·ces·sion·al,** *a.*—**suc·ces·sion·al·ly,** *adv.*

suc·ces·sive, suk·ses′iv, *a.* [M.L. *successivus*, < L. *succedere*, E. *succeed*.] Following in order or in uninterrupted course; as, four *successive* failures; following another in a regular sequence; as, on the second *successive* day; characterized by or involving succession.—**suc·ces·sive·ly,** *adv.*—**suc·ces·sive·ness,** *n.*

suc·ces·sor, suk·ses′ẽr, *n.* [L.] A person or thing that succeeds or follows; a person who takes the place which another has left, as: He was the president's *successor.*

suc·ci·nate, suk′si·nāt″, *n. Chem.* a salt of succinic acid.

suc·cinct, suk·singkt′, *a.* [L. *succinctus*, tucked or girded up, succinct—*sub*, up, and *cingo, cinctum,* to gird.] Compressed into few words; characterized by verbal brevity; brief; concise.—**suc·cinct·ly,** *adv.*—**suc·cinct·ness,** *n.*

suc·cin·ic ac·id, suk·sin′ik as′id, *n. Chem.* a water-soluble crystalline compound, $CO_2H(CH_2)_2CO_2H$, found naturally in amber and also produced synthetically for use in the manufacture of such products as dyes, perfumes, and pharmaceuticals.

suc·cor, *Brit.* **suc·cour,** suk′ẽr, *n.* [O.Fr. *sucurre, soucourre* (Fr. *secourir*), < L. *succurro,* to run up to the aid of—*sub,* under, and *curro,* to run.] Aid; help; assistance in difficulty or distress; the person or thing that brings relief.—*v.t.* To help in difficulty or distress; to assist; to aid or relieve.—**suc·cor·er,** *n.*

suc·co·ry, suk′o·rē, *n. pl.* **suc·co·ries.** [A corruption of *chicory.*] Chicory.

suc·co·tash, suk′o·tash″, *n.* [Algonquian.] A dish consisting of corn kernels cooked together with lima beans.

suc·cu·bus, suk′ya·bus, *n. pl.* **suc·cu·bi,** suk′ya·bī″. [M.L. *succubus.*] A female demon fabled to have sexual intercourse with men in their sleep; any devil or spirit of evil. Also **suc·cu·ba,** suk′ya·ba.

suc·cu·lent, suk′u·lent, suk′ya·lent, *a.* [L. *succulentus, suculentus,* < *succus, sucus,* juice.] Full of juice; juicy; rich in desirable qualities; affording mental nourishment; *bot.* having fleshy and juicy tissues.—*n.* A plant, such as a cactus, that has fleshy tissues.—**suc·cu·lence,** **suc·cu·len·cy,** *n.*—**suc·cu·lent·ly,** *adv.*

suc·cumb, su·kum′, *v.i.* [L. *succumbere,* < *sub,* under, and *-cumbere,* lie.] To give way to superior force; yield; yield to disease, wounds, old age, or the like; die.

suc·cur·sal, su·kụr′sal, *a.* [Fr. *succursale,* fem. (as in *église succursale,* succursal church) < M.L. *succursus,* aid, E. *succor, n.*] Subsidiary, esp. noting a religious establishment which is dependent upon a principal one.

suc·cus·sion, su·kush′an, *n.* [L. *succussio(n-).*] The act of vigorously shaking; *med.* a shaking of the patient to determine if fluid or gas is present in a body cavity.

such, such, *a.* [O.E. *swelc, swilc, swylc* = O.H.G. *sulīh* (G. *solch*) = Icel. *slīkr* = Goth. *swaleiks,* such; from the Teut. adv. (O.E. *swā,* etc.) represented by E. *so,* with termination related to E. *-ly* and *like*: cf. *which.*] Of the kind, character, degree, or

extent of that or those indicated or implied, as: *Such* a woman is dangerous. Like or similar in kind or quality; as, tea, coffee, and *such* commodities; being similar or the same as that last stated or indicated, as: *Such* nonsense is the case. Being the person or thing or persons or things indicated, as: If any member is late, *such* member shall be suspended. Of so extreme a degree or kind; as, *such* honor.—*pron.* Such a person or thing or persons or things; the person or thing or persons or things indicated; as, once a friend but no longer *such.*—*adv.* So, very, in such a manner, or to such a degree, used to precede an attributive adjective; as, *such* terrible deeds.—**as such,** as being what is indicated or implied, as: The leader, *as such,* is entitled to respect. In itself, as: Vice, *as such,* does not appeal to him.—**such as,** for example; of the indicated or implied kind; as, a picture *such as* this one.

such and such, *a.* Being definite or particular, but not named or specified, as: It happened in *such and such* a place.—*pron.* Someone or something not named or specified, as: If *such and such* should occur, be prepared.

such·like, such′līk″, *a.* Of a like kind; similar.—*pron.* Persons or things of a similar kind.

suck, suk, *v.t.* [O.E. *súcan,* to suck, also *súgan,* like G. *saugen,* Icel. *sjúga, súga,* Dan. *suge;* cogn. L. *sugo,* Gael. *sugaidh,* Ir. *suigim,* to suck.] To draw into the mouth by the action of the lips and tongue; to draw, as something, from with the mouth; to draw in or imbibe by suction; to inhale; to absorb; to draw in as a whirlpool; to swallow up; to engulf.—*v.i.* To draw fluid into the mouth; to draw milk from the breast; to draw in a substance by suction.—*n.* The act of drawing with the mouth; milk drawn from the breast by the mouth; the sound of sucking.—**suck in,** *slang,* to deceive or take advantage of.

suck·er, suk′ẽr, *n.* One who or that which sucks; an organ in animals for sucking; the piston of a suction pump; a fish of the family *Catostomidae,* whose mouth is designed for sucking; *bot.* a shoot or branch which proceeds from the roots or lower part of a stem; *slang,* a person easily duped, deceived, or cheated; *colloq.* a lollipop.—*v.t.* To strip off shoots or suckers from.—*v.i.* To produce or send out suckers.

suck·fish, suk′fish″, *n.* A remora; a fish, family *Gobiesocidae,* of the U.S. Pacific coast, having a suctorial disk on the under side of the body by which it adheres to the ocean floor.

suck·ing louse, *n.* A type of louse, order *Anoplura,* with a mouth opening modified to suck bodily fluids from mammals.

suck·le, suk′l, *v.t.*—**suckled, suckling.** [Freq. < *suck.*] To give suck to; to nurse at the breast; to nurture.—*v.i.* To nurse from the breast.

suck·ling, suk′ling, *n.* An unweaned young child or other mammal.

su·crase, sō′krās, *n. Biochem.* invertase.

su·crate, sō′krāt″, *n.* [Fr. *sucre,* sugar.] *Chem.* a compound of a metallic oxide with a sugar; as, calcium *sucrate.*

su·crose, sō′krōs, *n. Chem.* a crystalline compound, $C_{12}H_{22}O_{11}$, the ordinary sugar obtained from sugar cane, sugar beets, and sorghum.

suc·tion, suk′shan, *n.* [= Fr. *succion,* < L. *sugere* (pp. *suctus*), suck.] The act, process, or condition of sucking; the force which sucks or draws a substance into an interior space or causes the parts surrounding an interior space to adhere more firmly together when a partial vacuum is produced; the production of this force.

suc·tion pump, *n.* A pump for raising

liquid by suction, consisting of a vertical cylinder containing a moving piston, which draws up liquid and retains it by means of valves.

suc·tion stop, *n. Phon.* a click produced by withdrawing the tongue in a sucking action from contact with a part of the mouth.

suc·to·ri·al, suk·tōr′ē·al, suk·tạr′ē·al, *a.* Adapted for sucking or capable of adhering by sucking; having organs adapted for sucking; living by sucking fluids from plants or animals.

Su·dan grass, sö·dan′ gras″, *n.* A grass sorghum; a variety of sorghum, *Sorghum vulgare sudanensis,* introduced into the U.S. from the Sudan and grown for hay.

su·da·to·ri·um, sö″da·tōr′ē·um, sö″da·tạr′ē·um, *n. pl.* **su·da·to·ri·a,** sö″da·tōr′ē·a, sö″da·tạr′ē·a. [L.] A hot-air bath for inducing sweating.—**su·da·to·ry,** sö′da·tōr″ē, sö′da·tạr″ē, *n. pl.* **su·da·to·ries.**—*a.*

sudd, sud, *n.* [Ar.] Floating vegetation obstructing traffic in the White Nile River.

sud·den, sud′en, *a.* [O.Fr. *sodain, sudain, soubdain* (Fr. *soudain*), < L.L. *subitanus,* < L. *subitus,* sudden, < *subeo, subitum,* to steal upon—*sub,* under, and *eo,* to go.] Occurring without notice; coming unexpectedly; causing surprise or shock; hastily put in use, employed, or prepared; quick; rapid; hasty; rash.—**all of or on a sud·den,** unexpectedly; without warning.—**sud·den·ly,** *adv.*—**sud·den·ness,** *n.*

sud·den death, *n. Sports,* any of a number of established methods for settling a tie, usu. by extending the time limit until one of the contestants scores. An unanticipated death, usu. from a nonviolent cause.

su·dor·if·er·ous, sö″do·rif′ẽr·us, *a.* [L. *sudor,* sweat (akin to E. *sweat*), and *fero,* to bear.] Producing sweat; secreting perspiration.

su·dor·if·ic, sö″do·rif′ik, *a.* [L. *sudor,* and *facio,* to make.] Causing sweat.—*n.* A medicine that produces sweat.

suds, sudz, *n. pl., sing. or pl. in constr.* [From stem of *seethe;* cf. G. *sud,* a seething, < *sieden,* to seethe.] Water impregnated with soap and forming a froth or lather; soapy water; *slang,* beer.—*v.t.* To wash with suds.—*v.i.* To produce suds.—**suds·y,** sud′zē, *a.*—**sudsier, sudsiest.**

sue, sö, *v.t.*—**sued, suing.** [O.Fr. *suir, sewir, sivir* (Fr. *suivre*), < a form *sequere,* for L. *sequi,* to follow (whence *pursue, ensue, suit, suite*).] To seek justice or right from by legal process; to institute a process in law against; *archaic,* to seek in marriage.—*v.i.* To prosecute; to make legal claim; to seek by request; to petition; to plead; *archaic,* to woo.—**su·er,** *n.*

suede, suède, swād, *n.* [Fr. *Suède,* Sweden.] Kid or leather finished on the wrong or flesh side with a soft nap, or on the outer side after removal of a thin outer layer; undressed kid. A woolen fabric with a similar finish or appearance; also **suede cloth.**

su·et, sö′it, *n.* [O.Fr. *seu, sieu* (Fr. *suif*), < L. *sebum,* tallow, grease.] The fatty tissue situated about the loins and kidneys of the ox, sheep, deer, and other animals, which is harder than the fat from other parts and upon processing yields tallow.—**su·et·y,** *a.*

suf·fer, suf′ẽr, *v.t.* [O.Fr. *suffrir, sofferre* (Fr. *souffrir*), < L. *sufferre,* inf. of *suffero,* to suffer—*sub,* under and *fero,* to bear.] To feel or bear with painful, disagreeable, or distressing effects; to undergo, as pain; to be affected by; to allow.—*v.i.* To feel or undergo pain of body or mind; to undergo punishment, esp. capital punishment; to be injured; to sustain loss or damage. —**suf·fer·a·ble,** *a.*—**suf·fer·a·ble·ness,** *n.* —**suf·fer·a·bly,** *adv.*—**suf·fer·er,** *n.*— **suf·fer·ing,** suf′ẽr·ing, suf′ring, *n.*—**suf·fer·ing·ly,** *adv.*

suf·fer·ance, suf′ẽr·ans, suf′rans, n. Passive consent by not forbidding or hindering; tolerance; endurance; the state of suffering.

suf·fice, su·fīs′, su·fīz′, v.i.—sufficed, sufficing. [O.E. suffise, < Fr. suffire, suffisant, L. sufficio, to be sufficient—sub, under, and facio, to make.] To be enough or sufficient; to be equal to the end proposed.—v.t. To satisfy; to be equal to the wants or demands of.—suf·fic·er, n.

suf·fi·cien·cy, su·fish′en·sē, n. pl. suf·fi·cien·cies. The state of being sufficient or adequate; adequacy; capacity; adequate substance or means; a comfortable fortune; a supply equal to wants; self-confidence.

suf·fi·cient, su·fish′ent, a. [L. sufficiens, sufficientis, ppr. of sufficio.] Equal to the end proposed; adequate to wants; enough; archaic, capable or competent.—suf·fi·cient·ly, adv.

suf·fix, suf′iks, n. [N.L. suffixum, prop. neut. of L. suffixus, pp.] Gram. a letter or syllable or a number of letters or syllables affixed to the end of a word or to a verbal stem or root to qualify the meaning or form a derivative word; a terminal formative element of a word, as -th in warmth, -ly in godly, or -ation in flirtation. Something suffixed.—v.t. [L. suffixus, pp. of suffigere, fix below, fasten on, < sub, under, and figere, fix.] Gram. to add, as a syllable, as a suffix. To affix at the end of something.—suf·fix·al, suf′ik·sal, a.—suf·fix·ion, suf·fix·a·tion, su·fik′shan, n.

suf·fo·cate, suf′o·kāt′, v.t.—suffocated, suffocating. [L. suffoco, suffocatum—sub, under, and faux, faucis, the throat.] To choke or kill by stopping respiration; to stifle, as by depriving of air; to smother.—v.i. To become choked, stifled, or smothered.—suf·fo·cat·ing·ly, adv.—suf·fo·ca·tion, n.—suf·fo·ca·tive, a.

Suf·folk, suf′ok, n. [From Suffolk, an English county.] A variety of strongly-built English work horse; a breed of English sheep noted for top grade mutton.

suf·fra·gan, suf′ra·gan, n. [Fr. suffragant, L. suffragans, suffragantis, ppr. of suffragor, to vote for < suffragium, a vote.] Eccles. a bishop who assists or is subordinate to another bishop, an archbishop, or metropolitan in the administration of a diocese or a portion thereof.—a.

suf·frage, suf′rij, n. [Fr. suffrage, L. suffragium, a vote.] The right to vote; a vote given in deciding a question or chosing a person or measure; eccles. a prayer asking intercession.—suf·fra·gette, suf″ra·jet′, n. A woman who favors giving women the right to vote.—suf·fra·gist, suf′ra·jist, n. A supporter of some form of suffrage.

suf·fru·tex, suf′ru·teks, n. pl. suf·fru·ti·ces, su·frö′ti·sēz. Bot. an undershrub with a woody base, annually producing herbaceous shoots.

suf·fru·ti·cose, su·frö′ti·kōs″, a. Bot. Referring to a low, partially shrubby plant with a woody base; of the nature of a suffrutex.—suf·fru·tes·cent, suf″ru·tes′ent, a.

suf·fuse, su·fūz′, v.t.—suffused, suffusing. [L. suffundo, suffusum—sub, and fundo, to pour, to pour out.] To overspread, as with color, light, or fluid; to fill, as with something fluid, esp. from beneath; to cover; as, a face suffused with blushes.—suf·fu·sion, su·fū′zhan, n.—suf·fu·sive, su·fū′siv, a.

sug·ar, shug′ẽr, n. [O.Fr. cucre, zuchre (Fr. sucre), < Ar. sukkar, akin to Gr. sákchar, sákcharon, L. saccharon, M.L. saccharum, Pers. shakkar, all < Prakrit sakkara, Skt. carkara, sugar, orig. grit, gravel.] Sucrose, a sweet, white crystalline substance, $C_{12}H_{22}O_{11}$, obtained chiefly from the juice of the sugar cane and sugar beet, but also present in sorghum, the sugar maple, some palms, and various other plants, and having extensive nutritional, pharmaceutical, and industrial uses; any of the class of carbohydrates to which this substance belongs, as glucose, levulose, and lactose. Maple, or various other commercial sugars; a sugarlike substance; as, sugar of lead. Fig. a term of endearment; a pet name.—v.t. To cover, sprinkle, mix, or sweeten with sugar. Fig. to sweeten, as if with sugar; to make agreeable.—v.i. To form sugar; to make maple sugar.—sug·ar·less, a.—sug·ar·like, a.

sug·ar ap·ple, n. Sweetsop.

sug·ar beet, n. A species of beet, Beta vulgaris, whose thick, white root is a major source of sugar.

sug·ar·ber·ry, shug′ẽr·ber″ē, n. pl. sug·ar·ber·ries. Hackberry.

sug·ar·bush, shug′ẽr·bush″, n. A grove of sugar maple trees; an evergreen shrub, Rhus ovata, having yellow flowers and red fruit, found in the southwestern U.S.

sug·ar cane, n. A tall grass, Saccharum officinarum, of warm regions, having a stout, jointed stalk, containing sweet sap, and constituting the chief source of the commercial sugar, sucrose.

sug·ar-coat, shug′ẽr·kōt″, v.t. To put a coating of sugar on; fig. to surround with a deceptive aura of attractiveness or acceptability.

sug·ar·house, shug′ẽr·hous″, n. A building in which sugar is refined.

sug·ar·ing off, n. The completion of the boiling down of maple syrup in preparation for granulation into sugar; a party at which the guests often help in the making of maple sugar.

sug·ar loaf, n. A hard conical mass of refined sugar; anything shaped like a sugar loaf.—su·gar-loaf, shug′ẽr·lōf″, a.

sug·ar ma·ple, n. A tree of northern N. America, Acer saccharum, from the sap of which maple syrup and maple sugar are made; the hardwood from this tree, much used for furniture. Also rock maple.

sug·ar of lead, n. Lead acetate.

sug·ar or·chard, n. A grove or orchard of sugar maples; sugarbush.

sug·ar·plum, shug′ẽr·plum″, n. A small sweetmeat made of sugar with various flavoring and coloring ingredients; a bonbon.

sug·ar·y, shug′a·rē, a. Consisting of or containing sugar; pertaining to or resembling sugar; sweet; sometimes, excessively sweet; honeyed; cloying; deceitfully agreeable.

sug·gest, sug·jest′, su·jest′, v.t. [L. suggestus, pp. suggerere, put under, supply, suggest, < sub, under and gerere, bear.] To place or bring, as an idea, proposition, or plan, before a person's mind for consideration or possible action; to propose, as a person or thing, as suitable or possible; to prompt the consideration, making, or doing of, as: The success of his first book suggested a second. To bring before a person's mind indirectly or without plain expression; hint; intimate; to call up in the mind, as a thing, through association or natural connection of ideas: said of a thing.—sug·gest·er, n.

sug·gest·i·ble, sug·jes′ti·bl, su·jes′ti·bl, a. That may be suggested; capable of being influenced by suggestion.—sug·gest·i·bil·i·ty, n.

sug·ges·tion, sug·jes′chan, sug·jesh′chan, su·jes′chan, su·jesh′chan, n. [L. suggestio(n-).] The act of suggesting or the state of being suggested; the calling up of an idea before the mind for consideration or possible action; the idea thus called up, or a thing suggested; indirect conveyance of an idea, or intimation; a hint; a seeming indication; psychol. the insinuation of an idea, belief, or impulse into the mind of a subject, whether by words, gestures, or otherwise, but without the normal critical command, thought, or action.

sug·ges·tive, sug·jes′tiv, su·jes′tiv, a. That suggests; tending to suggest thoughts or ideas, or conveying a suggestion or intimation; giving a seeming indication of something, such as something improper or indecent.—sug·ges·tive·ly, adv.—sug·ges·tive·ness, n.

su·i·cid·al, sö″i·sīd′al, a. Pertaining to, involving, or suggesting suicide; tending or leading to suicide.—su·i·cid·al·ly, adv.

su·i·cide, sö′i·sīd″, n. [L. sui, of oneself, and -cida, -cidium.] One who intentionally takes his own life; the intentional taking of one's own life; destruction of one's own interests or prospects.—v.i.—suicided, suiciding. To commit suicide.—v.t. To kill (oneself).

su·i ge·ne·ris, sö′i jen′ẽr·is, L. sö′i ge′ne·Ris, a. [L.] Of his, her, its, or their own or peculiar kind; unique.

su·i ju·ris, sö′i jur′is, sö′ē, a. Law, having the legal right or capacity to deal with one's own affairs.

su·int, sö′int, swint, n. [Fr., < suer, < L. sudare, to sweat.] The natural grease of the wool of sheep, consisting of a mixture of fatty matter and potassium salts, used as a source of potash and in the preparation of ointments.

suit, söt, n. [A.Fr. sute, O.Fr. sieute (Fr. suite), through L.L. < L. sequi (pp. secutus), follow.] A set of garments, vestments, or armor, intended to be worn together, esp. a set of outer garments, as jacket, vest, and trousers; a livery, uniform, or garb. Law, the act or process of suing in a court of law; legal prosecution; a process instituted in a court of justice for the enforcement or protection of a right or claim, or for the redress of a wrong; a lawsuit; the act of making petition or appeal. One of the four sets or classes, spades, clubs, hearts, and diamonds, into which playing cards are divided; the aggregate of cards belonging to one of these sets held in a player's hand at one time; fig. forte. A succession, sequence, or order; a number of objects corresponding in general character or purpose and intended to be used together; the courting of a woman; solicitation in marriage; naut. a complete set of sails for a boat.—v.t. To arrange in proper order; to make appropriate, adapt, or accommodate, as one thing to another; be adapted or suitable for; be becoming to; to be or prove appropriate, satisfactory, agreeable, or acceptable to; to conform with; satisfy or please; to provide, as with something desired; provide with a suit of clothes, or clothe or array.—v.i. To be appropriate or suitable; accord; to be satisfactory, agreeable, or acceptable.—fol·low suit, to play a card of the suit led; to do as someone or something else has done; to follow example.

suit·a·ble, sö′ta·bl, a. Suiting or being in accordance; fitting; proper; becoming.—suit·a·bil·i·ty, suit·a·ble·ness, n.—suit·a·bly, adv.

suit·case, söt′kās″, n. A kind of flat, oblong valise used to carry clothing and other articles, esp. when traveling.

suite, swēt, söt, n. [Fr.] A number of things forming a series or set; a connected series of rooms to be used together by one person or a number of persons; a company of followers or attendants; a train or retinue, swēt. A matched set of furniture designed for a given room, swēt, söt. Mus. a definitely ordered series of instrumental dances, in the same key or related keys, commonly preceded by a prelude; an ordered series of instrumental movements of any character, swĕt.

suit·ing, sö′ting, *n.* Cloth for making suits of clothes.

suit·or, sö′tẽr, *n.* One who asks for a woman in marriage; a wooer. *Law,* a party to a lawsuit; a petitioner; an applicant; one who sues or entreats.

su·ki·ya·ki, sö″kē·yä′kē, su̧k″ē·yä′kē, skē·-yä′kē, *n.* A Japanese dish made of thinly sliced meat and vegetables, cooked, usu. at the table, with soy sauce, sugar, and sake.

Suk·koth, su̧k′ōth, su̧k′ōs, su̧k′os, *Heb.* sö·kät′, sö·kạs′, *n.* A Jewish harvest celebration and a remembrance of the wandering in the desert, held on the 15th day of Tishri in late September or early October. Also **Feast of the Tab·er·nac·les.**

sul·cate, sul′kāt, *a.* [L. *sulcatus,* < *sulcus,* a furrow.] *Biol.* Having long, narrow channels or flutes; furrowed or grooved, as a plant stem or a horse's hoof. Also **sul·cat·ed.—sul·ca·tion,** *n.*

sul·cus, sul′kus, *n.* pl. **sul·ci,** sul′sī. [L., a furrow.] A furrow or groove; *anat.* a fissure between two convolutions of the surface of the brain.

sul·fa, sul′pha, sul′fa, *a. Pharm.* Chemically related to sulfanilamide; of or concerning sulfa drugs; containing or consisting of a sulfa drug or drugs.—*n. Pharm.* sulfa drug.

sul·fa drug, *n. Pharm.* any of a family of bacteriostatic drugs which are closely related in chemical structure to sulfanilamide. Also *sulfa.*

sul·fa·nil·a·mide, sul·pha·nil·a·mide, sul″fa·nil′a·mīd″, sul″fa·nil′a·mid, *n. Pharm.* a colorless, crystalline compound, $C_6H_8N_2O_2S$, a derivative of sulfanilic acid, used for its therapeutic action in numerous bacterial infections, as in pneumonia and gonorrhea.

sul·fa·nil·ic ac·id, sul′fa·nil′ik as′id, sul″fa·nil′ik, *n. Chem.* a somewhat water-soluble, grayish-white crystal, $C_6H_7NO_3S$, used in dye making and medicine. Also **sul·pha·nil·ic ac·id.**

sulf·ar·se·nide, sulph·ar·se·nide, sul″-fär′se·nīd″, sul·fär′se·nid, *n. Chem.* any compound which contains a sulfide in addition to an arsenide.

sul·fate, sul·phate, sul′fāt, *n. Chem.* a salt of sulfuric acid.—*v.t.—sulfated, sulfating. Chem.* To combine, treat, or impregnate with sulfuric acid or with a sulfate or sulfates; convert into a sulfate; to form a deposit of lead sulfate on, as the lead plates of a storage battery.—*v.i. Chem.* to become sulfated.

sul·fide, sul·phide, sul′fīd, *n. Chem.* a compound of sulfur with a more electropositive element or radical. Also *sulfuret.*

sul·fi·nyl, sul·phi·nyl, sul′fi·nil, *n. Chem.* the bivalent radical group, SO.

sul·fite, sul·phite, sul′fīt, *n. Chem.* a salt composed of sulfurous acid with a base.—**sul·fit·ic,** sul·fit′ik, *a.*

sul·fon·a·mide, sul·phon·a·mide, sul″-fon′a·mīd″, sul″fo·nam′id, *n. Chem.* any of a class of organic compounds containing sulfanilamide.

sul·fo·nate, sul·pho·nate, sul′fo·nāt″, *n. Chem.* a salt composed of sulfonic acid with a base.—*v.t.—sulfonated, sulfonating. Chem.* To change or form into a sulfonic acid; to add the sulfonic group to.

sul·fone, sul·phone, sul′fōn, *n.* [G. *sulfon,* < *sulfur,* sulphur.] *Chem.* any of a class of organic compounds containing the bivalent SO_2 group united with two hydrocarbon radicals.

sul·fon·ic, sul·phon·ic, sul·fon′ik, *a. Chem.* Noting or pertaining to the group SO_2OH; noting or pertaining to any of the acids containing this group, as ethyl sulfonic acid, $C_2H_5SO_2OH$.

sul·fon·ic ac·id, *n. Chem.* any of the group of acids which contain the sulfonic radical and can be formed from sulfuric acid by replacing an OH group. Also **sul·phon·ic ac·id.**

sul·fo·ni·um, sul·pho·ni·um, sul·fō′-nē·um, *n.* [From (*sulph*)ur and amm-(*onium*).] *Chem.* the univalent radical, SH_3, present in certain organic compounds.

sul·fon·meth·ane, sul·phon·meth·an, sul″-fon·meth′än, *n.* A crystalline compound, $(CH_3)_2C(SO_2C_2H_5)_2$, used mainly in medicine as a hypnotic or sedative.

sul·fo·nyl, sul·pho·nyl, sul′fo·nil, *n. Chem.* sulfuryl.

sul·fur, sul·phur, sul′fẽr, *n.* [L. *sulfur, sulphur, sulpur,* sulphur.] *Chem.* A nonmetallic element existing in several forms, the ordinary one being a yellow crystalline solid which burns with a blue flame and a suffocating odor, and is used in medicine, in vulcanizing rubber, and in making matches and gunpowder. Sym. S, at. no. 16, at. wt. 32.064. See Periodic Table of Elements.—*v.t. Chem.* To treat with sulfur; sulfurize.

sul·fur but·ter·fly, *n.* Any of a number of butterflies of the family *Pieridae,* which have yellow or orange wings with black borders. Also **sul·phur but·ter·fly.**

sul·fur di·ox·ide, *n. Chem.* a heavy, suffocating, colorless, water-soluble gas, SO_2, obtained from burning sulfur and used in preserving foods, in bleaching and disinfecting, and in producing sulfuric acid. Also **sul·phur di·ox·ide.**

sul·fu·re·ous, sul·phu·re·ous, sul·fūr′-ē·us, *a.* Consisting of or having the qualities of sulfur; sulfurous.—**sul·fu·re·ous·ly,** sul·phu·re·ous·ly, *adv.*—**sul·fu·re·ous·ness, sul·phu·re·ous·ness,** *n.*

sul·fu·ret, sul·phu·ret, sul′fya·ret″, *n. Chem.* a sulfide.—*v.t.—sulfureted, sulfureting, Brit. sulfuretted, sulfuretting. Chem.* To combine, impregnate, or treat with sulfur; to sulfurize.

sul·fu·ric, sul·phu·ric, sul·fūr′ik, *a. Chem.* of, pertaining to, or containing sulfur, esp. in higher valence states.

sul·fu·ric ac·id, *n. Chem.* a colorless, oily, and strongly corrosive compound, H_2SO_4, used in manufacturing explosives, fertilizers, and chemicals. Also **sul·phu·ric ac·id,** *oil of vitriol, vitriol.*

sul·fu·rize, sul·phu·rize, sul′fya·rīz″, sul′fu·rīz″, *v.t.—sulfurized, sulfurizing, sulphurized, sulphurizing. Chem.* To combine, treat, or impregnate with sulfur; fumigate with the fumes of burning sulfur.

sul·fur·ous, sul·phur·ous, sul′fẽr·us, sul·fūr′us, *a.* [L. *sulfurosus.*] Full of sulfur; pertaining to or resembling sulfur; like the suffocating fumes or the heat of burning sulfur; pertaining to the fires of hell; hellish or satanic; fiery or heated; blasphemous or profane, as language; *chem.* containing sulfur, esp. in lower valence states.—**sul·fur·ous·ly, sul·phur·ous·ly,** *adv.*—**sul·fur·ous·ness, sul·phur·ous·ness,** *n.*

sul·fur·ous ac·id, *n. Chem.* a weak, colorless acid, H_2SO_3, known chiefly through its salts, the sulfites, and used as a bleach. Also **sul·phur·ous ac·id.**

sul·fur yel·low, *n.* A color ranging between yellow and brilliant green. Also **sul·phur yel·low.**

sul·fur·yl, sul·phur·yl, sul′fu·ril, sul′-fū·ril, *n. Chem.* the bivalent radical group, SO_2, formed from sulfuric acid. Also *sulfonyl.*

sulk, sulk, *v.i.* [Origin uncertain.] To hold oneself aloof in a sullenly ill-humored or offended mood; to maintain an attitude of ill-humored reserve; to be sulky.—*n.* A state or fit of sulking; *pl.* ill humor shown by sulking.

sulk·y, sul′kē, *a.—sulkier, sulkiest.* Sulking; sullenly ill-humored or resentful; marked by ill-humored aloofness or reserve; *fig.* gloomy, as of weather. *Brit. dial.* hard to work, as soil, stone, or timber.—*n.* pl. **sulk·ies.** [So called because the rider is alone.] A light two-wheeled, one-horse carriage carrying one person and commonly used for trials of speed between trotting horses.—**sulk·i·ly,** *adv.*—**sulk·i·ness,** *n.*

sul·lage, sul′ij, *n.* Sewage; waste or any refuse; silt; *metal.* scoria which floats in the ladle on metal that is molten.

sul·len, sul′en, *a.* [M.E. *soleyn,* solitary, unsociable, through O.Fr. < L. *solus,* alone, E. *sole.*] Showing ill humor by a gloomy silence or reserve; silently and persistently ill-humored; morose; indicative of gloomy ill humor. *Fig.* gloomy or dismal, as weather, places, or sounds; somber, as in aspect or hue; as, *sullen* skies; sluggish, as a stream.—**sul·len·ly.—sul·len·ness,** *n.*

sul·ly, sul′ē, *v.t.—sullied, sullying.* [Fr. *souiller* or O.E. *solian,* both meaning to soil.] To soil, spot, or tarnish; defile; to impair the purity or brilliance of.—*v.i.* To be soiled or tarnished.—*n.* Any spot or stain; blemish; defilement.

sul·tan, sul′tan, *n.* [Fr. *sultan* (O.Fr. *soldan*) = It. *sultano,* < Ar. *sultān,* sovereign, ruler, orig. power, dominion.] The sovereign of a Mohammedan country; (*cap.*) formerly, the sovereign of Turkey. (*l.c.*) any absolute ruler; a despot; a tyrant; one of a breed of domestic fowls of small size, having white plumage and the legs profusely feathered.—**sul·tan·ic,** sul′-tan′ik, *a.*

sul·tan·a, sul·tan′a, sul·tä′na, *n.* [It.] The wife, mother, sister, or daughter of a sultan; also **sul·tan·ess.** A concubine or mistress, esp. of any royal personage. A species of gallinule, *Porphyrula martinica,* belonging to the rail family and notable for its brilliant purple plumage; also **pur·ple gal·li·nule.** A kind of white, small, seedless grape cultivated esp. for raisins and the making of wine; a raisin from this kind of grape.

sul·tan·ate, sul′ta·nāt″, *n.* The rule or territory of a sultan. Also **sul·tan·ship.**

sul·try, sul′trē, *a.* [A form of *sweltry,* O.E. *sueltrie,* sultry, < *swelter.*] Very hot, burning, and oppressive; very hot and moist, or hot, close, and heavy; as, a *sultry* atmosphere; emitting or characterized by a sweltering heat; hot or burning, as with anger or passion.—**sul·tri·ly,** *adv.*—**sul·tri·ness,** *n.*

sum, sum, *n.* [O.Fr. *summe, somme* (Fr. *somme*), < L. *summa,* highest point, culmination, completion, issue, total amount, an amount, principal matter, substance, M.L. summary, prop. fem. of L. *summus,* highest, superl. of *superus,* being above.] The utmost degree or culmination. *Math.* the total amount or the whole; the aggregate of two or more numbers, magnitudes, quantities, or particulars as determined by the mathematical process of addition; an arithmetical problem to be solved or such a problem worked out; the limit of the sequence of partial sums of a given infinite series. An indefinite quantity or amount, esp. of money; as, to lend small *sums*; the substance, gist, or essence of a matter, comprehensively or broadly viewed; as, the *sum* and substance; a concise or brief form; as, in *sum*; the issue or conclusion; a summary.—*v.t.—summed, summing.* [O.Fr. Fr. *sommer,* < M.L. *summare,* < L. *summa.*] To combine into an aggregate; to ascertain the total, often with *up*; reckon, followed by *up*; to bring into or contain in a small compass, often with *up*; express in a concise form; summarize; to bring to completion or perfection.—*v.i.* To amount, as to a total; to do sums, as in arithmetic; to summarize facts or statements; recapitulate.

su·mac, su·mach, shŏ'mak, sŏ'mak, *n.* [Fr. *sumac,* Sp. *zumaque,* < Ar. *sumak, sumach.*] Any shrub or tree of the genus *Rhus,* the powdered leaves of certain species being used for tanning.

Su·me·ri·an, Su·mi·ri·an, sŏ·mēr'ē·-an, sŏ·mēr'ē·an, *a.* [From *Sumer,* ancient name of Babylonia or part of Babylonia.] Noting or pertaining to the primitive inhabitants of ancient Sumer or Babylonia, believed to have been of non-Semitic origin; noting or pertaining to a certain language preserved in cuneiform inscriptions, held to be non-Semitic and ascribed to the primitive inhabitants of Babylonia.— *n.* One of the Sumerian people; the Sumerian language.

sum·ma, sụm'a, sum'a, *n.* pl. **sum·mae, sum·mas,** sụm'ī, sum'ē. A treatise of large scope covering a particular field or area of knowledge, esp. one written by a scholastic philosopher.

sum·ma cum lau·de, sụm'a kụm lou'dā, sụm'a kụm lou'da, sụm'a kụm lou'dē, sụm'a kum lạ'dē, *adv.* With highest honors: used to denote the highest of three degrees of academic distinction. See *cum laude, magna cum laude.*

sum·ma·rize, sum'a·rīz", *v.t.—summarized, summarizing.* To make a summary of; to state or express in a concise form; to constitute a summary of.—**sum·ma·ri·za·tion,** *n.*—**sum·ma·riz·er, sum·mar·ist,** *n.*

sum·ma·ry, sum'a·rē, *a.* Reduced into few words; concise; quickly executed without ceremony; effected by a short way or method; *law,* of proceedings carried on by methods intended to facilitate the dispatch of business, esp. without the legal formalities.—*n.* pl. **sum·ma·ries.** [L. *summarium,* a summary.] An abridged or condensed statement or account; a compendium or recapitulation containing the sum or substance of a fuller statement.—**sum·mar·i·ly,** sum·mer'i·lē, sum'ẽr·i·lē, *adv.*—**sum·mar·i·ness,** *n.*

sum·ma·tion, su·mā'shan, *n.* [N.L. *summatio(n-),* < M.L. *summare.*] The process of summing; combination into or ascertainment of an aggregate or total; the result of this; an aggregate or total; a recapitulation or reviewing of previous arguments or facts, usu. expressing one or more final conclusions, as in any debate or court trial.—**sum·ma·tion·al,** *a.*

sum·mer, sum'ẽr, *n.* [O.E. *sumor* = D. *zomer* = G. *sommer* = Icel. *sumar* = Sw. *sommar* = Dan. *sommer,* summer.] The second and warmest season of the year, between spring and autumn, in N. America considered to comprise June, July, and August, and in Great Britain, May, June, and July; the period between the summer solstice and the autumnal equinox. *Fig.* a whole year represented by this season; as, seventeen *summers;* the period of finest development, perfection, or beauty, previous to any decline; as, the *summer* of life. Summer weather or warmth; a summerlike season or period, specif. a period of mild, fine weather in late autumn or early winter; as, Indian *summer.—a.* Of, pertaining to, or characteristic of summer; as, *summer* warmth, *summer* clothing; having the warmth of summer; of fruit, denoting a kind that ripens during the summer.—*v.i.* To spend or pass the summer.—*v.t.* To keep, manage, or feed during the summer; to make summerlike.—**sum·mer·ly, sum·mer·y,** *a.*

sum·mer, sum'ẽr, *n.* [O.Fr. *somier* (Fr. *sommier*), < M.L. *sagmarius,* packhorse, orig. *a.* < L.L. *sagma,* < Gr. *ságma,* packsaddle.] *Building.* A principal timber or beam; a girder; a lintel; a stone at the top of a pier or column.

sum·mer cy·press, *n.* A Eurasian herb, *Kochia scoparia,* common in N. America and belonging to the goosefoot family, densely branched and grown primarily for its ornamental foliage.

sum·mer·house, sum'ẽr·hous", *n.* A structure in a park or garden, usu. of simple and often rustic character, intended to provide a shady and cool place in the heat of summer.

sum·mer kitch·en, *n.* A usu. detached building next to a house for use as a kitchen in warm weather.

sum·mer·sault, sum'ẽr·sạlt", *n., v.i.* Somersault.

sum·mer school, *n.* A school or study program held during the summer, either in connection with a particular educational institution or independently, enabling a student to obtain a degree sooner, make up credits, or supplement his education.

sum·mer squash, *n.* Any of the garden squashes of the variety, *Cucurbita pepo melopepo,* which are eaten as vegetables before the seeds and rind harden.

sum·mer·time, sum'ẽr·tīm", *n.* The season of summer; *Brit.* daylight saving time.

sum·mer·wood, sum'ẽr·wụd", *n.* The harder, more compact part of a yearly ring of wood that is formed late in a season of growth.

sum·mit, sum'it, *n.* [O.Fr. *somete,* also *somet* (Fr. *sommet*), dim. of *som,* < L. *summum,* highest point, top, prop. neut. of *summus.*] The highest point or part, as of a hill, line of travel, or any object; the top or apex; the highest point of attainment or aspiration; as, the *summit* of success; the highest stage or degree; the culmination; the acme; the highest rank, as of officials in government.—*a.* Of or pertaining to diplomacy between chiefs of state or the highest ranking government officials; as, a *summit* meeting.—**sum·mit·al,** *a.*

sum·mon, sum'on, *v.t.* [O.E. *somone,* O.Fr. *somoner* (Fr. *semondre*), < L. *summonere, submonere—sub,* under, privately, and *moneo,* to remind.] To send for or ask the attendance of; to call or cite by authority to appear at a specified place, esp. before a court of justice; to call or order together; as, to *summon* congress; to call on for a particular action, as surrender; to call up, muster, or excite into action, usu. followed by *up,* as: *Summon up* your courage.—**sum·mon·er,** *n.*

sum·mons, sum'onz, *n.* pl. **sum·mons·es.** [O.E. *somons, somounce,* O.Fr. *semonce, semonse,* a summons, fem. forms of *semons,* pp. of *semondre.*] A call or command by authority to appear at a specific place or to attend to some public duty. *Law,* a call by authority to appear in a court; the written or printed document by which such a call is given.—*v.t.*

sum·mum bo·num, sum'um bō'num, *L.* sụm'ụm bō'nụm, *n.* [L.] The highest or chief good.

su·mo, sŏ'mō, *n.* A type of wrestling in Japan won by the contestant who forces his opponent out of the ring or causes any part of his opponent's body other than the feet to touch the ground.

sump, sump, *n.* [M.E. *sompe* = D. *somp* = M.L.G. *sump* = G. *sumpf,* swamp: cf. *swamp.*] A pit, well, or cesspool in which water or other liquid is collected; *mech.* a reservoir for oil situated at the lowest point of a crankcase in a circulating system; *min.* a space at the bottom of a shaft where water is allowed to collect; *Brit. dial.* a swamp, bog, or muddy pool.

sump pump, *n.* A pump used to remove excess liquid accumulated in a sump.

sump·ter, sump'tẽr, *n.* [O.Fr. *sommetier,* a packhorse driver; same origin as *summer,* beam.] A baggage horse or mule; a packhorse.

sump·tu·ar·y, sump'chŏ·er"ē, *a.* [L. *sumptuarius,* < *sumptus,* expense, < *sumo, sumptum,* to use, spend—*sub,* under, and *emo,* to buy, to take.] Relating to expense; regulating expense or expenditure; as, *sumptuary* laws.

sump·tu·ous, sump'chŏ·us, *a.* [L. *sumptuosus,* < *sumptus,* cost, expense.] Costly; having an impressively expensive appearance; luxurious; magnificent.—**sump·tu·ous·ly,** *adv.*—**sump·tu·ous·ness,** *n.*

sum to·tal, *n.* Complete or all-inclusive total, as of numbers, results, information, accomplishment, or the like.

sun, sun, *n.* [O.E. *sunne* = D. *zon* = G. *sonne* = Icel. *sunna* = Goth. *sunnō,* sun; < same root as L. *sol,* sun.] The central body of the solar system, a star around which the earth and other planets revolve and from which they receive light and heat, having a mean distance from the earth of about 93,000,000 miles, a diameter of about 864,000 miles, a mass about 330,000 times as great as the earth's, and a mean density of about one-fourth that of the earth; some similar celestial body; sunlight; as, to stay out of the *sun;* a figure or representation of the sun; something likened to the sun in brightness, splendor, or life-giving properties.—*v.t.—sunned, sunning.* To expose to the heat or light of the sun or of a sun lamp.—*v.i.* To expose oneself to the rays of the sun or a sun lamp.—**place in the sun,** favorable, usu. public, acknowledgment or recognition; prominence.—**under the sun,** anywhere on earth.

sun·baked, sun'bākt", *a.* Baked by exposure to the sun, as bricks; dried, made hot, or hardened by the heat of the sun.

sun bath, *n.* An exposure of the body to the direct rays of the sun or a sun lamp.

sun·bathe, sun'bāTH", *v.i.—sunbathed, sunbathing.* To lie exposed to the sun.—**sun·bath·er,** *n.*

sun·beam, sun'bēm", *n.* A ray of the sun perceived as a beam of visible light.

sun·bird, sun'bụrd", *n.* Any of several small, bright-colored songbirds, family *Nectariniidae,* of the African and Far East tropics, similar to the hummingbird.

sun·bon·net, sun'bon"it, *n.* A large bonnet of cotton or other light material shading the face and projecting down over the neck, worn outdoors by women and girls.

sun·bow, sun'bō", *n.* A rainbow formed by the refraction of light on the spray of waterfalls or on any rising vapor.

sun·burn, sun'bụrn", *n.* Inflammation of the skin, caused by prolonged exposure to the sun's rays; the discoloration or tan so produced.—*v.t., v.i.* To affect or be affected with sunburn.

sun·burst, sun'bụrst", *n.* A burst of sunlight; a sudden shining of the sun through rifted clouds; a firework, a piece of jewelry, a decorative ornament, or the like, resembling the sun with its rays issuing in all directions.

sun·dae, sun'dē", sun'dā, *n.* [Origin unknown.] An individual portion of ice cream with fruit or other syrup poured over it, and often with whipped cream, minced nuts, or other additions.

sun dance, *n.* A religious ceremony associated with the sun, practiced by N. American Indians of the Plains, consisting of dancing attended with various symbolic rites, commonly including self-torture.

Sun·day, sun'dē, sun'dā, *n.* [O.E. *sunnandaeg,* that is, day of the sun; G. *sonntag,* Dan. *söndag,* D. *zondag;* so called because this day was anciently dedicated to the *sun* or its worship.] The first day of the week; the Christian Sabbath; the Lord's day.—*a.*—**Sun·days,** sun'dēz, sun'dāz, *adv.* On Sundays; every Sunday.

Sun·day-go-to-meet·ing, sun'dē·gō"to·-mēt'in, sun'dē·gō"to·mē'ting, sun'dā·gō"-to·mēt'in, sun'dā·gō"to·mē'ting, *a. Colloq.* best looking; as, *Sunday-go-to-meeting* clothes.

Sun·day punch, *n. Boxing,* the punch used to gain a knockout; a boxer's most effective punch. Anything capable of striking a fast hard blow at an opponent.

Sun·day School, *n.* A school for religious instruction held on Sundays; the pupils and teachers collectively, of a Sunday School.

sun deck, *n.* A platform or surface used for sunbathing and having the best exposure to the sun, as a roof or terrace of a building or an upper deck of a ship.

sun·der, sun'dèr, *v.t., v.i.* [O.E. *sundrian, syndrian,* < *sundor, sunder,* asunder, apart; similarly Icel. *sundra,* Dan. *sōndre,* D. *zonderen,* G. *sondern,* to separate. Hence *sundry, asunder. Sound,* a channel, is closely allied.] To part; to divide; to disunite in almost any manner, as by rending, cutting, or breaking.—*n.* A separation or division into parts, usu. preceded by *in.*—**sun·der·-ance,** sun'dèr·ans, *n.*

sun·dew, sun'dō", sun'dū", *n.* [= D. *zonnedauw,* G. *sonnentau,* transl. < L. *ros solis,* 'dew of the sun.'] Any of several small, bog-inhabiting herbs of the genus *Drosera,* which have leaves covered with sticky hairs by which insects are caught.

sun·di·al, sun'dī"al, sun'dīl", *n.* An instrument that shows the time of day by means of a shadow cast by the sun onto a dial.

sun disk, *n.* A disklike figure or representation of the sun, esp. in religious symbolism.

sun·dog, sun'dag", sun'dog", *n.* A parhelion; a small or incomplete rainbow.

sun·down, sun'doun", *n.* Sunset; the time of sunset; a kind of broad-brimmed hat formerly worn by women.

sun·down·er, sun'dou"nèr, *n. Aust.* a tramp, esp. one who makes a practice of arriving at some station at sundown under the pretense of seeking work, so as to obtain food and a night's lodging.

sun·dries, sun'drēz, *n. pl.* Various small things, too minute or numerous to be individually specified.

sun·drops, sun'drops", *n. pl., sing. or pl. in constr.* One of various plants of the genus *Oenothera,* esp. *O. fruticosa,* related to the evening primrose but having yellow flowers that open by day.

sun·dry, sun'drē, *a.* [O.E. *sundrig, syndrig,* < *sundor,* separate.] Several; various; miscellaneous; being of an indeterminate number.

sun·fast, sun'fast", sun'fäst", *a.* Having the quality of retaining color in sunlight, as dyes or fabrics; resistant to fading from exposure to sun.

sun·fish, sun'fish", *n. pl.* **sun·fish, sun·-fish·es.** A large marine fish, *Mola mola,* with a deep body truncated behind, and with high anal and dorsal fins; any of various small fresh-water fishes of the family *Centrarchidae,* of N. America, with a deep, compressed body.

sun·flow·er, sun'flou"èr, *n.* Any of several tall herbs of the genus *Helianthus,* in the composite family, with large leaves and yellow-rayed flowers, the seeds of which contain an edible oil, are used as stock feed, and, when dried, are eaten as a snack.

sun·glass·es, sun'glas"iz, sun'glä"siz, *n. pl. sing. or pl. in constr.* Eyeglasses which have tinted or colored lenses for protecting the eyes from strong, glaring sunlight.

sun·glow, sun'glō", *n.* A diffused hazy light sometimes seen in the sky before the sun rises or after it sets, due to particles of

foreign matter in the atmosphere; the glow or warm light of the sun.

sun-god, sun'god", *n.* The sun considered or personified as a deity; a god identified or associated with the sun.

sun grebe, *n.* Any of various birds of the family *Heliornithidae,* found in tropical America and Africa, and related to the rails and coots.

sunk·en, sung'ken, *a.* Submerged; lying on the bottom of the sea or other water; hollow or recessed; lying below the normal level; constructed or located at a lower level.

sunk fence, *n.* A ditch with a retaining wall on one side, used for the purpose of dividing lands without altering the appearance of the landscape; a ha-ha.

sun lamp, *n.* An electric lamp which emits ultraviolet rays and is used mainly therapeutically or as an indoor source of sun tan.

sun·less, sun'lis, *a.* Without sun or sunlight; dark; dismal; cheerless or bleak.— **sun·less·ness,** *n.*

sun·light, sun'līt", *n.* The light of the sun; sunshine.—**sun·lit,** sun'lit", *a.* Lighted by the sun.

sunn, sun, *n.* [Hind. *san;* < Skt.] A tall East Indian leguminous shrub, *Crotalaria juncea,* with slender branches and yellow flowers, and an inner bark which yields a hemplike fiber used for making ropes and sacking; the fiber.

Sun·na, Sun·nah, sun'a, *n.* [Ar., lit. 'path.'] The traditional portion of Moslem law based on Mohammed's words and acts but not written by him, and accepted as authoritative by the Sunnites.

Sun·nite, sun'īt, *n.* One of the so-called orthodox Mohammedans who consider the Sunna of equal importance with the Koran: opposed to *Shiah, Shiite.* Also **Sun·ni,** sun'ē.

sun·ny, sun'ē, *a.*—*sunnier, sunniest.* Like the sun; shining or dazzling with light; bright; exposed to the rays of the sun; lighted up or warmed by the direct rays of the sun; cheery or pleasant; as, a *sunny* disposition.— **sun·ni·ly,** *adv.*—**sun·ni·ness,** *n.*

sun·ny-side up, sun'ē·sīd" up', *a.* Denoting an egg fried on only one side, with the yolk unbroken.

sun par·lor, *n.* A room or porch exposed to the sun's rays and enclosed by a full expanse of windows. Also **sun porch, sun·-room.**

sun·rise, sun'rīz", *n.* The ascent or appearance of the sun above the horizon; the time when this takes place.

sun·set, sun'set", *n.* The disappearance or seeming descent of the sun below the horizon; the time when the sun sets; *fig.* a close or decline.

sun·shade, sun'shād", *n.* Something used as a protection from the rays of the sun; a parasol; an awning.

sun·shine, sun'shīn", *n.* The light of the sun; a place, point, or surface on which the rays of the sun fall directly; something acting like the rays of the sun, as in exuding or creating warmth or cheerfulness; brightness or happiness.—**sun·shin·y,** *a.*

sun·spot, sun'spot", *n.* One of the relatively dark patches which appear periodically on the surface of the sun, and which are regarded as having a certain effect on terrestrial magnetism.

sun·stroke, sun'strōk", *n.* A type of heatstroke resulting from exposure to the direct rays of the sun.

sun·struck, sun'struk", *a.* Having sunstroke; affected by the sun.

sun·suit, sun'sōt", *n.* A short, one- or two-piece playsuit worn by women and children.

sun tan, *n.* A browning or darkening of the skin due to exposure to the sun or a sun lamp. Also **sun·tan.**

sun·up, sun'up", *n.* Sunrise.

sun·ward, sun'wèrd, *adv.* Toward the sun. Also **sun·wards.**—*a.* Turned toward the sun.

sun·wise, sun'wīz", *adv.* In the direction of the sun's apparent daily motion; clockwise.

sup, sup, *v.i.*—*supped, supping.* [O.Fr. *soper, super* (Fr. *souper.*)] To eat the evening meal; to take supper.—*v.t.* To provide with supper; to entertain at supper.

sup, sup, *v.t., v.i.*—*supped, supping.* [O.E. *sūpan,* to sup = Icel. *sūpa,* L.G. *supen,* D. *zuipen,* O.G. *sufan,* G. *saufen,* to sip or sup.] To take in small amounts into the mouth with the lips, as a liquid; to sip.—*n.* A little taken with the lips; a sip.

su·per, sō'pèr, *n. Colloq.* a shortened form of *superior, superintendent, supervisor;* an object of high quality or large size. *Entom.* the upper portion of a beehive where the honey is stored; *bookbinding,* the open-weave, starched cotton cloth used in reinforcing books.—*v.t. Bookbinding,* to strengthen, as a book, using super.—*a. Colloq.* Superfine; extremely good or excellent; of the greatest measure or degree; as, *super* spy; of an excessive measure or degree.

su·per·a·ble, sō'pèr·a·bl, *a.* [L. *superabilis,* < *supero,* to overcome.] Capable of being overcome or conquered.—**su·per·a·ble·-ness,** *n.*—**su·per·a·bly,** *adv.*

su·per·a·bound, sō"pèr·a·bound', *v.i.* To abound above or beyond measure.

su·per·a·bun·dant, sō"pèr·a·bun'dant, *a.* Abounding far above or beyond necessity.— **su·per·a·bun·dance,** *n.*—**su·per·a·bun·-dant·ly,** *adv.*

su·per·add, sō'pèr·ad', *v.t.* To add over and above; to add or join in addition.— **su·per·ad·di·tion,** sō"pèr·a·dish'an, *n.*

su·per·an·nu·ate, sō"pèr·an'ū·āt", *v.t.*— *superannuated, superannuating.* To allow to retire from service on a pension, on account of old age or infirmity; to give a retiring pension to; to discard or set aside as too old.—*v.i.* To become retired.— **su·per·an·nu·at·ed,** *a.* Retired due to old age; too old to be useful or efficient; outdated or obsolete.—**su·per·an·nu·a·tion,** sō"pèr·an"ū·ā'shan, *n.*

su·perb, su·purb', su·purb', *a.* [Fr. *superbe;* L. *superbus,* proud, < *super,* above.] Grand; august; stately; splendid; rich; sumptuous; showy; very fine; first-rate.—**su·perb·ly,** *adv.*—**su·perb·ness,** *n.*

su·per·cal·en·der, sō'pèr·kal"en·dèr, *v.t.* To give a high gloss or extra smoothness to, as paper, by passing it through an additional and special calender.—*n.*

su·per·car·go, sō"pèr·kär'gō, sō'pèr·kär"-gō, *n. pl.* **su·per·car·goes, su·per·car·-gos.** A person on a merchant ship whose business is to manage sales and superintend all the commercial concerns of the voyage.

su·per·charg·er, sō'pèr·chär"jèr, *n.* A device by which an increased quantity of air is supplied to the cylinders of an internal-combustion engine, producing greater power; *avi.* a compressor used to pressurize airplane cabins.—**su·per·-charge,** sō'pèr·chärj', *v.t.*—*supercharged, supercharging.*

su·per·cil·i·ar·y, sō"pèr·sil'ē·er"ē, *a.* [L. *supercilium,* the eyebrow; haughtiness or pride, as expressed by raising the brows.] Pertaining to the eyebrow; situated or being above the eyelid.—*n.*

su·per·cil·i·ous, sō"pèr·sil'ē·us, *a.* [L. *superciliosus.*] Having a haughty air or manner; disdainful; acting as if others were inferior; haughty; overbearing; arrogant. —**su·per·cil·i·ous·ly,** *adv.*—**su·per·cil·-i·ous·ness,** *n.*

su·per·class, sō'pèr·klas", sō'pèr·kläs", *n. Biol.* a group or category ranking above a class.

---

su·per·con·duc·tiv·i·ty, sō″pėr·kon″- duk·tiv′i·tē, *n. Phys.* the absence of almost all resistance in a metal at temperatures approximating absolute zero.—**su·per·- con·duc·tive,** sō″pėr·kon·duk′tiv, *a.*—**su·- per·con·duc·tor,** sō″pėr·kon·duk′tėr, *n.*

su·per·cool, sō″pėr·kōl′, *v.t. Physical chem.* to cool, as a liquid, below its freezing point without producing solidification.— *v.i.* To be so cooled. Also *subcool.*

su·per·dom·i·nant, sō″pėr·dom′i·nant, *n. Mus.* The note above the dominant; the sixth note of the diatonic scale; the submediant.

su·per·e·go, sō″pėr·ē′gō, sō″pėr·eg′ō, *n. Psychoanal.* A system within the mind which, acting consciously or unconsciously, brings perceived parental, social, or moral standards to bear upon the actions and decisions of the ego; the conscience plus a memory of perceived ideals.

su·per·em·i·nent, sō″pėr·em′i·nent, *a.* Eminent in a superior degree; surpassing others in excellence, power, or authority.— **su·per·em·i·nence,** *n.*—**su·per·em·i·- nent·ly,** *adv.*

su·per·er·o·ga·tion, sō″pėr·er″o·gā′shan, *n.* [L. *supererogo, supererogatum,* to pay over and above.] Performance of more than duty requires; superfluous action.—**su·- per·e·rog·a·to·ry,** sō″pėr·e·rog′a·tōr″ē, sō″pėr·e·rog′a·tar″ē, *a.*

su·per·fam·i·ly, sō″pėr·fam″i·lē, sō″pėr·- fam″lē, *n. pl.* **su·per·fam·i·lies.** *Biol.* a group or category ranking above a family.

su·per·fe·cun·da·tion, sō″pėr·fē″kun·- dā′shan, sō″pėr·fek″un·dā′shan, *n.* Fertil- ization of two ova during the same men- strual cycle by two different acts of coition.

su·per·fe·ta·tion, sō″pėr·fē·tā′shan, *n.* A second conception after a prior one, and by which two fetuses exist at once in the same womb.

su·per·fi·cial, sō″pėr·fish′al, *a.* [L. *super- ficialis.*] Lying on or pertaining to the surface; not penetrating the substance of a thing; not deep or profound as regards knowledge; not learned or thorough; not going to the heart of things; not genuine; of measurements, square.—**su·per·fi·ci·- al·i·ty,** sō″pėr·fish″ē·al′i·tē, *n. pl.* **su·- per·fi·ci·al·i·ties.**—**sup·er·fi·cial·ly,** *adv.*—**su·per·fi·cial·ness,** *n.*

su·per·fi·ci·es, sō″pėr·fish′ē·ēz″, sō″pėr·- fish′ēz, *n. pl.* **su·per·fi·ci·es.** [L.] The surface; the appearance; the exterior part or face of a thing, consisting of length and breadth without thickness, and therefore forming no part of the substance or solid content of a body.

su·per·fine, sō″pėr·fīn′, *a.* Very fine; surpassing others in fineness; excessively or faultily subtle.

su·per·flu·id, sō″pėr·flō′id, *n. Phys.* A condensed degenerate gas theoretically described by physicists Bose and Einstein; the low quantum energy, low entropy liquid state of a gas, such as helium, which has two liquid states at a temperature approximately absolute zero; any fluid which exhibits near frictionless movement, high capillarity, and high heat conductiv- ity.—**su·per·flu·id·i·ty,** *n.*

su·per·flu·i·ty, sō″pėr·flō′i·tē, *n. pl.* **su·per·flu·i·ties.** [Fr. *superfluité,* L. *superfluitas,* < *superfluus,* overflowing.] A quantity that is over and above what is necessary; a greater quantity than is wanted; an excess; redundancy; something for show or luxury rather than for necessity.

su·per·flu·ous, su·pur′flō·us, *a.* [L. *super- fluus.*] Being more than is wanted; more than sufficient or necessary; in excess; redundant.—**su·per·flu·ous·ly,** *adv.*— **su·per·flu·ous·ness,** *n.*

su·per·gal·ax·y, sō″pėr·gal″ak·sē, *n. pl.* **su·per·gal·ax·ies.** *Astron.* A galactic sys- tem; a group of galaxies.

su·per·heat, sō″pėr·hēt′, *v.t.* To heat to an extreme degree; specifically, to heat steam, apart from contact with water, until it resembles a perfect gas; to heat, as a liquid, above its boiling point without vaporiza- tion.—sō′pėr·hēt′, *n.*—**su·per·heat·er,** *n.*

su·per·het·er·o·dyne, sō″pėr·het′ėr·o·- din″, *a. Electron.* noting or pertaining to a method of receiving radio signals by which the incoming wave is changed by the heterodyne process to a lower frequency, the 'intermediate frequency,' which is inaudible but more easily amplified, and then submitted to a number of stages of radiofrequency amplification with sub- sequent detection and audiofrequency amplification.—*n.* A superheterodyne re- ceiver.

su·per·high fre·quen·cy, sō′pėr·hī″ frē′- kwen·sē, *n. Radio,* the electromagnetic frequencies in the radio band between 3,000 and 30,000 megacycles. Abbr. *shf, s.h.f., SHF, S.H.F.*

su·per·high·way, sō″pėr·hī′wā″, *n.* A high-speed, multilane highway often with safety medians and limited access inter- changes.

su·per·hu·man, sō″pėr·hū′man, sō″pėr·- ū′man, *a.* Above or beyond what is human; divine.—**su·per·hu·man·i·ty,** sō″pėr·hū″- man′i·tē, sō″pėr·ū″man′i·tē, *n.*—**su·per·- hu·man·ly,** *adv.*—**su·per·hu·man·ness,** *n.*

su·per·im·pose, sō″pėr·im·pōz′, *v.t.*— *superimposed, superimposing.* To lay or im- pose on something else; to add (something) over something else.—**su·per·im·pos·a·- ble,** *a.*—**su·per·im·po·si·tion,** sō″pėr·- im″po·zish′an, *n.*

su·per·in·cum·bent, sō″pėr·in·kum′- bent, *a.* Lying or resting on something else.—**su·per·in·cum·bence, su·per·in·- cum·ben·cy,** *n.*—**su·per·in·cum·bent·ly,** *adv.*

su·per·in·duce, sō″pėr·in·dōs′, sō″pėr·- in·dūs′, *v.t.*—*superinduced, superinducing.* To bring in or on as an addition to some- thing.—**su·per·in·duc·tion,** sō″pėr·in·- duk′shan, *n.*

su·per·in·tend, sō″pėr·in·tend′, sō″prin·- tend′, *v.t.* [L. *superintendo,* to have the oversight of.] To have the charge and oversight of; to oversee with the power of direction; to take care of with authority.— **su·per·in·tend·ence, su·per·in·tend·- en·cy,** sō″pėr·in·ten′den·sē, sō″prin·ten′- den·sē, *n.*

su·per·in·tend·ent, sō″pėr·in·ten′dent, sō″prin·ten′dent, *n.* One who super- intends or has the oversight and charge of something; a manager; a maintenance supervisor in an apartment building who acts as the agent of the owner. Abbr. *super., supt., Supt.*—*a.*

su·pe·ri·or, su·pēr′ē·ėr, su·pēr′ē·ėr, *a.* [L. compar. of *superus,* upper, high, < *super,* above.] More elevated in place; higher; upper; higher in rank, office, or quality; excellent; unaffected by some power or influence, usu. followed by *to*; as, *superior to* revenge; supercilious; as, putting on *superior* airs; *print.* superscript; *bot.* growing above or upon another, esp. denoting the ovary growing above the origin of the calyx and corolla.—**su·pe·ri·or·- i·ty,** su·pēr″ē·ar′i·tē, su·pēr″ē·or′i·tē, su·pēr″ē·ar′i·tē, su·pēr″ē·or′i·tē, *n.*— **su·pe·ri·or·ly,** *adv.*

su·pe·ri·or, su·pēr′ē·ėr, su·pēr′ē·ėr, *n.* One who is superior to another or others in social station, rank, power, excellence, or qualities of any kind; *eccles.* the chief of a monastery, convent, or abbey.

su·pe·ri·or con·junc·tion, *n. Astron.* the conjunction of a planet or other celestial body and the sun, in which the sun is interposed between the celestial body and the earth.

su·pe·ri·or court, *n.* A court of general jurisdiction; a court having original juris- diction in which proceedings with a jury are conducted.

su·pe·ri·or gen·er·al, *n. pl.* **su·pe·ri·- ors gen·er·al.** In a religious order or con- gregation, the ecclesiastical head.

su·pe·ri·or·i·ty com·plex, *n.* A feeling that one is generally superior to other people, often accompanied by a high degree of self-assertion. Also **su·pe·ri·or·i·ty feel·ing.**

su·pe·ri·or plan·et, *n. Astron.* any of those planets that are more distant from the sun than the earth is, as Mars, Jupiter, Saturn, Uranus, and Neptune.

su·per·ja·cent, sō″pėr·jā′sent, *a.* [L. *super,* above, and *jacens, jacentis,* ppr. of *jaceo,* to lie.] Lying directly above or upon.

su·per·la·tive, su·pur′la·tiv, su·pur′la·- tiv, *a.* [L. *superlativus,* < *superlatus—super,* over, and *latus,* carried.] Of the highest rank or degree; most eminent; surpassing all others; excessive; *gram.* referring to that form of an adjective or adverb which expresses the highest or utmost degree of comparison.—**su·per·la·tive·ly,** *adv.*— **su·per·la·tive·ness,** *n.*

su·per·la·tive, su·pur′la·tiv, su·pur′la·- tiv, *n.* That which is of the highest rank or degree. *Gram.* the superlative degree of adjectives or adverbs; a word in the super- lative degree.

su·per·lin·er, sō″pėr·lī″nėr, *n.* A luxury ocean liner of exceptional size and speed.

su·per·lu·nar, sō″pėr·lō′nėr, *a.* Beyond the moon, as opposed to *sublunary* or *earthly;* heavenly; celestial. Also **su·per·- lu·na·ry.**

su·per·man, sō″pėr·man″, *n. pl.* **su·per·- men.** [Transl. G. *übermensch.*] An ideal superior being conceived by the 19th century German philosopher Nietzsche as the product of human evolution, being in effect a ruthless egoist of superior strength, cunning, and force of will; a man who prevails by virtue of such characteristics; a man of seemingly more than human powers.

su·per·mar·ket, sō″pėr·mär″kit, *n.* A large retail market selling food and other household items and usu. operating on a self-service, cash-and-carry basis, esp. one of a chain of such markets.

su·per·nal, su·pur′nal, *a.* [L. *supernus,* < *super,* above.] Being or coming from above; lofty; relating to things above the world and worldly concerns; celestial; heavenly; ethereal; divine.—**su·per·nal·ly,** *adv.*

su·per·na·tant, sō″pėr·nāt′ant, *a.* [L.] Swimming or floating on the surface.—*n.*

su·per·nat·u·ral, sō″pėr·nach′ėr·al, *a.* Transcending actual or potentially natural phenomena; referring to divine, ghostly, or infernal transcendence or violation of what are assumed to be natural laws; miraculous; eerie.—*n.* Anything super- natural; supernatural beings, actions, or happenings, preceded by *the*; existence or forces above the natural, preceded by *the.*— **su·per·nat·u·ral·ly,** *adv.*—**su·per·nat·- u·ral·ness,** *n.*

su·per·nat·u·ral·ism, sō″pėr·nach′ėr·a·- liz″um, *n.* The state of being supernatural; belief in pervasive supernatural interven- tion.—**su·per·nat·u·ral·ist,** *n., a.*—**su·- per·nat·u·ral·is·tic,** *a.*

su·per·nor·mal, sō″pėr·nar′mal, *a.* Above or beyond what is normal; beyond average human intelligence or ability.—**su·per·- nor·mal·i·ty,** sō″pėr·nar·mal′i·tē, *n.*— **su·per·nor·mal·ly,** *adv.*

su·per·no·va, sō″pėr·nō′va, *n. pl.* **su·- per·no·vae,** sō″pėr·nō″vas, sō″pėr·nō′vē. *Astron.* a rarely observed, exploding star which achieves a brightness as much as 100 million times greater than that of the sun.

su·per·nu·mer·ar·y, sō″pĕr·nŏ″me·rer″ē, sō″pĕr·nū″me·rer″ē, *n.* pl. **su·per·nu·mer·ar·ies.** A person or thing beyond what is necessary or usual; an actor who appears briefly on stage, usu. in a nonspeaking role.—*a.* Exceeding a designated, necessary, or usual number; extra; superfluous.

su·per·or·der, sō″pĕr·ar″dĕr, *n. Biol.* a group or category ranking above an order and below a class.

su·per·or·di·nate, sō″pĕr·ar′di·nit, *a.* More elevated in rank, class, or condition; *logic,* referring to the relation of a universal proposition to a particular proposition with the same terms.—*n.*—sō″pĕr·ar′di·nāt′, *v.t.*—*superordinated, superordinating.*

su·per·or·di·na·tion, sō″pĕr·ar″di·nā′shan, *n. Logic,* a superordinate relationship; *eccles.* the ordination of his successor by a currently serving ecclesiastical official.

su·per·phos·phate, sō″pĕr·fos′fāt, *n.* A fertilizer consisting of a specially soluble mixture of calcium acid phosphate and calcium sulfate.

su·per·phys·i·cal, sō″pĕr·fiz′i·kal, *a.* Above or beyond what is physical; hyperphysical.

su·per·pose, sō″pĕr·pōz′, *v.t.*—*superposed, superposing.* [Fr. *superposer,* < L. *super,* over, and Fr. *poser,* put.] To place above or upon something else or one upon another; *geom.* to place, as one configuration over another, so that all corresponding parts coincide.—**su·per·pos·a·ble,** *a.*—**su·per·posed,** *a.*—**su·per·po·si·tion,** sō″pĕr·po·zish′an, *n.*

su·per·pow·er, sō″pĕr·pou″ĕr, *n.* Power on an extraordinary or extensive scale; a nation or bloc of nations having great political power, capable of influencing the actions of smaller countries; electric power on an extraordinary scale, secured by the linking together of a number of separate power systems with a view toward more efficiency and economy.—**su·per·pow·ered,** *a.*

su·per·sat·u·rate, sō″pĕr·sach′u·rāt″, *v.t.*—*supersaturated, supersaturating. Chem.* to saturate to excess or beyond normal, under known conditions of temperature and pressure; as, to *supersaturate* a solution.—**su·per·sat·u·ra·tion,** *n.*

su·per·scribe, sō″pĕr·skrīb′, sō″pĕr·skrīb″, *v.t.*—*superscribed, superscribing.* [L. *superscribo*—*super,* over or above, and *scribo,* to write.] To write on the top, outside, or surface of, as a name or address; to put an inscription on.

su·per·script, sō″pĕr·skript″, *n.* A sign, letter, or numeral positioned high on a line of writing, as the 2 in x^2.—*a.*

su·per·scrip·tion, sō″pĕr·skrip′shan, *n.* The act of superscribing; that which is written or engraved on the outside of or above something else; an address in a letter or parcel; *phar.* the symbol ℞ in a prescription, which means 'take.'

su·per·sede, sō″pĕr·sēd′, *v.t.*—*superseded, superseding.* [L. *supersedere* (pp. *supersessus*), sit above, be superior to, desist, M.L. stay, postpone.] To replace in power, authority, effectiveness, acceptance, or use, as by another person or thing; to set aside as void, useless, or obsolete, usu. in favor of something mentioned, as: The incompetent officer was *superseded* by another. To succeed to the position, function, or office of; to supplant.—**su·per·sed·er,** *n.*

su·per·se·de·as, sō″pĕr·sē′dĕ·as, sō″pĕr·sē′dē·as″, *n.* pl. **su·per·se·de·as.** [M.L., 'thou shalt stay.'] *Law,* a writ having the effect of a command to stay judicial proceedings.

su·per·se·dure, sō″pĕr·sē′jĕr, *n.* The act of superseding or the state of being superseded.

su·per·sen·si·ble, sō″pĕr·sen′si·bl, *a.* Beyond the awareness of the senses; spiritual.

su·per·sen·si·tive, sō″pĕr·sen′si·tiv, *a.* Extremely, excessively, or abnormally sensitive.—**su·per·sen·si·tive·ly,** *adv.*—**su·per·sen·si·tive·ness,** *n.*

su·per·sen·so·ry, sō″pĕr·sen′so·rē, *a.* Beyond or above the organs of sense; extrasensory.

su·per·serv·ice·a·ble, sō″pĕr·sur′vi·sa·bl, *a.* Too zealous or anxious to be of service; officious.—**su·per·serv·ice·a·ble·ness,** *n.*

su·per·ses·sion, sō″pĕr·sesh′an, *n.* [M.L. *supersessio(n-),* < L. *supersedere,* E. *supersede.*] The act of removing or setting aside; supersedure.—**su·per·ses·sive,** *a.*

su·per·son·ic, sō″pĕr·son′ik, *a. Aerodynamics,* pertaining to or attaining speeds greater than that of sound; as, a *supersonic* aircraft; *acoustics,* of or pertaining to frequencies above those that can be heard by the human ear. See *ultrasonic.*—**su·per·son·i·cal·ly,** *adv.*

su·per·son·ics, sō″pĕr·son′iks, *n.* pl. but sing. in constr. That branch of science that treats of supersonic speeds or other supersonic phenomena.

su·per·son·ic trans·port, *n. Aeron.* an airplane designed and built to transport passengers, cargo, or both great distances at speeds faster than the speed of sound.

su·per·sti·tion, sō″pĕr·stish′an, *n.* [O.Fr. *superstition,* < L. *superstitio(n-),* appar. orig. a standing still over a thing as in wonder or awe, < *superstare,* stand over or upon.] Irrational fear of what is unknown or mysterious, esp. in connection with religion; a religious system, belief, or practice founded on irrational fear or credulity; a particular instance or form of such belief; any ceremony or practice inspired by such belief; faith in magic or chance; reverence for charms, omens, signs; a belief or notion entertained, either popularly or by an individual, regardless of reason or knowledge, of the ominous significance of a particular thing, circumstance, occurrence, proceedings, or the like; as, the *superstitions* about Friday, the number 13, a black cat, a four-leaf clover; any blindly accepted belief or notion, as the divine right of kings.

su·per·sti·tious, sō″pĕr·stish′us, *a.* [O.Fr. Fr. *superstitieux,* < L. *superstitiosus.*] Full of or addicted to superstition; of the nature of, characterized by, or proceeding from superstition; pertaining to or connected with superstition.—**su·per·sti·tious·ly,** *adv.*—**su·per·sti·tious·ness,** *n.*

su·per·stra·tum, sō″pĕr·strā″tum, sō′pĕr·strat″um, *n.* pl. **su·per·stra·ta, su·per·stra·tums.** A stratum or layer above or overlying another.

su·per·struc·ture, sō″pĕr·struk″chĕr, *n.* Any structure built on something else, esp. all of a building above the basement or foundation; anything erected on some foundation or basis, as a concept; the rolling stock, rails, ties, and the like of a railroad, as distinguished from the roadbed; *naut.* the structure of a ship built above the main deck; as, the *superstructure* of an aircraft carrier.—**su·per·struc·tur·al,** *a.*

su·per·sub·tle, sō″pĕr·sut′l, *a.* Extremely or excessively subtle; oversubtle.—**su·per·sub·tle·ty,** *n.*

su·per·tank·er, sō″pĕr·tang″kĕr, *n. Naut.* a fast tanker with a minimum capacity of 75,000 tons.

su·per·tax, sō″pĕr·taks″, *n. Chiefly Brit.* an extra tax, usu. graduated, on incomes above a fixed amount. *U.S.* a surtax.

su·per·ton·ic, sō″pĕr·ton′ik, *n. Mus.* The tone next above the tonic or key note; the second tone of the diatonic scale.

su·per·vene, sō″pĕr·vēn′, *v.i.*—*supervened, supervening.* [L. *supervenio*—*super,* above, over, and *venio,* to come.] To take place or happen as something supplementary, extraneous, or unforeseen; to occur immediately after something.—**su·per·ven·tion,** *n.*

su·per·ven·ient, sō″pĕr·vēn′yent, *a.* Coming as something additional, extraneous, or unforeseen; arising or occurring soon afterward.—**su·per·ven·ience,** sō″pĕr·vēn′yens, *n.*

su·per·vise, sō″pĕr·vīz″, *v.t.*—*supervised, supervising.* [L.] To oversee in order to direct, as employees; to be charged with overseeing; to superintend; to inspect.—**su·per·vi·sion,** sō″pĕr·vizh′an, *n.*

su·per·vi·sor, sō″pĕr·vī″zĕr, *n.* One who supervises; an overseer; an inspector; a superintendent; an administrative official.—**su·per·vi·so·ry,** sō″pĕr·vī′zo·rē, *a.*

su·pi·nate, sō′pi·nāt″, *v.t.*—*supinated, supinating.* [L. *supinatus,* pp. of *supinare,* bend backward, lay on the back, < *supinus,* E. *supine, a.*] To render supine; rotate or place, as the hand or forelimb, so that the palmar surface is upward when the limb is stretched forward horizontally; to rotate, as a limb or joint, upward and away from the midline of the body.—*v.i.* To become supinated.

su·pi·na·tion, sō′pi·nā′shan, *n.* The position of the hand extended with palm upward; the rotating of a limb or joint upward and away from the midline of the body.

su·pi·na·tor, sō′pi·nā″tĕr, *n. Anat.* a muscle which aids in turning the palm of the hand upward.

su·pine, sō·pīn′, *a.* [L. *supinus,* bent backward, lying on the back, inactive, indolent.] Lying on the back, or with the face or front upward; having the palm of the hand upward. *Fig.* inactive; passive; inert; esp. inactive or passive from indolence or indifference.—sō′pīn, *n. Gram.* A part of the Latin verb, really a verbal noun, having two forms, an accusative used with verbs of motion, ending in -*um,* and an ablative used with adjectives, ending in -*u;* an analogous form in some other language.—**su·pine·ly,** *adv.*—**su·pine·ness,** *n.*

sup·per, sup′ĕr, *n.* [O.Fr. *soper* (Fr. *souper*), noun use of inf.] The evening meal; the last meal of the day, taken in the evening; any evening repast, often one forming a social entertainment.

sup·plant, su·plant′, su·plänt′, *v.t.* [L. *supplantare,* trip up, overthrow, < *sub,* under, and *planta,* sole of the foot.] To turn out or displace, as a person, esp. by treacherous or underhand means, in order to take his place; take the place of another, as in office or favor, through scheming or strategy. To displace or supersede, as one thing does another; replace, as a thing, by something else.—**sup·plan·ta·tion,** sup″lan·tā′shan, *n.*—**sup·plant·er,** *n.*

sup·ple, sup′l, *a.*—*suppler, supplest.* [O.Fr. Fr. *souple,* < L. *supplex* (*supplic-*), suppliant, lit. 'bending under' (as in kneeling), < *sub,* under, and -*plex,* akin to *plicare,* fold: cf. *supplicate.*] Bending readily without breaking or deformation; as, *supple* leather; pliant; flexible; characterized by ease in bending; as, *supple* joints; limber; lithe; characterized by ease and adaptability in mental action; as, a *supple* mind; conforming readily to circumstances or to the will or humor of others; compliant or yielding; obsequious; servilely or unscrupulously accommodating or complaisant.—*v.t., v.i.*—*suppled, suppling.* To make or become supple.—**sup·ple·ly,** **sup·ply,** *adv.*—**sup·ple·ness,** *n.*

sup·ple·jack, sup'l·jak″, *n.* A strong, pliant cane or walking stick; any of various climbing shrubs with strong stems suitable for making walking sticks.

sup·ple·ment, sup'le·ment, *n.* [L. *supplementum*, < *suppleo*, to fill up, to make full.] An addition to anything, esp. a book, magazine, or other publication, by which it is made fuller, more correct, up-to-date, or complete; that which adds or supplies what is lacking or insufficient; *math.* the quantity by which an arc or an angle falls short of 180° or a semicircle.—sup'le·ment', *v.t.*—To increase or complete by a supplement; to furnish what is lacking. —**sup·ple·men·tal,　su·ple·men·ta·ry,** sup″le·men'tal,　sup″le·men'ta·rē, *a.*— **sup·ple·men·ta·tion,** sup″le·men·tā'shan, *n.*—**sup·ple·to·ry,** sup'li·tōr″ē, sup'li·tạr″ē, *a.*

sup·ple·men·ta·ry an·gles, *n. pl.* Two angles which together equal 180°.

sup·ple·tion, su·plē'shan, *n. Gram.* the occurrence of an allomorph that fits into a paradigm with another allomorph but is not phonemically related to it, as the verb form 'hasten' of 'haste.'—**sup·ple·tive,** su·plē'tiv, sup'li·tiv, *a.*

sup·pli·ance, sup'lē·ans, *n.* Entreaty; an act of supplication. Also **sup·pli·an·cy.**

sup·pli·ant, sup'lē·ant, *a.* [Fr. *suppliant*, ppr. of *supplier*, to entreat, < L. *supplico*, to supplicate.] Entreating or begging earnestly; asking earnestly and humbly.—*n.* A humble petitioner.—**sup·pli·ant·ly,** *adv.*

sup·pli·cant, sup'li·kant, *n.* One who supplicates; a humble petitioner.—*a.* Earnestly entreating; suppliant.—**sup·pli·cat·ing·ly,** *adv.*

sup·pli·cate, sup'li·kāt″, *v.t.*—supplicated, supplicating. [L. *supplico, supplicatum*, < *supplex, supplicis*, suppliant, lit. 'bending under,' whence *supple*.] To entreat or beg humbly for; to seek by earnest prayer; as, to *supplicate* blessings; to petition humbly; as, to *supplicate* God.—*v.i.* To petition with earnestness; to implore.—**sup·pli·ca·tion,** sup″li·kā'shan, *n.*—**sup·pli·ca·to·ry,** sup'·li·ka·tōr″ē, sup'li·ka·tạr″ē, *a.*

sup·ply, su·plī', *v.t.*—supplied, supplying. [O.Fr. *supplier, soupleier* (Fr. *suppléer*), < L. *supplere* (pp. *suppletus*), fill up, complete, supply.] To furnish with what is lacking or requisite; as, to *supply* an army; to furnish or provide, followed by *with*; as, to *supply with* money; to afford; to make up, as a deficiency; to make up for or compensate for, as a loss, lack, or absence; to satisfy, as a want, need, or demand; to fill, as a place or vacancy; to occupy as a substitute; to make up for the want of, take the place of, or serve as a substitute for.—*v.i.* To fill the place of another, esp. to substitute for the minister of a church.—*n. pl.* **sup·plies.** The act of supplying, furnishing, providing, or satisfying; that which is supplied; a quantity of something provided or on hand, as for use; a stock or store; *usu. pl.* a provision, stock, or store of food or other things necessary for maintenance; as, *supplies* for an army. A sum of money provided by a national legislature to meet the expenses of government; one who supplies a vacancy or takes the place of another, esp. temporarily; a clergyman who officiates in a vacant charge or in the temporary absence of the pastor; *pol. econ.* the quantity of a commodity that is on the market and available for purchase at a particular price.—**sup·pli·a·ble,** *a.*—**sup·pli·er,** *n.*

sup·port, su·pōrt', su·pạrt', *v.t.* [O.Fr. Fr. *supporter*, < L. *supportare*, < *sub*, under, and *portare*, carry.] To bear or hold up, as a load, mass, part, or structure; to sustain or withstand without giving way; to undergo, endure, or bear with fortitude, patience, or submission; tolerate; to sustain, as a person, the mind, spirits, or courage, under trial or affliction; to maintain, as a person, family, or institution, by supplying with things necessary to existence; provide for; to uphold, as a person, cause, or policy, by aid or countenance; to maintain or advocate, as a theory or cause; to corroborate. *Theatr.* to act with or second, as a leading actor; to assist in any performance.—*n.* The act of supporting; the state of being supported; maintenance, as of a person or family, with necessities, means, or funds; a thing or a person that supports.— **sup·port·a·ble,** *a.*—**sup·port·a·ble·ness,** *n.*—**sup·port·a·bly,** *adv.*—**sup·port·ive,** *a.*

sup·port·er, su·pōr'tẽr, su·pạr'tẽr, *n.* One who aids, maintains, or supports another person, or a cause or thing; a defender; an advocate or adherent; something which holds or keeps up, as a prop or pillar; a garter or bind which supports some part of the clothing or body, as an elastic bandage; *her.* a figure on each side of a shield appearing to support it.

sup·pos·al, su·pō'zal, *n.* The act of supposing; a supposition; an idea; a surmise or conjecture.

sup·pose, su·pōz', *v.t.*—supposed, supposing. [Fr. *supposer*.] To lay down or regard as fact for the sake of argument or illustration, as: *Suppose* the shipment is delayed. To suggest or propose, as: *Suppose* we postpone our decision until next week. To assume or take for granted, as: I *suppose* he will go. To imagine, as: I *suppose* you want a definite answer. To demand or expect, used in the passive, as: Aren't you *supposed* to be at work? To imply or presuppose, as: Creation *supposes* a creator.— *v.i.* To make or form a supposition; to think.—**sup·pos·a·ble,** *a.*—**sup·pos·a·bly,** *adv.*—**sup·posed,** *a.*—**sup·pos·ed·ly,** *adv.*—**sup·pos·ing,** *conj.* Provided that; in the event that.

sup·po·si·tion, sup″o·zish'an, *n.* The act of supposing; what is assumed hypothetically; an assumption; a conjecture; hypothesis.—**sup·po·si·tion·al,** *a.*—**sup·po·si·tion·al·ly,** *adv.*—**sup·pos·i·tive,** su·poz'·i·tiv, *a.*—**sup·pos·i·tive·ly,** *adv.*

sup·pos·i·ti·tious, su·poz″i·tish'us, *a.* [L. *supposititius*, < *suppono, suppositum*—*sub*, under, and *pono*, to place.] Put by trick in the place belonging to another; substituted falsely; not genuine; spurious; based on hypothesis or supposition.— **sup·pos·i·ti·tious·ly,** *adv.*—**sup·pos·i·ti·tious·ness,** *n.*

sup·pos·i·to·ry, su·poz'i·tōr″ē, su·poz'i·tạr″ē, *n. pl.* **sup·pos·i·to·ries.** [M.L. *suppositorium*, prop. neut. of L.L. *suppositorius*, placed under, < L. *supponere* (pp. *suppositus*).] *Med.* a mass of some prepared substance, usu. in the form of a cone or cylinder, for introduction into the rectum, vagina, or urethra.

sup·press, su·pres', *v.t.*—[L. *supprimo, suppressum*—*sub*, under, and *premo, presum*, to press.] To overpower and crush; to put down; to quell, as a revolt, mutiny, or riot; to restrain from utterance; to conceal, as one's feelings; not to tell or reveal, as news; to retain without making public.— **sup·press·i·ble,** *a.*—**sup·pres·sor,** *n.*

sup·pres·sion, su·presh'an, *n.* The act of suppressing; the state of being suppressed; the deliberate, conscious retention of an utterance, action, impulse, or desire; the concealment or withholding of information or facts from public notice.—**sup·pres·sive,** *a.*

sup·pu·rate, sup'ya·rāt″, *v.i.*—suppurated, suppurating. [L. *suppuro, supuratum*.] To generate pus or matter; to contain pus; fester.—**sup·pu·ra·tion,** sup″ū·rā'shan, sup″ya·rā'shan, *n.*—**sup·pu·ra·tive,** *n.* Something that promotes suppuration, esp. a drug.—*a.*

su·pra·lim·i·nal, sö″pra·lim'i·nal, *a.* [L. *supra*, above, and *limen* (*limin-*), threshold.] *Psychol.* Above the limen or threshold of consciousness; of or in consciousness: opposed to *subliminal*.—**su·pra·lim·i·nal·ly,** *adv.*

su·pra·mo·lec·u·lar, sö″pra·mo·lek'ū·lẽr, *a. Chem.* Of greater complexity than a molecule; composed of an aggregation of molecules.

su·pra·na·tion·al, sö″pra·nash'a·nal, *a.* Outside the authority of any one nation or national government; as, *supranational* cooperation.

su·pra·or·bit·al, sö″pra·ạr'bi·tal, *a. Anat.* situated or being above the orbit of the eye.

su·pra·pro·test, sö·pra·prō'test, *n.* [N.L. *supra protestum*, for It. *sopra protesto*, upon protest.] *Law*, an acceptance or a payment of a bill by a third person for the honor of the drawer, after protest for nonacceptance or nonpayment by the drawee.

su·pra·re·nal, sö″pra·rēn'al, *a.* [L. *supra*, above, and *renes*, the kidneys.] *Anat.* Situated above the kidneys; pertaining to an adrenal gland.—*n. Anat.* an adrenal gland or other suprarenal part.

su·pra·re·nal gland, *n.* Adrenal gland.

su·prem·a·cy, su·prem'a·sē, su·prem'a·sē, *n. pl.* **su·prem·a·cies.** The state or character of being supreme; highest authority or power.—**su·prem·a·cist,** *n.*

su·preme, su·prēm', su·prēm', *a.* [L. *supremus*, < *superus*, upper, higher, < *super*, above.] Highest in authority; holding the highest place in government or power; sovereign; dominant; highest as to quality or degree; greatest possible; utmost; last or ultimate; final.—**su·preme·ly,** *adv.*—**su·preme·ness,** *n.*

Su·preme Be·ing, *n.* God.

Su·preme Court, *n.* The Federal court which is highest in the judicial system of the United States; the highest appellate court in most states.

su·ra, su·rah, sur'a, *n.* [Ar.] *Islam*, a chapter of the Koran.

su·rah, sur'a, *n.* [Appar. < *Surat*, city and district of northern Bombay, India.] A soft twilled fabric made of silk or rayon. *Islam*, sura.

sur·base, sur'bās″, *n. Arch.* The crowning molding or cornice of a pedestal or the like; a border or molding above the base.

sur·based, sur'bāst″, *a.* [Fr. *surbaissé*, < *sur-* and *baissé*, pp. of *bassier*, lower, < L.L. *bassus*, low, E. *base*.] *Arch.* Having a surbase; flattened or depressed; having a rise that is less than half the span, as an arch or vault.

sur·cease, sur·sēs', *v.i.*—surceased, surceasing. [O.Fr. Fr. *sursis*, pp. of *surseoir*, < L. *supersedere*, desist.] *Archaic*. To cease from some action, or desist; to come to an end.—*v.t. Archaic*. To cease from; leave off.—*n. Archaic*. End; a cessation.

sur·charge, sur'chärj″, *n.* An extra tax, charge, or cost; an overcharge; an excessive burden; an addition overprinted on a stamp which in some way differentiates it or changes its denomination; *law*, an act of surcharging.—sur·chärj', sur'chärj″, *v.t.*—surcharged, surcharging. To add on an extra charge, cost, or tax; to overcharge; to overload to mark with a surcharge or new denomination; to show credit for, as an amount previously omitted.

sur·cin·gle, sur'sing″gl, *n.* [O.Fr. *sursangle*.] A belt or girth encircling a horse's body and fastening a saddle, pack, or the like on a horse's back; a girdle, esp. around a cassock.

sur·coat, sur'kōt″, *n.* An outer garment or coat; a loose robelike garment worn over a suit of armor during the Middle Ages.

sur·cu·lose, sur'kū·lōs″, sur'kya·lōs″, *a.* [L. *surculosus*, < *surculus*, shoot, sprout, sucker.] *Bot.* having or producing suckers.

surd, surd, *a.* [L. *surdus,* deaf, not sounding, stupid (seen also in *absurd*).] *Phon.* uttered with breath and not with the voice, as opposed to *sonant. Math.* irrational; not capable of being expressed in rational numbers.—*n. Phon.* a voiceless or nonsonant speech sound. *Math.* an irrational quantity; a quantity that cannot be expressed in finite terms, as the square root of two.

sure, shur, *a.*—*surer, surest.* [Fr. *sûr,* O.Fr. *seur, seür,* Pr. *segur,* < L. *securus,* unconcerned. The same word as *secure.*] Perfectly confident; knowing and believing; certain; fully persuaded; certain to find or retain; to be depended on; unfailing; firm; stable; secure; infallible; inevitable; destined.—*adv.* Certainly; without doubt.—**be sure,** be or do as designated.—**for sure,** a certainty.—**make sure,** secure; clinch.—**sure e·nough,** *colloq.* might have been supposed or expected.—**to be sure,** without doubt; admittedly; certainly.—**sure·ly,** *adv.*—**sure·ness,** *n.*

sure-fire, shur'fī ẽr", *a. Colloq.* Sure to succeed or to meet expectations; dependable; unfailing.

sure-foot·ed, shur'fut'id, *a.* Not liable to stumble, slip, or fall; not liable to err.—**sure-foot·ed·ly,** *adv.* In a sure-footed manner.—**sure-foot·ed·ness,** *n.*

sure·ty, shur'i·tē, shur'tē, *n.* pl. **sure·ties.** One responsible for another, called the principal, who is primarily liable; one who binds himself to stand for another; security against loss, damage, or default of payment; certainty; security; ground of security or safety; guarantee; a bail.—**sure·ty·ship,** *n.*

sure·ty bond, *n.* A written statement guaranteeing execution of a contract or agreement.

surf, surf, *n.* [For old *suffe,* the same as *sough;* or < a forgotten word of Ind. origin.] The swell of the sea which breaks upon a shore or upon sandbanks or rocks; the strip of foamy water deposited along a shore by breaking waves.—*v.i.* To float one's body or to ride a surfboard toward shore on cresting waves.—**surf·y,** *a.*—*surfier, surfiest.*

sur·face, sur'fis, *n.* [Fr. *surface,* < L. *super,* and *facies.*] An exterior layer or boundary of anything that has length and breadth; as, the *surface* of a solid or liquid; any face of an object; as, the *surface* of a coin; the total area of the outside or superficial boundaries; *fig.* outward or external appearance, as: Beneath the *surface* the company is in turmoil. *Geom.* having length and breadth only, as a figure; *aeron.* an airfoil.—*a.* External; superficial, as appearances; denoting movement by land or sea, as opposed to underground or air travel.—*v.t.*—*surfaced, surfacing.* To apply a particular surface to; to work over the surface of; to raise or bring to the surface, as a submerged object.—*v.i.* To come to the surface, as: The diver *surfaced* far from shore. *Min.* to work ore at or near the surface.—**sur·face·less,** *a.*—**sur·fac·er,** *n.*

sur·face-ac·tive, sur'fis·ak"tiv, *a. Chem.* pertaining to a substance which lowers the surface tension of a liquid in which it is dissolved or weakens the interface tension between two adjoining liquids, as: Detergents are *surface-active* agents. Also **sur·fac·tant.**

sur·face of rev·o·lu·tion, *n. Math.* any surface generated by revolving a plane curve about a line in the same plane.

sur·face plate, *n. Mach.* A perfectly flat plate used by machinists as a standard for testing the flatness of other surfaces.

sur·face ten·sion, *n.* An intermolecular force causing the free surface of a liquid to contract to its minimum possible area, due to the attraction of molecules within the liquid for those at its surface, as shown by drops of water assuming spherical shape.

sur·fac·ing, sur'fi·sing, *n.* The procedure or method of applying an outer layer to something, as a roadbed; the material composing a surface or used to surface something; the occurrence of a buried or submerged object rising to the surface of a surrounding substance; *min.* the working of ore deposits upon or near the surface.

surf·bird, surf'burd", *n.* A shore-inhabiting bird, *Aphriza virgata,* of the Pacific coast, allied to the turnstone.

surf·board, surf'bōrd", surf'bard", *n.* An oblong, buoyant board used to ride incoming waves in the sport of surfboarding.—*v.i.* To ride a surfboard.—**surf·board·er,** *n.*

surf·boat, surf'bōt", *n.* A strong, buoyant rowboat built to ride through heavy surf.

surf cast·ing, *n.* A technique of rod and reel fishing consisting of casting out into the water from the beach.—**surf cast·er,** *n.*

surf·feit, sur'fit, *n.* [O.Fr. *surfait,* excess—*sur,* and (L. *super*), over, and *fait,* pp. of *faire,* L. *facere,* to do.] An excessive amount or supply; intemperance or overindulgence, esp. in eating or drinking; physical discomfort from overeating or too much drink; a reaction of disgust to gluttony or intemperance.—*v.t.* To satiate or overload; to stuff or gorge; to disgust by excess.—*v.i.* To do anything excessively; to suffer from overindulgence.—**sur·feit·er,** *n.*

surf·fish, surf'fish", *n.* pl. **surf·fish, surf·fish·es.** Any of the small fishes constituting the family *Embiotocidae,* which produce live young rather than laying eggs, and inhabit the shallow waters of the Pacific coast of N. America.

surf·rid·ing, surf'rī"ding, *n.* The sport of riding the crests of waves on a surfboard. Also **surf·board·ing, surf·ing.**—**surf·rid·er, surf·er,** *n.*

surge, surj, *n.* [O.Fr. *surgeon, sourgeon,* a spring, a spouting up, < L. *surgere,* to rise.] A sudden or powerful flow; a large wave or billow; a great rolling swell of water; a heaving or swelling up; an undulation; *elect.* a sudden increase or fluctuation of current.—*v.i.*—*surged, surging.* To swell; to flow suddenly or powerfully; to rise high and roll, as waves; *naut.* to slip, as a rope around a capstan.—*v.t. Naut.* to slacken, as a rope.

sur·geon, sur'jon, *n.* [O.E. *chirurgeon,* O.Fr. *surgien,* contr. for *chirurgien,* < L. *chirurgus,* Gr. *cheirourgos,* a surgeon—*cheir,* the hand, and *ergon,* work.] A medical man who specializes in the practice of surgery: distinguished from a *physician.*

sur·geon·cy, sur'jon·sē, *n.* pl. **sur·geon·cies.** The rank or office of surgeon.

sur·geon gen·er·al, *n.* pl. **sur·geons gen·er·al, sur·geon gen·er·als.** A medical officer of high rank in the army, navy, or public health service. (Cap.) in the U.S. Army, the chief of the Medical Department; in the U.S. Navy, the chief of the Bureau of Medicine and Surgery. Abbr. *Surg. Gen.*

sur·geon's knot, *n.* Any of the knots used by a surgeon in tying ligatures or stitches, esp. the knot adapted from a reef knot.

sur·ger·y, sur'je·rē, *n.* pl. **sur·ger·ies.** [For *surgeonry.*] The practice which involves the performance of operations on the human subject to cure diseases or injuries of the body; the operative branch of medicine; a room where surgical operations are performed; *Brit.* the office of a physician.—**sur·gi·cal,** sur'ji·kal, *a.*—**sur·gi·cal·ly,** *adv.*

su·ri·cate, sur'i·kāt", *n.* [S. Afr. name.] A burrowing carnivorous animal, *Suricata suricatta,* of South Africa, resembling the polecat, mongoose, or ferret.

sur·ly, sur'lē, *a.*—*surlier, surliest.* [Old form *sirly* or *syrly;* prob. for *sir-like,* that is, magisterial, arrogant.] Sternly sour; cross and rude; churlish; rough or tempestuous.—*adv.*—**sur·li·ly,** *adv.*—**sur·li·ness,** *n.*

sur·mise, ser·mīz', sur'mīz, *n.* [O.Fr. *surmise,* accusation, < *surmettre,* pp. *surmis, surmise,* to accuse, < prefix *sur,* L. *super,* upon, above, and *mettre,* L. *mittere,* to send.] A thought or supposition with little or no ground to go upon; a guess or conjecture.—ser·mīz', *v.t.*—*surmised, surmising.* To guess; to conjecture.

sur·mount, sur·mount', *v.t.* [Fr. *surmonter.*] To mount or rise above; to overcome; to surpass; to be located over, above, or on top of; to position on top of or above.—**sur·mount·a·ble,** *a.*

sur·mul·let, ser·mul'it, *n.* pl. **sur·mul·lets, sur·mul·let.** [Fr. *surmulet,* for *sormulet,* < O.Fr. *sor,* reddish brown, sorrel, and *mulet,* a mullet.] A goatfish or variety of mullet.

sur·name, sur'nām", *n.* A name held in common by a family; family name; last name; a name added to the Christian or given name.—sur'nām", sur·nām', *v.t.* To give a surname to.

sur·pass, ser·pas', ser·päs', *v.t.* [Fr. *surpasser.*] To exceed; to be more than; to outdo; as, to *surpass* expectation; to excel, as in a profession; to go beyond, as in distance, limit, degree, amount, or the like.—**sur·pass·a·ble,** *a.*—**sur·pass·ing,** ser·pas'ing, ser·päs'ing, *a.*—**sur·pass·ing·ly,** *adv.*

sur·plice, sur'plis, *n.* [Fr. *surplis,* L.L. *superpellicium,* < L. *super,* over, and *pellicium,* a coat or tunic.] A white garment worn by priests, deacons, and choristers, as in the Roman Catholic Church, over their other dress at religious services.

sur·plus, sur'plus, sur'plus, *n.* [Fr. *surplus.*] That which remains when use or need is satisfied; that which more than suffices.—*a.*—**sur·plus·age,** sur'plus·ij, *n.*

sur·plus val·ue, *n. Marxian econ.* the value of labor inputs of workers which exceeds the wages and is regarded by the entrepreneur as profit.

sur·print, sur'print", *n.* An overprint; any additional mark added by printing; printed matter changed by printing new information directly over it.—*v.t.*

sur·prise, ser·prīz', *n.* [Fr. *surprise,* < *surpris,* pp. of *surprendre,* to surprise—prefix *sur* (L. *super*), over, and *prendre,* L. *prendere, prehendere,* to seize.] The act of coming upon unawares, or of taking suddenly and without preparation; an emotion excited by something happening suddenly and unexpectedly; wonder; astonishment.—*v.t.*—*surprised, surprising.* To fall upon suddenly and unexpectedly; to attack or take unawares; to confuse or perplex; to strike with wonder or astonishment; to astonish; to lead, bring, or betray unawares.—**sur·pris·al,** ser·prī'zal, *n.*—**sur·pris·er,** *n.*—**sur·pris·ing,** ser·prī'zing, *a.*—**sur·pris·ing·ly,** *adv.*

sur·ra, sur'a, *n. Veter. pathol.* a disease in horses, dogs, camels, and elephants caused by parasite protozoa common to the Old World, transmitted by horseflies, and marked by fever and bleeding.

sur·re·al·ism, su·rē'a·liz"um, *n.* [Fr. *surréalisme.*] (*Sometimes cap.*) an early 20th century movement in literature and art based on the expression of nonrational thought, and seeking to suggest the activities of the subconscious mind by use of incongruous juxtapositions of ideas or images.—**sur·re·al·ist,** *n., a.*—**sur·re·al·is·tic,** *a.*—**sur·re·al·is·ti·cal·ly,** *adv.*

sur·re·but·tal, sur'ri·but'al, *n. Law,* the giving of evidence by the plaintiff to meet a defendant's rebuttal.

---

a- fat, fāte, fär, fâre, fall;   **e-** met, mē, mēre, hèr;   **i-** pin, pīne;   **o-** not, nōte, mōve;   **u-** tub, cūbe, bull;   **oi-** oil;   **ou-** pound.

sur·re·but·ter, sur″ri·but′ėr, *n. Law,* the plaintiff's reply to a defendant's rebutter.

sur·re·join·der, sur″ri·join′dėr, *n. Law,* the answer of a plaintiff to a defendant's rejoinder.

sur·ren·der, su·ren′dėr, *v.t.* [Fr. *surrendre.*] To yield to the power of another or relinquish possession of; to abandon; to give or deliver up upon compulsion or demand; as, to *surrender* stolen money; to resign in favor of another; to cease to claim or use; to yield to some influence or emotion, said esp. of the self; to forfeit; as, to *surrender* a game by default.—*v.i.* To give up or yield to another's supremacy or power.—*n.* A yielding or giving up; an abandonment without rebate, as of an insurance policy after partial payment of premiums.

sur·rep·ti·tious, sur″ep·tish′us, *a.* [L. *surreptitius,* < L. *surrepo,* to creep stealthily.] Done or acquired by stealth or without proper authority; made or produced fraudulently; secretive or clandestine, as actions.—**sur·rep·ti·tious·ly,** *adv.*—**sur·rep·ti·tious·ness,** *n.*

sur·rey, sur′ē, sure′ē, *n. pl.* **sur·reys.** [From *Surrey,* county in southeastern England.] A light, four-wheeled, two-seated carriage with or without a top, seating four persons.

sur·ro·gate, sur′o·gāt, sur′o·git, sur′o·gāt″, sur′o·git, *n.* [L. *surrogatus,* substituted, pp. of *surrogo, surrogatum,* to put in another's place—*sub,* under, and *rogo,* to ask.] Someone acting in place of another, as a deputy; a substitute; in some states, a judicial officer of probate court; the deputy of an ecclesiastical judge, most commonly of a bishop or his chancellor.—sur′o·gāt, sur′o·gāt″, *v.t.*—*surrogated, surrogating.*

sur·round, su·round′, *v.t.* [O.Fr. *suronder,* to overflow.] To encompass or enclose on all sides; to envelop or encircle, as a city, so as to cut off escape or aid.—*n.*—**sur·round·er,** *n.*

sur·round·ing, su·roun′ding, *n.* An act or movement of encompassing. *Usu. pl.* those things which surround; an environment.—*a.*

sur-roy·al, sur·roi′al, *n.* A stag's topmost antler. Also *crown antler.*

sur·sum cor·da, sur′sum kōr′dä, sur′sum kar′dä, *n. Eccles.* a short responsive verse of the words, "Lift up your hearts," preceding the preface of the Mass. An inspiriting or inciting cry; an exaltation, as of God or spirit.

sur·tax, sur′taks″, *n.* [Prefix *sur,* above, and *tax.*] A heightened or extra tax in addition to the usual levy, esp. on incomes exceeding a specified amount.—sur′taks″, sur·taks′, *v.t.* To charge with such a tax.

sur·tout, sėr·tö′, sėr·töt′, *Fr.* SYR·tö′, *n.* A long, fitted overcoat.

sur·veil·lance, sėr·vā′lans, sėr·väl′yans, *n.* [Fr., < *surveiller,* to watch over.] Watch kept over some person or thing, esp. in the case of spying or guarding; superintendence.—**sur·veil·lant,** sėr·vā′lant, sėr·val′yant, *a., n.*

sur·vey, sėr·vā′, *v.t.* [O.Fr. *surveer, surveoir—sur* (L. *super*), over, and *veer, veoir* (Fr. *voir*), L. *videre,* to see.] To inspect or take a view of; to view, as from a high place; to view with a scrutinizing eye; to examine; to examine with reference to condition, situation, or value; to inspect for a purpose; to determine the boundaries, extent, position, or natural features of, as any portion of the earth's surface, by means of measurements and the application of geometry and trigonometry.—*v.i.* To practice the surveying of land.—sur′vā, sėr·vā′, *n.* A general view; a look at or over; a close examination or inspection to ascertain condition, quantity, or quality; a random sampling of facts and figures; the determination of dimensions and other topo-

graphical particulars of any part of the earth's surface; the plan or account drawn up of such particulars.—**sur·vey·or,** sėr·-vā′ėr, *n.*

sur·vey·ing, sėr·vā′ing, *n.* The act of one who surveys; the operation of making a survey of a portion of the earth's surface by means of measurements and calculations.

sur·vey·or's lev·el, *n.* A tripod-mounted spirit level and attached telescope used for sighting a level line.

sur·vey·or's meas·ure, *n.* A system of units of length based on Gunter's chain used in surveying land: 7.92 inches being equivalent to one link, 100 links being equivalent to one chain of 66 ft.

sur·viv·al, sėr·vī′val, *n.* The act of surviving; a living beyond the life of another person or beyond any event; any habit, usage, or belief remaining from ancient times and existing merely from custom.

sur·viv·al of the fit·test, *n.* The principle of natural selection that the animals and plants best suited to their surroundings survive while the others die out.

sur·viv·al val·ue, *n.* Value as related to the struggle for existence, as of a biological character.

sur·vive, sėr·vīv′, *v.t.*—*survived, surviving.* [Fr. *survivre,* < L. *supervivo.*] To outlive; to live beyond the life of; to live longer than; to live beyond; as, to *survive* one's usefulness.—*v.i.* To remain alive; to live after the death of another or after anything else.—**sur·vi·vor,** sėr·vī′vėr, *n.*—**sur·vi·vor·ship,** sėr·vī′vėr·ship″, *n.*

sus·cep·ti·bil·i·ty, su·sep″ti·bil′i·tē, *n.* The state or quality of being susceptible; sensitiveness; capacity for feeling or emotional excitement; sensibility; *elect.* the ratio between the intensity of magnetization in a magnetic substance and the magnetizing force producing it.

sus·cep·ti·ble, su·sep′ti·bl, *a.* [Fr. *susceptible,* < L. *suscipio, susceptum.*] Capable of being acted on or affected in any way; admitting any change; capable of emotional impression; readily impressed; impressible; sensitive.—**sus·cep·ti·ble·ness,** *n.*—**sus·cep·ti·bly,** *adv.*

sus·cep·tive, su·sep′tiv, *a.* Readily admitting or being affected by influence; susceptible.—**sus·cep·tive·ness,** *n.*—**sus·cep·tiv·i·ty,** sus″ep·tiv′i·tē, *n.*

sus·lik, sus′lik, *n.* [Russ.] A little marmot or ground squirrel, *Citellus citellus,* found in eastern Europe and western Asia; the fur of a suslik. Also **sous·lik,** sös′lik.

sus·pect, su·spekt′, *v.t.* [L. *suspicio, suspectum.*] To have a vague belief or fear of the existence of; to imagine as probably existing; as, to *suspect* danger; to mistrust; to imagine to be guilty upon slight evidence or without proof; to hold to be uncertain; to doubt.—*v.i.* To hold certain suspicions.—sus′pekt, *n.*—sus′pekt, su·spekt′, *a.*

sus·pend, su·spend′, *v.t.* [L. *suspendo.*] To hang; to cause for a time; to interrupt temporarily; to hold in an undetermined state; to debar for a time from any privilege; to remove temporarily from an office; to cause to cease for a time from operation or effect; to postpone or defer, as in sentencing.—*v.i.* To cease to meet obligations; to cease for a while.

sus·pend·ed an·i·ma·tion, *n.* A temporary cessation of vital bodily functions, esp. from asphyxia.

sus·pend·er, su·spen′dėr, *n.* One that suspends; *usu. pl.* a pair of braces for trousers; *Brit.* a garter.—**sus·pend·er belt,** *Brit.* a garter belt.

sus·pense, su·spens′, *n.* [L. *suspensus,* suspended.] A state of uncertainty, with more or less apprehension or anxiety; a situation giving rise to such a state; a sense

of insecurity; indetermination; indecision; *law,* a temporary cessation.—**sus·pense·ful,** *a.*

sus·pense ac·count, *n. Bookkeeping,* an account where credits or charges of unknown final disposition are placed until such disposition becomes known.

sus·pen·sion, su·spen′shan, *n.* [L. *suspensio, suspensionis.*] The act of suspending or hanging up; the act of delaying, interrupting, or stopping for a time; a cessation of operation; a stoppage; temporary abeyance; the parts of an automobile or railway car by which the chassis is connected to the axles in such a way as to cushion the movements of the chassis; the state of being in the form of particles floating undissolved in a fluid; *mus.* a note of a chord which is prolonged into the next chord to creat an effect of temporary dissonance.

sus·pen·sion bridge, *n.* A bridge, the roadway of which is suspended from ropes, chains, or wire cables usu. hung between massive towers of masonry or steel and securely fastened at the extremities.

sus·pen·sion points, *n. pl. Print.* a series of dots or periods signifying an omission of words.

sus·pen·sive, su·spen′siv, *a.* In suspense; uncertain; doubtful; halting temporarily; characterized by or relating to suspension.—**sus·pen·sive·ly,** *adv.*—**sus·pen·sive·ness,** *n.*

sus·pen·soid, su·spen′soid, *n. Physical chem.* a colloidal mixture in which the dispersed phase is solid.

sus·pen·sor, su·spen′sėr, *n.* Something which suspends; *bot.* the cord by which the embryo of some plants is suspended from the opening of the seed.—**sus·pen·so·ry,** su·spen′so·rē, *a., n.*

sus·pen·so·ry lig·a·ment, *n. Anat.* any of several fibrous tissues that support certain anatomical parts, esp. the ring-shaped tissue holding the eye's lens.

sus·pi·cion, su·spish′an, *n.* [L. *suspicio, suspicionis.*] The act of suspecting; the feeling of one who suspects; the thought or impression that there is probably something wrong without clear proof or evidence.—*v.t. Substandard,* to suspect.

sus·pi·cious, su·spish′us, *a.* [L. *suspiciosus.*] Tending to arouse suspicion; questionable; inclined to suspect; as, a *suspicious* husband; entertaining suspicion; indicating or exhibiting suspicion; as, *suspicious* glares.—**sus·pi·cious·ly,** *adv.*—**sus·pi·cious·ness,** *n.*

sus·pire, su·spī′ėr, *v.i.*—*suspired, suspiring.* [L. *suspiro,* to sigh.] *Liter.* To breathe with a long, deep breath; to sigh.—**sus·pi·ra·tion,** sus″pi·rā′shan, *n.*

sus·tain, su·stān′, *v.t.* [O.Fr. *sustenir, sostenir* (Fr. *soutenir*), < L. *sustinere.*] To support or bear up, esp. from underneath; to bear up against; to suffer, undergo, or endure without failing or yielding; to keep from sinking in despondence; as, to *sustain* one's mind; to nourish or furnish sustenance for; to aid or keep from ruin; to hold valid in law or to establish by evidence; to confirm or corroborate.—**sus·tain·a·ble,** *a.*—**sus·tain·er,** su·stā′nėr, *n.*—**sus·tain·ment,** *n.*

sus·tain·ing pro·gram, *n.* A television or radio program with no sponsor.

sus·te·nance, sus′te·nans, *n.* [O.Fr. *sustenance.*] That which supports life, as food or provisions; subsistence; the act of sustaining; the state of being supported or maintained.

sus·ten·tac·u·lar, sus″ten·tak′ū·lėr, sus″ten·tak′ya·lėr, *a. Anat.* supporting or sustaining.

sus·ten·ta·tion, sus′ten·tā′shan, *n.* [L. *sustentatio, sustento,* intens. of *sustineo.*]

Support; sustenance; support of life. Also **sus·ten·tion,** su·sten'shan.—**sus·ten·ta·tive, sus·ten·tive,** sus'ten·tā"tiv, su·sten'ta·tiv, su·sten'tiv, *a.*

su·sur·rus, su·sur'us, *n.* pl. **su·sur·rus·es.** [L.] A soft, humming, murmuring sound; a whisper; a rustling.—**su·sur·rant, su·sur·rous,** su·sur'ant, su·sur'us, *a.*—**su·sur·ra·tion,** sŏ"su·rā'shan, *n.*

sut·ler, sut'lẽr, *n.* [O.D. *soeteler,* D. *zoetelaar,* a sutler, < *soetelen,* to perform menial offices or dirty work.] A person who follows an army and sells to the troops provisions, liquors, or the like.

su·tra, sŏ'tra, *n.* [Skt., string.] A collection or string of aphorisms in Hindu literature; any of the sermons or scriptures of Buddhism.

sut·tee, su·tē', sut'ē, *n.* [Skt. *sati,* < *sat,* good, pure; prop. a chaste and virtuous wife.] A Hindu widow who immolates herself on the funeral pyre of her husband; the voluntary self-immolation by fire of a Hindu widow. Also *sati.*—**sut·tee·ism,** *n.*

su·ture, sŏ'chẽr, *n.* [L. *sutura,* < *suo,* to sew.] The act of sewing; a seam; the line along which two things or parts are joined; *surg.* the uniting of the lips or edges of a wound or incision by stitching; *anat.* one of the seams uniting the bones of the skull; *bot.* the seam of a dehiscent pericarp where the valves unite.—*v.t.*—*sutured, suturing.* To join with or as with a suture.—**su·tur·al,** *a.*—**su·tur·al·ly,** *adv.*

su·ze·rain, sŏ'ze·rin, sŏ'ze·rān", *n.* [Fr.] Formerly, a feudal lord or baron; a ruler or state which exercises political control over the foreign relations of a locally autonomous vassal state.—**su·ze·rain·ty,** sŏ'ze·rin·tē, sŏ'ze·rān"tē, *n.*

svelte, svelt, sfelt, *a.*—*svelter, sveltest.* [Fr., < It. *svelto,* pp. of *svellere,* < L. *ex-,* out, and *vellere,* pluck.] Slender, esp. gracefully slender in figure; lithe; urbane.—**svelte·ly,** *adv.*—**svelte·ness,** *n.*

swab, swob, *n.* [Same as Sw. *swab,* a mop; akin to D. *zwabber,* G. *schwabber,* Dan. *svabre,* a mop; cf. Prov. E. *swab,* G. *schwabbeln,* to splash; allied to *sweep.*] A mop for cleaning floors, ships' decks, and the like; a small bit of cotton or other material attached to a stick used in cleansing or in medicine as an applicator; a cleaner or sponge for the bore of a cannon; *slang,* an awkward, clumsy fellow.—*v.t.*—*swabbed, swabbing.* To clean with a swab or mop. Also *swob.*—**swab·ber,** *n.*

swab·bie, swab·by, swo'bē, *n.* *Slang,* a sailor.

swad·dle, swod'l, *v.t.*—*swaddled, swaddling.* [< O.E. *swaethil, swethel,* a swaddling band; same origin as *swathe.*] To swathe, or wrap with strips of various kinds of cloth, as an infant; to bind with a bandage.—*n.* A cloth band or strip used for the purpose of swaddling.

swad·dling clothes, *n. pl.* Cloth strips or bands wrapped about an infant, esp. a new-born; the time or period of immaturity or infancy; any rigid restrictions, limitations, or control, as on those who are immature.

swag, swag, *n.* A festoon, as of flowers or foliage; *slang,* booty or plunder; *Brit. dial.* a swaying or lurching movement.—*v.i.*—*swagged, swagging.* [Prob. < Scand.: cf. Norw. *svaga,* sway, also E. *sway* and *swagger.*] *Brit. dial.* to move heavily or unsteadily from side to side or up and down. Sway; to hang loosely and heavily; sink down.—*v.t.* To cause to sway, sink, or sag.

swage, swāj, *n.* [O.Fr. *souage,* form, fashion.] A tool used by blacksmiths for stamping or molding heated metal into a required form.—*v.t.*—*swaged, swaging.* To shape by means of a swage.

swage block, *n.* A heavy iron block con-taining holes and grooves of various sizes, used for heading bolts and shaping or swaging metal objects not easily worked on an anvil.

swag·ger, swag'ẽr, *v.i.* [A freq. < *swag;* cf. Swiss *schwaggeln,* to stroll about.] To strut with a proud, defiant, or insolent air; to boast noisily; to bluster; to brag.—*v.t.* To influence by blustering or threats; bully.—*n.* Bravado or insolence in manner; an arrogant strut.—**swag·ger·er,** *n.*—**swag·ger·ing,** swag'ẽr·ing, *a.*—**swag·ger·ing·ly,** *adv.*

swag·ger stick, *n.* A short stick or cane, often leather-covered and sometimes carried by army officers or soldiers.

Swa·hi·li, swä·hē'lē, *n.* pl. **Swa·hi·li, Swa·hi·lis.** A Bantu language influenced by Arabic that is the official language in much of East Africa; the Bantu people on Zanzibar Island and the Tanganyikan coast who speak this language.

swain, swān, *n.* [Same as Icel. *sveinn,* a youth, a servant; O.E. *swén,* Sw. *sven,* Dan. *svend,* O.E. *swán.*] *Poet.* A lover; a young man dwelling in the country; a peasant or rustic; a country gallant.—**swain·ish,** *a.*—**swain·ish·ness,** *n.*

swale, swāl, *n.* [Origin obscure.] A low place in the surface of the ground; a slight depression in a tract of land, usu. more moist and often with ranker vegetation than the adjacent higher land.

swal·low, swol'ō, *n.* [O.E. *swalewe, swealwe* = D. *zwaluw,* Icel. and Sw. *svala,* Dan. *svale,* G. *schwalbe,* a swallow.] *Ornith.* Any of certain passerine birds, family *Hirundinidae,* usu. having forked tails and long slim wings, and noted for their swift flight and rigid migratory habits; any of certain similar unrelated birds, as a swift.

swal·low, swol'ō, *v.t.* [O.E. *swelgan,* to swallow (pret. *swealg,* pp. *swolgen*) = L.G. *swalgen,* D. *zwelgen,* Dan *svälge,* Icel. *svelgja,* G. *schwelgen,* to swallow.] To receive, as food or liquid, through the fauces, pharynx, and esophagus into the stomach by muscular contractions in the throat; to draw into, engulf, or absorb, often followed by *up,* as: The stampede *swallowed* them *up. Colloq.* to accept gullibly as true, as a falsehood or deception. To put up with; to bear or take patiently; as, to *swallow* an affront; to embrace, accept, or receive readily, as opinions; to forbear, suppress, or conceal, as one's wrath; to revoke, take back, or withdraw, as something said; to speak, as words, incoherently; to mumble.—*v.i.* To go through the action of swallowing.—*n.* Capacity for swallowing; the action of swallowing; an amount or quantity swallowed in one gulp; *naut.* the opening or hole in a block between the shell and the sheave, which the rope runs through.—**swal·low·er,** *n.*

swal·low·tail, swol'ō·tāl", *n.* A swallow's tail or something resembling it; any of certain butterflies, esp. of the genus *Papilio,* having large tapering wings resembling a swallow's tail; a swallow-tailed coat, or tail coat.—**swal·low·tailed,** swol'ō·tāld", *a.*

swal·low·wort, swol'ō·wurt", *n.* Any of various plants of the milkweed family; an herb, *Vincetoxicum officinale* or *Cynanchum vincetoxicum,* of Europe, with pods suggesting a flying swallow and an emetic root formerly esteemed as a counterpoison; the greater celandine, *Chilidonium majus.*

swa·mi, swa·my, swä'mē, *n.* pl. **swa·mis, swa·mies.** [Hind. *swāmī,* < Skt. *svāmin,* owner, master, lord.] A Hindu religious teacher; a Hindu title of great respect; anyone whose opinion or knowledge is respected or authoritative; a pundit.

swamp, swomp, *n.* [Closely akin to *sump,* a pond, and to O.E. *swamm,* Dan and Sw. *svamp,* Icel. *svôppr,* G. *schwamm,* a sponge; from root of *swim.*] A piece of spongy land, or low ground saturated with water; a bog, fen, marsh, or morass.—*v.t.* To plunge or sink in a swamp, or as in a swamp; to plunge into inextricable difficulties; to overwhelm; *naut.* to sink, or cause to become filled, as a boat, with water.—*v.i.* To sink or become submerged; to be overwhelmed.—**swamp·y,** swom'pē, *a.*—*swampier, swampiest.*—**swamp·i·ness,** *n.*

swamp·er, swom'pẽr, *n.* One who lives in or is an inhabitant of swamps; one who cuts trees in a swamp; a laborer, as a handyman; *logging,* one who works at clearing the ground of underbrush and trims fallen trees in order to clear a trail or skidway for moving logs.

swamp·land, swomp'land", *n.* An expanse or area of swampy land.

swan, swon, *n.* [O.E. *swan* = D. *zwaan,* Icel. *svanr,* Sw. *svan,* Dan. *svane,* G. *schwan;* prob. < same root as Skt. *svan,* L. *sono,* to sound.] A long-necked web-footed bird of the family *Cygninae,* similar to but larger than the goose, and noted for its grace and its usu. snowy white plumage; *fig.* anything which is suggestive of a swan because of its beauty, purity, or grace; (*cap.*), *astron.* the constellation Cygnus.

swan, swon, *v.i.*—*swanned, swanning.* To roam in a random manner, as: He *swanned* idly over the field.

swan, swon, *v.i.*—*swanned, swanning. Dial.* a euphemistic substitute for swear, as: I *swan* this road is rough.

swan dive, *n.* A forward dive characterized by an arched back and arms extended out from the sides of the body, before entering the water.

swan·herd, swon'hurd", *n.* One who tends swans.

swank, swangk, *v.i.* [Origin uncertain; orig. provinc. Eng.: cf. *swank.*] To move in a swaggering manner; behave ostentatiously; to make pretense.—*n. Colloq.* The action or manner of one who swanks; swagger; ostentatious behavior; dashing smartness, as in bearing or appearance; style; pretense.—*a. Colloq.* Ostentatious; fashionable.—**swank·er,** *n.*—**swank·i·ly,** *adv.*—**swank·i·ness,** *n.*—**swank·y,** swang'kē, *a.*—*swankier, swankiest.* Swanking; swaggering.

swan·ner·y, swon'e·rē, *n.* pl. **swan·ner·ies.** A place where swans are bred and reared, or kept.

swan's-down, swans·down, swonz'doun", *n.* The down or under feathers of the swan; a fine, soft, thick woolen cloth; a thick cotton with a soft nap on one side.

swan·skin, swon'skin", *n.* The feathered skin of a swan; a kind of fine-twilled, soft flannel having a downy surface.

swan song, *n.* The final accomplishment, work, or act, as of a composer, performer, civilization, or culture, based upon the ancient belief that a swan sings a song just before death.

swap, swop, *v.t.*—*swapped, swapping, swopped, swopping.* [Allied to *sweep* and *swoop;* cf. G. *schwappen,* to strike, to swap; cf. *to strike a bargain.*] To barter; to exchange.—*v.i.* To make a trade.—*n.* An exchange or trade.

swa·raj, swa·räj', *n.* [For Hind. *svarāj,* < Skt. *sva,* own, and *rāj-,* rule.] Self-government, in India; (*cap.*) the political principle advocated by natives of India that India should be governed by its own people, either as a part of the British Empire or, esp. in later use, with complete independence of British control.—*a.* Pertaining to swaraj or to the Swaraj party.—**swa·raj·ist,** *a., n.*

sward, sward, *n.* [O.E. *sweard,* D. *zwoord,* Dan. *svaer,* Icel. *svôrdr,* G. *schwarte,* all signifying the skin or rind of bacon, hence sward.] The grassy surface of land; turf; greensward.—*v.t.* To cover, as the ground, with sward. Also *swarth.*

swarf, swạrf, *n.* [Cf. O.E. *geswearf,* filings, and *sweorfan,* file, E. *swerve.*] The wet or greasy grit, mixed with particles of iron or steel, abraded from a grindstone or the like. Also *sludge.*

swarm, swạrm, *n.* [O.E. *swearm* = M.L.G. *swarm* = G. *schwarm,* swarm = Icel. *svarmr,* tumult.] A body of honeybees which emigrate from a hive and fly off together, with a queen, to start a new colony; a body of bees settled together, as in a hive; a great number of things or persons, esp. in motion; a group or aggregation of free-floating or free-swimming cells or organisms, as zoospores.—*v.i.* To fly off together in a body from a hive to start a new colony, as bees; to move about, along, or forth in great numbers, as things or persons; to congregate or occur in masses or multitudes; be exceedingly numerous, as in a place or area; to be thronged or overrun, as a place, followed by *with*; abound or teem, followed by *with*; to move or swim about in a swarm.—*v.t.* To swarm about, over, or in; to throng; overrun; to produce a swarm of.

swarm, swạrm, *v.i., v.t.* [Perh. akin to *swerve* or to *squirm.*] To climb by gripping with the arms and legs and pulling oneself up; to shin.

swarm·er, swạr'mẽr, *n.* One of a number that swarm; one of a swarm; *biol.* a swarm spore.

swarm spore, *n. Biol.* Any minute motile spore produced in great numbers; zoospore.

swart, swạrt, *a.* [O.E. *sweart* = D. *zwart* = G. *schwarz* = Icel. *svatr* = Goth. *swarts,* black.] Swarthy. Also *swarth.*—**swart·-ness,** *n.*

swarth, swạrth, *n.* [O.E. *swearth.*] Sward.

swarth, swạrth, *a.* Swart.

swarth·y, swạr'ᴛʜē, swạr'ᴛʜē, *a.*—*swarthier, swarthiest.* Being of a dark hue or dusky complexion; tawny; dark-colored. Also *swart·y.*—**swarth·i·ness,** *n.*

swash, swosh, swạsh, *v.i.* [Prob. from sound of splashing water; cf. Sw. *swassa,* to bluster, to swagger; akin *swish.*] To splash water; to dash or strike; to swagger.—*v.t.* To dash or strike with extreme force.—*n.* A dashing blow or the sound it makes; a dashing or splash of water or the sound it makes; a piece of ground over which water flows; *print.* a long ornamental flourish.—*a.* Noting or pertaining to an italic capital letter with a swash or long flourish.

swash·buck·ler, swosh'buk"lẽr, swạsh'-buk"lẽr, *n.* A swaggering fellow; a bravo; a daredevil. Also **swash·er.**—**swash·buck·-le,** *v.i.*—*swashbuckled, swashbuckling.*—**swash·buck·ling,** swosh'buk"ling, swạsh'-buk"ling, *a.*

swas·ti·ka, swos'ti·ka, *Brit.* swas'ti·ka, *n.* [Skt. *svastika,* < *svasti,* well-being, luck.] A figure used as a symbol or an ornament in the Old World and in America since prehistoric times, consisting of a cross with arms of equal length, each arm having a continuation at right angles, and all four continuations turning the same way; the Nazi party's official emblem.

swat, swot, *v.t.*—*swatted, swatting.* [Imit.] To hit with a smart or violent blow; *baseball,* to hit, as the ball, a long way.—*n.* A smart or violent blow; *baseball,* a very long hit, as a home run.—**swat·ter,** swä'tẽr, swạ'tẽr, *n.*

swatch, swoch, *n.* [Origin obscure.] A sample of cloth or other material; a specimen or distinguishing sample of anything.

swath, swoth, swạth, *n.* [O.E. *swaeth, swathu,* track, trace = D. *zwad,* G. *schwad,* swath.] The space covered by the stroke of a scythe or the cut of a mowing machine; the piece or strip so cut; a line or ridge of grass or grain, cut and thrown together by a scythe or mowing machine; a strip, belt, or long and relatively narrow extent of anything. Also **swathe.**—**cut a swath,** to make a pretentious display.

swathe, swoᴛʜ, swāᴛʜ, *v.t.*—*swathed, swathing.* [Icel. *svatha,* to swathe; O.E. *swethian,* to bind.] To bind or wrap with a band or bandage; to wrap or envelop. Also *swath.*—*n.* A bandage, band, or wrapping.—**swath·er,** *n.*

sway, swā, *v.i.* [Same as Icel. *sveggja,* to make to sway, *sveigja,* to swerve; Dan. *svaie,* D. *swaaijen,* to swing; akin *swing, swag.*] To swing backward and forward; to be drawn to one side by weight; to incline or hang; to move or advance to one side; to have the judgment or feelings inclining one way; to have weight or influence; to exercise rule; to govern.—*v.t.* To move backward and forward; to bias; to cause to incline to one side; to prejudice; to rule; to influence, govern, or direct; *naut.* to hoist, as a yard.—*n.* A swing or sweep; power exerted in governing; rule; influence; weight or authority that inclines to one side.—**sway·a·ble,** *a.*—**sway·er,** *n.*

sway-back, sway·back, swā'bak", *n. Veter. pathol.* an unnatural downward curving or sagging of the back, esp. of a horse.—**sway-backed,** *a. Veter. pathol.* having the back abnormally curved or sagged. Also **sway-back.**

swear, swâr, *v.i.*—past *swore,* pp. *sworn,* ppr. *swearing.* [O.E. *swerian,* to swear; same as the *swer* of *answer*; D. *zweren,* G. *schwōren,* Goth. *svaran,* Icel. *sverja,* Sw. *swarja,* Dan. *svärge,* to swear; same root as in *swarm.*] To utter a solemn declaration, with an appeal to God for the truth of what is affirmed; to declare or affirm in a solemn manner; to promise upon oath; to give evidence on oath; to use profane language; to utter profane oaths.—*v.t.* To affirm with an appeal to God; to utter on oath; to promise solemnly; to vow; to put to an oath; to bind by an oath; to utter in a profane manner.—**swear by,** to name someone as one's witness, as a god; to have faith or confidence in.—**swear in,** to induct into service or office by administering an oath.—**swear off,** to renounce or abstain from, as liquor.—**swear out,** to obtain, as a warrant for arrest, by making a charge or accusation under oath.—**swear·er,** *n.*

swear·word, swâr'wụrd", *n.* A profane word or oath used in swearing; an obscenity.

sweat, swet, *v.i.*—*sweat* or *sweated, sweating.* [O.E. *swaētan,* < *swāt* = D. *zweet* = G. *schweiss* = Icel. *sveiti,* sweat, perspiration; akin to L. *sudor,* Gr. *idos, idrōs,* sweat, Skt. *svid-,* to sweat.] To excrete watery fluid through the pores of the skin; to perspire, esp. profusely; to exude moisture; to gather moisture on the surface due to condensation; of liquids, to ooze out or be exuded like sweat; to ferment. *Colloq.* to labor or toil; to feel anxiety, impatience, or vexation; to suffer punishment, as: I'll make him *sweat* for that.—*v.t.* To emit, as moisture, through the pores of the skin; to exude in drops or small particles; to send forth or get rid of like or with sweat, often with *off* or *out*; as, to *sweat off* pounds; to wet or stain with sweat; to cause, as a person, horse, or the like, to sweat. *Colloq.* to cause to work hard, esp. an employee, at low wages during long hours or under other unfavorable conditions; to extract from by force or pressure, as money or payment. *Slang,* to subject to severe questioning or to the third degree. *Metal.* to heat, as alloyed metals, to the degree needed to remove the more readily fusible components; to heat, as solder, until it melts; to join, as metal parts, by heating and fusing with solder. To cause to ferment, as tobacco leaves.—*n.* The moisture excreted through the pores of the skin; perspiration; moisture exuded from something or collected on a surface due to condensation; a period or condition of sweating; a workout or run, as given to exercise a horse. *Colloq.* strenuous exertion or toil; a state of perturbation, anxiety, or impatience.—**no sweat,** *slang.* Causing no difficulty; easily handled.—**sweat blood,** *slang.* To be in a state of acute anxiety; to exert oneself to the utmost, esp. mentally.—**sweat out,** *slang.* To endure something through to the end; wait helplessly.—**sweat·ed,** *a.*—**sweat·i·ly,** *adv.*—**sweat·-i·ness,** *n.*—**sweat·less,** *a.*—**sweat·y,** *a.*—*sweatier, sweatiest.*

sweat·band, swet'band", *n.* A band of leather or other material fastened within a hat or cap to protect it against the sweat of the head; any piece of material worn across the forehead and around the head to keep sweat from the eyes.

sweat·box, swet'boks", *n.* A contrivance in which something is placed for sweating, as hides or fruit; a boxlike device or cell in which one is made to sweat, esp. a prisoner for the purpose of punishment.

sweat·er, swet'ẽr, *n.* A knitted or crocheted blouselike garment usu. for informal wear with skirts or trousers, orig. worn by athletes during or after strenous exercise; a person who or thing that sweats or induces sweating; an unreasonably demanding employer who overworks those in his employ.

sweat·er girl, *n. Slang,* a girl with a large and shapely bust, esp. one who wears snug sweaters to accentuate it.

sweat gland, *n. Anat.* one of the minute, coiled, tubular glands of the skin that secrete sweat.

sweat·ing sick·ness, *n.* An epidemic, frequently fatal within hours, which made its appearance in England and on the Continent in the 15th and 16th centuries, characterized by profuse sweating.

sweat pants, *n. pl.* Loose, heavy cotton trousers, used esp. by athletes to cause a sweat or avert chill, made with snug cuffs and a drawstring waist.

sweat shirt, *n.* A loose fitting, usu. collarless, heavy cotton jersey pullover, often worn by athletes when exercising.

sweat·shop, swet'shop", *n.* A usu. small factory or shop in which the workers are subjected to adverse conditions as to hours, wages, and environment.

Swede, swēd, *n.* An inhabitant or native of Sweden; *(usu. cap.), Brit.* a rutabaga.

Swed·ish, swē'dish, *a.* Of or pertaining to Sweden, its people, its culture, or its language.—*n.*

Swed·ish mas·sage, *n.* A massage including certain exercises that alternate between being moderately and slightly active. See *Swedish movements.*

Swed·ish move·ments, *n. pl.* A system of exercises which originated in Sweden and are used in connection with a Swedish massage for therapy or hygiene.

Swed·ish tur·nip, *n.* Rutabaga.

swee·ny, swē'nē, *n.* [Origin uncertain.] *Veter. pathol.* atrophy of the shoulder muscles in the horse.

sweep, swēp, *v.t.*—*swept, sweeping.* [M.E. *swepen,* for earlier *swopen,* < O.E. *swāpan* (pret. *swēop*) = O.Fries. *swēpa* = O.H.G. *sweifan* (G. *schweifen*) = Icel. *sveipa,* sweep: cf. *swoop, swipe,* and *swift.*] To move, drive, or bring by or as by passing a broom or brush over the surface occupied; to move, bring, or take by or as by a steady, driving stroke or with continuous forcible action, as: The waves *swept* the boat on the rocks. To pass or draw over a surface or along with a steady, continuous stroke or movement; to trail, as garments; to clear or clean, as a floor, of dirt or litter by or as by means of a broom; to make, as a path, by clearing a space; to clear, as a surface, of something on or in it; to clear or search, esp. water, by dragging; as, to *sweep* a harbor of or for submarine mines; to brush or rub against; as, garments that *sweep* the ground; to pass over with a steady, driving movement or with an unimpeded course, as winds. To direct the gaze over, as an area, with the unaided eye or with a telescope; to survey with a continuous view over the whole extent; to assail, as an area, with gunfire; to have within range of fire, as guns when suitably placed; to execute with a sweeping movement of the hand or body, as a bow or curtsy; *mus.* to pass the fingers over, as an instrument, to produce music.— *v.i.* To sweep an area with a broom, or as a broom does; to drag water, as for submarine mines; to move steadily and strongly or swiftly; to pass unimpeded, as wind or floods; to pass in a stately manner, as a funeral cortege; to walk in long, trailing garments; to move or pass in a continuous course, esp. in a wide curve or circuit, as: His glance *swept* about the room. To extend in a continuous or curving stretch, as a road.—*n.* The act or an act of sweeping, esp. a moving, removing, or clearing by or as by the use of a broom, often used figuratively; as, to make a clean *sweep* of incompetence; the steady driving motion or swift onward course of something moving unimpeded and with force; as, the *sweep* of the wind or waves; a trailing movement, as of garments; a swinging or curving movement or stroke, as of the arm or a weapon; the reach, range, or compass, as of something sweeping about; a curving course or circuit; as, the *sweep* of a road; a continuous extent or stretch, often curving, as of road, shore, or surrounding country; a curving, esp. a widely or gently curving, line, form, part, or mass; matter removed or gathered by sweeping, esp. that of an establishment where precious metals are worked; one who sweeps, esp. a chimney sweeper; something that sweeps or has a sweeping motion; a leverlike device for raising or lowering a bucket in a well, consisting essentially of a long pole pivoted on an upright post; a large oar used in small vessels, sometimes to assist the rudder in turning the vessel but usu. to propel the craft; *Brit.* one employed as a sweeper; *colloq.* sweepstakes. *Cards*, in the game of whist, the winning of all the tricks in a hand; in casino, a pairing or combining, and hence taking of all the cards on the board.—**sweep·er**, *n.*

sweep·back, swēp'bak", *n. Aeron.* The backward slant of a wing, horizontal tail, or other airfoil surface of an airplane; the backward slant of a leading or trailing edge of an airfoil; the amount of this slant.

sweep·ing, swē'ping, *a.* Wide of slope or area; including a large number in a single act or assertion; as, a *sweeping* accusation; comprehensive.—*n. Pl.* Things collected by sweeping; rubbish.—**sweep·ing·ly**, *adv.*—**sweep·ing·ness**, *n.*

sweep-sec·ond, swēp'sek"ond, *n.* A moving hand on a watch or clock, mounted to make a complete revolution in one minute. Also **sweep hand.**

sweep·stakes, swēp'stāks", *n. pl. but. sing. in constr.* Any gaming transaction, as a lottery or horserace, in which a number of persons contribute a certain stake or entry fee, the total amount becoming the property of one or several of the contributors under certain conditions; a prize made up of

several stakes; a contest or race with such a prize. Also **sweep·stake**, swēp'stāk".

sweep·y, swē'pē, *a.—sweepier, sweepiest.* Moving in sweeps; sweeping.

sweet, swēt, *a.* [O.E. *swéte* = D. *zoet*, G. *süss*, Icel. *sœtr, sōtr*, Goth. *sutis*; same root as L. *suavis* (for *suadvis*), whence *suave*; Skt. *svâdus*, sweet, *svad*, to taste.] Having a pleasant taste or flavor like that of sugar or honey: opposed to *bitter*; pleasing to the smell; fragrant; pleasing to the ear; soft; melodious; pleasing to the eye; beautiful; pleasing or agreeable to the mind; mild; gentle; kind; obliging; bland; not salt or salted; not stale; not sour or acid; as, *sweet* soil; not putrescent; fresh; as, *sweet* milk; not dry; as, a *sweet* wine.—*adv.*— **sweet on**, *colloq.* extremely fond of, or in love with.—**sweet·ly**, *adv.*—**sweet·ness**, *n.*

sweet, swēt, *n.* Sweet taste, flavor, smell, or sound; sweetness; that which is sweet; a sweet food or drink. *Usu. pl., chiefly Brit.* a sweet dish, as a pudding or tart; a sweetmeat or bonbon. Something having a sweet smell; a perfume; something pleasant to the mind or feelings, or yielding pleasure or enjoyment; the pleasant part of anything; a beloved person, darling, or sweetheart.

sweet a·lys·sum, *n.* A perennial belonging to the mustard family, *Lobularia maritima*, being a low, white or purple flowered herb common to the Mediterranean area.

sweet-and-sour, swēt'an·sour', swēt'an·-sou'ẽr, *a. Cooking.* Seasoned with lemon juice or vinegar and sugar; flavored with seasonings of vinegar, sugar, cornstarch, soy sauce, pepper, and garlic, esp. Oriental dishes.

sweet bay, *n.* A fragrant species of laurel, *Laurus nobilis*, common to the Mediterranean area; also **Eu·ro·pe·an bay, Eu·ro·pe·an lau·rel.** A magnolia, *Magnolia virginiana*, common to N. America.

sweet·bread, swēt'bred", *n.* The pancreas or thymus of an animal used as food.

sweet·bri·er, sweet·bri·ar, swēt'brī"ẽr, *n.* A native European species of wild rose, *Rosa eglanteria*, having hooked, bristly prickles, pink flowers which are single, and fragrant leaves. Also *eglantine.*

sweet cher·ry, *n.* A cherry, *Prunus avium*, with sweet heart-shaped fruit, common to Eurasia; the fruit of a sweet cherry tree.

sweet clo·ver, *n.* Melilot.

sweet corn, *n.* A variation of corn, *Zea mays saccharata*, which has translucent kernels and a sweet taste. Also **sug·ar corn.**

sweet·en, swēt'en, *v.t.* To make sweet to the taste; to make pleasing to the mind or senses; to make mild or kind; to increase the agreeable qualities of; to make pure and wholesome; to make mellow and fertile; to restore to purity.—*v.i.* To become sweet.— **sweet·en·er, sweet·en·ing**, swēt'e·ning, swēt'ning, *n.*

sweet fern, *n.* A small N. American shrub, *Comptonia peregrina*, with aromatic fern-like leaves.

sweet flag, *n.* A plant, *Acorus calamus*, growing in marshy places, the perennial rhizome of which is known as calamus and is used in medicines, confections, and perfumes.

sweet·heart, swēt'härt", *n.* [< *sweet* and *heart*.] A lover, either male or female; one who is a beloved person; a darling: often used as an expression of affection.

sweet·ie, swē'tē, *n.* [Dim. of *sweet*: orig. Sc.] A sweetheart; *colloq.* a term of endearment; *usu. pl., Brit.* a sweetmeat or sweet cake.

sweet·ing, swē'ting, *n.* A sweet-flavored variety of apple.

sweet·ish, swē'tish, *a.* Somewhat or rather sweet.—**sweet·ish·ly**, *adv.*

sweet mar·jo·ram, *n.* Marjoram.

sweet·meat, swēt'mēt", *n.* A delicate confection, candy, or preserve, prepared with

sugar or honey; *usu. pl.* any sweet delicacy of the confectionery or candy kind, as candied fruit, sugar-covered nuts, sugar-plums, bonbons, balls or sticks of candy.

sweet oil, *n.* An edible oil, as olive oil, used in cooking and in certain food preparations.

sweet pea, *n.* An annual climbing vetchling, *Lathyrus odoratus*, popular for its various colored, sweet-scented flowers.

sweet pep·per, *n.* Bell pepper.

sweet po·ta·to, *n.* A tropical plant, *Ipomoea batatas*, of the morning glory family, largely cultivated for its edible tuberous roots; the root, eaten as a vegetable; *colloq.* an ocarina.

sweet shop, *n. Brit.* a candy store.

sweet·sop, swēt'sop", *n.* [Cf. *sour-sop*.] A sweet pulpy fruit with a thick scaly rind, borne by a custard apple tree or shrub, *Annona squamosa*, native in tropical America; the tree or shrub. Also *sugar apple.*

sweet sor·ghum, *n.* Sorgo.

sweet-talk, swēt'tạk", *v.i. Colloq.* to use words that are cajoling or flattering.—*v.t. Colloq.* To cajole; to coax.

sweet tooth, *n.* A great liking for sweet things or sweetmeats.

sweet wil·liam, *n.* A flower of the pink family, *Dianthus barbatus*, common in old-fashioned gardens and bearing small flowers of various colors in dense clusters.

swell, swel, *v.i.—past swelled*, pp. *swelled* or *swollen*, ppr. *swelling.* [O.E. *swellan*, to swell = Icel. *svella*, D. *zwellen*, G. *schwellen*, to swell.] To grow bulkier; to dilate; to increase in size or extent; to rise or be driven into billows, as waves; to protuberate; to bulge out, as sails; to be puffed up with some feeling; to strut; to look big; to grow and increase in the mind; to become larger in amount; to increase in intensity or volume, as sound.—*v.t.* To increase the size of; **to** cause to dilate or increase; to aggravate; **to** heighten; to inflate; to puff up.—*n.* The act of swelling; gradual increase; an elevation of land; an undulation; a succession of long unbroken waves setting in one direction, as after a storm; a billow; a surge. *Mus.* a gradual increase or crescendo and decrease or diminuendo in the volume of musical sound; an arrangement in an organ whereby the player can increase or diminish the intensity of the sound.—*a. Colloq.* pleasant, excellent, enjoyable, or wonderful.

swell box, *n.* A box or chamber containing a set of pipes in a pipe organ or of reeds in a harmonium, and having movable slats or shutters which can be opened or closed by a pedal or a knee lever to increase or diminish the loudness of the tones.

swelled head, *n. Colloq.* a conceited attitude about oneself.—**swelled-head·ed**, *a.*—**swelled-head·ed·ness**, *n.*

swell·fish, swel'fish", *n.* pl. **swell·fish, swell·fish·es.** Any of various fishes capable of inflating the body; a puffer; blowfish. See *globefish.*

swell·head, swel'hed", *n. Colloq.* a person who is vain or conceited.—**swell·head·ed**, *a.*—**swell·head·ed·ness**, *n.*

swell·ing, swel'ing, *n.* The state of being swollen; that which is swollen; a protuberance or enlargement. *Pathol.* an abnormal protuberance; a tumor.—*a.* Having swells; turgid; bombastic; swelled, as with pride or pretense; pompous; grand.

swel·ter, swel'tẽr, *v.i.* [< O.E. *sweltan*, to die, Goth. *swiltan*, Icel. *svelta*, Sw. *svälta*, Dan. *sulte*, to die. Hence *sultry*, for *sweltery*.] To be overcome and faint with heat.—*v.t.* To oppress with heat.—*n.* A condition of intense heat.—**swel·ter·ing**, *a.*—**swel·ter·ing·ly**, *adv.*

swept, swept, *a.* Angled backward; slanted to the rear, as the wings of a jet airplane.

swept·back, swept'bak', *a.* Slanted backward obtusely, as wings or automobile fenders.

swerve, swŭrv, *v.i.*—*swerved*, *swerving*. [O.E. *sweorfan* = Icel. *svarfa*, D. *zwerven*, L.G. *swarven*, O.H.G. *suerban*, Goth. *svairban*—used of movements of various kinds.] To wander from any line prescribed, as a fast-moving car; to turn aside from a rule or duty; to deviate; to turn to one side; to incline; to waver.—*v.t.* To cause to swerve.—*n.* A swerving; deviation; that which swerves.

swift, swift, *a.* [O.E. *swift*, < *swifan*, to move quickly, to revolve; Icel. *svifa*, to glide, G. *schweifen*, to sweep.] Moving with great speed or rapidity; fleet; rapid; ready; prompt; coming suddenly or without delay; of short continuance; rapidly passing.—*adv.*—**swift·ly**, *adv.*—**swift·ness**, *n.*

swift, swift, *n.* Any of several small, plain, long-winged, rapid-flying birds of the family *Apodidae*, resembling the swallow but related to the hummingbird, esp. the chimney swift that nests in chimneys; any of various small lizards of the western U.S.; a piece of equipment for winding yarn from skeins; a part of a machine used for carding flax.

swig, swig, *n.* [Perh. < O.E. *swilgan*, to swallow.] *Colloq.* a large draft, esp. of an alcoholic drink.—*v.t.*, *v.i.*—*swigged*, *swigging*. *Colloq.* to drink rapidly, greedily, or in large drafts.—**swig·ger**, *n.*

swill, swil, *n.* [O.E. *swillan*, *swilian*, wash.] Liquid or partly liquid food for animals, esp. kitchen refuse given to swine; kitchen refuse in general; any liquid matter or slop; a deep draft of liquor or liquor drunk to excess.—*v.i.* To drink greedily or excessively.—*v.t.* To guzzle or drink greedily or to excess; to feed kitchen refuse to, as hogs; *chiefly Brit. colloq.* to wash or cleanse by flooding with water.—**swill·er**, *n.*

swim, swim, *v.i.*—past *swam* or archaic *swum*, pp. *swum*, ppr. *swimming*. [O.E. *swimman*, to swim = L.G. *swimmen*, Icel. *svimma*, G. *schwimmen*.] To move through water by the motion of the hands, feet, or fins; to be supported on water or other fluid; to float; to be suspended or move in the air, as a parachutist; to glide with a smooth motion; to be flooded or drenched; to overflow. *Fig.* to be dizzy or giddy; to seem to float or whirl.—*v.t.* To pass or cross, as water, by swimming; to execute or accomplish, as a certain stroke, in swimming; to cause to swim or float.—*n.* The act of swimming; period or extent of swimming; a smooth gliding motion like swimming; *fig.* a dizziness or giddiness.—**in the swim**, *colloq.* in the main stream or current of society, activity, or the like.—**swim·ma·ble**, *a.*—**swim·mer**, *n.*

swim blad·der, *n.* Air bladder.

swim fin, *n.* One of any pair of rubber fins or flippers. See *fin*, *flipper*.

swim·mer·et, **swim·mer·ette**, swim'e·-ret'', *n. Zool.* one of a number of abdominal limbs or appendages of many crustaceans, usu. adapted for swimming and for carrying eggs. Also *pleopod*.

swim·ming, swim'ing, *n.* The act or art of sustaining and propelling the body in water, esp. in sport; *fig.* dizziness.—*a.* Capable of or habituated to swimming, applied esp. to a natatorial web-footed or fin-footed bird; used for or in swimming; immersed in or overflowing with liquid, as the eyes with tears; *fig.* affected by giddiness or dizziness.—**swim·ming·ly**, *adv.* Without impediment or difficulty; with great success, or prosperously.

swim·ming hole, *n.* A deep place in which to swim, in a pond, creek, stream, or the like.

swim·ming pool, *n.* A tank or artificial basin, usu. made of concrete or plastic, placed either indoors or outdoors and filled with water for swimming.

swim·suit, swim'sŏt'', *n.* A garment which is designed and worn for bathing or swimming. Also **bath·ing suit**.

swin·dle, swin'dl, *v.t.*—*swindled*, *swindling*. [Borrowed < G. *schwindeln*, to cheat, *schwindler*, a swindler, < *schwindel*, dizziness, infatuation.] To cheat and defraud grossly, or with deliberate artifice.—*v.i.* To practice deception in order to acquire illegally the assets of another.—*n.* A fraudulent scheme intended to dupe people out of money or property.—**swin·dler**, *n.*

swine, swin, *n.* pl. **swine**. [O.E. *swin*, = D. *zwijn*, G. *schwein*, Dan. *sviin*, Icel. *svin*, Goth. *svein*, Pol. *swinia*, Bohem. *swine*; same root as *sow*, L. *sus*.] The domesticated hog or pig; any omnivorous mammal of the family *Suidae*, having a stout body and a long movable snout; *fig.* a coarse, greedy, or brutish person.

swine·herd, swin'hŭrd'', *n.* One who tends or keeps swine.

swing, swing, *v.t.*—past *swung* or rare *swang*, pp. *swung*, ppr. *swinging*. [O.E. *swingan*, strike, beat, whip, fly = O.Fries. *swinga* = O.H.G. *swingan* (G. *schwingen*): cf. *swinge*, *swingle*, and *swink*.] To cause to move to and fro, sway, or oscillate, as something suspended from above; to cause to move in alternate directions about a fixed point or line of support, as a door on its hinges; to move, as the fist or something held, with a sweeping or rotational movement; brandish; flourish; to transport by suspension from or rotation about a point of support; as, to *swing* a girder with a crane; to cause to move in a curve as if about a central point; as, to *swing* one's car around a corner; to suspend so as to hang freely, as a hammock. *Colloq.* to sway or influence as desired; as, to *swing* a district in an election; bring off; as, to *swing* a business deal.—*v.i.* To move to and fro or from side to side, as a pendulum or something suspended from above; to be suspended so as to hang freely. *Colloq.* to accept and conform to contemporary and progressive principles of moral and social conduct; to be pleasure-loving; to die by hanging. To ride in a swing; to move in alternate directions about a point or line of support, as a gate on its hinges; to move in a curve as if around a central point or around a corner; to change or fluctuate, as from one condition or opinion to another; to move with a free, swaying motion, as soldiers on the march; to convey or propel oneself by clutching a fixed support or one support after another; to strike at with a sweeping motion of the arm.—*n.* The act or manner of swinging; movement in alternate directions, or in a particular direction, as in suspension from above or about a point or line of support; the amount of such movement; the swinging, or a swinging movement, of something held; a curving movement or course; a change or fluctuation, as from one condition or opinion to another; an upward or downward trend in a variable cycle, as of business activity; a moving of the body or a part of the body with a free, swaying motion, as in walking; a steady marked rhythm, as of verse or music; insistently rhythmic dance music, influenced by jazz and played by large bands; the characteristic rhythm of such music; freedom of action; as, to have free *swing* in determining policy; something that is swung or that swings, esp. a contrivance consisting of a seat suspended from above, in which one may sit and swing to and fro for pleasure.—*a.* Denoting a swing; in swing, as a song.—**in full swing**, fully in progress.—**swing·a·ble**, *a.* —**swing·ing**, *a.*—**swing·er**, *n.*

swinge, swinj, *v.t.*—*swinged*, *swingeing*. [< *swing*; cf. *springe* < *spring*, *singe* < *sing*.] *Archaic.* To beat soundly; to whip; to chastise.—**swing·er**, swin'jĕr, *n.*

swinge·ing, swin'jing, *a. Chiefly Brit. slang*, very forcible, great, or large; as, a *swingeing* blow.—**swinge·ing·ly**, *adv.*

swin·gle·tree, swing'gl·trē'', *n.* A crossbar, pivoted at the middle, to which the traces of the harness are fastened in a cart, carriage, or plow. Also *whiffletree*, *whippletree*.

swing shift, *n.* A work shift from 4 p.m. until midnight, between the day and night shifts.

swin·ish, swi'nish, *a.* Like or befitting swine; hoggish; brutishly gross or sensual; beastly.—**swin·ish·ly**, *adv.*—**swin·ish·ness**, *n.*

swipe, swip, *v.t.*, *v.i.*—*swiped*, *swiping*. [Akin to *sweep*, *swoop*.] To strike with a sweeping blow; to strike or drive with great force; to hit with a glancing blow, as a car in an accident; *slang*, to steal.—*n.* A strong, sweeping, or glancing blow; a groom in a stable.

swipes, swips, *n. pl. Brit. colloq.* Poor watery beer; spoiled beer; malt liquor in general, esp. small beer.

swirl, swŭrl, *v.i.* [Akin to Dan. *svirre*, to whirl; same root as *swerve*.] To form eddies; to whirl in eddies; to reel or be giddy; to swim, as the head.—*v.t.* To cause to twist or curve.—*n.* A whirling motion; an eddy, as of water; a twist or curl, as in a grain of wood.—**swirl·ing·ly**, *adv.*—**swirl·y**, swŭr'lē, *a.*—*swirlier*, *swirliest*.

swish, swish, *v.i.* [Imit.] To move with or make a sibilant sound, as a slender rod or a bullet cutting sharply through the air, small waves washing on the shore, or an object passing swiftly in contact with water; to rustle, as silk.—*v.t.* To cause to swish; to flourish or whisk with a swishing movement or sound; to bring or take with or as with such a movement or sound; as, to *swish* off the tops of plants with a cane; to flog or whip.—*n.* A swishing movement or sound; a stick or rod for flogging, or a stroke given with this.—*a.* Making a swishing sound.—**swish·er**, *n.*—**swish·ing·ly**, *adv.* —**swish·y**, swish'ē, *a.*—*swishier*, *swishiest*.

Swiss, swis, *a.* [Fr. *Suisse*, < M.H.G. *Swiz.*] Of or pertaining to Switzerland or the Swiss.—*n.* A native or inhabitant of Switzerland; any light, sheer, crisp fabric made in Switzerland.—**Swiss cheese**, a firm, pale yellow or whitish cheese containing numerous holes and usually made from cow's milk.—**Swiss guard**, one of the Pope's household guards, all of whom are natives of Switzerland.

Swiss steak, *n.* A thick cut of round or other steak, floured and pounded, and braised with a sauce of tomatoes, onions, and spices.

switch, swich, *n.* [Same as O.D. *swick*, a switch; akin Icel. *svigi*, *sveigr*, a switch.] A small flexible twig or rod, esp. one used for whipping; an instance of whipping or lashing with a switch; a quick whisking or twitching movement; as, a *switch* of the tail; a sudden shift or changing; as, a *switch* of opinion; *elect.* a device for connecting or breaking an electric circuit or changing direction of current; *rail.* a device for moving a short section of rail and turning a railroad train from one set of tracks to another. A hairpiece consisting of long tresses tied together at one end; a tassel of hairs on the end of an animal's tail, as on a lion or cow.—*v.t.* To strike with a switch; to lash; to change over or shift, as votes, support, conversation, or the like; *elect.* to turn on or off or into a new circuit

---

by means of a switch; *rail*. to transfer or shunt, as a train, from one line of tracks to another.—*v.i.* To whisk or lash back and forth, as a tail or skirt; to shift or divert; to be turned or diverted.—**switch·er,** *n.*

switch·back, swich′bak″, *n.* An inclined road with many alternating turns, as one ascending a mountainside; a zigzag pattern of railroad track for climbing a steeply sloping hill; *Brit.* a roller coaster.

switch·blade knife, swich′blād″ nīf′, *n.* A weaponlike pocketknife with a blade which snaps open and locks when a button is pressed. Also **switch·knife.**

switch·board, swich′bōrd″, swich′bạrd″, *n.* An apparatus consisting of a frame or panel on which are mounted switches for making electric circuit connections, as for a series of lights in a building or for telephone wires in an exchange.

switch cane, *n.* A coarse grass, *Arundinaria tecta,* of grazing regions in southern parts of the U.S.

switch·er·oo, swich″e·rō′, swich′e·rō″, *n. Slang,* a substitution, esp. novel or unexpected, of one idea, thing, attitude, or action for another.

switch hit·ter, *n. Baseball,* a player who is able to bat from either side of the plate; *slang,* a person who can do something well in more than one way.

switch·man, swich′man, *n. pl.* **switch·men.** One who has charge of switches for the directing of trains on a railroad.

switch·yard, swich′yärd″, *n.* An area of track for the switching of railroad cars in making up or disassembling trains.

swith, swithe, swith, *adv. Dial.* quickly or immediately.

swiv·el, swiv′el, *n.* [M.E. *swyvel,* < O.E. *swīfan,* move.] A fastening device which allows the thing fastened to turn around freely; such a device consisting of two parts, each of which turns around independently, as a compound link of a chain, one part of which turns freely in the other by means of a headed pin or the like; a pivoted support for allowing a gun to turn around in a horizontal plane. A gun mounted on such a support; also **swiv·el gun.**—*v.t.*— swiveled, swiveling, *Brit.* swivelled, swivelling. To turn on or as on a swivel; to fasten by a swivel; to furnish with a swivel.—*v.i.* To turn on a swivel, pivot, or the like.

swiv·el chair, *n.* A chair whose seat rotates horizontally on a swivel base.

swiv·et, swiv′it, *n.* [Origin obscure.] *Dial.* A state of excitement; a hurry; a tizzy, usu. preceded by *in a.*

swiz·zle, swiz′l, *n.* [Origin unknown.] Any of various mixed intoxicating drinks containing some liquor, esp. rum, the juice of a lemon or lime, bitters, sugar, and ice.— *v.i.*—swizzled, swizzling. To drink to excess; to guzzle.—*v.t.* To stir or mix with or as with a swizzle stick.—**swiz·zler,** *n.*

swiz·zle stick, *n.* A small slender rod or stick, usu. made of glass or plastic, and used for mixing or stirring drinks.

swob, swob, *n.* Swab.—*v.t.*—swobbed, swobbing. Swab.

swoon, swōn, *v.i.* [< O.E. *swógan,* to sigh, M.E. *swowen,* to swoon.] To faint; to sink into a fainting fit; to become ecstatic or enraptured.—*n.* The act or state of one who swoons; a fainting fit; daze; rapture.— **swoon·er,** *n.*—**swoon·ing·ly,** *adv.*

swoop, swōp, *v.i.* [O.E. *swápan,* to sweep, to swoop.] To descend upon prey from a height; to descend upon suddenly.—*v.t.* To take with a sweep, often followed by *up, off,* or *away.*—*n.* The sudden pouncing of a rapacious bird on its prey; a falling on and seizing in the manner of a bird of prey.— **swoop·er,** *n.*

swoosh, swush, *v.i.* To ascend or descend with a rushing sound, as a flock of birds;

to make a gushing sound, as oil first rising from a well.—*v.t.* To cause to move with or make a rushing sound.—*n.* Any sudden rushing movement or sound.

swop, swop, *v.t., v.i.*—swopped, swopping. Swap.—*n.* Swap.

sword, sōrd, sạrd, *n.* [O.E. *sweord* = D. *zwaard* = G. *schwert* = Icel. *swerdh,* sword.] A weapon having various forms but consisting typically of a long, straight, or slightly curved blade, sharp-edged on one side or both sides, with one end pointed and the other fixed in a hilt or handle; this weapon as the symbol of warfare, military power, punitive justice, authority, rank, or honor; a cause of death or destruction; war, combat, or slaughter; military force or power.—**at swords' points,** with swords ready for mutual attack; in the position or relation of active enemies.—**put to the sword,** to kill by the sword; slay, as those conquered or taken in war.—**sword·like,** *a.*

sword cane, *n.* A cane or walking stick containing a blade, as in a scabbard.

sword dance, *n.* Any of various dances, as among the Scottish Highlanders, in which swords are featured either by being flourished or crossed on the ground to form a pattern for the dance steps.—**sword danc·er,** *n.*

sword fern, *n.* Any of various ferns with pinnate, long, and narrow fronds.

sword·fish, sōrd′fish″, sạrd′fish″, *n. pl.* **sword·fish, sword·fish·es.** A large marine food fish, *Xiphias gladius,* having the upper jaw elongated into a swordlike process.

sword grass, *n.* Any of various grasses or plants with swordlike or sharp leaves, as the sword lily.

sword knot, *n.* An ornamental loop, as of ribbon, leather, or cord, orig. fastened to the sword as a support for the wrist.

sword·play, sōrd′plā″, sạrd′plā″, *n.* The action or skill involved in handling a sword, esp. that of fencers in a match.—**sword·play·er,** *n.*

swords·man, sōrdz′man, sạrdz′man, *n. pl.* **swords·men.** A man armed with or skilled in the use of the sword, as one who fences with sabers. Also **sword·man,** sōrd′man, sạrd′man.—**swords·man·ship,** *n.*

sword·tail, sōrd′tāl″, sạrd′tāl″, *n.* A popular tropical fish, *Xiphophorous helleri,* bred in a variety of colors for the aquarium, the male having a swordlike elongation of the tail; any of several Central American, viviparous, fresh-water topminnows of the genus *Xiphophorous.*

swot, swot, *v.i.*—swotted, swotting. [Provinc. var. of *sweat.*] *Brit. slang.* To study or work hard; grind.—*n. Brit. slang.* One who studies hard; hard study at school; labor or toil; grind.—**swot·ter,** *n.*

swung dash, *n.* The symbol ~ used in printed material to represent a word or a part of a word spelled out earlier.

syc·a·mine, sik′a·min, sik′a·mīn″, *n.* [Gr. *sykaminos.*] *N.T.* the black mulberry, *Morus nigra.*

syc·a·more, sik′a·mōr″, sik′a·mạr″, *n.* [Fr. *sycomore,* L. *sycomorus,* < Gr. *sykomoros,* the fig mulberry—*sykon,* fig, *moron,* mulberry.] The plane tree or buttonwood, *Platanus occidentalis;* the sycamore maple, *Acer pseudo-platanus,* a common shade tree of Europe and Asia, with ornate yellow flowers; a tree, *Ficus sycomorus,* of Egypt and Southwest Asia, with an edible fruit similar to the common fig.

syce, sīs, *n.* A servant or groom in India. Also **sice, saice.**

sy·cee, sī·sē′, *n.* A fine silver of China, cast into ingots of various weights and used as a medium of exchange.

sy·co·ni·um, sī·kō′nē·um, *n. pl.* **sy·co·ni·a,** sī·kō′nē·a. [N.L., < Gr. *sykon,* fig.] *Bot.* a multiple fruit developed from a

hollow fleshy receptacle containing numerous flowers, as in the fig.

syc·o·phan·cy, sik′o·fan·sē, *n. pl.* **syc·o·phan·cies.** Self-seeking or servile flattery; the character or conduct of a sycophant.

syc·o·phant, sik′o·fant, *n.* [L. *sycophanta,* < Gr. *sykophántes,* false accuser, slanderer, false adviser, appar. < *sykon,* fig, and *phainein,* show; the original application of the term being in dispute.] A fawning, self-seeking flatterer; a servile parasite.— **syc·o·phan·tic, syc·o·phan·ti·cal, syc·o·phant·ish,** sik″o·fan′tik, *a.*—**syc·o·phan·ti·cal·ly, syc·o·phant·ish·ly,** *adv.*

sy·co·sis, sī·kō′sis, *n.* [Gr. *sykōsis,* < *sykon,* a fig.] A disease characterized by an eruption of tubercles on the hair of the beard and scalp.

sy·e·nite, sī′e·nīt″, *n.* [L. *(lapis) Syenites,* (stone) of *Syene,* a town (now *Assuan*) in Upper Egypt.] A granular igneous rock consisting principally of feldspar and containing some hornblende or biotite.— **sy·e·nit·ic,** sī″e·nit′ik, *a.*

syl·la·bar·y, sil′a·ber″ē, *n. pl.* **syl·la·bar·ies.** A list or set of syllables; a set of graphic symbols used to represent the syllables of a given language. Also **syl·la·bar·i·um.**

syl·lab·ic, si·lab′ik, *a.* Pertaining to or consisting of a syllable or syllables; distinguished by the articulation of syllables; of or relating to a type of verse in which the number of syllables is more important than rhythm or accent, as haiku.—*n.* The sound of a syllable.— **syl·lab·i·cal·ly,** *adv.*

syl·lab·i·cate, si·lab′i·kāt″, *v.t.*—syllabicated, syllabicating. To form into syllables; syllabify.—**syl·lab·i·ca·tion,** *n.*

syl·lab·i·fy, si·lab′i·fī″, *v.t.*—syllabified, syllabifying. To form into syllables.— **syl·lab·i·fi·ca·tion,** *n.*

syl·la·ble, sil′a·bl, *n.* [Fr. *syllable,* L. *syllaba,* < Gr. *syllabe.*] A sound or combination of sounds uttered together or at a single impulse of the voice, and constituting a word or part of a word; the least expression of language or thought; the closest representation in phonetics for such an expression; a particle; *fig.* the least observation, hint, or part.—*v.t.*—syllabled, syllabling. To utter distinctly; to articulate; to pronounce in syllables.—*v.i.* To utter syllables.

syl·la·bub, sil′a·bub″, *n.* A sillabub; a glass or dish for serving sillabub.

syl·la·bus, sil′a·bus, *n. pl.* **syl·la·bus·es, syl·la·bi,** sil′a·bī″. [L., < the same source as *syllable.*] A brief summary or outlined statement of the principal points of a discourse, legal brief, or course of lectures; an abstract; *Rom. Cath. Ch.* a summary enumeration of points decided by ecclesiastical authority. A document issued by Pope Pius IX in 1864, condemning various doctrines, institutions, and practices; also **Syl·la·bus of Er·rors.**

syl·lep·sis, si·lep′sis, *n. pl.* **syl·lep·ses,** si·lep′sēz. [L.L. < Gr. *syllepsis,* < *syllambánein,* take together.] *Gram.* the use of one word in a sentence to serve two or more purposes without equal appropriateness, as: Neither he nor we *are* willing. The use of one word to express more than one sense, as: He *fought* with desperation and a stout club.—**syl·lep·tic,** si·lep′tik, *a.*

syl·lo·gism, sil′o·jiz″um, *n.* [L. *syllogismus,* < Gr. *syllogismos,* a syllogism, < *syl* for *syn,* with, and *logizomai,* to reckon, < *logos,* word, reason, etc.] *Logic,* a form of reasoning or argument, consisting of three propositions, of which the two first are called the *premises, major* and *minor,* and the last the *conclusion,* the conclusion necessarily following from the premises, as: A plant does not have the power of locomotion; an oak is a plant; therefore, an oak does not have the power of locomotion.—**syl·lo·gist**, *n.*—**syl·lo·gis·tic**, **syl·lo·gis·ti·cal**, sil″*o*·jis′tik, *a.*—**syl·lo·gis·ti·cal·ly**, *adv.* —**syl·lo·gize**, sil′*o*·jīz″, *v.i.*, *v.t.*—*syllogized, syllogizing.*—**syl·lo·giz·er**, *n.*

sylph, silf, *n.* [Fr. *sylphe*, a sylphe, a sylph; a word coined by Paracelsus.] An elemental spirit of the air according to the system of Paracelsus; a woman of graceful and slender proportions.—**sylph·like**, *a.*

sylph·id, sil′fid, *n.* A young or small sylph.—*a.* Also **sylph·id·ine**, sil′fi·din, sil′fi·dīn″.

syl·va, sil′va, *n.* pl. **syl·vas**, **syl·vae**. Silva.

syl·van, **sil·van**, sil′van, *a.* [L. *silvanus*, *sylvanus* (as, n., *Silvanus*, god of the woods, *silvani*, pl. masc., and *silvanae*, pl. fem., woodland deities), < *silva*, *sylva*.] Of, pertaining to, or inhabiting the woods; consisting of or abounding in woods or trees; wooded; woody.—*n.* A person dwelling in a woodland region; a fabled deity or spirit of the woods.

syl·van·ite, sil′va·nīt″, *n.* [From *Tran-(sylvan)ia*, where it was found.] A mineral consisting of a telluride of gold and silver, (AuAg)Te₂, often occurring in crystals so arranged as to resemble written characters.

syl·vat·ic, sil·vat′ik, *a.* Referring to or found in forests or trees; affecting or carried by animals living in forests.

syl·vi·cul·ture, *n.* Silviculture.

syl·vite, sil′vīt, *n.* [N.L. (*sal digestivus*) *Sylvii*, '(digestive salt) of Sylvius,' an old name of potassium chloride.] The mineral potassium chloride, KCl, which crystallizes in cubes and octahedrons and is a primary source of potassium. Also **syl·vin**, **syl·vine**, sil′vin.

sym·bi·ont, sim′bī·ont″, sim″bē·ont″, *n.* [Gr. *symbiōn* (*symbiount-*), ppr. of *symbioun.*] *Biol.* an organism living in a state of symbiosis. Also **sym·bi·on**, **sym·bi·ot**, **sym·bi·ote.**—**sym·bi·on·ic**, **sym·bi·on·tic**, sim″bī·on′tik, sim″bē·on′tik, *a.*

sym·bi·o·sis, sim″bī·ō′sis, sim″bē·ō′sis, *n.* pl. **sym·bi·o·ses**, sim″bī·ō′sēz, sim″bē·ō′sēz. [Gr. *syn*, together, *bios*, life.] *Biol.* the state of two different organisms living in close relationship, each benefiting from such an association.—**sym·bi·ot·ic**, sim″bī·ot′ik, sim″bē·ot′ik, *a.*—**sym·bi·ot·i·cal·ly**, *adv.*

sym·bol, sim′bol, *n.* [L. *symbolum*, < Gr. *symbolon*, a symbol, < *symballō*, to infer, conclude—*sym*, for *syn*, with, and *ballō*, to throw or put.] Something standing for or calling up something else, esp. a concrete object which stands for an intangible object or idea; a character, letter, or cipher which by convention or arbitrary usage has come to represent something else, as the name of a chemical element; an image which embodies a web of interrelated meanings or which evokes a complex of emotions; *psychol.* an image which articulates a subconscious complex of meanings, as a dream image; *psychoanal.* an action or affect which takes the place of the gratification of a repressed desire or the resolution of unconscious conflict; *anthropol.*, *sociol.* culturally significant sounds, objects, or dramas which draw forth, externalize, or rationalize an individual or corporate response.—*v.t.*—*symboled, symboling, esp. Brit. symbolled, symbolling.* Symbolize.

sym·bol·ic, sim·bol′ik, *a.* Pertaining to a symbol or symbols; of the nature of a symbol; representative; *gram.* formerly, denoting a class of words expressing relation, as pronouns or prepositions. Also **sym·bol·i·cal.**—**sym·bol·i·cal·ly**, *adv.*

sym·bol·ic log·ic, *n.* A modern treatment of formal logic, using symbols to represent logical elements and their relationships, and manipulating these symbols according to precise rules. Also *mathematical logic.*

sym·bol·ism, sim′bo·liz″*u*m, *n.* The practice of representing things by symbols, or of investing things with a symbolic meaning or character; a set or system of symbols; symbolic meaning or character; the principles and practice of symbolists in art or literature; (*usu. cap.*) a movement in French and Belgian literature and art of the late 19th century.

sym·bol·ist, sim′bo·list, *n.* One who uses symbols or symbolism; one versed in the study or interpretation of symbols. *Liter., art*, a writer or artist who seeks to express, suggest, or evoke ideas or emotions by a written presentation of symbolic words, sounds, and objects or by a visual presentation of colors, textures, and objects; (*usu. cap.*) a member of a group of French and Belgian writers and artists of the late 19th century who rejected realism and expressed themselves by means of symbols. *Theol.* one who views the Eucharist as symbolic.—**sym·bol·is·tic**, *a.*

sym·bol·ize, sim′bo·līz″, *v.t.*—*symbolized, symbolizing.* To serve as a symbol of; to represent by a symbol or symbols; to regard or treat as symbolic.—*v.i.* To express or represent in symbols.—**sym·bol·i·za·tion**, *n.*—**sym·bol·iz·er**, *n.*

sym·bol·o·gy, sim·bol′o·jē, *n.* [Gr. *symbolon*, and *logos*, discourse.] The interpretation and study of symbols; the art of expressing by symbols.

sym·met·al·ism, sim·met′a·liz″*u*m, *n.* A monetary system using as a standard two or more metals, as gold and silver, combined in assigned proportions.

sym·met·ri·cal, si·met′ri·kal, *a.* Characterized by or exhibiting symmetry; well-proportioned, as a body or whole; exhibiting symmetry in the size, form, and arrangement of parts on opposite sides of a plane, line, or point; regular in form or arrangement of corresponding parts; well-balanced in the combination of parts or elements; *pathol.* affecting corresponding parts simultaneously, as certain diseases; *bot.* of a flower, having the same number of parts in each whorl. *Math.* denoting or having points that correspond in pairs such that the lines connecting each pair are bisected by an axis or plane; as, a curve *symmetrical* to the x-axis; being such that the variables may be consistently interchanged without mathematically altering the expression; as, a *symmetrical* equation. *Chem.* having a structural formula exhibiting symmetry. Also **sym·met·ric.**—**sym·met·ri·cal·ly**, *adv.*—**sym·met·ri·cal·ness**, *n.*

sym·me·trize, sim′i·trīz″, *v.t.*—*symmetrized, symmetrizing.* To make symmetrical. —**sym·me·tri·za·tion**, *n.*

sym·me·try, sim′i·trē, *n.* pl. **sym·me·tries.** [L. *symmetria*, < Gr. *symmetria*, < *symmetros*, commensurate, < *syn*, with, and *métron*, measure.] The correspondence in size, form, and arrangement of parts on opposite sides of a plane, line, or point, each part on one side having its counterpart on the other side; the proper or due proportion of the parts of a body or whole to one another with regard to size and form; excellence of proportion; the character of being well-proportioned; the beauty or regularity of form or arrangement with reference to corresponding parts; *math.* the property or quality of being symmetrical.

sym·pa·thec·to·my, sim″pa·thek′to·mē, *n.* pl. **sym·pa·thec·to·mies.** *Surg.* the excision or interruption of part of the sympathetic nerve pathways.

sym·pa·thet·ic, sim″pa·thet′ik, *a.* Expressive of, produced by, or exhibiting sympathy; having sympathy or common feeling with another; *physiol.* relating to that part of the nervous system that, with the para-

sympathetic nerves, makes up the autonomic nervous system.—**sym·pa·thet·i·cal·ly**, *adv.*

sym·pa·thet·ic nerv·ous sys·tem, *n. Anat.* the section of the autonomic nervous system originating in the thoracic and lumbar regions which stimulates the heart beat, dilates the pupils, contracts the blood vessels, and, in general, functions in opposition to the parasympathetic nervous system.

sym·pa·thet·ic strike, *n.* Sympathy strike.

sym·pa·thin, sim′pa·thin, *n. Biochem.* a substance produced at the nerve endings of the sympathetic nervous system having an effect similar to adrenalin.

sym·pa·thize, sim′pa·thīz″, *v.i.*—*sympathized, sympathizing.* [Fr. *sympathiser*, < *sympathie*, < L. *sympathia*, E. *sympathy.*] To be in sympathy or agreement of feeling, as one person with another; to share in a feeling or feelings, usu. followed by *with*; to share with another in his feelings over what affects him, esp. his sufferings or troubles; to feel a compassionate sympathy, usu. followed by *with*; to express sympathy or condole, usu. followed by *with*; to be in approving accord, as with a person, party, cause, or policy; to have a special natural sympathy, relation, or affinity, as one thing with another; to exhibit such a sympathy, as by some responsive action, usu. followed by *with*; to agree, correspond, or accord; *pathol.* to exhibit a sympathetic affection, induced affliction, or sympathetic disorder.—**sym·pa·thiz·er**, *n.*—**sym·pa·thiz·ing·ly**, *adv.*

sym·pa·thy, sim′pa·thē, *n.* pl. **sym·pa·thies.** [Fr. *sympathie*, L. *sympathia*, < Gr. *sympatheia*—*syn*, with, and *pathos*, suffering.] Feeling corresponding to that which another feels; a feeling that enables a person to enter into and in part share another's feelings; fellow feeling; compassion; commiseration.

sym·pa·thy strike, *n.* A strike by a body of workers, not due to grievances against their employer, but by way of endorsing and aiding another body of workers who are on strike or have been locked out. Also *sympathetic strike.*

sym·pat·ric, sim·pa′trik, sim·pā′trik, *a. Genetics, ecology*, occupying the same territory without losing genetic identity by interbreeding.—**sym·pat·ri·cal·ly**, *adv.*—**sym·pat·ry**, *n.*

sym·pet·al·ous, sim·pet′a·lus, *a. Bot.* having united petals. Also **gam·o·pet·a·lous.**

sym·phon·ic, sim·fon′ik, *a. Mus.* of, pertaining to, or having the character of a symphony. Of or pertaining to symphony or harmony of sounds; characterized by similarity of sound, as words.—**sym·phon·i·cal·ly**, *adv.*

sym·phon·ic po·em, *n. Mus.* a type of extended programmatic work for symphony orchestra based on a pictorial or literary subject and freer in form than the symphony, developed in the 19th century. Also *tone poem.*

sym·pho·ni·ous, sim·fō′nē·us, *a.* Agreeing in sound; harmonious.—**sym·pho·ni·ous·ly**, *adv.*

sym·pho·ny, sim′fo·nē, *n.* pl. **sym·pho·nies.** [L. *symphonia*, < Gr. *symphōnia*—*syn*, with, and *phōnē*, voice.] *Mus.* an elaborate composition for a full orchestra, consisting usu., like the sonata, of three or four contrasted but intimately related movements but usu. of greater scope, complexity, and size; a concert by a symphony orchestra. A consonance or harmony of sounds; any harmonious blending or agreeable combination.—**sym·pho·nist**, sim′fo·nist, *n.* A composer of symphonic works.

sym·pho·ny or·ches·tra, *n.* A large orchestra, composed usu. of string, woodwind, brass, and percussion instruments, that performs symphonic works.

sym·phy·sis, sim′fi·sis, *n. pl.* **sym·phy·ses**, sim′fi·sēz″. [N.L., < Gr. *symphyis*, < *symphyein*, cause to grow together, < *syn*, with, and *phnein*, produce.] *Anat., zool.* the growing together, or the fixed or movable union, of bones, as that of the two halves of the human lower jaw, or that of the two human pubic bones at the lower anterior point of the abdomen; a line of junction or articulation of other parts so formed. *Bot.* a coalescence or growing together of parts.—**sym·phys·e·al**, **sym·phys·i·al**, **sym·phys·tic**, sim·fiz′ē·al, sim·fis′tik, *a.*

sym·po·di·um, sim·pō′dē·um, *n. pl.* **sym·po·di·a**, sim·pō′dē·a. [N.L., < Gr. *sympous* (*sympod*-), having the feet together, < *syn*, with, and *pous* (*pod*-), foot.] *Bot.* an axis or stem which simulates a simple stem but is made up of the bases of a number of axes which arise successively as branches one from another. Also **pseud·ax·is**. Compare *monopodium*.—**sym·po·di·al**, *a.*—**sym·po·di·al·ly**, *adv.*

sym·po·si·arch, sim·pō′zē·ärk″, *n.* [Gr. *symposiarchos*, < *symposion*, E. *symposium*, and *archein*, lead, rule.] The president, director, or master of a symposium; the toastmaster at a banquet.

sym·po·si·um, sim·pō′zē·um, *n. pl.* **sym·po·si·a**, **sym·po·si·ums**, sim·pō′zē·a. [L., < Gr. *symposion*, a drinking party, < *sym*, with, + *posion*, related to *posis*, a drinking, and *pinein*, drink.] A meeting or conference for discussion of some subject; a collection of opinions expressed, or a series of articles contributed, by several persons on a given subject or topic; an account of such a meeting or of the conversation at it; among the ancient Greeks, a convivial meeting, usu. following a dinner, for drinking and intellectual talk.

symp·tom, simp′tom, *n.* [Gr. *symptōma*—*syn*, together, with *piptō*, to fall.] Any circumstance or condition which serves as evidence of something not seen; an indication, sign, or token; *pathol.* a circumstance or condition which results from or accompanies a disease, and by which the existence and the nature of a disease may be diagnosed.

symp·to·mat·ic, simp′to·mat′ik, *a.* Pertaining or relating to a symptom or symptoms; indicative, usu. followed by *of*; as, *symptomatic of* cancer; according to a symptom or symptoms; as, a *symptomatic* diagnosis of disease. Also **symp·to·mat·i·cal.**—**symp·to·mat·i·cal·ly**, *adv.*

symp·tom·a·tol·o·gy, simp′to·ma·tol′o·jē, *n.* That part of medicine which treats of the symptoms of diseases.

syn·aer·e·sis, si·ner′i·sis, *n.* Syneresis.

syn·aes·the·sia, sin″is·thē′zha, sin″is·thē′zhē·a, sin″is·thē′zē·a, *n.* Synesthesia.

syn·a·gogue, **syn·a·gog**, sin′a·gog″, sin′a·gag″, *n.* [Fr. *synagogue*, Gr. *synagōgē*—*syn*, together, and *agō*, to bring.] A congregation of Jews assembled for the purpose of worship; a Jewish place of worship.—**syn·a·gog·al**, **syn·a·gog·i·cal**, sin′a·gog″al, sin′a·ga″gal, sin′a·goj′i·kal, *a.*

syn·a·loe·pha, **syn·a·le·pha**, sin″a·lē′fa, *n.* [Gr. *synaloiphē*, *synaleiphō*, to melt together—*syn*, together, and *aleiphō*, to smear.] A suppression of some vowel or diphthong at the end of a word before another vowel or diphthong, as 'th' infantry' for 'the infantry.' Also **syn·a·le·phe**, sin″a·lē′fē.

syn·apse, sin′aps, si·naps′, *n.* The area in which contact takes place and where a neuron transmits nerve impulses to another neuron.

syn·ap·sis, si·nap′sis, *n. pl.* **syn·ap·ses**, si·nap′sēz. [Gr. *synapsis*, union.] *Biol.* a stage in meiosis at which homologous chromosomes pair up.—**syn·ap·tic**, si··nap′tik, *a.*

syn·ar·thro·sis, sin″är·thrō′sis, *n. pl.* **syn·ar·thro·ses**, sin″är·thrō′sēz. [Gr. *synarthrōsis*—*syn*, with, and *arthron*, a joint.] *Anat.* A union of two bones which prohibits either from moving; a fixed articulation. Also **syn·ar·thro·di·a**, sin″är·thrō′dē·a.—**syn·ar·thro·di·al**, *a.*—**syn·ar·thro·di·al·ly**, *adv.*

sync, singk, *n.* Synchronism; synchronization.—*a.*—*v.i.*, *v.t.*—**synced**, **syncing.** Synchronize.

syn·car·pous, sin·kär′pus, *a. Bot.* composed of or having united carpels.—**syn·car·py**, *n. Bot.* The state of having united carpels; sometimes the condition in which several pistils of one flower are partially united.

syn·chro, sing′krō, *n.* Selsyn.

syn·chro·cy·clo·tron, **syn·chro·cy·clo·tron**, sing″krō·sī′klo·tron″, sing″krō··sik′lo·tron″, *n. Phys.* a cyclotron which compensates for the increased mass of charged particles as they approach the speed of light by regulating the accelerating voltage.

syn·chro·flash, sing′kro·flash″, *a. Photog.* pertaining to the use of a flash lamp which is exactly synchronized with the camera shutter.

syn·chro·mesh, sing′kro·mesh″, *n.* An automobile transmission whose driving gears are synchronized to facilitate gear shifting.—*a.* Pertaining to such a mechanism.

syn·chron·ic, sin·kron′ik, *a.* Coinciding or agreeing in time; synchronous; *ling.* relating to a language feature or system considered at a particular point in time without reference to its historical background: distinguished from *diachronic.* Also **syn·chron·i·cal.**—**syn·chron·i·cal·ly**, *adv.*

syn·chro·nism, sing′kro·niz″um, *n.* Concurrence of two or more events or facts in time; simultaneousness; arrangement of contemporaneous events or persons in tabular form; *art*, the placement in a single picture of persons or events not coexistent in time. Also *sync.*—**syn·chro·nis·tic**, **syn·chro·nis·ti·cal**, *a.*—**syn·chro·nis·ti·cal·ly**, *adv.*

syn·chro·ni·za·tion, sing″kro·ni·zā′shan, *n.* The act of synchronizing. Also *sync.*

syn·chro·nize, sing′kro·nīz″, *v.i.*—**synchronized**, **synchronizing.** To concur or agree in time; to proceed or operate at exactly the same rate.—*v.t.* To make to agree in time; to cause to indicate the same time, as one timepiece with another; to cause to proceed or operate at exactly the same rate; as, to *synchronize* the movements of a dancer with the music. Also *sync.*—**syn·chro·niz·er**, *n.*

syn·chro·nous, sing′kro·nus, *a.* [Gr. *syn*, with, and *chronos*, time (whence also *chronic*, *chronicle*, etc.).] Happening at the same time or rate; contemporaneous; simultaneous; *phys.* having the same frequency and period, as electric currents. Also **syn·chro·nal**, sing′kro·nal.—**syn·chro·nous·ly**, *adv.*—**syn·chro·nous·ness**, *n.*

syn·chro·nous mo·tor, *n.* An electric motor whose speed is regulated proportionally to the frequency of the electric current.

syn·chro·ny, sing′kro·nē, *n.* Simultaneous events or actions; simultaneous patterns of events or actions.

syn·chro·scope, sing′kro·skōp″, *n. Elect.* an electrical device for measuring the degree of synchronization between two machines. Also **syn·chron·o·scope.**

syn·chro·tron, sing′kro·tron″, *n.* [(*Synchro*)nous and elect(*tron*).] *Phys.* a device

analogous to the betatron for imparting great speed to atomic particles.

syn·cli·nal, sin·klin′al, sing′kli·nal, *a.* [Gr. *syn*, together, and *klinō*, to incline or slope.] *Geol.* Sloping downward in opposite directions so as to meet in a common point or line; dipping toward a common line or plane; as, *synclinal* strata; formed by or pertaining to strata dipping in such a manner; as, a *synclinal* axis: opposed to *anticlinal.*

syn·cline, sing′klīn, sin′klīn, *n. Geol.* a synclinal fold.

syn·co·pate, sing′ko·pāt″, sin′ko·pāt″, *v.t.*—**syncopated**, **syncopating.** [M.L. *syncopatus*, pp. of *syncopare*, < L.L. *syncope*.] *Mus.* to modify, as a piece of music, by displacing normal accents to create rhythmic contradiction; *gram.* to contract, as a word, by taking one or more letters or syllables from the middle, as in reducing *Gloucester* to *Gloster*.—**syn·co·pa·tor**, *n.*

syn·co·pat·ed, sing′ko·pā″tid, sin′ko·pā″tid, *a.* Characterized by or manifesting syncopation; shortened; abbreviated.

syn·co·pa·tion, sing″ko·pā′shan, sin″ko··pā′shan, *n.* [M.L. *syncopatio(n*-).] The act of syncopating or the state of being syncopated; that which is syncopated; *mus.* a displacement of the normal accent of a piece of music, creating a rhythmic contradiction, esp. in jazz; *gram.* syncope.—**syn·co·pa·tive**, *a.*

syn·co·pe, sing′ko·pē, sing′ko·pē″, sin′ko··pē, sin′ko·pē″, *n.* [L.L., < Gr. *synkopē*, < *synkóptein*, cut up, cut short, < *syn*, with, and *kóptein*, cut.] *Gram.* the contraction of a word by taking one or more letters or syllables from the middle, as in the reduction of *never* to *ne'er*; also *syncopation. Pathol.* a temporary diminution or suspension of the heart's action, characterized chiefly by loss of consciousness; fainting.—**syn·co·pal**, **syn·cop·ic**, sin·kop′ik, *a.*

syn·cre·tism, sing′kri·tiz″um, sin′kri·tiz″um, *n.* [Gr. *synkrētismos.*] The attempted blending of irreconcilable principles or parties, as in philosophy or religion; *gram.* the merging of two or more different categories or inflectional forms into one.—**syn·cre·tis·tic**, **syn·cret·ic**, sing″kri·tis′tik, sin″kri·tis′tik, sin·kret′ik, *a.*—**syn·cre·tist**, *n., a.*

syn·cy·tium, sin·sish′um, sin·sish′ē·um, *n. pl.* **syn·cy·tia**, sin·sish′a, sin·sish′ē·a. *Biol.* a mass of multinucleate protoplasm, not definitely divided into cells.—**syn·cy·tial**, sin·sish′al, *a.*

syn·dac·tyl, **syn·dac·tyle**, sin·dak′til, *a.* [Gr. *syn*-, together, and *dáctylos*, finger or toe.] *Anat.* having certain digits partially or wholly united, as the kingfisher.—*n.* A syndactyl animal.—**syn·dac·tyl·ism**, sin··dak′ti·liz″um, *n.*

syn·de·sis, sin′di·sis, sin·dē′sis, *n. pl.* **syn·de·ses**, sin′di·sēz″, sin·dē′sēz″, sin′di·sēz, sin′dē·sēz. *Biol.* synapsis.

syn·des·mo·sis, sin″des·mō′sis, *n. pl.* **syn·des·mo·ses**, sin″des·mō′sēz. [N.L., < Gr. *syndesmos*, fastening, ligament, < *syndein*.] *Anat.* a connection of bones by ligaments, fasciae, or membranes other than those of the joints.—**syn·des·mot·ic**, sin″des·mot′ik, *a.*

syn·det·ic, sin·det′ik, *a.* [Gr. *syndetikos*, < *syndein*, bind together, < *syn*, with, and *dein*, bind.] Serving to unite or connect; connective; conjunctive; copulative. Also **syn·det·i·cal.**—**syn·det·i·cal·ly**, *adv.*

syn·dic, sin′dik, *n.* [Fr. *syndic* < L.L. *syndicus*, < Gr. *syndikos*, advocate, < *syn*, with, and *dikē*, right, justice.] A person chosen to represent and transact business for a corporation or the like, as a university; a council or committee so designated; a civil magistrate having different powers in different countries.

syn·di·cal, sin'di·kal, *a.* [Fr. *syndical,* < *syndic,* E. *syndic.*] Noting or pertaining to a union, for the protection of their interests, of persons engaged in a particular trade; of or pertaining to syndicalism.

syn·di·cal·ism, sin'di·ka·liz″um, *n.* [Fr. *syndicalisme.*] A form or development of trade unionism, originating in France, which aims at the possession of the means of production and distribution and ultimately at the control of society and government by the federated bodies of industrial workers, and which seeks to realize its purposes through general strikes, terrorism, sabotage, violence, or like means.—**syn·di·cal·ist,** *n.,* *a.*—**syn·di·cal·is·tic,** *a.*

syn·di·cate, sin'di·kit, *n.* [Fr. *syndicat,* < *syndic,* E. *syndic.*] A combination of bankers or capitalists formed for the purpose of carrying out some project requiring large resources of capital, as the underwriting of an issue of stock or bonds; any combination of persons, companies, or the like resembling this, esp. an association of publishers of newspapers or other periodicals in different places, for purchasing articles or stories and publishing them simultaneously; any agency which supplies articles for that purpose; an association of criminals in organized crime.—sin'di·kāt″, *v.t.*—*syndicated, syndicating.* To combine into a syndicate; to handle, manage, or effect through a syndicate or as a syndicate does; to publish simultaneously or supply for simultaneous publication in a number of newspapers or other periodicals in different places.—**syn·di·ca·tion,** *n.*—**syn·di·ca·tor,** *n.*

syn·drome, sin'drōm, sin'dro·mē″, *n.* [N.L., < Gr. *syndromē,* < *syn,* with, and *dramein,* run.] *Pathol.* the combination of symptoms in a disease; a number of symptoms occurring together. The set of circumstances characteristic of a certain social condition; a set or series of related things, happenings, or the like.—**syn·drom·ic,** sin·drom'ik, *a.*

syn·ec·do·che, si·nek'do·kē, *n.* [L., < Gr. *synekdochē,* < *synekdéchesthai,* understand with something else, < *syn,* with, and *ekdéchesthai,* take, understand, < *ek,* out of, and *déchesthai,* receive.] *Rhet., pros.* a figure of speech in which a part images the whole or the whole a part, the special the general or the general the special, as 'a fleet of ten sail' for 'ships,' or 'to eat of the tree,' for 'fruit,' or a 'Croesus' for a 'rich man,' or a 'marble on its pedestal' for a 'statue.'—**syn·ec·doch·ic, syn·ec·doch·i·cal,** sin″ik·dok'ik, *a.*—**syn·ec·doch·i·cal·ly,** *adv.*

syn·e·col·o·gy, sin″e·kol'o·jē, *n.* The branch of ecology concerned with communities rather than individual species: opposed to *autecology.*—**syn·ec·o·log·ic, syn·ec·o·log·i·cal,** sin″ek·o·loj'ik, *a.*—**syn·ec·o·log·i·cal·ly,** *adv.*

syn·er·e·sis, syn·aer·e·sis, si·ner'i·sis, *n.* [L.L. *synaeresis,* < Gr. *synairesis,* < *synairein,* take together, contract, < *syn,* with, and *airein,* take.] *Gram.* the contraction of two syllables or two vowels into one, esp. the contraction of two vowels to form a diphthong; *chem.* the contraction of a gel causing exudation of liquid, as the separation of serum from a blood clot.

syn·er·get·ic, sin'ér·jet'ik, *a.* [Gr. *synergētikós,* < *synergein,* work together, < *synergós.*] Synergistic; working together; cooperative; as, *synergetic* muscles. Also **syn·er·gic,** si·nur'jik.

syn·er·gism, sin'ér·jiz″um, si·nur'jiz·um, *n.* [Gr. *synergia.*] Any cooperative effort of discrete agencies that produces a more effective result than the sum of the results produced by the same agencies acting independently of one another, as two drugs;

theol. the doctrine that the human will cooperates with the Holy Spirit and the Word of God in the work of salvation.—**syn·er·gist,** sin'ér·jist, *n.*—**syn·er·gis·tic,** *a.*—**syn·er·gis·ti·cal·ly,** *adv.*

syn·er·gy, sin'ér·jē, *n.* pl. **syn·er·gies.** [Gr. *synergia,* cooperation, < *synergós,* working together, < *syn,* with, and *-ergós,* working: cf. *energy.*] Combined action; the cooperative action of two or more parts or organs of the body; the cooperative interaction of different drugs.

syn·e·sis, sin'i·sis, *n.* [N.L., < Gr. *synesis,* understanding, < *synienai,* put together, understand, < *syn,* with, and *ienai,* send.] *Gram.* construction according to the sense, rather than or in violation of strict syntax, as: If *anyone* asks, tell *them* he is out.

syn·es·the·sia, syn·aes·the·sia, sin″is·thē'zha, sin″is·thē'zhē·a, sin″is·thē'zē·a, *n.* [N.L.] Sensation produced in one part of the body when a stimulus is applied to another part; the bringing about, through a sensation produced by one stimulus, of a mental image corresponding to another, as when hearing a particular sound induces the visualization of a particular color.—**syn·es·thet·ic, syn·aes·thet·ic,** sin″is·thet'ik *a.*

syn·ga·my, sing'ga·mē, *n.* *Biol.* the union of female and male gametes during fertilization.—**syn·gam·ic,** sin·gam'ik, *a.*

syn·gen·e·sis, sin·jen'i·sis, *n. Biol.* Sexual reproduction; formerly, the theory that every sexually fertilized germ cell contains the germ cells of all generations to come from it: opposed to *epigenesis.*—**syn·ge·net·ic,** sin″je·net'ik, *a.*

syn·i·ze·sis, sin″i·zē'sis, *n.* [L.L. < Gr. *synizēsis,* < *synizánein,* sink in, collapse, < *syn-,* together, and *izánein,* settle down, < *izein,* seat, sit.] *Gram.* the combination into one syllable of two vowels that cannot form a diphthong, or of a vowel and a diphthong; *biol.* the massing of chromatin of the nucleus in the early stage of meiosis; *pathol.* closure or obliteration of the pupil of the eye. Also **syn·e·zi·sis.**

syn·od, sin'od, *n.* [L.L. *synodus,* < Gr. *synodos,* assembly, meeting, < *syn-,* together, and *odós,* way.] An assembly of ecclesiastics or other church delegates duly convoked, pursuant to the law of the church, for the discussion and decision of ecclesiastical affairs; an ecclesiastical council; a court in Presbyterian churches which ranks above the presbytery, and either is subordinate to a general assembly or is itself the supreme court of the church; an assembly, convention, or council of any kind.—**syn·od·al,** *a.*

syn·od·ic, si·nod'ik, *a.* [L.L. *synodicus,* < Gr. *synodikós.*] Of or pertaining to, done or made by, or proceeding from a synod; *astron.* pertaining to a conjunction or to two successive conjunctions of the same bodies. Also **syn·od·i·cal.**—**syn·od·i·cal·ly,** *adv.*

syn·oe·cious, syn·e·cious, si·nē'shus, *a.* [Gr. *syn-,* together, and *oikos,* house.] *Bot.* Having male and female flowers in one head, as in many composite plants; having sperm and egg producing structures in the same receptacle, as in mosses. Also **syn·oi·cous,** si·noi'kus.—**syn·oe·cious·ly,** *adv.*—**syn·oe·cious·ness,** *n.*

syn·o·nym, sin'o·nim, *n.* [= Fr. *synonyme,* < L. *synonymum,* < Gr. *synōnymon,* prop. neut. of *synōnymos,* synonymous, < *syn,* with, and *ónyma,* name.] A word that has the same meaning, or the same general meaning, as a particular word in the same language, or is in some applications a more or less satisfactory equivalent for it, as 'joyful,' 'happy,' 'elated,' and 'delighted' are synonyms of 'glad': opposed to *antonym;* a

word or expression accepted as another name for something or denoting or implying something, as 'arcadia' has become a synonym for 'pastoral simplicity' and 'contentment'; *biol.* an alternative but less approved scientific name, as for a species or genus.—**syn·o·nym·ic, syn·o·nym·i·cal,** *a.*—**syn·o·nym·i·ty,** sin″o·nim'i·tē, *n.*

syn·on·y·mize, si·non'i·mīz″, *v.t.*—*synonymized, synonymizing.* To give synonyms for, as a word or name; to furnish with synonyms.

syn·on·y·mous, si·non'i·mus, *a.* [Gr. *synōnymos.*] Having the character of synonyms or a synonym; of the same meaning, as words; equivalent in meaning; expressing or implying the same idea.—**syn·on·y·mous·ly,** *adv.*

syn·on·y·my, si·non'i·mē, *n.* pl. **syn·on·y·mies.** [L.L. *synonymia,* Gr. *synōnymia.*] The character of being synonymous; equivalence in meaning; the use or coupling of synonyms in discourse for emphasis or rhetorical amplification; the study of synonyms; a set, list, or system of synonyms; *biol.* a list of the alternative, less approved, scientific names used for a particular species or other group, or for various species with explanatory matter.

syn·op·sis, si·nop'sis, *n.* pl. **syn·op·ses,** si·nop'sēz. [L.L., < Gr. *synopsis,* < *syn-,* together, and *ap-,* see.] A brief or condensed statement giving a general view of some subject, as a novel, play, or movie; a compendium of heads or short paragraphs so arranged as to afford a view of the whole or principal parts of a matter under consideration; a conspectus.

syn·op·size, si·nop'sīz, *v.t.*—*synopsized, synopsizing.* To summarize in a synopsis.

syn·op·tic, si·nop'tik, *a.* [Gr. *synoptikos.*] Pertaining to or constituting a synopsis; affording or taking a general view of the whole or of the principal parts of a subject. (*Often cap.*) taking a common view, esp. applied to the first three Gospels (Matthew, Mark, and Luke) from their similarity in contents, order, and statements; pertaining to the Synoptic Gospels. Also **syn·op·ti·cal.**—*n.* (*Often cap.*) any one of the Synoptic Gospels or their authors.—**syn·op·ti·cal·ly,** *adv.*

syn·os·to·sis, sin″o·stō'sis, *n.* pl. **syn·os·to·ses,** sin″o·stō'sēz. [N.L., < Gr. *syn-,* together, and *ostéon,* bone.] *Anat.* Union by means of ossified cartilage or bone; ankylosis. Also **syn·os·te·o·sis,** si·nos″tē·ō'sis.—**syn·os·tot·ic,** sin″o·stot'ik, *a.*

syn·o·vi·a, si·nō'vē·a, *n.* [N.L.; a word coined by Paracelsus, of uncertain elements.] *Physiol.* a lubricating liquid resembling the white of an egg, secreted by certain membranes, as those of the joints.—**syn·o·vi·al,** *a.*

syn·o·vi·tis, sin″o·vī'tis, *n.* [N.L.] *Pathol.* inflammation of a synovial membrane.

syn·sep·al·ous, sin·sep'a·lus, *a. Bot.* having united or joined sepals.

syn·tac·tic, sin·tak'tik, *a.* [Gr. *syntaktikós.*] *Gram.* Of or pertaining to syntax; in accordance with the rules of syntax. Also **syn·tac·ti·cal.**—**syn·tac·ti·cal·ly,** *adv.*

syn·tac·tics, sin·tak'tiks, *n. pl. but sing. in constr. Logic, philos.* The study of the formal characteristics of symbol structures and systems, esp. languages; a branch of semiotics, along with semantics and pragmatics. Also **log·i·cal syn·tax.**

syn·tax, sin'taks, *n.* [L.L. *syntaxis,* < Gr. *syntaxis,* < *syntássein,* arrange together, < *syn,* with, and *tássein,* arrange.] *Gram.* the structure of sentences; the established rules of usage for arrangement of the words of sentences into their proper forms and relations. *Ling.* that branch of the study of languages which deals with the patterns of word arrangement; *logic,* the syntactics of calculi or of languages, as computer languages.

syn·the·sis, sin′thi·sis, n. pl. **syn·the·ses,** sin′thi·sēz″. [L., < Gr. *synthesis*, a putting together, composition, < *syntithénai*, put together, < *syn*, with, and *tithénai*, set, put.] The combination of parts or elements, as material substances or objects of thought, into a complex whole: opposed to *analysis*; a complex whole made up of parts or elements combined; a process of reasoning which consists in advancing in a direct manner from principles established or assumed and propositions already proved to the conclusion; *chem.* the forming or building up of a complex substance or compound by the union of elements or the combination of simpler compounds or radicals.—**syn·the·sist,** n.

syn·the·size, sin′thi·sīz″, v.t.—synthesized, synthesizing. To combine into a complex whole; treat synthetically; to make up by combining parts or elements. Also *synthetize.*—**syn·the·siz·er,** n.

syn·thet·ic, sin·thet′ik, a. [Gr. *synthetikos*.] Of, pertaining to, proceeding by, or involving synthesis: opposed to *analytic*; *chem.* noting or pertaining to compounds produced artificially by chemical reaction in a laboratory as opposed to those of natural origin; *ling.* characterized by the use of inflectional affixes rather than separate words as the standard means of expressing an idea, as in Latin, Greek, and Russian. Not authentic or genuine; man-made. n. Any product of synthesis.—**syn·thet·i·cal,** a.—**syn·thet·i·cal·ly,** adv.

syn·thet·ic res·in, n. Any of a number of semisolid or solid organic materials resembling natural resins and produced by polymerization; a natural resin which has been chemically modified.

syn·thet·ic rub·ber, n. Any of various elastic products, as neoprene, butyl rubber, and many others, which are produced by chemical process to resemble natural rubber and which have commercially important properties, as toughness or resistance to heat, oil, or weather: used in electrical insulation, tires, waterproof material for divers' suits or crepe soles, and the like.

syn·the·tize, sin′thi·tīz″, v.t.—synthetized, synthetizing. To synthesize.—**syn·the·tiz·er,** n.

syn·ton·ic, sin·ton′ik, a. [Gr. *syn-*, together, and *tonos*, E. *tone*.] *Elect.* adjusted to oscillations of the same or a particular frequency; *psychiatry*, of a personality, marked by emotional responsiveness to the environment. Also **syn·to·nous.**—**syn·ton·i·cal·ly,** adv.

syph·i·lis, sif′i·lis, n. [N.L., first used in a Latin poem (published 1530) by Girolamo Fracastoro, entitled "Syphilis, sive Morbus Gallicus" ("Syphilis, or the French Disease"), being the story of *Syphilis*, a shepherd infected with the disease.] *Pathol.* a chronic, infectious venereal disease, caused by the microorganism *Treponema pallidum*, either congenital or communicated by contact, and usu. having three stages: the first, 'primary syphilis,' in which a hard chancre forms at the point of inoculation, the second, 'secondary syphilis,' characterized by skin affections and constitutional disturbances, and the third, 'tertiary syphilis,' characterized by infections of the bones, muscles, and viscera.—**syph·i·lit·ic,** sif″i·lit′ik, a. Pertaining to or affected with syphilis.—n. One affected with syphilis.

syph·i·lol·o·gy, sif″i·lol′o·jē, n. The sum of scientific knowledge concerning syphilis. —**syph·i·lol·o·gist,** n.

sy·phon, sī′fon, n., v.t., v.i. Siphon.

Syr·ette, si·ret′, n. A disposable tube attached to a hypodermic needle for injecting medicines. (Trademark.)

sy·rin·ga, si·ring′ga, n. An ornamental shrub of the genus *Philadelphus*, having sweet-smelling, white or cream-colored blossoms; also *moçk orange*. The lilac belonging to the genus *Syringa*.

sy·ringe, si·rinj′, sir′inj, n. [= Fr. *seringue*, < M.L. *syringa*, for L.L. *syrinx* (pl. *syringes*), < Gr. *syrigx*, pipe.] A small, portable device for drawing in a quantity of a fluid and ejecting it in a stream, used for cleansing wounds or injecting fluids into the body, and commonly consisting of a tube, narrowed at its outlet, fitted with a piston or a rubber bulb; any of various similar pumplike devices, as for spraying plants or exhausting air from a closed vessel. —v.t.—syringed, syringing. To cleanse, wash, or inject by means of a syringe.

sy·rin·ge·al, si·rin′jē·al, a. *Ornith.* of, pertaining to, or connected with the syrinx.

sy·rin·go·my·e·li·a, si·ring″gō·mī·ē′lē-a, n. *Pathol.* a disease affecting the spinal cord in which liquid accumulates in abnormal cavities, replacing the nerve tissue and causing spasticity and muscle atrophy.—**sy·rin·go·my·el·ic,** si·ring″gō·mī·el′ik, a.

syr·inx, sir′ingks, n. pl. **sy·rin·ges, syr·inx·es,** si·rin′jēz. [L.L., < Gr. pipe, tube passage, tunnel: cf. *susurrus*.] *Ornith.* the vocal organ of birds, situated at or near the bifurcation of the trachea into the bronchi; *archaeol.* a narrow channel or tunnel cut in the rock, as in the burial vaults of ancient Egypt; *mythol.* panpipe.

syr·phid, sur′fid, n. [N.L. *Syrphidæ*, pl., < *Syrphus*, the typical genus, < Gr. *syrphos*, gnat.] Any of the *Syrphidæ*, a family of dipterous insects or flies, feeding on nectar and pollen of flowers, and esp. beneficial because their larvae feed on plant lice. Also **syr·phid fly, syr·phus fly, flow·er fly.**

syr·up, sir·up, sir′up, sur′up, n. [O.Fr. Fr. *sirop*, Ar. *sharāb*, drink, beverage, syrup: cf. *shrub* and *sherbet*.] Any of various sweet usu. viscous liquids; a preparation of water or fruit juice boiled down with sugar; the liquid yielding, or that separated from, crystallized sugar in the process of refining; a liquid prepared for table use from molasses or glucose. *Pharm.* the U.S.P. standard of 1000 cubic centimeters of 850 grams of sucrose dissolved in purified water, used as a vehicle in many prescriptions; also **sim·ple syr·up.**—v.t.—syruped, syruping. To cover, fill, or sweeten with or as with syrup.—**syr·up·y, sir·up·y,** a. Like syrup; sweet or thick; *fig.* cloyingly sweet or overly sentimental.

sys·sar·co·sis, sis″är·kō′sis, n. pl. **sys·sar·co·ses,** sis″är·kō′sēz. *Anat.* the union or connection of bones attached by muscle.

sys·tal·tic, si·stal′tik, si·stal′tik, a. [Gr. *systaltikos*—*syn*, with, and *stellō*, to put.] *Physiol.* Having alternate contraction and dilatation, as the heart; pulsating.

sys·tem, sis′tem, n. [L.L. *systema*, < Gr. *systēma*, an organized or complex whole, < *synistánai*, set together, combine, < *syn*, with, and *istánai*, cause to stand.] An assemblage or combination of things or parts forming a complex or unitary whole; as, a mountain *system* or a *system* of rivers or canals; a number of heavenly bodies associated and acting together according to certain natural laws; as, the solar *system*; any assemblage or set of correlated members; as, a *system* of weights and measures; an ordered and comprehensive assemblage of facts, principles, or doctrines in a particular field of knowledge or thought; as, a *system* of philosophy; a coordinated body of methods, or a complex scheme or plan of procedure; as, a *system* of government or taxation; any formulated, regular, or special method or plan of procedure; as, a *system* of numbering; government, business, politics,

or society in general, as: He rebelled against the *system*. Due method, or orderly manner of arrangement or procedure; as, work that shows *system*. *Biol.* an assemblage of parts or organs of the same or similar tissues, or concerned with the same function; as, the nervous *system*; the entire human or animal body as a physiological unity or anatomical whole; as, to expel poison from the *system*. *Geol.* a division in the classification of stratified deposits, usu. comprising those of a given geological period; *chem.* any substance or group of substances considered apart from their surroundings. *Mus.* a series of tones, as a mode or scale, serving as a basis for muscial composition; a set of two or more staves connected together for concerted music. *Astron.* a hypothesis or theory of the disposition and arrangements of the heavenly bodies by which their phenomena are explained; as, the Copernican *system*; *nat. hist.* a method or scheme of classification; *crystal.* any of the six general modes of crystallization.—**sys·tem·less,** a.

sys·tem·at·ic, sis″te·mat′ik, a. [Gr. *systēmatikós*.] Having, showing, or involving a system, method, or plan; as, a *systematic* course of reading; characterized by system or method, or methodical; as, *systematic* habits; arranged in or comprising an ordered system; as, *systematic* theology; pertaining to, based on, or in accordance with a system of classification; as, the *systematic* names of plants or animals; concerned with relationships in classification; as, *systematic* botany. Also **sys·tem·at·i·cal.**—**sys·tem·at·i·cal·ly,** adv.— **sys·tem·at·ic·ness,** n.

sys·tem·at·ics, sis″te·mat′iks, n. pl. but sing. in constr. The study of systems or of classification, as of plants and animals. See *taxonomy*.

sys·tem·a·tism, sis′te·ma·tiz″um, n. The practice of systematizing; adherence to system.

sys·tem·a·tist, sis′te·ma·tist, n. One who constructs a system or classifies according to a system; one who adheres to system.

sys·tem·a·tize, sis′te·ma·tīz″, v.t.—systematized, systematizing. To arrange in or according to a system; to reduce to a system; to make systematic. Also *systemize*.—**sys·tem·a·ti·za·tion,** n.—**sys·tem·a·tiz·er,** n.

sys·tem·ic, si·stem′ik, a. Of or pertaining to a system. *Physiol., pathol.* pertaining to a particular system of parts or organs of the body; pertaining to or affecting the entire bodily system or the body as a whole; as, a *systemic* disease.—**sys·tem·i·cal·ly,** adv.

sys·tem·ize, sis′te·mīz″, v.t.—systemized, systemizing. Systematize.—**sys·tem·i·za·tion,** n.—**sys·tem·iz·er,** n.

sys·tems a·nal·y·sis, n. The process of incorporating data from various fields of science into mathematical models to achieve an optimum solution to a problem; the analysis of a complex problem or situation using mathematical models so as to allow subsequent treatment of data by electronic computers or other data-processing equipment. Also **sys·tems de·sign,** **sys·tems en·gi·neer·ing.**—**sys·tems an·a·lyst,** one who analyzes systems, esp. a professional; a moderator for the various sciences or systems involved in a systems analysis.

sys·to·le, sis′to·lē″, sis′to·lē, n. [Gr. *systolé*, < *syn*, together, and *stello*, to put.] *Physiol.* the regularly repeated contraction of the heart that forces the blood through the circulatory system: opposed to *diastole*. The shortening of a long syllable, esp. as in classical prosody.—**sys·tol·ic,** si·stol′ik, a.

sys·tyle, sis′til, a. *Arch.* having a space between columns that is equal in length to twice the diameter of a column.

syz·y·gy, siz'i·jē, *n.* pl. **szy·y·gies.** [L.L. *syzygia,* < Gr. *syzygia,* < *syzygos,* yoked together, < *syn,* with, and *zeygnynai,* yoke, join.] *Astron.* the conjunction or opposition of two or more heavenly bodies within one gravitational system and forming a nearly straight line; a point in the orbit of a body, as the moon, at which it is in conjunction with or in opposition to the sun. *Anc. pros.* a group or combination of two feet in one verse. A pair or couple, as of connected or correlated things; a joining or conjunction of two things.—**sy·zyg·i·al,** si·zij'ē·al, *a.*

T

T, t, tē, *n.* The twentieth letter of the English alphabet and sixteenth consonant; the sound of the letter T as represented in speech; the delineation of the letter T or t in writing or printing; something designated by or having the shape of the letter T or t; a graphic device for printing the letter T or t; the Roman numeral representing 160.—**to a T,** to perfection; exactly.

't, t. A contracted form of the pronoun 'it,' usu. used before a verb; as, *'tis, 'twill, 'twas.*

T, tē. *Phys.* temperature, on an absolute scale; radioactive half life; surface tension. (*Usu. l.c.*) time.

tab, tab, *n.* [Origin uncertain.] A small flap, strap, loop, or similar appendage, as on a garment; a tag or label; a small addition or insert, as on a license plate; a small piece projecting from a card or folder to aid in filing; *aeron.* a small auxiliary control surface added to a larger control surface on an airplane. *Colloq.* a bill or statement of amount owed; a close watch, check, or account, usu. with *keep* and *on*; as, to *keep tabs on* someone.—*v.t.*— *tabbed, tabbing.* To furnish or ornament with a tab or tabs; to single out or name.

tab·a·nid, tab'a·nid, *n.* Any of a number of large, dipterous, bloodsucking insects belonging to the family *Tabanidae,* including horseflies and gadflies.—*a.*

tab·ard, tab'ērd, *n.* [O.Fr. *tabarde, tabart;* origin unknown.] A kind of coarse, heavy, short coat with or without sleeves, formerly used as an outdoor garment; a loose outer garment with short sleeves, or without sleeves, formerly worn by knights over their armor, and usu. emblazoned with the arms of the wearer; a similar garment forming the official dress of a herald, emblazoned with the arms of his lord.

Ta·bas·co, ta·bas'kō, *n.* [From *Tabasco,* state of southeastern Mexico.] A pungent condiment sauce prepared from the fruit of a variety of capsicum. (Trademark.)

tab·by, tab'ē, *n.* pl. **tab·bies.** [Fr. *tabis,* earlier *atabis,* silk fabric; < Ar., and named from a quarter of Bagdad where it was manufactured.] A cat with a striped or brindled coat; a domestic cat, esp. female; an old maid; spinster; any spiteful female gossip or tattler; a watered silk fabric, or some other watered material, as moreen.— *a.* Made of or resembling tabby; striped or brindled.—*v.t.*—*tabbied, tabbying.* To give a wavy or watered appearance to, as silk.

tab·er·nac·le, tab'ēr·nak"l, *n.* [O.Fr. Fr. *tabernacle,* < L. *tabernaculum,* tent, dim. of *taberna,* hut, shop.] A temporary habitation, as a tent or hut; a dwelling place; a tent used by the Israelites as a portable sanctuary in the wilderness during the

Exodus; any place or house of worship, esp. one designed for a large audience; a canopied niche or recess, as for an image or statue; formerly, the human body as the temporary abode of the soul; *eccles.* an ornamental receptacle for the pyx; *naut.* an elevated socket for a mast, or a post to which a mast may be hinged when fitted for lowering to pass beneath bridges.— *v.i., v.t.*—*tabernacled, tabernacling.* To dwell or place in, or as in, a tabernacle.— **tab·er·nac·u·lar,** tab'ēr·nak'ū·lėr, *a.*

ta·bes, tā'bēz, *n.* pl. **ta·bes.** [L., < *tabere,* melt, waste: cf. Gr. *tēkein,* melt.] *Pathol.* A gradually progressive emaciation accompanying a disease; tabes dorsalis.—**ta·-bet·ic,** ta·bet'ik, ta·bē'tik, *a. n.*

ta·bes dor·sa·lis, tā'bēz dạr·sā'lis, *n.* [N.L., 'tabes of the back.'] *Pathol.* a disease of the spinal cord caused by syphilis, marked by intense pain, difficulty in coordination and walking, and eventually paralysis. Also *locomotor ataxia.*

tab·la·ture, tab'la·chėr, *n.* [Fr. *tablature,* < L. *tabula,* E. *table.*] A tabular space, surface, or structure; *mus.* a system of notation using letters or figures to indicate finger position rather than tones to be produced; *anat.* the division between two plates of cranial bones.

ta·ble, tā'bl, *n.* [O.Fr. Fr. *table,* < L. *tabula,* board, plank, tablet, writing, list, picture, prob. akin to *taberna,* hut, shop.] An article of furniture consisting of a flat top resting on legs or on a pillar, on which to serve meals, play games, perform work, or set ornaments; the board at or around which persons sit at meals; the food placed on a table to be eaten; a company of persons at a table, as for a meal, game, or business transaction; a flat or plane surface; a level area; a tableland or plateau; *pl.* the tablets on which certain collections of laws were anciently inscribed, or the laws themselves. An arrangement of words, numbers, or signs, or combinations of them, as in parallel columns, to exhibit a set of facts or relations in a definite, compact, and comprehensive form; a synoptical statement; a list of items or particulars; a synopsis or scheme. *Jewelry,* the upper horizontal surface of a faceted gem, esp. a brilliant; a gem with such a surface. *Arch.* a flat, vertical, usu. rectangular surface forming a distinct feature in a wall, often ornamental; a stringcourse or other horizontal band of some size and weight. *Games,* a backgammon board, or either of its two parts.—*v.t.*—*tabled, tabling.* To place, as money or a card, upon a table; to postpone, as a proposal or resolution of an assembly, for discussion at some future, frequently unspecified time; to enter in or form into a table or list; *carp.* to fit together by alternate seams and projections.—**turn the ta·bles,** to bring about a complete reversal of circumstances or relations between two persons or parties.

tab·leau, tab'lō, ta·blō', *n.* pl. **tab·leaux, tab·leaus,** tab'lōz, ta·blōz'. [Fr. *tableau,* < *table,* a table.] A striking representation; a picture; an artistic arrangement or grouping. A picturelike representation of a scene by performers, often in costume, striking appropriate poses and remaining motionless; also **ta·bleau vi·vant.**

tab·leau cur·tain, *n. Theatr.* a curtain drawn to the side and upward to produce a draped appearance.

ta·ble·cloth, tā'bl·klạth", tā'bl·kloth", *n.* A cloth for covering a table before the dishes are set on it for meals.

ta·ble d'hôte, tab'l dōt', tä'bl dōt', *Fr.* tä·ble dōt', *n.* pl. **ta·bles d'hôte,** tab'lz dōt', tä'blz dōt', *Fr.* tä·ble dōt'. [Fr., 'host's table.'] A meal of prearranged courses served at a fixed time and price,

for guests at a hotel or restaurant, as distinguished from *à la carte.* Also *prix fixe.*

ta·ble-hop, tā'bl·hop", *v.i.*—*table-hopped, table-hopping. Colloq.* to go from one table to another visiting with people, as in any night club, restaurant, or the like.

ta·ble·land, tā'bl·land", *n.* A broad stretch of elevated flat land; a plateau.

ta·ble lin·en, *n.* The linen used for and at the table, as napkins and tablecloths.

ta·ble salt, *n.* Salt used for seasoning food in cooking and at the table.

ta·ble·spoon, tā'bl·spōn", tā'bl·spųn", *n.* A spoon larger than a teaspoon or a dessertspoon, used in serving food. A standard unit of measurement in cooking, equivalent to three teaspoons, or ½ fluid ounce; abbr. *T., tbs., tbsp.*

ta·ble·spoon·ful, tā'bl·spōn"fųl', tā'bl·-spųn"fųl", *n.* pl. **ta·ble·spoon·fuls.** The quantity that a tablespoon can hold.

tab·let, tab'lit, *n.* [Fr. *tablette,* dim. of *table.*] A pad of sheets of paper, as for notes or letters; a thin, flat piece or sheet, as of wood, ivory, or slate, used for writing or drawing; a small, flat surface, a slab of wood or stone, or a metal plate bearing a design or inscription; a small disk or lozenge of medicine, as of aspirin; a small flattish cake, as of soap.

ta·ble talk, *n.* Talk at meals; talk at a table, as conversation about the cards during a bridge game; a polite subject for conversation at meals.

ta·ble ten·nis, *n.* A game very similar to tennis, played by two or teams of two players on a rectangular table using wood paddles and a small plastic ball. Also *ping pong.*

ta·ble·top, tā'bl·top", *n.* The top surface of a table; a photograph of or a miniature arrangement of objects on a table.—*a.*

ta·ble·ware, tā'bl·wâr", *n.* Dishes and utensils used at the table or at meals.

ta·ble wine, *n.* A wine containing no more than 14 percent alcohol, served with meals.

tab·loid, tab'loid, *n.* [Prop. a trademark name for compressed drugs, etc.: cf. *tablet* and *-oid.*] A newspaper with pages half the standard size, containing condensed stories and articles and numerous pictures. (*Cap.*) a compressed tablet of various drugs; (Trademark.)—*a.* Compressed; condensed; in small form.

ta·boo, ta·bu, ta·bö', ta·bö', *a.* [Polynesian *tabu* (in Tonga Islands), also *tapu.*] Among the Polynesians and other races of the southern Pacific Ocean, separated or set apart as sacred, forbidden to general use, or placed under a prohibition or ban; forbidden, as by social usage; interdicted. —*n.* Among the Polynesians and related races, the system, practice, or act, whereby things are set apart as sacred, forbidden to general use, or placed under a prohibition or interdiction; the fact of being so set apart, forbidden, or placed; a prohibition or interdiction of something; exclusion from use or practice; exclusion from social intercourse; ostracism.—*v.t.*—*tabooed, tabooing.* To put under a taboo; to prohibit or forbid; to ostracize, as a person.

ta·bor, ta·bour, tā'bėr, *n.* [O.Fr. *tabor, tabour* (Fr. *tambour*), drum; prob. < Ar. or Pers.] A small kind of drum formerly used esp. as self accompaniment while playing a pipe or fife.—*v.i.* To play upon or as upon a tabor; drum.—**ta·bor·er, ta·bour·er,** *n.*

tab·o·ret, tab·ou·ret, tab'o·rit, tab"o·ret', *n.* [Fr. *tabouret,* orig. dim. of O.Fr. *tabour,* E. *tabor.*] A low seat without back or arms; a stool; a small stand of similar form; a frame for embroidery; a tabret.

tab·o·rin, tab'ėr·in, *n.* [Fr. *tabourin.*] A small tabor. Also **tab·o·rine,** tab'o·rēn, tab·o·rēn'.

tab·ret, tab'rit, *n.* [A dim. form.] A small tabor.

tab·u·lar, tab'ū·lẽr, *a.* [L. *tabularis,* < *tabula.*] Pertaining to or of the nature of a table or tabulated arrangement; ascertained from or computed by the use of tables; having the form of a table, tablet, or tablature; flat and expansive.—**ta·bu·lar·ly,** *adv.*

ta·bu·la ra·sa, tab'ū·la rā'sa, tab'ū·la rä'sa, L. tä'bŏ·lä" rä'sä, n. pl. **ta·bu·lae ra·sae,** tab'ū·lē rā'sē, tab'ū·lē" rä'sē, L. tä'bụ·lī" Räʼsī. [L.] The mind before outside impressions or experiences have affected it; a clean or empty slate.

tab·u·late, tab'ū·lāt", *v.t.—tabulated, tabulating.* [L. *tabula,* board, plank, tablet, list.] To put or form into a table, scheme, list, or synopsis; formulate tabularly; to give a flat surface to; make tabular.—**tab'ū·lit,** tab'ū·lāt", *a.* [N.L. *tabulatus,* table-shaped, L..boarded, floored, < L. *tabula.*] Shaped like a table or tablet; tabular; *zool.* having transverse dissepiments, as certain corals.—**tab·u·la·tion,** *n.*

tab·u·la·tor, tab'ū·lā"tẽr, *n.* One who or that which tabulates; an attachment to a typewriter for tabulating accounts or for aligning typewritten matter in columns.

tac·a·ma·hac, tak'a·ma·hak", *n.* [Mex.] Any of certain resinous substances used in incenses or ointments, as the gum obtained from *Terebinthus tomentosa,* a tropical American balsameaceous tree; the resin derived from the buds of *Populus balsamifera,* the balsam poplar; any tree yielding such a product, esp. in N. America, the balsam poplar. Also **tac·a·ma·hac·a,** tac·ma·hack, tak"a·ma·hak'a, tak'ma·hak".

ta·cet, tä'ket, tā'sit, *n.* [L., 'it is silent.'] *Mus.* an indication that an instrument or voice is to be silent for a time.

tach·i·na fly, tak'i·na flī", *n.* A dipterous insect of the *Tachinidae* family whose parasitic larvae are useful in control of caterpillars, beetles, and other pests.

ta·chis·to·scope, ta·kis'to·skōp", *n.* [Gr. *táchistos,* superl. of *tachys,* swift.] *Psychol.* an apparatus for testing visual perception which exposes to view, for a selected brief period of time, an object or group of objects, as letters or words.—**ta·chis·to·scop·ic,** ta·kis"to·skop'ik, *a.*—**ta·chis·to·scop·i·cal·ly,** *adv.*

ta·chom·e·ter, ·ta·kom'i·tẽr, ta·kom'i·tẽr, *n.* [Gr. *tachus,* swift, *metron,* measure.] An instrument for measuring velocity, as of running water or any flowing liquid; a device for indicating the revolutions per minute of an engine, esp. an automobile engine.—**tach·o·met·ri·cal·ly,** tak"o·me'trik·lē, *adv.*—**ta·chom·e·try,** *n.*

tach·y·car·di·a, tak"i·kär'dē·a, *n.* [N.L. (Gr. *chardia,* heart).] *Med.* excessively rapid heart action.

ta·chyg·ra·phy, ta·kig'ra·fē, ta·kig'ra·fē, *n.* [Gr. *tachys,* quick, and *graphō,* to write.] The art or practice of quick writing; shorthand; stenography, esp. that of the ancient Greeks and Romans.—**tach·y·graph·ic, tach·y·graph·i·cal,** tak"i·graf'ik, *a.*

tach·y·lyte, tach·y·lite, tak'i·līt", *n.* [Gr. *tachys,* swift, *lūō,* to loose.] Vitreous, black basalt, easily fused under a blowpipe.—**tach·y·lit·ic,** tak"i·lit'ik, *a.*

ta·chym·e·ter, ta·kim'i·tẽr, ta·kim'i·tẽr, *n.* *Surv.* an instrument, as a transit or theodolite, used for the rapid determination of points in a survey. Also **tach·e·om·e·ter.**—**ta·chym·e·try,** ta·kim'i·trē, ta·kim'i·trē, *n.*

tac·it, tas'it, *a.* [L. *tacitus,* silent, < *taceo,* to be silent; cogn. with Goth. *thahan,* to be silent.] Silent; unspoken; implied but not expressed in words; as, *tacit* consent; *law,* existing without express agreement or legislation.—**tac·it·ly,** *adv.*—**tac·it·ness,** *n.*

tac·i·turn, tas'i·tẽrn", *a.* [L. *taciturnus,* < *tacitus,* silent.] Speaking little or infrequently; habitually silent.—**tac·i·tur·ni·ty,** tas"i·tẽr'ni·tē, *n.*

tack, tak, *n.* [Of Celtic origin; Ir. *taca,* Armor. *tach,* a nail; seen also in *attach, attack, detach.*] A stubby, usu. tapered, sharp-pointed nail having a broad head; a loosely sewed stitch; basting; a slight fastening; the condition of being sticky before completely dried, as paint; a procedure or course of action, as of government or business administration, esp. when different from prior established practices; equipment, as a saddle and bridle, for a riding horse. *Naut.* a line secured to the lower leading corner of certain sails, as a studding sail; that part of the sail to which the line is attached; the lower leading corner of the fore-and-aft sail; the heading of a sailing ship in reference to the position or trim of the sails; a heading into the wind; a shift in direction; a back and forth or zigzag course.—*v.t.—tacked, tacking.* To fasten; to attach, as with tacks; to connect or join in a slight or hasty manner; to add on as a supplement or addition; to append. *Naut.* to bring about, as a sailboat, to a heading into the wind; to maneuver, as a sailboat, in a tack.—*v.i. Naut.* to alter a ship's course by tacking; to sail windward by tacking. To reverse, change, or modify abruptly one's ideas, conduct, or attitude; swing around; shift; to proceed along or pursue a zigzag course.—**tack·er,** *n.*

tack, tak, *n.* [Perh. another use of *tack.*] Food; fare: used in compounds; as, hardtack.

tack·le, tak'l, tä'kl, *n.* [From the stem of *take;* L.G. and D. *takel,* Dan. *takkel,* Sw. *tackel,* tackle.] Apparatus, appliances, or equipment for various kinds of work or sport; gear, as football suits, tak'l. An arrangement of one or more pulleys with rope or cable in a block, used for hoisting and lowering large, heavy weights, tä'kl. *Naut.* the ropes and rigging of a ship, tak'l. An act of grabbing and upsetting, as in football; *football,* one or the other of two players on a football team whose position in the line of scrimmage is usu. between a guard and an end, or the position of such a player, tak'l.—tak'l, *v.t.—tackled, tackling.* To take upon, as something difficult, to try to do, master, or resolve, as: He *tackled* the problem vigorously. To cope with; *football,* to throw to the ground, as an opposing ball carrier.—tak'l, *v.i. Football,* to tackle the opposing ball carrier.—**tack·ler,** *n.*—**tack·ling,** tak'ling, *n.*

tack·y, tak'ē, *a.—tackier, tackiest.* [From tack.] Adhesive; sticky.—**tack·i·ness,** *n.*

tack·y, tak'ē, *a.—tackier, tackiest.* [Origin obscure.] *Colloq.* Poor or shabby; dowdy; low-class; cheap; unnecessarily gaudy or showy.—**tack·i·ness,** *n.*

ta·co, tä'kō, *Sp.* tä'kạ, *n.* pl. **ta·cos,** tä'kōz, *Sp.* tä'kạs. A food of Mexican-Spanish origin, made by folding a fried tortilla over a spiced filling.

tac·o·nite, tak'o·nīt", *n.* A silica-hematite ore mined as a source of low-grade iron in the Lake Superior area.

tact, takt, *n.* [Fr. *tact,* touch, feeling, tact, < L. *tactus,* touch, < *tango, tactum,* to touch, < which also *tactile, tangent, tangible,* etc.] Skill or adroitness in doing or saying exactly what is required; a highly developed perception of what is tasteful, proper, or aesthetically pleasing; the sense of touch.—**tact·ful,** takt'ful, *a.*—**tact·ful·ly,** *adv.*—**tact·ful·ness,** *n.*

tac·tic, tak'tik, *a.* [N.L. *tacticus,* < Gr. *tacticós,* pertaining to arrangement, esp. in war, < *tássein,* arrange; as n., N.L. *tactica,*

< Gr. *tacticē,* the art of arranging, tactics, prop. fem. of *tacticós.*] Of or pertaining to arrangement or order; tactical.

tac·tic, tak'tik, *n.* A system of tactics; as, the *tactic* of any army; a tactical procedure.

tac·ti·cal, tak'ti·kal, *a.* Of or having to do with tactics, esp. as applied to military or naval combat tactics; pertaining to tactics in general; characterized by skillful tactics or adroit maneuvering or procedure; as, *tactical* movements or efforts, a *tactical* leader.—**tac·ti·cal·ly,** *adv.*

tac·tics, tak'tiks, *n. pl., sing. or pl. in constr.* [Fr. *tactique,* Gr. *taktikē* (*technē,* art), the art of drawing up soldiers, < *tassŏ, taxŏ,* to arrange (seen also in *syntax, taxidermy.*] *Milit.* the branch of military science that deals with the positioning and maneuvering of forces in a battle area and the practical application of weapons, for the purpose of achieving an advantage over the enemy or improving a disadvantage: distinguished from *strategy.* Any actions or methods employed to gain an objective or an end, as in business.—**tac·ti·cian,** tak·tish'an, *n.* One who is skilled, through experience or study, in tactics.

tac·tile, tak'til, tak'tīl, *a.* [Fr. *tactile,* < L. *tactilis,* < *tango,* to touch.] Pertaining to or possessing the sense of touch; capable of being touched or felt; tangible.—**tac·til·i·ty,** tak·til'i·tē, *n.*

tac·tile cor·pus·cle, *n. Anat.* any of numerous minute oval bodies, esp. of the fingers and toes, concerned with the sense of touch. Also **touch cor·pus·cle.**

tac·tion, tak'shan, *n.* [L. *tactio.*] The act of touching; touch.

tact·less, takt'lis, *a.* Without tact; characterized by lack of tact; as, a *tactless* person.—**tact·less·ly,** *adv.*—**tact·less·ness,** *n.*

tac·tu·al, tak'chŏ·al, *a.* Pertaining to the sense of touch; derived from touch.—**tac·tu·al·ly,** *adv.*

tad, tad, *n.* [Prob. for *tadpole.*] *Colloq.* a small child, esp. a boy.

tad·pole, tad'pōl", *n.* [Equiv. to *toadpoll,* that is toad with a big poll or head.] The young or aquatic larva of the frog or similar amphibian in its first stage from the spawn, prior to losing its tail and gills and before the development of legs. Also *polliwog.*

tae·di·um vi·tae, tē'dē·um vī'tē, *L.* tī'dē·ụm" wē'tī, *n.* [L.] The condition or state of feeling that life is tedious or tiresome.

tae·ni·a, tē'nē·a, *n.* pl. **tae·ni·ae,** tē'nē·ē". [L., < Gr. *tainia,* band, ribbon, fillet, also tapeworm.] A headband or fillet worn in ancient Greece; *arch.* the fillet or band on the Doric architrave, which separates it from the frieze; *anat.* a ribbonlike structure, as certain bands of white nerve or muscle fibers; *zool.* any of the various tapeworms of the genus *Taenia.* Also *tenia.*

tae·ni·a·cide, te·ni·a·cide, tē'nē·a·sīd", *n. Med.* a remedy that destroys tapeworms—*a.* Destructive of tapeworms; als **tae·ni·a·cid·al, te·ni·a·cid·al.**

tae·ni·a·sis, te·ni·a·sis, tē·nī'a·sis, *n.* [N.L.] *Pathol.* a diseased condition due to the presence of tapeworms. Also **te·ni·a·sis.**

taf·fe·ta, taf'i·ta, *n.* [Fr. *taffetas,* It. *taffetà,* < Pers. *tâftah,* pp. of verb *tâftan,* to weave.] A closely woven, stiff fabric of silk or synthetic fibers, esp. rayon or acetate, having a lustrous finish.—*a.*

taf·fe·ta weave, *n.* An alternate over and under weave which produces a tight, checkered pattern in the fabric. Also **plain weave.**

taff·rail, taf'rāl", *n.* [Earlier *tafferel,* < D. *tafereel,* panel, taffrail, dim. of *tafel,* L. *tabula,* E. *table.*] *Naut.* The upper part of the stern of a vessel; the rail around the stern.

taf·fy, taf'ē, *n.* A candy made of molasses or brown sugar and butter, boiled down and usu. drawn into strips until porous; also *Brit.* toffee, toffy. *Colloq.* flattery; cajolery.

Taf·fy, taf'ē, *n.* [W. *David.*] *Brit. slang*, a Welshman. Welsh pronunciation of David or Davy.

taf·fy pull, *n.* A type of party or informal social event at which the guests make and pull taffy.

taf·i·a, taf'ē·a, *n.* [Fr. from Malay.] A poor variety of West Indies rum distilled from sugarcane juice or a low grade of molasses.

tag, tag, *n.* [M.E. *tagge*: cf. Sw. *tagg*, prickle, spine, point, tooth.] A piece or strip, as of paper, leather, or plastic, used as a mark or label; as, a price or luggage *tag*; something appended, as by way of ornament or addition; a loose end or tatter; a point or binding, as of metal or plastic, as at the tip of a shoelace; any small appendage to a garment, as a loop or tassel; a bright piece of material around the shank of the hook on an artificial fly; a remnant or vestige; the tail of an animal, or the tip of the tail; a matted piece of sheep's wool; an addition to a speech or other writing, as the moral of a fable; a quotation added for special effect; a common phrase or expression; a cliché; an epithet; the last words of a speech in a play; an actor's cue.—*v.t.*—*tagged, tagging.* To furnish or label with a tag or tags; to append, as a tag; to shear tags from, as sheep. *Colloq.* to follow closely; to ticket for a traffic violation.—*v.i.* To follow closely, used with *after* and *along.*—**tag·like**, *a.*

tag, tag, *n.* [Origin uncertain.] A children's game in which one player chases the others until he touches one of them, who then takes his place as pursuer; *baseball*, the act or occurrence of touching a base runner. —*v.t.*—*tagged, tagging.* To touch in the game of tag; *baseball*, to touch and put out, as a sliding base runner, with the ball in the hand or with the glove holding the ball; *colloq.* to hit solidly, as a baseball or an opponent in boxing.

tag·board, tag'bōrd″, tag'bård″, *n.* A sturdy cardboard used as material for tags, posters, and the like.

tag day, *n.* A day on which contributions to a charity or special fund are solicited, each contributor receiving a tag as a distinguishing mark.

tag end, *n.* The last or concluding part; tail end; a scrap or fragment; as, a *tag end* of cloth.

tag line, *n.* The concluding line, as in a play, anecdote, or speech, esp. when used for clarification or dramatic effect; an identifying phrase or slogan.

tag up, *v.i. Baseball*, to touch the base one is occupying before advancing toward another following the catch of a fly ball.

Ta·hi·tian, ta·hē'shan, ta·hē'tē·an, tä·hē'shan, tä·hē'tē·an, *a.* Of or pertaining to the island of Tahiti in the Society Islands, its inhabitants, or their language.— *n.* A native or inhabitant of Tahiti, esp. a member of the native Polynesian race; the language of this race.

tah·sil·dar, ta·sēl·där′, *n. India*, a tax collector or officer for the revenue department. Also **tah·seel·dar**.

Tai, tī, *n., a.* Thai.

tai·ga, tī'ga, *n.* The coniferous, far northern forest in Siberia; the similar forests in far northern areas of N. America and Eurasia.

tail, tāl, *n.* [O.E. *tægel, tægl,* = O.H.G. *zagel* = Icel. *tagl,* tail, = Goth. *tagl,* hair.] The extreme rear part of an animal or organism that forms a distinct and usu. flexible appendage to the body; something

resembling or suggesting this in shape or position; as, the *tail* of a kite; the hinder, bottom, or concluding part of anything; the conclusion, as of a speech, book, play or event; the inferior or undesirable part of anything; *aeron.* the after portion or a rear part of an airplane; *astron.* the luminous train extending from the head of a comet. *Pl., colloq.* the reverse of a coin; a tailcoat; men's formal attire. The outer corner of the eye; a long braid or tress of hair; a line or file of people; a train of followers or attendants; retinue; the hind part of a cart or wagon; the lower part of a pool or stream. *Colloq.* someone who keeps close undercover surveillance of another; a shadow. *Slang*, the posterior or rump.— *v.t.* To form or furnish with a tail; to form or constitute the tail or end of, as a procession; terminate; *colloq.* to follow, as someone under surveillance. To join or attach at the tail or end of another; to remove or shorten the tail of; *carp.* to fasten, as a beam, by one of its ends, usu. followed by *in* or *into.*—*v.i.* To form, move, or pass in a line; *colloq.* to follow after; *naut.* to have or take a position with the stern of the boat leading, usu. followed by *in* or *into;* *carp.* to be fastened by the end, usu. followed by *in* or *into.*—*a.* Coming from, or being in, the rear.—**tail off**, to diminish or fade away gradually; as, a stream that *tails off* into a thicket.—**turn tail**, to flee or run from something.—**with the tail be·tween the legs**, completely defeated; cowed; abject.—**tailed**, *a.*—**tail·er**, tā'lėr, *n.*—**tail·less**, *a.*—**tail·like**, *a.*

tail, tāl, *n.* [O.Fr. Fr. *taille*, a cutting, cut, division, assessment, tax, < O.Fr. *taillier* (Fr. *tailler*), cut, shape, fix, < M.L. *taliare*, cut, < L. *talea*, rod, stick, twig, cutting (for planting): cf. *tally.*] *Law*, the limitation of an estate to a person and the heirs of his body, or some particular class of such heirs.—*a.* [O.Fr. *taillie*, pp. of *taillier.*] *Law*, Limited to a specified line of heirs; being in tail, or entailed.

tail·back, tāl'bak″, *n. Football*. An offensive player in the position farthest back from the scrimmage line; the position this team member plays.

tail·board, tāl'bōrd″, tāl'bård″, *n.* The rear section, or tailgate, esp. of a cart, wagon, or truck.

tail coat, *n.* A man's formal dress coat, or cutaway, with a swallowtail back. Also **tail·coat**, *tails, swallowtail.*

tail end, *n.* The hindmost, lowest, or concluding part of anything.

tail fin, *n.* The caudal fin of a fish; one of the two projections on an automobile formed by ornamental shaping of the rear fender.

tail·gate, tāl'gāt″, *n.* A rear mounted board or gate on a truck or station wagon, hinged or sliding in a frame to allow easy access for loading or unloading.—*v.i.*— *tailgated, tailgating.* To drive so closely behind another vehicle as to be hazardous. —*v.t.* To follow, as another vehicle, at a hazardous interval.

tail·ing, tā'ling, *n.* The part of a projecting stone or brick tailed or inserted in a wall. *Pl.* the residue of any product; leavings; remainders.

taille, tāl, *Fr.* tä'ye, *n.* pl. **tailles**, tālz, *Fr.* tä'ye. A former French tax, levied by the king or a feudal lord on his subjects and from which the nobles and clergy were usu. exempt; *dressmaking*, the bodice or waist of a dress.

tail·light, tāl'līt″, *n.* A light carried at the rear of a train, automobile, or truck. Also **tail lamp**.

tai·lor, tā'lėr, *n.* [O.Fr. *tailleor* (Fr. *tailleur*), lit. 'cutter,' < *taillier*, cut.] One whose business is to make or alter outer gar-

ments, as coats or suits.—*v.i.* To do the work of a tailor.—*v.t.* To make by tailor's work; to fit or furnish with clothing; to adjust or adapt to a particular need or use.

tai·lor·bird, tā'lėr·bụrd″, *n.* Any of various small Asiatic and African passerine birds of the warbler family which stitch leaves together to form and hide their nests.

tai·lored, tā'lėrd, *a.* Made by or as by a tailor; made with simplicity of cut and style, often from substantial fabric, usu. referring to women's garments; appearing neat and well-fitted.

tai·lor·ing, tā'lėr·ing, *n.* The business or work of a tailor; the workmanship or finished product of a tailor.

tai·lor·made, tā'lėr·mād′, *a.* Made by or as by a tailor; made with simplicity of cut and finish; made-to-order or well-fitted; made or adjusted to a particular need or purpose.

tail·piece, tāl'pēs″, *n.* A piece forming a tail or added to the end; an end piece; an appendage; *print.* a small picture or ornamental design at the end of a chapter or section in a book; *mus.* the triangular, wooden piece at the lower end of instruments belonging to the viol family, to which the strings are fastened. *Constr.* a rafter or beam, usu. short, tailed in the wall at one end and supported with a header at the other end; also **tail beam**.

tail·pipe, tāl'pīp″, *n.* A pipe which conveys the exhaust fumes from the engine to the rear of a vehicle or jet plane and discharges them.

tail plane, *n. Aeron.* The horizontal supporting plane or surface of the tail of the aircraft; a horizontal stabilizer on an airplane.

tail·race, tāl'rās″, *n.* The race, flume, lower section of the millrace, or channel which conducts the water away from a water wheel or the like: opposed to *headrace;* *min.* the channel for conducting tailings or refuse away in water.

tail·spin, tāl'spin″, *n. Aeron.* a downward movement of an aircraft with the nose foremost and the tail whirling in circles above, whether performed as a stunt or occurring as an accident, as when the airplane is out of control from stalling; *fig.* a sudden collapse into confusion, depression, failure, or the like, which often results in losing one's control. Also **tail spin**.

tail·stock, tāl'stok″, *n. Mech.* the movable sliding frame of a lathe which supports the dead center or spindle holding the work. Also **foot·stock**.

tail·wind, tāl'wind″, *n.* A wind coming from the rear, as of a moving airplane, ocean vessel, or vehicle.

taint, tānt, *v.t.* [O.Fr. *taindre*, pp. *taint;* (Mod.Fr. *teindre, teint*), < L. *tingere*, to wet or moisten; whence also *tinge, tincture, tint.*] To imbue or impregnate with something noxious, poisonous, or offensive; to infect; to corrupt; to sully or pollute, as one's name or honor.—*v.i.* To become infected, corrupted, or contaminated—*n.* Any trace of that which is bad, harmful, or offensive; something that infects or contaminates; infection; corruption; a stain; a blemish on one's reputation.— **taint·less**, tānt'lis, *a.*

Tai·ping, tī'ping′, *a.* [Chinese, *t'ai p'ing,* great peace.] Referring to the unsuccessful Chinese rebellion of 1850–64, or to the dynasty that was to be established.—*n.* A fighter in the rebellion.

take, tāk, *v.t.*—past *took,* pp. *taken,* ppr. *taking.* [< Icel. and O.Sw. *taka,* Sw. *taga,* Dan. *tage,* to take, to seize, etc.; same root as L. *tango, tactum,* to touch (whence *tangible, tact,* etc.) *Tackle* is akin.] To grasp; to lay hold of; to seize; to get into one's hand; to obtain; to lay hold of and remove;

to catch suddenly; to entrap; to surprise; to make prisoner of; to capture; to obtain possession of by force of arms; to enter into possession by renting or leasing; to win, as a prize. To choose and make one's own; to select; to receive or accept, as an offer; to assume, as a position or office; to bear or submit to; to put up with; to subject oneself to, as an oath. To understand or comprehend; to receive with good or ill will; to feel concerning; as, to *take* an act amiss; to look upon as; to suppose, regard, or consider; as, to *take* something to be right; to experience, indulge, or feel, as pride. To carry off; to put an end to, as one's life; to subtract; as, *take* five from ten; to captivate, attract, or allure; as, to *take* one's fancy; to be infected or seized with; as, to *take* a cold; fasten on, attack, or assail, as by a blast, a disease, or the like. To convey or carry; to use for conveyance; as, to *take* a train; to conduct or lead; as, a path that *takes* one through the woods; to guide or escort; to maneuver or negotiate; as, to *take* the stairs two at a time; to clear. To avail oneself of, as an opportunity; to employ for advantage or pleasure, as a nap, vacation, or the like; to have recourse to, as shelter; to form or adopt, as a plan; to use, as precaution; to place oneself in; to occupy, as space or time; to consume; to require or render necessary, as: This job *takes* patience. To receive and swallow, as medicine; to copy; to draw, as a sketch; to photograph; to put in writing; to note down; *baseball*, to refrain from swinging at, as a pitch; *slang*, to cheat.—*v.i.* To direct one's course; to betake oneself; to turn in some direction; to suit the public taste; to please; to have the intended effect, as medicine; to catch hold, as a mechanical device; to become; as, to *take* sick; to apply oneself, as to studies; to put forth roots, as a plant; to be absorbed, as dye.—*n.* The quantity of anything taken; the quantity of fish or game taken at one haul; *motion pictures*, an uninterrupted span of filming; *printing*, a short piece of copy to be set in type; *colloq.* receipts from a sport event, play, or the like.—**take af·ter**, to follow; to imitate; to resemble.—**take arms** or **take up arms**, to commence war or hostilities.—**take breath**, to stop in order to breathe or rest after exertion.—**take care**, to be watchful, vigilant, or careful.—**take care of**, to have the charge of; to keep watch over.—**take fire**, to become ignited or inflamed; *fig.* to become excited, as with anger or love.—**take from**, to derogate or detract from.—**take heart**, to become courageous or confident.—**take in vain**, to use or utter unnecessarily, carelessly, or profanely.—**take it**, to accept or assume; to endure punishment or hardship.—**take it out on**, to mistreat or abuse, as another, because of one's own adversity, suffering, or the like.—**take leave**, to bid farewell; to depart; to permit oneself; to use a certain license or liberty.—**take one's part**, to espouse one's cause; to defend one.—**take pains**, to use all one's skill, care, and the like.—**take part in**, to share; to partake of.—**take part with**, to join or unite with.—**take place**, to happen.—**take root**, to strike a root; to put forth roots and grow; to become firmly fixed or established.—**take the field**, to commence the operations of a military campaign.—**take thought**, to be solicitous or anxious.—**take to**, to become fond of; to resort to.—**take to heart**, to be keenly or deeply affected by; to feel sensibly.—**take up with**, to associate with. —**tak·er**, *n.* One that takes; one who catches; a captor.

take back, *v.t.*—past *took back*, pp. *taken back*, ppr. *taking back*. To withdraw or retract, as a statement; to return, as de-

fective goods to a store; to regain possession of; to permit to return, as a defector.

take down, *v.t.*—past *took down*, pp. *taken down*, ppr. *taking down*. To raze, as a building; to disassemble or dismantle; to write down or record; to lower; to guide to a lower level, as a submarine; *colloq.* to humiliate.—*v.i.*

take·down, take-down, tāk′doun″, *a.* Made or constructed so as to be easily taken down or apart.—*n.* A rifle or other firearm that can be quickly disassembled; *colloq.* the art of reprimanding, humiliating, or embarrassing someone.

take-home pay, tāk′hōm′ pā″, *n.* Colloq. net earned income for a pay period; wages or salary after all deductions, esp. of taxes, have been made.

take in, *v.t.*—past *took in*, pp. *taken in*, ppr. *taking in*. To admit or bring into one's house; to encompass or include; to comprehend; to make smaller, as a dress; to contract; to furl, as a sail; to receive into the mind; to visit, as a museum; *colloq.* to cheat.

take-in, tāk′in″, *n.* Colloq. A deception, fraud, or imposition; something that deceives or imposes on one; the amount gained by a fraud.

take off, *v.t.*—past *took off*, pp. *taken off*, ppr. *taking off*. To remove or lift from the surface, outside, or top; to divest oneself of, as a shirt; to remove to a different place; to copy or reproduce; to kill; to withdraw; to deduct; *colloq.* to mimic.—*v.i.* To become airborne, as an airplane; *colloq.* to leave.

take·off, tāk′af″, tāk′of″, *n.* The leaving of the ground in leaping or in beginning a flight in an airplane; the place or point at which this occurs; departure; a setting out, as on a journey; *colloq.* an imitation or caricature; *mech.* any device for transferring power from an engine to a working machine.

take on, *v.t.*—past *took on*, pp. *taken on*, ppr. *taking on*. To assume, as new duties; to undertake; to acquire; to hire; to deal with; to enter into competition with.—*v.i.* Colloq. to be violently emotional, as sorrowful or angry.

take out, *v.t.*—past *took out*, pp. *taken out*, ppr. *taking out*. To remove; to extract; to deduct; to remove by cleansing or the like; to obtain, as a license; *colloq.* to escort or conduct; *bridge*, to overcall, as one's partner, and change the suit.

take o·ver, *v.t.*—past *took over*, pp. *taken over*, ppr. *taking over*. To assume control or ownership of; to seize by force or craft.— *v.i.* To come into dominance, as a new religion.—**take·o·ver**, tāk′ō″vėr, *n.* The act or process of assuming control, management, or ownership, as of a corporation.

take up, *v.t.*—past *took up*, pp. *taken up*, ppr. *taking up*. To lift; to raise; to begin where another left off; to resume; to occupy, engross, or engage; to charge oneself with, as a quarrel; to enter upon; to adopt, as a trade; to pay, as a loan, mortgage, or the like; to accept, as an option; to tighten or shorten; to criticize.—**take-up**, tāk′ up″, *n.* Any device for tightening, closing spaces, or the like; the act of tightening.

tak·ing, tā′king, *n.* The act of one who or that which takes; the state of being taken; a seizing or capture; that which is taken; *pl., colloq.* receipts.—*a.* Captivating; winning; charming; *colloq.* infectious.—**tak·ing·ly**, *adv.*—**tak·ing·ness**, *n.*

ta·lar·i·a, ta·lâr′ē·a, *n. pl.* [L., prop. neut. pl. of *talaris*, pertaining to the ankles, < *talus*, ankle.] *Class. mythol.* the winged sandals of the gods Hermes or Mercury.

tal·bot, tal′bot, tal′bot, *n.* [Prob. < *Talbot*, Eng. family name.] A breed of large, usu. white hounds with broad mouths, long, pendulous ears, and great powers of scent.

talc, talk, *n.* [Fr. *talc*, Sp. and Pg. *talco*, < Ar. *talq*, talc.] A hydrous magnesium

silicate, $Mg_3Si_4O_{10}(OH)_2$, a soft mineral that occurs in laminated masses, which is smooth to the touch, and may be of a white, gray, or greenish color. Also **tal·cum**, tal′-kum.—*v.t.*—talced, talcing, talcked, talcking. To coat or treat with talc.—**talck·y**, **talc·-ose, talc·ous**, tal′kōs, tal·kōs′, tal′kus, *a.*

tal·cum pow·der, *n.* Talc in a refined, powdered form, often perfumed for cosmetic use.

tale, tāl, *n.* [O.E. *talu*, speech, number; Icel. *tal, tala*, a speech, a number; Dan. *tal*, number, *tale*, talk, to talk; D. *tal*, number, *taal*, speech; G. *zahl*, number; akin *tell*.] A narrative of events that have happened or are imagined to have happened; a short story, true or fictitious; a piece of information, esp. gossip; a rumor; a falsehood; a lie.

tale·bear·er, tāl′bâr″ėr, *n.* A person who tells tales or spreads rumors likely to breed trouble; a gossip.—**tale·bear·ing**, *a., n.*

tal·ent, tal′ent, *n.* [O.Fr. Fr. *talent*, < L. *talentum*, talent (weight, money), < Gr. *tálanton*, a balance, weight, sum of money, akin to *tlēnai*, bear.] A special natural ability or aptitude; a capacity for achievement or success; natural ability; cleverness; a person or a group of persons of ability. An ancient unit of weight of the Mediterranean area; this weight of gold, silver, or other metal used as an ancient monetary unit.— **tal·ent·ed**, *a.*

tal·ent scout, *n.* A person who finds and recruits people with great ability or talent, as for the fields of entertainment or sports.

tal·ent show, *n.* A show in which amateur entertainers perform in order to win recognition of their talent.

tales·man, tālz′man, tā′lēz·man, *n. pl.* **tales·men**, *Law*, a person selected, usu. from a group of bystanders in a court, to serve on a jury in order to make up a deficiency in the number of jurors.

tale·tell·er, tāl′tel″ėr, *n.* One who tells tales or stories; a talebearer.—**tale·tell·ing**, *a., n.*

tal·i·grade, tal′i·grād″, *a. Zool.* walking with the weight on the outer edge of the foot.

tal·i·pes, tal′i·pēz″, *n.* [L. *talus*, ankle, and *pes*, foot.] *Pathol.* clubfoot.

tal·i·pot, tal′i·pot″, *n.* [Singhalese name.] A palm, *Corypha umbraculifera*, of India, Ceylon, and the Philippines, having leaves used for covering houses, for making umbrellas and fans, and as a substitute for writing paper.

tal·is·man, tal′is·man, tal′iz·man, *n. pl.* **tal·is·mans**. [Fr. and Sp. *talisman*, < Ar. *telsamân*, pl. of *telsam*, a magical figure, < Byzantine Gr. *telesma*, incantation, < Gr. *teleō*, to accomplish, < *telos*, an end.] An object having an engraved figure or symbol which is thought to preserve the bearer from harm and bring good luck; something that produces extraordinary effects on human behavior; any charm or amulet.— **tal·is·man·ic, tal·is·man·i·cal**, tal′is-man′ik, tal′iz·man′ik, *a.*—**tal·is·man·i·cal·ly**, *adv.*

talk, tạk, *v.i.* [A word related to *tale, tell*, in much the same way as *hark* to *hear*, *smirk* to *smile*, and *walk* to *well*, *wallow*.] To utter words in exchanging or expressing thoughts; speak; to confer; to give a speech or a lecture; to gossip; to chatter or prate; to utter words; to sound as if speaking; to communicate in any way, as by signs or signals; to converse familiarly; *colloq.* to give secret information, as to the police.—*v.t.* To use as a means of conversation or communication; as, to *talk* French; to speak; to use as the subject of a conversation; as, to *talk* politics; to utter; as, to *talk* nonsense; to have a certain effect on by talking.—*n.* The act of talking; familiar or informal conversation; a discourse; an address or lecture, esp. when informal; report; rumor; gossip; a subject of discourse; a conference or discussion; as, peace *talks*; empty or pointless conversation; a dialect, lingo, or specialized kind of talk.—**talk a·round**, to persuade; bring around to one's opinions by talking.— **talk back**, to reply rudely, disrespectfully, or impertinently.—**talk big**, *slang*, to brag or boast.—**talk down**, to silence by force of argument, loudness, or persistency; to outtalk; to disparage or belittle. *Avi.* to aid, as an aircraft, in landing during fog or other restricting conditions by radioing instructions to the pilot; also **talk in.**— **talk down to**, to patronize by speaking condescendingly, as by using oversimplified statements or words.—**talk one's ear** or **head off**, *slang*, to annoy with incessant talk.—**talk out**, to gain clarity or agreement by discussion; *Brit.* to continue discussion of, as a bill in Parliament, until time for adjournment, thus preventing a vote on it. —**talk o·ver**, to discuss orally; consider; weigh; to win over; persuade by talking. —**talk shop**, to have a conversation about a common vocation, esp. at a social gathering when using technical terms or talking about technical details.—**talk tur·key**, *slang*, to speak candidly and directly.—**talk up**, to extole, praise, advocate, or promote in talking.—**talk·er**, *n.*

talk·a·tive, ta̧'ka·tiv, *a.* Tending to talk excessively; garrulous.—**talk·a·tive·ly**, *adv.*—**talk·a·tive·ness**, *n.*

talk·ie, ta̧'kē, *n. Colloq.* a motion picture with sound. Also **talk·ing pic·ture.**

talk·ing book, *n.* A tape recording or phonograph record of a reading of a magazine, book, or other literary piece, esp. as prepared for the blind.

talk·ing ma·chine, *n.* Formerly, a phonograph.

talk·ing point, *n.* A fact, feature, or approach which gives support for a position or belief, as in an argument or debate, or which is useful in selling.

talk·ing-to, ta̧'king·tö″, *n.* pl. **talk·ing-tos.** *Colloq.* A reproving talk addressed directly to a person; a reprimand; a scolding.

talk·y, ta̧'kē, *a.—talkier, talkiest.* Talkative; disposed to talk; loquacious; containing so much talk as to obscure meaning or to bore, as a novel or play.

tall, ta̧l, *a.* [< W. *tâl*, tall, towering.] High in stature; long and comparatively slender from top to bottom; having the height indicated, great or small; as, two feet *tall.* *Colloq.* fanciful; extravagant; as, a *tall* story; considerable in degree of difficulty or in extent or amount; as, to be given a *tall* order to fill.—*adv.* Straight; proudly; as, to stand or walk *tall.*—**tall·ish**, ta̧'lish, *a.* Rather tall.—**tall·ness**, *n.*

tal·lage, tal'ij, *n.* [O.Fr. *taillage*, < *taillier*.] A tax levied by the Norman and early Angevin kings of England upon the demesne lands of the crown and upon all royal towns; a tax, toll, duty, or levy.—*v.t.* —*tallaged, tallaging.* To assess or tax.

tall·boy, ta̧l'boi″, *n. Brit.* A tall chest of drawers, usu. in two sections, one on top of the other; a tall-stemmed glass or goblet; a tall chimney pot.

tal·lith, tä'lis, *Heb.* tä·lēt', *n.* pl. **tal·li·thim**, tä·lē'sim, *Heb.* tä·lē·tēm'. *n.* [Heb.] A mantle or a scarflike garment with fringes, worn by Jewish men at prayer.

tall oil, tä̧l' oil″, *n.* A resinous emulsifying agent obtained as a by-product of wood pulp production and used in the manufacture of soaps, coatings, paints, and the like.

tal·low, tal'ō, *n.* [Same as Dan., Sw., and G. *talg*, Icel. *tólg*, D. *talk*, tallow; cf. Goth. *tulgus*, firm.] The harder and less

fusible fat of cattle and sheep, melted and separated from the fibrous or membranous matter for use in candles, soap, and the like; a similar fatty substance obtained from plants.—*v.t.* To grease or smear with tallow.—**tal·low·y**, tal'ō·ē, *a.*

tal·ly, tal'ē, *n.* pl. **tal·lies.** [A.Fr. *tallie* = Fr. *taille*, < L. *talea*, rod, stick: cf. *tail.*] An account or reckoning; a record of debit and credit or of the score of a game; a notch or mark made in scoring; a mark made to register a certain number of objects in keeping account, as four verticals and a diagonal for a group of five; a number of objects serving as a unit of computation; a number or group of objects recorded; a stick of wood with notches cut transversely to indicate the amount of a debt or payment, and often cut lengthwise across the notches, the debtor retaining one piece and the creditor the other; anything on which a score or account is kept; a score kept on a notched stick or otherwise; a ticket, label, or mark used as a means of identification, as when attached to a plant or tree; anything corresponding to another thing as a counterpart or duplicate; correspondence or agreement.—*v.t.*— *tallied, tallying.* To mark on a tally; to register; record; to count or reckon up; to furnish with a tally or identifying label.— *v.i.* To correspond, as one part of a tally with the other; to accord or agree.

tal·ly·ho, tal″ē·hō′, *interj.* The huntsman's cry to urge on his hounds.—tal'ē·hō″, *n.* pl. **tal·ly·hos.** The cry of 'tallyho'; a four-in-hand coach.—tal'ē·hō″, *v.i., v.t.*— *tallyhoed* or *tallyho'd, tallyhoing.* To shout 'tallyho' or to urge on by this cry.

tal·ly·man, tal'ē·man, *n.* pl. **tal·ly·men.** One who keeps a tally, score, or account; *Brit.* one who sells goods on credit, to be paid for by installments.

Tal·mud, täl'mu̧d, täl'mud, tal'mu̧d, tal'-mud, *n.* [Chal. *talmûd*, instruction.] The body of Jewish civil and canonical laws, traditions, and explanations, or the book that contains them.—**Tal·mud·ic, Tal·mud·i·cal**, täl·mö'dik, täl·mû'dik, tal'-mu̧d'ik, täl·mud'ik, tal·mö'dik, tal·mū'dik, tal·mu̧d'ik, tal·mud'ik, *a.*—**Tal·mud·ism**, *n.*—**Tal·mud·ist**, täl'mu̧·dist, tal'-mu̧·dist, *n.*

tal·on, tal'on, *n.* [O.Fr. Fr. *talon*, < M.L. *talo(n-)*, heel, < L. *talus*, ankle, heel.] A claw, esp. of a bird of prey; any clawlike object or part; the shoulder of a bolt in a lock on which the key exerts pressure as it turns in sliding the bolt. *Cards*, the discard pile in solitaire; the remainder of the pack after the deal in some other card games.—**tal·oned**, *a.*

ta·lus, tā'lus, *n.* pl. **ta·li**, tā'lī. [L., ankle, heel.] *Anat.* The anklebone or astragalus; the ankle.

ta·lus, tā'lus, *n.* pl. **ta·lus·es.** [Fr. *talus*, O.Fr. *talu*, ult. < L. *talus.*] A slope. *Geol.* a sloping mass of rocky fragments lying at the base of a cliff; also *scree.* *Fort.* the sloping side or face of a wall, rampart, parapet, or the like.

tam, tam, *n.* A tam-o'-shanter.

ta·ma·le, ta·mä'lē, *n.* A highly seasoned Mexican dish made by combining ground meat and peppers, then rolling the mixture in a coating of cornmeal dough, wrapping it in cornhusks and steaming it.

ta·man·dua, tä″män·dwä′, *n.* [Brazil.] The four-toed anteater, *Tamandua tetradactyla*, an arboreal species of tropical America. Also **tam·an·du**, tam'an·dö″.

tam·a·rack, tam'a·rak″, *n.* The American larch, *Larix laricina*, or any of various related larches, found chiefly in the northern areas of N. America; wood from any of these tamaracks. Also *hackmatack.*

ta·ma·rau, tä″ma·rou′, *n.* A small, dark,

wild buffalo, *Bubalus mindorensis*, of Mindoro Island in the Philippines.

tam·a·rin, tam'a·rin, *n.* [Native name in Cayenne.] Any of various very small S. American marmosets.

tam·a·rind, tam'a·rind, *n.* [It. and Sp. *tamarindo*, Fr. *tamarin*, < Ar. *tamrhindī*, < *tamr*, fruit, date, and *hindī*, Ind.] A tropical leguminous tree, *Tamarindus indica*, having yellow flowers with red stripes; the fruit of this tree containing an acid pulp used in medicines and foods.

tam·a·risk, tam'a·risk, *n.* [L. *tamariscus.*] Any of the shrubs or small trees of the genus *Tamarix*, having slender branches with pinkish flowers, found chiefly in desert areas of southern Europe and Asia.

tam·bour, tam'bu̧r, *n.* [Fr. *tambour*, a drum, a tabor.] A drum; the circular vertical part of a cupola; a cylindrical stone, as in the shaft of a column; a circular frame on which cloth is stretched for embroidering; embroidery made on a tambour; a rolling desk top or cabinet door, consisting of narrow wooden strips set close together and glued on canvas.—*v.t.* To embroider, as cloth, using a tambour.—*v.i.* To work on a tambour frame.—**tam·bour·er**, *n.*

tam·bou·rine, tam″bo·rēn′, *n.* [Fr. *tambourin*, < *tambour.*] A musical instrument formed of a hoop over which parchment is stretched, and having small metal jingles inserted in the rim.

tame, tām, *a.—tamer, tamest.* [O.E. *tam*, tame = D., Dan., Sw., and Goth. *tam*, Icel. *tamr*, G. *zahm*, tame; same root as in L. *domo*, to subdue, *dominus*, a lord; Skt. *dam*, to subdue.] Having lost its native wildness and shyness; accustomed to man; domesticated; as, a *tame* deer; submissive; spiritless; unanimated; without liveliness or interest; listless; harmless or ineffectual; insipid; dull; flat; as, *tame* scenery; *agric.* cultivated.—*v.t.*—*tamed, taming.* To make tame; to reduce from a wild to a domestic state; to subdue; to bring under control, as water for a source of power; to crush; to depress; *agric.* to cultivate.—**tam·a·ble, tame·a·ble**, tā'-ma·bl, *a.*—**tame·less**, tām'lis, *a.*—**tame·ly**, *adv.*—**tame·ness**, *n.*—**tam·er**, *n.*

Tam·ma·ny Hall, tam'a·nē ha̧l′, *n.* [From a popular Indian chief of pre-Revolutionary times.] The headquarters and organization of the Democratic party in New York City.—**Tam·ma·ny·ism**, *n.* Corrupt political control by bossism.

tam-o'-shan·ter, tam'o·shan″tèr, *n.* A cap, usu. of woolen material, originating in Scotland and having a tight, often decorative headband and a round flat crown with a pompon at the center. Also *tam.*

tamp, tamp, *v.t.* [< Fr. *tamponner*; akin to *tampion.*] To force or drive down by successive light blows; to ram tight with tough clay or other substance, as a hole bored for blasting, after the charge is lodged.—*n.*

tam·pa·la, tam·pal'a, *n.* An ornamental annual herb, *Amaranthus tricolor*, sometimes grown as a potherb, esp. in the Orient.

tam·per, tam'pèr, *v.i.* [A form of *temper.*] To meddle or interfere; to make alterations by corruption or adulteration, usu. followed by *with*; as, to *tamper with* a document; to employ secret and unfair means, esp. to influence toward a certain course, usu. followed by *with*; as, to *tamper with* a witness.—*v.t.*—**tam·per·er**, *n.*

tam·pi·on, tam'pē·on, *n.* [< Fr. *tampon*, a nasalized form < *tapon*, a bung, < D. *tap* = E. *tap*, a plug.] The stopper, plug, or cover for a cannon or other piece of ordnance. Also *tompion.*

tam·pon, tam'pon, *n.* [Fr.] *Med.* a plug of cotton or the like inserted into an orifice or wound, as to stop hemorrhage.—*v.t. Med.* to fill or plug with a tampon.

tam-tam, tum′tum″, tam′tam″, *n.* [Hind., from sound of drum.] A large, disklike gong of oriental origin; a tom-tom.

tan, tan, *v.t.*—*tanned, tanning.* [Fr. *tanner,* to tan, < *tan,* oak bark, < Armor. *tann,* oak; akin *tawny.*] To convert into leather, as animal skins, by steeping in an infusion of oak or other tanbark; to make brown by exposure to the rays of the sun; *colloq.* to beat, flog, or thrash—*v.i.* To become tanned; to become tan-colored or sun-burned.—*n.* The bark of the oak, willow, or other trees, used for tanning; tanbark; a yellowish-brown color; a brown skin color resulting from exposure to the rays of the sun.—*a.*—**tan·nish,** *a.*

tan·a·ger, tan′a·jẽr, *n.* [Altered < Brazil. *tanagra.*] Any of a group of American birds of the finch family, remarkable for their bright colors, as the scarlet tanager, *Piranga olivacea.*

tan·bark, tan′bärk″, *n.* Tree bark, esp. hemlock or oak, which is rich in tannin and is used in the tanning of hides; spent tanbark used in covering a surface, as a racetrack or circus arena.

tan·dem, tan′dem, *adv.* [L., at length, that is, after some *time*; the E. sense is by a pun or joke.] One before the other.—*a.* Arranged one before the other.—*n.* A vehicle drawn by two horses harnessed one before the other; the horses themselves; any arrangement of persons, things, or parts situated one before the other; a truck having closely paired axles; a tandem bicycle.

tan·dem bi·cy·cle, *n.* A bicycle built for two or more persons, the seats and pedals being in tandem, one behind another.

tang, tang, *n.* [M.E. *tange, tongge,* prob. < Scand.: cf. Icel. *tangi,* projecting point, spit of land, tang of a knife, also E. *tongs.*] A strong taste or flavor; a taste of something extraneous to the thing itself; a pungent or distinctive odor; a smack, touch, or suggestion of something; a projecting point, or projection; a long and slender projecting strip, tongue, or prong forming part of an object, as a chisel, file, or knife, and serving as a means of attachment for another part, as a handle or stock.—*v.t.* To furnish with a tang.—**tanged,** *a.*—**tang·y,** tang′ē, *a.*—*tangier, tangiest.*

tang, tang, *n.* [Imit. of a sound, like *twang.*] A twang or sharp sound.—*v.i.* To ring; to twang.

Tang, täng, *n.* A Chinese dynasty, 618 to 907 A.D., noted for the development of high art forms and the invention of printing. Also **T'ang.**

tan·ge·lo, tan′je·lō″, *n.* pl. **tan·ge·los.** [< *tang(erine),* *n.,* and *(pom)-elo.*] A hybrid of the tangerine or orange tree with either the pomelo or grapefruit tree; the loose-skinned fruit produced from this cross.

tan·gent, tan′jent, *a.* [L. *tangens* (*tangent-*), ppr. of *tangere,* touch: cf. *tact, tangible, attain, contingent,* and *intact.*] Touching. *Geom.* touching at one point only and not intersecting, as a straight line in relation to a curve or surface, or two curves or surfaces in relation to each other, or a plane in relation to a sphere; in contact along a single line or element, as a plane with a cylinder.—*n. Geom.* a tangent line, plane, curve, or surface. *Trig.* a function of an acute angle in a right triangle, equal to the ratio of the opposite leg to the adjacent leg; a function of any angle, equal to the ordinate of a point on a line divided by its abscissa, when the angle is shown in Cartesian coordinates as the angle the line makes with the positive x-axis at the origin. Abbr. *tan., tgn.*—**fly,** or **go, off on,** or **at, a tan·gent,** *fig.* to go or pass with sudden

divergence from one line of movement, course of action, or train of thought to another.—**tan·gen·cy,** tan′jen·sē, *n.*—**tan·gen·tial,** tan·jen′shal, *a.* Pertaining to or of the nature of a tangent; being or moving in the direction of a tangent; merely touching; slightly connected; divergent or digressive. Also **tan·gen·tal,** tan·jen′tal.—**tan·gen·tial·ly,** tan·gen′tal·ly, *adv.*

tan·ge·rine, tan″je·rēn′, *n.* [*Tangier.*] A small shiny orange, *Citrus reticulata,* easily skinned and segmented; the tree producing this fruit; also *mandarin.* A reddish-orange color.

tan·gi·ble, tan′ji·bl, *a.* [Fr. *tangible,* L. *tangibilis,* < *tango,* to touch.] Capable of being touched or grasped; perceptible by the touch; material; capable of being possessed or realized by the mind; real; actual; evident; as, *tangible* proofs; having monetary value, as an asset.—*n. Usu. pl.* material or tangible assets.—**tan·gi·bil·i·ty, tan·gi·ble·ness,** *n.*—**tan·gi·bly,** *adv.*

tan·gle, tang′gl, *v.t.*—*tangled, tangling.* [Allied to Icel. *thöngull, thang,* Dan. and G. *tang,* tangle, seaweed; hence *entangle.*] To knit together confusedly; to interweave or interlace so as to be difficult to unravel; to entangle or entrap; to involve; to complicate.—*v.i.* To become or be tangled; *colloq.* to quarrel.—*n.* A knot of threads or other things confusedly interwoven; a perplexity or embarrassment; a state of complication; *colloq.* a quarrel.—**tan·gled, tan·gly,** *a.*—**tan·gle·ment,** *n.*

tan·gle, tang′gl, *n.* [< Scand.: cf. Icel. *thöngull, thang,* and E. *tang.*] Either of two large seaweeds, *Laminaria digitata* and *L. saccharina.*

tan·go, tang′gō, *n.* pl. **tan·gos.** [Sp.] A ballroom dance originated in Argentina and performed by couples gliding and dipping in slow tempo to an accented rhythm; the music to which it is danced.—*v.i.*—*tangoed, tangoing.* To perform the tango.

Tan·go, tang′gō, *n.* A communications code word to designate the letter T.

tank, tangk, *n.* [Prob. < Pg. *tanque,* pond, tank, = Sp. *estanque* = Fr. *étang,* < L. *stagnum,* pool, pond: cf. *stagnate.*] A large receptacle or structure for holding water or other liquid or a gas; *milit.* an armored vehicle having caterpillar treads which permit travel over rough terrain and containing cannon or machine guns fired from inside. A natural or artificial pool, pond, or lake; *slang,* a jail cell designed to hold a number of prisoners, usu. pending arraignment or processing.—*v.t.* To put or store in a tank.

tan·ka, täng′ka, *n.* pl. **tan·ka, tan·kas.** A five line Japanese form of verse, the first and third lines having five syllables and the rest having seven.

tank·age, tang′kij, *n.* The capacity of a tank or tanks; the act or process of storing liquid in a tank; the fee or price charged for tank storage; the dried residue from tanks in which fat has been rendered from animal carcasses or waste, much used as a fertilizer or animal feed.

tank·ard, tang′kẽrd, *n.* [O.Fr. *tanquart, tanquard,* O.D. *tanckaerd,* a tankard.] A large drinking vessel with a hinged lid and a handle, usu. of silver or pewter.

tank car, *n.* A railroad car equipped to carry gases or liquids.

tank de·stroy·er, *n. Milit.* a high-speed, highly mobile half-track protected by light armor and equipped with antitank guns.

tank·er, tang′kẽr, *n.* A vehicle designed to transport liquids, esp. gasoline or oil, as a ship, railroad car, or truck.

tank farm, *n.* An area containing a large number of storage tanks, as found near refineries.

tank farm·ing, *n.* Hydroponics.

tank town, *n. Colloq.* A town at which trains stop chiefly to be supplied with water; any small or unimportant town.

tank trail·er, *n.* A truck trailer designed to hold and transport gases or liquids.

tank truck, *n.* A truck having a tank trailer.

tan·nage, tan′ij, *n.* The operation of tanning; the result or product of tanning.

tan·nate, tan′āt, *n. Chem.* a salt of tannic acid.

tan·ner, tan′ẽr, *n.* One whose occupation is to tan hides.—**tan·ner·y,** tan′e·rē, *n.* pl. **tan·ner·ies.** A business establishment where hides are tanned.

tan·nic, tan′ik, *a. Chem.* derived from or relating to tannin.

tan·nic ac·id, *n.* Tannin.

tan·nin, tan′in, *n.* [Fr. *tanin, tannin,* < *tan.*] *Chem.* any of a group of astringent vegetable compounds having tanning properties, used commercially in manufacturing leather, inks, and dyes. Also *tannic acid.*

tan·ning, tan′ing, *n.* The operation and art of converting raw hides and skins of animals into leather, usu. through the use of various chemicals; a brown or tan color produced on the skin by the sun; *colloq.* a whipping.

Ta·no·an, tä′nō·an, *n.* A group of Indian languages spoken in the old pueblos of New Mexico and Arizona.—*a.*

tan·sy, tan′zē, *n.* pl. **tan·sies.** [O.Fr. *tanesie* (Fr. *tanaisie*), < M.L. *athanasia,* tansy, < Gr. *athanasia,* immortality.] Any plant or herb belonging to the genus *Tanacetum* esp. *T. vulgare,* a coarse, strong-scented herb with toothed pinnate leaves, corymbs of yellow flowers, and a bitter taste, formerly used in cookery and in medicine.

tan·sy rag·wort, *n.* An herb, *Senecio jacobaea,* which produces numerous yellow flowers and which is found in N. America and Europe.

tan·ta·late, tan′ta·lāt″, *n. Chem.* a salt of tantalic acid.

tan·tal·ic, tan·tal′ik, *a. Chem.* of or pertaining to tantalum, usu. in a pentavalent form.

tan·ta·lite, tan′ta·līt″, *n.* A heavy ore, $(FeMn)(NbTa)_2O_6$, a principal source of tantalum, occurring in black, lustrous crystals.

tan·ta·lize, *Brit.* **tan·ta·lise,** tan′ta·līz″, *v.t.*—*tantalized, tantalizing, Brit. tantalised, tantalising.* [From *Tantalus,* a mythical king of Lydia or Phrygia, who for divulging the secrets of his father Zeus was condemned to stand in water, which receded from him whenever he stooped to drink, while branches loaded with fruit, which always eluded his grasp, hung over his head.] To tease or torment by presenting something desirable to the view, but continually frustrating the expectations by keeping it out of reach; to excite by expectations or hopes which will not be realized.—**tan·ta·liz·er,** *n.*—**tan·ta·liz·ing,** tan′ta·li″zing, *a.*—**tan·ta·liz·ing·ly,** *adv.*

tan·ta·lum, tan′ta·lum, *n.* [Named from the *tantalizing* difficulties in analyzing the ore.] *Chem.* a rare, gray-white metallic element which is hard, ductile, and resistant to single acids. Sym. Ta, at. no. 73, at. wt. 180.948. See Periodic Table of Elements.

Tan·ta·lus, tan′ta·lus, *n.* [L., < Gr. *Tántalos.*] *Class. mythol.* a king and son of Zeus condemned, for revealing the secrets of the gods, to stand in Tartarus up to his chin in water under branches laden with fruit, the water or fruit receding whenever he tried to eat or drink; (*l.c.*) a stand containing decanters which are clearly visible but securely locked.

tan·ta·mount, tan′ta·mount″, *a.* [Fr. *tant,* L. *tantus,* so much, and E. *amount.*]

Equivalent, as in value, force, effect, or signification, followed by *to*.

tan·ta·ra, tan′tėr·a, tan·tar′a, tan·tär′a, *n.* [Imit] A blast of a trumpet or horn; any similar sound.

tan·tiv·y, tan·tiv′ē, *adv.* [From the sound of galloping horses, or the note of a hunting horn.] At a headlong gallop.—*a.* Fast; rapid.—*n. pl.* **tan·tiv·ies**. A rapid, violent gallop; a hunting cry urging speed.

tan·tra, tun′tra, *n.* [Skt., thread, warp, fundamental doctrine, < tan-, stretch.] (*Often cap.*) one of a class of Hindu religious books of comparatively late date, involved in the worship of Shakti, in which mysticism and magic play a great part.—**Tan·trism**, tun′triz·um, *n.*

tan·trum, tan′trum, *n.* [Origin obscure.] An outburst of anger or rage; a violent display of temper.

Tao·ism, dou′iz·um, tou′iz·um, *n.* [Chin. *tao*, way or path.] A nontheistic Chinese religion teaching simplicity and conformity to the Tao or Way; a philosophy derived from this religion but associated with belief in magic.—**Tao·ist**, *a.*, *n.*—**Tao·is·tic**, *a.*

tap, tap, *n.* [O.E. *taeppa* = L.G. *tappe*, D. and Dan. *tap*, Icel. *tappi*, G. *zapfen*, a tap, a faucet; akin *tip*, *top*, *tipple*, *tampion*, etc.] A pipe or hole through which liquor is drawn from a cask or other vessel; a spigot; a faucet; a cock; the liquor itself; a plug to stop a hole in a cask; *Brit.* a taphouse or taproom; *surg.* a procedure for removing fluid; *mech.* a small tool for cutting threads in drilled holes.—*v.t.*—**tapped**, **tapping**. [Same as L.G. and D. *tappen*, Icel. and Sw. *tappa*, G. *zapfen*.] To pierce or open, as a cask, so as to let out fluid from; to treat in any analogous way for the purpose of drawing something from; as, to *tap* a telephone, to *tap* a sugar maple, to *tap* a water main; to call upon, as a reserve; as, to *tap* a resource; *slang*, to borrow money from.—**on tap**, available for tapping, as of beer; having a tap; *colloq.* handy or readily available.—**tap·per**, tap′ėr, *n.* One who or that which taps the contents of something; a person or tool that cuts threads in a nut.

tap, tap, *v.t.*—**tapped**, **tapping**. [< Fr. *taper*, to tap, *tape*, a tap; < Prov. G. *tapp*, a blow, G. *tappen*, to grope; Icel. *tapsa*, to tap; imit. of sound, like *pat*.] To strike lightly, as with something small; to hit gently, as with a slight, audible blow; to pat gently.—*v.i.* To strike a gentle, audible blow.—*n.* A gentle blow; an audible pat; a slight blow with a small object; the sound produced by such a blow; a leather or metal piece on a shoe; as, a *tap* for dancing; a kind of drumbeat; a person or thing selected by being tapped.—**tap·per**, tap′ėr, *n.* One who or that which taps something, esp. repeatedly or insistently; as, a finger or pencil *tapper*.—**tap·ping**, tap′ing, *n.* The act of one who or that which taps or strikes lightly; the sound itself; as, *tappings* on a door. *Sports*, a pat or tip of a basketball; a gentle stroke in billiards.

ta·pa, tä′pa, *n.* [Polynesian.] The bark of a paper mulberry tree. An unwoven cloth of the Pacific islands, made by steeping and beating the inner bark of this kind of tree; also **ta·pa cloth**.

tap dance, *n.* A dance in which the dancer's special shoes cause the steps to be audible. —**tap-dance**, tap′dans″, tap′däns″, *v.i.*—**tap-danced**, **tap-dancing**.—**tap-danc·er**, *n.* —**tap-danc·ing**, *n.*

tape, tāp, *n.* [O.E. *taeppe*, a fillet; akin to *tapestry*, *tippet*.] A narrow woven band of cotton or linen, used for tying or fastening; a long strip or ribbon of paper, plastic, or metal; as, ticker *tape*, friction *tape*, magnetic *tape*; *sports*, a string stretched across the finishing line of a race.—*v.t.*, *v.i.*—**taped**,

taping. To tie or secure with tape; to measure with a tape measure; to record on magnetic tape; to cover with adhesive tape. —**tap·er**, *n.* One who or that which tapes. —**tape·like**, *a.*

tape deck, *n.* The mechanism for transporting tape between reels of a tape recorder, requiring an amplifier and speaker for sound playback.

tape grass, *n.* An underwater plant, *Vallisneria spiralis*, with long leaves resembling ribbons.

tape meas·ure, *n.* A long cloth, metal, or paper tape marked with inches or centimeters and used in measuring. Also **tape-line**, tāp′lin″.

ta·per, tā′pėr, *v.i.* [O.E. *tapor*, *taper*, a taper, < Ir. *tapar*, W. *tampr*, a taper; cf. Skt. *tap*, to burn.] To become gradually slenderer or less in diameter; to diminish; to grow gradually less.—*v.t.* To make smaller, esp. toward one particular end; to reduce gradually; to lessen.—*n.* Gradual diminution of thickness in an elongated object; gradual decrease in power or capacity; tapering form, as of an obelisk; a small candle, esp. one which is very slender; a long wick coated with wax or other suitable material, as used in lighting fires, candles, lamps, or pipes; a small, esp. feeble light.—*a.* Long and regularly becoming slenderer toward the point; becoming small toward one end.—**ta·per off**, to make or become smaller gradually; to decrease or diminish.—**ta·per·er**, *n.*—**ta·per·ing·ly**, *adv.*

tape-re·cord, tāp′ri·kȧrd″, *v.t.* To record, as music, on magnetic tape.—**tape re·cord·er**, *n.* A device for making recordings on magnetic tape.—**tape re·cord·ing**, *n.* Magnetic recording on tape.

tap·es·try, tap′i·strē, *n. pl.* **tap·es·tries**. [Fr. *tapisserie*, tapestry, < *tapis*, tapestry, a carpet, < L. *tapes*, *tapete*, < Gr. *tapēs*, *tapētos*, a carpet, a rug.] A colorful, handwoven, patterned or pictorial cloth usu. used as a wall hanging but occasionally as a furniture covering or a throw; the special handweave using a bobbin, distinguished by a coarse warp, fine weft, and a ribbed surface with fine slits at color separations; as, a Navaho Indian rug woven in *tapestry*; anything resembling tapestry.—*v.t.*—**tapestried**, **tapestrying**. To decorate or furnish with, or as with, tapestry; to weave in the manner of tapestry; to illustrate, as a story, by pictures in tapestry; to reproduce, as a painting, in tapestry.—**tap·es·tried**, tap′i·strēd, *a.* Having the appearance of tapestry.

tap·es·try car·pet, *n.* A machine-made carpet with patterns printed with dye on yarns before weaving; a trade designation for certain patterned uncut pile rugs, similar to Brussels carpet, and not to be confused with authentic tapestry weaving.

ta·pe·tum, ta·pē′tum, *n. pl.* **ta·pe·ta**, ta·pē′ta. [N.L., < L. *tapete*, < Gr. *tápēs* (*tapēt-*), carpet: cf. *tapis*.] *Bot.* a layer of cells often investing the archespore in a developing sporangium and absorbed as the spores mature; *anat.*, *zool.* any of certain membranous layers or the like, as in the retina.

tape·worm, tāp′wurm″, *n.* Any of various flat or tapelike cestode worms, as those belonging to the genus *Taenia*, parasitic when adult in the alimentary canal of man and other vertebrates, and usu. characterized by having the larval and adult stages in different hosts.

tap·hole, tap′hōl″, *n.* The hole for a tap; *metal.* a hole in the lower part or at the bottom of a furnace for drawing off metal or slag.

tap·i·o·ca, tap″ē·ō′ka, *n.* [Native Amer. name.] A nutritious substance prepared

from dried cassava starch, usu. in granular form, and used in making puddings or for thickening liquids.

ta·pir, tā′pėr, *n. pl.* **ta·pir**, **ta·pirs**. [From the native Brazil. name.] Any of several Central and South American or Malayan nocturnal ungulates, family *Tapiridae*, measuring three feet high and six feet long, and distinguished by a proboscis.

tap·pet, tap′it, *n* [A dim. < *tap*, to strike gently.] *Mech.* a small lever connected with a valve of a cylinder in an engine and operated by a small cam.

tap·room, tap′rōm″, tap′rum″, *n.* A room where beer is served from the tap; a common room for drinking in a tavern; a cocktail lounge; a barroom.

tap·root, tap′rōt″, tap′rut″, *n. Bot.* the main root of a plant which penetrates the earth downward and from which smaller lateral roots are given off.

taps, taps, *n. pl. but sing. in constr.* A bugle call or drum beat used esp. in the military to signal the putting out of lights at night; a bugle sounded at military funerals.

tap·ster, tap′stėr, *n.* A person employed in a tavern or barroom to draw, dispense, or serve liquor; bartender.

tar, tär, *n.* [O.E. *taro*, *tero*, tar = D. *teer*, Icel. *tjaro*, G. *theer*, tar; allied to *tree*.] A thick, dark-colored viscid product obtained by the destructive distillation of organic substances and bituminous minerals, as certain woods and coal.—*v.t.*—**tarred**, **tarring**. To smear with tar.—**knock the tar out of**, to beat severely.—**tar and feath·er**, to punish or humiliate, as a person, by coating first with tar and then with feathers; *fig.* to subject to any severe punishment.

tar, tär, *n.* [Contraction of *tarpaulin*.] *Colloq.* a sailor.

tar·a·did·dle, **tar·ra·did·dle**, tär″a·did′l, *n. Colloq.* A minor lie; a fib; an exaggeration.

tar·an·tel·la, tär″an·tel′a, *n.* [It.] A swift, whirling Italian dance in 6/8 time, formerly considered a remedy for tarantism; music for or suitable for this dance.

tar·ant·ism, tar′an·tiz″um, *n.* [It. *tarantismo*.] A disorder prevalent in later medieval Italy, characterized by manic, hysterical fits of dancing and popularly believed to result from a bite from the tarantula. Also **tar·ent·ism**.

ta·ran·tu·la, ta·ran′cha·la, *n. pl.* **ta·ran·tu·las**, **ta·ran·tu·lae**, ta·ran′cha·lē. [It. *tarantola*, < L. *Tarentum*, now *Taranto*, in the south of Italy.] Any of various spiders, usu. large and hairy, of the family *Theraphasidae*, which have a painful although not very poisonous bite and are common in the southwestern U.S.; a similar spider, *Lycosa tarantula*, the wolf spider of southern Europe whose bite was formerly believed to cause tarantism.

ta·rax·a·cum, ta·rak′sa·kum, *n.* [N.L.; through Ar. < Pers.] Any of the composite plants constituting the genus *Taraxacum*, as the dandelion, the dried roots of which are used as a tonic, diuretic, and gentle laxative.

tar·boosh, tär·bōsh′, *n.* [Ar. name.] A brimless headpiece, usu. tasseled and of red felt, worn either alone or under a turban by Muslim men. Also **tar·bush**.

tar·di·grade, tär′di·grād″, *a.* [L. *tardigradus*, < *tardus*, slow, and *gradi*, walk, go.] Slow in pace or movement; belonging or relating to the *Tardigrada*, a classification of microscopic arthropods living on damp mosses or in water.—*n.* Any member of the *Tardigrada*.

tar·do, tär′dō, *It.* tär′da, *a.* [It. < L. *tardus*, slow.] *Mus.* Slow; noting a passage to be performed slowly: used as a direction to the performer.

tar·dy, tär′dē, *a.—tardier, tardiest.* [Fr. *tardif*, tardy, as if from a form of *tardivus*, < L. *tardus*, slow.] Late; not punctual; moving at a slow pace; dilatory.—**tar·di·ly**, *adv.*—**tar·di·ness**, *n.*

tare, târ, *n.* [Origin obscure.] Any of several species of vetch, esp. *Vicia sativa*, or any seed of a vetch; a weed pest of grainfields.

tare, târ, *n.* [Fr. *tare*, < Sp. *tara*, < Ar. *tarha*, deduction.] *Com.* a deduction made from the gross weight of goods as an allowance for the weight of the container or conveyance.—*v.t.*—**tared, taring.** *Com.* to weigh, as packaged goods, to ascertain the amount of tare; to mark the tare of.

tar·get, tär′git, *n.* [O.Fr. *targuete*, var. of *targete*, dim. of *targe*, E. *targe*.] A disk, board, or other object, usu. marked with concentric circles, to be aimed at in shooting practice or contests; any object used for this purpose; anything fired at; anything aimed at; a goal; an object of abuse, scorn, derision, or the like; a butt; a disk-shaped signal, as at a railroad switch; *surv.* the sliding sight on a leveling rod; *electron.* the metallic surface within an x-ray tube which is the focus of cathode rays and which emits the x-rays. A small, round shield or buckler.—*v.t.* To designate or use as a goal; to cause to become the object of an attack.—**tar·get·eer**, tär′gi·tēr′, *n.* A soldier armed with a shield.

tar·get date, *n.* The date aspired to or set for the start or completion of some effort, project, or event.

Tar·gum, tär′gum, *Heb.* täR·gŏm′, *n.* pl. **Tar·gums**, *Heb.* **Tar·gu·mim**, *Heb.* täR′gö·mĕm′. [Chal. *targûm*, interpretation, < *targem*, to interpret; akin *dragoman*.] An ancient translation or paraphrase of a book or section of the Old Testament in Aramaic.—**Tar·gum·ic**, *a.*—**Tar·gum·ist**, *n.*

Tar·heel, tär′hēl′, *n. Colloq.* a native or inhabitant of North Carolina: used as a nickname.—**Tar·heel State**, the state of North Carolina: a nickname.

tar·iff, tar′if, *n.* [Fr. *tarif*, Sp. *tarifa*, < the Ar. *tarif*, explanation, information, a list of fees to be paid, < *arafa*, to inform.] A list or schedule of goods with the legal duties imposed on them when imported or exported; a duty as given in such a schedule; any table or scale of charges or prices.—*v.t.* To set a tax, duty, or charge on.

tar·la·tan, tar·le·tan, tär′la·tan, *n.* [Bengali *tarnatan*, a fine muslin.] A sheer, stiff cotton material with an open weave.

Tar·mac, tär′mak, *n.* [(*Tarmac*)adam.] A bituminous material used in paving roads, parking areas, or the like. (Trademark.)

tar·mac, tär′mak, *n.* A surface of tarmacadam or similar material, esp. in an airport, used for a runway or hangar apron.

tar·mac·ad·am, tär′ma·kad′am, *n.* A paving material consisting of crushed stone, with tar or a mixture of tar and bitumen used as a binder; a road or other pavement constructed of such material.

tarn, tärn, *n.* [Icel. *tjörn*, Sw. *tärn*, a tarn.] A small mountain lake or pool.

tar·nish, tär′nish, *v.t.* [Fr. *ternir*, ppr. *ternissant.* < O.H.G. *tarnjan*, to conceal; akin to O.E. *dernan*, Sc. *dern*, to hide.] To diminish or destroy the luster of; to discolor, as metal, by oxidation; to soil or sully; to disgrace.—*v.i.* To lose luster; become dull or discolored; to become soiled or sullied.—*n.* A discoloration, esp. on metal; a blot; a tarnished state.—**tar·nish·a·ble**, *a.*

ta·ro, tär′ō, târ′ō, *n.* pl. **ta·ros.** [Native name.] A plant, *Colocasia esculenta*, of the arum family, cultivated in the tropics for its edible tuberous roots; the root of this plant.

tarp, tärp, *n. Colloq.* tarpaulin.

tar·pa·per, tär′pā″pèr, *n.* A sturdy paper impregnated or coated with tar for use in roofing and siding.

tar·pau·lin, tär·pa̯′lin, tär′pa·lin, *n.* [Said to be < *tar* and *pall*, *v.*] A covering or sheet of canvas or other material, waterproofed with tar or paint and used to protect something exposed to weather or moisture; canvas or other material so waterproofed; a sailor's hat made of or covered with such material. Also *colloq. tarp.*

Tar·pe·ian, tär·pē′an, *a.* [L. *Tarpeius*.] Of or denoting the hillside or cliff in ancient Rome from which condemned criminals were thrown to their deaths.

tar·pon, tär′pon, *n.* pl. **tar·pons, tar·pon.** [Origin unknown.] A large, silver-scaled sport fish, *Megalops atlantica*, inhabiting the warm waters off the Florida coast and the Gulf of Mexico.

tar·ra·gon, tar′a·gon″, tar′a·gon, *n.* [Obs. Fr. *targon* (Mod.Fr. *estragon*); < Ar., and perh. ult. < Gr. *drákōn*, E. *dragon*.] A European plant, *Artemisia dracunculus*, in the composite family; the aromatic leaves of this plant, used for flavoring.

tar·ry, tar′ē, *v.i.—tarried, tarrying.* [M.E. *tarien*; origin obscure.] To delay or be tardy in acting, starting, or coming; to linger or loiter; to wait; to remain or stay in a place; to sojourn.—*n.* pl. **tar·ries.** A stay or sojourn.

tar·ry, tär′ē, *a.—tarrier, tarriest.* Of or resembling tar; coated or smeared with tar.

tar·sal, tär′sal, *a.* [N.L. *tarsalis*.] *Anat.* of or pertaining to the tarsus of the foot or to the tarsi of the eyelids.—*n.* A tarsal part, as a bone or joint.

tar·si·er, tär′sē·ėr, *n.* [Fr. *tarsier*, from the length of its *tarsus*.] Any of several small, arboreal, East Indian primates of the genus *Tarsius*, being nocturnal and insectivorous and having large eyes and a long, slender tail.

tar·so·met·a·tar·sus, tär″sō·met″a·tär′sus, *n.* pl. **tar·so·met·a·tar·si**, tär″sō··met″a·tär′sī. *Ornith.* a large bone above the toes of a bird, being a fusion of tarsal and metatarsal bones. Also *tarsus*, *shank.*

tar·sus, tär′sus, *n.* pl. **tar·si**, tär′sī. [N.L. < Gr. *tarsós*, flat surface, flat of the foot, edge of the eyelid.] *Anat.* the proximal segment of the foot; the instep; the collection of bones between the tibia and the metatarsus, entering into the construction of the ankle joint; the plate of connective tissue along the border of an eyelid. *Ornith.* the shank of a bird; *zool.* the distal segment of an insect's leg.

tart, tärt, *a.* [O.E. *teart*, severe.] Sharp to the taste; sour or acid; as, *tart* apples; sharp in character, spirit, or expression; cutting; caustic; as, a *tart* rejoinder.—**tart·ish**, *a.*—**tart·ish·ly**, *adv.*—**tart·ly**, *adv.*—**tart·ness**, *n.*

tart, tärt, *n.* [O.Fr. Fr. *tarte*; origin uncertain.] A small pastry shell filled with cooked fruit or other sweetened preparation, usu. without a top crust; *slang*, a prostitute.

tar·tan, tär′tan, *n.* [O.Fr. *tiretaine*, linsey-woolsey; of unknown origin.] A kind of woolen cloth, having stripes and crossbars in various colors, traditionally worn by Scottish Highlanders, each clan having its own pattern and colors; the pattern itself; a plaid; a garment of any such design or material.—*a.*

tar·tan, tär′tan, *n.* [Fr. *tartane*, It., Sp., and Pg. *tartana*; of Eastern origin.] A vessel used in the Mediterranean, with a single mast bearing a large lateen sail.

tar·tar, tär′tèr, *n.* [O.Fr. Fr. *tartre*, < M.L. *tartarum*; perh. from Ar.] The potassium bitartrate deposited from the juice of grapes in winemaking; a yellowish, hard substance deposited on the teeth consisting chiefly of calcium phosphate.—**tar·tar·ic**,

tär·târ′ik, tär·tär′ik, *a.*—**tar·tar·ous, tär′·tér·us**, *a.*

tar·tar, tär′tèr, *n.* [= *Tatar*. *Tartar* is the common and long-established form in literary and general use, *Tatar* being a more recent form with more precise ethnological application.] (*Sometimes cap.*) a savage, intractable person; a person of irritable temper; a person or thing that proves unexpectedly troublesome, strong, or formidable: used esp. in the phrase 'to catch a *tartar.*' (*Cap.*) a Tatar.—*a.* (*Cap.*) pertaining to the Tatars; also **Tar·tar·i·an**, tär·târ′ē·an.

tar·tar e·met·ic, *n. Chem., pharm.* potassium antimonyl tartrate, a poisonous, water-soluble salt, with a sweetish metallic taste, occurring as a white crystal or a granular powder, and used as an emetic, expectorant, and diaphoretic in medicine and as a mordant in dyeing.

tar·tar·ic ac·id, *n. Chem.* any of four optical isomers, existing as a water-soluble powder or a transparent crystal, commonly found in fruit juice and vegetable tissue and used in foods, medicine, photography, and tanning.

tar·tar sauce, *n.* A dressing, esp. for fish, composed of chopped olives, pickles, onions, and other relishes in a mayonnaise base. Also **tar·tare sauce.**

Tar·ta·rus, tär′tèr·us, *n.* [L., < Gr. *Tártaros*.] *Class. mythol.* a deep, sunless abyss far below Hades. The lower world in general.—**Tar·tar·e·an**, tär·târ′ē·an, *a.*

tart·let, tärt′lit, *n.* A small tart.

tar·trate, tär′trāt, *n. Chem.* a salt or ester of tartaric acid.

tar·trat·ed, tär′trā·tid, *a. Chem.* formed into a tartrate; combined with tartaric acid.

tar·tuffe, tar·tufe, tär·tuf′, tär·töf′, *Fr.* täR·tyf′, *n.* [From the principal character in Molière's comedy of that name.] A hypocritical pretender to religious piety; any hypocrite.

Tar·zan, tär′zan, tär′zan, *n.* [From Edgar Rice Burroughs' series of jungle novels.] A person of extraordinary agility and strength.

ta·sim·e·ter, ta·sim′i·tèr, *n.* [Gr. *tásis*, stretching, tension.] An electrical device for determining minute changes in temperature by means of the changes in pressure caused by an expanding or contracting solid.—**tas·i·met·ric**, tas″i·me′trik, *a.*—**ta·sim·e·try**, *n.*

task, task, täsk, *n.* [O.Fr. *tasque, tasche*, (Fr. *tâche*), a task, < L.L. *tasca*, by metathesis < *taxa* (= *tacsa*), < L. *taxare*, to tax.] A piece of work imposed upon a person by another; a piece of work to be done; that which duty or necessity imposes; an undertaking; a burdensome, difficult, or unpleasant chore or duty.—*v.t.* To impose a task upon; to oppress with severe labor.—**take to task**, to reprimand; to reprove.

task force, *n. Milit.* a temporary merging of units or individuals under one command with the purpose of accomplishing one specific mission or objective. An assemblage of specialists formed to investigate or solve a particular problem.

task·mas·ter, task′mas″tèr, täsk′mä″stèr, *n.* One who assigns or imposes tasks, esp. taxing, burdensome ones; one who rigorously oversees the work of others.—**task·mis·tress**, task′mis″tris, täsk′mis″tris, *n.* A female taskmaster.

task·work, task′wurk″, täsk′wurk″, *n.* Work imposed or performed as a task; hard work; piecework.

tas·sel, tas′el, *n.* [O.Fr. *tassel*, a fastening, as for a cloak; origin uncertain.] A pendent ornament consisting commonly of a bunch of threads, small cords, or strands hanging from a roundish knob or head; something resembling this, as the inflorescence of certain plants, esp. that at the summit of a stalk of corn.—*v.t.*—*tasseled, tasseling, tasselled, tasselling.* To furnish or adorn with or as with tassels; to form into a tassel or tassels; to remove the tassel from, as growing corn, in order to improve the crop.—*v.i.* To produce tassels, as corn.

taste, tāst, *v.t.*—*tasted, tasting.* [O.Fr. *taster* (Fr. *tâter*), try by touching, try, taste, appar. from a freq. of L. *taxare*, touch sharply.] To try the flavor or quality of, as food, by taking into the mouth; to eat or drink a little of; as, barely *tasted* the dishes before them; to perceive or distinguish the flavor of by the sense of taste; as, to *taste* the wine in a sauce; to have or get experience, esp. a slight experience; as, to *taste* freedom.—*v.i.* To try the flavor or quality of something by the sense of taste; to take a taste, as of food or drink; to eat or drink a small amount, often followed by *of*; to perceive or distinguish the flavor or taste of anything; to partake or have experience of something; to have a particular flavor or taste; as, milk that *tastes* sour; *fig.* to smack or savor, usu. followed by *of*.—*n.* The act or an act of tasting; the sense by which the flavor or savor of things is perceived when they are brought into contact with the taste buds in the mouth; a particular sensation excited in these taste buds by something; as, a pleasant *taste* left in the mouth; the flavor or quality of a thing as perceived by the sense of taste; a small quantity of something tasted, eaten, or drunk; a morsel, bit, or sip; a slight experience or a sample of something; a relish, liking, or predilection for something; as, a *taste* for music; the sense of what is harmonious, beautiful, or socially proper; the perception and appreciation of what constitutes excellence in the fine arts; a manner, style, or general character indicating perception, or lack of perception, of what is fitting or beautiful; the prevailing or characteristic style, as of a culture or period.

taste bud, *n.* One of the many tiny end organs of the sense of taste located in the epithelium of the tongue.

taste·ful, tāst′ful, *a.* Having, displaying, or being in accordance with good taste.—**taste·ful·ly,** *adv.*—**taste·ful·ness,** *n.*

taste·less, tāst′lis, *a.* Having no taste or flavor; insipid; dull or uninteresting; lacking in good taste.—**taste·less·ly,** *adv.*—**taste·less·ness,** *n.*

tast·er, tā′stēr, *n.* One who tastes; one who tests food, provisions, or liquors by tasting samples; a device or container with which something is tasted in order to judge its quality.

tast·y, tā′stē, *a.*—*tastier, tastiest.* Pleasing to the taste; savory; appetizing; as, a *tasty* supper; *colloq.* having or showing good taste.—**tast·i·ly,** *adv.*—**tast·i·ness,** *n.*

tat, tat, *v.i., v.t.*—*tatted, tatting.* To make tatting or make by tatting.—**tat·ter,** tat′ēr, *n.*

Ta·tar, tä′tēr, *a.* Of or pertaining to the Tatars.—*n.* A member of any of various Mongolian and other tribes who under the leadership of Genghis Khan overran parts of Asia and eastern Europe during the Middle Ages; a member of the descendants of these peoples, now inhabiting parts of the Soviet Union; any of their languages. Also *Tartar.*

'ta·ter, tā′tēr, *n. Dial.* potato.

tat·ter, tat′ēr, *n.* [M.E. *tater*; from Scand.] A torn piece hanging loose from the main part, as of a garment; a separate torn piece; *pl.* torn or ragged clothing.—*v.t.* To tear or wear into tatters.—*v.i.* To become ragged.

tat·ter·de·mal·ion, tat″ēr·di·māl′yon, tat″ēr·di·mal′yon, *n.* [Formation obscure.] A person in tattered clothing; a ragged fellow.

tat·tered, tat′ērd, *a.* Torn to tatters; ragged; wearing ragged clothing.

tat·ter·sall, tat′ēr·sal″, *n.* A pattern having intersecting colored lines forming squares against a contrasting background color; a fabric having such a pattern.

tat·ting, tat′ing, *n.* A kind of looped and knotted lace made by hand on a small shuttle; the act of making such lace.

tat·tle, tat′l, *v.i.*—*tattled, tattling.* [Cf. L.G. *tateln*, gabble, D. *tateren*, stammer.] To chatter, prate, or talk idly; to gossip or let out secrets.—*v.t.* To utter idly; to disclose by tattling.—*n.* The act of tattling; idle or frivolous talk; gossip.

tat·tler, tat′lēr, *n.* One who tattles; a tattletale. Any of various N. American shore birds of the genera *Totanus* and *Heteroscelus*, noted for their vociferous cries.

tat·tle·tale, tat′l·tāl″, *n.* One who is an informer; a talebearer.—*a.* Indicating or revealing; telltale.

tat·too, ta·tö′, *n. pl.* **tat·toos.** [D. *taptoe*, lit. 'tap to,' with reference to the turning off of taps of casks, as in the closing of public houses for the night.] A signal on a drum or bugle at night, for soldiers or sailors to repair to their quarters; military entertainment consisting of music and exercises by troops, usu. held outdoors at night; a beating of a drum; any beating or pulsation like the beating of a drum.—*v.i.* —*tattooed, tattooing.* To beat rhythmically. —*v.t.* To beat or tap on.

tat·too, ta·tö′, *n. pl.* **tat·toos.** [Polynesian.] The act or practice of marking the skin with indelible patterns, pictures, or legends by making punctures in it and inserting pigments; a pattern, legend, or picture so made.—*v.t.*—*tattooed, tattooing.* To mark, as the skin, with tattoos; to put, as tattoos, on the skin; *fig.* to mark, spot, or stain, esp. permanently.—**tat·too·er, tat·too·ist,** *n.*

tau, tä, tou, *n.* [Gr. *tau.*] The nineteenth letter of the Greek alphabet.

tau cross, *n.* A T-shaped cross, having no upright piece above the horizontal bar. Also *Saint Anthony's cross.*

taunt, tänt, tänt, *v.t.* [O.Fr. *tanter, tenter*, to tempt, to provoke, < L. *tentare, temptare*, to try.] To reproach with jeers or sarcasm; to upbraid; to twit; to provoke with scornful or insulting words.—*n.* A bitter or sarcastic challenge or reproach; insulting invective.—**taunt·er,** *n.*—**taunt·ing·ly,** *adv.*

taunt, tänt, tänt, *a.* [O.Fr. *tant,* L. *tantus,* so great.] *Naut.* high or tall: said of masts.

taupe, tōp, *n.* [Fr. < L. *talpa,* mole.] A medium to dark, brownish-gray color sometimes with a pinkish or yellowish cast.

tau·rine, tär′in, tär′in, *a.* [L. *taurinus,* < *taurus,* bull.] Of, pertaining to, or resembling a bull; bovine; pertaining to the zodiacal sign or constellation Taurus.

tau·rine, tär′ēn, tär′in, *n.* [G. *taurin* (first found in ox bile), < L. *taurus,* bull, ox.] *Chem.* a neutral crystalline substance, $C_2H_7NO_3S$, obtained from the bile of cattle and other animals, from muscles and lung tissue, and as a decomposition product of taurocholic acid.

tau·ro·cho·lic, tär″o·kō′lik, tär″o·kol′ik, *a.* [Gr. *tauros,* bull, and *cholē,* gall, bile.] *Chem.* noting or pertaining to a deliquescent acid, $C_{26}H_{45}NO_7S$, occurring as a sodium salt in the bile of man, the ox, and certain other carnivorous animals.

Tau·rus, tär′us, *n.* [L., a bull.] The Bull, a constellation containing the Pleiades; the second of the twelve signs of the zodiac, which the sun enters about the 20th of April.

taut, tät, *a.* [A form of *tight* or closely allied to it.] Tight; not slack; tense; highstrung, unrelaxed; as, *taut* nerves or muscles; correctly or neatly arranged; tidy. —**taut·en,** tät′en, *v.t., v.i.*—**taut·ly,** *adv.* —**taut·ness,** *n.*

tau·tog, ta·tog′, ta·täg′, *n.* [Pl. of *taut,* the Ind. name.] A black, edible fish, *Tautoga onitis,* caught along the New England coast. Also *blackfish.*

tau·tol·o·gy, ta·tol′o·jē, *n. pl.* **tau·tol·o·gies.** [Gr. *tautologia*—*tautos,* the same, and *logos,* word.] A useless repetition of the same idea or meaning in different words; needless redundancy; an example of this; *logic,* a statement which permits no other logical possibilities because of its structure, as 'Either you agree or you don't agree.'— **tau·to·log·i·cal, tau·tol·o·gous,** tat″o·loj′i·kal, ta·tol′o·gus, *a.*—**tau·to·log·i·cal·ly, tau·tol·o·gous·ly,** *adv.*

tau·to·mer, ta′to·mēr, *n. Chem.* A compound having the property of tautomerism; one of the isomeric forms of a tautomer.

tau·tom·er·ism, ta·tom′e·riz″um, *n.* [Gr. *tautó,* the same, and *méros,* part.] *Chem.* the property of certain compounds of reacting to form either of two isomeric structures coexisting in equilibrium.—**tau·to·mer·ic,** ta″to·mer′ik, *a.*

tau·to·nym, ta′to·nim, *n.* [Gr. *tautónymos,* of the same name, < *tautó* and *ónyma,* name.] A scientific name in which the generic and the specific names are the same, as *Histrionicus histrionicus,* the harlequin duck: a use forbidden in botany but common in zoology.—**tau·to·nym·ic, tau·ton·y·mous,** ta·ton′i·mus, *a.*—**tau·ton·y·my,** *n.*

tav·ern, tav′ērn, *n.* [Fr. *taverne,* Pr., Sp., and It. *taverna,* < L. *taberna,* a shed, a tavern, from root of *tabula,* a board.] A place where alcoholic beverages are sold by the drink; an inn.—**tav·ern·er,** tav′ēr·nēr, *n.* An owner of a tavern.

taw, tä, *n.* [Origin obscure.] A choice or fancy playing marble with which to shoot; ring taw; the line from which the players shoot in playing marbles.—*v.i.* To shoot a marble.

taw, tä, *v.t.* [O.E. *tāwian* = D. *touwen.*] To prepare or dress, as a raw material, for use or for further manipulation; to make into leather, as a hide, by soaking in a solution of alum and salt.

taw·dry, ta′drē, *a.*—*tawdrier, tawdriest.* [From *St. Audrey,* otherwise called St. Etheldreda, at whose fair, held on the Isle of Ely, laces and cheap gay ornaments are said to have been sold.] Showy, without taste or elegance; cheap; gaudy; tastelessly and showily ornamental.—**taw·dri·ly,** *adv.* —**taw·dri·ness,** *n.*

taw·ny, ta′nē, *a.*—*tawnier, tawniest.* [O.Fr. *tané,* Fr. *tanné,* tanned, tawny, pp. of *tanner,* to tan.] Of a yellowish-brown color. —*n.* A yellowish-brown color.—**taw·ni·ness,** *n.*

taws, tawse, taz, täz, *n. pl., sing. or pl. in constr.* [Appar. < *taw,* tanned leather.] *Sc.* a leather strap, usu. divided at the end into narrow strips, used as a whip by schoolmasters and others.

tax, taks, *n.* [Fr. *taxe,* < *taxer,* to tax, < L. *taxo, taxare,* to handle, to rate, to censure, from stem of *tango,* to touch (whence also *tangent, task, taste,* etc.).] A charge imposed by governmental authority upon property, individuals, or transactions to raise money for public purposes; a similar assessment on members of any organization; a strain, serious burden, or heavy demand; as, a *tax* on one's strength.—*v.t.* To impose a tax upon; to subject to a strain or make heavy demands upon; as, to *tax* one's patience; to accuse of, charge with, or impute to; as, to *tax* a man with rudeness; *law,* to settle judicially, as the charge or cost in any judicial matter.—**tax·a·bil·i·ty,** *n.*—**tax·a·ble,** *a.*—**tax·er,** *n.*

tax·a·tion, tak·sā′shan, *n.* [L. *taxatio, taxationis.*] The act of laying or imposing a tax or taxes; the state of being taxed; the money raised by taxes.

tax·back, taks′bak′, *a*. Pertaining to the allocation of federal funds to states and localities, often considered a return to local governments of U.S. taxes collected from their citizens; as, *taxback* grants, *taxback* funds.

tax·eme, tak′sēm, *n. Ling.* a feature of grammatical structure, as pitch modulation, stress modulation, word or morpheme order, phonetic modification, or word selection.—**tax·e·mic**, tak·sē′mik, *a*.

tax-ex·empt, taks′ig·zempt, *a*. Exempt from taxation; yielding interest that is not taxable; as, *tax-exempt* bonds.

tax·i, tak′sē, *n*. pl. **tax·is, tax·ies**. A taxicab. —*v.i.*—*taxied, taxiing* or *taxying*. To ride or travel in a taxicab; *avi.* to move over the surface of the ground or water under its own power, as an airplane preparing for takeoff.—*v.t. Avi.* to cause, as an airplane, to taxi.

tax·i·cab, tak′sē·kab′, *n*. [For *taximeter cab*.] A public vehicle for hire, esp. an automobile, fitted with a taximeter.

tax·i danc·er, *n*. A girl or woman employee of a carbaret or dance hall who is available to dance with customers for a fee, either by the dance or for a certain amount of time.

tax·i·der·my, tak′si·dur″mē, *n*. [Gr. *taxis*, an arranging, order, and *derma*, skin.] The art of treating, stuffing, and mounting the skins of animals so that they retain their natural appearance.—**tax·i·der·mic**, *a*.— **tax·i·der·mist**, *n*.

tax·i·me·ter, tak′sē·mē″tēr, tak·sim′i·tēr, *n*. [Fr. *taximètre*, < *taxe*, tax, charge, and Gr. *métron*, measure: cf. G. *taxameter*.] A device fitted to a public cab or other vehicle for automatically computing and indicating the fare due at any moment, in accordance with a fixed tariff of charges.

tax·ing, taks′ing, *a*. Wearing; imposing or constituting a strain or burden.

tax·is, tak′sis, *n*. pl. **tax·es**, tak′sēz. [N.L., < Gr. *taxis*, arrangement, order, position, < *tassein*, arrange.] *Surg.* the replacing of a displaced part, or the reducing of a hernial tumor or the like, by manipulation and without incision; *biol.* the exhibition by a cell or organism of movement in a particular direction in relation to an external stimulus.

tax·ite, tak′sīt, *n*. [Gr. *taxis*, arrangement.] *Petrog.* a lava having parts of different colors or textures, thus appearing to be formed from fragments.—**tax·it·ic**, tak·sit′ik, *a*.

tax·i·way, tak′sē·wā″, *n*. Any path or surface area, usu. paved, used for taxiing to or from a runway, parking apron, or the like of an airport.

tax·on, tak′son, *n*. pl. **tax·a**, tak′sa. Any formal unit or category in a taxonomic system, as class, family, or phylum.

tax·on·o·my, tak·son′o·mē, *n*. [Fr. *taxonomie*, < Gr. *taxis*, arrangement, and *nomia*, < *némein*, deal out, distribute.] Classification, esp. in relation to its principles or laws; the classification of plants and animals into established groups or categories on the basis of their natural relationships.—**tax·o·nom·ic, tax·o·nom·i·cal**, tak″so·nom′ik, *a*.—**tax·o·nom·i·cal·ly**, *adv*.—**tax·on·o·mist**, *n*.

tax·pay·er, taks′pā″ēr, *n*. One who pays a tax or is subject to a tax; a small building temporarily placed on property to meet taxes on the land.

tax stamp, *n*. A stamp placed upon a product, as cigarettes or alcohol, to indicate that tax has been paid on it.

tax·us, tak′sus, *n*. pl. **tax·us**. Any plant of the genus *Taxus* in the yew family.

taz·za, tät′sa, *It.* tät′tsä, *n*. pl. **taz·zas**, *It.* **taz·ze**, tät′tse. [It. = Fr. *tasse*, E. *tass*.] A shallow ornamental bowl or vase, esp. one having a foot or pedestal.

TB, T.B., tē′bē, *n*. Tuberculosis.

T-bar lift, tē′bär″ lift″, *n*. A ski lift in which two skiers stand on their skis and lean against a center crossbar as they are pulled uphill.

T-bone, tē′bōn″, *n*. A beefsteak taken from the loin and containing a T-shaped bone and some tenderloin. Also **T-bone steak**.

tea, tē, *n*. [= Fr. *thé*, G. *thee*, N.L. *thea*, < Chin. *te*, for *ch′a, ts′a*, tea.] The dried and prepared leaves of the shrub *Thea sinensis*, from which a somewhat bitter, aromatic beverage is prepared by infusion in hot water; the beverage so prepared; the shrub itself, which is extensively cultivated in China, Japan, and India, and which has fragrant white flowers; any of various infusions prepared from the leaves or flowers of other plants and used as beverages or medicines; any kind of leaves or flowers so used; a service of tea, with or without other food, in the late afternoon; an afternoon reception at which tea is served; *slang*, marijuana.

tea bag, *n*. A porous container of cloth or paper which holds enough tea leaves for one serving of tea.

tea ball, *n*. A perforated ball, usu. of metal, in which tea leaves are placed to be immersed in hot water to make tea.

tea·ber·ry, tē′ber″ē, tē′be·rē, *n*. pl. **tea·ber·ries**. The spicy red fruit of the American wintergreen, *Gaultheria procumbens*; the plant itself.

tea bis·cuit, *n*. A sweetened biscuit or cookie served with tea.

tea·cake, tē′kāk″, *n*. A light, simple cake or cookie for serving at tea; *Brit.* a kind of flat, light cake.

tea·cart, tē′kärt″, *n*. Tea wagon.

teach, tēch, *v.t.*—*taught, teaching*. [< O.E. *taecan*, to teach, show, command; allied to *tihan*, to accuse; Goth. G. *zeigen*, to point out; cogn. L. *dico*, to say; Gr. *deiknymi*, Skt. *diç*, to point out. *Token* is akin.] To give instruction to; to guide the studies of; as, to *teach* a class; to impart the knowledge of; as, to *teach* history; to train; to give skill in the use of; to instruct by implying; as, an experience that *teaches* a lesson.—*v.i.* To give instruction; to work as a teacher.

teach·a·ble, tē′cha·bl, *a*. Receptive or equal to learning; docile; impartable by teaching; as, *teachable* subject matter. —**teach·a·bil·i·ty, teach·a·ble·ness**, *n*.— **teach·a·bly**, *adv*.

teach·er, tē′chēr, *n*. One who teaches, esp one whose profession or occupation is teaching; a tutor; an instructor.

teach·ers col·lege, teach·ers′ col·lege, *n*. A college, usu. with a four-year course of studies, which prepares students for the teaching profession.

teach-in, tēch′in″, *n*. pl. **teach-ins**. An extended symposium on some issue of public concern conducted by faculty and students of a university, esp. when organized as a protest against government policies.

teach·ing, tē′ching, *n*. The act or business of instructing; instruction; *often pl.* doctrine.

teach·ing fel·low, *n*. A graduate student on a fellowship that obligates him to assume some teaching duties.

teach·ing ma·chine, *n*. An automatic device that allows a student to learn at his own rate by presenting a unit of information and questions as part of a planned sequence of such units, and requiring a satisfactory response before the next unit is presented; any of various similar devices, either automatic or hand-operated.

tea co·zy, *n*. A padded or quilted cover shaped to fit over a teapot and used for retaining the heat.

tea·cup, tē′kup″, *n*. A cup in which tea is served, usu. of small or moderate size; a

teacupful.—**tea·cup·ful**, tē′kup·fŭl″, *n*. pl. **tea·cup·fuls**. As much as a teacup will hold: sometimes taken as about four fluid ounces.

tea dance, *n*. Any dance held during teatime, in the late afternoon.

tea gar·den, *n*. A garden or open-air enclosure, usu. public, where tea and other refreshments are served to customers; a plantation where tea plants are grown.

tea gown, *n*. A woman's semiformal gown styled in flowing lines and made of fine material, for wearing at afternoon social gatherings, esp. when entertaining in one's home.

tea·house, tē′hous″, *n*. A house, restaurant, or place, usu. public, where tea and other light refreshments are served, esp. in China and Japan.

teak, tēk, *n*. [Tamil name.] A tree, *Tectona grandis*, growing in different parts of the East Indies, and yielding a strong, durable, and valuable timber. The wood obtained from this tree; also **teak·wood**.

tea·ket·tle, tē′ket″l, *n*. A portable kettle with a cover, spout, and handle, in which to boil water.

teal, tēl, *n*. pl. **teals, teal**. [Same as *tel* or *tal* in D. *teling, taling*, a teal; origin doubtful.] Any of several short-necked freshwater ducks, esp. the blue-winged teal and the green-winged teal. A dull, darkish color of a greenish-blue hue; also **teal blue**.

team, tēm, *n*. [O.E. *tēam*, progeny, family, team, from the root of *tēon*, draw, *togian*, drag, E. *tow*.] A number of persons associated in a joint action or endeavor; as, a *team* of reporters; one of the sides in a contest; as, a football *team*; two or more horses or other draft animals harnessed together to draw a wagon, other vehicle, or implement; these animals or one such animal, together with the harness and the vehicle drawn.—*v.t.* To harness or join together in a team; to convey or transport by means of a team.—*v.i.* To drive a team; to form a team, usu. followed by *up* or *together*.—*a*.

tea mak·er, *n*. A perforated spoon with a hinged lid, used as a container for tea when brewing tea in the cup.

team·mate, tēm′māt″, *n*. A fellow team member.

team·ster, tēm′stēr, *n*. One who drives a team or other vehicle, as a truck, esp. as an occupation.

team teach·ing, *n*. A method of teaching in which several teachers instruct one group of students, thus allowing each teacher to specialize.

team·work, tēm′wụrk″, *n*. The work of a team or number of persons acting together, esp. with reference to coordination of effort and collective efficiency.

tea par·ty, *n*. A party or other social gathering at which tea and light refreshments are served, esp. in the afternoon.

tea·pot, tē′pot″, *n*. A vessel with a lid, spout, and handle, in which tea is made and from which it is poured and served.

tea·poy, tē′poi, *n*. [Hind. *tipāī*, three-legged table.] A small three-legged table or stand; a small table for use in serving tea.

tear, tēr, *n*. [O.E. *teár*, a tear = Icel. *tár*, Dan. *taare*, G. *zähre*, Goth. *tager*; cogn. Gr. *dakry*, O.L. *dacryma*, L. *lacryma*, Ir. *dear*, W. *daiger*, Gael. *deur*; < a root meaning to bite.] A limpid, droplike liquid secretion of the lacrimal gland which moistens the surface of the eye and cleanses it of foreign particles; this liquid appearing in the eyes or flowing from them, esp. through excessive grief or joy; any transparent drop of fluid matter; a solid transparent drop, as of some resins. *Pl.* weeping; sorrow or misery.—*v.i.* To shed or emit tears.—**tear·y**, *a*.—*tearier, teariest*.

tear, târ, v.t.—past *tore*, pp. *torn*, ppr. *tearing*. [O.E. *teran*, tear, = D. *teren*, G. *zehren*, consume, = Goth. *-tairan*, tear, rend; akin to Gr. *dérein*, flay, Skt. *dar-*, burst, split.] To pull apart or in pieces by force, esp. so as to leave ragged or irregular edges; rend; produce or effect by rending; as, to *tear* a hole in one's coat; to wound or injure by or as by rending; to lacerate; to rend or divide, as: The state was *torn* by civil war. Distress greatly; as, to *tear* the heart with anguish; to pull or pluck violently; to remove by force; as, to *tear* oneself from a place.—v.i. To make a tear or rent; to become torn; to move or go with violence or great haste, as: He *tore* out of the house.—n. The act or an act of tearing; a rent or fissure; a rushing movement; a violent outburst, as of rage or enthusiasm; *slang*, a spree.—**tear a·round**, to go or move about in a wild or disorderly manner, as in anger or excitement.—**tear a·way**, to remove, as oneself, with reluctance or lack of enthusiasm, as: He could not *tear* himself *away* from the movie.—**tear down**, to take down or apart; to disassemble; to cast aspersions upon; as, to *tear down* one's friends.—**tear in·to**, *colloq*. to attack unrestrainedly, esp. verbally.—**tear off**, *slang*, to compose or perform quickly, as: He can *tear off* a novel in a week.—**tear up**, to damage or remove, esp. a bottom surface, as a street or floor; to tear or rip into shreds, as a sheet of paper.—**tear·er**, n.

tear·down, târ'doun″, n. A taking apart.

tear·drop, tēr'drop″, n. A tear; that which suggests or resembles a tear because of its shape.

tear·ful, tēr'ful, a. Weeping; causing or provoking tears.—**tear·ful·ly**, adv.—**tear·ful·ness**, n.

tear gas, tēr'gas″, n. A substance causing excessive tearing and therefore temporary partial blindness: used primarily by police in dispersing mobs.—**tear·gas**, v.t.—*teargassed*, *tear-gassing*.

tear-jerk·er, tear·jerk·er, tēr'jur″kér, n. *Colloq*. an overly sentimental song, play, story, or the like.—**tear·jerk·ing**, a.

tear·less, tēr'lis, a. Without tears; without weeping; unable to cry or weep.—**tear·less·ly**, adv.

tea·room, tē'röm″, tē'rụm″, n. A room or shop where tea and other refreshments are served to customers. Also **tea·shop**.

tea rose, n. Any of several varieties of cultivated rose descended primarily from the Chinese rose, *Rosa odorata*, bearing white, pink, and pale-yellow flowers and having a scent supposed to resemble that of tea; a yellow-pink color.

tear sheet, târ' shēt″, n. A page taken from a publication, as a magazine or newspaper, usu. for the purpose of proving to an advertiser that his advertisement has been published.

tear-stained, tēr'stānd″, a. Marked with tears; streaked or spotted from weeping.

tear strip, târ'strip″, n. The strip on a can, box, or wrapper which, when pulled, opens the container.

tease, tēz, v.t.—*teased*, *teasing*. [O.E. *tæsan* = D. *teezen* = M.L.G. *tēsen* = M.H.G. *zeisen*, tease (wool).] To pull apart or separate the adhering fibers of, as in combing or carding wool, or in preparing a specimen for microscopic examination; to comb or card, as wool; to comb, as the hair, toward the scalp to give body to a hairdo; shred; to raise a nap on, as cloth, with teasels; to teasel; to worry or irritate by persistent petty requests, trifling raillery, or other annoyance; to disturb by persistent petty annoyance, for mere sport; to exite sexually without the intention of satisfying.—v.i. To worry or disturb a person by importunity or persistent petty

annoyance.—n. The act of teasing, or the state of being teased; one who or that which teases or annoys.—**teas·a·ble**, a.—**teas·er**, tē'zér, n.—**teas·ing·ly**, adv.

tea·sel, tē'zel, n. Any of the herbs, genus *Dipsacus*, with prickly leaves and flower heads; the bur or dried flower head of these plants, covered with stiff, hooked bracts, used for teasing or teaseling cloth; any mechanical contrivance used for the same purpose.—v.t.—*teaseled*, *teaseling*, *esp. Brit. teaselled*, *teaselling*. To raise a nap on with teazels; to dress by means of teazels. Also *esp. Brit.* **tea·zel**, **tea·zle**.

tea serv·ice, n. Tea set.

tea set, n. A set of articles of chinaware or metalware used in serving tea, as a teapot, sugar bowl, cream pitcher, and sometimes cups, saucers, dessert plates, a waste bowl, and tray. Also *tea service*.

tea shop, n. A tearoom. *Brit.* any restaurant serving snacks or light meals; lunchroom.

tea·spoon, tē'spön″, tē'spụn″, n. The small spoon commonly used to stir tea, coffee, or the like; a teaspoonful. A unit of measurement in cooking equivalent to one-third of a tablespoon, or one and one-third fluid-drams; abbr. *t.*, *tsp.*

tea·spoon·ful, tē'spön·fụl″, tē'spụn·fụl″, n. pl. **tea·spoon·fuls**. As much as a teaspoon can hold.

teat, tēt, tit, n. [O.E. *tit*, *titt*, a teat = L.G. and O.D. *titte*, G. *zitze*, Ir. and Gael. *did*, a teat.] The projecting structure through which milk is drawn from the breast or udder of females; a nipple; a dug; a pap. —**teat·ed**, a.

tea ta·ble, n. A table at which tea is served or taken, or on which things are placed for tea.

tea·time, tē'tīm″, n. The time, customarily in the late afternoon, for serving or taking tea.

tea tow·el, n. Dishtowel.

tea tray, n. Any tray used to hold or carry the articles for serving tea.

tea wag·on, n. A small stand or table on wheels for holding articles for use in serving tea. Also *teacart*.

tech·ne·ti·um, tek·nē'shē·um, tek·nē'-shum, n. *Chem.* a silver-gray, metallic element produced artificially by bombardment of molybdenum, or produced in the fission of plutonium or uranium. Sym. Tc, at. no. 43, at. wt. 97. See Periodic Table of Elements.

tech·nic, tek'nik, tek·nēk′, n. [= Fr. *technique*, a. and n., < Gr. *technicós*, pertaining to art, skillful, technical, < *téchnē*, art, workmanly skill.] A technicality, tek'-nik. Technical skill; technique, tek·nēk′.— tek'nik, a. Technical.

tech·ni·cal, tek'ni·kal, a. Belonging or pertaining to an art or arts; as, a *technical* dictionary; characteristic of a particular art, science, profession, or trade; as, a *technical* term; using technical terms, as a writer or a book; familiar in a practical way with a particular art or trade, as a person; so considered from a technical point of view; as, a military engagement ending in a *technical* defeat; pertaining to or connected with the mechanical or industrial arts and the applied sciences; as, a *technical* school; *econ.* denoting a market or field in which the costs or prices are fixed by the availability of the products and speculators' demands. —**tech·ni·cal·ly**, adv.—**tech·ni·cal·ness**, n.

tech·ni·cal·i·ty, tek″ni·kal'i·tē, n. pl. **tech·ni·cal·i·ties**. A technical character; the use of technical methods or terms; something that is technical, or peculiar to an art, science, profession, or trade; a technical point or detail, esp. one significant only to an expert; a technical term or expression.

tech·ni·cal knock·out, n. A decision by the referee against a boxer who has been beaten to the extent that he is unable to continue fighting, his opponent in the contest being awarded the victory.

tech·ni·cal ser·geant, n. *U.S. Air Force and Marine Corps*, a noncommissioned officer immediately below master sergeant and immediately above staff sergeant; the rank or grade of this person.

tech·ni·cian, tek·nish'an, n. One highly trained in the technicalities of a subject, profession, or occupation; one skilled in the technique of an art, as sculpture, painting, ballet, or music; *armed forces*, a rank formerly given to an enlisted man having special skills in a particular technical field.

Tech·ni·col·or, tek′ni·kul'ér, n. A process for making color motion pictures by superposing the three primary colors to produce the finished print. (Trademark.)

tech·nics, tek'niks, n. pl., sing. or pl. in *constr.* The study or science of an art or of arts in general, esp. the industrial or mechanical arts; technology.

tech·nique, tek·nēk′, n. Method of performance; as, the *technique* of the poet; technical skill.

tech·noc·ra·cy, tek·nok'ra·sē, n. pl. **tech·noc·ra·cies**. [Gr. *téchnē*, art.] A theory of government, prominent in 1932, advocating control and management of industrial resources and reorganization of society by technologists and engineers.—**tech·no·crat**, tek'no·krat″, n.—**tech·no·crat·ic**, a.

tech·no·log·i·cal, tek″no·loj'i·kal, a. Pertaining to technology; influenced or caused by scientific or industrial advancement. Also **tech·no·log·ic**.—**tech·no·log·i·cal·ly**, adv.

tech·nol·o·gy, tek·nol'o·jē, n. [Gr. *téchnē*, art.] The branch of knowledge that deals with the industrial arts and sciences; utilization of such knowledge; the knowledge and means used to produce the material necessities of a society; the terminology of an art or science; technical nomenclature.— **tech·nol·o·gist**, n.

tech·y, tech'ē, a,—*techier*, *techiest*. Tetchy.

tec·ton·ic, tek·ton'ik, a. [L.L. *tectonicus*, < Gr. *tectonicós*, < *téctōn*, carpenter, builder, workman, maker.] Of or pertaining to building or construction; constructive; architectural. *Geol.* pertaining to the structure of the earth's crust; noting valleys or the like due chiefly to elevation or other changes in portions of the earth's crust, rather than to erosion.

tec·ton·ics, tek·ton'iks, n. pl. but sing. in *constr.* The science or art of assembling, shaping, or ornamenting materials in construction; the constructive arts in general; the study of the structure of the earth.

tec·trix, tek'triks, n. pl. **tec·tri·ces**, tek'-tri·sēz″, tek·trī'sēz. [< L. *tego*, *tectum*, to cover.] *Ornith.* a covert.—**tec·tri·cial**, tek·trish'al, a.

ted, ted, v.t.—*tedded*, *tedding*. [< W. *teddu*, to spread out.] To turn over and scatter after mowing, as hay, in order to dry by exposing to the air.

ted·der, ted'ér, n. One who teds; an implement that spreads newly mown hay to accelerate drying.

ted·dy bear, ted'ē bâr, n. [Named from 'Teddy' (Theodore) Roosevelt, from his well-known interest in hunting and animals.] A stuffed figure of a bear, used as a toy.

Te De·um, tā dā'um, tē dē'um, n. pl. **Te De·ums**. [L.; < the first words, *Te Deum laudamus*, 'thee, God, we praise.'] An ancient Latin hymn, in the form of a psalm, sung regularly in Latin or English at matins in the Roman Catholic Church and, in an English translation, at Morning Prayer in the Anglican Church, as well as for special occasions, as a service of thanksgiving; a musical setting of the hymn; a service of thanksgiving in which this hymn forms a prominent part.

te·di·ous, tē′dē·us, tē′jus, *a.* [O.Fr. *tedieux,* L. *taediosus.*] Involving or causing tedium; tiresome from continuance or slowness; wearisome; monotonous.—**te··di·ous·ly,** *adv.*—**te·di·ous·ness,** *n.*

te·di·um, tē′dē·um, *n.* [L. *taedium,* < *taedet,* it wearies.] Irksomeness; wearisomeness.

tee, tē, *n.* [Origin uncertain.] The mark aimed at in various games, as curling. *Golf,* the starting place, usu. a small heap of earth, from which the ball is driven at the beginning of play for each hole; a small peg of wood, plastic, rubber, or metal from which the ball is hit at the beginning of play for each hole; *Football,* a support to hold a football in place for kicking.—*v.t. teed, teeing. Golf,* to place on a tee, as the ball.—**tee off,** *golf,* to play, as a ball, from some tee; *colloq.* to begin; as, to *tee off* the banquet with a short speech.—**teed off,** indignant or disgusted, as: They were *teed off* because dinner was two hours late.

tee, tē, *n.* The letter T, t; something shaped like a T, as a pipe joint; a metal beam or bar which in cross section is like the letter T.—*a.* In the shape of a T.—**to a tee,** perfectly or precisely.

teem, tēm, *v.i.* [O.E. *teman, tyman,* to produce.] To be stocked to overflowing; to be prolific or abundantly fertile.—*v.t.* To produce; to bring forth.

teem, tēm, *v.i., v.t.* [M.E. *temen;* < Scand.; akin to E. *toom.*] To pour, as rain.

teen, tēn, *a.* Teen-age.—*n.* A teen-ager.

teen·ag·er, teen·ag·er, tēn′ā″jėr, *n.* A person from the age of 13 through 19.—**teen-age, teen·age,** *a.*

teens, tēnz, *n. pl.* The years from 13 through 19, esp. when listed consecutively, as in a person's age or years of a century; the numbers having the termination *-teen.*

tee·ny, tē′nē, *a.—teenier, teeniest. Colloq.* tiny.

tee·pee, tē′pē, *n.* Tepee.

tee shirt, *n.* T-shirt.

tee·ter, tē′tėr, *v.i.* [Var. of *titter.*] To seesaw; to move like a seesaw; to move unsteadily.—*v.t.* To cause to move with a seesaw motion.—*n.* A seesaw; a seesaw motion.

tee·ter·board, tē′tėr·bōrd″, tē″tėr·bård″, *n.* A seesaw. Also **tee·ter·tot·ter.**

teethe, tēŦH, *v.i.—teethed, teething.* [< *teeth.*] To grow teeth; to cut one's teeth.—**teeth·ing,** tē′ŦHing, *n.*

teeth·ing ring, *n.* A ring made of plastic, rubber, or the like, on which a baby who is teething may bite.

teeth·ridge, tēth′rij″, *n.* The inner gum surface of the upper jaw between the front teeth and the hard palate.

tee·to·tal, tē·tōt′al, *a.* [Extended form of *total,* appar. for emphasis.] Of or pertaining to, advocating, or pledged to total abstinence from intoxicating drink; *fig.* absolute, complete, or entire.—*v.i.—teetotaled, teetotaling, esp. Brit. teetotalled, teetotalling.* To adhere to teetotalism.—**tee·to·tal·er,** tē·tōt′a·lėr, **tee·to·tal·ist,** *n.*—**tee·to·tal··ism,** tē·tōt′a·liz″um, *n.*—**tee·to·tal·ly,** *adv.*

tee·to·tum, tē·tō′tum, *n.* [Orig. *T totum,* that is, L. *totum,* 'the whole,' preceded by its initial letter, *T,* this letter, representing L. *totum,* being inscribed on one side of the toy.] A kind of top having four sides, each marked with a different initial letter, spun with the fingers in an old game of chance; any small top spun with the fingers.

te·fil·lin, te·fil′in, *Heb.* te·fē·lēn′, *n. pl. Judaism,* the phylacteries. Also **te·phil·lin.**

Tef·lon, tef′lon, *n.* A waxy material, polytetrafluorethylene, used as a covering to prevent sticking on cooking utensils and industrial appliances. (Trademark.)

teg·men, teg′men, *n. pl.* **teg·mi·na,** teg′-mi·na. [L., a covering, < *tegere,* cover.] A cover, covering, or integument; *entom.* one of the forewings of an insect, esp. an orthopterous insect, when they form a protective covering for the posterior wings; *bot.* the delicate inner integument or coat of a seed.

teg·u·lar, teg′ū·lėr, *a.* [L. *tegula,* a tile, < *tego,* to cover.] Resembling a tile; pertaining to or consisting of tiles.—**teg·u·lar·ly,** *adv.*

teg·u·ment, teg′ū·ment, *n.* [L. *tegumentum,* < *tego,* to cover.] A cover or covering; a natural covering, as of an animal; an integument.—**teg·u·men·tal, teg·u·men··ta·ry,** teg″ū·men′tal, teg″ū·men′ta·rē, *a.*

teil, tēl, *n.* [Fr. *teil,* < L. *tilia,* a lime tree.] The lime or European linden tree. Also **teil tree.**

tek·tite, tĕk′tīt, *n. Geol.* any of various types of rounded, glassy masses, assumed to have come from outer space, found in Australia, Czechoslovakia, and Indonesia.

tel·aes·the·sia, tel″is·thē′zha, tel″is·the′-zhē·a, tel″is·thē′zē·a, *n.* Telesthesia.

tel·a·mon, tel′a·mon″, *n. pl.* **tel·a·mo·nes,** tel″a·mō′nēz. [Gr. *telamon,* a bearer.] *Arch.* a column or pilaster in the figure of a man. See *atlantes.*

tel·an·gi·ec·ta·sis, tel·an″jē·ek′ta·sis, *n. pl.* **tel·an·gi·ec·ta·ses,** tel·an″jē·ek′ta··sēz. [N.L., < Gr. *télos,* end, and *alleion,* vessel, and *éctasis,* extension.] *Pathol.* dilation of the capillaries and other small blood vessels, as caused by congenital defects, alcoholism, or cold weather, producing a form of angioma, usu. on the face. —**tel·an·gi·ec·tat·ic,** tel·an″jē·ek·tat′ik, *a.*

Tel·Au·to·graph, tel·a′to·graf″, tel·a′to·· gräf″, *n.* A form of telegraph for reproducing graphic material, as handwriting or drawings, the movements of a pen or pencil at one end of the line being reproduced in a pen or pencil at the other end by a system of electromagnets. (Trademark.)

tel·e·cast, tel′e·kast″, tel′e·käst″, *v.t., v.i.—telecast* or *telecasted, telecasting.* To broadcast by television.—*n.* A televised broadcast.—**tel·e·cast·er,** *n.*

tel·e·com·mu·ni·ca·tion, tel′e·ko·mū″-ni·kā′shan, *n. Often pl. but sing. in constr.* the science of communication by electronically transmitted waves, as by radio, television, radar, telephone, telegraph, and the like. Any communication transmitted in this manner.

tel·e·course, tel′e·kōrs″, tel′e·kårs″, *n.* A course of instruction presented through the medium of television.

tel·e·du, tel′i·dö″, *n.* [Native name.] A deep brown, small carnivorous mammal, genus *Mydaus,* native to the mountains of Sumatra, Java, and Borneo, and like the skunk in its ability to emit a foul-smelling secretion.

tel·e·film, tel′e·film″, *n.* A motion picture created for presentation on television.

tel·e·gen·ic, tel″e·jen′ik, *a.* [(*tele*)vision and *-genic.*] Televising well; suited for broadcasting by television. Also *videogenic.* —**tel·e·gen·i·cal·ly,** *adv.*

te·leg·o·ny, te·leg′o·nē, *n.* The supposed influence of a previous sire upon the progeny subsequently borne by the same mother to other sires.—**tel·e·gon·ic,** tel″e··gon′ik, *a.*

tel·e·gram, tel′e·gram″, *n.* [Gr. *tēle,* far, and *gramma,* what is written, < *graphō,* to write.] A communication sent by telegraph; a telegraphic message or dispatch.

tel·e·graph, tel′e·graf″, tel′e·gräf″, *n.* An apparatus, system, or process for transmitting messages or signals over a distance, esp. by means of an electrical device consisting essentially of a transmitting instrument and a distant receiving instrument

connected by a conducting wire; a message so transmitted.—*v.t.* To transmit or send, as a message, by telegraph; to send a message to by telegraph.—*v.i.* To send a message by telegraph.—**te·leg·ra·pher, te··leg·ra·phist,** te·leg′ra·fėr, *n.*

tel·e·graph·ic, tel″e·graf′ik, tel″e·gräf′ik, *a.* Pertaining to the telegraph; made by a telegraph; communicated by a telegraph; *fig.* succinct.—**tel·e·graph·i·cal·ly,** *adv.*

te·leg·ra·phone, te·leg′ra·fōn″, *n.* One of the first magnetic sound recorders; an apparatus which records a message when the telephone to which it is connected is unanswered.

tel·e·graph plant, *n. Bot.* a tick trefoil of East India, *Desmodium gyrans,* remarkable for the spontaneous jerking motions of its leaflets, suggesting signaling.

te·leg·ra·phy, te·leg′ra·fē, *n.* The art or practice of constructing or operating telegraphs.

tel·e·ki·ne·sis, tel″e·ki·nē′sis, tel″e·kī··nē′sis, *n.* [N.L., < Gr. *tēle,* afar, and *kinēsis,* movement.] The production of motion in objects with no physical cause in evidence; the ability claimed by mediums to cause such motions.—**tel·e·ki·net·ic,** tel″e·ki·net′ik, tel″e·kī·net′ik, *a.*

tel·e·mark, tel′e·märk″, *n.* (*Sometimes cap.*), *skiing,* a method of turning in which the outside ski is placed far in advance of the other, and then slowly angled into the turn.

te·lem·e·ter, te·lem′i·tėr, tel′e·mē″tėr, *n.* Any apparatus for computing distances from the measurement of angles; *electron.* an apparatus for determining or measuring quantities, as temperature or cosmic radiation, and converting them into transmissible signals that register at a distant station; *aerospace,* radio transmission of coded data between a ground station and a spacecraft or artificial satellite.—*v.t.* To transmit, as data, by telemeter.—*v.i.* to transmit the measurement of a quantity or other data.— **tel·e·me·ter·ing,** *n.* The science and use of telemeters.—**tel·e·met·ric,** tel″e·me′-trik, *a.*—**tel·e·met·ri·cal·ly,** *adv.*—**te··lem·e·try,** te·lem′i·trē, *n.*

tel·en·ceph·a·lon, tel″en·sef′a·lon″, *n. pl.* **tel·en·ceph·a·lons, tel·en·ceph·a·la,** tel″en·sef′a·la. *Anat.* the anterior division or section of the forebrain or prosencephalon. Also *endbrain.*—**tel·en·ce·phal··ic,** tel″en·se·fal′ik, *a.*

tel·e·o·log·i·cal, tel″ē·o·loj′i·kal, tē″lē··o·loj′i·kal, *a.* Of or pertaining to teleology; relating to final causes; pertaining to design or purpose in nature. Also **tel·e·o·log·ic.** —**tel·e·o·log·i·cal·ly,** *adv.*

tel·e·ol·o·gy, tel″ē·ol′o·jē, tē″lē·ol′o·jē, *n.* [Gr. *telos, teleos,* an end, and *logos,* discourse.] *Philos.* The doctrine of final causes; the study of evidence in nature indicating that final causes exist; an explanation of natural phenomena by final causes; the metaphysical doctrine that final goals and purposes rather than mechanical causes order reality.—**tel·e·ol·o·gist,** *n.*

tel·e·ost, tel′ē·ost″, tē′lē·ost″, *a.* [N.L. *Teleostei,* pl., < Gr. *téleos,* complete, and *ostéon,* bone.] Belonging or pertaining to the subclass *Teleostei,* a large group of fishes having a more or less completely ossified or bony skeleton, as the salmon, flounder, or mackerel.—*n.* Any teleost fish.—**tel·e·os··te·an,** *a., n.*

te·lep·a·thy, te·lep′a·thē, *n.* Communication of one mind with another by some means beyond normal sensory perception. —**tel·e·path·ic,** tel″a·path′ik, *a.*—**tel·e··path·i·cal·ly,** *adv.*—**te·lep·a·thist,** te·-lep′a·thist, *n.*

tel·e·phone, tel′e·fōn″, *n.* An apparatus, system, or process for the transmission of sound or speech to a distant point, esp. by an electrical device consisting essentially of a transmitter, a conducting wire, and a receiver. A similar communicating device or system in which there are no connecting wires; see *wireless.—v.t.—telephoned, telephoning.* To speak to, as a person, by means of a telephone; to summon by telephone; to send, as a message, by telephone.—*v.i.* To communicate or send a message by telephone.—**tel·e·phon·er,** *n.*

tel·e·phone book, *n.* A book which lists alphabetically the telephone subscribers in a certain area, their addresses, and their telephone numbers. Also **tel·e·phone di·rec·to·ry.**

tel·e·phone booth, *n.* A booth or enclosure equipped with a public telephone and usu. more or less soundproof.

tel·e·phone re·ceiv·er, *n.* The device within a telephone which converts the varying electric current or impulses into sound.

tel·e·phon·ic, tel″*e*·fon′ik, *a.* Of, conveyed by, or pertaining to the telephone; conveying or conducting sound, esp. to a distant point.—**tel·e·phon·i·cal·ly,** *adv.*

tel·e·pho·ni·tis, tel″*e*·fo·ni′tis, *n. Slang,* the obsessive use of the telephone.

te·leph·o·ny, te·lef′*o*·nē, *n.* The science dealing with the construction and operation of the various types of telephones and telephonic systems.

tel·e·pho·to, tel′*e*·fō′tō, *a.* Relating to telephotography; denoting a lens structure in a camera which permits large photographs to be taken of far-off objects.

tel·e·pho·tog·ra·phy, tel″*e*·fo·tog′ra·fē, *n.* The art of photographing objects too distant for the ordinary camera, by the use of telephoto lenses and a special camera; the art of electrically reproducing photographs or pictures at a distance by a special telegraphic process.—**tel·e·pho·to·graph·ic,** tel″*e*·fō″to·graf′ik, *a.*

tel·e·play, tel′*e*·plā″, *n.* A play which is created or rewritten esp. for television.

tel·e·print·er, tel′*e*·prin′tèr, *n.* Teletypewriter.

tel·e·proc·ess·ing, tel′*e*·pros′i·sing, *n.* That form of data processing involving the use of various communications media, as radio or wire, for the gathering of information.

Tel·e·prompt·er, tel′*e*·promp″tèr, *n.* An electronic text-enlarging device for television performers or speakers. (Trademark.)

tel·e·ran, tel′*e*·ran″, *n.* A navigational system for landing aircraft which combines the use of radar and television to give constant data to a pilot on the position of his plane in relation to others in the same area.

tel·e·scope, tel′i·skōp″, *n.* [N.L. *telescopium,* < Gr. *telescopos,* far-seeing.] An optical instrument used for making distant objects appear nearer and larger, of which there are two principal forms: one, a refracting telescope, consisting essentially of a lens or object glass for forming an image, and the other, a reflecting telescope, having a similar arrangement, but containing a concave mirror or speculum instead of an object glass.—*v.t.—telescoped, telescoping.* To force together, one into another, or to force into something else, after the manner of the sliding tubes of a jointed telescope; to shorten or compress.—*v.i.* To slide together, or into something else, after the manner of the tubes of a jointed telescope; to be driven one into another, as railroad cars in collision.

tel·e·scop·ic, tel′i·skop′ik, *a.* Of, pertaining to, or of the nature of a telescope; obtained by means of a telescope; as, a *telescopic* view of the moon; seen by means of a telescope; visible only through a

telescope; far-seeing; as, a *telescopic* eye; consisting of parts which slide one within another like the tubes of a jointed telescope, and thus capable of being extended or shortened. Also **tel·e·scop·i·cal.—tel·e·scop·i·cal·ly,** *adv.*

tel·es·the·sia, tel″is·thē′zha, tel″is·thē′zhē·a, tel″is·thē′zē·a, *n.* Ability to respond to a stimulus beyond or presumed to be beyond the usual range of the senses. Also *telaesthesia.*—**tel·es·thet·ic, tel·aes·thet·ic,** tel″is·thet′ik, *a.*

tel·e·ther·mom·e·ter, tel″*e*·thèr·mom′i·tèr, *n.* An apparatus that indicates the temperature at some distant point. Also **tel·e·ther·mo·scope.—tel·e·ther·mom·e·try,** *n.*

tel·e·thon, tel′*e*·thon″, *n.* A lengthy television program, usu. broadcast to raise funds for a charitable undertaking, a political campaign, or the like.

tel·e·tran·scrip·tion, tel″*e*·tran·skrip′shan, *n.* A recording on film made for presentation as a television program; kinescope; video tape.

Tel·e·type, tel′i·tīp″, *n.* A teletypewriter. (Trademark.)—*v.t.—teletyped, teletyping.* (*l.c.*) to transmit, as a message, by Teletype.—*v.i.* (*l.c.*) to operate or use a Teletype.—**tel·e·typ·ist,** tel′i·tī″pist, *n.*

Tel·e·type·set·ter, tel″i·tīp′set″èr, tel′i·tīp″set″èr, *n.* An apparatus resembling a typewriter, that perforates a tape which, either directly or by means of telegraphy, activates a typesetting machine. (Trademark.)

tel·e·type·writ·er, tel″i·tīp′rī″tèr, tel′i·tīp″rī″tèr, *n.* A telegraphic apparatus by which signals are sent by striking the letters of the keyboard of an instrument resembling a typewriter, and are received by a similar instrument which automatically prints them in type corresponding to the letters struck. Also *teleprinter.*

te·leu·to·spore, te·lö′to·spōr″, te·lö′to·spar″, *n. Bot.* teliospore.—**te·leu·to·spor·ic,** te·lö″to·spōr′ik, te·lö″to·spar′ik, *a.*

tel·e·view, tel′*e*·vū″, *v.t., v.i.* To observe through the medium of television.—**tel·e·view·er,** *n.*

tel·e·vise, tel′*e*·vīz″, *v.t., v.i.—televised, televising.* To transmit by television.

tel·e·vi·sion, tel′*e*·vizh″an, *n. pl.* **tel·e·vi·sion.** The transmission of scenes or moving pictures by conversion of light rays to electrical waves, which are reconverted to reproduce the original image; a set which receives television broadcasts; the industry of television broadcasting; television broadcasts collectively. Also *TV, video.—a.—***tel·e·vi·sion·al·ly,** *adv.*—**tel·e·vi·sion·ar·y,** tel″*e*·vizh′a·ner″ē, *a.*

tel·ic, tel′ik, *a.* [Gr. *telos,* end.] *Gram.* denoting end or purpose; perfective. Tending toward a purpose or end.—**tel·i·cal·ly,** *adv.*

te·li·o·spore, tē′lē·o·spōr″, tē′lē·o·spar″, tel′ē·o·spōr″, tel′ē·o·spar″, *n.* [Gr. *teleutē,* completion, and *sporá,* E. *spore.*] *Bot.* one of the resting, thick-walled spores of various rust fungi, formed usu. toward the end of fructification, which carries this fungus through the winter for germination in the spring.—**te·li·o·spor·ic,** *a.*

te·li·um, tē′lē·um, tel′ē·um, *n. pl.* **te·li·a,** tē′lē·a, tel′ē·a. *Bot.* a sorus bearing teliospores, its host plant being the rust fungus.—**te·li·al,** *a.*

tell, tel, *v.t.—told, telling.* [O.E. *tellan* (pret. *tealde*), state, recount, enumerate, reckon, = D. *tellen,* G. *zählen,* reckon, count, = Icel. *telja,* recount, say, speak, count.] To give an account or narrative of; to narrate; to relate; to make known by speech or writing, as a fact, news, or information; to communicate; to announce or proclaim; to utter, as the truth; to express in words, as

thoughts or feelings; to reveal or divulge, as something secret or private; to say plainly or positively; to discern so as to be able to say, as: Can you *tell* who that is over there? To inform or appraise, as a person, of something; to assure emphatically, as: I won't, I *tell* you! To bid, order, or command, as: Do as I *tell* you. To mention one after another, as in enumerating; to count one by one or in exact amount, with *off, out,* or *down;* as, to *tell off* five yards in measuring.—*v.i.* To give an account; to make a report; to give evidence or be an indication, usu. followed by *of;* to disclose something secret or private; to play the informer, usu. followed by *on;* to count, have force or effect, or operate effectively; as, a contest in which every stroke *tells;* to produce a marked or severe effect, as: The strain was *telling* on his health.—**tell off,** to set apart from a whole; *colloq.* to scold severely.

tell·er, tel′èr, *n.* One who or that which tells, relates, or communicates; a narrator; one who counts or enumerates, as one appointed to count votes in a legislative body; one employed in a bank to receive or pay out money over the counter.

tell·ing, tel′ing, *a.* Operating with great effect; highly effective; impressive; forceful or striking; expressive or revealing.—**tell·ing·ly,** *adv.*

tell·tale, tel′tāl″, *n.* One who heedlessly or maliciously reveals private, secret, or confidential matters; a tattler; a talebearer; a thing serving to reveal or disclose something; any of various indicating or registering devices, as a timer or time clock; a row of cords or strips hung over a track to warn brakemen on freight trains when they are approaching a low bridge or tunnel; an indicator showing the position of a ship's tiller or rudder; *mus.* an air pressure gauge as found on an organ.—*a.* Pertaining to anything that reveals or betrays what is not intended to be known; as, a *telltale* blush; giving notice or warning of something, as a mechanical device.

tel·lu·ri·an, te·lụr′ē·an, *a.* Characteristic of or pertaining to the earth or an inhabitant of the earth.—*n.* An inhabitant of the earth.

tel·lu·ri·an, te·lụr′ē·an, *n.* [L. *tellus* (*tellur-*), the earth.] An apparatus for showing how the diurnal rotation and annual revolution of the earth and the obliquity of its axis produce the alternation of day and night and the changes of the seasons. Also **tel·lu·ri·on,** te·lụr′ē·on″.

tel·lu·ric, te·lụr′ik, *a.* Of or pertaining to the earth; terrestrial; of or proceeding from the earth or soil; *chem.* of or containing tellurium.

tel·lu·ride, tel′ū·rīd″, tel′ū·rid, tel′ya·rīd″, tel′ya·rid, *n. Chem.* a compound of tellurium with an electropositive element.

tel·lu·rite, tel′ū·rīt″, tel′ya·rīt″, *n. Chem.* a salt of tellurous acid. A mineral, tellurium dioxide, usu. occurring in white or yellowish crystals.

tel·lu·ri·um, te·lụr′ē·um, *n.* [N.L., < L. *tellus* (*tellur-*), the earth.] *Chem.* a rare silver-white element resembling sulphur in its chemical properties, and usu. occurring in nature combined with gold, silver, or other metals. Sym. Te, at. no. 52, at. wt. 127.60. See Periodic Table of Elements.

tel·lu·rize, tel′ya·rīz″, *v.t.—tellurized, tellurizing. Chem.* to mix or cause to combine with tellurium.

tel·lu·rous, tel′yer·us, te·lụr′us, *a.* Pertaining to or obtained from tellurium.—**tel·lu·rous ac·id,** an acid, H_2TeO_3, derived from tellurium.

tel·ly, tel′ē, *n. pl.* **tel·lies.** *Brit. colloq.* a television.

tel·o·phase, tel'o·fāz", *n. Biol.* the last stage of mitotic division during which the formation of daughter nuclei occurs and processes leading to the formation of a cell membrane and cell wall are initiated.—**tel·o·pha·sic,** *a.*

tel·pher, tel·fer, tel'fèr, *n.* [Gr. *tēle,* afar, and *phérein,* bear.] A traveling unit, car, or carrier in a telpherage system.—*v.t.* To transport, as luggage, by telpher.

tel·pher·age, tel·fer·age, tel'fèr·ij, *n.* [Crude formation < *tele,* far, and *phero,* to carry.] A system of transportation consisting of light carriers or cars suspended from an aerial cable and propelled electrically.

tel·son, tel'son, *n.* [N.L., < Gr. *télson,* boundary, limit.] *Zool.* the last segment, or an appendage of the last segment, of certain crustaceans and arachnids, as the middle flipper of a lobster's tail or the sting of a scorpion.

Tel·star, tel'stär", *n.* The first artificial communications satellite, launched July 10, 1962 from Cape Canaveral (Kennedy); a second such satellite launched in 1963.

tem·blor, tem'blèr, tem'blạr, *Sp.* tem··blạr', *n. pl.* **tem·blors, tem·blo·res,** tem··blạ'Res. [Sp.] An earthquake.

tem·er·ar·i·ous, tem"e·râr'ē·us, *a.* [L. *temerarius.*] Rash; reckless; careless.—**tem·er·ar·i·ous·ly,** *adv.*—**tem·er·ar·i·ous·ness,** *n.*

te·mer·i·ty, te·mer'i·tē, *n.* [L. *temeritas,* rashness, < *temere,* rashly.] Extreme venturesomeness; recklessness; rashness.

tem·per, tem'pèr, *v.t.* [O.E. *temprian* < L. *temperare* (pp. *temperatus*), *v.t.* divide or proportion duly, mingle in due proposition, combine properly, qualify, regulate, *v.i.* observe proper measure, be moderate, perh. < *tempus,* time.] To bring to a proper, suitable, or desirable state by or as by blending or mingling with something else; to modify by or as by blending or admixture; as, to *temper* justice with mercy; to moderate or mitigate; to soften or tone down; to moisten, mix, and work up into proper consistency, as clay or mortar; to prepare, as colors, by mixing with oil or another solvent; to keep within due limits or bounds; to restrain, check, or curb; *metal.* to bring to a proper degree of hardness and elasticity, as steel. *Mus.* to adjust the pitch of, as a musical instrument; to tune, as a piano, so as to make the tones available in different keys or tonalities.—*v.i.* To be or become tempered.—*n.* Mental balance or composure, equanimity, or calmness; as, to keep one's *temper*; constitution or habit of mind, or natural disposition; habit of mind with respect to irritability, patience, outbursts of anger, or similar emotional reactions; a particular frame of mind, feeling, or humor; heat of mind or passion, shown in outbursts of anger or resentment; a substance added to something to modify its properties or qualities; *metal.* the particular degree of hardness and elasticity imparted to steel by tempering.—**tem·per·a·bil·i·ty,** *n.*—**tem·per·a·ble,** *a.* —**tem·per·er,** *n.*

tem·per·a, tem'pèr·a, *n.* [It.] A method of painting in which the colors are mixed with some water-soluble binding, esp. egg yolk or an egg and oil mixture, to achieve a quick-drying mat finish; a painting done by this method; the pigment so prepared. Also **tem·por·a.** See *distemper.*

tem·per·a·ment, tem'pèr·a·ment, tem'pra·ment, *n.* [L. *temperamentum,* admixture, moderation, etc., < *tempero.*] The mixture of elements or qualities which make up a personality; that individual peculiarity of physical organization by which the manner of acting, feeling, and thinking of each person is permanently

affected; disposition; *mus.* a certain adjustment of the tones or intervals of the scale of fixed-toned instruments, as the organ or piano, to fit the scale for use in all keys.—**tem·per·a·men·tal,** tem"pèr·a·men'tal, tem"pra·men'tal, *a.*—**tem·per·a·men·tal·ly,** *adv.*

tem·per·ance, tem'pèr·ans, tem'prans, *n.* [L. *temperantia,* moderation, sobriety, < *tempero,* to temper.] The observance of moderation in one's emotions, thoughts, or acts; customary moderation with regard to indulging the natural appetites and passions; restrained or moderate indulgence in, or abstinence from, intoxicating beverages; sobriety.

tem·per·ate, tem'pèr·it, tem'prit, *a.* [L. *temperatus.*] Showing self-restraint or moderation; moderate as regards the indulgence of the appetites or desires, esp. in using intoxicating liquors; abstemious; not violent, excessive, or extreme; calm; not going beyond due bounds; moderate as regards amount of heat or cold; not liable to excessive heat or cold; as, a *temperate* climate; *mus.* tempered, as a scale or interval.—**tem·per·ate·ly,** *adv.*—**tem·per·ate·ness,** *n.*

Tem·per·ate Zone, *n. Geog.* either of two latitudinal belts or zones on the earth between the tropics and the polar circles: the North Temperate Zone lies between the Arctic Circle and the Tropic of Cancer, the South Temperate Zone lies between the Antarctic Circle and the Tropic of Capricorn.

tem·per·a·ture, tem'pèr·a·chèr, tem'pra·chèr, *n.* [L. *temperatura,* due measure, temperature.] The degree or intensity of heat or cold as measured on a thermometric scale. *Med.* the body heat in animals, esp. man; any amount of body heat above a normal level, as above 98.4°F. in man.

tem·per·a·ture gra·di·ent, *n. Meteor.* rate of temperature change over a distance, esp. altitude.

tem·pered, tem'pèrd, *a.* Having a certain disposition or temper, usu. used in compounds; as, ill-*tempered*; moderated by the influence of some quality or by mixture with another ingredient; *mus.* tuned to conform to some temperament, esp. to a temperament of equal-interval semitones; *metal.* treated by tempering to the desired degree of hardness or elasticity.

tem·pest, tem'pist, *n.* [O.Fr. *tempeste,* < L. *tempestas,* time, season, a tempest, < *tempus,* time.] An extensive current of wind rushing with great velocity and violence, often accompanied by hail, rain, or snow; a storm of extreme violence; a violent tumult or commotion.—*v.t.* To cause a tempest to rise around or in; to disturb or stir up violently.

tem·pes·tu·ous, tem·pes'chö·us, *a.* [L. *tempestuosus.*] Belonging to, resembling, or characterized by a tempest; very stormy; violent; turbulent; subject to fits of stormy passion.—**tem·pes·tu·ous·ly,** *adv.*—**tem·pes·tu·ous·ness,** *n.*

Tem·plar, tem'plèr, *n.* [O.Fr. Fr. *templier,* < M.L. *templarius,* < L. *templum,* E. *temple.*] A member of a religious and military order, also called Knights Templars, founded at Jerusalem about 1118, chiefly for the protection of the Holy Sepulcher and of pilgrims to the Holy Land, and suppressed in 1312; a member of an order of freemasons in the U.S., calling themselves Knights Templars and claiming descent from the medieval order; a student of law or a barrister occupying chambers in the Temple in London.

tem·plate, tem'plit, *n.* [Cf. Fr. *temple,* *templet,* a mechanical appliance of several kinds.] A flat thin board or piece of sheet iron whose edge is shaped in some particular way, so that it may serve as a guide or

test in making an article with a corresponding contour; *building,* a short piece of timber or a stone placed in a wall to support a girder or beam; *shipbuilding,* a wedge in a block which serves to support the keel of a ship. Also **tem·plet.**

tem·ple, tem'pl, *n.* [O.E. *templ, tempel,* < L. *templum,* consecrated place, sanctuary, temple, orig. open space for augurial observations.] An edifice or place dedicated to the service or worship of a deity or deities; a synagogue, usu. of a Reformed Jewish congregation; a Protestant church, esp. in France; a Mormon church; a building of the order of freemasons known as Knights Templars; a building, usu. large or pretentious, devoted to some public use; any place or object regarded as occupied by the divine presence, as the body of a Christian. (*Cap.*) any of three successive buildings in ancient Jerusalem which were devoted to the worship of Jehovah; either of two establishments of the medieval Templars, one in London and the other in Paris; either of two groups of buildings on the site of the Templars' former establishment in London.—**tem·pled,** *a.*—**tem·ple·less,** *a.*—**tem·ple·like,** *a.*

tem·ple, tem'pl, *n.* [O.Fr. *temple* (Fr. *tempe*), < L. *tempora,* pl. of *tempus,* temple, head, face.] The flattened region on either side of the human forehead; a corresponding region in lower animals; either of the side-pieces of a pair of spectacles, extending back above the ears of the wearer.

tem·ple, tem'pl, *n.* [Fr. *temple,* also *tempia*: cf. L. *tempia,* temple of the head, *tempiale,* temple of a loom.] In a loom, a device for keeping the cloth stretched to the proper width during the process of weaving.

tem·po, tem'pō, *n. pl.* **tem·pos, tem·pi,** tem'pē. [It. *tempo,* time.] *Mus.* the relative speed or pace at which a piece, passage, or movement is to be played or sung, usu. indicated by a term such as 'allegro' or 'adagio,' and often by a metronome direction. Characteristic pace; rate of activity in general.

tem·po·ral, tem'pèr·al, tem'pral, *a.* [L. *temporalis,* < *tempus, temporis,* time or season (seen in *tense,* n., *contemporary, extempore*).] Pertaining to this life or this world; secular, civil, or lay; pertaining to measured or limited time, or limited by this life or state of things; having limited existence; *gram.* relating to verb tense.—*n.* Anything temporal or secular; a temporality.—**tem·po·ral·ly,** *adv.*—**tem·po·ral·ness,** *n.*

tem·po·ral, tem'pèr·al, tem'pral, *a.* [L.L. *temporalis,* < L. *tempora.*] *Anat.* Of or pertaining to the temple or temples of the head; noting or pertaining to either of a pair of complex bones which form part of the sides and base of the skull.—*n. Anat.* a temporal bone.

tem·po·ral bone, *n. Anat.* one of the two compound bones located on either side of the head.

tem·po·ral·i·ty, tem"po·ral'i·tē, *n. pl.* **tem·po·ral·i·ties.** The state or quality of being temporary or temporal; anything temporal; *pl.* a secular possession or the like, esp. revenue from ecclesiastical lands or tithes.

tem·po·rar·y, tem'po·rer"ē, *a.* [L. *temporarius.*] Lasting for a time only; existing or continuing for a limited time; transient.—**tem·po·rar·i·ly,** *adv.*—**tem·po·rar·i·ness,** *n.*

tem·po·rar·y du·ty, *n.* Duty performed away from the organization or station to which one is assigned or attached, usu. extending over a limited period of time, esp. military duty of this type. Abbr. *TDY.*

tem·po·rize, tem'po·riz", *v.i.*—*temporized, temporizing.* [F. *temporiser,* < L. *tempus (tempor-),* time.] To comply with the time or occasion, or yield temporarily or ostensibly to the current of opinion or circumstances; to act indecisively or use evasive means in order to gain time or delay matters; to treat or parley so as to gain time, usu. followed by *with*; to come to terms, usu. followed by *with*; to effect a compromise, usu. followed by *between*.—**tem·po·ri·za·tion**, *n.*—**tem·po·riz·er**, *n.*—**tem··po·riz·ing·ly**, *adv.*

tempt, tempt, *v.t.* [O.Fr. *tempter* (Fr. *tenter*), < L. *temptare*, *tentare*, to try, prove, test, incite, intens. of *tendo*, *tentum*, to stretch; same root as Gr. *teinō*, Skt. *tan*, to stretch. *Taunt* is of same origin.] To entice to an act which is evil, immoral, or unwise; to entice to something wrong by some specious argument or inducement; to seduce; to invite or allure; to try to entice or persuade; to try the patience of or provoke; to put to a test.—**tempt·a·ble**, *a.*—**tempt·er**, *n.* One who tempts; that which entices or allures.—**tempt·ing**, *a.*—**tempt·ing·ly**, *adv.*—**tempt·ing·ness**, *n.*—**tempt·ress**, *n.*

temp·ta·tion, temp·tā'shan, *n.* The act of tempting or state of being tempted; an enticement to evil; that which is presented as an inducement, enticement, or allurement.

tem·pu·ra, tem'pōō·rä, tem·pur'a, *n.* A Japanese dish of seafood or vegetables coated with batter and deep-fried.

ten, ten, *n.* [O.E. *ten*, *týn* = D. *tien*, Goth. *taihun*, G. *zehn*, Icel. *tiu*, Sw. *tio*, Dan. *ti*; cogn. L. *decem*, Gr. *deka*, Skt. *deçan*; W. *deg*, Armor. *dek*, Ir. *deag*, Gael. *deich*.] The cardinal number between nine and eleven; a symbol representing it; a set of ten persons or things; a playing card with ten spots. *Math.* the second place left of the decimal point in the base ten; also **ten's place**.—*a.*

ten·a·ble, ten'a·bl, *a.* [Fr. *tenable*, < *tenir*, L. *tenere*, to hold (seen also in *tenant*, *tenacious*).] Capable of being held, maintained, or defended, as against an assailant or against dispute.—**ten·a·bil·i·ty**, **ten··a·ble·ness**, *n.*—**ten·a·bly**, *adv.*

ten·ace, ten'ās", *n.* [Fr. *tenace*, a tenace, orig. *a.*, 'tenacious': cf. Fr. *demeurer tenace*, 'remain tenacious,' hold a tenace.] *Bridge*, *whist*, a combination of two high cards of the same suit in one hand, separated in rank by one card which the hand lacks, as a queen and an ace.

te·na·cious, te·nā'shus, *a.* [L. *tenax* (*tenac-*), < *tenere*, hold.] Holding fast, or characterized by keeping a firm hold; *fig.* clinging or adhering persistently to something, often followed by *of*; as, to be *tenacious* of one's opinions. Highly retentive; as, a *tenacious* memory; pertinacious, persistent, stubborn, or obstinate; adhesive or sticky; viscous or glutinous; holding together; cohesive; not easily pulled asunder; tough.—**te·na·cious·ly**, *adv.*—**te·na·cious·ness**, *n.*

te·nac·i·ty, te·nas'i·tē, *n.* The quality or property of being tenacious; firmness in holding fast; retentiveness; persistence or obstinacy; adhesiveness; cohesiveness; toughness.

te·nac·u·lum, te·nak'ū·lum, *n.* pl. **te··nac·u·la**, te·nak'ū·la. [L.L., instrument for holding, < L. *tenere*, hold.] *Surg.* a small, sharp-pointed hook set in a handle, used for picking up and maintaining a hold on parts, such as arteries, in operations and dissections.

ten·an·cy, ten'an·sē, *n.* pl. **ten·an·cies**. The state of being a tenant; a holding, as of lands, by any kind of title; tenure; occupancy of land, a house, or the like, under a lease or on payment of rent; the period of a tenant's occupancy; a holding; as, the *tenancy* of an advertising manager.

ten·ant, ten'ant, *n.* [Fr. *tenant*, holding, ppr. of *tenir*, L. *tenere*, to hold.] A person who holds or possesses lands or tenements

by any kind of title; one who occupies lands or houses for which he pays rent; one who has possession of any place; a dweller; an occupant.—*v.t.* To hold or possess as a tenant.—*v.i.* To live as a tenant; to dwell.—**ten·ant·a·ble**, *a.*—**ten·ant·less**, *a.*

ten·ant farm·er, *n.* One who farms land not his own and who pays rent with a portion of the crops or in cash.

ten·ant·ry, ten'an·trē, *n.* A body of tenants; tenancy.

ten-cent store, ten'sent" stōr", ten'sent', *n.* Five-and-ten.

tench, tench, *n.* pl. **tench**, **tench·es**. [O.Fr. *tenche* (Fr. *tanche*), < L.L. *tinca*.] A freshwater, carplike fish, *Tinca tinca*, of Europe.

Ten Com·mand·ments, *n. pl.* The moral precepts given by God to Moses which form the foundation of the Mosaic Law. Also *Decalogue.* Ex. xx. 1-17, Deut. v. 6-21.

tend, tend, *v.i.* [O.Fr. Fr. *tendre*, < L. *tendere* (pp. *tentus*, also *tensus*), *v.t.* stretch, extend, *v.i.* direct the course, go, strive, tend, akin to Gr. *teinein*, Skt. *tan-*, stretch.] To be directed or lead to or toward, as a journey or road; to be naturally disposed or impelled to move in a particular direction; as, to *tend* away from the center; *fig.* to incline or have a bent or drift in a particular direction, as in a course of progress, change, or action, as: Governments are *tending* toward democracy. To incline in operation or effect; to lead or conduce, as to some result, as: Exercise *tends* to health. To be disposed or inclined in action, operation, or effect, as: The particles *tend* to unite.

tend, tend, *v.t.* [For *attend*.] To attend to by work, services, or care; as, to *tend* a fire; to look after, as a flock; to watch over and care for, as an infant; to minister to or wait on.—*v.i.* To attend by action or care, usu. followed by *to*; to attend or wait with ministration or service, followed by *on*.

tend·ance, ten'dans, *n.* Attention or care; ministration, as to the weak or sick.

ten·den·cy, ten'den·sē, *n.* pl. **ten·den·cies**. [M.L. *tendentia*, < L. *tendens*, ppr. *tendere*, E. *tend*.] A natural or prevailing disposition to move, proceed, or act in some direction or toward some point, end, or result; as, the *tendency* of falling bodies toward the earth; an inclination, bent, or predisposition to something; drift or trend, as of discourse; a special and definite purpose in a novel or other literary work.

ten·den·tious, **ten·den·cious**, ten·den'shus, *a.* [After G. *tendenziös*.] Having or exhibiting a definite tendency, aim, or bias.—**ten·den·tious·ly**, **ten·den·cious·ly**, *adv.*—**ten·den·tious·ness**, **ten·den·cious··ness**, *n.*

ten·der, ten'dėr, *a.* [O.Fr. Fr. *tendre*, < L. *tener*, soft, delicate, tender: cf. L. *tenuis*, thin, fine.] Soft or delicate in substance, or not hard or tough; as, *tender* meat; yielding readily to force or pressure; easily broken; fragile; weak or delicate in constitution; unable to endure fatigue, hardship, or rough treatment; having the weakness and delicacy of youth; as, *tender* babes; young or immature; marked by the weakness of early childhood or youth; as, the *tender* years of infancy; delicate or soft in quality; as, a *tender* melody; delicate, soft, or gentle, as the touch or the hand in touching; soft or soft-hearted; easily touched or sympathetic, as the heart; kind; compassionate; affectionate or loving; sentimental or amatory; as, *tender* passion; fond, considerate, or careful, followed by *of*; acutely or painfully sensitive; as, a *tender* bruise; readily made uneasy, as the conscience; of a delicate or ticklish nature, or requiring careful or tactful handling, as a matter or subject; *naut.* apt to lean over.—*v.t.* To make tender.—**ten·der·ly**, *adv.*—**ten·der·ness**, *n.*

tend·er, ten'dėr, *n.* One who tends; one who attends to or takes charge of something; as, a bridge *tender*; a vessel employed to attend one or more larger vessels, as for supplying provisions; a rowboat or motorboat carried or towed by a yacht or other vessel and used for landing persons; a car attached to a locomotive on a railroad, for carrying coal, water, and other supplies.

ten·der, ten'dėr, *v.t.* [Fr. *tendre*, stretch, extend.] To present formally for acceptance; as, to *tender* one's resignation; to make a formal offer of; to offer or proffer; *law*, to offer, as money or goods, in payment of a debt or other obligation, esp. in exact accordance with the terms of the law and of the obligation.—*v.i.* To make a tender or offer.—*n.* The act of tendering; an offer of something for acceptance; that which is tendered or offered; as, legal *tender*; *law*, an offer, as of money or goods, in payment or satisfaction of a debt or other obligation, esp. in exact accordance with terms of the law and of the obligation; *com.* an offer made in writing by one party to another to execute certain work or supply certain commodities at a given cost.—**ten·der·er**, *n.*

ten·der·foot, ten'dėr·fut", *n.* pl. **ten·der··foots**, **ten·der·feet**. A novice or newcomer; one who is unaccustomed to the ways of a place, esp. one inexperienced in the rigors of the outdoor life in the ranching or mining areas of the western states; one in the beginning rank of the Boy Scouts of America.

ten·der-heart·ed, ten'dėr·här'tid, *a.* Easily affected by another's sorrow or misfortune; compassionate.—**ten·der-heart··ed·ly**, *adv.*—**ten·der-heart·ed·ness**, *n.*

ten·der·ize, ten'dė·rīz", *v.t.*—*tenderized*, *tenderizing*. To make tender or palatable, as meat, by breaking down connective tissues by mechanical or chemical means.—**ten·der·i·za·tion**, *n.*—**ten·der·iz·er**, *n.*

ten·der·loin, ten'dėr·loin", *n.* A strip of tender meat forming part of the loin of beef or pork, lying under the short ribs; a cut of beef lying between the sirloin and ribs. (*Cap.*), *colloq.* a district in New York City forming the center of night life, formerly noted for bribery and corruption of police; a similar district in other cities.

ten·di·nous, ten'di·nus, *a.* [Fr. *tendineux*.] Of, relating to, or full of tendons; sinewy.

ten·don, ten'don, *n.* [Fr. *tendon*, < L. *tendo*, to stretch.] *Anat.* a hard, tough cord or bundle of fibers by which a muscle is attached to a bone or other part which it serves to move.

ten·dril, ten'dril, *n.* [Cf. obs. Fr. *tendrillon*, dim. of *tendron*, shoot, sprout, < *tendre*, E. *tender*.] *Bot.* a filiform leafless organ of climbing plants, often growing in spiral form which attaches itself to or twines round some other body to support the plant. Something resembling this, as a curl or ringlet of hair.—**ten·driled**, **ten·drilled**, *a.* —**ten·dril·ly**, **ten·dril·ous**, *a.*

Ten·e·brae, ten'e·brä", *n. pl.*, *sing.* or *pl. in constr.* [L., pl. darkness.] *Eccles.* the office of matins and lauds, sung Wednesday, Thursday, and Friday of Holy Week, at which, in the past, lighted candles were gradually extinguished commemorating the Crucifixion.

ten·e·brif·ic, ten"e·brif'ik, *a.* [L. *tenebrae*, darkness, and *facio*, to make.] Producing darkness; gloomy.

ten·e·brous, ten'e·brus, *a.* [L. *tenebrosus*, < *tenebræ*, darkness.] Dark; gloomy; obscure. Also **te·neb·ri·ous**, te·neb'rē·us.—**ten·e·brous·ness**, **te·neb·ri·ous·ness**, *n.*

ten·e·ment, ten'e·ment, *n.* [O.Fr. *tenement* (Fr. *tenement*), < M.L. *tenementum*, a holding, < L. *tenere*, hold.] Any house or building to live in, or a dwelling house; any habitation or abode; a portion of a house or building occupied by a tenant as a separate dwelling; a tenement house. *Law*, any type of permanent property, as lands, houses, rents, an office, or a franchise, that may be held of another; *pl.* freehold interests in things immovable and considered as subjects of property.—**ten·e·men·ta·ry**, ten″e·men′ta·rē, *a.*

ten·e·ment house, *n.* A house or building divided into sets of rooms tenanted by separate families or individuals, esp. a badly maintained building occupied by families in crowded parts of large cities.

te·nes·mus, te·nez′mus, te·nes′mus, *n.* [L., < Gr. *teinesmos*, < *teinō*, to stretch to strain.] *Med.* an inclination to void the contents of the bowels or bladder, accompanied by straining, but without any discharge.

ten·et, ten′it, tē′nit, *n.* [L. *tenet*, he holds.] Any opinion, principle, dogma, or doctrine believed or maintained as true, esp. by an organized group or profession.

ten·fold, ten′fōld″, *a.* Comprising ten parts or members; ten times as great or as much.—ten′fōld′, *adv.* In tenfold measure.

te·ni·a, tē′nē·a, *n.* pl. **te·ni·ae**, tē′nē·ē″. Taenia.

te·ni·a·sis, ti·nī′a·sis, *n.* Taeniasis.

Ten·nes·see Walk·ing Horse, *n.* A large saddlehorse of Morgan and Standardbred ancestry, noted esp. for its easy-gaited running walk. Also **Ten·nes·see Walk·er**.

ten·nis, ten′is, *n.* [Said to be < Fr. *tenez*, take it (< *tenir*, L. *tenere*, to hold), a word which the Fr. use when the ball is struck.] A game with rackets in which the ball must pass back and forth over a net and land within a marked court, the player failing to return the ball losing the point.

ten·nis shoe, *n.* A lightweight sports shoe, usu. with a canvas upper and a flat, soft rubber sole. Also *sneaker*.

ten·on, ten′on, *n.* [Fr. *tenon*, < *tenir*, L. *tenere*, to hold.] *Carp.* a projecting part on the end of a piece of wood for insertion into a corresponding hole or mortise to form a joint.—*v.t.* To join or fit with a tenon.

ten·or, ten′ẽr, *n.* [L. *tenor*, a holding on, course, tenor, < *teneo*, to hold.] The prevailing course or progression; the general direction or drift of thought in written or spoken discourse; the general spirit or meaning conveyed by such discourse, or the substance of its message; *law*, a copy of the exact claims of a document, as a transcript; *rhet.* the subject of a metaphor. *Mus.* the highest of the adult male natural voices; in mixed four-part harmony, the next to lowest voice part, between alto and bass; one who sings a tenor part; a musical instrument normally played in the range between alto and bass, esp. a viola; the lowest toned of a set of bells, regardless of pitch.—*a.*

ten·pen·ny, ten′pen″ē, ten′pe·nē, *a.* Costing or valued at ten pennies; referring to a three-inch nail.

ten·pins, ten′pinz″, *n. pl. but sing. in constr.* A game in which players bowl a ball down a bowling alley at ten wooden pins placed in a triangle and attempt to knock them down. Also *bowling*.—**ten·pin**, *n.* A pin used in such a game.

ten·pound·er, ten′poun″dẽr, *n.* A large game and sport fish, *Elops saurus*, having silver scales and found in warm seas, related to the tarpon.

ten·rec, ten′rek, *n.* [Native Madagascar name.] An insect-eating mammal of the family *Tenrecidae*, native to the Malagasy Republic and typically long-snouted, some species being spiny-coated and tailless. Also **tan·rec**.

tense, tens, *a.*—*tenser, tensest.* [L. *tensus*, pp. of *tenao*, to stretch.] Stretched tight;

taut or rigid; in a strained nervous or emotional condition; referring to an instance of high mental pressure involving strain on emotions or nerves; *phon.* articulated with the tongue kept taut.—*v.t., v.i.* tensed, tensing.—**tense·ly**, *adv.*—**tense·ness**, *n.*—**ten·si·ty**, ten′si·tē, *n.*

tense, tens, *n.* [O.Fr. *tens*, Mod.Fr. *temps*, time, < L. *tempus*, time.] *Gram.* One of the forms which verbs take in the structure of many languages in order to express the time or length of the action or condition referred to; in languages with such verb structures, a particular time distinction, as past, present, future; collective reference to these constructions or their forms.—**tense·less**, *a.*

ten·sile, ten′sil, ten′sil, *Brit.* ten′sīl, *a.* Pertaining to tension; capable of tension or being extended; ductile.—**ten·sil·i·ty**, ten·sil′i·tē, *n.*

ten·sile strength, *n. Phys.* the capacity of a material to withstand longitudinal strain or rupture, measured by the maximum pounds of force per square inch the material can endure without separating.

ten·sim·e·ter, ten·sim′i·tẽr, *n.* [< *tension* and *-meter*.] An instrument for determining vapor pressure.

ten·si·om·e·ter, ten″sē·om′i·tẽr, *n.* An instrument which registers longitudinal tension in metal, concrete, or other material; a device for measuring liquid surface tension.

ten·sion, ten′shan, *n.* [L. *tensio, tensionis*.] The act of stretching or straining; the state of being stretched or strained; stiffness or tightness; mental or emotional strain, as in worry or excitement; an intense or uncomfortable feeling between people or groups of people. *Phys.* strain produced in a material by two balancing or opposing forces causing it to stretch or elongate; either of these forces, or a device that produces such a force. *Mach.* a regulating instrument maintaining proper tension, as in a loom; *elect.* potential.—*v.t.*—**ten·sion·al**, *a.*—**ten·sion·less**, *a.*—**ten·sive**, ten′siv, *a.*

ten·sor, ten′sẽr, ten′sar, *n.* [N.L., < L. *tendere*.] *Anat.* a muscle that stretches or tightens some part of the body; *math.* a vector quantity having sets of functional components in more than one coordinate system such that the components undergo a particular transformation with a change of the coordinate system.—**ten·so·ri·al**, ten·sōr′ē·al, ten·sar′ē·al, *a.*

ten-strike, ten′strīk″, *n.* A stroke which knocks down all ten pins in the game of tenpins; *fig.* any stroke or act which is completely successful.

tent, tent, *n.* [Fr. *tente*, L.L. *tenta*, a tent, lit. 'something stretched out or extended,' < L. *tendo, tentum*, to stretch.] A portable shelter consisting of some flexible covering, such as skins, matting, or canvas stretched and sustained by poles.—*v.t.* To lodge in or furnish with tents, as a group of men; to cover with a tent or with something resembling a tent.—*v.i.* To lodge or camp out in tents.—**tent·ed**, *a.* Covered or furnished with tents; tent-shaped.

tent, tent, *n.* [Fr. *tenter*, < L. *tentare*, to feel, to try.] *Surg.* a roll of lint or linen used to dilate an opening in the flesh, or keep open a sore from which matter is discharged.—*v.t. Surg.* To hold open with a tent or pledget; to probe.

ten·ta·cle, ten′ta·kl, *n.* [L.L. *tentaculum*, < L. *tento*, to handle, to feel.] *Zool.* an elongated appendage on the head or cephalic extremity of many of the lower forms of animals, used as an instrument of prehension or as a feeler; *bot.* a sensitive process or glandular hair on a plant, as the sundew.—**ten·ta·cled**, *a.*—**ten·tac·u·lar**, ten·tak′ū·lẽr, *a.*

tent·age, ten′tij, *n.* Tents collectively; equipment or supply of tents.

ten·ta·tive, ten′ta·tiv, *a.* [Fr. *tentatif*, < L. *tento, tentatum*, to try, to test.] Temporary, provisional, or unsure; hesitant; based on or consisting of trial or experiment; experimental.—**ten·ta·tive·ly**, *adv.*—**ten·ta·tive·ness**, *n.*

tent cat·er·pil·lar, *n.* Any of several caterpillars or larvae of moths of the genus *Malacosoma*, as *M. americanum*, which spin tentlike silken webs in which they live gregariously.

ten·ter, ten′tẽr, *n.* [< L. *tentus*, stretched, < *tendo, tentum*, to stretch.] A frame used in cloth manufacture to stretch pieces of cloth, causing them to set or dry evenly and squarely.—*v.t.*

ten·ter·hook, ten′tẽr·hụk″, *n.* A hook for stretching cloth on a tenter.—**on ten·ter·hooks**, in a condition of anxiety or painful suspense.

tenth, tenth, *a.* Following the ninth; being the ordinal of ten; being one of ten equal parts into which anything is divided.—*n.* One of ten equal parts; that which follows the ninth in a series. *Mus.* a tone separated from another tone by one and one third octaves; such an interval between tones.—**tenth·ly**, *adv.*

tent·mak·er, tent′mā″kẽr, *n.* One who makes tents.

tent stitch, *n.* A short embroidery stitch which slants to the right. See *petit point*.

ten·u·is, ten′ū·is, *n. pl.* **ten·u·es**, ten′ū·ēz″. [L., thin, used to render Gr. *psilós*, bare, not aspirated.] *Gr. gram.* any of the three surd stops, κ, π, or τ, (k, p, or t).

ten·u·i·ty, te·nō′i·tē, te·nū′i·tē, te·nō′i·tē, te·nū′i·tē, *n.* [L. *tenuitas*, < *tenuis*, thin, from root meaning to stretch, as in E. *thin*.] The state of being thin or fine; slenderness; rarity; thinness, as of a fluid.

ten·u·ous, ten′ū·us, *a.* Thin or slender; of little density; rare; weak, unsure, or vague.—**ten·u·ous·ly**, *adv.*—**ten·u·ous·ness**, *n.*

ten·ure, ten′yẽr, *n.* [Fr. *tenure*, L.L. *tenura*, < L. *teneo*, to hold.] The act, manner, or right of holding property, esp. real estate; the terms or conditions upon which anything is held or possessed; a status granted to one after serving a period of time in a particular position which assures him of his permanency in that position.—**ten·u·ri·al**, ten·ūr′ē·al, *a.*—**ten·u·ri·al·ly**, *adv.*

te·nu·to, te·nō′tō, *It.* te·nō′tä, *a.* [It., pp. of *tenere*, < L. *tenere*, hold.] *Mus.* held or sustained to its full time value, as a tone or chord.

te·o·cal·li, tē″o·kal′ē, *Sp.* te″ạ·kä′yē, *n. pl.* **te·o·cal·lis**, tē″o·kal′ēz, *Sp.* te″ạ·kä′yēs. [Lit. 'God's house.'] A temple among the aboriginal Indians of Mexico and Central America, usu. set on a pyramidal base.

te·o·sin·te, tē″o·sin′tē, *n.* [Mex.] A tall annual grass, *Euchlaena mexicana*, native in Mexico and Central America, closely related to Indian corn, and cultivated as a fodder plant.

te·pee, tē′pē, *n.* [Amer. Ind.] The American Indian cone-shaped tent, usu. of skins on a framework of poles. Also *teepee, tipi*.

tep·id, tep′id, *a.* [L. *tepidus*, warm, < *tepeo*, to be warm; same root as Skt. *tap*, to burn.] Moderately warm; lukewarm.—**te·pid·i·ty**, tep·id′i·tē, **tep·id·ness**, te·pid′i·tē, *n.*—**tep·id·ly**, *adv.*

te·qui·la, te·kē′la, *n.* An alcoholic liquor of Mexican origin distilled from the agave plant, *Agave tequilana*; the plant itself.

te·rai, te·rī′, *n.* A felt sun hat with a wide brim usu. worn in subtropic areas, as India.

ter·aph, ter′af, *n. pl.* **ter·a·phim**, ter′a·fim. [Heb.] A household deity or image reverenced by the ancient Hebrews.

ter·a·tol·o·gy, ter″a·tol′o·jē, *n.* [Gr. *teras, teratos*, a prodigy, and *logos*, discourse.]

Biol. the study of monstrosities or malformations in the plant and animal kingdoms.—**ter·a·to·log·i·cal,** ter″a·to·loj′i·kal, *a.*—**ter·a·tol·o·gist,** *n.*

ter·bi·um, tụr′bē·um, *n.* A metallic element of the rare-earth series. Sym. Tb, at. no. 65, at. wt. 158.924. See Periodic Table of Elements.

terce, tụrs, *n.* [= *tierce.*] *Eccles.* the third of the seven canonical hours or the service for it, orig. fixed for the third hour of the day, or 9 A.M. Also *tierce.*

ter·cel, tụr′sel, *n.* [Fr. *tiercelet,* tiercelet, a dim. < *tierce,* L. *tertius,* third—because it was said that every third falcon's egg produced a male.] A male hawk or falcon, esp. a peregrine falcon. Also *tiercel,* **terce·let,** tụrs′lit.

ter·cen·te·nar·y, tụr·sen′te·ner″ē, tụr″·sen·ten′e·rē, *n.* pl. **ter·cen·te·nar·ies.** [L. *ter,* thrice, and E. *centenary.*] The 300th anniversary of any event; the celebration of a tercentenary.—*a.* Also **ter·cen·ten·ni·al.**

ter·cet, tụr′sit, tụr·set′, *n.* [Fr.] *Poetry,* a group of three rhyming lines, or one of the triplets in terza rima; *mus.* a triplet.

ter·e·bene, ter′e·bēn″, *n. Chem.* a terpenic mixture used in medicine.

te·reb·ic, te·reb′ik, te·rē′bik, *a.* [< *tereb*(*inth*).] *Chem.* noting or pertaining to an acid, $C_7H_{10}O_4$, formed by the action of nitric acid on oil of turpentine.

ter·e·binth, ter′e·binth, *n.* [L. *terebinthus,* < Gr. *terébinthos,* earlier *términthos,* terebinth.] A Mediterranean tree, *Pistacia terebinthus,* in the cashew family and the orig. source of turpentine.

ter·e·bin·thine, ter″e·bin′thin, *a.* [L. *terebinthinus,* < Gr. *terebinthinos.*] Of or pertaining to terebinth; of, pertaining to, consisting of, or resembling turpentine.

te·re·do, te·rē′dō, *n.* pl. **te·re·di·nes,** te·rēd′i·nēz″. [L. < Gr. *terēdōn,* < *tereō,* to bore.] A wormlike molluscan animal, genus *Teredo;* the shipworm.

te·rete, te·rēt′, ter′ēt, *a.* [L. *teres* (teret-), rounded, < *terere,* rub. TRITE.] Slender and smooth, with a circular transverse section; cylindrical or slightly tapering.

ter·gi·ver·sate, tụr′ji·vẹr·sāt″, *v.i.*—*tergiversated, tergiversating.* [L. *tergiversor, tergiversatus,* < *tergum,* the back, and *versor,* to turn, < *verto,* to turn.] To change one's opinions; to turn against a cause formerly advocated; to practice evasion or subterfuge.—**ter·gi·ver·sa·tion,** *n.*—**ter·gi·ver·sa·tor,** *n.*

ter·gum, tụr′gum, *n.* pl. **ter·ga,** tụr′ga. [L., the back.] *Zool.* the convex upper plate on each segment of an arthropod.—**ter·gal,** tụr′gal, *a.*

term, tụrm, *n.* [Fr. *terme,* an end, end, word, speech, period, etc., < L. *terminus,* a boundary (whence *terminal, terminate, determine,* etc.); akin Gr. *terma,* limit; same root as L. *trans.* E. *through.*] A word or phrase by which something fixed and definite is expressed, esp. a word having a technical meaning; a limit; a boundary; the time for which anything lasts; a tenure; a time or period fixed in some way; a period during which instruction is regularly given to students in certain universities and colleges; a day on which rent or interest is regularly payable. *Law,* the space of time in which a court is held or open for the trial of causes; a specific amount of time allowed for discharge of a debt; a specified time period during which an estate may be held or retained. *Pl.* words or language used in a general way; as, to speak in vague *terms;* conditions or propositions stated and offered for acceptance; as, to state your *terms;* relative position or footing; as, to be on good *terms* with a person. *Logic,* the subject or the predicate of a proposition; one of the three substantive elements of a syllogism. *Math.* one of the members in an expression

composed of quantities, unitary or compound, combined by connecting plus or minus signs; the numerator or denominator of a fraction; *med.* parturition; *arch.* a pillar tapering downward, usu. surmounted by sculpture.—*v.t.* To name; to denominate.—**bring to terms,** to reduce to submission or to conditions.—**come to terms,** to agree.—**in terms of,** with regard to.—**term·less,** tụrm′lis, *a.*

ter·ma·gant, tụr′ma·gant, *n.* [O.Fr. *Tervagant,* It. *Tervagante, Trivagante;* prob. a name of Eastern origin. Termagant was a fabled deity of the Mohammedans introduced into the old moralities or other shows, in which he figured as a most violent personage.] A brawling, turbulent woman; a vixen; a shrew; a virago.—*a.*—**ter·ma·gant·ly,** *adv.*

term·er, tụr′mẹr, *n.* One who is serving a term, esp. in prison: used in compounds; as, a first-*termer.*

ter·mi·nal, tụr′mi·nal, *n.* That which terminates; an extremity; a terminus or station, as for railroad passengers or freight. *Elect.* a device, as a clamping screw, which facilitates the completion of a circuit in a battery or other apparatus; the point at which current enters or leaves a conducting element in a circuit.—*a.* Relating to or forming the end or extremity; placed at the end of something; pertaining to or occurring in a fixed time period; causing death, as a disease.—**ter·mi·na·ble,** tụr′mi·na·bl, *a.*—**ter·mi·na·ble·ness,** tụr′mi·na·bly, *adv.*—**ter·mi·nal·ly,** *adv.*

ter·mi·nal leave, *n.* The final or concluding leave due a person on leaving military or government service which amounts to his unused, accumulated leave.

ter·mi·nate, tụr′mi·nāt″, *v.t.*—*terminated, terminating.* [L. *termino, terminatum,* to bound, to terminate.] To bound; to limit; to form the extreme point or side of; to put an end to; to complete.—*v.i.* To be limited in space; to end; to come to a limit in time.—*a.* Capable of coming to an end; as, a *terminate* decimal.—**ter·mi·na·tive,** *a.*—**ter·mi·na·tive·ly,** *adv.*—**ter·mi·na·tor,** *n.*

ter·mi·na·tion, tụr″mi·nā′shan, *n.* The act of terminating; an ending or concluding; the end of a thing or point where it ends; limit in space; end in time; conclusion; result; issue. *Gram.* a part annexed to the root or stem of an inflected word; the syllable or letter that ends a word; suffix.—**ter·mi·na·tion·al,** *a.*

ter·mi·nol·o·gy, tụr″mi·nol′o·jē, *n.* pl. **ter·mi·nol·o·gies.** [< L. *terminus,* with meaning of term or appellation, and Gr. *logos,* discourse.] A set of terms used in an art, science, or the like; nomenclature; the science of technical terms as used in a particular field of knowledge.—**ter·mi·no·log·i·cal,** tụr″mi·no·loj′i·kal, *a.*—**ter·mi·no·log·i·cal·ly,** *adv.*

term in·sur·ance, *n.* A type of insurance designed to pay benefits for losses incurred during a specific period of time only, at the end of which the policy becomes void.

ter·mi·nus, tụr′mi·nus, *n.* pl. **ter·mi·ni,** ter·mi·nus·es, tụr′mi·nī″. [L.] The end or limit; the finishing point or goal; extremity; either termination point of a travel line; *Brit.* the station, town, or city at either extremity of a transportation route, as of a train, bus, or airplane. A boundary or landmark; (*cap.*), *Rom. mythol.* the god of landmarks and boundaries.

ter·mi·nus ad quem, tụr′mi·nus ad kwem′, *L.* teR′mi·nụs äd kwem′, *n. Latin.* The point toward which anything moves; aim or objective; conclusion or end.

ter·mi·nus a quo, tụr′mi·nus ā kwō′, *L.* teR′mi·nụs″ ä kwō′, *n. Latin.* The point from which anything begins; origin or starting point.

ter·mite, tụr′mīt, *n.* [N.L. *termes* (termit-), white ant, L.L. wood-worm, < the root of L. *terere,* rub.] Any of the pale-colored, soft-bodied, wood-eating, social insects belonging to the order *Isoptera,* often very destructive to buildings, furniture, and other wooden structures. Also *white ant.*

term pa·per, *n.* A long written report assigned to a student in a course at school during a semester or term.

tern, tụrn, *n.* [< Scand.: cf. Dan. *terne,* Sw. *tärna,* tern.] Any bird of the subfamily *Sterninae,* comprising numerous aquatic species allied to the gulls, but which have usu. a slenderer body and bill, smaller feet, and a long and deeply forked tail, esp. any of those constituting the genus *Sterna,* as *S. hirundo,* the common species of Europe and N. America.

ter·na·ry, tụr′na·rē, *a.* [L. *ternarius,* < *terni.*] Consisting of or involving three; threefold; triple; being the last of each successive group of three; third in order or rank. *Chem.* consisting of three different atoms, radicals, or elements; formerly, consisting of three atoms. *Math.* having three variables; based on the number three. *Metal.* having three constituents, as an alloy.—*n.* pl. **ter·na·ries.** A group of three.

ter·nate, tụr′nit, tụr′nāt, *a.* [L.L. *ternatus.*] Arranged in threes; composed of three; *bot.* having three in a group or whorl, as three leaflets to a compound leaf.—**ter·nate·ly,** *adv.*

terne·plate, tụrn′plāt″, *n.* [Fr. *terne,* dull: cf. *tarnish.*] Steel or sheet iron coated with a dull-finished kind of tin plate in which the tin used is alloyed with a large percentage of lead. Also *terne.*

ter·pene, tụr′pēn, *n.* [G. *terpen,* < *terpentin,* turpentine.] *Chem.* Any of certain unsaturated hydrocarbons with the formula $C_{10}H_{16}$, as occurring in essential oils of many plants; any of various analogous or related compounds.—**ter·pe·nic,** tụr·pē′nik, *a.*

ter·pin·e·ol, tụr·pin′ē·ōl″, tụr·pin′ē·ạl″, tụr·pin′ē·ol″, *n. Chem.* a tertiary unsaturated alcohol, $C_{10}H_{17}OH$, occurring naturally in some essential oils or made synthetically, and used mainly in the manufacture of perfumes.

terp·si·cho·re·an, tụrp″si·ko·rē′an, tụrp″·si·kōr′ē·an, tụrp″si·kạr′ē·an, *a.* [< *Terpsichore,* Greek Muse of dancing, < *terpsō,* to delight, and *chorós,* dancing.] Pertaining or relating to dancing. Also **terp·si·cho·re·al.** —*n. Colloq.* a dancer.

ter·ra al·ba, ter′a al′ba, *n.* [L. 'white earth.'] Any of various white, earthy or powdery substances, as pipe clay, gypsum, kaolin, or magnesia.

ter·race, ter′as, *n.* [O.Fr. *terrace* (Fr. *terrasse*), < L. *terra,* earth.] A raised level with a vertical or sloping front or sides faced with masonry, turf, or the like; one of a series of levels with vertical or sloping front, rising one above another; a natural formation resembling such a level; an open platform, promenade, or porch; balcony; an open, usu. paved area adjoining a house or building; patio; a nearly level strip of land with a more or less abrupt descent along the margin of the sea, a lake, or a river; a landscaped strip in the center of various paved streets, or a street having such an area; a row of houses running along the face or top of a slope, or a street with such a row or rows; the flat roof of a house, esp. of an Oriental or Spanish house.—*v.t.*—*terraced, terracing.* To form into or furnish with a terrace or terraces.

ter·ra cot·ta, ter′a kot′a, *n.* [It. lit. 'baked or cooked earth.'] A type of earthenware or clay, usu. unglazed, baked in a kiln to a durable hardness, and much used for statues, pottery, and architectural facings;

an object, as a piece of sculpture, made of such clay; its brownish or dull orange color, or a similar color.—**ter·ra·cot·ta,** *a.*

ter·ra fir·ma, ter′*a* fur′ma, *n.* [L.] Firm or solid earth, as opposed to air or water.

ter·rain, te·rān′, ter′ān, *n.* [Fr. *terrain,* < L. *terra,* earth.] A tract of land, esp. as considered with reference to its natural features or suitability for a certain purpose, as a military advantage; *geol.* a terrane.

ter·ra in·cog·ni·ta, ter′*a* in·kog′ni·ta, ter′*a* in″kog·nē′ta, L. teR′Rä in·kŏg′ni·tä″, *n. pl.* **ter·rae in·cog·ni·tae.** [L.] An unknown or unexplored region, territory, or land; an unexplored subject or field of knowledge.

Ter·ra·my·cin, ter″*a*·mī′sin, *n.* [L. *terra,* earth, and Gr. *mycēs,* fungus, and *-in.*] *Pharm.* an antibiotic derived from a soil mold, *Streptomyces rimosus,* effective against many disease-causing microorganisms. (Trademark.) Also **oxytetracycline.**

ter·rane, te·rān′, ter′ān, *n.* [= *terrain.*] *Geol.* Any formation or group of similar formations, esp. of rock; a region where a certain rock or rock formation is prevalent. Also *terrain.*

ter·ra·pin, ter′*a*·pin, *n. pl.* **ter·ra·pins, ter·ra·pin.** [N. Amer. Ind.] Any of various edible N. American tidewater or fresh-water turtles belonging to the family *Testudinidae,* notably the diamondback terrapin; any of a number of similar turtles.

ter·ra·que·ous, ter·ā′kwē·us, ter·ak′wē·us, *a.* [< L. *terra,* land, and *aqua,* water.] Consisting of land and water.

ter·rar·i·um, ter·râr′ē·um, *n. pl.* **ter·rar·i·ums, ter·rar·i·a,** te·râr′ē·a. [N.L. < L. *terra,* earth.] An enclosure, container, or vessel, usu. having glass sides for growing plants or keeping small land animals, often for study; a vivarium.

ter·raz·zo, te·raz′ō, te·rä′zō, *It.* teR·Rät′tsä, *n.* A polished mosaic flooring made of chips of marble or other stone which are set in cement.

ter·rene, te·rēn′, te·rĕn′, *a.* [L. *terrenus,* < *terra,* earth.] Pertaining to the earth; earthly; mundane or worldly.—*n.* The earth; a region.

terre·plein, ter′plān″, *n.* [Fr.] *Fort.* the flat section or platform of a rampart on which guns are placed or mounted.

ter·res·tri·al, te·res′trē·al, *a.* [L. *terrestris,* < *terra,* the earth.] Pertaining to or existing on the earth; pertaining to land, as opposed to water or air; *biol.* confined to or living on land, as opposed to *aquatic, aerial,* or *arboreal.* Pertaining to the world; mundane or worldly.—*n.* An inhabitant of the earth.—**ter·res·tri·al·ly,** *adv.*

ter·ret, ter′it, *n.* [M.E. *tyret, turet, toret,* < O.Fr. *toret,* dim. of *tor, tour,* E. *tour.*] One of the round loops or rings on the saddle of a harness, through which the driving reins pass; a ring, which is similar, for joining a leash to a collar or harness, as on a dog.

ter·ri·ble, ter′i·bl, *a.* [Fr. *terrible,* < L. *terribilis,* < *terreo,* to frighten.] Exciting fear or terror; dreadful; appalling; inspiring awe; imposing; excessive; extreme; severe or difficult; disagreeable or very bad; of inferior quality.—**ter·ri·ble·ness,** *n.*—**ter·ri·bly,** ter′i·blē, *adv.*

ter·ric·o·lous, te·rik′o·lus, *a.* [L. *terra,* earth, *colo,* to inhabit.] *Biol.* Inhabiting the earth; living in the soil.

ter·ri·er, ter′ē·ĕr, *n.* [Fr. *terrier,* the hole of a rabbit, < *terre,* L. *terra,* the earth; equiv. therefore to burrow dog.] Any of the various breeds of energetic dogs, now popular as pets, and orig. used to hunt small burrowing animals, as rabbits.

ter·ri·er, ter′ē·ĕr, *n.* [O.Fr. Fr. *terrier,* orig. *a.,* pertaining to the earth or to land,

< M.L. *terrarius,* < L. *terra,* earth, land.] *Law,* a book or roll in which the lands of private persons or corporations are described by their site, boundaries, acreage, and the like.

ter·rif·ic, te·rif′ik, *a.* [L. *terrificus.*] Extraordinarily fine or intense; extreme; great; astounding or awesome; causing or tending to cause fear or terror; terrifying; dreadful.—**ter·rif·i·cal·ly,** *adv.*

ter·ri·fy, ter′i·fī′, *v.t.*—**terrified, terrifying.** [L. *terreo,* to frighten, and *facio,* to make.] To cause or pervade with terror; frighten; to alarm or shock; to menace; intimidate.—**ter·ri·fy·ing·ly,** *adv.*

ter·rig·e·nous, te·rij′e·nus, *a.* [L. *terra,* the earth, and root *gen,* to bring forth.] Earthborn; produced of or by the earth; *geol.* derived or produced from the land, as sedimentary deposits in or near water, esp. on the bottom of the sea.

ter·ri·to·ri·al, ter′i·tōr′ē·al, ter′i·tar′ē·al, *a.* [L. *territorialis.*] Of or pertaining to territory or land, or its jurisdiction; of, pertaining to, associated with, or restricted to a particular territory, district, or region; local; (*cap.*) of or pertaining to a Territory of the U.S., or any similar district; (*cap.*), *milit.* designating an army or force, as in the British military system, which is organized on a local basis for home defense.—*n.* A person belonging to a territorial army or force; (*cap.*) a member of Great Britain's Territorial Army.—**ter·ri·to·ri·al·ly,** *adv.*

ter·ri·to·ri·al·ism, ter′i·tōr′ē·a·liz″um, ter′i·tar′ē·a·liz″um, *n.* The principle of the predominance of the landed classes; landlordism. *Eccles.* a church governmental system in which the subjects must have the same religion as their ecclesiastical ruler, who is also the civil power; also **ter·ri·to·ri·al sys·tem.**—**ter·ri·to·ri·al·ist,** *n.* —**ter·ri·to·ri·al·i·ty,** ter′i·tōr′ē·al′i·tē, ter′i·tar′ē·al′i·tē, *n.*

ter·ri·to·ri·al·ize, ter′i·tōr′ē·a·līz″, ter′i·tar′ē·a·līz″, *v.t.*—**territorialized, territorializing.** To enlarge by the acquisition of new territory; to associate with or restrict to a particular territory or territories; to put upon a territorial basis.—**ter·ri·to·ri·al·i·za·tion,** *n.*

ter·ri·to·ri·al wa·ters, *n. pl.* The waters bordering or within a state over which it claims jurisdiction, esp. waters within the distance to shore of three miles.

ter·ri·to·ry, ter′i·tōr″ē, ter′i·tar″ē, *n. pl.* **ter·ri·to·ries.** [L. *territorium,* the land around a town, domain, district, territory, < *terra,* earth, land.] Any tract of land, region, or district; the land and waters belonging to or under the jurisdiction of a state, sovereign, or other body. (*Cap.*) in the government of the U.S., a region or district not admitted to the Union as a State but with an organized government; some similar district elsewhere, as in Canada and Australia. *Fig.* the field of action or thought, or domain or province, of something. The region or district assigned to a representative, agent, or the like, to carry on work in, as in soliciting and making sales; an animal's area of control which is considered out of bounds to other animals of that species.

ter·ror, ter′ĕr, *n.* [O.Fr. Fr. *terreur,* < L. *terror,* < *terrere,* frighten.] Intense, sharp, overmastering fear, or a feeling or instance of this; a cause of intense fear; as, to be a *terror* to evil doers; intense fear caused for the purpose of coercing or subduing; as, to rule by *terror;* any period or program of violence or terror, as caused by political enemies or a terrorist group. *Colloq.* a person or thing that is esp. dreadful or unpleasant; nuisance.—**ter·ror·ism,** ter′o·riz″um, *n.*—**ter·ror·ist,** ter′ĕr·ist, *n.*—**ter·ror·is·tic,** *a.*—**ter·ror·less,** *a.*

ter·ror·ize, ter′o·rīz″, *v.t.*—**terrorized, ter-**

rorizing. To fill or overcome with terror; to dominate, coerce, or subdue by terror, or intimidation.—**ter·ror·i·za·tion,** *n.*—**ter·ror·iz·er,** *n.*

ter·ry, ter′ē, *n. pl.* **ter·ries.** [Origin obscure.] The loop formed by the pile of a fabric when left uncut. A fabric with uncut pile loops, esp. a cotton one used for turkish towels; also **ter·ry cloth.**

terse, turs, *a.*—**terser, tersest.** [L. *tersus,* pp. of *tergo,* to rub or wipe.] Free from superfluity; neat and concise; to the point and pithy: said of style or language.—**terse·ly,** *adv.*—**terse·ness,** *n.*

ter·tial, tur′shal, *a.* [L. *tertius,* third.] *Ornith.* denoting those flight feathers attached to the humerus bone on the inner edge of a bird's wing and nearest to the body.—*n. Ornith.* Any feather which is tertial; tertiary.

ter·tian, tur′shan, *a.* [L. *tertianus,* < *tertius,* third.] Recurring or repeating every other day (every third day when figured inclusively); as, a *tertian* fever.—*n. Pathol.* a tertian ague, esp. malaria.

ter·ti·ar·y, tur′shē·er″ē, tur′sha·rē, *a.* [L. *tertiarius,* < *tertius,* third.] Of the third order, rank, or formation; third; *ornith.* tertial; *eccles.* noting or pertaining to a branch or third order of certain religious orders. *Chem.* pertaining to a carbon atom which is joined to three similar carbon atoms; denoting the replacement of three radicals or atoms. (*Cap.*), *geol.* noting or pertaining to a geological period or a system of rocks which constitutes the earlier period of the Cenozoic era.—*n. pl.* **ter·ti·ar·ies.** *Ornith.* a tertial feather; *eccles.* a member of a tertiary branch of a religious order. (*Cap.*), *geol.* the Tertiary period; see Table of Geologic Time.

ter·ti·ar·y col·or, *n.* A color produced by the mixture of two secondary colors.

ter·ti·um quid, tur′shē·um kwid′, L. teR′tē·um kwid′, *n.* [L., 'third something.'] Something related in some way to two things, but distinct from both; an intermediate between two things or persons.

ter·va·lent, tur·vā′lent, *a.* Trivalent.

ter·za ri·ma, tert′sa rē′ma, *It.* teR′tsä Rē′mä, *n.* [It. *terza rima,* 'third rime.'] *Pros.* a verse form of interlocking tercets, the middle line of each rhyming with the first and third lines of the following.

tes·sel·lat·ed, tes′e·lā″tid, *a.* [L. *tessella,* a dim. of *tessera,* a square.] Formed by inlaying materials of different colors in little squares, triangles, or other geometrical figures, or by mosaic work.—**tes·sel·late,** tes′e·lāt″, *v.t.*—**tessellated, tessellating.** —**tes·sel·la·tion,** tes″e·lā′shan, *n.* The art, operation, or result of tessellating.

tes·ser·a, tes′ĕr·a, *n. pl.* **tes·ser·ae,** tes′-e·rē″. [L., a cube, a die.] A small cube of marble, precious stone, ivory, glass, wood, or the like, used in tessellated or mosaic work; a small square of bone, wood, or the like, used as a token or ticket in ancient Rome.

tes·si·tu·ra, tes″i·tur′a, *It.* tes″sē·tō′Rä, *n. pl.* **tes·si·tu·ras,** *It.* **tes·si·tu·re,** *It.* tes″sē·tō′Re. The average or natural range of a singer's voice or of some vocal part.

test, test, *n.* [O.Fr. Fr. (Fr. *têt*), < L. *testum,* an earthen vessel, < *testa,* a piece of earthenware, the shell of shellfish.] Any trial or examination; means of trial; a criterion; a standard; means of discrimination; a group of questions or problems to be answered or solved as a gauge of ability, knowledge, or aptitude. *Metal.* a vessel used in refining gold and silver; a cupel. *Chem.* a substance which is employed to detect the presence or identity of any ingredient in a compound, by causing it to exhibit some known property; a reagent.—*v.t.* To try; to subject to trial and examination;

to prove, as by experiment or by some fixed standard; *metal.* to refine, as gold or silver, in cupellation; *chem.* to examine, as by the application of some reagent.—*v.i.* To make, give, or achieve a certain rating or score from an examination; to undergo a trial; *chem.* to be analyzed or assayed.— **test·a·ble**, *a.*—**test·er**, *n.* One who or that which tests.

test, test, *n.* [L. *testa*, a shell, etc.] *Zool.* the hard protective outside covering or shell of certain invertebrates, as the sea urchin or the mollusk.

test·a, tes′ta, *n.* pl. **tes·tae**, tes′tē. [L.] *Bot.* the usu. hard integuments constituting the coat of a seed. Also *seed coat.*

tes·ta·cean, te·stā′shan, *a.* [N.L. *Testacea*, prop. neut. pl. of L. *testaceus*, E. *testaceous.*] *Zool.* Referring to an order of protozoa in the subclass *Rhizopoda;* having a test or shell-like covering. Testaceous.—*n.* A testacean animal.

tes·ta·ceous, te·stā′shus, *a.* [L. *testaceus.*] Having a molluscan shell; having the character of or derived from a test or shell. Brick-colored; of a dull reddish or brownish-yellow color.

tes·ta·cy, tes′ta·sē, *n.* The state of being testate.

tes·ta·ment, tes′ta·ment, *n.* [L. *testamentum*, < *testor*, to be a witness, to make a will, < *testis*, a witness; similarly *testify, testimony, attest, contest.*] *Law*, a document by which a person declares his will concerning the disposal of his personal property after his death; a will. Tangible evidence; a tribute; *Bib.* a covenant. (*Cap.*) either of the two general divisions of the Bible: the Old or the New Testament; the New Testament or a volume containing it.—**tes·ta·men·ta·ry**, tes·ta·men′ta·rē, *a.*

tes·tate, tes′tāt, *a.* [L. *testatus.*] Having made and left a will.

tes·ta·tor, tes′tā·tẽr, te·stā′tẽr, *n.* One who makes a will; one leaving a will at death. —**tes·ta·trix**, te·stā′triks, *n.* pl. **tes·ta·tri·ces**, tes·tā′tri·sēz. A female testator.

test ban, *n.* An agreement between nations to cease testing of nuclear weapons, esp. in the atmosphere.

test case, *n. Law.* A representative case, likely to establish a precedent; an action usu. initiated with the cooperation of the contending litigants to determine or interpret some matter of a law, esp. its constitutionality.

tes·ter, tes′tẽr, *n.* [O.Fr. *testiere*, a headpiece, < *teste* (Fr. *tête*) a head, < L. *testa*, an earthen pot, the skull, the head.] A flat canopy over a bed, altar, or tomb.

tes·ti·cle, tes′ti·kl, *n.* [L. *testiculus*, dim. of *testis*, a testicle.] *Anat., zool.* one of the two oval-shaped reproductive glands in the male, enclosed in the scrotum, which form and secrete the spermatozoa and several of the fluid elements of the semen. Also *testis.* —**tes·tic·u·lar**, te·stik′ya·lẽr, *a.*

tes·tic·u·late, te·stik′ū·lit, *a.* Shaped like a testicle; ovoid. *Bot.* testicle-shaped, as the tubers of certain orchids; having such tubers.

tes·ti·fy, tes′ti·fī′, *v.i.*—*testified, testifying.* [O.Fr. *testifier*, < L. *testificari—testis*, a witness, and *facio*, to make.] To make a solemn declaration; to support; to bear witness; to indicate; *law*, to give evidence under oath.—*v.t.* To affirm or declare solemnly; to state in support of; to bear witness to; *law*, to affirm under oath.— **tes·ti·fi·er**, *n.*

tes·ti·mo·ni·al, tes″ti·mō′nē·al, *n.* [L.L. *testimonialis.*] A writing certifying to the character, conduct, or qualifications of a person, or to the value or excellence of a thing; a letter of recommendation; something given or done as an expression of appreciation.—*a.* Relating to or serving as testimony or a testimonial.

tes·ti·mo·ny, tes′ti·mō″nē, *n.* pl. **tes·ti·mo·nies**. [L. *testimonium*, < *testari*, bear witness.] *Law*, the evidence given by a witness under oath or affirmation. Evidence given in support of a fact or statement; proof; open declaration or profession, as of faith; *Bib.* the Decalogue as inscribed on the two tables of the law, or the ark in which they were kept.

tes·tis, tes′tis, *n.* pl. **tes·tes**, tes′tēz. [L.] A testicle.

test match, *n.* A game or series of games to decide the championship between top-rated teams of different countries, esp. the cricket match between England and Australia.

tes·tos·ter·one, te·stos′te·rōn″, *n. Biochem.* a male testicular hormone, $C_{19}H_{28}O_2$, that promotes male secondary sex characteristics.

test pa·per, *n. Chem.* paper impregnated with a reagent as litmus which changes color when acted upon by certain substances, thus indicating their presence. A paper on which answers to an examination are written.

test pat·tern, *n. TV*, a telecast of a geometric arrangement of contrasting lines and circles to aid in tuning or in diagnosing and correcting faulty reception or signals.

test pi·lot, *n.* A pilot who flies a new or modified aircraft in order to test it or its equipment.

test tube, *n.* A hollow cylinder of thin glass with one end closed, used in testing liquids and other substances in scientific experiments.—**test-tube**, test′tōb″, test′tūb″, *a.* Experimental; produced as a result of artificial insemination.

tes·tu·di·nate, te·stöd′i·nit, te·stöd′i·nāt″, te·stūd′i·nit, te·stūd′i·nāt″, *a.* Resembling the back of a tortoise; arched; vaulted.—*n.* A turtle or tortoise.

tes·tu·do, te·stö′dō, te·stū′dō, *n.* pl. **tes·tu·di·nes**, te·stöd′i·nēz″, te·stūd′i·nēz″. A shelter on wheels having a heavy, fireproof roof, used by the ancient Romans to protect soldiers during siege operations; the overlapping of shields overhead, used by soldiers for defensive cover.

tes·ty, tes′tē, *a.*—*testier, testiest.* [O.Fr. *testu* (Fr. *têtu*), headstrong, willful, < *teste* (Fr. *tête*), the head, < L. *testa*, potsherd, shell.] Touchy; peevish; easily irritated or annoyed.—**tes·ti·ly**, *adv.*—**tes·ti·ness**, *n.*

tet·a·nus, tet′a·nus, *n.* [L., < Gr. *tétanos*, < *teinein*, stretch.] *Pathol.* an infectious, often fatal disease, due to a specific bacterium, *Clostridium tetani*, which gains entrance to the body through wounds, characterized by more or less violent tonic spasm and rigidity of many or all the voluntary muscles, esp. those of the neck and lower jaw; see *lockjaw. Bact.* the specific bacterium which causes this disease; *physiol.* the condition of prolonged contraction which a muscle assumes under rapidly repeated stimuli.—**tet·tan·ic**, te·tan′ik, *a.*—**tet·a·nize**, tet′a·nīz″, *v.t.*—*tetanized, tetanizing. Physiol.* to cause tetanus in, as a muscle.—**tet·a·ni·za·tion**, tet″a·ni·zā′shan, *n.*

tet·a·ny, tet′a·nē, *n.* [Fr. *tétanie*, < L. *tetanus.*] *Pathol.* a disorder or condition characterized by irregularly intermittent muscular spasms and pain, esp. in the extremities, and usu. occurring because of defective metabolism of calcium salts.

te·tar·to·he·dral, ti·tär″tō·hē′dral, *a.* [Gr. *tétartos*, fourth, and *édra*, seat, base.] *Crystal.* of a crystal, having one fourth the planes or faces required by the maximum symmetry of its system. Compare *holohedral.*—**te·tar·to·he·drism**, *n.*

tetched, techt, *a.* [< *touched.*] Somewhat crazy.

tetch·y, tech′ē, *a.*—*tetchier, tetchiest.* [< old *teche, tache*, a blemish, a vice, < Fr. *tache*, a spot.] Peevish; fretful; irritable; touchy. Also *techy.*—**tetch·i·ly**, *adv.*—**tetch·i·ness**, *n.*

tête-à-tête, tāt′a·tāt′, *Fr.* te·tä·tet′, *a.* [Fr., lit. 'head to head.'] Private; between or for two persons exclusively.—*n.* A private interview or talk between two people; a sofa formed in an S-shape, so that two persons may sit face to face.—*adv.* In private; engaged in private conversation.

tête-bêche, tet·besh′, *a. Philately*, denoting two adjoining stamps printed so that one is upside-down.

teth·er, teTH′ẽr, *n.* [Same as Icel. *tjóthr*, a tether, *tjóthra*, to tether; O.Fris. *tieder*, L.G. *tider*, O.Sw. *tiuther*, cord, tether.] A rope or chain by which an animal is confined within certain limits; *fig.* the range or farthest limits of one's powers, capabilities, or resources.—*v.t.* To confine with a tether.

teth·er·ball, teTH′ẽr·bạl″, *n.* A game for two players who use rackets to bat a ball hanging from the top of a pole, each one attempting to wrap the rope or chain around the pole in a direction opposite to that of his opponent.

tet·ra, te′tra, *n.* Any of various fresh-water tropical fishes of the family *Characidae*, often kept and bred in aquariums.

tet·ra·ba·sic, te″tra·bā′sik, *a. Chem.* of an acid, having four atoms of hydrogen replaceable by basic atoms or radicals.— **tet·ra·ba·sic·i·ty**, te″tra·bā·sis′i·tē, *n.*

tet·ra·bran·chi·ate, te″tra·brang′kē·it, te″tra·brang′kē·āt″, *a.* [N.L. *Tetrabranchiata*, pl., < Gr. *tetra-*, four, and *brágchia*, gills.] *Zool.* belonging to the *Tetrabranchiata*, a subclass of cephalopods with four gills, as the pearly nautilus.—*n.* Also **tet·ra·branch**.

tet·ra·chlo·ride, te″tra·klōr′īd, te″tra·klōr′id, te″tra·klạr′īd, te″tra·klạr′id, *n. Chem.* any compound having four atoms of chlorine.

tet·ra·chord, te′tra·kạrd″, *n.* [Gr. *tetrachordon—tetra-*, four, and *chordē*, a chord.] *Mus.* a series of four notes in a diatonic scale, of which the first is separated from the last by a perfect fourth.

te·trac·id, te·tras′id, *n. Chem.* a base capable of combining with four molecules of a monobasic acid.

tet·ra·cy·cline, te″tra·sī′klin, te″tra·sī′klin, *n. Pharm.* the antibiotic, $C_{22}H_{24}N_2O_8$, a yellow powder having a crystalline structure, and produced artificially by chemical synthesis or naturally by certain soil bacilli of the genus *Streptomyces.*

tet·rad, te′trad, *n.* [L.L. *tetras* (tetrad-), < Gr. *tetrás* (tetrad-), < *téttares*, four: cf. *tetra-*.] A group of four; the number four; *chem.* a tetravalent or quadrivalent element, atom, or radical; *biol.* the arrangement of four chromosomes, formed during meiosis by the splitting of paired chromosomes.— **te·trad·ic**, te·trad′ik, *n.*

te·trad·y·mite, te·trad′i·mīt″, *n.* [G. *tetradymit*, < Gr. *tetrádymos*, fourfold.] *Mineral.* a bismuth telluride, $Bi_2(TeS)_3$, usu. occurring in foliated masses, of a pale steel-gray color and a brilliant metallic luster.

tet·ra·dy·na·mous, te″tra·dī′na·mus, *a.* [Gr. *tetra-*, four, and *dynamis*, power.] *Bot.* of flowers, having six stamens, four longer than the other two.

tet·ra·eth·yl, te″tra·eth′il, *a. Chem.* having four ethyl groups.

tet·ra·eth·yl lead, te′tra·eth″il led′, *n. Chem.* a heavy liquid which is oily, colorless, and poisonous, $Pb(C_2H_5)_4$, used to prevent knocking in engines. Also **lead tet·ra·eth·yl.**

tet·ra·gon, te′tra·gon″, *n.* [Gr. *tetragōnon—tetra-* four, and *gōnia*, an angle.] *Geom.* A plane figure having four angles; a quadrangle.—te·trag·o·nal, te·trag′o·nal, a.—te·trag·o·nal·ly, adv.—te·trag·o·-nal·ness, n.

te·trag·o·nal sys·tem, n. Crystal. a crystal structure having square or rectangular faces, with axes which are perpendicular to each other, the two horizontal axes being equal in length and shorter than the vertical axis.

Tet·ra·gram·ma·ton, te″tra·gram′a·ton″, n. [Gr. tetragrámmaton < tetra-, four, and grámma (grammat-), character, letter, < gráphein, write.] The Hebrew word written JHVH or YHWH, representing without vowels Jahveh or Yahweh, commonly rendered in English as Jehovah, used as a substitute for the name of God, which is considered ineffable.

tet·ra·he·dral, te″tra·hē′dral, a. Having the form of a tetrahedron; having four sides.—tet·ra·he·dral·ly, adv.

tet·ra·he·drite, te″tra·hē′drīt, n. A steel-gray or blackish mineral with a brilliant metallic luster, consisting essentially of copper, antimony, and sulphur, but often containing other elements, as silver, occurring in tetrahedral crystals and massive, and forming an important ore of silver.

tet·ra·he·dron, te″tra·hē′dron, n. pl. **tet·ra·he·drons, tet·ra·he·dra,** te″tra·hē′dra. [Gr. tetra-, four, and hedra, a base.] Geom. a triangular pyramid having four plane faces.

tet·ra·hy·drate, te″tra·hī′drāt, n. Chem. a compound containing four water molecules.—tet·ra·hy·drat·ed, a.

tet·ra·hy·drox·y, te″tra·hī·drok′sē, a. Chem. of or pertaining to a molecule with four hydroxy groups.

te·tral·o·gy, te·tral′o·jē, n. pl. **te·tral·o·gies.** [Gr. tetralogia—tetra-, four, and logos, discourse.] A series of four interrelated works, as of literature, music, art, and the like; a collection of four dramatic compositions, three tragic and one satiric, exhibited together on the ancient Athenian stage during the festival of Dionysius.

tet·ra·mer, te′tra·mêr, n. Chem. a large molecule resulting from the union of four simpler, identical molecules.

te·tram·er·ous, te·tram′ér·us, a. [Gr. tetra- four, and meros, a part.] Having four parts; bot. having the floral parts in fours.

te·tram·e·ter, te·tram′i·tèr, n. [Gr. tetra-, four, and metron, measure.] Pros. A verse consisting of lines of four measures; a line of poetry having four measures.

te·tran·drous, te·tran′drus, a. Bot. having four stamens.

tet·ra·pet·al·ous, te″tra·pet′a·lus, a. [Gr. tetra-, four, and petalon, a leaf.] Bot. having four distinct petals.

tet·ra·ploid, te′tra·ploid″, a. With a chromosome number four times that of the haploid number.—n.—tet·ra·ploi·dic, a. —tet·ra·ploi·dy, n.

tet·ra·pod, te′tra·pod″, a. [< Gr. tetra-, four, and pous, foot.] Having four feet or footlike appendages.

te·trap·ter·ous, te·trap′tèr·us, a. Entom. having four wings; bot. having four appendages resembling wings, as some fruits.

te·trarch, tē′trärk, te′trärk, n. [Gr. te-trarchēs—tetra-, four, and archē, rule.] Anyone who governs or rules a fourth part, as of a district or province; one whose power is subordinate to another's; originally, a Roman governor of a fourth part of a province.—te·trarch·ate, te·trar·chy, tē′trär·kāt″, tē′trär·kit, te′trär·kāt″, te′trär·kit, tē′trär·kē, te′trär·kē, n.—te·trar·chic, ti·trär′kik, a.

tet·ra·spore, te′tra·spōr″, te″tra·spar″, n. [Gr. tetra-, four, and E. spore.] Bot. an asexual spore, of which there are four, produced in the sporangium of many red and brown algae after meiosis.—tet·-

ra·spor·ic, tet·ra·spor·ous, te″tra·spȯr′ik, te″tra·spȯr′us, te″tra·spar′us, te″tra·spȯr′-us, ti·tras′pêr·us, a.

te·tras·ti·chous, te·tras′ti·kus, a. [Gr. tetrastichos.] Bot. Arranged in a spike of four vertical rows, as flowers; having four such rows of flowers, as a spike.

tet·ra·tom·ic, te″tra·tom′ik, a. Chem. Having four atoms in the molecule; containing four replaceable atoms or groups; quadrivalent.

tet·ra·va·lent, te″tra·vā′lent, te·trav′a·-lent, a. Chem. quadrivalent.

tet·rode, te′trōd, n. Electron. a vacuum tube having four electrodes, usu. a cathode, two grids, and an anode.

te·trox·ide, te·trok′sīd, te·trok′sid, n. Chem. an oxide which contains in its molecule four atoms of oxygen.

tet·ryl, te′tril, n. Chem. a highly sensitive explosive, $C_7H_5N_5O_8$, occurring as pale yellow crystals, and used chiefly as a detonating agent and bursting charge.

tet·ter, tet′ér, n. [O.E. tetr, G. zitter, tetter; cf. Skt. dadru, tetter.] Any of several cutaneous diseases, as herpes, impetigo.

Teu·ton, töt′on, tūt′on, n. An ancient prob. Germanic people, living in Jutland north of Germany about 400 B.C.; one of the Teutonic peoples, esp. of Germany.

Teu·ton·ic, tö·ton′ik, tū·ton′ik, a. [L. Teutones, the Teutons; a Latinized form of their native name; akin Dutch.] Belonging or relating to the ancient tribe of Teutons; belonging, relating, or pertaining to peoples of northern Europe, as the Germans, British, Scandinavians, Dutch, and related groups; German; of or having to do with the Germanic languages.—n. The Germanic language.—Teu·ton·i·cal·ly, adv.

Teu·ton·ism, töt′o·niz″um, tūt′o·niz″um, n. The culture and civilization of the Teutons or Germans; a belief that the Teutonic or German race is superior. A custom or idiom that is characteristic of the Teutons or Germans; Germanism; also **Teu·ton·i·cism,** tö·ton′i·siz″um, tū·ton′i·siz″um.—**Teu·ton·ist,** töt′o·ni·zā′shan, tūt″o·ni·zā′shan, n.—**Teu·ton·ize,** töt′o·niz″, tūt′o·niz″, v.i., v.t.—Teutonized, Teutonizing. To become or make Teutonic or German; Germanize.

tex·as, tek′sas, n. [From the State of Texas.] A structure on the hurricane deck of a steamboat, containing officers' cabins and the like, and having the pilot house in front or on top.

Tex·as fe·ver, n. An infectious disease of cattle due to a parasitic protozoan which is transmitted from sick to healthy animals by the tick, Margaropus annulatus, and which multiplies in the blood and destroys the red blood corpuscles.

Tex·as lea·guer, n. [In allusion to the Texas League of baseball clubs.] Baseball, a pop fly ball that falls midway between infielders and outfielders and is a base hit.

Tex·as Rang·er, n. A member or an officer of the mounted police force of Texas; initially, any of a group of settlers banded together to protect the frontier from Indian attacks and lawlessness.

Tex·as Tow·er, n. A radar platform built upon a base sunk into the ocean bottom, and operated as part of an air attack warning network.

text, tekst, n. [Fr. texte, < L. textus, a tissue, a text, < texo, textum, to weave; seen also in texture, textile, context, pretext.] The main part of a printed or written work, as distinguished from index, pictures, notes, and the like; an author's own words, as distinct from commentary, translations, and the like; the exact wording of a printed or written work; a recension adopted by an editor as representative of the actual wording of the writer; a subject

or a theme; the words of a musical composition; a textbook; a passage of Scripture, esp. one selected as the theme of a sermon or discussion; the Scriptures or one of the forms or versions of the Scriptures; a bold-faced type; a large-size handwriting.

text·book, tekst′bụk″, n. A book used by students as a standard reference for a particular branch of study; a manual of instruction.—text·book·ish, tekst′bụk″ish, a.

text e·di·tion, n. An edition of a book published for use in educational institutions, and often offered at a discounted rate: distinguished from trade edition.

text hand, n. A type of handwriting distinguished by large, carefully formed characters.

tex·tile, teks′til, teks′tīl, a. [L. textilis, < texo, to weave.] Woven or capable of being woven; formed by weaving; pertaining to weaving.—n. A fabric made by weaving; any material, as a yarn or thread, which may be used for weaving.

tex·tu·al, teks′chŏ·al, a. [L. textus.] Of or pertaining to the text; as, textual criticism; based on or conforming to the text, as of the Scriptures; reproduced verbatim.—tex·tu·al·ly, adv.

tex·tu·al crit·i·cism, n. A literary study which seeks to determine the exact wording of original texts, esp. of the Bible; also lower criticism. A critical analysis based on careful study of the text of literary works. Compare new criticism.—tex·tu·al crit·ic, n.

tex·tu·al·ism, teks′chŏ·a·liz″um, n. Strict adherence to the text, esp. of the Scriptures; textual criticism, esp. of the Bible.

tex·tu·al·ist, teks′chŏ·a·list, n. One who is well versed in the text of the Scriptures; one who adheres closely to the text, esp. of the Scriptures.

tex·tu·ar·y, teks′chŏ·er″ē, n. pl. **tex·tu·ar·ies.** Textualist.—a. Textual.

tex·ture, teks′chèr, n. [L. textura, < texere, weave.] The characteristic disposition of the interwoven or intertwined threads, strands, or the like which make up a textile fabric; the characteristic disposition of the constituent parts of anything; as, soil of heavy texture, cake with a fine texture; structure or constitution in general. Fine arts, the representation of the surface structure of an object, esp. the skin, hair, fur, and the like; the surface structure of the work of art itself. The art or process of weaving; anything produced by weaving; a woven fabric.—v.t.—textured, texturing.—tex·tur·al, a.—tex·tur·al·ly, adv.—tex·tured, a.

T for·ma·tion, n. Football, an offensive formation in which the quarterback stands behind the center, the fullback behind the quarterback, and the halfbacks on either side of the fullback.

Thai, Tai, tī, tä′ē, n. A native of Siam or Thailand; the official and predominant language of Thailand; a branch of the Kadai family of languages which includes Lao, Shan, and the Thai.—a.

thal·a·men·ceph·a·lon, thal″a·men·-sef′a·lon″, n. pl. **thal·a·men·ceph·a·la, thal·a·men·ceph·a·lons,** thal″a·men·sef′-a·la. [N.L.] Anat. The segment of the brain behind the prosencephalon or forebrain, containing the optic thalami and the pineal gland; the between-brain.—thal·a·men·ce·phal·ic, thal″a·men″se·fal′ik, a.

thal·a·mus, thal′a·mus, n. pl. **thal·a·mi,** thal′a·mī″. [Gr. thalamos, a bedroom.] Anat. a part of the diencephalon composed of gray matter which relays sensory impulses to the cortex of the brain; rare, bot. the receptacle of a flower on which the carpels are placed.—**tha·lam·ic,** tha·lam′ik, a.—**tha·lam·i·cal·ly,** adv.

tha·las·sic, tha·las′ik, *a.* Of or pertaining to the sea, as distinguished from the open ocean; growing, living, or found in the sea; pelagic; marine.

thal·li·um, thal′ē·um, *n.* [Gr. *thallos,* a young green shoot— < the green line it gives in the spectrum.] *Chem.* a rare metallic element, soft and malleable, resembling lead, and having poisonous compounds. Sym. Tl, at. no. 81, at. wt. 204.37. See Periodic Table of Elements.—**thal·lic**, thal′ik, *a.*

thal·lo·phyte, thal′o·fīt″, *n.* [Gr. *thallos,* young shoot, *phyton,* plant.] Any one of the lowest phylum, *Thallophyta,* of plants, comprising the algae, bacteria, lichens, fungi, and some minor groups.—**thal·lo·phyt·ic**, thal″o·fit′ik, *a.*

thal·lous, thal′us, *a. Chem.* containing thallium in its lower valence. Also **thal·li·ous.**

thal·lus, thal′us, *n.* pl. **thal·lus·es, thal·li**, thal′ī. [N.L., < Gr. *thallós,* young shoot, young branch.] *Bot.* a vegetative body undifferentiated into true leaves, stem, and root, as the plant body of typical thallophytes.—**thal·loid**, thal′oid, *a.*

than, THan, *unstressed* THan, *conj.* [Orig. same as *then;* < O.E. *thonne.*] A particle used after certain adjectives and adverbs which express comparison or diversity, such as *more, better, other, otherwise, rather,* or *else,* for the purpose of introducing the second member of the comparison; when, as: He scarcely started *than* he had to leave.—*prep.* Compared with.

Than·a·tos, than′a·tos″, *n.* [From the god of death in Gr. mythol.] *Psychoanal.* in Freudian theory, the death instinct.

thane, thān, *n.* [M.E. *thane,* northern (Sc.) form of *thain, thein,* < O.E. *thegn, thegen,* servant, retainer, soldier, thane, = O.H.G. *degan,* boy, servant, soldier, = Icel. *thegn,* liegeman: cf. Gr. *téknon,* child.] *E. hist.* a member of any of several classes of men ranking between earls and ordinary freemen, and holding lands of the king or lord by military service. *Sc. hist.* a person, ranking with an earl's son, holding lands of the king; the chief of a clan, who became one of the king's barons. Also **thegn.**—**thane·ship**, *n.*

thank, thangk, *v.t.* [O.E. *thancian, thoncian.*] To give thanks or express gratitude to; to blame or hold accountable for, usu. used ironically, as: He is to *thank* for the team's loss.—**thank·er**, *n.*

thank·ful, thangk′ful, *a.* Expressive of gratitude; grateful; appreciative.—**thank·ful·ly**, *adv.*—**thank·ful·ness**, *n.*

thank·less, thangk′lis, *a.* Not feeling or expressing gratitude; ungrateful; not apt to be rewarded or appreciated with thanks.—**thank·less·ly**, *adv.*—**thank·less·ness**, *n.*

thanks, thangks, *n. pl.* [O.E. *thanc,* thanks, also thought, mind, will; Goth. *thagks,* Icel. *thökk,* D. and G. *dank,* thanks; < stem of *think.*] An expression of gratitude or acknowledgment of a benefit or favor; as, a smile of *thanks;* lit., 'I thank you,' as: *Thanks* for your help.—*interj.* I thank you. —**thanks to,** due to; because of.

thanks·giv·ing, thangks″giv′ing, *n.* The act of expressing thanks; grateful acknowledgment of benefits or favors; the act of giving thanks to God; a public celebration in acknowledgment of divine favor; *(cap.)* Thanksgiving Day.

Thanks·giv·ing Day, *n. U.S.* a national holiday in acknowledgment of divine favor, celebrated on the fourth Thursday of November; a similar national holiday in Canada, the second Monday in October.

thank·wor·thy, thangk′wur″THē, *a.* Worthy of thanks; deserving gratitude.

thank-you, thangk′yö, *a.* Expressing or transmitting thanks or appreciation; as, a *thank-you* letter.

that, THat, *unstressed* THat, *a.* pl. **those.** [O.E. *thæt,* neut. of the demonst. and def. art. *the* or *se* and = Goth. *thata,* Icel. *that,* D. *dat,* G. *das,* Skt. *tat.*] Being previously mentioned or otherwise understood; as, *that* man, *those* cities you spoke of; being more remote, as in place, time, or consideration, as opposed to *this,* as: I was talking about this year, but you were thinking about *that* year.—*pron.* pl. **those.** One or something previously mentioned or otherwise understood; a demonstrative pronoun, as: We talked about *that* yesterday. One or something more remote, as opposed to *this;* often used without a noun as a demonstrative pronoun, as: When this happens, *that* will surely follow. Something; an unspecified or unknown quality or object, as: *That* is the thing I don't like about him, What is *that*? Often used as a relative pronoun equivalent to *who, whom,* or *which,* esp. to introduce a restrictive or qualifying clause; as, the subject *that* we were talking about.—*adv.* To such an extent, degree, or amount; so, as: I will not go *that* far, I will not pay *that* much.— *conj.* Used chiefly to connect a subordinate to a principal clause, as to introduce a reason, purpose, consequence, or to supply any subject or object of the principal verb, as: He went *that* I might stay, Speak *that* I may hear, He is so weak *that* he cannot stand, We knew *that* he was gone. Used to introduce a wish, as: Would *that* I were there!

thatch, thach, *n.* [O.E. *thaec,* thatch, *theccan,* to thatch; Icel. *thak,* a roof, thatch; D. *dak,* G. *dach,* a roof; Dan. *daekke,* D. *dekken,* G. *decken,* to cover; same root as L. *tego, tectum,* to cover, Gr. *tegos, stegos,* a roof, Skt. *sthag,* to cover. Deck is allied.] Any of various natural materials, as straw, reeds, or palm leaves, used as roofing for a dwelling; also **thatch·ing.** Such a protective covering; something similar to such a covering; as, a *thatch* of white hair.—*v.t.* To cover with straw, reeds, or some similar substance.—**thatch·er**, *n.*—**thatch·y**, *a.*

thau·ma·tur·gy, thạ′ma·tur″jē, *n.* [Gr. *thaumatourgia*—*thauma, thaumatos,* a wonder, and *ergon,* work.] The act of performing something magical or miraculous; wonderwork; magic.—**thau·ma·turge,** thau·ma·tur·gist, thạ′ma·turj″, *n.*—**thau·ma·tur·gic, thau·ma·tur·gi·cal,** thạ″ma·tur′jik, *a.*

thaw, thạ, *v.i.* [O.E. *tháwan,* to thaw, Icel. *thá,* a thaw, *theyja,* to thaw; D. *dooi,* thaw, *dooijen,* to thaw; G. *thauen,* to melt, to thaw; cf. Gr. *tēkō,* to melt.] To be reduced from a frozen to a semiliquid or liquid state; to melt; to be relieved, as of stiffness or numbness, by warming, often followed by *out;* to become sufficiently warm to melt ice or snow, as the weather; *fig.* to become less reserved, formal, or tense.— *v.t.* To cause to thaw, as something frozen; to make less cold or reserved.—*n.* The process or occurrence of thawing; a period of warmer weather that causes ice and snow to melt; a reduction in tenseness or formality.

the, *stressed* THē, *unstressed before a consonant* THe, *unstressed before a vowel* THē, *def. art.* [O.E. *the* (for earlier *se,* fem. *sēo,* neut. *thæt*), art., orig. demonstrative pronoun, O. Fries. *thi,* D. *de,* O.H.G. G. *der,* Icel. *that,* Goth. *thata,* also in L. *iste,* that, Gr. *tó,* the, Skt. *tat,* it, that: cf. *that, then, thence, there, they, this, thither,* and *thus.*] Used, esp. before nouns, with a specifying or particularizing effect, as opposed to the indefinite or generalizing force of the indefinite article, *a* or *an;* as, *the* book you borrowed, *the* day we met; used to mark a noun as denoting something well-known or unique; as, *the* Alps; used with, or as part of, a title; as, *the* President of the U.S.; used to mark a noun as denoting a superlative example of its kind; as, *the* man for the job; used before a noun generically; as, a region inhabited by *the* lion; used to mark an adjective as substantive, and often, to render it abstract; as, to heal *the* sick, *the* sublime; used distributively, in place of *a, an, per,* or *each;* as, sold at one dollar *the* pound; used in place of a possessive pronoun, to denote a part of the body or clothing; as, a shot in *the* arm, a tug at *the* sleeve; *colloq.* used in place of a possessive pronoun, to denote a member of one's family; as, *the* wife.

the, THe, THē, *adv.* [O.E. *thē, thȳ,* instrumental case of *se.*] In or by that; on that account; in some degree; used to modify an adjective or adverb in the comparative degree, as: He is taking care of himself and looks *the* better, If you start now, you'll be back *the* sooner, His shirt is none *the* worse for wear. By how much; by so much; in what degree; in that degree: used correlatively, in one instance with relative force and in the other with demonstrative force; as, *the* more *the* merrier, *the* sooner *the* better.

the·ar·chy, thē′är·kē, *n.* pl. **the·ar·chies.** [Gr. *theos,* God, and *archē,* rule.] Government by God or another deity; theocracy; a body or order of deities or divine rulers.

the·a·ter, the·a·tre, thē′a·tėr, thēa′tėr, *n.* [Fr. *théâtre,* < L. *theatrum,* < Gr. *theatron,* < *theaomai,* to see, *thea,* a view.] A building, a part thereof, or a natural outdoor setting for the representation of dramatic spectacles, as plays, operas, or movies; a playhouse; a room with seats rising stepwise for lectures, anatomical demonstrations, surgical procedures, or the like; dramatic representation as a division of the performing arts; dramatic quality or impact; as, wonderful *theater;* the locality where important events take place; as, the European *theater* of war.

the·a·ter·go·er, the·a·tre·go·er, thē′a·tėr·gō″ėr, thēa′tėr·gō″ėr, *n.* One who goes to the theater, esp. habitually.— **the·a·ter·go·ing,** *n., a.*

the·a·ter-in-the-round, thē′a·tėr·in·THe·round′, thēa′tėr·in·THe·round′, *n.* Arena theater.

The·a·ter of the Ab·surd, *n.* (*Sometimes l.c.*) a genre of 20th century drama characterized by bizarre themes, characters, and conventions that illustrate the notion that reality is a meaningless accumulation of unrelated events made preposterous by man's futile attempts to interpret it or give it order.

the·at·ri·cal, thē·a′tri·kal, *a.* Pertaining to a theater or to scenic representations; bringing to mind the theater or a stage performance; as, to make a *theatrical* entrance; calculated for display; meretricious; artificial. Also **the·at·ric.**—**the·at·ri·cals,** *n. pl.* Dramatic presentations, esp. when given by amateurs.—**the·at·ri·cal·ism, the·at·ri·cal·i·ty,** thē·a″tri·kal′i·tē, *n.*— **the·at·ri·cal·ize,** thē·a′tri·ka·līz″, *v.t.* theatricalized, theatricalizing.—**the·at·ri·cal·ly,** *adv.*

the·at·rics, thē·a′triks, *n. pl. but sing. in constr.* The skill involved in the staging of a dramatic presentation; *pl. in constr.* affected, usu. emotional actions or speech indulged in for dramatic effect.

the·ca, thē′ka, *n.* pl. **the·cae,** thē′sē. [L., < Gr. *thēkē,* a case.] A sheath or hollow case; *zool.* caselike tissue enclosing anatomical structures, as the horny layer of an insect pupa; *bot.* a sac or cavity, as the pollen sac of an anther.—**the·cal, the·cate,** thē′kit, thē′kāt, *a.*

thee, THē, *pron.* [O.E. *thé,* dat. and accus. of *thu,* thou.] The objective and dative case of *thou*; among Quakers, thou as the subject of a sentence, as: *Thee* hears my prayer.

thee·lin, thē′lin, *n. Biochem.* estrone.

thee·lol, thē′lōl, thē′lạl, thē′lol, *n. Biochem.* estriol.

theft, theft, *n.* [O.E. *theŏfthe*, theft, < *theŏf*, a thief. Final *th* became *t* as in *height*.] The wrongful taking away of the goods of another; the act of stealing; larceny.

thegn, thän, *n.* Thane.—**thegn·ly**, *a.*

the·ine, thē′ēn, thē′in, *n.* [< *Thea*, the generic name of the tea plant.] An alkaloid found in tea, and chemically identical to caffeine in coffee. Also **the·in.**

their, THâr, *unstressed* THėr, *a.* [Icel. *theirra*, their = O.E. *thaera*, of them: the genitive pl. of which *the, that*, are nominatives.] Pertaining or belonging to them: the possessive case of the third person plural pronoun, *they*.

theirs, THârz, *pron.* That which pertains or belongs to a particular group, as: *Theirs* was lost, but I found mine. The possessive case of *they*, used predicatively, as: It was *theirs*, I took *theirs*.—**of theirs**, belonging or pertaining to a particular group; as, that cat *of theirs*.

the·ism, thē′iz·um, *n.* [Fr. *théisme*, < Gr. *theos*, God, seen also in *theocracy, theology, atheism*, etc.] A religious or philosophical doctrine utilizing the concept of deity to explain man's existence, as opposed to *atheism*; the doctrine that all things originate in a unitary God; monotheism, as opposed to *polytheism*; the doctrine that one God is the deep transcendent mystery in all reality and, at the same time, the creative immanent reality within all action, as opposed to *pantheism* and *deism*.—**the·ist**, thē′ist, *n., a.*—**the·is·tic, the·is·ti·cal,** *a.*—**the·is·ti·cal·ly,** *adv.*

them, THem, *unstressed* THem, *pron.* The objective case of *they*, as: I was with *them* last week.

theme, thēm, *n.* [Gr. *thema*, a proposition, a theme, a root word, < Gr. *tithēmi*, to place.] A subject of discourse or discussion; a subject or topic on which a person writes; a short dissertation composed by a student on a given subject. *Mus.* the leading subject in a composition or movement; a series of notes selected as the text or subject of a new composition; as, *theme* and variations. *Ling.* a stem.—**the·mat·ic,** *a.*—**the·mat·i·cal·ly,** *adv.*

theme song, *n.* A predominant melody in a muscial play or operetta that is symbolic of the entire production and its mood; a musical signature, as of a television or radio program, a performer, or the like.

them·selves, THem·selvz′, *pron. pl.* A reflexive or emphatic form of the third person plural pronoun, 'they,' as: They scolded *themselves*, The criminals *themselves* admitted their guilt. A denotation of a particular group's usual or customary state, as: They were not *themselves* all evening.

then, THen, *adv.* [O.E. *thanne, thonne, thaenne*, then, also than, = D. *dan*, then, than, = G. *dann*, then, *denn*, then, than; from the stem represented by E. *the*.] At that time, as: Clothing was cheaper *then*. Immediately or soon afterward, as: He stopped rowing, and *then* began again. Next in order of time, as: We'll have lunch, and *then* do our shopping. Next in place, as: He was first in line, *then* Jim, *then* Tom. In addition; besides; also, as: I enjoy sewing my own clothes, and *then* it's less costly. In that case; in those circumstances, as: If you are wet, *then* you must change your clothes. Since that is so or therefore, as: The rumor *then* is true.—*n.* That time, as: We

haven't taken a trip since *then*.—**then and there**, immediately; at that time and place.

the·nar, thē′när, *n.* [Gr. *thenar*, < *thenō*, to strike.] *Anat.* the fleshy part of the palm of the hand at the thumb's base.—*a.*—**the·nal**, thē′nal, *a.*

thence, THens, *adv.* [O.E. *thens, thennes, thannes*, genit. forms < O.E. *thanan, thonon*, thence.] From that place; from that time; for that reason; from this; out of this.

thence·forth, THens″fōrth′, THens″fạrth″, thens′fōrth″, thens′fạrth″, *adv.* From that time or place forward. Also **thence·for·ward, thence·for·wards.**

the·o·bro·mine, thē″o·brō′mēn, thē″o·brō′min, *n.* [< *Theobroma*, the generic name of the cacao tree < Gr. *theos*, God, and *brōma*, food.] *Chem.* a white, poisonous crystalline powder, $C_7H_8N_4O_2$, found in the seeds of cacao, and used primarily in medicine, as a vasodilator and diuretic.

the·o·cen·tric, thē″o·sen′trik, *a.* Having or regarding God as the center of all things; as, *theocentric* doctrines.—**the·o·cen·tri·cism, the·o·cen·tric·i·ty, the·o·cen·trism,** thē″ō·sen·tris′i·tē, *n.*

the·oc·ra·cy, thē·ok′ra·sē, *n. pl.* **the·oc·ra·cies.** [Gr. *theokratia—theos*, God, and *kratos*, power.] Government of a state claimed to be by the immediate direction of God or another deity; government by priests or by an ecclesiastical institution claiming to be divinely directed; a state thus governed. Also **thearchy.**—**the·o·crat**, thē′o·krat″, *n.*—**the·o·crat·ic, the·o·crat·i·cal,** thē″o·krat′ik, *a.*—**the·o·crat·i·cal·ly,** *adv.*

the·od·i·cy, thē·od′i·sē, *n. pl.* **the·od·i·cies.** [Gr. *theos*, God, and *dike*, justice.] A justification of the existence, justice, and goodness of God in light of the existence of evil.

the·od·o·lite, thē·od′o·līt″, *n.* [Origin doubtful; perh. < Gr. *thea*, a seeing, *hodos*, way, and *litos*, smooth.] A surveying instrument for measuring horizontal and vertical angles by means of a telescopic attachment.—**the·od·o·lit·ic**, thē·od″o·lit′ik, *a.*

the·og·o·ny, thē·og′o·nē, *n. pl.* **the·og·o·nies.** [Gr. *theogonia-theos*, a god, and *gone*, generation.] Any account or recitation dealing with the generation and descent of gods, as in myths or ancient poetry.—**the·o·gon·ic**, thē″o·gon′ik, *a.*—**the·og·o·nist**, *n.*

the·o·log·i·cal vir·tues, *n. pl.* Faith, hope, and love or charity, the three spiritual graces added to the cardinal virtues of Platonic philosophy by the Christian moralists.

the·o·logue, the·o·log, thē′o·lạg″, thē′o·lôg″, *n.* [L. *theologus*, < Gr. *theológos*, < *theós* god, and *légein*, speak.] *Colloq.* a theological student.

the·ol·o·gy, thē·ol′o·jē, *n. pl.* **the·ol·o·gies.** [Gr. *theologia—theos*, God, and *logos*, discourse.] The philosophical discipline, esp. in Western Civilization, dealing with the question of God in relation to other philosophical questions; the theoretic part of any religious activity; a branch of Christian systematics dealing with man's creatural state; an historical analysis of the doctrines and beliefs of a religion; a formal course of study of these disciplines; divinity.—**the·o·lo·gian**, thē″o·lō′jan, thē″o·lō′jē·an, *n.*—**the·o·log·ic, the·o·log·i·cal,** *a.*—**the·o·log·i·cal·ly,** *adv.*—**the·ol·o·gize**, thē·ol′o·jīz″, *v.i.—theologized, theologizing.*—**the·ol·o·giz·er,** *n.*

the·oph·a·ny, thē·of′a·nē, *n. pl.* **the·oph·a·nies.** [Gr. *theos*, God, and *phaninomai*, to appear.] A manifestation of God or a god to man in some visible form.—**the·o·phan·ic**, thē″o·fan′ik, *a.*

the·o·phyl·line, thē″o·fil′ēn, thē″o·fil′in,

n. Chem. a crystalline alkaloid, $C_7H_8N_4O_2$,—H_2O, which is an isomer of theobromine, produced synthetically or extracted from the leaves of tea, and used in medicines.

the·or·bo, thē·ạr′bō, *n. pl.* **the·or·bos.** [Fr. *théorbe, téorbe*, < It. *tiorba*.] An obsolete musical instrument of the lute class, having a neck that is double, one above the other, the lower bearing the melody strings, which are fretted, and the upper bearing the accompaniment strings.

the·o·rem, thē′o·rem, thēr′em, *n.* [Gr. *theōrēma*, < *theōreo*, to look, to view.] *Math.* A position to be proved as a logical development of other positions; a rule or property expressed by symbols or formulae. A position accepted as an acknowledged truth or established principle.—**the·o·re·mat·ic**, thē″ėr·e·mat′ik, thēr″e·mat′ik, *a.*—**the·o·re·mat·i·cal·ly,** *adv.*

the·o·ret·i·cal, thē″o·ret′i·kal, *a.* [Gr. *theorētikos*.] Pertaining to theory or theoretics; depending on theory or speculation; hypothetical; speculative; visionary; not practical. Also **the·o·ret·ic.**—**the·o·ret·i·cal·ly,** *adv.*

the·o·ret·ics, thē″o·ret′iks, *n. pl. but sing. in constr.* That part of a discipline or science which is theoretical.

the·o·rize, thē′o·rīz″, *v.i.—theorized, theorizing.* To form one or more theories; to form opinions solely by theory; to speculate.—**the·o·re·ti·cian**, thē″ėr·i·tish′an, thēr″i·tish′an, thē′o·rist, *n.*—**the·o·ri·za·tion**, *n.*—**the·o·riz·er,** *n.*

the·o·ry, thē′o·rē, thēr′ē, *n. pl.* **the·o·ries.** [L. *theoria*, a theory, < Gr. *theoria*, a looking at, theory, < *theōreð*, to see, < *theōros*, an observer.] A systematic arrangement of facts with respect to some real or hypothetical laws; a hypothetical explanation of phenomena; a hypothesis not yet empirically verified as law but accepted as the basis of experimentation; an exposition of the general or abstract principles of any science or humanity which have been derived from practice; a plan or system suggested as a method of action; an ideal arrangement of events, usu. preceded by *in*; a doctrine or scheme of things resting merely on speculation, contemplation, supposition, or conjecture; *math.* a presentation of all the axioms, theorems, lemmas, and principles relating to one subject.

the·os·o·phy, thē·os′o·fē, *n. pl.* **the·os·o·phies.** [M.L. *theosophia*, < L.Gr. *theosophia*, knowledge of divine things, < *theósophos.*] Any of various forms of philosophical or religious thought characterized by the belief in a transcendent reality which can be perceived or experienced mystically; *(often cap.)* the system of belief and doctrine of a religious sect, the Theosophical Society, based largely on Brahmanic and Buddhistic ideas.—**the·o·soph·ic, the·o·soph·i·cal,** thē″o·sof′ik, *a.*—**the·o·soph·i·cal·ly,** *adv.*—**the·os·o·phist,** *n.*

ther·a·peu·tic, ther″a·pū′tik, *a.* [Gr. *therapeutikos*, < *therapeuō*, to nurse, serve, or cure.] Curative; *med.* pertaining to therapeutics. Also **ther·a·peu·ti·cal.**—**ther·a·peu·ti·cal·ly,** *adv.*

ther·a·peu·tics, ther″a·pū′tiks, *n. pl. but sing. in constr. Med.* that branch or part of medicine dealing with the remedy or treatment of diseases.—**ther·a·peu·tist,** *n.*

ther·a·py, ther′a·pē, *n. pl.* **ther·a·pies.** [Gr. *therapeia*, service, care, medical treatment, < *therapeýein*.] *Med.* the treatment of disability or disease, as by some remedial or curative process: used in compounds; as, *serumtherapy*. Any soothing or curative device, process, or activity; curative or therapeutic quality or ability.—**ther·a·pist,** ther′a·pist, *n.*

there, THâr, *adv.* [O.E. *ther, thaer*, there, a locative case of the pronominal stem *the*, *that, then,* etc. In *thereafter, thereby,* etc., the dative case fem. sing. of the definite article.] In that place; at that place: opposed to *here,* as: She is *there.* To that place; thither, as: *There* goes the train. At that point, as in performance, song, or speech; as, to pause *there* for effect; in that particular instance or respect, as: Her attitude *there* is wrong.—*interj.* Used with an expression of greeting, as: Hello, *there*! An expression of consolation, as: *There, there.* An expression of defiance, usu. preceded by *so*; an expression of relief, as at a task completed; an expression of satisfaction or approval.—*pron.* Used to begin clauses or sentences before a verb when there is an inversion of the subject, as: *There* came a day of reckoning. That place, as previously designated, as: She lives near *there.*—*n.* That state, position, or point, as: It's your problem from *there* on.—*a.* In standard usage, only following the noun or pronoun, and usu. for emphasis, as: Do you see that girl *there*? In nonstandard usage, between the adjective and noun which it modifies, and usu. for emphasis; as, that *there* woman.

there·a·bout, THâr′*a*·bout′, *adv.* Near that place; about that time; near that number, degree, or quantity; approximately. Also **there·a·bouts.**

there·af·ter, THâr′af′tèr, THâr″äf′tèr, *adv.* After that, as in sequence or any specified time; afterward; *archaic,* accordingly.

there·at, THâr′at′, *adv.* At that place; at that time; on that account.

there·by, THâr″bī′, THâr″bī″, *adv.* By that; by that means; in connection or relation with that.

there·for, THâr″far′, *adv.* For that, this, or it.

there·fore, THâr′fōr′, THâr′far′, *adv., conj.* [*There,* the dat. sing. fem. of the old def. art., and *for.*] For that or this reason, referring to something previously stated; consequently.

there·from, THâr″frum′, THâr″from′, *adv.* From this or that; from this or that thing, place, or time.

there·in, THâr″in′, *adv.* Into or in that or this place, time, or thing; in that or this particular point or respect.

there·in·af·ter, THâr″in·af′tèr, THâr″in·äf′tèr, *adv.* Subsequently or later in that writing, speech, or the like.

there·in·to, THâr″in′tö, THâr″in·tö′, *adv.* Into that or that place; into it.

there·of, THâr″uv′, THâr″ov′, *adv.* Of that, this, or it; because of that reason or cause.

there·on, THâr″on′, THâr″an′, *adv.* On that or this; thereupon.

there·to, THâr″tö′, *adv.* To that or this, as thing or place; *archaic,* moreover, furthermore. Also **there·un·to,** THâr″un·tö′, THâr″un′tö.

there·to·fore, THâr″to·fōr′, THâr″to·far′, *adv.* Up to or before that time; prior to that.

there·un·der, THâr″un′dèr, *adv.* Under that or this, as in number; by that title, or under the provisions or authority of that.

there·up·on, THâr′*a*·pon″, THâr′*a*·pan″, THâr″*a*·pon′, THâr″*a*·pan′, *adv.* Upon that or this; in consequence of that; therefore; at once.

there·with, THâr″with′, THâr″wiTH′, *adv.* With that or this; moreover or besides that; thereupon or immediately following.— **there·with·al,** THâr″with·al′, THâr″wiTH·al′, *adv.*

the·ri·a·ca, the·rī′*a*·ka, *n.* [L. *theriac* (*a*), Gr. *thēriakē,* < *thērion,* a wild beast.] A name given formerly to a paste made of numerous drugs combined with honey, and considered effective against the effects of animal or other poison; treacle; molasses. Also **the·ri·ac,** thēr′ē·ak″.—**the·ri·a·cal,** *a.*

the·ri·o·mor·phic, thēr″ē·*o*·mar′fik, *a.* [Gr. *thērion,* animal, *morphē,* shape.] Having the form of an animal or beast, as of a god or deity. Also **the·ri·o·mor·phous.**

therm, thurm, *n.* [Gr. *thérmē,* heat, < *thermós,* hot, warm, < *thérein,* make hot.] *Phys.* a unit of heat or thermal capacity, as the small calorie, the large calorie, a unit equal to 1,000 large calories, or a unit equal to 100,000 Brit. thermal units. Also **therme.**

ther·mae, thur′mē, *n. pl.* [L., hot springs, hot baths, < Gr. *thérmai,* pl. of *thermē,* heat.] Hot springs; hot baths; a public bathing establishment of the ancient Greeks or Romans.

ther·mal, thur′mal, *a.* [Partly < L. *thermae,* hot springs or baths (see *thermae*), partly < Gr. *Oépun,* heat (see *therm*).] Of, caused by, or pertaining to heat; also *thermic.* Of, pertaining to, or of the nature of thermae, or hot springs.—*n. Meteor.* an ascending current of air caused by heat.— **ther·mal·ly,** *adv.*

ther·mal bar·ri·er, *n. Aeron.,* rocketry, a limit imposed on the velocity of airplanes or rockets due to heating caused by friction. Also **heat bar·ri·er.**

ther·mal spring, *n.* A spring which issues water of a higher temperature than that found in the surrounding locality.

ther·mal u·nit, *n.* Any of the various units, as of temperature or energy, for measuring heat.

ther·mic, thur′mik, *a.* See *thermal.*

therm·i·on, thurm′ī″on, thur′mē·on, *n.* [Gr. *thérmē,* heat, and E. *ion.*] *Phys., electron.* any of a class of electrically charged particles emitted by incandescent substances or materials, as metals.—**therm·i·on·ic,** thurm″ī·on·ik, thur″mē·on′ik, *a.*

therm·i·on·ic cur·rent, *n.* A current or directed flow of thermions.

therm·i·on·ics, thurm″ī·on′iks, thur″mē·on′iks, *n. pl. but sing. in constr.* That area of physics concerned with thermionic activity.

therm·i·on·ic tube, *n. Electron.* any electron or vacuum tube within which the emission of thermions from an electrode, usu. the cathode, is caused by the heating of that same electrode. Also *Brit.* **therm·i·on·ic valve.**

ther·mis·tor, thèr·mis′tèr, *n. Electron.* a small resistor in which the resistance varies over a wide range with temperature, composed of a special semiconducting material.

ther·mite, thur′mīt, *n.* [G. *thermit,* < Gr. *thérme,* heat.] A mixture of powdered aluminum and an oxide of another metal, usu. iron, which upon ignition produces an extremely high temperature as the result of the union of the aluminum with the oxygen of the oxide, as used in welding or incendiary munitions. Also **Ther·mit** (Trademark), **ther·mit,** thur′mit.

ther·mo·cou·ple, thur′mo·kup″l, *n. Phys.* a device consisting of the connection or junction of two pieces of dissimilar conductive metals kept at different temperatures to produce a current, which is thermoelectric, and used for measuring differences in temperature, as of a third metal. Also *thermoelectric couple.*

ther·mo·dur·ic, thur″mo·dur′ik, thur″mo·dūr′ik, *a. Bact.* resistant to high temperatures with the ability for survival, as through the process of pasteurization: said esp. of microorganisms.

ther·mo·dy·nam·ic, thur″mō·dī·nam′ik, *a.* Of or pertaining to thermodynamics; pertaining to or operated by force due to heat or to the conversion of heat into mechanical energy. Also **ther·mo·dy·nam·i·cal.**— **ther·mo·dy·nam·i·cal·ly,** *adv.*

ther·mo·dy·nam·ics, thur″mō·dī·nam′iks, *n. pl. but sing. in constr.* That area of physics which deals with heat and its relationship with various other forms of energy, esp. mechanical energy.

ther·mo·e·lec·tric, thur′mō·i·lek′trik, *a.* Involving, noting, or pertaining to any or various phenomena or operations in which heat and electricity are both involved; specif. of or pertaining to thermoelectricity. Also **ther·mo·e·lec·tri·cal.**—**ther·mo·e·lec·tri·cal·ly,** *adv.*

ther·mo·e·lec·tric cou·ple, *n.* Thermocouple.

ther·mo·e·lec·tric·i·ty, thur″mō·i·lek·tris′i·tē, thur″mō·ē″lek·tris′i·tē, *n.* Electricity produced directly from heat, as that generated by a thermocouple.

ther·mo·e·lec·tron, thur″mō·i·lek′tron, *n. Phys.* an electron given off in thermionic phenomena.—**ther·mo·e·lec·tron·ic,** *a.*

ther·mo·gen·e·sis, thur″mō·jen′i·sis, *n.* Heat created in the animal body by metabolic processes.

ther·mo·gram, thur′mō·gram″, *n.* A record that is made by means of a thermograph.

ther·mo·graph, thur′mo·graf″, thur′mo·gräf″, *n.* A thermometer which automatically makes a record of the temperature.

ther·mog·ra·phy, thèr·mog′ra·fē, *n. Print.* a process which imitates engraving by means of dusting wet print with a powder and heating it to produce raised letters.—**ther·mog·ra·pher,** *n.*—**ther·mo·graph·ic,** thur″mo·graf′ik, *a.*—**ther·mo·graph·i·cal·ly,** *adv.*

ther·mo·junc·tion, thur″mō·jungk′shan, *n. Phys.* the junction of the two dissimilar conductive metals where thermoelectric current is generated, as in a thermocouple.

ther·mo·la·bile, thur″mō·lā′bil, *a. Biochem.* subject to destruction or loss of characteristic properties through the action of moderate heat, as certain toxins and ferments: opposed to *thermostable.*—**ther·mo·la·bil·i·ty,** thur″mō·la·bil′i·tē, *n.*

ther·mol·y·sis, thèr·mol′i·sis, *n. Physiol.* the dispersion of heat from the body; *chem.* decomposition or dissociation by heat.— **ther·mo·lyt·ic,** thur″mo·lit′ik, *a.*

ther·mom·e·ter, thèr·mom′i·tèr, *n.* [Gr. *thermos,* warm, and *metron,* measure.] An instrument by which temperatures are measured, consisting usu. of a closed glass tube containing some liquid, most often mercury or alcohol, which expands or contracts with variations of temperature.— **ther·mo·met·ric, ther·mo·met·ri·cal,** thur″mo·me′trik, *a.*—**ther·mo·met·ri·cal·ly,** *adv.*

ther·mom·e·try, thèr·mom′i·trē, *n.* Temperature measurement; the science or technology of using and constructing thermometers.

ther·mo·nu·cle·ar, thur″mō·nö′klē·èr, thur″mō·nū′klē·èr, *a.* Of or pertaining to nuclear reactions or processes, esp. nuclear fusion, which in their inception require extremely high temperatures, as in various atomic weapons.

ther·mo·phile, thur′mo·fīl″, thur′mo·fil, *n. Biol.* a microorganism which grows only within a certain range of generally high temperatures, usu. above 45°C. and not beyond 75°C.—**ther·mo·phil·ic,** thur″mo·fil′ik, *a.*

ther·mo·pile, thur′mo·pīl″, *n. Phys.* a series of thermocouples joined to produce a combined effect, and used for generating currents, usu. thermoelectric, or for measuring small differences in temperature.

ther·mo·plas·tic, thur″mo·plas′tik, *a.* Becoming soft and supple when heated, as of various plastics: contrasted with *thermosetting.*—*n.* Any material or substance of this kind.—**ther·mo·plas·tic·i·ty,** thur″mō·pla·stis′i·tē, *n.*

ther·mos bot·tle, *n.* Vacuum bottle. Also **ther·mos,** thur′mos.

ther·mo·scope, thur'mo·skōp", *n.* An instrument by which changes of temperature are indicated, but not accurately measured, by any corresponding changes in a substance's volume.—**ther·mo·scop·ic**, **ther·mo·scop·i·cal**, thur"mo·skop'ik, *a.*

ther·mo·set·ting, thur"mō·set'ing, *a.* Pertaining to a material which, under the influence of heat, first softens and then becomes permanently set and infusible, as of various plastics: contrasted with *thermoplastic.*

ther·mo·sphere, thur'mo·sfēr", *n.* The outermost region of the earth's atmosphere, lying above the mesosphere, within which temperature increases steadily with altitude.

ther·mo·sta·ble, thur"mō·stā'bl, *a. Biochem.* able to undergo moderate heating without loss of characteristic properties, as certain toxins and ferments: opposed to *thermolabile.*—**ther·mo·sta·bil·i·ty**, *n.*

ther·mo·stat, thur'mo·stat", *n.* An automatic device for regulating temperature, as one in which the expansion of a piece of metal by heat closes an electric circuit, which in turn causes a ventilator or the like to open; a similar device for indicating a change in temperature, as by sounding an alarm.—**ther·mo·stat·ic**, *a.*—**ther·mo·stat·i·cal·ly**, *adv.*

ther·mo·tax·is, thur"mo·tak'sis, *n. Biol.* the property in a cell or organism of movement toward or away from a heat source; *physiol.* the regulation of the bodily temperature.—**ther·mo·tac·tic, ther·mo·tax·ic**, *a.*

ther·mot·ro·pism, thèr·mo'tro·piz"um, *n. Biol.* the property in organisms of turning or bending a part of the organism either toward or away from a certain heat source, as in growth.—**ther·mo·trop·ic**, thur"mo·trop'ik, *a.*

the·sau·rus, thi·sar'us, *n. pl.* **the·sau·ri**, **the·sau·rus·es**, thi·sar'ī. [L. *thesaurus*, < Gr. *thesauros*, < (ti)-*thēmi*, to place.] A lexicon or similar book of words or information, esp. one containing synonyms and antonyms; a treasury; a storehouse.

the·sis, thē'sis, *n. pl.* **the·ses**, thē'sēz. [L., < Gr. *thésis*, a setting or laying down, something laid down, thesis, < *tithenai*, set, put; akin to E. *do*.] A proposition, statement, or assertion laid down or stated, esp. one to be discussed and proved or to be maintained against objections; a subject propounded for a college composition or the essay itself; a dissertation, as one presented by a candidate for a diploma or degree; *prosody*, orig. the accented, later the unaccented part of a foot in verse: opposed to *arsis*; *mus.* the downbeat; *logic*, an unproved proposition, used esp. as a premise.

Thes·pi·an, thes'pē·an, *a.* Of or pertaining to Thespis, a Greek tragic poet and the traditional founder of Greek tragedy. (*Often l.c.*) pertaining to tragedy or to the dramatic art in general; tragic; dramatic.—*n.* A tragedian; an actor or actress. Also **thes·pi·an.**

the·ta, thā'ta, thē'ta, *n.* [L., < Gr. *thēta.*] The eighth letter, symbolized by Θ, θ, and ϑ, of the Greek alphabet which corresponds to *th* in the English alphabet.

thet·ic, thet'ik, *a.* [Gr. *thetikós*, < *tithénai.*] Positive; dogmatic; *pros.* starting with, pertaining to, or constituting a thesis. Also **thet·i·cal**—**thet·i·cal·ly**, *adv.*

the·ur·gy, thē'ur·jē, *n. pl.* **the·ur·gies.** [L.L. *theurgia*, < L.Gr. *theourgia*, divine work, miracle, theurgy, < *theourgós*, divinely working, < Gr. *theós*, god, and *-ergós*, working.] The working of some divine or supernatural agency in human affairs; the effects brought about among men by such an agency; any magical art professedly based on aid from beneficent, divine, or supernatural agencies; a system of

magic practiced by the Egyptian Platonists and others professing to have communication with and aid from beneficent deities.—**the·ur·gic, the·ur·gi·cal**, *a.*—**the·ur·gi·cal·ly**, *adv.*—**the·ur·gist**, *n.*

thew, thū, *n.* [Perh. same as O.E. *theáwas*, manners, habits.] *Usu. pl.* well-developed muscles or strong sinews; *pl.* strength or power, esp. muscular.—**thew·y**, *a.*

they, THā, *pron.*—*sing. nom. he, she*, or *it*, poss. *his, her*, or *its*, obj. *him, her*, or *it*; pl. nom. *they*, poss. *their* or *theirs*, obj. *them*; intens. and refl. *themselves.* [From Scand.: cf. Icel. *their* (gen. *theira*) = O.E. *thā* (dat. *thæm*), pl. of the demonstrative *se.*] Nominative plural of *he, she*, and *it* used in designating two or more persons, creatures, or things whose identity is already established; often used to denote persons indefinitely or people in general, as: *They* say he beats his wife.

they'd, THād. Contraction of they would or they had.

they'll, THāl. Contraction of they shall or they will.

they're, THār. Contraction of they are.

they've, THāv. Contraction of they have.

thi·a·mine, thī'a·mēn", thī'a·min, *n. Biochem.* a B-complex vitamin compound of white crystals, $C_{12}H_{17}ClN_4OS$, found in both animal and plant sources but also made synthetically, and necessary for proper activity of the nervous system and carbohydrate metabolism. Also *Vitamin B₁.* Also **thi·a·min**, thī'a·min.

thi·a·zine, thī'a·zēn", thī'a·zin, *n.* [< *thio-* and *azin.*] *Chem.* any of a class of compounds, which are organic, containing a ring composed of one atom each of sulphur and nitrogen and four atoms of carbon.

thi·a·zole, thī'a·zōl", *n.* [< *thio-* and *azole.*] *Chem.* A colorless liquid with a pungent odor, C_3H_3NS; any of various derivatives of this substance, esp. used in obtaining various dyes.

thick, thik, *a.* [O.E. *thicce* = D. *dik* = G. *dick* = Icel. *thykkr*, thick.] Having relatively great extent from one surface or side to its opposite; not thin; as, a *thick* slice of cake; having a specified measurement in depth or in a direction perpendicular to that of length and breadth; as, a board one inch *thick*; placed close together, dense, or compact; numerous, abundant, or plentiful; as, *thick* hair; filled, covered, or abounding, usu. followed by *with*; as, table *thick* with dust; having great consistency or density; as, *thick* syrup; containing much solid matter in suspension or solution; dense with mist, smoke, or haze, as the weather or atmosphere; muffled, husky, hoarse, or indistinct; as, a *thick* voice; pronounced; as, a *thick* Italian accent; dull, stupid, or slow in mental apprehension; *colloq.* close in friendship or intimate; *Brit. colloq.* excessive, esp. of that which is tolerable or proper.—*adv.* In a thick manner; so as to be thick; as, butter spread *thick.*—*n.* That which is thick; the thickest, densest, or most crowded part of anything; the place, time, or stage of greatest activity; as, in the *thick* of the fight.—**lay it on thick**, *colloq.* To exaggerate or overstate; to praise or flatter excessively.—**through thick and thin**, through good and bad circumstances; loyally; unwaveringly.—**thick·ish**, *a.*—**thick·ly**, *adv.*

thick·en, thik'en, *v.i., v.t.* To become or make thick or thicker; to become or make more involved, intense, or complicated, as the plot of a story.—**thick·en·er**, thik'e·nèr, *n.*

thick·en·ing, thik'e·ning, *n.* The process or act of becoming or making thick; something added esp. to a liquid to thicken; a thickened area, section, or part.

thick·et, thik'it, *n.* [O.E. *thiccet*, < *thicce*,

E. *thick.*] A thick or dense growth of shrubs, bushes, or small trees; a thick coppice; that which suggests a thicket, esp. in impenetrability.—**thick·et·ed, thick·et·y**, *a.*

thick·head·ed, thik'hed"id, *a.* Having a thick head; dull-witted or stupid, as of a person.—**thick·head**, *n.* One who is stupid; blockhead.—**thick·head·ed·ness**, *n.*

thick·ness, thik'nis, *n.* The state or quality of being thick; the third and usu. smallest dimension of a solid, distinct from length and width; the thick part of something; a layer, sheet, or ply, as of cloth or paper.

thick·set, thik'set', *a.* Of thick form or build, as a person; heavily or solidly built; stocky; stout; set or growing thickly, or in close arrangement; dense; as, a *thickset* hedge.—**thick'set**", *n.* A thicket.

thick-skinned, thik'skind', *a.* Having a thick skin or rind; not easily moved or irritated, as by criticism or ridicule; callous or insensitive.

thick-wit·ted, thik'wit'id, *a.* Deficient in wit or intelligence; stupid; dull.

thief, thēf, *n. pl.* **thieves.** [O.E. *theóf* = Icel. *thjófr*, Sw. *tjuf*, D. *dief*, G. *dieb*, Goth. *thjubs*, thief; root doubtful.] One who steals or deprives another of property secretly or without open force; a person who commits or is guilty of larceny or theft.

thieve, thēv, *v.t.*—*thieved, thieving.* To take by theft; to steal.—*v.i.* To steal; to commit or practice theft.

thiev·er·y, thē've·rē, *n. pl.* **thiev·er·ies.** The practice, an instance, or the act of stealing; theft.

thiev·ish, thē'vish, *a.* Given to stealing; of the nature of, or relating to, theft or a thief; furtive; stealthy.—**thiev·ish·ly**, *adv.*—**thiev·ish·ness**, *n.*

thigh, thī *n.* [O.E. *thēoh* = D. *dij* = O.H.G. *dioh* = Icel. *thjó*, thigh.] That part of the leg between the hip and the knee in man, or a homologous or apparently corresponding part of the hind limbs of other animals; the true femoral region, in birds, buried in the general integument of the body, or the segment below, containing the fibula and tibia; an insect's femur.

thigh·bone, thī'bōn", *n. Anat.* femur.

thig·mo·tax·is, thig"mo·tak'sis, *n.* [N.L., < Gr. *thigma*, touch, and *táxis*, arrangement.] *Biol.* A movement by a cell or organism toward or away from the stimulus of a mechanical contact; stereotaxis.—**thig·mo·tac·tic**, thig"mo·tak'tik, *a.*

thig·mo·tro·pism, thig·mo'tro·piz"um, *n.* [Gr. *thigma*, touch.] *Biol.* The involuntary change of position of a plant or other organism, esp. in its growth, by turning or bending toward or away, in reaction to mechanical contact; stereotropism.—**thig·mo·trop·ic**, thig"mo·trop'ik, *a.*

thill, thil, *n.* [Cf. O.E. *thille*, plank, flooring.] Either of the pair of shafts between which a single animal drawing a vehicle is harnessed.

thim·ble, thim'bl, *n.* [O.E. *thȳmel*, < *thūma*, E. *thumb.*] A usu. metal or plastic bell-shaped cap worn on the finger to push the needle in sewing; *mech.* any of various devices or attachments likened to a thimble, as a sleeve, tube, or bushing for joining the ends of pipes; *naut.* a metal ring with a concave groove on the outside, used to line the inside of a ring of rope forming an eye.

thim·ble·ber·ry, thim'bl·ber"ē, *n. pl.* **thim·ble·ber·ries.** Any of several American raspberries or other related plants with a thimble-shaped fruit, esp. the flowering raspberry, *Rubus odoratus.*

thim·ble·ful, thim'bl·fu̇l", *n.* As much as a thimble will hold; a small quantity.

thim·ble·rig, thim'bl·rig", *n.* A swindling game in which the operator apparently covers a small ball or pea with one of three thimblelike cups, and then, moving the cups about, offers to bet that no one can tell under which cup the ball or pea lies. A swindler, esp. one operating such a game; also **thim·ble·rig·ger.**—*v.t.*—*thimblerigged, thimblerigging.* To cheat or manipulate by or as by the thimblerig.

thim·ble·weed, thim′bl·wēd″, *n.* Any of several plants of the genera *Anemone* and *Rudbeckia* exhibiting thimble-shaped seed receptacles.

thi·mer·o·sal, thī·mur′o·sal″, thī·mer′o·sal″, *n.* A light-colored, water-soluble, crystalline powder, $NaOOCC_6H_4SHgC_2H_5$, used as a germicide and antiseptic.

thin, thin, *a.*—*thinner, thinnest.* [O.E. *thynne* = D. *dun* = G. *dunn* = Icel. *thunnr,* thin; akin to L. *tenuis,* Skt. *tanu,* thin, L. *tendere,* Gr. *teinein,* Skt. *tan-,* stretch: cf. *tend* and *tone.*] Having relatively little extent from one surface or side to its opposite, or not thick; as, *thin* paper; of small cross section in comparison with the length, or slender; as, a *thin* wire; having little flesh, spare, or lean; easily seen through, transparent, flimsy, or inadequate; as, a *thin* excuse; having the constituent parts or individuals relatively few and not close together; as, *thin* hair; not dense; sparse; scanty, as having few in attendance; having relatively slight consistency, as a liquid; fluid; rare or rarefied, as air; without solidity or substance, or unsubstantial, as a wisp or vapor; wanting depth or intensity, as color; wanting fullness or volume, as sound that is weak; faint, slight, poor, or feeble; meager or scanty, as diet; lacking body, richness, or strength, as of low alcoholic content in liquor; *photog.* lacking in opaqueness to produce prints without strong contrasts of light and shade, as a developed negative. —*adv.* In a thin manner; so as to be thin; thinly.—*v.t.*—*thinned, thinning.* [O.E. *thynnian.*] To make thin or thinner; reduce in thickness, density, numbers, or consistency, used with *down* or *out.*—*v.i.* To become thin or thinner, as: The woods *thin* toward the edge. Become reduced or diminished, go: used with *down, off,* or *away.*—**thin·-ly,** *adv.*—**thin·ness,** *n.*—**thin·nish,** *a.*

thine, THīn, *pron.* [O.E. *thin,* poss. a., also gen. of *thū,* E. thou.] *Archaic.* The possessive form of *thou* used predicatively or without a noun following, or attributively before a noun beginning with a vowel or *h*; that which relates or belongs to thee; thy.

thing, thing, *n.* [O.E. *thing,* thing, object, matter, affair, cause, assembly, = O.S. and O.Fries. *thing* = D. *ding* = O.H.G. G. *ding* = Icel. *thing,* akin to Goth *theihs,* time.] That which is or may become an object of thought, whether material or ideal, animate or inanimate, actual, possible, or imaginary; that which exists individually, whether in fact or in idea; a separate or individual entity; some entity, object, or creature which is not or cannot be specifically designated or precisely described; that which is signified or represented, as distinguished from a word, symbol, or idea representing it; a material object without life or consciousness, or an inanimate object; a living being or creature, applied to a person, as: She is a pretty little *thing.* Some object not precisely designated but more or less clearly understood; a specific kind of substance or material; *law,* anything that may be the subject of a property right. *Pl.* personal possessions or belongings; clothes or apparel, esp. articles of dress added to the ordinary clothing when going out of doors; implements, utensils, or other articles for service. A piece of literary or musical composition, artistic work, or the like, as: A little *thing* written for the occasion. A matter or affair, as: *Things* are going well

now. An action, deed, or performance; as, to do great *things*; an occurrence; as, many *things* have happened since; an objective or aim, as of some activity; an idea, notion, or statement; *colloq.* a phobia or obsession; as, to have a *thing* about cars.—**make a good thing of,** to gain or benefit by, as an experience or situation.—**see things,** to have one or more hallucinations.—**the thing,** the advisable, proper, or important result or act; that which is fashionable.

thing·a·ma·jig, thing·u·ma·jig, thing′-a·ma·jig″, *n. Colloq.* something, as a device or gadget, whose name has been forgotten or is not known. Also **thing·a·ma·bob, thing·u·ma·bob, thing·um·bob,** thing′a·-ma·bob″, thing′um·bob″.

thing-in-it·self, thing″in·it·self′, *n. pl.* **things-in-them·selves,** thingz″in·THem·-selvz′. *Philos.* the reality or phenomena, according to Kant, which is beyond human knowledge or experience, and cannot be known.

think, thingk, *v.t.*—*thought, thinking.* [O.E. *thencan* (pret. *thōhte*) = O.S. *thenkian* = O.H.G. *denchan* (G. *denken*), think, = Icel. *thekkja,* perceive, = Goth. *thagkjan,* think; orig. causative, from the same source as E. *think.*] To form or conceive mentally, as a thought; to create intellectually, as an idea or concept; to speculate upon, meditate, or ponder, usu. followed by *over* or *through*; as, to *think* it *over* before deciding; to examine or solve rationally, usu. followed by *out*; to concentrate on or be preoccupied with, as a particular subject; to call to mind, recollect, or remember; as, to *think* what has happened since then; to plan, devise, or contrive, used with *up*; intend or have as a purpose; to believe, opine, or suppose, as: They *thought* that the earth was flat. To consider or suppose as specified; as, to *think* the lecture interesting; to suspect; as, *thinking* no harm; to anticipate or expect; as, not *thinking* to see you here; to will; as, to *think* oneself into a state, condition, or action.—*v.i.* To exercise the intellectual faculties in forming ideas, decisions, judgments, or inferences; to reason; cogitate or meditate; to form or have an idea or mental image, used with *of* or *about*; to reflect upon the matter in question; as, to *think* carefully before beginning; to effect remembrance, usu. with *of,* as: I can't *think* of his name. To have consideration or regard, usu. with *of*; as, to *think* of others first; to make mental discovery or plan, usu. with *of*; as, to *think* of it first; to have a notion or plan, usu. with *of*; as, to *think* of selling; to have a belief or opinion as indicated; as, if you *think* so, to *think* well of a person; to have an anticipation or expectation, used with *of,* as: He little *thought of* what would happen. —*n. Colloq.* An act of thinking; an idea or thought; what one thinks about something. —*a.*—**think bet·ter of,** to reconsider or alter, as an intended action; to hold a higher opinion of.—**think fit,** to regard as desirable or appropriate.—**think·er,** thing′kėr, *n.* One who thinks, esp. one who has exercised or cultivated his powers of thinking to an extraordinary extent.

think·a·ble, thing′ka·bl, *a.* Capable of being thought; conceivable; possible.— **think·a·ble·ness,** *n.*—**think·a·bly,** *adv.*

think·ing, thing′king, *a.* Able to think; using the faculty of reasoning; rational.—*n.* The act or state of one who thinks; thought; cogitation.—**think·ing·ly,** *adv.*

think·ing cap, *n.* A condition characterized by thought, as: If you put on your *thinking cap,* you can answer the question.

think piece, *n. Journ., colloq.* an article to give background information, overall analysis, and usu. personal opinion concerning a news situation, often intended to be provocative.

think tank, *n.* A group of specialists from fields of science, orig. pooled together for collaboration in the computer and electronics programs of aerospace, working together as a unit in systems analysis for the solution of problems of government and industry, esp. in urban development and other sociological or economic projects.

thin·ner, thin′ėr, *n.* One who or that which thins; a volatile liquid used to thin paint, as turpentine.

thin-skinned, thin′skind′, *a.* Having a thin skin; unduly sensitive to censure or abuse; easily offended or irritated.

thi·o·a·ce·tic ac·id, thī″ō·a·sē′tik as′id, thī″ō·a·set′ik, *n. Chem.* an acrid, volatile, liquid reagent, CH_3COSH.

thi·o ac·id, thī′ō as′id, *n. Chem.* an acid in which sulfur has partly or wholly replaced oxygen.

thi·o·car·bam·ide, thī″ō·kär·bam′id, thī″ō·kär·bam′id, *n. Chem.* thiourea.

thi·o·cy·a·nate, thī″ō·sī′a·nāt″, *n. Chem.* a derivative of thiocyanic acid, in the form of an ester or salt.

thi·o·cy·an·ic, thī″ō·sī·an′ik, *a. Chem.* referring to or being the acrid, unstable, transparent liquid acid, HSCN.

Thi·o·kol, thī″ō·kōl″, thī′ō·kạl″, thī′ō·kol″, *n.* Any of several synthetic polysulfide rubber products. (Trademark.)

thi·o·nate, thī′o·nāt″, *n. Chem.* a derivative of a thionic acid, in the form of an ester or salt.

thi·on·ic, thī·on′ik, *a.* [Gr. *theion,* sulfur.] *Chem.* of, pertaining to, or composed of sulfur.

thi·on·ic ac·id, *n. Chem.* any of five unstable, sulfur-containing acids of the general formula, $H_2S_nO_6$, in which *n* may be any number from two to six.

thi·o·nyl, thī′o·nil, *n. Chem.* a bivalent radical consisting of a single atom each of sulfur and oxygen. Also *sulfinyl.*

thi·o·pen·tal, thī″o·pen′tal, *n. Pharm.* a barbiturate, $C_{11}H_{18}N_2O_2S$, administered intravenously as a sedative and hypnotic for surgical proceedings and psychotherapeutics. Also **thi·o·pen·tal so·di·um.**

thi·o·phene, thī′o·fēn″, *n.* [G. *thiophen.*] *Chem.* a colorless liquid, C_4H_4S, which is water-insoluble and similar to benzene, occurring in crude coal-tar benzene and used esp. for organic synthesis. Also **thi·o·phen,** thī′o·fen″.

thi·o·sul·fate, thī″ō·sul′fāt, *n. Chem.* any salt or ester of thiosulfuric acid, $H_2S_2O_3$, analogous to sulfuric acid, H_2SO_4.

thi·o·sul·fu·ric, thī″ō·sul·fūr′ik, *a. Chem.* noting or pertaining to an unstable acid, $H_2S_2O_3$, which may be regarded as sulfuric acid with one oxygen atom replaced by sulfur.

thi·o·u·ra·cil, thī″ō·ūr′a·sil, *n. Pharm.* an antithyroid agent, $C_4H_4N_2OS$, used in the treatment of thyrotoxicosis by reducing the production of hormones by the thyroid gland.

thi·o·u·re·a, thī″ō·ū·rē′a, thī″ūr′ē·a, *n. Chem.* a colorless crystalline substance, $(NH_2)_2CS$, with a bitter taste, regarded as urea with the oxygen replaced by sulfur, and used esp. in external medicines, organic synthesis, and photography. Also *thiocarbamide.*

third, thurd, *a.* [O.E. *thridda,* ordinal of *thrī,* E. *three.*] Following the second; being the ordinal of 3; being one of three equal parts into which anything is divided.—*n.* One of three equal parts; that which follows the second in series; in an automobile transmission, the third gear; *baseball,* third base. *Mus.* a tone on the third degree from a given tone, beginning the count with the first tone; the interval between such tones; the harmonic combination of such tones. *Usu. pl., law,* the third part of the personal property of a deceased husband, which under certain circumstances goes absolutely to the widow; loosely, a widow's dower.—**third·ly**, *adv.*

third base, *n. Baseball.* The base to which a base runner proceeds from second base; the position of the player defending the area around that base.—**third base·man**, *n.*

third class, *n.* The rank, class, or grade classified under second class; the cheapest accommodations, as on trains and ships; the U.S. postal classification which consists of printed matter as circulars and books, excluding regular periodicals and newspapers, weighing not more than 16 ounces and open to inspection.

third-class, thŭrd′klas′, thŭrd′kläs′, *a.* Of or belonging to the class next after the second; pertaining to the third grade of conveyances for travel.—*adv.*

third de·gree, *n.* The use of severe measures by the police or others in examining a person in order to get information or a confession; the degree of master in freemasonry.—**third-de·gree**, *a.*—*v.t.*—*third-degreed, third-degreeing.*

third-de·gree burn, *n.* A charring burn in which the epidermis is destroyed, exposing nerve endings.

third di·men·sion, *n.* Thickness or depth; the dimension that distinguishes a solid object from its two-dimensional representation or from a two-dimensional object; a quality or something that enhances reality or vividness.—**third-di·men·sion·al**, *a.*

third es·tate, *n.* The third order in a political hierarchy; traditionally, the common people, as distinguished from the nobility and clergy in England and France.

third force, *n.* A political power whose position is the middle ground between two political extremes.

third or·der, *n.* (*Often cap.*), *eccles.* a lay organization under the direction of a religious order.

third par·ty, *n.* A political party formed as an alternative to or independent from the two major political parties in a state having a two-party system; a person whose involvement in a legal suit or quarrel is not principal.

third per·son, *n. Gram.* A modification of a linguistic form, as a pronoun or verb, that is used by a writer or speaker in referring to the person or thing spoken about, as distinguished from the writer or speaker himself and from the one or ones spoken to; a set of such linguistic forms.—*a.* Being in such a linguistic form or pertaining to such a grammatical person, as: 'He,' 'it,' and 'they' are *third person* pronouns.

third rail, *n.* A conductor in the form of a supplementary rail, laid beside the rails of the track of an electric railroad, to carry the current.—**third-rail**, *a.*

third-rate, thŭrd′rāt′, *a.* Quite inferior.—**third-rat·er**, *n.*

thirl, thŭrl, *v.t., v.i.* [O.E. *thyrlian*] *Brit. dial.* To pierce; penetrate; to thrill.—*n. Brit. dial.* a hole or aperture.

thirst, thŭrst, *n.* [O.E. *thurst* = D. *dorst* = G. *durst*, thirst; akin to Goth. *thaurstei*, thirst, *thaursus*, dry, withered, also L. *torrere*, to dry, parch, Gr. *térsesthai*, become dry.] The distressing sensation of dryness in the mouth and throat caused by want or need of fluids; the physical condition resulting from this want; strong or eager desire; as, his *thirst* for power; a craving.—*v.i.* To feel thirst; be thirsty; to have a strong desire.—**thirst·er**, *n.*

thirst·y, thŭr′stē, *a.*—*thirstier, thirstiest.* [O.E. *thurstig.*] Having thirst; craving drink; wanting moisture, as land or plants; dry, parched, or arid; eagerly desirous, or eager.—**thirst·i·ly**, *adv.*—**thirst·i·ness**, *n.*

thir·teen, thŭr′tēn′, *n.* [O.E. *threótyne*, lit. 'three-ten.'] The cardinal number between twelve and fourteen; a symbol representing it; a set of thirteen persons or things.—*a.*

thir·teenth, thŭr′tēnth′, *a.* Following the twelfth; being the ordinal of 13; being one of 13 equal parts into which anything is divided.—*n.* One of 13 equal parts; that which follows the twelfth in a series.

thir·ti·eth, thŭr′tē·ith, *a.* Following the twenty-ninth; being the ordinal of 30; being one of 30 equal parts into which anything is divided.—*n.* One of 30 equal parts; that which follows the twenty-ninth in a series.

thir·ty, thŭr′tē, *n.* pl. **thir·ties**. [O.E. *thritting, thrítig*, < *threó, thré*, three, and *-tig*, ten = L. *decem*, Gr. *deka*, ten.] The cardinal number between 29 and 31; a symbol representing it; a set of 30 persons or things. *Pl.* the numbers between 30 and 39 inclusive; the years in the third decade of a lifetime or century.—*a.*

thir·ty-sec·ond note, thŭr′tē·sek′ond nōt″, *n. Mus.* a note with time value equaling $\frac{1}{32}$ of a whole note or semibreve. Also *demisemiquaver.*

thir·ty-three, thŭr′tē·thrē′, *n.* The cardinal number between 32 and 34; a symbol representing it; a set of 33 persons or things. An LP phonograph record; see *LP.*—*a.*

thir·ty-two-mo, thŭr″tē·tö′mō, *n.* pl. **thir·ty-two-mos**. A page size formed by folding a printer's sheet to give 32 leaves, and measuring about 3 × 5 inches; a book or page of this size.—*a.* Having pages of this size. Abbr. *32mo.* Also **tri·ges·i·mo-se·cun·do**.

this, THis, *pron.* pl. **these**. [O.E. *thes*, masc., *thēos*, fem., *this*, neut. (pl. *thās*, also *thǣs*) from the stem of *the* with suffix *-s* (earlier *-se, -si*) perh. identical with Goth. *sai*, see, behold.] A demonstrative term indicating or designating a person, thing, idea, or condition as being present, near, before mentioned, supposedly understood, or about to be mentioned; one of two persons, things, ideas, or conditions already mentioned, either referring to the one nearer in place, time, or thought, or implying mere contradistinction: opposed to *that.*—*a.*—*adv.* To the indicated extent or degree, used in place of the word *so* to modify adjectives and adverbs of quantity or extent; as, *this* much, *this* far, or *this* early.

this·tle, this′l, *n.* [O.E. *thistel* = D. and G. *distel* = Icel. *thistill*, thistle.] Any of numerous prickly plants of the genus *Carduus* and allied genera, esp. *Onopordum* and *Circium*, and belonging to the family *Compositae*, as *Circium arvense*, the 'Canada thistle,' an old world herb with small purple or white flower heads, which has spread to America and is one of the most troublesome of weeds; any of various other prickly plants.—**this·tly**, this′lē, this′e·lē, *a.*

this·tle·down, this′l·doun″, *n.* The silky down or pappus of the fruit of a thistle.

thith·er, THiTH′ėr, THITH′ėr, *adv.* [O.E. *thider*, Icel. *thathra*, thither, there; < demonst. stem seen in *the, that*, and suffix *ther = tra* in Skt. *tatra*, there, < root *tar*, to go.] To that place; toward, or in that direction.—*a.* Located on the other side; more distant.

thith·er·to, THiTH″ėr·tö′, THiTH″ėr·tö′, thiTH′ėr·tö″, THiTH′ėr·tö″, *adv.* Up to that time; until then.

thith·er·ward, THiTH′ėr·wėrd, THiTH′ėr·wėrd, *adv.* Toward that place. Also **thith·er·wards**.

thole, thōl, *n.* [O.E. *thol*, a thole-pin = Icel. *thollr*, a thole-pin, a wooden peg; L.G. *dolle*, D. *dol*, a thole.] A pin inserted into the gunwale of a boat to serve as a fulcrum for the oar in rowing. Also **thole·pin**, thōl′pin″.

tho·mi·sid, thō′mi·sid, *n.* One of the crab spiders of the family *Thomisidae.*

Tho·mist, tō′mist, thō′mist, *n.* A follower of the scholastic philosophy of Thomas Aquinas.—*a.*—**Tho·mism**, *n.*—**Tho·mis·tic**, *a.*

Thomp·son sub·ma·chine gun, tomp′son sub″ma·shēn′ gun″, tom′son, *n.* An automatic .45 caliber submachine gun. Also **tom·my gun**.

thong, thang, thong, *n.* [O.E. *thwang, thwong*, a thong; Icel. *thvengr*, a strap, a latchet.] A strap of leather used for fastening anything; a long narrow strip of leather or similar material; a whiplash.

tho·rac·ic duct, *n. Anat.* the largest lymphatic vessel in the body, located along the vertebral column and serving to convey lymph to the left subclavian vein, where it enters the circulatory system.

tho·ra·cos·to·my, thōr″a·kos′to·mē, thar″a·kos′to·mē, *n.* pl. **tho·ra·cos·to·mies**. *Surg.* the opening of the chest usu. for drainage.

tho·ra·cot·o·my, thōr″a·kot′o·mē, thar″a·kot′o·mē, *n.* pl. **tho·ra·cot·o·mies**. *Surg.* an incision of the chest wall.

tho·rax, thōr′aks, thar′aks, *n.* pl. **tho·rax·es**, **tho·ra·ces**, thōr′a·sēz″, thar′a·sēz″. [Gr. *thórax*, the chest, a breastplate.] The cavity of the body formed by the spine, ribs, and breastbone, and containing the lungs and heart; the chest; the corresponding portion of the body in animals; the portion of an insect between the head and abdomen. —**tho·rac·ic**, thō·ras′ik, tha·ras′ik, *a.*

tho·ri·a, thōr′ē·a, thar′ē·a, *n. Chem.* an oxide of thorium, ThO_2, a heavy white powder used in making incandescent mantles for gas burners and linings for crucibles. Also **tho·ri·um ox·ide, tho·ri·um di·ox·ide**.

tho·ri·a·nite, thōr′ē·a·nīt″, thar′ē·a·nīt″, *n.* A rare, radioactive mineral, occurring in small, black, cubic crystals, which consists largely of thorium oxide, but also contains the oxides of uranium, cerium, and similar rare metals.

tho·rite, thōr′īt, thar′īt, *n.* A mineral, thorium silicate, $ThSiO_4$, which occurs in black to brown or yellowish crystalline form.

tho·ri·um, thōr′ē·um, thar′ē·um, *n.* [From *Thor*, the Scand. deity.] *Chem.* a heavy, grayish, radioactive metallic element isolated from thorite and other rare minerals, used in alloys and for generating atomic energy. Sym. Th, at. no. 90, at. wt. 232.038. See Periodic Table of Elements.—**thor·ic**, thar′ik, thor′ik, *a.*

thorn, tharn, *n.* [O.E. *thorn* = D. *doorn* = G. *dorn* = Icel. *thorn* = Goth. *thaurnus*, thorn.] A sharp excrescence on a plant, esp. a sharp-pointed aborted branch; a spine; a prickle; a similar process on an animal; any of various thorny shrubs or trees, esp. the hawthorns of the genus *Crataegus*; something that wounds, or causes discomfort or annoyance. The Old English rune þ representing the Modern English sound of *th*, as in *thin*.—**thorn in the side**, the origin or cause of worry or annoyance.—**thorn·less**, *a.*—**thorn·like**, *a.*

thorn ap·ple, *n.* Certain poisonous plants belonging to the family *Solanaceae*, in the genus *Datura*, certain species of which bear capsules covered with prickly spines, esp. the jimson weed, *D. stramonium*; any fruit of various hawthorns belonging to the genus *Crataegus.*

thorn·back, tharn′bak″, *n.* A European ray, *Raia clavata*, with short spines on the back and tail; a ray, *Platyrhinoidis triseriatus*, found esp. in California, having spines along its back; a large crab, *Maia squinado*, of Europe.

---

thorn·y, thȧr'nē, *a.—thornier, thorniest.*
Full of thorns, spines, or prickles; prickly;
vexatious; harassing; full of problems or
difficulties.—**thorn·i·ness,** *n.*

tho·ron, thōr'on, thȧr'on, *n. Chem.* a gaseous
element which is produced from thorium
and is a radioactive isotope of randon.
Sym. Tn, at. no. 86. See Periodic Table of
Elements.

thor·ough, thur'ō, thur'ō, *a.* [Same deriv.
as *through.*] Carried completely through to
the end; as, a *thorough* study of the matter;
complete or perfect; as, *thorough* fulfillment;
marked by detailed and accurate attention;
as, *thorough* research; characterized as being
very careful and accurate; as, a *thorough*
housekeeper; being fully accomplished in a
field, as: He was a *thorough* artist. Also
colloq. **thor·o.—thor·ough·ly,** *adv.—***thor·-
ough·ness,** *n.*

thor·ough bass, *n. Mus.* The method of
expressing chords by means of figures
placed under a given bass line, indicating
the harmony through all the other parts of
each chord; the figured bass line.

thor·ough brace, *n.* Either of two strong
braces or bands of leather supporting the
body of a coach or other vehicle and usu.
serving as a spring.

thor·ough·bred, thur'ō·bred″, thur'o·-
bred″, thur'ō·bred″, thur'o·bred″, *a.* Of
pure or unmixed breed, stock, or race, as a
horse or other animal; bred from the purest
and best stock; (*usu. cap.*) pertaining to or
being one of an English breed of race
horses, having the pedigree officially recorded in the studbook for a given number
of generations. Having qualities characteristic of pure breeding; high-spirited;
mettlesome; elegant or graceful in form or
bearing; of a person, thoroughly educated,
trained, or accomplished.—*n.*

thor·ough·fare, thur'ō·fâr″, thur'o·fâr″,
thur'ō·fâr″, thur'o·fâr″, *n.* [O.E. *thurhfaru.*]
An unobstructed way, esp. an unobstructed
road or street for public traffic; passage or
the right of passing; a waterway that
affords passage.

thor·ough·go·ing, thur'ō·gō″ing, thur'o·-
gō″ing, thur'ō·gō″ing, thur'o·gō″ing, *a.*
Going or ready to go to all lengths; zealous;
absolute or unmitigated; as, a *thoroughgoing*
rascal.—**thor·ough·go·ing·ly,** *adv.—***thor·-
ough·go·ing·ness,** *n.*

thor·ough·paced, thur'ō·pāst″, thur'o·-
pāst″, thur'ō·pāst″, thur'o·pāst″, *a.* Trained
to go through all the paces, as a well-trained
horse; thoroughgoing; consummate.

thor·ough·pin, thur'ō·pin″, thur'o·pin″,
thur'ō·pin″, thur'o·pin″, *n. Veter. pathol.* a
swelling just above the hock of a horse, usu.
appearing on both sides of the leg so as to
resemble a pin passing through, and sometimes causing lameness.

thor·ough·wort, thur'ō·wurt″, thur'o·-
wurt″, thur'ō·wurt″, thur'o·wurt″, *n.* A
boneset.

thou, THou, *pron.—sing. nom. thou,* poss.
thy or *thine,* obj. *thee;* pl. nom. *you* or *ye,*
poss. *your* or *yours,* obj. *you* or *ye;* intens.
and refl. *thyself.* [O.E. *thú,* genit. *thin,* dat.
and acc. *thé,* nom. pl. *gé,* genit. *eówer,*
dat. and acc. *eów;* Icel. *thú,* Goth. *thu,* D.,
Dan., and G. *du;* L. *tu,* Gr. *su,* Goth. *tu,*
Slav. *ti,* W. *ti,* Gael. *tu,* thou.] The second
person singular personal pronoun in the
nominative, used to indicate the person
spoken to, now restricted to poetic, Biblical,
or ecclesiastic style, or to use among the
Friends or Quakers, the plural form *you*
being universally substituted for it.—*v.t.* To
use this form of address to.

thou, thou, *n.* pl. **thou, thous.** *Slang,* 1,000,
esp. of dollars.

though, THō, *conj.* [O.E. *theáh,* though =
Icel. *thó,* Dan. *dog,* D. and G. *doch,* Goth.
thauh, though; < stem of *that, the.*] Not-

withstanding that; while; although, as:
Though the sun shone, it was still cold.
Granting or allowing it to be the fact that,
often preceded by *even.* Also *colloq.* **tho.—**
adv. However; for all that.—**as though,** as if.

thought, thȧt, *n.* [O.E. *thoht, gethoht,* <
thencan, to think, pret. *thohte,* pp. *gethoht;*
Icel. *thótti,* G. *gedacht.*] The act or power
of thinking; cogitation; meditation; as, lost
in *thought;* that which is thought; an idea;
a conception; a judgment; a fancy; deliberation or reflection, as: It takes some *thought.*
Purpose or intention; as, have some *thought*
of moving; expectation; as, no *thought* of
recovering it; view or opinion; as, give my
thought on the matter.

thought·ful, thȧt'ful, *a.* Full of thought;
contemplative; meditative; attentive; careful; mindful; solicitous; considerate.—
thought·ful·ly, *adv.—***thought·ful·ness,** *n.*

thought·less, thȧt'lis, *a.* Exhibiting a lack
of thought or care; heedless; negligent;
inconsiderate.—**thought·less·ly,** *adv.—*
thought·less·ness, *n.*

thought-out, thȧt'out′, *a.* Produced by
deliberate, careful thought.

thou·sand, thou'zand, *n.* pl. **thou·sand,
thou·sands,** *n.* [O.E. *thusend* = Icel.
thus-hund, thus-hundrath, Dan. *tusind,* D.
duizend, Goth. *thusundi,* G. *tausend.*] The
cardinal number between 999 and 1,001;
a symbol representing this number; a set
of 1,000 persons or things; an unspecified
very large number or great amount.—*a.—*
thou·sandth, thou'zandth, *a., n.*

Thou·sand Is·land dress·ing, *n.* A salad
dressing made with mayonnaise, ketchup,
olives, pickles, and other seasonings.

thrall, thrȧl, *n.* [O.E. *thrael* = Icel. *thraell,*
Sw. *träl,* Dan. *trael,* a serf, a slave.] One in
bondage; slave; serf; the condition of enslavement.—*v.t. Archaic,* to put or hold in
bondage.

thrall·dom, thral·dom, thrȧl'dom, *n.* The
state or condition of being a thrall; bondage; servitude.

thrash, thrash, *v.t.* [O.E. *threscan, therscan,*
to thrash (corn), to beat = Icel. *threskja,*
Sw. *tröska,* Dan. *taerske,* D. *dorschen,* G.
dreschen, Goth. *thriskan;* cf. Lith. *trasketi,*
to rattle.] To beat soundly with a stick or
whip; to defeat completely; thresh.—*v.i.*
To toss about or move violently; thresh;
naut. to make one's way in opposition to the
tide or wind.—*n.* An instance or act of
thrashing; *swimming,* a kick used in the
crawl or backstroke.—**thrash o·ver** or **out,**
to go or talk over again and again in order
to reach a conclusion or solution.—
thrash·er, thrash'ėr, *n.—***thrash·ing,** *n.*

thrash·er, thrash'ėr, *n.* [Also *thrusher:* cf.
thrush.] *Zool.* Any of various long-tailed
thrushlike birds, esp. of the genus *Toxos-
toma,* allied to the mockingbird, as the
brown thrasher, *T. rufum,* an American
song bird commonly found in shrubbery;
the thresher shark.

thra·son·i·cal, thrȧ·son'i·kal, *a.* [From
Thraso, a boaster in old comedy.] Given to
bragging; boastful.—**thra·son·i·cal·ly,**
adv.

thread, thred, *n.* [O.E. *thraed,* lit. 'what is
twisted,' < *thráwan,* to twist, to throw;
similarly Icel. *thrádr,* Dan. *traad,* D. *draad,*
G. *draht,* thread.] A fine cord, esp. such as
is used for sewing; a cord consisting of the
twisted filaments of a fibrous substance,
such as cotton, flax, silk, or wool, spun out
into a slender line; anything resembling
this; any slender filament; continued
course or tenor; as, the *thread* of discourse; the prominent spiral part of a
screw.—*v.t.* To pass a thread through the
eye or aperture of; to pass or go through,
as a narrow way.—*v.i.—***thread·er,** *n.—*
thread·less, *a.—***thread·like,** *a.*

thread·bare, thred'bâr′, *a.* Having the nap

worn off so as to show the separate threads;
poor; shabby; trite; hackneyed.—**thread·-
bare·ness,** *n.*

thread·fin, thred'fin″, *n.* Any of the acanthopterygian fishes constituting the family
Polynemidae, as the barbudo, in which the
lower part of the pectoral fin is composed of
numerous separate slender filaments.

thread·worm, thred'wurm″, *n.* Any of
various nematode worms, esp. a pinworm.

thread·y, thred'ē, *a.—threadier, threadiest.*
Like thread; filamentous; containing
thread; stringy; feeble, as a pulse; without
fullness, as a voice.—**thread·i·ness,** *n.*

threat, thret, *n.* [O.E. *threat,* threat, punishment; < stem of O.E. *threotan,* to tire,
harass; Goth. *thriutan,* G. (*ver*) *drieszen,* to
annoy; allied to L. *trudo,* to thrust (in
intrude).] A menace, as a thing or person;
a declaration of an intention to inflict
punishment, loss, or pain on another; a
warning or sign of impending danger or
damage; as, a *threat* of a tornado.—*v.t., v.i.
Archaic,* to threaten.

threat·en, thret'en, *v.t.* To use threats
toward; to declare threats of, as injury; to
menace; to act menacingly towards; to
exhibit the appearance of bringing something evil or unpleasant on, as: The clouds
threaten us with rain. To show to be impending, as: The sky *threatens* a storm.—
v.i. To utter or employ threats or menaces.
—**threat·en·er,** *n.—***threat·en·ing·ly,** *adv.*

three, thrē, *n.* [O.E. *thri, threo* = Goth.
threis, Icel. *thrir,* Dan. *tre,* D. *drie,* G. *drei;*
cogn. W., Ir., and Gael. *tri,* Lith. *trys,* L.
tres, Gr. *treis,* Skt. *tri.*] The cardinal
number between two and four; the symbol
representing it; a set of three persons or
things.—*a.*

three-base hit, thrē'bās″ hit′, *n. Baseball,* a
hit ball which allows the batter to gain third
base. Also *triple.*

three-col·or, thrē'kul'ėr, *a.* Having, or
characterized by the use of, three colors;
specif. pertaining to a photomechanical
process for making reproductions of colored
pictures, usu. carried out by making three
plates or printing surfaces, each corresponding to a primary color, by the halftone
process, and then making superimposed
impressions from these plates in three
correspondingly colored inks.

3-D, thrē'dē′, *a. Colloq.* referring to something in three-dimensional form or appearance, as in motion pictures.—*n.*

three-deck·er, thrē'dek'ėr, *n.* Any ship
with three decks; formerly, a vessel of war
carrying guns on three decks; a sandwich
consisting of three pieces of bread and two
layers of filling; anything having three
decks, tiers, or layers.

three-di·men·sion·al, thrē'di·men'sha·-
nal, *a.* Referring to something which lies or
seems to lie in all three planes of height,
width, and depth.

three·fold, thrē'fōld″, *a.* Consisting of
three in one; triple.—*adv.—***three-fold,** *n.
Theater,* three flats joined by hinges to form
a unit.

three-gaited, thrē'gā'tid, *a.* Of a horse
trained to walk, trot, and canter.

three-leg·ged, thrē'leg'id, thrē'legd′, *a.*
Having or possessing three legs; as, a *three-
legged* swivel chair.

three-mile lim·it, thrē'mīl″ lim'it, *n.*
Three miles of coastal water extending from
the shoreline out, over which a state has
jurisdiction under international law.

three·pence, thrip'ens, threp'ens, thrup'ens,
thrē'pens″, *n.* A minor coin of Great
Britain.—**three·pen·ny,** thrip'e·nē, threp'-
e·nē, thrup'e·nē, thrē'pen″ē, *a.* Worth
three pence; of little worth.—*n. Carp.* a
nail, either one and one-fourth inches or
one and one-eighth inches in length.

three-phase, thrē'fāz″, *a. Elect.* pertaining

to a system of alternating current supply, in which there are three circuits differing in phase from each other by 120° or one third of a cycle or revolution.

three-piece, thrē'pēs', *a.* Pertaining to an ensemble or grouping of three coordinated pieces, as a set of furniture; in three parts.

three-ply, thrē'plī', *a.* Consisting of three strands, or three thicknesses.

three-point land·ing, thrē'point" lan'ding, *n. Aeron.* an airplane landing executed so that all three wheels of the craft simultaneously touch the runway; *fig.* any perfect completion or successful result.

three-quar·ter, thrē'kwar'tér, *a.* Consisting of or involving three quarters of a whole; as, a *three-quarter* portrait; pertaining to a facial view somewhat fuller than a profile but not full face.—*n.*

three-quar·ter bind·ing, *n. Bookbinding,* a binding in which the material covering the spine extends over a third of the front and back covers.

three-ring cir·cus, thrē'ring" sur'kus, *n.* A circus in which simultaneous acts occur in three rings; any occasion characterized by a confusion of simultaneously occurring activities. Also **three-ringed cir·cus.**

three R's, *n. pl.* An expression for reading, 'riting, and 'rithmetic, regarded as the fundamentals of education.

three·score, thrē'skōr', thrē'skar', *a.* Of or having three times twenty; sixty.

three·some, thrē'som, *a.* Consisting of three; threefold; performed or played by three persons.—*n.* Three forming a group; something in which three persons participate; *golf,* a match in which one player, playing his own ball, plays against two opponents with one ball, the latter playing alternate strokes.

three-square, thrē'skwâr', *a.* Having an equilateral triangular cross section, as certain files.

threm·ma·tol·o·gy, threm"a·tol'o·jē, *n.* [Gr. *thrémma* (*thremmat-*), nursling.] *Biol.* the science of breeding or propagating animals and plants under domestication.

thren·o·dy, thren'o·dē, *n. pl.* **thren·o·dies.** [Gr. *thrēnōdía,* < *thrēnos,* dirge, lament, and *aeidein,* sing.] A song of lamentation, esp. a lament for the dead; a funeral song. Also **thre·node.—thre·no·di·al, thre··nod·ic,** thri·nō'dē·al, thri·nod'ik, *a.—* **thren·o·dist,** thren'o·dist, *n.*

thre·o·nine, thrē'o·nēn", thrē'o·nin, *n. Biochem.* an amino acid, $C_4H_9NO_3$, considered to be essential to nutrition.

thresh, thresh, *v.t.* To beat out, as grain, by striking the stalks with a flail or by passing them through a threshing machine; to beat or whip; to thrash.—*v.i.* To thresh or beat grain; to thrash or toss about.

thresh·er, thresh'ér, *n.* One who or that which threshes; one who separates seeds from wheat or other grain by beating with a flail or using a threshing machine; a device or machine for this purpose; *zool.* a warm seas shark, *Alopias vulpes,* also known as a thresher shark or fox shark, with an elongated upper lobe of the tail used to thresh the water to round up small feeder fish. Also **thrash·er.**

thresh·ing ma·chine, *n. Agric.* a mechanical grain harvester which removes grain from the straw. Also **thrash·ing ma··chine.**

thresh·old, thresh'ōld, thresh'hōld, *n.* [O.E. *therscwald, therscold, therxold,* < *therscan,* to thrash or thresh, and apparently *wald,* a wood, timber, because this bar was threshed or trod upon by the feet.] A doorsill; the stone or piece of timber which lies under a door; entrance; beginning; outset; as, the *threshold* of an argument. *Psychol., physiol.* the point at which a stimulus to the sensory organism is just sufficiently intense to be

felt; as, the *threshold* of consciousness; also *limen.*

thrice, thrīs, *adv.* [O.E. *thries, thryes,* < *thrie,* three, with genit. term., like *once, twice.*] Three times; of threefold importance or amount; emphatically or intensely; as, *thrice* blessed.

thrift, thrift, *n.* [Cf. Icel. *thrift* and E. *thrive.*] Economical management, conservation of resources, economy, or frugality. *Bot.* any of the alpine and maritime plants, belonging to the genus *Armeria,* and in the family *Plumbaginaceae,* with pink or white flowers, esp. *A. maritima,* notable for its vigorous growth; see *statice.* Any of various allied plants; *rare,* vigorous growth, as of a plant.

thrift·shop, thrift'shop", *n.* A store selling secondhand merchandise usu. for charity at a reduced cost.

thrift·y, thrif'tē, *a.—***thriftier, thriftiest.** Practicing or having thrift; careful in conserving resources; frugal; economical; prosperous or thriving; growing with vigor. **—thrift·i·ly,** *adv.—***thrift·i·ness,** *n.*

thrill, thril, *v.t.* [O.E. *thyrlian, thyrelian* (< *thirl, thyrel,* a hole = *tril* of nos*tril*), to pierce = D. *drillen,* to bore, to drill troops (whence E. to *drill*); same root as *through.*] To affect with a keen emotion, as of delight or excitement; to cause to tremble or quiver. —*v.i.* To produce a tingling sensation; to act tremulously; to vibrate; to feel a shivering sensation running through the body; to shiver; to quiver or move with a tremulous movement.—*n.* A thrilling sensation; that which causes a thrilling sensation.—**thrill·er,** thril'ér, *n.* A mystery or suspense story.—**thrill·ful, thrill·ing,** thril'ing, *a.—***thrill·ing·ly,** *adv.*

thrips, thrips, *n. pl.* **thrips.** [L. < Gr. *thrips,* a woodworm.] Any of numerous small insects of the order *Thysanoptera,* characterized by long, narrow wings fringed with hairs; certain species, esp. those in the family *Thripidae,* which are destructive to many cultivated plants.

thrive, thrīv, *v.i.—*past *throve* or *thrived,* pp. *thrived* or *thriven,* ppr. *thriving.* [< Icel. *thrífask,* to thrive (a refl. verb, *sk* meaning self, as in *bask*), whence also *thrift;* Dan. *trives,* to thrive.] To prosper or succeed; to be fortunate; to increase in goods and estate; to keep increasing one's acquisitions; to be marked by prosperity; as, a business which *thrives;* to go on or turn out well; to have a good issue; to grow vigorously; to flourish.—**thriv·er,** *n.—* **thriv·ing,** *a.—***thriv·ing·ly,** *adv.*

throat, thrōt, *n.* [O.E. *throte;* akin to G. *drossel,* the throat, the throttle; cf. D. *strot,* throat; hence *throttle.*] The passage that leads from the nose and mouth to the lungs and stomach and includes the esophagus, the fauces, and pharynx; the front part of the neck; any of various narrow channels or parts, as the orifice or opening of a plant tubule, the curved opening between fireplace and chimney flue, or the section of a tennis racket where the handle meets the head.—*v.t.* To give a throat to; to express or give out gutturally, or from one's throat. **—cut one's own throat,** *colloq.* to be the cause of one's own downfall.—**cut some··one's throat,** *colloq.* to bring about another's ruin or downfall.—**jump down some·one's throat,** *colloq.* To be suddenly and vehemently critical; to berate.—**lump in one's throat,** a sensation of a constriction or obstruction in the throat, due to emotion.— **ram some·thing down one's throat,** *colloq.* to coerce another into agreement with or acceptance of something.—**stick in one's throat,** to resist expression, as words one hesitates to utter; to be painful or difficult to accept or, figuratively speaking, to swallow.—**throat·ed,** *a.*

throat·latch, thrōt'lach", *n.* A strap which passes under a horse's throat and helps to hold a bridle or halter in place.

throat·y, thrō'tē, *a.* Of utterances, having a husky or guttural sound.—**throat·i·ly,** *adv.—***throat·i·ness,** *n.*

throb, throb, *v.i.—*throbbed, throbbing. [O.E. *throbbe;* origin doubtful.] To beat, as the heart or pulse, with more than usual force or rapidity; to show, exhibit, or feel emotion; to palpitate, quiver, or vibrate.—*n.* A beat or strong pulsation; palpitation.— **throb·ber,** *n.*

throe, thrō, *n.* [M.E. *throwe, thrawe:* cf. O.E. *thrawu, thrēa,* oppression, affliction, *thrōwian,* suffer, also *thrāwan,* twist, rack, E. *throw.*] A violent spasm or pang; a paroxysm; a sharp attack of emotion. *Pl.* the pains of childbirth; the agony of death; any violent convulsion or struggle.

throm·bin, throm'bin, *n.* [Gr. *thrómbos,* lump, clot.] *Biochem.* The enzyme which causes the coagulation of blood; a preparation to control capillary bleeding. Also **throm·base.**

throm·bo·cyte, throm'bo·sīt", *n. Physiol.* any blood platelet.—**throm·bo·cyt·ic,** throm"bo·sit'ik, *a.*

throm·bo·em·bo·lism, throm"bō·em'bo·--liz"um, *n. Pathol.* an embolus which has dislodged from the thrombus and is blocking any blood vessel.

throm·bo·gen, throm'bo·jen", *n. Biochem.* prothrombin.

throm·bo·phle·bi·tis, throm"bō·fli·bī'tis, *n. Pathol.* the inflammation of any blood vessel accompanied by a thrombus.

throm·bo·plas·tic, throm"bo·plas'tik, *a. Biochem.* bringing about or speeding up the formation of blood clots.—**throm·bo··plas·ti·cal·ly,** *adv.*

throm·bo·plas·tin, throm"bo·plas'tin, *n. Biochem.* lipoprotein that promotes blood clotting and is esp. found in blood platelets. Also **throm·bo·ki·nase,** throm"bō·kī'nās, throm"bō·kin'ās.

throm·bo·sis, throm·bō'sis, *n. pl.* **throm··bo·ses.** [N.L., < Gr. *thrómbōsis,* a curdling, < *thrómbos,* E. *thrombus.*] *Pathol.* A coagulation of the blood in a blood vessel or in the heart during life; the formation or existence of a thrombus.—**throm·bot·ic,** throm·bot'-ik, *a.*

throm·bus, throm'bus, *n. pl.* **throm·bi,** throm'bī. [L. < Gr. *thrómbos,* a clot.] *Pathol.* a fibrinous clot of blood which forms in and obstructs a blood vessel.

throne, thrōn, *n.* [O.Fr. *trone* (Fr. *trône*), < L. *thronus,* < Gr. *thrónes,* seat, throne.] The chair or seat occupied by a sovereign, bishop, or other exalted personage on occasions of state, esp. the seat occupied by a sovereign on ceremonial occasions, being usu. more or less ornate and raised on a dais and covered with a canopy; the office or dignity of a sovereign; sovereign power or authority; episcopal office or authority; the occupant of a throne; a sovereign; *pl.* one of the orders of angels.—*v.t., v.i.—throned, throning.* To place or sit on or as on a throne.—**throne·less,** *a.*

throne room, *n.* A formal chamber or room which holds a sovereign's throne.

throng, thrang, throng, *n.* [O.E. *thrang, throng,* a crowd, < *thringan,* to crowd; Icel. *thröng,* G. *drang,* a crowd, distress; D. and G. *dringen,* to crowd.] A multitude of persons pressed into a close body; a crowd; a great number; a number of things crowded or close together.—*v.i.* To crowd together; to come in multitudes.—*v.t.* To crowd or press; to annoy with a crowd of living beings; to fill with a crowd.

thros·tle, thros'l, *n.* [A dim. corresponding to *thrush;* O.E. *throstle,* G. and Dan. *drossel,* a thrush.] *Brit., ornith.* a literary name for the song thrush, *Turdus ericetorum,* a European bird having a flutelike song; also **ma·vis.** A kind of spinning machine.

throt·tle, throt′l, *v.t.*—throttled, throttling. [M.E. *throtelen,* appar. < *throte,* E. *throat.*] To stop the breath of by compressing the throat; to strangle; to choke or suffocate in any way; to compress by fastening something tightly about; to silence or check as if by choking. *Mech.* to obstruct the flow of, as steam, by means of a valve; to decrease the speed of, as an engine, by diminishing the fuel supply in this way.—*v.i.* To undergo suffocation; to choke.—*n. Mech.* a handle, lever, or pedal for volume control of fuel or steam in an internal-combustion or steam engine; also **throt·tle valve.** *Mech.* the lever that controls this handle or valve; *rare,* the throat, gullet, or windpipe. —**throt·tler,** *n.*

through, thru, thrö, *prep.* [O.E. *thurh, thuruh,* = O.S. *thurh* = O.H.G. *duruh* (G. *durch*), through, akin to Goth. *thairh,* through: cf. *thirl* and *thorough.*] In at one end, side, or surface, and out at the other; as, to pass *through* a doorway; from one end or side to the other; as, to bore a hole *through* a board; with passage or course within the limits of, or between or among the individual members or parts of; as, *through* the water, trees, or grass; here and there, or everywhere, over the surface or within the limits of; as, to travel *through* a country; during the whole period of; as, to enjoy health *through* life; from the beginning to the end of or along the whole course of; as, *through* a book; having reached the farther end or the conclusion of; as, to be *through* one's work; having finished successfully; as, to get *through* an examination; by reason of or in consequence of; as, to run away *through* fear; by the means or instrumentality of, as: It was *through* him they found out.—*adv.* In at one end, side, or surface and out at the other; as, an apple with a knife stuck *through*; from one end or side of a thing to the other; as, to cut a thing *through*; all the way, or along the whole distance; as, this train goes *through* to Boston; through the whole extent, thickness, or substance, or throughout; as, chilled *through*; from the beginning to the end; as, to read a letter *through*; to the end or the purposed conclusion; as, to carry a matter *through*; to a favorable or successful conclusion; as, to pull *through*; having reached the farther end; having completed an action or process; being completed or finished, as an action.—*a.* Passing or extending from one end, side, or surface to the other, as a bolt; pertaining to that which extends, goes, or conveys through the whole of a long distance with little or no interruption; as, a *through* train; finished, as: He is *through* with my book.

through·out, thrö·out′, *prep.* In, or to every part of, as: There was rejoicing *throughout* the city. Everywhere in; from the beginning to the end of, as: It rained *throughout* the day.—*adv.* In or to every part; as, dark *throughout*; at every moment or point, as: The party was well planned *throughout.* Through the whole time or action, as: The troops fought courageously *throughout.*

through street, *n.* A thoroughfare on which vehicles do not have to yield the right of way to cross traffic.

through·way, thrö′wā″, *n.* Thruway.

throw, thrō, *v.t.*—past *threw,* pp. *thrown,* ppr. *throwing.* [O.E. *thrāwan,* twist, turn, rack, = D. *draaien* = G. *drehen,* turn: cf. *thread.*] To project or propel forcibly through the air by a sudden jerk or straightening of the arm; to fling or toss; to propel or cast in any way; to hurl or project, as a missile fired by a gun; to project or cast, as light or a shadow; to exert or use, as

influence or authority; as, to *throw* one's influence into the case; to direct, as a glance; to cause to go or come into some place, position, or condition, as if by throwing; as, to *throw* a man into prison, to *throw* a bridge across a river, to *throw* troops into action; to put on hastily; as, to *throw* a shawl over one's shoulders. *Mach.* to move, as a lever, in order to connect or disconnect parts of an apparatus or mechanism; to connect, engage, disconnect, or disengage by such a procedure. To shape, as clay, on a potter's wheel; to discharge, as a blow in a prize-fight; to play, as a card; to bring to the ground, as an opponent in a wrestling match; *colloq.* to permit an opponent to win, as a game, unnecessarily or in accordance with a previous agreement. To cast; as, to *throw* dice; to make, as a cast, at dice; to cause to fall off, as: That horse *throws* any rider. To give birth to, as the young of domestic animals; to twist into thread, as raw silk; *colloq.* to upset, as: Don't let the bad news *throw* you. *Slang,* to give or act as host for; as, to *throw* a party.—*v.i.* To cast, fling, or hurl something.—*n.* An act of throwing or casting; a cast or a fling; the distance to which anything is or may be thrown; as, a stone's *throw* away. *Mach.* the movement of a reciprocating part or the like from its control position to its extreme position in either direction, or the distance traversed; the radius of a crank to which an eccentric is equivalent. The distance traveled by the images from a projector to a movie screen, as in a movie theater; a cast at dice, or the number thrown; a hazard or venture; a lightweight cover or spread; as, a *throw* for a couch; a woman's scarf or boa; *wrestling,* the maneuver by which an opponent is thrown; *geol., min.* the amount of vertical displacement produced by a fault. —**throw cold wa·ter on,** to raise objections to the point of discouragement.—**throw in the sponge** or **tow·el,** to admit defeat.— **throw one·self at,** to make obvious attempts to win the romantic attentions of, as a woman toward a man.—**throw one·self in·to,** to attack enthusiastically, as a task.— **throw one·self on** or **up·on,** to seek the consideration or mercy of another, as that of a court.—**throw o·pen,** *fig.* to waive any restriction; as, to *throw open* a meeting for discussion.—**throw o·ver,** to cast off relations with; as, to *throw over* an admirer.—**throw to·geth·er,** to assemble or put together haphazardly, as a meal.—**throw·er,** thrō′ẽr, *n.*

throw a·way, *v.t.* To discard; to spend recklessly; squander; to waste, as an opportunity.

throw·a·way, thrō′a·wā″, *n.* A circular, leaflet, or handbill containing advertising matter, which is distributed door-to-door, or handed out on the street.

throw·back, thrō′bak″, *n.* An act of throwing back; a setback or check; reversion to an ancestral type or character.—**throw back,** *v.i.* To revert to an ancestral type or character; exhibit atavism.—*v.t.* To set back or check, as one's progress or accomplishment; to force to be dependent.

throw in, *v.t.* To put in as an addition; to add, esp. without charge, as in a sale or bargain; *mech.* to engage, as a clutch.—*v.i.* To come into close association, followed by *with.*

throw off, *v.t.* To cast off or aside; to discard; to reject; to elude by deception, as in a chase; to send forth, as heat; to bring forth effortlessly; to perplex or befuddle.—*v.i.* To make disparaging comments, followed by *on.*

throw out, *v.t.* To cast out; to reject or discard; to insinuate or utter; as, to *throw out* a hint; to emit; to disengage, as a mechanical part; *baseball,* to put out, as a runner or batter, by making a throw to a teammate. To eject, esp. by force.

throw rug, *n.* Scatter rug.

throw·ster, thrō′stẽr, *n.* One who throws or makes threads of silk or synthetic fibers.

throw up, *v.t.* To erect or build rapidly; to resign, usu. in haste and frustration; to abandon; to reproach; to vomit, as food.— *v.i.* To vomit.

thrum, thrum, *v.i.*—thrummed, thrumming. To play on a stringed instrument, as a guitar, by plucking the strings, esp. in an idle, monotonous, or unskillful manner; to sound when thrummed on, as a guitar; to drum or tap idly with the fingers.—*v.t.* To play, as a stringed instrument, by plucking the strings, esp. in an idle, monotonous, or unskillful manner; to recite or tell in a monotonous way; to drum or tap idly on.—*n.* The act or sound of thrumming; any dull, monotonous sound.—**thrum·mer,** *n.*

thrum, thrum, *n.* [M.E. *throm* = D. *drom* = G. *trumm,* thrum.] One of the ends of the warp threads in a loom, left unwoven and remaining attached to a loom when the web is cut off; any short piece of waste thread or yarn; a tuft, tassel, or fringe of threads, as at the edge of a piece of cloth; *pl.* the row or fringe of such threads; *pl., naut.* short bits of rope yarn used for roughening canvas or preventing chafing.—*v.t.*—thrummed, thrumming. *Naut.* to insert short pieces of rope yarn through, as a piece of canvas, and thus give it a rough surface, so that it may be wrapped around a part to prevent chafing.

thrush, thrush, *n.* [O.E. *thrisc,* a thrush; akin to Icel. *thröstr,* Sw. *trost,* Russ. *drozd*; same root as L. *turdus,* a thrush. *Throstle* is a dim. form.] A passerine bird, family *Turdidae,* of various species, esp. the wood thrush, robin, and hermit thrush, and celebrated as a songbird; any of several unrelated birds, as the water thrush.

thrush, thrush, *n.* [Cf. Dan. *tröske,* Sw. *torsk,* thrush.] *Pathol.* a disease, esp. in children, characterized by whitish spots and ulcers on the membranes of the mouth, fauces, or the like, due to a parasitic fungus, *Candida albicans; veter. pathol.* a diseased condition of the frog of a horse's foot.

thrust, thrust, *v.t.*—thrust, thrusting. [M.E. *thrusten, thristen,* < Scand.: cf. Icel. *thrýsta,* thrust, press.] To push forcibly, shove, or drive; to impel; to put or drive with force, as into some thing or opening; as, to *thrust* a knife into an apple; to put forth or extend in some direction; to put forcibly, as a person, into some position or condition; as, to *thrust* oneself into danger; to interpose, as: She *thrust* in her opinion. To stab or pierce, as with a sword.—*v.i.* To push against something; to push or force one's way, as against obstacles, through a crowd, or between persons; to make a thrust, lunge, or stab at something.—*n.* An act of thrusting; a forcible push or drive; a lunge or stab; *mech., arch.* a pushing force or pressure exerted by a thing or part against a contiguous one, specif. the force exerted in a lateral direction by an arch and tending to overturn the abutments; *geol.* a horizontal fault; *milit.* an attack.—**thrust·er,** thrus′tẽr, *n.*

thru·way, thrö′wā″, *n.* A divided, high-speed highway uninterrupted by grade crossings and with limited access and exit facilities. Also *throughway.*

thud, thud, *v.i., v.t.*—thudded, thudding. [Appar. imit.: cf. O.E. *thyddan,* strike, thrust.] To beat or strike with a dull sound of heavy impact.—*n.* A dull sound, as of a heavy blow or fall; a blow causing such a sound.

thug, thug, *n.* [Hind. *thag,* cheat, robber, thug.] (*l.c.*) a cutthroat; a ruffian. (*Often cap.*) one of a former body of professional robbers and murderers in India, who strangled their victims.—**thug·ger·y**, **thug·gism**, thug'e·rē, n.—**thug·gish**, a.

thug·gee, thug'ē, n. [Hind. thagī.] (Often cap.) The system or practices of the thugs.

thu·ja, thō'ja, n. [N.L. Thuja, Thuya, < Gr. thuia, thúia, kind of Afr. tree.] Any of the evergreen coniferous trees and shrubbery of the genus Thuja, esp. T. occidentalis, the common arborvitae which yields a medicinal oil. Also **thu·ya**, thō'ya.

thu·li·um, thō'lē·um, n. Chem. a metallic element of the rare-earth series. Sym. Tm, at. no. 69, at. wt. 168.934. See Periodic Table of Elements.

thumb, thum, n. [O.E. thūma = D. duim = G. daumen; thumb; prob. meaning orig. 'big or thick (finger),' and akin to L. tumere, swell.] The short, thick, opposable inner digit of the human hand, next to the forefinger; the pollex; the extension of a glove or mitten which covers the thumb. Ornith. the movable radial digit of a bird's wing; the hind toe of a bird. Arch. an ovolo.—v.t. To soil or wear with the thumbs in handling, as the pages of a book; to leaf through quickly, as the pages of a book; to handle, play, or perform clumsily; colloq. to signal, as a request for a ride in a passing car, by gesturing with the thumb.—v.i. Colloq. to hitchhike.—**all thumbs**, colloq. clumsy or awkward with the hands.—**thumbs down**, colloq. an expression of denial or disapproval.—**thumbs up**, colloq. an expression of acceptance or approval.—**un·der one's thumb, un·der the thumb of**, subject to the persuasion or power of.—**thumb one's nose**, to signal, as defiance or scorn, by putting the thumb to the nose and extending the fingers.—**thumb·less**, a.—**thumb·like**, a.

thumb in·dex, n. Notches scalloped from a book's fore edge which indicate sections or divisions.—**thumb-in·dex**, thum'in'deks, v.t.

thumb·nail, thum'nāl", n. The nail of the thumb; anything of the size of a thumbnail, or quite small or brief, as a drawing or a short essay.—a.—v.t.

thumb·print, thum'print", n. A mark, print, or impression of the thumb.

thumb·screw, thum'skrö", n. A screw that may be turned by the finger and thumb. Formerly, an instrument of torture for squeezing or pressing the thumb; also **thumb·kin**, thum'kin.

thumb·tack, thum'tak", n. A tack with a large, flat head, designed to be thrust into an object by the pressure of the thumb or a finger.

thump, thump, n. [Allied to Dan. dump, a plunge, dump, dull, low; D. dompen, to plunge; perh. of imit. origin; cf. bump, plump.] The sound made by the sudden fall of a heavy body; a heavy blow given with anything that is thick.—v.t. To strike or beat with something thick or heavy; colloq. to beat severely.—v.i. To strike or fall with a heavy blow; to pound, as heavy footsteps.

thump·ing, thum'ping, a. Like thumps, beating, or throbbing; colloq. of exceptional size, extent, or the like.

thun·der, thun'dèr, n. [O.E. thunor, thunder (with insertion of d. as in gender, jaundice); D. donder, G. donner; cogn. L. tonitru, Pers. tundur; same root as L. tonare, to sound, E. stun, G. stöhnen, to groan, Gr. stonos, a groaning.] The sound which follows a flash of lightning, caused by the sudden expansion of the air produced by the violent discharge of atmospheric electricity; any loud resounding noise; a loud or vehement utterance, as a threat or denunciation.—v.i. To emit thunder, usu. impersonal, as: It thundered yesterday. To emit a loud echoing noise; to utter loud or angry threats or denunciations.—v.t. To utter loudly or

vehemently, as a threat or denunciation.—**steal some·one's thun·der**, to appropriate without permission, as someone's creation, idea, or argument.—**thun·der·er**, n.

thun·der·bird, thun'dèr·bùrd", n. A large bird of N. American Indian folklore believed to be capable of producing lightning, thunder, and rain.

thun·der·bolt, thun'dèr·bōlt", n. An electrically produced discharge in the form of lightning followed by thunder; an imaginary or illusory dart or bolt cast from heaven to earth by lightning; someone or something which is a dreadful threat, denunciation, or censure; a fulmination.

thun·der·clap, thun'dèr·klap", n. A clap or burst of thunder. Also thunderpeal.

thun·der·cloud, thun'dèr·kloud", n. A cumulonimbus cloud of dark and dense appearance that produces lightning and thunder.

thun·der·head, thun'dèr·hed", n. One of the round swelling masses of cumulus clouds appearing when conditions are right for thunderstorms.

thun·der·ing, thun'dèr·ing, a. Producing or characterized by thunder or any other loud rumbling noise; colloq. large or extraordinary; as, a thundering success.—**thun·der·ing·ly**, adv.

thun·der·ous, thun'dèr·us, a. Producing thunder or a noise like thunder.—**thun·der·ous·ly**, adv.

thun·der·peal, thun'dèr·pēl", n. Thunderclap.

thun·der·show·er, thun'dèr·shou"ér, n. A shower of rain in conjunction with thunder and lightning.

thun·der·stick, thun'dèr·stik", n. Bullroarer.

thun·der·stone, thun'dèr·stōn", n. Any of a variety of stones once supposed to have fallen as thunderbolts.

thun·der·storm, thun'dèr·storm", n. A storm of thunder and lightning, and usu. precipitation and wind.

thun·der·struck, thun'dèr·struk", a. Struck by, or as if by lightning; amazed; confounded; stupefied. Also **thun·der·strick·en**, thun'dèr·strik"en.

thu·ri·ble, thur'i·bl, n. [L. thuribulum, < thus, thuris, frankincense.] Eccles. a censer.

thu·ri·fer, thur'i·fèr, n. Eccles. the attendant who carries the thurible in church services.

Thu·rin·gi·an, thu·rin'jē·an, thu·rin'jan, a. Of or pertaining to Thuringia, a region in Germany.—n. A native or inhabitant of Thuringia.

Thurs·day, thurz'dē, thurz'dā, n. [That is, Thor's day, the day consecrated to Thor, the old Scand. god of thunder.] The fifth day of the week; the day following Wednesday. Abbr. Th., Thur., Thurs.—**Thurs·days**, thurz'dēz, thurz'dāz, adv. On Thursdays; every Thursday.

thus, THus, adv. [O.E. thus, akin to thes, theos, this, this.] In this or that way, manner, or state; accordingly; things being so; to this degree or extent; so; therefore; hence.

thwack, thwak, v.t. [Modified < O.E. thaccian, to stroke gently; Icel. thjökka, to thwack. Whack is another form.] To strike, bang, beat, or thrash with a flat object.—n. A heavy blow with something flat or heavy; a bang.—**thwack·er**, n.

thwart, thwart, v.t. [M.E. thwert, < Scand: cf. Icel. thvert, neut. of thverr, adj., cross, transverse, = O.E. thweorh, cross, perverse; = G. zwerch-, cross, Goth. thwairhs, angry: cf. L. torquere, twist.] To oppose successfully, or prevent from accomplishing a purpose, as; to thwart his plans; to frustrate, as a purpose; to baffle.—a. Passing or lying crosswise or across; cross; traverse. Archaic, perverse; obstinate.—

adv., prep. Archaic, across.—**thwart·ed·ly**, adv.—**thwart·er**, n.

thwart, thwart, n. [Appar. a var. (due to association with thwart) of obs. or prov. thought, for earlier thoft, < O.E. thofte, rower's bench.] A seat across a boat, on which a rower sits; a transverse brace lying crosswise in a canoe.

thy, THĪ, pronominal a. Archaic, the possessive case of the pronoun thou, used in an attributive manner, as: Thy trust comforts me.

thy·la·cine, thī'la·sīn", thī'la·sin, n. [N.L. Thylacinus, < Gr. thylakos, pouch.] A nearly extinct carnivorous, wolflike marsupial, Thylacinus cynocephalus, of Tasmania having black stripes on its back. Also **Tas·ma·ni·an wolf, Tas·ma·ni·an ti·ger**.

thyme, tīm, thīm, n. [L. thymum < Gr. thymon, thyme, < thyō, to smell.] Any small, aromatic subshrub of the genus Thymus, as T. vulgaris and T. serphyllum, whose leaves are used as a seasoning in cooking.—**thym·ic**, **thym·y**, **thym·ey**, tī'mik, tī'mē, a.

thy·mol, thī'mōl, thī'mol, n. [< thyme, oleum, oil.] Chem., pharm. a crystalline substance, $C_{10}H_{13}OH$, obtained from the oil of thyme or synthetically prepared, being a strong antiseptic and disinfectant, and used in medicine and perfumery.

thy·mus, thī'mus, n. pl. **thy·mu·ses, thy·mi**, thī'mī. [< Gr. thymos, thyme, being compared to the flower of this plant by Galen.] Anat. a ductless gland of uncertain function in vertebrates situated in the upper thoracic cavity and in man attaining its maximum development at the end of the second year, becoming vestigial in adults.—**thy·mic**, thī'mik, a.

Thy·ra·tron, thī'ra·tron", n. Electron. an electron tube filled with gas in which a heated cathode initiates, but cannot limit, the electron current. (Trademark.)

thy·roid, thī'roid, a. [Prop. thyreoid, < Gr. thyreoeidēs, shield-shaped, < thyreōs, oblong shield, and eidos, form.] Anat. noting or pertaining to the principal cartilage of the larynx; noting or pertaining to a ductless gland adjacent to the larynx and upper trachea.—n. The thyroid cartilage; the thyroid gland; an artery, vein, or the like, of the thyroid region; a preparation made from the thyroid glands of certain domesticated animals and used for treating disorders of the thyroid.—**thy·roid·less**, a.

thy·roid car·ti·lage, n. Anat. the principal cartilage of the larynx, forming the projection known in men as the Adam's apple.

thy·roid·ec·to·my, thī'roi·dek'to·mē, n. pl. **thy·roid·ec·to·mies**. Surg. excision of the whole or a part of the thyroid gland.

thy·roid gland, n. Anat. a ductless two-lobed gland adjacent to the larynx and upper trachea, and furnishing an important secretion for regulating body development and metabolism.

thy·ro·tox·i·co·sis, thī"rō·tok"si·kō'sis, n. Pathol. An ailment caused by an overabundant secretion of the thyroid resulting usu. in an enlarged thyroid gland, bulging of the eyes, tremors, and rapid heartbeat; hyperthyroidism.

thy·rox·ine, thī·rok'sēn, thī·rok'sin, n. Biochem. an active iodine compound, $C_{15}H_{11}O_4NI_4$, of the thyroid gland that controls metabolism, and is used in treating hypothyroidism; a similar compound prepared synthetically or extracted from animals. Also **thy·rox·in**, thī·rok'sin.

thyr·sus, thur'sus, n. pl. **thyr·si**, thur'sī. [L. thyrsus, < Gr. thyrsos, a thyrsus.] Bot. a paniculate cluster or inflorescence having an indeterminate main axis and other parts determinate, as in the lilac and grape; also **thyrse**. A symbol of Bacchus and the celebrants of his rites, consisting of a staff wrapped with ivy and topped with a pine cone.—**thyr·soid, thyr·soi·dal,** thur′soid,*a*.

thy·sa·nu·ran, thĭ″sa′nur′an, thĭ″sa·nūr′an, this″*a*·nur′an, this″*a*·nūr′an, *a*. [N.L. *Thysanura,* pl., < Gr. *thysanos,* tassel, and *oyrá,* tail.] Belonging to the *Thysanura,* an order of wingless insects with long filamentous caudal appendages, comprising the bristletails.—*n.* A thysanuran insect.—**thy·sa·nu·rous,** *a*.

thy·self, THĭ·self′, *pron. Archaic.* Used after *thou,* to express distinction with emphasis, as: *Thou* knows *thyself* better than anyone else. Used reflexively without *thou,* its usage being similar to that of *yourself,* as: Control *thyself.*

ti, tē, *n.* pl. **tis.** *Mus.* the syllable representing the seventh or highest tone in a diatonic scale in solmization.

ti, tē, *n.* pl. **tis.** *Bot.* any of several trees or shrubs of Asia and the Pacific islands of the genus *Cordyline,* palmlike with terminal tufts of leaves.

ti·ar·a, tē·ar′a, tē·är′a, tē·âr′a, *n.* [L. and Gr. *tiara* < the Pers.] A woman's ornamental crown or coronet. *Rom. Cath. Ch.* the pope's triple crown; the papal dignity. A headdress worn in ancient Persia.—**ti·ar·aed,** *a*.

Ti·bet·an, Thi·bet·an, ti·bet′an, tib′ĭ·t*a*n, *a*. Of or pertaining to Tibet, its inhabitants, or their language.—*n.*

tib·i·a, tib′ē·a, *n.* pl. **tib·i·ae, tib·i·as,** tib′ē·ē″. [L., a musical pipe, the large bone of the leg.] *Anat.* the large bone of the lower leg; the shinbone. *Entom.* the fourth joint of the leg. A kind of pipe, the commonest musical instrument of the Greeks and Romans.—**tib·i·al,** *a*.

tic, tik, *n.* [Fr.: origin uncertain.] *Pathol.* A habitual spasmodic contraction of certain muscles, esp. of the face; tic douloureux.

tic dou·lou·reux, tik″ dŏ″lŏ·rŏ′, *Fr.* tĕk″ dö·lö·RŒ′, *n.* [Fr. *tic douloureux,* painful tic.] *Pathol.* severe facial neuralgia accompanied by convulsive twitchings of the facial muscles. Also **fa·cial neu·ral·gia, tri·gem·i·nal neu·ral·gia.**

tick, tik, *n.* [M.E. *tek,* light touch, = D. *tik,* touch, pat, tick (of watch); appar. imit.] A light, quick touch or tap; as, a *tick* of a clock; a slight, sharp sound or sounds, as made by a small hard body striking upon a hard surface; a recurring click or beat, as of a metronome; *Brit. colloq.* a moment or instant. A small dot or mark serving as a check or the like.—*v.i.* To emit or produce a tick, like that of a clock; to pass or announce a duration of time, as with ticks of a clock or a taximeter.—*v.t.* To mark or note, as on a list or series of things with pencil checks, dots, or ticks; to touch or tap lightly and quickly.

tick, tik, *n.* [M.E. *tyke, teke,* akin to D. *teek, tiek,* and G. *zecke,* tick.] Any of various mites or acarids which are parasitic on animals, as those of the genus *Ixodes,* which bury the head in the flesh of the host and suck the blood, and often serve as carriers of diseases; any of various blood-sucking diptera, as *Melophagus ovinus,* a wingless insect infesting sheep, *Hippobosca equina,* a blood-sucking fly troublesome to horses, and *Olfersia americana,* and other flies parasitic on birds.

tick, tik, *n.* [Same as D. *tijk,* G. *zieche,* a cover, a tick, < L. *theca,* Gr. *thēkē,* a case, a cover.] The cover or case which contains the feathers, wool, or other materials of a mattress or pillow; *colloq.* ticking.

tick, tik, *n.* [Contr. of *ticket.*] *Brit. colloq.* Trust; credit; as, to buy on *tick.*

tick·er, tik′ĕr, *n.* One who or that which ticks; a telegraphic instrument which automatically prints stock market reports or the like, on a narrow tape. *Slang,* a watch; the heart.

tick·er tape, *n.* A paper ribbon on which information is printed by a ticker.

tick·er-tape pa·rade, tik′ĕr·tăp″ pa·rād″, *n.* A parade held for a hero or other famous person during which ticker tape or pieces of paper are thrown from office windows into the street as the parade proceeds.

tick·et, tik′it, *n.* [Fr. *étiquette,* ticket, label.] A slip, usu. of paper or cardboard, serving as evidence or token of the holder's title, usu. by reason of payment, to some service or right; as, an admission *ticket;* a written or printed slip, as of paper or cardboard, affixed to something to indicate its nature or price; a label or tag; a list of candidates nominated or put forward by a political party or faction to be voted on; a summons given out to the violator of a traffic or parking law; the certificate licensing a mariner or the pilot of an airplane; *colloq.* the correct or proper thing, used with *the,* as: That's *the ticket.—v.t.* To attach a ticket to; to distinguish by means of a ticket or label; to furnish with a ticket, as for travel on a railroad.

tick·et a·gen·cy, *n.* An agency where tickets, esp. theater and travel tickets, are sold.—**tick·et a·gent,** *n.*

tick·et of·fice, *n.* An office where ticket sales and reservations are handled.

tick·et of leave, *n.* pl. **tick·ets of leave.** *Brit.* a permit or license giving a convict his liberty, subject to certain restrictions, before his sentence has expired. Also **tick·et-of-leave.**

tick fe·ver, *n. Pathol.* any fever transmitted to man or animals by a mite or acarid of the families *Ixodidae* and *Argasidae,* as Rocky Mountain spotted fever afflicting man and Texas fever occurring in some animals, esp. cattle.

tick·ing, tik′ing, *n.* A strong striped linen or cotton fabric, as used for the ticks of pillows or mattresses.

tick·le, tik′l, *v.t.*—*tickled, tickling.* [M.E. *tiklen, tikelen,* v.i. and v.t.] To touch or stroke lightly, as with the fingers or a feather, so as to excite a tingling or itching sensation; to titillate; to poke in some sensitive part of the body so as to excite spasmodic laughter; to excite agreeably or gratify; to excite amusement in; to touch or stir lightly, as a stringed instrument; to get or move, by or as by tickling.—*v.i.* To be affected with a tingling or itching sensation, as from light touches or strokes; to produce the sensation of titillation.—*n.* An act of tickling; a tickling sensation; *Canadian,* a narrow strait, passage, or inlet on the coast of Newfoundland or Labrador.

tick·ler, tik′lĕr, *n.* One who or that which tickles; a memorandum book or the like kept to tickle or jog the memory, as with reference to engagements or payments due; *electron.* a tickler coil.

tick·ler coil, *n. Electron.* the coil by which the plate circuit of a vacuum tube is inductively coupled with the grid circuit in the process of regeneration.

tick·lish, tik′lish, *a.* Sensitive to tickling; unstable or easily upset, as a boat; unsteady; unsettled or uncertain; easily offended; touchy; requiring careful handling or action; delicate; risky or hazardous; difficult.—**tick·lish·ly,** *adv.*—**tick·lish·ness,** *n.*

tick·seed, tik′sēd″, *n. Bot.* any of various plants having seeds resembling ticks, as a coreopsis or the bugseed; tick trefoil.

tick·seed sun·flow·er, *n. Bot.* any of various species of bur marigold, esp. *Bidens trichosperma* and *B. coronata,* with conspicuous yellow rays.

tick·tack, tic·tac, tik′tak″, *n.* [Imit.: cf. *tick.*] A recurring and often alternating sound, as that of ticking made by a clock or the sound of the heartbeat; a device for

making a ticking or tapping sound, as against a window in playing a practical joke.—*v.i.*

tick-tack-toe, tik″tak·tō′, *n.* A game played by two persons, one of whom marks crosses and the other ciphers, in alternate turns, in the nine spaces formed by two vertical lines drawn at right angles across two horizontal lines, the object being to place three marks of one kind in a row; a children's game consisting of trying, with the eyes shut, to bring a pencil down upon one of a set of numbers, as on a slate, the number hit being scored; the practical joke of using a ticktack. Also **tic-tac-toe,** *tit-tat-toe.*

tick·tock, tic·toc, tik′tok″, *n.* A ticking sound, as of a clock.—*v.i.* To make such a sound.

tick tre·foil, *n. Bot.* any of the plants constituting the leguminous genus *Desmodium,* having trifoliolate leaves and jointed pods with hooked hairs by which they adhere to objects.

ti·dal, tīd′al, *a.* Of or pertaining to tides; periodic or intermittent; dependent, as to departure or arrival time, on the state of the tide; as, a *tidal* steamer.—**tid·al·ly,** *adv.*

ti·dal wave, *n.* A dangerously large ocean wave produced by an earthquake, windstorm, or extraordinarily high tide; tsunami; *fig.* any overwhelming occurrence, esp. as a manifestation of popular sentiment or opinion; as, a *tidal wave* of letters supporting the president.

tid·bit, tid′bit″, *n.* [< *tit,* anything small, and *bit.*] A delicious morsel of food; any pleasing item, as of gossip. Also *Brit.* **titbit.**

tid·dly·winks, tid′lē·wingks″, *n. pl. but sing. in constr.* A game in which participants press plastic disks against the edges of smaller ones lying on a flat surface in an attempt to flick them into a cup. Also **tid·dle·dy·winks,** tid′l·dē·wingks″.

tide, tīd, *n.* [O.E. *tīd,* time = D. *tijd* = G. *zeit* = Icel. *tīdh,* time: cf. M.L.G. *getīde, tīde,* time, tide (of the sea), D. *tij,* tide.] The periodical rise and fall of the waters of the ocean and its estuaries about every 12 hours, due to the gravitational attraction of the moon and sun; flood tide; a stream or current; any rising or falling tendency; as, a rising *tide* of public indignation. *Archaic,* an extent of time; a suitable time. *Eccles.* an anniversary or festival of the church, used in compounds; as, Whitsun*tide.—v.i.—tided, tiding.* [Partly < O.E. *tīdan,* happen (< *tīd,* time), partly < E. *tide, n.*] To flow to and fro as the tide; to float or drift with the tide; *naut.* to navigate a ship by taking advantage of the tide; *archaic,* to happen, or befall.—*v.t.* To carry or buoy up as the tide does; to enable, as a person or family, to survive or endure a period of difficulty, usu. followed by *over;* as, a check to *tide* him *over* his illness.—**tide·ful,** *a.*—**tide·less,** *a.*—**tide·less·ness,** *n.*—**tide·like,** *a.*

tide·land, tīd′land″, *n.* Land inundated at high tide and dry at ebb tide.

tide·mark, tīd′märk″, *n.* A mark left by, or placed to indicate, the highest point of a tide, or the lowest point; any specified level of attainment or recession.

tide ta·ble, *n.* A table listing the expected heights of the tide at certain times of the day, prepared for each day of a year at a particular place.

tide·wait·er, tīd′wā″tĕr, *n.* Formerly, an official who boarded newly arrived ships to check for violations of customs regulations.

tide·wa·ter, tīd′wȧ″tĕr, tīd′wot″ĕr, *n.* Water at high tide that inundates tideland; water affected by the ordinary flow and ebb of the tide; an area, usu. a seacoast, where the waters are acted upon by tides.—*a.*

tide·way, tīd′wā″, *n.* A channel in which a tidal current runs.

ti·dings, tī′dingz, *n. pl.,* sing. or pl. in

constr. [Lit. 'events that happen or *betide*'; Icel. *títhindi* (pl.), tidings, news; Dan. *tidende*, D. *tijding*, G. *zeitung*.] News; information; intelligence.

ti·dy, tī′dē, *a.*—*tidier, tidiest.* [< *tide*, n.] In neat condition, orderly, or trim; as, a *tidy* room; given to keeping things neat and in order; as, a *tidy* woman. *Colloq.* considerable; as, a *tidy* sum; moderately or fairly satisfactory; as, a *tidy* agreement.—*v.t.*—*tidied, tidying.* To make tidy, orderly, or neat, often followed by *up,* as: She *tidied up* the room.—*v.i.*—*n.* pl. **ti·dies.** Any of various articles for keeping things, esp. small objects, arranged or in order; a covering for the backs or arms of upholstered furniture.—**ti·di·ly,** *adv.*—**ti·di·ness,** *n.*

ti·dy·tips, tī′dē·tips″, *n. pl.,* sing. or pl. in constr. *Bot.* an annual ornamental plant, *Layia elegans,* native to California and grown for its brilliant, yellow-rayed flowers.

tie, tī, *v.t.*—*tied, tying.* [O.E. *tīgan,* < *tēag,* band, rope, from the root of *tēon,* draw.] To bind or make fast with a cord, string, or the like, drawn together and knotted, as one thing to another or two things together; to draw together the parts of with a knotted string or the like; as, to *tie* a bundle; to fasten by tightening and knotting the string or strings of; as, to *tie* one's shoes; to draw together into a knot, as a cord or lace; to form by looping and interlacing, as a knot; to fasten, join, or connect in any way; to bind or join closely or firmly; to confine, restrict, or limit, as: His infirmities *tied* him to a wheelchair. To equal or make the same score as in a contest, as: Harvard *tied* Yale in football. *Colloq.* to unite in marriage; *mus.* to connect by a curved line, as notes.—*v.i.* To make a bond or connection; to become tied; to make the same score or be equal in a contest.—*n.* A cord, string, or the like with which something is tied; a necktie; a low shoe fastened with a lace; an ornamental knot or bow; anything that makes fast or secures; a uniting principle or bond of union; as, a *tie* of blood; a link or connection; a restraint or constraint; the act or method of tying or state of being tied; an equality achieved in points, votes, and the like, as: The match ended in a *tie.* A contest in which this occurs; a beam, rod, or the like that connects or holds together two or more parts; *mus.* a curved line connecting two notes on the same pitch to indicate that the sound is to be sustained, not repeated. *Railroad,* one of the transverse beams to which the rails that form a railroad track are fastened; also *sleeper.*—**tie down,** to hinder or limit; as, to *tie down* with responsibilities.

tie·back, tī′bak″, *n.* A strip of fabric, cord, metal, or the like, used to drape or hold curtains to the sides of a window; *usu. pl.* a curtain made to be tied back.

tie in, *v.t.*—*tied in, tying in.* To connect or coordinate.—*v.i.* To become connected or related.

tie-in, tī′in″, *a.* Relating to a sales offer in which the customer may or sometimes is required to buy two or more products together, often a combination of one popular item with less desirable merchandise, usu. at a reduced price; relating to one of the products sold in such a sale.—*n.* A sale or advertisement in which two or more products are sold together; a product sold in such a sale; a connection.

tie·mann·ite, tē′ma·nīt″, *n.* [G. *tiemannit;* named from W. *Tiemann,* who discovered it.] A mineral, a native selenide of mercury, HgSe, that occurs usu. in dark gray masses of metallic luster.

tie·pin, tī′pin″, *n.* A decorative straight pin with a clasp used to hold a necktie in place.

tier, tēr, *n.* [Fr. *tire,* a drawing, pull, continuous stretch, row, < *tirer,* draw: cf. *tire,* n.] One of a series of rows or ranks rising one behind or above another, as seats in an amphitheater; one of a number of galleries, as in a theater; a single level in any layered arrangement.—*v.t.* To arrange in tiers.—*v.i.* To rise in tiers.

ti·er, tī′ėr, *n.* One that ties; a type of apron worn by a child.

tierce, tērs, *n.* [O.Fr. Fr. *tierce,* fem. of *tiers,* third, < L. *tertius,* third, ordinal of *tres,* three.] An old measure of capacity equivalent to one third of a pipe, or 42 wine gallons; a cask or vessel holding this quantity; *fencing,* the third of a series of eight parries; *cards,* a sequence of three cards of the same suit; *eccles.* terce.

tier·cel, tēr′sel, *n.* Tercel.

tier·ta·ble, *n.* A stand consisting of two or more round shelves placed one over the other.

tie·tack, *n.* A pin with a decorative head pinned through the necktie to hold it in place.

tie·up, *v.t.*—*tied up, tying up.* To fasten securely; to bind or wrap up; to hinder; to bring to a stop or pause; to invest or place in such a way as to render unavailable; as, to *tie up* money; to place under such conditions or restrictions as to prevent sale or alienation; as, to *tie up* property; to moor, as, to *tie up* a boat.—*v.i.*

tie-up, tī′up″, *n.* A slowing or stoppage of business, transportation, telephone service, or the like, due to a strike, storm, accident, mechanical failure, or the like; a place where a boat may be moored; *colloq.* an association or connection; as, a political *tie-up.*

tiff, tif, *n.* [Origin obscure.] A slight or petty quarrel; a slight fit of ill humor.—*v.i.* To have a petty quarrel; to be in a tiff.

tif·fa·ny, tif′a·nē, *n. pl.* **tif·fa·nies.** [O.Fr. *tiffer,* to adorn.] A sheer, mesh gauze, formerly made from thin silk, but now usu. made from cotton or synthetic fabrics.

ti·ger, tī′gėr, *n. pl.* **ti·gers, ti·ger.** [O.Fr. Fr. *tigre,* < L. *tigris,* < Gr. *tigris,* tiger.] A large, carnivorous, Asiatic feline mammal, *Panthera tigris,* having a tawny-colored coat with vertical black stripes; broadly, one of several wild felines with tigerlike characteristics, as the jaguar; a person with fierce or aggressive traits; *colloq.* an additional yell, often the word *tiger,* at the end of a round of cheering. One of several powerful aggressive fishes.—**ti·ger·like,** *a.*

ti·ger bee·tle, *n.* Any of various highly active, predacious beetles of the family *Cicindelidae,* usu. having a definite, brightly colored pattern, and commonly found in open, sunny places, as on sandy beaches.

ti·ger cat, *n.* Any of various wildcats, smaller than the tiger, but resembling it in markings or ferocity, as the margay or ocelot; a domestic cat with striped, tigerlike markings.

ti·ger·eye, tī′gėr·ī″, *n.* A golden-brown chatoyant stone used for ornament consisting essentially of quartz colored by iron oxide. Also **ti·ger's-eye.**

ti·ger·ish, tī′gėr·ish, *a.* Concerning or resembling the tiger; having tigerlike characteristics, as ferociousness, cruelty, or courage. Also **ti·grish,** tī′grish.—**ti·ger·ish·ly,** *adv.*—**ti·ger·ish·ness,** *n.*

ti·ger lil·y, *n.* A lily, *Lilium tigrinum,* with flowers of an orange color spotted with black, and small bulbs or bulbils in the axils of the leaves; any of several lilies with flowers of similar appearance.

ti·ger moth, *n.* Any of numerous sturdy-bodied moths of the *Arctiidae* family, usu. having brightly spotted or striped wings.

tight, tīt, *a.* [M.E. *tight,* appar. a var. of *thight, thyht,* dense, solid, prob. < Scand.: cf. Icel. *thēttr,* tight, water-tight, close, Sw. *tät,* Dan. *tæt,* also D. and G. *dicht,* tight, close, dense.] Securely or closely fixed in place; as, a *tight* bolt; drawn or stretched so as to be tense or taut; fitting closely, esp. too closely; as, *tight* shoes; difficult to deal with or manage; as, to be in a *tight* place; compressed or packed full; of such close or compacted texture or fitted together so closely as to be impervious to water, steam, air, and the like; as, a *tight* roof; concise or succinct; as, a *tight* essay; firm or strict; as, to keep a *tight* rein over one's subordinates. *Colloq.* nearly even or close; as, a *tight* race; stingy or parsimonious. *Slang,* drunk. *Econ.* difficult to obtain and much in demand; as, *tight* money; characterized by scarcity or high demand; as, a *tight* market. *Dial.* neat, trim, or well-built; competent.—*adv.* Closely, firmly, or securely.—**tight·ly,** *adv.*—**tight·ness,** *n.*

tight·en, tīt′en, *v.t., v.i.* To make or become tight or tighter.—**tight·en·er,** *n.*

tight-fist·ed, tīt′fis′tid, *a.* Parsimonious; close-fisted.

tight-lipped, tīt′lipt′, *a.* Having tightly closed lips; saying very little; taciturn.

tight·rope, tīt′rōp″, *n.* A rope or cable tautly stretched above the ground, and used by acrobats while performing balancing acts.

tights, tīts, *n. pl.* A garment of close-fitting stretchable material covering the lower part of the body and the legs, or sometimes the whole body, worn esp. by dancers, acrobats, or gymnasts.

tight·wad, tīt′wod″, *n. Slang,* a close-fisted or stingy person.

ti·glon, tī′glon, *n.* An offspring resulting from the mating of a male tiger with a female lion.

ti·gress, tī′gris, *n.* A female tiger; a woman having a fierce nature.

tike, tīk, *n.* Tyke.

ti·ki, tē′kē, *n.* (*Usu. cap.*), *Polynesian.* A god represented in wood or stone; a mythological first man; a carved figurine representing an ancestor.

til, til, tēl, *n.* The sesame plant. Also **teel,** tēl.

til·ak, til′ak, *n. pl.* **til·ak, til·aks.** A Hindu religious symbol of colored paste or powder worn on the forehead.

til·bur·y, til′ber″ē, til′be·rē, *n. pl.* **til·bur·ies.** [From the name of the inventor, a London coach builder in the beginning of the 19th century.] A gig or two-wheeled carriage without a top or cover.

til·de, til′de, *n.* [Sp.] A diacritical mark (˜) signifying the nasal palatal sound *ny* and placed over a palatal *n* in Spanish, as in *señora,* or in Portuguese, over a vowel to be nasalized, as in *João.*

tile, til, *n.* [O.E. *tigele, tigule,* < L. *tegula,* tile, < *tegere,* cover.] A thin slab, plate, or shaped piece of baked clay, often glazed and ornamented, used for covering roofs, lining walls, paving floors, draining land, or in ornamental work; any of various similar slabs or pieces, as of stone or metal; the material of which clay tiles are made; tiles collectively; a hollow block of material, as burnt clay, used in building construction; *slang,* a stiff hat or a high silk hat.—*v.t. tiled, tiling.* To cover with or as with tiles.

tile·fish, til′fish″, *n. pl.* **tile·fish, tile·fish·es.** A large, brilliantly colored food fish, *Lopholatilus chamaeleonticeps,* of the Atlantic.

til·ing, tī′ling, *n.* The operation of covering with or as with tiles; something tiled; tiles collectively.

till, til, *prep.* [O.E. (Northumbrian) *til,* < Scand.: cf. Icel. *til,* Sw. *till,* Norw. and Dan. *til,* to till, also G. *ziel,* limit, end, goal, *zielen,* to aim, and E. *till.*] To the time of; up to the time of; until, as: We waited *till* noon. Before, used with the negative, as: He didn't come *till* evening. *Sc. and North. Eng.* to; unto.—*conj.* To the time that or when; until, as: I'll wait *till* they come. Before, used with the negative, as: They didn't come *till* I was gone.

till, til, *v.t.* [O.E. *tilian,* strive for, labor on, till, = D. *telen,* cultivate, breed, = G. *zielen,* aim: cf. *till.*] To do labor on, as by plowing, harrowing, and sowing upon, as the soil, for the raising of crops; to cultivate.—*v.i.* To cultivate the soil.—**till·a·ble,** *a.*

till, til, *n.* [M.E. *tylle;* origin uncertain.] A drawer or tray, as in a shop or bank, in which cash is kept; a compartment, as in a cabinet or chest, for keeping valuables.

till, til, *n.* [Origin obscure.] *Geol.* nonstratified glacial sediment, consisting of clay, gravel, and boulders; boulder clay.

till·age, til'ij, *n.* The operation or art of tilling land; the land under cultivation.

til·lands·i·a, ti·lan'dzē·a, *n.* [N.L. from E. *Tillands,* 17th century botanist in Finland.] Any of the tropical and subtropical American plants constituting the genus *Tillandsia,* of the pineapple family, most of which are epiphytic on trees, as the Floriba moss, *T. usneoides.*

till·er, til'ẽr, *n.* One who tills; a farmer.

till·er, til'ẽr, *n. Naut.* the bar or lever fitted to the head of a rudder to turn the helm of a boat in steering.

till·er, til'ẽr, *n.* [Cf. O.E. *telgor,* a plant, a shoot; akin D. *telen,* to breed.] The shoot of a plant, springing from the root; a sprout or sapling.—*v.i.* To put forth shoots from the root.

till·er·man, til'ẽr·man, *n. pl.* **till·er·men.** Someone responsible for steering or operating the tiller of a boat.

tilt, tilt, *v.t.* [M.E. *tylten,* < O.E. *tealt,* unsteady.] To cause to lean or incline from the vertical or horizontal; to slope or slant; to hold poised for attack, as a lance; to rush at or charge, as in a joust; to hammer or forge with a tilt hammer.—*v.i.* To move into or assume a sloping position or direction; to engage in a joust, tournament, or similar contest; to strike, thrust, or charge with or as if with a lance or the like, usu. followed by *at.*—*n.* The act of tilting, or the state of being tilted; a sloping position; a slope; a joust or some similar contest; the exercise of riding with a lance or the like at a mark; any encounter, combat, or contest; a dispute; a thrust of a weapon, as at a tilt or joust.—**at full tilt,** with full speed.—**tilt·er,** *n.*

tilt, tilt, *n.* [O.E. *teld,* a tent = Dan. and L.G. *telt,* Icel, *tjald,* G. *zelt,* tent.] The cloth covering of a cart or wagon; a canopy or awning, as over the after part of a boat.—*v.t.* To cover with a tilt or awning.

tilth, tilth, *n.* [O.E. *tilth,* < *tilian,* E. *till.*] The act or operation of tilling; tillage; cultivation; the state of being tilled; as, land in good or bad *tilth;* tilled land; land under cultivation.

tim·bal, tym·bal, tim'bal, *n.* [Fr. *timbale,* for earlier *attabale,* Moorish drum, = E. *atabal.*] A kettledrum; *entom.* a vibrating membrane in certain insects, as the cicada, by means of which a shrill chirring sound is produced.

tim·bale, tim'bal, *Fr.* taN·bäl', *n.* [Fr., lit. 'kettledrum.'] A preparation of minced meat, fish, or other food, often enclosed in paste, cooked in a mold; a pastry shell filled with such a mixture.

tim·ber, tim'bẽr, *n.* [O.E. *timber,* a building, edifice, building material, timber, = M.L.G. *timber,* timber, = D. *timmer,* G. *zimmer,* room, = Icel. *timbr,* timber, akin to Goth. *timrjan,* build, L. *domus,* Gr. *dómos,* Skt. *dama,* house, Gr. *démein,* build.] Wood suitable for building or for use in carpentry; the wood of growing trees suitable for structural uses; growing trees themselves; a single beam or piece of wood forming, or capable of forming, part of a structure. Personal character or quality. *Naut.* one of the curved pieces of wood in a ship's frame, which spring upward and out-

ward from the keel; a rib.—*v.t.* [O.E. *timbran, timbrian.*] To furnish with timber; to support with timber.—*interj.* A warning call from a lumberjack when a tree is cut and ready to fall.

tim·bered, tim'bẽrd, *a.* Made of or furnished with timber; covered with growing trees, or wooded; as, the *timbered* slopes.

tim·ber·head, tim'bẽr·hed", *n. Naut.* The top end of a timber, rising above the deck and serving for belaying ropes, or the like; the top of a post, projecting above a wharf, which is similar to this in both use and position.

tim·ber hitch, *n. Naut.* a kind of hitch or knot by which a rope is fastened around a spar or any similar object.

tim·ber·ing, tim'bẽr·ing, *n.* Building material of wood; timbers collectively; timberwork.

tim·ber·land, tim'bẽr·land", *n.* Land filled with forests, esp. when producing saleable timber.

tim·ber line, *n.* The elevation above sea level, as on mountains or in the polar areas, at which timber ceases to grow. Also *tree line.*—**tim·ber-line,** *a.*

tim·ber wolf, *n.* A gray wolf, *Canis lupus,* of northern U.S. and Canada.

tim·ber·work, tim'bẽr·wụrk", *n.* Work, esp. relating to a structural framework, formed of timbers.

tim·bre, tim'bẽr, *Fr.* taN'bre, *n.* [Fr., < L. *tympanum,* a drum.] That distinctive quality having to do with the mixture and intensity of harmonics in a sound which sets it apart from another sound of the same pitch and volume, as between vocal or instrumental tones in music or voiced sounds in speech.

tim·brel, tim'brel, *n.* [A. dim. of Fr. *timbre,* a bell, orig. a drum.] A type of hand drum; a tambourine.—**tim·brelled,** *a.*

time, tim, *n.* [O.E. *tīma* = Icel. *tīmi,* time, = Sw. *timme,* Dan. *time,* hour; akin to E. *tide.*] The system of those relations which any event has to any other as past, present, or future; indefinite continuous duration regarded as that in which events succeed one another; duration regarded as belonging to the present life as distinct from the life to come, or from eternity; a system or method of measuring or reckoning the passage of time; limited extent of time, as between two successive events; as, a long *time;* a particular period considered as distinct from other periods; as, for the *time* being. *Often pl.* a period in the history of the world, or contemporary with the life or activities of a notable person; as, in ancient *times;* the period or era now or then present; as, the indifference of the *times;* a period considered with reference to its events or prevailing conditions, tendencies, or ideas; as, hard *times.* A prescribed or allotted term or period, as of one's life, of apprenticeship, of pregnancy, or the like; a period with reference to personal experience of a specified kind; as, to have a good *time;* a period allowed, as for payment; a period of work of an employee, or the pay for it; *colloq.* a term of imprisonment; as, to do *time.* The period necessary for or occupied by something; as, to ask for *time* to consider; leisure or spare time; as, to have no *time;* a particular or definite point during the day, as: What *time* is it? A particular part of a year, day, or the like; as, spring-*time;* an appointed, fit, due, or proper moment; the right moment or opportunity; as, to watch one's *time;* each occasion of a recurring action; as, one thing at a *time;* *pl., math.* a multiplicative word in phrasal combinations expressing how many instances of a quantity or factor are taken together; as, four *times* five; *drama,* one of Aristotle's three unities; as, unity of *time,*

place, and action; *pros.* a unit or a group of units in the measurement of meter. *Mus.* the arrangement of the successive beats or measures, each kind of measure employed in music containing a certain number of these beats; tempo; the metrical duration of a note or rest; characteristic tempo; the general movement of a particular kind of musical composition with reference to its rhythm, metrical structure, and tempo; the movement of a dance or the like to music so arranged. *Milit.* the rate of marching, calculated on the number of paces taken per minute; as, double *time.*—*v.t.*—**timed,** **timing.** To appoint the time of or choose the moment or occasion for; to regulate as to time, as a train or a clock; *mus.* to mark the rhythm or measure of. To fix the duration of; as, to *time* an exposure in photography; to ascertain or record the time, duration, or rate of; as, to *time* a race.—*v.i.* To keep time; to, sound or move in unison or harmony.—*a.* Related or pertaining to time; planned to occur or happen within or at a desired time; payable or redeemable on or any time after some designated date or after some specified amount of time following purchase; pertaining to installment payments; as, a *time* loan.—**be·hind the times,** outmoded; passe; old-fashioned.—**keep time,** to indicate or record time correctly, as a timepiece or watch; *mus.* to conduct, play, or sing some composition while strictly adhering to the rhythm or tempo.—**time of one's life,** *colloq.* an experience or event of great enjoyment.

time and a half, *n.* The pay rate of one and one half times an employee's regular rate of payment which is given for working overtime.

time bill, *n.* A bill of exchange due at a certain date.

time bomb, *n.* A bomb built to explode at a preset time.

time cap·sule, *n.* A receptacle which holds typical records and objects from the current culture set into a cornerstone or in the earth to be uncovered in a future age.

time·card, tim'kärd", *n.* A sheet for recording, usu. mechanically, an employee's attendance and hours worked.

time chart, *n.* A diagram that shows corresponding times for different parts of the world.

time clock, *n.* A clock with an attachment by which a record, as on a tape or card, may be made of the time of an event, as of the arrival and departure of employees.

time-con·sum·ing, tim'kon·sö"ming, *a.* Requiring a great length of time to accomplish; time-wasting.

timed, timd, *a.* Planned to occur or happen within or at a specified time, as an explosion; occurring at a particular time; as, an ill-*timed* departure.

time de·pos·it, *n.* A type of bank deposit which is payable only after a given length of time, or requiring advance notice for withdrawal.

time draft, *n.* A draft that is payable a given number of days after presentation.

time ex·po·sure, *n. Photog.* An extended interval between the opening and closing of the shutter; a picture made by a comparatively long exposure—**time-ex·po·sure,** *a.*

time-hon·ored, tim'on"ẽrd, *a.* Venerable and worthy of honor by reason of antiquity and long continuance. Also *Brit.* **time-hon·oured.**

time im·me·mo·ri·al, *n.* Time so distant in the past as to predate memory or history; also **time out of mind.** *E. law,* time before the reign of Richard I, 1189, a fixed date beyond which legal memory does not extend.

time·keep·er, tim'kē"pẽr, *n.* One who or that which keeps time; one who records and

announces time of occurrence or time occupied, as in certain athletic events; a timepiece; a person employed to keep account of the hours of work done by others; one who beats time in music.—**time·keep·ing,** *n.*

time-lag, tīm'lag″, *n.* A time interval between two events or phenomena that are closely related, as a cause and its effect.

time-lapse, tīm'laps″, *a. Photog.* of or relating to the filming of a slow process, as the growth of a plant, by exposing each frame at an interval, so that during the projection of the motion picture the slow process appears to speed up.

time·less, tīm'lis, *a.* Not subject to or affected by time; eternal; unending; referring to no particular time.—**time··less·ly,** *adv.*—**time·less·ness,** *n.*

time lim·it, *n.* The time period within which a procedure must be completed.

time loan, *n.* A loan having a scheduled repayment date.

time lock, *n.* A lock controlled by clockwork so that when locked it cannot be unlocked before the expiration of a set interval of time.

time·ly, tīm'lē, *a.*—*timelier, timeliest.* Occurring at a fitting or suitable time; seasonable; opportune; well-timed.—*adv.*—**time·li·ness,** *n.*

time mon·ey, *n.* Money designated for loan on a predetermined repayment schedule.

time note, *n.* A note contracted to be repaid within a certain period of time.

time-out, tīm'out′, *n.* A temporary cessation of action, esp. in a sports contest; a recess or intermission; a rest break. Also **time out.**

time·piece, tīm'pēs″, *n.* An apparatus for measuring and recording the progress of time; a chronometer; a clock or watch.

tim·er, tī'mèr, *n.* One who measures or records time; a timekeeper; a device for recording time or intervals of time, as a stopwatch; in an internal-combustion engine, an automatic device which causes the spark for igniting the charge to occur at the instant required; a mechanism which allows a machine or appliance to operate automatically and then shut off at some predetermined time; as, an oven *timer.*

time·sav·ing, tīm'sā″ving, *a.* Enabling the performance of a task in less time; facilitating a speedy finish.—**time·sav·er,** *n.*

time·serv·er, tīm'sur″vèr, *n.* One who for his own ends adapts his opinions and manners to the times or complies with the ruling power.—**time·serv·ing,** *a., n.*

time-share, tīm'shâr″, *v.i.*—*time-shared, time-sharing.* To allocate or assign parts of the complete operating time, as of a computer, to at least two functions.—*v.t.*

time sheet, *n.* A record of employees' completed hours at work, kept on cards or ledger sheets, esp. indicating arrivals and departures.

time sig·na·ture, *n. Mus.* a fractional notation of intended meter found at the beginning of a musical composition, as $\frac{3}{4}$ or $\frac{6}{8}$.

time·ta·ble, tīm'tā″bl, *n.* A table or register of times, as of scheduled hours to be observed, of the arrival and departure of railroad trains or the like, or indicating an ordered sequence of events.

time·work, tīm'wurk″, *n.* Work performed for a unit wage, usu. hourly or by the day.—**time·work·er,** *n.*

time·worn, tīm'wōrn″, tīm'warn″, *a.* Worn or impaired by time; ancient or showing the effects of time; as, *timeworn* buildings; hackneyed or banal, as a cliché.

time zone, *n.* Any of 24 longitudinal segments of the globe, roughly divided by meridians 15° apart beginning at Greenwich, England, and differing by one hour before or after each adjoining segment.

tim·id, tim'id, *a.* [L. *timidus,* < *timeo,* to fear.] Fearful; lacking courage to meet danger; timorous; not bold.—**ti·mid·ly,** *adv.*—**tim·id·i·ty, tim·id·ness,** *n.*

tim·ing, tī'ming, *n. Theatr., sports, mus.* The adjusting of an action, phrase, or sound to occur at the instant of maximum effect, or to coordinate with other motions, sounds, or effects; the outcome of this coordinating; the act of measuring the time passed in a performance or contest, as with a stopwatch.

ti·moc·ra·cy, tī·mok'ra·sē, *n. pl.* **ti·moc·-ra·cies.** [= Fr. *timocratie,* < Gr. *timokratia,* < *timē,* honor, valuation, and *kratein,* rule.] A form of government in which love of honor is the dominant motive of the rulers; a form of government in which a certain amount of property is requisite as a qualification for office.—**ti·mo·crat·ic, ti·mo·crat·i·cal,** tī″mo··krat'ik, *a.*

tim·or·ous, tim'èr·us, *a.* [L.L. *timorosus,* < L. *timor,* fear, < *timeo,* to fear.] Fearful of danger; timid; destitute of courage; indicating or marked by fear.—**tim·or··ous·ly,** *adv.*—**tim·or·ous·ness,** *n.*

tim·o·thy, tim'o·thē, *n.* [From *Timothy* Hanson, who is said to have carried the seed from New York to the Carolinas about 1720.] *Bot.* a coarse grass, *Phleum pratense,* with cylindrical spikes, valuable as fodder. Also **tim·o·thy grass, herd's-grass.**

tim·pa·ni, tim'pa·nē, *n. pl., sing. or pl.* in *constr.* [It., < L. *tympanum.*] A set of orchestral kettledrums.—**tim·pa·nist,** *n.*

tin, tin, *n.* [O.E., D., Dan., and Icel. *tin,* Sw. *ten,* G. *zinn;* not connected with L. *stannum,* tin.] *Chem.* a silver-white, malleable, ductile metallic element, used as a protective coating and in alloys. Sym. Sn, at. no. 50, at. wt. 118.69. Also **stan·num.** See Periodic Table of Elements. A container, box, can, or vessel fashioned from tin or tin plate; *Brit.* a can, as for food; *Brit. slang,* money.—*v.t.*—**tinned,** *tinning.* To cover or plate with tin; *Brit.* to can.—*a.* Made of tin; counterfeit; cheap; valueless.

tin·a·mou, tin'a·mö″, *n.* Any of several members of a group of South and Central American game birds of the family *Tinamidae,* resembling gallinaceous birds but related to the ratite birds.

tin·cal, ting'käl, ting'kal, *n.* [Malay *tingkal,* Hind. and Pers. *tinkâr.*] Unrefined borax.

tin can, *n.* A sealed metal container, usu. constructed from tin-plated sheet steel, used to preserve food. *Navy slang,* a warship, esp. a destroyer; a depth charge.

tinct, tingkt, *a.* [L. *tinctus,* pp. of *tingere:* see *tinge.*] *Poet.* Tinged; colored; flavored.—*n. Poet.* Tint; tinge; coloring.

tinc·to·ri·al, tingk·tōr'ē·al, tingk·tar'ē·al, *a.* [< L. *tinctor,* a dyer.] Pertaining to or permeated with colors or dyes.—**tinc·to··ri·al·ly,** *adv.*

tinc·ture, tingk'chèr, *n.* [L. *tinctura,* < *tingo, tinctum.*] A tinge or shade of color; slight taste superadded to any substance; slight quality added to anything; *med.* an extract or solution of the active principles of some substance in a solvent, usu. alcohol; *her.* any of the colors, metals, or furs used in escutcheons.—*v.t.*—*tinctured, tincturing.* To tinge; to impart a slight color to; to impregnate; to imbue.

tin·der, tin'dèr, *n.* [O.E. *tynder, tender,* < *tyndan, tendan,* to kindle (Dan. *taende,* G. *zünden*) = Sw. and L.G. *tunder,* Icel. *tundr,* D. *tonder,* G. *zunder,* tinder.] Orig. an inflammable substance such as partially burned linen, used for kindling fire from a spark struck with a steel and flint; any highly combustible material.—**tin·der·y,** tin'dė·rē, *a.*

tin·der·box, tin'dèr·boks″, *n.* A box in which tinder is kept; anything extremely combustible; one who is overly excitable; a potential source of contagious violence.

tine, tīn, *n.* [O.E. *tinde, tind* = Icel. *tindr,* Dan. *tind, tinde,* L.G. and Sw. *tinne,* same root as *tooth.*] The spike of a fork; a prong; a point or prong of an animal's antler.—**tined,** *a.*

tin·e·a, tin'ē·a, *n.* [L., a gnawing worm, a bookworm, a moth.] *Pathol.* ringworm or any similar fungus infection of the skin.—**tin·e·al,** *a.*

tin fish, *n. Slang,* a torpedo.

tin·foil, tin'foil′, *n.* Tin, aluminum, or a tin-lead alloy, beaten and rolled into thin sheets, used for wrapping products. Also **tin foil.**—**tin-foil,** *a.*

ting, ting, *n.* [Imit., cf. *tinkle, jingle;* L. *tinnio,* to tinkle.] A clear, brief, ringing sound, as of a tiny bell.—*v.t., v.i.* To sound or cause to sound with a ting.

tinge, tinj, *v.t.*—*tinged, tingeing* or *tinging.* [L. *tingo, tinctum,* to moisten, stain, dye (seen also in *tincture, tint, taint, distain,* whence *stain*); cogn. Gr. *tenggō,* to wet.] To imbue with some substance so as to slightly affect or modify the color, taste, or qualities of; to give a certain shade, flavor, or quality to; to color.—*n.* A slight degree of color, taste, flavor, or quality infused or added to something; touch; tint; trace.

tin·gle, ting'gl, *v.i.*—*tingled, tingling.* [Prob. orig. a var. of *tinkle,* later associated with *ting.*] To have a sensation of slight stings, quivers, or prickles, as from a sharp blow or cold; to cause such a sensation.—*v.t.* To cause to tingle.—*n.* A tingling sensation.—**tin·gler,** *n.*—**tin·gling·ly,** *adv.*—**tin·gly,** ting'glē, *a.*—*tinglier, tingliest.*

tin hat, *n.* A hard hat, usu. metal, worn by many construction workers and soldiers.

tin·horn, tin'harn″, *n. Slang,* a noisy or pretentious person with little money or ability, as a gambler.—*a.*

tink·er, ting'kèr, *n.* [M.E. *tinkere;* origin uncertain.] A mender of pots, kettles, pans, and other metal household articles, esp. an itinerant mender of such articles; an unskilled or clumsy mender or worker; a bungler; one skilled in various minor kinds of mechanical work; a jack-of-all-trades. Also **tink·er·er.** An act or instance of tinkering. Any of various fishes, esp. a young mackerel.—*v.i.* To do the work of a tinker; to work unskillfully or clumsily at anything; to busy oneself with a thing without useful results.—*v.t.* To mend as a tinker; to repair in an unskillful, clumsy, or makeshift way.

tink·er's damn, tink·er's dam, *n.* [A tinker's curse or oath in allusion to the reputed addiction of tinkers to swearing.] *Colloq.* something insignificant; as, not worth a *tinker's damn.*

tin·kle, ting'kl, *v.i.*—*tinkled, tinkling.* [M.E. freq. < *tink, ting,* imit. of sound.] To make small, quick, sharp sounds, esp. by striking on metal, as a little bell; to jingle.—*v.t.* To cause to make sharp, quick, ringing sounds; to signal or make known by tinkling.—*n.* A small, quick, sharp, ringing noise or sound; any instance or act of this sound.—**tin··kling,** ting'kling, *n.*—**tin·kly,** ting'klē, *a.*—*tinklier, tinkliest.*

tin·man, tin'man, *n. pl.* **tin·men.** A manufacturer of, or dealer in, tinware; a tinsmith.

tin·ner, tin'èr, *n.* One who works in a tin mine; a tinman; a tinsmith.

tin·ni·tus, ti·nī'tus, *n.* [L., a ringing, a tingling, < *tinnio,* to ring.] *Pathol.* a ringing, buzzing, or other similar subjective or pathological sensation in the ears.

tin·ny, tin'ē, *a.*—*tinnier, tinniest.* Pertaining to or resembling tin; lacking in resonance; tasting like tin, as food packaged in a tin can.—**tin·ni·ly,** *adv.*—**tin·ni·ness,** *n.*

Tin-Pan Al·ley, tin'pan″ al'ē, *n.* A district

or street in a city or town, esp. New York City, in which many publishers or composers of popular music are located; the publishers and composers considered collectively.

tin plate, *n.* Thin sheet steel or iron coated with tin. Also **tin·plate.—tin-plate,** tin′plāt″, *v.t.*—tin-plated, tin-plating.—**tin·plat·er,** *n.*

tin·sel, tin′sel, *n.* [Fr. *étincelle,* O.Fr. *estincelle,* < L. *scintilla,* a spark (whence also *scintillate*).] Thin strips, pieces, or sheets of glittering metallic material used for inexpensive ornamentation; anything superficially showy or more glamorous than valuable.—*a.—v.t.—tinseled, tinseling, chiefly Brit.* tinselled, tinselling. To adorn with tinsel or anything showy and superficial.—**tin·sel·ly,** tin′se·lē, *a.*

tin·smith, tin′smith″, *n.* One who makes and repairs articles of tin, tin plate, or other light metal.

tin spir·it, *n.* Often *pl.* any of various solutions of tin compounds in strong acid, used as mordants in dyeing.

tin·stone, tin′stōn″, *n.* Cassiterite, SnO_2, one of the principal ores of tin.

tint, tint, *n.* [It. *tinta,* Fr. *teint,* < L. *tinctus,* pp. of *tingo.*] A slight coloring or tincture distinct from the ground or principal color; a hue; a tinge; degree of intensity of a color; hair dye; *print.* a pale color over which something in a darker shade of color is printed.—*v.t.* To tinge; to give a slight coloring to.—**tint·er,** *n.*—**tint·ing,** *n.*—**tint·less,** tint′lis, *a.*

tin·tin·nab·u·lar, tin″ti·nab′ū·lėr, tin″ti·nab′ya·lėr, *a.* [L. *tintinnabulum,* a bell, < *tintinno,* a freq. < *tinnio,* to ring, to jingle, a word imit. of sound.] Of or relating to bells or their sound. Also **tin·tin·nab·u·lar·y, tin·tin·nab·u·lous,** tin″ti·nab′ū·lėr″ē, tin″ti·nab′ya·lėr″ē.—**tin·tin·nab·u·la·tion,** tin″ti·nab′ū·lā″shan, tin″ti·nab″ya·lā′shan, *n.* The tinkling or ringing sound of bells.

tin·type, tin′tīp″, *n.* A photograph in the form of a positive taken on a sensitized sheet of enameled tin or iron; a ferrotype.

tin·ware, tin′wâr″, *n.* Articles made of tinned iron or tin plate.

tin·work, tin′wụrk″, *n.* Anything made of tin.

tin·works, tin′wụrks″, *n. pl., sing.* or *pl.* in *constr.* A mine or establishment where tin or tinware is processed or fabricated.

ti·ny, tī′nē, *a.—tinier, tiniest.* [M.E. *tyne,* tiny.] Very small; little; minute.—**ti·ni·ly,** *adv.*—**ti·ni·ness,** *n.*

tip, tip, *n.* [M.E. *tippe* = M.L.G. and D. *tip* = Sw. *tipp* = Dan. *tip* = M.H.G. *zipf,* *tip*: cf. G. *zipfel.*] A slender, pointed extremity or end, esp. of anything long or tapering; as, the *tip* of a leaf; the top, summit, or apex; a small piece or part, as of metal or leather, forming the extremity of something.—*v.t.—tipped, tipping.* To furnish with a tip; to serve as or form the tip of; to mark or adorn the tip of; to take off the ends of, as strawberries.—**tip in,** *bookbinding,* an extra leaf or insert, as a map or picture, attached to the binding edge of a book or magazine.—**tip·less,** *a.*

tip, tip, *v.t.—tipped, tipping.* [M.E. *tipen, typen*; origin uncertain.] To cause to assume a slanting or sloping position; incline; tilt; to overthrow, overturn, or upset, followed by *over*; to touch or lift, as the hat, in salutation. *Brit.* to empty by tilting; to dump.—*v.i.* To assume a slanting or sloping position; incline; to tilt up at one end and down at the other; to be overturned or upset; to tumble or topple, followed by *over,* as: The milk bottle *tipped over.*—*n.* The act of tipping; the state of being tipped. *Brit.* a place into which refuse or the like is tipped; a dump.—**tip·pa·ble,** *a.*—**tip·per,** *n.*

tip, tip, *n.* A small present of money bestowed for services, as to a porter, cab driver, or waiter; a gratuity; *colloq.* a piece of private or secret information, as for use in betting, speculation, or other action, often used with *off.* A useful hint, suggestion, or idea.—*v.t.—tipped, tipping.* To give a gratuity to; *colloq.* to give private or secret information to, often followed by *off.*—*v.i.* To give a gratuity.—**tip·less,** *a.*—**tip·pa·ble,** *a.*—**tip·per,** tip′ėr, *n.*

tip, tip, *v.t.—tipped, tipping.* [Cf. L.G. *tippen,* Sw. *tippa,* strike lightly, tap, also E. *tap.*] To strike or hit with a light, smart blow; tap; *baseball,* to hit, as the ball, obliquely with the bat.—*n.* A light, smart blow; a tap; *baseball,* a ball that has been tipped; as, a foul *tip.*

tip·cart, tip′kärt″, *n.* A cart which can be tilted up to empty its contents.

tip·cat, tip′kat″, *n.* A game in which a small pointed piece of wood called a cat is made to jump from the ground by being struck on the tip, batted, and fielded; the piece of wood used in the game.

ti·pi, tē′pē, *n. pl.* **ti·pis.** Tepee.

tip-off, tip′af″, tip′of″, *n. Colloq.* The act of disclosing confidential information; a tip or hint; a caution or warning.

tip·pet, tip′it, *n.* [M.E. *tipet,* perh. < *tippe,* E. *tip.*] An article of dress, usu. of fur or wool, for covering the neck or the neck and shoulders, and having ends hanging down in front; a long, narrow, pendent part of the dress, as part of a hood or sleeve; *eccles.* a band of silk or the like worn round the neck with the ends pendent in front.

tip·ple, tip′l, *v.i.—tippled, tippling.* [Freq. and dim. < *tip,* to tilt or turn up; akin *tipsy.*] To drink intoxicating liquors habitually.—*v.t.* To drink often, esp. in small amounts.—*n.* Intoxicating liquor.—**tip·pler,** tip′lėr, *n.*

tip·ple, tip′l, *n.* [Freq. of *tip.*] A place where, or structure by which, cars loaded with coal or the like are emptied by tipping.

tip·staff, tip′staf″, tip′stäf″, *n. pl.* **tip·staffs, tip·staves,** tip′stāvz″, tip′stavz″, tip′stävz″. [For *tipped staff.*] *Law,* an attendant in an English court. A staff tipped with metal formerly carried as a badge of office by certain English officials, as a constable or sheriff's officer; any of such officials.

tip·ster, tip′stėr, *n. Colloq.* one who is paid for supplying tips to gamblers or speculators.

tip·sy, tip′sē, *a.—tipsier, tipsiest.* [Appar. < *tip.*] Intoxicated, but not to complete drunkenness or stupor; characterized by or due to intoxication; as, a *tipsy* laugh; *fig.* tipping, unsteady, or tilted, as if from intoxication.—**tip·si·ly,** *adv.*—**tip·si·ness,** *n.*

tip·toe, tip′tō″, *n.* The tip or end of a toe; the tips of the toes collectively.—*v.i.—tiptoed, tiptoing.* To move or go about on tiptoe, as with caution or stealth.—*a.* Characterized by standing or walking on tiptoe; eagerly expectant; cautious or stealthy.—*adv.* On the tips of one's toes.—**on tip·toe,** straining upward; eager; expectant; cautious or stealthy.

tip·top, tip′top″, *n.* [< *tip* and *top,* or a reduplication of *top* (like *ding-dong, slipslop,* etc.).] The summit; *colloq.* the best.—*a. Colloq.* excellent.—*adv.* In tiptop fashion; very well.

ti·rade, tī′rād, ti·rād′, *n.* [Fr. *tirade,* < *tirer,* to draw, < the Germanic verb = E. to *tear.*] A long, violent speech, often censorious; a harangue.

tire, tīėr, *v.t.—tired, tiring.* [O.E. *teorian,* to tire; *tirian, tirigan,* to vex, annoy; D. *tergen,* to irritate.] To exhaust the strength of, as by labor; to fatigue; to weary; to exhaust the attention or patience of, as with

tediousness.—*v.i.* To become weary; to have the attention or patience exhausted.—**tire·less,** *a.*—**tire·less·ly,** *adv.*—**tire·less·ness,** *n.*

tire, tīėr, *n.* [For *tier* < *tie.*] A pneumatic structure that encircles the wheels of a vehicle, as a car or bicycle, usu. consisting of a discrete external covering of rubber reinforced with fabric protecting an inflated, cushioning, inner tube and providing traction; such an external covering, as opposed to *inner tube*; a band or hoop, as of steel or hard rubber, forming the tread of a vehicle wheel.—*v.t.—tired, tiring.* To furnish with a tire or tires. Also *Brit.* tyre.

tire, tīėr, *v.t.—tired, tiring. Archaic.* To attire; to dress, as the hair.—*n. Archaic.* Attire; a headdress.

tired, tīėrd, *a.* Exhausted, as by exertion; fatigued; weary. Hackneyed; trite; *colloq.* impatient or disgusted.—**tired·ly,** *adv.*—**tired·ness,** *n.*

tire·some, tīėr′som, *a.* Tending to tire; boring; tedious.—**tire·some·ly,** *adv.*—**tire·some·ness,** *n.*

ti·ro, tī′rō, *n. pl.* **ti·ros.** Tyro.

ti·sane, ti·zan′, *Fr.* tē·zän′, *n.* [Fr.] Ptisan.

Tish·ab b'Ab, tē·shä′ ba·äb′, *n.* A Jewish day of fasting in memory of the destruction of the temples in Jerusalem. Also **Tish·ah b'Av.**

tis·sue, tish′ö, *n.* [O.Fr. Fr. *tissu,* orig. pp. of O.Fr. *tistre* (later *tître*), < L. *texere,* weave.] *Biol.* in plants and animals, an aggregate of cells usu. of similar structure which perform the same or related functions; as, xylem or muscle *tissue.* Any of various woven or textile fabrics of light or gauzy texture; an interwoven or interconnected series; as, a *tissue* of falsehoods; any of various types of thin, soft paper; as, facial *tissue*; tissue paper; a variety of extremely fine typewriter paper.—*v.t.—tissued, tissuing.* To clothe or adorn with tissue.

tis·sue cul·ture, *n.* The science of growing a piece of tissue removed from an animal in a culture medium.

tis·sue pa·per, *n.* A semitransparent, soft paper used for wrapping delicate articles, covering illustrations in books, copying letters, or the like.

tit, tit, *n.* [Prob. detached from *titmouse* (recorded much earlier): cf. *tit.*] Any of various small birds, esp. a titmouse.

tit, tit, *n.* [O.E. *tit.*] A teat; a breast.

Ti·tan, tīt′an, *n.* [L., < Gr. *Titán.*] *Class. mythol.* one of a family of primordial deities, the children of Uranus or Heaven, and Gaea or Earth, conceived as lawless beings of gigantic size and enormous strength who overthrew Uranus, the ruler of the world, and raised Cronus, one of their number, to the throne, but were themselves overcome by Zeus, the son of Cronus; the sun-god, Helios or Sol, son of the Titan Hyperion. (*Usu. l.c.*), *fig.* a person or thing of enormous size or strength; (*cap.*), *milit.* a U.S. intercontinental ballistic missile.—*a.* Titanic; gigantic.—**Ti·tan·ess,** *n.* A female Titan.

ti·ta·nate, tīt′a·nāt″, *n. Chem.* a salt of titanic acid.

ti·tan·ic, tī·tan′ik, ti·tan′ik, *a.* Of or containing titanium, esp. in a higher valence.

Ti·tan·ic, tī·tan′ik, *a.* Pertaining to the Titans. (*l.c.*) Enormous in size or strength; colossal.—**ti·tan·i·cal·ly,** *adv.*

ti·tan·ic ac·id, *n. Chem.* one of various acids derived from titanium dioxide.

ti·tan·if·er·ous, tīt″a·nif′ėr·us, *a.* Containing or yielding titanium.

Ti·tan·ism, tīt′a·niz″um, *n.* (*Sometimes l.c.*) the state of having the spirit characteristic of a Titan, esp. in rebellion against traditional behavior or institutions.

ti·tan·ite, tīt′a·nīt″, *n.* A widespread mineral, calcium titanium silicate, $CaTiSi$-

---

ch- chain, G. na*ch*t;   **th-** THen, thin;   **w-** wig, hw as sound in whig;   **z-** zh as in azure, zeal.   *Italicized vowel* indicates schwa sound.

O₅, occurring in yellow, green, or brown crystals. Also *sphene*.

ti·ta·ni·um, tī·tā′nē·um, *n.* [So called in fanciful allusion to the *Titans*.] A very hard, silver to dark gray metallic element occurring in many rocks, mainly ilmenite and rutile, used chiefly in metallurgy, esp. steel-making, because of its light weight, its strength, and corrosion resistant properties. Sym. Ti, at. no. 22, at. wt. 47.90. See *Periodic Table of Elements*.

ti·ta·ni·um di·ox·ide, *n. Chem.* TiO_2, a white powder having various industrial uses, such as in paint pigments, lacquers, rubber, plastics, ceramics, and as a delustering agent for synthetic fibers.

ti·ta·ni·um white, *n.* A white paint pigment composed mainly of titanium dioxide.

ti·tan·o·saur, tī·tan′o·sạr″, tīt′a·no·sạr″, *n.* Any of the large, amphibious, plant-eating dinosaurs of the genus *Titanosaurus*, which lived during the Cretaceous period.

ti·tan·ous, tī·tan′us, tī·tan′us, *a. Chem.* of or pertaining to titanium compounds, esp. when trivalent.

tit·bit, tit′bit″, *n. Brit.* tidbit.

ti·ter, ti·tre, tī′tẽr, tē′tẽr, *n.* [Fr. *titre*, title, fineness, strength, < L. *titulus*, E. *title.*] *Chem.* the strength of a standard solution, or the concentration of a substance, as determined by titration.

tit for tat, *n.* [Cf. *tip.*] An equivalent given in return, as in retaliation, repartee, or the like; blow for blow.

tithe, tīTH, *n.* [O.E. *teogotha*, *tēotha*, tenth, akin to *tēn*, *tīen*, E. *ten.*] The tenth part of the annual produce or income due or paid as a tax for the support of the priesthood and religious institutions; any tax, levy, or the like of one tenth; a tenth part, or any indefinitely small part, of anything, as: Not one *tithe* of the sum was recovered.—*v.t. tithed, tithing.* [O.E. *teogothian*, *tēothian*.] To give or pay a tithe or tenth of, as for the support of the church; to pay tithes on; to exact a tithe from; to levy a tithe on.—*v.i.* To give or pay a tithe or tenth of.—**tith·a·ble**, *a.*—**tithe·less**, *a.*

tith·ing, tī′THing, *n.* [O.E. *tēothung*.] A tithe; *Eng.* an administrative district, formerly consisting of ten households.

ti·ti, tē·tē′, *n. pl.* **ti·tis**. [S. Amer.] *Zool.* any of various small monkeys of the genus *Callicebus*, of S. America.

ti·ti, tē′tē,, *n. pl.* **ti·tis**. [Origin uncertain.] *Bot.* A shrub or small tree, *Cliftonia monophylla*, or 'black titi,' with glossy leaves and racemes of white flowers, found in the southern U.S.; a related tree, *Cyrilla racemiflora*, of tropical America.

ti·tian, tish′an, *n.* [< *Titian* (c. 1477–1576), It. painter who used such a color in painting women's hair.] A reddish-brown or auburn color.—*a.*

tit·il·late, tit′i·lāt″, *v.t.*—**titillated, titillating.** [L. *titillatus*, pp. of *titillare*, tickle.] To tickle; to excite agreeably; as, to *titillate* the fancy.—**tit·il·la·tion**, *n.*—**tit·il·la-tive**, *a.*

tit·i·vate, tit′i·vāt″, *v.t.*—**titivated, titivating.** [Perh. < *tidy.*] *Colloq.* To put in order; to make look smart or spruce; to adorn.—*v.i.* Also **tit·ti·vate.**—**tit·i·va·tion**, *n.*

tit·lark, tit′lärk″, *n.* [< *tit*, a small bird, and *lark.*] Any of various small birds resembling a lark; a pipit.

ti·tle, tī′tl, *n.* [O.Fr. *title* (Fr. *titre*), < L. *titulus*, inscription, label, notice, title, appellation, sign, M.L. mark over a letter or word.] The distinguishing name of a book, poem, piece of music, picture, or other work; a descriptive heading or caption, as of a chapter, section, or other part of a book; a division of a statute or law book, esp. one larger than an article or section; all the matter on a title page, or the title page itself; the panel on the spine of a book,

giving its name; any descriptive or distinctive appellation; a distinguishing appellation belonging to a person by right of rank, office, or attainment, or assigned as a mark of respect or courtesy; an appellation indicating social rank, as in the nobility or peerage; established or recognized right to something; ground for a claim; anything affording ground for a claim. *Law*, legal right to the possession of property, esp. real property; the ground or evidence of such right. *Sports*, the championship, as: They won the *title*. *Pl.*, *cinematography*, credits; subtitles. *Eccles.* a fixed sphere of work and source of income, required as a condition of ordination; any of certain churches in Rome, the nominal incumbents of which are cardinals.—*v.t.*—*titled, titling.* To furnish with a title; to designate by an appellation; to call or style; to entitle.—**ti·tled**, tīt′ld, *a.*

ti·tle deed, *n. Law*, a deed constituting evidence of ownership.

ti·tle·hold·er, tīt′l·hōl″dẽr, *n.* One possessing a title, esp. in sports; champion.

ti·tle page, *n.* The page, at or near the beginning of a book, which contains its full title, usu. with particulars as to its authorship, publication, and the like.

tit·mouse, tit′mous″, *n. pl.* **tit·mice**, tit′mīs″. [< *tit*, a small thing, a small bird, and *mouse*, by corruption < O.E. *māse* (D. *mees*, G. *meise*), a titmouse.] Any of several birds of the family *Paridae*, esp. *Parus bicolor*, the tufted titmouse, distinguished by its crest and rusty flanks.

Ti·to·ism, tē′tō·iz″um, *n.* A nationalistic form of Communism, originated and practiced by Marshal Tito in Yugoslavia, stressing independence from, and opposition to, Soviet control of Communist countries.

ti·tra·tion, tī·trā′shan, tī·trā′shan, *n.* [Fr. *titrer*, < *titre*, fineness, strength.] *Chem.* a method to ascertain the quantity of a given constituent present in a solution by accurately measuring the volume of a liquid reagent of known strength necessary to convert the constituent into another form, the close of the reaction being marked by some definite phenomenon, as a change of color.—**ti·trat·a·ble, ti·tra·ble**, tī′tra·bl, *a.*—**ti·trate**, tī′trāt, tī′trāt, *v.t.*, *v.i.*—*titrated, titrating.*

tit·tat·toe, tit″tat·tō′, *n.* Tick-tack-toe.

tit·ter, tit′ẽr, *v.i.* [An imit. word, like *snigger*, *tattle*, etc.] To laugh with a stifled sound or with restraint; to laugh nervously.—*n.*—**tit·ter·er**, *n.*—**tit·ter·ing·ly**, *adv.*

tit·tle, tit′l, *n.* [O.Fr. *title*, a title, a tittle.] A particle; a jot; an iota; a diacritical mark.

tit·tle-tat·tle, tit′l·tat″l, *n.* [Varied redupl. of *tattle.*] Idle, trifling talk; petty gossip; one who engages in such talk or gossip.—*v.i.*—*tittle-tattled, tittle-tattling.* To talk tittle-tattle; gossip.—**tit·tle-tat·tler**, *n.*

tit·tup, tit′up, *n.* [Appar. imit.] A canter or easy gallop, as of a horse; a prancing movement; a curvet.—*v.i. tittuped, tittuping,* chiefly Brit. *tittupped, tittupping.* To go at a canter or easy gallop, as a horse or the rider; to go with an up-and-down movement suggesting this, as a boat on the waves or a person walking in an affected manner; to prance; spring; caper.

tit·u·lar, tich′a·lẽr, tit′ya·lẽr, *a.* [Fr. *titulaire*; < L. *titulus*, a title.] Having the title or name only; nominal; of, pertaining to, or constituting a title.—*n.* One who holds a title.—**tiv·u·lar·ly**, *adv.*

tiz·zy, tiz′ē, *n. pl.* **tiz·zies**. *Colloq.* an agitated state of mind; a dither. *Brit. slang*, a sixpence.

T-man, tē′man″, *n. pl.* **T-men**. *Colloq.* a nickname for a special agent of the Treasury Department.

tme·sis, ta·mē′sis, mē′sis, *n.* [Gr. *tmēsis*, < *temnō*, to cut.] *Gram.* the division of a compound word into two parts, with one or

more words between, as *what* place *soever* for *whatsoever*.

TNT, T.N.T., tē′en·tē′, *n.* Trinitrotoluene; *colloq.* anything likened to an explosive.

to, tō, *unstressed* tụ, to, *prep.* [O.E. *tō*, O.Fries. *tō* = D. *toe* = O.H.G. *zō*, *zuo* (G. *zu*) *to*.] Toward, specifying a point or person to be approached and reached, as: Come *to* the house. In the direction of, expressing motion toward; as, from north *to* south; to the degree that; as, rotten *to* the core; in contact or contiguity with, as: Apply varnish *to* the surface. Until, regarding a point in time; as, *to* this day; designated for, as: This note is addressed *to* you. For the purpose of; as, leaping *to* his defense; toward; concerning a destined or appointed end; as, sentenced *to* death; in direct contact with; as, person *to* person; in honor of, as: They drank *to* his success. To the limit of; as, punctual *to* the minute; in addition to, as: He added insult *to* injury. In adherence to, as: He held *to* his opinion. By comparison with, as: One man's wealth is nothing *to* another's. In agreement or accordance with; as, a position *to* one's liking; in reference or relation to, as: What will he say *to* this? Used to supply the place of the dative in other languages, connecting transitive verbs with their indirect or direct objects, and adjectives, nouns, and intransitive or passive verbs with a following noun which limits their action or application; used as the ordinary sign or accompaniment of the infinitive expressing orig. motion, direction, purpose, and the like, as in the ordinary uses with a substantive object, but now appearing in many cases as a mere meaningless sign.—*adv.* Toward a person, thing, or point implied or understood; *colloq.* to a point of contact, or a closed position, as: Pull the shutter *to*. To a matter, or to action or work, as: Fall *to*! To consciousness, or to one's senses; as, after he came *to*.—**to and fro**, to and from some place or thing; in opposite or different directions alternately.

toad, tōd, *n.* [O.E. *tādige*, *tādie*, toad; origin unknown.] *Zool.* any of various tailless amphibians, esp. the warty-skinned terrestrial species of the genus *Bufo*; *fig.* a person or thing as an object of disgust or aversion.

toad·eat·er, tōd′ē″tẽr, *n.* [Orig. a mountebank's attendant, who pretended to swallow toads, etc.] A fawning, obsequious person; a sycophant. Also *toady.*

toad·fish, tōd′fish″, *n. pl.* **toad·fish**, **toad·fish·es**. Any of the thick-headed, widemouthed fishes constituting the family *Batrachoididae*, as *Opsanus tau*, of the Atlantic coast of the U.S.

toad·flax, tōd′flaks″, *n.* A common European plant, *Linaria vulgaris*, having showy yellow and orange flowers and naturalized as a weed in the U.S.; any plant of the same genus. Also *butter-and-eggs.*

toad spit, *n.* Cuckoo-spit. Also **toad spit·tle.**

toad·stone, tōd′stōn″, *n.* Any of various stones or stonelike objects resembling a toad in shape or color, supposed to have been formed in the head or body of a toad, and formerly worn as jewels or amulets.

toad·stool, tōd′stōl″, *n.* Any of various fungi having a stalk with an umbrellalike cap, esp. those that are poisonous, as distinguished from the edible forms. See *mushroom.*

toad·y, tō′dē, *n. pl.* **toad·ies**. [Short for *toadeater*.] A sycophant; a flatterer; a toadeater.—*v.t.*—*toadied, toadying.* To fawn upon in a servile manner; to play the toady or sycophant to.—*v.i.* To act as a toady.—**toad·y·ism**, *n.*

to-and-fro, tō′an·frō′, *a.* Moving back-and-forth.—*n. pl.* **to-and-fros.** A backward and forward movement or motion.

---

a- fat, fāte, fär, fåre, fạll; e- met, mē, mēre, hẽr; i- pin, pīne; o- not, nōte, mōve; u- tub, cūbe, bụll; oi- oil; ou- pound.

toast, tōst, *v.t.* [O.Fr. *toster,* < L. *torrere* (pp. *tostus*) dry, parch, scorch.] To brown, as bread or cheese, by exposure to heat; to heat or warm thoroughly at a fire.—*v.i.* To become toasted.—*n.* Bread in slices superficially browned by heat.

toast, tōst, *n.* [Another use of *toast, n.,* with reference to a piece of toast put into a beverage to flavor it.] A person whose health is proposed; an event, sentiment, person, or the like, to which one drinks; a call on another or others to drink to some person or thing, or the act of thus drinking. —*v.t.* To propose as a toast; drink to the health of or in honor of.—*v.i.* To propose or drink a toast.

toast·er, tō'stẽr, *n.* One who toasts; an instrument for toasting bread or cheese.

toast·mas·ter, tōst'mas"tẽr, tōst'mä"stẽr, *n.* One who is appointed to propose or announce the toasts at a public dinner or the like; one who presides at a dinner and introduces the after-dinner speakers.— **toast·mis·tress,** tōst'mis"tris, *n.* Feminine of toastmaster.

to·bac·co, to·bak'ō, *n.* pl. **to·bac·cos, to·bac·coes.** [Sp. *tabaco,* from a W. Ind. name variously explained as meaning orig. a kind of pipe used in smoking, a roll of leaves smoked, or the plant.] Any plant of the solanaceous genus *Nicotiana,* esp. *N. tabacum,* whose leaves are prepared for smoking or chewing or as snuff; the leaves so prepared.

to·bac·co heart, *n. Pathol.* a functional disorder of the heart, characterized by a rapid and often irregular pulse, due to excessive use of tobacco.

to·bac·co·nist, to·bak'o·nist, *n.* A dealer in tobacco; one who sells smoking supplies at retail.

to-be, to·bē', *a.* Pertaining to that which is soon to be or is yet to come: used in combination; as, mother-*to-be.*

to·bog·gan, to·bog'an, *n.* [Corruption of Amer. Ind. *odabagan,* a sled.] A kind of flat-bottomed sled of thin wood turned up in front, usu. with low side rails, and used for sliding down snow-covered slopes.—*v.i.* To use such a sled; *fig.* to fall rapidly, as stock prices.—**to·bog·gan·er, to·bog·gan·ist,** *n.*

to·by, tō'bē, *n.* pl. **to·bies.** [From *Toby,* for *Tobiah* or *Tobias,* man's name.] A small ale jug or mug in the form of a stout old man wearing a three-cornered hat; also **To·by jug.** *Slang,* a cheap panetella.

toc·ca·ta, to·kä'ta, *It.* tạk·kä'tä, *n.* pl. **toc·ca·te,** to·kä'tē, *It.* tạk·kä'tē. [It., orig. pp. fem. of *toccare,* touch.] *Mus.* a composition in the style of an improvisation for a keyboard instrument, and frequently intended to exhibit the player's technique.

to·col·o·gy, to·kol'o·gy, tō·kol'o·jē, *n.* [Gr. *tókos,* birth, offspring.] Medicine as applied to parturition; obstetrics.

to·coph·er·ol, to·kof'e·rōl, tō·kof'e·rạl, tō·kof'e·rol", *n.* [< Gr. *tókos,* birth.] *Biochem.* any of four phenolic compounds obtained from oils of various plants, as wheat germ and cottonseed, and possessing the active principle of vitamin E.

toc·sin, tok'sin, *n.* [Fr. *tocsin,* O.Fr. *toquesin;* < *toque,* a stroke, and *sin, sein,* a bell, < L. *signum,* a sign.] An alarm bell; a bell rung as a signal or for the purpose of giving an alarm.

tod, tod, *n.* [M.E. *todde,* weight of wool; perh. < L.G.] An English unit of weight, chiefly for wool, usu. equal to 28 pounds but varying locally; a load; a bushy mass, esp. of ivy.

to-day, to-day, to·dā', *adv.* [O.E. *tō dæg.*] On this present day; at the present time; in these days.—*n.* This present day; this present time or age.

tod·dle, tod'l, *v.i.*—*toddled, toddling.* [Freq.

akin to *totter;* cf. G. *zotteln,* to toddle.] To walk with short steps in a tottering way, as a child or an old person.—*n.* The act of walking in this manner; an unsteady gait.— **tod·dler,** *n.*

tod·dy, tod'ē, *n.* pl. **tod·dies.** [Hind.] A drink made of a liquor, hot water, and sugar, often spiced with bitters, clove, or lemon peel; the sap of certain E. Indian palm trees used as a beverage.

to-do, to·dö', *n.* pl. **to-dos.** *Colloq.* Bustle; hurry; commotion; fuss, as: He made little *to-do* about his good fortune.

to·dy, tō'dē, *n.* pl. **to·dies.** [Cf. Fr. *todier* and N.L. *Todus,* < L. *todi,* pl., kind of small birds.] Any of the small insectivorous W. Indian birds, genus *Todus,* related to kingfishers, and having a brightly colored plumage.

toe, tō, *n.* [O.E. *tā* = M.L.G. *tē* = O.H.G. *zēha* (G. *zehe*) = Icel. *tā,* toe.] One of the terminal members or digits of the foot in man and other vertebrates; an analogous part in other animals; the forepart of the foot or hoof of a horse or the like; a part, as of a stocking or shoe, to cover the toes; a part resembling a toe or the toes in shape or position. *Mach.* a journal or part placed vertically in a bearing, as the lower end of a vertical shaft; an arm or projecting part on which a cam or the like strikes. *Golf,* the end of a golf club's head.—*v.t.*—*toed, toeing.* To furnish with a toe or toes; to touch or reach with the toes; to kick with the toe; *golf,* to strike, as the ball, with the toe or tip of the club. *Carp.* to fasten, as by nails driven obliquely; to drive, as a nail, obliquely.—*v.i.* To place or move the toes in a manner specified; as, to *toe* in, in walking; to tap with the toe, as in dancing.—**toe the mark** or **line,** to stand with the tips of the toes touching a certain mark or line; *fig.* to conform to a certain standard, as of duty or conduct.—**toe·less,** *a.*

toe box, *n.* A piece or small portion of hardened leather or similar substance which is put between a shoe's lining and toecap.

toe·cap, tō'kap", *n.* The leather or similar covering for a shoe's toe or tip.

toe crack, *n.* A sand crack on the toe of a horse's hoof.

toed, tōd, *a.* Having a toe or toes; as, a five-*toed* animal. *Carp.* driven obliquely, as a nail; fastened by nails driven in an oblique manner.

toe dance, *n.* A dance done on one's tiptoes.—**toe-dance,** tō'dans", tō'däns", *v.i.* —*toe-danced, toe-dancing.* To execute a toe dance.—**toe danc·er,** *n.*

toe hold, *n.* A small place or ledge used to support one's toes while climbing; a way of progress, an advantage, or a footing; as, to obtain a *toe hold* in the country; *wrestling,* a hold in which one's opponent's foot is bent back.

toe-in, tō'in", *n.* An adjustment for an automobile's front wheels which places the front of them closer together than the back and improves the steering.

toe·nail, tō'nāl", *n.* The nail growing on each of the toes of the human foot; *carp.* a nail driven obliquely.—*v.t. Carp.* to fasten or secure by nails obliquely driven.

toe·shoe, tō'shö", *n.* A ballet slipper having a leather-covered wooden toe and heelless, used to toe dance.

toff, tof, *n.* [Origin obscure.] *Brit. slang.* A person of stylish or smart appearance; a swell; a dandy; sometimes, in compliment, a good fellow or a gentleman.

tof·fee, tof·fy, tạ'fē, tof'ē, *n. Chiefly Brit.* a hard sweetmeat or candy made of sugar, butter, and flavoring, as rum, boiled together and sometimes mixed with nuts. See *taffy.*

toft, tạft, toft, *n.* [Late O.E. *toft;* < Scand.]

Brit. dial. The site of a house and its outbuildings; a homestead or messuage; a knoll or hillock.

tog, tog, *n.* [Origin obscure; first in vagabonds' and thieves' slang.] *Colloq.* coat; usu. *pl.* clothes.—*v.t.*—*togged, togging. Colloq.* to clothe or dress, often used with *out* or *up.*

to·ga, tō'ga, *n.* pl. **to·gas, to·gae.** [L., akin to *tegere,* cover.] The loose outer garment of the citizens of ancient Rome when appearing in public; a similar robe of office or some other distinctive garment.—**to·gaed,** tō'gad, *a.* Clad in a toga.

to·gat·ed, tō'gā·tid, *a.* Togaed; *fig.* stately and dignified.

to·ga vi·ri·lis, tō'ga vi·rī'lis, *L.* tō'gä wi·rē'lis, *n.* pl. **to·gae vi·ri·les,** tō'jē vi·ri'lēz, *L.* tō'gī wi·rē'les. [L., 'manly toga.'] The toga, usu. white, symbolizing manhood, assumed by Roman youths when they attained the age of fourteen.

to·geth·er, tụ·geTH'ẽr, *adv.* [O.E. *tōgaedere, tōgadore,* < *tō,* to, and *gador, geador,* together.] Into or in one gathering, company, mass, or body; as, to call the people *together;* into or in union, proximity, contract, or collision, as two or more things; as, to tie or sew things *together;* into or in relationship or association, as two or more persons; taken or considered collectively or conjointly, as: This one cost more than all the others *together.* Into or in a condition of unity or compactness, or so as to form a connected whole or compact body, as at the same time or simultaneously, as: You cannot have both *together.* Without intermission or interruption, continuously, or uninterruptedly; in cooperation, with united action, or conjointly; with mutual action, with one another, mutually, or reciprocally; as, to confer *together.*—**to·geth·er·ness,** *n.*

tog·ger·y, tog'e·rē, *n.* pl. **tog·ger·ies.** [Perh. humorously formed < L. *toga.*] *Colloq.* Togs; clothes; garments; a store which sells clothing.

tog·gle, tog'l, *n.* [Origin obscure.] A transverse pin, bolt, or rod placed through an eye of a rope or link of a chain for various purposes, as to fit into a bight, loop, or ring in another rope or chain, thus fastening the two ropes or chains together, or to serve as a hold for the fingers; a toggle joint, or a device furnished with one.—*v.t.*—*toggled, toggling.* To furnish with a toggle or toggles; to secure or fasten with a toggle or toggles.

tog·gle joint, *n. Mech.* a device consisting of two arms hinged together at their inner ends and hinged to other parts at their outer ends which creates pressure on the outer ends when the arms are made to open out into a position, more or less approaching a straight line, by force applied at the bend between them.

tog·gle switch, *n. Elect.* a switch composed of a lever which moves through a small arc to open or close an electrical circuit.

toil, toil, *v.i.* [A.Fr. *toiler,* dispute, contend, O.Fr. Fr. *touiller,* stir, mix, < L. *tudiculare,* stir, < *tudicula,* dim. of *tudes,* hammer, mallet, akin to *tundere,* beat.] To engage in severe and continuous work or exertion; to labor arduously; to move or travel with difficulty, weariness, or pain.—*v.t.* To bring, effect, or produce by toil.—*n.* Hard and continuous work or exertion; exhausting labor or effort; any struggle with difficulties; a laborious task; a period of arduous labor; something produced or accomplished by toil.—**toil·er,** *n.*

toil, toil, *n.* [O.Fr. Fr. *toile,* cloth, web, < L. *tela,* web, < *texere,* weave.] *Usu. pl.* a net or nets set about a space into which game is driven or within which game is known to be.

toile, twäl, *n.* Any of several sheer linen or linenlike fabrics.

toile de Jouy, *Fr.* twal de zhwē', *n.* A linen

or linenlike fabric distinguished by scenic designs of a single color printed on a light background and used extensively for draperies and upholstery.

toi·let, toi'lit, *n.* [Fr. *toilette,* dim. of *toile,* cloth.] A dressing room, esp. one with a bath: in a restricted sense, a bathroom or watercloset; a fixture in the bathroom with a seat and bowl containing water for feces and urine which are then flushed away. The act or process of dressing, including bathing and arranging the hair; the dress or costume of a person; also *toilette. Surg.* the cleansing of the part after an operation, esp. in the peritoneal cavity.—*a.*

toi·let pa·per, *n.* A light, soft paper, usu. wound around a roll, for bathroom use. Also **bath·room tis·sue, toi·let tis·sue.**

toi·let pow·der, *n.* Any fine powder used to sprinkle or rub over the skin, esp. after the bath, usu. scented and with antiseptic ingredients.

toi·let·ry, toi'li·trē, *n. pl.* **toi·let·ries.** Any article, as soap, cologne, or a comb, used in dressing or completing one's toilet.

toi·let soap, *n.* Any mild, fine soap, usu. colored and perfumed.

toi·lette, toi·let', *Fr.* twä·let' [Fr.] *n. pl.* **toi·lettes.** Act of dressing. See *toilet.*

toi·let wa·ter, *n.* A lightly perfumed liquid containing alcohol.

toil·ful, toil'ful, *a.* Full of or characterized by toil; laborious.—**toil·ful·ly,** *adv.*

toil·some, toil'som, *a.* Attended with toil; laborious; fatiguing.—**toil·some·ly,** *adv.*—**toil·some·ness,** *n.*

toil·worn, toil'wōrn", toil'wǎrn", *a.* Worn; worn out or exhausted by toil.

To·kay, tō·kā', *n.* A sweet dessert wine distinguished by its aromatic taste and deriving its name from Tokay in Hungary where it was first produced; a type of large white or reddish grape originating in the vicinity of Tokay.

to·ken, tō'ken, *n.* [O.E. *tácen, tácn,* a token = Icel. *tákn, teiken,* D. *teeken,* G. *zeichen,* Goth. *taikns*—a sign, a token; akin to *teach.*] Something intended or supposed to represent or indicate another thing or an event; a sign; a mark; indication; a memento of friendship or affection; a souvenir; something that serves by way of pledge of authenticity, good faith, or the like; a stamped metal disk or the like, used for payment of fares or similar purposes.—*a.*—*v.t.* To be a symbol of; to serve as a token of.

to·ken pay·ment, *n.* A payment, only partial and usu. small, made as an acknowledgement of the existence of a larger debt or other obligation.

tol·bu·ta·mide, tol·bū'ta·mīd", *n. Pharm.* a drug of the sulfonamide group, $C_{12}H_{18}N_2O_3S$, used to control some types of diabetes.

tole, tôle, tōl, *n.* A kind of metalware, usu. tin, enameled or lacquered and often displaying gilt designs on a black or dark green background, used esp. for trays, lamps, and small boxes.

To·le·do, to·lē'dō, *Sp.* tạ·le'ᴛнạ, *n.* (Often *l.c.*) a sword blade or sword from Toledo in Spain, formerly famous for its weaponry.

tol·er·a·ble, tol'ér·a·bl, *a.* [L. *tolerabilis.*] Capable of being borne or endured; sufferable; moderately good or agreeable; passable.—**tol·er·a·ble·ness, tol·er·a·bil·i·ty,** *n.*—**tol·er·a·bly,** *adv.*

tol·er·ance, tol'ér·ans, *n.* [L. *tolerantia.*] The state or fact of being tolerant; toleration; the act of, or capacity to endure; endurance; *med.* the capacity to endure or resist the action of a drug or poison; *mech.* an allowable variation in the dimensions of a mechanical part. *Coinage,* a legally permissible deviation in the weight and fineness of coins; also *remedy.*

tol·er·ant, tol'ér·ant, *a.* [L. *tolerans, tolerantis,* ppr. of *tolero.*] Inclined or disposed to tolerate; forbearing; *med.* capable of tolerance.—**tol·er·ant·ly,** *adv.*

tol·er·ate, tol'e·rāt", *v.t.*—*tolerated, tolerating.* [L. *toleratus,* pp. of *tolerare,* bear, support, endure.] To bear without repugnance; to put up with; to suffer to be, or to be practiced or done, without prohibition or hindrance; *med.* to endure or resist the action of, as a drug or poison.—**tol·er·a·tive,** *a.*—**tol·er·a·tor,** *n.*

tol·er·a·tion, tol"e·rā'shan, *n.* [L. *toleratio(n-).*] The act or practice of tolerating; forbearance; allowance, by a government, of the exercise of religions not officially established or recognized; *med.* tolerance.

tol·i·dine, tol'i·dēn", tol'i·din, *n.* [< *toluene.*] *Chem.* any of several isomeric basic derivatives of toluene, one of which is used in making dyes.

toll, tōl, *n.* [O.E. *toll, toln,* < L.L. *toloneum,* for *telonium* < Gr. *telōnion,* tollhouse, < *telōnēs,* collector of taxes, < *télos,* tax, toll.] A payment exacted for some right or privilege, esp. for the right of passage along a road or over a bridge; a compensation for services rendered, as for transportation or a long-distance telephone call; *fig.* the cost, as in damage or loss, incurred in any undertaking or happenstance; exaction, as: The epidemic took a heavy *toll* of lives.—*v.t.* To exact or collect as toll.—*v.i.* To exact or collect toll.

toll, tōl, *v.t.* [M.E. *tollen, tullen,* akin to O.E. *-tyllan* in *fortyllan,* draw away, seduce.] To cause, as esp. a large bell, to sound slowly and regularly, as for summoning a congregation to church, announcing a death, or on the occasion of a funeral. To lure or decoy, as game; also *tole.*—*v.i.* To sound slowly and regularly, as a bell.—*n.* The sound made by a tolling bell; the act of tolling a bell.

toll·booth, tōl'bōth", tōl'bōᴛн", *n. pl.* **toll·booths,** tōl'bōthz'. A booth or stall, as by a road or bridge, where tolls are collected; tollhouse.

toll call, *n.* A telephone call for which one pays a higher rate than is charged for local calls, esp. a long-distance call.

toll col·lec·tor, *n.* A person who collects tolls at a tollgate; a tollman. Also **toll·keep·er,** tōl'kēpér.

toll·gate, tōl'gāt", *n.* A gate, as across a road or at the approach to a bridge, where toll is taken.

toll·house, tōl'hous", *n. pl.* **toll·hous·es,** tōl'hou"ziz. A booth or house near a tollgate, where the toll collector is stationed; tollbooth.

toll·man, tōl'man, *n. pl.* **toll·men.** Toll collector.

toll road, *n.* A road, esp. a highway, on which toll is charged. Also **toll·way.**

Tol·tec, tol'tek, *a.* Pertaining to an Indian people who flourished in central Mexico previous to the advent of the Aztecs, and who were, according to tradition, the source of Aztec culture.—*n.* A member of the Toltecs.—**Tol·tec·an,** *a.*

to·lu, tạ·lō', to·lō', *n.* [From *Tolú* (or Santiago de *Tolú*), seaport of Colombia.] A fragrant yellowish-brown balsam obtained from a S. American tree, *Myroxylon balsamum,* used in medicine as a stomachic and expectorant, and in perfumery. Also *balsam of Tolu.*

tol·u·ate, tol'ū·āt", *n. Chem.* an ester or salt of toluic acid.

tol·u·ene, tol'ū·ēn", *n. Chem.* a colorless, flammable, mobile liquid hydrocarbon, $C_6H_5CH_3$, obtained from coal tar and petroleum, used in making explosives, dyes, and as a solvent. Also **meth·yl ben·zene.**

to·lu·ic ac·id, *n. Chem.* any of several isomeric acids, $C_6H_4CH_3COOH$, which are

derivatives of toluene.—**to·lu·ic,** to·lö'ik, tol'ū·ik, *a.*

to·lu·i·dine, to·lō'i·dēn", to·lö'i·din, *n. Chem.* any of three isomeric amines, $CH_3C_6H_4NH_2$, derived from compounds of toluene and used in manufacturing drugs and dyes.

tol·u·ol, tol·u·ole, tol'ū·ōl", *n. Chem.* the commercial or crude grade of toluene.

tol·yl, tol'il, *n. Chem.* a univalent hydrocarbon radical, $CH_3C_6H_4$, obtained from toluene.

tom, tom, *n.* The male of certain animals, often used in compounds; as, *tomcat.*

tom·a·hawk, tom'a·hǎk", *n.* [N. Amer. Ind.] A light ax used by the N. American Indians as a weapon and tool; any of various similar weapons or implements.—*v.t.* To strike, cut, or kill with a tomahawk.

tom·al·ley, tom'al"ē, *n. pl.* **tom·al·leys.** [Carib.] The liver of the lobster, which becomes green when cooked, and is a delicacy.

Tom and Jer·ry, *n.* A drink consisting of water or milk, rum, beaten eggs, sugar, and spices, and served hot.

to·ma·to, to·mā'tō, to·mä'tō, *n. pl.* **to·ma·toes.** [Sp. *tomate,* < Mex. *tomatl,* tomato.] A widely cultivated solanaceous plant, *Lycopersicon esculentum,* native to S. America, bearing a slightly acid, pulpy fruit, commonly red, sometimes yellow, used as a vegetable; the fruit itself; any plant of the same genus, or its fruit; *slang,* a female.

tomb, tōm, *n.* [O.Fr. Fr. *tombe,* < L.L. *tumba,* < Gr. *túmbos,* sepulchral mound, tomb: cf. *tumulus.*] An excavation in earth or rock for the reception of a dead body; a grave, chamber, or vault; a mausoleum; any sepulchral structure that receives or holds the remains of the dead or serves as a commemorative monument for them.—*v.t.* To place in or as in a tomb; bury.—**tomb·less,** *a.*—**tomb·like,** *a.*

tom·bac, tom·back, tom·bak, tom'bak, *n.* [Fr. *tombac,* < Malay *tambaga,* copper.] An alloy of copper and zinc, used as an imitation of gold for cheap jewelry. Also **tam·bac,** tam'bak.

tom·bo·lo, tom'bo·lō", *n. pl.* **tom·bo·los.** A bar of sand or gravel tying an island to the mainland or connecting two islands.

tom·boy, tom'boi", *n.* A boisterous, wild, romping girl; a hoyden.—**tom·boy·ish,** *a.*—**tom·boy·ish·ness,** *n.*

tomb·stone, tōm'stōn", *n.* A stone erected over a grave, usu. bearing an inscription; a marker.

tom·cat, tom'kat", *n.* A male cat.

tom·cod, tom'kod", *n.* [Perh. < N. Amer. Ind.] Any of various small edible cods of the genus *Microgadus,* esp. *M. tomcod,* of the Atlantic coast of N. America; any of various similar fishes.

Tom Col·lins, *n.* A drink made of gin, carbonated water, lime or lemon juice, and sugar.

Tom, Dick, and Har·ry, *n Colloq.* Men or persons indiscriminately, esp. of the common run; anybody; everybody, usu. preceded by *every.*

tome, tōm, *n.* [Fr. *tome,* < L. *tomus,* a portion of a book, a book, < Gr. *tomos,* a section, < *temnō,* to cut.] A volume, forming part of a larger work; a book, usu. a ponderous one.

to·men·tose, to·men'tōs, tō'men·tōs", *a.* [L. *tomentum,* down.] *Biol.* densely covered with short woolly or downy hairs. Also **to·men·tous.**

to·men·tum, to·men'tum, *n. pl.* **to·men·ta,** to·men'ta. [L.] A stuffing of wool, etc., for cushions.] *Bot.* pubescence consisting of longish, soft, entangled hairs pressed close to the surface; *anat.* a blood vessel network found within the brain's cortex and the pia mater's cerebral surface.

tom·fool, tom'fōl', *n.* [From *Tom Fool*, used as a name for a half-witted person.] A grossly foolish person; a silly fool.—*a.* Stupid, foolish, or doltish.

tom·fool·er·y, tom"fō'le·rē, *n.* pl. **tom·fool·er·ies.** Senseless or silly foolery; a silly or foolish performance, matter, or thing; nonsense.

tom·my, tom'ē, *n.* pl. **tom·mies.** [From the name *Thomas Atkins,* used casually in specimen forms given in Army Regulations.] (*Often cap.*) a private in the British army; also **Tom·my At·kins.** *Brit. colloq.* a piece or loaf of bread, esp. brown bread; provisions; rations; food.

Tom·my gun, *n. Colloq.* a Thompson submachine gun, or any similar weapon.

tom·my·rot, tom'ē·rot", *n. Colloq.* Foolishness; nonsense.

to·mog·ra·phy, to·mog'ra·fē, *n.* [Gr. *tōmos,* cutting, and *-graphy.*] *Med.* a special X-ray technique by which detailed images of a structure lying in a specific layer of tissue may be obtained, with images of structures in other layers eliminated or blurred.

to·mor·row, to-mor·row, to·mar'ō, to·mor'ō, *n.* [M.E. *to morwe.*] The morrow, or the day after this day, as: *Tomorrow* will be fair. A future time; as, the inventions of *tomorrow.*—*adv.* On the morrow; on the day after this day; as, come *tomorrow.*

tom·pi·on, tom'pē·on, *n.* Tampion.

Tom Thumb, *n.* A diminutive hero of a popular story; any diminutive person; a midget or dwarf.

tom·tit, tom'tit", *n. Brit.* a common name for various small birds, esp. certain tits or titmice. A name sometimes given to the chickadee and wren in the U.S.

tom-tom, tom'tom", *n.* [Also *tam-tam;* E. Ind.] A native Indian or African small-headed drum, usu. played with the hands; a gong having a metal disk which is sounded by striking with a padded hammer; a repetitious rhythm or beating sound. Also *tam-tam.*

ton, tun, *n.* [Var. of *tun.*] A unit of weight equivalent to 2,000 pounds avoirdupois, a 'short ton' in the U.S., and 2,240 pounds avoirdupois, a 'long ton' in Great Britain; a unit measuring displacement of ships, equal to 35 cubic feet; a unit measuring internal capacity of ships, equal to 100 cubic feet, a 'register ton'; a unit of volume for freight, being a ton in weight but varying in measure with the type of freight carried, a 'freight ton'; a unit of volume used in transportation by sea, commonly 40 cubic feet, a 'shipping ton'; in the metric system, a unit of weight equal to 1,000 kilograms or 2,204.6 pounds avoirdupois, a 'metric ton.' *Often pl., colloq.* a great number or quantity; a lot.

ton, *Fr.* taN, *n.* [Fr.] Tone; chic; stylishness.—**ton·ish,** *a.*—**ton·ish·ly,** *adv.*—**ton·ish·ness,** *n.*—**ton·y,** *a.*—*tonier, toniest.*

to·nal·i·ty, to·nal'i·tē, *n.* pl. **to·nal·i·ties.** *Mus.* a system of composition in which the tones and chords are related to a central keynote: distinguished from *atonality. Art,* the tone values of dark and light in a work as distinguished from, although often affected by, color values.

tone, tōn, *n.* [Fr. *ton,* tone, accent, style, manner, etc., L. *tonus,* a sound, a tone, < Gr. *tonos,* a stretching, a tone, note, strength, etc. < *teino,* to stretch, cogn. with L. *tendo,* to stretch, and E. *thin.* Tune is the same word.] Any sound that impresses the ear with its individual character, esp. pitch; quality of sound or timbre; strength or volume of sound; a modulation of the voice, as expressive of an emotion; a stress, accent, or inflection of voice; *ling.* the pitch used with stress, accent, or inflection sequentially to give one word different meanings, as in

a tone language. *Mus.* the distinctive sound of any voice or instrument; a pure or fundamental note without overtones or harmonics; precise pitch constituted of partial tones; a melody which is the basic of Gregorian Chants; a whole interval between certain contiguous notes, as of the diatonic scale; timbre. State of mind or disposition; mood; the general or prevailing character, as of morals, manners, or sentiments. *Paint.* a harmonious relationship of colors or their gradations of light and dark; the characteristic expression of a picture, as distinguished by its colors. *Physiol.* that condition of a vital body in which the parts have tension, the organs function normally, and the tissues are firm, sound, and resilient.—*v.t.*—*toned, toning.* To give certain tone to; to utter in an affected voice.—*v.i.* To adopt a certain tone.—**tone down,** to subdue or moderate, as a painting's color; to become softer.—**tone up,** to raise the strength or quality of; to gain in strength.—**ton·al,** *a.*—**ton·al·ly,** *adv.*—**tone·less,** *a.*—**tone·less·ly,** *adv.*—**tone·less·ness,** *n.*

tone arm, *n. Mus.* the pivoted pickup bar of a record player with a head consisting of a needle set into a cartridge, that follows the grooves of the record, converting the oscillations into electrical impulses.

tone-deaf, tōn'def", *a. Pathol.* lacking the capability to express or to discriminate distinctions in musical pitch.

tone lan·guage, *n. Ling.* a language in which pauses and pitch variations give identical words different meaning, as in Chinese.

ton·eme, tō'nēm, *n. Ling.* a phoneme with a discrete speech pattern in a tone language.—**to·ne·mic,** *a.*

tone po·em, *n.* Symphonic poem.

to·net·ic, tō·net'ik, *a. Ling.* pertaining to or having a relationship with meanings of intonations in speech, esp. to the pauses and pitch changes in a tone language.—**to·net·i·cal·ly,** *adv.*—**to·net·ics,** tō·net'-iks, *n. pl. but sing. in constr. Ling.* the science of phonetics as applied to intonations, esp. in a tone language.

tong, taŋg, tong, *v.t.* To seize, gather, hold, or handle with tongs, as ice or logs.—*v.i.* To use, or work with, tongs.

tong, taŋg, tong, *n.* [Chin.] A Chinese society or association; a secret Chinese society in the U.S.

ton·ga, tong'ga, *n.* [Hind. *tāṅgā.*] A light two-wheeled vehicle, usu. horse-drawn, used in India.

tongs, taŋgz, tongz, *n. pl., sing. or pl. in constr.* [O.E. *tange,* pl. *tangan,* tongs = D. and Dan. *tang,* Icel. *tŏng,* G. *zange,* tongs; same root as Gr. *daknō,* to bite.] An instrument of metal, a kind of large nippers with two hinged or pivoted arms, used for handling or grasping things.

tongue, tung, *n.* [O.E. *tunge,* a tongue, speech = L.G. and Dan. *tunge,* Icel. and Sw. *tunga,* Goth. *tuggo,* G. *zunge;* cogn. O.L. *dingua,* L. *lingua,* a tongue (whence *lingual, linguist*).] The freely moving organ within a man's and other vertebrate's mouth or the analogous organ of an invertebrate, with the power to shape itself for different purposes, as tasting, swallowing, and in man, articulation or speech; the tongue of an animal cooked for food; a receptor with taste buds and nerve endings; an articulator of speech in man; the power or act of speech; the whole sum of words used by a particular linguistic group or their dialect; anything formed, shaped, or exercised in the manner of a tongue; a point or strip of land, rock, or ice extruding from its surroundings, as a promontory or monolith; the closing pin of the clasp of an ornament or buckle; the taper of something, as a flame; a bell's clapper; *fox hunting,* the cry,

bark, or bay of a coursing dog. An utterance of divine inspiration; the pole with which a wagon is pulled; the sealing flap in back of the laced or buckled facing of a shoe; *carp.* the enclosed member of a tongue-and-groove joint; *mach.* a rib, blade, or flange; *mus.* the vibrating end of a reed in a wind instrument.—*v.t.*—*tongued, tonguing.* To investigate or touch with the tongue. *Archaic,* to articulate; to utter. *Colloq.* to scold; *mus.* to change the tones of, as notes or instruments; as, to *tongue* or in *tonguing* a trumpet. *Carp.* to cut or make a tongue on; to fit, as by a tongue-and-groove joint.—*v.i.* To project or extend, as a tongue; to talk; *mus.* to use one's tongue in playing one of the wind instruments.—**hold one's tongue,** to maintain silence.—**on the tip of one's tongue,** at the point of utterance; almost, but not quite, recollected.—**slip of the tongue,** the wrong word used.

tongue-and-groove joint, tung'an·gröv' joint", *n. Carp.* a means of joining two boards by inserting a ridge or tongue on the edge of one board into a groove in the other.

tongue in cheek, *adv.* With obvious insincerity for the purpose of sarcasm or humor, usu. preceded by *with.*

tongue-lash, tung'lash", *v.t., v.i. Colloq.* to rebuke harshly.—**tongue-lash·ing,** *n.*

tongue·less, tung'lis, *a.* Having no tongue; speechless; mute.

tongue-tie, tung'tī", *n.* Restricted movement of the tongue, esp. from a shortened frenum.—*v.t.*—*tongue-tied, tongue-tying.* To cause to be tongue-tied.

tongue-tied, tung'tīd", *a.* Unable to articulate distinctly; having an impediment in the speech or having tongue-tie; *fig.* unable to speak freely, as from surprise.

tongue twist·er, *n.* A phrase, word, or sentence which is difficult to utter rapidly due to the repetition of similar sounds or alliteration of the consonants, as 'rubber baby buggy bumpers.'

tongu·ing, tung'ing, *n. Mus.* the use of the tongue in playing a note on a wind instrument to divide the tone, producing a staccato or fluttering effect.

ton·ic, ton'ik, *a.* [Fr. *tonique,* < Gr. *tonikos,* < *tonos.*] *Med.* pertaining to, maintaining, increasing, or restoring the tone or healthy condition of the system or organs, as a medicine. Invigorating or bracing to the physical system, or to the mind or moral nature; as, a *tonic* experience. *Physiol., pathol.* pertaining to tension, as of the muscles; marked by continued muscular contraction; as, a *tonic* spasm. *Ling.* using alterations of pitch to distinguish words identical or nearly identical in form, as in certain languages; pertaining to tone or accent in speech. *Phon.* stressed, esp. by a principal accent. *Mus.* of or pertaining to a tone or tones; pertaining to or founded on the keynote, or first tone, of a scale; as, a *tonic* chord; a chord having the keynote for its root.—*n. Med.* a tonic agent or remedy. Anything invigorating or bracing, physically, mentally, or morally; *mus.* the keynote, or first tone, of a scale. Quinine water.—**ton·i·cal·ly,** *adv.*

ton·ic ac·cent, *n.* Vocal accent, or syllabic stress, in pronunciation or speaking. *Phon.* accent rendered by change of pitch rather than by altered stress; also **pitch ac·cent.**

to·nic·i·ty, tō·nis'i·tē, *n.* Tonic quality or condition; the property of possessing bodily tone; *physiol.* the normal elastic tension of living muscles, arteries, and other parts by which the tone of the system is maintained.

ton·ic sol-fa, *n. Mus.* a system of teaching music, esp. singing, in which tonality or key relationship is emphasized, the usual staff notation is replaced with special symbolization, and the tones are indicated by the sol-fa syllables or by their initial letters with *do* always denoting the tonic or keynote. See *sol-fa.*

to·night, to-night, to·nīt′, *n.* [Cf. *today, tomorrow.*] The present night; the night after the present day.—*adv.* On or in the present night, or the night after the present day.

ton·ka bean, tong′ka bēn″, *n.* [< *tonka,* the name of the bean in Guiana.] The fruit of the shrubby leguminous tree, *Dipteryx odorata,* containing a single seed with a pleasant odor, used in perfumes, as a vanilla substitute, and in flavoring tobaccos; the tree producing this fruit.

ton·nage, tun·nage, tun′ij, *n.* The carrying capacity of a merchant ship expressed in tons of 100 cubic feet; ships collectively considered with reference to carrying capacity or together with their cargoes; a duty on ships at so much per ton of cargo or freight, or according to the capacity in tons; the total weight or amount in tons of materials produced, shipped, or the like.

ton·neau, tu·nō′, *n.* pl. **ton·neaus, ton·neaux,** tu·nōz′. [Fr., lit. 'cask,' dim. of *tonne,* tun.] A rear body or compartment of an automobile, with seats for passengers; a complete automobile body having such a rear part.—**ton·neaued,** *a.*

to·nom·e·ter, tō·nom′i·tèr, *n.* [Gr. *tónos,* tension, tone.] An instrument for measuring the pitch of tones, esp. a tuning fork, or a graduated set of tuning forks, whose pitch has been exactly determined; *med.* any of various physiological instruments, as for measuring the tension of the eyeball, or for determining blood pressure within the vessels. An instrument for measuring vapor pressure.—**to·no·met·ric,** ton″o·me′trik, tō″no·me′trik, *a.*—**to·nom·e·try,** *n.*

ton·sil, ton′sil, *n.* [L. *tonsilla,* a tonsil, a mooring pole for a boat.] *Anat.* one of two oblong masses of lymphoid tissue, located on each side of the throat.—**ton·sil·lar, ton·sil·ar,** *a.*

ton·sil·lec·to·my, ton″si·lek′to·mē, *n.* pl. **ton·sil·lec·to·mies.** *Surg.* an operation for the removal of enlarged or inflamed tonsils.

ton·sil·li·tis, ton″si·li′tis, *n. Pathol.* inflammation of the tonsils.—**ton·sil·lit·ic,** ton″si·lit′ik, *a.*

ton·sil·lot·o·my, ton″si·lot′o·mē, *n.* pl. **ton·sil·lot·o·mies.** *Surg.* the operation of cutting away or incising a tonsil or the tonsils, wholly or in part.

ton·so·ri·al, ton·sōr′ē·al, ton·sär′ē·al, *a.* Of or pertaining to barbering or a barber, used humorously.

ton·sure, ton′shèr, *n.* [L. *tonsura,* the act of shaving or clipping.] The act of removing the hair of the head by clipping or shaving, esp. the custom of hair removal, as from the crown of the heads of those entering the priesthood or a monastic order; the state of being shaven in this way; that area of the head, usu. the crown, bared by such shaving.—*v.t.*—**tonsured, tonsuring.** To shave or clip the head of.

ton·tine, ton′tēn, ton·tēn′, *n.* [Fr. < Lorenzo *Tonti,* a Neapolitan banker who proposed the method in France in 1653.] An arrangement by which subscribers to a loan or common fund share an annuity, the shares of the survivors being increased as the subscribers die, until the whole goes to the last survivor; the annuity shared; the share of each subscriber; the number who share; any similar form of life insurance.

to·nus, tō′nus, *n.* [L.] *Physiol.* Tone; the normal condition of tension in muscles, enabling response to a stimulus; tonicity.

too, tö, *adv.* [A form of *to,* the preposition; O.E. *tó,* meaning both *to* and *too.* Cf. G. *zu,* to and too.] Likewise; also; in addition, as: Let him come *too.* More than enough, excessively; as, *too* long or *too* short; very; exceedingly; as, being only *too* glad to help;

over and above; as, a painter and a poet *too*; *colloq.* an emphatic affirmative, used to contradict a previous statement, as: I did *too* attend the meeting!

tool, töl, *n.* [O.E. *tól,* a tool, prob. from stem of *tawian,* to make, to prepare.] Any implement used by a craftsman or laborer at his work; an instrument employed in manual labor for facilitating mechanical operations; the cutting part on various machines driven by power, as a drill or lathe; a machine tool; the entire machine; a decoration or ornamentation stamped on a book cover; a person used by another as an instrument to accomplish certain ends. —*v.t.* To shape with a tool; to ornament, as a book cover; *colloq.* to drive, as a vehicle. —*v.i.* To use or employ tools; *colloq.* to drive in an automobile or other vehicle.

tool·box, töl′boks″, *n.* A chest or box for the storage of tools.

tool en·gi·neer·ing, *n.* That branch or part of engineering concerned with the planning of processes necessary for the manufacture of a product, providing proper machinery and tools, and with integrating required facilities with moderate expense.

tool·hold·er, töl′hōl″dèr, *n.* A device, usu. of steel, containing a shank and a clamp located at opposite ends to hold tools.

tool·house, töl′hous″, *n.* pl. **tool·hous·es,** töl′hou″ziz. A building used for tool storage. Also **tool·shed,** töl′shed″.

tool·mak·er, töl′mā″kèr, *n.* A workman who makes and repairs tools and related items.—**tool·mak·ing,** *n.*

tool·room, töl′röm″, töl′rụm″, *n.* A room in which implements and tools are kept, fixed, or made, esp. in a machine shop.

tool sub·ject, *n. Educ.* an academic subject that should be mastered as an aid in studying another subject or subjects.

toon, tön, *n.* The wood of an E. Indian tree, *Toona ciliata,* highly valued as a furniture wood; the tree yielding this wood.

toot, töt, *v.i.* [Same as D. *toeten,* G. *tuten,* Sw. *tuta,* to blow a horn, to toot; imit. of sound.] To make a noise like that of a pipe or horn, esp. in brief blasts; to sound or blow a whistle or horn.—*v.t.* To sound, as a horn.—*n.* A sound blown on a horn; a similar noise.—**toot·er,** *n.*

toot, töt, *n. Slang.* A spree; a drinking binge.

tooth, töth, *n.* pl. **teeth,** tēth. [O.E. *tóth* (pl. *tēth*) = D. *tand* = G. *zahn* = Icel. *tönn* = Goth. *tunthus,* tooth; akin to L. *dens* (*dent-*), Gr. *odous* (*odont-*), Skt. *dant-,* tooth.] One of the hard bodies or processes, in most vertebrates, usu. attached in a row to each jaw, serving for the prehension and mastication of food, as weapons of attack or defense, and in mammals typically composed chiefly of dentin surrounding a sensitive pulp and covered on the crown with enamel; any of various similar or analogous processes, in invertebrates, occurring in the mouth or alimentary canal; any projection resembling or suggesting a tooth; one of a series of projections, as on a comb, rake, or saw; *mach.* one of a series of projections on the edge of a wheel or gear which engage with corresponding parts of another wheel or body. A roughened surface, as of drawing paper; a sharp, distressing, or destructive attribute or agency; a taste, relish, or liking; *bot.* one of a series of projections around the edge of a leaf.—*v.t.*—**toothed, toothing,** tötht, tōтнd, tö′thing, tö′тнing. To furnish with teeth; to cut teeth upon; to bite or gnaw; to fix into (something) by means of or in the manner of teeth.—*v.i.* To interlock, as cogwheels.—**by the skin of one's teeth,** by a small margin.—**cut one's teeth on,** to begin an activity or career by doing.—**in one's teeth, in the teeth,** in direct opposition or conflict; to one's face or openly.—**in the teeth of,** so as to face or confront, or

straight against; in defiance of or in spite of; as, to persist *in the teeth of* warnings.— **put teeth in,** to make effective; as, to *put teeth in* a law.—**set one's teeth,** to resolve to do; to prepare for adversity.—**show one's teeth,** to show hostility or act in a threatening manner.—**to the teeth,** so as to be fully equipped; as, armed *to the teeth.*— **tooth·like,** *a.*

tooth·ache, töth′āk″, *n.* Pain in a tooth or in the teeth arising from decay.—**tooth·ach·y,** *a.*

tooth and nail, *adv.* With one's utmost power; by all possible means of attack and defense.

tooth·brush, töth′brush″, *n.* A small brush for cleaning the teeth.

toothed, töht, tōтнd, *a.* Having teeth or cogs; having projecting points somewhat like teeth; indented or notched.

toothed whale, *n.* Any whale having many cone-shaped teeth, belonging to the suborder *Odontoceti,* who feeds upon squid, fish, or the like.

tooth·less, töth′lis, *a.* Being without or showing absence of teeth; lacking effectiveness or power.—**tooth·less·ly,** *adv.*— **tooth·less·ness,** *n.*

tooth·paste, töth′pāst″, *n.* A dentifrice in paste form.

tooth·pick, töth′pik″, *n.* A small instrument, usu. pointed, for picking substances from between the teeth, and usu. made of wood or plastic.

tooth pow·der, *n.* A powdered dentifrice.

tooth shell, *n.* Any of the burrowing mollusks constituting the genus *Dentalium,* having a long tubular shell; the shell of this mollusk.

tooth·some, töth′som, *a.* Palatable; agreeable to the taste; desirable or attractive.— **tooth·some·ly,** *adv.*—**tooth·some·ness,** *n.*

tooth·wort, töth′wụrt″, *n.* Any plant of the genus *Dentaria,* in the crucifer family, having toothlike projections on the leaves; a European plant, *Lathraea squamaria,* of the family *Orobanchaceae,* having a rootstock covered with toothlike scales.

tooth·y, tö′thē, tö′тнē, *a.*—**toothier, toothiest.** Having or exhibiting large or conspicuous teeth; toothsome; having a rough surface.—**tooth·i·ly,** *adv.*—**tooth·i·ness,** *n.*

too·tle, töt′l, *v.i.*—**tootled, tootling.** [Freq. or dim. of *toot.*] To toot gently or repeatedly; to produce a succession of light modulated sounds as with a flute.—*v.t.* To toot repeatedly.—*n.* A tootling sound.—**too·tler,** *n.*

top, top, *n.* [O.E. *top* = D. *top* = G. *zopf* = Icel. *toppr,* top.] The highest or uppermost point, part, or surface of anything; the apex; the summit; the crest; a part considered as higher; as, the *top* of a street; a part serving as a cover or lid; as, a convertible *top*; the head, esp. the crown of the head; as, from *top* to toe; *bot.* the part of a plant above ground, as distinguished from *root*; as, a carrot *top*; *naut.* a platform surrounding the head of a lower mast. That part of anything which is first or foremost; the beginning; the highest or leading place, position, or rank; as, the *top* of his class; one who or that which occupies the highest or leading position; the highest pitch or degree; as, shouted at the *top* of his voice; the most perfect example or type; the choicest part; *card games,* high cards, esp. aces and kings in a hand. *Sports,* a stroke above the center of a ball; the forward spin given to a ball by such a stroke.—*a.* Pertaining to, situated at, or forming the top; highest; uppermost; upper; highest in degree; greatest; foremost; chief; principal. —*v.t.*—**topped, topping.** To remove, as the top of; to put on, as a top; to be at or constitute the top of, as the top of; to reach, as the top of; to rise above; to exceed in height, amount, or number; to surpass, excel, or outdo. *Sports*, to hit, as a ball, above the center; to make, as a stroke, by hitting a ball in this way.—*v.i.*—**blow one's top,** *slang*. To become very angry; to lose one's sanity.—**on top,** successful; victorious; dominant.—**on top of,** above and resting upon; upon; in addition to; close upon; following upon.—**o·ver the top,** in excess of a predetermined goal; *milit.* over trench fortifications, as troops beginning an attack. —**top off,** to complete by or as by putting a top on; to finish.—**top out,** *building,* to complete, as the framework of the top story; *stock market,* the gradual stabilizing of market prices following an upward movement, as opposed to *bottom out.*

top, top, *n.* [D. *top,* G. *topf*—perh. being named from whirling round on its top or point.] A child's toy of various shapes, but usu. conoidal, made to spin on a point usu. by the rapid unwinding of a string or uncoiling of a spring.

to·paz, tō′paz, *n.* [O.Fr. Fr. *topaze,* < L. *topazus,* < Gr. *tópazos,* topaz: cf. Skt. *tapas,* heat, fire.] A mineral, fluosilicate of aluminum, usu. occurring in prismatic crystals of various colors, and used as a gem; a yellow variety of sapphire; a yellow variety of quartz. Either of two tropical American hummingbirds, *Topaza pyra* and *T. pella,* with brightly colored plummage.— **to·paz·ine,** tō′pa·zēn″, tō′pa·zin, *a.*

top boot, *n.* A high boot having the top cuff of light-colored or of a different texture leather, and worn chiefly by equestrians.

top·coat, top′kōt″, *n.* A lightweight overcoat.

top cross, *n. Genetics,* the breeding of an inferior female stock with a male purebred to improve the quality of the offspring; the offspring so produced.

top dog, *n. Colloq.* a dominant individual or group, usu. by virtue of a victory over a rival or rivals.—**top-dog,** *a.*

top draw·er, *n. Colloq.* High quality; highest rank, priority, or authority.—*a.*

top-dress, top′dres″, *v.t.* To apply or spread a material on the surface of, as manure on land.—**top dress·ing,** top-dress·ing,** *n.*

tope, tōp, *v.i.*—*toped, toping.* To drink alcoholic beverages immoderately and frequently.—*v.t.*—**top·er,** tō′pér, *n.*

tope, tōp, *n.* [Orig. a Corn. word.] A small European shark, *Galeorhinus galeus.*

tope, tōp, *n.* [Skt. *stûpa,* a tope.] A dome-shaped Buddhist monument or shrine. Also *stupa.*

to·pee, to·pi, tō·pē′, tō′pē, *n.* A lightweight sun hat made of pith. Also **pith hel·met.**

top·flight, top′flīt′, *a. Colloq.* Superior; first-rate.

top·full, top·ful, top′ful′, *a.* Brimful.

top·gal·lant, top″gal′ant, *Naut.* to·gal′ant, *a. Naut.* above the topmast and below the royal mast.—*n. Naut.* a topgallant mast, sail, yard, or rigging.

top·ham·per, top′ham″pér, *n. Naut.* Light upper sails, spars, and rigging; any unnecessary weight either aloft or about the upper decks.

top hat, *n.* A man's tall, cylindrical, dress hat, usu. covered with silk. Also *high hat, silk hat, topper.*

top-heav·y, top′hev″ē, *a.*—*top-heavier, top-heaviest.* Having the top or upper part too heavy for the lower, 'esp. with the possibility of falling because of this; badly balanced or proportioned; *finance,* overcapitalized.—**top-heav·i·ly,** *adv.*—**top-heav·i·ness,** *n.*

To·phet, To·pheth, tō′fet, *n.* [Heb., lit. 'a place to be spit on.'] *Bib.* A place near Jerusalem where human sacrifice was offered to the fire god Moloch; a place of torment after death.

top-hole, top′hōl′, *a. Brit. slang,* excellent, first-rate.

to·phus, tō′fus, *n.* pl. **to·phi,** tō′fī. [L. *tophus,* tufa or tuff.] *Pathol.* a uratic or calcareous deposit formed in the fibrous tissue of the body, as around or at a joint or on the roots of teeth, esp. in gout.

to·pi, tō′pē, *n.* pl. **to·pis.** An antelope, *Damaliscus corrigum jimela,* native to central Africa with a purplish-brown coat.

to·pi·ar·y, tō′pē·er″ē, *a.* [L. *topiarius,* < *topia* (*opera*), ornamental gardening, < Gr. *topos,* a place.] Shaped, esp. ornamentally, by clipping, pruning, or training, as trees or shrubs.—*n.* pl. **to·pi·ar·ies.** Any work or art of this kind; a garden which contains topiary work.

top·ic, *n.* [As *a.,* L.L. *topicus,* < Gr. *topikos,* pertaining to a place, local, pertaining to commonplaces, < *topos,* place; as *n.,* L. *topica,* pl., < Gr. *topiká,* commonplaces (in title of a work of Aristotle), prop. neut. pl. of *topikos.*] The subject of a discourse, argument, or literary composition; a subject of speech or writing; an idea or consideration of general application or reference; a general rule or maxim; a consideration affording a ground of argument.

top·i·cal, top′i·kal, *a.* Pertaining to or dealing with matters of current or local interest; of or pertaining to any topic of speech or writing; of or pertaining to a place; local; *med.* pertaining or applied to a particular part of the body. —**top·i·cal·i·ty,** top′i·kal′i·tē, *n.* pl. **top·i·cal·i·ties.**

top·ic sen·tence, *n.* A sentence which expresses the main idea of a paragraph or larger written unit, usu. placed in an introductory position.

top kick, *n. Milit. slang,* first sergeant.

top·knot, top′not″, *n.* An ornamental knot of hair or bow of ribbon worn on the top of the head; the crest of a bird.

top·less, top′lis, *a.* Without a top, esp. without a part covering the breasts; as, a *topless* swimsuit; *fig.* seeming to extend infinitely upward; as, *topless* mountains.

top·loft·y, top′lôf″tē, top′lof′tē, *a.*—*toploftier, toploftiest. Colloq.* Haughty; pompous.—**top·loft·i·ly,** *adv.*—**top·loft·i·ness,** *n.*

top·mast, top′mast″, top′mäst″, *Naut.* top′mast, *n. Naut.* the mast next above the lower mast, usu. supporting the topsail rigging.

top·min·now, top′min″ō, *n.* pl. **top·min·now, top·min·nows.** Any small surface-feeding fish of the oviparous family *Cyprinodontidæ,* or the viviparous family *Poeciliidæ.*

top·most, top′mōst″, *Brit.* top′most, *a.* Highest; uppermost.

top·notch, top′noch′, *a. Colloq.* First-rate; excellent.—**top·notch·er,** *n.*

top·o·graph·i·cal, top″o·graf′i·kal, *a.* Pertaining to topography; descriptive of a place or country. Also **top·o·graph·ic,** top″o·graf′ik.—**top·o·graph·i·cal·ly,** *adv.*

to·pog·ra·phy, to·pog′ra·fē, *n.* pl. **to·pog·ra·phies.** [L.L. *topographia,* < Gr. *topographia,* < *topográphos,* a topographer.] The accurate and detailed description of any region; the features of a locality or region collectively; a comprehensive description of natural and synthetic elements of a given area, esp. in map or chart form. —**to·pog·ra·pher,** *n.*

to·pol·o·gy, to·pol′o·jē, *n.* pl. **to·pol·o·gies.** *Geom.* the study of the properties of figures that remain constant when the figures are transformed in such a manner that the points of the resultant figures are in a one-to-one correspondence with the originals, as when a figure is stretched; *geol.* the history of a region as determined from a study of its topography; *anat.* the

structure of a particular region or part of the body.—**top·o·log·ic, top·o·log·i·cal,** top″o·loj′ik, *a.*—**top·o·log·i·cal·ly,** *adv.*— **to·pol·o·gist,** *n.*

top·o·nym, top′o·nim, *n.* [Gr. *tópos,* place, and *ónoma,* name.] A place name; a regional name; a name derived from the name of a place, location, or origin, as in nomenclature, esp. zoological or botanical; the name of a particular region of the body, as contrasted with an *organ.*— **top·o·nym·ic, top·o·nym·i·cal,** top″o·nim′ik, *a.*

to·pon·y·my, to·pon′i·mē, *n.* pl. **to·pon·y·mies.** [Gr. *tópos,* a place, and *ónoma,* a name.] The study of toponyms; *anat.* regional nomenclature of the body.

top·per, top′ér, *n. Colloq.* one who tops or excels; anything superior. Someone who or something that removes tops; a woman's outer coat, usu. lightweight, loose-fitting, and short; *colloq.* a top hat.

top·ping, top′ing, *n.* The act of one who or that which tops; a distinct part forming a top to something; something put on a thing at the top to complete it, as any sauce or garnish; *pl.* that which is removed in topping or cropping plants, as branches.—*a.* Rising above something else, or overtopping; surpassing; very high in rank, degree, or the like; *Brit. colloq.* excellent or first-rate.

top·ple, top′l, *v.i.*—*toppled, toppling.* To fall forward, as from top-heaviness; to tumble down; to jut out, lean, or be on the point of falling; totter.—*v.t.* To overturn or cause to fall; overthrow.

top round, *n.* A cut of beef taken above the bottom round, and below the rump.

tops, tops, *a. Colloq.* Excellent; topmost.

top·sail, top′sāl″, *Naut.* top′sal, *n. Naut.* The second sail above the deck on any mast of a square-rigged vessel; a sail carried above the gaff of a lower sail on a fore-and-aft-rigged vessel. Also **top·s'l.**

top-se·cret, top′sē′krit, *a. Govt., milit.* classified as most highly secret, as a project or document accessible only to specially authorized personnel.

top ser·geant, *n. Milit. slang,* first sergeant.

top·side, top′sīd″, *n. Often pl., naut.* The upper part of a ship's side; the superstructure.—*adv. Naut.* on or toward the deck; also **top·sides.**

top·soil, top′soil″, *n.* The uppermost layer or surface of the soil.—*v.t.* To remove the topsoil from, as an area of land.

top spin, *n. Sports,* a forward rotation given to a projected object, esp. a ball.

top·stone, top′stōn″, *n.* Copestone.

top·sy-tur·vy, top′sē·tur′vē, *adv.* [Prob. < *top* (or pl. *tops*) and M.E. *terven, tirven,* turn, overturn; with second syllable (*-sy-*) possibly representing *so.*] With the top where the bottom should be; upside down; in or into a state of confusion or disorder.— *a.* Turned upside down; inverted; reversed; confused or disorderly.—*n.* pl. **top·sy-tur·vies.** Inversion of the natural order; a state of confusion or disorder.—**top-sy-tur·vi·ly,** *adv.*—**top·sy-tur·vi·ness,** *n.*—**top·sy-tur·vy·dom,** top′sē·tur′vē-dom, *n.*

toque, tōk, *n.* [Fr., < Armor. *tôk,* W. *toc,* a hat or bonnet.] A woman's close-fitting hat of soft material, brimless or with a narrow brim; a similar hat worn in the 16th century; a tuque.

tor, tar, *n.* [W. *tor,* a bulge, a hill; allied to L. *turris,* a tower.] A high pointed rock or rocky hill.

To·rah, Tor·a, tōr′a, tar′a, *Heb.* tō·rä′, *n.* [Heb. *tôrâh.*] The Pentateuch; Mosaic law; broadly, instruction, doctrine, or law contained in the Old Testament; a scroll on which the Pentateuch is written.

torch, tarch, *n.* [Fr. *torche,* It. *torcia,* < L.L.

tortia, < L. *torqueo, tortus,* to twist, to turn (whence *torture,* etc.), because the torch was made of a twisted roll of tow and the like.] A light to be carried in the hand, formed of some combustible substance, as of wood, twisted flax, hemp, or the like, soaked with tallow; a flambeau; *fig.* a guiding light from which inspiration emanates; as, the *torch* of freedom. Any readily carried device for the emission of an esp. hot flame, as for use in working with solder; *Brit.* flashlight.—**car·ry a** or **the torch for,** *slang,* to be intensely in love with, usu. without the possibility of reciprocation.—**torch·like,** *a.*

torch·bear·er, tȯrch′bâr″ẽr, *n.* One who carries a lighted torch; *fig.* a person in the vanguard of supporters of a cause or movement.

torch·light, tȯrch′līt″, *n.* The light of a torch or of torches.—*a.* Illuminated by torches; as, a *torchlight* parade.

tor·chon lace, tȧr′shon lās′, *Fr.* tȧr·shäN′, *n.* [Fr. *torchon,* dishcloth, duster, < *torcher,* wipe.] A bobbin linen lace with loosely twisted threads in simple, open patterns; a machine-made imitation of this.

torch song, *n.* A popular song telling of unrequited love or the painful memory of it.—**torch sing·er,** one whose forte is the torch song.

torch·wood, tȯrch′wu̇d″, *n.* Any of various resinous woods suitable for making torches, as wood of trees of the genus *Amyris,* esp. *A. balsamifera,* of Florida and the West Indies; any of the trees yielding these woods.

tor·e·a·dor, tȧr′ē·a·dȯr″, *Sp.* tȧ″Re·ä·THȧR′, *n.* [Sp., < *toro,* a bull.] A bullfighter.

to·re·ro, te·râr′ō, *Sp.* tȧ·Re′Rȧ, *n.* pl. **to·re·ros,** te·râr′ōz, *Sp.* tȧ·Re′Rȧs. A matador; a bullfighter.

to·reu·tics, to·rō′tiks, *n.* pl. but sing. in constr. [Gr. *toreutikos,* < *toreutēs,* an embosser, < *toreuō,* to emboss, to work in relief.] The art or technique of ornamental work sculptured in metal, esp. in relief.—**to·reu·tic,** to·rō′tik, *a.*

tor·ic, tȧr′ik, tōr′ik, *a.* Of or pertaining to a torus, esp. noting or pertaining to a lens with a surface forming a portion of a torus, used in eyeglasses.

to·ri·i, tōr′ē·ē″, tȧr′ē·ē″, *n.* pl. **to·ri·i.** [Jap.] A form of decorative gateway or portal in Japan, consisting of two upright wooden posts connected at the top by two horizontal crosspieces, and commonly found at the entrance to Shinto temples.

tor·ment, tȧr′ment, *n.* [O.Fr. *torment* (Fr. *tourment*), < L. *tormentum,* an engine for hurling missiles, a rack, torture, < *torqueo, tortum,* to twist.] Extreme pain; anguish of body or mind; torture; that which causes such pain.—tȧr·ment′, *v.t.* To put to extreme pain or anguish; to inflict excruciating pain on; to torture; to afflict; to tease, vex, or harass; to annoy.—**tor·ment·ing·ly,** *adv.*

tor·men·til, tȧr′men·til, *n.* [M.L. *tormentilla,* dim. < L. *tormentum,* E. *torment*; from its use medicinally to allay pain.] *Bot.* a low-growing plant of the rose family, *Potentilla tormentilla,* of Europe, with small bright yellow flowers, and a strongly astringent root used in medicine and in tanning and dyeing.

tor·men·tor, tor·ment·er, tȧr·men′tẽr, *n.* One who torments; *theatr.* a curtain or scenery structure placed at both stage sides toward the rear of a proscenium to obstruct the view into the wings; *motion pictures,* a silencing screen used to prevent any echoing and other related acoustical problems during filming.

tor·na·do, tȧr·nā′dō, *n.* pl. **tor·na·does, tor·na·dos.** [Appar. an altered form, by association with Sp. *tornar,* turn, of Sp. *tronada,* thunderstorm, < *tronar,* < L. *tonare,* thunder.] A destructive rotatory storm of the midwestern and southern U.S. appearing as a whirling, advancing funnel extending downward from a black cloud; a violent squall or whirlwind, as those occurring during the summer on the west coast of Africa. Compare *cyclone.*—**tor·nad·ic,** tȧr·nad′ik, *a.*

tor·nil·lo, tȧr·nil′ō, *Sp.* tȧr·nēl′yȧ, *n.* pl. **tor·nil·los.** Screw bean.

to·roid, tōr′oid, tȧr′oid, *n.* *Geom.* A surface generated by the revolution of any closed plane, curve, or contour about an axis lying in its plane; the solid enclosed by such a surface.—**to·roi·dal,** tō·roid′al, tȧ·roid′al, tōr′oid·al, tȧr′oid·al, *a.*—**to·roi·dal·ly,** *adv.*

to·rose, tōr′ōs, tȧr′ōs, tō·rōs′, tȧ·rōs′, *a.* [L. *torosus,* < *torus,* a bulge, protuberance: cf. *torus.*] Bulging; protuberant; knobbed; *bot.* cylindrical, with swellings or constrictions at intervals. Also **to·rous,** tōr′us, tȧr′us.—**to·ros·i·ty,** tȧ·ros′i·tē, *n.*

tor·pe·do, tȧr·pē′dō, *n.* pl. **tor·pe·does.** [L. *torpedo,* numbness, torpidity, torpedo (fish), < *torpere,* to numb: cf. *torpid.*] A submarine explosive device for destroying hostile ships, esp. a self-propelled cigar-shaped missile containing explosives which is launched from a tube in a submarine and explodes upon impact with the ship fired at; an explosive shell buried in the ground for destructive purposes; any of various other explosive devices, as a firework which consists of an explosive wrapped up with gravel in a piece of tissue paper, and which detonates when thrown forcibly on the ground or against a hard surface; a detonating device employed on a railroad as a signal, being placed on a rail and exploded by the wheels of a passing locomotive; a cartridge of gunpowder or dynamite exploded in an oil well to start or increase the flow of oil; an electric rayfish; *slang,* a hired gunman.—*v.t.*—**torpedoed, torpedoing.** To attack, hit, damage, or destroy with a torpedo or torpedoes; to lay, as a channel, with torpedoes or submarine mines, as against enemy ships; to explode a torpedo in, as an oil well, to start or increase the flow of oil.—*v.i.* To use, discharge, or explode torpedoes.

tor·pe·do boat, *n.* *Nav.* a war vessel of small size and high speed, armed with torpedo tubes.

tor·pe·do-boat de·stroy·er, tȧr·pē′dō-bōt″ di·stroi′ẽr, *n.* *Nav.* a vessel somewhat larger than a torpedo boat, used for destroying torpedo boats or as a more powerful type of torpedo boat.

tor·pe·do tube, *n.* A tube through which a torpedo boat or submarine launches a self-propelled torpedo, usu. by the explosion of a charge of powder.

tor·pid, tȧr′pid, *a.* [L. *torpidus,* < *torpeo,* to be numb, motionless.] Having lost motion or the power of motion and feeling; numb; dull; sluggish; inactive; listless.—**tor·pid·i·ty,** *n.*—**tor·pid·ly,** *adv.*

tor·por, tȧr′pẽr, *n.* [L., < *torpere,* be numb.] A state of suspended physical powers and activities; dormancy, as of a hibernating animal; sluggish inactivity or inertia; lethargic dullness or indifference; apathy.—**tor·por·if·ic,** tȧr″po·rif′ik, *a.* Causing torpor.

tor·quate, tȧr′kwit, tȧr′kwāt, *a.* [L. *torquatus,* wearing a torque, < *torques.*] *Zool.* Ringed about the neck, as with feathers or a color; collared.

torque, tȧrk, *n.* *Mech.* That which produces or tends to produce torsion or rotation; the moment of a system of forces which tends to cause rotation; the pressure, measured in foot-pounds, exerted by a rotating shaft.

torque, torc, tȧrk, *n.* [In part, < L. *torques, torquis,* a twisted neck-ring, < *torquere,* twist; in part, < L. *torquere.*] A collar, necklace, or similar ornament consisting of a twisted narrow band, usu. of precious metal, worn esp. by the ancient Gauls and Britons.

torque con·vert·er, *n.* A hydraulic device which amplifies torque by decreasing speed.

tor·re·fy, tor·ri·fy, tȧr′e·fī″, tȯr′e·fī″, *v.t.* —**torrefied, torrefying.** [Fr. *torréfier,* < L. *torreo,* to roast, and *facio,* to make.] To dry, roast, scorch, or parch by heat, as drugs or metallic ores.—**tor·re·fac·tion,** tȧr″e·fak′shan, tȯr″e·fak′shan, *n.*

tor·rent, tȧr′ent, tȯr′ent, *n.* [Fr. *torrent,* < *torrens* (torrent-), a torrent, prop. ppr., burning, boiling, rushing, < *torrere.*] A stream of water flowing with great rapidity and violence; a rushing, violent, or abundant and unceasing stream of anything; a violent downpour of rain; a violent, tumultuous, or overwhelming flow.—*a.* Torrential.

tor·ren·tial, tȧ·ren′shal, tȯ·ren′shal, to·ren′shal, *a.* Of, pertaining to, or of the nature of a torrent; resembling a torrent in rapidity or violence; falling in torrents; produced by the action of a torrent; violent, vehement, or impassioned; overwhelming; extraordinarily copious.—**tor·ren·tial·ly,** *adv.*

tor·rid, tȧr′id, tȯr′id, *a.* [L. *torridus,* < *torrere,* dry, parch, scorch, burn.] Subject to parching or burning heat, esp. of the sun; as, *torrid* deserts; parching or burning; oppressively hot, as climate, weather, or air. *Fig.* characterized by great heat of feeling; passionate.—**tor·rid·i·ty, tor·rid·ness,** *n.* —**tor·rid·ly,** *adv.*

Tor·rid Zone, *n.* The belt of the earth on both sides of the equator, between the Tropics of Capricorn and Cancer.

tor·sade, tȧr·sâd′, *n.* [Fr.] A twisted cord; any ornamental twist, as of velvet.

tor·sion, tȧr′shan, *n.* [Fr. *torsion,* < L.L. *torsio(n-), tortio(n-),* < L. *torquere,* twist.] The act of twisting or the resulting state; *mech.* the twisting of a body by two equal and opposite forces.—**tor·sion·al,** *a.*— **tor·sion·al·ly,** *adv.*

tor·sion bal·ance, *n.* An instrument for measuring small forces, as electrical attraction or repulsion, by determining the amount of torsion or twisting they cause in a slender wire or filament.

tor·so, tȧr′sō, *n.* pl. **tor·sos, tor·si,** tȧr′sē. [It., lit. 'a trunk or stump.'] The trunk of the human body; the trunk of a statue, esp. a statue consisting only of the trunk; anything dismembered or unfinished.

tort, tȧrt, *n.* [O.Fr. Fr. *tort,* < M.L. *tortum,* wrong, injustice, prop. neut. of L. *tortus,* twisted, crooked, pp. of *torquere,* twist.] *Law,* a wrong, other than a breach of contract, such as the law requires compensation for in damages.

torte, tȧrt, *Ger.* tȧr′te, *n.* pl. **tortes,** *Ger.* **tor·ten.** Any rich cake consisting of eggs, sugar, butter, and often nuts, fruit, and bread crumbs, usu. containing little flour.

tor·ti·col·lis, tȧr″ti·kol′is, *n.* [N.L., < L. *tortu,* twisted and *collum,* neck.] *Path.* An affliction in which the neck is twisted and the head inclined to one side, due to spasmodic muscular contraction; wryneck.

tor·til·la, tȧr·tē′a, *Sp.* tȧr·tē′yä, *n.* pl. **tor·til·las,** tȧr·tē′az, *Sp.* tȧr·tē′yäs. [Sp., dim. of *torta,* < L.L. *torta,* cake.] *Mex.* a thin, round, cornmeal cake baked on a flat plate of iron, earthenware, or the like, and eaten hot.

tor·tious, tȧr′shus, *a.* *Law,* of the nature of or pertaining to a tort.—**tor·tious·ly,** *adv.*

tor·toise, tȧr′tos, *n.* [M.E. *tortuce,* < M.L. *tortuca,* tortoise, said to be named from its crooked feet, < L. *tortus,* twisted, crooked, pp. of *torquere*, twist.] A turtle, esp. a terrestrial turtle, as distinguished from any of the aquatic species; *Rom. milit.* a testudo or movable shelter, or sheltering arrangement of shields; *colloq.* a person or thing that moves very slowly.

tor·toise bee·tle, *n.* Any of various usu. brightly colored small beetles of the subfamily *Cassidinæ*, broadly oval in shape and somewhat resembling tortoises.

tor·toise shell, *n.* The shell, or outer shell, of a tortoise; the horny substance, with the mottled or clouded yellow and brown coloration, composing the plates or scales that cover the carapace of certain marine turtles, as the hawksbill, used for making combs and other articles, inlaying, or the like.—**tor·toise-shell,** *n.* Any of several butterflies of the genus *Nymphalis*; a female cat with black and yellow fur in the configuration of a tortoise's shell.—**tor·toise-shell,** *a.* Yielding tortoise shell, as a turtle; made of tortoise shell; mottled or variegated like tortoise shell, esp. with yellow and black and sometimes other colors; as, a *tortoise-shell* cat, *tortoise-shell* ware.

tor·to·ni, tạr·tō′nē, *n.* An ice cream of rich, heavy cream and eggs, usu. containing cherries, minced almonds, crushed macaroons, or the like.

tor·tri·cid, tạr′tri·sid, *n.* [N.L. *Tortricidæ*, pl., < *Tortrix*, the typical genus, < L. *torquere*, twist.] Any of the *Tortricidae*, a family of small, stout-bodied moths with wide oblong wings, whose larvae are leaf rollers.—*a.* Belonging or pertaining to the *Tortricidae*.

tor·tu·os·i·ty, tạr″chö·os′i·tē, *n.* pl. **tor·-tu·os·i·ties.** The state of being tortuous; twisted form or course; crookedness; a twist, bend, or crook, as in the course of something; a twisting or winding part, passage, or thing.

tor·tu·ous, tạr′chö·us, *a.* [O.Fr. *tortuous* (Fr. *tortueux*), < L. *tortuosus*, < *tortus*, a twisting, winding, < *torquere*, twist.] Full of twists, turns, or bends; twisting, winding, or crooked. *Fig.* not direct or straightforward, as in a line or course of procedure, thought, speech, or writing; deceitfully indirect or devious, or morally crooked, as proceedings, methods, or policy; pursuing an indirect or devious course or policy, as persons.—**tor·tu·ous·ly,** *adv.*—**tor·tu·-ous·ness,** *n.*

tor·ture, tạr′chẽr, *n.* [Fr. *torture*, < L.L. *tortura*, a twisting, torture, < L. *torquere*, twist: cf. *torment*.] The act of inflicting excruciating pain from sheer cruelty or in hatred or revenge; the infliction of such pain by judicial or quasi-judicial authority, esp. in order to extort a confession or as part of punishment; a method of inflicting such pain; an instrument for inflicting it; subjection to any excruciating or severe pain, physical or mental; the pain or suffering caused or undergone; extreme anguish of body or mind; agony; torment; a cause of severe pain or anguish; violent distortion or perversion, as of language.—*v.t.*—**tortured, torturing.** To subject to torture, specif. to subject to judicial torture; to afflict with severe pain of body or mind; torment; to twist, force, or bring into some unnatural position or form; as, trees *tortured* by storms; distort or pervert, as language.—**tor·tur·a·ble,** *a.*—**tor·tured·ly,** *adv.*—**tor·tur·er,** *n.*—**tor·ture·some,** *a.*—**tor·tur·ing·ly,** *adv.*

tor·tur·ous, tạr′chẽr·us, *a.* Full of, involving, or causing torture.—**tor·tur·-ous·ly,** *adv.*

to·rus, tōr′us, tạr′us, *n.* pl. **to·ri,** tōr′ī, tạr′ī. [L., a bulge, protuberance, raised ornament, torus (molding), cushion, bed.] *Arch.* a large convex molding, more or less semicircular in profile, commonly forming the lowest member of the base of a column, or that directly above the plinth, when present, and sometimes occurring as one of a pair separated by a scotia and fillets; also **tore.** *Bot.* the receptacle of a flower; a plant's part bearing the floral leaves. *Anat.* a rounded ridge; a protuberant part. *Geom.* a surface generated by the revolution of a conic, esp. a circle, about an axis lying in its plane; the solid enclosed by such a surface; also **tore.**

To·ry, tōr′ē, tạr′ē, *n.* pl. **To·ries.** [Ir. *toiridhe*, pursuer.] A member of a political party in Great Britain during the 18th century and early 19th century, that favored conservation of the existing order in state and church, and known as the Conservative party since about 1832; (*often l.c.*) one advocating conservative principles. One who adhered to the British crown during the American Revolution; a loyalist; in the 17th century, one of a class of dispossessed Irish, nominally royalists, who became outlaws and were noted for their outrages and cruelties.—*a.* Of, pertaining to, or characteristic of the Tories; being a Tory; (*sometimes l.c.*) conservative.—**To·-ry·ism,** tōr′ē·iz″um, tạr′ē·iz″um, *n.*

tosh, tosh, *n.* [Origin obscure.] *Brit. slang.* Bosh; nonsense; rubbish.

toss, tạs, tos, *v.t.* [Origin uncertain: cf. Norw. *tossa*, strew, scatter.] To throw, pitch, or fling, esp. lightly or carelessly; as, to *toss* a bone to the dog; to throw or send, as a ball, from one to another; to throw, pitch, heave, or jerk about with irregular motions; as, ships *tossed* by a tempest; to agitate, disturb, or disquiet; to raise or jerk upward suddenly; as, to *toss* the head in impatience; to bandy or pass from one to another in discussion; discuss freely and casually; as, to *toss* in an idea; to throw, as a coin, into the air to decide something by the side turned up when it falls, often used with *up*; to mix gently, as a salad.—*v.i.* To pitch, rock, sway, or move irregularly, as a ship on a rough sea; to fling or jerk oneself or move restlessly about, esp. on a bed or couch; as, to *toss* in one's sleep; to throw something; to throw a coin into the air in order to decide something by the way it falls, often used with *up*; to go with a fling of the body, or flounce; as, to *toss* out of a room.—*n.* An act of tossing; the state of being tossed; a throw or pitch; or the distance to which something is or may be thrown; a tossup, as of a coin; a sudden fling or jerk of the body or backward movement of the head.—**toss off,** to do or accomplish casually and quickly; to drink rapidly, esp. in one draft.—**toss·er,** *n.*

toss·pot, tạs′pot″, tos′pot″, *n.* A heavy or habitual drinker; an inebriate; a toper.

toss·up, tạs′up″, tos′up″, *n.* *Colloq.* The tossing up of a coin in order to decide something by its fall; an even or fifty-fifty chance.

tot, tot, *n.* [Dan. *tot*, Icel. *tottr*, *tuttr*, applied to dwarfish persons; perh. allied to *tit*.] A young child; anything small or insignificant; a small quantity or drink of liquor.

tot, tot, *v.t.*, *v.i.*—**totted, totting.** [Abbr. of *total*.] To add or total, used with *up*.

to·tal, tōt′al, *a.* [O.Fr. Fr. *total*, < M.L. *totalis*, < L. *totus*, all, whole, entire.] Of or pertaining to the whole of something; as, a *total* eclipse; constituting or comprising the whole; entire; as, the *total* amount expended; complete in extent or degree; absolute, unqualified, or utter; as, a *total* failure.—*n.* The total amount, sum, or aggregate; the whole.—*v.t.*—**totaled, totaling,** *Brit.* **totalled, totalling.** To bring to a total; add up; to reach a total of; amount to.—*v.i.* To amount, often followed by *to.*

to·tal de·prav·i·ty, *n. Theol.* the Calvinist theory of the absolute sinfulness and corruption of man, due to original sin, which continues until rebirth through the Spirit of God.

to·tal e·clipse, *n.* An eclipse in which an entire celestial body is obscured by another celestial body.

to·tal·i·tar·i·an, tō·tal″i·târ′ē·an, *a.* Of or pertaining to a centralized form of government in which those in control grant neither recognition nor tolerance to parties of differing opinion.—*n.* An adherent of totalitarian principles.—**to·tal·i·tar·i·an·ism,** tō·tal″i·târ′ē·a·niz″um, *n.*—**to·tal·i·tar·i·an·ize,** tō·tal″i·târ′ē·a·nīz″, *v.t.*—**totalitarianized, totalitarianizing.**

to·tal·i·ty, tō·tal′i·tē, *n.* pl. **to·tal·i·ties.** The state of being total; entirety; that which is total; the total amount; a total or whole; *astron.* the state or phase of total eclipse.

to·tal·i·za·tor, tōt′a·li·zā″tẽr, *n.* [Fr. *totalisateur*.] An apparatus for registering and indicating the total of operations, measurements, and the like; a pari-mutuel machine.

to·tal·ize, tōt′a·līz″, *v.t.*—**totalized, totalizing.** [= Fr. *totaliser*.] To make total; combine into a total.

to·tal·iz·er, tōt′a·lī″zẽr, *n.* One who totalizes; a machine which adds and totals; a pari-mutuel machine.

to·tal·ly, tōt′a·lē, *adv.* In a total manner or degree; wholly; entirely; completely.

to·ta·quine, tō′ta·kwēn″, tō′ta·kwin″, *n. Pharm.* a blend of alkaloids extracted from the bark of cinchona trees and used in the treatment of malaria.

tote, tōt, *v.t.*—**toted, toting.** [Origin unknown.] *Colloq.* To carry or bear, as on the back or in the arms or hands, as a burden or load; to carry or have on the person, as for use; to transport or convey, as in a vehicle or boat.—*n. Colloq.* an act of toting; the burden or load toted. A woman's large handbag; also **tote bag.**—**tot·er,** *n.*

to·tem, tō′tem, *n.* [Algonquian.] Among primitive cultures, an object or thing in nature, often an animal, assumed as the token or emblem of a clan, family, or related group; a representation of such an object serving as the distinctive mark of the clan or group; a clan or group having a particular emblem or distinctive mark.—**to·tem·ic,** tō·tem′ik, *a.*

to·tem·ism, tō′te·miz″um, *n.* The practice of having totems; the system of tribal division according to totems; belief in relationships between people or groups and totems.—**to·tem·ist,** *n.*—**to·tem·is·tic,** *a.*

to·tem pole, *n.* A pole or post carved and painted with totemic figures, erected by Indians of the northwest coast of N. America, esp. in front of their houses.

tote road, *n.* An unsurfaced road used for transporting materials and supplies, as to a clearing or camp.

toth·er, t'oth·er, tuTH′ẽr, *pron., a. Dial.* The other; that other.

to·ti·pal·mate, tō″ti·pal′mit, tō″ti·pal′māt, *a.* [N.L. *totipalmatus*, < L. *totus*, all, whole, and *palma*, palm, sole.] *Ornith.* having all four toes fully webbed and joined, as pelicans.—**to·ti·pal·ma·tion,** *n.*

tot·ter, tot′ẽr, *v.i.* [M.E. *toteren*: cf. D. *touteren*, swing, O.E. *tealtrian*, be unsteady.] To walk or go with faltering steps, as if from extreme weakness; to sway or rock on the base or ground, as if about to fall; to shake or tremble.—*n.* The act of tottering; an unsteady movement or gait.—**tot·ter·er,** *n.*—**tot·ter·y,** tot′ẽ·rē, *a.*

tot·ter·ing, tot′ẽr·ing, *a.* Walking falteringly or shakily; unstable, as structures or conditions; insecure; precarious.—**tot·-ter·ing·ly,** *adv.*

tou·can, tö′kan, tö·kän′, *n.* [Fr.; from

Brazil. name.] Any of various fruit-eating birds of the family *Rhamphastidae*, in tropical America, with a very large beak and usu. a striking coloration.

touch, tuch, *v.t.* [O.Fr. *tochier, tuchier* (Fr. *toucher*), = Sp. and Pg. *tocar* = It. *toccare*, touch, strike; origin uncertain; commonly explained as from Teut. and akin to G. *zucken,* pluck, jerk, twitch, *ziehen,* draw, and E. *tow*.] To put the hand, finger, or the like on or into contact with; to come into contact with so as to feel or perceive; to bring into contact with something; to strike or hit gently; to be adjacent to; adjoin or border on; *geom.* to be tangent to, as a line or surface. To come up to; to compare with, often in the negative, as: *No* one can *touch* her cooking. To modify or improve, as a painting; to mark by strokes of a brush, pencil, or pen, used with *up*; to mark or relieve slightly, as with color; as, a black dress *touched* with red; to treat or affect in some way by contact; tinge or imbue; to affect with some feeling or emotion, as tenderness, pity, or gratitude; to handle, use, or have to do with in any way, usu. with a negative, as: He will *never touch* another card. To deal with or treat in speech or writing; to allude, pertain, or relate to. *Mus.* to strike the strings or keys of, as a musical instrument; to play, as a tune. *Metal.* to stamp, as metal, to indicate purity; *slang,* to succeed in getting money from.—*v.i.* To place the hand, finger, or part of the body on or in contact with something; to come into or be in contact.— *n.* The act of touching; the state or fact of being touched; that sense by which anything material is perceived by means of the contact with it of some part of the body; the sensation or effect imparted or experienced by touching something; as, a slimy *touch*; coming into or being in contact; mental sensitivity; a close relation of communication, agreement, or sympathy; as, to be in *touch* with public opinion; a slight stroke or blow; a slight attack, as of illness; a slight added action or effort in doing or completing any piece of work; the manner of execution in artistic work. *Mus.* the act or manner of striking a keyboard instrument; the mode of action of the keys of such an instrument. A detail in any artistic work; a slight amount of some quality or attribute; as, a *touch* of anger in his expression; a slight quantity or degree; as, a *touch* of garlic; a distinguishing characteristic or trait; as, his light *touch* with colors; the act of testing anything. *Slang,* the act of soliciting money, as a loan or gift; the money so obtained; a person easily victimized for a loan, often used in phrases; as, a soft *touch* or easy *touch*. *Metal.* an official mark of quality placed on fine metals.— **touch at,** to stop at or visit in passing, as a ship or those on board.—**touch off,** to cause to explode; to ignite; to cause to happen.— **touch on,** to relate or pertain to; to mention briefly or in passing.—**touch·a·ble,** *a.*— **touch·a·ble·ness,** *n.*—**touch·er,** *n.*

touch and go, *n.* A speedy movement or action; an uncertain, precarious, delicate, or ticklish state of affairs.—**touch-and-go,** *a.* Hasty, sketchy, or desultory; risky; precarious.

touch·back, tuch'bak″, *n. Football,* the act of a player in touching the ball to the ground on or behind his own goal line when it has been driven there by the opposing side.

touch·down, tuch'doun″, *n. Football,* the act or play of possessing the ball on or behind the opponent's goal line, thereby scoring six points; *aeron.* the moment when the aircraft's landing gear touches the landing surface.

tou·ché, tö·shā′, *interj.* [Fr.] *Fencing,* an exclamation indicating that an opponent

has been touched by the tip of the foil. An expression acknowledging that an opponent has been successful, as in an argument.

touched, tucht, *a.* Emotionally stirred or moved; unbalanced; mentally ill.

touch foot·ball, *n.* A type of informal football wherein tackling is replaced by touching, commonly with both hands, and protective equipment is not worn.

touch·hole, tuch'hōl″, *n.* A small tubular opening in the breech of an old-time firearm, esp. a cannon, through which the charge was ignited.

touch·ing, tuch'ing, *a.* Affecting; moving, pathetic; that touches.—*prep.* In reference or relation to; regarding; concerning.— **touch·ing·ly,** *adv.*—**touch·ing·ness,** *n.*

touch·line, tuch'lin″, *n. Rugby, soccer,* one of the side lines bounding a playing field.

touch mark, *n.* A mark of quality, stamped on pewter, which identifies the maker.

touch-me-not, tuch'mē·not″, *n. Bot.* any plant of the genus *Impatiens,* of the balsam family, whose ripe seed pods burst open when touched, as *I. balsamina,* an introduced garden flower, or the native wild-flower, *I. pallida,* the jewelweed.

touch·stone, tuch'stōn″, *n.* A gritty black stone, formerly used to test the purity of gold and silver by the color of the streak produced on it by rubbing it with the metals; any test or criterion by which the qualities of a thing are tried.

touch sys·tem, *n.* A typewriting system in which each finger is trained by touch to locate and use certain keys, thus allowing typing to be done without looking at the keyboard.

touch-tone tel·e·phone, tuch'tōn″ tel′e·fōn″, *n.* A push-button operated telephone.

touch-type, tuch'tip″, *v.t.*—**touch-typed,** touch-typing. To type without having to look at the keyboard, as in the touch system.—**touch-typ·ist,** *n.*

touch up, *v.t.* To improve or modify by slight additions or corrections, as a painting or other artistic work; to prod or rouse, as by striking.—**touch-up,** *n.*

touch·wood, tuch'wud″, *n.* The soft white substance into which wood is converted by the action of several fungi, making it suitable for use as tinder; punk.

touch·y, tuch'ē, *a.*—**touchier,** touchiest. [Appar. orig. a var. of *tetchy,* with form and later senses due to *touch.*] Apt to take offense on slight provocation; irritable; sensitive to touch; easily ignited, as tinder; precarious, risky, or ticklish, as a subject or situation.—**touch·i·ly,** *adv.*—**touch·i·ness,** *n.*

tough, tuf, *a.* [O.E. *tóh,* tough; akin to D. *taai,* G. *zähe,* Prov. G. *zach,* tough.] Strong; durable; yielding to force without breaking; firm but flexible without being brittle; difficult to cut or chew, as food; viscous in consistency; physically or mentally able to endure hardship; stubborn; hard to manage or deal with; difficult to achieve or perform; demanding or rigorous, as a task or game; strict, harsh, or severe. *Colloq.* rowdy; rough; belligerent; vicious; unfortunate, as bad luck.—*n. Colloq.* a rough, belligerent, or rowdy person.—**tough·ly,** *adv.*—**tough·ness,** *n.*

tough·en, tuf'en, *v.i.* To grow tough.—*v.t.* To make tough.—**tough·en·er,** *n.*

tough·ie, tough·y, tuf'ē, *n. Colloq.* A person with a loud, coarse, rough, or disorderly manner; a hard problem; a difficult situation.

tough-mind·ed, tuf'mīn'did, *a.* Characterized by a lack of sentimentality; realistic and practical in attitude or viewpoint; determined.—**tough-mind·ed·ly,** *adv.*— **tough-mind·ed·ness,** *n.*

tou·pee, tö·pā′, tö·pē′, *n.* [Fr. *toupet,* dim. of O.Fr. *toup, top,* tuft of hair; from Teut.,

and akin to E. *top.*] A patch of false hair or a partial wig worn to cover a bald spot; formerly, a curl or an artificial lock of hair on the top of the head, esp. as a crowning feature of a periwig.

tour, tụr, *n.* [Fr. *tour,* a turn, trip, or tour; same origin as *turn.*] A lengthy trip or excursion, as for sightseeing or business; a journey in a circuit; as, a theatrical *tour; milit.* a turn or period of service at one place.—*v.i.* To make a tour.—*v.t.* To make a tour of; to take or present on a tour, as a ballet or play.

tou·ra·co, tụr′a·kō′, *n.* pl. **tou·ra·cos.** [< F. *touraco;* said to be imit. of its cry.] An African bird, *Turacus fischeri,* in the family *Musophagidae,* notable for their large size, brilliant plumage, and helmetlike crest. Also **tu·ra·co,** tụr′a·kō″.

tour·bil·lion, tụr·bil'yon, *n.* [Fr. *tourbillion,* a whirlwind.] A spiraling type of sky-rocket; a vortex; a whirlwind.

tour de force, tụr″ de fōrs′, tụr″ de fạrs′, *Fr.* tör de fạrs′, *n.* pl. **tours de force,** tụr″ de fōrs′, tụr″ de fạrs′, *Fr.* tör de fạrs′. An achievement which requires ingenuity, great ability, or strength; an artistic work which cannot be equaled or surpassed.

tour·ing car, *n.* An open automobile with a folding top, designed for five or more passengers popular during the 1920's.

tour·ism, tụr'iz·um, *n.* The custom or practice of traveling for pleasure; the promotion by establishments or countries to attract tourists; the business or occupation of providing various services for tourists.

tour·ist, tụr'ist, *n.* One who makes a tour; one who travels for pleasure.—*a.*

tour·ist class, *n.* The most economic accommodations on airplanes and ships.

tour·ist court, *n.* A motel.

tour·ist home, *n.* A private home which provides lodging for tourists or other transients.

tour·ist trap, *n.* A business that overcharges tourists.

tour·ma·line, tụr'ma·lin, tụr'ma·lēn″, *n.* [Fr. < *toramalli,* a name given to it in Ceylon.] A complex silicate mineral of boron and aluminum, occurring in black and various colors, the clear varieties used as gemstones. Also **tour·ma·lin,** turmaline, tụr'ma·lin.

tour·na·ment, tụr'na·ment, *n.* [O.Fr. *tourneiment, tournoyement, < tourneier, tournoyer,* to turn or twirl about.] A contest of skill in which players compete in a series of games; as, a chess *tournament*; a series of games or athletic events in which teams or individuals compete against one another; a martial sport or type of combat in the Middle Ages performed by opposing armored knights on horseback for the purpose of exhibiting their courage, prowess, and skill, or in competition for a prize.

tour·ney, tụr'nē, *n.* pl. **tour·neys.** [O.Fr. *tournei.*] A tournament.—*v.i.* To tilt; to engage in a tournament.

tour·ni·quet, tụr'ni·kit, *n.* [Fr., < *tourner,* to turn.] *Surg.* a bandage which is tightened by twisting with a stick, or a pad pressed down with a screw or elastic, to arrest hemorrhage. A tool for pulling the parts of a piece of furniture together.

tou·sle, tou·zle, tou'zl, *v.t.*—*tousled, tousling, touzled, touzling.* To put into disorder; to dishevel; to rumple.—*n.* A disarrangement, as of clothing or a head of hair.

tout, tout, *v.i.* [M.E. *tuten,* var. of *toten,* peep, peer, < O.E. *tōtián,* peep out (to sight), protrude.] *Colloq.* To solicit employment, votes, or business importunately; to spy on a race horse to obtain information for betting purposes; to act as a tout.—*v.t. Colloq.* To solicit support for, importunately; to praise highly and insistently; to spy on, as a race horse, to gain information for betting purposes; to give a tip on, as a race horse, esp. for a fee.—*n. Colloq.* One who solicits employment, support, or business importunately; one who spies on race horses to gain information for betting purposes, or who gives tips on a horse or race as a business.—**tout·er,** tou′tẽr, *n.*

to·va·rich, tō·vär′ish, *Russ.* to·vä′rishch, *n. Russ.* Comrade, a title or term of address in the U.S.S.R., used for Communist Party members; any citizen of the Soviet Union. Also **to·va·rish, to·va·risch.**

tow, tō, *v.t.* [O.E. *togian,* drag, secondary form of *tēon* = O.H.G. *ziohan* (G. *ziehen*) = Goth. *tiuhan,* draw; akin to L. *ducere,* lead: cf. *team, tie, touch, tow,* and *tug.*] To drag or pull, as a trailer, boat, or car, by means of a rope, chain, or hitch; to haul.— *n.* The act of towing, or the state of being towed; a rope, chain, or hitch for towing; something towed; that which tows; a ski tow.—**in tow,** in the condition of being towed; under guidance or in charge; accompanying or following.—**tow·age,** tō′ij, *n.* The act of towing or the state of being towed; a charge for towing.

tow, tō, *n.* [M.E. *tow:* cf. O.E. *towlīc,* of spinning, *towhūs,* spinning-house, Icel. *tō,* tuft of wool.] The fiber of flax, hemp, or jute prepared for spinning by scutching; the coarse and broken parts of flax or hemp separated from the finer parts in hackling.— *a.*

to·ward, tōrd, tard, to·ward′, *prep.* [O.E. *tōweard, tōweardes—tō,* and *-weard,* expressing direction. *Towards* is an advbl. genit.] In the direction of; as, *toward* the house; facing; as, turned *toward* us; in expectation of or for; as, saving *toward* a new car; close to or near in time; aiding or contributing to; in regard or with respect to; as, an attitude *toward* war. Also **to·wards.**—tōrd, tard, *a.* Imminent; in progress or ongoing; favorable; ready to learn; apt; docile.

to·ward·ly, tōrd′lē, tard′lē, *a. Archaic.* Promising or apt; tractable or docile; friendly; favorable or propitious; seasonable or suitable.—**to·ward·li·ness,** *n.*

tow·boat, tō′bōt″, *n.* A small, rugged, steam- or diesel-powered boat used to tow or push ships and barges in harbors or inland waterways. Also *tugboat.*

tow car, *n.* A wrecker or tow truck.

tow·el, tou′el, *n.* [Fr. *touaille,* < O.H.G. *twahilla, dwahilla,* a towel, < *twahan,* O.E. *thweán* (for *thweahan*), Goth. *thvahan,* to wash.] A cloth or soft paper for drying or wiping anything, esp. the hands and face after washing.—*v.t., v.i.,* toweled, toweling, *Brit.* towelled, towelling. To wipe or dry with a cloth or towel.

tow·el·ing, chiefly *Brit.* **tow·el·ling,** tou′e·ling, *n.* Cloth or other material for making towels.

tow·er, tou′ẽr, *n.* [O.E. *tour,* < Fr. *tour,* a tower, < L. *turris,* a tower; cogn. Gr. *tyrris, tyrsis,* Ir. *túr,* W. *twr,* Gael. *torr,* a heap, a tower.] A structure or building, relatively tall and narrow, either standing alone or forming part of a church, castle, or other edifice; any tall thin structure; as, a television *tower*; a tall, movable wooden structure used in ancient warfare in storming a fortified place; a citadel; a fortress.— *v.i.* To rise or fly high; to soar; to be lofty; to stand sublime; to surpass all others.— **tow·ered,** *a.*

tow·er·ing, tou′ẽr·ing, *a.* Very high or lofty; as, a *towering* rage; outstanding; extreme; excessive.

tow·head, tō′hed″, *n.* A head of flaxen or light-colored hair, or a person with such hair; a sand bar, shoal, or newly formed island in a river.—**tow-head·ed,** *a.*

tow·hee, tou′hē, tō′hē, *n.* [Imit. of its note.]

Ornith. the chewink, *Pipilo erythrophthalmus,* in the finch family. Also **ground rob·- in, tow·hee bun·ting.**

tow·line, tō′lin″, *n.* A line, hawser, or the like, by which anything is or may be towed.

town, toun, *n.* [O.E. *tūn,* enclosure, yard, manor, village, town, = Icel. *tūn,* enclosure, homestead, house, = D. *tuin* garden, fence, = G. *zaun,* fence, hedge: cf. Celtic *dun,* appearing as *-dunum* in Latinized place-names, as L. *Lugdunum,* Lyons.] A collection of inhabited houses larger than a village and having more complete local government; a city or borough; the particular town or city under consideration; the chief town or city of a district or country; the central area of a city; a municipal corporation, in New England, with less elaborate organization and powers than a city; a township, in states excluding New England; the townspeople. *Brit.* a village or rural community which holds a periodic market.—*a.* Of or pertaining to a town; characteristic of a town.—**go to town,** *slang.* To achieve rapidly; to advance.—**on the town,** *slang.* Enjoying entertainment, esp. in nightclubs and the like; receiving public assistance from a municipality.—**paint the town red,** *slang,* to celebrate boisterously.

town car, *n.* A large automobile with the front seat separated from the passenger seat by a partition of glass.

town clerk, *n.* A clerk or official who keeps the records of a town.

town cri·er, *n.* A public official who formerly issued proclamations in a town, usu. by loud verbal announcement through the town's streets.

town hall, *n.* A hall or building belonging to a town, usu. containing offices of town officials, and used for the transaction of the town's business and often as a place of public assembly.

town house, *n.* A house or mansion in town, as distinguished from a country residence belonging to the same individual. A house or residence, occupied by a single family, usu. two-storied and connected by a common wall to the side of a similar house.

town meet·ing, *n.* A general meeting of the inhabitants of a town; a meeting of the qualified voters of a town for the transaction of public business.

towns·folk, tounz′fōk″, *n. pl.* Townspeople.

town·ship, toun′ship, *n.* [O.E. *tūnscipe.*] An administrative division of a county with varying corporate powers; a region or district, in surveys of public land, usu. six miles square, containing 36 sections, each one mile square; a local community, in the New England states, which a town meeting governs; *E. hist.* a manor, parish, or subdivision of a parish, or the people of any such place.

towns·man, tounz′man, *n. pl.* **towns·men.** An inhabitant of a town; an inhabitant of one's own or the same town, or a fellow townsman; a selectman, in New England.

towns·peo·ple, tounz′pē″pl, *n. pl.* The inhabitants of a town; people raised in an urban as opposed to a rural area. Also *townsfolk.*

towns·wom·an, tounz′wụm″an, *n. pl.* **towns·wom·en.** A woman who resides in a town.

town·wear, toun′wâr″, *n.* Dress, usu. conservative in color and style, which is proper for city wear.

tow·path, tō′path″, tō′päth″, *n.* A path along the bank of a canal or river for use, as by animals or men, in towing boats.

tow·rope, tō′rōp″, *n.* A rope, hawser, or the like, used esp. in towing boats. Also *towline.*

tow truck, *n.* A vehicle used for towing away stalled or wrecked automobiles. Also *tow car.* See *wrecker.*

tox·al·bu·min, tok″sal·bū′min, *n. Biochem.* a toxic albumin.

tox·a·phene, tok′sa·fēn″, *n. Chem.* a chlorinated waxy camphene, serving as a rodenticide and insecticide.

tox·e·mi·a, tox·ae·mi·a, tok·sē′mē·a, *n.* [N.L., < Gr. *toxikón,* poison and *aima,* blood.] *Pathol.* a form of blood poisoning, esp. one in which the toxins produced by certain microorganisms enter the blood.— **tox·e·mic, tox·æ·mic,** tok·sē′mik, tok·- sem′ik, *a.*

tox·ic, tok′sik, *a.* [M.L. *toxicus,* < L. *toxicum,* poison < Gr. *toxikón,* a. (with *phármakon,* drug, poison), in *toxikón phármakon,* poison for arrows, hence any poison: *toxikón,* neut. of *toxikós,* of or for the bow, < *tóxon,* bow.] Of, pertaining to, or caused by a toxin or poison; of the nature of a poison; poisonous. Also **tox·i·cal.—tox·i·cal·ly,** *adv.*

tox·i·cant, tok′si·kant, *a.* Being toxic or poisonous.—*n.* A poison; any toxic agent of a stimulating, narcotic, or anesthetic nature, as an intoxicant.—**tox·i·ca·tion,** tok″si·- kā′shan, *n.*

tox·ic·i·ty, tok·sis′i·tē, *n. pl.* **tox·ic·i·- ties.** Poisonous or toxic quality, or the degree or state of being toxic; poisonous-ness.

tox·i·co·gen·ic, tok″si·kō·jen′ik, *a.* [Gr. *toxikón* and *gen-,* bear, produce.] Generating or producing toxic products or poisons; caused or produced by poisonous or toxic substances.

tox·i·col·o·gy, tok″si·kol′o·jē, *n.* [Gr. *toxikón* and *-logia.*] The science of poisons, their effects, antidotes, detection, and the like.—**tox·i·co·log·ic, tox·i·co·log·i·cal,** tok″si·ko·loj′ik, *a.*—**tox·i·co·log·i·cal·ly,** *adv.*—**tox·i·col·o·gist,** *n.*

tox·i·co·sis, tok″si·kō′sis, *n. pl.* **tox·i·co·- ses.** [N.L., < Gr. *toxikón.*] *Pathol.* an abnormal or diseased condition produced by the action of a toxin or poison.

tox·in, tok′sin, *n.* Any of various usu. unstable organic poisons produced in living or dead organisms or their products, as a venom, or ptomaine; any of the specific poisonous products generated by pathogenic microorganisms, and constituting the causative agents in various diseases, as tetanus or diphtheria. Compare *antitoxin.*

tox·in-an·ti·tox·in, tok′sin·an″ti·tok′sin, tok′sin·an″tē·tok′sin, *n.* A mixture or combination of antitoxin and toxin for inducing, esp. formerly, active immunity in defense of various diseases, as diphtheria.

tox·i·pho·bi·a, tok″si·fō′bē·a, *n.* [N.L., < Gr. *toxikón* and *-phobia.*] *Psychol.* an abnormal or morbid fear of being poisoned.

tox·oid, tok′soid, *n.* A toxin whose toxic property has been eliminated, usu. by a chemical agent, but retaining its antigenic qualities that produce immunity on injection into the body by initiating anitibody production.

tox·oph·i·lite, tok·sof′i·līt″, *n.* [Gr. *toxon,* a bow, and *philos,* loving.] A lover of archery.—*a.*—**tox·oph·i·ly,** *n.*

tox·o·plas·mo·sis, tok″sō·plaz·mō′sis, *n.* A disease, esp. of the nervous system, resulting from infestation of tissue by *Toxoplasma gondii,* a parasitic protozoan, occurring sporadically in certain animals, and occasionally man.

toy, toi, *n.* [M.E. *toye,* toying, play; origin uncertain.] An object, often a small imitation of some familiar thing, for children or others to play with; a plaything; a thing or matter of little or no value or importance, or a trifle; a small article of little real value, but prized for some reason; a knickknack; a trinket; something diminutive like a plaything; a small variety of dog.—*a.* Designed as a toy, as for children or others to play with; being a small imitation of some familiar object, used as a plaything; of petty character or diminutive size.—*v.i.* To act idly or without seriousness; to trifle; to dally amorously; flirt.—**toy·er,** *n.*—**toy··like,** *a.*

to·yon, tō′yon, *n.* [Amer. Sp. *tollon.*] An evergreen shrub or small tree, *Heteromeles arbutifolia,* belonging to the rose family, with white flowers and bright red berries, and common to the Pacific coast of N. America. Also **tol·lon, Christ·mas ber·ry, Cal·i·for·nia hol·ly.**

tra·be·at·ed, trā′bē·ā″tid, *a.* [L. *trabs,* beam.] *Arch.* Constructed with horizontal beams, as a flat, unvaulted ceiling, or with a lintel or entablature, as an unarched doorway; pertaining to such construction, as distinct from the vaulted or arched kind. Also **tra·be·ate,** trā′bē·it, trā′bē·āt″.—**tra·be·a·tion,** *n.*

tra·bec·u·la, tra·bek′ya·la, *n.* pl. **tra··bec·u·lae,** tra·bek′ya·lē″. [L., dim of *trabs,* beam.] *Biol.* A structural part resembling a small beam or crossbar; the tissue supporting an organ in animals, or the projections extending across ducts in plants.—**tra·bec·u·lar,** *a.*—**tra·bec·u··late,** tra·bek′ya·lit, tra·bek′ya·lāt″, *a.*

trace, trās, *n.* [Fr. *trace,* trace, track, outline, < *tracer,* to trace, < L.L. *tractiare,* < L. *tractus,* pp. of *traho, trahere,* to draw; whence also *tract, tractable, train, trait, treat, abstract, detract, extract.* In last sense directly < O.Fr. *trais,* pl. of *trait,* the trace of a carriage, < *traire,* L. *trahere,* to draw.] Any mark, impression, or appearance left when the thing itself no longer exists; a minute quantity or insignificant particle; token; *chem.* a nearly immeasurable amount of a chemical ingredient or element. A track, path, or trail, as left by an object or a person; *biol., psychol.* an engram. A line or mark faintly drawn; a line made by an instrument or device which records, as a seismograph.—*v.t.*—*traced, tracing.* To follow by traces left; to track out; to follow by vestiges or indications; to discover or find by investigation; to draw or delineate with marks; to draw in outline; to decorate or embellish, as with designs; to imprint, as designs; to copy, as a drawing or engraving, by following the lines and marking them on a sheet superimposed through which they appear; to print or mark with a broken or wavy line, as a seismograph or other recording device.—*v.i.* To walk; to travel; to trace back in origin, time, or history.—**trace·a·ble,** trā′sa·bl, *a.*—**trace·a·ble··ness,** *n.*—**trace·a·bly,** *adv.*—**trace·less,** *a.*

trace, trās, *n.* [M.E. *trais, trays,* pl. < O.Fr. *trais,* pl. of *trait,* a drawing, line, trace.] Either of the two straps, ropes, or chains by which a carriage, wagon, or the like is drawn by a harnessed horse or other draft animal; a linking part, as a rod, in a machine, with a pivoting point at each of the ends, used to transfer movement to one part of the machine from another.—**kick o··ver the trac·es,** to cast aside control; to exhibit defiance or insubordination.

trace el·e·ment, *n. Biol.* an element which is utilized by plants and animals in extremely small amounts and which is necessary to their physiological functioning. Also **mi·cro·el·e·ment.**

trac·er, trā′sèr, *n.* One who or that which traces; one who traces missing property, as parcels, or baggage; an inquiry form sent to trace a missing shipment, parcel, or the like; any of various devices for tracing, as for drawings or plans; ammunition with the inclusion of a chemical to render the path of a projectile visible; a substance, as a radioactive atom used in biological or chemical research to trace the course of a process.

trac·er·y, trā′se·rē, *n.* pl. **trac·er·ies.** Ornamental work consisting of intersecting or ramified ribs, bars, or the like, as in the upper part of a Gothic window, or in panels or screens; any delicate interlacing work of lines or threads, as in carving or embroidery; network.

tra·che·a, trā′kē·a, *Brit.* tra·kē′a, *n.* pl. **tra·che·ae.** [M.L., for L.L. *trachia,* < Gr. *tracheia,* windpipe, lit. 'rough artery,' prop. fem. of *tracys,* rough.] *Anat.* the tube extending from the larynx to the bronchi, in man and other vertebrates, serving as the passage for conveying air to and from the lungs; the windpipe; one of the air-conveying tubes of the respiratory system in insects and other arthropods. *Bot.* a duct or vessel formed by a row of cells that have lost their protoplasm and their intervening walls, conducting water and minerals.—**tra·che·al,** trā′kē·al, *Brit.* tra·kē′al, *a.*

tra·che·ate, trā′kē·āt″, *Brit.* tra·kē′it, *a.* Breathing through trachea, as an arthropod.

tra·che·id, trā′kē·id, *n.* [G. *tracheïde.*] *Bot.* an elongated supporting and conducting xylem cell with a pitted wall.—**tra·che·i··dal,** tra·kē′i·dal, trā′kē·id′al, *a.*

tra·che·i·tis, trā″kē·ī′tis, *n.* [N.L.] *Pathol.* inflammation of the trachea.

tra·che·o·bron·chi·al, trā″kē·ō·brong′-kē·al, *a. Anat.* in the region of, related to, or acting upon both the bronchi and trachea.

tra·che·o·phyte, trā′kē·o·fīt″, *n. Bot.* a member of a division of embryo-forming plants, *Tracheophyta,* characterized by the presence of the vascular tissues, xylem and phloem, and containing the club mosses, horsetails, ferns, and seed plants.

tra·che·os·co·py, trā″kē·os′ko·pē, *n. Med.* examination of the interior of the trachea, as with a laryngoscope.—**tra·che·o·scop·-ic,** trā″kē·o·skop′ik, *a.*—**tra·che·os·co·-pist,** *n.*

tra·che·ot·o·my, trā″kē·ot′o·mē, *n.* pl. **tra·che·ot·o·mies.** [*Trachea,* and Gr. *tomē,* a cutting, < *temnō,* to cut.] *Surg.* the operation of incising the trachea.

tra·cho·ma, tra·kō′ma, *n.* [N.L., < Gr. *tráchōma,* roughness, < *trachys,* rough.] *Pathol.* a contagious inflammation of the conjunctiva of the eyelids, characterized by the formation of granulations or small rounded growths.—**tra·chom·a·tous,** tra··kom′a·tus, tra·kō′ma·tus, *a.*

tra·chy·car·pous, trā″kē·kär′pus, trak″ē·-kär′pus, *a.* Of a rough-skinned fruit.

tra·chy·sper·mous, trā″kē·spur′mus, trak″ē·spur′mus, *a. Bot.* having roughly coated seeds.

tra·chyte, trā′kīt, trak′īt, *n.* [Gr. *trachys,* rough.] A feldspathic rock, light in color, abundant among the products of volcanoes, and often containing crystals of glassy feldspar, sometimes with hornblende and mica.

tra·chyt·ic, tra·kit′ik, *a. Mineral.* Pertaining to trachyte or consisting of it; referring to volcanic rock with parallel feldspar crystal arrangement.

trac·ing, trā′sing, *n.* The act of one who or that which traces; that which is produced by tracing, marking, or drawing; the record traced by a self-registering instrument; a traced copy of a drawing or the like, made on a transparent material.

track, trak, *n.* [O.Fr. Fr. *trac.* track, trace; perhaps from Teut. and akin to D. *trekken.*] One or more pairs of parallel lines of rails with their ties for railroad vehicles; a wheel rut; the mark or series of marks left by something that has passed; *usu. pl.* a series of footprints or other marks left by an animal or a person. A way made or beaten by the feet of men or animals; a line of travel or motion; as, the *track* of a bird; a course followed; a course of action or conduct or a method of proceeding; as, to go on in the same *track* year after year; a path or course made or laid out for some particular purpose; a train or succession of ideas, occurrences, or events; something making a track, as the tread of a tire; the distance between the outside of the rims of the tires on a motor vehicle. *Sports,* a course laid out for running or racing; the collective sports taking place on a track, as hurdling and running. *Computer technology,* a sequence of cells on a memory device, as a drum or tape of a computer, which can be read one at a time.—*v.t.* To trace or pursue by or as by the track, traces, or footprints left; to follow, as a track or course; to make one's way through or traverse; to make a track of footprints on; to make a track with, as dirt, mud, snow, or tar, carried on the feet while walking; to furnish with a track or tracks, as for railroad vehicles; *aeron., rocketry,* to observe or follow the progress of, as an aircraft or rocket, by sighting and watching, esp. by means of radar, an optical instrument, or a radio direction finder.—*v.i.* To follow up a track or trail; to run in the same track, as the wheels of a vehicle; to be in alignment, as one gearwheel with another; to have a specific distance between wheels or rails.—**in one's tracks,** *colloq.* in the position where someone is.—**keep track of,** to follow the course or progress of.—**lose track of,** to neglect to keep advised of.—**make tracks,** *colloq.* to leave or go quickly.—**off the track,** going off from the subject or objective.—**on the track of,** in close pursuit of.—**on the wrong side of the tracks,** in a poor neighborhood. —**track·a·ble,** *a.*—**track·er,** *n.*

track·age, trak′ij, *n.* The collective tracks of a railroad or railway; the right of one railroad company to use the tracks of another company; the amount charged for this privilege or right.

track and field, *n.* A category of athletics including various running, jumping, and throwing events performed on a circular track and the field adjoining it.—**track-and-field,** trak′an·fēld′, *a.*

track·ing sta·tion, *n. Aerospace,* a station for tracking the path of a flying or orbiting object, esp. one of a series of such stations set up to maintain contact with a spacecraft or satellite by radio or radar.

track·less, trak′lis, *a.* Without a track or tracks; pathless; leaving no track or trace; not running on a track, or lines of rails.— **track·less·ly,** *adv.*—**track·less·ness,** *n.*

track·less trol·ley, *n.* Trolley bus.

track meet, *n.* An athletic competition involving track and field events.

track·walk·er, trak′wạ″kèr, *n. Rail.* a man employed to walk over and inspect a certain section of track at regular intervals. Also **track·man.**

tract, trakt, *n.* [L. *tractus,* a drawing, train, course, stretch, extent, tract, < *trahere,* draw: cf. *trait.*] A stretch or extent of land or water; a region; *anat.* a particular area of the body, esp. a system of related organs; as, the digestive *tract. Archaic,* an extent of time; duration; lapse.

tract, trakt, *n.* [Appar. < L. *tractatus.*] A brief treatise or pamphlet suitable for general distribution and usu. dealing with a religious, moral, or political topic.

tract, trakt, *n. Rom. Cath. Ch.* verses of Scripture said after the gradual, instead of the alleluia, in all masses from Septuagesima to Holy Saturday.

trac·ta·ble, trak′ta·bl, *a.* [L. *tractabilis,* < *tracto,* to handle, treat.] Capable of being easily trained or managed; very amenable to discipline; docile; governable; pliable.—**trac·ta·bil·i·ty, trac·ta·ble··ness,** *n.*—**trac·ta·bly,** *adv.*

Trac·tar·i·an, trak·târ′ē·an, *a.* Of or pertaining to the views expressed in or the writers of *Tracts for the Times*, a series of papers published in England between 1833 and 1841 as part of the Oxford movement; pertaining to any exponent, supporter, or tenet of the Oxford movement.—*n.*—**Trac·tar·i·an·ism**, trak·târ′ē·a·niz″um, *n.*

trac·tate, trak′tāt, *n.* A treatise; a tract.

trac·tile, trak′til, *a.* [L. *trahere* (pp. *tractus*), draw.] Capable of being drawn; that may be drawn out in length; ductile.—**trac·til·i·ty**, *n.*

trac·tion, trak′shan, *n.* [Fr. *traction*, < L. *traho, tractum*, to draw.] The act of drawing or pulling; the act of drawing a body along a plane, as when a vessel is towed in water; a body's friction on a surface, as an automobile tire on a highway; *med.* the action of pulling on an organ or a muscle to relieve or lessen pressure, or repair a dislocation.—**trac·tion·al, trac·tive**, trak′tiv, *a.*

trac·tion en·gine, *n.* A steam locomotive engine for dragging heavy loads on ground or roads.

trac·tor, trak′tēr, *n.* [M.L., < L. *trahere*, draw.] A strong, usu. heavy-treaded, motorized vehicle used for pulling or drawing heavy equipment and farm machinery; a truck which hitches to and hauls a trailer and consists of an engine and a cab one who or that which draws or pulls; something used for drawing or pulling. *Aeron.* an airplane with a propeller mounted at the front; also **trac·tor air·plane**.

trade, trād, *n.* [M.E. *trade*, < M.L.G. *trade*, track; akin to E. *tread*.] A line of work or form of occupation pursued as a business or calling, esp. some line of skilled mechanical work learned by apprenticeship, as distinguished from mercantile, professional, or agricultural occupations or from unskilled labor; as, the *trade* of a carpenter; anything practiced as a means of getting a living or money; a line of mercantile or commercial business or the traffic in a particular commodity or class of commodities; as, the silk *trade*; those engaged in a particular line of business; as, the sale of books to the *trade*; the buying and selling or exchanging of commodities either by wholesale or by retail, within a country or between countries; as, domestic or foreign *trade*; business, patronage, or custom; a particular commercial or business transaction; a purchase, sale, or exchange; a bargain or deal; *usu. pl.* a trade wind.—*v.t.*—*traded, trading.* To buy, sell, barter, or traffic in; to exchange, or give in exchange; as, to *trade* one thing for another.—*v.i.* To carry on trade; as, to *trade* with the Indians; to traffic, followed by *in*; as, to *trade* in wheat; to make an exchange; to make purchases or to shop.—*a.*—**trade in**, to exchange, as a used item, for credit toward the purchase of a similar one; as, to *trade in* one's old typewriter.—**trade on** or **up·on**, to use for personal gain; as, to *trade on* the family name.

trade ac·cep·tance, *n.* A bill of exchange, drawn on the purchaser by the person selling, having the acceptance of the purchaser for a future payment.

trade book, *n.* A book intended for the public, as distinct from an instruction or textbook or limited edition of that book.

trade coun·cil, *n.* A council made up of local trade unions.

trade dis·count, *n.* *Com.* A reduction of list price for a retailer or other large buyer allowed by someone in manufacturing or one dealing in wholesale goods.

trade dol·lar, *n.* A dollar which consisted of somewhat more silver than was standard, issued by the U.S. from 1873 to 1885 for trade or business with the Orient.

trade e·di·tion, *n.* A publication of a work, as a book, intended for sale to the general public, as distinguished from *text edition*.

trade-in, trād′in″, *n.* A used article, as a car

or radio, given in trade as part payment for a new article; an instance of business transacted in this manner.—*a.*—**trade in**, *v.t.*

trade-last, trād′last″, trād′läst″, *n. Colloq.* a compliment conveyed to the person so flattered by a third person who has heard it paid, in exchange for a similarly favorable comment heard about the latter. Abbr. *T.L.*

trade·mark, trād′märk″, *n.* A distinctive mark, wording, or device adopted by a manufacturer, business, or dealer, usu. registered with a government agency, and impressed on his goods and labels to distinguish them from those of others.—*v.t.* To stamp, as a trademark, on; to officially record, as a trademark.

trade name, *n.* A name invented or adopted as the distinctive name of some article of commerce; the name by which an article or substance is known to the trade; the name or style under which a firm does business.

trad·er, trā′dēr, *n.* One engaged in trade or commerce; a stock exchange broker who operates only for his own account; a vessel employed regularly in any particular trade.

trade route, *n.* A land or sea route traveled by traders, as in caravans or merchant ships.

trad·es·can·ti·a, trad″is·kan′shē·a, trad″-is·kan′sha, *n.* [N.L. from John *Tradescant* (died about 1638), gardener to Charles I.] Any plant of the genus *Tradescantia*, belonging to the spiderwort family.

trade school, *n.* A school teaching the theory and practice of a trade.

trade se·cret, *n.* A private formula or process used by a profession, trade, or manufacturer to their advantage.

trades·folk, trādz′fōk″, *n. pl.* Persons in business or trade. Also *tradespeople*.

trades·man, trādz′man″, *n. pl.* **trades·men**. A skilled laborer; craftsman; mechanic; *Brit.* a shopkeeper.—**trades·wom·an**, trādz′wụm″an, *n. pl.* **trades·wom·en**.

trades·peo·ple, trādz′pē″pl, *n. pl.* Tradesfolk.

trade un·ion, *n.* A labor union, comprised of workers in related fields or crafts, as distinct from a general labor union. Also *Brit.* **trades-un·ion**.—**trade un·ion·ism**, *Brit.* **trade-un·ion·ism**, *n.*—**trade un·ion·ist**, *Brit.* **trade-un·ion·ist**, *n.*

trade wind, *n.* [Cf. the obs. phrase *to blow trade*, of the wind, to blow in one regular course.] One of the winds prevailing over the oceans from about 30° north latitude to about 30° south latitude, and blowing from northeast to southwest in the northern hemisphere, and from southeast to northwest in the southern hemisphere, toward the equator.

trad·ing post, *n.* A post or station established for carrying on trade in an unsettled or thinly settled region by a trading company or trader.

trad·ing stamp, *n.* A printed stamp of a certain value, given by the dealer to the customer, a quantity of which may be redeemed for merchandise.

tra·di·tion, tra·dish′an, *n.* [Fr. *tradition*, < L. *trado*, to hand over, deliver.] The handing down of opinions, doctrines, practices, rites, and customs from father to son, or from ancestors to posterity by oral communication; that which is handed down from age to age by oral communication; a doctrine or statement of facts so handed down. *Theol.* an unwritten set of theories and laws, among the Jewish people, which are believed to have been obtained and orally handed down from Moses; similar Christian doctrines acquired and handed down orally. *Law,* a transference of something into the buyer's possession.—**tra·di·tion·less**, *a.*

tra·di·tion·al, tra·dish′a·nal, *a.* Pertaining to or derived from tradition; com-

municated from ancestors to descendants.—**tra·di·tion·al·ly**, *adv.*

tra·di·tion·al·ism, tra·dish′a·na·lizm, *n.* Adherence to or importance placed on tradition; a doctrine professing that divine revelation is the only valid source of religious truth.—**tra·di·tion·al·ist**, *n.*—**tra·di·tion·al·is·tic**, *a.*

trad·i·tor, trad′i·tēr, *n. pl.* **trad·i·to·res**, trad″i·tōr′ēz, trad″i·tar′ēz. A traitor of early Christian times who surrendered the scriptures or sacred vessels and betrayed other Christians during the Roman persecutions.

tra·duce, tra·dōs′, tra·dūs′, *v.t.*—*traduced, traducing.* [L. *traduco, traducere,* to lead along, exhibit, disgrace, defame—*trans,* over, and *duco,* to lead.] To misrepresent willfully; to defame; to falsely accuse; to vilify.—**tra·duce·ment**, *n.* **tra·duc·er**, *n.*

traf·fic, traf′ik, *n.* [Fr. *trafic*, It. *traffico,* prob. < L. *transfero,* to bear across, transport.] Goods or persons collectively passing along a road, railroad, boat route, or airway; the movement of these goods or persons; dealings; the transportation business; an interchange of goods or merchandise between countries, communities, or individuals; trade; commerce; a heavy exchange or buying and selling of anything, as goods; the business flow of a system of communication, as measured by the signals and messages transmitted; illegal trade, as in stolen merchandise.—*v.i.*—*trafficked, trafficking.* To do business, esp. illegally; to have business or dealings usu. followed by *with*.—**traf·fick·er**, *n.*

traf·fic cir·cle, *n.* See *rotary*. Also *Brit.* **round·a·bout**.

traf·fic court, *n.* A court whose jurisdiction is usu. limited to decisions on charges of violation of traffic ordinances or statutes.

traf·fic is·land, *n.* A prohibited spot in the roadway, used for some other purpose than vehicular traffic; a safety zone for pedestrians; a median strip.

traf·fic light, *n.* Color-coded lights that caution, stop, and start traffic; directional lights that show open or closed lanes; turn signals, as green arrows. Also **traf·fic sig·nal**.

trag·a·canth, trag′a·kanth″, *n.* [Fr. *tragacanthe*, the gum (now usu. *adragant, adragante*), also the plant yielding it, < L. *tragacantha,* < Gr. *trágos,* goat, and *ákantha,* thorn.] A mucilaginous substance derived from various old-world shrubs of the genus *Astragalus,* used in making pills, candies, and preserved foods, and in processing textiles and leather.

tra·ge·di·an, tra·jē′dē·an, *n.* [L. *tragœdus*.] A writer, or esp. an actor of tragedy.

tra·ge·di·enne, tra·jē″dē·en′, *n.* [Fr. *tragédienne*.] An actress of tragedy.

trag·e·dy, traj′i·dē, *n. pl.* **trag·e·dies**. [L. *tragoedia,* < Gr. *trago(i)dia,* tragedy—*trágos,* a he-goat, and *ōdē, o(i)de,* a song, < *aeidō,* to sing; because, it is said, a goat was the prize of the early tragic choirs in Athens.] A drama, usu. in verse, portraying the struggle of a strong-willed protagonist against fate, as predestined by mysterious, divine, social, or psychological forces culminating in disaster and usu. death, caused by a flaw, as envy or ambition, in the protagonist's character, usu. resolved by the protagonist's belated recognition and acceptance of fate, and in classical tragedy, according to Aristotle's dictum, arousing terror and pity; the genre to which such dramas belong, as opposed to *comedy*; a medieval didactic narrative in verse or prose concerning the fall of a great person; the perception of human existence conveyed by a tragedy; any disaster, misfortune, death, or sequence of interrelated disastrous events.

trag·ic, traj′ik, a. [L. *tragicus*.] Pertaining to tragedy; of the nature or character of tragedy; lamentable; dreadful. Also **trag·i·cal**—**trag·i·cal·ly**, adv.—**trag·i·cal·ness**, n.

trag·ic flaw, n. *Liter.* the characteristic fault or defect of a tragic protagonist, often ambition or pride, that leads to his downfall, although it may also have led to his rise.

trag·i·com·e·dy, traj″i·kom′i·dē, n. pl. **trag·i·com·e·dies**. [Fr. *tragi-comédie*, < L.L. *tragicomœdia*, for L. *tragicocomœdia*, < *tragicus*, E. *tragic*, and *comœdia*, E. comedy.] A drama or other literary work combining elements of tragedy and comedy; an incident or series of incidents of mixed tragic and comic character.—**trag·i·com·ic**, **trag·i·com·i·cal**, traj″i·kom′ik, a. —**trag·i·com·i·cal·ly**, adv.

trag·o·pan, trag′o·pan″, n. [L. < Gr. *tragópan*, a fabulous Ethiopian bird, < *trágos*, goat, and *Pán*, Pan.] Any of the Asiatic pheasants constituting the genus *Tragopan*, characterized by two fleshy hornlike structures on the head, and brightly colored feathers.

tra·gus, trā′gus, n. pl. **tra·gi**, trā′jī. [Gr. *trágos*, a goat, being sometimes furnished with a tuft of hair suggesting the beard of a goat.] *Anat.* a small cartilaginous eminence at the front entrance of the external ear.

trail, trāl, v.t. [< old *traile*, a sledge, < L. *tragula*, a sledge, a dragnet, *traho*, to draw.] To draw behind or along the ground; to drag; to cause to float after itself; as, to *trail* dust or smoke; to mark or track out; to follow, as a detective.—v.i. To sweep over a surface by being pulled or dragged; to grow with long slender and creeping shoots or stems, as a plant; to lag; to grow ineffectual or dwindle, usu. followed by *off*, as: The music *trailed* off.—n. A path or route created by the usu. repeated passage of men or animals, as through a wooded area; a track followed by a hunter, runner, horseback rider, or the like; anything drawn out behind; as, a *trail* of smoke; *milit.* the end of the stock of a gun carriage which rests upon the ground when a gun is in position for firing. Evidence of passage left behind by a moving object or body.—**trail arms**, *milit.* to carry the rifle obliquely, muzzle forward, butt near ground.

trail·blaz·er, trāl′blā″zèr, n. One who blazes a new trail through a wilderness; *fig.* any innovator who facilitates subsequent work in his field.—**trail·blaz·ing**, a. n.

trail·er, trā′lèr, n. One who or that which trails; any vehicle attached to, and drawn by, a car, tractor, or truck, as a van for freight or a conveyance for a boat for overland transportation; a house on wheels, attachable to an automobile and fitted with conveniences as for camping; a plant which creeps or trails along the ground; a short film shown in a movie theater, giving a preview of a forthcoming production.

trail·er camp, n. A parking area equipped with utility outlets for temporary or permanent use by house trailers, mobile campers, and similar vehicles. Also **trail·er court**, **trail·er park**.

trail·ing ar·bu·tus, n. Mayflower.

trail·ing edge, n. *Aeron.* that edge of an airfoil, as of a wing, propeller blade, or rotor blade, over which the airflow passes last.

train, trān, n. [O.Fr. *traine*, also *train* (Fr. *traîne*, *train*).] A connected series of railway cars; a line or procession of persons, vehicles, animals, or the like traveling together; a succession or series of proceedings, events, or circumstances; a succession of connected ideas or a continuous course of thought or reasoning; a line or succession of persons or things following after; a body of followers or attendants;

retinue; aftermath or consequence; as, famine following in the *train* of crop failure; a series or row of objects or parts; an elongated part of a skirt, robe, or the like trailing behind on the ground; a trail or stream of something from a moving object, as the trail of a comet or meteor; order, esp. proper order, for proceeding; a line of combustible material, as gunpowder, for leading fire to an explosive charge; *milit.* an aggregation of vehicles, animals, and men accompanying an army to carry supplies, baggage, ammunition, and other materials; *mach.* a series of connected parts, as wheels and pinions, through which motion is transmitted; *phys.* a group or series of successive waves, oscillations, or the like.—v.t. To form, as behavior, habits, and mental attitude, by discipline and instruction; to make proficient by instruction and practice, as in some art, profession, or work; to discipline and instruct, as an animal, in the performance of tasks or tricks; to make fit, as a person, by proper exercise, diet, or drill, as for some athletic feat or contest; to treat or manipulate so as to bring into some desired form, position, or direction; to bring to bear on some object, or to point, aim, or direct, as a firearm, camera, telescope, or eye; *hort.* to bring, as a plant, branch, or the like into a particular shape or position by bending, pruning, or other means.—v.i. To give the discipline and instruction, drill, or practice designed to impart proficiency; to undergo such discipline, instruction, or drill; to get oneself into condition, as for a contest or athletic event, by exercise, drill, or diet; to travel by train.—**train·a·ble**, a.—**train·er**, n.

train·band, trān′band″, n. [For *trained band*.] One of the trained bands or forces of citizen soldiery organized in London and elsewhere in the 16th, 17th, and 18th centuries.

train·ing, trā′ning, n. The act or process of one who or that which trains, or the resulting condition.—a. Of, relating to, or used for training.

train·ing col·lege, n. *Brit.* a college for training students to be teachers.

train·ing school, n. A school that offers training in some art, profession, or trade; a custodial institution where juvenile delinquents are detained for corrective training and education.

train·man, trān′man, n. pl. **train·men**. A man employed on a railroad train, esp. a brakeman or flagman who assists the conductor.

train oil, n. [D. and L.G. *traan*, Dan. and Sw. *tran*, G. *thran*, train oil; cf. D. *traan*, G. *thräne*, a tear, a drop.] The oil procured from the blubber or fat of whales.

train·sick, trān′sik″, a. Afflicted with nausea due to the motion of train travel; pertaining to motion sickness.—**train sick·ness**, n.

traipse, trāps, v.i.—*traipsed*, *traipsing*. [Perh. < O.Fr. *trespasser*, to pass across.] *Colloq.* to walk or gad about, esp. without definite purpose.—v.t. Also **trapes**.

trait, trāt, n. [Fr., a trait, a stroke, < L. *tractus*, a drawing.] A distinguishing or peculiar feature or quality; a characteristic; formerly, a stroke or touch.

trai·tor, trā′tèr, n. [O.Fr. *traitor* (Fr. *traître*), < L. *traditor*, < *trado*, to deliver up (whence *tradition*)—*trans*, over, and *do*, *datum*, to give.] One who violates his allegiance and betrays his country; one guilty of treason; one guilty of perfidy.—**trai·tor·ous**, trā′tèr·us, a.—**trai·tor·ous·ly**, adv.—**trai·tress**, trā′tris, n. Feminine of traitor.

tra·ject, tra·jekt′, v.t. [L. *trajicio*, *trajectum*—*trans*, across, over, and *jacio*, to

throw.] To throw or cast across, or through. —**tra·jec·tion**, n.

tra·jec·to·ry, tra·jek′to·rē, n. pl. **tra·jec·to·ries**. The curve in the vertical plane traced by a bullet or shell moving through space, esp. from expulsion at the muzzle to the impact area; the arc described by an object or body trajected by an applied exterior force; *geom.* a curve intersecting each of a given series of curves at an identical angle.

tram, tram, n. [It. *trama*, < L. *trama*, weft.] A silk thread of two strands twisted loosely together, and used for cross threads in weaving of silk and velvet fabrics.

tram, tram, n. [Cf. M.L.G. *trame*, crossbar, rung, L.G. *traam*, G. *tram*, beam.] *Brit.* a streetcar. A wheeled truck or car on which loads are transported in coal mines; a tramroad or tramway.—v.t., v.i.—*trammed, tramming*. To travel or convey by tram.

tram·car, tram′kär″, n. *Brit.* a streetcar.

tram·line, tram′līn″, n. *Brit.* a streetcar line or tracks.

tram·mel, tram′el, n. [Fr. *tramail, trémail*, a net, < L.L. *tramaculum, tremaculum*, a kind of fishing net, < L. *tres*, three, and *macula*, a mesh.] *Usu. pl.* anything that hinders, confines, or impedes activity, freedom, or progress. A mechanical instrument for describing ellipses; training shackles for teaching a horse to amble; fetters; a fish net having two nets of large mesh between which hangs a net of fine mesh; a net for trapping fowl; an instrument for adjusting or aligning machinery parts.—v.t.—*trammeled, trammeling, chiefly Brit. trammelled, trammelling*. To confine; to hamper; to shackle.—**tram·mel·er**, *Brit.* **tram·mel·ler**, n.

tra·mon·tane, tra·mon′tān, tram′on·tān″, a. [It. *tramontano*, < L. *transmontanus*—*trans*, beyond, and *mons*, mountain.] Lying or being beyond the mountains, originally applied by the Italians to those on the other side of the Alps; foreign; barbarous. —n. Also **trans·mon·tane**.

tramp, tramp, v.i. [M.E. *trampen* = M.L.G. and G. *trampen*, tramp, stamp: cf. Goth. *anatrimpan*, tread or press upon.] To tread or walk with a firm, heavy, resounding step; to tread heavily or trample, usu. followed by *on* or *upon*; as, to *tramp on* a person's toes; to walk heavily or steadily, march, or trudge; to go on a walking excursion or expedition; to go about as a vagabond.—v.t. To tread or trample underfoot; to walk heavily or steadily through or over; to traverse on foot.—n. A person who travels about on foot from place to place, esp. a vagabond who wanders about the country living on occasional gifts of money, food, or other temporary means of subsistence; the act of tramping; a firm, heavy, resounding tread; the sound made by a continuing heavy tread; a long, steady walk or trudge; a walking excursion or expedition; a freight vessel which does not run regularly between fixed ports, but takes its cargo wherever shippers desire; a plate of iron on the sole of a shoe to protect it from a spade while digging; *slang*, any sexually promiscuous female.—**tramp·er**, n.

tram·ple, tram′pl, v.i.—*trampled, trampling*. [Freq. of *tramp*.] To tread or step heavily and noisily, or stamp; to tread heavily, roughly, or crushingly, often followed by *on, upon*, or the like; as, to *trample* upon young plants; to act in a harsh, domineering, or cruel way, as if treading roughly, often followed by *on, upon*, or the like; as, to *trample on* an oppressed people or their rights.—v.t. To tread heavily, roughly, or carelessly on or over; *fig.* to trample on, domineer harshly over, or crush; as, to *trample* law and order. To put out, force, or reduce by trampling, usu. followed by *out*; as, to *trample out* a fire.—*n.* The act or sound of trampling.—**tram·pler,** *n.*

tram·po·line, tram″po·lēn′, tram′po·lin, *n.* [G. *trampolin,* a springboard.] A heavy canvas or net fastened by springs or elastic rope inside a horizontal rectangular frame and used in certain tumbling and acrobatic performances.—**tram·po·lin·er, tram·po·lin·ist,** *n.*

tram·road, tram′rōd″, *n.* A road or track formed of parallel lines of wooden beams, lengths of stone, iron plates, or rails, for wheeled conveyances, esp. in a mine.

tram·way, tram′wā″, *n.* A tramroad; a railroad in or at a mine; *Brit.* a streetcar line.

trance, trans, träns, *n.* [O.Fr. Fr. *transe,* orig. passage, esp. from life to death, hence deadly suspense or fear, < *transir,* < L. *transire,* go across, pass over.] A half-conscious state, as between sleeping and waking, characterized by involuntary functioning; an unconscious, cataleptic, or hypnotic condition; a dazed or bewildered condition; a condition of complete mental absorption or deep musing; *spirit.* a temporary state in which a medium, with suspension of personal consciousness, is controlled by an intelligence from without and used as a means of communication, as from the dead to the living.—*v.t.*—**tranced,** *trancing.* To entrance.

tran·quil, trang′kwil, *a.* [Fr. *tranquille,* < L. *tranquillus,* quiet, calm.] Quiet; calm; undisturbed; peaceful; as, a *tranquil* landscape; not easily agitated; as, a *tranquil* disposition.—**tran·quil·ly,** *adv.*—**tran·quil·ness,** *n.*

tran·quil·ize, tran·quil·lize, trang′kwi·līz″, *v.t.*—*tranquilized, tranquilizing, tranquillized, tranquillizing.* To render tranquil; to pacify when agitated, esp. by administering drugs; to compose; to calm.—*v.i.* To become tranquil or composed.

tran·quil·iz·er, tran·quil·liz·er, trang′kwi·lī″zẻr, *n.* That which tranquilizes or soothes; any of several drugs capable of relieving tension.

tran·quil·li·ty, tran·quil·i·ty, trang′kwil′i·tē, *n.* The property or condition of being tranquil; quietude; composure.

trans·act, tran·sakt′, tran·zakt′, *v.t.* [L. *transactus,* pp. of *transigere,* < *trans,* across, through, and *agere,* drive, do.] To conduct or carry through, as affairs or business, to a conclusion or settlement.—*v.i.* To carry through affairs or negotiations; to transact business.—**trans·ac·tor,** *n.*

trans·ac·tion, tran·sak′shan, tran·zak′shan, *n.* [L.L. *transactio(n-).*] The act of transacting, or the fact of being transacted; an instance or process of transacting something, or that which is transacted, as an affair or a piece of business; *pl.* records, often published, of the doings of a learned society or the like, or reports of papers read, addresses delivered, discussions, or the like, at the meetings.—**trans·ac·tion·al,** *a.*

trans·al·pine, trans·al′pin, trans·al′pīn, tranz·al′pin, tranz·al′pīn, *a.* [L. *transalpinus,* < *trans,* across, and *Alpes,* the Alps.] Across or beyond the Alps, esp. as viewed from Italy.—*n.* A native or inhabitant of a country beyond the Alps.

trans·am·i·nase, trans·am′i·nās″, tranz·am′i·nās″, *n.* *Biochem.* any enzyme causing transamination.—**trans·am·i·na·tion,** trans·am″i·nā′shan, tranz·am″i·nā′shan, *n.* A reaction in which an amino group from one compound is transferred to another.

trans·at·lan·tic, trans″at·lan′tik, tranz″at·lan′tik, *a.* Extending across the Atlantic; on the other side of the Atlantic.

trans·ceiv·er, tran·sē′vẻr, *n.* [< *trans*(*mitter*) and (*re*)*ceiver.*] *Electron.* a combined transmitter and receiver in one radio device, usu. portable.

tran·scend, tran·send′, *v.t.* [L. *transcendere,* < *trans,* across, over, and *scandere,* climb.] To go above or beyond, overpass, or exceed, as a limit; to go beyond in elevation, excellence, extent, or degree; to surpass, excel, or exceed; *theol.* of the Deity, to be above and independent of, as the universe.—*v.i.* To be transcendent.

tran·scend·ent, tran·sen′dent, *a.* [L. *transcendens,* (*-ent-*), ppr.] Going beyond ordinary limits; surpassing or excelling; superior or supreme; *theol.* of the Deity, transcending the material universe. *Philos.* in scholastic philosophy, transcending the Aristotelian categories; in Kantian philosophy, transcending experience and not realizable in human experience.—**tran·scend·ence, tran·scend·en·cy,** tran·sen′dens, *n.*—**tran·scend·ent·ly,** *adv.*

tran·scen·den·tal, tran″sen·den′tal, *a.* Transcendent, surpassing, or superior; transcending ordinary or common experience, thought, or belief; supernatural; abstract or metaphysical; idealistic, lofty, or extravagant. *Philos.* of certain theories, explaining what is objective as the product of the subjective mind; in Kantian philosophy, pertaining to, based upon, or concerned with a priori elements in experience, which are the basis of all human knowledge. *Math.* not producible by the algebraic operations of addition, subtraction, multiplication, and the extraction of roots, each performed a finite number of times, as pi.—**tran·scen·den·tal·ly,** *adv.*

tran·scen·den·tal·ism, tran″sen·den′ta·liz″um, *n.* Transcendental character, thought, or language. *Philos.* any philosophy based upon the doctrine that the principles of reality are to be discovered by the study of the processes of thought, or by emphasizing the intuitive and spiritual above the empirical; also **tran·scen·den·tal·phi·los·o·phy.**—**tran·scen·den·tal·ist,** *n.*

trans·con·ti·nen·tal, trans″kon·ti·nen′tal, *a.* Passing or extending across a continent; as, a *transcontinental* railroad; on the far or other side of a continent.

tran·scribe, tran·skrīb′, *v.t.*—*transcribed, transcribing.* [L. *transcribere* (pp. *transcriptus*), < *trans,* across, over, and *scribere,* write.] To make a handwritten or typed copy of, as the text of a document, shorthand notes, or lecture notes; *phon.* to represent the sounds of speech in phonetic symbols; *mus.* to arrange, as a composition, for a voice or instrument other than that for which it was originally written; *radio,* to record for later broadcasting, as a performance or announcement.—**tran·scrib·er,** *n.*

tran·script, tran′skript, *n.* [M.L. *transcriptum,* prop. neut. of L. *transcriptus,* pp.] Something transcribed or made by transcribing; a written or typed copy; a copy or reproduction; a form of something as rendered from one alphabet or language into another; an official school report which includes a student's courses, grades, and credits.

tran·scrip·tion, tran·skrip′shan, *n.* [L. *transcriptio(n-).*] The act of transcribing; a transcript or copy. *Mus.* the arrangement of a composition for a voice or instrument other than that for which it was originally written; a composition so arranged. *Radio,* a recording of a musical, dramatic, or other performance made for radio broadcasting.—**tran·scrip·tion·al, tran·scrip·tive,** tran·skrip′tiv, *a.*

trans·duc·er, trans·dō′sẻr, trans·dū′sẻr, tranz·dō′sẻr, tranz·dū′sẻr, *n.* [L. *trans,* across, and *ducere,* lead.] *Electron.* a device for converting the energy of one transmission system into the energy of another transmission system.

trans·duc·tion, trans·duk′shan, *n.* *Genet-*

ics, a means by which genetic determinants are transferred from one microscopic organism to another by an agent, as a virus.

tran·sect, tran·sekt′, *v.t.* [L. *trans,* and *sectus,* pp. of *secare,* cut.] To cut across; to divide by passing across; to dissect transversely.—**tran·sec·tion,** *n.*

tran·sept, tran′sept, *n.* [L. *trans,* across, and *septum,* an enclosure.] *Arch.* That portion of a church built in the form of a cross, which is between the nave and choir and projects externally on each side so as to form the short arms of the cross; either of the arms of the transept.—**tran·sep·tal,** *a.*—**tran·sep·tal·ly,** *adv.*

trans·fer, trans·fụr′, trans′fẻr, *v.t. transferred, transferring.* [L. *transferre,* bear across, bring over, transfer, translate, < *trans* across, and *ferre,* bear; cf. *translate.*] To convey or remove from one place or person, to another. *Law,* to make over the possession or control of; as, to *transfer* a title to land; to sell or give. To convey, as a drawing, design, or pattern, from one surface to another.—*v.i.* To transfer oneself; to be transferred; to change from one conveyance to another.—trans′fẻr, *n.* The act of transferring or the fact of being transferred; also **trans·fer·al, trans·fer·ral,** trans·fụr′al. That which is transferred, as a drawing, pattern, or the like; a point or place for transferring; a means or system of transferring; a ticket entitling a passenger to continue his journey on another conveyance.—**trans·fer·a·ble,** *a.* Capable of being transferred. *Law,* capable of being made over to another; negotiable.—**trans·fer·ee,** trans″fe·rē′, *n.* One to whom a transfer is made, as of property; one who is transferred or moved, as from one place to another.

trans·fer·ase, trans′fe·rās″, *n. Biochem.* an enzyme that acts as a catalyst in the transfer of an organic grouping from one molecule to another.

trans·fer·ee, trans″fe·rē′, *n. Law,* one to whom a transfer is made, as of property. One who is moved from one place or position to another.

trans·fer·ence, trans·fụr′ens, trans′fẻr·ens, *n.* The act of transferring or being transferred; *psychoanal.* the revival and transferal of emotions, esp. those related to forgotten childhood experiences, toward a different person from whom they were initially experienced, usu. a psychoanalyst.—**trans·fer·en·tial,** trans″fe·ren′shal, *a.*

trans·fer·or, trans·fụr′ẻr, *n. Law,* one who makes a transfer, as of property.

trans·fer pay·ment, *n.* Any public expenditure made for a purpose other than the procurement of materials, services, or goods.

trans·fig·u·ra·tion, trans″fig·ya·rā′shan, trans·fig″ya·rā′shan, *n.* [L. *transfiguratio(n-).*] The act of transfiguring, or the state of being transfigured. (*Cap.*) the change in the appearance of Christ on the mountain, Mat. xvii. 1-9; the church festival commemorating this, observed on Aug. 6.

trans·fig·ure, trans·fig′yẻr, *v.t.*—*transfigured, transfiguring.* [Fr. *transfigurer,* < L. *transfiguro*—*trans,* over, and *figura,* face.] To change the outward form or appearance of; to transform in appearance; to give an elevated or glorified appearance to; to elevate and glorify; to idealize.—**trans·fig·ure·ment,** *n.*

trans·fi·nite, trans·fī′nīt, *a.* Extending beyond or exceeding the finite.—**trans·fi·nite num·ber,** *math.* an infinite cardinal number or infinite ordinal number.

trans·fix, trans·fiks′, *v.t.*—*transfixed, transfixt, transfixing.* [L. *transfigo, transfixum*—*trans,* through, and *figo,* to fix.] To pierce through as with a pointed weapon;

to hold or make immovable, as with awe or terror.—**trans·fix·ion**, trans·fik′shan, n.

trans·form, trans·fŏrm′, v.t. [L. *transformare* (pp. *transformatus*), < *trans*, across, over, and *formare*, E. *form*.] To change in form or appearance; metamorphose; to change in condition, nature, or character; convert; to change into another substance; transmute; *elect.* to change, as a current, in potential, as from high to low voltage, or in type, as from alternating to direct; *math.* to change the form of, as a figure or expression, without changing the value; *phys.* to change, as one form of energy, into another.—v.i. To change in form, appearance, or character; to become transformed.—**trans′fŏrm**, n. *Math.* A transformed figure or expression; a transformation.—**trans·form·a·ble**, a.—**trans·form·a·tive**, trans·fŏr′ma·tiv, a.

trans·for·ma·tion, trans″fĕr·mā′shan, n. [L.L. *transformatio(n-).*] The act of transforming or the state of being transformed. *Math.* a change of one figure or expression to an equivalent figure or expression; a formula that determines such a change. *Ling.* a syntactic or phonetic change of a phrase or word, as by adjunction, deletion, or substitution, often effecting a semantic change, as in the tense or mood of a verb. A woman's wig.—**trans·for·ma·tion·al**, a.—**trans·for·ma·tion·al·ly**, adv.

trans·for·ma·tion·al gram·mar, n. *Ling.* a grammar that uses transformations, as adjunction, deletion, or substitution of words or phrases, to account for linguistic relationships, esp. a grammar that posits the existence of a deep structure of abstract syntactic relationships from which a surface structure, functional and grammatically correct for a given language, is generated by means of transformations of semantic and phonetic components introduced from a lexicon into the syntax of the deep structure.

trans·form·er, trans·fŏr′mĕr, n. *Elect.* an appliance in alternating current circuits for changing high voltage current to a lower voltage, or low voltage current to a higher voltage.

trans·fuse, trans·fūz′, v.t.—*transfused, transfusing.* [Fr. *transfuser*, < L. *transfundo, transfusum—trans*, over, and *fundo, fusum*, to pour.] To transfer by pouring; to cause to be instilled or imbibed; to instill or impart; *surg.* to transfer, as blood, from the veins or arteries of one person or animal to those of another.—**trans·fus·i·ble, trans·fus·a·ble**, a.

trans·fu·sion, trans·fū′shan, n. The act of transfusing; *surg.* the transmission of blood from the veins of one person or animal into those of another, as from those of one man into another man.

trans·gress, trans·gres′, tranz·gres′, v.t. [Fr. *transgresser*, < L. *transgredior, transgressus—trans*, across, and *gradior*, to pass.] To overpass, as some law or rule prescribed; to break or violate; to infringe.—v.i. To offend by violating a law; to sin.—**trans·gres·sive**, a.—**trans·gres·sor**, n.

trans·gres·sion, trans·gresh′an, tranz·gresh′an, n. The act of transgressing; the breaking or violation of any law; an offense.

trans·hu·mance, trans·hū′mans, trans·ū′mans, n. The seasonal drive of livestock, esp. between mountains and lowlands, as other pastures become better suited for grazing.—**trans·hu·mant**, a.

tran·sience, tran′shens, tran′zhens, n. The state or quality of being transient. Also **tran·sien·cy**.

tran·sient, tran′shent, tran′zhent, a. [L. *transiens*, ppr. of *transeo*, to pass away—*trans*, across, and *eo*, to go. Akin *transition, transit, trance.*] Passing quickly away; of short duration; not permanent, lasting, or durable; momentary; passing.—n. A transient or temporary person or thing; as, a room for a *transient*.—**tran·sient·ly**, adv.

tran·sil·i·ent, tran·sil′ē·ent, tran·sil′yent, a. Moving quickly from one condition or thing to another.

trans·il·lu·mi·nate, trans″i·lö′mi·nāt″, tranz″i·lö′mi·nāt″, v.t.—*transilluminated, transilluminating.* To cause light to pass through; *med.* to throw a strong light through, as an organ or part, as a means of diagnosis.—**trans·il·lu·mi·na·tion**, n.

tran·sis·tor, tran·zis′tĕr, n. *Electron.* a device using a semiconductor, such as germanium or silicon, that performs many of the functions of an electron tube but without having its requirements for space or power, thus allowing new circuitry and miniaturization.—**tran·sis·tor·ize**, tran·zis′to·rīz″, v.t.—*transistorized, transistorizing.* To furnish or design with transistors.

trans·it, tran′sit, tran′zit, n. [L. *transitus*, a passing across, < *transeo, transitum*, to go over. *Trance* is a doublet of this word.] The act of passing; a passing over or through; the process of conveying; passage, change, or alteration; conveyance; as, the *transit* of goods through a country. *Astron.* the passage of a heavenly body across the meridian of any place; the passage of one heavenly body over the disk of a larger one, as of the planets Mercury or Venus over the sun's disk; a theodolite.—v.t., v.i.

trans·it in·stru·ment, n. An astronomical instrument consisting essentially of a telescope so fixed as to move only in the plane of the meridian, and used chiefly to determine the exact moment when a celestial body passes the meridian of the place of observation; a theodolite.

tran·si·tion, tran·zish′an, tran·sish′an, n. [L. *transitio.*] Passage from one place or state to another; change or process of change; *mus.* a change in the course of a composition from one key to another, or from one passage to another; *rhet.* turning from one subject to another.—**tran·si·tion·al**, a.—**tran·si·tion·al·ly**, adv.

tran·si·tive, tran′si·tiv, tran′zi·tiv, a. *Gram.* denoting a verb whose action passes directly to a complement from its subject and requires this direct object to express the full meaning of the predicate. Having the power of passing or making transition.—**tran·si·tive·ly**, adv.—**tran·si·tive·ness**, **tran·si·tiv·i·ty**, n.

tran·si·to·ry, tran′si·tŏr″ē, tran′si·tạr″ē, tran′zi·tŏr″ē, tran′zi·tạr″ē, a. [L. *transitorius*, < *transeo*.] Passing away without continuance; unstable; fleeting; transient; temporary.—**tran·si·to·ri·ly**, adv.—**tran·si·to·ri·ness**, n.

trans·late, trans·lāt′, tranz·lāt′, trans′lāt, tranz′lāt, v.t.—*translated, translating.* [O.Fr. *translater*, < L. *translatus—trans*, across, and *latus*, borne or carried.] To render into another language; to interpret; to express in other terms or words; to transform, as one medium or condition into another; as, to *translate* enthusiasm into accomplished tasks. *Eccles.* to remove, as a bishop, from one see to another; to transfer, as relics of a saint; to take up to heaven without death. *Teleg.* to relay, as a message.—v.i. To be engaged in or practice translation; to be able to be translated.—**trans·lat·a·bil·i·ty**, n.—**trans·lat·a·ble**, a., **trans·lat·or**, n.

trans·la·tion, trans·lā′shan, tranz·lā′shan, n. The act of translating, esp. the act or process of turning into another language; that which is produced by turning into another language; a version. *Eccles.* the removal of a bishop from one see to another; the transfer of the relics of a saint from one place to another; the removal of a person to heaven without subjecting him to death. *Mech.* a motion during which particles of any body move in parallel paths at the same velocity; *teleg.* the relaying of a message; *aerospace*, movement in a straight line without rotation.—**trans·la·tion·al**, **trans·la·tive**, a.

trans·lit·er·ate, trans·lit′e·rāt″, tranz·lit′e·rāt″, v.t.—*transliterated, transliterating.* [L. *trans*, across, over, and *litera*, a letter.] To express or represent in the alphabetic characters of another language; to spell in different characters intended to express the same sound.—**trans·lit·er·a·tion**, n.

trans·lo·cate, trans·lō′kāt, tranz·lō′kāt, v.t.—*translocated, translocating.* To remove from one place to another; to cause to change place; to displace; to dislocate.—**trans·lo·ca·tion**, n.

trans·lu·cent, trans·lö′sent, tranz·lö′sent, a. [L. *translucens, translucentis—trans*, through, and *luceo*, to shine.] Allowing light to pass through, but not so as to render the form or color of objects beyond distinctly visible.—**trans·lu·cence, trans·lu·cen·cy**, n.—**trans·lu·cent·ly**, adv.

trans·lu·cid, trans·lö′sid, tranz·lö′sid, a. [L. *translucidus*.] Translucent.

trans·ma·rine, trans″ma·rēn′, tranz″ma·rēn′, a. [L. *transmarinus—trans*, across, and *mare*, the sea.] Lying or being beyond the sea; traversing an ocean or sea.

trans·mi·grate, trans·mī′grāt, tranz·mī′grāt, v.i.—*transmigrated, transmigrating.* [L. *transmigro, transmigratum—trans*, across, and *migro*, to migrate.] To migrate; to pass from one country or region to another; to pass from one body into another, as the soul after death.—**trans·mi·gra·tion**, trans″mī·grā′shan, tranz″mī·grā′shan, n.—**trans·mi·gra·tor**, n.—**trans·mi·gra·to·ry**, a.

trans·mis·sion, trans·mish′an, tranz·mish′an, n. [L. *transmissio.*] The act of transmitting, or the state of being transmitted; transference; a passing through, as of light through glass or other transparent body; *mech.* a device or unit that transmits power from an engine to a driven component, as in an automobile; *phys.* the process by which radiant flux is propagated through a medium or a body.—**trans·mis·si·bil·i·ty**, **trans·mis·siv·i·ty**, n. Transmittance.—**trans·mis·si·ble, trans·mis·sive**, trans·mis′a·bl, tranz·mis′a·bl, trans·mis′iv, tranz·mis′iv, a.

trans·mit, trans·mit′, tranz·mit′, v.t.—*transmitted, transmitting.* [L. *transmitto, transmissum—trans*, across, through, and *mitto*, to send.] To cause to pass or be conveyed from one point to another, as by post, wire, rail, conduit, or air; to communicate by sending; to send from one person or place to another; to hand down, as by heredity; to spread, as disease; to allow, as light, sound, heat, or the like, to pass through.—v.i. *Electron.* to send out electrical energy with its concurrent reception shaped to be meaningful in a signal, as radio, radar, television, or any other electromagnetic broadcast wave; *mech.* to transfer movement from one part of a machine to another, often changing ratios of power delivery and sometimes direction, as in automobile transmission systems.—**trans·mit·ta·ble**, a.—**trans·mit·tal**, trans·mit′al, tranz·mit′al, n.

trans·mit·tance, trans·mit′ans, tranz·mit′ans, n. The act of transmitting; transmission of a message or signal; *phys.* the ratio of the radiant flux transmitted through a medium or a body to the incident flux.—**trans·mit·tan·cy**, n. The transmission capability.

trans·mit·ter, trans·mit′ĕr, tranz·mit′ĕr, n. One who or that which transmits; the sending or transmittal equipment; *electron.* that portion of the equipment which includes circuits designed to generate, amplify, and shape radio and television frequency energy for broadcast.

trans·mog·ri·fy, trans·mog′ri·fī″, tranz·mog′ri·fī″, *v.t.*—transmogrified, transmogrifying. [A fanciful or humorous formation from *trans.*] To transform into some other person or thing; to change entirely the appearance of.—**trans·mog·ri·fi·ca·tion,** *n.*

trans·mon·tane, trans·mon′tān, tranz·mon′tān, *a.* Tramontane.

trans·mu·ta·tion, trans″mū·tā′shan, tranz″mū·tā′shan, *n.* [L. *transmutatio.*] The act of transmuting; change into another substance, form, or nature; *alchemy,* the supposed changing of base metals into gold or silver.—**trans·mut·a·ble, trans·mu·ta·tive,** trans·mū′ta·tiv, tranz·mū′ta·tiv, *a.*

trans·mute, trans·mūt′, tranz·mūt′, *v.t.*—transmuted, transmuting. [L. *transmuto—trans,* across, through, and *muto,* to change, from same root as *moveo,* to move.] To change from one nature, form, or substance into another; to change into another thing or body; to metamorphose; to transform.—*v.i.*—**trans·mut·er,** *n.*—**trans·mut·a·ble·ness, trans·mut·a·bil·i·ty,** *n.*—**trans·mut·a·bly,** *adv.*

trans·na·tion·al, trans·nash′a·nal, tranz·nash′a·nal, *a.* Transcending national boundaries or narrow national interests.

trans·o·ce·an·ic, trans″ō·shē·an′ik, tranz″ō·shē·an′ik, *a.* Across, beyond, or passing over the ocean.

tran·som, tran′som, *n.* [Short for *transommer, transummer,* < *trans,* across, and *summer,* a beam; or < L. *transtrum,* a transom.] A small window above a door or larger window usu. hinged to permit easy adjustment for ventilation; the crossbar separating a window or door from such a window; a horizontal crosspiece dividing a window into sections; *naut.* a strengthening beam across the stern of a ship; *artillery,* the piece of wood or iron joining the cheeks of gun carriages.—**tran·somed,** *a.*

tran·son·ic, tran·son′ik, *a. Aeron.* pertaining to the speeds between subsonic and supersonic, and the phenomena which occur within this range. Also **trans·son·ic.**

trans·pa·cif·ic, trans″pa·sif′ik, *a.* Passing or extending across the Pacific; beyond, or on the other side of, the Pacific.

trans·par·ence, trans·pâr′ens, trans·par′ens, *n.* See transparency.

trans·par·en·cy, trans·pâr′en·sē, trans·par′en·sē, *n. pl.* **trans·par·en·cies.** The quality or condition of being transparent; also *transparence.* Something transparent; a picture painted on transparent or semi-transparent materials, to be viewed by light shining through it; *photog.* the amount of light sent through developing fluid onto an image.

trans·par·ent, trans·pâr′ent, trans·par′ent, *a.* [Fr. *transparent,* < L. *trans,* across, through, and *parens, parentis,* ppr. of *pareo,* to appear (seen also in *apparent, appear*).] Having the property of transmitting rays of light through the material of which it is made so that bodies behind or beyond can be distinctly seen; diaphanous; pellucid; easily seen through; guileless or frank; unable to hide underlying feelings. Also *transpicuous.*—**trans·par·ent·ly,** *adv.*—**trans·par·ent·ness,** *n.*

tran·spic·u·ous, tran·spik′ū·us, *a.* [L. *trans,* through, and *specio,* to see] Transparent.

trans·pierce, trans·pērs′, *v.t.*—transpierced, transpiercing. [Prefix *trans,* and *pierce.*] To pierce through.

tran·spi·ra·tion, tran″spi·rā′shan, *n.* The

act or process of transpiring; exhalation of moisture through the skin; see *perspiration. Bot.* emission of water vapor from the stomata of the leaves of plants.

tran·spire, tran·spīēr′, *v.t.*—transpired, transpiring. [Fr. *transpirer,* L. *trans,* across, and *spiro,* to breathe.] To excrete, as waste matter, in the form of perspiration, through the pores of the skin; to emit, as water vapor, from the stomata of plants.—*v.i.* To be emitted through the pores of the skin; to be emitted through the stomata of plants; to become public gradually; to come to light; to take place; to happen.—**tran·spir·a·ble,** *a.*—**tran·spir·a·to·ry,** tran·spīēr′a·tŏr″ē, tran·spīēr′a·tar″ē, *a.*

trans·plant, trans·plant′, trans·plänt′, *v.t.* [L.L. *transplantare* (pp. *transplantatus*), < L. *trans,* across, over, and *plantare,* E. *plant, v.*] To remove, as a plant, from one place and plant in another; to remove from one place to another, esp. to bring from one country to another for settlement, as a colony; *surg.* to transfer, as an organ or a portion of tissue, from one part of the body to another or from one person or animal to another.—*v.i.* To undergo transplanting, esp. in a manner specified.—**trans′plant″,** trans′plänt″, *n.* The act of transplanting; something that has been transplanted.—**trans·plant·a·ble,** *a.*—**trans·plan·ta·tion,** *n.*—**trans·plant·er,** *n.*

tran·spon·der, tran·spon′dèr, *n. Electron.* a radio or radar device, as used in aeronautics, meteorology, and navigation, that, on receiving a pulse emitted by an interrogator, automatically emits a signal in response.

trans·pon·tine, trans·pon′tin, trans·pon′tīn, *a.* [L. *trans,* beyond, and *pons, pontis,* bridge.] Situated beyond the bridge or across the bridge; pertaining to a section in London on the Surrey side of the Thames and London Bridge.

trans·port, trans·pōrt′, trans·part′, *v.t.* [Fr. *transporter,* < L. *transportare—trans,* across, and *porto,* to carry.] To carry or convey from one place to another; to carry away with pleasurable emotion; to send away in banishment.—**trans′pōrt″, trans′part″,** *n.* A vessel engaged in transporting goods and passengers; a ship employed for carrying soldiers or war equipment; transportation; conveyance; a vehement emotion; passion; rapture; ecstasy.—**trans·port·a·bil·i·ty,** *n.*—**trans·port·a·ble,** *a.*—**trans·port·er,** *n.*

trans·por·ta·tion, trans″pèr·tā′shan, *n.* The act of transporting; the means of conveyance from one place to another; a ticket purchased to travel on some public carrier, as a bus, train, boat, or airplane; the charge for such conveyance; *geol.* the conveyance or shifting of materials along the earth's surface by the movement of ice, air, or water, and the action of gravity.—**trans·por·ta·tion·al,** *a.*

trans·pose, trans·pōz′, *v.t.*—transposed, transposing. [Fr. *transposer,* prefix *trans,* and *poser,* to place.] To change the place or order of, as words or phrases, by putting each in the place of the other; to cause to change places; *alg.* to bring, as any term of an equation, over from one side to the other side; *gram.* to change the natural order of, as words; *mus.* to change the key of, either higher or lower than the original.—*v.i.*—**trans·pos·a·ble,** *a.*

trans·po·si·tion, trans″po·zish′an, *n.* The act of transposing or state of being transposed; *alg.* the bringing over of any term of an equation from one side to the other side.—**trans·po·si·tion·al,** *a.*

trans·ship, trans·ship′, *v.t.*—transshipped, transshipping. To convey or transfer from one ship, or other vehicle, to another. Also **tran·ship.**—**trans·ship·ment,** *n.*

tran·sub·stan·ti·ate, tran″sub·stan·shē·āt″, *v.t.*—transubstantiated, transubstantiating. [L. *trans,* over, and *substantia,* substance.] To change to another substance; *relig.* to cause, as by consecrating bread and wine, to undergo transubstantiation.—**tran·sub·stan·tial,** *a.*—**tran·sub·stan·tial·ly,** *adv.*

tran·sub·stan·ti·a·tion, tran″sub·stan″shē·ā′shan, *n. Theol.* the doctrine, subscribed to by Roman Catholics and others, that bread and wine consecrated in the Eucharist become the actual body and blood of Christ, although the appearance of bread and wine remains. Any change of substance; transmutation.

tran·su·da·tion, tran″su·dā′shan, *n.* The act or process of transuding; a fluid or substance which has transuded. Also **tran·su·date,** trans′su·dāt″.

tran·sude, tran·sōd′, *v.i.*—transuded, transuding. [L. *trans,* across, through, and *sudo,* to sweat; allied to E. *sweat.*] To pass or ooze through the pores of a substance.

trans·u·ran·ic, trans″ū·ran′ik, tranz″ū·ran′ik, *a. Chem.* pertaining to any of several elements possessing a higher atomic number than that of uranium, No. 92. See Periodic Table of Elements. Also **trans·u·ra·ni·an, trans·u·ra·ni·um,** trans″ū·rā′nē·an, tranz″ū·rā′nē·an.

trans·val·ue, trans·val′ū, tranz·val′ū, *v.t.*—transvalued, transvaluing. To reevaluate according to new principles, usu. repudiating the current prevailing standards.—**trans·val·u·a·tion,** *n.*

trans·ver·sal, trans·vur′sal, tranz·vur′sal, *a.* Transverse; lying crosswise.—*n. Geom.* a line intersecting a group of lines.—**trans·ver·sal·ly,** *adv.*

trans·verse, trans·vurs′, tranz·vurs′, trans′vurs, tranz′vurs, *a.* [L. *transversus—trans,* across, and *versus,* turned.] Lying athwart; being in a cross direction; being across.—*n.* A transverse object. *Geom.* the axis passing through both foci of a hyperbola; also **trans·verse ax·is.**—**trans·verse·ly,** *adv.*

trans·verse co·lon, *n. Anat.* the part of the colon which extends across the abdominal cavity from right to left, as distinguished from the ascending and descending parts on the right and left sides of the abdomen respectively.

trans·verse proc·ess, *n. Anat.* a lateral extension of a vertebra.

trans·ves·tism, trans·ves′tiz·um, tranz·ves′tiz·um, *n. Psychol.* the practice of wearing or compulsion to wear clothes appropriate to the other sex. Also **trans·ves·ti·tism.**—**trans·ves·tite,** trans·ves′tīt, tranz·ves′tīt, *a., n.*

trap, trap, *n.* [O.E. *traeppe* (recorded in composition), *treppe,* trap; cf. Med.L. *trappa,* O.Fr. *trape,* Fr. *trappe,* trap, < Teut.] A contrivance used for taking game, as a pitfall; a mechanical device that shuts suddenly by means of a spring, or a snare; any device, stratagem, or the like for catching one unawares; any of various contrivances for preventing the passage of steam, water, and the like; a device in a pipe, as a double curve or a U-shaped section in which liquid remains and forms a seal, for preventing the passage or escape of air or gases through the pipe from behind or below; a device for suddenly releasing or tossing into the air objects to be shot at, as pigeons or clay targets; the piece of wood, shaped somewhat like a shoe hollowed at the heel, and moving on a pivot, used in playing the game of trapball; the game itself; *golf,* a golf course hazard, as a depression filled with sand; *Brit. colloq.* a carriage, esp. a light two-wheeled carriage. Any trap door. *Slang,* mouth; as, never closes her *trap;* a night club.—*v.t.*—trapped, trapping. To catch in a trap; to catch as if in a trap; to take by stratagem; to lead by artifice or wiles; to furnish or set with traps; to provide, as a drain, with a trap; to stop and hold by or as by a trap, as air or gas in a pipe.—*v.i.* To set traps for game; to practice catching animals in traps for their furs; to work the trap in trapshooting.—**trap·per,** trap′ẽr, *n.*

trap, trap, *v.t.*—*trapped, trapping.* [O.E. *trappe,* a horse-cloth; same word as Sp. *trapo,* L.L. *trapus,* cloth, Fr. *drap,* cloth; akin *drape.*] To adorn; to dress with ornaments; to caparison.

trap, trap, *n.* [Dan. *trap,* Sw. *trapp,* G. *trapp,* the rock, < Dan. *trappe,* Sw. *trappa,* G. *treppe,* a stair, stairs; akin to *trap* above. The rock was named from the terraced or steplike arrangement seen in many of these rocks.] *Geol.* Any of several igneous rocks that are dark in color and often columnar in structure, as basalt and diabase. Also *traprock.*

trap door, *n.* A door flush, or nearly so, with the surface of a floor, ceiling, or roof.

tra·peze, tra·pēz′, *n.* A sort of swing, consisting of one or more crossbars suspended by two cords at some distance from the ground, on which various feats are performed; *geom.* a trapezium.—**tra·pez·ist,** *n.*

tra·pe·zi·um, tra·pē′zē·um, *n.* pl. **tra·pe·zi·ums, tra·pe·zi·a,** tra·pē′zē·a. [L., < Gr. *trapézion,* a little table, dim. of *trapeza,* a table, for *tetrapeza,* lit. 'four-footed thing.'] *Geom.* a plane figure contained by four straight lines, no two of them parallel; *Brit.* a trapezoid; *anat.* a bone of the wrist, so named from its shape.

tra·pe·zi·us, tra·pē′zē·us, *n.* pl. **tra·pe·zi·us·es.** [N.L., < *trapezium.*] *Anat.* each of a pair of large flat triangular muscles of the back of the neck and adjacent parts serving to draw the head back or to the side and move the shoulders.

tra·pe·zo·he·dron, tra·pē″zo·hē′dron, trap″i·zo·hē′dron, *n.* pl. **tra·pe·zo·he·drons, tra·pe·zo·he·dra,** tra·pē″zo·hē′dra, trap″i·zo·hē′dra. [Gr. *trapézion,* trapezium, and *édra,* seat, base.] *Crystal.* a solid whose faces are all trapeziums.—**tra·pe·zo·he·dral,** *a.*

trap·e·zoid, trap′i·zoid″, *n. Geom.* a four-sided plane figure having two of its opposite sides parallel; *Brit.* trapezium; *anat.* an irregularly shaped bone at the base of the forefinger.—**trap·e·zoi·dal,** *a.*

trap·pings, trap′ingz, *n. pl.* Ornamental accessories, esp. as put on horses; general ornaments of dress; finery.

Trap·pist, trap′ist, *a.* [From the abbey of La Trappe, in Normandy, the former headquarters of the Order.] *Rom. Cath. Ch.* of or pertaining to the Order of Cistercians of the Stricter Observance, remarkable for the austere life led by the monks.—*n.*

trap·rock, trap′rok″, *n. Geol.* trap.

traps, trapz, *n. pl.* The types of percussion instruments used by a dance or jazz band, as drums and cymbals. *Slang,* luggage; personal possessions, esp. clothes.

trap·shoot·ing, trap′shö″ting, *n.* The sport of shooting at clay targets thrown into the air by a machine called a trap.—**trap·shoot·er,** *n.*

tra·pun·to, tra·pun′tō, *n.* pl. **tra·pun·tos.** A quilting design worked with a combination of stitching and padding so as to create an embossed or relief effect.

trash, trash, *n.* [Cf. Icel. *tros,* rubbish, leaves and twigs picked up for fuel.] Waste or worthless matter; rubbish; refuse; pointless or vulgar writing or ideas; worthless art; a worthless person or persons; as, white *trash;* loppings of trees; sugar cane from which the juice has been squeezed.—*v.t.* To free from superfluous twigs or branches; to lop.—**trash·i·ly,** *adv.*—

trash·i·ness, *n.*—**trash·y,** trash′ē, *a.*—*trashier, trashiest.*

trass, tras, *n.* [Prov. G. *trass, tarrass,* trass, < Fr. *terrasse,* earthwork, < L. *terra,* earth.] A volcanic material consisting of ashes and scoriae and used in the manufacture of hydraulic cement.

trat·to·ri·a, trä·tō′rē·ä, *n.* [It.] An Italian eating house; a restaurant.

trau·ma, trou′ma, trä′ma, *n.* pl. **trau·ma·ta, trau·mas,** trou′ma·ta, trä′ma·ta. [N.L., < Gr. *trauma,* wound.] *Pathol.* a wound; a bodily injury produced by violence or some kind of shock; the condition produced by this; traumatism; *psychol.* a disordered or disturbed state, either mental or behavioral, which is an effect of some kind of stress or injury, and which sometimes has a lifelong effect; a shock.—**trau·mat·ic,** tra·mat′ik, trą·mat′ik, trou·mat′ik, *a.*—**trau·mat·i·cal·ly,** *adv.*

trau·ma·tism, trą′ma·tiz″um, trou′ma·tiz″um, *n. Pathol.* Any morbid condition produced by a trauma; the trauma or wound itself.—**trau·ma·tize,** trą′ma·tīz″, trou′ma·tīz″, *v.t.*—*traumatized, traumatizing. Pathol.* to damage, as tissues, by some kind of force or by chemical or other agents; *psychol.* to produce a trauma or shock in, as in a person's brain.

tra·vail, tra·vāl′, trav′āl, trav′al, *n.* [< Fr. *travailler,* to labor, *travail,* labor, toil; orig. an apparatus of bars to restrain a vicious horse, < L. *trabs,* a beam. *Travel* is the same word.] Extremely difficult, strenuous work; toil; physical or mental hardship; pain and suffering; the pain and labor involved in childbirth.—*v.i.* To toil; to suffer the pangs of childbirth.

trave, trāv, *n.* [O.Fr. *traf, tref,* It. *trave,* a beam, < L. *trabs, trabis,* a beam.] A wooden frame to confine an unruly horse while shoeing; *arch.* a crossbeam or an area enclosed by crossbeams.

trav·el, trav′el, *v.i.*—*traveled, traveling,* Brit. *travelled, travelling.* [A different orthography and application of *travail.*] To go from place to place or make a journey, as by airplane or car; to go from one location to another; to proceed or advance in any way; to go from place to place for business purposes; to keep company; as, to *travel* with a fast crowd; *colloq.* to go swiftly; *basketball,* to walk. To go in a set course, as a mechanical part; to pass or be conveyed, as: Sounds *travel* clearly over water.—*v.t.* To journey over or pass through, as a city or a street; to journey a certain distance; as, to *travel* 25 miles.—*n.* The act of traveling or journeying to different countries; a motion or advance; the traffic or number of vehicles or people passing through a place or along a road; the action of a moving segment of a mechanism, esp. a back-forth movement; the distance of the movement. *Pl.* journeys or trips; an account of occurrences and observations made during journeys or trips.

trav·el a·gen·cy, *n.* An establishment which gives information, arranges reservations and sells tickets to travelers. Also **trav·el bu·reau.**

trav·el a·gent, *n.* One who is employed in a travel agency and takes care of giving travelers information, reservations, and tickets.

trav·eled, *Brit.* **trav·elled,** trav′eld, *a.* Having made many journeys; experienced by much travel; much utilized by travelers.

trav·el·er, *Brit.* **trav·el·ler,** trav′e·lẽr, trav′lẽr, *n.* One who travels; one who visits or has visited foreign countries; *Brit.* a traveling salesman or a person who travels for commercial purposes. *Naut.* a mechanical device made to go in a set course; a ring of metal that slips along a ship's spar, rope, or rod; the spar, rope, or rod; a device for conveying sideward.

trav·el·er's check, *n.* A check or draft issued by an express company or bank bearing the signature of the purchaser and to be cashed when countersigned in the presence of a payee.

trav·el·ing bag, *n.* A piece of hand luggage for holding the personal articles and attire of a traveler.

trav·el·ing sales·man, *n.* A salesman or representative of a company with a designated territory to sell the firm's services or products or secure orders for them.

trav·e·logue, trav·e·log, trav′e·ląg″, trav′e·log″, *n.* [With *-logue* as in *monologue, dialogue.*] A lecture describing travel, usu. illustrated, as with slides or movies.

trav·erse, trav′ẽrs, tra·vụrs′, *v.t.*—*traversed, traversing.* [O.Fr. *travers, transvers,* < L. *transversus.*] To go across, over, through, or along; to move or go back and forth along or over; to stretch over or across; to move across, up, or down on an angle; as, to *traverse* a mountain; to cause to go sideward; to inspect or survey carefully; to deny, resist, or thwart; to contradict; *naut.* to brace along a line from the front to the back of the boat; *gun.* to turn sideward and point in any direction. *Law,* to formally deny, as what the opposite party has alleged; to disagree or take issue with or upon; as, to *traverse* an important point in an indictment.—*v.i.* To go across, over, or up and down; to turn, as on a pivot; to turn sideward, as some weapon or gun; *fencing,* to slip the blade in the direction of an opponent's foil handle.—*n.* The process of moving over, across, or through; a thing that crosses or blocks; an obstruction; a transverse object, as a crossbar, or line; a place to go across; a crossing; *arch.* a gallery or loft of communication in a church or other large building. Something which forms a barrier, as a curtain, railing, or screen; *geom.* any intersecting or transversal line. *Naut.* the zigzag track of a ship when compelled to sail on different courses; each run in one direction in such a maneuver. *Gun.* the sideward movement of a gun to make it aim in any direction; *surv.* a line fixed by surveying a tract of ground; *law,* a denial of what the opposite party has advanced. *Fort.* a barrier for defense or parapet set crosswise; a parapet thrown across a covered way at certain points. *Mech.* the sideward motion of some contrivance, esp. of a lathe tool, moving across the work; the contrivance for producing such a motion.—*a.* Going or reaching across; transverse; relating to the hanging or operating of draperies that can be pulled apart or together with a cord.—**tra·vers·a·ble,** tra·vụrs′a·bl, *a.*—**tra·vers·al,** *n.*—**tra·vers·er,** *n.*

trav·erse ju·ry, *n. Law,* petit jury.

trav·er·tine, trav′ẽr·tin, trav′ẽr·tēn″, *n.* [It. *travertino, tibertino, tiburtino,* L. *lapis Tiburtinus,* from being formed by the waters of the *Anio,* now Aniene at *Tibur,* now Tivoli.] A white concretionary limestone deposited from the waters of springs holding carbonate of lime in solution. Also **trav·er·tin,** trav′ẽr·tin.

trav·es·ty, trav′i·stē, *n.* pl. **trav·es·ties.** [Fr. *travesti,* pp. of *travestir* < It. *travestire,* disguise < L. *trans,* across, over, and *vestire,* clothe.] A literary composition or artistic work characterized by burlesque or ludicrous treatment of a serious work or subject; a composition so bad that it seems to be of this kind; any grotesque or debased likeness or imitation; as, a *travesty* on humanity.—*v.t.*—*travestied, travestying.* To make a travesty on; to turn, as a serious work or subject, to ridicule by burlesque imitation or treatment; to imitate grotesquely or absurdly.

tra·vois, tra·voi′, *n.* pl. **tra·vois·es,** tra·voiz′, **tra·vois′,** tra·voi′ziz. A carrying frame which the Plains Indians of N. America used, constructed from two poles which supported a net or lashed crosspieces, and drawn by a dog or horse with the poles trailing. Also **tra·voise,** tra·voiz′.

trawl, trạl, n. [< Fr. trôler, to lead, to drag.] A long line from which short lines with baited hooks are suspended, used in sea fishing; also **trawl line.** A fishing net which a boat drags along the bottom of the sea; also **trawl net.**—v.i. To fish with a trawl net.—v.t. To catch, as fish, with a trawl.

trawl·er, trạ′lẽr, n. One who trawls; a fishing vessel which uses a trawl net.

tray, trā, n. [O.E. treg, a tray; connected with trough.] A shallow receptacle of metal, wood, or the like with rimmed edge on which a variety of objects may be carried, presented, or displayed.

treach·er·ous, trech′ẽr·us, a. [O.Fr. tricheor (Fr. tricheur), a trickster, < O.Fr. tricher, trecher, to cheat, to trick; of Germanic origin, and akin to trick.] Characterized by treason or violation of allegiance or faith pledged; faithless; deceptive; uncertain or unreliable; as, treacherous waters; precarious; risky.—**treach·er·ous·ly,** adv. **treach·er·ous·ness,** n.

treach·er·y, trech′e·rē, n. pl. **treach·er·ies.** [Fr. tricherie, trickery.] Violation of allegiance, or of faith and confidence; treason; an act or instance of perfidy.

trea·cle, trē′kl, n. [O.Fr. triacle, corrupted < L. theriaca, < Gr. thēriaka (pharmaka, drugs, understood), antidotes against the bites of venomous animals, < thērion, a wild beast, dim of thēr, an animal.] Brit. molasses, esp. that which is a by-product of sugar refining. A medicinal compound of various ingredients, formerly believed to be capable of curing or preventing the effects of poison, esp. that of a snake; excessive sentiment and sweetness.—**trea·cly,** trē′klẽ, a.

tread, tred, v.t.—past trod, pp. trod or trodden, ppr. treading. [O.E. tredan, pret. traed, to tread = O.Fris. treda, D. and L.G. treden, Dan. traede, Icel. trotha, G. treten, Goth. trudan, to tread; root same as tramp. Trade is from this verb.] To step or walk on, along, in, or over; to crush under the feet; to form by stepping or tramping upon; as, to tread a trail through the field; to treat with contempt or brutality; to oppress; to perform or follow with feet motions; as, to tread a rhythm; ornith. to copulate with, as said of male birds.—v.i. To set the feet down in stepping; to walk; to press or trample with the feet, usu. followed by on or upon; ornith. to copulate, as said of male birds.—n. The act, sound, or way of stepping or walking; a step; one of several objects on which a person walks or an object moves, as the portion of a shoe sole that contacts the ground or the section of a tire or wheel that moves on rail or ground; the design or pattern made on a tire; the horizontal part of a stair step.—**tread on some·one's toes,** to irritate, insult, or affront someone.—**tread wa·ter,** swimming, to hold oneself upright in the water and one's head above water by making walking motions with the legs and sometimes moving the arms.—**tread·er,** n.

trea·dle, tred′l, n. A foot lever of a loom or other machine used to produce motion, esp. rotary motion.—v.i.—treadled, treadling.

tread·mill, tred′mil″, n. A mechanism consisting of a belt wound around two cylinders, kept in motion by a man forced to tread it, and formerly used as an instrument of torture; a similar mechanism operated by a beast of burden, as to operate a mill; fig. a monotonous and futile routine.

trea·son, trē′zon, n. [O.Fr. traison (Fr. trahison), < L. traditio, a delivering up,

< trado, to deliver up—trans, over and do, to give. Treason and tradition are doublets.] Disloyalty or treachery to one's country; the illegal act of giving aid and comfort to the enemies of one's country.—**trea·son·a·ble, trea·son·ous,** trē′zo·na·bl, trē′zo·nus, a.—**trea·son·a·bly,** adv.

treas·ure, trezh′ẽr, n. [O.E. tresoure, Fr. trésor, L. thesaurus, < Gr. thēsauros, a store, treasure, < root of tithēmi, to put or place (whence also thesis, theme, etc.).] Any form of wealth accumulated, particularly a stock or store of money in reserve; something or someone very much valued.—v.t. treasured, treasuring. To hoard; to collect or store for future use; to retain carefully in the mind; to cherish; to regard as precious or valuable; to prize.—**treas·ur·a·ble,** a.

treas·ure hunt, n. A game played by following a series of clues, usu. written, which have been left in different places, the last clue leading to a prize which is given to the first player to find it.

treas·ur·er, trezh′ẽr·ẽr, n. One who has the care of a treasure or treasury; one who has the charge of collected funds, such as those belonging to incorporated companies, associations, or private societies; a public officer who receives and disburses the money collected from taxes and other revenue sources.—**treas·ur·er·ship,** n.

treas·ure-trove, trezh′ẽr·trōv″, n. [O.Fr. trové, Mod.Fr. trouvé, found.] Law, money, bullion, or the like found hidden in the earth or in any private place, the owner of which is not known. Any valuable discovery.

treas·ur·y, trezh′a·rē, n. pl. **treas·ur·ies.** A place where the revenues of a government or group are deposited and debts discharged; (often cap.) that department of a government, corporation, or the like which has charge of the finances; (cap.) a department of the U.S. federal government which has charge of collection and disbursement of funds. (l.c.) a place where valuable articles are kept; a collection of treasures or things of value; a group of written works, information, facts, or the like considered valuable.

treas·ur·y note, n. A note issued by the U.S. Treasury Department, legal tender at its face value for all debts, public and private.

treas·ur·y of the Church, n. A spiritual fund composed of the infinite merits of Christ, the Virgin Mary, and the saints, upon which the Roman Catholic Church may draw in granting indulgences. Also **treas·ur·y of mer·its.**

treat, trēt, v.t. [Fr. traiter, O.Fr. traicter, to handle, to treat, < L. tractare, a freq. of traho, tractum, to draw (whence also tract, trace, trait, train, etc.).] To act or behave toward; as, to treat elderly people with kindness; to look upon or view in a particular way; to deal with by applying remedies; as, to treat a patient; to handle in writing, speaking, or any medium of art; to subject to the action of a substance or agent in order to alter or improve; to entertain without expense to the guest; to give food and drink to.—v.i. To handle a topic in writing or speaking, usu. followed by of; to provide or pay for entertainment; to discuss settlement terms; to negotiate.—n. An entertainment given as a compliment or expression of regard; anything that affords much pleasure; the process of treating; one person's turn to entertain.—**treat·a·ble,** a.—**treat·er,** n.

trea·tise, trē′tis, n. [O.Fr. tretis, traitis.] A written formal composition on some subject, in which the principles of it are discussed or systematically explained.

treat·ment, trēt′ment, n. The act or the manner of treating; characteristic style or

method in art, music, or literature; conduct or behavior toward a person; manner of proceeding in applying medicinal remedies or surgery to cure an illness.

trea·ty, trē′tē, n. pl. **trea·ties.** [Fr. traité.] A formally negotiated settlement of differences, or an agreement, between nations; a document containing an agreement or contract between two or more nations or sovereigns.

trea·ty port, n. Any of the sea or river ports in China, Japan, and Korea of the 19th century in which foreign commerce was allowed under a special treaty.

tre·ble, treb′l, a. [O.Fr. treble, < L. triplus, triple.] Threefold; triple. Mus. pertaining to the highest or most acute sounds; playing or singing the highest part or most acute sounds; having shrillness or high pitch.—n. Mus. The highest vocal or instrumental part in a piece of music; a soprano voice, singer, or instrument; a shrill or high-pitched sound or voice; the upper range of musical pitch.—v.t.—trebled, trebling. To make thrice as much; to triple.—v.i. To become threefold.—**tre·bly,** treb′lē, adv.

tre·ble clef, n. Mus. a symbol at the beginning of a staff to indicate the position of G above middle C on the second of the five lines in ascending order, used chiefly in scores for high-pitched voices or instruments.

tre·ble staff, n. Mus. a staff having a treble clef upon it.

treb·u·chet, treb′ū·shet″, n. [O.Fr. trebuchet, trebuket, engine of war, trap (Fr. trébucher, trap, balance), < O.Fr. trebuchier, overturn (Fr. trébucher, stumble, trip), < L. trans, over, and O.Fr. buc, trunk of the body (< Teut., and akin to G. bauch, belly).] A medieval military engine for hurling stones and other missiles. Also **tre·buck·et,** trē′buk″it.

tre·cen·to, trā·chen′tō, It. trɛ·chen′tạ, n. [It., three hundred, short for mille trecento, one thousand three hundred.] The 14th century, with reference to Italy, esp. to the Italian art or literature of that period.—**tre·cen·tist,** n.

tre·de·cil·lion, trē″di·sil′yon, n. pl. **tre·de·cil·lions.** A cardinal number indicated by 1 followed by 42 zeros in the American and French numbering systems, and by 1 followed by 78 zeros in the British and German systems.

tree, trē, n. [O.E. treów, treó, a tree = Icel. tré, Dan. trae, Sw. trä, O.D. tree, Goth. triu, tree, wood; cogn. W. derw, an oak; Gr. drus, an oak, doru, a spear; Skt. dru, a tree. Tar is allied.] A perennial plant having a woody trunk of considerable size, from which spring branches, or, in the palms, fronds; something resembling a tree, consisting of a stem or stalk and branches; as, a genealogical tree; a generic name for many wooden pieces in machines or structures; as, axletree, saddletree.—v.t.—treed, treeing. To drive to a tree, as: A dog trees a squirrel.—v.i. To take refuge in a tree, as a wild animal—**up a tree,** colloq. Cornered; in a difficult situation.—**tree·less,** a.—**tree·less·ness,** n.—**tree·like,** a.

tree farm, n. A forested area, commercially owned and managed, to guarantee a continuous supply of timber.

tree fern, n. Any of various ferns, mostly tropical, and belonging to the families Cyatheaceae, Polypodiaceae, and Dicksoniaceae, many of which attain the appearance and size of trees, sending up a straight trunklike stem with foliage at the summit.

tree frog, n. Any of various small, brightly colored arboreal frogs of the family Hylidae, usu. having adhesive suckers on the ends of the toes. Also tree toad.

tree heath, n. A tall shrub, Erica arborea, of

ch- chain, G. nacht;   th- THen, thin;   w- wig, hw as sound in whig;   z- zh as in azure, zeal.   Italicized vowel indicates schwa sound.

tree·hop·per, trē'hop″ẽr, *n.* Any of various hemipterous insects, suborder *Homoptera,* chiefly those of the family *Membracidae,* which includes numerous small oddly shaped leaping species; as, the buffalo *treehopper,* which damages apple trees.

tree house, *n.* A children's small playhouse constructed among a tree's branches.

tree line, *n.* Timber line.

tree·nail, tre·nail, trē'nāl″, tren'al, trun'al, *n.* A hardwood cylindrical pin or peg that swells when moistened, used in joining timbers, esp. in furniture making and shipbuilding. Also *trunnel.*

tree of heav·en, *n.* Ailanthus.

tree shrew, *n.* One of the small, arboreal mammals of the family *Tupaiidae,* squirrellike in appearance and habits, and found in southern Asia and nearby islands.

tree sur·ger·y, *n.* The professional treatment and care of diseased, damaged, or decayed trees.—**tree-sur·geon,** *n.*

tree toad, *n.* Tree frog.

tree·top, trē'top″, *n.* The topmost branches or highest part of a tree.

tref, trāf, *a.* Forbidden according to Jewish law; not kosher.

tre·foil, trē'foil, *n.* [A.Fr. *trifoil* = O.Fr. *trefeuil* (Fr. *trèfle*), < L. *trifolium,* < *tri-,* three, and *folium,* leaf.] Any of the herbs constituting the genus *Trifolium,* usu. having digitate leaves of three leaflets, and reddish, purple, yellow, or white flower heads, and including the common clovers; any of various similar plants; *arch.* an ornamental figure or structure resembling a trifoliate leaf.—**tre·foiled,** *a.*

tre·ha·lose, trē'ha·lōs″, *n. Biochem.* a disaccharide, $C_{12}H_{22}O_{11}$, in crystalline form which is stored for food by many fungi.

treil·lage, trā'lij, *n.* [Fr., < *treille,* arbor, trellis, < L. *trichila,* arbor.] Latticework; a lattice or trellis.

trek, trek, *v.i.*—**trekked, trekking.** [D. *trekken,* draw, pull, go, travel: cf. *track.*] *S. Africa,* to pull or haul, as a vehicle or load, by a draft animal.—*v.i. S. Africa,* to travel, by ox wagon; migrate. To travel slowly.—*n.* [D.] *S. Africa,* the act of trekking; a journey by ox wagon or otherwise; a migration or expedition, as by ox wagon; a stage of a journey. A journey, as a slow or difficult one.—**trek·ker,** *n.*

trel·lis, trel'is, *n.* [O.Fr. Fr. *treillis,* trellis, lattice (with form and sense prob. affected by *treille:* see *treillage*), orig. adj. O.Fr. *treliz,* < L. *trilix (trilic-),* woven with three threads, < *tri-,* three, and *licium,* thread.] A frame or structure of latticework, as a summerhouse or gate; a lattice; a framework of this kind used for the support of growing vines.—*v.t.* To furnish with a trellis; to enclose in a trellis; to train or support on a trellis; to form into or like trelliswork.—**trel·lised,** trel'ist, *a.*—**trel·lis·work,** trel'-is·wụrk″, *n.*

trem·a·tode, trem'a·tōd″, trē'ma·tōd″, *n.* [N.L. *Trematoda,* pl., < Gr. *trēmatōdēs,* having holes, < *trēma (tremat-),* hole, and *eīdos,* form.] Any member of the *Trematoda,* a class of flatworms having two or more suckers, and living as parasites on or in various animals.—*a.*—**trem·a·toid,** *a.*

trem·ble, trem'bl, *v.i.*—**trembled, trembling.** [O.Fr. Fr. *trembler,* < M.L. *tremulare,* < L. *tremulus,* shaking, E. *tremulous.*] To shake involuntarily with quick, short movements, as from fear, excitement, weakness, or cold; to quake, quiver, or shiver; to be agitated with fear or apprehension; to be affected with vibratory motion; to be tremulous, as light or sound. —*n.* The act of trembling; a state or fit of trembling.—**trem·bles,** *n. pl. but sing. in*

constr. Pathol. any condition or disease characterized by continuing trembling or shaking, as ague; milk sickness, a cattle disease due to ingestion of white snakeroot. —**trem·bler,** trem'blẽr, *n.*—**trem·bly,** trem'blē, *a.*—**trem·bling·ly,** *adv.*

tre·men·dous, tri·men'dus, *a.* [L. *tremendus,* lit. to be trembled at, < *tremo,* to tremble.] *Colloq.* such as may astonish by magnitude, force, greatness, or superiority; exceptional. Sufficient to excite fear or terror; terrible; awful; dreadful.—**tre·men·dous·ly,** *adv.*—**tre·men·dous·ness,** *n.*

trem·o·lant, trem'o·lant, *a. Mus.* having a vibration or tremolo in sound.—*n. Mus.* a pipe in an organ which produces a tremolant sound.

trem·o·lite, trem'o·līt″, *n.* [< Val *Tremola,* valley in Switzerland.] A white or grayish variety of amphibole, consisting essentially of a silicate of calcium and magnesium, $Ca_2Mg_5(OH)_2(Si_8O_{22})$.

trem·o·lo, trem'o·lō″, *n. pl.* **trem·o·los.** [It., < L. *tremulus,* E. *tremulous.*] *Mus.* A tremulous or vibrating effect produced on certain instruments and in the human voice, as to express emotion; a mechanical device in a musical instrument by which such an effect is produced.

trem·or, trem'ẽr, trē'mẽr, *n.* [L. *tremor,* < *tremere,* shake, tremble, = Gr. *trémein,* tremble.] Involuntary shaking of the body or limbs, as from fear, weakness, or fever; a fit of trembling; any tremulous or vibratory movement, as of the earth; a vibration; a trembling or quivering effect, as of light; a tremulous sound or note.— **trem·or·ous,** *a.*

trem·u·lant, trem'ya·lant, trem'ū·lant, *a.* Tremulous; trembling.

trem·u·lous, trem'ya·lus, trem'ū·lus, *a.* [L. *tremulus,* < *tremere,* shake, tremble.] Characterized by trembling, as from fear, nervousness, or weakness; fearful or timorous; done with a trembling hand or minutely wavy, as of writing; vibratory or quivering, as of things.—**trem·u·lous·ly,** *adv.*—**trem·u·lous·ness,** *n.*

trench, trench, *n.* [O.Fr. *trenchier* (Fr. *trancher*), cut, through L.L. < L. *truncare,* reduce by cutting, cut off, cut apart.] A narrow excavation of considerable length cut into the ground; a deep furrow; a ditch; *milit.* a long narrow excavation, the earth from which is thrown up in front to serve as a shelter from the enemy's fire or as an obstruction to an advancing force.—*v.t.* To cut; to divide by cutting; to cut or make a linear depression in; to cut a trench or trenches in; to form, as a furrow or ditch, by cutting into or through something. —*v.i.* To dig a trench; to encroach or infringe, used with *on* or *upon.*

trench·ant, tren'chant, *a.* [O.Fr. ppr. of *trenchier,* cut.] Incisive or keen, as language, or a person speaking or writing; thoroughgoing; vigorous, or effective; as, a *trenchant* policy; clearly or sharply defined, as an outline.—**trench·an·cy,** *n.*—**trench·ant·ly,** *adv.*

trench coat, *n.* A double-breasted, waterproof outer coat of military origin, belted at the waist and usu. having shoulder straps.

trench·er, tren'chẽr, *n.* [O.Fr. *trencheor,* < *trenchier,* cut.] A square or circular flat piece of wood on which food was formerly served or cut.—*a.*

trench·er, trench'ẽr, *n.* One who or that which digs trenches or ditches.

trench·er·man, tren'chẽr·man, *n. pl.* **trench·er·men.** An eater, esp. one who has a hearty appetite; *archaic,* a hanger-on.

trench fe·ver, *n. Pathol.* a recurrent rickettsial fever spread by body lice that occurred commonly among the troops during World War I.

trench foot, *n. Pathol.* a condition of the feet resembling frostbite, frequently terminating in gangrene, and caused by exposure to wet and cold, as in trench warfare.

trench knife, *n.* A daggerlike military knife for use in hand-to-hand combat.

trench mouth, *n.* Vincent's angina.

trend, trend, *n.* [O.E. *trendan,* turn, roll, akin to M.L.G. *trent,* ring, circumference, Sw. and Dan. *trind,* round.] A general course, drift, or tendency; as, the *trend* of events, a *trend* in literature; the direction of such a course, drift, or tendency.—*v.i.* To have a general tendency, as events; to tend to take a particular direction; to turn off in a specified direction, as a road or coastline.

trente et qua·rante, tränt' ā ka·ränt', *Fr.* träN tä kä·räNt', *n.* Rouge et noir.

tre·pan, tri·pan', *n.* [O.Fr. *trepan* (Fr. *trépan*), < M.L. *trepanum,* < Gr. *trúpanon,* boring instrument, terpan, < *trupan,* bore.] A boring tool in the form of a crown saw, used in cutting shafts in rock; a similar tool for cutting disks from metal plate or the like; an early form of trephine, a surgical instrument.—*v.t.*—**trepanned, trepanning.** To cut with a trepan.—**trep·an·a·tion,** trep″a·nā'shan, *n.*

tre·pan, tri·pan', *n.* [Earlier *trapan:* cf. *trap.*] *Archaic.* One who ensnares or entraps others; one who decoys others into some disadvantageous course or position; a stratagem; a trick; a trap. Also **tra·pan.**—*v.t.*—**trepanned, trepanning.** *Archaic.* To ensnare or entrap; to entice; to beguile or lure; to cheat or swindle. Also **tra·pan.**

tre·pang, tri·pang', *n.* [Malay name]. Any of several sea cucumbers gathered in the waters of northern Australia and the E. Indies, and used as food in China.

tre·phine, tri·fīn', tri·fēn', *n.* [Orig. *trafine,* explained by the inventor as < L. *tres,* three, and *finis,* end.] An improved form of surgical trepan for removing disks of bone from the skull, having a transverse handle, and a center pin which is fixed in the bone to steady the instrument during operation.—*v.t.*—**trephined, trephining.** To operate upon with a trephine.—**treph·i·na·tion,** tref″i·nā'shan, *n.*

trep·i·da·tion, trep″i·dā'shan, *n.* [L. *trepidatio(n-),* < *trepidare,* hurry or tremble with alarm, < *trepidus,* E. *trepid.*] Tremulous alarm, agitation, or perturbation; utter dread; trembling of the limbs, as in paralytic affections; a vibratory movement. Also **tre·pid·i·ty.**

trep·o·ne·ma, trep″o·nē'ma, *n. pl.* **trep·o·ne·mas, trep·o·ne·ma·ta,** trep″o·nē'-ma·ta. Any spirochete of the genus *Treponema,* parasitic on man and other mammals, as the organism which causes syphilis.—**trep·o·ne·mal, trep·o·nem·a·tous,** trep″o·nem'a·tus, *a.*

tres·pass, tres'pas, *v.i.* [O.Fr. *trespasser,* pass over, pass, die, transgress (Fr. *trepasser,* die), < L. *trans,* across, over, and M.L. *passare,* E. *pass,* v.] To commit a transgression or offense; to transgress; to offend; to sin; to make an improper inroad on a person's presence, time, or privacy; to encroach or infringe, followed by *on;* law, to commit a trespass.—*v.t.* To commit, as a transgression; to transgress or violate.—*n.* [O.Fr. *trespas* (Fr. *trépas*).] A breach of law or duty; a transgression; an offense, sin, or wrong; an encroachment or intrusion. *Law,* any transgression of the law constituting an injury to the person, property, or rights of another, committed with force or violence, actual or implied, esp. a wrongful entry upon the lands of another; the action to recover damages for such an injury.— **tres·pass·er,** *n.*

tress, tres, *n.* [O.Fr. *trece* (Fr. *tresse*), < M.L. *trecia, tricia,* a plait, a braid; cf. Gr.

tricha, threefold.] *Archaic*, a plait or braid of human hair of the head; *usu. pl.* long locks or curls of hair, esp. of a woman, not plaited or braided.—**tressed**, trest, *a.*

tres·tine, tres'tin, *n.* The third branch next below the crown antler of a stag. Also **roy·al ant·ler.**

tres·tle, tres'l, *n.* [O.Fr. *trestel* (Fr. *tréteau*), dim. < L. *transtrum*, crossbeam.] A frame used as a support, consisting typically of a horizontal beam or bar fixed at each end to a pair of spreading legs; *civil engin.* a supporting framework composed chiefly of vertical or inclined pieces with or without diagonal braces, used for various purposes, as for carrying railroad tracks across a gap.

tres·tle·tree, tres'l·trē", *n. Naut.* either of two horizontal fore-and-aft timbers or bars secured at a masthead to support the cross-trees.

tres·tle·work, tres'l·wurk", *n. Civil engin.* Structural work consisting of a trestle or trestles; a support, bridge, or the like, of such structure. Also **tres·tling.**

trews, trōz, *n. pl.* The tight-fitting tartan trousers or breeches of the Scottish Highlander dress, now worn chiefly by soldiers in Highland regiments.

trey, trā, *n.* [O.Fr. *trei*, Fr. *trois*, L. *tres*, three.] The three of any of the four suits in a deck of playing cards or the face of any die or domino having three dots.

tri·a·ble, trī'a·bl, *a.* That may be tried; *law*, subject or liable to judicial trial.—**tri·a·ble·ness**, *n.*

tri·ac·id, trī·as'id, *a. Chem.* Capable of combining with three molecules of a monobasic acid, said of bases; containing three replaceable hydrogen atoms, said of acid salts or acids.—*n.* An acid containing three replaceable hydrogen atoms.

tri·ad, trī'ad, *n.* [L.L. *trias* (triad-), < Gr. *triás* (triad-), < *treis*, three.] A group of three, esp. of three closely related or associated persons or things; *mus.* a chord of three tones, esp. one consisting of a given tone with its major or minor third and its perfect, augmented, or diminished fifth. *Chem.* an element, atom, or radical having a valence of three; a set of three elements with similar properties.—**tri·ad·ic**, *a.*—**tri·ad·i·cal·ly**, *adv.*

tri·al, trī'al, trīl, *n. Law*, the examination of a cause in controversy between parties before a proper tribunal and the determination thereof. The act of trying or testing; an attempt; an experiment; proof through experience; that which tries or afflicts, as suffering or misfortune; that which tests strength of character, faith, fact, or principle; temptation; the state of being tried; a process for testing qualification; an examination.—*a.* Of, relating to, or used by way of trial, proof, experiment, or sample; as, a *trial* run.

tri·al and er·ror, *n.* That form of experimentation or problem solving in which a variety of methods or theories are tried and discarded before arriving at the one which produces the desired result or correct answer to the problem.

tri·al bal·ance, *n.* A listing of items of debit and credit in each open account made preparatory to balancing the accounts in double entry bookkeeping.

tri·al bal·loon, *n.* A small balloon sent up to determine the direction of the wind; a device, program, or scheme designed to test public opinion.

tri·al ju·ry, *n.* Petit jury.

tri·al law·yer, *n.* A lawyer specializing in trying cases before courts of law.

tri·al run, *n.* A preliminary test of something conducted to check performance, esp. of a vehicle such as a racing car or an ocean vessel.

tri·an·gle, trī'ang"gl, *n.* [Fr. *triangle*, < L.

triangulum—tres, tria, three, and *angulus*, an angle.] *Geom.* a polygon bounded by three sides and containing three angles. Anything shaped or arranged in such a manner, as a corner of land; a flat, three-cornered, straightedged implement used for drawing geometric figures or lines; a triad or group of three; an emotional situation involving three people, as in one in which two women are in love with the same man; *mus.* an instrument of percussion, made of a rod of steel bent into the shape of a triangle and open at one of the angles.

tri·an·gu·lar, trī·ang'gū·lẽr, trī·ang'gya·-lẽr, *a.* Pertaining to, resembling, or having the form of a triangle; three-cornered; having a base or surface in the form of a triangle; of, pertaining to, or containing three members, elements, or persons.—**tri·an·gu·lar·i·ty**, trī·ang"gū·lar'i·tē, trī·ang"gya·lar'i·tē, *n.*—**tri·an·gu·lar·ly**, *adv.*

tri·an·gu·late, trī·ang'gū·lāt", trī·ang'gya·lāt", *v.t.*—*triangulated, triangulating.* [L. *triangulus*.] To make triangular; to divide into triangles; to survey or map out, as a region or area, by dividing into triangles; as, to *triangulate* the height of a mountain.—trī·ang'gū·lit, trī·ang'gū·lāt", trī·ang'gya·lit, trī·ang'gya·lāt", *a.* Triangular; composed of or marked with triangles.

tri·an·gu·la·tion, trī·ang"gū·lā'shan, trī·ang"gya·lā'shan, *n. Surv., navig.* A technique for accurately measuring a large distance or finding a specific position or location by dividing a region into a network of triangular areas along a base line of determined length and computing the unknown distance or position using trigonometry; the series of triangles thus laid out and measured.

tri·ar·chy, trī'är·kē, *n. pl.* **tri·ar·chies.** [Gr. *treis*, three, and *archē*, rule.] Government by three persons; a triumvirate; a country governed by three rulers.

Tri·as·sic, trī·as'ik, *a. Geol.* noting or pertaining to the geological period or system of rocks constituting the earliest principal division of the Mesozoic era.—*n.* The Triassic period or system. See Table of Geologic Time.

tri·at·ic stay, trī·at'ik stā', *n.* [Origin obscure: cf. *tri-.*] *Naut.* a rope device attached to the foremast and mainmast heads, used to attach tackles for hoisting boats or other heavy weights.

tri·a·tom·ic, trī"a·tom'ik, *a.* [Gr. *treis*, three, and *atomos*, an atom.] Having three atoms in the molecule; having three hydroxyl groups.

tri·ax·i·al, trī·ak'sē·al, *a.* Having three axes.

tri·a·zine, trī'a·zēn", trī'a·zin, trī·az'ēn, trī·az'in, *n. Chem.* One of a group of three compounds having the formula $C_3H_3N_3$, and containing a six-membered ring of three nitrogen atoms and three carbon atoms; any of various derivatives of these compounds.

tri·a·zole, trī'a·zōl", trī·az'ōl, *n. Chem.* One of a group of four compounds having the formula, $C_2H_3N_3$, and containing a five-membered ring of three nitrogen atoms and two carbon atoms; any of various derivatives of these compounds.—**tri·a·zol·ic**, trī"a·zol'ik, *a.*

trib·al, trī'bal, *a.* Belonging to a tribe; characteristic of a tribe.—**trib·al·ly**, *adv.*—**trib·al·ism**, trī'ba·liz"um, *n.*

tri·ba·sic, trī·bā'sik, *a.* [Gr. *treis*, three, and *basis*, base.] *Chem.* Applied to acids which combine with three equivalents of a base; applied to salts which contain three basic atoms each having a chemical valence of one.—**tri·ba·sic·i·ty**, trī"bā·sis'i·tē, *n.*

tribe, trīb, *n.* [L. *tribus*, one of the three bodies into which the Romans were orig.

divided, < *tres*, three.] A division, class, or distinct portion of a people or nation; a family or race descending from the same progenitor, and kept distinct; as, the 12 *tribes* of Israel; a political category among the Romans denoting one of the three primitive Roman tribes, the Sabine, Latin, or Etruscan; a nation or family of primitive people forming a subdivision of a race; a number of persons of any character or profession, often used disparagingly. *Biol.* a division of animals or plants of various ranks usu. either below a suborder or below a subfamily.

tribes·man, trībz'man, *n. pl.* **tribes·men.** A man belonging to a tribe; a member of a tribe.

tri·bo·e·lec·tric·i·ty, trī"bō·i·lek·tris'i·-tē, trī"bō·ē"lek·tris'i·tē, trib"ō·i·lek·tris'-i·tē, trib"ō·ē"lek·tris'i·tē, *n. Elect.* static electricity produced by friction, as by walking across a wool carpet.—**tri·bo·e·lec·tric**, trī"bō·i·lek'trik, trib"ō·i·lek'trik, *a.*

tri·bo·lu·mi·nes·cence, trī"bō·lō"mi·-nes'ens, trib"ō·lō"mi·nes'ens, *n. Phys.* luminescence, usu within a crystal, generated by friction.—**tri·bo·lu·mi·nes·cent**, *a.*

tri·brach, trī'brak, trib'rak, *n.* [Gr. *tribrachys—treis*, three, and *brachys*, short.] *Pros.* a poetic foot of three short syllables.—**tri·brach·ic**, *a.*

tri·bro·mo·eth·a·nol, trī·brō"mō·eth'-a·nōl", trī·brō"mō·eth'a·nal", trī·brō"mō·eth'a·nol", *n. Pharm.* a white crystalline bromine compound of ethyl alcohol, CBr_3CH_2OH, used as a general basal anesthetic.

trib·u·la·tion, trib"ū·lā'shan, trib"ya·-lā'shan, *n.* [Eccles. L. *tribulatio*, distress, < L. *tribulo, tribulatum*, to thrash, < *tribulum*, a threshing sledge for dragging over corn; akin *tero, tritum*, to rub (whence *trite, contrite* heart).] That which occasions affliction or distress; severe affliction; distress; trouble; trial.—**trib·u·late**, *v.t.*

tri·bu·nal, trī·būn'al, tri·būn'al, *n.* [L. *tribunal*, < *tribunus*, a tribune.] A court of justice; the seat occupied by a judge or magistrate when presiding in a court.

trib·une, trib'ūn, *Brit.* trī'būn, *n.* [L. *tribunus*, a tribune, magistrate, or officer, < *tribus*, tribe; in latter senses short for *tribunal*.] A person who champions the rights of the people; a title applicable to several types of officials in ancient Rome, esp. to the magistrates chosen by the plebeians to represent their interests in opposition to those of the patricians; one of six military officers rotating annually the command of a Roman legion.—**trib·une·ship, trib·u·nate**, *n.*

trib·une, trib'ūn, *n.* [Fr. *tribune*, < It. and M.L. *tribuna*, for L. *tribunal*, E. *tribunal*.] A raised platform, dais, or rostrum, orig. the platform for magistrates in a Roman basilica; a raised part or gallery with seats, as in a church; in a Christian basilica, the bishop's throne in a corresponding recess or apse, or the apse itself.

trib·u·tar·y, trib'ū·ter"ē, trib'ya·ter"ē, *a.* [L. *tributarius*.] Flowing into a larger stream or other body of water; furnishing subsidiary aid; contributory; auxiliary; paying or required to pay tribute; paid as tribute.—*n. pl.* **trib·u·tar·ies.** A stream contributing its flow to a larger stream or other body of water; one who pays tribute. —**trib·u·tar·i·ly**, *adv.*

trib·ute, trib'ūt, *n.* [Fr. *tribut*, L. *tributum*, < *tribuo*, to give, to bestow, perh. < *tribus*, a tribe.] Anything said or done in commemoration of a person or event, given as a token of gratitude or esteem; as, a *tribute* to one's predecessors; an annual or stated sum paid by one head of state to another, either as acknowledgment of submission or by virtue of some treaty; a rent or tax, as that imposed in the feudal system, on a liegeman by his lord; any exorbitant payment obtained by coercion; the obligation or necessity of complying with such a demand.

tri·car·pel·lar·y, trī·kär′pe·ler″ē, a. Bot. having three carpels.

trice, trīs, v.t.—triced, tricing. [Same as M.E. trisen, Dan. tridse, to hoist, tridse, a pulley; Sw. trissa, a pulley.] Naut. To haul by means of a small rope or line; to hoist and lash with a rope, usu. followed by up.

trice, trīs, n. [< M.E. trisen, to pull, hoist.] A very short time; a moment: now used chiefly in the phrase in a trice.

tri·ceps, trī′seps, n. pl. **tri·ceps·es**, tri-ceps, trī′sep·siz. [L. triceps, three-headed, threefold, < tri-, three and caput, head.] Anat. a muscle having three heads or points of origin, esp. one extending along the humerus at the back of the upper arm. —a.

tri·cer·a·tops, trī·ser′a·tops″, n. [N.L. < Gr. tri, three, and ceras (cerat-), horn, and ops, eye, face.] Paleon. any dinosaur of the genus Triceratops, with a large horn above each eye, a smaller horn on the nose, and a kind of bony collar extending backward and upward from the skull.

tri·chi·a·sis, tri·kī′a·sis, n. Pathol. an inversion or ingrowth of an eyelid, causing irritation of the eyeball by the eyelashes.

tri·chi·na, tri·kī′na, n. pl. **tri·chi·nae**, tri·kī′nē. [N.L. < Gr. trichinos, of hair, < thrix (trich-), hair.] Any of the nematode worms constituting the genus Trichinella, esp. T. spiralis, a parasite sometimes present as an encysted larva in the muscular tissues of man and certain animals, esp. pigs and rats.—**tri·chi·nal**, a.—**trich·i·nize**, trik′a·nīz″, v.t.—trichinized, trichinizing. To infect with trichinae.—**trich·i·ni·za·tion**, n.

trich·i·no·sis, trik″i·nō′sis, n. [N.L.] Pathol. a disease due to the presence of the trichina worm, Trichinella spiralis, in the intestines and muscular tissues. Also **trich·i·ni·a·sis**, trik″i·nī′a·sis.

trich·i·nous, trik′i·nus, a. Infected with trichinae; pertaining to or of the nature of trichinosis.

trich·ite, trik′īt, n. [G. trichit, < Gr., thrix (trich-), hair.] Geol. any of various minute hairlike mineral bodies occurring in certain vitreous igneous rocks, esp. obsidian.—**tri·chit·ic**, tri·kit′ik, a.

tri·chlo·ride, trī·klōr′īd, trī·klôr′īd, trī-klạr′īd, trī·klạr′id, n. Chem. a chloride having three atoms of chlorine per molecule.

trich·o·cyst, trik′o·sist″, n. [Gr. thrix, trichos, a hair, and kystis, a bag.] Zool. a cell capable of emitting threadlike filaments, found in some protozoans.—**trich·o·cyst·ic**, a.

trich·o·gyne, trik′o·jīn″, trik′o·jin″, n. [Gr. thrix, and gynē, a woman.] Bot. a threadlike projection from the female sex organ that receives a male gamete, in some algae, fungi, and lichens.

trich·oid, trik′oid, a. [Gr. trichoeidēs, < thrix (trich-), hair, and eidos, form.] Hairlike; capillary.

tri·chome, trī′kōm, trik′ōm, n. Bot. a hair or similar outgrowth from the epidermis of a plant.—**tri·chom·ic**, tri·kom′ik, a.

trich·o·mo·nad, trik″o·mon′ad, n. Any flagellate protozoan, genus Trichomonas, parasitic in many animals and certain species in human beings.—**a.—trich·o·mon·a·dal**, **trich·o·mon·al**, trik″o·mon′-a·dal, trik″o·mon′al, trik″o·mōn′al, tri-kom′o·nal, a.

trich·o·mo·ni·a·sis, trik″o·mo·nī′a·sis, n. Pathol. A trichomonadal infection; vaginitis or urethitis in humans caused by Trichomonas vaginalis infestation, resulting

in an inflammatory reaction characterized by tenacious discharging. Veter. pathol. a disease afflicting cattle causing aborting and sterility; a disease of birds.

tri·chot·o·mous, trī·kot′o·mus, a. [Gr. tricha, in three parts, and -tomos, < témnein, cut: cf. dichotomous.] Divided or dividing into three parts; branching into three parts; giving off shoots by threes.—**tri·chot·o·mous·ly**, adv.—**tri·chot·o·my**, trī·kot′o·mē, n.

tri·chro·mat, trī′krō·mat″, trī′kro·mat″, n. A person having normal color or trichromatic vision.

tri·chro·mat·ic, trī″krō·mat′ik, trī″kro·mat′ik, a. [Prefix tri-, and Gr. chroma, color.] Having or pertaining to the combining or using of three colors, as in printing; characterized by or pertaining to three colors.—**tri·chro·mat·ic vi·sion**, a normal condition in which the retina perceives all colors.

tri·chro·ma·tism, trī·krō′ma·tiz″um, n. Trichromatic condition; the use or combination of three different colors.

trick, trik, n. [O.Fr. trique, var. of triche, < trichier (Fr. tricher), deceive, deceit, < trichier (Fr. tricher), deceive, cheat, trick.] A crafty or fraudulent device; an artifice, stratagem, ruse, or wile; a deceptive or illusory appearance; a roguish or mischievous performance, or prank; a practical joke; as, to play a trick on someone; a hoax; a foolish, disgraceful, or mean performance or action; a clever device, ingenious shift, or dodge; as, a rhetorical trick; the art or knack of doing something; a clever or dexterous feat, as for exhibition or entertainment; a feat of jugglery or legerdemain; a peculiar habit, practice, or way of acting; a peculiar quality, feature, trait, or characteristic; colloq. a child or young girl. Naut. the period of duty of a man at the helm; a spell or turn of duty. Cards, the cards collectively which are played and won in one round.—v.t. To deceive by trickery; to cheat; to cheat or swindle, used with out of; to beguile by trickery, used with into.—v.i. To practice trickery or deception; to cheat; to play tricks; to trifle.—a.—**trick·er**, n.

trick·er·y, trik′e·rē, n. pl. **trick·er·ies**. The practice of tricks; cheating; artifice.

trick·ish, trik′ish, a. Given to tricks; artful; knavish.—**trick·ish·ly**, adv.—**trick·ish·ness**, n.

trick·le, trik′l, v.i.—trickled, trickling. [M.E. triklen; origin uncertain.] To flow or fall by drops or in a small, broken stream, as: Tears trickle down the cheeks. To come, go, pass, or proceed as if by drops or in a small stream, as: Subscriptions are trickling in.—v.t. To let or cause to flow by drops or in a gentle stream.—n. A trickling flow or stream; a quantity of anything coming, going, or proceeding as if by drops or in a small stream; as, a trickle of visitors to a house.

trick or treat, n. A practice on Halloween in which children go to neighbors' homes and ask for candy and other treats while threatening a trick if a treat is not given.

trick·ster, trik′stėr, n. A person who plays tricks on others; a deceiver; a cheat.

trick·sy, trik′sē, a.—tricksier, tricksiest. Full of tricks; given to pranks; tricky.—**trick·si·ness**, n.

trick-track, **tric·trac**, trik′trak″, n. A game similar to backgammon that utilizes both pegs and counters.

trick·y, trik′ē, a.—trickier, trickiest. Given to or characterized by deceitful tricks; crafty; wily; shifty; skilled in clever tricks or dodges; deceptive; uncertain.—**trick·i·ly**, adv.—**trick·i·ness**, n.

tri·clin·ic, trī·klin′ik, a. [Gr. treis, three, klinō, to incline.] Crystal. having three unequal axes intersecting obliquely.

tri·clin·i·um, trī·klin′ē·um, n. [L., < Gr. triklinion.] Among the ancient Romans, a divided couch placed around three sides of a table, for reclining on at meals; the dining room in which such a couch was laid.

tric·o·lette, trik″o·let′, n. A silklike knitted fabric used chiefly in the manufacture of women's garments.

tri·col·or, Brit. **tri·col·our**, trī′kul″ėr, n. [Fr. tricolore, of three colors—L. tres, three, and color, color.] A flag having three colors, usu. arranged in equal stripes, as in the flag of France.—a.—**tri·col·ored**, Brit. **tri·col·oured**, a. Consisting of three colors.

tri·corn, trī′kȯrn, a. [= Fr. tricorne, < L. tricornis, three-horned, < tri-, three, and cornu, horn.] Having three horns, hornlike projections, or corners.—n. A hat with the brim turned up on three sides. Also **tri·corne**.—**tri·cor·nered**, trī·kạr′nėrd, a.

tri·cos·tate, trī·kos′tāt, a. [L. tri = tres, three, and costa, a rib.] Biol. Having three ribs or ridges; three-ribbed.

tri·cot, trē′kō, Fr. trē·kō′, n. [Fr., < tricoter, knit; origin uncertain.] A knitted fabric made by hand or machine of wool, nylon, cotton, or silk; a kind of woolen cloth.

tric·o·tine, trik″o·tēn′, n. [Fr., < tricot.] A kind of woolen, cotton, or worsted cloth with a twilled face.

tri·crot·ic, trī·krot′ik, a. [Gr. tri-, three, and crótos, beat: cf. dicrotic.] Physiol. Having a threefold beat, as of the arterial pulse; pertaining to such a pulse.—**tri·cro·tism**, trī′kro·tiz″um, trik′ro·tiz″um, n.

tric·trac, trik′trak″, n. Tricktrack.

tri·cus·pid, trī·kus′pid, a. [L. tricuspis (tricuspid-), three-pointed, < tri-, three, and cuspis, point, E. cusp.] Having three cusps or points, as a tooth; anat. pertaining to the tricuspid valve. Also **tri·cus·pi·dal**.—n. Anat. A tricuspid tooth; the tricuspid valve.

tri·cus·pi·date, trī·kus′pi·dāt″, a. [L. tri = tres, three, and cuspis, cuspidis, a point.] Having three cusps; three-pointed; tricuspid.

tri·cus·pid valve, n. Anat. a valve of three cusps or folds which prevents the back flow of blood coursing from the right auricle into the right ventricle of the heart.

tri·cy·cle, trī′si·kl, n. [Gr. tri-treis, three, and kyklos, a circle, a wheel.] A three-wheeled vehicle, esp. one having two wheels parallel to each other in the rear and one large wheel in front propelled by two pedals and designed for a child.

tri·cy·clic, trī·sī′klik, trī·sik′lik, a. Relating to or composed of three cycles.

tri·dac·tyl, trī·dak′til, trī·dak′til, a. [Gr. tridáctylos, < tri- three, and dáctylos, finger or toe.] Zool. having three fingers, claws, or toes.

tri·dent, trīd′ent, n. [L. tridens, tridentis—tri = tres, three, and dens, dentis, a tooth.] An instrument having the form of a fork with three prongs, esp. the scepter or spear with three barbed prongs with which Poseidon or Neptune, the sea god, is represented.—a.—**tri·den·tate**, trī·den′tāt, a.—**tri·den·tal**, trī·den′tal, a.

Tri·den·tine, trē·den′tin, trē·den′tīn, trī-den′tin, trī·den′tīn, a. [L. Tridentum, Trent.] Pertaining to Trent, or to the ecumenical council which met in that city in 1545.

tri·di·men·sion·al, trī″di·men′sha·nal, a. [Prefix tri, three, and dimension.] Having three dimensions; having length, width, and depth.—**tri·di·men·sion·al·i·ty**, n.

tried, trīd, a. Tested; proved; dependable; as, tried friends; having withstood hardship or distress.

tri·en·ni·al, trī·en′ē·al, a. [L. triennis, tri-, three, and annus, year.] Occurring every three years; lasting three years.—n.

Something that occurs every three years; a third anniversary; a period of three years.—**tri·en·ni·al·ly**, *adv.*

tri·en·ni·um, trī·en′ē·um, *n. pl.* **tri·en·ni·ums, tri·en·ni·a**, trī·en′ē·a. [L.] A period of three years.

tri·er, trī′ér, *n.* One who or that which tries or attempts.

tri·er·arch, trī′e·rärk″, *n.* [L. *trierarchus*, < Gr. *triērarchos*, < *triērēs*, trireme, and *árchein*, lead, rule.] *Gr. antiq.* The commander of a trireme; in Athens, a citizen who, singly, or jointly with other citizens, was required to fit out a trireme for the public service.

tri·er·ar·chy, trī′e·rär″kē, *n. pl.* **tri·er·ar·chies.** [Gr. *triērarchía*.] *Gr. Hist.* The office of a trierarch; the duty of ancient Athenians to fit out and maintain triremes for the public service.

tri·eth·yl, trī·eth′il, *a. Chem.* having three ethyl groups.

tri·fa·cial, trī·fā′shal, *a.* Trigeminal.

tri·fid, trī′fid, *a.* [L. *trifidus*—*tri* = *tres*, three, and *findo, fidi*, to divide.] Split into three lobes or parts by clefts.

tri·fle, trī′fl, *n.* [O.Fr. *trufle, truffle*, for *trufe*, mockery, deception; origin uncertain.] A matter of slight importance, or a trivial or insignificant affair or circumstance; a toy, trinket, or knickknack; a literary work, or musical composition of light or trivial character; a small quantity or amount of anything; a small inconsiderable sum of money; a kind of pewter of medium hardness. *Brit.* cookery a dish consisting of whipped cream or some substitute, as beaten whites of eggs, and usu. containing cake soaked in wine or liqueur, and jam or fruit.—*v.i.*—**trifled, trifling.** To deal lightly or without due seriousness or respect, followed by *with*; amuse oneself or play for mere diversion or in idle dalliance, followed by *with*; play or toy by handling or fingering, followed by *with*; to act or talk in an idle or frivolous way; pass time idly or frivolously; waste time; idle.—*v.t.* To utter lightly or idly; to pass, as time, idly or frivolously, followed by *away*.—**trif·ler**, *n.*

tri·fling, trī′fling, *a.* Acting idly or frivolously; frivolous, shallow, or light; of slight importance, trivial, or insignificant; of small value, cost, or amount; inconsiderable; small; paltry.—**tri·fling·ly**, *adv.* —**tri·fling·ness**, *n.*

tri·fo·cal, trī·fō′kal, *a. Opt.* having three focal distances.—**tri·fo·cals**, trī·fō′kalz, trī″fō″kalz, *n. pl.* Eyeglasses having a segmented lens for adjustment to three distances.

tri·fo·li·ate, trī·fō′lē·it, trī·fō′lē·āt″, *a.* [L. *tri* = *tres*, three, and *folium*, a leaf.] *Bot.* having three leaves, as a trillium. Also **tri·fo·li·at·ed.**

tri·fo·li·ate or·ange, *n.* A Chinese orange tree, *Poncirus trifoliata*, esp. grown for use as stock for grafting.

tri·fo·li·o·late, trī·fō′lē·o·lāt″, *a. Bot.* having three leaflets, as a clover leaf.

tri·fo·li·um, trī·fō′lē·um, *n.* Any herbaceous plant, genus *Trifolium*, of the legume family.

tri·fo·ri·um, trī·fōr′ē·um, trī·far′ē·um, *n. pl.* **tri·fo·ri·a**, trī·fōr′ē·a, trī·far′ē·a. [L. *tri* = *tres*, three and *foris*, pl. *fores*, a door.] *Arch.* an arcaded passage in a wall above the arches of the nave of a church.— **tri·fo·ri·al**, *a.*

tri·form, trī′farm″, *a.* [L. *triformis*—*tri* = *tres*, three, and *forma*, shape.] Having or consisting of a triple form or shape. Also **tri·formed.**

tri·fur·cate, trī·fur′kit, trī·fur′kāt, *a.* [L. *tri* = *tres*, three, and *furca*, a fork.] Having three branches or forks; trichotomous. Also **tri·fur·cat·ed.**—*v.i.*—**trifurcated, trifurcating.**—**tri·fur·ca·tion**, *n.*

trig, trig, *a.* [< Scand.: cf. Icel. *tryggr*, trusty, faithful, true, and E. *true*.] *Chiefly Brit. dial.* Neat, trim, smart, or spruce; in good physical condition; sound; true, faithful, or trustworthy.—*v.t.*—**trigged, trigging.** *Chiefly Brit. dial.* to make trig, trim, or smart, often followed by *out* or *up*.—**trig·ness**, *n.*

trig, trig, *v.t.*—**trigged, trigging.** [Origin uncertain.] *Dial.* To stop or prevent the moving of, as wheels or barrels, by means of a wedge or block set beneath; to support or prop, as with a wedge.—*n.* A wedge or block used as a brake.

tri·gem·i·nal, trī·jem′i·nal, *a.* [L. *trigeminus*, born three at a birth, < *tri-*, three, and *geminus*, twin.] *Anat.* noting or pertaining to the pair of fifth cranial nerves, each of which divide into three main branches to supply the sensory nerves to the face and head. Also *trifacial.*—*n.* A trigeminal nerve.

tri·gem·i·nal neu·ral·gia, *n.* Tic douloureux.

trig·ger, trig′ér, *n.* [Earlier *tricker*, < D. *trekker*, trigger, < *trekken*, draw, pull: cf. *trek*.] A small fingerlike projection, esp. in a shoulder gun or pistol, actuating the weapon's firing mechanism when pulled or depressed by a finger; a device, as a lever, the pulling or pressing of which releases a detent or spring; an act or happening which incites, stimulates, or influences action or emotion.—*v.t.* To shoot, as a gun; to start or set off; initiate.—**quick on the trig·ger**, *colloq.* Quick to shoot a gun; quick to respond, understand, or act; alert.—**trig·ger·less**, *a.*

trig·ger·fish, trig′ér·fish″, *n. pl.* **trig·ger·fish, trig·ger·fish·es.** Any of various moderately compressed, deep-bodied fishes of the genus *Balistes*, and allied genera, chiefly of tropical seas, having an anterior dorsal fin with two or three stout spines, the first of which cannot be pressed down until the second is depressed.

trig·ger-hap·py, trig′ér·hap″ē, *a. Colloq.* Having a tendency to fire a gun heedlessly; heedless and irresponsible in advocating situations and actions that might lead to war; bellicose in attitude.

trig·ger·man, trig′ér·man, trig′ér·man″, *n. pl.* **trig·ger·men**, trig′ér·men, trig′ér·men″. *Slang*, A professional killer, esp. of the underworld; a gangster's bodyguard.

tri·glyph, trī′glif″, *n.* [L. *triglyphus*, < Gr. *triglyphos*, < *tri-*, three, and *glyphein*, carve.] *Arch.* a structural member of a Doric frieze, separating two consecutive metopes, and consisting typically of a rectangular block with vertical lines formed by two grooves or glyphs and two chamfers or half-grooves at the sides, together counting as a third glyph.—**tri·glyph·ic**, *a.*

tri·gon, trī′gon, *n.* [L. *trigonum*, < Gr. *trigōnon*, triangle, prop. neut. of *trigōnos*, triangular, *tri-*, three, and *gōnia*, angle.] *Astrol.* one of the four sets of three signs of the zodiac; trine. An ancient triangular lyre or harp; *archaic*, a triangle.

trig·o·nal, trig′o·nal, *a.* Of, relating to, or in the shape of a triangle; triangular; containing three angles; *crystal.* of a crystal system, having threefold symmetry.

trig·o·no·met·ric func·tion, *n. Math.* a function of an angle or arc, as sine, cosine, tangent, cotangent, secant, or cosecant, expressed as a ratio of two sides of a right triangle. Also **cir·cu·lar func·tion.**

trig·o·nom·e·try, trig″o·nom′i·trē, *n.* [N.L. *trigonometria*, < Gr. *trigōnon*, triangle, and *-metria*, measurement.] The branch of mathematics that deals with the relations between the sides and angles of plane or spherical triangles and the calculations based on these relations.— **trig·o·no·met·ric**, trig″o·no·mé′trik, *a.*

—**trig·o·no·met·ri·cal**, *a.*—**trig·o·no·met·ri·cal·ly**, *adv.*

trig·o·nous, trig′o·nus, *a.* [L. *trigonus*, < Gr. *trigōnos*, triangular.] Having three angles or corners; triangular, esp. as stems or seeds.

tri·graph, trī′graf, trī′gräf, *n.* [Gr. *tri-*, three, and *graphē*, writing.] A group of three letters representing a single speech sound, as *eau* in *beau*.—**tri·graph·ic**, *a.*

tri·he·dral, trī·hē′dral, *a. Geom.* having three planes.—*n. Geom.* a figure formed by three intersecting lines, each of which is in a different plane.

tri·he·dron, trī·hē′dron, *n. pl.* **tri·he·drons, tri·he·dra**, trī·hē′dra. *Geom.* a figure formed by three intersecting lines, each of which is in a different plane.

tri·hy·drate, trī·hī′drāt, *n. Chem.* a hydrated compound having three molecules of water.—**tri·hy·drat·ed**, *a.*

tri·hy·drox·y, trī″hī·drok′sē, *a. Chem.* pertaining to a molecule having three hydroxyl groups.

tri·ju·gate, trī′ju·gāt″, trī·jö′git, trī·jö′gāt, *a.* [L. *tri* = *tres*, three, *jugum*, yoke.] *Bot.* in three pairs, as a pinnate leaf with three pairs of leaflets. Also **tri·ju·gous**, trī′ju·gus, trī·jö′gus.

tri·lat·er·al, trī·lat′ér·al, *a.* [L. *tri* = *tres*, three, *latus, lateris*, a side.] Having three sides, as a triangle.—**tri·lat·er·al·i·ty**, *n.* —**tri·lat·er·al·ly**, *adv.*

tril·by, tril′bē, *n. pl.* **tril·bies.** *Brit.* a man's hat made of soft felt and having an indented crown.

tri·lin·e·ar, trī·lin′ē·ér, *a.* [L. *tri* = *tres*, three, and *linea*, a line.] Composed of, or having three lines.

tri·lin·gual, trī·ling′gwal, *a.* [L. *tri* = *tres*, three, and *lingua*, a tongue.] Consisting of or pertaining to three languages; able to speak or skilled in speaking three languages.—**tri·lin·gual·ly**, *adv.*

tri·lit·er·al, trī·lit′ér·al, *a.* [L. *tri-*, three, and *litera*, letter.] Consisting of three letters, esp. of three consonants, as most Semitic roots.—*n.* A triliteral word or root. —**tri·lit·er·al·ism**, trī·lit′ér·a·liz″um, *n.* The characteristic occurrence of triliteral roots, as in the Semitic languages.

trill, tril, *v.t.* [It. *trillare*; perh. imit.] To sing or play with a vibratory or tremulous effect; *phon.* to articulate with a rapid vibration of one vocal organ against another, as the tongue against the alveolar ridge for the Spanish *rr*.—*v.i.* To resound tremulously or vibrantly; *mus.* to execute a shake or trill.—*n.* The sound of trilling or a succession of such sounds, as made by a bird, an insect, or a person singing. *Mus.* a rapid alternation of two consecutive tones; a shake. *Phon.* the articulation of a speech sound by trilling; a speech sound so articulated.

trill, tril, *v.t.* [M.E. *trillen*, turn, roll: cf. Sw. *trilla*, Dan. *trille, trilde*, roll.] *Archaic*, to cause to roll down or trickle.—*v.i. Archaic*, to trickle or flow.

tril·lion, tril′yon, *n. pl.* **tril·lions** or when after a numeral, **tril·lion.** [Formed < *tri-*, three, and *million*.] In the U.S. and France, a million times a million or a thousand billions; a digit followed by twelve zeros as 1,000,000,000,000. In Great Britain or Germany, a million billions or a digit followed by eighteen zeros as, 1,000,000,-000,000,000,000.—*a.*—**tril·lionth**, *n., a.*

tril·li·um, tril′ē·um, *n.* [N.L., < L. *tri-*, three.] Any of the herbs constituting the liliaceous genus *Trillium*, characterized by a whorl of three leaves from the center of which rises a solitary flower.

tri·lo·bate, trī·lō′bāt, trī′lo·bāt″, *a.* [Gr. *tri* = *treis*, three, and *lobos*, a lobe.] Having three lobes, as certain leaves. Also **tri·lo·bat·ed, tri·lobed**, trī·lō′bā′tid, trī′lō·bā″tid, trī′lōbd″.—**tri·lo·ba·tion,** *n.*

tri·lo·bite, trī′lo·bīt″, *n.* [N.L. *Trilobita,* pl., < Gr. *tri-,* three, and *lobós,* lobe: with reference to the three lobes or divisions into which the body is divided by longitudinal dorsal furrows.] *Paleon.* any of the *Trilobita,* a group of extinct marine arthropods of the Paleozoic era, with a flattened oval segmented body varying in length from an inch or less to two feet.—**tri·lo·bit·ic,** trī″lo·bit′ik, *a.*

tri·loc·u·lar, trī·lok′ū·lėr, trī·lok′ya·lėr, *a.* [L. *tri = tres,* three, and *loculus,* a cell, dim. of *locus,* a place.] *Biol.* Three-celled; having three cells or compartments.

tril·o·gy, tril′o·jē, *n.* pl. **tril·o·gies.** [Gr. *trilogia,* < *treis, tria,* three, and *logos,* speech, discourse.] A series of three dramas, operas, or novels, each in a certain sense complete in itself, yet together forming one connected whole; a term, esp. relating to the Greek drama, denoting three tragedies together forming a myth or legend.

trim, trim, *v.t.*—**trimmed, trimming.** [Appar. < O.E. *trymman, trymian,* make strong, strengthen, arrange, array (troops), < *trum,* firm, strong.] To reduce to a neat or orderly state by clipping, paring, pruning, lopping, or otherwise removing superfluous waste or used parts; as, to *trim* a person's hair; to remove by clipping, paring, or pruning, often followed by *off*; to modify, as opinions, according to expediency; *archaic,* to dress or array, usu. followed by *up; carp.* to bring, as a piece of timber, to the required smoothness or shape; *aeron.* to adjust the controls of (some vehicle, as an airplane), so that the craft is in horizontal movement. *Naut.* to distribute the load so that a ship sits well on the water; to stow or arrange, as cargo; to adjust, as sails or yards, with reference to the direction of the wind and the course of the ship. To adjust or adapt; to deck with ornaments; as, to *trim* a Christmas tree; to put into condition for burning or use by removing ashes or exhausted matter and renewing the fuel or any necessary parts; as, to *trim* a lamp. *Colloq.* to rebuke or reprove; to beat or thrash; to defeat, as in a game.—*v.i. Naut.* to assume a particular position or trim in the water, as a vessel; to adjust the sails or yards with reference to the direction of the wind and the course of the ship. To pursue a neutral, cautious, or time-serving course or policy between parties; to adapt one's course of action in order to get on under conflicting conditions or to stand well with both or all parties.—*n.* Proper conditions or order; as, to find everything in *trim. Naut.* the set of a ship in the water, esp. the most advantageous one; the condition of a ship when properly balanced; the difference between the draft at the bow of a vessel and that at the stern; the adjustment of the sails, with reference to the direction of the wind and the course of the ship; the condition of a ship with reference to her fitness for sailing. Dress, array, or equipment; as, in one's Sunday *trim;* decorative trimming or a style of trimming; as, a military *trim;* the decorative merchandise in a store window; trimming by cutting or clipping, as a type of haircut; *aeron.* the position or attitude of any aircraft relative to the proper horizontal plane necessary for balanced flight; *carp.* the visible woodwork on the interior of a building. Decorations of furnishings on the exterior and interior of some vehicle, as a car.—*a.*—**trimmer, trimmest.** Pleasingly neat or smart in appearance; as, *trim* lawns; in good condition or order; *archaic,* properly prepared or equipped.— **trim·ly,** *adv.*—**trim·ness,** *n.*

tri·mer, trī′mėr, *n. Chem.* a molecule formed by three less complex identical molecules.—**tri·mer·ic,** trī·mer′ik, *a.*

trim·er·ous, trim′ėr·us, *a.* [Gr. *trimerēs,* < *tri-,* three, and *méros,* part.] Consisting of or divided into three parts. *Bot.* having three members in each whorl, as of a flower; also **3·mer·ous.** *Entom.* having three joints or segments.

tri·mes·ter, tri·mes′tėr, *n.* [Fr. *trimestre,* < L. *trimestris*—prefix *tri,* three, and *mensis,* a month.] A term or period of three months; one of three equal periods or terms into which some colleges and universities divide the year: contrasted with *quarter* or *semester.*—**tri·mes·tral, tri·mes·tri·al,** *a.*

trim·e·ter, trim′i·tėr, *n.* [Gr. *tri = treis,* three, and *metron,* a measure.] A line or verse of poetry having three measures or feet.

tri·met·ric, trī·me′trik, *a.* Consisting of, or relating to a trimeter; *crystal.* orthorhombic. Also **tri·met·ri·cal.**

tri·met·ro·gon, trī·me′tro·gon″, *n.* A method of aerial photography in which three high-speed cameras, one aimed directly downward and each of the others aimed at oblique angles, are used for topographic mapping of wide areas.—*a.*

trim·mer, trim′ėr, *n.* One who or that which trims; a tool or machine for trimming or clipping, paring, or pruning; a machine for trimming lumber; an apparatus for stowing, arranging, or shifting cargo, coal, or the like; a person who trims in his course of action, as in politics; one who pursues a cautious policy between parties, accommodating himself to one side or another as expediency may dictate; *building,* a timber or beam into which one of the ends of a header is fitted in the framing about an opening or a chimney.

trim·ming, trim′ing, *n.* Anything used or serving to trim or decorate; as, the *trimmings* of a Christmas tree; a decorative fitting or finish; a garnish; the act of one who or that which trims; *colloq.* a rebuking or reproving, a beating or thrashing, or a defeat. *Pl.* agreeable accompaniments or additions to plain or simple dishes or food; pieces cut off in trimming, clipping, paring, or pruning.

tri·mo·lec·u·lar, trī″mo·lek′ya·lėr, *a. Chem.* composed of, or relating to, three molecules.

tri·month·ly, trī·munth′lē, *a.* Taking place or performed every three months, as a payment on a loan.

tri·morph, trī′mạrf, *n.* [Gr. *trimorphos,* having three forms, < *tri-,* three, and *morphē,* form.] *Crystal.* A substance existing in three distinct forms; any one of the three forms.

tri·mor·phism, trī·mạr′fiz·um, *n. Zool.* the occurrence of three forms distinct in coloration or structure among animals of the same species; *bot.* the occurrence of three different forms of flowers or leaves on the same plant or on distinct plants of the same species; *crystal.* the property of some substances to crystallize in three distinct forms.—**tri·mor·phic, tri·mor·phous,** *a.*

tri·mo·tor, trī·mō′tėr, *n.* An airplane which is run by three motors.

trim size, *n.* The final dimensions of an article after the removal of all excess parts.

Tri·mur·ti, tri·mụr′tē, *n.* [Skt. *trimūrti,* < *tri,* three, and *mūrti,* shape.] The Hindu triad or trinity, Brahma, Vishnu, and Siva regarded respectively as the creative, the preserving, and the destroying principles, represented as one body with three heads.

tri·nal, trīn′al, *a.* [L. *trinus,* threefold, < *tres,* three.] Threefold; triple; consisting or made of three parts.

tri·na·ry, trī′na·rē, *a.* Ternary.

trin·dle, trin′dl, trin′l, *v.t., v.i.*—**trindled,** trindling. [M.E. *trindel, trendel,* < O.E. *trendel,* ring, circle, disk, akin to *trendan,* turn, roll: cf. *trundle.*] *Brit. dial.* to trundle, make round, or roll.—*n. Bookbinding,* one of many flat rectangular wooden or metal instruments used to flatten the front and back book edges before trimming. *Brit. dial.* a wheel, esp. of a wheelbarrow; a trundle.

trine, trīn, *a.* [L. *trinus,* threefold, pl. *trini,* three each, < *tres (tri-),* three.] Threefold; triple; *astrol.* noting or pertaining to the favorable aspect of two planets distant from each other 120°, or the third part of the zodiac.—*n.* A set or group of three; a triad; *(cap.)* the Trinity; *(l.c.), astrol.* the trine aspect of two planets.

trine im·mer·sion, *n.* Baptism administered by fully immersing the candidate three times, denoting each member of the Trinity in sequence.

Trin·i·tar·i·an, trin″i·târ′ē·an, *a.* [N.L. *trinitarius,* < L.L. *trinitas,* E. *trinity.*] Of or pertaining to the Trinity; believing in the doctrine of the Trinity; pertaining to believers in the doctrine of the Trinity; belonging or pertaining to the religious order of Trinitarians. *(l.c.)* forming a trinity; threefold; triple.—*n.* One who believes in the doctrine of the Trinity; a member of a religious order, the Order of the Holy Trinity, founded in 1198 to redeem Christian captives from Mohammedans.—**Trin·i·tar·i·an·ism,** trin″i·târ′-ē·a·niz″um, *n.*

tri·ni·tro·cre·sol, trī·nī″trō·krē′sōl, trī·-nī″trō·krē′sạl, trī·nī″trō·krē′sol, *n. Chem.* an organic yellow crystal, the compound $(NO_2)_3C_6H(CH_3)OH$, used in explosive charges.

tri·ni·tro·glyc·er·in, trī·nī″trō·glis′ėr·-in, *n. Chem.* nitroglycerin.

tri·ni·tro·tol·u·ene, trī·nī″trō·tol′ū·ēn″, *n.* [< *tri-* and *nitro-* and *toluene.*] *Chem.* a high explosive nitro derivative of toluene used in explosives and chemical synthesis. Also *TNT,* **tri·ni·tro·tol·u·ol,** *trotyl,* trī·nī″trō·tol′ū·ōl″, trī·nī″trō·tol′ū·ạl″, trī·nī″trō·tol′ū·ol″.

Trin·i·ty, trin′i·tē, *n.* [O.Fr. *trinite* (Fr. *trinité*), < L.L. *trinitas,* < L. *trinus,* threefold.] *Theol.* the union of three distinct persons, Father, Son, and Holy Spirit, in one Godhead; also **Bless·ed Trin·i·ty, Ho·ly Trin·i·ty.** A feast day celebrated on the first Sunday after Pentecost; also **Trin·i·ty Sun·day.** A work of art symbolically depicting the Trinity. *(l.c.)* the state of being triple; a group of three; triad; pl. **trin·i·ties.**

trin·ket, tring′kit, *n.* [Prob. a nasalized form of *tricket,* < *trick,* to dress out.] A small ornament, as a jewel, a ring, and the like; a thing of no great value; a trifle.—*v.i.* To hold secret communication or dealings; to intrigue.—**trin·ket·er,** tring′ki·tėr, *n.* Someone who holds secret or clandestine meetings.

trin·ket·ry, tring′ki·trē, *n.* Trinkets collectively.

trin·kums, tring′kumz, *n.* pl. *Brit. dial.* trinkets.

tri·no·mi·al, trī·nō′mē·al, *a.* [< *tri-* and *-nomial* as in *binomial.*] *Alg.* consisting of or pertaining to three terms connected by the sign +, the sign −, or both of these; *biol.* noting a name comprising three terms, as of genus, species, and subspecies or variety, or characterized by the use of such names.—*n. Alg.* a trinomial expression, as $a + b - c$; *biol.* a trinomial name, as *Cannabis sativa indica,* Indian hemp.

tri·o, trē′ō, *n.* pl. **tri·os.** [Fr., < It. *trio,* < L. *tres (tri-),* three.] A musical composition for three voices or instruments; a subordinate division of a minuet, scherzo, march, or the like, usu. in a contrasted key and

a- fat, fāte, fär, fâre, fall; **e-** met, mē, mēre, hėr; **i-** pin, pīne; **o-** not, nōte, möve; **u-** tub, cūbe, bųll; **oi-** oil; **ou-** pound.

style, perhaps orig. written for three instruments or in three parts; a company of three singers or players; any group of three persons or things.

tri·ode, trī′ōd, *n. Electron.* a three-electrode vacuum tube, containing a control grid, cathode, and anode.

tri·oe·cious, tri·e·cious, trī·ē′shus, *a.* [Gr. *tri-*, three, and *oikos*, house.] *Bot.* having male, female, and hermaphrodite flowers on different plants.—**tri·oe··cious·ly**, *adv.*

tri·o·let, trī′ō·lit, *n.* [Fr.: cf. *trio.*] *Pros.* an eight-line poem of fixed form having the first line repeated as the fourth and seventh, and the second as the eighth, with *abaaabab* as the rhyme scheme.

tri·ose, trī′ōs, *n. Chem.* any of a class of simple sugars containing three atoms of carbon.

tri·ox·ide, trī·ok′sīd, trī·ok′sid, *n. Chem.* an oxide containing three oxygen atoms.

trip, trip, *n.* [O.Fr. *tripper, triper, treper,* strike the ground, etc., with the foot, skip, dance; < Teut., and akin to D. *trippen, trippelen,* G. *trippeln,* trip.] A journey or voyage; a journey, voyage, or run made by a boat, train, or the like, from one point to another; a journey made from one point to another and back again; as, a round *trip;* a journey, jaunt, or excursion for pleasure or health; a tripping, stumbling, or loss of footing; a sudden impeding or catching of a person's foot so as to throw him down, as a move made in wrestling; the act of tripping or stepping lightly; a light or nimble movement of the feet; a light quick tread. *Fig.* a slip, mistake, or blunder; a wrong step in conduct. *Mach.* a projecting part or catch for starting or checking some movement; *colloq.* an experience resulting from the use of psychedelic drugs.—*v.i.* —tripped, tripping. To make a journey, excursion, or trip; to strike the foot against something or have the foot suddenly impeded or caught, so as to stagger or fall; as, to *trip* over a curb; to stumble; to falter or stumble in speech; to step lightly or nimbly, skip, or dance; to tip or tilt; *horol.* of a tooth of a watch's escape wheel, to slip past the pallet without catching or locking. *Fig.* to make a slip, or a mistake, as in a statement; to behave improperly; to commit a fault or moral error.—*v.t.* To cause to trip, stumble, or fall by suddenly impeding or catching the foot; to cause to lose the footing or to upset; to tip or tilt. *Fig.* to overthrow or bring into confusion; to cause to make a slip or error, followed by *up;* as, to *trip up* a witness. *Naut.* to lift, as an anchor, clear of the bottom; to lift, as a mast, before lowering; to tip or turn from a horizontal to a vertical position. *Mach.* to release or operate suddenly, as a catch or a clutch; to operate or set free by suddenly releasing a catch or a clutch.—**trip·ping·ly**, *adv.*

tri·par·tite, trī·pär′tīt, *a.* [L. *tripartitus—tri = tres,* three, and *partitus,* pp. of *partior,* to part.] Divided into three parts; having three corresponding parts; made between or including three parties; as, a *tripartite* treaty; *bot.* divided into three parts almost down to the base, but not wholly separate. —**tri·par·tite·ly**, *adv.*

tri·par·ti·tion, trī″pär·tish′an, trip″ər·tish′an, *n.* A division into three parts, or a division by three.

tripe, trīp, *n.* [O.Fr. Fr. *tripe;* origin uncertain.] The first and second divisions of the stomach of a ruminant, esp. of oxen or goats, prepared for use as food; *slang,* anything poor or worthless, as an off-color novel.

tri·pet·al·ous, trī·pet′a·lus, *a. Bot.* having three petals.

trip·ham·mer, trip′ham″ər, *n.* A power-operated heavy hammer with a massive head that is repeatedly raised and then let fall by a cam or other tripping device.—*a.* Pertaining to or resembling the repeated blows of a triphammer. Also **trip ham·mer.**

tri·phen·yl·meth·ane, trī·fen″il·meth′-ān, trī·fēn″il·meth·ān, *n. Chem.* a colorless hydrocarbon compound of crystalline structure, $(C_6H_5)_3CH$, used in making certain dyes.

tri·phib·i·an, trī·fib′ē·an, *a.* Equally skilled or ready for combat on land or sea, or in the air; of aircraft, capable of operating from water, ice, snow, or land; triphibious.—*n.* One who or that which is triphibian.

tri·phib·i·ous, trī·fib′ē·us, *a.* Composed of, or using, air, land, and sea forces in a coordinated effort; designating a ground vehicle or aircraft that operates on land, water, snow, or ice.

triph·thong, trif′thong, trif′thong, trip′-thang, trip′thong, *n.* [Gr. *tri = treis,* three, and *phthongē,* sound.] A complex combination of three vowel sounds in a single syllable, as in the pronunciation of the word 'flour'; a trigraph.—**triph·thong·al**, trif·thang′gal, trif·thong′gal, trip·thang′-gal, trip·thong′gal, *a.*

triph·y·lite, trif′i·līt″, *n.* [Gr. *tri-*, three, and *phylē*, tribe; from the three metallic bases.] A mineral, a phosphate of lithium, iron, and manganese, usually occurring in masses of a bluish or greenish color. Also **triph·y·line**, trif′i·lēn″, trif′i·lin.

tri·pin·nate, trī·pin′āt, *a.* [Prefix *tri-*, three, and *pinnate, pinnatifid, pinnatisect.*] *Bot.* trebly pinnate, as when the leaflets of a bipinnate leaf are themselves pinnate. Also **tri·pin·nat·ed.**—**tri·pin·nate·ly**, *adv.*

tri·plane, trī′plān″, *n.* An airplane with three wings or supporting planes placed one above another.

tri·ple, trip′l, *a.* [Fr. *triple,* < L. *triplus,* < *tri-* three, and *-plus.*] Threefold; consisting of three parts; of three kinds; three times as great.—*n.* A triad; something triple or threefold; *baseball,* a hit which allows the batter to get to third base.—*v.t.*—**tripled, tripling.** To make triple; to treble.—*v.i.* To become triple.—**tri·ply**, trip′lē, *adv.*

tri·ple coun·ter·point, *n. Mus.* a counterpoint in which the melodies are transposed among three voices or parts.

tri·ple-nerved, trip′l·nurvd′, *a. Bot.* of a leaf, characterized by the presence of two prominent veins situated on opposite sides of the midrib near its base.

tri·ple play, *n. Baseball,* a play resulting in three base runners being removed in one play of the ball.

tri·ple-space, trip′l·spās′, *v.t.*—**triple-spaced, triple-spacing.** To type so that an interval of two blank lines is left between the lines of copy.—*v.i.*

tri·plet, trip′lit, *n.* [Dim. < *triple.*] One of three children born at the same birth; a collection or combination of three, esp. of a kind; *pros.* three verses or lines of poetry succeeding each other and often rhyming. *Mus.* a group of three notes of equal time value to be performed in the time of two, indicated by a slur and the figure 3; also *tercet.*

tri·ple-tail, trip′l·tāl″, *n.* A large food fish, *Lobotes surinamensis,* which is found in warm seas and whose dorsal and anal fins extend backward so that with the caudal fin it appears to have a three-lobed tail.

tri·ple threat, *n.* Anyone possessing three special skills, esp. within a single field; *football,* a back who can run, punt, and pass with skill.

tri·plex, trip′leks, trī′pleks, *a.* [L. *triplex,* < *tri-*, three, and *-plex.*] Threefold; triple.

—*n.* Something triple, as a housing unit; *mus.* triple time or meter.

trip·li·cate, trip′li·kāt″, *v.t.*—**triplicated, triplicating.** [L. *triplicatus,* pp. of *triplicare,* < *triplex.*] To make threefold; triple; make or produce a third time or in units of three. —trip′li·kit, trip′li·kāt″, *a.* Threefold; triple; tripartite.—trip′li·kit, trip′li·kāt″, *n.* —**trip·li·ca·tion**, *n.*

tri·plic·i·ty, trī·plis′i·tē, *n. pl.* **tri·plic·i·ties.** [M.L. *triplicitas,* < L. *triplex.*] The state of being triple; triple character; a group or combination of three; a triad; *astrol.* a trigon, or set of three signs of the zodiac.

trip·lite, trip′līt, *n.* [G. *triplit,* < Gr. *triplóos,* threefold; from its three cleavages.] A mineral, essentially a phosphate of iron and manganese containing fluorine, occurring in dark-brown or blackish masses.

trip·lo·blas·tic, trip″lō·blas′tik, *a. Zool.* having three embryonic germ layers, developing into the vertebrate endoderm, mesoderm, and ectoderm.

trip·loid, trip′loid, *a. Biol.* having three times the number of chromosomes that exist in a gamete.—*n.*—**trip·loi·dy**, *n.*

tri·pod, trī′pod, *n.* [L. *tripus* (*tripod-*), < Gr. *tripous* (*tripod-*), tripod, orig. an adj.; three-footed, < *tri-*, three, and *poús* (*pod-*), foot.] A vessel, as a pot, caldron, or vase, with three feet or legs; a stool or the like with three legs; a three-legged frame or stand of any kind, as one for supporting a camera; *Gr. antiq.* the three-legged seat from which the priestess of Apollo at Delphi delivered the oracles.—*a.*—**trip·o·dal**, trip′o·dal, *a.*—**tri·pod·ic**, trī·pod′ik, *a.*

trip·o·li, trip′o·lē, *It.* trē′pạ·lē, *n.* A kind of siliceous rottenstone composed of the shields of microscopic infusorians and diatoms and used in polishing metals, marble, glass, and the like.

tri·pos, trī′pos, *n. pl.* **tri·pos·es.** [Cf. Gr. *tripos,* poetic var. of *tripous,* tripod.] At Cambridge University, England, any of various final honors examinations, orig. in mathematics, but now also in other subjects.

trip·per, trip′ər, *n.* One who or that which trips. *Mach.* a tripping device; a trip. *Brit. colloq.* one who goes on a pleasure trip or excursion; an excursionist.

trip·pet, trip′it, *n.* [< *trip.*] *Mach.* a projection, cam, or the like, for striking some other part at regular intervals.

trip·tane, trip′tān, *n. Chem.* a liquid, colorless fuel additive, $CH_3C(CH_3)_2\text{-}CH(CH_3)CH_3$, used as an antiknock ingredient in aviation gasoline.

trip·tych, trip′tik, *n.* [Gr. *tri = treis,* three, and *ptychē,* a fold or folding.] A painting or carving on three adjacent panels, esp. such a representation of a religious subject often used for an altarpiece; a writing tablet, usu. used in ancient times, having three hinged or folding leaves.

tri·que·trous, trī·kwē′trus, trī·kwe′trus, *a.* [L. *triquetrus,* < *tri-*, three.] Threesided; triangular; having a triangular cross-section.

tri·ra·di·ate, trī·rā′dē·āt″, *a.* [L. *tri = tres,* three, and *radius,* a ray.] Having three rays or radially arranged branches. Also **tri·ra·di·at·ed.**—**tri·ra·di·ate·ly**, *adv.*

tri·reme, trī′rēm, *n.* [L. *triremis—tri = tres,* three, and *remus,* an oar.] An ancient Mediterranean warship with three tiers, banks, or rows of oars on each side.

tri·sac·cha·ride, trī·sak′a·rīd″, trī·sak′ər·id, *n. Chem.* a sugar compound composed of three molecules which hydrolyze to monosaccharide units.

tri·sect, trī·sekt′, *v.t.* [L. *tri = tres,* three, and *seco, sectum,* to cut.] To cut or divide into three usu. equal parts.—**tri·sec·tion**, tri·sek′shan, *n.*—**tri·sec·tor**, *n.*

---

tri·sep·tate, trī·sep′tāt, *a. Biol.* possessing or consisting of three septa or membranes.

tris·kel·i·on, tri·skel′ē·on″, tri·skel′ē·on, *n.* pl. **tris·kel·i·a,** tri·skel′ē·a. [N.L., < Gr. *triskelēs,* three-legged, < *tri-,* three, and *skélos,* leg.] A symbolic figure consisting of three legs, arms, or branches radiating from a common center. Also **tris·kele,** tris′kēl.

tris·mus, triz′mus, tris′mus, *n.* pl. **tris·mus·es.** [Gr. *trismos,* gnashing of the teeth, < *trizō,* to gnash.] *Pathol.* a species of tetanus affecting the under jaw with spastic rigidity; lockjaw.

tris·oc·ta·he·dron, tris·ok″ta·hē′dron, *n.* pl. **tris·oc·ta·he·drons, tris·oc·ta·he·dra,** tris·ok″ta·hē′dra. [Gr. *tris,* three times, *oktō,* eight, and *hedra,* face.] A solid bounded by 24 equal faces in units of three, with each of these units corresponding to each face of an octahedron.—**tris·oc·ta·he·dral,** *a.*

tri·so·mic, trī·sō′mik, *a. Genetics,* possessing one or more triploid chromosomes in a normally diploid organism.—*n.* A trisomic individual. Also **tri·some,** trī′sōm.—**tri·so·my,** trī′sō·mē, *n.*

triste, trēst, *a.* [O.Fr. *triste,* < L. *tristis.*] Sad; sorrowful; melancholy.—**tris·tesse,** *n.* Sorrow.

trist·ful, trist′ful, *a. Archaic.* Melancholy; gloomy; sad.—**trist·ful·ly,** *adv.*

tri·sty·lous, trī·stī′lus, *a. Bot.* having or existing in three styles.—**tri·sty·ly,** trī′·stī·lē, *n.*

tri·sul·fide, trī·sul′fīd, trī·sul′fid, *n. Chem.* a sulfide containing three sulfur atoms.

tri·syl·la·ble, trī·sil′a·bl, trī·sil′a·bl, *n.* [L. *tri = tres,* three, and *syllaba,* syllable.] A word consisting of three syllables.—**tri·syl·lab·ic, tri·syl·lab·i·cal,** trī″si·lab′ik, tris″i·lab′ik, *a.*—**tri·syl·lab·i·cal·ly,** *adv.*

trite, trīt, *a.* [L. *tritus,* pp. of *terere,* to rub, to wear (seen also in *triturate, contrite, detritus*); root *tar, tra,* to pierce, as in prep. *trans.*] Used so commonly as to have lost its novelty and interest; commonplace; hackneyed; stale. *Archaic,* useless, ruined by much use, or worn.—**trite·ly,** *adv.*—**trite·ness,** *n.*

tri·the·ism, trī′thē·iz″um, *n.* [Gr. *tri = treis,* three, and *Theos,* God.] The belief in the existence of three Gods, esp. the belief that the Father, Son, and Holy Spirit of Christianity are three truly distinct beings.—**tri·the·ist,** *n.*—**tri·the·is·tic, tri·the·is·ti·cal,** *a.*

trit·i·um, trit′ē·um, trish′um, *n.* [< Gr. *tritos,* third.] *Phys.* a radioactive hydrogen isotope with an atomic weight of three.

tri·ton, trīt′on, *n.* [L., < Gr. *Triton.*] *Zool.* any of various marine gastropods of the family *Tritonidae,* esp. of the genus *Triton,* having a large trumpet-shaped shell; the shell of such an animal. (*Cap.*), *Gr. mythol.* a sea god, the son of Poseidon, represented as having the head and trunk of a man and the tail of a fish, and bearing a conch-shell trumpet which he blows to raise or calm the waves; one of a race of subordinate sea deities similarly represented.

tri·ton, trī′ton, *n. Phys.* the nucleus of a tritium atom composed of two neutrons and a proton.

tri·tone, trī′tōn″, *n.* [Gr. *tritonos,* of three tones, < *tri-,* three, and *tónos,* E. *tone.*] *Mus.* an interval consisting of three whole tones.

trit·u·rate, trich′a·rāt″, *v.t.*—*triturated, triturating,* [L.L. *trituratus,* pp. of *triturare,* thresh, < L. *tritura,* a rubbing, threshing, < *terere,* rub.] To reduce to fine particles or powder by rubbing, grinding, bruising, or the like; pulverize.—*n.* A triturated substance; a trituration.—**trit·u·ra·ble,** trich′·ér·a·bl, *a.*—**trit·u·ra·tor,** *n.*

trit·u·ra·tion, trich″a·rā′shan, *n.* [L.L. *trituratio(n-).*] The act of triturating, or the state of being triturated. *Phar.* any triturated substance, esp. a mixture of a medicinal substance with sugar of milk, triturated to an impalpable powder; also *triturate.*

tri·umph, trī′umf, *n.* [O.Fr. *triumphe* (Fr. *triomphe*), < L. *triumphus,* triumphal procession, victory: cf. Gr. *thriambos,* hymn sung in procession in honor of Bacchus.] The action or fact of being victorious; a victory; a conquest; a distinguished success or achievement; the exultation of victory; joy over success; elation or exultant gladness. *Rom. hist.* the ceremonial entrance into ancient Rome of a victorious commander with his army, spoils, and captives in honor of an important military or naval achievement.—*v.i.* To gain a victory or be victorious; to gain mastery; to exult over victory; to rejoice over success; to be elated or glad; to celebrate a triumph, as a Roman commander.—**tri·um·phal,** trī·um′fal, *a.* Of or pertaining to a triumph; celebrating or commemorating a triumph or victory; as, a *triumphal* arch.—**tri·um·phal·ly,** *adv.*—**tri·um·phant,** trī·um′fant, *a.* Victorious; successful; exulting or rejoicing over victory or success; exultant.—**tri·um·phant·ly,** *adv.*—**tri·umph·er,** *n.*

tri·um·vir, trī·um′vér, *n.* pl. **tri·um·virs, tri·um·vi·ri,** trī·um′ve·rī″. [L. pl. *triumviri,* < *trium virorum,* of three men: *trium,* gen. of *tres,* three; *virorum,* gen. pl. of *vir,* man.] One of three persons associated in an office, esp. in a triumvirate of ancient Rome.—**tri·um·vi·ral,** *a.*

tri·um·vi·rate, trī·um′vér·it, trī·um′ve·rāt″, *n.* [L. *triumviratus.*] *Rom. hist.* the joint government of three officers or magistrates. Any association of three in office or authority; the position of a triumvir; any group or set of three.

tri·une, trī′ūn, *a.* [L. *tri = tres,* three, and *unus,* one.] Three in one; pertaining to the Trinity.—*n.* (*Cap.*) the Trinity.—**tri·u·ni·ty,** trī·ū′ni·tē, *n.*

tri·va·lent, trī·vā′lent, triv′a·lent, *a.* [Prefix *tri-,* three, and L. *valeo,* to be worth.] *Chem.* having a valence of three. Also *tervalent.*—**tri·va·lence, tri·va·len·cy,** trī·vā′lens, trī·vā′len·sē, *n.*

tri·valve, trī′valv″, *n.* [Prefix *tri-,* three, and *valve.*] Anything having three valves, esp. a shell with three valves.—*a.*

triv·et, triv′it, *n.* [Corruption of *three-feet* or *three-foot,* or of Fr. *trépied,* < L. *tripes, tripedis,* a three-footed stool—*tres,* three, and *pes, pedis,* a foot.] A three-legged stand; a kind of iron frame or stand on which to place vessels for cooking; a short-footed metal stand on which to place hot dishes at the table.

triv·i·a, triv′ē·a, *n. pl.* Insignificant matters; trifles; unimportant things.

triv·i·al, triv′ē·al, *a.* [Fr. *trivial,* < L. *trivialis,* belonging to the public streets, hence common, < *trivium,* a place where three roads meet, a crossroad—*tri = tres,* three, and *via,* a way, a road.] Commonplace; trifling; insignificant; of little worth or importance; inconsiderable.—**triv·i·al·i·ty,** triv′ē·al′i·tē, *n.* pl. **triv·i·al·i·ties.**—**triv·i·al·i·za·tion,** *n.*—**tri·vi·al·ize,** triv′ē·a·līz″, *v.t.*—*trivialized, trivializing*—**triv·i·al·ly,** *adv.*

triv·i·um, triv′ē·um, *n. pl.* **triv·i·a,** triv′ē·a. [M.L. use of L. *trivium,* place where three ways meet, cross-road, public street, < *tri = tres,* three, and *via,* way: cf. *trivial.*] During the Middle Ages, the lower division of the seven liberal arts, comprising grammar, rhetoric, and logic. Compare *quadrivium.*

tri·week·ly, trī·wēk′lē, *a.* Occurring or appearing once every three weeks; happen-

ing or appearing three times each week.—*n.* pl. **tri·week·lies.** A publication issued triweekly.—*adv.*

tro·car, tro·char, trō′kär, *n.* [Fr. *trocar,* < *trois,* three, and *carre,* a square, a face, the instrument having a triangular face.] *Med.* a perforating surgical instrument, specif. a sharp-tipped rod used to insert a cannula for drawing off fluid from a body cavity.

tro·cha·ic, trō·kā′ik, *a.* [L. *trochaicus,* < Gr. *trochaikós.*] *Pros.* Pertaining to the trochee; consisting of or employing a trochee or trochees.—*n. Pros.* A trochee; a verse or poem consisting of trochees.

tro·chal, trō′kal, *a.* [Gr. *trochós,* wheel.] *Zool.* resembling a wheel; as, the *trochal* disk.

tro·chan·ter, trō·kan′tèr, *n.* [N.L. < Gr. *trochantér, tréchein,* run.] *Anat., zool.* a prominence or process on the upper part of the femur in many vertebrates, to which a muscle is attached; *entom.* the second segment of an insect's leg, between the coxa and femur.—**tro·chan·ter·al, tro·chan·ter·ic,** trō″kan·ter′ik, *a.*

tro·che, trō′kē, *n.* [Gr. *trochos,* something circular, a round ball or cake.] A small usu. circular medicinal cake or lozenge made of sugar, mucilage, and some drug, to be gradually dissolved in the mouth.

tro·chee, trō′kē, *n.* [L. *trochaeus,* < Gr. *trochaios,* prop. a., 'running,' < *tróchos,* a running, < *tréchein,* run.] *Pros.* a metrical foot of two syllables, a long followed by a short, or an accented followed by an unaccented.

troch·i·lus, trok′i·lus, *n.* pl. **troch·i·li,** trok′i·lī″. [L. < Gr. *trochílos,* < *tréchein,* run.] *Ornith.* The crocodile bird, *Pluvianus aegyptius;* any of several Old World warblers; any of certain hummingbirds.

troch·le·a, trok′lē·a, *n.* pl. **troch·le·ae,** trok′lē·ē″. [L. *pulley,* < Gr. *trochilia,* sheave, roller.] *Anat.* a pulleylike structure or arrangement of parts affording a smooth surface upon which another part glides, as the surface of the inner condyle of the humerus, with which the ulna articulates.

troch·le·ar, trok′lē·ér, *a. Anat.* belonging to or connected with a trochlea; forming a trochlea; pulleylike. *Bot.* circular and contracted in the middle so as to resemble a pulley.

tro·choid, trō′koid, *n.* [Gr. *trochoeidés,* < *trochós,* wheel, and *eidos,* form.] *Geom.* the plane curve traced by a point fixed to and in the plane of a circle as the circle rolls along a tangent line.—*a.* Rotating about its axis, as a joint or wheel.—**tro·choi·dal,** *a.*—**tro·choi·dal·ly,** *adv.*

troch·o·phore, trok′o·fōr″, trok′o·far″, *n. Zool.* a free-swimming invertebrate, appearing in ciliate larval form.

trof·fer, trof′ér, *n.* An inverted trough-shaped lighting fixture suspended from a ceiling and usu. holding fluorescent tubes.

trog·lo·dyte, trog′lo·dīt″, *n.* [Gr. *tröglodytēs,* a troglodyte < *trôglē,* a cavern, and *dyō,* to enter.] A cave dweller, esp. a prehistoric or primitive man; one living in seclusion; a hermit; a brutish or primitive person; an ape belonging to the anthropoids, as a gorilla.—**trog·lo·dyt·ic,** trog″lo·dit′ik, *a.*

tro·gon, trō′gon, *n.* [N.L. < Gr. *trôgōn,* ppr. of *trôgein,* gnaw, nibble.] Any bird of the family *Trogonidae,* esp. of the genus *Trogon,* of tropical and subtropical regions, notable for its brilliant plumage.—**tro·gon·oid,** trō′go·noid″, *a.*

troi·ka, troi′ka, *n.* [Russ.] *Russ.* A team of three horses abreast; the vehicle drawn by them; the vehicle and horses together; any group of three related or acting together, as a ruling triumvirate.

troi·lus but·ter·fly, trō′i·lus but′ér·flī″,

n. A large swallowtail butterfly, *Papilio troilus*, of N. America, having black wings spotted with yellow and blue. Also **spice‌·bush swal‌·low‌·tail.**

Tro‌·jan, trō′jan, *a.* Pertaining or relating to ancient Troy and its civilization.—*n.* A native or inhabitant of Troy. *Colloq.* a boon companion, or good fellow; one who shows pluck, determination, or energy, as: They all worked like *Trojans.*

Tro‌·jan Horse, *n.* [From the wooden horse presented to the city of Troy by the Greeks and used as a means of getting Greek soldiers inside the gates.] Any person, process, or device which is intended to weaken, subvert, or destroy from within.

Tro‌·jan War, *n. Class. mythol.* a ten year war, described in Homer's *Iliad*, which was caused by the kidnapping of Helen, wife of Menelaus, by Paris.

troll, trōl, *v.t.* [M.E. *trollen*, roll, ramble, stroll: cf. O.Fr. *traller*, *troller*, ramble, Fr. *trôler*, ramble, drag about (prob. from Teut. and akin to G. *trollen*, roll).] To sing or utter in a full, rolling voice; to sing in the manner of a round or catch; to fish for or in, by moving or dragging the hook and line; to move in doing this; as, to *troll* the line; to cause to turn round and round; roll; revolve.—*v.i.* To sing with a full, rolling voice; give forth full, rolling tones; to be uttered or sounded in such tones; to fish with a moving line, as one worked up and down with a rod, esp. one trailed behind a boat; to roll or turn round and round.—*n.* A song whose parts are sung in succession; a round; the act of trolling; the method of trolling for fish; a lure used in trolling for fish.—**troll‌·er,** *n.*

troll, trōl, *n.* [Icel. and Sw. *troll* = Dan. *trold.*] *Scand. folklore*, one of a race of supernatural beings conceived as giants or dwarfs, inhabiting caves or subterranean dwellings.

trol‌·ley, trol′ē, *n. pl.* **trol‌·leys.** [Cf. *troll*, v.] A streetcar; a pulley or a truck traveling on an overhead track and serving to support and move a suspended object; a grooved metallic wheel or pulley carried on the end of a pole by an electric car or locomotive and held in contact with an overhead conductor, usu. a suspended wire, from which it collects the current for the propulsion of the car or locomotive; any of various other devices for collecting current for such a purpose, as a bowlike structure sliding along an overhead wire, or a device for taking current from the underground wire or conductor employed by some electric railways; a low truck that runs on a track; *Brit.* any of various kinds of low carts or vehicles. Also **trol‌·ly.**—*v.t.*, *v.i.*—**trolleyed, trolleying.** To convey or go by trolley. Also **trol‌·ly.**

trol‌·ley bus, *n.* A bus run on electricity drawn from overhead wires. Also **trackless trolley.**

trol‌·ley car, *n.* A street railway car propelled electrically by current taken from a conductor by means of a trolley.

trol‌·lop, trol′op, *n.* [Cf. Sc. *trollop*, *trallop*, a loose hanging rag; Armor. *trul*, a rag or tatter, *trulen*, a slatternly woman; Ir. *troll*, corruption; Gael. *truaill*, to pollute; G. *trulle*, a trull. *Trull* is allied.] A sloppily dressed woman; a slattern; a prostitute; a lascivious woman.

trom‌·bi‌·di‌·a‌·sis, trom″bi‌·di′a‌·sis, *n. Pathol.* a state or condition of being overrun with chiggers. Also **trom‌·bi‌·di‌·o‌·sis,** trom″bi‌·di‌·o′sis.

trom‌·bone, trom‌·bōn′, trom′bōn, *n.* [It. *trombone*, aug. of *tromba*, trumpet, = E. *trump.*] A large brass musical instrument of the trumpet class, the 'slide trombone' having a long U-shaped sliding piece for varying the length of the tube in order to produce a desired note, the 'valve trombone'

having valves for changing notes and tuning.—**trom‌·bon‌·ist,** trom′bō‌·nist, trom‌·bō′nist, *n.*

trom‌·mel, trom′el, *n.* A cylindrical screen for separating rocks, coal, ore, or the like, by size.

tro‌·mom‌·e‌·ter, trō‌·mom′i‌·tėr, *n.* [Gr. *trómos*, a trembling.] An instrument for measuring or detecting very slight earthquake tremors.

tro‌·na, trō′na, *n.* [Sw. *trona*, said to be < Ar.: cf. *natron*.] A grayish or yellowish hydrous carbonate of sodium, Na_2CO_3. $HNaCO_3 \cdot 2H_2O$.

troop, trōp, *n.* [Fr. *troupe*, < M.L. *troppus*, flock; origin uncertain.] A body of soldiers. *Pl.* armed forces; soldiers collectively. *Milit.* a cavalry unit corresponding in organization to an infantry. An assemblage of persons or things; company; a herd, flock, or swarm; a unit of Girl Scouts or Boy Scouts under the supervision of an adult.—*v.i.* To gather or move in a company; to go or come in great numbers; to associate or consort, usu. followed by *with.*

troop car‌·ri‌·er, *n.* A military transport plane used for moving troops and equipment.

troop‌·er, trō′pėr, *n.* A cavalryman; a member of the mounted police; *Brit.* a troopship.

troop‌·ship, trōp′ship″, *n.* A ship for the conveyance of troops; a transport.

troost‌·ite, trō′stīt, *n.* [From Dr. G. *Troost*, geologist, of Nashville, Tenn.] A reddish variety of willemite, in which the zinc is partly replaced by manganese.

tro‌·pae‌·o‌·lum, trō‌·pē′o‌·lum, *n. pl.* **tro‌·pae‌·o‌·lums, tro‌·pae‌·o‌·la,** trō‌·pē′o‌·la. [Gr. *tropaion*, a trophy, the leaves being shield-shaped, the flowers helmet-shaped.] *Bot.* any member of the genus *Tropaeolum*, a group of S. American trailing or climbing plants of the family *Tropaeolaceae*, as the nasturtium.

trope, trōp, *n.* [Fr. *trope*, < L. *tropus*, < Gr. *tropos*, a trope or figure, a turn, < *trepō*, to turn.] *Rhet.* a word or expression intentionally used in a different sense from that which it ordinarily possesses; a figure of speech. *Rom. Cath. Ch.* the interpolation of words, phrases, and verses into the liturgy of the medieval church.

troph‌·ic, trof′ik, *a.* [Gr. *trophikós*, < *trophē*, nourishment, < *tréphein*, nourish.] *Physiol.* Of or pertaining to nutrition; concerned in nutritive processes.—**troph‌·i‌·cal‌·ly,** *adv.*

troph‌·o‌·blast, trof′o‌·blast″, *n. Embryol.* a special layer of cells external to the ectoderm of the embryo in many mammals and having to do with embryonic nutrition.—**troph‌·o‌·blas‌·tic,** *a.*

troph‌·o‌·plasm, trof′o‌·plaz″um, *n. Biol.* a kind of protoplasm which is regarded as forming the nutritive part of a cell.—**troph‌·o‌·plas‌·mat‌·ic, troph‌·o‌·plas‌·mic,** trof″o‌·plaz‌·mat′ik, *a.*

troph‌·o‌·zo‌·ite, trof″o‌·zō′īt, *n. Zool.* a protozoan in an active growing stage.

tro‌·phy, trō′fē, *n. pl.* **tro‌·phies.** [Fr. *trophée*, < L. *trophaeum*, for *tropaeum*. < Gr. *tropaion*, trophy, < *tropē*, a turning, rout, < *trepein*, turn, put to flight, defeat.] Anything taken in war, hunting, or the like, esp. when preserved as a memento; a spoil or prize; anything serving as a token or evidence of victory, valor, or skill; a carving, painting, or other representation of objects associated with or symbolical of victory or achievement; any memento or memorial; a memorial erected by the ancient Greeks or Romans in commemoration of a victory in war, consisting of arms or other spoils taken from the enemy and hung upon a tree, pillar, or the like; *arch.* an ornament which represents weaponry.

trop‌·ic, trop′ik, *n.* [Fr. *tropique*, L. *tropicus*,

Gr. *tropikos*, turning, pertaining to a turn, < *tropē*, a turning, < *trepō*, to turn; < the turning back of the sun at each tropic.] *Geog.* either of two corresponding parallels of latitude, each 23°27′ from the equator, the northern one being called the tropic of Cancer, and the southern, the tropic of Capricorn, and including between them that portion of the globe called the Torrid Zone, which has the equator for its central line. *Pl.* the regions lying between these parallels or near them on either side; the Torrid Zone. *Astron.* either of two circles on the celestial sphere, each 23°27′ from the equator.

trop‌·ic, trop′ik, *a.* Characteristic of, pertaining to, or taking place in the tropics.

trop‌·i‌·cal, trop′i‌·kal, trō′pi‌·kal, *a.* Pertaining to the tropics; being within the tropics; incident to the tropics; as, *tropical* diseases, trop′i‌·kal. Denoting or relating to a trope; metaphorical, trō′pi‌·kal.—**trop‌·i‌·cal‌·ly,** *adv.*

trop‌·i‌·cal cy‌·clone, *n.* A cyclonic storm originating in the tropics with wind usu. above 75 miles per hour, called a hurricane in the United States and West Indies, a typhoon in the Pacific, and various other names elsewhere.

trop‌·i‌·cal fish, *n.* Any of several small, exotic, beautifully colored fish from warm waters of the world, bred for living display in aquariums.

trop‌·i‌·cal storm, *n. Colloq.* a general term sometimes applied to a tropical cyclone in which the surface wind speed is below that of a hurricane.

trop‌·ic bird, *n.* Any of the web-footed sea birds, genus *Phaethon*, of the tropical oceans, being usu. white with some black markings, and having a pair of greatly elongated central tail feathers.

tro‌·pism, trō′piz‌·um, *n. Biol.* the natural tendency of an organism to respond to an external stimulus, as light or gravity, by growth curvature toward or away from the stimulus source.—**tro‌·pis‌·tic,** trō‌·pis′tik, *a.*

tro‌·pol‌·o‌·gy, trō‌·pol′o‌·jē, *n. pl.* **tro‌·pol‌·o‌·gies.** [L.L. *tropologia*, < Gr. *tropologia* < *tropos*, trope, and *-logia*, < *légein*, speak.] The use of tropes or figures of speech in speech or writing; a treatise on tropes or figures of speech; the use of a Scripture text so as to give it a moral interpretation or significance apart from its direct meaning.—**trop‌·o‌·log‌·ic, trop‌·o‌·log‌·i‌·cal,** trop″o‌·loj′ik, *a.*—**trop‌·o‌·log‌·i‌·cal‌·ly,** *adv.*

trop‌·o‌·pause, trop′o‌·paz″, *n.* [Gr. *tropē*, a turning, change, and *pause.*] *Meteor.* the layer of transition between the troposphere and the stratosphere.

tro‌·poph‌·i‌·lous, trō‌·pof′i‌·lus, *a.* [Gr. *tropē*, a turning, change, and *philos*, loving.] *Ecology*, adapted to a climate that experiences marked changes of conditions, as of warmth or moisture, esp. said of plants.

trop‌·o‌·sphere, trop′o‌·sfēr″, *n.* [Gr. *tropos*, turn, and *sphere.*] *Meteor.* the layer of the atmosphere nearest the earth, varying in depth from seven to twelve miles, in which temperature falls as the altitude increases, clouds form, and weather conditions occur. —**trop‌·o‌·spher‌·ic,** trop″o‌·sfer′ik, *a.*

trot, trot, *v.i.*—**trotted, trotting.** [O.Fr. *troter* (Fr. *trotter*); origin uncertain.] To go at a gait between a walk and a canter, in which the legs of a mammal, esp. a horse, move in diagonal pairs but not quite simultaneously, so that, when the movement is slow at least one foot is on the ground, and, when the movement is fast, all feet are momentarily off the ground; to go at a quick, steady gait; to move briskly, bustle, or hurry.—*v.t.* To cause to trot; to ride at a trot; to lead at a trot; *colloq.* to bring forward for, or as for inspection, followed by *out.—n.* The gait of a horse or the like when trotting; a trotting sound; a jogging gait between a walk and a run; quick, continuous movement; as, to be on the *trot*; *colloq.* a toddling child; *slang*, a crib, translation, or other illicit aid made use of by a student.

troth, trạth, trŏth, *n.* [A form of *truth.*] *Archaic*. Truth; faith; fidelity; veracity.— *v.t. Archaic*, to pledge.

troth·plight, trạth′plīt″, trŏth′plīt″, *a. Archaic*. Engaged by troth or promise, esp. of marriage; betrothed.—*v.t. Archaic*. To troth; betroth.—*n. Archaic*. A solemn troth or promise, esp. of marriage; betrothal.

trot·line, trot′līn″, *n.* A heavy fishing line set out across a river or stream with many smaller lines and baited hooks hanging from it.

Trot·sky·ite, trot′skē·īt″, *a.* Relating to the social, political, and economic doctrines advocated by the Russian revolutionary leader, Leon Trotsky (1879–1940), esp. his form of communism including the concept of a necessary world-wide proletariat revolution.—*n.*—**Trot·sky·ist,** *a., n.* Trotskyite.—**Trot·sky·ism,** trot′skē·iz″um, *n.*

trot·ter, trot′ér, *n.* A horse bred and gaited to trot, esp. in harness races; the foot of an animal, esp. of a sheep or pig, used for food.

tro·tyl, trō′til, trō′tēl, *n.* Trinitrotoluene, TNT.

trou·ba·dour, trö′ba·dōr″, trō′ba·dạr″, trö′ba·dụr″, *n.* [Fr. *troubadour*, < Pr. *trobador*, a troubadour (Sp. *trovador*, It. *trovatore*), < *trobar*, Fr. *trouver*, to find, orig. to invent or compose new poems, < L.L. *tropare*, to sing, < L. *tropus*, a song, a trope.] One of the early lyrical poets of southern France and neighboring areas of Italy and Spain during the 11th through the 13th centuries, who wrote of courtly love; any writer or singer of love songs.

trou·ble, trub′l, *v.t.—troubled, troubling.* [Fr. *troubler*, by metathesis and alteration < L. *turbula*, dim. of *turba*, a crowd, confusion; akin *turbid, turbulent, disturb, perturb.*] To disturb or distress; to put to some slight labor or pains; to afflict or discomfort; to annoy; to disturb or put into confused motion, as wine or water.—*v.i.* To worry; to bother.—*n.* Distress of mind; that which causes such distress; grief; worry; affliction; anxiety; annoyance; pains, labor, or exertion, as: Don't go to a lot of *trouble* in preparing dinner. A distressing physical condition or ailment; as, foot *trouble*; a difficulty or unfortunate state or condition. —**in trou·ble,** in difficulties; *colloq.* being unmarried and pregnant.—**trou·bler,** *n.*

trou·ble·mak·er, trub′l·mā″kér, *n.* A person causing distress or difficulties for others, intentionally or unintentionally.

trou·ble·shoot·er, trou·ble-shoot·er, trub′l·shö″tér, *n.* One who is skillful in locating and repairing malfunctions in machines and mechanical equipment; one who resolves or eliminates business or political disputes or problems.

trou·ble·some, trub′l·som, *a.* Giving or causing trouble; harassing; annoying; vexatious.—**trou·ble·some·ly,** *adv.*— **trou·ble·some·ness,** *n.*

trou·blous, trub′lus, *a.* Full of civil commotion, disturbance, or disorder; unsettled; as, *troublous* times.—**trou·blous·ly,** *adv.*— **trou·blous·ness,** *n.*

trou-de-loup, trödʺe·lö′, *n.* pl. **trous-de-loup,** trödʺe·lö′. [Fr. *trou de loup*, 'hole of wolf.'] *Milit.* a conical or pyramidal pit with a pointed stake fixed vertically in the center, rows of which are dug in front of an installation to hinder an enemy's approach.

trough, traf, trof, *dial.* trạth, troth, *n.* [O.E. *trog, troh* = Icel., D., and G. *trog*, Dan.

trug, a trough; akin *tray*.] A vessel, generally rather long and not very deep, for holding water, foodstuff for animals, or the like; a channel or spout for conveying water; anything resembling a trough in shape, as a depression between two ridges or between two waves; *meteor.* an oblong area having lower barometric pressure than its surroundings; *econ.* a relatively slow or inactive period in a cycle of business.— **trough·like,** *a.*

trounce, trouns, *v.t.—trounced, trouncing.* [O.Fr. *troncer, troncir*, to cut or break off into pieces, < L. *truncus*, a trunk.] To beat or punish severely; *colloq.* to defeat by a wide margin.

troupe, tröp, *n.* [Fr.; same as *troop.*] *Theatr.* A troop; a company, particularly, a touring band of players, dancers, acrobats, or the like.—*v.i.—trouped, trouping.* To tour as a member of a traveling company. —**troup·er,** trö′pér, *n.* A member of a troupe; an experienced actor; *colloq.* a person faithful to a cause or duty, as a conscientious worker.

troup·i·al, trö′pē·al, *n.* [Fr. *troupiale,* < *troupe,* E. *troop*; from the habit of going in flocks.] Any of the birds of the American family *Icteridae,* including the American blackbirds, orioles, and grackles, esp. one with brilliant plumage, as the large tropical oriole, *Icterus icterus.*

trou·sers, trou′zèrz, *n. pl.* [For older *trouses, trowses,* a kind of drawers, < O.Fr. *trousses,* a kind of hose, < *trousse,* a truss, case, or cover.] An outer garment worn usu. by men and boys, extending from the waist to the ankles and covering each leg separately.—**trou·ser,** trou′zér, *a.*

trous·seau, trö′sō, trö·sō′, *n. pl.* **trous·seaux, trous·seaus,** trö′sōz, trö·sōz′. [Fr., < *trousse,* a bundle, a truss.] The collection of clothes, other items of personal attire, and linens for the household, which a bride assembles in anticipation of her marriage.

trout, trout, *n. pl.* **trout, trouts.** [O.E. *truht,* < L. *tructa, tructus,* trout = Gr. *trōctēs,* kind of sea fish, < *trōgein,* gnaw, nibble.] A food and game fish of the family *Salmonidae,* found in cold fresh waters of Europe and the Americas; as, in Europe, the brown or salmon *trout,* or, in the Americas, the cutthroat *trout,* rainbow *trout,* and brook or speckled *trout*; any of various similar fishes not of the salmon family.

trout·perch, trout′pùrch″, *n. pl.* **trout·perch·es, trout·perch.** Any of the small fresh-water fishes of the family *Percopsidae,* of the cooler parts of North America, as *Percopsis omiscomaycus,* found in the central and eastern parts of the U.S.

trou·vère, trö·vâr′, *Fr.* TRÖ·veR′, *n. pl.* **trou·vères,** trö·vârz′, *Fr.* TRÖ·veR′. [Fr. *trouver,* to find.] One of a class of chiefly narrative poets of northern France who wrote during the 11th to 14th centuries in langue d'oïl, composing typically the chansons de geste. Also **trou·veur,** trö·vụr′, *Fr.* TRÖ·VŒR′.

trove, trōv, *n.* A valuable find. Also *treasure-trove.*

tro·ver, trō′vèr, *n.* [Noun use of O.Fr. *trover,* find, invent, compose (Fr. *trouver,* find); origin uncertain: cf. *troubadour* and *trouvère.*] *Law,* an action at law for the recovery of the value of personal property illegally converted by another to his own use.

trow, trō, *v.i.* [O.E. *treówian, treówan,* to believe, lit. 'to believe to be true.'] *Archaic,* to think or suppose.

trow·el, trou′el, *n.* [Fr. *truelle,* < L. *trulla,* a small ladle, dim. of *trua,* a stirring spoon, a ladle.] A tool resembling a small, flat spade, used for spreading and dressing mortar and plaster; a scooplike gardener's

tool, used in taking up plants and turning over dirt.—*v.t.—troweled, troweling, Brit. trowelled, trowelling.* To dress or form with a trowel.—**trow·el·er, trow·el·ler,** *n.*

troy, troi, *a.* Expressed by means of troy weight.

troy weight, *n.* [From *Troyes,* in France.] A weight used chiefly in weighing gold and silver. See Measures and Weights table.

tru·an·cy, trö′an·sē, *n. pl.* **tru·an·cies.** The act or an act of playing truant; truant conduct or habit. Also **tru·ant·ry.**

tru·ant, trö′ant, *n.* [O.Fr. *truant* (Fr. *truand*), vagabond, beggar; prob. < Celtic.] One who shirks or neglects his duty; a child who stays away from school without leave.—*a.* Staying away from school without leave, as a child; pertaining to or characteristic of a truant.—*v.i.* To be truant.—**tru·ant·ly,** *adv.*

tru·ant of·fic·er, *n.* An employee of the public schools who officially investigates absences of pupils.

truce, trös, *n.* [M.E. *trewes,* pl. of *trewe,* < O.E. *trēow,* truth, good faith, engagement, = O.H.G. *triuwa* (G. *treue*) truth, faith, = Goth. *triggwa,* covenant; akin to E. *true.*] A suspension of hostilities, as between armies, for a specified period, by agreement; an armistice; an agreement or treaty establishing this; respite, intermission, or freedom, as from trouble or pain.

truck, truk, *n.* [Perh. < *truckle.*] Any of a class of self-propelled vehicles of various sizes and designs for transporting goods, either a single conveyance or, for larger loads, a motorized cab with a separate trailer unit attached; any of various wheeled frames or conveyances for moving heavy articles; also *motor truck.* A barrow with two very low front wheels, on which sacks, bales, boxes, or luggage are moved; also **hand truck.** A low rectangular frame on which heavy loads are moved; a group of two or more pairs of wheels in one frame, for supporting one end of a railway car or locomotive; *naut.* a circular or square piece of wood fixed on the head of a mast or the top of a flagstaff, usu. containing small holes for halyards.—*v.t.* To put on a truck; to transport by a truck or trucks—*v.i.* To convey articles or goods on a truck; to drive a truck.

truck, truk, *n.* [O.Fr. Fr. *troquer*; origin unknown.] *U.S.* vegetables raised for the market. Articles of miscellaneous or worthless character; odds and ends; *colloq.* dealings. Barter; a bargain or deal. The payment of wages in goods instead of money; also *truck system.*—*v.t.* To exchange, trade, or barter; to peddle or hawk.—*v.i.* To exchange commodities; to barter; to traffic or have dealings.

truck·age, truk′ij, *n.* Conveyance by a truck or trucks; the charge for this.

truck·er, truk′ér, *n.* One, as a person or company, that is in the business of conveying articles or goods on a truck or trucks. One who drives a truck; also **truck·driv·er.**

truck·er, truk′ér, *n.* One who barters; *U.S.* a truck farmer.

truck farm, *n. U.S.* a farm devoted to the growing of vegetables for market. Also **truck gar·den,** *Brit.* **mar·ket gar·den,** *n.*— **truck farm·er,** *n.*—**truck farm·ing,** *n.*

truck·ing, truk′ing, *n.* The act or business of conveying articles or goods on trucks.

truck·le, truk′l, *v.i.—truckled, truckling.* [Dim. of *truck,* to barter; or < *truckle bed,* because inferiors slept in them.] To yield or bend obsequiously to the will of another.— **truck·ler,** *n.*

truck·le, truk′l, *n.* [Dim. of *truck,* a wheel.] A small wheel or caster; a truckle bed.

truck·le bed, *n.* Trundle bed.

truck·load, truk′lōd″, *n.* A load filling a truck; the required minimum weight for shipping at a reduced bulk rate or truckload rate.

truck·man, truk'man, *n.* pl. **truck·men.** One who drives a truck; one who works in the trucking business.

truck sys·tem, *n.* The method of making wage payments in goods rather than in money.

truck trail·er, *n.* A motorless highway vehicle designed to be hauled by a motor truck or tractor.

truc·u·lent, truk'ya·lent, trö'kya·lent, *a.* [L. *truculentus,* < *trux, trucis,* fierce, savage.] Fierce; savage; inspiring terror; bellicose; quarrelsome in manner or tone; inordinately severe; defiantly rude and contemptuous.—**truc·u·lence, truc·u·len·cy,** *n.*—**truc·u·lent·ly,** *adv.*

trudge, truj, *v.i.*—*trudged, trudging.* [Origin obscure.] To make one's way on foot; walk; esp. to walk laboriously or wearily.—*v.t.* To walk wearily along.—*n.* An act of trudging; a laborious walk.—**trudg·er,** *n.*

trudg·en stroke, *n.* [From J. *Trudgen,* English swimmer, who learned the stroke in S. Amer.] A stroke in swimming, in which a double overarm motion and a scissor kick are used. Also **trudg·en,** truj'en.

true, trö, *a.*—*truer, truest.* [O.E. *trēowe, trȳwe,* = D. *trouw* = G. *treu* = Icel. *tryggr* = Goth. *triggws,* true, faithful: cf. *trow, truce,* and *trust.*] Steadfast or adhering, as to a friend, a cause, or a promise; firm in allegiance; loyal; faithful; trusty; honest, honorable, or upright; free from deceit; sincere; as, *true* interest in a person's welfare; telling the truth; truthful; being consistent with the actual state of things; as, a *true* story; conforming to fact; not false; agreeing with a standard, pattern, rule, or the like; as, a *true* copy; exact, correct, or accurate; as, a *true* balance; exactly or accurately shaped, formed, fitted, or placed, as a surface, an instrument, or a part of a mechanism; reliable, unfailing, or sure; as, a *true* sign; of the right kind, such as it should be, or proper; legitimate or rightful; real or genuine; as, *true* gold; correctly called or answering to a description; *biol.* conformable to the type or the accepted character of a class, genus, or the like, as: An amoeba is a *true* animal. Not hybrid or mongrel; as, a *true* Siamese cat.—*n.* Exact or accurate information, position, or adjustment; that which is true, used with *the.*—*v.t.*—*trued, trueing* or *truing.* To make true; shape, adjust, or place exactly or accurately; make perfectly straight, level, square, or the like.—*adv.* In a true manner; truly or truthfully; exactly or accurately; in agreement with the ancestral or genetic type; as, to breed *true.*—**true·ness,** *n.*

true bill, *n. Law,* a bill of indictment endorsed by a grand jury, after investigation, as being sufficiently supported by evidence to justify a hearing of the case.

true blue, *n.* A colorfast blue dye; the color adopted by 17th century Scotch Covenanters to contrast with the royal red; one who is true-blue.

true-blue, trö'blö', *a.* Loyal; unwavering; staunch; true.

true·born, trö'bôrn', *a.* Authentically such by birth.

true-false, trö'fals', *a.* Designating a statement or series of statements, as an examination or personality inventory, to be answered as true or false.

true·heart·ed, trö'här'tid, *a.* Faithful or loyal; honest or sincere.—**true·heart·ed·ness,** *n.*

true·love, trö'luv", *n.* One truly loving or loved; a sweetheart. *Bot.* the herb, *Paris quadrifolia,* which has a whorl of four leaves with a single flower or berry in the center suggesting a truelover's knot; also **Par·is.**

true·lov·er's knot, *n.* A kind of double knot, made with two bows on each side, interlacing each other, considered as an emblem of affection. Also **true·love knot, true-lov·er's knot.**

true rib, *n. Anat.* one of the seven upper ribs in man directly attached by cartilages to the sternum.

truf·fle, truf'l, trö'fl, *n.* [Fr. *truffle, trufle,* obs. var. of *truffe,* truffle, perhaps < L. *tuber.*] Any of various subterranean edible fungi of the genus *Tuber,* commonly with a brown or black warty exterior; any of various similar edible fungi of other genera. —**truf·fled,** *a.*

tru·ism, trö'iz·um, *n.* An undoubted or self-evident truth.—**tru·is·tic,** *a.*

trull, trul, *n.* [Of similar origin with *trollop.*] A strumpet; a promiscuous woman; a prostitute.

tru·ly, trö'lē, *adv.* In a true manner; exactly; honestly; legitimately; in reality; in fact; *archaic,* faithfully.

trump, trump, *n.* [*Contr.* < *triumph,* which formerly had sense of *trump.*] *Cards,* one of the suit of cards which temporarily ranks above the other suits; *often pl.* such a suit of cards. A powerful asset or resource; *colloq.* a good fellow.—*v.t. Cards,* to take, as a trick, with a trump. To surpass; outdo; beat.—*v.i. Cards,* to play a trump; ruff.— **trump up,** to invent or concoct in order to deceive; fabricate.

trump, trump, *n.* [Fr. *trompe,* a trumpet or horn; Sp. and Pg. *trompa,* It. *tromba,* a trumpet; cf. O.H.G. *trumba, trumpa,* a drum; Lith. *truba,* a herdsman's horn. Akin *trombone.* Hence *trumpet.*] *Archaic, poet.* a trumpet or its sound; *Sc.* a jew's-harp.

trump·er·y, trum'pe·rē, *n.* pl. **trump·er·ies.** [Fr. *tromperie,* fraud; trumpery is what deceives by false show.] That which is showy but of no value; rubbish; nonsense. —*a.*

trum·pet, trum'pit, *n.* [O.Fr. Fr. *trompette,* dim. of *trompe,* E. *trump.*] *Mus.* any of a class of musical wind instruments with a penetrating, powerful tone, consisting of a long, metallic tube, commonly once or twice curved round upon itself, having a cup-shaped mouthpiece at one end and a flaring bell at the other; an organ stop having a tone resembling that of a trumpet; a trumpeter. A sound like that of a trumpet; the loud cry of the elephant or other animal; any article or device shaped like a trumpet; an ear trumpet; *pl.* a pitcher plant, *Sarracenia flava.*—*v.i.* To blow or sound a trumpet; to emit a sound like that of a trumpet, as an elephant.—*v.t.* To sound on a trumpet; to utter with a sound like that of a trumpet; to proclaim loudly or widely.— **trum·pet·like,** *a.*

trum·pet creep·er, *n.* Any of the climbing plants of the genus *Campsis,* of the bignonia family, esp. *C. radicans,* a native of the southern U.S., with large red trumpet-shaped flowers. Also *trumpet flower,* **trum·pet vine.**

trum·pet·er, trum'pi·tėr, *n.* One who sounds or plays a trumpet; *fig.* one who proclaims or announces something loudly or widely. *Ornith.* any of the large S. American birds allied to the cranes and rails, constituting the genus *Psophia,* esp. *P. crepitans,* the golden-breasted trumpeter; a large wild swan of N. America, *Olor buccinator,* having a sonorous cry; one of a breed of domestic pigeons.

trum·pet flow·er, *n.* Any of various plants bearing large tubular flowers, as *Bignonia capreolata,* a climbing vine with red or yellow flowers; the trumpet creeper, *Campsis radicans,* a vine bearing scarlet flowers.

trum·pet·weed, trum'pit·wēd", *n.* Joe-pye weed.

trun·cate, trung'kāt, *v.t.*—*truncated, trun-*

cating. [L. *trunco, truncatum,* to cut short, < *truncus,* mutilated, and as substantive, the trunk of a tree.] To shorten by cutting abruptly; to cut short.—*a.* Truncated. *Biol.* appearing as if cut short at the tip; as, a *truncate* leaf; without an apex, as certain shells.—**trun·ca·tion,** trung·kā'shan, *n.*

trun·cat·ed, trung'kā·tid, *a.* Shortened by the cutting off of a part; *geom.* having the apex, vertex, or end cut off by a plane; as, a *truncated* cone or pyramid; *crystal.* having angles or edges cut off or replaced by planes; *biol.* truncate; *pros.* lacking one or more unstressed syllables at the beginning or end, as a line of verse.

trun·cheon, trun'chon, *n.* [O.Fr. *tronchon,* Fr. *tronçon,* < *tronche, tronce,* a trunk, staff, etc., L. *truncus.*] A club; a heavy short stick; a baton, esp. one symbolizing authority; *Brit.* a policeman's billy club. A tree whose branches have been lopped off to produce rapid growth.—*v.t.*—**trun·cheoned,** *a.*

trun·dle, trun'dl, *v.t.*—*trundled, trundling.* [O.E. *tryndel, trendel,* a circle, a wheel; akin Sw. and Dan. *trind,* round.] To cause to roll; as, to *trundle* a hoop; to move in a wheeled vehicle.—*v.i.* To roll on; to rotate; to move along on wheels.—*n.* A little wheel, as a caster; a lantern wheel or each of its bars; a small carriage or truck with low wheels.—**trun·dler,** *n.*

trun·dle bed, *n.* A low bed, usu. on trundles or casters, which can be pushed under a high bed when not in use. Also *truckle bed.*

trunk, trungk, *n.* [O.Fr. Fr. *tronc,* < L. *truncus,* trunk (of tree, body, etc.), stock, shaft, < *truncus,* mutilated, deprived of parts.] The main stem of a tree, as distinct from the branches and roots; a large box, chest, or case for holding clothes and other articles, as for use on a journey; a large automobile compartment for the storage of a spare tire, tools, luggage, or the like; the body of a human being or other animal, considered apart from the head and limbs; the torso; the thorax of an insect; *arch.* the shaft of a column. The main line of a river, railroad, or canal; the main line of a telephone or telegraph line; also *trunk line. Anat.* the main body of an artery, nerve, or the like, as distinct from the branches; *pl.* short, tight-fitting breeches or shorts, as worn by athletes, swimmers, or the like. The long, flexible, cylindrical nasal appendage of the elephant, having the nostrils at the extremity; *mach.* the tube or hollow cylinder replacing the piston rod in a trunk engine; *naut.* a large enclosed passage through the decks or bulkheads of a vessel, for cooling, ventilation, or the like; any of various watertight casings in a vessel, as the vertical one above the slot for a centerboard in the bottom of a boat.—*a.* Noting or pertaining to the main line, as of a railroad.

trunk·fish, trungk'fish", *n.* pl. **trunk·fish, trunk·fish·es.** Any of various small fishes constituting the family *Ostraciontidae,* having a boxlike body encased in bony polygonal plates.

trunk hose, *n. pl.* Full, baglike breeches covering the person from the waist to the middle of the thigh or lower, worn in the 16th and 17th centuries.

trunk line, *n.* See *trunk.*

trun·nel, trun'el, *n.* Treenail.

trun·nion, trun'yon, *n.* [Fr. *trognon,* core, stump; origin uncertain.] Either of the two cylindrical projections on a cannon, one on each side, which support it on its carriage; any of various similar supports, gudgeons, or pivots.—**trun·nioned,** *a.*

truss, trus, *v.t.* [O.Fr. *trusser, trosser, torser* (Fr. *trousser*); origin uncertain.] To tie, bind, or fasten, as with a rope; to secure; to furnish or support, as a bridge, with a truss or trusses; to bolster; to make fast with skewers or string, as wings of a turkey, prior to roasting; to confine or enclose, as the body, with snug clothes.—*n. Constr.* a combination of beams, bars, or ties arranged in a triangle or series of triangles to form a rigid framework, and used in bridges and roofs to give support and rigidity to part or all of the structure; *med.* a belt with an affixed pad, used to support a hernia; *naut.* an iron fitting by which a lower yard is secured to a mast; *bot.* a terminal cluster of flowers growing on a single stalk. A collection of things bundled together; a package; *Brit.* a bundle of hay or straw, containing either 56 pounds of old or 60 pounds of new hay, or 36 pounds of straw.—**truss·er,** *n.*

truss bridge, *n.* A bridge braced or supported essentially by trusses.

trust, trust, *n.* [M.E. *trust, trost,* < Scand: cf. Icel. *traust,* trust, confidence; akin to E. *true.*] Reliance on the integrity or justice of a person or confidence in some quality, feature, or attribute of a thing; confident expectation or hope; as, a *trust* in tomorrow; credit or confidence in the ability or intention of a person to pay at some future time for goods, property, or services received; as, buying on *trust*; a person or thing that one relies on; the state of one to whom something is entrusted; the obligation or responsibility imposed on one in whom confidence or authority is placed; care, safe-keeping, or custody; *law,* a confidence reposed in a person by conveying to him the legal title to property which he is to hold for the benefit of another. *Com.* an illegal grouping or combination of industrial or commercial companies having a board of trustees controlling the stock of the constituent companies, thus making it possible to minimize expenses, regulate production, control prices, and defeat competition; a combination of industrial or commercial companies or a large corporation exercising a semimonopolistic control over some service or the manufacture of some product.—*a.* Of or pertaining to trust or a trust; held in trust; as, a *trust* fund.—*v.i.* To have faith or confidence in something or someone; to hope; to sell goods on credit.—*v.t.* To have trust or confidence in; to rely on; to believe; to allow to be somewhere or do something without fear of consequences; to give credit to, as a person, for goods or services supplied; to expect confidently or to hope, usu. followed by a clause or infinitive, as: *Trusting* to complete the first job, he began another.—**trust·er,** *n.*—**trust·less,** *a.*

trust bust·er, *n.* One who seeks or advocates the dissolution of industrial or commercial trusts, esp. a federal official who vigorously enforces antitrust laws. Also **trust·bust·er.—trust bust·ing,** *n.*

trust com·pa·ny, *n.* pl. **trust com·pa·nies.** A company or corporation organized to exercise the functions of a trustee, and which also engages in banking and other financial activities.

trus·tee, tru·stē′, *n.* One to whom property or funds have been legally entrusted to be administered for the benefit of another; a person, usu. one of a body of persons, appointed to administer the affairs of a company, institution, or the like.—*v.t.—trusteed, trusteeing.* To place in the hands of a trustee or trustees; law, to attach by trustee process.—**trus·tee proc·ess,** *law,* the attachment of property by garnishment. —**trus·tee·ship,** *n.*

trust·ful, trust′ful, *a.* Full of trust; trusting; confiding.—**trust·ful·ly,** *adv.*—**trust·ful·ness,** *n.*

trust fund, *n.* Any estate, esp. stock, securities, or money, which is held in trust.

trust ter·ri·to·ry, *n.* pl. **trust ter·ri·to·ries.** A territory that is not self-governing

and that is administered by a member of the United Nations Trusteeship Council.

trust·wor·thy, trust′wῠr″тНē, *a.* Worthy of trust or confidence; reliable.—**trust·wor·thi·ly,** *adv.*—**trust·wor·thi·ness,** *n.*

trust·y, trus′tē, *a.—trustier, trustiest.* Deserving confidence or trust; reliable.—*n.* pl. **trust·ies.** A person who is trusted, esp. a convict granted special liberties and privileges because he is well-behaved and reliable.—**trust·i·ness,** *n.*

truth, trōōth, *n.* pl. **truths,** trōōтHz. [O.E. *treōwthe,* < *treōwe,* true. Formed similarly to *sloth, filth,* etc.] Conformity to fact or reality; veracity or honesty; a true statement; a verified or accepted fact; the state or quality of being true; fidelity; constancy; that which is true or actual; (*often cap.*) a spiritual or philosophical verity.—**in truth,** actually; in fact.—**truth·less,** *a.*

truth·ful, trōōth′ful, *a.* Speaking the truth, either by habit or by nature; true; in accordance with reality or the facts.—**truth·ful·ly,** *adv.*—**truth·ful·ness,** *n.*

truth se·rum, *n.* A drug, as scopolamine or one of certain barbiturates, used to induce a state in which a subject will talk freely when questioned, as about criminal involvement or about repressed memories in psychotherapy.

try, trī, *v.t.—tried, trying.* [O.Fr. Fr. *trier,* pick, cull, sort; origin uncertain.] To attempt to do or accomplish; as, easy until you *try* it; to test the effect or result of; as, to *try* an experiment or new method; to endeavor to ascertain by experiment; to put to the proof or test in order to determine the quality, value, fitness, or accuracy of; to attempt to open, as a door or window, in order to find out whether it is locked or fastened; to put to a severe test or to strain the endurance or patience of; to render or melt, as fat, in order to obtain oil. *Law,* to examine and determine judicially, as a cause; to determine judicially the guilt or innocence of, as of a person.—*v.i.* To make an attempt or effort.—*n.* pl. **tries.** An attempt, endeavor, or effort; *rugby,* a three-point score gained by crossing the opposing goal line with the ball.—**the old col·lege try,** a vigorous attempt or effort.—**try out,** to test the effect of.—**try out for,** to engage in competition for, as for a position or a part in a play.—**try up,** *carp.* to plane the entire length of, as of a board.

try·ing, trī′ing, *a.* That tests severely; hard to endure; annoying.—**try·ing·ly,** *adv.*—**try·ing·ness,** *n.*

try·ma, trī′ma, *n.* pl. **try·ma·ta,** trī′ma·ta. [N.L., < Gr. *tryma,* hole, < *tryein,* rub down, wear out.] *Bot.* a drupaceous nut having a fibrous or fleshy exocarp which at maturity dehisces, as in the walnut and hickory.

try on, *v.t.* To put on, as a garment, in order to test the fit and appearance.

try·out, trī′out″, *n. Colloq.* a trial or test made to determine the fitness of a person or thing for a particular purpose; as, *tryouts* for football.

tryp·a·no·some, trip′a·no·sōm″, tri·pan′o·sōm″, *n.* [N.L. *Trypanosoma,* < Gr. *trypanon,* boring instrument and *sōma,* body.] Any of the minute, flagellate protozoans constituting the genus *Trypanosoma,* parasitic in the blood of man and other vertebrates, and often causing serious diseases, as sleeping sickness and tsetse fly disease, the infection being transmitted by the bite of a tsetse fly; any of various related protozoans. Also **tryp·a·no·so·ma.**—

tryp·a·no·so·mi·a·sis, trip″a·nō·sō·mī′a·sis, tri·pan″ō·sō·mī′a·sis, *n.* [N.L.] *Pathol.* any disease due to infection with trypanosomes.

tryp·sin, trip′sin, *n.* [Appar. formed, after *pepsin,* < Gr. *tryein,* rub down, wear out.]

Biochem. the protein-splitting enzyme of the pancreatic juice, capable of converting proteins into peptone, used in medicine and to peptonize milk.—**tryp·tic,** *a.*

tryp·sin·o·gen, trip·sin′o·jen, *n. Biochem.* a pancreatic secretion converted into trypsin by enzyme action.

tryp·to·phan, trip′to·fan″, *n.* [Gr. *truein,* to rub down, *phainein,* to show.] *Biochem.* an essential amino acid, $C_{11}H_{12}N_2O_2$, in proteins and requisite in the nutrition of humans and animals. Also **tryp·to·phane,** trip′to·fān″.

try·sail, trī′sāl″, *naut.* trī′sal, *n. Naut.* a small fore-and-aft sail set with a gaff on the foremast or mainmast of a ship or on a small mast abaft the foremast or mainmast, used esp. for heavy weather.

try square, *n.* A carpenter's square, usu. consisting of a metal blade set at a right angle to a wooden block, used to test the squareness of something built or for laying off right angles.

tryst, trist, trīst, *n.* [Closely akin to *trust*; Icel. *treysta,* to trust.] An appointment to meet; a rendezvous; an appointed meeting place.

tsar, zär, tsär, *n.* Czar.—**tsa·ri·na.—tsar·dom.—tsar·e·vitch.—tsa·rev·na.—tsar·ism.—tsar·ist.**

tset·se, tset′sē, tsēt′sē, *n.* pl. **tset·se, tset·ses.** A fly of southern Africa, the genus *Glossina,* which is the intermediate host or transmitter of the trypanosomes causing sleeping sickness and other diseases in man and domestic animals. Also **tset·se fly.**

T-shirt, tē′shῠrt″, *n.* A collarless, lightweight, short-sleeved pullover shirt of cotton, worn by men as an undershirt; a similar outer shirt. Also **tee shirt.**

T square, *n.* A T-shaped ruler for making parallel lines, the crosspiece acting as a guide as it slides along the edge of a table or drawing board.

tsu·na·mi, tsῠ·nä′mē, *n.* A huge sea wave resulting from a seaquake or submarine volcanic eruption; a tidal wave.—**tsu·na·mic,** tsῠ·nä′mik, tsῠ·nam′ik, *a.*

tsu·tsu·ga·mu·shi dis·ease, tsö′tsa·ga·mö′shē di·zēz′, tsö″tsa·ga·mö′shē, *n. Pathol.* an infectious rickettsial disease usu. occurring in the Orient, caused by the microorganism, *Rickettsia tsutsugamushi,* or *R. orientalis,* and transmitted by mites. Also *scrub typhus.*

tu·a·ta·ra, tö″a·tä′ra, *n.* A spiny reptile, *Sphenodon punctatum,* inhabiting islands close to New Zealand.

tub, tub, *n.* [M.E. *tubbe* = M.L.G. *tubbe* = D. *tobbe,* tub.] A round, open wooden vessel, broad in proportion to height, usu. made of staves held together by hoops and fitted around a flat bottom; any similar vessel or container; a vessel or receptacle for bathing in; a bathtub; *chiefly Brit.* the act or practice of bathing in a tub, or a bath in a tub; *mining,* a bucket, box, or the like in which material is brought up from or conveyed in a mine; *colloq.* a slow, clumsy ship or boat.—*v.t.—tubbed, tubbing.* To put or set in a tub; *chiefly Brit.* to wash or bathe in a tub or bath.—*v.i. Chiefly Brit.* To wash oneself in a tub or bath; to undergo washing in a tub.—**tub·ba·ble,** *a.*—**tub·ber,** *n.*

tu·ba, tö′ba, tū′ba, *n.* pl. **tu·bas, tu·bae,** tö′bē, tū′bē. [L. trumpet, akin to *tubus,* E. *tube.*] A brass musical instrument of very large size and low pitch; a reed stop in an organ of powerful eight-foot pitch.

tu·bal, tö′bal, tū′bal, *a.* Of or pertaining to a tube or tubes; tubular.

tu·bate, tö′bāt, tū′bāt, *a.* Forming or having a tube or tubes; tubate.

tub·by, tub′ē, *a.—tubbier, tubbiest.* Tub-shaped; round like a tub; corpulent; having a sound like that of an empty tub when struck; having a dull sound; without resonance.—**tub·bi·ness,** n.

tube, tōb, tūb, n. [Fr. tube, < L. tubus, tube, pipe: cf. tuba.] A hollow, usu. cylindrical body, as of metal, glass, rubber, or plastic, used for conveying or containing fluids or acting as a form for solids; material of tubular form; any tubelike instrument, piece, part, organ, or duct; a test tube; a small collapsible metal or plastic cylinder closed at one end with the other end open and being provided with a cap or lid and used for holding and dispensing material, as paint, toothpaste, or other semiliquids; a pneumatic tunnel for transmission of materials; the tubular tunnel in which a subway train runs; anat. any hollow cylindrical vessel or organ; bot. any hollow elongated part or body, esp. the united lower portion of a sympetalous corolla.—v.t.—tubed, tubing. To furnish or fit with a tube or tubes; to cause to pass through or enclose in a tube; to make tubular.

tube foot, n. pl. **tube feet.** One of the many small tubelike appendages by means of which the starfish and most other echinoderms move and hold their food.

tube·less, tōb'lis, tūb'lis, a. Pertaining to a tire without an inner tube whose performance is designed to duplicate that of one with a pneumatic tube and usu. having a cost or self-sealing advantage.

tu·ber, tō'bėr, tū'bėr, n. [L., hump, swelling, knob, truffle, prob. akin to tumere, swell.] Bot. a fleshy, usu. oblong or rounded thickening or outgrowth of a subterranean stem, bearing minute scalelike leaves with buds or eyes in their axils, from which new plants may arise, as the potato. Anat. a rounded swelling or protuberance; a tuberosity; a tubercle.

tu·ber·cle ba·cil·lus, tō'bėr·kl, tū'bėr·kl, n. [L. tuberculum, dim. of tuber.] Biol. a small rounded projection or excrescence, as on a bone, on the surface of the body in various animals, or on a plant. Pathol. a small, firm, rounded nodule or swelling; the characteristic lesion of tuberculosis.

tu·ber·cle ba·cil·lus, n. pl. **tu·ber·cle ba·cil·li.** A short, slender, rodlike, often slightly curved bacterium, Mycobacterium tuberculosis, the cause of tuberculosis.

tu·ber·cu·lar, tụ·bụr'kū·lėr, tụ·bụr'kya·lėr, tū·bụr'kū·lėr, tū·bụr'kya·lėr, a. Of, pertaining to, or of the nature of a tubercle or tubercles; characterized by tubercles. Pathol. pertaining to or characterized by small rounded nodules or tubercles; pertaining to tuberculosis; tuberculous.—n. A person afflicted with tuberculosis.—**tu·ber·cu·lar·ly,** adv.

tu·ber·cu·late, tụ·bụr'kū·lit, tụ·bụr'kya·lit, tụ·bụr'kū·lāt, tụ·bụr'kya·lāt, tū·bụr'kū·lit, tū·bụr'kya·lit, tū·bụr'kū·lāt, tū·bụr'kya·lāt, a. Having tubercles; tubercled; tubercular. Also **tu·ber·cu·lat·ed.**—**tu·ber·cu·la·tion,** n. The formation of tubercles; the disposition or arrangement of tubercles; a growth or set of tubercles.—**tu·ber·cu·late·ly,** adv.

tu·ber·cu·lin, tụ·bụr'kya·lin, tụ·bụr'kū·lin, tū·bụr'kya·lin, tū·bụr'kū·lin, n. [G. tuberkulin, < L. tuberculum, E. tubercle.] Med. a sterile liquid prepared from cultures of the tubercle bacillus, used in the diagnosis and treatment of tuberculosis.

tu·ber·cu·lin test, n. A test for a hypersensitive reaction to tuberculin indicating a present or past tubercular disease.

tu·ber·cu·loid, tụ·bụr'kya·loid', tụ·bụr'kū·loid', tū·bụr'kya·loid', tū·bụr'kū·loid', a. Resembling tuberculosis or a tubercle.

tu·ber·cu·lo·sis, tụ·bụr"kya·lō'sis, tụ·bụr"kū·lō'sis, tū·bụr"kya·lō'sis, tū·bụr"kū·lō'sis, n. [N.L., < L. tuberculum, E. tubercle.] Pathol. an infectious disease affecting any of various tissues of the body, due to the tubercle bacillus, and characterized by the production of tubercles; this disease when affecting the lungs; consumption. Abbr. TB, T.B.

tu·ber·cu·lous, tụ·bụr'kya·lus, tụ·bụr'kū·lus, tū·bụr'kya·lus, tū·bụr'kū·lus, a. Tubercular; pertaining to or of the nature of tuberculosis; affected with tuberculosis.—**tu·ber·cu·lous·ly,** adv.

tube·rose, tōb'rōz", tūb'rōz", tō'be·rōz", tū'be·rōz", n. [L. tuberosa, fem. of tuberosus, E. tuberose, tuberous.] A bulbous plant of the amaryllis family, Polianthes tuberosa, cultivated for its fragrant, waxy white flowers.

tu·ber·os·i·ty, tō"be·ros'i·tē, tū"be·ros'i·tē, n. pl. **tu·ber·os·i·ties.** The state of being tuberous; anat. a rough projection or protuberance of a bone, as for the attachment of a muscle.

tu·ber·ous, tō'bėr·us, tū'bėr·us, a. [Fr. tubéreux, < L. tuberosus, having lumps or protuberances, < tuber, E. tuber.] Covered with or characterized by rounded or wartlike prominences or tubers; of the nature of such a prominence. Bot. bearing tubers; of the nature of or resembling a tuber; as, a tuberous root.—**tu·ber·ous·ly,** adv.

tu·ber·ous root, n. A true root so thickened as to resemble a tuber but bearing no buds or eyes.—**tu·ber·ous-root·ed,** a.

tu·bi·fex, tō'bi·feks, tū'bi·feks, n. pl. **tu·bi·fex, tu·bi·fex·es.** A slender, aquatic, tube-dwelling worm, genus Tubifex, used as a food worm for tropical or aquarium fish.

tub·ing, tō'bing, tū'bing, n. The act of making or providing with tubes; a series of tubes; a piece of tube or tubing; material for tubes, as plastic, copper, glass, or aluminum.

tu·bu·lar, tō'bya·lėr, tū'bya·lėr, a. [L. tubulus, E. tubule.] Of or pertaining to a tube or tubes; characterized by or consisting of tubes; of the nature or form of a tube; tube-shaped; med. noting a respiratory sound resembling that produced by a current of air passing through a tube.—**tu·bu·lar·ly,** adv.—**tu·bu·lar·i·ty,** n.

tu·bule, tō'būl, tū'būl, n. [L. tubulus, dim. of tubus, E. tube.] A small tube; a minute tubular structure.

tu·bu·li·flo·rous, tō"bya·li·flōr'us, tō"bya·li·flȧr'us, tū"bya·li·flōr'us, tū"bya·li·flȧr'us, a. [L. tubulus, tubule, and flos (flor-), flower.] Bot. having the corolla tubular in all the perfect flowers of a head, as certain composite plants.

tu·bu·lous, tō'bya·lus, tū'bya·lus, a. Having the form of a tube; tubular; containing or composed of tubes; bot. containing tubular flowers.—**tu·bu·lous·ly,** adv.

tu·bu·lure, tō'bya·lėr, tū'bya·lėr, n. [Fr., < L. tubulus, E. tubule.] A short tubular opening, as in a glass jar or at the top of a retort.

tu·chun, dö'jyn', n. Chin. hist. A provincial military governor; a warlord.

tuck, tuk, v.t. [M.E. tukken, pull, pluck, tuck up; = M.L.G. tucken = G. zucken, pluck, jerk.] To pull up into a fold or a folded arrangement; to thrust the edge or end of, as a garment or covering, closely into place between retaining parts or things, followed by in or up; as, to tuck in one's shirt; to cover snugly; to thrust into a close, concealing, or safe place; as, to tuck money into a purse; to sew tucks in; colloq. to eat or drink, followed by in or away; as, to tuck away a whole pie.—v.i. To draw together; contract; to make tucks.—n. A tucked piece or part; a fold stitched in fabric or a garment to decorate or to control the fit; naut. that part of a vessel where the after ends of the outside planking unite at the sternpost; Brit. slang, food, esp. sweets or pastries.

tuck, tuk, n. [< Fr. estoc, It. stocco, a rapier, < G. stock, a stick.] Archaic, a rapier.

tuck·a·hoe, tuk'a·hō", n. [N. Amer. Ind.] An edible underground fungus, Poria cocos, occurring in tuberlike masses on the roots of trees in the southern U.S. Also **In·di·an Bread.**

tuck·er, tuk'ėr, n. One who or that which tucks; a device in a sewing machine for making tucks; a piece of linen, muslin, or other material worn by women about the neck and shoulders.

tuck·er, tuk'ėr, v.t. [Cf. tuck.] Colloq. to weary, tire, or exhaust, often with out.

tuck·er-bag, tuk'ėr·bag, n. Aust. a bag used by bush travelers or outdoors men to carry food.

tuck·et, tuk'it, n. [< It. toccata, a prelude, < toccare, to touch.] A flourish on a trumpet; a fanfare.

tuck-point, tuk'point", v.t. To fill or finish, as the mortar joints in masonry work, with a fillet of fine mortar or putty.—**tuck-point·er,** n.—**tuck point·ing,** n.

tuck-shop, tuk'shop", n. Brit. slang, a shop for pastries or sweets.

Tu·dor, tō'dėr, tū'dėr, a. Of or pertaining to the line of English sovereigns which reigned from 1485 to 1603; designating, relating to, or characteristic of various facets of this period, esp. the architecture.

Tu·dor arch, n. A distinctive four-centered arch of flattened appearance.

Tues·day, tōz'dē, tōz'dā, tūz'dē, tūz'dā, n. [O.E. Tiwesdaeg, that is, Tiw's day, the day of Tiw, the northern Mars, or god of war; so Icel. týsdagr, tyrsdagr, Sw. tisdag, Dan. tirsdag, G. dienstag. Cf. Thursday = Thor's day.] The third day of the week; the day following Monday.—**Tues·days,** adv.

tu·fa, tō'fa, tū'fa, n. [It. tufa, tufo, < L. tofus, tophus.] Geol. A variety of porous limestone deposited by springs; tuff.—**tu·fa·ceous,** tō·fā'shus, tū·fā'shus, a.

tuff, tuf, n. [Fr. tuf, < It. tufo.] Geol. a fragmental rock consisting of the smaller kinds of volcanic detritus, usu. more or less stratified.—**tuff·a·ceous,** tuf·ā'shus, a.

tuf·fet, tuf'it, n. A tuft, as of grass; a low stool or hassock.

tuft, tuft, n. [Appar. < O.Fr. tuffe, toffe (Fr. touffe), tuft, prob. from Teut. and akin to E. top.] A bunch or clump of small, usu. soft and flexible things, as feathers, hair, and the like, fixed at the base and with the upper ends loose; any like cluster; a clump of threads tightly drawn through a mattress, cushion, quilt, or upholstery at regular intervals, to hold the stuffing secure, or as a decoration.—v.t. To furnish with or arrange in a tuft or tufts; to decorate with a tuft or tufts.—v.i. To form a tuft or tufts; to grow in tufts.—**tuft·er,** n.—**tuft·y,** tuf'tē, a.—**tuftier, tuftiest.**

tug, tug, v.t.—tugged, tugging. [M.E. tuggen, toggen; akin to E. tow.] To pull at with force or effort; to move by pulling forcibly; drag or haul; to tow, as a vessel, by means of a tugboat.—v.i. To pull with force or effort; as, to tug at a heavy carton; to strive hard; to labor or toil.—n. The act of tugging; a strong pull; a strenuous contest; a struggle; a tugboat; a harness trace; that by which something is pulled, as a rope, chain, or strap.—**tug·ger,** n.

tug·boat, tug'bōt", n. A small, strongly built, and powerful boat designed for pulling or pushing other craft, as ocean-going vessels or barges. Also **towboat.**

tug of war, n. An athletic contest between two teams pulling at the opposite ends of a rope, each team endeavoring to drag the other over a line marked between them; a severe or critical struggle, as between contending forces.

tu·i, tō'ē, n. Ornith. a New Zealand honey eater, Prosthemadera novae-zealandiae, a glossy black bird with white spottings on neck, breast, throat, and wings. Also **par·son bird.**

tuille, twēl, n. [O.Fr. *tieule* (Fr. *tuile*), tile, < L. *tegula*, E. *tile.*] One of the steel plates protecting the thighs in a suit of armor.

tu·i·tion, tö·ish′an, tū·ish′an, n. [L. *tuitio, tuitionis,* guardianship, < *tueor, tuisus,* to see, to look to.] The amount charged for instruction at an educational institution; instruction; the profession of teaching.— **tu·i·tion·al, tu·i·tion·ar·y,** a.

tu·la·re·mi·a, tu·la·rae·mi·a, tö″la··rē′mē·a, n. [N.L., < E. *Tulare,* county in California, and Gr. *aima,* blood.] A disease of rabbits, squirrels, and other rodents, caused by a bacterium, *Pasteurella tularensis,* transmitted to man by insects or by the handling of infected animals, and causing prolonged intermittent fever and swelling of the lymph nodes. Also *rabbit fever.*— **tu·la·re′mic,** a.

tu·le, tö′lē, *Sp.* tö′le, n. pl. **tu·les,** tö′lēz, *Sp.* tö′les. [Mex.] Either of two large bulrushes, *Scirpus lacustris,* or *S. acutus,* which in California and adjacent regions occupy water-inundated land and marshes.

tu·lip, tö′lip, tū′lip, n. [= Fr. *tulipe,* earlier *tulipan,* < Turk. *tulband,* for Pers. *dulband,* turban (cf. *turban*); from the shape of the flower.] Any of the liliaceous plants constituting the genus *Tulipa,* cultivated in many varieties, and having large, showy, usu. erect, cup-shaped or bell-shaped flowers of various colors; a flower or bulb of such a plant.—**tu·lip·like,** a.

tu·lip·o·ma·ni·a, tö″li·po·mā′nē·a, tö″li·po·mān′ya, tū″li·po·mā′nē·a, tu″li·po·mān′ya, n. A passion or mania for the cultivation or acquisition of tulip bulbs, esp. that occurring during the early 17th century in Holland.

tu·lip tree, n. A N. American magnoliaceous tree, *Liriodendron tulipifera,* with tuliplike flowers and a wood that is used in cabinetwork, furniture, and other wood products. Also **tu·lip pop·lar,** *yellow poplar.*

tu·lip·wood, tö′lip·wụd, tū′lip·wụd″, n. The wood of the tulip tree; whitewood; any of various striped or variegated woods of other trees; any of these trees.

tulle, töl, *Fr.* tӱl, n. A thin, delicate net of silk, nylon, or rayon, orig. manufactured in France, and used for millinery, veils, evening gowns, and ballet costumes.

tul·li·bee, tul′i·bē″, n. Any of various whitefishes, esp. the edible, commercial cisco common in the Great Lakes.

tum·ble, tum′bl, v.i.—**tumbled, tumbling.** [M.E. *tumblen,* freq. < O.E. *tumbian,* dance, tumble: cf. O.Fr. *tumber,* let fall, overturn, Fr. *tomber,* fall (< L.G.).] To perform leaps, springs, somersaults, or other feats of bodily agility; to roll about; to toss; to fall headlong or precipitately; to stumble or fall over; to fall or collapse, as a structure, government, or the like; to fall suddenly or rapidly, as prices or stocks; to lose a position of authority; as, to *tumble* from power; to go or come, in a precipitate or hasty way; to come upon by chance; *colloq.* to become suddenly aware of some fact or circumstance, followed by *to.*—v.t. To disorder by or as by tossing about; to rumple; to induce tumbling or falling; to throw over or down; to throw, cast, put or send in a precipitate, hasty, or rough manner; to subject to the action of a tumbling barrel.—n. An act of tumbling; a fall; a downfall; a tumbled condition; a confused heap; *colloq.* an indication of interest and encouragement.

tum·ble·bug, tum′bl·bug″, n. Any of various dung beetles which roll up globular masses of dung in which they deposit their eggs and in which the larvae develop.

tum·ble-down, tum′bl·doun″, a. In a tumbling or falling condition; dilapidated; rickety.

tum·bler, tum′blėr, n. One who or that which tumbles; one who performs leaps, somersaults, and other bodily feats; one of a breed of dogs resembling small greyhounds, formerly used in hunting rabbits; one of a breed of domestic pigeons having the habit of turning over backward in their flight; a glass with a flat bottom and without a stem or handle; a toy, usu. representing a fat, squatting figure, with a weighted and rounded base, so as to rock when touched; a tumbling box; the revolving drum in a clothes dryer; in a lock, any locking or checking part which, when in the proper position, prevents the movement of the bolt, and which, when lifted or released by the action of a key allows the bolt to move; in a gunlock, a leverlike piece which by the action of a spring forces the hammer forward when released by the trigger; a tumbrel or cart. *Mach.* a device in a selective transmission which moves a gear into place; a cam.

tum·ble·weed, tum′bl·wēd″, n. Any of various plants, esp. *Amarantus graecizans,* having a branching upper part which in autumn becomes detached from the roots and is driven about by the wind.

tum·bling, tum′bling, n. Acrobatics; leaps, springs, somersaults and other feats of bodily agility performed as a skill in sports competition or for exercise.

tum·bling bar·rel, n. A revolving drum in which articles or substances are tumbled, as for the purpose of polishing, mixing, or coating.

tum·brel, tum·bril, tum′brel, n. [O.Fr. *tumberel* (Fr. *tombereau*), tipcart, < *tumber,* let fall, overturn; cf. *tumble.*] A tipcart or dump cart, esp. one for carrying dung; one of the carts used during the French Revolution to convey victims to the guillotine.

tu·me·fac·tion, tö″me·fak′shan, tū″me··fak′shan, n. [Fr. *tuméfaction.*] The act of tumefying or swelling, or the state of being tumefied; a swollen part; a swelling.— **tu·me·fac·tive,** a.

tu·me·fy, tö′me·fī, v.t., v.i.—*tumefied, tumefying.* [Fr. < L. *tumefacere,* < *tumere,* swell, and *facere,* make.] To become or cause to become swollen or tumid.

tu·mes·cent, tö·mes′ent, tū·mes′ent, a. [L. *tumescens* (-ent-), ppr. of *tumescere,* begin to swell, < *tumere,* swell.] Becoming swollen; swelling; slightly tumid.—**tu··mes·cence,** n.

tu·mid, tö′mid, tū′mid, a. [L. *tumidus,* < *tumere,* to swell, < root *tu,* producing also *tumulus, tumultus, tumor, tuber,* etc. (whence *tumult, tumor,* etc.). Akin *tomb.*] Swollen, enlarged, or distended, as a body organ or part; protuberant; pompous or bombastic in language or style.—**tu·mid··i·ty, tu·mid·ness,** n.—**tu·mid·ly,** adv.

tum·my, tum′ē, n. pl. **tum·mies.** *Colloq.* stomach.

tu·mor, *Brit.* **tu·mour,** tö′mėr, tū′mėr, n. [L. *tumor,* < *tumere,* swell; cf. *tumid.*] *Pathol.* an abnormal or morbid swelling in any part of the body; a more or less circumscribed morbid growth of new tissue, not due to inflammation, and differing in structure from the part in which it grows. A swollen part.—**tu·mor·ous,** a.—**tu··mor·like,** a.

tump, tump, tụmp, n. [Cf. W. *twmp,* round mass, hillock.] *Brit. dial.* A hillock; a mound; a heap; a clump, as of trees or other vegetation growing in a swamp.

tump·line, tump′lin″, n. [With *tump-* prob. of Algonquian origin.] A strap passing across the forehead or chest, helping to support a pack carried on the back.

tu·mult, tö′mult, tū′mult, n. [L. *tumultus,* < *tumere,* to swell.] The commotion, disturbance, or agitation of a multitude; an uproar; violent commotion or agitation, with confusion of sounds; irregular or confused motion; an uprising or riot; emotional or mental agitation.

tu·mul·tu·ar·y, tö·mul′chö·er″ē, tū··mul′chö·er″ē, a. [L. *tumultuarius.*] Tumultuous; disorderly; confused; unsystematic.

tu·mul·tu·ous, tö·mul′chö·us, tū·mul′chö·us, a. [Fr. *tumultueux,* < L. *tumultuosus.*] Full of or marked by tumult, violent disorder, or uproar; making a tumult or uproar; turbulent or riotous; loud and confused, as sounds or cries; rough or tempestuous, as waters or winds; disturbed or agitated, as the mind or feelings.—**tu·mul·tu·ous·ly,** adv.—**tu·· mul·tu·ous·ness,** n.

tu·mu·lus, tö′mya·lus, tū′mya·lus, n. pl. **tu·mu·lus·es, tu·mu·li,** tö′mya·lī″, tū′mya·lī″. [L., mound, esp. sepulchral mound, < *tumere,* swell: cf. *tumid* and *tomb.*] A mound or elevation, esp. of artificial origin; such a mound, raised over or enclosing a tomb or sepulchral chamber; a barrow.

tun, tun, n. [O.E. *tunne* = D. *ton* = G. *tonne,* tun: cf. O.Fr. Fr. *tonne,* tun, and E. *tunnel.*] A large cask for holding liquids, esp. wine, ale, or beer; a measure of liquid capacity, usu. equivalent to 252 gallons.— v.t.—*tunned, tunning.*

tu·na, tö′na, n. pl. **tu·na, tu·nas.** Any of various large game and food fishes, as the bluefin tuna, the yellowfin tuna, and the albacore, belonging to the mackerel family and found in warm waters of the Atlantic Ocean, Pacific Ocean, and the Mediterranean Sea; also *tunny.* The processed flesh of these fish, used as food; also **tu·na fish.**

tu·na, tö′na, tū′na, n. [Sp.; from Haitian.] Any of various prickly pears, esp. an erect, treelike species, *Opuntia tuna,* a native of Mexico and the West Indies, bearing a sweet, edible fruit; the fruit itself.

tun·a·ble, tune·a·ble, tö′na·bl, tū′na·bl, a. Capable of being tuned; in tune.— **tun·a·ble·ness, tune·a·ble·ness,** n.—**tun·· a·bly, tune·a·bly,** adv.

tun·dra, tun′dra, tụn′dra, n. [Russ.] One of the vast level or rolling treeless plains of the arctic regions of Europe, Asia, and N. America, having the ground frozen beneath the surface even in summer.

tune, tön, tūn, n. [M.E. *tune,* var. of *tone,* E. *tone.*] A pleasing rhythmical succession of musical sounds; an air or melody, with or without the harmony accompanying it; a musical setting of a hymn or psalm, usu. in four-part harmony; the state of being in the proper pitch; agreement in pitch, unison, or harmony; as, many voices or instruments sounding in *tune*; accord or harmony in relationships; correct adjustment, as of wireless instruments or circuits with respect to frequency.—v.t.—*tuned, tuning.* To adjust the tones of, as of a musical instrument, to a correct or given standard of pitch; to put in tune; to adapt the voice or a song to a particular tone or to the expression of a particular feeling; to put into a proper or a particular condition or mood; to bring into harmony; to adjust mechanisms or motors into proper condition. *Radio,* to adjust, as a circuit, so as to bring into resonance with another circuit or a given frequency; to establish contact with, as a source of transmission, with *in.*—v.i. To put a musical instrument in tune; to sound or be in harmony; to give forth a musical sound. —**call the tune,** to make final decisions or to control.—**change one's tune,** to change one's stated opinions or actions.—**sing a dif·fer·ent tune,** to alter behavior or ideas.

—to the tune of, *colloq.* at the cost of, as: She wrecked her car *to the tune of* a thousand dollars.—**tune in,** *radio,* to adjust a receiving apparatus so as to accord in frequency with a sending apparatus whose signals are to be received.—**tune out,** *radio,* to shut out the signals of a sending station by altering the frequency of the circuit or circuits of a receiving apparatus.—**tune up,** *mus.* To bring a musical instrument to the proper pitch; to put in tune; *mech.* to put a machine or motor into proper working condition.

tune·ful, tōn′fưl, tūn′fưl, *a.* Full of tune or melody; melodious; producing musical sounds.—**tune·ful·ly,** *adv.*—**tune·ful·ness,** *n.*

tune·less, tōn′lis, tūn′lis, *a.* Without tune or melody; unmelodious or unmusical; producing no music; silent.

tun·er, tō′nẽr, tū′nẽr, *n.* A person or thing that tunes; one whose occupation is the tuning of musical instruments; *radio,* a receiver part which can be adjusted to pick up a particular signal or frequency.

tune-up, tōn′up″, tūn′up″, *n.* The process of putting a machine or motor in working order.

tung oil, tung′ oil″, *n.* A yellow to brown pungent oil processed from the seeds of the Chinese tung tree, *Aleurites fordii,* used as a drying agent in varnishes and paints and in waterproofing.

tung·state, tung′stāt, *n.* *Chem.* a salt of tungstic acid.

tung·sten, tung′sten, *n.* [Sw. *tungsten,* < *tung,* heavy, and *sten,* stone.] *Chem.* a rare, metallic element having a bright-gray color, a metallic luster, and a high melting point and found in wolframite, tungstite, and scheelite: used in the manufacture of high-speed steel tools, electric lamp filaments, and other products. Sym. W, at. no. 74, at. wt. 183.85. Also *wolfram.* See Periodic Table of Elements.—**tung·sten·ic,** tung·sten′ik, *a.*

tung·sten lamp, *n.* An incandescent electric lamp in which the filament is made of tungsten.

tung·sten steel, *n.* A hard steel alloy containing tungsten.

tung·stic, tung′stik, *a.* *Chem.* of or containing tungsten, esp. with a valence of six.

tung·stic ac·id, *n.* *Chem.* A yellowish acid, H_2WO_4, produced by combining tungstic trioxide, WO_3, with water; a whitish acid, $H_2WO_4 \cdot H_2O$, produced by combining tungstate solutions with acid.

tung·stite, tung′stīt, *n.* *Chem.* native tungsten trioxide, WO_3, a yellow or yellowish-green mineral occurring usu. in a powdered form. Also **tung·stic o·cher.**

tung tree, tung′ trē″, *n.* Any of various trees, genus *Aleurites,* in the spurge family, the seeds of which yield tung oil, esp. *Aleurites fordii.*

Tun·gus·ic, tựn·gụz′ik, *a.* Of or pertaining to the Tunguses, a Mongoloid people of eastern Siberia; noting or pertaining to a division of the Ural-Altaic family of languages including Tungus and Manchu. Also **Tun·gus·i·an,** tựn·gụ′zē·an.—*n.* The language of the Tunguses; the Tungusic division of the Ural-Altaic family of languages. Also **Tun·gus·i·an.**

tu·nic, tō′nik, tū′nik, *n.* [L. *tunica,* undergarment, integument, membrane.] A garment like a shirt or gown, worn by both sexes among the ancient Greeks and Romans; a woman's garment, either loose or close-fitting, extending below the waist and over the skirt; *chiefly Brit.* a body coat worn as part of a military or other uniform; *eccles.* a tunicle. *Anat., zool.* any covering or investing membrane or part, as of an organ; also *tunica.* *Bot.* a natural integument or seed coat; also *tunica.*

tu·ni·ca, tō′ni·ka, tū′ni·ka, *n.* pl. **tu·ni·cae,** tō′ni·sē″, tū′ni·sē″. [L.] *Anat., biol.* a tunic.

tu·ni·cate, tō′ni·kit, tō′ni·kãt″, tū′ni·kit, tū′ni·kãt″, *a.* [L. *tunicatus,* pp. of *tunicare,* clothe with a tunic, < *tunica,* E. *tunic.*] Having a tunic or covering; *zool.* of or relating to a small marine chordate, subphylum *Tunicata,* having a cylindrical body resembling a sac covered with a thick membrane or tunic; *bot.* having or consisting of a series of concentric layers, as a bulb.—*n.* *Zool.* a tunicate animal.—**tu·ni·cat·ed,** *a.*

tu·ni·cle, tō′ni·kl, tū′ni·kl, *n.* [L. *tunicula,* dim. of *tunica,* E. *tunic.*] *Eccles.* a vestment worn over the alb by subdeacons, as at the celebration of the Mass, and also by bishops. Also *tunic.*

tun·ing fork, *n.* A steel instrument with two prongs producing a musical sound of a certain fixed pitch when set in vibration, and serving as a guide to tune musical instruments.

Tu·ni·sian, tō·nē′zhan, tō·nē′shan, tō·nizh′an, tō·nish′an, *a.* Of or pertaining to the republic of Tunisia, in northern Africa, or to Tunis, its capital city; of or pertaining to the inhabitants of Tunis or Tunisia or to their language.—*n.* A resident or native of Tunis or Tunisia; the language of this area.

tun·nel, tun′el, *n.* [O.Fr. Fr. *tonnelle,* arbor, semicircular vault, < *tonne,* tun, large cask, akin to E. *tun.*] A subterranean passage; a roadway beneath the ground, as through a hill or mountain, or under the bed of a stream, esp. one for automobiles or trains; an approximately horizontal passage, as in a mine; the burrow of an animal.—*v.t.* *tunneled, tunneling,* Brit. *tunnelled, tunnelling.* To make or form like a tunnel; as, to *tunnel* a passage under a river; to make or form a tunnel through or under; to perforate, as with tunnels; as, wood *tunneled* by shipworms.—*v.i.* To make a tunnel or tunnels; as, to *tunnel* through the Alps.—**tun·nel·er,** Brit. **tun·nel·ler,** *n.*—**tun·nel·like,** *a.*

tun·ny, tun′ē, *n.* pl. **tun·ny, tun·nies.** [It. *tonno,* Fr. *thon,* < L. *thynnus,* < Gr. *thynnos,* a tunny, < *thynō,* to dart.] A tuna.

tup, tup, *n.* [M.E. *tuppe, tupe;* origin uncertain.] *Chiefly Brit.* The male of the sheep; a ram.—*v.t.*—*tupped, tupping.* *Chiefly Brit.* of the ram, to copulate with.—*v.i.* *Chiefly Brit.* of the ram, to copulate with the ewe.

tup, tup, *n.* The striking head of a power-operated hammer.

tu·pe·lo, tō′pe·lō″, *n.* pl. **tu·pe·los.** [N. Amer. Ind.] Any of several trees of the family *Nyssaceae,* genus *Nyssa,* as *N. sylvatica,* the black gum or sour gum found in N. America, and *N. aquatica,* found only in the swamps of the southern U.S.; the wood of these trees, often used commercially, as for flooring.

Tu·pi·an, tō·pē′an, *a.* Of or pertaining to a tribe or a widespread group of tribes of S. American Indians of a distinct linguistic stock, believed to have lived orig. along the lower Amazon, but afterward extending southward along the Brazilian coast and through Brazil, Paraguay, and Uruguay; of or pertaining to the language of these Indians.—*n.*—**Tu·pi,** tō·pē′, tō′pē, *n.* pl. **Tu·pis, Tu·pi.** A member of a Tupian tribe; the language of the Tupian Indians.

Tu·pi-Gua·ra·ni·an, tō′pē·gwa·rä′nē·an, *a.* Pertaining to a family of Indian languages indigenous to central S. America.—*n.* This family of languages. Also **Tu·pi-Gua·ra·ni,** tō·pē′gwär″a·nē′, tō′pē·gwär″a·nē′.

tuque, tök, tūk, *n.* [Canadian Fr., for Fr. *toque.*] A knitted cap resembling a stocking in shape, worn in Canada for winter sports.

tu quo·que, tö kwō′kwē, tū kwō′kwē, L. tö kwō′kwe, *n.* [L., 'thou too.'] A retort

charging an accuser with a fault or crime similar or identical to that with which he has charged his adversary.

Tu·ra·ni·an, tụ·rä′nē·an, tū·rä′nē·an, *a.* [Pers. *Tūrān,* name of a region of Asia northeast of Iran (Persia).] Belonging or pertaining to a group of Asiatic peoples or languages comprising all or nearly all those which are neither Aryan nor Semitic.—*n.* A member of any of the races speaking a Turanian, esp. a Ural-Altaic, language.

tur·ban, tụr′ban, *n.* [Fr. *turban,* < Turk. *tulband, dulbend,* < Pers. *dulband,* turban: cf. *tulip.*] A headdress of Mohammedan origin worn by men of eastern Mediterranean and Oriental countries, consisting of a long scarf of silk, linen, or cotton, wound directly around the head or around a cap; a headdress resembling this; a small hat, either brimless or with the brim turned up close against the crown, worn by women and children.—**tur·baned,** *a.*

tur·ba·ry, tụr′ba·rē, *n.* pl. **tur·ba·ries.** [L.L. *turbaria,* < O.H.G. *turba,* E. *turf.*] A place where turf or peat is dug; *law,* the right or liberty of cutting turf from public or private lands.

tur·bel·lar·i·an, tụr″be·lâr′ē·an, *a.* [N.L. *Turbellaria,* pl., < L. *turbella,* bustle, stir, dim. of *turba,* disorder, tumult; from the currents produced in water by their vibratile cilia.] Belonging to the *Turbellaria,* a class of platyhelminths or flatworms, mostly aquatic and having cilia whose motions produce small currents in water.—*n.* A turbellarian platyhelminth.

tur·bid, tụr′bid, *a.* [L. *turbidus,* < *turba,* a crowd, or *turbare,* to trouble (as in *disturb, perturb, turbulent*).] Having the lees or sediment disturbed; muddy; foul with extraneous matter; not clear; muddled or confused.—**tur·bid·i·ty,** tụr·bid′i·tē, **tur·bid·ness,** *n.*—**tur·bid·ly,** *adv.*

tur·bi·dim·e·ter, tụr″bi·dim′i·tẽr, *n.* A device used to measure a liquid's turbidity. —**tur·bi·di·met·ric,** tụr″bi·di·me′trik, *a.*—**tur·bi·di·met·ri·cal·ly,** *adv.*—**tur·bi·dim·e·try,** *n.*

tur·bi·nal, tụr′bi·nal, *a.* [L. *turbo* (*turbin-*), top.] Top-shaped; spiral; scroll-like; turbinate.—*n.* *Anat.* a turbinate bone.

tur·bi·nate, tụr′bi·nit, tụr′bi·nāt″, *a.* [L. *turbinatus,* < *turbo.*] Shaped like a spinning top; inversely conical; spiral, as some shells; scroll-like or whorled; *anat.* noting or pertaining to certain scroll-like spongy bones of the nasal passages in the higher vertebrates. Also **tur·bi·nat·ed.**—*n.* A turbinate shell; *anat.* a turbinate bone.—**tur·bi·na·tion,** *n.*

tur·bine, tụr′bin, tụr′bīn, *n.* [Fr. *turbine,* < L. *turbo* (*turbin-*), something that whirls, whirlwind, top, spindle, < *turbare,* disturb.] Any of a class of engines which deliver power created by a continuous flow or jets of steam, air, water, or other liquids, against the curved blades or vanes of a rotor or series of rotors.

tur·bit, tụr′bit, *n.* [Origin unknown.] One of a breed of domestic pigeons with a stout, roundish body, a short head and beak, and a ruffled breast and neck.

tur·bo, tụr′bō, *n.* pl. **tur·bos.** A turbine, as in a turbojet airplane; a turbosupercharger.

tur·bo·car, tụr′bō·kär″, *n.* An automotive vehicle, esp. a racing car, powered by a gas turbine.

tur·bo·charg·er, tụr″bō·chär′jẽr, *n.* *Aeron.* a turbosupercharger.

tur·bo·fan, tụr′bō·fan″, *n.* *Aeron.* the fan or fans driven by a turbine in a ducted fan jet engine; a turbofan engine.

tur·bo·jet, tụr′bō·jet″, *n.* *Aeron.* a turbojet engine; an airplane propelled by a turbojet engine.

tur·bo·jet en·gine, *n.* *Aeron.* an airplane engine consisting of an air intake, a compressor driven by a turbine, a combustion chamber, and a cone-shaped exhaust from which the blast of a jet of hot gases produced in the combustion chamber causes a thrust.

tur·bo·prop, tur′bō·prop″, *n. Aeron.* A turbo-propeller engine; an airplane with turbo-propeller engines.

tur·bo·pro·pel·ler en·gine, tur′bō·pro·pel′ẽr en′jin, *n. Aeron.* a jet engine which provides power chiefly by a turbine-driven propeller.

tur·bo·ram·jet en·gine, tur′bō·ram′jet″ en″jin, *n. Aeron.* a jet engine capable of operating as a turbojet engine or a ramjet engine.

tur·bo·su·per·charg·er, tur′bō·sō′pẽr·chär″jẽr, *n. Aeron.* a supercharger operated by a turbine which is powered by the exhaust gases of the engine.—**tur·bo·su·per·charged**, tur″bō·sō′pẽr·chärjd″, *a.*

tur·bot, tur′bot, *n.* pl. **tur·bot, tur·bots.** [O.Fr. *tourbout* (Fr. *turbot*): origin uncertain.] A large European flatfish, *Psetta maxima,* much esteemed as food; any of various similar flatfishes, as certain flounders.

tur·bu·lence, tur′byạ·lens, *n.* A turbulent state or condition; *meteor.* an irregular condition of the atmosphere, characterized by updrafts, downdrafts, and gusts; *phys.* a state of fluid flow in which the instantaneous velocities and pressures exhibit irregular and random fluctuations, as produced by an obstruction or friction. Also **tur·bu·len·cy.**

tur·bu·lent, tur′byạ·lent, *a.* [L. *turbulentus,* < *turba,* disorder, tumult, disturbance: cf. *trouble* and *turbid.*] Disposed or given to violent disturbances, disorder, or agitation; tumultuous; obstreperous, unruly, or insubordinate.—**tur·bu·lent·ly,** *adv.*

tur·bu·lent flow, *n.* The motion of a fluid where velocity and pressure are not constant at any given point; *aerodynamics,* the airflow around a wing or other airfoil in which the layers of air travel at different speeds involving lateral movements, with resulting variations in pressure.

Tur·co·man, tur′kō·man, *n.* pl. **Tur·co·mans.** Turkoman.

tu·reen, tụ·rēn′, tū·rēn′, *n.* [< Fr. *terrine,* a tureen, lit. 'an earthen vessel,' < *terre* = L. *terra,* earth.] A rather large, deep, covered vessel for holding and serving soup or other food.

turf, turf, *n.* pl. **turfs,** *Brit.* **turves.** [O.E. *turf* = D. *turf* = O.H.G. *zurf* = Icel. *torf,* turf, peat: cf. *turbary.*] The covering of grass and other plants with their matted roots forming the upper or surface layer of certain land; a piece cut from this; sod; a block of peat, esp. to be burned as fuel; a grass course or dirt track used for racing horses, usu. preceded by *the*; the racing of horses, preceded by *the*; *slang,* the territory ruled by gangsters or youthful street gangs. —*v.t.* To cover, as barren ground, with turf or sod.—**turf·y,** tur′fē, *a.*—**turfier, turfiest.**

turf·man, turf′man, *n.* pl. **turf·men.** A man interested in or devoted to horse racing.

tur·ges·cent, tur·jes′ent, *a.* [L. *turgescens.*] Growing turgid; in a swelling state.— **tur·ges·cence, tur·ges·cen·cy,** *n.*

tur·gid, tur′jid, *a.* [L. *turgidus,* < *turgeo.*] Swollen; distended beyond its natural state; inflated; bombastic or pompous; as, a *turgid* style.—**tur·gid·i·ty, tur·gid·ness,** tur·jid′i·tē, *n.*—**tur·gid·ly,** *adv.*

tur·gor, tur′gẽr, *n.* [L.L. < L. *turgere,* swell out.] The state of being swollen or filled out; *plant physiol.* the normal distention or rigidity of plant cells, resulting from the pressure exerted from within by the watery contents against the cell walls;

physiol. the normal fullness or pressure of animal cells.

tur·key, tur′kē, *n.* pl. **tur·keys, tur·key.** [So called because it was erroneously believed to have come from *Turkey.*] A large gallinaceous bird, *Meleagris gallopava,* native to N. America and domesticated in much of the world, having a bare head and red, yellow, and brown plumage; the bird's flesh, eaten as food; *slang,* an unsuccessful stage production; *bowling slang,* three strikes in a row.—**talk tur·key,** *colloq.* to discuss a situation bluntly.

tur·key buz·zard, *n.* A common species of the vulture family, *Cathartes aura,* somewhat resembling a turkey.

tur·key cock, *n.* A male turkey; *fig.* a conceited, vain man.

Tur·key red, *n.* [Because orig. produced by madder from Turkey.] A brilliant red color from alizarin, now produced synthetically; cotton fabric of such a color.

tur·key shoot, *n.* A contest of riflery using turkeys as targets and usu. as prizes.

tur·key trot, *n.* A round dance, danced by couples properly to ragtime, the step being a springy walk with little or no bending of the knees, and accompanied by a swinging motion of the body with shoulder movements up and down.

Tur·ki, tur′kē, *a.* [Pers. *Turki,* < *Turk,* Turk.] Of or pertaining to the several Turkic languages spoken in central Asia, Turkey, and Iran; of or pertaining to the people speaking them.—*n.*

Tur·kic, tur′kik, *a.* Noting or pertaining to a subdivision of the Altaic family of languages including Turkish; noting or pertaining to the people using these languages. —*n.* The Turkic languages.

Turk·ish, tur′kish, *a.* Of, pertaining to, or derived from the Turks or Turkey; of or pertaining to the Turkic language.—*n.* The language spoken by the Turks, esp. Osmanli.

Turk·ish bath, *n.* A kind of bath in which, after a copious perspiration in a heated room, the body is soaped, washed, massaged, and the like.

Turk·ish de·light, *n.* A rich, fruit-flavored, jellylike confection, usu. cubed and having a coating of fine confectioners' sugar. Also **Turk·ish paste.**

Turk·ish to·bac·co, *n.* A strain of tobacco raised in Greece and Turkey having a fragrant flavor and smell, and used esp. in blending with other cigarette tobaccos.

Turk·ish tow·el, turk·ish tow·el, *n.* A kind of thick cotton towel or toweling with a long nap which is usu. composed of uncut loops.

Turk·ism, tur′kiz·um, *n.* The Turkish way of life, culture, customs, and the like.

Tur·ko·man, tur′kō·man, *n.* pl. **Tur·ko·mans.** [Pers. *Turkuman,* one resembling a Turk.] A member of a Turkic people consisting of a group of tribes which inhabit the Turkmen, Uzbek, and Kazakh republics of the U.S.S.R.; the language of this people. Also *Turcoman.—a.*

Turk's-head, turks′hed″, *n. Naut.* a knot shaped like a turban and made by weaving turns of small cord around a larger rope.

tur·ma·line, tur′ma·lēn″, *n.* Tourmaline.

tur·mer·ic, tur′mẽr·ik, *n.* [Fr. *terre merite,* < L. *terra merita,* a deserving earth, from the earthy appearance of the prized rhizomes.] An East Indian plant of the ginger family, *Curcuma longa,* whose rhizomes are used as a condiment, a yellow dye, and as a chemical test for the presence of alkalis; the powder from this rhizome; one of several similar plants or substances.

tur·moil, tur′moil, *n.* [Origin doubtful; cf. *tumult* and *moil.*] A state or condition of extreme commotion, upset, tumult, or confusion.

turn, turn, *v.t.* [O.E. *tyrnan, turnian,* also O.Fr. *torner, tourner* (Fr. *tourner*), < L. *tornare,* turn in a lathe, round off, < *tornus,* lathe, < Gr. *tórnos,* turner's chisel, akin to *teirein,* rub.] To cause to move around on an axis or about a center; rotate; as, to *turn* a wheel; to cause to move around or partly around, as for opening, closing, or tightening; as, to *turn* a key, door knob, or screw; to change the position of by or as if by rotating; as, to *turn* a box on its side; to reverse the position of; as, to *turn* a page; to bring the under layers of, as sod or soil, to the surface, as in plowing; to reverse, as a garment, so that the inner side becomes the outer; to revolve in the mind or ponder, often with *over*; to twist or sprain; as, to *turn* an ankle while going downstairs; to cause, as the stomach, to feel upset; to shape, as a piece of wood, into rounded form, as on a lathe; to bring into rounded or curved form; to form or express gracefully; as, to *turn* a sentence; to execute, as a cartwheel, by rotating or revolving; to bend back or blunt, as the edge of a knife; to change or alter the nature, character, or appearance of, usu. followed by *in* or *into*; as, to *turn* stocks *into* cash; to change from one language or form of expression to another usu. followed by *into*; as, to *turn* verse *into* prose; to apply to some use or purpose; as, to *turn* something to good use; to direct, avert, aim, or set going toward or away from something specified; as, to *turn* one's eyes from an accident, to *turn* a hose on a burning house, to *turn* one's steps to the north; to change the color of, as leaves; to cause to ferment or become sour; as, milk *turned* by warm weather; to change or reverse the course of; divert; deflect; as, to *turn* an army's flank; to go around, as a corner; to get past; as, to *turn* twenty-one; to cause to go away; send; drive; as, to *turn* a stranger from one's door; to alienate; as, to *turn* a child against his parents; to disturb the mental balance of; distract; infatuate; as to *turn* someone's head; *archaic,* to pervert.—*v.i.* To move around on an axis or about a center; rotate; revolve; to move partly around, as a door on a hinge; to shift about; as, to toss and *turn*; to change or reverse course or direction; as, to *turn* to the right, *turn* to the north; to change position so as to face in a different or the opposite direction; to direct one's thought, attention, or desire toward or away from something; to hinge or depend, usu. followed by *on* or *upon*, as: The question *turns on* a crucial point. To have a sensation of whirling; be affected with giddiness; to take an attitude or policy of hostility or opposition; as, to *turn* against one's friends; to change position in order to resist or attack, as: The animal *turned* on its owner. To change or alter in nature, character, or appearance, followed by *to* or *into*; to change so as to be or become; as, to *turn* pale; to undergo a change of color, as leaves; to become sour or fermented, as milk or wine; to shape material into rounded form on a lathe; to assume a curved form; bend.—*n.* A total or partial rotation; revolution; something that revolves or rotates, as a lathe; the act or an act of changing or reversing course or direction; as, a *turn* to the right; a place or point where such a change occurs; a bend, as on a river or road; an opportunity or time for one of a number of persons acting in rotation or succession; as, a *turn* at bat; round; spell; rounded or curved form; shape, form, mold, or style; as, a happy *turn* of expression; natural inclination, bent, tendency, or aptitude; as, of a philosophical *turn* of mind; change or a change in nature, condition, circumstance, or character; as a *turn* for the better in the weather; direction, drift, or trend; as, a rightward *turn* in his politics; an act of service or disservice; requirement, exigency, or need, as: This will serve your *turn*. A short walk or ride that includes a going and a returning; as, a *turn* in the park; a single round, as of a wound or coiled rope; a passing or twisting of one thing around another, as of a rope around a mast; *mus.* an ornament consisting of a principal tone alternating with two auxiliary tones, one above and the other below the principal tone; *theatr.* a short act or individual performance; *colloq.* a nervous shock, as from fright or astonishment; *stock market,* a transaction including both the sale and purchase of securities; *milit.* a maneuver in drilling by which a formation changes the direction of its front.—**at eve‧ry turn,** everywhere; every time; constantly.—**by turns,** one after another; alternately or in rotation.—**in turn,** in due order of succession.—**on the turn,** at the turning point; on the point of or in process of change or reversal.—**out of turn,** out of due order of succession.—**take turns,** to follow one another, alternately or in rotation.—**to a turn,** to perfection.—**turn an hon‧est dol‧lar,** to earn or gain money by honest means.—**turn one's hand to,** to turn one's energies to; set to work at.—**turn tail,** to run away; flee.

turn‧a‧bout, turn′a‧bout″, *n.* The act or an act of facing another direction or turning about, as in opinion, direction, or allegiance.

turn‧a‧round, turn′a‧round″, *n.* A complete or round trip, as of a vehicle, ship, or aircraft, and the time consumed in such a trip; an area large enough to allow a vehicle to completely turn around; a turnabout.

turn back, *v.t.* To cause to return the same way; to drive back; to fold, as a paper, back on itself.—*v.i.* To return; to be folded back.

turn‧buck‧le, turn′buk″l, *n. Mach.* a link or sleeve with a swivel at one end and an internal screw thread at the other, or with an internal screw thread at each end, used as a means of uniting or coupling and tightening two parts, as the ends of two rods.

turn‧coat, turn′kōt″, *n.* One who changes his party or principles, usu. to opposite or opposing positions; a renegade; a traitor.

turn down, *v.t.* To fold or double down; to diminish the force of, as the volume on a radio; *colloq.* to reject, as a proposal.—**turn‧down,** turn′doun″, *n. Colloq.* a refusal; as, a *turndown* to a request.

turn‧down, turn′doun″, *a.* That is or may be turned down; folded or doubled down; as, a *turndown* collar.

turn‧er, turn′nėr, *n.* One who or that which turns; one who fashions objects on a lathe.

turn‧er, turn′nėr, *n.* [G., < *turnen,* perform gymnastic exercises, < Fr. *tourner,* turn.] A gymnast; a member of a gymnastic society; someone belonging to a turnverein.

turn‧er‧y, turn′ne‧rē, *n. pl.* **turn‧er‧ies.** The art or work of forming objects on a lathe; the articles made on a lathe; the shop where such articles are made.

turn in, *v.t.* To fold or bend inward; to inform on or deliver over; to submit, as a thesis.—*v.i.* To bend or point inward; to turn and enter; *colloq.* to go to bed.

turn‧ing, turn′ning, *n.* The act of someone or something which turns; an act of changing or reversing position; the point of bending or reversal, as in a road; the art or operation of shaping something, as in a lathe.

turn‧ing point, *n.* A point at which a decisive change takes place; a critical point; a crisis; a point at which something turns or changes position or direction.

tur‧nip, turnip, *n.* [Formerly *turnepe,* <

tur- (possibly for *turn,* as suggesting roundness) and *nepe, neep,* turnip.] The thick, fleshy edible root of various cultivated varieties of *Brassica rapa;* any one of these plants.

turn‧key, turn′kē″, *n. pl.* **turn‧keys.** [One who *turns* the *key* in locks.] A person who has charge of the keys of a prison; a jailer.

turn off, *v.t.* To shut off the flow of, as water, by turning a faucet or stopcock; to put out, as an electric light; to deflect, as an insult; *Brit.* to dismiss, as an employee; *slang,* to bore, annoy, or arouse dislike in, as: That viewpoint *turns* me *off.*—*v.i.* To turn and go off, as from one road onto another.—**turn‧off,** turn′af″, turn′of″, *n.* A road or ramp curving off from a main road.

turn on, *v.t.* To bring on the flow of, as by turning a faucet; to switch on, as an electrical device; to produce as if by switching on, as charm; *slang,* to cause to become involved, excited, or interested.—*v.i.* To begin taking a narcotic or psychedelic drug, or smoking marijuana; to be in a state influenced by a narcotic, a psychedelic drug, or marijuana.

turn out, *v.t.* To eject, evict, dismiss, expel, or discharge; to turn off, as an electric light; to produce, esp. with toil or with machinelike speed or frequency; to bend or point outward; to carefully equip, fit out, dress, finish, or supply; to empty by turning inside out.—*v.i.* To prove to be in the result; to issue; to result. *Colloq.* to get out of bed; to appear publicly or assemble, as for a performance or event.

turn‧out, turn′out″, *n.* An instance or act of turning out; the number of persons present at an event or spectacle; an amount produced; output; mode of dress; configuration of equipment or supplies; a short passing lane of a highway; a switching configuration of a railroad track which permits movement of a train to a branching or parallel track. *Brit.* a strike in a labor dispute; a striking worker.

turn o‧ver, *v.t.* To turn, as an object, so that another side or face is uppermost; to hand over; to consider; to transfer; as, to *turn over* the business to someone else; to start, as an automobile motor. *Commerc.* to invest and reacquire, as capital; to buy and later on, sell in the course of business, as goods.—*v.i.* To turn upside down; roll over; capsize; of a motor, to start.

turn‧o‧ver, turn′ō″vėr, *n.* The act or result of turning over; an upending or overthrow; the flow of people through a checkpoint; the replacement rate of employees in a firm or the total number of workers replaced; business volume or rate of sales in a given period; the aggregate number of capital or stock replacements in a given time; the scope of an operation, measured by its rate of processing; a reversal of position or belief; a restructuring of an organization or hierarchy; a triangular filled pastry.—*a.* Able to be turned over, as a cuff.

turn‧pike, turn′pīk″, *n.* [Orig. a turning frame with *pikes* or *spikes* projecting.] A road designed for high-speed travel on which a toll for maintenance is collected at regular intervals; formerly, a movable gate set across a road to stop travelers until a toll was paid; a tollgate.

turn‧sole, turn′sōl″, *n.* [Fr. *tournesol,* < *tourner,* to turn, and L. *sol,* the sun.] Any plant whose flower turns with the sun during the course of one day, as the sunflower.

turn‧spit, turn′spit″, *n.* A rotating spit, as used for roasting meat; a person who turns a spit; a dog used formerly to drive a wheel to turn a spit for roasting.

turn‧stile, turn′stīl″, *n.* A device consisting of a post surmounted by four horizontal arms which revolve as a person pushes by

them, placed in a gateway to control passage through it; such a device used at entrances to public transportation to admit a passenger on payment of a fare or to confine his movement to a single direction, as at an exit.

turn‧stone, turn′stōn″, *n.* Any of several birds of the plover family, genus *Arenaria,* so called because they turn over small stones in search of worms and other small animals, esp. *A. interpres.*

turn‧ta‧ble, turn′tā″bl, *n.* The circular revolving platform of a record player; *rail.* a large platform used for reversing locomotives or cars on the same track or to another. Any rotating stand, such as used in pottery making or for displaying objects.

turn to, *v.i.* To apply or direct oneself to some task; to work vigorously.

turn up, *v.t.* To fold up or over, esp. in order to shorten, as a garment; to give an upward turn or direction to; to bring, as sod or soil, to the surface; to dig up; to turn or to place with the face upward, as a playing card; to find; to increase the force of by turning a handle or similar control.—*v.i.* To be directed upward; to make one's appearance; to occur, as: We'll see what *turns up.*

turn‧up, turn′up″, *n.* The act or fact of turning up; that which is turned up or which turns up. *Brit.* a trouser cuff; a fight, a row, or disturbance.—*a.* That is or may be turned up.

turn‧ver‧ein, turn′ve‧rīn″, *G.* tųrn′feR‧ɪn″, *n.* [G., < *turnen,* perform gymnastic exercises, and *verein,* union, society: cf. *turner.*] An association of turners or gymnasts.

tur‧pen‧tine, tur′pen‧tīn″, *n.* [O.Fr. *terbentine* (Fr. *térébenthine*), < M.L. *terebinthina,* prop. fem. of L. *terebinthinus,* of or from the terebinth, E. *terebinthine.*] Any of various oleoresins derived from various coniferous trees and yielding a volatile oil, as oil of turpentine, and a resin when distilled; an oleoresin exuding from the terebinth, *Pistacia terebinthus.*—*v.t.*—*turpentined, turpentining.* To treat with turpentine; to apply turpentine to; to gather or take crude turpentine from.—**oil of tur‧pen‧tine,** a colorless, volatile oil, obtained by distilling the oleoresin of coniferous trees, used in the preparation of paints, varnishes, and the like, and in medicine. Also *spirits of turpentine.*—**tur‧pen‧tin‧ic, tur‧pen‧tin‧ous,** tur′pen‧‐ tin′ik, tur′pen‧tin″us, tur′pen‧ti″nus, *a.*

tur‧pi‧tude, tur′pi‧tōd″, tur′pi‧tūd″, *n.* [L. *turpitudo,* < *turpis,* foul, base.] Inherent baseness or vileness of principle, words, or actions; shameful wickedness; moral depravity.

tur‧quoise, tur‧quois, tur′koiz, tur′kwoiz, *n.* [Fr. *turquoise,* O.Fr. *turquoyse,* orig. a 'Turkish' (stone); because first brought from (or through) Turkey.] A sky-blue or greenish-blue mineral, essentially a hydrous phosphate of aluminum containing a little copper and iron, valuable as a gemstone. A light blue color with a greenish tinge; also **tur‧quoise blue.**

tur‧ret, tur′it, tur′it, *n.* [O.Fr. *tourete,* dim. of *tour,* tower.] A small tower, usu. one forming part of a larger structure; a small tower at an angle of a building, frequently beginning some distance above the ground. *Mach.* an attachment on a lathe or similar machine for holding a number of tools, each of which can be brought to the work by a simple rotation; also **tur‧ret‧head.** *Nav.,* *milit.* a low, towerlike, heavily armored structure, usu. revolving horizontally, within which guns are mounted. A tall structure, usu. moved on wheels, formerly employed in breaching or scaling a fortified place or a wall.—**tur‧ret‧ed,** tur′i‧tid, *a.*

tur′i·tid, *a.* Furnished with a turret or turrets; having a turretlike part or parts; *zool.* having whorls in the form of a long or towering spiral, as certain shells.

tur·tle, tur′tl, *n.* Archaic, turtledove.

tur·tle, tur′tl, *n.* pl. **tur·tles, tur·tle.** [Appar. a corruption of obs. *tortue,* < F. *tortue,* < M.L. *tortuca,* E. *tortoise.*] Any of the *Chelonia,* an order of reptiles having the body enclosed in a shell consisting of a carapace and a plastron, from between which the head, tail, and four legs protrude; an aquatic species, as distinguished from a tortoise, or terrestrial species; the flesh of some edible species of turtle used or prepared for food.—*v.i.*—*turtled, turtling.* To catch turtles; to make a practice or business of catching turtles.—**turn tur·tle,** to capsize.

tur·tle·back, tur′tl·bak″, *n.* Naut. an arched protection erected over the deck of a steamer at the bow and often at the stern, to guard against damage from heavy seas; also **tur·tle·deck.** Archaeol. a rude stone implement having one or both faces slightly convex.

tur·tle·dove, tur′tl·duv″, *n.* [O.E. *turtle,* a corruption of L. *turtur,* a turtledove, whence also D. *tortel,* G. *turtel,* Icel. *turtil.*] An old-world bird of the dove family, *Streptopelia turtur,* smaller than the ordinary domestic pigeon, celebrated in poetry for its cooing and the constancy of its affection. See *mourning dove.*

tur·tle·head, tur′tl·hed″, *n.* Any of the N. American herbs constituting the genus *Chelone,* having large white, red, or purple flowers. Also **snake·head.**

tur·tle·neck, tur′tl·nek″, *n.* A high, rolled-over, tight-fitting collar, found esp. on a sweater; a sweater or shirt having this type of collar.

Tus·can, tus′kan, *a.* Of or pertaining to Tuscany, its dialects, or its people; *arch* noting or pertaining to a classical Roman order of architecture, distinguished by a plain, unfluted column and the absence of decorative detail.—*n.* A native or inhabitant of Tuscany; the form of the Italian language spoken in Tuscany, regarded as the standard form of Italian.

tusch·e, tush, G. tush′e, *n.* Print. a grease-like substance used in the lithographic process for painting a design, which repels water and receives lithographic ink, and used in the silkscreen process and etching as a resistant.

tush, tush, *n.* [A form of *tusk.*] A long pointed tooth; a tusk.—**tushed,** *a.*

tush, tush, *interj.* An exclamation indicating rebuke, impatience, or contempt.

tusk, tusk, *n.* [O.E. *tusc, tux,* a tusk; prob. for *twisc,* < *twá,* two.] The long, pointed, and often protruding tooth on each side of the jaw of certain animals, as in the elephant; the canine tooth of various animals, as the bear, walrus, and hippopotamus; any sharp, tusklike projection; *carp.* a projecting part formed at the end of a piece of wood to fit into a mortise in another piece to form a joint and strengthen its tenon.—*v.t.* To dig, tear, or gore with the tusks or tusk; to furnish with tusks or tusklike projections.—**tusked,** *a.*—**tusk·er,** *n.*—**tusk·like,** *a.*

tusk ten·on, *n.* Carp. a tenon strengthened by having one or more shoulders, steps or tusks on the lower side.

tus·sah, tus′a, *n.* [Hind. *tasar,* shuttle; perh. from the form of the cocoon.] A coarse brown silk obtained from the cocoon of various Asiatic silkworms, as the larvae of *Antheraea mylitta;* a fabric made from this; the silkworm itself, or its moth. Also **tus·sore,** tus′ōr, tus′ar.

tus·sive, tus′iv, *a.* Pathol. of or relating to a cough. Also **tus·sal.**—**tus·sis,** *n.*

tus·sle, tus′l, *v.i.*—*tussled, tussling.* [A form of *tousle,* to pull about roughly.] To struggle; to scuffle; to wrestle.—*n.* A struggle; a conflict; a scuffle.

tus·sock, tus′ok, *n.* [Modified from older *tuske, tushe,* a tuft, a bush; Dan. *dusk,* a tuft, a tassel.] A clump, tuft, or small hillock of grass or sedge; hassock; any tuft, as of hair.—**tus·socked,** tus·sock·y, tus′o·-kē, *a.*

tus·sock moth, *n.* A medium-sized, dull-colored moth of the family *Liparidae,* characterized by larvae with tussocks, or tufts of hairs.

tut, tut, *interj.* An exclamation used to check or rebuke or to express impatience or contempt. Also **tut-tut,** tut′tut′.

tu·te·lage, tōt′e·lij, tūt′e·lij, *n.* [< L. *tutela,* protection, < *tueor,* to defend (whence also *tutor, tuition*).] Guardianship; protection bestowed; the state of being under a guardian or a tutor; instruction; guidance.

tu·te·lar·y, tōt′e·ler″ē, tūt′e·ler″ē, *a.* [L. *tutelaris.*] Having the guardianship or charge of protecting a person, place, or thing; pertaining to guardianship or a guardian.—*n.* pl. **tu·te·lar·ies.** One with tutelary powers, as, a person, deity, saint, or the like. Also **tu·te·lar,** tōt′e·lēr, tūt′e·lēr.

tu·tor, tō′ter, tū′ter, *n.* [O.Fr. *tutour* (Fr. *tuteur*), < L. *tutor,* guardian, < *tueri,* look after, guard, keep.] One employed to instruct another privately in some branch or branches of learning; a private instructor; one of a class of officers in a university or college, esp. at Oxford and Cambridge, England, having immediate supervision, in studies or otherwise, of undergraduates assigned to them; a teacher subordinate to a professor in some American universities and colleges; *law,* the guardian of a boy or girl from birth to puberty.—*v.t.* To act as a tutor to; to teach or instruct, esp. privately; to train, school, or discipline.—*v.i.* To act as a tutor or private instructor; to study under a tutor.—**tu·tor·ship,** *n.*

tu·tor·age, tō′ter·ij, tū′ter·ij, *n.* A tutor's position, function, or authority; a tutoring fee.

tu·to·ri·al, tō·tōr′ē·al, tō·tar′ē·al, tū-tōr′ē·al, tū·tar′ē·al, *a.* Belonging to a tutor or instructor.—*n.* A class given by an instructor or tutor.

tu·toy·er, tō″twä·yā′, tū″twä·yā′, Fr. tY·-twä·yā′, *v.t.*—*tutoyered* or *tutoyed, tutoyering.* Fr. to address with the French familiar second person singular pronouns, *tu, te,* and *toi,* rather than the formal second person plural pronoun, *vous;* to address in a familiar manner.

tut·ti, tō′tē, It. töt′tē, *a.* [It. < L. *totus,* pl. *toti,* all.] Mus. All; pertaining to a direction to every performer to take part in the execution of the passage or movement, esp. after any passage which does not include all instruments.—*n.* pl. **tut·tis.** Mus. A movement or other composition for every performer; the tonal effect of such a performance.

tut·ti-frut·ti, tō·tē·frö′tē, *n.* [It., 'all fruits.'] A preserve of mixed fruits; ice cream or some other confection containing a variety of fruit flavorings or fruits, usu. candied and minced.

tut·ty, tut′ē, *n.* [Fr. *tutie,* Pg. *tutia,* < Ar. *tútiya.*] An impure protoxide of zinc, collected from the chimneys of smelting furnaces, and used as a polishing powder.

tu·tu, tō′tō, Fr. tY·tY′, *n.* pl. **tu·tus,** tō′tōz, Fr. tY·tY′. A full, very short skirt, usu. of layers of tulle or other thin fabric, worn by a ballet dancer.

tu·whit tu·whoo, tu·hwit′ tu·hwō′, tu·-wit′ tu·hwō′, tu·hwit tu·wō′, tu·wit′ tu·wō′, *n., interj.* [Imit.] An owl's cry.

tux·e·do, tuk·sē′dō, *n.* pl. **tux·e·dos.** [For *Tuxedo coat,* named from a country club at Tuxedo Park, N.Y.] (*Often cap.*) A dress coat for evening wear; an entire suit of semi-formal clothing including trousers, a tuxedo jacket, shirt, black bow tie, and vest or cummerbund. Also *dinner jacket,* **tux.**

tu·yère, twē·yâr′, tö·yâr′, twēr·yâr′, Fr. tY·yeR′, *n.* pl. **tu·yères.** [Fr. *tuyère,* akin to *tuyau,* a pipe.] Metal. a nozzle or pipe that forces a blast of air into a blast furnace or forge. Also **tu·yer,** twē·yâr′, tö·yâr′, twēr·yâr′.

TV, tē′vē′, *n.* pl. **TVs, TV's.** Television.

TV din·ner, *n.* A commercially packaged, frozen meal, usu. placed on an aluminum, partitioned tray, that is ready to be served when heated.

twad·dle, twod′l, *n.* [Older form *twattle,* also *twittle, twittle-twattle;* an imit. word like *tattle, twitter,* etc.] Empty, trivial, or silly talk or writing.—*v.i., v.t.*—*twaddled, twaddling.* To talk in a weak, silly, or tedious manner; to prate.—**twad·dler,** *n.*

twain, twān, *a.* [O.E. *tweyne, tweyen, twegen,* < *twá,* two- O.Fris. *twêne,* Dan. *tvende,* G. *zween.*] Archaic, two.—*n.* The two-fathom or twelve-foot mark on a river-boat sounding line; *poet.* a pair.

twang, twang, *v.i.* [Imit. of a resonant sound; akin to *tang.*] To sound with a quick, sharp, vibrating noise; to be released with a sharp, vibrating sound; to speak with a harsh, nasal tone.—*v.t.* To cause to sound with a quick, vibrating noise; to utter with a harsh, nasal tone; to cause to emit a vibrating sound by pulling and suddenly releasing, as a bowstring.—*n.* A sharp, quick, vibrating sound, as of a plucked banjo string; a plucking action; a harsh, nasal tone of voice; a sound similar to this; the speech typical of a region or people, esp. when characterized by nasal intonations.—**twang·y,** twang′e, *a.*

tway·blade, twā′blād″, *n.* Any of various plants of the orchid family of the genus *Liparis,* esp. L. *liliifolia,* characterized by two nearly opposite broad leaves.

tweak, twēk, *v.t.* [O.E. *twiccian,* to twitch = L.G. *twikken,* D. *zwikken,* G. *zwicken;* an older form of *twitch.*] To pinch and pull with a sudden twist and jerk.—*n.* An abrupt, twisting pinch.

tweed, twēd, *n.* [Orig. called *tweels,* that is *twills,* but this name was misread into *tweeds,* when the goods were sent to London, the idea being that they were so called from the river *Tweed.*] A coarse, twilled woolen fabric, used esp. for coats, jackets, and suits; *pl.* clothing made of tweed.—**tweed·y,** twē′dē, *a.*—*tweedier, tweediest.*—**tweed·i·ness,** *n.*

Twee·dle·dum and Twee·dle·dee, twēd″-l·dum′ an twēd″l·dē′, *n.* [Coinage imit. of musical tones < *On the Feuds between Handel and Bononcini* (1723) by John Byrom.] Two nearly identical individuals, groups, or things.

'tween, tween, twēn, *prep.* Poet. contraction of between.

tweet, twēt, *n.* A weak chirping note of a young bird.—*v.i.* To utter weak chirps.

tweet·er, twē′ter, *n.* A small loudspeaker that reproduces high-frequency sounds in high-fidelity audio equipment.

tweez·ers, twē′zerz, *n. pl.* [Formerly *tweezes,* < *tweeze,* a surgeon's box of instruments, a case containing scissors, penknife, or similar articles, < Fr. *étuis,* pl. of *étui,* O.Fr. *estui,* a case or sheath (of Germanic origin).] Small pincers used to pluck out hairs and to pick up or hold small objects. Also **tweez·er, pair of tweez·ers.**—**tweeze,** *v.t.*—*tweezed, tweezing.*

twelfth, twelfth, *a.* Following the eleventh;

being the ordinal of 12; being one of 12 equal parts into which anything is divided. —*n.* One of 12 equal parts; that which follows the eleventh in a series. *Mus.* an interval of 12 diatonic scale degrees; a tone that is 12 degrees above or below a specified tone.

Twelfth-day, twelfth′dā″, *n.* Epiphany.

Twelfth-night, twelfth′nīt″, *n.* The evening before Epiphany or the evening of Epiphany, formerly the last festivity of the Christmas season.

twelve, twelv, *n.* [O.E. twelf = *twelif*, O. Fris. *twelef*, D. *twaalf*, Icel. *tólf* Goth. *tvalif*, O.H.G. *zwelif*, Mod.G. *zwölf*. Formed similarly to *eleven*, the elements being *two*, O.E. *twá*, and a suffix = *ten*.] The cardinal number between 11 and 13; a symbol representing it; a set of 12 persons or things; a dozen.—*a.*—**the Twelve**, the disciples of Christ.

twelve·mo, twelv′mō, *n.* Duodecimo.—*a.*

twelve·month, twelv′munth″, *n.* A year.

twelve-tone, twelv′tōn, *a. Mus.* of or referring to the modern technique of composition that uses all 12 notes of the chromatic scale arranged in the order selected for the particular work and treated equally in an atonal manner.

twen·ti·eth, twen′tē·ith, *a.* Following the nineteenth; being the ordinal of 20; being one of 20 equal parts.—*n.* One of 20 equal parts; that which follows the nineteenth in a series.

twen·ty, twen′tē, *n. pl.* **twen·ties.** [O.E. *twéntig*, < *twegen*, two, *twain*, and *-tig*, ten; *-tig* being cogn. with L. *decem*, ten; so D. and L.G. *twintig*, G. *zwanzig*, Goth. *tvaitigjus*.] The cardinal number between 19 and 21; a symbol representing it; a set of 20 persons or things.

twen·ty-one, twen′tē·wun′, *n.* [Fr. *vingt-et-un*, twenty and one.] The cardinal number between 20 and 22; a symbol representing it; a set of 21 persons or things. *Cards*, a gambling game played by any number of persons, in which the object of each player is to obtain from the dealer cards adding up to 21, or as near as possible to this number without exceeding it; also *blackjack, vingt-et-un.*

twerp, twurp, *n. Slang.* A contemptible person, esp. an insignificant or obnoxious boy or man; a jerk.

twice, twīs, *adv.* [O.E. *twiges* (with adverbial suffix *-es*), < *twiga, twiwa,* twice, < *twi-*, two.] Two times, as in succession; as, to write *twice* a week; on two occasions; in two instances; in twofold quantity or degree, or doubly; as, *twice* as much or as fast.

twice-laid, twīs′lād′, *a.* Made out of strands or other pieces of old rope; made from any scraps or worn material.

twice-told, twīs′tōld′, *a.* Told or related twice or before; often told; trite.

twid·dle, twid′l, *v.t.*—**twiddled, twiddling.** [Origin obscure: cf. *twirl* and *fiddle*.] To twirl or turn round and round, esp. with the fingers; to play with idly.—*v.i.* To play with something idly, as by touching or handling; to turn round and round; to twirl.—*n.* The act or an act of twiddling; a twirl.—**twid·dle one's thumbs**, to keep turning one's thumbs or fingers idly about each other; to do nothing; to be idle.—**twid·dler,** *n.*

twig, twig, *n.* [O.E. *twigge, twig,* akin to D. *twijg,* G. *zweig,* twig, branch.] A slender shoot of a tree or other plant; a small offshoot from a branch or stem; a small dry, woody piece fallen from a branch; *anat.* one of the minute branches of a blood vessel or nerve.—**twig·gy,** twig′ē, *a.*—**twiggier, twiggiest.**

twig, twig, *v.t.*—**twigged, twigging.** [Ir. and Gael. *tuig,* to perceive, discern.] *Brit. colloq.*

To take notice of; to observe keenly; to see. —*v.i.* To apprehend or understand.

twi·light, twī′līt″, *n.* [M.E. *twylyghte*.] The light from the sky when the sun is below the horizon in the morning and esp. in the evening; the time during which this light prevails; any dim light or partial illumination; a condition or period following full development or glory.—*a.* Of, pertaining to, or resembling twilight; crepuscular, as a bat or moth.

twi·light sleep, *n. Med.* a state of semiconsciousness produced by the hypodermic injection of scopolamine and morphine, usu. to effect relatively painless childbirth.

twill, twil, *n.* [M.E. *twyll, twylle,* < O.E. *twili,* woven with two threads, < *twi-*, two: cf. O.E. *thrili,* also L. *trilix,* woven with three threads.] A fabric woven with the weft threads so crossing the warp as to produce an effect of parallel diagonal lines, as in serge; the characteristic weave of such fabrics, or the diagonal line or pattern formed.—*v.t.* To weave in the manner of a twill.—**twilled,** *a.*

twin, twin, *n.* [O.E. *twinn, getwinn,* a., *getwinn,* n., < *twi-*, two.] One of two young brought forth at a birth; either of two persons or things closely related, connected, or resembling each other; *crystal.* a compound crystal consisting of two or more crystals or parts, esp. with one or more parts in a reversed position in relation to another.—*a.* Being two, or one of two, young born at the same birth; as, *twin* sisters; being two persons or things closely related or associated or much alike, or forming a pair or couple; being one of two such persons or things, or forming one of a couple or pair; as, a *twin* peak; consisting of two similar parts or elements joined or connected; as, a *twin* vase; *biol.* occurring in pairs or didymous; *crystal.* of the nature of a twin.—*v.t.*—**twinned, twinning.** To conceive or bring forth as twins or as a twin; to pair or couple; to unite or combine; to furnish a counterpart to; *crystal.* to form, as crystals or crystal forms, into twins.— *v.i.* To bring forth twins.

twin·ber·ry, twin′ber″ē, twin′be·rē, *n. pl.* **twin·ber·ries.** The partridgeberry, *Mitchella repens*; a shrub, *Lonicera involucrata,* of the honeysuckle family having purple flowers.

twin bill, *n.* Doubleheader.

twin·born, twin′barn″, *a.* Born at the same birth.

twine, twīn, *n.* [O.E. *twīn,* a double thread, < *twi-*, two: cf. *twist*.] Strong thread or string composed of two or more strands twisted together, esp. of hemp, manila, or the like; the act of twining; the state of being twined; a twisted thing or part; a convolution or coil; a twist or turn; a knot or tangle.—*v.t.*—**twined, twining.** [M.E. *twinen*.] To twist together to form a thread, string, or the like; as, to *twine* a wreath; interwind; intertwine; to twist, as one strand with that of another; to bring in or into by twisting or winding, as: She *twined* ribbons in her hair. To put, encircle, or wreathe, about or around by winding; as to *twine* ivy about the head, to *twine* a statue with garlands.—*v.i.* To become twined or twisted together; to wind itself about or around something; to grow in convolutions about a support, as in plants, stems, or the like; to wind in a sinuous or meandering course.— **twin·er,** *n.*

twin·flow·er, twin′flou″ er, *n.* A slender, creeping, evergreen herb, *Linnaea borealis,* of Europe or a N. American variety, *L. borealis* var. *americana,* belonging to the honeysuckle family, with pink, white, or purple flowers borne in pairs on threadlike peduncles.

twinge, twinj, *n.* [O.E. *twengan,* pinch.] A sudden, sharp pain; as, a *twinge* of rheumatism; a pain or pang in the mind; as, a *twinge* of remorse.—*v.t.*—**twinged, twinging.** To affect with sudden, sharp pain or pains, as in body or mind.—*v.i.* To have or feel a twinge or twinges.

twi-night, twī′nīt″, *a. Baseball,* denoting a doubleheader that begins a little before evening and continues after dark under artificial lighting.—**twi-night·er,** *n.* A twi-night baseball doubleheader. Also **twi-night dou·ble·head·er.**

twin·kle, twing′kl, *v.i.*—**twinkled, twinkling.** [O.E. *twinclian,* to twinkle, a dim. and freq. corresponding to *twinken,* G. *zwinken,* to wink with the eyes; nasalized forms corresponding to *twitch*.] To open and shut the eyes rapidly; to gleam; to sparkle: said of the eyes; to shine with a tremulous intermitted light; to scintillate.—*v.t.* To give off, as light, in intermittent flashes.—*n.* A wink or quick motion of the eye; a gleam or sparkle of the eye or of a star; a twinkling.— **twin·kler,** *n.*

twin·kling, twing′kling, *n.* The act of that which twinkles; a quick movement of the eye; the time taken up in winking the eye; an instant.

Twins, twinz, *n. pl. Astron.* the zodiacal constellation or sign Gemini.

twin-screw, twin′skrō′, *a. Naut.* having two screw propellers on either side of the keel, which usu. revolve in opposite directions: said of a vessel.

twirl, twurl, *v.t.* [Perh. a var. of obs. or prov. *tirl,* transposed form of *trill*.] To cause to rotate rapidly; spin; whirl; twiddle; *baseball slang,* to pitch.—*v.i.* To rotate rapidly; spin; whirl; *baseball slang,* to pitch.—*n.* A twirling action or motion; twist; curl; coil; whorl.—**twirl·er,** twurl′lẽr, *n.*—**twirl·y,** *a.*

twirp, twurp, *n. Slang,* twerp.

twist, twist, *v.t.* [M.E. *twisten,* < O.E. *twi-*, two: cf. *twine*.] To combine, as two or more strands or threads, by winding together; intertwine; entangle; to form by or as by winding strands together; to entwine, wind, or twine about a thing; to encircle with something wound about; to alter in shape, as by turning the ends in opposite directions, so that parts previously in the same straight line are located in a spiral; to wring out of shape or place, or sprain; as to *twist* one's ankle; to force awry; to contort; as, to *twist* a facial expression; to distort; to force down, into, off, or out, by a turning movement; to wrest from the proper form or meaning; to pervert; to perplex; to emotionally warp; to form into a coil, knot, or the like, by winding or rolling; as, to *twist* the hair into a knot; to bend tortuously; to cause to move with a rotary motion, as a ball pitched in a curve; to turn so as to face in another direction; to turn, as on an axis. —*v.i.* To be or become intertwined; to wind or twine about something; writhe or squirm; to take a spiral form or course; to wind, curve, or bend; to turn or rotate as on an axis; to revolve about something; to turn so as to face in another direction; to change shape with a spiral movement; to wind or meander, as a stream; to move with a progressive rotary motion, as a ball pitched in a curve; to perform the dance called the twist.—*n.* Any deviation, curve, turn, or bend; a turning or rotating as on an axis; rotary motion; spin; anything formed by or as by twisting or twining parts together, as in thread, yarn, or rope; a twisting awry or askew; a wresting or perverting, as of meaning; a peculiar turn, bent, bias, or the like, as in mind or nature; a spiral movement, course, or arrangement; an irregular bend; a sudden change of events or of mind; the altering of the shape of anything by or as by turning the ends in opposite directions, or the resulting shape; a twisting action, force, or stress; a wrench; a strong, twisted silk thread, heavier than ordinary sewing silk, used for buttonholes or the like; thread, cord, or the like; a fast, vigorous dance with rhythm.

twist drill, *n. Mach.* a drill with one or more deep spiral grooves in the body.

twist·er, twis'tẽr, *n.* One who or that which twists; a ball pitched or moving with a spinning motion, as in baseball or cricket; *colloq.* a whirlwind or tornado.

twit, twit, *v.t.—twitted, twitting.* [O.E. *atwite, atwiten, atwiten*, to twit, reproach— *aet,* at, and *witan,* to blame; Sc. *wite,* blame; akin to Icel. *vita,* to fine.] To vex or annoy by bringing to remembrance a fault, imperfection, or the like; to taunt; to upbraid, as for some previous act.—*n.* A twitting action; a reproach.

twitch, twich, *v.t.* [A form of *tweak.*] To pull with an abrupt motion; to jerk.—*v.i.* To be suddenly contracted, as a muscle; to move or make a motion with a jerk.—*n.* A brief involuntary contraction of the muscles; a short quick pull; a jerk.—**twitch·er,** *n.*

twitch grass, *n.* Couch grass.

twit·ter, twit'ẽr, *v.i.* [Imit. of sound, like G. *zwitschern,* D. *kwetteren,* to twitter.] To utter a succession of small, tremulous, intermitted notes, as certain birds; to chatter; to tremble from eagerness or excitement.—*v.t.* To say, as with a twitter.—*n.* A small intermitted noise or series of chirpings, as the sound made by a swallow; a twittering action; an excited state.— **twit·ter·er,** *n.*—**twit·ter·y,** *a.*

'twixt, twikst, *prep. Poetic.* contraction of betwixt.

two, tö, *n.* [O.E. *twá* = Icel. *tveir, tvö,* Goth. *tvai,* D. *twee,* G. *zwei,* Rus. *dwa,* Lith. *du,* L. and Gr. *duo,* Ir. and Gael. *da, do.* Pers. *do,* Hind. *do, doo,* Skt. *dvi, dvau.* Twin, *twine, twill, twain, twist,* etc., are connected.] The cardinal number between one and three; a symbol representing it; a set of two persons or things.—*a.*—**in two,** into two parts.—**put two and two to·geth·er,** to come to the obviously correct conclusion.

two-base hit, tö'bās" hit', *n. Baseball,* a base hit on the strength of which the hitter is enabled to reach second base. Also *double,* **two-bag·ger.**

two-bit, tö'bit", *a. Slang.* Worth 25 cents; petty; small-time; cheap.

two bits, *n. pl. but sing. in constr. Slang,* 25 cents.

two-by-four, tö'bī-fōr", tö'bī-fạr", tö'bī- fōr", tö'bī-fạr", *a.* Indicating a thickness of two units and a width of four units, usu. in inches. *Colloq.* small; cramped. *Slang,* trifling; insignificant.—*n.* A cut piece of timber or lumber widely used in building, usu. measuring slightly less than two inches by four inches.

two-cy·cle, tö'sī"kl, *n.* A cycle in an internal-combustion engine in which one piston stroke out of every two is a working stroke.—*a.*

two-di·men·sion·al, tö'di·men'sha·nal, *a.* Having only two dimensions.

two-faced, tö'fāst", *a.* Having two faces. *Fig.* deceitful; hypocritical.—**two-fac·ed·- ly,** tö'fā'sid·lē, tö'fāst'lē, *adv.*—**two-fac·- ed·ness,** *n.*

two-fist·ed, tö'fis'tid, *a. Colloq.* Strong; vigorous; manly; aggressive.

two-fold, tö'fōld", *a.* Double; composed of two members or parts; multiplied by two.—*adv.*

2, 4-D, *n. Chem.* a white or yellowish crystalline compound, $Cl_2C_6H_3OCH_2COOH$, used to kill weeds. Also **di·chlo·ro·phe·- nox·y·a·ce·tic ac·id.**

2, 4, 5-T, *n. Chem.* a compound, $C_6H_2Cl_3-$

OCH_2CO_2H, used principally as a weed killer. Also **tri·chlo·ro·phe·nox·y·a·ce·- tic ac·id.**

two-hand·ed, tö'han'did, *a.* Entailing the use of both hands; requiring or needing two persons for use; as, a *two-handed* saw; ambidextrous.

two·pence, tup·pence, tup'ens, *n., sing. or pl. in constr. Brit.* The sum or value of two pennies; a small silver coin minted only as alms money for Maundy Thursday; a copper coin during the time of George III; a trifle.

two·pen·ny, tup·pen·ny, tup'e·nē, *a. Brit.* Of the price or value of twopence; of small worth, or paltry.

two-phase, tö'fāz', *a. Elect.* diphase.

two-ply, tö'plī', *a.* Having two strands, as cord, or two thicknesses, as cloth or carpets.

two-sid·ed, tö'sī'did, *a.* Having or consisting of two sides or aspects; bilateral.— **two-sid·ed·ness,** *n.*

two·some, tö'som, *n.* Two together or in company; *golf,* a match between two persons.

two-step, tö'step", *n.* A round dance in duple rhythm, characterized by sliding steps; a piece of music for, or in the rhythm of, this dance.—*v.i.*—**two-stepped,** *two-stepping.*

two-time, tö'tīm", *v.t.—two-timed, two- timing. Slang.* To be secretly unfaithful to, as a spouse or lover; to double-cross.

two-way, tö'wā', *a.* Allowing traffic to simultaneously move in opposite directions; as, a *two-way* street; allowing or involving a reciprocal arrangement or exchange; as, a *two-way* communication; both sending and receiving; as, a *two-way* radio; having two passages by which a fluid may be channeled to either of two branches; as, a *two-way* cock; usable in two ways.

ty·coon, tī·kön', *n.* [Jap. *Tai-koon,* great lord.] *Colloq.* an exceptionally wealthy and powerful businessman. A shogun.

tyke, tike, tīk, *n. Colloq.* any small or young child. A dog; a cur.

tym·bal, tim'bal, *n.* [Fr. *timbale,* It. *timballo, taballo,* < Ar. *thabal,* a drum.] Timbal.

tym·pan, tim'pan, *n.* [Fr. *tympan,* L. *tympanum,* < Gr. *tympanon, tympanon,* a drum < *typtō,* to beat.] *Print.* a frame attached to a handpress or platen machine and covered with parchment or cloth on which the blank sheets are put in order to be laid on the form to be impressed; *arch.* tympanum. A tightly stretched membrane, as a drumhead.—**tym·pan·ic,** tim·pan'ik, *a.*

tym·pan·ic bone, tim·pan'ik bōn', *n. Anat.* a bone of the skull of mammals, supporting the tympanic membrane and enclosing part of the tympanum or middle ear.

tym·pan·ic mem·brane, *n. Anat.* a membrane separating the tympanum or middle ear from the passage of the external ear. Also *eardrum.*

tym·pa·nist, tim'pa·nist, *n. Mus.* a drummer, esp. one who plays kettledrums.

tym·pa·ni·tes, tim"pa·nī'tēz, *n. Pathol.* a distention of the abdomen from a collection of air or gas in the intestines or inside the peritoneum.—**tym·pa·nit·ic,** tim"pa·nit'ik, *a.*

tym·pa·num, tim'pa·num, *n. pl.* **tym·- pan·a,** tim'pa·nums, tim'pa·na. [L., drum, drumlike part, tympanum of a pediment, M.L. drum of the ear, < Gr. *tympanon,* orig. kettledrum, < *typtein,* strike.] *Anat., zool.* the middle ear; the tympanic membrane. *Arch.* the recessed, usu. triangular space enclosed between the horizontal and sloping cornices of a pediment, often adorned with sculpture; a similar space between an arch and the horizontal head of a door or window below. *Electron.* the diaphragm of a telephone. A

drum or similar instrument; the stretched membrane forming a drumhead, or any similar membrane, thin sheet, or plate.

tym·pa·ny, tim'pa·nē, *n. pl.* **tym·pa·nies.** *Pathol.* tympanites. Inflation of language; bombast.

tyne, tīn, *n.* Tine.

ty·pal, tī'pal, *a.* Pertaining to, serving as, or forming a type; typical.

type, tīp, *n.* [L. *typus,* < Gr. *typos,* impression, image, figure, form, model, type, < *typtein,* strike.] A kind, class, or group as distinguished by a particular character; a representative or typical specimen; a person or thing embodying the characteristic qualities of a kind, class, or group; as, the athletic *type;* the standard or model. *Biol.* a taxonomic division, as a genus or species, which most nearly exemplifies the essential characteristics of a higher group and usu. gives it its name; a representative or typical individual specimen, as of an animal or plant genus or species. *Print.* a rectangular piece or block, usu. of metal, having on its upper surface a letter or character in relief for use in printing; such pieces or blocks collectively; a printed character, or esp. printed characters. A distinguishing mark or sign; the principal figure or device on either side of a coin or medal; *theol.* a prefiguring symbol, esp. as an Old Testament event prefiguring a New Testament event.—*v.t.—typed, typing.* To typewrite; to reproduce in type or print; to designate the particular type of, as a blood sample; to identify; to serve as an example or specimen of. *Theol.* to prefigure; to foreshadow, as a symbol. *Theatr.* to type-cast.—*v.i.* To typewrite.—**typ·a·ble, type·- a·ble,** *a.*

type·cast, tīp'kast", tīp'käst", *v.t.—typecast, typecasting. Theatr.* To cast, as an entertainer, in the part of a character similar to himself in personality, appearance, or the like; to cast or hire, as an entertainer, in or for the same type of role in which he has sustained continued success.

type·face, tīp'fās", *n. Print.* face.

type found·er, *n.* A person whose occupation is the casting of printing type.— **type·found·ing,** *n.*—**type·found·ry,** *n.*

type ge·nus, *n. Biol.* a genus that is typical of the family or other higher group to which it belongs.

type-high, tīp'hī, *a. Print.* of the same height as type. See *height-to-paper.*—*adv.*

type met·al, *n. Print.* an alloy, usu. of lead, tin, antimony, and copper, and used in the manufacture of printing type.

type·script, tīp'skript", *n.* Matter produced by a typewriter.

type·set·ter, tīp'set"ẽr, *n.* One who sets type; a compositor; a typesetting machine. —**type·set,** tīp'set", *v.t.—typeset, typeset- ting.—n., a.*

type spe·cies, *n. Biol.* a species considered most typical or illustrative of its genus, and whose name is therefore given to the genus.

type spec·i·men, *n. Taxonomy,* an individual plant or animal whose characteristics determine the basic description of a species. See *holotype.*

type·write, tīp'rīt", *v.t., v.i.—past type- wrote,* pp. *typewritten,* ppr. *typewriting.* To print by a typewriter. Also *type.*

type·writ·er, tīp'rī"tẽr, *n.* A keyboard machine for producing writing resembling type impressions; *archaic,* one who uses such a machine.

type·writ·ing, tīp'rī"ting, *n.* The act or art of using a typewriter; work done on a typewriter.

typh·lol·o·gy, tif·lol'o·jē, *n. pl.* **typh·- lol·o·gies.** [Gr. *typhlós,* blind.] *Med.* the area of scientific knowledge concerning blindness.

ty·phoid, tī'foid, *n. Pathol.* an infectious,

often fatal, febrile disease, characterized by intestinal inflammation and ulceration, due to a specific bacillus, *Salmonella typhosa*, which is usu. introduced with food or drink. Also **ty·phoid fe·ver.**—*a. Pathol.* of or pertaining to typhoid fever.

ty·phoon, ti·fön′, *n.* [Pg. *tufao*, < Ar. *tufan*, tempest, hurricane; perh. also, in part, Chin. *t'ai fung,* 'great wind.'] A hurricane occurring in the China Sea and western Pacific, chiefly during the summer and fall.

ty·phus, tī′fus, *n.* [N.L., < Gr. *typhos*, smoke, vapor, stupor from fever; < *typhein*, smoke, smolder.] *Pathol.* an acute infectious disease characterized by great prostration, severe nervous symptoms, and a peculiar eruption of reddish spots on the body, caused by the microorganism, *Rickettsia prowazeki*, and transmitted by fleas and lice. Also **ty·phus fe·ver.**—**ty·phous,** *a.*

typ·i·cal, tip′i·kal, *a.* [L.L. *typicalis.*] Of the nature of or serving as an emblem; symbolic; of the nature of or serving as a representative specimen; conforming to some type; characteristic. Also **typ·ic.**—**typ·i·cal·ly,** *adv.*—**typ·i·cal·ness, typ·i·cal·i·ty,** *n.*

typ·i·fy, tip′i·fī″, *v.t.*—**typified, typifying.** To represent by a type or symbol; prefigure; signify; symbolize; to constitute or serve as the typical specimen of; to exemplify.—**typ·i·fi·ca·tion,** *n.*

typ·ist, tī′pist, *n.* An operator of a typewriter.

ty·po, tī′pō, *n. pl.* **ty·pos.** *n. Colloq.* typographical error.

ty·po., tī′pō. Abbreviation for printer, compositor, typography. Also **ty·pog.,** tī′pog.

ty·pog·ra·pher, ti·pog′ra·fėr, *n.* One skilled or engaged in typography; a printer.

ty·pog·ra·phy, ti·pog′ra·fē, *n.* [Fr. *typographie,* < N.L. *typographia,* < Gr. *typos,* impression and *-graphia,* < *gráphein,* write.] The art or process of printing with types; the work of setting and arranging types and of printing from them; the general character or appearance of printed matter. —**ty·po·graph·ic,** tī″po·graf′ik, *a.*—**ty·po·graph·i·cal,** *a.*—**ty·po·graph·i·cal·ly,** *adv.*

ty·pol·o·gy, tī·pol′o·jē, *n. pl.* **ty·pol·o·gies.** The study or classification of types; the study of types or symbols in literature.—**ty·po·log·i·cal,** tī″po·loj′i·kal, *a.*—**ty·po·log·i·cal·ly,** *adv.*—**ty·pol·o·gist,** *n.*

ty·poth·e·tae, tī·poth′i·tē″, tī″po·thē′tē, *n. pl. but sing. in constr.* [N.L., < Gr. *typos,* impression and *phetēs,* one who places, < *tiphenai,* set, put.] Printers collectively; as in the names of associations of master printers.

ty·ran·ni·cal, ti·ran′i·kal, tī·ran′i·kal, *a.* Of, pertaining to, or befitting a tyrant; arbitrary; despotic; severely oppressive. Also **ty·ran·nic.**—**ty·ran·ni·cal·ly,** *adv.* —**ty·ran·ni·cal·ness,** *n.*

tyr·an·ni·cide, ti·ran′i·sīd″, tī·ran′i·sīd″, *n.* [L. *tyrannus,* and *caedo,* to kill.] The act of killing a tyrant; one who kills a tyrant.

tyr·an·nize, tir′a·nīz″, *v.i.*—**tyrannized, tyrannizing.** [Fr. *tyranniser,* < *tyran.*] To exercise power or control cruelly or oppressively, often followed by *over*; to reign as a tyrant.—*v.t.* To rule or treat tyrannically.—**tyr·an·niz·er,** *n.*

ty·ran·no·saur, ti·ran′o·sȯr, tī·ran′o·sȯr, *n.* [N.L. < Gr. *tyrannos,* absolute ruler, tyrant, and *sauros,* lizard.] A huge carnivorous dinosaur, *Tyrannosaurus rex,* of the Cretaceous period in N. America, which walked erect on its hind limbs. Also **ty·ran·no·sau·rus.**

tyr·an·nous, tir′a·nus, *a.* Tyrannical.— **tyr·an·nous·ly,** *adv.*—**tyr·an·nous·ness,** *n.*

tyr·an·ny, tir′a·nē, *n. pl.* **tyr·an·nies.** [O.Fr. *tirannie* (Fr. *tyrannie*), < M.L.

tyrannia, < Gr. *tyrannia,* < *týrannos,* E. *tyrant.*] The government or rule of a tyrant or absolute ruler, as in ancient Greece; a state ruled by a tyrant; oppressive or unjust government by any ruler; despotic abuse or authority; undue severity or harshness; a tyrannical act or proceeding.

ty·rant, tī′rant, *n.* [O.Fr. *tyrant* (Fr. *tyran*), < L. *tyrannus,* < Gr. *tyrannos,* absolute ruler, despot, tyrant.] An absolute ruler, as in ancient Greece, owing his office to usurpation; a king or ruler who uses his power oppressively or unjustly; any person who exercises power or authority despotically or oppressively.

ty·rant fly·catch·er, *n.* Any bird of the American family *Tyrannidae,* esp. the kingbird.

tyre, tī′ėr, *n. Brit.* tire.

Tyr·i·an pur·ple, tir′ē·an pur′pl, *n.* A purple dye, prob. crimson, used by the ancient Greeks and Romans, prepared at Tyre from certain mollusks; a purplish-red color now made synthetically. Also **Tyr·i·an dye.**

ty·ro, ti·ro, tī′rō, *n.* [L. *tiro,* a raw recruit, a novice.] A beginner in learning; any novice.

ty·ro·ci·dine, tī″ro·sīd′in, tī′ro·si′dēn, *n. Pharm.* a complex crystalline antibiotic produced by the bacterium, *Bacillus brevis,* used in the treatment of bacterial infections. Also **ty·ro·ci·din,** tī″ro·sīd′in.

ty·ro·si·nase, tī′rō·si·nās″, tir′ō·si·nās″, *n. Biochem.* a catalytic enzyme containing copper and contained in plant and animal tissue, which acts in the oxidation of tyrosine in the natural production of pigments, as melanin.

ty·ro·sine, tī′ro·sēn″, tī′ro·sin, tir′o·sēn″, tir′o·sin, *n. Biochem.* a common amino acid, $C_6H_4OHCH_2CHNH_2COOH$, isolated by protein hydrolysis.

tzar, zär, tsär, *n.* Czar.—**tza·ri·na,** zä·rē′na, tsä·rē′na, *n.* Czarina.

Tzi·gane, tsi·gän′, *n.* [Hung.] A Hungarian Gypsy.—*a. (Often l.c.)* of or pertaining to the Hungarian Gypsies; as, *Tzigane* songs. Also **Tzigany.**

Tzi·ga·ny, tsi·gä·nē, *n. pl.* **Tzi·ga·nies.** Tzigane.—*a.*

U

U, u, ū, *n.* The twenty-first letter of the English alphabet and the fifth vowel; the sound of the letter U as represented in speech; the delineation of the letter U or u in writing or printing; something designated by or having the shape of the letter U or u; a graphic device for printing the letter U or u.—*pron. Colloq.* you, as: All U Can Eat.

U, ū. *Chem.* uranium; *math.* union.

U·ban·gi, ū·bang′gē, ȯ·bäng′gē, *n.* A woman of the Central African Republic characterized by pierced lips which are distended by the insertion of platelike wooden disks.

u·biq·ui·tous, ū·bik′wi·tus, *a.* [< L. *ubique,* everywhere.] Existing or being everywhere simultaneously; omnipresent. Also **u·biq·ui·tar·y.**—**u·biq·ui·tous·ly,** *adv.*—**u·biq·ui·tous·ness,** *n.*

u·biq·ui·ty, ū·bik′wi·tē, *n.* The capacity or state of being present everywhere; existing in numerous places or everywhere at the same time; omnipresence.

u·bi su·pra, ū′bī sȯ′pra, *L.* ȯ′bē sȯ′prä, *adv. Latin,* where mentioned above. Abbr. *u.s.*

U-boat, ū′bōt″, *n.* A German submarine.

ud·der, ud′er, *n.* [O.E. *ūder* = O.H.G. *ūtar* (G. *euter*), akin to L. *uber,* Gr. *outhar,* Skt. *ūdhar,* udder.] A mamma or mam-

mary gland, esp. when large and baggy with more than one teat, as in cows.

UFO, ū′ef′ō′, *n.* Abbreviation for an unidentified flying object.

U·ga·rit·ic, ȯ″ga·rit′ik, *a.* Characteristic of or referring to the ancient city, people, or language of Ugarit in Syria.—*n.* The written and spoken Semitic language of the people of Ugarit, related to and resembling Hebrew and Phoenician, the Semitic language of Phoenicia.

ugh, öch, uch, u, ụ, *spelling* ug, *interj.* An exclamation of horror, recoil, disgust, or the like, often accompanied by a shudder.—*n.* A representation of the sound of a grunt or cough.

ug·li·fy, ug′li·fī″, *v.t.*—**uglified, uglifying.** To make ugly.—**ug·li·fi·ca·tion,** *n.*

ug·ly, ug′lē, *a.*—**uglier, ugliest.** [M.E. *ugly,* *uglike,* < Scand.: cf. Icel. *uggligr,* fearful, dreadful, *ugga,* to fear.] Repulsive or displeasing in appearance; offensive to the sense of beauty; disagreeable, unpleasant, or objectionable; as, *ugly* duties to perform; morally revolting; base; vile; discreditable or disgraceful; as, an *ugly* tale of treachery; troublesome; as, an *ugly* wound; threatening disadvantage or danger; as, an *ugly* omen; *colloq.* ill-natured, quarrelsome, or vicious; as, an *ugly* disposition. Rough or turbulent conditions; as, *ugly* weather.— **ug·li·ly,** *adv.*—**ug·li·ness,** *n.*

ug·ly duck·ling, *n.* An unattractive or unpromising child who grows up to be a beautiful or much-admired person: in allusion to the despised young bird among a brood of ducklings that turned out to be a swan in Hans Christian Andersen's tale by the same name.

U·gri·an, ȯ′grē·an, ū′grē·an, *a.* [From *Ugria* or *Ugra,* district about the Ural Mountains.] Noting or pertaining to a race or ethnological group including the Magyars and related Finno-Ugric peoples of western Siberia and usu. Hungary. Pertaining to the languages of these peoples; also *Ugric.*—*n.* A member of any of the Ugrian peoples; also *Ugric.*

U·gric, ȯ′grik, ū′grik, *n.* A portion of the Finno-Ugric group of the Uralic languages native to western Siberia and Hungary composed of the Hungarian, Ostyak, and Vogul tongues.—*a.* See *Ugrian.*

uh·lan, ȯ′län, ū′lan, *n.* [G. *uhlan,* < Polish *ulan,* a lancer.] A mounted lancer, usu. in light cavalry units, formerly prominent in the armies of Poland; a German cavalryman.

u·in·tah·ite, u·in·ta·ite, ū·in′ta·īt″, *n.* [From the *Uintah* or *Uinta* Mountains, in Utah.] A very pure variety of black asphalt found esp. in Utah. Also *gilsonite.*

uit·land·er, īt′lan″dėr, oit′lan″dėr, *D.* œit′län″dėr, *n.* [D., 'outlander.'] *(Sometimes cap.)* An outlander; a foreigner, esp. one of the British who settled in the former Boer republics of southern Africa.

u·kase, ū′kās, ū·kāz′, *n.* [Rus., < *kasati,* to show.] Formerly, a Russian edict or order, esp. during the Czarist regimes, having the force of law; any decree or order issued by an authority or official.

U·krain·i·an, ū·krā′nē·an, ū·krī′nē·an, *a.* Of or pertaining to the Ukraine, a district in southwest European Russia, its inhabitants, or the language.—*n.* A native or inhabitant of the Ukraine. The slavic language of its people; also **Lit·tle Rus·sian.**

u·ku·le·le, ū″ka·lā′lē, *Hawaiian* ȯ″kụ·lä′lä, *n.* [Hawaiian, lit. 'flea.'] A musical instrument, usu. four-stringed, similar to a guitar but smaller in size. Also *colloq.* uke.

ul·cer, ul′sėr, *n.* [O.Fr. *ulcere* (Fr. *ulcère*), < L. *ulcus* (*ulcer-*), akin to Gr. *helkos,* wound, sore, ulcer.] *Pathol.* a sore open either to the surface of the body or to a natural cavity, and accompanied by the disintegration of

---

tissue and usu. the formation of pus; *fig.* a corrupting condition or influence, likened to an open sore.

ul·cer·ate, ul′se·rāt″, *v.t.*, *v.i.*—*ulcerated*, *ulcerating*. [L. *ulceratus*, pp. of *ulcerare*, < *ulcus*.] To make or to become ulcerous.

ul·cer·a·tion, ul″se·rā′shan, *n.* [L. *ulceratio(n-)*.] The action or progress of ulcerating, or the state of being ulcerated; an ulcer or a group of ulcers.—**ul·cer·a·tive**, ul′se·rā″tiv, ul′sėr·a·tiv, *a.*

ul·cer·ous, ul′sėr·us, *a.* Pertaining to or of the nature of an ulcer or ulcers; characterized by the formation of ulcers; affected with an ulcer or ulcers.—**ul·cer·ous·ly**, *adv.*—**ul·cer·ous·ness**, *n.*

u·le·ma, ö′le·mä″, *n. pl.* (Ar. 'ulamā, pl. of 'ālim, learned, scholar.] The Moslem doctors or scholars of religion and sacred law, esp. in Turkey; *sing. in constr.* a council of such doctors in a Moslem country. Also **u·la·ma**.

ul·lage, ul′ij, *n.* [O.Fr. *eullage*, the filling up of leaky wine vessels, < *oeil*, the eye, the bunghole, < L. *oculus*, the eye.] The quantity, esp. of a liquid, that a container, as any barrel or cask, lacks or wants of being full, as often caused by seepage, evaporation, or use.

ul·na, ul′na, *n. pl.* **ul·nae**, **ul·nas**, ul′nē. [N.L. use of L. *ulna*, elbow, arm.] *Anat.* In man, that one of the two long bones of the forearm which is on the side opposite to the thumb; a corresponding bone in the forelimb of other vertebrates.—**ul·nar**, *a.*

u·lot·ri·chous, ū·lo′tri·kus, *a.* [Gr. *oulotrichos*, < *oulos*, crisp or curly, and *thrix*, *trichos*, hair.] Pertaining to the crispy- or woolly-haired groups of people; having such hair.—**u·lot·ri·chy**, ū·lo′tri·kē, *n.*

ul·ster, ul′stėr, *n.* A heavy, long, loose overcoat, often having a belt, orig. made of frieze cloth in Ulster, Ireland.

ul·te·ri·or, ul·tēr′ē·ėr, *a.* [L., compar. adj. (superl. *ultimus*), connected with *ultra*, beyond: cf. *ultra* and *ultima*.] Being beyond what is seen or avowed, or intentionally kept concealed; as, *ulterior* motives; being beyond what is immediate or present, or coming at a subsequent time or stage, as: What *ulterior* action will be taken is uncertain. Being or situated beyond, or on the farther side, as of a certain boundary.—**ul·te·ri·or·ly**, *adv.*

ul·ti·ma, ul′ti·ma, *n.* [L. *ultimus*, last, furthest, superl. of *ulter*, further.] The last syllable of a word.

ul·ti·mate, ul′ti·mit, *a.* [M.L. *ultimatus*, < L. *ultimus*, farthest, last.] Farthest or most remote; extreme; last, as in a series; coming at the end, as of a course of action or a process; coming as a final result; final and decisive; as, an *ultimate* check to progress; forming the final aim or object; as, his *ultimate* goal or purpose; beyond which it is impossible to proceed, as by investigation or analysis; as, *ultimate* principles; fundamental; elemental.—*n.* The final point; the final result; the conclusion; a fundamental fact or principle.—**ul·ti·mate·ly**, *adv.*—**ul·ti·mate·ness**, *n.*

ul·ti·ma·tum, ul″ti·mā′tum, ul″ti·mä′tum, *n. pl.* **ul·ti·ma·tums**, **ul·ti·ma·ta**, ul″ti·mā′ta, ul″ti·mä′ta. In any dispute, the final proposal or statement of terms or conditions for settlement offered by either of the parties involved; in diplomatic negotiations, the final offer or demand submitted by the negotiator, which, if rejected, will usu. end negotiations and may have other serious consequences.

ul·ti·mo, ul′ti·mō″, *adv.* [L. *ultimo mense*, in the last month.] In or concerning the last or preceding month, as distinguished from the current month. Abbr. *ult.*, *ulto.*

ul·ti·mo·gen·i·ture, ul″ti·mō·jen′i·chėr, *n.* The custom or practice by which the youngest child succeeds to an inheritance, as opposed to *primogeniture*.

ul·tra, ul′tra, *a.* [L., *adv.* and *prep.*, beyond: cf. *ulterior*.] Going beyond what is usual or ordinary; immoderate; excessive; extreme.—*n.* One who goes to extremes, as in fashion, conduct, or politics; an extremist.

ul·tra·cen·tri·fuge, ul″tra·sen′tri·fūj″, *n.* A centrifuge of extremely high speed used to settle out particles of a colloid or various solutions by graduated concentrations according to their molecular weight.—*v.t.*—*ultracentrifuged, ultracentrifuging.* To stratify by the use of an ultracentrifuge.—**ul·tra·cen·trif·u·gal**, ul″tra·sen·trif′ya·gal, *a.*—**ul·tra·cen·trif·u·ga·tion**, *n.*

ul·tra·con·serv·a·tive, ul″tra·kon·sur′va·tiv, *a.* Excessively conservative.—*n.* One who is extremely conservative.

ul·tra·high fre·quen·cy, ul′tra·hī″ frē′kwen·sē, ul′tra·hī′, *n. pl.* **ul·tra·high fre·quen·cies**. *Radio*, any frequency in the range of 300 to 3000 megacycles per second. Abbr. *uhf*, *UHF*.

ul·tra·ism, ul′tra·iz″um, *n.* The principles or views of those advocating extreme measures; an act or instance of these views.—**ul·tra·ist**, *a.*, *n.*—**ul·tra·is·tic**, *a.*

ul·tra·ma·rine, ul″tra·ma·rēn′, *a.* [M.L. *ultramarinus*, < L. *ultra*, beyond, and *mare*, sea.] Situated beyond the sea; of a deep blue color called ultramarine.—*n.* A blue pigment consisting of powdered lapis lazuli; a similar blue pigment artificially prepared; any of various other related pigments; a deep blue color.

ul·tra·mi·cro·chem·is·try, ul″tra·mī″krō·kem′i·strē, *n.* That branch of chemistry concerned with substances having quantities equal to or less than one microgram.

ul·tra·mi·cro·scope, ul″tra·mī′kro·skōp″, *n.* An instrument for rendering visible, by means of diffractive effects, objects too small to be seen by the ordinary microscope.

ul·tra·mi·cro·scop·ic, ul″tra·mī″kro·skop′ik, *a.* Beyond the power of, or too small to be seen with, a regular microscope; of or pertaining to an ultramicroscope. Also **ul·tra·mi·cro·scop·i·cal**.—**ul·tra·mi·cros·co·py**, ul″tra·mī·kros′ko·pē, *n.*

ul·tra·mod·ern, ul″tra·mod′ėrn, *a.* Advanced beyond the modern; extremely modern or advanced, as in techniques, styles, or ideas.—**ul·tra·mod·ern·ism**, *n.*—**ul·tra·mod·ern·ist**, *n.*

ul·tra·mon·tane, ul″tra·mon·tān′, *a.* [L. *ultra*, and *mons*, mountain.] Being or lying beyond the mountains, esp. Italy or south of the Alps; tramontane. *Rom. Cath. Ch.* belonging or pertaining to the party favoring papal supremacy; holding the doctrines of ultramontanism.—*n.*

ul·tra·mon·ta·nism, ul″tra·mon′ta·niz″um, *n.* (Often cap.), *Rom. Cath. Ch.* the policy and principles of those in the Church favoring absolute papal authority and power, as opposed to the theory called 'Gallicanism' which restricts papal authority and the authority of the Church with regard to the state.

ul·tra·mun·dane, ul″tra·mun′dān, ul″tra·mun·dān′, *a.* [L. *ultra*, and *mundus*, world.] Being beyond the world, or beyond the limits of our planetary system; beyond or outside the present life.

ul·tra·na·tion·al·ism, ul″tra·nash′a·na·liz″um, *n.* Extraordinary ardor for and devotion to a nation and its pursuits, esp. with little regard for the effect on other nations.—**ul·tra·na·tion·al**, *a.*—**ul·tra·na·tion·al·ist**, ul″tra·nash′a·na·list, *a.*, *n.*—**ul·tra·na·tion·al·is·tic**, *a.*

ul·tra·red, ul″tra·red′, *a.* Infrared.

ul·tra·son·ic, ul″tra·son′ik, *a. Phys.* of or pertaining to frequencies above the range of human audibility, or above 20,000 vibrations per second.—**ul·tra·son·ics**, *n. pl. but sing. in constr.* That branch of physics, esp. the area of acoustics, dealing with ultrasonic frequencies.

ul·tra·struc·ture, ul′tra·struk″chėr, *n. Biol.* the submicroscopic, basic arrangement of protoplasm.

ul·tra·vi·o·let, ul″tra·vī′o·lit, *a.* Beyond the end that is violet in the visible spectrum, as of light rays with very short wavelengths: contrasted with *infrared*; producing or pertaining to these rays.—*n.* Radiation that is ultraviolet.

ul·tra vi·res, ul′tra vī′rēz, *a.*, *adv. Law*, beyond or exceeding the legal authority or power, as of some corporation.

ul·tra·vir·us, ul″tra·vī′rus, *n. pl.* **ul·tra·vir·us·es**. Any filterable, ultramicroscopic virus.

ul·u·late, ūl′ya·lāt″, ul′ya·lāt″, *v.i.*—*ululated, ululating.* To howl, as a dog or wolf; to hoot; to wail loudly; to lament shrilly.—**ul·u·lant**, ūl′ya·lant, ul′ya·lant, *a.* Howling.—**ul·u·la·tion**, *n.*

um·bel, um′bel, *n.* [L. *umbella*, a little shade, dim. of *umbra*, a shade.] *Bot.* an inflorescence, which consists of a number of flower stalks or pedicels, nearly equal in length and spreading from a common center, somewhat like umbrella ribs, as in plants belonging to the carrot family, *Umbelliferae*.—**um·bel·lar**, **um·bel·late**, **um·bel·lat·ed**, um′be·lit, um′be·lāt″, *a.*—**um·bel·late·ly**, *adv.*

um·bel·lif·er·ous, um″be·lif′ėr·us, *a. Bot.* Producing or bearing one or more umbels; pertaining to or of the family *Umbelliferae*, including various edible plants as parsley, celery, and carrots, and several poisonous herbs, as poison hemlock.

um·bel·lule, um′bel·ūl″, um·bel′ūl, *n.* [Dim. of *umbel*.] *Bot.* one of a number of secondary umbels within a larger compound umbel. Also **um·bel·let**, um′be·lit.—**um·bel·lu·late**, um·bel′ya·lit, um·bel′ya·lāt″, *a.*

um·ber, um′bėr, *n.* [Fr. *ombre*, for *terre d'ombre*, lit. 'earth of Umbria' (Fr. *Ombrie*), in Italy.] An earth consisting chiefly of a hydrated oxide of iron and some oxide of manganese, used in its natural state as a brown pigment or, after heating, as a reddish-brown pigment; the color of such a pigment; *ichth.* the grayling, *Thymallus thymallus*, of Europe. *Ornith.* the hammerhead, *Scopus umbretta*; also **um·ber bird**, **um·brette**, um·bret′.—*a.* Of the color of umber.—*v.t.* To color with or as with umber.

um·bil·i·cal, um·bil′i·kal, *a.* [L. *umbilicus*, the navel; akin to G. *omphalos*, the navel.] Pertaining to the navel or umbilicus; formed or located in the middle, like a navel; central, esp. relating to the abdomen.

um·bil·i·cal cord, *n. Anat.* a cordlike structure which passes from the navel of the fetus or embryo to the mother's placenta, supplying nourishment to and carrying wastes from the fetus. *Aerospace*, any of the servicing electrical or fluid lines between the ground or a tower and a rocket vehicle before the launch; a life line between an astronaut in space and his space vehicle which supplies air and some system of communication to him.

um·bil·i·cate, um·bil′i·kit, um·bil′i·kāt″, *a.* Navel-shaped; having a navel or umbilicus. Also **um·bil·i·cat·ed**.—**um·bil·i·ca·tion**, um·bil″i·kā′shan, *n.*

um·bil·i·cus, um·bil′i·kus, um″bi·lī′kus, *n. pl.* **um·bil·i·ci**, um·bil′i·sī″, um″bi·lī′sī. [L.] *Anat.* the navel; *biol.* a navellike or circular depression, as a seed's hilum or the indentation in the lower whorl of many spiral univalves.

um·bles, um′belz, *n. pl.* The entrails of some animals, esp. deer, used primarily as food. See *humble pie.*

um·bo, um′bō, *n.* pl. **um·bo·nes, um·bos,** um·bō′nēz. [L. *umbo,* a boss on a shield, any boss or knob.] The boss or protuberant part of a shield, as one located at the center; something similar to or resembling this; *zool.* a protuberance or rounded elevation, as the projection situated immediately above the hinge of a bivalve shell; *anat.* an external depression of the tympanic membrane at the point of its attachment to the malleus.—**um·bo·nal, um·bon·ic,** um′bo·nal, um·bon′ik, *a.*—**um·bo·nate,** um′bo·nit, um′bo·nāt′, *a.*

um·bra, um′bra, *n.* pl. **um·bras, um·brae,** um′brē. [L. a shadow.] Any area of total shadow; shade. *Astron.* The conical portion of a shadow cast by a celestial body that cuts off all light from a particular source, as the total shadow of the earth or moon in an eclipse; the dark central portion of a sunspot. See *penumbra.*

um·brage, um′brij, *n.* [O.Fr. *umbrage,* Fr. *ombrage,* < L. *umbra,* a shade (whence also *umbel, umbrella, adumbrate*).] Resentment; offense; suspicion or doubt; shade caused by foliage; *poetic,* shade or shadow; *archaic,* any semblance or appearance that is shadowy.—**um·bra·geous,** um·brā′jus, *a.*—**um·bra·geous·ly,** *adv.*—**um·bra·geous·ness,** *n.*

um·brel·la, um·brel′a, *n.* [It. *ombrella,* an umbrella, dim. of *ombra,* a shade, < L. *umbra,* a shade.] A portable fabric screen or canopy extended on an expandable or collapsible radial frame fastened to a rod or stick and used for shelter from sun or rain; *zool.* the gelatinous, saucer-shaped, inflatable bell forming the body of jellyfish; *milit.* a cover of aircraft protecting surface forces or operations.—*a.* Having the qualities or shape of an umbrella; all-embracing, as applied to a group of related items or elements.—**um·brel·la·like,** *a.*

um·brel·la bird, *n.* A South American bird, *Cephalopterus ornatus,* which has a radiating umbrellalike crest on the head; any of certain other birds of the genus *Cephalopterus.*

um·brel·la leaf, *n.* A N. American perennial herb, *Diphylleia cymosa,* in the barberry family, bearing either a large, peltate, umbrellalike, lobed, basal leaf, or two smaller similar leaves on a flowering stem.

um·brel·la plant, *n.* An African herb, *Cyperus alternifolius,* in the sedge family, having long umbrella-shaped leaves.

um·brel·la tree, *n.* A N. American magnolia, *Magnolia tripetala,* a tree with large leaves in umbrellalike clusters; any of various other trees suggesting an umbrella, as in arrangement or shape of the leaves.

Um·bri·an, um′brē·an, *a.* Of or pertaining to Umbria, a region in central Italy, or its inhabitants.—*n.* A native or inhabitant of Umbria, as in ancient or modern times; the ancient and now extinct Italic language of Umbria.

u·mi·ak, ōō′mē·ak″, *n.* [Eskimo.] An open, flat-bottomed Eskimo boat consisting of hides stretched over a wooden framework, usu. operated with paddles, and used esp. by women. Also **oo·mi·ac, oomiak.**

um·laut, ụm′lout, *n.* [Gr., from prefix *um,* indicating alteration, and *laut,* sound-change of sound.] *Gram.* A common feature in many of the Germanic tongues marking the change of a vowel in one syllable through the influence of a semivowel or a vowel in the syllable immediately following; a vowel so changed by an umlaut; a diacritical mark (¨) over a vowel, as ä, ö, ü, used to mark a change in vowel sound from the original notation, esp. in the German language.—

v.t. To alter with an umlaut; to mark an umlaut over.

um·pire, um′pī·ėr, *n.* [< O.E. *noumpere, nowmpere, nompere,* and with loss of initial *n* (as in *apron*), *owmper,* etc., < O.Fr. *nonper,* not equal, odd—L. *non,* not, and *par,* equal, a pair. Lit. 'an odd person,' in addition to a pair.] An official who enforces the rules of play in baseball and other games; any person to whose sole decision a controversy or question between parties is referred.—*v.t., v.i.—umpired, umpiring.*—**um·pir·age,** *n.* The authority or post of an umpire; the act of one who arbitrates, as an umpire; arbitrament.

ump·teen, ump′tēn′, *a. Colloq.* Numerous, but of an indeterminate number; many. Also **ump·steen,** ump′stēn′.—**ump·teenth,** ump′tēnth′, *a.*

un·a·bashed, un″a·basht′, *a.* Not abashed or daunted; not embarrassed or put to shame.—**un·a·bash·ed·ly,** un″a·bash′id·lē, *adv.*

un·a·bat·ed, un″a·bā′tid, *a.* Not diminished in strength, force, or vigor.—**un·a·bat·ed·ly,** *adv.*

un·a·ble, un·ā′bl, *a.* Not having sufficient ability or knowledge; incompetent, as for some task; not able.

un·a·bridged, un″a·brijd′, *a.* Not abridged, as a dictionary; not shortened; complete and comprehensive.

un·ac·a·dem·ic, un″ak·a·dem′ik, *a.* Not academic; unconventional, as in literature or art.

un·ac·cep·ta·ble, un″ak·sep′ta·bl, *a.* Not acceptable, pleasing, or adequate; not welcome.—**un·ac·cept·ed,** *a.*

un·ac·com·mo·dat·ed, un″a·kom′o·dā″tid, *a.* Not accommodated; not adapted or adjusted; not having accommodations; not supplied with necessary provisions or conveniences.

un·ac·com·mo·dat·ing, un″a·kom′o·dā″ting, *a.* Not obliging or helpful.

un·ac·com·pa·nied, un″a·kum′pa·nēd, *a.* Having no attendants or companions; alone; *mus.* performed or written without an accompaniment.

un·ac·com·plished, un″a·kom′plisht, *a.* Not accomplished; not performed completely; not having accomplishments or achievements; inexpert.

un·ac·count·a·ble, un″a·koun′ta·bl, *a.* Not explicable; such that no reason or explanation can be given; strange; not responsible or accountable for.—**un·ac·count·a·ble·ness,** *n.*—**un·ac·count·a·bly,** *adv.*—**un·ac·count·ed-for,** *a.* Not explained, accounted for, or understood.

un·ac·cred·it·ed, un″a·kred′i·tid, *a.* Not accredited; not authorized or certified; not attributed to or believed.

un·ac·cus·tomed, un″a·kus′tomd, *a.* Uncommon; not usual or familiar; not accustomed; not habituated.

un·ac·knowl·edged, un″ak·nol′ijd, *a.* Not acknowledged or recognized; not declared or admitted.

u·na cor·da, ō′na kạr′da, *It.* ō′nä kạr′dä, *adv., a.* [It.] *Mus.* with the depression of the soft pedal: used as a direction, esp. in piano playing.

u·na cor·da ped·al, *n.* The soft pedal, as of a piano.

un·ac·quaint·ed, un″a·kwān′tid, *a.* Not having formed an acquaintance; unfamiliar; not having knowledge, usu. followed by *with.*

un·a·dapt·a·ble, un″a·dap′ta·bl, *a.* Not adaptable; incapable of adjustment.—**un·a·dapt·ed,** *a.*

un·a·dorned, un″a·dạrnd′, *a.* Not adorned; not decorated or embellished.

un·a·dul·ter·at·ed, un″a·dul′te·rā″tid, *a.* Not adulterated; genuine; pure.—**un·a·dul·ter·at·ed·ly,** *adv.*

un·ad·vis·a·ble, un″ad·vī′za·bl, *a.* Not advisable or recommended; not expedient; not prudent.—**un·ad·vis·a·bly,** *adv.*

un·ad·vised, un″ad·vīzd′, *a.* Without advice or due consideration; rash; imprudent.—**un·ad·vis·ed·ly,** un″ad·vī′zid·lē, *adv.*—**un·ad·vis·ed·ness,** *n.*

un·af·fect·ed, un″a·fek′tid, *a.* Not showing affectation; natural; not artificial; simple; sincere; unchanged; not influenced.—**un·af·fect·ed·ly,** *adv.*—**un·af·fect·ed·ness,** *n.*

un·a·fraid, un″a·frād′, *a.* Not afraid; fearless or without reluctance.

un·al·lied, un″a·līd′, *a.* Having no alliance or connection, as by nature, marriage, or treaty; not related.

un·al·loyed, un″a·loid′, *a.* Not alloyed; not mixed; pure; without disturbing elements, or unqualified; as, *unalloyed* happiness.

un·al·ter·a·ble, un·al′tėr·a·bl, *a.* Not alterable; unchangeable; immutable.—**un·al·ter·a·ble·ness,** *n.*—**un·al·ter·a·bly,** *adv.*—**un·al·tered,** un·al′tėrd, *a.*

un·am·bi·tious, un″am·bish′us, *a.* Free from ambition; without aspirations; without a strong desire to attain some end.

un-A·mer·i·can, un″a·mer′i·kan, *a.* Not American; not characteristic of or proper to the United States; considered disregardful of or antagonistic toward American customs, ideals, or institutions; unpatriotic; treasonous.

un·a·mi·a·ble, un·ā′mē·a·bl, *a.* Not amiable or friendly; unobliging; surly.

un·a·neled, un″a·nēld′, *a.* [< *un,* not, old *an-* for *on,* and O.E. *elan,* to oil, < *ele,* oil.] *Archaic,* not having received extreme unction.

u·nan·i·mous, ū·nan′i·mus, *a.* [L. *unanimus,* of one mind—*unus,* one, and *animus,* mind.] Being of one mind; agreeing in opinion or determination; showing or formed by complete accord.—**u·na·nim·i·ty,** ū″na·nim′i·tē, *n.*—**u·nan·i·mous·ly,** *adv.*—**u·nan·i·mous·ness,** *n.*

un·an·swer·a·ble, un·an′sėr·a·bl, *a.* Not to be satisfactorily answered; having no known answer; not capable of refutation.—**un·an·swer·a·bly,** *adv.*—**un·an·swered,** un″a·nsėrd, *a.*

un·ap·peal·a·ble, un″a·pē′la·bl, *a.* Not able to be carried to a higher court by appeal; not to be appealed from, as a decision or judgment.

un·ap·peas·a·ble, un″a·pē′za·bl, *a.* Not to be appeased or pacified.—**un·ap·peas·a·bly,** *adv.*—**un·ap·peased,** un″a·pēzd′, *a.*

un·ap·pe·tiz·ing, un·ap′i·tī″zing, *a.* Not appetizing; without appeal.

un·ap·pre·ci·at·ed, un″a·prē′shē·ā″tid, *a.* Not appreciated; not properly valued or esteemed.—**un·ap·pre·ci·a·tive,** un″a·prē′sha·tiv, un″a·prē′shē·ā″tiv, *a.*

un·ap·proach·a·ble, un″a·prō′cha·bl, *a.* That cannot be approached; inaccessible; difficult to know or get acquainted with; aloof; not to be equaled or rivaled; unmatched.—**un·ap·proach·a·ble·ness,** *n.*—**un·ap·proach·a·bly,** *adv.*—**un·ap·proached,** *a.*

un·ap·pro·pri·at·ed, un″a·prō′prē·ā″tid, *a.* Not appropriated; not applied or set apart for any specific use or purpose, as money; not granted to, or taken into possession by, any person, company, or corporation; as, *unappropriated* lands.

un·ap·proved, un″a·prōvd′, *a.* Not having received approval or approbation.

un·apt, un·apt′, *a.* Unfit or unsuitable; not inclined or likely; dull or slow.—**un·apt·ly,** *adv.*—**un·apt·ness,** *n.*

un·armed, un·ärmd′, *a.* Not having armor or weapons; of animals or plants, lacking hard, sharp projections, as scales, claws, or thorns.—**un·arm,** un·ärm′, *v.t.* Disarm.

un·a·shamed, un″a·shāmd′, a. Not ashamed; devoid of shame; unabashed.

un·asked, un·askt′, un·äskt′, a. Not asked; not invited; unsolicited.

un·a·spir·ing, un″a·spī′ėr·ing, a. Not aspiring; unambitious.

un·as·sail·a·ble, un″a·sā′la·bl, a. Incapable of being assailed; not open to question, disapproval, or attack.—**un·as·sail·a·ble·ness,** n.—**un·as·sail·a·bly,** adv.—**un·as·sailed,** a.

un·as·ser·tive, un″a·sur̥′tiv, a. Not assertive; not aggressive; shy.

un·as·sist·ed, un″a·sis′tid, a. Not assisted; unaided.

un·as·sum·ing, un″a·sö′ming, a. Not bold, forward, or arrogant; modest; unpretentious.—**un·as·sum·ing·ly,** adv.—**un·as·sum·ing·ness,** n.

un·at·tached, un″a·tacht′, a. Not attached; unmarried or unengaged; not associated with or committed to a certain person, organization, or task; law, not seized on account of a judgment.

un·at·tain·a·ble, un″a·tā′na·bl, a. Not able to be gained, obtained, or arrived at.—**un·at·tained,** a.

un·at·tempt·ed, un″a·temp′tid, a. Not attempted; not tried; not subjected or exposed to an attempt.

un·at·tend·ed, un″a·ten′did, a. Having no attendance; as, an unattended performance; not escorted or accompanied; not carried out or attended, often followed by to; as, work remaining unattended to; neglected; as, an unattended child.

un·au·thor·ized, un·ä′tho·rīzd″, a. Not warranted by proper authority; not formally sanctioned, or justified.

un·a·vail·a·ble, un″a·vā′la·bl, a. Not available or accessible; not suitable or ready for use.—**un·a·vail·a·bil·i·ty,** un″a·vā″la·bil′i·tē, n.—**un·a·vail·a·bly,** adv.—**un·a·vail·ing,** un″a·vā′ling, a. Ineffectual.

un·a·void·a·ble, un″a·void′a·bl, a. Not avoidable; not to be shunned; inevitable; not voidable.—**un·a·void·a·bil·i·ty,** un·a·void·a·ble·ness,** un″a·void″a·bil′i·tē, n.—**un·a·void·a·bly,** adv.

un·a·ware, un″a·wâr′, a. Not aware; not knowing; not cognizant; heedless.—adv. Unawares.—**un·a·ware·ness,** n.

un·a·wares, un″a·wârz′, adv. [An advbl. genit.; like betimes, etc.] Without being aware, or unknowingly; inadvertently; without previous preparation, premeditation, or warning; unexpectedly.

un·backed, un·bakt′, a. Without backing or support; not endorsed or wagered on; never having been mounted by a rider, as a horse; not having a back, as some stools.

un·bal·ance, un·bal′ans, v.t.—unbalanced, unbalancing. To throw out of balance; to disorder or derange, as the mind.—n. An unbalanced situation or state.

un·bal·anced, un·bal′anst, a. Not balanced or not properly balanced; lacking mental balance, or steadiness and soundness of judgment; mentally disordered or deranged; not adjusted, or not brought to an equality of debits and credits, as of an account.

un·bal·last·ed, un·bal′a·stid, a. Not ballasted, as a ship; not properly steadied or regulated; wavering.

un·bar, un·bär′, v.t.—unbarred, unbarring. To remove a bar or bars from; to unfasten; to unlock or open.

un·bat·ed, un·bā′tid, a. Not abated, lessened, or diminished; archaic, not blunted, or lacking a button, as a sword or lance.

un·bear·a·ble, un·bâr′a·bl, a. Unable to be borne or endured; intolerable.—**un·bear·a·ble·ness,** n.—**un·bear·a·bly,** adv.

un·beat·en, un·bēt′en, a. Not beaten; not struck or pounded; not mixed by beating; untrodden; as, unbeaten paths; not defeated or surpassed; as, an unbeaten competitor.—**un·beat·a·ble,** un·bēt′a·bl, a.

un·be·com·ing, un″bi·kum′ing, a. Unattractive; not becoming or suitable, esp. to a place or person; improper; indecorous.—**un·be·com·ing·ly,** adv.—**un·be·com·ing·ness,** n.

un·be·fit·ting, un″bi·fit′ing, a. Not fitting or suitable; unbecoming; improper.

un·be·known, un″bi·nōn′, a. Unknown; unperceived; without a person's knowledge, usu. followed by to. Also **un·be·knownst,** un″bi·nōnst′.

un·be·lief, un″bi·lēf′, n. Incredulity; skepticism; the absence of belief, esp. in religious faith or doctrines.

un·be·liev·a·ble, un″bi·lēv′a·bl, a. Unable to be believed; incredible.—**un·be·liev·a·bly,** adv.

un·be·liev·er, un″bi·lē′vėr, n. One who does not believe; skeptic; doubter; one unaccepting of or not believing in some particular religion; one who lacks religious beliefs; an infidel.—**un·be·liev·ing,** un″bi·lē′ving, a.—**un·be·liev·ing·ly,** adv.—**un·be·liev·ing·ness,** n.

un·bend, un·bend′, v.t.—unbent or archaic unbended, unbending. To relax, set at ease, or release, as from strain, exertion, or formality; as, to unbend the mind; to straighten out or up from a bent condition; to free from tension or flexure, as a bow. Naut. to unfasten from the spars or stays, as various sails; to loose; to untie, as any line or rope.—v.i. To become relaxed or unbent; to rid oneself of constraint or to act with freedom; to give up stiffness or austerity of manner; unwind.

un·bend·ing, un·ben′ding, a. Unyielding; stiff; resolute, as in character; rigid; inflexible.—n. Ease; relaxation.—**un·bend·ing·ly,** adv.—**un·bend·ing·ness,** n.

un·be·seem·ing, un″bi·sē′ming, a. Unbecoming; not befitting, appropriate, or suitable.

un·bi·ased, Brit. also **un·bi·assed,** un·bi′ast, a. Free from bias or prejudice; impartial.—**un·bi·ased·ly,** adv.

un·bid·den, un·bid′en, a. Not commanded; spontaneous; uninvited; not requested or summoned. Also **un·bid.**

un·bind, un·bīnd′, v.t.—unbound, unbinding. To release or free from shackles or restraints; to untie; to unfasten; to loose.

un·bit·ted, un·bit′id, a. Not bitted or bridled; uncontrolled.

un·bleached, un·blēcht′, a. Not bleached; not whitened, as by bleaching.

un·blem·ished, un·blem′isht, a. Not blemished or marred; untarnished; pure; spotless; as, an unblemished reputation.

un·blenched, un·blencht′, a. Archaic. Not disconcerted; undaunted.

un·blessed, **un·blest,** un·blest′, a. Not blessed; excluded from a blessing; unhallowed, unholy, or evil; unhappy or wretched.

un·blush·ing, un·blush′ing, a. Not blushing; destitute of shame; immodest.—**un·blush·ing·ly,** adv.

un·bod·ied, un·bod′ēd, a. Having no body; incorporeal; disembodied; formless.

un·bolt, un·bōlt′, v.t. To withdraw a bolt from, as a window or door; to unfasten or unlock; to open.—**un·bolt·ed,** a. Not fastened or freed from fastening, as with bolts.

un·bolt·ed, un·bōl′tid, a. Not bolted or sifted, as meal or flour.

un·bon·net, un·bon′it, v.i. To take off the bonnet; to uncover the head, as in respect.—v.t. To take off the bonnet from.—**un·bon·net·ed,** un·bon′i·tid, a. Bareheaded.

un·born, un·bärn′, a. Not yet born; future; still to come; not yet brought into existence or life; existing with no beginning or birth.

un·bos·om, un·bu̠z′om, un·bō′zom, v.t. To reveal, esp. in confidence; to disclose, as one's personal opinions or feelings, often used with reflexive pronouns; as, to unbosom himself.—v.i. To disclose or reveal one's opinions or feelings, esp. in confidence.—**un·bos·om·er,** n.

un·bound, un·bound′, a. Not bound, as pages in a book; untied; freed, as from shackles or bonds; unconfined; unattached, as chemically not in a bond.

un·bound·ed, un·boun′did, a. Having no bounds; unlimited in extent; very great; without restraint or control.—**un·bound·ed·ly,** adv.—**un·bound·ed·ness,** n.

un·bowed, un·boud′, a. Not bowed or bent; as, with unbowed head. Fig. not forced to yield or submit, esp. to defeat; unsubdued.

un·brace, un·brās′, v.t.—unbraced, unbracing. To remove the braces from; to free from tension; to loosen; to relax; to weaken.

un·braid, un·brād′, v.t. To separate, as anything braided, into the several strands; unravel.

un·branched, un·brancht′, un·bräncht′, a. Being without branches; not having branched divisions.

un·break·a·ble, un·brāk′a·bl, a. Not breakable.

un·bred, un·bred′, a. Untaught; untrained; never or not yet bred or mated, as a stock animal; ill-bred or unmannerly.

un·bri·dled, un·brīd′ld, a. Not harnessed with a bridle; as, an unbridled mule. Fig. unrestrained; ungoverned; unruly; as, an unbridled imagination.—**un·bri·dle,** un·brīd′l, v.t.—unbridled, unbridling.

un·bro·ken, un·brō′ken, a. Not broken; not violated, as a promise; intact or whole; not interrupted; continuous; not subdued; not tamed and rendered tractable, as a colt; not impaired or disordered.—**un·bro·ken·ly,** adv.

un·buck·le, un·buk′l, v.t.—unbuckled, unbuckling. To unfasten the buckle or buckles of.

un·build, un·bild′, v.t.—unbuilt, unbuilding. To demolish or tear down, as anything built; destroy; raze.

un·bur·den, un·bur̥′den, v.t. To rid of or free from a load or burden; to relieve the mind, heart, or the like of, as by making a confession or disclosure.

un·but·ton, un·but′on, v.t. To unfasten one or more buttons of; to open or undo as if by unfastening buttons.—v.i. To unfasten or undo one or more buttons.—**un·but·toned,** a.

un·called-for, un·käld′fär″, a. Not called for or required; unnecessary and improper; unwarranted; as, an uncalled-for remark; gratuitous.

un·can·ny, un·kan′ē, a.—uncannier, uncanniest. [Sc. and occasionally in E.] Suggesting the intervention of inexplicable or supernatural influences; as, his uncanny foresight; eerie; mysterious; strange in an uncomfortable way; beyond the normal or extraordinary, as in accuracy.—**un·can·ni·ly,** adv.—**un·can·ni·ness,** n.

un·cap, un·kap′, v.t.—uncapped, uncapping. To remove the cap or similar covering from, as a person's head; to remove a cap or cover from, as a jar or bottle.—v.i. To remove the cap from one's head, as in respect.

un·car·pet·ed, un·kär′pi·tid, a. Not carpeted, as a floor.

un·caused, un·käzd′, a. Not caused; being without cause; self-existent.

un·ceas·ing, un·sēs′ing, a. Not ceasing; perpetual; continual.—**un·ceas·ing·ly,** adv.—**un·ceas·ing·ness,** n.

un·cer·e·mo·ni·ous, un″ser·e·mō′nē·us, *a.* Not using ceremony; informal; abrupt or curt; rude or discourteous.—**un·cer·e·mo·ni·ous·ly,** *adv.*—**un·cer·e·mo·ni·ous·ness,** *n.*

un·cer·tain, un·sụr′tan, *a.* Not sure or certain; doubtful; not certainly known; indeterminate; ambiguous; not having certain knowledge; unreliable; not to be depended on; undecided; not having the mind made up; vague; not steady; fitful; fickle; variable; inconstant; capricious.—**un·cer·tain·ly,** *adv.*—**un·cer·tain·ness,** *n.*

un·cer·tain·ty, un·sụr′tan·tē, *n.* pl. **un·cer·tain·ties.** The quality or state of being uncertain; doubtfulness; hesitation; something not exactly known or uncertain; a contingency.

un·cer·tain·ty prin·ci·ple, *n. Phys.* the principle, pertaining to quantum mechanics, which states the impossibility of experimental accuracy in determining more than one observable quantity, as position or velocity, at any specified time or point, as of an electron. Also *indeterminacy principle*.

un·cer·ti·fied, un·sụr′ti·fīd″, *a.* Not certified; without certification.

un·chain, un·chān′, *v.t.* To free from chains; to let loose; set free.—**un·chain·a·ble,** *a.*—**un·chained,** *a.*

un·chal·lenged, un·chal′injd, *a.* Not challenged, demanded, or objected to; not called in question.

un·change·a·ble, un·chān′ja·bl, *a.* Not capable of change; not subject to variation; immutable.—**un·change·a·bly,** *adv.*—**un·changed,** *a.*—**un·chang·ing,** *a.*

un·chap·er·oned, un·shap′e·rōnd″, *a.* Without a chaperon.

un·charged, un·chärjd′, *a.* Not charged or having a charge, esp. electrically; as, an *uncharged* automobile battery.

un·char·i·ta·ble, un·char′i·ta·bl, *a.* Not charitable; ungenerous; unforgiving; harsh; censorious; severe in judging.—**un·char·i·ta·ble·ness,** *n.*—**un·char·i·ta·bly,** *adv.*

un·chart·ed, un·chär′tid, *a.* Not indicated or recorded, as on a map or chart; unknown; as, an *uncharted* island.

un·chaste, un·chāst′, *a.* Not chaste; lacking in virtue; impure; indecent or bawdy.—**un·chaste·ly,** *adv.*—**un·chaste·ness,** **un·chas·ti·ty,** un·chas′ti·tē, *n.*

un·chris·tian, un·kris′chan, *a.* Contrary to the laws of Christianity; opposed to the Christian principles or spirit; uncharitable; not Christian.

un·church, un·chụrch′, *v.t.* To expel, as a person, from a church; excommunicate; to deprive of the character and rights of a church.—**un·churched,** un·chụrcht′, *a.* Not belonging to or connected with a church.

un·ci·al, un′shē·al, un′shal, *a.* [L. *uncialis*, of an inch, < *uncia*, twelfth part, inch, ounce: cf. *inch* and *ounce*.] Designating, written in, or pertaining to a variety of ancient majuscule letters distinguished from modern capital majuscules by relatively greater roundness, and found esp. in the Latin and Greek manuscripts written between the 4th and 8th centuries A.D.—*n.* An uncial letter; uncial writing; a manuscript written in unicials.—**un·ci·al·ly,** *adv.*

un·ci·form, un′si·fạrm″, *a.* [L. *uncus*, a hook, and *forma*, form.] Hooklike; having a curved or hooked shape.—*n. Anat.* the unciform bone of the wrist, being wedge-shaped and with a hooked process.

un·ci·na·ri·a·sis, un″si·na·rī′a·sis, *n.* [N.L., < *Uncinaria*, genus of hookworms, < L. *uncinus*, hook.] *Pathol.* Ancylostomiasis; hookworm disease.

un·ci·nate, un′si·nit, un′si·nāt′, *a.* [L. *uncinatus*, < *uncinus*, hook, barb, < *uncus*, hook.] *Biol.* Hooked; bent at the end like a hook. Also **un·ci·nal,** **un·ci·nat·ed.**

un·ci·nus, un·sī′nus, *n.* pl. **un·ci·ni.** That which is formed, shaped, or structured like a hook.

un·cir·cum·cised, un·sụr′kum·sīzd″, *a.* Not circumcised; non-Jewish.—**un·cir·cum·ci·sion,** un″sụr·kum·sizh′an, *n.* The condition or state of not being circumcised; *scrip.* those who are uncircumcised, esp. the Gentiles.

un·civ·il, un·siv′il, *a.* Not courteous; ill-mannered; rude; uncivilized.—**un·civ·il·ly,** *adv.*

un·civ·i·lized, un·siv′i·līzd″, *a.* Not civilized; wild; barbarous; savage; not enlightened.

un·clad, un·klad′, *a.* Not clad; unclothed; naked.

un·clasp, un·klasp′, un·kläsp′, *v.t.* To loosen or undo the clasp of; to release or open from a grasp or clasp.—*v.i.* To become released or unfastened from a grasp or clasp; to relax a hold.

un·clas·si·fi·a·ble, un·klas′i·fī″a·bl, *a.* Not classifiable.—**un·clas·si·fied,** *a.*

un·cle, ung′kl, *n.* [O.Fr. *uncle* (Fr. *oncle*), < L. *avunculus*, an uncle, a dim. of *avus*, a grandfather.] The brother of one's father or mother; the husband of one's aunt; an elderly man, used as a term of direct address; *slang*, pawnbroker.—**say un·cle,** *slang.* To admit defeat; submit.

un·clean, un·klēn′, *a.* Not clean; foul or dirty; filthy; unchaste; spiritually or morally impure; wicked; evil; ceremonially impure, esp. according to the Jewish law.—**un·cleaned,** *a.*—**un·clean·ly,** un·klēn′lē, *adv.*—**un·clean·ness,** *n.*

un·clean·ly, un·klen′lē, *a.*—*uncleanlier, uncleanliest.* Impure; unclean.—**un·clean·li·ness,** *n.*

un·clear, un·klēr′, *a.* Not clear; clouded; obscure; indistinct; uncertain.—**un·cleared,** *a.*

un·clench, un·klench′, *v.t.*, *v.i.* To open or become opened from a clenched state; relax. Also **un·clinch,** un·klinch′.

Un·cle Sam, *n.* A personification or representation of the government or the people of the United States, as a tall, thin man having white chin whiskers and wearing red-and-white-striped trousers, a blue tailcoat, and a tall top hat with a band of stars.

Un·cle Tom·ism, un′kl tom′iz·um, *n.* A submissive or subservient attitude of some Negroes toward a patronizing or paternalistic position held by some whites, as involving a gradual, compromising approach toward obtaining civil rights, a term originating from the main character, Uncle Tom, in *Uncle Tom's Cabin*, by Harriet Beecher Stowe.

un·cloak, un·klōk′, *v.t.* To remove or shed the cloak or similar covering from; to reveal or unmask.—*v.i.* To divest oneself of a cloak or similar outer garments.

un·close, un·klōz′, *v.t.*, *v.i.*—*unclosed, unclosing.* To open or lay open; to disclose.

un·clothe, un·klōᴛʜ′, *v.t.*—*unclothed* or *unclad, unclothing.* To strip of clothes; to divest of covering; undress; uncover.—**un·clothed,** *a.*

un·clut·tered, un·klut′ẽrd, *a.* Neat; orderly; without litter.

un·coil, un·koil′, *v.t.* To unwind, as a rope which has been coiled.—*v.i.* To become released or unwound from any coiled position, as a snake.

un·coined, un·koind′, *a.* Not coined; natural; not fabricated; not minted.

un·com·fort·a·ble, un·kumf′ta·bl, un·kum′fẽr·ta·bl, *a.* Affording no comfort; causing bodily discomfort; uneasy; ill at ease; disquieting.—**un·com·fort·a·ble·ness,** *n.*—**un·com·fort·a·bly,** *adv.*

un·com·mit·ted, un″kọ·mit′id, *a.* Not committed; not obligated by any pledge to

hold to certain beliefs, loyalties, or any course of action.

un·com·mon, un·kom′ọn, *a.* Not common; not usual; infrequent; rare; remarkable; extraordinary.—**un·com·mon·ly,** un·kom′ọn·lē, *adv.*—**un·com·mon·ness,** *n.*

un·com·mu·ni·ca·tive, un″ko·mū′ni·kā″tiv, un″ko·mū′ni·ka·tiv, *a.* Not inclined to communicate with others, as feelings, information, or opinions; reserved.—**un·com·mu·ni·ca·tive·ly,** *adv.*—**un·com·mu·ni·ca·tive·ness,** *n.*

un·com·plet·ed, un″kom·plē′tid, *a.* Not completed or entire; unfinished; imperfect.

un·com·pli·men·ta·ry, un″kom·pli·men′ta·rē, un″kom·pli·men′trē, *a.* Not complimentary; unflattering; disparaging; derogatory.

un·com·pre·hend·ing, un″kom·pri·hen′ding, *a.* Not comprehending or understanding; not perceiving; not embracing or including.—**un·com·pre·hend·ed,** *a.*—**un·com·pre·hen·si·ble,** un″kom·pri·hen′si·bl, *a.*

un·com·pro·mis·ing, un·kom′pro·mī″zing, *a.* Not accepting or making of any compromise; not agreeing to terms; inflexible; unyielding; making no exceptions; strict or undeviating.—**un·com·pro·mised,** *a.*—**un·com·pro·mis·ing·ly,** *adv.*—**un·com·pro·mis·ing·ness,** *n.*

un·con·cern, un″kon·sụrn′, *n.* Want of interest or concern; indifference; freedom from solicitude; cool and undisturbed state of mind.

un·con·cerned, un″kon·sụrnd′, *a.* Feeling no concern or solicitude; easy in mind; having or taking no interest; not affected; indifferent.—**un·con·cern·ed·ly,** un″kon·sụr′nid·lē, *adv.*—**un·con·cern·ed·ness,** *n.*

un·con·di·tion·al, un″kon·dish′a·nal, *a.* Not limited by any conditions; absolute.—**un·con·di·tion·al·ly,** *adv.*

un·con·di·tioned, un″kon·dish′and, *a.* Not subject to, or without, conditions. *Philos.* absolute; infinite. *Psychol.* not conditioned or acquired; natural; unlearned.

un·con·fined, un″kon·find′, *a.* Not confined or limited; free from restraint or control; not having narrow limits; wide and comprehensive.

un·con·firmed, un″kon·fụrmd′, *a.* Not firmly established; not ratified; not strengthened or established by additional testimony; unverified; not confirmed according to religious rites.

un·con·form·a·ble, un″kon·fạr′ma·bl, *a.* Not consistent; not conforming; not conformable. *Geol.* exhibiting unconformity or discontinuous, irregular stratigraphic sequence.—**un·con·form·a·bil·i·ty,** *n.*—**un·con·form·a·bly,** *adv.*

un·con·form·i·ty, un″kon·fạr′mi·tē, *n.* pl. **un·con·form·i·ties.** Lack of conformity; incongruity; inconsistency; *geol.* a lack of continuity in succeeding layers of rocks often accompanied by erosion.

un·con·nect·ed, un″ko·nek′tid, *a.* Not connected; separate; not related, as logically; not coherent.—**un·con·nect·ed·ly,** *adv.*—**un·con·nect·ed·ness,** *n.*

un·con·quer·a·ble, un·kong′kẽr·a·bl, *a.* Not conquerable; not to be overcome in contest; incapable of being subdued or brought under control; insuperable.—**un·con·quered,** *a.*

un·con·scion·a·ble, un·kon′sha·na·bl, *a.* Contrary to the dictates of conscience; unscrupulous or unprincipled; exceeding that which is reasonable or customary; inordinate; unjustifiable.—**un·con·scion·a·ble·ness,** *n.*—**un·con·scion·a·bly,** *adv.*

un·con·scious, un·kon′shus, *a.* Not conscious or aware, often used with *of*;

temporarily devoid of consciousness or not having the mental faculties awake; not endowed with consciousness or knowledge of one's existence, condition, or situation; not known to or perceived by oneself; as, an *unconscious* mistake; unintentional; as, an *unconscious* slight.—*n. Psychol.* a general name for the mental processes which are not conscious.—**un·con·scious·ly,** *adv.*—**un·con·scious·ness,** *n.*

un·con·sid·ered, un″kon·sid′ẽrd, *a.* Not considered or reflected on; not taken into consideration; not esteemed or highly regarded.

un·con·sti·tu·tion·al, un″kon·sti·tö′sha-nal, un″kon·sti·tū′sha·nal, *a.* Not consistent or in accordance with the basic laws or constitution, esp. of a nation.—**un·con·sti·tu·tion·al·i·ty,** *n.*—**un·con·sti·tu·tion·al·ly,** *adv.*

un·con·strained, un″kon·strānd′, *a.* Free from constraint; voluntary; having no feeling that checks one's words or actions; natural.

un·con·test·ed, un″kon·tes′tid, *a.* Not contested; not disputed or contended; unchallenged.

un·con·trol·la·ble, un″kon·trō′la·bl, *a.* That cannot be controlled, ruled, or restrained; ungovernable.—**un·con·trol·la·bly,** *adv.*—**un·con·trolled,** *a.*

un·con·ven·tion·al, un″kon·ven′sha·nal, *a.* Not bound by or conforming to convention, rule, or precedent; out of the ordinary; free from conventionality; nonconformist.—**un·con·ven·tion·al·i·ty,** un″kon·ven″sha·nal′i·tē, *n.*—**un·con·ven·tion·al·ly,** *adv.*

un·con·vinced, un″kon·vinst′, *a.* Not persuaded or brought to belief; not proven or satisfied, as by evidence.—**un·con·vinc·ing,** *a.*

un·cork, un·kẏrk′, *v.t.* To draw the cork from; *colloq.* to release or let go, esp. unexpectedly.—**un·corked,** *a.*

un·cor·rect·ed, un″ko·rek′tid, *a.* Not corrected; not revised, rectified, or amended; not punished, restrained, or rebuked.

un·count·ed, un·koun′tid, *a.* Not counted; innumerable.

un·cou·ple, un·kup′l, *v.t.*—**uncoupled,** *uncoupling.* To unfasten or release, as anything coupled; to loose or unleash, as a dog; to disconnect.—*v.i.* To become loose or unfastened.

un·cour·te·ous, un·kẏr′tē·us, *a.* Not courteous; uncivil; not polite.

un·couth, un·kōth′, *a.* [O.E. *uncúth,* unknown—*un,* not, and *cúth,* pp. of *cunnan,* to know.] Lacking in manners or social graces; crude; awkward or ungainly; strange or odd, esp. in appearance; unusual; *archaic,* unknown or unfamiliar.—**un·couth·ly,** *adv.* —**un·couth·ness,** *n.*

un·cov·er, un·kuv′ẽr, *v.t.* To lay bare or make known; to disclose; to remove a cover or covering from; to remove a head covering from, esp. a hat as in showing respect.—*v.i.* To take off a cover or covering; to take off one's hat, as in showing respect.

un·cov·ered, un·kuv′ẽrd, *a.* Without a cover or covering; without insurance coverage or collateral protection; bareheaded.

un·cre·at·ed, un″krē·ā′tid, *a.* Not created or produced by creation; self-existent or existing eternally; not yet created.

un·crit·i·cal, un·krit′i·kal, *a.* Not critical; wanting in critical powers or discrimination; not according to the rules of criticism or analysis.—**un·crit·i·cal·ly,** *adv.*

unc·tion, ungk′shan, *n.* [= Fr. *onction,* < L. *unctio(n-),* an anointing, an ointment, < *ungere, unguere,* smear, anoint: cf. *unguent* and *ointment.*] The act of anointing, esp. for medical purposes or as a religious

rite; that which is applied or used in anointing; an unguent or ointment. *Eccles.* the oil used in religious rites, as in anointing the sick or dying; see *extreme unction.* Something soothing or comforting, as a soothing thought; a soothing, sympathetic, and persuasive quality in discourse, esp. in religious subjects; a moving or appealing force in public delivery; a professional, conventional, or affected earnestness or fervor in utterance.

unc·tu·ous, ungk′chö·us, *a.* [= Fr. *onctueux,* < M.L. *unctuosus,* < L. *unctum,* ointment, < *ungere:* see *unction.*] Of the nature of, resembling, or characteristic of an unguent or ointment; oily; greasy; having an oily or soapy feel, as certain minerals; rich, esp. in matter that is organic and workable, as of soil; plastic, as of clay; characterized by religious unction or fervor, esp. of an affected kind; as, an *unctuous* preacher; smug; excessively smooth or suave.—**unc·tu·os·i·ty,** unc·tu·ous·ness, ungk′chö·os′i·tē, *n.*—**unc·tu·ous·ly,** *adv.*

un·cul·ti·vat·ed, un·kul′ti·vā′tid, *a.* Not cultivated or tilled; not produced or developed by cultivation; not refined; not cultured.—**un·cul·ti·va·ble, un·cul·ti·vat·a·ble,** *a.*

un·curl, un·kẏrl′, *v.t.* To straighten out, as something curled.—*v.i.* To become straight from a curled state.

un·cut, un·kut′, *a.* Not cut; unabridged; not shortened; not cut open at the edges, as the leaves of a book; not cut to shape, or not ground; as, an *uncut* gem.

un·daunt·ed, un·dạn′tid, *a.* Not daunted; not discouraged or dismayed; fearless; intrepid.—**un·daunt·ed·ly,** *adv.*—**un·daunt·ed·ness,** *n.*

un·de·ceive, un″di·sēv′, *v.t.*—*undeceived, undeceiving.* To free from deception, misunderstanding, illusion, or mistake.—**un·de·ceiv·a·ble,** *n.*

un·de·cid·ed, un″di·sī′did, *a.* Not decided or determined; not settled; not having the mind made up; irresolute.—**un·de·cid·ed·ly,** *adv.*—**un·de·cid·ed·ness,** *n.*

un·de·cil·lion, un″di·sil′yan, *n.* The number which, in Great Britain and Germany, is the eleventh power of a million, represented by 1 followed by 66 ciphers, and in the U.S. and France, is a thousand decillions, represented by 1 followed by 36 ciphers.—*a.* —**un·de·cil·lionth,** *a., n.*

un·de·fined, un″di·fīnd′, *a.* Not defined; not having fixed limits; indefinite; not defined or explained.—**un·de·fin·a·ble,** *a.*

un·de·mon·stra·tive, un″de·mon′stra·tiv, *a.* Not demonstrative; not inclined to outwardly express the feelings; reserved.—**un·de·mon·stra·tive·ly,** *adv.*—**un·de·mon·stra·tive·ness,** *n.*

un·de·ni·a·ble, un″di·nī′a·bl, *a.* Incapable of being denied; indisputable; evidently true; unquestionably good.— **un·de·ni·a·ble·ness,** *n.*—**un·de·ni·a·bly,** *adv.*—**un·de·nied,** *a.*

un·de·pend·a·ble, un″di·pen′da·bl, *a.* Not dependable; unreliable; untrustworthy. —**un·de·pend·a·bil·i·ty, un·de·pend·a·ble·ness,** *n.*

un·der, un′dẽr, *prep.* [O.E. *under* = D. *onder* = G. *unter* = Icel. *undir* = Goth. *undar,* under: cf. Skt. *adhara,* lower, *adhas,* below, L. *inferior,* lower, *infra,* below.] Beneath and covered by; below the surface of; as, *under* the ground; at a point or position lower than; in the position or state of bearing, supporting, sustaining, or undergoing; as, to be *under* heavy expense; beneath, or included in, as a classification; as designated, indicated, or represented by; as, *under* a new name; below in degree, amount, price, or the like; less than; below in rank, dignity, or the like; subject to the

rule, direction, guidance, or instruction of; as, *under* orders; subject to the influence or conditioning force of; as, *under* an impression; with the favor or aid of; as, *under* protection; authorized, warranted, or attested by; as, *under* one's seal; in accordance with; during the regime, government, or political system of.—*adv.* Below or beneath something; beneath the surface; in a lower place; in a lower degree or amount, esp. than is required; in a subordinate position or condition; in or into subjection or submission.—*a.* Situated beneath; lower in position; lower in degree or amount, esp. than is required or desired; lower in rank or condition; subordinate; inferior; restrained or controlled, as by some force or person.—**go un·der,** to be drowning; to succumb, as in a struggle; to fail, esp. in business.

un·der·a·chiev·er, un″dẽr·a·chē′vẽr, *n.* One whose performance is low compared to his theoretical potential, esp. in schoolwork. —**un·der·a·chieve·ment,** *n.*

un·der·act, un″dẽr·akt′, *v.t., v.i.* To act or perform inadequately, or without sufficient energy or force; underplay.

un·der·age, un″dẽr·āj′, *a.* Not having reached a requisite or legal age; immature, esp. legally.—un′dẽr·ij′, *n.* Shortage.

un·der·arm, un′dẽr·ärm′, *a.* Under the arm; as, an *underarm* seam of a garment; *sports,* executed or delivered with the hand below the shoulder, or underhand.—*adv. Sports,* underhand.—*n.* The armpit.

un·der·bel·ly, un′dẽr·bel″ē, *n. pl.* **un·der·bel·lies.** The lower area of the abdomen; *fig.* any area that is unprotected or vulnerable, as to attack.

un·der·bid, un″dẽr·bid′, *v.t.*—*underbid, underbidding.* To bid less than, as at a letting of contracts or in other competitions; *contract bridge,* to bid, as a hand, so as to arrive at a contract short of a makable game or slam.—**un·der·bid·der,** *n.*

un·der·bod·y, un′dẽr·bod″ē, *n. pl.* **un·der·bod·ies.** The underside, as of an animal, machine, or vehicle.

un·der·bred, un″dẽr·bred′, *a.* Of inferior breeding or manners; ill-bred; not thoroughbred or of pure breed; as, an *underbred* dog.

un·der·brush, un′dẽr·brush″, *n.* Shrubs and small trees in a wood, growing under taller trees; undergrowth. Also **un·der·bush,** un′dẽr·bush″.

un·der·car·riage, un′dẽr·kar″ij, *n.* The supporting framework beneath the body of an automobile or other vehicle; the portions of an airplane beneath the body, serving as a landing gear.

un·der·charge, un″dẽr·chärj′, *v.t.*—*undercharged, undercharging.* To charge less than a fair or usual price for; to take too low a price from; to put into or load with an inadequate charge, esp. a gun.—*n.* Too low a charge or price; any load or charge that is insufficient or inadequate.

un·der·class·man, un″dẽr·klas′man, un″dẽr·kläs′man, *n. pl.* **un·der·class·men.** A student belonging to the class of freshmen or sophomores, as in a college or secondary school.

un·der·clothes, un′dẽr·klōz″, un′dẽr·klōthz″, *n. pl.* Underwear. Also **un·der·cloth·ing,** un′dẽr·klōthing″.

un·der·coat, un′dẽr·kōt″, *n.* A coat that is worn under another; underfur. A coat or layer of varnish, paint, or another surface-sealing compound over which a finishing coat may be applied; also **un·der·coat·ing,** un′dẽr·kō″ting.—*v.t.* To apply any undercoating or undercoat to, as in furniture finishing.

un·der·col·ored, un″dẽr·kul′ẽrd, *a.* Having too little color, esp. when needed or suitable.

un·der·cool, un″dẽr·kōl′, v.t. Supercool.

un·der·cov·er, un″dẽr·kuv′ẽr, un′dẽr·-kuv″ẽr, a. Done or acting in secret, esp. working as a spy or secret investigator; secret.

un·der·croft, un′dẽr·krȧft″, un′dẽr·kroft″, n. [Under, and croft, a corruption of crypt.] A vault or room that is underground, esp. a crypt of a church.

un·der·cur·rent, un′dẽr·kur″ent, un′dẽr·-kur″ent, n. A current below the upper or surface currents, or below the surface, as of a body of water or air; fig. an underlying tendency more or less different from what is visible or apparent.

un·der·cut, un′dẽr·kut″, v.t.—undercut, undercutting. To cut under or beneath; to cut away material from so as to leave a portion overhanging, as in carving or sculpture; to undersell, or to work for wages or payment lower than, as some competitor; sports, to give, as a ball, a backspin, slice, or cut by an oblique or underhand stroke, esp. in golf or tennis.—v.i. To undercut any person or thing.—n. A cut, or a cutting away, underneath; a notch cut in a tree to determine the direction in which the tree is to fall and to prevent its splitting. Chiefly Brit. the tenderloin or fillet of beef; sports, a backspin, esp. in golf, or a slice or cut, esp. in tennis, given to the ball.—a. Cut away underneath or resulting from such a cut.

un·der·de·vel·oped, un″dẽr·di·vel′apt, a. Insufficiently or incompletely developed; econ. insufficiently or incompletely industrialized; photog. lacking a proper degree of contrast because of insufficient developing or other factors, as of any negative.—**un·der·de·vel·op**, **un·der·de·-vel·ope**, v.t.—underdeveloped, underdeveloping.

un·der·do, un″dẽr·dö′, v.t., v.i.—past underdid, pp. underdone, ppr. underdoing. To do less thoroughly than is requisite or normal.

un·der·dog, un″dẽr·dȧg″, un′dẽr·dog″, n. One, esp. a contestant, who is pitted against a presumably superior opponent in any struggle or conflict; any predicted loser; a victim of neglect or oppression, esp. by society.

un·der·done, un′dẽr·dun′, a. Not sufficiently or fully cooked; rare; as, underdone meat.

un·der·draw·ers, un′dẽr·drȧrz″, n. pl. An article of underclothing, as shorts or briefs, which covers one's lower body and usu. the upper parts of one's legs. Also drawers.

un·der·es·ti·mate, un″dẽr·es′ti·māt″, v.t., v.i.—underestimated, underestimating. To estimate at too low a rate.—un″dẽr·es′-ti·mit, un″dẽr·es′ti·māt″, n. An estimate at too low a rate.—**un·der·es·ti·ma·tion**, n.

un·der·ex·pose, un″dẽr·ik·spōz′, v.t.—underexposed, underexposing. To expose, as to light, for too short a time, as in photography.—**un·der·ex·po·sure**, un″dẽr·ik·-spō′zhẽr, n.

un·der·feed, un″dẽr·fēd′, un′dẽr·fēd″, v.t.—underfed, underfeeding. To feed insufficiently, un″dẽr·fēd′. To feed or supply with fuel from underneath, as a furnace, un′dẽr·fēd′.

un·der·foot, un′dẽr·fut′, adv., a. Under the foot or feet; on the ground; below or underneath; in the way.

un·der·fur, un′dẽr·fur″, n. The fur, or fine, soft, thick, hairy coating, underlying the longer and coarser outer hair in certain animals, as seals, otters, and beavers. Also undercoat.

un·der·gar·ment, un′dẽr·gär″ment, n. A garment worn under another garment, esp. under an outer garment.

un·der·gird, un″dẽr·gurd′, v.t.—under-

girded or undergirt, undergirding. To support, secure, or strengthen, as by a rope passed beneath; to strengthen at the base, or provide with fundamental support.

un·der·glaze, un′dẽr·glāz″, a. Ceram. applied or suitable for application before the glaze is put on, as decoration or colors in porcelain painting.—n.

un·der·go, un″dẽr·gō′, v.t.—past underwent, pp. undergone, ppr. undergoing. To be subjected to; to experience; to pass through; to bear; to endure; to suffer.

un·der·grad·u·ate, un″dẽr·graj′ö·it, n. A student of a university or college who has not received his first degree.—a. Having the position or status of such a student; of, characteristic of, or pertaining to undergraduates.

un·der·ground, un′dẽr·ground′, adv. Beneath the surface of the ground. Fig. in concealment or secrecy; not openly.—un′dẽr·ground′, a. Existing, situated, operating, or taking place beneath the surface of the ground. Fig. hidden; secret; clandestine.—un′dẽr·ground″, n. The place or region beneath the surface of the ground; any underground space or passage; a clandestine organization or movement engaged in subversive or disruptive activity against the established governmental authority, esp. in an occupied country; Brit. a subway.

un·der·ground rail·road, n. A railroad running through a continuous tunnel, as under the streets of a city; subway; also **un·der·ground rail·way**. (Cap.) in the United States before the abolition of slavery, a cooperative arrangement among certain opponents of slavery for helping fugitive slaves to escape into Canada or some other place of safety.

un·der·grown, un′dẽr·grōn″, un″dẽr·grōn′, a. Not fully grown; of low stature; undersized; having undergrowth.

un·der·growth, un′dẽr·grōth″, n. Shrubs, small trees, and other vegetation growing among or under larger trees, as in forests; also underbrush. The state or condition of being undersized or undergrown; the dense growth of fine, short hair forming the underfur in animal pelts.

un·der·hand, un′dẽr·hand″, a. Secret or covert; sly; not open, esp. secret and crafty or dishonorable. Sports, done or delivered underhand; as, underhand pitching or bowling; underarm.—adv. Secretly; stealthily; slyly; not openly or aboveboard. Sports, with the hand below the shoulder, as in pitching or bowling a ball; underarm.

un·der·hand·ed, un′dẽr·han′did, a. Underhand; short-handed.—**un·der·hand·-ed·ly**, adv.—**un·der·hand·ed·ness**, n.

un·der·hung, un″dẽr·hung′, a. Anat. projecting beyond the upper jaw, as applied to the under or lower jaw; having this projection of the jaw. Running or resting on some rail or track supported from beneath, as certain sliding doors; mech. underslung.

un·der·laid, un″dẽr·lād′, a. Lying or laid beneath; supporting; having something lying or laid beneath.

un·der·lay, un″dẽr·lā′, v.t.—underlaid, underlaying. To lay, as one thing under or beneath another; to provide with something laid underneath; to raise or support with something laid underneath; to traverse or cover the bottom of.—un″dẽr·lā′, n. Something underlaid; print. a piece or pieces of paper put under cuts or types to bring them to the proper height for printing.

un·der·let, un″dẽr·let′, v.t.—underlet, underletting. To let or lease below the actual value; to sublet.

un·der·lie, un″dẽr·li′, v.t.—past underlay, pp. underlain, ppr. underlying. To lie beneath; to be situated under; to be at the

basis of; to support; to form the foundation of; to be subject or liable to; finance, to constitute the first lien or security over.

un·der·line, un″dẽr·lin″, un″dẽr·lin′, v.t.—underlined, underlining. To mark underneath or below with a line; to underscore; to emphasize; to stress.—un′dẽr·lin″, n. A line beneath a word or phrase to denote emphasis.

un·der·ling, un′dẽr·ling, n. [Late O.E. underling.] A subordinate, used esp. in disparagement; an inferior.

un·der·lip, un′dẽr·lip″, n. Lower lip.

un·der·ly·ing, un′dẽr·li″ing, a. Lying under or beneath; basic or fundamental; discoverable or evident only by close inspection; anterior and prior in claim to another one, as of a mortgage.

un·der·mine, un″dẽr·min′, un′dẽr·min″, v.t.—undermined, undermining. To form a mine or passage or make an excavation under, as in military operations, un″dẽr·-min′. To wear away and weaken the foundations or base of; as, a river undermining its banks; to affect injuriously or weaken by secret or underhand means; to weaken or destroy insidiously or gradually; as, to undermine his health, un′dẽr·min″, un″dẽr·min′.—**un·der·min·er**, n.

un·der·most, un′dẽr·mōst″, a., adv. Lowest in position, place, rank, condition, or the like.

un·der·neath, un″dẽr·nēth′, prep. [Under, and -neath, as in beneath.] Under; beneath or below; under the power or control of; under the appearance, form, or disguise of.—adv. Beneath; below; in or at a lower place or level; on the underside.—a. Lower; positioned under or below.—n. Underside; the lower part.

un·der·nour·ish, un″dẽr·nur′ish, un″dẽr·nur′ish, v.t. To supply with an inadequate amount of food or nourishment for proper growth and health.—**un·der·-nour·ish·ment**, n.

un·der·pants, un′dẽr·pants″, n. pl. An undergarment for the lower part of the body; drawers.

un·der·part, un′dẽr·pärt″, n. The lower or under side, or a part on a lower side.

un·der·pass, un′dẽr·pas″, un′dẽr·päs″, n. A passage running underneath, esp. a passage for pedestrians or vehicles, or both, crossing under a railway or road.

un·der·pin, un″dẽr·pin′, v.t.—underpinned, underpinning. To pin or support underneath; to place something, as a prop, under for support or foundation, esp. when a previous support is removed; to substantiate or corroborate.

un·der·pin·ning, un′dẽr·pin″ing, n. The solid construction or other supports introduced beneath a wall or building, esp. one already constructed; a support or prop; pl., colloq. legs.

un·der·play, un″dẽr·plā′, un′dẽr·plā″, v.t. To project or present with restraint, as in acting a role with less than customary or requisite overt emotion; underact.—v.i. To act a role in a low-key or subtle manner; to underact; to fail to make full use of assets or advantages, as in playing cards.

un·der·plot, un′dẽr·plot″, n. A plot subordinate to another plot, as in a play or a novel.

un·der·priv·i·leged, un′dẽr·priv′i·lijd, un′dẽr·priv′lijd, a. Denied access by restrictive economic or social conditions to the fundamental privileges or rights to which all members of a society are entitled.

un·der·pro·duc·tion, un′dẽr·pro·duk″-shan, n. Production that is less than normal or inadequate to the demand.

un·der·proof, un′dẽr·pröf′, a. Containing a smaller proportion of alcohol than proof spirit.

un·der·rate, un″dẽr·rāt′, v.t.—underrated,

underrating. To rate too low; to undervalue; to underestimate.

un·der·ripe, un″dẽr·rīp′, *a.* Not entirely or sufficiently ripe, as fruits.

un·der·run, un″dẽr·run′, *v.t.*—past *underran,* pp. *underrun,* ppr. *underrunning.* To run, pass, or go under; *naut.* to pass under, as a cable in a boat for the purpose of examining.—*n.* That which runs or passes underneath, as an undercurrent.

un·der·score, un″dẽr·skōr′, un″dẽr·skạr′, *v.t.*—*underscored, underscoring.* To underline or draw a line or lines under; to accentuate or emphasize.—un′dẽr·skōr″, un′dẽr·skạr″, *n.* An underline.

un·der·sea, un′dẽr·sē″, *a.* Located, adapted for use, or carried on beneath the sea's surface; submarine; as, an *undersea* vessel. —*adv.* Beneath the sea's surface. Also **un·der·seas,** un′dẽr·sēz′.

un·der·sec·re·tar·y, un″dẽr·sek′ri·ter″ē, *n.* pl. **un·der·sec·re·tar·ies.** A secretary subordinate to the principal secretary, as in a department of the government.

un·der·sell, un″dẽr·sel′, *v.t.*—*undersold, underselling.* To sell merchandise at a lower price than, as a competitor; to sell for less than the actual price or value.—**un·der·- sell·er,** *n.*

un·der·shirt, un′dẽr·shụrt″, *n.* A collarless inner shirt, either with or without sleeves, worn beneath another shirt and next to the skin.

un·der·shoot, un″dẽr·shöt′, un′dẽr·shöt″, *v.t.*—*undershot, undershooting.* To shoot below or short of, as a target; to fail to reach in aiming at; *aeron.* to drop a bomb or land an aircraft short of, as a designated spot.—*v.i.* To shoot or fall short of some designated mark or target.

un·der·shot, un′dẽr·shot″, *a.* Having the lower incisor teeth projecting beyond the upper ones when the mouth is closed, as a dog; having a lower jaw that protrudes; driven by water passing beneath, as a water wheel.

un·der·shrub, un′dẽr·shrub″, *n.* A low shrub.

un·der·side, un′dẽr·sīd″, *n.* The lower side or surface underneath.

un·der·sign, un″dẽr·sīn′, un′dẽr·sīn″, *v.t.* To sign or write one's name at the foot or end of, as any document or letter.—**un·- der·signed,** un″dẽr·sīnd′, *a.* Having one's name signed at the bottom or end of any document or letter; signed or subscribed at the bottom or end, as of some writing.—**the un·der·signed,** the person or persons signing any document.

un·der·sized, un′dẽr·sīzd″, *a.* Being of a size or stature less than normal, usual, or average. Also **un·der·size.**

un·der·skirt, un′dẽr·skụrt″, *n.* A skirt worn under an outer skirt or dress; petticoat; the skirt used as a foundation under a draped gown.

un·der·slung, un′dẽr·slung′, *a. Mech.* pertaining to a vehicle frame suspended below, rather than supported by, the axles of the vehicle; underhung. Having the center of gravity low; squat.

un·der·soil, un′dẽr·soil″, *n.* Subsoil.

un·der·song, un′dẽr·sạng″, un′dẽr·song″, *n. Mus.* an accompaniment of a song; a subordinate strain or melody. An underlying or suggested meaning.

un·der·spin, un′dẽr·spin″, *n.* Backspin.

un·der·stand, un″dẽr·stand′, *v.t.*—*understood, understanding.* [O.E. *understandan.*] To perceive the meaning of, grasp the idea of, or comprehend; to be thoroughly acquainted or familiar with, as a subject; to apprehend clearly the character or nature of, as a person; to comprehend, as by knowing the symbols or words employed; as, to *understand* French; to interpret; as, to try to *understand* his remarks; to take as

a fact or as settled; as, to *understand* payment is due immediately; to gain knowledge of, come to know, or learn by hearing, as: I *understand* my neighbor is vacationing. To accept as truth or to believe; to conceive the meaning of in a particular way; as, to *understand* the phrase literally; to supply mentally, as an unexpressed word, phrase, or idea necessary to the complete meaning.— *v.i.* To perceive what is meant; to have information or knowledge about something; as, to *understand* about a matter; to be informed; to believe; to accept with tolerance or sympathy, as: If you fail, she will *understand.*—**un·der·stand·a·bil·i·ty,** *n.* —**un·der·stand·a·ble,** un″dẽr·stan′da·bl, *a.*—**un·der·stand·a·bly,** *adv.*

un·der·stand·ing, un″dẽr·stan′ding, *n.* The act of one who understands; the ability or power to acquire and interpret knowledge; comprehension; intelligence; mental faculties, or power of discernment; personal interpretation; as, his *understanding* of the situation; knowledge of a particular field; ability to cope or deal with something; a state of mutually friendly relations between persons; a mutual agreement, usu. of a private or unannounced kind; as, an *understanding* about who drives to work; an agreement involving a joint action or settling differences, as: The two disputing factions reached an *understanding.* *Philos.* the power of abstract thought; logical power.—*a.* Possessing or showing intelligence, comprehension, or discernment; tolerant.—**un·der·stand·ing·ly,** *adv.*

un·der·state, un″dẽr·stāt′, *v.t.*—*understated, understating.* To state or represent less strongly than the truth will bear; to state in a deliberately restrained manner, esp. to imply approval or praise by calling attention to a contrast between the tone of the statement and the significance of its content.

un·der·state·ment, un′dẽr·stāt″ment, *n. Rhet., liter.* The act or an instance of understating; an unemphatic statement devised to heighten the effect of its content. See *meiosis.*

un·der·stood, un″dẽr·stụd′, *a.* Agreed upon or consented to; assumed; unexpressed but implied or supplied mentally; as, an *understood* meaning.

un·der·strap·per, un′dẽr·strap″ẽr, *n.* [Cf. *strapper,* in local sense of groom.] An underling; a subordinate of little importance.

un·der·stud·y, un′dẽr·stud″ē, *v.t.*—*understudied, understudying.* To study, as a part, in order to replace the regular actor or actress when necessary.—*v.i.* To act as an understudy to an actor or actress.—*n.* pl. **un·der·stud·ies.** One trained and retained to act as a substitute for an actor or actress.

un·der·sur·face, un′dẽr·sụr″fis, *n.* Underside.—*a.* Beneath the surface; submerged or moving about in a submerged area.

un·der·take, un″dẽr·tāk′, *v.t.*—past *undertook,* pp. *undertaken,* ppr. *undertaking.* To take on oneself, as a task or performance; to attempt; to assume responsibility for, as by a formal promise or agreement; to warrant or guarantee.

un·der·tak·er, un″dẽr·tā′kẽr, un′dẽr·tā″kẽr, *n.* One who undertakes something, un″dẽr·tā′kẽr. One whose business it is to prepare the dead for burial and to take charge of funerals, un′dẽr·tā″kẽr; also *mortician.*

un·der·tak·ing, un″dẽr·tā′king, un′dẽr·- tā″king, *n.* The act of one who undertakes any task or responsibility; a task, enterprise, or something undertaken; a promise, pledge, or guarantee, un″dẽr·tā′king. The business of an undertaker or funeral director, un′dẽr·tā″king.

un·der·ten·ant, un′dẽr·ten″ant, *n.* A subtenant; a subleassee.

un·der-the-coun·ter, un′dẽr·THe·koun′- tẽr, *a.* Sold or transacted surreptitiously; illegal; illicit.

un·der·tone, un′dẽr·tōn″, *n.* A low or subdued tone, as of speech or sound; an underlying quality or element; an undercurrent; a subdued tone or color; a color seen through some superimposed color or colors.

un·der·tow, un′dẽr·tō″, *n.* The backward, subsurface flow of a wave breaking on a beach; a forceful current of water below the surface in a direction different from that at the surface.

un·der·trick, un′dẽr·trik″, *n. Cards,* a trick which the declarer needs but fails to win to make the number bid.

un·der·trump, un′dẽr·trump′, *v.i. Cards,* to play a lower trump than has already been played.—*v.t. Cards,* to play a lower trump than, as another player.

un·der·val·ue, un″dẽr·val′ū, *v.t.*—*undervalued, undervaluing.* To value below the real worth; to put too low a value on; to diminish in value or make of less value; to esteem lightly or too low.—**un·der·val·- u·a·tion,** *n.*

un·der·vest, un′dẽr·vest″, *n. Brit.* an undershirt.

un·der·waist, un′dẽr·wāst″, *n.* A waist worn under another waist.

un·der·wa·ter, un′dẽr·wạ′tẽr, un′dẽr·- wot′ẽr, *a.* Being or occurring under water; designed to be used under water; as, an *underwater* boat or a submarine; lying below a boat's water line.—*adv.*—*n.*

un·der·wear, un′dẽr·wâr″, *n.* Garments or clothing worn under the outer clothing, esp. those nearest the skin. Also *underclothes, underclothing.*

un·der·weight, un′dẽr·wāt″, *n.* Weight deficiency; weight below average.—un′dẽr·- wāt′, *a.* Having a weight deficiency.

un·der·wing, un′dẽr·wing″, *n. Entom.* A posterior wing; any of the genus *Catocala,* of relatively large moths having the hind wings brightly colored with red, yellow, or orange concentric bands.

un·der·wood, un′dẽr·wụd″, *n.* Small trees or bushes that grow among taller trees; underbrush; undergrowth.

un·der·world, un′dẽr·wụrld″, *n.* A social stratum of persons engaged in vice or crime; organized criminals; racketeers. *Gr. and Rom. mythol.* the region inhabited by the dead; Hades. The antipodes. *Archaic,* the sublunary world; the earth.

un·der·write, un′dẽr·rīt″, *v.t.*—past *underwrote,* pp. *underwritten,* ppr. *underwriting.* To write below or under; to subscribe; to set one's name to, as a statement with which one agrees; to commit oneself to contribute money to or finance, as a project to be implemented by others; to guarantee to assume financial responsibility for, as a business enterprise. *Insurance,* to sign, as a policy, thereby becoming answerable for specific losses stated in the policy; to insure; to assume liability for, by insurance, as losses to a certain amount. *Finance,* to guarantee the sale of, as a new issue of stock or other securities to be presented for public subscription.—*v.i.* To engage in the business of underwriting.

un·der·writ·er, un′dẽr·rī″tẽr, *n.* A person or company engaged in the insurance business; one who calculates the risk and determines the cost of the premium on an insurance policy; a person or corporate body that underwrites issues of stocks, bonds, or other securities.

un·de·served, un″di·zụrvd′, *a.* Not deserved; not merited.—**un·de·serv·ing,** un″- di·zụr′ving, *a.*

un·de·signed, un″di·zīnd′, *a.* Not previously planned; unintentional.—**un·de·-sign·ed·ly,** *adv.*

un·de·sign·ing, un″di·zī′ning, *a.* Not having any underhand plan, purpose, or motive; artless.—**un·de·sign·ing·ly,** *adv.*

un·de·sir·a·ble, un″di·zī′ér·a·bl, *a.* Not desirable; not to be wished; objectionable. —*n.*—**un·de·sir·a·bil·i·ty, un·de·sir·a·ble·ness,** *n.*—**un·de·sir·a·bly,** *adv.*

un·de·ter·mined, un″di·tụr′mind, *a.* Not determined; not decided, fixed, or settled.

un·de·vi·at·ing, un·dē′vē·āt″ing, *a.* Not departing from a rule, principle, or purpose; steady; not swerving.—**un·de·vi·at·ing·ly,** *adv.*

un·dies, un′dēz, *n. pl. Colloq.* underwear, esp. women's or children's.

un·dig·ni·fied, un·dig′ni·fīd″, *a.* Not dignified.

un·dine, un·dēn′, un′dēn, un′dīn, *n.* [< L. *unda,* a wave.] A nymph inhabiting water who, according to Paracelsus, a Swiss alchemist, could receive a soul upon marrying a mortal and bearing his child.

un·dip·lo·mat·ic, un″dip·lo·mat′ik, *a.* Not diplomatic; wanting in diplomacy; tactless.—**un·dip·lo·mat·i·cal·ly,** *adv.*

un·di·rect·ed, un″di·rek′tid, un″di·rek′tid, *a.* Not directed; not guided; unaddressed, as a letter.

un·dis·cern·ing, un″di·sụr′ning, un″di·zụr′ning, *a.* Not discerning; wanting judgment or discrimination.—**un·dis·cern·i·ble,** *a.*

un·dis·ci·plined, un·dis′i·plind, *a.* Not disciplined; not properly trained.

un·dis·closed, un″di·sklōzd′, *a.* Not exposed; not revealed.

un·dis·cov·er·a·ble, un″di·skuv′ér·a·bl, *a.* Not able to be discovered or found out.— **un·dis·cov·ered,** un″di·skuv′érd, *a.*

un·dis·crim·i·nat·ing, un″di·skrim′i·nā″ting, *a.* Not discriminating or distinguishing; disregarding or not perceiving differences.

un·dis·posed, un″di·spōzd′, *a.* Not sold, allocated, or otherwise settled, usu. followed by *of;* as, goods *undisposed of.*

un·dis·put·ed, un″di·spū′tid, *a.* Not disputed; not called in question. Also **un·dis·put·a·ble,** un″di·spū′ta·bl.

un·dis·so·ci·at·ed, un″di·sō′shē·ā·tid, un″di·sō′sē·ā″tid, *a. Chem.* not dissociated, esp. by electrolysis.

un·dis·tin·guished, un″di·sting′gwisht, *a.* Not having any distinguishing mark or characteristic; mediocre; as, an *undistinguished* speaker.

un·di·vid·ed, un″di·vīd′id, *a.* Not divided; unbroken; whole; as, one's *undivided* attention.

un·do, un·dö′, *v.t.*—pres. sing. *undo, undo, undoes;* pres. pl. *undo;* past. sing. *undid, undid, undid;* past pl. *undid;* pp. *undone;* ppr. *undoing.* [With *un-* in sense of reversal.] To reverse, as something which has been done; to annul; to untie or unfasten; to unravel; to open up; to bring ruin or distress upon; to ruin the morals, reputation, or prospects of; to destroy; to impoverish.—*v.i.*—**un·do·er,** *n.*

un·do·ing, un·dö′ing, *n.* The reversal of what has been done; ruin; destruction; the process of opening or unfastening.

un·dou·ble, un·dub′l, *v.t., v.i.*—*undoubled, undoubling.* To make no longer double or doubled, as by unfolding or unclenching.

un·doubt·ed, un·dou′tid, *a.* Not doubted; not called in question; indubitable; indisputable.—**un·doubt·ed·ly,** *adv.*—**un·doubt·ing,** *a.*

un·drape, un·drāp′, *v.t.*—*undraped, undraping.* To uncover; to remove drapery from.

un·draw, un·drá′, *v.t.*—past, *undrew,* pp. *undrawn,* ppr. *undrawing.* To draw aside or open.—*v.i.* To be drawn aside or opened.

un·dress, un·dres′, *v.t.*—*undressed* or *undrest, undressing.* To divest of clothes; to strip; to disrobe; to remove the dressing or bandages from.—*v.i.* To take off one's clothes.—*n.* A loose, comfortable dress or robe; an ordinary dress, as opposed to full dress or uniform.

un·dressed, un·drest′, *a.* Divested of dress; not attired; not prepared, as leather; in a naked state.

un·due, un·dö′, un·dū′, *a.* Not due; not yet demandable by right; not right; as, *undue* punishment; not lawful; improper; excessive; inordinate; as, an *undue* attachment to ritual.

un·du·lant, un′ja·lant, un′da·lant, un′dya·lant, *a.* Waving; wavy.

un·du·lant fe·ver, *n.* A disease produced by a bacterium of the genus *Brucella,* affecting man and transferred through milk of infected goats and cows. Also *brucellosis, Malta fever.*

un·du·late, un′ja·lāt, un′da·lāt″, un′dya·lāt″, *v.i.*—*undulated, undulating.* [L.L. *undulo, undulatum,* < L. *undula,* a little wave, dim. of *unda,* a wave (seen also in *inundate, abundant, redundant*); < a root seen also in E. *water.*] To have a wavy motion; to rise and fall in waves; to move in curving or bending lines; to wave.—*v.t.* To cause to wave, or move with a wavy motion.—un′ja·lit, un′ja·lāt″, un′da·lit, un′da·lāt″, un′dya·lit, un′dya·lāt″, *a.* Wavy or having a wavy edge. Also **un·du·lat·ed.**

un·du·la·tion, un′ja·lā′shan, un″da·lā′shan, un″dya·lā′shan, *n.* The act of undulating; a waving motion; a wavy form, alternately rising and falling in waves or curved lines. *Phys.* a vibratory motion transmitted through some fluid medium by impulses communicated to the medium; any one vibration of such a fluid.

un·du·la·to·ry, un′ja·la·tōr″ē, un′ja·la·tạr″ē, un′da·la·tōr″ē, un′da·la·tạr″ē, un′dya·la·tōr″e, un′dya·la·tạr″ē, *a.* Pertaining to undulation; having an undulating character; moving in the manner of waves.

un·du·la·to·ry the·o·ry, *n.* Wave theory.

un·du·ly, un·dö′lē, un·dū′lē, *adv.* Excessively; immoderately; unjustifiably; improperly; unlawfully.

un·du·ti·ful, un·dö′ti·ful, un·dū′ti·ful, *a.* Not dutiful; not performing or not in accordance with duty.—**un·du·ti·ful·ly,** *adv.*—**un·du·ti·ful·ness,** *n.*

un·dy·ing, un·dī′ing, *a.* Not ending or dying; not subject to death; immortal.

un·ea·ger, un·ē′gér, *a.* Not eager.

un·earned, un·ụrnd′, *a.* Not merited by labor or services; undeserved.

un·earned in·cre·ment, *n.* The increase in the value of holdings, esp. land, as when it arises from growth of population and not due to any expenditure on the part of the owner.

un·earth, un·ụrth′, *v.t.* To dig up or bring forth from the earth; to bring to light; to discover or find out.

un·earth·ly, un·ụrth′lē, *a.* Not earthly; divine; supernatural or weird; unreal; completely absurd or ridiculous.—**un·earth·li·ness,** *n.*

un·eas·y, un·ē′zē, *a.*—*uneasier, uneasiest.* Not easy in body or mind; uncomfortable; restless; disturbed; perturbed; not easy in manner; embarrassed; constrained; not conducive to ease; causing bodily discomfort.—**un·ease,** *n.*—**un·eas·i·ly,** *adv.* —**un·eas·i·ness,** *n.*

un·eat·a·ble, un·ē′ta·bl, *a.* Not eatable; not fit to be eaten.—**un·eat·en,** un·ēt′en, *a.*

un·ed·u·cat·ed, un·ej′ụ·kā″tid, un·ed′ū·kā″tid, *a.* Not educated.—**un·ed·u·ca·ble,** *a.* Incapable of being educated.

un·e·mo·tion·al, un″i·mō′sha·nal, *a.* Not emotional; impassive.

un·em·ploy·a·ble, un″em·ploi′a·bl, *a.* Unable to be employed; lacking qualifications for employment.—*n.* One who is not able to be employed.

un·em·ployed, un″em·ploid′, *a.* Not employed; not in use; not kept busy or at work; out of work; without work or employment.—**the un·em·ployed,** persons without jobs.

un·em·ploy·ment, un″em·ploi′ment, *n.* Lack of employment; an unemployed condition.

un·em·ploy·ment com·pen·sa·tion, *n.* Payments made by a federal or state office, a union, or an employer, usu. by the week, to a worker who is unemployed, for a part or the whole term of his unemployment.

un·em·ploy·ment in·sur·ance, *n.* An insurance system providing unemployment compensation to unemployed workers from funds to which employers and employees contribute.

un·en·cum·bered, un″en·kum′bérd, *a.* Not encumbered; free from encumbrance.

un·end·ing, un·en′ding, *a.* Not ending; having no end; perpetual.

un·en·joy·a·ble, un″en·joi′a·bl, *a.* Not able to be enjoyed.

un·en·light·ened, un″en·līt′end, *a.* Not enlightened; not mentally illuminated.

un·en·ter·pris·ing, un·en′tér·prī″zing, *a.* Not enterprising; not adventurous; lacking initiative.

un·en·ter·tain·ing, un″en·tér·tā′ning, *a.* Not entertaining or amusing.

un·en·thu·si·as·tic, un″en·thö″zē·as′tik, *a.* Not enthusiastic; devoid of enthusiasm. —**un·en·thu·si·as·ti·cal·ly,** *adv.*

un·en·vi·a·ble, un·en′vē·a·bl, *a.* Not enviable; not to be envied or viewed with envy; as, an *unenviable* notoriety.—**un·en·vied,** *a.* Not envied; exempt from envy.

un·e·qual, un·ē′kwal, *a.* Not equal; not of the same type, size, quantity, quality, or the like; inadequate; insufficient; not uniform; unbalanced or unevenly distributed.—*n.*—**un·e·qual·ly,** *adv.*

un·e·qualed, un·ē′kwald, *a.* Not to be equaled; unparalleled; unrivaled.

un·e·quiv·o·cal, un″i·kwiv′o·kal, *a.* Not equivocal; not doubtful; clear; evident; not ambiguous.—**un·e·quiv·o·cal·ly,** *adv.*

un·err·ing, un·ụr′ing, un·er′ing, *a.* Not erring; incapable of missing the mark; committing no mistake; incapable of error; certain or exact.—**un·err·ing·ly,** *adv.*

un·es·sen·tial, un″e·sen′shal, *a.* Not essential; not absolutely necessary; not of prime importance.—*n.* Something not essential.

un·eth·i·cal, un·eth′i·kal, *a.* Not ethical; not in accordance with the rules for right conduct or practice.—**un·eth·i·cal·ly,** *adv.*

un·e·ven, un·ē′ven, *a.* Not level, smooth, or flat; rough; not straight, parallel, or equally balanced; irregular or not uniform; not fair or just; as, an *uneven* match or game. *Math.* odd; not divisible by two without a remainder, as: The numbers 11, 13, and 15 are *uneven.*—**un·e·ven·ly,** *adv.*—**un·e·ven·ness,** *n.*

un·e·vent·ful, un″i·vent′ful, *a.* Not eventful; lacking in important or striking occurrences.—**un·e·vent·ful·ly,** *adv.*—**un·e·vent·ful·ness,** *n.*

un·ex·am·pled, un″ig·zam′pld, un″ig·zäm′pld, *a.* Having no example or similar case; unprecedented; unparalleled.

un·ex·cep·tion·a·ble, un″ik·sep′sha·na·bl, *a.* Not liable to any exception or objection; unobjectionable; faultless.—**un·ex·cep·tion·a·ble·ness,** *n.*—**un·ex·cep·tion·a·bly,** *adv.*

un·ex·pect·ed, un″ik·spek′tid, *a.* Not expected; not looked for; unforeseen.—**un·ex·pect·ed·ly,** *adv.*—**un·ex·pect·ed·ness,** *n.*

un·ex·plored, un″ik·splōrd′, un″ik·splärd′, *a.* Not explored; not examined for geographical purposes; not investigated.

un·ex·pres·sive, un″ik·spres′iv, *a.* Not expressive; lacking in expression of meaning or feeling.—**un·ex·pres·sive·ly,** *adv.*—**un·ex·pres·sive·ness,** *n.*

un·fad·ing, un·fā′ding, *a.* Not liable to fade; not losing strength or freshness of coloring; not liable to wither or to decay.—**un·fad·a·ble,** *a.*

un·fail·ing, un·fā′ling, *a.* Not failing or liable to fail; always fulfilling a hope, promise, or want; inexhaustible or never ending; as, an *unfailing* supply; sure, certain, or infallible.—**un·fail·ing·ly,** *adv.*—**un·fail·ing·ness,** *n.*

un·fair, un·fâr′, *a.* Not fair; not honest, just, or ethical; unequal or disproportionate; as, an *unfair* portion; dishonest; not conforming to regular, lawful, or ethical business practices.—**un·fair·ly,** *adv.*—**un·fair·ness,** *n.*

un·faith·ful, un·fāth′ful, *a.* Not faithful; not observant of promises, vows, allegiance, or duty; disloyal; violating the marriage vow; as, an *unfaithful* wife; inexact, incomplete, or inaccurate; as, an *unfaithful* reproduction of the original painting; violating trust or confidence.—**un·faith·ful·ly,** *adv.*—**un·faith·ful·ness,** *n.*

un·fal·ter·ing, un·fąl′tėr·ing, *a.* Not faltering; unhesitating; unwavering.—**un·fal·ter·ing·ly,** *adv.*

un·fa·mil·iar, un″fa·mil′yėr, *a.* Not familiar; not well known by frequent use; having an element of strangeness.—**un·fa·mil·i·ar·i·ty,** un″fa·mil″ē·ar′i·tē, *n.*—**un·fa·mil·iar·ly,** *adv.*

un·fash·ion·a·ble, un·fash′a·na·bl, *a.* Not complying in dress or manners with the prevailing fashion, mode, or custom.

un·fast·en, un·fas′en, un·fä′sen, *v.t.* To loosen; to detach; to unbind; to untie.—*v.i.* To become loosened, detached, or untied.—**un·fas·ten·a·ble,** *a.*—**un·fas·ten·er,** *n.*

un·fa·thered, un·fä′THėrd, *a.* Having no father; fatherless; having no known or acknowledged father; illegitimate or bastard; of unknown origin or source.

un·fath·om·a·ble, un·faTH′om·a·bl, *a.* Incapable of being fathomed or sounded; too deep to be measured; incapable of being interpreted.

un·fa·vor·a·ble, *Brit.* **un·fa·vour·a·ble,** un·fā′vėr·a·bl, *a.* Not favorable; not propitious; discouraging; giving an adverse judgment or opinion; somewhat prejudicial. —**un·fa·vor·a·ble·ness,** *Brit.* **un·fa·vour·a·ble·ness,** *n.*—**un·fa·vor·a·bly,** *Brit.* **un·fa·vour·a·bly,** *adv.*

un·feath·ered, un·feTH′ėrd, *a.* See *un-fledged.*

un·feel·ing, un·fē′ling, *a.* Devoid of feeling; insensible; without sensibility; devoid of sympathy for others; hardhearted.—**un·feel·ing·ly,** *adv.*—**un·feel·ing·ness,** *n.*

un·feigned, un·fānd′, *a.* Not feigned; not counterfeit; not hypocritical; real; sincere. —**un·feign·ed·ly,** un·fā′nid·lē, *adv.*

un·fem·i·nine, un·fem′i·nin, *a.* Not feminine; not possessing delicacy; not according to the female image or manners.

un·fet·ter, un·fet′ėr, *v.t.* To loose from fetters; to unchain; to free from restraint; to set at liberty.—**un·fet·tered,** *a.*

un·fil·i·al, un·fil′ē·al, *a.* Unsuitable to a son or daughter; neglectful of the customary obligations to a parent.

un·fin·ished, un·fin′isht, *a.* Not finished; incomplete; imperfect; lacking some further treatment; as, *unfinished* furniture.

un·fit, un·fit′, *a.* Not fit; improper; unsuitable; lacking suitable physical or moral qualifications; not suited or adapted; not competent.—*v.t.* To render unfit; to make

unsuitable; to disqualify.—**un·fit·ly,** *adv.* —**un·fit·ness,** *n.*—**un·fit·ting,** *a.*

un·fix, un·fiks′, *v.t.*—*unfixed* or *unfixt, unfixing.* To make no longer fixed or firm; to loosen from any fastening; to detach; to unsettle, as habits.

un·flat·ter·ing, un·flat′ėr·ing, *a.* Not flattering; not affording a favorable prospect.

un·fla·vored, *Brit.* **un·fla·voured,** un·flā′vėrd, *a.* Without extrinsic flavoring; having no additives.

un·fledged, un·flejd′, *a.* Not yet furnished with feathers, esp. flight feathers; also *unfeathered.* *Fig.* undeveloped; inexperienced; callow.

un·flinch·ing, un·flin′ching, *a.* Not flinching; not shrinking.—**un·flinch·ing·ly,** *adv.*

un·fold, un·fōld′, *v.t.* To open, as the folds of something; to expand; to spread out; to lay open, as for viewing or contemplation; to disclose; to reveal; to expose, as verbally. —*v.i.* To become gradually expanded; to open out; to become disclosed; to become unwrapped.

un·fore·see·a·ble, un″fōr·sē′a·bl, un″far·sē′a·bl, *a.* Not foreseeable; incapable of being foreseen.—**un·fore·see·a·ble·ness,** *n.*—**un·fore·see·a·bly,** *adv.*

un·fore·seen, un″fōr·sēn′, un″far·sēn′, *a.* Not foreseen; not foreknown.

un·for·get·ta·ble, un″fėr·get′a·bl, *a.* Not forgettable; never to be forgotten.—**un·for·get·ta·bly,** *adv.*

un·for·giv·a·ble, un″fėr·giv′a·bl, *a.* Incapable of being forgiven; unpardonable.

un·formed, un·farmd′, *a.* Not having been formed; not fashioned; not molded into regular shape.

un·for·ti·fied, un·far′ti·fīd, *a.* Not fortified; not having fortifications; not strengthened by the addition of spirits, as wine.

un·for·tu·nate, un·far′cha·nit, *a.* Not fortunate; not having good fortune; unlucky or unhappy; not attended with good fortune; ill-fated; sad; deplorable.—*n.* An unfortunate person.—**un·for·tu·nate·ly,** *adv.*—**un·for·tu·nate·ness,** *n.*

un·found·ed, un·foun′did, *a.* Having no real foundation; groundless; baseless; not confirmed.—**un·found·ed·ly,** *adv.*—**un·found·ed·ness,** *n.*

un·fre·quent·ed, un·frē′kwen·tid, *a.* Rarely visited; seldom resorted to by human beings; solitary.

un·friend·ed, un·fren′did, *a.* Lacking friends; friendless; not befriended.

un·friend·ly, un·frend′lē, *a.*—*unfriendlier, unfriendliest.* Not friendly; not kind or benevolent; hostile; not favorable.—*adv.* In an unkind manner; not as a friend.—**un·friend·li·ness,** *n.*

un·frock, un·frok′, *v.t.* To deprive or divest of a frock; to deprive of the function and privileges of a priest or clergyman.

un·fruit·ful, un·frōt′ful, *a.* Not producing fruit or offspring; barren; unproductive; not fertile; as, an *unfruitful* soil; fruitless; ineffectual.—**un·fruit·ful·ly,** *adv.*—**un·fruit·ful·ness,** *n.*

un·fund·ed, un·fun′did, *a.* Not funded, as a debt; having no permanent fund established for the payment of its interest.

un·furl, un·fŭrl′, *v.t.* To spread or shake out from a furled state, as a sail or a flag; to unfold.—*v.i.* To become unfurled.

un·fur·nished, un·fŭr′nisht, *a.* Not furnished; not supplied with furnishings or furniture; as, an *unfurnished* house.

un·gain·ly, un·gān′lē, *a.* [< *un-,* not, and old *gainly, geinly,* < Icel. *gegn,* ready, serviceable; akin to -*gain* in *again.*] Clumsy; awkward; uncouth; ill-shaped, as a person. —*adv.* In a clumsy, ungainly manner.—**un·gain·li·ness,** *n.*

un·gal·lant, un·gal′ant, *a.* Not gallant; uncourtly; unchivalrous.—**un·gal·lant·ly,** *adv.*

un·gath·ered, un·gaTH′ėrd, *a.* Not gathered; not culled; not picked.

un·gen·er·ous, un·jen′ėr·us, *a.* Not generous; illiberal; mean; stingy; harsh; not showing generosity or liberality of mind or sentiments.—**un·gen·er·ous·ly,** *adv.*

un·gen·tle, un·jen′tl, *a.* Not gentle; harsh; rude.

un·gift·ed, un·gif′tid, *a.* Not gifted; not endowed with natural gifts or talents.

un·gird, un·gŭrd′, *v.t.*—*ungirded* or *ungirt, ungirding.* To loosen, divest, or free from a girdle or band; to unbind.

un·girt, un·gŭrt′, *a.* Having any confining or restraining apparel loosened or taken off; loose; relaxed or slack.

un·glazed, un·glāzd′, *a.* Not furnished with glass, as window frames in a new building; lacking windows; not covered with vitreous matter; as, *unglazed* pottery.

un·glue, un·glōō′, *v.t.*—*unglued, ungluing.* To separate, as anything that is glued or cemented.—**un·glued,** *a.*

un·god·ly, un·god′lē, *a.*—*ungodlier, ungodliest.* Not godly; godless; wicked; impious; sinful. *Colloq.* preposterous; outrageous.—**un·god·li·ness,** *n.*

un·gov·ern·a·ble, un·guv′ėr·na·bl, *a.* Incapable of being governed, ruled, or restrained; refractory; unruly; wild.—**un·gov·ern·a·ble·ness,** *n.*—**un·gov·ern·a·bly,** *adv.*

un·gov·erned, un·guv′ėrnd, *a.* Not governed; not controlled or curbed; not guided.

un·grace·ful, un·grās′ful, *a.* Not graceful; lacking grace and elegance; clumsy.—**un·grace·ful·ly,** *adv.*—**un·grace·ful·ness,** *n.*

un·gra·cious, un·grā′shus, *a.* Unmannerly; not pleasing; rude; offensive; disagreeable.—**un·gra·cious·ly,** *adv.*—**un·gra·cious·ness,** *n.*

un·grad·ed, un·grād′id, *a.* Not graded; not arranged in grades or classes.

un·gram·mat·i·cal, un″gra·mat′i·kal, *a.* Not according to the rules of grammar; grammatically awkward; contrary to accepted usage.—**un·gram·mat·i·cal·ly,** *adv.*

un·grate·ful, un·grāt′ful, *a.* Not grateful; not feeling thankful or showing gratitude; making poor or no returns for kindness; unpleasing; disagreeable.—**un·grate·ful·ly,** *adv.*—**un·grate·ful·ness,** *n.*

un·ground·ed, un·groun′did, *a.* Having no foundation or support; groundless; baseless; unfounded.

un·grudg·ing, un·gruj′ing, *a.* Not grudging; freely giving; liberal; without malice or envy.—**un·grudg·ing·ly,** *adv.*

un·gual, ung′gwal, *a.* [< L. *unguis,* a nail, claw, or hoof.] Pertaining to a nail, claw, or hoof; having a nail, claw, or hoof.

un·guard·ed, un·gär′did, *a.* Not guarded; unprotected or undefended; incautious; imprudent; having no guard; as, an *unguarded* door.—**un·guard·ed·ly,** *adv.*—**un·guard·ed·ness,** *n.*

un·guent, ung′gwent, *n.* [L. *unguentum,* < *unguere,* smear, anoint.] Any soft preparation or salve, either liquid or semiliquid, applied to sores and wounds; an ointment.

un·guic·u·late, ung·gwik′ya·lit, ung·gwik′ya·lāt″, *a. Zool.* having nails or claws, as distinguished from hoofs; *bot.* having a clawlike base, as certain petals.—*n.* An unguiculate animal.

un·guid·ed, un·gī′did, *a.* Not guided, led, or conducted; not regulated; uncontrolled.

un·guis, ung′gwis, *n.* pl. **un·gues,** ung′gwēz. [L.*, nail or claw.] A nail, claw, or hoof of an animal; *bot.* a clawlike portion of a petal.

un·gu·late, ung′gya·lit, ung′gya·lāt″, *a.* [L.L. *ungulatus,* having claws or hoofs, < L. *ungula.*] Of the nature of a hoof; hooflike; having hoofs; belonging or pertaining to the *Ungulata,* a former order of mammals containing all hoofed species.—*n.* An ungulate mammal.

un·hair, un·hâr′, *v.t.* To free from hair; to remove or strip hair from, as an animal hide.—*v.i.* To lose hair; become hairless.

un·hal·lowed, un·hal′ōd, *a.* Not hallowed, consecrated, or dedicated to sacred purposes; unholy; profane; impious; immoral.—**un·hal·low**, *v.t. Archaic*, to make unholy or profane.

un·ham·pered, un·ham′pėrd, *a.* Not hampered, hindered, or restricted; unimpeded.

un·hand, un·hand′, *v.t.* To take the hand or hands from; to release from a grasp; to let go.

un·hand·some, un·han′som, *a.* Not handsome or physically attractive; homely; not beautiful; not generous or becoming; mean; rude; unpleasant.—**un·hand·some·ly**, *adv.*—**un·hand·some·ness**, *n.*

un·hand·y, un·han′dē, *a.*—*unhandier, unhandiest.* Not handy; inconvenient; cumbersome; not skillful in the use of the hands; awkward; not dexterous.

un·hap·py, un·hap′ē, *a.* Not happy, cheerful, or gay; miserable or wretched; marked by ill fortune or mishap; ill-omened; inappropriate or unsuitable.—**un·hap·pi·ly**, *adv.*—**un·hap·pi·ness**, *n.*

un·harmed, un·härmd′, *a.* Not harmed or injured; unscathed; sound.

un·har·ness, un·här′nis, *v.t.* To strip of harness, as a horse; to divest of armor; to release, as power or strength.—*v.i.* To remove harness or gear.

un·hatched, un·hacht′, *a.* Not hatched; as, an *unhatched* egg; having failed to come into existence; as, an *unhatched* plan, plot, or scheme.

un·health·y, un·hel′thē, *a.*—*unhealthier, unhealthiest.* Not healthy; wanting health; not sound and vigorous of body; habitually weak or indisposed; sickly; unfavorable to the preservation of health, as insanitary living conditions; likely to generate disease; unwholesome; corrupt; insalubrious; not indicating health; resulting from bad health; morbid; risky.—**un·health·i·ly**, *adv.*—**un·health·i·ness**, *n.*

un·heard, un·hûrd′, *a.* Not heard; not perceived by the ear; not granted an audience.

un·heard-of, un·hûrd′uv″, un·hûrd′ov″, *a.* Never known before; unprecedented; not known to fame; unknown.

un·heat·ed, un·hē′tid, *a.* Without heat.

un·heed·ed, un·hē′did, *a.* Not heeded; disregarded; unnoticed.—**un·heed·ful**, *a.* Not heedful; inattentive; inconsiderate.—**un·heed·ing**, *a.* Not heeding; careless; negligent.

un·her·ald·ed, un·her′al·did, *a.* Not proclaimed or announced beforehand; undeclared.

un·hes·i·tat·ing, un·hez′i·tā″ting, *a.* Not hesitating; unfaltering; not remaining in doubt; prompt; ready; steady.—**un·hes·i·tat·ing·ly**, *adv.*

un·hinge, un·hinj′, *v.t.*—*unhinged, unhinging.* To take from the hinges; to take off the hinges of; to unfasten and remove; to disconnect; to disturb the calm of; to unsettle; to render unstable or wavering; to discompose or disorder, as the mind or opinions; disarrange.

un·hitch, un·hich′, *v.t.* To untie or unloosen, as a dog from a chain; unfasten; untether; release.

un·ho·ly, un·hō′lē, *a.*—*unholier, unholiest.* Not holy; not sacred; not hallowed or consecrated; impious; wicked; evil. *Colloq.* ungodly; outrageous.—**un·ho·li·ly**, *adv.*—**un·ho·li·ness**, *n.*

un·hon·ored, un·on′ėrd, *a.* Not honored; not regarded with veneration; not celebrated.

un·hood, un·hud′, *v.t.* To divest of a hood; to remove the hood from, as a hawk in falconry.

un·hook, un·huk′, *v.t.* To loosen from a hook; to undo the hook or hooks of.—*v.i.* To become or be unhooked, as a dress.

un·hoped, un·hōpt′, *a. Archaic.* Not hoped for; not so probable as to excite hope.

un·hoped-for, un·hōpt′far″, *a.* Not hoped for or expected; as, an *unhoped-for* victory.

un·horse, un·hârs′, *v.t.*—*unhorsed, unhorsing.* To throw from, or as if from, a horse; unseat; dislodge, as from an appointed office; *archaic*, to remove a horse or horses from, as a carriage.

un·hur·ried, un·hur′ėd, un·hur′ēd, *a.* Not hurried; without haste; leisurely.

un·hurt, un·hurt′, *a.* Not hurt; not harmed; free from wound or injury.—**un·hurt·ful**, *a.*

U·ni·at, ū′nē·at″, *a.* [Russ. *uniyat*, < *uniya*, part of an Eastern Christian church in communion with Rome, < L. *unus*, one.] Pertaining to any of various communities of Greek and other Eastern Christians, or a member of such a community, that accept the authority of the Pope but retain their own liturgy and discipline.—*n.* Also **U·ni·ate**, ū′nē·it, ū′nē·āt″.

u·ni·ax·i·al, ū″nē·ak′sē·al, *a.* Having one axis; *crystal.* having one line or direction in which no double refraction occurs; *bot.* having a primary stem which does not branch and which terminates in a flower.—**u·ni·ax·i·al·ly**, *adv.*

u·ni·cam·er·al, ū″ni·kam′ėr·al, *a.* [L. *unus*, one, *camera*, a chamber.] Consisting of a single lawmaking or legislative chamber.—**u·ni·cam·er·al·ly**, *adv.*

u·ni·cel·lu·lar, ū″ni·sel′ya·lėr, *a.* [L. *unus*, one, and E. *cellular*.] *Biol.* Consisting of a single cell; exhibiting only a single cell, as a protozoan.—**u·ni·cel·lu·lar·i·ty**, *n.*

u·ni·corn, ū′ni·karn″, *n.* [L. *unicornis*, one-horned—*unus*, one, and *cornu*, horn.] A legendary animal having the head, neck, and body of a horse, the hind legs of a stag, the tail of a lion, and a long spiral horn growing out of the forehead: a symbol of fierceness, purity, or chastity in myth and literature.

u·ni·cy·cle, ū′ni·sī″kl, *n.* A vehicle with only one wheel, esp. one propelled or driven by pedals and used chiefly by acrobats. Also *monocycle.*—**u·ni·cy·clist**, *n.*

un·i·den·ti·fied, un″ī·den′ti·fīd″, un″i·den′ti·fīd″, *a.* Not identified.

u·ni·di·rec·tion·al, ū″ni·di·rek′sha·nal, ū″ni·dī·rek′sha·nal, *a.* Having, or moving in, only one direction.

u·ni·fi·a·ble, ū′ni·fī″a·bl, *a.* That may be unified.

u·ni·fi·ca·tion, ū″ni·fi·kā′shan, *n.* The act of uniting; the state of being allied or united.

u·ni·fied field the·o·ry, *n. Phys.* any theory expressed as a unified set of equations that generalizes inclusively from two or more theories and yields predictions not inferable from any single theory, esp. any of various attempts, as by Einstein, to unify the electromagnetic theory with the relativity theory and the gravitation theory.

u·ni·fi·lar, ū″ni·fī′lėr, *a.* [L. *unus*, one, and *filum*, a thread.] Having only one thread, fiber, or the like.

u·ni·fo·li·ate, ū″ni·fō′lē·it, ū″ni·fō′lē·āt″, *a.* [L. *unus*, one, and *folium*, leaf.] *Bot.* One-leafed; unifoliolate.

u·ni·fo·li·o·late, ū″ni·fō′lē·o·lāt″, *a. Bot.* Compound in structure yet having but one leaflet, the other leaflets abortive, as the leaf of the orange tree; bearing such leaves, as a plant.

u·ni·form, ū′ni·farm″, *a.* [Fr. *uniforme*, L. *uniformis—unus*, one, and *forma*, form.] Having always the same form; not changing in shape, appearance, or character; not varying in degree or rate; equable; invariable; of the same kind or matter throughout; homogeneous; consistent at all times; conforming to one rule or mode. A style of clothing of the same general appearance as that worn by other members of the same body; as, a naval *uniform*; a suit or ensemble of such distinctive dress.—*v.t.* To bring about uniformity in; to equip with or array in a uniform.—**u·ni·formed**, ū′ni·farmd″, *a.*—**u·ni·form·ly**, *adv.*—**u·ni·form·i·ty**, **u·ni·form·ness**, ū″ni·far′mi·tē, *n.*

U·ni·form, ū′ni·farm″, *n.* A communications code word to designate the letter U.

u·ni·form·i·tar·i·an, ū″ni·far″mi·târ′ē·an, *a.* Pertaining to uniformity or a doctrine of uniformity; *geol.* noting or pertaining to the doctrine that certain geological changes in the earth's history were caused by processes still active rather than by catastrophes.—*n.*—**u·ni·form·i·tar·i·an·ism**, *n.*

u·ni·fy, ū′ni·fī″, *v.t.—unified, unifying.* [L. *unus*, one, and *facio*, to make.] To form into one; to reduce to unity by resolving differences; to consolidate.—**u·ni·fi·er**, *n.*

u·nij·u·gate, ū·nij′a·gāt″, ū′ni·jö″git, ū″ni·jö′gāt, *a.* [L. *unus*, one, and *jugrum*, yoke.] *Bot.* a single pair of leaflets, as on a pinnate leaf. Also **u·ni·ju·gous.**

u·ni·lat·er·al, ū″ni·lat′ėr·al, *a.* [L. *unus*, one, and *latus, lateris*, side.] One-sided; pertaining to one side; undertaken for the benefit of one side or faction; showing or containing one side only. *Law*, pertaining to a one-sided contract; not reciprocal. *Bot.* growing chiefly to one side. Tracing family descent through one side, as either the father or mother. *Phon.* formed by air passage on one side of the tongue.—**u·ni·lat·er·al·ly**, *adv.*—**u·ni·lat·er·al·ism**, *n.*

u·ni·loc·u·lar, ū″ni·lok′ya·lėr, *a.* [L. *unus*, one, and *loculus*, cell, dim. of *locus*, a place.] *Bot.* Having one cell or chamber only; not divided into cells; as, a *unilocular* fruit.

un·im·ag·i·na·ble, un″i·maj′i·na·bl, *a.* Not capable of being imagined, conceived, or thought of; inconceivable.—**un·im·ag·i·na·tive**, un″i·maj′i·na·tiv, un″i·maj′i·nā″tiv, *a.* Lacking in imagination.

un·im·paired, un″im·pârd′, *a.* Not impaired; not diminished; not enfeebled by time or injury.

un·im·pas·sioned, un″im·pash′ond, *a.* Not impassioned; not moved or actuated by passion; dispassionate.

un·im·peach·a·ble, un″im·pē′cha·bl, *a.* Not impeachable; not to be called in question; blameless; irreproachable.—**un·im·peach·a·bly**, *adv.*

un·im·por·tance, un″im·par′tans, *n.* Lack of importance, consequence, or significance.—**un·im·por·tant**, *a.*

un·im·pres·sion·a·ble, un″im·presh′a·na·bl, un″im·presh′na·bl, *a.* Not impressionable; not easily impressed or influenced.

un·im·proved, un″im·prövd′, *a.* Not used advantageously; not brought to a more desirable condition; unameliorated; lacking development leading to full potentialities and profits, as real estate; not put in a better condition for ease of travel, as a country road; not made better by instruction or study, as one's mind; not bred selectively to enhance the species, as plants or animals.

un·in·cor·po·rat·ed, un″in·kar′po·rā″tid, *a.* Not constituted as a legal corporation; not chartered by the state for self-government; as, an *unincorporated* village; not blended or combined into one body; disassociated from.

un·in·flu·enced, un·in′flö′enst, *a.* Not influenced; not affected; not persuaded or moved; free from bias or prejudice.

un·in·formed, un″in·fạrmd′, *a.* Not informed; uninstructed, uneducated, or ignorant; without information on some matter.

un·in·hab·it·a·ble, un″in·hab′i·tạ·bl, *a.* Not inhabitable; unfit to be the residence of man.—**un·in·hab·it·ed,** un″in·hab′i·tid, *a.*

un·in·hib·it·ed, un″in·hib′i·tid, *a.* Not inhibited, esp. heedless of conventional proscriptions or constraints in personal conduct; open.—**un·in·hib·it·ed·ly,** *adv.*

un·in·spired, un″in·spī′ẽrd, *a.* Without vigor or imagination; dull; flat.

un·in·tel·li·gent, un″in·tel′i·jent, *a.* Lacking in or not showing intelligence; dull; ignorant; stupid; unwise.—**un·in·tel·li·gence,** *n.*—**un·in·tel·li·gent·ly,** *adv.*

un·in·tel·li·gi·ble, un″in·tel′i·ji·bl, *a.* Not intelligible; not capable of being understood; meaningless.—**un·in·tel·li·gi·ble·ness,** *n.*—**un·in·tel·li·gi·bly,** *adv.*

un·in·ten·tion·al, un″in·ten′shạ·nal, *a.* Not intentional; done or happening without design.—**un·in·ten·tion·al·ly,** *adv.*

un·in·ter·est·ed, un·in′tẽr·i·stid, un··in′tris·tid, un·in′te·res″tid, *a.* Not interested; indifferent; not personally concerned; not having the mind or feelings engaged.—**un·in·ter·est·ing,** *a.*

un·in·ter·rupt·ed, un″in·te·rup′tid, *a.* Not interrupted; incessant; continual.—**un·in·ter·rupt·ed·ly,** *adv.*—**un·in·ter·rupt·ed·ness,** *n.*

un·in·vit·ed, un″in·vī′tid, *a.* Not having received an invitation; unbidden.

un·in·vit·ing, un″in·vī′ting, *a.* Not attractive; not alluring; not enticing.

un·ion, ūn′yon, ūnyon′, *n.* [Fr. *union,* < L.L. *unio*(n-), the number one, unity, union, L. a single large pearl, a kind of single onion, < L. *unus,* one: cf. *onion.*] The act of uniting or the state of being united; junction; combination; something formed by uniting; a number, as of persons, societies, states, or nations, joined or associated together for a common purpose; a labor union; a combination of states or nations into one political body; (*cap.*) the United States of America, preceded by *the.* A device emblematic of union used in a flag or ensign, usu. occupying the upper inside corner or the entire field. Marriage; sexual intercourse. (*Cap.*) an organization providing recreational facilities at a college or university; the building used by such an organization, preceded by *the. Mech.* any of various devices for connecting parts, as a coupling for pipes or tubes. *Brit.* formerly, a number of parishes united for the administration of the poor laws; a workhouse maintained by such a union. *Textiles,* a fabric of two or more materials woven together.—*a.* Of or pertaining to a union, esp. a labor union; (*cap.*) of or pertaining to the U.S., esp. during the Civil War, as opposed to *Confederate.*

un·ion card, *n.* An identification card that certifies the person named as a member of the specified labor union.

un·ion·ism, ūn′ya·niz″um, *n.* The principle of union; trade unionism; (*cap.*) loyalty to the federal union of the United States of America at the time of the American Civil War.

un·ion·ist, ūn′ya·nist, *n.* One who promotes or advocates unionism; a member of a trade union; (*cap.*) an adherent of the federal union of the United States of America at the time of the American Civil War; (*cap.*), *Brit. politics,* an upholder of the legislative union of Great Britain opposing home rule in Ireland.—**un·ion·is·tic,** *a.*

un·ion·ize, ūn′ya·nīz″, *v.t.*—*unionized, unionizing.* To form into or cause to join a union, esp. a labor union; to subject

to the rules of a labor union.—**un·ion·i·za·tion,** *n.*

un·ion jack, *n.* A jack or marine flag consisting of the union of a national flag or ensign; (*often cap.*) the national flag of Great Britain.

un·ion shop, *n.* An industrial establishment where employment is limited to members of a labor union or to those who agree to become members within a specified time. See *closed shop.*

un·ion suit, *n.* A suit of underwear for men and boys consisting of a shirt and drawers in one piece.

u·nip·a·rous, ū·nip′ẽr·us, *a.* [L. *unus,* one, and *parere,* bring forth.] *Zool.* producing only one offspring at each birth; *bot.* producing only one axis at each branching, as a cyme.

u·ni·per·son·al, ū″ni·pụr′so·nal, *a.* Consisting of or existing as only one person; *gram.* used in only one person, esp. the third person singular, as certain verbs.

u·ni·pet·al·ous, ū″ni·pet′a·lus, *a. Bot.* having only one petal.

u·ni·pla·nar, ū″ni·plā′nẽr, *a.* Lying or taking place in one plane; as, *uniplanar* motion.

u·ni·pod, ū′ni·pod″, *n.* A support consisting of a single rod or staff, as for a camera.

u·ni·po·lar, ū″ni·pō′lẽr, *a.* [L. *unus,* one, *polus,* a pole.] *Phys.* having only one polarity; *anat.* pertaining to a nerve cell having a single pole or process, esp. those of the spinal column—**u·ni·po·lar·i·ty,** ū″ni·pō·lar′i·tē, *n.*

u·nip·o·tent, ū·nip′o·tent, *a. Biol.* said of a cell, having the ability to develop into only one kind of cell or tissue.

u·nique, ū·nēk′, *a.* [Fr. *unique,* < L. *unicus,* < *unus,* one.] Without a like or equal; unmatched; unequaled; single in its kind; uncommon or rare.—**u·nique·ly,** *adv.*—**u·nique·ness,** *n.*

u·ni·sep·tate, ū″ni·sep′tāt, *a Biol.* having only one septum or partition, as a silicle.

u·ni·sex·u·al, ū″ni·sek′shö·al, *a.* Of or pertaining to one sex only; having only male or female organs in one individual, as an animal or a flower; not hermaphroditic.—**u·ni·sex·u·al·i·ty,** *n.*—**u·ni·sex·u·al·ly,** *adv.*

u·ni·son, ū′ni·son, ū′ni·zon, *n.* [Fr. *unisson,* unison, < M.L. *unisonus,* having one or the same sound, < L. *unus,* one, and *sonus,* sound.] Coincidence in pitch of two or more tones or voices, as in speaking. *Mus.* the interval between any tone and a tone of exactly the same pitch; a sounding together at the same pitch or in octaves, as of different voices or instruments performing the same part.—**in u·ni·son,** in accord or agreement; simultaneity of like actions or sounds.

u·nis·o·nous, ū·nis′o·nus, *a.* Being in unison; concordant. Also **u·nis·o·nal.**

u·nit, ū′nit, *n.* [< *unity.*] A single thing or person; any group of things or persons regarded as an individual; one of the individuals or groups making up a whole, or into which a whole may be analyzed; any magnitude regarded as an independent whole; any standard quantity or amount, as of length, area, volume, force, value, or time, with which another quantity of the same kind is compared for measurement or estimation; a piece of machinery or group of machines with a specified function; as, an air conditioning *unit. Math.* the least positive whole number or one; the position to the immediate left of the decimal point. *Educ.* a portion of a course organized around a specific theme and often crossing traditional course divisions; as, a *unit* in historical geography; a specific quantity of hours of work used to determine student credits.

Med. the measure of a medicine or drug necessary to yield a specific effect, as immunization; *milit.* a group of soldiers organized as a subdivision of a larger group of soldiers.

u·nit·age, ū′ni·tij, *n.* The specification of the quantity used as a unit of measurement.

u·ni·tar·i·an, ū″ni·târ′ē·an, *n.* [N.L. *unitarius,* < L. *unitas,* E. *unity:* cf. *Trinitarian.*] One who maintains that God is only one being in opposition to the doctrine of the Trinity; (*cap.*) a member of a Christian denomination founded upon the doctrine that God is only one being and emphasizing freedom in religious thought, tolerance of other religious beliefs, importance of individual character, and autonomy of each congregation. An advocate of unity or centralization, as in government.—*a.* (*Cap.*) of the Unitarians, or pertaining to their doctrines; adhering to Unitarian beliefs. Unitary.

u·ni·tar·i·an·ism, ū″ni·târ′ē·a·niz″um, *n.* (*Cap.*) the doctrines and beliefs of Unitarians. Any unitary system, as of government.

u·ni·tar·y, ū′ni·ter″ē, *a.* [< *unit* or *unity* and *-ary.*] Of or pertaining to a unit or units; pertaining to, characterized by, or based on unity; of the nature of a unit or having the character of a unit; *govt.* advocating or directed toward national unity or centralization in government.

u·nit char·ac·ter, *n. Genetics,* a character inherited as a unit and transmitted by a single gene or a certain set of genes.

u·nite, ū·nīt′, *v.t.*—*united, uniting.* [L. *unitus,* pp. of *unire unus,* one.] To join, combine, or incorporate so as to form one connected whole; to cause to hold together or adhere; as, to *unite* bricks with cement; to join in marriage; to associate by some bond or tie; as, to *unite* nations by treaty; to join in action, interest, opinion, or feeling; to have or exhibit in union or combination; as, a building which *unites* two different styles of architecture.—*v.i.* To become joined together so as to form one connected whole; to become one; to become joined in marriage; to enter into alliance or association; to join in action, opinion, or feeling.—**u·nit·a·ble, u·nite·a·ble,** *a.*—**u·nit·er,** *n.*

u·nit·ed, ū·nī′tid, *a.* Joined together; combined; made one; formed or produced by a combination or union of two or more things or persons; in accord or agreement.—**u·nit·ed·ly,** *adv.*

U·nit·ed King·dom, *n.* The geographical and political entity consisting of England, Wales, Scotland, Northern Ireland, Isle of Man, and the Channel Islands. Abbr. U.K. Also The **U·nit·ed King·dom of Great Brit·ain and North·ern Ire·land.**

U·nit·ed Na·tions, *n.* The international organization of nations established by permanent charter in San Francisco, California, in 1945, to promote and maintain international peace and security; the coalition of nations that pledged themselves in Washington in 1942, to employ full resources against the Axis powers and not to make a separate peace. Abbr. UN, U.N.

U·nit·ed States, *n.* A federal republic of N. America comprising 50 states, the District of Columbia, and various possessions. Abbr. *U.S., US.* Also **A·mer·i·ca, U·nit·ed States of A·mer·i·ca.**

u·nit fac·tor, *n. Genetics,* a gene functioning in the transmission of a unit character.

u·ni·tive, ū′ni·tiv, *a.* Having the power of, involving, or characterized by uniting.

u·ni·tize, ū′ni·tīz, *a.* To arrange as or into one unit.

u·nit mag·net·ic pole, *n. Phys.* the amount of strength in a magnetic pole capable of repelling with a one dyne force another like magnetic pole of the same strength placed in a vacuum one centimeter away.

u·nit rule, *n.* In a Democratic national convention, a rule requiring all members of some State delegations to vote for the candidate the majority prefers.

u·ni·ty, ū″ni·tē, *n. pl.* **u·ni·ties.** [O.Fr. *unite* (Fr. *unité*), < L. *unitas*, < *unus*, one.] The state or fact of being one; oneness; one single thing; something complete in itself or regarded as such; the oneness of a complex, organic whole or of an interconnected series; the fact or state of being united or combined into a whole or totality, as a group of related parts; freedom from diversity or variety; oneness of mind or feeling, as among a number of persons; concord, harmony, or agreement. *Math.* the number one; a quantity regarded as one; a number which leaves unchanged any other number or quantity on which it is operating. *Art, liter.* a relation of all the parts or elements of a work constituting a harmonious whole and producing a single general effect; *drama,* any of the three unities of time, place, and action derived from Aristotle's *Poetics,* which state that a drama should consist of a single action occurring within a single day at a single locality.

u·ni·va·lent, ū″ni·vā′lent, ū·niv′a·lent, *a.* [L. *unus,* one, *valere,* to be strong.] *Chem.* having a valence of one; monovalent. *Genetics,* relating to or designating a single chromosome which has no synaptic mate.—**u·ni·va·lence, u·ni·va·len·cy,** ū″ni·vā′lens, ū″niv′a·lens, *n.*

u·ni·valve, ū″ni·valv″, *a.* [L. *unus,* one, and E. *valve.*] Having one valve only, as a snail shell; also **u·ni·valved, u·ni·val·vu·lar,** ū″ni·val′vya·lẽr.—*n.* A shell having one valve only; a mollusk with a shell composed of a single piece, as a snail; a gastropod.

u·ni·ver·sal, ū″ni·vẽr′sal, *a.* [L. *universalis,* < *universus,* all together.] Of, pertaining to, or characteristic of all or the whole; as, the *universal* experience of mankind; affecting, concerning, or involving all; as, *universal* military service; used or understood by all; as, a *universal* language; existing or prevailing in all parts; embracing all subjects or fields; as, a *universal* culture; of, or pertaining to the universe, all nature, or all existing things. *Logic,* applicable to many individuals or general, as a generic trait, characteristic, or pattern of behavior; relating or applicable to all the members of a class or genus: contrasted with *particular. Mech.* adapted or adaptable for all or various uses, angles, or sizes; allowing free movement in all directions within certain limits; as, a *universal* joint.—*n.* A widely applicable principle, judgment, or idea. *Logic,* a universal proposition; any of the five Aristotelian predicables; a general term or concept, or the general nature which such a term signifies, as realism.—**u·ni·ver·sal·ly,** *adv.*—**u·ni·ver·sal·ness,** *n.*

u·ni·ver·sal·ism, ū″ni·vẽr′sa·liz″um, *n.* Universal character; universality; universal range of knowledge, interests, or activities, as opposed to *specialism; (cap.), theol.* the doctrine or belief in the universality of God and redemption for everyone; *philos.* the belief that each man should strive for the good of all.—**u·ni·ver·sal·ist,** *n. Philos.* one whose goal is well-being for all mankind; *(cap.), theol.* one who believes in Universalism.—*a.*

u·ni·ver·sal·i·ty, ū″ni·vẽr·sal′i·tē, *n. pl.* **u·ni·ver·sal·i·ties.** The character or state of being universal; relation, extension, or applicability to all; existence or prevalence everywhere; universal character or range of knowledge or interests.

u·ni·ver·sal·ize, ū″ni·vẽr′sa·līz″, *v.t.*—

universalized, universalizing. To make universal.—**u·ni·ver·sal·i·za·tion,** *n.*

u·ni·ver·sal joint, *n. Mech.* a coupling system or joint used to join two rotating shafts not in a straight line with each other, one shaft being connected to the power unit and conveying rotation to the other. Also **u·ni·ver·sal coup·ling.**

u·ni·ver·sal quan·ti·fi·er, *n. Philos.* a term in formal logic expressing that a given formula with a free variable *x* holds for all values of *x* usu. within a specific range. See *existential quantifier.*

u·ni·verse, ū″ni·vẽrs″, *n.* [L. *universum,* the universe, prop. neut. of *universus,* all together, whole, universal, lit. 'turned into one,' < *unus,* one, and *versus,* pp. of *vertere,* turn.] The totality of existing or created things, including the earth with all on or in it, the heavenly bodies, and all else throughout space; the cosmos or the macrocosm; all creation; the whole world; mankind; a system of heavenly bodies or an indefinitely great expanse of space conceived as a single world analogous to the great universe; a world or sphere in which something exists or prevails; *logic,* universe of discourse.

u·ni·verse of dis·course, *n. Logic,* the aggregate of an area of ideas or class of things accepted as a subject for thought or discourse; the collection of all the objects to which any discourse refers.

u·ni·ver·si·ty, ū″ni·vẽr′si·tē, *n. pl.* **u·ni·ver·si·ties.** [O.Fr. *universite* (Fr. *université*), < L. *universitas,* the whole, the universe, a community, society, or corporation, < *universus,* all together.] An institution concerned with the higher branches of learning, having various undergraduate schools awarding bachelor's degrees, and also graduate and professional schools authorized to confer master's or doctorate degrees; in Europe, an institution consisting of professional or graduate schools, or consisting of both; the faculty and students of a university collectively; the grounds, equipment, and buildings of a university. Abbr. *U., Univ.*

u·niv·o·cal, ū·niv′o·kal, *a.* [L.L. *univocus,* < L. *unus,* one, and *vox (voc-),* voice, speech.] Having one meaning only; not equivocal; capable of but one interpretation. —*n.*—**u·niv·o·cal·ly,** *adv.*

un·just, un·just′, *a.* Not just; contrary to justice and right; unfair.—**un·just·ly,** *adv.* —**un·just·ness,** *n.*

un·jus·ti·fi·a·ble, un·jus′ti·fī″a·bl, un·jus″ti·fī′a·bl, *a.* Not justifiable; not to be vindicated or defended.—**un·jus·ti·fi·a·ble·ness,** *n.*—**un·jus·ti·fi·a·bly,** *adv.*

un·kempt, un·kempt′, *a.* Uncombed; untidy, as in dress; disheveled; rough; unpolished; unrefined.

un·ken·nel, un·ken′el, *v.t.*—unkenneled, unkenneling, *esp. Brit.* unkennelled, unkennelling. To drive or force from a lair or hiding place, as an animal; to turn loose from a kennel, as hunting dogs; *fig.* to reveal or disclose.—*v.i.* To emerge from a kennel or hiding place.

un·kind, un·kind′, *a.* Wanting in kindness; without consideration; cruel.—**un·kind·ness,** *n.*

un·kind·ly, un·kind′lē, *a.*—unkindlier, unkindliest. Unkind; ungracious.—*adv.*—**un·kind·li·ness,** *n.*

un·knit, un·nit′, *v.t.*—unknitted or unknit, unknitting. To unravel, undo, or untie, as knitting or a knot; to smooth out, as a wrinkled sweater.—*v.i.* To become unraveled or unknit.

un·knot, un·not′, *v.t.*—unknotted, unknotting. Untie; to free from knots; to bring out of a knotted state.

un·know·a·ble, un·nō′a·bl, *a.* Not knowable; incapable of being known; transcending human knowledge.—**the Un·know·a·**

ble, *philos.* the postulated reality lying behind all phenomena but exceeding the limits of human comprehension.—**un·know·a·ble·ness,** *n.*—**un·know·a·bly,** *adv.*

un·know·ing, un·nō′ing, *a.* Not knowing; ignorant.—**un·know·ing·ly,** *adv.*—**un·know·ing·ness,** *n.*

un·known, un·nōn′, *a.* Not known; unfamiliar; strange; not ascertained, discovered, or identified.—*n.* One who or that which is unknown; *math.* an unknown quantity, usu. represented by a symbol.—**Un·known Sol·dier,** an unidentified soldier killed in action in World War I and enshrined to symbolize or represent the nation's unknown dead of all its wars.

un·lace, un·lās′, *v.t.*—unlaced, unlacing. To loosen the lacing or fastening of; to unfasten by untying the lace of.

un·lade, un·lād′, *v.t.*—unladed, unlading. To take off the cargo from, as a vessel; to discharge, as a load.—*v.i.* To discharge a load.

un·la·dy·like, un·lā′dē·līk″, *a.* Not ladylike; not like or befitting a lady.

un·la·ment·ed, un″la·men′tid, *a.* Not lamented.

un·lash, un·lash′, *v.t.* To loosen or unfasten, as something lashed or tied fast.

un·latch, un·lach′, *v.t.* To open by lifting the latch.—*v.i.* To become unlocked.

un·laun·dered, un·lạn′dẽrd, un·län′dẽrd, *a.* Not laundered.

un·law·ful, un·lạ′ful, *a.* Contrary to law; illegal; not born in wedlock; illegitimate.— **un·law·ful·ly,** *adv.*—**un·law·ful·ness,** *n.*

un·lay, un·lā′, *v.t., v.i.*—unlaid, unlaying. To untwist, as a rope.

un·lead·ed, un·led′id, *a.* Not leaded; not separated or spaced with leads, as lines of type or printed matter.

un·learn, un·lụrn′, *v.t.*—unlearned or unlearnt, unlearning. To put aside or dismiss, as certain knowledge; to forget the knowledge of.

un·learn·ed, un·lụr′nid, un·lụrnd′, *a.* Not learned or erudite; ignorant; illiterate, un·lụr′nid. Not gained through instruction, un·lụrnd′.—**un·learn·ed·ly,** *adv.*

un·leash, un·lēsh′, *v.t.* To free from, as a leash; to let go of.

un·leav·ened, un·lev′end, *a.* Not leavened; not raised by yeast or other leavening agent.

un·less, un·les′, *conj.* [For earlier *onlesse, on lesse than* (or *that*), 'on less than' (with specification of some condition).] If it not be, or were the case that, as: We can expect her, *unless* she is delayed.—*prep.* Except.

un·let·tered, un·let′ẽrd, *a.* Without education; untaught; ignorant; without letters, as a tombstone.

un·li·censed, un·lī′senst, *a.* Not having a license or legal permission; done or undertaken without due license; uncontrolled.

un·light·ed, un·lī′tid, *a.* Not lighted; not illuminated; not kindled or ignited.

un·lik·a·ble, un·like·a·ble, un·lī′ka·bl, *a.* Incapable of inspiring a friendly feeling. —**un·lik·a·ble·ness, un·like·a·ble·ness,** *n.*—**un·lik·a·bly, un·like·a·bly,** *adv.*

un·like, un·līk′, *a.* Not like; different or dissimilar; having no resemblance.—*prep.* Different from; not like or typical of.—**un·like·ness,** *n.*

un·like·li·hood, un·līk′lē·hụd″, *n.* The state of being unlikely; improbability.

un·like·ly, un·līk′lē, *a.*—unlikelier, unlikeliest. Not likely; improbable; holding little prospect of success; unpromising.—*adv.*—**un·like·li·ness,** *n.*

un·lim·ber, un·lim′bẽr, *v.t.* To unhitch, as a howitzer, from its tractor or prime mover; to prepare for action or use.—*v.i.* To work at a task which prepares something for action.

un·lim·it·ed, un·lim′i·tịd, *a.* Not limited;

boundless; infinite, vast, unconfined; not restrained.

un·lined, un·līnd', *a.* Not lined; having no lining or inner layer, as a garment; without any lines on the surface, as paper; unwrinkled.

un·link, un·lingk', *v.t.* To separate the links of; to loose, as something fastened by a link; to disconnect.—*v.i.*

un·list·ed, un·lis'tid, *a.* Not listed; not entered in a list; pertaining to securities in the stock exchange which are not entered in the regular list of those admitted for dealings.

un·lit, un·lit', *a.* Not lit; unlighted.

un·liv·a·ble, un·live·a·ble, un·liv'a·bl, *a.* Lacking in comfort, uninhabitable; intolerable or unbearable; difficult to get along with, or disagreeable, often followed by *with*.

un·live, un·liv', *v.t.*—*unlived, unliving.* To undo or nullify, as past life or experiences; to live so as to undo the consequences of.

un·load, un·lōd', *v.t.* To take the load from; to remove the burden, cargo, or freight from; to remove or discharge, as a load; to get rid or dispose of, as stock and securities, by sale in large quantities; to relieve of anything burdensome; to withdraw the charge from, as a firearm.—*v.i.* To unload something.—**un·load·er**, *n.*

un·lock, un·lok', *v.t.* To unfasten, as something which has been locked; to open; to lay open or disclose.—*v.i.*

un·looked-for, un·lukt'far", *a.* Not looked for or expected; unforeseen.

un·loose, un·lös', *v.t.*—*unloosed, unloosing.* To loosen; to untie; to undo; to set free; to unfasten; to release.—**un·loos·en**, un·lö'sen, *v.t.* To unloose, as a rope.

un·lov·a·ble, un·love·a·ble, un·luv'a·bl, *a.* Not lovable; unendearing; not inspiring love.

un·loved, un·luvd', *a.* Not loved.

un·love·ly, un·luv'lē, *a.* Not lovely; not beautiful or attractive; unpleasant or repellent.—**un·love·li·ness**, *n.*

un·lov·ing, un·luv'ing, *a.* Not loving; without love.—**un·lov·ing·ly**, *adv.*—**un·lov·ing·ness**, *n.*

un·luck·y, un·luk'ē, *a.*—*unluckier, unluckiest.* Not lucky or fortunate; not successful in one's undertakings; resulting in failure, disaster, or misfortune; illomened or inauspicious, as an event.—**un·luck·i·ly**, *adv.*—**un·luck·i·ness**, *n.*

un·make, un·māk', *v.t.*—*unmade, unmaking.* To cause to be as if never made; to reduce to the original matter, elements, or state; to take to pieces; to destroy; to ruin or undo; to depose from office or authority. —**un·mak·er**, *n.*

un·man, un·man', *v.t.*—*unmanned, unmanning.* To deprive of the character or qualities of a man; to deprive of manly courage and fortitude; to dishearten; to emasculate.

un·man·age·a·ble, un·man'i·ja·bl, *a.* Not manageable; not easily restrained or directed; not controllable.

un·man·ly, un·man'lē, *a.* Not manly; effeminate; unbecoming in a man; cowardly; timid.—**un·man·li·ness**, *n.*

un·manned, un·mand', *a.* Deprived of human control; as, an *unmanned* spacecraft; rendered effeminate or weak; lacking manly qualities.

un·man·ner·ly, un·man'ér·lē, *a.* Not mannerly; not having good manners; discourteous; rude.—*adv.*—**un·man·nered**, *a.*—**un·man·nered·ly**, *adv.*—**un·man·ner·li·ness**, *n.*

un·mar·ket·a·ble, un·mär'ki·ta·bl, *a.* Not fit for the market; not saleable.

un·mask, un·mask', un·mäsk', *v.t.* To strip of a mask or disguise; to expose in the true character; *milit.* to reveal the presence of, as guns, by firing.—*v.i.* To put off a mask or disguise.

un·matched, un·macht', *a.* Matchless; having no equal.

un·mean·ing, un·mē'ning, *a.* Having no meaning or signification; mindless; senseless.—**un·mean·ing·ly**, *adv.*—**un·mean·ing·ness**, *n.*—**un·meant**, *a.*

un·meas·ured, un·mezh'érd, *a.* Not measured; beyond measure; immense; infinite; excessive; immoderate.—**un·meas·ur·a·ble**, *a.*

un·med·i·tat·ed, un·med'i·tā"tid, *a.* Not contemplated or planned.

un·meet, un·mēt', *a.* Not meet or fit; not worthy or suitable.

un·men·tion·a·ble, un·men'sha·na·bl, *a.* Unfit to be mentioned or noticed.—*n.* A thing unfit to be mentioned or noticed. *Pl.* articles of dress not to be mentioned in polite circles; underwear: used humorously.

un·mer·ci·ful, un·múr'si·ful, *a.* Not merciful; relentless; cruel; merciless; unconscionable; extreme or excessive.—**un·mer·ci·ful·ly**, *adv.*

un·mer·it·ed, un·mer'i·tid, *a.* Not merited or deserved.

un·mind·ful, un·mīnd'ful, *a.* Not mindful; not heedful; careless; without regard; not attentive; not aware.

un·mis·tak·a·ble, un"mi·stā'ka·bl, *a.* Not capable of being mistaken or misunderstood; clear; evident.—**un·mis·tak·a·bly**, *adv.*

un·mit·i·gat·ed, un·mit'i·gā'tid, *a.* Not mitigated; not softened or toned down; having no redeeming feature or qualification; as, an *unmitigated* scoundrel; unmodified.—**un·mit·i·gat·ed·ly**, *adv.*

un·mo·lest·ed, un"mo·les'tid, *a.* Not molested or disturbed.

un·moor, un·múr', *v.t. Naut.* to loose from anchorage or moorings.—*v.i. Naut.* to become unanchored or free from moorings.

un·mor·al, un·mar'al, un·mor'al, *a.* Nonmoral; having no moral aspect; neither moral nor immoral.—**un·mo·ral·i·ty**, un"mo·ral'i·tē, un"ma·ral'i·tē, *n.*

un·moved, un·mövd', *a.* Not moved; not changed in purpose or resolution; firm; not touched by passion or emotion.—**un·mov·a·ble, un·move·a·ble**, *a.*

un·muf·fle, un·muf'l, *v.t.*—*unmuffled, unmuffling.* To uncover, as by removing what muffles or conceals.—*v.i.* To free oneself of a muffle; to take off a muffle.

un·muz·zle, un·muz'l, *v.t.*—*unmuzzled, unmuzzling.* To remove a muzzle from, as a dog; to free from restraint, as to allow someone to talk openly.

un·nat·u·ral, un·nach'ér·al, *a.* Not natural; contrary to the laws of nature; contrary to natural feelings or instincts; contrary to normal behavior; acting without the affections of our common nature; perverse; cruel in the extreme; forced; affected; artificial.—**un·nat·u·ral·ly**, *adv.*—**un·nat·u·ral·ness**, *n.*

un·nec·es·sar·y, un·nes'i·ser"ē, *a.* Not necessary; needless; not required by the circumstances of the case.—**un·nec·es·sar·i·ly**, *adv.*

un·neigh·bor·ly, un·nā'bér·lē, *a.* Not neighborly; not kind and friendly.

un·nerve, un·núrv', *v.t.*—*unnerved, unnerving.* To deprive of nerve, force, or strength; to deprive of composure, as with shock.

un·no·ticed, un·nō'tist, *a.* Not observed; not regarded.—**un·no·tice·a·ble**, *a.*

un·num·bered, un·num'bérd, *a.* Not numbered; innumerable or countless; without numbers for identification or position; not counted.

un·ob·jec·tion·a·ble, un"ob·jek'sha·na·bl, *a.* Not liable to objection; not likely to be condemned as faulty, false, or improper.—**un·ob·jec·tion·al**, *a.*

un·ob·serv·a·ble, un"ob·zúr'va·bl, *a.* Not observable; not discoverable.—**un·ob·serv·ant, un·ob·serv·ing, un·ob·served**, un"ob·zúr'vant, *a.*

un·ob·struct·ed, un"ob·struk'tid, *a.* Not obstructed; not blocked by obstacles; not hindered.

un·ob·tru·sive, un"ob·trö'siv, *a.* Not obtrusive; not forward; modest.—**un·ob·tru·sive·ly**, *adv.*—**un·ob·tru·sive·ness**, *n.*

un·oc·cu·pied, un·ok'ya·pīd", *a.* Not occupied; empty, uninhabited, or vacant; as, an *unoccupied* building; not inhabited or in the control of enemy forces; not employed; idle or inactive.

un·of·fi·cial, un"o·fish'al, *a.* Not official; not in an official manner or capacity.—**un·of·fi·cial·ly**, *adv.*

un·o·pened, un·ō'pend, *a.* Not opened; closed.

un·op·posed, un"o·pōzd', *a.* Not opposed; not resisted; not meeting with any obstruction or opposition.—**un·op·pos·a·ble**, *a.*

un·or·gan·ized, un·ar'ga·nīzd", *a.* Not organized; without organic structure; inorganic; not formed into an organized or systematized whole; not unionized.

un·o·rig·i·nal, un"o·rij'i·nal, *a.* Not original; copied.

un·or·tho·dox, un·ar'tho·doks", *a.* Not orthodox; unconventional or unacceptable in doctrine or procedure.

un·owned, un·ōnd", *a.* Having no known owner; not acknowledged or admitted.

un·pack, un·pak', *v.t.* To take from a package; to remove a wrapper from; to remove the contents from, as from a package, box, or suitcase; to unload.—*v.i.* To unpack a suitcase.

un·paid, un·pād', *a.* Not paid; not discharged, as a debt; not having received what is due; not receiving a salary or wages.

un·pal·at·a·ble, un·pal'a·ta·bl, *a.* Not palatable; not pleasing to the taste; disagreeable to the feelings.

un·par·al·leled, un·par'a·leld", *a.* Having no parallel or equal; unequaled; matchless; unprecedented.

un·par·don·a·ble, un·pär'do·na·bl, *a.* Not to be forgiven; incapable of being pardoned.

un·par·lia·men·ta·ry, un"pär·la·men'ta·rē, *a.* Not parliamentary; contrary to the rules of procedure of parliamentary bodies. —**un·par·lia·men·ta·ri·ly**, *adv.*—**un·par·lia·men·ta·ri·ness**, *n.*

un·paved, un·pāvd', *a.* Not paved; having no pavement.

un·peg, un·peg', *v.t.*—*unpegged, unpegging.* To remove the peg or pegs from; to open, unfasten, or unfix by removing a peg or pegs.

un·peo·ple, un·pē'pl, *v.t.*—*unpeopled, unpeopling.* To remove the inhabitants from; to depopulate.

un·per·ceiv·a·ble, un"pér·sēv'a·bl, *a.* Incapable of being perceived; unseen; unnoticed; incomprehensible.

un·per·fect, un·púr'fikt, *a.* Imperfect.

un·per·turbed, un"pér·túrbd', *a.* Not perturbed; free from perturbation; undisturbed; calm; composed.

un·pile, un·pīl', *v.t.*—*unpiled, unpiling.* To remove or take from a heap or a pile.

un·pin, un·pin', *v.t.*—*unpinned, unpinning.* To loose from pins; to unfasten or undo by taking out a pin or pins; to detach.

un·pleas·ant, un·plez'ant, *a.* Not pleasing; disagreeable.—**un·pleas·ant·ly**, *adv.*

un·pleas·ant·ness, un·plez'ant·nis, *n.* The quality or condition of being unpleasant; an unpleasant incident or situation, as an argument.

---

a- fat, fāte, fär, fâre, fall; **e-** met, mē, mēre, hér; **i-** pin, pīne; **o-** not, nōte, möve; **u-** tub, cūbe, bull; **oi-** oil; **ou-** pound.

un·plumbed, un·plumd′, *a.* Not plumbed or measured by a plumb line, esp. as to depth; unfathomed; not investigated; not having plumbing facilities.

un·pop·u·lar, un·pop′ya·lèr, *a.* Not popular; generally disapproved; not having the public favor.—**un·pop·u·lar·i·ty,** un″·pop·ya·lar′i·tē, *n.*—**un·pop·u·lar·ly,** *adv.*

un·prec·e·dent·ed, un·pres′i·den′tid, *a.* Having no precedent; not matched by any previous instance; unexampled; unheard of. —**un·prec·e·dent·ed·ly,** *adv.*

un·pre·dict·a·ble, un″pri·dik′ta·bl, *a.* Not predictable.—**un·pre·dict·a·bil·i·ty,** *n.*—**un·pre·dict·a·bly,** *adv.*

un·prej·u·diced, un·prej′a·dist, *a.* Not prejudiced; free from bias; unbiased; impartial.

un·pre·pared, un″pri·pârd′, *a.* Not prepared; not fitted or made suitable or ready; not brought into a right or suitable condition in view of a future event, contingency, danger, or the like.—**un·pre·par·ed·ness,** *n.*

un·pre·sent·a·ble, un″pri·zen′ta·bl, *a.* Not fit for being presented to company or society.

un·pre·ten·tious, un″pri·ten′shus, *a.* Not pretentious; modest; not ostentatious.— **un·pre·ten·tious·ly,** *adv.*—**un·pre·ten··tious·ness,** *n.*

un·prin·ci·pled, un·prin′si·pld, *a.* Not having moral principles; unscrupulous.

un·print·a·ble, un·prin′ta·bl, *a.* Unacceptable for printed publication, usu. due to obscenity; offensive.

un·pro·duc·tive, un″pro·duk′tiv, *a.* Not productive; not producing large crops; not making profitable returns for labor; not producing profit or interest; not producing articles for consumption or distribution; not producing any effect.—**un·pro·duc··tive·ly,** *adv.*—**un·pro·duc·tive·ness,** *n.*

un·pro·fes·sion·al, un″pro·fesh′a·nal, *a.* Not pertaining to one's profession; contrary to the rules or standards of a profession; not belonging to a profession; lacking professional qualifications or competence.— **un·pro·fes·sion·al·ly,** *adv.*

un·prof·it·a·ble, un·prof′i·ta·bl, *a.* Not profitable; bringing no profit; serving no useful end; useless; profitless; futile.— **un·prof·it·a·ble·ness,** *n.*—**un·prof·it·a··bly,** *adv.*

un·pro·nounce·a·ble, un″pro·nouns′a·bl, *a.* Incapable of being pronounced properly; unfit for being named; unmentionable.

un·pro·voked, un″pro·vōkt′, *a.* Not provoked; not proceeding from provocation or just cause.

un·pub·lished, un·pub′lisht, *a.* Not made public; not published or issued from the press to the public, as a manuscript or book.

un·qual·i·fied, un·kwol′i·fīd″, *a.* Not having the requisite qualifications; without sufficient education, abilities, or accomplishments; not legally competent to act; not modified by conditions or exceptions; as, *unqualified* praise; absolute.—**un·qual··i·fied·ly,** *adv.*

un·quench·a·ble, un·kwench′a·bl, *a.* Incapable of being quenched or extinguished.

un·ques·tion·a·ble, un·kwes′cha·na·bl, *a.* Not questionable; not open to question; beyond dispute or doubt; as, an *unquestionable* fact; certain; indisputable; indubitable; beyond criticism.—**un·ques··tion·a·bly,** *adv.*

un·ques·tioned, un·kwes′chand, *a.* Not questioned; not interrogated; not inquired into; not called in question; undisputed.

un·ques·tion·ing, un·kwes′cha·ning, *a.* Not questioning, disputing, or objecting.— **un·ques·tion·ing·ly,** *adv.*

un·qui·et, un·kwī′it, *a.* Not calm or tranquil; restless; agitated; disturbed.—**un··qui·et·ly,** *adv.*—**un·qui·et·ness,** *n.*

un·quote, un·kwōt′, *v.i.—unquoted, unquoting.* To end a quotation.—*v.t.*

un·rat·i·fied, un·rat′i·fīd″, *a.* Not ratified, as a treaty; unsanctioned.

un·rav·el, un·rav′el, *v.t.—unraveled, unraveling, esp. Brit. unravelled, unravelling.* To free from a raveled or tangled state; disentangle; disengage the threads or fibers of, as a woven or knitted fabric. *Fig.* to free from complication or difficulty; to solve; as, to *unravel* a mystery.—*v.i.* To become unraveled.—**un·rav·el·ment,** *n.*

un·read, un·red′, *a.* Not read or perused, as a book; not having gained knowledge by reading.

un·read·a·ble, un·rē′da·bl, *a.* Not readable; illegible; not suitable for reading; not interesting to read; incomprehensible.

un·read·i·ness, un·red′ē·nis, *n.* The state of not being ready.

un·read·y, un·red′ē, *a.* Not prepared; not fit or ready; not prompt or alert.

un·re·al, un·rē′al, un·rēl′, *a.* Not real; not substantial; imaginary; not authentic; artificial; unpractical or visionary.

un·re·al·i·ty, un″rē·al′i·tē, *n.* pl. **un··re·al·i·ties.** Lack of reality; nonexistence; the quality of being unreal; illusoriness; an impractical or visionary character; something unreal.

un·rea·son, un·rē′zon, *n.* Lack of reason; irrationality; that which is devoid of or contrary to reason; absurdity; madness.

un·rea·son·a·ble, un·rē′zo·na·bl, *a.* Not guided by or agreeable to reason or sound judgment; irrational; exceeding the bounds of reason; immoderate or exorbitant.— **un·rea·son·a·ble·ness,** *n.*—**un·rea·son··a·bly,** *adv.*

un·rea·son·ing, un·rē′zo·ning, *a.* Not reasoning or exercising reason; thoughtless; hasty.—**un·rea·son·ing·ly,** *adv.*

un·rec·om·pensed, un·rek′om·penst″, *a.* Not rewarded or requited; not paid.

un·rec·on·ciled, un·rek′on·sīld″, *a.* Not reconciled; not made consistent; not restored to friendship or favor; still at enmity.

un·re·con·struct·ed, un″rē·kon·struk′tid, *a.* Refusing to adjust to altered circumstances. *U.S. hist.* refusing to accede to or comply with Reconstruction.

un·re·cord·ed, un″ri·kar′did, *a.* Not recorded or registered, esp. in official record books; not kept in remembrance by public monuments; not mentioned in any historical document.

un·reel, un·rēl′, *v.t.* To unwind, as a fishing line or a film, from a reel; *fig.* to unwind, as a story, as if from a reel.—*v.i.*

un·reeve, un·rēv′, *v.t.—past unreeved or unrove, pp. unreeved or unroven, ppr. unreeving. Naut.* to withdraw, as a rope, from a block, thimble, or the like.—*v.i.* To unreeve a rope; to become unreeved.

un·re·fined, un″ri·fīnd′, *a.* Not purified; not converted into a finished product; as, *unrefined* sugar; not polished in language, taste, or behavior.

un·re·gen·er·ate, un″ri·jen′er·it, *a.* Not regenerated or renewed in heart or spirit; not having reformed; unreconstructed; sinful. Also **un·re·gen·er·at·ed.**—**un··re·gen·er·a·cy,** un″ri·jen′ér·a·sē, *n.*— **un·re·gen·er·ate·ly,** *adv.*

un·re·lat·ed, un″ri·lā′tid, *a.* Not connected by blood or affinity; having no connection of any kind.

un·re·lent·ing, un″ri·len′ting, *a.* Not becoming lenient, gentle, or merciful; pitiless; not slackening; unflagging.—**un··re·lent·ing·ly,** *adv.*

un·re·li·a·ble, un″ri·lī′a·bl, *a.* Not reliable; not to be relied or depended on.— **un·re·li·a·bil·i·ty,** un·re·li·a·ble·ness, *n.*—**un·re·li·a·bly,** *adv.*

un·re·li·gious, un″ri·lij′us, *a.* Irreligious;

having no connection with or relation to religion; neither religious nor irreligious, being a neutral attitude.

un·re·mit·ted, un″rē·mit′id, *a.* Not remitted, as debt; not forgiven; not having any relaxation.—**un·re·mit·ting,** un″ri·mit′·ing, *a.* Not abating; not relaxing; incessant; continued.—**un·re·mit·ting·ly,** *adv.*

un·re·pair, un″ri·pâr′, *n.* Disrepair.— **un·re·paired,** *a.*

un·re·pent·ant, un″ri·pen′tant, *a.* Not penitent; not contrite for having sinned.

un·re·port·ed, un″ri·pōr′tid, *a.* Not reported; unrecorded.

un·rep·re·sent·a·tive, un″rep·ri·zen′ta·tiv, *a.* Not representative; failing to represent adequately; not typical; not standing for someone or something.—**un·rep·re··sent·ed,** *a.*

un·re·serve, un″ri·zurv′, *n.* Absence of reserve; frankness.—**un·re·served,** un″·ri·zurvd′, *a.* Not reserved; without reservation; full or entire; as, *unreserved* obedience; free from reserve; frank or open; as, to be *unreserved* in one's speech.—**un·re·serv··ed·ly,** *adv.*—**un·re·serv·ed·ness,** *n.*

un·re·spon·sive, un″ri·spon′siv, *a.* Not responsive or inclined to respond.—**un··re·spon·sive·ness,** *n.*—**un·re·spon·sive··ly,** *adv.*

un·rest, un·rest′, *n.* Mental restlessness; disquiet; uneasiness; anxiety; a state of public restlessness; agitation; turmoil.

un·re·strained, un″ri·strānd′, *a.* Not restrained or controlled; not limited; uncontrolled; loose; free.—**un·re·strain·ed··ly,** *adv.*—**un·re·straint,** *n.* Freedom from restraint.

un·re·strict·ed, un″ri·strik′tid, *a.* Without restriction; not limited or confined; having freedom of choice.

un·re·venged, un″ri·venjd′, *a.* Not having obtained revenge; not having taken vengeance.

un·re·ward·ed, un″ri·war′did, *a.* Not having received a reward; not compensated by a reward; unrequited.—**un·re·ward··ing,** *a.*

un·rid·dle, un·rid′l, *v.t.—unriddled, unriddling.* To solve, as a riddle; to explain, as a mystery; to interpret.

un·rig, un·rig′, *v.t.—unrigged, unrigging.* To strip of rigging, as a ship; to strip of equipment.

un·right·eous, un·rī′chus, *a.* Not righteous; not just; not fair; wicked; sinful; not upright and honest.—**un·right·eous·ly,** *adv.*—**un·right·eous·ness,** *n.*

un·right·ful, un·rīt′ful, *a.* Not equitable; not right; unjust; not fair; wrong.

un·rip, un·rip′, *v.t.—unripped, unripping.* To undo by ripping; cut or tear open; rip; to disclose.

un·ripe, un·rīp′, *a.* Not ripe, as of fruit; not mature; not fully prepared; not completed. —**un·ripe·ness,** *n.*—**un·ri·pened,** *a.* Immaturity.

un·ri·valed, *Brit.* **un·ri·valled,** un·rī′vald, *a.* Having no rival, competitor, or equal; peerless; incomparable.

un·robe, un·rōb′, *v.t.—unrobed, unrobing.* To undress; to disrobe.—*v.i.*

un·roll, un·rōl′, *v.t.* To open out, as something rolled; to lay open or display.—*v.i.* To unfold; to uncoil; to become uncoiled or unrolled.

un·ro·man·tic, un″rō·man′tik, *a.* Not romantic; not given to romantic fancies; having nothing of romance connected with it.

un·roof, un·rōf′, un·ruf′, *v.t.* To strip off, as a roof; to uncover.

un·root, un·rōt′, un·rut′, *v.t.* To tear up or pull up, as by the roots; to uproot.

un·round, un·round′, *v.t. Phon.* to pronounce or articulate without rounding the lips, as in the pronunciation of the vowel 'e' in the word 'she.'—**un·round·ed,** un·-roun'did, a.

un·ruf·fled, un·ruf'ld, a. Calm; tranquil; not agitated; smooth; not disturbed; possessing aplomb.

un·ru·ly, un·rö'lē, a.—*unrulier, unruliest.* Disregarding restraint; disposed to violate laws; lawless; turbulent; ungovernable; disorderly.—**un·ru·li·ness,** n. Disregard of restraint; turbulence.

un·sad·dle, un·sad'l, v.t.—*unsaddled, unsaddling.* To take the saddle from; to unseat; to unhorse; to unburden, as of a task or duty.—v.i. To remove a saddle from an animal.

un·safe, un·sāf', a. Not affording or accompanied by complete safety; perilous; hazardous.—**un·safe·ly,** adv. Not without danger.—**un·safe·ty,** un·sāf'tē, n.

un·said, un·sed', a. Not spoken; not uttered.

un·salt·ed, un·sal'tid, a. Not salted; fresh.

un·sanc·ti·fied, un·sangk'ti·fīd", a. Unholy; profane; wicked; not consecrated; sinful.

un·san·i·tar·y, un·san'i·ter"ē, a. Not sanitary; unhealthful.

un·sat·is·fac·to·ry, un"sat·is·fak'to·rē, a. Not satisfactory; not satisfying; not giving satisfaction; not adequate.—**un·sat·is·-fac·to·ri·ly,** adv.—**un·sat·is·fac·to·ri·-ness,** n.

un·sat·is·fied, un·sat'is·fīd", a. Not having enough; not gratified to the full; not content; not pleased; not convinced or fully persuaded; unpaid.

un·sat·u·rat·ed, un·sach'a·rā"tid, a. Not saturated; having the power to dissolve or absorb still more of something; *chem.* capable of taking on an element by direct chemical combination without the liberation of other elements or compounds; as, an *unsaturated* compound.—**un·sat·u·rate,** un·sach'ėr·it, un·sach'a·rāt", n.

un·sa·vor·y, Brit. **un·sa·vour·y,** un·-sā'vo·rē, a. Not savory; unappealing; disagreeable to the taste or sense of smell; unpleasing; offensive; *fig.* morally objectionable; as, an *unsavory* character.

un·say, un·sā', v.t.—*unsaid, unsaying.* To recant or recall after having been said; to retract, as a statement; to take back.

un·scathed, un·skāтнd', a. Not scathed; uninjured.

un·sched·uled, un·skej'ōld, un·skej'ụld, un·skej'ö·ld, Brit. un·shed'ūld, un·shej'-öld, a. Not scheduled or arranged in advance.

un·schooled, un·sköld', a. Not schooled; not taught; untrained; natural; not artificial.

un·sci·en·tif·ic, un"sī·en·tif'ik, a. Not scientific; not in accordance with the requirements of science; not conforming to the principles or methods of science; unfamiliar with scientific procedure.—**un·sci·en·tif·i·cal·ly,** adv.

un·scram·ble, un·skram'bl, v.t.—*unscrambled, unscrambling.* To bring out of a scrambled condition; to reduce from confusion to order; to make intelligible, as a scrambled message.

un·screw, un·skrö', v.t. To draw the screws from; to unfasten by removing screws; to undo, as a jar cap, by rotating or turning.—v.i. To become unscrewed.

un·scru·pu·lous, un·skrö'pya·lus, a. Having no scruples; having no principles.—**un·scru·pu·lous·ly,** adv.—**un·scru·pu·lous·ness,** n.

un·seal, un·sēl', v.t. To break a seal of; to open after having been sealed.

un·seam, un·sēm', v.t. To open the seam or seams of; to rip apart; to undo.

un·search·a·ble, un·sụr'cha·bl, a. Incapable of being discovered or understood by search; not able to be explored or

researched; inscrutable; mysterious; hidden.—**un·search·a·bly,** adv.

un·sea·son·a·ble, un·sē'zo·na·bl, a. Not seasonable; not agreeable to the time of the year; not seasonal; ill-timed; untimely; not suited to the time or occasion; inappropriate.—**un·sea·son·a·ble·ness,** n.—**un·sea·son·a·bly,** adv.

un·sea·soned, un·sē'zond, a. Not seasoned; unripe; not matured; inexperienced; not inured; not flavored with seasoning.

un·seat, un·sēt', v.t. To remove from a seat; to throw from a seat on horseback; to depose from a political position.

un·sea·wor·thy, un·sē'wụr"тнē, a. Not fit for a sea voyage.—**un·sea·wor·thi·-ness,** n.

un·se·cured, un"si·kūrd', a. Not secured; not insured against loss, as by a bond or pledge; unfastened.

un·seem·ly, un·sēm'lē, a. Not seemly; not becoming; not conforming to accepted behavior modes; indecorous; indecent; inappropriate.—adv.—**un·seem·li·ness,** n.

un·seen, un·sēn', a. Not seen; invisible; unperceived; unobserved; unstudied, as a musical composition.

un·seg·re·gat·ed, un·seg're·gā"tid, a. Not segregated, esp. not racially segregated; integrated.

un·self·ish, un·sel'fish, a. Not selfish; not unduly attached to one's own interests or welfare; generous.—**un·self·ish·ly,** adv.—**un·self·ish·ness,** n.

un·sen·ti·men·tal, un"sen·ti·men'tal, a. Not apt to be swayed by sentiment; matter-of-fact.—**un·sen·ti·men·tal·ly,** adv.

un·set, un·set', a. Not set; not firm or solid, as gelatin or asphalt when first poured; unmounted, as gems.

un·set·tle, un·set'l, v.t.—*unsettled, unsettling.* To change or displace from a settled state; to make uncertain or unstable; disrupt, disturb, or upset.—v.i. To become disordered or unsettled.

un·set·tled, un·set'ld, a. Not settled; not fixed or stable; without established order; not fixed in a place or abode; wavering or uncertain, as opinions or actions; undetermined or doubtful; not populated; as, a region; not adjusted or disposed of, as an account or estate.—**un·set·tled·ness,** n.

un·sex, un·seks', v.t. To deprive of qualities of sex, esp. the femininity of a woman.

un·shack·le, un·shak'l, v.t.—*unshackled, unshackling.* To unfetter; to set free from restraint.

un·shaped, un·shāpt', a. Not shaped; not having definite shape or form.

un·shap·en, un·shā'pen, a. Not shaped; shapeless; imperfectly shaped; misshapen.

un·sheathe, un·shēтн', v.t.—*unsheathed, unsheathing.* To draw from a sheath, as a sword, knife, or the like; to bring or put forth from a covering, threateningly or otherwise.

un·shed, un·shed', a. Not shed, as tears, hair, or feathers; not dropped, as leaves.

un·shel·tered, un·shel'tėrd, a. Not sheltered; without shelter or protection.

un·ship, un·ship', v.t.—*unshipped, unshipping.* To put or take off from a ship, as persons or goods; to remove from the proper place for use on a boat, as an oar or tiller.—v.i. To become removed or be removable.

un·shod, un·shod', a. Without shoes.

un·shorn, un·shōrn', un·shạrn', a. Not shorn; not sheared or clipped.

un·shrink·ing, un·shringk'ing, a. Not withdrawing from danger; difficult problems, work, or duty; not recoiling.—**un·-shrink·ing·ly,** adv.

un·sift·ed, un·sif'tid, a. Not separated by a sieve; not critically examined.

un·sight, un·sīt', a. [Appar. a contr. of *unsighted.*] Not seen; without inspection or

examination; as, to buy a thing *unsight, unseen.*

un·sight·ly, un·sīt'lē, a.—*unsightlier, unsightliest.* Disagreeable to the eye; repulsive; ugly.—**un·sight·li·ness,** n.

un·sing·a·ble, un·sing'a·bl, a. Not singable; not suited or adapted for being sung.

un·sized, un·sīzd', a. Not sized; not marked with a specific size; not stiffened with sizing, as paper or fabric.

un·skilled, un·skild', a. Not skilled; untrained; not demanding skill; as, *unskilled* labor; manifesting an unskillful execution.

un·skill·ful, Brit. **un·skil·ful,** un·skil'ful, a. Not skillful; inexpert; inept.—**un·-skill·ful·ly,** Brit. **un·skil·ful·ly,** adv.—**un·skill·ful·ness,** Brit. **un·skil·ful·-ness,** n.

un·slaked, un·slākt', a. Not slaked or quenched; not mixed with water and so reduced to powder; as, *unslaked* lime.

un·sling, un·sling',v.t.—*unslung, unslinging.* To remove, as a hammock, from a position in which it has been slung. *Naut.* to take off the slings of; release from slings.

un·smil·ing, un·smī'ling, a. Not smiling; grave; serious.—**un·smil·ing·ly,** adv.

un·snap, un·snap', v.t.—*unsnapped, unsnapping.* To loosen or undo by, or as if by, unfastening snap closings.

un·snarl, un·snärl', v.t. To bring out of a snarled condition; disentangle.

un·so·cia·ble, un·sō'sha·bl, a. Not sociable; not inclined to friendly association with people; not companionable; withdrawn.—**un·so·cia·bil·i·ty,** un·so·cia·ble·ness, n.—**un·so·cia·bly,** adv.

un·so·cial, un·sō'shal, a. Not social; not caring to seek or associate with people.—**un·so·cial·ly,** adv.

un·soiled, un·soild', a. Not soiled; not tainted or polluted; not sullied.

un·so·lic·it·ed, un"so·lis'i·tid, a. Not solicited; unasked; unsought.

un·so·lic·i·tous, un"so·lis'i·tus, a. Not solicitous; unconcerned; indifferent.

un·so·phis·ti·cat·ed, un"so·fis'ti·kā"tid, a. Not sophisticated; not adept in or restrained by social conventions; naïve; uncomplicated; plain; not adulterated; pure; genuine.—**un·so·phis·ti·cat·ed·ly,** adv.—**un·so·phis·ti·cat·ed·ness,** un·so·-phis·ti·ca·tion, n.

un·sought, un·sạt', a. Not searched for; unasked for; unsolicited.

un·sound, un·sound', a. Not strong or reliable; diseased; impaired; defective; not solid or firm; not well-founded or valid; fallacious; specious.—**un·sound·ly,** adv.—**un·sound·ness,** n.

un·spar·ing, un·spâr'ing, a. Not sparing; liberal; profuse. Unmerciful; ruthless.—**un·spar·ing·ly,** adv.—**un·spar·-ing·ness,** n.

un·speak·a·ble, un·spē'ka·bl, a. Incapable of being spoken or uttered; unutterable; ineffable; so bad as to preclude description.—**un·speak·a·bly,** adv.

un·spec·i·fied, un·spes'i·fīd", a. Not specified; not fully or explicitly mentioned.

un·sphere, un·sfēr', v.t.—*unsphered, unsphering.* To remove from its or one's sphere; to displace.

un·spo·ken, un·spō'ken, a. Not spoken or uttered; unexpressed but understood; as, *unspoken* criticism.

un·spot·ted, un·spot'id, a. Free from spots or blemishes; free from moral stain or guilt.

un·sprung, un·sprung', a. Not sprung; having no springs; not released, as a trap.

un·sta·ble, un·stā'bl, a. Not stable; irresolute; lacking in emotional control; *chem.* subject to easy decomposition or spontaneous change.—**un·sta·ble·ness,** n.—**un·sta·bly,** adv.

un·states·man·like, un·stāts'man·līk", a.

Not statesmanlike; unlike or unbefitting a statesman.

un·stead·y, un·sted′ē, *a.—unsteadier, unsteadiest.* Not steady; shaky; staggering; reeling; wavering; fluctuating; not constant in mind; fickle; unsettled; not regular, equable, or uniform; varying.—*v.t. unsteadied, unsteadying.*—**un·stead·i·ly,** *adv.*

un·step, un·step′, *v.t.—unstepped, unstepping. Naut.* to remove, as a mast, from its step.

un·stint·ed, un·stin′tid, *a.* Not stinted; bestowed abundantly; rather profuse or lavish.

un·stop, un·stop′, *v.t.—unstopped, unstopping.* To free from obstruction, as a drain; to open, as a bottle, by drawing out its stopper or cork; *mus.* to pull out the stops of, as an organ.

un·strap, un·strap′, *v.t.—unstrapped, unstrapping.* To loosen, remove, or unfasten a strap of.

un·stressed, un·strest′, *a.* Not stressed; unaccented.

un·string, un·string′, *v.t.—unstrung, unstringing.* To remove the string or strings from; to relax or untune the strings of; to take from a string; to relax the tension of; to weaken, as the nerves.

un·stud·ied, un·stud′ēd, *a.* Not premeditated; not labored; natural; not learned through study; unversed, followed by *in.*

un·sub·stan·tial, un″sub·stan′shal, *a.* Not substantial or solid; not having substance; fanciful or unreal.—**un·sub·stan·ti·al·i·ty,** un″sub·stan″shē·al′i·tē, *n.*—**un·sub·stan·tial·ly,** *adv.*

un·sub·stan·ti·at·ed, un″sub·stan′shē·ā″tid, *a.* Not substantiated; not established by evidence.—**un·sub·stan·ti·a·tion,** *n.*

un·suc·cess·ful, un″suk·ses′ful, *a.* Not successful; having met with no success.—**un·suc·cess·ful·ly,** *adv.*

un·suit·a·ble, un·sö′ta·bl, *a.* Not suitable, fit, or adapted; improper.—**un·suit·a·ble·ness,** *n.*—**un·suit·a·bly,** *adv.*

un·sung, un·sung′, *a.* Not sung; not celebrated in song or poem; unacclaimed.

un·sur·passed, un″sėr·past′, un″sėr·päst′, *a.* Not excelled, exceeded, or outdone.

un·sus·pect·ed, un″sa·spek′tid, *a.* Not suspected; not an object of suspicion; not supposed or imagined.

un·swathe, un·swäTH′, *v.t.—unswathed, unswathing.* To take a swathe from; to free from a bandage or bandages.

un·swear, un·swâr′, *v.t.—past unswore,* pp. *unsworn,* ppr. *unswearing.* To retract, esp. in a formal manner; recant by a subsequent oath; to abjure.—*v.i.*

un·swerv·ing, un·swur′ving, *a.* Not deviating from any rule or standard; unwavering; firm.—**un·swerv·ing·ly,** *adv.*

un·sym·met·ri·cal, un″si·me′tri·kal, *a.* Without symmetry or due proportion of parts.—**un·sym·met·ri·cal·ly,** *adv.*

un·tan·gle, un·tang′gl, *v.t.—untangled, untangling.* To bring out of a tangled state; disentangle; unsnarl, straighten out or clear up, as anything confused or perplexing.

un·taught, un·tat′, *a.* Not instructed, educated, or schooled; ignorant; natural or innate.

un·teach, un·tēch′, *v.t.—untaught, unteaching.* To cause to forget, disbelieve, or give up what has been taught; to teach the opposite of.

un·teach·a·ble, un·tēch′a·bl, *a.* Incapable of being taught; resisting instruction.

un·ten·a·ble, un·ten′a·bl, *a.* Not tenable; that cannot be maintained by argument; not defensible.—**un·ten·a·bil·i·ty,** *n.*

un·teth·er, un·teTH′ẽr, *v.t.* To release from a tether, as a cow.

un·thanked, un·thangkt′, *a.* Not having received thanks.

un·thank·ful, un·thangk′ful, *a.* Ungrateful; thankless; not welcome.

un·think, un·thingk′, *v.t.—unthought, unthinking.* To retract in thought; to change one's mind about.—*v.i.* To end or change a line of thought.

un·think·a·ble, un·thing′ka·bl, *a.* Not within the grasp of the mind; inconceivable; not to be made an object of thought or consideration.

un·think·ing, un·thing′king, *a.* Not heedful; inconsiderate; not indicating thought or reflection; having no power to think.—**un·think·ing·ly,** *adv.*

un·thread, un·thred′, *v.t.* To draw out or take out the thread from; as, to *unthread* a needle; to thread one's way out of; as, to *unthread* a labyrinth.

un·throne, un·thrōn′, *v.t.—unthroned, unthroning.* To dethrone.

un·ti·dy, un·tī′dē, *a.—untidier, untidiest.* Not tidy or neat; slovenly or disordered; disorganized.—**un·ti·di·ly,** *adv.*—**un·ti·di·ness,** *n.*

un·tie, un·tī′, *v.t.—untied, untying.* To loose or unfasten, as anything tied; to let or set loose by undoing a knot; to undo the string or cords of; to undo, as a cord or a knot; to free from restraint; to resolve, as perplexities.—*v.i.* To become untied.

un·til, un·til′, *conj.* [M.E. *until,* < *un-* and *til,* E. *till.*] Up to the time that or when; till; before, usu. with negatives, as: He did *not* come *until* the meeting was half over.—*prep.* Onward to or till, as a specified time; before, usu. with negatives, as: He did *not* go *until* night. *Sc., N. Brit.,* to or unto.

un·time·ly, un·tīm′lē, *a.* Not timely; not done or happening in the right season; inopportune; premature.—*adv.* Before the natural time; unseasonably.—**un·time·li·ness,** *n.*

un·tir·ing, un·tī′ėr·ing, *a.* Not becoming tired or exhausted; unwearied.—**un·tir·ing·ly,** *adv.*

un·tit·led, un·tīt′ld, *a.* Having no title; without right or claim.

un·to, un′tö, *unstressed* un′to, *prep. Archaic, poet.* To: in all uses except the infinitive; until; till.

un·told, un·tōld′, *a.* Not told, related, or revealed; not numbered or counted; as, *untold* plates of food; not expressible.

un·touch·a·ble, un·tuch′a·bl, *a.* Not near enough to be touched; inaccessible; interdicted or forbidden to the touch; unpleasant or dangerous to touch; *fig.* not subject to bribery, interference, control, or criticism.—*n.* A member of the lowest caste in India whose touch was formerly considered a defilement by Hindus of higher caste.—**un·touch·a·bil·i·ty,** un″tuch·a·bil′i·tē, *n.*—**un·touch·a·bly,** *adv.*

un·to·ward, un·tōrd′, un·tạrd′, *a.* Unlucky; adverse; not easily guided or taught; vexatious; intractable.—**un·to·ward·ly,** *adv.*—**un·to·ward·ness,** *n.*

un·trained, un·trānd′, *a.* Not trained; not disciplined; not instructed.—**un·train·a·ble,** *a.*

un·trav·eled, *Brit.* **un·trav·elled,** un·trav′eld, *a.* Not traversed by vehicles or travelers; not having traveled; not having gained experience by or as by travel; unsophisticated.

un·tread, un·tred′, *v.t.—past untrod,* pp. *untrodden* or *untrod,* ppr. *untreading.* To retrace.

un·treat·ed, un·trē′tid, *a.* Not treated; not under treatment, as a disease or disorder.

un·tried, un·trīd′, *a.* Not tried; not attempted or tested; not heard and tried in a court of law.

un·trimmed, un·trimd′, *a.* Not trimmed; not decorated; not clipped; not pruned; not sheared.

un·trou·bled, un·trub′ld, *a.* Free from

trouble; not disturbed by care, sorrow, or worry; not agitated or ruffled; of bodies of water, not raised into waves.

un·true, un·trö′, *a.* Not true; not faithful, as to a cause, pledge, or person; disloyal; false; contrary to the fact; incorrect.—**un·true·ness,** *n.*—**un·tru·ly,** *adv.*

un·truss, un·trus′, *v.t., v.i. Archaic,* to loosen from or as from a truss; to unfasten or untie. *Obs.* to undress.

un·trust·wor·thy, un·trust′wur″THē, *a.* Not worthy of being trusted; not deserving of confidence.—**un·trust·wor·thi·ly,** *adv.* —**un·trust·wor·thi·ness,** *n.*

un·truth, un·tröth′, *n.* The state or quality of being untrue; contrariety to truth; want of veracity; a false assertion; a lie. *Obs.* unfaithfulness; want of fidelity.

un·truth·ful, un·tröth′ful, *a.* Wanting in truth or veracity; not truthful; false.—**un·truth·ful·ly,** *adv.*—**un·truth·ful·ness,** *n.*

un·tuck, un·tuk′, *v.t.* To release from or bring out of a tucked condition.

un·tun·a·ble, un·tön′a·bl, un·tūn′a·bl, *a.* Not capable of being tuned; discordant; not musical.

un·tune, un·tön′, un·tūn′, *v.t.—untuned, untuning.* To put out of tune; to upset; to confuse.

un·tu·tored, un·tö′tẽrd, un·tū′tẽrd, *a.* Untaught; uninstructed; rude; naïve.

un·twine, un·twīn′, *v.t.—untwined, untwining.* To untwist, unwind, or disentangle. —*v.i.* To become untwisted, unwound, or disentangled.

un·twist, un·twist′, *v.t.* To separate and open, as twisted threads; to turn back from being twisted.—*v.i.* To become untwisted or untwined.—**un·twist·ed,** *a.*

un·used, un·ūzd′, un·ūst′, *a.* Not used; not put to use; never having been used, un·ūzd′. Not accustomed or habituated, followed by *to;* as, hands *unused* to labor, un·ūst′.

un·u·su·al, un·ū′zhö·al, *a.* Not usual; not common; rare.—**un·u·su·al·ly,** *adv.*—**un·u·su·al·ness,** *n.*

un·ut·ter·a·ble, un·ut′ẽr·a·bl, *a.* Incapable of being uttered or expressed; ineffable; inexpressible; unspeakable.—**un·ut·ter·a·bly,** *adv.*—**un·ut·tered,** *a.*

un·val·ued, un·val′ūd, *a.* Not valued or prized; unimportant; not appraised.

un·var·ied, un·vâr′ēd, *a.* Not varied; not altered; not diversified; always the same.—**un·var·y·ing,** *a.* Not altering; uniform.

un·var·nished, un·vär′nisht, *a.* Not overlaid with varnish; not artfully embellished; plain; straightforward.

un·veil, un·vāl′, *v.t.* To remove a veil from; to disclose to view.—*v.i.* To remove one's veil; to reveal or disclose oneself.

un·ven·ti·lat·ed, un·ven′ti·lā″tid, *a.* Not ventilated.

un·versed, un·vụrst′, *a.* Not versed or skilled, followed by *in;* inexperienced, followed by *in.*

un·vo·cal, un·vō′kal, *a.* Not forceful or persuasive of voice; not outspoken; restrained.

un·voice, un·vois′, *v.t.—unvoiced, unvoicing. Phon.* To make, as a voiced sound, voiceless; to utter without vocal quality.

un·voiced, un·voist′, *a.* Not spoken; unuttered; unexpressed. *Phon.* not uttered with voice as distinct from breath; voiceless.

un·want·ed, un·won′tid, un·wạn′tid, *a.* Not wanted or desired.

un·war·rant·a·ble, un·wạr′an·ta·bl, un·wor′an·ta·bl, *a.* Not defensible; not justifiable; improper.—**un·war·rant·a·bly,** *adv.*

un·war·rant·ed, un·wạr′an·tid, un·wor′an·tid, *a.* Not justified.

un·war·y, un·wâr′ē, *a.* Not wary; not cautious; careless; unguarded.—**un·war·i·ly,** *adv.*—**un·war·i·ness,** *n.*

un·washed, un·wosht′, un·wȧsht′, *a.* Not washed; not cleansed by water; not washed by waves or flowing water.—*n. Liter.* the lower classes or the ignorant, usu. preceded by *the.*

un·wa·ver·ing, un·wā′vẽr·ing, *a.* Not wavering; not fluctuating; fixed; steadfast.—*un·wa·ver·ing·ly, adv.*

un·wear·able, un·wâr′a·bl, *a.* That cannot be worn; unsuitable for wearing.

un·wea·ried, un·wēr′ēd, *a.* Not tired; not fatigued; indefatigable.

un·weave, un·wēv′, *v.t.*—past *unwove,* pp. *unwoven,* ppr. *unweaving.* To undo or unravel, as something which has been woven; to disentangle; unsnarl.

un·wed, un·wed′, *a.* Not married. Also **un·wed·ded.**

un·weed·ed, un·wē′did, *a.* Not cleared of weeds.

un·wel·come, un·wel′kom, *a.* Not welcome; not well received; not pleasing or agreeable.

un·well, un·wel′, *a.* Indisposed; not in good health; ailing.

un·wept, un·wept′, *a.* Not wept for; not lamented; not mourned; not shed, as tears.

un·whole·some, un·hōl′som, *a.* Not wholesome; unhealthful; deleterious to health or well-being, physically or morally; not sound in health; unhealthy, esp. in appearance; suggestive of disease; disgusting; detestable.—**un·whole·some·ly**, *adv.*—**un·whole·some·ness**, *n.*

un·wield·y, un·wēl′dē, *a.* [< *un,* not, and old *weldy, wieldy,* active.] Movable with difficulty; too bulky and awkward to move or be moved easily; unmanageable from weight; cumbersome; clumsy; ponderous.—**un·wield·i·ness**, *n.*

un·willed, un·wild′, *a.* Not willed; involuntary; not premeditated.

un·will·ing, un·wil′ing, *a.* Not willing; loath; reluctant.—**un·will·ing·ly**, *adv.*—**un·will·ing·ness**, *n.*

un·wind, un·wīnd′, *v.t.*—*unwound, unwinding.* To undo or uncoil, as something wound; wind off; loosen or untwist, as what is wound; to disentangle; to lessen the tension of.—*v.i.* To become unwound; to become less tense; as, to *unwind* after work.

un·wink·ing, un·wingk′ing, *a.* Not winking; not opening and closing the eyes.

un·wis·dom, un·wiz′dom, *n.* [O.E. *unwīsdōm.*] Lack of wisdom; unwise action; folly.

un·wise, un·wīz′, *a.* [O.E. *unwīs.*] Not wise; foolish; as, an *unwise* thing to do; imprudent; injudicious; indiscreet.—**un·wise·ly**, *adv.*

un·wish, un·wish′, *v.t.* To withdraw or revoke, as a thing wished; to stop wishing for.

un·wished, un·wisht′, *a.* Not wished; undesired; unwanted. Also **un·wished-for**, un·wisht′fȧr.

un·wit·nessed, un·wit′nist, *a.* Not witnessed; not seen; not attested by witnesses; as, an *unwitnessed* signature.

un·wit·ting, un·wit′ing, *a.* Not knowing; unconscious; unaware; accidental.—**un·wit·ting·ly**, *adv.*

un·wom·an·ly, un·wum′an·lē, *a.* Not womanly; unbecoming to a woman.

un·wont·ed, un·wōn′tid, un·wȧn′tid, un·wun′tid, *a.* Not wonted; not customary, habitual, or usual; *obs.* unaccustomed or unused.—**un·wont·ed·ly**, *adv.*—**un·wont·ed·ness**, *n.*

un·work·a·ble, un·wur′ka·bl, *a.* Not workable; incapable of being worked; unmanageable; impracticable, as a scheme.

un·worked, un·wurkt′, *a.* Not worked; not developed or exploited, as a field of operations.

un·world·ly, un·wurld′lē, *a.* Not influenced by worldly or sordid motives; naïve; spiritual or unearthly.—**un·world·li·ness**, *n.*

un·worn, un·wōrn′, un·wȧrn′, *a.* Not worn; not impaired by wear; fresh.

un·wor·thy, un·wur′THē, *a.* Not worthy; lacking worth or excellence; not commendable or creditable; not of adequate merit or character; of a kind not worthy, followed by *of;* beneath the dignity, followed by *of;* undeserving.—**un·wor·thi·ly**, *adv.*—**un·wor·thi·ness**, *n.*

un·wound·ed, un·wōn′did, *a.* Not hurt; not wounded; intact.

un·wrap, un·rap′, *v.t.*—*unwrapped, unwrapping.* To take off a wrapper from; to open or undo.—*v.i.* To become unwrapped.

un·wreathe, un·rēTH′, *v.t.*—*unwreathed, unwreathing.* To untwist or untwine.

un·wrin·kle, un·ring′kl, *v.t.*—*unwrinkled, unwrinkling.* To eliminate wrinkles from; to smooth.

un·writ·ten, un·rit′en, *a.* Not reduced to writing; traditional; oral; not written upon; blank.

un·writ·ten con·sti·tu·tion, *n.* A constitution not expressed in a single document but implied in customs and accepted statutes and based upon precedent.

un·writ·ten law, *n.* A law which, although it may be reduced to writing, rests on custom or judicial decision for its authority, as distinguished from law originating in written statutes or decrees; the principle, often popularly accepted as valid, of the right of an individual to avenge wrongs against personal or family honor, esp. in cases involving relations between the sexes, usu. preceded by *the.*

un·wrought, un·rȧt′, *a.* Not manufactured; not processed; raw; natural.

un·yield·ing, un·yēl′ding, *a.* Unbending; not pliant; stiff; firm; obstinate.

un·yoke, un·yōk′, *v.t.*—*unyoked, unyoking.* To free from or as from a yoke; to part or disjoin, as by removing a yoke.—*v.i.* To remove a yoke; *archaic,* to cease work.

un·zip, un·zip′, *v.t.*—*unzipped, unzipping.* To open by or as by a zipper.—*v.i.* To become unzipped or unfastened.

up, up, *adv.* [O.E. *up, upp,* = O.S. *ūp* = O.H.G. *ūf* (G. *auf*) = Icel. *upp,* akin to Goth. *iup,* up, and prob. ult. to E. *over.*] To, toward, or in a more elevated position; as, to climb *up* to the top of a ladder; to or in an erect position; as, to stand *up;* out of bed; as, to get *up;* above the horizon; to or at any point that is considered higher; as, *up* north; to or at a source, origin, center, or the like; to follow a stream *up* to its head; to or at a higher point or degree in a scale, as of rank, size, value, or pitch; to or at a point of equal advance or extent; as, to catch *up* in a race; in continuous awareness; as, keeping *up* with the times; into or in activity or operation; as, to stir *up* rebellion; into existence; as, a deed drawn *up* in an office; into view, prominence, or consideration, as: The lost papers have turned *up.* Into or in a place of safekeeping, storage, or retirement; as, to put *up* preserves; into or in a state of union or contraction; as, to fold or shrivel *up;* to the required or final point; as, to pay *up* one's debts, burned or used *up;* to or at an end; *naut.* toward the windward side; *baseball,* at bat; *golf,* ahead of an opponent a specified number of holes. *Sports,* ahead; as, came *up* from behind; apiece or each, as: The score stood at six *up.*—*a.* Relatively high; going or directed up or higher; as, the *up* conveyor belt; tending or inclining upward; *colloq.* informed or aware, as: They are *up* on recent discoveries. Abreast; finished, ended, or over, as: The joke is *up. Colloq.* happening or taking place, as: What's *up?* In any higher state, condition, or position; erect or standing; out of bed; as, to be *up;* above a surface, the ground, or the horizon; being above the normal or former degree,

amount, or the like, as water nearing flood level; in an agitated, excited, or active state, as: His ire was *up.* Prepared or ready for operation, use, or the like; being considered, or presented for consideration, as: The proposal is *up* before the voters. On trial or charged; as, *up* for theft. *Sports, games,* being ahead or in advance of any opponent; equal, used in combination with a numeral, as: The score was *6-up. Baseball,* at bat. At stake, wagered, or bet in gambling.—*prep.* To, toward, or at a higher place or rank on or in; as, *up* the stairs; to, toward, or at a point of considered as higher; as, *up* the street; toward the source or origin of; as, *up* the stream; toward or in the interior of, as a region or country, as: The explorers went *up* country. In an opposite direction to, used in compounds; as, *upwind.*—*n.* An upward movement; an ascent; a rise of fortune; as, *ups* and downs.—*v.t.*—*upped, upping. Colloq.* To put or take higher; to make better; increase.—*v.i. Colloq.* To get or start up; to begin something quickly, usu. followed by *and* and a verb, as: He *upped and* left school.—**all up with,** near the end for; near defeat for.—**up a·gainst**, *colloq.* faced with; as, *up against* a dilemma.—**up a·gainst it**, *colloq.* in a troublesome situation, esp. regarding finances.—**up on** or **in.** *Colloq.* Well supplied with information on; aware of.—**up to,** equal to or capable of; *colloq.* scheming or doing, as: What's the baby *up to* now? Incumbent or dependent upon, as: The decision is *up to* us.

up-and-down, up′an·doun′, *a.* Moving successively upward and downward; pertaining to a surface which is not level; as, *up-and-down* terrain; likely to change; as, an *up-and-down* existence; vertical.

U·pan·i·shad, ö·pan′i·shad″, ö·pä′ni·shäd″, *n.* [Skt.] *Hinduism,* a philosophical treatise found in the third division of the Vedas which contains metaphysical, ethical, and ontological speculations.

u·pas, ū′pas, *n.* [Malay. *upas,* poison.] An evergreen tree of Southeastern Asia and the E. Indies, *Antiaris toxicaria,* yielding a poison; the poison itself, used on arrowheads by the natives; *fig.* something extremely harmful.

up·beat, up′bēt″, *n. Mus.* The last beat in a musical measure; any unaccented beat in a measure; the upward movement of the conductor's hand which indicates an unaccented beat.

up·beat, up′bēt″, *a. Colloq.* Happy or optimistic; entertaining.

up-bow, up′bō″, *n. Mus.* a stroke of the bow in playing stringed instruments in which the movement is toward the bow's heel.

up·braid, up·brād′, *v.t.* [< *up,* and *braid,* in old sense of to scold.] To criticize or scold for some fault or offense; to reprove with severity; to chide; to be a reproach to.—**up·braid·er**, *n.*—**up·braid·ing**, up·brā′ding, *n.*—**up·braid·ing·ly**, *adv.*

up·bring·ing, up′bring″ing, *n.* The process of bringing up; training; education; care.

up·build, up·bild′, *v.t.*—*upbuilt, upbuilding.* To build up; enlarge; establish.—**up·build·er**, *n.*

up·cast, up′kast″, up′käst″, *a.* Cast up; thrown or turned upward; directed up.—*n.* The ventilating shaft of a mine through which the air passes upward after circulating in the mine; anything cast up.

up·chuck, up′chuk″, *v.i., v.t. Slang,* to vomit.

up·com·ing, up′kum″ing, *a.* Forthcoming; ready to occur.

up·coun·try, up′kun″trē, *a.* Being or living far away from the coast or border; interior; as, an *upcountry* village.—*n.* The interior of a country.—*adv.* Toward or in the interior of a country.

up·date, up·dāt′, up′dāt″, v.t.—updated, updating. To make modern or up-to-date.

up·do, up′dō″, n. pl. **up·dos.** An upswept hairdo.

up·draft, up′draft″, up′dräft″, n. An upward movement of air or other gas.

up·end, up·end′, v.t. To set on end, as a barrel; to upset, defeat, or overthrow.—v.i. To stand or turn on end.

up·grade, up′grād″, n. An ascending slope or road; an increase, as of status, rank, or quality, usu. preceded by on the, as: His fortunes are on the upgrade.—up″grād′, v.t.—upgraded, upgrading. To elevate the rank or status of; to increase or raise the quality of, as livestock, by breeding selectively.—up′grād′, a. Uphill; upward; pertaining to or along an upgrade.—adv. Uphill.

up·growth, up′grōth″, n. The process of growing up; development; something that grows up.

up·heav·al, up·hē′val, n. The act of upheaving; the condition of being upheaved; an abrupt change or violent disturbance; geol. a lifting up of a portion of the earth's crust by some expansion or elevating power from below.

up·heave, up·hēv′, v.t.—upheaved or up-hove, upheaving. To heave or lift up; to raise up or aloft.—v.i. To be lifted up; to rise as if thrust up.—**up·heav·er**, n.

up·hill, up′hil′, adv. Upward, as on an ascending slope or incline; against obstacles.—a. Going up, as on a rising slope; situated on a high level or high ground; difficult; fatiguing.—n. A rising incline.

up·hold, up·hōld′,v.t.—upheld, upholding. To raise or hold up; to keep elevated or prevent from sinking; to support against opposition; to sustain.—**up·hold·er**, n.

up·hol·ster, up·hōl′stėr, v.t. [Back-formation from upholsterer.] To provide, as chairs or sofas, with coverings, cushions, stuffings, and springs; to furnish, as rooms, with hangings, curtains, carpets, or the like.—**up·hol·ster·er**, up·hōl′stėr·ėr, a·pōl′stėr·ėr, n.

up·hol·ster·y, up·hōl′ste·rē, a·pōl′ste·rē, n. pl. **up·hol·ster·ies.** The fabrics, fittings, or decorations supplied by an upholsterer, as cushions, furniture coverings, curtains, hangings, or the like; the business or craft of an upholsterer.

up·keep, up′kēp″, n. The process of keeping up or maintaining; the maintenance, or keeping in operation, due condition, and repair, of an establishment, a machine, or the like; the cost of this.

up·land, up′land, up′land″, n. The higher ground of a district or region; ground elevated above meadows, valleys, and rivers.—a.

up·land cot·ton, n. (Sometimes cap.) a short-staple cotton, Gossypium hirsutum, and various other cottons derived from it which are usu. cultivated in the U.S.

up·land plov·er, n. Ornith. a large sand-piper, Bartramia longicauda, of eastern N. America, resembling a plover in habit and appearance and inhabiting fields and uplands. Also **Bar·tra·mi·an sand·pi·per.**

up·lift, up·lift′, v.t. To lift up; to raise or elevate; to raise socially, morally, or culturally; as, to uplift the masses; to exalt emotionally or spiritually.—v.i.—up′lift″, n. The act of lifting up or raising; elevation; the process or work of raising socially, morally, or culturally; emotional or spiritual exaltation; a type of brassiere which lifts up the breasts; geol. an upheaval.—**up·lift·er**, up·lif′tėr, n.

up·most, up′mōst″, Brit. up′most, a. Uppermost.

up·on, u·pon′, u·pan′, prep. [O.E. uppon, upon—upp, up, and on, on.] On: used synonymously with on in all its meanings, primarily to achieve a desired rhythm or euphony. Sometimes upon is used to emphasize an upward movement onto something, whereas on connotes rest.—adv. On: used to extend or complete a verbal idea; as, a page that has been scribbled upon.

up·per, up′ėr, a. [Compar. of up.] Higher, as in place or position, or in a scale; as, the upper lip, the upper notes of a singer's voice; superior, as in rank, dignity, or station; as, the upper house of a legislature; of places, situated at a higher level or farther from the sea; geol. noting a later division of a period or system, or a later formation.—n. The upper part of a shoe or boot, above the sole, comprising the vamp and the quarters. Pl. cloth gaiters; upper teeth or a dental plate for the upper jaw. Colloq. a berth or bunk above another.—**on one's up·pers**, colloq. to be reduced to extreme shabbiness or poverty.

up·per case, n. Print. The top case or tray used by compositors to hold capital letters, reference marks, and other less used type; the capital letters.

up·per-case, up′ėr·kās′, a. Relating to a capital letter; capital; print. pertaining to or belonging in the upper case.—n.—v.t.—upper-cased, upper-casing. To set or put in capital letters.

up·per-class, up′ėr·klas′, up′ėr·kläs′ a. Pertaining to the highest social class; pertaining to the junior and senior classes in a high school or college.

up·per·class·man, up″ėr·klas′man, up″·ėr·kläs′man, n. pl. **up·per·class·men.** A junior or senior in a high school or college.

up·per crust, n. Colloq. the highest class of society.

up·per·cut, up′ėr·kut″, n. An upward swinging blow, as in boxing.—v.t., v.i.—uppercut, uppercutting. To strike with, or use, an uppercut.

up·per hand, n. The superior position; the advantage, as: He has the upper hand in the group.

up·per·most, up′ėr·mōst″, Brit. up′ėr·most, a. Highest in place or position; highest in power or authority; first, as in thought or time. Also upmost.—adv. In the topmost place, position, or power; first.

up·pish, up′ish, a. Colloq. Proud; arrogant; self-assertive; snobbish. Also uppity.—**up·pish·ly**, adv.—**up·pish·ness**, n.

up·pi·ty, up′i·tē, a. Colloq. uppish.

up·raise, up·rāz′, v.t.—upraised, upraising. To raise or lift up.

up·rear, up·rēr′, v.t. To rear up; to raise; to construct or erect.—v.i. To rise.

up·right, up′rīt″, a. [That is right, or directly, up.] Vertical; perpendicular; erect on one's feet; of inflexible honesty and moral rectitude.—n. Something standing erect; the state of being vertical or upright.—adv.—**up·right·ly**, adv.—**up·right·ness**, n.

up·right pi·an·o, n. A piano having a rectangular upright body and vertically arranged strings.

up·rise, up·rīz′, v.i.—past uprose, pp. uprisen, ppr. uprising. To rise up, as from bed or from a seat; to ascend above the horizon; to slope upward; to revolt or engage in rebellion; to increase in size or intensity; to come into being or importance.—up′rīz″, n. The act of rising up; a slope inclining upward.—**up·ris·er**, n.

up·ris·ing, up′rī″zing, up·rī′zing, n. The act of rising up; a riot; a rebellion; a rise; an ascent.

up·roar, up′rōr″, up′rȧr″, n. [< D. oproer, uproar, tumult = Dan. uprör, Sw. upror, G. aufruhr, < op, up, auf, up, and D. roeren, Dan. röre, Sw. röra, G. ruhren, to stir; the spelling being affected by roar.] A violent disturbance and noise; commotion; clamor; tumult; a state of such disturbance.

up·roar·i·ous, up·rōr′ē·us, up·rȧr′ē·us, a. Making an uproar or tumult; noisy; confused; very humorous or comical.—**up·roar·i·ous·ly**, adv.—**up·roar·i·ous·ness**, n.

up·root, up·rōt′, up·rut′, v.t. To tear up by the roots, or as if by the roots; to eradicate; to tear away, as from a homeland or tradition.—**up·root·er**, n.

ups and downs, n. pl. Interchanging ascents and descents of fortune; prosperous and poor times.

up·set, up·set′, v.t.—upset, upsetting. To overturn; as, to upset a glass of water; to perturb or mentally, physically, or emotionally disturb, as: The news of the accident upset her. To disturb or derange completely; to put out of order, or to throw into disorder; as, to upset a house; to overthrow or defeat unexpectedly, as an opponent in sports, contests, or elections. Mech. to shorten and thicken by hammering on the end, as a heated piece of iron; to swage; to shorten, as a metal tire of a wheel, in resetting it.—v.i. To become upset or overturned.—up′set″, n. An upsetting or the condition of being upset; an overturn; an overthrow, esp. the defeat of a contestant favored to win; a state of mental, physical, or emotional agitation or disturbance; a disturbance, derangement, or disorder. Mech. A tool or swage utilized for upsetting; a part, section, or segment which has been upset.—up·set′, a. Overturned; disturbed or disordered; mentally, physically, or emotionally agitated or disturbed.—**up·set·ter**, n.

up·set price, n. The lowest price at which anything is exposed to sale by auction.

up·shot, up′shot″, n. Final issue; conclusion.

up·side, up′sīd″, n. The upper side or portion.

up·side down, adv. With the upper part undermost; in complete disorder.—**up·side-down**, a.

up·side-down cake, n. A cake which is baked with the batter placed over a surface of fruit so that, when served, the fruit forms the top of the cake.

up·si·lon, ūp′si·lon″, up′si·lon″, Brit. ūp·sī′lon, n. [Gr. upsilón, 'simple u.'] The twentieth letter of the Greek alphabet, Υ, υ, having the sound of English u or y.

up·spring, up·spring′, v.i.—past upsprang or upsprung, pp. upsprung, ppr. upspringing. To spring up as from the soil; to come into existence.

up·stage, up′stāj′, adv. [From the phrase up stage, in theatrical use, that is, toward the back of the stage, or back from the audience, as with reference to the position of an actor.] On, near, or toward the rear of a stage.—a. Of or relating to the rear section of a stage; colloq. haughty, haughtily aloof, or supercilious.—v.t.—upstaged, upstaging. To cause, as another actor, to lose audience attention and diminish his performance by standing directly in his way or by compelling him to perform with his back toward the audience; to steal the scene or the show from; colloq. to treat in a supercilious or haughty way.

up·stairs, up′stârz′, a. Pertaining or relating to an upper story or floor.—adv. In, toward, or on an upper story or floor.—n. pl., usu. sing. in constr. An upper story or floor.—**kick up·stairs**, to promote to a seemingly better post or position so as to be free of, as of an objectionable or unruly employee.

up·stand·ing, up·stan′ding, a. Standing erect; erect and tall; of a fine, vigorous type; upright or honorable.—**up·stand·ing·ness**, n.

up·start, up'stärt", *n.* One that suddenly rises from a humble position to wealth, power, or consequence; a parvenu.—*a.*—up·start', *v.i.* To start or spring up suddenly.

up·state, up'stāt', *a.* Of, denoting, or from the northern part of a state, esp. an area lying north of a major city.—*n.* The northern part of a state, esp. of New York State.—**up·stat·er,** *n.*

up·stream, up'strēm', *adv.* Toward the higher or upper part of a stream, or at its source; against the current.—*a.*

up·stroke, up'strōk", *n.* An upward line, as made by the pen or pencil in writing.

up·surge, up'surj', *v.i.*—*upsurged, upsurging.* To surge up; to rise.—up'surj", *n.*

up·sweep, up'swēp', *v.t.*, *v.i.*—*upswept, upsweeping.* To sweep, brush, or arrange upward.—up'swēp', *n.* A sweeping or curving upward, as in the lower jaw of a bulldog; a hairdo in which the hair is brushed upward toward the top of the head.

up·swept, up'swept', *a.* Swept upward; of hair, swept or brushed upward on or toward the top part of the head.

up·swing, up'swing", *n.* An upward swing or swinging movement, as of a pendulum; an increase, rise, or improvement; as, an *upswing* in business.—up·swing', *v.i.*—*upswung, upswinging.*

up·take, up'tāk", *n.* The act of taking up; a lifting; perception or understanding; as, quick on the *uptake*; a pipe or passage leading upward from below, as for conducting smoke, a current of air, or the like.

up·throw, up'thrō", *n.* A throwing up or being thrown up; an upheaval; *geol.* an upward displacement of rock on one side of a fault: opposed to *downthrow.*

up·thrust, up'thrust", *n.* A thrust in an upward direction; *geol.* an upheaval or uplift.

up·tilt, up·tilt', *v.t.* To tilt up.

up-to-date, up'to·dāt', *a.* Extending to the present time, or including the latest facts; as, an *up-to-date* account or record; in accordance with the latest or newest standards, ideas, or style; abreast of the times, as in information, ideas, methods, or style.—**up-to-date·ly,** *adv.*—**up-to-date·ness,** *n.*

up·town, up'toun', *adv.* To or in the upper part of a city or town.—*a.* Moving toward, situated in, or pertaining to the upper part of a city or town.—*n.* The uptown part of a city or town.

up·trend, up'trend", *n.* An improvement or upward tendency, esp. in economic matters.

up·turn, up·turn', *v.t.* To turn up or over; as, to *upturn* earth with a plow; to turn or direct upward.—*v.i.* To turn upward.—up'turn", *n.* An increase or rise, esp. in prices or economic conditions.

up·ward, up'wèrd, *adv.* [O.E. *upweard, upweardes,* the latter being an adverbl. genit., like *toward,* etc.] Toward a higher position or place; toward a higher amount, degree, or rank; with respect to the upper or higher part; as, from the foot *upward*; toward the source or origin; more. Also **up·wards.**—*a.* Tending or directed upward; as, on *upward* wing.—**up·ward** or **up·wards of,** more or higher than.—**up·ward·ly,**—**up'ward·ness,** *n.*

up·wind, up'wind', *adv.* Against or toward the wind; in a direction opposing that of the wind.—*a.*—up'wind", *n.*

u·ra·cil, ūr'a·sil, *n. Biochem.* a crystalline heterocyclic compound, $C_4H_4N_2O_2$, obtained usu. by hydrolysis of nucleic acid and used in growth research.

u·rae·us, ū·rē'us, *n.* pl. **u·rae·us·es, u·rae·i.** [N.L., < Egypt. *ouro,* asp (cobra), lit. 'king.'] The sacred asp or cobra, as represented upon the headdress of divinities

and royal personages of ancient Egypt, usu. directly over the forehead, as an emblem of supreme power.

U·ral-Al·ta·ic, ūr'al·al·tā'ik, *a.* Pertaining to a large family of agglutinative languages spoken in portions of northern and eastern Europe and nearly the whole of northern and central Asia, containing the Finno-Ugrian, Turkic, Samoyedic, Tungusic, and Mongolian subfamilies or branches; noting or pertaining to the peoples using these languages; referring to a large Asiatic region between the Ural Mountains and the Altai Mountains.—*n.*

U·ra·li·an, ū·rā'lē·an, *a.* Of or pertaining to the Ural Mountains, or of the people of the region; of or pertaining to a language family comprised of the Finno-Ugric and Samoyed subfamilies.—*n.* Also **U·ral·ic,** ū·ral'ik.

u·ral·ite, ūr'a·līt", *n.* [G. *uralit;* named from the Ural Mountains, where it was found.] A green, usu. fibrous, variety of amphibole.—**u·ral·it·ic,** ūr'a·lit'ik, *a.*

u·ran·ic, ū·ran'ik, *a.* Pertaining to the heavens; celestial; *chem.* pertaining to uranium compounds in the higher valences.

u·ran·i·nite, ū·ran'i·nīt", *n.* A blackish mineral, UO_2, similar to pitchblende, containing uranium, radium, cerium, thorium, lead and various other elements: an important ore of uranium and radium.

u·ra·ni·um, ū·rā'nē·um, *n.* [N.L.; named from the planet *Uranus.*] *Chem.* a heavy, radioactive metallic element, occurring in uraninite, pitchblende, and several other minerals, silvery in appearance, ductile and malleable. Sym. U, at. no. 92, at. wt. 238.04. See Periodic Table of Elements. See *uranium 235, uranium 238.*

u·ran·i·um 235, *n.* The isotopic form of uranium that undergoes fission by chain reaction in atomic bombs and reactor fuels.

u·ran·i·um 238, *n.* The common isotope of uranium, used in making plutonium 239 and in hardening steel.

u·ra·nog·ra·phy, ūr"a·nog'ra·fē, *n.* The branch of astronomy concerned with the description and mapping of the heavens, and esp. of the fixed stars. Also *uranology.*—**u·ra·nog·ra·pher,** *n.*—**u·ra·no·graph·ic, u·ra·no·graph·i·cal,** ūr"a·no·graf'ik, *a.*

u·ra·nol·o·gy, ūr"a·nol'o·jē, *n.* pl. **u·ra·nol·o·gies.** *Astron.* Uranography; a treatise on uranography.—**u·ra·no·log·i·cal,** ūr"a·no·loj'i·kal, *a.*

u·ra·nom·e·try, ūr"a·nom'i·trē, *n. Astron.* A chart, map, or catalog of the heavens, esp. one showing the positions of the visible fixed stars; the measurement of distances between celestial bodies and determination of their positions.

u·ra·nous, ūr'a·nus, *a.* Containing uranium in chemical union, esp. in the lower valences.

U·ra·nus, ūr'a·nus, ū·rā'nus, *n.* [L., < Gr. *Ouranós,* personification of *ouranós,* heaven, sky.] *Astron.* the seventh major planet from the sun which has an orbit between Saturn and Neptune, a sidereal period of 84 years, and five satellites; *Gr. mythol.* the personification of Heaven, ruler of the world, son and husband of Gaea, and father of the Titans, Cyclops, and Furies who confined his children in Tartarus and was dethroned by his son Cronus at the instigation of Gaea.

u·ra·nyl, ūr'a·nil, *n.* [< *uranium* and *-yl.*] *Chem.* the bivalent radical UO_2, present in many compounds of uranium; as, *uranyl* bromide, UO_2Br_2.

u·rate, ūr'āt, *n. Chem.* a salt of uric acid.—**u·rat·ic,** ū·rat'ik, *a.*

ur·ban, ur'ban, *a.* [L. *urbanus,* < *urbs,* a city (seen also in *suburb*).] Belonging to or included in a town or city; characteristic of cities; citified.

ur·bane, ur·bān', *a.* Possessing or characterized by worldliness, sophistication, and refinement; polished; suave: opposed to *rustic.*—**ur·bane·ly,** *adv.*—**ur·bane·ness,** *n.*

ur·ban·ism, ur'ba·niz"um, *n.* The characteristic mode of life in cities or urban areas.—**ur·ban·ist,** ur'ba·nist, *n.*—**ur·ban·is·tic,** ur"ba·nis'tik, *a.*—**ur·ban·is·ti·cal·ly,** *adv.*

ur·ban·ite, ur'ba·nīt", *n.* A resident of a city or urban area.

ur·ban·i·ty, ur·ban'i·tē, *n.* pl. **ur·ban·i·ties.** An urbane state or quality; politeness; *pl.* courtesies, amenities, or civilities.

ur·ban·ize, ur'ba·nīz", *v.t.*—*urbanized, urbanizing.* To render urban, as in character; as, to *urbanize* a district or its people.—**ur·ban·i·za·tion,** *n.*

ur·bi·cul·ture, ur'bi·kul"chèr, *n.* Problems and characteristics unique to cities or urban life.

ur·ce·o·late, ur'sē·o·lit, ur'sē·o·lāt", *a.* [< L. *urceolus,* dim. of *urceus,* a pitcher.] Shaped like a pitcher or urn, as the corolla of a flower.

ur·chin, ur'chin, *n.* [Prov.Fr. *hurchon, hirchon,* Fr. *hérisson,* O.Fr. *ericon,* < L.L. *ericio, ericionis,* < L. *ericius,* a hedgehog, < *er* = Gr. *chēr,* hedgehog.] A mischievous, roguish boy or child; a sea urchin; a roller used in carding; *Brit. dial.* a hedgehog.

urd, urd, *n.* [Hind.] A bean, *Phaseolus mungo,* highly esteemed and largely cultivated throughout India. Also **black gram.**

u·re·a, ū·rē'a, ur'ē·a, *n.* [N.L., < Gr. *ouron,* urine.] *Chem.* a colorless, soluble, crystalline substance, $CO(NH_2)_2$, present in the urine of mammals, and produced synthetically for use in medicine and industry.—**u·re·al, u·re·ic,** *a.*

u·re·a-form·al·de·hyde res·in, ū·rē'a·far·mal'de·hīd" rez'in, ūr'ē·a·far·mal'de·hīd", *n. Chem.* any of several synthetic resins containing urea and formaldehyde, used for making molded plastic products, adhesives, and enamels.

u·re·ase, ūr'ē·ās", ūr'ē·āz", *n. Biochem.* an enzyme which decomposes urea with the formation of ammonium carbonate, used in measuring the amount of urea in urine and blood. Also **u·rase.**

u·re·din·i·um, ūr"i·din'ē·um, *n.* pl. **u·re·din·i·a,** ūr"i·din'ē·a. *Bot.* a sorus of a rust fungus. Also *uredium.*—**u·re·din·i·al,** *a.*

u·re·di·um, ū·rē'dē·um, *n,* pl. **u·re·di·a,** ū·rē'dē·a. Uredinium.

u·re·do, ū·rē'dō, *n.* [L. blight of plants, < *uro,* to burn.] *Pathol.* A skin disease characterized by itching and reddish wheals; hives; urticaria.

u·re·do·spore, yu·rē'do·spōr", yu·rē'do·spar", *n. Bot.* a unicellular spore developed in the summer by rust fungi.

u·re·do stage, *n. Bot.* the stage in the life cycle of rust fungi characterized by the development of uredospores.

u·re·ide, ūr'ē·īd", ūr'ē·id, *n. Chem.* any of a group of nitrogenous derivatives of urea, many of which are sedatives.

u·re·mi·a, u·rae·mi·a, ū·rē'mē·a, *n.* [N.L., < Gr. *ouron,* urine, and *aima,* blood.] *Pathol.* a condition resulting from the retention in the blood of waste products that should normally be eliminated in the urine.—**u·re·mic, u·rae·mic,** ū·rē'mik, *a.*

u·re·ter, ū·rē'tèr, *n.* [Gr. *ourētēr,* < *oureo,* to make water.] *Anat.* the duct or tube that conveys the urine from the kidney to the bladder.—**u·re·ter·al,** *a.*—**u·re·ter·ic,** ūr'i·ter'ik, *a.*

u·re·thane, ūr'ē·than", *n.* [< *urea* and *ether* and *-ane.*] *Chem.* a white crystalline substance, $NH_2CO_2C_2H_5$, used in making

---

a- fat, fāte, fär, fâre, fall;   **e-** met, mē, mēre, hèr;   **i-** pin, pīne;   **o-** not, nōte, möve;   **u-** tub, cūbe, bull;   **oi-** oil;   **ou-** pound.

medicines and fungicides. Also **eth·yl car·ba·mate, u·re·than.**

u·re·thra, ū·rē′thra, *n.* pl. **u·re·thrae, u·re·thras,** ū·rē′thrē. [L.L., < Gr. *ourēthra,* < *ourein,* urinate, < *ouron,* urine.] *Anat.* in most mammals, including man, a tube extending from the bladder that serves to convey and discharge urine and that, in the male, discharges semen also.—**u·re·thral,** *a.*

u·re·thri·tis, ūr″e·thrī′tis, *n.* [N.L.] *Pathol.* inflammation of the urethra.—**u·re·thrit·ic,** ūr″e·thrit′ik, *a.*

u·re·thro·scope, ū·rē′thro·skōp″, *n. Med.* an instrument providing an illuminated view of the urethra for examination.—**u·re·thro·scop·ic,** ū·rē″thro·skop′ik, *a.*—**u·re·thros·co·py,** ūr″e·thros′ko·pē, *n.*

urge, ụrj, *v.t.*—*urged, urging.* [L. *urgere,* press, push, drive, urge.] To push or force along; impel with force or vigor; to drive with incitement to speed or effort; spur; hurry; to impel, constrain or move to some action; stimulate; provoke; incite; to endeavor to induce or persuade, as by entreaties or earnest recommendations; to press by persuasion or recommendation, as for acceptance, performance, or use; advocate earnestly.—*v.i.* To exert a driving or impelling force; to press arguments or allegations; to make entreaties or earnest recommendations.—*n.* An involuntary, natural, or instinctive impulse; the act or action of urging.—**urg·er,** *n.*—**urg·ing·ly,** *adv.*

ur·gen·cy, ụr′jĕn·se, *n.* pl. **ur·gen·cies.** The fact or quality of being urgent; imperativeness; insistence; importunateness; an urgent requirement or need.

ur·gent, ụr′jent, *a.* [L. *urgens, urgentis.*] Pressing; necessitating or calling for immediate action; earnestly insistent; importunate.—**ur·gent·ly,** *adv.*

u·ric, ūr′ik, *a.* [Gr. *ouron,* urine.] Pertaining to or obtained from urine; as, *uric* acid.

ur·ic ac·id, *n. Biochem.* a nitrous, soluble, crystalline acid, $C_5H_4N_4O_3$, found in urine, used in its natural state for agriculture, and extracted or synthesized for both agriculture and industry.

u·ri·nal, ụr′i·nal, *n.* [L. *urinal.*] A wall fixture with flushing facilities used by men for urination; a room or other structure equipped with one or more such fixtures; a vessel used as a receptacle for urine, esp. that of a bedridden person.

u·ri·nal·y·sis, ụr″i·nal′i·sis, *n.* pl. **u·ri·nal·y·ses,** ụr″i·nal′i·sēz. The chemical analysis of urine. Also **u·ra·nal·y·sis.**

u·ri·nar·y, ūr′i·ner″e, *a.* Of or pertaining to urine or to the organs connected with its secretion and discharge.—*n.* pl. **u·ri·nar·ies.** A storage receptacle for animal urine, the contents of which are used as a fertilizing agent; a urinal.

u·ri·nar·y blad·der, *n.* The distensible membranous organ or sac that receives, holds, and discharges urine.

u·ri·nate, ụr′i·nāt″, *v.i.*—*urinated, urinating.* To discharge or pass urine.—**u·ri·na·tion,** *n.*

u·rine, ūr′in, *n.* [O.Fr. Fr. *urine,* L. *urina,* akin to Gr. *ouron,* urine: cf. Skt. *vār,* water, O.E. *waer,* sea.] The liquid secretion of the kidneys, which in most mammals is conducted to the bladder by the ureters, and discharged through the urethra.—**u·ri·nous,** ūr′i·nus, *a.* Of, pertaining to, or resembling urine or its qualities, as color or odor.

u·ri·nif·er·ous tu·bule, ūr″i·nif′ĕr·us tö′bul, *n. Biol.* in vertebrates, a tubule of the kidney that carries urine.

urn, ụrn, *n.* [L. *urna,* < *uro,* to burn, as being made of burned clay.] A large, footed vase or vessel of various shapes, in which the ashes of the dead are preserved; a closed

container with a spigot, available in several sizes, for brewing and serving hot beverages, often in large quantities; *bot.* the spore case of a moss capsule.

u·ro·chord, ūr′o·kạrd″, *n.* [Gr. *ourá,* tail, and *chordē,* string.] *Zool.* the notochord of a tunicate, found mostly in the larva, and confined chiefly to the caudal region.—**u·ro·chor·dal,** *a.*

u·ro·chrome, ūr′o·krōm″, *n. Biochem.* the yellow pigment that colors urine.

u·ro·dele, ūr′o·dēl, *a.* [N.L. *Urodela,* pl. < Gr. *ourá,* tail, and *dēlos,* visible.] Belonging to the *Urodela,* an order of amphibians which retain the tail throughout life, as the salamanders and newts.—*n.* A urodele amphibian.

u·ro·gen·i·tal, ūr″ō·jen′i·tal, *a.* Noting or pertaining to the urinary and genital organs; genitourinary. Also **u·ri·no·gen·i·tal.**

u·ro·lith, ūr′o·lith, *n. Pathol.* a urinary calculus.—**u·ro·lith·ic,** *a.*

u·rol·o·gy, ū·rol′o·jē, *n.* The field of medicine devoted to the study, diagnosis, and treatment of any malfunction or disease of the urinary tract.—**u·ro·log·ic,** **u·ro·log·i·cal,** ūr″o·loj′ik, *a.*—**u·rol·o·gist,** *n.*

u·ro·pod, ūr′o·pod″, *n.* [Gr. *oura,* tail, and *pous, podos,* foot.] *Zool.* one of the footlike posterior appendages on the abdomen of some crustaceans, as the lobsters.—**u·rop·o·dal, u·ro·po·dous,** ū·rop′o·dal, *a.*

u·ro·pyg·i·al, ūr″o·pij′ē·al, *a. Ornith.* of or pertaining to the uropygium.

u·ro·pyg·i·al gland, *n. Ornith.* a gland, at the base of a bird's tail, secreting oil with which the bird preens and waterproofs his feathers. Also **oil gland.**

u·ro·pyg·i·um, ūr″o·pij′ē·um, *n.* [N.L., < Gr. *ouropygion,* for *orrogygion,* < *órros,* end of the sacrum, and *pygē,* rump.] *Ornith.* the projecting terminal part of the body of a bird from which the tail feathers grow.

Ur·sa Ma·jor, ụr′sa mā′jĕr, *n.* [L., 'greater bear': *ursa,* fem. of *ursus,* bear.] *Astron.* the Great Bear, the most prominent constellation in the northern heavens, containing the seven bright stars that form the Big Dipper. Also *Charles's Wain, the Plow.*

Ur·sa Mi·nor, ụr′sa mī′nĕr, *n.* [L., 'lesser bear.'] *Astron.* the Little Bear, a northern constellation containing the stars forming the Little Dipper, the outermost one of the handle being Polaris, the polestar.

ur·si·form, ụr′si·fạrm″, *a.* [L. *ursus,* bear.] Having the form of a bear.

ur·sine, ụr′sīn, ụr′sin, *a.* [L. *ursinus,* < *ursus,* bear.] Of, resembling, or pertaining to a bear or bears; bearlike; *entom.* clothed with bristlelike hairs, as certain caterpillars.

Ur·spra·che, ụr′shprä″che, G. ör′shprä″che, *n.* A parent or original language hypothetically reconstructed through linguistics into the Indo-European languages.

ur·ti·cant, ụr′ti·kant, *a. Pathol.* inducing itching or stinging.—*n.*

ur·ti·car·i·a, ụr″ti·kâr′ē·a, *n.* [N.L., < L. *urtica,* nettle.] *Pathol.* A disorder of the skin characterized by transient eruptions of itching wheals, caused by an allergy; nettle rash; hives.—**ur·ti·car·i·al,** *a.*

ur·ti·cate, ụr′ti·kāt″, *v.t.*—*urticated, urticating.* [M.L. *urticatus,* pp. of *urticare,* < L. *urtica,* nettle.] To sting with or as with nettles; to whip with nettles.—*v.i.* To sting as or like a nettle.

ur·ti·ca·tion, ụr″ti·kā′shan, *n. Med.* The former practice of whipping a paralyzed limb or part with nettles to restore sensation; a stinging sensation; the formation or development of urticaria.

u·rus, ūr′us, *n.* pl. **u·rus·es.** [L. < Teut.:

cf. *aurochs.*] An extinct species of wild ox, *Bos primigenius,* common in Europe at the time of Julius Caesar. Also **au·rocks.**

u·ru·shi·ol, ụr′ö·shē·ōl″, ụr′ö·shē·ạl″, ụr′ö·shē·ol″, *n.* A toxic liquid constituting the irritant principle found in various species of the genus *Rhus,* as poison ivy or poison sumac.

u.s., ū′es′. *Latin.* Ubi supra; ut supra.

us, us, *pron.* [O.E. *ūs,* pl., dat. and acc. (gen. *ūre*), = O.S. *ūs* = O.H.G., G. *uns* = Icel. *oss* = Goth. *uns,* us.] The objective case of *we,* employed as the object of a preposition, as: He is going with *us.* Used as an indirect object of a verb, as: He gave *us* a painting. Employed as the direct object of a verb, as: She called *us.*

us·a·ble, use·a·ble, ū′za·bl, *a.* In suitable condition or convenient for use.—**us·a·ble·ness, use·a·ble·ness,** *n.*—**us·a·bly, use·a·bly,** *adv.*—**us·a·bil·i·ty, use·a·bil·i·ty,** *n.*

us·age, ū′sij, ū′zij, *n.* [O.Fr. Fr. *usage,* < *user,* E. *use,* v.] Habitual or customary use or practice; a custom or practice; the customary or established mode of using the sounds, words, and phrases of a language; a particular instance of such a use of language; a way of using a person or thing; treatment; the act of using.

us·ance, ū′zans, *n.* [O.Fr. Fr. *usance,* < *user,* E. *use,* v.] *Com.* the length of time allowed by custom or usage for the payment of foreign bills of exchange; *econ.* income derived from the ownership of wealth. *Obs.* use; employment; usury; custom.

use, ūz, *v.t.*—*used, using.* [O.Fr. Fr. *user,* < M.L. *usare,* freq. of L. *uti* (pp. *usus*), make use of.] To employ for some purpose; put into service; make use of; utilize; as, to *use* a knife; to avail oneself of; employ; to make a practice of; as, to *use* common sense; to expend or consume in use, often followed by *up;* to act or behave toward; treat; to practice habitually or customarily; to habituate; accustom; inure, now used only in the past participle; as, to be *used* to hardships; to consume; to partake of, as drugs, regularly or habitually.—*v.i.* To be accustomed, wont, or customarily found, now used only in the past tense with an infinitive expressed or understood, as: He *used* to go everyday.

use, ūs, *n.* [O.Fr. Fr. *us,* use, usage, < L. *usus,* use, employment, usage, practice, < *uti,* make use of, employ, practice, enjoy, have; also, in legal use, O.Fr. *ues, oes, oeps,* work, service, benefit, < L. *opus,* work, need; cf. *opus.*] The act of using or putting into service; as, the *use* of tools; the state of being used; an instance or way of using something; as, a poor *use* of good material; a purpose for which something is used; object; function; the power, right, or privilege of using something; as, to have the *use* of a car; service or advantage in or for being used; as, too late to be of *use;* occasion or need; as, to have *use* for a watch; continual, habitual, or customary employment or practice; custom. *Law,* the enjoyment of property, as by the employment, occupation, or exercise of it; the benefit or profit of property, as lands and tenements, in the possession of another who simply holds them for the beneficiary; the trust or legal arrangement by which these benefits are established. *Relig.* the distinctive form of ritual or of any liturgical observance used in a particular church, diocese, or community; as, Roman *use.*—**have no use for,** *colloq.* to have no liking or tolerance for.—**make use of,** to employ; to use for one's own purposes or advantage.—**of no use,** of no service, advantage, or help.

used, ūzd, *a.* Utilized or employed for some accomplishment or function; having undergone use; secondhand.

use·ful, ūs′fụl, *a.* Valuable for use or service; suited or adapted to some purpose; helpful or of practical use; beneficial; utilitarian.—**use·ful·ly**, *adv.*—**use·ful·ness**, *n.*

use·less, ūs′lis, *a.* Of no use; not serving the purpose or any purpose; without useful qualities; of no practical good; unavailing or futile.—**use·less·ly**, *adv.*—**use·less·ness**, *n.*

us·er, ū′zẽr, *n.* One who uses.

us·er, ū′zẽr, *n.* [O.Fr. n. use of *user*, inf.] *Law*, the use or enjoyment of property or a right to that use.

use up, *v.t.* To consume entirely by using; to use all of; to exhaust of strength or energy, as by overwork or strain.

ush·er, ush′ẽr, *n.* [O.Fr. *ussier, uissier, hussier*, Fr. *huissier*, a doorkeeper, < O.Fr. *uis, huis*, < L. *ostium*, a door.] One who guides people to seats, as in a theatre, auditorium, or church; an officer or servant who has care of the entrance door, as of a court, hall, or chamber; an officer whose duty is to introduce strangers or to walk before a person of rank; a male who attends a groom at the marriage ceremony; *Brit. archaic*, an underteacher or assistant to a schoolmaster or principal teacher.—*v.t.* To act as an usher toward; to escort; as, to *usher* members of an audience to their seats; to introduce, as a forerunner or harbinger, usu. followed by *in* or *forth*, as: He *ushered in* the new fishing season.

u·su·al, ū′zhŏ·al, ū′zhwal, *a.* [L. *usualis*, Fr. *usuel*.] In common or general use; commonly occurring; customary; ordinary; prevalent; conventional.—**u·su·al·ly**, *adv.* —**u·su·al·ness**, *n.*

u·su·fruct, ū′zụ·frukt″, ū′sụ·frukt″, ūz′ū·frukt″, ūs′ū·frukt″, *n.* [L. *ususfructus* (abl. *usufructu*), for *usus et fructus*, 'use and enjoyment.'] *Law*, the right of enjoying all the advantages derivable from the use of something which belongs to another, so far as is compatible with the substance of the thing not being destroyed or harmed.

u·su·fruc·tu·a·ry, ū′zụ·fruk′chö·er″ē, ū′sụ·fruk′chö·er″ē, ūz′ū·fruk′chö·er″ē, ūs′ū·fruk′chö·er″ē, *n.* pl. **u·su·fruc·tu·ar·ies**. [L. *usufructuarius*.] *Law*, a person who has the usufruct of property.—*a.* Of, pertaining to, or of the nature of a usufruct.

u·su·rer, ū′zhẽr·er, *n.* One who lends money at an exorbitant or unlawful rate of interest.

u·su·ri·ous, ū·zhụr′ē·us, *a.* Practicing usury; taking exorbitant or unlawful interest for the use of money; pertaining to or of the nature of usury.—**u·su·ri·ous·ly**, *adv.*—**u·su·ri·ous·ness**, *n.*

u·surp, ū·sụrp′, ū·zụrp′, *v.t.* [Fr. *usurper*, < L. *usurpare*, < *usus*, use, and *rapio*, to seize.] To seize and hold possession of, as an office or rights, by force or without lawful right; to appropriate or assume illegally or wrongfully.—*v.i.* To commit an act of unlawful seizure and possession; to encroach.—**u·sur·pa·tion**, ū″sẽr·pā′shan, ū″zẽr·pā′shan, *n.*—**u·surp·er**, *n.*

u·su·ry, ū′zhu·rē, *n.* pl. **u·su·ries**. [O.E. *usure*, later, *usurie*, < Fr. *usure*, L. *usura*, interest for money lent, lit. 'a using,' < *utor*, to use.] An excessive or inordinate interest for the use of money borrowed; extortionate interest; the practice of taking exorbitant or unlawful interest.

ut, ut, öt, *n. Mus.* The first syllable of the solmization system of Guido d'Arezzo; the tone *C*: now superseded by *do*.

u·ten·sil, ū·ten′sil, *n.* [Fr. *utensile*, < L. *utensilis*, fit for use, < *utor*, to use.] An implement or receptacle for domestic use; as, kitchen *utensils*; an instrument or tool designed for a particular purpose, as for mining or farming.

u·ter·ine, ū′tẽr·in, ū′tẽ·rīn″, *a.* [L. *uterinus*,

< *uterus*, the womb.] Pertaining to the uterus or womb; born of the same mother but of a different father.

u·ter·us, ū′tẽr·us, *n.* pl. **u·ter·i**, ū′te·rī″. [L.] *Anat.* The organ in female mammals which serves as a protective place for the ovum while it develops into an embryo or fetus; the womb; loosely, a corresponding part in other animals.

u·til·i·tar·i·an, ū·til″i·târ′ē·an, *a.* [< *utility.*] Consisting in or pertaining to utility; holding forth utility as a standard, esp. as more important than luxury or beauty; adhering to utilitarianism.—*n.*

u·til·i·tar·i·an·ism, ū·til″i·târ′ē·a·niz″um, *n. Philos.* the ethical view that right conduct is determined by useful consequences, esp. as it tends to promote the most good for the largest number of persons.

u·til·i·ty, ū·til′i·tē, *n.* pl. **u·til·i·ties**. [L. *utilitas*, < *utilis*, useful, < *utor*, to use.] The state or quality of being useful; usefulness; something of use; something providing a beneficial service, esp. to the public, as a telephone or electric power system; *econ.* the capacity of a product or service to add to the enjoyment of mankind. The principle of promoting the most good for the largest number; *pl.* stock issued by a utility company, as a telephone company.—*a.* Intended for general rather than limited use; planned to be functional rather than esthetic; *baseball*, having ability to play several positions; as, a *utility* outfielder.

u·ti·lize, ūt′i·līz″, *v.t.*—*utilized, utilizing.* To make useful; to adapt to some useful purpose; to turn to profitable account.— **u·ti·liz·a·ble**, *a.*—**u·ti·li·za·tion**, *n.*— **u·ti·liz·er**, *n.*

ut·most, ut′mōst″, *Brit.* ut′most, *a.* [O.E. *útemest*, uttermost, outmost, a double superl., being from *utema*, which itself is a superl., and *mest*, also a superl. termination; similarly *aftermost*. *Outmost* is another form; *utter* is the compar.] Of or in the greatest or highest degree, number, or quantity; as, a message of the *utmost* significance; being at the farthest point or extremity; as, the *utmost* mountain peak in the range. Also *uttermost.*—*n.* The extreme extent or farthest possible point; as, the *utmost* in fashion; the most of one's power or effort; as, to try your *utmost.* Also *uttermost.*

U·to·pi·a, ū·tō′pē·a, *n.* [Lit. 'the land of Noplace,' < Gr. *ou*, not, and *topos*, a place.] An imaginary island, the setting for Sir Thomas More's *Utopia*, where the highest degree of social and political organization is experienced; (*l.c.*) an ideally perfect situation or place; an idealistic or impracticable plan for improving society.

U·to·pi·an, ū·tō′pē·an, *a.* Of or pertaining to Utopia; (*l.c.*) founded upon or involving imaginary or ideal perfection.—*n.* An inhabitant of Utopia; (*l.c.*) an ardent but impractical reformer.—**u·to·pi·an·ism**, **u·to·pism**, *n.*—**u·to·pist**, *n.*—**u·to·pis·tic**, *a.*

u·to·pi·an so·cial·ism, *n.* An economic theory that voluntary relinquishment of individual ownership of the powers of production would result in ultimate well-being for all.

u·tri·cle, ū′tri·kl, *n.* [L. *utriculus*, dim. of *uter*, bag or bottle made of skin: cf. L. *utriculus*, dim. of *uterus*, E. *uterus.*] *Bot.* a small sac or baglike body, as an air cell in a seaweed; a thin bladderlike pericarp or fruit. *Anat.* the larger of two sacs in the membranous labyrinth of the inner ear. Also *utriculus.*

u·tric·u·lar, ū·trik′ya·lẽr, *a.* Pertaining to or of the nature of a utricle; baglike; having a utricle or utricles. Also **u·tric·u·late**, ū·trik′ya·lit, ū·trik′ya·lāt″, *a.*

u·tric·u·lus, ū·trik′ya·lus, *n.* pl. **u·tric·u·li**, ū·trik′ya·lī. Utricle.

ut su·pra, ut sö′pra, *L.* ụt sö′prä, *adv.* Latin, as above. Abbr. *u.s., ut sup.*

ut·ter, ut′ẽr, *a.* [O.E. *utor, uttor.* compar. of *ut*, out. Outer is the same word.] Complete, total, or entire; as, *utter* refusal; absolute; as *utter* nonsense.

ut·ter, ut′ẽr, *v.t.* [From the above word; cf. as also from comparatives; the verbs to *lower*, to *better.*] To give expression to with the voice; to give vent to by the vocal organs; to pronounce; *law*, to put, as money, notes, or base coin, into circulation, esp. counterfeit money.—**ut·ter·a·ble**, *a.* —**ut·ter·er**, *n.*

ut·ter·ance, ut′ẽr·ans, *n.* The act of uttering; expression with the voice; manner or power of speaking; something spoken, uttered, or written; *ling.* a meaningful speech sequence grammatically independent of the context in which it appears.

ut·ter·most, ut′ẽr·mōst″, *Brit.* ut′ẽr·most, *a., n.* Utmost.

u·va·rov·ite, ö·vär′o·vīt″, ū·var′o·vīt″, *n.* [From Count S. S. *Uvarov* (1785–1855), Russ. statesman.] An emerald-green variety of garnet containing chromium, to which the color is due.

u·ve·a, ū′vē·a, *n.* [< L. *uva*, a grape—from resembling a grape skin.] *Anat.* the vascular, or middle layer of the eye, consisting of the ciliary muscle, choroid, and the iris. —**u·ve·al**, **u·ve·ous**, *a.*

u·ve·i·tis, ū″vē·i′tis, *n.* [N.L.] *Pathol.* inflammation of the uvea.

u·vu·la, ū′vya·la, *n.* pl. **u·vu·las**, **u·vu·lae**, ū′vya·lē″. [L., dim. of *uva*, a grape, the uvula.] *Anat.* A small, conical, fleshy projection suspended from the soft palate over the root of the tongue; any similar structure, esp. at the neck of the bladder.

u·vu·lar, ū′vya·lẽr, *a.* Relating to the uvula; *phon.* sounded with the back part of the tongue placed near the uvula.—*n.* —**u·vu·lar·ly**, *adv.*

ux·o·ri·al, uk·sōr′ē·al, uk·sạr′ē·al, ug·zōr′ē·al, ug·zạr′ē·al, *a.* Pertaining to or characteristic of a wife.

ux·o·ri·cide, uk·sōr′i·sīd″, uk·sạr′i·sīd″, ug·zōr′i·sīd″, ug·zạr′i·sīd″, *n.* [L. *uxor*, and *caedo*, to kill.] The murder of a wife by her husband; a husband who murders his wife.

ux·o·ri·ous, uk·sōr′ē·us, uk·sạr′ē·us, ug·zōr′ē·us, ug·zạr′ē·us, *a.* [L. *uxorius*, < *uxor, uxoris*, a wife.] Excessively or foolishly fond of one's wife; doting on one's wife.—**ux·o·ri·ous·ly**, *adv.*—**ux·o·ri·ous·ness**, *n.*

V

V, v, vē, *n.* The twenty-second letter of the English alphabet and eighteenth consonant; the sound of the letter V as represented in speech; the delineation of the letter V or v in writing or printing; something designated by, or having the shape of the letter V or v; a graphic device for printing the letter V or v; the Roman numeral representing 5.

V, vē. Victory, esp. by the Allies during World War II; *chem.* vanadium; *math.* vector; *phys.* velocity; (*sometimes l.c.*), *elect.* volt; *colloq.* a five-dollar bill.

va·can·cy, vā′kan·sē, *n.* pl. **va·can·cies**. The state or condition of being vacant; vacuity; an unoccupied place or vacant quarters, as in an apartment building, a motel, or an office building; an unoccupied post, position, or office; an empty space, gap, break, or other opening; a lack of sense or ideas. *Archaic*, an unoccupied interval of time; leisure.

---

a- fat, fāte, fär, fâre, fạll;　**e-** met, mē, mēre, hẽr;　**i-** pin, pīne;　**o-** not, nōte, mŏve;　**u-** tub, cūbe, bụll;　**oi-** oil;　**ou-** pound.

va·cant, vā′kant, *a.* [O.Fr. Fr. *vacant*, < L. *vacans* (*vacant-*), ppr. of *vacare*, be empty.] Having no contents; empty or void; devoid or destitute, usu. followed by *of*; as, *vacant of* all normal emotions; unoccupied, empty, or unfilled; as, a *vacant* seat on a bus; untenanted, as a house or apartment; not in use, as a room; not filled or occupied by an incumbent or official, as an office or position; free from work, business, or other employment; as, *vacant* time; unoccupied with thought or reflection; as, the *vacant* mind of a fool; characterized by, showing, or proceeding from lack of thought or intelligence; as, a *vacant* stare. *Law*, unoccupied or unutilized, as land; without any heir or claimant, as an abandoned estate.—**va·cant·ly**, *adv.*—**va·cant·ness**, *n.*

va·cate, vā′kāt, *v.t.*—*vacated, vacating.* To make vacant or unoccupied; to give up or quit, as a position; as, to *vacate* one's job; to relinquish the occupancy or possession of; as, to *vacate* a house; to make void or annul.—*v.i.* To make a position or post vacant; to give up occupancy of a place or residence. *Colloq.* to leave; to go away.

va·ca·tion, vā·kā′shən, va·kā′shən, *n.* [O.Fr. Fr. *vacation*, < L. *vacatio*(*n-*), a being free from duty, etc., exemption, < *vacare*.] Freedom or release from some regular activity; a period of suspension of study, work, or other regular duty, as for travel, recreation, or relaxation; a recess, intermission, or holiday; a regularly scheduled part of the year when the activities of courts of law are suspended; the act of vacating.—*v.i.* To take a vacation; to spend a vacation, as at a particular place.—**va·ca·tion·less**, *a.*

va·ca·tion·ist, vā·kā′shə·nist, va·kā′shə·nist, *n.* One who is taking a vacation or holiday. Also **va·ca·tion·er**.

va·ca·tion·land, vā·kā′shən·land″, va·kā′shən·land″, *n.* A place or area providing relaxation, recreation, interesting and beautiful sights, and other pleasurable features for vacationists.

vac·ci·nate, vak′si·nāt″, *v.t.*—*vaccinated, vaccinating.* [L. *vaccinus*, pertaining to a cow, < *vacca*, a cow.] To inoculate with the cowpox vaccine to produce immunity from smallpox or mitigate its attack; to inoculate with microorganisms of any other disease. —*v.i.* To practice or perform vaccination, as a preventive action.—**vac·ci·na·tor**, vak′si·nā″tĕr, *n.*

vac·ci·na·tion, vak″si·nā′shən, *n.* The act of vaccinating; inoculation with vaccine.

vac·cine, vak·sēn′, vak′sēn, vak′sin, *n.* [L. *vaccinus*, of or from cows, < *vacca*, cow; as n., Fr. *vaccin*, vaccine virus, < L. *vaccinus*.] The virus of cowpox, obtained from the vesicles of an affected cow or person, and used in vaccination; modified microorganisms of any of various other diseases, used for preventive inoculation.— *a.* Pertaining to vaccinia or vaccination; of, pertaining to, or derived from cows.— **vac·ci·nal**, vak′si·nal, *a.* Pertaining or due to vaccine or vaccination.

vac·cin·i·a, vak·sin′ē·a, *n.* [N.L., < L. *vaccinus*.] Cowpox.—**vac·cin·i·al**, *a.*

vac·il·late, vas′i·lāt″, *v.i.*—*vacillated, vacillating.* [L. *vacillatus*, pp. of *vacillare*, sway, waver: cf. Skt. *vañc-*, totter, go crookedly.] To sway unsteadily; waver; stagger; fluctuate; to waver in mind or opinion; to be irresolute, indecisive or, inconstant.— **vac·il·la·tion**, vas″i·lā′shən, *n.*—**vac·il·la·tor**, *n.*

vac·il·lat·ing, vas′i·lā″ting, *a.* Wavering or oscillating; characterized by vacillation; irresolute; fluctuating. Also **vac·il·lant**, **vac·il·la·to·ry**, vas′i·lant, vas′i·la·tōr″ē, vas′i·la·tär″ē.—**vac·il·lat·ing·ly**, *adv.*

va·cu·i·ty, va·kū′i·tē, *n.* pl. **va·cu·i·ties.** [L. *vacuitas*, < *vacuus*, empty.] The state

of being empty or unfilled; emptiness; a space unfilled or unoccupied; a vacuum; freedom from mental exertion; absence of thought; absence of intelligence; an inane or stupid thing.

vac·u·o·late, vak′ū·o·lit, vak′ū·o·lāt″, *a.* Containing a vacuole or vacuoles. Also **vac·u·o·lat·ed.**—**vac·u·o·la·tion**, vak″ū·o·lā′shən, *n.* The formation of vacuoles; the state of being vacuolate; a system of vacuoles.

vac·u·ole, vak′ū·ōl″, *n.* [A dim. < *vacuum*.] *Biol.* A space or cavity within the protoplasm of a cell, as in many plants, containing a watery solution; a minute cavity containing fluid or air and found in organic tissue.—**vac·u·o·lar**, vak″ū·ō′lĕr, vak′ū·o·lĕr, vak′yo·lĕr, *a.*

vac·u·ous, vak′ū·us, *a.* [L. *vacuus*, empty, akin to *vacare*, be empty.] Empty; without contents; lacking or void of ideas or intelligence; stupid; unintelligent; inane; showing mental vacancy; as, a *vacuous* look; purposeless; unoccupied or idle.—**vac·u·ous·ly**, *adv.*—**vac·u·ous·ness**, *n.*

vac·u·um, vak′ū·um, vak′ūm, *n.* pl. **vac·u·ums**, **vac·u·a**, vak′ū·a. [L., an empty space, neut. sing. of *vacuus*, empty.] Space devoid of molecules and atoms; an enclosed space from which matter, esp. air has been more or less removed; the degree to which air has been removed from an area; the condition of being isolated from outside environmental factors; pl. **vac·u·ums**, **vac·u·a**. A vacuum cleaner; pl. **vac·u·ums**.—*a.* Pertaining to, using, or causing a vacuum; partly emptied of air; as, a *vacuum* container; referring to a packaging process in which some of the air is removed from a container before it is sealed.—*v.t.* To subject to a vacuum instrument; to apply a vacuum cleaner to.—*v.i.* To operate a vacuum cleaner.

vac·u·um bot·tle, *n.* A bottle or flask protected by a vacuum jacket which prevents the escape of heat from hot contents or the entrance of heat to cold contents. Also *thermos.*

vac·u·um clean·er, *n.* An apparatus for cleaning carpets, floors, and furniture by suction.

vac·u·um gauge, *n.* A gauge for measuring the degree of vacuum produced, as in steam condensers.

vac·u·um-packed, vak′ū·um·pakt″, vak′ūm·pakt″, *a.* Pertaining to a sealed container from which all or most of the air has been removed.

vac·u·um pump, *n.* A pump or device by which a partial vacuum can be produced; a pump in which a partial vacuum is utilized in raising water.

vac·u·um tube, *n. Electron.* A sealed, partially evacuated, glass envelope used to generate, amplify, rectify, or detect oscillations and which contains a cathode heated to emit electrons, an anode consisting of a metal plate kept at a positive potential, and a control grid which regulates the flow of electrons from cathode to anode; a sealed glass tube, as a Crookes tube, containing a partial vacuum or a highly rarefied gas and which is used to observe the effects of a discharge of electricity. Also *electron tube*, *Brit.* **vac·u·um valve**, *valve.*

va·de me·cum, vā′dē mē′kum, vä′dē mē·kum, *n.* pl. **va·de me·cums.** [L. *vade mecum*, go with me.] A book or other thing that a person regularly carries with him for frequent use; a manual; a guide book.

va·dose, vā′dōs, *a.* [L. *vadosus*, < *vadum*, a shallow.] *Geol.* noting or pertaining to certain underground waters, springs, or the like, situated a comparatively short distance below the surface of the earth and above the water table.

vag·a·bond, vag′a·bond″, *a.* [O.Fr. Fr. *vagabond*, < L. *vagabundus*, < *vagari*, wander, roam, < *vagus*, wandering, E. *vague.*] Wandering from place to place without settled habitation; nomadic; leading an irregular, disreputable, or unsettled life; good-for-nothing, worthless, or disreputable; of or pertaining to a vagabond or vagrant; as, *vagabond* habits; aimlessly moving about without certain direction.— *n.* One who is without a fixed habitation and wanders from place to place, esp. an idle wanderer without visible means of support; a tramp or vagrant; an idle, worthless fellow; a scamp or rascal.—**vag·a·bond·ish**, *a.*—**vag·a·bond·ism**, *n.*

vag·a·bond·age, vag′a·bon″dij, *n.* The state or condition of a vagabond; vagabonds collectively.

va·gal, vā′gal, *a.* Of or pertaining to the vagus.

va·gar·y, va·gâr′ē, vā′ga·rē, *n.* pl. **va·gar·ies.** [< It. *vagare*, to wander, or directly < L. *vagari*, to wander (whence *vagabond*, etc.).] A wild, unpredictable, or odd notion or action; a whim; a whimsical idea.—**va·gar·i·ous**, va·gâr′ē·us, *a.* Erratic; whimsical; capricious.—**va·gar·i·ous·ly**, *adv.*

vag·ile, vaj′il, *Brit.* vaj′īl, *a. Biol.* possessing freedom of motion.—**va·gil·i·ty**, va·jil′i·tē, *n.*

va·gi·na, va·ji′na, *n.* pl. **va·gi·nas**, **va·gi·nae**, va·ji′nē. [L., a sheath.] *Anat.* the canal in female mammals leading from the exterior genital orifice to the uterus; an organ or a part having sheathlike characteristics. *Bot.* the tubular part formed by the base portion of leaves where they envelope the stem.—**vag·i·nal**, vaj′i·nal, *a.*

vag·i·nate, vaj′i·nit, vaj′i·nāt″, *a.* Possessing a sheath; sheathed; enveloped by a sheath. Also **vag·i·nat·ed.**

vag·i·ni·tis, vaj″i·ni′tis, *n.* [N.L.] *Pathol.* inflammation of the vagina.

va·gran·cy, vā′gran·sē, *n.* pl. **va·gran·cies.** A state of wandering without a settled home; the condition of being a vagrant; a vagrant's conduct or mode of life; any wandering in speech or thought.

va·grant, vā′grant, *n.* [Formerly *vagarant*, same origin as *vagary*.] One without a settled home or habitation; an idle wanderer or stroller; a vagabond; a tramp; *law*, an idle, and often disorderly, person with no visible or lawful means of support, as a prostitute, beggar, or drunkard; rover; wanderer.—*a.* Wandering without any settled habitation; pertaining to one who wanders; nomadic; unsettled; wayward; moving without any certain direction or at random. Also *archaic*, **va·grom**, vā′grom.— **va·grant·ly**, *adv.*

vague, vāg, *a.*—*vaguer, vaguest.* [Fr. *vague*, < L. *vagus*, wandering.] Unclear as regards meaning, scope, or the like; indefinite; hazy; uncertain; doubtful; of uncertain authority, origin, or foundation. —**vague·ly**, *adv.*—**vague·ness**, *n.*

va·gus, vā′gus, *n.* pl. **va·gi**, vā′jī. [L., wandering.] *Anat.* either of the tenth pair of cranial nerves extending down through the neck and thorax to the upper part of the abdomen, providing sensory, motor, or secretory impulses through its branches to the larynx, lungs, heart, stomach, and abdominal viscera. Also *pneumogastric nerve*, **va·gus nerve.**

vail, vāl, *v.t.* [For obs. *avale*, < O.Fr. *avaler*, bring or let down, also go down.] To allow to sink; to lower; *archaic*, to take off, as a hat, in respect or submission.

vail, vāl, *v.i., v.t. Archaic.* To be useful; avail.—*n. Archaic*, a gratuity or a tip.

vain, vān, *a.* [Fr. *vain*, vain, empty, vainglorious, etc. < L. *vanus*, empty, void (whence also *vanish, evanescent*); same root as to *wane, want*.] Displaying excessive admiration for one's own personal appearance, possessions, qualities, or attainments; unduly proud or conceited; having no real value, worth, or importance; as, a *vain* promise; ineffectual, fruitless, or unsuccessful; as, a *vain* endeavor.—**in vain,** without success or effect; as, to try *in vain*; in a light, irreverent, or profane way; as, to use God's name *in vain*.—**vain·ly,** *adv.*—**vain·ness,** *n.*

vain·glo·ri·ous, vān·glōr′ē·us, vān·glạr′ē·ūs, *a.* Feeling or proceeding from vainglory; boastful.—**vain·glo·ri·ous·ly,** *adv.* —**vain·glo·ri·ous·ness,** *n.*

vain·glo·ry, vān′glōr″ē, vān′glạr″ē, vān·glōr′ē, vān·glạr′ē, *n.* pl. **vain·glo·ries.** Glory, pride, or boastfulness that unduly exalts oneself or one's own performances; vain or empty pomp or show.

vair, vâr, *n.* [O.Fr. *vair,* < L. *varius,* various, variegated.] A kind of fur used in the Middle Ages, said to have been the skin of a species of squirrel with a gray back and white belly; *her.* one of the furs, represented by bell-shaped figures, usu. alternately silver and blue.

val·ance, val′ans, vā′lans, *n.* [< Norm. *valaunt,* O.Fr. *avalant,* descending, hanging down, < *avaler,* to let down.] A drapery hanging from a bed frame or from the edge of a shelf, canopy, or the like; a short, decorative drapery or the like covering curtain fixtures along the top of a window. —**val·anced,** *a.*

vale, vāl, *n.* [Fr. *val,* < L. *vallis,* a valley.] A tract of low ground between hills; a valley; *fig.* earthly life and its afflictions.

va·le, vä′lā, vā′lē, wä′lā, *interj., n.* [L., impv. of *valere,* be strong, be well.] *Latin,* an expression of farewell.

val·e·dic·tion, val″i·dik′shan, *n.* [L. *valedicere* (pp. *valedictus*), say farewell, < *vale* and *dicere,* say.] A bidding farewell; a leave-taking; an utterance at leave-taking; a valedictory.

val·e·dic·to·ri·an, val″i·dik·tōr′ē·an, val″i·dik·tạr′ē·an, *n.* A student, usu. the one ranking highest in scholarship, who delivers the valedictory or farewell oration at the graduating or commencement exercises of his or her class.

val·e·dic·to·ry, val″i·dik′to·rē, *a.* Bidding farewell; pertaining to an occasion of leave-taking.—*n.* pl. **val·e·dic·to·ries.** A farewell or valedictory address or oration, esp. the oration delivered by the valedictorian.

va·lence, vā′lens, *n.* [L. *valentia,* strength, < *valens* (*valent-*), ppr. of *valere,* be strong, have force or effect.] *Chem.* The quality which determines the number of atoms or radicals with which any single atom or radical will unite chemically; the relative combining capacity of an atom or radical compared with the standard hydrogen atom; as, a *valence* of one, the capacity to unite with one atom of hydrogen or its equivalent. Also **va·len·cy.**

Va·len·ci·ennes, va·len″sē·enz′, *Fr.* välän·syen′, *n.* A fine, handmade, floral patterned lace made orig. at Valenciennes, France. Also **Va·len·ci·ennes lace,Val lace.**

val·en·tine, val′en·tīn″, *n.* [From St. *Valentine.*] A sentimental, sometimes satirical, printed card or a token or gift of regard, sent by one person to another on St. Valentine's Day; a sweetheart chosen on St. Valentine's Day; an affectionate written message or work.

Val·en·tine's Day, Val·en·tine Day, *n.* Saint Valentine's Day, Feb. 14th.

va·le·ri·an, va·lēr′ē·an, *n.* [O.Fr. *valeriane* (Fr. *valériane*), < M.L. *valeriana,* appar. < L. *Valerianus* or *Valerius,* personal name.] Any of the perennial herbs constituting the genus *Valeriana,* as *V. officinalis,* the garden

heliotrope, a plant with white or pink flowers and a root yielding a drug formerly used as a nerve sedative and an agent to check spasms; the drug obtained from the root of *Valeriana officinalis.*—**va·ler·ic,** va·ler′ik, va·lēr′ik, *a.* Of, obtained from, or relating to valerian.

va·ler·ic ac·id, *n. Chem.* an acid, $CH_3(CH_2)_3COOH$, extracted from the roots of the valerian plant or made synthetically, and used in perfumery and medicines.

val·et, val′it, val′ā, va·lā′, *Fr.* vä·le′, *n.* [Fr. *valet,* O.Fr. *vallet, vaslet,* also *varlet;* akin to E. *vassal.*] A manservant who is his master's personal attendant; one employed, as by a hotel, to perform various personal services for the guests.—*v.t., v.i.—valeted, valeting.* To attend or act as a valet.

va·let de cham·bre, vä·le *de* shän′bRe, *n.* pl. **va·lets de cham·bre,** vä·le *de* shän′bRe. [Fr., 'valet of chamber.'] *French,* a valet.

val·e·tu·di·nar·i·an, val″i·tōd″i·nâr′ēan, val″i·tūd″i·nâr′ē·an, *n.* [L. *valetudinarius,* < *valetudo,* good or ill health, < *valeo,* to be well.] A person of an infirm or sickly constitution; one who is seeking to recover health; one who is overly concerned with poor health.—*a.* In a poor state of health; seeking to recover health.

val·e·tu·di·nar·i·an·ism, val″i·tōd″inâr′ē·a·niz″um, val″i·tūd″i·nâr′ē·a·niz″um, *n.* The state of being a valetudinarian.

val·e·tu·di·nar·y, val″i·tōd″i·ner″ē, val″i·tūd″i·ner″ē, *n.* pl. **val·e·tu·di·nar·ies.** Valetudinarian.—*a.* Valetudinarian.

val·gus, val′gus, *n.* pl. **val·gus·es.** [L., bow-legged.] *Pathol.* a condition of turned or twisted leg or foot bones, as knock-knee or formerly, bowleg; one so afflicted.—*a.* Knock-kneed; formerly, bowlegged.

val·ian·cy, val′yan·sē, *n.* The quality of being valiant; bravery, courage, or valor. Also **val·iance.**

val·iant, val′yant, *a.* [Fr. *vaillant,* < *valoir,* L. *valere,* to be strong.] Brave; courageous; intrepid in danger; performed with valor; heroic.—**val·iant·ly,** *adv.*—**val·iant·ness,** *n.*

val·id, val′id, *a.* [Fr. *valide,* L. *validus,* strong, powerful, < *valeo,* to be strong, to be well.] Sufficiently supported by actual fact; well grounded, sound, or just; good or effective; having sufficient legal strength or force; good or sufficient in point of law; *logic,* derived correctly from premises already accepted.—**val·id·ly,** *adv.*—**val·id·ness,** *n.*

val·i·date, val′i·dāt″, *v.t.—validated, validating.* [M.L. *validatus,* pp. of *validare,* < L. *validus.*] To make valid; to confirm; to give legal force to; to legalize.—**val·i·da·tion,** *n.*

va·lid·i·ty, va·lid′i·tē, *n.* pl. **va·lid·i·ties.** The state or quality of being valid; legal strength or force; soundness.

val·ine, val′ēn, val′in, vā′lēn, vā′lin, *n. Biochem.* an amino acid, $(CH_3)_2CHCH$-$(NH_2)COOH$, occurring as white, water-soluble crystals derived from the hydrolysis of proteins and used as a dietary supplement in medicine.

va·lise, va·lēs′, *Brit.* va·lēz′, *n.* [Fr.] A small bag or case for holding a traveler's clothes and related articles.

val·late, val′āt, *a.* [L. *vallatus,* pp. of *vallare,* surround with a rampart, < *vallum,* palisade, wall, rampart, < *vallus,* stake, pale: cf. *wall.*] Having a surrounding ridge or elevation.

val·la·tion, va·lā′shan, *n.* [L.L. *vallatio(n-).*] A rampart or entrenchment, usu. for military defenses; the skill and method of designing, planning, and building fortifications.

val·lec·u·la, va·lek′ya·la, *n.* pl. **val·lec·u·lae,** va·lek′ya·lē″. [L.L., for L. *vallicula,*

dim. of *vallis, valles,* valley.] *Anat.* a furrow, as on the back of the tongue; *bot.* a furrow or depression.—**val·lec·u·lar,** *a.*—**val·lec·u·late,** va·lek′ya·lāt″, *a.* Having a vallecula or valleculae.

val·ley, val′ē, *n.* pl. **val·leys.** [Fr. *vallée,* O.Fr. *valee,* < *val,* a vale, < L. *vallis,* a valley.] Any hollow or surface depression of the earth bounded by hills or mountains, and usu. traversed by a stream or river; the great extent of land drained by a river; *arch.* the angle formed by the meeting of the two inclined sides of a roof.

va·lo·ni·a, va·lō′nē·a, *n.* [It. *vallonia,* < Mod.Gr. *balania,* the holm oak, < Gr. *balanos,* an acorn, an oak.] The acorn cups of a species of oak, *Quercus macrolepis,* exported from the Mediterranean region for use in tanning and dyeing.

val·or, *Brit.* **val·our,** val′ėr, *n.* [O.Fr. *valor,* Mod.Fr. *valeur,* L.L. *valor,* worth, < L. *valeo,* to be strong.] That quality which enables a man to encounter danger with firmness; personal bravery, esp. in fighting; intrepidity; prowess.

val·or·ize, val′o·rīz″, *v.t.—valorized, valorizing.* [Pg. *valorizar,* < *valor,* value, < L.L. *valor.*] To assign a value to; of a government, to fix and maintain the value or price of, as a commercial commodity, by purchase of the commodity at the fixed price or by subsidy.—**val·or·i·zation,** *n.*

val·or·ous, val′ėr·us, *a.* Brave; courageous; valiant; intrepid; possessing or characterized by valor.—**val·or·ous·ly,** *adv.*—**val·or·ous·ness,** *n.*

valse, väls, *n.* pl. **valses.** [Fr.] *French,* a waltz, esp. a concert waltz.

val·u·a·ble, val′ū·a·bl, val′ya·bl, *a.* Having great value or monetary worth; expensive; having estimable or worthy qualities; of considerable use, service, or importance.—*n.* Usu. *pl.* valuable articles, as of personal property or of merchandise, esp. articles of comparatively small size.— **val·u·a·ble·ness,** *n.*—**val·u·a·bly,** *adv.*

val·u·ate, val′ū·āt″, *v.t.—valuated, valuating.* To put a value on; to appraise.—**val·ua·tor,** val′ū·a″tėr, *n.*

val·u·a·tion, val″ū·ā′shan, *n.* The act of estimating or fixing the value of a thing; a value estimated or fixed; the estimation or appreciation of the worth or qualities of a person or thing.—**val·u·a·tion·al,** *a.*— **val·u·a·tion·al·ly,** *adv.*

val·ue, val′ū, *n.* [O.Fr. *value,* orig. pp. fem. of *valoir,* be worth, < L. *valere.*] The worth, merit, usefulness, or importance of a thing; as, the *value* of an education; material or monetary worth, as in business; the worth of a thing as measured by the amount of other things for which it can be exchanged, or as estimated in terms of a medium of exchange; equivalent worth or adequate return; estimated or assigned worth; valuation; force; import, or significance; as, the *value* of a word; esteem or regard; *math.* the number or amount represented by a figure or symbol; *mus.* the relative duration of a tone signified by a note; *paint.* the relative effect of color, esp. with reference to the degree of lightness and darkness; *phon.* the characteristic sound quality of a letter; *pl., sociol.* the qualities, customs, standards, and principles of a people regarded as desirable.—*v.t.—valued, valuing.* To estimate the value of; appraise; to place a certain value or price on; to consider with respect to worth, excellence, usefulness, or importance; to regard or esteem highly.—**val·ue·less,** *a.*—**val·ue·less·ness,** *n.*—**val·u·er,** *n.*

val·ued, val′ūd, *a.* Highly regarded or esteemed; estimated or appraised; having a specified value.

va·lu·ta, va·lō′ta, *n.* The value given to a

currency as expressed in its exchange rate in another currency.

val·var, val′vẽr, *a.* Valvular.

val·vate, val′vāt, *a.* [L. *valvatus,* having folding doors.] Furnished with or opening by a valve or valves; serving as or resembling a valve. *Bot.* opening by valves, as certain capsules and anthers; meeting without overlapping, as the parts of certain buds; composed of or characterized by such parts.

valve, valv, *n.* [Fr. *valve,* < L. *valvae,* folding doors, from same root *volvo,* to roll (whence *voluble,* etc.).] Any apparatus or device used to regulate the admission or escape of water, gas, or steam; a movable lid or partition formed in such an apparatus as to open a passage in one direction and to close it in the other; *anat.* a structure within a hollow organ that opens to allow the passage of a fluid in one direction or shuts to prevent its return; as, the *valves* of the heart; *mus.* an apparatus in some brass instruments that changes the length of the air column and alters the pitch; *zool.* one of the separable portions of the shell of a mollusk. *Bot.* one of the divisions of any dehiscent body; one of the lidlike coverings of various anthers. *Brit.* a vacuum or electron tube.—*v.t.*—*valved,* *valving.* To furnish with valves to control the flow of, as fluid, gas, and the like, by the use of a movable lid.—**valve·less,** *a.*

valve-in-head en·gine, valv′in·hed′ en″jin, *n.* An internal-combustion engine with inlet and exhaust valves contained in the cylinder, rather than in the engine block, as in some cars.

val·vu·lar, val′vya·lẽr, *a.* Containing valves; having the character of, pertaining to, or acting as a valve.

val·vule, val′vūl, *n.* [Dim. < *valve.*] A little valve or a similar structure.

val·vu·li·tis, val″vya·lī′tis, *n.* [N.L.] *Pathol.* inflammation of a valve, esp. a valve of the heart.

va·moose, va·mös′, *v.i.,* *v.t.*—*vamoosed,* *vamoosing. Slang.* To depart hastily; to quit Also **va·mose,** va·mōs′.

vamp, vamp, *n.* [Formerly *vampey,* < Fr. *avant-pied*—*avant,* before, and *pied.* the foot.] The section of a boot or shoe that overlays the instep and sometimes the toes; a thing that has been pieced together or patched; *mus.* an improvised accompaniment.—*v.t.* To supply with a vamp; to repair or piece together; to fabricate or concoct, usu. followed by *up; mus.* to improvise; as, to *vamp* a tune.—*v.i. Mus.* to improvise tunes, accompaniments, and the like.—**vamp·er,** *n.*

vamp, vamp, *n. Colloq.* a seductive woman who unscrupulously beguiles and exploits men.—*v.t.* To beguile and seduce; as, to *vamp* men.—*v.i.* To act the part of a vamp.

vam·pire, vam′pīẽr, *n.* [Fr. *vampire;* < Slav.] A preternatural being, in the common belief a reanimated corpse, supposed to suck the blood of sleeping persons at night; one who preys ruthlessly on others; an extortioner, esp. a woman who preys on men; a woman who uses her feminine charms or seductions to extract profit from male victims, or feeds her vanity at their expense; a self-seeking or unscrupulous flirt. *Zool.* any of various South and Central American bats, genera *Desmodus* and *Diphylla,* which suck blood; any of various large frugivorous bats, genus *Phyllostomus,* of the Old World.—**vam·pir·ic,** vam·pir′ik, *a.*—**vam·pir·ism,** vam′pĩr·iz″um, vam′pi·riz″um, *n.* Belief in the existence of prenatural vampires; the supposed existence of vampires; the acts or practices of vampires; the practice of preying on others.

van, van, *n.* [Fr. *van,* < L. *vannus,* a van or fan for winnowing.] *Archaic,* a winnowing machine or fan; *poet.* a wing.

van, van, *n.* Vanguard.

van, van, *n.* [Abbrev. < *caravan.*] A large, covered vehicle, usu. a truck or wagon, used to move furniture, commercial goods, livestock, and the like; *Brit.* a covered railway car for freight or luggage.—*v.t.*—*vanned,* *vanning.* To transport by van.

van·a·date, van′a·dāt″, *n. Chem.* a salt or an ester of vanadic acid. Also **va·na·di·ate,** va·nā′dē·āt″.

va·nad·ic, va·nad′ik, va·nā′dik, *a. Chem.* referring to a compound containing vanadium, esp. in its higher valences.

va·nad·ic ac·id, *n. Chem.* any of certain acids containing vanadium, esp. one with the formula, H_3VO_4, that does not exist in a pure state.

va·nad·i·nite, va·nad′i·nīt″, *n.* A mineral consisting of lead vanadate and chloride, $Pb_5(VO_4)_3Cl$, occurring in yellow, brown, or red crystals; an important ore of vanadium and lead.

va·na·di·um, va·nā′dē·um, *n.* [From *Vanadis,* a surname of the Scand. goddess Freya, < its being discovered in a Sw. ore.] A silvery white hard metallic element, used in certain steels to add toughness and tensile strength, and to form many compounds used in chemical manufacturing. Sym.V, at. no. 23, at. wt. 50.942. See Periodic Table of Elements.—**va·na·di·ous, van·a·dous,** va·nā′dē·us, van′a·dus, *a.*

Van Al·len belt, van al′en belt″, *n.* Either of two high-intensity radiation zones surrounding the earth beginning at an altitude of approximately 1,000 kilometers. Also **Van Al·len ra·di·a·tion belt.**

van·da, van′da, *n.* Any of various epiphytic orchids, genus *Vanda,* found in tropical areas of the eastern hemisphere, and bearing large, often showy flowers in colors of lilac, white, blue, and green.

van·dal, van′dal, *n.* [L. *Vandali, Vinduli,* the Vandals.] (*Cap.*) A member of a Teutonic tribe that invaded Gaul, Spain, and North Africa in the 4th and 5th centuries and pillaged Rome in 455 A.D.; (*l.c.*) one who willfully or ignorantly damages or destroys property, either public or private. —*a.* Pertaining to or resembling the Vandals; (*l.c.*) willfully destructive.— **Van·dal·ic, van·dal·ic,** van·dal′ik, *a.*

van·dal·ism, van′da·liz″um, *n.* Willful or ignorant destruction of public or private property.—**van·dal·is·tic,** *a.*—**van·dal·ize,** van′da·līz″, *v.t.*—*vandalized, vandalizing.*

Van de Graaf gen·er·a·tor, van′ de graf″ jen′e·rā″tẽr, *n. Elect., phys.* an electrostatic generator that uses a rapidly moving conveyor belt between terminals to charge an insulated electrode to high potential, and frequently using the voltage in the conductor for particle acceleration.

Van·dyke, van·dīk′, *a.* [From Sir Anthony *Van Dyck* (or *Vandyke*), Flem. painter, 1599–1641.] Relating to or like the style of Van Dyck; relating to or like the mode of dress shown in Van Dyck's paintings.—*n.* A painting or portrait by Van Dyck.

Van·dyke beard, *n.* A small pointed beard. Also *Vandyke,* **van·dyke.**

Van·dyke brown, *n.* A brown pigment used in Sir Anthony Van Dyck's paintings; one of several similar brown pigments.

Van·dyke col·lar, *n.* A very wide pointed collar of lace and linen. Also *Vandyke,* *vandyke,* **van·dyke col·lar.**

vane, vān, *n.* [O.E. *fane,* a banner, a weathercock, < *fana* = O.H.G. *fano,* G. *fahne,* D. *vaan,* a flag; Goth. *fana,* cloth; cogn. L. *pannus,* cloth.] A contrivance made of a thin strip of metal or wood, usu. in the shape of a cock or arrow, placed on a spindle at the top of a spire, tower, or similar elevation for the purpose of showing by its turning the direction of the wind; also *weathercock, weathervane.* Any of several bladelike surfaces radially connected to a central shaft moved by air, as the sail of a windmill, or moved by a fluid, as the blade of a turbine engine; *rocketry,* any of the surfaces affixed to the outside or in the tail of a missile to control and guide it; *ornith.* the broad or weblike part of a feather on either side of the shaft. *Surv.* a sliding target on a leveling rod; a sight on an instrument, as a quadrant. *Archery,* one of the feathers attached to the arrow's nock.—**vaned,** *a.*—**vane·less,** *a.*

van·guard, van′gärd″, *n.* The troops who march in the van or front division of an army; the advance guard; the group at the forefront of any field, movement, or activity, as in politics, art, or literature; also *van.* (*Cap.*) a type of rocket used for launching satellites.

va·nil·la, va·nil′a, *n.* [< Sp. *vainilla,* dim. of *vaina,* a scabbard; < L. *vagina,* a scabbard; the pod resembles a scabbard.] Any of a number of climbing orchids of the genus *Vanilla,* esp. *V. planifolia,* native to tropical regions, and having a podlike fruit which yields a fragrant extract used in flavoring foods and making medicines and perfumes. The bean or podlike fruit of this plant; also **va·nil·la bean.** The flavorful extract made from the podlike fruit.

va·nil·lic, va·nil′ik, *a.* Pertaining to, derived from, or resembling vanilla or vanillin.

van·il·lin, van′i·lin, va·nil′in, *n. Chem.* a white crystalline compound, $C_8H_8O_3$, the active principle of vanilla, extracted from the vanilla bean or prepared artificially from wood pulp. Also **va·nil·lic al·de·hyde, van·il·line,** van′i·lin, van′i·lēn″, va·nil′in, va·nil′ēn.

van·ish, van′ish, *v.i.* [< L. *vanesco, evanesco,* to vanish, to pass away (through the old French), < *vanus,* vain.] To disappear; to pass from a visible to an invisible state; to pass beyond the limit of vision; to be annihilated or lost; to be no more; *math.* to become less and less until the value is zero.—*n. Phon.* the weaker, end part of some vowel sounds, as the weak *e* sound completing the vowel sound in *main.* —**van·ish·er,** *n.*

van·ish·ing cream, *n.* A cosmetic cream resembling cold cream, usu. used as a foundation for facial powder.

van·ish·ing point, *n. Art,* the point in a view or picture at which all parallel lines in the same plane appear to meet. The point at which something ceases or disappears, as: *Her tolerance had reached the vanishing point.*

van·i·ty, van′i·tē, *n. pl.* **van·i·ties.** [Fr. *vanité,* L. *vanitas.*] The quality or condition of being vain; excessive or overweening pride in one's personal appearance, possessions, qualities, or attainments; lack of worth, usefulness, or true value; the quality or thing about which a person is vain; something that is worthless, useless, or without value; a small piece of luggage or cosmetic case; a dressing table.

van·i·ty fair, *n.* [From the vain show of worldly folly, frivolity, and ostentation sketched in Bunyan's *Pilgrim's Progress* and in Thackeray's novel, *Vanity Fair.*] A group, society, or place, as the world of high society, dominated by folly, frivolity, and ostentation.

van·quish, vang′kwish, van′kwish, *v.t.* [< Fr. *vaincre,* pret. *vainquis,* subj. *vainquisse,* O.Fr. *veinquir,* < L. *vincere,* to conquer.] To conquer, overcome, or subdue in battle; to defeat in any contest or struggle; to overpower.—**van·quish·a·ble,** *a.*—**van·quish·er,** *n.*

van, van, *n.* [Fr. *van,* < L. *vannus,* a van or

van·tage, van′tij, vän′tij, n. [M.E. *vantage*, by reduction < O.Fr. *advantage*, E. *advantage*.] A position or condition affording superiority, as for action or defense; an opportunity likely to give superiority; an advantage.

van·ward, van′wėrd, a., adv. Toward or in the van or front.

vap·id vap′id, a. [L. *vapidus*, vapid, having lost spirit, same root as *vapor*.] Having lost life, spirit, or flavor; insipid or flat; dull, unanimated, or spiritless; as, *vapid* remarks. —**va·pid·i·ty**, **vap·id·ness**, n.—**vap·id·ly**, adv.

va·por, Brit. **va·pour**, vā′pėr, n. [L. *vapor*, steam; vapor; akin to *vapidus*, vapid, having lost flavor, *vappa*, vapid wine.] Any visible, diffused substance or hazy matter floating in the atmosphere, as fog, mist, dust, or smoke; an exhalation or fume, as of steam or a gas; a substance which has been vaporized for use in industry or, as an inhalant in medicine. *Phys.* the gaseous form which any solid or liquid assumes when heated; a gas below its critical temperature. Something unsubstantial, fleeting, or transitory; an unreal fancy.—*v.t.* To vaporize. —*v.i.* To emit vapor; to brag or boast.— **va·por·er**, Brit. **va·pour·er**, n.—**va·por·ish**, Brit. **va·pour·ish**, vā′pėr·ish, a.— **va·por·ish·ness**, Brit. **va·pour·ish·ness**, n.

va·por·if·ic, Brit. **va·pour·if·ic**, vā″po·rif′ik, a. [L. *vapor*, and *facio*, to make.] Forming vapor; converting into vapor or a volatile form; vaporous.

va·por·ing, Brit. **va·pour·ing**, vā′pėr·ing, a. Boasting; tending to boast or brag.—n. Boastful or windy talk.

va·por·ize, vā′po·rīz″, v.t.—vaporized, vaporizing, Brit. vapourized, vapourizing. To convert into vapor, esp. by the application of heat; to cause to evaporate.—v.i. To be changed into vapor.—**va·por·iz·a·ble**, Brit. **va·pour·iz·a·ble**, a.—**va·por·i·za·tion**, Brit. **va·pour·i·za·tion**, vā″pėr·i·zā′shan, n.

va·por·iz·er, Brit. **va·pour·iz·er**, vā′po·rī″zėr, n. A person or thing that vaporizes; a mechanism for converting a liquid, esp. a medication for respiratory ailments, into a very fine spray or vapor.

va·por lock, n. *Mech.* a blocking of the fuel flow to an internal combustion engine, resulting from vaporization or air bubbles in the fuel.

va·por·ous, Brit. **va·pour·ous**, vā′pėr·us, a. Being in the form of or having the characteristics of vapor; full of, emitting, or producing vapors; cloudlike; unsubstantial or ethereal; vainly imaginative, fanciful, or whimsical.—**va·por·ous·ly**, Brit. **va·pour·ous·ly**, adv.—**va·por·ous·ness**, Brit. **va·pour·ous·ness**, **va·por·os·i·ty**, Brit. **va·pour·os·i·ty**, vā″po·ros′i·tė, n.

va·por pres·sure, n. *Phys.* the pressure which a confined vapor exerts at a given temperature when in equilibrium with its solid or liquid state. Also **va·por ten·sion**.

va·por trail, n. Condensation trail.

va·por·y, Brit. **va·pour·y**, vā′po·rē, a. Vaporous; full of vapor.

va·que·ro, vä·kâr′ō, *Sp.* bä·ke′ʀạ, n. pl. **va·que·ros**. [Sp., a cowherd, < *vaca*, L. *vacca*, a cow.] *Western U.S.* a cattle herdsman or a cowboy.

va·ra, vär′a, *Sp.* bä′ʀä, *Pg.* vä′ʀa, n. pl. **va·ras**. Any of various units of length in Spain, Portugal, or their former colonies, measuring from about 32 to about 43 inches.—**square va·ra**, the length of a vara squared as a unit of area.

var·i·a, vâr′ē·a, n. pl. A miscellaneous collection, esp. of literary pieces.

var·i·a·ble, vâr′ē·a·bl, a. [O.Fr. Fr. *variable*, < L. *variabilis*.] Apt or liable to vary or change; changeable; inconstant or fickle, as a person; capable of being varied or changed; alterable; diverse; *astron.* of a star, changing in brightness; *biol.* deviating from the strict type, as a species or a specific character; *meteor.* of a wind, tending to change in direction.—n. Something variable; *math.* a quantity or symbol which has no fixed value and is considered with reference to its different possible values; *astron.* a variable star. *Meteor.* a shifting wind, as contrasted with a *trade wind*; *pl.* a region where such winds occur. —**var·i·a·bil·i·ty**, **var·i·a·ble·ness**, n.— **var·i·a·bly**, adv.

var·i·a·ble cost, n. *Econ.* cost to a business or industry that varies with changes in the number of transactions or in the volume of output.

var·i·a·ble star, n. *Astron.* a star whose brightness varies at fairly regular intervals due to alternate contractions and expansions.

var·i·ance, vâr′ē·ans, n. [O.Fr. *variance*, < L. *variantia*, < *varians*, ppr.] The state or fact of varying; difference or discrepancy; disagreement, discord, or dissension. *Law*, a discrepancy between two parts of a legal proceeding, as between allegations and proof, that satisfy the requirements of law only when entirely consonant; legal permission to deviate from the standard regulations, usu. of a zoning law. *Statistics*, the standard deviation squared; *phys.*, *chem.* any one or all of the variable factors, as pressure, temperature, or concentration, required to define the state of a material system.—**at var·i·ance**, not in agreement or harmony.

var·i·ant, vâr′ē·ant, a. [O.Fr. Fr. *variant*, < L. *varians* (*variant*-), ppr. of *variare*, E. *vary*.] Exhibiting or characterized by variation; varying; differing; tending to change or alter; variable; being an altered or different form of something; as, a *variant* spelling.—n. A variant form, esp. in the pronunciation or spelling of a word or in the interpretation or reading of a passage or text; *ling.* the form assumed by a linguistic unit as determined by its position or context, as an allophone or allomorph.

var·i·ate, vâr′ē·it, n. Any variable or variant. *Statistics*, a variable quantity whose probable numerical values are determined by a given sample; also **ran·dom var·i·a·ble**.

var·i·a·tion, vâr″ē·ā′shan, n. [O.Fr. Fr. *variation*, < L. *variatio(n-)*, < *variare*, E. *vary*.] The act, process, or result of varying in condition, character, or degree; diversity, alteration, or modification; amount or rate of change; deviation or divergence; a different form of something; variant; *mus.* the repetition of a melody or theme with changes or elaborations, usu. as one of a series of such changes; *astron.* any deviation from the mean orbit or mean motion of a celestial body; *navig.* the declination of a magnetic needle; *math.* a formula for the measurement of change in a variable or function. *Biol.* deviation in structure or function of an organism from that of parent organisms or others of the same species or group; an organism exhibiting such deviation. *Gram.* inflection.—**var·i·a·tion·al**, a.—**var·i·a·tion·al·ly**, adv.

var·i·a·tive, vâr′ē·ā″tiv, a. Of, pertaining to, or exhibiting variation.—**var·i·a·tive·ly**, adv.

var·i·cel·la, var″i·sel′a, n. [Dim. of *variola*, the smallpox.] *Pathol.* chicken pox. —**var·i·cel·lar**, a.

var·i·co·cele, var′i·kō·sēl″, n. [L. *varix*, a dilated vein, and Gr. *kēlē*, a tumor.] *Pathol.* a varicose enlargement of the spermatic cord veins of the scrotum.

var·i·col·ored, Brit. **var·i·col·oured**, vâr′i·kul″ėrd, a. [L. *varius*, various, and *color*, color.] Having various colors; variegated; motley.

var·i·cose, var′i·kōs″, vâr′i·kōs″, a. [L. *varicosus*, < *varix* (*varic*-) varix.] Abnormally dilated, as a vein; pertaining to or affected with varicose veins.

var·i·cos·i·ty, var″i·kos′i·tē, n. pl. **var·i·cos·i·ties**. *Pathol.* the state or condition of being varicose; a varix.

var·ied, vâr′ēd, a. Diversified or characterized by variety; as, a *varied* assortment; changed or altered; as, a *varied* form of a word; variegated, as in color.—**var·ied·ly**, adv.—**var·ied·ness**, n.

var·i·e·gate, vâr′ē·e·gāt″, vâr′e·gāt″, v.t. —variegated, variegating. [L. *variegatus*, pp. of *variegare*, < *varius*, various, and *agere*, drive, do.] To render varied in appearance, esp. by differences in color or texture; to give variety to; diversify.— **var·i·e·ga·tor**, n.

var·i·e·gat·ed, vâr′ē·e·gā″tid, vâr′e·gā″-tid, a. Varied in appearance or color; marked with blots or specks of different colors; varied; diversified.

var·i·e·ga·tion, vâr″ē·e·gā′shan, vâr″e·gā′shan, n. The act of variegating; the state of being variegated; varied coloration.

va·ri·e·tal, va·rī′i·tal, a. Of, pertaining to, or characteristic of a variety; constituting a variety.—**va·ri·e·tal·ly**, adv.

va·ri·e·ty, va·rī′i·tē, n. pl. **va·ri·e·ties**. [Fr. *variété*, < *varietas*, < *varius*, E. *various*.] The state or character of being various or varied; diversity or absence of uniformity; difference or discrepancy; a number of things of different kinds; a varied assortment of something; a different form, condition, or phase of something; a kind or sort. *Biol.* a subdivision of a species; a form of plant originating in nature or under cultivation, based on a slight hereditary difference from that of the type species; a group or race of animals produced by artificial selection. *Theatr.* entertainment of a mixed character, consisting of a number of individual performances, as of singing, dancing, acrobatic exhibitions, or playlets; also **va·ri·e·ty show**.

va·ri·e·ty meat, n. Meat, as sweetbread or tongue, not cut from the skeletal muscles.

va·ri·e·ty store, n. A retail store that carries a wide variety of inexpensive merchandise.

var·i·form, vâr′i·fạrm″, a. [L. *varius*, various, and *forma*, form.] Varied in form; having various forms.

var·i·o·cou·pler, vâr″ē·ō·kup′lėr, n. [L. *variare*, to vary, and E. *coupler*.] *Elect.* a transformer with coils having a mutual impedance, adjustable by changing one coil in relation to the other, while the self-impedance remains essentially constant.

va·ri·o·la, va·rī′o·la, n. [Fr. *variole*, Mod.L. *variola*, smallpox, < L. *varius*, spotted.] *Pathol.* smallpox.—**va·ri·o·lar**, **va·ri·o·lous**, va·rī′o·lėr, va·rī′o·lus, a.

var·i·ole, vâr′ē·ōl″, n. [M.L. *variola*.] A shallow pit or depression like the mark left by a smallpox pustule; *petrog.* one of the spherules of variolite.

var·i·o·lite, vâr′ē·o·līt″, n. [M.L. *variola*, smallpox; from the appearance.] *Petrog.* any of certain basic igneous rocks containing embedded light-colored spherules, that give them a pock-marked appearance. —**var·i·o·lit·ic**, vâr″ē·o·lit′ik, a.

var·i·o·loid, vâr′ē·o·loid″, a. *Pathol.* resembling smallpox; pertaining to a mild form of smallpox.—n. *Pathol.* a mild form of smallpox, esp. as occurring in persons who have been vaccinated or who have previously had smallpox.

var·i·om·e·ter, vâr″ē·om′i·tėr, n. *Elect.* an instrument used to measure inductance, composed of an inductor with coils that may be changed in position with respect to each other to alter the inductance; an instrument that designates changes of magnetic force.

var·i·o·rum, vâr″ē·ôr′um, vâr″ē·ạr′um, a. [L. (gen. pl. of *varius*, E. *various*), as in *editio cum notis variorum*, edition with notes of various persons.] Of or pertaining to an edition containing various versions of the text or numerous commentaries and notes by editors or critics.—*n.* An edition having various versions or commentaries and notes.

var·i·ous, vâr′ē·us, a. [L. *varius*, diverse, manifold, variegated, various, varying, changeable.] Differing one from another or being of different kinds; exhibiting or marked by variety or diversity; exhibiting or possessing different characters or qualities; varied in color or variegated; dissimilar or presenting different aspects; separate or individual; as, approval by the *various* offices; several or many; *archaic*, inconstant or changeable.—**var·i·ous·ly,** *adv.*—**var··i·ous·ness,** *n.*

var·i·sized, vâr′i·sīzd″, a. Of different or various sizes.

var·is·tor, va·ris′tẽr, va·ris′tẽr, n. *Elect.* a resistor whose resistance varies proportionately with the voltage applied to it.

var·ix, vâr′iks, n. pl. **var·i·ces,** vâr′i·sēz″. [L., a dilated vein, varix.] *Pathol.* an abnormal dilation of a vein or other vessel of the body, usu. accompanied by distortion; a varicose vein. *Zool.* a mark or scar on the surface of a shell denoting a former position of the lip of the aperture.

var·let, vär′lit, n. [O.Fr. *varlet*, var. of *vallet*, E. *valet*.] *Archaic.* A manservant, valet, or attendant; an attendant or page attached to a knight; a low fellow, knave, or rascal.

var·let·ry, vär′li·trē, n. *Archaic.* Varlets collectively; the mob or rabble.

var·mint, var·ment, vär′mint, n. [Var. of *vermin*.] *Dial.* Vermin; a noxious or objectionable animal; an objectionable or troublesome person.

var·nish, vär′nish, n. [O.Fr. *vernis, verniz* (Fr. *vernis*); origin unknown.] A preparation consisting of resinous matter, as copal or lac, dissolved in oil, alcohol, or other volatile liquid, which when applied to the surface of wood or metal dries and leaves a hard, glossy, usu. transparent coating; the sap of certain trees used for the same purpose; any of various other preparations similarly used, as one having India rubber, pyroxylin, or asphalt for the chief constituent; a coating or surface of varnish; something resembling a coating of varnish; a gloss; superficial embellishment or external show, esp. to cover a defect. —*v.t.* To lay varnish on; to invest with a glossy appearance; to give an improved appearance to; to embellish; to adorn; to cover with a specious or deceptive appearance.—**var·nish·er,** *n.*—**var·nish·y,** *a.*

var·nish tree, n. Any of various trees yielding sap or other substances used for varnish, as *Rhus verniciflua*, of Japan.

var·si·ty, vär′si·tē, n. pl. **var·si·ties.** The principal or first team, esp. in athletics, representing a college, university, school, or the like, in competition; *Brit. colloq.* university.

var·us, vâr′us, n. pl. **var·us·es.** [L. *varus*.] *Pathol.* a deformity of a bone or joint, esp. bowleg.

varve, värv, n. *Geol.* any annual stratified deposit generally comprised of two layers of seasonal sedimentation.

var·y, vâr′ē, v.t.—*varied, varying.* [Fr. *varier*, < L. *variare*, to vary, < *varius*, variegated, diverse, various.] To alter in form, appearance, substance, or position; to

make different by a partial change; to diversify; *mus.* to embellish, as a melody or theme, with passing notes or arpeggios.— *v.i.* To alter or be altered in any manner; to suffer change; to appear in different forms; to differ or be different; to change, as in purpose or opinion; to deviate; *math.* to be subject to continual increase or decrease; *biol.* to have or be subject to variation.— **var·i·er,** *n.*—**var·y·ing·ly,** *adv.*

var·y·ing hare, n. Any of the hares whose fur becomes white in winter, esp. the snowshoe rabbit, *Lepus americanus*.

vas, vas, n. pl. **va·sa,** vā′sa. [L., vessel: cf. *vase*.] *Biol.* a vessel or duct.

vas·cu·lar, vas′kya·lẽr, a. [L. *vasculum*, a vessel, dim. of *vas*, a vessel.] *Biol.* pertaining to or containing the system of vessels or ducts which convey fluid, as blood in animals and water and food materials in plants.—**vas·cu·lar·i·ty,** *n.* The condition of being vascular.

vas·cu·lar bun·dle, n. *Bot.* a strand of conducting and strengthening tissues including phloem, xylem, and fibers, found in all parts of a plant.

vas·cu·lar cyl·in·der, n. *Bot.* stele.

vas·cu·lar plant, n. *Bot.* a plant which possesses a vascular system, characteristic of higher plants.

vas·cu·lar ray, n. *Bot.* a radial strand of parenchymatous cells in stems which stores and transfers nutrients.

vas·cu·lar tis·sue, n. *Bot.* a complex tissue made up principally of xylem and phloem conducting water and food respectively.

vas·cu·lum, vas′kya·lum, n. pl. **vas·cu·la,** vas·cu·lums, vas′kya·la. A case used by a botanist for carrying plant specimens as he collects them.

vas de·fe·rens, vas def′e·renz″, n. pl. **va·sa de·fe·ren·ti·a,** vā′sa def″e·ren′- shē·a. *Anat.* the duct that transfers sperm from the testis into the urethra for ejaculation.

vase, vās, vāz, *Brit.* väz, n. [Fr. *vase*, < L. *vas*, vessel: cf. *vas*.] A hollow vessel, generally high in proportion to its horizontal diameter, used as a holder for flowers or as a decoration.

vas·ec·to·my, va·sek′to·mē, n. pl. **vas·ec·to·mies.** [L. *vas*, vessel, and Gr. *ek*, out of, and *-tomia*, < *temnein*, cut.] *Surg.* excision of the vas deferens or of a portion of it.

Vas·e·line, vas′e·lēn″, vas″e·lēn′, n. [Irreg. < G. *wasser*, water, and Gr. *elaion*, oil.] A translucent, yellow or whitish, semisolid petroleum product, or a form of petrolatum, used in various preparations for medicinal and other purposes. (Trademark.) Also **vas·e·line.**

vas·o·con·stric·tor, vas″ō·kon·strik′tẽr, a. *Physiol.* serving, when stimulated, to constrict blood vessels, as certain nerves.— *n. Physiol.* a drug, nerve, or other agent causing constriction of blood vessels.—**vas··o·con·stric·tion,** *n.*—**vas·o·con·stric··tive,** *a.*

vas·o·di·la·tor, vas″ō·dī·lā′tẽr, vas″ō·di·lā′tẽr, a. *Physiol.* serving, when stimulated, to dilate or relax blood vessels.—*n. Physiol.* a drug, nerve, or other agent which causes relaxation or dilatation of blood vessels.—**vas·o·dil·a·ta·tion, vas·o·di·la·tion,** vas″ō·dil″a·tā′shan, vas″ō·dī′la·tā′shan, vas″ō·dī·lā·lā′shan, vas″ō·di·lā′shan, *n.*

vas·o·in·hib·i·tor, vas″ō·in·hib′i·tẽr, n. A drug or other agent which inhibits vasomotor nerve action.—**vas·o·in·hib··i·to·ry,** vas″ō·in·hib′i·tōr″ē, vas″ō·in·hib′i·tạr″ē, a.

vas·o·mo·tor, vas″ō·mō′tẽr, a. [L. *vas*, a vessel, and *motor*, a mover.] Applied to the system of nerves distributed over the mus-

cular coats of the blood vessels, which regulates their size.

va·so·pres·sor, vas′ō·pres″ẽr, n. Adrenalin or other substances producing a blood pressure rise by causing a constriction of artery muscles.—*a.*

vas·sal, vas′al, n. [O.Fr. Fr. *vassal*, < M.L. *vassallus*, < *vassus*, servant, retainer, vassal; < Celtic.] In the feudal system, a person holding lands under the obligation to render military service or its equivalent to his superior; a feudal tenant; a subject, follower, or retainer; a servant or serf.—*a.* —**vas·sal·age,** vas′a·lij, n. The state of being a vassal; homage or service due from a vassal to his superior; dependence, subjection, or servitude; a territory held by a vassal; a body of vassals.

vast, vast, väst, a. [Fr. *vaste*, < L. *vastus*, waste, desert, vast, huge (hence, *vasto*, to lay waste, to *devastate*); allied to G. *wüste*, a desert.] Of great extent; boundless; huge in bulk and size; immense; very great in numbers or amount; very great as to degree or intensity.—*n. Poet.* A boundless waste or space; immensity.—**vast·ly,** *adv.* —**vast·ness,** *n.*—**vast·y,** vas′tē, vä′stē, a.— *vastier, vastiest. Poet.* vast.

vas·ti·tude, vas′ti·tõd″, vas′ti·tūd″, vä′- sti·tõd″, vä′sti·tūd″, n. [L. *vastitudo*.] Vastness or immensity; a vast expanse or space. Also **vas·ti·ty,** vas′ti·tē, vä′sti·tē.

vat, vat, n. [Also *fat*, a vat, < O.E. *faet*, a vat-D, *vat*, Icel. and Sw. *fat*, a vat, G. *fass*, a cask.] A large vessel for holding liquids, as a tank, tub, or cistern; *chem.* a liquid containing dye reduced to a soluble state.—*v.t.* —*vatted, vatting.* To put in a vat.

vat dye, n. *Chem.* any of a series of dyes which can be reduced to a soluble, usu. colorless form for impregnating fibers and can be regenerated into insoluble, fast colors by oxidation.—**vat-dyed,** *a.*

vat·ic, vat′ik, a. [L. *vates*, a prophet.] Of or pertaining to a prophet; prophetic; oracular. Also **vat·i·cal.**

Vat·i·can, vat′i·kan, a. [L. *Vaticanus*.] Of or pertaining to the palace of the popes or papal government.—*n.* The palace of the popes, situated on the Vatican Hill in Rome and including a library, art museum, living quarters, and offices; the papal power or government.—**Vat·i·can Coun·cil,** an ecumenical council of 1869–1870, that promulgated the dogma of papal infallibility.

Vat·i·can·ism, vat′i·ka·niz″um, n. *Usu. pejorative.* The doctrine of papal infallibility or supremacy; ultramontanism.— **Vat·i·can·ist,** *n.*

va·tic·i·nate, va·tis′i·nāt″, v.t., v.i.— *vaticinated, vaticinating.* [L. *vaticinor, vaticinatus*, to prophesy, < *vates*, a prophet.] To prophesy, or to practice prediction; to foretell.—**va·tic·i·nal,** va·tis′i·nal, a.— **vat·i·ci·na·tion,** vat″i·si·nā′shan, n.— **va·tic·i·na·tor,** n.

vaude·ville, vạd′vil, võd′vil, vạ′de·vil, n. [Fr. *vaudeville*, orig. a kind of song, for *chanson du vau de Vire*, 'song of the valley of Vire' (in Normandy).] A stage entertainment consisting of a number of individual acts, as singing, dancing, prestidigitation, comic sketches, and performances by animals, most popular in the U.S. from about 1890 to about 1930; sometimes, a light play or sketch with musical interludes; a satirical or topical ballad.—**vaude·vil·lian,** vạd·vil′yan, võd·vil′yan, vạ″de·vil′yan, n. One associated with vaudeville, esp. a performer or writer.

vault, vôlt, v.i. [O.Fr. *volter*, turn, leap, < It. *voltare*, turn, < L. *volutare*, freq. of *volvere*, roll, turn: cf. *revolt*.] To leap or spring, as over something; to leap with the aid of the hands supported on something, as a brace or pole.—*v.t.* To leap over, or clear by jumping, as an obstacle.—*n.* The

vault

act or an act of bounding with the aid of the hands supported on something.—**vault·er**, *n.*—**vault·ing**, *a.* Of or pertaining to the sport of a vaulter; as, a *vaulting* pit or pole; jumping or leaping over; *fig.* overreaching, as a desire to succeed.

vault, vạlt, *n.* [O.Fr. *volte, voute* (Fr. *voûte*), < M.L. *volta,* < L. *volvere* (pp. *volutus*), roll, turn; cf. *volute.*] An arched structure, commonly made of stones or bricks, usu. forming a ceiling or roof; something resembling an arched roof; as, the *vault* of heaven; an arched space, chamber, or passage, esp. one underground; an underground chamber, as a cellar or a division of a cellar; a chamber or structure, usu. wholly or partly underground, for receiving the bodies of the dead; any room specially constructed for the safekeeping of things; a cavern or natural cavity, as in a glacier; *anat.* an arched roof of a cavity.—*v.t.* To construct or cover with a vault; to make in the form of a vault; to arch; to set or extend over like a vault.—**vault·ed**, *a.* Constructed or covered with a vault, as a building, chamber, or passage; made in or having the form of a vault or vaults, as below the surface of the ground.—**vault·ing**, *n.* Vaulted construction; the act or art of constructing a vault or vaults.

vaunt, vạnt, vänt, *v.i.* [< Fr. *vanter,* to vaunt, < L.L. *vanitare,* to boast, < L. *vanus,* vain.] To boast; to talk with ostentation; to brag; to glory; to exult.—*v.t.* To boast of; to display or put forward boastfully.—*n.* A boastful display; a brag.—**vaunt·er**, *n.*—**vaunt·ful**, *a.*—**vaunt·ing·ly**, *adv.*

vaunt-cour·i·er, vạnt′kụr″ē·ẽr, vänt′kụr″ē·ẽr, *n. Archaic,* a precursor or a herald.

vav·a·sor, vav′a·sor″, vav′a·sạr″, *n.* [O.Fr. *vavassor,* L.L. *vavassor, vasvassor,* probably a contr. of *vassus vassorum,* the vassal of vassals.] In the feudal system, a vassal holding lands of a great lord, and having vassals subordinate to him. Also **vav·a·sour,** vav′a·sụr″.

va·ward, vä′wạrd″, vou′ạrd, *n. Archaic,* vanguard.

V-Day, vē′dā″, *n.* A day on which final military victory is achieved, formalized, or celebrated.

've, *ve.* Contraction of have, used in compounds, as: *I've* seen it before.

veal, vēl, *n.* [O.Fr. *veel* (Fr. *veau*), calf, < L. *vitellus,* dim. of *vitulus,* calf: cf. *vellum* and *wether.*] The flesh of the calf as used for food. A calf, esp. as intended or used for food; also **veal·er,** vē′lẽr.

vec·to·graph, vek′to·graf″, vek′to·gräf″, *n.* A composite picture of two superimposed images which is viewed as three-dimensional through polarized lenses.—**vec·to·graph·ic,** *a.*

vec·tor, vek′tẽr, *n.* [L. a bearer or carrier, < *veho,* to carry.] An entity which has direction as well as magnitude, such as a force or velocity; a line segment that represents an entity; *aeron.* the direction of an object, such as an airplane or missile from one point to another, usu. in a given interval of time; *med.* a carrier of a disease-producing microorganism, as an insect. —**vec·to·ri·al,** vek·tōr′ē·al, vek·tạr′ē·al, *a.*

vec·tor prod·uct, *n. Math.* a vector whose magnitude is equal to the product of the magnitudes of any two given vectors and the sine of the angle between their positive directions. Also **cross prod·uct.**

vec·tor sum, *n. Math.* the resultant vector equivalent to two or more vectors occurring simultaneously, which for any two vectors has the magnitude and direction of the diagonal of the parallelogram formed when the vectors are placed so as to issue from a common point.

Ve·da, vā′da, vē′da, *n.* [Skt., < *vid,* to know; cogn. L. *video,* E. *wit,* to know.] The complete body of sacred Hindu writings, divided into four distinct collections: the Rig-Veda, containing praises and hymns, the Sama-Veda, containing chants, the Yajur-Veda, containing prayers, and the Atharva-Veda, containing spells and incantations; also **Ve·das.** Each of the four distinct collections.—**Ve·da·ic,** vi·dā′ik, *a.*—**Ve·da·ism,** vā′da·iz″um, vē′da·iz″um, *n.*

ve·da·lia, vi·dāl′ya, vi·dā′lē·a, *n. Entom.* a ladybug, *Rodolia cardinalis,* in the beetle order, native to Australia, having been brought into several other countries for the control of scale or plant-sucking insects.

Ve·dan·ta, vi·dän′ta, vi·dan′ta, *n.* A system of Hindu philosophy based primarily upon the Upanishadic doctrine of the unifying relation between Atman, man's individual soul, and Brahman, the world soul or supreme spirit.—**Ve·dan·tic,** *a.*—**Ve·dan·tism,** *n.*—**Ve·dan·tist,** *n.*

ve·dette, ve·det′, *n.* [Fr. *vedette,* < It. *vedetta,* a vedette, < *vedere,* L. *videre,* to see.] *Nav.* a small boat used in scouting; also *vidette,* **ve·dette boat.** *Milit.* formerly, a sentinel on horseback; also *vidette.*

Ve·dic, vā′dik, vē′dik, *a.* Of or pertaining to the Veda or the Vedas, or its language; of or relating to Hindu culture or history between 1500 B.C. and 500 B.C.—*n.* The language of the Veda. Also **Ve·dic San·skrit.**

veep, vēp, *n.* [< V.P., an abbreviation.] *Colloq.* any vice-president.

veer, vẽr, *v.i.* [Fr. *virer,* to turn, veer, or tack; < L.L. *virare,* to turn, < L. *viria,* a ring, a bracelet; akin *environ.*] To shift or change direction, as the wind; to change the direction of its course by turning, as a ship; to turn around, vary, be otherwise minded: said in regard to persons, feelings, or intentions; *naut.* to turn into a different course.—*v.t. Naut.* To direct, as a ship, as into a different course; to wear or cause, as a ship, to change course.—*n.* A change in direction.—**veer·ing·ly,** *adv.*

veer, *v.t.* [D. *vieren,* let out (a cable, etc.).] *Naut.* to allow to run out to a greater extent, as a sheet, line, or cable.

veer·y, vẽr′ē, *n.* pl. **veer·ies.** [Perh. imit.] A cinnamon-brown thrush with a faintly spotted breast, *Hylocichla fuscescens,* of the eastern U.S. Also **Wil·son's thrush.**

veg·e·ta·ble, vej′ta·bl, vej′i·ta·bl, *n.* [O.Fr. *vegetable* (Fr. *végétable*) vegetable, < L.L. *vegetabilis,* animating, enlivening, < L. *vegetare.*] An herb whose fruit, shoots or stems, leaves, roots, or other parts are used for food, as the cucumber, asparagus, spinach, cabbage, beet, potato, and onion; the edible part of such a plant; loosely, any member of the plant kingdom; *fig.* a person having a passive and unthinking personality.—*a.* Of, consisting of, or made from vegetables; as, a *vegetable* diet; pertaining to or characteristic of plants; as, *vegetable* growth; derived from plants or some parts of plants; as, *vegetable* oils; consisting of or containing the substance or remains of plants; as, decomposing *vegetable* matter; of the nature of a plant; as, a *vegetable* organism; similar to the life of a plant, as passive or dull.—**veg·e·ta·bly,** vej′ta·blē, vej′i·ta·blē, *adv.*

veg·e·ta·ble but·ter, *n.* Any of various concrete fixed vegetable fats which are solid at ordinary temperatures.

veg·e·ta·ble i·vo·ry, *n.* The ivory nut's hard endosperm used in making buttons and other ornaments. See *ivory nut.*

veg·e·ta·ble mar·row, *n.* Any of the edible squashes of oblong shape; the fruit of this squash, as of the zuccini, used as a vegetable.

veg·e·ta·ble oil, *n.* An oil derived from fruit or plant seeds, having various uses in medicine, cooking, and as a lubricant.

veg·e·ta·ble silk, *n.* A silklike fiber obtained from various plants, esp. from the seedcoats of a S. American tree, *Chorisia speciosa,* used for stuffing pillows and similar purposes.

veg·e·ta·ble sponge, *n.* Any gourd of the genus *Luffa,* the dried, netlike interior of which may be used as a sponge, strainer, or dishcloth. Also *dishcloth gourd, loofa, loofah.*

veg·e·ta·ble tal·low, *n.* Any of several tallowlike, fatty substances of vegetable origin, used in making candles, soap, or the like.

veg·e·ta·ble wax, *n.* A wax or waxlike substance obtained from various plants, as the wax palm.

veg·e·tal, vej′i·tal, *a.* Having the characteristics or nature of a plant or vegetable; vegetative; pertaining to that class of vital functions common to plants and animals, as nutritive and growth processes.

veg·e·tar·i·an, vej″i·târ′ē·an, *n.* One who, for moral or nutritional reasons, abstains from eating meat, fowl, or fish, or in some instances any animal product, and instead lives solely on vegetables, grain, fruit, and nuts.—*a.* Of, characteristic of, or relating to vegetarians; advocating or dedicated to vegetarianism; consisting exclusively of vegetables.

veg·e·tar·i·an·ism, vej″i·târ′ē·a·niz″um, *n.* The theory, practices, and beliefs of a vegetarian.

veg·e·tate, vej′i·tāt″, *v.i.* —*vegetated, vegetating.* [L. *vegetatus,* pp. of *vegetare,* animate, enliven, quicken, < *vegetus,* lively, active, < *vegere,* move, excite, quicken: cf. *vigor.*] To grow in the manner of plants; to live in an inactive, passive, or unthinking way; *pathol.* to grow or increase by abnormal growth, as an excrescence.

veg·e·ta·tion, vej″i·tā′shan, *n.* [L. *vegetatio(n-).*] The act or process of vegetating; plant life collectively, esp. the plant life of an area or region; as, the *vegetation* of the mountaintops; an inactive, passive, or unthinking existence; *pathol.* an abnormal growth or excrescence.—**veg·e·ta·tion·al,** *a.*—**veg·e·ta·tion·less,** *a.*

veg·e·ta·tive, vej′i·tā″tiv, *a.* Growing or developing as or like plants; pertaining to or connected with vegetation or vegetable growth; noting or pertaining to those involuntary or unconscious bodily functions, such as growth or nutrition, as differentiated from *sexual reproduction;* not involving sexual reproductive processes; having the power to produce or support growth in plants; as, *vegetative* mold; inactive, passive, or unthinking; as, a *vegetative* way of life. Also **veg·e·tive,** vej′i·tiv.—**veg·e·ta·tive·ly,** *adv.*—**veg·e·ta·tive·ness,** *n.*

ve·he·mence, vē′e·mens, *n.* [Fr. *véhémence,* L. *vehementia.*] The character or quality of being vehement; violent ardor; fervor; violence. Also **ve·he·men·cy.**

ve·he·ment, vē′e·ment, *a.* [Fr. *véhément,* < L. *vehemens, vehementis,* eager, vehement, lit. 'carried out of one's mind,' < *veho,* to carry, and *mens, mentis,* the mind.] Characterized by impetuosity of feeling; fervent or passionate; acting with great force or energy; as, *vehement* wind or fire; energetic; violent; very forcible.—**ve·he·ment·ly,** *adv.*

ve·hi·cle, vē′i·kl, *n.* [L. *vehiculum,* a vehicle, a carriage, < *veho,* to carry (seen also in *inveigh, vehement*) < a root seen also in E. *wagon, way.*] Any means of transporting something from one place to another, as on wheels, tracks, or runners; a conveyance; an instrument of transmission

---

a- fat, fāte, fär, fâre, fạll;   **e-** met, mē, mẽre, hẽr;   **i-** pin, pīne;   **o-** not, nōte, mōve;   **u-** tub, cūbe, bụll;   **oi-** oil;   **ou-** pound.

or communication, as: Language is a *vehicle* for conveying ideas. *Med.* an innocuous substance used as a medium for medical ingredients; an excipient. *Paint.* a solution used for mixing pigments.—**ve·hic·u·lar**, vē·hik′ya·lẽr, *a.*

V-eight, vē′āt′, *a.* Of, pertaining to, or denoting an internal-combustion engine having two opposing banks of four cylinders apiece, set at an angle to one another in the form of an upright V.—*n.* A V-eight engine; an automobile with a V-eight engine.

veil, vāl, *n.* [O.Fr. *veile*, *voile* (Fr. *voile*), < L. *vela*, pl. of *velum*, covering, curtain, veil, sail: cf. *velum* and *voile*.] A piece of light and usu. transparent material worn over the head to protect, conceal, or decorate the face; a piece of material worn so as to fall over the head and shoulders on each side of the face, as the outer part of the headdress of a nun; the vows made or the life chosen by a novice or nun; something that covers, screens, or conceals; as, a *veil* of smoke; a mask, disguise, or pretense; as, the criminal's *veil* of honesty; *biol.* a velum; *dial.* a caul.—*v.t.* To cover or conceal with or as with a veil; to hide the real nature of, mask, or disguise.—*v.i.* To wear a veil.—**take the veil**, to become a nun.

veiled, vāld, *a.* Having or covered with a veil; wearing a veil; concealed or hidden with a veil; as, a *veiled* woman; not openly expressed; as, a *veiled* threat; indistinct or muffled; as, a *veiled* noise.

veil·ing, vā′ling, *n.* The act of covering or concealing with a veil; a veil; material for making veils.

vein, vān, *n.* [O.Fr. Fr. *veine*, < L. *vena*, vein.] One of the system of branching vessels or tubes conveying blood from various parts of the body to the heart; loosely, any blood vessel; a nervure of an insect's wing; one of the strands or bundles of vascular tissue forming the principal framework of a leaf; a body of ore or coal with definite boundaries; as, a *vein* of gold; a lode; a body or mass of igneous rock or deposited mineral occupying a crevice or fissure in rock; a small natural channel or watercourse within the earth; the water running through such a watercourse; a streak or marking, as of a different shade or color, running through marble, wood, or other natural material; a particular state of mind, humor, or mood; a strain or intermixture of some quality traceable in character, conduct, or writing; a particular style of language or expression; as, in a poetic *vein*; some line or course suggestive of a vein.—*v.t.* To furnish with veins; to mark with lines or streaks suggesting veins; to extend over or through in the manner of veins.—**vein·al**, *a.*—**vein·y**, vā′nē, *a.*—**veinier**, **veiniest**.

veined, vānd, *a.* Having or showing veins; characterized by venation; streaked.

vein·ing, vā′ning, *n.* An arrangement of veins or veinlike markings.

vein·let, vān′lit, *n.* A smaller vein branching off from a large vein.

vein·stone, vān′stōn″, *n.* Gangue.

ve·la·men, vē·lā′min, *n.* pl. **ve·lam·i·na**, vē·lam′e·na. [L. *velare*, cover, E. *veil*, *v.*] *Anat.* a membranous covering; a velum. *Bot.* the thick, spongy integument or epidermis covering the aerial roots of epiphytic orchids.—**ve·la·men·tous**, *a.*

ve·lar, vē′lẽr, *a.* Of or pertaining to a velum or veil, esp. of the palate; *phon.* produced with the tongue near or touching the soft palate.—*n.*

ve·lar·i·um, vē·lâr′ē·um, *n.* pl. **ve·lar·i·a**, vē·lâr′ē·a. An awning stretched over an ancient Roman theater or amphitheater, these buildings being open to the sky.

ve·lar·ize, vē′la·rīz″, *v.t.*—*velarized*, *velar-*

izing. *Phon.* to produce, as a vowel, with velar sounds or articulation.

ve·late, vē′lit, vē′lāt, *a.* [L. *velatus*, pp. of *velare*, E. *veil*, *v.*] *Biol.* having a velum.—**ve·la·tion**, vē·lā′shan, *n.*

veld, **veldt**, velt, felt, *n.* [D. *veld*.] The open country, bearing grass, bushes, or shrubs, or thinly forested, characteristic of southern Africa.

vel·i·ta·tion, vel″i·tā′shan, *n.* [L. *velites*, light-armed soldiers.] A skirmish; a slight controversy.

vel·le·i·ty, ve·lē′i·tē, *n.* pl. **vel·le·i·ties**. [Fr. *velléité*, < L. *velle*, to will.] *Philos.* Volition in the weakest form; a slight wish or inclination toward a thing.

vel·lum, vel′um, *n.* [O.Fr. *veelin* (Fr. *vélin*), < *veel*, calf, E. *veal*.] A fine parchment, usu. of treated kidskin or calfskin, used for writing, printing, painting, and binding; a manuscript on such parchment; a kind of paper resembling such parchment.—*a.*

ve·lo·ce, ve·lā′che, *adv. Mus.* in a quick tempo.—*a.*

ve·loc·i·pede, ve·los′i·pēd″, *n.* [< L. *velox*, and *pes*, *pedis*, a foot.] A light vehicle or conveyance, usu. two- or three-wheeled, and driven or impelled by the feet of the rider, esp. a bicycle or tricycle of an early type; a tricycle for a child; a handcar, esp. the type used on tracks on a railroad.

ve·loc·i·ty, ve·los′i·tē, *n.* pl. **ve·loc·i·ties**. [Fr. *vélocité*, < L. *velocitas*, < *velox* (*veloc-*), swift.] Rapidity of motion or operation; swiftness; quickness. *Mech.* the rate of motion; the change of position of a point per unit of time; the rate of motion in which direction as well as speed is considered.

vel·ours, **vel·our**, ve·lʊr′, Fr. ve·lör′, *n.* pl. **vel·ours**, ve·lʊrz′. [Fr. *velours*, L. *villosus*.] A velvety fabric with a nap or pile used in making overcoats, upholstery, hats, or the like.

ve·lou·té, ve·lö·tā′, *n.* [Fr.] *Cookery*, a smooth white sauce made with chicken or veal stock. Also **ve·lou·té sauce**.

ve·lum, vē′lum, *n.* pl. **ve·la**, vē′la. [N.L. use of L. *velum*, curtain, veil: cf. *veil*, *n.*] *Biol.* any of various veillike membranous coverings or partitions; *anat.* the soft palate.

ve·lure, ve·lʊr′, *n.* Velvet or a similar fabric; a silk or velvet pad with which to smooth or brush a silk hat.—*v.t.*—*velured*, *veluring*. To brush or smooth with a velure.

ve·lu·ti·nous, ve·löt′i·nus, *a.* [N.L. *velutinus*, < M.L. *velutum*, velvet.] Having a soft, velvety surface, as certain plants.

vel·vet, vel′vit, *n.* [M.E. *velvet*, *veluett*, *velwet*: cf. O.Fr. *velve*, *velvel*, *velute* (M.L. *velutum*), velvet, *velut*, velveteen, *velu*, *velut*, hairy, shaggy, having the pile of velvet, ult. < L. *villus*, shaggy hair, nap: cf. *velours*.] A fabric of silk, cotton, nylon, or rayon, having a thick, soft pile formed of warp thread loops either cut at the outer end or left uncut, and a plain backing; something likened to the fabric velvet, as in softness; the soft deciduous covering of a growing antler. *Slang*, money gained through gambling or speculation; clear gain or profit.—*a.* Made of or covered with velvet; also **vel·vet·ed**. Resembling velvet; also **vel·vet·like**.

vel·vet ant, *n.* Any brightly colored wasp of the family *Mutillidae*, members of which are covered with downy hairs and resemble ants in appearance.

vel·vet·een, vel″vi·tēn′, *n.* A cloth made of cotton having a short pile in imitation of velvet; *pl.* clothes, usu. men's trousers, made or fashioned of velveteen.—*a.* Made or fashioned of velveteen; as, a *velveteen* dress.

vel·vet sponge, *n.* The commercial name of a large, soft sponge, *Hippospongia gossypina*, found off the shores of the West Indies.

vel·vet·y, vel′vi·tē, *a.* Resembling velvet; smooth, soft, or delicate in texture; smooth or mellow tasting, usu. said of liquors; as, *velvety* bourbon.

ve·na, vē′na, *n.* pl. **ve·nae**, vē′nē. [L.] *Anat.* a vein.

ve·na ca·va, vē′na kā′va, *n.* pl. **ve·nae ca·vae**, vē′nē kā′vē. [L., 'hollow vein.'] *Anat.* either of two large veins discharging into the right atrium of the heart.

ve·nal, vēn′al, *a.* [L. *venalis*, < *venus*, *venum*, sale: cf. *vend*.] Purchasable like merchandise, as things not properly bought and sold; as, *venal* votes; ready to sell one's services or influence basely or unscrupulously; accessible to bribery; corruptly mercenary; characterized by venality.—**ve·nal·i·ty**, vē·nal′i·tē, ve·nal′i·tē, *n.*—**ve·nal·ly**, *adv.*

ve·nat·ic, vē·nat′ik, *a.* [L. *venaticus*, < *venatus*, hunting, < *venari*, hunt.] Of, used in, or pertaining to hunting. Also **ve·nat·i·cal**.—**ve·nat·i·cal·ly**, *adv.*

ve·na·tion, vē·nā′shan, ve·nā′shan, *n.* [< L. *vena*, a vein.] *Biol.* the manner in which veins are arranged, as in leaves or insect wings.—**ve·na·tion·al**, *a.*

vend, vend, *v.t.* [< L. *vendo*, to sell, < *venum*, sale, and *do*, to give.] To sell, often by peddling; to express publicly, as ideas or opinions; to publish.—*v.i.* To sell merchandise, often as a peddler; to be bought or sold.

ven·dace, ven′dis, ven′dās, *n.* pl. **ven·dac·es**, **ven·dace**. [O.Fr. *vendese*, Fr. *vandoise*, the dace; origin unknown.] A finely flavored whitefish, *Coregonus vandesius*, found in some lakes of Great Britain and Sweden.

vend·ee, ven·dē′, *n. Law.* The person to whom a thing is sold; purchaser; buyer.

vend·er, ven′dẽr, *n.* One who or that which vends or sells; a seller; any vending machine. Also **vendor**.

ven·det·ta, ven·det′a, *n.* [It., < L. *vindicta*, revenge.] Any prolonged and vehement dispute, rivalry, or feud; a blood feud in which the nearest of kin executes vengeance on the murderer of a relative.

vend·i·ble, ven′di·bl, *a.* Capable of being sold; salable; marketable.—*n.* Usu. pl. vendible items.—**vend·i·bil·i·ty**, **vend·i·ble·ness**, *n.*—**vend·i·bly**, *adv.*

vend·ing ma·chine, *n.* A coin-operated, mechanical device which sells gum, candy, or other small articles.

ven·di·tion, ven·dish′an, *n.* [L. *venditio(n-)*, < *vendere*, E. *vend*.] The act of vending or selling; sale.

ven·dor, ven′dẽr, ven·dar′, *n.* Vender.

ven·due, ven·dö′, ven·dū′, *n.* [O.Fr. *vendue*, < *vendre*, to sell.] A sale by public auction.

ve·neer, ve·nēr′, *n.* [< G. *furnier*, a veneer, *furnieren*, to veneer, < Fr. *fournir*, to furnish (which see).] A thin piece of wood or other substance laid upon a less valuable surface; one of the many thin pieces of wood joined together to construct plywood; a superficial appearance or show; as, to hide one's shortcomings under a *veneer* of self-confidence; *building*, a facing of some substance, as stone or brick, superimposed on a less durable or ornamental surface, as wood.—*v.t.* To overlay or face, as a surface, with veneer for decoration or protection; to cover, as something unattractive or displeasing, with a more desirable surface; to join together, as pieces of wood, to construct plywood; to conceal with a superficial appearance.—**ve·neer·er**, *n.*

ve·neer·ing, ve·nēr′ing, *n.* The act or process of applying veneer; the material utilized as veneer; the surface resulting from the use of veneers.

ven·er·a·ble, ven′ẽr·a·bl, *a.* [L. *venerabilis*.] Worthy of veneration or reverence, because of high character or office; used in the Anglican Church as a title for an archdeacon; in the Roman Catholic Church used as the title for those who have attained the first degree in the process of canonization; commanding respect by reason of age and dignity of appearance; hallowed by religious, historic, or other lofty associations, as places, buildings, or cities; impressive or interesting from age or antique appearance; as, a *venerable* castle; aged, old, or ancient: used ironically.—**ven·er·a··bil·i·ty**, **ven·er·a·ble·ness**, *n.*—**ven·er·a·bly**, *adv.*

ven·er·ate, ven′e·rāt″, *v.t.*—**venerated**, *venerating*. [L. *veneror*, *veneratus*, to venerate, < the stem of *Venus*, *Veneris*, *Venus*, love; allied to Skt. *van*, to worship, to love.] To regard with respect and reverence; to revere.—**ven·er·a·tor**, *n.*

ven·er·a·tion, ven″e·rā′shan, *n.* [L. *veneratio*.] An act expressing reverence; a feeling of high respect and reverence; the state or condition of being venerated.

ve·ne·re·al, ve·nēr′ē·al, *a.* [L. *venereus*, < *Venus*: see *venery*.] Of or pertaining to venery; arising from or connected with sexual intercourse with an infected person; as, *venereal* diseases; pertaining to diseases so arising; adapted to the cure of such diseases; as, a *venereal* remedy; infected with or suffering from venereal disease.

ve·ne·re·al dis·ease, *n. Pathol.* any disease contracted from an infected person by means of sexual intercourse. Abbr. *V.D.*

ve·ne·re·ol·o·gy, ve·nēr″ē·ol′o·jē, *n.* An area of medical science concerned with studying and treating venereal disease. Also **ven·er·ol·o·gy**, ven″e·rol′o·jē.—**ve··ne·re·ol·o·gist**, *n.*

ven·er·y, ven′e·rē, *n.* pl. **ven·er·ies**. [M.E. *venerie*, < *Venus* (*Vener-*), Venus (goddess of love), also, sexual love, venery.] *Archaic*, the gratification of sexual desire.

ven·er·y, ven′e·rē, *n.* pl. **ven·er·ies**. [Fr. *vénerie*, < O.Fr. *vener*, L. *venari*, to hunt, whence also *venison*.] *Archaic*. The act or practice of hunting; the sport of the chase.

ven·e·sec·tion, ven″i·sek′shan, vē″ni·sek′shan, *n.* [L. *vena*, vein, and *sectio*, a cutting.] Phlebotomy. Also **ven·i·sec·tion**.

Ve·ne·tian, ve·nē′shan, *a.* Relating to Venice, its residents, or its culture.—*n.* A resident or native of Venice.

Ve·ne·tian blind, *n.* A blind, as one hung on a window, made of thin, narrow transverse slips of wood, metal, or the like, so connected as to overlap each other when closed, and to show a series of open spaces for the admission of light and air when in the open position.

Ve·ne·tian glass, *n.* Fine, ornate, often colored glass tableware, vases, and the like, made in Italy, mostly in or around Venice.

Ve·ne·tian red, *n.* A burnt ocher or red pigment whose color comes from iron oxide; a dark reddish-orange color.

Ven·e·zue·lan, ven″i·zwā′lan, ven″i·zwē′lan, *Sp.* be″ne·swe′län, *a.* Of or pertaining to Venezuela.—*n.* An inhabitant of Venezuela, a republic in S. America.

venge, venj, *v.t.*—**venged**, *venging*. [O.Fr. *vengier* (Fr. *venger*), < L. *vindicare*, avenge.] *Archaic*, to avenge.

ven·ge·ance, ven′jans, *n.* [O.Fr. Fr. *vengeance*.] The avenging of a wrong or injury; retribution; revenge.—**with a ven·ge·ance**, with extreme force or violence; with surprising or disconcerting effect.

venge·ful, venj′ful, *a.* Showing vindictiveness; retributive; revengeful.—**venge·ful·ly**, *adv.*—**venge·ful·ness**, *n.*

V-en·gine, vē·en′jin, *n.* An internal-combustion engine with pairs of cylinders arranged in a 'V' configuration.

ve·ni·al, vē′nē·al, vēn′yal, *a.* [L. *venialis*, < L. *venia*, pardon; akin to *Venus* (which see).] Excusable; trivial; *theol.* that may be forgiven or pardoned, as a sin: opposed to *mortal*.—**ve·ni·al·i·ty**, **ve·ni·al·ness**, *n.*—**ve·ni·al·ly**, *adv.*

ven·in, ven′in, vē′nin, *n. Biochem.* any one of the poisonous constituents of snake venom.

ven·i·punc·ture, **ven·e·punc·ture**, ven′i·pungk″chèr, vē′ni·pungk″chèr, *n. Med.* the puncturing of a vein, either for intravenous medication or feeding, or for drawing a blood sample for analysis.

ve·ni·re fa·ci·as, vi·nī′rē fā′shē·as″, *n.* [L. 'that you cause to come.'] *Law*, a writ directed to a sheriff requiring him to summon citizens to jury duty. Also **ve·ni·re**.

ve·ni·re·man, vi·nī′rē·man, *n.* pl. **ve·ni·re·men**. *Law*, one of the jurors summoned under a writ of venire facias.

ven·i·son, ven′i·son, ven′i·zen, *Brit.* ven′zen, *n.* [O.Fr. *venison* (Fr. *venaison*), < L. *venatio*, a hunting, < *venari*, to hunt (whence *venery*, hunting).] Deer flesh as it is used as human food.

Ve·ni·te, vi·nī′tē, *n.* [L., 2d pers. pl. impv. of *venire*, come: being the first word of the psalm in Latin.] The 95th psalm, 94th in the Vulgate and Douay, used as a canticle at matins or morning prayer; a musical setting of this psalm.

ven·om, ven′om, *n.* [O.E. *venim*, *venime*, O.Fr. *venim*, *venin*, Mod.Fr. *venin*, < L. *venenum*, poison.] The poisonous fluid secreted by certain animals and introduced into the bodies of other animals by biting, as in the case of snakes, and stinging, as in the case of scorpions, wasps, or bees. *Fig.* spite; malice; malignity. *Rare*, any poisonous substance.—*v.t. Archaic*, to envenom.

ven·om·ous, ven′o·mus, *a.* Provided with a venom-producing gland or glands; as, a *venomous* insect; capable of causing a poisonous bite or sting; full of venom. *Fig.* malignant, malicious, or spiteful; as, a *venomous* denunciation.—**ven·om·ous·ly**, *adv.*—**ven·om·ous·ness**, *n.*

ve·nose, vē′nōs, *a.* Having numerous branched veins, as leaves; venous.

ve·nos·i·ty, vi·nos′i·tē, *n.* The state or quality of being venous or venose.

ve·nous, vē′nus, *a.* [L. *venosus*, < *vena*, a vein.] Of, pertaining to, or full of veins; *physiol.* pertaining to the blood that is traveling back to the heart through veins, characterized by the absence of oxygen and the presence of carbon dioxide, and of a darker color than arterial blood.—**ve·nous·ly**, *adv.*—**ve·nous·ness**, *n.*

vent, vent, *n.* [< Fr. *vent*, wind, air, < L. *ventus*, wind (in *ventilate*), so that the original meaning would be airhole; or same as *fent*.] A small aperture, outlet, or opening; a hole for the release or elimination of something, as a vent for carbon monoxide and dioxide resulting from coal or natural gas combustion; a flue, exhaust passage, or pipe; a slit, as in a back seam in a piece of clothing; a means of expression; as, giving *vent* to anger; *zool.* the external excretory opening, as the anus, esp. in birds and fish.—*v.t.*—**vented**, *venting*. To let out; to give passage to; to emit; to release, as a repressed feeling or emotion; to pour forth; to utter; to excrete.

vent·age, ven′tij, *n.* [< Fr. *vent*, L. *ventus*, wind.] A small hole, as of a flute.

ven·tail, ven′tāl, *n.* [Fr. *ventail*, L.L. *ventaculum*, < L. *ventus*.] The movable front section of a medieval helmet located below the visor.

ven·ter, ven′tèr, *n.* [L., belly, womb; in legal use, through A.Fr. *ventre*.] *Anat.*, *zool.* The abdomen or belly; a bellylike cavity or concavity, as of bones; a bellylike

protuberance, as of muscles; *law*, the womb, or a wife or mother as a source of offspring.

ven·ti·late, ven′ti·lāt″, *v.t.*—**ventilated**, *ventilating*. [L. *ventilo*, *ventilatum*, to winnow, to ventilate, < *ventus*, wind; same root as Skt. *vâ*, to blow, E. *wind*.] To supply with fresh air for and remove vitiated air from, as an office building; to combine with oxygen, as blood in the lungs in breathing; to blow through and make fresh the air of, as a sea breeze; to expose to the free passage of air or wind; to open up for mutual or public consideration; to let be freely discussed; to provide with a small opening or vent, as for the removal of noxious gases.—**ven·ti·la·tive**, ven′ti·lā″tiv, *a.*—**ven·ti·la·tor**, ven′ti·lā″tèr, *n.*—**ven·ti·la·to·ry**, ven′ti·la·tōr″ē, ven′ti··la·tar″ē, *a.*

ven·ti·la·tion, ven″ti·lā′shan, *n.* [L. *ventilatio*.] The act of ventilating; the condition of being ventilated; the operation and equipment involved in supplying confined places, as buildings or mines, with the necessary quantity of fresh air; public examination or discussion of questions or topics.

ven·tral, ven′tral, *a. Anat.* belonging or pertaining to the belly or the abdomen, or to the surface of the body opposite to the dorsal or back side; *bot.* situated on or being the under or lower side, as of a leaf.—*n.* A ventral fin.—**ven·tral·ly**, *adv.*

ven·tral fin, *n.* One of a pair of fins on the underside of a fish.

ven·tri·cle, ven′tri·kl, *n.* [L. *ventriculus*, dim. of *venter*, belly.] *Anat.* Any of various hollow organs or parts in an animal body, esp. one of the two cavities of the heart which receives the blood from the auricles and propels it into the arteries; one of a series of connecting cavities of the brain, continuous with the central cavity of the spinal cord.—**ven·tric·u·lar**, ven·trik′ya··lèr, *a.*

ven·tri·cose, ven′tri·kōs″, *a.* [L. *ventricosus*.] Swelled out, esp. unequally on one side; possessing a protruding abdomen.—**ven·tri·cos·i·ty**, ven″tri·kos′i·tē, *n.*

ven·tric·u·lus, ven·trik′ya·lus, *n.* pl. **ven·tric·u·li**, ven·trik′ya·lī″. A hollow organ for digestion, esp. a bird's gizzard or an insect's stomach.

ven·tril·o·quism, ven·tril′o·kwiz″um, *n.* [L. *ventriloquus*, a ventriloquist—*venter*, and *loquor*, to speak, the notion being that the voice proceeded from the belly.] The act, art, or practice of speaking or uttering sounds with barely visible lip movement, by employing the vocal chords in such a manner that the voice appears to come not from the actual speaker, but from some distant source. Also **ven·tril·o·quy**, ven··tril′o·kwē,—**ven·tri·lo·qui·al**, ven″tri·lo′kwē·al, *a.*—**ven·tri·lo·qui·al·ly**, *adv.*

ven·tril·o·quist, ven·tril′o·kwist, *n.* One who practices or is skilled in ventriloquism.—**ven·tri·lo·quis·tic**, *a.*

ven·tril·o·quize, ven·tril′o·kwīz″, *v.i.*, *v.t.*—**ventriloquized**, *ventriloquizing*. To produce, as words or vocal sounds, by employing ventriloquism.

ven·ture, ven′chèr, *n.* [Abbrev. of *aventure*, old form of *adventure*, < Fr. *aventure*, L. *ad*, to, and *venturus*, about to come, < *venio*, to come (seen also in *advene*, *advent*, *convene*, *convent*, *covenant*, *event*, *invent*, *prevent*, *revenue*, etc.).] An undertaking of chance, danger, or hazard, esp. a commercial speculation; that which is risked or exposed to hazard, as funds or property.—*v.t.*—**ventured**, *venturing*. To expose to hazard; to risk; to undertake or run the risk and danger of; to brave; to offer or express, risking denial, objection, or censure.—*v.i.* To dare; to undertake or run a risk.—**at a**

ven·ture, at random; by chance.—**ven·-tur·er**, *n.*

ven·ture cap·i·tal, *n. Econ.* money invested, or earmarked for investment in speculative businesses, esp. in stocks of new corporations. Also *risk capital.*

ven·ture·some, ven'chĕr·som, *a.* Inclined to undertake or court hazard or risk; venturous; daring; involving or accompanied by risk.—**ven·ture·some·ly**, *adv.*—**ven·-ture·some·ness**, *n.*

Ven·tu·ri tube, ven·tur'ē tōb", *n.* A device or contrivance which measures the flow of a fluid, consisting of a tube constricted in the middle and flared at the ends which operates on the principle that the fluid's velocity will increase and its pressure will decrease while passing through the constricted section of the tube; *mech.* a similar section in a carburetor which draws fuel by the suction it creates.

ven·tur·ous, ven'chĕr·us, *a.* Daring; bold; intrepid; adventurous; risky; dangerous.—**ven·tur·ous·ly**, *adv.*—**ven·tur·ous·ness**, *n.*

ven·ue, ven'ō, ven'ū, *n.* [Fr. *venue*, a coming, < *venir*, L. *venire*, to come.] *Law.* The locality in which cause for legal action occurs; the locality or county in which a case is tried and from which a jury is impaneled; the part of a declaration designating the county where a particular action is pending.

ven·ule, ven'ūl, *n.* [L. *venula*, a small vein.] A small vein; any of the tiny branches of a vein in an insect's wing. Also **vein·ule.**—**ven·u·lar**, *a.*

Ve·nus, vē'nus, *n.* [L. *Venus, Veneris* (hence *venereal*), cogn. with O.E. *wine*, Icel. *vinr*, O.G. *wini*, a friend, Skt. *van*, to love, to worship.] *Astron.* the second planet from the sun and sixth largest in the solar system; *Rom. mythol.* the goddess of love and beauty, often identified with the Greek goddess, Aphrodite; *poet, colloq.* a beautiful woman.—**Ve·nu·si·an**, ve·nō'sē·an, ve·nō'shē·an, ve·nō'shan, ve·nū'sē·an, ve·nū'shē·an, ve·nū'shan, *a., n.*

Ve·nus's-fly·trap, vē'nu·siz·flī'trap", *n.* An insectivorous plant, *Dionaea muscipula*, of the sundew family, and a native of southeastern U.S., having leaf blades with spiny margins which close when certain hairs are touched, entrapping insects. Also **Ve·nus fly·trap.**

Ve·nus's-hair, vē'nu·siz·hâr, *n.* A delicate maidenhair fern, *Adiantum capillus-veneris*, having brown or black stipes. Also **Ven·us·hair.**

ve·ra·cious, ve·rā'shus, *a.* [L. *verax, veracis*, < *verus*, true.] Habitually disposed to speak truth; characterized by truth; true; exact; accurate.—**ve·ra·cious·ly**, *adv.*—**ve·ra·cious·ness**, *n.*

ve·rac·i·ty, ve·ras'i·tē, *n. pl.* **ve·rac·i·ties.** Habitual regard to or observance of truth; truthfulness; agreement with actual fact; exactness or precision; a truth.

ve·ran·da, ve·ran·dah, ve·ran'da, *n.* [Pg. *varanda*, < Skt. *varanda*, a veranda, < *vri*, to cover.] A kind of open portico, usu. having a roof, and attached to the outside of a building; a porch.

ve·rat·ri·dine, ve·ra'tri·dēn", ve·ra'tri·din, *n.* [< *veratrine.*] *Chem.* an amorphous alkaloid, $C_{36}H_{51}O_{11}N$, occurring with veratrine in the seeds of the sabadilla.

ver·a·trine, ver'i·trēn", ver'i·trin, *n.* [L. *veratrum*, hellebore.] *Chem.* a poisonous alkaloid, $C_{32}H_{49}NO_9$, found in sabadilla seeds, and formerly used as an external application in treating neuralgia and rheumatism. Also **ve·ra·tri·a, ve·rā'trē·a, ve·ra'trē·a.**

verb, vụrb, *n.* [Fr. *verbe*, < L. *verbum*, a word, a verb; same root as E. *word.*] *Gram.* that part of speech whose essential function

is to express existence, action, or occurrence; a particular word or phrase that functions as a verb, as *be, eat up, perceive. Ling.* a linguistic form identifiable on the basis of certain morphological and syntactic criteria, as various inflections that indicate person, tense, aspect, voice, or mood, and syntactic position relative to other units of meaning.

ver·bal, vụr'bal, *a.* [O.Fr. Fr. *verbal*, < L.L. *verbalis*, < L. *verbum*, word, verb.] Of, pertaining to, or consisting of words; pertaining to or concerned with words only, rather than ideas, facts, or realities; as, a *verbal* solecism; expressed in spoken words; oral; as, a *verbal* agreement; corresponding word for word; verbatim; as, a *verbal* translation; *gram.* of, pertaining to, or derived from a verb; as, a *verbal* noun or *verbal* auxiliary.—*n. Gram.* a part of speech derived from a verb, that functions as a noun, as a gerund or infinitive, or as an adjective, as a present or past participle, but retains some of its original characteristics. Also *verbid.*—**ver·bal·ly**, *adv.*

ver·bal·ism, vụr'ba·liz"um, *n.* Representation of an idea by means of words; the phrasing of such an expression; a verbal expression lacking meaning; undue stress on wording over meaning.

ver·bal·ist, vụr'ba·list, *n.* One proficient in word usage; one who shows a preference for words over ideas or actuality.—**ver·bal·is·tic**, *a.*

ver·bal·ize, vụr'ba·līz", *v.t.*—*verbalized, verbalizing.* To express in spoken or written language; to articulate; *gram.* to convert into a verb.—*v.i.* To use words in excess; to be verbose; to express something in spoken or written language.—**ver·bal·i·za·tion**, *n.*—**ver·bal·iz·er**, *n.*

ver·bal noun, *n. Gram.* a noun obtained or derived from a verb and usu. sharing with it its sense and construction, as many English gerunds and infinitives.

ver·ba·tim, vĕr·bā'tim, *adv., a.* [L.] Word for word; in the same words.

ver·be·na, vĕr·bē'na, *n.* [N.L. use of L. *verbena*, usu. pl., *verbenæ*, leaves or branches used in ceremonies, also plants used as cooling remedies: cf. *vervain.*] Any plant of the genus *Verbena*, characterized by elongated spikes of sessile flowers.—**ver·be·na·ceous**, vụr"be·nā'shus, *a.* Pertaining to any plant of the vervain family *Verbenaceae.*

ver·bi·age, vụr'bē·ij, *n.* [Fr.] The use of excessive or unnecessary words; verbosity.

ver·bid, vụr'bid, *n.* Verbal.

ver·bi·fy, vụr'bi·fī", *v.t.*—*verbified, verbifying. Gram.* to convert into or use as a verb.—**verb·i·fi·ca·tion**, *n.*

ver·bose, vĕr·bōs', *a.* [L. *verbosus.*] Abounding in words; using or containing more words than are necessary; wordy; prolix.—**ver·bose·ly**, *adv.*—**ver·bose·ness, ver·bos·i·ty**, vĕr·bos'i·tē, *n.*

ver·bo·ten, vĕr·bōt'en, G. fĕr·bōt'en, *a.* [G., pp. of *verbieten*, forbid.] *G.* Forbidden, as by law; prohibited.

ver·bum sap, vụr'bum sap'. [Abbr. for L. *verbum sapienti sat est.*] A word to the wise is sufficient; enough said. Also **ver·bum sat**, vụr'bum sat'.

ver·dant, vụr'dant, *a.* [Fr. *verdir*, to grow green, O.Fr. *verd*, green L. *viridis*, green.] Green with herbage or foliage; covered with growing plants or grass; green in color or hue; inexperienced or naïve.—**ver·dan·cy**, *n.*—**ver·dant·ly**, *adv.*

verd an·tique, verde an·tique, vụrd'an·tĕk', *n.* [Fr., < *verd*, green, *antique*, ancient.] *Mineral.* An aggregate of serpentine and white crystallized marble having a greenish color; a green porphyry used as marble.

ver·der·er, ver·de·ror, vụr'dĕr·er, *n.*

[A.Fr. *verderer*, for *verder*, O.Fr. *verdier*, < M.L. *viridarius*, < L. *viridis*, green.] An English judicial officer in charge of the royal forests.

ver·dict, vụr'dikt, *n.* [L.L. *verdictum*; *veredictum*, < L. *vere*, truly, and *dictum*, something declared, < *dico, dictum*, to say.] *Law*, the answer of a jury given to the court concerning any matter committed to their examination and judgment. A decision, judgment, or opinion.

ver·di·gris, vụr'di·grēs", vụr'di·gris, *n.* [O.Fr. *verdegrice, vert de Grece* (Fr. *vert-de-gris*), 'green of Greece.'] A green or bluish-green poisonous compound, a basic acetate of copper, used as a pigment, drug, or the like; a green or bluish coating formed on copper, brass, or bronze surfaces exposed to the air for a long time.

ver·din, vụr'din, *n. Ornith.* a tiny titmouse with a yellow head, *Auriparus flaviceps*, found in northern Mexico and the southwestern section of the U.S.

ver·di·ter, vụr'di·tĕr, *n.* [O.Fr. *verd* (Fr. *vert*) *de terre*, 'green of earth.'] Either of two pigments, consisting usu. of carbonate of copper made by crushing blue verditer or azure and green verditer or malachite.

ver·dure, vụr'jĕr, *n.* [Fr. *verdure*, greenness, green vegetation; < *verd, vert*, green, < L. *viridis*, green.] Greenness or freshness of vegetation; green plants or foliage; a flourishing condition; vigor.—**ver·dured**, *a.*—**ver·dur·ous**, vụr'jĕr·us, *a.* Covered with verdure; verdant.—**ver·dur·ous·ness**, *n.*

verge, vụrj, *n.* [O.Fr. Fr. *verge*, < L. *virga*, a slender green branch, switch, rod.] The edge, rim, or margin of something; the limit or point beyond which something begins or occurs; as, on the *verge* of total collapse; a limiting belt, strip, or border of something; the grass edging of a bed or border, as in a garden; the edge of a structural part or similar object; space within boundaries; room or scope; an area or district subject to a particular jurisdiction; a rod, wand, or staff, esp. one carried as an emblem of authority or as a sign of office; *hist.* an area or district in England, being the compass of the jurisdiction of the Marshalsea Court and embracing the royal palace; *print.* a triggerlike device for releasing the matrices of a Linotype machine; *horol.* the spindle of a balance wheel of a watch. *Arch.* the edge of the tiling projecting over the gable of a roof; the shaft portion of a column.—*v.i.*—*verged, verging.* To be on the verge or border; to touch at the border; to border on or approach.

verge, vụrj, *v.i.*—*verged, verging.* [L. *vergere*, bend, incline.] To incline, slope, turn, or extend in course or direction; to tend, used with *to* or *toward.*

ver·ger, vụr'jĕr, *n. Brit.* An attendant who bears the verge or staff of office before a bishop, dean, or other dignitary; the official who takes charge of the interior of a church, esp. during the service; an usher.

Ver·gil·i·an, Vir·gil·i·an, vĕr·jil'ē·an, vĕr·jil'yan, *a.* Of or pertaining to the Latin poet Virgil or his works.

ver·glas, ver·glä', *n. pl.* **ver·glases**, ver·glä', ver·gläz'. A thin sheet or film of ice, esp. on rock.

ve·rid·i·cal, ve·rid'i·kal, *a.* [L. *veridicus=verum*, truth, and *dico*, to say.] Veracious; telling the truth; truthful; real or genuine. Also **ve·rid·ic.**—**ve·rid·i·cal·ly**, *adv.*

ver·i·fi·ca·tion, ver"i·fi·kā'shan, *n.* [Fr. *vérification.*] The act of verifying or the state of being verified; a formal assertion of the truth of something; ascertainment of correctness, as by examination or comparison; *law*, a short confirmatory affidavit at the end of a pleading or petition.—**ver·i·fi·ca·tive, ver·i·fi·ca·to·ry**, *a.*

ver·i·fy, ver'i·fī″, v.t.—verified, verifying. [Fr. vérifier, < L. verus, true, and facio, to make.] To prove to be true; to confirm; to establish the truth of; to examine or test the correctness or authenticity of. Law, to assert under oath; to append a confirmation to.—**ver·i·fi·a·bil·i·ty**, **ver·i·fi·a·ble·ness**, n.—**ver·i·fi·a·ble**, a.—**ver·i·fi·er**, n.

ver·i·ly, ver'i·lē, adv. [< very.] Archaic. In truth; certainly; really.

ver·i·sim·i·lar, ver″i·sim'i·lėr, a. [L. verisimilis—verus, true, and similis, like.] Having the appearance of truth; probable; likely.—**ver·i·sim·i·lar·ly**, adv.

ver·i·si·mil·i·tude, ver″i·si·mil'i·tŏd″, ver″i·si·mil'i·tūd″, n. [L. verisimilitudo.] The appearance of truth; anything having only the semblance of truth; probability; likelihood.

ver·ism, vĕr'iz·um, ver'iz·um, n. A theory or style in the creation of a work of art, esp. grand opera, holding that truth and realism are a part of art and often using contemporary material, as opposed to romanticism.—**ver·ist**, n., a.—**ve·ris·tic**, a.

ver·i·ta·ble, ver'i·ta·bl, a. [Fr. véritable.] True; agreeable to truth or fact; real; actual.—**ver·i·ta·ble·ness**, n.—**ver·i·ta·bly**, adv.

ver·i·ty, ver'i·tē, n. pl. **ver·i·ties**. [Fr. vérité, < L. veritas, < verus, true.] The quality of being true or real; reality; truth; fact; a true assertion or tenet.

ver·juice, vur'jŏs″, n. [Fr. verjus, < verd, vert, L. viridis, green, and jus, juice.] An acid liquor derived from crab apples, unripe grapes, and other green fruits, orig. used for culinary and other purposes; sourness or acidity of temper, manner, or expression.

ver·meil, vur'mil, n. [Fr. vermeil.] A bright red, as the color of vermilion; metal that is gilded, as silver, copper, or bronze.—a. Bright red or vermilion in color.

ver·mi·cel·li, vur″mi·sel'ē, vur″mi·chel'ē, n. [It., lit. 'little worms,' pl. of vermicello, < L. vermiculus, dim. of vermis, a worm.] A certain food paste or pasta made of wheat flour in the form of long, slender threads, thinner than, but similar to spaghetti.

ver·mi·cide, vur'mi·sĭd″, n. [L. vermis, a worm, and caedo, to kill.] A substance which kills or destroys worms; med. an agent or drug which is used to destroy intestinal worms, esp. those which are parasitic.—**ver·mi·cid·al**, a.

ver·mic·u·lar, vėr·mik'ya·lėr, a. [< L. vermiculus, a little worm, dim. of vermis, a worm.] Pertaining to worms; resembling a worm, esp. in shape or movement; having wormlike, wavy tracks; vermiform.

ver·mic·u·late, vėr·mik'ya·lit, vėr·mik'ya·lāt″, a. Wormlike in shape, markings, movement, or appearance; vermicular; squirming; winding; tortuous; worm-eaten. Also **ver·mic·u·lat·ed**, vėr·mik'ya·lā″tid.—vėr·mik'ya·lāt″, v.t.—vermiculated, vermiculating. To ornament or decorate with markings resembling winding or wavy worm tracks; to infest or overrun with worms.—**ver·mic·u·la·tion**, n.

ver·mic·u·lite, vėr·mik'ya·lĭt″, n. [L. vermiculus, and Gr. lithos, a stone.] Any of various complex hydrous silicates formed by alteration of the common micas, and used chiefly in thermal insulation.

ver·mi·form, vur'mi·fȧrm″, a. [L. vermis, and forma, form.] Having the shape of a worm; wormlike.

ver·mi·form ap·pen·dix, n. Anat., zool. a fingerlike vestigial appendage projecting from the end of the cecum, varying in length from three to six inches, and present in man and some other mammals. Also appendix.

ver·mi·fuge, vur'mi·fūj″, n. A medicine or agent that expels parasitic intestinal worms.—a. Also **an·thel·min·tic**, an″thel·min'-tik.

ver·mil·ion, **ver·mil·lion**, vėr·mil'yan, n. [Fr. vermillon, < vermeil, vermilion, red, < L. vermiculus (dim. of vermis, a worm), a little worm, the kermes insect, hence a scarlet color such as that obtained from the kermes insect.] The bright red pigment composed of mercuric sulfide, formerly obtained from cinnabar, now artificially made from a preparation of sulfur and mercury; a color similar to that of such a pigment.—a. Of the bright red color of vermilion.—v.t. To color as with or with vermilion.

ver·min, vur'min, n. pl. **ver·min**. [Fr. vermine, vermin, parasitic insects, < L. vermis, a worm (seen also in vermicular, vermilion, vermicelli, etc.) cogn. E. worm.] Any of certain undesirable, noxious small mammals, as rats or mice, and various parasitic insects, which are destructive to mankind and difficult to control; any obnoxious human being.—**ver·min·ous**, vur'mi·nus, a. Infested with, pertaining to, caused by, or characteristic of vermin.—**ver·min·ous·ly**, adv.

ver·miv·o·rous, vur·miv'ėr·us, a. [L. vermis, worm, and vorare, devour.] Feeding on worms, as certain birds.

ver·mouth, **ver·muth**, vėr·mŏth', Fr. veR·mŏt', n. [Fr. vermout, vermouth, < G. wermuth, absinthe.] A white wine spiced with aromatic herbs and used as an ingredient in cocktails and as an aperitif.

ver·nac·u·lar, vėr·nak'ya·lėr, a. [L. vernaculus, domestic, native, indigenous, < verna, a slave born in the master's house, a native.] Native or originating in the place of its occurrence or use, as language or words, as opposed to literary or learned language; expressed or written in the native language of a place, as literary works; using such a language, as a speaker or a writer; pertaining to such a language; native or peculiar to a place or to fashionable taste, as a style of architecture; noting the common animal or plant name rather than the scientific name.—n. The native speech or language of a place; the common language people use every day; the language or phraseology peculiar to a class or profession; the common animal or plant name rather than the scientific name.—**ver·nac·u·lar·ly**, adv.

ver·nac·u·lar·ism, vėr·nak'ya·la·riz″um, n. A vernacular word or expression; the use of the vernacular.

ver·nal, vur'nal, a. [L. vernalis, < ver, spring; cogn. Icel. vár, Dan. vaar, the spring; < root signifying to be bright, to burn, seen in Vesta, Vesuvius, etc.] Belonging to spring; appearing in spring; suggestive of spring; as, vernal temperatures; belonging to youth.—**ver·nal·ly**, adv.

ver·nal·ize, vur'na·lĭz″, v.t.—vernalized, vernalizing. To reduce the growth period of and hasten the blossoming or fruit production of, as of a plant, by exposing the bulb or seed to chilling temperatures.—**ver·nal·i·za·tion**, vur″na·li·zā'shan, n.

ver·na·tion, vėr·nā'shan, n. [L. verno, vernatum, to be spring-like.] Bot. the disposition of the leaves within the bud.

Ver·ner's law, vur'nėrz la′, n. [From Karl Verner, who developed this law in 1846.] Ling. a postulate or consonantal development of the Germanic languages, which recognized that the placement of the primary accent was responsible for variations from Grimm's law.

ver·ni·er, vur'nē·ėr, n. [From the inventor, Peter Vernier, of Brussels, who died 1637.] A small sliding scale parallel with some fixed scale, as on a barometer, theodolite, or other instrument, and used for measuring fractional parts of the divisions on the fixed graduated scale; also **ver·ni·er scale**. Mech. an accessory device used to achieve a higher level of adjustment accuracy in a precision apparatus.—a. Equipped with or having a vernier.

ver·ni·er cal·i·per, n. A caliper consisting of two L-shaped sliding pieces, the outer being calibrated with a graduated scale and the inner with a vernier scale.

Ver·o·nal, ver'o·nal, n. Pharm. barbital. (Trademark.)

ve·ron·i·ca, ve·ron'i·ka, n. [From a supposed female saint of the name of Veronica.] Bot. a genus Veronica, of subshrubs and herbs including the many species of speedwell.

ve·ron·i·ca, ve·ron'i·ka, n. [M.L. veronica (the cloth), Veronica (the saint), a name identical with L. Berenice, Macedonian Gr. Berenicē, for Gr. Pherenicē, < phérein, bear, and nicē, victory.] The representation of the face of Christ which, according to Christian tradition, was miraculously impressed on a cloth which St. Veronica offered to Him to wipe His brow as He carried His cross to Calvary; the cloth itself; any similar picture of Christ's face, as on a garment or ornament.

ver·ru·ca, ve·rŏ'ka, ve·rŏ'ka, n. pl. **ver·ru·cae**, ve·rŏ'sē, ve·rŏ'sē. Med. any wart; biol. any wartlike prominence or projection, as found on animals or the leaves of some plants.

ver·ru·cose, ver'u·kōs″, a. [L. verrucosus, warty, < verruca, a wart.] Warty; having little knobs or warts on the surface. Also **ver·ru·cous**, ver'u·kus.—**ver·ru·cos·i·ty**, ver″u·kos'i·tē, n.

ver·sant, vur'sant, n. [Fr., a slope shedding water, < verser, pour, overturn, < L. versare: see versed.] A slope of a mountain or mountain chain; the general slope of a country or region.

ver·sa·tile, vur'sa·til, Brit. vur'sa·tĭl″, a. [Fr. versatile, < L. versatilis, < versare, turn about: see versed.] Capable of or adapted for turning with ease from one to another of various tasks or subjects; variable or changeable, esp. in feeling, purpose, or policy; capable of being used in many ways; bot. attached at or near the middle so as to swing or turn freely, as an anther; zool. turning either forward or backward; as, a versatile toe of a bird.—**ver·sa·tile·ly**, adv.—**ver·sa·tile·ness**, **ver·sa·til·i·ty**, n.

vers de so·ci·é·té, ver'di sō″sē·i·tā′, Fr. veR de sa·syä·tā′, n. French, light verse treating contemporary fashions and frailties with wit and irony.

verse, vurs, n. [O.E. fers, also O.Fr. Fr. vers, < L. versus, furrow, line, verse, so called from the turning to begin a new furrow or line, < vertere, turn.] A stanza or associated group of metrical lines; a succession of metrical feet written or printed as one line; a particular type of metrical composition; as, iambic verse; twentieth-century verse; a piece of poetry; poem; metrical composition; poetry: opposed to prose; inferior or trivial metrical composition; doggerel; a short division of a chapter in the Bible, usu. one sentence or part of a long sentence; mus. a portion of an anthem or song to be sung by a single voice or by soloists rather than by the choir.—a.—v.i., v.t.—versed, versing. Archaic, to versify.

verse, vurs, v.t.—versed, versing. To cause to be thoroughly acquainted with or skilled in; to familiarize; to school: usu. followed by in.—versed, vurst, a.

versed sine, n. Trig. one minus the cosine of an angle. Also **ver·sine**, ver'sĭn, **ver·sin**, vur'sĭn.

ver·si·cle, vur'si·kl, n. [L. versiculus, dim. of versus.] A little verse; eccles. a short passage in a church service spoken or chanted by the priest or minister followed by a response by the people or congregation.—**ver·sic·u·lar**, vẽr·sik′ya·lẽr, *a.*

ver·si·col·or, *Brit.* **ver·si·col·our**, vur′si·kul″ẽr, *a.* [L. *versicolor*, < *vertere* (pp. *versus*), turn, and *color*, E. *color.*] Changeable in color; of various colors.

ver·si·fy, vur′si·fī″, *v.i.*—*versified*, *versifying.* [Fr. *versifier*, L. *versificare*—*versus*, a verse, and *facio*, to make.] To make verses. —*v.t.* To relate in verse; to turn into verse. —**ver·si·fi·er**, *n.*—**ver·si·fi·ca·tion**, vur″si·fi·kā′shan, *n.*

ver·sion, vur′zhan, vur′shan, *n.* [Fr. *version*, < M.L. *versio(n-)*, < L. *vertere*, turn.] A translation; (*often cap.*) a translation of the Bible or some part of it. A particular account or description, esp. as contrasted with another or others; a form or variant; as, an earlier *version* of an invention, the movie *version* of a novel. *Med.* the spontaneous or manual turning of a fetus in the uterus, as to facilitate delivery; a condition in which the uterus is turned from its normal position.—**ver·sion·al**, *a.*

vers li·bre, veR lē′bRe, *n. pl.* **vers li·bres.** *Fr.* free verse.—**vers-li·brist**, vâr·lē′brist, *n.*

ver·so, vur′sō, *n. pl.* **ver·sos.** [L., abl. of *versus*, pp. of *vertere*, turn.] *Print.* the back of a leaf, or the left-hand page of a book: opposed to *recto.* The reverse, back, or other side of some object.

verst, vurst, verst, *n.* A Russian measure of length equal to 1.067 kilometers or two-thirds of a mile.

ver·sus, vur′sus, *prep.* [M.L. *versus*, against, L. toward, prop. pp. of L. *vertere*, turn: cf. *-ward.*] *Law*, against, used to indicate an action brought by one party against another; *sports*, against, used to denote a contest between two teams or players. Contrasted with or considered as one of two alternatives; as, peace *versus* war. Abbr. *v.* or *vs.*

vert, vurt, *n.* [O.Fr. Fr. *vert*, < L. *viridis*, green.] *Brit. forest law*, everything bearing green leaves in a forest and capable of serving as cover for deer; the right to cut trees or shrubs in a forest. *Her.* the tincture green.

ver·te·bra, vur′te·bra, *n. pl.* **ver·te·brae**, ver′te·bras, vur′te·brē″. [L., joint, vertebra, < *vertere*, turn.] *Anat.*, *zool.* any of the bones or segments composing the spinal column in man and other vertebrates, consisting typically of a more or less cylindrical body and an arch with various processes, forming a foramen through which the spinal cord passes.

ver·te·bral, vur′te·bral, *a.* [N.L. *vertebralis.*] Of or pertaining to a vertebra or the vertebrae; spinal; composed of vertebrae, as the spinal column; having vertebrae, as an animal.—**ver·te·bral·ly**, *adv.*

ver·te·bral col·umn, *n.* Spinal column.

ver·te·brate, vur′te·brāt″, vur′te·brit, *a.* [L. *vertebratus.*] Having vertebrae, a backbone, a spinal column, or, in the embryo, a notochord; belonging to the *Vertebrata*, a division of animals, comprising fishes, amphibians, reptiles, birds, and mammals, all of which have a segmented spinal column.—*n.* A vertebrate animal.

ver·te·bra·tion, vur″te·brā′shan, *n.* A vertebrate development; a segmented backbone.

ver·tex, vur′teks, *n. pl.* **ver·tex·es**, **ver·ti·ces**, vur′ti·sēz″. [L. *vertex* (*vertic-*), a whirl, whirlpool, vortex, crown of the head (from the disposition of the hair there), pole of the heavens, summit, highest point, < *vertere*, turn: cf. *vortex.*] The highest point of something; the apex; the top; the summit, *anat.*, *zool.* the crown or top of the head; *astron.* the point of the heavens toward which a group of stars is oriented. *Geom.* the point, as in a triangle, which is opposite to and most distant from the base;

the point where the two sides of some angle or plane figure intersect; a point where three or more faces, sides, or edges of a polyhedron intersect.

ver·ti·cal, vur′ti·kal, *a.* [Fr. *vertical*, < L.L. *verticalis.*] Of, pertaining to, or situated at the vertex; being in a position or direction perpendicular to the plane of the horizon; upright; plumb; *anat.* pertaining or related to the top of the head; *bot.* having the blade in a perpendicular plane, as a leaf, so that neither of the surfaces can be called upper or under; *econ.* of or concerned with a consolidated group of businesses that handle the total process of manufacture and sale of some commodity.—*n.* A vertical line or plane; a vertical or upright position; a vertical element in any truss.—**ver·ti·cal·i·ty**, **ver·ti·cal·ness**, *n.*—**ver·ti·cal·ly**, *adv.*

ver·ti·cal cir·cle, *n. Astron.* a great circle of the celestial sphere, passing through the zenith and nadir of an observer and perpendicular to the horizon.

ver·ti·cal file, *n.* A group of clippings, pamphlets, and other ephemera, placed upright and which is kept, as in a library, for easy reference.

ver·ti·cal un·ion, *n.* Industrial union.

ver·ti·cil, vur′ti·sil, *n.* [N.L. *verticillus*, verticil, L. whorl of a spindle, dim. of L. *vertex*, a whirl.] *Biol.* a whorl or circle, as of leaves or hairs, arranged around a point on an axis.

ver·ti·cil·las·ter, vur″ti·si·las′tẽr, *n.* [N.L., < *verticillus*, E. *verticil.*] *Bot.* a cluster or false whorl of flowers formed of two nearly sessile cymes arising from the axils of two opposite leaves, as in many mints.—**ver·ti·cil·las·trate**, vur′ti·si·las″trāt, vur′ti·si·las″trit, *a.*

ver·tic·il·late, vẽr·tis′i·lit, vẽr·tis′i·lāt″, vur′ti·sil′āt, *a.* [N.L. *verticillatus*, < *verticillus*, E. *verticil.*] *Biol.* Disposed in or forming verticils or whorls, as flowers, leaves, hairs, or a shell; having flowers, leaves, hairs, or a shell so arranged or disposed, as in plants or animals. Also **ver·tic·il·lat·ed.**—**ver·tic·il·late·ly**, *adv.*—**ver·tic·il·la·tion**, vẽr·tis″i·lā′shan, *n.*

ver·tig·i·nous, vẽr·tij′i·nus, *a.* [L. *vertiginosus*, < *vertigo*, E. *vertigo.*] Whirling or rotary; as, *vertiginous* motion; affected with vertigo; liable to cause vertigo. *Fig.* apt to change quickly; marked by inconstancy or instability.—**ver·tig·i·nous·ly**, *adv.*—**ver·tig·i·nous·ness**, *n.*

ver·ti·go, vur′ti·gō″, *n. pl.* **ver·ti·goes**, **ver·tig·i·nes**, vẽr·tij′i·nēz″. [L. *vertigo* (*vertigin-*), a turning or whirling round, vertigo, < *vertere*, turn.] *Pathol.* A disordered condition in which an individual feels that he or his immediate environment is whirling about; dizziness.

ver·tu, vẽr·tö′, vur′tö, *n.* Virtu.

ver·vain, vur′vān, *n.* [O.Fr. Fr. *verveine*, < L. *verbena.*] Any plant of the genus *Verbena*, having elongated spikes of sessile flowers.

verve, vurv, *n.* [Fr.] Poetical or artistic vitality or enthusiasm; great spirit; energy; rapture; *archaic*, talent.

ver·vet, vur′vit, *n.* [Fr., < *vert*, green, and (*gri*)*vet*, grivet.] An African monkey, *Cercopithecus pygerythrus*, allied to the green monkey and the grivet, but distinguished by a rusty patch at the root of the tail.

ver·y, ver′ē, *adv.* [O.Fr. *verai* (Fr. *vrai*), ult. < L. *verus*, true.] In a high degree; extremely, or exceedingly; as, *very* soon, *very* tired; actually or truly, used as an intensive emphasizing superlatives or stressing identity or oppositeness; as, the *very* best thing to be done, in the *very* same place.—*a.*—*verier*, *veriest.* Precise or identical; as, the *very* thing you should not have

done; mere, as: The *very* thought is distressing. Sheer; as, to weep for *very* joy; actual; as, caught in the *very* act; true, genuine, or real; as, the *very* God; with emphatic or intensive force, being such in the true or full sense of the term, or absolute; as, the *very* heart of the matter; used as an intensive for emphasis of what is specified, as: The *very* ground trembled. *Archaic*, rightful or legitimate; truthful or veracious.

ver·y high fre·quen·cy, *n. Telecommunication*, the frequency band including wave frequencies between 30 and 300 megacycles per second. Abbr. *VHF.*

Ver·y light, *n.* [After Lieut. *Very*, the inventor.] *Milit.* a signal flare or light shot from a Very pistol.

ver·y low fre·quen·cy, *n. Telecommunication*, any radio frequency below 30 kilocycles. Abbr. *VLF.*

Ver·y pis·tol, *n. Milit.* a flare pistol having a relatively short barrel, used esp. for signaling.

Ver·y Rev·er·end, *n.* A title for high church officials, as superiors of religious houses and cathedral deans.

ve·si·ca, ve·sī′ka, *n. pl.* **ve·si·cae**, ve·sī′sē. [L., bladder, blister.] *Anat.* A bladder, esp. the urinary bladder; a sac.—**ves·i·cal**, ves′i·kal, *a.*

ves·i·cant, ves′i·kant, *n.* A blistering substance or agent; *chemical warfare*, any chemical agent that burns and blisters the skin and other tissue. Also **ves·i·ca·to·ry**, ves′i·ka·tōr″ē, ves′i·ka·tạr″ē, ve·sik′a·tōr″ē, ve·sik′a·tạr″ē, *pl.* **ves·i·ca·to·ries.**—*a.* Producing blisters.

ves·i·cate, ves′i·kāt″, *v.t.*—*vesicated*, *vesicating.* To raise vesicles or blisters on; to blister.—**ves·i·ca·tion**, ves″i·kā′shan, *n.*

ves·i·cle, ves′i·kl, *n.* [L. *vesicula*, dim. of *vesica*, bladder, blister.] A small bladderlike structure or cavity; a little sac or cyst; *anat.*, *zool.* a small bladder or bladderlike air cavity; *pathol.* a circumscribed elevation of the epidermis containing serous fluid; *geol.* a small, usu. spherical cavity in a rock or mineral, due to gas or vapor.

ve·sic·u·lar, ve·sik′ya·lẽr, *a.* Of or pertaining to vesicles; having the form of a vesicle; characterized by or consisting of vesicles.—**ve·sic·u·lar·ly**, *adv.*

ve·sic·u·late, ve·sik′ya·lit, ve·sik′ya·lāt″, *a.* Characterized by or covered with vesicles; of the nature of a vesicle.—**ve·sic′ya·lāt″**, *v.t.*, *v.i.*—*vesiculated*, *vesiculating.* To make or become vesiculate or vesicular.—**ve·sic·u·la·tion**, ve·sik″ya·lā′shan, *n.*

ves·per, ves′pẽr, *n.* [L., akin to Gr. *Hesperos*, the evening, the evening star; same root as *west.*] An evening bell, esp. one that calls to vespers; also **ves·per bell.** Evening worship or service; (*cap.*) the evening star; *archaic*, the evening.—*a.*

ves·per·al, ves′pẽr·al, *n. Eccles.* A book or part of a book which contains the chants and office for vespers; a protective covering placed on the altar when it is not in use to prevent the altar cloths from becoming soiled.

ves·pers, ves′pẽrz, *n. (Often cap.), eccles.* The sixth of the seven canonical hours, or the service for it, occurring in the late afternoon or the evening; a religious service held in the late afternoon or the evening; evensong.

ves·per·tine, ves′pẽr·tin, ves′pẽr·tīn″, *a.* [L. *vespertinus*, < *vesper*, evening.] Of, pertaining to, or occurring in the evening; *bot.* opening or expanding in the evening, as certain flowers; *zool.* appearing or flying in the early evening, as certain moths. Also **ves·per·ti·nal**, ves″pẽr·tīn′al.

ves·pi·ar·y, ves′pē·er″ē, *n. pl.* **ves·pi·ar·ies.** [< L. *vespa*, a wasp.] A nest or colony of social wasps.

---

ch- chain, G. na**ch**t;   **th-** T**H**en, **th**in;   **w-** **w**ig, **hw** as sound in **wh**ig;   **z-** **z**h as in a**z**ure, **z**eal.   *Italicized vowel* indicates schwa sound.

ves·pid, ves′pid, n. [N.L. *Vespidae*, pl., < L. *vespa*, wasp.] *Entom.* any member of the *Vespidae*, a widely distributed family of wasps, consisting of both the solitary and the social wasps, and including the hornets and yellowjackets, which live like bees in communities composed of males, females, and workers.—a.—**ves·pine**, ves′pin, vḗs′-pin, a.

ves·sel, ves′el, n. [O.Fr. *vessel, vaissel* (Fr. *vaisseau*), < L. *vascellum*, dim. of *vasculum*, small vessel, dim. of *vas*, vessel.] Any craft designed to move through water carrying persons or goods, esp. one larger than an ordinary rowboat; ship; airship; boat; a hollow or concave article, as a cup or tub, esp. for holding liquid; as, a drinking *vessel*; receptacle; container; *anat., zool.* a tube or duct, as an artery, vein, or the like, containing or conveying blood or some other bodily fluid; *bot.* a duct formed of connected cells which have permeable intervening partitions, as for containing or conveying sap. A person regarded as a receptacle or container or as made for some use or end; as, a *vessel* of holiness.

vest, vest, n. [Fr. *veste*, < It. *veste*, < L. *vestis*, garment, clothing; akin to E. *wear*.] A waistcoat, or short sleeveless garment worn by men under a suit coat reaching from the base of the neck down to or below the waistline; a similar garment, or a part of trimming simulating the front of such a garment, worn by women; *Brit.* an undershirt. *Archaic,* clothing; garment; dress; robe; a cassocklike, long, sometimes ecclesiastical vestment, popular during the reign of Charles II.—v.t. [O.Fr. *vestir* (Fr. *vêtir*), < L. *vestire*, clothe, < *vestis*.] To clothe, dress, or robe; to dress, as in ecclesiastical vestments; to invest formally, as with a garment or dress; to cover or drape, as an altar; to cover or surround, as if with, or like, a garment; to invest or endow, as a person, with something, esp. with powers or functions; to put or establish, as in the possession of something, or in some office or position; to place or settle, as something, esp. property, rights, or powers, in the possession or control of a person or persons, followed by *in.—v.i.* To put on vestments; to become vested in a person or persons, as a right; to pass into possession; to devolve upon a person as possessor.—**vest·like**, a. —**vest·less**, a.

Ves·ta, ves′ta, n. [L., akin to Gr. *Estia* (lit. 'hearth'), the Greek goddess Hestia, of like attributes.] Among the ancient Romans, the goddess of the hearth and hearth fire, worshipped in a temple containing an altar on which a sacred fire was kept perpetually burning under the care of vestal virgins; (*l.c.*), *Brit.* a short match of wax or wood.

ves·tal, ves′tal, a. [L. *Vestalis*.] Of or pertaining to Vesta; as, a *vestal* virgin; pertaining to, characteristic of, or resembling a vestal virgin; virgin; chaste.—n. A vestal virgin; a virgin; a chaste unmarried woman; a nun.

ves·tal vir·gin, n. One of the four, then later six, virgins consecrated to Vesta and to the service of watching the sacred fire on her altar and keeping it burning; a chaste woman.

vest·ed in·ter·est, n. A special interest in the continued existence of systems or institutions that confer or protect personal benefits or privileges; *usu. pl.* those whose favorable economic, political, or social position depends on the continued existence of current systems or institutions; *law,* a right or title that permits disposal of property, as by sale or gift, but postpones enjoyment or possession to some future time.

vest·ee, ves·tē′, n. Any decorative blouse-front worn by women to fill in a neckline or jacket opening; a dickey or vest, esp. one simulating a vest worn by men.

ves·ti·ar·y, ves′tē·er″ē, a. [L. *vestiarius*, a. (as n., *vestiarium*, neut. of *vestiarius*), < *vestis*, garment, clothing.] Of or pertaining to vestments, garments, or dress.—n. pl. **ves·ti·ar·ies.** A room or place for keeping garments or clothes, as a cloakroom or dressing room; a vestry.

ves·ti·bule, ves′ti·būl″, n. [Fr. *vestibule*, < L. *vestibulum*, entrance court before a house.] A hall or antechamber between the outer door and the interior of a building; lobby; an enclosed passage between railroad passenger cars; *anat., zool.* any of various cavities or channels regarded as forming an approach or entrance to another cavity or space; as, the *vestibule* of the ear.—v.t. *vestibuled, vestibuling.* To provide with a vestibule or vestibules; to unite by means of vestibules, as a train.—**ves·tib·u·lar,** ves·ti·bu·late, ve·stib′ya·lẽr, a.—**ves- ti·buled,** a.

ves·ti·bule school, n. A department of an industrial plant in which new employees are trained.

ves·tige, ves′tij, n. [Fr. *vestige*, < L. *vestigium*, footstep, footprint, trace.] A mark, trace, or visible evidence of something which is no longer present or in existence; as, the *vestiges* of a fire; a surviving evidence or memorial of some condition, practice, or the like; as, *vestiges* of a custom; a very slight trace or amount of something. *Biol.* a degenerate or imperfectly developed organ or structure having little or no utility, but which in an earlier stage of the individual or in ancestral forms performed a useful function.—**ves·tig·i·al,** ve·stij′ē·al, a.— **ves·tig·i·al·ly,** adv.

vest·ment, vest′ment, n. [O.Fr. *vestement* (Fr. *vêtement*), < L. *vestimentum*, clothing, garment, < *vestire*, clothe, E. *vest*, v.] A garment, esp. an outer garment, robe, or gown; an official or ceremonial robe; *fig.* something that clothes or covers like a garment. *Eccles.* one of the garments worn by the clergy and their assistants during divine service and on other ceremonial occasions; one of the garments worn by the celebrant, deacon, and subdeacon during the celebration of the Eucharist.—**vest·ment·al,** a. —**vest·ment·ed,** a.

vest-pock·et, vest′pok″it, a. Of a size that fits in a vest pocket; tiny; miniature; *fig.* relatively small; as, a *vest-pocket* battleship.

ves·try, ves′trē, n. pl. **ves·tries.** [M.E. *vestrye,* for *vestiarie,* E. *vestiary,* n.] *Eccles.* a room in a church building where vestments and the paraphernalia of worship are kept; sacristy; a room in a church building used as a chapel, for meetings, and for Sunday School. *Episcopal Ch.* an elective governing committee; *Ch. of Eng.* a meeting of parishioners for the dispatch of official business.—**ves·try·man,** ves′trē·man, n. pl. **ves·try·men.** A member of a vestry.

ves·ture, ves′chẽr, n. [O.Fr. *vesture.*] *Archaic,* garments; clothing; apparel; something that envelops or covers like a garment; covering. *Law,* everything except trees growing on the surface of land, as crops.— v.t.—*vestured, vesturing. Archaic.* To cover; to clothe.

ve·su·vi·an, ve·sō̄′vē·an, n. A kind of match or fusee, as for lighting cigars; *mineral.* vesuvianite.—a. (*Cap.*) Of, pertaining to, or resembling Mount Vesuvius, a volcano near Naples; volcanic.

ve·su·vi·an·ite, ve·sō̄′vē·a·nīt″, n. [< *vesuvian.*] *Mineral.* a basic silicate of aluminum and calcium, containing small amounts of iron and magnesium, commonly crystalline in form, and usu. of a brown to green color. Also *idocrase, vesuvian.*

vet, vet, n. *Colloq.* veterinarian.—v.t.— *vetted, vetting. Colloq.* to examine, treat, or provide care for as any veterinarian does; *Brit.* to examine or scrutinize as an expert. —v.i. *Colloq.* to practice veterinary medicine or surgery.

vet, vet, n., a. *Colloq.* veteran.

vetch, vech, n. [O.Fr. *veche, vesse,* Fr. *vesce,* It. *veccia,* < L. *vicia,* a vetch, cogn. Gr. *bikas,* a vetch. *Fitch* is another form.] Any of various usu. climbing leguminous plants, genus *Vicia,* allied to the bean, some of them, as the common vetch, *V. sativa,* cultivated for fodder for cattle and to build soil; a leguminous plant of Europe, *Lathyrus sativa,* grown for its edible seeds.— **vetch·like,** a.—**bit·ter vetch,** a species of vetch, *V. ervilia,* bearing poisonous seeds.

vetch·ling, vech′ling, n. Any of several small plants of the genus *Lathyrus,* esp. *L. pratensis,* in the legume family.

vet·er·an, vet′ẽr·an, vē′tran, n. [L. *veteranus,* < *vetus, veteris,* old; same root as Gr. (*v*)*etos,* a year, seen also in L. *vitulus,* a calf.] One who has become thoroughly experienced in a profession, occupation, or position through long service; one who has served his country in the armed forces, esp. in time of war.—a. Experienced through length of participation in a profession or activity; of or pertaining to former members of the armed forces. Abbr. *vet.*

Vet·er·ans Day, n. A national holiday observed in the U.S. on November 11, commemorating the end of World War I and honoring all veterans of the armed services; formerly, Armistice Day. Also *Vet·er·ans′ Day.*

vet·er·ans′ pref·er·ence, n. A special consideration in the civil service examination given an armed forces veteran applying for a job.

vet·er·i·nar·i·an, vet″ẽr·i·nâr′ē·an, ve″tri·nâr′ē·an, n. One who practices veterinary medicine or surgery. Abbr. *vet.* Also *vet.*

vet·er·i·nar·y, vet′ẽr·i·ner″ē, ve′tri·ner″ē, n. pl. **vet·er·i·nar·ies.** [L. *veterinarius,* < *veterinus,* belonging or pertaining to cattle.] A veterinarian.—a. Of or pertaining to the medical or surgical treatment of cattle, horses, and other animals, esp. those which are domesticated. Abbr. *vet., veter.*

vet·er·i·nar·y med·i·cine, n. The branch or division of medical science concerned with the prevention, diagnosis, treatment, and general study of the diseases of animals, esp. domesticated.

vet·er·i·nar·y sur·geon, n. *Brit.* veterinarian.

vet·i·ver, vet′i·vẽr, n. An East Indian grass, *Vetiveria zizanioides,* raised in many warm regions of the world for its aromatic roots, which are used in mat-making and as a source of an oil used in perfumes; this plant's root.

ve·to, vē′tō, n. pl. **ve·toes.** [L. *veto,* I forbid.] The executive power of governors and of the President of the U.S. to interdict a measure passed by their legislatures. A message or official paper stating the reasons of the President of the U.S. or other executive for refusing or vetoing a bill; also **ve·to mes·sage.** Any prohibition by an authority.—v.t.—*vetoed, vetoing.* To forbid; to interdict; as, to *veto* an act of legislature. —**ve·to·er,** n.

vex, veks, v.t. [O.Fr. Fr. *vexer,* < L. *vexare* (pp. *vexatus*), shake, disturb, molest, annoy.] To irritate, annoy, provoke, or make angry, esp. with trivial or petty irritations, as: His awkwardness *vexes* his friends. To torment, plague, or worry; to agitate, discuss, or debate, as a subject, with vigor, as: They *vexed* the issue. To disturb by motion, stir up, or throw into commotion, as: Storms *vex* the water.—**vex·er,** n.—**vex·ing·ly,** adv.

vex·a·tion, vek·sā′shan, *n.* The act of vexing or state. of being vexed; irritation; annoyance; that which or one who vexes; any cause of irritation, distress, or annoyance; affliction.

vex·a·tious, vek·sā′shus, *a.* Full of or causing vexation; vexing; annoying; harassing; *law,* instituted without sufficient grounds, and serving only to cause annoyance to the defendant, as of legal actions. —**vex·a·tious·ly,** *adv.*—**vex·a·tious·ness,** *n.*

vexed, vekst, *a.* Disturbed; irritated; troubled; annoyed; much discussed or disputed, as a question.—**vex·ed·ly,** vek′sid·lē, *adv.*—**vex·ed·ness,** vek′sid·nes, *n.*

vex·il·lar·y, vek′si·ler″ē, *n. pl.* **vex·il·lar·ies.** A member of a group of veteran soldiers in ancient Rome serving under a special standard; a standard-bearer.—*a. Bot.* pertaining to or having a vexillum; also **vex·il·lar.** Pertaining to an ensign or standard.

vex·il·lum, vek·sil′um, *n. pl.* **vex·il·la,** vek·sil′a. [L., standard, company, troop, < *vehere,* carry.] A military standard or flag carried by ancient Roman troops; a body of men serving under such a standard. *Bot.* the large upper petal of a leguminous flower; also *standard. Ornith., rare,* the web of a feather.—**vex·il·late,** vek′si·lit, vek′si·lāt″, *a.*

vi·a, vī′a, vē′a, *prep.* [L., a way or road.] By way of; as, to drive to California *via* the Grand Canyon in Arizona; *colloq.* by means of; as, to travel *via* airplane.

vi·a·ble, vī′a·bl, *a.* [Fr., likely to live, < *vie,* L. *vita,* life.] Capable of sustaining independent life, as of a normal newborn child; possessing the ability to grow and develop; as *viable* spores, seeds, or eggs; pertaining to an idea, design, or plan that will lead to a productive end result.— **vi·a·bil·i·ty,** *n.*—**vi·a·bly,** *adv.*

vi·a·duct, vī′a·dukt″, *n.* [L. *via,* way, and *ductus,* a leading, a duct.] A long bridge or series of arches conducting a railroad or road over a valley or other area of low level.

vi·al, vī′al, vīl, *n.* [A modification of *phial.*] A small glass vessel or bottle which holds liquids. Also *phial.*—*v.t.*—vialed, vialing, *Brit.* vialled, vialling. To keep or put in a vial.

vi·a me·di·a, vī′a mē′dē·a, L. wē′ä me′di·ä″, *n.* Latin, a middle way.

vi·and, vī′and, *n.* [Fr. *viande,* viands, food, < L.L. *vivanda,* provisions, < L. *vivo,* to live.] An item of food. *Usu. pl.* stocks of food; victuals; food, esp. of high quality.

vi·at·i·cum, vī·at′i·kum, *n. pl.* **vi·at·i·cums, vi·at·i·ca,** vī·at′i·ka. [L. *viaticus,* pertaining to a way or road, < *via,* way.] Provisions for a journey; in ancient Rome, a magistrate's travel allowance; *eccles.* the communion or eucharist given to a dying person.

vi·a·tor, vī·ā′tar, *n. pl.* **vi·a·to·res,** vī″a·tōr′ēz, vī″a·tar′ēz. One who travels; a wayfarer.

vi·brant, vī′brant, *a.* Vibrating; moving to and fro rapidly; vibrating so as to produce sound, as a string; of sounds, characterized by perceptible vibration; resonant; throbbing or pulsating with energy, vitality, or vigor.—**vi·bran·cy,** *n.*—**vi·brant·ly,** *adv.*

vi·bra·phone, vī′bra·fōn″, *n.* A musical instrument similar to the xylophone, but which has metal rather than wooden bars, and electric valved resonators to produce a vibrato. Also **vi·bra·harp,** vī′bra·härp″.— **vi·bra·phon·ist,** vī′bra·fō″nist, vī·brof′o·nist, *n.*

vi·brate, vī′brāt, *v.i.*—vibrated, vibrating. [L. *vibratus,* pp. of *vibrare,* shake, vibrate.] To move to and fro, as a pendulum; to oscillate; to move to and fro or up and down quickly and repeatedly; to quiver; to

tremble; of sounds, to produce or have a quivering or vibratory effect; to resound; to thrill, as in emotional response; to fluctuate, vacillate, or move between extremes. —*v.t.* To cause to move to and fro, to swing, or to oscillate; to cause to move to and fro or up and down quickly and repeatedly; to cause to quiver or shake tremulously; to give forth or emit, as sound, by or as by vibratory motion; to measure or indicate by vibration or oscillation; as, a pendulum *vibrating* seconds.

vi·bra·tile, vī′bra·til, vī′bra·tīl″, *a.* Capable of vibrating or being vibrated; having a vibratory motion; pertaining to or of the nature of vibration.—**vi·bra·til·i·ty,** vī″bra·til′i·tē, *n.*

vi·bra·tion, vī·brā′shan, *n.* [L. *vibratio(n-).*] The act or state of vibrating or being vibrated; a single vibrating motion; an oscillation; a quiver or tremor. *Phys.* the oscillating, reciprocating, or other stationary motion of a body forced from a position or state of equilibrium; the analogous motion of the particles of a mass, as of air, whose state of equilibrium has been disturbed, as in transmitting sound; a single complete motion of any of these kinds, from the position of equilibrium until the motion begins to repeat itself.—**vi·bra·tion·al,** *a.*

vi·bra·to, vi·brä′tō, vī·brä′tō, *n. pl.* **vi·bra·tos.** [It., pp. of *vibrare,* vibrate, < L. *vibrare.*] *Mus.* a pulsating effect, produced in singing by the rapid reiteration of emphasis on a tone, and on bowed instruments by a rapid change of pitch corresponding to the vocal tremolo.

vi·bra·tor, vī′brā·tèr, *n.* That which vibrates; any of various instruments or devices causing or having a vibratory motion or action; an electrical device which vibrates and is used for massage. *Elect.* an oscillator; an electromagnetic device for changing a direct current to an alternating or oscillating current.

vi·bra·to·ry, vī′bra·tōr″ē, vī′bra·tar″ē, *a.* Consisting in or belonging to vibration; causing to vibrate; vibrating; concerned with vibration. Also **vi·bra·tive.**

vib·ri·o, vib′rē·ō″, *n. pl.* **vib·ri·os.** [N.L., < L. *vibrare,* vibrate.] Any of the motile bacteria constituting the genus *Vibrio,* characterized by a lively motion and usu. having a comma or S shape.—**vib·ri·oid,** vib·ri·on·ic,** vib′rē·oid″, vib″rē·on′ik, *a.*

vib·ri·o·sis, vib″rē·ō′sis, *n. Veter. pathol.* a disease caused by the bacterium *Vibrio fetus,* which infects cattle and sheep.

vi·bris·sa, vī·bris′a, *n. pl.* **vi·bris·sae,** vī·bris′ē. [L. *vibrissae,* the hairs in the nostrils.] One of many stiff, long, bristle-like hairs located around the mouth and nostrils of many mammals, often performing the function of tactile organs, as a cat's whisker; one of many bristlelike feathers about the mouth of certain birds, as the flycatchers.—**vi·bris·sal,** *a.*

vi·bro·graph, vī′bro·graf″, vī′bro·gräf″, *n.* An instrument for measuring and recording vibrations. Also **vi·brom·e·ter,** vī·brom′i·tèr.

vi·bur·num, vī·bur′num, *n.* [L., the wayfaring-tree.] Any of several shrubs or small trees in the genus *Viburnum,* of the honeysuckle family, many of which are cultivated for ornament.

vic·ar, vik′èr, *n.* [Fr. *vicaire,* < L. *vicarius,* forming a substitute, < *vicis,* change (whence prefix *vice* in *viceroy,* etc., *vicissitude*).] *Anglican Ch.* the priest of a parish who receives only a small salary or stipend, while a layman or church corporation receives the main portion of tithes collected; a parish clergyman not holding the office of rector. *Prot. Episcopal Ch.* a clergyman who usu. has charge of a chapel but not the church proper; a bishop's deputy,

usu. in charge of a mission or church. *Rom. Cath. Ch.* a cleric who exercises an ecclesiastical office as a deputy or substitute for another. Any substitute in office; a representative.—**vi·car·i·al,** vī·kâr′ē·al, *a.*— **vic·ar·ship,** *n.*

vic·ar·age, vik′èr·ij, *n.* The position, duties, or benefice of a vicar; the house or residence of a vicar.

vic·ar ap·os·tol·ic, *n. pl.* **vic·ars ap·os-tol·ic.** *Rom. Cath. Ch.* a titular bishop who possesses no diocese, but who, by direct authority of the pope, exercises jurisdiction over a certain district, usu. where a see has not yet been established or where the succession has been interrupted.

vic·ar fo·rane, vik′èr fō·rān′, fa·rān′, *n. pl.* **vic·ars fo·rane.** *Rom. Cath. Ch.* a priest appointed by a bishop to supervise a section of the diocese containing several parishes; a dean.

vic·ar-gen·er·al, vik′èr·jen′èr·al, *n. pl.* **vic·ars-gen·er·al.** The official assistant of a bishop or archbishop, usu. a layman in the Anglican Church or a priest in the Roman Catholic Church, who serves as an administrative aid.

vi·car·i·ate, vī·kâr′ē·it, vī·kâr′ē·āt″, vī·kâr′ē·it, vī·kâr′ē·āt″, *n.* The office or authority of a vicar; a district under the charge of a vicar. Also **vic·ar·ate,** vik′èr·it, vik′a·rāt″.

vi·car·i·ous, vī·kâr′ē·us, vī·kâr′ē·us, *a.* [L. *vicarius.*] Performed or suffered for, or instead of, another; filling the place of another; serving as a substitute or deputy; delegated; felt or realized, as sensations or emotions, by imagining one is taking part in someone else's experiences; *physiol.* pertaining to a body organ assuming a function which it does not normally perform.—**vi·car·i·ous·ly,** *adv.*—**vi·car·i·ous·ness,** *n.*

Vic·ar of Christ, *n. Rom. Cath. Ch.* the pope, as the representative of Christ in matters of teaching and governing the church on earth.

vice, vīs, *n.* [Fr. *vice,* < L. *vitium,* vice, blemish, fault, error, crime, < root *vi,* to twist.] Any specific immoral or evil habit or practice; an inconsequential personal fault; foible; a defect or blemish; a physical imperfection or bad trick, as of a horse. (*Cap.*), *drama,* a stock character in English morality plays, usu. the instigator and butt of ribald and slapstick comedy; clown.

vi·ce, vī′sē, *prep.* [L. *vice,* in the room of, ablative of *vicis,* change, turn, etc., the stem being seen also in *vicar, vicissitude.*] In the place of; instead of; succeeding.

vice-ad·mi·ral, vīs′ad′mèr·al, *n. Navy,* an officer next in rank and command to the admiral.—**vice-ad·mi·ral·ty,** *n.*

vice chan·cel·lor, vice-chan·cel·lor, vīs′chan′se·lèr, vīs′chän′se·lèr, *n.* An officer who ranks next to a chancellor; a judge in the chancery courts assisting or substituting for the chancellor; an officer of a university serving as assistant to the chancellor.— **vice-chan·cel·lor·ship,** *n.*

vice con·sul, vice-con·sul, vīs′kon′sul, *n.* One who acts as substitute for a consul; a consul of subordinate rank.— **vice-con·su·lar,** *a.*—**vice-con·su·late,** *n.* —**vice-con·sul·ship,** *n.*

vice·ge·ren·cy, vīs·jēr′en·sē, *n. pl.* **vice-ge·ren·cies.** The office of a vicegerent; the district a vicegerent rules.

vice·ge·rent, vīs·jēr′ent, *n.* [Fr. *vicegerent* —*vice,* and L. *gerens, gerentis,* ppr. of *gero,* to act.] An officer who is deputized to exercise the powers of another; a substitute; one having a delegated power.—*a.*

vi·cen·ni·al, vī·sen′ē·al, *a.* [L. *viceni,* twenty, and *annus,* a year.] Lasting or continuing 20 years; happening once in every 20 years.

vice-pres·i·dent, vice pres·i·dent, vīs′-prez′i·dent, *n.* An officer next in rank to a president and assuming his duties in the event of the president's absence or incapacity; an officer, as in a large corporation, ranking below the president, and in charge of a specific department, function, or location; (*cap.*), *U.S. Govt.* the officer next in rank to, and elected at the same time as, the President, succeeding to the presidential office on the resignation, removal, death, or disability of the President. Abbr. *V.P., Vice-Pres., V. Pres.*—**vice-pres·i·den·cy,** *n.*—**vice-pres·i·den·tial,** *a.*

vice·re·gal, vīs·rē′gal, *a.* Pertaining to a viceroy.—**vice·re·gal·ly,** *adv.*

vice-re·gent, vīs′rē′jent, *n.* An individual delegated to act as deputy to a regent.—vīs·rē′jent, *a.*

vice·reine, vīs′rān, *n.* [Fr. *vice-reine,* < L. *vice* and Fr. *reine,* < L. *regina,* queen.] The wife of a viceroy; a woman exercising the powers of a viceroy.

vice·roy, vīs′roi, *n.* [Fr. *vice-roi,* < L. *vice* and Fr. *roi,* < L. *rex,* king.] One appointed to rule a country or province as the deputy of the sovereign; as, the *viceroy* of India; *entom.* a N. American butterfly, *Limenitis archippus,* of an orange-red color with black markings and closely resembling the monarch butterfly.—**vice·roy·al,** *a.*

vice·roy·al·ty, vīs·roi′al·tē, vīs′roi″al·tē, *n.* pl. **vice·roy·al·ties.** The dignity, office, or period of office of a viceroy; a country or province ruled by a viceroy. Also **vice·roy·ship.**

vice squad, *n.* A police unit charged with enforcement of laws dealing with public morality.

vi·ce ver·sa, vī′se vur′sa, vī′sē, vīs′, *adv.* [L.] Conversely; in reverse; with the terms or the case being reversed.

vi·chy·ssoise, vish″ē·swäz′, *n.* A creamed, usu. cold soup of potatoes flavored with onions or leeks.

vi·chy wa·ter, vish′ē wạ′tẽr, *n.* A naturally occurring mineral water coming from springs in Vichy, France; a similar, artificial or natural, mineral water. Also **Vi·chy, vi·chy.**

vic·i·nage, vis′i·nij, *n.* [O.Fr. *veisinage* (Fr. *voisinage*), neighborhood, < L. *vicinus,* neighboring, < *vicus,* a village, akin to Gr. (*v*)*oikos,* Skt. *veca,* a house.] Neighborhood or proximity; the place or places adjoining or near; the vicinity.

vic·i·nal, vis′i·nal, *a.* [L. *vicinalis,* < *vicinus.*] Belonging to a neighborhood or district; neighboring; adjacent; *crystal.* noting planes whose position varies very little from certain prominent fundamental planes which they replace.

vi·cin·i·ty, vi·sin′i·tē, *n.* pl. **vi·cin·i·ties.** [L. *vicinitas,* < *vicinus,* neighboring.] The adjoining district, space, or country; nearness in place; neighborhood; the quality of being near; propinquity; proximity.

vi·cious, vish′us, *a.* [O.Fr. *vitious* (Fr. *vicieux*), < L. *vitiosus,* < *vitium,* E. *vice.*] Addicted to or characterized by vice or immorality; depraved or profligate; given or disposed to evil; reprehensible, blameworthy, or wrong; as, a *vicious* practice; spiteful or malignant; as, *vicious* lies; unpleasantly severe or intense; as, a *vicious* headache; characterized or marred by faults or defects; as, *vicious* reasoning; having an ugly disposition; savage; as, a *vicious* temper.—**vi·cious·ly,** *adv.*—**vi·cious·ness,** *n.*

vi·cious cir·cle, *n.* A situation in which a solution to a problem begins a chain of progressively more difficult problems, each created by a solution to a previous problem; *logic,* a fallacy in which a premise is used to establish a proposition or define a term that is subsequently used to establish or define

the premise; *pathol.* a condition in which one disease causes or allows a second to develop that subsequently worsens the first.

vi·cis·si·tude, vi·sis′i·tõd″, vi·sis′i·tūd″, *n.* [L. *vicissitudo,* < *vicis,* a change.] A passing from one state or condition to another; *pl.* changes, esp. in regard to the affairs of life or the world. Mutation; an alternating or successive change, as from winter to spring and summer to fall.—**vi·cis·si·tu·di·nar·y, vi·cis·si·tu·di·nous,** vi·sis″i·tõd′i·nẽr″ē, vi·sis″i·tūd′i·nẽr″ē, *a.*

vic·tim, vik′tim, *n.* [Fr. *victime,* < L. *victima,* a victim, lit. 'a well-grown beast'; same root as *vigour, wax* (to grow).] A person destroyed, sacrificed, or injured by another, or by some condition or agency; one who is cheated or duped; a living being sacrificed to some deity, or in the performance of a religious rite.

vic·tim·ize, vik′ti·mīz, *v.t.*—*victimized, victimizing.* To make a victim of; to expose or subject to swindle or deception; to sacrifice.—**vic·tim·i·za·tion,** *n.*—**vic·tim·iz·er,** *n.*

vic·tor, vik′tẽr, *n.* [< L. *victus,* pp. *vincere* to conquer (seen also in *convince, evince, invincible, vanquish*).] One who wins or gains the advantage in a contest, struggle, or battle.—*a.*

Vic·tor, vik′tẽr, *n.* A communications code word to designate the letter V.

vic·to·ri·a, vik·tōr′ē·a, vik·tạr′ē·a, *n.* [L. *victoria,* E. *victory.*] A low, light, four-wheeled carriage with a folding top, a seat for two passengers, and a raised seat in front for the driver; a kind of touring car with a folding top, commonly covering only the rear seat.

vic·to·ri·a, vik·tōr′ē·a, vik·tạr′ē·a, *n.* A water lily, *Victoria amazonica,* a native of S. America, with leaves often over six feet in diameter, and white- to rose-colored nocturnal flowers.

Vic·to·ri·a Cross, *n. Brit.* a naval and military decoration awarded for exceptional bravery in the face of the enemy. Abbr. *V.C.*

Vic·to·ri·an, vik·tōr′ē·an, vik·tạr′ē·an, *a.* Of or pertaining to the time of Queen Victoria's reign over Great Britain, 1837–1901; exhibiting what are conceived to have been the prevalent morals, manners, and tastes of Queen Victoria's reign; prudish; narrow; pompous; hypocritical. Ornate; eclectic; massive; as, *Victorian* architecture.—*n.* One who lived during Queen Victoria's reign, esp. an author.—**Vic·to·ri·an·ism,** vik·tōr′ē·a·niz″um, vik·tạr′ē·a·niz″um, *n.*

vic·to·ri·ous, vik·tōr′ē·us, vik·tạr′ē·us, *a.* [Fr. *victorieux,* < L. *victoriosus.*] Having conquered or won victory in battle or contest; being victor; conquering; characterized by or indicating victory.—**vic·to·ri·ous·ly,** *adv.*—**vic·to·ri·ous·ness,** *n.*

vic·to·ry, vik′to·rē, *n.* pl. **vic·to·ries.** [L. *victoria.*] The defeat of an enemy in battle, or of an antagonist in a contest; the superiority or state of triumph gained in any contest or endeavor.

vic·tress, vik′tris, *n.* A female that conquers or is victor. Also **vic·trix,** pl. **vic·tri·ces.**

Vic·tro·la, vik·trō′la, *n.* A phonograph. (Trademark.)

vict·ual, *colloq.* **vit·tle,** vit′l, *n.* [O.Fr. *vitaille,* Fr. *victuaille,* < L.L. *victualia,* provisions, *victualis,* pertaining to food, < L. *victus,* food, < *vivo, victum,* to live.] (*Usu. pl.*) provisions of any kind. Food for human beings, prepared for eating.—*v.t.*—*victualed, victualing, Brit. victualled, victualling.* To supply or store with victuals; to provide with stores of food.—*v.i.* To store food or provisions; *archaic,* to eat.

vict·ual·er, *Brit.* **vict·ual·ler,** vit′a·lẽr, *n.*

One who furnishes victuals; a ship carrying provisions; *Brit.* an inn or tavern keeper.

vi·cu·ña, vi·kõ′na, vi·kū′na, vi·kõ′na, vi·kū′na, vi·kõ′nya, *n.* [Sp. *vicuña,* from native name.] A S. American ruminant, *Lama vicugna,* related to the llama, with soft, silken wool used for making fabrics; cloth made from vicuña wool or a substitute material. Also **vi·cu·na.**

vi·de, vī′dē, *L.* wē′de, *v. impv.* [L.] See: used in making reference to parts of a text. Abbr. *v.*

vi·del·i·cet, vi·del′i·sit, *L.* wi·dā′li·ket′, *adv.* [L., for *videre licet,* 'it is permitted to see.'] *Latin.* That is to say; namely. Abbr. *viz.*

vid·e·o, vid′ē·ō″, *a. Electron.* Of or pertaining to the conversion of certain electronic impulses into wave lengths that can be seen on a TV screen; connected with the display or presentation of such objects on a TV screen, as distinguished from *audio.*

vid·e·o, vid′ē·ō″, *n.* The visual component of TV, as distinguished from *audio.*

vid·e·o·gen·ic, vid″ē·ō·jen′ik, *a.* Telegenic.

vid·e·o tape, *n. TV,* magnetic tape that records the complete intelligence of a TV signal, both video impulses and synchronized audio impulses, and is available for instant replay. See *magnetic tape.*—*v.t.*—*video taped, video taping.* To record on video tape.

vi·dette, vi·det′, *n.* Vedette.

vid·i·con, vid′i·kon″, *n. TV,* a photoconductive electron tube that scans with an optical lens to collect discrete data for transmission, as a picture or configuration.

vi·du·i·ty, vi·dõ′i·tē, vi·dū′i·tē, *n.* Widowhood.

vie, vī, *v.i.*—*vied, vying.* [Contr. < old *envie, envye* (accent on last), < Fr. *envier,* to invite, to vie in games, < L. *invitare.*] To strive for superiority or to contend, used with *for* or *with.*—*v.t. Archaic,* to match or put forward in rivalry.—**vi·er,** *n.*

Vi·en·na sau·sage, vē·en′a sạ′sij, *n.* A thinly-cased, blunt-ended, small sausage of the frankfurter type, often served as an appetizer.

Vi·et·minh, vē″et·min′, vē·et″min′, vyet″-min′, *a.* Of or denoting a communist, nationalist, politico-military organization in Indochina that fought the Japanese invaders during World War II and the French colonialists afterwards under the leadership of Ho Chi Minh, a Vietnamese nationalist and communist who, after the partition of Viet Nam following the French defeat, became Premier of the People's Republic of North Vietnam. Also **Vi·et Minh.**—*n.* pl. **Vi·et·minh.** This politico-military organization; *pl.* members and supporters of this organization.

Vi·et·nam·ese, vē·et″nä·mēz′, vē·et″nä·mēs′, vē·et″na·mēz′, vē·et″na·mēs′, vyet″nä·mēz′, vyet″nä·mēs′, vyet″na·mēz′, vyet″na·mēs′, *a.* Of or pertaining to the countries of North or South Vietnam or their inhabitants.—*n.* pl.**Vi·et·nam·ese.** A native or an inhabitant of North or South Vietnam; the predominant language of Vietnam.

view, vū, *n.* [O.Fr. *veue* (Fr. *vue*), < *veü, veu,* L.L. participle *vidutus,* < L. *video, videre,* to see.] The act of looking, seeing, or beholding; a visual survey; power of seeing or perception; sight; range of vision; that which is viewed, seen, or beheld, as a sight, picture, or spectacle; a representation of a landscape or other scene; a mental survey; consideration; a particular manner of looking at things; judgment, opinion, or way of thinking; something looked toward or forming the subject of consideration; intention; purpose.—*v.t.* To see; to look on; to examine or inspect; to survey intellectually; to consider.—**in view,** in the scope of vision; under consideration, as an object or goal.—**in view of,** in consideration of; because of.—**on view,** openly presented for inspection or examination, as by the public. —**with a view to,** with the purpose or intention of; with the hope of; as, to act *with a view to* happiness.

view·er, vū′ėr, *n.* A person who views or watches anything, esp. television programs; an optical device for viewing photographic transparencies.

view hal·loo, *n. Fox hunting,* the shout uttered by a huntsman on seeing a fox break cover. Also **view hal·lo, view hal·-loa.**

view·less, vū′lis, *a.* Furnishing no view; having no opinion or point of view; *obs.* invisible.—**view·less·ly,** *adv.*

view·point, vū′point″, *n.* An opinion, attitude, or point of view; an observation point.

view·y, vū′ē, *a.*—*viewier, viewiest. Colloq.* Given to or full of fanciful or unpractical views; visionary; having an ostentatious appearance.

vi·ges·i·mal, vī·jes′i·mal, *a.* [L. *vigesimus, vicesimus,* twentieth, ordinal of *viginti,* twenty.] Pertaining to or based upon twenty; twentieth; proceeding by twenties.

vig·il, vij′il, *n.* [O.Fr. Fr. *vigile,* < L. *vigilia,* wakefulness, watch, < *vigil,* awake, alert, akin to *vigere,* be lively. WAKE.] A keeping awake for any purpose during the natural hours of sleep; a watch kept by night or at other times; a course or period of watchful attention; a period of wakefulness from inability to sleep. *Eccles.* a devotional watching, or keeping awake, during the customary hours of sleep; the eve, or day and night, before a church festival, esp. an eve which is a fast; *usu. pl.* a nocturnal devotional exercise or service, esp. on the eve of, or before, a church festival.

vig·i·lance, vij′i·lans, *n.* The state or quality of being vigilant; watchfulness; circumspection.

vig·i·lance com·mit·tee, *n. U.S. hist.* An extralegal body of volunteers organized to maintain order by the summary punishment of an offense or a crime, esp. in areas of the western territories where legal authorities were unsatisfactory or nonexistent; an organization of terrorists in the southern states who sought to maintain the subjugation of Negroes through intimidation and violence.

vig·i·lant, vij′i·lant, *a.* [L. *vigilans, vigilantis,* ppr. of *vigilo,* to watch.] Watchful; on the alert for danger; wary.—**vig·i·lant·-ly,** *adv.*

vig·i·lan·te, vij″i·lan′tē, *n. U.S. hist.* one of the members of a vigilance committee.— **vig·i·lan·tism,** vij′i·lan·tiz″um, *n.*

vig·il light, *n.* A candle or other similar light which is kept burning before a statue, shrine, or memorial; *Rom. Cath. Ch.* a candle lit, and usu. left burning, before some statue or shrine by any worshiper for the purpose of devotion.

vi·gin·til·lion, vī″jin·til′yon, *n. pl.* **vi·-gin·til·lions, vi·gin·til·lion.** In the U.S. and France, a thousand novemdecillions, represented by 1 followed by 63 ciphers; in Great Britain and Germany, the twentieth power of a million, represented by 1 followed by 120 ciphers.—**vi·gin·til·lionth,** *a.*

vi·gnette, vin·yet′, *n.* [Fr., dim. of *vigne,* L. *vinea,* a vine.] A small running design, as one representing vine leaves, tendrils, and grapes, used on title pages or as a headpiece or tailpiece in books; a photograph, picture, or engraving not enclosed within a definite border; a small photographic portait; a short literary sketch or description.—*v.t.*—*vignetted, vignetting.*—**vi·gnett·er,** vin·-yet′ėr, *n. Photog.* a contrivance used to shade

or blur the background edges of a picture in making vignettes.—**vi·gnett·ist,** *n.*

vig·or, *Brit.* **vig·our,** vig′ėr, *n.* [L. *vigor,* vigor, < *vigeo,* to be strong; < root also seen in *vigil, vegetable, victim.*] Active strength or force of body; physical strength; strength of mind; energy; vitality; strength in animal or vegetable nature or action; *law,* validity or effectiveness.

vi·go·ro·so, vig″o·rō′sō, *It.* vē″gạ·Rạ′zạ, *a. Mus.* Vigorous; spirited or energetic in manner or style, used as the direction to one who is performing.—*adv.*

vig·or·ous, vig′ėr·us, *a.* Possessing vigor or physical strength; strong; exhibiting or resulting from vigor, energy, or strength of either body or mind; powerful; energetic; forceful.—**vig·or·ous·ly,** *adv.*—**vig·or·-ous·ness,** *n.*

vi·king, vī′king, *n.* [Icel. *vikingr,* lit. 'one who frequents bays and fjords'—*vik,* a bay, and term. *-ing,* one who belongs to or is descended from (*r* being the masc. art.).] (*Cap.*) one of the Scandinavian warriors whose seaborne raiding parties ravaged the European coasts from the 8th to the 10th centuries; (*l.c.*) any sea rover.

vile, vil, *a.*—*viler, vilest.* [O.Fr. Fr. *vil,* < L. *vilis,* cheap, poor, mean, vile.] Wretchedly bad; as, *vile* weather; highly offensive or objectionable; repulsive or disgusting, as to the senses or feelings; morally base, depraved, or despicable; as, *vile* thoughts; foul, as language; poor, wretched, or sorry, as in quality or state; mean or menial, as tasks; low, degraded, or ignominious, as a condition; as, *vile* servitude; of little value or account; paltry.—**vile·ly,** *adv.*—**vile·-ness,** *n.*

vil·i·fy, vil′i·fī″, *v.t.*—*vilified, vilifying.* [L. *vilifico*—*vilis,* vile, and *facio,* to make.] To attempt to degrade by slander; to defame; to malign.—**vil·i·fi·ca·tion,** *n.*—**vil·i·fi·-er,** *n.*

vil·i·pend, vil′i·pend″, *v.t.* [L. *vilipendo,* to hold in slight esteem—*vilis,* worthless, vile, and *pendo,* to weigh, to value.] To express a disparaging or mean opinion of; to slander; to think of or treat with contempt.

vill, vil, *n.* [A.Fr. and O.Fr. *vile* (Fr. *ville,* town), < L. *villa*.] *Archaic,* a village.

vil·la, vil′a, *n.* [L. *villa,* a country house, farm, villa, a contr. of *vicula,* < *vicus,* a village.] A country residence, usu. of some size and pretension; a rural or suburban mansion; *chiefly Brit.* a middle class suburban home.

vil·la·dom, vil′a·dom, *n. Brit.* suburban villas and suburban society.

vil·lage, vil′ij, *n.* [O.Fr. Fr. *village,* < L. *villaticum,* neut. of *villaticus,* belonging to a country house or farm, E. *villatic.*] A small assemblage of houses in a country district, being larger than a hamlet and smaller than a town; a sometimes incorporated municipality, as in parts of the U.S.; the village inhabitants collectively; a collection of animal habitations.—**vil·lag·er,** *n.*—**vil·-lage·ry,** *n.*

vil·lain, vil′an, *n.* [A.Fr. and O.Fr. *vilain, vilein,* < M.L. *villanus,* < L. *villa.*] A malevolent or harmful person; scoundrel; a character who functions as an evil antagonist in the plot of a literary work; a villein.—**vil·lain·ess,** vil′a·nis, *n.* Feminine of villain.

vil·lain·ous, vil′a·nus, *a.* Having the character of, pertaining to, or befitting a villain; wicked; depraved; *fig.* unpleasant; as, *villainous* weather.—**vil·lain·ous·ly,** *adv.*—**vil·lain·ous·ness,** *n.*

vil·lain·y, vil′a·nē, *n. pl.* **vil·lain·ies.** The conduct or actions of a villain; the quality of being villainous; depravity; wickedness.

vil·la·nel·la, vil″a·nel′a, *It.* vēl″lä·nel′lä, *n. pl.* **vil·la·nel·le,** vil″a·nel′ē, *It.* vil″a·-

nel′le. [It., < *villano,* rustic, < M.L. *villanus,* E. *villain.*] An Italian rustic part song without accompaniment.

vil·la·nelle, vil″a·nel′, *n.* [Fr. < It. *villanella.*] A short poem of fixed form usu. written in five tercets with a final quatrain and all based on two rhymes.

vil·lat·ic, vi·lat′ik, *a.* [L. *villaticus,* belonging to a country house or farm, < *villa.*] Of or pertaining to a village or farm; rural.

vil·lein, vil′en, *n.* [O.Fr. *villein.*] One of a feudal class of persons who served as serfs to their lords but who possessed the rights of free men with respect to all other persons. Also *villain.*

vil·lein·age, vil′e·nij, *n.* A feudal tenure of lands and tenements by villeins at the will of a lord; the status, condition, or class of a villein. Also **vil·lain·age, vil·len·age.**

vil·li·form, vil′i·farm″, *a.* Having the form of villi; so shaped and closely set as to resemble the pile of velvet, as the teeth of certain fishes.

vil·los·i·ty, vi·los′i·tē, *n. pl.* **vil·los·i·-ties.** *Biol.* The condition of being villous; a villous surface or coating; a number of villi together; a villus.

vil·lous, vil′us, *a.* [L. *villosus,* < *villus,* hair.] *Biol.* Abounding with villi; having the surface covered with fine hairs or woolly substance. Also **vil·lose,** vil′ōs.—**vil·lous·-ly,** *adv.*

vil·lus, vil′us, *n. pl.* **vil·li,** vil′ī. [L., shaggy hair, tuft of hair, nap: cf. *velvet.*] *Anat., zool.* one of the minute, hairlike, vascular processes on certain animal membranes, esp. on the mucous membrane of the small intestine, where they serve in absorbing nutriment; *bot.* one of the long, soft, straight hairs covering the fruit, flowers, and other parts of certain plants.

vim, vim, *n.* [L. acc. of *vis,* strength.] Vigor; vitality; forceful enthusiasm.

vi·min·e·ous, vi·min′ē·us, *a.* Made or composed of twigs; *bot.* of, producing, or resembling shoots or twigs that are long and flexible.

vim·pa, vim′pa, *n. Rom. Cath. Ch.* a silk shoulder veil worn during a Pontifical Mass by the acolyte who bears the staff and miter.

vi·na, vē′nä, *n.* [Skt. and Hind. *vīnā.*] A musical instrument of India having seven strings stretched over a long bamboo fingerboard which rests on two gourds.

vi·na·ceous, vī·nā′shus, *a.* [L. *vinaceus,* < *vinum,* wine.] Belonging to or concerned with wine or grapes; of the red color of wine.

vin·ai·grette, vin″a·gret′, *n.* [Fr., < *vinaigre,* vinegar.] A small box or bottle for holding aromatic vinegar or smelling salts. Also **vin·e·gar·ette.**—*a.* Served, as a food, with vinaigrette sauce.

vin·ai·grette sauce, *n.* A sauce consisting of vinegar, herbs, oil, and additional seasoning, and served on cold fish and meats.

vin·ca, ving′ka, *n. Bot.* periwinkle.

Vin·cen·tian, vin·sen′chan, *a. Rom. Cath. Ch.* of or relating to St. Vincent de Paul or to the Congregation of the Mission, an order he established in 1625 in France.—*n.* A member of this order. Also **Laz·a·rist.**

Vin·cent's an·gi·na, vin′sentz an·jī′na, *n. Pathol.* acute inflammation of the tonsils, floor of the mouth, and esp. the gums, characterized by ulceration, swelling, fever, and other fever symptoms, often resulting in deterioration of the gums and loss of teeth. Also **Vin·cent's in·fec·tion,** *trench mouth.*

vin·ci·ble, vin′si·bl, *a.* [< L. *vinco,* to conquer.] Capable of being conquered or subdued.—**vin·ci·bil·i·ty, vin·ci·ble·-ness,** *n.*

vin·cu·lum, ving′kya·lum, *n. pl.* **vin·cu·-la, vin·cu·lums,** ving′kya·la. [L., < *vincio,* to bind.] A bond of union; a tie;

math. a line over a quantity of two or more terms in order to connect them together as one quantity, as $\overline{x + y}$.

vin·di·cate, vin'di·kāt", *v.t.*—**vindicated, vindicating.** [L. *vindico, vindicatum*, to lay claim to, to avenge or revenge, < *vindex, vindicis*, one who lays claim, perh. < root meaning desire, love (in *Venus*), and *dico*, to declare. Of same origin are *vengeance, avenge, revenge.*] To exonerate from charges or absolve from suspicions or guilt; to justify or support, as a legal action; to prove to be just or valid, as a claim; to support, maintain, or defend against denial, censure, or objections. *Obs.* to avenge; to free or liberate.—**vin·di·ca·ble**, vin'di·ka·bl, *a.*—**vin·di·ca·tion**, vin"di·kā'shan, *n.*—**vin·di·ca·tor**, *n.*

vin·di·ca·to·ry, vin'di·ka·tōr"ē, vin'di·ka·tạr"ē, *a.* Tending to vindicate; justificatory; retributive. Also **vin·dic·a·tive**, vin·dik'a·tiv.

vin·dic·tive, vin·dik'tiv, *a.* [L. *vindicta*, revenge.] Revengeful; given to revenge. Also *rare*, **vin·dic·a·tive.**—**vin·dic·tive·ly**, *adv.*—**vin·dic·tive·ness**, *n.*

vine, vīn, *n.* [O.Fr. *vine, vigne*, (Fr. *vigne*), < L. *vinea*, vineyard, vine, < *vinum*, wine, grapes, the vine.] Any plant with a long, slender stem that trails or creeps on the ground or climbs by winding itself about a support or holding fast with tendrils or claspers; the stem of any such plant; the grapevine, esp. the common European species, *Vitis vinifera*, commonly known as the wine grape.

vine·dress·er, vīn'dres"ẽr, *n.* One who trims, prunes, or cultivates vines, esp. grapevines.

vin·e·gar, vin'e·gẽr, *n.* [Fr. *vinaigre*, < *vin*, L. *vinum*, wine, and *aigre*, L. *acer*, sharp, sour.] Dilute and impure acetic acid, usu. obtained by the souring or acetification of fermented fruit juices, used as a preservative or condiment; *med.* a dilute acetic acid preparation. Sourness of temper. *Slang*, excess energy; vitality.

vin·e·gar eel, *n.* A minute nematode worm, *Anguillula aceti*, found in vinegar and similar acetic fermenting matter. Also **vin·e·gar worm.**

vin·e·gar·roon, vin"e·ga·rön', *n.* A large whip scorpion, *Mastigoproctus giganteus*, of the southern U.S. and Mexico which emits a vinegarlike odor when alarmed. Also **vin·e·ge·rone.**

vin·e·gar·y, vin'e·ga·rē, *a.* Of the nature of or resembling vinegar; sour like vinegar in manner or temper. Also **vin·e·gar·ish**, vin'e·gẽr·ish.

vin·er·y, vī'ne·rē, *n. pl.* **vin·er·ies.** A kind of greenhouse where vines, esp. grapevines, are cultivated by artificial heat; vines collectively.

vine·yard, vin'yẽrd, *n.* A plantation of vines producing grapes, esp. wine grapes; *fig.* a field for religious mission work or similar spiritual activity.—**vine·yard·ist**, *n.*

vingt-et-un, *Fr.* vaN·tā·œN', *n. Cards*, twenty-one.

vi·nic, vī'nik, vin'ik, *a.* [L. *vinum*, wine.] Of, pertaining to, found in, or extracted from wine.

vin·i·cul·ture, vin'i·kul"chẽr, *n.* [L. *vinum*, wine grapes, the vine, and *cultura*, culture.] The cultivation of vines, esp. grapevines, usu. with reference to wine making. Also *viticulture.*—**vin·i·cul·tur·al**, *a.*—**vin·i·cul·tur·ist**, *n.*

vi·nif·er·ous, vī·nif'ẽr·us, *a.* [L.L. *vinifer*, < L. *vinum*, wine, and *ferre*, bear.] Suitable for, yielding, or producing wine.

vi·no, vē'nō, *n. pl.* **vi·nos.** *Colloq.* wine.

vi·nous, vī'nus, *a.* [L. *vinosus*, < *vinum*, wine.] Of the nature of or resembling wine; pertaining to or characteristic of wine; produced by, indicative of, or given to indul-

gence in wine; as, *vinous* gaiety; wine-colored, esp. of shades of red; vinaceous.—**vi·nos·i·ty**, vī·nos'i·tē, *n.*

vin·tage, vin'tij, *n.* [Partly < *vintner*, partly < Fr. *vendange*, vintage, < L. *vindemia*, the vintage—*vinum*, wine, and *demo*, to take away.] The crop of grapes or wine produced from one season; a high quality wine from a superior crop; the gathering of a crop of grapes; a type of person or thing well-known during a past era; as, a dance of jazz-age *vintage*.

vin·tage, vin'tij, *a.* Referring to wine, esp. a particular wine, or to a season of wine making; outmoded; *fig.* referring to a period, age, make, or the like; as, a *vintage* automobile.

vin·tag·er, vin'ta·jẽr, *n.* One who harvests wine grapes.

vin·tage year, *n.* The year of a certain vintage wine's production; any year in which success is outstanding.

vint·ner, vint'nẽr, *n.* [O.E. *viniter*, O.Fr. *vinetier*, < L.L. *vinitarius*, < L. *vinum*, wine.] *Chiefly Brit.* One who deals in wine; wine merchant.

vin·y, vī'nē, *a.*—**vinier, viniest.** Pertaining to, of the nature of, or resembling vines; abounding in or producing vines; as, a *viny* area.

vi·nyl, vī'nil, vīn'il, vin'il, vin'il, *n.* [L. *vinum*, wine.] *Chem.* the univalent radical, CH_2CH, present in many organic compounds; as, the *vinyl* resins. A type of plastic made from these resins.

vi·nyl·i·dene, vī·nil'i·dēn", *n. Chem.* a bivalent radical, $H_2C=C$, obtained from ethylene.

vi·nyl·i·dene res·in, *n.* Any of a group of thermoplastic resins obtained by the polymerization of vinylidene compounds, and used chiefly for molded items, films, and the like.

Vi·nyl·ite, vīn'i·līt", vin'i·līt", *n.* A thermoplastic resin which is formed by the polymerization of a vinyl compound, and used for molded items, films, coatings, and the like. (Trademark.)

vi·nyl res·in, *n.* A thermoplastic resin obtained chiefly from polymers of vinyl compounds.

vi·ol, vī'ol, *n.* [Fr. *viole*, It. *viola*, Pr. *viola, viula*, L.L. *vidula*, a viol, < L. *vitulari*, to celebrate a festival (perh. by killing a calf—*vitulus*, a calf).] A medieval, usu. five- to seven-stringed musical instrument of various sizes and shapes, and ancestor of the modern violin. See *double bass.*

vi·o·la, vē·ō'la, vī·ō'la, *n.* [It.] A musical instrument similar to the violin, but somewhat larger and with the strings tuned a fifth lower, producing a more sonorous tone; an organ stop, usu. of four- or eight-foot pitch producing stringlike tones.—**vi·o·list**, vē·ō'list, vī·ō'list, *n.*

vi·o·la, vī'o·la, vī·ō'la, *n.* [L.] One of the plants of the genus *Viola*, including pansies and violets, esp. one of many cultivated plants yielding small, varicolored blossoms.

vi·o·la·ble, vī'o·la·bl, *a.* Capable of being violated.—**vi·o·la·bil·i·ty**, **vi·o·la·ble·ness**, *n.*—**vi·o·la·bly**, *adv.*

vi·o·la·ceous, vī"o·lā'shus, *a.* [L. *violaceus*.] *Bot.* of or relating to the violet family, *Violaceae.* Having a violet color.—**vi·o·la·ceous·ly**, *adv.*

vi·o·la da brac·cio, vē·ō'la da brä'chō, vī·ō'la, *n. pl.* **vi·o·la da brac·cios.** [It., 'arm viol.'] An early musical instrument of the viol class, held resting on the shoulder, superseded by the modern viola.

vi·o·la da gam·ba, vē·ō'la da gäm'ba, vē·ō'la da gam'ba, vī·ō'la, *n. pl.* **vi·o·la da gam·bas.** [It., 'leg viol.'] An old musical instrument of the viol family, held between or against the knees, superseded by the modern violoncello; a bass fiddle; an

organ stop having a string tone similar to that of the viola da gamba.

vi·o·la d'a·mo·re, vē·ō'la dä·mōr'ā, vē·ō'la dä·mạr'ā, vī·ō'la, *n. pl.* **vi·o·la d'a·mo·res.** A viol having sympathetic strings beneath the bowed ones, producing full, silvery tones in a tenor range.

vi·o·late, vī'o·lāt", *v.t.*—**violated, violating.** [L. *violo, violatum*, to violate; akin to *vis*, force.] To infringe or transgress; to break in upon; to disturb; to desecrate; to treat with irreverence; to profane or profanely meddle with; to ravish or rape; to do injury to; to outrage.—**vi·o·la·tive**, vī'o·lā"tiv, vī'o·la·tiv, *a.*—**vi·o·la·tor**, *n.*

vi·o·la·tion, vī"o·lā'shan, *n.* The act of violating; the condition of being violated; desecration or profanation; an infringement or transgression; rape.

vi·o·lence, vī'o·lens, *n.* [L. *violentia*, < *violentus*, violent.] Intense or severe force; severe or injurious treatment or action; an unfair exercise of power or force; an act of violence; an inordinate vehemence of expression or feeling; a distortion or misrepresentation of content, meaning, or intent.

vi·o·lent, vī'o·lent, *a.* [L. *violentus*, violent; akin *violate*.] Characterized by or acting with extremely rough physical force; characterized or caused by harsh, destructive force; marked by intensity of force or effect; as, a *violent* cough; exhibiting or caused by intense emotional or mental force; sudden, intense energy; as, a *violent* rush; tending to misrepresent or distort.—**vi·o·lent·ly**, *adv.*

vi·o·let, vī'o·lit, *n.* [O.Fr. *violete* (Fr. *violette*), dim. of O.Fr. *viole*, < L. *viola*, violet.] Any herbaceous plant of the genus *Viola*, chiefly low, stemless, or leafy-stemmed with purple, blue, yellow, white, or variegated flowers, as *V. odorata*, a fragrant species common in gardens, and *V. tricolor*, the pansy, whose flowers are often variegated in coloring; a bluish-purple color.—*a.* Of the color called violet; bluish-purple.

vi·o·let ray, *n.* The shortest ray of the visual spectrum, producing the color violet; an ultraviolet ray.

vi·o·lin, vī"o·lin', *n.* [It. *violino*, a dim. of *viola*.] A treble instrument of wood, having four strings stretched by means of a bridge over a hollow body, held under the chin resting horizontally on the shoulder, and played with a bow; a violinist.—**vi·o·lin·ist**, vī"o·lin'ist, *n.* A person who plays the violin.

vi·o·lon·cel·lo, vē"o·lon·chel'ō, *n.* [It., a dim. of *violone*, which is an augmentative of *viola*, a viol.] A cello.—**vi·o·lon·cel·list**, vē"o·lon·chel'ist, *n.*

vi·os·ter·ol, vī·os'te·rōl", vī·os'te·rạl", vī·os'te·rol", *n.* A vitamin D preparation used in medicine, made of irradiated ergosterol dissolved in oil.

VIP, V.I.P., vē'ī'pē', *n. Colloq.* very important person.

vi·per, vī'pẽr, *n.* [Fr. *vipère*, < L. *vipera*, < *vivus*, alive, and *pario*, to bring forth, as bringing forth its young alive.] Any of the family *Viperidae*, poisonous old-world snakes, esp. the common viper, *Vipera berus*; a bit viper; any poisonous or reputedly poisonous snake; a malevolent or spiteful person.—**vi·per·ine**, **vi·per·ish**, **vi·per·ous**, vī'pẽr·in, vī'pe·rīn", vī'pẽr·ish, vī'pẽr·us, *a.*—**vi·per·ous·ly**, *adv.*

vi·per's bu·gloss, *n.* A bristly plant, *Echium vulgare*, having pink buds and bright blue flowers. Also *blueweed.*

vi·ra·go, vi·rā'gō, vi·rä'gō, *n. pl.* **vi·ra·goes**, vi·ra·gos. [L., a heroic maiden, a heroine, a female warrior, < *vir*, a man.] A bold, turbulent, loud, bad-tempered woman; a shrew; *archaic*, an unusually large woman who has great strength and courage.

vi·ral, vī′ral, *a.* Of, relating to, or as a result of a virus.

vir·e·lay, vir·e·lai, vir′e·lā″, *n.* [O.Fr. Fr. *virelai,* earlier *vireli;* origin uncertain.] An old French form of short poem, with short lines running on two rhymes, and having the two opening lines recurring at intervals; any of various similar or other forms of poem, as one consisting of stanzas made up of longer and shorter lines, the lines of each kind rhyming together in each stanza, and having the rhyme of the shorter lines of one stanza forming the rhyme of the longer lines of the next stanza.

vir·e·o, vir′ē·ō″, *n.* pl. **vir·e·os.** [L., kind of bird.] Any of the small American insectivorous birds constituting the family *Vireonidae,* having plumage more or less tinted with olive and green. Also **green·let.—vir·e·o·nine,** *a., n.*

vi·res·cence, vī·res′ens, *n.* The condition or process of turning green; *bot.* this condition in plant parts not usu. green, caused by the presence of chlorophyll not normally present.

vi·res·cent, vi·res′ent, *a.* [L. *virescens, virescentis,* ppr. of *viresco,* to grow green, incept, verb < *vireo,* to be green.] Slightly green; beginning to be green.

vir·ga, vur′ga, *n. Meteor.* streaks of precipitation from clouds that evaporate before reaching the ground.

vir·gate, vur′git, vur′gāt, *a.* [L. *virga,* a rod.] Having the shape of a rod or wand; straight and slender; *bot.* bearing numerous small twigs.

vir·gate, vur′git, vur′gāt, *n.* [L. *virga,* a rod, in L.L. a measure of land, like *rod, pole,* or *perch.*] An early English unit of land measure, varying in extent, but usu. equal to about 30 acres.

vir·gin, vur′jin, *n.* [O.Fr. *virgine,* L. *virgo, virginis,* a virgin, root as *virga,* a twig.] A person, esp. a girl or young woman, who has not had sexual intercourse; a chaste woman; a maiden; a female animal that has not copulated; *entom.* female insect producing fertile eggs parthenogenetically; *astrol., astron.* the sign or the constellation Virgo; *eccles.* an unmarried, religious woman who has taken a chastity vow. (*Cap.*), *eccles.* Mary, mother of Jesus, usu. preceded by *the;* also **Bless·ed Vir·gin,** *Virgin Mary.* **—a.** Being or pertaining to a virgin; composed of virgins; characteristic of or suitable for a virgin; maidenly; chaste; untouched, unsullied; in a pure or natural state; unused or uncultivated; unprocessed; occurring for the first time; as, his *virgin* speech; taken from the first pressing, as oil from olives, without the aid of heat; taken directly from ore or at the initial smelting.**—vir·gin·al,** vur′ji·nal, *a.***—vir·gin·al·ly,** *adv.*

vir·gin·al, vur′ji·nal, *n.* [Appar. a noun use of *virginal,* perh. as denoting an instrument suitable for virgins or girls.] *Often pl.* a spinet or small harpsichord, usu. without legs, set on a table, popular in the 16th and 17th centuries.

vir·gin birth, *n. Theol.* the dogma that Jesus Christ was miraculously conceived and born of a virgin mother, Mary, as distinguished from *Immaculate Conception; zool.* parthenogenesis.

Vir·gin·ia cow·slip, vur·jin′ya kou′slip, *n.* A perennial herb, *Mertensia virginica,* found in eastern North America, having clusters of showy, blue flowers. Also **Vir·gin·ia blue·bell.**

Vir·gin·ia creep·er, vur·jin′ya krē′pẽr, *n.* A vitaceous, climbing plant, *Parthenocissus quinquefolia,* of N. America, having palmate leaves with five leaflets, and bluish-black berries. Also *American ivy, woodbine.*

Vir·gin·ia fence, vur·jin′ya fens″, *n.* A snake fence. Also **Vir·gin·ia rail fence,** *worm fence.*

Vir·gin·ia reel, vur·jin′ya rēl′, *n.* An American country dance in which the partners begin by facing each other in two lines, and dance a series of figures, called out by the caller.

vir·gin·i·ty, vur·jin′i·tē, *n.* pl. **vir·gin·i·ties.** [L. *virginitas.*] The state of being a virgin; the state of being pure, unused, untouched, or the like.

vir·gin·i·um, vur·jin′ē·um, *n. Chem.* a former name for the element now known as francium.

Vir·gin Mar·y, *n.* Mary, the mother of Jesus Christ, usu. preceded by *the.*

vir·gin's-bow·er, vur′jinz·bou′ẽr, *n.* Any of several climbing varieties of clematis with small white flowers in large clusters, as *Clematis virginiana,* of the U.S.

vir·gin wool, *n.* Wool that has yet to be processed.

vir·gu·late, vur′gya·lit, vur′gya·lāt″, *a.* [L. *virgula,* dim. of *virga,* rod.] Rod-shaped; virgate.

vir·gule, vur′gūl, *n.* A slanted line (/) used to denote two alternatives (as in and/or), to replace the word 'per' (50 cents/lb), to divide fractions or dates, and to separate lines of poetry. Also *diagonal.*

vi·ri·cide, vī′ri·sīd″, *n.* Virucide.**—vi·ri·ci·dal,** *a.* Virucidal.

vir·id, vir′id, *a.* Bright green, esp. the green color of vegetation.

vir·i·des·cent, vir″i·des′ent, *a.* [L.L. *viridescens (-ent-),* ppr. of *viridescere,* grow green, < L. *viridis,* green.] Somewhat green; greenish.**—vir·i·des·cence,** *n.*

vi·rid·i·an, vi·rid′ē·an, *n.* [L. *viridis,* green.] A bluish-green pigment of great permanency, consisting of a hydrated oxide of chromium.

vi·rid·i·ty, vi·rid′i·tē, *n.* pl. **vi·rid·i·ties.** [L. *viriditas,* < *viridis,* green.] Greenness; verdure.

vir·ile, vir′il, *Brit.* vir′īl, *a.* [L. *virilis,* < *vir,* man; akin to Skt. *vīra,* Goth. *wair,* O.E. *wer,* man; cf. *werewolf.*] Of, pertaining to, or characteristic of a man; masculine or manly; natural to or befitting a man; having or exhibiting in a marked degree masculine strength, vigor, or forcefulness; characterized by a vigorous, masculine spirit; pertaining to or capable of procreation.**—vi·ril·i·ty,** vi·ril′i·tē, *n.* The state or quality of being virile; manhood; the power of procreation.

vir·i·lism, vir′i·liz″um, *n.* A disorder in which secondary sexual male characteristics, as facial hair growth, develop in a female.

vi·rol·o·gy, vī·rol′o·jē, vi·rol′o·jē, *n.* [*vir(us)* and *-ology.*] The science which deals with viruses and the diseases they cause.**—vi·ro·log·i·cal,** vī″ro·loj′i·kal, *a.***—vi·rol·o·gist,** *n.*

vi·ro·sis, vi·rō′sis, *n.* pl. **vi·ro·ses.** An infection or disease due to a virus.

vir·tu, ver·tu, vẽr·tō′, vur′tō, *n.* [It. *virtù,* virtue, excellence, < L. *virtus,* E. *virtue.*] Such excellence or merit in objects of art, curios, and the like, as recommends them to the taste of connoisseurs and collectors; as, articles of *virtu;* such objects or articles collectively; a taste for or knowledge of such objects.

vir·tu·al, vur′chō·al, *a.* [Fr. *virtuel.*] Being in essence or effect, not in fact; not actual but equivalent, so far as result is concerned; as, a *virtual* denial of a statement.**—vir·tu·al·i·ty,** *n.*

vir·tu·al fo·cus, *n. Opt.* a point from which light rays appear to diverge, as the reflection of a light source on a plane mirror.

vir·tu·al im·age, *n. Opt.* an image, formed of virtual focuses, from which reflected or refracted light rays appear to diverge, as the reflection of an object on a plane mirror.

vir·tu·al·ly, vur′chō·a·lē, *adv.* In efficacy or effect if not in actuality; mostly or almost entirely, as: The movie was *virtually* successful.

vir·tue, vur′chō, *n.* [O.Fr. *virtu. vertu* (Fr. *verta*), < L. *virtus,* manly excellence, strength, courage, worth, virtue, < *vir,* man.] Moral excellence or goodness; conformity of conduct to moral laws; rectitude; chastity, esp. in women; a particular moral excellence; as, one of the cardinal or theological *virtues;* any praiseworthy quality or trait; merit; inherent power to produce effects; potency; *pl., theol.* an order of angels. *Archaic,* manly excellence; valor.**—by vir·tue of** or **in vir·tue of,** by the power, force, or authority of.**—make a vir·tue of ne·ces·si·ty,** to resign oneself to an unpleasant obligatory action by focusing one's attention on whatever fortuitous benefits might be derived from it.**—vir·tue·less,** *a.*

vir·tu·os·i·ty, vur″chō·os′i·tē, *n.* pl. **vir·tu·os·i·ties.** The technique or skill of a virtuoso; an interest in the fine arts.

vir·tu·o·so, vur″chō·ō′sō, *n.* pl. **vir·tu·o·sos, vir·tu·o·si,** vur″chō·ō′sē. [It., orig. *a.* virtuous, excellent, < L.L. *virtuosus,* E. *virtuous.*] One who has special knowledge or skill in any field, as in music; one who excels in musical technique or execution; one who has a cultivated appreciation of artistic excellence; a connoisseur of works or objects of art, or a collector of objects of art, curios, antiquities, or the like.**—a.—vir·tu·o·sic,** vur″chō·os′ik, vur″chō·ō′sik, *a.*

vir·tu·ous, vur′chō·us, *a.* [O.Fr. *vertuous* (Fr. *vertueux*), < L.L. *virtuosus,* < L. *virtus,* E. *virtue.*] Conforming to moral laws; upright; righteous; moral; chaste; *archaic,* potent or efficacious.**—vir·tu·ous·ly,** *adv.***—vir·tu·ous·ness,** *n.*

vi·ru·cide, vī′ru·sīd″, *n.* An agent capable of stopping the activity of or destroying viruses. Also *viricide.***—vi·ru·ci·dal,** *a.* Pertaining to a virucide. Also *viricidal.*

vir·u·lence, vir′ya·lens, vir′a·lens, *n.* The quality of being virulent; an actively poisonous or malignant quality; *bact.* a microorganism's ability to produce disease. Venomous hostility. Also **vir·u·len·cy.**

vir·u·lent, vir′ya·lent, vir′a·lent, *a.* [Fr. *virulent,* < L. *virulentus,* poisonous, < *virus,* poison.] Extremely poisonous, venomous, noxious, or baneful; as, a *virulent* snake bite; very actively or spitefully injurious to life; very bitter in enmity. *Med.* malignant; actively or highly poisonous or infectious. *Bact.* having the ability to produce disease, as a bacterium.**—vir·u·lent·ly,** *adv.*

vi·rus, vī′rus, *n.* pl. **vi·rus·es.** [L., poison; allied to Gr. *ios* (for *vios, visos*), Skt. *visha,* Ir, *fi,* poison.] Any of a class of submicroscopic filterable pathogens which cause disease in all life forms and are dependent upon the host's living cells for their growth and reproduction, considered to be either living organisms or borderline nucleoprotein units which can generally penetrate a fine filter; a virus disease; vaccine lymph, obtained from infectious blisters and used as vaccine against diseases, as smallpox; loosely, any substance formed by an organism that can cause an infectious disease; *rare,* venom, as of a poisonous snake. *Fig.* a poisoning of the mind, soul, or morals.

vis, vis, *L.* wēs, *n.* pl. **vi·res,** vī′rēz, *L.* wē′Res. [L.] Power, might, or strength.

vi·sa, vē′za, *n.* pl. **vi·sas.** [Fr. *visé,* pp. of *viser,* to put a visé to, < L. *visus,* seen, *video, visum,* to see.] An endorsement made upon a passport by an authorized official representing a country which the bearer wishes to visit and denoting that it has been examined, found correct, and entry permission has been granted. Also *visé.*—*v.t.*—*visaed, visaing.* To indicate approval of a visa for; to affix a visa to. Also *visé.*

vis·age, viz′ij, *n.* [O.Fr. Fr. *visage,* < L. *visus,* sight, look, appearance, < *videre,* see.] The face, esp. of a human being, and commonly with reference to shape, features, expression, or the like; the countenance; aspect; appearance.—**vis·aged,** *a.* Having a visage, as a kind which is specified, used in compounds; as, grim-*visaged.*

vis-à-vis, vē″za·vē′, *Fr.* vē·zä·vē′, *adv., a.* [Fr., face to face (*vis,* face, < L. *visus.*)] Face to face.—*prep.* In relation to, or compared with; face to face with; opposite to. —*n.* pl. **vis-à-vis.** One face to face with, or situated opposite to, another; counterpart; a carriage in which the occupants sit face to face; a kind of sofa or double chair in the general shape of the letter S, with seats for two persons thus enabled to face each other, or tête-à-tête.

Vi·sa·yan, vi·sī′an, *a.* Of, relating to, or pertaining to the largest native race inhabiting the Visayan Islands in the Philippines, the Malayan language they speak, or to their culture. Also **Bi·sa·yan.**—*n.* pl. **Vi·sa·yans, Vi·sa·yan.** A member of this race. Also **Bi·sa·yan.**

vis·ca·cha, vis·kä′cha, *n.* Any of various large-sized burrowing rodents, genera *Lagostomus* and *Lagidium,* native to S. America. Also *vizcacha.*

vis·cer·a, vis′ẽr·a, *n. pl.* [L., pl. of *viscus.*] *Anat.* the soft interior organs contained in the cavities of the body, esp. such of these as are confined to the abdomen and thorax, including the lungs, heart, stomach, and intestines; in popular use, the intestines or bowels.

vis·cer·al, vis′ẽr·al, *a.* Of or pertaining to the viscera; affecting or located within the viscera; having the character of viscera; proceeding from feeling or intuition that is intense or deep.—**vis·cer·al·ly,** *adv.*

vis·cid, vis′id, *a.* [L.L. *viscidus,* clammy, < L. *viscum,* the mistletoe, birdlime.] Sticking or adhering, and having a glutinous consistency; *bot.* covered, as leaves, with a sticky material.—**vis·cid·i·ty, vis·cid·ness,** vis·id′i·tē, *n.*—**vis·cid·ly,** *adv.*

vis·co·e·las·tic, vis″kō·i·las′tik, *a. Phys.* of or pertaining to matter containing elastic and viscous qualities.

vis·com·e·ter, vi·skom′i·tẽr, *n.* An instrument for ascertaining the extent of viscosity of fluids. Also *viscosimeter.*

vis·cose, vis′kōs, *n.* [L.L. *viscosus,* E. *viscous.*] A sticky plastic substance prepared by treating cellulose with caustic soda and carbon disulfide, used in manufacturing rayon or artificial silk, in making a product resembling celluloid, and for sizing and other purposes.—*a.*

vis·co·sim·e·ter, vis″kō·sim′i·tẽr, *n.* Viscometer.—**vis·co·si·met·ric,** vis″kō·si·me′trik, vi·skos″i·me′trik, *a.*

vis·cos·i·ty, vi·skos′i·tē, *n.* pl. **vis·cos·i·ties.** The state or quality of being viscous. *Phys.* the resistance of a fluid to the motion of its molecules among themselves; the capability in a solid of changing shape gradually under the action of force.

vis·count, vī′kount″, *n.* [O.Fr. *visconte* (Fr. *vicomte*), < M.L. *vicecomes* (*vicecomit-*), < L. *vice-* and *comes,* E. *count.*] A nobleman ranking next below an earl or count and next above a baron; *hist.* a deputy of a count or earl. A sheriff in England.—**vis·count·cy,** vī′kount″sē, *n.* pl. **vis·count·cies.**—**vis·count·y,** vī′koun″tē, *n.* pl. **vis·count·ies.**

vis·count·ess, vī′koun″tis, *n.* A viscount's widow or wife; a woman having a corresponding or similar title to a viscount.

vis·cous, vis′kus, *a.* [L.L. *viscosus,* < L.

viscum, mistletoe, birdlime.] Sticky, adhesive, thick, or glutinous; of a glutinous character or consistency; *phys.* having the property of viscosity.—**vis·cous·ly,** *adv.*—**vis·cous·ness,** *n.*

vise, *Brit.* **vice,** vīs, *n.* [O.Fr. Fr. *vis,* winding stair, screw, < L. *vitis,* vine.] Any of various devices having two jaws which may be brought together or separated by means of a screw or lever, used to hold an object firmly while work is being done upon it.—*v.t.*—**vised, vising,** *Brit.* **viced, vicing.** To hold, press, or squeeze with or as with a vise.

vi·sé, vē′zā, vē·zā′, *v.t.*—**viséed, viséing.** Visa.—*n.*

Vish·nu, vish′nö, *n.* [Skt. *Vishnu,* < *vish,* to pervade.] The Hindu deity, called 'the Preserver', who belongs to the *Trimurti* or trinity, composed also of Brahma and Shiva, and whose many incarnations include one as Krishna.—**Vish·nu·ism,** *n.*—**Vish·nu·ite,** *n.*

vis·i·bil·i·ty, viz″i·bil′i·tē, *n.* pl. **vis·i·bil·i·ties.** The state or quality of being visible; the relative ease with which objects can be seen through the atmosphere under various conditions; the capability of giving an unobstructed range of vision.

vis·i·ble, viz′i·bl, *a.* [O.Fr. Fr. *visible,* < L. *visibilis,* < *videre* (pp. *visus*), see.] Capable of being seen; perceptible by the eye; constructed so as to be open to sight or view; perceptible by the mind; apparent, manifest, or obvious; conspicuous.—**vis·i·ble·ness,** *n.*—**vis·i·bly,** *adv.*

vis·i·ble speech, *n.* A system of phonetical characters or symbols designed to represent every possible speech sound in a manner suggesting its mode of articulation; the representation of a speech sequence on a sound spectrogram.

vi·sion, vizh′an, *n.* [O.Fr. Fr. *vision,* < L. *visio(n-),* < *videre* (pp. *visus*), see.] The act, power, or faculty of seeing; sight; the ability to imagine and prepare for the future, as: He had a *vision* of things to come. Foresight; the act or power of perceiving abstract or invisible subjects as clearly as if they were visible objects; a sight such as might be seen in a dream or vision, esp. when conceived of as revelation or prophecy; a vivid imaginative conception or anticipation; as, *visions* of wealth or glory; a sight, esp. when beautiful or satisfying.—*v.t.* To envision.—**vi·sion·al,** vizh′a·nal, *a.*—**vi·sion·al·ly,** *adv.*—**vi·sion·less,** *a.*

vi·sion·ar·y, vizh′a·ner″ē, *a.* Given to or characterized by fanciful or impracticable ideas or plans; purely idealistic or speculative; utopian; given to or characterized by imagining or dreaming; given to or concerned with seeing visions; unreal; imaginary.—*n.* pl. **vi·sion·ar·ies.** One who sees visions; an impractical theorist or enthusiast; a dreamer.—**vi·sion·ar·i·ness,** *n.*

vis·it, viz′it, *v.t.* [O.Fr. Fr. *visiter,* < L. *visitare,* freq. of *visere,* go to, go to see, freq. of *videre,* see.] To come or go to see, as a person or place, in the way of friendship, ceremony, duty, business, or the like; to make a stay or sojourn with as a guest; to go to for the purpose of official inspection or examination; to come in order to comfort or aid; to come upon or assail; to inflict punishment for or upon.—*v.i.* To make a visit or visits; *colloq.* to talk casually.—*n.* [Fr. *visite.*] An act of visiting; the act of going to see a person or place; *colloq.* a friendly talk. A stay or sojourn as a guest; the action of going to a place to make an official inspection or examination; visitation, as of a neutral vessel by a naval officer of a belligerent nation.

vis·it·a·ble, viz′i·ta·bl, *a.* Capable of or suitable for being visited; liable or subject to official visitation.

vis·i·tant, viz′i·tant, *n.* A visitor or guest; a temporary resident; a spirit believed to have returned from the afterworld; a migrating bird staying temporarily in a region; as, a summer *visitant,* a winter *visitant.*—*a.*

vis·i·ta·tion, viz″i·tā′shan, *n.* [L. *visitatio.*] A visit; a formal visit by a superior or superintendent in order to inspect; a special dispensation or judgment from heaven; a communication of divine favor or of divine indignation and retribution; (*cap.*), *eccles.* a feast day, July 2, commemorating the visit of the Virgin Mary to Elizabeth, her cousin.—**vis·it·a·tion·al,** *a.*

vis·it·a·to·ri·al, viz″i·ta·tōr′ē·al, viz″i·ta·tạr′ē·al, *a.* Pertaining to an official visitor or to official inspection or visitation; having the power of visitation. Also **vis·i·to·ri·al,** viz″i·tōr′ē·al, viz″i·tạr′ē·al.

vis·it·ing, viz′i·ting, *a.* Giving specialized or professional assistance in the home for brief periods of time; as, a *visiting* nurse.

vis·it·ing card, *n.* A calling card.

vis·it·ing fire·man, *n. Colloq.* an influential, official, or big-spending visitor, as to a city or organization, who is usu. given special tours, or impressively entertained.

vis·it·ing nurse, *n.* A nurse who is employed by a service establishment or hospital to care for a sick person in his home.

vis·it·ing pro·fes·sor, *n.* A professor asked by a university to join its staff for a short time, usu. one semester or academic year, while on leave from his own university.

vis·it·ing teach·er, *n.* A public school teacher who instructs handicapped or sick students in their homes.

vis·i·tor, viz′i·tẽr, *n.* One who visits for business, social, or other reasons; a caller.

vi·sor, vi·zor, vī′zẽr, viz′ẽr, *n.* [Fr. *visière,* a visor, < O.Fr. *vis,* the face or visage.] The movable face guard of a helmet; a shield, usu. projecting from a cap, worn above the eyes to protect them from glare; a movable part over a car windshield which can be pulled down to shield the driver's eyes from glare; a mask used to conceal the face or disguise the wearer.—*v.t.* To shield or protect with a visor.—**vi·sor·less,** *a.*

vis·ta, vis′ta, *n.* [It., sight, view, < L. *video, visum,* to see.] A view or prospect through an avenue, as between rows of trees; the trees that form the avenue; a mental view stretching over an extensive range of time or sequence of events.—**vis·taed,** vis′tad, *a.*

vis·u·al, vizh′ö·al, *a.* [Fr. *visual,* now *visuel,* < L.L. *visualis,* < L. *visus,* sight, vision, < *videre,* see.] Of or pertaining to vision; used in sight; perceptible by sight; visible; perceptible by the mind, or of the nature of a mental vision.

vis·u·al a·cu·i·ty, *n. Ophthalm.* sharpness of vision as formulated from a comparison of the distance, usu. 20 feet, from a chart at which the patient sees the smallest letters possible for him, with the distance at which a normal eye would see those same letters. Abbr. *V.*

vis·u·al aid, *n. Often pl.* any of a variety of devices and materials which rely on the sense of sight to inform, as maps, motion pictures, and filmstrips: used to supplement the basic text in the teaching of a course.

vis·u·al·ize, vizh′ö·a·līz″, *v.t.*—*visualized, visualizing.* To make perceptible to the mind or imagination; to form a mental image of.—*v.i.* To call up or form mental images.—**vis·u·al·i·za·tion,** *n.*—**vis·u·al·iz·er,** *n.*—**vis·u·al·ly,** *adv.*

vis·u·al pur·ple, *n. Biochem.* rhodopsin.

vi·ta, vī′ta, L. wē′tä, *n.* pl. **vi·tae,** vī′tē, L. wē′tī. A curriculum vitae.

vi·tal, vīt′al, *a*. [O.Fr. Fr. *vital*, < L. *vitalis*, < *vita*, life, < *vivere*, live: see *quick*.] Of or pertaining to life; as, *vital* functions or processes; filled with life; being the seat or source of life; as, the *vital* parts or organs; necessary to life; as, *vital* air; necessary to the existence, continuance, or well-being of something; as, a *vital* necessity; indispensable; essential; affecting the existence, well-being, truth, or the like, of something; as, a *vital* error; of critical importance; as, *vital* problems, a *vital* contribution to modern thought; imparting life or vigor; vitalizing or invigorating; as, the *vital* sunlight; affecting life; destructive to life; as, a *vital* wound.—**vi·tal·ly**, *adv.*—**vi·tal·ness**, *n*.

vi·tal·ism, vīt′a·liz″um, *n*. *Biol.*, *philos*. the doctrine that ascribes the functions of a living organism to a vital principle and considers them only partly controlled by chemical and physical forces: opposed to *mechanism*.—**vi·tal·ist**, *n*.—**vi·tal·is·tic**, *a*.

vi·tal·i·ty, vi·tal′i·tē, *n*. pl. **vi·tal·i·ties**. The state of showing vital force; energy; as, full of *vitality*; vigor; the principle of life; animation; the ability to live or a capacity for lasting; continuance.

vi·tal·ize, Brit. **vi·tal·ise**, vīt′a·līz″, *v.t.* —*vitalized, vitalizing,* Brit. *vitalised, vitalising.* To give life to; to furnish with vital force; to invigorate.—**vi·tal·i·za·tion**, Brit. **vi·tal·i·sa·tion**, *n*.

Vi·tal·li·um, vi·tal′ē·um, *n*. An electrically neutral alloy of chromium, cobalt, and molybdenum, used esp. in dentistry, orthopedics, and reconstructive surgery of certain organs. (Trademark.)

vi·tals, vī′talz, *n. pl.* Internal parts or organs of animal bodies essential to life, as the heart and lungs; the part of a complex whole essential to its life, existence, or to a sound state.

vi·tal sta·tis·tics, *n. pl.* Facts or figures relating to significant aspects of human existence, either individually or collectively, as births, deaths, and incidence of disease.

vi·ta·mer, vī′ta·mėr, *n. Biochem.* one of several similar compounds that are able to carry out a definite vitamin function.— **vi·ta·mer·ic**, vī″ta·mer′ik, *a*.

vi·ta·min, vī′ta·min, *n*. [L. *vita*, life, and *amine*.] *Biochem.* one of several organic substances occurring in minute quantities in natural foods and necessary for proper metabolism in man and other animals, the lack of which causes various diseases.

vi·ta·min A, *n. Biochem.* a terpene, fat-soluble alcohol, obtained from egg yolk and certain other animal products, administered for the condition of night blindness and for protecting epithelial tissue.

vi·ta·min Bc, *n. Biochem.* folic acid.

vi·ta·min B com·plex, *n. Biochem.* an important group of B vitamins containing vitamin B$_1$, vitamin B$_2$, and others which are water-soluble.

vi·ta·min B$_1$, *n. Biochem.* thiamine.

vi·ta·min B$_2$, *n. Biochem.* riboflavin.

vi·ta·min B$_6$, *n. Biochem.* pyridoxine.

vi·ta·min B$_{12}$, *n. Biochem.* a water-soluble, crystalline vitamin, C$_{63}$H$_{90}$N$_{14}$O$_{14}$PCo, obtained from milk, eggs, liver, fish, and meat, which treats pernicious and other forms of anemia and is used as a nutriment, esp. for animals.

vi·ta·min C, *n. Biochem.* ascorbic acid.

vi·ta·min D, *n. Biochem.* any of a group of fat-soluble vitamins often prescribed for treatment of rickets and whose common sources are oil from the livers of fish, milk products, eggs, and ultraviolet irradiation of ergosterol.

vi·ta·min E, *n. Biochem.* a vitamin found in wheat germ and other grains and used in treating sterility.

vi·ta·min G, *n. Biochem.* riboflavin.

vi·ta·min H, *n. Biochem.* biotin.

vi·ta·min K, *n. Biochem.* a vitamin which occurs in many green vegetables and is necessary for normal blood clotting.

vi·ta·min P, *n. Biochem.* a vitamin found in paprika and citrus fruits which helps to maintain capillary and cell wall permeability. Also **bi·o·fla·vo·noid**.

vi·ta·scope, vī′ta·skōp″, *n*. One of the earliest types of motion-picture projectors. —**vi·ta·scop·ic**, vī″ta·skop′ik, *a*.

vi·tel·lin, vi·tel′in, vī·tel′in, *n*. [< *vitellus*.] *Biochem.* a protein in the yolk of eggs.

vi·tel·line, vi·tel′in, vī·tel′in, *a*. Of or relating to the yolk of an egg; having the color of the yolk of an egg.

vi·tel·lus, vi·tel′us, vī·tel′us, *n. pl.* **vi·tel·lus·es**. [L., the yolk of an egg.] The yolk of an egg.

vi·ti·ate, vish′ē·āt″, *v.t.*—*vitiated, vitiating.* [L. *vitio, vitiatum*, < *vitium*, a fault, vice.] To render faulty or imperfect; to injure the quality or substance of; to impair; to spoil or pollute; to render base or corrupt; to pervert; to render legally invalid or of no effect; to invalidate.—**vi·ti·a·tion**, *n*.—**vi·ti·a·tor**, *n*.

vit·i·cul·ture, vit′i·kul′chėr, vī′ti·kul″chėr, *n*. Viniculture.—**vit·i·cul·tur·al**, *a*. —**vit·i·cul·tur·er**, **vit·i·cul·tur·ist**, *n*.

vit·i·li·go, vit″i·lē′gō, *n*. [L., tetter.] *Pathol.* a disease in which smooth white patches form on various parts of the body due to loss of the natural pigment. Also **leu·ko·der·ma**.

vit·re·ous, vi′trē·us, *a*. [L. *vitreus*, < *vitrum*, glass.] Pertaining to or obtained from glass; consisting of glass; resembling glass; of or pertaining to the vitreous humor of the eye.—**vit·re·ous·ly**, *adv.*— **vit·re·ous·ness**, **vit·re·os·i·ty**, vi″trē·os′i·tē, *n*.

vit·re·ous e·nam·el, *n*. Porcelain enamel.

vit·re·ous hu·mor, *n. Anat.* the transparent gelatinous substance filling the body of the eyeball behind the crystalline lens. Also **vit·re·ous bod·y**.

vit·ri·fy, vi′tri·fī″, *v.t.*—*vitrified, vitrifying.* [L. *vitrum*, and *facio*, to make.] To convert into glass by fusion or the action of heat; to make vitreous.—*v.i.* To become vitreous; to be converted into glass.—**vit·ri·fi·a·ble**, *a*.—**vit·ri·fi·ca·tion**, vi″tri·fi·kā′shan, *n*.

vit·ri·ol, vi′trē·ol, *n*. [O.Fr. Fr. *vitriol*, < M.L. *vitriolum*, prop. neut. of *vitriolus*, for L.L. *vitreolus*, of glass, dim. of L. *vitreus*, E. *vitreous*.] *Chem.* any of certain metallic sulfates of glassy appearance, as of copper, iron, or zinc; sulfuric acid. *Fig.* something highly caustic or severe in its effects, as criticism.—*v.t.*—*vitrioled, vitrioling,* Brit. *vitriolled, vitriolling.* To subject to the effect of vitriol, esp. to dip in dilute sulfuric acid; to injure or burn with vitriol or sulfuric acid.—**vit·ri·ol·ic**, vi″trē·ol′ik, *a*.

vit·ta, vit′a, *n. pl.* **vit·tae**, vit′ē. [L., fillet.] *Bot.* a tube or receptacle for oil, found in the fruits of most umbelliferous plants; *biol.* a streak or stripe, as of color.

vit·tate, vit′āt, *a*. Provided with or having a vitta or vittae; striped longitudinally.

vit·tle, vit′l, *n., v.t., v.i.* Colloq. victual.

vi·tu·per·ate, vī·tö′pe·rāt″, vī·tū′pe·rāt″, vi·tö′pe·rāt″, vi·tū′pe·rāt″, *v.t.*—*vituperated, vituperating.* [Fr. *vituperer*, < L. *vitupero, vituperatum—vitium*, a vice, fault, and *paro*, to prepare.] To censure with abusive language; to abuse; to berate.—

vi·tu·per·a·tive, vī·tö″pe·rā′tiv, vī·tö′pėr·a·tiv, vi·tū″pe·rā′tiv, vi·tū′pėr·a·tiv, vī·tö′pe·rā″tiv, vi·tö′pėr·a·tiv, vi·tū′pe·rā″tiv, *a*.—**vi·tu·per·a·tive·ly**, *adv.*—**vi·tu·per·a·tor**, *n*.

vi·tu·per·a·tion, vī·tö″pe·rā′shan, vī·tū″pe·rā′shan, vi·tö″pe·rā′shan, vi·tū″pe·rā′shan, *n*. [L. *vituperatio*.] The act of vituperating; abusive railing.

vi·va, vē′va, vē′vä, *interj*. [It.: cf. *vive* and *vivat*.] Long live, usu. used with a specified someone in compounds, as: *Viva Romeo!* An acclamation, applause, or salute exclaimed.—*n*. A shout of 'viva!'

vi·va·ce, vi·vä′chä, *It.* vē·vä′che, *a*. [It.] *Mus.* Vivacious; lively; spirited: used as a performer's direction.—*adv*.

vi·va·cious, vi·vā′shus, vī·vā′shus, *a*. [L. *vivax, vivacis*, < *vivus*, alive.] Lively; active; sprightly in temper or conduct.— **vi·va·cious·ly**, *adv.*—**vi·va·cious·ness**, *n*.

vi·vac·i·ty, vi·vas′i·tē, vī·vas′i·tē, *n. pl.* **vi·vac·i·ties**. [L. *vivacitas*.] The quality or condition of being vivacious; liveliness of manner or character; sprightliness of temper or behavior; animation; briskness; cheerfulness; spirit.

vi·van·diè·re, vē·vaN·dyeR′, *n. pl.* **vi·van·dières**, vē·vaN·dyeR. [Fr.] Formerly, a female attached to French and other continental regiments, who sold provisions and liquor.

vi·var·i·um, vī·vâr′ē·um, *n. pl.* **vi·var·i·a**, vi·vâr′ē·a, **vi·var·i·ums**, vī·vâr′ē·a. [L., < *vivus*, alive.] A place artificially prepared for keeping animals and plants alive, in as near their natural state as possible.

vi·va vo·ce, vī′va vō′sē, *adv*. [L., by the living voice.] By word of mouth; orally.— *n. Chiefly Brit.* any examination carried on viva voce.—**vi·va-vo·ce**, *a*.

vive, vēv, *interj. Fr.* long live, usu. used with a specified person or thing in compounds, as: *Vive Molière!* An acclamation or exclamation of approval or salute.

vi·ver·rine, vī·ver′īn, vī·ver′in, vi·ver′īn, vi·ver′in, *a*. [L. *viverra*, a ferret.] Of or pertaining to the *Viverridae*, a family of small carnivorous mammals including the civet cat and the mongoose.—*n*. A viverrine animal.

viv·id, viv′id, *a*. [L. *vividus*, < *vivus*, alive.] Extremely bright, distinct, or intense; as, a dress of *vivid* red; lively; vigorous; spirited; exhibiting the appearance of life or freshness; realistic; perceived intensely and clearly by the senses; forming clear, strong mental images; as, his *vivid* description of the accident.—**viv·id·ly**, *adv.*— **viv·id·ness**, *n*.

viv·i·fy, viv′i·fī″, *v.t.*—*vivified, vivifying.* [Fr. *vivifier*, L. *vivificare—vivus*, alive, and *facio*, to make.] To endue with life; to animate; to make, as a story, more exciting, vivid, or lively.—**viv·i·fi·ca·tion**, viv″i·fi·kā′shan, *n*.—**viv·i·fi·er**, *n*.

vi·vip·ar·ous, vi·vip′er·us, *a*. [L. *vivus*, alive, and *pario*, to bear.] *Zool.* producing young in a living state, as most mammals, distinguished from *oviparous*; *bot.* bringing forth bulbs or seeds that begin to develop while still on the plant.—**vi·vip·a·rous·ly**, *adv.*—**vi·vip·a·rism**, *n*.—**vi·vi·par·i·ty**, **vi·vip·a·rous·ness**, viv″i·par′i·tē, *n*.

viv·i·sect, viv′i·sekt″, viv″i·sekt′, *v.t.* [Back-formation < *vivisection*.] To dissect the living body of, as some animal.—*v.i.* To practice vivisection.—**viv·i·sec·tor**, *n*.

viv·i·sec·tion, viv″i·sek′shan, *n*. [< L. *vivus*, alive, and *sectio, sectionis*, a cutting.] The dissection of, or otherwise experimenting on, a living animal, esp. for the purpose of ascertaining or demonstrating some fact in physiology or pathology.— **viv·i·sec·tion·al**, *a*.—**viv·i·sec·tion·al·ly**, *adv.*—**viv·i·sec·tion·ist**, viv″i·sek′sha·nist, *n*.

vix·en, vik′sen, *n*. [O.E. *fixen, fyxen*, a she-fox, fem. of fox (with change of *f* to *v*); cf. G. *füchsin*, a she-fox, *fuchs*, a fox.] A turbulent, quarrelsome, or shrewish woman; a fox belonging to the female sex.—**vix·en·ish**, *a*.—**vix·en·ish·ly**, *adv.*—**vix·en·ish·ness**, *n*.—**vix·en·ly**, *a., adv*.

viz·ard, **vis·ard**, viz′ėrd, *n*. [Var. of *vizor*.] A visor or mask.—**viz·ard·ed**, *a*.

viz·ca·cha, vis·kä′cha, *n.* Viscacha.

vi·zier, vi·zir, vi·zēr′, viz′yẽr, *n.* [Fr. *vizir,* < Ar. *wazir,* a vizier, lit. 'a bearer of burdens,' a porter, < *wazara,* to bear a burden.] The title of high political officers in the former Turkish Empire and in Moslem countries; a minister of state.—**vi·zier·ate, vi·zir·ate,** vi·zēr′it, vi·zēr′āt, viz′yẽr·it, viz′ya·rāt″, *n.*—**vi·zier·ship, vi·zir·ship,** *n.*—**vi·zier·i·al, vi·zir·i·al,** *a.*

vi·zor, vī′zẽr, viz′ẽr, *n., v.t.* Visor.

V-mail, vē′māl″, *n.* A service dispatching letters which had been microfilmed and which were in turn enlarged before delivery to U.S. armed forces outside the continental U.S. during World War II.

V neck, *n.* A V-shaped neckline, as on a dress or sweater.

vo·ca·ble, vō′ka·bl, *n.* [L. *vocabulum,* < *voco,* to call.] A word; a term; a word without regard to its meaning, but looked upon only as a certain combination of letters or sounds.—*a.* Having the capacity for being spoken or voiced.

vo·cab·u·lar·y, vō·kab′ya·ler″ē, *n.* pl. **vo·cab·u·lar·ies.** [M.L. *vocabularium,* < *vocabulum,* word.] The stock of words used by a people, or by a particular class or person; a list or collection of the words of a language, book, author, branch of science, or the like, usu. in alphabetical order and defined; the words of a language; a word-book, glossary, dictionary, or lexicon; the sum or scope of one's expressive techniques, as in the arts.

vo·cab·u·lar·y en·try, *n.* In any dictionary, any word, phrase, symbol, term, abbreviation, name, or the like, entered alphabetically and explained by the use of definition, word origin, or words having similar or opposite meanings.

vo·cal, vō′kal, *a.* [L. *vocalis,* uttering sound, vocal (as n., a vowel), < *vox* (*voc-*), voice: cf. *vowel.*] Of or pertaining to the voice; uttered with the voice, or oral; rendered by or intended for singing, as music; having a voice; expressing oneself in a free manner of speech; giving forth sound with or as with a voice. *Phon.* voiced; sonant; pertaining to or having the character of a vowel.—*n. Phon.* a vocal sound.—**vo·cal·i·ty,** vō·kal′i·tē, *n.*—**vo·cal·ly,** *adv.*

vo·cal cords, *n. pl. Anat.* either of two pairs of membranous ligaments projecting into the cavity of the larynx, the edges of which can be drawn together and made to vibrate by the passage of air from the lungs, thus producing vocal sound.

vo·cal·ic, vō·kal′ik, *a.* Of, pertaining to, or of the nature of a vowel; containing or constructed of vowels.—**vo·cal·i·cal·ly,** *adv.*

vo·cal·ism, vō′ka·liz″um, *n.* The use of the voice, as in speech or song; vocalization, specif. the technique or act of singing. *Phon.* the vowel tones used in a given language; the vocalic nature of a sound.

vo·cal·ist, vō′ka·list, *n.* A singer, esp. a trained one.

vo·cal·ize, vō′ka·līz″, *v.t.*—*vocalized, vocalizing.* To make vocal; to utter or articulate; sing; to endow with voice or make articulate. *Phon.* to utter, as speech sounds, with the voice, and not merely with the breath; to use as a vowel; to supply with vowel points or vowels, as an Arabic or Hebrew text.—*v.i.* To use the voice, as in speech or song; to exercise the vocal cords, as in voice warm-up, using note patterns and arpeggios; *phon.* to become altered to a vowel.—**vo·cal·i·za·tion,** vō″kal·i·zā′shan, *n.*—**vo·cal·iz·er,** *n.*

vo·ca·tion, vō·kā′shan, *n.* [L. *vocatio(n-),* < *vocare,* call.] A particular occupation, business, profession, trade, or calling; a summons to, or predilection for, a par-

ticular activity or career; a divine call to God's service or to the Christian life; a function or station to which one is called by God.

vo·ca·tion·al, vō·kā′sha·nal, *a.* Pertaining to a vocation or occupation; as, *vocational* schools; pertaining to guidance or training in the development of skills required by different trades; as, a *vocational* guidance counselor.—**vo·ca·tion·al·ly,** *adv.*

vo·ca·tive, vok′a·tiv, *a.* [L. *vocativus,* < *voco,* to call.] *Gram.* denoting or relating to the case in inflected languages, as Latin, that designates a person or object indicated or addressed. Relating to or used in addressing or calling.—*n. Gram.* The vocative case; any word which is in this form or case.

vo·cif·er·ance, vō·sif′ẽr·ans, *n.* Vociferant utterance; vociferation.

vo·cif·er·ant, vō·sif′ẽr·ant, *a.* Noisy; vociferating.—*n.* One who vociferates.

vo·cif·er·ate, vō·sif′e·rāt″, *v.i., v.t.*—*vociferated, vociferating.* [L. *vocifero, vociferatum—vox, vocis,* the voice, and *fero,* to bear.] To cry out with a loud voice; to clamor; to shout.—**vo·cif·er·a·tor,** *n.*

vo·cif·er·a·tion, vō·sif″e·rā′shan, *n.* The act of vociferating; outcry; clamor.

vo·cif·er·ous, vō·sif′ẽr·us, *a.* Making a loud outcry; clamorous; noisy.—**vo·cif·er·ous·ly,** *adv.*—**vo·cif·er·ous·ness,** *n.*

vod·ka, vod′ka, *n.* An intoxicating liquor distilled from potatoes or various cereals, orig. made and much used in Russia.

vogue, vōg, *n.* [Fr. *vogue,* fashion, lit. 'rowing of a ship,' < It. *voga,* a rowing, < G. *wogen,* to wave, akin E. *wag, wave.*] The prevalent mode or fashion, often preceded by *in*; popular favor; acceptance.

voice, vois, *n.* [O.Fr. *vois, voiz* (Fr. *voix*), < L. *vox* (*voc-*), voice, sound, word, speech, akin to *vocare,* call, Skt. *vac-,* say, *vacas,* speech, Gr. *épos,* word, tale.] The sound or sounds uttered by the mouth of living creatures, esp. of human beings in speaking, shouting, or singing; the sounds naturally uttered by a single person in speech or vocal utterance, often as characteristic of the utterer; such sounds considered with reference to their character or quality; as, a manly *voice*; the condition of the voice for speaking or singing, as: She was in poor *voice*. Any sound likened to vocal utterance; as, the *voice* of the wind; anything likened to speech; as, the *voice* of nature; the faculty of uttering sounds with the mouth, esp. articulate sounds; speech; expression in spoken or written words, or by other means; as, to give *voice* to one's disapproval by a letter; expressed opinion or choice; as: His *voice* was for compromise. The right to express an opinion or choice; as, to have no *voice* in the matter; expressed wish or injunction; as, obedient to the *voice* of God; the person or other agency by which something is expressed or revealed; a singer; a voice part; a musical sound caused by vocal cord vibration and throat and oral resonance; *phon.* sound uttered with the resonance of the vocal cords and not by mere emission of breath; *gram.* distinctive form of a verb indicating the relation of the subject to the action expressed by the verb, or any of the groups of forms of a verb serving to indicate this; as, the active or passive *voice.*—*v.t.*—*voiced, voicing.* To give voice, utterance, or expression to; to declare or proclaim. *Mus.* to regulate the tone of, as the pipes of an organ; to write the voice parts for, as music. *Phon.* to utter with voice or vocal sound, as distinguished from *breathe.*—**in voice,** in good or fit condition as for speaking or singing.—**with one voice,** unanimously.

voice box, *n.* The larynx.

voiced, voist, *a.* Having a voice or type of voice; as, low-*voiced*; expressed or stated

with the voice. *Phon.* uttered with voice or vocal vibration, as the consonants *b, d,* and *g*; sonant; vocal.—**voic·ed·ness,** voi′sid-nis, voist′nis, *n.*

voice·ful, vois′ful, *a.* Having a voice, esp. a loud voice; sounding; sonorous.—**voice·ful·ness,** *n.*

voice·less, vois′lis, *a.* Having no voice; mute; uttering no speech or words; silent; not having a musical voice; having no voice or vote; unspoken or unuttered. *Phon.* uttered without voice or vocal sound, as the consonants *p, t,* and *k*; surd.—**voice·less·ly,** *adv.*—**voice·less·ness,** *n.*

voice part, *n. Mus.* the melody or succession of tones for one of the voices or instruments in a harmonic or concerted composition.

voice·print, vois′print″, *n.* A spectographic record of modulation, amplitude, and duration of human speech sounds, used chiefly in criminological identification.

voice vote, *n.* An estimation of a vote by the relative strength of the ayes and noes, instead of by roll call or individual ballot.

void, void, *a.* [O.Fr. *voide, vuide* (Fr. *vide*), empty, void, < L. *viduus,* widowed, bereaved; allied to E. *widow.*] *Law,* having no legal or binding force; null. Empty or not containing matter; having no holder or possessor; vacant; unoccupied; devoid; destitute; as, *void* of learning; not producing any effect; ineffectual; in vain.—*n.* An empty space; a vacuum.—*v.t.* To make or leave vacant; to nullify; to emit or discharge.—**void·a·ble,** voi′da·bl, *a.*—**void·a·ble·ness,** *n.*—**void·er,** *n.*—**void·ness,** *n.*

void·ance, void′ans, *n.* The act of voiding, ejecting, or vacating; vacancy, as of a benefice.

void·ed, voi′did, *a.* Of or pertaining to being empty or made void; *her.* having the center cut out with only a framework left round the edge.

voile, voil, *Fr.* vwäl, *n.* A fabric of rayon, silk, cotton, or wool, which is sheer and used for curtains, women's dresses, or the like.

voir dire, vwär′ dēr′, *Fr.* vwär dēr′, *n.* [O.Fr., 'to say the truth': cf. *verdict.*] *Law.* An oath administered to a proposed witness or juror by which he is sworn to speak the truth in an examination for the purpose of ascertaining his competence; the examination itself.

voix cé·leste, vwä sä·lest′, *n.* A certain organ stop which for each note consists of two pipes, one whose pitch is slightly sharp, yielding a soft tone of tremulous quality, similar to the vox angelica. Also *vox caelestis.*

vo·lant, vō′lant, *a.* [Fr. *volant,* flying, < *voler,* L. *volare,* to fly.] Having the ability to fly; flying; nimble; rapid; *her.* represented as flying.

vo·lan·te, vō·län′tä, *It.* va·län′te, *a. Mus.* quick and light, used as a performer's direction.

Vo·la·pük, vō″la·pɥk′, *n.* [An invented name based on the words *world* and *speak*; world speech.] An artificial language intended for universal use, based primarily on English, invented by Johann Schleyer of Germany around 1879.

vo·lar, vō′lẽr, *a.* [L. *vola,* palm.] Relating to the palm of the hand or the sole of the foot.

vo·lar, vō′lẽr, *a.* Of or pertaining to flight.

vol·a·tile, vol′a·til, vol′a·til, *Brit.* vol′a·til″, *a.* [Fr. *volatil,* < L. *volatilis,* < *volo, volatum,* to fly.] Having the quality of passing off quickly by evaporation; able to vaporize freely in the air; fickle; apt to change; lively; explosive.—**vol·a·tile·ness,** **vol·a·til·i·ty,** vol′a·til′i·tē, *n.*

vol·a·tile oil, *n.* Any oil that evaporates quickly and completely, without leaving a mark; essential oil.

vol·a·til·ize, vol′*a·*ti·līz″, *v.t.*—*volatilized, volatilizing.* [Fr. *volatiliser.*] To cause to evaporate; to cause to pass off in vapor. —*v.i.* To become volatile.—**vol·a·til·i·za·tion,** vol″*a·*til*·i·*zā′shan, *n.*

vol-au-vent, vō·lō·vän′, *n.* [Fr., for *vole-au-vent,* lit. 'fly-in-the-wind.'] A baked pastry shell of light puff paste filled with a preparation of meat or fish.

vol·can·ic, vol·kan′ik, *a.* Pertaining to or characteristic of volcanoes; emitted or discharged from volcanoes.—**vol·can·i·cal·ly,** *adv.*

vol·can·ic glass, *n.* A natural glass produced when molten lava cools very rapidly; obsidian.

vol·can·ic tuff, *n.* Tuff.

vol·can·ism, vol′ka·niz″um, *n.* The phenomena connected with volcanoes and volcanic activity. Also **vol·can·ic·i·ty,** vul·can·ic′i·ty, *vulcanism,* vol″ka·nis′i·tē. —**vol·can·ist,** *n.* One who specializes in the study of volcanoes.

vol·can·ize, vol′ka·nīz″, *v.t.*—*volcanized, volcanizing.* To subject to volcanic heat.

vol·ca·no, vol·kā′nō, *n.* pl. **vol·ca·noes, vol·ca·nos.** [It. *volcano, vulcano,* < L. *Volcanus, Vulcanus,* the fire-god Vulcan, or Hephaestus, whose workshop was fabled to be under Mount Etna.] A vent in the earth's crust through which molten rock, steam, ashes, and the like, are expelled from within, gradually forming a conical heap or mountain, commonly with a cup-shaped hollow or crater around the vent; a mountain or hill having an opening or vent through which heated matter is expelled from the interior of the earth.

vol·can·ol·o·gy, vol″ka·nol′o·jē, *n.* The scientific study of volcanoes and volcanic phenomena. Also *vulcanology.*—**vol·can·o·log·ic,** vol″ka·no·loj′ik, *a.*—**vol·can·ol·o·gist,** *n.*

vole, vōl, *n.* [Also called *vole-mouse,* perh. for *wold-mouse.*] Any of several small rodents belonging to the genus *Microtus,* resembling mice. Also *field mouse, meadow mouse.*

vole, vōl, *n.* [Fr., < *voler,* to fly.] *Cards.* The winning or taking of all the tricks in various card games; a grand slam.—**go the vole,** *colloq.* To go all out for a big win; to go for broke.

vo·li·tion, vō·lish′an, *n.* [L. *volitio,* < *volo,* to will; same root as E. *will.*] The act of willing; the exercise of the will; the power of willing; will; that which has been decided or chosen by will.—**vo·li·tion·al,** *a.*—**vo·li·tion·al·ly,** *adv.*

vol·i·tive, vol′i·tiv, *a.* Originating in the will; relating or pertaining to volition; *gram.* expressing a wish or permission; as, a *volitive* proposition.

Volks·lied, fạlks′lēt″, *n.* pl. **Volks·lied·er,** fạlks″lē′dᴇʀ. [G.] A folk song.

vol·ley, vol′ē, *n.* pl. **vol·leys.** [Fr. *volée,* a flight, < *voler,* L. *volare,* to fly.] A flight of missiles, as of shot or arrows; a simultaneous discharge of a number of missile weapons, as small arms; a discharge or burst of numerous things at one time; as, a *volley* of ideas; a return of the ball before it touches the ground, as in tennis or soccer; *cricket,* a ball bowled in such a way that it reaches the wicket before it reaches the ground.—*v.t.*—*volleyed, volleying.* To discharge with a volley, or as if with a volley; *sports,* to return, as a ball, before it touches the ground.—*v.i.* To be discharged at once or with a volley; to return a ball before it touches the ground, as in tennis or soccer. —**vol·ley·er,** *n.*

vol·ley·ball, vol′ē·bạl″, *n.* A game, usu. played by two teams in a gymnasium, the object of which is to keep a large ball in motion, from side to side over a high net, by striking it with the hands before it touches the ground; the ball so used.

vol·plane, vol′plān, *v.i.*—*volplaned, volplaning. Avi.* to glide downward in an aircraft.—*n.* Any such glide, as in an aircraft.

Vol·scian, vol′shan, *a.* Belonging or pertaining to the Volsci, a people of ancient Italy dwelling southeast of Rome, or to their language.—*n.* One of the Volsci or their language.

volt, vōlt, *n.* [From *Volta,* the discoverer of voltaism.] *Elect.* the practical unit of electromotive force or potential difference in a conductor which has one ampere as a constant or steady current against a resistance of one ohm, thus expending one watt of power.

volt, vōlt, *n.* [Fr. *volte,* < L. *volvo, volutum,* to turn.] *Horsemanship,* a gait executed in side steps about a center point; the circle formed by this gait. *Fencing,* a sudden movement or leap to avoid a thrust.

volt·age, vōl′tij, *n.* Electromotive force as expressed and measured in volts.

volt·age di·vid·er, *n. Elect.* a sequence of resistors or a resistor having taps at various points to reduce the applied voltage to desired variances.

vol·ta·ic, vol·tā′ik, *a. Elect.* Pertaining to or denoting electricity created by chemical activity, as in an automobile battery; galvanic.

vol·ta·ic bat·ter·y, *n. Elect.* a battery consisting of a combination of voltaic or primary cells. Also *galvanic battery.*

vol·ta·ic cell, *n. Elect.* a primary cell. Also **gal·van·ic cell.**

vol·ta·ic cou·ple, *n. Elect.* the pair of substances, commonly two dissimilar metallic plates, which, when placed in dilute acid or other electrolyte, give rise to the electric current. Also *galvanic couple.*

vol·ta·ic pile, *n. Elect.* pile. Also **Vol·ta's pile.**

vol·ta·ism, vol′ta·iz″um, *n.* The chemically activated production of electricity. See *galvanism.*

vol·tam·e·ter, vol·tam′i·tėr, *n.* [*Voltaic,* and Gr. *metron,* measure.] An electrolytic means for measuring the quantity and strength of a current. Also **cou·lom·e·ter.** —**vol·ta·met·ric,** vol″ta·me′trik, *a.*

volt·am·me·ter, vōlt′am′mē″tėr, *n.* An instrument used for measuring volts or amperes.

volt-am·pere, vōlt′am′pēr, *n. Elect.* an electrical unit equal to the product of one volt and one ampere, which with continuous currents is equivalent to one watt in direct current and an apparent power unit for a system of alternating current.

volte-face, volt·fäs′, *Fr.* vạlt·*e·*fäs′, *n.* pl. **volte-face.** [Fr., for It. *volta-faccia,* lit. 'turn-face.'] A turning so as to face in the opposite direction, as a reversal of opinion or policy.

volt·me·ter, vōlt′mē″tėr, *n.* [After A. *Volta,* Gr. *metron,* a measure.] *Elect.* an instrument for measuring electrical force, or difference of potential, in volts between two different points.

vol·u·ble, vol′ya·bl, *a.* [Fr. *voluble,* L. *volubilis,* revolving, fluent, voluble, < *volvo, volutum,* to roll (whence also *vault, volume, revolve, involve, convolution,* etc.); cogn. E. *wallow, walk.*] Having a great flow of words or glibness of utterance; speaking with great fluency; overly fluent; *bot.* twisting, applied to stems which twist or twine around other bodies.—**vol·u·bly,** *adv.*—**vol·u·bil·i·ty, vol·u·ble·ness,** vol″-ya·bil′i·tē, *n.*

vol·ume, vol′ūm, vol′yam, *n.* [O.Fr. Fr. *volume,* < L. *volumen* (volumin-), a roll (as of manuscript), book, < *volvere,* roll.] A collection of written or printed sheets bound together and constituting a book; a book forming one of a related set or series; the size, measure, or amount of anything in

three dimensions; as, the *volume* of a gas; cubic magnitude; bulk; amount; as, the *volume* of travel on a railroad; a mass or quantity, esp. a large quantity, of anything; *hist.* the ancient form of a book or manuscript, usu. a roll of papyrus or parchment. Intensity or loudness of tone or sound.— *v.t.*—*volumed, voluming.* To send up in volumes.—*a.*—**vol·umed,** vol′-yamd, *a.*

vo·lu·me·ter, vo·lö′mi·tėr, *n.* [< *volume* and *-meter:* cf. Fr. *volumètre.*] Any of various instruments or devices for measuring volume, as of gases, liquids, or solids.

vol·u·met·ric, vol″ya·me′trik, *a. Chem.* pertaining to measuring the volume of a substance.—**vol·u·met·ri·cal·ly,** *adv.*

vol·u·met·ric a·nal·y·sis, *n. Chem.* a method of analysis in which the quantity of a substance present in a solution is estimated by the amount of a standard solution required to produce a certain reaction.

vo·lu·mi·nous, vo·lö′mi·nus, *a.* [L.L. *voluminosus,* < L. *volumen* (volumin-), E. *volume.*] Forming, filling, or writing a large volume or volumes; as, a *voluminous* literary work; sufficient to fill a volume or volumes; as, a *voluminous* correspondence; of great volume, size, or extent; as, a *voluminous* flow of lava; of ample size, extent, or fullness; as, a *voluminous* robe; *archaic,* having many coils, convolutions, or windings.—**vo·lu·mi·nous·ly,** *adv.*—**vo·lu·mi·nos·i·ty, vo·lu·mi·nous·ness,** vo·lö″mi·nos′i·tē, *n.*

vol·un·ta·rism, vol′an·ta·riz″um, *n. Philos.* any theory that regards the will, rather than the intellect, as the fundamental agency or principle of reality.—**vol·un·ta·rist,** *n.*—**vol·un·ta·ris·tic,** *a.*

vol·un·tar·y, vol′an·ter″ē, *a.* [L. *voluntarius,* acting or done of one's own will, < *voluntas,* will, choice, < *volo,* I will, inf. *velle.*] Done, made, brought about, or undertaken of one's own accord or by free choice; having the power of willing or choosing; as, a *voluntary* agent; exercising one's own will or choice; as, a *voluntary* substitute; pertaining to or depending on voluntary action; as, *voluntary* schools; proceeding from a natural impulse; spontaneous; as, a *voluntary* burst of song; *physiol.* subject to or controlled by the will; as, *voluntary* muscles. *Law,* acting or done without compulsion or obligation; done by intention and not by accident; made without valuable consideration; as, a *voluntary* conveyance or settlement.—*n.* pl. **vol·un·tar·ies.** Something done voluntarily; *mus.* an organ solo, frequently extemporized, performed as a prelude to, during, or after a church service.—**vol·un·tar·i·ly,** vol′an·ter″i·lē, vol′an·târ′i-lē, *adv.*—**vol·un·tar·i·ness,** *n.*

vol·un·tar·y·ism, vol′un·ter″ē·iz″um, *n.* The principle or system of supporting churches, schools, or the like, by voluntary contributions or aid, independently of the state.—**vol·un·tar·y·ist,** *n.*

vol·un·teer, vol″un·tēr′, *n.* [Fr. *volontaire,* orig. *a.,* < L. *voluntarius,* E. *voluntary.*] One who enters into any service or undertakes anything of his own free will; *milit.* one who enters the service voluntarily rather than through conscription or draft, esp. for special or temporary service rather than as a member of the regular or permanent army; *agric.* a plant, other than a weed, which springs up spontaneously or without being planted. *Law,* one to whom a voluntary conveyance or property transfer is made before there is valuable or good consideration; an outside or disinterested party who participates in some legal transaction.—*a.* Being or consisting of volunteers; pertaining to voluntary entrance into any service; *agric.* of crops springing up spontaneously or from self-sown seed; as, a *volunteer* growth.—*v.i.* To offer oneself for some service or undertaking; to enter into a service or enlist as a volunteer.—*v.t.* To offer, as one's services or self, for some duty or purpose; to offer to give, show or share voluntarily; to offer in speech or communication; as, to *volunteer* an explanation.

vo·lup·tu·ar·y, vo·lup'chŏ·er"ē, *n.* pl. **vo·lup·tu·ar·ies.** [L. *voluptuarius,* < *voluptas,* pleasure, akin to *volo,* to wish.] One primarily interested in sensual pleasure and luxury; a sensualist.—*a.*

vo·lup·tu·ous, vo·lup'chŏ·us, *a.* [L. *voluptuosus.*] Pertaining to, characterized by, exciting, or producing sensual pleasure; gratifying to the senses; concerned with or indulging in sensuous pleasures and luxuries; tending to excite sensual desires, as a woman's full, shapely form.—**vo·lup·tu·ous·ly,** *adv.*—**vo·lup·tu·ous·ness,** *n.*

vo·lute, vo·lōt', *n.* [Fr. *volute,* < L. *voluta,* prop. fem. of *volutus.*] A spiral or twisted formation or object; *arch.* a spiral scroll-like ornament, esp. one forming the distinctive feature of the Ionic capital or a more or less important part of the Corinthian and Composite capitals. *Zool.* a turn or whorl of a spiral shell; any of the *Volutidae,* a family of marine gastropods of tropical seas, many of the species of which have shells prized for their beauty.—*a.* Rolled up; having the form of a volute.—**vo·lut·ed,** *a.*—**vo·lu·tion,** *n.*

vol·va, vol'va, *n.* [L., a wrapper.] *Bot.* a membrane that envelops certain fungi when young.—**vol·vate,** vol'vit, vol'vāt, *a.*

vol·vox, vol'voks, *n.* Any of the fresh-water flagellates, genus *Volvox,* that aggregate to form green hollow spherical colonies and usu. classed with the green algae.

vol·vu·lus, vol'vya·lus, *n.* pl. **vol·vu·lus·es.** [N.L., < L. *volvere,* roll, turn.] *Pathol.* a torsion or twisting of the intestine causing intestinal obstruction.

vo·mer, vō'mer, *n.* [N.L. use of L. *vomer,* plowshare.] *Anat.* a bone of the skull in most vertebrates, forming a large part of the nasal septum, or partition between the right and left nasal cavities.—**vo·mer·ine,** vō'me·rīn", vō'mer·in, vom'e·rīn", vom'ĕr·in, *a.*

vom·it, vom'it, *v.i.* [L. *vomitus,* pp. of *vomere,* vomit, discharge, akin to Gr. *emein,* vomit.] To eject the contents of the stomach through the mouth; to throw up; to be ejected or come out with force or violence.—*v.t.* To eject from the stomach through the mouth; to spew; to cast out or eject as if in vomiting; to send out copiously with force; to cause, as a person, to vomit.—*n.* The act of vomiting; matter ejected in vomiting; an emetic.—**vom·i·ter,** *n.*—**vom·i·tous,** *a.*

vom·i·to·ry, vom'i·tŏr"ē, vom'i·tar"ē, *a.* [L. *vomitorius, a.* (as n., *vomitorium,* prop. neut. of *vomitorius*), < *vomere.*] Inducing vomiting; emetic; pertaining to vomiting. —*n.* pl. **vom·i·to·ries.** An emetic; an opening through which something is ejected or discharged. One of the openings in a theater, amphitheater, or stadium allowing mass entry or exit; also **vom·i·to·ri·um,** vom"i·tŏr'ē·um, vom"i·tar'ē·um.

vom·i·tu·ri·tion, vom"i·chụ·rish'an, *n.* Ineffectual efforts to vomit; the vomiting of but little matter.

vom·i·tus, vom'i·tus, *n.* pl. **vom·i·tus·es.** The matter ejected in vomiting.

voo·doo, vō'dŏ, *n.* pl. **voo·doos.** [Creole Fr. *vaudou,* prob. of Afr. origin.] A religion of African origin characterized by mysterious rites or practices of the nature of sorcery, witchcraft, or conjuration, prevalent among the negroes of the West Indies; one who practices such rites; a fetish; a charm.—*a.* Pertaining to, associated with, or practicing voodoo or voodooism.—*v.t.*—*voodooed, voodooing.* To affect by voodoo sorcery or conjuration.

voo·doo·ism, vō'dō·iz"um, *n.* The voodoo rites or practices; voodoo sorcery; the voodoo superstition.—**voo·doo·ist,** *n.*—**voo·doo·is·tic,** *a.*

vo·ra·cious, vō·rā'shus, va·rā'shus, vo·rā'shus, *a.* [L. *vorax, voracis,* < *voro,* to devour; same root as Gr. *bora,* food; Skt. *gar,* to swallow.] Greedy for eating; eating food in large quantities; rapacious; ready to devour or swallow up.—**vo·ra·cious·ly,** *adv.*—**vo·ra·cious·ness,** *n.*—**vo·rac·i·ty,** vō·ras'i·tē, va·ras'i·tē, vo·ras'i·tē, *n.*

vor·lage, fōr'lä"ge, *n.* pl. **vor·la·ge.** *German,* the posture of a skier, assumed by leaning forward but maintaining a position in which the heels touch the skis.

vor·tex, vạr'teks, *n.* pl. **vor·tex·es, vor·ti·ces,** vạr'ti·sēz". [L. *vortex* (*vortic-*), var. of *vertex,* a whirl, a whirlpool, vortex, also summit.] A whirling mass of water or air, as a whirlpool or whirlwind; a state of affairs likened to a whirlpool, as for violent activity or irresistible force; in the Cartesian philosophy, a rapid rotary movement of cosmic matter about a center, regarded as accounting for the origin or phenomena of bodies or systems of bodies in space.

vor·ti·cal, vạr'ti·kal, *a.* Of, pertaining to, causing, moving in, or resembling a vortex. —**vor·ti·cal·ly,** *adv.*

vor·ti·cel·la, vạr"ti·sel'a, *n.* pl. **vor·ti·cel·lae,** vạr"ti·sel'ē. Any ciliate, bell-shaped, stalked protozoan of the genus *Vorticella.*

vor·tic·i·ty, vạr·tis'i·tē, *n.* pl. **vor·tic·i·ties.** *Phys.* a measurement of a fluid's circulation or rotation in a vortexlike motion.

vor·ti·cose, vạr'ti·kōs", *a.* [L. *vorticosus.*] Vortical; whirling.

vor·tig·i·nous, vạr·tij'i·nus, *a.* [Var. of *vertiginous,* after *vortex.*] Whirling; vortical; like or similar to a vortex.

vo·ta·ress, vō'tĕr·is, *n.* A female devoted to any service, worship, or way of life. Also **vo·tress,** vō'tris.

vo·ta·ry, vō'ta·rē, *n.* pl. **vo·ta·ries.** [L. *votum,* a vow: see *vote.*] One who is bound by a vow, esp. one bound by vows to a religious life; a monk or a nun; a devoted worshiper, as of God; a devotee of some form of religious worship; one devoted to any pursuit or study; a devoted follower or admirer, as of some person. Also **vo·ta·rist.**—*a.* Characterized by a vow.

vote, vōt, *n.* [L. *votum,* a vow, wish, desire, < *vovere,* promise solemnly, vow.] A formal expression of will, wish, or choice in some matter, whether of a single individual or of a body of individuals; the means by which such an expression is made, as a ballot or ticket; the right to such expression; the decision reached by voting, as by a majority of ballots cast; a number of votes collectively; as, the labor *vote.* *Archaic,* vow; wish; prayer.—*v.i.*—*voted, voting.* To cast a vote or votes.—*v.t.* To enact, establish, or determine by vote; to support or advocate by one's vote; as, to *vote* Republican; *colloq.* to declare by general consent.—**vote down,** to defeat, as a referendum, by vote. —**vote in,** to elect.

vote·less, vōt'lis, *a.* Having no vote, esp. not entitled to vote in political elections.

vot·er, vō'tĕr, *n.* One who votes; one who has a right to vote; an elector.

vot·ing ma·chine, *n.* A machine whose operation by a succession of voters in an election furnishes a record and tally of votes cast.

vo·tive, vō'tiv, *a.* [L. *votivus,* < *votum,* a vow, wish.] Offered, given, or dedicated in accordance with a vow; as, a *votive* offering; performed or undertaken in consequence of a vow; of the nature of or expressive of a wish or desire; *Rom. Cath. Ch.* optional, or not prescribed; as, a *votive* Mass.—**vo·tive·ly,** *adv.*—**vo·tive·ness,** *n.*

vo·tive Mass, *n. Rom. Cath. Ch.* a Mass which does not correspond with the office of the day, but is said at the choice of the priest.

vouch, vouch, *v.i.* [O.Fr. *vochier,* call, invoke, declare, < L. *vocare,* call: cf. *avouch.*] To support as being true, certain, reliable, or justly asserted, usu. used with *for,* as: His grades *vouch for* his capabilities. To give warrant or attestation; to give one's own assurance, as surety or sponsor, usu. used with *for,* as: The judge would *vouch for* his character.—*v.t.* To warrant, attest, or confirm; to sustain or uphold by some practical proof or demonstration, or as such proof does; to adduce or quote in support, as extracts from a book or author; to cite in warrant or justification, as authority, instances, or facts; *law,* to call or summon, as a person, into court to make good a warranty of title; *obs.* to call or take to witness, as a person.

vouch·ee, vou'chē, *n. Law,* one summoned to defend or warrant a title, esp. concerning common recoveries.

vouch·er, vou'chĕr, *n.* One who or that which vouches, as for something; a book, document, stamp, or the like which serves to prove the truth of something; a receipt or other written evidence, as of the payment of money.

vouch·safe, vouch·sāf', *v.t.*—*vouchsafed, vouchsafing.* [< *vouch* and *safe,* to vouch or attest as safe; formerly often as two words.] To grant, often condescendingly; to permit.—*v.i.* To condescend; to deign.— **vouch·safe·ment,** *n.*

vous·soir, vō·swär', *n.* [Fr., ult. < L. *volvere,* roll, turn.] *Arch.* any of the pieces in the shape of a truncated wedge which form an arch or vault.

vow, vou, *n.* [O.Fr. *vou,* Mod.Fr. *voeu,* a vow, < L. *votum,* a vow.] A solemn promise; an engagement solemnly entered into; an oath made to God or to some deity to perform some act on the fulfillment of certain conditions; a promise to follow out some line of conduct, or to devote oneself to some act or service.—*v.t.* To promise solemnly; to give, consecrate, or dedicate by a solemn promise, as to a divine power; to threaten solemnly or upon oath, as: I *vow* vengeance.—*v.i.* To make a promise or vow.—**take vows,** to enter a religious order. —**vow·er,** *n.*

vow·el, vou'el, *n.* [O.Fr. *vouel, voyeul* (Fr. *voyelle*), < L. *vocalis,* lit. 'vocal (letter).'] One of the more or less open and resonant speech sounds, used alone or in combination with consonants to form syllables: distinguished from *consonant;* a letter or character representing such a sound, as, in English, *a, e, i, o, u,* and sometimes *y.*—*a.*

vow·el·ize, vou'e·līz", *v.t.*—*vowelized, vowelizing.* To provide with vowel points or symbols, as a Hebrew text.—**vow·el·i·za·tion,** *n.*

vow·el point, *n.* Any of certain marks placed above or below consonants in certain languages, as Arabic or Hebrew, to represent vowel sounds.

vox an·gel·i·ca, voks' an·jel'i·ka, *n.* An organ stop with a soft, delicate tone, similar to the voix céleste.

vox cae·les·tis, voks' si·les'tis, *n.* Voix céleste.

vox hu·ma·na, voks' hū·mā'na, *n.* [L., lit. 'human voice.'] An organ stop designed to produce tones resembling those of the human voice.

vox po·pu·li, voks' pop'ya·lī", *n.* [L.] The voice of the people; the expression of the popular will.

---

a- fat, fāte, fär, fâre, fạll; **e-** met, mē, mēre, hėr; **i-** pin, pīne; **o-** not, nōte, mŏve; **u-** tub, cūbe, bụll; **oi-** oil; **ou-** pound.

voy·age, voi′ij, *n.* [Fr. *voyage,* a journey; It. *viaggio,* Sp. *viage;* < L. *viaticum,* < *viaticus,* pertaining to a journey, < *via,* a way (seen also in *viaduct, deviate, obviate, obvious, previous, convey,* etc.); same root as E. *way.*] A journey by sea from one place, port, or country to another, esp. a journey by water to a distant place or country; formerly, a journey by sea or by land; a journey in a space vehicle or airplane; an account written about a voyage.—*v.i. voyaged, voyaging.* To take a journey or voyage; to sail or pass by water.—*v.t.* To travel; to pass over.—**voy·ag·er,** *n.*

vo·ya·geur, vwä″yä·zhụr′, voi·*a·*zhụr′, *Fr.* vwä·yä·zhųrz′, *n.* pl. **vo·ya·geurs,** vwä″yä·zhụrz′, voi·*a·*zhụrz′, *Fr.* vwä·yä·zhœR′. [Fr. 'traveler.'] One of a class of men in Canada hired by some fur company to travel through unsettled regions, esp. by canoe, to transport men and goods and to maintain communications with various stations.

vo·yeur, vwä·yụr′, voi·yụr′, *Fr.* vwä·yœR′, *n.* pl. **vo·yeurs,** vwä·yụrz′, voi·yụrz′, *Fr.* vwä·yœR′. One who obtains sexual satisfaction from the sight of sexual actions or objects.—**vo·yeur·ism,** *n.*—**voy·eur·is·tic,** vwä″ye·ris′tik, voi″ye·ris′tik, *a.*—**voy·eur·is·ti·cal·ly,** *adv.*

V-par·ti·cle, vē′pär·ti·kl, *n.* Former term for hyperon.

vrouw, vrou, *D.* frou, *n. Dutch.* Wife; a woman; a title for a married woman.

V sign, *n.* A gesture symbolizing victory, or peace, or expressing approval, made by raising one's middle and index fingers into the form of a V.

VTOL, vē′tạl″, *n.* [(*V*)ertical (*T*)ake-(*O*)ff and (*L*)anding.] *Aeron.* an airplane, other than a helicopter, that takes off and lands vertically, used esp. in reference to a fixed-wing airplane.

vug, vugg, vugh, vug, vụg, *n.* [Corn.] *Min.* a small hollow or cavity in a mineral vein, often lined with crystals.—**vug·gy,** *a.*

Vul·can·i·an, vul·kā′nē·an, *a.* Pertaining to Vulcan, the Roman metalworking and fire god, or to metalwork. (*l.c.*), *geol.* volcanic; pertaining to vulcanism.

vul·can·ism, vul′ka·niz″um, *n. Geol.* volcanism.

vul·can·ite, vul′ka·nīt″, *n.* A form of hard rubber, vulcanized at a high temperature and containing a large proportion of sulfur, used for making combs, electrical insulating equipment, and the like; ebonite.

vul·can·i·zate, vul′ka·ni·zāt″, *n.* A vulcanized material or product.

vul·can·ize, vul′ka·nīz″, *v.t.*—*vulcanized, vulcanizing.* [From *Vulcan.*] To treat, as rubber, with sulfur or some compound of sulfur, and subject to a moderate heat, in order to render nonplastic and give greater elasticity or durability, or, when a large amount of sulfur and a more extensive heat treatment are employed, in order to make it very hard, as in the case of vulcanite; to treat, as rubber, similarly with sulfur or sulfur compounds, but without the action of heat, in which case the effects are only superficial; to subject, as substances other than rubber, to some analogous process, as to harden.—**vul·can·i·za·tion,** vul″ka·ni·zā′shan, *n.*—**vul·can·iz·er,** *n.*

vul·can·ized fi·ber, *n.* A tough, pliable material produced by the action of zinc chloride on cellulose, and used esp. in low-voltage insulation.

vul·can·ol·o·gy, vul″ka·nol′o·jē, *n.* Volcanology.—**vul·can·ol·o·gist,** *n.*

vul·gar, vul′gẽr, *a.* [Fr. *vulgaire,* < L. *vulgaris,* < *vulgus,* the common people, the crowd.] Lacking in good taste, cultivation, or refinement; somewhat coarse; boorish; crude; indecent or obscene; pertaining to the common people, or the multitude;

plebeian; popular or current; expressed in the language of the common people, or vernacular; as, the *vulgar* tongue; ordinary, or deficient in distinction.—*n. Archaic,* the multitude, or common people; *obs.* the vernacular.—**vul·gar·ly,** *adv.*—**vul·gar·ness,** *n.*

vul·gar·i·an, vul·gâr′ē·an, *n.* A vulgar person, esp. a prominent or wealthy individual with coarse or conspicuous tastes and manners.

vul·gar·ism, vul′ga·riz″um, *n.* Vulgarity; a vulgar phrase or expression used in colloquial speech.

vul·gar·i·ty, vul·gar′i·tē, *n.* pl. **vul·gar·i·ties.** The quality of being vulgar; coarseness; a vulgar expression, habit, or action.

vul·gar·ize, vul′ga·rīz″, *v.t.*—*vulgarized, vulgarizing.* To make vulgar; coarsen; to debase; to make generally acceptable; to popularize.—**vul·gar·i·za·tion,** *n.*—**vul·gar·iz·er,** *n.*

Vul·gar Lat·in, *n.* Latin used by the common people of ancient Rome and from which developed the Romance Languages: as opposed to the literary language of the time.

vul·gate, vul′gāt, vul′git, *a.* [L. *vulgatus,* common, ordinary, pp. of *vulgare,* spread among the multitude, make common, < *vulgus,* the multitude: cf. *vulgar.*] Common, or in common use; as, a *vulgate* text or version; (*cap.*) of or pertaining to the Vulgate.—*n.* (*Cap.*) the Latin version of the Scriptures prepared by Jerome about the close of the 4th century, accepted as the authorized version of the Roman Catholic Church; any vulgate text or version.

vul·gus, vul′gus, *n.* pl. **vul·gus·es.** The masses of common people. A short Latin writing exercise, once required of students in English public schools.

vul·ner·a·ble, vul′nẽr·a·bl, *a.* [Fr. *vulnerable,* < L. *vulnero,* to wound, < *vulnus, vulneris,* a wound.] Capable of being wounded; liable to injury or criticism; subject to being affected injuriously or attacked; as, a *vulnerable* nation; *bridge,* pertaining to the team which has won a game of the rubber and which can receive increases in bonuses or penalties.—**vul·ner·a·bil·i·ty, vul·ner·a·ble·ness,** *n.*—**vul·ner·a·bly,** *adv.*

vul·ner·ar·y, vul′ne·rer″ē, *a.* [L. *vulnerarius.*] Used in healing or curing wounds. —*n.* pl. **vul·ner·ar·ies.** Any agent useful in the healing of wounds.

vul·pine, vul′pīn, vul′pin, *a.* [L. *vulpinus,* < *vulpes,* a fox.] Pertaining to the fox; resembling the fox; cunning.

vul·ture, vul′chẽr, *n.* [O.Fr. *voltour* (Fr. *vautour*), < L. *vulturius, vultur,* vulture.] Any of certain large raptorial birds allied to the eagles, hawks, and falcons, either of the Old World belonging to the family *Accipitridae,* or any of the similar birds of the New World constituting the family *Cathartidae,* which feed chiefly or wholly on carrion, and which have the head and neck more or less bare of feathers and the beak and claws less powerful than in most birds of prey; *fig.* a person or thing that preys ravenously and ruthlessly.

vul·tur·ine, vul′che·rīn″, vul′chẽr·in, *a.* [L. *vulturinus.*] Pertaining to or characteristic of a vulture; of the nature of a vulture; resembling a vulture. Also **vul·tur·ous,** vul′chẽr·us.

vul·va, vul′va, *n.* pl. **vul·vae, vul·vas,** vul′vē. [L. *vulva,* a wrapper, the womb, < *volvo,* to roll.] *Anat.* the female external genital organs.—**vul·val, vul·var,** *a.*—**vul·vate,** vul′vāt, vul′vit, *a.*

vul·vi·form, vul′vi·fạrm″, *a.* Having the shape or appearance of a vulva, esp. as related to plants.

vul·vi·tis, vul·vī′tis, *n. Pathol.* an inflamed condition of the vulva.

W

W, w, dub′l·ū″, *n.* The twenty-third letter of the English alphabet and the eighteenth consonant, although often referred to as a semivowel, esp. when followed immediately by a vowel; the sound of the letter W as represented in speech; the delineation of the letter W or w in writing or printing; something designated by or having the shape of the letter W or w; a graphic device for printing the letter W or w.

W, dub′l·ū″. Symbol for tungsten or wolfram.

W, w, dub′l·ū″. *Elect.* watt; watts. West; western.

wab·ble, wob′l, *v.i., v.t.*—*wabbled, wabbling.* Wobble.—*n.* A wobble.—**wab·bler,** *n.*

WAC, Wac, wak, *n.* [From the initials.] A member of the Women's Army Corps.

WAC, W.A.C., wak. Abbreviation for Women's Army Corps.

wack·y, wak′ē, *a.*—*wackier, wackiest. Slang.* Erratic or eccentric; seemingly quite irrational; crazy. Also *whacky.*—**wack·i·ly,** *adv.*—**wack·i·ness,** *n.*

wad, wod, *n.* [Same word as Sw. *vadd,* Dan. *vat,* G. *watte,* wad.] A soft mass of fibrous material, as cotton, used for stuffing, stopping an aperture, and the like; a lump, mass, or ball of something; a plug used to hold powder or shot in place in a gun, cartridge, or cannon; *slang,* a roll of paper currency, esp. a large sum.—*v.t.*—*wadded, wadding.* To mold into a wad by rolling, crumpling, compressing, and the like; to plug with a wad; to stuff or line with wadding.—*v.i.* To form into a wad.—**wad·der,** *n.*

wad·ding, wod′ing, *n.* Wads of soft material used for stuffing or padding; material used as wads for guns, cartridges, and the like.

wad·dle, wod′l, *v.i.*—*waddled, waddling.* [A dim. and freq. formed < *wade.*] To sway or rock from side to side in walking; to walk in a tottering manner.—*n.* A characteristic walk; as, the *waddle* of a duck.—**wad·dler,** *n.*—**wad·dly,** *a.*

wad·dy, wod′ē, *n.* pl. **wad·dies.** *Aust.* A short, heavy, wooden club used as a weapon by the aborigines; a walking stick.—*v.t.*—*waddied, waddying. Aust.* to beat with a waddy.

wade, wād, *v.i.*—*waded, wading.* [O.E. *wadan,* to go, to wade = L.G. *waden,* Icel. and Sw. *vada,* D. *waden,* G. *waten,* to wade; same root as L. *vado,* to go.] To walk through any substance that impedes or hinders the free motion of the legs, as water, snow, or high grass; *fig.* to move or proceed with difficulty; as, to *wade* through the required reading assignment.—*v.t.* To pass or cross by wading; to ford.—*n.* The act of wading; as, to go for a *wade* along the beach.—**wade·in** or **wade in·to,** *colloq.* To make a vigorous start; as, to *wade* right *in;* to attack verbally, as: The boss *waded into* the employee for being late.—**wad·a·ble, wade·a·ble,** *a.*

wad·er, wā′dẽr, *n.* One who wades; any long-legged bird, as the stork, heron, snipe, or rail, that wades in water searching for food; *pl.* high, waterproof boots used by hunters and fishermen for wading.

wa·di, wä′dē, *n.* pl. **wa·dis, wa·dies.** [Ar. *wādi.*] *Southwestern Asia, North Africa.* The channel of a watercourse that is dry, except in the rainy season; a watercourse or stream running through this channel; any oasis. Also **wa·dy.**

wad·ing bird, *n.* A water bird that wades. See *wader.*

wad·mal, wod′mal, *n.* [Icel. *vad-mál,* Sw.

vadmal, Dan. *vadmel.*] A coarse woolen cloth formerly used extensively in the manufacture of warm winter clothing in both England and the Scandinavian countries. Also **wad·maal, wad·mel, wad·-mol.**

WAF, Waf, waf, *n.* A member of the Women in the Air Force.

WAF, W.A.F., waf. Abbreviation for Women in the Air Force.

wa·fer, wā′fėr, *n.* [O.Fr. *waufre* (Fr. *gaufre*), wafer, < G. *waffel,* D. *wafel,* a thin cake, a wafer.] A small, crisp, sweet cake, biscuit, or cracker; *eccles.* a circular piece of unleavened bread, as used in the Roman Catholic Church in the celebration and administration of the Eucharist. A small thin disk of an adhesive substance, used in the sealing of letters and documents; *med.* a thin coating of dried paste or the like covering a powdered drug to be swallowed. —*v.t.* To fasten, seal, or attach with a wafer.

waf·fle, wof′l, *n.* [D. *wafel,* G. *waffel, waffer.*] A crisp batter cake, having deep latticelike indentations on both sides, baked in a waffle iron.

waf·fle i·ron, *n.* A metal utensil with two indented or studded hinged parts which, when shut together, impress a pattern on the baking batter.

waft, waft, wäft, *v.t.* [Closely akin to *wave,* and to Sw. *vefta,* to waft, Dan. *vifte,* to waft, to fan; *vift,* a puff.] To convey or carry lightly through, or as if through, water or air, as objects or odors; to make to sail or float.—*v.i.* To sail or float, as through air.—*n.* The act of one who or that which wafts; any wafting movement or motion; anything, as a sound or odor, conveyed gently through the air; a breath or current, as of wind. *Naut.* a small flag or pennant for signaling or to show wind direction; the signal made with such a flag or pennant; also *waif.*—**waft·age,** waf′tij, wäf′tij, *n.*—**waft·er,** *n.*

waf·ture, waf′chėr, wäf′chėr, *n.* The act of wafting; something wafted; as, *waftures* of sound; a waving movement or wave of something; as, with an angry *wafture* of your hand.

wag, wag, *v.t.*—**wagged, wagging.** [M.E. *waggen,* akin to O.E. *wagian,* move, *wegan,* carry, move: see *weigh.*] To move from side to side, forward and backward, or up and down, esp. rapidly and repeatedly, as a dog's tail; to move, as the head, in agreement or denial; to move, as the tongue, in talk or gossip.—*v.i.* To be moved from side to side or one way and the other, esp. rapidly and repeatedly, as the head, the tail, or the tongue; to travel, go, or proceed; to walk with a sway or waddle; *Brit. slang,* to play hooky, as from school.—*n.* An act of wagging.—**wag·ger,** *n.*

wag, wag, *n.* [Most likely a shortening of the old term *waghalter,* one likely to *wag* in a *halter* or gallows. Comp. Sc. *hempte,* a gallows bird, a frolicsome fellow, lit. 'one fitted for the hempen rope.'] A person who is full of mischievous humor; a wit; a joker.—**wag·gish,** wag′ish, *a.*—**wag·gish·ly,** *adv.*—**wag·gish·ness,** *n.*

wage, wāj, *n.* [O.Fr. *wage, guage* (Fr. *gage*), pledge, security; < Teut., and akin to E. *wed.*] *Often pl.* money paid for labor or services, usu. according to specified intervals of work, as by the hour, day, or week; *pl., econ.* the share of a national product received by labor for its work, as distinct from the share going to capital. *Pl., sing.* or *pl. in constr.* recompense; requital; as: The *wages* of sin is death.—*v.t.*—**waged, waging.** To carry on, as a battle, conflict, or argument; as, to *wage* war against a nation. —**wage·less,** *a.*

wage earn·er, *n.* One who is paid wages for working. Also *wageworker.*

wa·ger, wā′jėr, *n.* [O.Fr. *wageure* (Fr. *gageure*), < *wagier,* E. *wage, v.*] A bet; the subject of a bet; something staked or hazarded on an uncertain event.—*v.t.* To hazard, as money or property, on the issue of a contest or any uncertain event or matter; to stake; to bet.—*v.i.* To make or offer a wager; to bet.—**wa·ger·er,** *n.*

wage scale, *n.* A schedule of wages paid to workers in a particular type of job, industry, or plant; the wage schedule of a single employer.

wage·work·er, wāj′wur″kėr, *n.* Wage earner.

wag·ger·y, wag′e·rē, *n.* pl. **wag·ger·ies.** The manner, action, or attitude of a wag; jocular, mischievous pleasantry; a prank or joke.

wag·gle, wag′l, *v.i.*—**waggled, waggling.** [A freq. and dim. < *wag.*] To move with a wagging motion; to sway or move from side to side; to wobble or totter.—*v.t.* To cause to wag or move rapidly and with short motions.—*n.* A waggling movement.—**wag·gling·ly,** *adv.*—**wag·gly,** wag′lē, *a.*

Wag·ne·ri·an, väg·nēr′ē·an, *a.* Of or pertaining to Richard Wagner, 1813–1883, the celebrated German composer, or his works; pertaining to or in accordance with the ideas or the style of Wagner, being highly dramatic, stressing the leitmotif, and with increasing emphasis on the orchestra.—*n.* An admirer or advocate of Wagnerian music. Also **Wag·ner·ite,** väg′ne·rīt″.—**Wag·ner·ism,** väg′ne·riz″um, *n.* The theory or style as exemplified in Richard Wagner's music dramas.—**Wag·ner·ist,** *n.*

wag·on, *Brit.* **wag·gon,** wag′on, *n.* [< D. *wagen,* rather than < O.E. *waegen,* a wagon (whence *wain*); Icel. and Sw. *vagn,* Dan. *vogn,* G. *wagen;* lit. 'what carries,' < stem of *weigh;* cogn. Skt. *vah,* L. *veho,* to carry (whence *vehicle*); akin also *way, wag,* etc.] A four-wheeled vehicle for the transport of heavy loads; a delivery wagon; a low, four-wheeled cart for children's use; a small cart or table on wheels, from which food and beverages are served; a station wagon; *Brit.* a railroad freight car; *astron.* the constellation Charles's Wain; *colloq.* a patrol wagon.—*v.t.* To transport or carry in a wagon.—*v.i.* To transport goods or freight by wagon.—**hitch one's wag·on to a star,** to pursue an ambitious course.—**off the wag·on,** *slang,* no longer giving up all alcoholic beverages.—**on the wag·on,** *slang,* to give up all alcoholic beverages.

wag·on·er, wag′o·nėr, *n.* One who drives a wagon; also *Brit.* **wag·gon·er.** (*Cap.*), *astron.* the constellation Charles's Wain or Ursa Major; the constellation Auriga containing the bright star Capsella.

wag·on·ette, *Brit.* **wag·gon·ette,** wag″o·net′, *n.* [Dim. of *wagon.*] A light, usu. open, four-wheeled vehicle having two lengthwise facing seats behind the front cross seat.

wa·gon-lit, *Fr.* vä·gaN·lē′, *n. pl.* **wa·gons-lits, wa·gon-lits,** vä·gaN·lē′. [Fr., 'bed car.'] *Europe,* a railroad sleeping car.

wag·on train, *n.* A group or train of wagons traveling together for a common purpose or for transporting supplies.

wag·tail, wag′tāl″, *n.* Any of many small European birds, genus *Motacilla,* related to the pipits, which wags its tail continuously; the yellow wagtail, *Motacilla flava,* of Alaska.

wa·hi·ne, wä·hē′nä, *n.* Hawaiian, a woman.

wa·hoo, wä·hö′, wä′hö, *n. pl.* **wa·hoos.** [N. Amer. Ind.] A shrub or small tree, *Euonymus atropurpureus,* of N. America, with purple flowers and pendulous capsules which in dehiscing reveal the bright scarlet arils of the seeds; also *burning bush.* Loosely any of various N. American shrubs or trees, as the winged elm, *Ulmus alata,* and the white basswood, *Tilia heterophylla.*

waif, wāf, *n.* [O.Fr. *waif, gaif,* a waif; of Scand. origin, like E. *waive.*] A neglected, homeless person, esp. a young child; a wanderer; any stray or abandoned animal; anything found, as goods, of which the owner is not known, or that no one claims; *law,* stolen goods that are thrown away or abandoned by the fleeing thief. *Naut.* a small pennant or flag used for signaling; also *waft.*

wail, wāl, *v.i.* [M.E. *wailen, weilen,* prob. from Scand.: cf. Icel. *væla,* to wail, *væ, vei,* interj., woe, and E. *woe.*] To utter a prolonged, inarticulate, mournful cry, usu. high-pitched or clear-sounding, as in grief or suffering; to cry piteously; to lament or mourn bitterly; to give forth a mournful or plaintive sound suggesting a cry, as musical instruments or the wind; to sound mournfully, as music.—*v.t.* To wail over, bewail, or lament; as, to *wail* the dead; to cry or say in lamentation.—*n.* The act or sound of wailing; a wailing cry, as of lamentation, grief, or pain; any mournful sound; as, the *wail* of an old tune.—**wail·er,** *n.*—**wail·ing·ly,** *adv.*

wail·ful, wāl′ful, *a.* Full of wailing or lamentation; characterized by or resembling wails; mournful; plaintive.—**wail·ful·ly,** *adv.*

Wail·ing Wall, *n.* A stone wall in Jerusalem which is reputed to be a remnant of Solomon's temple, and to which Jews address themselves with prayer and lamentation.

wain, wān, *n.* [O.E. *waen,* a contracted form of *waegen,* a wagon, < *wegan,* to carry.] A four-wheeled farm wagon for the transportation of heavy goods; (*cap.*), *astron.* Charles's Wain, a constellation.

wain·scot, wān′skot, wān′skot, *n.* [< D. *wagenschot,* wainscot, for *wageschot,* < *waeg,* a wall, and *schot,* boarding, a covering of boards.] A wooden lining for the walls of rooms, usu. made in panels; *Brit.* high quality oak, imported from Baltic nations to be used in fine woodwork. The wood-paneled lower portion of a wall, the upper portion of which is finished in some other material.—*v.t.*—*wainscoted, wainscoting,* *Brit.* *wainscotted, wainscotting.* To line with wainscot.—**wain·scot·ing,** *Brit.* **wain·scot·ting,** wān′skō·ting, wān′skot·ing, wān′skot·ing, *n.*

wain·wright, wān′rīt″, *n.* A wagon maker.

waist, wāst, *n.* [M.E. *wast,* prob. orig. 'growth,' 'size': cf. O.E. *waestm,* growth, stature, form, *weaxan,* grow, E. *wax.*] The part of the human body between the ribs and the hips; the part of a garment covering the waist; a garment or a part of a garment covering the body from the neck or shoulders to the waistline, esp. in women's or children's dress; a bodice, blouse, or the like, separate from the skirt or other garments; an undergarment or undershirt for children, esp. to which additional garments may be fastened or attached; that part, often the narrowest, of an object, esp. a central or middle part, which bears some analogy to the human waist; as, the *waist* of a violin. *Naut.* the central part of a ship; that part of the deck between the forecastle and the quarter-deck. *Aeron.* the middle section of an airplane's fuselage; *entom.* the constricted or narrow basal portion of the abdomen of various insects, as the wasp.

waist·band, wāst′band″, wāst′band, *n.* A band for encircling the waist, esp. such a band forming part of a skirt or trousers.

waist·coat, wes′kot, wāst′kōt″, *n. Chiefly Brit.* A sleeveless body garment for men, now reaching only a short distance below the waist, worn underneath the coat; a vest. A similar garment sometimes worn by women; a body garment for men, usu. ornamental, formerly worn under the doublet.—**waist·coat·ed,** *a.*

waist·er, wā′stẽr, *n.* An inexperienced or incapacitated seaman posted in a ship's waist, as on a whaling ship.

waist·line, wāst′līn″, *n.* The line of the waist, between the chest and hip portions of the human body; the measurement of this line; the narrow part on clothing to which the skirt or lower portion attaches.

wait, wāt, *v.i.* [O.Fr. *waitier, guaitier* (Fr. *guetter*), watch; < Teut., and akin to *wake* and *watch*.] To stay or rest in expectation, often followed by *for, till,* or *until*; to be in readiness; to remain neglected or be postponed for a time; as, a matter that can *wait*; to perform the duties of an attendant, esp. as a waiter or waitress.—*v.t.* To remain stationary or inactive in expectation of; to await; as, to *wait* one's turn; to postpone in expectation of; to defer; as, to *wait* dinner for someone; *archaic,* to attend or escort.—*n.* [O.Fr. *waite, guaite* (Fr. *guette*).] An act or interval of waiting; delay; *Brit.* one of a band of musicians and carolers who play and sing in the streets during the Christmas season; *archaic,* watchman.—**lie in wait,** to watch for from a place of concealment, esp. with hostile intent.—**wait on** or **wait up on,** to act as attendant or servant to; to make a formal, usu. deferential, call upon; as, to *wait on* the King.—**wait up,** to postpone going to bed in expectation of someone or something.

wait-a-bit, wāt′a·bit″, *n.* [Orig. S. Afr., tr. S. Afr. D. *wacht-een-beetje,* name applied to various plants.] Any of various plants bearing thorns or prickly appendages, as a procumbent herb, *Harpagophytum procumbens,* of southern Africa.

wait·er, wā′tẽr, *n.* A male attendant who waits upon the guests in a hotel, restaurant, or similar place; one who waits or awaits something or someone; a salver or tray for carrying something, as dishes.

wait·ing, *n.* The act of a person who waits. —*a.* Expecting; attending.—**in wait·ing,** in attendance, esp. on a person of royalty.

wait·ing game, *n.* A ploy in which an action is postponed in the expectation of a more favorable opportunity in the future.

wait·ing list, *n.* A list of those who are waiting, as for admission, selection, or appointment.

wait·ing room, *n.* A room provided for the use of persons waiting, as in a railroad station or a physician's office.

wait·ress, wā′tris, *n.* A girl or woman who waits on tables, esp. in a restaurant.

waive, wāv, *v.t.*—**waived, waiving.** [The verb corresponding to the noun *waif*; lit. 'to leave loose or unregarded'; comp. Icel. *veifa,* to swing loosely, to vibrate.] To refrain from claim or insistence upon; to relinquish; to forgo; to put aside, postpone, or dismiss; *law,* to relinquish, give up, or abandon voluntarily, as a right or claim.

waiv·er, wā′vẽr, *n.* [A.Fr. *weyver,* inf., used as noun.] *Law.* An intentional relinquishment of a known right, interest, or advantage; an express or written statement of such relinquishment.

wake, wāk, *v.i.*—past *waked* or *woke,* pp. *waked* or *woken,* ppr. *waking.* [O.E. *wacan* (pret. *wōc,* pp. *wacen*), wake, arise, also *wacian* (pret. *wacode,* pp. *wacod*), be awake, watch; akin to D. *waken,* G. *wachen,* Icel. *vaka,* Goth. *wakan,* wake, watch, also L. *vigil,* awake, alert: cf. *wait* and *watch*.] To become roused from sleep, often followed by *up,* as: He *woke up* suddenly. To awake; to be or continue to be awake; as, *waking* or sleeping; to become roused from a quiescent or inactive state; to become aware, as of something perceived; as, to *wake* to the truth; to remain awake for some purpose or duty; *colloq.* to hold a wake.—*v.t.* To rouse from sleep, often followed by *up,* as: *Wake* me *up* for breakfast. To awaken; to

rouse from quiescence, inactivity, lethargy, or unconsciousness; to stir up or excite, as feelings; *colloq.* to hold a wake over, as a corpse.—*n.* A watching or a watch kept, esp. for some solemn or ceremonial purpose; an all-night watch over the body of a dead person before burial; an annual festival formerly held in England to commemorate the dedication of the parish church, beginning with an all-night watch in the church and followed by a holiday with merrymaking and amusements; the state of being awake; as, between sleep and *wake.*—**wak·er,** *n.*—**wake·less,** wāk′lis, *a.*

wake, wāk, *n.* [< Scand.: cf. Icel. *vök* (*vak-*), hole, opening in ice (affording passage for ships), Sw. *vak,* Dan. *vaage.*] The track left by a ship or other object moving in the water; the path, track, or course of anything that has passed or preceded.—**in the wake of,** following closely; as a consequence or result of, as: Arrests increased *in the wake of* the robbery.

wake·ful, wāk′fu̇l, *a.* Indisposed or unable to sleep, as a person; characterized by absence of sleep; as, a *wakeful* night; sleeplessly alert, watchful, or vigilant; as, a *wakeful* enemy.—**wake·ful·ly,** *adv.*—**wake·ful·ness,** *n.*

wak·en, wā′ken, *v.t.* [O.E. *waecnan,* to become awake, < *wacan,* to wake.] To awake, or rouse from sleep; to awaken; to excite to action; to rouse; to stir; to call forth; as, to *waken* love or fear.—*v.i.* To wake; to cease to sleep; to awaken.—**wak·en·er,** *n.*

wake-rob·in, wāk′rob″in, *n.* Any of various plants of the genus *Trillium,* as *T. erectum,* a species with rank-smelling purple or pink flowers; the cuckoopint, *Arum maculatum,* of Europe.

Wal·dorf sal·ad, wal′dȧrf sal′ad, *n.* A salad consisting of diced apples, nuts, and celery, with a mayonnaise dressing.

wale, wāl, *n.* [O.E. *walu.*] A stripe or ridge produced on the skin, as by the stroke of a whip; a welt; a ridge or rib in the weave of cloth; *naut.* any of certain strakes of thick outside planking on the sides of a wooden ship.—*v.t.*—**waled, waling.** To raise wales on; to weave wales into; to protect, reinforce, or hold together with wales.

wale, wāl, *n.* [M.E. *wale, wal,* < Scand.: cf. Icel. *val* = O.H.G. *wala,* G. *wahl,* choice, < the root of E. *will.*] *Brit. dial., Sc. dial.* Choice; the choicest or best selection.—*v.t.* —**waled, waling.** *Brit. dial., Sc. dial.* To choose; to select.—*a. Brit. dial., Sc. dial.* well-chosen.

Wa·ler, wā′lẽr, *n.* (*Sometimes l.c.*) A sturdy horse bred in New South Wales, Australia, exported in large numbers to India for military use during the days of the British empire.

walk, wak, *v.i.* [O.E. *wealcan,* roll, turn, = O.H.G. *walchan,* G. *walken,* full (cloth), = Icel. *valka,* roll.] To go or travel on foot at a moderate pace; to proceed by steps; to proceed by advancing the feet in turn so that there is always one foot on the ground in bipedal locomotion, and two or more feet on the ground in quadrupedal locomotion; to go on foot for enjoyment or exercise; to go about on the earth as a ghost; of inanimate objects, to move in a manner suggestive of walking, as through repeated vibrations; to conduct oneself in a particular manner or pursue a particular course of life; as, to *walk* with God; *baseball,* to be advanced one base after four balls are pitched; *basketball,* to advance more than two steps, while in possession of the ball, without passing or dribbling.—*v.t.* To proceed through, over, or upon, on foot at a moderate pace; as, to *walk* the streets; to pass, as hours, while walking, usu. followed by *away*; to perform or accomplish in

walking; to lead, drive, or ride at a walk, as an animal; to force or help to walk, as a person; to conduct on a walk; as, to *walk* the neighbors around the street; to move, as an inanimate object, in a manner suggestive of walking; *baseball,* to advance by one base, as a batter, by pitching four balls; *basketball,* to advance more than two steps while in possession of, as the ball, without passing or dribbling; to measure, survey, or otherwise examine, as property, by inspecting on foot.—*n.* An act of walking or going on foot; a time or interval of walking for exercise or pleasure; a distance walked or to be walked, often in terms of the time required; as, a ten minutes' *walk* to school; the gait or pace of a person or animal that walks; a manner of walking; as, her figure and her *walk*; a particular profession, activity, or position; as, various *walks* of life; a place prepared or set apart for walking, as a path in a garden; a path for pedestrians on a street; a sidewalk; *baseball,* advancement to first base after four pitched balls. An enclosed area in which domestic animals exercise and are fed; the route of a tradesman or hawker; *Brit.* a division of a forest under the charge of a forester; *sports,* a walking race.—**walk off,** to depart suddenly; *colloq.* to rid oneself of, by walking, as a heavy meal.—**walk off with,** *colloq.* To obtain surreptitiously; to win in competition, as honors. —**walk out,** *colloq.* to go on strike.—**walk out on,** *colloq.* To desert; abandon; forsake. —**walk o·ver,** *colloq.* to trounce, as one team over the other.—**walk through,** *theatr.* to run through, as a play rehearsal, adding stage positions to the first reading. —**win in a walk,** to gain an easy victory.

walk·a·way, wak′a·wā″, *n.* An easily won competition.

walk·er, wak′ẽr, *n.* A device moving on casters designed to enclose and support a child during his early attempts at walking; a similar framework which may be rigid or movable, with arm supports, to aid an invalid or elderly person in walking; one who walks, esp. one fond of walking.

walk·ie-talk·ie, wak′ē·tȧ′kē, *n.* A mobile or portable two-way radio-telephone system with a receiver and microphone, which is operated by a battery and compact enough for one person to carry, usu. on his back. Also **walk·y-talk·y.**

walk-in, wak′in″, *a.* Pertaining to that which can be entered on foot; as, a *walk-in* closet; of or pertaining to one who enters a place of business casually or without prior planning to make a major purchase, as of a car.

walk-in, wak′in″, *n.* A space large enough to be entered on foot; a cold storage room; an easily won victory, as in an athletic event or an election.

walk·ing, wak′ing, *a.* Pertaining to that which walks; proceeding on foot at a walk; used for walking; as, a *walking* stick; not confined, as to bed; as, a *walking* patient; ambulatory; pertaining to a mechanical device that traverses back and forth; as, a *walking* crane.—*n.* The act of walking; gait; carriage; the condition or suitability of that on which one walks, as: The *walking* is difficult on an icy street.

walk·ing del·e·gate, *n.* An official appointed by a trade-union to go from place to place in the interests of the union, as to see that the rules are obeyed, and to represent the union in dealings with other organizations and with employers: a term now infrequently used.

walk·ing fern, *n. Bot.* a fern of the genus *Camptosorus,* with fronds tapering into a slender prolongation which frequently takes root at the apex, esp. *C. rhizophyllus,* a small, hardy species of eastern N. America.

walk·ing leaf, *n. Entom.* an insect of the order *Orthoptera,* found in southern Asia and the E. Indies, whose wings and legs resemble a leaf.

walk·ing pa·pers, *n. pl. Colloq.* notification that one has been dismissed or discharged.

walk·ing stick, *n.* A cane or stick carried in the hand, usu. to assist in walking. *Entom.* any insect of the family *Phasmidae,* with a long, twiglike body; also **stick in·sect.**

walk-on, wǎk'on″, wǎk'ạn″, *n.* A small part, as in a play or film, usu. without lines; a performer who plays such a part.

walk·out, wǎk'out″, *n.* A workers' strike; an expression of disapproval by departure or absence, as from a meeting.

walk·o·ver, wǎk'ō″vẽr, *n.* A race, esp. a horse race, won by the entry who is the only starter; *colloq.* any easy victory.

walk-up, wǎk'up″, *n. Colloq.* An apartment on the second floor or above in a building in which there is no elevator; such a building.—*a.*

walk·way, wǎk'wā″, *n.* Any passage used by one walking; a sidewalk; path; promenade.

wall, wǎl, *n.* [O.E. *weall,* a wall, a rampart = O. Fris., and D. *wal,* Dan. *val,* Sw. *vall,* G. *wall,* a rampart; < L. *vallum,* a fence of stakes, a rampart (seen also in *interval),* < *vallus,* a stake.] A vertical structure of stone, brick, wood, or other materials which serves to enclose a space, form a division, support superincumbent weights, retain earth or water, or perform similar functions; the side of a building or room; a solid and permanent enclosing fence; something similar to a wall; a means of security or protection; a rampart; *usu. pl.* a fortified enclosure or barrier; *bot.* an outer layer of enclosing and protective material; as, a cell *wall.*—*v.t.* To enclose or separate with a wall; to fortify or protect by walls; to fill up with a wall, as an opening.— *a.* Of or concerned with a wall; growing, placed, or hanging on a wall.—**go to the wall,** to get the worst of a contest; to be overpowered.—**push to the wall,** to crush; to humiliate or force into a desperate state.— **wall-like,** *a.*

wal·la·by, wol'a·bē, *n. pl.* **wal·la·bies, wal·la·by.** [Native Aust.] Any of various small and medium-sized kangaroos, esp. of the genera *Macropus* and *Petrogale,* some of which are no larger than rabbits.

wal·lah, wal·la, wä'lä, *n.* [Hind. *-wālā,* a suffix.] *Anglo-Ind.* a person employed at or concerned with a specified occupation or thing: used esp. in compounds; as, a punkah-*wallah,* one who operates a ceiling fan.

wal·la·roo, wol″a·rö′, *n. pl.* **wal·la·roos, wal·la·roo.** Any of several large kangaroos of western Australia, reddish gray to black, esp. *Macropus robustus.* Also **eu·ro.**

wall·board, wǎl'bōrd″, wǎl'bȧrd″, *n.* An artificially prepared board or sheet material for use in making or covering walls and ceilings, as a substitute for wooden boards or plaster.

walled, wǎld, *a.* Possessing walls or a wall; surrounded or closed in by a wall.

wal·let, wol'it, wǎ'lit, *n.* [Prob. a corruption of old *watel,* a bag.] A small case carried in a pocket or handbag for holding money, identification and credit cards, pictures, or the like; also *billfold. Brit.* a bag or sack for personal articles and provisions which a person carries with him on a journey.

wall·eye, wǎl'ī, *n. pl.* **wall·eye, wall·eyes.** [Back-formation < *wall-eyed.*] An eye in which the iris is of a very light gray or whitish color, such as is seen in a walleyed person or other animal. *Pathol.* strabismus in which there is a turning outward of the eye; leukoma. Any of various game fishes with large, staring eyes, as a pikeperch, *Stizostedion vitreum.*

wall·eyed, wǎl'īd″, *a.* [From Scand.: cf. Icel. *vagleygr,* walleyed, < *vagl,* beam in the eye, and *eygr,* adj. < *auga,* eye.] Having an eye or the eyes presenting little or no color, as the result of a light-colored or white iris or of white opacity of the cornea; having eyes in which there is an abnormal amount of the white showing, because of divergent strabismus; having large, staring eyes, as some fishes.

wall fern, *n.* The common polypody, *Polypodium vulgare.*

wall·flow·er, wǎl'flou″ẽr, *n.* Any plant of the genus *Cheiranthus,* in the mustard family, esp. a European perennial, *C. cheiri,* growing wild on old walls, cliffs, and similar places, and also cultivated in several varieties, bearing sweet-scented yellow, red, or purple flowers; also *gillyflower.* Any of various similar plants, as *Erysimum asperum,* of western U.S. *Colloq.* a person, esp. a woman or girl, who is left stranded at the side in a social situation, as at a dance, either from shyness or failure to obtain a partner.

wal·lop, wol'op, *v.t.* [Origin uncertain: cf. *wallop.*] *Colloq.* To beat soundly; thrash; to strike with a vigorous blow; to defeat thoroughly, as in a game.—*v.i. Colloq.* To move in a clumsy manner; to flounder; to boil vigorously, as water.—*n. Colloq.* A forceful blow; an ability to deliver such blows, as in boxing.—**wal·lop·er,** wol'o·pẽr, *n.*

wal·lop·ing, wol'o·ping, *a. Colloq.* Big; powerful; strong.—*n. Colloq.* A beating; a defeat.

wal·low, wol'ō, *v.i.* [O.E. *wealwian* = Goth. *walwjan,* roll; akin to L. *volvere,* roll, turn.] To roll the body about, or lie in water, snow, mud, dust, or the like, as for refreshment, as a pig in mud; to live self-indulgently or luxuriously, as in some form of pleasure, manner of life, or the like; as, to *wallow* in wealth; to flounder about or along clumsily or with difficulty, as a vessel on the waves; to surge forth, as smoke or heat.—*n.* The act of wallowing; a place where an animal wallows.—**wal·low·er,** wol'ō·ẽr, *n.*

wall·pa·per, wǎl'pā″pẽr, *n.* Paper, usu. colored and decorated, for covering the walls of rooms.—*v.t.* To put wallpaper on the walls of.

wall pel·li·to·ry, *n.* An old-world herb, *Parietaria officinalis,* of the nettle family that grows on old walls: formerly used as a diuretic.

wall plate, *n. Arch.* a piece of timber fixed horizontally in or on a wall, under the ends of girders, joists, and other timbers; see *plate. Mech.* a plate fastened vertically to the wall for supporting a bracket; *min.* one of the main timbers on the side of a shaft.

wall plug, *n.* A wall outlet for electricity.

wall rock, *n. Min.* the rock forming the walls of a vein.

wall rock·et, *n. Bot.* a European perennial plant, *Diplotaxis tenuifolia,* bearing yellow flowers, and usu. found growing along walls and fences.

wall rue, *n. Bot.* a small fern, *Asplenium rutamuraria,* growing on stone walls, rocks, and similar places.

Wall Street, *n.* A street in the southern part of the borough of Manhattan, in the city of New York, following the line of the early wall of the city, and now famous as the chief financial center of the U.S.; the center for the financiers and financial interests of the U.S.

wal·nut, wǎl'nut, wǎl'nut, *n.* [O.E. *wealhhnut,* a walnut, lit. 'a foreign nut'—*wealh,* foreign, and *hnut,* nut; so G. *walnuss,* D. *walnoot.*] One of several trees, genus *Juglans,* bearing fruit containing an edible kernel; the nut of these trees; the timber from such a tree, esp. the black walnut, *Juglans nigra,* valued for cabinetwork and gunstocks; a shade of dark brown similar to the heartwood of the black walnut tree.

Wal·pur·gis Night, väl·pur'gis nīt′, *n.* [From St. *Walpurgis,* an E. missionary who became an abbess in Germany, died 777, and whose feast day falls on May 1.] The eve on which, according to superstition in medieval Germany, witches rode to some appointed rendezvous, esp. the Brocken, the highest of the Harz Mountains, to hold revels with their master, the Devil.

wal·rus, wǎl'rus, wol'rus, *n. pl.* **wal·rus·es, wal·rus.** [D. *walrus,* a walrus, lit. 'a whale-horse'—*wal,* a whale, and *ros,* a horse; so G. *wallross,* Dan. *valros,* Sw. *vallross,* O.E. *hors-hwael,* Icel. *hross-hvalr,* horse-whale.] Either of two large marine carnivorous mammals, genus *Odobenus,* of the arctic regions, related to the seals and hunted for the tough hide, the ivory of the tusks, and the oil derived from the blubber.

waltz, wǎlts, *n.* [Short for G. *walzer,* < *walzen,* to roll, to waltz; akin to *welter.*] A ballroom dance in which the couples glide in a revolving motion around the floor to music in three-quarter time; the music for such a dance.—*a.* Of or pertaining to the waltz; as, a *waltz* gown.—*v.i.* To dance to waltz time; *colloq.* to perform a task effortlessly, followed by *through;* as, to *waltz through* a math assignment.—*v.t.* To lead, as a partner, in a waltz; *colloq.* to move or propel briskly; as, to *waltz* a misbehaving child out of the classroom.— **walt·zer,** *n.*

wam·ble, wom'l, wam'l, *v.i.*—*wambled, wambling.* [Same as Dan. *vamle,* to nauseate; akin Icel. *vaema,* to loathe, *vaema,* nausea.] *Chiefly dial.* To turn or twist about; to move unsteadily; to be upset, as the stomach.—*n. Chiefly dial.* An unsteady walk or a rolling gait; a sensation of nausea.—**wam·bly,** *a.*

wam·pum, wom'pum, wam'pum, *n.* [Amer. Ind.; said to mean white.] Small beads made of shells strung together, formerly used by the N. American Indians as a medium of exchange or for ornamentation: applied to two varieties, the white, or the more valuable black or dark purple; also **peag.** *Colloq.* money.

wam·pum·peag, wom'pum·pēg″, wam'pum·pēg″, *n.* [Algonquin *wampompeag,* 'white strings (of shell beads).'] Wampum, properly white wampum.

wan, won, *a.*—*wanner, wannest.* [O.E. *wan, won, wann,* dark, dusky.] Having a pale or sickly color; pallid; indicative of or showing fatigue, emotional distress, illness, or the like; languid; gloomy.—*v.t., v.i.*—*wanned, wanning. Poet.* to make or grow wan.— **wan·ly,** *adv.*—**wan·ness,** *n.*

wand, wond, *n.* [Same as Dan. *vaand,* O.Sw. *wand,* Icel. *vondr,* Goth. *wandus,* a twig, a wand; prob. akin to *wind* (v.), from its flexibility.] A long, slender stick or rod used by magicians or diviners; a rod or staff indicative of the bearer's office or authority; a musician's baton; a slim twig or branch; *archery,* a six foot by two inch slat employed as a target.

wan·der, won'dẽr, *v.i.* [O.E. *wandrian,* to wander = O.D. *wanderen,* Dan. *vandre,* Sw. *vandra,* G. *wandern,* to wander; freq. forms akin to *wend.*] To ramble or travel here and there without a specific goal or destination; roam; to go indirectly or casually; stroll; to go or extend in an irregular direction or course; meander; to deviate or stray morally; err; to stray in one's thoughts; to be irrational or incoherent in speech or thought.—*v.t.* To travel over.—*n.* A ramble or stroll.— **wan·der·er,** *n.*

wan·der·ing, won′dẽr·ing, *a.* Given to wander; roaming; winding, as a river, path, or road; nomadic.—*n. Often pl.* Travel without a set course; meandering, irrational thought or speech.—**wan·der·ing··ly,** *adv.*

Wan·der·ing Jew, *n.* Any of various trailing or creeping plants, as *Zebrina pendula,* and *Tradescantia fluminensis,* of the spiderwort family; also **wan·der·ing Jew, Wan·der·ing-jew.** In medieval legend, one who was condemned to wander over the earth as punishment for refusing to permit Christ to rest before his house on the way to the Crucifixion.

wan·der·lust, wän′dẽr·lust″, G. vän′-dẽR·lụst″, *n.* [G.] Desire to wander; a longing or impulse to rove or travel about; a compulsion to visit faraway places.

wan·der·oo, won′dẽ·rö′, *n.* [Singhalese.] Any of several species of langur, esp. *Presbytis cephalopterus,* inhabiting Ceylon; a macaque, *Macaca silenus,* of southern India.

wane, wān, *v.i.*—**waned, waning.** [O.E. *wanian,* to diminish, become less, < *wan,* deficient; akin *want.*] To diminish; to decrease or grow less: particularly applied to the illuminated part of the moon, as opposed to *wax;* to decline, as in importance or power; to approach its end, as: The autumn *wanes.*—*n.* A waning period; the decrease of the illuminated part of the moon to the eye of the spectator; a decline; a defective beveled or slanting edge on a board, denoted by bark or a lack of wood. —**on the wane,** in a decreasing period; waning.

wan·ey, wan·y, wā′nē, *a.*—**wanier, waniest.** Diminished or decreased; having a defective beveled or slanting edge, as sawed timber.

wan·gle, wang′gl, *v.t.*—**wangled, wangling.** *Colloq.* To accomplish or obtain by irregular or devious methods or means; as, to *wangle* an extra ticket; to manipulate, esp. fraudulently; to wriggle.—*v.i. Colloq.* to gain one's ends by devious or unscrupulous methods. —*n. Colloq.* an act of wangling.—**wan··gler,** *n.*

wan·i·gan, wan·ni·gan, won′i·gon, *n.* [N. Amer. Ind.] *North. U.S., Canada.* A lumberjack's trunk or chest; a place or receptacle in lumber camps for small supplies and miscellaneous stores; a shack mounted on wheels, treads, or a boat, as for a kitchen, office, or shelter. Also **wan·gan, wan·gun,** wang′gan.

wan·ion, won′yon, *n.* [M.E. *waniand,* the waning moon (regarded as unlucky), prop. ppr. of *wanien,* < O.E. *wanian,* E. *wane.*] *Archaic.* Ill luck; vengeance: used in imprecatory or emphatic phrases; as, with a *wanion.*

want, wont, wạnt, *v.t.* [< Icel. *vant,* neut. of *vanr,* lacking, wanting, *vanta,* to be lacking; akin *wane, wan-* in *wanton.*] To feel a desire for; long, wish, need, or crave, often followed by an infinitive, as: I *want* to sleep. To be without; to lack; as, to *want* experience; to require or need, as: The lawn *wants* cutting. To be short of, as a specified extent or amount.—*v.i.* To be needy or impoverished; to have need, usu. followed by *for;* to be inclined, often followed by *to,* as: Stay home if you *want to.* —*n.* Absence or scarcity of something needed or desired; lack; the state of being in need; poverty; a desire for something. —**want in** or **want out,** *colloq.* To desire to come in or go out; to wish to be included in or to reject some undertaking or plan.—**want·er,** *n.*

want ad, *n.* Classified ad.

want·ing, won′ting, wạn′ting, *a.* Lacking or absent; as, an apparatus with some of the parts *wanting;* deficient in some part, thing,

or respect, usu. used with *in;* as, to be *wanting in* courtesy.—*prep.* Lacking or without; less; minus; as, a century, *wanting* three years.

wan·ton, won′ton, *a.* [O.E. *wantowen, wantoun,* undisciplined, dissolute, < *wan,* prefix denoting want or deficiency (*wan,* lacking), and *towen, togen,* pp. of *teón,* to draw, to educate.] Licentious or lustful; indulging unrestrainedly in natural impulses or appetites; dissipated; unprovoked or unjustified; spiteful; arising from recklessness or disregard of right or consequences; excessive or immoderate; overly luxurious or lavish, as a style of living. *Chiefly liter.* playful or fun loving; free, unbound, or without constraint; as, *wanton* ringlets of hair. Growing luxuriantly or without restraint, as weeds or other plants. —*n.* A lustful person, esp. a woman; a person or other animal inclined to excess frolic or play.—*v.t.* To waste or expend wantonly.—*v.i.* To frolic unrestrainedly or carouse; to indulge in lewdness.—**wan··ton·ly,** *adv.*—**wan·ton·ness,** *n.*

wap·en·take, wop′en·tāk″, wap′en·tāk″, *n.* [Lit. 'a *weapontaking* or weapon-touching' —from the men of a district touching the arms of a superior in token of fealty.] In some northern shires of England, a former division of a county corresponding to the 'hundred.'

wap·i·ti, wop′i·tē, *n. pl.* **wap·i·tis, wap··i·ti.** [N. Amer. Ind.] A N. American species of deer, *Cervus canadensis,* with long slender antlers; elk.

wap·pen·shaw, wop′en·shạ″, wap′en·shạ″, *n.* [Lit. 'a *weapon-show.*'] *Sc.* Formerly a periodic review of the men and arms in each district of Scotland; muster. Also **wap·in·schaw, wap·pen·schaw·ing.**

wap·per·jaw, wop′ẽr·jạ″, *n. Colloq.* an undershot, crooked, or deformed jaw.— **wap·per·jawed, wap·per-jawed,** *a.*

war, wạr, *n.* [O.E. *wár,* O.D. *werre,* O.H.G. *werra,* war (whence Fr. *guerre,* war); akin to G. *wirren,* to embroil, confuse; D. *war,* entanglement; perh. allied to *worse.*] An armed clash between nations or factions in the same nation; a state of hostility or military conflict; an act of enmity or contention; the profession, science, or art of military operations.—*v.i.*—**warred, warring.** To make or carry on war; to carry on hostilities; to be in a state of forceful opposition.—*a.* Of, relating to, used in, or caused by war.—**war·less,** *a.*

war·ble, wạr′bl, *v.t.*—**warbled, warbling.** [O.Fr. *werbler,* < O.H.G. *hwerbalôn,* G. *wirbeln,* to whirl, to warble.] To sing, as any selection, melodiously in a trilling, quavering, or vibrating manner; to modulate with turns or variations; to sing or carol generally.—*v.i.* To have a trilling, quavering, or vibrating sound; to carol or sing with melodious turns or variations; to yodel. —*n.* A flow of melodious sounds, or a trilling, flexible melody; the act or sound of warbling; a trill; a carol or song.

war·ble, wạr′bl, *n.* [Origin uncertain.] *Veter. pathol.* a small, hard tumor or swelling on a horse's back, produced by the galling of the saddle; a tumor or small swelling found under the skin on an animal's back, as cattle, caused by the larva of a warble fly. A warble fly, or its larva.— **war·bled,** *a.*

war·ble fly, *n. pl.* **war·ble flies.** *Entom.* any of various flies of the families *Oestridae* and *Hypodermatidae,* the larvae of which cause swellings or warbles under the skins of cattle and other animals.

war·bler, wạr′blẽr, *n.* One who or that which warbles. *Ornith.* any of the vividly colored, small, chiefly insectivorous birds of N. and S. America constituting the family *Parulidae,* as the yellow warbler, water thrushes,

and the redstart; any of numerous European singing birds of the family *Sylviidae,* including the reed warbler and the whitethroat.

war bon·net, *n.* A ceremonial headdress made of feathers attached to a headband or cap and to an extension trailing down the back, worn by the N. American Plains Indians.

war chest, *n.* Money kept available to finance an expected or planned war; *fig.* money reserved for any future enterprise, as a political campaign.

war club, *n.* A club, usu. having one end weighted with iron or stone, formerly used by American Indians as a weapon.

war crime, *n. Often pl.* a violation of international agreements or ethical standards concerning the conduct of war, esp. a crime against persons, as genocide, slave labor, or mistreatment of prisoners.

war cry, *n.* A battle cry or phrase shouted by fighters in charging an enemy; a slogan or phrase used to unite or rally people in any contest or campaign.

ward, wạrd, *v.t.* [O.E. *weardian* to guard, *weard,* a guard, a watch; G. *wart,* Icel. *vörthr,* Goth. *vards,* guard. < the G. *are,* Fr. *garder,* E. *guard, regard, reward.* Akin to *wary.*] To fend off; to turn aside, as a blow, often followed by *off.*—*n.* The act of guarding; a defensive motion or position in fencing or the like; the state of being under a guard; confinement; custody; guardianship; one who is guarded, specif. a minor or a mental incompetent who is under guardianship; a certain division or section of a town or city, formed for the convenient transaction of civic business and for political purposes; one of the divisions in a prison or hospital; a curved ridge of metal inside a lock to oppose the passage of a key which has no corresponding notch; the notch in the key; a territorial division of the Mormon church; an open court within the walls of a castle or fortification; a division of counties in areas of Britain and Scotland.—**ward·ed,** wạr′did, *a.*

war dance, *n.* A dance engaged in by primitive tribes, either before a battle or afterward, as a celebration of victory.

ward·ed, wạr′did, *a.* Having or provided with wards or notches, as locks or keys.

war·den, wạr′den, *n.* [O.Fr. *wardein,* var. *guardein, gardien,* E. *guardian.*] One who guards, protects, or defends; one charged with the care or custody of something, as a keeper; the chief official of a prison; a public official charged with superintendence, as over a forest or wild game; a person in charge of enforcing regulations for public safety, as for fire or air raids; the chief executive officer of a borough in some states, esp. Connecticut; *Brit.* the head of certain colleges or schools. A member of the governing body of a guild; a churchwarden.—**war·den·ship,** *n.*

ward·er, wạr′dẽr, *n.* One who wards or guards something; a keeper or watchman; a soldier or other person set to guard an entrance. *Chiefly Brit.* an official having charge of prisoners in a jail; a warden.— **ward·er·ship,** *n.*

ward·er, wạr′dẽr, *n.* A truncheon or staff of office or authority formerly carried by a king, commander in chief, or the like, and used by him in giving signals.

ward heel·er, *n. Slang,* a subordinate in a political ward who does such tasks as canvassing votes and soliciting small contributions, usu. in return for a patronage job when his party is in office.

ward·ress, wạr′dris, *n. Chiefly Brit.* a female prison warden.

ward·robe, wạr′drōb, *n.* A place in which clothes are kept, often a piece of furniture resembling a cupboard or cabinet; a large upright trunk; wearing apparel in general belonging to any one person; the costumes and other apparel of a theatrical company; a room keeping these clothes; the department charged with caring for clothes or jewelry in a household of royalty or nobility.

ward·room, wạrd′rŏm″, wạrd′rṳm″, *n.* In a warship, the space or area constituting the living quarters, and esp. the dining room or messroom, of commissioned officers other than the commanding officer; these officers in total, or collectively.

ward·ship, wạrd′ship, *n.* Guardianship; custody; the state or condition of being a ward, or under a legal guardian; *law,* guardianship over a ward.

ware, wâr, *a.* [O.E. *waer = war =* Icel. *varr =* Goth. *wars,* wary, cautious: cf. *wary, aware, beware, ward, n.,* and *warn.*] *Archaic.* Watchful, wary, or cautious; aware or conscious.—*v.t.—wared, waring. Archaic,* to look out for or beware of, used usu. in the imperative, as: *Ware* the dog.

ware, wâr, *n.* [O.E. *waru =* D. *waar,* Icel. *vara,* Dan. *vare,* G. *waare,* ware, merchandise; perh. connected with *worth* (value), *wary.*] *Usu. pl.* articles of merchandise; goods; a service or a salable item produced by artistic or intellectual endeavor. A special type of manufactured item, usu. used in a compound word; as, china*ware;* pottery, or a special type of pottery.

ware·house, wâr′hous″, *n.* A building in which wares or goods are kept or stored; *Brit.* a large store where wholesale goods are sold.—wâr′houz″, wâr′hous″, *v.t.—warehoused, warehousing.* To deposit or secure in a warehouse, esp. one which is bonded or government owned.—**ware··house·man,** wâr′hous″man, *n. pl.* **ware·· house·men.**

ware·room, wâr′rŏm″, wâr′rṳm″, *n.* A room in which goods are stored or are displayed for sale.

war·fare, wạr′fâr″, *n.* The act of military hostilities between nations, political units, or the like; war; any struggle or conflict.

war·far·in, wạr′fa·rin, *n. Chem.* a complex hydrocarbon compound, $C_{19}H_{16}O_4$, used to poison rats and mice and as an anticoagulant medicine.

war foot·ing, *n.* The state of preparedness of an organization, esp. some military force, to maintain or undertake war, or to operate under a state of war.

war game, *n.* A simulated battle or a series of simulated military moves by two opposing forces, undertaken to test the validity of a war plan or of an operational concept.

war·head, wạr′hed″, *n. Milit.* that part of a bomb, guided missile, ballistic missile, torpedo, or other missile, containing an explosive, chemical, or atomic charge intended to damage the enemy.

war-horse, wạr′hạrs″, *n.* A horse used in war; a charger; *colloq.* a veteran of numerous campaigns and battles, as a politician or soldier. An artistic work, as a play or a song, which has become trite through constant repetition.

war·i·son, wạr′i·son, *n.* [O.Fr. *warison,* defense, provision, store, goods, var. of *garison.*] A note sounded as a signal for assault.

war·like, wạr′līk″, *a.* Fit or prepared for war; disposed or inclined to war; military; pertaining to or suggestive of war; openly antagonistic or hostile.

war·lock, wạr′lok″, *n.* [O.E. *waerloga,* deceiver.] A male witch; a magician; a wizard or sorcerer.

war lord, war·lord, *n.* A military leader in a militaristic government or nation; a military ruler, as in the Orient, exerting civil authority in a local area.

warm, wạrm, *a.—warmer, warmest.* [O.E. *wearm =* D. and G. *warm =* Icel. *varmr,* warm; akin to Goth. *warmjan,* to warm, and perh. to L. *formus,* warm, Gr. *thermós,* warm, hot, Skt. *gharma,* heat.] Having or communicating a moderate degree of heat; of or at a moderately high temperature; characterized by a comparatively high temperature; as, a *warm* climate; having a sensation of bodily heat, as from exercise or exertion; producing such a sensation; as, *warm* clothes; characterized by or showing lively feelings, passions, emotions, or sympathies; as, a *warm* heart; cordial or hearty; as, a *warm* welcome; strongly attached or intimate; as, *warm* friends; heated, irritated, or angry; as, to become *warm* when criticized; animated, lively, brisk, or vigorous; as, a *warm* contest; strong or fresh; as, a *warm* scent; suggestive of warmth, as the colors red or yellow. *Colloq.* close to a concealed object or fact, as in various games; uncomfortable or unpleasant; as, a debate too *warm* for comfort.—*v.t.* To make warm; to excite ardor, enthusiasm, or animation in; to affect with kindly feelings.—*v.i.* To become warm; to become ardent, enthusiastic, or animated, followed by *up* or *to;* as, to *warm to* a task; to grow kindly disposed, followed by *to* or *toward,* as: My heart *warmed toward* her.—*n. Colloq.* a warming or heating.—**warm·ish,** *a.*—**warm·ly,** *adv.*—**warm·ness,** *n.*

warm-blood·ed, wạrm′blud′id, *a. Zool.* having warm blood; noting or pertaining to mammals and birds, whose blood temperatures remain relatively constant regardless of the temperature of their surroundings; homoiothermal. Having an ardent, impetuous, or passionate nature.—**warm-blood·· ed·ness,** *n.*

warmed-o·ver, wạrmd′ō′vẽr, *a.* Heated over again, as food not consumed after the first cooking; redone with no new concepts or material and lacking the enthusiasm engendered by the orig.; as, a *warmed-over* production of a once-popular play.

warm·er, wạrm′ẽr, *n.* One who warms; a device for warming or retaining the heat of food already cooked; as, a bun *warmer* or a coffee *warmer;* a device for warming a part of the body; as, a hand *warmer.*

warm front, *n. Meteor.* the irregular forward edge separating an advancing mass of warm air from the cold air it will replace.

warm-heart·ed, warm·heart·ed, wạrm′-här′tid, *a.* Having or showing a genuine interest in or affectionate concern for others; cordial; hearty.—**warm-heart·ed·· ly, warm·heart·ed·ly,** *adv.*—**warm-heart·· ed·ness, warm·heart·ed·ness,** *n.*

warm·ing pan, *n.* A long-handled, covered, flat vessel, usu. of brass, for holding hot coals or the like, formerly in common use for warming beds.

war·mong·er, wạr′mung″gẽr, wạr′mong″-gẽr, *n.* One who advocates or seeks to bring about war; a jingo.—**war·mon·ger·ing,** wạr′mung″gẽr·ing, wạr′mong″gẽr·ing, *n.*

warm spot, *n. Fig.* a feeling of tender attachment to someone or something; as, to have a *warm spot* in one's heart for a good neighbor.

warmth, wạrmth, *n.* The quality or state of being warm; the sensation of heat; gentle heat; hearty kindness or affection; ardor; zeal; fervor; earnestness; slight anger or irritation; *paint.* a bright, cheerful effect which arises from the use of warm colors.

warm up, *v.i.* To become warm; to practice or rehearse before taking part in an athletic effort or a performance; *fig.* to become increasingly intense, as a situation or conflict.—*v.t.* To make warm; to heat; as, to *warm up* yesterday's soup; to run, as an automobile engine, until warm enough to operate properly.—**warm-up,** wạrm′up″, *n.* An act, procedure, or time of warming up.

warn, wạrn, *v.t.* [O.E. *warnian, wearnian,* to warn, to take heed, < *wearn,* refusal, denial; Icel. and Sw. *varna,* G. *warnen,* to warn; of same origin as *ware, wary.*] To give notice of approaching or probable danger or evil; to caution against anything that may prove injurious; to advise; to expostulate with; to inform previously; to give notice to, as a person or persons, to leave or stay away, often followed by *off* or *away.*—*v.i.* To give caution or warning; as: A storm usu. *warns* before it hits.—**warn·er,** *n.*

warn·ing, wạr′ning, *n.* The act of giving notice or intimation of danger or of cautioning, admonishing, or notifying; notice of this kind given or received; something serving to warn, caution, or admonish.—*a.* Serving as a caution.—**warn·ing·ly,** *adv.*

war of nerves, *n.* A conflict in which each antagonist seeks to break the other's will through psychological tricks, as threats and bluffs.

warp, wạrp, *v.t.* [< O.E. *weorpan,* pret. *wearp,* to throw, to cast; Icel. *verpa,* to throw, and reflexively, to warp or shrink, also *varpa,* to throw; Dan. *varpe,* to warp a vessel; Goth. *vairpan,* G. *werfen,* to throw. Akin *wrap.* As to first meaning cf. *cast* in sense of twist.] To change the shape, as of something; to turn or twist out of shape, or out of a straight direction, as by heat or contraction, as: The sun *warps* boards. To turn aside from the true direction; to pervert, as the mind or judgment; *naut.* to tow or move, as a ship into a required position; *aeron.* to bend or twist, as a wing, at the end or ends in order to bank or turn the airplane; *agric.* to fertilize by artificial inundation from rivers which hold large quantities of earthy matter in suspension.—*v.i.* To twist, or be twisted from straightness; to turn from a straight, true, or proper course; to deviate; to swerve; *naut.* to work forward by means of a rope.—*n.* A twist or distortion, as of wood in drying; a mental quirk, aberration, twist, or bias; *weaving,* the threads which are extended lengthwise in the loom and crossed by the woof. *Naut.* a rope used in moving a ship by attachment to an anchor or post; a towline. *Agric.* a deposit of silt artificially introduced upon low lands.—**warp·er,** wạr′pẽr, *n.*

war paint, *n.* Paint applied to the face and parts of the body by American Indians upon going to war. *Colloq.* cosmetics or make-up; full dress; finery; official or ceremonial costume.

warp and woof, *n.* Basic structure, as the criss-crossing threads of woven cloth; foundation; base.

war·path, wạr′path″, wạr′päth″, *n. pl.* **war·paths.** The path or course taken by American Indians on a warlike expedition. **—on the war·path,** looking for, preparing for, or on a warlike or hostile expedition; in an aggressive, angry, or hostile state of mind.

warp beam, *n. Weaving,* the roller in the rear of the loom around which the warp is twisted or wound.

war·plane, wạr′plān″, *n.* An airplane for use in warfare.

war·rant, wạr′ant, wor′ant, *n.* [O.Fr. *warant, guarant,* warrant, security, protection; < Teut., and akin to G. *gewähr,* warrant, guaranty: cf. *guaranty.*] Authorization, sanction, or justification; that which serves to give reliable or formal assurance of something; a security, promise, or guarantee; something having the force of a guarantee or positive assurance of a thing; *law,* an instrument issued by a magistrate authorizing an officer to make an arrest, seize property, conduct a search, or carry a judgment into execution. A writing or document certifying or authorizing something, as a certificate, receipt, license, or commission; *milit.* the certificate of authority or appointment issued to an officer below the rank of a commissioned officer. A written statement authorizing the payment or receipt of money; as, a treasury *warrant.—v.t.* To give authority to or authorize; to justify or afford warrant or sanction for; as, circumstances which do not *warrant* such measures; to give a formal assurance, guarantee, or promise to; as, to *warrant* proper care; to guarantee the reliability, quality, or other claims of, as an appliance or product; to guarantee compensation against loss; to vouch for or give one's word for, often used with a clause to assert emphatically, as: I'll *warrant* he did. **—war·rant·a·ble,** wạr'an·ta·bl, wor'an·-ta·bl, *a.*—**war·rant·a·bly,** *adv.*

war·ran·tee, wạr''an·tē', wor'an·tē', *n. Law,* one to whom a warranty is made.

war·rant of·fic·er, *n. Milit.* an officer ranking below a commissioned officer, serving under a warrant and not a commission.

war·ran·tor, wạr'an·tạr', wor'an·tạr', *n. Law,* one who warrants or makes a warranty. Also **war·rant·er.**

war·ran·ty, wạr'an·tē, wor'an·tē, *n.* pl. **war·ran·ties.** [O.Fr. *warantie, guarantie;* cf. *guaranty.*] The act of warranting; warrant; assurance; authorization. *Law,* an engagement, implied or explicit, assuring that some particular fact in connection with a contract is or will be as it is expressed or assured to be; as, an implied *warranty* of the quality of goods. *Law,* a covenant by which the grantor of an estate assures the grantee that there will be no interference by other persons claiming the land; also **cov·e·nant of war·ran·ty.** *Insurance law,* a statement or promise made by the party insured, included in a policy as an essential part of the contract, falsity or nonfulfillment of which renders the policy void. A written statement or guarantee made by the manufacturer of a product, such as an automobile or appliance, assuring the purchaser that repairs or replacement of defective parts will be done without charge for a specified period of time.

war·ran·ty deed, *n. Law,* a deed which possesses a formal agreement or covenant of warranty.

war·ren, wạr'en, wor'en, *n.* [O.Fr. *warenne, guarenne* (Fr. *garenne*); < Teut.] A place where rabbits breed in burrows or abound; a piece of land or enclosure for the keeping and breeding of small game; *fig.* a building or collection of buildings containing many tenants in limited quarters.

war·ren·er, wạr'e·nẻr, wor'e·nẻr, *n.* The keeper of a warren.

war·ri·or, wạr'ē·ẻr, wạr'yẻr, wor'ē·ẻr, wor'yẻr, *n.* [M.E. *werreour,* < an O.Fr. derivative of *werre, guerre,* E. *war.*] A man engaged or experienced in warfare; a soldier, esp. a brave or veteran soldier.

war risk in·sur·ance, *n.* Government term insurance for U.S. armed services personnel.

war·saw, wạr'sạ, *n.* [Sp. *guasa.*] *Ichth.* a large grouper, *Epinephelus nigritus,* of the southern Atlantic and Gulf coasts of the U.S.

war·ship, wạr'ship'', *n.* A ship built or armed for war. Also *war vessel.*

wart, wạrt, *n.* [O.E. *wearte,* a wart = Icel. *varta,* Dan. *vorte,* D. *wrat,* G. *warze;* same root as L. *verruca,* a wart.] A small, dry, hard, nonmalignant lesion of the skin; *bot.* a roundish, small gland on the surface of a plant.—**wart·ed,** *a.*—**wart·y,** *a.*

wart hog, *n.* Any of several species of African wild swine of the genus *Phacochoerus,* esp. *P. aethiopicus,* notable for the warty growths or excrescences on the face and the large curving tusks.

war·time, wạr'tīm'', *n.* A time when a nation is at war.—*a.* As a result of or occurring in a time of war; as, *wartime* experiences.

war ves·sel, *n.* Warship.

war whoop, *n.* A whoop or yell uttered, as by N. American Indians, when attacking or making war.

war·y, wâr'ē, *a.*—**warier, wariest.** [Formed < *ware,* wary, aware (the *-ware* of *a-ware, be-ware*), < O.E. *waer,* cautious = Icel. *varr,* Dan. and Sw. *var,* Goth. *vars;* < root of L. *vereor,* to regard, to dread. Of kindred origin are *warn, warrant, ward, guard,* etc.] Carefully watching to detect and avoid deception or danger; on one's guard; careful; marked by prudence or caution; as, a *wary* glance.—**war·i·ly,** wâr'i·lē, *adv.*—**war·i·ness,** wâr'ē·nis, *n.*

war zone, *n.* Any surface area or airspace where hostile actions are being conducted by belligerents; an area, esp. at sea, where neutral ships are subject to search and seizure by a nation at war.

was, wuz, woz, *unstressed* waz. [O.E. *ic waes,* I was; *hé waes,* he was, *thú waere,* thou wert, pl. *waeron,* were; inf. *wesan,* to be; Icel. *vesa* or *vera,* to be; G. *wesen,* to be, *war,* I was; Dan. *vaere,* Sw. *vara,* to be; allied to Goth. *visan,* to dwell, to be; Skt. *vas,* to dwell.] The past tense of the first and third person singular of the verb *to be,* as: I was, he was.

wash, wosh, wạsh, *v.t.* [O.E. *wascan,* to wash = L.G. *wasken,* Dan. *vaske,* Sw. *vaska,* G. *waschen;* same root as *water.*] To immerse in or apply water or other liquid to, for the purpose of cleansing; to scour, scrub, or the like, with water or other liquid; to cleanse from guilt, sin, or ceremonial defilement; to wet or bathe with water or another liquid; to cover with water; to flow against or through, as: The sea *washed* the sand. To sweep away in a rush of water; as, to *wash,* as a helmsman, overboard; to transport, remove, or deposit by the flow of water or other liquid, usu. followed by *away* or *off;* to wear or weaken by flowing; to make a stream, river, or channel by flowing; to erode; *min.* to separate, as ore, from earth by the action of water; as, to *wash* gold. To purify, as a gaseous material, by liquid flow; to cover with a watery or thin coat of color; to overlay with a thin coat of metal.—*v.i.* To wash oneself; to wash clothes or other items in water; to withstand washing without being injured, spoiled, or destroyed; as, a dress that *washes; chiefly Brit.* to stand being put to the proof, as: His tale won't *wash.* To be driven or transported by water; to move in waves or beat against; as, water *washing* against the shore; to be damaged or eroded by water.—*n.* The act of washing; the clothes or other items washed on one occasion; a liquid used for washing or wetting; a thin coat of color spread over surfaces, as water color; the rush, flow, or sweep of water; the sound caused by this; as, the *wash* of the ocean or tide; the broken, choppy water following a boat; a wake; *aeron.* the air turbulence caused by an airplane. A liquid or lotion used for cosmetic purposes; as, hair *wash; min.* mineral with valuable materials extractable by washing. Erosion on or wearing away of land by water; a channel, shallow river, marsh, or stream; *geol.* alluvial material; as, dry *wash.* Waste liquid containing food refuse, often fed to pigs; swill; the fermented wort from which spirit is extracted during distillation.—*a.* Washable; capable

of being undamaged in washing; as, *wash* materials.—**wash down,** to clean thoroughly by washing; as, to *wash down* a window.—**wash out,** to wash; to cleanse; to destroy by force of water, as: The flood *washed out* the road. *Slang,* to fail; to be eliminated; as, to *wash out* of school.—**wash up,** to wash the hands or face; to wash the dishes.—**wash·a·ble,** wosh'a·bl, wạ'sha·bl, *a.*

wash and wear, *a.* Denoting a fabric or article of clothing which, after washing, requires hardly any or no ironing.

wash·ba·sin, wosh'bā''sin, wạsh'bā''sin, *n.* Washbowl.

wash·board, wosh'bōrd'', wosh'bạrd'', wạsh'bōrd'', wạsh'bạrd'', *n.* A board with a ribbed surface, usu. metallic on which to rub clothes in the washing process; a board around the bottom of the walls of a room; baseboard; *naut.* a broad thin board on a boat's gunwale or sill of a deck port to prevent the sea from breaking over.

wash·bowl, wosh'bōl'', wạsh'bōl'', *n.* A sink or basin for washing the face and hands. Also *washbasin.*

wash·cloth, wosh'klạth'', wosh'kloth'', wạsh'klạth'', wạsh'kloth'', *n.* A square, small cloth which is used to wash one's body. Also **wash·rag.**

washed-out, wosht'out', wạsht'out', *a.* Showing a loss of color, as from repeated laundering. *Colloq.* extremely tired; listless; pallid.

washed-up, wosht'up', wạsht'up', *a. Colloq.* Having lost the ability or strength to continue, as in professional sports; having failed utterly; exhausted.

wash·er, wosh'ẻr, wạ'shẻr, *n.* One who or that which washes; a washing machine; a flat ring or perforated piece of leather, rubber, or metal, used to give tightness to a joint, to prevent leakage, or to distribute pressure, as under the head of a bolt or nut.

wash·er·man, wosh'ẻr·man, wạ'shẻr·man, *n.* pl. **wash·er·men.** A man whowashes clothes or other laundry for hire; a laundryman.

wash·er·wom·an, wosh'ẻr·wụm''an, wạ'shẻr·wụm''an, *n.* pl. **wash·er·wom·en.** A woman who washes clothes or other laundry for hire. Also *washwoman.*

wash·ing, wosh'ing, wạ'shing, *n.* The act of cleansing with water, usu. with soap or a detergent; articles, as clothes, washed at one time; a material, as gold, obtained after washing soil; the process of applying a coating, as dipping an automobile frame in rustproof paint; *often pl.* liquid which has been used for washing something.

wash·ing ma·chine, *n.* A machine for washing clothes and other laundry. Also *washer.*

wash·ing so·da, *n.* Hydrated sodium carbonate.

Wash·ing·ton pie, wosh'ing·ton pī', wạ'shing·ton, *n.* A layer cake with a filling of jelly or jam.

wash·out, wosh'out'', wạsh'out'', *n.* The washing out or away of earth, esp. from a roadbed by heavy rains or a flood; *aeron.* a warp in an airplane's wing giving a decrease in the angle of attack toward the tip; *slang,* a complete failure, esp. socially or in sports; *milit. slang,* a person, esp. an air force student pilot, eliminated from further training through failure.

wash·room, wosh'rōm'', wosh'rụm'', wạsh'rōm'', wạsh'rụm'', *n.* A room containing one or more washbowls and various other toilet facilities, esp. found in public places; a rest room. See *lavatory.*

wash·stand, wosh'stand'', wạsh'stand'', *n.* A piece of furniture which holds a basin, pitcher, and other articles for use in washing the face and hands; a permanent fixture having faucets with running water, for use in washing the face and hands.

wash·tub, wosh'tub", wạsh'tub", _n._ A tub for use in washing clothes.

wash·wom·an, wosh'wụm"an, wạsh'wụm"-an, _n._ pl. **wash·wom·en.** A washerwoman.

wash·y, wosh'ē, wạ'shē, _a.—washier, washiest._ Watery; excessively diluted; thin; weak; pale or pallid.

was·n't, wuz'ant, woz'ant. Contraction of was not.

wasp, wasp, _n._ [O.E. _wæsp_, by metathesis for _wæps_; D. _wesp_, G. _wespe_; cogn. L. _vespa_ (for _vepsa_) a wasp, Lith. _wapsa_, a gadfly.] _Entom._ any of various stinging hymenopterous insects, esp. of the families _Vespoidea_ and _Sphecoidea_, usu. having the waist or base portion of the abdomen narrowly constricted, and many of which live in societies; _fig._ a person characterized by ill nature, irritability, or petty malignity.—**wasp·ish**, wos'pish, _a._—**wasp·ish·ly**, _adv._—**wasp·ish·ness**, _n._

wasp waist, _n._ An exceptionally slender waist, esp. of a woman.—**wasp-waist·ed**, _a._

was·sail, wos'al, wos'āl, was'al, was'āl, wo·sāl', _n._ [O.E. _wes hael, waes hael_, be hale, that is, health be to you, an old pledge or salutation in drinking—_wes_, imper. of _wesan_, to be.] An ancient English drinking toast; a festive occasion where drinking and pledging of healths are indulged in; the liquor used on such occasions, esp. wine or spiced ale on Christmas or New Year's.—_v.i._ To hold a merry drinking meeting; to carouse.—_v.t._ To toast or pledge in drinking.—**was·sail·er**, _n._

Was·ser·mann test, wä'sèr·man test", G. väs'ềr·män", _n._ [From August von _Wassermann_, 1866–1925, a German bacteriologist.] A test used for the detection of syphilis. Also **Was·ser·mann re·ac·tion.**

wast·age, wā'stij, _n._ The act of wasting; loss by use, wear, decay, or leakage; that which is lost.

waste, wāst, _v.t.—wasted, wasting._ [O.Fr. _wast_, also _guast, gast_, < L. _vastus_, empty, unoccupied, waste, vast: cf. _vast._] To consume, spend, or employ uselessly or without adequate return; as, to _waste_ money, time, efforts, or words; to squander; to use to no avail; to fail or neglect to use; as, to _waste_ an opportunity; to destroy or consume gradually; to wear down or reduce in bodily substance, health, or strength; to emaciate or enfeeble; to lay waste, devastate, ór ruin.—_v.i._ To become gradually consumed, used up, or worn away; to diminish gradually or dwindle; to become physically wasted, lose flesh or strength, or become emaciated or enfeebled; to pass gradually, as time.—_n._ The act of wasting or the state of being wasted; useless consumption or expenditure or use without adequate return; as, _waste_ of material, money, or time; neglect, instead of use; as, _waste_ of opportunity; gradual destruction, impairment, or decay; as, the _waste_ and repair of bodily tissue; devastation or ruin, as from war or fire; a region or place laid waste or in ruins; anything unused, unproductive, or not properly utilized; an uncultivated or unused tract of land; a tract of uninhabited, desolate country or desert; an empty, desolate, or dreary tract or extent of anything; anything left over or superfluous, as excess material or byproducts; not of use for the work in hand; refuse from the working of cotton used for wiping machinery and for other purposes; steam, heat, or water allowed to pass off without being put to use; anything rejected as useless or worthless; refuse; _pl._ excrement; _phys. geog._ material derived by mechanical and chemical disintegration.—_a._ Not used or in use; as, _waste_ energy; of land or regions, uninhabited, desolate, barren, or desert; of regions, towns, or habitations, in a state of desolation and ruin, as from devastation or decay; left over or superfluous; as, _waste_ materials; having served a purpose and no longer of use; rejected as useless, worthless, or refuse; as, _waste_ paper; used for carrying off or holding waste material.—**waste·ful**, wāst'-ful, _a._—**waste·ful·ly**, _adv._—**waste·ful·-ness**, _n._

waste·bas·ket, wāst'bas"kit, wāst'bä"skit, _n._ A basket or other container used for wastepaper and other small waste items. Also **waste·pa·per bas·ket.**

waste·land, wāst'land", _n._ An area of uncultivated or devastated land; _fig._ any locality, period of history, or institution considered barren of intellectual or imaginative vigor.

waste·ness, wāst'nis, _n._ The state of being waste; desolation.

waste·pa·per, waste pa·per, wāst'pā"pèr, _n._ Spoiled or used paper which is thrown away.

waste pipe, _n._ A pipe for carrying away water or other liquids.

waste prod·uct, _n._ Anything left over and rejected as useless after a manufacturing process; superfluous material excreted from a living body, as feces or urine.

wast·er, wā'stèr, _n._ One who wastes; a squanderer; a prodigal or wastrel; an article spoiled in the making.

wast·ing, wā'sting, _a._ Desolating; laying waste; sapping the bodily strength; as, a _wasting_ disease.—**wast·ing·ly**, _adv._

wast·rel, wā'strel, _n._ [< _waste._] A wasteful person or spendthrift; an idler or good-for-nothing; _chiefly Brit._ a waif.

watch, woch, _v.i._ [O.E. _waecce_, a watch, a watching, < stem of _wacan_, to wake.] To be or continue without sleep; to keep vigil; to be attentive or vigilant; to be closely observant; to give heed; to act as a watchman, guard, or sentinel; to look forward with expectation, often followed by _for_; to wait.—_v.t._ To look with close attention at or on; to keep under close examination or observation; to keep a sharp lookout for; to regard with vigilance and care; to tend; to guard; to look for; to wait for.—_n._ A keeping awake for the purpose of attending, guarding, or preserving a vigil; vigilant attention; a guard or number of guards; the time during which a person or body of persons are on guard; a small timepiece, either worn or carried in the pocket. _Naut._ the period of time occupied by each part of a ship's crew alternately while on duty; a certain part of the officers and crew who together attend to working the ship for an allotted time.—**on the watch**, alert, cautious.—**watch out**, to be cautious or on guard.—**watch o·ver**, to oversee for protection.—**watch·er**, woch'ẻr, _n._

watch·band, woch'band", _n._ The strap or band of a wrist watch, made of metal, leather, or various fabrics, which holds the watch on one's wrist.

watch cap, _n._ A knitted cap made of wool, worn in cold weather by enlisted personnel of the U.S. navy.

watch·case, woch'kās", _n._ The case or outer covering for the works of a watch.

watch·dog, woch'dȧg", woch'dog", _n._ A dog kept to watch or guard premises and property; a person acting as a guardian, as against illegal activities.—_v.t._ To act as a guardian or watchdog for.

watch fire, _n._ A fire kept up in the night as a signal or for use by a guard.

watch·ful, woch'ful, _a._ Closely or intently observant; giving wary attention; alert; vigilant. _Archaic_, wakeful; not sleeping.—**watch·ful·ly**, _adv._—**watch·ful·ness**, _n._

watch·mak·er, woch'mā"kèr, _n._ One whose occupation is to make and repair watches.—**watch·mak·ing**, _n._

watch·man, woch'man, _n._ pl. **watch·men.** A person paying heedful attention or keeping watch over something; anyone employed to keep watch or guard, as over an estate or building, esp. during the night; formerly, one who patrolled streets during the night.

watch night, _n._ The last night of the year. Religious services held on New Year's Eve; also **watch meet·ing.**

watch·tow·er, woch'tou"ẻr, _n._ A tower upon which a sentinel is placed or posted to watch or keep guard, as over prisoners, or for enemies, fires in a forest, or the like.

watch·word, woch'wụrd", _n._ A word, phrase, or signal given to a guard or the like, used to ascertain whether an unknown person is friendly or hostile; a countersign; a password; a motto, esp. used as a rallying cry or slogan.

wa·ter, wạ'tèr, wot'èr, _n._ [O.E. _wæter_ = D. _water_ = G. _wasser_, akin to Icel. _vatn_, Goth. _watō_, water, also to Gr. _udōr_, Skt. _udan_, water, L. _unda_, a wave, water; all < the same root as E. _wet_: cf. _hydra_, _otter_, _undine_, and _wash_.] The liquid which in a more or less impure state constitutes rain, oceans, lakes, and rivers, and which in a pure state is a transparent, odorless, tasteless liquid, a compound of hydrogen and oxygen, H_2O, freezing at 32° F. or 0° C. and boiling at 212° F. or 100° C.; a special form or variety of this liquid, as rain; _often pl._ the liquid obtained from a mineral spring; _pl._ flowing water, or water moving in waves. The water of a river or the like with reference to its relative height, esp. as dependent on tide; as, the high-_water_ mark; water, referring to its surface level; as, below _water_; a particular body of water; as, the _waters_ off Alaska; any liquid or aqueous organic secretion, exudation, humor, or the like, as tears, perspiration, or saliva; a liquid solution or preparation; as, toilet _water_; any of various solutions of volatile or gaseous substances in water; as, ammonia _water_; the degree of transparency and brilliancy of a diamond or other precious stone; as, a diamond of the first _water_; a kind of wavy, lustrous pattern or marking, as on silk fabrics; _finance_, additional shares or securities created by watering the stock or other securities of a company.—_v.t._ To sprinkle, moisten, or drench with water; as, to _water_ a road; to supply with water, as by irrigation; to furnish water to, as a region, as with streams; to supply, as animals, with water for drinking; to furnish with a supply of water, as a ship; to produce a wavy, lustrous pattern, marking, or finish on, as fabrics; to dilute or adulterate with water, often with _down_; as, to _water down_ soup; _finance_, to increase, as stock or other securities, by the issue of additional shares or securities without a corresponding increase in capital or assets.—_v.i._ To discharge, fill with, or secrete water or liquid, as the eyes with tears, or as the mouth at the sight or thought of tempting food; to drink water, as an animal; to take in a supply of water, as a ship.—**a·bove wa·ter**, out of embarrassment or trouble, esp. financial trouble.—**hold wa·ter**, to prove sound, tenable, or valid, as a theory.—**in hot wa·ter**, in trouble, in difficulty.—**like wa·ter**, abundantly; freely, as: The beer flowed _like water_.—**wa·ter·er**, _n._—**wa·ter·like**, _a._

wa·ter back, _n._ A reservoir, combination of pipes, or the like, at the back of a stove or fireplace, for providing a supply of heated water.

wa·ter bal·let, _n._ A presentation of synchronized, dancelike patterns in water by swimmers.

wa·ter bee·tle, _n._ Any of various aquatic beetles of the family _Dytiscidae_, or related

---

a- fat, fāte, fär, fâre, fạll; **e-** met, mē, mēre, hèr; **i-** pin, pīne; **o-** not, nōte, mōve; **u-** tub, cūbe, bụll; **oi-** oil; **ou-** pound.

families, having the hind legs broad and fringed so as to be well adapted for swimming.

wa·ter bird, *n.* An aquatic bird, or bird that frequents the water; a swimming or wading bird; a waterfowl.

wa·ter bis·cuit, *n.* A type of biscuit or cracker prepared from water, flour, and often shortening.

wa·ter blis·ter, *n.* A blister that contains a fluid which is clear and watery, and devoid of blood or pus.

wa·ter boat·man, *n. pl.* **wa·ter boat·men.** Any of various aquatic insects of the family *Corixidae*, which swim by means of oarlike legs.

wa·ter·borne, wạ′tẽr·bōrn″, wạ′tẽr·bạrn″, wot′ẽr·bōrn″, wot′ẽr·bạrn″, *a.* Supported by the water; carried by the water; conveyed by ship or boat, as goods.

wa·ter boy, *n.* One who carries and distributes drinking water, as to a work gang or football team.

wa·ter·brain, wạ′tẽr·brān″, wot′ẽr·brān″, *n. Veter. pathol.* A disease in sheep; gid.

wa·ter brash, *n. Pathol.* heartburn.

wa·ter·buck, wạ′tẽr·buk″, wot′ẽr·buk″, *n.* Any of various African antelopes of the genus *Kobus*, frequenting marshes and reedy places, esp. *K. ellipsiprymnus*, of southern and central Africa.

wa·ter buf·fa·lo, *n.* An Asiatic buffalo, *Bubalus bubalis*, frequently domesticated for draft use. Also *water ox, carabao.*

wa·ter bug, *n.* Any of various aquatic hemipterous insects, esp. of the family *Belostomatidae*, which live chiefly beneath the surface of the water. A small light-brown cockroach, *Blatella germanica*, common near moisture; also **Cro·ton bug, Ger·man cock·roach.**

wa·ter chest·nut, *n.* Any of the aquatic plants constituting the genus *Trapa*, bearing an edible, nutlike fruit, esp. *T. natans*, of the Old World. The fruit of these plants; also **wa·ter cal·trop.**

wa·ter chin·qua·pin, *n.* A N. American lotus, *Nelumbo lutea*, with an edible nutlike seed; the seed of this plant.

wa·ter clock, *n.* One of various devices, as a clepsydra, for measuring time by the flow of water.

wa·ter clos·et, *n.* A room or enclosed compartment having a toilet bowl or similar contrivance for carrying off the discharges through a waste pipe below by flushing with water; the contrivance itself; *dial.* a privy. *Abbr. w.c.*

wa·ter·col·or, wạ′tẽr·kul′ẽr, wot′ẽr·kul′ẽr, *n.* A paint in which the pigment is dissolved in water instead of oil; the art of painting with water colors; a painting done in water colors.—**wa·ter·col·or,** *a.*—**wa·ter·col·or·ist,** *n.*

wa·ter·cool, wạ′tẽr·kōl″, wot′ẽr·kōl″, *v.t.* To cool by means of water, esp. by water circulating in pipes or a water jacket.

wa·ter cool·er, *n.* An apparatus or vessel which holds and cools drinking water and dispenses it.

wa·ter·course, wạ′tẽr·kōrs″, wạ′tẽr·kạrs″, wot′ẽr·kōrs″, wot′ẽr·kạrs″, *n.* A stream of water; a river; a brook; a natural channel conveying water, as a stream bed; a channel or canal made for the conveyance of water.

wa·ter·craft, wạ′tẽr·kraft″, wạ′tẽr·kräft″, wot′ẽr·kraft″, wot′ẽr·kräft″, *n.* Skill in aquatic sports, as boating; a ship or boat of any type; boats or ships as a whole.

wa·ter crake, *n.* The spotted crake, *Porzana porzana*, a small European rail; the European water ouzel, *Cinclus aquaticus*.

wa·ter·cress, wạ′tẽr·kres″, wot′ẽr·kres″, *n.* A perennial cress, *Nasturtium officinale*, of the mustard family, usu. growing in clear, running water, and bearing pungent leaves which are used for salad and as a garnish.

wa·ter cure, *n.* Treatment of disease by some method of using water; hydropathy; hydrotherapy; *colloq.* torture by means of forcing great quantities of water into the victim's stomach.

wa·ter dog, *n.* A dog accustomed to swimming in the water or trained to go into the water to retrieve game, as a water spaniel; the mudpuppy; *colloq.* a person at home on or in the water, as a sailor or an experienced swimmer.

wa·ter·fall, wạ′tẽr·fạl″, wot′ẽr·fạl″, *n.* A fall or perpendicular descent of the water of a river or stream; a cascade; a cataract.

wa·ter flea, *n.* Any of various small or minute crustaceans, esp. *Daphnia*, which swim about in the water like fleas.

wa·ter·fowl, wạ′tẽr·foul″, wot′ẽr·foul″, *n. pl.* **wa·ter·fowls, wa·ter·fowl.** A water bird, esp. a swimming bird; such birds collectively, esp. swimming game birds.

wa·ter·front, wạ′tẽr·frunt″, wot′ẽr·frunt″, *n.* Land abutting on a body of water; a section of a city or town, as a dock, abutting on a harbor.

wa·ter gap, *n.* A gap in a mountain ridge, giving passage to a stream.

wa·ter gas, *n.* A poisonous gas consisting of a mixture of various gases, chiefly carbon monoxide and hydrogen, which is made by passing steam over incandescent coal or other carbon fuel: used for illuminating purposes and as a fuel.—**wa·ter-gas,** *a.*

wa·ter gate, *n.* A gate serving to control the flow of water; a floodgate; a gate by which access is gained to a body or supply of water.

wa·ter gauge, *n.* An instrument for measuring or ascertaining the depth or quantity of water, as in the boiler of a steam engine.

wa·ter glass, *n.* A glass vessel or container used to hold water, as for drinking; a water clock or clepsydra; a device for observing objects beneath the surface of the water, consisting essentially of an open tube or box with a glass bottom; a glass water gauge. A solution, esp. one similar to a sodium silicate preparation, used to produce a transparent coating on objects in order to protect, preserve, or fireproof them; also **sol·u·ble glass, liq·uid glass.**

wa·ter gum, *n.* A tupelo, *Nyssa sylvatica*, of the southern U.S.; also *black gum, sour gum.* Any of several Australian trees of the myrtle family growing near water.

wa·ter ham·mer, *n.* The concussion or sound of concussion, of moving water against the sides of a pipe, esp. a steam pipe when steam is present.

wa·ter heat·er, *n.* A large appliance for the home used to heat and store water.

wa·ter hem·lock, *n.* Any of the poisonous plants constituting the genus *Cicuta*, as *C. virosa*, of Europe, and *C. maculata*, of N. America, growing in swamps and marshy places.

wa·ter hen, *n.* The moorhen, *Gallinula chloropus*, of Europe; the N. American coot, *Fulica americana*.

wa·ter hole, *n.* A hole or hollow in the ground in which water collects; a natural pool or small pond of water, as one used by animals for drinking.

wa·ter hy·a·cinth, *n.* A floating aquatic plant, *Eichhornia crassipes*, with violet or blue flowers and ovate leaves with inflated bladderlike petioles, native in tropical S. America, and cultivated elsewhere, but a troublesome weed in inland waters of Florida and other places.

wa·ter ice, *n.* A sherbetlike frozen dessert, prepared with water, fruit juice, and sugar; solid ice formed by the direct freezing of fresh or salt water, and not by the compacting of snow.

wa·ter-inch, wạ′tẽr·inch′, wot′ẽr·inch′, *n. Hydraulics,* the quantity of water, about 500

cubic feet, discharged in 24 hours through a circular opening of one-inch diameter leading from a reservoir in which the water is constantly only high enough to cover the orifice.

wa·ter·ing place, *n.* A place where water is available, as for cattle; a resort where people go for therapeutic mineral waters or waterside recreational facilities.

wa·ter·ing pot, *n.* A hand vessel for sprinkling water on plants, esp. one having an extended spout with perforations on the head. Also **wa·ter·ing can, sprin·kling can.**

wa·ter·ish, wạ′tẽr·ish, wot′ẽr·ish, *a.* Resembling water, as in consistency; watery. —**wa·ter·ish·ness,** *n.*

wa·ter jack·et, wạ′tẽr·jak″it, wot′ẽr·jak″it, *n.* An outer casing containing water which surrounds something, as an internal-combustion engine cylinder, for its cooling.

wa·ter jump, *n.* A stream, pond, ditch, or other water obstacle over which a horse running in a steeplechase must jump.

wa·ter·leaf, wạ′tẽr·lēf″, wot′ẽr·lēf″, *n. pl.* **wa·ter·leafs, wa·ter·leaves,** wạ′tẽr·lēvz″, wot′ẽr·lēvz″. [Said to be so called from a supposed cavity for water in each leaf.] Any of the N. American woodland herbs of the genus *Hydrophyllum*, esp. *H. virginianum*, a species with white or purple flowers.

wa·ter·less, wạ′tẽr·lis, wot′ẽr·lis, *a.* Destitute of water, or dry; requiring no water, esp. in cooking.—**wa·ter·less·ly,** *adv.*—**wa·ter·less·ness,** *n.*

wa·ter lev·el, *n.* Still water's surface height or water line; a leveling instrument in which water is employed in a bent glass tube; *geol.* a water table; *naut.* the water line on a ship.

wa·ter lil·y, *n. pl.* **wa·ter lil·ies.** Any of the aquatic plants constituting the genus *Nymphaea*, characterized by large, disklike floating leaves and showy, fragrant flowers, esp. *N. odorata*, of N. America or *N. alba*, of Europe; the flower of any such plant.

wa·ter line, *n. Naut.* Any of several lines marked or indicated on the hull of a ship, showing the depth to which it sinks when unloaded and when partially or fully loaded; the surface level of any body of water; also *water level.* Any of a series of lines on the hull, parallel with the surface of the water, as in a naval architect's drawing or model.

wa·ter·log, wạ′tẽr·lạg″, wạ′tẽr·lọg″, wot′ẽr·lạg″, wot′ẽr·lọg″, *v.t.*—*waterlogged, waterlogging.* To make heavy and unmanageable by flooding, as a ship; to soak with water so as to become unserviceable. —*v.i.* To become soaked with water.

wa·ter·logged, wạ′tẽr·lạgd″, wạ′tẽr·lọgd″, wot′ẽr·lạgd″, wot′ẽr·lọgd″, *a.* So filled with water as to be heavy or unmanageable, as a ship; excessively saturated with water, as a log, field, or the like.

Wa·ter·loo, wạ′tẽr·lö″, wot′ẽr·lö″, wạ″tẽr·lö′, wot″ẽr·lö′, *n.* [From the battle near the village of *Waterloo*, in Belgium, in which Napoleon was decisively defeated, June 18, 1815.] A decisive or crushing defeat.

wa·ter main, *n.* A main or principal pipe or conduit in a system for conveying water, as one that is installed underground.

wa·ter·man, wạ′tẽr·man, wot′ẽr·man, *n. pl.* **wa·ter·men.** One who works on boats; a boatman; a ferryman.

wa·ter·man·ship, wạ′tẽr·man·ship″, wot′ẽr·man·ship″, *n.* The business or ability of a waterman; proficiency, as in boating or swimming.

wa·ter·mark, wạ′tẽr·märk″, wot′ẽr·märk″, *n.* A mark indicating the height to which water rises or has risen, as in a river. A faint letter, design, or the like, often marked in the fabric of paper during the process of manufacture by pressure on the moist pulp, usu. visible only when the sheet is held against strong light.—*v.t.* To mark, as paper, with a watermark; to impress as a watermark, esp. a design.

wa·ter·mel·on, wạ'tẽr·mel″on, wot'ẽr··mel″on, *n.* The large, roundish or elongated edible fruit of a trailing cucurbitaceous vine, *Citrullus vulgaris,* having a hard, green rind and a sweet, watery usu. pink or red pulp; the plant or vine.

wa·ter me·ter, *n.* An instrument that measures and indicates the quantity of water that passes through an outlet or pipe.

wa·ter mil·foil, *n.* Any of various aquatic plants, of the genus *Myriophyllum,* the submersed leaves of which are very finely divided: used in aquariums.

wa·ter mill, *n.* A mill whose machinery is moved by water.

wa·ter moc·ca·sin, *n.* A large venomous viper, *Agkistrodon piscivorus,* allied to the copperhead, having a dark crossband pattern and found in swampy areas in the southern part of the U.S.; also *cottonmouth.* Any of various similar but harmless water snakes, esp. of the genus *Natrix.*

wa·ter nymph, *n. Mythol.* a nymph of the water, as a naiad.

wa·ter oak, *n.* An oak, *Quercus nigra,* of the southern U.S. growing chiefly along streams and swamps.

wa·ter of crys·tal·li·za·tion, *n. Chem.* water of hydration, formerly thought to be necessary to crystallization, but now usu. regarded as affecting crystallization only in so far as it forms new molecular combinations.

wa·ter of hy·dra·tion, *n. Chem.* that portion of a hydrate which is represented as, or can be driven off as water, now usu. regarded as being in true molecular combination with the other atoms of the compound, and not existing in the compound as water.

wa·ter ou·zel, wa·ter ou·sel, *n. Ornith.* two species of oily-plumaged birds, *Cinclus aquaticus,* of Europe and *C. mexicanus,* of western N. America, having the habit of flying through mountain streams and walking and feeding on the bottom of these streams. Also **dip·per.**

wa·ter ox, *n.* Water buffalo.

wa·ter part·ing, *n.* See *watershed.*

wa·ter pep·per, *n.* Any of various plants of the genus *Polygonum,* growing in wet places, esp. the smartweed, *P. hydropiper.*

wa·ter pim·per·nel, *n.* Brookweed.

wa·ter pipe, *n.* A conduit for conveying water. A type of tobacco pipe; also *hookah.*

wa·ter pis·tol, *n.* A toy pistol, usu. made of plastic, that shoots a jet of water. Also **wa·ter gun.**

wa·ter plan·tain, *n.* Any of the aquatic herbs of the genus *Alisma,* esp. *A. plantago-aquatica,* a species growing in shallow water throughout the temperate regions of the northern hemisphere, and having leaves suggesting those of the common plantain.

wa·ter po·lo, *n.* A game played in the water by two teams, each having seven swimmers, the object of which is to propel an inflated ball into a defended goal.

wa·ter pow·er, *n.* The power of water used, or capable of being used, as to drive machinery; a fall or descent in a stream, capable of being so used; the right of a mill for the use of water.

wa·ter·proof, wạ'tẽr·prŏf″, wot'ẽr·prŏf″, *a.* Impervious to water; rendered impervious to water by some special process, as coating or treating with rubber or the like. —*n.* A waterproof material; a fabric which has been specially treated to render it impervious to water. *Brit.* an outer garment of waterproof material; a raincoat.—*v.t.* To render waterproof.—**wa·ter··proof·er,** *n.*

wa·ter·proof·ing, wạ'tẽr·prŏ″fing, wạ'tẽr·prŏ′fing, wot'ẽr·prŏ″fing, wot'ẽr·prŏ′fing, *n.* The act or process of rendering waterproof; a substance, as rubber or oil, used to render something waterproof.

wa·ter rat, *n.* The American muskrat; any of the rats constituting the subfamily *Hydromyinae,* native to Australia, New Guinea, and the Phillipines; any of various other aquatic rodents, as a European vole; *slang,* a thief, thug, or other undesirable person on a waterfront.

wa·ter·re·pel·lent, wạ'tẽr·ri·pel″ent, wot'ẽr·ri·pel″ent, *a.* Consisting of a finish which resists water, but is not entirely impermeable to it.

wa·ter·re·sist·ant, wạ'tẽr·ri·zis″tant, wạ'tẽr·ri·zis′tant, wot'ẽr·ri·zis″tant, wot'ẽr··ri·zis′tant, *a.* Able to resist, although not completely, water's penetration.

wa·ter right, *n.* A right to use water from a specific source, as for power or irrigation.

wa·ter sap·phire, *n.* A variety of cordierite, transparent, blue or violet, found in Ceylon and Madagascar and sometimes used as a gemstone.

wa·ter·scape, wạ'tẽr·skāp″, wot'ẽr·skāp″, *n.* [With *-scape* as in *landscape.*] A picture or view of the sea or other body of water.

wa·ter scor·pi·on, *n.* Any of the aquatic hemipterous insects in the family *Nepidae,* having a taillike, tubular process through which respiration is effected.

wa·ter·shed, wạ'tẽr·shed″, wot'ẽr·shed″, *n.* An elevated line that forms the division between two areas drained by separate streams, systems, or bodies of water; also *divide, water parting.* An area drained by a particular stream, system, or body of water; *fig.* an occurrence or time after which a significant change, as in international relations or public opinion, is noticeable.

wa·ter shield, *n.* An aquatic plant, *Brasenia schreberi,* belonging to the water lily family, with peltate floating leaves, the undersurfaces of which are coated with a jellylike material. Plants of the genus *Cabomba,* esp. *C. caroliniana;* also fanwort.

wa·ter·side, wạ'tẽr·sīd″, wot'ẽr·sīd″, *n.* The bank or margin of a river, ocean, stream, or lake; the shore.—*a.* Of, referring to, or on the shore; working on or along the shore.

wa·ter-ski, wạ'tẽr·skē″, wot'ẽr·skē″, *v.i.*—*water-skied, water-skiing.* To ski on water, achieving and maintaining motion by holding on to a towline pulled by a motorboat.—*n.* **wa·ter-skis, wa·ter-ski.** A ski used in water-skiing; also **wa·ter ski. wa·ter-ski·er,** *n.*—**wa·ter-ski·ing,** *n.*

wa·ter snake, *n.* Any of various snakes living in or near water, esp. any of the harmless snakes of the genus *Natrix,* family *Colubridae,* found in or near fresh water.

wa·ter-soak, wạ'tẽr·sōk″, wot'ẽr·sōk″, *v.t.* To soak with water.

wa·ter sof·ten·er, *n.* Any of several chemical substances used in the treatment of hard water to counteract the soap-precipitating property of the metals, magnesium and calcium, present in it, in order to facilitate the formation of suds.

wa·ter-sol·u·ble, wạ'tẽr·sol″ū·bl, wot'ẽr·sol″ū·bl, *a.* Having the property of dissolving in water, as many organic compounds.

wa·ter span·iel, *n.* A curly-haired spaniel of either of two varieties which take readily to water and are often trained for the retrieval of game birds living on or near the water.

wa·ter·spout, wạ'tẽr·spout″, wot'ẽr·spout, *n. Meteor.* a tornadolike storm over the sea that forms a spinning funnel of air laden with mist and spray, presenting the appearance of a solid column of water reaching upward to the clouds. A pipe or spout from which water is discharged, esp. a drainpipe on the side of a house descending from a gutter.

wa·ter sprite, *n.* A sprite, nymph, or spirit inhabiting the water.

wa·ter strid·er, *n.* Any of the aquatic hemipterous insects of the family *Gerridae,* having long, slender legs, and able to dart about on the surface of water with great rapidity. Also **skat·er.**

wa·ter sup·ply, *n.* The amount of water accessible to a commnuity; the treating, storage, and distribution system necessary to dispense water to a community.

wa·ter sys·tem, *n.* A river and its tributaries; a water supply.

wa·ter ta·ble, *n. Arch.* a projecting stringcourse or similar member so placed as to throw off water; *geol.* the level below which the ground is saturated with water.

wa·ter thrush, *n.* Either of two N. American warblers, *Seiurus noveboracensis,* the northern water thrush, or *S. motacilla,* the Louisiana water thrush; the European water ouzel, *Cinclus aquaticus.*

wa·ter·tight, wạ'tẽr·tīt″, wot'ẽr·tīt″, *a.* So tight as to retain or not to admit water; staunch or foolproof.—**wa·ter·tight·ness,** *n.*

wa·ter tow·er, *n.* A standpipe, with a similar function as that of a reservoir, used to sustain equal pressure for water systems; a fire-extinguishing apparatus for throwing a stream of water on the upper parts of a tall burning building, consisting of a towerlike structure supporting a vertical pipe at the top of which is a movable nozzle from which the water issues.

wa·ter tur·key, *n.* Snakebird.

wa·ter va·por, *n.* Water in a gaseous condition, esp. below the point of boiling, and present in varying quantities in the atmosphere.

wa·ter-vas·cu·lar sys·tem, wạ″tẽr·vas′·kyạ·lẽr sis′tem, wot″ẽr·vas′kyạ·lẽr, *n. Zool.* a kind of hydraulic-pressure mechanism in echinoderms, as starfish, in which water, drawn into and expelled from a series of tube feet in their arms, provides locomotion.

wa·ter wave, *n.* A hairdo created by moist hair set into a wave with combs and dried by a drier; a wave or billow of water.—**wa·ter·waved,** *a.*

wa·ter·way, wạ'tẽr·wā″, wot'ẽr·wā″, *n.* A way or channel for water; a river, canal, or other body of water as a way of travel or transport.

wa·ter·weed, wạ'tẽr·wēd″, wot'ẽr·wēd″, *n.* A submerged aquatic plant, *Anacharis canadensis,* native to N. America, common in fresh-water streams and ponds, and used in aquariums; any of various other aquatic plants without showy flowers.

wa·ter wheel, *n.* A wheel turned by the action of water and used to perform mechanical work; a wheel for raising water, as a noria.

wa·ter wings, *n. pl.* Two inflatable balloonlike devices joined together and worn under one's arms and extending back from the shoulders, used to keep a person afloat.

wa·ter witch, *n.* One claiming the power or ability to discover water which is underground by the use of some device, as the divining rod.—**wa·ter witch·ing,** *n.*

wa·ter·works, wạ'tẽr·wụrks″, wot'ẽr··wụrks″, *n. pl.* An aggregate of apparatus and structures by which water is obtained, preserved, purified, and distributed for the use of a city or town; an ornamental fountain or waterfall; *slang,* tears; as, to turn on the *waterworks.*

wa·ter·worn, wạ'tẽr·wạrn″, wot'ẽr·wạrn″, *a.* Worn by the action of water; smoothed, as to a shine, by the action of running water.

wa·ter·y, wạ'te·rē, wot'e·rē, a. [O.E. waeterig.] Full of or abounding in water; consisting of water; as, a watery grave; of the nature of water; as, watery vapor; pertaining to or connected with water; resembling water in appearance or color; pale as if diluted with water; resembling water in consistency; as, a watery fluid; containing too much water, as liquid food; containing a large proportion of moisture, as fruits; fig. weak, thin, washy, vapid, or poor; as, a watery smile. Discharging, filled with, or secreting some aqueous organic liquid; tearful, as the eyes; exuding tears as the result of weakness or disease of the lachrymal organs.—wa·ter·i·ness, n.

watt, wot, n. [After James Watt.] The unit of electric power equal to one joule per second, or a current of one ampere under an electrical pressure of one volt. Abbr. W, w.

watt·age, wot'ij, n. An amount of power reckoned in watts; an amount of watts requisite for the operation of an appliance.

Wat·teau, wo·tō', wot'ō, Fr. vä·tō', a. Pertaining to or in the style of the French painter, Jean Antoine Watteau, 1684–1721, or his paintings; as, a Watteau shepherdess. —Wat·teau back, a long, loose, full back of a woman's gown, held in, in folds, only at the neckline.

watt-hour, wot'our", wot'ou"ẽr, n. A unit of energy or work equal to one watt operating for one hour. Abbr. wh., whr., w.-hr.

wat·tle, wot'l, n. [O.E. watel, watul, a wattle, a hurdle, etc.] A hurdle or fence made of interwoven rods, branches, or reeds; the poles, branches, or other such materials used to build such a fence; pl. rods to support thatch on a roof. Brit. dial. a stick, twig, rod, or wand; a hurdle. The fleshy lobe that grows under the throat of certain reptiles and some birds, as the turkey; the barbel of a fish; any Australian tree of the genus Acacia.—v.t.—wattled, wattling. To twist, interweave, or interlace, as twigs or branches, to form a fence; to plait.—a. Made from or covered with wattles.—wat·tled, a.

wat·tle·bird, wot'l·bụrd", n. One of several big Australian honey eaters of the genus Anthochaera, having wattles hanging below the ear.

watt·me·ter, wot'mē"tẽr, n. [Watt, Gr. metron, a measure.] An instrument for measuring electrical energy in watts.

wave, wāv, n. [O.E. wawe, a wave of the sea, < waeg, a wave (akin to wag).] A moving swell or ridge on the surface of water or other liquid; a billow; a widespread surge of emotion or opinion; one of a series of curves on a surface; an undulation; a swelling outline; a spell of extremely hot or cold weather; a signal made by waving the hand, flag, or the like, back and forth; a curved or wavelike condition of the hair. Phys. a vibration propagated from one set of particles of an elastic medium to the adjoining set, as in heat or light transmission; a graphic representation of such a vibration.—v.i.—waved, waving. [< O.E. wafian, to waver or hesitate through astonishment; Icel. veifa, to wave, to vibrate; O.G. waben, to fluctuate. Waver, waft, are derived forms.] To move loosely up and down, or backward and forward; to float or flutter; to undulate; to be moved as a signal; to beckon.—v.t. To move one way and the other; to brandish, as a flag; to signal to, by waving the hand or the like; to beckon; to give a wave to, as hair.— wave·less, a.—wave·like, a.

Wave, wāv, n. A member of the WAVES, the corps of the U.S. Navy open to women enlistees.

wave band, n. Phys. the group of waves situated about an assigned frequency, esp. in radio or television transmitting.

waved, wāvd, a. Having a wavy or undulating form or outline; marked with wavy lines.

wave front, n. Phys. a surface in a wave disturbance traced by all those oscillations in the same phase at any given instant.

wave guide, n. Elect. metal tubing for transmitting and channeling high-frequency electromagnetic waves.

wave·length, wave length, wāv'length", n. The distance between crests of two adjacent water waves; phys. the least distance between particles moving in the same phase of oscillation in a wave disturbance.

wave·let, wāv'lit, n. A small wave; a ripple on water.

wave me·chan·ics, n. pl., sing. or pl. in constr. Phys. an aspect of quantum mechanics that identifies elementary particles by their wavelike properties.

wa·ver, wā'vẽr, v.i. [A freq. corresponding to the verb to wave, to fluctuate = Icel. vafra, to hover.] To sway or move to and fro; to flutter; to be in danger of failing or collapsing; to shake involuntarily; to be unsettled in opinion; to be irresolute; to vacillate; to hesitate; to fluctuate; to totter; to reel.—n. An act of wavering.—wa·ver·er, n.—wa·ver·ing·ly, adv.—wa·ver·y, a.

wave the·o·ry, n. Phys. the theory that light is transmitted as waves similar to electromagnetic oscillations. Also undulatory theory.

wave train, n. Phys. a series of successive waves spaced at equal intervals.

wav·y, wā'vē, a.—wavier, waviest. Rising or swelling in waves; characteristic of or full of waves; undulating on the border or on the surface, as hair or a leaf; sinuous; wavering; unsteady.—wav·i·ly, adv.— wav·i·ness, n.

wax, waks, n. pl. wax·es. [O.E. weax, wax = G. wachs, Icel. and Sw. vax, Dan. vox, D. vas; cogn. Pol. voska, vosk, Russ. Lith. waszkas, wax.] A solid, yellowish secretion discharged by bees, with which they construct their honeycombs; also beeswax. Any of numerous substances secreted by some plants and animals, as carnauba and spermaceti; a solid, plastic mineral substance, as paraffin; any of various waxlike materials made from hydrocarbon compounds; cerumen or earwax; a resinous material used by shoemakers; sealing wax. Fig. a person or thing that is easily influenced; as, the mind of a young child.—v.t.—waxed, waxing. To coat, rub, or polish with wax; colloq. to record on a phonograph recording.—a. Made of, covered with, or resembling wax. —wax·er, n.

wax, waks, v.i.—past, waxed; pp. waxed or poet. waxen; ppr. waxing. [O.E. weaxen, to grow, to become = Icel. vaxa, Dan. voxe, Sw. vaxa, G. wachsen, D. wassen, to wax; allied to L. augeo (whence augment), Skt. vakshami, to increase, to wax.] To increase in size or strength; to grow in any manner; to become larger or to develop toward fullness, esp. the moon, as opposed to wane. —n.

wax, waks, n. Chiefly Brit. Rage; a tantrum.

wax bean, n. A variety of the string bean, Phaseolus vulgaris, having waxy, pale yellow pods. Also butter bean.

wax·ber·ry, waks'ber"ē, waks'be·rē, n. pl. wax·ber·ries. The wax myrtle, Myrica cerifera, or its waxy fruit; the snowberry.

wax·bill, waks'bil", n. Any of various weaverbirds of Asia and Africa, esp. of the genus Estrilda, having white, pink, or red bills of waxlike appearance, and including many well-known cage birds; the Java sparrow, Padda orizvora, of the East Indies.

wax·en, wak'sen, a. Made of, or covered with wax; pallid or pale, as one's complexion; adaptable or impressionable, as the mind of a child.

wax in·sect, n. Any of various homopterous insects, as a Chinese scale insect, Ericerus pe-la, that secretes a wax or waxlike substance.

wax myr·tle, n. A shrub or tree of the genus Myrica, as M. cerifera, that bears small berries coated with a waxy substance that may be used for making candles. Also bayberry, candleberry.

wax palm, n. A S. American palm tree, Ceroxlon andicola, that exudes a resinous wax from the leaves and trunk; a tree, Copericia cerifera, of Brazil, which has wax-coated leaves, yielding carnauba wax.

wax pa·per, n. A paper treated or coated with wax or paraffin to make it waterproof. Also waxed pa·per.

wax·wing, waks'wing", n. Any of several crested passerine birds of America and Eurasia, of the genus Bombycilla, having sleek brown plumage with tiny horny appendages on their wings the color of red sealing wax.

wax·work, waks'wụrk", n. Work in wax; figures formed of wax in imitation of real beings; pl., sing. or pl. in constr. a place where a collection of such figures is exhibited, or the exhibition itself.—wax·work·er, n.

wax·y, wak'sē, a.—waxier, waxiest. Resembling wax, as in substance or appearance; pertaining to, abounding in, covered with, or made of wax; fig. pliable, yielding, or impressible. Pathol. pertaining to the degeneration of body tissue resulting from a buildup of waxlike, insoluble protein deposits in some organs; characteristic of amyloid. Brit. colloq. angry.—wax·i·ness, n.

way, wā, n. [O.E. weg = D. and G. weg = Icel. vegr = Goth. wigs, way; akin to L. via, way (cf. via); < the root of E. weigh.] Manner, mode, or fashion; as, a new way of looking at a matter; characteristic or habitual manner, as: That is only his way. A course, plan, or means for attaining an end; as, to find a way to reduce friction; respect or particular; as, a plan defective in several ways; direction, as: Look this way. Passage or progress on a course; as, to lead the way; distance; as, a long way off; a path or course leading from one place to another; a road, route, passage, or channel; as, a highway; any line of passage or travel used or available; space for passing or advancing; as, to make way; law, a right of way; often pl. a habit or custom, as: I don't like his ways. One's preferred course or mode of procedure; as, to have one's own way; condition, as to health or prosperity; as, to be in a bad way; range of experience or notice; as, the best device that ever came in my way; course of life, action, or experience; colloq. calling or business; as, in the grocery way; pl., ship-building, the timbers on which a ship is launched; mech. a longitudinal guiding slide or strip for a moving carriage or work table; naut. movement or passage through the water.—adv. Colloq. away. Also 'way.— by way of, by the route of; via; through; as a way, method, or means of; as, to number articles by way of distinguishing them.—in a way, in a manner; after a fashion; to some extent.—make way, to give room for passing; to stand aside.—out of the way, out of the road or path; so as not to obstruct or hinder; off one's hands; apart from what is usual or proper; unusual, improper, or amiss.—un·der way, in motion, or moving along, as a ship that has weighed anchor; in progress, as an enterprise.—way·less, a.

way·bill, wā'bil", n. A list of goods sent in

the care of a common carrier, as a railroad, with shipping directions for the same.

way·far·er, wā′fâr″ẽr, n. One who journeys or travels; a traveler.—**way·far·ing**, wā′fâr″ing, a. Traveling, esp. by foot.—n.

way·lay, wā-lā′, v.t.—**waylaid, waylaying.** [*Way* and *lay.*] To await or intercept in order to seize, rob, or slay; to beset in ambush.—**way·lay·er**, n.

way-out, wā′out′, a. *Slang.* Experimental, esp. in the arts; unconventional. Also **far-out.**

ways and means, n. pl. Methods and means of accomplishing something; methods and means, as in legislation, of raising revenue for the use of the government; as, the Committee of *Ways and Means* of the U.S. House of Representatives.

way·side, wā′sīd″, n. The side, border, or edge of a road or highway.—a. Growing, situated, or being by or near the side of the way; as, *wayside* flowers.—**go by the way·side, let go by the way·side,** to put aside or postpone due to a more urgent matter.

way sta·tion, n. A station situated between principal stations, as on a railroad.

way·ward, wā′wẽrd, a. [For obs. *awayward,* turned away, turned from the proper course, wayward, < *away* and *-ward* (cf. *froward*); the sense in later use being colored by association with *way* ('one's own way').] Turned or turning away from what is right or proper; froward; disposed to turn willfully from what is proper, reasonable, or expected, in order to follow one's own impulses or whims, or willfully or capriciously perverse; disobedient; swayed or prompted by caprice, or capricious; as, a *wayward* fancy; turning or changing irregularly, or irregular; as, a *wayward* stream, path, or breeze; untoward or unfavorable; as, some *wayward* star.—**way·ward·ly**, adv.—**way·ward·ness**, n.

way·worn, wā′wōrn″, wā′wŏrn″, a. Worn or wearied by travel; as, a *wayworn* traveler.

we, wē, pron.—pl. nom. *we,* poss. *our* or *ours,* obj. *us;* intens. and refl. *ourself* or *ourselves.* [O.E. *wé, we, wi,* Icel. *vér, vaer,* Dan. and Sw. *vi,* D. *wij,* G. *wir,* Goth. *weis;* cogn. Skt. *vayam,* we.] The nominative pl. of 'I'; used to refer to the speaker and one or more other persons; used to refer to people in general, as: *We* are all mortal beings. Used by sovereigns and high officials or by editors and writers in place of 'I'; *colloq.* used familiarly, esp. in talking to a child.

weak, wēk, a. [M.E. *weik, waik:* cf. Icel. *veikr* = O.H.G. *weih* (G. *weich*) = O.E. *wāc,* weak; all < the Teut. verb represented by O.E. *wícan,* G. *weichen,* give way: cf. Gr. *eikein,* yield, give way, Skt. *vij-,* move suddenly.] Not strong; liable to yield, break, or collapse under pressure or strain; as, a *weak* fortress; deficient in bodily strength or vigor either constitutionally, or from age or sickness; feeble; infirm; deficient in political strength, governing power, or authority; as, a *weak* nation; wanting in force, potency, or efficacy; impotent; ineffectual or inadequate; as, a *weak* battery; wanting in rhetorical force or effectiveness; as, a *weak* literary style; wanting in logical or legal force or soundness; as, a *weak* argument; deficient in mental power, intelligence, or judgement; as, a *weak* intellect; deficient in moral strength or firmness, resolution, or force of character; as, to prove *weak* under temptation; deficient in amount, volume or intensity; as, *weak* tones or vibrations; deficient, wanting, or poor in something specified; as, *weak* in punctuation; deficient in the essential or desirable properties or ingredients; as, *weak* broth; *phon.* unstressed or unaccented, as sounds or syllables. *Gram.* pertaining to Germanic verbs which are inflected without change of the

root vowel, as in English verbs which form the past tense by the addition of *-ed, -d,* or *-t,* as *work, worked;* pertaining to Germanic nouns and adjectives inflected with the less marked distinctions characteristic of stems ending in *n. Photog.* not dense; as, a *weak* negative; *com.* tending downward in price, as the stock market.—**weak·ish**, a.—**weak·ish·ly**, adv.—**weak·ish·ness**, n.

weak·en, wē′ken, v.t. To make weak or weaker.—v.i. To become weak or weaker. —**weak·en·er**, n.

weak·fish, wēk′fish″, n. pl. **weak·fish, weak·fish·es.** Any of the sciaenoid food fishes constituting the genus *Cynoscion,* as *C. regalis,* inhabiting the waters of the Atlantic and Gulf coasts of the U.S. Also squeteague.

weak·heart·ed, wēk′här′tid, a. Without moral strength or courage.—**weak·heart·ed·ly**, adv.—**weak·heart·ed·ness**, n.

weak·kneed, wēk′nēd′, a. Yielding readily to opposition or intimidation; showing lack of moral firmness or resolution.

weak·ling, wēk′ling, n. One without physical or moral strength.—a. Weak; lacking strength or character.

weak·ly, wēk′lē, a.—**weaklier, weakliest.** Feeble or sickly; of a frail or delicate constitution.—adv. In a weak manner.— **weak·li·ness**, n.

weak-mind·ed, wēk′mīn′did, a. Irresolute; having or showing mental vacillation; having or showing a feeble intellect.— **weak·mind·ed·ness**, n.

weak·ness, wēk′nis, n. The state or quality of being weak; feebleness; a defect; a failing; a particular fondness, followed by *for;* the object of such fondness.

weal, wēl, n. [O.E. *wela,* prosperity, lit. 'the state of being well,' < *wel,* well; Dan. *vel,* Sw. *väl.*] *Archaic.* A sound, healthy, prosperous state; welfare; prosperity.

weal, wēl, n. Wheal, welt, or wale.

weald, wēld, n. [O.E. *weald,* a forest tract; akin G. *wald,* a wood or forest. It is a form of *wold.*] *Chiefly Brit.* An area of open forest land; an uncultivated area, esp. an open upland.

wealth, welth, n. [< *well,* and suffix *th;* cf. *health, sloth,* etc.] A collective term for riches; material possessions in all their variety; affluence; profusion or abundance of something; *econ.* all objects which have both utility and the ability of being appropriated and therefore exchanged.

wealth·y, wel′thē, a.—**wealthier, wealthiest.** Having wealth; affluent; rich; opulent; ample.—**wealth·i·ly**, adv.—**wealth·i·ness**, n.

wean, wēn, v.t. [O.E. *wenian,* to accustom, whence *áwenian,* to wean; Icel. *venja,* to accustom; Dan. *vaenne,* to accustom, *vaenne fra brystet,* to wean, lit. 'to accustom from the breast'; < stem seen in *wont.*] To accustom to do without the mother's milk as food, as a young child or animal; to detach or alienate, as a person, from any object of desire, affection, or habit.—**wean·er**, n. One who undertakes weaning; a guard used over the mouth in weaning animals.

wean·ling, wēn′ling, n. A child or animal newly weaned.—a. Newly weaned.

weap·on, wep′on, n. [O.E. *waepen,* a weapon = Icel. *vápon,* Dan. *vaaben,* Sw. *vapen,* D. *wapen,* G. *waffe,* a weapon, Goth. *wepna* (pl.), arms.] Any instrument of offense or defense in combat; an instrument or means for combating enemies or an opponent; *zool.* the sting, horns, claws, or the like which animals employ for attack or defense.—v.t. To provide or arm with a weapon or weapons.—**weap·on·less**, a.

weap·on·ry, wep′on·rē, n. An aggregation of assorted weapons; the origination, design, and manufacture of weapons.

wear, wâr, v.t.—past *wore,* pp. *worn,* ppr. *wearing.* [O.E. *werian,* clothe, wear, =

O.H.G. *werjan* = Icel. *verja* = Goth. *wasjan,* clothe; akin to L. *vestis,* Gr. *esthēs,* clothing, Skt. *vas-,* put on.] To carry or have on the body or about the person, as a covering, equipment, ornament, or the like; as, to *wear* a coat, badge, or ring; to have or use on the person habitually; as, to *wear* a beard; to bear or have the aspect or appearance of; as, to *wear* a smile; to impair, deteriorate, or consume gradually by use or any continued process; to waste or diminish gradually by rubbing, scraping, or washing, as: The waves *wear* the rocks away. To bring, reduce, or render, as specified, by wear, use, or rubbing; as, to *wear* clothes to rags; to fly or show, as a flag on a ship; to weary or exhaust, as one's patience or strength; to pass, as time, gradually or tediously, used with *away* or *out;* as, to *wear away* the hours; *naut.* to bring, as a vessel, on another tack by turning with the stern toward the wind.—v.i. To undergo gradual impairment, diminution, or reduction from wear, use, attrition, or other causes, followed by *away, down, out,* or *off;* to withstand or last under wear, use, or any continued strain, as: The rug *wore* well for many years. To become or react, as specified, from use or strain; as, patience *worn* thin; to pass, as time, slowly or tediously, often with *away, down, out,* or *off; naut.* to come around on another tack by turning away from the wind.—n. The act of wearing or the state of being worn, as garments; use; clothing, garments, or other articles for wearing, esp. that which is fashionable or for a particular use, often used in compounds; as, sports*wear* or beach*wear;* gradual impairment, wasting, or diminution, as from use; as, cuffs showing *wear;* the ability to endure use; durability.— **wear down**, to reduce or deteriorate by heavy use; to exhaust; to overcome by persistence.—**wear off**, to lessen gradually; disappear.—**wear out**, to become or cause to become unstable through constant wear or use; to use up; to exhaust.—**wear·a·ble**, wâr′a·bl, a.—**wear·er**, n.

wear and tear, n. Loss or deterioration by wearing or ordinary use.

wea·ri·ful, wēr′ē·ful, a. Wearisome; tiresome; tedious; dreary.—**wea·ri·ful·ly**, adv.—**wea·ri·ful·ness**, n.

wea·ri·less, wēr′ē·lis, a. Unwearying; tireless.

wear·ing, wâr′ing, a. Pertaining to articles intended for or capable of being worn. Causing impairment or wear; wearying; fatiguing.

wea·ri·some, wēr′ē·som, a. Causing weariness; tiresome; irksome; monotonous.— **wea·ri·some·ly**, adv.—**wea·ri·some·ness**, n.

wea·ry, wēr′ē, a.—**wearier, weariest.** [O.E. *wérig,* weary, perhaps < *wór,* a swampy place, the word orig. having reference to the fatigue of walking on wet ground.] Having the strength exhausted by work, violent exertion, pain, or distress; tired; fatigued; caused by or indicating weariness; as, a *weary* droop to his shoulders; impatient, disgusted, or unhappy with the continuance of something painful, irksome, or boring.— v.t.—**wearied, wearying.** To make weary; to exhaust or harass.—v.i. To become weary; to tire.—**wea·ri·ly**, a.—**wea·ri·ness**, n.

wea·sand, wē′zand, n. [O.E. *wásend,* the windpipe; O.Fris. *wasende,* O.H.G. *weisunt.*] *Archaic.* The windpipe; the gullet; the throat.

wea·sel, wē′zel, n. pl. **wea·sels, wea·sel.** [O.E. *wesle* = D. *wezel* = G. *wiesel* = Icel. *vísla,* weasel.] Any of certain small, carnivorous mammals of the genus *Mustela,* having a long slender body, feeding on rodents and small birds, and noted for cunning and ferocity; a self-propelled, tracked vehicle capable of traveling over snow, ice, sand, or swampy areas; *fig.* a cunning, sneaky person.—*v.i.* To be deceptive or evasive in actions or speech; to renege on or escape from a commitment or duty, followed by *out.*

wea·sel word, *n.* An ambiguous or misleading word used intentionally to evade a direct statement, commitment, or position.

weath·er, weTH′ẽr, *n.* [O.E. *weder* = D. and L.G. *weder,* Icel. *vethr,* Sw. *väder,* G. *wetter;* supposed to be from same root as *wind. Wither* is a derivative.] The state of the atmosphere at any particular time with respect to conditions of temperature, pressure, humidity, or other meteorological phenomena; a storm or period of intense heat, high winds, or other disagreeable conditions.—*v.t.* To expose to the effects of the weather; to change, as a result of exposure to the weather; to bear up against and come through, as danger or difficulty; *arch.* to cause to slope, so as to allow water to run off; as, to *weather* a roof; *naut.* to sail to the windward of; as, to *weather* an island.—*v.i.* To undergo change, as disintegration or discoloration, by exposure to the weather; to show resistance to weathering.—*a. Naut.* Toward the wind; windward.—**keep one's weath·er eye o·pen,** *colloq.* to be vigilant, attentive, or observant.—**un·der the weath·er,** *colloq.* Ailing, or ill; slightly drunk; having a hangover.—**weath·er·a·bil·i·ty,** weTH″ẽr·a·bil′i·tē, *n.*

weath·er-beat·en, weTH′ẽr·bēt″en, *a.* Beaten, damaged, or worn by the weather; toughened or seasoned by exposure to every kind of weather; as, a *weather-beaten* complexion.

weath·er·board, weTH′ẽr·bōrd″, weTH′ẽr·bard″, *n.* A board used as siding; clapboard; *naut.* the windward side of a ship.—**weath·er·board·ing,** weTH′ẽr·bōr″ding, weTH′ẽr·bar″ding, *n.* Siding.

weath·er-bound, weTH′ẽr·bound″, *a.* Delayed, checked, or halted by bad weather.

Weath·er Bu·reau, *n.* A bureau of the U.S. Department of Commerce, serving as a center for assembling meteorological reports in order to forecast the weather, issue warnings of severe or hazardous weather, and prepare statistical records.

weath·er·cock, weTH′ẽr·kok″, *n.* A vane, often in the figure of a cock, which turns with and shows the direction of the wind; a fickle, inconstant person.—*v.i. Aeron.* to tend to veer into the wind.

weath·er deck, *n. Naut.* a deck with no protection from the weather.

weath·ered, weTH′ẽrd, *a.* Altered, worn, or discolored by exposure to atmospheric influences, or to artificial means inducing the same effects; seasoned; *arch.* sloped, as to allow water to run off.

weath·er eye, *n.* The ability to detect and predict weather changes; *fig.* close observance, esp. of any change in a situation.

weath·er·glass, weTH′ẽr·glas″, weTH′ẽr·gläs″, *n.* An instrument to indicate the current state or impending changes of the atmosphere; a barometer.

weath·er·ing, weTH′ẽr·ing, *n. Geol.* the action of the natural elements which alter the shape, color, or texture of rocks or earth surfaces.

weath·er·ly, weTH′ẽr·lē, *a. Naut.* able to sail close to the wind with very little leeward drift.—**weath·er·li·ness,** *n.*

weath·er·man, weTH′ẽr·man″, *n.* pl. **weath·er·men.** A person forecasting and reporting weather conditions, esp. a Weather Bureau employee.

weath·er map, *n.* A map or chart showing weather conditions over a wide area at a particular time, compiled from simultaneous observations at different places within the area.

weath·er·proof, weTH′ẽr·prōf″, *a.* Able to withstand exposure to all kinds of weather. —*v.t.* To make weatherproof.—**weath·er·proof·ness,** *n.*

weath·er ship, *n.* A ship positioned to observe, record, and report weather conditions in its area.

weath·er sta·tion, *n.* A facility with specialized equipment for observing, recording, and transmitting data on meteorological conditions.

weath·er strip, *n.* A narrow strip of material inserted between a door or window and the jamb or casing to exclude wind, rain, and the like.—**weath·er-strip,** weTH′ẽr·strip″, *v.t.*—*weather-stripped, weatherstripping.* To fit with weather strips.—**weath·er strip·ping,** *n.*

weath·er·tight, weTH′ẽr·tīt′, *a.* Impenetrable by cold, wind, or rain.

weath·er vane, *n.* A vane for indicating the direction of the wind; a weathercock.

weath·er-wise, weTH′ẽr·wiz″, *a.* Skillful in prognosticating changes, as of the weather, of public feeling, opinion, or response.

weath·er·worn, weTH′ẽr·wōrn″, weTH′ẽr·warn″, *a.* Worn by the action of the weather.

weave, wēv, *v.t.*—past *wove* or *weaved,* pp. *woven* or *wove,* ppr. *weaving.* [O.E. *wefan* = D. *weven* = G. *weben* = Icel. *vefa,* weave; akin to Gr. *uphainein,* wave.] To form by interlacing threads, yarns, strands, or strips of some materials; as, to *weave* cloth; to interlace, as threads, yarns, strips, or fibrous material, so as to form a fabric or texture; to form by combining various elements or details into a connected whole; as, to *weave* a tale; to introduce as an element or detail into a connected whole, followed by *in* or *into;* as, to *weave* an incident *into* a story; to move, as the body or a vehicle, in a zigzag or winding fashion. —*v.i.* To make cloth; to become woven or interwoven; to move in a zigzag fashion or from side to side.—*n.* The manner of weaving; a particular style of weaving.

weav·er, wē′vẽr, *n.* One who or that which weaves; one whose occupation is weaving; a weaverbird.

weav·er·bird, wē′vẽr·bụrd″, *n.* Any of numerous, chiefly African and Asian passerine birds of the family *Ploceidae,* related to the finches and noted for their elaborately woven nests.

wea·ver's hitch, *n. Naut.* sheet bend. Also **wea·ver's knot.**

web, web, *n.* [O.E. *webb* = D. *web* = O.H.G. *weppi* (cf. G. *gewebe*) = Icel. *vefr,* web; < the verb represented by E. *weave.*] That which is formed by or as by weaving; a woven fabric, esp. a whole piece of cloth in the course of being woven or after it comes from the loom; something resembling or suggesting a woven fabric; webbing; the structure of delicate threads or filaments spun by a spider and by the larvae of certain insects; a cobweb; a sheet or plate on a steel girder which connects the upper and lower laterally extending portions; the corresponding part between the head and the foot of a rail; *zool.* a membrane which connects the digits of an animal, esp. that which connects the toes of aquatic birds and mammals; *ornith.* the series of barbs on either or both sides of the shaft of a feather; *arch.* the surface between the ribbing of a ribbed vault; *print.* a long continuous roll of paper used on a press. *Fig.* something formed as by weaving or interweaving; as, the *web* of life; a network. —*v.t.*—*webbed, webbing.* To envelop or surround with a web; to ensnare.—*v.i.* To form or build a web.—**web·by,** *a.*—*webbier, webbiest.*—**web·like,** *a.*

web·bing, web′ing, *n.* Woven material of hemp or cotton, in bands of various widths,

for use where strength is required, as for supporting the seats of upholstered chairs or sofas, for brake lining, seat belts, and the like; something forming a web or webs.

we·ber, vā′bẽr, wē′ber, web′ẽr, *n.* [From Wilhelm Edouard *Weber,* a German physicist.] *Phys.* The meter-kilogram-second unit of magnetic flux equal to the flux which, in linking a single turn, produces one volt of electromotive force when the flux is decreased uniformly to zero in one second; 10^8 maxwells.

web·foot, web′fụt″, *n.* pl. **web·feet.** A foot in which the toes are joined by a web; an animal that has webbed feet.—**web·foot·ed,** *a.*

web mem·ber, *n. Civil engin.* any of several structural elements connecting the upper and lower flanges of a lattice girder or a truss.

web press, *n.* A printing press which is automatically supplied with its paper from a long, continuous roll.

web spin·ner, *n.* Any of various slender, long insects of the order *Embioptera,* that spin tunnels or galleries in which to live under bark, rocks, or debris.

web·ster, web′stẽr, *n.* [O.E. *webbestre,* female weaver.] *Archaic,* a weaver.

web·worm, web′wụrm″, *n.* Any of several caterpillars which spin large webs encasing foliage from which they feed, as the garden webworm, *Loxostege similalis.*

wed, wed, *v.t.*—*wedded* or *wed, wedding.* [O.E. *weddian,* to engage, to pledge, wed, a pledge; similarly Goth. *(ga)wadjan,* to pledge, to betroth, < *wadi,* a pledge. Akin *gage, wage, wager.*] To marry; to take for husband or for wife; to join in marriage, as a couple; to unite closely or inseparably.— *v.i.* To marry; to contract matrimony.

we'd, wēd. Contraction of we should, we had, or we would.

wed·ding, wed′ing, *n.* [O.E. *weddung.*] The act or ceremony of marrying; marriage; nuptials; a celebration of an anniversary of a marriage; the action or an example of uniting closely.

wed·ding march, *n.* A slow, stately march played during a bridal procession.

wed·ding ring, *n.* A plain band or ring, commonly of gold, platinum, or silver, given during the wedding ceremony to the bride by the groom; a similar ring often given to the groom by the bride.

wedge, wej, *n.* [O.E. *wecg,* a wedge = Icel. *veggr,* Dan. *vaegge,* Sw. *vigg,* D. *wig,* G. *weck,* wedge; perh. akin to *wag, way, weigh,* and signifying lit. 'the mover.'] A piece of wood or metal, thick at one end and tapering to a thin edge at the other, used for splitting wood or rocks, for tightening or securing objects, or for raising or levering weights; anything in the form of a wedge; as, a *wedge* of apple pie; a tactical formation arranged like a wedge, as of troops or football players; an initiatory move or action; an idea, action, policy, or procedure resulting in change, disruption, or breach; a triangular-shaped character in cuneiform writing; *golf,* an iron club with an extremely angled face, used for lofting the ball; *meteor.* a long, triangular area of high pressure.—*v.t.*—*wedged, wedging.* To split with or as with a wedge; to fasten or fix with a wedge; to crowd or compress into a confined space.—*v.i.* To jam in like a wedge; to become wedged.—*wedged, wejd,* *a.*—**wedg·y,** wej′ē, *a.*—*wedgier, wedgiest.*

Wedg·ie, wej′ē, *n.* A woman's shoe in which a thick wedge, serving as the heel, tapers down to the front of the shoe, forming a flat, unbroken sole. (Trademark.) Also *colloq.* **wedg·ie.**

Wedg·wood ware, wej′wụd wâr″, *n.* [After Josiah *Wedgwood,* 1730-1795, the English inventor.] A superior, hard pottery displaying delicate, classical motifs orig. in white cameo relief on an unglazed background tinted blue or black.

wed·lock, wed′lok, *n.* [O.E. *wedlāc,* a pledging, < *wed,* a pledge, and *lāc,* sport, a gift, latterly used as a mere termination of abstract nouns.] Matrimony; marriage.—**out of wed·lock,** born of natural parents who have not married one another.

Wednes·day, wenz′dē, wenz′dā, *n.* [O.E. *Wódnesdaeg,* that is Woden's day.] The fourth day of the week; the next day after Tuesday.—**Wednes·days,** wenz′dēz, wenz′dāz, *adv.* On Wednesdays.

wee, wē, *a.*—**weer, weest.** [A form of *way,* its present meaning being due to its frequent usage in the phrase 'a little *we*' (or *wea*) = a little way, a little bit.] Tiny; small; extremely early, as the hours of early morning.

weed, wēd, *n.* [O.E. *weód,* a weed. D. *wiede,* weeds; affinities doubtful.] Any plant that is useless, troublesome, or injurious to any cultivated plant or crop; an undesired plant of rank or profuse growth; any worthless or useless object or animal, esp. an animal unfit for breeding. *Slang,* tobacco, used with *the*; a cheap cigar; marijuana. *Colloq.* a cigarette.—*v.t.* To free from weeds; as, to *weed* the roses; to remove, as weeds, followed by *out*; as, to *weed out* the clover in the lawn; to free from anything harmful or undesirable; to remove as undesirable, used with *out*; as, to *weed out* one's wardrobe.—*v.i.* To remove weeds.—**weed·ed,** *a.* Free of weeds; weedy.—**weed·less,** *a.*

weed, wēd, *n.* [O.E. *waed, waede,* a garment; O.Fris. *wede,* D. *(ge)waad,* Icel. *vád*; < same root as Goth. *ga-widan,* to bind, and as E. *withy.*] A black band, worn on a man's coat sleeve or hat as a symbol of mourning; *pl.* a woman's mourning garments; as, widow's *weeds*; *archaic,* a garment or clothing.

weed·er, wē′dėr, *n.* One who weeds; a tool used for removing weeds.

weed·y, wē′dē, *a.*—**weedier, weediest.** Consisting of weeds; abounding with weeds; pertaining to or resembling weeds, as in growth that is rank or rapid; *colloq.* lanky, scrawny, or ungainly, esp. of an animal or person; as, a *weedy* horse.—**weed·i·ly,** *adv.* —**weed·i·ness,** *n.*

week, wēk, *n.* [O.E. *wice,* a week = D. *week,* Icel. *vika,* a week; akin G. *woche,* a week; root doubtful.] A period of seven consecutive days, esp. one beginning with Sunday; such a period beginning with or including a specific holiday or event; as, *Easter Week*; a week devoted to the recognition of a cause or institution; as, *National Secretaries Week*; the portion of a week devoted to work, school, or business; work-week; a seven-day period before or after a specified day; as, a *week* from Saturday. Abbr. *w., wk.*

week·day, wēk′dā″, *n.* Any day of the week except Saturday and Sunday.—**week·days,** wēk′dāz″, *adv.* On any weekday; during weekdays.

week·end, wēk′end″, *n.* The end of the week; the period from Friday night or Saturday to Monday morning.—*v.i.* To pass the weekend, as at a place.—**week·ends,** wēk′endz″, *adv.* During weekends; on weekends.

week·end·er, wēk′en″dėr, *n.* One who travels on weekends. A travel case or bag in which to carry the toilet articles and clothing for a weekend; also **week·end bag.**

week·ly, wēk′lē, *a.* Pertaining to a week or weekdays; happening or done once a week; determined or reckoned according to intervals of any week; as, the *weekly* rate.—*adv.* Once a week.—*n. pl.* **week·lies.** A periodical, as a newspaper, appearing once a week.

ween, wēn, *v.t., v.i.* [O.E. *wēnan,* < *wēn,* expectation, belief, = D. *waan,* G. *wahn,* delusion, = Icel. *vān,* Goth. *wēns,* expecta-tion: cf. *overween.*] *Archaic,* to expect, think, or suppose.

wee·nie, wee·ny, wē′nē, *n. Colloq.* A frankfurter or wiener; a hot dog.

wee·ny, wē′nē, *a.*—**weenier, weeniest.** Exceptionally tiny; very small; wee. Also **ween·sy.**

weep, wēp, *v.i.*—**wept, weeping.** [O.E. *wépan,* to weep, < *wóp,* clamor, outcry; O.E. *wopian,* Goth. *wopjan,* to cry; cogn. Rus. *vopit,* Lith. *vapiti,* to weep; L. *vox,* voice; Skt. *vach,* to speak.] To manifest grief or other strong passion by shedding tears; to drop or flow like tears; to drip; to give out moisture.—*v.t.* To lament, bewail, or bemoan; to shed tears for; to shed or let fall drop by drop; to ooze; to pour forth in drops, as if tears; to arrive at a certain state by weeping, usu. followed by *away* or *out.* —*n.* An act or period of weeping.—**weep·y,** wē′pē, *a.*—**weepier, weepiest.**

weep, wēp, *n. Brit. dial.* the lapwing.

weep·er, wē′pėr, *n.* One who weeps, or sheds tears; a hired mourner at a funeral; something worn as a badge of mourning, as a widow's long black veil or a long scarflike hatband formerly worn by men at funerals; that which hangs loose like a streamer, as a moss tendril suspended from a tree; any hole, as in a wall or floor, that allows water to drip through.

weep·ing, wē′ping, *a.* Expressive of sorrow or grief; tearful; exuding moisture; having slim, drooping branches, as trees.

weep·ing wil·low, *n.* A large, widely cultivated willow, *Salix babylonica,* native to Asia, with very long, slender, pendulous branches.

wee·ver, wē′vėr, *n.* [Cf. Fr. *vive,* weever, for *vivre,* O.Fr. *wivre,* viper.] Any of the small marine food fishes of the genus *Trachinus,* found in European waters, notable for their sharp, poisonous, dorsal spines; any fish of the family *Trachinidae.*

wee·vil, wē′vil, *n.* [O.E. *wifel,* L.G. and D. *wevel,* G. *wiebel*; cogn. Lith. *wabalas,* a beetle.] Any of various snout beetles, family *Curculionoidae,* destructive to field and garden crops, fruit and shade trees, and to stored products, and whose larvae burrow into and infest nuts, twigs, and grain. —**wee·vil·y, wee·vil·ly, wee·viled, wee·villed,** wē′vi·lē, wē′vild, *a.*

weft, weft, *n.* [O.E. *weft,* the woof, < *wefan,* to weave; so Icel. *veftr.*] *Textiles,* the threads that are carried in the shuttle across the warp; the woof; an item or article made of woven fabric.

wei·ge·la, wī·gē′la, wī·jē′la, wī′ge·la, *n.* [N.L. *Weigela,* also *Weigelia*; named from C. E. *Weigel,* German botanist.] Any of various shrubby plants of the honeysuckle family, genus *Weigela,* with showy, funnel-shaped white, pink, or crimson flowers. Also **wei·ge·li·a,** wi·gē′lē·a, wi·jē′lē·a.

weigh, wā, *v.t.* [O.E. *wegan,* to lift, to weigh, to move; *waeg,* a balance, a pair of scales; D. *wegen,* to weigh; Icel. *vega,* to bear, lift, move; G. *wiegen,* to rock; same root as *way, wain, wag,* etc.] To measure the weight of or gravitational pull on, as an article, with a balance or scale; to raise or bear up in balancing or estimating the weight of, as with the shoulder or hand; to pay, allot, or measure by weight, usu. followed by *out*; as, to *weigh out* a pound of nuts; to consider, compare, or evaluate; as, to *weigh* the alternatives; to oppress or burden with weight or heaviness, followed by *down*; *naut.* to lift or hoist; as, to *weigh* anchor.— *v.i.* To have weight; to be equal in weight to; as, to *weigh* a pound; to be considered important; to rest or press upon as a burden, duties or worries, usu. followed by *on* or *upon*; to consider or evaluate; *naut.* to hoist anchor.—**weigh in,** to weigh one's baggage before a flight. *Sports,* to have one's weight recorded preceding a boxing match or race; to be of the weight measured.— **weigh one's words,** to speak with deliberation.—**weigh·a·ble,** *a.*—**weigh·er,** *n.*

weigh, wā, *n.* Way, esp. as used nautically in the phrase *under weigh.*

weight, wāt, *n.* [O.E. *wiht, gewiht,* akin to D. and G. *gewicht,* Icel. *vaett,* weight; < the root of E. *weigh.*] An amount of heaviness; the measure of a body's tendency to move toward the center of the earth or other celestial body, determined by multiplying the mass of the body by its gravitational acceleration; a unit for measuring weight or mass; a system of such units; as, avoirdupois *weight*; a quantity of a substance determined by weighing; as, a small *weight* of sugar; any heavy mass or object, esp. an object used because of its heaviness, as for holding something down, to drive a mechanism, or as a counterpoise. *Fig.* a burden, as of responsibility; pressure; importance, consequence, or effective influence. *Math.* the value assigned to an item in order to increase or decrease its importance relative to the other items in a compilation. The relative lightness or heaviness of fabrics, esp. in regard to suitability for a particular season; as, a summer *weight* suit; a classification into which boxers or wrestlers are placed according to individual body weight; the specific poundage a horse must carry in a handicap race.—*v.t.* To add weight to; to load with additional weight; to attach a weight or weights to; to burden with or as with weight; *math.* to give or assign a weight to; *textiles,* to load or treat, as fabrics, with chemical matter in order to increase the weight and bulk.—**by weight,** measure according to weight.—**carry weight,** to have importance, influence, or authority.—**pull one's weight,** to do one's fair share of any work.—**throw one's weight a·round,** to make unnecessary use of one's power, authority, or influence.— **weight·ed,** wā′tid, *a.*—**weight·less,** wāt′-lis, *a.*—**weight·less·ly,** *adv.*—**weight·less·ness,** *n.* Abbr. *w., wt.*

weight lift·ing, *n.* The lifting of barbells as a competitive sport according to prescribed rules or as an exercise for body conditioning. —**weight lift·er,** *n.*

weight·y, wā′tē, *a.*—**weightier, weightiest.** Having great weight; heavy; ponderous; oppressive, troublesome, or burdensome; as, a *weighty* problem; important or momentous; as, *weighty* decisions; forcible or convincing; grave or serious.—**weight·i·ly,** *adv.*—**weight·i·ness,** *n.*

Wei·mar·an·er, vī′ma·rä″nėr, wī′ma·rä″nėr, *n.* A German breed of large hunting dog with short, smooth gray hair and blue or amber eyes.

weir, wēr, *n.* [O.E. *waer, wer,* a fence, an enclosure for fish; G. *wehr,* weir, dam; lit. 'a fence or defense' being akin to *ward, ware, wary, warren.*] A dam across a stream to raise the water, or to convey it to a mill, or irrigation ditches; a fence of twigs or stakes set in a stream to catch or retain fish.

weird, wērd, *a.*—**weirder, weirdest.** [O.E. *wyrd, wird,* fate, destiny < stem of *weorthan,* G. of *werden,* Goth. *wairthan,* to become, to be.] Pertaining to the supernatural or unearthly; uncanny; eerie; relating to or resulting from magic or witchcraft; mysterious; fantastic or bizarre; as, a *weird* theory; odd or strange; *archaic,* pertaining to or connected with fate or destiny, or to the Fates.—*n. Chiefly Sc.* The Fates; destiny.—**weird·ly,** *adv.*—**weird·ness,** *n.*

Weird Sis·ters, *n. pl.* The Fates.

weis·en·heim·er, wī′zen·hī″mėr, *n.* Wisenheimer.

Weis·mann·ism, vīs′män·iz″um, *n. Biol.* a theory propounded by the German biologist

August Weismann, 1834–1914, that regards the germ plasm as continuous from generation to generation and as the basis of heredity, but as having no interaction with the somatic cells, thereby denying the possibility of the transmission of acquired characteristics.

we·ka, wā′kä, wē′ka, *n.* [Maori.] Any of several large, flightless New Zealand rails of the genus *Ocydroma*.

welch, welch, welsh, *v.i.* Welsh.—**welch·er,** welch′ér, welsh′ér, *n.* Welsher.

Welch, welch, welsh, *a.* Welsh.

wel·come, wel′kom, *a.* [Equiv. to *well come*.] Received with gladness; admitted willingly to one's house and company; producing gladness or pleasure; pleasing; made free to have, use, or enjoy; pertaining to phrases of courtesy.—*n.* A warm salutation to a newcomer or guest.—*v.t.*—*wel·comed,* welcoming. To receive hospitably and cheerfully; to accept or receive with gladness.—*interj.* An expression of cordial greeting.—**wear out one's wel·come,** to visit so frequently or stay so long that it becomes unpleasant to the host.—**wel·-come·ly,** *adv.*—**wel·come·ness,** *n.*—**wel·com·er,** *n.*

wel·come wag·on, *n.* A motor vehicle driven by a person employed to welcome newcomers to a community, to answer questions about goods and services available, and to offer gifts from, and coupons redeemable at, local stores; (*sometimes cap.*) the organization responsible for this service.

weld, weld, *n.* [O.E. *welde, wolde,* Sc. *wald*; origin unknown.] An herb, *Reseda luteola,* of southern Europe, the source of a yellow dye; the dye itself. Also *wold*.

weld, weld, *v.t.* [O.E. *welle,* Sc. *waul* (the final *d* has been added) = G. and D. *wellen*, to boil, to weld; Sw. *walla,* to weld; same word as *well,* to boil, to bubble up.] To unite or join into firm union, as pieces of metal, by heating the edges and applying pressure, hammering, or with the addition of a fusible filler; to unite closely or bring into harmony.—*v.i.* To be welded.—*n.* The union of metals by welding; the section or joint formed.—**weld·a·bil·i·ty,** weld″a·bil′i·tē, *a.*—**weld·a·ble,** *a.*—**weld·er, wel·dor,** *n.*

weld·ment, weld′ment, *n.* A unit consisting of an assembly of welded pieces.

wel·fare, wel′fâr, *n.* [Lit. 'a state of *faring well*.'] A state or condition of well-being, as of health, happiness, or prosperity; welfare work.—*a.* Of or pertaining to welfare work. —**on wel·fare,** relying or depending on government relief.

wel·fare state, *n.* A state whose government is responsible for the welfare of its citizens through such measures as social security, free medical care, old-age pensions, and providing education, housing, and the like; the social system characteristic of such a state.

wel·fare work, *n.* A program devoted to the betterment of underprivileged people, undertaken by government or private organizations, and providing funds, better housing, hospitalization, jobs, or the like.— **wel·fare work·er,** *n.*

wel·far·ism, wel′fâr″iz·um, wel′fâ·riz″um, *n.* The theories of, or attitudes and practices associated with the welfare state.

wel·kin, wel′kin, *n.* [O.E. *wolcen, wolcn,* a cloud, pl. the sky; G. *wolke,* O.H.G. *wolchan,* a cloud.] *Poetic.* The sky; the air; the vault of heaven.

well, wel, *n.* [O.E. *wella, wylla*.] A spring or natural source of water; a fountain; a hole, pit, or shaft sunk in the ground by digging or boring to obtain a supply of water, brine, petroleum, or natural gas; any sunken or deep, enclosed space, as a shaft for air or

light, or for stairs, an elevator, or the like, extending vertically through the floors of a building; a compartment or enclosure around a ship's pumps to render them easily accessible and protect them from being injured by the cargo; a water-filled tank aboard a fishing boat used to preserve fish; an enclosed space before the judges' bench in English courts of law, for the lawyers and their assistants; a vessel, receptacle, or reservoir for a liquid; as, an ink*well*; a reservoir or source, as of emotions, vigor, knowledge, and the like.—*v.i.* [O.E. *wellan, wyllan,* secondary form of *weallan* = O.E. and O.H.G. *wallan* (G. *wallen*), boil, well up.] To rise, spring, or gush from the earth or some source, as water, often followed by *up, out,* or *forth,* as: Tears *welled up* in his eyes.—*v.t.* To send welling up or forth.—*a.*

well, wel, *adv.*—*better, best.* [O.E. *wel* = D. *wel* = Icel. *vel* = O.H.G. *wela,* later *wola* (G. *wohl*), = Goth. *waila,* well, orig. 'as wished': < the root of E. *will*.] In a satisfactory, favorable, or advantageous manner, as: Affairs are going *well*. Prosperously; beneficially; conveniently; fortunately or happily; approvingly or kindly; as, to be *well* treated; in a good manner; commendably, meritoriously, or excellently; as, to reason *well*; properly or fittingly; admirably or finely; with propriety, justice, or reason, as: I could not *well* refuse. In satisfactory or good measure, adequately, or sufficiently; as, to think *well* before acting; heartily; to a considerable extent or degree; as, to dilute the acid *well*; personally or intimately, as: He knows her *well*. Considerably; thoroughly.—*a.* Satisfactory or good; as: All is *well* with us. Right, proper, or fitting; advisable, as: Is it *well* to act so hastily? In a satisfactory or comfortable condition; prosperous; in good health, or sound in body and mind; as, a *well* man.— *interj.* An expression indicating surprise, expectation, doubt, or the like; an expression used as an introduction to or in resuming a conversation.—**as well,** also; in addition; with equal consequence or effect.— **as well as,** moreover; in addition to; as satisfactorily as.

we'll, wel. Contraction of we will or we shall.

well-ad·vised, wel′advīzd′, *a.* Acting or done with due or careful consideration; prudent.

well-be·ing, wel′bē′ing, *n.* Welfare; the condition of happiness, prosperity, and good health.

well-be·lov·ed, wel′bi·luv′id, wel′bi·luvd′, *a.* Loved with much sincerity and depth; highly or deeply respected, often used in forms of ceremonial address.

well·born, wel′bârn′, *a.* Born of a noble or respectable family.

well·bred, wel′bred′, *a.* Showing or being of good breeding; polite, as in conduct or manners; cultivated; refined; of good breed, stock, or pedigree, as animals.

well-dis·posed, wel′di·spōzd′, *a.* Favorably, benevolently, or sympathetically inclined or disposed, as toward some person or to a certain idea; having a pleasant or good disposition.

well-done, wel′dun′, *a.* Accomplished with diligence and skill; completely cooked, esp. as meats: opposed to *rare*.

well-fa·vored, *Brit.* **well-fa·voured,** wel′-fā′vèrd, *a.* Handsome; comely; pleasing to the eye; pretty.—**well-fa·vored·ness,** *Brit.* **well-fa·voured·ness,** *n.*

well-fixed, wel′fikst′, *a. Colloq.* Prosperous or moneyed; well-to-do.

well-found, wel′found′, *a.* Well furnished with supplies or necessaries.

well-found·ed, wel′foun′did, *a.* Founded on good and valid reasons, facts, or evidence.

well-groomed, wel′grömd′, *a.* Well-dressed with meticulous attention to the cleanliness of one's clothing, hair, and skin, resulting in an exceptionally neat appearance; made trim in appearance by proper feeding, bathing, and brushing, as a dog entered in competition; tidy and carefully tended, as a lawn.

well-ground·ed, wel′groun′did, *a.* Based on good grounds or reasons; well-founded; well or thoroughly instructed in the fundamental principles of a subject.

well-han·dled, wel′han′dld, *a.* Showing evidence of much use or handling; well or efficiently completed or managed.

well·head, wel′hed″, *n.* A natural source of water, as of a well or stream; a protective structure over a well. *Fig.* any principal source; fountainhead.

well-heeled, wel′hēld′, *a. Slang,* wealthy.

Wel·ling·ton boot, wel′ing·ton böt′, *n.* A high boot having a loose front flap which extends to the top of the knee. Also **wel·ling·ton.**

well-knit, wel′nit′, *a.* Firmly or closely linked or joined; close-knit; sturdily constructed.

well-known, wel′nōn′, *a.* Fully known; generally known or acknowledged; familiar; famous.

well-mean·ing, wel′mē′ning, *a.* Well-intentioned; stemming from good intentions. Also **well-meant,** wel′ment′.

well-nigh, wel′nī′, *adv.* Very nearly; almost.

well-off, wel′af′, wel′of′, *a.* In a fortunate position; in comfortable circumstances; financially secure.

well-or·dered, wel′ar′dèrd, *a.* Ordered or arranged well; well-regulated.

well-read, wel′red′, *a.* Having read a great deal; conversant and knowledgeable.

well-spo·ken, wel′spō′ken, *a.* Said well, fittingly, or with propriety; spoken courteously or in a pleasant manner.

well·spring, wel′spring″, *n.* A stream's source; fountainhead; *fig.* an unflagging source of supply; as, a *wellspring* of knowledge.

well-thought-of, wel′that′uv″, wel′that′ov″, *a.* Highly regarded; held in high esteem.

well-timed, wel′tīmd′, *a.* Fittingly timed; opportune; timely.

well-to-do, wel′to·dö′, *a.* Well-off; prosperous; wealthy.

well-turned, wel′turnd′, *a.* Turned or shaped well, as with rounded or curving form; gracefully, appropriately, or concisely expressed; as, a *well-turned* thought.

well-wish·er, wel′wish′èr, *n.* One who wishes well to a person, a cause, or the like. —**well-wish·ing,** *a., n.*

well-worn, wel′wörn′, wel′warn, *a.* Much worn or affected by wear or use; as, *well-worn* garments; trite, hackneyed, or stale; as, a *well-worn* saying or theme; *fig.* fittingly or becomingly worn; as, *well-worn* honors.

Wels·bach burn·er, welz′bak bur′nèr, *G.* vels′bäch, *n.* A gas burner devised by the Austrian chemist, Karl von Welsbach, 1859–1929, consisting essentially of a Bunsen burner with an incombustible mantle, composed of thoria with a trace of ceria, CeO_2, a compound of cerium, which becomes incandescent and emits a brilliant light when heated. (Trademark.)

welsh, welch, welsh, welch, *v.i.* [Origin uncertain; perh. from *Welsh,* personal name, or from *Welsh*.] *Slang.* To cheat by failing to pay a bet; to evade the payment of a debt or the fulfilment of any obligation.— **welsh·er, welch·er,** *n.* One who welshes, as on a bet.

Welsh, welsh, welch, *a.* [O.E. *welisc, waelisc,* lit. 'foreign,' < *waelh,* a foreigner; similarly G. *wälsch, welsch,* is foreign, esp. Fr. or It., and *Wälschland* is Italy. So *walnut* is the welsh or foreign nut. Akin to *Walloon, Cornwall.*] Pertaining to Wales, its culture, people, or their language. Also *Welch.—n.* The inhabitants of Wales and their offspring who live elsewhere; also **Cym·ry.** The Celtic language of Wales; also **Cym·ric.** Also *Welch.*—**Welsh·man,** *n.* An inhabitant of Wales.

Welsh cor·gi, welsh kạr′gē, *n.* Either one of two breeds of sturdy Welsh working dogs distinguished by short legs, a long body, and a head resembling that of a fox.

Welsh rab·bit, *n. Cookery,* a preparation of melted cheese, usu. seasoned and mixed with ale or beer and milk or cream, poured over toast or sometimes crackers while still hot. Also **Welsh rare·bit.**

Welsh spring·er span·iel, *n.* A medium-sized, red and white Welsh-bred spaniel used for hunting.

Welsh ter·ri·er, *n.* A Welsh breed of medium-sized terriers, similar to an Airedale, with a wiry, brindle coat, used for hunting.

welt, welt, *n.* [Prob. < W. *gwald,* a hem, a welt.] A decorative or reinforcing seam or edging; a strip of leather sewed around the edge of the upper part of a boot or shoe and the inner sole, to which the outer sole is afterward attached. An inflamed stripe raised on the skin by a blow; also *wale, weal, wheal.—v.t.* To furnish or decorate with a welt; to strike or thrash as to raise welts on the skin.

Welt·an·schau·ung, velt′än′shou″ụng, *n.* pl. **Welt·an·schau·ungs, Welt·an·schau·ung·en,** [Lit. 'world viewing.'] *German,* a systematized or consistent conception of all existence, as that of a philosopher, nation, or era.

wel·ter, wel′tẽr, *v.i.* [< O.E. *wealtan,* to roll; L.G. *weltern,* Sw. *vältra,* G. *wälzen,* to roll, to wallow, to welter; same root as *walk, wallow.* Akin *waltz.*] To roll or toss, as waves; to wallow or tumble about; to be doused in or covered with a liquid, esp. blood; to become deeply absorbed.—*n.* A disordered mass; a state of confusion or turmoil; a rolling and tossing motion, as by waves.

wel·ter, wel′tẽr, *n.* Welterweight.

wel·ter·weight, wel′tẽr·wāt″, *n.* A boxer or wrestler who competes at a weight between 136 and 147 pounds. Also *welter.*

Welt·schmerz, velt′shmeRts″, *n.* [Lit. 'world pain.'] *German.* A state of melancholy brought about by belief in inevitable disappointment; world-weariness; romantic pessimism.

wen, wen, *n.* [O.E. *wenn,* D. *wen,* L.G. *ween,* Prov. G. *wenne,* a swelling, a wart.] *Pathol.* a nonmalignant tumor, esp. of the scalp, without inflammation and caused by blockage of a sebaceous gland.—**wen·nish, wen·ny,** wen′ē, *a.*

wen, wen, *n.* A rune in Old English replaced by the *w* in Modern English.

wench, wench, *n.* [O.E. *wenche,* < *wenchel,* a child, *wencel,* weak; allied to G. *wanken,* to totter.] A woman, esp. a young woman. *Archaic,* a maid; a girl from a rural area; a promiscuous woman.—*v.i. Archaic,* to seek out or consort with promiscuous women.—**wench·er,** *n.*

wend, wend, *v.i.—wended* or archaic *went, wending.* [O.E. *wendan,* to turn, to go = Icel. *venda,* Dan. *vende,* D. and G. *wenden,* to change, to turn: a caus. of the verb to *wind,* to turn, to twist.] *Archaic.* To go; to pass to or from a place; to travel.—*v.t. Archaic.* To pursue; to direct; as, to *wend* one's way.

Wend·ish, wen′dish, *a.* Of or concerning the Wends, a Slavic people living in eastern Germany, or the language used by them.— *n.* The West Slavic language used by the Wends. Also **Sorb·i·an, Lu·sa·tian.**

wen·tle·trap, wen′t'l·trap″, *n.* [D. *wenteltrap,* a winding staircase.] Any of the usu. white, high-spired, marine snails of the family *Epitoniidae.*

were, wụr, *unstressed* wẽr, *Brit.* wâr. The past indicative plural and second person singular, and past subjunctive singular and plural of *be.*

we're, wẽr. Contraction of we are.

weren't, wụrnt, wụr′ont. Contraction of were not.

were·wolf, wer·wolf, wẽr′wụlf″, wụr′- wụlf″, wâr′wụlf″, *n.* pl. **were·wolves,** wẽr′wụlvz″, wụr′wụlvz″, wâr′wụlvz″. [O.E. *werewulf,* lit. man-wolf, < *wer* (Icel. *verr,* Goth. *wair*), a man, and *wulf,* wolf; *wer* is cogn. with L. *vir,* a man.] A man transformed into a wolf or having the power to assume a wolf's form; a lycanthrope.

wer·geld, wụr′geld, *n.* [O.E. *wergild—wer,* man, and *gild, geld,* a payment.] A compensation received, in old Teutonic and Anglo-Saxon law, by the family or lord of a slain or injured man, paid by the offender and freeing him of further obligation or punishment. Also **wer·gelt, were·gild, wer·gild,** wụr′gelt, wụr′gild.

wes·kit, wes′kit, *n.* A waistcoat, usu. one worn by women.

Wes·ley·an, wes′lē·an, *Brit.* wez′lē·an, *a.* Of or pertaining to John or Charles Wesley, or to Methodism, the Protestant denomination they established—*n.* One who adheres to the religious teachings of John Wesley.— **Wes·ley·an·ism,** wes′lē·a·niz″um, *Brit.* wez′lē·a·niz″um, *n.*

west, west, *n.* [O.E. *west,* adv. akin to D. *west,* adv. G. *west,* n. Icel. *vestr,* n. and perh. to L. *vesper,* evening, the west, and Gr. *ésperos,* of or at evening, western.] The cardinal point of the compass directly opposite to east; the point where the sun is seen to set at the equinox; the general direction in which this point lies, or the direction to one's left when facing north; (*usu. cap.*) a region west of a specified or implied point of reference, as the part of the U.S. west of the Mississippi River. (*Cap.*) those nations west of Asia, more or less united by common traditions and institutions of European origin: distinguished from the *East* or the *Orient*; the Occident. —*a.* Lying toward or situated in the west; western; coming from the west, as the wind. —*adv.* Toward or in the west; westward. Abbr. *w, w., W, W.*

west·bound, west′bound″, *a.* Directed or traveling westward.

west by north, *n. Navig.* a point on the navigator's compass, 281° 15′, indicating a direction north of due west by one point. Abbr. *WbN.*

west by south, *n. Navig.* a point on the navigator's compass, 258° 45′, indicating a direction south of due west by one point. Abbr. *WbS.*

west·er, wes′tẽr, *v.i.* To move or tend toward the west.—*n.* A weather disturbance, as a storm, from the west.

west·er·ly, wes′tẽr·lē, *a.* Of or toward the west; situated in the western region; coming from the west, as a breeze.—*adv.* Tending, going, or moving toward the west; from the west.—*n.* pl. **west·er·lies.** A wind from the west.

west·ern, wes′tẽrn, *a.* Being in the west, or in the direction of west; as, a *western* state; moving or directed to the west; proceeding from the west; as, a *western* breeze; (*often cap.*) pertaining to or being of the west; as, a *Western* pine tree; (*cap.*) referring to the Western Church.—*n.* A westerner; a novel, movie, or play of the western U.S., esp. relating to Indians, pioneers, and cowboys.

West·ern Church, *n.* The Roman Catholic Church; broadly, the Christian churches of western Europe and the U.S.: as distinguished from the *Eastern Orthodox Church.*

west·ern·er, wes′tẽr·nẽr, *n.* A native or inhabitant of the West, esp. of the U.S.

West·ern Hem·i·sphere, *n.* The part of the earth which includes the continents of North and South America, the surrounding islands, and the adjacent waters.

west·ern·ize, wes′tẽr·nīz″, *v.t.—westernized, westernizing.* To render western in character, ideas, or ways.—*v.i.—*west·ern·- i·za·tion, wes′tẽr·ni·zā′shan, *n.*

west·ern·most, wes′tẽrn·mōst″, *Brit.* wes′- tẽrn·most, *a.* Farthest west.

West High·land white ter·ri·er, *n.* A small Scottish breed of terrier having short legs and a long, rather stiff, white coat.

west·ing, wes′ting, *n. Navig.* the distance westward which a ship travels; the distance reckoned from one point, as a meridian, to another westward from it.

west-north·west, west′nạrth″west′, *Naut.* west′nạr″west′, *n. Navig.* the point on the navigator's compass, 292° 30′, indicating a direction half the distance between due west and northwest; this direction.—*a.* Lying toward or situated in the west-northwest. —*adv.* Toward, in, or from the west-northwest. Abbr. *wnw, w.n.w., WNW, W.N.W.*

West Sax·on, *n.* The Old English dialectal language of Wessex, an ancient kingdom in southern England, and the primary literary language of England from Alfred the Great's time to the Norman Conquest; one of the Saxons who inhabited Wessex before the Norman Conquest.

west-south·west, west′south″west′, *Naut.* west′sou″west′, *n. Navig.* the point on the navigator's compass, 247° 31′, indicating a direction half the distance between due west and southwest; this direction.—*a.* Lying toward or situated in the west-southwest.—*adv.* Toward, in, or from the west-southwest.

west·ward, west′wẽrd, *adv.* [O.E. *west,* and -*weard,* denoting direction. *Westwards* is an adverbial genitive.] Toward the west. Also **west·wards.—***n.* A westward region or direction.—*a.*

wet, wet, *a.—wetter, wettest.* [O.E. and Sc. *weet,* O.E. *waet,* Icel. *vátr,* Dan. *vaad,* wet; akin to *water.*] Containing water; soaked with water; rainy; very damp; not totally dry, as: The paint is still wet. *Colloq.* permitting the manufacturing and selling of alcoholic drinks. Bottled or preserved, as food in a sweetened liquid, as syrup.—*n.* Water or wetness; moisture or humidity in considerable degree; rainy weather; rain; *colloq.* a person opposing prohibition.—*v.t.—past wet* or *wetted,* pp. *wet* or *wetted,* ppr. *wetting.* To make wet; to moisten; drench; or soak with water or other liquid; to make wet, as by urinating. —*v.i.* To become wet.—**wet be·hind the ears,** inexperienced or immature.—**wet·ly,** *adv.*—**wet·ness,** *n.*—**wet·ta·ble,** *a.*—**wet·- ter,** *n.*—**wet·tish,** *a.*

wet·back, wet′bak″, *n. Colloq.* a Mexican citizen who illegally enters the U.S., often by swimming the Rio Grande.

wet blan·ket, *n. Colloq.* a person or thing that dampens enthusiasm or has a discouraging or depressing effect.—**wet-blan·ket,** *v.t.* To put out, as a fire, using a blanket or the like made damp by water; to lessen the enthusiasm of a person, enterprise, or the like.

weth·er, weTH′ẽr, *n.* [O.E. *wether,* a ram; a word common to the Teut. tongues, and allied to L. *vitulus,* a calf, lit. 'a yearling.'] A castrated ram.

wet·land, wet′land″, *n. Usu. pl.* a piece of land whose soil is moist and spongy, as a swamp or marsh.

wet nurse, *n.* A woman who suckles and nurses a child not her own.—**wet-nurse,** wet′nụrs″, *v.t.*

wet·ta·bil·i·ty, wet″*a*·bil′i·tē, *n.* The quality of being wettable; the degree to which a fabric or the like can be made absorbent or wet.

wet·ting a·gent, *n. Chem.* any substance which, with its absorption by a liquid, reduces the surface tension and increases the spreading or penetrating ability of that liquid over a surface.

wet wash, *n.* Clean, damp, unironed laundry.

we've, wēv. Contraction of we have.

whack, hwak, wak, *v.t.* [THWACK.] *Colloq.* to thwack; to give a hearty or resounding blow to. *Slang,* to divide or share, often followed by *up.*—*v.i. Colloq.* to strike or continue striking anything with smart blows. —*n. Colloq.* A hearty or resounding blow; a chance or attempt, as: She had a *whack* at being class president. *Slang,* a share or section.—**whack·er,** *n.*

whack·ing, hwak′ing, wak′ing, *a. Chiefly Brit., colloq.* extremely large.

whack·y, hwak′ē, wak′ē, *a.* Wacky.

whale, hwāl, wāl, *n.* [O.E. *hwæl* = Icel. *hvair* = Sw. and Dan. *hval* = O.H.G. G. *wal,* whale: cf. *walrus.*] Any of various pelagic animals of the order *Cetacea,* the members of which, though of fishlike form, are air-breathing viviparous mammals, esp. one of the larger cetaceans: as distinguished from the *dolphins* and *porpoises*; see *right whale, whalebone whale. Fig.* something extraordinarily big, great, or fine of its kind, followed by *of*; as, a *whale* of a finish; (*cap.*), *astron.* the constellation Cetus.—*v.i.* —*whaled, whaling.* To carry on the work of taking whales.

whale, hwāl, wāl, *v.t.*—*whaled, whaling.* [Cf. *wale, v.*] To whip, thrash, or beat soundly.—*v.i.* To strike vigorous blows, often with *away*; as, to *whale away* at a person.

whale·back, hwāl′bak″, wāl′bak″, *n.* That which has a shape similar to a whale's back; *naut.* a vessel having a rounded deck which meets the sides in a continuous curve, sometimes with upper works, formerly much used on the Great Lakes in N. America.

whale·boat, hwāl′bōt″, wāl′bōt″, *n.* A long, narrow boat, sharp at both ends, formerly much used in whaling, and presently carried by sea vessels for a lifeboat.

whale·bone, hwāl′bōn″, wāl′bōn″, *n.* An elastic horny substance growing in place of teeth in the upper jaw of certain whales, and forming a series of thin, parallel plates on each side of the palate; baleen; a thin strip of this material, used for stiffening corsets or other garments.

whale·bone whale, *n.* Any of the large whales constituting the suborder *Mysticeti,* having no dorsal fin, and in which in the adult have whalebone in place of teeth in the upper jaw.

whal·er, hwā′lèr, wā′lèr, *n.* A person or ship employed in the whale fishery.

whal·ing, hwā′ling, wā′ling, *n.* The work or industry of taking whales and processing them; whale fishing.

wham, hwam, wam, *n.* The sound, usu. loud, produced by any hard impact; a hard blow or impact.—*v.t.*—*whammed, whamming.* To beat or hit, as some object, with hard impact, usu. causing a loud noise.— *v.i.* To explode or strike with hard impact, usu. accompanied by loud sound.

wham·my, hwam′ē, wam′ē, *n.* pl. **wham·· mies.** *Slang.* A hex; the evil eye, as: He put the *whammy* on me.

whang, hwang, wang, *n.* [Imit.] *Colloq.* A resounding blow, bang, or such a noise or sound; whack.—*v.t. Colloq.* to strike with a resounding blow or bang.—*v.i. Colloq.* to resound with or make such a bang or blow.

whang, hwang, wang, *n. Dial.* a thong, esp.

made of leather, as buckskin. *Brit. dial.* a large slice or piece, as of cheese or bread; a chunk.—*v.t. Dial.* to thrash, as with any thong; to beat or lash violently. *Brit. dial.* to slice or chop, esp. in chunks or large pieces.—*v.i. Dial.* to beat with violence or great force.

whang·ee, hwang·ē′, wang·ē′, *n. Bot.* any of several Chinese bamboos of the genus *Phyllostachys.* A cane or walking stick made from the stalk of such a plant.

whap, hwop, wop, *v.t., v.i.*—*whapped, whapping.* Whop.—*n.*

whap·per, hwop′ér, wop′ér, *n.* Whopper.

whap·ping, hwop′ing, wop′ing, *a.* Whopping.

wharf, hwarf, warf, *n.* pl. **wharves, wharfs,** hwarvz, warvz. [O.E. *hwearf, hwerf,* bank, embankment, prob. orig. as turning back water, < *hweorfan,* turn.] A structure, as of stone or timber, built on the shore of, or projecting out into, a harbor, stream, or the like, so that vessels may be moored alongside to load or unload or to lie at rest; a quay; a pier; *obs.* a bank, as of some river, or shore.—*v.t.* To provide with a wharf or wharves; to place or store on a wharf; to bring, as a ship, to a wharf.—*v.i.* To dock.

wharf·age, hwar′fij, war′fij, *n.* The use of a wharf; storage of goods at a wharf; the charge or payment for the use of a wharf; wharves collectively.

wharf·in·ger, hwar′fin·jèr, war′fin·jèr, *n.,* [For *wharfager,* < *wharfage.*] One who owns, or has charge of, a wharf.

wharf rat, *n.* The common brown rat, *Rattus norvegicus,* when living in or about a wharf; *colloq.* a man or boy who loafs about wharves and may sometimes steal from shipments.

wharve, hwarv, warv, *n.* [O.E. *hweorfa,* < *hweorfan* = Icel. *hverfa* = O.H.G. *hwerban* = Goth. *hwairban,* turn, go about: cf. *wharf, whorl,* and *whirl.*] *Spinning,* a wheel or round piece of wood on a spindle, serving as a flywheel or as a pulley.

what, hwut, hwot, wut, wot, *unstressed* hwut, wot, *pron.* pl. **what.** [O.E. *hwaet,* neut. of *hwa,* E. *who.*] Used in asking for the specifying of something, as: *What* did he do? Used to inquire as to the nature, character, class, origin, or the like, of a thing or person, as: *What* is he by birth? Used to inquire as to the worth, usefulness, force, or importance of something, as: *What* is wealth without health? Used in asking, often elliptically, for repetition or explanation of some word or words, as: Five *what*? That which, as many or as much as, as: Send *what* was promised. The kind of thing or person that, or such as; as, just *what* it professes to be; anything that, or whatever, as: Come *what* may. How much, as: *What* do you want for your car? Used in parenthetic clauses meaning something that, as: He went, and *what* is more surprising, gained a hearing. *Brit.* used with a general or vague interrogative force, esp. at the end of a sentence, as: He's a good fellow, *what*? Used with intensive force in exclamatory or interrogative phrases, as: *What,* two more? An incorrect usage as a simple relative meaning 'that,' 'which,' or 'who'; as, a bird *what* sings.—*a.* Asking for specification between persons or things, as: *What* book does he mean? Whatever, as: Take *what* time you need. How much, as: *What* money can you borrow? Used with intensive force in exclamatory phrases, as: *What* luck!—*adv.* To what extent or degree, or how much, as: *What* does it matter? For what reason or purpose, or why, usu. followed by *for*; in what or some manner or measure, or partly, usu. followed by *with,* as: *What with* accidents, his return was delayed.—*conj.* That, as used incorrectly in the phrase *but what,* as: I don't

know *but what* I will. *Colloq.* to the extent that, as, as much as, or so far as, as: He helps me *what* he can.—*interj.* Used to express surprise, disbelief, indignation, and the like, as: *What!* You shot him?—**and what not,** any other similar things which do not have to be enumerated; and the like.—**what for,** *slang.* Bodily punishment or chastisement; a severe scolding; any painful lesson or experience; as, to give one *what for.*— **what have you,** *colloq.* Any other similar things; and the like; as, an assortment of candies, nuts, and *what have you.*—**what if,** what would the final result or outcome be if; supposing.—**what it takes,** *colloq.* that which is needed or a prerequisite for success or for the achievement of one's goal.— **what's what,** the true or actual nature of things or situation.

what·ev·er, hwut·ev′ér, hwot·ev′ér, wut·· ev′ér, wot·ev′ér, hwat·ev′ér, wat·ev′ér, *pron.* Anything that, usu. found in relative clauses, as: Do *whatever* you like. What not; as, pins, needles, and *whatever*; any amount or measure, as of something, or that, used relatively, as: Keep *whatever* pleases you. No matter what, as: Do it, *whatever* happens. What ever, or what, used interrogatively, as: *Whatever* do you mean? —*a.* Any that, as: Ask *whatever* person you like. No matter what; being what or who it may be, as: He is unwilling, for no reason *whatever.*

what·not, hwut′not″, hwot′not″, wut′not″, wot′not″, *n.* A stand with shelves, as for bric-à-brac or books; a trivial or unspecified article or object.

what·so·ev·er, hwut″sō·ev′ér, hwot″sō·· ev′ér, wut″sō·ev′ér, wot″sō·ev′ér, *pron., a.* Whatever, used emphatically; as, anything, *whatsoever* it be, in any place *whatsoever.*

whaup, hwäp, hwap, wäp, wap, *n.* [Imit. of its cry.] *Brit. dial.* a curlew.

wheal, hwēl, wēl, *n.* [In part, M.E. *whele,* pustule (cf. O.E. *hwelian,* suppurate); in part, var. of *weal, wale.*] A small, burning or itching swelling on the skin, as from a mosquito bite or from urticaria; a ridge raised on the skin by a stroke, as of a rod or whip; a wale. Also *weal.* See *welt.*

wheat, hwēt, wēt, *n.* [O.E. *hwǣte* = Icel. *hveiti* = O.H.G. *weizzi* (G. *weizen*) = Goth. *hwaiteis,* wheat; akin to E. *white.*] The grain of a widely distributed cereal grass of the genus *Triticum,* esp. *T. œstivum,* used extensively in the form of flour for making bread and other foods; the plant, which bears the grain in dense spikes.

wheat cake, *n.* A type of pancake having wheat flour as the basic ingredient.

wheat·ear, hwēt′ēr″, wēt′ēr″, *n.* [O.E. *hwit,* white, *aers,* posteriors.] *Ornith.* any of a group of small birds of the northern hemisphere, related to the thrushes, esp. *Oenanthe oenanthe,* having a brownish-gray upper body with white on the underside and a black and white tail pattern.

wheat·en, hwēt′en, wēt′en, *a.* Made of, or relating to, wheat.

wheat germ, *n.* The embryo or germ of a grain of wheat, used particularly as a vitamin source.

wheat rust, *n. Plant pathol.* any of various fungus diseases affecting wheat.

Wheat·stone's bridge, hwēt′stōnz″ brij″, wēt′stōnz″, *Brit.* hwēt′stonz″, wēt′stonz″, *n.* [After Sir Charles *Wheatstone,* inventor.] *Elec.* a bridge or similar instrument for measuring the resistance, as of an electrical conductor. Also **Wheat·stone bridge.**

wheat·worm, hwēt′wùrm″, wēt′wùrm″, *n.* A small nematode worm, *Anguina tritici,* often causing extensive damage to growing wheat.

whee, hwē, wē, *interj.* An expression showing exuberance or delight.

---

ch- chain, G. na*ch*t; **th-** Then, thin; **w-** wig, hw as sound in whig; **z-** zh as in azure, zeal. *Italicized vowel* indicates schwa sound.

whee·dle, hwēd′l, wēd′l, v.t.—wheedled, wheedling. [Origin uncertain: cf. O.E. wǣdlian, be poor, beg.] To endeavor to influence or to influence by smooth, flattering, or beguiling words; to coax; to cajole; to get from a person by artful persuasion.—v.i. To use beguiling or artful persuasion.—whee·dler, n.—whee·dling·ly, adv.

wheel, hwēl, wēl, n. [O.E. hwēol, hweogul, = D. wiel = Icel. hjōl, wheel; akin to Gr. cyklos, ring, circle, wheel, and Skt. cakra, wheel: cf. cycle.] A circular frame or solid disk arranged to turn on an axis, as in vehicles or machinery; any instrument, machine, or apparatus shaped like this or having such a frame or disk as an essential feature; as, a potter's wheel; a circular frame with projecting handles and an axle connecting with the rudder for steering a ship; an old instrument of torture in the form of a circular frame on which the victim was stretched while his limbs were broken with an iron bar; a rotating instrument which the goddess Fortune is represented as turning in order to bring about changes or reverses in human affairs; a circular firework which revolves while burning; anything resembling or suggesting a wheel in shape or movement; colloq. a bicycle. A circular or revolving movement; formerly, a movement of troops or ships, drawn up in line, as if turning on a pivot; pl. moving, propelling, or animating agencies; slang, a person who is important or influential, esp. in politics or business. —v.t. To cause to turn, rotate, or revolve, as on an axis; to perform, as a course or flight, in a circular or curving direction; to move or roll, as a vehicle or piece of furniture, on wheels or casters; to provide with a wheel or wheels.—v.i. To turn on or as on an axis or about a center; to rotate; to revolve; to execute a rotating movement through part or all of a circle, as a line of troops pivoting on one end; to turn or change in direction or in procedure or opinion, used with about or around; to move in a circular or curving course; to roll along on wheels; to travel along smoothly.—at the wheel, steering or driving, as a boat or car.—wheel and deal, colloq. to act or transact independently and without restraints, esp. in business.—wheels with·in wheels, complex interconnections, as of motives or operations, reacting together toward an ultimate end.

wheel and ax·le, n. A simple machine consisting typically of a cylindrical axle on which a wheel, concentric with the axle, is firmly fastened, as to lift a weight attached to a rope by causing the rope to wind up on the axle as the wheel is turned.

wheel an·i·mal·cule, n. A rotifer.

wheel·bar·row, hwēl′bar″ō, wēl′bar″ō, n. A frame or box for conveying a load, supported at one end on a wheel on which to run, and having at the other end two legs on which to rest and two shafts by which a person may lift the legs from the ground and push or pull it along; some similar vehicle with more than one wheel.—v.t. To convey, transport, or move by means of a wheelbarrow.

wheel·base, hwēl′bās″, wēl′bās″, n. The distance, usu. in inches, from the front axle's center to the rear axle's center, in a motor vehicle.

wheel bug, n. An insect of southern U.S., Arilus cristatus, which feeds upon the blood of other insects, named for a notched crest on its prothorax.

wheel·chair, hwēl′châr″, wēl′châr″, n. A chair mounted on wheels and used by invalids.

wheeled, hwēld, wēld, a. Having or furnished with a wheel or wheels, often used in compounds; as, three-wheeled; moving or mounted on wheels; as, a wheeled conveyance.

wheel·er, hwē′lẽr, wē′lẽr, n. One who or that which wheels; a maker of wheels; something provided with a wheel or wheels, used in compounds; as, a side-wheeler, a stern-wheeler; a wheel horse.

wheel horse, n. A horse, or one of the horses, harnessed behind others and next to the fore wheels of a vehicle; also wheeler. A plodding worker; one who labors steadily and obediently under the direction of a leader.

wheel·house, hwēl′hous″, wēl′hous″, n. pl. **wheel·hous·es**. The pilothouse of a vessel, which shelters the steering wheel.

wheel·ing, hwē′ling, wē′ling, n. The act of one who or that which wheels, or travels on wheels, esp. the practice of riding on a bicycle or tricycle; a circular, turning, or rotating movement; the condition or state of a highway or road in regard to traveling by means of wheeled vehicles.

wheel lock, n. An old type of gunlock in which sparks are produced by the friction of a small steel wheel against a piece of iron pyrites or the like.

wheel·man, hwēl′man, wēl′man, n. pl. **wheel·men**. The man at the steering wheel of a vessel; a steersman; also **wheels·man**. A rider of a bicycle, tricycle, or the like.

wheel·work, hwēl′wụrk″, wēl′wụrk″, n. The combination of wheels and gears in machinery.

wheel·wright, hwēl′rīt″, wēl′rīt″, n. A man whose occupation is to repair or make wheels.

wheen, hwēn, wēn, n. [Cf. O.E. hwēne, somewhat.] Brit. dial. A few; a number or quantity.

wheeze, hwēz, wēz, v.i.—wheezed, wheezing. [O.E. hwēsan.] To breathe with difficulty and with a whistling sound; to make a similar sound.—v.t. To utter with a sound of wheezing.—n. A wheezing breath or sound; slang, a humorous saying or anecdote, or a theatrical gag, usu. a trite one.

wheez·y, hwē′zē, wē′zē, a.—wheezier, wheeziest. Affected with or characterized by wheezing.—wheez·i·ly, adv.—wheez·i·ness, n.

whelk, hwelk, welk, n. [O.E. weoloc, wioloc.] Any of various large marine gastropods of the family Buccinidae, having a spiral shell, as Buccinum undatum, which is used for food in Europe.

whelk, hwelk, welk, n. [Dim. < wheal, a pustule.] A pustule or pimple.

whelm, hwelm, welm, v.t. [M.E. whelmen, akin to whelven, roll, O.E. hwylfan, turn over, O.E. hwealf, Icel. hvalf, a vault, G. wölben, to vault, arch.] To cover or bury beneath a mass of something, as of water or snow; to submerge; to engulf; to overcome utterly or overwhelm.

whelp, hwelp, welp, n. [O.E. hwelp = D. welp = Icel. hvelpr = Dan. hvalp, whelp.] The young of the dog, wolf, bear, lion, tiger, or seal; a puppy; a youth: used contemptuously. Mech. any of a series of longitudinal projections or ridges of iron or the like on the barrel of a capstan or windlass; one of the teeth of a sprocket wheel.— v.i., v.t. To bring forth, as young, as a dog or lioness.

when, hwen, wen, adv. [O.E. hwaenne, hwonne, = O.H.G. wanne (G. wann) = Goth. hvan, when; from the pronominal stem represented by E. who.] At what time: used interrogatively, as: When are you coming? When, did you say? On or at what occasion: used interrogatively.—conj. At what time; as, to know when to be silent; at the time that; as, to rise when one's name is called, when we were young; at any time that, if, or whenever, as: He is impatient when he is kept waiting. Upon or after which, as: They had just left when company arrived. While on the contrary, although, or whereas.—pron. What time, as: Since when have you known this? Which time, as: They left on Monday, since when we have heard nothing.—n. The time of anything; as, the when and the where of an act.

when·as, hwen·az′, wen·az′, conj. Archaic. When; while; whereas.

whence, hwens, wens, adv. [M.E. whennes (with adverbial suffix -s), < whenne, < O.E. hwanan, whence, akin to hwaenne, E. when.] From what place; from what source or origin; from what cause.—conj. From what place, source, or cause, as: He told me whence he came. From which place, source, or cause, or whensefrom.

whence·so·ev·er, hwens″sō·ev′ẽr, wens″-sō·ev′ẽr, conj., adv. From whatsoever place, source, or cause.

when·ev·er, hwen·ev′ẽr, wen·ev′ẽr, conj. At whatever time; at any time when, as: Come whenever you like.—adv. Colloq. when: used emphatically, as: Whenever did he tell you that?

when·so·ev·er, hwen″sō·ev′ẽr, wen″sō·-ev′ẽr, adv., conj. At whatsoever time; whenever.

where, hwâr, wâr, adv. [O.E. hwǣr, hwār, = O.H.G. hwār (G. wo) = Icel. hvar = Goth. hwar, where; from the pronominal stem represented by E. who.] In or at what place, as: Where is he? In what part, or at what point, as: Where is the pain? In what position or circumstances, as: Where do you stand on this question? In what particular, respect, or way, as: Where does this affect us? To what place, point, or end, as: Where are you going? From what source or whence, as: Where did you get such a notion?—conj. In or at what place, part, or point, as: Find where he is. In or at the place, part, point, at which, as: The book is where you left it. In a position or case in which; in any place, position, or case, in which, or wherever, as: Use the lotion where pain is felt. To what or whatever place, or to the or any place to which, as: Go where you will. In or at which place or there, as: They came to the town where they lodged for the night.—n. The place of something; as, the where of this occurrence.

where·a·bouts, hwâr′a·bouts″, wâr′a·-bouts″, adv. About where; where.—conj. Near or in what place.—n. pl., sing. or pl. in constr. The place where a person or thing is; the locality of a person or thing.

where·as, hwâr·az′, wâr·az′, conj. The fact or case really being that; when in fact; considering that things are such that.—n. pl. **where·as·es**. A prefatory or qualifying clause or statement in a legal or other formal document or disputation starting with 'whereas.'

where·at, hwâr·at′, wâr·at′, adv. Archaic. At which; as, whereat one eats; at what, as: Whereat was she annoyed?—conj. Archaic. At which; whereupon.

where·by, hwâr·bī′, wâr·bī′, adv., conj. By or by way of which; as, the door whereby she left; by what.

where·fore, hwâr′fōr, hwâr′fạr, wâr′fōr, wâr′fạr, adv., conj. Archaic. For what; why.—conj. Archaic. for what or which cause or reason.—n. The cause, reason, or purpose.

where·from, hwâr·frum′, hwâr·from′, wâr·frum′, wâr·from′, conj., adv. From which; whence.

where·in, hwâr·in′, wâr·in′, adv. In what; how, as: Wherein did he fail?—conj. In what or which; as, the place wherein he works.

where·in·to, hwâr·in′tö, wâr·in′tö, hwâr″-in·tö′, wâr″in·tö′, conj. Into what or which.

where·of, hwâr·uv′, hwâr·ov′, wâr·uv′, wâr·ov′, adv., conj. Archaic, of what, which, or whom.

where·on, hwâr·on′, hwâr·ạn′, wâr·on′, wâr·ạn′, adv. Archaic. On what; where-upon.—conj. Archaic, on what or which.

where·so·ev·er, hwâr″sō·ev′ẽr, wâr″sō·-ev′ẽr, adv., conj. Archaic. In or to whatsoever place; wherever.

where·through, hwâr·thrō′, wâr·thrō′, conj. Archaic, through which.

where·to, hwâr·tō′, wâr·tō′, adv. To what; whither. Also archaic **where·un·to.**—conj. To what or which. Also archaic **where·-un·to.**

where·up·on, hwâr″a·pon′, hwâr″a·pạn′, wâr″a·pon′, wâr″a·pạn′, adv. Archaic. Upon what; whereon.—conj. Upon what or which; at or after which.

wher·ev·er, hwâr·ev′ẽr, wâr·ev′ẽr, adv. Where, as: Wherever did you find that?—conj. In, at, or to whatever place.

where·with, hwâr·with′, hwâr·wiTH′, wâr·-with′, wâr·wiTH′, adv. With what.—conj. With what or which; by which.—pron. Archaic, the thing by which, used with an infinitive, as: She has not wherewith to accomplish it.—n. Archaic, wherewithal.

where·with·al, hwâr′wiTH·al″, wâr′wiTH·-al″, n. Resources, esp. financial, needed to accomplish some purpose, preceded by the; as, to have the wherewithal to go around the world.—adv., pron. Archaic, wherewith.

wher·ry, hwer′ē, wer′ē, n. pl. **wher·ries.** [Origin unknown.] A kind of light rowboat used chiefly in England for carrying passengers and goods on rivers; any of certain larger boats, as barges, used locally in Great Britain; a kind of light rowboat for one person, as used for racing.—v.i. wherried, wherrying. To carry in, or make use of a wherry.—v.t.

whet, hwet, wet, v.t.—whetted, whetting. [O.E. hwettan = D. wetten = G. wetzen, sharpen, whet; akin to O.E. hwaet, keen, bold.] To sharpen, as a knife or tool, by grinding or friction. Fig. to make keen or eager; as, to whet the appetite; to stimulate. —n. The act of whetting; something that whets; an appetizer; an alcoholic appetizer. Dial. a short time; a while; a period of work.—**whet·ter**, n.

wheth·er, hweTH′ẽr, weTH′ẽr, conj. [O.E. hwaether = O.H.G. hwedar = Icel. hvárr = Goth. hwathar, whether; from the pronominal stem represented by E. who.] A term introducing the first of two or more alternatives, and sometimes repeated before the second or later alternative, usu. used in correlation with or, as: It matters whether we go or stay. Used to introduce a single alternative, the other being implied or understood, or a clause or element not involving alternatives, as: See whether·he has come.—pron. Archaic. Which one of the two; whichever.—**wheth·er or no**, whether or not; under whatever circumstances; in any case, as: He threatens to go, whether or no.

whet·stone, hwet′stōn″, wet′stōn″, n. A stone for sharpening cutlery or tools by friction.

whew, hwū, interj. A whistling exclamation or sound expressing astonishment, dismay, or relief upon the avoidance of some pitfall or the accomplishment of a difficult task.—n. An utterance of 'whew.'

whey, hwā, wā, n. [O.E. hwaeg = D. wei, hui, L.G. wey, whey.] The watery part of milk separated from the more coagulable part, particularly in the process of making cheese.—**whey·ey**, hwā′ē, wā′ē, a.

whey·face, hwā′fās″, wā′fās″, n. A face white or pale, as from fear; a person with this type of face.—**whey·faced**, a.

which, hwich, wich, pron. [O.E. hwilc, hwylc, hwelc, = O.H.G. hwelīh (G. welcher) = Goth. hwileiks, lit. 'of what form or sort'; from the pronominal stem represented by E. who, with termination related

to E. -ly and like: cf. such.] What one, as of a certain number mentioned or implied, as: Which do you want? That or which, referring to things or animals, formerly to persons: used relatively with an antecedent expressed, in clauses conveying an additional idea, as: I read the book, which was short. Used in clauses defining or restricting the antecedent, regularly after that, as: That which must be, will be. Used after a preposition, as; the horse on which I rode; the one or thing that; as, the book which I gave you; the fact or occurrence that, as: She cooked the dinner and which was unusual for her, cleaned the house.—a. What one, as: Which house is yours? Whichever, as: Take which book you want.

which·ev·er, hwich·ev′ẽr, wich·ev′ẽr, a. No matter which.—pron. Anyone. Also **which·so·ev·er**, hwich″sō·ev′ẽr, wich″sō·-ev′ẽr.

whid·ah, hwid′a, wid′a, n. Whydah.

whiff, hwif, wif, n. [Imit. of the sound of blowing; cf. puff, W. chwif, a whiff, a puff, chwaf, a quick gust.] A sudden expulsion of air, smoke, or the like from the mouth; a puff; a gust of air conveying some smell; an inhaling or exhaling.—v.t. To puff; to throw out in whiffs; to smoke.—v.i. To emit puffs or inhale puffs, as of smoke; to move or blow in puffs or whiffs.

whif·fet, hwif′it, wif′it, n. [Dim. of whiff, n.: cf. whippet.] Colloq. an insignificant person; a whippersnapper. A small dog; a little whiff.

whif·fle, hwif′l, wif′l, v.i.—whiffled, whiffling. [Prob. < whiff; but cf. D. weifelen to waver; Icel. veifla, to shake often.] To veer about or blow in gusts, as the wind; to change from one opinion or course to another.—v.t. To blow with puffs or gusts.

whif·fler, hwif′lẽr, wif′lẽr, n. One who shifts about in thought, opinion, or intention; a shifty or evasive person.

whif·fler, hwif′lẽr, wif′lẽr, n. [M.E. wifle, spear, battle-ax < O.E. wifel, javelin, spear.] Hist. an attendant armed with a spear, battle-ax, or staff, employed to clear the way, as for a procession.

whif·fle·tree, hwif′l·trē″, wif′l·trē″, n. Swingletree.

Whig, hwig, wig, n. [Appar. < whiggamores, a name applied to a body of Covenanters who marched from the southwest of Scotland to Edinburgh in 1648, said to be < whiggam, a word used in southwestern Scotland in driving horses.] U.S. hist. a native supporter of the American Revolution, as opposed to Tory; a member of a political party formed in 1834 in opposition to the Democratic Party, succeeded in 1855 by the Republican Party. Eng. hist. a member of a relatively liberal political party in the 1700's and 1800's, more recently known as the Liberal Party, as opposed to Tory, now Conservative.—a.—**Whig·gish**, hwig′ish, wig′ish, a.—**Whig·gish·ly**, adv.—**Whig·gish·ness**, n.

Whig·ger·y, hwig′e·rē, wig′e·rē, n. pl. **Whig·ger·ies.** Whig principles or policies. Also **Whig·gism**, hwig′iz·um, wig′iz·um.

whig·ma·lee·rie, **whig·ma·lee·ry**, hwig″ma·lēr′ē, wig″ma·lēr′ē, n. A whim or fancy; an ornament of whimsical or fanciful nature; a gimcrack.

while, hwīl, wīl, n. [O.E. hwīl = D. wijl = G. weile = Goth. hweila, a while, time, = Icel. hvīla, place of rest, bed, = Sw. hvila, Dan. hvile, rest; perh. akin to L. quies, rest.] A space of time; as, all the while, a long while, a while ago; one's time, as well-spent on something; as, worth one's while; a particular time or occasion.—conj. During or in the time that; as long as; at the same time, as implying opposition or contrast, as: While he appreciated the honor conferred, he could not accept the position.—v.t.—

whiled, whiling. To cause time to pass, esp. in some easy or pleasant manner, usu. used with away.—prep.

whiles, hwīlz, wīlz, conj. Archaic, while.—adv. Dial. sometimes.

whilst, hwilst, wilst, conj. Chiefly Brit. while.

whim, hwim, wim, n. [Prob. akin to Icel. hvima, to wander with the eyes; Sw. hvimsa, to be unsteady; Dan. vimse, to skip about. Cf. also W. chwim, motion.] A sudden turn of the mind; a freakish or capricious notion; mining, a kind of large, vertical windlass worked by horse power or steam, formerly used for raising ore or water from the bottom of a mine.

whim·brel, hwim′brel, wim′brel, n. [Perh. from its cry resembling a whimpering.] A European bird, Numenius phaeopus phaeopus, having a long downwardly curving bill, related to the curlews but smaller and with a striped crown.

whim·per, hwim′pẽr, wim′pẽr, v.i. [Akin to G. wimmern, to whimper, and to whine, both being imit. words.] To cry with a low, whining, broken voice, as a dog.—v.t. To utter in a low, whining, or crying tone.—n. A low, peevish, broken cry.—**whim·per·er**, n.—**whim·per·ing**, n.

whim·si·cal, hwim′zi·kal, wim′zi·kal, a. [< whimsey.] Full of whims; freakish; capricious; odd; fantastic; changing rapidly and without warning.—**whim·si·cal·i·ty**, **whim·si·cal·ness**, hwim″zi·kal′i·tē, wim″-zi·kal′i·tē, n.—**whim·si·cal·ly**, adv.

whim·sy, **whim·sey**, hwim′zē, wim′zē, n. pl. **whim·sies.** [Related to whim.] An odd or fanciful notion; anything odd or fanciful; a product of a quirk or playful fancy, as a humorous literary work.

whim-wham, hwim′hwam″, wim′wam″, n. [Appar. a varied redupl. of whim. although recorded earlier.] Any odd or fanciful object or thing; a gimcrack. Pl., colloq. jitters; uneasiness.

whin, hwin, win, n. [M.E. whynne, quyn; origin uncertain.] Chiefly Brit. furze.—**whin·ny**, a.

whin, hwin, win, n. [Origin uncertain.] Whinstone.

whin·chat, hwin′chat″, win′chat″, n. A small old-world bird, Saxicola rubetra, having a brown back and buff breast.

whine, hwīn, wīn, v.i.—whined, whining. [O.E. hwīnan, to whiz; Icel. hvína, Dan. hvine, to whiz; imit. words like whiz, whir, etc.] To express distress or complaint by a plaintive drawling cry; to complain in an infantile, petty, or ill-humored way.—v.t. To express with a whine.—n. A drawling plaintive tone or cry; a petty, ill-humored complaint.—**whin·er**, n.—**whin·ing·ly**, adv.

whin·ny, hwin′ē, win′ē, v.i.—whinnied, whinnying. [Imit. and akin to whine; cf. L. hinnio, to whinny.] To neigh.—v.t. To utter with a neigh.—n. pl. **whin·nies.** The neigh or cry of a horse; a horse-like sound.

whin·stone, hwin′stōn″, win′stōn″, n. Basaltic rock; any of various other hard, dark-colored rocks. Also whin.

whip, hwip, wip, v.t.—whipped or whipt, whipping. [Allied to D. wippen, to skip or toss; wip, a swing, a swipe; O.D. wippe, a whip; L.G. wippen, Dan vippe, to see-saw; G. wippen to rock, to see-saw, etc.; cf. also W. chwip, a quick turn; chwipiaw, to move briskly.] To strike quickly with a lash or with anything thin and flexible; to lash or flog, esp. as punishment; to tongue-lash or treat with cutting severity; to drive on, as with lashes of a whip, followed by up, on; to hit or strike in a whiplike fashion, as: The wind whipped the young saplings. Colloq. to defeat, as in a competition. To take, seize, or move with a sudden, rapid motion, followed by away, in, out, off; to beat into a froth or thick foam, as eggs or cream; to overlay or wrap, as the end of a rope, with a cord, twine, or thread; to wrap, as thread, about something, as to reinforce or prevent excessive wear. To sew loosely or overcast, as in hemming or seaming; also *whipstitch. Naut.* to raise, as a sail, by using a rope and an overhead pulley or whip. To fish(water)by casting with a rod and line.—*v.t.* To turn or start suddenly and rapidly, followed by *away, around, off, out*; to thrash about violently; as, girl's hair *whipping* in the wind; to cast repeatedly with rod and line, as in fishing.—*n.* An instrument for driving animals, as horses, or for correction or punishment, usu. consisting of a rod to which is attached a thong of leather or the like; a person who is expert in using a whip; anything having the flexibility or form of a whip, as the arm of a windmill or a fishing rod; *mach.* a type of hoisting device, esp. one used to lift objects which are not too heavy. A dessert of whipped egg whites or cream combined with fruit. *Naut.* an overhead pulley or hoist for raising light objects. *Fox hunting,* a huntsman's assistant who keeps hounds from wandering; also *whipper-in. Polit.* a member of a parliament or other legislative body who disciplines and secures the attendance of as many members of his party as possible at important proceedings; also **par·ty whip;** a call made by a whip upon members to be in their places at the time of a vote.—**whip in,** to keep from scattering, as hounds in a hunt; to bring the members of a political party together.—**whip up,** to stir or arouse, as the emotions of a crowd; *colloq.* to put together quickly, or prepare, as a meal.—**whip·like,** *a.*—**whip·per,** *n.*—**whip·py,** *a.*

whip·cord, hwip'k̇ard″, wip'k̇ard″, *n.* A hard-twisted cord of which lashes for whips are made; a hard-woven, diagonally ribbed fabric, often used for making riding habits or sportswear; a cord made of catgut.

whip hand, *n.* The hand that holds the whip in riding or driving; advantage; mastery of a situation.

whip·lash, hwip'lash″, wip'lash″, *n.* The lash or striking end of a whip.

whip·lash, hwip'lash″, wip'lash″, *n.* An injury to the neck, caused by the head being suddenly jerked forward or back.

whip·per-in, hwip'ėr·in′, wip'ėr·in′, *n.* pl. **whip·pers-in.** A political party whip. *Fox hunting,* a hunt staff member who helps the huntsman by whipping in wandering hounds; see *whip.*

whip·per·snap·per, hwip'ėr·snap″ėr, wip'ėr·snap″ėr, *n.* An impertinent, insignificant person, esp. a young person.

whip·pet, whip'it, wip'it, *n.* A breed of dog resembling the greyhound but smaller and used chiefly for coursing and racing. A quick-moving, light tank used during World War I; also **whip·pet tank.**

whip·ping, hwip'ing, wip'ing, *n.* Punishment with a whip; flagellation. A cord, string, or other material used for binding or tying things together.

whip·ping boy, *n.* Anyone who takes undeserved punishment; a scapegoat; orig. a boy educated with a prince and punished in his stead.

whip·ping post, *n.* A post to which offenders are tied when whipped.

whip·ple·tree, hwip'l·trē″, wip'l·trē″, *n.* Swingletree.

whip·poor·will, hwip'ėr·wil″, wip'ėr·wil″, hwip″ėr·wil′, wip″ėr·wil′, *n.* A N. American bird, *Caprimulgus vociferus,* of the goatsucker family, having a brown patterned body, a black throat, tiny feet, a wide bill, and, in the male, white tail feathers: named for its cry.

whip·ray, hwip'rā″, wip'rā″, *n.* Stingray.

whip·saw, hwip'sᶐ″, wip'sᶐ″, *n.* A hand saw used for cutting small curves, consisting of a narrow blade stretched in a frame; a large,

two-man log cutting saw, as a pitsaw.—*v.t.* —past *whipsawed,* pp. *whipsawn,* ppr. *whipsawing.* To cut with a whipsaw. To win two bets, as from a person, at one turn or play, as in faro or other games of chance; to easily defeat in two ways at once.

whip scor·pi·on, *n.* Any of various arachnids belonging to the order *Pedipalpida,* which resemble the scorpion and has an abdomen ending in a stingless, slender, whiplike part.

whip·stall, hwip'stᶐl″, wip'stᶐl″, *n. Aeron.* a stall in which a vertically climbing airplane momentarily slips backward, then whips forward suddenly and drops with its nose downward, usu. executed intentionally.—*v.i., v.t.*

whip·stitch, hwip'stich″, wip'stich″, *v.t.* To sew with stitches passing successively over the edge of a fabric.—*n.* A stitch made in such a manner; *colloq.* an instant, or brief space of time.

whip·stock, hwip'stok″, wip'stok″, *n.* The handle of a whip.

whip·worm, hwip'wᶙrm″, wip'wᶙrm″, *n.* Any of certain parasitic nematode worms, of the genus *Trichuris,* having a long body tapered to a whiplike front end.

whir, whirr, hwᶙr, wᶙr, *v.t., v.i.—whirred, whirring.* [From the sound, partly influenced in meaning by *whirl;* cf. *whiz.*] To whiz; to fly, dart, revolve, or otherwise move quickly with a whizzing or buzzing sound.—*n.* The buzzing sound made by a quickly revolving wheel, or the like.

whirl, hwᶙrl, wᶙrl, *v.i.* [M.E. *whirlen,* appar. < Scand.: cf. Icel. and Sw. *hvirfla,* Dan. *hvirvle,* whirl, akin to G. *wirbeln,* whirl, and O.E. *hweorfan,* turn.] To turn round, spin, or rotate rapidly; to turn about or aside quickly; to move, travel, or be carried rapidly along on wheels or similar means; to have the sensation of turning round rapidly.—*v.t.* To cause to turn round, spin, or rotate rapidly; as, to *whirl* a wheel or a top; to send, drive, or carry in a circular or curving course; to send or carry along with great or dizzying rapidity.—*n.* The act of whirling; rapid rotation or gyration; a whirling movement; a quick turn or swing; a short drive, run, or walk; a spin; something that whirls; a whirling current or mass; *colloq.* a tentative or experimental try. *Fig.* a rapid round of events or affairs; as, a *whirl* of social festivities; a state marked by a dizzying succession or mingling of feelings, thoughts, or ideas.—**whirl·er,** *n.*

whirl·i·gig, hwᶙr'li·gig, wᶙr'li·gig, *n.* Something that whirls, revolves, or goes around; a circling motion; a continuous round or succession; a toy for whirling or spinning, as a top; a merry-go-round or carousel.

whirl·i·gig bee·tle, *n.* Any of the aquatic beetles of the family *Gyrinidae,* which are commonly seen circling rapidly about in large numbers on the surface of the water.

whirl·pool, hwᶙrl'pōl″, wᶙrl'pōl″, *n.* A circular eddy or current in a river or sea produced by the configuration of the channel, by meeting currents, by winds meeting tides, or the like; a vortex.

whirl·wind, hwᶙrl'wind″, wᶙrl'wind″, *n.* A mass of air spiraling upward around a more or less vertical axis, and having a progressive motion over the surface of land or water, as a dust devil, tornado, or water spout; *fig.* anything resembling a whirlwind, as in violent activity or effect.—*a. Fig.* any short, aggressive effort; as, a *whirlwind* campaign.

whirl·y, hwᶙr'le, wᶙr'le, *n.* pl. **whirl·ies.** A violent whirlwind snow storm, occurring in Antarctica.—*a.—whirlier, whirliest.* Characterized by a whirlwind movement.

whirl·y·bird, hwᶙr'le·bᶙrd″, wᶙr'le·bᶙrd″, *n. Colloq.* a helicopter.

whir·ry, hwᶙr'ē, wᶙr'ē, *v.t., v.i.—whirried, whirrying. Sc.* to hurry.

whish, hwish, wish, *v.i.* [Imit.] To make, or move with the sound of something rushing rapidly through the air; to whiz; to whistle; to swish.—*n.* A whishing sound.

whisht, hwist, wist, hwisht, wisht, *interj.* Hush: an expression calling for silence.—*n. Sc.* a whisper.—*v.t. Sc.* to silence or hush.—*v.i. Sc.* to be quiet or taciturn.

whisk, hwisk, wisk, *v.t.* [Appar. < Scand.: cf. Icel. *visk,* wisp (of hay, etc.), Sw. *viske,* wisp, brush, whisk, O.H.G. *wisc,* G. *wisch,* brush, duster.] To sweep from(a surface)with a whisk broom or brush; as, to *whisk* crumbs from the table; to whip to a froth with a whisk or beating implement; as, to *whisk* eggs; to move with a rapid, sweeping stroke; to draw, snatch, or carry lightly and rapidly.—*v.i.* To sweep, pass, or go lightly and rapidly.—*n.* A small bunch of grass, straw, hair, or like material, esp. for use in brushing; a whisk broom; an implement composed of a bunch of loops of wire held together in a handle and used for beating or whipping eggs or cream; an act of whisking; a rapid, sweeping stroke; a light, rapid movement.

whisk broom, *n.* A short-handled, small broom used esp. for brushing clothes.

whisk·er, hwis'kėr, wis'kėr, *n. Pl.* the hair growing on the side of a man's face, esp. when worn long and with the chin cleanshaven; the beard generally; orig. the mustache. A single hair of the beard; one of the long, stiff, bristly hairs growing about the mouth of certain animals, as the cat or the rat; a vibrissa; anything having a thin, thread-like form, as a crystal filament. *Naut.* either of two bars of wood or iron projecting laterally one from each side of the bowsprit, to give more spread to the guys which support the jib-boom; also **whisk·er boom.—whisk·ered,** hwis'kėrd, wis'kėrd, *a.—whisk·er·y,* *a.*

whis·key, whis·ky, hwis'kē, wis'kē, *n.* pl. **whis·keys, whis·kies.** [Gael. and Ir. *uisge,* water, in *uisgebeatha,* 'water of life,' E. *usquebaugh.*] A distilled alcoholic liquor made from grain, as barley, malt, rye, or corn, commonly having 40 to 50 percent of alcohol; a single drink of whiskey.—*a.* Made of, related to, or resembling whiskey.

Whis·key, hwis'kē, wis'kē, *n.* A communications code word for the letter 'W.'

whis·key-Jack, hwis'kē·jak″, wis'kē·jak″, *n.* Canada jay.

whis·key sour, *n.* A cocktail consisting of lemon juice, whiskey, and sugar.

whis·per, hwis'pėr, wis'pėr, *v.i.* [O.E. *hwisprian,* akin to O.H.G. *hwispalōn,* G. *wispeln, wispern,* D. *wispelen,* whisper; orig. imit.] To speak with soft, low sounds, using the breath and lips, without vibration of the vocal cords; to talk softly and privately, often with implication of gossip, slander, or plotting; to make a soft, rustling sound, esp. of trees, water, breezes, and the like; *phon.* to speak, using breath rather than phonation.—*v.t.* To utter with soft, low sounds, using the breath and lips; to speak or tell privately; as, to tell a person in a *whisper; phon.* to speak using breath rather than phonation.—*n.* The mode of utterance, or the voice, of one who whispers; as, to speak in a *whisper;* a sound, word, or remark uttered by whispering; as, low *whispers;* something said or repeated privately; a soft, rustling sound, as of leaves moving in the wind.—**whis·per·er,** hwis'pėr·er, wis'pėr·er, *n.*

whis·per·ing, hwis'pėr·ing, wis'pėr·ing, *n.* Whispered utterance or speech; insinuations, rumors, or gossip; a low, sibilant sound.—*a.* Speaking in a whisper; making secret insinuations of evil; making a low, sibilant sound.—**whis·per·ing·ly,** *adv.*

whis·per·ing cam·paign, *n.* A propaganda effort or informational distribution intended, through vilification, to bring discredit upon or raise doubts about a product, cause, or person, and accomplished largely by means of the spoken word.

whis·per·y, hwis′pe·rē, wis′pe·rē, *a.* Similar to a whisper; having many whispering sounds; as, a cool, *whispery* forest glade.

whist, hwist, wist, *n.* [First recorded as *whisk*, explained as referring to the whisking or sweeping of the cards from the table; later associated with *whist*, as if expressing a call for silence during the game.] A card game played by four players, two against two, with a pack of 52 cards, resembling bridge, which it preceded.

whist, hwist, wist, *interj.* [M.E. *whist*, a natural utterance calling for silence: cf. *hush, v.,* and *hist.*] Hush! silence! be still! —*a.* Hushed; silent; still.—*v.i.* To be silent.

whis·tle, hwis′l, wis′l, *v.i.*—*whistled, whistling.* [O.E. *hwistlian,* akin to Sw. *hvissla,* Dan. *hvisle,* whistle, Icel. *hvīsla,* whisper; orig. imit.] To make a clear musical sound, or a series of such sounds, by the forcible expulsion of the breath through a small orifice formed by contracting the lips, or through the teeth with the aid of the tongue; to make such a sound or series of sounds otherwise, as by blowing on a device; to produce a similar sound through a device operated by steam or the like; as, a noisy factory *whistle*; to emit similar sounds from the mouth, as birds do; to move, go, or pass with a whizzing or whistling sound, as a bullet, strong winds, or a missile.—*v.t.* To produce by whistling; as, to *whistle* a happy tune; to call, direct, or signal by or as by whistling; as, to *whistle* a cab to the curb; to send with a whistling or whizzing sound. —*n.* [O.E. *hwistle,* whistle, pipe.] An instrument for producing whistling sounds, as by the force of breath, steam, or the like; a sound produced by or as by whistling; a whistling sound intended as a signal, direction, or summons.—**wet one's whis·tle,** *colloq.* to quench one's thirst.—**whis·tle for,** *colloq.* to be unsuccessful in a claim or demand, as for payment.—**whis·tle·a·ble,** *a.*

whis·tler, hwis′lėr, wis′lėr, *n.* A person or a thing that whistles; one of several birds whose wings whistle when they fly, esp. the European widgeon and the N. American goldeneye; a big marmot, *Marmota caligata,* found in the northwestern N. American mountains; a horse suffering from wheezing; *phys.* a low frequency radio signal produced by a discharge of lightning.

whis·tle stop, *n. Colloq.* A town too small for inclusion in a schedule of train stops, but where a train may stop on signal; one of a series of brief appearances at small towns by a campaigning political candidate, esp. to give a speech from the rear platform of his train.—**whis·tle-stop,** hwis′l·stop″, wis′-l·stop″, *v.i.*—*whistle-stopped, whistle-stopping.* To make a series of whistle stops on a political campaign.

whis·tling, hwis′ling, wis′ling, *n.* The act of one who or that which whistles, or the sound which is produced; *veter. pathol.* a form of roaring,affecting horses, characterized by a peculiarly shrill sound.

whit, hwit, wit, *n.* [By metathesis < O.E. *wiht,* a creature, a wight, a whit.] The smallest part or particle; an iota: used generally with a negative; as, not a *whit* better.

white, hwīt, wīt, *a.*—*whiter, whitest.* [O.E. *hwit* = D. *wit* = G. *weiss* = Icel. *hvītr* = Goth. *hweits,* white: cf. *wheat.*] Of the color of pure snow; reflecting the rays of sunlight or similar light, as: The *white* beaches were dazzling in the sunlight. Light or comparatively light in color; having a light-colored skin, as a Caucasian; noting, pertaining to, or controlled by the Caucasian race, as schools, housing and the like; pallid or pale, as from fear or other strong emotion; as, *white* with suppressed anger; silvery, gray, or hoary, as hair; accompanied by or covered with snow; reactionary or conservative in political views: opposed to *red*; blank, as unoccupied space in printed matter; not burnished, as silverware; wearing white clothing; as, a *white* friar; free from spot or stain; pure or innocent; not intending harm; as, a *white* lie; light-colored or yellowish, as wine: opposed to *red. Slang,* honorable; fair; decent; dependable.—*n.* A luminous achromatic color, devoid of intensity or hue: opposite to *black*; the condition or characteristic of being white; a Caucasian; something white, as a material or substance; a white part of something, as the viscous albumen which surrounds an egg yolk, or the white part of the eyeball; white fabric; white wine; a white species or breed of animal. *Pl.* white articles of clothing, esp. as a uniform; the finest grade of white flour; a blank space in printing. *Pathol.* leukorrhea; *archery,* the outermost ring on the target and a hit or score on this area; *chess,* the white pieces, and the player using them; (*often cap.*) one who is a conservative in politics.—*v.t.*— *whited, whiting.* [O.E. *hwitan.*] *Print.* to create white spaces in, as in copy or around artwork, followed by *out*; *archaic,* to make white.—**whit·ish,** hwī′tish, wī′tish, *a.*— **white·ly,** *adv.*

white ant, *n.* Termite.

white·bait, hwīt′bāt″, wīt′bāt″, *n. pl.* **white·bait.** Any of several very small, silvery fish, the young of various food fishes, esp. of sprats and herrings, considered a delicacy in Europe.

white bass, *n.* A freshwater food fish, *Lepibema chrysops,* silvery-white and yellow, marked with black stripes, found in lakes in the central part of the U.S.

white·beard, hwīt′bērd″, wīt′bērd″, *n.* An old man, esp. a man having a white or grayish beard.

white blood cell, *n.* Leukocyte.

white book, *n.* An official government report, so named because it was originally bound in white.

white·cap, hwīt′kap″, wīt′kap″, *n.* A wave with a broken, foamy crest; (*cap.*) formerly, a member of a secret organization who, by terrorism and coercion, pretended to protect a community from people the organization deemed evil or harmful: so called from the white hoods some of them wore.

white ce·dar, *n.* Any of various N. American evergreen trees, esp. *Chamaecyparis thyoides,* found in the swampland along the Atlantic coast, and yielding valuable timber; the wood of this tree; the arborvitae, *Thuja occidentalis.*

white-col·lar, hwīt′kol′ėr, wīt′kol′ėr, *a.* Of, pertaining to, or designating the class of salaried employees, as clerks or salesmen, whose jobs do not usu. include manual labor, and whose mode of dress therefore is more or less formal, as distinguished from *blue-collar.*

white cor·pus·cle, *n. Anat.* A white blood cell; a leukocyte.

white crap·pie, *n.* A small, edible, freshwater sunfish, *Pomoxis annularis,* found in lakes of the central U.S.

whit·ed, hwī′tid, wī′tid, *a.* White covered, as a whitewashed fence; made white, as by bleaching.

whit·ed sep·ul·cher, *n.* [From the scriptural expression used in Matt. xxiii. 27.] A person having a virtuous outward appearance that covers corruption within; a hypocrite.

white dwarf, *n. Astron.* one of a class of small stars having a high density and surface temperature and a low luminosity, believed to be the remnants of supernovae.

white el·e·phant, *n.* An Asian elephant of an abnormally pale color, venerated in some sections of Central and Southeast Asia. *Fig.* a possession of great value but entailing great expense to maintain; anything ostensibly desirable but burdensome to have.

white·face, hwīt′fās″, wīt′fās″, *n.* An animal having a white face, esp. Hereford cattle; white face make-up, as often worn by a clown.

white-faced, hwīt′fāst′, wīt′fāst′, *a.* Having a white or pale face; marked with white on the front of the head, as a horse; having a white front or surface.

white feath·er, *n.* [Orig. from a white feather in a gamecock's tail taken as a sign of inferior breeding and hence of poor fighting qualities.] A symbol of cowardice. —**show the white feath·er,** to behave in a cowardly manner.

white·fish, hwīt′fish″, wīt′fish″, *n. pl.* **white·fish·es, white·fish.** Any fish of the genus *Coregonus,* in the salmon family, esp. the common whitefish, *C. clupeiformis,* an edible fish of the Great Lakes region of the U.S., having a bluish-back and silvery-white sides; the beluga, a white whale; an edible tropical marine fish, *Caulolatilus princeps,* of California.

white flag, *n.* A white banner or piece of cloth raised to indicate surrender, esp. in battle, or as a token of truce.

white·fly, hwīt′flī″, wīt′flī″, *n. pl.* **white·flies.** Any of various small, whitish, homopterous insects of the family *Aleyrodidae,* destructive in citrus groves and greenhouses.

White Fri·ar, *n.* A Carmelite friar: so named from the distinctive white cloak.

white gas·o·line, *n.* Gasoline having no tetraethyl lead. Also **white gas.**

white gold, *n.* One of various gold alloys, given a white color by its platinum or nickel content.

white goods, *n.* Linens, as towels, sheets, and tablecloths; major appliances used in the home, as refrigerators, washing machines, stoves, and the like, usu. finished in white.

White·hall, hwīt′hạl″, wīt′hạl″, *n.* [From *Whitehall,* a London street where the principal government offices are located.] A former palace belonging to the royalty; *fig.* the British government.

white-head·ed, hwīt′hed′id, wīt′hed′id, *a.* Having white or very light-colored hair, fur, or feathers on the head; white-haired; flaxen-haired. *Ir.* specially favored; darling.

white heat, *n.* The very high temperature, surpassing red heat, at which iron or the like becomes incandescent and emits a dazzling white light; a stage of intense activity, excitement, feeling, or the like; as, to work at a *white heat.*

white-hot, hwīt′hot′, wīt′hot′, *a.* Heated to a glowing, white heat, as metal; *colloq.* excessively angry, ardent, impassioned, or the like.

White House, *n.* The official residence of the President of the U.S. in Washington, D.C., a large two-story freestone building painted white, usu. preceded by *the*; also *Executive Mansion.* The executive branch of the U.S. government.

white lead, *n.* A basic carbonate of lead, $2PbCO_3 \cdot Pb(OH)_2$, widely used as a pigment in paints, and also used in medical salves for burns and in putty; cerussite.

white leath·er, *n.* Leather prepared with alum and salt. Also **whit·leath·er.**

white lie, *n.* A lie told with a kind or polite

intention; a harmless or non-malicious falsehood concerning something trivial.

white line, *n.* Any white border, edge, or margin; the white stripe which is painted down the middle of a highway or road for the purpose of traffic control.

white-liv·ered, hwīt′liv′ẻrd, wīt′liv′ẻrd, *a.* [From an old notion that pusillanimous persons had pale-colored or bloodless livers.] Cowardly; dastardly; sickly or pale.

white man's bur·den, *n.* [From the poem, "The White Man's Burden" (1899) by Rudyard Kipling.] The presumed duty of the white peoples native to industrially and militarily powerful nations to enforce their conception of civilization upon the non-white peoples native to lands rich in natural resources.

white mat·ter, *n. Anat.* nerve tissue, esp. of the brain and spinal cord, containing mostly myelinic nerve fibers, and which is nearly white in color: distinguished from *gray matter.*

white met·al, *n.* Any of several alloys in which tin or lead is used, giving it a whitish color, as Babbitt metal, pewter, or britannia metal.

whit·en, hwīt′en, wīt′en, *v.t.* To make white; to bleach; to blanch.—*v.i.* To turn or become white or whiter.

whit·en·er, hwīt′e·nẻr, wīt′e·nẻr, *n.* One who or that which whitens; a bleach, polish, or other substance used to whiten something.

white·ness, hwīt′nis, wīt′nis, *n.* The state of being white; paleness; purity; cleanness; white color or substance.

whit·en·ing, hwīt′e·ning, wīt′e·ning, *n.* The operation or act of making or becoming white; a substance or agent used to whiten something.

white noise, *n.* A sound which is random, but having uniform intensity and covering a wide range of frequencies.

white oak, *n.* A large oak tree, *Quercus alba,* of eastern N. America, having a light gray bark and a hard, durable wood; any of several other species of oak, as *Q. garryana,* of western N. America, or *Q. robur,* of Great Britain; the wood of any of these trees.

white·out, hwīt′out″, wīt′out″, *n.* A condition occurring in arctic regions when approximately equal intensities of light coming from above and reflected from below cause clouds and snow-covered surface to blend into one vast whiteness so that no object casts a shadow, and only very dark objects are visible.

white pa·per, *n.* An official government publication, usu. treating a subject less extensively than would a blue book or white book.

white perch, *n.* A small, edible fish, *Roccus americanus,* found in Atlantic coastal streams or inland waters of N. America.

white pine, *n.* A tall pine, *Pinus strobus,* of eastern N. America, yielding a white soft wood of great commercial importance; the wood itself; any of various other similar species of pine, as the western white pine.

white plague, *n. Pathol.* tuberculosis, esp. pulmonary tuberculosis.

white po·ta·to, *n.* See *potato.*

white pri·ma·ry, *n.* A primary election, formerly held in various southern parts of the U.S., in which Caucasians were the only persons allowed to vote.

White Rus·sian, *n.* A native of Belorussia; the language spoken by its inhabitants. Also *Belorussian.*

white sale, *n.* A sale of towels, sheets, pillowcases, and other, similar white merchandise.

white sauce, *n.* A sauce made of flour, butter, seasonings, and milk or cream, or sometimes chicken or veal stock.

white slave, *n.* A woman or girl who is sold or forced to serve as a prostitute.—**white-slave,** *a.*

white slav·er, *n.* A person engaged in white slavery.

white slav·er·y, *n.* The condition of or the traffic in white slaves.

white·smith, hwīt′smith″, wīt′smith″, *n.* A tinsmith; a worker in iron who finishes or polishes the work.

white su·prem·a·cy, *n.* The doctrine that whites are entitled, by virtue of self-proclaimed racial superiority, to subordinate Negroes.—**white su·prem·a·cist,** *n.*

white-tailed deer, hwīt′tāld″ dēr′, wīt′tāld″, *n.* A widely distributed, N. American deer, *Odocoileus virginianus,* whose tail has a white underside. Also **white·tail deer, white·tail, Vir·gin·ia deer.**

white·throat, hwīt′thrōt″, wīt′thrōt″, *n.* A common sparrow of N. America, *Zonotrichia albicollis,* which has a white patch on its throat; also **white-throated spar·row.** One of several small European warblers, esp. *Sylvia communis,* with a whitish throat and belly.

white tie, *n.* A bow tie, white in color, worn by men dressed in formal evening clothes; formal evening clothes for men, as contrasted with *black tie.*

white·wall, hwīt′wạl″, wīt′wạl″, *n.* A tire used on automobiles and other vehicles whose sidewall is white in color.

white·wash, hwīt′wosh″, hwīt′wạsh″, wīt′-wosh″, wīt′wạsh″, *n.* A wash or liquid composition for whitening something, esp. a composition, as of lime and water or of whiting, size, and water, used for whitening walls, woodwork, or the like; *colloq.* anything used as a means of covering up defects, glossing over faults or errors, rehabilitating reputation, or imparting a specious semblance of respectability or honesty; *colloq., sports,* a defeat in which the loser fails to score.—*v.t.* To whiten with whitewash; *colloq.* to cover up or gloss over the defects, faults, or errors of by some special means; *colloq., sports,* to subject to a whitewash.—**white·wash·er,** *n.*

white wa·ter, *n.* Frothy, foamy water, as the water in rapids or breakers.

white whale, *n.* See beluga.

white·wing, hwīt′wing″, wīt′wing″, *n.* A street cleaner or other person wearing a white uniform.

white·wood, hwīt′wụd″, wīt′wụd″, *n.* Any of several trees, as the tulip tree or the linden, having a white or light-colored wood; the wood of such trees.

whith·er, hwiTH′ẻr, wiTH′ẻr, *adv.* [O.E. *hwidre,* whither, < stem of *who, what,* and suffix *-ther;* closely akin to *whether.*] *Archaic.* To what place; where. To what point, end, or situation: used interrogatively.—*conj. Archaic.* to which place.—**whith·er·so·ev·er,** *adv. Archaic,* to whatever place.—**whith·er·ward,** *adv. Archaic,* toward or in what direction.

whit·ing, hwī′ting, wī′ting, *n. pl.* **whit·ings, whit·ing.** A common European food fish, *Merlangus merlangus,* abundant off the coast of Great Britain; the silver hake of N. America, *Merluccius bilincaris;* any of various food fishes, genus *Menticirrhus,* abundant in the Atlantic waters of N. America.

whit·ing, hwī′ting, wī′ting, *n.* A material made from naturally occurring chalk or calcite, both being forms of calcium carbonate, $CaCO_3$, used in making putty, whitewash, pigments, detergents, and polishes.

whit·low, hwit′lō, wīt′lō, *n.* [A corruption of *whickflaw* for *quick-flaw,* lit. 'flaw or sore of the *quick.*'] *Pathol.* An inflammation affecting the skin around or under the nail of a finger or toe, generally terminating in pus; felon.

Whit·mon·day, Whit-Mon·day, hwit′-mun′dē, hwit′mun′dā, wit′mun′dē, wit′-mun′dā, *n.* The Monday following Whitsunday, generally observed as a holiday in England.

Whit·sun·day, hwit′sun′dē, hwit′sun′dā, wit′sun′dē, wit′sun′dā, hwit′sun′dā, wit′-sun′dā, *n.* [Lit. 'white Sunday.' The name was given because Pentecost was formerly a great season for christenings, in which white robes are a prominent feature.] The seventh Sunday after Easter, observed as a church festival in commemoration of the descent of the Holy Spirit on the day of Pentecost.

Whit·sun·tide, hwit′sun·tīd″, wit′sun·tīd″, *n.* [*Whitsun,* and *tide,* time, season.] The week, esp. the first three days, following Whitsunday or Pentecost. Also **Whit·-sun Tide.**—**Whit·sun,** hwit′sun, wit′sun, *a.*

whit·tle, hwit′l, wit′l, *v.t.*—*whittled, whittling.* [O.E. *thwitel,* dim. < O.E. *thwitan,* to cut; O.E. and Sc. *white,* to cut with a knife.] To cut, dress, or shape, as a block or stick of wood, by removing small chips with a knife; to cut down the amount of or gradually eliminate as if by removing small bits with a knife, usu. followed by *away, down,* or *off.*—*v.i.* To cut or shape wood by removing small chips with a knife, esp. as a diversion or a pastime.—*n. Brit. dial.* a knife.—**whit·tler,** *n.*—**whit·tling,** hwit′-ling, wit′ling, *n.*

whiz, whizz, hwiz, wiz, *v.i.*—*whizzed, whizzing.* [An imit. word; cf. *wheeze, whistle, whir,* etc.] To make a humming or hissing sound, as the sound made by an arrow or ball flying through the air; to rush, speed by, or move quickly with a similar sound.—*v.t.* To cause or induce to whiz.—*n. pl.* **whiz·zes.** A sound between hissing and humming; quick movement causing a similar sound. *Slang,* one who or that which is regarded as very able, attractive, proficient, or excellent, as: Where math is concerned, she is a real *whiz.*

whiz, hwiz, wiz, *n.* See *wizard.*

whiz-bang, whizz-bang, hwiz′bang″, wiz′-bang″, *n. Slang.* A small high-velocity shell which bursts as soon as the sound or report of the shell's flight is heard; a firecracker producing an effect resembling this.—hwiz′bang′, wiz′bang′, *a. Slang,* excellent, skillful, or notable.

whiz·zer, hwiz′ẻr, wiz′ẻr, *n.* A machine using centrifugal force to dry various things, as clothes, sugar, grain, or the like; something that or one who whizzes.

who, hö, *pron.*—nom. *who,* poss. *whose,* obj. *whom.* [O.E. *hwā* (gen. *hwaes,* dat. *hwǣm, hwām,* acc. *hwone;* neut. *hwaet,* E. *what*), akin to O.H.G. *hwer* (G. *wer*), Icel. *hverr,* Goth. *hwas,* also to L. *qui, quis,* Skt. *kas,* who.] What person, as: *Who* told you so? Of a person, what as to character, origin, position, or importance, as: *Who* do they think they are? Used as a simple relative with an expressed antecedent, as a person, sometimes an animal, or a personified thing, in clauses conveying an additional idea, as: We saw several men *who* were at work. Any person that, used as a simple relative in clauses defining or restricting the antecedent, as: Release all *who* have served their term. The or any person that, used as a compound relative (with an antecedent not expressed), as: *Who* procrastinates may suffer later.

whoa, hwō, wō, *interj.* Stop! stand still! used as a command, esp. to horses.

who·dun·it, hö·dun′it, *n. Colloq.* a novel or play which is concerned with the detection of a crime, esp. murder.

who·ev·er, hö·ev′ẻr, *pron.*—nom. *whoever,* poss. *whosoever,* obj. *whomever.* Anyone who; whatever person, as: *Whoever* comes will be welcome. No matter who, as: *Whoever* she may be, the president will not see her. What person. Also *whoso, whosoever.*

whole, hōl, *a.* [O.E. *hole, hool* (the *w* being erroneous, as in *whore*), < O.E. *hál,* whole, sound, safe; D. *heel,* Icel. *heill,* G. *heil,* Goth. *hails,* healthy, sound, whole.] In a healthy state; sound; well; restored to a sound state; healed; unimpaired; uninjured; not broken or fractured; not defective or imperfect; entire, complete; intact; comprising all parts or units that make up an aggregate; all; total; as, the *whole* city; having the same mother and father; as, a *whole* sister; *math.* not a fraction; as, a *whole* number.—*n.* An entire thing; a thing complete in itself; the entire or total assemblage of parts making a complete system; unity.—**as a whole,** altogether; all things considered.—**on the whole,** as a rule, all things considered.—**out of whole cloth,** fictitious; without foundation or fact.—**whole·ness,** *n.*

whole gale, *n. Meteor.* A wind that registers 10 on the Beaufort scale; a wind with a velocity of 55 to 63 miles per hour.

whole·heart·ed, hōl'här'tid, *a.* Hearty; enthusiastic; earnest; sincere.—**whole·heart·ed·ly,** *adv.*—**whole·heart·ed·ness,** *n.*

whole hog, *n. Slang.* The farthest limit; entirety or completeness.—**go the whole hog,** *slang.* To do anything thoroughly or in its entirety; to become involved completely or to the limit.

whole note, *n. Mus.* A note sustained for the same duration as four quarter notes; a semibreve.

whole num·ber, *n. Math.* A number consisting of one or more units, as 30, as distinguished from a fraction or a mixed number; an integer.

whole·sale, hōl'sāl', *n.* The sale of commodities in large quantities, and esp. for the purpose of resale, as to retailers or jobbers rather than to consumers directly: opposed to *retail.*—*a.* Of, pertaining to, or engaged in sale by wholesale; extensive and indiscriminate; as, *wholesale* discharge of workers.—*adv.* In bulk or large quantities; on a large scale and without discrimination.—*v.t., v.i.*—*wholesaled, wholesaling.* To sell at or by wholesale.—**whole·sal·er,** *n.*

whole·some, hōl'som, *a.* [Whole, and affix-*some.*] Tending to promote health; beneficial to physical well-being; healthful; favorable·to morals, religion, or prosperity; salutary; free from risk.—**whole·some·ly,** *adv.*—**whole·some·ness,** *n.*

whole-souled, hōl'sōld', *a.* Wholehearted; generous; hearty; devoted.

whole step, *n. Mus.* An interval equal to the sum of two semitones; two half steps. Also **whole tone.**

whole-wheat, hōl'hwēt', hōl'wēt', *a.* Made with the entire wheat grain, as flour; prepared with such flour; as, *whole-wheat* bread.

whol·ly, hō'lē, hōl'lē, *adv.* To the whole amount or extent; so as to comprise or involve all; entirely; totally; altogether; quite.

whom, hōm, *pron.* The objective case of *who.*

whom·ev·er, hōm·ev'ėr, *pron.* The objective case of *whoever.*

whomp, hwomp, womp, *n. Colloq.* a blow delivered with great force and characterized by the volume of its sound.—*v.t. Colloq.* To win a decisive victory over; to beat soundly or trounce; to strike, bang, or slap.

whomp up, *v.t. Colloq.* To stimulate, as excitement; to produce, create, or conjure up, esp. hastily; to throw together.

whom·so, hōm'sō, *pron.* Objective case of *whoso.*

whom·so·ev·er, hōm"sō·ev'ėr, *pron.* Objective case of *whosoever.*

whoop, hōp, hwōp, wōp, *n.* [O.Fr. Fr. *houper,* < *houp,* interj. used in shouting]. A cry or shout, as of a hunter, warrior, or the like; the cry of an owl, crane, or other bird; the whooping or gasping sound characteristic of whooping cough.—*v.i.* To utter a loud cry or shout; to cry, as an owl or certain other birds; to make the characteristic sound accompanying the deep inspiration after a series of coughs in whooping cough.—*v.t.* To utter, as with a whoop or whoops; to whoop to or at; to call, urge, pursue, or drive with whoops; as, to *whoop* the dogs on.—*interj.* An expression of joy, excitement, or defiance.—**whoop it up,** *colloq.* To take part in a noisy, riotous celebration; to promote enthusiasm.—**not worth a whoop,** *colloq.* to have little or no value.

whoop-de-do, whoop-de-doo, hōp'dē··dō", hōp'dē·dō", hwōp'dē··dō", wōp'dē·dō", wōp'dē·dō", *n.* pl. **whoop-de-dos, whoop-de-doos.** *Colloq.* A noisy celebration; heated or excited public debate; elaborate, unrestrained display or promotion.

whoop·ee, hwup'ē', wup'ē', hwö'pē, wö'pē', *interj., n. Slang.* a cry of joy or excitement.—**make whoop·ee,** *slang,* to take part in uproarious festivity.

whoop·ing cough, hō'ping kaf, hup'ing, *n. Pathol.* an infectious disease of the respiratory mucous membrane, esp. of children, characterized by a series of short, convulsive coughs followed by a deep inspiration accompanied by a whooping sound. Also **chin·cough,** *pertussis.*

whoosh, hwösh, wösh, hwush, wush, *v.i.* To move quickly with a hissing, whistling sound; as, wind *whooshing* through the leaves.—*v.t.* To move, as an object, with such a sound.—*n.* A rushing, whistling sound.

whop, hwop, wop, *v.t.*—*whopped, whopping.* [Also *whap, wap, wop*; M.E. *whappen, wappen*; origin obscure.] *Colloq.* To strike forcibly; to beat; to defeat soundly, as in a contest; to pull out. Also *whap.*—*v.i. Colloq.* To plump suddenly down; to flop. Also *whap.*—*n. Colloq.* A heavy blow or impact; the sound made by it; a bump; a heavy fall. Also *whap.*

whop·per, hwop'ėr, wop'ėr, *n. Colloq.* Something uncommonly large of its kind; a big lie. Also *whapper.*

whop·ping, hwop'ing, wop'ing, *a. Colloq.* Very large of its kind; thumping; huge. Also *whapping.*

whore, hōr, har, hur, *n.* [O.E. *hóre,* Icel. *hóra,* Dan. *hore,* D. *hoer,* G. *hure,* a whore; same root as L. *carus,* dear; Skt. *kâma,* love. The *w* has intruded as in *whole.*] A prostitute; a promiscuous woman.—*v.i.*—*whored, whoring.* To have sexual intercourse with a prostitute; to associate with whores; to be a whore.—**whor·ish,** hōr'ish, har'ish, hur'ish, *a.*

whore·dom, hōr'dom, har'dom, hur'dom, *n.* Whoring; prostitution; *Bib.* idolatry.

whore·house, hōr'hous", har'hous", hur'hous", *n.* pl. **whore·hous·es,** hōr'hou"ziz, har'hou"ziz, hur'hou"ziz. A house or place where prostitutes are accessible for hire; a brothel.

whore·mong·er, hōr'mung"gėr, hōr'-mong"gėr, har'mung"gėr, har'mong"gėr, hur'mung"gėr, hur'mong"gėr, *n.* One who associates with, or has to do with whores; a fornicator; a lecher. Also **whore·mas·ter.**

whore·son, hōr'son, har'son, hur'son, *n. Archaic.* A bastard; a coarse term of contempt or abuse for a person.—*a. Archaic.* Bastardly; mean; scurvy.

whorl, hwurl, hwarl, wurl, warl, *n.* [A form of *whirl,* which is also used in the same sense.] *Bot.* a set of leaves or other organs of a plant, all on the same plane, disposed in a circle; *zool.* a single turn of a univalve shell; *textile mach.* a flywheel on the spindle of a spinning or weaving machine. Any of the circular ridges of a fingerprint; anything having the shape or appearance of a coil.—**whorled,** *a.* Having whorls; arranged in whorls, as leaves.

whor·tle·ber·ry, hwur'tl·ber"ē, wur'tl·ber"ē, *n.* pl. **whor·tle·ber·ries.** [< O.E. *wyrtil,* a small shrub, dim. of *wort,* a wort.] A European shrub, *Vaccinium myrtillus,* of the blueberry family, bearing edible, black berries; the berry itself. Also *bilberry,* **hur·tle·ber·ry, whort, whor·tle,** hwurt, wurt, hwur'tl, wur'tl.

whose, hōz, *pron.* The possessive case of *who,* and sometimes of *which.*

whose·so·ev·er, hōz"sō·ev'ėr, *pron.* The possessive case of *whosoever.*

who·so, hō'sō, *pron.*—nom. *whoso,* poss. *whoseso,* obj. *whomso.* Whoever; whatever person.

who·so·ev·er, hō"sō·ev'ėr, *pron.*—nom. *whosoever,* poss. *whosoever,* obj. *whomsoever.* Whoever; any person whatever.

why, hwī, wī, *adv.* [O.E. *hwí, hwý,* the instrumental case of *hwá,* who, *hwæt,* what. *How* is a form of the same word.] For what cause, reason, or purpose; wherefore.—*interj.* Used emphatically or to denote surprise or hesitation.—*n.* pl. **whys.** The reason; as, the how and the *why.*—*conj.* The reason for which, as: His outgoing personality is *why* he is so popular.

whyd·ah, whid·ah, hwid'a, wid'a, *n.* [For *widow-bird* (after Pg. *viuva,* widow-bird, lit. 'widow'), from the black and white plumage of some species.] Any of the small weaverbirds of Africa which constitute the subfamily *Viduinae,* the males of which have elongated, drooping tail feathers throughout the breeding season. Also *widow bird.*

wick, wik, *n.* [O.E. *weoca, wecca,* a wick; D. *wiek,* a wick, a plug for a wound; Sw. *veke,* Dan. *vaege,* a wick; allied to *weak* (being pliant) and to *wicker.*] A band or piece of fabric, tape, cord, or loosely twisted threads, as in an oil lamp, candle, cigarette lighter, or the like, which serves to absorb and convey the oil, tallow, or other fuel to the flame.—**wick·ing,** wik'ing, *n.*

wick·ed, wik'id, *a.* [< old *wicke, wikke,* wicked (cf. *wretched*), apparently < O.E. *wicca,* a wizard, *wicce,* a witch.] Evil in principle or practice; sinful; vicious; iniquitous; disposed to mischief; malicious; unpleasant or offensive; as, a *wicked* stench; painful or harmful; as, a *wicked* blow; *slang,* excellent; as, a *wicked* tennis player.—**wick·ed·ly,** *adv.*—**wick·ed·ness,** *n.*

wick·er, wik'ėr, *n.* [O.E. *wikir, wiker,* a withy, < stem of *weak;* cf. Sw. *wika,* to plait, to bend; Dan. *vegre,* a withy, G. *wickel,* a roll.] A small pliant twig or shoot; a withe or osier; wickerwork.—*a.* Made of plaited or woven twigs or osiers; covered with such woven work.—**wick·er·work,** wik'ėr·wurk", *n.* Wicker woven together, as used in furniture or baskets; articles made of such material.

wick·et, wik'it, *n.* [O.Fr. *wiket* (Fr. *guichet*), < Icel. *víkja,* to turn, to bend, same word as O.E. *wícan,* to yield.] A small gate or door, esp. one made within or next to a larger one; a small window, often having a protective screen or grille, as in a ticket booth; a gate controlling the flow of water, as in a channel, pipe, or canal lock. *Cricket,* the object at which the bowler aims, consisting of two sets of three upright rods, having two small pieces lying in grooves along their tops; the area on which the wickets are set up; a player's turn at the wicket; an inning not started or one unfinished. *Croquet,* a wire hoop.—**wick·et·keep·er,** wik'it·kē"pėr, *n. Cricket,* the player positioned behind the wicket.

wick·i·up, wik·i·up, wik'ē·up", *n.* [N. Amer. Ind.] A N. American Indian hut having a crudely constructed framework covered with brushwood or mats made of grass or reeds which were built by certain nomadic tribes of the western U.S.

wic·o·py, wik'o·pē, *n*. pl. **wic·o·pies.** [Algonquian.] The leatherwood, *Dirca palustris*; any of various willow herbs, as *Epilobium angustifolium*; a basswood.

wid·der·shins, wid'ẽr·shinz", *adv.* Withershins.

wide, wīd, *a.*—*wider*, *widest*. [O.E. *wid*, wide, broad, extensive = D. *wijd*, Icel. *vidr*, Sw. and Dan. *vid*, G. *weit*, wide; connections doubtful.] Having a great or considerable distance or extent between the sides; broad: opposed to *narrow*; having the extent from side to side limited to a certain degree; as, three feet *wide*; having a great extent every way; vast; extensive; as, the *wide* skies of the West; pertaining to a great scope or variety; as, a *wide* choice of job offers; open to the fullest extent; loose, comfortable, or non-binding; as, *wide*-leg trousers; failing to hit a mark; *fig.* remote or distant from anything, as truth or propriety. *Phon.* of a sound, produced with relaxed muscles; also **lax.**—*adv.* Over a considerable distance or expanse; as, to broadcast far and *wide*; over a specified or limited distance, used in compounds; as, to campaign state-*wide*; to the full extent; as, to open a door *wide*; apart from or to one side of a mark, as: The shot went *wide*.—**wide·ly**, *adv.*—**wide·ness**, *n.*—**wid·ish**, wī'dish, *a.*

wide-an·gle, wīd'ang'gl, *a. Photog.* pertaining to or designating a lens which allows for an angle or range of view wider than that provided by an ordinary lens.

wide-a·wake, wīd'a·wāk', *a.* Fully or totally awake; alert; knowing.—*n.* A broad-brimmed hat made of soft felt. Also **wide-a·wake hat.**—**wide-a·wake·ness**, *n.*

wide-eyed, wīd'īd", *a.* With one's eyes opened fully or widely, as in astonishment or wonder; naive or innocent.

wide-mouthed, wīd'mouтHd", wīd'moutht", *a.* Possessing a wide mouth, as an object or a person; with one's mouth widely open, as in surprise.

wid·en, wīd'en, *v.t.* To make wide or wider; to extend the breadth of.—*v.i.* To grow wide or wider; to extend in breadth.—**wid·en·er**, *n.*

wide-o·pen, wīd'ō'pen, *a.* Opened wide; lacking law enforcement, as a city.

wide·spread, wīd'spred', *a.* Spread to a great distance; extending far and wide; covering a vast area; broadly accepted; as, *widespread* reforms; comprehensive.—**wide-spread·ing**, *a.* Extending over or affecting a large area.

widg·eon, **wig·eon**, wij'on, *n.* pl. **widg·-eons**, **widg·eon.** [Fr. *vigeon*, *vingeon*, names of ducks; cf. L. *vipio*, *vipionis*, a small crane.] A medium-sized N. American freshwater duck, *Mareca americana*, having a short bill; also **bald·pate.** A similar duck of Europe, *Mareca penelope*.

wid·get, wij'it, *n.* A small device or object, esp. something whose name is unknown or forgotten; a gadget.

wid·ow, wid'ō, *n.* [O.E. *widuwe*, *wuduwe*, a widow = D. *weduwe*, L.G. *wedewe*, G. *wittwe*, Goth. *widuwo*; cogn. Rus. *vdová*, L. *vidua*, < *viduus*, deprived; Skt. *vidhavâ*, a widow.] A woman who has lost her husband by death and who remains unmarried; a woman whose husband is often away from home, usu. preceded by a word indicating the absence; as, golf or baseball *widow*; a hand dealt to the table in certain card games. *Print.* a short line of type left hanging at the end of a paragraph or carried over to the next column.—*v.t.* To reduce, as one, to the state of a widow; to bereave of a husband; to divest of anything good.

wid·ow bird, *n.* Whydah.

wid·ow·er, wid'ō·ẽr, *n.* A man who has lost his wife by death and has not remarried.

wid·ow·hood, wid'ō·hụd", *n.* The state or time of being a widow, or occasionally, a widower. Also *viduity*.

wid·ow's mite, *n.* A small but freely given contribution from a person of limited means. Mark xii. 42.

wid·ow's peak, *n.* A point that is formed on the hairline of the forehead, usu. in the middle, by the hair's growth.

wid·ow's walk, *n.* A railed porch like area at the top of certain houses on the seacoast, esp. those built during the era of sailing vessels, from which incoming ships could be more easily sighted.

width, width, *often* with, *n.* [Cf. *breadth*, *length*.] A measure taken from one side to the other of an object; a portion of the full breadth of something; as, a *width* of material.

width·wise, width'wīz", with'wīz, *adv.* Toward the width; in the direction of the width. Also **width·ways**, width'wāz", with'-wāz".

wield, wēld, *v.t.* [O.E. *welden*. O.E. (ge)*weldan*, (ge)*wyldan*, < *wealdan*, to rule; Icel. *valda*, G. *walten*, to rule; Goth. *valdan*, to govern; same root as L. *valeo*, to be strong.] To exert or exercise, as influence, power, or authority; to use in the hand or hands, as a weapon or tool, with full command or power.—**wield·a·ble**, *a.* —**wield·er**, *n.*—**wield·y**, wēl'dē, *a.*—*wieldier*, *wieldiest*.

wie·ner, wē'nẽr, *n.* Frankfurter; Vienna sausage. Also **wee·nie**, **wee·ny**, **wie·nie**, **wie·ner·wurst**, wē'nẽ, wē'nẽr·wụrst".

Wie·ner schnit·zel, vē'nẽr shnit'sel, vē'-nẽr shnit'sel, *n.* [G., 'Vienna cutlet.'] A breaded veal cutlet, variously seasoned or garnished.

wife, wīf, *n.* pl. **wives**, wīvz. [O.E. *wif*, a woman, a wife = D. *wijf*, Icel. *vif*, Dan. *viv*, G. *weib*, a woman; root doubtful. This word gives the first syllable of *woman*.] A woman who is united to a man in wedlock; *dial.* any woman of mature age: still so used in compounds; as, fish*wife*, house*wife*.— **take to wife**, to marry, as a certain woman. —**wife·hood**, *n.*—**wife·less**, *a.*—**wife·ly**, *a.*

wife·like, wīf'līk", *adv.* In the manner typical of a wife.—*a.* Wifely; suitable or relating to a wife.

wig, wig, *n.* [The final syllable of *periwig*.] An artificial covering of hair for the head, used esp. to conceal baldness, but now also worn as an article of fashion or part of a costume; *Brit. colloq.* a harsh scolding.— *v.t.*—*wigged*, *wigging*. To provide with a wig or wigs; *Brit. colloq.* to scold.—**wigged**, *a.* Wearing a wig.

wig·an, wig'an, *n.* [From *Wigan* in Lancashire, Eng.] A stiff canvaslike fabric used for stiffening certain parts of clothing as lapels, hems, or seams.

wig·gle, wig'l, *v.i.*—*wiggled*, *wiggling*. [M.E. *wigelen* = M.L.G. and D. *wiggelen*, shake, totter; a freq. form akin to E. *wag*, *waggle*, and *weigh*.] To move or go with short, quick, irregular movements from side to side; wriggle.—*v.t.* To cause to wiggle; to move quickly and irregularly from side to side.—*n.* A wiggling movement or course; *cookery*, a creamed dish of peas with fish or various shellfish.—**get a wig·gle on**, *slang*, to move fast, or hurry up.—**wig·gly**, wig'lē, *a.*—*wigglier*, *wiggliest*. Wiggling; wavy, as a line.

wig·gler, wig'lẽr, *n.* One who or that which wiggles; the larva of a mosquito, or a wriggler.

wight, wīt, *n.* [O.E. *wiht*, *wuht*, a creature, a thing; D. *wicht*, a baby; G. *wicht*, creature, fellow; Goth. *waihts*, *waiht*, a thing. Perh. orig. 'moving creature,' allied to *wag*, *weigh*.

Whit is the same word, and it is also contained in *aught*, *naught* or *nought*.] *Archaic.* A being; a human being; a creature.

wig·let, wig'lit, *n.* A type of woman's small wig or hairpiece used as a partial hair covering, or to change or create a hair style.

wig·mak·er, wig'mā"kẽr, *n.* A person making or selling wigs.

wig·wag, wig'wag', *v.t.*, *v.i.*—*wigwagged*, *wigwagging*. [Varied redupl. of *wag*.] To move to and fro; *naut.* to signal by movements of flags or lights waved by the signaler according to a code.—*n. Naut.* The act of signaling by movements of flags or lights; a message so signaled.—**wig·wag·-ger**, *n.*

wig·wam, wig'wom, wig'wạm, *n.* [Algonquian.] An American Indian hut or lodge, usu. of rounded or conical shape, formed of poles overlaid with bark, mats, or skins; *colloq.* a structure, esp. of large size, used for political conventions or meetings.

wil·co, wil'kō, *interj.* Will comply: used esp. in radio communication to acknowledge an order or directive.

wild, wīld, *a.* [O.E. *wilde* = D. and G. *wild* = Icel. *villr* = Goth. *wiltheis*, wild.] Living in a state of nature, as animals that have not been tamed or domesticated; as, *wild* beasts; feral; growing or produced without cultivation or the care of man, as plants or flowers; uncultivated, uninhabited, or waste, as land; uncivilized or barbarous, as tribes or savages; undisciplined, unruly, lawless, or turbulent; as, a *wild* gang; disregardful of moral restraints as to pleasurable indulgence; as, to be *wild* during youth; of unrestrained violence, fury, or intensity; as, *wild* storms; violent; furious; tempestuous; unrestrained, untrammeled, or unbridled; as, *wild* orgies; unrestrained by reason or prudence; as, a *wild* venture; extravagant or fantastic; as, *wild* fancies; disorderly or disheveled; as, *wild* locks; violently excited; as, *wild* with rage; characterized by or indicating violent excitement, as actions; frantic; distracted, crazy, or mad; wide of the mark; as, a *wild* throw; *colloq.* intensely eager or enthusiastic; as, *wild* about baseball; *cards*, having a value determined by the holder, as a card.— *adv.* In a wild or unruly manner; wildly.— *n. Often pl.* An uninhabited region or place; wilderness or desert.—**run wild**, to live as a wild animal or as an animal escaped from domestication; to grow unchecked, as a wild plant; to go about freely without discipline or restraint.—**the wild**, an uncultivated, uninhabited, or desolate region or tract; a waste; a wilderness; a desert.— **wild·ly**, *adv.*—**wild·ness**, *n.*

wild all·spice, *n. Bot.* A spicebush, *Lindera benzoin*.

wild boar, *n.* An old-world hog, *Sus scrofa*, thought to be the ancestor of the domesticated swine.

wild car·rot, *n. Bot.* a weed, *Daucus carota*, of the parsley family, having a woody taproot, common in fields and waste places: the garden carrot is derived from it. Also *Queen Anne's lace*.

wild·cat, wīld'kat", *n.* pl. **wild·cat**, **wild·-cats.** A wild European cat, *Felis sylvestris*, resembling the common domestic cat but larger; any of various other small or medium-sized wild feline animals of Europe and Africa; any of various similar feline animals of the New World, as the ocelot; felines of the genus *Lynx*, of the northern hemisphere; the bobcat, *Lynx rufus*, of N. America; a violent or quick-tempered person; *rail.* a locomotive in operation, but not hauling cars, as one in a switch yard. An oil well which is drilled as an exploratory one; an unsound or unsafe business undertaking.—*a.* Wild, reckless, or irresponsible, esp. characterized by or proceeding from recklessly unsound or unsafe business methods; as, *wildcat* banks, *wildcat* companies or stocks; referring to an illegal business venture; running without control or regulation, as a locomotive, or apart from the regular schedule, as a train.—*v.t., v.i.*—*wildcatted, wildcatting.* To prospect, as for oil or ore, as an independent prospector, esp. in an area of uncertain resources.

wild·cat strike, *n.* An unauthorized violation of an agreement with a labor union by striking workers.

wild·cat·ter, wīld′kat″ėr, *n. Colloq.* A person who drills an oil well, gambling on a strike, usu. on land unknown to have oil; a promoter, esp. of shady business ventures.

wild cel·er·y, *n. Bot.* tape grass.

wil·de·beest, wil′de·bēst″, *D.* vil′de·bāst″, *n. pl.* **wil·de·beests, wil·de·beest.** [S. Afr. D., 'wild beast.'] A gnu.

wil·der, wil′dėr, *v.t.* [< the *wilder-* of *wilderness;* hence *bewilder.*] *Archaic.* To cause to lose the way or track; to puzzle with mazes or difficulties; to bewilder.—*v.i.*—**wil·der·ment,** *n.*

wil·der·ness, wil′dėr·nis, *n.* [M.E. *wildernesse,* < O.E. *wilder, wildēor,* wild animal, < *wilde,* E. *wild,* and *dēor,* E. *deer.*] A wild region, as of forest or desert, inhabited only by wild animals; a waste; any desolate tract, as of water; a part of a garden set apart for plants to grow wild; *fig.* a bewildering mass or multitude.

wild-eyed, wīld′īd″, *a.* Appearing angry or enraged; having radical or irrational viewpoints, as in politics.

wild fig, *n.* Caprifig.

wild·fire, wīld′fīr″, *n.* A highly inflammable composition, as Greek fire, formerly used in warfare; *fig.* something that runs or spreads with extraordinary rapidity, as: The news spread like *wildfire.* Lightning unaccompanied by thunder; ignis fatuus; *veter. pathol.* an inflammatory disease of the skin of sheep.

wild flax, *n.* Gold-of-pleasure.

wild flow·er, *n.* The flower of a plant that grows in the wild without cultivation; the plant itself.

wild·fowl, wīld′foul″, *n.* A game bird, esp. a waterfowl, as a duck or a goose.—**wild··fowl·er,** *n.*—**wild·fowl·ing,** *n.*

wild gin·ger, *n.* A perennial herb, *Asarum canadense,* of N. America with short stems bearing purplish-brown flowers.

wild-goose chase, wīld′gōs″ chās″, *n.* The earnest pursuit of a non-existent or unattainable object.

Wild Hunts·man, *n.* A spectral huntsman who, in European, esp. German, folklore, with a phantom host of followers, runs through woods, fields, and villages during the night, accompanied by shouts of huntsmen and baying of hounds.

wild hy·a·cinth, *n.* A camass, *Camassia scilloides,* of eastern N. America, bearing purplish or white flowers in racemes; the wood hyacinth, *Scilla nonscripta,* of Europe.

wild in·di·go, *n. Bot.* any of the leguminous N. American plants constituting the genus *Baptisia,* esp. *B. tinctoria,* a species with yellow flowers.

wild·ing, wīl′ding, *n.* Any plant that grows wild, or its fruit, esp. a wild apple tree or the apple itself; an escape, or any plant formerly under cultivation and now growing wild; a wild animal; a person who is unconventional or unrestrained.—*a.* Not cultivated or domesticated; wild.

wild·life, wīld′līf″, *n.* Animals or plants that exist in a wild, undomesticated state, as: We must provide adequate sanctuary for the native *wildlife* of the world.

wild·ling, wīld′ling, *n.* A wild thing in nature, as an animal or plant, esp. a plant transplanted to a garden.

wild mad·der, *n.* Any of various old-world

and S. American plants of the genus *Rubia,* esp. *R. tinctorum* or its root; see *madder.* Either of two N. American bedstraw plants, *Galium mollugo* or *G. tinctorium.*

wild mus·tard, *n.* The charlock, *Brassica arvensis.*

wild oat, *n. Bot.* weeds and grasses of the genus *Avena,* esp. *A. fatua,* a common European species.—**sow one's wild oats,** to perform youthful excesses or indiscretions.

wild ol·ive, *n.* The wild variety of the olive, *Olea europaea oleaster.* Also *oleaster.*

wild pan·sy, *n.* A common European violet, *Viola tricolor,* the uncultivated form of the garden pansy. Also **John·ny-jump-up.**

wild pink, *n. Bot.* a small plant, *Silene caroliniana,* of the pink family, growing wild in the southeastern U.S. and bearing five-petaled pink flowers.

wild pitch, *n. Baseball,* an errant pitch that allows a base runner to advance and that, in the judgment of the official scorer, could not have been caught by the catcher. Compare *passed ball.*

wild rice, *n.* An aquatic, tall grass, *Zizania aquatica,* found in N. America and having a grain which is edible.

wild rye, *n. Bot.* any of the grasses of the genus *Elymus,* somewhat resembling rye.

wild type, *n. Biol.* an organism in its typical or natural form in the wild state, as distinguished from mutants.

wild va·nil·la, *n. Bot.* a plant in the composite family, *Trilisa odoratissima,* of the southeastern U.S., bearing leaves with a persistent vanillalike fragrance.

Wild West, *n.* The western U.S., esp. when it was unruly frontier territory.

wild·wood, wīld′wụd″, *n.* Natural or wild woods or forest land.

wile, wīl, *n.* [O.E. *wile, wil,* wile; Icel. *vél, vael,* artifice, craft, trick; connections doubtful. *Guile* is the same word, but has come to us directly from the French.] A trick or stratagem practiced for ensnaring or deceiving; an enticing artifice; guile or cunning.—*v.t.*—*wiled, wiling.* To draw or turn away, as by diverting the mind; to pass leisurely or divertingly, as time, followed by *away.*—**wil·i·ly,** *adv.*—**wil·i·ness,** *n.*—**wil·y,** *a.*—*wilier, wiliest.* Crafty; cunning.

will, wil, *aux. v.*—past *would;* archaic second person sing. pres. *wilt;* archaic second person sing. past *wouldst.* [O.E. *willan* (past *wolde*) = D. *willen* = O.H.G. *wellan* (G. *wollen*) = Icel. *vilja* = Goth. *wiljan,* wish, will; akin to L. *velle,* wish, will.] Used before the infinitive or with the infinitive understood. Used to express futurity, as: We *will* arrive tomorrow. Used to express inevitability, as: People *will* talk. Used to express disposition or willingness, as: I *will* go if you do. Used to express determination or insistence, as: You *will* go, if I have to drag you by the ears. Used to express customary or frequent activity, as: He *will* write for hours at a time. Used to express capability, as: This car *will* go eighty miles an hour. Used to express probability, as: I think this *will* be my brother at the door.—*v.t., v.i.* To wish or desire; to like, as: Go where you *will.*

will, wil, *n.* [O.E. *willa.*] The faculty or power of conscious and esp. of deliberate action; the act, experience, or process of exercising this power or faculty; choice; wish; desire; volition; process or determination; self-control; emphatic determination; inclination; disposition toward another or others; discretionary or arbitrary power. *Law,* a legal declaration of a person's wishes as to the disposition of his property after his death; the document containing such a declaration; a testament. *Archaic,* command; request.—*v.t.* To purpose, determine on, or elect by act of will; to

choose; to decide upon or ordain; to influence by exerting will power; to give by will or testament; to bequeath. *Archaic,* to wish; to desire.—*v.i.* To exercise the will; to determine, decide, or ordain, as by act of will; to choose.—**at will,** as one wishes or desires; at one's pleasure, option, or discretion; at one's command.—**will·a·ble,** wil′a·bl, *a.*

willed, wild, *a.* Having a will, usu. used in compounds; as, strong-*willed.*

wil·lem·ite, wil′e·mīt″, *n.* [From *Willem* (William) I, king of the Netherlands 1815-40.] A mineral, Zn_2SiO_4, a native silicate of zinc, occurring in hexagonal prisms or granular masses, and varying much in color.

wil·let, wil′it, *n. pl.* **wil·lets, wil·let.** [Imit. of its cry.] A large N. American bird, *Catoptrophorus semipalmatus,* of the sandpiper family, having a distinct black and white pattern on the wings.

will·ful, wil·ful, wil′ful, *a.* Governed by one's own will without yielding to reason; obstinate, unyielding, or exceptionally stubborn; headstrong; done by design, or intentional; as, *willful* murder; voluntary.—**will·ful·ly,** *adv.*—**will·ful·ness,** *n.*

wil·lies, wil′ēz, *n. pl. Slang.* Uneasiness; nervousness; the jitters or creeps, usu. preceded by *the.*

will·ing, wil′ing, *a.* Having the mind inclined, or consenting; as, *willing* to go home; not averse; desirous or ready; as, a *willing* employee; compliant; gladly or readily borne, done, or accepted; voluntary; relating or pertaining to the power or process of choice; volitional.—**will·ing·ly,** *adv.*—**will·ing·ness,** *n.*

wil·li·waw, wil·ly·waw, wil′i·wạ″, *n.* A sudden strong blast of cold air blowing seaward off coastal mountains, esp. found in the Magellan Strait.

will-less, wil′lis, *a.* Lacking or not exerting the will or will power; involuntary.

will-o'-the-wisp, wil′o·THe·wisp′, *n.* [Cf. *wisp,* in the sense of 'torch' or 'candle,' also *jack-o'-lantern.*] The ignis fatuus; anything that deludes or misleads.—**will·o'-the-wisp·ish,** *a.*

wil·low, wil′ō, *n.* [O.E. *welig, wilig,* D. *wilg,* L.G. *wilge,* a willow.] A shrub or tree of the genus *Salix,* and belonging to the willow family, *Salicaceae,* typically having pliable branches used for a variety of purposes, as basketmaking; the wood of a willow; *colloq.* that which is made from the wood of a willow, esp. a cricket or baseball bat. A machine consisting essentially of a cylinder armed with spikes revolving within a spiked casing, for opening and cleaning cotton or other fiber; also *willower, willy.*—*v.t.* To treat, as fibers, with the willow.—**wil·low·er,** *n.* A machine or some person who willows.—**wil·low·ish,** *a.*—**wil·low··like,** *a.*

wil·low herb, *n.* Any perennial herb of the genus *Epilobium,* belonging to the evening-primrose family, esp. *E. angustifolium* having pinkish-purple flowers and long, willowlike leaves; a species of loosestrife, *Lythrum salicaria,* having purple flowers.

wil·low oak, *n.* An oak, *Quercus phellos,* of the eastern U.S., with narrow, lanceolate leaves suggesting those of the willow.

wil·low pat·tern, *n.* A well-known design, usu. in white and blue, used on stoneware and porcelain dishes, and originating in 1780 in England in imitation of a Chinese design which includes a bridge and a willow tree.

wil·low·ware, wil′ō·wâr″, *n.* China having the willow pattern on it as decoration.

wil·low·y, wil′ō·ē, *a.* Abounding with willows; resembling a willow; slender and graceful; pliant.

will pow·er, *n.* Strength of mind; determination; resoluteness; self-control.

---

ch- chain, G. na*ch*t;   **th-** THen, thin;   **w-** wig, hw as sound in whig;   **z-** zh as in azure, zeal.   *Italicized vowel* indicates schwa sound.

wil·ly, wil′ē, *n.* pl. **wil·lies.** A machine for cleaning and opening fiber, as cotton. See *willow.*—*v.t.*—**willied, willying.** To willow.

wil·ly-nil·ly, wil′ē-nil′ē, *adv.* [For *will he, nill he.*] Willingly or unwillingly, as: She'll have to go *willy-nilly.*—*a.* Shilly-shallying; vacillating; indecisive; irresolute.

wilt, wilt, *v.i.* [Altered form of *welk.*] To become limp and drooping, as a fading flower; to wither; *fig.* to lose strength, vigor, assurance, or courage.—*v.t.* To cause to wilt.—*n.* The action of wilting or the condition of being wilted; languor. *Pathol.* any of a number of plant diseases, often caused by a fungus, characterized by a wilting and a loss or turgidity of the leaves due to faulty or inadequate absorption of moisture; a virus in some caterpillars causing shriveling and liquefaction of the body; also **wilt dis·ease.**

Wil·ton, wil′ton, *n.* [From *Wilton*, town in southern England, where such carpet was first made.] A kind of carpet woven like Brussels carpet but having the loops cut to form a velvet pile. Also **Wil·ton car·pet, Wil·ton rug.**

Wilt·shire, wilt′shēr, wilt′shēr, *n.* A sheep of an English breed having a pure-white fleece, a long head, and horns that curve spirally.

wim·ble, wim′bl, *n.* [Same (with inserted *b*) as Sc. *wimmle* or *wummle*, Dan. *vimmel*, an auger; akin D. *wemelen*, to bore, *weme*, an auger; Sw. *wimla*, G. *wimmeln*, to be in tremulous movement. *Gimlet* is a dim. form.] An instrument used for boring holes, as the gimlet, auger, brace, or bit; a device used to remove rubbish from any hole that is bored, as in mining.—*v.t.*—**wimbled, wimbling.** To bore using or as if using a wimble.

wim·ple, wim′pl, *n.* [O.E. *winpel*, a wimple = D. *wimpel*, Icel. *vimpill*, Dan. *vimpel*, G. *wimpel*, a pennon; perh. akin to *whip, gimp.*] A woman's cloth headdress laid in plaits over the head and around the chin, sides of the face, and neck, orig. used as outdoor wear and commonly worn by nuns. —*v.t.*—**wimpled, wimpling.** To cover, as with a veil or wimple; to veil; to fold or lay in plaits; to make to ripple, as water.—*v.i.* To lie or fall in plaits; to undulate or ripple; as, a brook that *wimples.*

win, win, *v.i.*—**won, winning.** [O.E. *winnan*, labor, strive, suffer (*gewinnan* = G. *gewinnen*, gain, win), = O.H.G. *winnan*, strive = Icel. *vinna*, labor, suffer, gain, win, = Goth. *winnan*, suffer: cf. Skt. *van-*, hold dear, desire, seek, get, win.] To gain the victory; as, to *win* in a context; so succeed in attaining some specified end or state by striving or effort, sometimes followed by *out*; to get, often used with *in, out, through, to*, or the like.—*v.t.* To get by effort, as through labor, competition, or conquest; to gain, as a livelihood, prize, stake, or fame; to be successful in, as a game or battle; to make, as one's way, as by effort, ability, or the like; to attain or reach, as a point or goal; as, to *win* the summit of a mountain; to gain, as favor, love, sympathy, consent, or the heart, as by qualities or influence; to gain the favor, regard, or adherence of; to bring to favor or consent, often followed by *over*; as, to *win over* persons opposed to a plan; persuade; to persuade to love or marriage, or gain in marriage. *Min.* to take out, as ore or coal; to prepare, as a vein, bed, or mine, for working, as by means of shafts.—*n.* An act of winning; a success; a victory, as in a game; profit or winnings; first place position in some race, esp. a horse race: distinguished from *place, show.* —**win·na·ble**, *a.*

wince, wins, *v.i.*—**winced, wincing.** [Formerly also *winch*, < O.Fr. *guinchir, guenchir, winchir* (?), < O.G. *wenken*, to start

aside. Akin to *wink.*] To recoil or flinch, as in pain; to shrink or start back, esp. suddenly.—*n.* The act of one who winces; a sudden start.—**winc·er**, *n.*

winch, winch, *n.* [O.E. *wince*, a winch, a reel for thread; akin *vince, wink, winkle.*] A hoisting machine in which a cylinder, as a drum or barrel, is turned by a crank so that a rope or chain winding around it raises a weight; windlass; a crank having a handle and used for turning an axle, as to operate a grindstone.—*v.t.* To move or hoist with or as with a winch.—**winch·er**, *n.*

wind, wind, *n.* [O.E. *wind* = D. and G. *wind*, Dan. and Sw. *vind*, Icel. *vindr*, Goth. *winds*; cogn. L. *ventus*, W. *gwynt*, wind. The root is in Goth. *waian*, Skt. *vâ*, to blow. *Weather* is from same root.] Air naturally in motion, esp. in a horizontal flow; a current of air; air artificially put in motion, as from a fan; a current of air coming from a particular direction, as from one of the four cardinal points of the compass; the direction from which it comes; a fast-moving, damaging flow of air, as a tornado or gale; a current of air conveying a scent, as of some animal or person; the power of respiration; breath; empty or idle utterance; conceit; intestinal gas. *Pl.* the wind instruments in an orchestra; the players of these instruments.—*v.t.* To detect and follow the scent of; to expose to the wind, as for drying; to make short of breath; to allow recovery of breath, as by resting.—**get wind of**, *colloq.* to hear or learn of.—**have or get the wind up**, *colloq.* to become alarmed, excited, or upset.—**how the wind blows**, *colloq.* public tendencies or opinion.—**in the wind**, *colloq.* afoot, or about to happen. —**sail close to the wind**, to sail directly into the wind; to be frugal or economical; to take a foolish risk.

wind, wind, *v.i.*—**wound** or rare **winded, winding.** [O.E. *windan* = D. and G. *winden* = Icel. *vinda* = Goth. *-windan*, wind: cf. *wend.*] To change direction; to bend or turn; to take a frequently bending course; to meander; to have a circular or spiral course or direction; to coil or twine about something, as: A vine *winds* around a pole. To be twisted or warped, as a board; to proceed circuitously or indirectly; to undergo winding, or winding up, as a clock. —*v.t.* To bend or turn about; as, to *wind* a ship to reverse its position; to encircle or wreathe, as with something twined, wrapped, or placed about; to roll or coil, as thread onto a spool; to bring out of a rolled or coiled state, usu. followed by *off* or *from*; to twine, fold, wrap, or place about something; to adjust, as a mechanism, for operation by some turning or coiling process, often followed by *up*; as, to *wind up* a clock; to haul or hoist by means of a winch, windlass, or the like, often followed by *up*; to make, as one's or its way, in a winding or frequently bending course; to make, as the way, by indirect or insidious methods; as, to *wind* his way into another's personal business.—*n.* A winding; a bend or turn; a twist producing an uneven surface.— **wind·a·ble**, *a.*

wind, wind, wind, *v.t.*—**winded** or **wound, winding.** [< *wind*, the noun, pronounced as *wind*; the strong conjugation has been introduced through confusion with *wind*, to twist.] To blow, as a horn; to sound by blowing.

wind·age, win′dij, *n.* The influence of the wind in deflecting a bullet or other missile; the amount or extent of such deflection; the amount of adjustment necessary to a gunsight to compensate for wind deflection; a difference between the diameter of a projectile and that of the gunbore, for the escape of gas and the prevention of friction; the air friction against a mechanism in

motion; the disturbance of air caused by any fast-moving object; *naut.* that portion of a vessel's surface upon which the wind acts.

wind·bag, wind′bag″, *n. Colloq.* a voluble, pretentious talker who communicates little of real worth or interest.

wind·blown, wind′blōn″, *a.* Blown or scattered by the wind; shaped or growing in a certain way due to prevailing winds, as trees; denoting a woman's hairstyle in which the hair is cut short and brushed forward.

wind·bound, wind′bound″, *a.* Detained by contrary or high-velocity winds, as a ship or sailboat.

wind·break, wind′brāk″, *n.* A growth of trees, a fence, or a similar protective structure serving as a shelter from the wind.

Wind·break·er, wind′brā″kėr, *n.* A short jacket of tightly-woven fabric or leather with elastic hip band and cuffs, and usu. having a collar, worn outdoors in cold weather. (Trademark.)

wind-brok·en, wind′brō″ken, *a. Veter. pathol.* Having impaired breathing, as a horse; affected with heaves.

wind·burn, wind′burn″, *n.* Skin discoloration or inflammation caused by excessive wind exposure.—**wind·burned**, *a.*

wind cone, wind′kōn″, *n.* Windsock.

wind·ed, win′did, *a.* Out of breath.

wind·er, win′dėr, *n.* One who or that which winds yarn or the like; an instrument or machine for winding; a twining or coiling plant; any winding staircase step; a key, appliance, or knob used to wind a spring.

wind·fall, wind′fal″, *n.* Fruit or timber, blown down by the wind; an unexpected legacy or piece of good fortune.

wind-flaw, wind′fla″, *n.* A strong wind that comes without warning; a gust.

wind·flow·er, wind′flou″ėr, *n.* Any plant of the genus *Anemone*; an anemone.

wind·gall, wind′gal″, *n. Veter. pathol.* a soft tumor or swelling on the fetlock joint of a horse.—**wind·galled**, *a.*

wind gap, wind′gap″, *n.* An indentation in a mountain crest without the depth necessary for a stream.

wind harp, wind′härp″, *n.* Aeolian harp.

wind·hov·er, wind′huv″ėr, wind′hov″ėr, *n. Ornith.* the kestrel.

wind·ing, win′ding, *n.* A turn, curve, or bend, as of a path or road; a spiral; a coiling of some material around an object; one such complete turn; the action of one who or that which winds. *Elect.* a conducting wire wound into a coil; the way or manner in which it is wound.—*a.* Having curves or bends; twisting, as a road or river; spiral, as a stairway.

wind·ing sheet, *n.* A sheet in which a corpse is wrapped; a shroud.

wind in·stru·ment, wind′in″stru·ment, *n. Mus.* an instrument played by breath or air, as the flute, horn, or organ.

wind·jam·mer, wind′jam″ėr, win′jam″ėr, *n. Naut.* a sailing ship or one of its crew; *slang*, a loquacious or chatty person.

wind·lass, wind′las, *n.* [Partly < D. *windas*, or Icel. *vindass*, lit. 'winding-beam'; partly < O.E. *windle*, a wheel or reel, a dim. < the verb to *wind.*] A hoisting or hauling apparatus, operated mechanically or by hand, consisting of a horizontal barrel or drum on which is wound the rope or chain attached to the object to be raised or moved.—*v.t.* To raise or move with a windlass.

win·dle·straw, win′dl·stra″, win′l·stra″, *n.* [O.E. *windelstreow*, prop. straw for plaiting, < *windel*, a basket, < *windan*, to wind.] *Brit. dial.* A name given to various species of grasses; a stalk of grass, esp. a dried one used in making baskets or ropes; any weak or slender person or thing.

wind·mill, wind'mil", *n.* A mill or similar machine for grinding or pumping, operated by the wind acting on a set of arms, vanes, sails, or slats attached to a horizontal axis so as to form a revolving wheel; something resembling or similar to a windmill. An imaginary opponent, wrong, or evil, in allusion to the adventure of Cervantes' Don Quixote who attacked windmills which he mistook for giants, used usu. in the phrases 'to fight windmills' or 'to tilt at windmills.'

win·dow, win'dō, *n.* [M.E. *windowe, windoge,* < Scand.: cf. Icel. *vindauga,* window, lit. 'wind-eye'.] An opening in the wall of a building, the cabin of a boat, or the like, for the admission of air or light, or both, commonly fitted with a frame in which are set movable sashes containing panes of glass; such an opening together with the frame, sashes, and panes of glass, or any other device, by which it is closed; the frame, sashes, and panes of glass, or the like, intended to fit such an opening; a windowpane; a section of an envelope which is transparent, through which the address is seen; *aerospace,* the code name for strips of metal or metal foil dropped from aircraft as a radar jamming device.—*v.t.* To furnish with a window or windows.

win·dow box, *n.* A box for growing plants, placed at or in a window; one of the hollows at the sides of a window frame for the weights counterbalancing the sash.

win·dow dress·ing, *n.* Merchandise attractively displayed in a shop window or the art of arranging this merchandise; a statement or action made with the intention of giving unfavorable facts an attractive appearance.—**win·dow dress·er,** *n.*

win·dow·pane, win'dō·pān", *n.* One of the plates of glass used in a window.

win·dow seat, *n.* A seat built beneath a recessed or other window.

win·dow shade, *n.* A covering for a window, usu. made of sturdy treated paper or cloth attached to a spring roller.

win·dow-shop, win'dō·shop", *v.i.—window-shopped, window-shopping.* To gaze at articles in the windows of shops, instead of going in to do actual shopping.—**win·dow-shop·per,** *n.*

win·dow sill, *n.* The sill beneath a window.

wind·pipe, wind'pīp", *n.* The trachea.

wind-pol·li·nat·ed, wind'pol"*i*·nā"tid, *a. Bot.* pollinated by pollen carried on air currents.

wind·proof, wind'prōf", *a.* Resistant to the wind; as, a *windproof* jacket.

wind rose, wind'rōz", *n.* A diagram showing relative frequency and average strength of winds from different directions in a given area, sometimes showing the average relation between wind direction and the occurrence of other meteorological phenomena.

wind·row, wind'rō", win'rō", *n.* A row or line of hay raked together to dry before being made into cocks or heaps; any similar row, as of sheaves of grain, made for the purpose of drying; a row of dry leaves or dust, swept together by the wind; a deep, narrow channel or furrow dug for planting.—*v.t.* To arrange in a windrow or windrows. —**wind·row·er,** *n.*

wind scale, wind'skāl", *n.* A scale in numbers or descriptive terms for indicating the relative strength of the wind, as the Beaufort scale.

wind-screen, wind'skrēn", win'skrēn", *n. Brit.* windshield.

wind shake, wind'shāk", *n.* A flaw in wood supposed to be caused by the action of strong winds upon the trunk of the tree; such flaws collectively. Also *cup shake.*— **wind-shak·en,** wind'shā"ken, *a.*

wind·shield, wind'shēld", win'shēld", *n.* A framed shield of glass, in one or more sections, projecting above the dashboard of an automobile; also *Brit.* wind-screen. Any shield or protection against the force of the wind.

wind·sock, wind'sok", *n.* A tapered sleeve-like device made of cloth, pivoted at one end from a standard so that the wind catches it, showing the wind direction. Also *air sleeve, air sock, wind cone, wind sleeve.*

Wind·sor chair, win'zėr chār', *n.* A strong, plain chair, popular in the 18th century, made entirely of wood, with outward-slanting legs and a spindle back.

Wind·sor knot, win'zėr not', *n.* A wide, rather loose knot used in tying a four-in-hand necktie.

Wind·sor tie, win'zėr tī', *n.* A wide necktie, usu. of black silk cut on the bias, loosely tied in a bow.

wind sprint, wind'sprint", *n.* A sprint run as an exercise to develop the capacity to maintain normal breathing during strenuous exertion, esp. in an athletic event.

wind·storm, wind'stȧrm", *n.* A storm with strong wind, but little or no precipitation.

wind-suck·ing, wind'suk"ing, *n. Veter. pathol.* a harmful habit in which a horse swallows large amounts of air while biting on its manger. Also *cribbing, crib-biting.*— **wind·suck·er,** wind'suk"ėr, *n.*

wind-swept, wind'swept", *a.* Exposed or subjected to the wind.

wind tee, wind'tē", *n.* A large weather vane, in the form of a T, usu. found on or close to an airfield.

wind tun·nel, wind'tun"el, *n. Aeron.* a long chamber through which air may be forced at selected velocities to test the aerodynamic properties of objects, as airplane parts, models, or the like.

wind up, wind up, *v.t.—wound up, winding up.* To wind; to bring to a conclusion or final settlement.—*v.i.* To come to a conclusion or final settlement; *baseball,* to swing the arm preparatory to delivering a pitch; *colloq.* to arrive at a particular place or in a particular condition or situation.— **wind·up,** wind'up", *n.* The act of bringing to a conclusion or end; a final or concluding part or act; *baseball,* the preliminary arm and body movements prior to pitching a ball.

wind·ward, wind'wėrd, *n.* The point or direction from which the wind blows.—*a.* Being on the side toward which the wind blows.—*adv.* Toward the wind: opposed to *leeward.*—**to wind·ward,** in a favorable position.

wind·way, wind'wā", *n.* An air passage, as for ventilation; airway.

wind·y, win'dē, *a.—windier, windiest.* Abounding in or characterized by wind; windswept or laid open to the wind; resembling the wind; empty or with little substance; verbose or prone to inflated and pretentious talk; producing or characterized by flatulence.—**wind·i·ly,** *adv.*— **wind·i·ness,** *n.*

wine, wīn, *n.* [O.E. *wīn,* < L. *vinum,* wine, grapes, the vine, akin to Gr. *oînos,* wine, *oinē,* the vine.] The fermented juice of the grape, containing up to 15 per cent alcohol by volume, used as a beverage and in cooking; the juice, fermented or unfermented, of various other fruits or plants, used as a beverage; a dark red color, as of some red wines; *fig.* something that invigorates, cheers, or intoxicates like wine; *phar.* vinum.—*v.t.—wined, wining.* To supply or entertain with wine, usu. in the phrase *wine and dine,* as: He *wined and dined* his visiting relatives.—*v.i.* To drink wine.

wine cel·lar, *n.* A cellar or other storage place for wine; wines, stored or stocked.

wine-cool·er, wīn'kö"lėr, *n.* An ornamental bucket or similar container used for chilling a bottle of wine.

wine·glass, wīn'glas", wīn'gläs", *n.* A small stemmed glass from which wine is drunk.

wine-grow·er, wīn'grō"ėr, *n.* One who cultivates a vineyard and makes wine.

wine palm, *n.* Any of several palm trees from whose sap palm wine is made.

wine press, *n.* A machine in which the juice is pressed out of grapes. Also **wine press·-er.**

win·er·y, wī'ne·rē, *n.* pl. **win·er·ies.** An establishment for making wine.

wine·shop, wīn'shop", *n.* A shop or tavern where wine is sold.

wine·skin, wīn'skin", *n.* A vessel made of the nearly complete skin of a goat, hog, or the like, and used, esp. in the East, for holding wine.

wine-tast·er, wīn'tās"tėr, *n.* One who judges the quality of wine by tasting it.

wing, wing, *n.* [M.E. *winge, wenge,* prob. < Scand: cf. Icel. *vaengr,* Sw. and Dan. *vinge, wing.*] Either of the two anterior extremities or appendages of the scapular arch or shoulder girdle of most birds and of bats, which constitute the forelimbs and correspond to the human arms, but are adapted for flight; either of two corresponding but functionless parts in certain other birds; any of various analogous but structurally different appendages, by means of which insects fly; something resembling or likened to a wing, as a vane or sail of a windmill; a means or instrument of flight, travel, or progress; the act or manner of flying; a faction or group within a political party or other organized body. *Bot.* any leaflike expansion, as of a samara; one of the two side petals of a papilionaceous flower. *Arch.* a part of a building projecting on one side of, or subordinate to, a central or main part; *aeron.* that portion of a main supporting surface confined to one side of an airplane; *milit.* either of the two side portions of an army or fleet, usu. called right wing and left wing, and distinguished from the center; *furniture,* a projecting sidepiece at the top of an armchair; *colloq.* an arm of a human being, esp. the arm used for pitching in baseball. *Theatr.* the platform or space on either side of the stage proper; one of the long, narrow side pieces of scenery. *Sports,* a player or position on either side of the center position or line; *anat.* an ala, or wing of the nose; *Brit.* a fender of an automotive vehicle.—*v.t.* To equip with wings; to enable to fly; to transport on or as on wings; to traverse in flight; to supply with a winglike part; to wound or disable the wing of; to wound superficially.—*v.i.* To travel on or as on wings; to fly.—**on the wing,** in flight or motion.—**take wing,** to fly; depart hurriedly.—**un·der one's wing,** under one's care or protection.—**wing·like,** *a.*

wing and wing, *adv. Naut.* with a sail fully extended on each side.

wing·back, wing'bak", *n. Football.* An offensive back positioned behind or outside of an end in some formations; the position played by such a back.

wing·bow, wing'bō", *n. Ornith.* a distinctive marking or coloration on the bend of a bird's wing.

wing case, *n. Entom.* The hard case which covers the wings of beetles and some other insects; the elytron. Also **wing cov·er.**

wing chair, *n.* A large, completely upholstered armchair having winglike, projecting side pieces.

wing cov·erts, *n. pl. Ornith.* the feathers which cover the bases of the quill feathers of the wing in birds.

wing-ding, wing'ding", *n. Slang,* a large social gathering or celebration, usu. on an elaborate scale, marked by the loud merry-making of the participants. Also *whing-ding.*

---

winged, wingd, *poetic* wing′id, *a.* Having wings; swift; rapid; passing quickly; lofty; *bot.* having winglike parts; as, a *winged* seed.

wing-foot·ed, wing′fut″id, *a.* Having winged feet; rapid; swift.

wing·less, wing′lis, *a.* Having imperfectly developed or no wings.—**wing·less·ness**, *n.*

wing·let, wing′lit, *n.* A little wing; the bastard wing of a bird.

wing load·ing, *n. Aeron.* the stress analysis of an airplane, arrived at by dividing the gross weight by the wing area. Also **wing load**.

wing nut, *n.* A type of nut which has two small wings which can be easily gripped by the finger and thumb.

wing·o·ver, wing′ō″vėr, *n. Avi.* a maneuver in which an airplane is put into a climbing turn until almost stalled, the nose then being allowed to fall, followed by a halfroll, but returning to normal flight after the ensuing dive in an approximately reverse direction from that in which the maneuver was begun.

wings, wingz, *n. pl. Avi.* a metal emblem or badge, worn on the uniform, consisting of spread silver wings bearing distinctive center designs signifying a particular rating or flight service. Also **a·vi·a·tion badge**.

wing shoot·ing, *n.* The practice or action of shooting at flying birds or other flying targets.

wing·span, wing′span″, *n.* The overall distance from wing tip to wing tip, as of an airplane.

wing·spread, wing′spred″, *n.* The distance between the outermost extremities of the wings, when fully extended, of a bird, other winged creature, or airplane; wingspan.

wing tip, *n.* A cap covering the toe of a shoe, sometimes with a perforated design, having a center point and extending back along the sides to the shank; a shoe having such a tip.

wing·y, wing′ē, *a.*—**wingier, wingiest**. Having or resembling wings; swift.

wink, wingk, *v.i.* [O.E. *wincian*, to wink; akin to *wancol*, unsteady; D. *winken*, *wenken*, Icel. *vanka*, to wink; Dan. *vinke*, Sw. *vinka*, to wink or nod; G. *winken*, to beckon; root perh. same as in *weak*, G. *weichen*, to yield or turn aside. Akin *wince*, *winch*.], To close and open one eyelid rapidly, as in a signal or hint; to close and open the eyelids quickly and involuntarily; to blink; to gleam or twinkle.—*v.t.* To close and open rapidly, as an eye or the eyes; to convey or signify by winking; to move or force by winking, followed by *away* or *back*; as, to *wink away* the tears.—*n.* The act of winking; the time necessary for winking; an instant; a hint or signal conveyed by winking; *colloq.* a brief nap.—**wink at**, to ignore deliberately, as corruption or connivance.

wink·er, wing′kėr, *n.* One who winks; a blinder used on a horse; a blinker; *colloq.* an eyelash or an eye.

win·kle, wing′kl, *n.* [Appar. an abbr. of *periwinkle*.] Any of various marine gastropods; a periwinkle.

win·kle, wing′kl, *v.t.*—**winkled, winkling**. To extract, remove, or expel, usu. followed by *out*, as: The test run *winkled out* the defects in the engine.

win·ner, win′ėr, *n.* One who wins; a champion or victor.

win·ner's cir·cle, *n.* A small space or enclosure at racetracks where, after a race, the winning horse and jockey are presented with awards and photographed.

win·ning, win′ing, *n.* The act of one who wins; *usu. pl.* the sum won by success in a contest or competition; as, golf tournament *winnings*. *Min.* a newly opened pit or shaft; any section of a mine ready to be worked. —*a.* Successful in competition with others;

as, a *winning* season; charming or engaging; as a *winning* manner.—**win·ning·ly**, *adv.*

win·now, win′ō, *v.t.* [O.E. *windwian*, akin to *wind*, E. *wind*.] To free, as grain, from chaff or refuse by means of wind or driven air; to fan; to drive or blow, as chaff, away by fanning; to subject to some process of separating or distinguishing; to analyze critically; sift; as, to *winnow* a mass of statements; to separate or distinguish, as good from bad, often followed by *out*; to fan or stir, as the air, as with the wings in flying; to pursue, as a course, with flapping wings in flying.—*v.i.* To free grain from chaff by wind or driven air; to fly with flapping wings; to flutter.—*n.* A device used for winnowing grain; the act of winnowing.—**win·now·er**, *n.*

win·o, wī′nō, *n. pl.* **win·oes, win·os**. *Slang*, one who is constantly drunk from cheap wine.

win·some, win′som, *a.* [O.E. *wynsum*, pleasant, delightful, < *wynn*, delight, joy (akin to *win*), and term. *sum*, later *-some*.] Attractive; agreeable; engaging.—**win·some·ly**, *adv.*—**win·some·ness**, *n.*

win·ter, win′tėr, *n.* [O.E. *winter*, winter = D. and G. *winter*, Sw. and Dan. *winter*, Icel. *vetr*, *vitr* (for *vintr*), Goth. *vintrus*; allied to *wind* or to *wet*.] The cold season of the year, which in the northern latitudes is the period of time between the winter solstice and the vernal equinox, approximately December, January, and February; a time characterized by decline, decay, or cheerlessness; one year of life; as, a woman of seventy *winters*.—*a.* Relating to, or occurring in the winter; of a type that is planted in autumn; as, *winter* wheat.—*v.i.* To spend the winter; as, to *winter* in the South.—*v.t.* To care for or feed during the winter, esp. plants and cattle.—**win·ter·er**, *n.*—**win·ter·ish**, *a.*—**win·ter·less**, *a.*

win·ter ac·o·nite, *n.* A small, low-growing herb of Europe and Asia, *Eranthis hyemalis*, belonging to the buttercup family, often cultivated for its bright yellow flowers, which appear in late winter or early spring.

win·ter·ber·ry, win′tėr·ber″ē, *n. pl.* **win·ter·ber·ries**. Any of several N. American species of holly, genus *Ilex*, with red berries that are persistent through the winter. The N. American evergreen shrub, *Ilex glabra*, of the holly family, having black berries; also *inkberry*.

win·ter·bourne, win′tėr·bōrn″, win′tėr·burn″, *n.* A stream flowing only when the source of water exceeds a certain level due to excessive rainfall, chiefly in winter.

win·ter crook·neck, *n.* A squash, *Cucurbita moschata*, having a long, curving neck, maturing late in the autumn.

win·ter floun·der, *n.* A food fish, *Pseudopleuronectes americanus*, found on the Atlantic coast of N. America.

win·ter·green, win′tėr·grēn″, *n.* A N. American evergreen shrub, *Gaultheria procumbens*, of the heath family, having scarlet berries, and yielding a fragrant oil used in confections and medicines; also *checkerberry*. Any of several somewhat similar plants of the heath family.

win·ter·ize, win′te·rīz″, *v.t.*—**winterized, winterizing**. To equip or put in readiness for cold winter weather, as a car, by adding an antifreeze to the contents of the radiator.—**win·ter·i·za·tion**, win″te·ri·zā′shan *n.*

win·ter·kill, win′tėr·kil″, *v.t.*, *v.i.* To kill by or die from exposure to the cold of winter, as wheat.—*n.*

win·ter·ly, win′tėr·lē, *a.* Wintry; cheerless.

win·ter mel·on, *n.* A large, sweet, edible muskmelon, *Cucumis melo inodorus*, which keeps well in cold weather.

win·ter squash, *n.* Any of several squashes of the genus *Cucurbita*, as *C. maxima*, which

ripen in late autumn, esp. the varieties Hubbard and Boston Marrow.

win·ter·tide, win′tėr·tīd″, *n. Poet.* the winter season.

win·try, win′trē, *a.*—**wintrier, wintriest**. Suitable to or characteristic of winter; brumal; cold; stormy; bleak or cheerless. Also **win·ter·y**, win′te·rē.—**win·tri·ly**, *adv.*—**win·tri·ness**, *n.*

win·y, wī′nē, *a.*—**winier, winiest**. Of the nature of or resembling wine.

winze, winz, *n.* [Icel. *vinza*, to winnow, < *vindr*, wind.] *Min.* a small shaft, often inclined, sunk from one level to another.

wipe, wīp, *v.t.*—**wiped, wiping**. [O.E. *wīpian*, wipe: cf. *wisp*.] To rub lightly, as a surface, with a cloth, towel, paper, or the hand, in order to clean or dry; to remove by rubbing with or on something, usu. followed by *away* or *off*; as, to *wipe away* tears; to blot out, as from existence or memory; to rub or draw, as something, over a surface, as in cleaning or drying. *Plumbing*, to apply, as solder, by spreading with a pad of leather or cloth; to form, as a joint, in this manner. —*n.* The act or an act of wiping; a rub, as of one thing over another; *colloq.* a gibe; *slang*, a handkerchief; *mach.* a wiper.—**wipe out**, to completely destroy; *slang*, to murder.

wip·er, wī′pėr, *n.* One who or that which wipes; that with which anything is wiped, as a towel or handkerchief; *mach.* a projecting piece, as on a rotating axis, acting on another part, esp. for the purpose of raising it so that it may fall by its own weight; *elect.* a moving part in an electrical device that serves as a contact with the terminals.

wire, wīėr, *n.* [O.E. *wir* = L.G. *wire*, Icel. *virr*, Dan. *vire*, wire; allied to L. *viriae*, bracelets; of same root as *wind*, to twist, *withe*.] A flexible thread of metal; a fine, slender filament or metal rod of various thicknesses or lengths; such metal threads collectively; a cable; a telegraph or telephone wire; the wire or cable used to transmit electricity; *colloq.* a telegram. Something made of wire, as a fence, a snare, a cage, or the like; the wire over the finish line at a racetrack; the metal screen used in a papermaking machine; *pl.* the network of wires used in operating puppets.—*a.* Of or resembling wire.—*v.t.*—**wired, wiring**. To bind or fasten with wire; to equip with wire. *Colloq.* to send by telegraph; to send a telegram to.—*v.i. Colloq.* to telegraph.— **pull wires**, *colloq.* to use devious and secret means to influence or control others.— **un·der the wire**, *colloq.* at the very last moment.—**wir·a·ble**, *a.*—**wire·like**, *a.*

wire cloth, *n.* A fabric or mesh of fine, woven wire used in the manufacture of paper, and in making strainers, screens, and the like.

wire coat, *n.* The coarse, thick, outer hair of many breeds of dogs.

wired, wīėrd, *a.* Of or constructed with wire; fastened or bound with wire; equipped with wire, as for electrical use; supported or reinforced with wire, as an article of furniture.

wire·draw, wīėr′drạ″, *v.t.*—past *wiredrew*, pp. *wiredrawn*, ppr. *wiredrawing*. To form, as metal, into wire by forcibly pulling through a series of holes, each decreasing in size; to draw or spin out, as a discussion, to great length and excessive detail.—**wire·draw·er**, *n.*

wire·draw·ing, wīėr′drạ″ing, *n.* The act or art of extending ductile metals into wire; the practice of drawing out an argument or discussion by useless distinctions or digressions.

wire·drawn, wīėr′drạn″, *a.* Lengthened or drawn out, as a wire; subtly or excessively refined; lengthy; intricately detailed.

wire gauge, *n.* A standard set of sizes for measuring the diameter of wire; a plate or disk edged with various-sized notches for determining wire diameter.

wire gauze, *n.* A stiff closely woven fabric made of fine wire.

wire glass, *n.* Glass having wire netting embedded within it to increase its strength.

wire grass, *n. Bot.* a European meadow grass, *Poa compressa*, with wiry culms, naturalized in N. America; any of various similar grasses.

wire-haired, wīer′hârd″, *a.* Having coarse, stiff, wirelike hair; as, a *wire-haired* terrier. **—wire·hair,** wīer′hâr″, *n.* A wire-haired or fox terrier, whose hair is stiff, wiry, and coarse; also **wire-haired ter·ri·er.**

wire-haired point·ing grif·fon, *n.* A medium-sized European-bred dog, having a coarse, wiry grey coat, used in hunting birds.

wire·less, wīer′lis, *a.* Having no wire; operated without a wire or wires, esp. pertaining to telegraph or telephone systems, in which signals are transmitted through space by electromagnetic waves; *Brit.* radio.—*n.* Wireless telegraphy or telephony; a wireless telegraph or telephone; a wireless message; *Brit.* a radio set.—*v.t.*, *v.i.* To communicate with by wireless.

wire·less te·leg·ra·phy, *n.* Telegraphy by electromagnetic waves.

wire·less tel·e·phone, *n.* Radiotelephone.

wire·man, wīer′man, *n. pl.* **wire·men.** A man who installs or repairs wire, as for a telegraph, telephone, or electric power system; a lineman.

wire net·ting, *n.* A fine wire mesh or netting used for light fencing, screens, and the like.

Wire·pho·to, wīer′fō″tō, *n. pl.* **Wire·pho·tos.** A machine and process by which photographs are reproduced by electric signals transmitted over great distances by wire; a photograph produced by this process. (Trademark.)—*v.t.* (*l.c.*) to transmit by Wirephoto.

wire·pull·er, wīer′pul″ẽr, *n.* One who pulls the wires, as of puppets; one who secretly or deviously influences the actions of others; an intriguer.—**wire·pull·ing,** *n.*

wir·er, wīer′ẽr, *n.* A trapper who uses wire snares to catch game; one who wires or uses wire in his work.

wire re·cord·er, *n. Electron.* a machine by which sound is recorded on a moving, magnetized, steel wire, the recorded sound being reproduced as the wire passes through a receiver.—**wire re·cord·ing,** *n.* The act or process of recording on wire; a recording made in this manner.—**wire-re·cord,** *v.t.*

wire rope, *n.* A strong rope made of iron or steel wire twisted together.

wire serv·ice, *n.* An agency for the collection and distribution of news that sends its syndicated copy to subscribers by wire.

wire·tap, wīer′tap″, *v.t.*—**wiretapped, wiretapping.** To connect a monitoring device to, as a telephone or telegraph wire; to monitor, as a telephone conversation, by means of such a device.—*n.* A concealed device connected, as to a telephone or telegraph wire, to intercept information; the act or practice of using a wiretap.—**wire·tap·per,** wīer′tap″ẽr, *n.*—**wire·tap·ping,** *n.*

wire·work, wīer′wûrk″, *n.* An article or fabric made of wire.

wire·works, wīer′wûrks″, *n. pl.*, *sing. or pl. in constr.* A factory or other place in which wire or articles made of wire are manufactured.

wire·worm, wīer′wûrm″, *n.* The slim, hard larva of the click beetle which is destructive to the roots of crops; a millipede.

wir·ing, wīer′ing, *n.* The act of one who wires; an arrangement, system, or aggregate of wires.

wir·ra, wir′a, *interj. Ir.* an outcry of grief or sorrow.

wir·y, wīer′ē, *a.*—**wirier, wiriest.** Made of wire; like wire, as in form, texture, or flexibility; tough; lean and sinewy.— **wir·i·ly,** *adv.*—**wir·i·ness,** *n.*

wis, wis, *v.t.* [A spurious verb form corresponding to *wist* (< *wit*, *v.*), due to misunderstanding of *iwis*, *adv.*] *Archaic*, to know.

wis·dom, wiz′dom, *n.* [O.E. *wisdóm*, < *wis*, and term. *-dóm* = Icel. *vísdómr*, Sw. *visdom*, Dan. *viisdom*.] The quality of being wise; the faculty to discern right and truth and to judge or act accordingly; sound judgment; sagacity; discretion; common sense; extensive knowledge.

wis·dom tooth, *n.* A large back molar, so named because it usu. appears when a person is nearing or has reached adulthood.— cut one's **wis·dom teeth,** to attain maturity.

wise, wīz, *a.*—**wiser, wisest.** [O.E. *wís*, wise, prudent = D. *wijs*, Icel. *viss*, Dan. *viis*, G. *weise*, wise; < same root as *wit*, *wot*, L. *video*, to see. The wise man is therefore the man that sees and knows.] Having the power of discerning and judging correctly; possessed of discernment, judgment, and discretion; prudent; sensible; judicious; sage; having extensive knowledge; learned; shrewd; *slang*, informed or aware of.—*v.t.* —*wised, wising. Slang.* To learn of; to make or become aware of.—**get wise,** *slang.* To learn the true facts; to be sarcastic, bold, or insolent.—**wise up,** *slang.* to become enlightened as to the truth of facts, conditions, or a situation.—**wise·ly,** *adv.*—**wise·ness,** *n.*

wise, wīz, *n.* [O.E. *wíse*, manner = D. *wijs*, Icel. *vís*, *vísa*, Dan. *viis*, G. *weise*; orig., knowledge or known way; akin to *wise*, *a. Guise* is the same word.] Manner; method or way: used in phrases; as, in any *wise*, in no *wise*.—*adv.* Denoting or indicating direction, position, or manner: used in combination; as, gears moving clock*wise*; *colloq.* with reference to: used in combination; as, time*wise*, market*wise*, dollar*wise*.

wise·a·cre, wīz′ā″kẽr, *n.* [Corrupted < G. *weissager*, a soothsayer, < O.H.G. *vizzago*, *vizago*, a seer = O.E. *witega*, a seer, lit. 'one who is wise or knowing'; akin to *wit* and *wise*.] One who makes pretensions to great wisdom.

wise·crack, wīz′krak″, *n. Slang*, a smart or facetious remark.—*v.i. Slang*, to make wisecracks.—**wise·crack·er,** *n.*

wise guy, *n. Slang*, a conceited, smart-aleck person.

wis·en·heim·er, weis·en·heim·er, wī′zen·hī″mẽr, *n.* One who contends he knows everything; wiseacre.

wi·sent, vē′zent, *n.* The European bison, *Bison bonasus.*

wish, wish, *v.t.* [O.E. *wische*, *wusche*, *wýscan*, to wish, < *wúsc*, a wish; D. and G. *wunsch*, a wish; allied to Skt. *van*, to love, *vanchh*, to desire, L. *Venus*, the goddess, *veneror*, to venerate.] To desire or to long for: often used with an infinitive or a clause; as, *wish to be* free; to frame or express desires concerning; to desire, as someone or something, to be as stated; as, to *wish* one well; to invoke upon; as, to *wish* them good luck; to order or command, as: I never *wish* to see you again.—*v.i.* To desire or long, usu. used with *for*; to formulate or make a wish; to wish.—*n.* A desire; a longing; an expression of desire; a request; a petition; the thing desired.—**wish on,** to impose upon, as something undesirable.—**wish·er,** *n.*

wish·bone, wish′bōn″, *n.* [From the belief that the one who, having broken the wishbone with another person, holds the longer piece will have his wish fulfilled.] The forked bone, which is a united pair of clavicles, in front of the breastbone in most birds; the furcula.

wish·ful, wish′ful, *a.* Having a desire; desirous; showing desire; longing.—**wish·ful·ly,** *adv.*—**wish·ful·ness,** *n.*

wish·ful·fill·ment, *n. Psychoanal.* the gratification symbolically of a wish, as the satisfaction in a dream of an unconscious or repressed desire. A gratification of a wish.

wish·ful think·ing, *n.* Interpreting statements, actions, or the like as being what one desires them to be, not as they are in actuality.

wish-wash, wish′wosh″, wish′wash″, *n.* [A reduplication of *wash*, thin or waste liquor.] Any sort of weak, thin drink.

wish·y-wash·y, wish′ē·wosh″ē, wish′ē·wa″shē, *a.* Very thin and weak; diluted; feeble; wanting in substantial qualities or character.

wisp, wisp, *n.* [O.E. *wispe*, *wesp*, *wips*; akin to L.G. *wiep*, *vippa*, a wisp, also to *whip*.] A small bunch of straw or like substance; a thin bunch, tuft, or mass, as of fibrous matter, hair, or smoke; someone or something delicate or tiny; an ignis fatuus or will-o'-the-wisp.—*v.t.* To form or fold into a wisp.—**wisp·ish, wisp·like,** *a.*—**wisp·y,** wis′pē, *a.*—**wispier, wispiest.**

wis·te·ri·a, wis·tēr′ē·a, *n.* [N.L., orig. *Wisteria* (given as genus name), but prop. *Wistaria*; in honor of Caspar *Wistar*, 1761-1818, Amer. anatomist.] Any of the climbing shrubs, genus *Wisteria*, of the legume family, with pendent racemes of purple, blue, or white flowers and pinnate leaves. Also **wis·tar·i·a,** wi·stēr′ē·a, wi·stâr′ē·a.

wist·ful, wist′ful, *a.* [Modified < old *wistly*, observantly, < *wist*, known, pp. of *wit*, to know.] Longing; pensive because of absence or lack of something.—**wist·ful·ly,** *adv.*—**wist·ful·ness,** *n.*

wit, wit, *n.* [O.E. *wit*, *witt*.] Intelligence; understanding; sagacity; the keen perception and apt expression of surprising, incongruous, subtle, or ludicrous relations between phenomena, ideas, or words; speech or writing showing such perception and expression; a person endowed with or noted for such perception and expression, esp. one having a talent for witty conversation. *Pl.* the combined abilities of observation, perception, and comprehension; the proper balance of such abilities; as, to lose one's *wits*.—**at one's wits' end,** having exhausted or lost one's powers of perceiving or thinking; befuddled.

wit, wit, *v.t.*—pres. sing. *wot*, *wost*, *wot*; pres. pl. *wit*; past *wist*; pp. *wist*; ppr. *witting.* [O.E. *witan* = O.H.G. *wizzan* (G. *wissen*) = Icel. *vita* = Goth. *witan*, know; akin to L. *videre*, see, Gr. *idein*, see, *oida*, I know (lit. 'I have seen'), Skt. *vid-*, know, perceive.] *Archaic.* To learn; to know.— *v.i. Archaic*, to know.—**to wit,** that is to say; namely.

wit·an, wit′an, *n. pl.* [O.E. pl. of *wita*, wise man, councilor, < *witan*, know, E. *wit*.] The members of the national council or witenagemot in Anglo-Saxon England; the witenagemot.

witch, wich, *n. pl.* **witch·es.** [O.E. *wicca*, masc. *wicce*, fem.: cf. O.E. *wītega*, *wītga*, O.H.G. *wizago*, prophet, Icel. *vitki*, wizard (all akin to O.E. *witan*, know, E. *wit*, *v.*), also E. *wiseacre*.] A woman who professes or is supposed to practice magic; a sorceress; an ugly or malignant old woman; a hag; a bewitching or fascinating woman or girl.— *v.t.* To affect by or as by witchcraft; to bewitch; to bring about by or as by witchcraft; to fascinate; to enchant.

witch·craft, wich′kraft″, wich′kräft″, *n.* The practices of witches; sorcery; black magic; enchantment; fascination.

witch doc·tor, *n.* A medicine man, esp. among primitive groups or tribes, who tries to heal others by practicing sorcery.

witch·er·y, wich′e·rē, *n. pl.* **witch·er·ies.** Witchcraft; sorcery; fascination; entrancing influence.

witch·es'-broom, wich'iz·bröm", wich'iz·-brŭm", *n.* A peculiar, abnormal, broomlike growth on various trees and shrubs, as on hackberry trees, consisting of a dense mass of branching twigs, due to irritation set up by certain fungi. Also **hex·en·be·sen.**

witch·es' Sab·bath, *n.* The sabbat.

witch grass, *n.* [Cf. *quitch, quitch-grass.*] A panic grass, *Panicum capillare,* with a brushlike compound panicle, common as a weed in N. America.

witch ha·zel, *n.* A N. American shrub, *Hamamelis virginiana,* with yellow flowers; an alcoholic solution of an extract obtained from the bark of this shrub, used on bruises and sprains and as an astringent. Also **wych-ha·zel.**

witch hunt, witch-hunt, *n.* A public investigation ostensibly conducted to detect subversion, used as a forum for arbitrary accusations by the investigators against unpopular or powerless individuals in order to acquire a reputation for vigilant patriotism.—**witch-hunt·er,** *n.*—**witch-hunt·ing,** *a., n.*

witch·ing, wich'ing, *n.* The use of sorcery or witchcraft.—*a.* Bewitching; suited to enchantment or witchcraft.

witch moth, *n.* Any of various moths of the genus *Erebus,* of the family *Noctuidae,* esp. *E. odora,* the largest witch moth in the U.S. Also **black witch.**

witch·y, wich'ē, *a.*—**witchier, witchiest.** Relating to or like a witch; suggesting witchcraft.

wit·e·na·ge·mot, wit'e·na·ge·mōt", *n.* [O.E. *witena,* gen. pl. of *wita,* a wise man. *(ge)mót,* a meeting, a moot.] The national council of Anglo-Saxon England, consisting of about 100 noblemen, prelates, and other notables, called at various times to advise the king. Also **witan.**

with, wiᴛн, with, *prep.* [O.E. *with,* against, toward, to, with (Icel. *vidh*), beside *wither,* against, akin to O.H.G. *widar,* G. *wider,* Icel. *vidhr,* Goth. *withra,* against.] Accompanied by or accompanying, as: I will go *with* you. In some particular relation to, esp. implying interaction, company, combination, association, or connection; as, to deal, talk, sit, or rank *with,* to blend the milk *with* the eggs; characterized by or having; as, a man *with* initiative; by means or use of; as, to cut *with* a knife; using or showing; as, to work *with* diligence; in correspondence or proportion to, as: Their power increased *with* their number. In regard to; as, to be pleased *with* a thing; because of or owing to; as, to die *with* pneumonia; in the course of; as, *with* time; in the same direction as; as, *with* the current; in spite of; as: *With* all his misfortunes, he seemed happy. From; as, to part *with* a thing; against, as in opposition or competition; as, to fight or vie *with;* in the keeping or charge of; as: Leave it *with* me. Immediately after, as: *With* that, he left. Of the same belief or opinion as, as: Is he *with* us in our conclusion? On the side of, as: She voted *with* the majority. Equal to, as: He golfs *with* the pros.

with·al, wiᴛн·al', with·al', *adv.* [*With* and *all.*] *Archaic.* With the rest; besides; together with that; likewise.—*prep. Archaic.* with: used after relatives or equivalent words, and transposed to the end of a sentence or clause.

with·draw, wiᴛн·drạ', with·drạ', *v.t.*—past *withdrew,* pp. *withdrawn,* ppr. *withdrawing.* [Prefix *with,* against, opposite to, and *draw.*] To draw back; to pull out; to remove, as: He *withdrew* his watch from his pocket. To lead, bring, or take back; as, to *withdraw* troops; to recall; to retract; as, *withdrawing* an offer.—*v.i.* To move from or quit a place; to retire; to go away; to retreat. —**with·drawn,** *a.*—**with·drawn·ness,** *n.*

with·draw·al, wiᴛн·drạ'al, with·drạ'al *n.* Act of withdrawing or taking back; a retraction.

with·draw·ing room, *n. Archaic.* A room for withdrawing or retiring to; a parlor; a drawing room.

withe, with, wiᴛн, wīᴛн, *n.* [O.E. *withig,* willow, withe; Icel. *vithja, vith,* a withy, a withe; Dan. *vidie,* Sw. *vide, vidja,* G. *weide,* a willow; allied to Gr. *itea* (for *vitea*), a willow; < a root meaning to twist or bend, seen also in L. *vimen,* a withe, *vitis,* a vine.] A willow or osier twig; a flexible twig used to bind something; a fastening of plaited or twisted twigs; a flexible tool handle.—*v.t.*—*withed, withing.* To tie with withes.

with·er, wiᴛн'er, *v.i.* [Lit. 'to *weather,*' to suffer from or expose to the weather.] To dry and shrivel up, as a plant from loss of moisture; to fade or decline; to lose freshness and vigor.—*v.t.* To cause to fade and shrivel; to embarrass or disconcert, as with a contemptuous glance.—**with·ered,** *a.*—**with·er·ing,** *a.*

with·er·ite, wiᴛн'e·rīt", *n.* [From Dr. W. *Withering,* E. scientist, who described it in 1784.] A white or grayish mineral, barium carbonate, $BaCO_3$, occurring in crystals and in columnar or granular masses.

withe rod, *n.* Either of two N. American species of viburnum, *Viburnum cassinoides* and *V. nudum,* having tough, osierlike shoots.

with·ers, wiᴛн'erz, *n. pl.* [Lit. the parts that act against or resist, < O.E. *wither,* against, < prep. *with,* against.] The junction of the shoulder bones of a horse or other mammal, the highest part of the back.

with·er·shins, wiᴛн'er·shinz", *adv.* [O.E. *withersȳnes,* < *wither,* against.] *Sc.* In the reverse or wrong direction; in a direction contrary to the apparent course of the sun. Also **widdershins.**

with·hold, with·hōld', wiᴛн·hōld', *v.t.*—*withheld, withholding.* [*With,* in sense of against, and *hold.*] To hold back; to restrain; to keep from action; to keep back; not to grant.—*v.i.* To forbear; to refrain.—**with·hold·er,** *n.*

with·hold·ing tax, *n.* An installment of an income tax levy deducted from an employee's wages or salary by his employer, and sent to a government department of revenue.

with·in, wiᴛн·in', with·in', *prep.* [O.E. *withinnan—with,* against, towards, and *innan,* within, inwardly, < *in,* in.] In the inner or interior part or parts of; as, *within* this room; inside of: opposed to *without;* in the limits, range, reach, or compass of; not beyond; inside or comprehended by the scope, limits, reach, or influence of; as, *within* his grasp; not exceeding, not overstepping.—*adv.* In the interior or center; inwardly; internally; in the mind, heart, or soul; in the house or dwelling; indoors; inside; at home.—*n.* The inside part of a building, place, space, or the like.

with·in·doors, wiᴛн·in'dōrz", wiᴛн·in'darz", with·in'dōrz", with·in'darz", *adv. Archaic.* Indoors; inside.

with·out, wiᴛн·out', with·out', *prep.* [O.E. *withútan, without—with,* toward, against, and *út,* out.] On or at the outside or exterior of; out of: opposed to *within;* out of the limits, compass, range, or reach of; as, *without* being heard; beyond; not having or not being with; in absence, with avoidance, or in destitution of; deprived of; not having; as, *without* enough money.—*conj. Dial.* unless.—*adv.* On the outside; outwardly; externally; out of doors; lacking or not having something; as, can do *without.*—*n.* An outer room, area, place, or the like.

with·out·doors, wiᴛн·out'dōrz", wiᴛн·out'darz", with·out'dōrz", with·out'darz", *adv. Archaic.* Out of doors; outside.

with·stand, with·stand', wiᴛн·stand', *v.t., v.i.*—*withstood, withstanding.* [*With,* in sense of against, and *stand.*] To resist, as a physical or moral force; to oppose.—**with·stand·er,** *n.*

with·y, wiᴛн'ē, with'ē, *n.* pl. **with·ies.** [O.E. *withig,* beside *withthe,* akin to G. *weide,* willow, osier, Icel. *vidh, vidhja,* withy: cf. L. *vitis,* vine.] A willow or osier; a flexible twig or a withe; a band or halter made of withes.—*a.*—*withier, withiest.* Made of withes; slender and flexible.

wit·less, wit'lis, *a.* Being without sense or understanding; silly; foolish.—**wit·less·ly,** *adv.*—**wit·less·ness,** *n.*

wit·ling, wit'ling, *n.* [Dim. < *wit.*] *Archaic,* a person who tries to seem witty.

wit·loof, wit'lōf, *n.* A salad foliage, chicory or endive.

wit·ness, wit'nis, *n.* [O.E. *witnes,* testimony, lit. 'what one knows,' < *witan,* to know.] One who personally sees or observes anything; that which furnishes evidence or proof; attestation of a fact or event; testimony. *Law,* a person who gives testimony or evidence in a judicial proceeding; one who sees the execution of an instrument, as a will, and subscribes to it for confirmation of its authenticity. (*Cap.*), *relig.* a Jehovah's Witness.—*v.t.* To see or know by personal presence; as, to *witness* a burglary; to formally attest or testify; to give or serve as evidence of; to subscribe as witness; *fig.* to be the scene of an action, as: The gymnasium has *witnessed* many games.—*v.i.* To give evidence; to testify.—**wit·ness·er,** *n.*

wit·ness stand, *n.* A courtroom enclosure, stand, or chair where the witness discloses his evidence or testimony.

wit·ted, wit'id, *a.* Having wit or understanding, usu. used in combination; as, a quick-*witted* boy.

wit·ti·cism, wit'i·siz"um, *n.* [< *witty;* cf. such words as *Atticism, Gallicism.*] A witty sentence, phrase, or remark.

wit·ting, wit'ing, *a.* Having knowledge about something; aware; conscious.—*n.*—**wit·ting·ly,** *adv.*

wit·tol, wit'ol, *n.* [Var. of *witwall, woodwall,* CUCKOLD.] *Archaic,* a man who knows and tolerates his wife's infidelity.

wit·ty, wit'ē, *a.*—*wittier, wittiest.* [O.E. *witig.*] Possessed of wit; smartly or cleverly facetious; bright and amusing. *Brit. dial.* possessing intelligence; clever.—**wit·ti·ly,** *adv.*—**wit·ti·ness,** *n.*

wive, wiv, *v.t.*—*wived, wiving.* [< *wife.*] To take, as a woman, for a wife.—*v.i.* To marry or take a wife.

wi·vern, wi'vern, *n. Her.* wyvern.

wiz·ard, wiz'erd, *n.* [< *wise,* and term.] A person who is adept in or practices magic; a magician; an enchanter; a conjurer. An accomplished person; as, a *wizard* at mathematics; also *whiz.*—*a.* Pertaining to a wizard or wizardry; *chiefly Brit.* praiseworthy or superior.—**wi·zard·ly,** *a.*—**wiz·ard·ry,** wiz'er·drē, *n.*

wiz·en, wiz'en, *dial.* wē'zen, *a.* [O.E. *wisnian,* to become dry, akin to Icel. *visna,* to wither, < *visinn,* withered, palsied.] Dried out and shriveled; withered; shrunken.—*v.t., v.i.* To shrivel, shrink, or wither.—**wiz·ened,** *a.*

woad, wōd, *n.* [O.E. *wád,* D. *weede,* Dan. *vaid, veid,* G. *waid, weid,* woad; connected with L. *vitrum,* woad.] A plant of the mustard family, *Isatis tinctoria,* formerly grown for its leaves, which yield a blue dye; any of various other members of the genus *Isatis.*—**woad·ed,** wō'did, *a.*

wob·ble, wob'l, *v.i.*—*wobbled, wobbling.* [Akin to L.G. *wabbeln,* G. *wabern, weibeln, weiben,* to move to and fro.] To move unsteadily in rotating or spinning; to rock from side to side; to vacillate; to tremble or falter.—*v.t.* Also *wabble.*—A wavering;

rocking motion; a fluctuating emission, as in vocal sound. Also *wabble*.—**wob·bler,** *n.* —**wob·bling·ly,** *adv.*—**wob·bly,** *a.*—*wob-blier, wobbliest.*

woe, wō, *n.* [O.E. *wá;* often as an interjection, as in *wá lá wá,* woe lo woe! wellaway! D. *wee,* Icel. *vei,* Dan. *vee,* G. *weh,* Goth. *vai;* a natural sound of grief, like L. *vae!* Gr. *ouai!* alas.] Grief; sorrow; misery; heavy calamity.—*interj.* An expression of distress or sorrow.

woe·be·gone, wo·be·gone, wō′bi·gạn″, wō′bi·gon″, *a.* [That is, surrounded or overwhelmed with woe, *begone* being < O.E. *began,* to surround—*be,* by, and *gán,* to go.] Having a mournful, dejected, or doleful appearance; *archaic,* overwhelmed with woe.—**woe·be·gone·ness, wo·be-gone·ness,** *n.*

woe·ful, wo·ful, wō′fụl, *a.* Full of woe; afflicted with or expressing woe; doleful; piteous; miserable; wretched.—**woe·ful·ly, wo·ful·ly,** *adv.*—**woe·ful·ness, wo·ful-ness,** *n.*

wold, wōld, *n.* [O.E. *wald, weald,* a wood; O.E., O.Fris., and G. *wald,* a wood or forest. *Weald* is the same word.] A region of unforested, hilly, open country; a moor.

wold, wōld, *n.* Weld.

wolf, wụlf, *n.* pl. **wolves,** wụlvz. [O.E. *wulf* = D. and G. *wolf* = Icel. ūlfr = Goth. *wulfs,* wolf; akin to L. *lupus,* Gr. *lýkos,* wolf.] Any of several wild carnivorous mammals of the genus *Canis,* as *C. nubilus,* the gray wolf of N. America, or *C. lupus,* the common European wolf, belonging to the dog family; the fur of any such animal; a swift-footed, crafty, rapacious animal; certain wolflike animals not of the dog family, as the thylacine or Tasmanian wolf, *Thylacinus cynocephalus; slang,* a philanderer; *fig.* a cruelly rapacious person; *entom.* the larva of various insects, esp. those infesting granaries; *(cap.), astron.* the constellation Lupus; *mus.* a jarring, discordant sound in chords produced by a keyboard instrument tuned to unequal temperament.—*v.t.* To gulp down, as food; to devour or swallow ravenously.—*v.i.* To hunt for wolves.—**cry wolf,** to give a false alarm.—**keep the wolf from the door,** to keep out hunger or want. —**wolf in sheep's cloth·ing,** a hypocrite.— **wolf·ish,** *a.*—**wolf·ish·ly,** *adv.*—**wolf-ish·ness,** *n.*—**wolf·like,** *a.*

wolf·ber·ry, wụlf′ber″ē, wụlf′be·rē, *n.* pl. **wolf·ber·ries.** A shrub of the honeysuckle family, *Symphoricarpos occidentalis,* of N. America, cultivated for ornament because of its pink flowers and white berries.

wolf dog, *n.* Any of various dogs of several breeds, orig. bred for hunting wolves; a wolfhound; a cross between a wolf and a domestic dog; an Eskimo dog.

Wolff·i·an bod·y, wụl′fē·an bod′ē, *n.* [Named after Kasper Friedrich *Wolff,* 1733–1794, G. anatomist and physiologist.] *Embryol.* the mesonephros.

wolf·fish, wụlf′fish″, *n.* pl. **wolf·fish·es, wolf·fish.** An edible fish, *Anarhichas lupus,* about six feet long, having powerful jaws and large teeth; any of several other fish of the same genus.

wolf·hound, wụlf′hound″, *n.* A hound of any of various breeds, formerly used in hunting wolves, as the Russian wolfhound or borzoi, resembling the deerhound in general build, but having much softer hair, or the Irish wolfhound, a very large and powerful dog.

wolf pack, *n. Warfare,* a number of submarines working together hunting down and attacking enemy shipping, esp. convoys; a flight of two or more fighter planes in a coordinated attack against an air or ground target. A pack of wolves.

wolf·ram, wụl′fram, *n.* [G. said to be <

wolf, wolf, and *rahm,* cream, froth.] Tungsten; wolframite.

wolf·ram·ite, wụl′fra·mīt″, vạl′fra·mīt″, *n.* [G. *wolframit,* < *wolfram.*] A mineral consisting of a tungstate of iron and manganese, $(Fe,Mn)WO_4$, usu. of a brownish or grayish black color, occurring massive and in crystals, that is a leading source of tungsten.—**wolf·ram·ic,** wụl·fram′ik, *a.*

wolfs·bane, wụlfs′bān″, *n.* Aconite.

wolf spi·der, *n.* Any member of a large and widely distributed group of spiders of the family *Lycosidae,* notable for hunting its prey rather than catching it in a web. Also **ground spi·der.**

wol·las·ton·ite, wụl′a·sto·nīt″, *n.* [From W. H. *Wollaston,* 1766–1828, E. chemist and physicist.] A mineral consisting of a silicate of calcium, $CaSiO_3$, usu. occurring in fibrous masses, and used in making paints, ceramics, cements, and fertilizers.

wol·ver·ine, wol·ver·ene, wụl′ve·rēn′, *n.* A carnivorous mammal of the weasel family, *Gulo luscus,* noted for its strength, ferocity, cunning, and voracity, living in northern forests of N. America; also *carcajou,* **quick·hatch.** *(Cap.)* an inhabitant of Michigan, known as the Wolverine State.

wom·an, wụm′an, *n.* pl. **wom·en.** [O.E. *wifman,* later *wimman,* < *wif,* wife, and *man,* in its primitive sense of human being, person.] The female of the human race; an adult or grownup female, as distinguished from a man; a female attendant on a person of rank; a female domestic; a mistress or sweetheart; a man having effeminate qualities, as timidity.—*a.* Womanly; feminine; female; as, a *woman* chemist.— **wom·an·like, wom·an·ly,** wụm′an·līk″ wụm′an·lē, *a.*—**wom·an·ly,** *adv.*—**wom-an·li·ness,** *n.*

wom·an·hood, wụm′an·hụd″, *n.* The state, character, or collective qualities of a woman; women in general.

wom·an·ish, wụm′a·nish, *a.* Suitable to a woman; feminine; effeminate: in a contemptuous sense.—**wom·an·ish·ly,** *adv.*— **wom·an·ish·ness,** *n.*

wom·an·ize, wụm′a·nīz″, *v.t.*—*womanized, womanizing.* To give feminine traits to.— *v.i. Colloq.* to be in constant, esp. illicit, pursuit of women.—**wom·an·iz·er,** wụm′-a·nī″zėr, *n. Colloq.* a man who habitually indulges himself in the pursuit of women.

wom·an·kind, wụm′an·kīnd″, *n.* Women in general; the female sex.

wom·an suf·frage, *n.* The political right of woman to vote; female suffrage.— **wom·an suf·fra·gist,** *n.*

womb, wōm, *n.* [O.E. *wamb, womb,* the belly = D. *wam,* Icel. *vómb,* Dan. *vom,* G. *wamme, wampe,* Goth. *wamba,* the belly.] *Anat.* the uterus. *Fig.* a place where something is engendered or developed; matrix; an enclosure likened to a womb, as for security. *Archaic,* the belly.—**wombed,** *a.*

wom·bat, wom′bat, *n.* [Corruption of the native name *womback* or *wombach.*] A marsupial mammal, family *Vombatidae,* of Australia and Tasmania, resembling a small bear, inhabiting a burrow, and feeding on vegetation.

wom·en·folk, wim′in·fōk″, *n. pl.* Women. Also **wom·en·folks.**

wom·en's rights, *n. pl.* The rights of women to the same legal protections, privileges, and occupational opportunities as men. See *feminism.* Also **wom·an's rights.**

won, wun, wụn, wōn, *v.i.*—*wonned, wonning.* [O.E. *wunian,* dwell, remain, *gewunian,* be accustomed, akin to D. *wonen,* G. *wohnen,* dwell, G. *gewohnen,* become accustomed, also to E. *wean:* cf. *wont, a.*] *Brit. archaic,* to dwell, abide, or stay.

won·der, wun′dėr, *v.i.* [O.E. *wundor* = D. *wonder* = G. *wunder* = Icel. *undr,* a

wonder.] To think or speculate with curiosity; as, to *wonder* about a thing; to marvel; to be surprised; to entertain some doubt.— *v.t.* To speculate about, with a clause; as, to *wonder* what happened; to feel wonder at, with a clause, as: I *wonder* that you went.— *n.* Something strange and surprising; a cause of surprise, astonishment, or admiration; as, to see the *wonders* of a city; the emotion excited by something strange and surprising; a feeling of surprised or puzzled interest, sometimes tinged with admiration; a marvel; a prodigy; a miracle or a miraculous deed or event.—**do won·ders,** to do wonderful things; to achieve or produce extraordinary results.—**for a won·der,** as a surprising thing or circumstance, as: *For a wonder,* everybody was satisfied.—**nine days' won·der,** a subject of general surprise and interest for a short time.—**sev·en won-ders of the world,** the seven most remarkable structures of ancient times, as commonly given: the Egyptian pyramids, the Mausoleum erected by Artemisia at Halicarnassus, the temple of Artemis at Ephesus, the walls and hanging gardens of Babylon, the Colossus of Rhodes, the statue of Zeus by Phidias at Olympia, and the Pharos or lighthouse at Alexandria.—**won·der·er,** *n.*

won·der·ful, wun′dėr·fụl, *a.* Capable of exciting wonder; astonishing; marvelous.— **wond·er·ful·ly,** *adv.*—**won·der·ful·ness,** *n.*

won·der·land, wun′dėr·land″, *n.* An enchanted or imaginary land; any comparable region or setting; as, a water *wonderland.*

won·der·ment, wun′dėr·ment, *n.* Wonder; surprise; astonishment; something causing surprise or wonder.

won·der·work, wun′dėr·wụrk″, *n.* A prodigy; a miracle; a marvel.—**won·der-work·er,** wun′dėr·wụr″kėr, *n.*—**won·der-work·ing,** *a.*

won·drous, wun′drus, *a. Liter.* Wonderful; marvelous.—*adv. Archaic.* To a wonderful degree; remarkably; as, *wondrous* wise.— **won·drous·ly,** *adv.*—**won·drous·ness,** *n.*

won·ky, wong′kē, *a.*—*wonkier, wonkiest. Brit. slang.* Weak; unsteady; frail; ailing.

wont, wōnt, wạnt, wunt, *a.* [For older *woned,* a participle or participial adjective, < O.E. *wuna, gewuna,* custom, habit, or < the kindred *wunian,* to dwell; akin Icel. *vani,* custom, *vanr,* accustomed.] Accustomed; having a certain habit or custom; using or doing customarily.—*n.* [< O.E. *wuna,* habit, custom, and M.E. *wone.*] Custom; habit; use.—*v.i.*—past *wont,* pp. *wont* or *wonted,* ppr. *wonting.* [For old *wone,* to be accustomed, to dwell. The past and pp. *wont* are thus put for *woned,* and *wonted* is a doubled form.] To be accustomed or habituated; to be used.—*v.t.* To habituate.

won't, wōnt, wunt. Contraction of will not.

wont·ed, wōn′tid, wạn′tid, wun′tid, *a.* Customary or familiar from use or habit; usual; accustomed; made or having become familiar by using or frequenting.—**wont-ed·ly,** *adv.*—**wont·ed·ness,** *n.*

woo, wō, *v.t.*—*wooed, wooing.* [O.E. *wógian,* to woo, < *wóh,* genit. *wóges,* bent, bending; the meaning is therefore to bend or incline another toward one's self.] To court; to solicit in love; to invite, as a circumstance; as, to *woo* destruction; to seek to gain or bring about.—*v.i.* To make love.—**woo-ing,** *n.*

wood, wụd, *n.* [O.E. *wudu, widu,* = O.H.G. *witu* = Icel. *vidhr,* wood.] The hard fibrous substance, xylem, composing most of the stem and branches of a tree or shrub, and lying beneath the bark; the trunks or main stems of trees as suitable for architectural and other purposes; timber or lumber; firewood; the cask, barrel, or keg: distinguished from the *bottle;* as, wine aged and drawn from the *wood; print.* a wood block or woodcut. *Mus.* a wooden wind instrument; such instruments collectively in a band or orchestra. *Usu. pl.* a large and thick collection of growing trees; a grove or forest. *Golf*, a club having a wooden head. —*a.* Consisting of or produced from wood; suitable or made for storing, using, or shaping wood; growing or living in woods. —*v.t.* To forest or plant with trees; to supply with wood.—*v.i.* To take in or get supplies of wood.—**out of the woods,** *colloq.* Free of danger or difficulties; safe.— **wood·less,** *a.*

wood, wụd, *a.* [O.E. *wōd* = Icel. *ōdhr* = Goth. *wōds*, mad, furious: cf. G. *wut*, fury, rage, also E. *Woden.*] *Archaic.* Mad; frantic; furious; wild, as with rage or excitement.

wood·al·co·hol, *n.* Methanol.

wood a·nem·o·ne, *n.* A small N. American plant, *Anemone quinquefolia*, having white, purple, or rose flowers; any of various old-world anemones, as *A. nemorosa*.

wood bet·o·ny, *n.* The lousewort, *Pedicularis canadensis*, a plant of eastern N. America having yellow or red flowers and long, deeply indented leaves; any of various similar plants of the same genus.

wood·bin, wụd′bin″, *n.* A container for firewood.

wood·bine, wụd′bin″, *n.* [Also *woodbind*, < O.E. *wudubinde*, < *wudu*, wood, and *bindan*, bind; with reference to its twining about trees.] The common European honeysuckle, *Lonicera periclymenum*, which is cultivated in the U.S. The N. American woodbine, *Parthenocissus quinquefolia*, having five palmately arranged leaves; also *Virginia creeper.*

wood block, *n.* Woodcut.—**wood-block,** *a.* Printed or made from wood blocks.

wood-bor·ing, wụd′bōr″ing, wụd′bạr″ing, *a.* Of or pertaining to boring in wood; as, a *wood-boring* tool, a *wood-boring* insect.

wood carv·ing, *n.* The art of creating objects out of wood or of cutting designs into wood by the use of sharp hand tools; such a creation.—**wood-carv·er,** wụd′-kär″vèr, *n.*

wood·chat, wụd′chat″, *n.* Any of several shrikes of the genus *Lanius*, native to Europe and N. Africa.

wood·chuck, wụd′chuk″, *n.* A burrowing, hibernating marmot, *Marmota monax*, common in N. America, having a reddish-brown coat. Also *ground hog.*

wood coal, *n.* Charcoal; lignite or brown coal.

wood·cock, wụd′kok″, *n.* pl. **wood·cocks, wood·cock.** A popular game bird, *Scolopax rusticola*, found throughout Europe, distinguished by its long bill and short legs; a related bird, *Philohela minor*, inhabiting eastern N. America; *archaic*, a fool.

wood·craft, wụd′kraft″, wụd′kräft″, *n.* Skill in anything which pertains to woods or forests; skill in hunting, trapping, or camping, esp. as related to woods; the ability to make or construct objects out of wood; woodworking.

wood·cut, wụd′kut″, *n.* A block of wood engraved for use in making prints; a print from such engraving. Also *wood block, woodprint.*

wood·cut·ter, wụd′kut″ér, *n.* A person who cuts wood; one who engraves on wood to make woodcuts.—**wood·cut·ting,** *n.*

wood·ed, wụd′id, *a.* Covered with living trees, as a hillside.

wood·en, wụd′en, *a.* Made of wood; consisting of wood; without spirit or expression; ungainly; awkward.—**wood·en·ly,** *adv.*— **wood·en·ness,** *n.*

wood en·grav·ing, *n.* The art of engraving with special cutting tools a design or picture in relief on the surface of a block of wood from which impressions can be taken by means of an ink or pigment; an engraved wood block; the impression or print itself; a woodcut.—**wood en·grav·er,** *n.* A person skilled in the art of wood engraving.

wood·en·head, wụd′en·hed″, *n. Colloq.* A blockhead; a dull or stupid person.— **wood·en·head·ed,** wụd′en·hed″id, *a.*— **wood·en·head·ed·ness,** *n.*

wood·en In·di·an, *n.* A likeness of a N. American Indian carved out of wood and colorfully painted, formerly placed on the sidewalk to identify a cigar store; *colloq.* an emotionally unresponsive person.

wood·en·ware, wụd′en·wâr″, *n.* Vessels or utensils, made of wood, as bowls, spoons, rolling pins, and the like.

wood hy·a·cinth, *n. Bot.* a European plant of the lily family, *Scilla nonscripta*, having blue or white bell-shaped flowers. Also **Eng·lish blue·bell.**

wood i·bis, *n.* A large wading bird, *Mycteria americana*, of storklike appearance, inhabiting the wooded swamps of the southern U.S. and regions southward. Also **flint·head.**

wood·land, wụd′land″, wụd′land, *n.* Land covered with an abundance of trees and shrubs.—wụd′land, *a.* Pertaining to or dwelling in the woods; sylvan.—**wood·land·er,** *n.*

wood lot, *n.* A section of land used for the cultivation of trees, or consisting of native woods.

wood louse, *n.* pl. **wood lice.** *Zool.* any of certain small terrestrial crustaceans of the order *Isopoda*, found in decaying wood and other damp places, and having a flattened elliptical body which in some species, as the sowbug, *Oniscus asellus*, is capable of being rolled up into a ball; any of certain small wingless insects of the family *Psocidae*, found in the woodwork of houses and under bark of trees.

wood·man, wụd′man, *n.* pl. **wood·men.** Woodsman.

wood·note, wụd′nōt″, *n.* A wild or natural musical tone, as that of a forest bird.

wood nymph, *n.* A goddess of the woods; a dryad; a butterfly of the family *Satyridae*, usu. brown in color and with eyespots; any of several S. American hummingbirds of the genera *Thalurania* and *Cyanophaia.*

wood·peck·er, wụd′pek″èr, *n. Ornith.* any of numerous birds constituting the family *Picidae*, having a hard, chisellike bill adapted for boring into wood in search of grubs and the like, rigid and sharply pointed tail feathers to assist in climbing and usu. a striking patterned plumage.

wood pe·wee, *n. Ornith.* a pewee.

wood·pile, wụd′pil″, *n.* A stack of piled-up wood, esp. that which has been cut for fuel.

wood·print, wụd′print″, *n.* Woodcut.

wood pulp, *n.* Pulp from wood widely used in making paper.

wood pus·sy, *n. Colloq.* skunk.

wood rat, *n.* Any of numerous forest-dwelling rats, esp. those of the genus *Neotoma*, as *N. cimera*, the pack rat of N. America.

wood ray, *n.* Xylem ray.

wood·ruff, wụd′ruf″, wụd′ruf″, *n.* [O.E. *wuderofe, wudurofe*, the latter part of doubtful meaning.] Any of various members of the genus *Asperula*, of the madder family, a group of Old World plants, esp. *A. odorata*, cultivated in gardens for the beauty of its whorled leaves and white blossoms, as well as for its fragrance.

wood·shed, wụd′shed″, *n.* A shed for storing wood, esp. firewood.

woods·man, wụdz′man, *n.* pl. **woods·men.** One accustomed to life in the woods and skilled in the arts connected with it, as woodcraft, hunting, and trapping; a lumberman.

wood sor·rel, *n.* A small species of sorrel, *Oxalis montana*, having three leaflets on each stem, and supposed by some to be the Irish shamrock; also *oxalis.* Any plant of the genus *Oxalis*, as *O. oregana* of western N. America, which bears pink flowers.

wood spir·it, *n.* Methanol.

wood sug·ar, *n. Chem.* a white powdery sugar, $C_5H_{10}O_5$, obtained by hydrolyzing cellulose material, as wood, straw, or corn cobs, used in diabetic foods and in dyeing and tanning. Also *xylose.*

woods·y, wụd′zē, *a.*—**woodsier, woodsiest.** Of, like, suggestive of, or associated with the woods; as, a *woodsy* fragrance.

wood tar, *n.* A dark-colored viscid product obtained from wood by distillation or burning slowly without flame: used in its natural state to preserve timber, rope, and the like, or subjected to further destructive distillation, when it yields creosote, various oils, and a final residuum, wood pitch.

wood thrush, *n.* A large thrush, *Hylocichla mustelina*, noted for its sweet musical songs, common in forests of eastern N. America.

wood turn·ing, *n.* The craft of turning wood blocks into different shapes by use of a lathe.—**wood·tur·ner,** wụd′tụr″nèr, *n.* One who works at wood turning.

wood·wax·en, wụd′wak″sen, *n.* An ornamental leguminous plant, *Genista tinctoria*, distinguished by clumps of brilliant yellow flowers which were formerly used in producing a yellow dye. Also **wood·wox·en.**

wood·wind, wụd′wind″, *n. Mus.* One of the wind instruments that are blown directly or through a reed and constitute a group comprising the flutes, oboes, clarinets, bassoons, and saxophones; *pl.* a section or group of woodwind instruments in an orchestra or band.—*a.*

wood·work, wụd′wụrk″, *n.* Work formed of wood; the part of any structure that is made of wood, as the doors of a house.— **wood·work·er,** wụd′wụr″kèr, *n.*—**wood·work·ing,** wụd′wụr″king, *n., a.*

wood·worm, wụd′wụrm″, *n.* A worm or larva that is bred in or bores in wood.

wood·y, wụd′ē, *a.*—**woodier, woodiest.** Abounding with wood; consisting of wood; resembling or pertaining to woods.— **wood·i·ness,** *n.*

woo·er, wö′èr, *n.* Someone who woos; a lover.

woof, wụf, wöf, *n.* [O.E. *oof, owef*, < *ōwef*, < prefix *ō*, for *on*, and *wefan*, to weave.] The threads that cross the warp in weaving; the weft; texture.

woof, wụf, wöf, *n.* A low growling sound, as that made by a dog; any comparable sound.

woo·fer, wụf′èr, *n. Electron.* a loudspeaker in a sound-reproducing apparatus which picks up low sound frequencies.

wool, wụl, *n.* [O.E. *wull* = D. *wol* = G. *wolle* = Icel. *ull* = Goth. *wulla*, wool: cf. L. *vellus*, fleece, Skt. *ūrnā*, wool.] The fine, soft, curly hair that forms the fleece of sheep and certain other animals, characterized by minute, overlapping surface scales, to which its felting property is mainly due; cloth or garments made of wool; woolen yarn used for knitting, crocheting, and ornamental needlework; worsted; any of various substances used commercially as substitutes for the wool of animals such as sheep; a kind of woollike yarn or material made from cellulose by a process similar to that used in manufacturing rayon or artificial silk; any of certain plant fibers, such as cotton or flax, used as a substitute for wool, esp. after preparation by a special process; any finely fibrous or filamentous matter suggestive of the wool of sheep; as, glass *wool*; any coating of short, fine hairs or hairlike processes, as on a caterpillar or a plant; pubescence; short, thick, curly or kinky hair on the head of a human being.—**pull the wool o·ver one's eyes,** to deceive or delude one.—**wooled,** *a.*

wool clip, *n.* The quantity of wool shorn from sheep in one season in a given region.

wool·en, wooll·en, wụl'en, *a.* Made of wool; consisting of wool; pertaining to wool.—*n. Usu. pl.* cloth or clothing made of wool, such as blankets, serges, flannels, and the like.

wool·er, wụl'ẽr, *n.* Any wool-bearing animal raised specifically for its wool.

wool fat, *n.* Refined wool grease; lanolin.

wool·fell, wụl'fel", *n.* The skin of a wool-bearing animal with the fleece still on it.

wool·gath·er·ing, wụl'gaTH"ẽr·ing, *n.* Indulgence in idle fancies; wandering of the mind resulting in lack of attention.—*a.*—**wool-gath·er,** *v.i.*—**wool·gath·er·er,** *n.*

wool grease, *n.* An oily or greasy substance obtained from unwashed sheep's wool.

wool·ly, wool·y, wụl'ē, *a.*—*woolier, wooliest.* Consisting of or containing wool; similar to or resembling wool; fleecelike; clothed or covered with wool; wool-bearing; *bot.* covered with a pubescence resembling wool; *colloq.* of or like the old western frontier of America: used in the phrase 'wild and woolly.'—**wool·li·ness,** *n.*

wool·ly, wool·ie, wool·y, wụl'ē, *n. pl.* **wool·lies, wool·ies.** *Usu. pl.,* *colloq.* a piece of wool clothing, esp. underwear. Sheep, esp. in western U.S.

wool·ly a·phid, *n. Entom.* any of a large group of aphids of the family *Eriosomátidae,* having a woolly appearance because of a mass of waxy fibers covering their bodies.

wool·ly bear, *n.* The larva of any of various moths, esp. tiger moths, which are covered with a dense coat of woolly hairs.

wool·ly-head·ed, wụl'ē-hed'id, *a.* Having hair which is similar to wool in appearance or texture; characterized by disorderly or jumbled thinking.

wool·pack, wụl'pak", *n.* A large sack or wrapper of some coarse material, as canvas, into which wool is packed for shipping; such a bundle or bale weighing 240 pounds; *meteor.* a cumulus cloud of fleecy appearance.

wool·sack, wụl'sak", *n.* A sack or bag for wool. *Brit.* the chair of the Lord Chancellor or one assigned to any judge summoned to the House of Lords, distinguished by a large square seat stuffed with wool without back or arms; the Lord Chancellorship itself.

wool·shed, wụl'shed", *n.* A building for shearing sheep and preparing the wool for market.

wool·sort·er's dis·ease, wụl'sạr"tẽrz di·-zēz', *n.* Pulmonary anthrax which is acquired when one inhales spores of the bacterium, *Bacillus anthracis,* contained in contaminated hair, esp. wool.

wool sponge, *n.* A sponge, *Hippiospongia lachne,* of the Gulf of Mexico and adjacent waters, valued for commercial use because of its softness and durability.

wool sta·pler, *n.* A dealer in wool; a sorter of wool.—**wool-sta·pling,** *a.,* *n.*

wooz·y, wŏ'zē, wụz'ē, *a.*—*woozier, wooziest.* [Origin obscure.] Muddled, or stupidly confused; in a confused or uncertain condition, as from alcohol; out of sorts physically, as from nausea.—**wooz·i·ly,** *adv.*—**wooz·i·ness,** *n.*

Worces·ter chi·na, wụs'tẽr chī'na, *n.* A very fine translucent china made at Worcester, England, since 1751. Also **Worces·ter por·ce·lain.**

Worces·ter·shire sauce, wụs'tẽr·shẽr"·sạs", wụs'tẽr·shẽr, *n.* A sharp, tangy sauce which originated in Worcester, England, consisting of vinegar, soy, and various other ingredients.

word, wụrd, *n.* [O.E. *word* = D. *woord* = G. *wort* = Icel. *ordh* = Goth. *waurd,* word; akin to L. *verbum,* word, E. *verb.*] A speech sound or combination of speech sounds, or its representation, used as the smallest unit of meaningful communication by language; any single linguistic unit that forms a grammatical part of speech; something said; a vocable. A short talk or conversation; as, to have a *word* with someone; an expression or utterance; as, a *word* of praise; an authoritative utterance; command; as, the father's *word* was law; assurance; promise; as, to give one's *word;* news; information; as, to send *word* of an occurrence; rumor; a verbal signal; watchword; password. (*Cap.*) Logos; the Scriptures, preceded by *the.* *Pl.* speech; talk; discourse; conversation; the text of a song or other vocal musical composition; contentious or angry speech; as to have *words* with someone.—*v.t* To express in words; to phrase.—**be as good as one's word,** to act in accord with what one has promised or said.—**by word of mouth,** orally.—**in a word,** in a brief statement; in short.—**take one at his word,** to take seriously another's words as spoken and act accordingly.—**the last word,** *colloq.* the latest thing.—**word for word,** verbatim.

word·age, wụr'dij, *n.* Words collectively; verbiage; a particular number of words, as in a book; wording.

word-blind, wụrd'blīnd", *a. Pathol.* unable to understand written or printed words, even while able to see, write, and speak, and to understand spoken words.—**word blind·ness,** *n. Pathol.* alexia.

word·book, wụrd'bụk", *n.* A vocabulary; a dictionary; a lexicon; a libretto.

word-deaf, wụrd'def", *a. Pathol.* unable to comprehend heard speech, due to cortical lesions.—**word deaf·ness,** *n.*

word for word, *adv.* In the exact words or terms; verbatim; exactly.—**word-for-word,** wụrd'fẽr·wụrd', *a.*

word·ing, wụr'ding, *n.* Expression in words; form of expression; phraseology.

word·less, wụrd'lis, *a.* Not speaking; silent; unexpressed.—**word·less·ly,** *adv.*—**word·less·ness,** *n.*

word-of-mouth, wụrd'ov·mouth', *a.* Made known or disclosed by oral communication.

word or·der, *n.* The sequence of words in the syntax of a clause, phrase, or sentence.

word·play, wụrd'plā", *n.* An exercise or exchange of verbal wit; repartee; punning.

word square, *n.* A set of words of equal length which, when arranged one beneath another in the form of a square read the same horizontally and vertically.

word·y, wụr'dē, *a.*—*wordier, wordiest.* Using many more words than are necessary; verbose; consisting of words; verbal.—**word·i·ly,** *adv.*—**word·i·ness,** *n.*

work, wụrk, *n.* [O.E. *weorc* = D. and G. *werk* = Icel. *verk,* work; akin to Goth. *waurkjan,* to work, also to Gr. *ergon,* work, *organon,* instrument, E. *organ.*] Exertion directed to produce or accomplish something; labor; toil; productive or operative activity; as, to make a machine do *work;* activity undertaken in return for payment, as in wages; employment; a job; a place where one is employed; as, not at home but at *work;* that on which exertion or labor is expended; a product of activity or labor; as, a literary *work;* needlework or embroidery; an engineering structure, as a bridge or dock; workmanship; as, to do good *work;* a task or undertaking; as, one's life's *work;* a deed or act; *pl., theol.* righteous deeds or acts. *Pl. but usu. sing. in constr.* a place or establishment for carrying on some form of labor or industry; as, an iron *works;* the working parts of a mechanical apparatus; as, the *works* of a clock. A froth produced during fermentation, as in making cider or vinegar; *phys.* the transfer of energy from one body or system to another.—*v.i.* *worked* or archaic *wrought, working.* [O.E. *wyrcan* (past *worhte*).] To do work; to labor; to toil; to be employed, as a person; to be in operation, as a machine; to act or operate effectively; to have an effect or influence; as, to *work* on one's conscience; to make way with effort or difficulty; as, a ship *working* to windward; to become as specified by or as by continuous effort; as, to *work* loose; to move in agitation, as the features reflecting strong emotion; to ferment; *naut.* to give slightly at the joints, as a vessel under strain at sea; *mech.* to move improperly, as from defective fitting of parts or from wear.—*v.t.* To bring about by or as by work or effort; to cause; to effect; to operate, as a mine or farm; to manipulate or treat, as dough or butter; to adjust, repair, or be in the process of producing, followed by *on;* as, to *work on* an engine or a novel; to use or manage, as a machine, in operation; to put into effective operation; to keep, as a person or animal, at work; to achieve by work or effort; as, to *work* one's way through college; to make or decorate by needlework; to find the solution to, as an arithmetic problem; to move, stir, or excite, usu. followed by *up;* to cause to ferment; to influence or persuade, esp. insidiously; to seek to influence or persuade, usu. followed by *on;* *colloq.* to use flattery or other inducements upon, in order to obtain some profit or favor; as, to *work* someone for a loan.—*a.* Of, proper to, or used for work. Used to form nouns denoting a product of a particular material or method of production; as, woodwork, needlework; used to form nouns denoting a particular kind of work; as, paperwork, piecework; used to form nouns denoting work done at a particular place; as, housework.—**at work,** working.—**out of work,** having no employment.—**the works,** *slang,* everything possible.—**work off,** to rid oneself of by work or effort, as a debt. —**work up,** to develop or concoct.

work·a·ble, wụr'ka·bl, *a.* Able to be worked; achievable, feasible, or possible, as a project.—**work·a·bil·i·ty,** wụr"ka·bil'-i·tē, **work·a·ble·ness,** *n.*

work·a·day, wụr'ka·dā", *a.* Relating or pertaining to a working day; prosaic; everyday; commonplace.

work·bag, wụrk'bag", *n.* A bag for work materials and tools, esp. for needlework.

work bas·ket, *n.* A basket in which sewing materials are kept.

work·bench, wụrk'bench", *n.* A solidly built table at which a carpenter or other artisan works.

work·book, wụrk'bụk", *n.* A book used by students which includes exercises and questions to be worked on directly in the book; a handbook of instructions on operating procedures; a book for keeping a record of planned or completed work.

work·box, wụrk'boks", *n.* A small box for holding work materials and implements, esp. those used in needlework.

work camp, *n.* A prison camp for those sentenced to spend time doing physical labor; a short program or project staffed by volunteers from religious organizations.

work·day, wụrk'dā", *n.* A day on which work is accomplished; the part of, or hours in, one day during which work is accomplished. Also *working day.*—*a.* Workaday.

worked, wụrkt, *a.* That has been made, developed, or treated through various processes.

worked-up, wụrkt'up', *a.* Excited. Also *wrought-up.*

work·er, wụr'kẽr, *n.* One who works; a laborer; a toiler; a member of the working class; *entom.* a sterile female working member of an insect colony, as that of bees or termites; *print.* an electrotyped plate.

work farm, *n. Penology,* a farm to which a court may assign a person, usu. a minor, for a period to work.

work·folk, wŭrk'fōk", *n. pl.* Workpeople, esp. agricultural laborers. Also **work·folks.**

work force, *n.* All the workers of a business, factory, or other activity; the total number, both employed and unemployed, of workers.

work·horse, wŭrk'hars", *n.* A horse, as one on a farm used for heavy work in the fields: differentiated from one used for riding for pleasure; a person who derives satisfaction from hard work, esp. one who may be counted upon to assume the arduous part of any task as well as additional responsibilities as they arise.

work·house, wŭrk'hous", *n.* A house of correction where petty offenders are incarcerated and put to work; *Brit.* a poorhouse or almshouse which houses the poor and supplies them with work.

work in, *v.t.* To include or insert, usu. in a subtle way, as: The speaker managed to *work in* a reference to honors recently bestowed upon him. To include by special arrangement, as: The boss has a full schedule today but he may be able to *work* you *in*.

work·ing, wŭr'king, *a.* Engaged in bodily toil or other active employment; concerning or used in work; of a sufficient size or quality for action or use; as, having a *working* knowledge of mathematics; performing a facilitating function; as, a *working* diagram; twitching or moving jerkily, as facial muscles under emotional strain.—*n.* The act of working; operation; movement; fermentation, as of wine or yeast; *pl.* the part of a quarry, mine, or tunnel where digging has been done or is being done.

work·ing as·set, *n. Accounting*, any asset as differentiated from capital asset.

work·ing cap·i·tal, *n.* Cash and other current assets used by a business enterprise to carry on operations; *accounting*, current assets in excess of current liabilities.

work·ing class, *n. pl.* **work·ing class·es.** A class of people whose social status is determined by the economic dependence of its members on manual or industrial employment; the proletariat.—**work·ing·class**, wŭr'king·klas", wŭr'king·kläs", *a.*

work·ing day, *n.* Workday.

work·ing draw·ing, *n.* A drawing, as of the whole or a part of a structure or machine, made ,to scale and in such detail as to form a guide for the workmen in the construction of the object represented.

work·ing·man, wŭr'king·man", *n. pl.* **work·ing·men.** A male member of the working class; a man who earns wages for work, as a manual laborer or a worker in a plant or factory.

work·ing pa·pers, *n. pl.* Documentary evidence entitling a person, esp. a minor, to be legally employed.

work·ing sub·stance, *n. Mech.* the substance, as steam, air, or a fluid, which under pressure operates a prime mover.

work load, *n.* The expected performance of a machine, individual worker, department, or business, in a given time.

work·man, wŭrk'man, *n. pl.* **work·men.** A man engaged in manual or mechanical work, as in labor and industry; often used in reference to his work; as, a skilled *workman.*

work·man·like, wŭrk'man·lĭk", *a.* Like or worthy of a workman; skillful; wellperformed. Also **work·man·ly.**

work·man·ship, wŭrk'man·ship", *n.* The art or skill of a workman; the quality or character of work performed; operative skill; the result or objects produced by a workman, artisan, or operator.

work·men's com·pen·sa·tion in·sur·ance, *n.* Insurance prescribed by statutes in most states, which protects an employer against an employee's job-connected injury or death, the law stipulating the amount of the settlement.

work of art, *n.* An artistic production, as a sculpture, esp. one of superior quality; something likened to an artistic production.

work out, *v.t.* To bring about by, or as by labor and exertion; to exhaust, as soil or a mine, by working; to solve; to discharge, as a debt, by working rather than paying money; work off; to develop; formulate, as a scheme.—*v.i.* To eventuate successfully or suitably; to eventuate as specified; as, to *work out* badly; to exercise or practice, esp. in order to develop skills in or prepare for an athletic activity or event.

work·out, wŭrk'out", *n. Colloq.* An exercise or practice session for the development of skills in or in preparation for an athletic activity or event; any rigorous or tiring activity.

work·peo·ple, wŭrk'pē"pl, *n. pl.* People engaged in labor, particularly manual labor; employees; workers.

work·room, wŭrk'rōm", wŭrk'rum", *n.* A room in which work is carried on.

work·shop, wŭrk'shop", *n.* A shop or building where any work or handicraft is carried on; a discussion or seminar held for the purpose of intensive study, discussion, and application of some subject or topic.

work stop·page, *n.* A discontinuance or ceasing of work, esp. in industry, usu. brought about by employees in sympathy with a cause.

work·ta·ble, wŭrk'tā"bl, *n.* A table at which one works, often with drawers or receptacles for materials, as for sewing.

work-up, wŭrk'up", *n. Print.* an unintentional imprint of metal word or line spacers on a printed sheet.

work·week, wŭrk'wēk", *n.* The total of hours or days worked or needed to be worked during the period of a week.

work·wom·an, wŭrk'wum"an, *n. pl.* **work·wom·en.** A woman engaged in any work, esp. in that which requires manual or mechanical skills, as in industry.

world, wŭrld, *n.* [O.E. *woruld, weorold,* = D. *wereld* = O.H.G. *werald* (G. *welt*) = Icel. *veröld,* world; a compound word, lit. 'age of man,' < Teut. elements represented by O.E. *wer,* man, and *yldu,* age.] The planet earth; the universe; any period, state, or sphere of existence; as, the next *world*; (*often cap.*) a particular division of the earth; as, the New *World.* The earth, with its inhabitants, affairs, and characteristic form of existence during a particular period; as, the prehistoric *world*; mankind; the public generally, as: The whole *world* knows it. A particular class or association of people having common interests and aims; as, the sports *world*; any sphere, realm, or domain, with all that pertains to it; as, the *world* of dreams; the insect *world*; the course of affairs or experience, as: How goes the *world* with you? *Often pl.* a great quantity or extent; as, *worlds* of difference. Any celestial body, esp. a planet.—**for all the world,** in every respect.—**in the world,** anywhere; at all; ever: used to add emphasis, as: What *in the world* is that?—**on top of the world,** *colloq.* Very happy; elated.—**out of this world,** *colloq.* Very good; superb.

world-beat·er, wŭrld'bē"ter, *n. Slang,* one who or that which goes beyond all others of like grouping in degree of excellence, capabilities, or performance.

World Day of Pray·er, *n.* The first Friday during Lent, on which prayer services for foreign missions are conducted.

world fed·er·al·ism, *n.* Federalism, as applied to the whole world; (*cap.*) a movement begun shortly after World War II to promote world peace through the con-

federation of all nations.—**world fed·er·al·ist,** *n.*

world·ling, wŭrld'ling, *n.* One who is devoted exclusively to the affairs and interests of this life.

world·ly, wŭrld'lē, *a.*—*worldlier, worldliest.* Belonging to the world or present state of man's existence; secular; desirous of temporal benefit or enjoyment; earthly, as opposed to *heavenly* or *spiritual.*—**world·li·ness,** *n.*

world·ly-mind·ed, wŭrld'lē·mĭn'dĭd, *a.* Devoted to worldly aims.—**world·ly-mind·ed·ness,** *n.*

world·ly-wise, wŭrld'lē·wīz', *a.* Wise as to the affairs of this world.

world pow·er, *n.* A state, institution, or corporate body possessing such powers as to have great influence throughout the world.

World Se·ries, *n. pl.* **World Se·ries.** *Baseball,* a post season series of games played every October in the U.S. by the pennant winners in each major league until one team wins four games and is declared world champion. Also **World's Se·ries.**

world-shak·ing, wŭrld'shā"king, *a.* Of such great importance or consequence that the whole world is affected.

world soul, *n. Philos.* a supposed spiritual aspect of the material universe, conceived as analogous to the soul of a human being.

World War I, *n.* A war carried on from 1914 to 1918 with the chief contestants being on the one side the Central Powers of Germany, Austria-Hungary, Turkey, and Bulgaria, and on the other side Great Britain, France, Belgium, Russia, and the U.S., and fought mainly in Europe. Abbr. *W.W.I.*

World War II, *n.* A war carried on from 1939 to 1945 with the chief contestants being on the one side the Axis made up of Germany, Italy, and Japan, and on the other side the Allies made up of Great Britain, France, the Soviet Union, and the U.S., culminating in the surrender of Germany and Japan. Abbr. *W.W.II.*

world-wea·ry, wŭrld'wēr"ē, *a.* Weary of the world, existence, or material pleasures. —**world-wea·ri·ness,** *n.*

world-wide, wŭrld'wīd', *a.* Extending or spread throughout the world.

worm, wŭrm, *n.* [O.E. *wyrm, wurm* = O.H.G., G. *wurm* = Icel. *ormr* = Goth. *waurms,* akin to L. *vermis,* worm.] Any of various small invertebrates with more or less slender elongated bodies and without limbs, including the platyhelminths, nemahelminths, and annelids; any of various small creeping or boring animals, as an insect larva or a shipworm; something resembling or suggesting a worm in appearance or movement; something that penetrates, injures, or consumes slowly or insidiously; a groveling, abject, or contemptible person; wretch; the thread of a screw; the spiral pipe in a still in which the vapor is condensed; a wormlike part of the body, as the vermiform process of the cerebellum or the lytta of a dog; *pl., pathol.* a disease or disorder arising from the presence of parasitic worms in the intestines.—*v.t.* To make, as one's way, by creeping or crawling; to insinuate, followed by *in* or *into*; as, to *worm* oneself *into* someone's good graces; to get by persistent, insidious efforts, followed by *out of* or *from. Med.* to cure of worms; to remove the lytta of. *Naut.* to wind yarn or the like spirally around, as a rope, so as to fill the spaces between the strands.—*v.i.* To move or advance slowly or stealthily; to get by insidious means, followed by *in* or *into*; to avoid or escape by insidious means, followed by *out of.*—**worm·er.**

worm-eat·en, wŭrm'ēt'en, *a.* Eaten into or gnawed by worms; as, *worm-eaten* timbers; impaired by time or decayed; antiquated.

worm fence, *n.* Snake fence.

worm gear, *n. Mech.* A gear wheel which engages with a revolving worm, or endless screw, in order to receive or impart motion; a worm wheel; a gear wheel together with the endless screw, forming a device by which the rotary motion of one shaft can be transmitted to another shaft at right angles to it.

worm·hole, wُrm'hōl″, *n.* A hole made by a burrowing or gnawing worm, as in timber or nuts.

worm·root, wُrm'rōt″, wُrm'rُt″, *n.* A pinkroot.

worm·seed, wُrm'sēd″, *n.* The dried, unexpanded flower heads of santonica, *Artemisia cina,* of the composite family, used as a vermifuge; the fruit of certain goosefoots, esp. *Chenopodium ambrosioides anthelminticum,* used as a vermifuge.

worm snake, *n.* Any of several small snakes which resemble worms.

worm wheel, *n.* A wheel which gears with an endless screw.

worm·wood, wُrm'wُd″, *n.* [O.E. *wermōd* = O.H.G. *wermuota* (G. *wermut*): cf. *vermouth.*] Any plant of the genus *Artemisia,* of the composite family; a bitter, aromatic European herb, *Artemisia absinthium,* formerly much used as a vermifuge and a tonic, but now chiefly used in making absinthe; something bitter, grievous, or extremely unpleasant; bitterness.

worm·y, wُrm'ē, *a.*—*wormier, wormiest.* Containing a worm or worms; infested with worms; worm-eaten; wormlike; groveling; low.

worn, wōrn, *a.* Impaired by wear or use; as, *worn* clothing; wearied or exhausted; showing the wearing effects of toil, care, suffering, or the like.

worn-out, wōrn'out′, wٔrn'out′, *a.* Destroyed or much injured by wear; wearied; exhausted with toil.

wor·ri·ment, wُr'ē·ment, wٔr'ē·ment, *n. Colloq.* Harassing annoyance; worry; anxiety.

wor·ri·some, wُr'ē·som, wٔr'ē·som, *a.* Worrying, annoying, or disturbing; causing worry; inclined to worry or be anxious.—**wor·ri·some·ly,** *adv.*

wor·ry, wُr'ē, wٔr'ē, *v.i.*—*worried, worrying.* [M.E. *worowen,* < O.E. *wyrgan* = G. *würgen,* strangle.] To torment oneself with or suffer from disturbing thoughts; to fret; *colloq.* to move by constant effort, in spite of difficulties or troubles, used with *along* or *through.*—*v.t.* To cause to feel uneasy or anxious; to trouble; to torment with annoyances, cares, or anxieties; to plague, pester, or bother; to seize, as by the throat, with the teeth and shake or mangle, as one animal does another; to harass by repeated biting or snapping.—*n.* pl. **wor·ries.** A worried condition or feeling; harassing care, uneasiness, or anxiety; a cause of uneasiness or anxiety; a trouble; the act of worrying.—**wor·ri·er,** *n.*—**wor·ry·ing·ly,** *adv.*

wor·ry·wart, wُr'ē·wٔrt, wٔr'ē·wٔrt, *n.* One who worries constantly and often without good reason.

worse, wُrs, *a.,* irreg. compar. of *bad* and *ill.* [O.E. *wiersa, wyrsa* (akin to Icel. *verri,* O.H.G. *wirsire,* Goth. *wairsiza,* worse), a compar. form, with superl. *wiersta, wyrsta,* associated with *yfel,* E. *evil,* as positive; perh. from the same root as E. *war.*] Bad or ill in a greater or higher degree; inferior in excellence, quality, or character; more faulty, unsatisfactory, or objectionable; more unfavorable or injurious; in less good condition; in poorer health.—*n.* That which is worse; a worse thing or state.—*adv.* [O.E. *wiers, wyers.*] In a worse manner or one which is more evil or wicked; with greater violence or intensity; as: It is raining *worse* than ever.

wors·en, wُr'sen, *v.t., v.i.* To become or cause to become worse.

wor·ship, wُr'ship, *n.* [From *worth,* and term. *-ship;* O.E. *weorthscipe,* honor.] The performance of devotional acts in honor of a deity, as a church service; the act of paying divine honors to the Supreme Being or other divine power; religious exercises; reverence; submissive respect; loving or admiring devotion; *chiefly Brit.* a title used when one addresses certain magistrates and others of rank or station.—*v.t.*—*worshiped, worshiping, esp. Brit. worshipped, worshipping.* To pay divine honors to; to reverence with supreme respect and veneration; to perform religious service to; to adore; to idolize.—*v.i.* To perform acts of adoration; to perform religious service.—**wor·ship·er, wor·ship·per,** *n.*—**wor·ship·less,** *a.*

wor·ship·ful, wُr'ship·ful, *a.* Worthy of honor; honorable; of or pertaining to a reverent feeling, as to a person; *chiefly Brit.* a term of respect, as applied to magistrates or certain other high officials.—**wor·ship·ful·ly,** *adv.*—**wor·ship·ful·ness,** *n.*

worst, wُrst, *a.,* irreg. superl. of *bad* and *ill.* [O.E. *wiersta, wyrsta.*] Bad or ill in the greatest or highest degree; most faulty, unsatisfactory, or objectionable; most evil or wicked; most unfavorable or injurious; in the poorest condition.—*n.* That which is worst; the worst thing or state.—*adv.* In the worst manner; as, to fare *worst;* with the greatest violence or intensity; as, to hate one *worst* of all.—*v.t.* To give, as a person, the worst of a contest or struggle; defeat; beat. —**at worst,** under the most unfavorable conditions.—**get the worst of something,** to be the loser, undergo defeat.—**if worst comes to worst,** if the very worst happens.

wor·sted, wُs'tid, wُr'stid, *n.* [From *Worsted,* now *Worstead,* town in Norfolk, England.] Firmly twisted yarn or thread spun from combed long-staple wool, used for weaving, knitting, crocheting, and the like; any kind of cloth woven of such yarn.—*a.*

wort, wُrt, *n.* [O.E. *wyrte,* wort, must; Icel. *virtr,* O.D. *wort,* G. *würze,* wort; prob. akin to above word.] The unfermented sweet infusion of malt that constitutes beer when fermented.

wort, wُrt, *n.* [O.E. *wyrt* = O.H.G., G. *wurz,* plant, root, = Goth. *waurts,* root; akin to E. *root.*] A plant, herb, or vegetable, usu. used in compounds; as, liver*wort* or milk*wort.*

worth, wُrth, *n.* [O.E. *weorth, wurth,* price, value, honor, or as an adj. valuable, honorable, with similar forms in the other Teut. languages; perh. from root meaning to guard, as in *wary,* beware.] That quality of a thing which renders it valuable or useful; value, esp. of a monetary nature; value or merit in respect to excellence of mental or moral qualities; wealth or riches of any sort; a certain amount or number of something which may be acquired for a particular sum; as, a nickel's *worth* of jelly beans.—*a.* Equal in value or price to; deserving of; as, a cause *worth* defending; possessing specified value, as: He is *worth* at least two million.—**for all one is worth,** *colloq.* To the utmost; to the limits of one's capabilities.—**put in one's two cents worth,** *slang,* to contribute one's opinion or views to a discussion or argument.—**worth·ful,** *a.* Honorable; esteemed; having worth.

worth, wُrth, *v.i. Archaic,* to befall or happen, as: Woe *worth* the day!

worth·less, wُrth'lis, *a.* Having no value; having no dignity or excellence; not deserving.—**worth·less·ly,** *adv.*—**worth·less·ness,** *n.*

worth·while, wُrth'hwīl′, wُrth'wīl′, *a.* Such as to repay one's time, attention,

interest, work, or trouble.—**worth·while·ness,** *n.*

wor·thy, wُr'ᴛʜē, *a.*—*worthier, worthiest.* Having worth; valuable; deserving praise; estimable or having merit; deserving, usu. followed by *of,* or an infinitive; as, *worthy* of love or hatred.—*n.* pl. **wor·thies.** A person of high position, great influence, or distinction, as: Doctors and lawyers are usually town *worthies.* A local character or celebrity, often humorous or derogatory in usage.—**wor·thi·ly,** *adv.*—**wor·thi·ness,** *n.*

would, wُd, *unstressed* wud, *aux. v.* The past and pp. of *will.* Used in conveying a mood, as to express a desire or wish, as: *Would* it were true! Used to express intent; as, those who *would* wage war; used to express customary action, as: She *would* go there daily. Used to express condition, as: He *would* if asked. Used to express uncertainty, as: *Would* that be all right? Used in expressing preference, as: He *would* rather win than lose. Used in expressing the future, as: They said they *would* come tomorrow. Used to make a statement or question less direct and blunt, as: *Would* you be so kind?

would-be, wُd'bē″, *a.* Wishing, aspiring, or pretending to be; as, a *would-be* wit; intended to be; as, *would-be* kindness.

would·n't, wُd'nt. Contraction of would not.

wound, wȯnd, *n.* [O.E. *wund,* a wound; also, as an adjective, wounded, < *winnan,* to fight; D. *wonde,* Icel. *und,* Dan. *vunde,* G. *wunde,* a wound.] A cut, breach, or rupture in the skin and flesh of a person or an animal caused by violence; a similar injury to a plant; any injury, hurt, or pain, as to the feelings.—*v.t.* To inflict a wound on; to cut, slash, or lacerate; to hurt the feelings of; to pain.—*v.i.* To inflict hurt or injury.—**wound·less,** *a.*

wound·ed, wȯn'did, *n. pl.* Persons suffering from a wound or wounds, often used with *the,* as: *The wounded* filled the aid station.—*a.*

wound·wort, wȯnd'wُrt″, *n.* Any of several plants having soft leaves formerly used for dressing wounds.

wove pa·per, *n.* Writing paper made with a surface of uniform appearance, without the markings found on laid paper.

wow, wou, *interj. Colloq.* an exclamation of surprise, wonder, pleasure, or dismay.—*n. Slang.* Something that proves an extraordinary success; an unqualified hit, as: The new play is a *wow.*—*v.t. Slang.* To raise great enthusiasm; to please greatly; as, to *wow* an audience.

wow, wou, wō, *n.* A wavering distortion or fluctuation of a reproduced sound due to variations of the speed of the reproduction apparatus, as a turntable or tape reel.

wrack, rak, *n.* [A form of *wreck;* the seaweed is so called as being cast up by the waves. Cf. Dan. *vrag,* wreck, *vrage,* to reject, Sw. *vrak,* wreck, refuse, *vraka,* to reject.] Seaweed, esp. when thrown ashore by the waves; *Brit. dial.* weeds. A wreck, esp. of a ship; a piece of wreckage; ruin.—*v.t., v.i. Archaic.* To ruin; to wreck; to be wrecked.—**wrack·ful,** *a.*

wrack, rak, *n.* A thin, flying cloud or a mass of such clouds; a rack.—*v.i.* To float or scud before a strong wind, as clouds.

wraith, rāth, *n.* [Origin unknown.] An apparition in the exact likeness of a person, seen before or soon after the person's death; a ghost; an apparition or insubstantial appearance.

wran·gle, rang'gl, *v.i.*—*wrangled, wrangling.* [A freq. < *wring, wringan,* pret. *wrang,* to press.] To dispute angrily; to brawl; to altercate; to engage in discussion and disputation.—*v.t.* To argue; to debate; to

ch- chain, G. na*ch*t; **th-** THen, thin; **w-** wig, hw as sound in whig; **z-** zh as in azure, zeal. *Italicized vowel indicates schwa sound.*

round up or herd, as cattle.—*n.* An angry dispute; a noisy quarrel.

wran·gler, rang′glẻr, *n.* One who wrangles; an angry or noisy disputant; a cowboy or herdsman; a student who has received the highest honors in the field of mathematics at Cambridge University, England.

wrap, rap, *v.t.*—*wrapped*—*wrapping.* [M.E. *wrappen*; origin uncertain.] To enclose, envelop, or muffle in something wound or folded about, often with *up*; as, to *wrap up* an injured hand; to enclose and fasten, as an article or package, within a covering of paper or the like, often with *up*; as, to *wrap up* a dress for delivery; to wind, fold, or bind, as something, about as a covering; to protect with coverings or outer garments, often with *up*; to surround, envelop, shroud, or hide; to involve.—*v.i.* To wrap oneself, used with *up*; to become wrapped, as about something; to fold.—*n.* Something to be wrapped about the person, as a shawl, scarf, cloak, or robe; *pl.* outdoor garments or coverings.—**wrapped up in,** *colloq.* Involved, engrossed, or absorbed in, as work, a project, or situation; bound up with, as children or family.—**keep un·der wraps,** *colloq.* to keep concealed or secret.

wrap·a·round, rap′*a*·round″, *a.* Overlapping or curving around, or appearing to overlap or curve around, esp. designating a garment, as a dress or robe, open to the hem, and wrapped around one's body before fastening.—*n.* A wraparound garment.

wrap·per, rap′ẻr, *n.* One who wraps; that in which anything is wrapped; an outer covering; a paper in which a magazine or newspaper is wrapped and mailed; a loose outer garment; a lady's dressing gown, negligee, or robe; the paper jacket of a book; the high-grade leaf of tobacco which covers a cigar.

wrap·ping, rap′ing, *n. Often pl.* that in which something is wrapped.

wrap up, *v.t.* To complete or conclude, as a business deal, project, or any undertaking.—**wrap-up,** rap′up″, *n.* A concise presentation of the news.

wrasse, ras, *n.* [W. *wrach.*] Any of the thalassic fishes belonging to the family *Labridae,* having oblong, prickly-spined, and brightly colored bodies and inhabiting temperate waters, some species of which are food fish.

wrath, rath, räth, *Brit.* rạth, *n.* [O.E. *wraeththo, wrath,* < *wráth,* wrathful, wroth; Icel. *reithi,* wrath, < *reithr,* wroth, < *ritha,* for *vritha,* to writhe or twist; Sw. and Dan. *vrede,* wrath; akin to *writhe, wreathe, wrest.*] Violent anger; vehement exasperation; indignation; rage; an angry act, esp. one of punishment.

wrath·ful, rath′ful, räth′ful, *Brit.* rạth′ful, *a.* Full of wrath; greatly incensed; raging; furious; indicating wrath. Also **wrath·y,** rath′ē, rä′thē, *Brit.* rạ′thē.—**wrath·ful·ly,** *adv.*—**wrath·ful·ness,** *n.*

wreak, rēk, *v.t.* [O.E. *wrecan,* to punish, to revenge, orig. to banish or drive away = D. *wreken,* to avenge or revenge; Icel. *reka,* to repel; G. *rächen,* to revenge; Goth. *wrikan,* to persecute; same root as L. *urgeo,* E. to *urge. Wretch, wreck,* are closely akin.] To inflict or cause to take effect; as, to *wreak* vengeance; to carry out the free expression of, as rage or rancor, on an object or person.

wreath, rēth, *n. pl.* **wreaths,** rēTHz. [O.E. *wraeth,* < *writhan,* to twist.] Something twisted or curled; a garland, as of flowers for a grave; a chaplet; an ornamental twisted band or bandage, worn on the head, or used for some other decorative purpose; a twist or curl.—**wreath·y,** *a.*

wreathe, rēTH, *v.t.*—*wreathed, wreathing.* To form into a wreath; to make or fashion by twining or twisting the parts together; to entwine; to intertwine; to surround with a wreath; to encircle or envelop.—*v.i.* To move or twine circularly; to be interwoven or entwined as a wreath.

wreck, rek, *n.* [M.E. *wrek, wrak,* appar. from Scand.: cf. Icel. *rek,* a thing drifted ashore, Sw. *vrak,* Dan. *vrag,* wreckage, wreck, refuse, Icel. *reka,* drive, also O.E. *wrecan,* drive, *wraec,* exile, misery.] Any building, structure, or thing reduced to a state of ruin; that which is cast ashore by the sea, as the remains of a ruined vessel or of its cargo; the ruin or destruction of a vessel in the course of navigation; shipwreck; a vessel in a state of ruin from disaster at sea, on rocks, or the like; the ruin or destruction of anything; someone of poor mental or physical health.—*v.t.* To cause the wreck of, as a vessel, as in the course of navigation; to shipwreck; to involve in a wreck; to cause the ruin or destruction of; as, to *wreck* a bank.—*v.i.* To suffer wreckage; to act as a wrecker; to engage in wrecking.—**wreck·ing,** *n., a.*

wreck·age, rek′ij, *n.* The act of wrecking; the condition of being wrecked; the materials or parts remaining from anything demolished, either by design or accident, as a building or vehicle.

wreck·er, rek′ẻr, *n.* A machine or person which wrecks; one engaged in the business of tearing down buildings to clear the sites; one who removes wreckage, as damaged automobiles or trains, from a right of way. A specially equipped automobile or truck used in removing such wreckage; also *tow car, tow truck.* A person or ship employed to recover cargo or goods from wrecked vessels, as well as the wrecked vessels; one who causes shipwrecks in order to plunder the wrecked ships; a plunderer of any kind.

wreck·ing bar, *n.* Pinch bar.

wren, ren, *n.* [O.E. *wrenna,* a wren; allied perh. to *wraene,* lascivious.] Any of various small passerine birds, family *Troglodytidae,* as the N. American house wren, *Troglodytes aedon,* and the European wren, *Troglodytes troglodytes.*

wrench, rench, *n.* [Same as O.E. *wrence, wrencan,* deceit, fraud (a figurative meaning); allied to G. *renken,* to sprain, to wrench; O.D. *wronck,* contortion; akin *wring, wrong, wrinkle.*] A violent twist, or a pull with twisting; a sprain; an injury by twisting, as in a joint; an emotional shock; a twisting, as of meaning; *mech.* any of various tools having jaws or a socket adapted to grip the head of a bolt or a nut to turn it.—*v.t.* To pull with a sudden, sharp, violent jerk; to twist, jerk, or tear from the normal position, as a ligament of the body; *fig.* to distort the meaning of, as something said.—*v.i.* To twist or give a turn or twist.

wrest, rest, *v.t.* [O.E. *wraestan,* to writhe, to twist; Icel. *reista* (for *vreista*), Dan. *vriste,* to wrest, to twist; akin to *writhe, wreathe, wrist; wrestle* is a derivative.] To twist; to wrench; to apply a violent twisting force to; to extort or bring out, as by a twisting, painful force; to force, as by torture; to turn from truth or twist from the natural meaning by violence; to pervert.—*n.* A wrench or twist; a wrestling action; a key with which to tune stringed musical instruments.—**wrest·er,** *n.*

wres·tle, res′l, *v.i.*—*wrestled, wrestling.* [A freq. of *wrest;* O.E. *wraestlian,* D. *wrastelen, worstelen,* to wrestle.] To contend by grappling and trying to throw down an adversary; to struggle, strive, or contend, followed by *with;* as, to *wrestle with* rising costs.—*v.t.* To contend with in wrestling; to strive for control over, as if by force; as, to *wrestle* a problem to its conclusion; *western U.S.* to throw to the ground for

branding, as young cattle.—*n.* A wrestling match; any struggle for mastery.—**wres·tler,** *n.*

wrest·ling, res′ling, *n.* A contact sport in which each of two opponents attempts to force the shoulders of the other to the mat or ground.

wrest pin, *n.* A pin of metal or wood in any stringed instrument on which the strings are twined or coiled and which is tightened or loosened in tuning the instrument.

wretch, rech, *n.* [O.E. *wraecca,* an outcast, an exile, < *wrecan,* to banish, to weak.] A miserable person; one who is supremely unhappy; a mean, base, or vile person.

wretch·ed, rech′id, *a.* [< *wretch;* similar in formation to *wicked.*] Miserable or unhappy; sunk into deep affliction or distress; causing unhappiness or misery; worthless; very poor or mean in quality; despicable.—**wretch·ed·ly,** *adv.*—**wretch·ed·ness,** *n.*

wrig·gle, rig′l, *v.i.*—*wriggled, wriggling.* [Freq. < older *wrig, wrigge,* to wriggle; so D. *wriggelen,* to wriggle, a freq. < *wrikken,* Dan. *vrikke,* to wriggle; akin *wry, wrench, wring, wrong.*] To move the body to and fro with short motions like a worm or an eel; to move with writhing or twisting of the body; to work by paltry shifts or schemes; as, to *wriggle* into one's confidence.—*v.t.* To cause, as a person, to wriggle.—*n.* The motion of one who wriggles; a quick twisting motion like that of a worm or an eel.—**wrig·gly,** rig′lē, *a.*—*wrigglier, wriggliest.*

wrig·gler, rig′lẻr, *n.* One who or that which wriggles. The larva of a mosquito; also *wiggler.*

wright, rīt, *n.* [O.E. *wyrhta,* a worker, a maker, < *wyrht,* a work, < *wyrcan,* to work.] An artisan or artificer; a worker in wood or a carpenter: chiefly used in compounds; as, ship*wright,* wheel*wright,* play*wright.*

wring, ring, *v.t.*—*wrung, wringing.* [O.E. *wringan,* to wring, strain, press = L.G. and D. *wringen,* Dan. *vraenge,* Sw. *vränga,* G. *ringer,* to wring, twist, etc., all nasalized forms of stem seen in *wriggle,* and in O.E. *wrigian,* to bend (whence *wry*), and akin to *wrong.*] To twist and squeeze or compress; to forcibly twist out of shape or into an awkward position; to pain, as if by twisting or squeezing; to torture or distress; as, to *wring* one's heart; to squeeze or press out, as a liquid, esp. by twisting; to extort or force as if by twisting; as, to *wring* a confession or money from a person; to force off by twisting, as a bottle cap; to grip tightly with or without twisting, as the hands.—*v.i.* To writhe or twist, as with anguish.—*n.* A twisting or wringing.

wring·er, ring′ẻr, *n.* One who wrings; an apparatus for forcing water from clothes, after they have been washed, by compression between rollers.

wrin·kle, ring′kl, *n.* [O.E. *wrincle* a wrinkle = O.D. *wrinckle,* a wrinkle; a dim. form corresponding to Dan. *rynke,* Sw. *rynka,* a wrinkle; akin to *wring, wrench,* etc.] A small ridge or a furrow, formed by the folding, shrinking, or contraction of any smooth substance; a small crease or fold in the skin, as caused by age.—*v.t.*—*wrinkled, wrinkling.* To contract into wrinkles or furrows; to furrow or crease.—*v.i.* To become contracted into wrinkles.—**wrin·kly,** ringk′lē, *a.*—*wrinklier, wrinkliest.*

wrin·kle, ring′kl, *n. Colloq.* an innovative or ingenious method, device, or idea.

wrist, rist, *n.* [O.E. *wrist, handwrist,* the wrist; lit. 'the turning joint,' < *writhan,* to twist; Dan. and Sw. *vrist,* Icel. *rist* (for *vrist*), the instep; G. *rist,* the wrist, the instep.] The joint by which the hand is united to the arm, and by means of which the hand moves on the forearm; the carpus;

the section on a glove or other garment which is a covering for the wrist; *mech.* a wrist pin.

wrist·band, rist'band", *n.* The band or part of a sleeve, esp. of a shirt sleeve, which covers the wrist.

wrist·let, rist'lit, *n.* A band worn around the wrist, esp. to protect it from cold; a bracelet; *slang*, a handcuff.

wrist·lock, rist'lok", *n.* A hold upon a wrestler's wrist which makes it impossible for him to use his arms and hands.

wrist pin, *n. Mech.* a stud or pin projecting from the side of a piston for attachment to a connecting rod. Also *gudgeon pin.*

wrist watch, *n.* A watch which is attached to a band and fastened on the wrist.

writ, rit, *n.* [O.E. *writ, gewrit,* a writing, a writ; < *writan,* to write.] *Law,* a written order or precept issued by a judicial court or official in the name of a sovereign power, commanding the person to whom it is addressed to perform or cease the performance of a specified act.

write, rit, *v.t.*—past *wrote* or archaic *writ*; pp. *written* or archaic *writ*; ppr. *writing.* [O.E. *writan,* pret. *wrat,* pp. *writen,* to write = Icel. *rita,* to scratch, write; Sw. *rita,* to draw, to trace; D. *rijten,* G. *reissen,* to tear. Orig. it meant to scratch marks with something sharp.] To form or trace; as, to *write* the alphabet on the blackboard; to communicate or describe in writing; as, to *write* a report on the meeting; to fill out the blank places of; as, to *write* a money order; to set down as letters, words, numbers, or the like; as, to *write* several copies of the math assignment; to communicate with, by writing a letter; to create by writing; to create, as by an author or composer; to cover with writing; as, to *write* several full sheets of paper; to impress deeply and durably; to draft or draw up, as a will; to underwrite; to spell as specified; to designate or call in writing, as: He *writes* himself 'Admiral.'—*v.i.* To trace or form characters with a pen, pencil, or the like; to work as an author or writer; to set forth ideas or facts in writing; to produce or communicate by a letter or letters; to produce a certain kind of writing.—**writ·a·ble,** *a.*

write down, *v.t.* To set forth in writing; to record; to belittle or injure in writing; to appeal in writing to an uncultivated readership.—**write-down,** rit'doun", *n. Accounting,* a reduction of the recorded value of an asset.

write in, *v.t.* To cast a vote for, as a candidate not listed on an official ballot, usu. by writing a name in a space provided; to write, as an application or request, usu. in response to an advertisement or other public appeal; to make a written insertion in, as a manuscript or document.

write-in, rit'in", *a.* Of, pertaining to, or designating votes written in; as, a *write-in* candidate.—*n.* A vote for a candidate whose name is not printed on the ballot.

write off, *v.t.* To note or record the deduction or canceling of; to depreciate; to drop or dismiss from mind or consideration.—**write-off,** rit'af", rit'of", *n.*

write out, *v.t.* To set forth in writing; to state fully in writing; to exhaust the literary capacity of by too much writing: used reflexively.

writ·er, ri'ter, *n.* A person who writes, esp. one who has written a particular item; as, the *writer* of the letter; one who writes as an occupation; an author.

writ·er's cramp, *n.* A spasmodic muscle contraction affecting the fingers or hand of persons who have been writing excessively.

write up, *v.t.* To report fully in a written account; to update in writing; to praise highly in a general publication; *accounting,*

to set an excessive value upon.—**write-up,** rit'up", *n.*

writhe, riTH, *v.i.*—*writhed, writhing.* [O.E. *writhan,* to writhe, wreath, twist = Icel. *ritha* (for *vritha*), Dan. *vride,* Sw. *vrida,* to writhe; < same root as *worth* (verb), L. *verto,* to turn. Akin *wrath, wreath, wrist, wrest.*] To twist the body about, as in pain; to suffer mental distress, as from acute anguish.—*v.t.* To twist with violence; as, to *writhe* the body; to distort.—*n.* A writhing action; a twisted shape or contortion.—**writh·er,** *n.*

writ·ing, ri'ting, *n.* The act of one who or that which writes; the state of being written, or written form; as, to obtain a statement in *writing*; that which is written; characters or matter written with a pen or similar instrument; as, paper bearing *writing*; such characters or matter with respect to style, kind, or quality; as childish *writing*; an inscription; a letter; any written or printed paper or document; literary work with respect to style, kind, or quality; as, allegorical *writing*; a literary composition or production; as, novels, poems, and miscellaneous *writings*; the occupation or profession of a writer or author.

writ·ing desk, *n.* A desk or piece of furniture for use in writing, commonly with drawers and pigeonholes, for holding materials, papers, or the like; a portable case for holding materials for writing, and affording, when opened, a surface to rest the paper on in writing.

writ·ing pa·per, *n.* Paper of suitable kinds and sizes for writing on.

writ of as·sis·tance, *n. Law,* a writ that is issued to an officer, as a marshal, to enforce a search or an order of the court.

writ of cer·ti·o·ra·ri, *n.* Certiorari.

writ of e·lec·tion, *n.* A writ issued by an executive authority, ordering an election to be held, esp. a special election so that a vacancy in an elective office may be filled.

writ of er·ror, *n. Law,* a writ which any appellate court may issue that allows a record of some former legal action to be examined and the decision corrected or reversed, if an alleged error is found to exist.

writ of ex·tent, *n. Law,* a writ, formerly issued in England for the recovery of debts that were owed to the English crown, which authorized the seizure of property, goods, and the like, from the debtor.

writ of pro·hi·bi·tion, *n. Law,* a writ that any superior court issues to arrest the prosecution and proceedings of some inferior court because the matter, or some part of the matter, it is considering rests outside or in excess of its jurisdiction.

writ of right, *n. Law,* a writ that restores or establishes real estate ownership in a land dispute.

wrong, rang, rong, *a.* [A participial form < *wring*; Dan. *vrang,* Icel. *rangr, vrangr,* wrong; D. *wrang,* sour, harsh (lit. twisting the mouth).] Not right; not according to rule, wish, design, or the like; not what ought to be; not according to moral law or right; not according to facts or truth; inaccurate; erroneous; being in error; mistaken; designed to be worn inward, as: That is the *wrong* side of the dress.—*n.* What is not right, esp. morally; a wrong, unfair, or unjust act; any injury, hurt, pain, or damage; *law,* a violation of a person's rights.—*adv.* In a wrong direction or manner.—*v.t.* To treat with injustice; to deal harshly or unfairly with; to do injustice to by imputation; to think ill of unfairly.— **go wrong,** to fail or go awry.—**wrong·ly,** *adv.*—**wrong·ness,** *n.*

wrong·do·er, rang'dö"er, rang'dö"er, rong'- dö"er, rong'dö"er, *n.* One who does wrong or evil.—**wrong·do·ing,** *n.*

wronged, rangd, rongd, *a.* Suffering from an injustice; harmed.

wrong font, *n. Print.* a type, not of the proper font, size, or style, for its place. Abbr. *wf, w.f.*

wrong·ful, rang'ful, rong'ful, *a.* Injurious; unjust; unfair; contrary to law or justice.— **wrong·ful·ly,** *adv.*—**wrong·ful·ness,** *n.*

wrong-head·ed, wrong·head·ed, rang'- hed'id, rong'hed'id, *a.* Stubbornly holding to misguided views or opinions; perversely wrong.—**wrong-head·ed·ly, wrong·head·- ed·ly,** *adv.*—**wrong-head·ed·ness, wrong·- head·ed·ness,** *n.*

wroth, rath, roth, *Brit.* rōth, *a.* [O.E. *wrath,* angry, enraged (whence *wrath*), lit. 'twisted,' < *writhan,* to twist or writhe.] Very angry; much exasperated; wrathful.

wrought, rat, *a.* Worked; elaborated; not rough or crude; beaten and shaped with a hammer or other tool, as metal articles.— **wrought-up,** rat'up', *a.* Excited; as, to be *wrought-up* over a trifle; also *worked-up.*

wrought i·ron, *n.* A comparatively pure form of iron, as that produced from pig iron, which contains almost no carbon, and which is easily forged and welded.— **wrought-i·ron,** rat'i"ern, *a.*

wry, ri, *a.*—*wrier, wriest.* [O.E. *wrigian,* to bend, to turn, to incline; akin to *wriggle.*] Abnormally bent or turned to one side; twisted; distorted; crooked; perverse; warped or distorted, as in subject or meaning; ironically or bitterly humorous; as, wry wit.—*v.t.*—*wried, wrying.* To twist.— **wry·ly,** *adv.*—**wry·ness,** *n.*

wry·neck, ri'nek", *n. Pathol.* torticollis; *colloq.* a person having a twisted or distorted neck. A small bird, genus *Jynx,* allied to the woodpeckers: so called from the manner in which it twists its neck.

wul·fen·ite, wul'fe·nit", *n.* [G. *wulfenit*; named from Baron F. X. von *Wulfen* (1728–1805), Austrian scientist.] A mineral consisting of lead molybdate, occurring usu. in tabular crystals, and varying in color from grayish to bright yellow or red. Also **yel·low lead ore.**

wurst, wurst, *n.* See *sausage.*

Wy·an·dotte, wi'an·dot", *n.* [From the *Wyandotte,* or *Wyandot,* Indians.] One of an American breed of medium-sized, domestic fowls, raised for eggs and meat.

Wyc·lif·fite, Wyc·lif·ite, wik'li·fit", *a.* Of or pertaining to the English theologian, John Wycliffe, c1320–84, his principles, or his followers.—*n.* A follower of John Wycliffe. Also **Lol·lard, Lol·ler.**

wy·vern, wi·vern, wi'vern, *n.* [O.Fr. *wivre, vivre* (with *n* added as in *bittern*), a viper, a dragon, < L. *vipera,* a viper.] *Her.* a representation of a winged dragon with two legs and a body tapering to a snakelike form.

X

X, x, eks, *n.* The twenty-fourth letter of the English alphabet and eighteenth consonant; the sound of the letter X as represented in speech; the delineation of the letter X or x in writing or printing; something designated by or having the shape of the letter X or x; a graphic device for printing the letter X or x.

X, eks, *n.* Christ; Christian. (*Sometimes l.c.*) the Roman numeral representing 10; an indication of a location on maps or diagrams, as: *X* marks the spot. A movie rating denoting a film for adult viewing only.

x, eks, *n.* A term often used to designate a person, thing, agency, factor, or the like whose true name is unknown or withheld. *Math.* an unknown quantity; abscissa; a sign of multiplication, as: $5 x 5 = 25$. A symbol for a kiss, esp. at the end of a letter; a sign used between numbers in dimensions; as, a room 8 feet x 12 feet; (*often cap.*) the signature of an illiterate. An indication of choice, as on a ballot; often an indication of error, as in test scoring.

x, eks, *v.t.*—x-ed, x-ing, x'd, x'ing. To take out, excise, or cancel, as a word or line of written material, usu. followed by *out*; to choose by the use of an *x*, as an item on a multiple-choice questionnaire.

xan·thate, zan'thāt, *n. Chem.* a salt or ester of xanthic acid.

xan·thic, zan'thik, *a.* [Gr. *xanthós*, yellow.] Yellow, applied esp. to a series of colors in flowers including the yellows and all colors which tend toward yellow. *Chem.* of or pertaining to xanthine or xanthic acid; pertaining to or denoting an organic acid occurring as a colorless, oily liquid with a penetrating smell, its copper salts having a bright yellow color.

xan·thin, zan'thin, *n.* [Gr. *xanthós*, yellow.] That part of the yellow coloring matter in yellow flowers which is insoluble in water; a yellow coloring matter contained in madder.

xan·thine, zan'thēn, zan'thin, *n.* [Gr. *xanthós*, yellow.] *Biochem.* A crystalline nitrogenous compound, $C_5H_4N_4O_2$, closely related to uric acid, found in urine, blood, and certain animal and plant tissues; any derivative of this substance.

Xan·thip·pe, Xan·tip·pe, zan·tip'ē, *n.* [Wife of Socrates.] A shrewish female, esp. a wife.

xan·tho·chroid, zan'thō·kroid″, *a.* [Gr. *xanthóchroos*, yellow-skinned, < *xanthós*, yellow, and *chróa*, skin, complexion.] *Ethnol.* belonging or pertaining to light-complexioned or light-haired Caucasoid peoples.—*n.*

xan·tho·ma, zan·thō'ma, *n.* pl. **xan·tho·mas, xan·tho·ma·ta.** *Pathol.* a skin condition marked by small, yellow, raised plates or nodules, esp. in the eyelids.—**xan·tho·ma·tous,** *a.*

xan·tho·phyll, xan·tho·phyl, zan'thō·fil *n.* [Gr. *xanthós*, yellow, *phyllon*, a leaf.] *Biochem.* Any of a group of yellow carotene derivatives, esp. a pigment, $C_{40}H_{54}(OH)_2$, found in withering leaves; lutein.—**xan·tho·phyll·ous,** zan'thō·fil'us, *a.*

x-ax·is, eks'ak″sis, *n.* pl. **x-ax·es,** eks'ak″-sēz. *Math.* The horizontal axis of the two axes in a two-dimensional Cartesian coordinate system for locating points in a plane; the abscissa; one axis of three axes in the Cartesian coordinate system of three dimensions for locating points in space. Compare *y-axis, z-axis.*

X-chro·mo·some, eks'krō″mo·sōm, *n. Genetics,* the sex chromosome carrying or associated with female characteristics, which occurs in a paired state in the female cell and zygote, and with one Y-chromosome in the male cell and zygote.

X-dis·ease, eks'di·zēz″, *n. Veter. pathol.* hyperkeratosis.

xe·bec, ze·bec, zē'bek, *n.* [Sp. *xabeque,* < Turk. *sumbeki,* a xebec; Ar. *sumbûk,* a small vessel.] A small three-masted vessel having both square and lateen sails, formerly used by Barbary pirates, and still in limited use in Mediterranean commercial traffic.

xe·ni·a, zē'nē·a, *n.* [N.L., < Gr. *xénios,* pertaining to a guest or to hospitality, < *xénos,* guest.] *Bot.* in hybrid fertilization, the immediate influence or effect of pollen on the seed or fruit which is pollinated rather than on the embryo.

xen·o·di·ag·no·sis, zen″o·dī″ag·nō'sis, *n. Med.* a means of detecting a parasitic disease, as in humans, by feeding an unin-fected insect or other host on material believed to be infected and later checking it for the disease or infection.—**xen·o·di·ag·nos·tic,** zen″o·dī″ag·nos'tik, *a.*

xen·o·gen·e·sis, zen″o·jen'i·sis, *n.* [Gr. *xenos,* strange, and *genesis,* birth.] *Biol.* the supposed production of offspring entirely unlike the parents. Also **xe·nog·e·ny,** ze·noj'e·nē.—**xen·o·ge·net·ic, xen·o·gen·ic,** zen″ō·je·net'ik, *a.*

xen·o·lith, zen'o·lith, *n. Geol.* rock fragments not related to the rock in which they occur.—**xen·o·lith·ic,** *a.*

xe·non, zē'non, zen'on, *n.* [Gr. *xenos,* stranger.] *Chem.* a colorless, odorless, gaseous element in the atmosphere, very rare and chemically inactive. Sym. Xe, at. no. 54, at. wt. 131.30. See Periodic Table of Elements.

xen·o·pho·bi·a, zen″o·fō'bē·a, *n.* Hatred, distrust, or contempt of foreigners, esp. as reflected in foreign policy or political opinion; *psychol.* a morbid or abnormal fear of unfamiliar persons.—**xen·o·phobe,** zen'o·fōb″, *n.*—**xen·o·pho·bic,** *a.*

xe·rarch, zēr'ärk, *a. Ecology,* indigenous to a dry locality or site.

xe·ric, zēr'ik, *a.* Pertaining to or adjusted to a dry climate.—**xe·ri·cal·ly,** *adv.*

xe·rog·ra·phy, zi·rog'ra·fē, *n. Print.* the application of negatively charged resin powder to a metal plate sensitized with static electricity to form an image which is thermally fused onto a printing surface.—**xe·ro·graph·ic,** zēr″o·graf'ik, *a.*—**xe·ro·graph·i·cal·ly,** *adv.*

xe·roph·i·lous, zi·rof'i·lus, *a.* [Gr. *xērós,* dry, and *philos,* loving.] *Biol.* growing in, or adapted for existence in dry, esp. dry and hot regions, as some animals and plants.—**xe·roph·i·ly,** *n.*

xe·roph·thal·mi·a, zēr″of·thal'mē·a, *n.* [Gr. *ophthalmos,* the eye.] A dry, red soreness or itching of the eyes, caused by an insufficiency of vitamin A.—**xe·roph·thal·mic,** *a.*

xe·ro·phyte, zēr'o·fīt″, *n.* [Gr. *xēros,* dry, *phyton,* a plant.] *Bot.* a plant adapted to live in surroundings of extreme drought and heat.—**xe·ro·phyt·ic,** zēr″o·fit'ik, *a.*—**xe·ro·phyt·i·cal·ly,** *adv.*—**xe·ro·phyt·ism,** zēr'o·fī″tiz·um, zēr'o·fi·tiz″um, *n.*

x-height, eks'hīt″, *n. Typography,* the height of the small letter *x.*

xi, zī, sī, *Gr.* ksē, *n.* [Gr. *xi.*] The fourteenth letter, Ξ, ξ, of the Greek alphabet; the English *X, x.*

xiph·i·ster·num, zif″i·stųr'num, *n.* pl. **xiph·i·ster·na,** zif″i·stųr'na. [N.L., < Gr. *xiphos,* sword, and N.L. *sternum.*] *Anat.* the lowermost portion of the sternum. Also *xiphoid.*

xiph·oid, zif'oid, *a.* [Gr. *xiphos,* a sword, and *eidos,* likeness.] Ensiform, or shaped like or resembling a sword; *anat.* related or referring to the xiphisternum.

xiph·oid, zif'oid, *n.* Xiphisternum.

xiph·o·su·ran, zif″o·sų̨r'an, *a. Zool.* relating to any arthropod of the order *Xiphsura,* which comprises the horseshoe crabs.—*n.*

Xmas, eks'mas, *n.* [*X,* symbol for Christ; *mas,* contraction of Mass.] Christmas.

X·ray, eks'rā″, *n.* A communications code word to designate the letter X.

X-ray pho·to·graph, *n.* A picture produced by x-rays.

X-rays, x-rays, eks'rāz″, *n. pl.* High frequency electromagnetic rays of short wave length, generated by the impact of high speed electrons on a metal target, capable of penetrating solid masses, destroying living tissue, and affecting a photographic plate; *sing.* an X-ray photograph, esp. one used in medical diagnosis.—**X-ray, x-ray,** eks'rā″, *v.t.* To examine or treat, as a person, with X-rays; to photograph with X-rays.

X-ray star, *n.* A certain astronomical body, as a star, which emits X-rays.

X-ray ther·a·py, *n.* Treatment of certain diseases, as cancer, by the use of X-rays.

X-ray tube, *n.* A vacuum tube containing a metal target, on which X-rays are produced by impact of electrons.

xy·lan, zī'lan, *n.* A gummy pentosan, found in cell walls of plants and woody tissue, and yielding xylose with the occurrence of hydrolysis.

xy·lem, zī'lem, zī'lem, *n.* [G., < Gr. *xylon,* wood.] *Bot.* that part of a vascular bundle which consists of tracheids, parenchyma cells, vessels, and woody fibers, which forms the woody tissue, and functions in conducting water and minerals. Compare *phloem.*

xy·lem ray, *n. Bot.* a band of vascular rays that are in or reach radially into the secondary xylem: distinguished from *phloem ray.* Also *wood ray.*

xy·lene, zī'lēn, *n.* [Gr. *xylon,* wood.] *Chem.* any of three isomeric hydrocarbons of the benzene series, $C_6H_4(CH_3)_2$, occurring as oily, colorless liquids obtained chiefly from coal tar, and used mainly in the manufacture of dyes. Also **xy·lol,** zī'lōl, zī'lol.

xy·lic ac·id, zī'lik as'id, *n. Chem.* any of six crystalline or isomeric acids obtained from xylene.

xy·li·dine, zī'li·dēn″, zī'li·din, zil'i·dēn″, zil'i·din, *n. Chem.* Any of six isomeric compounds, $(CH_3)_2C_6H_3NH_2$, derivatives of xylene, which resemble aniline; an oily liquid consisting of a mixture of certain of these compounds, used commercially in the manufacture of dyes.

xy·lo·graph, zī'lo·graf″, zī'lo·gräf″, *n.* [Gr. *xylon,* and *graphō,* to write or engrave.] A wood engraving or a print taken from it.—**xy·log·ra·pher,** zī·log'ra·fẽr, *n.*

xy·log·ra·phy, zī·log'ra·fē, *n.* Wood engraving or printing from a wood engraving; a process of decorative painting.—**xy·lo·graph·ic, xy·lo·graph·i·cal,** zī″lo·graf'ik, *a.*—**xy·lo·graph·i·cal·ly,** *adv.*

xy·loph·a·gous, zī·lof'a·gus, *a.* Boring into or feeding on wood, as certain mollusks, fungi, and larvae.

xy·lo·phone, zī'lo·fōn″, *n.* A musical instrument consisting of a graduated series of wooden bars, usu. sounded by striking with small wooden hammers.—**xy·lo·phon·ist,** zī'lo·fō″nist, zī·lof'o·nist, zī'lo·fō″nist, zī·lof'o·nist, *n.*

xy·lose, zī'lōs, *n. Chem.* a crystalline, white pentose powder, $C_5H_{10}O_5$, obtained by the hydrolysis or fermentation of corn cobs, wood, or straw, and used in dyeing and tanning.

xy·lot·o·mous, zī·lot'o·mus, *a.* Adapted or able to cut or bore wood, as various insects.

xy·lot·o·my, zī·lot'o·mē, *n.* [Gr. *xylon,* wood, and *-tomia,* a cutting, < *témnein,* cut.] The art of cutting sections of wood, as with a microtome, for microscopic examination.—**xy·lo·tom·ic, xy·lo·tom·i·cal,** zī″lo·tom'ik, *a.*—**xy·lot·o·mist,** *n.*

Y

Y, y, wī, *n.* The twenty-fifth letter of the English alphabet; a semivowel; the sound of the letter Y as represented in speech; the delineation of the letter Y or y in writing or printing; something designated by or having the shape of the letter Y or y; a graphic device for printing the letter Y or y; (*cap.*), *chem.* yttrium; (*cap.*) yen, the monetary unit of Japan; (*cap.*), *colloq.* Y.M.C.A and similar organizations whose title bears an initial Y.

y, wī. *Math.* An unknown, used esp. following *x* to form a set; an ordinate.

yacht, yot, *n*. [D. *jacht*, yacht, fast-sailing vessel, also chase, hunting (= G. *jagd*), < *jagen* (= G. *jagen*), drive, chase, hunt.] A boat propelled by sail or motor, and used for pleasure trips, private cruising, racing, or the like.—*v.i.* To sail, voyage, or race in a yacht.

yacht·ing, yot'ing, *n*. The practice or sport of navigating, sailing, or voyaging in a yacht.

yachts·man, yots'man, *n*. pl. **yachts·men**. One who owns or sails a yacht.—**yachts·man·ship**, **yacht·man·ship**, *n*.

ya·ger, yā'gér, *n*. Jaeger.

ya·gi, yä'gē, yag'ē, *n*. A type of television or radio antenna, consisting of a horizontal conductor with insulated dipoles arranged parallel to and on the same plane as the conductor. Also **ya·gi an·ten·na**.

ya·hoo, yä'hö, yā'hö, yä·hö', *n*. pl. **ya·hoos**. [From *Yahoo*, one of the creatures depicted by Jonathan Swift in *Gulliver's Travels* as an emblem of man's bestiality.] A brutish, crude, or rowdy person.

Yah·weh, yä'we, *n*. The God of Biblical Israel: a transliteration of the Tetragrammaton. Also **Jah·ve**, **Jah·veh**, **Jah·we**, **Jah·weh**, **Yah·ve**, **Yah·veh**, **Yah·we**, yä've. Compare *Jehovah*.

Yah·wism, yä'wiz·um, *n*. The monotheistic religion of the ancient Hebrews.

Yah·wis·tic, yä·wis'tik, *a*. Characterized by the use of the name Yahweh, esp. of or pertaining to the Yahwist or Jehovist, the author of early Biblical texts using the Tetragrammaton, as opposed to *Elohistic*; of or pertaining to Yahwism. Also **Je·ho·vis·tic**.

yak, yak, *n*. pl. **yaks**, **yak**. [Tibetan.] A large, stocky ox, *Bos grunniens*, with long, silky hair, living in the mountain regions of Tibet, in both the wild and the domesticated state.

yak, **yack**, yak, *v.i.*—*yakked*, *yakking*, *yacked*, *yacking*. *Slang*. To talk rapidly and continually; to laugh loudly.—*n*. *Slang*. Incessant chatter; joke.

yam, yam, *n*. [Pg. *inhame* or Sp. *igname*, *ñame*, = Fr. *igname*; prob. of Afr. origin.] The starchy, tuberous root of any of various vines of the genus *Dioscorea*, much cultivated for food in the warmer regions of both hemispheres; any of these plants; a large sweet potato.

ya·men, yä'men, *n*. [Chin.] The residence or office of a Chinese official, as a mandarin, or a department headquarters, in the Chinese Empire. Also **ya·mun**.

yam·mer, yam'ér, *v.i.* [O.E. *geomrian*, mourn, complain, < *gēomor*, sad, mournful; akin to G. *jammer*, lamentation, misery.] *Colloq*. To lament, wail, whine, or complain; to make an outcry or clamor; to talk loudly and persistently.—*v.t. Colloq*. to utter or say in complaint.—*n*. An act of lamenting or complaining.—**yam·mer·er**, *n*.

Yang, yäng, yang, *n*. (*Sometimes l.c.*), *Chin. philos.* the active male force or principle in nature whose manifestations are opposite and complementary to those of Yin in their joint perpetual replication of the universe.

yank, yangk, *v.t.*, *v.i.* [Origin obscure.] To pull with a sudden, vigorous, jerking motion; to jerk.—*n*. A sudden jerking pull; a jerk.

Yan·kee, yang'kē, *n*. [Of disputed origin; commonly referred to an Indian corruption of the word *English*; also conjectured to be from D. *Janke*, dim. of *Jan*, *John*.] A native or inhabitant of any of the northern

states of the U.S.; a northern soldier in the American Civil War; any native or inhabitant of the U.S. Also *colloq.* **Yank**.—*a*. Of, pertaining to, or characteristic of the Yankees. Also *colloq.* **Yank**.—**Yan·kee·dom**, yang'kē·dom, *n*.—**yan·kee·ism**, yang'kē·iz"um, *n*.

Yan·kee, yang'kē, *n*. A communications code word to designate the letter Y.

Yan·kee Doo·dle, *n*. A famous tune, popular in the time of the American Revolution, now regarded as American and national.

yap, yap, *v.i.*—*yapped*, *yapping*. [Imit.] To yelp; to bark snappishly; *colloq.* to talk snappishly, noisily, or foolishly.—*v.t.* To utter by yapping.—*n*. A yelp; a snappish bark. *Colloq*. snappish, noisy, or foolish talk; the mouth.

ya·pok, **ya·pock**, ya·pok', *n*. An opossum of S. America, *Chironectes minimus*, aquatic in its habits, and resembling a small otter. Also **wa·ter o·pos·sum**.

Yar·bor·ough, yär'bur"ō, yär'bur"ō, *Brit.* yär'bér·o, *n*. [From the Second Earl of *Yarborough* (d. 1897), who is said to have lost a bet at odds of 1000 to 1 that such a hand would not be dealt.] A hand in bridge or whist with all cards lower than a ten.

yard, yärd, *n*. [O.E. *gyrd*, *gird*, a rod, a yard measure = D. *garde*, G. *gerte*, a rod, a twig; Goth. *gazds*, a goad; cogn. with L. *hasta*, a spear.] The British and American standard measure of length, equal to 3 feet or 36 inches, or 0.9144 meter; abbr. *yd.*, *y*. *Naut.* a long cylindrical piece of timber in a ship, slung crosswise to a mast, and supporting and extending a sail.

yard, yärd, *n*. [O.E. *geard* = D. and Dan. *gaard* = Icel. *gardhr*, yard, = Goth. *gards*, house; akin to L. *hortus*, garden, *cohors*, enclosure, Gr. *chórtos*, yard: cf. *garth*, *garden*, *court*, and *gird*.] The ground adjoining or surrounding a house or other buildings; a court or an outdoor area, frequently paved, near to or surrounded by a building; an enclosed area outdoors, designed for use by residents, students, and the like; an outdoor area surrounded by buildings; as, a campus *yard*; an area of enclosed ground used for animals; as, a poultry *yard*; an enclosure within which any work or business is carried on; as, a ship*yard*; an outdoor storage or assembly area; a space with tracks adjacent to a railroad terminal used for the switching or making up of trains; an outdoor area used for a garden; the winter pasture or browsing ground of moose and deer.—*v.t.* To put into or enclose in a yard. —*v.i.* To assemble as in a yard.—**the Yard**, Scotland Yard.

yard·age, yär'dij, *n*. The use of a yard or enclosure in loading or unloading livestock at a railroad station; the charge made for such use.

yard·age, yär'dij, *n*. Measurement or the amount measured in yards.

yard·arm, yärd'ärm", *n*. *Naut.* either end of a yard of a square sail.

yard·bird, yärd'burd", *n*. *Slang*. A new inductee in the army; an armed serviceman who is bungling, inefficient, or under punishment; a prison convict.

yard goods, *n*. Fabrics or other goods for sale by the yard. Also *piece goods*.

yard grass, *n*. A coarse, spiked, annual grass, *Eleusine indica*, common in dooryards and fields.

yard·man, yärd'man, *n*. pl. **yard·men**. A man employed in yard or service work, as in a railroad yard or boatyard.

yard·mas·ter, yärd'mas"tér, yärd'mä"stér, *n*. One in charge of a railroad yard.

yard·stick, yärd'stik", *n*. A stick a yard long, commonly marked with subdivisions, used for measuring; any standard of measurement.

yare, yâr, yär, *a*. [O.E. *gearu* = *garu* = O.H.G. *garo* (G. *gar*) = Icel. *görr*, ready.] Brisk; quick; answering quickly to the helm, as a ship, yâr, yär; also *yar. Archaic*, ready or prepared, yâr.—**yare·ly**, *adv*.

yar·mul·ke, yär'mul·ke, yä'mul·ke, *n*. A skullcap worn by observant male Jews of the Orthodox or Conservative tradition during religious services, sacred study, or occasions when respect for religious representation is called for. Also **yar·mel·ke**, **yar·mul·kah**.

yarn, yärn, *n*. [O.E. *gearn* = D. *garen* = G. *garn* = Icel., Sw., and Dan. *garn*, yarn.] Thread spun from wool or other fibrous material, esp. that prepared for weaving or for knitting; the thread, in the form of a loosely twisted aggregate of fibers, as of hemp, of which rope is made; thread, as of plastic, metal, silk, or the like, of which several fibers twisted together form a strand; *colloq.* a story or tale of adventure, extraordinary occurrences, or the like, esp. a tale that is highly improbable.—*v.i. Colloq.* To spin a yarn; to tell stories.

yarn-dyed, yärn'did", *a*. *Textiles*, pertaining to yarn dyed before weaving, as distinguished from *piece-dyed*.

yar·row, yar'ō, *n*. [O.E. *gearwe* = D. *gerw* = G. *garbe*, yarrow.] A common perennial plant, *Achillea millefolium*, of Europe and N. America, with finely divided leaves, white flowers, and a strong scent; any of various herbs of the same genus. Also *milfoil*.

yash·mak, **yash·mac**, yäsh·mäk', yash'mak, *n*. [Ar.] A thick or double veil worn in public by Moslem women to conceal the face. Also **yas·mak**.

yat·a·ghan, **yat·a·gan**, yat'a·gan", yat'a·gan, *Turk.* yä'tä·gän', *n*. [Turk.] A Turkish dagger or scimitar with the blade curved twice and without a cross guard to the handle. Also *ataghan*.

yau·pon, ya'pon, *n*. A tall shrub of the holly family, *Ilex vomitoria*, growing wild in the southern U.S., the leaves of which were formerly used to make tea and medicines. Also **ya·pon**.

yaw, yä, *v.i.* [Cf. prov. G. *gagen*, to rock, to move unsteadily.] *Naut.* to deviate wildly from course, as a ship; *aerospace*, to swerve from course by rotating about the vertical axis, as an aircraft, rocket, or the like.—*v.t.* To cause to rotate about a vertical axis.—*n*. A sudden deviation of a ship from its course; the rotational movement of an aircraft, rocket, or the like about a vertical axis; the amount of this movement or the angle of yaw.

yawl, yäl, *n*. [D. *jol*.] A ship's small boat, usu. rowed by four or six oars; a fore-and-aft rigged vessel with a large mainmast nearer the bow, and a much smaller mast nearer the stern and set far aft, usu. behind the rudder.

yawn, yän, *v.i.* [O.E. *gánian*, to yawn, to gape; akin Sc. *gant*, to yawn; Gr. *gāhnen*, to yawn; < root seen in Gr. *chainō*, L. *hio*, to gape; also in G. *gans*, E. *gander*, goose. From same root are *chasm*, *chaos*.] To have the mouth open involuntarily with a long inhalation of air, through drowsiness or dullness; to open wide; to stand open, as a chasm, gulf, or the like.—*v.t.* To say or express with a yawn.—*n*. An involuntary opening of the mouth from drowsiness; a gaping or opening wide.—**yawn·er**, *n*.

yawn·ing, ya'ning, *a*. Wide open; gaping; expressing boredom or tiredness by a yawn.

yawp, **yaup**, yäp, yäp, *v.i.* [Imit.: cf. *yap* and *yelp*.] *Colloq.* to utter a loud, harsh cry or sound; to yelp; to bawl. *Slang*, to talk noisily and foolishly.—*n. Colloq.* a noisy cry; any harsh or raucous sound. *Slang*, a noisy, foolish utterance.—**yawp·er**, *n*.— **yawp·ing**, *n*.

yaws, yạz, *n. pl. but sing. in constr.* [Afr. *yaw,* a raspberry.] *Pathol.* an infectious tropical disease caused by the spirochete, *Treponema pertenue,* and characterized by skin eruptions resembling raspberries. Also **fram·be·sia,** fram·bē″zha.

y-ax·is, wī′ak″sis, *n. pl.* **y-ax·es,** wī′ak″sēz. *Math.* The vertical axis of the two axes in a two-dimensional Cartesian coordinate system for locating points in a plane; the ordinate; one of three axes in a three-dimensional Cartesian coordinate system for locating points in space. Compare *x-axis, z-axis.*

Y-chro·mo·some, wī′krō″mo·sōm, *n. Genetics,* the sex chromosome carrying or associated with male characteristics, occurring with one X-chromosome in males.

ye, yē, *pron.* [O.E. *ge* = *gē,* O.H.G. *īr* (G. *ihr*) = Icel. *ēr* = Goth. *jus,* ye; akin to Gr. Skt. *yūyam,* ye.] *Archaic,* nom. pl. of 'thou'; nom. second person sing., as: Are *ye* one of us ? *Archaic,* obj. second person sing. or pl., as: Lo, the days of joy have come to *ye.*

ye, THē, *spelling pronunciation* yē, *def. art. Archaic,* a written or printed form of 'the'; as, *Ye Olde Pub.*

yea, yā, *adv.* [O.E. *gēa* = O.H.G. *jā* (G. *ja*) = Icel. *jā* = Goth. *ja,* yes: cf. *yes.*] Yes: used in affirmation or assent only in oral voting. *Archaic,* indeed or truly: used to introduce a sentence or clause; not only so, but also: used in adding something which intensifies and amplifies.—*n.* An affirmative reply or vote; one who votes in the affirmative.

yean, yēn, *v.t., v.i.* [O.E. *eánian, eacnian,* < *eácen,* gravid, lit. 'increased,' being pp. of *eacan,* to increase, to *eke.*] To bring forth young, as a goat or sheep.

yean·ling, yēn′ling, *n.* A lamb; a sheep's or goat's young.—*a.*

year, yēr, *n.* [O.E. *gēar* = D. *jaar* = G. *jahr* = Icel. *ār* = Goth. *jēr,* year; akin to Gr. *hōra,* time, season, E. *hour.*] The period of the earth's revolution around the sun, a period of 365 or 366 days, divided into 12 calendar months and now considered as beginning January 1 and ending December 31; also **cal·en·dar year.** A period of approximately the same length in other calendars; a space of 12 calendar months considered from any point; as, to be gone a *year.* A period consisting of 12 lunar months; also **lu·nar year..** The period of one complete apparent circuit of the ecliptic by the sun, being equal to about 365 days, 5 hours, 48 minutes, and 46 seconds; also **as·tro·nom·i·cal year, so·lar year, trop·i·cal year.** The true period of the earth's revolution around the sun, being about 20 minutes longer than the astronomical year due to the apparent traveling of the sun from a given star and back to it; also **si·de·re·al year.** The time in which any planet completes a revolution around the sun; as, the Jupiter *year;* a period out of every 12 months devoted to a certain activity; as, an academic *year. Pl.* age; as, big for one's *years;* old age; as, a man of *years.*—**a year and a day,** *law,* a period specified as the limit of time in various legal matters to allow for a full year by whatever way of counting.—**year by year,** during or with each succeeding year.—**year in, year out,** from the beginning to the end of each succeeding year; always.

year·book, yēr′bụk″, *n.* A book giving facts about the year, its seasons, festivals, dates, or the like; as, a high school *yearbook;* a book published annually, each issue containing new or additional information, of general or special nature, in regard to matters pertaining to the year preceding or the year following publication.

year·ling, yēr′ling, *n.* An animal one year old or in the second year of its age; a horse one year old, dating from January 1st of the year of foaling.—*a.* A year old.

year·long, yēr′lạng′, yēr′long′, *a.* Lasting for a year.

year·ly, yēr′lē, *a.* [O.E. *gēarlīc.*] Pertaining to a year, or to each year; done, made, happening, appearing, or coming once a year, or every year; as, a *yearly* trip; annual; continuing for a year; lasting but a year.—*adv.* Once a year; annually; every year.

yearn, yụrn, *v.i.* [O.E. *geornian, gyrnan,* to yearn, < *georn,* desirous; Icel. *gjarn,* eager, whence *girna,* to desire; Goth. *gairns,* desirous, *gairnjan,* to long for; Dan. *gierne,* D. *gaarne,* G. *gern,* willingly.] To feel a deep desire; to be filled with eager longing; to have a wistful feeling.—**yearn·er,** *n.*—**yearn·ing,** *n.*—**yearn·ing·ly,** *adv.*

year-round, yēr′round′, *a.* Continuing, lasting, or operating the entire year; as, a resort open *year-round.*

yeast, yēst, *n.* [O.E. *gist, gyst,* = D. *gest, gist,* = G. *gäscht, gischt,* = Icel. *jastr,* yeast; akin to Gr. *zein,* boil.] A yellowish, somewhat viscid, semifluid substance consisting of the aggregated cells of certain minute fungi, esp. of the genus *Saccharomyces,* which appears in saccharine liquids such as fruit juices or malt worts, used to induce fermentation in the manufacture of alcoholic liquors, esp. beer, and as a leaven to render bread light and spongy; a similar commercial substance; spume or foam; a foaming mass; ferment or agitation.—*v.i.* To leaven; to ferment; to spume.

yeast cake, *n.* A compacted mixture of yeast cells with starch, used in baking.

yeast·y, yē′stē, *a.*—*yeastier, yeastiest.* Of, containing, or resembling yeast; spumy, frothy, or foamy; as, *yeasty* waves; light, trifling, or frivolous.

yegg, yeg, *n.* [Prob. < John *Yegg,* said to have been the first to use nitroglycerine in blowing safes.] *Slang.* A safecracker; any thief, esp. an itinerant one. Also **yegg·man.**

yell, yel, *v.i.* [O.E. *giellan,* yell, akin to *galan,* sing: cf. *nightingale.*] To cry out with a strong, loud, clear sound; to scream with pain, fright, rage, or the like; to cheer.—*v.t.* To utter or tell by yelling.—*n.* A cry uttered by yelling; a chant or shout of fixed words or sounds, adopted by a college, group, or the like.

yel·low, yel′ō, *a.* [O.E. *geolu* = D. *geel* = G. *gelb,* yellow; akin to L. *helvus,* light-bay, Gr. *khlōrós,* greenish-yellow, green, Skt. *hari,* yellow: cf. *gold.*] Of a bright color like that of gold, butter, or lemons; having the yellowish skin characteristic of Mongolians; noting or pertaining to the Mongolian race; jaundiced; *colloq.* cowardly; as, a man with a *yellow* streak. Sensational, esp. morbidly or offensively sensational: said of newspapers and the like; as, *yellow* journalism; envious.—*n.* A yellow color, between orange and green on the spectrum; a yellow pigment or dye; the yolk of an egg; *pl., bot.* a variety of plant diseases resulting in stunted growth and leaf yellowing; *pl.* jaundice.—*v.t., v.i.* To make or become yellow.—**yel·low·ish,** yel′ō·ish, *a.*

yel·low a·lert, *n. Milit.* the earliest alert put into effect when hostile aircraft are over, or enroute to, a defended territory.

yel·low-bird, yel′ō·bụrd″, *n.* The yellow warbler, *Dendroica petechia,* or the goldfinch, *Spinus tristis,* both of N. America.

yel·low dai·sy, *n.* A black-eyed Susan.

yel·low-dog con·tract, yel′ō·dạg′ kon′trakt, yel′ō·dog′, *n.* A contract, now illegal, by which an employer could make employment conditional upon a worker's forgoing union membership while employed.

yel·low fe·ver, *n. Pathol.* an acute, dangerous, often fatal, infectious disease of warm climates, transmitted by the bite of a mosquito of the genus *Aedes,* and characterized by jaundice, vomiting, hemorrhages, and fever. Also *yellow jack.*

yel·low-fe·ver mos·qui·to, yel′ō·fē′vėr mo·skē′tō, *n.* A dark-colored and small mosquito, *Aedes aegypti,* which carries and can transmit dengue and yellow fever.

yel·low-green al·ga, *n.* Any of various aquatic plants of the phylum *Chrysophyta,* having a yellowish-green or brownish-green color.

yel·low·ham·mer, yel′ō·ham″ėr, *n.* [Cf. G. *ammer,* bunting.] A European bunting, *Emberiza citrinella,* the male of which is marked with bright yellow; *colloq.* the flicker, *Colaptes auratus,* of N. America.

yel·low jack, *n. Pathol.* yellow fever. A flag flown by ships that are under quarantine; *ichth.* a carangoid fish, usu. found in Florida and the West Indies, esp., *Caranx bartholomaei.*

yel·low·jack·et, yel′ō·jak″it, *n.* A small, social wasp, family *Vespidae,* having bright yellow stripes or markings, and usu. nesting in the ground.

yel·low jas·mine, *n.* Gelsemium.

yel·low·legs, yel′ō·legz″, *n. pl. but sing. in constr. Ornith.* A N. American sandpiper, *Totanus melanoleucus,* having long, bright yellow legs; also **great·er yel·low·legs.** A similar but smaller bird, *T. flavipes;* also **less·er yel·low·legs.**

yel·low per·il, Yel·low Per·il, *n.* The supposed danger of a predominance of the yellow race, with its enormous numbers, over the white race and Western civilization generally; the yellow race regarded as presenting such a danger.

yel·low pine, *n.* One of several N. American coniferous trees of the genus *Pinus,* which yields timber or other useful products; the wood which comes from this tree.

yel·low pop·lar, *n.* Tulip tree.

yel·low spot, *n. Anat.* a small, circular yellowish area on the retina, opposite the pupil.

yel·low streak, *n.* Cowardice as a trait.

yel·low·tail, yel′ō·tāl″, *n. pl.* **yel·low·tail, yel·low·tails.** Any of various fishes with a yellowish tail, as a carangoid fish, *Seriola dorsalis,* or a rockfish, *Sebastodes flavidus,* of the coast of California. A snapper, *Ocyurus chrysurus;* also **yel·low·tail snap·per.**—**yel·low·tailed,** *a.*

yel·low·throat, yel′ō·thrōt″, *n.* Any of several N. American warblers of the genus *Geothlypis,* having a yellow throat, esp. *G. trichas,* the Maryland yellowthroat.—**yel·low·throat·ed,** yel′ō·thrō″tid, *a.*

yel·low war·bler, *n.* A small American warbler, *Dendroica petechia,* the male of which has a bright yellow plumage streaked with brown on the under parts.

yel·low·weed, yel′ō·wēd″, *n.* Any of certain coarse species of goldenrod; a type of European ragwort; the plant weld.

yel·low·wood, yel′ō·wụd″, *n.* The hard, yellow wood of *Cladrastis lutea,* a leguminous tree found locally in the southern U.S., which bears showy white flowers and yields a yellow dye; this tree; any of various other yellow woods as that of *Schaefferia frutescens,* a small tree of southern Florida and neighboring regions; any of the trees yielding yellow woods.

yelp, yelp, *v.i.* [O.E. *gielpan,* boast, = Icel. *gjālpa,* yelp: cf. *yap* and *yawp.*] To give a quick, sharp, shrill cry, as dogs, foxes, or the like; to call or cry out sharply, as from surprise, pain, or excitement.—*v.t.* To utter or express by or as by yelps.—*n.* A quick, sharp bark or cry.—**yelp·er,** *n.*

yen, yen, *n. Colloq.* An intense desire or longing; a craving or want.—*v.i.—yenned, yenning. Colloq.* To crave; to long; to yearn.

yeo·man, yō′man, *n. pl.* **yeo·men.** [M.E. *yoman, yeman;* origin uncertain: cf. M.E.

yong man, servant, attendant, lit. 'young man' (O.E. *geong man*), also O.Fries. *gāman*, villager, *gāfolk*, village people, *gā*, *gō*, D. *gouw*, G. *gau*, Goth. *gawi*, district, province, country.] A petty officer in the Navy; *Brit.* one of the landowning farmer class. Formerly, a servant, attendant, or subordinate official in a royal or other great household; formerly, a subordinate or assistant, as of a sheriff or other official or in a craft or trade; *hist.* one of a class of lesser freeholders, ranking below the gentry, who cultivated their own land and were early admitted in England to political rights.

yeo·man·ly, yō′man·lē, *a.* Of the condition or rank of a yeoman; pertaining to or befitting a yeoman.—*adv.* Like or as befits a yeoman; bravely.

yeo·man of the guard, *n.* A member of the bodyguard of the English sovereign, consisting of 100 men retaining the ornate uniform of the Tudor era, carrying a halberd, and performing ceremonial duties.

yeo·man·ry, yō′man·rē, *n.* Yeomen collectively; *Brit.* a cavalry force made up of volunteer yeomen which was organized for home defense in 1761 and later became part of the Territorial Army.

yeo·man's serv·ice, *n.* Good, useful, or substantial service. Also **yeo·man serv·ice.**

yer·ba ma·té, yâr′ba mä′tā, yur′ba, *n.* [Sp. < L. *herba*, E. *herb*.] *Bot.* maté.

yes, yes, *adv.* [O.E. *gese*, *gise*, < *geá*, yea, and *sí*, *sý*, be it so, let it be, 3rd sing. pres. subj. of the substantive verb in O.E. = G. *sei*, let it be; akin to L. *sim*, may it be; from root *as*.] Used for expressing agreement or consent: opposed to *no*, as: *Yes*, I will go. Used in contradicting a preceding negative request or assertion, as: He didn't go there. Oh, *yes* he did! Used, usu. interrogatively, to express doubt, hesitation, or inquisitiveness, as: *Yes?* Who's there? What is more; moreover, as: The painting is good, *yes*, very good.—*n.* pl. **yes·es.** An affirmative approval; aye.

ye·shi·va, ye·shi·vah, ye·shē′va, *Heb.* ye·shē′vä, *n.* pl. **ye·shi·vas, ye·shi·vahs, ye·shi·voth,** ye·shē′vōt. A Jewish educational institution, as an orthodox seminary, a school for studying the Talmud, or a day school in which both secular and religious subjects are studied.

yes man, *n.* *Colloq.* A subordinate who ingratiatingly agrees with or supports all suggestions or proposals of his superior; a sycophant.

yes·ter, yes′tėr, *a.* [O.E. *geostra, giestra, gystra,* yesterday's, *geostran daeg,* yesterday; *gystran niht,* yesternight; D. *gisteren,* G. *gestern,* yesterday; Goth. *gistra, gistra dagis,* tomorrow. These are compar. forms, applied to L. *hesternus,* of yesterday, and to Gr. *chthes,* Skt. *hyas,* yesterday.] *Archaic,* pertaining to the day preceding the present.

yes·ter·day, yes′tėr·dē, yes′tėr·dā″, *n.* The day next before the present; time not long gone by.—*a., adv.*

yes·ter·year, yes′tėr·yēr′, *n.* Last year; some time just recently past.—*adv.*

yet, yet, *adv.* [O.E. *get, git,* yet, still; equiv. etymologically to *yea* to or *yea too*.] At this time or now; as, while *yet* young; thus far; hitherto, often accompanied by *as,* as: I have not met him *as yet.* At or before some future time; before all is done, as: He'll suffer *yet.* Still, used esp. with comparatives; as, *yet* more surprising; in addition; over and above; further; though the case be such; nevertheless.—*conj.* Nevertheless; notwithstanding; however, as: He looks fine, *yet* he is not well.

yet·i, yet′ē, *n.* Abominable snowman.

yew, ū, *n.* [O.E. *īw, ēow,* = O.H.G. *īwa* (G. *eibe*) = Icel. *ȳr,* yew.] An evergreen tree, *Taxus baccata,* of moderate height, a native of the Old World, having a thick,

dark foliage; the fine-grained, elastic wood of such a tree; a bow for shooting, made of this wood.

Yg·dra·sil, ig′dra·sil, Yg′dra·sil, *n.* *Norse mythol.* an enormous ash tree which, by its branches and roots, binds the universe together. Also **Ygg·dra·sill, Ygg·dra·sil.**

YHWH, wī′ảch′dub′l·ū″ảch′, *n.* Yahweh. Also **YHVH, JHVH, JHWH.**

Yid·dish, yid′ish, *a.* [G. *jūdisch,* Jewish.] Of or pertaining to the Yiddish language; expressed in Yiddish.—*n.* A language of High German derivation containing vocabulary additions from the Hebrew and Slavic languages, written in Hebrew characters, and spoken by Jews of eastern Europe, their descendants in other countries, and by Jewish emigrants.

yield, yēld, *v.t.* [O.E. *gieldan, geldan,* = O.H.G. *geltan* = Icel. *gjalda* = Goth. *-gildan,* pay, yield: cf. *geld.*] To give forth or produce by a natural process or in return for cultivation or labor; as, land *yielding* a good crop; to produce or furnish as payment, profit, or interest; as, an investment *yielding* six per cent; to give up, as to superior power or authority; as, to *yield* a military position to the enemy; to give up or surrender, as oneself; as, to *yield* oneself to the temptation to sleep late; to give up or over; relinquish; as, to *yield* one's place in line; to give as due or required; as, to *yield* obedience; to furnish, afford, or cause, as: The bridge game *yielded* two high scores.—*v.i.* To give a return, as for labor expended; produce or bear; to surrender or submit, as to superior power, as: The enemy *yielded* in surrender. To give way to influence, entreaty, argument, or the like, as: He *yielded* to the arguments of the other jurors. To give place or precedence, followed by *to*; as, to *yield to* a rival; to give way to force or pressure, so as to move, bend, collapse, or the like.—*n.* The act of yielding or producing; that which is yielded; the quantity or amount yielded; the return or profit from a financial transaction or investment; the energy of a nuclear explosion as measured in units of weight of TNT.—**yield·er,** *n.*

yield·ing, yēl′ding, *a.* Ready to submit, comply, or yield; compliant; unresisting; flexible; productive.—**yield·ing·ly,** *adv.*

Yin, yin, *n.* (*Sometimes l.c.*), *Chin. philos.* the passive, female force or principle in nature. Compare *Yang.*

yip, yip, *v.i.*—**yipped, yipping.** To yelp or bark sharply, as a puppy.—*n.* The sound made by young dogs.

Yip·ee, Yip·pie, yip′ē, *n.* A member of the Youth International Party, a radical group founded in 1966 that seeks to completely change U.S. society.

yip·pee, yip′ē, *interj.* An exclamation of elation, delight, or joy.

y·lang-y·lang, ē′läng·ē′läng, *n.* A large tree, *Canaga odorata,* of the Philippines and Java, from whose flowers a perfume oil is obtained; also *ilang-ilang.* The oil itself; also **a·no·na oil.**

Y.M.C.A., YMCA, wī′em′sē′ā′, *n.* Abbreviation for Young Men's Christian Association.

yo·del, yo·dle, yōd′el, *v.t., v.i.*—**yodeled, yodeling, yodled, yodling,** *Brit.* **yodelled, yodelling.** [G. Swiss.] To sing like the Swiss and Tyrolese mountaineers, by suddenly changing from the natural voice to the falsetto, and vice versa; to yell or call in the same manner.—*n.*—**yo·del·er, yo·dler,** *Brit.* **yo·del·ler,** *n.*

yo·ga, yō′ga, *n.* [Hind. *yoga,* < Skt. *yoga,* union.] (*Sometimes cap.*), *Hindu philos.* The mystical union of the human soul with the universal spirit; a system of physical and mental exercises devised to effect such a union or to develop physical and spiritual

health through the withdrawal of the senses from all external objects and the unbroken meditation upon some principle or esp. significant object.—**yo·gic,** yō′gik, *a.*

yo·gi, yō′gē, *n.* pl. **yo·gis,** yō′gēz. [Hind. *yogī.*] One who practices or teaches yoga. Also **yo·gin,** yō′gin.

yo·gurt, yo·ghurt, yo·ghourt, yō′gėrt, *n.* [Turk. *yôghurt.*] A thickened, fermented milk product made by treatment with bacteria cultures and usu. eaten as a health or diet food.

yo·him·bine, yō·him′bēn″, *n.* An alkaloid, $C_{21}H_{26}O_3N_2$, obtained from the bark of the tree, *Corynanthe yohimbe,* formerly used as an aphrodisiac.

yoicks, hīk, *spelling pronunciation* yoiks, *interj.* An old fox hunting cry of excitement and encouragement to the dogs.

yoke, yōk, *n.* pl. **yokes, yoke.** [O.E. *geoc* = O.H.G. *joh* (G. *joch*) = Icel. *ok* = Goth. *juk,* yoke; akin to L. *jugum,* Gr. *zygon,* Skt. *yuga,* yoke; < a root seen in E. *join.*] A contrivance for joining together a pair of draft animals, esp. oxen, usu. consisting of a crosspiece with two bow-shaped pieces beneath, one at each end, each bow enclosing the head of an animal; a pair of draft animals fastened together by a yoke; something resembling a yoke or a bow of a yoke in form or use; a frame fitting the neck and shoulders of a person, for carrying a pair of buckets or the like, one at each end; *mech.* a device, as a clamp or slot, used to guide a moving mechanical part; *naut.* a crossbar on the head of a boat's rudder. The part of a horse's double harness supporting a wagon tongue; a shaped piece in a garment, fitted about or below the neck, or about the hips, from which the rest of the garment hangs; an emblem or token of subjection, servitude, or slavery, as one under which prisoners of war were compelled to pass by the ancient Romans and others; something that couples or binds together, or a bond or tie; as, the *yoke* of matrimony; *Brit. dial.* the time during which a plowman and his team work at one stretch, a period of steady work, or a part of the working day in which work is carried on without interruption.—*v.t.*—**yoked, yoking.** To put a yoke on; to join or couple by means of a yoke; to attach, as a draft animal, to a plow or vehicle; to join, couple, link, or unite.—*v.i.* To be or become joined, linked, or united.

yoke·fel·low, yōk′fel″ō, *n.* One associated with another in labor; one connected with another by marriage; a partner; a mate. Also **yoke·mate.**

yo·kel, yōkel, *n.* [Perh. < *yoke* = one who drives yoked animals, or akin to *gawk.*] A rustic or countryman; a country bumpkin. —**yo·kel·ish,** *a.*

yolk, yōk, yōlk, *n.* [O.E. *geolōca,* lit. 'the yellow of the egg,' < *geolu,* yellow.] *Biol.* The yellow part of an egg suspended in the white portion or albumen; food material in the form of protein and fat granules in the ovum of animals, which supplies nourishment to the growing embryo; an oily secretion from the skin of sheep which renders the pile soft and pliable.—**yolk·y,** *a.*—*yolkier, yolkiest.*

yolk sac, *n.* *Biol.* a saclike structure of membranous tissue in reptiles, birds, or the like, containing yolk which is connected to an embryo, the yolk-filled space communicating with the intestine of the embryo furnishing nourishment and blood during embryonic development and, in mammals, terminating from the embryo at birth.

Yom Kip·pur, yam kip′er, *Heb.* yōm′ kē·pör′, *n.* Day of Atonement.

yon, yon, *a., adv.* [O.E. *geon,* yon, that; Goth. *jains,* G. *jener,* that; of pronominal origin, and akin to Skt. *yas,* who.] *Poet.*

yonder.—*pron. Poet.* that or those, as referring to an object at a distance.

yond, yond, *a., adv.* [O.E. *geond* (= Goth. *jaind*), < *geon*, E. *yon*.] *Archaic,* yonder.

yon·der, yon′dẽr, *a.* [A compar. form < *yon*; cf. Goth. *jaindre*, there.] Being at a distance within view or indicated.—*adv.* At or in that place, as one relatively distant or indicated; there.

yo·ni, yō′nē, *n.* The symbol for the female's external reproductive parts, in Indian religion, used in the worship of Shakti. Compare *lingam.*

yoo-hoo, ū′hö″, *interj.* An exclamation utilized in attracting the attention of or in calling another person.

yore, yōr, yạr, *n.* [O.E. *gēara*, of old, formerly, orig. gen. pl. of *gēar*, E. *year*.] Many years ago; the distant past, usu. preceded by *of*; as, castles *of yore*.

York·ist, yạr′kist, *a.* Of or pertaining to the English house of York, the reigning members of which were Edward IV, Edward V, and Richard III.—*n.* A supporter or member of the house of York, esp. during the Wars of the Roses, 1455–1485, the contention for the English throne between the houses of York and Lancaster.

York rite, *n.* The rituals or practices of one of the two upper ranking Masonic orders, offering the ultimate degree of Commander of the Knights Templar. Compare *Scottish rite.*

York·shire, yạrk′shẽr, yạrk′shẽr, *n.* A type of white swine orig. from Yorkshire, England.

York·shire pud·ding, *n.* [From the county of *Yorkshire* in northern England.] A pudding made of unsweetened batter, baked under meat, so as to catch the drippings.

York·shire ter·ri·er, *n.* An English toy terrier with a straight, long, silky coat of grayish-blue having tan on the chest and head.

you, ū, *unstressed* yụ, *pron.*—*poss. your* or *yours.* [O.E. *ēow*, dat. and acc. of *gē*, E. *ye*.] The pronoun of the second person, orig. the objective plural of *ye*, but now used regularly as either objective or nominative and with either plural or singular meaning but always, when used as subject, taking a plural verb; one, or persons generally, as: *You* can get there by bus.

you-all, ū·ạl′, yạl, *pron. Chiefly south. U.S.* you: usu. used for two or more people in direct address.

you'd, ūd. Contraction of you had or you would.

you'll, ūl, *unstressed* yụl. Contraction of you will or you shall.

young, yung, *a.* [O.E. *geong, giung, iung* = D. *jong*, G. *jung*, Goth. *juggs*, Icel. *ungr, jungr*, Dan. and Sw. *ung*; cogn. L. *juvenis* (whence *juvenile*), Skt. *juvan*, young.] Being in the first or early stage of life or growth; not old; having the appearance of early life; fresh or vigorous; pertaining to or characteristic of early life or youth; having little experience; raw; green; being younger or junior to another having the same name; being in the early part of existence; as, the *young* corporation; new; symbolizing or representing new or progressive political or social views or aims, used with proper names; as, the *Young* Liberals.—*n.* Young people or youth, collectively; the offspring of animals.—**with young,** pregnant.— **young·ish,** *a.*

young·ber·ry, yung′ber″ē, yung′be·rē, *n.* pl. **young·ber·ries.** *Hort.* a large hybrid berry, a combination of a dewberry and a blackberry, developed by B. M. Young in 1900.

young·ling, yung′ling, *n.* A young person; an animal in the first part of life; a novice; one with little or no experience.—*a.* Young.

young·ster, yung′stẽr, *n.* A young person; a lad; a young plant or animal; a second year midshipman at the U.S. Naval Academy; *Brit. colloq.* a junior-ranking officer in the military.

Young Turk, *n.* [From *Young Turk*, a member of a revolutionary and nationalistic political party in Turkey, active in the late 19th and early 20th centuries.] An insurgent or reformist member of an organization, esp. one of a group of insurgents within a political party.

youn·ker, yung′kẽr, *n.* [< D. *jonker, jonkherr*, lit. 'young sir' (heer = G. *herr*, sir, gentleman).] A lad; a youngster; orig. a young man of noble birth.

your, yụr, yōr, yạr, *unstressed* yẽr, *pronominal a.* [O.E. *ēower* = D. *uwer*, G. *euer*; the poss. corresponding to *ye, you*, and therefore prop. pl. (*thy* being the singular), but now like *you* used as singular or plural.] Pertaining or belonging to you; a possessive of *you.*

you're, ūr, *unstressed* yẽr. Contraction of you are.

yours, yụrz, yōrz, yạrz, *pron.* That or those which belong to you; a possessive of *you:* used predicatively, with or without direct reference to a preceding noun, as: That coat is *yours*, which is *yours*?—**yours tru·ly,** a phrase which is often used in closing a letter, preceding the signature; *colloq.* I, me, or myself.

your·self, yụr·self′, yōr·self′, yạr·self′, yẽr·self′, *pron.* pl. **your·selves,** yụr·selvz′, yōr·selvz′, yạr·selvz′, yẽr·selvz′. You, not another or others; you, in your own person or individually: used reflexively, as: Did you make that *yourself*? Used for distinctiveness or emphasis, as: Only you *yourself* can find the right answer.

youth, ūth, *n.* pl. **youth, youths,** ūths, ūTHz. [O.E. *geóguth*, for *geonguth* (= *youngth, young* and *-th*), < *geong*, young.] The state or quality of being young; youthfulness; the part of life between childhood and manhood; a young individual, esp. a young man; a stripling or lad; young persons collectively.

youth·ful, ūth′fụl, *a.* Being in the early stage of life; young; characteristic of or pertaining to youth; fresh or vigorous, as in youth; *geol.* having undergone only slight erosion.—**youth·ful·ly,** *adv.*—**youth·ful·ness,** *n.*

youth hos·tel, *n.* See *hostel.*

you've, ūv, *unstressed* yụv. Contraction of you have.

yowl, youl, *v.i.* [Akin to *yell*.] To give a long distressful or mournful cry, as a dog.—*n.* A long distressful or mournful cry, as that of a dog; a howl.

Yo-Yo, yō′yō, *n.* pl. **Yo-Yos.** A toy made of two wheellike disks joined by a center piece holding a string which winds and unwinds while the player holds an end of the string. (Trademark.)

yt·ter·bi·um, i·tụr′bē·um, *n. Chem.* a metallic element, one of the lanthanide or rare earth metals, occurring in either bivalent or trivalent form, found chiefly in gadolinite. Sym. Yb, at. no. 70, at. wt. 173.04. See Periodic Table of Elements.— **yt·ter·bic, yt·ter·bous,** *a.*

yt·tri·um, i′trē·um, *n. Chem.* a rare, grayish metallic element, found in trivalent form in combination with rare earth elements, and used in nuclear technology, metallurgy, and other industrial applications. Sym. Y, at. no. 39, at. wt. 88.905. See Periodic Table of Elements.

Yu·ca·tec·an, yö″ka·tek′an, *a.* [Sp. *Yucateco.*] Belonging or pertaining to Yucatan, a peninsula of southeastern Mexico.—**Yu·ca·tec,** yö′ka·tek″, *n.*

yuc·ca, yuk′a, *n.* [From some Amer. Ind. tongue.] *Bot.* a genus of plants, *Yucca*, in the lily family, native to N. America, all of considerable size, some being small trees, with white or violet flowers in large panicles, and long rigid pointed leaves.

Yu·ga, yụg′a, *n.* pl. **Yu·gas.** [Skt., age, orig. yoke.] *Hindu philos.* an age of time, esp. one of the four ages that successively deteriorate in quality of life during a cycle of the world's existence. Also **Yug.**

Yu·go·sla·vi·an, yö′gō·slä′vē·an, *a.* Pertaining to Yugoslavia, its language, or its residents. Also *Jugoslav, Jugoslavic*, **Yu·go·slav, Yu·go·slav·ic.**—*n.*

Yu·kon time, ū′kon tīm″, *n.* One of the U.S. time zones including some of southern Alaska and the Yukon Territory.

yule, ūl, *n.* [O.E. *geól, giúl, iúl, geóhol*, Christmas; Icel. *jól*, Dan. *juul*, Sw. *jul*; orig. a pagan festival; etymol. doubtful. *Jolly* is from this through the French.] Christmas, or the festival of Christmas.

yule log, *n.* Traditionally, a large log of wood forming the basis of a Christmas Eve fire.

yule·tide, ūl′tīd″, *n.* (*Often cap.*) the time or season of Yule or Christmas.

Yu·man, ū′man, *a. Ling.* referring to the classification for the common tongue of the Mohave Indians and Yuma Indians of the northwestern part of Mexico and the southwestern part of the U.S.—*n.* The Yuman language.

yum·my, yum′ē, *a.*—**yummier, yummiest.** *Colloq.* Delicious; delectable; appealing to the various senses.

yurt, yụrt, *n.* A domed, portable cylindrical tent, constructed from skins or felt stretched onto a framework made of branches, and used by various nomadic peoples of central Asia and Siberia.

Y.W.C.A., YWCA, wī′dub'l·ū″sē′ā″, *n.* Abbreviation for Young Women's Christian Association.

Z

Z, z, zē, *Brit.* zed, *archaic* iz′ẽrd, *n.* The twenty-sixth and final letter of the English alphabet and the nineteenth consonant; the sound of the letter Z as represented in speech; the delineation of the letter Z or z in writing or printing; something designated by or having the shape of the letter Z or z; a graphic device for printing the letter Z or z.

Z, zē, *Brit.* zed, *archaic,* iz′ẽrd. *Chem.* atomic number; *elect.* impedance; *astron.* zenith distance.

z, zē, *Brit.* zed, *archaic,* iz′ẽrd. *Math.* An unknown; the *z*-axis.

za·ba·glio·ne, zä″bal·yō′nē, *It.* dzä″bä— lyạ′ne, *n.* A frothy dessert served either hot or cold, made by beating a mixture of egg yolks, sugar, and Marsala wine over hot water.

zaf·fer, zaf·fre, zaf′ẽr, *n.* [Fr. *zafre, safre*: cf. *sapphire*.] An impure oxide of cobalt used esp. to produce a blue color in glass and porcelain, and in the manufacture of smalt.

za·mi·a, zā′mē·a, *n.* [N.L.] Any of the plants of the cycad family, genus *Zamia*, chiefly of tropical America, having a short, thick stem, a crown of palmlike pinnate leaves, and oblong cones.

za·min·dar, ze·min·der, za·mēn·där′, *n.* [Hind. and Pers. *zamīndār*, landholder.] *Mogul Ind.* a farmer of the revenue, required to pay a fixed sum on the tract or district assigned to him; *Anglo-Ind.* a native landlord responsible to the British government for the tax on the land under his jurisdiction.

zan·der, zan′dẽr, *n.* pl. **zan·ders**, **zan·der**. A European fresh-water fish, *Lucioperca sandra*, of the perch family.

za·ny, zā′nē, *n.* pl. **za·nies**. [Fr. *zani*, < It. *zanni*, zany, orig. a familiar form of *Giovanni*, John.] Orig. a comic performer on the Italian stage who mimicked the actions of the professional clown; any apish buffoon; a clown; a silly person or simpleton.—*a.*—*zanier*, *zaniest*. Characteristic of or pertaining to a zany; crazy; humorous in a slapstick or outlandish manner.—**za·ni·ly**, *adv.*—**za·ni·ness**, *n.*—**za·ny·ism**, *n.*

za·re·ba, **za·ree·ba**, za·rē′ba, *n.* [Ar. *zarībah*, enclosure for cattle, etc.] An enclosure in the Sudan and adjoining regions, as of thorn bushes or the like, built about a camp or village for protection against enemies or wild animals.

zar·zue·la, zär·zwä′la, zär·zwē′la, *Sp.* thär·thwe′lä, sär·swe′lä, *n.* pl. **zar·zue·las**, zär·zwä′laz, zär·zwē′laz, *Sp.* thär·thwe′läs, sär·swe′läs. A form of Spanish opera which includes dialogue, often of a comical or satirical nature.

z-ax·is, zē′ak″sis, *n.* pl. **z-ax·es**, zē′ak″sēz. *Math.* one of the three axes in a three-dimensional Cartesian coordinate system for locating points in space. See *x-axis*, *y-axis*.

zeal, zēl, *n.* [Fr. *zèle*, < L. *zelus*, Gr. *zēlos*, zeal; < stem of *zeō*, to boil, which is akin to E. *yeast*, jealous.] Passionate ardor in the pursuit of anything; eagerness in any cause or behalf; earnestness; fervency; enthusiasm.

zeal·ot, zel′ǒt, *n.* [Fr. *zélote*, L. *zelotes*, < Gr. *zēlōtēs*.] One who is zealous or full of zeal; one carried away by excess of zeal; a fanatical partisan; (*cap.*) one who belonged to the fanatical Judean group, A.D. 6–70, who were consistently opposed to and in rebellion against the Romans, esp. in the matter of Roman domination and jurisdiction in Palestine.

zeal·ot·ry, zel′o·trē, *n.* pl. **zeal·ot·ries**. Excessive zeal; fanaticism.

zeal·ous, zel′us, *a.* [< *zeal*. *Jealous* is really the same word.] Inspired with zeal; ardent in the pursuit of a goal or cause; fervent; eager; earnest.—**zeal·ous·ly**, *adv.*—**zeal·ous·ness**, *n.*

ze·bra, zē′bra, *n.* pl. **ze·bras**, **ze·bra**. [A native Afr. word.] An African mammal, genus *Equus*, related to the horse and ass, and having a whitish body striped with numerous brownish-black or black bands.—**ze·brine**, zē′brīn, zē′brin, *a.*—**ze·broid**, zē′broid, *a.*

ze·bra·fish, zē′bra·fish″, *n.* pl. **ze·bra·fish·es**, **ze·bra·fish**. A small, oviparous, tropical fish of India, *Brachydanio rerio*, striped in silver and blue, in demand for home aquariums. Also **ze·bra dan·i·o**.

ze·bra·wood, zē′bra·wụd″, *n.* A striped, light brown wood from a S. American tree, *Connarus guianensis*, used by cabinetmakers; the tree itself.

ze·bu, zē′bū, *n.* [Fr. *zébu*; origin obscure.] A bovine animal, *Bos indicus*, having a large hump over the shoulders and a very large dewlap, widely domesticated in Asia and Africa.

zed, zed, *n.* [Fr. *zède*, < L. *zeta*, < Gr. *zēta*, E. *zeta*.] *Brit.* a name for the letter Z.

ze·in, zē′in, *n.* *Biochem.* a protein obtained from corn, used principally in making textile fibers, coatings, and plastics.

Zeit·geist, tsīt′gīst″, *n.* [G., 'time-spirit.'] German. The spirit of the time; the general inclination of thought or feeling characteristic of a particular period of time.

ze·min·dar, ze·mēn″där′, *n.* Zamindar.

Zen, zen, *n.* *Buddhism*, a form of Mahayana Buddhism practiced in China and Japan which asserts that enlightenment can be reached directly through self-discipline, meditation, and intuition rather than through the study of the scriptures.

ze·na·na, ze·nä′na, *n.* [Hind. and Pers. *zanāna*, < Pers. *zan*, woman.] In India, that part of the house in which the women and girls of a family are secluded.

ze·nith, zē′nith, *Brit.* zen′ith, *n.* [Fr. *zenith*, < Sp. *zenit*, zenith, a corruption of Ar. *samt*, *sent*, abbreviated for *samt-ur-ras*, *samt-er-ras*, way of the head, zenith, *samt* being a way (*ras*, head). Akin *azimuth*.] *Astron.* the vertical point of the heavens at any place, or the point right above a spectator's head. *Fig.* the highest point, as of a person's career; the culminating point. Compare *nadir*.

ze·nith·al, zē′ni·thal, *Brit.* zen′i·thal, *a.* *Astron.* pertaining to or in a position near the zenith; *cartography*, indicating direction from the center point to any surrounding point.

ze·o·lite, zē′o·līt″, *n.* [Sw. *zeolit*, < Gr. *zein*, boil, and *lithos*, stone; so called from its swelling up under the blowpipe.] Any of a group of hydrated silicates of aluminum with alkali metals or alkaline earth metals or both, and commonly occurring as secondary minerals in cavities in igneous rocks.—**ze·o·lit·ic**, zē″o·lit′ik, *a.*

Zeph·i·ran, zef′i·ran″, *n.* A solution of ammonium chloride derivatives, used as an antiseptic and disinfectant. (Trademark.)

zeph·yr, zef′ẽr, *n.* [L. *Zephyrus*, < Gr. *Zephyros*.] The west wind; any soft, mild breeze; a light, fine fabric or yarn for knitting; any of various things of fine, light quality.

zep·pe·lin, tsep″e·lēn′, *n.* [From Count Ferdinand von *Zeppelin*, 1838–1917, G. designer of the zeppelin.] (*Often cap.*) a rigid dirigible with internal gas cells supporting the long, cylindrical body.

ze·ro, zēr′ō, *n.* pl. **ze·ros**, **ze·roes**. [Fr. *zéro*, < It. *zero*, contr. of *zefiro*, < Ar. *çifr*, cipher, lit. 'empty.'] The symbol 0; a cipher. *Math.* the number that indicates the absence of quantity; the origin of any kind of measurement; the point from which all divisions of a scale are measured in either a positive or negative direction, as on a thermometer. A temperature registering zero on a thermometer; a setting of a gunsight that can be adjusted for accuracy according to varying conditions; a person or thing of no importance; nonentity; the lowest point or degree; nadir; nothing; nil. —*a.* Of, pertaining to, or being zero; nonexistent; absent, lacking; having limited or no visibility, as an atmospheric ceiling.— *v.t.*—*zeroed, zeroing*. To calibrate to a zero point.—**ze·ro in**, to adjust, as the zero of a rifle, to a calibration determined by previous firings to be more appropriate to conditions; *fig.* to move toward or focus the attention, used with *on* or *upon*.

ze·ro hour, *n.* *Milit.* the time set for the beginning of an attack or any planned maneuver; also **H-hour**. *Colloq.* the time or moment at which anything critical or decisive takes place.

ze·ro-ze·ro, zēr′ō-zēr′ō, *a.* *Meteor.* characterized by weather conditions in which the ceiling and visibility are zero.

zest, zest, *n.* [Fr. *zeste*, the peel of an orange or lemon; < L. *schistus*, Gr. *schistos*, split, divided < *schizō*, to split (whence also *schism*, *schist*).] Orig. a piece of orange or lemon peel, used to give flavor to liquor; that which serves to enhance enjoyment or to add flavor; relish; keen enjoyment; gusto, usu. followed by *for*.—*v.t.* To give relish, gusto, or zest to.—**zest·ful**, *a.*—**zest·ful·ly**, *adv.*—**zest·ful·ness**, *n.*—**zest·y**, *a.*—**zestier**, **zestiest**.

ze·ta, zā′ta, zē′ta, *n.* [L., < Gr. *zēta*.] The sixth letter of the Greek alphabet, Z, ζ, equivalent to Z, z in English.

zeug·ma, zŏg′ma, *n.* [L., < Gr. *zeugma* < *zeugnynai*, yoke, join.] *Gram.*, *rhet.* a figure in which a verb is associated with two subjects or objects, or an adjective with two nouns, although appropriate to but one of the two, as 'to wage war and peace.'

zib·el·ine, **zib·el·line**, zib′e·lin″, zib′e·lin, *n.* [Fr. *zibeline*, earlier *zibelline*, < It. *zibellino*; of Slavic origin, and akin to E. *sable*.] A lustrous woolen cloth with a flattened hairy nap; the fur of the sable. —*a.* Of or pertaining to the sable or its pelt.

zib·et, zib′it, *n.* [= *civet*.] A species of civet cat, *Viverra zibetha*, of India and Asia. Also **zib·eth**.

zig, zig, *v.i.*—*zigged, zigging*. To turn in one of the directions of a zigzag course.—*n.* An abrupt turn in a zigzag course.

zig·gur·at, zig′ụ·rat″, *n.* [Babylonian (Akkadian).] A temple used by the ancient Babylonians and Assyrians, constructed in the form of a pyramidal tower with a number of stories, and having about the outside a broad ascent winding round and round the structure and presenting the appearance of a series of terraces. Also **zik·ku·rat**, zik′ụ·rat″.

zig·zag, zig′zag″, *n.* [Fr. *zigzag*, perh. < G. *zickzack*, zigzag: cf. G. *zacke*, a sharp projection.] A line, course, or progression characterized by sharp turns first to one side and then to the other; one of a series of such turns, as in a line or a path.—*a.* Proceeding or formed in a zigzag.—*adv.* In a zigzag manner.—*v.i.*—*zigzagged*, *zigzagging*. To proceed in a zigzag line or course.—*v.t.* To make, as something, zigzag, as in form or course.

zil·lion, zil′yon, *n.* pl. **zil·lions**, **zil·lion**. *Colloq.* a very large indefinite number.

zinc, zingk, *n.* [Fr. *zinc*, G., Sw., and Dan. *zink*; allied to G. *zinn*, tin.] A bluish-white metallic element occurring in combination, used as a protective covering or coating, as a component in alloys, as a reducing agent, and as an electrode in a voltaic battery. Sym. Zn, at. no. 30, at. wt. 65.37. See Periodic Table of Elements.—*v.t.*—*zincked, zincking, zinced, zincing*. To coat with zinc. —**zinc·ic**, **zinc·oid**, **zinc·ous**, *a.*—**zinck·y**, **zinc·y**, *a.*

zinc·ate, zing′kāt, *n.* *Chem.* a salt resulting from the replacement of the hydrogen in zinc hydroxide, H_2ZnO_2, by a very strongly electropositive metal such as the potassium or sodium in alkali solutions.

zinc blende, *n.* Sphalerite.

zinc·ite, zing′kīt, *n.* A brittle mineral of deep-red to orange-yellow color, native zinc oxide, ZnO, usu. occurring in translucent masses of granular form, constituting an important ore of zinc.

zin·co·graph, zing′ko·graf″, zing′ko·gräf″, *n.* A zinc plate produced by zincography; a print from such a plate.

zin·cog·ra·phy, zing·kog′ra·fē, *n.* The art or process of producing a printing surface on a zinc plate, esp. of producing one in relief by etching away unprotected parts with acid.—**zin·cog·ra·pher**, *n.*—**zin·co·graph·ic**, **zin·co·graph·i·cal**, zing″ko·graf′ik, *a.*

zinc oint·ment, *n.* *Pharm.* a preparation consisting of 20 percent zinc oxide in a base of white petroleum and paraffin, used to treat skin disorders.

zinc ox·ide, *n.* *Chem.* an amorphous white powder, ZnO, primarily used in paint pigments, cosmetics, and as an antiseptic or astringent in medicine. Also *zinc white*.

zinc white, *n.* Oxide of zinc used as a white paint pigment.

zin·fan·del, zin′fan·del″, *n.* A kind of red,

claret type wine made from a black California grape of the same name.

zing, zing, *n.* A sharp, high-pitched whining sound, as of an object moving swiftly through the air; vitality; enthusiasm.—*v.i.* To make a sharp, high-pitched sound.

Zin·jan·thro·pus, zin·jan′thro·pus, *n.* pl. **Zin·jan·thro·pi, Zin·jan·thro·pus·es.** *Anthropol.* one of a genus, *Zinjanthropus*, of early men, identified from fossil remains believed to be about 2,000,000 years old, discovered in Tanganyika.

zin·ken·ite, zinck·en·ite, zing′ke·nīt″, *n.* [G. *zinkenit*; named from J. K. L. *Zincken*, 1790–1862, G. metallurgist and mining official.] A steel-gray mineral with a metallic luster, consisting of the sulfides of lead and antimony, $PbSb_2S_4$, occurring in crystals and masses.

zin·ni·a, zin′ē·a, *n.* [N.L.; named from J. G. *Zinn*, 1727–59, of Göttingen.] Any American plant of the genus *Zinnia*, of the composite family, cultivated in many varieties for its showy flowers in a wide range of color; the most commonly cultivated zinnia, *Z. elegans.*

Zi·on, zī′on, *n.* [L.L. *Sion*, < Gr. *Siōn*, < Heb. *Tsīyōn*, orig. a hill.] A hill in Jerusalem, site of David's palace and temple, and the center of ancient Hebrew worship; the house or household of God, as consisting of the chosen people; the Israelites; the theocracy, or church of God; the church in general; heaven as the final gathering place of true believers; a church or chapel of some Christian denominations.

Zi·on·ism, zī′o·niz″um, *n.* A modern plan or movement to colonize Hebrews in Palestine, the land of Zion; a movement to secure for such Jews as cannot or will not be assimilated in the country of their adoption a national homeland in Palestine, part of which now forms the state of Israel.—**Zi·on·ist,** *n., a.*—**Zi·on·is·tic,** zī′o·nis′tik, *a.*—**Zi·on·ite,** zī′o·nīt″, *n.*

zip, zip, *n.* [Imit.] A sudden, brief, hissing sound, as of a flying bullet; *colloq.* energy or vim.—*v.i.*—*zipped, zipping.* To make or move with a zipping or hissing sound; *colloq.* to proceed or act with energy and rapidity; as, to *zip* to the store and back.—*v.t.* To convey with or give speed or force to; *colloq.* to add or impart interest or zest to, used with *up*; as, to *zip up* a room with bright color.

zip, zip, *v.t.*—*zipped, zipping.* To fasten or unfasten with a zipper, as garments, luggage, wallets, and the like; to enclose or release by opening or closing a zipper; as, to *zip* papers into a briefcase.—*v.i.* To become fastened or unfastened through the use of a zipper.

ZIP Code, Zip Code, *n.* [(*Z*)one (*I*)mprovement (*P*)lan.] The system to simplify mail sorting and delivery, consisting of a number of five digits for identification of the state, the city or district, and the postal zone in U.S. delivery areas.

zip gun, *n.* A homemade pistol usu. made of a length of pipe attached to a piece of wood and having a firing pin triggered by a rubber band.

zip·per, zip′ėr, *n.* A fastener consisting of metal or plastic toothed tracks set along each of two facing edges and interlocked or separated when an attached piece which slides between them is pulled; also *slide fastener.* (*Cap.*) a rubber and fabric boot or overshoe fastened up the leg by a slide fastener. (Trademark.)—**zip·pered,** zip′-ėrd, *a.*

zip·py, zip′ē, *a.*—*zippier, zippiest.* Colloq. Energetic; peppy; lively; full of vim; brisk.

zir·con, zur′kon, *n.* [Pers. *zargun*, Ar. *zarqun*, gold-colored.] A common tetragonal mineral, $ZrSiO_4$, which occurs in small, opaque or transparent prismatic crystals, naturally colorless, reddish-orange, brownish-red, gray, violet-gray, or green, and which when treated with heat, turns bluish-white: translucent specimens are classified and used as gems.

zir·con·ate, zur′ko·nāt″, *n. Chem.* a salt produced by heating a metal oxide or carbonate with acidic zirconium oxide.

zir·co·ni·um, zėr·kō′ni·um, *n. Chem.* a hard, grayish metallic element obtained from the mineral zircon, used in the metallurgic, ceramic, and chemical industries, as an abrasive, and as structural material for nuclear reactors. Sym. Zr, at. no. 40, at. wt. 91.22. See Periodic Table of Elements.—**zir·con·ic,** zėr·kon′ik, *a.*

zir·co·ni·um ox·ide, *n. Chem.* a white powdery compound, ZrO_2, used in paints, glazes, abrasives, and insulation. Also **zir·co·ni·a,** zėr·kō′nē·a.

zith·er, zith′ėr, *n.* [G., < L. *cithara.*] A flat, stringed musical instrument consisting of a sounding box with 30 to 40 strings, played with the fingertips and a plectrum. Also **zith·ern,** zith′ėrn.—**zith·er·ist,** *n.*

zi·zith, tsit′sis, *Heb.* tsē·tsēt′, tsi′tsis, *n. pl.* [Heb. *tsītsith.*] *Judaism,* the fringes or tassels of entwined blue and white threads at the four corners of the tallith worn by males during prayer.

zo·di·ac, zō′dē·ak″, *n.* [O. Fr. Fr. *zodiaque*, < L. *zodiacus*, < Gr. *zōdiakós*, zodiac, prop. a. < *zōdion*, small figure or image (in painting, etc.), sign of the zodiac, dim. of *zōion*, living being, animal, figure or image.] An imaginary belt encircling the heavens, extending about eight degrees on each side of the ecliptic, and containing twelve constellations and their twelve astrological signs, each sign, however, because of the precession of the equinoxes, now containing the constellation west of the one from which it took its name; a circular or elliptical diagram representing this belt, and usu. containing pictures of the animals and other symbols associated with the constellations and signs; a picture representing this belt; a complete circuit or round.—**zo·di·a·cal,** zō·dī′a·kal, *a.*

zo·di·a·cal light, *n. Astron.* a luminous, nearly ecliptic tract on the horizon, seen either in the west after sunset or in the east before sunrise.

zo·e·trope, zō′ē·trōp″, *n.* A drumlike contrivance having a series of slits opposite a sequence of images, the latter appearing as one moving image when viewed through the slits as the drum is whirled.

zois·ite, zoi′sīt, *n.* [Named (1805) from Baron von *Zois*, who first observed it.] A mineral, $Ca_2Al_3O(OH)(SiO_4)(Si_2O_7)$, consisting of a hydroxylic calcium aluminum silicate, occurring in orthorhombic crystals and related to the mineral epidote.

zom·bie, zom·bi, zom′bē, *n.* A snake deity of West African, Haitian, and southern U.S. voodoo cults; according to voodoo belief, the supernatural power of reanimating a corpse; a human body made an automaton by such a power or by having its soul stolen by sorcery; a person who looks or behaves like a zombie. A mixed drink concocted of various kinds of fruit juice, rum, and liqueur.—**zom·bi·ism,** *n.*

zon·al, zōn′al, *a.* Having the character of or pertaining to a zone. Also **zon·a·ry,** zō′-na·rē.—**zon·al·ly,** *adv.*

zon·ate, zō′nāt, *a.* Marked with zones or concentric bands of color; arranged in rows or zones. Also **zo·nat·ed.**—**zo·na·tion,** zō·nā′shan, *n.*

zone, zōn, *n.* [Fr. *zone*, < L. *zona*, < Gr. *zōnē*, girdle, belt, zone, < *zōnnunai*, gird.] Any continuous tract or area, usu. forming a belt about an object or extending about a point, which differs in some respect or is distinguished for some purpose from ad-joining tracts or areas, or within which certain distinguishing circumstances exist or are established; as, a wheat *zone*; a surrounding area or one of a series of such areas about a particular place, to all points within which a uniform charge is made for transportation or some similar service; such an area, in the parcel post system, to all points within which the same rate of postage prevails for parcel post shipments from a particular place; a numbered division of a metropolitan area, so designated to aid in the sorting and distribution of mail; an area or district in a city or town under special restrictions as to buildings; the total sum of railroad stations located within a given area encircling a designated shipping center; *geog.* any of five great divisions of the earth's surface, bounded by lines parallel to the equator and named according to the prevailing temperature; *biogeography,* an area or region distinguished by more or less uniform and characteristic plant or animal life; *geom.* a part of a sphere's surface which is included between two planes which are parallel; *sports,* a particular area on a playing field; *archaic,* a girdle, belt, or cincture. —*v.t.*—*zoned, zoning.* To encircle with or surround as with a zone, girdle, or belt; to mark with zones or bands; to divide into zones, tracts, or areas, as according to existing characteristics, or as distinguished for some purpose; to divide, as a city or town, into areas or districts subject to special restrictions as to buildings, as with respect to their purpose or use, their maximum height, and the amount of the lot that may be covered.—*v.i.* To be formed into a zone or zones.—**zone·less,** *a.*

zone rate, *n.* A rate schedule for a public utility which divides territories into zones usu. according to different costs in different areas, the rates being the same within a particular zone, but differing between zones.

zon·ing laws, zō′ning laz, *n.* Ordinances set up by towns or cities which restrict or limit the use of certain areas of land, as a section specified as only industrial or only residential.

zon·ule, zōn′ūl, *n.* A little zone, band, or belt.—**zon·u·lar,** zōn′ya·lėr, *a.*

zoo, zō, *n.* pl. **zoos.** A park or other area, usu. with both an indoor and outdoor display of various living animals.

zo·o·ge·og·ra·phy, zō″o·jē·og′ra·fē, *n.* The science concerned with the geographical distribution of animals; the study of effects and relationships in these distributions.—**zo·o·ge·og·ra·pher,** *n.*—**zo·o·-ge·o·graph·ic, zo·o·ge·o·graph·i·cal,** zō″o·jē″o·graf′ik, *a.*—**zo·o·ge·o·graph·-i·cal·ly,** *adv.*

zo·o·gloe·a, zō″o·glē′a, *n.* [N.L., < Gr. *zōion,* animal, and *gloia,* glue.] *Bact.* a jellylike mass or aggregate of bacteria formed when the cell walls swell through absorption of water and become contiguous.—**zo·o·-gloe·al,** *a.*

zo·og·ra·phy, zō·og′ra·fē, *n.* [Gr. *zōion,* an animal, and *graphō,* to describe.] A description of animals, their forms, and habits.—**zo·og·ra·pher,** *n.*—**zo·o·graph·ic, zo·o·graph·i·cal,** zō″o·graf′ik, *a.*

zo·oid, zō′oid, *n.* [Gr. *zōion,* an animal, and *eidos,* likeness.] *Biol.* An organic body, either animal or plant, capable of life and movement independent of the generating body, as a gamete or a tapeworm; any motile life form that can exist separately from the parent body and is produced by gemmation, fission, or other type of asexual reproduction; a single distinct animal of a colony or aggregate.—*a.* Pertaining to or having the nature of an animal; also **zo·oi·dal,** zō′oid′l.

zooks, zuks, zōks, *interj.* An exclamation equivalent to some mild oath.

zo·ol·a·try, zō·ol'a·trē, *n.* pl. **zo·ol·a·tries.** [Gr. *zōion*, an animal, and *latreia*, worship.] The worship of animals.— **zo·ol·a·ter,** *n.*—**zo·ol·a·trous,** *a.*

zo·o·log·i·cal gar·den, *n.* A garden or other area in which a collection of living animals is kept, usu. for display.

zo·ol·o·gy, zō·ol'o·jē, *n.* pl. **zo·ol·o·gies.** [Gr. *zōion*, an animal, and *logos*, discourse.] That science which treats of the natural history of animals or their structure, physiology, classification, habits, and distribution; a treatise about zoology; animal life of a specific area.—**zo·o·log·i·cal,** zō''o·loj'i·kal, *a.*—**zo·o·log·i·cal·ly,** *adv.*—**zo·ol·o·gist,** zō·ol'o·jist, *n.*

zoom, zōm, *v.i.* [Imit.] To make a continuous humming sound; to drive an airplane suddenly and very sharply upward at great speed for a short distance, as in regaining altitude, clearing an obstacle, signaling, or the like; *motion pictures, TV,* to go rapidly away from or toward a subject with the camera, keeping the subject in focus, giving the effect of greater or lesser distance.— *v.t.* To cause, as an airplane, to zoom; to fly over or surmount, as an obstacle, by zooming.—*n.* An act or sound of zooming; a sudden, very sharp upward movement of an airplane.

zo·om·e·try, zō·om'i·trē, *n.* The measurement of the dimensions and individual sections of animals to determine by comparison the relative bulk.—**zo·o·met·ric,** **zo·o·met·ri·cal,** zō''o·me'trik, *a.*

zoom lens, *n.* A lens, usu. on a motion picture or television camera, that allows a rapid enlargement or diminution of an image without losing focus.

zo·o·mor·phic, zō''o·mąr'fik, *a.* Representing or using animal forms; as, *zoomorphic* ornament; ascribing animal form or attributes to beings or things not animal; representing a deity under the form of an animal; characterized by or involving such ascription or representation.

zo·o·mor·phism, zō''o·mąr'fiz·um, *n.* Zoormorphic representation, as in ornaments or art; zoomorphic conception, as of a deity.

zo·on, zō'on, *n.* pl. **zo·a,** zō'a. [N.L., < Gr. *zōion*, living being, animal, akin to *zōē*, life, and *zēn*, live.] *Zool.* any of the individuals of an animal colony.—**zo·on·al,** zō·on'al, *a.*

zo·on·o·sis, zō·on'o·sis, zō''o·nō'sis, *n. Pathol.* a communicable disease from animals to man.

zo·oph·a·gous, zō·of'a·gus, *a.* [Gr. *zōophágos,* < *zōion*, animal, and *phagein,* eat.] Feeding on animals; carnivorous.

zo·oph·i·lous, zō·of'i·lus, *a.* Loving animals; *bot.* adapted to pollination by the agency of animals. Also **zo·o·phil·ic,** zō''o·fil'ik.

zo·o·pho·bi·a, zō''o·fō'bē·a, *n. Psychol.* morbid fear of animals.

zo·o·phyte, zō'o·fīt'', *n.* [Fr. *zoophyte,* < Gr. *zōóphyton,* < *zōion*, animal, and *phytón,* plant.] Any of various invertebrate animals resembling a plant, as a coral or a sea anemone.—**zo·o·phyt·ic,** **zo·o·phyt·i·cal,** zō''o·fit'ik, *a.*

zo·o·plank·ton, zō''o·plangk'ton, *n.* Planktonic animals, as distinguished from *phytoplankton.*—**zo·o·plank·ton·ic,** zō''o·plangk·ton'ik, *a.*

zo·o·plas·ty, zō'o·plas''tē, *n. Surg.* transplantation to the human body of lower animal tissue.—**zo·o·plas·tic,** *a.*

zo·o·sperm, zō'o·spųrm'', *n.* Spermatozoon; *bot., obs.* a zoospore.—**zo·o·sper·mat·ic,** zō''o·spėr·mat'ik, *a.*

zo·o·spo·ran·gi·um, zō''o·spo·ran'jē·um, *n.* pl. **zo·o·spo·ran·gi·a,** zō''o·spo·ran'jē·a. [N.L.] *Bot.* a sporangium or spore case in which zoospores are produced. —**zo·o·spo·ran·gi·al,** *a.*

zo·o·spore, zō'o·spōr'', zō'o·spąr'', *n. Bot.* an asexual spore produced by certain algae and some fungi, capable of moving about by means of cilia; *zool.* any of the minute motile flagelliform or amoeboid bodies which issue from the sporocyst of certain protozoans.—**zo·o·spor·ic,** **zo·os·por·ous,** zō''o·spąr'ik, zō''o·spor'ik, zō·os'·pėr·us, zō''o·spōr'us, zō''o·spąr'us, *a.*

zo·ot·o·my, zō·ot'o·mē, *n.* The dissection of the bodies of animals, other than man, for the purposes of study; comparative anatomy.—**zo·o·tom·ic,** **zo·o·tom·i·cal,** zō''o·tom'ik, *a.*—**zo·ot·o·mist,** *n.*

zoot suit, zōt'sōt'', *n. Slang,* an egregiously flashy men's suit, esp. such a suit popular in the beginning of the 1940's, having a long coat with wide lapels and large padded shoulders, and high-waisted baggy pants which taper to a narrow cuff.—**zoot-suit·er,** *n.*

zor·il, ząr'il, zor'il, *n.* A small African mammal, *Ictonyx striatus,* resembling a skunk.

zos·ter, zos'tėr, *n.* [L., < Gr. *zōstēr,* girdle, < *zonnynai,* gird.] *Pathol.* herpes zoster; *Gr. antiq.* a belt or girdle.

Zou·ave, zō·äv', zwäv, *n.* [Fr. *zouave;* from the name of a Kabyle tribe in Algeria.] (*Sometimes l.c.*) One of a body of infantry in the French army, composed orig. of Algerians, wearing a picturesque Oriental uniform; a member of any body of soldiers wearing a similar dress.

zounds, zoundz, *interj.* [Also *swounds;* reduced form of *God's wounds.*] *Archaic,* a mild oath, used as a mere emphatic exclamation, as of surprise, indignation, or anger.

zoy·si·a, zoi'sē·a, *n.* A creeping grass, genus *Zoisia,* used as a lawn grass in warm climates, distinguished by its thin, wiry leaves.

zuc·chet·to, zō·ket'ō, *It.* tsōk·ket'ta, *n.* pl. **zuc·chet·tos,** *It.* **zuc·chet·ti,** *It.* tsōk·ket'tē. [It., dim. < *zucca,* gourd.] A small, round skullcap worn by Roman Catholic ecclesiastics, a priest's being black, a bishop's violet, a cardinal's red, and the Pope's white.

zuc·chi·ni, zō·kē'nē, *n.* pl. **zuc·chi·ni,** **zuc·chi·nis.** A variety or kind of cylindrical slender summer squash, the skin of which is dark green and smooth.

Zu·lu, zō'lō, *a.* Pertaining to a member of a people of southeastern Africa or to their language.—*n.*

Zu·lu, zō'lō, *n.* A communications code word to designate the letter Z.

Zu·ñi·an, zō'nyē·an, zō'nē·an, sō'nyē·an, sō'nē·an, *a.* Pertaining to the Zuñi Indian tribe of New Mexico or to their language.— *n.* The Zuñi people or language.

zwie·back, zwī'bak'', zwī'bäk'', zwē'bak'', zwē'bäk'', swī'bak'', swī'bäk'', *G.* tsvē'bäk'', *n.* [G., 'twice-baked': for the meaning, cf. *biscuit.*] A kind of bread or biscuit, baked, cut into slices, and toasted.

zwit·ter·i·on, tsvit'ėr·ī''on, *n. Physical chem.* an ion or atom, possessing a negative and positive charge.—**zwit·ter·i·on·ic,** tsvit''ėr·ī·on'ik, *a.*

zyg·a·poph·y·sis, zig''a·pof'i·sis, zī''ga·pof'i·sis, *n.* pl. **zyg·a·poph·y·ses,** zig''a·pof'i·sēz', zī''ga·pof'i·sēz''. *Anat.* one of the articular processes upon the neural arch of a vertebra, usu. occurring in two pairs, one anterior and the other posterior, and serving to interlock each vertebra with the one above and below.—**zyg·ap·o·phys·e·al,** **zyg·ap·o·phys·i·al,** zig''ap·o·fiz'ē·al, *a.*

zy·go·dac·tyl, zī''go·dak'til, zig''o·dak'til, *a.* [N.L. *zygodactylus,* < Gr. *zygon,* yoke, and *dáctylos,* finger or toe.] *Ornith.* of a bird or a bird's foot, having the toes disposed in pairs, one pair before and one pair behind

on each foot. Also **zy·go·dac·tyl·ous.** —*n.*—**zy·go·dac·tyl·ism,** *n.*

zy·go·ma, zī·gō'ma, zī·gō'ma, *n.* pl. **zy·go·ma·ta,** zī·gō'ma·ta, zī·gō'ma·ta. [Gr. *zygōma,* < *zygon,* a yoke.] *Anat.* The prominence of the cheekbone, or the part that joins it with the cranium; zygomatic arch; zygomatic bone.—**zy·go·ma·tic,** zī''go·mat'ik, zig''o·mat'ik, *a.*

zy·go·mat·ic arch, *n. Anat.* the arch in the bone beneath the skull's orbit extending along its front or side.

zy·go·mat·ic bone, *n. Anat.* a bone on both sides of the face which helps form a section of the zygomatic arch and its orbit.

zy·go·mat·ic proc·ess, *n.* One of the bony processes which is joined to the zygomatic bone.

zy·go·mor·phic, zī''go·mąr'fik, zig''o·mąr'fik, *a. Biol.* capable of being halved in one plane only, with each half being identical to each other, as of organisms, organs, or parts of organs. Also **zy·go·mor·phous.** —**zy·go·mor·phism,** **zy·go·mor·phy,** zī''go·mąr''fē, *n.*

zy·go·phyte, zī'go·fīt, zig'o·fīt, *n.* A plant that reproduces by means of zygospores.

zy·go·sis, zī·gō'sis, zi·gō'sis, *n. Biol.* The union of two cells or gametes; conjugation. —**zy·gose,** zī'gōs, zig'ōs, *a.*

zy·go·spore, zī'go·spōr'', zī'go·spąr'', zig'o·spōr'', zig'o·spąr'', *n.* [Gr. *zeugos,* a pair, *sporos,* fruit.] *Bot.* a cell or spore formed by union of two similar gametes.—**zy·go·spor·ic,** zī''go·spąr'ik, zī''go·spor'ik, zig''o·spąr'ik, zig''o·spor'ik, *a.*

zy·gote, zī'gōt, zig'ōt, *n.* [Gr. *zygōtós,* yoked, < *zygoyn,* to yoke.] *Biol.* A cell formed by the union of two gametes; the organism produced from this type of cell. —**zy·got·ic,** zī·got'ik, zi·got'ik, *a.*—**zy·got·i·cal·ly,** *adv.*

zy·go·tene, zī'go·tēn'', zig'o·tēn'', *n. Biol.* the first division of meiosis during which homologous chromosomes are paired with formation of bivalents.

zy·mase, zī'mās, *n.* [Gr. *zymē,* leaven.] *Biochem.* an enzyme in yeast which causes the decomposition of sugar into alcohol and carbon dioxide, and which may be obtained in the form of an extract.

zy·mo·gen, zī'mo·jen, *n. Biochem., biol.* any of various substances which by internal change may give rise to an enzyme. Also *proenzyme.*—**zy·mo·gen·e·sis,** zī''mo·jen'i·sis, *n.* The change of a zymogen into an enzyme.—**zy·mo·gen·ic,** zī''mo·jen'ik, *a.*

zy·mol·o·gy, zī·mol'o·jē, *n. Biochem.* the branch of science which deals with ferments and fermentation.—**zy·mo·log·ic,** zī''mo·loj'ik, *a.*

zy·mol·y·sis, zī·mol'i·sis, *n.* The fermentative action of enzymes; the resulting fermentation.—**zy·mo·lyt·ic,** zī''mo·lit'ik, *a.*

zy·mo·plas·tic, zī''mō·plas'tik, *a. Biol.* producing an enzyme or enzymes.

zy·mo·scope, zī'mo·skōp, *n.* A device that measures yeast's fermenting power.

zy·mo·sis, zī·mō'sis, *n.* pl. **zy·mo·ses,** zī·mō'sēz. [Gr., fermentation.] Fermentation. *Med.* a zymotic disease; the infective process by which certain diseases were once believed to evolve.

zy·mos·then·ic, zī''mos·then'ik, *a.* Intensifying functional activity of enzymes.

zy·mot·ic, zī·mot'ik, *a.* [Gr. *zymōtikos,* < *zymoō,* to ferment, < *zymē,* ferment.] Pertaining to or relating to fermentation; *pathol.* denoting an infectious disease.— **zy·mot·i·cal·ly,** *adv.*

zy·mur·gy, zī'mųr·jē, *n.* [Gr. *zymē,* leaven, and *ergon,* work.] *Chem.* the principles and methods of fermentation, esp. as applied to brewing, distilling, winemaking, and the preparation of yeast and vinegar.

DICTIONARY OF SYNONYMS AND ANTONYMS

abandon, *v.* SYN.—abdicate, abjure, relinquish, renounce, resign, surrender, vacate, waive; desert, forsake, leave, quit. ANT.—defend, maintain, uphold; stay, support.

abate, *v.* SYN.—assuage, decrease, diminish, lessen, lower, moderate, reduce, suppress. ANT.—amplify, enlarge, increase, intensify, revive.

abbey, *n.* See cloister.

abbreviate, *v.* See shorten.

abbreviation, *n.* SYN.—abridgement, contraction, reduction, shortening. ANT.—amplification, enlargement, expansion, extension.

abdicate, *v.* See abandon.

aberrant, *a.* See irregular.

abet, *v.* SYN.—aid, assist, encourage, help, incite. ANT.—discourage, hinder, oppose, resist.

abhor, *v.* See hate.

abhorrence, *n.* See aversion, hatred.

ability, *n.* SYN.—aptitude, aptness, capability, capacity, dexterity, efficiency, faculty, power, qualification, skill, talent. ANT.—disability, incapacity, incompetency, unreadiness.

abject, *a.* See vile.

able, *a.* See capable.

abnormal, *a.* See irregular.

abolish, *v.* SYN.—destroy, end, eradicate, obliterate, overthrow; abrogate, annul, cancel, invalidate, revoke. ANT.—continue, establish, promote, restore, sustain.

abominable, *a.* SYN.—detestable, execrable, foul, hateful, loathsome, odious, revolting, vile. ANT.—agreeable, commendable, delightful, pleasant.

aboriginal, *a.* See primitive.

abridge, *v.* See shorten.

abridgement, *n.* See abbreviation.

abrogate, *v.* See cancel.

abrupt, *a.* SYN.—hasty, precipitate, sudden, unannounced, unexpected; blunt, brusque, curt, rude; craggy, harsh, precipitous, rough, rugged, sharp, steep. ANT.—anticipated, expected; courteous, gradual, smooth.

absent, *a.* SYN.—abroad, away, departed; absent-minded, abstracted, distracted, inattentive, preoccupied. ANT.—attending, present; attentive, watchful.

absolute, *a.* SYN.—actual, complete, entire, perfect, pure, ultimate, unconditional, unqualified, unrestricted; arbitrary, authoritative, despotic, tyrannous. ANT.—accountable, conditional, contingent, dependent, qualified.

absolve, *v.* See pardon.

absorb, *v.* SYN.—assimilate, consume, engulf, imbibe, swallow up; engage, engross, occupy. ANT.—discharge, dispense, emit, expel, exude.

abstain, *v.* See refrain.

abstention, *n.* See abstinence.

abstinence, *n.* SYN.—abstention, continence, fasting, forbearance, moderation, self-denial, sobriety, temperance. ANT.—excess, gluttony, greed, intoxication, self-indulgence.

abstract, *v.* SYN.—draw from, part, remove, separate; appropriate, purloin, steal;

---

abridge, summarize. ANT.—add, replace, restore, return, unite.

absurd, *a.* SYN.—foolish, inconsistent, irrational, nonsensical, preposterous, ridiculous, self-contradictory, silly, unreasonable. ANT.—consistent, rational, reasonable, sensible, sound.

abundant, *a.* SYN.—ample, bountiful, copious, overflowing, plenteous, plentiful, profuse, rich, teeming. ANT.—deficient, insufficient, scant, scarce.

abuse, *n.* SYN.—aspersion, defamation, desecration, dishonor, disparagement, insult, invective, maltreatment, misuse, outrage, perversion, profanation, reproach, reviling, upbraiding. ANT.—approval, commendation, laudation, plaudit, respect.

abuse, *v.* SYN.—asperse, defame, disparage, ill-use, malign, revile, scandalize, traduce, vilify; misapply, misemploy, misuse. ANT.—cherish, honor, praise, protect, respect.

academic, *a.* SYN.—bookish, erudite, formal, learned, pedantic, scholarly, scholastic, theoretical. ANT.—common-sense, ignorant, practical, simple.

accede, *v.* See yield.

accelerate, *v.* SYN.—dispatch, expedite, facilitate, forward, hasten, hurry, push, quicken, rush, speed. ANT.—block, hinder, impede, retard, slow.

accept, *v.* See admit, receive.

acceptable, *a.* See agreeable.

accessible, *a.* See available.

accessory, *n.* See accomplice.

accident, *n.* SYN.—calamity, casualty, contingency, disaster, fortuity, misfortune, mishap. ANT.—calculation, design, intention, purpose.

accidental, *a.* SYN.—casual, chance, contingent, fortuitous, incidental, undesigned, unintended. ANT.—calculated, decreed, intended, planned, willed.

accommodate, *v.* See adapt.

accompany, *v.* SYN.—associate with, attend, chaperone, consort with, convoy, escort, go with. ANT.—abandon, avoid, desert, leave, quit.

accomplice, *n.* SYN.—abettor, accessory, ally, assistant, associate, confederate. ANT.—adversary, enemy, opponent, rival.

accomplish, *v.* SYN.—achieve, attain, complete, consummate, do, effect, execute, finish, fulfill, perfect, perform. ANT.—block, defeat, fail, frustrate, spoil.

accordance, *n.* See agreement.

account, *n.* SYN.—chronicle, description, detail, history, narration, narrative, recital, relation; computation, reckoning, record. ANT.—caricature, confusion, distortion, misrepresentation.

account, *v.* SYN.—believe, consider, deem, esteem, estimate, hold, judge, rate, reckon, regard, think, view; elucidate, explain, expound.

accountability, *n.* See responsibility.

accountable, *a.* See liable, responsible.

accumulate, *v.* SYN.—accrue, amass, collect, gather, heap, hoard, increase, store. ANT.—diminish, disperse, dissipate, scatter, waste.

accuracy, *n.* See fidelity.

---

accurate, *a.* See correct, precise.

accusation, *n.* SYN.—arraignment, charge, imputation, incrimination, indictment. ANT.—exculpation, exoneration, pardon.

accuse, *v.* SYN.—arraign, censure, charge, incriminate, indict. ANT.—absolve, acquit, exonerate, release, vindicate.

accustom, *v.* See use.

ache, *n.* See pain.

achieve, *v.* SYN.—accomplish, acquire, do, effect, execute, gain, obtain, realize, win. ANT.—fail, fall short, lose, miss.

achievement, *n.* SYN.—deed, exploit, feat; accomplishment, attainment, completion, performance, realization. ANT.—neglect, omission; defeat, failure.

acknowledge, *v.* See admit, recognize.

acquaintance, *n.* SYN.—cognizance, companionship, familiarity, fellowship, friendship, intimacy, knowledge. ANT.—ignorance, inexperience, unfamiliarity.

acquiesce, *v.* See yield.

acquire, *v.* SYN.—assimilate, attain, earn, get, obtain, procure, secure, win. ANT.—forego, forfeit, lose, miss, surrender.

acquit, *v.* See pardon.

acquittal, *n.* See pardon.

acrid, *a.* See bitter, sharp.

act, *n.* SYN.—accomplishment, action, deed, doing, execution, feat, operation, performance, transaction; decree, edict, law, statute. ANT.—cessation, deliberation, inactivity, inhibition, intention.

act, *v.* See behave, pretend.

action, *n.* SYN.—achievement, activity, deed, exercise, exploit, feat, motion, movement, performance, play, procedure. ANT.—idleness, inactivity, inertia, repose, rest.

active, *a.* SYN.—operative, working; busy, industrious; agile, alert, brisk, lively, nimble, quick, sprightly, supple. ANT.—dormant, inactive; indolent, lazy, passive.

activity, *n.* SYN.—action, agility, briskness, energy, enterprise, exercise, intensity, liveliness, motion, movement, quickness, rapidity, vigor. ANT.—dullness, idleness, inactivity, inertia, sloth.

actual, *a.* See real.

actuate, *v.* See move.

adage, *n.* See proverb.

adapt, *v.* SYN.—accommodate, adjust, conform, fit, suit. ANT.—disturb, misapply, misfit.

add, *v.* SYN.—adjoin, affix, append, attach, augment, increase, sum, total. ANT.—deduct, detach, reduce, remove, subtract.

address, *v.* SYN.—accost, approach, greet, hail, speak to. ANT.—avoid, pass by.

adept, *a.* See skillful.

adequate, *a.* SYN.—ample, capable, commensurate, enough, fitting, satisfactory, sufficient, suitable. ANT.—deficient, lacking, scant.

adherent, *n.* See disciple.

adjacent, *a.* See close, touching.

adjust, *v.* See adapt.

admirable, *a.* See honorable.

admire, *v.* SYN.—appreciate, approve, esteem, respect, venerate, wonder. ANT.—abhor, despise, dislike.

admissible, *a.* SYN.—allowable, fair, justifiable, permissible, probable, tolerable.

warranted. ANT.—inadmissible, irrelevant, unsuitable.

admit, v. SYN.—accept, acknowledge, agree, allow, assent, concede, confess, grant, permit, welcome. ANT.—deny, dismiss, reject, shun.

admonition, n. See **advice.**

adopt, v. See **take.**

adore, v. See **revere.**

adorn, v. SYN.—beautify, bedeck, decorate, embellish, garnish, gild, ornament, trim. ANT.—deface, deform, disfigure, mar, spoil.

adroit, a. See **clever.**

adulterate, v. See **debase.**

advance, v. SYN.—aggrandize, elevate, forward, further, promote; adduce, allege, assign, bring forward, offer, propose, propound; improve, proceed, progress, rise, thrive; augment, enlarge, increase. ANT.—hinder, oppose, retard, retreat, withhold.

advantage, n. SYN.—edge, mastery, superiority; benefit, good, profit, service, utility. ANT.—detriment, handicap, harm, impediment, obstruction.

advantageous, a. See **beneficial.**

adventurous, a. SYN.—bold, chivalrous, daring, enterprising, foolhardy, precipitate, rash. ANT.—cautious, hesitating, timid.

adversary, n. See **enemy, rival.**

adverse, a. SYN.—antagonistic, contrary, hostile, opposed, opposite; counteractive, disastrous, unfavorable, unlucky. ANT.—benign, favorable, fortunate, lucky, propitious.

adversity, n. See **misfortune.**

advertisement, n. See **announcement.**

advice, n. SYN.—admonition, caution, counsel, exhortation, instruction, recommendation, suggestion, warning; information, intelligence, notification.

advise, v. See **inform.**

affable, a. See **social.**

affect, v. SYN.—alter, change, influence, modify, transform; concern, interest, regard; impress, melt, move, soften, subdue, touch; adopt, assume, feign, pretend.

affected, a. See **theatrical.**

affection, n. SYN.—attachment, endearment, fondness, kindness, love, tenderness; disposition, emotion, feeling, inclination. ANT.—aversion, hatred, indifference, repugnance, repulsion.

affiliate, v. See **associate.**

affirm, v. SYN.—assert, aver, declare, maintain, protest, state, swear. ANT.—contradict, demur, deny, dispute, oppose.

affix, v. See **apply, attach.**

afflict, v. See **burden.**

affluence, n. See **wealth.**

affluent, a. See **rich.**

affront, n. See **insult.**

afraid, a. SYN.—apprehensive, fainthearted, fearful, frightened, scared, timid, timorous. ANT.—assured, bold, composed, courageous, sanguine.

age, n. SYN.—dotage, senescence, senility, seniority; antiquity, date, epoch, era, generation, period, time. ANT.—childhood, infancy, youth.

agent, n. See **instrument.**

aggravate, v. SYN.—heighten, increase, intensify, magnify; annoy, chafe, embitter, exasperate, inflame, irritate, nettle, provoke, vex. ANT.—appease, mitigate, palliate, soften, soothe.

aggregate, n. SYN.—amount, collection, conglomeration, entirety, sum, total, whole. ANT.—element, ingredient, part, particular, unit.

agile, a. See **nimble.**

agitate, v. SYN.—arouse, disconcert, disturb, excite, jar, perturb, rouse, ruffle, shake, trouble. ANT.—calm, ease, placate, quiet.

agitated, a. See **restless.**

agony, n. SYN.—ache, anguish, distress, misery, pain, suffering, throe, torment, torture, woe. ANT.—comfort, ease, mitigation, relief.

agree, v. SYN.—accede, acquiesce, assent, comply, consent; coincide, concur, conform, tally. ANT.—contradict, differ, disagree, dissent, protest.

agreeable, a. SYN.—acceptable, amiable, charming, gratifying, pleasant, pleasing, pleasurable, suitable, welcome. ANT.—disagreeable, obnoxious, offensive, unpleasant.

agreement, n. SYN.—accordance, coincidence, concord, concurrence, harmony, understanding, unison; bargain, compact, contract, covenant, pact, stipulation. ANT.—difference, disagreement, discord, dissension, variance.

agriculture, n. SYN.—agronomy, cultivation, farming, gardening, horticulture, husbandry, tillage.

aid, n. See **assistance.**

aid, v. See **assist, help.**

ailment, n. See **disease.**

aim, n. See **ambition, purpose.**

aim, v. See **direct.**

ajar, a. See **open.**

alarm, n. SYN.—affright, apprehension, consternation, dismay, fright, signal, terror, warning. ANT.—calm, composure, quiet, security, tranquility.

alarm, v. See **frighten.**

alert, a. See **vigilant.**

alien, a. SYN.—adverse, contrasted, extraneous, foreign, irrelevant, remote, strange, unconnected. ANT.—akin, germane, kindred, relevant.

alike, a. See **analogous.**

allege, v. SYN.—advance, affirm, assign, cite, claim, declare, maintain. ANT.—contradict, deny, disprove, gainsay, refute.

allegiance, n. See **loyalty.**

alleviate, v. SYN.—abate, allay, assuage, diminish, extenuate, mitigate, relieve, soften, solace, soothe. ANT.—aggravate, agitate, augment, increase, irritate.

alliance, n. SYN.—association, coalition, combination, confederacy, entente, federation, league, partnership, union; compact, covenant, marriage, treaty. ANT.—divorce, schism, separation.

allocate, v. See **allot.**

allot, v. SYN.—apportion, deal, dispense, distribute, divide, mete; allocate, appropriate, assign, give, grant, measure. ANT.—confiscate, keep, refuse, retain, withhold.

allotment, n. See **part.**

allow, v. SYN.—let, permit, sanction, suffer, tolerate; authorize, give, grant, yield; acknowledge, admit, concede. ANT.—forbid, object, protest, refuse, resist.

allowable, a. See **admissible.**

allude, v. SYN.—advert, hint, imply, insinuate, intimate, refer, suggest. ANT.—declare, demonstrate, specify, state.

alluring, a. See **charming.**

alone, a. SYN.—deserted, desolate, isolated, lonely, secluded, unaided; lone, only, single, sole, solitary. ANT.—accompanied, attended, surrounded.

aloof, a. See **distant.**

also, adv. SYN.—besides, furthermore, in addition, likewise, moreover, similarly, too.

alter, v. See **change.**

alteration, n. See **change.**

alternate, n. See **substitute.**

alternative, n. See **choice.**

always, adv. SYN.—constantly, continually, eternally, ever, evermore, forever, incessantly, perpetually, unceasingly. ANT.—fitfully, never, occasionally, rarely, sometimes.

amass, v. See **gather.**

amateur, n. SYN.—apprentice, beginner, dabbler, dilettante, learner, neophyte, novice. ANT.—adept, authority, expert, master, professional.

amazement, n. See **wonder.**

ambiguity, n. See **doubt.**

ambiguous, a. SYN.—dubious, enigmatical, equivocal, obscure, uncertain, vague. ANT.—clear, explicit, obvious, plain, unequivocal.

ambition, n. SYN.—aspiration, eagerness, emulation, goal, incentive, pretension. ANT.—contentment, indifference, indolence, resignation, satisfaction.

ambush, n. See **trap.**

amend, v. See **correct.**

amiable, a. SYN.—agreeable, engaging, friendly, good-natured, gracious, pleasing. ANT.—churlish, disagreeable, hateful, ill-natured, surly.

amicable, a. See **friendly.**

amid, prep. See **among.**

among, prep. SYN.—amid, amidst, between, betwixt, mingled, mixed.

amount, n. SYN.—aggregate, number, quantity, sum, total, whole.

ample, a. SYN.—broad, extensive, great, large, spacious, wide; abundant, bountiful, copious, full, generous, liberal, plentiful, profuse, rich. ANT.—constricted, limited, small; insufficient, lacking, meager.

amplify, v. See **increase.**

amusement, n. See **recreation.**

analogous, a. SYN.—akin, alike, allied, comparable, correlative, correspondent, corresponding, like, parallel, similar. ANT.—different, dissimilar, divergent, incongruous, opposed.

analyze, v. See **examine.**

ancestry, n. See **race.**

ancient, a. See **old.**

anecdote, n. See **story.**

anger, n. SYN.—animosity, choler, exasperation, fury, indignation, ire, irritation, passion, petulance, rage, resentment, temper, wrath. ANT.—conciliation, forbearance, patience, peace, self-control.

angry, a. SYN.—enraged, exasperated, furious, incensed, indignant, irate, maddened, provoked, wrathful, wroth. ANT.—calm, happy, pleased, satisfied.

anguish, n. SYN.—agony, distress, grief, misery, suffering, torment, torture. ANT.—comfort, joy, relief, solace.

animosity, n. SYN.—bitterness, enmity, grudge, hatred, hostility, malevolence, rancor, spite. ANT.—friendliness, good will, love.

annihilate, v. See **destroy.**

announce, v. SYN.—advertise, declare, give out, herald, make known, notify, proclaim, promulgate, publish, report. ANT.—bury, conceal, stifle, suppress, withhold.

announcement, *n.* SYN.—advertisement, bulletin, declaration, notification, promulgation. ANT.—hush, muteness, silence, speechlessness.

annoy, *v.* SYN.—bother, chafe, disturb, inconvenience, irk, irritate, molest, pester, tease, trouble, vex. ANT.—accommodate, console, gratify, soothe.

annoying, *a.* See **troublesome.**

annul, *v.* See **abolish, cancel.**

answer, *n.* SYN.—rejoinder, reply, response, retort; defense, rebuttal. ANT.—inquiry, questioning, summoning; argument.

antagonistic, *a.* See **adverse, hostile.**

anticipation, *n.* SYN.—contemplation, expectation, foresight, forethought, hope, preconception, prescience, presentiment. ANT.—doubt, dread, fear, worry.

antipathy, *n.* See **enmity.**

antiquated, *a.* See **obsolete.**

anxiety, *n.* SYN.—apprehension, care, concern, disquiet, fear, solicitude, trouble, worry. ANT.—assurance, confidence, contentment, equanimity, nonchalance.

anxious, *a.* See **eager.**

apathy, *n.* See **indifference.**

apex, *n.* See **climax.**

apology, *n.* SYN.—alibi, confession, defense, excuse, explanation, justification. ANT.—accusation, complaint, denial, dissimulation.

apparatus, *n.* See **instrument.**

apparel, *n.* See **clothes.**

apparent, *a.* SYN.—clear, evident, manifest, obvious, palpable, plain, self-evident, transparent, unambiguous, unmistakable, visible; illusory, ostensible, seeming. ANT.—ambiguous, dubious, indistinct, real, uncertain.

appear, *v.* SYN.—look, seem; arise, arrive, emanate, emerge, issue. ANT.—be, exist; disappear, vanish, withdraw.

appearance, *n.* SYN.—advent, apparition, arrival; air, aspect, demeanor, look, manner, mien; fashion, guise, pretense, semblance.

appease, *v.* SYN.—allay, alleviate, assuage, calm, compose, lull, pacify, placate, quell, quiet, relieve, satisfy, soothe, still, tranquilize. ANT.—arouse, excite, incense, inflame.

appetite, *n.* SYN.—hunger, relish, stomach, thirst, zest; craving, desire, inclination, liking, longing, passion. ANT.—disgust, distaste, renunciation, repugnance, satiety.

apply, *v.* SYN.—administer, affix, allot, appropriate, assign, attach, avail, devote, direct, employ, use; bear, pertain, refer, relate; appeal, petition, request.

appoint, *v.* See **name.**

apportion, *v.* See **share.**

appraise, *v.* See **assess.**

appreciate, *v.* SYN.—admire, cherish, enjoy, esteem, prize, regard, value; appraise, estimate, evaluate, rate; apprehend, comprehend, understand; go up, improve, rise. ANT.—belittle, degrade, depreciate; misapprehend, misunderstand.

appreciative, *a.* See **grateful.**

apprehend, *v.* See **catch.**

apprehension, *n.* See **worry.**

apprehensive, *a.* See **afraid.**

appropriate, *a.* SYN.—applicable, apt, becoming, fitting, particular, proper, suita-

ble. ANT.—contrary, improper, inappropriate.

appropriation, *n.* See **grant.**

approval, *n.* SYN.—approbation, assent, commendation, consent, endorsement, praise, sanction, support. ANT.—censure, reprimand, reproach, stricture.

approve, *v.* SYN.—appreciate, commend, like, praise; authorize, confirm, endorse, ratify, sanction. ANT.—criticize, disparage; condemn, nullify.

apropos, *a.* See **relevant.**

aptitude, *n.* See **ability, skill.**

arbitrate, *v.* See **judge.**

arbitrator, *n.* See **judge.**

archetype, *n.* See **example.**

ardent, *a.* SYN.—eager, enthusiastic, fervent, fervid, fiery, glowing, hot, impassioned, intense, keen, passionate, vehement, zealous. ANT.—apathetic, cool, indifferent, nonchalant.

ardor, *n.* SYN.—devotion, eagerness, enthusiasm, fervor, fire, passion, rapture, spirit, zeal. ANT.—apathy, disinterest, indifference, unconcern.

arduous, *a.* See **difficult, hard.**

area, *n.* See **location.**

argue, *v.* SYN.—debate, discuss, dispute, plead, reason, wrangle; denote, imply, indicate, prove, show. ANT.—ignore, overlook, reject, spurn.

argument, *n.* See **dispute.**

arid, *a.* See **dry.**

aroma, *n.* See **smell.**

arrange, *v.* SYN.—adjust, assort, classify, dispose, organize, place, regulate; devise, organize, plan, prepare. ANT.—confuse, disorder, disturb, jumble, scatter.

arrangement, *n.* See **system.**

array, *n.* See **clothes.**

arrest, *v.* SYN.—apprehend, check, detain, hinder, interrupt, obstruct, restrain, seize, stop, withhold. ANT.—activate, discharge, free, liberate, release.

arrive, *v.* SYN.—appear, attain, come, emerge, land, reach, visit. ANT.—depart, exit, leave.

arrogant, *a.* See **proud.**

art, *n.* SYN.—adroitness, aptitude, cunning, knack, skill, tact; artifice, duplicity, guile, shrewdness, subtlety. ANT.—clumsiness, unskillfulness; forthrightness, honesty, innocence.

article, *n.* See **object.**

artificial, *a.* SYN.—affected, assumed, bogus, counterfeit, ersatz, fake, feigned, fictitious, phony, sham, spurious, synthetic, unreal. ANT.—genuine, natural, real, true.

ascend, *v.* SYN.—climb, mount, rise, scale, soar, tower. ANT.—descend, fall, sink.

ascertain, *v.* See **discover.**

asinine, *a.* See **foolish.**

ask, *v.* SYN.—beg, claim, demand, entreat, invite, request, solicit; inquire, interrogate, query, question. ANT.—command, dictate, insist, order, reply.

asperse, *v.* See **abuse.**

aspiration, *n.* SYN.—aim, ambition, craving, desire, goal, hope, longing, objective, passion.

aspire, *v.* See **try.**

assail, *v.* See **attack.**

assassinate, *v.* See **kill.**

assault, *v.* SYN.—assail, attack, bombard, charge, invade, pound, storm, strike. ANT.—defend, oppose, protect.

assembly, *n.* See **group.**

assent, *v.* See **agree.**

assert, *v.* SYN.—affirm, allege, aver, claim, declare, express, maintain, state; defend, support, uphold, vindicate. ANT.—contradict, deny, refute.

assess, *v.* SYN.—appraise, assign, calculate, compute, estimate, evaluate, fix, levy, reckon, tax.

assessment, *n.* See **tax.**

assign, *v.* SYN.—allot, apportion, appropriate, ascribe, attribute, cast, designate, distribute, specify. ANT.—discharge, release, relieve, unburden.

assimilate, *v.* See **absorb.**

assist, *v.* SYN.—abet, aid, back, further, help, promote, serve, support, sustain. ANT.—hamper, hinder, impede, prevent.

assistance, *n.* SYN.—aid, alms, backing, furtherance, help, patronage, relief, succor, support. ANT.—antagonism, counteraction, defiance, hostility, resistance.

associate, *n.* See **companion.**

associate, *v.* SYN.—affiliate, ally, combine, conjoin, connect, join, link, mingle, mix. ANT.—disrupt, divide, estrange, separate.

association, *n.* See **connection.**

assorted, *a.* See **miscellaneous.**

assortment, *n.* See **variety.**

assuage, *v.* See **abate.**

assume, *v.* SYN.—appropriate, arrogate, take, usurp; adopt, affect, pretend, simulate, wear; postulate, presume, suppose. ANT.—concede, grant, surrender; doff; demonstrate, prove.

assurance, *n.* SYN.—assuredness, certainty, confidence, conviction, courage, firmness, security, self-reliance, surety; pledge, promise, word; assertion, declaration, statement. ANT.—bashfulness, humility, modesty, shyness, suspicion.

assure, *v.* See **confirm.**

astonishment, *n.* See **wonder.**

astound, *v.* See **surprise.**

attach, *v.* SYN.—adjoin, affix, annex, append, connect, join, stick, unite; assign, associate, attribute. ANT.—detach, disengage, separate, unfasten, untie.

attachment, *n.* SYN.—adherence, affection, affinity, devotion, friendship, liking, regard. ANT.—alienation, aversion, estrangement, opposition, separation.

attack, *n.* SYN.—aggression, assault, criticism, denunciation, invasion, offense, onslaught; convulsion, fit, paroxysm. ANT.—defense, opposition, resistance, surrender, vindication.

attack, *v.* SYN.—assail, assault, besiege, charge, encounter, invade; abuse, censure, impugn. ANT.—aid, defend, protect, repel, resist.

attain, *v.* SYN.—accomplish, achieve, acquire, arrive, effect, gain, get, obtain, procure, reach, secure, win. ANT.—abandon, desert, discard, relinquish.

attempt, *n.* SYN.—effort, endeavor, essay, experiment, trial, undertaking. ANT.—inaction, laziness, neglect.

attend, *v.* SYN.—accompany, escort, follow, guard, lackey, protect, serve, tend, watch; be present, frequent.

attention, *n.* SYN.—alertness, care, circumspection, consideration, heed, mindfulness, notice, observance, watchfulness; application, contemplation, reflection, study. ANT.—disregard, indifference, negligence, omission, oversight.

attentive, *a.* SYN.—alert, alive, awake,

aware, careful, considerate, heedful, mindful, observant, thoughtful, wary, watchful; assiduous, diligent, studious. ANT.—apathetic, indifferent, oblivious, unaware.

attire, n. See clothes.

attitude, n. SYN.—disposition, standpoint, viewpoint; aspect, pose, position, posture, stand.

attract, v. SYN.—allure, captivate, charm, enchant, entice, fascinate, lure. ANT.—alienate, deter, repel, repulse.

attractive, a. SYN.—alluring, charming, enchanting, engaging, inviting, magnetic, pleasant, pleasing, seductive, winning. ANT.—forbidding, obnoxious, repellent, repulsive.

attribute, n. See quality.

audacious, a. See bold.

audacity, n. SYN.—boldness, effrontery, fearlessness, hardihood, temerity. ANT.—circumspection, fearfulness, humility, meekness.

audience, n. See company.

augment, v. See increase.

august, a. See majestic.

austere, a. See rigid.

authentic, a. SYN.—genuine, pure, real, true, verifiable; accurate, authoritative, correct, reliable, trustworthy. ANT.—counterfeit, erroneous, false, spurious.

author, n. SYN.—composer, creator, father, inventor, maker, originator, writer.

authoritarian, a. See dogmatic.

authority, n. SYN.—control, domination, dominion, force, justification, power, supremacy; authorization, license, permission, sanction; ground, importance, influence, prestige, weight. ANT.—impotence, incapacity, weakness; denial, prohibition.

autonomous, a. See free, independent.

auxiliary, a. SYN.—ancillary, assisting, conducive, furthering, helping, instrumental, subsidiary. ANT.—cumbersome, obstructive, opposing, retarding.

available, a. SYN.—accessible, handy, obtainable, prepared, ready, usable. ANT.—inaccessible, unavoidable.

avaricious, a. See greedy.

avenge, v. See revenge.

aver, v. See affirm.

average, a. SYN.—fair, intermediate, mean, median, mediocre, medium, middling, moderate, ordinary. ANT.—exceptional, extraordinary, outstanding.

averse, a. See reluctant.

aversion, n. SYN.—abhorrence, antipathy, disgust, disinclination, dislike, distaste, dread, hatred, loathing, repugnance, repulsion, reluctance. ANT.—affection, attachment, devotion, enthusiasm.

avert, v. See avoid.

avoid, v. SYN.—avert, dodge, escape, eschew, elude, forbear, forestall, free, shun, ward. ANT.—confront, encounter, meet, oppose.

aware, a. SYN.—apprised, cognizant, conscious, informed, mindful, observant, perceptive, sensible. ANT.—ignorant, insensible, oblivious, unaware.

away, a. See absent.

awful, a. SYN.—appalling, dire, dreadful, frightful, horrible, terrible; awe-inspiring, imposing, majestic, solemn. ANT.—commonplace, humble, lowly, vulgar.

awkward, a. SYN.—clumsy, gauche, inept, rough, unpolished, untoward. ANT.—adroit, graceful, neat, polished, skillful.

axiom, n. SYN.—adage, aphorism, apothegm, byword, fundamental, maxim, principle, proverb, saw, saying, theorem, truism.

B

backward, a. SYN.—regressive, retrograde, revisionary; dull, sluggish, stupid; disinclined, hesitating, indisposed, loath, reluctant, unwilling, wavering. ANT.—advanced, civilized, progressive.

bad, a. SYN.—baleful, base, deleterious, evil, immoral, iniquitous, noxious, pernicious, sinful, unsound, unwholesome, villainous, wicked. ANT.—excellent, good, honorable, moral, reputable.

badger, v. See tease.

baffle, v. See frustrate.

balance, n. SYN.—composure, equilibrium, poise, stability, steadiness; proportion, symmetry; excess, remainder, remains, residue, rest. ANT.—fall, imbalance, instability, unsteadiness.

balance, v. See suspend.

bald, a. See naked.

ban, v. See prohibit.

banal, a. SYN.—commonplace, hackneyed, inane, insipid, trite, vapid. ANT.—fresh, novel, original, stimulating, striking.

banish, v. SYN.—deport, dismiss, dispel, eject, exclude, exile, expatriate, expel, ostracize, oust. ANT.—accept, admit, harbor, receive, shelter.

banquet, n. SYN.—celebration, dinner, entertainment, feast, festival, regalement.

barbaric, a. See barbarous.

barbarous, a. SYN.—barbarian, barbaric, brutal, crude, cruel, inhuman, merciless, remorseless, rude, ruthless, savage, uncivilized, uncultured, unrelenting. ANT.—civilized, humane, kind, polite, refined.

bargain, n. See contract.

barren, a. See empty.

base, a. SYN.—abject, contemptible, despicable, dishonorable, groveling, ignoble, ignominious, low, lowly, mean, menial, servile, sordid, vile, vulgar. ANT.—esteemed, exalted, honored, lofty, noble, righteous.

base, n. See foundation.

bashful, a. SYN.—abashed, coy, diffident, embarrassed, humble, modest, recoiling, shamefaced, sheepish, shy, timid, timorous. ANT.—adventurous, daring, fearless, gregarious, outgoing.

basic, a. See elementary.

basis, n. SYN.—base, bottom, foundation, ground, groundwork, support, underpinning; assumption, postulate, premise, presumption, presupposition, principle. ANT.—derivative, implication, superstructure, trimming.

bathe, v. See wash.

battle, n. SYN.—combat, conflict, contest, fight, fray, skirmish, strife, struggle. ANT.—agreement, concord, peace, truce.

battle, v. See fight.

bear, v. SYN.—support, sustain, uphold; allow, brook, endure, permit, stand, suffer, tolerate, undergo; carry, convey, take, transport; produce, spawn, yield. ANT.—avoid, dodge, evade, refuse, shun.

beat, v. SYN.—belabor, buffet, dash, hit, knock, pound, pummel, punch, smite, strike, thrash, thump; conquer, defeat, overpower, overthrow, rout, subdue, vanquish; palpitate, pulsate, pulse, throb. ANT.—defend, shield, stroke; fail, surrender.

beautiful, a. SYN.—beauteous, charming, comely, elegant, fair, fine, handsome, lovely, pretty. ANT.—foul, hideous, homely, repulsive, unsightly.

beauty, n. SYN.—attractiveness, charm, comeliness, elegance, fairness, grace, handsomeness, loveliness, pulchritude. ANT.—deformity, disfigurement, eyesore, homeliness, ugliness.

because, conj. SYN.—as, for, inasmuch as, since.

bed, n. SYN.—berth, bunk, cot, couch, cradle; accumulation, deposit, layer, stratum, vein.

befoul, v. See contaminate.

beg, v. SYN.—adjure, ask, beseech, crave, entreat, implore, importune, petition, pray, request, solicit, supplicate. ANT.—bestow, cede, favor, give, grant.

beget, v. SYN.—breed, create, engender, father, generate, originate, procreate, produce, propagate, sire. ANT.—abort, destroy, extinguish, kill, murder.

beggar, n. SYN.—mendicant, pauper, ragamuffin, scrub, starveling, tatterdemalion, vagabond, wretch.

begin, v. SYN.—arise, commence, enter, inaugurate, initiate, institute, open, originate, start. ANT.—close, complete, end, finish, terminate.

beginner, n. See amateur.

beginning, n. SYN.—commencement, inception, opening, origin, outset, source, start. ANT.—close, completion, consummation, end, termination.

behalf, n. See benefit.

behave, v. SYN.—act, bear, carry, comport, conduct, demean, deport, interact, manage, operate.

behavior, n. SYN.—action, bearing, carriage, conduct, deed, demeanor, deportment, disposition, manner.

behold, v. See see.

belief, n. SYN.—certitude, confidence, conviction, credence, faith, feeling, opinion, persuasion, reliance, trust. ANT.—denial, doubt, heresy, incredulity.

believe, v. SYN.—accept, apprehend, conceive, credit, fancy, hold, imagine, support, suppose. ANT.—distrust, doubt, question, reject.

belittle, v. SYN.—decry, depreciate, disparage, minimize, underrate. ANT.—admire, appreciate, esteem.

below, prep. SYN.—beneath, lower, under, underneath. ANT.—above, aloft, over, overhead.

bend, v. SYN.—bow, crook, curve, deflect, incline, lean, stoop, turn, twist; influence, mold; submit, yield. ANT.—break, resist, stiffen, straighten.

beneath, prep. SYN.—below, under, underneath. ANT.—above, over.

beneficial, a. SYN.—advantageous, good, helpful, profitable, salutary, serviceable, useful, wholesome. ANT.—deleterious, destructive, detrimental, harmful, injurious.

benefit, n. SYN.—account, advantage, avail, behalf, favor, gain, good, interest, profit, service. ANT.—calamity, distress, handicap, trouble.

benefit, v. See serve.

benevolence, n. SYN.—altruism, beneficence, charity, generosity, humanity, kindness, liberality, magnanimity, philanthropy, tenderness. ANT.—cruelty, inhumanity, malevolence, selfishness, unkindness.

benevolent, *a.* SYN.—altruistic, benign, charitable, friendly, generous, humane, kind, liberal, merciful, obliging, philanthropic, tender, unselfish. ANT.—greedy, harsh, malevolent, wicked.

bent, *n.* See **inclination.**

belittle, *v.* See **disparage.**

belongings, *n.* See **property.**

beloved, *a.* See **dear.**

bequest, *n.* See **grant.**

berate, *v.* See **scold.**

besides, *prep.* See **also.**

bestial, *a.* See **brutal.**

bestow, *v.* See **give.**

better, *v.* See **improve.**

bevy, *n.* See **crowd.**

bewilder, *v.* See **puzzle.**

bewildered, *a.* See **confused.**

bias, *n.* SYN.—bent, disposition, inclination, leaning, partiality, penchant, predilection, predisposition, prejudice, proclivity, proneness, propensity, slant, tendency, turn. ANT.—equity, fairness, impartiality, justice.

bicker, *v.* See **dispute.**

big, *a.* SYN.—august, bulky, colossal, enormous, grand, great, huge, hulking, immense, large, majestic, massive, monstrous. ANT.—little, petite, small, tiny.

bigoted, *a.* SYN.—dogmatic, fanatical, illiberal, intolerant, narrow-minded, prejudiced. ANT.—liberal, progressive, radical, tolerant.

bind, *v.* SYN.—attach, connect, engage, fasten, fetter, join, link, oblige, restrain, restrict, tie. ANT.—free, loose, unfasten, untie.

binding, *a.* See **valid.**

bit, *n.* See **piece.**

bite, *v.* SYN—champ, chew, crunch, gnash, gnaw, nibble, nip, pierce, rend, tear.

bitter, *a.* SYN.—acrid, biting, distasteful, pungent, sour, tart; galling, grievous, painful, poignant; cruel, fierce, relentless, ruthless; acrimonious, caustic, harsh, sardonic, severe. ANT.—delicious, mellow, pleasant, sweet.

bizarre, *a.* See **odd, strange.**

black, *a.* See **dark.**

blackball, *v.* See **exclude.**

blame, *v.* SYN.—accuse, censure, condemn, implicate, rebuke, reproach, upbraid. ANT.—absolve, acquit, exonerate.

blameless, *a.* See **perfect.**

blaze, *n.* See **fire.**

bleak, *a.* See **dismal.**

bleakness, *n.* See **gloom.**

blemish, *n.* SYN.—blot, speck, stain; defect, disgrace, fault, flaw, imperfection. ANT.—adornment, embellishment, perfection, purity.

blend, *v.* SYN.—amalgamate, coalesce, combine, commingle, conjoin, consolidate, fuse, mingle, mix, merge, unify, unite. ANT.—analyze, decompose, disintegrate, separate.

bless, *v.* SYN.—adore, celebrate, delight, exalt, extol, gladden, glorify. ANT.—blaspheme, curse, denounce, slander.

blind, *a.* SYN.—ignorant, oblivious, sightless, undiscerning, unmindful, unseeing; headlong, heedless, rash. ANT.—aware, calculated, discerning, perceiving, sensible.

bliss, *n.* SYN.—blessedness, blissfulness, ec-

stasy, felicity, happiness, joy, rapture. ANT.—grief, misery, sorrow, woe, wretchedness.

blithe, *a.* See **buoyant.**

block, *v.* See **obstruct.**

blond, *a.* See **fair.**

blot, *n.* See **blemish.**

blunt, *a.* SYN.—dull, edgeless, obtuse, pointless, stolid, thick-witted, unsharpened; abrupt, bluff, brusque, impolite, outspoken, plain, rough, rude, unceremonious. ANT.—polished, polite, suave, subtle, tactful.

blustery, *a.* See **stormy.**

boast, *v.* SYN.—brag, crow, flaunt, glory, vaunt. ANT.—apologize, deprecate, humble, minimize.

bodily, *a.* See **carnal.**

body, *n.* SYN.—carcass, corpse, remains; form, frame, torso; bulk, corpus, mass; aggregate, association, company, society. ANT.—intellect, mind, soul, spirit.

bold, *a.* SYN.—adventurous, audacious, brave, courageous, daring, dauntless, fearless, intrepid; brazen, forward, impudent, insolent, pushy, rude; abrupt, conspicuous, prominent, striking. ANT.—cowardly, flinching, timid; bashful, retiring.

boldness, *n.* See **audacity.**

bolt, *v.* See **lock.**

bond, *n.* See **link.**

bondage, *n.* SYN.—captivity, confinement, imprisonment, serfdom, servitude, slavery, thralldom, vassalage. ANT.—freedom, liberation.

bonus, *n.* See **reward.**

book, *n.* SYN.—booklet, brochure, compendium, handbook, manual, monograph, pamphlet, textbook, tract, treatise, volume, work.

border, *n.* SYN.—boundary, brim, brink, edge, fringe, frontier, limit, margin, outskirts, rim, termination, verge. ANT.—center, core, interior, mainland.

boredom, *n.* SYN.—doldrums, dullness, ennui, tedium, weariness. ANT.—activity, excitement, motive, stimulus.

boring, *a.* See **dull.**

bother, *v.* SYN.—annoy, disturb, harass, haunt, inconvenience, molest, perplex, pester, plague, tease, trouble, upset, worry. ANT.—gratify, please, relieve, soothe.

bottom, *n.* SYN.—base, basis, foot, foundation, fundament, groundwork. ANT.—apex, peak, summit, top.

boulder, *n.* See **stone.**

bound, *v.* See **enclose.**

boundary, *n.* See **border, edge.**

bountiful, *a.* See **abundant.**

bow, *v.* See **bend.**

brag, *v.* SYN.—bluster, boast, crow, flaunt, flourish, vaunt. ANT.—debase, degrade, demean, denigrate.

brand, *n.* See **mark.**

brave, *a.* SYN.—adventurous, audacious, bold, chivalrous, courageous, daring, dauntless, fearless, gallant, heroic, intrepid, magnanimous, valiant, valorous. ANT.—cowardly, cringing, fearful, timid, weak.

bravery, *n.* See **courage.**

brazen, *a.* See **bold.**

break, *v.* SYN.—burst, crack, crush, demolish, destroy, fracture, infringe, pound, rack, rend, rupture, shatter, smash, squeeze; disobey, transgress, violate. ANT.

—join, mend, renovate, repair, restore.

breed, *n.* See **variety.**

breed, *v.* SYN.—bear, beget, conceive, engender, generate, procreate, propogate; foster, nurture, raise, rear, train.

breeding, *n.* See **culture.**

breeze, *n.* See **wind.**

brief, *a.* SYN.—compendious, concise, curt, laconic, pithy, short, succinct, terse; fleeting, momentary, passing, transient. ANT.—extended, lengthy, long, prolonged, protracted.

bright, *a.* SYN.—brilliant, clear, gleaming, lucid, luminous, lustrous, radiant, shining, translucent, transparent; clever, intelligent, witty. ANT.—dark, dull, gloomy, murky, sullen.

brightness, *n.* See **radiance.**

brilliant, *a.* See **bright.**

bring, *v.* See **carry.**

brisk, *a.* See **fresh.**

brittle, *a.* SYN.—breakable, crisp, crumbling, delicate, fragile, frail, splintery. ANT.—enduring, thick, tough, unbreakable.

broad, *a.* SYN.—expanded, extensive, large, sweeping, vast, wide; liberal, tolerant. ANT.—confined, narrow, restricted.

broken, *a.* SYN.—crushed, destroyed, flattened, fractured, interrupted, reduced, rent, ruptured, separated, shattered, smashed, wrecked. ANT.—integral, repaired, united, whole.

brotherhood, *n.* SYN.—brotherliness, fellowship, kindness, solidarity; association, clan, fraternity, society. ANT.—acrimony, discord, opposition, strife.

brutal, *a.* SYN.—barbarous, bestial, brute, brutish, carnal, coarse, cruel, ferocious, gross, inhuman, merciless, remorseless, rough, rude, ruthless, savage, sensual. ANT.—civilized, courteous, gentle, humane, kind.

build, *n.* See **shape.**

build, *v.* SYN.—construct, erect, establish, found, raise, rear. ANT.—demolish, destroy, overthrow, raze, undermine.

bulletin, *n.* See **announcement.**

bum, *n.* See **vagrant.**

bunch, *n.* See **group.**

buoyant, *a.* SYN.—effervescent, light, resilient; animated, blithe, cheerful, elated, hopeful, jocund, lively, spirited, sprightly, vivacious. ANT.—dejected, depressed, despondent, hopeless, sullen.

burden, *v.* SYN.—afflict, encumber, load, oppress, overload, tax, trouble, weigh. ANT.—alleviate, console, ease, lighten, mitigate.

burdensome, *a.* See **tedious.**

burglarize, *v.* See **steal.**

burglary, *n.* See **robbery.**

burn, *v.* SYN.—blaze, char, consume, incinerate, scald, scorch, sear, singe. ANT.—extinguish, put out, quench.

bury, *v.* SYN.—conceal, cover, entomb, hide, immure, inhume, inter. ANT.—display, expose, open, reveal.

business, *n.* SYN.—art, commerce, employment, engagement, enterprise, job, occupation, profession, trade, trading, vocation, work. ANT.—avocation, hobby, pastime.

busy, *a.* See **active, diligent.**

butchery, *n.* See **massacre.**

buy, *v.* SYN.—acquire, get, obtain, procure, purchase. ANT.—dispose of, sell, vend.

by, *prep.* SYN.—beside, near, next to; by means of, through, with; according to; from.

C

cabal, *n.* See **conspiracy**.

calamity, *n.* See **disaster**.

calculate, *v.* SYN.—compute, consider, count, estimate, figure, reckon. ANT.—conjecture, guess, miscalculate.

caliber, *n.* See **quality**.

callous, *a.* SYN.—hard, impenitent, indurate, insensible, insensitive, obdurate, tough, unfeeling. ANT.—compassionate, sensitive, soft, tender.

calm, *a.* SYN.—composed, dispassionate, imperturbable, pacific, peaceful, placid, quiet, serene, still, tranquil, undisturbed, unruffled. ANT.—excited, frantic, stormy, turbulent, wild.

calm, *n.* See **quiet**.

calm, *v.* See **appease**.

calumny, *n.* See **slander**.

cancel, *v.* SYN.—cross out, delete, eliminate, erase, expunge, obliterate; abolish, abrogate, annul, invalidate, nullify, quash, repeal, rescind, revoke. ANT.—confirm, enact, enforce, perpetuate.

candid, *a.* SYN.—frank, free, honest, ingenuous, open, plain, sincere, straightforward, truthful; fair, impartial, just, unbiased. ANT.—contrived, scheming, sly, wily.

candor, *n.* See **honesty**.

calamity, *n.* See **accident**.

capability, *n.* See **capacity**.

capable, *a.* SYN.—able, clever, competent, efficient, fitted, qualified, skillful. ANT.—inadequate, incapable, incompetent, unfitted.

capacity, *n.* SYN.—ability, capability, faculty, power, skill, talent; magnitude, size, volume. ANT.—impotence, inability, incapacity, stupidity.

capitulate, *v.* See **surrender**.

caprice, *n.* See **whim**.

capricious, *a.* See **fickle**.

captivity, *n.* See **bondage**.

capture, *v.* See **catch**.

carcass, *n.* See **body**.

care, *n.* SYN.—anxiety, concern, solicitude, worry; attention, caution, regard, vigilance, wariness; charge, custody, guardianship, ward. ANT.—disregard, indifference, neglect, negligence.

careful, *a.* SYN.—attentive, heedful, prudent, scrupulous, thoughtful; cautious, circumspect, discreet, guarded, vigilant, wary. ANT.—forgetful, improvident, indifferent, lax.

careless, *a.* SYN.—heedless, imprudent, inattentive, inconsiderate, indiscreet, reckless, thoughtless, unconcerned; desultory, inaccurate, lax, neglectful, negligent, remiss. ANT.—accurate, careful, meticulous, nice.

carelessness, *n.* See **neglect**.

caress, *v.* SYN.—coddle, cuddle, embrace, fondle, hug, kiss, pet. ANT.—annoy, buffet, spurn, tease, vex.

carnal, *a.* SYN.—animal, base, bodily, corporeal, fleshly, gross, lustful, sensual, voluptuous, worldly. ANT.—exalted, intellectual, refined, spiritual, temperate.

carping, *a.* See **critical**.

carry, *v.* SYN.—bring, convey, transmit, transport; bear, support, sustain. ANT.—abandon, drop.

caste, *n.* See **class**.

casual, *a.* SYN.—accidental, chance, fortuitous, unexpected; incidental, informal, nonchalant, offhand, relaxed, unconcerned, unpremeditated. ANT.—expected, intended; formal, planned, pretentious.

casualty, *n.* See **accident**.

catastrophe, *n.* See **disaster, misfortune**.

catch, *v.* SYN.—apprehend, arrest, capture, clutch, grasp, grip, lay hold of, seize, snare, trap. ANT.—liberate, lose, release, throw.

catching, *a.* See **contagious**.

category, *n.* See **class**.

cause, *n.* SYN.—agent, determinant, incentive, inducement, motive, origin, principle, reason, source. ANT.—consequence, effect, end, result.

cause, *v.* SYN.—create, effect, evoke, incite, induce, make, occasion, originate, prompt.

caustic, *a.* See **sarcastic**.

caution, *n.* SYN.—care, heed, prudence, vigilance, wariness, watchfulness; admonition, counsel, injunction, warning. ANT.—abandon, carelessness, recklessness.

cautious, *a.* See **careful**.

cease, *v.* See **quit, stop**.

celebrate, *v.* SYN.—commemorate, honor, keep, observe, solemnize; commend, extol, glorify, honor, laud, praise. ANT.—disregard, overlook; decry, disgrace, dishonor, profane.

celestial, *a.* See **divine**.

censure, *v.* See **condemn**.

center, *n.* SYN.—core, heart, middle, midpoint, midst, nucleus. ANT.—border, boundary, outskirts, periphery, rim.

ceremonious, *a.* See **formal**.

ceremony, *n.* SYN.—formality, observance, parade, pomp, protocol, rite, ritual, solemnity.

certain, *a.* SYN.—assured, definite, fixed, indubitable, inevitable, positive, secure, sure, undeniable, unquestionable. ANT.—doubtful, probable, questionable, uncertain.

certainty, *n.* See **assurance**.

challenge, *v.* SYN.—object to, question; brave, dare, defy; call, invite, summon; demand, require.

chance, *a.* See **accidental**.

chance, *n.* See **accident, opportunity**.

chance, *v.* See **happen**.

change, *n.* SYN.—alteration, alternation, modification, mutation, substitution, variation, variety, vicissitude. ANT.—monotony, stability, uniformity.

change, *v.* SYN.—exchange, substitute; alter, convert, modify, shift, transfigure, transform, vary, veer. ANT.—retain; continue, establish, preserve, settle, stabilize.

changeable, *a.* See **variable**.

chaos, *n.* SYN.—anarchy, confusion, disorder, disorganization, jumble, muddle. ANT.—order, organization, system.

chaperone, *v.* See **accompany**.

character, *n.* SYN.—class, description, disposition, individuality, kind, nature, reputation, repute, sort, standing; mark, sign, symbol.

characteristic, *n.* SYN.—attribute, feature, mark, peculiarity, property, quality, trait.

charge, *n.* See **accusation**.

charge, *v.* See **accuse**.

charitable, *a.* See **benevolent**.

charity, *n.* See **benevolence**.

charming, *a.* SYN.—alluring, attractive, bewitching, captivating, enchanting, engaging, fascinating, winning. ANT.—repugnant, repulsive, revolting.

chart, *n.* See **plot**.

chase, *v.* See **pursue**.

chaste, *a.* See **pure**.

chastise, *v.* See **punish**.

chat, *n.* See **conversation**.

chat, *v.* See **talk**.

chatter, *n.* See **talk**.

cheap, *a.* SYN.—inexpensive, low-priced, poor; beggarly, common, inferior, mean, shabby. ANT.—costly, dear, expensive; dignified, honorable, noble.

cheat, *n.* See **fraud**.

cheat, *v.* SYN.—bilk, circumvent, deceive, defraud, dupe, fool, gull, hoax, hoodwink, outwit, swindle, trick, victimize.

check, *v.* See **examine, hinder**.

cheer, *v.* See **comfort**.

cheerful, *a.* SYN.—gay, glad, happy, jolly, joyful, lighthearted, merry, sprightly. ANT.—depressed, glum, mournful, sad, sullen.

cherish, *v.* SYN.—appreciate, hold dear, prize, treasure, value; foster, nurture, sustain. ANT.—dislike, disregard, neglect; abandon, reject.

chief, *a.* See **principal**.

chief, *n.* SYN.—captain, chieftain, commander, head, leader, master, principal, ruler. ANT.—attendant, follower, servant, subordinate.

chilly, *a.* See **cold**.

choice, *n.* SYN.—alternative, election, option, preference, selection.

choose, *v.* SYN.—cull, elect, opt, pick, select. ANT.—refuse, reject.

chronicle, *n.* See **account**.

cinema, *n.* See **picture**.

circuitous, *a.* See **devious**.

circular, *a.* See **round**.

circumspection, *n.* See **care**.

circumstance, *n.* SYN.—condition, event, fact, happening, incident, occurrence, position, situation.

cite, *v.* See **allege, quote**.

civil, *a.* See **polite**.

civilization, *n.* See **culture**.

claim, *v.* See **assert, state**.

clamor, *n.* See **noise**.

clan, *n.* See **brotherhood**.

clandestine, *a.* See **secret**.

clarify, *v.* See **explain**.

clasp, *v.* See **hold**.

class, *n.* SYN.—caste, category, denomination, genre, kind; grade, order, rank, set; elegance, excellence.

clean, *v.* SYN.—cleanse, mop, purify, scrub, sweep, wash. ANT.—dirty, pollute, soil, stain, sully.

cleanse, *v.* See **clean, wash**.

clear, *a.* SYN.—cloudless, fair, sunny; limpid, transparent; apparent, distinct, evident, intelligible, lucid, manifest, obvious, plain, unmistakable, visible; open, unobstructed. ANT.—cloudy, foul, overcast; ambiguous, obscure, unclear, vague.

clemency, *n.* See **mercy**.

clever, *a.* SYN.—adroit, apt, dexterous, quick, quick-witted, skillful, talented, witty; bright, ingenious, sharp, smart. ANT.—awkward, bungling, clumsy, slow, unskilled; dull, foolish, stupid.

cleverness, *n.* See **wit**.

climax, *n.* SYN.—acme, apex, consummation, culmination, height, peak, summit, zenith. ANT.—anticlimax, base, depth, floor.

climb, v. See **ascend.**

cloak, v. See **cover.**

cloister, n. SYN.—abbey, convent, hermitage, monastery, nunnery, priory.

close, a. SYN.—abutting, adjacent, adjoining, immediate, impending, near, nearby, neighboring; confidential, dear, devoted, intimate. ANT.—afar, distant, faraway, removed.

close, n. See **conclusion.**

close, v. SYN.—occlude, seal, shut; clog, obstruct, stop; cease, complete, conclude, end, finish, terminate. ANT.—open, unbar, unlock; begin, commence, inaugurate, start.

clothes, n. SYN.—apparel, array, attire, clothing, drapery, dress, garb, garments, raiment, vestments, vesture. ANT.—nakedness, nudity.

clothing, n. See **clothes.**

cloudy, a. SYN.—dark, dim, indistinct, murky, mysterious, obscure, overcast, shadowy. ANT.—bright, clear, distinct, limpid, sunny.

clumsy, a. See **awkward.**

coalition, n. See **alliance.**

coarse, a. SYN.—crude, impure, rough, rugged, unrefined; gross, gruff, immodest, indelicate, rude, unpolished, vulgar. ANT.—fine, polished, refined, smooth; cultivated, cultured, delicate.

coerce, v. See **compel.**

coercion, n. See **force.**

cognizant, a. See **aware.**

coincide, v. See **agree.**

cold, a. SYN.—arctic, chilly, cool, freezing, frigid, frozen, icy, wintry; passionless, phlegmatic, stoical, unfeeling. ANT.—burning, fiery, heated, hot, torrid; ardent, passionate.

collapse, v. See **fall.**

colleague, n. See **companion.**

collect, v. SYN.—accumulate, amass, assemble, concentrate, congregate, consolidate, gather, heap, hoard, mass, pile. ANT.—assort, disperse, distribute, divide, dole.

collected, a. See **composed.**

collection, n. See **aggregate.**

collision, n. See **conflict.**

collusion, n. See **conspiracy.**

color, n. SYN.—complexion, dye, hue, paint, pigment, shade, stain, tincture, tinge, tint. ANT.—achromatism, paleness, transparency.

colossal, a. See **enormous.**

combat, n. See **conflict.**

combat, v. See **fight.**

combination, n. See **alliance.**

combine, v. See **join, unite.**

comfort, n. SYN.—consolation, contentment, ease, enjoyment, relief, solace, succor. ANT.—affliction, discomfort, misery, suffering, torment, torture.

comfort, v. SYN.—cheer, console, encourage, gladden, solace, soothe, sympathize. ANT.—antagonize, aggravate, depress, dishearten.

comfortable, a. SYN.—acceptable, agreeable, convenient, cozy, gratifying, pleasing, pleasurable, relaxed, restful, welcome. ANT.—distressing, miserable, troubling, uncomfortable, wretched.

comical, a. See **funny.**

command, n. See **order.**

command, v. See **direct.**

commemorate, v. See **celebrate.**

commence, v. See **begin.**

commencement, n. See **beginning.**

commend, v. See **approve, praise.**

commensurate, a. See **equal.**

comment, n. See **remark.**

commerce, n. See **business.**

commit, v. SYN.—do, perform, perpetrate; commend, consign, entrust, relegate, trust; bind, obligate, pledge. ANT.—fail, miscarry, neglect; mistrust, release, renounce; free, loose.

commodious, a. See **convenient.**

common, a. SYN.—familiar, frequent, general, ordinary, popular, prevalent, universal, usual; low, mean, vulgar. ANT.—exceptional, extraordinary, odd, scarce; noble, refined.

commotion, n. See **confusion.**

communicable, a. See **contagious.**

communicate, v. SYN.—confer, convey, disclose, divulge, impart, inform, notify, relate, reveal, tell, transmit. ANT.—conceal, hide, withhold.

communion, n. SYN.—association, fellowship, intercourse, participation, sacrament, union. ANT.—alienation, nonparticipation.

compact, a. See **tight.**

compact, n. See **agreement.**

companion, n. SYN.—associate, attendant, colleague, comrade, consort, crony, friend, mate, partner. ANT.—adversary, enemy, stranger.

company, n. SYN.—assemblage, band, crew, group, horde, party, throng, troop; association, fellowship, society; corporation, firm. ANT.—dispersion, individual, seclusion, solitude.

comparable, a. See **analogous.**

compare, v. See **contrast.**

compassion, n. See **pity, sympathy.**

compassionate, a. See **kind, merciful.**

compatible, a. See **consistent.**

compel, v. SYN.—coerce, constrain, drive, enforce, force, impel, oblige. ANT.—allure, convince, induce, persuade, prevent.

compensation, n. See **pay.**

competent, a. See **capable.**

competitor, n. See **adversary.**

complain, v. SYN.—grouch, grumble, lament, murmur, protest, regret, remonstrate, repine, whine. ANT.—applaud, approve, praise, rejoice.

complete, a. SYN.—concluded, consummate, ended, entire, finished, full, perfect, thorough, total, unbroken, undivided. ANT.—imperfect, lacking, unfinished.

complete, v. See **finish.**

complex, a. SYN.—complicated, compound, intricate, involved, perplexing. ANT.—plain, simple, uncompounded.

complexion, n. See **color.**

complicated, a. See **complex.**

compliment, n. SYN.—adulation, commendation, eulogy, flattery, praise, tribute. ANT.—affront, criticism, insult, taunt.

comply, v. See **agree.**

component, n. See **part.**

compose, v. See **form.**

composed, a. SYN.—calm, collected, cool, imperturbable, peaceful, placid, quiet, sedate, tranquil, unmoved. ANT.—agitated, aroused, excited, perturbed, violent.

composer, n. See **author.**

composure, n. See **poise.**

compound, v. See **mix.**

comprehend, v. See **understand.**

comprehension, n. See **perception.**

comprise, v. See **contain.**

compulsion, n. See **force.**

compute, v. See **calculate.**

comrade, n. See **companion.**

conceal, v. See **cover, hide.**

concede, v. See **allow.**

conceit, n. SYN.—complacency, egotism, pride, self-esteem, vanity; caprice, conception, fancy, idea, imagination, notion, whim. ANT.—diffidence, humility, meekness, modesty.

conceited, a. See **vain.**

conceive, v. See **invent.**

concentrated, a. See **dense.**

concept, n. See **idea.**

conception, n. See **thought.**

concern, n. SYN.—affair, business, matter, transaction; anxiety, care, solicitude, worry. ANT.—apathy, indifference, negligence, unconcern.

concise, a. See **brief, terse.**

conclude, v. See **close, finish.**

conclusion, n. SYN.—close, completion, end, finale, issue, settlement, termination; decision, deduction, inference, judgment. ANT.—beginning, commencement, inception, prelude, start.

conclusive, a. See **final.**

concord, n. See **agreement.**

concur, v. See **agree.**

condemn, v. SYN.—blame, censure, denounce, reprehend, reproach, reprobate, reprove, upbraid; convict, sentence. ANT.—approve, commend, condone, forgive, praise; absolve, acquit, exonerate, pardon.

condition, n. SYN.—case, circumstance, plight, predicament, situation, state; provision, requirement, stipulation, term.

condition, v. See **prepare.**

conditional, a. See **dependent.**

condolence, n. See **sympathy.**

conduct, n. See **behavior.**

conduct, v. SYN.—direct, escort, guide, lead, steer; control, manage, regulate, supervise.

confederate, n. See **accomplice.**

confederation, n. See **alliance.**

confer, v. See **talk.**

confess, v. SYN.—acknowledge, admit, allow, avow, concede, divulge, grant, own, reveal. ANT.—conceal, deny, disclaim, disown, renounce.

confession, n. See **apology.**

confidence, n. See **assurance.**

confine, n. See **enclose.**

confirm, n. SYN.—corroborate, substantiate, verify; acknowledge, assure, establish, settle; approve, fix, ratify, sanction; strengthen.

confirmation, n. See **proof.**

confiscate, v. See **take.**

conflagration, n. See **fire.**

conflict, n. SYN.—battle, collision, combat, duel, encounter, fight, struggle; contention, controversy, discord, inconsistency, interference, opposition, variance. ANT.—amity, concord, consonance, harmony.

confront, v. See **oppose.**

confuse, v. See **puzzle.**

confused, a. SYN.—bewildered, deranged, disconcerted, disordered, disorganized, indistinct, mixed, muddled, perplexed. ANT.—clear, lucid, obvious, organized, plain.

confusion, n. SYN.—agitation, chaos, commotion, disarrangement, disarray, disorder, ferment, jumble, stir, tumult, turmoil. ANT.—certainty, order, peace, tranquility.

congruous, *a.* See **consistent.**

conjecture, *n.* See **hypothesis.**

conjecture, *v.* See **hazard.**

connect, *v.* See **attach, join.**

connection, *n.* SYN.—affinity, alliance, association, bond, conjunction, link, relationship, tie, union. ANT.—disunion, isolation, separation.

conquer, *v.* SYN.—beat, crush, defeat, humble, master, overcome, quell, rout, subdue, subjugate, surmount, vanquish. ANT.—capitulate, cede, lose, retreat, surrender.

conquest, *n.* See **triumph.**

conscious, *a.* See **aware.**

consecrate, *v.* See **glorify.**

consecrated, *a.* See **holy.**

consent, *n.* See **permission.**

consent, *v.* See **agree.**

consequently, *adv.* See **therefore.**

consider, *v.* SYN.—contemplate, deliberate, examine, heed, meditate, ponder, reflect, study, weigh; esteem, regard, respect. ANT.—ignore, neglect, overlook.

considerate, *a.* See **thoughtful.**

consideration, *n.* See **attention.**

consistent, *a.* SYN.—accordant, agreeing, compatible, conforming, congruous, consonant, constant, correspondent. ANT.—contradictory, discrepant, incongruous, inconsistent, paradoxical.

consolation, *n.* See **comfort.**

console, *v.* SYN.—allay, assuage, comfort, solace, soothe. ANT.—annoy, distress, worry.

consort, *n.* See **companion.**

conspicuous, *a.* SYN.—clear, distinguished, manifest, noticeable, obvious, prominent, salient, striking, visible. ANT.—common, hidden, inconspicuous, obscure.

conspiracy, *n.* SYN.—cabal, collusion, combination, intrigue, machination, plot, treachery, treason.

constant, *a.* SYN.—abiding, ceaseless, continual, enduring, faithful, fixed, immutable, invariant, permanent, perpetual, persistent, unalterable, unchanging, unwavering. ANT.—fickle, mutable, vacillating, wavering.

constantly, *adv.* See **always.**

constrain, *v.* See **necessity.**

construct, *v.* SYN.—build, erect, fabricate, form, frame, make, raise. ANT.—demolish, destroy, raze.

construe, *v.* See **interpret.**

consult, *v.* See **talk.**

consummate, *a.* See **complete.**

consummation, *n.* See **climax.**

contagious, *a.* SYN.—catching, communicable, infectious, pestilential, virulent. ANT.—healthful, hygienic, noncommunicable.

contain, *n.* SYN.—accommodate, comprise, embody, embrace, hold, include; repress, restrain. ANT.—discharge, emit, exclude; encourage, yield.

contaminate, *v.* SYN.—befoul, corrupt, defile, infect, poison, pollute, sully, taint. ANT.—disinfect, purify.

contaminated, *a.* See **corrupt.**

contamination, *n.* See **infection.**

contemplate, *v.* See **think.**

contemplative, *a.* See **thoughtful.**

contemporary, *a.* See **modern.**

contempt, *n.* SYN.—contumely, derision, detestation, disdain, hatred, scorn. ANT.—awe, esteem, regard, respect, reverence.

contemptible, *a.* See **mean.**

contented, *a.* See **happy.**

contention, *n.* See **conflict.**

contentment, *n.* See **happiness.**

contest, *v.* See **dispute.**

continence, *n.* See **abstinence.**

contingent, *a.* See **dependent.**

continual, *a.* SYN.—ceaseless, constant, continuous, endless, everlasting, incessant, perennial, perpetual, unceasing, uninterrupted, unremitting. ANT.—interrupted, occasional, periodic, rare.

continue, *n.* SYN.—advance, extend, proceed; endure, last, remain; persevere, persist, prolong, pursue. ANT.—arrest, check, interrupt; cease, defer, halt, stop, suspend.

contract, *n.* SYN.—agreement, bargain, compact, covenant, pact, promise, stipulation, treaty.

contract, *v.* See **shorten.**

contradict, *v.* SYN.—confute, controvert, counter, dispute, gainsay, oppose. ANT.—agree, confirm, support, verify.

contradictory, *a.* See **inconsistent.**

contrary, *a.* See **adverse.**

contrast, *v.* SYN.—compare, differentiate, discriminate, distinguish, oppose.

contrite, *a.* See **penitent.**

contrition, *n.* See **regret.**

contrive, *v.* See **plan.**

control, *n.* See **discipline.**

control, *v.* SYN.—command, direct, dominate, govern, manage, regulate, rule, superintend; bridle, check, curb, repress, restrain. ANT.—abandon, follow, forsake, ignore, submit.

controversy, *n.* See **dispute.**

convenient, *a.* SYN.—accessible, adapted, advantageous, appropriate, commodious, favorable, fitting, handy, suitable, timely. ANT.—awkward, inconvenient, inopportune, troublesome.

conversation, *n.* SYN.—chat, colloquy, conference, dialogue, interview, parley, talk.

converse, *v.* See **talk.**

convert, *v.* See **change.**

convey, *v.* See **carry.**

convict, *n.* See **criminal.**

convict, *v.* See **sentence.**

conviction, *n.* See **belief.**

convince, *v.* See **persuade.**

copious, *a.* See **abundant.**

copy, *n.* SYN.—duplicate, exemplar, facsimile, imitation, replica, reproduction, transcript. ANT.—original, prototype.

copy, *v.* See **imitate.**

cordial, *a.* SYN.—ardent, earnest, gracious, hearty, sincere, sociable, warm. ANT.—aloof, cool, reserved, taciturn.

core, *n.* See **center.**

corporal, *a.* See **physical.**

corporation, *n.* See **company.**

corpse, *n.* See **body.**

correct, *a.* SYN.—accurate, exact, faultless, impeccable, precise, proper, right, strict. ANT.—erroneous, false, faulty, untrue, wrong.

correct, *v.* SYN.—amend, mend, rectify, reform, right; admonish, discipline, punish. ANT.—aggravate, ignore, spoil; condone, indulge.

correction, *n.* See **discipline.**

correlative, *a.* See **analogous.**

correspondent, *a.* See **analogous.**

corrupt, *a.* SYN.—contaminated, corrupted, crooked, debased, depraved, dishonest, impure, profligate, putrid, spoiled, tainted, unsound, venal, vitiated.

corrupt, *v.* See **debase.**

corrupted, *a.* See **corrupt.**

cost, *n.* See **price.**

council, *n.* See **advice.**

counsel, *v.* See **suggest.**

count, *v.* See **calculate.**

counterfeit, *a.* See **artificial.**

courage, *n.* SYN.—boldness, bravery, chivalry, fearlessness, fortitude, intrepidity, mettle, prowess, resolution. ANT.—cowardice, fear, pusillanimity, timidity.

courageous, *a.* See **brave.**

course, *n.* See **way.**

courteous, *a.* See **polite.**

covenant, *n.* See **agreement.**

cover, *v.* SYN.—cloak, clothe, conceal, curtain, disguise, envelop, guard, hide, mask, protect, screen, shield, shroud, veil. ANT.—bare, divulge, expose, reveal, unveil.

covert, *a.* See **hidden.**

covetousness, *n.* See **envy.**

cowardice, *n.* See **fear.**

crafty, *a.* See **sly.**

crass, *a.* See **crude.**

craving, *n.* See **appetite.**

crazy, *a.* SYN.—delirious, demented, deranged, foolish, idiotic, imbecilic, insane, mad, maniacal. ANT.—rational, reasonable, sane, sensible, sound.

create, *v.* SYN.—cause, engender, fashion, form, formulate, generate, invent, make, originate, produce; appoint, constitute, ordain. ANT.—annihilate, demolish, destroy; disband, terminate.

creative, *a.* See **imaginative, original.**

creed, *n.* See **doctrine.**

crest, *n.* See **head.**

crime, *n.* See **offense.**

criminal, *n.* SYN.—convict, culprit, delinquent, felon, malefactor, offender, transgressor.

crippled, *a.* See **lame.**

crisis, *n.* SYN.—acme, conjuncture, contingency, emergency, exigency, juncture, pass, pinch, strait. ANT.—calm, equilibrium, normality, stability.

crisp, *a.* See **brittle.**

criterion, *n.* SYN.—gauge, law, measure, principle, proof, rule, standard, test, touchstone. ANT.—chance, fancy, guess, supposition.

critical, *a.* SYN.—accurate, discerning, discriminating, exact, fastidious, particular; captious, carping, caviling, censorious, faultfinding, hypercritical; acute, crucial, decisive, hazardous, important, momentous. ANT.—cursory, shallow, superficial, uncritical; appreciative, approving, commendatory, encouraging; insignificant, unimportant.

criticize, *v.* SYN.—analyze, appraise, evaluate, examine, inspect, scrutinize; blame, censure, reprehend. ANT.—approve, neglect, overlook.

critique, *n.* See **review.**

crony, *n.* See **companion.**

crooked, *a.* See **corrupt.**

crop, *n.* See **harvest.**

crowd, *n.* SYN.—bevy, crush, horde, host, masses, mob, multitude, populace, press, rabble, swarm, throng.

crown, *n.* See **top.**

crucial, *a.* See **critical.**

crude, *a.* SYN.—coarse, green, harsh, ill-prepared, raw, rough, unfinished, unpolished, unrefined; crass, uncouth, unrefined. ANT. —finished, well-prepared; cultivated, refined.

cruel, *a.* SYN.—barbarous, brutal, ferocious, inhuman, malignant, merciless, ruthless, savage. ANT.—benevolent, compassionate, forbearing, gentle, humane, kind, merciful.

crumb, *n.* See **particle.**

cuddle, *v.* See **caress.**

cull, *v.* See **choose.**

culmination, *n.* See **climax.**

culprit, *n.* See **criminal.**

cultivation, *n.* See **agriculture.**

culture, *n.* SYN.—breeding, civilization, cultivation, education, enlightenment, refinement. ANT.—boorishness, ignorance, illiteracy, vulgarity.

cultured, *a.* See **sophisticated.**

cunning, *a.* See **devious.**

cunning, *n.* See **ingenuity.**

curb, *v.* See **restrain.**

cure, *n.* See **remedy.**

curious, *a.* SYN.—inquiring, inquisitive, interrogative, meddling, nosy, peeping, peering, prying, searching, snoopy; odd, peculiar, queer, strange, unusual. ANT.—incurious, indifferent, unconcerned, uninterested; common, ordinary.

curiosity, *n.* See **wonder.**

current, *a.* See **modern.**

cursory, *a.* See **superficial.**

curt, *a.* See **abrupt.**

curtail, *v.* See **shorten.**

curve, *v.* See **bend.**

custody, *n.* See **care.**

custom, *n.* See **habit.**

customary, *a.* See **usual.**

cylindrical, *a.* See **round.**

D

dainty, *a.* See **delicate.**

damage, *n.* See **harm.**

damage, *v.* SYN.—deface, harm, hurt, impair, injure, mar, spoil. ANT.—ameliorate, benefit, enhance, mend, repair.

damaging, *a.* See **detrimental.**

danger, *n.* SYN.—hazard, jeopardy, peril, risk. ANT.—defense, immunity, protection, safety.

dangerous, *a.* SYN.—critical, hazardous, insecure, menacing, perilous, precarious, risky, threatening, unsafe. ANT.—firm, protected, safe, secure.

dare, *v.* See **challenge.**

daring, *a.* See **adventurous.**

dark, *a.* SYN.—black, dim, gloomy, murky, obscure, shadowy, unilluminated; dusky, opaque, sable, swarthy; dismal, gloomy, mournful, somber, sorrowful; evil, sinister, sullen, wicked; hidden, mystic, occult, secret. ANT.—light; bright, clear; pleasant; lucid.

dead, *a.* SYN.—deceased, defunct, departed, dull, gone, inanimate, insensible, lifeless, spiritless, unconscious. ANT.—alive, animate, living, stirring.

deafening, *a.* See **loud.**

deal, *n.* See **transaction.**

dear, *a.* SYN.—beloved, esteemed, precious, valued; costly, expensive, valuable. ANT.—despised, unwanted; cheap.

debase, *v.* SYN.—abase, adulterate, alloy, corrupt, defile, degrade, deprave, depress, humiliate, impair, lower, pervert, vitiate. ANT.—enhance, improve, raise, restore, vitalize.

debate, *v.* See **argue, dispute.**

decay, *v.* SYN.—decline, decompose, decrease, disintegrate, dwindle, ebb, putrefy, rot, spoil, wane, waste. ANT.—flourish, grow, increase, luxuriate, rise.

deceased, *a.* See **dead.**

deceit, *n.* SYN.—beguilement, cheat, chicanery, cunning, deceitfulness, deception, duplicity, fraud, guile, sham, trick, wiliness. ANT.—candor, honesty, openness, sincerity, truthfulness.

deceitful, *a.* See **deceptive.**

decent, *a.* SYN.—adequate, becoming, befitting, comely, decorous, fit, proper, respectable, seemly, suitable, tolerable. ANT.—coarse, gross, indecent, reprehensible, vulgar.

deception, *n.* See **deceit.**

deceptive, *a.* SYN.—deceitful, delusive, delusory, fallacious, false, illusive, misleading, specious. ANT.—authentic, genuine, honest, real, truthful.

decide, *v.* SYN.—adjudicate, close, conclude, determine, end, resolve, settle, terminate. ANT.—doubt, hesitate, suspend, vacillate, waver.

decipher, *v.* See **interpret.**

declaration, *n.* See **statement.**

declare, *v.* SYN.—affirm, announce, assert, aver, broadcast, express, make known, proclaim, profess, promulgate, protest, state, tell. ANT.—conceal, repress, suppress, withhold.

decline, *v.* SYN.—incline, slant, slope; descend, sink, wane; decay, decrease, degenerate, depreciate, deteriorate, diminish, dwindle, weaken; refuse, reject. ANT.—ameliorate, appreciate, ascend, increase; accept.

decorate, *v.* SYN.—adorn, beautify, deck, embellish, enrich, garnish, ornament, trim. ANT.—debase, defame, expose, strip, uncover.

decoration, *n.* See **ornament.**

decrease, *v.* SYN.—abate, curtail, decline, deduct, diminish, dwindle, lessen, reduce, remove, shorten, subtract, wane. ANT.—amplify, enlarge, expand, grow, increase.

dedicated, *a.* See **devoted.**

dedication, *n.* See **devotion.**

deduct, *v.* See **decrease.**

deed, *n.* See **act.**

defame, *v.* See **abuse.**

default, *n.* See **failure.**

defeat, *v.* See **conquer.**

defect, *n.* See **fault.**

defend, *v.* SYN.—fortify, guard, protect, safeguard, screen, shield; assert, espouse, justify, maintain, uphold, vindicate. ANT.—assault, attack, deny, oppose, submit.

defense, *n.* See **protection.**

deficient, *a.* SYN.—defective, inadequate, incomplete, insufficient, lacking, scanty, short. ANT.—adequate, ample, enough, satisfactory, sufficient.

definite, *a.* SYN.—certain, correct, determined, exact, explicit, fixed, precise, prescribed, specific. ANT.—ambiguous, confused, dubious, equivocal, indefinite.

defy, *v.* See **resist.**

degenerate, *v.* See **decline.**

degrade, *v.* See **debase, humble.**

delay, *v.* SYN.—defer, postpone, procrastinate; arrest, detain, hinder, impede, retard, stay; dawdle, linger, loiter, tarry. ANT.—expedite, hasten, precipitate, quicken.

delectable, *a.* See **delicious.**

deliberate, *a.* See **intentional.**

deliberate, *v.* See **consider.**

delicate, *a.* SYN.—dainty, elegant, exquisite, fastidious, feeble, frail, sensitive, slender, slight, weak; pleasant, pleasing, savory. ANT.—brutal, coarse, rude, tough, vulgar.

delicious, *a.* SYN.—delectable, delightful, luscious, palatable, savory, sweet, tasty. ANT.—acrid, distasteful, nauseous, unpalatable, unsavory.

delight, *n.* SYN.—bliss, ecstasy, enjoyment, gladness, happiness, joy, pleasure, rapture, transport. ANT.—annoyance, dejection, melancholy, misery, sorrow.

delighted, *a.* See **happy.**

deliver, *v.* SYN.—commit, give, impart, transfer, yield; announce, communicate, impart, proclaim, publish; emancipate, free, liberate, release, rescue, save. ANT.—confine, withhold; capture, imprison, restrict.

delusion, *n.* See **illusion.**

demand, *v.* SYN.—ask, ask for, challenge, claim, exact, require; inquire, necessitate. ANT.—give, offer, present, tender.

demolish, *v.* See **destroy.**

demonstrate, *v.* SYN.—display, exhibit, show; establish, evince, manifest, prove. ANT.—conceal, hide.

denounce, *v.* See **condemn.**

dense, *a.* SYN.—close, compact, compressed, concentrated, crowded, thick; dull, obtuse, slow, stupid. ANT.—dispersed, dissipated, sparse; clever, quick.

deny, *v.* SYN.—contradict, contravene, gainsay, refute; abjure, disavow, disown, forbid, refuse, repudiate, withhold. ANT.—affirm, assert, concede, confirm.

depart, *v.* See **leave.**

dependable, *a.* See **reliable.**

dependent, *a.* SYN.—conditional, contingent, depending, relying, subject, subordinate. ANT.—absolute, autonomous, casual, independent, original.

depict, *v.* See **describe, portray.**

depreciate, *v.* See **decline.**

depression, *n.* See **despair.**

derision, *n.* See **ridicule.**

derivation, *n.* See **origin.**

descend, *v.* See **decline.**

describe, *v.* SYN.—characterize, depict, explain, narrate, portray, recount, relate.

description, *n.* See **account.**

desert, *v.* See **abandon.**

design, *n.* SYN.—delineation, draft, drawing, outline, plan, sketch; artfulness, contrivance, cunning, plotting, scheming; intent, intention, objective, purpose. ANT.—result; candor, sincerity; accident, chance.

design, *v.* SYN.—contrive, create, devise, invent, plan, scheme; intend, mean, purpose; draw, sketch.

designate, *v.* See **indicate.**

desire, *n.* SYN.—appetite, aspiration, craving, hungering, longing, lust, urge, wish, yearning. ANT.—abomination, aversion, distaste, hate, loathing.

desire, *v.* See **want.**

desist, *v.* See **stop.**

desolate, *a.* SYN.—abandoned, bare, bleak, deserted, forlorn, forsaken, lonely, solitary, uninhabited, waste, wild. ANT.—attended, cultivated, fertile.

despair, *n.* SYN.—depression, desperation, despondency, discouragement, gloom, hopelessness, pessimism. ANT.—confidence, elation, hope, optimism.

desperate, *a.* SYN.—audacious, daring, despairing, despondent, determined, hopeless, reckless, wild. ANT.—assured, composed, confident, hopeful, optimistic.

desperation, *n.* See **despair.**

despicable, *a.* See **mean.**

despise, *v.* See **hate.**

despondent, *a.* See **melancholy.**

despotic, *a.* See **absolute.**

destiny, *n.* See **fate.**

destitute, *a.* See **poor.**

destroy, *v.* SYN.—annihilate, demolish, devastate, eradicate, exterminate, extinguish, obliterate, ravage, raze, ruin, wreck. ANT.—construct, establish, make, preserve, save.

destroyed, *a.* See **broken.**

destructive, *a.* SYN.—baneful, deadly, deleterious, detrimental, devastating, fatal, injurious, noxious, pernicious, ruinous. ANT.—beneficial, constructive, creative, profitable, salutary.

detail, *n.* SYN.—circumstance, item, minutia, part, particular; detachment, party, squad. ANT.—generality.

detain, *v.* See **delay.**

detect, *v.* See **discover.**

determinant, *n.* See **cause.**

determination, *n.* See **resolution.**

determine, *v.* SYN.—conclude, decide, end, fix, resolve, settle; ascertain, verify; incline, induce, influence; condition, define, limit; compel, necessitate.

detest, *v.* See **hate.**

detestable, *a.* See **abominable.**

detriment, *n.* See **harm.**

detrimental, *a.* SYN.—damaging, deleterious, harmful, hurtful, injurious, mischievous. ANT.—advantageous, beneficial, helpful, profitable, salutary.

develop, *v.* SYN.—amplify, create, elaborate, enlarge, evolve, expand, mature, unfold. ANT.—compress, contract, restrict, stunt, wither.

development, *n.* SYN.—elaboration, expansion, unfolding, unraveling; evolution, growth, maturing, progress. ANT.—abbreviation, compression, curtailment.

deviate, *v.* SYN.—bend, crook, deflect, digress, diverge, divert, sidetrack, stray, wander. ANT.—continue, follow, persist, preserve, remain.

device, *n.* See **instrument.**

devious, *a.* SYN.—circuitous, crooked, distorted, erratic, indirect, roundabout, swerving, tortuous, wandering, winding; crooked, cunning, tricky. ANT.—direct, straight; honest, straightforward.

devoted, *a.* SYN.—addicted, affectionate, ardent, attached, dedicated, disposed, earnest, faithful, fond, given up to, inclined, loyal, prone, true, wedded. ANT.—detached, disinclined, indisposed, untrammeled.

devotion, *n.* SYN.—affection, ardor, attachment, consecration, dedication, devoutness, fidelity, love, loyalty, piety, religiousness, zeal. ANT.—alienation, apathy, aversion, indifference, unfaithfulness.

devout, *a.* See **religious.**

dexterity, *n.* See **ability, skill.**

dialect, *n.* See **language.**

dialogue, *n.* See **conversation.**

dictator, *n.* See **tyrant.**

die, *v.* SYN.—cease, decay, decease, decline,

depart, expire, fade, languish, perish, sink, wane, wither. ANT.—begin, flourish, grow, live, survive.

difference, *n.* SYN.—disparity, dissimilarity, distinction, separation, variety; disagreement, discord, dissension. ANT.—identity, resemblance, similarity; agreement, harmony.

different, *a.* SYN.—contrary, dissimilar, distinct, divergent, diverse, incongruous, opposite, unlike, variant; divers, miscellaneous, sundry, various. ANT.—alike, congruous, identical, same, similar.

differentiate, *v.* See **discern.**

difficult, *a.* SYN.—arduous, complicated, demanding, hard, intricate, involved, laborious, obscure, perplexing, toilsome, trying. ANT.—easy, effortless, facile, simple.

digress, *v.* See **deviate.**

dilate, *v.* See **enlarge.**

dilemma, *n.* See **predicament.**

diligent, *a.* SYN.—active, assiduous, busy, careful, hard-working, industrious, patient, perseverant. ANT.—apathetic, careless, indifferent, lethargic, unconcerned.

dim, *a.* See **faint.**

diminish, *v.* See **abate, decrease.**

din, *n.* See **noise.**

diplomacy, *n.* See **tact.**

diplomatic, *a.* See **tactful.**

direct, *a.* See **straight.**

direct, *v.* SYN.—aim, level, point, train; conduct, govern, guide, manage, regulate, rule; bid, command, instruct, order. ANT.—deceive, distract, misdirect, misguide.

direction, *n.* SYN.—course, inclination, tendency, trend, way; administration, management, superintendence; guidance, instruction, order.

dirty, *a.* SYN.—filthy, foul, grimy, muddy, soiled, squalid; indecent, nasty, obscene; base, contemptible, despicable, low, mean, pitiful, shabby. ANT.—clean, neat, presentable; pure, wholesome.

disabled, *a.* See **lame.**

disagreement, *n.* See **dissent, quarrel.**

disaster, *n.* SYN.—adversity, calamity, casualty, catastrophe, mishap, ruin. ANT.—advantage, fortune, welfare.

disavow, *v.* See **renounce.**

discern, *v.* SYN.—descry, detect, differentiate, discriminate, distinguish, observe, perceive, recognize, see, separate. ANT.—confound, confuse, mingle, omit, overlook.

discerning, *a.* See **critical.**

discernment, *n.* See **insight.**

discharge, *v.* See **dismiss, emit.**

disciple, *n.* SYN.—adherent, devotee, follower, supporter, votary; learner, pupil, scholar, student.

discipline, *n.* SYN.—control, order, regulation, restraint, self-control; exercise, instruction, practice, training; correction, punishment. ANT.—chaos, confusion, turbulence.

disclaim, *v.* See **renounce.**

disclose, *v.* See **reveal.**

disconsolate, *a.* See **sad.**

discontinue, *v.* See **suspend.**

discourteous, *a.* See **rude.**

discover, *v.* SYN.—ascertain, detect, devise, expose, find, find out, invent, learn, originate, reveal. ANT.—cover, hide, lose, mask, screen.

discreet, *a.* See **tactful.**

discrepant, *a.* See **inconsistent.**

discriminate, *v.* See **discern.**

discriminating, *a.* See **critical.**

discrimination, *n.* See **judgment.**

discuss, *v.* See **talk.**

discussion, *n.* See **talk.**

disdain, *n.* See **contempt.**

disease, *n.* SYN.—ailment, complaint, disorder, illness, infirmity, malady, sickness. ANT.—health, healthiness, soundness, vigor.

diseased, *a.* See **sick.**

disgrace, *n.* See **shame.**

disgraceful, *a.* SYN.—discreditable, dishonorable, disreputable, ignominious, scandalous, shameful. ANT.—esteemed, honorable, renowned, respectable.

disguise, *n.* See **pretense.**

disguise, *v.* See **hide.**

dishonest, *a.* See **corrupt.**

dishonor, *n.* See **shame.**

disintegrate, *v.* See **decay.**

dislike, *n.* See **aversion, hatred.**

dislike, *v.* See **hate.**

disloyal, *a.* SYN.—apostate, faithless, false, perfidious, recreant, traitorous, treacherous, treasonable. ANT.—constant, devoted, loyal, true.

dismal, *a.* SYN.—bleak, cheerless, dark, doleful, dreary, dull, funereal, gloomy, lonesome, melancholy, sad, somber. ANT.—cheerful, gay, joyous, lively.

dismiss, *v.* SYN.—banish, discard, discharge, eject, exile, oust, remove, send off. ANT.—accept, detain, recall, retain.

disobedient, *a.* SYN.—defiant, forward, insubordinate, rebellious, refractory, undutiful, unruly. ANT.—compliant, dutiful, obedient, submissive.

disobey, *v.* See **violate.**

disorder, *n.* See **chaos, confusion.**

disorganization, *n.* See **chaos.**

disorganized, *a.* See **confused.**

disparage, *v.* SYN.—belittle, decry, depreciate, derogate, discredit, lower, minimize, undervalue. ANT.—aggrandize, commend, exalt, magnify, praise.

dispatch, *v.* See **send.**

dispel, *v.* See **disperse.**

dispense, *v.* See **allot.**

disperse, *v.* SYN.—diffuse, dispel, disseminate, dissipate, scatter, separate. ANT.—accumulate, amass, assemble, collect, gather.

displace, *v.* See **remove.**

display, *v.* SYN.—exhibit, expose, flaunt, parade, reveal, show, spread out. ANT.—conceal, cover, disguise, hide.

disposition, *n.* See **behavior, bias.**

dispute, *n.* SYN.—argument, contention, controversy, debate, disagreement, quarrel, squabble. ANT.—agreement, concord, decision, harmony.

dispute, *v.* SYN.—altercate, argue, bicker, contend, contest, debate, discuss, quarrel, squabble, wrangle. ANT.—agree, allow, assent, concede.

disregard, *v.* See **ignore.**

disreputable, *a.* See **disgraceful.**

dissent, *n.* SYN.—challenge, difference, disagreement, dissentience, noncompliance, nonconformity, objection, protest, recusancy, rejection, remonstrance, variance. ANT.—acceptance, agreement, assent, compliance.

dissimilar, *a.* See **different.**

dissipate, *v.* See **waste.**

distant, *a.* SYN.—far, faraway, remote, removed; aloof, cold, reserved, stiff, unfriendly. ANT.—close, near, nigh; cordial, friendly.

distinct, *a.* See **clear.**

distinction, *n.* See **quality, renown.**

distinctive, *a.* See **peculiar, special.**

distinguish, *v.* See **discern.**

distinguished, *a.* See **eminent.**

distress, *n.* See **anguish.**

distribute, *v.* SYN.—allot, apportion, deal, dispense, divide, dole, mete, scatter, spread; classify, group, sort.

district, *n.* See **territory.**

distrust, *v.* See **doubt.**

disturb, *v.* SYN.—agitate, annoy, confuse, decompose, derange, interrupt, perplex, perturb, rouse, trouble, unsettle, vex, worry. ANT.—order, pacify, quiet, settle, soothe.

diverse, *a.* See **different.**

diversity, *n.* See **variety.**

divert, *v.* See **turn.**

divide, *v.* SYN.—part, separate, sever, sunder; allot, deal out, dispense, distribute, share. ANT.—combine, convene, gather, join; unite.

divine, *a.* SYN.—celestial, godlike, heavenly, holy, superhuman, supernatural, transcendent. ANT.—blasphemous, diabolical, mundane, profane, wicked.

divulge, *v.* See **reveal.**

do, *v.* SYN.—accomplish, complete, conclude, consummate, effect, execute, finish, fulfill, perform, settle, terminate; carry on, conduct, discharge, transact; observe, perform, practice; make, produce, work; answer, serve, suffice.

docile, *a.* SYN.—compliant, obedient, pliant, submissive, tame, teachable, tractable, yielding. ANT.—mulish, obstinate, stubborn, ungovernable, unruly.

doctrinaire, *a.* See **dogmatic.**

doctrine, *n.* SYN.—belief, creed, dogma, precept, teaching, tenet. ANT.—conduct, deed, performance, practice.

document, *n.* See **record.**

dogma, *n.* See **doctrine.**

dogmatic, *a.* SYN. — arrogant, authoritarian, dictatorial, doctrinaire, domineering, magisterial, opinionated, overbearing, positive; authoritative, doctrinal, formal. ANT.—fluctuating, indecisive, open-minded, questioning, skeptical.

dole, *v.* See **distribute.**

doleful, *a.* See **dismal.**

domain, *n.* See **territory.**

dominate, *v.* See **control.**

domination, *n.* See **supremacy.**

donation, *n.* See **gift, grant.**

dormant, *a.* See **idle, latent.**

doubt, *n.* SYN.—ambiguity, distrust, hesitation, incredulity, scruple, skepticism, suspense, suspicion, unbelief, uncertainty. ANT.—belief, certainty, conviction, determination, faith.

doubt, *v.* SYN.—hesitate, question, waver; distrust, mistrust, suspect. ANT.—believe, confide, decide, rely on, trust.

dour, *a.* See **morose.**

draw, *v.* SYN.—drag, haul, pull, tow, tug; extract, remove, take out, unsheathe; allure, attract, entice, induce, lure, persuade; delineate, depict, sketch, trace; compose, draft, formulate, write; deduce, derive, get, infer, obtain; extend, lengthen, prolong, protract, stretch. ANT.—alienate, contract, drive, propel, shorten.

drawing, *n.* See **picture.**

dread, *n.* SYN.—alarm, apprehension, awe, fear, foreboding, horror, reverence, terror. ANT.—assurance, boldness, confidence, courage.

dreadful, *a.* See **horrible.**

dreary, *a.* See **dismal.**

dress, *n.* See **clothes.**

drill, *n.* See **exercise.**

drive, *v.* See **compel.**

droll, *a.* See **funny.**

drop, *v.* See **fall.**

drunk, *a.* See **intoxicated.**

dry, *a.* SYN.—arid, dehydrated, desiccated, drained, parched, thirsty; barren, dull, insipid, plain, tedious, tiresome, uninteresting, vapid. ANT.—damp, moist; fresh, interesting, lively.

dull, *a.* SYN.—dense, slow, stupid; blunt, obtuse; boring, commonplace, dismal, dreary, monotonous, sad, tedious. ANT.—animated, lively, sharp; clear, interesting.

dumb, *a.* See **stupid.**

dunk, *v.* See **immerse.**

duplicate, *n.* See **copy.**

duplicate, *v.* See **repeat.**

durability, *n.* See **strength.**

durable, *a.* See **permanent.**

duration, *n.* See **term.**

duty, *n.* See **obligation, tax.**

dwelling, *n.* See **home.**

E

eager, *a.* SYN.—anxious, ardent, avid, enthusiastic, fervent, hot, impassioned, impatient, keen, yearning. ANT.—apathetic, indifferent, unconcerned, uninterested.

early, *adv.* SYN.—beforehand, betimes, shortly, soon. ANT.—belated, late, overdue, tardy.

earn, *v.* SYN.—achieve, acquire, attain, deserve, gain, get, merit, obtain, win. ANT.—consume, forfeit, lose, spend, waste.

earned, *a.* See **merited.**

earnest, *a.* See **sincere.**

earth, *n.* See **land.**

ease, *v.* SYN.—allay, alleviate, assuage, calm, comfort, facilitate, lighten, mitigate, pacify, relieve, soothe. ANT.—confound, distress, disturb, trouble, worry.

easy, *a.* SYN.—facile, light, pleasant, relaxed, simple, uncomplicated. ANT.—arduous, demanding, difficult, hard.

eccentric, *a.* See **odd, peculiar.**

economical, *a.* SYN.—frugal, niggardly, provident, saving, sparing, thrifty. ANT.—extravagant, improvident, lavish, prodigal, wasteful.

ecstasy, *n.* SYN.—delight, exaltation, gladness, rapture, transport; frenzy, madness, trance. ANT.—depression, melancholy.

edge, *n.* SYN.—border, boundary, brim, brink, extremity, hem, margin, periphery, rim, verge; intensity, keenness, sharpness, sting. ANT.—center, interior; bluntness, dullness.

edict, *n.* See **act.**

educate, *v.* See **teach.**

education, *n.* SYN.—cultivation, development, instruction, knowledge, learning, schooling, study, training, tutoring.

effect, *v.* See **accomplish.**

effective, *a.* See **efficient.**

efficacy, *n.* See **efficiency.**

efficiency, *n.* SYN.—ability, capability, competency, effectiveness, efficacy, potency, skillfulness. ANT.—inability, ineptitude, wastefulness.

efficient, *a.* SYN.—adept, capable, competent, effective, effectual, efficacious, proficient, skillful. ANT.—incompetent, ineffectual, inefficient, unskilled.

effort, *n.* SYN.—attempt, endeavor, essay, exertion, trial; labor, pains, strain, strife, struggle, toil, trouble.

effrontery, *n.* See **impudence.**

egotism, *n.* See **conceit.**

elastic, *a.* See **flexible.**

elect, *v.* See **choose.**

elegance, *n.* See **beauty.**

elegant, *a.* See **beautiful.**

elementary, *a.* SYN.—basic, fundamental, primary, rudimentary, simple. ANT.—abstract, abstruse, complex, elaborate, intricate.

elevate, *v.* See **raise.**

elevated, *a.* See **high.**

eliminate, *v.* SYN.—dislodge, eject, eradicate, erase, exclude, expel, extirpate, oust, remove. ANT.—accept, admit, include, involve.

elongate, *v.* See **stretch.**

elude, *v.* See **avoid, escape.**

emanate, *v.* See **emit.**

emancipate, *v.* See **liberate.**

embarrass, *v.* SYN.—abash, discomfit, distress, entangle, fluster, hamper, hinder, mortify, perplex, rattle, trouble. ANT.—cheer, encourage, help, relieve.

embellish, *v.* See **decorate.**

embody, *v.* See **contain.**

embrace, *v.* SYN.—clasp, hug; accept, adopt, espouse, receive, welcome; comprehend, comprise, contain, embody, include, incorporate, subsume. ANT.—reject, renounce, repudiate, scorn, spurn.

emerge, *v.* See **appear.**

emergency, *n.* SYN.—crisis, exigency, juncture, pass, pinch, strait, urgency.

eminent, *a.* SYN.—conspicuous, distinguished, elevated, famous, glorious, illustrious, noted, prominent, renowned. ANT.—common, obscure, ordinary, unimportant, unknown.

emit, *v.* SYN.—belch, breathe, discharge, eject, emanate, expel, hurl, shed, shoot, spurt, vent.

emotion, *n.* SYN.—affection, agitation, feeling, passion, perturbation, sentiment, trepidation, turmoil. ANT.—calm, dispassion, indifference, restraint, tranquility.

employ, *v.* SYN.—apply, avail, busy, devote, occupy, use, utilize. ANT.—banish, discard, discharge, reject.

employment, *n.* SYN.—business, engagement, function, occupation, service, vocation, work. ANT.—idleness, leisure, slothfulness.

empty, *a.* SYN.—barren, devoid, hollow, senseless, unfilled, unfurnished, unoccupied, vacant, vacuous, vain, void, worthless. ANT.—full, inhabited, occupied, replete, supplied.

enclose, *v.* SYN.—bound, circumscribe, confine, encompass, envelop, fence, limit, surround. ANT.—develop, distend, enlarge, expand, expose, open.

encounter, *n.* See **conflict.**

encounter, *v.* See **meet.**

encourage, *v.* SYN.—animate, cheer, countenance, embolden, exhilarate, favor, hearten, impel, incite, inspirit, urge; foster, promote, sanction, stimulate, support. ANT.—deject, deter, discourage, dispirit, dissuade.

encroach, v. See invade.

end, n. SYN.—aim, cessation, close, completion, conclusion, expiration, extremity, finish, object, purpose, result, termination, terminus, tip. ANT.—beginning, commencement, inception, introduction.

end, v. See finish.

endanger, v. See risk.

endeavor, n. See effort.

endless, a. See infinite.

endorsement, n. See approval.

endurance, n. See patience.

endure, v. SYN.—bear, brook, experience, suffer, sustain, tolerate, undergo; abide, continue, last, persist, remain. ANT.—fail, falter, succumb; disperse, wane.

enduring, a. See constant, stable.

enemy, n. SYN.—adversary, antagonist, competitor, foe, opponent, rival. ANT.—accomplice, ally, comrade, confederate, friend.

energetic, a. See lively.

energy, n. See force.

engender, n. See create.

engross, v. See absorb.

enigma, n. See riddle.

enjoyment, n. See delight, pleasure.

enlarge, v. SYN.—amplify, augment, broaden, dilate, distend, expand, increase, magnify, widen. ANT.—abridge, contract, diminish, restrict, shrink.

enlighten, v. See illuminate.

enmity, n. SYN.—animosity, antagonism, antipathy, hatred, hostility, ill-will, invidiousness, malignity. ANT.—affection, cordiality, friendliness, good will, love.

ennoble, v. See exalt.

enormous, a. SYN.—colossal, elephantine, gargantuan, gigantic, huge, immense, large, prodigious, vast. ANT.—diminutive, little, minute, small, tiny.

enough, a. See adequate.

ensue, v. See follow.

entangle, v. See involve.

entente, n. See alliance.

enterprise, n. See business.

enterprising, a. See adventurous.

entertain, v. SYN.—consider, contemplate, harbor, hold; amuse, beguile, cheer, delight, divert, gladden, please, regale. ANT.—annoy, bore, disgust, disturb, repulse.

entertainment, n. See recreation.

enthusiasm, n. SYN.—ardor, devotion, earnestness, excitement, fanaticism, fervency, fervor, inspiration, intensity, vehemence, warmth, zeal. ANT.—apathy, detachment, ennui, indifference, unconcern.

enthusiastic, a. See eager.

entice, v. See attract.

entire, a. See whole.

entrance, n. SYN.—doorway, entry, inlet, opening, portal. ANT.—departure, exit.

entreaty, n. See prayer.

entrust, v. See commit.

envy, n. SYN.—covetousness, jealousy, spitefulness. ANT.—generosity, geniality, indifference.

episode, n. See event.

epoch, n. See age.

equal, a. SYN.—alike, commensurate, equitable, equivalent, even, identical, like, same, uniform, unvarying. ANT.—different, disparate, dissimilar, diverse.

equilibrium, n. See balance.

equip, v. See furnish.

equitable, a. See fair.

equity, n. See justice.

equivalent, a. See identical.

equivocal, a. See ambiguous.

era, n. See age.

eradicate, v. See eliminate.

erase, v. See cancel.

erect, a. See straight.

erect, v. See build.

erroneous, a. See wrong.

error, n. SYN.—blunder, fallacy, fault, inaccuracy, mistake, slip. ANT.—accuracy, precision, truth.

erudite, a. See academic.

erudition, n. See wisdom.

escape, v. SYN.—abscond, decamp, flee, fly; avert, avoid, elude, evade, shun. ANT.—catch, confront, face, invite, meet.

eschew, v. See avoid.

escort, v. See accompany, attend.

essay, n. See theme.

essential, a. SYN.—basic, fundamental, important, indispensable, intrinsic, necessary, requisite, vital. ANT.—expendable, extrinsic, optional, peripheral.

establish, v. SYN.—form, found, institute, organize, raise; confirm, fix, ordain, sanction, settle, strengthen; prove, substantiate, verify. ANT.—abolish, demolish, overthrow, unsettle, upset; disprove, refute.

estate, n. See property.

esteem, v. SYN.—admire, appreciate, honor, prize, regard, respect, revere, reverence, value, venerate; consider, deem, hold, regard, think. ANT.—abhor, depreciate, dislike, scorn.

esteemed, a. See dear.

estimate, v. See assess, calculate.

eternal, a. SYN.—ceaseless, deathless, endless, everlasting, immortal, infinite, perpetual, timeless, undying. ANT.—ephemeral, finite, mortal, temporal, transient.

eternally, adv. See always.

ethereal, a. See spiritual.

ethical, a. See moral.

evade, v. See escape.

evaluate, v. See assess, criticize.

event, n. SYN.—circumstance, episode, happening, incident, issue; consequence, end, occurrence, outcome, result.

ever, adv. See always.

everlasting, a. See eternal.

every, a. SYN.—all, each.

evidence, n. See proof.

evident, a. SYN.—apparent, clear, conspicuous, indubitable, manifest, obvious, open, overt, patent, unmistakable. ANT.—concealed, covert, hidden, obscure.

evil, a. See bad.

evil, n. See sin.

evolve, v. See develop.

exact, a. See precise.

exaggerate, v. SYN.—amplify, caricature, embroider, enlarge, expand, heighten, magnify, overstate, stretch. ANT.—belittle, depreciate, minimize, understate.

exalt, v. SYN.—aggrandize, consecrate, dignify, elevate, ennoble, erect, extol, glorify, hallow, raise. ANT.— debase, degrade, dishonor, humble, humiliate.

exalted, a. See noble.

examination, n. See inquiry.

examine, v. SYN.—analyze, assess, audit, check, contemplate, dissect, inquire, interrogate, notice, question, quiz, review, scan, scrutinize, survey, view, watch. ANT.—disregard, neglect, omit, overlook.

example, n. SYN.—archetype, illustration, instance, model, pattern, prototype, sample, specimen. ANT.—concept, precept, principle, rule.

exasperate, v. See aggravate.

exasperation, n. See vexation.

excellent, a. See good, perfect.

exception, n. SYN.—exclusion, omission, preclusion; anomaly, deviation, unusual case; affront, objection, offense. ANT.—inclusion, rule, standard.

exceptional, a. See rare.

excess, n. SYN.—extravagance, immoderation, intemperance, profusion, superabundance, superfluity, surplus. ANT.—dearth, deficiency, lack, paucity, want.

excessive, a. See profuse.

exchange, v. See change.

excite, v. SYN.—agitate, arouse, awaken, disquiet, disturb, incite, irritate, provoke, rouse, stimulate, stir up. ANT.—allay, calm, pacify, quell, quiet.

exclaim, v. SYN.—call out, cry, cry out, ejaculate, shout, vociferate. ANT.—intimate, whisper, write.

exclude, v. SYN.—bar, blackball, except, expel, hinder, omit, ostracize, prevent, prohibit, restrain, shut out. ANT.—accept, admit, include, welcome.

excuse, n. See apology.

excuse, v. SYN.—absolve, acquit, condone, exculpate, exempt, forgive, free, justify, overlook, pardon, remit. ANT.—convict, prosecute, punish, retaliate, revenge.

execrable, a. See abominable.

execution, n. See act.

exemplar, n. See copy.

exemplary, a. See ideal.

exercise, n. SYN.—activity, application, drill, employment, exertion, lesson, operation, performance, practice, task, training, use. ANT.—idleness, indolence, relaxation, repose, rest.

exhaust, v. See tire.

exhausted, a. See weary.

exhaustion, n. See fatigue.

exhibit, v. See display, show.

exhibition, n. See show.

exile, n. SYN.—banishment, deportation, expatriation, expulsion, extradition, ostracism, proscription. ANT.—admittance, recall, reinstatement, retrieval, welcome.

existence, n. See life.

expand, v. See grow.

expanse, n. See extent.

expansion, n. See development.

expatriation, n. See exile.

expect, v. SYN.—anticipate, await, contemplate, hope for. ANT.—despair of.

expectation, n. See anticipation, hope.

expedite, v. See accelerate.

expedition, n. See journey.

expel, v. SYN.—banish, discharge, dismiss, disown, excommunicate, exile, expatriate, ostracize, oust, proscribe; dislodge, eject, eliminate, void. ANT.—admit, favor, include, recall.

expend, v. See use.

expense, n. See price.

expensive, a. See valuable.

expert, a. See skillful.

expire, v. See die, terminate.

explain, v. SYN.—clarify, decipher, elucidate, expound, illustrate, interpret, resolve, unfold, unravel. ANT.—baffle, confuse, darken, obscure.

explanation, n. See apology.

explicit, a. SYN.—clear, definitive, express, lucid, manifest, specific. ANT.—ambiguous, equivocal, implicit, obscure, vague.

exploit, n. See **achievement.**

exploit, v. See **use.**

exposed, a. See **open.**

expound, v. See **explain.**

express, a. See **explicit.**

express, v. See **state.**

expressive, a. See **vivid.**

extend, v. See **stretch.**

extended, a. See **long.**

extensive, a. See **broad.**

extent, n. SYN.—amount, area, compass, degree, expanse, length, magnitude, measure, range, reach, scope, size, stretch.

exterior, n. See **face.**

extol, v. See **celebrate, exalt.**

extract, v. See **withdraw.**

extradition, n. See **exile.**

extraneous, a. See **alien.**

extraordinary, a. SYN.—exceptional, marvelous, peculiar, rare, remarkable, singular, uncommon, unusual, wonderful. ANT.—common, frequent, ordinary, usual.

extravagance, n. See **excess.**

extravagant, a. See **profuse.**

extreme, a. See **severe.**

F

fable, n. See **legend.**

fabricate, v. See **construct.**

face, n. SYN.—countenance, mug, visage; assurance, audacity; cover, exterior, front, surface. ANT.—timidity; back, interior, rear.

facilitate, v. See **ease.**

facility, n. See **skill.**

facsimile, n. See **copy.**

fact, n. SYN.—actuality, certainty, reality, truth; act, circumstance, deed, event, incident, occurrence. ANT.—fiction, supposition, theory; delusion, falsehood.

faction, n. See **part.**

faculty, n. See **ability, capacity.**

faded, a. See **faint.**

failure, n. SYN.—fiasco, miscarriage; default, dereliction, omission; decay, decline; deficiency, lack, loss, want. ANT.—achievement, success, victory; sufficiency.

faint, a. SYN.—dim, faded, indistinct, pale; feeble, languid, wearied; irresolute, timid, weak. ANT.—conspicuous, glaring; strong, vigorous; brave, forceful.

fair, a. SYN.—bright, clear, light; attractive, blond, comely, lovely; equitable, honest, impartial, just, reasonable, unbiased; average, mediocre, passable. ANT.—foul, ugly; dishonorable, fraudulent, partial; excellent, first-rate, worst.

fairness, n. See **justice.**

faith, n. SYN.—confidence, credence, dependence, reliance, trust; belief, creed, doctrine, dogma, persuasion, religion, tenet; constancy, fidelity, loyalty. ANT.—doubt, incredulity, mistrust, skepticism; infidelity.

faithful, a. SYN.—constant, devoted, loyal, staunch, steadfast, true; accurate, reliable, trusty. ANT.—disloyal, false, fickle, treacherous, untrustworthy.

faithless, a. See **disloyal.**

fake, a. See **artificial.**

fall, v. SYN.—collapse, decline, decrease, descend, diminish, drop, sink, subside; stumble, topple, tumble; droop, extend downward, hang. ANT.—arise, ascend, climb, mount, soar; steady.

fallacy, n. See **error.**

false, a. See **wrong.**

falsehood, n. See **lie.**

falsify, v. See **refute.**

falter, v. See **hesitate.**

fame, n. SYN.—acclaim, credit, distinction, eminence, glory, honor, notoriety, renown, reputation. ANT.—disrepute, ignominy, infamy, obscurity.

familiar, a. SYN.—acquainted, aware, cognizant, conversant, intimate, knowing, versed; affable, amicable, close, courteous, friendly, informal, sociable, unreserved. ANT.—affected, cold, distant, reserved, unfamiliar.

familiarity, n. SYN.—acquaintance, fellowship, friendship, sociability; frankness, informality, intimacy, liberty, unreserve. ANT.—constraint, distance, haughtiness, presumption, reserve.

family, n. See **kindred.**

famished, a. See **hungry.**

famous, a. SYN.—celebrated, distinguished, eminent, glorious, illustrious, noted, renowned, well-known. ANT.—hidden, ignominious, infamous, obscure, unknown.

fanciful, a. See **romantic.**

fancy, n. See **imagination.**

fantasy, n. SYN.—caprice, dream, fancy, hallucination, illusion, imagination, whim.

far, a. See **distant.**

farewell, n. SYN.—departure, good-by, leave-taking, valediction. ANT.—greeting, salutation, welcome.

farming, n. See **agriculture.**

fascinate, v. See **attract.**

fascinating, a. See **charming.**

fashion, v. See **form.**

fast, a. SYN.—expeditious, fleet, quick, rapid, speedy, swift; constant, firm, inflexible, secure, solid, stable, steadfast, steady, unswerving, unyielding. ANT.—slow, sluggish; insecure, loose, unstable, unsteady.

fasten, v. See **fix.**

fastidious, a. See **critical.**

fat, a. SYN.—chubby, corpulent, obese, paunchy, plump, portly, pudgy, rotund, stocky, stout, thickset. ANT.—gaunt, lean, slender, slim, thin.

fatal, a. See **mortal.**

fate, n. SYN.—consequence, doom, fortune, lot, portion; destiny, issue, necessity, outcome, result.

father, v. See **beget.**

fatigue, n. SYN.—enervation, exhaustion, languor, lassitude, tiredness, weariness. ANT.—freshness, rejuvenation, restoration, vigor, vivacity.

fatigued, a. See **weary.**

fault, n. SYN.—blemish, defect, error, failure, flaw, imperfection, mistake, omission, shortcoming, vice. ANT.—completeness, correctness, perfection.

faultless, a. See **perfect.**

favor, n. See **privilege.**

favor, v. See **encourage.**

favorite, a. See **popular.**

fealty, n. See **fidelity.**

fear, n. SYN.—alarm, apprehension, consternation, cowardice, dismay, dread, fright, horror, panic, scare, terror, timidity, trepidation. ANT.—assurance, boldness, bravery, courage, fearlessness.

fearful, a. See **afraid.**

fearless, a. See **bold.**

feasible, a. See **possible.**

feast, n. See **banquet.**

feature, n. See **characteristic.**

fecund, a. See **fertile.**

feeble, a. SYN.—decrepit, delicate, enervated, exhausted, faint, forceless, impaired, infirm, languid, powerless, puny, weak. ANT.—forceful, lusty, stout, strong, vigorous.

feeling, n. SYN.—sensation; affection, emotion, passion, sensibility, sentiment, tenderness; impression, opinion. ANT.—anesthesia; coldness, imperturbability, insensibility; fact.

feign, v. See **pretend.**

felicity, n. See **happiness.**

fellowship, n. See **brotherhood.**

felon, n. See **criminal.**

female, a. See **feminine.**

feminine, a. SYN.—female, girlish, ladylike, maidenly, womanish, womanly. ANT.—male, manly, mannish, masculine, virile.

ferment, n. See **confusion.**

ferocious, a. See **brutal.**

fertile, a. SYN.—bountiful, fecund, fruitful, luxuriant, plenteous, productive, prolific, rich, teeming. ANT.—barren, impotent, sterile, unproductive.

fervent, a. See **ardent.**

fervor, n. See **enthusiasm.**

festive, a. See **merry.**

fetter, v. See **bind.**

feud, n. See **quarrel.**

fickle, a. SYN.—capricious, changeable, fitful, inconstant, restless, unstable, variable. ANT.—constant, reliable, stable, steady, trustworthy.

fiction, n. SYN.—allegory, fable, fabrication, falsehood, invention, narrative, novel, romance, story, tale. ANT.—fact, history, reality, truth, verity.

fictitious, a. See **artificial.**

fidelity, n. SYN.—allegiance, constancy, devotion, faithfulness, fealty, loyalty; accuracy, exactness, precision. ANT.—disloyalty, faithlessness, perfidy, treachery.

field, n. See **land.**

fierce, a. See **violent.**

fiery, a. See **hot.**

fight, v. SYN.—battle, brawl, combat, conflict, contend, dispute, encounter, quarrel, scuffle, skirmish, squabble, struggle, wrangle.

figure, n. See **shape.**

figure, v. See **calculate.**

fill, v. SYN.—fill up, occupy, pervade; furnish, replenish, stock, store, supply; content, glut, gorge, sate, satiate, satisfy, stuff. ANT.—deplete, drain, empty, exhaust, void.

film, n. See **picture.**

filthy, a. See **dirty.**

final, a. SYN.—concluding, conclusive, decisive, ending, eventual, last, latest, terminal, ultimate. ANT.—first, inaugural, incipient, original, rudimentary.

find, v. See **discover.**

fine, a. SYN.—choice, dainty, delicate, elegant, exquisite, nice, pure, refined, splendid, subtle; beautiful, handsome, pretty; minute, powdered, pulverized, sharp, slender, small, thin. ANT.—blunt, coarse, large, rough, thick.

finish, v. SYN.—accomplish, achieve, close, complete, conclude, consummate, do, end, execute, fulfill, get done, perfect, perform, terminate.

finished, a. See **complete.**

fire, n. SYN.—blaze, burning, combustion, conflagration, flame, glow, heat, warmth;

ardor, fervor, intensity, passion, vigor. ANT.—cold; apathy, quiescence.

firm, *a.* See **stable, tough.**

firm, *n.* See **company.**

first, *a.* SYN.—beginning, earliest, initial, original, primary, prime, primeval, primitive, pristine; chief, foremost. ANT.—hindmost, last, latest; least, subordinate.

fit, *a.* See **decent.**

fit, *v.* See **adapt.**

fitting, *a.* See **appropriate.**

fix, *v.* SYN.—affix, attach, bind, fasten, link, place, set, stick, tie; define, determine, establish, limit, set, settle; adjust, mend, rectify, regulate, repair. ANT.—displace, remove, unfasten; alter, change, disturb, modify; damage, mistreat.

fixed, *a.* See **constant.**

flame, *n.* See **light.**

flat, *a.* SYN.—even, horizontal, level, plane, smooth; dull, insipid, stale, tasteless, vapid. ANT.—broken, hilly, irregular, sloping; exciting, racy, savory, tasty.

flattery, *n.* See **compliment.**

flaunt, *v.* See **boast.**

flavor, *n.* See **taste.**

flaw, *n.* See **blemish, fault.**

flee, *n.* SYN.—abscond, decamp, escape, fly, hasten, run away. ANT.—appear, arrive, remain, stay.

fleet, *a.* See **fast.**

fleeting, *a.* See **temporary.**

flexible, *a.* SYN.—compliant, ductile, elastic, lithe, pliable, pliant, resilient, supple, tractable. ANT.—brittle, hard, rigid, stiff, unbending.

flow, *v.* SYN.—gush, run, spout, spurt, stream; come, emanate, issue, originate, proceed, result; abound, be copious.

flowing, *a.* See **full.**

fluctuate, *v.* SYN.—change, hesitate, oscillate, undulate, vacillate, vary, waver. ANT.—adhere, decide, persist, resolve, stick.

fluid, *a.* See **liquid.**

fluster, *v.* See **embarrass.**

fly, *v.* SYN.—flit, float, flutter, glide, hover, mount, sail, soar; dart, rush, shoot, spring; abscond, decamp, escape, flee, run away. ANT.—descend, fall, plummet, sink.

foil, *v.* See **frustrate.**

follow, *v.* SYN.—succeed, come next; comply, heed, obey, observe; adopt, copy, imitate; accompany, attend; chase, pursue, trail; ensue, result. ANT.—precede; guide, lead; avoid, elude, flee; cause.

follower, *n.* SYN.—adherent, attendant, devotee, disciple, henchman, partisan, successor, supporter, votary. ANT.—chief, head, leader, master.

folly, *n.* SYN.—foolishness, imbecility, silliness; absurdity, extravagance, imprudence, indiscretion. ANT.—sense, wisdom; judgment, prudence, reasonableness.

fond, *a.* See **devoted.**

fondle, *v.* See **caress.**

fondness, *n.* See **affection.**

food, *n.* SYN.—diet, edibles, fare, feed, meal, nutriment, provisions, rations, repast, sustenance, viands, victuals. ANT.—drink, hunger, starvation, want.

fool, *n.* SYN.—buffoon, clown, harlequin, jester; blockhead, dolt, dunce, idiot, imbecile, nincompoop, numbskull, oaf, simpleton. ANT.—genius, philosopher, sage, scholar.

foolish, *a.* SYN.—absurd, asinine, brainless, crazy, idiotic, irrational, nonsensical,

preposterous, ridiculous, senseless, silly, simple. ANT.—judicious, prudent, sagacious, sane, wise.

forbear, *v.* See **refrain.**

forbid, *v.* See **prohibit.**

force, *n.* SYN.—dint, emphasis, energy, intensity, might, potency, power, strength, vigor; coercion, compulsion, constraint, violence. ANT.—feebleness, frailty, impotence, weakness; persuasion.

force, *v.* See **compel.**

forceful, *a.* See **strong.**

foreign, *a.* See **alien.**

foreigner, *n.* See **stranger.**

foresight, *n.* See **anticipation.**

forever, *adv.* See **always.**

forgive, *v.* See **pardon.**

forgiveness, *n.* See **pardon.**

forlorn, *a.* See **miserable.**

form, *v.* SYN.—construct, create, fashion, forge, make, mold, produce, shape; compose, constitute, make up; arrange, combine, organize; devise, frame, invent. ANT.—destroy, disfigure, dismantle, misshape, wreck.

formal, *a.* SYN.—affected, ceremonious, correct, decorous, exact, methodical, precise, proper, regular, solemn, stiff; external, outward, perfunctory. ANT.—easy, natural, unconstrained, unconventional; heartfelt.

former, *a.* See **previous.**

formulate, *v.* See **create.**

forsake, *v.* See **abandon.**

fortitude, *n.* See **courage, strength.**

fortuity, *n.* See **accident.**

fortunate, *a.* SYN.—advantageous, auspicious, benign, favored, felicitous, fortuitous, happy, lucky, propitious, successful. ANT.—cheerless, condemned, ill-fated, persecuted, unlucky.

forward, *n.* See **introduction.**

forward, *v.* See **advance.**

foster, *v.* See **cherish.**

foul, *a.* See **dirty.**

found, *v.* See **establish.**

foundation, *n.* SYN.—base, basis, bottom, ground, groundwork, root, substructure, support, underpinning. ANT.—building, cover, superstructure, top.

fracture, *v.* See **break.**

fragile, *a.* SYN.—breakable, brittle, delicate, feeble, frail, infirm, weak. ANT.—durable, hardy, strong, sturdy, tough.

fragment, *n.* See **part.**

fragrance, *n.* See **smell.**

frail, *a.* See **fragile.**

frame, *v.* See **construct.**

frank, *a.* See **candid.**

fraternity, *n.* See **brotherhood.**

fraternize, *v.* See **mix.**

fraud, *n.* SYN.—artifice, cheat, chicanery, deceit, deception, duplicity, guile, imposition, imposture, swindle, trick. ANT.—fairness, honesty, integrity, sincerity.

free, *a.* SYN.—autonomous, emancipated, exempt, freed, independent, liberated, unconfined, unrestricted; clear, loose, open, unfastened, unobstructed; immune; careless, easy, familiar, frank; artless, bounteous, bountiful, generous, liberal, munificent. ANT.—confined, restrained, restricted; blocked, clogged, impeded; subject; illiberal, parsimonious, stingy.

free, *v.* See **liberate.**

freedom, *n.* SYN.—exemption, familiarity, immunity, independence, liberation, liberty, license, privilege, unrestraint. ANT.—bondage, compulsion, constraint, necessity, servitude.

freezing, *a.* See **cold.**

frenzied, *a.* See **wild.**

frequent, *a.* SYN.—common, general, habitual, often, persistent, usual. ANT.—exceptional, rare, scanty, solitary, unique.

frequently, *adv.* See **often.**

fresh, *a.* SYN.—modern, new, novel, recent; additional, further; brisk, cool, refreshing; artless, green, inexperienced, natural, raw. ANT.—decayed, faded, hackneyed, musty, stagnant.

fretful, *a.* See **peevish.**

friend, *n.* SYN.—companion, comrade, crony, intimate; advocate, defender, patron, supporter, well-wisher; ally, associate. ANT.—adversary, enemy, stranger.

friendly, *a.* SYN.—affable, amicable, companionable, genial, kindly, neighborly, sociable, social. ANT.—antagonistic, cool, distant, hostile, reserved.

friendship, *n.* See **acquaintance.**

fright, *n.* See **alarm, fear.**

frighten, *v.* SYN.—affright, alarm, appal, astound, daunt, dismay, horrify, intimidate, scare, startle, terrify, terrorize. ANT.—allay, compose, embolden, reassure, soothe.

frightened, *a.* See **afraid.**

frigid, *a.* See **cold.**

frivolous, *a.* See **superficial.**

frolic, *v.* See **play.**

frontier, *n.* See **border.**

frozen, *a.* See **cold.**

frugal, *a.* SYN.—economical, parsimonious, provident, saving, sparing, stingy, temperate, thrifty. ANT.—extravagant, intemperate, self-indulgent, wasteful.

frustrate, *v.* SYN.—baffle, balk, circumvent, defeat, disappoint, foil, hinder, outwit, prevent, thwart. ANT.—accomplish, fulfill, further, promote.

fulfill, *v.* See **satisfy.**

full, *a.* SYN.—crammed, filled, gorged, packed, replete, satiated, soaked; ample, complete, copious, entire, extensive, perfect, plentiful, sufficient; baggy, flowing, loose, voluminous; circumstantial, detailed, exhaustive. ANT.—depleted, devoid, empty, vacant; insufficient, lacking, partial.

fund, *n.* See **supply.**

fundamental, *a.* See **elementary, essential.**

funny, *a.* SYN.—amusing, comical, droll, farcical, humorous, laughable, ludicrous, ridiculous, witty; curious, odd, queer. ANT.—melancholy, sad, serious, sober, solemn.

furious, *a.* See **angry.**

furnish, *v.* SYN.—endow, equip, fit, fit out, provide, supply; afford, give, produce, yield. ANT.—denude, despoil, divest, strip.

further, *v.* See **advance.**

fury, *n.* See **anger.**

fusion, *n.* See **union.**

futile, *a.* See **vain.**

G

gain, *n.* See **benefit, profit.**

gain, *v.* SYN.—achieve, acquire, attain, earn, get, obtain, procure, reach, secure, win; benefit, net, profit. ANT.—forfeit, lose, surrender.

game, *n.* SYN.—amusement, contest, diversion, fun, match, merriment, pastime, play, recreation, sport. ANT.—business, drudgery, hardship, labor, work.

gap, *n.* See **hole.**

garb, *n.* See **clothes.**

garments, *n.* See **clothes.**

garnish, *v.* See **decorate.**

garrulous, *a.* See **talkative.**

gather, *v.* SYN.—accumulate, amass, assemble, collect, congregate, convene, muster; cull, garner, glean, harvest, pick, reap; conclude, deduce, infer, judge. ANT.—disband, disperse, distribute, scatter, separate.

gaunt, *a.* See **thin.**

gay, *a.* See **cheerful.**

general, *n.* SYN.—common, customary, ordinary, popular, prevalent, regular, universal, usual; indefinite, inexact, vague. ANT.—exceptional, rare, singular; definite, particular, specific.

generate, *v.* See **yield.**

generation, *n.* See **age.**

generous, *a.* SYN.—beneficent, bountiful, giving, liberal, magnanimous, munificent, openhanded, unselfish. ANT.—covetous, greedy, miserly, selfish, stingy.

genial, *a.* See **friendly.**

genius, *n.* SYN.—ability, aptitude, creativity, faculty, gift, inspiration, intellect, originality, sagacity, talent; adept, intellectual, master, proficient. ANT.—ineptitude, obtuseness, shallowness, stupidity; dolt, dullard, moron.

genre, *n.* See **class.**

gentle, *a.* SYN.—benign, calm, docile, mild, peaceful, placid, relaxed, serene, soft, soothing, tame, tractable. ANT.—fierce, harsh, rough, savage, violent.

genuine, *a.* SYN.—authentic, bona fide, legitimate, proven, real, sincere, true, unadulterated, unaffected, veritable. ANT.—artificial, bogus, counterfeit, false, sham.

germ, *n.* See **infection.**

gesture, *n.* See **sign.**

get, *v.* SYN.—achieve, acquire, attain, earn, gain, obtain, procure, receive, secure. ANT.—forfeit, leave, lose, renounce, surrender.

ghost, *n.* SYN.—apparition, phantom, shade, spectre, spirit, spook.

gift, *n.* SYN.—benefaction, bequest, boon, charity, donation, endowment, favor, grant, gratuity, largess, present; aptitude, faculty, genius, talent. ANT.—deprivation, earnings, loss, purchase; incapacity, ineptitude, stupidity.

gigantic, *a.* See **enormous.**

giggle, *n.* See **laugh.**

gist, *n.* See **meaning.**

give, *v.* SYN.—bestow, confer, contribute, deliver, donate, furnish, grant, impart, present, provide, supply. ANT.—keep, retain, seize, withdraw.

glad, *a.* SYN.—cheerful, delighted, exulting, gratified, happy, joyous, lighthearted, merry, pleased. ANT.—dejected, depressed, despondent, melancholy, sad.

gladness, *n.* See **happiness.**

glance, *n.* See **look.**

gleam, *v.* See **shine.**

glib, *a.* See **smooth.**

gloom, *n.* SYN.—blackness, bleakness, darkness, obscurity, shadow; dejection, depression, despondency, melancholy, misery, sadness, woe. ANT.—exultation, frivolity, joy, light, mirth.

gloomy, *a.* See **dismal, melancholy.**

glorify, *v.* SYN.—adore, consecrate, dignify, enshrine, enthrone, exalt, extol, hallow, honor, revere, venerate. ANT.—abuse, debase, degrade, dishonor, mock.

glorious, *a.* See **sublime.**

glory, *n.* See **honor.**

glow, *v.* See **shine.**

glum, *a.* See **morose.**

glut, *v.* See **fill.**

go, *v.* SYN.—depart, exit, fade, flee, leave, move, proceed, quit, retire, vanish, walk, withdraw. ANT.—arrive, come, enter, stand, stay.

goal, *n.* See **aspiration, purpose.**

godlike, *a.* See **divine.**

good, *a.* SYN.—conscientious, exemplary, honest, moral, pure, reliable, virtuous, worthy; admirable, commendable, excellent, genuine, precious, safe, sound, valid; benevolent, gracious, humane, kind; agreeable, cheerful, friendly, genial, pleasant; fair, honorable, immaculate; auspicious, beneficial, favorable, profitable, useful; able, capable, efficient, expert, proficient, skillful; adequate, ample, sufficient.

govern, *v.* SYN.—administer, command, control, direct, manage, oversee, regulate, reign, rule, supervise, sway. ANT.—acquiesce, assent, obey, submit, yield.

graceful, *a.* SYN.—beautiful, comely, elegant, flowing, fluid, lithe, natural, supple. ANT.—awkward, clumsy, deformed, gawky, ungainly.

gracious, *a.* See **amiable, cordial.**

grade, *n.* See **class, quality.**

gradual, *a.* See **slow.**

grandiose, *a.* See **majestic.**

grant, *n.* SYN.—allowance, appropriation, benefaction, bequest, boon, bounty, concession, donation, endowment, gift, subsidy.

grant, *v.* See **allot, yield.**

graph, *n.* See **plot.**

grasp, *v.* See **catch.**

grateful, *a.* SYN.—appreciative, beholden, indebted, obliged, thankful. ANT.—thankless, unappreciative.

gratifying, *a.* See **comfortable.**

grave, *a.* SYN.—consequential, important, momentous, serious, weighty; dignified, sedate, sober, solemn, staid, thoughtful. ANT.—insignificant, trifling, trivial; flighty, frivolous, light, merry.

great, *a.* SYN.—big, enormous, gigantic, huge, immense, large, vast; numerous, countless; celebrated, eminent, famed, illustrious, prominent, renowned; critical, important, momentous, serious, vital, weighty; august, dignified, elevated, grand, majestic, noble; excellent, fine, magnificent. ANT.—diminutive, little, minute, small; common, obscure, ordinary, unknown; menial, paltry.

greedy, *a.* SYN.—avaricious, covetous, grasping, rapacious, selfish; devouring, gluttonous, insatiable, ravenous, voracious. ANT.—generous, munificent; full, satisfied.

green, *a.* See **fresh.**

greet, *v.* See **address.**

gregarious, *a.* See **social.**

grief, *n.* SYN.—affliction, anguish, distress, heartache, lamentation, misery, mourning, sadness, sorrow, trial, tribulation, woe. ANT.—comfort, consolation, happiness, joy, solace.

grievance, *n.* See **injury.**

grieve, *v.* SYN.—bemoan, bewail, deplore, lament, mourn, suffer, weep. ANT.—carouse, celebrate, rejoice, revel.

grieved, *a.* See **sorry.**

grip, *v.* See **catch.**

gross, *a.* SYN.—aggregate, entire, total, whole; brutal, enormous, glaring, grievous, manifest, plain; coarse, crass, earthy, indelicate, obscene; rough, rude, vulgar; big, bulky, fat, great, large. ANT.—proper, refined; appealing, comely, delicate.

grouch, *v.* See **complain.**

group, *n.* SYN.—aggregation, assembly, band, brood, bunch, class, cluster, collection, crowd, flock, herd, horde, lot, mob, pack, party, set, swarm, throng, troupe.

grow, *v.* SYN.—advance, develop, distend, enlarge, expand, extend, germinate, increase, mature, swell. ANT.—atrophy, contract, decay, diminish, shrink, wane.

growth, *n.* See **development.**

gruff, *a.* See **rough.**

guarantee, *n.* SYN.—bail, bond, earnest, guaranty, pawn, pledge, security, surety, token, warrant.

guard, *n.* See **protection.**

guard, *v.* See **cover, defend.**

guess, *v.* SYN.—assume, believe, conjecture, estimate, reason, reckon, speculate, suppose, surmise, think.

guide, *v.* See **conduct, direct.**

guile, *n.* See **deceit.**

H

habit, *n.* SYN.—custom, fashion, practice, routine, usage, use, wont.

habitual, *a.* See **frequent.**

hackneyed, *a.* See **trite.**

hallow, *v.* See **exalt.**

hallucination, *n.* SYN.—aberration, fantasy, illusion, phantasm, vision.

halt, *v.* See **stop.**

handicap, *n.* See **inability, penalty.**

handsome, *a.* See **beautiful.**

handy, *a.* See **convenient.**

happen, *v.* SYN.—bechance, befall, betide, chance, occur, take place, transpire.

happiness, *n.* SYN.—beatitude, blessedness, bliss, contentment, delight, felicity, gladness, pleasure, satisfaction, well-being. ANT.—despair, grief, misery, sadness, sorrow.

happy, *a.* SYN.—blessed, cheerful, contented, delighted, fortunate, gay, glad, joyful, joyous, lucky, merry, opportune, propitious. ANT.—blue, depressed, gloomy, morose.

harass, *v.* See **tease.**

hard, *a.* SYN.—compact, firm, impenetrable, rigid, solid; arduous, burdensome, difficult, onerous, tough; intricate, perplexing, puzzling; cruel, harsh, rigorous, severe, stern, strict, unfeeling. ANT.—elastic, flabby, fluid, plastic, soft; easy, effortless, facile; simple; gentle, lenient, tender.

hardship, *n.* See **trial, trouble.**

harm, *n.* SYN.—damage, detriment, evil, hurt, ill, infliction, injury, mischief, misfortune, mishap, wrong. ANT.—benefit, boon, favor, kindness.

harm, *v.* See **injure.**

harmful, *a.* See **detrimental.**

harmless, *a.* See **safe.**

harmony, *n.* See **agreement.**

harsh, *a.* SYN.—blunt, coarse, grating, gruff, jarring, rigorous, rough, rugged, severe, strict, stringent. ANT.—gentle, melodious, mild, smooth, soft.

harvest, *n.* SYN.—crop, fruit, proceeds, produce, product, reaping, result, store, yield.

harvest, *v.* See **reap.**

hasten, *v.* See **hurry.**

hasty, *a.* See **abrupt, quick.**

hate, *v.* SYN.—abhor, abominate, despise, detest, dislike, loathe. ANT.—admire, approve, cherish, like, love.

hateful, *a.* See **abominable.**

hatred, *n.* SYN.—abhorrence, animosity, detestation, dislike, enmity, hostility, ill will, malevolence, rancor. ANT.—affection, attraction, friendship, love.

haughty, *a.* See **proud.**

have, *v.* See **possess.**

hazard, *n.* See **danger.**

hazard, *v.* SYN.—chance, conjecture, dare, endanger, imperil, jeopardize, peril, risk, venture. ANT.—determine, guard, insure, know.

hazardous, *a.* See **dangerous.**

hazy, *a.* See **vague.**

head, *n.* SYN.—chief, commander, director, leader, master, principal; acme, crest, pinnacle, summit, top; crisis, culmination. ANT.—follower, subordinate, underling; base, bottom, foot.

healthy, *a.* SYN.—hale, hearty, robust, sound, strong, well; hygienic, salubrious, salutary, wholesome. ANT.—delicate, diseased, frail, infirm; injurious, noxious.

hear, *v.* SYN.—harken, heed, listen, regard.

heart, *n.* See **center.**

heartache, *n.* See **grief.**

heartbroken, *a.* See **miserable.**

hearten, *v.* See **encourage.**

hearty, *a.* See **cordial, healthy.**

heavenly, *a.* See **divine.**

heavy, *a.* SYN.—massive, ponderous, weighty; burdensome, cumbersome, grievous, trying; gloomy, grave, serious; dull, sluggish. ANT.—animated, brisk, light.

heed, *n.* See **attention.**

heed, *v.* See **consider.**

heedless, *a.* See **blind, impulsive.**

height, *n.* See **climax.**

heighten, *v.* See **aggravate, raise.**

help, *n.* See **assistance.**

help, *v.* SYN.—abet, aid, assist, succor, support, uphold; facilitate, further, promote; mitigate, relieve, remedy. ANT.—impede, resist, thwart; hinder; afflict.

helpful, *a.* See **beneficial.**

hence, *adv.* See **therefore.**

heretic, *n.* SYN.—apostate, dissenter, nonconformist, schismatic, sectarian, sectary, unbeliever.

heroic, *a.* See **brave.**

hesitant, *a.* See **reluctant.**

hesitate, *v.* SYN.—delay, demur, doubt, falter, pause, scruple, stammer, stutter, vacillate, waver. ANT.—continue, decide, persevere, proceed, resolve.

hesitation, *n.* See **doubt.**

hidden, *a.* See **latent, secret.**

hide, *v.* SYN.—cloak, conceal, cover, disguise, mask, screen, secrete, suppress, veil, withhold. ANT.—disclose, divulge, expose, reveal, show, uncover.

high, *a.* SYN.—lofty, tall, towering; elevated, eminent, exalted, proud. ANT.—small, stunted, tiny; base, low, mean.

hinder, *v.* SYN.—block, check, hamper, impede, obstruct, prevent, resist, restrain, retard, stop, thwart. ANT.—assist, expedite, facilitate, further, promote.

hint, *n.* SYN.—allusion, implication, insinuation, intimation, reminder. ANT.—affirmation, declaration, statement.

hint, *v.* See **allude.**

hire, *v.* See **employ.**

hit, *v.* SYN.—beat, hurt, knock, pound, pummel, smite, strike.

hoax, *n.* See **trick.**

hold, *v.* SYN.—adhere, clasp, clutch, grasp, grip; have, keep, maintain, occupy, possess, retain, support; check, confine, curb, detain, restrain; accommodate, carry, contain, receive, stow. ANT.—abandon, relinquish, surrender, vacate.

hole, *n.* SYN.—abyss, aperture, cavity, chasm, gap, gulf, opening, pore, void.

hollow, *a.* SYN.—depressed, empty, unfilled, vacant, void; hypocritical, insincere, vain. ANT.—full, solid, sound; genuine, sincere.

holy, *a.* SYN.—blessed, consecrated, devout, divine, hallowed, pious, religious, sacred, saintly, spiritual. ANT.—evil, profane, sacrilegious, secular, worldly.

home, *n.* SYN.—abode, domicile, dwelling, habitat, hearth, quarters, residence, seat.

homely, *a.* See **ugly.**

honest, *a.* SYN.—candid, conscientious, fair, honorable, ingenuous, just, scrupulous, sincere, trustworthy, truthful, upright. ANT.—deceitful, dishonest, fraudulent, lying, tricky.

honesty, *n.* SYN.—candor, fairness, frankness, integrity, justice, openness, rectitude, responsibility, sincerity, trustworthiness, uprightness. ANT.—cheating, deceit, dishonesty, fraud, trickery.

honor, *n.* SYN.—admiration, adoration, deference, dignity, esteem, fame, glory, homage, praise, renown, respect, reverence, worship. ANT.—contempt, derision, disgrace, dishonor, reproach.

honor, *v.* See **celebrate, respect.**

honorable, *a.* SYN.—admirable, eminent, fair, honest, noble, respectable, true, trusty, upright, virtuous; creditable, esteemed, proper, reputable. ANT.—disgraceful, ignominious, infamous, shameful.

hope, *n.* SYN.—anticipation, expectancy, expectation; confidence, faith, optimism, trust. ANT.—despair, despondency, pessimism.

hopelessness, *n.* See **despair.**

horde, *n.* See **crowd.**

horrible, *a.* SYN.—appalling, awful, dire, dreadful, fearful, frightful, ghastly, hideous, horrid, repulsive, terrible. ANT.—beautiful, enchanting, enjoyable, fascinating, lovely.

horrid, *a.* See **horrible.**

horror, *n.* See **dread.**

hostile, *a.* SYN.—adverse, antagonistic, inimical, opposed, unfriendly, warlike. ANT.—amicable, cordial, favorable.

hostility, *n.* See **animosity, hatred.**

hot, *a.* SYN.—burning, scalding, scorching, torrid, warm; ardent, fervent, fiery, hot-blooded, impetuous, intense, passionate; peppery, pungent. ANT.—cold, cool, freezing, frigid; apathetic, impassive, indifferent, passionless, phlegmatic; bland.

however, *adv.* SYN.—but, nevertheless, notwithstanding, still, yet.

hue, *n.* See **color.**

hug, *v.* See **caress.**

huge, *a.* See **large.**

humane, *a.* See **merciful.**

humanity, *n.* See **benevolence.**

humble, *a.* SYN.—compliant, lowly, meek, modest, plain, simple, submissive, unassuming, unostentatious, unpretentious. ANT.—arrogant, boastful, haughty, proud, vain.

humble, *v.* SYN.—abase, abash, break, crush, degrade, humiliate, mortify, shame, subdue. ANT.—elevate, exalt, honor, praise.

humiliation, *n.* See **shame.**

humor, *n.* SYN.—facetiousness, irony, jocularity, joke, sarcasm, satire, waggery, wit; disposition, mood, temper, temperament. ANT.—gravity, seriousness, sorrow.

humorous, *a.* See **funny.**

hunger, *n.* See **appetite.**

hungry, *a.* SYN.—craving, famished, ravenous, starved, thirsting, voracious; avid, greedy, longing. ANT.—full, gorged, sated, satiated; satisfied.

hunt, *n.* See **search.**

hurl, *v.* See **throw.**

hurry, *v.* SYN.—accelerate, expedite, hasten, precipitate, quicken, rush, speed. ANT.—delay, detain, hinder, retard, tarry.

hurt, *n.* See **injury.**

hurt, *v.* See **injure.**

hygienic, *a.* See **healthy.**

hypocrisy, *n.* SYN.—cant, deceit, dissimulation, pretense, sanctimony. ANT.—candor, frankness, honesty, openness, truth.

hypothesis, *n.* SYN.—conjecture, law, supposition, theory. ANT.—certainty, fact, proof.

I

idea, *n.* SYN.—abstraction, concept, conception, fancy, image, impression, notion, opinion, sentiment, thought. ANT.—entity, matter, object, substance, thing.

ideal, *a.* SYN.—exemplary, fancied, faultless, imaginary, perfect, supreme, unreal, utopian, visionary. ANT.—actual, faulty, imperfect, material, real.

idealistic, *a.* See **romantic.**

identical, *a.* SYN.—coincident, equal, equivalent, indistinguishable, like, same. ANT.—contrary, disparate, dissimilar, distinct, opposed.

identify, *v.* See **recognize.**

idiot, *n.* See **fool.**

idiotic, *a.* See **foolish.**

idle, *a.* SYN.—dormant, inactive, indolent, inert, lazy, slothful, unemployed, unoccupied. ANT.—active, employed, industrious, occupied, working.

ignominious, *a.* See **base.**

ignorant, *a.* SYN.—illiterate, uncultured, uneducated, uninformed, unlearned, unlettered, untaught. ANT.—cultured, educated, erudite, informed, literate.

ignore, *v.* SYN.—disregard, neglect, omit, overlook, skip, slight. ANT.—include, notice, regard.

ill, *a.* See **sick.**

illegal, *a.* SYN.—criminal, illegitimate, illicit, outlawed, prohibited, unlawful. ANT.—honest, lawful, legal, permitted.

illicit, *a.* See **illegal.**

illness, *n.* See **disease.**

illuminate, *v.* SYN.—brighten, clarify, elucidate, enlighten, illumine, illustrate, irradiate. ANT.—complicate, confuse, darken, obfuscate, obscure.

illusion, *n.* SYN.—delusion, dream, fantasy, hallucination, mirage, phantom, vision. ANT.—actuality, reality, substance.

FLAGS FROM WORLD HISTORY

CHARLEMAGNE

WILLIAM I (THE CONQUEROR) OF ENGLAND

PEASANTS' WAR (16TH-CENTURY GERMANY)

PETER I (THE GREAT) OF RUSSIA

HUDSON'S BAY COMPANY

JOSÉ DE SAN MARTIN

CHINA UNDER THE CH'ING DYNASTY
(19TH-CENTURY)

FLAG PROPOSED BY CECIL RHODES
FOR BRITISH AFRICA

FLAGS FROM AMERICAN HISTORY

VIKINGS

CHRISTOPHER COLUMBUS

HENRY HUDSON

BRITISH EXPLORERS AND SETTLERS
(FIRST UNION JACK)

FRENCH EXPLORERS AND SETTLERS
(17TH AND 18TH CENTURIES)

CONTINENTAL COLORS (1776)

FIRST STARS AND STRIPES (1777-95)

ESEK HOPKINS, FIRST COMMANDER IN
CHIEF OF THE CONTINENTAL NAVY

FIRST STAR-SPANGLED BANNER (1795-1818)

OLIVER HAZARD PERRY
(WAR OF 1812)

BEAR FLAG REPUBLIC (1846)

STARS AND BARS OF THE
CONFEDERACY (1861-63)

FORT SUMTER FLAG (1861)

FLAGS OF AFRICA

ALGERIA

ANGOLA

BENIN

BOTSWANA

BURUNDI

CAMEROON

CAPE VERDE

CENTRAL AFRICAN REPUBLIC

CHAD

COMOROS

CONGO

DJIBOUTI

EGYPT

EQUATORIAL GUINEA

ETHIOPIA

GABON

GAMBIA

GHANA

GUINEA

GUINEA-BISSAU

IVORY COAST

FLAGS OF AFRICA (continued)

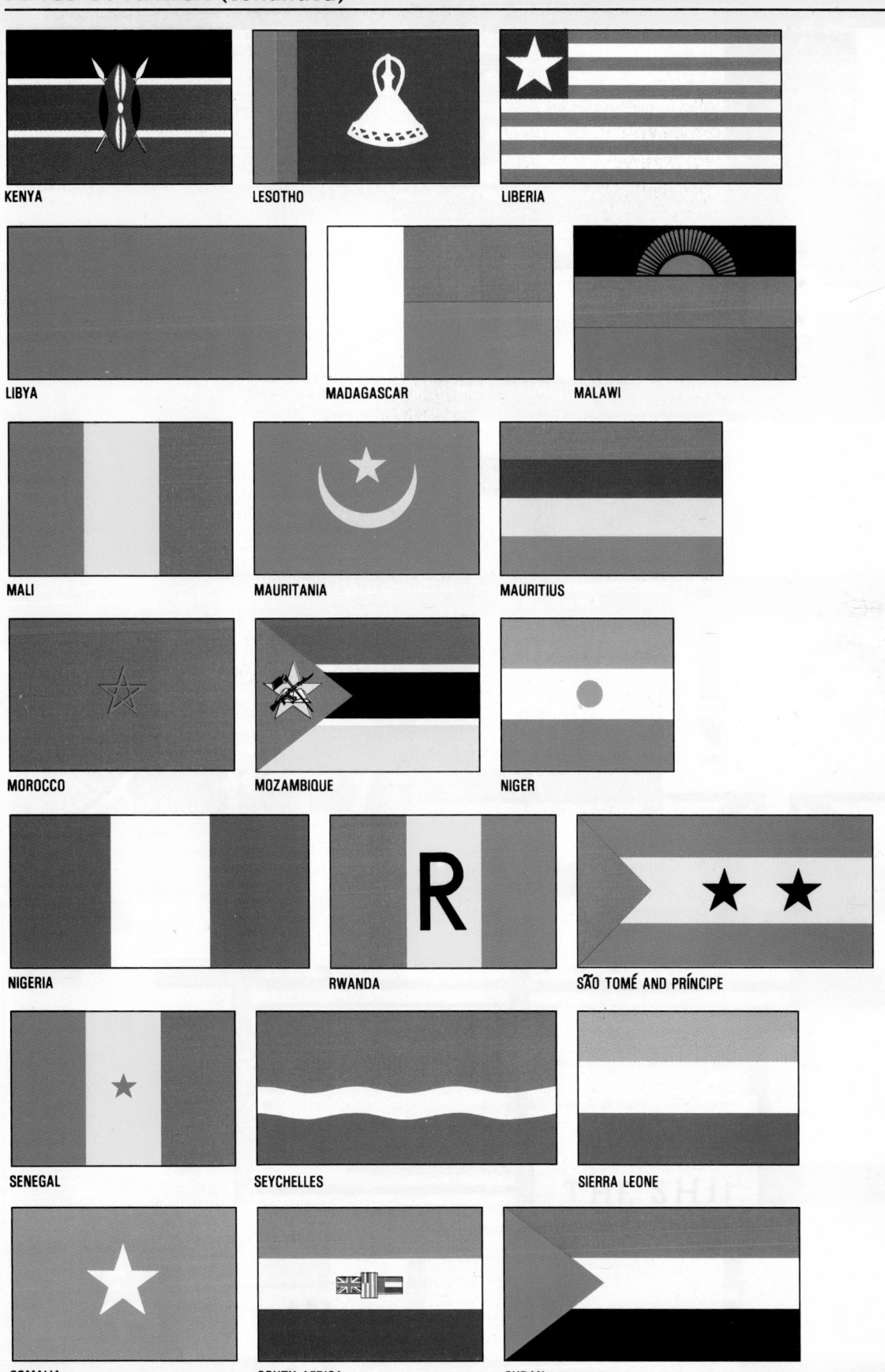

KENYA

LESOTHO

LIBERIA

LIBYA

MADAGASCAR

MALAWI

MALI

MAURITANIA

MAURITIUS

MOROCCO

MOZAMBIQUE

NIGER

NIGERIA

RWANDA

SÃO TOMÉ AND PRÍNCIPE

SENEGAL

SEYCHELLES

SIERRA LEONE

SOMALIA

SOUTH AFRICA

SUDAN

FLAGS OF AFRICA (continued)

SWAZILAND

TANZANIA

TOGO

TUNISIA

UGANDA

UPPER VOLTA

ZAIRE

ZAMBIA

ZIMBABWE

FLAGS OF ASIA

AFGHANISTAN

BAHRAIN

BANGLADESH

BHUTAN

BRUNEI

BURMA

CHINA, PEOPLE'S REPUBLIC OF

CHINA, REPUBLIC OF (TAIWAN)

CYPRUS

INDIA

INDONESIA

IRAN

FLAGS OF ASIA (continued)

IRAQ

ISRAEL

JAPAN

JORDAN

KAMPUCHEA

KOREA, NORTH

KOREA, SOUTH

KUWAIT

LAOS

LEBANON

MALAYSIA

MALDIVES

MONGOLIA

NEPAL

OMAN

PAKISTAN

PHILIPPINES

QATAR

SAUDI ARABIA

FLAGS OF ASIA (continued)

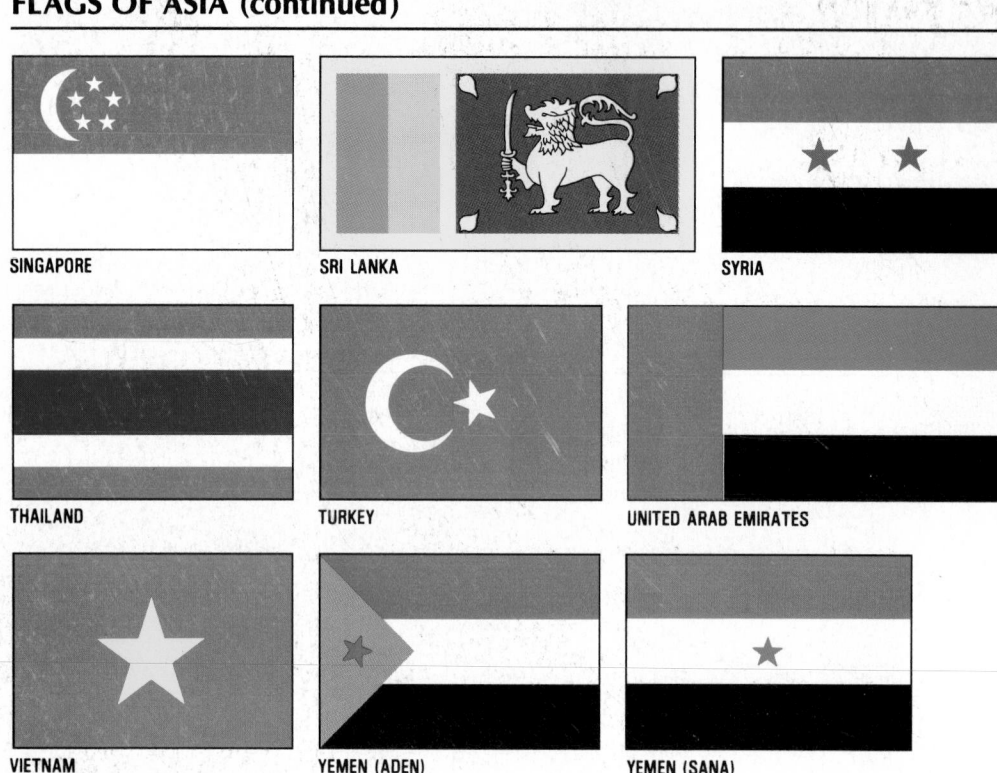

SINGAPORE

SRI LANKA

SYRIA

THAILAND

TURKEY

UNITED ARAB EMIRATES

VIETNAM

YEMEN (ADEN)

YEMEN (SANA)

FLAGS OF EUROPE

ALBANIA

ANDORRA

AUSTRIA

BELGIUM

BULGARIA

CZECHOSLOVAKIA

DENMARK

FINLAND

FRANCE

GERMAN DEM. REP. (EAST)

GERMANY, FED. REP. OF (WEST)

GREECE

HUNGARY

FLAGS OF EUROPE (continued)

ICELAND

IRELAND

ITALY

LIECHTENSTEIN

LUXEMBOURG

MALTA

MONACO

NETHERLANDS

NORWAY

POLAND

PORTUGAL

ROMANIA

SAN MARINO

SPAIN

SWEDEN

SWITZERLAND

UNION OF SOVIET SOCIALIST REPUBLICS

UNITED KINGDOM

VATICAN CITY

YUGOSLAVIA

FLAGS OF NORTH AMERICA

CANADA

MEXICO

UNITED STATES

FLAGS OF THE CARIBBEAN

ANTIGUA AND BARBUDA

BAHAMAS

BARBADOS

CUBA

DOMINICA

DOMINICAN REPUBLIC

GRENADA

HAITI

JAMAICA

SAINT KITTS-NEVIS

SAINT LUCIA

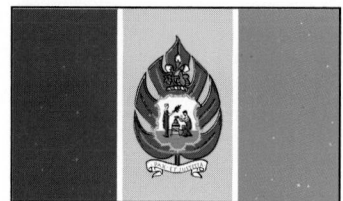

SAINT VINCENT AND THE GRENADINES

TRINIDAD AND TOBAGO

FLAGS OF CENTRAL AMERICA

BELIZE

COSTA RICA

EL SALVADOR

GUATEMALA

HONDURAS

NICARAGUA

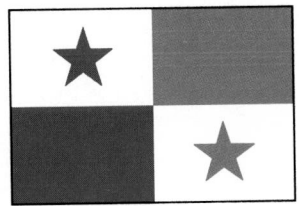
PANAMA

FLAGS OF SOUTH AMERICA

ARGENTINA

BOLIVIA

BRAZIL

CHILE

COLOMBIA

ECUADOR

GUYANA

PARAGUAY

PERU

SURINAME

URUGUAY

VENEZUELA

FLAGS OF OCEANIA

AUSTRALIA

FIJI

KIRIBATI

NAURU

NEW ZEALAND

PAPUA NEW GUINEA

SOLOMON ISLANDS

TONGA

TUVALU

VANUATU

WESTERN SAMOA

FLAGS OF AUSTRALIA

NEW SOUTH WALES

NORFOLK ISLAND

NORTHERN TERRITORY

QUEENSLAND

SOUTH AUSTRALIA

TASMANIA

VICTORIA

WESTERN AUSTRALIA

FLAGS OF CANADA

ALBERTA

BRITISH COLUMBIA

MANITOBA

NEW BRUNSWICK

NEWFOUNDLAND

NORTHWEST TERRITORIES

NOVA SCOTIA

ONTARIO

PRINCE EDWARD ISLAND

QUEBEC

SASKATCHEWAN

YUKON TERRITORY

FLAGS OF THE UNITED STATES

ALABAMA

ALASKA

ARIZONA

ARKANSAS

CALIFORNIA

COLORADO

CONNECTICUT

DELAWARE

DISTRICT OF COLUMBIA

FLORIDA

GEORGIA

HAWAII

IDAHO

ILLINOIS

INDIANA

IOWA

KANSAS

KENTUCKY

LOUISIANA

MAINE

MARYLAND

MASSACHUSETTS

MICHIGAN

MINNESOTA

MISSISSIPPI

MISSOURI

MONTANA

FLAGS OF THE UNITED STATES (continued)

NEBRASKA

NEVADA

NEW HAMPSHIRE

NEW JERSEY

NEW MEXICO

NEW YORK

NORTH CAROLINA

NORTH DAKOTA

OHIO

OKLAHOMA

OREGON

PENNSYLVANIA

RHODE ISLAND

SOUTH CAROLINA

SOUTH DAKOTA

TENNESSEE

TEXAS

UTAH

VERMONT

VIRGINIA

WASHINGTON

WEST VIRGINIA

WISCONSIN

WYOMING

FLAGS OF THE U.S. GOVERNMENT

PRESIDENT

VICE-PRESIDENT

SECRETARY OF STATE

DEPT. OF THE TREASURY

SECRETARY OF DEFENSE

ATTORNEY GENERAL

DEPT. OF THE INTERIOR

DEPT. OF AGRICULTURE

SECRETARY OF COMMERCE

DEPT. OF LABOR

DEPT. OF TRANSPORTATION

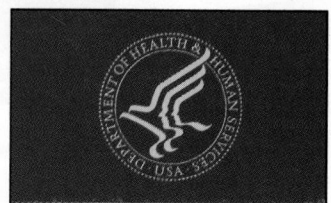

DEPT. OF HEALTH AND
HUMAN SERVICES

DEPT. OF HOUSING AND
URBAN DEVELOPMENT

DEPT. OF ENERGY

DEPT. OF EDUCATION

U.S. ARMY

U.S. MARINE CORPS

U.S. NAVY

U.S. AIR FORCE

U.S. COAST GUARD

JACK OF U.S. WARSHIPS

FLAGS OF UNITED STATES TERRITORIES

AMERICAN SAMOA

PALAU (BELAU)

GUAM

NORTHERN MARIANAS

MARSHALL ISLANDS

FEDERATED STATES OF MICRONESIA

PUERTO RICO

U.S. VIRGIN ISLANDS

FLAGS OF INTERNATIONAL ORGANIZATIONS

UNITED NATIONS

RED CROSS

RED CRESCENT

RED MAGEN DAVID

OLYMPICS

NATO

ORG. OF AMERICAN STATES

COMECON

ORG. OF AFRICAN UNITY

ARAB LEAGUE

INTERNATIONAL CODE FLAGS

INTERNATIONAL CODE PENNANTS

Code pennants and repeater pennants are used for signaling messages.

CODE PENNANT   1st REPEATER   2d REPEATER   3d REPEATER

WEATHER BUREAU FLAGS

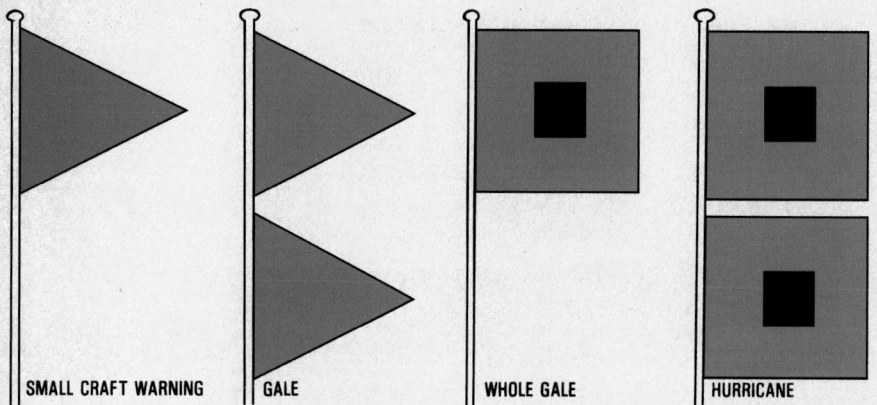

SMALL CRAFT WARNING   GALE   WHOLE GALE   HURRICANE

MONOCHROMATIC MESSAGE FLAGS

DEATH   DANGER   QUARANTINE   PROCEED   TRUCE   DISTRESS illusive, a. See deceptive.

illustration, n. See picture.

illustrious, a. See great.

imagination, n. SYN.—conception, creation, fancy, fantasy, idea, invention, notion.

imaginative, a. SYN.—clever, creative, fanciful, inventive, mystical, poetical, visionary. ANT.—dull, literal, prosaic, unromantic.

imagine, v. SYN.—conceive, dream, fancy, picture, pretend; assume, believe, conjecture, guess, opine, suppose, surmise, think.

imbecile, n. See fool.

imbibe, v. See absorb.

imitate, v. SYN.—ape, copy, counterfeit, duplicate, impersonate, mimic, mock, simulate. ANT.—alter, distort, diverge, invent.

imitation, n. See copy.

immature, a. See youthful.

immeasurable, a. See infinite.

immediately, adv. SYN.—directly, forthwith, instantaneously, instantly, now, presently, promptly, straightaway. ANT.—distantly, hereafter, later, shortly, sometime.

immense, a. See enormous.

immerse, v. SYN.—dip, douse, dunk, plunge, sink, submerge; absorb, engage, engross. ANT.—elevate, recover, uplift.

immigration, n. SYN.—colonization, settlement. ANT.—emigration, exodus.

imminent, a. See impending.

immoderation, n. See excess.

immoral, a. SYN.—anti-social, bad, corrupt, dissolute, indecent, licentious, profligate, sinful, unprincipled, vicious, wicked. ANT.—chaste, high-minded, noble, pure, virtuous.

immortal, a. See eternal.

immune, a. See free.

immutable, a. See constant.

impair, v. See damage.

impart, v. See communicate.

impartial, a. See fair.

impartiality, n. See indifference.

impede, v. SYN.—bar, block, check, clog, delay, encumber, frustrate, hamper, hinder, interrupt, obstruct, restrain, retard, stop, thwart. ANT.—advance, assist, further, help, promote.

impediment, n. See obstacle.

impel, v. See compel.

impending, a. SYN.—approaching, imminent, menacing, nigh, overhanging, threatening. ANT.—afar, distant, improbable, remote, retreating.

impenetrable, a. See hard.

imperative, a. See urgent.

imperceptible, a. See invisible.

imperfection, n. See fault.

impersonate, v. See imitate.

impertinence, n. See impudence.

impertinent, a. See insolent.

impetuous, a. See impulsive.

implicate, v. See blame.

implore, v. See beg, plead.

imply, v. SYN.—connote, insinuate, involve, mean, signify, suggest. ANT.—assert, express, state.

impolite, a. See rude.

import, n. See weight.

important, a. SYN.—consequential, critical, decisive, grave, influential, material, momentous, pressing, prominent, relevant, significant, weighty. ANT.—insignificant, irrelevant, mean, petty, trivial.

imposing, a. See majestic.

impression, n. See feeling.

impressive, a. SYN.—affecting, arresting, august, commanding, exciting, forcible, grandiose, imposing, majestic, moving, overpowering, remarkable, splendid, stirring, striking, thrilling, touching. ANT.—commonplace, ordinary, regular, unimpressive.

improve, v. SYN.—ameliorate, amend, better, help, rectify, reform. ANT.—corrupt, damage, debase, impair, vitiate.

improvement, n. See progress.

imprudent, a. See careless.

impudence, n. SYN.—assurance, audacity, boldness, effrontery, impertinence, insolence, presumption, rudeness, sauciness. ANT.—diffidence, politeness, subserviency, truckling.

impudent, a. See bold.

impulsive, a. SYN.—careless, hasty, heedless, impetuous, passionate, quick, rash. ANT.—calculating, cautious, reasoning.

impure, a. See corrupt.

inability, n. SYN.—disability, handicap, impotence, incapacity, incompetence, weakness. ANT.—ability, capability, power, strength.

inaccurate, a. See wrong.

inactive, a. See idle.

inadequate, a. See deficient.

inanimate, a. See dead.

inattentive, a. See absent.

incapacity, n. See inability.

inception, n. See beginning.

incessant, a. See continual.

incident, n. See circumstance.

incinerate, v. See burn.

incisive, a. See terse.

incite, v. SYN.—arouse, cause, encourage, foment, goad, induce, instigate, provoke, stimulate, urge. ANT.—bore, pacify, quiet, soothe.

inclination, n. SYN.—bending, incline, leaning, slope; affection, attachment, bent, bias, desire, disposition, penchant, predilection, preference. ANT.—apathy, aversion, distaste, nonchalance, repugnance.

include, v. See contain.

incongruous, a. See inconsistent.

inconsistency, n. See conflict.

inconsistent, a. SYN.—contradictory, contrary, discrepant, illogical, incompatible, incongruous, irreconcilable, paradoxical, unsteady, vacillating, wavering. ANT.—compatible, congruous, consistent, correspondent.

inconstant, a. See variable.

increase, v. SYN.—accrue, amplify, augment, enhance, enlarge, expand, extend, grow, heighten, intensify, magnify, multiply, raise, wax. ANT.—atrophy, contract, decrease, diminish, reduce.

indebted, a. See grateful.

indecent, a. See obscene.

independence, n. See freedom, liberty.

independent, a. SYN.—autonomous, free, self-reliant, uncontrolled, unrestrained, unrestricted, voluntary. ANT.—contingent, dependent, enslaved, restricted.

indestructible, a. See permanent.

indicate, v. SYN.—denote, designate, disclose, imply, intimate, manifest, reveal, show, signify, specify. ANT.—conceal, distract, divert, falsify, mislead.

indication, n. See sign.

indictment, n. See accusation.

indifference, n. SYN.—apathy, disinterestedness, impartiality, insensibility, neutrality, unconcern. ANT.—affection, ardor, fervor, passion.

indigence, n. See poverty.

indigenous, a. See native.

indigent, a. See needy.

indignation, n. See anger.

indignity, n. See insult.

indirect, a. See devious.

indiscretion, a. See folly.

indispensable, a. See essential.

indistinct, a. See obscure.

individual, a. SYN.—distinctive, marked, particular, separate, singular, special, specific, unique. ANT.—common, general, ordinary, universal.

individuality, n. See character.

indomitable, a. See invincible.

induce, v. See cause.

inducement, n. See motive.

indurate, a. See callous.

industrious, a. See diligent.

inebriated, a. See intoxicated.

ineffective, a. See weak.

inequity, n. See injustice.

inevitable, a. See certain.

inexpensive, a. See cheap.

inexplicable, a. See mysterious.

infect, v. See contaminate.

infection, n. SYN.—contagion, germ, pest, virus; ailment, contamination, disease, poison, pollution, taint.

infectious, a. See contagious.

inference, n. SYN.—conclusion, consequence, corollary, deduction, judgment, result. ANT.—assumption, foreknowledge, preconception, presupposition.

inferior, a. SYN.—lower, minor, poorer, secondary, subordinate. ANT.—better, greater, higher, superior.

infinite, a. SYN.—boundless, endless, eternal, illimitable, immeasurable, immense, interminable, unbounded, unlimited, vast. ANT.—bounded, circumscribed, confined, finite, limited.

infirm, a. See feeble.

infirmity, n. See disease.

inflexible, a. See obstinate.

influenced, v. SYN.—actuate, affect, bias, control, impel, incite, stir, sway.

influential, a. See important.

inform, v. SYN.—acquaint, advise, apprise, enlighten, impart, instruct, notify, teach, tell, warn. ANT.—conceal, delude, distract, mislead.

informal, a. SYN.—easy, familiar, natural, simple, unofficial. ANT.—distant, formal, proper, reserved.

informality, n. See familiarity.

infrequent, a. See rare.

ingenious, a. See clever.

ingenuity, n. SYN.—aptitude, cleverness, cunning, faculty, ingeniousness, inventiveness, resourcefulness, skill. ANT.—clumsiness, dullness, ineptitude, stupidity.

ingenuous, a. See candid.

inhabit, v. See occupy.

inherent, a. See intrinsic.

inhibit, v. See restrain.

inhuman, a. See cruel.

iniquitous, a. See bad.

iniquity, n. See injustice.

initial, a. See first.

initiate, v. See begin.

injure, v. SYN.—damage, disfigure, harm,

hurt, impair, mar, spoil, wound; abuse, affront, dishonor, insult, wrong. ANT.—ameliorate, benefit, help, preserve; compliment, praise.

injurious, *a.* See **detrimental.**

injury, *n.* SYN.—damage, detriment, harm, mischief; grievance, injustice, prejudice, wrong. ANT.—benefit, improvement, repair.

injustice, *n.* SYN.—grievance, iniquity, injury, unfairness, wrong. ANT.—equity, justice, lawfulness, righteousness.

innate, *a.* See **intrinsic.**

innocent, *a.* SYN.—blameless, faultless, innocuous, lawful, naive, pure, sinless, virtuous. ANT.—corrupt, culpable, guilty, sinful, unrighteous.

innocuous, *a.* See **innocent.**

inquire, *v.* See **ask, demand.**

inquiring, *a.* See **curious.**

inquiry, *n.* SYN.—examination, exploration, interrogation, investigation, query, quest, question, research, scrutiny. ANT.—disregard, inactivity, inattention, negligence.

inquisitive, *a.* See **curious.**

insane, *a.* See **crazy.**

insanity, *n.* SYN.—aberration, craziness, delirium, dementia, derangement, frenzy, lunacy, madness, mania, psychosis. ANT.—rationality, sanity, stability.

insensitive, *a.* See **callous.**

insight, *n.* SYN.—acumen, discernment, intuition, penetration, perspicuity. ANT.—obtuseness.

insignificant, *a.* See **trivial.**

insinuate, *v.* See **imply.**

insipid, *a.* See **flat.**

insolence, *n.* See **impudence.**

insolent, *a.* SYN.—abusive, arrogant, brazen, contemptuous, impertinent, impudent, insulting, offensive, rude. ANT.—considerate, courteous, polite, respectful.

inspect, *v.* See **look.**

inspection, *n.* See **review.**

inspiration, *n.* See **genius.**

instantaneous, *a.* See **sudden.**

instantly, *adv.* See **immediately.**

instinctive, *a.* See **spontaneous.**

institute, *v.* See **establish.**

instruct, *n.* See **teach.**

instruction, *n.* See **advice.**

instrument, *n.* SYN.—agent, apparatus, channel, device, means, medium, tool, utensil, vehicle. ANT.—hindrance, impediment, obstruction, preventive.

insubordinate, *a.* See **disobedient.**

insulation, *n.* See **isolation.**

insult, *n.* SYN.—abuse, affront, indignity, insolence, offense. ANT.—apology, homage, salutation

insult, *v.* See **injure.**

insufficient, *a.* See **short.**

integrity, *n.* See **honesty.**

intellect, *n.* SYN.—ability, intelligence, mind, reason, sense, understanding. ANT.—emotion, feeling, passion.

intelligence, *n.* See **intellect.**

intelligent, *a.* SYN.—alert, astute, bright, clever, discerning, quick, smart; enlightened, intellectual, knowledgeable, well-informed. ANT.—dull, foolish, insipid, obtuse, slow, stupid.

intend, *v.* See **plan.**

intense, *a.* See **vivid.**

intensify, *v.* See **increase.**

intent, *n.* See **design.**

intention, *n.* See **design.**

intentional, *a.* SYN.—contemplated, deliberate, designed, intended, premeditated, studied, voluntary, wilful. ANT.—accidental, fortuitous.

interfere, *v.* See **meddle.**

interior, *a.* SYN.—inmost, inner, internal, inward. ANT.—adjacent, exterior, external, outer.

interject, *v.* See **interpose.**

interminable, *a.* See **infinite.**

interpose, *v.* SYN.—inject, insert, interject, introduce, intrude; arbitrate, intercede, interfere, intervene, meddle, mediate. ANT.—avoid, disregard, overlook.

interpret, *v.* SYN.—construe, decipher, decode, elucidate, explain, explicate, render, solve, translate, unravel. ANT.—confuse, distort, falsify, misconstrue, misinterpret.

interrogate, *v.* See **examine, question.**

interrupt, *v.* See **suspend.**

intervene, *v.* See **interpose.**

intimacy, *n.* See **familiarity.**

intimate, *a.* SYN.—affectionate, chummy, close, confidential, familiar, friendly, loving, near. ANT.—ceremonious, conventional, distant, formal.

intimation, *n.* See **hint.**

intolerant, *a.* See **bigoted.**

intoxicated, *a.* SYN.—drunk, drunken, high, inebriated, tight, tipsy. ANT.—clearheaded, sober, temperate.

intricate, *a.* See **complex.**

intrigue, *n.* See **plot.**

intrinsic, *a.* SYN.—congenital, inborn, inbred, inherent, innate, native, natural, real. ANT.—acquired, external, extraneous, extrinsic.

introduction, *n.* SYN.—beginning, forward, overture, preamble, preface, prelude, prologue, start. ANT.—completion, conclusion, end, epilogue, finale.

intrude, *v.* See **invade.**

intuition, *n.* See **insight.**

invade, *v.* SYN.—attack, encroach, infringe, intrude, penetrate, trespass, violate. ANT.—abandon, evacuate, relinquish, vacate.

invasion, *n.* See **attack.**

invective, *n.* See **abuse.**

invent, *v.* SYN.—conceive, concoct, contrive, design, devise, fabricate, frame. ANT.—copy, imitate, reproduce.

inventive, *a.* See **imaginative.**

inventiveness, *n.* See **ingenuity.**

invert, *v.* See **reverse.**

investigate, *v.* See **search.**

investigation, *n.* See **inquiry.**

invincible, *a.* SYN.—impregnable, indomitable, insurmountable, invulnerable, unassailable, unconquerable. ANT.—powerless, puny, vulnerable, weak.

invisible, *a.* SYN.—imperceptible, indistinguishable, undiscernible, unseen. ANT.—evident, perceptible, seen, visible.

involve, *v.* SYN.—embrace, embroil, entangle, envelop, implicate, include, incriminate. ANT.—disconnect, disengage, extricate, separate.

involved, *a.* See **complex.**

invulnerable, *a.* See **invisible.**

ire, *n.* See **anger.**

irk, *v.* See **annoy.**

irrational, *a.* See **absurd.**

irregular, *a.* SYN.—aberrant, abnormal, capricious, devious, eccentric, unnatural, unusual, variable. ANT.—fixed, methodical, ordinary, regular, usual.

irrelevant, *a.* See **alien.**

irresolute, *a.* See **weak.**

irritable, *a.* SYN.—choleric, excitable, fiery, hasty, hot, irascible, peevish, petulant, snappish, testy, touchy. ANT.—agreeable, calm, composed, tranquil.

irritate, *v.* See **annoy, worry.**

irritation, *n.* See **vexation.**

isolated, *a.* See **alone.**

isolation, *n.* SYN.—alienation, insulation, loneliness, quarantine, retirement, seclusion, segregation, separation, solitude, withdrawal. ANT.—association, communion, connection, fellowship, union.

issue, *v.* See **flow.**

J

jargon, *n.* See **language.**

jealousy, *n.* SYN.—covetousness, envy, invidiousness, resentfulness, suspicion. ANT.—geniality, indifference, liberality, tolerance.

jeer, *v.* See **sneer.**

jeering, *n.* See **ridicule.**

jeopardize, *v.* See **hazard.**

jester, *n.* See **fool.**

job, *n.* SYN.—chore, labor, stint, task, toil, work, undertaking; business, employment, occupation, position, post, situation.

join, *v.* SYN.—accompany, adjoin, associate, attach, combine, conjoin, connect, couple, go with, link, unite. ANT.—detach, disconnect, disjoin, separate.

jolly, *a.* See **cheerful.**

jolt, *v.* See **shake.**

journey, *n.* SYN.—cruise, expedition, jaunt, passage, pilgrimage, tour, travel, trip, voyage.

journey, *v.* See **travel.**

joy, *n.* SYN.—bliss, delight, ecstasy, felicity, happiness, pleasure, rapture, transport; elation, exultation, festivity, glee, merriment, mirth. ANT.—affliction, depression, despair, grief, sorrow.

joyful, *a.* See **happy.**

joyous, *a.* See **merry.**

judge, *n.* SYN.—adjudicator, arbitrator, critic, justice, magistrate, referee, umpire.

judge, *v.* SYN.—decide, decree, determine; adjudicate, arbitrate, condemn, try, umpire; appreciate, consider, estimate, evaluate, measure, think.

judgment, *n.* SYN.—discernment, discrimination, intelligence, perspicacity, sagacity, understanding, wisdom. ANT.—arbitrariness, senselessness, stupidity, thoughtlessness.

jumble, *n.* See **confusion.**

jumble, *v.* See **mix.**

jump, *v.* SYN.—bound, caper, hop, jerk, leap, skip, spring, start, vault.

just, *a.* See **honest.**

justice, *n.* SYN.—equity, fairness, impartiality, justness, law, rectitude, right. ANT.—inequity, partiality, unfairness, wrong.

justifiable, *a.* See **admissible.**

justify, *v.* See **vindicate.**

K

keen, *a.* See **quick, sharp.**

keep, *v.* SYN.—conserve, continue, maintain, preserve, save; confine, detain, hold, reserve, restrain, retain; execute, obey; celebrate, commemorate, honor, observe; guard, protect; support, sustain. ANT.—discard, reject; dismiss, relinquish; disobey, ignore; abandon, forsake, neglect.

kill, *v.* SYN.—assassinate, butcher, execute, massacre, murder, put to death, slaughter, slay. ANT.—animate, protect, resuscitate, save, vivify.

kind, *a.* SYN.—affable, benevolent, benign, compassionate, forbearing, gentle, good, humane, indulgent, kindly, merciful, sympathetic, tender, thoughtful. ANT.—cruel, inhuman, merciless, severe, unkind.

kind, *n.* SYN.—breed, character, family, genus, race, sort, species, stock, strain, type, variety.

kindred, *n.* SYN.—affinity, consanguinity, family, kinsfolk, relations, relationship, relatives. ANT.—disconnection, foreigners, strangers.

kiss, *v.* See **caress.**

knack, *n.* See **skill, talent.**

know, *v.* SYN.—apprehend, ascertain, cognize, comprehend, discern, distinguish, perceive, recognize, understand. ANT.—dispute, doubt, ignore, suspect.

knowledge, *n.* SYN.—apprehension, cognizance, erudition, information, learning, lore, scholarship, science, understanding, wisdom. ANT.—ignorance, illiteracy, misunderstanding, stupidity.

L

labor, *n.* SYN.—drudgery, effort, endeavor, exertion, striving, task, toil, travail, work; childbirth, parturition. ANT.—idleness, indolence, leisure, recreation.

lacking, *a.* See **deficient.**

lame, *a.* SYN.—crippled, defective, deformed, disabled, feeble, halt, hobbling, limping, maimed, unconvincing, unsatisfactory, weak. ANT.—agile, athletic, robust, sound, vigorous.

lament, *v.* SYN.—bemoan, bewail, deplore, grieve, mourn, repine, wail, weep.

lamp, *n.* See **light.**

land, *n.* SYN.—continent, country, earth, field, ground, island, plain, region, soil, tract; domain, estate, farm, realm.

language, *n.* SYN.—cant, dialect, diction, idiom, jargon, lingo, phraseology, slang, speech, tongue, vernacular. ANT.—babble, drivel, gibberish, nonsense.

languish, *v.* See **wither.**

larceny, *n.* See **robbery.**

large, *a.* SYN.—ample, big, capacious, colossal, extensive, great, huge, immense, vast, wide. ANT.—little, mean, short, small, tiny.

last, *a.* SYN.—concluding, extreme, final, hindmost, latest, terminal, ultimate, utmost. ANT.—beginning, first, foremost, initial, opening.

late, *a.* SYN.—delayed, overdue, slow, tardy; advanced, new, recent. ANT.—early, timely.

latent, *a.* SYN.—concealed, dormant, hidden, inactive, potential, quiescent, secret, undeveloped, unseen. ANT.—conspicuous, evident, explicit, manifest, visible.

laugh, *n.* SYN.—cackle, chuckle, giggle, guffaw, jeer, mock, roar, scoff, snicker, titter.

lavish, *v.* See **waste.**

law, *n.* See **act.**

lawful, *a.* SYN.—allowable, authorized, constitutional, legal, legitimate, permissible, rightful. ANT.—criminal, illegal, illegitimate, illicit, prohibited.

lay, *a.* See **secular.**

lay, *v.* See **place.**

lax, *a.* See **careless.**

lazy, *a.* SYN.—idle, inactive, indolent, inert, slothful, sluggish, supine, torpid. ANT.—active, alert, assiduous, diligent.

lead, *v.* See **conduct.**

leader, *n.* See **chief, head.**

league, *n.* See **alliance.**

lean, *v.* SYN.—bend, incline, sag, slant, slope, tend; depend, rely, trust. ANT.—erect, raise, rise, straighten.

leaning, *n.* See **tendency.**

leap, *v.* See **jump.**

learned, *a.* See **wise.**

learning, *n.* See **knowledge.**

leave, *v.* SYN.—abandon, depart, desert, forsake, give up, go, quit, relinquish, renounce, retire, withdraw. ANT.—abide, remain, stay, tarry.

lecture, *v.* See **talk.**

legal, *a.* See **lawful.**

legend, *n.* SYN.—allegory, chronicle, fable, fiction, myth, parable, saga. ANT.—fact, history.

legitimate, *a.* See **genuine.**

leisure, *n.* See **rest.**

leisurely, *a.* See **slow.**

lengthen, *v.* See **draw.**

leniency, *n.* See **mercy.**

lenient, *a.* See **merciful.**

lessen, *v.* See **decrease.**

lethargy, *n.* See **stupor.**

letter, *n.* See **note.**

level, *a.* See **flat.**

levy, *n.* See **tax.**

lewd, *a.* See **obscene.**

liable, *a.* SYN.—accountable, amenable, answerable, exposed to, responsible, subject to. ANT.—exempt, free, immune, independent.

libel, *n.* See **slander.**

liberal, *a.* See **broad.**

liberate, *v.* SYN.—deliver, discharge, emancipate, free, let go, release, set free. ANT.—confine, imprison, oppress, restrict, subjugate.

liberated, *a.* See **free.**

liberty, *n.* SYN.—autonomy, freedom, independence, self-government; license, permission, privilege. ANT.—captivity, imprisonment, submission; constraint.

license, *n.* See **freedom, privilege.**

lie, *n.* SYN.—delusion, equivocation, falsehood, fib, fiction, illusion, untruth. ANT.—axiom, canon, fact, truism.

life, *n.* SYN.—animation, being, buoyancy, existence, liveliness, spirit, vigor, vitality, vivacity. ANT.—death, demise, dullness, languor, lethargy.

lifeless, *a.* See **dead.**

lift, *v.* See **raise.**

light, *a.* See **buoyant.**

light, *n.* SYN.—beam, brightness, dawn, flame, gleam, illumination, incandescence, lamp, luminosity, radiance, shine; enlightenment, insight, knowledge, understanding. ANT.—darkness, gloom, obscurity, shadow.

like, *a.* See **identical.**

likeness, *n.* See **similarity.**

limit, *n.* SYN.—border, bound, boundary, confine, edge, extent, limitation, restraint, restriction, terminus. ANT.—boundlessness, endlessness, extension, infinity, vastness.

limpid, *a.* See **clear.**

lineage, *n.* See **race.**

linger, *v.* See **wait.**

link, *n.* SYN.—bond, connection, connective, coupler, juncture, tie, union. ANT.—break, gap, interval, opening, split.

link, *v.* See **join.**

liquid, *a.* SYN.—flowing, fluent, fluid, juicy, watery. ANT.—congealed, gaseous, solid.

listen, *v.* SYN.—attend to, hear, hearken, heed, list, overhear. ANT.—be deaf to, disregard, ignore, reject, scorn.

little, *a.* See **small.**

lively, *a.* SYN.—active, animated, blithe, brisk, energetic, frolicsome, spirited, sprightly, supple, vigorous, vivacious; bright, clear, fresh, glowing, vivid. ANT.—dull, insipid, listless, stale, vapid.

load, *v.* See **burden.**

loathe, *v.* See **hate.**

loathsome, *a.* See **abominable.**

locality, *n.* See **neighborhood.**

location, *n.* SYN.—area, locale, locality, place, region, site, situation, spot, station, vicinity.

lock, *n.* SYN.—bar, bolt, clasp, fastening, hook, latch, padlock; curl, ringlet, tress, tuft.

lofty, *a.* See **majestic.**

logical, *a.* See **valid.**

lone, *a.* See **alone.**

loneliness, *n.* See **solitude.**

lonely, *a.* See **alone.**

long, *a.* SYN.—drawn out, elongated, extended, lasting, lengthy, lingering, prolix, prolonged, protracted, tedious, wordy. ANT.—abridged, brief, concise, short, terse.

look, *v.* SYN.—behold, discern, eye, gaze, glance, scan, see, stare, survey, view, watch, witness; appear, seem; examine, inspect, observe, regard. ANT.—avert, hide, miss, overlook.

loose, *a.* SYN.—disengaged, free, indefinite, lax, limp, slack, unbound, unfastened, untied, vague; careless, dissolute, heedless, unrestrained, wanton. ANT.—fast, tied, tight; inhibited, restrained.

lost, *a.* SYN.—adrift, astray, missing; consumed, destroyed, forefeited, misspent, used, wasted; absorbed, bewildered, confused, dazed, distracted, perplexed, preoccupied. ANT.—anchored, found, located.

lot, *n.* See **fate.**

loud, *a.* SYN.—clamorous, deafening, noisy, resounding, sonorous, stentorian, vociferous. ANT.—dulcet, inaudible, quiet, soft, subdued.

love, *n.* SYN.—adoration, affection, attachment, devotion, endearment, fondness. ANT.—aversion, dislike, enmity, hatred, indifference.

loveliness, *n.* See **beauty.**

lovely, *a.* See **beautiful.**

loving, *a.* See **intimate.**

low, *a.* See **base.**

lower, *a.* See **inferior.**

lower, *v.* See **debase.**

loyal, *a.* See **devoted.**

loyalty, *n.* SYN.—allegiance, constancy, devotion, faithfulness, fealty, fidelity. ANT.—disloyalty, falseness, perfidy, treachery.

lucid, *a.* See **clear.**

lucky, *a.* See **fortunate.**

luminous, *a.* See **bright.**

lunacy, *n.* See **insanity.**

lure, *v.* See **draw.**

luscious, *a.* See **delicious.**

lust, *n.* See **desire.**

luster, *n.* See **radiance.**

lustful, a. See carnal.
lusty, a. See masculine.
luxuriant, a. See rich.
luxurious, a. See plentiful.
luxury, n. See wealth.

M

mad, a. SYN.—angry, enraged, exasperated, furious, incensed, provoked, wrathful; crazy, delirious, demented, insane, lunatic, maniacal. ANT.—calm, happy, pleased; healthy, sane, sensible.

madness, n. See insanity.

magic, n. SYN.—black art, charm, conjuring, enchantment, legerdemain, necromancy, sorcery, voodoo, witchcraft, wizardry.

magnanimous, a. See generous.

magnify, v. See exaggerate, increase.

magnitude, n. See size.

main, a. See principal.

maintain, v. SYN.—continue, keep, preserve, support, sustain, uphold; affirm, allege, assert, claim, contend, declare; defend, justify, vindicate. ANT.—discontinue, neglect; deny, oppose, resist.

majestic, a. SYN.—august, dignified, grand, grandiose, high, imposing, lofty, magnificent, noble, pompous, stately, sublime. ANT.—common, humble, lowly, ordinary, undignified.

make, v. SYN.—assemble, build, cause, compel, construct, create, establish, execute, fashion, form, gain, manufacture, mold, produce, shape. ANT.—break, demolish, destroy, undo, unmake.

makeshift, n. See substitute.

malady, n. See disease.

malevolence, n. See malice.

malice, n. SYN.—animosity, enmity, grudge, ill will, malevolence, malignity, rancor, spite. ANT.—affection, kindness, love, toleration.

malicious, a. SYN.—bitter, evil-minded, hostile, malevolent, malignant, rancorous, spiteful, virulent, wicked. ANT.—affectionate, benevolent, benign, kind.

malign, v. See abuse.

malleable, a. See soft.

manage, v. See control, direct.

maneuver, n. See operation.

manifest, a. See clear.

manifest, v. See indicate.

manner, n. SYN.—custom, fashion, habit, method, mode, practice, style, way; air, behavior, conduct, demeanor, deportment.

many, a. SYN.—divers, manifold, multifarious, multitudinous, numerous, several, sundry, various. ANT.—few, infrequent, meager, scanty, scarce.

mar, v. See damage.

marine, a. SYN.—maritime, nautical, naval, ocean, oceanic.

mark, n. SYN.—brand, scar, stain, stigma, trace, vestige; badge, label, sign; characteristic, feature, indication, property, symptoms, trait.

mark, v. See notice.

marriage, n. SYN.—espousal, matrimony, nuptials, union, wedding, wedlock. ANT.—celibacy, divorce, virginity.

marvelous, a. See extraordinary.

masculine, a. SYN.—bold, hardy, lusty, male, manly, mannish, robust, strong, vigorous, virile. ANT.—effeminate, emasculated, feminine, unmanly, weak, womanish.

mask, v. See hide.

mass, n. See body.

massacre, n. SYN.—butchery, carnage, pogrom, slaughter.

massacre, v. See kill.

massive, a. See heavy.

master, n. SYN.—chief, commander, employer, head, leader, lord, manager, overseer, ruler, teacher; holder, owner, proprietor; adept, expert. ANT.—servant, slave; amateur.

mastery, n. See supremacy.

mate, n. See companion.

material, a. SYN.—bodily, corporeal, palpable, physical, sensible, tangible; essential, germane, important, momentous, relevant. ANT.—mental, metaphysical, spiritual; immaterial, insignificant.

material, n. See matter.

matrimony, n. See marriage.

matter, n. SYN.—material, stuff, substance; cause, concern, occasion, subject, theme, thing, topic; consequence, importance, moment. ANT.—immateriality, phantom, spirit.

mature, a. See ripe.

mature, v. SYN.—age, develop, perfect, ripen, season.

mean, a. SYN.—average, medium, middle; base, contemptible, despicable, low, sordid, vile, vulgar; malicious, nasty, offensive, selfish. ANT.—admirable, dignified, exalted, generous, noble.

meaning, n. SYN.—acceptation, connotation, drift, explanation, gist, implication, import, intent, interpretation, purport, purpose, sense, significance, signification.

means, n. See instrument.

measure, n. See criterion.

meddle, v. SYN.—interfere, interpose, interrupt, mix in, monkey, tamper.

mediocre, a. See average.

meditate, v. See think.

meek, a. See tame.

meet, v. SYN.—collide, confront, encounter, engage, find, greet, intersect; answer, fulfill, gratify, satisfy; experience, suffer, undergo. ANT.—cleave, disperse, part, scatter, separate.

melancholy, a. SYN.—dejected, depressed, despondent, disconsolate, dismal, dispirited, doleful, gloomy, glum, moody, sad, somber, sorrowful; grave, pensive. ANT.—cheerful, happy, joyous, merry.

melodramatic, a. See theatrical.

melody, n. See tune.

mellow, a. See ripe.

member, n. See part.

memorandum, n. See note.

memorial, n. SYN.—commemoration, memento, monument, remembrance, souvenir.

memory, n. SYN.—recollection, remembrance, reminiscence, retrospection; fame, renown, reputation. ANT.—forgetfulness, oblivion.

mend, v. SYN.—fix, patch, refit, repair, restore, sew; ameliorate, better, correct, improve, rectify, reform, remedy. ANT.—deface, destroy, hurt, injure, rend.

mentality, n. See mind.

mercenary, a. SYN.—avaricious, corrupt, greedy, sordid, venal. ANT.—generous, honorable, liberal.

merciful, a. SYN.—clement, compassionate, forbearing, forgiving, humane, kind, lenient, tender, tolerant. ANT.—brutal, cruel,

pitiless, remorseless, unfeeling.

merciless, a. See brutal.

mercy, n. SYN.—charity, clemency, compassion, forgiveness, grace, leniency, mildness, pity. ANT.—cruelty, punishment, retribution, vengeance.

merge, v. See blend, unite.

merit, n. See virtue.

merit, v. See earn.

merited, a. SYN.—adequate, condign, deserved, earned, proper, suitable. ANT.—improper, undeserved, unmerited.

merry, a. SYN.—blithe, cheerful, festive, gay, gleeful, hilarious, jolly, jovial, joyous, lively, mirthful, sprightly. ANT.—gloomy, melancholy, morose, sad, sorrowful.

message, n. See note.

mete, v. See allot.

method, n. SYN.—design, fashion, manner, mode, order, plan, procedure, system, way. ANT.—confusion, disorder.

methodical, a. See precise.

mettle, n. See courage.

microscopic, a. See minute.

middle, n. See center.

midst, n. See center.

might, n. SYN.—ability, force, potency, power, strength, vigor. ANT.—inability, weakness.

mighty, a. See strong.

mild, a. SYN.—bland, gentle, kind, meek, moderate, soft, soothing, tender. ANT.—bitter, fierce, harsh, rough, severe.

mimic, v. See imitate.

mind, n. SYN.—brain, faculties, intellect, intelligence, judgment, mentality, psyche, reason, soul, spirit, understanding, wit; disposition, inclination, intention, liking, purpose, will, wish. ANT.—body, corporeality, materiality, matter.

mingle, v. See blend.

minor, a. See inferior.

minute, a. SYN.—fine, microscopic, tiny; detailed, exact, particular, precise. ANT.—enormous, huge, large; general.

miraculous, a. See supernatural.

mirage, n. illusion, vision.

miscarriage, n. See failure.

miscellaneous, a. SYN.—assorted, diverse, heterogeneous, indiscriminate, mixed, motley, sundry, varied. ANT.—alike, classified, homogeneous, ordered, selected.

mischief, n. See harm.

miserable, a. SYN.—comfortless, disconsolate, distressed, forlorn, heartbroken, pitiable, wretched; abject, contemptible, despicable, low, mean, paltry, worthless. ANT.—contented, fortunate, happy; noble, significant.

miserly, a. SYN.—acquisitive, avaricious, greedy, niggardly, parsimonious, penurious, stingy, tight. ANT.—altruistic, bountiful, extravagant, generous, munificent.

misery, n. SYN.—agony, anguish, distress, grief, sorrow, suffering, torment, tribulation, woe; calamity, disaster, evil, misfortune, trouble. ANT.—delight, elation, fun, joy, pleasure.

misfortune, n. SYN.—accident, adversity, affliction, calamity, catastrophe, disaster, distress, hardship, mishap, ruin. ANT.—blessing, comfort, prosperity, success.

misleading, a. See deceptive.

mistake, n. See error, oversight.

mistaken, a. See wrong.

misuse, v. See abuse, waste.

mitigate, v. See alleviate.

mix, *v.* SYN.—alloy, amalgamate, blend, combine, commingle, compound, concoct, confound, fuse, jumble, mingle; associate, consort, fraternize, join. ANT.—dissociate, divide, segregate, separate, sort.

mixture, *n.* See **variety.**

mob, *n.* See **crowd.**

mock, *v.* See **sneer.**

mockery, *n.* See **ridicule.**

model, *n.* SYN.—archetype, copy, example, mold, pattern, prototype, specimen, standard, type. ANT.—imitation, production, reproduction.

modern, *a.* SYN.—contemporary, current, new, novel, present, recent. ANT.—ancient, antiquated, bygone, old, past.

modest, *a.* SYN.—bashful, humble, meek, reserved, shy, unassuming, unpretentious, virtuous. ANT.—arrogant, bold, conceited, forward, immodest, ostentatious, proud.

modification, *n.* See **change.**

modify, *v.* See **change.**

mold, *v.* See **form.**

molest, *v.* See **annoy.**

momentary, *a.* See **brief.**

momentous, *a.* See **important.**

monastery, *n.* See **cloister.**

monotonous, *a.* See **tedious.**

monument, *n.* See **memorial.**

moral, *a.* SYN.—chaste, decent, ethical, good, honorable, just, pure, right, righteous, scrupulous, virtuous. ANT.—amoral, libertine, licentious, sinful, unethical.

morality, *n.* See **virtue.**

morose, *a.* SYN.—crabbed, dour, fretful, gloomy, glum, moody, sulky, surly. ANT.—amiable, gay, joyous, merry, pleasant.

mortal, *a.* SYN.—deadly, destructive, fatal, final; human. ANT.—life-giving; divine, immortal.

motion, *n.* SYN.—action, activity, change, gesture, move, movement; proposal, proposition. ANT.—equilibrium, immobility, stability, stillness.

motive, *n.* SYN.—cause, impulse, incentive, incitement, inducement, principle, purpose, reason, spur, stimulus. ANT.—action, attempt, deed, effort, result.

motley, *a.* See **miscellaneous.**

mount, *v.* See **ascend.**

mourn, *v.* See **grieve.**

move, *v.* SYN.—actuate, agitate, drive, impel, induce, instigate, persuade, propel, push, shift, stir, transfer. ANT.—deter, halt, rest, stay, stop.

movement, *n.* See **motion.**

muddled, *a.* See **confused.**

multitude, *n.* SYN.—army, crowd, host, legion, mob. ANT.—few, handful, paucity, scarcity.

mundane, *a.* See **secular.**

murder, *v.* See **kill.**

music, *n.* SYN.—consonance, harmony, melody, symphony.

muster, *v.* See **gather.**

mute, *a.* See **silent.**

mutiny, *n.* See **revolution.**

mutual, *a.* SYN.—common, correlative, interchangeable, joint, reciprocal, shared. ANT.—dissociated, separate, unrequited, unshared.

mysterious, *a.* SYN.—cabalistic, cryptic, dark, dim, enigmatical, hidden, incomprehensible, inexplicable, inscrutable, mystical, obscure, occult, recondite, secret. ANT.—clear, explained, obvious, plain, simple.

mystery, *n.* See **riddle.**

mystical, *a.* See **mysterious.**

myth, *n.* See **legend.**

N

nag, *v.* See **tease.**

naive, *a.* SYN.—artless, candid, frank, ingenuous, innocent, natural, open, simple, unsophisticated. ANT.—crafty, cunning, sophisticated, worldly.

naked, *a.* SYN.—bare, exposed, nude, stripped, unclad, uncovered; bald, barren, unfurnished; mere, plain, simple; defenseless, open, unprotected. ANT.—clothed, covered, dressed; concealed; protected.

name, *n.* SYN.—appellation, denomination, designation, epithet, style, surname, title; character, reputation, repute; distinction, eminence, fame, renown. ANT.—misnomer, namelessness; anonymity.

name, *v.* SYN.—appoint, call, christen, denominate, entitle, mention, specify. ANT.—hint, miscall, misname.

nap, *n.* See **sleep.**

narrate, *v.* See **recite.**

narrative, *n.* See **account.**

narrow, *a.* See **bigoted.**

nasty, *a.* See **mean.**

nation, *n.* SYN.—commonwealth, community, kingdom, nationality, people, realm, state.

native, *a.* SYN.—aboriginal, domestic, endemic, inborn, indigenous, inherent, innate, natural.

natural, *a.* SYN.—characteristic, inherent, innate, native, original; normal, regular; genuine, ingenuous, real, simple, spontaneous, unaffected. ANT.—abnormal, artificial, irregular; forced, formal.

nature, *n.* See **character.**

nautical, *a.* See **marine.**

near, *a.* SYN.—adjacent, bordering, close, neighboring, nigh, proximate; approaching, imminent, impending; dear, familiar, intimate. ANT.—distant, far, removed.

neat, *a.* SYN.—clear, nice, orderly, precise, spruce, tidy, trim. ANT.—dirty, disheveled, sloppy, slovenly, unkempt.

necessary, *a.* SYN.— inevitable, unavoidable; essential, expedient, indispensable, needed, requisite. ANT.—accidental, casual; contingent, nonessential, optional.

necessity, *n.* SYN.—compulsion, constraint, destiny, fate; requirement, requisite; exigency, indigence, need, poverty, want. ANT.—choice, freedom, luxury, option, uncertainty.

need, *v.* SYN.—claim, covet, crave, demand, desire, lack, require, want, wish.

neglect, *n.* SYN.—carelessness, default, disregard, failure, heedlessness, negligence, omission, oversight, slight, thoughtlessness. ANT.—attention, care, diligence, watchfulness.

neglect, *v.* SYN.—disregard, ignore, omit, overlook, slight. ANT.—do, guard, perform, protect, satisfy.

negligence, *n.* See **neglect.**

negligent, *a.* See **careless.**

neighborhood, *n.* SYN.—district, environs, locality; adjacency, nearness, vicinity. ANT.—distance, remoteness.

neighborly, *a.* See **friendly.**

new, *a.* SYN.—fresh, late, modern, newfangled, novel, original, recent. ANT.—ancient, antiquated, archaic, obsolete, old.

news, *n.* SYN.—advice, copy, information, intelligence, message, report, tidings.

niggardly, *a.* See **miserly.**

nimble, *a.* SYN.—active, agile, alert, brisk, flexible, lively, quick, spry, supple. ANT.—clumsy, heavy, inert, slow, sluggish.

noble, *a.* SYN.—dignified, elevated, eminent, exalted, grand, illustrious, lofty, majestic, stately. ANT.—base, low, mean, plebian, vile.

noise, *n.* SYN.—babel, clamor, cry, din, outcry, racket, row, sound, tumult, uproar. ANT.—hush, quiet, silence, stillness.

noisy, *a.* See **loud.**

nonsensical, *a.* See **absurd.**

normal, *a.* See **regular.**

nosy, *a.* See **curious.**

note, *n.* SYN.—indication, mark, sign, symbol, token; annotation, comment, letter, memorandum, message, observation, remark.

noted, *a.* See **famous.**

notice, *n.* See **attention.**

notice, *v.* SYN.—attend to, behold, descry, heed, mark, note, observe, perceive, recognize, regard, remark, see. ANT.—disregard, ignore, overlook, skip.

notify, *v.* See **inform.**

novel, *n.* See **fiction.**

novice, *n.* See **amateur.**

now, *n.* See **present.**

nude, *a.* See **naked.**

nullify, *v.* See **cancel.**

number, *n.* See **quantity.**

numerous, *a.* See **many.**

nuptials, *n.* See **marriage.**

nurture, *v.* See **cherish.**

nutriment, *n.* See **food.**

O

obdurate, *a.* See **callous.**

obedient, *a.* SYN.—compliant, deferential, dutiful, submissive, tractable, yielding. ANT.—insubordinate, intractable, obstinate, rebellious.

obese, *a.* See **fat.**

object, *n.* SYN.—article, particular, thing; aim, design, end, goal, intention, mark, objective, purpose. ANT.—shadow, spirit, vision; consequence, result.

object, *v.* SYN.—abominate, disagree, disapprove, oppose, protest, reject, remonstrate. ANT.—acquiesce, approve, assent, comply, concur.

objection, *n.* See **dissent.**

objective, *n.* See **aspiration, purpose.**

obligate, *v.* See **commit.**

obligation, *n.* SYN.—accountability, bond, compulsion, contract, duty, engagement, responsibility. ANT.—choice, exemption, freedom.

oblige, *v.* See **compel.**

obliterate, *v.* See **destroy.**

oblivious, *a.* See **blind.**

obscene, *a.* SYN.—coarse, dirty, disgusting, filthy, gross, impure, indecent, lewd, offensive, pornographic, smutty. ANT.—decent, modest, pure, refined.

obscure, *a.* SYN.—abstruse, ambiguous, cloudy, cryptic, dark, dim, dusky, enigmatic, indistinct, mysterious, unintelligible, vague. ANT.—bright, clear, distinct, lucid.

observance, *n.* See **ceremony.**

observant, *a.* See **attentive, vigilant.**

observe, *v.* SYN.—behold, detect, discover, examine, eye, inspect, mark, note, notice, perceive, see, view, watch; keep, celebrate, commemorate; express, mention, remark, utter. ANT.—disregard, ignore, neglect, overlook.

obsolete, *a.* SYN.—ancient, antiquated, archaic, obsolescent, old, out-of-date, venerable. ANT.—current, extant, fashionable, modern, recent.

obstacle, *n.* SYN.—bar, barrier, block, check, difficulty, hindrance, impediment, obstruction, snag. ANT.—aid, assistance, encouragement, help.

obstinate, *a.* SYN.—contumacious, determined, dogged, firm, headstrong, immovable, inflexible, intractable, obdurate, pertinacious, stubborn, uncompromising, unyielding. ANT.—amenable, compliant, docile, submissive, yielding.

obstruct, *v.* SYN.—bar, barricade, block, clog, close, stop; delay, impede; hinder. ANT.—clear, open; aid, further, promote.

obtain, *v.* See **acquire.**

obtuse, *a.* See **dull.**

obvious, *a.* SYN.—apparent, clear, distinct, evident, manifest, palpable, patent, plain, self-evident, unmistakable. ANT.—abstruse, concealed, hidden, obscure.

occupation, *n.* See **business.**

occupy, *v.* SYN.—absorb, busy, dwell, fill, have, hold, inhabit, keep, possess. ANT.—abandon, release, relinquish.

occur, *v.* See **happen.**

occurrence, *n.* See **event.**

odd, *a.* SYN.—bizarre, curious, eccentric, peculiar, quaint, queer, singular, strange, unique, unusual; remaining, single, uneven, unmatched. ANT.—common, familiar, normal, regular, typical; even, matched.

odious, *a.* See **vile.**

odor, *n.* See **smell.**

offense, *n.* SYN.—affront, atrocity, indignity, insult, outrage; aggression, crime, injustice, misdeed, sin, transgression, trespass, vice, wrong. ANT.—gentleness, innocence, morality, right.

offer, *n.* See **proposal.**

offer, *v.* SYN.—advance, exhibit, extend, present, proffer, propose, sacrifice, tender, volunteer. ANT.—accept, receive, reject, retain, spurn.

office, *n.* See **position.**

often, *adv.* SYN.—commonly, frequently, generally, recurrently, repeatedly. ANT.—infrequently, occasionally, rarely, seldom, sporadically.

old, *a.* SYN.—aged, ancient, antiquated, antique, archaic, elderly, obsolete, old-fashioned, senile, superannuated, venerable. ANT.—modern, new, young, youthful.

omen, *n.* See **sign.**

omission, *n.* SYN.—default, deletion, failure, neglect, oversight. ANT.—attention, inclusion, insertion, notice.

omit, *v.* SYN.—cancel, delete, disregard, drop, eliminate, exclude, ignore, miss, neglect, overlook, skip. ANT.—enter, include, insert, introduce, notice.

onslaught, *n.* See **attack.**

open, *a.* SYN.—agape, ajar, unclosed, uncovered, unlocked; clear, passable, unobstructed; available, disengaged, free, unoccupied; accessible, exposed, public, unrestricted; candid, frank, honest, overt, plain.

open, *v.* SYN.—exhibit, expand, spread, unbar, unfasten, unfold, unlock, unseal. ANT.—close, conceal, hide, shut.

opening, *n.* See **hole.**

operate, *v.* See **behave, use.**

operation, *n.* SYN.—action, agency, effort, enterprise, execution, instrumentality, maneuver, performance, proceeding, working. ANT.—cessation, inaction, inactivity, rest.

operative, *a.* See **active.**

opinion, *n.* SYN.—belief, conviction, decision, feeling, idea, impression, judgment, notion, persuasion, sentiment, view. ANT.—fact, skepticism, misgiving, knowledge.

opinionated, *a.* See **dogmatic.**

opponent, *n.* See **rival.**

opportunity, *n.* SYN.—chance, contingency, occasion, opening, possibility. ANT.—disadvantage, hindrance, obstacle.

oppose, *v.* SYN.—bar, combat, confront, contradict, counteract, defy, hinder, obstruct, resist, thwart, withstand. ANT.—agree, cooperate, submit, succumb, support.

opposed, *a.* See **adverse.**

opposition, *n.* See **conflict.**

oppress, *v.* See **persecute.**

optimism, *n.* See **hope.**

option, *n.* See **choice.**

opulence, *n.* See **wealth.**

oral, *a.* See **verbal.**

ordain, *v.* See **create.**

ordeal, *n.* See **trial.**

order, *n.* SYN.—arrangement, class, method, plan, rank, regularity, sequence, series, succession, system; bidding, command, decree, dictate, injunction, instruction, mandate, requirement. ANT.—confusion, disarray, disorder, irregularity; consent, license, permission.

order, *v.* See **direct.**

ordinary, *a.* SYN.—accustomed, common, conventional, customary, familiar, habitual, normal, plain, regular, typical, usual, vulgar. ANT.—extraordinary, marvelous, remarkable, strange, uncommon.

organization, *n.* See **system.**

organize, *v.* See **arrange.**

origin, *n.* SYN.—beginning, birth, commencement, cradle, derivation, foundation, inception, source, spring, start. ANT.—end, harvest, issue, outcome, product.

original, *a.* SYN.—first, initial, primary, primeval, primordial, pristine; creative, fresh, inventive, new, novel. ANT.—derivative, later, modern, subsequent, terminal; banal, plagiarized, trite.

originate, *v.* See **create, start.**

ornament, *n.* SYN.—adornment, decoration, embellishment, garnish, ornamentation.

oscillate, *v.* See **fluctuate.**

ostentation, *n.* SYN.—boasting, display, flourish, pageantry, parade, pomp, show, vaunting. ANT.—humility, modesty, reserve, unobtrusiveness.

ostracize, *v.* See **exclude.**

outline, *n.* SYN.—brief, contour, delineation, draft, figure, form, plan, profile, silhouette, sketch.

outsider, *n.* See **stranger.**

outspoken, *a.* See **blunt.**

overcast, *a.* See **cloudy.**

overcome, *v.* See **conquer.**

overload, *v.* See **burden.**

overlook, *v.* See **omit.**

overseer, *n.* See **master.**

oversight, *n.* SYN.—error, inadvertence, inattention, mistake, neglect, omission; charge, control, inspection, management, superintendence, supervision, surveillance. ANT.—attention, care, observation, scrutiny.

overturn, *v.* See **overthrow.**

overthrow, *v.* SYN.—demolish, destroy, overcome, overturn, rout, ruin, supplant, upset, vanquish. ANT.—build, conserve, construct, preserve, uphold.

P

pacific, *a.* See **calm, peaceful.**

pacify, *v.* See **appease.**

packed, *a.* See **full.**

pact, *n.* See **agreement.**

pain, *n.* SYN.—ache, pang, paroxysm, throe, twinge; agony, anguish, distress, grief, suffering. ANT.—comfort, ease, relief; happiness, pleasure, solace.

painful, *a.* See **bitter.**

painting, *n.* See **picture.**

panic, *n.* SYN.—alarm, apprehension, dread, fear, fright, horror, terror, trembling. ANT.—calmness, composure, serenity, tranquility.

parade, *n.* See **procession.**

paradoxical, *a.* See **inconsistent.**

parallel, *a.* See **analogous.**

parched, *a.* See **dry.**

pardon, *n.* SYN.—absolution, acquittal, amnesty, forgiveness, remission. ANT.—conviction, penalty, punishment, sentence.

pardon, *v.* SYN.—absolve, acquit, condone, excuse, forgive, overlook, release, remit. ANT.—accuse, chastise, condemn, convict, punish.

parley, *n.* See **conversation.**

part, *n.* SYN.—allotment, apportionment, division, fragment, moiety, piece, portion, scrap, section, segment, share; component, element, ingredient, member, organ; concern, faction, interest, party, side; character, lines, role. ANT.—entirety, whole.

part, *v.* See **divide.**

partake, *v.* See **share.**

partiality, *n.* See **prejudice.**

participation, *n.* See **communion.**

particle, *n.* SYN.—atom, bit, corpuscle, crumb, grain, iota, jot, mite, scrap, shred, smidgen, speck. ANT.—aggregate, bulk, mass, quantity.

particular, *a.* SYN.—characteristic, distinctive, individual, peculiar, specific; singular, unusual; circumstantial, detailed, exact, minute, specific; careful, fastidious, squeamish. ANT.—comprehensive, general, universal; ordinary; general, rough; undiscriminating.

particular, *n.* See **detail.**

partisan, *n.* See **follower.**

partner, *n.* See **companion.**

passable, *a.* See **fair.**

passion, *n.* See **emotion.**

passionate, *a.* SYN.—ardent, burning, excitable, fervent, fervid, fiery, glowing, hot, impetuous, irascible, vehement. ANT.—apathetic, calm, cool, deliberate, quiet.

passive, *a.* SYN.—idle, inactive, inert, quiet, relaxed; enduring, patient, stoical, submissive. ANT.—active, aggressive, dynamic.

pastime, *n.* See **game.**

patent, *a.* See **evident.**

path, *n.* See **way.**

pathetic, *a.* SYN.—affecting, moving, piteous, pitiable, poignant, sad, touching. ANT.—comical, funny, ludicrous.

patience, *n.* SYN.—composure, endurance, forbearance, fortitude, long-suffering, perseverence, resignation. ANT.—impatience, nervousness, restlessness, unquiet.

patient, *a.* SYN.—assiduous, composed, forbearing, indulgent, long-suffering, passive, resigned, stoical, uncomplaining. ANT.—chafing, clamorous, high-strung, hysterical, turbulent.

pause, *v.* See **hesitate.**

pay, *n.* SYN.—allowance, compensation, earnings, fee, payment, recompense, salary, stipend, wages. ANT.—gift, gratuity, present.

peace, *n.* See **quiet.**

peaceful, *a.* SYN.—calm, gentle, mild, pacific, placid, quiet, serene, still, tranquil, undisturbed. ANT.—agitated, disturbed, noisy, turbulent, violent.

peak, *n.* See **climax.**

peculiar, *a.* SYN.—eccentric, exceptional, extraordinary, odd, rare, singular, strange, striking, unusual; characteristic, distinctive, individual, particular, special. ANT.—common, general, normal, ordinary.

peculiarity, *n.* See **characteristic.**

pedantic, *a.* See **academic.**

peevish, *a.* SYN.—fractious, fretful, ill-natured, ill-tempered, irritable, petulant, snappish, testy, touchy, waspish. ANT.—affable, genial, good-natured, good-tempered, pleasant.

penalty, *n.* SYN.—chastisement, fine, forfeiture, punishment, retribution; disadvantage, handicap. ANT.—compensation, pardon, remuneration, reward.

penetrating, *a.* See **profound.**

penitent, *a.* SYN.—contrite, regretful, remorseful, repentant, sorrowful, sorry. ANT.—obdurate, remorseless.

pensive, *a.* See **thoughtful.**

perceive, *v.* SYN.—conceive, discern, note, notice, observe, recognize, see; apprehend, comprehend, understand. ANT.—ignore, miss, overlook.

perceptible, *a.* See **sensible.**

perception, *n.* SYN.—apprehension, cognizance, comprehension, conception, discernment, insight, understanding. ANT.—ignorance, insensibility, misapprehension, misconception.

perceptive, *a.* See **aware.**

perfect, *a.* SYN.—complete, entire, finished, full, utter, whole; blameless, faultless, holy, immaculate, pure, sinless; complete, consummate, excellent, ideal, superlative, supreme; absolute, downright, unqualified, utter. ANT.—deficient, incomplete, lacking; blemished, defective, faulty, imperfect.

perform, *v.* See **play.**

performance, *n.* See **show.**

perfunctory, *a.* See **formal.**

peril, *n.* See **danger.**

perilous, *a.* See **dangerous.**

period, *n.* See **time.**

perish, *v.* See **die.**

permanent, *a.* SYN.—abiding, changeless, constant, durable, enduring, fixed, indestructible, lasting, stable, unchangeable. ANT.—ephemeral, temporary, transient, transitory, unstable.

permeate, *v.* See **pervade.**

permissible, *a.* See **admissible.**

permission, *n.* SYN.—authority, authorization, consent, leave, liberty, license, permit. ANT.—denial, opposition, prohibition, refusal.

permit, *v.* See **allow, suffer.**

perpetrate, *v.* See **commit.**

perpetual, *a.* See **eternal.**

perpetually, *adv.* See **always.**

perplex, *v.* See **puzzle.**

perplexed, *a.* See **confused.**

perplexing, *a.* See **complex.**

persecute, *v.* SYN.—afflict, annoy, badger, harass, harry, hound, oppress, pester, plague, torment, torture, vex, worry. ANT.—aid, assist, comfort, encourage, support.

persevere, *v.* See **persist.**

perseverance, *n.* SYN.—constancy, industry, persistence, persistency, pertinacity, steadfastness, tenacity. ANT.—cessation, idleness, laziness, rest, sloth.

persist, *v.* SYN.—abide, continue, endure, last, persevere, remain. ANT.—cease, desist, discontinue, vacillate, waver.

persistence, *n.* See **perseverance.**

persistent, *a.* SYN.—constant, enduring, fixed, immovable, indefatigable, lasting, persevering, steady; dogged, obstinate, perverse, stubborn. ANT.—hesitant, unsure, vacillating, wavering.

persuade, *v.* SYN.—allure, coax, convince, entice, exhort, incite, induce, influence, prevail upon, urge, win over. ANT.—coerce, compel, deter, dissuade, restrain.

persuasion, *n.* See **opinion.**

pertain, *v.* See **apply.**

pertinent, *a.* See **relevant.**

pervade, *v.* SYN.—diffuse, fill, infiltrate, penetrate, permeate, run through, saturate.

perverse, *a.* SYN.—contrary, disobedient, fractious, peevish, petulant; forward, intractable, obstinate, stubborn, ungovernable, untoward; perverted, sinful, wicked. ANT.—agreeable, obliging; docile, tractable.

perverted, *a.* See **perverse.**

pester, *v.* See **annoy.**

petition, *n.* See **prayer, request.**

petty, *a.* See **trivial.**

petulant, *a.* See **peevish.**

philanthropy, *n.* See **benevolence.**

phlegmatic, *a.* See **cold.**

phony, *a.* See **artificial.**

phrase, *n.* See **term.**

physical, *a.* SYN.—bodily, carnal, corporal, corporeal, somatic; material, natural. ANT.—mental, spiritual.

pick, *v.* See **choose.**

picture, *n.* SYN.—appearance, cinema, drawing, effigy, engraving, etching, film, illustration, image, likeness, painting, panorama, photograph, portrait, portrayal, print, representation, resemblance, scene, sketch, view.

piece, *n.* SYN.—amount, bit, fraction, fragment, morsel, part, portion, scrap. ANT.—all, entirety, sum, total, whole.

pigment, *n.* See **color.**

pinnacle, *n.* See **top.**

pious, *a.* See **holy.**

pitch, *v.* See **throw.**

pitfall, *n.* See **ambush.**

pitiable, *a.* See **pathetic.**

pity, *n.* SYN.—commiseration, compassion, condolence, mercy, sympathy. ANT.—brutality, cruelty, hardness, inhumanity, ruthlessness.

place, *v.* SYN.—arrange, deposit, dispose, lay, put, set. ANT.—disarrange, disturb, mislay, misplace, remove.

placid, *a.* See **calm.**

plain, *a.* SYN.—even, flat, level, smooth; apparent, clear, distinct, evident, manifest, obvious, palpable, visible; candid, frank, open, simple, sincere, unpretentious; absolute, unqualified. ANT.—abrupt, broken, rough, undulatory, uneven; abstruse, ambiguous, enigmatical, obscure; adorned, embellished, feigned, insincere.

plan, *n.* See **design, method.**

plan, *v.* SYN.—contrive, delineate, design, devise, intend, outline, plot, prepare, project, scheme, sketch.

plausible, *a.* See **possible.**

play, *n.* See **recreation.**

play, *v.* SYN.—caper, frolic, gamble, gambol, revel, romp, sport, stake, toy, wager; execute, perform; act, impersonate, pretend.

plea, *n.* See **prayer.**

plead, *v.* SYN.—appeal, ask, beg, beseech, entreat, implore, petition, supplicate; argue, defend, discuss, rejoin. ANT.—deny, deprecate, refuse.

pleasant, *a.* See **agreeable.**

please, *v.* See **satisfy.**

pleasing, *a.* See **sweet.**

pleasure, *n.* SYN.—amusement, comfort, delight, enjoyment, felicity, gladness, gratification, happiness, joy. ANT.—affliction, pain, suffering, trouble, vexation.

pledge, *n.* See **assurance, promise.**

pledge, *v.* See **commit.**

plentiful, *a.* SYN.—abundant, ample, bounteous, bountiful, copious, luxurious, plenteous profuse, replete. ANT.—deficient, insufficient, rare, scanty, scarce.

pliable, *a.* See **flexible.**

plight, *n.* See **predicament.**

plot, *n.* SYN.—cabal, conspiracy, design, intrigue, machination, plan, scheme, stratagem; chart, diagram, graph, sketch.

plotting, *n.* See **design.**

ploy, *n.* See **trick.**

plump, *a.* See **fat.**

poignant, *a.* See **touching.**

point, *v.* See **direct.**

pointed, *a.* See **sharp.**

poise, *n.* SYN.—balance, calmness, carriage, composure, equanimity, equilibrium, self-possession. ANT.—agitation, anger, excitement, rage, turbulence.

poise, *v.* See **suspend.**

poison, *v.* See **contaminate.**

polished, *a.* See **refined, smooth.**

polite, *a.* SYN.—accomplished, civil, considerate, courteous, cultivated, genteel, refined, urbane, well-bred, well-mannered. ANT.—boorish, impertinent, rude, uncivil, uncouth.

pollute, *v.* See **contaminate.**

pomp, *n.* See **ostentation.**

ponder, *v.* See **study, think.**

poor, *a.* SYN.—destitute, impecunious, indigent, needy, penniless, poverty-stricken; bad, deficient, inferior, scanty, shabby, unfavorable, wrong. ANT.—affluent, opulent, rich, wealthy; ample, good, right, sufficient.

popular, *a.* SYN.—common, familiar, favorite, general, prevailing, prevalent. ANT.—esoteric, exclusive, restricted, unpopular.

portal, *n.* See **entrance.**

portion, *n.* SYN.—bit, division, fragment, parcel, part, piece, section, segment, share. ANT.—bulk, whole.

portray, *v.* SYN.—delineate, depict, describe, draw, paint, picture, represent, sketch. ANT.—caricature, misrepresent, suggest.

position, *n.* SYN.—locality, place, site, situation, station; caste, condition, place, rank, standing, status; berth, incumbency, job, office, post, situation; attitude, bearing, pose, posture.

positive, *a.* See **certain.**

possess, *v.* SYN.—control, have, hold, occupy, own; affect, obtain, seize. ANT.—abandon, lose, renounce, surrender.

possessions, *n.* See **property.**

possible, *a.* SYN.—credible, feasible, likely, plausible, practicable, practical, probable. ANT.—impossible, impracticable, visionary.

possibility, *n.* See **opportunity.**

post, *n.* See **position.**

postpone, *v.* See **suspend.**

postulate, *n.* See **axiom.**

potency, *n.* See **efficiency.**

pound, *v.* See **beat.**

poverty, *n.* SYN.—destitution, indigence, necessity, need, penury, privation, want. ANT.—abundance, affluence, plenty, riches, wealth.

power, *n.* SYN.—ability, capability, competency, faculty, potency, talent, validity; cogency, energy, force, might, strength, vigor; authority, command, control, dominion, influence, predominance, sovereignty, sway. ANT.—disablement, impotence, incapacity, ineptitude; debility, fatigue, weakness.

powerful, *a.* See **strong.**

practical, *a.* See **sensible.**

practice, *n.* SYN.—custom, drill, exercise, habit, manner, training, usage, use, wont. ANT.—disuse, idleness, inexperience, speculation, theory.

praise, *n.* SYN.—acclaim, adulation, applause, approval, commendation, compliment, eulogy, flattery, laudation. ANT.—abuse, censure, condemnation, disapproval.

praise, *v.* SYN.—acclaim, applaud, commend, compliment, eulogize, extol, flatter, glorify, laud. ANT.—censure, condemn, criticize, disparage, reprove.

prayer, *n.* SYN.—appeal, entreaty, invocation, petition, plea, request, suit, supplication.

preamble, *n.* See **introduction.**

precarious, *a.* See **dangerous.**

precept, *n.* See **doctrine.**

precious, *a.* See **valuable.**

precise, *a.* SYN.—accurate, correct, definite, distinct, exact, strict, unequivocal; ceremonious, formal, prim, rigid, stiff. ANT.—erroneous, loose, rough, vague; careless, easy, informal.

preclude, *v.* See **prevent.**

preclusion, *n.* See **exception.**

predicament, *n.* SYN.—condition, difficulty, dilemma, fix, plight, scrape, situation, strait. ANT.—calmness, comfort, ease, satisfaction.

predilection, *n.* See **inclination.**

predominant, *a.* See **principal.**

preference, *n.* See **choice.**

prejudice, *n.* SYN.—bias, bigotry, partiality, preconception, predisposition. ANT.—fairness, impartiality, proof, reason.

prejudiced, *a.* See **bigoted.**

premeditated, *a.* See **intentional.**

premeditation, *n.* SYN.—deliberation, forecast, forethought, intention. ANT.—acci-

dent, extemporization, hazard, impromptu.

premise, *n.* See **basis.**

preoccupied, *a.* See **absent.**

prepare, *v.* SYN.—concoct, condition, contrive, equip, fit, furnish, get ready, make ready, predispose, provide, qualify, ready.

preposterous, *a.* See **absurd.**

prerogative, *n.* See **right.**

present, *n.* SYN.—boon, donation, gift, grant, gratuity, largess; now, today.

present, *v.* See **offer.**

preserve, *v.* SYN.—conserve, defend, guard, keep, maintain, protect, rescue, safeguard, save, secure, spare, uphold. ANT.—abandon, abolish, destroy, impair, injure.

press, *v.* See **push.**

pressing, *a.* See **urgent.**

pressure, *n.* SYN.—compression, force; constraint, influence; compulsion, exigency, hurry, press, stress, urgency. ANT.—ease, lenience, recreation, relaxation.

presume, *v.* See **suppose.**

presumption, *n.* See **impudence.**

pretend, *v.* SYN.—act, affect, assume, feign, profess, sham, simulate. ANT.—display, exhibit, expose, reveal.

pretense, *n.* SYN.—affection, cloak, disguise, excuse, garb, mask, pretension, pretext, semblance, show, simulation, subterfuge. ANT.—actuality, fact, reality, sincerity, truth.

pretty, *a.* See **beautiful.**

prevalent, *a.* See **common, general.**

prevent, *v.* SYN.—forstall, hinder, impede, obstruct, obviate, preclude, thwart. ANT.—aid, encourage, expedite, permit, promote.

previous, *a.* SYN.—aforesaid, antecedent, anterior, foregoing, former, preceeding, prior. ANT.—consequent, following, later, subsequent, succeeding.

price, *n.* SYN.—charge, cost, expense, value, worth.

pride, *n.* SYN.—arrogance, conceit, haughtiness, self-esteem, self-respect, superciliousness, vainglory, vanity. ANT.—humility, lowliness, meekness, modesty, shame.

primary, *a.* See **first.**

primitive, *a.* SYN.—aboriginal, ancient, antiquated, early, old, primary, primeval primordial, pristine. ANT.—civilized, late, modern, modish, sophisticated.

principal, *a.* SYN.—cardinal, chief, essential, first, foremost, highest, leading, main, paramount, predominant, supreme. ANT.—auxiliary, minor, subordinate, subsidiary, supplemental.

principal, *n.* See **head.**

principle, *n.* See **rule.**

prior, *a.* See **previous.**

private, *a.* See **secret.**

privilege, *n.* SYN.—advantage, exemption, favor, immunity, liberty, license, prerogative, right, sanction. ANT.—disallowance, inhibition, prohibition, restriction.

prize, *n.* See **reward.**

probe, *v.* See **reach.**

procedure, *n.* See **way.**

proceed, *v.* See **advance.**

proceeding, *n.* See **transaction.**

procession, *n.* SYN.—cavalcade, cortege, file, parade, retinue, sequence, succession, train.

proclaim, *v.* See **declare.**

procure, *v.* See **buy, gain.**

prodigious, *a.* SYN.—amazing, astonishing,

astounding, enormous, huge, immense, marvelous, monstrous, monumental, remarkable, stupendous, vast. ANT.—commonplace, insignificant, small.

produce, *n.* See **harvest.**

produce, *v.* SYN.—bear, breed, conceive, generate, hatch, procreate, yield; fabricate, fashion, make, manufacture, supply; bring forward, exhibit, show; accomplish, cause, effect, occasion, originate. ANT.—consume, destroy, reduce, waste; conceal, hide.

productive, *a.* See **fertile.**

profane, *v.* See **violate.**

profess, *v.* See **declare.**

proficient, *a.* See **skillful.**

profit, *n.* SYN.—advantage, avail, benefit, emolument, gain, improvement, service, use. ANT.—damage, detriment, loss, ruin, waste.

profligate, *a.* See **corrupt.**

profound, *a.* SYN.—abstruse, deep, penetrating, recondite, solemn. ANT.—shallow, slight, superficial, trivial.

profuse, *a.* SYN.—abundant, copious, excessive, extravagant, exuberant, immoderate, improvident, lavish, luxuriant, overflowing, plentiful, prodigal, wasteful. ANT.—economical, meager, poor, skimpy, sparse.

profusion, *n.* See **excess.**

progress, *n.* SYN.—advance, advancement, betterment, development, growth, improvement, progression. ANT.—decline, delay, regression, relapse, retrogression.

progress, *v.* See **advance.**

progression, *n.* See **sequence.**

prohibit, *v.* SYN.—ban, debar, forbid, hinder, inhibit, interdict, prevent. ANT.—allow, permit, sanction, tolerate.

project, *n.* SYN.—contrivance, design, device, plan, scheme. ANT.—accomplishment, performance, production.

prolific, *a.* See **fertile.**

prolong, *v.* See **draw.**

prominent, *a.* SYN.—celebrated, conspicuous, distinguished, eminent, famous, illustrious, influential, noteworthy, outstanding, remarkable, renowned. ANT.—common, humble, low, ordinary, vulgar.

promise, *n.* SYN.—agreement, assurance, bestowal, contract, engagement, fulfillment, guarantee, oath, pledge, undertaking, vow.

promote, *v.* SYN.—advance, aid, assist, encourage, facilitate, forward, foster. ANT.—demote, discourage, hinder, impede, obstruct.

prompt, *a.* See **punctual.**

prompt, *v.* See **cause.**

promptly, *adv.* See **immediately.**

promulgate, *v.* See **declare.**

proof, *n.* SYN.—confirmation, corroboration, demonstration, evidence, experiment, test, testimony, trial, verification. ANT.—failure, fallacy, invalidity.

propel, *v.* See **move.**

propensity, *n.* See **tendency.**

proper, *a.* SYN.—appropriate, befitting, correct, fit, legitimate, meet, right, seemly, suitable; conventional, correct, decent, formal, respectable; individual, peculiar, special.

property, *n.* SYN.—belongings, commodities, effects, estate, goods, merchandise, possessions, stock, wares, wealth; attribute, characteristic, peculiarity, quality, trait. ANT.—depravation, destitution, poverty, privation, want.

propogate, v. See breed.

proportion, n. See balance.

proposal, n. SYN.—offer, overture, proposition, suggestion, tender. ANT.—acceptance, denial, rejection, withdrawal.

propose, v. SYN.—design, intend, move, offer, present, proffer, propound, purpose, suggest. ANT.—effect, fulfill, perform.

propound, v. See advance.

proprietor, n. See master.

prosper, v. See succeed.

prosperous, a. See rich.

protect, v. See preserve.

protection, n. SYN.—bulwark, fence, refuge, safeguard, shelter, shield; defense, guard, security.

protest, n. See dissent.

protest, v. See object.

prototype, n. See example.

protract, v. See stretch.

proud, a. SYN.—arrogant, disdainful, haughty, overbearing, stately, supercilious, vain, vainglorious. ANT.—ashamed, humble, lowly, meek.

prove, v. SYN.—confirm, corroborate, demonstrate, establish, manifest, test, try, verify. ANT.—contradict, disprove, refute.

proverb, n. SYN.—adage, aphorism, apothegm, byword, maxim, motto, saw, saying.

provide, v. See furnish.

provident, a. See economical.

provision, n. See supply.

provoke, v. See excite, incite.

prowess, n. See courage.

proxy, n. See substitute.

prudence, n. See caution.

prudent, a. See sensible.

prying, a. See curious.

psychosis, n. See madness.

pull, v. See draw.

pulsate, v. See beat.

punctual, a. SYN.—exact, nice, precise, prompt, ready, timely. ANT.—dilatory, late, slow, tardy.

punish, v. SYN.—castigate, chastise, correct, discipline, pummel, strike. ANT.—acquit, exonerate, free, pardon, release.

punishment, n. See discipline, penalty.

puny, a. See feeble.

purchase, v. See buy.

pure, a. SYN.—clean, clear, genuine, immaculate, spotless, unadulterated, untainted; chaste, guiltless, innocent, modest, sincere, undefiled, virgin; absolute, bare, sheer. ANT.—foul, polluted, sullied, tainted, tarnished; corrupt, defiled.

purified, a. See refined.

purify, v. See clean.

purpose, n. SYN.—aim, design, drift, end, goal, intent, intention, object, objective. ANT.—accident, fate, hazard.

pursue, v. SYN.—chase, follow, hunt, persist, track, trail. ANT.—abandon, elude, escape, evade, flee.

push, v. SYN.—crowd, drive, force, impel, jostle, press, propel, shove; hasten, promote, urge. ANT.—drag, falter, halt, pull, retreat; ignore, oppose.

puzzle, n. See riddle.

puzzle, v. SYN.—bewilder, confound, confuse, dumfound, mystify, nonplus, perplex. ANT.—clarify, explain, illumine, instruct, solve.

Q

quaint, a. See queer.

qualified, a. See capable.

quality, n. SYN.—attribute, characteristic, distinction, feature, peculiarity, property, trait; caliber, grade, value. ANT.—being, essence, nature, substance.

quantity, n. SYN.—content, extent, measure, portion; aggregate, amount, number, sum, volume. ANT.—nothing, nothingness, zero.

quarrel, n. SYN.—affray, altercation, argument, bickering, contention, disagreement, dispute, feud, spat, squabble, wrangle. ANT.—agreement, friendliness, harmony, peace, reconciliation.

queer, a. SYN.—curious, droll, eccentric, odd, peculiar, quaint, singular, strange, unusual, whimsical. ANT.—common, familiar, normal, ordinary, usual.

quest, n. See inquiry.

question, v. SYN.—ask, examine, inquire, interrogate, pump, query, quiz; challenge, dispute, doubt. ANT.—answer, reply, respond, state; accept.

quick, a. SYN.—active, brisk, fast, hasty, lively, nimble, precipitate, rapid, speedy, swift; excitable, impatient, irascible, sharp, testy, touchy; acute, clever, discerning, keen, sensitive, shrewd. ANT.—slow, sluggish; dull, inattentive, unaware.

quicken, v. See accelerate.

quiet, a. SYN.—hushed, motionless, peaceful, placid, quiescent, still, tranquil, undisturbed; calm, gentle, meek, mild, modest, passive, patient, silent. ANT.—loud, strident; agitated, disturbed, perturbed.

quiet, n. SYN.—calm, calmness, hush, peace, quiescence, quietude, repose, rest, serenity, silence, stillness, tranquility. ANT.—agitation, disturbance, excitement, noise, tumult.

quiet, v. See appease.

quit, v. SYN.—abandon, cease, desist, discontinue, stop; give up, relinquish, resign, surrender; abandon, depart, leave, withdraw. ANT.—continue, endure, occupy, persist, stay.

quiz, v. See question.

quote, v. SYN.—adduce, cite, extract, paraphrase, plagiarize, recite, repeat. ANT.—contradict, misquote, refute, retort.

R

race, n. SYN.—ancestry, clan, folk, lineage, nation, people, stock, strain, tribe.

racket, n. See noise.

radiance, a. SYN.—brightness, brilliance, brilliancy, effulgence, luster, splendor. ANT.—darkness, dullness, gloom, obscurity.

radiant, a. See splendid.

radical, a. SYN.—complete, extreme, insurgent, total, thorough, ultra, uncompromising; basic, constitutional, fundamental, inherent, innate, intrinsic, natural, organic, original. ANT.—conservative, moderate, superficial; extraneous.

rage, n. See anger.

raging, a. See violent.

raise, v. SYN.—elevate, erect, exalt, heave, heighten, hoist, lift, uplift; breed, cultivate, grow, produce; gather, levy, muster. ANT.—abase, depreciate, depress, destroy, lower.

ramble, v. See wander.

rancor, n. See malice.

rank, n. SYN.—hue, range, row, series; blood, class, degree, estate, grade, quality, standing, station, status; dignity, distinction, eminence. ANT.—disrepute, humiliation, shame, stigma.

rapid, a. See fast, quick.

rapture, n. See bliss, ecstasy.

rare, a. SYN.—infrequent, occasional, strange, unusual; choice, exceptional, incomparable, precious, scarce, singular, uncommon, unique. ANT.—customary, frequent, ordinary, usual; abundant, commonplace, numerous, worthless.

rash, a. See blind, impulsive.

rational, a. SYN.—intelligent, judicious, reasonable, sensible, wise; sane, sober, sound. ANT.—absurd, foolish; irrational, insane.

rationality, n. See reason.

ravage, v. See waste.

ravish, v. See violate.

raw, a. See crude.

raze, v. See destroy.

reach, v. SYN.—extend, stretch; arrive at, attain, come to, overtake. ANT.—fail, fall short, miss.

react, v. See respond.

ready, a. See ripe.

ready, v. See prepare.

real, a. SYN.—actual, authentic, certain, genuine, positive, substantial, true, veritable. ANT.—apparent, fictitious, imaginary, supposed, unreal.

realize, v. See understand.

reap, v. SYN.—acquire, gain, garner, gather, glean, harvest. ANT.—lose, plant, sow, squander.

reaping, n. harvest.

rear, v. See breed.

reason, n. SYN.—argument, basis, cause, ground, motive, sake; aim, design, purpose, intelligence, mind, rationality, sense, understanding.

reason, v. SYN.—argue, conclude, deduce, deliberate, discuss, infer, judge, reflect. ANT.—bewilder, confuse, guess.

reasonable, a. See sensible.

rebel, v. SYN.—mutiny, revolt, strike.

rebellion, v. SYN.—See revolution.

rebellious, a. See disobedient.

rebuild, v. See restore.

rebuttal, n. See answer.

recall, v. See remember.

receive, v. SYN.—accept, gain, get, take; admit, shelter; entertain, welcome. ANT.—bestow, give, impart, reject; discharge, turn away.

recent, a. See new.

recite, v. SYN.—declaim, deliver, describe, detail, mention, narrate, recapitulate, rehearse, relate, repeat, tell.

reckless, a. See careless.

recognize, v. SYN.—apprehend, identify, perceive, recollect, remember; acknowledge, avow, concede, confess, own. ANT.—forget, ignore, overlook; disown, renounce, repudiate.

recollection, n. See memory.

recommend, v. See suggest.

recommendation, n. See advice.

reconsider, v. See review.

record, n. SYN.—account, archive, chronicle, document, memorandum, minute, note, report, register; mark, memorial, trace, vestige; achievement, career, history.

recount, v. See relate.

recover, v. SYN.—cure, rally, recuperate, re-

SYNONYMS AND ANTONYMS

store, revive; recapture, recoup, redeem, regain, repossess, retrieve. ANT.—regress, relapse, revert, weaken; forfeit, lose.
recreation, *n.* SYN.—amusement, diversion, entertainment, fun, game, pastime, play, sport. ANT.—boredom, labor, toil, work.
rectify, *v.* See **correct.**
recuperate, *v.* See **recover.**
reduce, *v.* See **abate, decrease.**
refined, *a.* SYN.—courtly, cultivated, cultured, genteel, polished, polite, well-bred; clarified, purified. ANT.—boorish, coarse, crude, rude, vulgar.
refinement, *n.* See **culture.**
reflect, *v.* See **think.**
reflection, *n.* See **thought.**
reform, *v.* See **correct, improve.**
refrain, *v.* SYN.—abstain, desist, forbear, withhold. ANT.—continue, indulge, persist.
refreshing, *a.* See **fresh.**
refuge, *n.* See **shelter.**
refuse, *v.* SYN.—decline, deny, rebuff, reject, repudiate, spurn, withhold. ANT.—accept, grant, welcome.
refute, *v.* SYN.—confute, controvert, disprove, falsify, rebut. ANT.—accept, affirm, confirm, establish, prove.
regain, *v.* See **recover.**
regal, *a.* See **stately.**
regard, *n.* SYN.—attention, care, concern, consideration, notice, observation; affection, esteem, liking. ANT.—antipathy, disgust, disaffection, neglect.
regard, *v.* SYN.—esteem, honor, respect, value; behold, contemplate, look, mark, notice, observe, see, view, watch; account, believe, deem, hold, imagine, reckon, suppose, think. ANT.—insult, mock; ignore, neglect, overlook.
region, *n.* See **location, zone.**
regret, *n.* SYN.—compunction, contrition, grief, penitence, qualm, remorse, repentance, self-reproach, sorrow. ANT.—complacency, impenitence, obduracy, self-satisfaction.
regular, *a.* SYN.—customary, methodical, natural, normal, orderly, ordinary, periodical, steady, systematic, uniform, unvaried. ANT.—abnormal, erratic, exceptional, rare, unusual.
regulation, *n.* See **discipline, rule.**
rehabilitate, *v.* See **restore.**
reiterate, *v.* See **repeat.**
reject, *v.* See **refuse.**
rejection, *n.* See **dissent.**
relate, *v.* SYN.—describe, narrate, recite, recount, rehearse, report, tell; apply, beat, connect, correlate, pertain, refer.
relation, *n.* See **alliance.**
relationship, *n.* See **connection.**
relatives, *n.* See **kindred.**
relaxed, *a.* See **casual, comfortable.**
release, *v.* See **liberate.**
relent, *v.* See **yield.**
relevant, *a.* SYN.—applicable, apposite, appropriate, apropos, apt, fit, germane, material, pertinent, related, relating, to the point. ANT.—alien, extraneous, foreign, unrelated.
reliable, *a.* SYN.—certain, dependable, safe, secure, sure, tried, trustworthy, trusty. ANT.—dubious, fallible, questionable, uncertain, unreliable.
reliance, *n.* See **faith.**
relief, *n.* See **assistance.**
relieve, *v.* See **alleviate, ease.**

religion, *n.* See **faith.**
religious, *a.* SYN.—devout, divine, godly, holy, pietistic, pious, reverent, sacred, sanctimonious, spiritual, theological. ANT.—atheistic, impious, profane, secular, skeptical.
religiousness, *n.* See **devotion.**
relinquish, *v.* See **surrender.**
reluctance, *n.* See **aversion.**
reluctant, *a.* SYN.—averse, disinclined, hesitant, loath, slow, unwilling. ANT.—disposed, eager, inclined, ready, willing.
remain, *v.* SYN.—abide, dwell, halt, rest, stay, tarry, wait; continue, endure, last, survive. ANT.—depart, go, leave; dissipate, finish, terminate.
remains, *n.* See **rest.**
remark, *n.* SYN.—annotation, assertion, comment, declaration, observation, statement, utterance.
remark, *v.* See **observe.**
remarkable, *a.* See **impressive.**
remedy, *n.* SYN.—antidote, cure, help, medicant, restorative; redress, relief, reparation.
remedy, *v.* See **mend.**
remember, *v.* SYN.—mind, recall, recollect, remind, reminisce. ANT.—disregard, forget, ignore, overlook.
remembrance, *n.* See **memorial.**
remonstrate, *v.* See **complain.**
remorse, *n.* See **regret.**
remote, *a.* See **distant.**
remove, *v.* SYN.—dislodge, displace, move, shift, transfer, transport; discharge, dismiss, eject, oust, vacate; extract, withdraw. ANT.—leave, remain, stay; retain.
renounce, *v.* SYN.—abandon, forego, forsake, quit, relinquish, resign, sacrifice; deny, disavow, disclaim, disown, reject, retract, revoke. ANT.—defend, maintain, uphold; acknowledge, assert, recognize.
renovate, *v.* See **restore.**
renown, *n.* SYN.—acclaim, distinction, eminence, fame, honor, luster, notability, reputation. ANT.—disgrace, disrepute, obscurity.
renowned, *a.* See **famous.**
repair, *v.* SYN.—correct, darn, fix, mend, patch, refit, renew, renovate, restore, tinker with; amend, redress, remedy, retrieve. ANT.—break, destroy, harm.
repeal, *v.* See **cancel.**
repeat, *v.* SYN.—quote, recite, rehearse, relate; duplicate, iterate, recapitulate, reiterate, reproduce.
repentance, *n.* See **regret.**
repentant, *a.* See **penitent.**
repine, *v.* See **complain.**
replica, *n.* See **copy.**
reply, *n.* See **answer.**
reply, *v.* See **respond.**
report, *v.* See **announce.**
repose, *n.* See **quiet.**
represent, *v.* See **portray.**
representation, *n.* See **picture.**
repress, *v.* See **restrain.**
reprimand, *v.* See **scold.**
reproduction, *n.* See **copy.**
repugnance, *n.* See **aversion.**
repulsive, *a.* See **ugly.**
reputation, *n.* See **character.**
repute, *n.* See **character.**
request, *v.* SYN.—appeal, ask, beg, beseech, desire, entreat, implore, importune, petition, pray, seek, sue, supplicate. ANT.—demand, require.

require, *v.* SYN.—call for, claim, command, demand, exact, order, prescribe; lack, necessitate, need, want.
requisite, *a.* See **essential, necessary.**
rescind, *v.* See **cancel.**
research, *n.* See **inquiry.**
resemblance, *n.* See **similarity.**
reserve, *n.* See **supply.**
reserved, *a.* See **distant, shy.**
residence, *n.* See **home.**
resign, *v.* See **quit.**
resignation, *n.* See **patience.**
resigned, *a.* See **patient.**
resist, *v.* SYN.—attack, confront, defy, hinder, impede, obstruct, oppose, thwart, withstand. ANT.—accede, allow, cooperate, relent, yield.
resolution, *n.* SYN.—courage, decision, determination, firmness, fortitude, persistence, resolve, steadfastness. ANT.—inconstancy, indecision, vacillation.
resolve, *n.* See **resolution.**
resolve, *v.* See **decide, determine.**
respect, *v.* SYN.—admire, consider, heed, honor, regard, revere, reverence, value, venerate. ANT.—abuse, despise, disdain, neglect, scorn.
respectable, *a.* See **decent.**
respond, *v.* SYN.—answer, react, rejoin, reply. ANT.—disregard, ignore, overlook.
response, *n.* See **answer.**
responsibility, *n.* SYN.—accountability, amenability, liability, obligation, trustworthiness; duty, trust.
responsible, *a.* SYN.—accountable, amenable, answerable, liable; reliable, trustworthy. ANT.—exempt, free, immune; careless, negligent.
rest, *n.* SYN.—sleep, slumber; calm, ease, leisure, peace, quiet, relaxation, repose, tranquility; cessation, intermission, pause, respite; balance, remainder, remains, residue, surplus. ANT.—agitation, commotion, disturbance, motion, tumult.
restless, *a.* SYN.—agitated, disquieted, disturbed, irresolute, sleepless, uneasy, unquiet; active, roving, transient, wandering. ANT.—at ease, peaceable, quiet, tractable.
restore, *v.* SYN.—rebuild, reconstruct, reestablish, refresh, rehabilitate, renew, renovate, repair; cure, heal, recover, rejuvenate, revive; reinstate, replace, return.
restrain, *v.* SYN.—bridle, check, constrain, curb, hinder, hold back, inhibit, limit, repress, stop, suppress. ANT.—aid, encourage, incite, loosen.
restraint, *n.* See **discipline.**
result, *n.* SYN.—conclusion, consequence, determination, effect, end, eventuality, issue, resolution, resolve.
retaliation, *n.* See **revenge.**
retard, *v.* See **delay, hinder.**
retort, *n.* See **answer.**
retribution, *n.* See **revenge.**
return, *v.* SYN.—go back, recur, retreat, revert; repay, replace, requite, restore. ANT.—appropriate, keep, retain, take.
reveal, *v.* SYN.—betray, disclose, discover, divulge, expose, impart, show, uncover. ANT.—cloak, conceal, cover, hide, obscure.
revelation, *n.* See **vision.**
revenge, *n.* SYN.—reparation, reprisal, requital, retaliation, retribution, vengeance, vindictiveness. ANT.—mercy, pardon, reconciliation, remission, forgiveness.

revenge, *v.* SYN.—avenge, requite, retaliate, vindicate. ANT.—forgive, pardon, pity, reconcile.

revere, *v.* SYN.—adore, esteem, honor, venerate, worship. ANT.—despise, hate, ignore.

reverence, *n.* See **honor**.

reverse, *v.* SYN.—invert, transpose, turn about; overthrow, overturn, subvert, unmake, upset; annul, countermand, repeal, rescind, revoke. ANT.—endorse, maintain, stabilize; affirm, confirm, vouch.

revert, *v.* See **return**.

review, *n.* SYN.—commentary, criticism, critique, examination, inspection, reconsideration, retrospect, retrospection, revision, survey, synopsis; digest, journal, periodical.

review, *v.* SYN.—consider, examine, inspect, reconsider, revise, survey; analyze, criticize, discuss, edit. ANT.—ignore, reject.

revision, *n.* See **review**.

revoke, *v.* See **cancel**.

revolting, *a.* See **abominable**.

revolution, *n.* SYN.—coup, insurrection, mutiny, overthrow, rebellion, revolt, uprising.

revolve, *v.* SYN.—circle, gyrate, rotate, spin, turn, twirl, wheel, whirl. ANT.—proceed, stop, stray, travel, wander.

reward, *n.* SYN.—award, bonus, bounty, compensation, premium, prize, recompense, remuneration, requital. ANT.—assessment, charge, earnings, punishment, wages.

rich, *a.* SYN.—abundant, affluent, ample, bountiful, copious, costly, exorbitant, luxurious, opulent, plentiful, prosperous, sumptuous, wealthy, well-to-do; fecund, fertile, fruitful, luxuriant, prolific. ANT.—beggarly, destitute, indigent, needy, poor; barren, sterile, unfruitful, unproductive.

riddle, *n.* SYN.—conundrum, enigma, mystery, problem, puzzle. ANT.—answer, clue, key, resolution, solution.

ridicule, *n.* SYN.—banter, derision, gibe, irony, jeering, mockery, raillery, sarcasm, satire, sneering.

right, *a.* SYN.—ethical, fair, just, lawful, legitimate; accurate, correct, real, true; appropriate, fit, proper, seemly, suitable; direct, erect, straight, upright. ANT.—bad, false, improper, wrong.

right, *n.* SYN.—authority, grant, liberty, license, prerogative, privilege; equity, honor, justice, propriety, virtue. ANT.—encroachment, injustice, violation, wrong.

righteous, *a.* See **moral**.

rigid, *a.* SYN.—austere, harsh, rigorous, severe, stern, strict, stringent, unyielding; inflexible, stiff, unbending. ANT.—compassionate, lax, lenient, mild, yielding; elastic, flexible, resilient, supple.

rigorous, *a.* See **hard, harsh**.

rim, *n.* See **border**.

rip, *v.* See **tear**.

ripe, *a.* SYN.—complete, consummate, finished, full-grown, mature, matured, mellow, ready, seasonable. ANT.—crude, green, immature, raw, undeveloped.

rise, *v.* See **advance, ascend**.

risk, *n.* See **danger**.

risk, *v.* SYN.—endanger, expose, hazard, jeopardize, peril; speculate, venture. ANT.—insure, protect, secure.

risky, *a.* See **dangerous**.

rite, *n.* See **ceremony**.

ritual, *n.* See **ceremony**.

rival, *n.* SYN.—adversary, antagonist, competitor, contestant, enemy, foe, opponent. ANT.—ally, comrade, confederate, teammate.

roam, *v.* See **wander**.

rob, *v.* SYN.—despoil, fleece, loot, pilfer, pillage, plunder, sack, steal, strip.

robbery, *n.* SYN.—burglary, depredation, larceny, pillage, plunder, theft.

robust, *a.* See **healthy**.

rock, *n.* See **stone**.

role, *n.* See **part**.

romantic, *a.* SYN.—dreamy, extravagant, fanciful, fantastic, fictitious, ideal, idealistic, imaginative, maudlin, mawkish, picturesque, poetic, sentimental. ANT.—factual, literal, matter-of-fact, practical, prosaic.

roomy, *a.* See **spacious**.

root, *n.* See **foundation**.

rot, *v.* See **decay**.

rotate, *v.* See **turn**.

rotund, *a.* See **round**.

rough, *a.* SYN.—craggy, irregular, jagged, rugged, scabrous, scratchy, uneven; approximate, coarse, crude, cursory, imperfect, incomplete, unfinished, unpolished; harsh, severe, stormy, tempestuous, turbulent, violent; blunt, brusque, churlish, gruff, rude, uncivil. ANT.—even, level, sleek, slippery, smooth; fine, finished, polished, refined; calm, placid, tranquil, unruffled; civil, courteous, gentle, mild.

round, *a.* SYN.—bulbous, chubby, circular, complete, curved, cylindrical, entire, globular, plump, rotund, spherical.

roundabout, *a.* See **devious**.

rout, *v.* See **conquer**.

route, *n.* See **way**.

routine, *n.* See **habit**.

royal, *a.* SYN.—courtly, dignified, grand, imperial, kingly, lordly, majestic, monarchial, noble, princely, regal, ruling, sovereign, stately, supreme. ANT.—common, humble, low, plebian, proletarian, servile, vulgar.

rude, *a.* SYN.—blunt, boorish, discourteous, gruff, impolite, impudent, insolent, rough, saucy, surly, uncivil, vulgar; coarse, crude, ignorant, illiterate, primitive, raw, rough, savage, unpolished, untaught; fierce, harsh, inclement, tumultuous, violent. ANT.—civil, genteel, polished; courtly, dignified, noble, stately; calm, mild, peaceful.

rugged, *a.* See **rough**.

ruin, *v.* See **destroy**.

ruinous, *a.* See **destructive**.

rule, *n.* SYN.—axiom, canon, formula, guide, law, maxim, method, order, precept, principle, propriety, regulation, standard, statute, system; authority, control, direction, dominion, government, jurisdiction, mastery, reign, sovereignty, sway. ANT.—chance, deviation, exception, hazard, irregularity; anarchy, chaos, misrule.

rule, *v.* See **control**.

rupture, *v.* See **break**.

rural, *a.* See **rustic**.

ruse, *n.* See **trick**.

rush, *v.* See **hurry**.

rustic, *a.* SYN.—country, pastoral, rural; coarse, homely, plain, simple; boorish, bucolic, uncouth, unsophisticated. ANT.—cultured, elegant, polished, refined, urbane.

ruthless, *a.* See **brutal**.

S

sacrament, *n.* See **communion**.

sacred, *a.* See **holy**.

sad, *a.* SYN.—cheerless, dejected, depressed, despondent, disconsolate, dismal, doleful, downcast, gloomy, lugubrious, melancholy, mournful, somber, sorrowful. ANT.—cheerful, glad, happy, joyous, merry.

safe, *a.* SYN.—certain, dependable, harmless, protected, reliable, secure, snug, trustworthy. ANT.—dangerous, hazardous, insecure, perilous, unsafe.

safeguard, *n.* See **protection**.

sagacity, *n.* See **wisdom**.

sage, *n.* See **scholar**.

salary, *n.* See **pay**.

salient, *a.* See **conspicuous**.

salutary, *a.* See **beneficial**.

same, *a.* See **identical**.

sample, *n.* SYN.—case, example, illustration, instance, model, pattern, prototype, specimen.

sanction, *n.* See **approval**.

sanction, *v.* See **allow**.

sanctuary, *n.* See **shelter**.

sarcastic, *a.* SYN.—acrimonious, biting, caustic, cutting, derisive, ironic, sardonic, satirical, sneering, taunting. ANT.—affable, agreeable, amiable, pleasant.

sardonic, *a.* See **bitter**.

satiate, *v.* See **satisfy**.

satire, *n.* See **wit**.

satirical, *a.* See **sarcastic**.

satisfactory, *a.* See **adequate**.

satisfy, *v.* SYN.—appease, compensate, content, fulfill, gratify, please, remunerate, satiate, suffice. ANT.—annoy, displease, dissatisfy, frustrate, tantalize.

saturate, *v.* See **pervade**.

sauciness, *n.* See **impudence**.

savage, *a.* See **brutal**.

save, *v.* See **preserve**.

savory, *a.* See **delicious**.

say, *v.* See **speak**.

saying, *n.* See **proverb**.

scandal, *n.* See **shame**.

scandalize, *v.* See **abuse**.

scandalous, *a.* See **disgraceful**.

scarce, *a.* See **rare**.

scare, *v.* See **frighten**.

scared, *a.* See **afraid**.

scatter, *v.* See **disperse**.

scent, *n.* See **smell**.

scheme, *v.* See **plan**.

scheming, *n.* See **design**.

scholar, *n.* SYN.—disciple, intellectual, learner, pupil, sage, savant, student. ANT.—dolt, dunce, fool, idiot, ignoramus.

scholarly, *a.* See **academic**.

scholarship, *n.* See **knowledge**.

science, *n.* SYN.—discipline, enlightenment, knowledge, learning, scholarship. ANT.—ignorance, nescience, superstition.

scold, *v.* SYN.—admonish, berate, blame, censure, lecture, rate, rebuke, reprehend, reprimand, upbraid, vituperate. ANT.—approve, commend, praise.

scope, *n.* See **extent**.

scorch, *v.* See **burn**.

scorn, *n.* See **contempt**.

scrub, *v.* See **clean**.

scrutinize, *v.* See **criticize, examine**.

search, *n.* SYN.—examination, exploration, inquiry, investigation, pursuit, quest. ANT.—abandonment, cession, resignation.

search, *v.* SYN.—examine, explore, ferret (out), hunt, investigate, look, probe, ransack, rummage, scour, scrutinize, seek.

searching, *a.* See **curious.**

secluded, *a.* See **alone.**

seclusion, *n.* See **isolation.**

secondary, *a.* See **inferior.**

secret, *a.* SYN.—clandestine, concealed, covert, hidden, latent, private, surreptitious, unknown. ANT.—conspicuous, disclosed, exposed, known, obvious.

secrete, *v.* See **cover.**

section, *n.* See **territory.**

secular, *a.* SYN.—earthly, laic, lay, mundane, profane, temporal, worldly. ANT.—ecclesiastical, religious, spiritual, unworldly.

secure, *a.* See **certain.**

secure, *v.* See **get.**

security, *n.* See **guarantee.**

see, *v.* SYN.—behold, contemplate, descry, discern, distinguish, espy, glimpse, inspect, look at, notice, observe, perceive, scan, scrutinize, view, watch, witness.

seek, *v.* See **search.**

seem, *v.* See **appear.**

segment, *n.* See **part.**

seize, *v.* See **arrest.**

select, *v.* See **choose,**

selection, *n.* See **choice.**

selfish, *a.* SYN.—egoistic, illiberal, mercenary, narrow, parsimonious, self-centered, self-seeking, stingy, ungenerous. ANT.—altruistic, charitable, liberal, magnanimous.

send, *v.* SYN.—cast, discharge, dispatch, emit, impel, propel, throw, transmit. ANT.—bring, get, hold, receive, retain.

seniority, *n.* See **age.**

sensation, *n.* SYN.—apprehension, feeling, image, impression, perception, sense, sensibility. ANT.—apathy, insensibility, stupor, torpor.

sense, *n.* See **meaning.**

senseless, *a.* See **stupid.**

sensible, *a.* SYN.—appreciable, apprehensible, perceptible; alive, awake, aware, cognizant, comprehending, conscious, perceiving, sentient; discreet, intelligent, judicious, practical, prudent, reasonable, sagacious, sage, sober, sound, wise. ANT.—absurd, impalpable, imperceptible, stupid, unaware.

sensitive, *a.* SYN.—impressionable, perceptive, prone, responsive, sentient, susceptible, tender. ANT.—callous, dull, hard, indifferent, insensitive.

sensual, *a.* SYN.—carnal, earthy, lascivious, lecherous, lewd, licentious, sensory, voluptuous, wanton. ANT.—abstemious, ascetic, chaste, continent, virtuous.

sentence, *v.* See **condemn.**

sentiment, *n.* See **feeling.**

sentimental, *a.* See **romantic.**

separate, *v.* See **divide.**

separation, *n.* See **isolation.**

sequence, *n.* SYN.—arrangement, chain, following, gradation, order, progression, series, string, succession, train.

serene, *a.* See **calm.**

serenity, *n.* See **quiet.**

series, *n.* See **sequence.**

serious, *a.* SYN.—great, important, momentous, weighty; earnest, grave, sedate, sober, solemn, staid; alarming, critical, dangerous, risky. ANT.—small, trifling, trivial; informal, relaxed.

serve, *v.* SYN.—aid, assist, attend, help, oblige, succor; advance, benefit, forward, promote; answer, content, satisfy, suffice; distribute, supply, wait on. ANT.—command, dictate, direct, rule.

servile, *a.* See **base.**

servitude, *n.* See **bondage.**

set, *v.* See **place.**

settle, *v.* See **decide.**

settlement, *n.* See **conclusion.**

sever, *v.* See **divide.**

severe, *a.* SYN.—acute, arduous, distressing, exacting, extreme, hard, harsh, intense, relentless, rigid, rigorous, sharp, stern, stringent, unmitigated, unyielding, violent. ANT.—considerate, genial, indulgent, merciful, yielding.

shabby, *a.* See **poor.**

shade, *n.* See **color.**

shadowy, *a.* See **dark.**

shake, *v.* SYN.—agitate, flutter, jar, jolt, quake, quaver, quiver, rock, shiver, shudder, sway, totter, tremble, vibrate, waver.

shallow, *a.* See **superficial.**

shame, *n.* SYN.—abashment, chagrin, humiliation, mortification; disgrace, dishonor, disrepute, ignominy, odium, opprobrium, scandal. ANT.—dignity, glory, honor, praise, renown.

shameful, *a.* See **disgraceful.**

shape, *n.* SYN.—appearance, build, cast, configuration, contour, cut, figure, form, frame, guise, image, mould, outline, pattern. ANT.—contortion, deformity, distortion, mutilation.

shape, *v.* See **form.**

share, *n.* See **portion.**

share, *v.* SYN.—allot, apportion, appropriate, assign, dispense, distribute, divide, parcel, partake, partition, portion. ANT.—aggregate, amass, combine, condense.

shared, *a.* See **mutual.**

sharp, *a.* SYN.—acute, cutting, keen, pointed; acrid, biting, bitter, pungent; penetrating, piercing, severe, shrill; astute, clever, cunning, quick, shrewd, wily, witty. ANT.—bland, blunt, gentle, shallow, stupid.

shatter, *v.* See **break.**

shattered, *a.* See **broken.**

shelter, *n.* SYN.—asylum, harbor, haven, refuge, retreat, sanctuary; cover, protection, safety, security. ANT.—danger, exposure, hazard, jeopardy, peril.

shelter, *v.* See **cover, defend.**

shield, *v.* See **cover.**

shift, *v.* See **change.**

shifting, *a.* See **variable.**

shine, *v.* SYN.—beam, blaze, flash, flicker, glare, glaze, gleam, glimmer, glisten, glitter, glow, radiate, scintillate, shimmer, sparkle, twinkle.

shining, *a.* See **splendid.**

shock, *v.* See **surprise.**

shocking, *a.* See **terrible.**

short, *a.* SYN.—dumpy, dwarfed, little, low, pudgy, small, squat, undersized; abrupt, brief, compendious, concise, curt, laconic, succinct, summary, terse; deficient, inadequate, insufficient, lacking, limited. ANT.—abundant, ample, big, extended, protracted.

shorten, *v.* SYN.—abbreviate, abridge, condense, contract, curtail, diminish, lessen, limit, reduce, restrict. ANT.—elongate, extend, lengthen.

shout, *v.* See **exclaim.**

show, *n.* SYN.—array, display, exhibition, exposition; demonstration, flourish, ostentation, parade, spectacle, splurge; entertainment, movie, performance, production.

show, *v.* SYN.—disclose, display, exhibit, expose, indicate, manifest, parade, present, reveal, unfold; demonstrate, evidence, manifest, prove, verify; conduct, direct, guide, usher; inform, instruct, teach. ANT.—conceal, confuse, hide.

showy, *a.* See **theatrical.**

shred, *v.* See **tear.**

shrewd, *a.* See **sly.**

shrill, *a.* See **sharp.**

shrivel, *v.* See **wither.**

shun, *v.* See **avoid.**

shut, *v.* See **close.**

shy, *a.* SYN.—bashful, cautious, chary, demure, diffident, fearful, modest, reserved, retiring, sheepish, shrinking, timorous, wary. ANT.—audacious, bold, brazen, forward, immodest.

sick, *a.* SYN.—ailing, diseased, ill, indisposed, infirm, morbid, unhealthy, unwell. ANT.—healthy, robust, sound, strong, well.

sickness, *n.* See **disease.**

sign, *n.* SYN.—emblem, gesture, indication, mark, note, omen, portent, proof, signal, symbol, symptom, token.

signal, *n.* See **alarm.**

significance, *n.* See **meaning.**

significant, *a.* SYN.—critical, grave, important, indicative, material, momentous, telling, weighty. ANT.—insignificant, irrelevant, meaningless, negligible, unimportant.

signify, *v.* See **indicate.**

silence, *n.* See **quiet.**

silent, *a.* SYN.—calm, dumb, hushed, mute, noiseless, peaceful, quiet, still, taciturn, tranquil. ANT.—clamorous, loud, noisy, raucous.

silly, *a.* See **foolish.**

similar, *a.* See **analogous.**

similarity, *n.* SYN.—analogy, correspondence, likeness, parity, resemblance, similitude. ANT.—difference, distinction, variance.

simple, *a.* SYN.—easy, effortless, elementary, facile, mere, pure, single, uncompounded, unmixed; homely, humble, plain; artless, frank, naive, natural, open, unsophisticated; asinine, credulous, foolish, silly. ANT.—adorned, artful, complex, intricate, wise.

simulate, *v.* See **imitate.**

sin, *n.* SYN.—crime, evil, guilt, iniquity, offense, transgression, ungodliness, vice, wickedness, wrong. ANT.—goodness, innocence, purity, righteousness, virtue.

sincere, *a.* SYN.—candid, earnest, frank, genuine, heartfelt, honest, open, straightforward, true, truthful, unfeigned, upright. ANT.—affected, dishonest, hypocritical, insincere, untruthful.

sincerity, *n.* See **honesty.**

sinful, *a.* See **immoral.**

sing, *v.* SYN.—carol, chant, croon, hum, intone, lilt, warble.

singe, *v.* See **burn.**

single, *a.* See **individual.**

singular, *a.* See **peculiar, unique.**

sire, *v.* See **beget.**

site, *n.* See **position.**

situation, *n.* See **condition.**

size, *n.* SYN.—amplitude, area, bigness, bulk, dimensions, expanse, extent, greatness, largeness, magnitude, mass, volume.

skeptic, *n.* SYN.—agnostic, deist, doubter, freethinker, infidel, questioner, unbeliever. ANT.—adorer, believer, follower, worshiper.

skepticism, *n.* See **doubt.**

sketch, *n.* See **outline.**

sketch, *v.* See **draw.**

skill, *n.* SYN.—ability, adroitness, cleverness, cunning, deftness, dexterity, facility, ingenuity, knack, readiness, skillfullness, ANT.—awkwardness, clumsiness, inability, ineptitude.

skilled, *a.* See **skillful.**

skillful, *a.* SYN.—able, accomplished, adept, clever, competent, cunning, expert, ingenious, practiced, proficient, skilled, versed. ANT.—awkward, bungling, clumsy, inexpert, untrained.

slack, *a.* See **loose.**

slander, *n.* SYN.—aspersion, backbiting, calumny, defamation, libel, scandal, vilification. ANT.—applause, commendation, defense, flattery, praise.

slavery, *n.* See **bondage.**

slaughter, *n.* See **massacre.**

slaughter, *n.* See **kill.**

sleek, *a.* See **smooth.**

sleep, *n.* SYN.—catnap, doze, drowse, nap, nod, repose, rest, slumber, snooze.

slender, *a.* See **thin.**

slight, *a.* See **thin.**

slip, *n.* See **error.**

slope, *n.* See **inclination.**

slothful, *a.* See **lazy.**

slow, *a.* SYN.—dawdling, delaying, deliberate, dull, gradual, laggard, leisurely, sluggish, tired. ANT.—fast, quick, rapid, speedy, swift.

sluggish, *a.* See **slow.**

slumber, *n.* See **sleep.**

sly, *a.* SYN.—artful, astute, clandestine, covert, crafty, cunning, foxy, furtive, guileful, insidious, shrewd, stealthy, subtle, surreptitious, tricky, underhand, wily. ANT.—candid, frank, ingenuous, open, sincere.

small, *a.* SYN.—diminutive, insignificant, little, miniature, minute, petty, puny, slight, tiny, trivial, wee. ANT.—big, enormous, huge, immense, large.

smart, *a.* See **clever, intelligent.**

smash, *v.* See **break.**

smell, *n.* SYN.—aroma, fetidness, fragrance, fume, incense, odor, perfume, redolence, scent, stench, stink.

smooth, *a.* SYN.—flat, level, plain, polished, sleek, slick; glib, diplomatic, suave, urbane. ANT.—bluff, blunt, harsh, rough, rugged.

snare, *v.* See **catch.**

sneer, *v.* SYN.—deride, fleer, flout, gibe, jeer, mock, scoff, taunt. ANT.—compliment, flatter, laud, praise.

sneering, *n.* See **ridicule.**

snoopy, *a.* See **curious.**

snug, *a.* See **tight.**

soar, *v.* See **fly.**

sober, *a.* See **solemn.**

sobriety, *n.* See **abstinence.**

social, *a.* SYN.—affable, civil, communicative, friendly, gregarious, hospitable, outgoing, sociable. ANT.—antisocial, disagreeable, hermitic, inhospitable.

soft, *a.* SYN.—compassionate, flexible, gentle, lenient, malleable, meek, mellow, mild, subdued, supple, tender, yielding. ANT.—hard, rigid, rough, tough, unyielding.

soil, *n.* See **land.**

soil, *v.* See **stain.**

solace, *n.* See **comfort.**

sole, *a.* See **alone.**

solemn, *a.* SYN.—august, awe-inspiring, ceremonious, formal, imposing, impressive, majestic, reverential, ritualistic; earnest, grave, sedate, serious, sober, staid. ANT.—boisterous, informal, joyful, ordinary.

solicitude, *n.* See **care.**

solitary, *a.* See **alone.**

solitude, *n.* SYN.—alienation, asylum, concealment, isolation, loneliness, privacy, refuge, retirement, retreat, seclusion. ANT.—exposure, notoriety, publicity.

somber, *a.* See **dismal.**

soon, *adv.* See **early.**

soothe, *n.* See **comfort.**

soothing, *a.* See **gentle.**

sophisticated, *a.* SYN.—blase, cultivated, cultured, worldly, worldly-wise. ANT.—crude, ingenuous, naive, simple, uncouth.

sorcery, *n.* See **magic.**

sordid, *a.* See **vile.**

sorrow, *n.* See **grief.**

sorry, *a.* SYN.—afflicted, grieved, hurt, pained, sad, sorrowful, vexed; contrite, penitent, remorseful, repentant; beggarly, contemptible, mean, paltry, pitiable, pitiful, poor, shabby, vile, worthless, wretched. ANT.—cheerful, delighted, impenitent, splendid, unrepentant.

sort, *n.* See **type.**

sound, *a.* See **valid.**

sound, *n.* SYN.—din, noise, note, tone. ANT.—hush, quiet, silence, stillness.

sour, *a.* SYN.—acid, acrimonious, bitter, glum, morose, peevish, rancid, sharp, sullen, tart. ANT.—genial, kindly, sweet, wholesome.

source, *n.* See **cause.**

sovereignty, *n.* See **power.**

spacious, *a.* SYN.—ample, broad, capacious, extensive, large, roomy, vast, wide. ANT.—confined, cramped, limited, narrow.

sparkle, *v.* See **shine.**

speak, *v.* SYN.—articulate, converse, declare, discourse, express, harangue, say, talk, tell, utter. ANT.—be silent, hush, refrain.

special, *a.* SYN.—distinctive, exceptional, extraordinary, individual, particular, peculiar, uncommon, unusual. ANT.—broad, comprehensive, general, prevailing, widespread.

specific, *a.* SYN.—definite, explicit, limited, precise; categorical, characteristic, especial, peculiar. ANT.—general, generic, vague.

specify, *v.* See **name.**

specimen, *n.* See **sample.**

spectacle, *n.* See **show.**

speculate, *v.* See **suppose.**

speech, *n.* See **talk.**

speed, *v.* See **accelerate.**

spherical, *a.* See **round.**

spirit, *n.* SYN.—apparition, ghost, phantom, soul, specter; courage, enthusiasm, fortitude, liveliness, temper, verve, vigor, vitality, zeal. ANT.—body, flesh, substance; languor, listlessness.

spiritual, *a.* SYN.—divine, ethereal, ghostly, holy, immaterial, incorporeal, religious, sacred, supernatural, unearthly, unworldly. ANT.—carnal, corporeal, material, mundane, physical.

spiteful, *a.* See **ugly.**

splendid, *a.* SYN.—brilliant, bright, dazzling, effulgent, glorious, gorgeous, grand, illustrious, magnificent, radiant, resplendent, shining, showy, sumptuous, superb. ANT.—dull, mediocre, modest, ordinary, unimpressive.

splendor, *n.* See **radiance.**

split, *v.* See **tear.**

spoil, *v.* See **decay.**

spoken, *a.* See **verbal.**

spontaneous, *a.* SYN.—automatic, extemporaneous, impulsive, instinctive, offhand, voluntary, willing. ANT.—compulsory, forced, planned, prepared, rehearsed.

sport, *n.* See **game.**

sport, *v.* See **play.**

spread, *v.* See **open.**

sprightly, *a.* See **buoyant.**

spur, *n.* See **motive.**

squabble, *v.* See **dispute.**

squalid, *a.* See **dirty.**

squander, *v.* See **waste.**

stable, *a.* SYN.—constant, durable, enduring, established, firm, fixed, immovable, immutable, lasting, permanent, secure, staunch, steadfast, steady, unwavering. ANT.—changeable, erratic, irresolute, vacillating, variable.

staid, *a.* See **solemn.**

stain, *v.* SYN.—befoul, blemish, blight, defile, discolor, disgrace, soil, spot, sully, tarnish; color, dye, tinge, tint. ANT.—bleach, cleanse, decorate, honor, purify.

stale, *a.* See **flat.**

stand, *v.* SYN.—abide, bear, continue, endure, suffer, sustain, tolerate; halt, pause, remain, rest, stay, stop. ANT.—advance, progress, run, submit, yield.

standard, *n.* See **criterion.**

start, *n.* See **beginning.**

start, *v.* SYN.—arise, begin, commence, establish, found, inaugurate, initiate, institute, organize, originate. ANT.—complete, end, finish, terminate.

startle, *v.* See **surprise.**

starved, *a.* See **hungry.**

state, *n.* See **condition, nation.**

state, *v.* SYN.—affirm, assert, avow, claim, declare, explain, express, propound, recite, recount, say, specify, tell, utter. ANT.—conceal, deny, imply, retract.

stately, *a.* See **royal.**

statement, *n.* SYN.—allegation, announcement, declaration, mention, report, assertion, proposition, thesis.

status, *n.* See **position, rank.**

statute, *n.* See **act.**

stay, *v.* SYN.—abide, arrest, check, delay, halt, hinder, linger, obstruct, remain, sojourn, stand, tarry, wait. ANT.—advance, expedite, hasten, leave, progress.

steadfast, *a.* See **fast.**

steal, *v.* SYN.—burglarize, embezzle, loot, pilfer, pillage, plagiarize, plunder, purloin, rob, snitch, swipe. ANT.—buy, refund, repay, restore, return.

steep, *a.* SYN.—abrupt, hilly, precipitous, sharp, sheer, sudden. ANT.—flat, gradual, level.

steer, *v.* See **conduct.**

stench, *n.* See **smell.**

stern, *a.* See **severe.**

stiff, *a.* See **rigid.**

stigma, *n.* See **mark.**

still, *a.* See **quiet, silent.**

stimulate, *v.* See **excite.**

stimulus, *n.* SYN.—arousal, encouragement, goad, incentive, motive, provocation, stimulant. ANT.—depressant, discouragement, dissuasion, response.

stingy, *a.* See **miserly.**

stock, *n.* See **supply.**

stock, *v.* See **fill.**

stoical, *a.* See **patient.**

stone, *n.* SYN.—boulder, gravel, jewel, pebble, rock.

stop, *v.* SYN.—abstain, arrest, bar, cease, check, close, cork, desist, discontinue, end, halt, hinder, impede, interrupt, obstruct, plug, seal, terminate. ANT.—begin, proceed, promote, speed, start.

stormy, *a.* SYN.—blustery, gusty, inclement, roaring, rough, tempestuous, turbulent, windy. ANT.—calm, clear, peaceful, quiet, tranquil.

story, *n.* SYN.—account, anecdote, chronicle, fable, fabrication, falsehood, fiction, history, narration, narrative, novel, report, tale, yarn.

stout, *a.* See **fat.**

straight, *a.* SYN.—direct, right, undeviating, unswerving; erect, unbent, upright, vertical; fair, honest, honorable, just, square. ANT.—circuitous, winding; bent, crooked; dishonest.

strain, *n.* See **variety.**

strange, *a.* SYN.—abnormal, bizarre, curious, eccentric, extraordinary, grotesque, irregular, odd, mysterious, peculiar, queer, singular, surprising, uncommon, unusual. ANT.—common, conventional, familiar, ordinary, regular.

stranger, *n.* SYN.—alien, foreigner, immigrant, newcomer, outsider. ANT.—acquaintance, associate, countryman, friend, neighbor.

stray, *v.* See **wander.**

stream, *v.* See **flow.**

strength, *n.* SYN.—durability, force, fortitude, intensity, lustiness, might, potency, power, stamina, stoutness, sturdiness, toughness, vigor. ANT.—feebleness, frailty, infirmity, weakness.

strengthen, *v.* See **confirm.**

stress, *n.* See **pressure.**

stretch, *v.* SYN.—distend, distort, elongate, expand, extend, lengthen, protract, spread, strain. ANT.—contract, loosen, shrink, slacken, tighten.

strict, *a.* See **harsh.**

strike, *v.* See **hit.**

striking, *a.* See **impressive.**

stringent, *a.* See **harsh.**

strive, *v.* See **try.**

strong, *a.* SYN.—athletic, cogent, concentrated, enduring, firm, forceful, forcible, fortified, hale, hardy, impregnable, mighty, potent, powerful, robust, sinewy, sturdy, tough. ANT.—brittle, delicate, feeble, fragile, insipid.

struggle, *n.* See **battle.**

struggle, *v.* See **fight.**

stubborn, *a.* See **obstinate.**

student, *n.* SYN.—disciple, learner, observer, pupil, scholar.

study, *v.* SYN.—contemplate, examine, investigate, scrutinize, weigh; cogitate, meditate, muse, ponder, reflect; learn, master.

stuff, *n.* See **matter.**

stuff, *v.* See **fill.**

stumble, *v.* See **fall.**

stun, *v.* See **surprise.**

stupid, *a.* SYN.—brainless, crass, dense, dull, dumb, foolish, obtuse, senseless, witless. ANT.—alert, bright, clever, discerning, intelligent.

stupor, *n.* SYN.—daze, drowsiness, insensibility, languor, lethargy, numbness, stupefaction, torpor. ANT.—activity, alertness, liveliness, readiness, wakefulness.

sturdy, *a.* See **strong, tough.**

subdue, *v.* See **conquer.**

subject, *n.* SYN.—citizen, dependent, inferior, liegeman, subordinate, vassal; argument, matter, point, theme, thesis, topic; case, object, patient.

sublime, *a.* SYN.—elevated, exalted, glorious, grand, high, lofty, majestic, noble, raised, splendid, supreme. ANT.—base, ignoble, low, ordinary, ridiculous.

submerge, *v.* See **immerse.**

submissive, *a.* See **obedient.**

submit, *v.* See **yield.**

subordinate, *a.* See **inferior.**

subordinate, *n.* See **subject.**

substantiate, *v.* See **confirm.**

substitute, *n.* SYN.—agent, alternate, deputy, lieutenant, proxy, representative, understudy; equivalent, expedient, makeshift. ANT.—head, master, principal, sovereign.

substitution, *n.* See **change.**

subterfuge, *n.* See **pretense.**

subtract, *v.* See **decrease.**

succeed, *v.* SYN.—achieve, flourish, gain, prevail, prosper, thrive, win; ensue, follow, inherit, supersede, supplant. ANT.—fail, miscarry, miss; anticipate, precede.

succession, *n.* See **sequence.**

succinct, *a.* See **brief.**

succor, *n.* See **comfort.**

sudden, *a.* SYN.—abrupt, hasty, immediate, instantaneous, rapid, unexpected. ANT.—anticipated, gradual, slowly.

suffer, *v.* SYN.—bear, endure, feel, stand, sustain, tolerate; allow, indulge, let, permit, tolerate; feel, undergo. ANT.—banish, discard, exclude, overcome.

suffering, *n.* See **agony.**

sufficient, *a.* See **adequate.**

suggest, *v.* SYN.—advise, allude, counsel, hint, imply, insinuate, intimate, offer, propose, recommend, refer. ANT.—declare, demand, dictate, insist.

suggestion, *n.* See **advice.**

suitable, *a.* See **agreeable.**

sullen, *a.* See **morose.**

sum, *n.* SYN.—aggregate, entirety, total, whole. ANT.—fraction, ingredient, part, sample.

sum, *v.* See **add.**

summarize, *v.* See **abstract.**

summit, *n.* See **top.**

sundry, *a.* See **different.**

sunny, *a.* See **clear.**

superficial, *a.* SYN.—cursory, exterior, flimsy, frivolous, imperfect, shallow, slight. ANT.—abstruse, complete, deep, profound, thorough.

superintend, *v.* See **control.**

superiority, *n.* See **advantage.**

supernatural, *a.* SYN.—marvellous, metaphysical, miraculous, other-worldly, preternatural, spiritual, superhuman, unearthly. ANT.—common, human, natural, physical, plain.

supervise, *v.* See **control.**

supervision, *n.* See **oversight.**

supplant, *v.* See **overthrow.**

supple, *a.* See **flexible.**

supply, *n.* SYN.—accumulation, fund, hoard, provision, reserve, stock, store.

supply, *v.* See **furnish.**

support, *n.* SYN.—base, basis, brace, buttress, foundation, groundwork, prop, stay; aid, assistance, backing, comfort, encouragement, favor, help, patronage, succor; livelihood, living, maintenance, subsistence; confirmation, evidence. ANT.—attack, enmity, opposition.

support, *v.* SYN.—advocate, assist, back, bear, brace, encourage, foster, further, help, keep, maintain, preserve, prop, sustain, uphold. ANT.—abandon, betray, destroy, discourage, oppose.

supporter, *n.* See **follower.**

suppose, *v.* SYN.—apprehend, assume, believe, conjecture, deduce, guess, imagine, presume, speculate, surmise, think. ANT.—ascertain, conclude, demonstrate, know, prove.

supremacy, *n.* SYN.—ascendancy, domination, mastery, predominance, sovereignty, sway, transcendence. ANT.—inferiority.

supreme, *a.* See **principal.**

sure, *a.* See **certain.**

surly, *a.* See **ugly.**

surplus, *n.* See **excess.**

surprise, *n.* See **wonder.**

surprise, *v.* SYN.—alarm, amaze, astonish, astound, disconcert, dumbfound, flabbergast, shock, startle, stun, take aback. ANT.—admonish, caution, forewarn, prepare.

surrender, *v.* SYN.—abandon, acquiesce, capitulate, cede, relinquish, renounce, resign, sacrifice, submit, yield. ANT.—conquer, overcome, resist, rout.

surround, *v.* See **enclose.**

suspect, *v.* See **doubt.**

suspend, *v.* SYN.—adjourn, defer, delay, discontinue, interrupt, postpone, stay; balance, dangle, hang, poise, swing. ANT.—continue, maintain, persist, proceed, prolong.

suspicion, *n.* See **doubt.**

sustain, *v.* See **support.**

sustenance, *n.* See **food.**

sway, *v.* See **influence.**

swear, *v.* See **affirm.**

sweeping, *a.* See **broad.**

sweet, *a.* SYN.—agreeable, delightful, engaging, gentle, honeyed, luscious, mellifluous, melodious, pleasing, saccharine, sugary, winning. ANT.—acrid, bitter, offensive, repulsive, sour.

swift, *a.* See **fast.**

swindle, *n.* See **fraud.**

swindle, *v.* See **cheat.**

symbol, *n.* See **character.**

sympathetic, *a.* See **kind.**

sympathize, *v.* See **comfort.**

sympathy, *n.* SYN.—affinity, agreement, commiseration, compassion, concord, condolence, congeniality, empathy, harmony, pity, tenderness, warmth. ANT.—antipathy, harshness, indifference, malevolence, unconcern.

synthetic, *a.* See **artificial.**

system, *n.* SYN.—arrangement, method, mode, order, organization, plan, process, regularity, rule, scheme. ANT.—chance, chaos, confusion, disarrangement, disorder, irregularity.

T

tact, *n.* SYN.—address, adroitness, dexterity, diplomacy, finesse, knack, poise, savoir faire, skill. ANT.—awkwardness, blunder, incompetence, rudeness, vulgarity.

tactful, *a.* SYN.—adroit, diplomatic, discreet, discriminating, judicious, politic. ANT.—boorish, churlish, coarse, gruff, rude.

tainted, *a.* See **corrupt.**

take, *v.* SYN.—appropriate, capture, catch, confiscate, ensnare, gain, purloin, remove, steal; clasp, clutch, grasp, grip, seize; accept, get, obtain, receive; bear, endure, stand, tolerate; bring, carry, convey, escort; attract, captivate, charm, delight, interest; claim, demand, necessitate, require; adopt, assume, choose, espouse, select.

tale, *n.* See **story.**

talent, *n.* SYN.—ability, aptitude, capability, cleverness, endowment, faculty, genius, gift, knack, skill. ANT.—incompetence, ineptitude, stupidity.

talented, *a.* See **clever.**

talk, *n.* SYN.—chatter, conference, conversation, dialogue, discourse, discussion, gossip, lecture, report, rumor, speech. ANT.—correspondence, meditation, silence, writing.

talk, *v.* SYN.—blab, chat, converse, gossip, jabber, mutter, prattle, speak, tattle; argue, comment, declaim, discourse, harangue, lecture, plead, preach, rant, spout; confer, consult, deliberate, discuss, reason.

talkative, *a.* SYN.—chattering, chatty, communicative, garrulous, glib, loquacious, verbose, voluble. ANT.—laconic, reticent, silent, taciturn, uncommunicative.

tall, *a.* See **high.**

tame, *a.* SYN.—docile, domestic, domesticated, gentle; meek, subdued, submissive; dull, flat, insipid, tedious. ANT.—fierce, savage, spirited, wild; animated, exciting, lively, spirited.

tangible, *a.* See **material.**

tarnish, *v.* See **stain.**

tart, *a.* See **bitter.**

taste, *n.* SYN.—flavor, relish, savor, tang; discernment, disposition, inclination, judgment, liking, predilection, sensibility, zest. ANT.—antipathy, disinclination, indelicacy, insipidity.

taunt, *v.* See **sneer, tease.**

taunting, *a.* See **sarcastic.**

taut, *a.* See **tight.**

tax, *n.* SYN.—assessment, custom, duty, exaction, excise, impost, levy, rate, toll, tribute; burden, strain. ANT.—gift, remuneration, reward, wages.

tax, *v.* See **assess.**

teach, *v.* SYN.—educate, inculcate, inform, instill, instruct, school, train, tutor. ANT.—misguide, misinform.

tear, *v.* SYN.—cleave, disunite, lacerate, rend, rip, rive, sever, shred, slit, split, sunder, wound. ANT.—join, mend, repair, sew, unite.

tease, *v.* SYN.—aggravate, annoy, badger, bother, disturb, harass, harry, irritate, molest, nag, pester, plague, provoke, tantalize, taunt, torment, vex, worry. ANT.—comfort, delight, gratify, please, soothe.

tedious, *a.* SYN.—boring, burdensome, dilatory, dreary, dull, humdrum, irksome, monotonous, slow, sluggish, tardy, tiresome, uninteresting, wearisome. ANT.—amusing, entertaining, exciting, interesting, quick.

tedium, *n.* See **boredom.**

tell, *v.* SYN.—describe, narrate, recount, rehearse, relate, report; communicate, express, mention, publish, speak, state, utter; announce, betray, confess, disclose, divulge, reveal; discern, discover, distinguish, recognize; acquaint, apprise, inform, instruct, notify; direct, order, request.

temerity, *n.* SYN.—audacity, boldness, foolhardiness, precipitancy, rashness, recklessness. ANT.—caution, hesitation, prudence, timidity, wariness.

temper, *n.* See **anger.**

temperament, *n.* See **humor.**

temperance, *n.* See **abstinence.**

tempest, *n.* See **wind.**

temporal, *a.* See **secular.**

temporary, *a.* SYN.—brief, ephemeral, evanescent, fleeting, momentary, short-lived, transient. ANT.—abiding, immortal, lasting, permanent, timeless.

tenacity, *n.* See **perseverance.**

tend, *v.* See **attend.**

tendency, *n.* SYN.—aim, bent, bias, drift, inclination, leaning, predisposition, proclivity, proneness, propensity, trend. ANT.—aversion, deviation, disinclination.

tender, *a.* See **mild, soft.**

tenderness, *n.* See **affection, sympathy.**

tenet, *n.* See **doctrine.**

term, *n.* SYN.—boundary, duration, limit, period, time; condition, expression, name, phrase, word.

terminal, *a.* See **final.**

terminate, *v.* SYN.—abolish, cease, close, complete, conclude, end, expire, finish, stop. ANT.—begin, commence, establish, initiate, start.

terrible, *a.* SYN.—appalling, awful, dire, dreadful, fearful, frightful, gruesome, hideous, horrible, horrid, severe, shocking. ANT.—happy, joyous, pleasing, safe, secure.

terrify, *v.* See **frighten.**

territory, *n.* SYN.—country, district, division, domain, dominion, land, place, province, quarter, region, section.

terror, *n.* SYN.—alarm, consternation, dismay, dread, fear, fright, horror, panic. ANT.—assurance, calm, peace, security.

terse, *a.* SYN.—brief, compact, concise, condensed, incisive, neat, pithy, succinct, summary. ANT.—lengthy, prolix, verbose, wordy.

test, *v.* SYN.—assay, examine, experiment, inspect, prove, try, verify.

testimony, *n.* SYN.—attestation, confirmation, declaration, evidence, proof, witness. ANT.—argument, contradiction, disproof, refutation.

testy, *a.* See **peevish.**

theatrical, *a.* SYN.—affected, artificial, ceremonious, dramatic, histrionic, melodramatic, showy, stagy. ANT.—modest, subdued, unaffected, unemotional.

theft, *n.* See **robbery.**

theme, *n.* SYN.—composition, essay, motive, subject, text, thesis, topic.

theory, *n.* SYN.—conjecture, doctrine, hypothesis, opinion, postulate, presupposition, speculation. ANT.—fact, practice, proof, verity.

therefore, *adv.* SYN.—accordingly, consequently, hence, so, then, thence.

thick, *a.* See **dense.**

thin, *a.* SYN.—attenuated, diaphanous, diluted, emaciated, fine, flimsy, gaunt, gauzy, gossamer, lank, lean, meager, narrow, rare, scanty, scrawny, skinny, slender, slight, slim, spare, tenuous. ANT.—broad, bulky, fat, thick, wide.

think, *v.* SYN.—conceive, imagine, picture, recall, recollect, remember; cogitate, contemplate, deliberate, meditate, muse, ponder, reason, reflect, speculate; apprehend, believe, consider, deem, esteem, judge, opine, reckon, regard, suppose; devise, intend, mean, plan, purpose. ANT.—conjecture, forget, guess.

thorough, *a.* See **complete, radical.**

thought, *n.* SYN.—cogitation, conception, consideration, contemplation, deliberation, fancy, idea, imagination, impression, judgment, meditation, memory, notion, opinion, recollection, reflection, regard, retrospection, sentiment, view.

thoughtful, *a.* SYN.—attentive, careful, cautious, concerned, considerate, heedful, provident, prudent; comtemplative, dreamy, introspective, meditative, pensive, reflective. ANT.—heedless, inconsiderate, precipitous, rash, thoughtless.

thoughtless, *a.* See **careless.**

threatening, *a.* See **impending.**

thrifty, *a.* See **frugal.**

throb, *v.* See **beat.**

throng, *n.* See **crowd.**

throw, *v.* SYN.—cast, fling, hurl, pitch, propel, thrust, toss. ANT.—draw, haul, hold, pull, retain.

thrust, *v.* See **push.**

thwart, *v.* See **frustrate, hinder.**

tidings, *n.* See **news.**

tidy, *a.* See **neat.**

tie, *n.* See **connection, link.**

tie, *v.* See **bind.**

tight, *a.* SYN.—close, compact, constricted, contracted, firm, narrow, snug, stretched, taut, tense; closefisted, niggardly, parsimonious, penny-pinching, stingy. ANT.—lax, loose, open, relaxed, slack.

time, *n.* SYN.—age, date, duration, epoch, era, interim, period, season, span, spell, tempo, term.

timid, *a.* See **afraid, bashful.**

tiny, *a.* See **small.**

tire, *v.* SYN.—bore, exhaust, fatigue, jade, tucker, wear out, weary. ANT.—amuse, invigorate, refresh, restore, revive.

tired, *a.* See **weary.**

title, *n.* SYN.—appellation, denomination, designation, epithet, name; claim, due, privilege, right.

toil, *n.* See **work.**

tolerant, *a.* See **broad, merciful.**

tolerate, *v.* SYN.—allow, permit; abide, bear, brook, endure, stand. ANT.—forbid, prohibit; protest.

toll, *n.* See **tax.**

too, *prep.* See **also.**

tool, *n.* See **instrument.**

top, *n.* SYN.—apex, chief, crest, crown, head, pinnacle, summit, zenith. ANT.—base, bottom, foot, foundation.

topic, *n.* See **subject, theme.**

torment, *n.* See **agony.**

torment, *v.* See **tease, worry.**

torpor, *n.* See **stupor.**

torrid, *a.* See **hot.**

torture, *n.* See **agony.**

torture, *v.* See **persecute.**

toss, *v.* See **throw.**

total, *a.* See **complete, whole.**

total, *n.* See **aggregate.**

total, *v.* See **add.**

touching, *a.* SYN.—affecting, heart-rending, impressive, moving, pitiable, poignant, sad, tender; adjacent, adjunct, bordering, tangent. ANT.—animated, enlivening, exhilarating, removed.

touchy, *a.* See **irritable.**

tough, *a.* SYN.—cohesive, firm, hardy, stout, strong, sturdy, tenacious; difficult, formidable, hard, laborious, troublesome, trying; callous, incorrigible, obdurate, stubborn, vicious. ANT.—brittle, fragile, frail; easy, facile; compliant, forbearing, submissive.

toughness, *n.* See **strength.**

tour, *v.* See **travel.**

tow, *v.* See **draw.**

train, *v.* See **direct, teach.**

training, *n.* See **education, exercise.**

trait, *n.* SYN.—attribute, characteristic, feature, mark, peculiarity, property, quality.

traitorous, *a.* See **disloyal.**

tramp, *n.* See **vagrant.**

tranquil, *a.* See **calm, composed.**

tranquility, *n.* See **quiet.**

transact, *v.* SYN.—carry on, conduct, execute, manage, negotiate, perform, treat.

transaction, *n.* SYN.—affair, business, deal, deed, negotiation, occurrence, proceeding.

transfer, *v.* SYN.—convey, dispatch, send, transmit, transport; remove, transplant; assign, consign, relegate.

transform, *v.* See **change.**

transient, *a.* See **temporary.**

translate, *v.* See **interpret.**

transmit, *v.* See **communicate, send.**

transparent, *a.* SYN.—clear, crystalline, limpid, lucid, thin, translucent; evident, explicit, manifest, obvious, open. ANT.—muddy, opaque, thick, turbid; ambiguous, questionable.

transpire, *v.* See **happen.**

transport, *v.* SYN.—bear, carry, convey, move, remove, shift, transfer; enrapture, entrance, lift, ravish, stimulate.

trap, *n.* SYN.—ambush, artifice, bait, intrigue, lure, net, pitfall, ruse, snare, stratagem, trick, wile.

travel, *v.* SYN.—go, journey, ramble, roam, rove, tour. ANT.—stay, stop.

treachery, *n.* See **conspiracy.**

treason, *n.* See **conspiracy.**

treasure, *v.* See **cherish.**

treat, *v.* See **use.**

treaty, *n.* See **alliance.**

tremble, *v.* See **shake.**

trespass, *v.* See **invade.**

trial, *n.* SYN.—examination, experiment, ordeal, proof, test; attempt, effort, endeavor, essay; affliction, hardship, misery, misfortune, suffering, tribulation, trouble. ANT.—alleviation, consolation.

trick, *n.* SYN.—antic, artifice, cheat, deception, device, fraud, guile, hoax, imposture, ploy, ruse, stratagem, stunt, subterfuge, wile. ANT.—candor, exposure, honesty, openness, sincerity.

tricky, *a.* See **sly.**

trifling, *a.* See **trivial.**

trim, *v.* See **adorn.**

trip, *n.* See **journey.**

trite, *a.* SYN.—banal, common, hackneyed, ordinary, stale, stereotyped, ANT.—fresh,

modern, momentous, novel, stimulating.

triumph, *n.* SYN.—achievement, conquest, jubilation, ovation, victory. ANT.—defeat, failure.

trivial, *a.* SYN.—frivolous, insignificant, paltry, petty, small, trifling, unimportant. ANT.—important, momentous, serious, weighty.

trouble, *n.* SYN.—affliction, anxiety, calamity, distress, grief, hardship, misery, pain, sorrow, woe; annoyance, bother, care, embarrassment, irritation, pains, torment, worry; disorder, disturbance, problem; care, effort, exertion, labor, toil.

trouble, *v.* See **annoy, disturb.**

troublesome, *a.* SYN.—annoying, bothersome, distressing, disturbing, irksome, trying, vexatious; arduous, burdensome, difficult, laborious, tedious. ANT.—accommodating, amusing, easy, gratifying, pleasant.

true, *a.* SYN.—accurate, actual, authentic, correct, exact, genuine, real, veracious, veritable; constant, faithful, honest, loyal, reliable, sincere, steadfast, trustworthy. ANT.—counterfeit, erroneous, false, fictitious, spurious; faithless, false, fickle, inconstant.

trust, *n.* See **faith.**

trust, *v.* SYN.—depend on, reckon on, rely on; believe, credit, hope; commit, confide, intrust. ANT.—doubt, impugn, question, suspect.

trustworthy, *a.* See **reliable.**

truth, *n.* SYN.—accuracy, actuality, authenticity, correctness, exactness, fact, honesty, rightness, truthfulness, veracity, verisimilitude, verity. ANT.—falsehood, falsity, fiction, lie, untruth.

truthful, *a.* SYN.—candid, frank, honest, open, sincere, true, veracious; accurate, correct, exact, reliable. ANT.—deceitful, misleading, sly.

try, *v.* SYN.—attempt, endeavor, strive, struggle, undertake; afflict, prove, test, torment, trouble; aim, aspire, design, intend, mean. ANT.—abandon, decline, ignore, neglect, omit; comfort, console.

trying, *a.* See **troublesome.**

tumult, *n.* See **confusion, noise.**

tune, *n.* SYN.—air, concord, harmony, melody, strain.

turbulent, *a.* See **stormy.**

turmoil, *n.* See **confusion.**

turn, *v.* SYN.—circle, circulate, invert, revolve, rotate, spin, twirl, twist, wheel, whirl; avert, deflect, deviate, divert, swerve; alter, change, transmute. ANT.—arrest, fix, stand, stop; continue, proceed; endure, perpetuate.

twist, *v.* See **bend, turn.**

type, *n.* SYN.—emblem, mark, sign, symbol; category, character, class, description, kind, nature, sort, stamp; exemplar, model, pattern. ANT.—deviation, eccentricity, monstrosity, peculiarity.

typical, *a.* See **ordinary.**

tyrant, *n.* SYN.—autocrat, despot, dictator, oppressor, persecutor.

U

ugly, *a.* SYN.—deformed, hideous, homely, plain, repellent, repulsive, uncomely; disagreeable, ill-natured, spiteful, surly, vicious. ANT.—attractive, beautiful, fair, handsome, pretty.

ultimate, *a.* See **last.**

unadulterated, *a.* See **pure.**

unassuming, *a.* See **humble.**

uncertain, *a.* See **vague.**

uncertainty, *n.* See **doubt.**

uncompromising, *a.* See **obstinate.**

unconcern, *n.* See **indifference.**

unconditional, *a.* See **absolute.**

uncouth, *a.* See **crude.**

uncover, *v.* See **reveal.**

under, *prep.* See **beneath.**

undergo, *v.* See **suffer.**

understand, *v.* SYN.—appreciate, apprehend, comprehend, conceive, discern, grasp, know, learn, perceive, realize, see. ANT.—ignore, misapprehend, mistake, misunderstand.

understanding, *n.* See **agreement.**

understudy, *n.* See **substitute.**

undertaking, *n.* See **attempt.**

undivided, *a.* See **whole.**

undying, *a.* See **eternal.**

unearthly, *a.* See **supernatural.**

uneducated, *a.* See **ignorant.**

unemployed, *a.* See **idle.**

unexpected, *a.* See **sudden.**

unfasten, *v.* See **open.**

unfavorable, *a.* See **adverse.**

unfold, *v.* See **develop.**

uniform, *a.* See **regular.**

uninteresting, *a.* See **tedious.**

union, *n.* SYN.—combination, concurrence, fusion, incorporation, joining, solidarity, unification; agreement, concord, harmony, unanimity; alliance, amalgamation, coalition, concert, confederacy, league, marriage. ANT.—division, schism, separation; disagreement, discord.

unique, *a.* SYN.—choice, distinctive, exceptional, matchless, peculiar, rare, singular, sole, solitary, uncommon, unequaled. ANT.—common, commonplace, frequent, ordinary, typical.

unison, *n.* See **agreement.**

unite, *v.* SYN.—amalgamate, associate, attach, blend, combine, conjoin, connect, consolidate, embody, fuse, join, link, merge, unify. ANT.—disconnect, disrupt, divide, separate, sever.

universal, *a.* See **common.**

unlawful, *a.* See **illegal.**

unlike, *a.* See **different.**

unlimited, *a.* See **infinite.**

unobstructed, *a.* See **free.**

unsafe, *a.* See **dangerous.**

unselfish, *a.* See **generous.**

unsophisticated, *a.* See **naive.**

unstable, *a.* See **fickle.**

untainted, *a.* See **pure.**

untamed, *a.* See **wild.**

unusual, *a.* See **irregular.**

unyielding, *a.* See **fast.**

upbraid, *v.* See **scold.**

uphold, *v.* See **defend.**

upright, *a.* See **straight.**

upset, *v.* See **bother.**

urge, *n.* See **desire.**

urge, *v.* See **persuade.**

urgency, *n.* See **emergency, pressure.**

urgent, *a.* SYN.—cogent, compelling, critical, crucial, exigent, impelling, imperative, important, importunate, insistent, instant, necessary, pressing, serious. ANT.—insignificant, petty, trifling, trivial, unimportant.

use, *n.* See **practice.**

use, *v.* SYN.—apply, avail, employ, exploit, manipulate, operate, utilize; exercise, exert, practice; consume, exhaust, expend; handle, manage, treat; accustom, familiarize, inure, train. ANT.—ignore, neglect, overlook, waste.

useful, *a.* See **beneficial.**

usefulness, *n.* See **worth.**

useless, *a.* See **vain.**

usual, *a.* SYN.—accustomed, common, customary, every-day, familiar, general, habitual, normal, ordinary. ANT.—abnormal, exceptional, extraordinary, irregular, rare.

utensil, *n.* See **instrument.**

utilize, *v.* See **employ.**

V

vacant, *a.* SYN.—bare, barren, blank, empty, unoccupied, vacuous, void. ANT.—busy, employed, engaged, full, replete.

vacate, *v.* See **abandon.**

vacillate, *v.* See **fluctuate.**

vacillating, *a.* See **inconsistent.**

vagabond, *n.* See **beggar.**

vagrant, *n.* SYN.—beggar, bum, hobo, rover, tramp, vagabond, wanderer. ANT.—gentleman, laborer, worker.

vague, *a.* SYN.—ambiguous, dim, hazy, indefinite, indistinct, obscure, uncertain, unclear, undetermined, unsettled. ANT.—clear, explicit, lucid, precise, specific.

vain, *a.* SYN.—abortive, bootless, empty, fruitless, futile, idle, ineffectual, pointless, unavailing, useless, valueless, vapid, worthless; conceited, proud, vainglorious. ANT.—effective, potent, profitable; meek, modest.

vainglory, *n.* See **pride.**

valiant, *a.* See **brave.**

valid, *a.* SYN.—binding, cogent, conclusive, convincing, effective, efficacious, legal, logical, powerful, sound, strong, telling, weighty. ANT.—counterfeit, null, spurious, void, weak.

valuable, *a.* SYN.—costly, expensive, precious; dear, esteemed; profitable, useful. ANT.—cheap, mean, poor; trashy, worthless.

value, *n.* See **worth.**

value, *v.* See **cherish.**

vanity, *n.* See **conceit, pride.**

vanquish, *v.* See **conquer.**

variable, *a.* SYN.—changeable, fickle, fitful, inconstant, shifting, unstable, vacillating, wavering. ANT.—constant, stable, steady, unchanging, uniform.

variant, *a.* See **different.**

variation, *n.* See **change.**

variety, *n.* SYN.—assortment, change, difference, dissimilarity, diversity, heterogeneity, medley, miscellany, mixture, multifariousness, variousness; breed, kind, sort, stock, strain, subspecies. ANT.—homogeneity, likeness, monotony, sameness, uniformity.

various, *a.* See **different.**

vary, *v.* See **change.**

vassalage, *n.* See **bondage.**

vast, *a.* See **large.**

vehement, *a.* See **passionate.**

veil, *v.* See **cover.**

venerate, *v.* See **admire.**

vengeance, *n.* See **revenge.**

vent, *v.* See **emit.**

venture, *v.* See **risk.**

verbal, *a.* SYN.—literal, oral, spoken, vocal. ANT.—documentary, recorded, written.

verbose, *a.* See **talkative.**

verbosity, *n.* SYN.—long-windedness, redundancy, talkativeness, verboseness, wordiness. ANT.—conciseness, laconism, terseness.

verification, *n.* See **proof.**

verify, *v.* See **confirm, determine.**

veritable, *a.* See **true.**

vertical, *a.* SYN.—erect, perpendicular, plumb, straight, upright. ANT.—horizontal, inclined, level, oblique, prone.

vex, *v.* See **aggravate.**

vexation, *n.* SYN.—annoyance, chagrin, exasperation, irritation, mortification, pique. ANT.—appeasement, comfort, gratification, pleasure.

vibrate, *v.* See **shake.**

vice, *n.* See **sin.**

vicinity, *n.* See **neighborhood.**

victory, *n.* See **triumph.**

view, *n.* SYN.—observation, regard, review, sight, survey; outlook, panorama, perspective, prospect, range, scene, vista; belief, conception, impression, judgment, opinion, sentiment.

view, *v.* See **look.**

viewpoint, *n.* See **attitude.**

vigilant, *a.* SYN.—alert, anxious, attentive, careful, cautious, circumspect, observant, wakeful, wary, watchful. ANT.—careless, inattentive, lax, neglectful, oblivious.

vigor, *n.* See **spirit.**

vigorous, *a.* See **lively.**

vile, *a.* SYN.—base, debased, depraved, foul, loathsome, obscene, odious, revolting, sordid, vicious, vulgar, wicked; abject, despicable, ignoble, low, mean, worthless, wretched. ANT.—attractive, decent, laudable; honorable, upright.

vilify, *v.* See **abuse.**

villainous, *a.* See **bad.**

vindicate, *v.* SYN.—absolve, acquit, assert, clear, defend, excuse, exonerate, justify, support, uphold. ANT.—abandon, accuse, blame, convict.

violate, *v.* SYN.—break, disobey, infringe, invade, transgress; defile, desecrate, dishonor, pollute, profane; debauch, deflower, ravish.

violence, *n.* See **force.**

violent, *a.* SYN.—boisterous, fierce, forceful, furious, impetuous; passionate, powerful, raging, raving, turbulent, vehement, wild; acute, extreme, intense, severe. ANT.—calm, feeble, gentle, quiet, soft.

virgin, *a.* See **pure.**

virtue, *n.* SYN.—chastity, goodness, integrity, morality, probity, purity, rectitude, virginity; effectiveness, efficacy, force, power, strength; excellence, merit, worth. ANT.—corruption, lewdness, sin, vice; fault.

virtuous, *a.* See **moral.**

visible, *a.* See **clear.**

vision, *n.* SYN.—apparition, daydream, dream, ghost, hallucination, mirage, phantasm, phantom, prophecy, revelation, specter. ANT.—reality, substance, verity.

visionary, *a.* See **ideal.**

vital, *a.* SYN.—alive, animate, living; basic, cardinal, essential, indispensable, necessary, paramount, urgent. ANT.—inanimate, inert, lifeless; nonessential, unimportant.

vitality, *n.* See **life.**

vitiate, *v.* See **debase.**

vitiated, *a.* See **corrupt.**

vivid, *a.* SYN.—bright, brilliant, intense, striking; animated, clear, expressive, fresh, graphic, lively, lucid. ANT.—dull, vague; dim, dreary, dusky.

vocation, *n.* See **business.**

void, *a.* See **vacant.**

volatile, *a.* See **buoyant.**

volition, *n.* See **will.**

volume, *n.* See **capacity.**

voluntary, *a.* See **spontaneous.**

volunteer, *v.* See **offer.**

vulgar, *a.* SYN.—common, general, ordinary, plebian, popular; base, coarse, gross, low, obscene, ribald, rude, unrefined. ANT.—esoteric, select; aristocratic, polite, refined.

W

wages, *n.* See **pay.**

wait, *v.* SYN.—abide, bide, delay, linger, remain, rest, stay, tarry; await, expect, watch; attend, minister, serve. ANT.—act, expedite, hasten, leave.

wander, *v.* SYN.—deviate, digress, err, ramble, range, roam, rove, saunter, stray, stroll, traipse. ANT.—halt, linger, settle, stay, stop.

want, *v.* SYN.—covet, crave, desire, long for, wish; lack, need, require.

wariness, *n.* See **caution.**

warm, *a.* See **cordial.**

warn, *v.* SYN.—admonish, advise, apprise, inform, notify.

warning, *n.* SYN.—admonition, advice, caution; indication, information, notice, portent, sign.

wary, *a.* See **attentive, vigilant.**

wash, *v.* SYN.—bathe, clean, cleanse, launder, rinse, scrub, wet. ANT.—dirty, foul, soil, stain.

waste, *a.* See **desolate.**

waste, *v.* SYN.—despoil, destroy, devastate, pillage, plunder, ravage, ruin, sack, strip; consume, corrode, dissipate, lavish, misuse, scatter, spend, squander, wear out; decay, diminish, dwindle, pine, wither. ANT.—accumulate, conserve, economize, preserve, save.

watch, *v.* See **see.**

waver, *v.* See **doubt.**

wavering, *a.* See **variable.**

wax, *v.* See **increase.**

way, *n.* SYN.—avenue, channel, course, passage, path, road, route, street, thoroughfare, track, trail, walk; fashion, form, habit, manner, method, mode, plan, practice, procedure, process, style, system.

weak, *adj.* SYN.—bending, fragile, frail, pliant, tender, yielding; debilitated, decrepit, delicate, feeble, impotent, infirm, illogical, inadequate, ineffective, lame, poor, vague; irresolute, pliable, vacillating, wavering; assailable, defenseless, exposed, vulnerable. ANT.—potent, powerful, robust, strong, sturdy.

weakness, *n.* See **inability.**

wealth, *n.* SYN.—abundance, affluence, fortune, luxury, money, opulence, plenty, possessions, riches. ANT.—indigence, need, poverty, want.

wealthy, *a.* See **rich.**

wearied, *a.* See **faint.**

weary, *a.* SYN.—bored, exhausted, faint, fatigued, jaded, spent, tired, wearied, worn. ANT.—fresh, hearty, invigorated, rested.

weary, *v.* See **tire.**

wedlock, *n.* See **marriage.**

weigh, *v.* See **consider.**

weight, *n.* SYN.—burden, gravity, heaviness, load, pressure; emphasis, import, importance, influence, significance, stress, value. ANT.—buoyancy, levity, lightness; insignificance, triviality.

well, *a.* SYN.—hale, happy, healthy, hearty, sound; beneficial, convenient, expedient, good, profitable. ANT.—depressed, feeble, infirm, weak.

whim, *n.* SYN.—caprice, fancy, humor, inclination, notion, quirk, vagary, whimsy.

whole, *a.* SYN.—all, complete, entire, intact, integral, perfect, total, undivided, unimpaired; hale, healed, healthy, sound, well. ANT.—defective, deficient, imperfect, incomplete, partial.

wholesome, *a.* See **healthy.**

wicked, *a.* See **bad, malicious.**

wide, *a.* See **broad.**

wild, *a.* SYN.—barbarous, fierce, outlandish, rude, savage, uncivilized, undomesticated, untamed; desert, desolate, rough, uncultivated, waste; frantic, frenzied, impetuous, irregular, mad, turbulent, wanton, wayward; boisterous, stormy, tempestous; extravagant, foolish, giddy, rash, reckless. ANT.—civilized, gentle; calm, placid, quiet.

wilful, *a.* See **intentional.**

will, *n.* SYN.—choice, decision, desire, determination, intention, pleasure, preference, resolution, testament, volition, wish. ANT.—coercion, compulsion, disinterest, indifference.

win, *v.* See **succeed.**

wind, *n.* SYN.—blast, breeze, draft, gale, gust, hurricane, squall, storm, tempest, zephyr.

wisdom, *n.* SYN.—discretion, erudition, foresight, information, insight, intelligence, judgment, knowledge, learning, prudence, reason, sagacity, sageness, sense. ANT.—foolishness, ignorance, imprudence, nonsense, stupidity.

wise, *a.* SYN.—deep, discerning, enlightened, intelligent, penetrating, profound, sagacious, sound; erudite, informed, knowing, learned, scholarly; advisable, expedient, prudent. ANT.—foolish, shallow, simple.

wish, *n.* See **desire.**

wish, *v.* SYN.—covet, crave, desire, hanker, hunger, long, thirst, want, yearn. ANT.—decline, despise, reject, repudiate, scorn.

wit, *n.* SYN.—comprehension, intellect, intelligence, mind, perspicacity, reason, sagacity, sense, understanding; banter, cleverness, fun, humor, irony, pleasantry, raillery, sarcasm, satire, witticism. ANT.—commonplace, platitude, sobriety, solemnity, stupidity.

witchcraft, *n.* See **magic.**

withdraw, *v.* See **leave, remove.**

wither, *v.* SYN.—droop, dry, sear, shrink, shrivel, waste, wilt, wizen; decline, fail, languish, sink, weaken. ANT.—refresh, rejuvenate, renew, revive.

withhold, *v.* See **refrain.**

witness, *n.* See **testimony.**

witty, *a.* See **clever, funny.**

wonder, *n.* SYN.—curiosity, marvel, miracle, phenomenon, prodigy, rarity, spectacle; admiration, amazement, astonishment, awe, bewilderment, curiosity, surprise, wonderment. ANT.— familiarity, triviality; apathy, expectation, indifference.

word, *n.* See **term.**

work, *n.* SYN.—achievement, business, drudgery, effort, employment, labor, occupation, opus, performance, production; task, toil, travail. ANT.—ease, leisure, play, recreation, vacation.

worldly, *a.* See **carnal.**

worn, *a.* See **weary.**

worry, *n.* SYN.—anxiety, apprehension, concern, disquiet, fear, trouble, uneasiness. ANT.—contentment, equanimity, peace, satisfaction.

worry, *v.* SYN.—annoy, bother, disturb, gall, harass, harry, haze, irritate, pain, persecute, tease, torment, trouble, vex; fret, fume, fuss. ANT.—comfort, console, solace.

worship, *v.* SYN.—adore, deify, honor, idolize, respect, revere, reverence, venerate. ANT.—blaspheme, curse, despise, loathe, scorn.

worth, *n.* SYN.—excellence, merit, price, usefulness, utility, value, virtue, worthiness. ANT.—cheapness, uselessness, valuelessness.

worthless, *a.* See **vain.**

wound, *v.* See **injure.**

wrap, *v.* See **cover.**

wrath, *n.* See **anger.**

wreck, *v.* See **destroy.**

wretched, *a.* See **miserable, sorry.**

writer, *n.* See **author.**

wrong, *a.* SYN.—amiss, askew, awry, erroneous, fallacious, false, faulty, inaccurate, incorrect, mistaken, unprecise, untrue; improper, inappropriate, unsuitable; aberrant, bad, criminal, evil, immoral, iniquitous, reprehensible. ANT.—correct, right, true; suitable; proper.

Y

yearning, *n.* See **desire.**

yield, *n.* See **harvest.**

yield, *v.* SYN.—afford, bear, bestow, breed, generate, impart, pay, produce, supply; accord, allow, concede, grant, permit; abdicate, accede, acquiesce, capitulate, cede, quit, relent, relinquish, resign, submit, succumb, surrender, waive. ANT.—deny, dissent, oppose, refuse; assert, resist, strive, struggle.

yielding, *a.* See **obedient.**

young, *a.* See **youthful.**

youthful, *a.* SYN.—boyish, callow, childish, childlike, girlish, immature, juvenile, puerile, young. ANT.—aged, elderly, mature, old, senile.

Z

zeal, *n.* See **enthusiasm.**

zealous, *a.* See **ardent.**

zenith, *n.* See **climax.**

zone, *n.* SYN.—belt, climate, locality, region, sector, tract.

aal, äl [D.] Eel.

Aal, äl [G.] Eel.

Aalsuppe, äl′söp″pe [G.] Eel soup.

abaisse, a·bes′ [Fr.] Pie crust.

abajo, ä·bä′hō [Sp.] Down, under, underneath, below, downstairs.

à bas, a bä′ [Fr.] Down, down with.

abatido, ä·bä·tē′dō [Sp.] Dejected, discouraged, abject.

abatis or **abattis,** a·bä·tē′ [Fr.] Giblets.

abatis de dinde, a·bä·tē′ de daNd′ [Fr.] Turkey giblets.

abatis en ragoût, a·bä·té′ oN rä·gö′ [Fr.] Giblet stew.

abbraciamento, ä·brä·chä·men′tō [It.] A hug, an embrace.

A beau jeu beau retour, a bō zhŒ′ bō Re·tör′ [Fr.] One good turn deserves another.

à bientôt, a byaN′tō [Fr.] Until soon; see you soon.

abierto, ä·bē·âr′tō [Sp.] Open, frank.

ab initio, äb i·ni′tē·ō [L.] From the beginning.

ab intra, äb in′trä [L.] From within.

ab invito, äb in·wē′tō, ab in·vē′tō [L.] Unwillingly.

abogado, ä·bō·gä′dō [Sp.] Lawyer.

A bon appétit il ne faut point de sauce, a bōN ä·pä·tē′ ēl ne fō pwaNe de sōs′ [Fr.] A good appetite needs no sauce.

à bon chat, bon rat, a bōN shä′ bōN rä″ [Fr.] Tit for tat.

à bon compte, a bōN kōnt′ [Fr.] Cheap, at little cost.

à bon droit, a bōN dRwä′ [Fr.] With good reason.

à bon marchê, a bōN mär·shä′ [Fr.] At a cheap price or bargain.

ab origine, äb ō·Rig′i·nä″ [L.] From the origin.

ab ovo, äb ō′wō, ab ō′vō [L.] From the egg; from the beginning.

abricot, ä·bRē·kō′ [Fr.] Apricot.

abrigo, ä·bRē′gō [Sp.] Overcoat; wrap, cover.

absit invidia, äb′sit in·wē′dē·ä, ab′sit in·vē′dē·a [L.] Let there be no ill will; all envy aside.

Ab uno disce omnes, äb ō′nō dēs′kä ōm′näs [L.] From one specimen judge all the rest.

a caballo, ä″kä·bä′yō [Sp.] On horseback.

a capella, ä″käp·pel′lä [It.] In the style of old church music; without musical accompaniment.

accelerando, ät·chel″e·rän′dō [It.] Accelerating; increasing the tempo of music.

acciuga, ät·chö′gä [It.] Anchovy.

accompli, a·kōn·plē′ [Fr.] Accomplished, fulfilled, perfect, complete.

aceite, ä·sā′tä [Sp.] Oil.

aceituna, ä·sä·tö′nä [Sp.] Olive.

acera, ä·sā′Rä [Sp.] Sidewalk.

aceto, ät·che′tō [It.] Vinegar.

aceto-dolce, ät·chet′ō·dōl′che [It.] Sour-sweet.

à cheval, a she·väl′ [Fr.] On horseback.

Achtung! ach·tong′ [G.] Attention.

à contre coeur, a kōntr″ kŒr′ [Fr.] Against one's will.

acqua, äk′kwä [It.] Water.

acqua vite, äk′kwä vē′te [It.] Brandy.

acre, äkr [Fr.] Sharp; sour.

adagio, ä·dä′jō [It.] Slowly; a slow musical movement.

addio, ä·dē′ō [It.] Farewell, good-bye.

addolorato, äd·dō·lō·Rä′tō [It.] Sorrowful, melancholy, sad.

adelante, ä·da·län′tä [Sp.] Forward, onward, ahead.

ademas, ä·da·mäs′ [Sp.] Besides, furthermore.

adentro, ä·dan′trō [Sp.] Inside; within.

adeus, ä·dā′ös [Pg.] Good-bye.

ad extremum, äd ek·strä′mum, ad ek·strē′mum [L.] To the end.

ad finem, äd fē′nem [L.] To the end.

ad hoc, äd hōk′, ad hok′ [L.] For this special object or occasion.

adieu, a·dŒ′, a·dū′ [Fr.] Farewell, good-bye.

ad infinitum, äd in·fi·nē′tum, ad in·fi·nī′tum [L.] To infinity.

ad interim, ad in′te·rim [L.] In the interim; for the meantime, temporarily.

adios, ä dē′ōs [Sp.] Farewell, good-bye.

a discrétion, a dēs·kRä·siōN′ [Fr.] At discretion, unrestricted, at will.

ad libitum, äd lib′i·tum, ad lib′i·tum [L.] At pleasure.

ad litem, äd li′tem, ad lī′tem [L.] For or during legal process. A representative is selected *ad litem* to speak and act in behalf of a person who is incompetent.

ad nauseam, äd na′sē·äm″, ad na′shē·am [L.] To the point of causing disgust.

adonde, ä·dōn′dä [Sp.] Where.

ad rem, äd Rem′ [L.] To the purpose; to the point.

Adsum, äd′sum, ad′sum [L.] I am present; here.

ad summam, äd sum′mäm, ad sum′mum [L.] In short.

ad valorem, äd wä·lōr′cm, ad va·lōr′em [L.] According to the value.

ad verbum, äd weR′bum, ad vur′bum [L.] Word for word, verbatim.

advocatus diaboli, äd·wō·kä′tüs dē·ä′bō·lē, äd·vō·kä′tus dē·ä′bo·lē [L.] The devil's advocate; a detractor.

aeg, eg [Dan.] Egg.

affaire d'amour, a·fâr′ da·mör′ [Fr.] Love affair.

affaire d'honneur, ä·fâr′ don·Œr′ [Fr.] An affair of honor; a duel.

affresco, ä·fRäs′kō [It.] Fresco.

a fortiori, ä fōr′tē·ō·Rē, ä fōr′shē·ōr·ē [L.] With stronger reason.

aga, a′gä [Turk.] Commander; leader; lord; a title of respect.

Age quod agis, ä′gä kwōd ä′gis [L.] Attend to what you are about.

ager publicus, a′gâr pö′blē·kus [L.] Public domain.

ägg, eg [Sw.] Egg.

aggregatio mentium, ä·grä·gä′tē·ō men′tē·um [L.] A meeting of minds.

agha. *See* aga.

aglio, a′glē·ō [It.] Garlic.

agneau, än·yō′ [Fr.] Lamb.

agnello, än·yä′lō [It.] Lamb.

Agnus Dei, äg′nus dä′ē, ag′nus dē′ī [L.] The Lamb of God.

à grands frais, a gRäN fre′ [Fr.] At great expense.

à haute voix, a ōt vwä′ [Fr.] Aloud.

ahí, ä·hē′ [Sp.] There.

Aide-toi, le ciel t'aidera, ed·twä′ le sē·el′ ted·e·Rä′ [Fr.] God helps those who help themselves.

aïeul, ä·yŒl′ [Fr.] Grandfather.

aigre-doux, egr·dö′ [Fr.] Sour-sweet.

ail, äy [Fr.] Garlic.

aillade, ä·yäd′ [Fr.] Garlic sauce.

à jamais, a zhä·me′ [Fr.] Forever.

ají, ä·hē′ [Sp.] Chili.

ajo, a′hō [Sp.] Garlic.

à la, a la [Fr.] In the manner or style of.

à la bayonnaise, a la be·ya·nez′ [Fr.] In the style of Bayonne; garnished with anchovy fillets, gherkins, and braised onions.

à la béarnaise, a la bä·är·nez′ [Fr.] In the style of Béarn; served with a thick sauce made of eggs, onion, and butter.

à la bigarade, a la bē·ga·räd′ [Fr.] Orange sauce, served usually on poultry or wild game.

à la bordelaise, a la bard·lez′ [Fr.] Served with a thickened wine sauce.

à la boulangère, a la bö·län·zhâr′ [Fr.] In the style of the baker's wife; served with chopped potatoes and onions.

à la broche, a la bRash′ [Fr.] Skewered or cooked on a spit.

à la carte, a la kärt′ [Fr., lit. 'according to the menu'.] Ordering each dish in a meal separately.

à la casserole, a la käs·ʀạl′ [Fr.] Served in casserole style.

à la cordon bleu, a la kạʀ·dạn blœ′ [Fr.] In blue-ribbon style; served in the style of an exquisite cook.

à la créole, a la kʀā·ạl′ [Fr.] In the créole style; served with a sauce of green peppers, onion, and tomatoes.

à la flamande, a la flä·mänd′ [Fr.] In the Flemish style; served with braised cabbage, potatoes, carrots, and cuts of pork.

à la francaise, a la fʀän·sez′ [Fr.] In the French style; garnished with mixed, diced vegetables.

à la grecque, a la gʀek′ [Fr.] In Greek style.

à la hollandaise, a la ạ·län·dez′ [Fr.] In the Dutch style; served with a sauce of butter, eggs, and lemon juice.

à la Holstein, a la hạl′stēn [Fr.] In the style of Schleswig-Holstein; food served with fried eggs and pickles.

à la julienne, a la zhɥl·yen′ [Fr.] Served with thin-sliced vegetables.

à l'allemande, a lal·mänd′ [Fr.] In the German style; garnished with potatoes; noodles, or sauerkraut.

à la maître d' hotel, a la metʀ′ dō·tel′ [Fr.] Served with a sauce of butter, parsley, and lemon juice.

à la mode, a la mạd′ [Fr., lit. 'in the fashion of'.] In America, served with ice cream; in France, braised beef.

à la parisienne, a la paʀ·ēz·yen′ [Fr.] Garnished with vegetables which usually include tiny sauteed potatoes.

à la provençale, a la pʀạ·vän·sạl′ [Fr.] Cooked with garlic or onions.

à l'armenienne, a lär·män·yen′ [Fr.] In the Armenian style; served with rice.

à la russe, a la ʀys′ [Fr.] In the Russian style; cooked with horseradish, beets, or sour cream.

à la soubise, a la sö·bēz′ [Fr.] Served with a sauce of butter and onion.

à la tartare, a la tär·tär′ [Fr.] In the Tartary style; served raw with a cold mustard sauce.

à la Vichy, a la vē·shē′ [Fr.] Served with sliced and creamed carrots.

alba, äl′bä [It.] Daybreak, dawn.

al dente, äl den′te [It.] Descriptive cooking phrase which means spaghetti or macaroni is still somewhat firm, rather than cooked to a mushy softness.

al fine, äl fē′ne [It.] To the end; a term used in music.

al fresco, äl fʀes′kō [It.] In the open air; dining outdoors.

algodón, äl·gō·dōn′ [Sp.] Cotton; the cotton plant itself.

à l'huile, a lwēl′ [Fr.] In olive oil.

aliéné, äl·yā·nā′ [Fr.] Mad, lunatic, deranged.

alimento, äl·ē·men′tō [Sp.] Food; nutrition; nourishment.

à l'indienne, a laɴ·dyen′ [Fr.] In the Indian style; served with curried rice.

aliquis in omnibus, nullis in singulis, al′i·kwis in ōm′ni·bụs nụl′is in sin′gụ·lis [L.] Jack of all trades, but master of none.

allégresse, äl·lā·gʀes′ [Fr.] Joyousness, gladness, mirth, cheerfulness.

allegro, äl·le′gʀä [It.] Brisk, sprightly, lively; a musical piece done in quick time.

allemand, äl·män′ [Fr.] German; the German language; (Cap.) a German.

allemande, äl·mänd′ [Fr.] A German dance, or the music for it; a sauce of egg yolk, veal stock, flour, and butter.

Allez-vous-en! äl·ā·vö·zän′ [Fr.] Away with you; go away.

Allons! äl·ōɴ′ [Fr.] Let us go; come on; come.

allumette, äl·ɥ·met′ [Fr.] A short rectangular puff pastry, served either plain or stuffed with chopped meat or fish.

almeja, äl·mä′hä [Sp.] Clam.

almendra, äl·men′dʀä [Sp.] Almond.

almôço, äl·mō′sō [Pg.] Lunch.

almôndega, äl·mōn·dā′gä [Pg.] Meatball.

almuerzo, äl·mwâʀ′sō [Sp.] The first major meal of the day, usually lunch.

aloha, ä·lō′hä [Hawaiian, lit. 'love'.] Hello; good-bye; a salutation of the Hawaiian Islands.

aloyau, äl·wä·yō′ [Fr.] Sirloin.

al pomodoro, äl pō·mō·dō′ʀō [It.] Served in tomato sauce or with tomatoes.

al sangue, äl sän′gwe [It.] Rare (meat).

alter ego, ạl′ter ā′gō, ạl′tér ē′gō [L.] Another self.

amande, a·mänd′ [Fr.] Almond.

amant, a·män′ [Fr.] Sweetheart, lover.

amante, ä·män′te [It.] Lover.

A maximis ad minima, ä mäk′sē·mēs äd mē′nē·mä [L.] From the greatest to the least.

ambigu, äɴ·bē·gy′ [Fr.] Buffet of various cold dishes.

ambos, äm′bōs [Sp.] Both.

amende honorable, ä·mänd′ ạ·nạ·ʀäbl′ [Fr.] Satisfactory apology; reparation.

à merveille, a meʀ·vāy′ [Fr.] To a wonder; marvelously; well done.

a mezzo voce, ä met′sō vō′che [It.] In moderate voice or musical tone.

ami, a·mē′ [Fr., fem., **amie,** a·mē′] Friend.

Amici probantur rebus adversis, ä·mē′kē prō·bän′töʀ ʀä′bụs äd·vâʀ′sis [L.] Friends are tested by adversity.

amicus curiae, ä·mē′kụs kö′ʀē·ī′′ [L.] A friend of the court; a person appointed by a judge as an impartial adviser.

amore, ä·mōʀ′e [It.] Love, affection.

Amore è cieco, ä·mōʀ′e ā chä′kō [It.] Love is blind.

Amor omnia vincit (or vincit omnia), ä′mōʀ ōm′nē·ä wēng′kit [L.] Love conquers all things.

amor patriae, ä′mōʀ pä′tʀē·ī′′ [L.] Love of country.

amour propre, a·möʀ′ pʀạpʀ [Fr.] Self-love, vanity.

ananas, ä·nä·nä′ [Fr., It.] Pineapple.

Anathema sit, a·nath′a·ma sit [L.] Let him be accursed. From *Vulgate*, Galatians 1, 8 and I Corinthians 16, 22.

anchoa, än·chō′ä [Sp.] Anchovy.

anchois, än·shwä′ [Fr.] Anchovy.

ancien régime, äɴ·sēäɴ′ ʀä·zhēm′ [Fr.] The old regime; period before the French Revolution of 1789.

âne, än [Fr., fem., **anesse,** ä·nes′] Ass; donkey.

anglaise, äɴ·glez′ [Fr.] In the English style; served without sauce, usually boiled.

anguila, än·gwē′lä [Sp.] Eel.

anguilla, än·gwē′lä [It.] Eel.

anguille, äɴ·gēy′ [Fr.] Eel.

animo et fide, ä·nē·mō′ et fē′dä [It.] With courage and fidelity.

anitra, ä·nē′tʀä [It.] Duck.

Anno Domini, ä′nō dō′mi·ne [L.] In the year of our Lord. Abbr. A.D.

Annuit Coeptis, än′nö·it koip′tis, an′yö·it sep′tis [L.] He (God) has favored our beginning. (Motto for the reverse side of the great seal of the U.S.)

año, än′yō [Sp.] Year.

Anschluss, än′shlụs [G.] Junction; union; connection; annexation.

ante, än′tā, an′tē [L.] Before.

ante bellum, an′tē bel′um [L.] Before the war.

ante diluvium, än′tä dē·lö′wē·ụm, an′tē di·lö′vē·um [L.] Before the flood.

antes, än′tās [Sp.] Formerly, before.

antipasto, än·tē·päs′tō [It., lit. 'before the meal'.] A side dish; usually the first dish served.

ape, ä′pe [It.] Bee.

apelkaka, ä′pel·kä′kä [Sw.] Apple cake.

apéritif, a·pä·ʀē·tēf′ [Fr.] Appetizer.

Apfelmus, äp′fel·mụs′ [G.] Applesauce.

Apfelwein, äp′fel·vīn′′ [G.] Cider.

à pied, a pyā′ [Fr.] On foot.

a poco a poco, ä pō′kō ä pō′kō [It.] Little by little.

a posteriori, ā′′ po·stēr′′ē·ôr′ī, ä′′ po·stēr′′ē·ôr′ē [L.] From the effect to the cause; reasoning sequence opposed to *a priori.*

appelbol, äp′pel·bol′′ [D.] Apple dumpling.

appeltaart, äp′pel·tärt′′ [D.] Apple tart, apple pie.

appétit, äp·pä·tē′ [Fr.] Appetite; craving.

après, a′pʀe [Fr.] After, afterwards; behind.

Après moi le déluge, a′pʀe mwä le dä·lyzh [Fr.] After me, the deluge, (Louis XV).

a priori, ā′′prī·ôr′ī, ä′′pʀe·ō′ʀe [L.] Reasoning sequence from cause to effect.

à propos, a pʀō·pō′ [Fr.] Apt; to the purpose; at the right moment.

aragosta, ä·ʀä·gōs′tä [It.] Lobster.

arancia, ä·ʀän′chä [It.] Orange.

arbiter elegantiarum, är′bi·teʀ′′ ā′′le·gän′′tē·ä′ʀụm [L.] A judge or supreme authority in matters of taste.

árbol, äʀ′bōl [Sp.] Tree.

argumentum ad absurdum, äʀ′′gö·men′tụm äd äb·söʀ′dụm, äʀ′′gü·men′tum ad ab·sụr′dum [L.] An argument proving the absurdity of an opponent's argument.

argumentum ad hominem, äʀ′′gö·men′tụm äd hō′mē·nem, äʀ′′gü·men′tum ad hä′mi·nem [L.] An argument to the individual man; *i.e.* to his interests and prejudices.

argumentum ad ignorantiam, äʀ′′gö·men′tụm äd ig′′nō·ʀän′tē·äm, äʀ′′gü·men′tum ad ig′′na·ran′sham [L.] An argument based on the ignorance of an opponent.

argumentum ad judicium, äʀ′′gö·men′tụm äd yö·dik′ē·ụm, äʀ′′gü·men′tum ad jö·dish′um [L.] An argument appealing to common sense and judgment.

arigato, ä·ʀē·gä′tō [Jap.] Thank you.

aringa, ä·ʀēn′gä [It.] Herring.

arista, ä·ʀēs′tä [It.] Roast loin of pork.

a rivederci, ä ʀē·ve·deʀ′chē [It.] Until we meet again.

arrière, ar·yer′ [Fr.] Backwards; back; behind.

arrière-garde, ar·yer″gard′ [Fr.] Rear guard.

arroba, är·ō′bä [Sp.] A weight of approximately 25 pounds; a liquid measure of approximately 4 gallons.

arroz, ä·rōs [Sp.] Rice.

Ars longa, vita brevis, ärs lōng′gä wē′tä bre′wis, ärz lạng′ga vē′ta brē′vis [L.] Art (is) long, life (is) short.

artichaut, är·tē·shō′ [Fr.] Artichoke.

Artium Magister, är′tē·ụm mä·gis′târ [L.] Master of Arts.

artrite, är·trē′te [It.] arthritis.

asado, ä·sä′dō [Sp.] Roast.

ascella, äs·chel′ä [It.] Armpit.

asparago, äs·pär′ä·gō [It.] Asparagus.

asperge, as·pârzh′ [Fr.] Asparagus.

Asperges, as·pûr′jēs [L.] Thou shalt sprinkle; the ceremony of sprinkling holy water in High Mass.

assez bien, ä·sā byan′ [Fr.] Pretty well, well enough.

até a vista, ä′tä ä vēs′tä [Pg.] Until we meet again.

à toutes jambes, a töt zhänb′ [Fr.] As fast as one's legs can carry one.

attendez! a·tän·dā′ [Fr.] Wait; wait a minute; stay.

attereau, at·e·rō′ [Fr.] Chunks of meat cooked on a skewer.

atún, ä·tön′ [Sp.] Tuna.

au, ō [Fr.] In; with.

aubergine, ō·bâr·zhēn′ [Fr.] Eggplant.

au beurre fondu, ō bœr fōn·dy′ [Fr.] In melted butter.

au beurre noir, ō bœr nwär′ [Fr.] Served in brown butter sauce.

au beurre roux, ō bœr rō′ [Fr.] In browned butter sauce.

au bleu, ō blœ′ [Fr.] Fish which has turned blue by cooking in vinegar or white wine.

au contraire, ō kōn·trâr′ [Fr.] On the contrary.

au fait, ō fe′ [Fr.] Well-acquainted with; expert; skilled.

Auflauf, ouf′louf [G.] Souffle.

au fond, ō fōn′ [Fr.] At bottom, basically.

Auf Wiedersehen, ouf vē′der·zä″en [G.] Until we meet again, good-bye.

au gras, ō grä′ [Fr.] Cooked in gravy or juices.

au gratin, ō grä·tan′ [Fr.] Sprinkled with cheese or bread crumbs and cooked to form a crust.

au jus, ō zhy′ [Fr.] Served in its own juice or gravy.

au lait, ō le′ [Fr.] With milk.

au maigre, ō megr′ [Fr.] Served lean.

au naturel, ō na·ty·rel′ [Fr.] Plainly cooked.

au pis aller, ō pē·za·lā′ [Fr.] At the worst.

aurea mediocritas, ou′rā″ä me″dē·ōk′-ri·täs″ [L.] The golden mean.

au reste, ō rest′ [Fr.] Moreover, besides.

Au revoir, ō re·vwär′ [Fr.] Until we meet again; farewell for the present.

aurora australis, ạ·rō′rạ ạ·strä′lis [L., lit. 'southern dawn'.] A luminous phenomenon of the South Polar region similar to the northern lights.

au soleil, ō sō·lāy′e [Fr.] In the sun.

aut Caesar, aut nihil, out kī′sär out ni′-hil [L.] Either Caesar or nothing.

autobus, ō·tō·bys′ [Fr.] Bus.

auto-da-fé, ạ″tō·de·fä′ [Sp.] An act of faith; a sentencing during the Inquisition, or the actual act of burning a heretic.

Aut vincere aut mori, out win′ke·re out mō′rē [L.] Either to conquer or to die.

Aux armes! ō zärm′ [Fr.] To arms.

aux choux, ō shō′ [Fr.] With cabbage.

aux oignons, ō zạn′yạn [Fr.] With onions.

avant-garde, a·vän·gard′ [Fr.] The vanguard; this name is also given to very new art forms.

avant-hier, a·vän·yâr′ [Fr.] The day before yesterday.

avant propos, a·vän prạ·pō′ [Fr.] Preliminary matter; preface.

Ave Maria, ä′vä mä·rē′ä [L.] Hail Mary; thus the angel Gabriel greeted the Virgin Mary.

avena, ä·vä′nä [It.] Oats.

avion, a·vyōn′ [Fr.] Airplane.

avondeten, ä·vōn·dä′ten [D.] Supper.

à votre santé, a vạtr sän·tā′ [Fr.] To your health.

a vuestra salud, ä vwä′strä sä·lōd′ [Sp.] To your health.

ayer, ä·yâr′ [Sp.] Yesterday.

azúcar, ä·zö′kär [Sp.] Sugar.

azul, ä·zōl′ [Sp.] Blue.

azzurro, ät·zö′rō [It.] Blue, azure, sky blue.

B

baba, bä·bä′ [Fr.] A spongy cake, usually eaten with rum or rum sauce poured over it.

baba, bä′bä [Hind.] A child, a baby.

babbo, bä′bō [It.] Dad, daddy, papa, pa.

babeurre, ba·bœr′ [Fr.] Buttermilk.

bacalao, bä·kä·lä′ō [Sp.] Codfish.

baciare, bä·chär′e [It.] To kiss.

bacio, bä′chō [It.] A kiss.

bahia, bä·hē′ä [Sp.] Bay; harbor.

baile, bä·ē·le [Sp.] A dance; a ball.

bain-marie, ban·mä·rē′ [Fr.] Double saucepan or boiler.

baklava, bä′klä·va″ [Turk.] A dessert made of thin pastry layers rolled and filled with honey and nuts.

ballotin, bal·lō·tan′ [Fr.] Meat or fish from which the bones are removed and which is rolled into a ball.

balon, bä·lōn′ [Sp.] Football; football game; balloon; tire.

baloo, bạ·lö′ [Anglo-Ind.] Bear.

bambina, bäm·bē′nä [It.] Little girl.

bambino, bäm·bē′nō [It.] Little boy.

banane, ba·nan′ [Fr.] Banana.

bananes flambées, ba·nan′ flän·bā′ [Fr.] A dessert of sliced bananas, with rum poured over them and set afire just before serving.

bandar, bän·där′ [Hind.] Ape, monkey.

bandarlog, bän′där·log [Hind.] Monkey people; group of monkeys.

banderilla, bän·dä·rē′yä [Sp.] A small dart, which usually has a banner or streamer attached, used in bullfighting to provoke the bull.

banderillero, bän·dä·rē·yä′rō [Sp.] Wielder of the banderillas in a bullfight.

banzai, bän·zī′ [Jap.] A battle cry meaning 'live forever'.

baptême du feu, ba·tem″ dy fœ′ [Fr.] Baptism of fire.

barbabietola, bär″bä·bē·ä·tō′lä [It.] Beet.

bardé, bär·dā′ [Fr.] Covered with thin strips of bacon.

bar de mer, bär de mâr′ [Fr.] Sea bass.

barrio, bär·ē′ō [Sp.] District, precinct, ward.

bas bleu, bä blœ′ [Fr.] A bluestocking; a literary woman.

basso buffo, bä′sō bö′fō [It.] An actor in comic opera with a bass voice.

Basta! bäs′tä [It.] Stop; enough.

bastante, bä·stän′tä [Sp.] Enough, sufficient.

batata, bä·tä′tä [Sp.] Sweet potato.

bateau, ba·tō′ [Fr.] Boat.

baton, ba·tōn′ [Fr.] Stick; cane; breadstick.

Bauernbrot, bou′ern·brōt″ [G., lit. 'farmer's bread'.] A coarse, dark brown bread.

beaucoup, bō·kö′ [Fr.] A great deal, many, much.

beau geste, bō zhest′ [Fr.] A fine or handsome gesture.

beaux yeux, bō zyœ′ [Fr.] Fine eyes; good looks.

béchamel, bā·sha·mel′ [Fr.] A white cream sauce of milk, flour, butter, and meat stock.

bêche-de-mer, besh·de·mâr′ [Fr.] Sea slug, trepang; a delicacy to Orientals and Pacific islanders.

bel air, bel âr′ [Fr.] The air, manner, or appearance of aristocratic society.

bellino, bā·lē′nō [It.] Pretty, cute.

bello, bā′yō [Sp.] Beautiful, lovely; fair; gracious.

Benedicite Domino! ben·e·di′ki·tä″dō′-mi·nō″ [L.] Praise the Lord.

ben venuto, bān vā·nö′tō [It.] Welcome.

berretta, ber·ret′ä [It.] Cap, hat, bonnet.

beso, bā′sō [Sp.] Kiss.

bête noir, bet nwär′ [Fr.] A black beast; a bugbear, a personal aversion.

betterave, bet·räv′ [Fr.] Beet.

beurre, bœr [Fr.] Butter.

beurre fondu, bœr fōn·dy′ [Fr.] Melted butter.

beurre noir, bœr nwär′ [Fr.] Browned butter sauce, seasoned with parsley, onion, or lemon juice.

bhalu. See baloo.

bhangi, bän·gē′ [Hind.] A lower Hindu caste made up of scavengers; any member of that caste.

bibliothèque, bē·blē·ō·tek′ [Fr.] Library.

bien, byan [Fr.] Good, well.

bien-aimé, byan·ne·mā′ [Fr.] Beloved, darling.

bien entendu, byan nän·tän·dy′ [Fr.] Of course.

Bier, ber [G.] Beer.

bière, byer [Fr.] Beer.

Bierhaus, ber′hous [G.] Alehouse, beerhouse, public house.

Bierstube, ber′sty·be [G.] Taproom, bar.

biffstek, bif·stek′ [Sw.] Beefsteak.

biftec, bef′tek [Sp.] Beefsteak.

bifteck, bef·tek′ [Fr.] Beefsteak.

bijou, bē·zhö′ [Fr.] Jewel, gem.

bimbo, bēm′bō [It.] Baby.

biondo, bē·ạn′dō [It.] Fair, blonde.

birra, bē′rä [It.] Beer.

biscotin, bēs·kạ·tan′ [Fr.] Hard biscuit.

bistec, bē·stek′ [Sp.] Beefsteak.

bistecca, bē·stä′kä [It.] Beefsteak.

bitte, bi′te [G.] Please.

blanc d'oeuf, blän dœf′ [Fr.] Egg white.

Blutwurst, blyt'vyrst [G.] Pork blood sausage.

boa noite, bō'ä noi'tä [Pg.] Good night, good evening.

boa tarde, bō'ä tär'dä [Pg.] Good afternoon.

boca, bō'kä [Sp.] Mouth, entrance.

Bockwurst, bäch'vyrst [G.] A heavy frankfurter.

bodega, bō-dä'gä [Sp.] Wine cellar; storeroom.

bœuf, bœf [Fr.] Beef; ox; prepared meat.

bœuf braisé, bœf bre-zä' [Fr.] Braised beef.

bœuf épicé, bœf ā-pē-sä' [Fr.] Spiced beef.

bœuf fumé, bœf fy-mä' [Fr.] Smoked beef.

bœuf rôti, bœf rō-tē' [Fr.] Roast beef.

bœuf salé, bœf sa-lä' [Fr.] Corned beef.

bois, bwä [Fr.] Woods, forest; wood.

boisson, bwä-sōn' [Fr.] Drink, beverage.

bolero, bō-le'rō [Sp.] Spanish dance.

bombe, bạnb [Fr.] Bombshell; ball-shaped confection.

bombilla, bōm-bē'yä [Sp.] A small tube used to drink maté.

bona fide, bō'nä fē'dä, bon'a fīd'' [L.] In good faith.

bon ami, bōn a-mē' [Fr.] Good friend.

Bon gré, mal gré, bōn'grä mal'grä [Fr.] With good or ill will; willing or unwilling.

bonito, bō-nē'tō [Sp.] Pretty.

bonjour, bōn-zhōr' [Fr.] Good day; good morning.

bon marché, bōn mär-shä' [Fr.] Inexpensive; cheap.

bon mot, bōn mō' [Fr.] A clever saying, a witticism.

bonne et belle, bạn ā bel [Fr.] Good and beautiful.

bonne foi, bạn fwä' [Fr.] Good faith.

bonnet rouge, bạ-ne rōzh' [Fr., lit. 'red cap'.] The red cap worn by participants in the French Revolution; a revolutionary or extremist.

bonsoir, bōn-swär' [Fr.] Good evening.

bon ton, bōn tōn' [Fr.] Good form or fashion.

bon vivant, bōn vē-vän' [Fr.] One who enjoys a life of luxury and pleasure.

bon voyage! bōn vwä-yäzh' [Fr.] Have a good trip.

bordelais, bạr-de-le' [Fr.] Of or from Bordeaux.

bordello, bōr-del'lō [It.] Brothel.

Borgen macht Sorgen, bōr'gen mächt sōr'gen [G.] He who goes borrowing goes sorrowing.

borscht, bạrsht [Russ.] Soup of red beets, cabbage, onions, and parsnips, often served with sour cream.

bosque, bōs'kä [Sp.] Woods, forest.

bouche, bōsh [Fr.] Mouth.

bouchée, bō-shä' [Fr.] Mouthful.

bouillabaisse, bō-ē-ya-bes' [Fr.] Provençal soup of fish and vegetables.

bouilli, bō-yē' [Fr.] Boiled beef.

bouillon, bō-ē-yōn' [Fr.] Broth.

boulanger, bō-län-zhä' [Fr.] Baker.

boulangerie, bō-län-zhrē' [Fr.] Bakery.

boulette, bōl-et' [Fr.] Meatball.

bourgeois, bōr-zhwä' [Fr.] Common; conventional; middle-class.

bourgeoisie, bōr-zhwä-zē' [Fr.] The middle class.

bragas, brä'gäs [Sp.] Wide, loose breeches.

braten, brä'ten [G.] To grill, fry, or roast.

Bratwurst, brät'verst [G.] A mild link sausage that is usually fried.

Braunschweiger, broun'shvī-ger [G.] Smoked liver sausage.

brève, bre'vä [It.] Short, brief.

breveté, brev-tä' [Fr.] Patented.

brioche, brē'ạsh [Fr., lit. 'blunder'.] A light dinner roll usually shaped like a ball.

broccio, brō'chō [It.] Corsican goat's-milk cheese.

broche, brạsh [Fr.] A spit or skewer.

brochet, brạ-she' [Fr.] Pike fish.

brochette, brạ-shet' [Fr.] Small skewer for broiling chunks of meat.

bröd, brœd [Sw.] Bread.

brut, bryt [Fr., lit. 'dry, crude'.] Very dry wine or champagne.

Buch, bōch [G.] Book.

budino, bō-dē'nō [It.] Pudding.

bue, bō'ä [It.] Beef.

Buena suerte! bwä'nä swâr'tä [Sp.] Good luck.

bueno, bwä'nō [Sp.] Good, well, kind.

buisson, bwē-sōn' [Fr.] Bush, shrub, thicket.

Bund, bönd [G.] League, alliance, confederacy.

Bundesrat, bön'des-rät [G.] Federal council of the German Republic.

buñuelo, bōn-wä'lō [Sp.] Fritter.

Buon Natale! bwōn nä-tä'le [It.] Merry Christmas.

buono, bwō'nō [It.] Good, favorable.

Buon viaggio! bwōn vē-äj'jō [It.] Happy journey.

burro, bōr'ō [It.] Butter.

Burschenschaft, bör'shen-shäft'' [G.] German Students' Association.

C

caballa, kä-bä'yä [Sp.] Mackerel.

caballero, kä-bä-yä'rō [Sp.] Rider, horseman; knight.

caballo, kä-bä'yō [Sp.] Horse.

cabeza, kä-bā'sä [Sp.] Head.

cabillaud, kä-bē-yō' [Fr.] Cod.

cacahuete, kä-kä-hwä'tä [Sp.] Peanut.

cacciatore, kät-chä-tō're [It.] Hunter.

cacerola, kä-sär-ō'lä [Sp.] Casserole.

cacio, kä'chō [It.] Cheese.

cacoethes scribendi, ka-kō-ē'thēz skrī-ben-dē [L.] The itch to write.

cada, kä'dä [Sp.] Each, every.

Cada uno es hijo de sus obras, kä'dä ō'nō äs hē'yō dä sös ō'bräs [Sp.] Every man is the product of his own works. (Cervantes.)

café au kirsch, ka-fä' ō kērsh' [Fr.] A drink made from coffee, egg whites, and cherry brandy, served over ice.

café au lait, ka-fä' ō le' [Fr.] Coffee with milk.

café con leche, ka-fä' kōn lä'chä [Sp.] Coffee with milk.

café crème, ka-fä' krem' [Fr.] Coffee with cream.

café frappé, ka-fä' fra-pä' [Fr.] Iced coffee.

café noir, ka-fä' nwär' [Fr.] Black coffee.

cafetal, kä-fä'täl [Sp.] Coffee plantation.

calabozo, kä-lä-bō'sō [Sp.] Cell, jail, dungeon.

caldo, käl'dō [It.] Hot; heat.

caldo de gallina, käl'dō dä gä-lēn'ä [Sp.] Chicken soup.

caliente, käl-ē-en'tä [Sp.] Warm, hot.

calle, kä'yä [Sp.] Street; passage.

camarão, kä-mä'rou [Pg.] Shrimp.

camarón, kä-mä-rōn' [Sp.] Shrimp.

camino, kä-mē'nō [Sp.] Road; path; highway.

cammino, kä-mē'nō [It.] Road; way.

campagne, kän-pän'ye [Fr.] Country; estate; campaign.

canapé, ka-na-pä' [Fr.] Couch, sofa; bread slice fried in butter, usually served with a spread or meat topping.

canard rôti, ka-när' rō-tē' [Fr.] Roast duck.

canard sauvage, ka-när' sō-väzh' [Fr.] Wild duck.

candide, kän-dēd' [Fr.] Frank, open.

caneton, kan-tōn' [Fr.] Duckling.

cangrejo, kän-grä'hō [Sp.] Crab.

caniche, ka-nēsh' [Fr.] Poodle.

canneberge, kan-bârj' [Fr.] Cranberry.

cannelon, kan-lōn' [Fr.] Rolled pastry, usually filled with meat.

cantare, kän-tä're [It.] To sing or chant.

cantina, kän-tē'nä [Sp.] Saloon, barroom.

capellini d'angelo, kä-pel-ē'nē dän'je-lō [It.] Long, thin noodles.

capello, kä-pel'lō [It.] Hair.

capias, kä'pē-äs [L., lit. 'that you take'.] General name for writs of arrest.

capo, kä'pō [It.] Head; origin, beginning.

caracol, kär-ä-kōl' [Sp.] Snail.

caramba! kär-äm'bä [Sp.] An exclamation of amazement.

cara sposa, kär'ä spō'zä [It.] Dear wife.

carciofo, kär-chō'fō [It.] Artichoke.

carne, kär'nä [It., Sp.] Meat.

carne asado, kär'nä ä-sä'dō [Sp.] Roasted meat.

carne fiambre, kär'nä fē-äm'brä [Sp.] Cold meat, cold cuts.

caro, kä'rō [It.] Dear, beloved; expensive.

caro sposo, kä'rō spō'zō [It.] Dear husband.

Carpe diem, kär'pä dē'em [L.] Enjoy the present day.

carrelet, kar-le' [Fr.] A flounder, fluke.

carrote, kar-at' [Fr.] Carrot.

carte blanche, kart blänsh' [Fr.] Full power or authorization.

carte de vins, kart de van' [Fr.] List of wines.

carte du jour, kart dy zhōr' [Fr.] Menu of the day; bill of fare.

casa, kä'sä [Sp.] House, home.

castrato, kä-strä'tō [It.] Mutton.

casus fortuitus, kä'sus far-tō'i-tus [L.] A matter of chance.

Caveat emptor, kä'we-ät'' emp'tōr, kä'-vē-at'' emp'tar [L.] Let the buyer beware.

Caveat venditor, kä'we-ät'' wen'di-tōr'', kä'vē-at'' ven'di-tar'' [L.] Let the seller beware.

Cave canem, kä'we kä'nem, kä've kä'nem [L.] Beware of the dog.

caviale, kä-vē-ä'le [It.] Caviar.

cavolo, kä-vō'lō [It.] Cabbage.

cebolla, sä-bō'ya [Sp.] Onion.

cece, chä'che [It.] Chickpea.

cédrat, sä-drä' [Fr.] Citron.

célèbre, sä-lebr' [Fr.] Famous, celebrated, eminent.

céleri, säl-rē' [Fr.] Celery.

cena, sä'nä [Sp.] Supper.

Cena Domini, sā'nä dō'mi·nē'' [L.] The Lord's Supper.

cenote, sā·nō'tä [Sp.] A reservoir of water in a natural cave.

Cepi corpus, se'pē kạr'pis [L., lit. 'I have taken the body'.] A sheriff's endorsement upon a writ of arrest after having made that arrest.

cerdo, seʀ'dō [Sp.] Hog.

cerise, se·ʀēz' [Fr.] Cherry.

certiorari, sèr·tē·ō·rä'rē [L.] A writ calling for a case in a lower court, or records of that case, to be brought before a higher court.

certo, cheʀ'tō [It.] Positive, sure, certain.

cervelle, sâʀ·vel' [Fr.] Brains; intelligence; mind.

cerveza, sâʀ·vā'sä [Sp.] Beer.

c'est à dire, se·ta dēʀ' [Fr.] That is to say.

C'est entendu, se·tän·tän·dy' [Fr.] It is agreed; settled.

C'est la guerre, se lä gâʀ' [Fr.] It is (due to) the war.

C'est la vie, se lä vē' [Fr.] Such is life; that's life.

C'est magnifique, se man·yē·fēk' [Fr.] It is magnificent.

Cetera desunt, kā'te·rä de'sunt, set'èr·a dē'sunt [L.] The rest are missing. (Found at the end of old segments of manuscripts, indicating that the remainder has never been located.)

ceteris paribus, kā'te·rēs pä'ri·bus, set'ar·is par'i·bus [L.] Other things being equal.

cetriolo, chä''trē·ō'lō [It.] Cucumber.

Chacun à son goût, sha·kạn' a sōN gö' [Fr.] Everyone to his taste.

chair blanche, shâʀ blänsh' [Fr.] White meat.

chair noir, shâʀ nwäʀ' [Fr.] Game; dark meat.

chambre meublée, shänbʀ' mœ·blä' [Fr.] Furnished room.

champignon, shän·pēn·yōN' [Fr.] Mushroom.

chanson de geste, shän·sōN' de zhest' [Fr.] An epic poem about medieval times.

chaparral, shä·pä·ʀäl' [Sp., lit. 'evergreen oak'.] A thicket or dense growth of evergreen oaks or other scrub trees.

chaparreras, shä·pä·ʀä'ʀäs [Sp.] Protective leather or sheepskin leggings worn by cowboys; chaps.

chapeau, sha·pō' [Fr.] Hat, cap.

chapeaux bas! sha·pō bä' [Fr.] Hats off.

chapon, sha·pōN' [Fr.] Capon.

châteaubriand, shä·tō·bʀē·än' [Fr.] Broiled filet of beef, served with a sauce, fried potatoes, and mushrooms.

chaud, shō [Fr.] Hot, warm.

chausson, shō·sōN' [Fr.] Turnover, pastry.

cher, shâʀ [Fr.] Dear, precious, beloved; expensive.

chère amie, shâʀ a·mē' [Fr.] A dear (female) friend.

Che sarà sarà, kä sa·ʀä' sa·ʀä' [It.] What will be, will be.

chevreuil, sha·vʀœ'ye [Fr.] Male of the roedeer; venison.

chiche, shēsh [Fr.] Chickpea.

chicote, chē·kō'te [Sp.] A long, wooden-handled whip.

chignon, shēn·yōN' [Fr.] Hair worn in a bun at the back of the neck.

chili con carne, chē'lē kōn käʀ'ne [Sp.] Spanish dish of chili pepper sauce, meat,

and usually beans.

chili relleno, chē'lē ʀe·yä'nō [Sp.] Chili pepper stuffed with meat or rice.

Chi lo sa? kē lō sä' [It.] Who knows?

choisi, shwä·zē' [Fr.] Chosen, selected.

chorizo, chō·ʀē'sō [Sp.] Pork sausage.

chou, shö [Fr.] Cabbage.

choucroute, shö·kʀōt' [Fr.] Sauerkraut.

chou-fleur, shö·flœʀ' [Fr.] Cauliflower.

choux de Bruxelles, shöd bʀy·sel' [Fr.] Brussels sprouts.

Christe eleïson, kʀē'stä ā·lā·e·zōn' [Gr.] Christ have mercy.

churrasco, chö·ʀäs'kō [Sp.] Broiled or barbecued meat.

Chut! sht [Fr.] Hush; be silent.

Ciao, chä'ō [It.] Hello; greetings; farewell.

cicoria, chē·kō'ʀē·ä [It.] Endive.

ciel, sē·yel' [Fr.] Sky; the heavens.

ci-git, sē·zhē' [Fr.] Here lies.

ciliegia, chē·lē·ä'jē·ä [It.] Cherry.

cioppino, chō·pē'nō [It.] A stew of fish and shellfish.

cipolla, chē·pō'lä [It.] Onion.

circum, kēʀ'kụm, sụr'kam [L.] Around; about.

ciruela pasa, sē·ʀō·ā'lä pä'sä [Sp.] Prune.

citoyen, sē·twä·yaN' [Fr.] Citizen.

citroen, sē·tʀō'en [D.] Lemon.

citronné, sē·tʀo·nā' [Fr.] Lemon-flavored.

ciudad, sē·ö·däd' [Sp.] City.

civet, sē·ve' [Fr.] Stew made of wild game meat and wine.

Civis Romanus sum, kē'wis ʀō·man'ụs sụm [L.] I am a Roman citizen.

clair de lune, klâʀ de lyn' [Fr.] Moonlight.

clairet, klâ·ʀe' [Fr.] Light red wine.

clara, klä'ʀä [Sp.] Egg white.

coche comedor, kō'chä kō·mä·dōʀ' [Sp.] Dining car.

cochon de lait, kạ·shōN'' de le' [Fr.] Suckling pig.

cocotte, kạ·kạt' [Fr.] Stew pan or casserole dish; served in such a dish.

Cogito, ergo sum, kō'gi·tō eʀ'gō sụm, ko'ji·tō ụr'gō sum [L.] I think, therefore I am (Descartes).

coiffeur, kwäf·fœʀ' [Fr.] Hairdresser, hair stylist.

coiffure, kwäf·fyʀ' [Fr.] Hair style.

coliflor, kō·lē·flōʀ' [Sp.] Cauliflower.

comal, kō·mäl' [Sp.] A flat stone or earthenware pan for cooking tortillas and maize cake.

comedor, kō·mä·dōʀ' [Sp.] Dining room.

comer, kō·mâʀ' [Sp.] Eat; feed.

comida, kō·mē'dä [Sp.] Meal; food; dinner.

compagnon de voyage, koN·pan·yōN' de vwä·yäzh' [Fr.] A traveling companion.

compatibile, kom·pä·tē'bē·le [It.] Compatible.

compatible, kōN·pa·tēbl' [Fr.] Compatible.

compos mentis, kōm'pōs men'tis, kom'-pos men'tis [L.] Of sound mind.

compote, kōN·pạt' [Fr.] Stewed fruit.

compte rendu, kōNt ʀän·dy' [Fr.] An account rendered, a report, a review.

con, kōn [Sp.] With.

coñac, kōn'yäk [Sp.] Brandy, cognac.

con amore, kōn ä·mō'ʀe [It.] With love.

concombre, kōN·kōNbʀ' [Fr.] Cucumber.

concordia, kōn·kōʀ'dē·ä [Sp.] Harmony; good will; agreement.

conditio sine qua non, kōn·di'tē·ō si'ne kwä nōn', kạn·di'shē·ō sī'nē kwä non' [L.] A necessary condition.

condottiere, kōn·dō·tē·âʀ'e [It.] An army leader.

conejo, kō·nä'hō [Sp.] Rabbit.

coniglio, kō·nē'glē·ō [It.] Rabbit.

con mucho gusto, kōn mō'chō gös'tō [Sp.] With great pleasure.

conocer, kō·nō·sâʀ' [Sp.] Know; meet; be acquainted with.

conocido, kō·nō·sē'dō [Sp.] An acquaintance.

Conquiescat in pace, kōn·kwē·es'kät in pä'chä [L.] Rest in peace.

Conseil d'Etat, kōn·sä'ya dä·tä' [Fr.] Council of state.

consommé, kōn·sạ·mā' [Fr.] Clear soup; broth.

Consummatum est, kōn·sụm·ä'tụm est' [L.] It is finished. (Last words of Christ on the cross.)

contra, kōn'trä [Sp.] Against.

coq, kạk [Fr.] Cock, rooster.

coq au vin, kạk ō vaN' [Fr.] Chicken cooked in wine.

cordero, kōʀ·dâ'ʀō [Sp.] Lamb.

cordon bleu, kạʀ·dōN blœ' [Fr., lit. 'blue ribbon'.] A first-rate chef or cook.

cornichon, kạʀ·nē·shōN' [Fr.] Gherkin.

coro, kō'ʀō [It.] Choir, chorus.

corps, kạʀ [Fr.] Substance, mass, body.

corpus, kạʀ'pus [L.] Body, matter.

Corpus Christi, kạʀ'pus kris'tē [L.] The body of Christ.

corpus delecti, kạʀ'pus di·lik'tī [L.] The body or object of a crime, as the corpse in a homicide or stolen goods in a theft.

Corpus Juris Civilis, kạʀ'pus jör'is si·vī'lis [L.] The body of Roman civil law.

correo, kōʀ·ā'ō [Sp.] Mail; post office.

corrida de toros, kō·ʀē'dä dä tō'ʀōs [Sp.] Bullfight.

côte à côte, kōt ä kōt' [Fr.] Side by side.

côte de bœuf, kōt da bœf' [Fr.] Beef rib.

coup, kö [Fr.] A stroke.

coup de grâce, kö da gräs' [Fr.] A finishing, merciful stroke.

coup de main, kö da maN' [Fr.] A sudden, unexpected attack or enterprise.

coup de maître, kö da metʀ' [Fr.] A master stroke.

coup de pied, kö da pyä' [Fr.] A kick.

coup de soleil, kö da sạ·lä'ya [Fr.] Sunstroke.

coup d'essai, kö de·sä' [Fr.] First attempt.

coup d'état, kö dä·ta' [Fr.] A sudden decisive blow in politics.

coup de théâtre, kö da tä·ätʀ' [Fr.] A dramatic theatrical effect.

coup d'œil, kö dœ'ya [Fr.] A glance.

courge, körj [Fr.] Gourd.

court bouillon, köʀ bö·ē·yōN' [Fr.] A wine sauce in which fish or meat is cooked.

couvert, kö·veʀ' [Fr.] Restaurant cover charge for a place setting.

crabe, kʀäb [Fr.] Crab.

crédit mobilier, kʀä·dē mạ·bēl·yä' [Fr.] A corporation which makes loans upon personal estates.

creer, kʀä·eʀ' [Sp.] To believe or think.

crème, kʀem [Fr.] Cream, custard.

crème de cacao, kʀem de ka·ka'ō [Fr.] A chocolate-flavored liqueur.

crème de café, kʀem de ka·fä' [Fr.] A coffee-flavored liqueur.

crème de menthe, kʀem de mänt' [Fr.] A green, mint-flavored liqueur.

crème de noyau, ᴋʀem de nwa·yō′ [Fr.] A cherry-flavored liqueur.

crème fouettée, ᴋʀem fö·we·tā′ [Fr.] Whipped cream.

crêpe, ᴋʀep [Fr.] A thin pancake, often served stuffed and rolled up.

cresson, ᴋʀe·sōɴ′ [Fr.] Cress.

crève-cœur, ᴋʀev·ᴋœʀ′ [Fr.] Heartbreak.

crevette, ᴋʀe·vet′ [Fr.] Shrimp.

criollo, ᴋʀē·ō′yō [Sp.] Creole.

croissant, ᴋʀwä·säɴ′ [Fr.] A light crescent-shaped roll, traditionally served in France at breakfast.

croquette, ᴋʀa·ket′ [Fr.] A ball of minced meat, fish, or vegetable dipped in batter and fried.

crouton, ᴋʀö·tōɴ′ [Fr.] Bread crust served in soup.

crudités, ᴋʀy·dē·tā′ [Fr.] Vegetables or fruit served raw.

cuadrilla, kwä·dʀē′yä [Sp.] Crew; party; gang; troop.

cuanto, kwän′tō [Sp.] How many, how much.

cucina, kö·chē′nä [It.] Kitchen; cookery.

cucinare, kö·chē·nä′ʀe [It.] To cook.

Cui bono? kwē bō′nō [L.] For whose advantage? To what end?

Cuidado! kwē·dä′dō [Sp.] Beware; look out.

cuiller, kwē·yâʀ′ [Fr.] Spoon; scoop.

cuique suum, kwē′kwä sö′um [L.] To each his own.

cuit à point, kwēt a pwaɴ′ [Fr.] Cooked just right.

cul-de-sac, ᴋʏl·de·sak′ [Fr.] Blind alley, dead end, passage with only one outlet.

culpa, ḳul′pä [L.] Fault, guilt.

cum grano salis, ḳum grä′nō sä′lis [L.] With a grain of salt.

cum laude, ḳum lou′dä [L.] With praise.

cum privilegio, ḳum pʀi·wi·lā′gē·ō, ḳum pri·vi·le′jō [L.] With privilege.

cuoco, kwa′kō [It.] Cook.

D

da capo, dä kä′pō [It.] From the beginning; again.

d'accord, da·ḳaʀ′ [Fr.] Agreed.

dactylographe, dak·tēl·ō·gʀaf′ [Fr.] Typist.

dame d'honneur, dam da·nœʀ′ [Fr.] Maid of honor.

Damnant quod non intelligunt, däm′nänt kwōd nōn in·tel′i·g̣unt′′, dam′nant kwod non in·tel′i·gant [L.] They condemn what they do not understand.

Danke schön, dän′ke shyn [G.] Thank you. Thank you very much.

darne, daʀn [Fr.] Slice of fish.

das heisst, däs hīst′ [G.] That is; that is to say.

das ist, däs ist′ [G.] That is; this is.

datte, dat [Fr.] Date fruit.

débâcle, dä·bäkl′ [Fr.] The breaking up of ice on a waterway; ruin; collapse.

de facto, dē fak′tō [L.] In fact; actually.

déglacer, dä·gla·sā′ [Fr.] Dilution of juices in a pan, usually through adding wine or clear broth.

De gustibus non est disputandum, de g̣us′ti·ḅus′′ nōn est dis′′pu·tän′dum, dē g̣us′ta·ḅas non est dis′′pū·tan′dum [L.] There is no disputing about tastes.

de haut en bas, de ō äɴ bä′ [Fr.] Contemptuously; with a condescending air.

Dei gratia, dā′ē gʀä′tē·ä [L.] By the grace of God.

déjà vu, dä·zhä vʏ′ [Fr., lit. 'already seen'.] A mental condition in which new scenes or sights seem familiar.

déjeuner, dā·zhœ·nä′ [Fr.] Lunch, luncheon.

déjeuner à la fourchette, dā·zhœ·nä′ a la föʀ·shet′ [Fr.] Late breakfast or brunch which includes meat.

de jure, de ūʀ′e, dē jö′ʀē [L.] From the law; by right.

Delenda est Carthago, de·len′dä est käʀ·tä′gō, di·len′da est käʀ·thä′gō [L.] Carthage must be destroyed (Cato the Elder).

delgado, del·gä′dō [Sp.] Thin, lean, slender.

delirium tremens, di·lēr′ē·um trē′menz [L.] A nervous disorder characterized by delusion, hallucination, and uncontrollable trembling of limbs: due to excessive alcoholic consumption followed by abstinence.

de luxe, de lʏks′ [Fr.] Luxurious, particularly elegant.

de mal en pis, de mal äɴ pē′ [Fr.] From bad to worse.

démarche, dä·maʀsh′ [Fr.] Walk; march; measure; course of action.

demasiado, dā·mä′′sē·ä′dō [Sp.] Too much, too many, excessive amount of.

demi-mondaine, de·mē′mōɴ·den′ [Fr.] A woman of ill repute.

demi-tasse, de·mē·täs′ [Fr., lit. 'half-cup'.] Half a cup; a small cup.

De mortuis nil nisi bonum, dā mōʀ′tö·is nil nē′sē bō′num, dē maʀ′chö·is nil nī′sī bō′nam [L.] (Say) nothing but good of the dead.

de nouveau, de nö·vō′ [Fr.] Again.

de novo, dä nō′wō, dē nō′vō [L.] Anew.

Deo gratias, dā′ō gʀä′tē·äs′′ [L.] Thanks to God.

de oídas, dā ō·ē′däs [Sp.] By hearsay.

Deo volente, dā′ō wō·len′tä [L.] God willing; by God's will.

de profundis, dä prō·fun′dis [L.] Out of the depths.

der Führer, dâʀ fʏ′ʀeʀ [G.] The leader; head of the Nazi party in Germany, Adolf Hitler.

Der Mensch ist was er isst, dâʀ mench ist väs âʀ ist′ [G.] Man is what he eats.

désaveu, dä·za·vœ′ [Fr.] Denial, repudiation, retraction.

desayuno, däs·ä·yö′nō [Sp.] Breakfast.

desideratum, di·sid′′a·rä′tam [L.] Something desired or needed.

despacio, däs·pä′syō [Sp.] Slowly.

de temps en temps, de täɴ′ zäɴ täɴ′ [Fr.] From time to time.

Deus nobiscum, quis contra? dā′us nō·bēs′kum kwēs kōn′tʀä [L.] If God is with us, who is against us?

Deus vobiscum, dā′us wō·bēs′kum [L.] God be with you.

Deus vult, dā′us wult [L.] God wishes it.

Deutsches Reich, doit′ches ʀīch [G.] Germany; the German Empire.

Deutschland, Deutschland über alles, doitch′länt, doitch′länt, ʏ′bâr äl′les [G., lit. 'Germany, Germany over all'.] German national anthem.

dharma, dä′rma [Skr.] Hindu religious law; religious duty or obligation.

día, dē′ä [Sp.] Day.

Dicho y hecho, dē′chō ē ā′chō [Sp.] No sooner said than done.

die schöne Welt, dē sʜʏ′na velt [G.] The beautiful world.

Dieu et mon droit, dyœ ā mōɴ dʀwä′ [Fr.] God and my right.

Dieu vous garde, dyœ vö gaʀd′ [Fr.] God protect you.

difficile, dē·fē·sēl′ [Fr.] Difficult, hard.

di molto, dē mōl′tō [It.] Greatly, very.

dinde, daɴd [Fr.] Turkey, turkey hen.

dindon, daɴ·dōɴ′ [Fr.] Turkey cock.

dindonneau, daɴ·da·nō′ [Fr.] Young turkey.

dîner, dē·nä′ [Fr.] Dinner.

dinero, dē·nâʀ′ō [Sp.] Money, currency.

Dios me libre de hombre de un libro, dē′ōs mä lē′bʀe dä ōm′bʀe dä ön lē′bʀō [Sp.] God deliver me from a man of one book.

Dirigo, dē′ʀi·gō′′, dir′i·gō′′ [L.] I direct. (The state motto of Maine.)

dispensa, dēs·pen′sä [It.] Pantry; distribution.

distingué, dēs·taɴ·gā′ [Fr.] Distinguished, noted, eminent.

Divide et impera, dē′wi·dē′′ et im′pe·rä′′, div′a·dē′′ et im′pa·ra [L.] Divide and rule.

Dixi, dik′sē [L.] I have spoken.

Doctor Mirabilis, dak′tōʀ miʀ·ä′bi·lēs′′, dok′tar mir·a′ba·lis′′ [L., lit. 'The Admirable Doctor'.] Roger Bacon.

Doctor Subtilis, dak′tōʀ söb·ti′lēs′′, dok′tar sub·ti′lis [L., lit. 'The Subtle Doctor'.] John Duns Scotus.

dolce, dōl′che [It.] Sweet.

dolce vita, dōl′che vē′tä [It.] The sweet life; a life of ease and pleasure.

dolente, dō·len′te [It.] Unhappy, doleful.

dolma, dōl′mä [Ar.] A vegetable or vegetable leaf stuffed with meat, rice, and herbs.

dolmades, dōl·mä′dēs [Gr.] Greek-style dolma; grape leaves wrapped around dolma stuffing.

dolor, dō·lōʀ′ [Sp.] Pain, ache; sorrow, grief.

dolore, dō·lō′ʀe [It.] Pain, grief, sorrow.

Dominus vobiscum, dō′mi·nus′′ wō·bēs′kum [L.] The Lord be with you.

don, dan [Sp.] Sir; Mister; a Spanish nobleman.

dona, da′nä [Pg.] Madame; Miss; a Portuguese lady.

doña, dōn′yä [Sp.] Madame; a Spanish lady.

dònna, dō′nä [It.] Madame; an Italian lady; woman.

Donner und Blitz, dun′neʀ unt blits′′ [G.] Thunder and lightning.

dono, dō′nō [It.] Gift, present.

dormido, daʀ·mē′dō [Sp.] Asleep.

dramatis personae, dram′a·tis paʀ·sō′nē [L.] The persons or characters in a drama.

duce, dö′che [It.] Commander, leader.

duchesse, dʏ·shes′ [Fr.] Duchess.

du jour, dy zhöʀ′ [Fr.] Food of the day.

Dum spiro spero, dum spē′ʀō spä′ʀō, dum spī′rō spē′rō [L.] While I breathe I hope. (South Carolina state motto.)

Dum vita est, spes est, dum wē′tä est späs est, dum vī′ta est spēs est [L.] While there is life, there is hope.

Dum vivimus, vivamus, dum wē·wē′mus wē·wä′mus, dum viv′i·mus vi·vä′mus

durazno, dö·räs′nō [Sp.] Peach.

duxelles, dу·sel′ [Fr.] Finely minced and sauteed mushrooms, used to garnish food or included in sauces and stuffings.

E

eau, ō [Fr.] Water.

eau de seltz, ōd selts′ [Fr.] Seltzer water.

Ecce homo, ek′ā hō′mō, ek′sē hō′mō [L.] Behold the man.

éclat, ā·kla′ [Fr.] A burst; an uproar; a flash; a brilliance; a radiance.

écrevisse, ā·kRe·vēs′ [Fr.] Crayfish.

edad, ā·däd′ [Sp.] Age; era.

editio princeps, e·dit′ē·ō′′ pRing′keps, i·dish′ē·ō′′ prin′seps [L.] The first printed edition of a book.

Edo, ergo sum, ā′dō eR′gō sum [L.] I eat, therefore I am.

égalité, ā·gal·ē·tā′ [Fr.] Equality; uniformity.

Eh bien! ā byaN′ [Fr.] Oh well.

Eine feste Burg ist unser Gott, ī′ne fes′ta börg ist ön′seR gat [G.] A mighty fortress is our God. (Martin Luther's great hymn.)

ein Helles, īn hel′es [G.] A glass of light ale.

Eisenbahn, ī′zen·bän [G.] Railway, railroad.

Eisen und Blut, ī′zen unt blöt′′ [G.] Iron and blood.

élan, ā·läN′ [Fr.] Enthusiasm; energy.

élan vital, ā·läN′′ vē·tal′ [Fr.] Vital energy.

Eli, eli, loma azavtani? ā′lē ā′lē lam′a o·zov·tä′nē [Aram.] My God, my God, why hast thou forsaken me? Matt. 27:46.

ella, ā′yä [Sp.] She.

ello, ā′yō [Sp.] It.

emeritus, i·mer′i·tus [L.] Retired after long and worthy service.

empanada, em·pä·nä′dä [Sp.] Meat pie.

empanada de pescado, em·pä·nä′dä dä pes·kä′dō [Sp.] Fish pie.

en ami, äN na·mē′ [Fr.] As a friend.

en arrière, äN naR·yâR′ [Fr.] In the rear; behind; back.

En avant! äN na·väN′ [Fr.] Forward; march.

en bloc, äN blak′ [Fr.] In a single group.

En boca cerrada no entran moscas, en bō′kä seR·ä′dä nō en′tRän mōs′käs [Sp.] Flies do not enter a closed mouth.

en brochette, äN bRa·shet′ [Fr.] Skewered.

enchiladas de gallina, en·chē·lä′däs dä gä·yē′nä [Sp.] Chicken enchiladas.

enchiladas de pescado, en·chē·lä′däs dä pes·kä′dō [Sp.] Fish enchiladas.

en famille, äN fa·mē′ye [Fr.] With one's family; in a domestic state.

enfants perdus, äN·fän peR·dу′ [Fr.] Lost children; a group of men forming a forlorn hope.

enfant terrible, äN·fän teR·ēbl′ [Fr.] A child who is always making inopportune and embarrassing remarks; an incorrigible child.

en garde, äN gaRd′ [Fr.] On guard; to the alert.

en masse, äN mas′ [Fr.] In a body; as a group.

en papillote, äN pa·pē·yat′ [Fr.] Wrapped in paper to retain juices while being cooked.

en rapport, äN Ra·paR′ [Fr.] In relation; in sympathy or accord.

en route, äN Rōt′ [Fr.] On the way.

ensalada, en·sä·lä′dä [Sp.] Salad.

ensenada, en·se·nä′dä [Sp.] Cove, small bay.

Ente, en′te [G.] Duck.

entente cordiale, äN·täNt′ kaR·djal′ [Fr.] Cordial understanding, especially between two states.

entonces, en·tōn′ses [Sp.] Then.

entre nous, äN′′tRe nö′ [Fr.] Between ourselves.

épinard, ā·pē·näR′ [Fr.] Spinach.

E pluribus unum, ā plö′Ri·bus′′ ö′num, ē′ plu′ri·bus yö′num [L.] One out of many; one composed of many.

épouser, ā·pö·zā′ [Fr.] To marry.

Erbse, eRb′sa [G.] Pea.

ergo, eR′gō, ur′gō [L.] Therefore, consequently.

Erin go bragh, âr′in gō bRä′ [Ir.] Ireland forever.

Errare humanum est, e·Rä′Re hö·mä′num est′, e·râ′rē hū·mā′num est′ [L.] To err is human.

Ersatz, eR′säts [G.] Substitute; imitation.

escadrille, es·ka·dRē′ye [Fr.] Squadron; flotilla.

escargot, es·kaR·gō′ [Fr.] Snail.

esercito, es·eR·chē′tō [It.] Army.

España, es·pän′yä [Sp.] Spain.

español, es·pän·yōl′ [Sp.] Spanish; Spaniard.

espinaca, es·pē·nä′kä [Sp.] Spinach.

esprit de corps, es·pRē′′ de kaR′ [Fr.] The animating spirit of a collective body, as a regiment.

esse quam videri, es′se kwäm wi′de·Rē, es′ē kwam vi·dâr′ī [L.] To be rather than to seem.

Est modus in rebus, est mō′dus in Re′bus, est mō′dus in rē′bus [L.] There is a medium in all things.

étal, ā·tal′ [Fr.] Butcher shop.

et cetera, et set′er·a, et se′tra [L.] And so forth; and the rest. Abbr. *etc.*

et nunc et semper, et nunk et sem′per [L.] Now and always.

Et tu, Brute! et tö′brö′tā [L.] And thou also, Brutus.

étude, ā·tуd′ [Fr.] Study.

Eureka! yu·rē′ka [Gr.] I have found it.

ex animo, eks ä′ni·mō′′, eks an′i·mō′′ [L.] Heartily; sincerely.

ex cathedra, eks ka·thē′dra, eks kath′i·dra [L.] With authority: since 1870 the Pope has claimed to be infallible when speaking ex cathedra.

excelsior, ek·sel′si·ōr′′, ik·sel′sē·ōr′′ [L.] Higher, upward.

Exeat, ek·sā′ät, ek′sē·at′′ [L.] Let him leave; a permit granting a student permission for temporary absence.

exempli gratia, ek·sem′plē gRä′tē·ä′′, ig·zem′plī grä′shē·a [L.] By way of example. Abbr. *e.g.*

exeunt, ek·sā′unt, ek′sē·unt [L.] They go out.

exit, ek′sit [L.] He [or she] goes out.

ex libris, eks lē′bris, eks lī′bris [L.] From the books of.

Ex nihilo nihil fit, eks nē′hi·lō nē′hil fit, eks nī′hi·lō nī′hil fit [L.] Out of nothing, nothing comes.

ex officio, eks a·fish′ē·ō′′ [L.] By virtue of office.

ex parte, eks pär′tē [L.] From one side only.

expatrier, eks·pa′′tRē·yä′ [Fr.] To expatriate, to exile.

ex post facto, eks·pōst′′fak′tō [L.] After the deed is done; retrospective.

ex tempore, ik·stem′po·rē [L.] Without preparation; impromptu.

extra muros, ek′strä mö′Rōs, ek′stra mū′rōs [L.] Beyond the walls.

extranjero, eks·tRän·hä′Rō [Sp.] Foreign; foreigner; stranger.

F

fácil, fä·sēl′ [Sp.] Easy.

facilidad, fä·sēl·ē·däd′ [Sp.] Easiness, facility.

Facilis descensus Averno, fä′ki·lis des··ken′sus ä·weR′nō, fas′a·lis di·sen′sas a·vur′nō [L.] The descent to hell is easy.

facta, non verba, fäk′tä nōn weR′bä, fak′ta non vėr′ba [L.] Deeds, not words.

factotum, fäk·tō′tum [It.] Handyman.

factum est, fak′tum est [L.] It is done.

fagiolino, fä·jō·lē′nō [It.] String bean.

fagottino, fä·gō·tē′nō [It.] Small bundle.

faisan, fa·zäN′ [Fr.] Pheasant.

faisán, fä·ē·sän′ [Sp.] Pheasant.

fait accompli, fe·ta·kaN·plē′ [Fr.] A thing already done.

fakir, fa·kēr′, fā′kir [Hind.] Mendicant of the Mohammedan religion.

Falsus in uno, falsus in omnibus, fal′sus in ö′nō fal′sus in ōm′ni·bus [L.] False in one thing, false in everything. Legally, the entire testimony of a witness may be disregarded if some part of it is found to be false.

fama semper vivat! fä′mä sem′peR wē′wät [L.] May his fame live forever.

fanciulla, fän·chō′lä [It.] Young girl.

fanciullo, fän·chō′lō [It.] Young boy.

farce, faRs [Fr.] Stuffing, forcemeat.

farouche, fa·Rösh′ [Fr.] Shy; unsociable; fierce.

fascio, fäs′chō [It.] Bunch, mass, group.

Fascismo, fäs·chēz′mō [It.] Fascism.

Fascista, fäs·chēz′tä [It.] Fascist.

faux-filet, fō·fē·le′ [Fr.] Sirloin.

faux pas, fō pä′ [Fr.] A false step; a social blunder.

felix culpa, fā′liks kul′pä, fē′liks kul′pa [L.] A fortunate mistake; a happy fall.

feliz, fä·lēs′ [Sp.] Happy.

femme, fam [Fr.] Woman; wife; lady.

femme fatale, fam fa·tal′ [Fr.] Seductive woman.

ferrocarril, feR·ō·kä·Rēl′ [Sp.] Railroad, railway.

festina lente, fes·tē′nä len′te, fe·stī′na len′tē [L.] Hasten slowly.

fettucine, fet·ö·chē′ne [It.] Egg noodles.

fiambre, fē·äm′bRe [Sp.] Cold food; a meal served cold.

Fiat lux, fē′ät luks′, fī′at luks′ [L.] Let there be light.

fiat voluntas tua, fē′ät wō·lun′täs tö′ä, fī′at vol′un·tas tö′a [L.] Thy will be done. Matt. 6:10.

fidei defensor, fē′dä·ē′′ de·fen′sōR, fī′dē·ī′′ di·fen′sar [L.] Defender of the faith.

fide, non armis, fē′dä nōn äR′mēs, fī′dē non är′mis [L.] By faith, not arms.

fides et justitia, fē′däs et ūs·ti′ti·ä, fī′dēs et jus·ti′sha [L.] Faith and justice.

fiesta, fē·äs′tä [Sp.] Festival; feast; party.

fille de joie, fē′ye de zhwä′ [Fr.] A prostitute.

fils, fēs [Fr.] Son.

finis, fē′nis, fĭ′nis [L.] The end.

fisk, fisk [Dan., Norw.] Fish.

Flagellum Dei, flä·gel′ŭm dā′ē, fla·jel′um dē′ī [L.] The scourge of God: name given to Attila the Hun.

flambant, fläɴ·bäɴ′ [Fr.] Flaming.

flambé, fläɴ·bā′ [Fr.] Served in flames.

flétan, flā·täɴ′ [Fr.] Halibut.

fleur, flœʀ [Fr.] Flower; blossom.

fleur-de-lis, flœʀ·de·lēs′ [Fr.] Lily; heraldic emblem of French royalty.

foie, fwä [Fr.] Liver.

fondu, fôɴ·dʏ′ [Fr.] Melted.

formaggio, fạr·mä′jō [It.] Cheese.

forno, fōʀ′nō [It.] Bakery shop; oven.

forte, fạr′tä [It.] Loud; mighty; vigorous.

fortiter in re, fōʀ′ti·teʀ in ʀä′, fạr′ta·tèr in rē′ [L.] With firmness in acting.

fragola, fʀä·gō′lä [It.] Strawberry.

fraise, fʀez [Fr.] Strawberry.

frappé, fʀa·pā′ [Fr.] Beverage served iced.

frater, fʀä′teʀ, fʀä′tèr [L.] Brother.

Frau, fʀou [G.] Wife; woman; lady.

Fräulein, fʀoi′līn [G.] Young lady; unmarried lady.

fréjol, fʀā′hạl [Sp.] Kidney bean.

fresa, fʀä′sä [Sp.] Strawberry.

fríjol, fʀē′hạl [Sp.] Bean.

frio, fʀē′ō [Sp.] Cold.

frit, fʀē [Fr.] Fried.

frito, fʀē′tō [Sp.] Fried.

frittata, fʀē·tä′tä [It.] Omelet.

fritto, fʀē′tō [It.] Fried.

Fröhliche Weihnachten! fʀʏ′li·che vī′näch·ten [G.] Merry Christmas.

froid, fʀwä [Fr.] Cold.

fromage, fʀạ·mazh′ [Fr.] Cheese.

fromage à la crème, fʀạ·mazh′ a la kʀem′ [Fr.] Cream cheese.

fromage bleu, fʀạ·mazh blœ′ [Fr.] Blue cheese.

fromage de chèvre, fʀạ·mazh′ de shevʀ′ [Fr.] Goat's milk cheese.

Frucht, fʀukt [G.] Fruit.

Frühstück, fʀʏ′styk [G.] Breakfast.

fruit frais, fʀwē fʀe′ [Fr.] Fresh fruit.

frumento, fʀö·mänʹtō [It.] Wheat.

fruta, fʀö′tä [Sp.] Fruit.

frutta, fʀö′tä [It.] Fruit.

fuego, fwä′gō [Sp.] Fire.

fuerza, fweʀ′sä [Sp.] Force, strength, might, power.

fugu, fö′gö [Jap.] Blowfish; the blowfish, or puffer, is served as a delicacy in Japan after removal of its poison.

Führer, fʏ′ʀèʀ [G.] Leader; head of the German Nazi Party, Adolf Hitler.

Führerschaft, fʏ′ʀèʀ·shäft′′ [G.] Leadership; command; guidance.

fumé, fʏ·mä′ [Fr.] Smoked.

fumer, fʏ·mä′ [Fr.] To smoke.

fungo, fön′gō [It.] Mushroom.

G

gallina, *It.* gä·lē′nä, *Sp.* gä·yē′nä [It., Sp.] Hen.

galuska, gä·lös′kä [Hung.] Soft noodles.

Gans, gäns [G.] Goose.

ganso, gän′sō [Pg., Sp.] Gander; goose.

garbanzo, gär·bän′sō [Sp.] Chickpea.

garbure, gaʀ·bʏʀ′ [Fr.] Soup of cabbage, bacon, and seasoning.

garçon, gaʀ·sôɴ′ [Fr.] Boy; waiter.

Gardez la foi, gaʀ·dä′ la fwä′ [Fr.] Keep the faith.

garni, gaʀ·nē′ [Fr.] Garnished; furnished.

Gasthaus, gäst′hous [G.] Restaurant; tavern; inn.

Gasthof, gäst′hôf [G.] Hotel.

gâteau, gä·tō′ [Fr.] Cake.

gauche, gōsh [Fr.] Left; ugly; awkward.

Gaudeamus igitur, gou′′dā·ä′mụs ig′i·tụr′′ [L.] Let us then be glad.

gaufre, gōfʀ [Fr.] Waffle; wafer.

gazpacho, gäs·pä′chō [Sp.] A salad of bread, onion, and garlic in a dressing of oil and vinegar.

geboren, ge·baʀ′en [G.] Born.

Geheime Staatspolizei, ge·hī′me stäts′′·pō·lit·sī′ [G.] The Nazi Secret State Police; Gestapo.

Geist, gīst [G.] Spirit; intellect.

gelé, je·lä′ [Fr.] Frozen; ice-cold.

gelée, je·lä′ [Fr.] Frost; jelly.

généralissime, jā·nä·ʀal′′ē·sēm′ [Fr.] Commander-in-chief.

genièvre, je·nyevʀ′ [Fr.] Juniper; gin.

genre, jäɴʀ [Fr.] Genus; kind; style; sort.

gens d'armes, jäɴ daʀm′ [Fr.] Men at arms; policemen.

gente, chen′te [Sp.] People.

gentilhomme, jäɴ·tē·ạm′ [Fr.] A gentleman; nobleman.

Gesagt, getan, ge·sägt′ ge·tän′ [G.] No sooner said than done.

Geschichte, ge·shich′te [G.] History.

Gesu, jä′zō [It.] Jesus, Jesus Christ.

gesundheit, ge·sönt′hīt [G.] (To your) health: said to a person sneezing.

ghiaccio, gē·ä′chō [It.] Ice.

gibelotte, jēb·lạt′ [Fr.] Rabbit stew.

gigot, jē·gō′ [Fr.] Leg of lamb.

gingembre, jaɴ·jäɴbʀ′ [Fr.] Ginger.

glace, glas [Fr.] Ice; icing, frosting.

Glocke, glạk′e [G.] Bell.

Glockenspiel, glạk′en·shpēl′′ [G.] Chimes; the ringing of chimes.

Gloria in Excelsis, glōr′ē·ä in ek·sel′sis [L.] Glory (to God) in the highest.

Gloria Patri, glōr′ē·ä pä′trē [L.] Glory be to the Father.

Gnothi seauton, ge·nä′thē se·ä′tōn [Gr.] Know thyself.

gomma, gō′mä [It.] Gum.

Gott sei Dank! gạt′′ tsī dänk′ [G.] Thank God.

gracias, gʀä′sē·äs [Sp.] Thanks, thank you.

granada, gʀä·nä′dä [Sp.] Pomegranate.

grande, gʀän′de [Sp.] Big, great, large.

grande dame, gʀäɴd dam′ [Fr.] A great lady; an aged lady of social distinction.

grand prix, gʀäɴ pʀē′ [Fr.] A great or grand prize.

grano, gʀä′nō [It.] Grain; corn.

grappa, gʀä′pä [It.] A dry brandy.

grasa, gʀä′sä [Sp.] Fat, grease, oil.

gratin, gʀa·taɴ′ [Fr.] The surface of a dish of food which has been browned or crusted before serving.

gré, gʀä [Fr.] Pleasure; will; inclination.

groentesoep, gʀœn′te·sœp′′ [D.] Vegetable soup.

gruau, gʀʏ·ō′ [Fr.] Wheat flour.

guayaba, gä·yä′bä [Sp.] Guava fruit.

guerra, gâ′ʀä [Sp.] War.

gueule, gœl [Fr.] Mouth.

guineo, gē·nä′ō [Sp.] Banana.

guisado, gē·sä′dō [Sp.] Stew.

Gurke, gör′ke [G.] Cucumber; gherkin.

guru, gö′rö [Hind., Skr.] Hindu religious teacher; spiritual or intellectual guide.

guten Abend, gö′ten ä′bend [G.] Good evening.

gute Nacht, gö′te nächt′ [G.] Good night.

guten Morgen, gö′ten mōʀ′gen [G.] Good morning.

guten Tag, gö′ten täg′ [G.] Good day.

gyu, gē′yö [Jap.] Beef.

H

habeas corpus, hä′bē·as kạr′pus [L.] You have the body. Several legal writs begin with these words, and all generally call for bringing the party in custody before the court.

habla, ä′blä [Sp.] Speech; talk; language; dialect.

hablar, ä·bläʀ′ [Sp.] To talk, to speak.

Hakenkreuz, hä′ken·kʀoits′′ [G.] Swastika; symbol of the German Nazi Party.

halle, al [Fr.] Market, marketplace.

hanche, äɴsh [Fr.] Hip; haunch.

haricot, aʀ·ē·kō′ [Fr.] Kidney bean.

hasta, äs′tä [Sp.] Until, till.

hasta la vista, äs′tä lä vē′stä [Sp.] Until we meet again; so long.

hasta luego, äs′tä lwä′gō [Sp.] Until later; until then.

hasta mañana, äs′tä män·yän′ä [Sp.] Until tomorrow.

Hausfrau, hous′fʀou [G.] Housewife; woman of the house.

Hausherr, hous′häʀ [G.] Man of the house; head of the house.

Haus und Hof, hous ụnt haf [G.] One's all; one's house and home.

haut, ō [Fr.] High; uplifted; tall; upper.

haute couture, ōt kö·tʏʀ′ [Fr.] High fashion; the art of designing high fashion clothes.

haute école, ōt ä·kạl′ [Fr.] High horsemanship.

hazan, chä′zan [Heb.] A cantor who sings the liturgy in a Jewish worship service.

heder, chä′dèr [Heb.] A parochial school in which Jewish culture, the Pentateuch, and the Hebrew language are taught.

He dicho, ā dē′chō [Sp.] I have spoken.

hein, aɴ [Fr.] Huh? Hey!

helado, e·lä′dō [Sp.] Ice cream; sherbet.

Herr, häʀ [G.] Master; lord; sir; mister.

Herrenhaus, häʀ′en·hous′′ [G.] Manor house; country mansion.

Herrenvolk, häʀ′en·vōlk′′ [G.] Master race.

Herzog, häʀ′tsōg [G.] Duke.

Heute Deutschland, morgen die ganze Welt, hoi′te doitch′ländt maʀ′gen dē gän′ze velt [G.] Today Germany, tomorrow all the world.

hibachi, hē·bä′chē [Jap.] Brazier; small container of hot coals used primarily for warming hands and the water for tea.

hic et ubique, hēk′ et ö·bē′kwe, hik′ et yö·bī′kwē [L.] Here and everywhere.

hic jacet, hēk yä′ket, hik jä′set [L.] Here lies.

hidalgo, ē·däl′gō [Sp.] Noble, nobleman.

hielo, yä′lō [Sp.] Ice; frost.

higado, ē·gä′dō [Sp.] Liver.

higo, ē′gō [Sp.] Fig.

hija, ē′hä [Sp.] Daughter.

hijo, ē′hō [Sp.] Son.

hoi polloi, hoi′ po·loi′ [Gr.] The many; the vulgar; the rabble.

hollandaise, ạ·läɴ·dez′ [Fr., lit. 'Dutch style'.] A sauce of lemon juice, egg yolks, and butter.

hombre, ōm'bRe [Sp.] Man.

homme de lettres, ạm de letr' [Fr., lit. 'man of letters'.] A literary man; a statesman; an official.

honneur, ạ·nŒR' [Fr.] Honor; virtue; respect.

honneur et patrie, ạ·nŒR' ā pa·trē' [Fr.] Honor and country.

hora fugit, hō'Rä fö'git, hạ'rä fū'jit [L.] The hour flies; time flies.

hors-d'oeuvre, ạR·dŒvR' [Fr.] A dish served at the commencement of a meal; an appetizer.

huevo, wā'vō [Sp.] Egg.

huevos duros, wā'vōs dö'Rōs [Sp.] Hard-boiled eggs.

huevos y tocino, wā'vōs ē tō·sē'nō [Sp.] Eggs and bacon.

huile, hwēl [Fr.] Oil.

Humanum est errare, hö·mä'nụm est eR·Rä're, hū·mā'nụm est ē·rär'ē [L.] To err is human.

I

ibidem, i·bē'dem, ib'i·dem [L.] At the same place, as in a book. Abbr. *ibid.*

Ich dien, ich dēn' [G.] I serve. (Motto of the Prince of Wales.)

Ici on parle francais, ē·sē' ạn paRl fRän·se' [Fr.] French is spoken here.

idem, ī'dem, id'em [L.] The same. Abbr. *id.*

id est, id est' [L.] That is. Abbr. *i.e.*

Iesus Nazarenus, Rex Iundaeorum, yā'sös nä·zä·Rā'nös, Reks ūn·dē·ōr'öm [L.] Jesus of Nazareth, King of the Jews. Abbr. *I.N.R.I.*

iglesia, ē·glä'sē·ä [Sp.] Church.

Il Duce, ēl dö'che [It.] The leader; head of the Italian Fascist Party during World War II, Benito Mussolini.

il penseroso, ēl pen·se·Rō'sō [It.] The pensive man.

imperméable, aN·pâR·mā·abl' [Fr.] Raincoat.

importe, im·pạr'te [Sp.] Value; price; amount.

imprévu, aN·pRä·vy' [Fr.] Unexpected.

in absentia, in ab·sen'sha, in ab·sen'shē·a [L.] In or during absence.

in articulo mortis, in är·tik'ụ·lō mōr'tis, in är·tik'yu·lō mạr'tis [L.] At the point of death.

incroyable, aN·kRä·yabl' [Fr.] Incredible, unbelievable.

in curia, in kụ'rē·a [L.] In court.

in esse, in es'e, in es'ē [L.] In being; in actuality; in existence.

in excelsis, in ek·sel'sis [L.] In the highest; on high.

in extremis, in ek·stRe'mēs, in ik·strē'-mis [L.] At the point of death.

in futuro, in fụ·tō'Rō, in fū·tụ'rō [L.] In the future; henceforth.

ingénu, aN·zhä·ny' [Fr.] Simple; ingenuous; a simple or ingenuous person.

in loco, in lō'kō [L.] In place; in the natural or proper place.

in loco parentis, in lō'kō pä·Ren'tēs, in lō'kō pa·ren'tis [L.] In the place of a parent.

in memoriam, in me·mōr'ē·am [L.] To the memory of; in memory.

in nomine, in nō'mi·nā'', in nom'i·nē', in nom'i·nā'' [L.] In the name of.

in omnia paratus, in ōm'nē·ä'' pä·Rä'tụs, in om'nē·a pa·rä'tus [L.] Prepared for all things.

in perpetuum, in peR·pet'ö·ụm'', in per·pech'ö·um [L.] Forever.

in re, in rē', in rā' [L.] In the matter of; regarding.

insalata, ēn·sä·lä'tä [It.] Salad.

inseguro, ēn·se·gö'Rō [Sp.] Unsure; unsafe.

in situ, in sit'ö, in sī'tō [L.] In its original situation.

in statu quo, in stä'tö kwō', in stä'työ kwō', in stäch'ö kwō' [L.] In the former state.

inter, in'teR, in'ter [L.] Amid, among, between.

inter alia, in'teR ä'li·ä'', in'ter ā'lē·a [L.] Among other things.

interés, ēn·te·rās' [Sp.] Interest; attraction; appeal.

intingolo, in·tēng·ō'lō [It.] Stew, ragout.

in toto, in tō'tō [L.] In the whole; entirely.

intra muros, in'tRä mö'Rōs, in'tra myö'-rōs [L.] Within the walls.

Ipse dixit, ip'se dik'sit, ip'sē dik'sit [L.] He himself said it; a dogmatic saying or assertion.

ipso facto, ip'sō fak'tō [L.] By the fact itself; in the nature of the case.

J

ja, yä [G.] Yes.

jabón, hä·bōn' [Sp.] Soap.

jacinto, hä·sēn'tō [Sp.] Hyacinth.

jaiba, hä·ē'bä [Sp.] Crab.

jambon, zhän·bōn' [Fr.] Ham.

jamón, hä·mōn' [Sp.] Ham.

jardin, zhaR·daN' [Fr.] Garden.

jatte, zhat [Fr.] Bowl.

jaune, zhōn [Fr.] Yellow.

ja wohl, yä vōl' [G.] Yes, indeed; certainly.

je ne sais pas, zhe ne se pä' [Fr.] I don't know.

Jerez, heR·äs' [Sp.] Sherry wine.

Jesus Hominum Salvator, hā'sös hō'-mē·nöm'' säl·vä'tōR, jē'zus hä'mi·num'' sal·vā'tor [L.] Jesus, Savior of Men.

jeune fille, zhŒn fē'ye [Fr.] Girl; young woman.

judicium Dei, ū·dik'ē·ụm dā'ē, jö·dik'ē-um dē'ī [L.] The judgment of God.

juego, hwā'gō [Sp.] Sport, gaming, play; gambling.

jugo de naranja, hö'gō dä nä·Rän'hä [Sp.] Orange juice.

jugo de piña, hö'gō dä pēn'yä [Sp.] Pineapple juice.

jugo de tomate, hö'gō dä tō·mä'te [Sp.] Tomato juice.

Junker, yöng'kėR [G.] Nobleman; country squire; landowner.

Junkerschaft, yöng'kėR·shäft'' [G.] The collective body of young German squires and noblemen.

jus, zhy [Fr.] Gravy; juice.

jus canonicum, ūs' kä·nō'nē·kụm'', jus' ka·non'i·kum [L.] Canon law.

jus civile, jus' si·vī'lē [L.] Civil law.

jus de fruit, zhy de fRwē' [Fr.] Fruit juice.

jus de tomate, zhy de tạ·mat' [Fr.] Tomato juice.

jus divinum, ūs' dē·wē'nụm, jus' di·vī'num [L.] Divine law.

jus d'orange, zhy dạR·äNzh' [Fr.] Orange juice.

jus gladii, ūs' glä'dē·ē, jus' gla'dē·ī [L.] The right of the sword.

jus sanguinis, jus sang'gwi·nis [L.] The right of blood; legal right of heritage or descent.

juste milieu, zhyst mē·lyŒ' [Fr.] The golden mean.

juvenil, hö·ven·ēl' [Sp.] Youthful, juvenile.

juventud, hö·ven·töd' [Sp.] Youth, youthfulness.

K

kabab, kä·bäb' [Hind., Pers.] Roasted cubes of meat, usually skewered.

Kaffeeklatsch, kä'fä·kläch'' [G.] Gossipy conversation while participants are drinking coffee.

Kaffeekuchen, kä'fä·kō''chen [G.] Coffee cake.

kakemono, kä·kē·mō'nō [Jap.] A painting or text on a long, narrow piece of silk paper, mounted on a roller, and usually displayed hanging.

kapusta, kä·pös'tä [Pol.] Cabbage.

Katzenjammer, kät''sen·yäm'ėR [G.] Hangover.

khidmatgar, kid'mat·gär'' [Hind.] One who does service; a waiter.

kiblah, kib'lä [Ar.] The direction which Mohammedans face to pray; East, toward the shrine of Mecca.

Kirsch, kēRsh [G.] Cherry

knish, ke·nish' [Heb.] Pastry dough wrapped around meat or cheese filling.

Kohl, kōl [G.] Cabbage, kale.

Krieg, kRēg [G.] War, warfare.

kringle, kRing'gel [Norw.] A ring-shaped or twisted pastry.

Küche, Kirche, und Kinder, kŒ'ke kēR'ke ụnt kin'der [G.] Kitchen, church, and children; Nazi Germany's official policy regarding the place of women.

Kulturkampf, köl'töR·kämpf'' [G., lit. 'culture conflict'.] The clash between Germany under Bismarck, and the Catholic church.

kvass, ke·väs' [Russ.] Russian beer.

Kyrie eleison, kir'ē·ā'' e·lā'i·san'' [Gr.] Lord have mercy upon us.

L

Labor omnia vincit, lä'bōR ōm'nē·ä'' wēng'kit, lä'bor om'nē·a vin'sit [L.] Labor conquers everything.

lago, lä'gō [It., Pg., Sp.] Lake.

laguna, lä·gö'nä [Sp.] Lagoon.

laine, len [Fr.] Wool.

laissez faire, les·sä feR' [Fr.] Leave (them) alone: policy of noninterference.

lait, le [Fr.] Milk.

laitue, le·ty' [Fr.] Lettuce.

l'allegro, läl·lä'gRō [It.] The cheerful man.

lana, lä'nä [Sp.] Wool, fleece.

la perfide Albion, la peR·fēd'' al·bē·yōN' [Fr.] Treacherous England.

lapin, la·paN' [Fr.] Rabbit.

lapis, lä'pēs, la'pis [L.] A stone.

lápiz, lä'pēs [Sp.] Lead; lead pencil; crayon.

lapsus linguae, läp'sụs ling'wī, lap'sus ling'gwē [L.] A slip of the tongue.

lapsus memoriae, läp'sụs me·mō'Rē·ē'', lap'sus me·mōr'ē·ē'' [L.] A slip of the memory.

lard, laR [Fr.] Fat; bacon.

lástima, lä'stē·mä [Sp.] Pity.

latigo, lä·tē'gō [Sp.] Whip; cinch strap.

Latine dictum, lä·tē'ne dēk'tụm [L.] Spoken in Latin.

latte, lät'te [It.] Milk.

latugga, lä·tö′gä [It.] Lettuce.

lavar, lä·väʀ′ [Sp.] To wash.

le beau monde, le ′bō mōɴd′ [Fr.] The fashionable world.

Lebensraum, lā′bens·ʀoum′′ [G.] Living space; environment; room in which to live.

Leber, lā′beʀ [G.] Liver.

Leberwurst, lā′beʀ·vörst′ [G.] Liver sausage.

leche, lā′chä [Sp.] Milk.

lechuga, le·chö′gä [Sp.] Lettuce.

Légion étrangère, lā·zhōɴ′ ā·tʀäɴ·zhâʀ′ [Fr.] The Foreign Legion.

le Grand Monarque, le gʀäɴ ma̧·naʀk′ [Fr.] The great monarch: Louis XIV of France.

legumbre, le·göm′bʀä [Sp.] Vegetables.

légume, lā·gym′ [Fr.] Vegetable.

Leierkastenmann, lī′′eʀ·käs′ten·män′′ [G.] Organ grinder.

lejos, lā′hōs [Sp.] Far.

lengua, läng′wä [Sp.] Tongue; language.

lentamente, len·tä·men′te [It.] Slowly.

le pas, le pä′ [Fr.] Step; stride; gait.

Le roi est mort; vive le roi! le ʀwä e ma̧ʀ′ vēv le ʀwä′ [Fr.] The king is dead; long live the king.

le tout ensemble, le tö täɴ·säɴbl′ [Fr.] The whole together.

lettre, letʀ [Fr.] Letter; note.

lettre de cachet, letʀ de ka·she′ [Fr.] A sealed letter containing a royal warrant of imprisonment.

levée en masse, le·vä′′ äɴ mas′ [Fr.] A general uprising.

lex, leks [L.] Law.

lex loci, leks lō′kē, leks lō′sī [L.] The law or custom of the place.

lex non scripta, leks nōn skʀēp′tä, leks non skrip′ta [L.] Unwritten law; common law.

lex scripta, leks skʀēp′tä, leks skrip′ta [L.] Written law; statute law.

liberté, égalité, fraternité, lē·beʀ·tā′ ā·gal′′ē·tā′ fʀa·teʀ′′nē·tā′ [Fr.] Liberty, equality, fraternity. (Motto of the French Republic.)

Liederkranz, lē′deʀ·kʀänts′′ [G.] A collection of songs; a German male singing society.

Litera scripta manet, lit′eʀ·ä skʀēp′tä mä′net [L.] The written word remains.

livre, lēvʀ [Fr.] Book; pound.

llanero, yä·nä′ʀō [Sp.] Plainsman.

llano, yä′nō [Sp.] The plains.

lluvia, yö′vē·ä [Sp.] Rain.

lobo, lō′bō [Sp.] Wolf.

loco, lō′kō [Sp.] Crazy, insane.

loco citato, lō′kō kē·tä′tō, lō′kō sī·tä′tō [L.] In the place cited. Abbr. *loc. cit.*

loma, lō′mä [Sp.] Small hill.

longe de veau, lōɴj de vō′ [Fr.] Loin of veal.

los Estados Unidos, lōs e·stä′dōs ö·nē′dōs [Sp.] The United States.

luego, lwä′gō [Sp.] Presently; afterwards; later.

luna, lö′nä [Sp.] Moon.

lune, lyn [Fr.] Moon.

luz, lös [Sp.] Light; daylight.

lycée, lē·sä′ [Fr.] French public grammar school or high school.

M

macédoine, ma·sä·dwan′ [Fr.] Salad.

ma chère, ma shâʀ′ [Fr.] My dear, my precious (referring to women).

macho, mä′chō [Sp.] Male.

Macht ist Recht, mächt ist ʀecht [G.] Might is right.

madame, ma·dam′ [Fr.] Madam; Mrs.; lady.

Mädchen, mäd′chen [G.] Girl; maiden; sweetheart.

mademoiselle, mad·mwa·zel′ [Fr.] Miss, young lady.

madre, mä′dʀä [Sp.] Mother; matron.

maestro, mä·äs′tʀō [It.] Master; teacher; director; instructor.

Ma foi! ma fwä′ [Fr.] To be sure.

magna cum laude, mäg′na ku̧m lou′dä [L.] With great praise.

magni nominis umbra, mäg′nē nō′mi·nis′′ u̧m′bʀa [L.] The shadow of a great name.

magnum opus, mag′nu̧m ō′pu̧s [L.] A great work.

maharaja, ma·hä′ʀä′ja [Hind., Skr.] Hindu ruling prince.

maharani, ma·hä′ʀä′nē [Hind., Skr.] Wife of a maharaja; Hindu ruling princess.

maiale, mä·ē·ä′le [It.] Hog, pig; pork.

maïs, mä·ēs′ [Fr.] Maize; Indian corn.

maître d'hotel, metʀ dō·tel′ [Fr.] A house steward.

maíz, mä·ēs′ [Sp.] Maize, Indian corn.

mal, *Fr.* mal, *Sp.* mäl [Fr., Sp.] Bad, evil; illness; misfortune.

mala fide, mä′lä fē′de, mä′la fī′dē [L.] With bad faith; treacherously.

mal à propos, mal a pʀa̧·pō′ [Fr.] Inopportunely or improperly timed.

mal de mer, mal de mâʀ′ [Fr.] Seasickness.

malentendu, mal·äɴ·täɴ·dy′ [Fr.] A misunderstanding; mistake.

malgré, mal·gʀä′ [Fr.] In spite of.

malgré soi, mal·gʀä swa′ [Fr.] In spite of himself.

malheur, mal·œʀ′ [Fr.] Misfortune; disaster; bad luck.

mañana, män·yän′ä [Sp.] Tomorrow; in the morning.

mandorla, män·dōʀ′lä [It.] Almond.

manger, mäɴ·zhä′ [Fr.] To eat, to consume.

mano, mä′nō [Sp.] Hand.

manqué, mäɴ·kä′ [Fr.] Unsuccessful, abortive; defective.

máquina, mä′kē·nä [Sp.] Machine; engine.

mar, mäʀ [Sp.] Sea.

Märchen, mäʀ′chen [G.] A fairy tale, legend, fable.

Mardi gras, maʀ·dē′′ gʀä′ [Fr.] Shrove Tuesday.

Mare Nostrum, mä′ʀe nōs′tʀu̧m, mâ′rē nos′tru̧m [L., lit. 'our sea'.] Roman name for Mediterranean Sea.

margaritas ante porcos, mäʀ′′gä·rē′täs än·ta pa̧ʀ′kōs [L.] Pearls before swine.

marinara, mäʀ′′ē·nä′ʀä [It.] Heavily spiced tomato sauce.

marito, mäʀ·ē′tō [It.] Husband.

mas, mäs [Sp.] Most, more; plus.

maschio, mäs′kē·ō [It.] Male; masculine; virile.

maté, mä·tä′ [Sp.] Paraguay tea.

mea culpa, mä′ä ku̧l′pä, mē′a kul′pa [L.] My fault; by fault of my own.

mein Herr, mīn hâʀ [G.] Sir.

Mein Kampf, mīn kämpf [G.] My battle; title of a book by Adolf Hitler.

mejor, mä·haʀ′ [Sp.] Better, best.

me judice, mä yō′dē·kä′′ [L.] I being judge; in my opinion.

mela, mä′lä [It.] Apple.

mem-sahib, mem′sä′′ib, mem′sä′′hēb [Anglo-Ind.] A white woman living in India; the wife of a European official assigned to India.

menos, mä′nōs [Sp.] Less, least; minus.

mens sana in corpore sano, mens sä′nä in kōʀ′pō·ʀe′′ sä′nō, menz sä′na in ka̧ʀ′po·rē′′ sä′nō [L.] A sound mind in a sound body.

menthe, mäɴt [Fr.] Mint.

mer, mâʀ [Fr.] Sea.

merci, mâʀ·sē′ [Fr.] Thanks; mercy; pleasure.

mes, mäs [Sp.] Month.

mesa, mä′sä [Sp.] Table; plateau.

metate, me·tä′te [Sp.] A stone slab used for grinding corn and maize.

meum et tuum, mä′u̧m et tö′u̧m, mē′um et tö′um [L.] Mine and thine.

miedo, mē·ä′dō [Sp.] Fear, dread.

mignon, mēn·yōɴ′ [Fr.] Delicate; dainty; pretty.

minestrone, mē·ne·stʀō′ne [It.] A thick soup of vegetables and macaroni.

mirabile dictu, mē·ʀäb′i·le′′ dik′tö, mi·rab′i·lē′′ dik′tö [L.] Wonderful to relate.

misericordia, mis′′eʀ·i·kōʀ′dē·ä′′, miz′′er·i·ka̧r′dē·a [L.] Compassion, pity, mercy.

mismo, mēs′mō [Sp.] Same, like, similar.

Missa cantata, mēs′sä kän·tä′tä, mis′a kan·tä′ta [L.] Mass sung by a single priest.

mit Gewalt, mit ge·vält′ [G.] By force.

mitzvah, mits·vä′, mits′va [Heb.] Fulfillment of a religious obligation; a good deed; privilege of assisting in the synagogue's ritual.

modus operandi, mō′du̧s ō′′pe·rän′dē, mō′dus op′′e·ran′dī [L.] Manner of working.

modus vivendi, mō′du̧s wē·wen′dē, mō′dus vi·ven′dī [L.] Mode of living.

moelle de boeuf, mwal de bœf′ [Fr.] Beef marrow.

mon ami, mō·na·mē′ [Fr.] My friend.

mon cher, mōɴ shâʀ′ [Fr.] My dear (referring to men).

Mon Dieu! mōɴ dyœ [Fr.] My God.

montaña, mōn·tän′yä [Sp.] Mountain.

motu proprio, mō′tö prō′pri·ō′′ [L.] Of his own accord.

moussaka, mös·sä′kä [Gr.] A dish of alternating layers of eggplant and meat filling.

mousse, mös [Fr.] A chilled, molded dish stiffened with egg white, gelatin, or whipped cream; may be made of a meat base as a main course, or made of custard to create a dessert.

mouton, mö·tōɴ′ [Fr.] Sheep, mutton.

mozzarella, mōt′′sä·ʀel′lä [It.] A white cheese used in pizza.

muchacha, mö·chä′chä [Sp.] Girl; female servant.

muchacho, mö·chä′chō [Sp.] Boy.

mucho, mö′chō [Sp.] Many, much.

mujer, mö·hâʀ′ [Sp.] Woman; wife.

mundial, mu̧n·dyäl′ [Sp.] Global, worldwide.

mundo, mu̧n′dō [Sp.] World.

mutatis mutandis, mö·tä′tēs mö·tän′dēs, mū·tä′tis mū·tan′dis [L.] With the necessary changes.

Mütterchen, mүт′тeʀ·chen′′ [G.] Mommy, dear mother.

muy, mwē [Sp.] Very, greatly.

N

nada, nä′dä [Sp.] Nothing.

nappe, nap [Fr.] Tablecloth; cover.

naranja, nä·ʀän′hä [Sp.] Orange.

nariz, nä·ʀēs′ [Sp.] Nose; nostrils.

Navidad, nä·vē·däd′ [Sp.] Christmas; Nativity.

Nec habeo, nec careo, nec curo, nek hä′bā·ō nek käʀ′ā·ō nek köʀ′ō [L.] I have not, I want not, I care not.

nein, nīn [G.] No.

ne quid nimis, ne kwid ni′mis [L.] Nothing to excess.

Nescit vox missa reverti, nes′kit voks mi′sa re·vėr′tē [L.] The spoken word can never be recalled.

n′est-ce pas? nes′′e pä′ [Fr.] Is it not so? Right?

nevado, ne·vä′dō [Sp.] Snow-capped, white as snow.

nicht wahr? nicht väʀ′ [G.] Is it not so? True?

nieve, nē·ā′ve [Sp.] Snow.

nihil, nē′hil, nī′hil [L.] Nothing.

nihil ad rem, nē′hil äd ʀem′′, nī′hil ad rem′′ [L.] Nothing to the point.

ni l′un ni l′autre, nē lœn′ nē lōtʀ′ [Fr.] Neither the one nor the other.

N′importe, naN·paʀt′ [Fr.] It matters not, it makes no difference.

niño, nēn′yō [Sp.] Child.

Nisi Dominus frustra, nē′sē dō′mē·nus fʀö′stʀä [L.] Unless God (be with us) all is in vain.

noblesse, na̱·bles′ [Fr.] Nobility.

noblesse oblige, na̱·bles′′ a̱·blēzh′ [Fr.] Rank imposes obligation.

noche, nō′che [Sp.] Night, evening; darkness.

nochebuena, nō′′che·bwā′nä [Sp.] Christmas eve.

Noël, nō·el′ [Fr.] Christmas.

no es verdad? nō′′es veʀ·däd′ [Sp.] Isn′t it true? Right?

noix, nwä [Fr.] Walnut.

nolens volens, nō′lens vō′lens [L.] Whether willing or not; unwilling.

Noli me tangere, nō′lē mä tän′ge·ʀe [L.] Touch me not.

Nolo contendere, nō′lō kon·ten′de·ʀē [L., lit. ′I will not contest it′.] A plea of a defendant by which he submits to conviction, but without necessarily admitting his guilt.

nombre, nōm′bʀe [Sp.] Name; title.

nom de guerre, nōN de gâʀ′ [Fr.] Assumed name, pseudonym.

nom de plume, nōN de plүm′ [Fr.] Pen name, literary pseudonym.

nom de théâtre, nōN de tā·ätʀ′ [Fr.] Stage name; a theatrical pseudonym.

non compos mentis, nōn kŏm′pŏs men′tis, non kom′pos men′tis [L.] Not of sound mind.

non culpabilis, nōn ku̱l·pä′bi·lis′′ [L.] Not guilty.

non obstante, nōn ōb·stän′te, non ob·stan′tē [L.] Notwithstanding.

non possumus, nōn pōs′u̱·mu̱s, non pos′-u·mus [L.] We cannot (comply).

non sequitur, nōn se′kwi·tu̱ʀ′′, non se′-kwi·tur [L.] It does not follow.

Nosce te ipsum, nōs′ke tä ip′su̱m, nō′sē tē ip′sum [L.] Know thyself.

Nota bene, nō′tä be′ne, nō′ta bē′nē [L.] Mark well, take note.

Notre Dame, na̱tʀ dam′ [Fr.] Our Lady; the Virgin Mary.

nouveau riche, nö·vō ʀēsh′ [Fr.] One newly rich; a wealthy upstart.

nozze, nōt′se [It.] Wedding, marriage.

nuestro, nwäs′tʀō [Sp.] Our, ours.

nuevo, nwä′vō [Sp.] New, modern.

nulla nuova, buona nuova, nö′lä nwō′vä bwō′nä nwō′vä [It.] No news, good news.

nulli secundus, nö′lē sä·ku̱n′du̱s, nu′lē se·kun′dus [L.] Second to none.

nunca, nön′kä [Sp.] Never.

nunc aut nunquam, nu̱ngk out nu̱n′kwäm [L.] Now or never.

nunquam non paratus, nu̱n′kwäm nōn pä·ʀä′tu̱s [L.] Never unprepared; always ready.

nutritif, nү′′tʀē·tēf′ [Fr.] Nutritious, nourishing.

O

obiit, ō′bi·it, ō′bē·it [L.] He (she) died.

obispo, ō·bēs′pō [Sp.] Bishop.

obiter dictum, ob′i·ter dik′tum [L.] A thing said by the way.

objet d′art, a̱b′′zhe daʀ′ [Fr.] An object of art.

oca, ō′kä [It.] Goose.

odeur, ō·dœʀ′ [Fr.] Smell, scent; perfume.

odium theologicum, ō′dē·um thē·o·loj′i·kum′′ [L.] The hatred of theologians for one another; the bitterness of theological controversy.

oeste, ō·äs′te [Sp.] West.

oeuf, œf [Fr.] Egg.

oeufs au plat, œ zō pla′ [Fr.] Fried eggs.

oeufs brouillés, œ bʀwö·ē·yä′ [Fr.] Scrambled eggs.

oeufs pochés, œ pa̱·shä′ [Fr.] Poached eggs.

oie, wä [Fr.] Goose.

oignon, a̱·nyōN′ [Fr.] Onion.

ojo, ō′hō [Sp.] Eye.

öl, œl [Sw.] Beer, ale.

olio, ō′lē·ō [It.] Oil.

olla, ō′yä [Sp.] Kettle, stewpot.

omelette, a̱m·let′ [Fr.] Omelet.

Omnia vincit amor, ōm′nē·ä′′ wēng′kit ä′mōʀ, om′nē·a vin′sit ä′ma̱ʀ [L.] Love conquers all things.

Omnia vincit labor, ōm′nē·ä′′ wēng′kit lä′bōʀ, om′nē·a vin′sit lä′bo̱ʀ [L.] Labor overcomes all things.

onus probandi, ō′nu̱s pʀō·bän′dē, ō′nus pʀō·ban′dī [L.] The burden of proof.

oomiak. *See* umiak.

oporto, ō·pa̱ʀ′tō [Sp.] Port wine.

opus, ō′pus [L.] A work.

ora, ō′ʀä [It.] Hour; time.

orge, a̱ʀj [Fr.] Barley.

origo mali, ō·ʀē′gō mä′lē [L.] Origin of the evil.

ortaggio, aʀ·tä′jō [It.] Vegetables, greens.

orzo, aʀ′tsō [It.] Barley.

os, a̱s [Fr.] Bone.

osteria, ōs·teʀ·ē′ä [It.] Tavern, inn.

ostra, ōs′tʀä [Sp.] Oyster.

ostrica, ōs·tʀē′kä [It.] Oyster.

O tempora! O mores! ō tem′pō·ʀä′′ ō mō′-ʀäs, ō tem′po·ra ō mōr′ēz [L.] O the times. O the customs.

oubliette, ö·blē·et′ [Fr.] A secret dungeon with a trap door entrance from above.

oui, wē [Fr.] Yes.

ovo, ō′vō [Pg.] Egg.

Oyez! a̱·yä′ [Fr.] Hear ye. Listen.

P

pace, pä′ke, pä′sē [L.] By or with the leave of.

pace tua, pä′ke tö′ä, pä′sē chö′a [L.] By your leave.

padella, pä·del′ä [It.] Pan, frying pan.

padre, pä′dʀe [Sp.] Father; priest.

paella, pä·e′yä [Sp.] Spanish dish consisting of rice mixed with meat or poultry.

pain, paN [Fr.] Bread; loaf.

pain de seigle, paN de segl′ [Fr.] Rye bread.

pain grillé, paN gʀē·yä′ [Fr.] Toast.

país, pä·ēs′ [Sp.] Nation; region; land.

paisano, pä·ē·sä′nō [Sp.] Fellow countryman, compatriot.

palabra, pä·lä′bʀä [Sp.] Word.

pamplemousse, pän′′ple·mös′ [Fr.] Grapefruit.

pan, pän [Sp.] Bread; loaf; crust.

pan de maíz, pän dä mä·ēs′ [Sp.] Corn bread.

pane, pä′ne [It.] Bread; loaf.

panna, pä′nä [It.] Cream.

pão, pouN [Pg.] Bread; loaf of bread.

papa, pä′pä [Sp.] Potato.

papas rellenas, pä′päs ʀe·yä′näs [Sp.] Stuffed potatoes.

papel, pä·pel′ [Sp.] Paper; document; role.

papier, pa·pyä′ [Fr.] Paper.

Parbleu! paʀ·blœ′ [Fr.] Of course. By Jove.

pardonnez-moi, paʀ·da̱·nä·mwa′ [Fr.] Pardon me.

par excellence, paʀ ek′′sel·äNs′ [Fr.] By excellence; above all others; preeminently.

parfum, paʀ·fœN′ [Fr.] Perfume; scent; fragrance.

parole d′honneur, pa·ʀa̱l′′ da̱n·œʀ′ [Fr.] Word of honor.

pars pro toto, pärz pʀō tō′tō [L.] Part for the whole.

partim, pär′tim [L.] In part; partly.

pas, pä [Fr.] Step; pace; stride.

paseo, pä·sä′ō [Sp.] A walk; a stroll; a ride.

pasha, pa·shä′, pä′sha [Turk.] Title of honor or rank.

passé, pa·sä′ [Fr.] Past, gone, finished.

passim, pas′im [L.] Everywhere; throughout; here and there.

pasta, päs′tä [It.] Paste; dough; paste foods, such as spaghetti and macaroni.

pastel, päs·tel′ [Sp.] Pie; pastries.

pastel de carne, päs·tel′ dä käʀ′ne [Sp.] Meat pie.

patata, pä·tä′tä [It., Sp.] Potato.

patata bollita, pä·tä′tä ba̱·lē′tä [It.] Mashed potato.

patata triturate, pä·tä′tä tʀē·tö·ʀä′te [It.] Mashed potato.

pater, pä′teʀ, pä′ter [L.] Father.

paterfamilias, pä′′teʀ·fä·mē′lē·äs, pä′′-ter·fa·mil′ē·as [L.] Father of a family; household head.

Pater Noster, pä′ter nos′ter [L.] Our Father, the first words of the Lord′s Prayer.

pater patriae, pä′teʀ pä′tʀē·ī′′, pä′ter pä′tʀē·ē′′ [L.] Father of his country.

pâteux, pä·tœ′ [Fr.] Pasty; sticky;

doughy; cloudy.

pâtisserie, pä·tē·se·Rē′ [Fr.] Pastry.

pato, pä′tō [Pg., Sp.] Duck.

patois, pa·twä′ [Fr.] A local dialect; jargon.

patres conscripti, pä′tRes kōn·skRēp′tē, pä′trēz kon·skrip′tī [L.] Conscript fathers; Roman senators.

pavo, pä′vō [Sp.] Turkey.

pax, päks, paks [L.] Peace.

Pax Romana, päks′ Rō·mä′nä, paks′ rō·mä′na [L.] Roman peace; peace established by Roman might and security.

pax vobiscum, päks′ wō·bēs′kụm, paks′ vō·bis′kum [L.] Peace be with you.

paz, päs [Sp.] Peace; tranquillity.

pêche, pesh [Fr.] Peach; fishing.

peligroso, pe·lē·gRō′sō [Sp.] Perilous, risky, dangerous.

pelo, pä′lō [Sp.] Hair.

pelota, pe·lō′tä [Sp.] Ball; ball game.

pensée, päN·sā′ [Fr.] A thought.

peón, pe·ōn′ [Sp.] Unskilled laborer; pedestrian; foot soldier.

peor, pe·ōR′ [Sp.] Worse, worst.

pepe, pe′pä [It.] Pepper.

pequeño, pe·kän′yō [Sp.] Little; small.

per annum, per an′um [L.] By the year; annually.

per capita, per kap′i·ta [L.] By the head; for each person.

per centum, per sen′tum [L.] By the hundred.

per diem, per dē′em, per dī′em [L.] By the day; daily.

periculum in mora, pe·rik′ū·lum in ma̧′ra [L.] Danger in delay.

per mensum, peR men′sụm, per men′sum [L.] By the month.

pero, peR′ō [Sp.] But.

per se, peR sē′, per sā′ [L.] By or in itself.

persona grata, peR·sō′nä grä′tä, per·sō′na grä′ta [L.] An acceptable or welcome person.

persona non grata, peR·sō′nä nōn grä′tä, per·sō′na non grä′ta [L.] An unacceptable person.

pesca, pes′kä [Sp.] Catch of fish; fishing.

pescado, pes·kä′dō [Sp.] A fish which has been caught; a dead fish.

pesce, pes′chä [It.] Fish.

peso, pā′sō [Sp.] Weight; load; Spanish monetary unit.

petit, pe·tē′ [Fr.] Little, small, slight.

petite-fille, pe·tēt′′fē′ye [Fr.] Granddaughter.

petit-fils, pe·tē′′fēs [Fr.] Grandson.

petits pois, pe·tē′′ pwä′ [Fr.] Green peas.

Pickelhaube, pik′′el·hou′be [G.] Spiked helmet.

pièce de résistance, pyes de Rä·zē·stäNs′ [Fr.] The main feature or strong point of anything; the most substantial dish of a meal.

pietà, pē′′ä·tä′, pyä·tä′ [It.] A sculpture or drawing of the Virgin Mary holding the body of Christ.

pieuvre, pyŒvR [Fr.] Octopus.

pilau, pē·lō′ [Fr.] Pilaf, a rice dish with fish, meat, or poultry.

piment, pē·mäN′ [Fr.] Pimento; red or green pepper.

pimiento, pē·mē·en′tō [Sp.] Green or red pepper.

piña, pēn′yä [Sp.] Pineapple; pine cone.

pince-nez, paNs·nā′ [Fr.] Folding eyeglasses.

pis aller, pē·zal·ä′ [Fr.] The worst; the last shift; the last resource.

pisello, pē·sel′ō [It.] Pea.

plata, plä′tä [Sp.] Silver; silver currency; money.

playa, plä′yä [Sp.] Shore; coast; beach.

pobre, pō′bRe [Sp.] Poor, needy; poor person, pauper.

poco, pō′kō [Sp.] Little; small; few.

poco a poco, pō′kō ä pō′kō [It., Sp.] Little by little.

poco tiempo, pō′kō tyem′pō [Sp.] Short time, soon.

poêle, pwäl [Fr.] Frying pan; stove.

poire, pwaR [Fr.] Pear.

pois, pwä [Fr.] Pea, peas.

poisson, pwa·sōN′ [Fr.] Fish.

poivre, pwavR [Fr.] Pepper.

politesse, pa̧·lē·tes′ [Fr.] Politeness; good breeding.

pollo, *It.* pō′lō, *Sp.* pō′yō [It., Sp.] Chicken.

pollo alla cacciatore, pō′lō ä′lä kä·chä·tō′Re [It.] Chicken cooked in 'hunter's style', stewed in tomatoes and wine.

pollo arrosto, pō′lō är·ō′stō [It.] Roast chicken.

pollo in vino bianco, pō′lō en vē′nō bē··äng′kō [It.] Chicken cooked in white wine.

polpetta, pōl·pe′tä [It.] Meatball.

porc, paR [Fr.] Pork; pig, swine.

por ciento, pōR syen′tō [Sp.] Percent.

por favor, pōR fä·vōR′ [Sp.] Please.

porto, pōR′tō [Pg.] Port, harbor.

post hoc, ergo propter hoc, pōst hōk′eR′·gō prōp′teR hōk′′, pōst hok′ ụr′gō prop′ter hok′′ [L.] After this, therefore on account of this.

post meridiem, pōst′ me·rid′ē·em [L.] After noon; afternoon.

post mortem, pōst ma̧r′tem [L.] After death; an autopsy.

postre, pōs′·tRä [Sp.] Last in order; dessert.

potage, pa̧·tazh′ [Fr.] Soup.

pot-au-feu, pa̧·tō·fŒ′ [Fr.] Beef broth.

potiron, pa̧·tē·RōN′ [Fr.] Pumpkin.

pouding, pö·daN′ [Fr.] Pudding.

pouding au pain, pö·daN′′ō paN′ [Fr.] Bread pudding.

poularde, pö·laRd′ [Fr.] Fat pullet.

poule, pöl [Fr.] Hen.

poulette, pö·let′ [Fr.] Young hen.

pour toujours, pöR tö·zhöR′ [Fr.] For always, forever.

pousse-café, pös·ka·fä′ [Fr.] After-coffee liqueur.

poussin, pö·saN′ [Fr.] Newly hatched chicken; chick.

pregunta, pRe·gön′tä [Sp.] Question.

premio, pRe·mē′ō [It.] Prize; award; reward.

presidio, pRe·sē′dē·ō [Sp.] Garrison, fortress, citadel.

presto, pRes′tō [It., Sp.] Quick, soon.

prima facie, prī′ma fä′shē·ē′′, prī′ma fä′shē [L.] At first appearance; at first glance.

primo, prē′mō [L.] In the first place, in the beginning, at first.

principia, non homines, pRin·kēp′ē·ä nōn hō′mi·näs′′, prin·sip′ē·a non ho′mi·nēz′′ [L.] Principles, not men.

prix, pRē [Fr.] Price, cost; reward, prize.

pro bono publico, pRō bō′nō pö′bli·kō′′, prō bō′nō pub′li·kō′′ [L.] For the good of the public.

pro et contra, prō et con′tra [L.] For and against.

pronto, pRōn′tō [Sp.] Prompt, soon; promptly, quickly.

pro patria, pRō pä′tRē·ä′′, prō′ pä′trē·a [L.] For country.

propter hoc, prōp′teR hōk′, prop′ter hok′ [L.] On account of this, because of this.

pro rata, prō rä′ta, prō rä′ta [L.] According to this current rate; proportionately.

pro rege, lege, et grege, pRō Rä′gä lä′gä et gRä′gä [L.] For the king, the law, and the people.

prosciutto, pRō·shö′tō [It.] Ham.

pro tempore, pRō tem′pō·Re′′, prō tem′po·rē′′ [L.] For the time; temporarily.

provocateur, pRa̧·va̧·ka·tŒR′ [Fr.] One who provokes trouble or causes a disturbance; an aggressor.

puchero, pö·cher′ō [Sp.] Stew.

pueblo, pwä′blō [Sp.] Town, settlement, village; people, population.

puerco, pwer′kō [Sp.] Filthy, foul, base; wild boar; base person.

purée, pY·Rä′ [Fr.] Thick soup.

pur-sang, pYR·säN′ [Fr.] A thoroughbred.

Putsch, pụtch [G.] Uprising, riot.

Q

quam proxime, kwäm prok′si·me [L.] As nearly as possible.

quasi, kwä′zī, kwä′sī, kwä′sē, kwä′zē [L.] As if; as it were.

que, kā [Sp.] That, which, who; what.

Que hora es? kā ō′Rä es [Sp.] What time is it?

queijo, kā′zō [Pg.] Cheese.

queso, kā′sō [Sp.] Cheese.

Que voulez-vous? ke vö·lä·vö′ [Fr.] What would you have? What do you want?

quid nunc? kwid′′ nunk′ [L.] What now?

quid pro quo, kwid′′ prō kwō′ [L.] Something in return; compensation.

Quien es? kyen es′ [Sp.] Who is it?

Quien sabe? kyen sä′be [Sp.] Who knows?

quignon, kēn·yōN′ [Fr.] Large hunk of bread.

Quis custodiet ipsos custodes? kwis kụ·stō′dē·et′′ ip′sōs kụ·stō′des, kwis kụ·stō′dē·it ip′sōs kụ·stō′dēz [L.] Who shall keep the keepers themselves? Who shall guard the guards?

qui va là? kē va la′ [Fr.] Who goes there?

quoad hoc, kwō′äd hōk′, kwō′ad hok′ [L.] To this extent; as to this; as far as this is concerned.

quo animo, kwō ä′ni·mō′′, kwō an′i·mō′′ [L.] With what intention or motive.

quo vadis? kwō vä′dis [L.] Whither goest thou?

R

raconteur, Ra·kon·tŒR′ [Fr.] Storyteller, narrator.

ragoût, Ra·gö′ [Fr.] Stew.

raifort, Re·faR′ [Fr.] Horseradish.

raison d'état, Re·zōN′′ dä·ta′ [Fr.] Justification; reason of state; legal grounds.

raison d'être, Re·zōN′′ detR′ [Fr.] The reason for existence.

raja, rä′ja [Hind.] Hindu ruling prince; any dignitary or official.

rajah. *See* **raja.**

Rajput, räj′pöt [Hind.] Member of a Hindu military caste.

Ramadan, ra′′ma·dän′ [Ar.] Ninth month of the Mohammedan year, during which fasting is observed from dawn to dusk.

ranchero, rän·chä′ro [Sp.] Small farmer; herdsman; rancher.

rapprochement, ra·prᴀsh·män′ [Fr.] Bringing together; drawing closer; reconciliation.

Raskolnik, räs·köl′nik [Russ.] Dissenter; nonconformist; one who seceded from the Russian Orthodox Church.

Ratskeller, rät′skel″er [G.] A town hall cellar: in Germany these came to be used as restaurants and beer halls.

re, rā, rē [L.] In the matter of, concerning the case of.

real, rä·äl′ [Sp.] Royal, noble, regal.

Realpolitik, rä″äl·pō·li·tēk′ [G.] Practical, realistic politics.

rebozo, re·bō′sō [Sp.] A shawl worn by women in Latin American countries.

réchaud, rā·shō′ [Fr.] Chafing dish; portable food warmer.

reductio ad absurdum, re·duk′tē·ō äd äb·sôr′dum, ri·duk′shē·ō ad ab·sur′dum [L.] Reduction (of an argument or proposition) to an absurdity.

refresco, re·frās′kō [Sp.] Refreshment; cold drink.

regina, re·gē′nä, ri·jī′na, ri·jē′na [L.] Queen.

Reichsbank, rīchs′bänk [G.] The German National Bank.

Reichsmark, rīchs′märk [G.] The mark, Germany's monetary unit.

Reichsrat, rīchs′rät [G.] Federal Council, the upper house of the German Parliament.

Reichstag, rīchs′täg [G.] Lower house of German legislature; the German Diet, or House of Representatives.

Reichswehr, rīchs′ver [G.] The total German military force.

relleno, rel·yä′nō [Sp.] Stuffed, filled, stuffing; forcemeat.

reloj, re·lach′ [Sp.] Watch, clock, timepiece.

remuda, re·mö′dä [Sp.] Change; replacement; total collection of horses available as remounts on a ranch.

repas, re·pä′ [Fr.] Repast, meal.

repollo, re·pōl′yō [Sp.] Cabbage.

répondez, s'il vous plaît, rā·pōn·dā′ sēl vö ple′ [Fr.] Respond (answer) if you please. Abbr. *R.S.V.P.*

requiescat in pace, re″kwē·es′kät in pä′chä [L.] May he (she) rest in peace. Abbr. *R.I.P.*

res gestae, rēz jes′tē, räs jes′tē [L.] Things done; exploits; accomplishments.

res judicata, rēz′ jö″di·kä′ta, räs′ jö″di·kä′ta [L.] A suit already judged; a settled case.

rex, reks, reks [L.] King.

Rex non potest peccare, reks′ nōn pō′test pe·kä′re [L.] The king can do no wrong.

rey, rā [Sp.] King.

rincón, rēn·kōn′ [Sp.] Nook; corner; angle.

río, rē′ō [Sp.] River.

rishi, rish′ē [Skr.] Hindu sage; seer; one poetically inspired.

risorgimento, rē·sōr″jē·men′tō [It.] Resurrection, revival.

riz, rē [Fr.] Rice.

riz au lait, rē″zō le′ [Fr.] Rice pudding.

ron, rōn [Sp.] Rum.

ropa, rō′pä [Sp.] Fabric, cloth; clothing, apparel.

rosbif, rᴀs·bēf′ [Fr., Sp.] Roast beef.

rôti, rō·tē′ [Fr.] Roast; roasted meat.

roux, rö [Fr.] Reddish-brown; brown butter sauce.

rue, ry [Fr.] Street.

ruidoso, rö·ē·dō′sō [Sp.] Noisy, loud.

russinkaka, rö′sin·kä′kä [Sw.] Raisin cake.

S

sábado, sä′bä·dō [Sp.] Saturday.

sabio, sä′bē·ō [Sp.] Wise, learned, scholarly; a scholar, wise man, sage.

sacré, sa·krä′ [Fr.] Sacred, holy; damned, cursed.

sahib, sä′ib, sä′ēb [Hind.] Sir, lord, master; title of respect and status; title used by natives referring to a European representative or official in their country.

sahibah, sä·ē′bä [Hind.] A lady; madam.

sake, sä′kē [Jap.] An alcoholic beverage of the Orient made from fermented rice and usually served hot.

sal, säl [Sp.] Salt; wit.

salaam, sä·läm′ [Ar.] Peace unto you; a salutation; a very low bow of obeisance.

salamoia, sä·lä·mō·ē′ä [It.] Pickle; brine.

salsa, säl′sä [Sp.] Gravy; dressing; sauce.

salsiccia, säl·sē′chē·ä [It.] Sausage.

salve! säl′wä, sal′vē [L.] Hail.

samadh, se·mäd′ [Hind.] Tomb or shrine erected on the grave site of a religious mendicant.

sanctum sanctorum, sangk′tum sangk·tᴀr′um [L.] The holy of holies.

sandía, sän·dē′ä [Sp.] Watermelon.

sang, sän [Fr.] Blood; gore.

sang froid, sän frwä′ [Fr.] Cold blood; coolness; composure.

sans doute, sän döt′ [Fr.] Without doubt, doubtless.

sans peine, sän pen′ [Fr.] Without pain; without trouble; with ease.

sans souci, sän sö·sē′ [Fr.] Without care; carefree; trouble-free.

saucisse, sö·sēs′ [Fr.] Sausage.

Sauerbraten, zou′er·brät″en, sour′brät″en [G.] Beef that has been pickled and then stewed.

savant, sa·vän′ [Fr.] A learned person.

savoir-faire, sa·vwär·fâr′ [Fr.] Knowing how to act; tact; wise to the ways of the world.

savoir-vivre, sa·vwär·vēvr′ [Fr.] Good breeding; refined behavior.

sayonara, sä·yō·nä′rä [Jap.] Farewell, good-bye.

scarole, ska·rᴀl′ [Fr.] Escarole.

Schloss, shlᴀs [G.] Castle, palace.

Schmerz, shmârts [G.] Pain, ache, suffering.

Schmierkäse, shmir·kä′ze [G.] Soft cheese.

schnell, shnel [G.] Rapid, quick, brisk, sudden.

Scusatemi! skö·sä′te·mē′ [It.] Excuse me. Pardon me.

sec, sek [Fr.] Dry; lacking sweetness, as wines.

sedano, sä·dä′nō [It.] Celery.

seguro, sä·gö′rō [Sp.] Secure, safe, certain.

Se habla español, sä äb′lä es·pän·yōl′ [Sp.] Spanish is spoken here.

seigle, segl [Fr.] Rye.

sel, sel [Fr.] Salt; wit.

semper fidelis, sem′per fi·dā′lis, sem′per fi·dä′lis [L.] Always faithful.

semper idem, sem′per ē′dem, sem′per ī′dem [L.] Always the same.

semper paratus, sem′per pä·rä′tus, sem′per pa·rä′tus [L.] Always ready.

senape, sä·nä′pe [It.] Mustard, mustard seed.

senhor, se·nᴀr′ [Pg.] Sir, Mister.

senhora, se·nᴀ′rä [Pg.] Ma'am, Mrs.

senhorita, se·nᴀ·rē′tä [Pg.] Miss, young lady.

señor, sän·yōr′ [Sp.] Sir, Mister; gentleman.

señora, sän·yōr′ä [Sp.] Mrs., Madam; lady, woman.

señorita, sän″yōr·ē′tä [Sp.] Miss; young lady.

sequitur, se′kwi·tur, sek′wi·tur [L.] It follows. Abbr. *seq.*

shalom alekhem, shä·lōm′ ä·lä′chem, sha·lōm′ a·lä′chem [Heb.] Peace unto you.

shikari, shi·kär′ē [Hind.] Big game hunter.

si, sē [Sp.] If, whether.

sí, sē [Sp.] Himself, itself, herself; yes.

sic, sēk, sik [L.] Thus; thus in the original copy: used parenthetically to point out errors in a quotation.

sic passim, sēk päs′sim, sik pas′im [L.] Thus everywhere; the same here and there throughout the text.

Sic semper tyrannis, sēk sem′per ti·rän′nis, sik sem′per ti·ran′is [L.] May it always be so to tyrants.

Si Deus nobiscum, quis contra nos? sē dä′us nō·bēs′kum kwēs kōn′trä nōs [L.] If God is with us, who can be against us?

Sieg Heil! zēg hīl′ [G.] Hail, victory. Hurrah, victory. A Nazi greeting.

siempre, sē·em′pre [Sp.] Always.

siesta, sē·es′tä [Sp.] An afternoon nap, traditional in Spanish and Latin American countries.

s'il vous plaît, sēl vö ple′ [Fr.] If you please; please.

Si monumentum requiris, circumspice, sē mō·nū·men′tum re·kwir′is sur″kum·spē′sē [L.] If you seek his monument, look around you.

sin, sēn [Sp.] Without.

sine, si′ne, sī′nē [L.] Without.

sine cura, si′ne kö′rä, sī′nē kū′ra [L.] Without care; without duty or responsibility.

sine dubio, si′ne dö′bē·ō, sī′nē dö′bē·ō [L.] Without any doubt.

sine mora, si′ne mō′rä, sī′nē ma′ra [L.] Without delay.

sine qua non, si′ne kwä nōn′, sī′nē kwä non′ [L.] Without which, not; a necessity.

skål, skōl [Dan., Norw., Sw.] A toast to one's health.

sla, slä [D.] Lettuce; salad.

smørre brød, smœr′re brœd [Dan.] A sandwich.

sobre, sō′bre [Sp.] About, on, over, concerning.

soirée, swa·rä′ [Fr.] Evening; evening party.

sol, sōl [Sp.] Sun; sunlight.

solomillo, sō·lō·mē′yō [Sp.] Sirloin.

sopa, sō′pä [Pg., Sp.] Soup.

sopa de cebollas, sō′pä dä se·bō′yäs [Sp.] Onion soup.

sopa de legumbres, sō′pä dä le·göm′bräs [Sp.] Vegetable soup.

sopa de pollo, sō′pä dā pō′yō [Sp.] Chicken soup.

sotto, sō′tō [It.] Below, under, beneath.

sotto voce, sō′tō vō′che [It.] In a low voice; muttered or whispered.

souci, sö·sē′ [Fr.] Care, anxiety, worry, trouble.

soupe à l'oignon, söp a la̱·nyōN′ [Fr.] Onion soup.

sparago, spä·ʀä′gō [It.] Asparagus.

spes, spās [L.] Hope.

spezzatino di manzo, spet·sä·tē′nō dē män′zō [It.] Beef stew.

spinace, spē·nä′che [It.] Spinach.

Spinat, shpi·nät′ [G.] Spinach.

sponte sua, spōn′te sö′ä [L.] Of one's own accord.

Stadt, shtät [G.] City, town.

status quo, stā′tu̇s kwō′, sta′tu̇s kwō′ [L., lit. 'the state in which'.] The existing condition or state of affairs at some particular time.

status quo ante bellum, stä′tu̇s kwō än′tä bel′lu̇m, stā′tu̇s kwō an′tē bel′lu̇m [L.] In the state in which things were before the war.

Strasse, shtʀäs′se [G.] Street, road, highway.

Stube, shtö′be [G.] Room; apartment.

stufato, stö·fä′tō [It.] Stew.

Sturm und Drang, shtu̇ʀm″ u̇nt dʀäng′ [G.] Storm and stress: reference to late 18th century period during which the tone and intellectual content of German literature changed radically.

su, sö [Sp.] His, her, its, your.

suave, swä′ve [Pg., Sp.] Smooth, soft, delicate.

suave, swav [Fr.] Agreeable; bland; soft.

suaviter in modo, fortiter in re, swä′wi·teʀ″ in mō′dō fōʀ′ti·teʀ″ in ʀä′, swav′i·ter in mō′dō fa̱r′ti·ter in rē′ [L.] Gentle in manner, firm in action.

sub judice, su̇b ū′di·ke″, sub jö′di·sē″ [L.] Under (judicial) consideration.

sub poena, sub poi′na, sub pē′na [L.] Under penalty; a legal writ ordering court appearance under penalty of punishment.

sub rosa, sub rō′za [L., lit. 'under the rose'.] Secretly, confidentially, privately.

succoso, sö·kō′zō [It.] Juicy.

sucre, sʏkʀ [Fr.] Sugar.

sud, söd [Sp.] South.

sueño, swä′nyō [Sp.] Sleep, sleepiness, drowsiness.

suerte, sweʀ′te [Sp.] Chance, luck, fate.

sui generis, sö′i ge′ne·ʀis, sö′ī jen′er·is [L.] Of its own unique kind; in a class of its own.

summa cum laude, su̇m′a ku̇m lou′dä [L.] With highest praise.

summum bonum, sum′u̇m bō′nu̇m, sum′um bō′num [L.] The chief good.

sur, söʀ [Sp.] South

suum cuique, sö′u̇m kwē′kwe, sö′um kī′kwē [L.] To each his own.

suyo, sö′yō [Sp.] His, hers, yours, one's.

svelto, svel′tō [It.] Quick, nimble, lively.

T

tabac, ta·ba′ [Fr.] Tobacco; snuff.

tabula rasa, tä′bö·lä″ ʀä′sä, tab′yu·la rä′sa [L.] A clean, blank tablet; John Locke theorized that at birth, the mind was just such a blank tablet.

tacchino, tä·kē′nō [It.] Turkey.

taco, tä′kō [Sp.] A tortilla filled with beans, meat, cheese, or fowl.

tamale, tä·mä′lā [Sp.] A Mexican dish consisting of a cornmeal roll filled with spicy ground meat.

también, täm·byen′ [Sp.] Also, too.

tant mieux, tän myœ′ [Fr.] So much the better.

tant pis, tän pē′ [Fr.] So much the worse.

tarde, täʀ′dä [Sp.] Afternoon; late.

tasse, täs [Fr.] Cup.

té, tā [Sp.] Tea.

Te Deum Laudamus, tā dā′u̇m lou·dä′mu̇s, tē dē′um lou·dä′mus [L.] We praise thee, O God; a hymn sung in both Roman Catholic and Protestant churches.

te judice, tē jö′di·sē [L.] You being the judge; in your opinion.

tel père, tel fils, tel pâr′tel fēs′ [Fr.] Like father, like son.

tempori parendum, tem′pō·ri pa·ren′dum [L.] One must yield to the times.

tempus fugit, tem′pu̇s fö′git, tem′pus fū′jit [L.] Time flies.

tempus omnia revelat, tem′pu̇s ōm′nē·ä ʀe·wel′ät, tem′pus om′nē·a re·vel′at [L.] Time reveals all things.

te nosce, tā nōs′ke, tē nos′ke [L.] Know thyself.

terra firma, ter′a fu̇r′ma [L.] The solid earth; dry land.

terra nova, ter′a nō′va [L.] A new land.

tête-à-tête, tet·a·tet′ [Fr., lit. 'head to head'.] A private conversation.

thon, tän [Fr.] Tuna.

tirailleur, tē·ʀä·yœʀ′ [Fr.] A sniper; skirmisher.

tocino, tō·sē′nō [Sp.] Bacon.

todo, tō′dō [Sp.] All, every, whole.

to kalon, tō kä′lon [Gr.] The beautiful.

tomate, ta̱·mat′ [Fr.] Tomato.

Tomatensaft, tō·mät′en·säft [G.] Tomato juice.

tonno, tō′nō [It.] Tuna.

torero, tō·ʀä′ʀō [Sp.] Bullfighter.

torlo, tōʀ′lō [It.] Yolk.

toro, tō′ʀō [Sp.] Bull.

torta, ta̱ʀ′tä [Sp.] Cake; loaf.

tortilla, ta̱ʀ·tē′yä [Sp.] A pancake, usually made of corn meal and cooked on a hot iron or flat stone.

tostado, tō·stä′dō [Sp.] Toasted, roasted.

totum, tō′tu̇m [L.] The whole; all.

touché, tö·shā′ [Fr.] Touched; hit, as by one's opponent in a fencing match.

toujours l'amour, tö·zhöʀ′ la·möʀ′ [Fr.] Love forever.

tour de force, töʀ de fa̱ʀs′ [Fr.] A feat of strength.

tournedos, töʀ·ne·dō′ [Fr.] Fillet steak.

tout à fait, tö·ta·fe′ [Fr.] Entirely; quite.

tout à l'heure, tö·ta·lœʀ′ [Fr.] Instantly; presently.

tout au contraire, tö·tō·ka̱N·tʀâʀ′ [Fr.] Quite the contrary.

tout à vous, tö·ta·vö′ [Fr.] Wholly yours; sincerely yours.

tout ensemble, tö·tän·sänbl′ [Fr.] The whole together.

tout le monde, tö·le·ma̱Nd′ [Fr.] All the world.

trabajo, tʀä·bä′hō [Sp.] Work, labor.

Träumerei, tʀoi′me·ʀī′ [G.] Dreaming; musing; reverie.

trefah, tʀä·fä′, trä′fa [Heb.] Foods not ritually cleaned and prepared, and thus forbidden by Jewish law; any violation of the Jewish dietary laws.

très, tʀe [Fr.] Very; very much.

très bien, tʀe byaN′ [Fr.] Very well.

triste, tʀēst [Fr.] Sad; melancholy; gloomy.

trota, tʀō′tä [It.] Trout.

trucha, tʀō′chä [Sp.] Trout.

truite, tʀwēt [Fr.] Trout.

tu, tö [Fr.] Your.

tú, tö [Sp.] You.

tuum, tö′u̇m [L.] Thine.

U

Übermensch, ʏ′beʀ·mench″ [G.] Superhuman; a person of superhuman powers or faculties.

último, öl′tē·mō [Sp.] Last; latest; ultimate.

umiak, ö′mē·ak″ [Esk.] An Eskimo boat made of hide stretched over a wooden frame.

un, una, ön, ö′nä [Sp.] A, an, one.

una voce, ö′nä wō′ke, ū′na vō′sē [L.] With one voice; of one accord, unanimously.

und, u̇nt [G.] And.

Universität, ö″ni·veʀ·si·tät′ [G.] University.

uno animo, ö′nō ä′ni·mō [L.] With one mind; of one accord, unanimously.

un poco, ön pō′kō [It., Sp.] A little; somewhat; a small quantity.

uovo, wō′vō [It.] Egg.

uovo bollito, wō′vō bō·lē′tō [It.] Boiled egg.

uovo fritto, wō′vō fʀē′tō [It.] Fried egg.

uovo sodo, wō′vō sō′dō [It.] Hard-boiled egg.

us supra, u̇s sö′pʀä [L.] As above.

usted, ö·sted′ [Sp.] You.

ut infra, u̇t in′fʀä [L.] As (stated) below.

uva, ö′vä [It., Pg., Sp.] Grape.

V

vaca, vä′kä [Sp.] Cow.

vade in pace, wä′dä in pä′kä, vä′dē in pä′chē [L.] Go in peace.

vale, wä′lä, vä′lä [L.] Good-bye, farewell.

valer, vä·leʀ′ [Sp.] To be worth; worth, value.

valor, vä·lōʀ′ [Sp.] Value, price; valor, courage.

valoroso, vä·lō·ʀō′sō [It.] Brave, bold.

vand, vänd [Dan.] Water.

vann, vän [Norw.] Water.

vaquero, vä·kâ′ʀō [Sp.] Cowboy.

vatten, vä′ten [Sw.] Water.

Vaya con Dios, vä′yä kōn dē′ōs [Sp.] Go with God; farewell.

Veni, vidi, vici, wä′nē wē′dē wē′kē, ve′nē vē′dē vē′chē [L.] I came, I saw, I conquered.

verboten, feʀ·bō′ten [G.] Forbidden; prohibited; illegal.

verdad, veʀ·däd′ [Sp.] Truth.

verdura, veʀ·dö′ʀä [Sp.] Foliage; greens; vegetables.

Verein, feʀ·īn′ [G.] Association; club; society.

Vereinigte Staaten, feʀ·īn′ig·te shtä′ten [G.] United States.

veritas, wä′ʀi·täs″, ver′i·tas″ [L.] Truth.

vertu, veʀ·tʏ′ [Fr.] Virtue.

vez, väs [Sp.] Turn; time.

viaje, vyä′hä [Sp.] Trip, journey, voyage.

viajero, vyä·heʀ′ō [Sp.] Traveler.

via media, wē′ä me·dē·ä″, vī′a mē′dē·a [L.] A middle course.

viande, vē·änd′ [Fr.] Meat.

vida, vē′dä [Sp.] Life.

vide et crede, wē'dä et kʀä'dā, vī'dē et krē'dē [L.] See and believe.

vide infra, wē·dä in'fʀä, vī'dē in'fra [L.] See below.

vide post, wē'dä pōst', vī'dē pōst' [L.] See after; see the following.

vide supra, wē'dä sö'pʀä, vī'dē sö'pra [L.] See above.

viejo, vyä'hō [Sp.] Old, aged; old person.

vi et armis, wē et är'mēs, vī et ar'mis [L.] By force and arms; by main force.

vin, vaɴ [Fr.] Wine.

vin, vēn [Scand.] Wine.

viña, vēn'yä [Sp.] Vineyard.

vin blanc, vaɴ blän' [Fr.] White wine.

vincit omnia veritas, wēng'kit ōm'nē·ä'' we'ʀi·täs'', vin'sit om'nē·a ver'i·tas'' [L.] Truth conquers all things.

vin coupé, vaɴ kö·pä' [Fr.] Diluted wine.

vin du Rhin, vaɴ dy ʀaɴ' [Fr.] Rhine wine.

vino bianco, vē'nō bē·än'kō [It.] White wine.

vino blanco, vē'nō blän'kō [Sp.] White wine.

vino dolce, vē'nō dōl'che [It.] Sweet wine.

vino rosso, vē'nō ʀōs'sō [It.] Red wine.

vin rosé, vaɴ ʀa̤·zā' [Fr., lit. 'pale pink'.] Light-red wine.

virtute et labore, wiʀ·tö'te et lä·bōʀ'e, vir·tö'tē et lä·bar̤'ē [L.] By virtue and labor.

virtute, non verbis, wiʀ·tö'te nōn weʀ'bēs, vir·tö'tē non vṳr'bis [L.] By virtue, not by words.

vis, wēs, vis [L.] Force; might; strength.

vis vitae, wēs wē'tī, vis vī'tē [L.] Vital force; the life force.

Vita brevis, ars longa, wē'tä bʀe'wēs äʀs lōn'gä vī'ta bre'vis ars lan̤'ga [L.] Life is short, art (is) long.

vitello, vē·tel'lō [It.] Veal; calf; calfskin.

voilà, vwä·lä' [Fr.] See there, behold; there is.

volaille, va̤·lä'ye [Fr.] Poultry.

vol-au-vent, va̤l·ō·vänˈ [Fr.] A meat and vegetable pie.

volo, non valeo, wō'lō nōn wä'lä·ō, vō'lō non val'ē·ō [L.] I am willing, but not able.

von, fon [G.] From; of; by.

vous, vö [Fr.] You.

vox, wōks, voks [L.] Voice.

vox et praeterea nihil, wōks' et pʀī·te'- ʀe·ä'' nē'hil, voks' et pri·ter'ē·a nī'hil [L.] A voice and nothing more.

vox populi, wōks pō'pṳ·lē'', voks' pop'- yṳ·lī'' [L.] The voice of the people.

vox populi, vox Dei, wōks pō'pṳ·lē'' wōks de'ē, voks pop'yṳ·lī'' voks dē'ī [L.] The voice of the people is the voice of God.

voz, vōs [Sp.] Voice.

vulgo, wöl'gō, vul'gō [L.] Commonly.

W

Wahrheit, väʀ'hīt [G.] Truth, reality.

Weinbrand, vīn'bʀänt [G.] Brandy, cognac.

Weintraube, vīn'tʀou''be [G.] Grapes, bunch of grapes.

Wein, Weib, und Gesang, vīn vīb ṳnt ge·säng' [G.] Wine, woman, and song.

Weltanschauung, velt'än'shou''ṳng [G.] A world view; ideology.

Weltmacht, velt'mächt'' [G.] A world power (said of a nation).

Weltpolitik, velt'pō·li·tēk' [G.] World policy; politics of a global scale.

Weltschmerz, velt'shmâʀts'' [G., lit. 'world-pain'.] Pessimism; discontent with life in general.

wohl, vōl [G.] Indeed, well, yes, certainly.

Wurst, vöʀst [G.] Sausage.

X

xérès, kä·ʀes' [Fr.] Sherry.

Y

y, ē [Sp.] And.

yaourt, ya·öʀt' [Fr.] Yogurt.

yo, yō [Sp.] I.

yoga, yō'ga [Hind.] A union; Hindu philosophy stressing need to distinguish between separate body and mental self, in order to achieve union with the supreme soul. A discipline, usually consisting of structured exercises, designed to achieve separation of mind and body.

yogi, yō'gē [Hind.] One who practices yoga.

Z

Zahlen, bitte, tsäl'en bit'te [G.] The bill, please.

zapato, sä·pä'tō [Sp.] Shoe.

Zeitgeist, tsīt'gīst'' [G.] The spirit of the time.

zu Befehl, tsö be'fel [G.] At your command; yes, sir.

zucca, tsö'kä [It.] Pumpkin, gourd.

zucchero, tsö'kâ·ʀō [It.] Sugar.

zum Beispiel, tsöm bī'shpēl [G.] For example. Abbr. *z.B.*

zumo, sö'mō [Sp.] Juice, sap.

zumo de uvas, sö'mō dä ö'väs [Sp.] Grape juice.

zuppa, tsö'pä [It.] Soup.

Zwieback, tsvē'bäk [G., lit. 'twice baked'.] Rusk.

Zwiebelsuppe, tsvē'bel·söp'pe [G.] Onion soup.

A

a *ante* (L.), before.

a. about; accepted; acre; active; adjective; afternoon; aged, alto; ampere; *annus* (L.), year; answer; *ante* (L.), before; (Metric System) are; (Sports) assists; at.

A (Chem.) argon.

A. Academician; Academy; Alberta (Canada); America; American; Artillery.

a.a. author's alteration.

A.A. Antiaircraft Artillery; Associate in Accounting; Associate in, or of, Arts; Alcoholics Anonymous.

A.A.A. Agricultural Adjustment Administration; Amateur Athletic Association; American Automobile Association.

A.A.A.L. American Academy of Arts and Letters.

A.A.A.S. American Association for the Advancement of Science.

A.A.C. *anno ante Christum* (L.), in the year before Christ.

A.A.G. Assistant Adjutant General.

A.A.P.S.S. American Academy of Political and Social Science.

a.a.r. against all risks.

A.A.S. *Academiae Americanae Socius* (L.), Fellow of the American Academy (of Arts and Sciences); Associate in Applied Science.

A.A.U. Amateur Athletic Union.

ab. about (times); (Baseball) at bat.

Ab (Chem.) alabamine.

A.B. able-bodied seaman; *Artium Baccalaureus* (L.), Bachelor of Arts.

A.B.A. American Bar Association; American Booksellers Association; Associate in Business Administration.

abbr. or **abbrev.** abbreviation; abbreviated.

ABC atomic, biologic and chemical (warfare); American Bowling Congress; American Broadcasting Co.; Australian Broadcasting Co.

A.B.C. Alcoholic Beverage Control; Argentina, Brazil, and Chile; (usually in reference to their mediation between the United States and Mexico in 1914.)

abd. abdicated.

A.B.F.M. American Board of Foreign Missions.

ab init *ab initio* (L.), from the beginning.

abl. ablative.

ABM Anti-ballistic missile.

Abp. Archbishop.

abr. abridged; abridgement.

abs. absent; absolute; abstract.

A.B.S. American Bible Society; American Bureau of Shipping.

abs. re. *absente reo* (L.), the defendant being absent.

abt. about.

Abyss. Abyssinia; Abyssinian.

ac. account; acre.

a.c. account current; alternating current; *ante cibum* (L.), before meals (in prescriptions).

Ac (Chem.) actinium; acetate; acetyl.

A.C. *ante Christum* (L.), before Christ; Army Corps; Athletic Club; Automobile Club.

ACAA Agricultural Conservation and Adjustment Administration.

acad. academic; academy.

acc. accelerate; acceptance; accompanied; according; account; accusative.

accel. *accelerando* (It.), increasing in speed; (music) accelerate.

acct. account.

AC/DC alternating current or direct current.

ack. acknowledge.

A.C.L.U. American Civil Liberties Union.

A.C.P. American College of Physicians.

A.C.S. American Cancer Society; American Chemical Society.

act. active.

actg. acting.

ACW (Radio) alternating continuous waves.

ad. (pl. **ads.**) adapted; advertisement.

a.d. after date; *ante diem* (L.), before the day; average deviation.

AD (Mil.) Active Duty.

A.D. *anno Domini* (L.), in the year of our Lord.

A.D.A. American Dairy Association; American Dental Association; Americans for Democratic Action.

A.D.C. Aide-de-Camp; Aid to Dependent Children.

ad eund. *ad eundem gradum* (L.), to the same degree.

ad fin. *ad finem* (L.), to, or at, the end.

ad inf. *ad infinitum* (L.), to infinity.

ad init. *ad initium* (L.), to, or at, the beginning.

ad int. *ad interim* (L.), in the meantime.

adj. adjacent; adjective; adjourned; (Banking) adjustment.

Adj. or **Adjt.** Adjutant.

Adj.Gen. or **Adjt. Gen.** Adjutant General.

ad lib. *ad libitum* (L.), at pleasure, as one wishes, to the amount desired.

ad loc. *ad locum* (L.), to, or at, the place.

ad val. *ad valorem* (L.), according to value.

adm. administration; administrator; admission.

Adm. Admiral; Admiralty.

admr. administrator.

adv. *ad valorem* (L.), according to value; adverb; adverbial; *ad versus* (L.) against; advertisement; advertising; advise; advocate.

Adv. Advent.

advt. advertisement.

ae. *aetatis* (L.), of age; aged.

A.E. Aeronautical Engineer; Agricultural Engineer; Associate in Education; Associate in Engineering.

A.E.A. Actor's Equity Association.

A. E. & P. Ambassador Extraordinary and Plenipotentiary.

A.E.F. American Expeditionary Forces.

aeron. aeronautics.

aet. or **aetat.** *aetatis* (L.), of age; aged.

a.f. audio frequency.

AF. or **A.F.** Anglo-French; Air-Force.

A.F.A.M. or **A.F. & A.M.** Ancient Free and Accepted Masons.

AFB air force base.

AFC automatic flight control; automatic frequency control.

aff. affectionate; affirmative; affirmatively.

afft. affidavit.

Afg. or **Afgh.** Afghanistan.

A.F.L. or **A.F. of L.** American Federation of Labor.

AFL-CIO American Federation of Labor-Congress of Industrial Organizations.

AFM American Federation of Musicians.

A.F.M. Air Force Medal (Brit.).

A.F. of L. See A.F.L.

Afr. Africa; African.

A. Fr. Anglo-French.

aft. afternoon.

A.F.T. American Federation of Teachers.

AFTRA American Federation of Television and Radio Artists.

Ag *argentum* (L.), (Chem.) silver.

Ag. August.

A.G. Adjutant General; Agent General; Attorney General.

AGCT Army General Classification Test.

agcy. agency.

agric. agricultural; agriculture.

agt. agent.

Ah or **a.h.** ampere

A.H. *anno Hejirae.* (L.), in the year of, or from, the Hejirae A.D. 622.

A.H.A. American Historical Association; American Hospital Association.

AHQ air headquarters; army headquarters.

A.I. artificial insemination.

A.I.A. American Institute of Architects.

AID Agency for International Development; American Institute of Decorators; artificial insemination by donor (Brit.).

A.I.E.E. American Institute of Electrical and Electronic Engineers.

A.I.M.E. American Institute of Mining Engineers.

AJ Associate Justice.

A.K.C. American Kennel Club.

Al (Chem.) aluminum.

Al. *alia* (L.), other things; *alii* (L.), other people.

A.L. (Baseball) American League; American Legion; Anglo-Latin.

Ala. Alabama.

A.L.A. American Library Association; Author's League of America; Association of Liberal Arts; Automobile Legal Association.

Alas. Alaska.

Alb. Albania; Albany; Albert.

Alba. Alberta (Canada).

ALBM air-launched ballistic missile.

alchem. alchemy.

ald. alderman.

alg. algebra.

Alg. Algeria; Algiers.

A.L.P. American Labor Party.

alt. alteration; alternate; altitude; alto.

Alta. Alberta (Canada).

a.m. *ante meridiem* (L.), before noon.

Am (Chem.) americium.

Am. America; American.

A.M. amplitude modulation; *anno mundi* (L.), in the year of the world; *ante meridiem* (L.), before noon; *Artium Magister* (L.), Master of Arts; *Ave Maria* (L.), Hail Mary.

A.M.A. American Management Association; American Medical Association

Amb. Ambassador.

A.M.D.G. *ad majorem Dei gloriam* (L.), for the greater glory of God.

A.M.E. African Methodist Episcopal.

Amer. America; American.

AMORC Ancient Mystic Order Rosae Crucis.

amp. ampere.

AMPAS Academy of Motion Picture Arts and Sciences.

A.M.S. Army Medical Staff.

amt. amount.

amu atomic mass unit.

an. *anno* (L.), in the year; anonymous.

An (Chem.) actinon.

A.N. Anglo-Norman; Associate in Nursing.

anal. analogous; analogy; analysis; analytic; analytical; analyze.

anat. anatomical; anatomy.

anc. ancient.

ANC Army Nurse Corps.

Angl. Anglican; Anglicized.

ANG Air National Guard.

ann. *anni* (L.), years; annual; annuity.

annot. annotated; annotation; annotator.

anon. anonymous.

ANPA American Newspaper Publishers Association.

ans. answer.

ant. antiquary; antiquities; antonym.

anth. anthology.

anthro. or **anthrop.** or **anthropol.** anthropological; anthropology.

antiq. antiquary; antiquities; antiquity.

a/o account of.

AOL absent over leave.

aor. aorist; aoristic.

ap. *apud* (L.), in the writings of; as quoted by.

Ap. Apostle; apothecaries; April.

a/p account paid; account payable; authority to pay or purchase.

a.p. additional premium; author's proof.

A.P. Associated Press.

A.P.A. American Pharmaceutical Association; American Philological Association; American Protective Association; American Protestant Association; American Psychological Association; American Psychiatric Association; Associate in Public Administration.

apo. apogee.

APO Army Post Office.

Apoc. Apocalypse; Apocrypha.

app. apparatus; apparent; apparently; appeal; appendix; applied; appointed; apprentice; approximate.

appar. apparent; apparently.

approx. approximately.

appx. appendix.

Apr. April.

A.P.S. American Peace Society; American Philatelic Society; American Philosophical Society; American Protestant Society.

A.P.S.A. American Political Science Association.

apt. (pl. **apts.**) apartment.

apx. appendix.

aq. *aqua* (L.), water

aq. dest. *aqua destillata* (L.), distilled water.

ar. arrival; arrived; arrives.

Ar (Chem.) argon.

a.r. (Insurance) all risks; analytical reagent.

Ar. Arabic; Aramaic.

A.R. *anno regni* (L.), in the year of the reign; annual return; Army Registration.

A.R.A. American Railway Association; Associate of the Royal Academy.

Arab. Arabia; Arabian; Arabic.

Aram. Aramaic.

A.R.A.M. Associate of the Royal Academy of Music.

A.R.C. American Red Cross.

arch. archaic; archaism; archery; archipelago; architect; architectural; architecture; archives.

Arch. Archbishop.

archaeol. archaeological; archaeology.

Archd. Archdeacon; Archduke.

A.R.C.M. Associate of the Royal College of Music.

A.R.C.S. Associate of the Royal College of Science; Associate of the Royal College of Surgeons.

Arg. Argentina.

A.R.I.B.A. Associate of the Royal Institute of British Architects.

arith. arithmetic; arithmetical.

Ariz. Arizona.

Ark. Arkansas.

Arm. Armenian; Armoric.

arr. arranged; arrival; arrived; arrives.

A.R.R. *anno regni Regis* or *Reginae* (L.), in the year of the reign of the King or Queen.

ars. arsenal.

A.R.S.A. Associate of the Royal Scottish Academy.

a.s. at sight.

As (Chem.) arsenic.

As. or **A.S.** Anglo-Saxon.

A.S. *anno salutis* (L.), in the year of salvation.

A.S.A. American Standards Association; American Statistical Association.

ASCAP American Society of Composers, Authors and Publishers.

A.S.C.E. American Society of Civil Engineers.

A.S.M.E. American Society of Mechanical Engineers.

A.S.P.C.A. American Society for the Prevention of Cruelty to Animals.

ass. assistant; association; assorted.

assd. assessed; assigned; assured.

assn. association.

assoc. associate; associated; association.

ASSR Autonomous Soviet Socialist Republic.

asst. assistant.

astr. astronomer; astronomical; astronomy.

astrol. astrologer; astrological; astrology.

at. airtight; atmosphere; atomic; attorney.

At (Chem.) astatine.

ATC Air Traffic Control; Air Transport Command.

Atl. Atlantic.

at. no. atomic number.

att. attaché; attention; attorney.

attrib. attribute; attributive; attributively.

atty. attorney.

Atty. Gen. Attorney General.

at. wt. atomic weight.

Au *aurum* (L.), (Chem.) gold.

AU astronomical unit.

A.U.A. American Unitarian Association.

A.U.C. *ab urbe condita* or *anno urbis conditae* (L.), in the year since the founding of the city (Rome, 735 B.C.).

aud. auditor.

Aufl. *Auflage* (G.), edition.

aug. augmentative; augmented.

Aug. August; Augustus.

Aus. Austria; Austrian.

Ausg. *Ausgabe* (G.), edition.

Aust. Austria; Austrian.

Austral. Australasia; Australasian; Australia; Australian.

auth. author; authorized.

Auth. Ver. Authorized Version (of the Bible).

auto. automatic, automobile; automotive.

aux. or **auxil.** auxiliary.

av. avenue; average; avoirdupois.

a.v. *ad valorem* (L.), at the value; *annos vixit* (L.) he or she lived so many years; audio visual.

A.V. Authorized Version (of the Bible).

avdp. avoirdupois.

ave. avenue.

avg. average.

avn. aviation.

avoir. avoirdupois.

AW article of war.

A.W.L. absent with leave.

A.W.O.L. absent without leave.

ax. axiom.

A.Y.H. American Youth Hostels.

az. azimuth; azure.

B

b. base; (Sports) base or baseman; bass; book; born; brother.

B (Chem.) boron; (Chess) bishop.

B. Baron; Bay; Bible; British; brotherhood.

Ba (Chem.) barium.

B.A. Bachelor of Arts; British America.

B.A.A. Bachelor of Applied Arts.

bact. bacteriology.

B.A.E. Bachelor of Aeronautical Engineering; Bachelor of Agricultural Engineering; Bachelor of Architectural Engineering; Bachelor of Art Education; Bachelor of Arts in Education.

B. Ag. or **B. Agr.** Bachelor of Agriculture.

Bah. Bahamas.

bal. balance.

Bal. Baluchistan.

Balt. Baltic.

bap. baptized.

Bapt. Baptist.

bar. barometer; barometric; barrel; barrister.

Bar. Baruch (Apocrypha).

BAR Browning Automatic rifle.

Barb. Barbados.

barr. barrister.

Bart. Baronet.

B.A.S. Bachelor of Agricultural Sciences; Bachelor of Applied Science.

batt. battalion; battery.

Bav. Bavaria; Bavarian.

bb (Baseball) base on balls.

b.b. bill book.

B.B. bail bond; Blue Book; B'nai B'rith; Bureau of the Budget; ball bearing; best of breed.

B.B.C. British Broadcasting Corporation.

bbl. (pl. **bbls.**) barrel.

BBT basal body temperature.

B.C. Bachelor of Chemistry; before Christ; British Columbia.

BCD (Mil.) bad conduct discharge; (Computer Technology) binary-coded decimal.

B.C.E. Bachelor of Christian Education; Bachelor of Civil Engineering.

B. Ch. Bachelor of Chemistry; *Baccalaureus Chirurgiae* (L.), Bachelor of Surgery.

B.C.L. Bachelor of Civil Law.

B.C.M. Bachelor of Church Music.

B.C.P. Bachelor of City Planning.

B.C.S. Bachelor of Chemical Science.

bd. board; bond; bound.

B.D. Bachelor of Divinity; bills discounted.

B/D bank draft; (Accounting) brought down.

bd. or **bdl.** (pl. **bdls.**) bundle.

bdry. boundary.

Be (Chem.) beryllium.

b.e. bill of entry; bill of exchange.

B.E. Bachelor of Education; Bachelor of Engineering; Bank of England; Board of Education; Buddhist Era.

Bech. Bechuanaland.

Beds. Bedfordshire.

B.E.E. Bachelor of Electrical Engineering.

bef. before.

B.E.F. British Expeditionary Forces.

Belg. Belgian; Belgium.

B.E.M. Bachelor of Engineering of Mines.

Beng. Bengal; Bengali.

B.E.P. Bachelor of Engineering Physics.

Berks. Berkshire.

B.E.S. Bachelor of Engineering Science.

bet. between.

bf. (Legal) brief.

b.f. (Printing) bold-face.

B/F (Accounting) brought forward.

B.F. Bachelor of Finance; Bachelor of Forestry.

B.F.A. Bachelor of Fine Arts.

B.F.S. Bachelor of Foreign Service.

B.F.T. Bachelor of Foreign Trade.

bg. (pl. **bgs.**) background; bag; being.

B.G. bonded goods.

B.G.E. Bachelor of Geological Engineering.

B. Gen. Ed. Bachelor of General Education.

bh. (Baseball) base hits.

B.H. base hospital; bill of health.

bhp brake horse power.

Bi (Chem.) bismuth.

B.I. British India.

Bib. Bible; Biblical.

bibliog. bibliographical; bibliography.

b.i.d. *bis in die* (L.), twice a day (in prescriptions).

B.I.D. Bachelor of Industrial Design.

B.I.E. Bachelor of Industrial Engineering.

biochem. biochemistry.

biog. biographer; biographical; biography.

biol. biological; biologist; biology.

B.I.S. Bank for International Settlements; British Information Service.

bk. (pl. **bks.**) bank; bark; black; block; book; brake.

BK (Chem.) berkelium.

bkcy. (Legal) bankruptcy.

bkg. banking.

Bklyn. Brooklyn.

bkpr. bookkeeper.

bkry. bakery.

bkt. (pl. **bkts.**) basket; bracket; bucket.

bl. (pl. **bls.**) bale; barrel; block; blue.

B/L bill of lading.

B.L. Bachelor of Laws; Bachelor of Letters.

B.L.A. Bachelor of Landscape Architecture; Bachelor of Liberal Arts.

bldg. (pl. **bldgs.**) building.

bldr. builder.

B. Lit. or **B. Litt.** *Baccalaureus Lit(t)erarum* (L.), Bachelor of Letters or Literature.

blk. black; block; bulk.

B.LL. *Baccalaureus Legum* (L.), Bachelor of Laws.

BLR breech-loading rifle.

bls. bales; barrels.

BLS Bureau of Labor Statistics.

B.L.S. Bachelor of Library Science.

blvd. boulevard.

BM basal metabolism; *Beatae Memoriae* (L.), of blessed memory; bench mark.

B.M. Bachelor of Medicine; Bachelor of Music; British Museum.

B.M.A. British Medical Association.

B. Mar. E. Bachelor of Marine Engineering.

B.M.E. Bachelor of Mechanical Engineering; Bachelor of Mining Engineering; Bachelor of Music Education.

B. Met. Bachelor of Metallurgy.

BMEWS (Mil.) ballistic missile early warning system.

B. Mgt. E. Bachelor of Management Engineering.

B. Min. E. Bachelor of Mining Engineering.

B.M.R. basal metabolic rate.

B.M.S. Bachelor of Marine Science.

B.M.T. Bachelor of Medical Technology.

B. Mus. Bachelor of Music.

B.M.V. *Beata Maria Virgo* (L.), Blessed Mary the Virgin.

B.N. Bachelor of Nursing.

B.N.S. Bachelor of Naval Science.

b.o. back order; branch office; broker's order; buyer's option.

B/O (accounting) brought over.

B.O. Board of Ordinance; (Informal) body odor; (Theatre) box office.

B.O.D. biochemical oxygen demand.

B. of E. Board of Education.

B. of H. Board of Health.

B. of T. Board of Trade.

Boh. or **Bohem.** Bohemia; Bohemian.

Bol. Bolivia.

bor. borough.

bot. botanical; botanist; botany; bought.

B.O.T. Board of Trade.

boul. boulevard.

bp. baptized; birthplace.

Bp. Bishop.

b.p. (Com.) bills payable; (Phys., Chem.) boiling point; *Ebonum publicum* (L.), the public good.

B.P. Bachelor of Pharmacy; Bachelor of Philosophy; blood pressure.

B.P.A. Bachelor of Professional Arts.

B.P.E. Bachelor of Physical Education.

B. Pet. E. Bachelor of Petroleum Engineering.

B.P.H. Bachelor of Public Health.

B. Pharm. Bachelor of Pharmacy.

B. Phil. Bachelor of Philosphy.

b.p.d. barrels per day.

bpl. birthplace.

B.P.O.E. Benevolent and Protective Order of Elks.

Br (Chem.) bromine.

br. branch; brig; brother.

b.r. (Com.) bills receivable.

Br. Britain; British.

Braz. Brazil; Brazilian.

brev. brevet; brevetted.

brig. brigade; brigadier.

Brig. Gen. Brigadier General.

Brit. Britain; British.

Brit. Mus. British Museum.

bro. (pl. **bros.**) brother.

b.s. (Com.) balance-sheet; bill of sale.

B.S. Bachelor of Science; Bachelor of Surgery; British Standard.

B.S.A. Bachelor of Science in Agriculture; Boy Scouts of America.

B.S.A.A. Bachelor of Science in Applied Arts.

B.S. Adv. Bachelor of Science in Advertising.

B.S.A.E. Bachelor of Science in Aeronautical Engineering; Bachelor of Science in Agricultural Engineering; Bachelor or Science in Architectural Engineering.

B.S. Arch. Bachelor of Science in Architecture.

B.S. Art Ed. Bachelor of Science in Art Education.

B.S.B.A. Bachelor of Science in Business Administration.

B.S. Bus. Bachelor of Science in Business.

B. Sc. Bachelor of Science.

B.S.C. Bachelor of Science in Commerce.

B.S.C.E. Bachelor of Science in Civil Engineering.

B.S. Ch. Bachelor of Science in Chemistry.

B.S. Ch. E. Bachelor of Science in Chemical Engineering.

B.S.D. Bachelor of Science in Design.

B.S.E. Bachelor of Science in Education; Bachelor of Science in Engineering.

B.S. Ec. Bachelor of Science in Economics.

B.S.E.M. Bachelor of Science in Engineering of Mines.

B.S.E.P. Bachelor of Science in Engineering Physics.

B.S.F. Bachelor of Science in Forestry.

bsh. bushel

B.S.H.A. Bachelor of Science in Hospital Administration.

B.S.H.E. Bachelor of Science in Home Economics.

B.S.I.E. Bachelor of Science in Industrial Education; Bachelor of Science in Industrial Engineering.

B.S.I.R. Bachelor of Science in Industrial Management.

B.S.J. Bachelor of Science in Journalism.

bskt. basket.

B.S.L. Bachelor of Science in Law.

B.S.L.S. Bachelor of Science in Library Science.

B.S.M. Bachelor of Science in Sacred Music; Bachelor of Science in Music.

B.S. Met. E. Bachelor of Science in Metallurgical Engineering.

B.S. Min. Bachelor of Science in Minerology.

bsmt. basement.

B.S.M.T. Bachelor of Science in Medical Technology.

B.S.N. Bachelor of Science in Nursing.

B.S.O.T. Bachelor of Science in Occupational Therapy.

B.S.P. Bachelor of Science in Pharmacy.

B.S.P.A. Bachelor of Science in Public Administration.

B.S.P.E. Bachelor of Science in Physical Education.

B.S.P.H. Bachelor of Science in Public Health.

B.S.P.H.N. Bachelor of Science in Public Health Nursing.

B.S.P.T. Bachelor of Science in Physical Therapy.

B.S.R.T. Bachelor of Science in Radiological Technology.

B.S.S.S. Bachelor of Science in Social Science.

bt. bought.

Bt. Baronet.

B. Th. Bachelor of Thelogy.

B.T.U. British thermal unit.

btwn. between.

bty. battery.

bu. bureau; bushel; bushels.

Bucks. Buckinghamshire.

bul. bulletin.

Bulg. Bulgaria; Bulgarian.

bull. bulletin.

bus. bushel; bushels; business; busmen.

b.v. book value.

B.V. *Beata Virgo* (L.), Blessed Virgin; *bene vale* (L.), farewell.

B.V.E. Bachelor of Vocational Education.

B.V.M. *Beata Virgo Maria* (L.), Blessed Virgin Mary.

bvt. brevet.

BW bacteriological warfare; biological warfare; bonded warehouse.

B.W.I. British West Indies.

bx. (pl. **bxs.**) box.

C

c *circa, circiter,* or *circum* (L.), about; cycle; cycles.

c. carat; case; (Baseball) catcher; cathode; cent; (Football) center; centime; centimeter; century; chapter; child; *circa, circiter, circum* (L.), about; copyright; cost; coupon; cubic; current; cycle.

C calorie; carbon; Roman numeral for 100.

C. Cape; Catholic; Celsius; Centigrade; Chairman; Chancellor;

Chancery; Church; Code; Commission; Congress; Conservative; Consult; Court.

ca. case; cathode; centiare; *circa* (L.), about.

Ca (Chem.) calcium.

CA chronological age.

C/A (Banking) capital account; cash account; credit account; current account.

C.A. Central America; Chartered Accountant; Chief Accountant; Commercial Agent; Consular Agent; Controller of Accounts; Court of Appeals.

CAA Civil Aeronautics Administration.

CAB Civil Aeronautics Board.

C.A.F. cost and freight; cost assurance and freight.

cal. calendar; calends; caliber; calorie.

Cal. California.

calc. calculate.

Calif. California.

c & sc (Printing) capitals and small capitals.

Camb. Cambridge.

can. canceled; cannon; canto.

Can. Canada; Canadian.

c. & f. cost and freight

Cant. Canterbury; Canticles.

Cantab. *Cantabrigiensis* (L.), of Cambridge.

C.A.O. Civil Administrative Officer.

cap. (pl. **caps.**) capital; capital letter; capitalize; *capitulum* or *caput* (L.), chapter or section.

C.A.P. Civil Air Patrol.

caps. capital letters.

Capt. Captain.

car. carat.

Card. Cardinal.

Carib. Caribbean.

carp. carpenter; carpentry.

C.A.S. Certificate of Advanced Studies.

cash. cashier.

cat. catalogue; catechism.

Cat. Catalan.

cath. cathedral.

Cath. Catholic.

caus. causative.

cav. cavalry; caveat; cavity.

CAVU (Aeron.) ceiling and visibility unlimited.

c.b. cash book; (Mil.) confined to barracks; (Com.) currency bond.

Cb (Chem.) columbium.

C.B. *Chirurgiae Baccalaureus* (L.), Bachelor of Surgery; Common Bench; Companion of the Bath (Brit.).

C.B.C. contraband control; Canadian Broadcasting Corporation.

C.B.D. Central Business District.

C.B.E. Commander of the Order of the British Empire.

cc. cubic centimeter; chapters.

c.c. carbon copy; cash credit; cubic centimeter.

C.C. cashier's check; chief clerk; Chamber of Commerce; Circuit Court; City Councilor; Civil Code; Civil Court; Common Councilman; Country Club; County Clerk; County Commissioner; County Court.

C.C.A. Chief Clerk of the Admiralty; Circuit Court of Appeals; County Court of Appeals.

C.C.P. Code of Civil Procedure; Court of Common Pleas.

CCR Commission on Civil Rights.

cd. cord; could.

Cd (Chem.) cadmium.

C/D (Banking) certificate of deposit.

C.D. Civil Defense; Coast Defense; *corps diplomatique* (F.), diplomatic corps.

C.D.S.O. Companion of the Distinguished Service Order (Brit.).

c.e. *caveat emptor* (L.), buyer's risk; compass error.

Ce (Chem.) cerium.

C.E. Chief Engineer; Church of England; Civil Engineer; Common Era; customs and excise.

CEA Council of Economic Advisors; County Education Authority.

CED Committee for Economic Development.

C.E.F. Canadian Expeditionary Forces.

Celt. Celtic.

cen. central; century.

cent. centigrade; central; century.

CENTO Central Treaty Organization.

cert. certificate; certify.

certif. certificate; certificated.

cet. par. *ceteris paribus* (L.), other things being equal.

Cf (Chem.) californium.

cf. (Baseball) center fielder; *confer* (L.), compare.

C/F (Accounting) carried forward.

C.F. cost and freight.

c.f.i. cost, freight and insurance.

cg. centigram.

C.G. Captain of the Guard; Center of Gravity; Coast Guard; Consul-General.

cge. carriage.

C.G.H. Cape of Good Hope.

C.G.M. Conspicuous Gallantry Medal (Brit.).

c.g.s. (Scale of Units) centimeter-gram-second.

ch. chain; chapter; chief; child; church.

Ch. Champion; Chancery; Church; China.

C.B. Clearing House; Courthouse; Customs House; Companions of Honour (Brit.).

Chal. or **Chald.** Chaldaic; Chaldee.

Chanc. Chancellor; Chancery.

chap. chapel; chapter.

Chap. Chaplain.

Ch. H. *Chirurgiae Baccalaureus* (L.), Bachelor of Surgery.

Ch. E. Chemical Engineer.

chem. chemical; chemist; chemistry.

Ches. or **Chesh.** Cheshire.

Chev. Chevalier; Chevron.

chg. change.

chf. chief.

Chi. or **Chic.** Chicago.

Chin. China; Chinese.

Ch. J. Chief Justice.

Chmn. or **Chn.** Chairman.

CHQ Corps Headquarters.

Chr. Christian.

chron. chronological; chronology.

Chron. Chronicles.

CI cast iron; cephalic index; certificate of insurance; cast and insurance.

C.I. Channel Islands; Chief Inspector; Counter Intelligence; Imperial Order of the Crown of India (Brit.).

Cia. *Compañia* (Sp.), Company.

C.I.A. Central Intelligence Agency.

CIC Counter Intelligence Corps.

C.I.D. Criminal Investigation Department (Brit.).

Cie. *Compagnie* (Fr.), Company.

C.I.E. Companion of the Order of the Indian Empire (Brit.).

c.i.f. cost, insurance, and freight.

c.i.f. & c. cost, insurance, freight and commission.

c.i.f.c. & i. cost, insurance, freight, commission, and interest.

c.i.f.i. & e. cost, insurance, freight, interest, and exchange.

Cin. Cincinnati.

C. in C. Commander-in-Chief.

C.I.O. Congress of Industrial Organizations.

cir. *circa, circiter,* or *circum* (L.), about; circle.

circ. *circa, circiter,* or *circum* (L.), about; circuit, circulation, circumference.

cit. citation; cited; citizen; citrate.

C.J. Chief Justice.

ck. cask; check.

cl. carload; centiliter; class; clause; clergyman; cloth.

Cl (Chem.) chlorine.

class. classic; classical; classification; classified.

cld. called; canceled; cleared; colored; cooled.

C.L.I. cost of living index.

clk. clerk, clock.

CLU Civil Liberties Union.

cm. centimeter.

Cm (Chem.) curium.

C.M. Certificated Master; Certificate of Merit; *Chirurgiae Magister* (L.), Master of Surgery; Church Missionary; Corresponding Member; court martial.

C.M.G. Companion of the Order of St. Michael and St. George, (Brit.).

cml. commercial.

C.M.S. Church Missionary Society (Brit.).

CNO Chief of Naval Operations.

CNS central nervous system.

c/o care of; carried over.

Co (Chem.) cobalt.

Co. Company, county.

C.O. Colonial Office; Commanding Officer; conscientious objector.

coch. *cochlear* or *cochleare* (L.), spoonful (in prescriptions).

C.O.D. cash, or collect, on delivery.

C. of C. Chamber of Commerce.

C. of M. certificate of merit.

C. of S. Chief of Staff.

cog. or **cogn.** cognate.

col. colonial; colony; color; column.

Col. Colonel; Colorado; Colossians; Colombia.

C.O.L. cost of living.

coll. collated; collateral; colleague; collected; collection; collective; collector; college; collegiate; colloquial.

collat. collateral.

colloq. colloquial; colloquialism; colloquially.

Colo. Colorado.

com. comedy; commentary; commerce; common; commonly; communication.

Com. commander; commission; commissioner; committee; commodore.

comb. combination; combined.

comdg. commanding.

Comdr. Commander.

Comdt. Commandant.

Com.-in-Chf. Commander-in-Chief.

comp. comparative; compiler; composer; composition; compositor; compound; comprising.

compar. comparative.

Compy. company.

Comr. commissioner.

Com. Ver. Common Version (of the Bible).

con. concerto; consolidated; continued; *contra* (L.), against.

Con. conformist; consul.

cong. *congius* (L.), gallon; congregation.

Cong. Congregational; Congress; Congressional.

conj. conjugation; conjunction; conjunctive.

conn. connected; connotation.

Conn. Connecticut.

consgt. consignment.

consol. consolidated.

const. constable; constant; constituent; constitution; constitutional; construction.

constr. construction; construed.

cont. containing; contents; continent; continental; continued.

Cont. continental.

contd. continued.

contemp. contemporary.

contr. contracted; contraction; contractor; contralto; contrary; control.

conv. convalescent; convene; convenient; convention; convert; convertible; convocation.

coop. cooperation; cooperative.

cor. corner; corpus; corrected; correction; correlative; correspondent; corresponding.

Cor. Corinthians; coroner.

Corn. Cornish; Cornwall.

coroll. corollary.

corp. corporal; corporation.

corr. corrected; correspond; corrupt; corruption.

correl. correlative.

Cors. Corsica.

cor. sec. corresponding secretary.

cos cosine.

cosec cosecant.

cot cotangent.

covers. coversed sine.

cox. coxswain.

cp. compare; coupon.

c.p. candle power; carriage paid; cerebal palsy; charter party; chemically pure.

C.P. Chief Patriarch; Common Pleas; Common Prayer; Communist Party; Court of Probate.

C.P.A. Certified Public Accountant.

CPI Consumer Price Index.

Cpl. Corporal.

C.P.O. Chief Petty Officer.

cps cycles per second.

CQ (Radio) a signal sent at the beginning of radiograms, or sent by an amateur as an invitation for another amateur to reply.

cr. center; circular; created; credit; creditor; creek; crown; crowned.

Cr (Chem.) chromium.

CR conditioned reflex; critical ratio.

C.R. Costa Rica

craniol. craniology.

craniom. craniometry.

cres. or **cresc.** *crescendo* (It.), (Music) increasing in volume.

crit. critical; criticism.

CRT cathode ray tube.

cryst. or **crystal.** crystalline; crystallography.

cs. case; census; consciousness.

c.s. capital stock; current series.

Cs (Chem.) caesium.

C.S. Chief of Staff; Christian Science; Civil Service; Clerk of Session; Confederate States; court of sessions.

C.S.A. Confederate States of America; Confederate States Army.

csc cosecant.

CSC Civil Service Commission.

C.S.C. Conspicuous Service Cross (Brit.).

csk. cask.

C.S.O. Chief Signal Officer; Chief Staff Officer.

CST Central Standard Time.

ct. (pl. **cts.**) carat; cent; certificate; court; current.

c.t. cable transfer.

Ct. Connecticut; Count.

C.T. Central Time.

ctf. certificate.

ctge. cartage.

ctl. central.

cts. centimes; cents; certificates.

cu. cubic; cumulus.

Cu *cuprum* (L.), (Chem.) copper.

cur. currency; current (the current month).

C.V. Common Version (of the Bible).

C.V.O. Commander of the Royal Victorian Order (Brit.).

C.W. chemical warfare; child welfare; churchwarden; continuous wave.

C.W.A. Civil Works Administration.

c.w.o. cash with order.

C.W.O. Chief Warrant Officer.

cwt. hundredweight (for L. *centum,* and E. *weight*).

cy. capacity; currency; cycle.

cyc. cycle; cyclopedia; cyclorama.

C.Z. Canal Zone.

Czech. Czechoslovakia.

D

d. date; daughter; day; dead; degree; *denarius* or *denarii* (L.), penny or pence; deputy; died; dime dividend; dollar; dose.

D Roman numeral for 500; (Chem.) deuterium.

D. Deacon; Democrat; *Deus* (L.), God; *Dominus* (L.), *Dom.* (Pg.) *Don,* (Sp.), Lord; Dowager; Duchess; Duke; Dutch.

d.a. days after acceptance; deposit account.

D.A. District Attorney.

DAB Dictionary of American Biography.

Dan. Daniel; Danish.

D.A.R. Daughters of the American Revolution.

dat. dative.

DATA Defense Air Transportation Administration.

dau. daughter.

DAV Disabled American Veterans.

db decibel.

d.b. day book.

D.B. Bachelor of Divinity; Doomsday Book.

D&B Dun and Bradstreet.

DBA doing business as.

D.B.E. Dame Commander of the Order of the British Empire.

D. Bib. Douay Bible.

dbk. drawback.

dbl. double.

d.c. direct current.

D.C. (Music) *da capo* (It.), repeat from the beginning; Dental Corps; Deputy Consul; District Court; District of Columbia.

D.C.L. Doctor of Civil Law.

D.C.M. Distinguished Conduct Medal (Brit.).

D. Cn. L. Doctor of Canon Law.

D.C.S. Deputy Clerk of Session; Doctor of Christian Science.

dd. delivered.

d.d. days after date; days after delivery; delayed delivery; demand draft.

DD dishonorable discharge.

D.D. Doctor of Divinity.

D.D.S. Doctor of Dental Surgery.

DE destroyer escort.

D.E. Doctor of Engineering.

Dea. Deacon.

deb. debenture; debutante.

dec. deceased; declension; (Music) *decrescendo* (It.), decrease.

Dec. December.

decd. deceased; declared; decreased.

decl. declension.

decres. or **decresc.** (Music) *decrescendo* (It.), decreasing in volume.

ded. dedicated; dedication.

def. defective; defendant; deferred; definite; definition.

deft. defendant.

deg. degree.

del. delegate; delete; *delineavite* (L.), he or she drew (it); deliver.

Del. Delaware.

Dem. Democrat; Democratic.

Den. Denmark.

D. Eng. Doctor of Engineering.

dent. dental; dentist; dentistry.

dep. departed; department; departs; deponent; depot; deputy.

dept. department.

der. derivation; derivative; derived.

deriv. derivation; derivative.

D. és L. *Docteur es Lettres* (Fr.), Doctor of Letters.

D. és S. *Docteur es Sciences* (Fr.), Doctor of Sciences.

det. detachment.

Deut. Deuteronomy.

Dev. Devonshire.

DEW Distant Early Warning.

DF (Telecom.) direction finding.

D.F. Dean of Faculty; *Defensor Fidei* (L.), Defender of the Faith; *Distrito Federal* (Sp.), Federal District, (Mexico); Doctor of Forestry.

D.F.A. Doctor of Fine Arts.

D.F.C. Distinguished Flying Cross (Brit.).

dft. defendant; draft.

dg decigram.

D.G. *Dei gratia* (L.), by the grace of God; *Deo gratias* (L.), thanks to God; Director-General.

d.h. *das heisst* (G.), that is to say.

D.H. Doctor of Humanities.

D.H.L. Doctor of Hebrew Letters.

d.i. *das ist* (G.), that is.

Di (Chem.) didymium.

dial. dialect; dialectical.

diam. diameter.

dict. dictator; dictation; dictionary.

diff. difference; different.

dig. digest.

dim. (Music) *diminuendo* (It.), decreasing in volume; diminutive.

dioc. diocesan; diocese.

dipl diploma; diplomatic.

dir. direction; director.

dis. discount; distance; distant; distribute.

disc. discount; discovered.

disp. dispatch; dispensary; dispensatory; dispenser.

diss. dissertation.

dist. distance; distinguish; district.

Dist. Atty. District Attorney.

Dist. Ct. district court.

div. divide; divided; dividend; divine; divinity; division; divisor; divorced.

D.J. (Colloq.) disc jockey; District Judge; *Doctor Juris* (L.), Doctor of Law.

dk. deck; dock.

dl deciliter.

D. Lit. or **D. Litt** *Doctor Lit(t)erarum* (L.), Doctor of Letters or Literature.

D.L.O. dead letter office.

dlr. dealer.

D.L.S. Doctor of Library Science.

dly. daily; delivery.

dm decimeter.

D.M. *destra mano* (It.), right hand; Deutsche mark.

D.M.D. *Dentariae Medecinae Doctor* (L.), Doctor of Dental Medicine.

D.M.S. Doctor of Medical Science.

D. Mus. Doctor of Music.

DMZ demilitarized zone.

DNA deoxyribonucleic acid.

D.N.B. Dictionary of National Biography (Brit.).

do. ditto.

d.o. delivery order.

D.O. district officer; Doctor of Optometry; Doctor of Osteopathy; duty officer.

D.O.A. dead on arrival.

doc. (pl. **docs.**) document.

dol. (pl. **dols.**) dollars; (Music) *dolce* (It.), soft, sweet.

dom. domestic; dominion.

D.O.M. *Deo Optimo Maximo* (L.), to God, the Best, the Greatest.

dom. econ. domestic economy.

Dor. Dorian; Doric.

D.O.R.A. Defense of the Realm Act (Brit.).

Dow. dowager.

doz. dozen; dozens.

D.P. displaced person.

D.P.A. Doctor of Public Administration.

D. Ph. Doctor of Philosophy.

D.P.H. Doctor of Public Health.

dpt. department; deponent.

D.P.W. Department of Public Works.

dr. debtor; drachma; dram; draw; drawer.

d.r. dead reckoning; deposit receipt; differential rate.

Dr. Doctor; Drive (in street names).

D.R. Daughters of the (American) Revolution; District Registry; Dutch Reformed (Church).

dram. pers. *dramatis personae* (L.), the persons (characters) in the drama.

d.s. daylight saving; (Com.) days after sight.

D.S. (Music) *dal segno* (It.), repeat from the sign; Doctor of Science.

D. Sc. Doctor of Science.

D.S.C. Distinguished Service Cross (Brit.); Doctor of Surgical Chiropody.

D.S.M. Distinguished Service Medal (Brit.); Doctor of Sacred Music.

D.S.O. Distinguished Service Order (Brit.).

d.s.p. *decessit sine prole* (L.), died without issue.

D.S.T. Daylight Saving Time.

d.t. (usu. pl. **d.t.'s**) (Colloq.) delirium tremens.

D.T. or **D. Th.** Doctor of Theology.

Du. Duke; Dutch.

duo. duodecimo.

D.V. *Deo volente* (L.), God willing; Douay Version (of the Bible).

D.V.M. Doctor of Veterinary Medicine.

D.V.M.S. Doctor of Veterinary Medicine and Surgery.

d.v.p. *decessit vita patris* (L.), died in his, or her, father's lifetime.

dwt. pennyweight (from L. *denarius*, penny and E. *weight*).

d.w.t. deadweight tonnage.

DX (Radio) distance.

Dy (Chem.) dysprosium.

dyn. or **dynam.** dynamics.

dz. dozen; dozens.

E

e. eldest; entrance; (Baseball) errors.

E. Earl; earth; east; eastern; English; excellent.

ea. each.

e.a. educational age; enemy aircraft.

e. & o.e. errors and omissions excepted.

E.C. East Central (postal district of London); Engineering Corps; Established Church.

E.C.A. Economic Commission for Africa; Economic Cooperation Administration.

ECAFE Economic Commission for Africa and the Far East.

eccl. or **eccles.** ecclesiastical.

Eccl. or **Eccles.** Ecclesiastes.

Ecclus. Ecclesiasticus (Apocrypha).

ECG electrocardiogram.

econ. economic; economics; economy.

ECOSOC Economic and Social Council (of UN).

ECT electroconvulsive therapy.

E.C.U. English Church Union.

Ecua. Ecuador.

ed. (pl. **eds.**) edited; edition; editor; educated.

E.D. election district; ex dividend.

Ed. B. Bachelor of Education.

Ed. D. Doctor of Education.

edit. edited; edition; editor.

Ed. M. Master of Education.

EDP electronic data processing.

eds. editors.

EDT. Eastern Daylight Time.

educ. educated; educational.

e.e. errors excepted.

E.E. early English; Electrical Engineer.

E.E. & M.P. Envoy Extraordinary and Minister Plenipotentiary.

EEC European Economic Community.

EEG electroencephalogram.

e.g. *exempli gratia* (L.), for example.

Eg. Egypt.

Egyptol. Egyptology.

E.I. East India; East Indies.

EKG (Med.) electrocardiogram.

elec. or **elect.** electric; electrical; electricity.

elem. element; elements; elementary.

Eliz. Elizabethan.

E. long. east longitude.

Em. (Physical Chem.) emanation.

EM electromagnetic; enlisted man.

E.M. Earl Marshall; Engineer of Mines.

embryol. embryology.

e.m.f. electromotive force.

e.m.h. educable mentally handicapped.

Emp. Emperor; Empire; Empress.

EMR electro magnetic response.

EMU electro magnetic unit.

ency. or **encyc.** encyclopedia.

E.N.E. east-northeast.

eng. engineer; engineering; engraver; engraving.

Eng. England; English.

enl. enlarged; enlisted.

Ens. Ensign.

entom. entomology.

E.O. errors and ommissions; executive officer; ex officio.

e.o.m. end of the month.

Ep. epistle.

Eph. Ephesians.

epil. epilogue.

Epiph. Epiphany.

Epis. or **Episc.** Episcopal; Episcopalian.

epit. epitaph; epitome.

EPNS electroplated nickel silver.

eq. equal; equation; equivalent.

EQ educational quotient.

equiv. equivalent.

Er (Chem.) erbium.

E.R. East Riding (Yorkshire); East River (New York); *Eduardus Rex* (L.), King Edward; *Elizabeth Regina* (L.), Queen Elizabeth.

ERA (Baseball) earned run average.

erron. erroneous; erroneously.

E.R.V. English Revised Version (of the Bible).

Es (Chem.) einsteinium.

Esd. Esdras (Apocrypha).

E.S.E. east-southeast.

esp. especially.

e.s.p. extrasensory perception.

espec. especially.

est. established; estate; estimated; estuary.

E.S.T. Eastern Standard Time.

estab. established.

Esth. Esther; Esthonia.

Et (Chem.) ethyl.

E.T. Eastern Time; English Translation.

ETA estimated time of arrival.

et al. *et alibi* (L.), and elsewhere; *et alii* (L.), and others.

etc. *et cetera* (L.), and others; and so forth.

Eth. Ethiopia.

ethnog. ethnography.

ethnol. ethnological; ethnology.

et. seq. (pl. **et seqq.** or **et sqq.**) *et sequens* (L.), and the following.

etym. or **etymol.** etymological; etymology.

Eu (Chem.) europium.

E.U. (Thermodynamics) entropy unit.

Eur. Europe; European.

E.V. English Version (of the Bible).

Evang. Evangelical.

evg. evening.

ex. examination; examined; example; except; exception; exchange; excursion; executed; executive; *exit* (L.), he or she goes out; *exeunt* (L.), they go out; export; extra; extract.

Ex. Exodus.

exam. examination; examined.

exc. excellent; except; exception; *excuit* (L.), he or she struck out, fashioned, or engraved (it); excursion.

Exc. Excellency.

exch. exchange; exchecquer.

excl. exclamation; exclamatory; excluding; exclusive.

ex d. or **ex div.** ex (without) dividend.

exec. executed; executive.

ex. gr. *exempli gratia* (L.), for example.

ex int. without interest.

ex lib. *ex libris* (L.), from the library (of).

Exod. Exodus.

ex off. *ex officio* (L.), by virtue of his office; officially.

exp. expense; expired; export; exporter; express.

exr. executor.

exrx. executrix.

ext. extended; extension; exterior; external; extinct; extra; extract; extreme.

Ez. Ezra.

Ezek. Ezekiel.

F

F. Fahrenheit; February; Fellow; folio; French; Friday.

FA Field Artillery.

FAA Federal Aviation Agency; Federal Alcohol Administration.

F.A.A.A.S. Fellow of the American Academy of Arts & Sciences; Fellow of the American Association for the Advancement of Science.

Fab. Soc. Fabian Society (Brit.).

fac. facsimile; factor; factory.

facet. facetious.

facsim. or **facsm.** facsimile.

Fahr. Fahrenheit.

F.A.I.A. Fellow of the American Institute of Architects.

fam. familiar; family.

F.A.M. or **F.&A.M.** Free and Accepted Masons.

FAO Food Agricultural Organization.

F.A.P.S. Fellow of the American Physical Society.

far. farad; farthing.

fath. fathom.

f.b. (Football) fullback.

F.B.A. Fellow of the British Academy.

F.B.I. Federal Bureau of Investigation.

F.B.S. Fellow of the Botanical Society (Brit.).

f.c. (Baseball) fielders choice; (Printing) follow copy.

F.C. Free Church (of Scotland).

F.C.A. Farm Credit Administration; Fellow of the Institute of Chartered Accountants (Brit.).

fcap. foolscap.

F.C.C. Federal Communications Commission; first-class certificate.

FCIC Federal Crop Insurance Corporation.

fco. *franco* (It.), franked, postage free.

fcp. foolscap.

F.C.P. Fellow of the College of Preceptors (Brit.).

F.C.S. Fellow of the Chemical Society (Brit.).

fd. fiord; fund.

F.D. *Fidei Defensor* (L.), Defender of the Faith; Fire Department; focal distance.

FDA Food and Drug Administration.

F.D.I.C. Federal Deposit Insurance Corporation.

Fe *ferrum* (L.); (Chem.) iron.

Feb. February.

fec. *fecit* (L.), he or she made (it).

Fed. Res. Bd. Federal Reserve Board.

Fed. Res. Bk. Federal Reserve Bank.

fem. female; feminine.

FEPC Fair Employment Practices Committee.

F.E.T. Federal Excise Tax.
feud. feudal, feudalism.
ff. folios; following (pages, chapters, verses, etc.); (Music) *fortissimo* (It.), very loud.
FFA Future Farmers of America.
fff. (Music) *fortississimo* (It.), very, very loud.
f.g. (Sports) field goal.
fgn. foreign.
F.G.S. Fellow of the Geological Society (Brit.).
F.G.S.A. Fellow of the Geological Society of America.
FHA Future Homemakers of America.
F.H.A. Federal Housing Administration.
F.I. Falkland Islands.
f.i.b. free into bunker.
F.I.C.A. Federal Insurance Contributions Act.
fict. fiction.
FIDO (Aeron) Fog Investigation Dispersal Operation.
FIFO (Indust.) First-in, First-out.
fig. figurative; figuratively; figure.
fin. financial.
Fin. Finland, Finnish.
fir. firkin.
fl. florin; *floruit* (L.), flourished; fluid.
Fl. Flanders, Flemish.
Fla. Florida.
F.L.B. Federal Land Banks.
fld. field; fluid.
fl dr fluid dram, fluid drams.
Flem. Flemish.
F.L.N. Front de Libération Nationale (Algerian Nationalists).
flor. *floruit* (L.), flourished.
fl oz fluid ounce; fluid ounces.
F.L.S. Fellow of the Linnean Society (Brit.).
fm. fathom; from.
Fm (Chem.) fermium.
F.M. Field Marshal; Foreign Mission; frequency modulation.
FMB Federal Maritime Board.
FMCS Federal Mediation and Conciliation Service.
fn. footnote.
fo. folio.
F.O. Field Officer; Foreign Office.
f.o.b. free on board.
F.O.E. Fraternal Order of Eagles.
fol. folio; following.
for. foreign; forester.
fort. fortification; fortified.
f.p. foot-pound; *forte-piano*, (It.), (Music) loud then soft; freezing point; fully paid.
F.P.C. Federal Power Commission.
FPHA Federal Public Housing Authority.
F.Ph.S. Fellow of the Philosophical Society (Brit.).
FPO field post office; fleet post office.
f.p.m. feet per minute.
f.p.s. feet per second.
Fr. *folio recto* (L.), on the front of the page.
fr. (pl. **fr** or **frs.**); fragment; franc; from.
Fr (Chem.) francium.
Fr. Father; France; Frau (G.); French; Friar; Friday.
F.R.A.M. Fellow of the Royal Academy of Music.
F.R.A.S. Fellow of the Royal Astronomical Society.
F.R.B. Federal Reserve Bank; Federal Reserve Board.
F.R.C.O. Fellow of the Royal College of Organists.

F.R.C.M. Fellow of the Royal College of Music.
F.R.C.P. Fellow of the Royal College of Physicians.
F.R.C.S. Fellow of the Royal College of Surgeons.
F.R.C.V.S. Fellow of the Royal College of Veterinary Surgeons.
freq. frequent; frequentative; frequently.
F.R.G.S. Fellow of the Royal Geographical Society.
F.R.S. Fellow of the Royal Horticultural Society.
Fri. Friday.
F.R.I.B.A. Fellow of the Royal Institute of British Architects.
F.R.I.C. Fellow of the Royal Institute of Chemistry.
Fris. Frisian.
Frl. Fraulein (G.).
F.R.Met.S. Fellow of the Royal Meteorological Society.
frs. francs.
FRS Federal Reserve System.
F.R.S. Federal of the Royal Society.
F.R.S.A. Fellow of the Royal Society of Arts.
F.R.S.L. Fellow of the Royal Society of Literature.
F.R.S.S. Fellow of the Royal Statistical Society.
frt. freight.
f.s. foot-second.
F.S.A. Fellow of the Society of Antiquaries (Brit.).
FSH follicle-stimulating hormone.
FSR Field Service Regulations.
F.S.S. Fellow of the Royal Statistical Society.
ft. feet; foot; fort.
FTC Federal Trade Commission.
fth. or **fthm.** fathom.
ft-lb. foot-pound.
fur. furlong; furlongs.
furl. furlough.
fut. future.
f.v. *folio verso* (L.), on the back of the page.
fwd. forward.
FWD four-wheel drive.
FYI (chiefly Mil.) for your information.
F.Z.S. Fellow of the Zoological Society (Brit.).

G

g. gauge; gender; genitive; (Sports) goalie; gram; guide; guinea.
G (Psychol. general intelligence; (Slang) sum of one thousand dollars (Abbr. of Grand).
G. German; (specific) gravity; Gulf.
g.a. general average.
Ga (Chem.) gallium.
Ga. Gallic; Georgia.
G.A. General Assembly.
Gael. Gaelic.
gal. (pl. **gals.**) gallon.
Gal. Galatians.
galv. galvanism; galvanized.
G.A.R. Grand Army of the Republic.
GATT General Agreement on Tariffs and Trades.
Gaul. Gaulish.
G.A.W. guaranteed annual wage.
gaz. gazette; gazetteer.
G.B. Great Britain.
G.B.E. Knight, or Dame, Grand Cross of the Order of the British Empire.
GCA (Aeron.) ground controlled approach.
G.C.B. Knight Grand Cross of the Bath.

g.c.d. greatest common divisor.
g.c.f. greatest common factor.
G.C.I.E. Knight Grand Commander of the Indian Empire.
g.c.m. greatest common measure.
GCM (Mil.) General Court Martial.
G.C.M.G. Knight Grand Cross of St. Michael and St. George.
G.C.S.I. Knight Grand Commander of the Star of India.
G.C.T. (Navigation) Greenwich civil time.
G.C.V.O. Knight Grand Cross of the Royal Victorian Order.
Gd (Chem.) gadolinium.
g.d. granddaughter.
G.D. Grand Duchess; Grand Duchy; Grand Duke.
gdn. garden, guardian.
gds. goods.
Ge (Chem.) germanium.
geb. *geboren* (G.), born.
gen. gender; general; genitive; genus.
Gen. General; Genesis; Geneva.
geneal. genealogical; genealogy.
genit. genitive.
Genl. General.
gent. gentleman.
geod. geodesy; geodetic.
geog. geographer; geographical; geography.
geol. geological; geologist; geology.
geom. geometrical; geometry.
ger. gerund.
Ger. German; Germany.
gest. *gestorben* (G.), died, deceased.
G.F.A. General Freight Agent.
G.F.T.U. General Federation of Trade Unions.
GG gamma globulin.
g.gr. great gross (144 dozen).
GHA (Navigation) Greenwich hour angle.
GHQ (Mil.) general headquarters.
gi. gill; gills.
G.I. galvanized iron; gastrointestinal; general issue; government issue; a member of the U.S. armed forces, especially an enlisted man.
Gib. Gibraltar.
gl. glass; gloss.
Gl (Chem.) glucinum.
G.L. grand lodge.
Glasg. Glasgow.
Glos. Gloucestershire.
gloss. glossary.
gm gram; grams.
G.M. general manager; grand marshal; grand master; guided missile.
G.M. & S. General Medical & Surgical.
GMT (Navigation) Greenwich mean time.
gn. (pl. **gns.**) guinea.
G.N. graduate nurse.
GNP gross national product.
G.O. general office; general order.
G.O.P. Grand Old Party (Republican Party).
Goth. Gothic.
gov. government.
Gov. Governor.
Gov. Gen. Governor General.
govt. government.
G.P. general practitioner; *Gloria Patri* (L.), Glory to the Father; Graduate in Pharmacy; Grand Prix.
gpd gallons per day.
gpm gallons per minute.
G.P.O. General Post Office; Government Printing Office.
G.Q. general quarters.
gr. grain; grand; great; gross.
Gr. Grecian; Greece; Greek.

G.R. *Georgius Rex* (L.), King George.
grad. (Math.) gradient; graduate; graduated.
gram. grammar; grammatical.
Gr. Br. or **Gr. Brit.** Great Britain.
gro. gross.
gr. wt. gross weight.
g.s. grandson.
G.S. general secretary; general staff.
G.S.A. General Services Administration; Girl Scouts of America.
G.S.R. galvanic skin response.
gt. gilt; great, *gutta* (L.), a drop (in prescriptions).
Gt. Br. or **Gt. Brit.** Great Britain.
g.t.c. good till canceled, or countermanded.
gtd. guaranteed.
gtt. (singular **gt.**) *guttae* (L.), drops (in prescriptions).
Guat. Guatemala.
Gui. Guiana.
Guin. Guinea.
gun. gunnery.

H

h. harbor; height; heller; heir; high; (Baseball) hits; hour; husband.
H (Phys.) enthalpy, intensity of magnetic field; (Chem.) hydrogen; (Slang) heroin.
H¹ (Chem.) protium.
H² (Chem.) deuterium.
H³ (Chem.) tritium.
ha. hectare.
H.A. *hoc anno* (L.), this year; horse artillery.
Hab. Habakkuk.
hab. corp. *habeas corpus* (L.), you may have the body.
Hag. Haggai.
Hal (Chem.) halogen.
Hants. Hampshire.
hb. (Football) halfback.
Hb. (Biochem.) hemoglobin.
H.B.M. His, or Her, Britannic Majesty.
H.C. Holy Communion; House of Commons.
h.c.f. highest common factor.
h.c.l. (Colloq.) high cost of living.
H.C.M. His, or Her, Catholic Majesty.
hd. hand; head.
hdkf. handkerchief.
hdqrs. headquarters.
He (Chem.) helium.
H.E. high explosive; His Eminence; His Excellency.
Heb. Hebrew; Hebrews.
her. heraldic; heraldry.
Heref. Herefordshire.
herp. or **herpet.** herpetology.
H.E.W. Department of Health Education and Welfare.
hf. half.
Hf (Chem.) hafnium.
HF high frequency.
hg. hectogram.
Hg (Chem.) *hydrargyrum* (L.), mercury.
H.G. High German; His, or Her, Grace; Home Guards (Brit.).
hgt. height.
H.H. His, or Her, Highness; His Holiness.
hhd. hogshead; hogsheads.
HHFA Housing and Home Finance Agency.
H.I. Hawaiian Islands.
H.I.H. His, or Her, Imperial Highness.
H.I.M. His, or Her, Imperial Majesty.

Hind. Hindustan; Hindustani.

hist. histology; historian; historical; history.

H.J. *hic jacet* (L.), here lies.

H.J.S. *hic jacet sepultus* (L.), here lies buried.

hl. hectoliter; hectoliters.

H.L. House of Lords.

hm. hectometer; hectometers.

H.M. His, or Her, Majesty.

H.M.G. His, or Her, Majesty's Government.

H.M.S. His, or Her, Majesty's Service; His, or Her, Majesty's Ship.

H.M.S.O. His, or Her, Majesty's Stationery Office.

ho. house.

Ho (Chem.) holmium.

H.O. head office; home office.

H.O.L.C. Home Owners' Loan Corporation.

Hon. Honorable; Honorary.

Hond. Honduras.

horol. horology.

hort. horticultural; horticulture.

Hos. Hosea.

hosp. hospital.

H.P. high pressure; hire purchase; horsepower; House of Parliament.

H.Q. headquarters.

hr. (pl. **hrs.**) hour.

Hr. Herr (G.).

H.R. Home Rule; House of Representatives.

H.R.E. Holy Roman Emperor; Holy Roman Empire.

H.R.H. His, or Her, Royal Highness.

H.R.I.P. *hic requiescit in pace* (L.), here rests in peace.

h.s. *hoc sensu* (L.), in this sense.

H.S. *hic sepultus* (L.), here is buried; *hic situs* (L.), here lies; High School, House Surgeon.

H.S.H. His, or Her, Serene Highness.

H.S.M. His, or Her, Serene Majesty.

ht. height.

HUAC House Un-American Activities Committee.

Hun. or **Hung.** Hungarian; Hungary.

hund. hundred.

Hunts. Huntingdonshire.

H.V. high voltage.

h.w.m. high water mark.

hyd. or **hydr.** hydraulics; hydrostatics.

hyp. hypotenuse; hypothesis; hypothetical.

I

i incisor; interest; intransitive.

I (Chem.) iodine; Roman numeral for 1.

I. *Imperator* (L.), Emperor; *Imperatrix* (L.), Empress; independent; island; isle.

Ia. Iowa.

IAEA International Atomic Energy Agency.

I. & R. intelligence and reconnaissance.

I.A.S. Institute of Advanced Studies; Institute of the Aeronautical Sciences.

IAS indicated air speed.

IATA International Air Transport Association.

ib. or **ibid.** *ibidem* (L.), in the same place.

i.b. invoice book.

IBT International Brotherhood of Teamsters.

I.C. *Iesus Christus* (L.), Jesus Christ.

I.C.A.A.A.A. Intercollegiate Association of Amateur Athletes of America.

ICBM intercontinental ballistic missile.

I.C.C. International Control Commission; Interstate Commerce Commission.

Ice. or **Icel.** Iceland; Icelandic.

ICFTU International Confederation of Free Trade Unions.

ich. or **ichth.** ichthyology.

I.CH. TH.U.S. or **ICHTHUS** representing the initial letters of Gr. *Iesous Christs Theou Vios Soter*, Jesus Christ, Son of God, the Savior: the Gr. word *ichthus* meaning fish, and the fish having been used among the early Christians as a symbol for Christ.

ICJ International Court of Justice.

I.C.S. Indian Civil Service; International Correspondence School.

id. *idem* (L.), the same.

Id. Idaho.

I.D. identification; (Mil.) infantry division; Intelligence Department.

Ida. Idaho.

IDA International Development Association.

i.e. *id est* (L.), that is.

I.E. Indo-European; Industrial Engineer.

IFC International Finance Corporation; International Fisheries Commission (U.S. and Canada); International Freighting Corporation.

IFF (Mil.) identification, friend or foe.

I.F.S. Irish Free State.

I.G. Indo-Germanic; inspector general.

ign. ignition; *ignotus* (L.), unknown.

i.h.p. indicated horsepower.

I.H.S. *IESOUS* (Gr.), Jesus; also taken to represent *Iesus Hominum Salvator* (L.), Jesus, Saviour of Men; *In Hoc Signo (vinces)* (L.), in this sign the cross (shalt thou conquer); *In Hoc Salus* (L.), in this cross is salvation; and I (Christ) Have suffered.

Il (Chem.) Illinium.

ILA International Law Association; International Longshoremen's Association.

I.L.G.W.U. International Ladies' Garment Workers Union.

ill. illustrated; illustration.

Ill. Illinois.

illus. or **illust.** illustrated; illustration.

ILO International Labor Organization.

I.L.P. International Labour Party (Brit.).

ILS (Aeron.) instrument landing system.

I.M. Isle of Man.

IMF International Monetary Fund.

imit. imitative.

imp. imperative; imperfect; imperial; impersonal; import; important; imported; importer; *imprimatur* (L.), let it be printed; imprint; improve.

Imp. *Imperator* (L.), Emperor; *Imperatri* (L.), Empress.

imperf. imperfect.

impers. impersonal.

impv. imperative.

Impx. *Imperatrix* (L.), Empress.

in. (pl. **in.** or **ins.**) inch.

In (Chem.) indium.

inc. include; income; incorporated; increase; incumbent.

incl. inclosure; including; inclusive.

incog. incognito.

incor. incorporated.

ind. independent; index; indicative; indirect; industry.

Ind. India; Indian; Indiana; Indies.

I.N.D. *in nomine Dei* (L.), in the name of God.

indecl. indeclinable.

indef. indefinite.

indic. indicating; indicative.

indiv. individual.

inf. infantry; inferior, infinitive; information; *infra* (L.), below, after.

in f. *in fine* (L.), at the end of a title, law, or paragraph quoted.

infin. infinitive.

infl. influenced.

infra dig. *infra dignitatem* (L.), (Colloq.) beneath one's dignity.

in. Hg (Chem.) inch of mercury.

in loc. cit. *in loco citato* (L.), in the place cited.

in mem. *in memoriam* (L.), in memory (of).

in pr. *in principio* (L.), in or at the beginning.

I.N.R.I. *Iesus Nazarenus Rex Iudaeorum* (L.), Jesus of Nazareth, King of the Jews.

ins. inches; inscribed; inspector; insulated; insurance.

I.N.S. International News Service.

insp. inspector.

Insp. Gen. Inspector General.

inst. instant (the present month); instantaneous; institute; institution; instrument.

instr. instructor; instrumental.

int. interest; interior; interjection; internal; international; interpreter; intransitive.

intens. intensive.

inter. intermediate; interrogation; interrogative.

interj. interjection.

internat. international.

interrog. interrogation; interrogative; interrogatively.

intr. intransitive; introduce; introductory.

in trans. *in transitu* (L.), in transit, on the way.

Int. Rev. Internal Revenue.

intro. or **introd.** introduction; introductory.

inv. *invenit* (L.), he, or she, designed (it); inventor; inventory; invoice.

invt. inventory.

Io (Chem.) ionium.

Io. Iowa.

I.O.F. Independent Order of Foresters.

Ion. Ionic.

I.O.O.F. Independent Order of Odd Fellows.

I.O.R.M. Improved Order of Red Men.

I O U I owe you (an acknowledgment of indebtedness).

IPA International Phonetic Alphabet; International Phonetic Association; International Press Association.

IPBM interplanetary ballistic missile.

i.q. *indem quod* (L.), the same as.

I.Q. (Psychol.) intelligence quotient.

I.Q.E.D. *id quod erat demonstrandum* (L.), that which was to be demonstrated.

Ir (Chem.) iridium.

Ir. Ireland; Irish.

I.R. Inland Revenue; Intelligence Ratio; Internal Revenue.

I.R.A. Irish Republican Army.

IRBM intermediate range ballistic missile.

IRC International Red Cross.

Ire. Ireland.

I.R.O. Internal Revenue Office; Internal Revenue Officer; International Refugee Organization.

iron. ironical; ironically.

irreg. irregular; irregularly.

IRS Internal Revenue Service.

is. island; isle.

Is. Isaiah; Island.

I.S.C. interstate commerce.

ISG imperial standard gallon (Brit.).

isl. (pl. **isls.**) island; isle.

I.S.O. Imperial Service Order (Brit.).

iss. issue.

isth. isthmus.

It. Italian; Italy.

ITA Initial Teaching Alphabet.

ital. italic.

Ital. Italian.

ITO International Trade Organization.

ITU International Telecommunication Union.

i.v. increased value; initial velocity; intravenous; invoice value.

i.w. isotopic weight.

I.W. Isle of Wight.

I.W.W. Industrial Workers of the World.

J

j (Physics) joule.

J. (pl. **J.J.**) Journal; Judge; Justice.

j.a. joint account.

J.A. Joint Agent; Judge Advocate.

J.A.G. Judge Advocate General.

Jam. Jamaica.

J.A.M.A. Journal of the American Medical Association.

Jan. January.

Jap. Japan; Japanese.

Jas. James.

Jav. Javanese.

J.C. Jesus Christ; Julius Caesar; *juris consultus* (L.), jurisconsult.

J.C.C. Junior Chamber of Commerce.

J.C.B. *Juris Canonici Baccalaureus* (L.), Bachelor of Canon Law; *Juris Civilis Baccalaureus* (L.), Bachelor of Civil Law.

J.C.D. *Juris Canonici Doctor* (L.), Doctor of Canon Law; *Juris Civilis Doctor* (L.), Doctor of Civil Law.

J.C.L. *Juris Canonici Licentiatus* (L.), Licentiate in Canon Law.

J.C.S. Joint Chief of Staff.

Jct. Junction.

J.D. *Juris Doctor* (L.), Doctor of Jurisprudence, Doctor of Law; *Jurum Doctor* (L.), Doctor of Laws; juvenile delinquency; juvenile delinquent.

Je. June.

Jer. Jeremiah; Jersey; Jerusalem.

j.g. junior grade.

JJ. judges; justices.

Jl. July.

Jno. John.

jnt. joint.

Josh. Joshua.

jour. or **journ.** journal; journalism.

J.P. Justice of the Peace.

Jr. junior.

jt. joint.

Jud. Judges; Judith (Apocrypha).

J.U.D. *Juris Utriusque Doctor* (L.), Doctor of Both Laws (canon and civil).

Judg. Judges.

Judge Adv. Judge Advocate.

Jun. June; Junior.

Junc. Junction.

JV Junior Varsity.

J.W.V. Jewish War Veterans.

K

k. (Elect.) capacity; karat; kilogram; knot.

K (Chem.) *kalium* (L.), potassium; (Chess) king.

K. Kaiser; Kelvin; King; Kings; Knight; krone; kronen.

kal. kalands, calends.

Kan. or **Kans.** Kansas.

K.B. King's Bench; Knight Bachelor (Brit.).

K.B.E. Knight Commander of the Order of the British Empire.

kc kilocycle.

K.C. King's Counsel; Knight Commander; Knight of Columbus.

K.C.B. Knight Commander of the Bath (Brit.).

K.C.I.E. Knight Commander of the Order of the Indian Empire (Brit.).

K.C.M.G. Knight Commander of St. Michael and St. George (Brit.).

K.C.S.I. Knight Commander of the Star of India (Brit.).

K.C.V.O. Knight Commander of the Royal Victorian Order (Brit.).

KD (Com.) knocked down.

Ken. Kentucky.

kg. keg; kilogram.

K.G. Knight of the Garter (Brit.).

Ki. Kings.

KIA (Mil.) killed in action.

KIAS (Aeron.) knot indicated airspeed.

kil. kilogram; kilometer.

kilom. kilometer; kilometers.

K.J.V. King James' Version (of the Bible).

K.K.K. Ku Klux Klan.

kl. kiloliter.

km. kilometer; kingdom.

Knt. Knight.

K.O. (Pugilism) knock-out.

K. of C. Knights of Columbus.

K. of P. Knights of Pythias.

K.P. kitchen police; Knight of the Order of St. Patrick (Brit.); Knight of Pythias.

kr. kreutzer; krona, kronor (Sweden and Faroe Isles.); krona, kronur (Iceland); krona, kroner (Denmark and Norway).

Kr (Chem.) krypton.

kt. karat; carat; knot.

Kt (Chess) Knight.

Kt. Knight.

K.T. Knight of the Order of the Thistle (Brit.); Knights Templars.

K.V. *Kochel-Verzeichnis* (G.), (Music) the chronological listing of Mozart's works used with numbers to identify them.

kw. kilowatt.

Ky. Kentucky.

L

l. (pl. **ll.**) leaf; league; left; length; *liber*(L.), book; *libra* or *librae*(L.), pound, or pounds (British money); line; link; lira; liter; long; lost.

L elevated railroad, or railway; Roman numeral for 50; longitude.

L. lady; lake; Late; Latin; latitude; law; liberal; London; lord; (Theater) stage left.

La (Chem.) lanthanum.

La. Louisiana.

L.A. Latin America; law agent; library association; local agent; Los Angeles.

lab. laboratory.

Lab. Labrador.

lam. laminated.

Lam. Lamentations.

Lancs. Lancashire.

lang. language.

Lap. Lapland.

lat. latitude.

Lat. Latin; Latvia.

lb. (pl. **lbs.**) *libra* (L.), (weight) pound.

L.B. *Litterarum Baccalaureus*, (L.), Bachelor of Letters or Literature; local board.

l.c. letter of credit; *loco citato* (L.), in the place cited; (Printing) lower-case.

L.C. Library of Congress; Lord Chamberlain; Lord Chancellor.

L.C.C. London County Council.

l.c.d. lowest common denominator.

LCI (Mil.) landing craft infantry.

L.C.J. Lord Chief Justice.

l.c.m. least common multiple.

LCT (Mil.) landing craft tanks.

ld. land; limited.

Ld. Lord.

L.D. Low Dutch.

ldg. landing.

Ldp. Ladyship; Lordship.

L.D.S. Latter-Day Saints; Licentiate of Dental Surgery.

l.e. (Football) left end.

lea. league.

leath. leather.

lect. lecture; lecturer.

leg. legal; (Music) *legato* (It.), connected, smooth; legend; legislative; legislature.

legg. (Music) *leggiero* (It.) light and rapid.

Leic. or **Leics.** Leicestershire.

Lev. Leviticus.

lex. lexical; lexicon.

lexicog. lexicographer; lexicographical; lexicography.

lf low frequency.

lf. (Baseball) left fielder.

l.g. (Football) left guard.

LG. or **L.G.** Low German.

L.G. life guard.

LGr. or **L.Gr.** Late Greek.

l.h. left hand.

L.H. lighthouse.

L.H.A. Lord High Admiral.

l.h.b. (Football) left halfback.

L.H.C. Lord High Chancellor.

L.H.D. *Litterarum Humaniorum Doctor* (L.), Doctor of Humane Letters; Doctor of the Humanities.

L.H.T. Lord High Treasurer.

Li (Chem.) lithium.

L.I. Light Infantry (Brit.); Long Island.

lib. *liber* (L.), book; librarian; library.

Lib. Liberal.

Lieut. Lieutenant.

LIFO (Ind.) Last-In, First-Out.

lin. lineal; linear; liniment.

Linc. or **Lincs.** Lincolnshire.

ling. linguistics.

l.i.p. life insurance policy.

liq. liquid; liquor.

lit. liter; literal; literally; literature.

Lit.B. *Lit(t)erarum Baccalaureus* (L.), Bachelor of Letters; Bachelor of Literature.

Lit. D. *Lit(t)erarum Doctor* (L.), Doctor of Letters; Doctor of Literature.

liter. literature; literary.

Lith. Lithuania, Lithuanian.

lithog. lithograph; lithography.

L.J. Lord Justice.

ll. lines.

l.l. *loco laudato* (L.), in the place cited; loose-leaf.

L.L. Late Latin; Lord Lieutenant; Low Latin.

LL.B. *Legum Baccalaureus* (L.), Bachelor of Laws.

LL.D. *Legum Doctor* (L.), Doctor of Laws.

LL.L. *Legum Licentiatus* (L.), Licentiate of Laws.

LL.M. *Legum Magister* (L.), Master of Laws.

L.M. Licentiate in Medicine; Licentiate in Midwifery; Lord Mayor.

L.M.T. local mean time.

loc. cit. *loco citato* (L.), in the place cited.

log. logarithm.

lon. longitude.

Lond. London.

long. longitude.

L.O.O.M. Loyal Order of Moose.

loq. *loquitur* (L.), he, or she, speaks.

L.P. Lord Provost; low pressure.

L.P.S. Lord Privy Seal.

L.R. Lloyd's Register.

LRBM long-range ballistic missile.

L.R.C.P. Licentiate of the Royal College of Physicians.

L.R.C.S. Licentiate of the Royal College of Surgeons.

l.s. left side; lord speaker.

L.S. Linnean Society (Brit.); *locus sigilli* (L.), the place of the seal.

L.S.A. Licentiate of the Society of Apothecaries (Brit.).

l.s.c. *loco supra citato* (L.), in the place cited above or before.

l.s.d. *librae solidi denarii* (L.), pounds, shillings, pence.

LSD lysergic acid diethylamide; (U.S. Navy) landing ship deck.

L.S.E. London School of Economics.

L.S.T. Local Standard Time.

l.t. (Football) left tackle; long ton.

Lt. Lieutenant.

Lt. Col. Lieutenant Colonel.

ltd. limited.

Lt. Gen. Lieutenant General.

Lt. Gov. Lieutenant Governor.

L. Th. Licentiate in Theology.

Lt. Inf. Light Infantry.

Lu (Chem.) lutetium.

Luth. Lutheran.

lv. leaf; leaves; livre; livres.

Lw (Chem.) lawrencium.

l.w.m. low-water mark.

lwop leave without pay.

lwp leave with pay.

LXX Septuagint.

M

m. male; married; masculine; medium; meter; mile; minim; minute; molar; month; moon; morning; mouth.

M Roman numeral for 1000.

M. (pl. **MM.**) Majesty; Manitoba; mark (German money); Marquis; Marquess; Master; Medieval; Member; *meridies*(L.), noon; Middle; Monday; Monsieur (Fr.); mountain.

Ma (Chem.) masurium.

MA (Psychol.) mental age.

M.A. Master of Arts; Military Academy.

Mac. Maccabees (Apocrypha).

M. Ac. Master of Accounting.

Maced. Macedonia.

mach. machinery; machinist.

Mad. Madam; Madrid.

Madag. Madagascar.

M.A.E. Master of Aeronautical Engineering; Master of Art Education.

M.A. Ed. Master of Arts in Education.

mag. magazine; magnetism; magnitude.

M. Agr. Master of Agriculture.

Maj. Major.

Maj. Gen. Major General.

Mal. Malachi; Malayan.

M.A.L.D. Master of Arts in Law and Diplomacy.

man. manual.

Man. Manila; Manitoba.

Manit. Manitoba.

manuf. manufacturer; manufacturing.

mar. maritime; married.

Mar. March.

M.A.R. Master of Arts in Religion.

M. Arch. Master of Architecture.

March. Marchioness.

M. Arch. E. Master of Architectural Engineering.

marg. margin.

Marq. Marquis; Marquess.

mas. or **masc.** masculine.

Mass. Massachusetts.

mat. matins; matured.

M.A.T. Masters of Arts in Teaching.

math. mathematical; mathematician, mathematics.

MATS Military Air Transport Service.

Matt. Matthew.

max. maximum.

M.B. *Medicinae Baccalaureus* (L.), Bachelor of Medicine.

M.B.A. Master of Business Administration.

M.B.E. Member of the Order of the British Empire.

M.B.S. or **M.B. Sc.** Master of Business Science.

M.C. Marine Corps; Master Commandant; Master of Ceremonies; Medical Corps; Member of Congress; Military Cross (Brit.).

M.C.E. Master of Civil Engineering.

M. Ch. *Magister Chirurgiae* (L.), Master of Surgery.

M. Ch. E. Master of Chemical Engineering.

mcht. merchant.

M.C.J. Master of Comparative Jurisprudence.

M.C.L. Master of Civil Law.

M.C.P. Master of City Planning.

M.C.R. Master of Comparative Religion.

Md (Chem.) mendelevium

Md. Maryland.

m.d. *mano destra* (It.), (Music) right hand; memorandum of deposit; months after date.

M.D. *Medicinae Doctor* (L.), Doctor of Medicine; Middle Dutch.

Mdlle. Mademoiselle (Fr.).

Mdme. Madame (Fr.)

M.D.S. Master in Dental Surgery.

mdse. merchandise.

Me (Chem.) methyl.

Me. Maine.

M.E. Managing Editor; Master of Education; Master of Engineering; Mechanical Engineer; Methodist Episcopal; Middle English; Mining Engineer; Most Excellent.

M.E.A. Master of Engineering Administration.

meas. measure.

mech. mechanical; mechanics.

med. medical; medicine; medieval; medium.

Medit. Mediterranean.

Med. L. Medieval Latin.

Melan. Melanesia.

mem. member; memoir; memorandum; memorial.

memo. memorandum.

mensur. mensuration.

M.E.P. Master of Engineering Physics.

M.E.P.A. Master of Engineering and Public Administration.

mer. meridian; meridional.

merc. mercantile; mercurial; mercury.

Mesop. Mesopotamia.

Messrs. Messieurs (Fr.).

met. metaphor; metaphysics; Metropolitan.

metal. Metallurgical; metallurgy.

metaph. metaphysical; metaphysics.

Met. E. metallurgical engineer.

meteor. or **meteorol.** meteorological; meteorology.

Meth. Methodist.

Mex. Mexican; Mexico.

mf. *mezzo forte* (It.), (Music) moderately loud; microfarad.

M.F. Master of Forestry; Middle French.

M. Fr. Middle French.

M.F.A. Master of Fine Arts.

mfg. manufacturing.

M.F.H. Master of Fox Hounds.

mfr. (pl. **mfrs.**) manufacturer.

mg. milligram; milligrams.

Mg (Chem.) magnesium.

mgr. manager.

Mgr. *Monseigneur* (Fr.); (Eccles.) Monsignor.

MGr. or **M. Gr.** Middle Greek.

M.H. Medal of Honor.

M.H.E. Master of Home Economics.

M.H.A. Master in Hospital Administration.

MHG magnetohydrodynamics generation.

MHG or **M.H.G.** Middle High German.

M.H.L. Master of Hebrew Literature.

M.H.R. Member of the House of Representatives.

mi. mile; miles; mill; mills.

M.I. military intelligence; mounted infantry.

M.I.A. Master of International Affairs.

Mic. Micah.

M.I.C.E. Member of the Institution of Civil Engineers (Brit.).

Mich. Michaelmas; Michigan.

micros. microscopy.

mid. middle.

Mid. Midshipman.

M.I.D. Master of Industrial Design; Military Intelligence Division.

M.I.E. Master of Industrial Engineering; Master of Irrigation Engineering.

M.I.E.E. Member of the Institution of Electrical Engineers (Brit.).

mil. military.

M.I. Mar.E. Member of the Institution of Marine Engineers (Brit.).

M.I. Mech.E. Member of the Institution of Mechanical Engineers (Brit.).

min. mineralogical; mineralogy; minim; minimum; mining; minister; minor; minute.

M.I.N.A. Member of the Institution of Naval Architects (Brit.).

mineral. mineralogical; mineralogy.

Minn. Minnesota.

Min. Plen. Minister Plenipotentiary.

m.i.p. marine insurance policy.

M.I.S. Master of International Service.

misc. miscellaneous; miscellany.

Miss. Mississippi.

M.I.T. Massachusetts Institute of Technology.

M.J. Master of Journalism.

mks meter-kilogram-second (scale of units).

mkt. market.

ml. mail; milliliter.

M.L. *Magister Legum* (L.), Master of Laws; Middle Latin; muzzle-loading.

M.L.A. Master of Landscape Architecture; Modern Language Association.

MLB Maritime Labor Board.

MLF multilateral nuclear force.

M.L.G. Middle Low German.

M.L.S. Master of Library Science.

MLW mean low water.

mm. millimeter; *millia* (L.), thousands.

m.m. *mutatis mutandis* (L.), the necessary change being made.

MM. Messieurs (Fr.).

M.M. (Music) Maelzel's Metronome; Master Mason; Master Mechanic; Master of Music; Merchant Marine.

Mme. (pl. **Mmes.**) Madame (Fr.).

M.M.E. Master of Mechanical Engineering; Master of Mining Engineering; Master of Music Education.

MMRBM mobile mid-range ballistic missile.

M. Mus. Master of Music.

Mn (Chem.) manganese.

M.N.A. Master of Nursing Administration.

M.N.A.S. Member of the National Academy of Science.

M.N.E. Master of Nuclear Engineering.

mng. managing.

Mngr. Monsignor.

M.N.S. Master of Nutritional Science.

mo. (pl. **mos.**) month.

Mo (Chem.) molybdenum.

Mo. Missouri; Monday.

M.O. mail-order; manually operated; Medical Officer; *modus operandi* (L.), method of working; money order.

mod. moderate; *moderato* (It.), (Music) in moderate time; modern.

Mod. Fr. Modern French.

Mod. Gr. Modern Greek.

Mod. Heb. Modern Hebrew.

M.O.H. Medical Officer of Health.

Moham. Mohammedan.

mol. wt. molecular weight.

mon. monastery; monetary.

Mon. Monday; Monmouthshire; Monsignor.

Mons. Monsieur.

Mont. Montana.

Mor. Morocco.

morph. morphological; morphology.

mp. *mezzo piano* (It.) (Music), medium soft.

m.p. melting point.

M.P. Member of Parliament (Brit.); Minister Plenipotentiary; military police; mounted police.

M.P.A. Master of Professional Accounting; Master of Public Administration; Master of Public Affairs.

M.P.E. Master of Physical Education.

m.p.g. miles per gallon.

M.Ph. Master of Philosophy.

m.p.h. miles per hour.

M.P.H. Master of Public Health.

M.P.C. Member of Parliament, Canada.

M.P.P. Member of the Provincial Parliament.

Mr. (pl. **Messrs.**) Mister.

M.R. Master of the Rolls; motivation research.

MRA Moral Re-Armament.

M.R.A.S. Member of the Royal Academy of Science; Member of the Royal Asiatic Society.

MRBM medium-range ballistic missile.

M.R.C. Medical Reserve Corps.

M.R.C.P. Member of the Royal College of Physicians.

M.R.C.S. Member of the Royal College of Surgeons.

M.R.E. Master of Religious Education.

M.R.P. Master of Regional Planning.

Mrs. (pl. **Mmes.**) Mistress, Missis, a title prefixed to the name of a married woman.

ms. *mano sinistra* (It.), (Music).

Ms. or **ms.** (pl. **Mss.** or **mss.**) manuscript.

M.S. Master of Science; Master of Surgery; *memoriae sacrum* (L.), sacred to the memory (of); metric system; motor ship; multiple sclerosis.

M.S.A. Master of Science in Agriculture.

M.S.A.E. Master of Science in Aeronautical Engineering.

M.S.A.M. Master of Science in Applied Mathematics.

M.S. Arch. Master of Science in Architecture.

M.S.B.A. Master of Science in Business Administration.

M.S.B.C. Master of Science in Building Construction.

M.S. Bus. Master of Science in Business.

M.Sc. Master of Science.

M.Sc.D. Doctor of Medical Science.

M.S.C.E. Master of Science in Civil Engineering.

M.S.Ch.E. Master of Science in Chemical Engineering.

M.S.C.P. Master of Science in Community Planning.

MSD most significant digit.

M.S.D. Master of Science in Dentistry.

M.S.E. Master of Science in Education; Master of Science in Engineering.

M.S. Ed. Master of Science in Education.

M.S.E.E. Master of Science in Electrical Engineering.

M.S.E.M. Master of Science in Engineering Mechanics.

M.S. En. Master of Science in Entymology.

M.S.F. Master of Science in Forestry.

MSG monosodium glutamate.

M.S.G.M. Master of Science in Government Management.

Msgr. Monsignor.

MSH (Biochem.) melanocyte-stimulating hormone; Mohs scale of hardness.

M.S.H. Master of Staghounds.

M.SH.A. Master of Science in Hospital Administration.

M.S.H.E. Master of Science in Home Economics.

M.S. Hort. Master of Science in Horticulture.

M.S. Hyg. Master of Science in Hygiene.

M.S.I.E. Master of Science in Industrial Engineering.

M.S.J. Master of Science in Journalism.

m.s.l. mean sea level.

M.S.L. Master of Science in Linguistics.

M.S.M. Master of Sacred Music.

M.S.M.E. Master of Science in Mechanical Engineering.

M.S.N. Master of Science in Nursing.

M.S.P.E. Master of Science in Physical Education.

M.S.P.H. Master of Science in Public Health.

M.S. Phar. Master of Science in Pharmacy.

M.S.S. Master of Social Service.

M.S. Sc. Master of Social Science.

M.S.T. Master of Science in Teaching; Mountain Standard Time.

Ms-Th (Chem.) mesothorium.

MSTS (U.S. Navy) Military Sea Transport Service.

M.S.W. Master of Social Welfare; Master of Social Work.

mt. (pl. **mts.**) mount; mountain.

MT mechanical translation; megation; megatons.

M.T. metric ton.

mtg. meeting; mortage.

mtgd. mortgaged.

mtge. mortgage.

M.Th. Master of Theology.

M T I moving target indicator.

Mt. Rev. Most Reverend.

mun. municipal.

M.U.P. Master of Urban Planning.

mus. museum; music; musical; musician.

Mus. B. *Musicae Baccalaureus*, (L.), Bachelor of Music.

Mus. D. *Musicae Doctor* (L.), Doctor of Music.

Mus. M. *Musicae Magister* (L.), Master of Music.

m.v. market value; mean variations; *mezza voce* (It.), (Music) with half the power of the voice, softly.

Mv (Elect.) megavolt; (Chem.) mendelevium.

MVA megavolt ampere.

MVD. *Ministerstvo Vnutrennikh Del* (R.), Ministry of Internal Affairs, Secret Police of U.S.S.R. since 1943, formerly NKVD.

M.V. Ed. Master of Vocational Education.

M.V.O. Member of the Royal Victorian Order.

Mw (Elect.) megawatt; megawatts.

M.W. Most Worshipful; Most Worthy.

M.W.A. Modern Woodmen of America.

Mx. Middlesex.

myl. myrialiter; myrialiters.

mym. myriameter; myriameters.

myth. or **mythol.** mythological; mythology.

N

n neutron.

n. *natus* (L.) born; nephew; net; neuter; new; night; nominative; note; noun; number.

N (Chem.) nitrogen; (Math) an indefinite constant whole number; (Chess) knight.

N. Nationalist; New; Noon; (Chem.) normal (strength solution); Norse; North; Northern; November.

Na *natrium* (L.), (Chem.) sodium.

N.A. National Academician; National Academy; National Army; Nautical Almanac; North America; North American; nursing auxiliary.

NAA National Aeronautic Association; National Automobile Association.

NAACP National Association for the Advancement of Colored People.

NAB National Association of Broadcasters; Naval Air Base.

N.A.D. National Academy of Design.

Nah. Nahum.

NAM National Association of Manufacturers.

N.Amer. North America; North American.

N.A.S. National Academy of Sciences.

NASA National Aeronautics and Space Administration.

nat. national; native; natural; naturalist.

nat. phil. natural philosophy.

natl. national.

NATO North Atlantic Treaty Organization.

nat. sc. natural science.

naut. nautical.

nav. naval; navigation.

navig. navigation.

Nb (Chem.) niobium.

NB Naval Base; (Sports) no ball; *nota bene* (L.), note well, take notice.

N.B. New Brunswick.

NBA National Basketball Association; National Boxing Association.

N.B.S. National Bureau of Statistics.

NC (Mil.) Nurse Corps.

N.C. North Carolina.

N.C.A.A. National Collegiate Athletic Association.

N.C.C.J. National Conference of Christians and Jews.

N.C.C.M. National Council of Catholic Men.

N.C.C.W. National Council of Catholic Women.

N.C.O. noncommissioned officer.

n.c.v. no commercial value.

n.d. no date.

Nd (Chem.) Neodymium.

N.D. or **N. Dak.** North Dakota.

NDAC National Defense Advisory Commission.

Ne (Chem.) neon.

N.E. New England; northeast; northeastern.

N.E.A. National Editorial Association; National Education Association.

Neb. or **Nebr.** Nebraska.

N.E.B. New English Bible.

N.E.D. New English Dictionary (Oxford English Dictionary).

neg. negative; negatively.

Neh. Nehemiah.

nem. con. *nemine contradicente* (L.), no one contradicting, unanimously.

nem. diss. *nemine dissentiente* (L.), no one dissenting, unanimously.

N. Eng. New England; Northern England.

n.e.s. not elsewhere specified.

Neth. Netherlands.

neut. neuter.

Nev. Nevada.

Newf. Newfoundland.

n.f. no funds.

N.F. National Formulary; Newfoundland; Norman French.

Nfld. Newfoundland.

n.g. (Colloq.) no good.

NG (Chem.) nitroglycerin.

N.G. National Guard; New Guinea.

N. Gr. New Greek.

N.H. New Hampshire.

NHG. or **N.H.G.** New High German.

N.H.S. National Health Service (Brit.)

Ni (Chem.) nickel.

N.I. Northern Ireland.

Nicar. Nicaragua.

ni. pri. *nisi prius* (L.), unless before.

N.I.R.A. National Industrial Recovery Act.

N.J. New Jersey.

NKVD *Narodni Kommisariat Vnutrennikh Del,* People's Commissariat for Internal Affairs, the secret police of the Soviet Union (1935-1942).

n.l. (Printing) new line; *non licet* (L.), it is not permitted; *non liquet* (L.), it is not clear or evident.

N.L. (Baseball) National League; Neo-Latin; New Latin.

N. Lat. north latitude.

N.L.F. National Liberation Front.

N.L.R.B. National Labor Relations Board.

nm nautical mile.

N.M. or **N. Mex.** New Mexico.

N.M.U. National Maritime Union.

N.N.E. north-northeast.

NNP net national product.

N.N.W. north-northwest.

no. north; northern; *numero* (L.), number (pl. **nos.**).

No (Chem.) nobelium.

nol. pros. *nolle prosequi* (L.), to be unwilling to prosecute.

nom. nominative.

noncom. noncommissioned officer.

non obst. *non obstante* (L.), notwithstanding.

non pros. *non prosequitur* (L.), he does not prosecute.

non seq. *non sequitur* (L.), it does not follow.

n.o.p. not otherwise provided for.

nor. north; northern.

Nor. Norman; North; Norway; Norwegian.

Norf. Norfolk.

Norm. Norman.

Norw. Norway, Norwegian.

nos. numbers.

n.o.s. not otherwise specified.

Notts. Nottinghamshire.

Nov. November.

np (Physics) neper; (Chem.) neptunium.

N.P. new paragraph; *nisi prius* (L.), no protest; Notary Public.

n.p. or d. no place or date (of publication).

n.p.t. normal pressure and temperature.

nr. near; number.

N.R. North Riding (Yorkshire); North River (New York).

N.R.A. National Recovery Act; National Recovery Administration.

N.R.C. National Research Council.

N.S. not specified; not sufficient funds.

N.S. new series; new style (in reckoning time); *Notre Seigneur* (F.), Our Lord; Nova Scotia.

NSA National Shipping Authority; National Standards Association; National Students Association.

NSC National Security Council.

n.s.f. not sufficient funds.

NSF National Science Foundation.

N.S.P.C.A. National Society for the Prevention of Cruelty to Animals.

N.S.P.C.C. National Society for the Prevention of Cruelty to Children.

N.S.W. New South Wales.

Nt (Chem.) niton.

N.T. National Trust (Brit.); New Testament; Northern Territory (Australia).

nt. wt. net weight.

n.u. name unknown.

Num. Numbers.

numis. numismatic; numismatics.

N.U.R. National Union of Railway Men.

N.U.T. National Union of Teachers.

N.W. North Wales; northwest; northwestern.

N.W.T. Northwest Territories (Canada).

N.Y. New York.

N.Y.C. New York City.

NYP not yet published.

N.Z. New Zealand.

O

o. *octarius* (L.), pint (in prescriptions); old; only; (Baseball) out, outs.

O (Elect.) ohm; (Chem.) oxygen.

O. ocean; octavo; October; Ohio; old; Ontario; order; Oregon.

o.a. on account.

OAS Organization of American States.

ob. *obiit.* (L.), he, or she, died.

Obad. Obadiah.

obdt. obedient.

O.B.E. Officer of the Order of the British Empire.

obj. object; objection; objective.

obl. oblique; oblong.

obs. observation; observatory; obsolete; obstetrics.

o.b.s.p. *obiit sine prole* (L.), he, or she, died without issue.

obstet. obstetrical; obstetrics.

oc. ocean.

occas. occasional; occasionally.

OCDM Office of Civil and Defense Mobilization.

OCS (Mil.) officer candidate school.

oct. or **8vo.** octavo.

Oct. October.

o.d. on demand; outside diameter; over-drive.

O.D. Officer of the Day; Old Dutch; olive drab (of military uniform); overdraft; Doctor of Optometry.

ODT Organization of Defense Transportation.

o.e. omissions expected.

OE. or **O.E.** Old English.

OECD Organization for Economic Cooperation and Development.

O.E.D. Oxford English Dictionary.

O.E.E.C. Organization for European Economic Community.

OEO Office of Economic Opportunity.

O.E.S. Order of the Eastern Star.

OF. or **O.F.** Old French.

off. office; officer; official.

O. Flem. Old Flemish.

O.F.M. *Ordo Fratrum Minorum* (L.), Order Friars Minor (Franciscan).

O.F.S. Orange Free State.

O.G. Officer of the Guard; (Philat.) original gum.

O.G.O. orbiting geophysical observatory.

OHG. or **O.H.G.** Old High German.

O.H.M.S. On His, or Her, Majesty's Service.

O.K. (Colloq.) all right; correct.

Okla. Oklahoma.

OL. or **O.L.** Old Latin.

OLG. or **O.L.G.** Old Low German.

O.M. Order of Merit (Brit.).

ON. or **O.N.** Old Norse.

ONI Office of Naval Intelligence.

Ont. Ontario.

op. opera; operation; opposite; *opus* (L.), work.

o.p. out of print.

O.P. *Ordo Praedicatorum* (L.), Order of Preachers (Dominican).

OPA Office of Price Administration, (1941-46).

op. cit. *opere citato* (L.), in the work cited.

ophthalm. ophthalmology.

opp. opposed; opposite.

opt. optative; optical; optician; optics; optional.

o.r. owner's risk.

O.R.C. Officers' Reserve Corps.

ord. ordained; order; ordinal; ordinance; ordinary; ordnance.

ordn. ordnance.

Oreg. Oregon.

org. organic; organized.

orig. original; originally.

ornith. ornithological; ornithology.

o.s. out of stock.

Os (Chem.) osmium.

O.S. *oculus sinister,* (L.), the left eye (in prescriptions); Old Saxon; Old Series; Old Style (in reckoning time); ordinary seaman.

O.S.A. Order of St. Augustine (Augustinian).

O.S.B. Order of St. Benedict (Benedictine).

O.S.D. Order of St. Dominic (Dominican).

O.S.F. Order of St. Francis (Franciscan).

OSRD Office of Scientific Research and Development.

OSS Office of Strategic Services.

O.T. occupational therapy; Old Testament; overtime.

O.T.C. Officer Training Corps.

Oxf. Oxford; Oxfordshire.

Oxon. *Oxonia* (L.), Oxford, Oxfordshire; *Oxoniensis* (L.), of Oxford.

oz. (pl. **oz.** or **ozs.**) ounce.

P

p. (pl. **pp.**) page; part; participle; *partim* (L.), in paft; past; *piano* (It.), (Music) soft; pint; pipe; (Baseball) pitcher; pole; population; *post* (L.), after; purl; peseta; peso.

P (Chess) pawn; (Chem.) phosphorus.

P. *Papa* (L.), Pope; *Pater* (L.), Father; President; pressure; Priest; Prince; progressive; Province.

p.a. participial adjective; *per annum* (L.), by the year.

Pa (Chem.) protactinium.

Pa. Pennsylvania.

PA public address system.

P.A. power of attorney; press agent; purchasing agent.

PABA (Chem.) para-aminobenzoic acid.

Pac. Pacific.

Pal. Palestine.

paleog. paleography.

paoleon. paleontology.

pam. or **pamph.** pamphlet.

Pan. Panama.

p. & l. profit and loss.

par. paragraph; parallel; parenthesis; parish.

Para. Paraguay.

paren. parenthesis.

Parl. Parliament; Parliamentary.

part. participle; particle; particular.

pass. passenger; *passim* (L.), here and there; passive.

pat. patent; patented.

PAT (Football) point, or points, after touchdown.

path. or **pathol.** pathological, pathology.

Pat. Off. patent office.

P.A.U. Pan American Union.

P.A.Y.E. Pay as you earn.

payt. payment.

p.b. (Baseball) passed ball.

Pb *plumbum* (L.), (Chem.) lead.

P.B. *Pharmacopoeia Britannica* (L.), British Pharmacopoeia; Prayer Book; Primitive Baptist.

PBA Public Buildings Administration.

PBX Private Branch Exchange (a telphone system for private use, as for routing interoffice calls, usually having outside lines.)

pc. (pl. **pcs.**) piece; price.

p.c. per cent; petty cash; *post cibum* (L.), after meals; post card; price current.

P.C. Penal Code; Perpetual Curate; Police Constable; Privy Council; Privy Councilor.

pd. paid.

Pd (Chem.) palladium.

P.D. *per diem* (L.), by the day; Police Department.

Pd. B. Bachelor of Pedagogy.

Pd. D. Doctor of Pedagogy.

Pd. M. Master of Pedagogy.

p.d.q. (Slang) pretty damned quick.

P.E. Physical Education; Presiding Elder; printer's error; probable error (statistics); Protestant Episcopal.

ped. (Music) pedal; pedestal.

P.E.I. Prince Edward Island.

pen. peninsula.

P.E.N. International Association of Poets; Playwrights, Editors, Essayists, and Novelists.

Penn. or **Penna.** Pennsylvania.

Pent. Pentecost.

per an. *per annum* (L.), by the year.

perf. perfect; perforated.

perh. perhaps.

perp. Perpendicular.

per pro. or **per proc.** *per procurationem* (L.), by procuration, by the agency of another.

pers. person; personal.

Pers. Persia: Persian.

persp. perspective.

pert. pertaining.

Pet. Peter.

petrog. petrography.

petrol. petrology.

pf. perfect; pfennig; preferred (of stock).

p.f. *pu forte* (It.), (Music) louder.

Pfc. (Mil.) private first class.

pfd. preferred (of stock).

pfg. pfennig, or *phennig* (G.), penny.

pg. page.

Pg. Portugal; Portuguese.

P.G. paying guest; postgraduate.

PGA Professional Golfer's Association.

P.G.M. Past Grand Master.

Ph (Chem.) phenyl.

P.H. Public Health.

PHA Public Housing Administration.

phar. or **pharm.** pharmaceutical; pharmacology; pharmacopoeia; pharmacy.

Phar. D or **Pharm. D.** Doctor of Pharmacy.

Phar. or **Pharm.** of Pharmacy.

Ph. B. *Philosophiae Baccalaureus* (L.), Bachelor of Philosophy.

Ph. D. *Philosophiae Doctor* (L.), Doctor of Philosophy.

phil. philosophical; philosophy.

Phil. Philadelphia; Philemon; Philip; Philippians; Philippine.

Phila. Philadelphia.

Philem. Philemon.

philol. philological; philology.

philos. philosopher; philosophical; philosophy.

phon. phonetics.

phonol. phonology.

phot. or **photog.** photographic; photography.

photom. photometry.

phr. phrase.

phren. or **phrenol.** phrenological; phrenology.

PHS Public Health Service.

phys. physical; physician; physics; physiological; physiology.

physiol. physiological; physiologist; physiology.

P.I. Philippine Islands.

pinx. *pinxit* (L.), he or she, painted (it).

PIO (Mil.) public information office or offices.

pizz. *pizzicato* (It.), pinched; (Music) played by plucking with the finger.

pk. (pl. **pks.**) pack; park; peak; peck.

PK psychokinesis.

pkg. (pl. **pkgs.**) package.

pkt. (pl. **pkts.**) packet.

pl. place; plate; plural.

P.L. Poet Laureate.

plat. plateau; platoon.

plf. or **plff.** plaintiff.

plupf. pluperfect.

plur. plural; plurality.

pm. premium.

Pm (Chem.) promethium.

P.M. Past Master; Paymaster; Postmaster; *post meridiem* (L.), afternoon; post mortem; Prime Minister; Provost Marshal.

P.M.G. Paymaster General; Postmaster General.

PMLA Publication of the Modern Language Association.

p.n. please note; promissory note.

PNA (Biochem.) pentose nucleic acid.

pneum. pneumatic; pneumatics.

pnxt. *pinxit* (L.), he, or she, painted (it).

po. (Baseball) put-outs.

Po (Chem.) polonium.

P.O. Petty Officer; postal order; post office; Province of Ontario.

P.O.B. post office box.

poet. poetic; poetry.

POGO polar orbiting geophysical observatory.

pol. political; politics.

Pol. Poland; Polish.

pol. econ. political economy.

polit. political; politics.

poly. polytechnic.

pop. popular; population.

P.O.P. print-out paper.

Port. Portugal; Portuguese.

pos. position; positive; possession; possessive.

poss. possessive; possible.

pot. potential.

POW prisoner of war.

p.p. past participle; *per procurationem* (L.), by procuration, by the agency of another; post-paid or prepaid.

P.P. parcel post; Parish Priest.

P.P.C. *pour prendre conge* (F.), to take leave.

pph. pamphlet.

ppr. or **p. pr.** present participle.

P.P.S. *post postscriptum* (L.), a second postscript.

P.Q. previous question; Province of Quebec.

pr. (pl. **prs.**) pair; preference; preferred; present; price; priest; printing; pronoun.

Pr (Chem.) praseodymium.

Pr. Prince; Provencal.

P.R. Parliamentary Reports; *populus Romanus* (L.), Roman people; Press Release; proportional representation; Public Relations; Puerto Rico.

PRA Public Roads Administration.

P.R.B. Pre-Raphaelite Brotherhood.

prec. preceding.

pred. predicate.

pref. preface; prefatory; preference; preferred; prefix.

prelim. preliminary.

prem. premium.

Prem. Premier.

prep. preparation; preparatory; preposition.

pres. present; pressure; presumptive.

Pres. President.

Presb. Presbyterian.

pret. preterit.

prin. principal; principally; principle.

print. printing.

priv. private; privative.

p.r.n. *pro re nata* (L.), as the occasion may require (in prescriptions).

PRO Public Relations Officer.

prob. probable; probably; problem.

proc. procedure; proceedings; process; proclamation; proctor.

prod. produced; production.

Prof. Professor.

Prog. Progressive.

prom. promontory; promoted.

pron. pronominal; pronoun; pronounced; pronunciation.

prop. proper; properly; property; proposition; proprietor.

propr. proprietor.

pros. proscenium; prosody.

Pros. Atty. Prosecuting Attorney.

Prot. Protestant.

pro. tem. *pro tempore* (L.), for the time, temporarily.

prov. provident; province; provincial; provisional.

Prov. Provencal; Proverbs; Province; Provost.

prox. *proximo (mense)* (L.), of the next or coming month.

prs. pairs.

P.R.S. President of the Royal Society.

Prus. Prussia; Prussian.

ps. pieces, pseudonym.

Ps. Psalms.

P.S. Permanent Secretary; *postscriptum* (L.), postscript; Privy Seal; (Theat.) prompt side; Public School; Public Service.

PSAT Preliminary Scholastic Aptitude Test.

PSC Public Service Commission.

pseud. pseudonym.

P.S.T. Pacific Standard Time.

psych. or **psychol.** psychological; psychologist; psychology.

psychoanal. psychoanalysis.

pt. (pl. **pts.**) part; payment; pint; point; port; preterit.

p.t. past tense; *pro tempore* (L.), for the time, temporarily.

Pt (Chem.) platinum.

P.T. patrol torpedo boat; physical therapist; Physical Training; pupil teacher.

P.T.A. Parent-Teacher Association.

p.t.o. please turn over.

Pu (Chem.) plutonium.

pub. public; publication; published; publisher; publishing.

punct. punctuation.

PVC polyvinyl chloride.

Pvt. private.

P.W.A. Public Works Administration.

P.W.D. Public Works Department.

pwt. pennyweight.

PX post exchange.

pxt. *pinxit* (L.), he, or she, painted (it).

Q

q. *quadrans* (L.), farthing; quart, quasi; query; question; quintal; quire.

Q. quarto; Quebec; Queen; Queensland; query; question.

q.b. (Football) quarterback.

Q.B. Queen's Bench.

Q.C. Queen's Counsel.

q.d. *quasi dicat* (L.), as if one should say; *quasi dictum* (L.), as if said; *quaque die* (L.) daily (in prescriptions).

q.e. *quod est* (L.), which is.

Q.E.D. *quod erat demonstrandum* (L.), which was to be demonstrated.

Q.E.F. *quod erat faciendum* (L.), which was to be done.

ql. quintal.

q.l. or **q. lib.** *quantum libet* (L.), as much as you please (in prescriptions).

Q.M. Quartermaster.

Q.M.C. Quartermaster Corps.

Q.M.G. Quartermaster General.

q.p. or **q.pl.** *quantum placet* (L.), as much as you please (in prescriptions).

qq. v. *quae vide* (L.), which (words, etc.) see.

qr. (pl. **qrs.**) *quadrans* (L.), farthing; quarter; quire.

q.s. quarter section.

qt. (pl. **qts.**) quart; quality.

q.t. (Slang) quiet.

qu. query; question.

qu. quadrangle.

quar. or **quart.** quarter; quarterly.

Que. Quebec.

ques. question.

quot. quotation.

q.v. *quantum vis* (L.), as much as you wish (in prescriptions); *quod vide* (L.), which see.

qy. query.

R

r. (pl. **rs.**) radius; railroad; railway; rare; received; *recto* (L.), right-hand page; residence; resides; retired; right; rises; rod; rood; ruble; (Baseball) runs; rupee.

R (Chem.) radical; (Math.) ratio; (Elect.) resistance; (Theat.) stage right; (Physics) roentgen; (Chess) rook.

R. *Réaumur* (L.), thermometer; *recipe* (L.), take (in prescriptions); *Regina* (L.), Queen; Republican; response; *Rex* (L.), king; River; ruble.

Ra (Chem.) radium.

R.A. Rear Admiral; (Astron.) right ascension; Royal Academician; Royal Academy; Royal Artillery.

R.A.A.F. Royal Australian Air Force.

rad. (Math.) radical; radix.

Rad. Radical.

R.A.F. Royal Air Force.

rail. railroad; railways.

rall. (Music) *rallentando* (It.), slackening; becoming slower.

R & D research and development.

R. & I. *Regina et Imperatrix* (L.), Queen and Empress; *Rex et Imperator* (L.), King and Emperor.

Rb (Chem.) rubidium.

R.B.I. (Baseball) run, or runs, batted in.

R.C. Reserve Corps; Red Cross; Roman Catholic.

R.C.A.F. Royal Canadian Air Force.

R.C.M.P. Royal Canadian Mounted Police.

R.C.P. Royal College of Physicians.

R.C.S. Royal College of Surgeons.

Rct. (Mil.) recruit.

rd. rendered; road; rod; round.

r.d. (Banking) refer to drawer.

Rd (Chem.) radium.

R.D. Royal Naval Reserve Decoration (Brit.); Rural Dean; rural delivery.

Rd Ac (Chem.) radio actinium.

RDF radio direction finder.

Re (Chem.) rhenium.

r.e. (Football) right end.

Re rupee.

R.E. Reformed Episcopal; Royal Engineers.

R.E.A. Railway Express Agency; Rural Electrification Administration.

Réaum. Réaumur (thermometer).

rec. receipt; recipe; record; recorded; recorder.

recd. received.

Recit. (Music) recitative.

rec. sec. recording secretary.

rect. receipt; rectangle; rector; rectory.

redupl. reduplicated; reduplication.

ref. referee; reference; referred; refined; reformation; reformed; refund.

Ref. Ch. Reformed Church.

refl. reflex; reflexive.

refrig. refrigeration.

reg. region; register; registered; regular.

Reg. Regent; Regiment; *Regina* (L.), Queen.

regd. registered.

Reg. Prof. Regius Professor.

regr. registrar.

regt. regiment.

rel. relative; relatively; religion; religious.

relig. religion.

rep. repair; repeat; report; reporter; representative; republic.

Rep. Republican.

repr. represented; representing; reprint; reprinted.

repts. reports.

Repub. Republican.

res. reserve; residence; resides; resigned.

ret. or **retd.** retained; returned.

rev. revenue; reverse; review; revised; revision; revolution; revolving.

Rev. Revelation; Reverend.

Rev. Stat. or **Rev. Stats.** Revised Statutes.

Rev. Ver. Revised Version (of the Bible).

rf. (Baseball) right fielder.

r.f. radio frequency; range finder; rapidfire; (Baseball) right field.

R.F. *Republique Francaise* (F.); Reserve Force.

R.F.A. Royal Field Artillery.

R.F.C. Reconstruction Finance Corporation; Royal Flying Corps.

R.F.D. rural free delivery.

r.g. (Football) right guard.

R.G.S. Royal Geographical Society.

Rh (Chem.) rhodium.

R.H. Royal Highlanders; Royal Highness.

r.h. relative humidity; right hand.

r.h.b. (Football) right halfback.

rhet. rhetoric; rhetorical.

R.H.S. Royal Historical Society; Royal Horticultural Society; Royal Humane Society.

R.I. Religious Instructions; Rhode Island; Royal Institute of Painters in Water Colours; Royal Institution of Great Britain.

R.I.B.A. Royal Institutes of British Architectures.

R.I.I.A. Royal Institute of International Affairs.

R.I.P. *requiescat* (or *requiescant*) *in pace* (L.), may he or she (or they) rest in peace.

rit. or **retard.** *ritardando* (It.), (Music) retarding.

riv. river.

rm. (pl. **rms.**) ream; room.

R.M. Resident Magistrate; Royal Mail; Royal Marines.

R.M.A. Royal Marine Artillery; Royal Military Academy; Royal Military Asylum.

R.M.C. Royal Military College (Sandhurst).

R.M.S. Railway Mail Service; Royal Mail Steamer.

Rn (Chem.) radon.

R.N. Registered Nurse; Royal Navy.

RNA (Biochem.) ribonucleic acid.

R.N.A.S. Royal Naval Air Service.

R.N.R. Royal Naval Reserve.

ro. *recto* (L.), the right-hand page; rood.

R.O. Royal Observatory.

Rom. Roman; Romance; Romans.

Rom. antiq. Roman antiquities.

Rom. Cath. Roman Catholic.

R.O.T.C. Reserve Officers Training Corps.

R.P. Reformed Presbyterian; Reguis Professor.

R.P.D. *Rerum Politicarum Doctor* (L.), Doctor of Political Science.

r.p.m. revolutions per minute.

R.P.O. Railway Post Office.

RPQ (Commercial) request for price quotation.

rpt. report.

R.R. railroad; Right Reverend.

r.s. right side.

R.S. Recording Secretary; reformed spelling; revised statutes.

R.S.A. Royal Scottish Academician; Royal Scottish Academy; Royal Society of Arts.

R.S.F.S.R. Russian Soviet Federated Socialist Republic.

R.S.P.C.A. Royal Society for the Prevention of Cruelty to Animals.

R.S.V.P. *repondez s'il vous plait* (F.), reply, if you please.

rt. right.

r.t. (Football) right tackle.

Rt. Hon. Right Honorable.

Rt. Rev. Right Reverend.

Ru (Chem.) ruthenium.

Rum. Rumania; Rumanian.

Russ. Russia; Russian.

R.V. Revised Version (of the Bible).

R.W. Right Worshipful; Right Worthy.

R.W.S. Royal Watercolour Society

Rwy. Railway.

R.Y.S. Royal Yacht Squadron.

S

s. (pl. **ss.**) second; section; series; *siercle* (Fr.), century; see; singular; *solidus*, or *solidi* (L.), shilling or shillings; son; soprano; substantive; succeeded; sun.

S (Chem.) sulfur.

S. (pl. **SS.**) Sabbath; Saint; Saskatchewan; Saturday; Saxon; school; sea; senate; September; *signa* (L.), mark; (Phar.) label; Signor (It.); Socialist; Society; *Socius* (L.), Fellow; south; southern; Sunday; surplus.

s.a. *sine anno* (L.), without year or date; subject to approval.

Sa (Chem. Obs.) samarium.

S.A. Salvation Army; sex appeal; *Son Altesse* (Fr.), His, or Her, Highness; *Societe anonym* (Fr.); South Africa; South African; South America; South American; South Australian.

Sab. Sabbath.

S.A.E. Society of Automotive Engineers.

S. Afr. South Africa; South African.

Salv. Salvador.

Sam. or **Saml.** Samuel.

SAM Surface-to-air-missile.

S. Amer. South American.

Sans. Sanskrit.

Sar. Sardinia.

S.A.R. Sons of the American Revolution.

Sask. Saskatchewan.

Sat. Saturday; Saturn.

SAT Scholastic Aptitude Test.

Sax. Saxon; Saxony.

sb. substantive.

Sb *stibium* (L.), (Chem.) antimony.

S.B. *Scientiae Baccalaureus* (L.), Bachelor of Science; South Britain (England and Wales).

SBA Small Business Administration.

sc. scale; scene; science; scientific; *scilicet* (L.), to wit, namely, that is to say; screw; scruple; *sculpsit* (L.), he, or she, carved (it).

s.c. small capitals.

Sc (Chem.) scandium.

Sc. Scotch; Scotland; Scots; Scottish.

S.C. Security Council (of U.N.); Signal Corps; South Carolina; Staff Corps; Supreme Court.

Scand. Scandinavia; Scandinavian.

s. caps. small capitals.

Sc. B. *Scientiae Baccalaureus* (L.), Bachelor of Science.

Sc. D. *Scientiae Doctor* (L.), Doctor of Science.

sch. school; schooner.

sci. science; scientific.

scil. *scilicet* (L.), to wit, namely.

Sc. M. *Scientiae Magister* (L.), Master of Science.

Scot. Scotch, Scotland; Scottish.

scr. scruple.

Script. Scriptural; Scripture.

SCS Soil Conservation Service.

sculp. sculptor; sculpture.

sd. sound.

s.d. sight draft; *sine die* (L.), without day, without day fixed for meeting again.

S.D. *Scientiae Doctor* (L.), Doctor of Science; South Dakota; (Statistics) Standard Deviation.

S.D.A. Seventh Day Adventists.

S. Dak. South Dakota.

S.D.S. Students for a Democratic Society.

Se (Chem.) selenium.

SE southeast; southeastern.

SEATO South East Asia Treaty Organization.

sec secant.

sec. second; secondary; secretary; section; sector; *secundum* (L.), according to.

S.E.C. Securities and Exchange Commission.

sec. art. *secundum artem* (L.), according to rule.

sect. section.

secy. secretary.

Sem. Seminary; Semitic.

Sen. Senate; Senator; Senior.

sep. sepal; separate.

Sept. September; Septuagint.

seq. (pl. **seqq.**) sequel; *sequens* (L.), the following.

ser. series; sermon.

Serb. Serbian.

Serg. or **Sergt.** Sergeant.

s.f. sinking fund.

SF science fiction.

S.F. San Francisco.

Sfc (Mil.) sergeant first class.

sfz. *sforzando* (It.), (Music) with force or emphasis.

s.g. specific gravity.

S.G. Solicitor General.

sgd. signed.

Sgt. Sergeant.

sh. share; shilling; shillings.

SHA (Navig.) sidereal hour angle.

Shp shaft house power.

shpt. shipment.

Si (Chem.) silicon.

S.I. Sandwich Island; Staten Island.

Sib. Siberia; Siberian.

Sic. Sicilian; Sicily.

sig. *signa* (L.), mark, label (in prescriptions); signature.

Sig. *Signore* (It.) Signor.

sin sine.

sing. singular.

S.J. Society of Jesus (Jesuit).

S.J.D. *Scientiae Juridicae Doctor* (L.), Doctor of Juridicial Science.

Skr. or **Skt.** Sanskrit.

s.l. *sine loco* (L.), without place (of publication).

S. lat. south latitude.

Slav. Slavic; Slavonic.

SLBM satellite-launched ballistic missile.

sld. sailed; sealed; sold.

Sm (Chem.) samarium.

S.M. *Santa Maria* (It.), Saint (or Holy) Mary; *Scientiae Magister* (L.), Master of Science; Sergeant Major; State Militia.

sm. c. or **sm. caps.** small capitals.

s.n. *sine nomine* (L.), without name.

Sn *stannum* (L.), (Chem.) tin.

so. south; southern.

s.o. seller's option; shipping order.

soc. socialist; society.

sociol. sociological; sociology.

S. of Sol. Song of Solomon.

sol. solicitor; solution.

Sol. Solomon.

Som. Somersetshire.

sop. soprano.

SOP Standard Operating Procedure.

SOS the letter represented by the radio telegraphic signal (... --- ...) used especially by ships in distress as an internationally recognized call for help.

sou. south; southern.

sp. special; species; specific; specimen; spelling; spirit.

s.p. *sine prole* (L.), without issue.

Sp. Spain; Spaniard.

S.P. Shore Patrol; Socialist party; submarine patrol.

S.P.A.S. *Societatis Philosophicae Americanae Socius* (L.), Member of the American Philosophical Society.

S.P.C.A. Society for the Prevention of Cruelty to Animals.

S.P.C.C. Society for the Prevention of Cruelty to Children.

S.P.C.K. Society for Promoting Christian Knowledge (Brit.).

spec. special; specially; specific; specifically.

S.P.G. Society for the Propagation of the Gospel.

sp. gr. specific gravity.

Spgs. Springs.

S.P.Q.R. *Senatus Populusque Romanus* (L.), the Senate and the People of Rome.

S.P.R. Society for Physical Research (Brit.).

spt. seaport.

sq. (pl. **sqq.**) *sequens* (L.), the following; squadron; square.

Sq. Squadron; Square.

Sr (Chem.) strontium.

Sr. Senior; *Señor* (Sp.).

Sra. *Señora* (Sp.).

SRBM short-range ballistic missile.

S.R.N. State Registered Nurse. (Brit.).

S.R.O. standing room only.

Srta. *Señorita* (Sp.).

SS. *scilicet* (L.), to wit; namely; sections; (Baseball) shortstop.

SS. Saints.

S.S. Secret Service; steamship; Sunday School.

S.S.C. Solicitor Before the Supreme Courts (Scotland).

S.S.D. *Sanctissimus Dominus* (L.), Most Holy Lord (a title of the Pope).

S.S.D. *Sacrae Scripturae Doctor* (L.), Doctor of the Sacred Scripture.

S.S.E. south-southeast.

S.S.L. *Sacrae Scripturae Licentiatus* (L.), Licentiate of Sacred Scripture.

SSM surface-to-surface missile.

SSS Selective Service System.

SST supersonic transport.

S.S.W. south-southwest.

st. stanza; statute; (Printing) *stet* (L.), let it stand or remain; (pl. **st.**, weight) stone; (pl. **sts.**) strait; (pl. **sts.**) street.

s.t. short ton.

St. Saint; Strait; Street.

sta. station.

Sta. *Santa* (It.), Saint (female); Station.

stacc. *staccato* (It.), (Music) detached, disconnected.

Staff. or **Staffs.** Staffordshire.

stat. statute.

S.T.B. *Sacrae Theologiae Baccalaureus* (L.), Bachelor of Sacred Theology; *Scientiae Theologicae Baccalaureus* (L.), Bachelor of Theology.

std. standard.

S.T.D. *Sacrae Theologiae Doctor* (L.), Doctor of the Sacred Theology.

Ste. *Sainte* (F.), Saint (female).

ster. sterling.

St. Ex. Stock Exchange.

stg. sterling.

str. steamer.

sub. subaltern; subscription; substitute; suburb; suburban; subway.

subj. subject; subjunctive.

subst. substantive; substantively; substitute.

suff. suffix.

Suff. Suffolk; Suffragan.

Suffr. Suffragan.

Sun. or **Sund.** Sunday.

sup. superior; superlative; supine; supplement; *supra* (L.), above, before.

Sup. Ct. Superior Court; Supreme Court.

superl. superlative.

supp. supplement.

supt. superintendent.

Sur. Surrey.

surg. surgeon; surgery; surgical.

surv. surveying; surveyor; surviving.

Sus. Sussex.

sus. per. coll. *suspendatur* (or *suspensio*, or *suspensus*) *per collum* (L.), let him be hanged (or hanging, or hanged) by the neck.

s.v. *sub verbo* or *sub voce* (L.), under the word or heading.

S.V. *Sancta Virgo* (L.), Holy Virgin.

S.V.P. *s'il vous plaît* (F.), if you please.

Sw. Sweden; Swedish; Swiss.

S.W. South Wales; southwest; southwestern.

Swed. Sweden, Swedish.

S.W.G. standard wire guage.

Switz. Switzerland.

syll. syllable; syllabus.

sym. symbol.

syn. synonym; synonymous.

synop. synopsis.

Syr. Syria; Syriac.

syst. system.

T

t. teaspoon; temperature; *tempore* (L.), in the time of; tenor; tense; *tome* (F.), volume; ton; town; transitive; tun.

T. Tablespoon; Territory; Testament; Tuesday; Turkish.

Ta (Chem.) tantalum.

tab. *tabella* (L.), tablet (in prescriptions); table.

TAC (Mil.) Tactical Air Command.

tan tangent.

Tasm. Tasmania.

TAT Thematic Apperception Test.

t.b. torpedo boat; trial balance.

Tb (Chem.) terbium.

T.B. tubercle bacillus; tuberculosis.

tbs. or **tbsp.** tablespoon, tablespoons.

Tc (Chem.) technetium.

TCBM transcontinental ballistic missile.

TD touchdown; touchdowns.

T.D. Territorial Decoration (Brit.); Traffic Director; Treasury Department.

Te (Chem.) tellurium.

tech. technical; technology.

technol. technology.

tel. telegram; telegraph; telephone.

teleg. telegram; telegraph; telegraphy.

teleph. telephony.

temp. temperature; temporary; *tempore* (L.), in the time of.

ten. tenor; *tenuto* (It.), (Music) held, sustained.

Tenn. Tennessee.

ter. terrace; territory.

term. terminal; termination.

Test. Testament.

Teut. Teutonic.

Tex. Texas.

t.g. (Biol.) type genus.

Th (Chem.) thorium.

Th. Thursday.

T.H. Territory of Hawaii.

Th.D. *Theologiae Doctor* (L.), Doctor of Theology.

theat. theatrical.

theol. theologian; theological; theology.

theor. theorem.

theos. theosophical; theosophy.

therap. therapeutic; therapeutics.

Thes. or **Thess.** Thessalonians.

T.H.I. temperature-humidity index.

Thos. Thomas.

Thurs. Thursday.

Ti (Chem.) titanium.

Tim. Timothy.

tinct. tincture.

tit. title.

Tit. Titus.

TKO (Boxing) technical knockout.

Tl (Chem.) thallium.

t.l.o. (Insurance) total loss only.

Tm (Chem.) thulium.

tn. ton.

Tn (Chem.) thoron.

TNT or **T.N.T.** trinitrotoluene; trinitrotoluol.

t.o. telegraph office; turn over.

Tob. Tobit (Apocrypha).

tonn. tonnage.

topog. topographical; topography.

tox. toxicology.

tp. township; troop.

t.p. title page.

tr. tincture; trace; train; transaction; transitive; translated; transpose; treasurer; *trillo* (It.), (Music) trill; trustee.

Tr (Chem.) terbium.

T.R. *tempore regis* (L.), in the time of the King; tons registered; trust receipts.

trans. transactions; transfer; transformer; transitive; translation; transparent; transportation; transpose; transverse.

transf. transferred.

trav. traveler; traveling.

treas. treasurer; treasury.

trig. or **trigon.** trigonometric; trigonometry.

trop. tropic; tropical.

T. Sgt. (Mil.) Technical Sergeant.

tsp. teaspoon; teaspoons.

T.T. telegraphic transfer; tuberculin tested.

Tu. Tuesday.

T.U. trade union; training unit.

Tues. Tuesday.

Turk. Turkey; Turkish.

TV television.

T.V.A. Tennessee Valley Authority.

twp. township.

ty. territory.

typ. or **typog.** typographer; typographical; typography.

U

u. uncle; *und* (G.), and; uniform; unit; upper.

U (Chem.) uranium.

U, Union; Unionist; University.

UAM underwater to air missile.

u. & l.c. (Print.) upper and lower case.

U.A.R. United Arab Republic.

UAW United Automobile Workers.

U.B. United Brethren.

u.c. *una corda* (It.), (Music) one string, soft pedal; (Print.) upper case.

U.C. Upper Canada; under construction.

UCMJ (Mil.) Uniform Code of Military Justice.

U.C.V. United Confederate Veterans.

U.D.C. United Daughters of the Confederacy; Urban District Council (Brit.).

U.E.L. United Empire Loyalists.

U.F.C. United Free Church (of Scotland).

UFO unidentified flying object.

UHF ultra high frequency.

U.J.D. *Utriusque Juris Doctor* (L.), Doctor of Civil and Canon Law.

U.K. United Kingdom.

Ukr. Ukraine.

ult. ultimate; ultimately; *ultimo mense* (L.), of the last month.

UMW United Mine Workers.

UN or **U.N.** United Nations.

UNESCO United Nations Educational, Scientific and Cultural Organization.

UNICEF United Nations International Children's Emergency Fund.

Unit. Unitarian.

univ. universal; universally; university.

Univ. Universalist.

UNRRA United Nations Relief and Rehabilitation Agency.

U. of S. Afr. Union of South Africa.

up. upper.

U.P. United Press.

U.P.I. United Press International.

Uru. Uruguay.

u.s. *ubi supra* (L.), in the place above (mentioned); *ut supra* (L.), as above.

U.S. United States.

U.S.A. United States Army; United States of America.

U.S.A.E.C. United States Atomic Energy Commission.

U.S.A.F. United States Air Force.

U.S.A.R. United States Army Reserve.

U.S.C.G. United States Coast Guard.

U.S.D.A. United States Department of Agriculture.

U.S.I.A. United States Information Agency.

U.S.I.S. United States Information Service.

U.S.M. United States Mail; United States Marine(s); United States Mint.

U.S.M.A. United States Military Academy.

U.S.M.C. United States Marine Corps; United States Maritime Commission.

U.S.N. United States Navy.

U.S.N.A. United States National Army; United States Naval Academy.

U.S.N.G. United States National Guard.

U.S.O. United Service Organization.

U.S.P. or **U.S. Pharm.** United States Pharmacopoeia.

U.S.P.O. United States Post Office.

U.S.P.H.S. United States Public Health Service.

U.S.S. United States Senate; United States Service; United States Ship.

U.S.S.B. United States Shipping Board.

U.S.S.R. Union of Soviet Socialist Republics.

U.S.S.S. United States Steamship.

usu. usual; usually.

U.S.V. United States Volunteers.

Ut. Utah.

ut dict. *ut dictum* (L.), as directed (in prescriptions).

UV ultraviolet.

ux. *uxor* (L.), wife.

V

v. (pl. **vv.**) vector; verb; verse; version; verso; *versus* (L.), against; *vert* (L.), turn over; vice; *vide* (L.), see; village; violin; vocative; volt; volume; *von* (G.), of (in personal names).

V (Chem.) vanadium; Roman numeral for 5.

V. Valve; Venerable; Vicar; Village; Viscount; Volunteers.

v.a. verb active; verbal adjective.

Va. Virginia.

V.A. Royal Order of Victoria and Albert (Brit.); Veterans Administration; Vicar Apostolic; Vice-Admiral.

val. valuation.

var. variant; variation; variety; various.

Vat. Vatican.

v. aux. verb auxiliary.

vb. verb.

vb.n. verbal noun.

V.C. Veterinary Corps; Vice-Chairman; Vice-Chancellor; Vice-Consul; Victoria Cross (Brit.); Viet Cong.

v.d. various dates.

V.D. venereal disease; Volunteer Officers' Decoration (Brit.).

Ven. Venerable; Venice.

Venez. Venezuela.

verb. sap., or **verb. sat**, or **verbum sap.** *verbum sapienti sat est* (L.), a word to the wise is sufficient.

vers (Math.) versed sine.

vet. veteran; veterinarian; veterinary.

V.F. Vicar Forane; video frequency; voice frequency.

V.F.W. Veterans of Foreign Wars.

v.g. *verbi gratia* (L.), for example.

V.G. Vicar General.

VHF very high frequency.

v.i. verb intransitive; *vide infra* (L.), see below.

Vi (Chem.) virginium.

V.I. Vancouver Island; Virgin Islands.

Vic. Vicar; Vicarage; Victoria.

vil. village.

Visc. Viscount; Viscountess.

VISTA Volunteer in Service to America.

viz. *videlicet* (L.), to wit; namely; that is to say.

v.l. (pl. **vv.ll.**) *varia lectio* (L.), variant reading.

V.L. Vulgar Latin.

V.M.D. *Veterinariae Medecinae Doctor*, (L.), Doctor of Veterinary Medicine.

v.n. verb neuter.

vo. *versa* (L.), left-hand page.

VOA Voice of America; Volunteers of America.

voc. vocative.

vocab. vocabulary.

vocat. vocative.

vol. (pl. **vols.**) volcanic; volcano; volume; volunteer.

v.p. verb passive.

V.P. or **V. Pres.** Vice-President.

v.r. verb reflexive.

V.R. *Victoria Regina* (L.), Queen Victoria.

V.Rev. Very Reverend.

vs. verse; *versus* (L.), against.

v.s. *vide supra* (L.), see above.

V.S. Veterinary Surgeon.

v.t. verb transitive.

Vt. Vermont.

Vte. *Vicomte* (Fr.), Viscount.

Vtesse. *Vicomtesse* (Fr.), Viscountess.

VTO (Aeron.) vertical take-off.

VTOL (Aeron.) vertical take-off and landing.

Vul. or **Vulg.** Vulgate.

vulg. vulgar; vulgarly.

vv. verses; violins.

v.v. *vice versa* (L.), the order being changed.

vv. ll. *variae lectiones* (L.), variant readings.

v.y. various years.

W

w. wanting; warehouse; watt; week; wide; width; wife; with; won; (Physics) work.

W *wolframium* (L.), (Chem.) tungsten.

W. Wales; Warden; Washington; Wednesday; Welsh; west; western.

W.A. West Africa; Western Australia.

W.A.A.C. Women's Army Auxiliary Corps (Brit.).

War. or **Warw.** Warwickshire.

Wash. Washington.

w.b. warehouse book; water ballast; waybill.

w.c. water-closet; without charge.

W.C. West Central (postal district, London).

WCC World Council of Churches.

W.C.T.U. Woman's Christian Temperance Union.

wd. ward, word.

W.D. War Department.

Wed. Wednesday.

Westm. Westminster.

wf (Printing) wrong font.

WFTU World Federation of Trade Unions.

W. Ger. West Germany.

W. Gmc. West Germanic.

whf. wharf.

WHO World Health Organization.

w.i. (Finance) when issued.

W.I. West Indian; West Indies.

Wilts. Wiltshire.

Wis. or **Wisc.** Wisconsin.

Wisd. Wisdom of Solomon (Apocrypha).

wk. (pl. **wks.**) week; work.

wkly. weekly.

w.l. water line; wave length.

W.L. or **W. long.** west longitude.

Wm. William

WMO World Meteorological Organization.

W.N.W. west-northwest.

W.O. warrant officer; War Office (Brit.).

Worc. or **Worcs.** Worcestershire.

wp. (Baseball) wild pitch; wild pitches.

W.R. West Riding (Yorkshire).

WRAC Women's Royal Army Corps.

WRAF Women's Royal Air Force.

WRNS Women's Royal Naval Service (Brit.).

W.S. Writer to the Signet; West Saxon.

W. Sax. West Saxon.

W.S.W. west-southwest.

wt. weight.

W. Va. West Virginia.

W.V.S. Women's Voluntary Service (Brit.).

w.w. warehouse warrant.

WW world war.

Wy. or **Wyo.** Wyoming.

X

X (Chem.) xenon; Christ; Christian; Roman numeral for 10.

xc. or **xcp.** (Stock Exchange) ex (without) coupon.

xd. or **xdiv.** (Stock Exchange) ex (without) dividend.

Xe (Chem.) xenon.

xi. or **xint.** (Stock Exchange) ex (without) interest.

XL extra large.

Xmas Christmas.

Xn. Christian.

Xnty. Christianity.

XP *Christos* (Gr.), Christ.

x pr (Stock Exchange) without privileges.

xr (Stock Exchange) without rights.

Xt. Christ.

Xtian. Christian.

Xty. Christianity.

Y

y. yard; yards; year; years.

Y (Chem.) yttrium.

Y. Young Men's Christian Association; Young Men's Hebrew Association; Young Women's Christian Association; Young Women's Hebrew Association.

Yb (Chem.) ytterbium.

Y.B. yearbook.

yd. (pl. **yds.**) yard.

yeo. yeoman; yeomanry.

YHA Youth Hostels Association.

Y.M.C.A. Young Men's Christian Association.

Y.M.C.U. Young Men's Christian Union.

Y.M.H.A. Young Men's Hebrew Association.

Yorks. Yorkshire.

Y.P.S.C.E. Young People's Society of Christian Endeavor.

yr. (pl. **yrs.**) year; younger; your.

yrs. years; yours.

Yt (Chem.) yttrium.

Y.T. Yukon Territory.

Yugo. Yugoslavia.

Y.W.C.A. Young Women's Christian Association.

Y.W.H.A. Young Women's Hebrew Association.

Z

z. zero; zinc.

Zach. Zacharias (Douay Version).

z.B. *zum Beispiel* (G.), for example.

Zech. Zechariah.

Zeph. Zephaniah.

Zn (Chem.) zinc.

zod. zodiac.

zoochem. zoochemical; zoochemistry.

zoogeog. zoogeographical; zoogeography.

zool. zoological; zoologist; zoology.

Zr (Chem.) zirconium.

Z.S. Zoological Society (London).

MUSICAL SIGNS AND ABBREVIATIONS

 The sign of the treble or G clef. It represents the S of *Sol* (G). The second line from the bottom is the G above middle C.

 The sign of the bass or F clef. It represents the F of *Fa* (F). The fourth line from the bottom is the F below middle C.

♯ *Sharp.* Indicates a note is to be played one half step higher than written.

♭ *Flat.* Indicates a note is to be played one half step lower than written.

♮ *Natural.* Indicates a note previously sharped or flatted is to be played as written.

× *Double sharp.* Indicates a note is to be played two half steps (one full step) higher than written.

♭♭ *Double flat.* Indicates a note is to be played two half steps (one full step) lower than written.

♮♯ *Single sharp.* Indicates a note previously double-sharped is to be sharped.

♮♭ *Single flat.* Indicates a note previously double-flatted is to be flatted.

NOTES:

𝅝 Whole; semibreve.   ♩ Quarter; crotchet.

𝅗𝅥 Half; minim.   ♪ Eighth; quaver.

𝅘𝅥𝅯 Sixteenth; semiquaver.

𝅘𝅥𝅰 Thirty-second; demisemiquaver.

𝅘𝅥𝅱 Sixty-fourth; hemidemisemiquaver.

RESTS:

▬ Whole.   ▬ Half.   𝄽 Quarter.   𝄾 Eighth.

𝄿 Sixteenth.   𝅀 Thirty-second.   𝅁 Sixty-fourth.

$\frac{4}{4}, \frac{3}{4}$, etc. *Time signatures.* The lower figure indicates the kind of note having unit beat; the upper figure the number of such notes per measure, e.g., each measure of $\frac{6}{8}$ time has a time value of six eighth notes.

𝄴 *Common time.* $\frac{4}{4}$.

ORNAMENTS:

〰 *Mordent.* The rapid alternation of the written note with the note above.

Written   Played

∾ *Turn.* The sequence of four notes beginning with the note above, followed by the written note and the note below, and ending with the written note.

Written   Played

𝆖〰 *Trill.* The repeated alternation of the written note with the note above.

Written   Played

𝅘𝅥 *Staccato.* A dot over a note indicating the note is to be played short and detached.

>𝅘𝅥 *Accent mark.* Indicates a stressed note.

◁ *Crescendo.* Gradually louder.

▷ *Diminuendo.* Gradually softer.

⌣ , ⌣ *Legato.* Smoothly and connectedly.

𝄋 *Segno.* A sign marking the beginning or end of a passage to be repeated.

 Double bar. Placed at the beginning and end of a passage, indicating the marked section is to be repeated.

𝄐 *Fermata.* Indicates a long pause on a note or rest.

accel. Accelerando. Gradually increasing speed.
cresc. Crescendo. Gradually increasing loudness.
D.C. Da capo. From the beginning: return to beginning of composition and repeat to double bar marked *fine* (end).
decresc. Decrescendo. Same as diminuendo.
dim. Diminuendo. Gradually decreasing loudness.
f. Forte. Loudly, strongly.
ff. Fortissimo. Very loud.
fff. As loudly as possible.
fp. Forte-piano. Loud, then immediately soft.
leg. Legato. With smooth connection between notes.
marc. Marcato. Marked: played prominently.
mf. Mezzo forte. Moderately loud.
M.M. Maelzel's metronome. Found at the beginning of a composition, together with the number of metronome beats per minute at which the piece is to be played, e.g., M.M. = 80, or 80 quarter notes per minute.
mp. Mezzo piano. Moderately soft.
8va. Ottava. An octave. *Ottava alta* (appearing above the notes): to be played an octave higher than written. *Ottava bassa* (appearing below the notes): to be played an octave lower.
p. Piano. Softly.
pizz. Pizzicato. Direction to string players to pluck the string with the fingers instead of bowing.
pp. Pianissimo. Very soft.
ppp. As softly as possible.
rall. Rallentando. Gradually slower.
rf., rfz., rinf. Rinforzando. With additional stress.
rit. Ritardando. Holding back in speed: gradually slower.
sf., sfz. Sforzando. With a strong accent.
sost. Sostenuto. Sustained: prolonging the tone for the full duration indicated.
trem. Tremolo. Tremblingly: a note or chord reiterated with great rapidity, so as to produce such an effect.

POPULAR QUOTATIONS

ABSENCE

Absence is to love what wind is to fire; it extinguishes the small, it enkindles the great. (L'absence est a l'amour ce qu'est au feu le vent; il éteint le petit, il allume le grand.)

> COMTE DE BUSSY-RABUTIN
> *Histoire Amoureuse des Gaules* "Maximes d'Amours"

Absence makes the heart grow fonder.

> ANONYMOUS
> (Davison, *Potential Rhapsody*)

ACCIDENT

Between the mouth and the morsel many things may happen. (Inter os atque offam multa intervenire posse.)

> CATO THE CENSOR
> "On the Improper Election Aediles." (Aulus Gellius, *Noctes Atticae* Bk. xiii, ch. 18, sec. 1)

Accidents will occur in the best-regulated families.

> CHARLES DICKENS
> *David Copperfield* Ch. 28

Great actions speak great minds.

> JOHN FLETCHER
> *The Prophetess* Act ii, sc. 3

Nothing under the sun is accidental.

> GOTTHOLD EPHRAIM LESSING
> *Emilia Galotti* Act iv, sc. 3

At first laying down, as a fact fundamental,
That nothing with God can be accidental.

> HENRY WADSWORTH LONGFELLOW
> *The Golden Legend* Pt. vi

Let us, then, be up and doing,
With a heart for any fate;
Still achieving, still pursuing,
Learn to labour and to wait.

> HENRY WADSWORTH LONGFELLOW
> *A Psalm of Life* St. 9

ANCESTRY

Gentility is nothing else but ancient riches.

> LORD BURGHLEY: WILLIAM CECIL BARON BURGHLEY
> (Peck, *Desiderata Curiosa* 48)

Noblesse oblige. (Birth compels it. Noble birth imposes the obligation of noble actions.)

> DUC DE LEVIS
> *Maxims* No. 73

I don't know who my grandfather was; I am much more concerned to know what his grandson will be.

> ABRAHAM LINCOLN
> (Gross, *Lincoln's Own Stories*)

He who boasts of his descent, praises the deeds of another. (Qui genus jactat suum, Aliena laudat.)

> SENECA
> *Hercules Furens*

ANGER

The angry man always thinks he can do more than he can. (Iratus semper plus putat posse facer quam possit.)

> ALBERTANO OF BRESCIA
> *Liber Consolationis*

Anger edgeth valour.

> JOHN CLARKE
> *Paroemiologia* 178

Beware the fury of a patient man.

> JOHN DRYDEN
> *Absalom and Achitophel* Pt. i

It is very difficult to get up resentment towards persons whom one has never seen.

> JOHN HENRY, CARDINAL NEWMAN
> *Apologia pro Vita Sua*
> "Mr. Kingsley's Method of Disputation"

Anger is momentary madness. (Ira furor brevis est.)

> HORACE
> *Epistles* Bk. i, epis, ii

When angry, count ten before you speak; if very angry, an hundred.

> THOMAS JEFFERSON
> *Writings* Vol. xvi

A soft answer turneth away wrath: but grievous words stir up anger.

> Proverbs xv, 1

ART

Art is a jealous mistress.

> RALPH WALDO EMERSON
> *Conduct of Life* "Wealth"

Fine art is that in which the hand, the head, and the heart of man go together.

> JOHN RUSKIN
> *The Two Paths* Lecture ii

The true artist will let his wife starve, his children go barefoot, his mother drudge for his living at seventy, sooner than work at anything but his art.

> GEORGE BERNARD SHAW
> *Man and Superman* Act i

ASPIRATION

No bird soars too high if he soars with his own wings.

> WILLIAM BLAKE
> *Proverbs of Hell*

Hitch your wagon to a star. Let us not fag in paltry works which serve our pot and bag alone. Let us not lie and steal. No god will help. We shall find all their teams going the other way: every god will leave us. Work rather for those interests which the divinities honor and promote,— justice, love, freedom, knowledge, utility.

> RALPH WALDO EMERSON
> *Society and Solitude* "Civilization"

The thing we long for, that we are
For one transcendent moment.

> JAMES RUSSELL LOWELL
> *Longing*

I have Immortal longings in me.

> WILLIAM SHAKESPEARE
> *Antony and Cleopatra* Act v, sc. 2

BEAUTY

There is no excellent beauty that hath not some strangeness in the proportion.

FRANCIS BACON
Essays "Of Beauty"

Rugged the breast that beauty cannot tame.

JOHN CODRINGTON BAMPFYLDE
"Sonnet in Praise of Delia"

Marke it welle:
There are flowers, and there are weeds—
But mostly weeds.

SCOTT ORVILLE BERGREN
God's Teeth "Song of Manona"

If you get simple beauty and naught else,
You get about the best thing God invents.

ROBERT BROWNING
Fra Lippo Lippi

She walks in beauty, like the night
Of cloudless climes and starry skies;
And all that's best of dark and bright
Meet in her aspect and her eyes:
Thus mellow'd to that tender light
Which heaven to gaudy days denies.

GEORGE GORDON, LORD BYRON
Hebrew Melodies "She Walks in Beauty"

All heiresses are beautiful.

JOHN DRYDEN
King Arthur, I, i

Beauty rests on necessities. The line of beauty is the line of perfect economy.

RALPH WALDO EMERSON
Conduct of Life "Beauty"

Beauty in things exists in the mind which contemplates them.

DAVID HUME
Essays "Of Tragedy"

Beauty is in the eye of the beholder.

MARGARET WOLFE HUNGERFORD
Quoted in *Molly Bawn*

A thing of beauty is a joy forever:
Its loveliness increases; it will never
Pass into nothingness; but still will keep
A bower quiet for us, and a sleep
Full of sweet dreams, and health,
and quiet breathing.

JOHN KEATS
Endymion Bk. i, I

"Beauty is truth, truth beauty,"—that is all
Ye know on earth, and all ye need to know.

JOHN KEATS
"Ode on a Grecian Urn"

Beauty from order springs.

WILLIAM KING
Art of Cookery

What is your sex's earliest, latest care,
Your heart's supreme ambition?—To be fair.

GEORGE LYTTELTON
Advice to a Lady

Beauty is the purgation of superfluities.

MICHELANGELO
(Emerson, *Conduct of Life* "Beauty")

'Tis now a lip, or eye, we beauty call,
But the joint force and full result of all.

ALEXANDER POPE
An Essay on Criticism

What a strange illusion it is to suppose that beauty is goodness.

LEO TOLSTOY
The Kreutzer Sonata Ch. 5

It is better to be beautiful than to be good, but... it is better to be good than to be ugly.

OSCAR WILDE
The Picture of Dorian Gray Ch. 17

BELIEF

Men willingly believe what they wish. (Fere libenter homines id quod volunt credunt.)

JULIUS CAESAR
De Bello Gallico iii, 18

Belief consists in accepting the affirmations of the soul; unbelief, in denying them.

RALPH WALDO EMERSON
Representative Men "Montaigne"

BOOKS

Some books are to be tasted, others to be swallowed, and some few to be chewed and digested; that is some books are to be read only in parts; others to be read but not curiously; and some few to be read wholly, and with diligence and attention. Some books may also be read by deputy, and extracts made of them by others.

FRANCIS BACON
Essays "Of Studies"

Books will speak plain, when counsellors blanch.

FRANCIS BACON
Essays "Of Counsel"

A good book is the purest essence of a human soul.

THOMAS CARLYLE
Speech 1840

Some books leave us free and some books make us free.

RALPH WALDO EMERSON
Journals December 22, 1839

Never read any book that is not a year old.

RALPH WALDO EMERSON
Society and Solitude "Books"

A man ought to read just as inclination leads him; for what he reads as a task will do him little good.

SAMUEL JOHNSON
(Boswell, *Life*)

Every age hath its book.

Koran Ch. xiii

Books are not absolutely dead things, but do contain a progeny of life in them to be as active as that soul was whose progeny they are; nay, they do preserve as in a vial the purest efficacy and extraction of that living intellect that bred them.

> JOHN MILTON
> *Areopagitica* Sec. 6

As good almost kill a man as kill a good book; who kills a man kills a reasonable creature, God's image; but he who destroys a good book, kills reason itself, kills the image of God, as it were, in the eye.

> JOHN MILTON
> *Areopagitica* Sec. 6

A good book is the best of friends, the same to-day and forever.

> MARTIN FARQUHAR TUPPER
> *Proverbial Philosophy* "Of Reading"

There is no such thing as a moral or immoral book. Books are well written, or badly written. That is all.

> OSCAR WILDE
> *Picture of Dorian Gray* "Preface"

BREVITY

Not that the story need be long, but it will take a long while to make it short.

> HENRY DAVID THOREAU
> *Letter to a Friend*

CERTAINTY

If a man will begin with certainties, he shall end in doubts; but if he will be content to begin with doubts, he shall end in certainties.

> FRANCIS BACON
> *Advancement of Learning* Bk. i

But in this world nothing can be said to be certain, except death and taxes.

> BENJAMIN FRANKLIN
> *Writings* Vol. x "Letter to Jean Baptiste Le Roy"

CHANCE

We do not what we ought,
What we ought not, we do,
And lean upon the thought
That Chance will bring us through.

> MATTHEW ARNOLD
> *Empedocles on Etna*

Chance fights ever on the side of the prudent.

> EURIPIDES
> *Pirithous*

Chance is perhaps the pseudonym of God when He did not want to sign. (Le hasard c'est peut-être le pseudonyme de Dieu, quand il ne veut pas signer.)

> ANATOLE FRANCE
> *Le Jardin d'Epicure*

Chances rule men and not men chances.

> HERODOTUS
> *History* Bk. vii, ch. 49

What chance has made yours is not really yours. (Non est tuum, fortuna quod fecit tuum.)

> LUCILIUS
> (Seneca, *Epistulæ ad Lucilium* Epis. viii, sec. 10)

Chance dispenses life with unequal justice. (Fortuna arbitriis tempus dispensat iniquis.)

> OVID
> *Consolatio ad Livium*

There is no chance which does not return. (Il n'est pas chance qui ne retourne.)

> FRENCH PROVERB

To a sensible man, there is no such thing as chance. (Für den vernünftigen Menschen gibt es keinen Zufall.)

> LUDWICK TIECK
> *Fortunat*

Chance is a word void of sense; nothing can exist without a cause.

> VOLTAIRE
> *A Philosophical Dictionary*

CHANGE

Constancy is the foundation of virtues.

> FRANCIS BACON
> *De Augmentis Scientiarum* Pt. i, bk. vi, sec. 23

It is sufficiently clear that all things are changed, and nothing really perishes, and that the sum of matter remains absolutely the same.

> FRANCIS BACON
> *De Natura Rerum*

The world's a scene of changes, and to be Constant, in Nature were inconstancy.

> ABRAHAM COWLEY
> *Inconstancy*

Change is inevitable in a progressive country. Change is constant.

> BENJAMIN DISRAELI
> *Speech* October 20, 1867

There is danger in reckless change; but greater danger in blind conservatism.

> HENRY GEORGE
> *Social Problems*

There is nothing permanent except change.

> HERACLITUS
> (Rogers, *Students' History of Philosophy*)

There is a certain relief in change, even though it be from bad to worse; as I have found in travelling in a stage-coach, that it is often a comfort to shift one's position and be bruised in a new place.

> WASHINGTON IRVING
> *Tales of a Traveller* "To the Reader"

New opinions are always suspected, and usually opposed, without any other reason but because they are not already common.

> JOHN LOCKE
> *Essay on Human Understanding*

CIVILIZATION

Civilization degrades the many to exalt the few.

> AMOS BRONSON ALCOTT
> *Table-Talk* "Pursuits"

Increased means and increased leisure are the two civilizers of man.

> BENJAMIN DISRAELI
> *Speech* April 3, 1872

Every prison is the exclamation point and every asylum is the question mark in the sentences of civilization.

> S. W. DUFFIELD
> *Essays* "Righteousness"

There is nothing so fragile as civilization, and no high civilization has long withstood the manifold risks it is exposed to.

HAVELOCK ELLIS
Impressions and Comments Ser. i

As long as our civilization is essentially one of property, of fences, of exclusiveness, it will be mocked by delusions.

RALPH WALDO EMERSON
Representative Men "Napoleon"

The highest civilty has never loved the hot zones. Wherever snow falls there is usually civil freedom. Where the banana grows, man is usually sensual and cruel.

RALPH WALDO EMERSON
Society and Solitude "Civilization"

The true test of civilization is, not the census, nor the size of cities, nor the crops,—no, but the kind of man the country turns out.

RALPH WALDO EMERSON
Society and Solitude "Civilization"

Civilization is paralysis.

PAUL GAUGUIN

The true civilization is where every man gives to every other every right that he claims for himself.

R. G. INGERSOLL
Interview November 14, 1880

A decent provision for the poor is the true test of civilization.

SAMUEL JOHNSON
(Boswell, *Life* ii)

COMMON SENSE

Common sense is the most widely shared commodity in the world, for every man is convinced that he is well supplied with it. (Le bon sens est la chose du monde la mieux partagée, car chacun pense en être bien porvu.)

RENE DESCARTES
Le Discours de La Methode

Common sense is not so common. (Le sens commun n'est pas si commun.)

VOLTAIRE
A Philosophical Dictionary "Self-Love"

COMPROMISE

All government—indeed, every human benefit and enjoyment, every virtue and every prudent act—is founded on compromise and barter.

EMUND BURKE
Speech March 22, 1775

Every compromise was surrender and invited new demands.

RALPH WALDO EMERSON
Miscellanies "American Civilization"

A lean compromise is better than a fat lawsuit.

GEORGE HERBERT
Jacula Prudentum

Life cannot subsist in society but by reciprocal concessions.

SAMUEL JOHNSON
Letter to Boswell 1766

All great alterations in human affairs are produced by compromise.

SYDNEY SMITH
Essays "The Catholic Question"

CONCEIT

The world tolerates conceit from those who are successful, but not from anybody else.

JOHN BLAKE
Uncommon Sense

Conceit may puff a man up, but never prop him up.

JOHN RUSKIN
True and Beautiful "Morals and Religion"

CONFIDENCE

Confidence does more to make conversation than wit. (La confiance fournit plus à la conversation que l'esprit.)

FRANCOIS LA ROCHEFOUCAULD
Maximes No. 421

Confidence placed in another often compels confidence in return. (Habita fides ipsam plerumque obligat fidem.)

LIVY
History Bk. xxii, ch. 22, sec. 20

Confidence, like the soul, never returns whence it has once departed.

PUBLILIUS SYRUS
Sententiœ No. 206

CONSCIENCE

The man who acts never has any conscience; no one has any conscience but the man who thinks.

GOETHE
Sprüche in Prosa

A man's conscience and his judgement is the same thing, and as the judgement, so also the conscience, may be erroneous.

THOMAS HOBBES
Leviathan Pt. ii, ch. 29

No guilty man is acquitted at the bar of his own conscience, though he win his cause by a juggling urn, and the corrupt favor of the judge. (Judice nemo nocens absolvitur, improba quamvis Gratia fallaci praetoris vicerit urna.)

JUVENAL
Satires Sat. xiii

Labour to keep alive in your breast that little spark of celestial fire, called conscience.

GEORGE WASHINGTON
Rules of Civility and Decent Behaviour
(Spark, *Life of Washington* Vol ii)

CONSERVATISM

The healthy stomach is nothing if not conservative. Few radicals have good digestions.

SAMUEL BUTLER
Mind and Matter "Indigestion"

Conservatism discards Prescription, shrinks from Principle, disavows Progress; having rejected all respect for antiquity, it offers no redress for the present, and makes no preparation for the future.

BENJAMIN DISRAELI
Coningsby Bk. ii, ch. 5

Men are conservatives when they are least vigorous, or when they are most luxurious. They are conservatives after dinner.

RALPH WALDO EMERSON
Essays, Second Series "New England Reformers"

What is conservatism? Is it not adherence to the old and tried, against the new and untried?

ABRAHAM LINCOLN
Speech February 27, 1860

CONVERSATION

Method is not less requisite in ordinary conversation than in writing, provided a man would talk to make himself understood.

JOSEPH ADDISON
The Spectator No. 476

Debate is masculine; conversation is feminine.

AMOS BRONSON ALCOTT
Concord Days "May"

You may talk of all subjects save one, namely, your maladies.

RALPH WALDO EMERSON
Conduct of Life "Behavior"

Conversation is a game of circles.

RALPH WALDO EMERSON
Essays, First Series "Circles"

Conversation is the vent of character as well as of thought.

RALPH WALDO EMERSON
Society and Solitude "Clubs"

Conversation is an art in which a man has all mankind for his competitors, for it is that which all are practising every day while they live.

RALPH WALDO EMERSON
Conduct of Life "Considerations by the Way"

He that converses not, knows nothing.

THOMAS FULLER
Gnomologia No. 3136

All discourses but my own afflict me; they seem harsh, impertinent, and irksome.

BEN JONSON
Epicaene; Or, The Silent Woman Act ii, sc. 1

Silence and modesty are very valuable qualities in the art of conversation. (Le silence et la modestie sont qualités très commodes à la conversation.)

MONTAIGNE
Essays Bk. i, ch. 25

COURAGE

A stout man's heart breaks bad luck.

CERVANTES
Don Quixote Pt. ii, ch. 10

Courage consists in equality to the problem before us.

RALPH WALDO EMERSON
Society and Solitude "Courage"

A great part of courage is the courage of having done the thing before.

RALPH WALDO EMERSON
Society and Solitude "Courage"

The greatest test of courage on earth is to bear defeat without losing heart.

R. G. INGERSOLL
The Declaration of Independence

Courage is the most common and vulgar of the virtues.

HERMAN MELVILLE
(Cournos, *Modern Plutarch*)

Being a man, ne'er ask the gods for life set free from grief, but ask for courage that endureth long.

MENANDER
Fragments No. 549

Fortune favors the brave. (Fortis fortuna adjuvat.)

TERENCE
Phormio Act i, sc. 4

COWARDICE

To see what is right and not to do it is want of courage.

CONFUCIUS
Analects Bk. ii, ch. 24

Ever will a coward shew no mercy.

SIR THOMAS MALORY
Morte d'Arthur Bk. xviii, ch. 24

Cowards die many times before their deaths: The valiant never taste of death but once.

WILLIAM SHAKESPEARE
Julius Caesar Act ii, sc. 2

Make a coward fight and he will kill the devil.

UNKNOWN
New Help to Discourse 151

CRITICISM

A man must serve his time to ev'ry trade,
Save censure—critics are all ready made.

GEORGE GORDON, LORD BYRON
English Bards and Scotch Reviewers

Whoever thinks a faultless piece to see
Thinks what ne'er was, nor is, nor e'er shall be.

ALEXANDER POPE
An Essay on Criticism

CURIOSITY

Too much curiosity lost Paradise.

APHRA BEHN
The Lucky Chance Act iii, sc. 3

Curiosity is little more than another name for hope.

J. C. AND A. W. HARE
Guesses at Truth

Curiosity is one of the most permanent and certain characteristics of a vigorous intellect.

SAMUEL JOHNSON
The Rambler No. 103

Curiosity is born of jealousy. (La curiosité naît de la jalousie.)

MOLIERE
Dom Garcie de Navarre Act ii, sc. 5

DEATH

I do not believe that any man fears to be dead, but only the stroke of death.

FRANCIS BACON
An Essay on Death 3

Though boys throw stones at frogs in sport, the frogs do not die in sport, but in earnest.

> BION
> (Plutarch, *Water and Land Animals* Sec. 7)

It costs a lot of money to die comfortably.

> SAMUEL BUTLER
> *Note Books* "A Luxurious Death"

The crash of the whole solar and stellar systems could only kill you once.

> THOMAS CARLYLE
> *Letter to John Carlyle*

Far happier are the dead, methinks, than they
Who look for death and fear it every day.

> WILLIAM COWPER
> *On Invalids*

For dust thou art, and unto dust shalt thou return.

> Genesis iii, 19

Death forseen comes not.

> GEORGE HERBERT
> *Jacula Prudentum*

If I go by land, and miscarry, then I go the way of all flesh.

> THOMAS HEYWOOD
> *Golden Age* Act iii

Dead as a door nail.

> WILLIAM LANGLAND
> *Piers Plowman* Pt. ii

Let the dead bury their dead.

> Matthew viii, 22

Whom the gods love die young.

> MENANDER
> *Dis Exapaton* Frag. 125

Death pays all debts. (La mort nous acquitte de toutes nos obligations.)

> MONTAIGNE
> *Essays* Bk. i, ch. 7

We shall die alone.

> BLAISE PASCAL
> *Pensées* Sec. iii

Earth to earth, ashes to ashes, dust to dust,
In sure and certain hope of the resurrection.
Book of Common Prayer "Burial of the Dead"

How I was born I do not remember. How I will die, I do not know.

> RUSSIAN PROVERB

CALPHURNIA: When beggars die, there are no comets seen:
The heavens themselves blaze forth the death of princes.
CAESAR: Cowards die many times before their deaths:
The valiant never taste of death but once.
Of all the wonders that I yet have heard,

It seems to me most strange that men should fear,
Seeing that death, a necessary end,
Will come when it will come.

> WILLIAM SHAKESPEARE
> *Julius Caesar* Act ii, sc. 2

Death is fortunate for the child, bitter to the youth, too late to the old. (Mors infanti felix, juveni acerba, nimis sera seni.)

> PUBLILIUS SYRUS
> *Sententiæ* No. 394

'Twere best to knock them in the head ...
The dead do tell no tales.

> JOHN WILSON
> *Andronicus Commenius* Act i, sc. 4

DILIGENCE

Diligence is the mother of good fortune, and idleness, its opposite, never brought a man to the goal of any of his best wishes. (La diligencia es madre de la buena ventura y la pereza, su contrario, jamas llego al termino que pide un buen deseo.)

> CERVANTES
> *Don Quixote*

'Tis a lesson you should heed,
Try, try again.
If at first you don't succeed,
Try, try again.

> WILLIAM EDWARD HICKSON
> *Try and Try Again*

DIPLOMACY

International arbitration may be defined as the substitution of many burning questions for a smouldering one.

> AMBROSE BIERCE
> *The Devil's Dictionary*

"Frank and explicit"—that is the right line to take when you wish to conceal your mind and to confuse the minds of others.

> BENJAMIN DISRAELI
> *Sybil* Bk. vi, ch. 1

The public weal requires that a man should betray, and lie, and massacre. (Le bien public requiert qu'on trahisse, et qu'on mente, et qu'on massacre.)

> MONTAIGNE
> *Essays* Bk. iii, ch. 1

DISAPPOINTMENT

The best-laid schemes o' mice an' men
Gang aft agley,
An' lea'e us nought but grief an' pain,
For promis'd joy!

> ROBERT BURNS
> *To a Mouse*

Like to the apples on the Dead Sea's shore,
All ashes to the taste.

> GEORGE GORDON, LORD BYRON
> *Childe Harold* Canto iii, st. 34

Nothing is so good as it seems beforehand.

> GEORGE ELIOT
> *Silas Marner* Ch. 18

DISCRETION

Cowardice?
I only know we don't live twice,
Therefore—shun death, is my advice.

ROBERT BROWNING
Arcades Ambo

To retire is not to flee, and there is no wisdom waiting when danger outweighs hope, and it is the part of wise men to preserve themselves today for tomorrow, and not risk all in one day.

CERVANTES
Don Quixote Pt. i, ch. 23

Valour would fight, but discretion would run away.

THOMAS FULLER
Gnomologia No. 5344

The man who runs away may fight again.

MENANDER
Monostikoi No. 45

The better part of valour is discretion.

WILLIAM SHAKESPEARE
I Henry IV Act v, sc. 4

It is an old saw, he fighteth well that flyeth fast.

UNKNOWN
Gesta Romanorum "The Wolf and Hare"

DISGRACE

Come, Death, and snatch me from disgrace.

BULWER-LYTTON
Richelieu Act iv, sc. 1

A wise and good man can suffer no disgrace.

FABIUS MAXIMUS
(Plutarch, *Lives*)

Disgrace is deathless. (Immortalis est infamia.)

PLAUTUS
Persa Act iii, sc. 1

It is better not to live at all than to live disgraced.

SOPHOCLES
Peleus Frag. 445

DOCTORS

God heals, and the Doctor takes the Fee.

BENJAMIN FRANKLIN
Poor Richard's Almanack

A physician can sometimes parry the scythe of death, but has no power over the sand in the hourglass.

HESTER LYNCH PIOZZI
Letter to Fanny Burney

DREAMS

Life and love are all a dream.

ROBERT BURNS
The Lament

After a dream of weddings comes a corse.

JOHN CLARKE
Paroemiologia 236

Dreams are the true interpreters of our inclinations, but art is required to sort and understand them.

MONTAIGNE
Essays Bk. iii, ch. 13

It is the fault of dreamers to fear fate.

STEPHEN PHILLIPS
Herod Act i

All that we see or seem
Is but a dream within a dream.

EDGAR ALLEN POE
"A Dream Within a Dream"

Man is but an ass if he go about to expound this dream.

WILLIAM SHAKESPEARE
A Midsummer-Night's Dream Act iv, sc. 1

I have had a dream, past the wit of man to say what dream it was.

WILLIAM SHAKESPEARE
A Midsummer-Night's Dream Act iv, sc. 1

The eye of man hath not heard, the ear of man hath not seen, man's hand is not able to taste, his tongue to conceive, nor his heart to report, what my dream was.

WILLIAM SHAKESPEARE
A Midsummer-Night's Dream Act iv, sc. 1

EATING

Tell me what you eat, and I will tell you what you are. (Dis-moi ce que tu manges, je te dirai ce que tu es.)

BRILLAT-SAVARIN
Physiologie du Gout Ch. 36

Till we have eat him out of house and home.

JOHN DAY
Blind Beggar Act iv, sc. 1

The way to a man's heart is through his stomach.

FANNY FERN
Willis Parton

To lengthen thy life, lessen thy meals.

BENJAMIN FRANKLIN
Poor Richard's Almanack

The proof of the pudding is in the eating.

HENRY GLAPTHORNE
The Hollander Act iii

Let us eat and drink; for tomorrow we shall die.

Isaiah xxii, 13

What is food to one man may be fierce poison to others.

LUCRETIUS
De Rerum Natura Bk. iv

Take no thought for your life, what ye shall eat, nor what ye shall drink.

Matthew vi, 25

One should eat to live, not live to eat. (Il faut manger pour vivre et non pas vivre pour manger.)

MOLIERE
L'Avare

Food for the gods. (Deorum Cibus.)

NERO

Other men live to eat, while I eat to live.

SOCRATES
(Diogenes Laertius, *Socrates* Bk. ii, sec. 34)

EGOTISM

Every man is of importance to himself.

SAMUEL JOHNSON
Works Vol. iv

The egoist does not tolerate egoism.

JOSEPH ROUX
Meditations of a Parish Priest Pt. ix, no. 11

There is nothing so monstrous but we can believe it of ourselves.

ROBERT LOUIS STEVENSON
Virginibus Puerisque Ch. ii

Other people are quite dreadful. The only possible society is oneself.

OSCAR WILDE
An Ideal Husband Act iii

EQUALITY

Your abundance may be a supply for their want, that their abundance also may be a supply for your want: that there may be equality.

II Corinthians vii, 14

As a man is equal to the Church and equal to the State, so he is equal to every other man.

RALPH WALDO EMERSON
Essays, Second Series "New England Reformers"

Men are made by nature unequal. It is vain, therefore, to treat them as if they were equal.

JAMES ANTHONY FROUDE
Short Studies on Great Subjects "Party Politics"

We hold these truths to be self-evident, that all men are created equal.

THOMAS JEFFERSON
Declaration of Independence

I leave you, hoping that the lamp of liberty will burn in your bosoms, until there shall no longer be a doubt that all men are created free and equal.

ABRAHAM LINCOLN
Speech July 10, 1858

Four score and seven years ago, our fathers brought forth on this continent a new nation, conceived in liberty, and dedicated to the proposition that all men are created equal.

ABRAHAM LINCOLN
Gettysburg Address

EVIL

No one becomes at once completely vile. (Nemo repente fuit turpissimus.)

JUVENAL
Satires Sat. ii

We believe no evil till the evil's done. (Nous ne croyons le mal que quand il est venu).

LA FONTAINE
Fables Bk. i, fab. 8

The best known evil is the most tolerable. (Notissimum quodque malum maxime tolerabile.)

LIVY
History Bk. xxiii, sec. 3

There is no evil that does not offer inducements. Avarice promises money; luxury, a varied assortment of pleasures; ambition, a purple robe and applause. Vices tempt you by the rewards which they offer.

SENECA
Epistulæ ad Lucilium Epis. lxix, 4

EVOLUTION

I have called this principle, by which each slight variation, if useful, is preserved, by the term of Natural Selection.

CHARLES DARWIN
The Origin of Species Ch. 3

Evolution is not a force but a process; not a cause but a law.

JOHN MORLEY
On Compromise

This survival of the fittest, which I have here sought to express in mechanical terms, is that which Mr. Darwin has called "natural selection, or the preservation of favoured races in the struggle for life."

HERBERT SPENCER
Principles of Biology Pt. iii, ch. 12, sec. 165

EXAMPLE

Example is the school of mankind, and they will learn at no other.

EDMUND BURKE
On a Regicide Peace

Why doth one man's yawning make another yawn?

ROBERT BURTON
Anatomy of Melancholy Pt. 1, sec. 2

They do more harm by their evil example than by their actual sin. (Plus exemplo quam peccato nocent.)

CICERO
De Legibus Bk. iii, sec. 14

EXPERIENCE

Experience teaches slowly, and at the cost of mistakes.

JAMES ANTHONY FROUDE
Short Studies on Great Subjects "Party Politics"

Nothing ever becomes real till it is experienced—even a proverb is no proverb to you till your life has illustrated it.

JOHN KEATS
Letters

EYES

In a moment, in the twinkling of an eye.

I Corinthians xv, 52

He kept him as the apple of his eye.

Deuteronomy xxxii, 10

She has eyes in the back of her head.

PERCY FITZGERALD
Comediettas

The eyes have one language everywhere.

GEORGE HERBERT
Jacula Prudentum

The light of the body is the eye.

Matthew vi, 22

She hath an eye behind her.

> WILLIAM STEVENSON
> *Gammer Gurton's Needle* Act ii, sc. 2

FACTS

In this life we want nothing but facts, Sir; nothing but facts.

> CHARLES DICKENS
> *Hard Times* Bk. 1, ch. 1

No facts to me are sacred; none are profane.

> RALPH WALDO EMERSON
> *Essays, First Series* "Circles"

FAILURE

They never fail who die
In a great cause: the block may soak their gore;
Their heads may sodden in the sun; their limbs
Be strung to city gates and castle walls—
But still their spirit walks abroad.

> GEORGE GORDON, LORD BYRON
> *Marino Faliero* Act ii, sc. 2

A fool often fails because he thinks what is difficult is easy, and a wise man because he thinks what is easy is difficult.

> CHURTON COLLINS
> *Aphorisms*

There is not a fiercer hell than the failure in a great object.

> JOHN KEATS
> *Endymion* "Preface"

To fail at all is to fail utterly.

> J. R. LOWELL
> *Among My Books* "Dryden"

In the lexicon of youth, which Fate reserves
For a bright manhood, there is no such word
As—fail! ... Never say *"Fail"* again.

> BULWER-LYTTON
> *Richelieu* Act ii, sc. 2

FAME

Let us now praise famous men.

> *Apocrypha*
> Ecclesiasticus xliv, 1

If you would be known, and not know, vegetate in a village; if you would know, and not be known, live in a city.

> CHARLES CALEB COLTON
> *Lacon* Vol. i, no. 334

It's a fine thing to have a finger pointed at one, and to hear people say, "That's the man." (At pulchrum est digito monstrari et dicier, "Hic est.")

> PERSIUS
> *Satires* Sat. i

If you will observe, it doesn't take
A man of giant mould to make
A giant shadow on the wall;
And he who in our daily sight
Seems but a figure mean and small,
Outlined in Fame's illusive light,
May stalk, a silhouette sublime,
Across the canvas of his time.

> J. T. TROWBRIDGE
> *Author's Night* St. 17

FANATICISM

Earth's fanatics make
Too frequently heaven's saints.

> ELIZABETH BARRETT BROWNING
> *Aurora Leigh* Bk. ii

There is no strong performance without a little fanaticism in the performer.

> RALPH WALDO EMERSON
> *Journals* Vol. ix

FATE

Fate holds the strings, and men like children move
But as they're led; success is from above.

> GEORGE GRANVILLE
> *Heroic Love* Act v, sc. 2

It lies not in our power to love or hate,
For will in us is over-ruled by fate.

> CHRISTOPHER MARLOWE
> *Hero and Leander* Sestiad 1

Our wills and fates do so contrary run
That our devices still are overthrown;
Our thoughts are ours, their ends none of our own.

> WILLIAM SHAKESPEARE
> *Hamlet* Act iii, sc. 2

FEAR

Fear of danger is ten thousand times more terrifying than danger itself.

> DANIEL DEFOE
> *Robinson Crusoe*

Whom they fear they hate. (Quem metuunt, oderunt.)

> QUINTUS ENNIUS
> *Thyestes* (Cicero, *De Officiis* ii, 7)

Fear is the parent of cruelty.

> JAMES ANTHONY FROUDE
> *Short Studies on Great Subjects* "Party Politics"

Fear is stronger than love.

> THOMAS FULLER
> *Gnomologia* No. 1513

Fear not.

> Genesis xlii, 23

Fear, the beadle of the law.

> GEORGE HERBERT
> *Jacula Prudentum*

Let me assert my firm belief that the only thing we have to fear is fear itself.

> FRANKLIN DELANO ROOSEVELT
> *First Inaugural Address* March 4, 1933

FOOL

An erudite fool is a greater fool than an ignorant fool. (Un sot savant est sot plus qu'un sot ignorant.)

> MOLIERE
> *Les Femmes Savantes* Act iv, sc. 3

The learn'd is happy nature to explore,
The fool is happy that he knows no more.

> ALEXANDER POPE
> *An Essay on Man*

For fools rush in where angels fear to tread.

> ALEXANDER POPE
> *An Essay on Criticism* Pt. iii

It is better to be a fool than to be dead.

> ROBERT LOUIS STEVENSON
> *Virginibus Puerisque* "Crabbed Age and Youth"

FORGIVENESS

They who forgive most shall be most forgiven.

> P. J. BAILEY
> *Festus* "Home"

"I can forgive, but I cannot forget," is only another way of saying "I cannot forgive."

> HENRY WARD BEECHER
> *Life Thoughts*

He who forgives readily only invites offense. (Qui pardonne aisément invite à l'offenser.)

> PIERRE CORNEILLE
> *Cinna* Act iv, sc. 4

The offender never pardons.

> GEORGE HERBERT
> *Jacula Prudentum*

It is just that he who asks forgiveness for his offenses should give it in turn. (Aequum est Peccatis veniam poscentem reddere rursus.)

> HORACE
> *Satires* Bk. i, sat. 3

Forgive others often, yourself never. (Ignoscito saepe alter, nunquam tibi.)

> PUBLILIUS SYRUS
> *Sententiæ* No. 325

FREEDOM

None can love freedom heartily, but good men; the rest love not freedom, but licence.

> JOHN MILTON
> *Tenure of Kings and Magistrates*

In the future days, which we seek to make secure, we look forward to a world founded upon four essential freedoms. The first is freedom of speech and expression—everywhere in the world. The second is freedom of every person to worship God in his own way—everywhere in the world. The third is freedom from want... The fourth is freedom from fear.

> FRANKLIN DELANO ROOSEVELT
> *Speech* January 6, 1941

Man is born free, and everywhere he is in chains. (L'homme est né libre, et partout il est dans les fers.)

> JEAN-JACQUES ROUSSEAU
> *Du Contrat Social* Ch. 1

No human being, however great, or powerful, was ever so free as a fish.

> JOHN RUSKIN
> *The Two Paths* Lecture V

FRIENDSHIP

It redoubleth joys and cutteth griefs in half.

> FRANCIS BACON
> *Essays* "Of Friendship"

Friendship is Love without his wings!

> LORD GEORGE BYRON
> *Hours of Idleness* "L'Amitié"

There is a Spanish proverb, which says very justly, Tell me whom you live with, and I will tell you who you are.

> PHILIP DORMER STANHOPE, EARL OF CHESTERFIELD
> *Letter to his Son*

Love and friendship exclude each other.

> LA BRUYERE
> *Les Caractères* Ch. 5

Friendship is equality.

> PYTHAGORAS
> (Diogenes Laertius, *Pythagoras* Sec. 10)

What is love? two souls and one flesh; friendship? two bodies and one soul.

> JOSEPH ROUX
> *Meditations of a Parish Priest* Pt. ix, no. 31

To desire the same things and to reject the same things, constitutes true friendship. (Idem velle atque idem nolle, ea demum firma amicitia est.)

> SALLUST
> *Catilina* Ch. 20, sec. 4

FUTILITY

To attack windmills. (Acometer molinos de viento.)

> CERVANTES
> *Don Quixote* Bk. i, ch. 8

With useless endeavor,
Forever, forever,
Is Sisyphus rolling
His stone up the mountain!

> HENRY WADSWORTH LONGFELLOW
> *The Masque of Pandora* Pt. v

GAIN

Of good ill got The third heir joyeth not.

> JOSEPH BURROUGHS
> *Sermons* "On Hosea"

Ill gotten gains will be ill spent. (Mala parta, male dilabuntur.)

> CICERO
> *Philippicoe* No. ii, sec. 27

No man should so act as to make a gain out of the ignorance of another. (Neminem id agere, ut ex alterius praedetur inscitia.)

> CICERO
> *De Officiis* Bk. iii, ch. 17, sec. 72

Desire of gain, the basest mind's delight.

> "A.W."
> (Davison, *Rhapsody* Sonnet I)

Better it is to have more of profit and less of honour.

> UNKNOWN
> *Melusine* Ch. 34

No one was ever ruined by taking a profit.

> UNKNOWN

GENIUS

Doing easily what others find difficult is talent; doing what is impossible for talent is genius.

HENRI-FREDERIC AMIEL
Journal December 17, 1856

There was never a great genius without a tincture of madness. (Nullam magnum ingenium sine mixtura dementiae fuit.)

ARISTOTLE
(Seneca, *De Tranquilitate Animi* Bk. i, sec. 15)

Genius is mainly an affair of energy.

MATTHEW ARNOLD
Essays in Criticism "Literary Influence of Academies"

Genius, that power which dazzles mortal eyes,
Is oft but perseverance in disguise.

HENRY AUSTIN
Perseverance Conquers All

Improvement makes straight roads; but the crooked roads without improvement are the roads of Genius.

WILLIAM BLAKE
Proverbs of Hell

Genius is patience. (Le Génie, c'est la patience.)

BUFFON
(Stevens, *Study of the Life and Times of Madame de Staël* Ch. 3)

Genius ... has been defined as a supreme capacity for taking trouble ... It might be more fitly described as a supreme capacity for getting its possessors into trouble of all kinds and keeping them therein so long as the genius remains.

SAMUEL BUTLER
Notebooks "Genius"

Genius is fostered by industry. (Ingenium industria alitur.)

CICERO
Pro Coelio Ch. xix, sec. 45

The first and last thing required of genius is the love of truth. (Das erste und letzte, was vom Genie gefordert wird, ist Wahrheits-liebe.)

GOETHE
Sprüche in Prosa Pt. iii

Rules and models destroy genius and art.

WILLIAM HAZLITT
Sketches and Essays "On Taste"

Gift, like genius, I often think only means an infinite capacity for taking pains.

JANE ELLICE HOPKINS
Work Amongst Working Men

Genius is the capacity of evading hard work.

ELBERT HUBBARD
The Philistine Vol. xi

Genius is the ability to act rightly without precedent— the power to do the right thing the first time.

ELBERT HUBBARD
A Thousand and One Epigrams

Men of genius are often dull and inert in society, as the

blazing meteor when it descends to the earth is only a stone.

HENRY WADSWORTH LONGFELLOW
Kavanagh Ch. 13

The lamp of genius burns more rapidly than the lamp of life. (Das Licht des Genie's bekam weniger Fett, als das Licht des Lebens.)

FRANZ SCHILLER
Fiesco Act ii, sc. 17

Hunger is the handmaid of genius.

MARK TWAIN
Pudd'nhead Wilson's New Calendar

GOD

God is no respecter of persons.

Acts x, 34

For science, God is simply the *stream of tendency by which all things seek to fulfill the law of their being.*

MATTHEW ARNOLD
Literature and Dogma

That we devote ourselves to God, is seen
In living just as though no God were there.

ROBERT BROWNING
Paracelsus Pt. i

An apology for the Devil: It must be remembered that we have only heard one side of the case. God has written all the books.

SAMUEL BUTLER
Note Books "Higgledy-Piggledy. An Apology for the Devil"

God doth not need
Either man's work or his own gifts; who best
Bear his mild yoke, they serve him best; his state
Is kingly. Thousands at his bidding speed
And post o'er land and ocean without rest:
They also serve who only stand and wait.

JOHN MILTON
On His Blindness

I am Alpha and Omega, the beginning and the end, the first and the last.

Revelations xxii, 13

If God did not exist, it would be necessary to invent Him. (Si Dieu n'existait pas, il faudrait l'inventer.)

VOLTAIRE
Epîtres xcvi "A l'Auteur du Livre des Trois Imposteurs"

God for his service needeth not proud work of human skill.

WILLIAM WORDSWORTH
Poet's Dream

GOODNESS

He cannot long be good that knows not why he is good.

RICHARD CAREW
Survey of Cornwall

Inability to tell good from evil is the greatest worry of man's life. (Ignoratione rerum bonarum et malarum, maxime hominum vita vexetur.)

CICERO
De Finibus Bk. i, ch. 13, sec. 43

True goodness springs from a man's own heart. All men are born good.

CONFUCIUS
Analects

None deserves praise for being good who has not spirit enough to be bad: goodness, for the most part, is nothing but indolence or weakness of will. (Nul ne mérite d'être loué de bonté, s'il n'a pas la force d'être méchant, toute autre bonté n'est le plus souvent qu'une paresse ou une impuissance de la volonté.)

FRANCOIS LA ROCHEFOUCAULD
Maximes No. 237

Every country can produce good men. (Alle Länder gute Menschen tragen.)

GOTTHOLD EPHRAIM LESSING
Nathan der Weise Act ii, sc. 5

It is hard to be good.

PITTACUS
(Diogenes Laertius, *Pittacus* Bk. i, sec. 76)

The larger part of goodness is the will to become good. (Itaque pars magna bonitatis est velle fieri bonum.)

SENECA
Epistulæ ad Lucilium Epis. xxxiv, 3

Be good and you will be lonesome.

MARK TWAIN
Following the Equator

He can never be good that is not obstinate.

BISHOP THOMAS WILSON
Maxims of Piety

GOSSIP

Gossip is a vice enjoyed vicariously.

ELBERT HUBBARD
The Philistine Vol. xix

I believe that there is nothing amongst mankind swifter than rumor. (Nullam rem citiorem apud homines esse, quam famam, reor.)

PLAUTUS
Fragment

There is only one thing in the world worse than being talked about, and that is not being talked about.

OSCAR WILDE
Picture of Dorian Gray Ch. 1

GOVERNMENT

The essence of a free government consists in an effectual control of rivalries.

JOHN ADAMS
Discourses on Davila

Royalty is a government in which the attention of the nation is concentrated on one person doing interesting actions. A Republic is a government in which that attention is divided between many, who are all doing uninteresting actions. Accordingly, so long as the human heart is strong and the human reason weak, Royalty will be strong because it appeals to diffused feeling, and Republics weak because they appeal to the understanding.

WALTER BAGEHOT
The English Constitution "The Monarchy"

If any ask me what a free government is, I answer, that, for any practical purpose, it is what the people think so.

EDMUND BURKE
Letter to the Sheriffs of Bristol

Government is a contrivance of human wisdom to provide for human wants. Men have a right that these wants should be provided for by this wisdom.

EDMUND BURKE
Reflections on the Revolution in France

A state without the means of some change is without the means of its conservation.

EDMUND BURKE
Reflections on the Revolution in France

An oppressive government is more to be feared than a tiger.

CONFUCIUS
Analects

Every country has the government it deserves. (Toute nation a le gouvernement qu'elle mérite.)

JOSEPH DE MAISTRE
Lettres et Opuscules Inédits Ch. I

A Conservative Government is an organized hypocrisy.

BENJAMIN DISRAELI
Speech March 17, 1845

The divine right of kings may have been a plea for feeble tyrants, but the divine right of government is the keystone of human progress, and without it government sinks into police and nation into a mob.

BENJAMIN DISRAELI
Lothair "Preface"

No Government can be long secure without a formidable Opposition.

BENJAMIN DISRAELI
Coningsby Bk. ii, ch. 1

The teaching of politics is that the Government, which was set for protection and comfort of all good citizens, becomes the principal obstruction and nuisance with which we have to contend ... The cheat and bully and malefactor we meet everywhere is the Government.

RALPH WALDO EMERSON
Journal 1860

An institution is the lengthened shadow of one man.

RALPH WALDO EMERSON
Essays, First Series "Self-Reliance"

Every actual State is corrupt.

RALPH WALDO EMERSON
Essays, Second Series "Politics"

I would not give half a guinea to live under one form of government rather than another. It is of no moment to the happiness of an individual.

SAMUEL JOHNSON
(Boswell, *Life* Ch. II)

Freedom of men under government is to have a standing rule to live by, common to every one of that society, and made by the legislative power vested in it; a liberty to follow my own will in all things, when the rule prescribes not, and not to be subject to the inconstant, uncertain, un-known, arbitrary will of another man.

JOHN LOCKE
On Government Bk. x, ch. 4

He that would govern others, first should be
The master of himself.

PHILLIP MASSINGER
The Bondman I, iii

Government, even in its best state, is but a necessary evil; in its worst state, an intolerable one.

THOMAS PAINE
Common Sense Ch. I

A hated government does not endure long. (Invisa numquam imperia, retinentur diu.)

SENECA
Phoenissae

In general, the art of government consists in taking as much money as possible from one class of citizens to give it to the other.

VOLTAIRE
A Philosophical Dictionary "Money"

GRATITUDE

What soon grows old? Gratitude.

ARISTOTLE

Next to ingratitude, the most painful thing to bear is gratitude.

HENRY WARD BEECHER
Proverbs From Plymouth Pulpit

Gratitude is a fruit of great cultivation; you do not find it among gross people.

SAMUEL JOHNSON
Tour to the Hebrides

I thank you for nothing, because I understand nothing.

JOHN LYLY
Mother Bombie

And name it gratitude, the word is poor.

GEORGE MEREDITH
The Sage Enamoured

One good turn deserves another. (Manus manum lavat.)

PETRONIUS
Satyricon Sec. 45

Let the man, who would be grateful, think of repaying a kindness, even while receiving it. (Qui gratus futurus est, statim, dum accipit, de reddendo cogitet.)

SENECA
De Beneficiis Bk. ii, ch. 25, sec. 3

GREATNESS

No great man lives in vain. The history of the world is but the biography of great men.

THOMAS CARLYLE
Heroes and Hero-Worship "The Hero as Divinity"

Man is only truly great when he acts from the passions.

BENJAMIN DISRAELI
Coningsby Bk. iv, ch. 13

GUILT

It is better that ten guilty persons escape than that one innocent suffer.

SIR WILLIAM BLACKSTONE
Commentaries Vol. iv, ch. 27

Guilt is present in the very hesitation, even though the deed be not committed. (In ipsa dubitatione facinus inest, etiamsi ad id non pervenerint.)

CICERO
De Officiis Bk. iii, ch. 8, sec. 37

Guilt has very quick ears to an accusation.

HENRY FIELDING
Amelia Bk. iii, ch. 11

It is so natural and easy to despise heavenly witnesses of our guilt, if only no mortal knows of it. (Tam facile et pronum est superos contemnere testes, Si mortalis idem nemo sciat!)

JUVENAL
Satires Sat. xiii, ch. 75

He that knows no guilt can know no fear.

PHILIP MASSINGER
The Great Duke of Florence Act iv, sc. 2

Suspicion always haunts the guilty mind.

WILLIAM SHAKESPEARE
III Henry VI Act v, sc. 6

HABIT

Men acquire a particular quality by constantly acting in a particular way.

ARISTOTLE
Nicomachean Ethics Bk. iii

A nail is driven out by another nail, habit is overcome by habit. (Clabus clavo pellitur, consuetudo consuetudine vincitur.)

ERASMUS
Diluculum

Habit is second nature.

MONTAIGNE
Essays Bk. iii

But when the fox hath once got in his nose,
He'll soon find means to make the body follow.

WILLIAM SHAKESPEARE
III Henry VI Act iv, sc. 7

HAPPINESS

That action is best, which procures the greatest happiness for the greatest number.

FRANCIS HUTCHESON
Concerning Moral Good and Evil Sec. 3, 8

One is never so happy or so unhappy as one thinks. (On n'est jamais si heureux ni si malheureux qu'on s'imagine.)

FRANCOIS LA ROCHEFOUCAULD
Maximes 49

Happiness is no laughing matter.

RICHARD WHATELY
Apophthegms

HELL

Hell is more bearable than nothingness.

P. J. BAILEY
Festus "Heaven"

Hell is paved with infants' skulls.

RICHARD BAXTER

Hell is a circle about the unbelieving.

The Koran

What you Kansas farmers ought to do is to raise less corn and raise more hell.

MRS. MARY ELIZABETH CLYENS LEASE
Speech 1890

The way to Hell's a seeming Heav'n.

FRANCIS QUARLES
Emblems Bk. ii

Hell is paved with good intentions.

JOHN RAY
English Proverbs

If I owned Texas and Hell, I would rent out Texas and live in Hell.

GENERAL PHILIP H. SHERIDAN

That's the greatest torture souls feel in hell:
In hell, that they must live, and cannot die.

DANIEL WEBSTER
Duchess of Malfi Act iv, sc. 1

HEROISM

I am convinced that a light supper, a good night's sleep, and a fine morning, have sometimes made a hero of the same man, who by an indigestion, a restless night, and rainy morning, would have proved a coward.

LORD CHESTERFIELD
Letters April 26, 1748

No man is a hero to his valet.(Il n'y a point de héros pour son valet de chambre.)

MADAME CORNUEL
Letters de Mlle. Aisse

To believe in the heroic makes heroes.

BENJAMIN DISRAELI
Coningsby Bk. iii, ch. 1

Each man is a hero and an oracle to somebody.

RALPH WALDO EMERSON
Letters and Social Aims "Quotation and Originality"

Every hero becomes a bore at last.

RALPH WALDO EMERSON
Representative Men "Uses of Great Men"

It is fortune (or chance) chiefly that makes heroes.

THOMAS FULLER
Gnomologia

The greatest obstacle to being heroic is the doubt whether one may not be going to prove one's self a fool; the truest heroism is to resist the doubt, and the profoundest wisdom to know when it ought to be resisted, and when to be obeyed.

NATHANIEL HAWTHORNE
The Blithedale Romance Ch. 2

There are heroes in evil as well as in good. (Il y a des héros en mal comme en bien.)

FRANCOIS LA ROCHEFOUCAULD
Maximes No. 185

See the conquering hero comes!
Sound the trumpets, beat the drums!

DR. THOMAS MORELL

One brave deed makes no hero.

JOHN GREENLEAF WHITTIER
The Hero

HISTORY

Even God cannot change the past.

AGATHON
(Aristotle, *Nicomachean Ethics*)

Happy is the nation without a history.

BECCARIA
Trattato dei Delitti e Delle Pene

It has been said that although God cannot alter the past, historians can; it is perhaps because they can be useful to Him in this respect that He tolerates their existence.

SAMUEL BUTLER
Erewhon Ch. 14

History, a distillation of Rumour.

THOMAS CARLYLE
The French Revolution Pt. i, bk. vii, ch. 5

Historians ought to be precise, faithful, and unprejudiced; and neither interest nor fear, hatred nor affection, should make them swerve from the way of the truth.

CERVANTES
Don Quixote Pt. 1, ch. 9

History is only a confused heap of facts.

LORD CHESTERFIELD
Letters February 5, 1750

Read no history: nothing but biography, for that is life without theory.

BENJAMIN DISRAELI
Contarini Fleming Pt. i, ch. 23

There is properly no history; only biography.

RALPH WALDO EMERSON
Essays "History"

History is bunk.

HENRY FORD

Sin writes histories, goodness is silent.

GOETHE
Table-Talk

History owes its excellency more to the writer's manner, than to the material of which it is composed.

OLIVER GOLDSMITH
Life of Richard Nash

The historian is a sort of talking ghost from out of the past.

ERNST HOFFMAN
Doge and Dogaressa

Seldom any splendid story is wholly true.
SAMUEL JOHNSON
Works Vol. ii

Had Cleopatra's nose been shorter, the whole history of the world would have been different. (Le nez de Cléopâtre, s'il eût été plus court, toute la face de la terre aurait changé.)
BLAISE PASCAL
Pensées

History is the crystallisation of popular beliefs.
DONN PIATT
Memories of Men Who Saved the Union "Abraham Lincoln"

History, however it is written, always pleases. (Historia quoquo moda scripta delectat.)
PLINY THE YOUNGER
Epistles Bk. v, epis. 8

Ancient histories, as one of our wits has said, are but fables that have been agreed upon. (Toutes les histoires anciens, comme le disait un de nos beaux esprits, ne sont que des fables convenues.)
VOLTAIRE
Jeannot et Colin

The history of the great events of this world is scarcely more than the history of crimes. (L'histoire des grands évènements de ce monde n'est guère que l'histoire des crimes.)
VOLTAIRE
Essai sur les Moeurs

Anybody can make history. Only a great man can write it.
OSCAR WILDE
Aphorisms

HOME

Whom God loves, his house is sweet to him.
CERVANTES
Don Quixote Pt. ii, ch. 43

For a man's house is his castle. (Et domus sua cuique tutissimum refugium.)
SIR EDWARD COKE
Institutes "Commentary upon Littleton"

My idea of a home is a house in which each member of the family can on the instant kindle a fire in his or her private room.
RALPH WALDO EMERSON
Journals

Home is where the heart is.
PLINY

HOSPITALITY

Hospitality consists in a little fire, a little food, and an immense quiet.
RALPH WALDO EMERSON
Journal 1856

Be not forgetful to entertain strangers: for thereby some have entertained angels unawares.
Hebrews xiii, 2

Wherever the storm carries me, I go a willing guest. (Quo me cumque rapit tempestas, deferor hospes.)
HORACE
Epistles Bk. i, epis. i

The first day a man is a guest, the second a burden, the third a pest.
EDOUARD LABOULAYE
Abdallah Ch. 9

It is more disgraceful to turn out a guest than not to admit him. (Turpius ejicitur, quam non admittitur hospes.)
OVID
Tristia Bk. v, eleg. 6

HOPE

Hope springs eternal in the human breast:
Man never is, but always to be, blest.
The soul, uneasy and confin'd from home,
Rests and expatiates in a life to come.
ALEXANDER POPE
Essay on Man Epis. i

HYPOCRISY

Your cold hypocrisy's a stale device,
A worn-out trick; wouldst thou be thought in earnest,
Clothe thy feign'd zeal in rage, in fire, in fury!
JOSEPH ADDISON
Cato Act i, sc. 3

An ill man is always ill, but he is worst of all when he pretends to be a saint. (Malus ubi bonum se simulat, tunc est pessimus.)
FRANCIS BACON
Ornamenta Rationalia No. 28

The only vice that cannot be forgiven is hypocrisy. The repentance of a hypocrite is itself hypocrisy.
WILLIAM HAZLITT
Characteristics No. 256

Hypocrisy is a homage which vice pays to virtue. (L'hypocrisie est un hommage que le vice rend à la virtue.)
FRANCOIS LA ROCHEFOUCAULD
Maximes No. 218

I hate a bad man saying what is good.
MENANDER
Fragments No. 767

IGNORANCE

To be ignorant of one's ignorance is the malady of the ignorant.
AMOS BRONSON ALCOTT
Table Talk "Discourse"

Ignorance is not innocence, but sin.
ROBERT BROWNING
The Inn Album Canto v

The truest characters of ignorance
Are vanity, and pride, and arrogance.
SAMUEL BUTLER
Miscellaneous Thoughts

If there are two things not to be hidden—love and a cough—I say there is a third, and that is ignorance, when once a man is obliged to do something besides wagging his head.

GEORGE ELIOT
Romola

Ignorance of one's misfortunes is clear gain.

EURIPIDES
Antiope Frag. 204

Where ignorance is bliss,
'Tis folly to be wise.

THOMAS GRAY
Ode on a Distant Prospect of Eton College

Better unborn than untaught.

JOHN HEYWOOD
Proverbs Bk. i, ch. 10

The recipe for perpetual ignorance is: be satisfied with your opinions and content with your knowledge.

ELBERT HUBBARD
The Philistine Vol. v

There is no slavery but ignorance.

R. G. INGERSOLL
Liberty of Man, Woman, and Child

He that voluntarily continues in ignorance, is guilty of all the crimes which ignorance produces.

SAMUEL JOHNSON
Letter to Mr. W. Drummond

Ignorance is a voluntary misfortune.

UNKNOWN
Politeuphuia

IMAGINATION

The human race is governed by its imagination. (C'est l'imagination qui gouverne le genre humain.)

NAPOLEON BONAPARTE
(Bourrienne, *Life*)

Imagination is not a talent of some men but is the health of every man.

RALPH WALDO EMERSON
Letters and Social Aims "Poetry and Imagination"

Them that build castles in the air.

SIR PHILIP SIDNEY
Apology for Poetry

INNOCENCE

Innocence is no protection.

THOMAS FULLER
Gnomologia No. 3100

The exactest vigilance and caution can never maintain a single day of unmingled innocence.

SAMUEL JOHNSON
The Rambler No. 14

INTELLIGENCE

The only means of strengthening one's intellect is to make up one's mind about nothing—to let the mind be a thoroughfare for all thoughts. Not a select party.

JOHN KEATS
Letters 156 September 17, 1819

To perceive things in the germ is intelligenced.

LAO-TSZE
The Simple Way No. 52

JUSTICE

Justice is truth in action.

BENJAMIN DISRAELI
Speech February 11, 1851

The most fluent talkers or most plausible reasoners are not always the justest thinkers.

WILLIAM HAZLITT
Sketches and Essays "On Prejudice"

A lawyer has no business with the justice or injustice of the cause which he undertakes, unless his client asks his opinion, and then he is bound to give it honestly. The justice or injustice of the cause is to be decided by the judge.

SAMUEL JOHNSON
(Boswell, *Tour to the Hebrides*)

Justice is the constant and perpetual wish to render to every one his due. (Justitia est constans et perpetua voluntas jus suum cuique tribuens.)

EMPEROR JUSTINIAN
Institutiones

KNOWLEDGE

Knowledge is of two kinds. We know a subject ourselves, or we know where we can find information upon it.

SAMUEL JOHNSON
(Boswell, *Life*)

The trouble with people is not that they don't know but that they know so much that ain't so.

HENRY WHEELER SHAW
Josh Billings' Encyclopedia of Wit and Wisdom

LANGUAGE

Language is called the garment of thought: however it should rather be, language is the flesh-garment, the body, of thought.

THOMAS CARLYLE
Sartor Resartus Bk. i, ch. 11

Language is the dress of thought.

SAMUEL JOHNSON
(Hill, *Lives of the English Poets* Vol. i)

LAWS

Bad laws are the worst sort of tyranny.

EDMUND BURKE
Speech 1780

Necessity has no law; I know some attorneys of the same.

BENJAMIN FRANKLIN
Poor Richard's Almanack

A man may as well open an oyster without a knife, as a lawyer's mouth without a fee.

BARTEN HOLYDAY
Technogamia Ch. ii

Laws were made to be broken.

CHRISTOPHER NORTH (JOHN WILSON)
Noctes Ambrosianae No. 24 May, 1830

Ignorance of the law excuses no man; not that all men know the law, but because 'tis an excuse every man will plead, and no man can tell how to confute him.

JOHN SELDON
Table Talk "Law"

The New England folks have a saying that three Philadelphia lawyers are a match for the very devil himself.

UNKNOWN
Salem Observer

We expect legislation to conform to public opinion, not public opinion to yield to legislation.
Report of Wickersham Commission

LIBERTY

Abstract liberty, like other mere abstractions, is not to be found.

EDMUND BURKE
Speech March 22, 1775

Is life so dear, or peace so sweet, as to be purchased at the price of chains and slavery? Forbid it, Almighty God! I know not what course others may take; but, as for me, give me liberty, or give me death!

PATRICK HENRY
Speech March 23, 1775

We can never be sure that the opinion we are endeavouring to stifle is a false opinion; and if we were sure, it would be an evil still.

JOHN STUART MILL
Liberty Ch. 2

If all mankind minus one, were of one opinion, and only one person were of the contrary opinion, mankind would be no more justified in silencing that one person, than he, if he had the power, would be justified in silencing mankind.

JOHN STUART MILL
Liberty Ch. 2

The liberty of the individual must be thus far limited; he must not make himself a nuisance to other people.

JOHN STUART MILL
Liberty Ch. 3

Liberty consists in doing what one desires.

JOHN STUART MILL
Liberty Ch. 5

LIES

Liars ought to have good memories.

ALGERNON SIDNEY
Discourses on Government Ch. 2

The cruelest lies are often told in silence.

ROBERT LOUIS STEVENSON
Virginibus Puerisque "Truth of Intercourse"

LIFE

Life is one long process of getting tired.

SAMUEL BUTLER
Note Books "Life"

Life is the art of drawing sufficient conclusions from insufficient premises.

SAMUEL BUTLER
Note Books "Life"

Youth is a blunder; Manhood a struggle; Old Age a regret.

BENJAMIN DISRAELI
Coningsby Bk. iii, ch. 1

At twenty years of age, the will reigns; at thirty, the wit; and at forty, the judgment.

BENJAMIN FRANKLIN
Poor Richard's Almanack

Life is a jest; and all things show it.
I thought so once; but now I know it.

JOHN GAY
My Own Epitaph

Custom, then, is the great guide of human life.

DAVID HUME
Inquiry Concerning Human Understanding Sec. v

The chess-board is the world; the pieces are the phenomena of the universe; the rules of the game are what we call the laws of Nature. The player on the other side is hidden from us. We know that his play is always fair, just, and patient. But also we know, to our cost, that he never overlooks a mistake, or makes the smallest allowance for ignorance.

THOMAS HENRY HUXLEY
Lay Sermons "A Liberal Education"

Into each life some rain must fall,
Some days must be dark and dreary.

HENRY WADSWORTH LONGFELLOW
The Rainy Day

Man shall not live by bread alone.

Matthew iv, 4

This world is a comedy to those that think, a tragedy to those who feel.

HORACE WALPOLE
Letters to the Countess of Upper Ossory

LOVE

It's love, it's love that makes the world go round.

ANONYMOUS
Chansons Nationales et Populaires de France Vol. ii

Nuptial love maketh mankind; friendly love perfecteth it; wanton love corrupteth and debaseth it.

FRANCIS BACON
Essays "Of Love"

'Tis impossible to love and be wise.

FRANCIS BACON
Essays "Of Love"

Love is a fiend, a fire, a heaven, a hell,
Where pleasure, pain, and sad repentance dwell.

RICHARD BARNFIELD
The Shepherd's Content St. 38

Of all the paths that lead to a woman's love
Pity's the straightest.

BEAUMONT AND FLETCHER
The Knight of Malta Act i, sc. 1

Thou shalt love thy neighbor.

Leviticus xix, 19

The only victory over love is flight.

NAPOLEON BONAPARTE
(O'Meara, *Napoleon in Exile*)

The first sigh of love is the last of wisdom. (Le premier soupir de l'amour est le dernier de la sagesse.)

ANTOINE BRET
Ecole Amoureuse Sc. 7

O, my Luve's like a red red rose
That's newly sprung in June:
O my Luve's like the melodie
That's sweetly played in tune.

ROBERT BURNS
A Red Red Rose

'Tis better to have loved and lost, than never to have lost at all.

SAMUEL BUTLER
The Way of All Flesh Ch. 77

For money has a power above
The stars and fate, to manage love.

SAMUEL BUTLER
Hudibras Ch. 3

Man's love is of man's life a thing apart,
'Tis woman's whole existence: man may range
The court, camp, church, the vessel and the mart,
Sword, gown, gain, glory, offer in exchange
Pride, fame, ambition, to fill his heart,
And few there are whom these cannot estrange;
Men have all these resources, we but one,
To love again, and be again undone.

LORD GEORGE BYRON
Don Juan C. I, 194

In all her first passion woman loves her lover,
In all the others all she loves is love.

LORD GEORGE BYRON
Don Juan C. III, 3

Better be courted and jilted,
Than never be courted at all.

THOMAS CAMPBELL
The Jilted Nymph

Love is ever the beginning of Knowledge as fire is of light.

THOMAS CARLYLE
Essays "Death of Goethe"

There is no love lost between us.

CERVANTES
Don Quixote Bk. iv, ch. 23

For love is blind all day and may not see.

GEOFFREY CHAUCER
The Marchantes Tale

Say what you will, 'tis better to be left than never to have been loved.

WILLIAM CONGREVE
The Way of the World II, i

But love's a malady without a cure.

JOHN DRYDEN
Palamon and Arcite Bk. ii

All mankind love a lover.

RALPH WALDO EMERSON
Essays "Love"

Love and scandal are the best sweeteners of tea.

HENRY FIELDING
Love in Several Masques IV, xi

Youth's the season made for joys,
Love is then our duty.

JOHN GAY
The Beggar's Opera Act I, sc. 4

It is the special quality of love not to be able to remain stationary, to be obliged to increase under pain of diminishing.

ANDRE GIDE
The Counterfeiters Pt. iii, ch. 5

If I love you, what business is that of yours? (Wenn ich dich lieb habe, was geht's dich an?)

GOETHE
Wilhelm Meister Bk. iv, ch. 9

The love of liberty is the love of others; the love of power is the love of ourselves.

WILLIAM HAZLITT
Political Essays

If you would be loved, love. (Si vis amari, ama.)

HECATO
Fragments No. 27 (Seneca, *Epistuloe ad Lucilium* Epis. ix, sec. 6)

Love and a cough cannot be hid.

GEORGE HERBERT
Jacula Prudentum

In love, there are these evils: first war, and then peace. (In amore haec sunt mala: bellum, Pax rursum.)

HORACE
Satires Bk. ii, sat. 3

A woman's whole life is a history of the affections.

WASHINGTON IRVING
The Sketch Book "The Broken Heart"

Love's like the measles—all the worse when it comes late in life.

DOUGLAS WILLIAM JERROLD
Wit and Opinions of Douglas Jerrold

Greater love hath no man than this, that a man lay down his life for his friends.

St. John xv, 13

Love is only one of many passions . . . and has no great influence on the sum of life.

SAMUEL JOHNSON
Works Vol. ix

Love is the wisdom of the fool and the folly of the wise.

SAMUEL JOHNSON
"Johnsonian Miscellanies" (William Cooke, *Life of Samuel Foote*)

Young men make great mistakes in life; for one thing, they idealize love too much.

BENJAMIN JOWETT
Letters

There are many people who would never have been in love if they had never heard love spoken of. (Il y a des gens qui n'auraient jamais été amoureux, s'ils n'avaient jamais entendu parler de l'amour.)

> FRANCOIS LA ROCHEFOUCAULD
> *Maximes* No. 136

There is only one kind of love, but there are a thousand imitations. (Il n'y a que d'une sorte d'amour, mais il y en a mille differentes copies.)

> FRANCOIS LA ROCHEFOUCAULD
> *Maximes* No. 74

The reason why lovers and their mistresses never tire of being together is because they are always talking of themselves. (Ce qui fait que les amants et les maîtresses ne s'ennuient point d'être ensemble, c'est qu'ils parlent toujours d'eux-mêmes.)

> FRANCOIS LA ROCHEFOUCAULD
> *Maximes* No. 312

Take love away from life and you take away its pleasures. (Otez l'amour de la vie, Vous en ôtez les plaisirs.)

> MOLIERE
> *Le Bourgeois Gentilhomme*
> Dialogue between acts i and ii

To live without loving is not really to live. (Vivre sans aimer n'est pas proprement vivre.)

> MOLIERE
> *La Princesse d'Elide* Act ii, sc. 1

Love is nothing else but an insatiate thirst of enjoying a greedily desired object.

> MONTAIGNE
> *Essays* Bk. iii, ch. 5

That you may be loved, be lovable. (Ut ameris, amabilis esto.)

> OVID
> *Ars Amatoria* Bk. ii

By habit love enters the mind; by habit is love unlearnt. (Intrat amor mentes usu, dediscitur usu.)

> OVID
> *Remediorum Amoris*

Whom we love best, to them we can say least.

> JOHN RAY
> *English Proverbs* 47

The sight of lovers feedeth those in love.

> WILLIAM SHAKESPEARE
> *As You Like It* Act iii, sc. 4

Love sought is good, but given unsought is better.

> WILLIAM SHAKESPEARE
> *Twelfth Night* Act iii, sc. 1

But love is blind, and lovers cannot see
The pretty follies that themselves commit.

> WILLIAM SHAKESPEARE
> *The Merchant of Venice* Act ii, sc. 4

Love is the salt of life.

> JOHN SHEFFIELD
> "Ode on Love" Canto v

All's fair in love and war.

> F. E. SMEDLEY
> *Frank Farlegh* ch. 50

Love is commenced at the mind's bidding, but is not cast off by it. (Amor animi arbitrio sumitur, non ponitur.)

> PUBLILIUS SYRUS
> *Sententiæ* No. 5

Man is the hunter; woman is his game.

> ALFRED LORD TENNYSON
> *The Princess*

The less my hope the hotter my love. (Quanto minus spei est tanto magis amo.)

> TERENCE
> *Eunuchus* Act v, sc. 4

Yet each man kills the thing he loves,
By each let this be heard,
Some do it with a bitter look,
Some with a flattering word.
The coward does it with a kiss,
The brave man with a sword!

> OSCAR WILDE
> *The Ballad of Reading Gaol* Pt. i, vii

MAN

It is the common wonder of all men, how among so many millions of faces, there should be none alike.

> SIR THOMAS BROWNE
> *Religio Medici* Pt. ii, sec. 2

Man is a tool-using animal ... Without tools he is nothing, with tools he is all.

> THOMAS CARLYLE
> *Sartor Resartus* Bk. i, ch. 5

Man does not live by bread alone, but by faith, by admiration, by sympathy.

> RALPH WALDO EMERSON
> *Lectures and Biographical Sketches*
> "The Sovereignty of Ethics"

Whoso would be a man would be a nonconformist.

> RALPH WALDO EMERSON
> *Essays* "Self-Reliance"

No doubt but ye are the people and wisdom shall die with you.

> *Job* xii, 2

The human species, according to the best theory I can form of it, is composed of two distinct races, the men who borrow, and the men who lend.

> CHARLES LAMB
> *Essays of Elia* "The Two Races of Men"

The Lord prefers common-looking people. That is the reason He makes so many of them.

> ABRAHAM LINCOLN

Men are never so good or so bad as their opinions.

> SIR JAMES MACKINTOSH
> (Bentham, *Ethical Philosophy*)

Blessed are the poor in spirit: for their's is the kingdom of heaven.
Blessed are they that mourn: for they shall be comforted.

Blessed are the meek: for they shall inherit the earth.
Blessed are they which do hunger and thirst after righteousness: for they shall be filled.
Blessed are the merciful: for they shall obtain mercy.
Blessed are the pure in heart: for they shall see God.
Blessed are the peacemakers: for they shall be called the children of God.

St. Matthew v, 3

Man is only a reed, the weakest thing in nature; but he is a thinking reed. (L'homme n'est qu'un roseau, le plus faible de la nature; mais c'est un roseau pensant.)

BLAISE PASCAL
Pensées vi

Men are generally more careful of the breed of their horses and dogs than of their children.

WILLIAM PENN
Reflexions and Maxims Pt. i, no. 85

Out—out are the lights—out all!
And, over each quivering form,
The curtain, a funeral pall,
Comes down with the rush of a storm,
And the angels, all pallid and wan,
Uprising, unveiling, affirm
That the play is the tragedy, "Man,"
And its hero, the Conqueror Worm.

EDGAR ALLEN POE
The Conqueror Worm St. 5

Know then thyself, Presume not God to scan,
The proper study of mankind is man.
Placed on this isthmus of a middle state,
A being darkly wise, and rudely great:
With too much knowledge for the sceptic's side,
With too much weakness for the stoic's pride,
He hangs between; in doubt to act or rest;
In doubt to deem himself a god, or beast;
In doubt his mind or body to prefer;
Born but to die, and reasoning but to err;
Alike in ignorance, his reason such,
Whether he thinks too little or too much;
Chaos of thought and passion, all confused;
Still by himself abused, or disabused;
Created half to rise and half to fall;
Great lord of all things, yet a prey to all;
Sole judge of truth, in endless error hurled;
The glory, jest, and riddle of the world!

ALEXANDER POPE
An Essay on Man Ep. ii

The mass of men lead lives of quiet desperation.

HENRY DAVID THOREAU
Walden "Economy"

I think I could turn and live with animals, they are so placid and self-contain'd,
I stand and look at them long and long.
They do not sweat and whine about their condition,
They do not lie awake in the dark and weep for their sins,
They do not make me sick discussing their duty to God,
Not one is dissatisfied, not one is demented with the mania of owning things,
Not one kneels to another, nor to his kind that lived thousands of years ago,
Not one is respectable or unhappy over the whole earth.

WALT WHITMAN
Song of Myself

At thirty man suspects himself a fool;
Knows it at forty, and reforms his plan;
At fifty chides his infamous delay,
Pushes his prudent purpose to resolve;
In all the magnanimity of thought
Resolves; and re-resolves; then dies the same.

EDWARD YOUNG
The Complaint; Night Thoughts

MARRIAGE

Certainly, the best works and of greatest merit for the public, have proceeded from the unmarried and childless men.

FRANCIS BACON
Essays "Of Marriage and Single Life"

Marriage: the state or condition of a community consisting of a master, a mistress, and two slaves, making in all, two.

AMBROSE BIERCE
Devil's Dictionary

One was never married, and that's his hell; another is and that's his plague.

ROBERT BURTON
Anatomy of Melancholy Pt. i, sec. ii

There are but two objects in marriage, love or money. If you marry for love, you will certainly have some very happy days, and probably many very uneasy ones; if for money, you will have no happy days and probably no uneasy ones.

LORD CHESTERFIELD
Letters

Oh! how many torments lie in the small circle of a wedding-ring!

COLLEY CIBBER
Double Gallant Act i, sc. 2

The first bond of society is marriage. (Prima societas in ipso conjugio est.)

CICERO
De Officiis Bk. i, ch. 17

The most happy marriage I can picture or imagine to myself would be the union of a deaf man to a blind woman.

SAMUEL TAYLOR COLERIDGE
(Allsop, *Recollections*)

Marry in haste, repent at leisure.

WILLIAM CONGREVE
Old Batchelor Act v, sc. 8

Marry first and love will follow.

HANNAH COWLEY
The Belle's Stratagem Act iii, sc. 1

Misses! the tale that I relate
This lesson seems to carry—
Choose not alone a proper mate,
But proper time to marry.

WILLIAM COWPER
Pairing Time Anticipated "Moral"

Every woman should—and no man.

BENJAMIN DISRAELI
Lothair Ch. 30

It is a maxim that man and wife should never have it in their power to hang one another.

> GEORGE FARQUHAR
> *The Beaux' Stratagem* Act iv, sc. 2

Where there's marriage without love, there will be love without marriage.

> BENJAMIN FRANKLIN
> *Poor Richard's Almanack*

The woes of wedlock with the joys, we mix;
'Tis best repenting in a coach and six.

> SAMUEL GARTH
> *Cato* "Prologue"

Therefore shall a man leave his father and his mother, and shall cleave unto his wife: and they shall be one flesh.

> Genesis ii, 24

Such as marry but to a fair face, tie themselves oft to a foul bargain.

> ROBERT GREENE
> *Works* Vol. viii

Marry your son when you will, your daughter when you can.

> GEORGE HERBERT
> *Jacula Prudentum*

Husband and wife come to look alike at last.

> O. W. HOLMES
> *The Professor at the Breakfast-Table* Ch. 7

No man likes to live under the eye of perpetual disapprobation.

> SAMUEL JOHNSON
> (Boswell, *Life*)

Marriage has many pains, but celibacy has no pleasures.

> SAMUEL JOHNSON
> *Rasselas* Ch. 26

Marriage, if one will face the truth, is an evil, but a necessary evil.

> MENANDER
> *Fragments* No. 651

'Tis unlucky to marry in the month of May. (Mense malum Maio nubere.)

> OVID
> *Fasti* Eleg. v

Marry in Lent, live to repent.

> JOHN RAY
> *English Proverbs*

Marry in May, repent alway.

> JOHN RAY
> *English Proverbs*

Wedlock is a padlock.

> JOHN RAY
> *English Proverbs*

She who is born handsome is born married.

> JOHN RAY
> *English Proverbs*

Of all actions of a man's life, his marriage does least concern other people; yet of all of our actions of our life, 'tis most meddled with by other people.

> JOHN SELDEN
> *Table-Talk* "Marriage"

You may think you had a conscience, but what is a conscience to a wife?... To marry is to domesticate the Recording Angel.

> ROBERT LOUIS STEVENSON
> *Virginibus Puerisque* Pt. ii

Remember, it is as easy to marry a rich woman as a poor woman.

> WILLIAM MAKEPEACE THACKERAY
> *Pendennis* Ch. 28

Monday for wealth, Tuesday for health,
Wednesday the best day of all:
Thursday for crosses, Friday for losses,
Saturday no luck at all.

> UNKNOWN
> (Brand, *Popular Antiquities*)

Marriage is the only adventure open to the cowardly.

> VOLTAIRE
> *Pensées d'un Philosophe*

The one charm of marriage is that it makes a life of deception absolutely necessary for both parties.

> OSCAR WILDE
> *Picture of Dorian Gray* Ch. 1

Men marry because they are tired; women because they are curious. Both are disappointed.

> OSCAR WILDE
> *A Woman of No Importance* Act iii

One should always be in love. That is the reason one should never marry.

> OSCAR WILDE
> *A Woman of No Importance* Act iii

Nowadays all the married men live like bachelors, and all the bachelors live like married men.

> OSCAR WILDE
> *Picture of Dorian Gray* Ch. 15

MELANCHOLY

Melancholy men of all others are most witty.

> ARISTOTLE
> (Burton, *Anatomy of Melancholy* Pt. 1)

There is no greater cause of melancholy than idleness; "no better cure than business," as Rhasis holds.

> ROBERT BURTON
> *Anatomy of Melancholy* "Democritus to the Reader"

MISERY

It is a miserable state of mind to have few things to desire, and many things to fear.

> FRANCIS BACON
> *Essays* "Of Empire"

It is misery enough to have once been happy.

> JOHN CLARKE
> *Paroemiologia*

He beareth his misery best that hideth it most.

> GABRIEL HARVEY
> *Marginalia*

Misery is but the shadow of happiness. Happiness is but the cloak of misery.

LAO-TSZE
The Simple Way No. 58

Misery loves company.

JOHN RAY
English Proverbs

MONEY

A fool and his money are soon parted.

GEORGE BUCHANAN
tutor to James VI of Scotland

If you would know the value of money, go and try to borrow some.

BENJAMIN FRANKLIN
Poor Richard's Almanak

The love of money is the root of all evil.

Timothy vi, 10

MORALITY

Not the whiteness of years but of morals is to be praised. (Non annorum canities est laudanda, sed morum.)

AMBROSIUS
Epistles Bk. i, epis. 18

All good moral philosophy is but an handmaiden to religion.

FRANCIS BACON
Advancement of Learning xxii, 14

The foundations of morality are like all other foundations: if you dig too much about them the superstructure will come tumbling down.

SAMUEL BUTLER THE YOUNGER
Note-books

"Tut, tut, child!" said the Duchess. "Every thing's got a moral, if only you can find it."

LEWIS CARROLL
Alice's Adventures in Wonderland Ch. 9

The moral system of the universe is like a document written in alternate ciphers, which change from line to line.

JAMES ANTHONY FROUDE
Short Studies on Greag Subjects "Calvanism"

There are many religions, but there is only one morality.

JOHN RUSKIN
Lectures on Art Lect. ii, sec. 37

If thy morals make thee dreary, depend upon it they are wrong.

ROBERT LOUIS STEVENSON
A Christmas Sermon

There is no such thing as morality; it is not immoral for the tiger to eat the wolf, or the wolf the cat, or the cat the bird, and so on down; that is their business ... It is not immoral to create the human species—with or without ceremony; nature intended exactly these things.

MARK TWAIN
(Paine, *Mark Twain*)

Morality is simply the attitude we adopt towards people we personally dislike.

OSCAR WILDE
An Ideal Husband Act ii

NATIONS

States, like men, have their growth, their manhood, their decrepitude, their decay.

WALTER SAVAGE LANDOR
Imaginary Conversations "Leonora di Este and Panigarola"

In the field of world policy, I would dedicate this nation to the policy of the good neighbor.

FRANKLIN DELANO ROOSEVELT
First Inaugural Address March 4, 1933

NATURE

Nature is cruel, man is sick of blood;
Nature is stubborn, man would fain adore;
Nature is fickle, man hath no need of rest;
Nature forgives no debt, and fears no grave.

MATTHEW ARNOLD
Man and Nature

Nature is not governed except by obeying her.

FRANCIS BACON
De Augmentis Scientiarum Pt. ii, bk. 1

Nature means Necessity.

P. J. BAILEY
Festus "Dedication"

Nature does nothing in vain. (Natura nihil agit frustra.)

SIR THOMAS BROWNE
Religio Medici Pt. i, sec. 19

Whatever befalls in accordance with Nature should be accounted good. (Omnia autem, quaesecundum naturam fiunt, sunt habenda in bonis.)

CICERO
De Senectute Ch. xix, sec. 71

Nature tells every secret once.

RALPH WALDO EMERSON
Conduct of Life "Behavior"

When nature has work to be done, she creates a genius to do it.

RALPH WALDO EMERSON
Method of Nature

Nature is the true law.

JOHN FLORIO
First Fruites

To be beautiful and to be calm is the ideal of nature.

RICHARD JEFFERIES
The Pageant of Summer

Nature does not proceed by leaps. (Natura non facit saltus.)

CARL LINNAEUS
Philosophia Botanica Sec. 77

Nature abhors a vacuum. (Natura abhorret vacuum.)

FRANCOIS RABELAIS
Works Bk. i, ch. 5

I have no enthusiasm for nature which the slightest chill will not instantly destroy.

GEORGE SAND

Nature subjects the weak to the strong. (Naturae est enim potioribus deteriora summittere.)

SENECA
Epistulœ ad Lucilium Epis. xc, sec. 4

Nature speaks in symbols and in signs.

JOHN GREENLEAF WHITTIER
To Charles Sumner

NEED

Necessity never made a good bargain.

BENJAMIN FRANKLIN
Poor Richard's Almanack

What this country really needs is a good five cent cigar.

THOMAS R. MARSHALL

NIGHT

The night shows stars and women in a better light.

GEORGE GORDON, LORD BYRON
Don Juan C. ii, st. 152

What hath night to do with sleep?

JOHN MILTON
Comus

Night brings our troubles to the light, rather than banishes them. (Nox exhibet molestiam, non tollit.)

SENECA
Epistulœ ad Lucilium Epis. lvi, sec. 6

OFFENCE

Neither give offence to others, nor take offence from them.

ST. AMBROSE
Letter to St. Augustine (Taylor, *Ductor Dubitantium*)

The offender never pardons.

GEORGE HERBERT
Jacula Prudentum

If their "offence be rank" should mine be *rancour*?

THOMAS HOOD
Ode to Rae Wilson

O, my offence is rank, it smells to heaven.

WILLIAM SHAKESPEARE
Hamlet Act iii, sc. 3

The rankest compound of villainous smell that ever offended nostril.

WILLIAM SHAKESPEARE
The Merry Wives of Windsor Act iii, sc. 5

There are offences given and offences not given but taken.

IZAAK WALTON
The Compleat Angler "Preface"

OPTIMISM

Optimist: A proponent of the doctrine that black is white.

AMBROSE BIERCE
Devil's Dictionary

Whatever is is right.

DEMOCRITUS
(Diogenes Laertius, *Democritus* Bk. ix, sec. 45)

ORDER

Chaos often breeds life, when order breeds habit.

HENRY ADAMS
Education of

Good order is the foundation of all good things.

EDMUND BURKE
Reflections on the Revolution in France

PARENTS

Lovers grow cold, men learn to hate their wives,
And only parents' love can last our lives.

ROBERT BROWNING
Pippa Passes

Honour thy father and thy mother: that thy days may be long upon the land which the Lord thy God giveth thee.

Exodus xx, 12

The virtue of parents is a great dowry. (Dos est magna parentium Virtus.)

HORACE
Odes·Bk. iii, ode 24

It is wise father that knows his own child.

WILLIAM SHAKESPEARE
The Merchant of Venice Act ii, sc. 2

Everything is dear to its parent.

SOPHOCLES
Oedipus Coloneus

PAST

You can never plan the future by the past.

EDMUND BURKE
Letter to a Member of the National Assembly

The dogmas of the quiet past are inadequate to the stormy present.

ABRAHAM LINCOLN
Second Annual Message to Congress

Consult the dead upon things that were,
But the living only on things that are.

HENRY WADSWORTH LONGFELLOW
The Golden Legend Pt. i

Let bygans be bygans.

FRANCES NETHERSOLE
Parables

Past and to come seems best; things present, worst.

WILLIAM SHAKESPEARE
II Henry IV Act i, sc. 3

PATRIOTISM

Let us therefore brace ourselves to our duties, and so bear ourselves that, if the British Empire and its Commonwealth last for a thousand years, men will still say: "This was their finest hour."

WINSTON CHURCHILL
Speech June 18, 1940

Our country! In her intercourse with foreign nations may she always be in the right; but our country, right or wrong!

STEPHEN DECATUR
Toast April, 1816

I only regret that I have but one life to lose for my country.

NATHAN HALE

Patriotism is the last refuge of a scoundrel.

SAMUEL JOHNSON
(Boswell, *Life* Vol. ii)

To plunder, to slaughter, to steal, these things they misname empire; and where they make a desert, they call it Peace. (Atgui ubi solitudinem faciunt, pacem appelant.)

CALGACUS
(Tacitus, *Agricola* Sec. 30.)

Peace is liberty in tranquillity.

CICERO
Philippicoe No. ii, sec. 44

The only foes that threaten America are the enemies at home, and these are ignorance, superstition, and incompetence.

ELBERT HUBBARD
The Philistine Vol. xx

They shall beat their swords into ploughshares, and their spears into pruning hooks: nation shall not lift up sword against nation, neither shall they learn war any more.

Isaiah ii, 4

We love peace, as we abhor pusillanimity; but not peace at any price. There is a peace more destructive of the manhood of living man than war is destructive of his material body. Chains are worse than bayonets.

DOUGLAS WILLIAM JERROLD
Specimens of Jerrold's Wit "Peace"

It is mutual cowardice that keeps us in peace. Were one-half of mankind brave, and one-half cowards, the brave would be always beating the cowards. Were all brave, they would lead a very uneasy life; all would be continually fighting: but being all cowards, we go on very well.

SAMUEL JOHNSON
(Boswell, *Life*)

Peace at any price. (Paix à tout prix.)

ALPHONSE DE LAMARTINE
(Arthur Hugh Clough, *Letters and Remains*)

Glory to God in the highest, and on earth, peace, good will toward men.

Luke ii, 14

Peace be within thy walls and prosperity within thy palaces.

Psalms cxxii, 7

If I must choose between peace and righteousness, I choose righteousness.

THEODORE ROOSEVELT
Unwise Peace Treaties

Peace with honor.

THEOBALD, COUNT OF CHAMPAGNE
(Walter Map, *De Nugis Curialium*)

He had rather spend £ 10,000 on Embassies to keep or procure peace with dishonour than £ 10,000 on an army that would have forced peace with honour.

SIR ANTHONY WELDON
The Court and Character of King James

Peace is always beautiful.

WALT WHITMAN
The Sleepers

There is a price which is too great to pay for peace, and that price can be put in one word. One cannot pay the price of self-respect.

WOODROW WILSON
Speech February 1, 1916

It must be a peace without victory.

WOODROW WILSON
Address January 22, 1917

Open covenants of peace openly arrived at...Absolute freedom of navigation upon the seas outside territorial waters alike in peace and in war...The removal, so far as possible, of all economic barriers and the establishment of an equality of trade conditions among all nations ...Adequate guarantees given and taken that national armaments will be reduced to the lowest point consistent with domestic safety.

WOODROW WILSON
Address January 8, 1918

PITY

Compassion will cure more sins than condemnation.

HENRY WARD BEECHER
Proverbs From Plymouth Pulpit

More helpful than all wisdom is one draught of simple human pity that will not forsake us.

GEORGE ELIOT
Mill on the Floss Bk. vii, ch. 1

He that pities another remembers himself.

GEORGE HERBERT
Jacula Prudentum

PLEASURE

One half of the world cannot understand the pleasures of the other.

JANE AUSTEN
Emma Ch. 9

Let us have wine and women, mirth and laughter, Sermons and soda-water the day after.

GEORGE GORDON, LORD BYRON
Don Juan C. II, clxxviii

Pleasure's a sin, and sometimes sin's a pleasure.

GEORGE GORDON, LORD BYRON
Don Juan C. I, cxxxiii

The great source of pleasure is variety.

SAMUEL JOHNSON
(Hill, *Lives of the English Poets* Vol. i)

A cigarette is the perfect type of a perfect pleasure. It is exquisite, and it leaves one unsatisfied. What more can one want?

OSCAR WILDE
Picture of Dorian Gray Ch. 6

POETRY

The eternal objects of poetry, among all nations, and at all times, are actions; human actions; possessing an inherent interest in themselves, and which are to be communicated in an interesting manner by the art of the poet.

MATTHEW ARNOLD
Sohrab and Rustum "Preface"

Poetry is simply the most beautiful, impressive, and widely effective mode of saying things, and hence its importance.

MATTHEW ARNOLD
Essays in Criticism "Heine"

Poetry is devil's wine. (Poesis est vinum daemonum.)

ST. AUGUSTINE
Contra Academicos Sec. 1

All poets are mad.

ROBERT BURTON
Anatomy of Melancholy "Democritus to the Reader"

Poetry which has been defined as the harmonious unison of man with nature.

SIR THOMAS CARLYLE
Essays "Early German Literature"

The freer utterances of the poet's license. (Poetarum licentiae liberiora.)

CICERO
De Oratore Bk. iii, ch. 38

A man may be an admirable poet without being an exact chronologer.

JOHN DRYDEN
Aeneid "Dedication"

All men are poets at heart.

RALPH WALDO EMERSON
Nature, Addresses, and Lectures "Literary Ethics"

There are great arts now, but no poetry celebrates them.

RALPH WALDO EMERSON
Journals 1864

The poet's business is not to save the soul of man but to make it worth saving.

JAMES ELROY FLECKER
(Untermeyer, *Modern British Poetry*)

Painters and poets always had an equal licence to dare anything. (Pictoribus atque poetis Quidlibet audendi semper fuit aequa potestas.)

HORACE
Ars Poetica

Poetry is the bill and coo of sex.

ELBERT HUBBARD
Epigrams

Poetry should surprise by a fine excess, and not by singularity; it should strike the reader as a wording of his own highest thoughts, and appear almost a remembrance. Its touches of beauty should never be halfway, thereby making the reader breathless, instead of content. The rise, the progress, the setting of imagery should, like the sun, come natural to him.

JOHN KEATS
Letters February 27, 1818

A prize poem is like a prize sheep...In general, prize sheep are good for nothing but to make tallow candles, and prize poems are good for nothing but to light them.

THOMAS MACAULAY
On the Royal Society of Literature

As civilization advances, poetry almost necessarily declines.

THOMAS MACAULAY
Essays "Milford's History of Greece"

Perhaps no person can be a poet, or can even enjoy poetry, without a certain unsoundness of mind.

THOMAS MACAULAY
Edinburgh Review

Using, as his habit, a poet's licence. (Usas Poetae, ut moris est, licentia.)

PHAEDRUS
Fables Bk. iv, fab. 25

I would define, in brief, the Poetry of words as the Rhythmical Creation of Beauty. Its sole arbiter is Taste.

EDGAR ALLAN POE
The Poetic Principle

What is poetry? The suggestion, by the imagination, of noble grounds for the noble emotions.

JOHN RUSKIN
Modern Painters Vol. iii

Rosalind: But are you so much in love as your rhymes speak?
Orlando: Neither rhyme nor reason can express how much.

WILLIAM SHAKESPEARE
As You Like It Act iii, sc. 2

Poetry is the record of the best and happiest moments of the happiest and the best minds.

PERCY BYSSHE SHELLEY
A Defence of Poetry

Poetry is the spontaneous overflow of powerful feelings: it takes its origin from emotion recollected in tranquillity.

WILLIAM WORDSWORTH
Lyrical Ballads "Preface"

POLITICS

Man is a political animal.

ARISTOTLE
Politics Bk. i, ch. 1

A shadow has fallen upon the scenes so lately lighted by the Allied victory. From Stettin in the Baltic to Trieste in the Adriatic, an iron curtain has descended across the continent.

WINSTON CHURCHILL
Speech March 5, 1946

The ballot is stronger than the bullet.

ABRAHAM LINCOLN
Speech May 19, 1856

I have not permitted myself, gentlemen, to conclude that I am the best man in the country; but I am reminded in this connection of a story of an old Dutch farmer, who remarked to a companion that it was not best to swap horses when crossing a stream.

ABRAHAM LINCOLN
Speech June 9, 1864

From each according to his abilities, to each according to his needs. (Jeder nach seinen Fähigkeiten, jedem nach seinen Bedürfnissen.)

KARL MARX
Randglossen zum Programm der Deutschen Arbeiter Partei

I pledge you, I pledge myself, to a new deal for the American people.

FRANKLIN DELANO ROOSEVELT
Speech June 3, 1932

I am reminded of four definitions; A radical is a man with both feet firmly planted—in the air; a conservative is a man with two perfectly good legs who, however, has never learned to walk; a reactionary is a somnambulist walking backwards; a liberal is a man who uses his legs and his hands at the behest of his head.

FRANKLIN DELANO ROOSEVELT
Speech October 26, 1939

My hat's in the ring. The fight is on and I'm stripped to the buff.

THEODORE ROOSEVELT
February 21, 1912

I will not accept if nominated, and will not serve if elected.

WILLIAM TECUMSEH SHERMAN
June 5, 1884

Politics make strange bedfellows.

CHARLES DUDLEY WARNER
My Summer in a Garden Ch. 15

If it is reorganization, a new deal, and a change you are seeking it is Hobson's choice. I am sorry for you, but it is really vote for me or not vote at all.

WOODROW WILSON
Speech October 24, 1910

POSSESSIONS

As much as thou hast, so much art thou worth.

CERVANTES
Don Quixote Pt. ii, ch. 20

I carry all my possessions with me. (Omnia mea porto mecum.)

BIAS
(Cicero, *Paradoxa* i, 2)

The feeling of satiety, almost inseparable from large possessions, is a surer cause of misery than ungratified desires.

BENJAMIN DISRAELI
Lothair Ch. 25

I can't, I trow,
Both eat my cake and have it too.

ROBERT HEATH
Occasional Poems

Unto everyone that hath shall be given, and he shall

have abundance: but from him that hath not shall be taken away even that which he hath.

Matthew xxv, 29

What is thine is mine, and all mine is thine. (Quod tuomst meumst, omne meum est autem tuom.)

PLAUTUS
Trinummus Act ii, sc. 2

What is mine is dear to me, as his own is dear to every man. (Meus mihi, suos cuique est carus.)

PLAUTUS
Captivi Act ii, sc. 2

It is better to have a little than nothing.

PUBLILIUS SYRUS
Sententiæ

No man can lose what he never had.

IZAAK WALTON
The Compleat Angler Ch. 5

POVERTY

I want there to be no peasant in my kingdom so poor that he is unable to have a chicken in his pot every Sunday. (Je veux qu'il n'y ait si pauvre paysan en mon royaume qu'il n'ait tous les dimanches sa poule au pot.)

HENRY IV
(Péréfixe, *Hist. de Henri le Grand*)

Few, save the poor, feel for the poor.

LETITIA ELIZABETH LANDON
The Poor

Poverty is no disgrace to a man, but it is confoundedly inconvenient.

REV. SYDNEY SMITH
His Wit and Wisdom

As for the virtuous poor, one can pity them, of course, but one cannot possibly admire them.

OSCAR WILDE
Soul of Man Under Socialism

POWER

Give me a lever long enough, and a fulcrum strong enough, and single-handed I can move the world.

ARCHIMEDES OF SYRACUSE
(Alexander, *Collectio* viii, 10)

The greater the power, the more dangerous the abuse.

EDMUND BURKE
Speech 1771

Increase of power begets increase of wealth.

WILLIAM COWPER
The Task Bk. iv

The depositary of power is always unpopular.

BENJAMIN DISRAELI
Coningsby Bk. iv, ch. 13

To be out of place is not necessarily to be out of power.

SAMUEL JOHNSON
Works "Debates"

Unlimited power is apt to corrupt the minds of those who possess it.

WILLIAM PITT, EARL OF CHATHAM
Speech January 9, 1770

PRAISE

We are all imbued with the love of praise. (Trahimur omnes laudis studio.)

CICERO
Pro Archia Poeta Ch. 11, sec. 26

He wants worth who dares not praise a foe.

JOHN DRYDEN
Conquest of Granada Act ii, sc. 1

It is as great a spite to be praised in the wrong place, and by a wrong person, as can be done to a noble nature.

BEN JONSON
Explorata "Non Vulgi Sunt"

Out of the mouths of babes and sucklings thou hast perfected praise.

Matthew xxi, 16

Their silence is sufficient praise. (Tacent, satis laudant.)

TERENCE
Eunuchus Act iii, sc. 2

PREJUDICE

A prejudice is a vagrant opinion without visible means of support.

AMBROSE BIERCE
The Devil's Dictionary

Prejudice is the child of ignorance.

WILLIAM HAZLITT
Sketches and Essays "On Prejudice"

To be prejudiced is always to be weak.

SAMUEL JOHNSON
Taxation No Tyranny

Remember, when the judgment's weak the prejudice is strong.

KANE O'HARA
Midas Act i, sc. 4

It is never too late to give up our prejudices.

HENRY DAVID THOREAU
Walden Ch. 1

PROGRESS

All that is human must retrograde if it does not advance.

EDWARD GIBBON
Decline and Fall of the Roman Empire Ch. 71

A single breaker may recede; but the tide is evidently coming in.

THOMAS MACAULAY
Essays "Southey's Colloquies"

Every step of progress that the world has made has been from scaffold to scaffold and from stake to stake.

WENDELL PHILLIPS
Speech October 15, 1851

PUNS

A man who could make so vile a pun would not scruple to pick a pocket.

JOHN DENNIS
Gentleman's Magazine Vol. li

It often happens a bad pun
Goes farther than a better one.

W. S. LANDOR
Last Fruit Off An Old Tree No. 92

QUOTATIONS

The wisdom of the wise, and the experience of ages, may be preserved by quotations.

ISAAC D'ISRAELI
Curiosities of Literature "Quotations"

Next to the originator of a good sentence is the first quoter of it.

RALPH WALDO EMERSON
Letters and Social Aims "Quotation and Originality"

Quotation confesses inferiority.

RALPH WALDO EMERSON
Letters and Social Aims "Quotation and Originality"

Always verify your quotations.

DR. MARTIN JOSEPH ROUTH
(Burgon, *Memoir of Dr. Routh*)

REFORM

Most reformers wore rubber boots and stood on glass when God sent a current of Commonsense through the Universe.

ELBERT HUBBARD
Epigrams

Moralists on the scent of evil will perpetrate any villainy in the name of God.

GEORGE WILLIAM RUSSELL

REGRET

The mind longs for what it has missed. (Animus quod perdidit optat.)

PETRONIUS ARBITER
Satyricon

For all sad words of tongue or pen,
The saddest are these: 'It might have been!'

JOHN GREENLEAF WHITTIER
Maud Muller

RELIGION

Superstition is the religion of feeble minds.

EDMUND BURKE
Reflections on the Revolution in France

From the age of fifteen, dogma has been the fundamental principle of my religion: I know no other religion; I cannot enter into the idea of any other sort of religion; religion, as a mere sentiment, is to me a dream and a mockery.

JOHN HENRY, CARDINAL NEWMAN
Apologia pro Vita Sua
"History of My Religious Opinions from 1833-1839"

Religion is the opium of the people. (Die Religion ... ist das Opium des Volkes.)

KARL MARX
Kritik der Hegelschen Rechtsphilosophie "Introduction"

REPENTANCE

In all my life, I have never repented but of three things: that I trusted a woman with a secret, that I went by sea when I might have gone by land, and that I passed a day in idleness.

MARCUS CATO
(Plutarch, *Lives* "Marcus Cato" Ch. 9, sec. 6)

Repentance is but want of power to sin.

JOHN DRYDEN
Palamon and Arcite Bk. iii

Repentance is the virtue of weak minds.

JOHN DRYDEN
The Indian Emperor

There's no repentance in the grave.

ISAAC WATTS
Solemn Thoughts

REPUTATION

To disregard what the world thinks of us is not only arrogant but utterly shameless. (Neglegere quid de se quisque sentiat, non solum arrogantis est, sed etiam omnino dissoluti.)

CICERO
De Officiis Bk. i, ch. 28

The solar system has no anxiety about its reputation.

RALPH WALDO EMERSON
Conduct of Life "Worship"

A man has a reputation, and is no longer free, but must respect it.

RALPH WALDO EMERSON
Society and Solitude "Works and Days"

I consider him of small account who esteems himself just as the popular breath may chance to raise him. (Ich halte nichts von dem, der von sich denkt wie ihn das Volk vielleicht erheben möchte.)

GOETHE
Iphigenia auf Tauris Act ii, sc. 1

The contempt of good reputation is called impudence.

THOMAS HOBBES
Leviathan Pt. i, ch. 6

Reputation is but a synonym of popularity: dependent on suffrage, to be increased or diminished at the will of the voters.

MRS. ANNA JAMESON
Memoirs and Essays "Washington Allston"

Most people judge men only by their vogue or by their fortune. (La plupart des gens ne jugent des hommes que par la vogue qu'ils ont, ou par leur fortune.)

FRANCOIS LA ROCHEFOUCAULD
Maximes No. 212

REWARD

The reward of a thing well done is to have done it.

RALPH WALDO EMERSON
Essays "New England Reformers"

The deed is everything, the glory naught. (Die That ist alles, nichts der Ruhm,)

GOETHE
Faust Pt. ii, act iv, sc. 1

Service without reward is punishment.

GEORGE HERBERT
Jacula Prudentum

The labourer is worthy of his reward.

I Timothy v, 18

RIGHTEOUSNESS

The humblest citizen of all the land, when clad in the armor of a righteous cause, is stronger than all the hosts of error.

WILLIAM JENNINGS BRYAN
Speech 1896

I had rather be right than be President.

HENRY CLAY

RIGHT-WRONG

The absent are always in the wrong. (Les absents ont toujours tort.)

PHILLIPPE NÉRICAULT DESTOUCHES
L'Obstacle Imprévu

SATIRE

He that hath a satirical vein, as he maketh others afraid of his wit, so he had need be of others' memory.

FRANCIS BACON
Essays "Of Discourse"

I'll publish, right or wrong:
Fools are my theme, let Satire be my song.

GEORGE GORDON, LORD BYRON
English Bards and Scotch Reviewers

Sarcasm I now see to be, in general, the language of the devil.

THOMAS CARLYLE
Sartor Resartus Bk. ii, ch. 4

The arrows of sarcasm are barbed with contempt . . . It is the sneer of the satire, the ridicule, that galls and wounds.

WASHINGTON GLADDEN
Things Old and New "Taming the Tongue"

It is difficult *not* to write satire. (Difficile est satiram non scribere.)

JUVENAL
Satires Sat. i

Satire is a sort of glass, wherein beholders do generally discover everybody's face but their own.

JONATHAN SWIFT
The Battle of the Books "Preface"

Satire, being levelled at all, is never resented for an offence by any.

JONATHAN SWIFT
A Tale of a Tub "Preface"

SCIENCE

Science is the labour and handicraft of the mind; poetry can only be considered its recreation.

FRANCIS BACON
Description of the Intellectual Globe Ch. 1

Science is the topography of ignorance.

O. W. HOLMES
Medical Essays

Science is nothing but trained and organized common sense, differing from the latter only as the veteran may differ from a raw recruit: and its methods differ from those of common sense only as far as the guardsman's cut and thrust differ from the manner in which the savage wields his club.

THOMAS HENRY HUXLEY
Collected Essays "The Method of Zadig"

Every science has been an outcast.

R. G. INGERSOLL
The Liberty of Man, Woman, and Child

Human science is uncertain guess.

MATTHEW PRIOR
Solomon Bk. i

Science is organized knowledge.

HERBERT SPENCER
Education Ch. 2

To define it rudely but not inaptly, engineering is the art of doing that well with one dollar which any bungler can do with two after a fashion.

ARTHUR M. WELLINGTON
The Economic Theory of Railway Location "Introduction"

SELF-CONTROL

I count him braver who overcomes his desires than him who conquers his enemies; for the hardest victory is the victory over self.

ARISTOTLE
(Stobaeus, *Florilegium*)

Coolness and absence of heat and haste indicate fine qualities.

RALPH WALDO EMERSON
Essays, Second Series "Manners"

Nothing gives one person so much advantage over another as to remain always cool and unruffled under all circumstances.

THOMAS JEFFERSON
Writings Vol. xix

Than self-restraint there is nothing better.

LAO-TSZE
The Simple Way No. 5

SELF-DETERMINATION

It matters not how strait the gate,
How charged with punishments the scroll,
I am the master of my fate:
I am the captain of my soul.

WILLIAM ERNEST HENLEY
Invictus

SELF-INTEREST

It is your own interest that is at stake when your neighbor's wall is ablaze. (Nam tua res agitur, paries cum proximus ardet.)

HORACE
Epistles xviii, 80

SELF-KNOWLEDGE

And these few precepts in thy memory
Look thou character. Give thy thoughts no tongue,
Nor any unproportion'd thought his act.
Be thou familiar, but by no means vulgar.
Those friends thou hast, and their adoption tried,
Grapple them to thy soul with hoops of steel;

But do not dull thy palm with entertainment
Of each new-hatch'd, unfledg'd courage. Beware
Of entrance to a quarrel; but, being in,
Bear't that th' opposed may beware of thee.
Give every man thine ear, but few thy voice;
Take each man's censure, but reserve thy judgment.
Costly thy habit as thy purse can buy,
But not express'd in fancy; rich, not gaudy;
For the apparel oft proclaims the man;
And they in France of the best rank and station
Are of a most select and generous choice in that.
Neither a borrower nor a lender be;
For loan oft loses both itself and friend,
And borrowing dulls the edge of husbandry.
This above all—to thine own self be true,
And it must follow, as the night the day,
Thou canst not then be false to any man.
Farewell; my blessing season this in thee!

WILLIAM SHAKESPEARE
Hamlet Act i, sc. 3

No one knows what it is that he can do till he tries.

PUBLILIUS SYRUS

Know thyself.

THALES
(Diogenes Laertius, *Thales* Sec. 40)

SELF-RELIANCE

The greatest thing in the world is to know how to be sufficient unto oneself. (La plus grande chose du monde c'est de savoir être à soi.)

MONTAIGNE
Essais I, xxxix

SELF-RESPECT

Self-respect—that corner-stone of all virtue.

SIR JOHN HERSCHEL
Speech January 20, 1833

SILENCE

Deep vengeance is the daughter of deep silence. (Alta vendetta D'alto silenzio è figlia).

ALFIERI
La Congiura de' Puzzi Act i, sc. 1

Silence is the virtue of fools, so he rightly said to the silent man: "If you are wise, you are a fool; if you are a fool, you are wise."

FRANCIS BACON
De Augmentis Scientiarium "Loquacitas"

Silence gives consent. (Qui tacet, consentire videtur.)
Canon Law "Decretals" Bk. v, ch. 12

Silence is more eloquent than words.

THOMAS CARLYLE
Heroes and Hero-Worship Lect. ii

Under all speech that is good for anything there lies a silence that is better. Silence is deep as Eternity; speech is shallow as Time.

THOMAS CARLYLE
Critical and Miscellaneous Essays "Sir Walter Scott"

There are haunters of the silence, ghosts that hold the heart and brain.

MADISON CAWEIN
Haunters of the Silence

When you have nothing to say, say nothing.

C. C. COLTON
Lacon "Reflections"

There be
Three silent things:
The falling snow ... the hour
Before the dawn ... the mouth of one
Just dead.

ADELAIDE CRAPSEY
Triad

Silence is the mother of Truth.

BENJAMIN DISRAELI
Tancred Bk. iv, ch. 4

It is safer to keep silence than to speak.

EPICTETUS
Enchiridion Frag. 29

Silence is true wisdom's best reply.

EURIPEDES
Fragments Frag. 947

Silence seldom hurts.

THOMAS FULLER
Gnomologia No. 4170

The most silent people are generally those who think most highly of themselves.

WILLIAM HAZLITT
Characteristics No. 91

There is the silent criticism of silence, worth all the rest.

SIR ARTHUR HELPS
Friends in Council Bk. ii, ch. 2

Three Silences there are: the first of speech,
the second of desire, the third of thought.

HENRY WADSWORTH LONGFELLOW
The Three Silences of Molinos

Three things are ever silent—Thought, Destiny, and the Grave.

BULWER-LYTTON
Harold Bk. x, ch. 2

Eternal silence be their doom.

JOHN MILTON
Paradise Lost Bk. vi

Silence is man's chief learning.

PALLADAS
Greek Anthology Bk. x, epig. 46

SIN

There is often a sin of omission as well as of commission.

MARCUS AURELIUS
Meditations Bk. ix, sec. 5

There is no sinner like a young saint.

APHRA BEHN
The Rover Pt. i, act i, sc. 2

Sin makes its own hell, and goodness its own heaven.

MARY BAKER EDDY
Science and Health

That which we call sin in others is experiment for us.

RALPH WALDO EMERSON
Essays, Second Series "Experience"

All that defiles comes from within.

MENANDER
Fragments No. 540

For the wages of sin is death.

Romans vi, 23

Fools make a mock at sin.

Proverbs xiv, 9

He who does not forbid sin when he can, encourages it. (Qui non vetat peccare cum possit, jubet.)

SENECA
Troades

More men abstain from forbidden actions because they are ashamed of sinning, than because their inclinations are good. (Plures enim pudore peccandi quam bona voluntate prohibitis abstinent.)

SENECA
Epistulæ ad Lucilium Epis. 83, 20

If we desire to judge all things justly, we must first persuade ourselves that none of us is without sin.

SENECA
De Ira Bk. ii, sec. 28

Few love to hear the sins they love to act.

WILLIAM SHAKESPEARE
Pericles Act i, sc. 1

There is no sin except stupidity.

OSCAR WILDE
The Critic as Artist 2

SLAVERY

It is far better to be a mortal free man than an immortal slave.

R. G. INGERSOLL
Voltaire

'A house divided against itself cannot stand.' I believe this government cannot endure permanently half-slave and half-free. I do not expect the Union to be dissolved—I do not expect the house to fall—but I do expect it will cease to be divided. It will become all one thing, or all the other. Either the opponents of slavery will arrest the further spread of it, and place it where the public mind shall rest in the belief that it is in the course of ultimate extinction; or its advocates will push it forward, till it shall become alike lawful in all the States, old as well as new—North as well as South.

ABRAHAM LINCOLN
Speech June 17, 1858

Whenever I hear anyone arguing for slavery, I feel a strong impulse to see it tried on him personally.

ABRAHAM LINCOLN
Speech March, 1865

Better the devil's than a woman's slave.

PHILIP MASSINGER
Parliament of Love Act ii, sc. 2

Slavery enchains a few; more enchain themselves to slavery. (Paucos servitus, piures servitutem tenet.)

SENECA
Epistulæ ad Lucilium Epis. 22, 11

SLEEP

We sleep, but the loom of life never stops and the pattern which was weaving when the sun went down is weaving when it comes up tomorrow.

HENRY WARD BEECHER
Life Thoughts

O sleep! it is a gentle thing,
Beloved from pole to pole!
To Mary Queen the praise be given!
She sent the gentle sleep from Heaven
That slid into my soul.

SAMUEL TAYLOR COLERIDGE
The Ancient Mariner Pt. v

I shall sleep like a top.

SIR WILLIAM D'AVENANT
The Rivals Act iii

Blessed are the sleepy, for they shall soon drop off.

NIETZSCHE
Thus Spake Zarathustra "Of the Chairs of Virtue"

I am going to the land of Nod.

JONATHAN SWIFT
Polite Conversation Dial. iii

SOCIETY

Man seeketh in society comfort, use, and protection.

FRANCIS BACON
Advancement of Learning Bk. ii

I live in the crowds of jollity, not so much to enjoy company as to shun myself.

SAMUEL JOHNSON
Rasselas Ch. 16

The Don Quixote of one generation may live to hear himself called the savior of society by the next.

JAMES RUSSELL LOWELL
Essays "Don Quixote"

Society is the union of men and not the men themselves. (La Société est l'union des hommes, et non pas les hommes.)

CHARLES LOUIS MONTESQUIEU
L'Esprit des Lois Bk. x, sec. 3

Society exists for the benefit of its members; not the members for the benefit of society.

HERBERT SPENCER
Principles of Ethics Sec. 222

What men call social virtue, good fellowship, is commonly but the virtue of pigs in a litter, which lie close together to keep each other warm.

HENRY DAVID THOREAU
Journal October 23, 1852

SOLITUDE

I am never less alone than when alone. (Minus solum, cum quam solus esset.)

SCIPIO AFRICANUS
(Cicero, *De Officiis* Bk. iii, ch. 1)

The worst solitude is to be destitute of sincere friendship.

FRANCIS BACON
De Dignitate et Augmentis Scientiarium
Pt. I, bk. vii, ch. 37

It had been hard for him that spake it to have put more truth and untruth together, in few words, than in that speech: "Whosoever is delighted in solitude is either a wild beast, or a god".

FRANCIS BACON
Essays "Of Friendship"

Solitude affects some people like wine; they must not take too much of it, for it flies to the head.

MARY COLERIDGE
Gathered Leaves

Alone, alone, all, all alone,
Alone on a wide wide sea!
And never a saint took pity on
My soul in agony.

SAMUEL TAYLOR COLERIDGE
The Ancient Mariner Pt. IV

The time when, most of all, you should withdraw into yourself is when you are forced to be in a crowd.

EPICURUS
Fragments No. 209

Ships that pass in the night, and speak each other in passing;
Only a signal shown and a distant voice in the darkness;
So on the ocean of life we pass and speak one another,
Only a look and a voice; then darkness again and a silence.

HENRY WADSWORTH LONGFELLOW
Tales of a Wayside Inn
Pt. III "The Theologian's Tale" "Elizabeth" IV

You will be sad if you are alone. (Tristis eris si solus eris.)

OVID
Remediorum Amoris

Overbearing austerity is always the companion of solitude.

PLATO
Epistle to Dion

Solitude prompts us to all kinds of evil. (Omnia nobis mala solitudo persuadet.)

SENECA
Epistulae ad Lucilium Epis. xxv

Why should I feel lonely? is not our planet in the Milky Way?

HENRY DAVID THOREAU
Walden "Solitude"

I never found the companion that was so companionable as solitude.

HENRY DAVID THOREAU
Walden "Solitude"

Avoid the reeking herd,
Shun the polluted flock,
Live like that stoic bird
The eagle of the rock.

ELINOR WYLIE
The Eagle and the Mole

SORROW

Nothing comes to us too soon but sorrow.

PHILIP JAMES BAILEY
Festus "Home"

Sorrow preys upon Its solitude ...
The busy have no time for tears.

GEORGE GORDON, LORD BYRON
The Two Foscari Act iv, sc. 1

Sorrow is knowledge.

GEORGE GORDON, LORD BYRON
Manfred Act i, sc. 1

Sing away sorrow, cast away care.

CERVANTES
Don Quixote Pt. i, ch. 8

All sorrows are less with bread. (Los duelos con Pan son menos.)

CERVANTES
Don Quixote Pt. ii, ch. 13

There is no greater sorrow than to recall a time of happiness in misery. (Nessun maggior delore, Che ricordarsi del tempo felice Nella miseria.)

DANTE ALIGHIERI
Divine Comedy "Inferno"

When sorrow is asleep wake it not.

THOMAS FULLER
Gnomologia No. 5569

Sorrow is good for nothing but sin.

THOMAS FULLER
Gnomologia No. 4232

The world will never be long without some good reason to hate the unhappy.

SAMUEL JOHNSON
The Adventure No. 99

Sorrow is a kind of rust of the soul, which every new idea contributes in its passage to scour away.

SAMUEL JOHNSON
The Rambler No. 47

We often console ourselves for being unhappy by a certain pleasure in appearing so. (On se console souvent d'être malheureux par un certain plaisir qu'on trouve á le paraitre.)

FRANCOIS LA ROCHEFOUCAULD
Maximes Supprimées No. 573

Sorrow, the great idealizer.

JAMES RUSSELL LOWELL
Among My Books "Spenser"

Humanity is fortunate, because no man is unhappy except by his own fault. (Bono loco res humanae sunt, quod nemo nisi vitio suo miser est.)

SENECA
Epistulæ ad Lucilium Epis. ixx

Pure and complete sorrow is as impossible as pure and complete joy.

LEO TOLSTOY
War and Peace Bk. xv, ch. I

Where there is sorrow, there is holy ground.

OSCAR WILDE
De Profundis

SPEECH

Speech is human, silence is divine, yet also brutish and dead: therefore we must learn both arts.

THOMAS CARLYLE
Journal

I disapprove of what you say, but I will defend to the death your right to say it.

(Attributed to) VOLTAIRE

STARS

Surely the stars are images of love.

PHILIP JAMES BAILEY
Festus "Garden and Bower by the Sea"

Eat, speak, and move, under the influence of the most received star; and though the devil lead the measure, such are to be followed.

WILLIAM SHAKESPEARE
All's Well That Ends Well Act ii, sc. 1

He that strives to touch the stars,
Oft stumbles at a straw.

EDMUND SPENSER
Shepheardes Calender, July

STRENGTH

Let our strength be the law of justice: for that which is feeble is found to be nothing worth.

Apocrypha
Wisdom of Solomon ii, 11

Such strength as a man has he should use. (Quod est, eo decet uti.)

CICERO
De Senectute Ch. 9, sec. 27

Success to the strongest, who are always, at last, the wisest and best.

RALPH WALDO EMERSON
Uncollected Lectures "Public and Private Education"

He who has great strength should use it lightly. (Minimum decet libere cui multum licet.)

SENECA
Troades

SUCCESS

I have found it! I have found it! (Eureka! Eureka!)

ARCHIMEDES
(Vitruvius, *De Architectura* ix, 215)

Success is full of promise till men get it; and then it is a last-year's nest from which the birds have flown.

HENRY WARD BEECHER
Life Thoughts

Knowledge may give weight, but accomplishments give lustre, and many more people see than weigh.

PHILIP DORMER STANHOPE, EARL OF CHESTERFIELD
Letter May 8, 1750

Success is the child of Audacity.

BENJAMIN DISRAELI
Iskander Ch. 4

The secret of success is constancy to purpose.

BENJAMIN DISREALI
Speech June 24, 1870

Nothing succeeds like success. (Rien ne réussit comme le succès.)

ALEXANDRE DUMAS
Ange Pitou Bk. i

If a man write a better book, preach a better sermon, or make a better mouse-trap than his neighbour, tho' he build his house in the woods, the world will make a beaten path to his door.

RALPH WALDO EMERSON
(Yule, *Borrowings*)

Nothing great was ever achieved without enthusiasm.
RALPH WALDO EMERSON
Essays x "Circles"

Success is never blamed.
THOMAS FULLER
Gnomologia No. 4273

Are you in earnest? seize this very minute—
What you can do, or dream you can, begin it,
Boldness has genius, power, and magic in it.
Only engage, and then the mind grows heated—
Begin it, and the work will be completed!
(Das Mögliche soll der Entschluss
Beherzt sogleich beim Schopfe fassen;
Er will es dann nicht fahren lassen,
Und wirket weiter, weil er muss.)

GOETHE
Faust "Vorspiel auf dem Theater"

The success of most things depends upon knowing how long it will take to succeed. (Le succes de la plupart des choses depend de voir combien il faut de temps pour reussir.)

CHARLES LOUIS MONTESQUIEU
Pensées Diverses

I have always observed that to suceed in the world one should seem a fool, but be wise. (J'ai toujours vu que, pour reussir dans le monde, il fallait avoir l'air fou et être sage.)

CHARLES LOUIS MONTESQUIEU
Pensées Diverses

Either attempt it not, or succeed. (Aut non temptaris, aut perfice.)

OVID
Ars Amatoria Bk. i

Nothing is so impudent as Success—unless it be those she favours.

J. R. PLANCHE
Success

His head was turned by too great success. (Motum illi felicitate nimia caput.)

SENECA
Epistulae ad Lucilium Epis. cxiv

SUICIDE

What, does he who is at liberty to leave the banquet when he will, and play the game no longer, keep on annoying himself by staying?

EPICTETUS
Discourses Bk. ii, ch. 16, sec. 37

Nine men in ten are suicides.

BENJAMIN FRANKLIN
Poor Richard's Almanack

It is the role of cowardice, not of courage, to crouch in a hole, under a massive tomb, to avoid the blows of fortune. (C'est le rôle de la couardise, non de la vertu, de s'en aller tapir dans un creux, sous un tombe massive, pour éviter les coups de la fortune.)

MONTAIGNE
Essays Bk. ii, ch. 3

Just as I shall select my ship when I am about to go on a voyage, or my house when I propose to take a residence, so I shall choose my death when I am about to depart from life.

SENECA
Epistulae ad Lucilium Epis. lxx, 11

SUSPICION

Superabundance of suspicion is a kind of political madness.

FRANCIS BACON
De Augmentis Scientarium "Suspicio"

Always suspect that which seems probable, and begin by believing what appears incredible.

EMILE GABORIAU
Monsieur Lecoq Ch. 8

The losing side is full of suspicion. (Ad tristem partem strenua est suspicio.)

PUBLILIUS SYRUS
Sententiae No. 7

All persons, as they grow less prosperous, grow more suspicious. (Omnes, quibus res sunt minus secundae magis sunt, nescio quomodo, Suspiciosi.)

TERENCE
Adelphi Act iv, sc. 3

SYMPATHY

Needs there groan a world in anguish just to teach us sympathy?

ROBERT BROWNING
La Saisiaz

We sink as easily as we rise, through sympathy.
RALPH WALDO EMERSON
Essays "Society and Solitude"

People in distress never think that you feel enough.
SAMUEL JOHNSON
(Boswell, *Life* ii)

A man should keep his heart strings tightly drawn. (Misericordia se abstinere hominem oportet.)

PLAUTUS
Mostellaria Act iii, sc. 2

Rejoice with them that do rejoice, and weep with those who weep.

Romans xii, 15

TALENT

To do easily what is difficult for others is the mark of talent.

HENRI-FREDERIC AMIEL
Journal December 17, 1856

Each man has his own vocation. The talent is the call.
RALPH WALDO EMERSON
Essays, First Series "Spiritual Laws"

Hidden talent counts for nothing. (Occultae musicae nullam esse respectum.)

NERO
(Suetonius, *Lives* Ch. 20, sec. 2)

TALK

Talking and eloquence are not the same: to speak and to speak well, are two things. A fool may talk, but a wise man speaks.

BEN JONSON
Explorata "Praecept"

But words once spoke can never be recall'd.

WENTWORTH DILLON, EARL OF ROSCOMMON
Art of Poetry

TIME

Time which is the author of authors.

FRANCIS BACON
Advancement of Learning Bk. i

Time is the greatest innovator.

FRANCIS BACON
Essays "Of Innovations"

To choose time is to save time.

FRANCIS BACON
Essays 25 "Of Dispatch"

Time ripens all things. No man is born wise.

CERVANTES
Don Quixote Pt. ii, ch. 33

"The time has come," the Walrus said,
 "To talk of many things:
Of shoes—and ships—and sealing-wax—
Of cabbages—and kings—
And why the sea is boiling hot—
 And whether pigs have wings."

LEWIS CARROLL
Through the Looking Glass

To every thing there is a season, and a time to every purpose under the heaven:
 A time to be born, and a time to die; a time to plant, and a time to pluck up that which is planted;
 A time to kill, and a time to heal; a time to break down, and a time to build up;
 A time to weep, and a time to laugh; a time to mourn, and a time to dance;
 A time to cast away stones, and a time to gather stones together;
 A time to embrace, and a time to refrain from embracing;
 A time to get, and a time to lose; a time to keep, and a time to cast away;
 A time to rend, and a time to sew; a time to keep silence, and a time to speak;
 A time to love, and a time to hate; a time of war, and a time of peace.

Ecclesiastes iii, 1-8

Dost thou love life? Then do not squander time, for that's the stuff life is made of.

BENJAMIN FRANKLIN
Poor Richard's Almanack

Remember, that time is money.

BENJAMIN FRANKLIN
Writings Vol. ii "Advice to Young Tradesman"

Time is itself an element. (Die Zeit ist selbst ein Element.)

GOETHE
Sprüche in Prosa Pt. iii

One would think that time stood still, so slowly does it move. (Stare putes, adeo procedunt tempora tarde.)

OVID
Tristia Bk. v, eleg. 10

Nothing is ours except time. (Omnia aliena sunt, tempus tantum nostrum est.)

SENECA
Epistulae ad Lucilium Epis. i, sec. 3

TOBACCO

For this you've my word, and I never yet broke it.
So put that in your pipe, my Lord Otto, and smoke it.

RICHARD HARRIS BARHAM
The Lay of St. Odille St. 14

Herein is not only a great vanity, but a great contempt of God's good gifts, that the sweetness of man's breath, being a good gift of God, should be willfully corrupted by this stinking smoke.... A custom loathsome to the eye, hateful to the nose, harmful to the brain, dangerous to the lungs, and in the black, stinking fume thereof nearest resembling the horrible Stygian smoke of the pit that is bottomless.

JAMES I OF ENGLAND

TRUTH

Be so true to thyself as thou not be false to others.

FRANCIS BACON
Essays 23 "Of Wisdom For a Man's Self"

Truth can never be told so as to be understood, and not be believ'd.

WILLIAM BLAKE
Marriage of Heaven and Hell "Proverbs of Hell"

'Tis strange—but true; for truth is always strange;
Stranger than fiction.

GEORGE GORDON, LORD BYRON
Don Juan c. xiv

Truth, ever lovely—since the world began
The foe of tyrants, and the friend of man.

THOMAS CAMPBELL
Pleasures of Hope Pt. ii

Irrationally held truths may be more harmful than reasoned errors.

THOMAS HENRY HUXLEY
Science and Culture xii
"The Coming of Age of the Origin of Species"

A thing is not necessarily true because a man dies for it.

OSCAR WILDE
Sebastian Melmoth

Truth is never pure, and rarely simple.

OSCAR WILDE
The Importance of Being Earnest Act i

VICTORY

I came, I saw, I conquered. (Veni, vidi, vici.)

JULIUS CAESAR
(Suentonius, *Divus Julius* xxxvii, 2)

Victory at all costs, victory in spite of all terror, victory however long and hard the road may be; for without victory there is no survival.

WINSTON CHURCHILL
Speech May 13, 1940

When there is no peril in the fight, there is no glory in the triumph. (A vaincre sans péril, on triomphe sans gloire.)

PIERRE CORNEILLE
Le Cid ii, 2

The race is not to the swift, nor the battle to the strong.

Ecclesiastes ix, 11

To the victor belong the spoils of the enemy.

WILLIAM LEARNED MARCY
(Patron, *Life of Jackson* Vol. iii)

VIRTUE

Prosperity doth best discover vice, but adversity doth best discover virtue.

FRANCIS BACON
Essays 5 "Of Adversity"

Virtue seldom walks forth without Vanity at her side.

SIR WILLIAM GURNEY BENHAM
Proverbs

Virtue has always been conceived of as victorious resistance to one's vital desire to do this, that or the other.

JAMES BRANCH CABELL
Beyond Life

The highest virtue is always against the law.

RALPH WALDO EMERSON
Conduct of Life "Worship"

The virtue which requires to be ever guarded is scarcely worth the sentinel.

OLIVER GOLDSMITH
The Vicar of Wakefield Ch. 5

But if he does really think that there is no distinction between virtue and vice, why, Sir, when he leaves our houses let us count our spoons.

SAMUEL JOHNSON
(Boswell, *Life*)

Virtue is often merely local.

SAMUEL JOHNSON
The Idler No. 53

Assume a virtue, if you have it not.

WILLIAM SHAKESPEARE
Hamlet Act iii, sc. 4

Anybody can be good in the country.

OSCAR WILDE
Picture of Dorian Gray Ch. 19

WAR

War is not sparing of the brave, but of cowards.

ANACREON
"Epigram" (*Greek Anthology* Bk. vii, No. 160)

In war events of importance are the result of trivial causes. (In bello parvis momentis magni casus intercedunt.)

JULIUS CAESAR
De Bello Gallico Bk. i, sec. 21

In war, whichever side may call itself the victor, there are no winners, but all are losers.

NEVILLE CHAMBERLAIN
Speech July 3, 1938

I would say to the House, as I said to those who have joined this Government, 'I have nothing to offer but blood, toil, tears, and sweat.'

WINSTON CHURCHILL
Speech May 13, 1940

We shall not flag or fail. We shall fight in France, we shall fight on the seas and oceans, we shall fight with growing confidence and growing strength in the air, we shall defend our island, whatever the cost may be, we shall fight on the beaches, we shall fight on the landing grounds, we shall fight in the fields and in the streets, we shall fight in the hills; we shall never surrender.

WINSTON CHURCHILL
Speech June 4, 1940

Never in the field of human conflict was so much owed by so many to so few.

WINSTON CHURCHILL
Speech August 20, 1940

We do not covet anything from any nation except their respect.

WINSTON CHURCHILL
Speech October 21, 1940

Let me, however, make this clear, in case there should be any mistake about it in any quarter. We mean to hold our own. I have not become the King's First Minister in order to preside over the liquidation of the British Empire.

WINSTON CHURCHILL
Speech November 10, 1942

The empires of the future are empires of the mind.

WINSTON CHURCHILL
Speech September 16, 1943

God is generally for the big squadrons against the little ones. (Dieu est ordinairement pour le gros escadrons contre les petits.)

ROGER, COMTE DE BUSSY-RABUTIN
Letters October 18, 1677

By the rude bridge that arched the flood,
Their flag to April's breeze unfurled,
Here once the embattled farmers stood,
And fired the shot heard 'round the world.

RALPH WALDO EMERSON
Hymn Sung at the Completion of the Concord Monument

Praise the Lord and pass the ammunition.

LT. COMMANDER HOWELL FORGY

There never was a good war, or a bad peace.

BENJAMIN FRANKLIN

Guns will make us powerful, butter will only make us fat.

FIELD MARSHALL HERMANN GOERING
July, 1936

War is death's feast.

GEORGE HERBERT
Jacula Prudentum

One can resist the invasion of armies, but not the invasion of ideas. (On résiste á l'invasion des armées; on ne resiste pas á l'invasion des idées.)

VICTOR HUGO
Histoire d'un Crime "Conclusion: La Chute"

There is no such thing as an inevitable war. If war comes it will be from failure of human wisdom.

ANDREW BONAR LAW
Speech July, 1914

Military glory—that attractive rainbow that rises in showers of blood, that serpent's eye that charms to destroy.

ABRAHAM LINCOLN
Speech January 12, 1848

I shall return.

GEN. DOUGLAS MACARTHUR

War should be the only study of a prince. He should consider peace only as a breathing-time, which gives him leisure to contrive, and furnishes ability to execute military plans.

MACHIAVELLI
The Prince

War hath no fury like a non-combatant.

CHARLES EDWARD MONTAGUE
Disenchantment

Two armies are two bodies which meet and try to frighten each other.

NAPOLEON I
Sayings of Napoleon

We shall attack and attack until we are exhausted, and then we shall attack again.

MAJOR GENERAL GEORGE S. PATTON JR.

We have met the enemy, and they are ours.

OLIVER HAZARD PERRY

We must be the great arsenal of democracy.

FRANKLIN DELANO ROOSEVELT
Speech December 29, 1940

We check manslaughter and isolated murders; but what of war and the much-vaunted crime of slaughtering whole peoples? . . . Deeds which would be punished by loss of life when committed in secret, are praised by us because uniformed generals have carried them out.

SENECA
Epistulœ ad Lucilium Epis. xcv, 30

Dying is more honorable than killing. (Quanto honestius mori discunt homines quam occidere.)

SENECA
Epistulœ ad Lucilium Epis. lxx, 27

Worse than war is the fear of war. (Pejor est bello timor ipse belli.)

SENECA
Thyestes

War is the statesman's game, the priest's delight,
The lawyer's jest, the hired assassin's trade.

PERCY BYSSHE SHELLEY
Queen Mab Pt. lv

There is many a boy here today who looks on war as all glory, but, boys, it is all hell. You can bear this warning voice to generations yet to come. I look upon war with horror.

WILLIAM TECUMSEH SHERMAN
Speech August 11, 1880

"Forward the Light Brigade."
Was there a man dismay'd?
Not tho' the soldier knew
Some one had blunder'd.
Theirs not to make reply,
Theirs not to reason why,
Theirs but to do and die.
Into the valley of Death
Rode the six hundred.

ALFRED LORD TENNYSON
The Charge of the Light Brigade

Cannon to the right of them,
Cannon to the left of them,
Cannon in front of them
Volley'd and Thunder'd;
Storm'd at with shot and shell,
Boldly they rode and well,
Into the jaws of Death,
Into the mouth of hell
Rode the six hundred.

ALFRED LORD TENNYSON
The Charge of the Light Brigade

Mad I take arms, yet little reason is there in arms. (Arma amens capio; nec sat rationis in armis.)

VERGIL
Aeneid Bk. i

All the business of war, and all the business of life, is to endeavour to find out what you don't know by what you do; that's what I called 'guessing what was at the other side of the hill'.

ARTHUR WELLESLEY, DUKE OF WELLINGTON
Croker Papers Vol. iii

As long as war is regarded as wicked, it will always have its fascination. When it is looked upon as vulgar, it will cease to be popular.

OSCAR WILDE
The Critic as Artist Pt. 2

The world must be made safe for democracy.

WOODROW WILSON
War Address to Congress April 2, 1917

WIFE

Wives are young men's mistresses, companions for middle age, and old men's nurses.

FRANCIS BACON
Essays "Of Marriage and Single Life"

To take a wife merely as an agreeable and rational companion, will commonly be found to be a grand mistake.

PHILIP DORMER STANHOPE, EARL OF CHESTERFIELD
Letters

He that takes a wife takes care.

BENJAMIN FRANKLIN
Poor Richard's Almanack

A man is in general better pleased when he has a good dinner upon his table, than when his wife talks Greek.

SAMUEL JOHNSON
Miscellanies Vol. ii

Give up all hope of peace so long as your mother-in-law is alive. (Desperanda tibi salva concordia socru.)

JUVENAL
Satires Sat. vi

Heaven deprives me of a wife who never caused me any other grief than that of her death. (Le ciel me prive d'une épouse qui ne m'a jamais donné d'autre chagrin que celui de sa mort.)

LOUIS XIV

WINE

Wine is one thing, drunkenness another. (Aliud vinum, aliud ebrietas.)

ROBERT BURTON
Anatomy of Melancholy

It has become quite a common proverb that in wine there is truth. (In vino veritas.)

PLINY
Historia Naturalis Bk. xiv, sec. 14

WISDOM

Wisdom cometh by suffering.

AESCHYLUS
Agamemnon

Wisdom consists in rising superior both to madness and to common sense, and in lending oneself to the universal illusion without becoming its dupe.

HENRI-FREDERIC AMIEL
Journal December 11, 1872

The wise learn many things from their foes.

ARISTOPHANES
The Birds

Their hindsight was better than their foresight.

HENRY WARD BEECHER

A sadder and wiser man,
He rose the morrow morn.

SAMUEL TAYLOR COLERIDGE
The Ancient Mariner Pt. vii

There is this difference between happiness and wisdom: he that thinks himself the happiest man, really is so; but he that thinks himself the wisest is generally the greatest fool.

C. C. COLTON
Lacon Vol. i, no. 326

The wisdom of this world is foolishness with God.

Corinthians I iii, 19

Knowledge is proud that he has learn'd so much;
Wisdom is humble that he knows no more.

WILLIAM COWPER
The Task Bk. vi
"The Winter Walk at Noon"

After the event, even a fool is wise.

HOMER
Iliad Bk. xvii

Wisdom denotes the pursuing of the best ends by the best means.

FRANCIS HUTCHESON
Inquiry into the Original of our ideas of Beauty and Virtue Treatise I, sec. v, 18

The wise man does not lay up treasure.

LAO-TSZE
The Simple Way No. 81

Nine-tenths of wisdom is being wise in time.

THEODORE ROOSEVELT
Speech June 14, 1917

Knowledge comes, but wisdom lingers.

ALFRED LORD TENNYSON
Locksley Hall

I have lived some thirty years on this planet, and I have yet to hear the first syllable of valuable or even earnest advice from my seniors.

HENRY DAVID THOREAU
Walden "Economy"

WIT

Wit without an employment is a disease.

ROBERT BURTON
Anatomy of Melancholy Pt. i, sec. ii

A witty thing never excited laughter; it only pleases the mind, and never distorts the countenance.

PHILIP DORMER STANHOPE, EARL OF CHESTERFIELD
Letters

Nothing more smooth than glass, yet nothing more brittle;
Nothing more fine than wit, yet nothing more fickle.

THOMAS FULLER
Gnomologia No. 6472

There must be more malice than love in the hearts of all wits.

BENJAMIN ROBERT HAYDON
Table Talk

Impromptu is truly the touchstone of wit. (L'impromptu est justement la pierre de touche de l'esprit.)

MOLIERE
Les Precieuses Ridicules Sc. ix

True wit is to nature to advantage dressed,
What oft was thought, but ne'er so well express'd

ALEXANDER POPE
An Essay on Criticism

There's no possibility of being witty without a little ill-nature; the malice of a good thing is the barb that makes it stick.

RICHARD SHERIDAN
The School for Scandal Act i, sc. 1

WOLF

The Boy . . . would be crying *a Wolf, a Wolf,* when there was none.

SIR ROGER L'ESTRANGE
Fables No. 360

The wolf from the door.

JOHN SKELTON
Colyn Cloute

WOMEN

The woman that deliberates is lost.

JOSEPH ADDISON
Cato Act iv, sc. 1

Women wish to be loved without a why or a wherefore; not because they are pretty, or good, or well-bred, or graceful, or intelligent, but because they are themselves.

HENRI-FREDERIC AMIEL
Journal March 17, 1868

With women the heart argues, not the mind.

MATTHEW ARNOLD
Merope

A compliment for a woman in love is like a sudden warmth falling around her—it is intoxication—it is like strong wine, one grows drunk with it.

HENRY BERNSTEIN
The Thief Act ii

Let men say what'er they will
Woman, woman, rules them still.

ISAAC BICKERSTAFFE
The Sultan Act ii, sc. 1

Here's to woman! Would that we could fall into her arms without falling into her hands.

AMBROSE BIERCE
(Grattan, *Bitter Bierce*)

And her *Yes,* once said to you,
Shall be Yes for evermore.

ELIZABETH BARRETT BROWNING
The Lady's Yes

Nothing is so delicate as the reputation of a woman; it is at once the most beautiful and most brittle of all human things.

FANNY BURNEY
Evelina

She generally gave herself very good advice (though she very seldom followed it.)

LEWIS CARROLL
Alice's Adventures in Wonderland

The woman who is resolved to be respected can make herself so even amidst an army of soldiers. (La mujer que se determina a ser honrada entre un ejército de soldados lo puede ser.)

CERVANTES
La Gitanilla

A woman's advice has little value, but he who won't take it is a fool.

CERVANTES
Don Quixote Pt. ii, ch. 7

Woman is made of glass. (Es de vidrio la mujer.)

CERVANTES
Don Quixote Pt. i, ch. 33

A man of sense only trifles with them [women], plays with them, humours and flatters them, as he does with a sprightly and forward child; but he neither consults them about, nor trusts them with, serious matters.

PHILIP DORMER STANHOPE, EARL OF CHESTERFIELD
Letter

Women are much more like each other than men: they have, in truth, but two passions, vanity and love; these are their universal characteristics.

PHILIP DORMER STANHOPE, EARL OF CHESTERFIELD
Letter

A man with a bad heart has been sometimes saved by a strong head; but a corrupt woman is lost forever.

SAMUEL TAYLOR COLERIDGE
Table-Talk

What attracts us in a woman rarely binds us to her.

CHURTON COLLINS
Aphorisms No. 101

A man is as old as he's feeling,
A woman as old as she looks.

MORTIMER COLLINS
The Unknown Quantity

Heav'n has no rage like love to hatred turn'd
Nor hell a fury like a woman scorn'd.

WILLIAM CONGREVE
The Mourning Bride Act iii, sc. 8

Women are like tricks of slight of hand,
Which, to admire, we should not understand.

WILLIAM CONGREVE
Love for Love

Women are never stronger than when they arm themselves with their weaknesses.

MADAME DU DEFFAND
Letter to Voltaire

There's no music when a woman is in the concert.

THOMAS DEKKER
The Honest Whore Act iv, sc. 1

The only useless life is woman's.

BENJAMIN DISRAELI
Coningsby Bk. iv, ch. 15

The happiest women, like the happiest nations, have no history.

GEORGE ELIOT
The Mill on the Floss Bk. vi, ch. 3

How a little love and good company improves a woman!

GEORGE FARQUHAR
The Beaux' Stratagem Act iv, sc. 1

No woman can be a beauty without a fortune.

GEORGE FARQUHAR
The Beaux' Stratagem Act ii, sc. 2

Women are like pictures: of no value in the hands of a fool till he hears men of sense bid high for the purchase.

GEORGE FARQUHAR
The Beaux' Stratagem Act ii, sc. 1

A woman's friendship ever ends in love.

JOHN GAY
Dione iv, 6

A noble man is led far by woman's gentle words. (Ein edler Mann wird durch ein gutes Wort der Frauen weit geführt.)

GOETHE
Iphigenia auf Tauris Act i, sc. 2

Women and music should never be dated.

OLIVER GOLDSMITH
She Stoops to Conquer Act iii

Nature is in earnest when she makes a woman.

OLIVER WENDELL HOLMES
The Autocrat of the Breakfast Table Ch. 12

Man has his will—but woman has her way.

OLIVER WENDELL HOLMES
The Autocrat of the Breakfast Table Ch. I

When a woman writes her confession she is never further from the truth.

JAMES HUNEKER
Pathos of Distance

Sir, a woman's preaching is like a dog's walking on his hinder legs. It is not done well; but you are surprised to find it done at all.

SAMUEL JOHNSON
(Boswell, *Life* Vol. i)

Nothing is as unbearable as a woman of wealth. (Intolerabilius nihil est quam femina dives.)

JUVENAL
Satires Sat. vi

Women are ever in extremes; they are either better or worse than men.

JEAN DE LA BRUYERE
Les Caractères "Des Femmes"

Women, like princes, find few real friends:
All who approach them their own ends pursue;
Lovers and ministers are seldom true.

GEORGE LYTTELTON
Advice to a Lady

He who teaches a woman letters feeds more poison to a frightful asp.

MENANDER
Fragments No. 72

I expect that woman will be the last thing civilized by man.

GEORGE MEREDITH
Richard Feverel Ch. 1

Never take No for an answer.

JOHN F. MITCHELL

Whether they give or refuse, it delights women to be asked. (Quae dant, quaeque negant, gaudent tamen esse rogatae.)

OVID
Ars Amatoria Bk. i

A woman is a foreign land,
Of which, though there he settle young
A man will ne'er quite understand
The customs, politics, and tongue.

COVENTRY PATMORE
The Angel in the House "The Foreign Land"

Any woman will love any man that bothers her enough.

HENRY WALLACE PHILLIPS
Mr. Scroggs

There's no such thing as picking out the best woman; it's only a question of comparative badness. (Nam optuma nulla potest eligi; Alia alia pejor est.)

PLAUTUS
Aulularia

Frailty, thy name is woman!

WILLIAM SHAKESPEARE
Hamlet Act i, sc. 2

No is no negative in a woman's mouth.

SIR PHILIP SIDNEY
Arcadia Bk. iii

A woman . . . always feels herself complimented by love, though it may be from a man incapable of winning her heart, or perhaps even her esteem.

ABEL STEVENS
Life of Madame de Staël Ch. 3

God made the woman for the man,
And for the good and increase of the world.

ALFRED LORD TENNYSON
Edwin Morris

What woman, however old, has not the bridal-favours
And raiment stowed away, and packed in lavender,
In the inmost cupboards of her heart.

WILLIAM MAKEPEACE THACKERAY
Lovel the Widower Ch. 28

Man's work lasts till set of sun;
Woman's work is never done.

UNKNOWN
(*Roxburghe Ballads* iii, 302)

Yet will the woman have the last word.

UNKNOWN
School House of Women

Very learned women are to be found, in the same manner as female warriors; but they are seldom or never inventors.

VOLTAIRE
A Philosophical Dictionary "Women"

There's no social differences—till women come in.

H. G. WELLS
Kipps Bk. ii, ch. 4

One should never trust a woman who tells one her real age. A woman who would tell one that, would tell one anything.

OSCAR WILDE
A Woman of No Importance Act i

A woman with a past has no future.

OSCAR WILDE

All women become like their mothers. That is their tragedy. No man does. That's his.

> OSCAR WILDE
> *The Importance of Being Earnest* Act i

THE WORLD

The world's a bubble.

> FRANCIS BACON
> *The World*

The world!—it is a wilderness,
Where tears are hung on every tree.

> THOMAS HOOD
> *Ode to Melancholy*

There are two worlds; the world that we can measure with line and rule, and the world that we feel with our hearts and imaginations.

> LEIGH HUNT
> *Men, Women, and Books* "Fiction and Matter-of-Fact"

It takes all sorts of people to make a world.

> DOUGLAS WILLIAM JERROLD
> *Story of a Feather* Ch. 28

The world meets nobody half-way.

> CHARLES LAMB
> *Essays of Elia* "Valentine's Day"

The world is but a perpetual see-saw. (Le monde n'est qu'une bransloire perenne.)

> MONTAIGNE
> *Essays* Bk. iii, ch. 2

I hold the world as but world, Gratiano—
A stage, where every man must play a part.

> WILLIAM SHAKESPEARE
> *The Merchant of Venice* Act i, sc. 1

The world is a mirror of infinite beauty, yet no man sees it. It is a Temple of Majesty, yet no man regards it. It is a region of Light and Peace, did not men disquiet it. It is the Paradise of God.

> THOMAS TRAHERNE
> *Centuries of Meditations*

WRITING

Talent alone cannot make a writer. There must be a man behind the book.

> RALPH WALDO EMERSON
> *Representative Men* "Goethe"

Nobody can write the life of a man, but those who have eat and drunk and lived in social intercourse with him.

> SAMUEL JOHNSON
> (Boswell, *Life*)

Beneath the rule of men entirely great,
The pen is mightier than the sword.

> BULWER-LYTTON
> *Richelieu* Act ii, sc. 2

True ease in writing comes from art, not chance,
As those move easiest who have learned to dance.
'Tis not enough no harshness gives offence,
The sound must seem an echo to the sense.
Soft is the strain when zephyr gently blows,
And the smooth stream in smoother numbers flows;
But when loud surges lash the sounding shore,

The hoarse, rough verse should like the torrent roar:
When Ajax strives some rock's vast weight to throw,
The line too labours, and the words move slow:
Not so, when swift Camilla scours the plain,
Flies o'er th' unbending corn, and skims along the main.

> ALEXANDER POPE
> *An Essay on Criticism*

YOUTH

Young men are fitter to invent than to judge, fitter for execution than for counsel, and fitter for new projects than for settled business.

> FRANCIS BACON
> *Essays* 42 "Of Youth and Age"

A boy's will is the wind's will,
And the thoughts of youth are long, long thoughts.

> HENRY WADSWORTH LONGFELLOW
> *My Lost Youth*

MISCELLANY

From ghoulies and ghosties and long-leggety beasties
And things that go bump in the night,
Good Lord, deliver us!

> ANONYMOUS

A wise man will make more opportunities than he finds.

> FRANCIS BACON
> *Essays* 52 "Of Ceremonies and Respects"

Riches are for spending.

> FRANCIS BACON
> *Essays* 28 "Of Expense"

Prudence is a rich, ugly, old maid courted by Incapacity.

> WILLIAM BLAKE
> *Marriage of Heaven and Hell* "Proverbs of Hell"

It is at home, not in public, one washes one's dirty linen. (C'est en famille, ce n'est pas en publique, qu'on lave son linge sale.)

> NAPOLEON BONAPARTE
> *Speech* 1815

Education makes a people easy to lead, but difficult to drive; easy to govern, but impossible to enslave.

> HENRY, BARON BROUGHAM
> *Speech* January 29, 1828

No man can justly censure or condemn another, because indeed, no man truly knows another.

> SIR THOMAS BROWNE
> *Religio Medici* 4

Charity begins at home, is the voice of the world.

> SIR THOMAS BROWNE
> *Religio Medici* 4

I shall not help crucify mankind upon a cross of gold. I shall not aid in pressing down upon the bleeding brow of labor this crown of thorns.

> WILLIAM JENNINGS BRYAN
> *Speech* December 22, 1894

Because half a dozen grasshoppers under a fern make the field ring with their importunate chink, whilst thousands of great cattle, reposed beneath the shadow of the British oak, chew the cud and are silent, pray do not imagine that those who make the noise are the only inhabitants of the field; that, of course, they are many in number, or that, after all, they are other than the little, shrivelled, meagre, hopping, though loud and troublesome *Insects* of the hour.

> EDMUND BURKE
> *Reflections on the Revolution in France*

Love is a boy, by poets styl'd,
Then spare the rod, and spoil the child.

> SAMUEL BUTLER
> *Hudibras* Pt. ii, c. 1

Sweet is revenge—especially to women.

> GEORGE GORDON, LORD BYRON
> *Don Juan* c. 1, cxxiv

Romances paint at full length people's wooings,
But only give a bust of marriages:
For no one cares for matrimonial cooings,
There's nothing wrong in a connubial kiss:
Think you, if Laura had been Petrarch's wife,
He would have written sonnets all his life?

> GEORGE GORDON, LORD BYRON
> *Don Juan* C. III, viii

Man, being reasonable, must get drunk;
The best of life is but intoxication.

> GEORGE GORDON, LORD BYRON
> *Don Juan* C. 1, clxix

Now hatred is by far the longest pleasure;
Men love in haste, but they detest at leisure.

> GEORGE GORDON, LORD BYRON
> *Don Juan* C. XIII, vi

The best sauce in the world is hunger. (La mejor del mundo es el hambre.)

> CERVANTES
> *Don Quixote* Pt. ii, ch. 5

Said the pot to the kettle, "Get away, blackface!" (Dijo la sartén a la caldera, quítate allá ojinegra.)

> CERVANTES
> *Don Quixote* Pt. ii, ch. 67

An injury is much sooner forgotten than an insult.

> PHILIP DORMER STANHOPE, EARL OF CHESTERFIELD
> *Letter to his Son*

Advice is seldom welcome; and those who want it the most always like it the least.

> PHILIP DORMER STANHOPE, EARL OF CHESTERFIELD
> *Letter to his Son*

Water, water every where,
And all the boards did shrink,
Water, water every where,
Nor any drop to drink.
The very deep did rot: O Christ!
That ever this should be!
Yea, slimy things did crawl with legs
Upon the slimy sea.
About, about, in reel and rout,
The death-fires danced at night;
The water, like a witch's oils,
Burnt green, and blue and white.

> SAMUEL TAYLOR COLERIDGE
> *The Ancient Mariner*

Examinations are formidable even to the best prepared, for the greatest fool may ask more than the wisest man can answer.

> CHARLES CALEB COLTON
> *Lacon* Vol. i, no. 183

Music has charms to soothe a savage breast.

> WILLIAM CONGREVE
> *The Mourning Bride*

The business of America is business.

> CALVIN COOLIDGE
> *Speech* January 17, 1925

When I was a child, I spake as a child, I understood as a child, I thought as a child: but when I became a man, I put away childish things. For now we see through a glass, darkly; but then face to face: now I know in part; but then shall I know even as also I am known. And now abideth, faith, hope, charity, these three; but the greatest of these is charity.

> I Corinthians xiii, 11

To follow foolish precedents, and wink
With both our eyes, is easier than to think.

> WILLIAM COWPER
> *Tirocinium*

When a dog bites a man that is not news, but when a man bites a dog that is news.

> CHARLES ANDERSON DANA
> "What is News?" *The New York Sun* 1882

The sun shines on both sides of the hedge.

> SIR JOHN DENHAM
> *Proverbs* 49

Society is infested with persons who, seeing that the sentiments please, counterfeit the expression of them. These we call sentimentalists—talkers who mistake the description for the thing, saying for having.

> RALPH WALDO EMERSON
> *Letters and Social Aims* "Social Aims"

Let there be no inscription upon my tomb. Let no man write my epitaph. No man can write my epitaph. I am here ready to die. I am not allowed to vindicate my character; and when I am prevented from vindicating myself, let no man dare to calumniate me. Let my character and motives repose in obscurity and peace, till other times and other men can do them justice.

> ROBERT EMMET
> *Speech* 1803

Taste is the feminine of genius.

> EDWARD FITZGERALD
> *Letter* October, 1877

Three may keep a secret, if two of them are dead.

> BENJAMIN FRANKLIN
> *Poor Richard's Almanack*

A little neglect may breed mischief, . . . for want of a nail, the shoe was lost; for want of a shoe the horse was lost; and for want of a horse the rider was lost.

> BENJAMIN FRANKLIN
> *Poor Richard's Almanack*

Wilful waste brings woeful want.

> THOMAS FULLER
> *Gnomologia* No. 5755

Men are not hanged for stealing horses, but that horses may not be stolen.

> GEORGE SAVILE, MARQUIS OF HALIFAX
> *Political Thoughts and Reflections* "Of Punishment"

Treason doth never prosper: what's the reason?
For if it prosper, none dare call it treason.

> SIR JOHN HARINGTON
> *Epigrams* Bk. iv, no. 5

Laughter is nothing else but sudden glory arising from some sudden conception of some eminency in ourselves, by comparison with the infirmity of others, or with our own formerly.

> THOMAS HOBBES
> *On Human Nature* ix

A law made to be habitually and openly violated is a frightful demoralizer of society. A law notoriously despised by many that appear as its public advocates, which takes many a vote from the same hand that an hour later is lifted trembling to the voter's lips with the draught that quiets at once his nerves and his conscience.

> OLIVER WENDELL HOLMES
> *Speech* December, 1885

In laboring to be brief, I become obscure. (Brevis esse laboro, obscurus fio.)

> HORACE
> *Ars Poetica*

A tart temper never mellows with age, and a sharp tongue is the only edged tool that grows keener with constant use.

> WASHINGTON IRVING
> *Rip Van Winkle*

A little rebellion now and then is a good thing.

> THOMAS JEFFERSON
> *Letter* January 30, 1787

Integrity without knowledge is weak and useless, and knowledge without integrity is dangerous and dreadful.

> SAMUEL JOHNSON
> *Rasselas* Ch. 41

It is great cleverness to know how to conceal one's cleverness. (C'est une grand habileté de savoir comment cacher son habileté.)

> FRANCOIS LA ROCHEFOUCAULD
> *Maximes* No. 245

There is no good in arguing with the inevitable. The only argument available with an east wind is to put on your overcoat.

> JAMES RUSSELL LOWELL
> *Democracy and Addresses* "Democracy"

Population, when unchecked, increases in a geometrical ratio. Subsistence only increases in an arithmetical ratio.

> THOMAS ROBERT MALTHUS
> *The Principle of Population*

If a house be divided against itself, that house cannot stand.

> St. Mark iii, 25

Follow your own bent no matter what people say.

> KARL MARX
> *Capital* "Preface"

But the children of the kingdom shall be cast out into outer darkness: there shall be weeping and gnashing of teeth.

> St. Matthew viii, 12

Judge not, that ye be not judged.

> St. Matthew vii, 1

Give not that which is holy unto the dogs, neither cast ye your pearls before swine, l'est they trample them under their feet, and turn again and rend you.

> St. Matthew vii, 6

A prophet is not without honor, save in his own country, and in his own house.

> St. Matthew xiii, 57

No man can serve two masters.

> St. Matthew vi, 24

Taxation without representation is tyranny.

> JAMES OTIS

The sublime and the ridiculous are often so nearly related, that it is difficult to class them separately. One step above the sublime, makes the ridiculous; and one step above the ridiculous, makes the sublime again.

> THOMAS PAINE
> *Age of Reason* Pt. ii

These are the times that try men's souls.

> THOMAS PAINE
> *The American Crisis* No. 1

The heart has its reasons, which reason does not know. (Le coeur a ses raisons, que la raison ne connaît pas.)

> BLAISE PASCAL
> *Pensées* Pt. ii, art. xvii

The man who makes no mistakes does not usually make anything.

> EDWARD JOHN PHELPS
> *Speech* January 24, 1899

Where'er you walk cool gales shall fan the glade;
Trees, where you sit, shall crowd into a shade;
Where'er you tread, the blushing flowers shall rise,
And all things flourish where you turn your eyes.

> ALEXANDER POPE
> *Pastorals* "Summer"

Pride goeth before destruction, and an haughty spirit before the fall.

> Proverbs xvi, 18

There is a homely adage which runs: "Speak softly and carry a big stick; you will go far."

> THEODORE ROOSEVELT
> *Speech* September 2, 1901

He is well payed that is well satisfied.

> WILLIAM SHAKESPEARE
> *The Merchant of Venice* Act iv, sc. 1

Friends, Romans, countrymen, lend me your ears;
I come to bury Caesar, not to praise him.
The evil that men do lives after them;
The good is oft interred with their bones;
So let it be with Caesar. The noble Brutus

Hath told you Caesar was ambitious.
If it were so, it was a grievous fault;
And grievously hath Caesar answer'd it.

WILLIAM SHAKESPEARE
Julius Caesar Act iii, sc. 2

Since brevity is the soul of wit,
And tediousness the limbs and outward flourishes,
I will be brief.

WILLIAM SHAKESPEARE
Hamlet Act ii, sc. 2

Doctor Livingstone, I presume?

HENRY M. STANLEY

His remedies were more grievous than the offence.
(Graviour remediis quam delicta erant.)

TACITUS
Annais Bk. iii, sec. 28

Sweet April showers
Do spring May flowers.

THOMAS TUSSER
Five Hundred Points of Good Husbandry
ch. 38 "April's Husbandry"

Faith consists in believing when it is beyond the power of reason to believe. It is not enough that a thing be possible for it to be believed. (La foi consiste à croire ce que la raison ne croit pas.... Il ne suffit pas qu'une chose soit possible pour le croire.)

VOLTAIRE
Questions sur l'Encyclopedie

Jesus loves me—this I know,
For the Bible tells me so.

SUSAN WARNER
The Love of Jesus

Honesty is the best policy; but he who is governed by that maxim is not an honest man.

RICHARD WHATELY, ARCHBISHOP OF DUBLIN
Apophthegms

Children begin by loving their parents. After a time they judge them. Rarely, if ever, do they forgive them.

OSCAR WILDE
A Woman of No Importance Act ii

CECIL GRAHAM: What is a cynic? LORD DARLINGTON: A man who knows the price of everything, and the value of nothing.

OSCAR WILDE
Lady Windemere's Fan Act iii

A man cannot be too careful in the choice of his enemies.

OSCAR WILDE
Picture of Dorian Gray Ch. I

A little sincerity is a dangerous thing, and a great deal of it is absolutely fatal.

OSCAR WILDE
The Critic as Artist

The only way to get rid of a temptation is to yield to it.

OSCAR WILDE
Picture of Dorian Gray Ch. 2

STUDENTS' AND WRITERS' GUIDE

When editors and publishers speak of style, they are usually not referring to the author's choice of words or the length of his sentences, but to the way a manuscript will look in print—capitalization, punctuation, spacing, and typesetting. However, even in this limited sense, style cannot be reduced to a set of comprehensive rules, for it may change over the years, according to the subject matter or the type of publication. Thus, newspaper style differs from that used in books, and the style of the United States Constitution is different from that of the 1970's: in the Constitution, all the nouns were capitalized, the trend today is to keep capitalization to a minimum. There is no objective standard for comparing the two.

The style suggested in this guide is based on the standards accepted by the majority of editors today. It is intended not only for students writing term papers, but also for secretaries and businessmen preparing communications which must be rendered in clear, correct English. The rules here, therefore, are thorough but not overly technical. They are meant as a guide in preparing typewritten manuscripts and reports.

Questions which are not answered by this style manual, such as margin widths and page numbering, usually have common-sense solutions; often solutions to unusual problems are found in the literature on the subject of the paper or manuscript being prepared. A dictionary is an invaluable aid, especially in solving questions of spelling, syllabication, and hyphenation.

Contents

Section IV
NUMBERS

Section V
FOOTNOTES

Section VI
BIBLIOGRAPHIES

Section VII
BASIC REFERENCE WORKS

Students' and Writers' Guide

Section I
PUNCTUATION
INTRODUCTION

1a. Punctuation in written material is often as important as the correct placement of signs and symbols in mathematical calculations. While 3(2 + 3) is equal to 15, 3(2) + 3 is equal to 9; yet the only difference in the two problems is in the placement of the parentheses. In writing, as in mathematics, the proper placement of commas, parentheses, periods, and other punctuation makes the difference between a clear, well-constructed statement and a muddled, confusing series of meaningless symbols. The following sections give basic rules for proper punctuation.

PERIOD

2a. A period (.) is placed at the end of declarative and imperative sentences and immediately after abbreviations and initials:
She walks ten miles every day.
Send a letter to Mr. D. M. Green.
Hand me a 1½ in. nail.

2b. No period is used, however, at the end

of a sentence contained within a longer sentence:
The defendant's reply, "I never saw this man before," surprised everyone.

2c. A period is placed after numbers or letters which precede items in a list or outline:
1. the early period before 1800
b. parrots and their allies
No period is used following numbers or letters used to list items in a paragraph; these should be enclosed in parentheses. See PARENTHESES.

QUESTION MARK

3a. A question mark (?) is placed after a direct question:
Where will you be this summer?
"Can you come too?" she asked.

3b. A question mark follows an interrogative sentence even when part of a larger sentence:
How can this be done? immediately occurred to me.

3c. If intended interrogatively, a declarative or imperative sentence is terminated with a question mark:
This is what we've been waiting for?

Do this?

3d. A question mark is not used after an indirect question:
He asked how long we'd been staying there.

3e. A question mark enclosed in parentheses is used to indicate uncertainty:
He said he'll be back on September 20 (?).

EXCLAMATION POINT

4. An exclamation point (!) is used after interjections and at the end of a sentence for emphasis or to indicate surprise, admiration, incredulity, or other strong emotion:
Aha! I caught you.
Hello! What's this?
There he goes!
How can you believe that!
That's incredible!
He walked three blocks in the pouring rain before missing his umbrella!

APOSTROPHE

5a. An apostrophe (') is used in contractions to indicate omitted letters or words, and in dates to indicate omitted numerals:
It's an interesting book.

I've never heard of him.
He didn't understand at all.
Come at eight o'clock.
He graduated in '06.

5b. An apostrophe with an *s* ('s) is added to form the possessive case of most singular nouns; exceptions are such words as *conscience, righteousness,* etc., and certain ancient or Biblical names, which take an apostrophe without *s:*

man's hat
boy's toy
girl's dolls
dress's length
fox's den
Joyce's stream-of-consciousness technique
Marx's theories
Strauss's tone poem
appearance' sake
Moses' tablet
Sophocles' trilogy

5c. An apostrophe only is added to form the possessive case of plural nouns ending in *s;* plural nouns not ending in *s* take an apostrophe with *s:*

boys' fathers
girls' homes
ladies' husbands
men's ties
geese's grain
the Smiths' farms
the Joneses' estates

5d. An apostrophe with *s* is added to form the possessive case of indefinite pronouns not ending in *s;* indefinite pronouns ending in *s* take an apostrophe only:

somebody's scarf
everyone's situation
others' rights

5e. An apostrophe with *s* is used to form the plural of letters, signs, symbols, and numbers; plurals of years, however, are commonly formed with *s* alone:

"Occurred" is spelled with two "r's."
Insert "$'s" in front of all these totals.
The number should be written as "3" followed by four "8's."
the 1890s (or 1890's)

QUOTATION MARKS

6a. Quotation marks (" ") are used to enclose direct quotations; if the quotation is interrupted, each separate part should be enclosed between quotation marks:

Peter cried, "Let's go!"
"When," the children asked, "are we going to the circus?"
"I think it's stopped raining," Don remarked. "I'm going to leave now."

6b. Quotation marks are used to enclose ironic and slang expressions, misnomers and nicknames, titles of short works, and titles of sections of longer works. For treatment of other titles see ITALICS:

Our "leader," it seems, had disappeared.
The gang split up when the "coppers" came.
William H. Bonney was known as "Billy the Kid."
She used to watch "Bonanza."
Chapter 2 is titled "Music in Ancient Greece."
He sang "The Wanderer," by Schubert.
Have you read Freud's essay, "The Moses of Michelangelo"?

6c. Quotation marks are used to enclose words, phrases, etc., referred to in a sentence:

The word "supersede" is frequently misspelled.
When I first read her card, I thought she said it was a "lovely" rather than a "lonely" place.
The words "once upon a time" are used to begin many children's stories.

6d. Single quotation marks (' ') are used to enclose quotations within quotations:

"I was certain," Steve said, "that George answered, 'No, I'm not going.' "
"I thought you asked me to spell 'leisure,' " he replied.

6e. Philosophical and theological terms having a special meaning are frequently enclosed in single quotation marks:

'being for itself'
'beatific vision'

ELLIPSIS POINTS

7a. Ellipsis points (. . .) are used to indicate material which has been omitted from a quoted passage. Use three dots to indicate an omission within a sentence; punctuation marks may be retained on either side of the ellipsis points if they help the sense of the sentence or show better what has been omitted, but their use is optional. The resulting extract should always be a complete sentence:

Samuel Johnson said, "Praise . . . owes its value only to its scarcity."
As Mark Twain put it, "Habit is . . . not to be flung out of the window . . ., but coaxed downstairs a step at a time."

7b. Use four dots—a period followed by three dots—if the omitted material is (1) the end of a sentence, (2) the beginning of the next sentence, (3) the whole next sentence or more, or (4) the whole next paragraph or more; if the sentence ends with a question mark or exclamation point rather than a period, use this punctuation followed by three dots. The quoted matter preceding that and following an ellipsis of four dots should always be a complete sentence; if the beginning of a sentence is omitted, the sentence will usually begin with a lower-case letter:

In Samuel Johnson's opinion, "Few things are impossible. . . ."
In *Walden* Thoreau observed: "Public opinion is a weak tyrant. . . . What a man thinks of himself . . . determines . . . his fate."
As Thoreau advised: "Love your life, poor as it is. . . . The setting sun is reflected from the window of the almshouse as brightly as from the rich man's abode."
As George Bernard Shaw remarked: "Liberty means responsibility. . . . most men dread it."

COMMA

8a. Series of three or more items joined by *and, or,* or *nor* are separated by commas (,); *etc.,* when used, should be set off by commas:

Marcia, Tony, and Judy went downtown yesterday.
The fish he bought was either mackerel, perch, or cod.

Neither chains, salt, nor sand kept us from skidding.
Pins, earrings, lockets, etc., are on sale this month.

8b. Commas should not be used if the items are all joined by conjunctions and are relatively simple:

I don't know whether to divide by 2 or 3 or 6.

8c. Direct quotations and expressions preceding a quotation are punctuated by commas as follows:

"It's a terrible book," he said.
Edward said doubtfully, "How much will it cost?"

8d. A quotation which is the subject or predicate nominative of a sentence is not set off by a comma:

"We shall overcome" was his motto.
His motto was "We shall overcome."

8e. Words designating a title or position following a proper name are set off by commas:

Mr. H. L. Hughes, director of public relations for Klein Products, Inc., will speak at the luncheon.
James Horton, president of Acme Corporation, is on the committee.

8f. Appositives are set off by commas:

The janitor, Mr. Brown, is sick today.
The timpani, or kettledrums, are used very effectively in this work.

8g. Words of direct address and interjections are set off by commas:

Charles, go to the back door.
My friends, I wish to thank you for your support.
No, I'm afraid that won't do.
Well, I think we'll have to try a different approach.

8h. Two or more adjectives preceding a noun are separated by a comma, except when adjective and noun appear as a unit:

A big, bright moon shone on the lake.
We had a short, rainy spring that year.
All the large electric lights were burned out.

8i. Two or more phrases referring to a single following word should be separated by commas:

These shocking, though not entirely unexpected, events could precipitate widespread panic.
The audience had expected to see Sir Laurence Olivier, not an understudy, play Hamlet.

8j. Conjunctions that join two independent clauses in compound sentences are preceded by commas, except when the clauses are short and closely related:

A shot rang out over the valley, but we could not determine who had fired the gun.
The committee prepared a report, the president reviewed it, and the board adopted the proposals it urged.
That is an interesting city, but it's so crowded that I wouldn't want to live there.
Tom walked down the road and his brother followed him.

8k. Dependent clauses at the beginning of a sentence and participial phrases at the beginning of a sentence, unless forming part of the verb, are set off by commas:

If you'll ask Harry, I'm sure he'll be able to help you.

Although we advised her not to, she went to California.

Judging by her handwriting, I decided she was exceptionally intelligent.

Walking beside the road was an old man.

8l. Dependent clauses at the end of a sentence are set off by commas if they are not essential to the basic meaning of the sentence:

She went to California, although we advised her not to.

We kept traveling after the storm, though most of the party would have preferred to go home.

We finally agreed to return if we could meet again during the next week.

She was surprised when we told her the news.

8m. Introductory adverbial phrases, unless quite brief, are followed by a comma except when they immediately precede the verb:

While closing the curtains, she noticed a man hurrying down the street.

Because of the enthusiasm shown, the show was extended another week.

After dinner we went for a walk.

Into the room rushed several children shouting noisily.

8n. Adverbial clauses or phrases occurring between the subject and verb are set off by commas:

Barton, after consulting with several authorities, proposed changes.

The group, due to unexpected difficulties, decided to drop the project.

John, because of illness, was unable to attend.

8o. An adjectival clause or phrase is set off by commas if dropping the clause or phrase does not change the meaning of the noun:

The winning bicycle, which weighed only 12 pounds, was made in France.

The bicycle that won the race weighed only 12 pounds.

8p. Elements occurring parenthetically in a sentence, if not remote enough to require parentheses or dashes, are set off by commas:

This month there have been, as far as we know, two accidents.

Jane, at least in the opinion of her sister, had always seemed quite stable.

Mr. Gregg (he worked here for many years) is said to have set up the system.

8q. Words or phrases such as "however," "therefore," "after all," etc., are set off by commas if they distinctly break the continuity of thought; if such elements are used so as not to break the continuity and not to require a pause in reading, commas should not be used:

By the same token, industry has not done all it could have.

The answer, perhaps, is to send out a questionnaire.

We should, however, consider ourselves quite fortunate.

All these cases, in fact, show similar symptoms.

I therefore demand that you remain here.

Tonight's performance has indeed been canceled.

COMMA (Special Uses)

9a. Inverted names, as in a list, have a comma between the last and first name:

Day-Lewis, Cecil

Whitman, Walt

Whittier, John Greenleaf

Wordsworth, William

9b. Words which together might be misunderstood or be awkward to read are separated by commas:

She watched him as he walked around the room, and then quickly left.

Where he is, is not known.

To Frank, Jones was most polite.

9c. Expressions such as *i.e., e.g., namely,* and *that is* are set off by commas; sometimes a semicolon or other punctuation should precede such expressions if the break is greater than that indicated by a comma:

There are three people on the commission who have done all the work, namely, Smith, Jones, and Pierce.

The discussion centered on the ancient Greek tragic playwrights, i.e., Aeschylus, Sophocles, and Euripedes.

The ruling does not apply to full-time employees, but only to part-time employees; that is, employees working fewer than thirty hours weekly.

Several states (e.g., Pennsylvania, New York, and Illinois) are "swing" states in every national election.

9d. Interrelated contrasting clauses should be separated by a comma:

The bigger they are, the harder they fall.

The more Tom worked, the hungrier he became.

9e. Words which are omitted but understood in context are indicated by the use of a comma:

He had a thousand friends when he was rich; when poor, none.

We did not do enough for him yesterday; today, too much.

9f. A comma is used to separate an interrogative clause from a declarative clause that it follows:

You'll be here tomorrow night, won't you?

That's the year you went to Europe, isn't it?

9g. The separate parts of addresses and place names are separated by commas:

He lives at 1414 Whitehall Drive, Brighton, Maryland.

Calcutta, India

Cook County, Illinois

9h. Dates are punctuated by commas as follows:

On September 12, 1959, the . . .

Thursday, April 25, is . . .

June 1947 (no comma)

12 September 1959 (no comma)

9i. Numbers of four or more digits contain commas to separate thousands, millions, etc.; commas are not used in ZIP codes, telephone numbers, serial numbers, etc.:

3,421 miles

a population of 20,590,120

part no. 73248593

page 2189

Chicago, Il. 60602 (note: there is no comma between state and ZIP code)

9j. A comma is used to separate two sets of figures:

In 1940, 159 people died of that disease.

Our school ordered 48, 34-inch pointers.

COLON

10a. Series and lists are introduced by colons (:):

Questionnaires were mailed to city managers in three states: Minnesota, California, and Florida.

The area of a triangle may be expressed in terms of three variables: the base, one of the sides, and the included angle.

Appalachian trail:

Northern region

the Adirondacks (New England states)

the Alleghenies (Middle Atlantic states)

Southern region

the Shenandoahs (Virginia)

the Blue Ridge (the Carolinas and Georgia)

The steps are as follows:

1. Construct the perpendicular bisector to . . .

2. Connect points . . .

10b. A complete sentence, question, or long quotation is introduced by a colon:

One rule is paramount: Do not fire until the order is given.

This question was discussed: Should the debate be methodological or teleological?

I quote from his recent speech: "In times such as ours . . . caution is our best policy. . . . Recent events . . . have shown this to be true."

10c. A colon follows the names of speakers in a dialogue and the introductory address of a speaker:

The father: Has he asked you to marry him?

Julie: Oh no, he . . .

Ladies and Gentlemen:

10d. Time indications, Bible references, volume and page references, and ratios are punctuated by colons as follows; many Catholic Bibles, however, now have a comma in place of a colon:

at exactly 3:48 in the afternoon

4:00 P.M.

I Kings 1:20 (or I Kings 1,20)

Ruth 4:18-22 (or Ruth 4,18-22)

American Psychologist 10:17-25

in the ratio of 7:5

SEMICOLON

11a. Items in a series are separated by a semicolon (;) when the items themselves contain a comma or other internal punctuation:

The number of games played this season is: team A, 3; team B, 5; team C, 2; team D, 4.

Some of those at the party were Franco Lorenzini, the leading tenor; Mrs. J. R. Grant, the president of the women's committee; and William Macklin, the assistant conductor.

The assignment for next Sunday is Matthew 2:17-19; 3:5-14; and 4:1,5,9.

11b. Two independent clauses in a compound sentence which are not joined by a conjunction are separated by a semicolon:

Everyone knew the banks were out of cash; yet depositors were lined up outside waiting to make withdrawals. (*yet* is an adverb, not a conjunction)

I washed the car yesterday; already it's dirty again.

The old buildings I liked; the new ones were atrocious.

11c. In a compound sentence containing long or internally punctuated clauses connected by a conjunction, a semicolon should be used between them, before the conjunction:

The girls, who had been waiting hours backstage for a chance to see their idol, pressed forward eagerly when he finally appeared; but their disappointment was great when he swiftly darted into the nearest cab without even acknowledging their presence.

11d. A semicolon should be used between the independent parts of a sentence that contains a comma indicating an omitted word or words (see COMMA, 9e); if another construction is used, and the comma avoided, do not use a semicolon:

In Illinois we have thirteen delegates; in Indiana, nine; in Michigan, eight.

He claims mental labor is tiring; physical labor, relaxing.

He claims mental labor is tiring, but finds physical labor relaxing.

DASH

12a. A sudden break in thought is indicated by a dash (–):

He said–to everyone's amazement– that the Chinese were stationed along the border.

If the car has rolled into the canal–God forbid!–then all we can do is take the train.

12b. Dashes may be used to set off a phrase or word repeated for emphasis:

And that's the price for one volume– one volume only–not for the set.

Note that the following figures are based on data obtained from men only–men only–and do not necessarily apply to the membership as a whole.

12c. An unfinished word or sentence is indicated by the use of a dash:

"I'm going to snee–," she cried.

Just before he was shot he cried, "We cannot continue–"

12d. A phrase which introduces a series and is understood to be repeated before each item is followed by a dash:

The committee decided–
1. to abolish three vice-presidencies;
2. to create a new office in the sales department for Jones;
3. to submit a list of thirty recommendations to Smith.

12e. To clarify the meaning of a sentence, a dash is used in place of commas or parentheses:

The basic ingredients of a cake–flour, sugar, milk, and eggs–were sitting on the counter.

12f. A final clause summarizing a series of ideas in a sentence, and a final clause which is an expansion of something in the main clause are set off by a dash:

I always use the dictionary, the thesaurus, and a grammar book–three indispensable aids when writing.

After lunch we all toured the caves– the same caves where just a week before three men had disappeared.

12g. A short dash (–) is used to indicate inclusive or continuing numbers, dates, etc. Do not use the dash with such words as *from* and *between:*

the period 1952–59
February–May 1970
11:00 A.M.–9:00 P.M.
pp. 197–210
September 25, 1962–June 6, 1963
Luke 2:4–3:22
A History of Europe, 1945–1970
Jean Paul Sartre (1905–   )
from 1952 to 1959 (*not* from 1952–59)
between 11:00 A.M. and 9:00 P.M. (*not* between 11:00 A.M.–9:00 P.M.)

PARENTHESES

13a. An independent part of a sentence or paragraph not directly related to the main statement, as a comment or explanation, is enclosed in parentheses [( )]:

Three people (all in the last row) were snoring so loudly that the lecturer stopped.

We'll have plenty of opportunity to go swimming since the pool will be open until Labor Day. (Last summer it closed on August 20, I think.)

13b. Letters and numbers enumerating the items in a series are enclosed in parentheses:

He traced the development of the symphony using examples from works by (1) Haydn, (2) Mozart, (3) Beethoven, and (4) Schubert.

The impedance of an electric circuit can be considered as consisting of (a) resistance, (b) inductance, and (c) capacitance.

13c. Numerals or other symbols when occurring appositively are enclosed in parentheses:

With each order of twelve (12), enclose a check for two dollars ($2.00).

It was decided that except in titles all ampersands (&) should be spelled out.

13d. A place name which is not part of an official name, but is necessary information in a sentence, is enclosed in parentheses:

The Pittsburg (Kansas) Historical Society should not be confused with the Pittsburgh (Pennsylvania) Historical Society.

BRACKETS

14a. Editorial comments or corrections in material are set off with brackets ([ ]):

On that day the president [Wilson] took a walk through the garden.

He said, "All those left [mostly women and children] must move back out of the way."

D[j]akarta was our last stop in Indonesia.

This book says Thomas Edison was a very ingenuous [*sic*] man.

14b. Parenthetical material within parentheses is enclosed in brackets:

After writing several novels (mostly about war experiences [such stories were quite popular at the time]), he began writing plays.

MULTIPLE PUNCTUATION

15a. If a sentence requires a question mark or exclamation point in the same place as a period or comma, only the question mark or exclamation point should be used; if a sentence requires a question mark in the same place as an exclamation point, only the exclamation point should be used:

"Did you see him?" she asked.

Who was it that said, "The British are coming!"

15b. Multiple punctuation often occurs when abbreviations are used; omit an abbreviating period only if it coincides with a period terminating a sentence:

Dan's boat measures only 21 ft.; Jim's is much longer.

The Sherman Co., on Third Ave., was closed.

When did you get your Ph.D.?

Every office in the building was closed, including Cartwright and Webb, Inc.

15c. Multiple punctuation often occurs at the end of quotations within quotations:

She said, "He stood up and shouted, 'Peter did it!' "

The teacher told him, "In your paper you repeatedly misspelled the word 'their.' "

15d. Periods are placed within quotation marks except in the case of single quotation marks setting off special terms:

Murray replied, "I intend to do that tomorrow."

For an encore he sang "Dream at Twilight."

We were clearly told, "Do nothing until Bill says 'Throw the line.' "

Here he introduces the term 'ontological entity'.

15e. A comma, when called for at the end of material within quotation marks, is placed inside the quotation marks:

"I'll do that tomorrow," George replied.

"The Unanswered Question," a short work of Charles Ives, was recently performed on campus.

"By," "with," "from," "in," "on," and "to" are some commonly used prepositions.

The lockers labeled "Tom," "Charles," and "George" have been empty all semester.

15f. Question marks and exclamation points should be placed inside quotation marks and parentheses when they are part of the quoted or parenthetical material; otherwise they are placed outside:

The woman shrieked, "Look out!"

Why did he answer, "That's not for me to say"?

When Margaret arrived at the station (had she been here before?), she immediately knew which bus to take.

Jack was so nervous about the speech that he showed up the day before (Thursday)!

15g. Colons and semicolons are placed outside quotation marks and parentheses; a colon or semicolon terminating quoted matter is dropped:

There are three main sections comprising chapter 5, "Alcidine Sea Birds": "Auks," "Guillemots and Murres," and "Puffins."

Joyce is planning a big party for next

Saturday (after Jane's graduation); yet I know she's flat broke.

The sentence beginning "The ingredients are these" mentions, among other things, two eggs and sugar.

15h. A comma is placed outside parentheses and brackets when the context calls for it; it is not used with the dash except to separate a quotation from the speaker:

Several homes were destroyed in the hurricane (especially along the west edge of town), but no one was killed.

Despite criticism from certain persons [Doyle and his followers], Michael continued to publish his views.

After living many years in Paris—this period in his life will be discussed later—Dupin settled in Italy.

"I came to ta—," he started to say.

15i. Periods are placed outside parentheses and brackets except when the parentheses or brackets enclose an entire sentence, in which case the period is placed inside:

This habit of his was well known (though I had never before been witness to it).

Mr. Whipple put on his coat, hat, and gloves. (Indeed, he had a remarkable way of performing the task.)

HYPHEN

16a. The dictionary is always an invaluable aid in all questions concerning hyphenation. This guide gives only general rules, and each specific use of a hyphen should be verified in the dictionary. Correct placement of hyphens, whether for syllabication of a word at the end of a line or for compounding, is indicated in each entry in the dictionary.

16b. A hyphen (-) is used to divide a word at the end of a line where the word continues over onto the next line. Correct syllabication should always be observed:

Joan worked the problems but had considerable difficulty.

16c. A hyphen is used to form most compound words containing the following word elements:

cross-eyed   single-space
cross-fertilization   single-valued
great-grandmother   double-edged
great-hearted   double-talk
light-handed   ill-suited
light-headed   ill-mannered
heavy-armed   well-balanced
heavy-laden   well-prepared

16d. Hyphens are used between the words of a compound modifier when it occurs before the noun but are usually omitted when the modifier follows the noun or when it is used in other ways. Do not hyphenate a compound modifier if it contains an adverb ending in *ly*:

a word-for-word translation
The translation was word for word.
word-of-mouth advertising
I heard about it by word of mouth.
a hand-to-mouth salary
We were living hand to mouth.
a well-known author
He is well known.
a tight-fitting sweater
a tightly fitting sweater
a well-prepared lesson
a carefully prepared lesson

16e. A hyphen is used to join nouns in forming compound nouns that show a combination of qualities or functions. Do not hyphenate chemical compounds:

counselor-psychologist
director-producer
city-state
secretary-treasurer
hydrogen peroxide

16f. Hyphens are used to form compound nouns made up of different parts of speech. Do not hyphenate compound nouns denoting military rank or certain governmental positions:

stick-to-it-iveness
an old stick-in-the-mud
a good-for-nothing
an eighth-grader
editor-in-chief
mother-in-law
counselor-at-law
sergeant at arms
postmaster general
lieutenant colonel
justice of the peace

16g. A hyphen is used to join certain prefixes, as *anti* and *non*, to proper nouns and adjectives; such prefixes are usually combined with common nouns and adjectives to form a single word unless the second element is compound:

un-American   neo-Nazi
anti-Semite   midwinter
mid-December   unpatriotic
non-Catholic   anticlimax
pro-Hellenic   un-self-righteous

16h. A hyphen is used to form many compound words containing certain prefixes or suffixes:

self-complacent   ex-president
self-doubt   senator-elect
ex-housewife   twenty-odd

16i. A hyphen may be used after a prefix if the prefix causes doubling of a vowel:

re-echo   pre-establish
re-enlist   anti-intellectual
re-examine   anti-imperialism
co-operative   extra-atmospheric

16j. A hyphen is used to distinguish a relatively unusual usage of a word from its customary usage by separating a prefix:

to re-cover a couch
an un-ionized gas

16k. A hyphen is used to separate the parts of a compound number under one hundred when written out:

a board divided into sixty-four squares
West Seventy-second Street
twenty-seven cubic feet in a cubic yard
eighteen hundred and ninety-eight

16l. A hyphen is used to separate the numerator and denominator of a fraction used as an adjective when written out; use of the hyphen is optional for fractions used as nouns. Do not use a hyphen if either part of the fraction is itself hyphenated:

one-half cup of sugar
a two-thirds majority
one fourth of those present (or one-fourth)
six hundredths of one percent (or six-hundredths)
thirteen fifty-seconds
thirty-seven fiftieths
thirty-nine fifty-seconds

16m. A hyphen is used in spelling out or syllabicating a word:

Hyphen is spelled h-y-p-h-e-n and syllabicated hy-phen.
a-e-r-i-a-l   L-a-o-s
aer-i-al   La-os

Section II
ITALICS

17. Introduction. Italics are generally used either to add emphasis to a word or phrase or to set off a word, phrase, or title from the rest of a sentence.

Italics used for emphasis should be avoided whenever possible. Instead, sentences should be constructed so that the importance of a word is immediately clear to a reader. Constructing a sentence which achieves this effect is often more difficult than italicizing, but is both easier to read and less offending to the reader to whom the emphasis is clear without the italics.

Italics are mandatory, however, when they are necessary for clarity or required by convention. Italics are indicated in typed manuscripts by underlining.

18. Titles of Single Works as books, newspapers, magazines, and other periodicals, poetry collections and anthologies, and long poems are italicized. Titles of theses, manuscripts, and other unpublished works should be in roman type and enclosed in quotation marks. For treatment of other titles see QUOTATION MARKS:

The Old Curiosity Shop by Dickens
Encyclopaedia Britannica
New York Times
New York Times Book Review
Christian Science Monitor
Newsweek
Foreign Affairs Quarterly
Master Poems of the English Language
Idylls of the King
Troilus and Criseyde by Chaucer
in a master's thesis, "German Expressionist Drama and the Theatre of the Absurd," . . .

19. Titles of Plays, whether published separately or as part of a collection, are italicized:

Desire Under the Elms
Man and Superman

20. Titles of Motion Pictures are italicized:

The Jazz Singer
Citizen Kane
Gone With the Wind

21. Titles of Paintings, statues, etc., are italicized:

Monet's *Water Lilies*
Gainsborough's *Blue Boy*
Michelangelo's *David*
Rodin's *The Thinker*

22. Titles of Musical Compositions such as operas and tone poems are italicized. When the title of a musical work is the name of a musical form with a number or key, it should be in roman type. If such a title also has a descriptive name, the name is italicized if the work is long or quoted in roman type if the work is short:

Carmen
Das Rheingold

Night on Bald Mountain
Scheherazade
La Mer
The Creation
the *Messiah* (not *The Messiah*)
Prelude in C-sharp Minor
Symphony no. 1 in C Major
Piano Sonata no. 8 in C Minor
Mass in B Minor
Trio in B-flat opus 97 (*Archduke*)
Symphony no. 36 (*Linz*)
the *Eroica* Symphony
Rienzi Overture
Devil's Trill Sonata
Tchaikovsky's Sixth Symphony
Etude op. 25 no. 11 ("Winter Wind")
"St. Anne" Fugue

23. Scientific Names for plants and animals are italicized. Plants and animals are placed in taxonomic categories which are, respectively, from largest to smallest: kingdom, phylum, class, order, family, genus, species, and variety. The genus name is capitalized and the species name (and subspecies or variety name when used) is lower-cased. Divisions larger than the genus, and their intermediate groupings, are capitalized and may be in roman type:

Acer rubrum
Populus deltoides
Anthus spinoletta rubescens
the phylum Nematoda (or *Nematoda*)
the suborder Oscines (or *Oscines*)
the family Sciuridae (or *Sciuridae*)

24. Names of Specific Ships, spacecraft, etc., are italicized, but such abbreviations as S.S., U.S., etc., are not:

S.S. *United States*
U.S.S. *Virginia*
H.M.S. *Victoria*
Mariner III
Apollo 10

25. Names of Legal Cases are italicized, but not the *v.* separating the two parties involved:

Preston v. *City of Chicago*
Thomas v. *Wilson Freight Lines*
the *Preston* case (*but* Preston's case)

26. Foreign Words and Phrases which are probably not familiar to the reader are italicized. Those which are more common or more familiar and the well-known abbreviations for Latin words should be in roman type; *sic*, however, is always italicized:

The university's motto is *Quaecumque sunt vera.*
Russians eat black bread (*khleb*).
stadium generale – the medieval university
a priori
ménage à trois
deus ex machina
la dolce vita
i.e.
e.g.
et al.
etc.
ca.
sic

27. Letters Used as Words, individually or in combination, are italicized. Alternatively these may be enclosed in quotation marks:

the letter *b* (or "b")
a lower-case *u*

Such words normally end in *ing*.
It is spelled with a capital *R*.
Is this plural formed with *s* or *es*?
Let us use *x* to stand for the independent variable.

28. Words Used as Words are italicized. Alternatively, especially in more informal writing, these may be enclosed in quotation marks. See QUOTATION MARKS:

He used *affect* in place of *effect*.
She was continually using words such as *nice* and *adorable*.

29. Key Terms, or other special terms to which the reader's attention should be directed, are italicized when first used; subsequent usage need not be italicized:

Let us consider what is meant by *level of significance.*
As will become apparent in this discussion, these thinkers were *empiricists* and *positivists*, taking a strong stand against *vitalism*.

30. Emphasized Words are italicized if italicization is the only way to make the emphasis clear:

The teacher told him that the problem is he doesn't *listen*.
His superior used to *tell* him how to do his job.

31. Letters in Enumerations are italicized when the enumerated items are contained within the text:

Samples were obtained using (*a*) incoming freshmen only and (*b*) students currently enrolled who have lived on campus for at least two semesters.
Subjects were randomly assigned to three groups: (*a*) those learning lists of categorically related words, (*b*) those learning lists of unrelated words, and (*c*) those learning mixed lists of words both related and unrelated.

Section III
CAPITALIZATION

INTRODUCTION

32. This guide provides some basic rules for capitalization and examples of the most commonly questioned instances of capitalization. It would be impractical to formulate exhaustive rules or to make a complete list of words and phrases which should be capitalized because capitalization in many instances is determined by convention, personal preference, or context. For example, both a.m. and A.M. are correct, and historical periods or events are in some instances capitalized while in others they are lower-cased. In such cases consistency is more important than whether an *up* (capitalized) or *down* (lower-case) style is chosen. The trend, however, is towards a *down* style. If a specific instance of capitalization cannot be found or extrapolated from the rules and examples below, and does not appear in any other source, it is usually best not to capitalize.

CONVENTIONAL USAGE

33a. The first word of every sentence should be capitalized:

He rang the bell.
It rained for a while this morning.

33b. The words "I" and "O" (but not "oh") are always capitalized:

Hear me, O Lord!
Why, oh, why did I do it?

33c. The first word of a direct quotation should be capitalized:

She said, "When it warms up a bit, I'm going shopping."
John asked, "Where are we going?"

33d. Do not capitalize the first word of indirect quotations or the first word of parts or fragments of direct quotations which are part of the sentence structure:

She said he traveled west after the disaster.
She said he traveled west "once the disaster was over."
"I traveled west," he said, "once the disaster was over."

33e. The first, last, and major words in titles of books, plays, magazines, articles, movies, songs, etc., should be capitalized; generally do not capitalize prepositions and coordinate conjunctions of fewer than five letters, or the articles *a, an,* or *the,* unless they are the first word of a title:

I liked the chapter "The Grand Inquisitor" in Dostoevsky's novel *The Brothers Karamazov.*
The Return of the Native
A Tale of Two Cities
Of Human Bondage
Murder in the Cathedral
Desire Under the Elms
The Saturday Evening Post
"How to Control Your Weight"
Walt Disney's *Fantasia*
Never on Sunday
"The Star-Spangled Banner"
"Meet the Press"
Swan Lake
Sound of Music

NAMES AND TITLES

34a. Personal names and initials are capitalized:

George Washington
John L. Lewis
W. H. Auden
T. S. Eliot
JFK

34b. Names of European derivation containing such particles as *de, de la, della, van, von,* etc., should be capitalized according to accepted usage; if in doubt about the spelling of a personal name, consult one of the biographical references listed in the section "BASIC REFERENCE WORKS"; when used alone, the surname generally retains the particle unchanged; when such names are Anglicized, the particle is frequently capitalized:

Catherine de Medici
the de Medici family
Vincent van Gogh; van Gogh
Luca della Robbia; della Robbia
Manuel de Falla; de Falla
von Steuben (or Von Steuben)
Johann Wolfgang von Goethe; Goethe
Ludwig van Beethoven; Beethoven
Alexis de Tocqueville; Tocqueville
Van Buren
Agnes De Mille
Thomas De Quincey
Eva Le Gallienne

34c. Familial names should not be capitalized unless followed by a given proper name:

I talked to mother.
her cousin
I saw Uncle Ted.
I met Cousin Alice.
the Greene brothers

34d. Names used as personifications and fictitious names should be capitalized except in certain slang expressions:

John Doe
Richard Roe
John Henry
Joe Blow
Sam Hill
every Tom, Dick, and Harry
plain jane (or plain Jane)
merry-andrew
by george

34e. An epithet used with or instead of a personal name should be capitalized:

Stonewall Jackson
Richard the Lion-Hearted
the Swedish Nightingale
Eric the Red
Ivan the Terrible
the Young Pretender

34f. Titles preceding a personal name should be capitalized; titles following a name and titles used without a name are capitalized only in formal usage, such as formal introductions and acknowledgements:

Secretary of Labor Maurice H. Stans
Pope Paul VI
Cardinal Spellman
Senator Dirksen
Doctor Watson
Professor Wright
President Nixon
Richard Nixon, president of the United States
the president
John Marshall, attorney general
General Custer
Let us give thanks to the Chairman of the Legal Committee.
I wish to express my indebtedness to Geoffrey Caxton, Chairman of the Classics Department.

34g. Words denoting occupation or role that are not used as titles should *not* be capitalized:

defense attorney William Reed
bricklayer George Mason
author Schwartz

34h. Academic degrees and distinctions following a name should be capitalized; such general terms as "doctorate" and "bachelor's" should, however, be lower-cased as should the terms for academic years:

Harold Walters, Ph.D.
Lyle Carlson, Master of Education
L. H. Hodgkins, Fellow of Trinity College, Cambridge
master's thesis
doctorate in sociology
sophomore

PROPER NOUNS

35a. Nationalities and groupings of people based on race, language, religion, etc., are capitalized:

Slavic	Semite
Cherokee	Teutonic
American	Inca
Negro	Aryan

35b. Names of countries, major political or geographical divisions, and popular names of places should be capitalized; words that are not part of an accepted name are not capitalized:

France	New York City
East Germany	Ridgeview Township
Central America	Tenth Ward
North Pole	Deep South
Antarctica	Corn Belt
the Orient	the Beaver State
the Midwest	Right Bank
the States	the north of Italy
Temperate Zone	central Asia
East-West conflict	the equator
Great Plains	Kansas plains

35c. Words which come from proper names and retain the original meaning of the root word should be capitalized:

Italian cooking
Hussite follower
Freudian slip of the tongue

35d. Words which are derived from proper names but now have an independent meaning or are frequently used should *not* be capitalized:

pasteurized milk	philistine
french fries	dutch door
quixotic	gargantuan

35e. Names of specific rivers, seas, oceans, mountains, forests, etc., should be capitalized; a generic term, such as *river* or *lake*, should only be capitalized when part of a name:

Cape Cod	Rocky Mountains
Sherwood Forest	Straits of Mackinac
Black Sea	Arctic Ocean
Long Island	Chesapeake Bay
Isle of Man	Mojave Desert
Gulf of Mexico	Illinois prairies
Snake River	the Atlantic coast
Yosemite Creek	Rhine valley
Lake of the Woods	the river Elbe

35f. When a term such as *river* or *mountain* is used in the plural following two or more names, it is *not* capitalized; when used preceding two or more names, it should be capitalized:

at the junction of the Mississippi and Missouri rivers
between the Aegean and Ionian seas
Lakes Erie, Ontario, and Huron
Mounts Vesuvius and Etna

35g. Points of the compass are not capitalized:

traveling east
facing north

35h. Names of buildings, roads, monuments, and various public places should be capitalized. Capitalize words such as *street, bridge,* and *square* only when part of a proper name; if such a word follows two or more names, it should be lower-cased:

Brooklyn Bridge
Clark Street
First Ave.
Orchestra Hall
Jackson Park
Times Square
room 23 is the Empire Room
Arc de Triomphe
the Midway Plaisance
Route 66
the Federal Building
Clark and Division streets

35i. Important words in full names of societies, governmental bodies, companies, committees, organizations, institutions, and other groups should be capitalized:

National Audubon Society
United States Congress
House of Representatives
Union Pacific Railroad
General Motors
Cook County Board of Health
Atomic Energy Commission
University of Texas
Harvard School of Business
Department of Physics
Cleveland Orchestra
Institute for Psychoanalysis

35j. Common nouns and adjectives used to refer to organizations should not be capitalized when the full name is not used except for abbreviations and special cases designating preeminence or distinction, as with federal government bodies:

Pennsylvania Assembly; the assembly
Augustinian Academy; the academy
Naval Academy; the Academy
the French army
the U.S. Army; the Army
Allied forces
the armed services
the county board
circuit court
U.S. Congress; Congress
United Nations; the U.N.

35k. Legal cases, acts, treaties, wars, battles, awards, and political parties and their members should be capitalized:

Rogers v. *People of Illinois*
Monroe Doctrine
First World War
World War I
Battle of Bunker Hill
Nobel Peace Prize
Iron Cross
the Socialist party
a Fascist

35l. Words such as "nationalist," "communist," "republican," and "democratic" should not be capitalized unless used to designate a member of a party or as part of an official name or title:

He was a French nationalist.
No country has a truly democratic form of government, but several have republican systems.
The ballots contained the names of many independents.
Some people think of all leftists as communists.
Polyansky had heard that the Communist leaders were planning to expel him from the party.
the Republican convention
a National Socialist

RELIGIOUS TERMINOLOGY

36a. All names given to the one supreme God as well as the names of other gods and titles of religious writings and their major subdivisions should be capitalized:

the Almighty	Artemis
Heavenly Father	Vishnu
the Lord	Bible
Son of God	Koran
King of Kings	the Gospels
Lamb of God	Genesis
Yahweh	Old Testament
Allah	Douay Version

36b. Appellations referring to revered persons, such as saints and prophets, are usually capitalized:

John the Baptist
the Blessed Virgin
Messiah (Jewish)
the Prophet (Muhammad)
Our Lady
the Apostle to the Gentiles

36c. Pronouns referring to God should not be capitalized except when necessary to avoid ambiguity:

the Lord who is in heaven
Jesus and his followers
Give alms to Him.

36d. Names of religions, denominations, sects, and religious movements, events, and concepts of major importance should be capitalized:

Muslim	the Reformation
Judaism	the Crucifixion
Anglicanism	Diaspora
Presbyterian	the Nicene Creed
Zen	Exodus
Christian Science	the Resurrection

36e. "Church" should not be capitalized unless part of a name of a building or organization or when referring to the universal body of believers:

the church on Main Street
to attend church
the First Baptist Church on Main Street
Greek Orthodox Church
Christ is the Church's foundation.

HISTORICAL TERMINOLOGY

37a. Months of the year, days of the week, and holidays should be capitalized; the four seasons are not capitalized unless personified:

January	Yom Kippur
Wednesday	Good Friday
Christmas Eve	spring fever
Father's Day	winter solstice
Labor Day	Winter's icy
April Fool's Day	breath

37b. Specially designated days or other time periods are usually capitalized:

National Youth Week
Law Day
Clean Up Week

37c. Time zones and designations are not capitalized when written out but are abbreviated in capitals:

central standard time (CST)
daylight saving time (DST)

37d. Historical or cultural periods, events, or movements should not be capitalized unless they come from proper nouns or are easily confused with the same word used in a general sense; there are many exceptions, however, particularly with events, and repeated usage of a term should of course be consistent:

surrealism	Wagnerism
the space age	the Middle Ages
the gold rush	Stoicism
classical period	Age of Reason
cubism	Dark Ages
ancient Rome	Renaissance
Edwardian age	Seattle World's Fair

SCIENTIFIC TERMINOLOGY

38a. Latin names for plants and animals that indicate genus are italicized and capitalized; Latin names for species and subspecies are not capitalized even if they are derivatives of proper names. If the person who proposed a species or subspecies name is added, his name is capitalized and appears in roman type:

Hydrophilus triangularis
Falco columbarius aesalon
Dendroica auduboni, Audubon's warbler
Dianthus deltoides Linnaeus or *Dianthus deltoides* L.

38b. Scientific names for groupings broader than the genus and their various subdivisions are capitalized and may be in roman type:

the family Hydrophilidae (or *Hydrophilidae*)
the phylum Platyhelminthes (or *Platyhelminthes*)
the suborder Ruminantia (or *Ruminantia*)

38c. After having been first used, a genus name may subsequently be denoted by its initial letter used as an abbreviation:

A bird similar to the downy woodpecker, *Dendrocopos pubescens*, is the hairy woodpecker, *D. villosus.*

38d. English names derived from scientific names of plants and animals are *not* capitalized:

amoeba
marsupial
carnivores
chrysanthemum

38e. Most common names of plants and animals are *not* capitalized; exceptions occur with proper nouns or adjectives that retain their original reference and with certain special names of domestic breeds or varieties:

red maple	rhesus monkey
white-tailed deer	benjamin bush
Virginia deer	timothy grass
Canada goose	johnny-jump-up
Brewer's blackbird	Black Angus cow
Irish wolfhound	Rhode Island Red

38f. "Sun" and "moon" should not be capitalized; nor should "earth" unless used in association with names of other planets:

During a solar or lunar eclipse, the earth, moon, and sun form an approximately straight line.
We live on the earth.
Mercury, Venus, and Earth are the planets closest to the sun; of these only Earth has a moon.

38g. Names of constellations, stars, planets and their satellites, and other particular celestial objects should be capitalized; for treatment of "sun," "earth," and "moon," see above:

Ursa Major	Saturn
Big Dipper	Deimos
the Dragon	the Milky Way
the Dog Star	Halley's Comet
Rigel	the Great Nebula in
North Star	Andromeda
Uranus	other galaxies

38h. Geologic time periods should be capitalized:

Pliocene epoch
Jurassic period
Precambrian era

38i. Names of diseases, symptoms, organisms, and tests and other medical terms should *not* be capitalized unless they contain or derive from proper names:

carcinoid syndrome	leukocytosis
Wilson's syndrome	plethora
deficiency symptom	measles
Wolffian body	streptomyces
foot and mouth disease	Schiff's test

38j. Generally drugs should be referred to by their generic names which are lowercase; when a generic term is first used, it may be followed by a trade or brand name, capitalized and within parentheses:

penicillin
She is dieting and taking dextroamphetamine (Dexedrine).

38k. Names of chemical compounds and elements should not be capitalized when written out; if chemical symbols are used, however, they should be capitalized:

hydrochloric acid; HCl
sodium carbonate; Na_2CO_3
barium; Ba

38l. Names of scientific or mathematical laws, theories, constants, and the like are not capitalized except for those words that are proper names:

general theory of relativity
Avogadro's number
Taylor series
Planck's constant
atomic number
quantum theory
Gaussian distribution
law of conservation of energy
Newton's law of gravitation

Section IV
NUMBERS

INTRODUCTION

39. One of the commonest and most vexatious questions confronting the writer is when to use figures and when to spell out numbers. Unfortunately there is no simple, single system for the use of numbers in textual matter. This guide provides a concise set of principles that should help guide the writer in the consistent use of numbers in their various forms. At the end of this section is a table of roman numerals together with an explanation of the principles governing their formation.

GENERAL PRINCIPLES

40a. Generally in ordinary text matter, whole numbers under one hundred should be spelled out and larger numbers expressed in figures, but see below for exceptions:

This sweater comes in four colors.
John just had his twenty-first birthday.
Tickets range from two to five dollars.
There are sixteen girls and twenty boys in my class.
His grandfather is eighty-eight years old.
Next year has 366 days.
Last year there were 1,214 subscribers.
The population of the city is 107,920.

40b. When numbers appear together in the same series, sentence, or paragraph, and are categorically related, they should be treated alike; if any have three or more digits, they should all appear as figures:

The company currently employs 112 women and 60 men.

Our school recently opened two new cafeterias. The larger one, for students, seats 220 people. A smaller room, for faculty members only, seats 48.

Three games were played that lasted 20, 44, and 102 moves.

40c. Normally numbers in dates, page numbers, decimal fractions, and percentages should be expressed in figures. Do not use *th, st,* or *d* after figures in dates:

26 B.C.

July 10, 1944 (*not* July 10th)

page 3

p. 126

an average of 10.105

a total of 19.6

6 percent interest

a maximum error of 20%

40d. A number that would ordinarily be expressed in figures should be spelled out if it occurs at the beginning of a sentence:

Thirty-seven percent of the sample returned their applications.

Forty men and 106 women were hired during the year.

40e. Approximate or indefinite numbers in hundreds or thousands should be spelled out:

At least ten thousand people were present.

a flock of over five hundred sheep

a twenty-five-hundred-word essay

40f. Very large round numbers may be expressed in figures followed by the appropriate unit spelled out:

a budget of $6.8 million

approximately 4.5 billion stars

over 10 billion possible combinations

40g. In technical, scientific, and statistical material, measurements and physical quantities are expressed in figures; in ordinary text such numbers may be spelled out:

110 volts   9 square feet

14 liters   17.5° C.

an angle of 30°   2.0 light-years

38 miles   3 angstroms

We drove seventy miles an hour.

She lives six miles from here.

The temperature is supposed to rise to ninety degrees today.

a three-by-four-by-six-inch box

40h. Fractional quantities, however, are usually expressed in figures:

We walked for 3½ miles.

These ceilings are 10¼ feet high.

40i. If an abbreviation or symbol is used for a unit of measure, the quantity should always be expressed in figures. Repeat the symbol after each usage:

12 in.   3'

48 cu. cm.   15° 30'

90° F.   200 mi.

16 oz.   a 3 x 5 in. card

12"   a 3" x 4" x 6" box

40j. When amounts of money are referred to in text, the unit of currency should be spelled out if the amount is spelled out; if the amount is expressed in figures, it should be preceded by the symbol "$":

We each contributed ten dollars to the fund.

He earns seventy-five dollars a week.

Mr. Jones won $450.

The bus fare is now forty-five cents.

40k. Amounts of money containing decimal fractions should be expressed in figures; if an amount which ordinarily would be spelled out occurs together or in series with a fractional amount, it should be expressed in figures:

The price went up from $5.00 to $5.50.

The three sizes sell for $35.00, $59.50, and $89.50.

40l. Time designations with A.M. or P.M. should be expressed in figures. Do not use words like *morning* or *afternoon* with A.M. or P.M.:

8:00 A.M. (*not* 8:00 A.M. in the morning)

3:00 P.M. (*not* 3:00 P.M. in the afternoon)

9:00 P.M. (*not* 9:00 P.M. in the evening)

12:00 P.M. (*not* 12:00 P.M. midnight)

40m. When A.M. or P.M. is not used, the time of day should be expressed in figures only if the exact time is indicated; otherwise the time of day is usually spelled out when occurring in text. Spell out the time when using *o'clock:*

The train leaves at 4:40 this afternoon.

My class starts at 3:00. (*not* 3:00 o'clock)

The alarm clock is set for 7:00. (*not* 7:00 o'clock)

My favorite program starts at eight o'clock.

We have to be at work by 8:30 in the morning.

I go to bed at half-past ten.

We usually get back from coffee break around twenty after three.

She went shopping at four o'clock.

40n. Spell out particular centuries and decades except when expressed in terms of a year number:

nineteenth century   the 1920s

the twenties   the 1600s

the gay nineties   the 1890s

40o. Generally ordinal numbers should be spelled out except when awkward or difficult to read:

This is his third try.

His name is seventeenth on the list.

the Twenty-sixth District

Fifth Avenue

Fifty-ninth Street

2430 West 111th Street

PLURALS OF FIGURES

41. Plurals of figures are usually formed by adding an apostrophe and *s*. Plurals of years, however, are commonly formed with *s* alone:

I got two 100's and a 95 on my tests.

the 1890s (or 1890's)

the 1940s (or 1940's)

For internal punctuation of figures, see COMMA.

INCLUSIVE NUMBERS

42. Inclusive numbers should be treated consistently and the following principles and examples illustrate an acceptable, commonly used system:

First Number	Second Number	Digits used in second number	Examples
1–99	any	all digits	pp. 1–12
			pp. 33–36
			pp. 88–112
100	any		pp. 100–109
200	any	all digits	pp. 200–220
:	:		pp. 600–678
etc.	etc.		the years 1900–1910
101–109	102–109		pp. 106–9
201–209	202–209	last digit only	pp. 201–5
:	:		pp. 1506–7
etc.	etc.		the years 1901–9
101–199	110–199		pp. 109–15
201–299	210–299	last two digits only	pp. 231–57
:	:		pp. 1387–91
etc.	etc.		the years 1945–47
			(but 350–330 B.C., *not* 350–30 B.C.)
101–199	200 or more		pp. 190–221
201–299	300 or more	all digits	pp. 277–518
:	:		pp. 598–601
etc.	etc.		the years 1890–1910

ROMAN NUMERALS

43a. Roman numerals in capitals are used to distinguish kings, queens, popes, or male members of a family with the same name. Lower-case roman numerals are used to number preliminary pages of a book or other manuscript. Roman numerals in outlines are usually capitalized but lower-case roman numerals may be used if the outline is elaborate with many subdivisions:

Louis XVI   Edward VII

Elizabeth II   Adlai Stevenson III

Pius XII   refer to pp. xii–xviii

I. Introduction

II. Class *Insecta*

  A. Order *Zoraptera*

  B. Order *Orthoptera*

    1. Structural characteristics

    2. Injurious grasshoppers

      a) Family *Tridactylidae*

      b) Family *Acrididae*

        (1) Subfamily *Acridinae*

        (2) Subfamily *Cyrtacanthacridinae*

          (a) Genus *Melanoplus*

            i) *M. bivittatus*, the two-striped grasshopper

            ii) *M. mexicanus*, the migratory grasshopper

            iii) Etc. . . .

          (b) Etc. . . .

43b. The following principles and table illustrate the formation of roman numerals:

1. A letter immediately preceding a letter of equal or lesser value adds to it:
   VI = 6; XX = 20; CX = 110
2. A letter immediately preceding a letter of greater value subtracts from it:
   IV = 4; XC = 90; CD = 400
3. A letter occurring between two letters, each of greater value, subtracts from the letter following, the difference then being added to the first letter:

$$\begin{array}{l} \text{XIV} = 14 \\ \underline{\begin{array}{l} \text{V} = 5 \\ -\text{I} = -1 \\ +\text{X} = 10 \end{array}} \\ \text{XIV} = 14 \text{ (since } I \text{ occurs between } X \text{ and } V) \end{array}$$

$$\begin{array}{l} \text{XLIV} = 44 \\ \underline{\begin{array}{l} \text{V} = 5 \\ -\text{I} = -1 \\ +\text{L} = 50 \end{array}} \\ \text{LIV} = 54 \text{ (since } I \text{ occurs between } L \text{ and } V) \\ \underline{-\text{X} = -10} \\ \text{XLIV} = 44 \text{ (by rule 2)} \end{array}$$

$$\begin{array}{l} \text{CDXCIX} = 499 \\ \underline{\begin{array}{l} \text{X} = 10 \\ -\text{I} = -1 \\ +\text{C} = 100 \end{array}} \\ \text{CIX} = 109 \text{ (since } I \text{ occurs between } C \text{ and } X) \\ \underline{\begin{array}{l} -\text{X} = -10 \\ +\text{D} = 500 \end{array}} \\ \text{DXCIX} = 599 \text{ (since } X \text{ occurs between } D \text{ and } C) \\ \underline{-\text{C} = -100} \\ \text{CDXCIX} = 499 \text{ (by rule 2)} \end{array}$$

$$\begin{array}{l} \text{MCM} = 1,900 \\ \text{M} = 1,000 \\ -\text{C} = -100 \\ \underline{+\text{M} = 1,000} \\ \text{MCM} = 1,900 \text{ (since } C \text{ occurs between } M \text{ and } M) \end{array}$$

4. A bar over a letter multiplies it by 1,000:
   $\overline{\text{V}} = 5,000$; $\overline{\text{L}} = 50,000$

43c. Table of Roman Numerals

Arabic Numeral	Roman Numeral	Arabic Numeral	Roman Numeral
1	I	50	L
2	II	60	LX
3	III	70	LXX
4	IV	80	LXXX
5	V	90	XC
6	VI	100	C
7	VII	200	CC
8	VIII	300	CCC
9	IX	400	CD
10	X	500	D
11	XI	600	DC
12	XII	700	DCC
13	XIII	800	DCCC
14	XIV	900	CM
15	XV	1,000	M
16	XVI	4,000	$\text{M}\overline{\text{V}}$
17	XVII	5,000	$\overline{\text{V}}$
18	XVIII	10,000	$\overline{\text{X}}$
19	XIX	15,000	$\overline{\text{X}}\overline{\text{V}}$
20	XX	20,000	$\overline{\text{X}}\overline{\text{X}}$
30	XXX	100,000	$\overline{\text{C}}$
40	XL	1,000,000	$\overline{\text{M}}$

Section V
FOOTNOTES

INTRODUCTION

44a. Most people who write papers, reports, and other nonfictional works depend partly on other sources. It is both common courtesy and good research practice to acknowledge these sources. This is usually done by using footnotes. Footnotes are also used to provide additional information or explanatory comments that would disrupt the flow of material in the main text if included in the body of the paper. Excessive use of footnotes, however, can be distracting and discouraging to the reader, especially if the amount of material in footnotes approaches or exceeds that in text. It should always be remembered that footnotes are provided for the reader's benefit; footnoting beyond what is necessary to aid the reader will probably seem merely pedantic and detract from the quality of the work.

USES OF FOOTNOTES

44b. Every statement, fact, or concept used in a paper that is not the writer's own should be acknowledged, either in a footnote or within the body of the paper. If a citation can be easily worked into the text of the paper without disrupting the continuity of the material, it is usually better to do this than to include a footnote since the reader's attention will not be diverted from what he is reading. In most cases this cannot be done, however, and the use of footnotes is necessary.

Citations are necessary for (1) material quoted or paraphrased from another work, (2) facts taken from some other source, and (3) ideas or opinions encountered in another work that the writer feels had a distinct influence on the paper and, although not used directly, were of primary importance in the formulation of concepts expressed in the paper.

In addition to being used to cite other sources, footnotes are sometimes necessary to provide additional or explanatory material or to expand on something in the text. In these cases the inclusion of the material within the body of the paper would interrupt the thought being expressed in the main text and it is more appropriate to use footnotes. If there is a citation necessary for the explanatory material, it can either be written into the text of the footnote or included at the end following the terminal punctuation of the note. Footnotes are also used to refer the reader to another page or part of the paper or to another footnote.

NUMBERING AND PLACEMENT

44c. All footnotes should be numbered using arabic numerals. It is best to number the footnotes consecutively throughout the paper, starting over at 1 for each chapter of a book. Do not number footnotes separately for each page since any subsequent addition or deletion of material may necessitate renumbering many of the footnotes. The footnote number should be placed at the end of the material cited in the text immediately after any punctuation, but before a dash, and again just before the footnote itself. The number should be placed slightly above the typed line without an intervening space and should appear alone without a period or other punctuation.

Footnotes may be placed either at the bottom of the page where the cited material appears or together on a separate sheet at the end of the paper. If they are placed at the bottom of the page, rule a line below the text extending from the left to the right margins and skip a line before beginning the first footnote for that page. Footnotes should be single-spaced with the first line indented like paragraphs within the text and subsequent lines beginning at the left margin. Double-space between successive footnotes.

FIRST CITATION FORM

44d. The following paragraphs describe the general form for the first citation of a book or other source giving the information in the order in which it should appear. The sample footnotes that follow show the exact form for various types of sources.

The author's name, as well as the name of an editor or translator, appears in normal order in as full a form as possible. Use the information on the title page; but if only initials are given, the first name should be supplied if it is known. Full names should not be supplied, however, in the case of well-known writers who only use initials, such as T. S. Eliot and C. P. Snow. Do not include degrees or affiliations following the name.

A comma separates the author's name from the title following.

The title of a book appears in italics (underlined) and should be taken from the title page. Capitalize the first word of the title and capitalize all other important words except *a, an, the,* and prepositions and conjunctions of four letters or less. If the book has a subtitle, use a colon to separate it from the main title and capitalize the first word following the colon. A long title may be abbreviated using three dots to indicate the omission of words, but always give the first few words of the title.

The title of a chapter in a book, or of an article in a collection, magazine, encyclopedia, or newspaper should be in quotation marks followed by the title of the work in which the article was found in italics (underlined). Include a comma after the title of the article, just before the final quotation mark.

If there is an editor or translator in addition to an author, his name follows the title of the book separated from the title by a comma and the abbreviation "ed." or "trans."

The place of publication, the publisher's name, and the date of publication of a book are shown in this order within one set of parentheses. The place of publication and name of the publisher can usually be found on the title page; if more than one city is shown, use only the home office, usually the first place listed. A colon follows the place of publication and a comma follows the publisher's name.

In citing a well-known reference book, such as an encyclopedia or dictionary, the facts of publication are usually omitted, but the edition or year of publication should be indicated without parentheses, set off by commas. If the reference is to a periodical, the volume number in capital roman numerals follows the title of the periodical separated by a comma, and the only information included in parentheses is the month and year of the volume. In citing a newspaper article give the full date of the newspaper, following the title of the newspaper and set off by commas, and include a column reference with the page reference if one is necessary to locate the article. It is unnecessary to give the title of an ordinary unsigned newspaper article as long as the reader can easily locate the article.

A comma follows the final parenthesis after the publication information and before the page reference.

Page references are in arabic numerals. Use "p." for one page, "pp." for more than one. Do not use "p." or "pp." if the page reference is preceded by a volume number in roman numerals; use only a comma between the volume and page reference.

SAMPLE FOOTNOTES

44e. The following sample footnotes illustrate the correct form for the first citation of the various sources usually encountered.

A book by one author:

[1]Martin Meisel, *Shaw and the Nineteenth-Century Theater* (Princeton, N.J.: Princeton University, 1963), p. 78.

[2]William Cullen Bryant, *Prose Writings of William Cullen Bryant* (New York: Russell and Russell, 1964), II, 350.

A book by two authors:

[3]John Kaplan and Jon R. Waltz, *The Trial of Jack Ruby* (New York: Macmillan, 1965), p. 27.

A book by three authors:

[4]Richard Hofstadter, William Miller, and Daniel Aaron, *The American Republic* (Englewood Cliffs, N.J.: Prentice-Hall 1959), II, 376–77.

A book by more than three authors:

[5]Karl W. Deutsh *et al., France, Germany, and the Western Alliance* (New York: Charles Scribner's Sons, 1967), p. 244.

A book having an editor and no author:

[6]William Rose Benét, ed., *The Reader's Encyclopedia* (New York: Thomas Y. Crowell, 1955), p. 328.

[7]Stanley J. Kunitz and Howard Haycraft, eds., *Twentieth Century Authors* (New York: H. W. Wilson, 1942), p. 461.

A book having an editor and an author:

[8]Henry David Thoreau, *Walden and Other Writings of Henry David Thoreau,* ed. Brooks Atkinson (New York: The Modern Library, 1950), p. 123.

A book having a translator:

[9]Rolf Hochhuth, *Soldiers,* trans. Robert David MacDonald (New York: Grove Press, 1968), p. 231.

A book in an edition other than the first:

[10]Merle Curti, *The Growth of American Thought,* 3rd ed. (New York: Harper and Row, 1964), p. 360.

A book in several volumes:

[11]Edward Gibbon, *The Decline and Fall of the Roman Empire* (New York: The Modern Library, 1932), III, 153.

A book in a series:

[12]Lawrence Henry Gipson, *The Triumphant Empire,* The British Empire Before the American Revolution, XIII (New York: Alfred A. Knopf, 1967), p. 31. [In this case the roman numeral is a number in a series, not a volume number of this work; therefore "p." must be included with the page reference.]

[13]Erich Fromm, *The Revolution of Hope: Toward a Humanized Technology,* World Perspectives, ed. Ruth Nanda Anshen, XXXVIII (New York: Harper and Row, 1968), p. 44.

An article or selection in a collection:

[14]Robert Lowell, "Where the Rainbow Ends," in *American Poetry,* ed. Gay Wilson Allen, Walter B. Rideout, and James K. Robinson (New York: Harper and Row, 1965), p. 1000. [Here "ed." means "edited by"—do not use "eds." in this case. Compare this with footnote 7.]

An article in a journal or magazine:

[15]Robert Penn Warren, "Whittier," *The Sewanee Review,* LXXIX (January–March, 1971), 94.

[16]Mark Schorer, "John Dos Passos: A Stranded American," *The Atlantic,* CCXXVII (March, 1971), 93.

A signed article in an encyclopedia:

[17]David Eugene Smith, "Abacus," *Encyclopaedia Britannica,* 1960, I, 6.

An unsigned article in an encyclopedia:

[18]"Alimony," *Encyclopaedia Britannica,* 1960, I, 635–36.

A signed article in a newspaper:

[19]Tom Wicker, "A Slaughter of Innocents," *The New York Times,* February 21, 1971, sect. 4, p. 11.

An unsigned article in a newspaper:

[20]"Posturing in the Middle East," *The Christian Science Monitor,* February 24, 1971, p. 14.

[21]*Chicago Sun-Times,* March 4, 1971, p. 8:5. [The number after the colon is the column number.]

SUBSEQUENT REFERENCES

44f. After the first footnote reference to a work containing the complete bibliographic information, it is unnecessary to repeat all this information in subsequent references to the same work. In most cases it is sufficient to give the author's surname followed by a comma and the appropriate page reference. For example, a subsequent reference to the book in footnote 1 above would appear like this:

[22]Meisel, p. 80.

If more than one work by the same author is cited in the footnotes, a subsequent reference to such a work should include the author's surname and the title of the work together with the page reference. The title used should usually be a shortened form of the main title containing the key word or words only, but with the words always in the same order as they appear in the title and without abbreviations. If the reference is to an article in a journal or magazine, the usual practice is to cite the journal rather than the title of the article. The following footnotes illustrate these cases:

[23]Stanley J. Kunitz, ed. *Twentieth Century Authors: First Supplement* (New York: H. W. Wilson, 1955), p. 689.

[24]Stanley J. Kunitz, ed. *British Authors of the Nineteenth Century* (New York: H. W. Wilson, 1936), p. 99.

[25]Kunitz, *British Authors,* p. 100.

[26]Robert Penn Warren, *Selected Essays* (New York: Random House, 1958), p. 22.

[27]Warren, *Sewanee Review,* 97. [This refers to footnote 15.]

[28]Warren, *Essays,* p. 24.

If the work cited is the same as that cited in the footnote immediately preceding, *Ibid.* (Latin *ibidem,* "in the same place") may be used in place of the author's name and other bibliographic information and is followed by a comma and the page reference. If the reference is to a different volume of the work cited in the preceding footnote, the volume number must be included too. When the reference is to the same page, *Ibid.* alone is used. *Ibid.* may be used repeatedly in footnotes as long as no other reference intervenes. The following examples refer to the work cited in footnote 11 above.

[29]Gibbon, III, 160.

[30]*Ibid.*, I, 195.

[31]*Ibid.*, 206. [The same volume number as the preceding footnote.]

[32]*Ibid.* [The same page as the preceding footnote.]

Section VI
BIBLIOGRAPHIES

INTRODUCTION

45a. The bibliography lists, alphabetically, by the author's last name, all works cited in the footnotes of the paper and any other relevant sources consulted. It is not necessary to list every book examined, but any that were directly helpful in some way should be included.

FORM FOR ENTRIES

45b. The author's last name should begin flush with the left margin of the page and succeeding lines for that entry should be indented at least two spaces. Bibliography entries are usually typed single-space, skipping a line between entries.

The form for a bibliography entry for a book is similar to that for a full footnote citation but with the following differences:

1. The author's last name comes first followed by the given name or names separated by a comma. If there is more than one author, only the first author's name is written in inverted order, any other names appearing in normal order.
2. Each part of the bibliographic information—name, title, and publication information—as well as the indication of a second or later edition, is set off by periods rather than commas. If the reference is to an article in a collection, give the title of the article in quotation marks followed by a comma and the book title in italics as in footnotes. In listing a work of more than one volume, indicate the total number of volumes after the period following the title using the abbreviation "vols."
3. The publication information is not enclosed in parentheses.
4. There is no page reference.

The bibliographic entry for an article in an encyclopedia or periodical differs from the full footnote form in only two respects. First, of course, the author's last name comes first, followed by the given name or names and a period. Secondly, the entry must contain the inclusive pages of the article—it is not enough to give merely the page or pages referred to in the footnotes.

If a work has no author or editor, it should be listed in the bibliography alphabetically by the first word of the title (excluding "A," "An," or "The"). If two or more works are by the same author, the author's name need only be given for the first entry. Begin each subsequent entry with a dash three to six spaces long in place of the name and follow the dash with a period. Entries by the same author should be alphabetized by title.

A SAMPLE BIBLIOGRAPHY

45c. The following sample bibliography lists the various references used in the footnote examples above.

"Alimony," *Encyclopaedia Britannica*, 1960, I, 635–36.

Benét, William Rose, ed. *The Reader's Encyclopedia*. New York: Thomas Y. Crowell, 1955.

Bryant, William Cullen. *Prose Writings of William Cullen Bryant*. 2 vols. New York: Russell and Russell, 1964.

Chicago Sun-Times, March 4, 1971, p. 8:5.

Curti, Merle. *The Growth of American Thought*. 3rd ed. New York: Harper and Row, 1964.

Deutsh, Karl W., *et al. France, Germany, and the Western Alliance*. New York: Charles Scribner's Sons, 1967.

Fromm, Erich. *The Revolution of Hope: Toward a Humanized Technology*. World Perspectives, ed. Ruth Nanda Anshen, XXXVIII. New York: Harper and Row, 1968.

Gibbon, Edward. *The Decline and Fall of the Roman Empire*. 3 vols. New York: The Modern Library, 1932.

Gipson, Lawrence Henry. *The Triumphant Empire. The British Empire Before the American Revolution*, XIII. New York: Alfred A. Knopf, 1967.

Hochhuth, Rolf. *Soldiers*, trans. Robert David MacDonald. New York: Grove Press, 1968.

Hofstadter, Richard, William Miller, and Daniel Aaron. *The American Republic*. 2 vols. Englewood Cliffs, N. J.: Prentice-Hall, 1959.

Kaplan, John, and Jon R. Waltz. *The Trial of Jack Ruby*. New York: Macmillan, 1965.

Kunitz, Stanley J., ed. *British Authors of the Nineteenth Century*. New York: H. W. Wilson, 1936.

———. *Twentieth Century Authors: First Supplement*. New York: H. W. Wilson, 1955.

Kunitz, Stanley J., and Howard Haycraft, eds. *Twentieth Century Authors*. New York: H. W. Wilson, 1942.

Lowell, Robert. "Where the Rainbow Ends," in *American Poetry*, ed. Gay Wilson Allen, Walter B. Rideout, and James K. Robinson. New York: Harper and Row, 1965.

Meisel, Martin. *Shaw and the Nineteenth-Century Theater*. Princeton, N. J.: Princeton University, 1963.

"Posturing in the Middle East," *The Christian Science Monitor*, February 24, 1971, p. 14.

Schorer, Mark. "John Dos Passos: A Stranded American," *The Atlantic*, CCXXVII (March, 1971), 93–96.

Smith, David Eugene. "Abacus," *Encyclopaedia Britannica*, 1960, I, 5–7.

Thoreau, Henry David. *Walden and Other Writings of Henry David Thoreau*, ed. Brooks Atkinson. New York: The Modern Library, 1950.

Warren, Robert Penn. *Selected Essays*. New York: Random House, 1958.

———. "Whittier," *The Sewanee Review*, LXXIX (January–March, 1971), 86–135.

Wicker, Tom. "A Slaughter of Innocents," *The New York Times*, February 21, 1971, sect. 4, p. 11.

Section VII
BASIC REFERENCE WORKS

46a. Introduction. A reference book may be consulted for specific, limited information. It is not written to be read consecutively for comprehensive information.

Reference books provide two useful services: they are a quick and convenient source of information in themselves, and they point the way toward sources with more comprehensive information on particular subjects.

46b. General Types of Reference Books A good reference book is an indexed tool of research, arranged alphabetically. It is only a preliminary source, however. Because of its general nature, it should not be regarded as a final authority.

There are several different types of reference books:

ENCYCLOPEDIAS, which usually give a brief, concise outline of a subject and a bibliography of sources for further information;

DICTIONARIES, which deal with the construction, pronunciation, meaning, and derivation of words;

ATLASES and GAZETTEERS, which provide geographical information, including maps and listings of the sizes and locations of geographical areas;

YEARBOOKS and ALMANACS, which furnish a compendium of facts and figures on a variety of topics; and

INDEXES, which provide a classified listing of more detailed reference on a particular topic, and which are issued periodically, usually monthly or yearly.

Besides the basic reference works, there are a number of reference books in almost every specialized field.

In order to conduct almost any type of research, the student must first familiarize himself with the basic tools of reference, so that he can find materials which will be of the greatest help to him.

46c. Atlases and Gazetteers

Britannica World Atlas
Chicago: Encyclopaedia Britannica, Inc.

Hammond Medallion World Atlas
Maplewood, N.J.: Hammond Inc.

Historical Atlas
New York: Barnes and Noble.

McGraw-Hill International Atlas
New York: McGraw-Hill Book Co.

National Geographical Atlas of the World
Washington: National Geographic Society.

Odyssey World Atlas
New York: Western Publishing Co.

Pergamon World Atlas
New York: Pergamon Press, Inc.

Rand McNally New Cosmopolitan World Atlas
Chicago: Rand McNally & Co.

Times Atlas of the World
London: Times Newspapers, Ltd.

Webster's Geographical Dictionary
Springfield, Massachusetts: G. & C. Merriam Co.

World Book Atlas
Chicago: Field Enterprises Educational Corp.

46d. Biographical References

Biography Index (quarterly)
New York: H. W. Wilson Co. 1946 to date

Current Biography (monthly)
New York: H. W. Wilson Co. 1940 to date

Dictionary of American Biography (deceased Americans)
New York: Charles Scribner's Sons.

Dictionary of National Biography (deceased British)
Oxford: Oxford University Press, Inc.

The International Who's Who (annual)
London: Europa Publications, Ltd.

Twentieth Century Authors (annual)
New York: H. W. Wilson Co.

Webster's Biographical Dictionary
Springfield, Massachusetts: G. & C. Merriam Co.

Who's Who (living British)
London: A. & C. Black, Ltd.

Who's Who in America (living Americans)
Chicago: A. N. Marquis Co. 1899 to date

46e. Business and Professional References

Business Periodicals Index
New York: H. W. Wilson Co.

Education Index
New York: H. W. Wilson Co.

Vertical File Index
New York: H. W. Wilson Co.

46f. Dictionaries

American College Dictionary
New York: Random House, Inc.

Funk & Wagnalls Standard College Dictionary
New York: Funk & Wagnalls Co.

The Living Webster Encyclopedic Dictionary of the English Language
Chicago: The English-Language Institute of America, Inc.

Oxford English Dictionary
London: Oxford University Press, Inc.

Random House Dictionary
New York: Random House, Inc.

Webster's New World Dictionary—College Edition
Cleveland: World Publishing Co.

Webster's Third New International Dictionary
Springfield, Massachusetts: G. & C. Merriam Co.

World Book Dictionary
Chicago: Field Enterprises Educational Corp.

46g. Encyclopedias

Collier's Encyclopedia
New York: Crowell-Collier Educational Corp. 24 volumes

Columbia Encyclopedia
New York: Columbia University Press. 1 volume

Compton's Encyclopedia
Chicago: F. E. Compton Co. 24 volumes

Encyclopaedia Britannica
Chicago: Encyclopaedia Britannica, Inc. 24 volumes

The Encyclopedia Americana
New York: The Americana Corp. 30 volumes

Merit Students Encyclopedia
New York: Crowell-Collier Educational Corp. 20 volumes

The New Book of Knowledge
New York: Grolier, Inc. 20 volumes

Universal World Reference Encyclopedia
Chicago: Consolidated Book Publishers. 16 volumes

The World Book Encyclopedia
Chicago: Field Enterprises Educational Corp. 20 volumes

46h. Guides to Books and Periodicals

Book Review Digest
New York: H. W. Wilson Co. 1905 to date

Books in Print (annual)
New York and London: R. R. Bowker Co.

Cumulative Book Index
New York: H. W. Wilson Co.

Essay and General Literature Index
New York: H. W. Wilson Co. 1900 to date

New York Times Index
New York: New York Times. 1913 to date

Poole's Index to Periodical Literature
Boston: Houghton-Mifflin Co. 1802–1908

The Publisher's Trade List Annual
New York: Publisher's Weekly. 1873 to date

The Reader's Guide to Periodical Literature (semi-monthly)
New York: H. W. Wilson Co. 1905 to date

Short Story Index
New York: H. W. Wilson Co.

46i. Historical References

Cambridge Modern History
New York: Cambridge University Press. 13 volumes

Concise Dictionary of American History
New York: Charles Scribner's Sons. 1 volume

Dictionary of American Biography
New York: Charles Scribner's Sons. 20 volumes plus index and supplement

Dictionary of American History
New York: Charles Scribner's Sons. 7 volumes

Encyclopedia of American History
New York: Harper and Row. 1 volume

McGraw-Hill Illustrated World History
New York: McGraw-Hill Book Co. 1 volume

46j. Scientific References

Applied Science & Technology Index
New York: H. W. Wilson Co.

Biological & Agricultural Index
New York: H. W. Wilson Co.

Encyclopedia of the Social Sciences
New York: P. F. Collier, Inc.

Handbook of Physics and Chemistry
Cleveland: Chemical Rubber Co.

McGraw-Hill Basic Bibliography of Science and Technology
New York: McGraw-Hill Book Co.

McGraw-Hill Encyclopedia of Science and Technology
New York: McGraw-Hill Book Co.

Social Sciences & Humanities Index
New York: H. W. Wilson Co.

46k. Special Dictionaries

Dictionary of American Slang
New York: Thomas Y. Crowell.

Fowler's Dictionary of Modern English Usage
Oxford: Oxford University Press

Roget's Thesaurus of English Words and Phrases
New York: St. Martin's Press.

Webster's New Dictionary of Synonyms
Springfield, Massachusetts: G. & C. Merriam Co.

46l. Special References

American Negro Reference Book
Englewood Cliffs, New Jersey: Prentice-Hall, Inc.

Art Index
New York: H. W. Wilson Co.

The Bibliographic Index
New York: H. W. Wilson Co.

Cambridge History of American Literature
New York: Macmillan Company.

Cambridge History of English Literature
London: Cambridge University Press.

The Catholic Peoples Encyclopedia
Chicago: The Catholic Press.

Encyclopedia of Religion and Ethics
New York: Charles Scribner's Sons.

Familiar Quotations (John Bartlett)
Boston: Little, Brown, and Co.

Granger's Index to Poetry
New York: Columbia University Press.

Index to Reproductions of European Paintings
New York: H. W. Wilson Co.

International Cyclopedia of Music and Musicians
New York: Dodd, Mead.

Play Index
New York: H. W. Wilson Co.

Statistical Abstracts of the U.S. (U.S. Bureau of the Census)
Washington: Government Printing Office. 1879 to date

Twentieth Century Authors
New York: H. W. Wilson Co.

World Almanac and Book of Facts
New York: Newspaper Enterprise Association, Inc.

PERPETUAL CALENDAR

This calendar will give you the day of the week on which a date falls during the two centuries from 1901 to the year 2100. To locate the day, first look at the proper year in the list below. A letter follows this year which indicates the calendar in use during that year.

Year		Year		Year		Year		Year		Year		Year	
1901	C	1930	D	1959	E	1988	M	2017	A	2046	B	2075	C
1902	D	1931	E	1960	M	1989	A	2018	B	2047	C	2076	K
1903	E	1932	M	1961	A	1990	B	2019	C	2048	K	2077	F
1904	M	1933	A	1962	B	1991	C	2020	K	2049	F	2078	G
1905	A	1934	B	1963	C	1992	K	2021	F	2050	G	2079	A
1906	B	1935	C	1964	K	1993	F	2022	G	2051	A	2080	I
1907	C	1936	K	1965	F	1994	G	2023	A	2052	I	2081	D
1908	K	1937	F	1966	G	1995	A	2024	I	2053	D	2082	E
1909	F	1938	G	1967	A	1996	I	2025	D	2054	E	2083	F
1910	G	1939	A	1968	I	1997	D	2026	E	2055	F	2084	N
1911	A	1940	I	1969	D	1998	E	2027	F	2056	N	2085	B
1912	I	1941	D	1970	E	1999	F	2028	N	2057	B	2086	C
1913	D	1942	E	1971	F	2000	N	2029	B	2058	C	2087	D
1914	E	1943	F	1972	N	2001	B	2030	C	2059	D	2088	L
1915	F	1944	N	1973	B	2002	C	2031	D	2060	L	2089	G
1916	N	1945	A	1974	C	2003	D	2032	L	2061	G	2090	A
1917	B	1946	C	1975	D	2004	L	2033	G	2062	A	2091	B
1918	C	1947	D	1976	L	2005	G	2034	A	2063	B	2092	J
1919	D	1948	L	1977	G	2006	A	2035	B	2064	J	2093	E
1920	L	1949	G	1978	A	2007	B	2036	J	2065	E	2094	F
1921	G	1950	A	1979	B	2008	J	2037	E	2066	F	2095	G
1922	A	1951	B	1980	J	2009	E	2038	F	2067	G	2096	H
1923	B	1952	J	1981	E	2010	F	2039	G	2068	H	2097	C
1924	J	1953	E	1982	F	2011	G	2040	H	2069	C	2098	D
1925	E	1954	F	1983	G	2012	H	2041	C	2070	D	2099	E
1926	F	1955	G	1984	H	2013	C	2042	D	2071	E	2100	F
1927	G	1956	H	1985	C	2014	D	2043	E	2072	M		
1928	H	1957	C	1986	D	2015	E	2044	M	2073	A		
1929	C	1958	D	1987	E	2016	M	2045	A	2074	B		

Reference calendars A through N.

CONVERSION FACTORS

There are two systems of measurement used in the world today—the metric system, based on the centimeter, gram, and second, and the imperial or United States system, based on the foot, pound, and second. The conversion factors listed below are used to change from one unit to another. Figures with the units given in the first column are multiplied by the numbers in the third column to obtain figures with units shown in the middle column. For example, to determine the number of cubic inches in 2 U.S. dry barrels multiply 7,056.0 (from the third column) by 2 (the number of U.S. dry barrels). Thus, 2 U.S. dry barrels equal 14,112.0 cubic inches.

Many of the numbers in the right column are written in scientific notation—a method used to simplify the arithmetic involved in multiplying large numbers. If a number in any part of the problem is not in scientific notation already, it may be put in scientific notation. This is done as follows: 1) Move the decimal place either to the left or right until the number is between 1 and 10, dropping insignificant zeros to the right of the decimal point. 2) For each decimal point moved to the left in the step above, multiply the new number by 10^1. This means for each decimal place moved to the left, the exponent (the small superscript to the right) of the 10 is increased by 1. Thus 1,000,000 is written as 1×10^6. 3) For each decimal place moved to the right multiply the resultant number by 10^{-1}. Thus 0.000001 is written as 1×10^{-6}. Numbers not in scientific notation are imagined to be multiplied by 10^0, e.g., 2 may be thought of as 2×10^0.

To multiply two numbers written in scientific notation the following steps are taken: 1) Multiply the left halves of the problem's two factors as usual (That is, the half to the left of the multiplication sign for scientific notation). 2) Add the exponents of the tens appearing on the right half of each factor. (A negative and a positive number added result in subtraction; two negative numbers added always result in another negative number.) Note: the tens are not added; only one ten appears in the final answer. Thus, when 2×10^6 is multiplied by 4×10^4, the answer is 8×10^{10}. After the multiplication is performed, the decimal place in the left half should be moved so the answer is a number between 1 and 10, with the exponent adjusted accordingly. For example: $(2 \times 10^6)(12 \times 10^{-4})$; and, $(3 \times 10^{-4})(4.02 \times 10^{-9}) = 12.06 \times 10^{-13} = 1.206 \times 10^{-12}$.

To Convert	Into	Multiply by
A		
acre	sq chain (Gunter's)	10.0
acre	rods	160.0
acre	sq links (Gunter's)	1×10^5
acre	hectare or sq hectometer	0.4047
acres	sq feet	43,560.0
acres	sq meters	4,047.0
acres	sq miles	1.562×10^{-3}
acres	sq yards	4,840.0
acre-feet	cu feet	43,560.0
acre-feet	gallons	3.259×10^5
ampere-hours	coulombs	3,600.0
ampere-hours	faradays	0.03731
ampere-turns	gilberts	1.257
angstrom unit	inch	$3,937 \times 10^{-9}$
angstrom unit	meter	1×10^{-10}
angstrom unit	micron	1×10^{-4}
astronomical unit	kilometers	1.495×10^8
atmospheres	ton/sq inch	0.007348
atmospheres	cms of mercury	76.0
atmospheres	ft of water (at 4° C)	33.90
atmospheres	in of mercury (at 0° C)	29.92
atmospheres	kgs/sq cm	1.0333
atmospheres	kgs/sq meter	10,332.0
atmospheres	pounds/sq in	14.70
atmospheres	tons/sq ft	1.058
B		
barrels (U.S., dry)	cu inches	7,056.0
barrels (U.S., dry)	quarts (dry)	105.0
barrels (U.S., liquid)	gallons	31.5
barrels (oil)	gallons (oil)	42.0
bars	atmospheres	0.9869
bars	dynes/sq cm	1×10^6
bars	kgs/sq meter	1.020×10^4
bars	pounds/sq ft	2,089.0
bars	pounds/sq in	14.50
bolt (U.S. cloth)	meters	36.576
Btu	ergs	1.0550×10^{10}
Btu	foot-lbs	778.3
Btu	gram-calories	252.0
Btu	horsepower-hrs	3.931×10^{-4}
Btu	joules	1,054.8
Btu	kilogram-calories	0.2520
Btu	kilogram-meters	107.5
Btu	kilowatt-hrs	2.928×10^{-4}
Btu/hr	foot-pounds/sec	0.2162
Btu/hr	gram-cal/sec	0.0700
Btu/hr	horsepower-hrs	3.929×10^{-4}

To Convert	Into	Multiply by
Btu/hr	watts	0.2931
Btu/min	foot-lbs/sec	12.96
Btu/min	horsepower	0.02356
Btu/min	kilowatts	0.01757
Btu/min	watts	17.57
Btu/sq ft/min	watts/sq in	0.1221
bucket (British dry)	cubic cm	1.818×10^4
bushels	cu ft	1.2445
bushels	cu in.	2,150.4
bushels	cu meters	0.03524
bushels	liters	35.24
bushels	pecks	4.0
bushels	pints (dry)	64.0
bushels	quarts (dry)	32.0
C		
calories, gram (mean)	Btu (mean)	3.9685×10^{-3}
candle/sq cm	lamberts	3.142
candle/sq inch	lamberts	0.4870
centares (centiares)	sq meters	1.0
centigrade	Fahrenheit	$(C° \times 9/5) + 32$
centigrams	grams	0.01
centiliter	ounce fluid (U.S.)	0.3382
centiliter	cubic inch	0.6103
centiliter	drams	2.705
centiliters	liters	0.01
centimeters	feet	3.281×10^{-2}
centimeters	inches	0.3937
centimeters	kilometers	1×10^{-5}
centimeters	meters	0.01
centimeters	miles	6.214×10^{-6}
centimeters	millimeters	10.0
centimeters	mils	393.7
centimeters	yards	1.094×10^{-2}
centimeter-dynes	cm-grams	1.020×10^{-3}
centimeter-dynes	meter-kgs	1.020×10^{-8}
centimeter-dynes	pound-feet	7.376×10^{-8}
centimeter-grams	cm-dynes	980.7
centimeter-grams	meter-kgs	1×10^{-5}
centimeter-grams	pound-feet	7.233×10^{-5}
centimeters of mercury	atmospheres	0.01316
centimeters of mercury	feet of water	0.4461
centimeters of mercury	kgs/sq meter	136.0
centimeters of mercury	pounds/sq ft	27.85
centimeters of mercury	pounds/sq in	0.1934
centimeters/sec	feet/min	1.1969
centimeters/sec	feet/sec	0.03281
centimeters/sec	kilometers/hr	0.036
centimeters/sec	knots	0.1943
centimeters/sec	meters/min	0.6

To Convert	Into	Multiply by
centimeters/sec	miles/hr	0.02237
centimeters/sec	miles/min	3.728×10^{-4}
centimeters/sec/sec	feet/sec/sec	0.03281
centimeters/sec/sec	kms/hr/sec	0.036
centimeters/sec/sec	meters/sec/sec	0.01
centimeters/sec/sec	miles/hr/sec	0.02237
chain	inches	792.00
chain	meters	20.12
chains (surveyors' or Gunter's)	yards	22.00
circular mils	sq cms	5.067×10^{-6}
circular mils	sq mils	0.7854
circular mils	sq inches	7.854×10^{-7}
circumference	radians	6.283
cords	cord feet	8.0
cord feet	cu feet	16.0
coulomb	statcoulombs	2.998×10^9
coulombs	faradays	1.036×10^{-5}
coulombs/sq cm	coulombs/sq in	64.52
coulombs/sq cm	coulombs/sq meter	1×10^4
coulombs/sq in	coulombs/sq cm	0.1550
coulombs/sq in	coulombs/sq meter	1,550.0
coulombs/sq meter	coulombs/sq cm	1×10^{-4}
coulombs/sq meter	coulombs/sq in	6.452×10^{-4}
cubic centimeters	cu feet	3.531×10^{-5}
cubic centimeters	cu inches	0.06102
cubic centimeters	cu meters	1×10^{-6}
cubic centimeters	cu yards	1.308×10^{-6}
cubic centimeters	gallons (U.S. liq.)	2.642×10^{-4}
cubic centimeters	liters	0.001
cubic centimeters	pints (U.S. liq.)	2.113×10^{-3}
cubic centimeters	quarts (U.S. liq.)	1.057×10^{-3}
cubic feet	bushels (dry)	0.8036
cubic feet	cu cms	28,320.0
cubic feet	cu inches	1,728.0
cubic feet	cu meters	0.02832
cubic feet	cu yards	0.03704
cubic feet	gallons (U.S. liq.)	7.48052
cubic feet	liters	28.32
cubic feet	pints (U.S. liq.)	59.84
cubic feet	quarts (U.S. liq.)	29.92
cubic feet/min	cu cms/sec	472.0
cubic feet/min	gallons/sec	0.1247
cubic feet/min	liters/sec	0.4720
cubic feet/min	pounds of water/min	62.43
cubic feet/sec	million gals/day	0.646317
cubic feet/sec	gallons/min	448.831
cubic inches	cu cms	16.39
cubic inches	cu feet	5.787×10^{-4}
cubic inches	cu meters	1.639×10^{-5}
cubic inches	cu yards	2.143×10^{-5}
cubic inches	gallons	4.329×10^{-3}
cubic inches	liters	0.01639
cubic inches	mil-feet	1.061×10^5
cubic inches	pints (U.S. liq.)	0.03463
cubic inches	quarts (U.S. liq.)	0.01732
cubic meters	bushels (dry)	28.38
cubic meters	cu cms	1×10^6
cubic meters	cu feet	35.31
cubic meters	cu inches	61,023.0
cubic meters	cu yards	1.308
cubic meters	gallons (U.S. liq.)	264.2
cubic meters	liters	1,000.0
cubic meters	pints (U.S. liq.)	2,113.0
cubic meters	quarts (U.S. liq.)	1,057.0
cubic yards	cu cms	7.646×10^5
cubic yards	cu feet	27.0
cubic yards	cu inches	46,656.0
cubic yards	cu meters	0.7646
cubic yards	gallons (U.S. liq.)	202.0
cubic yards	liters	764.6
cubic yards	pints (U.S. liq.)	1,615.9
cubic yards	quarts (U.S. liq.)	807.9
cubic yards/min	cubic ft/sec	0.45
cubic yards/min	gallons/sec	3.367
cubic yards/min	liters/sec	12.74

D

To Convert	Into	Multiply by
days	seconds	86,400.0
decigrams	grams	0.1
deciliters	liters	0.1
decimeters	meters	0.1
degrees (angle)	quadrants	0.01111
degrees (angle)	radians	0.01745
degrees (angle)	seconds	3,600.0

To Convert	Into	Multiply by
degrees/sec	radians/sec	0.01745
degrees/sec	revolutions/min	0.1667
degrees/sec	revolutions/sec	2.778×10^{-3}
dekagrams	grams	10.0
dekaliters	liters	10.0
dekameters	meters	10.0
drams (apothecaries' or troy)	ounces (avoirdupois)	0.1371429
drams (apothecaries' or troy)	ounces (troy)	0.125
drams (U.S., fluid or apothecaries')	cubic cm	3.6967
drams	grams	1.7718
drams	grains	27.3437
drams	ounces	0.0625
dyne/cm	erg/sq millimeter	0.01
dyne/sq cm	atmospheres	9.869×10^{-7}
dyne/sq cm	inch of mercury at 0° C	2.953×10^{-5}
dyne/sq cm	inch of water at 4° C	4.015×10^{-4}
dynes	grams	1.020×10^{-3}
dynes	joules/cm	1×10^{-7}
dynes	joules/meter (newtons)	1×10^{-5}
dynes	kilograms	1.020×10^{-6}
dynes	poundals	7.233×10^{-5}
dynes	pounds	2.248×10^{-6}
dynes/sq cm	bars	1×10^{-6}

E

To Convert	Into	Multiply by
ell	cm	114.30
ell	inches	45.0
em, pica	inch	0.167
em, pica	cm	0.4233
erg/sec	dyne-cm/sec	1.000
ergs	Btu	9.480×10^{-11}
ergs	dyne-centimeters	1.0
ergs	foot-pounds	7.3670×10^{-8}
ergs	gram-calories	0.2389×10^{-7}
ergs	grams-cms	1.020×10^{-3}
ergs	horsepower-hrs	3.7250×10^{-14}
ergs	joules	1×10^{-7}
ergs	kg-calories	2.389×10^{-11}
ergs	kg-meters	1.020×10^{-8}
ergs	kilowatt-hrs	0.2778×10^{-13}
ergs	watt-hours	0.2778×10^{-10}
ergs/sec	Btu/min	$5,688 \times 10^{-9}$
ergs/sec	ft-lbs/min	4.427×10^{-6}
ergs/sec	ft-lbs/sec	7.3756×10^{-8}
ergs/sec	horsepower	1.341×10^{-10}
ergs/sec	kg-calories/min	1.433×10^{-9}
ergs/sec	kilowatts	1×10^{-10}

F

To Convert	Into	Multiply by
farads	microfarads	1×10^6
faraday/sec	ampere (absolute)	9.6500×10^4
faradays	ampere-hours	26.80
faradays	coulombs	9.649×10^4
fathoms	meter	1.828804
fathoms	feet	6.0
feet	centimeters	30.48
feet	kilometers	3.048×10^{-4}
feet	meters	0.3048
feet	miles (naut.)	1.645×10^{-4}
feet	miles (stat.)	1.894×10^{-4}
feet	millimeters	304.8
feet	mils	1.2×10^4
feet of water	atmospheres	0.02950
feet of water	in of mercury	0.8826
feet of water	kgs/sq cm	0.03048
feet of water	kgs/sq meter	304.8
feet of water	pounds/sq ft	62.43
feet of water	pounds/sq in	0.4335
feet/min	cms/sec	0.5080
feet/min	feet/sec	0.01667
feet/min	kms/hr	0.01829
feet/min	meters/min	0.3048
feet/min	miles/hr	0.01136
feet/sec	cms/sec	30.48
feet/sec	kms/hr	1.097
feet/sec	knots	0.5921
feet/sec	meters/min	18.29
feet/sec	miles/hr	0.6818
feet/sec	miles/min	0.01136
feet/sec/sec	cms/sec/sec	30.48
feet/sec/sec	kms/hr/sec	1.097

To Convert	Into	Multiply by
feet/sec/sec	meters/sec/sec	0.3048
feet/sec/sec	miles/hr/sec	0.6818
feet/100 feet	per cent grade	1.0
foot-candle	lumen/sq meter	10.764
foot-pounds	Btu	1.286×10^{-3}
foot-pounds	ergs	1.356×10^{7}
foot-pounds	gram-calories	0.3238
foot-pounds	hp-hrs	5.050×10^{-7}
foot-pounds	joules	1.356
foot-pounds	kg-calories	3.24×10^{-4}
foot-pounds	kg-meters	0.1383
foot-pounds	kilowatt-hrs	3.766×10^{-7}
foot-pounds/min	Btu/min	1.286×10^{-3}
foot-pounds/min	foot-pounds/sec	0.01667
foot-pounds/min	horsepower	3.030×10^{-5}
foot-pounds/min	kg-calories/min	3.24×10^{-4}
foot-pounds/min	kilowatts	2.260×10^{-5}
foot-pounds/sec	Btu/hr	4.6263
foot-pounds/sec	Btu/min	0.07717
foot-pounds/sec	horsepower	0.818×10^{-3}
foot-pounds/sec	kg-calories/min	1.01945
foot-pounds/sec	kilowatts	1.356×10^{-3}
furlongs	miles (U.S.)	0.125
furlongs	rods	40.0
furlongs	feet	660.0

G

To Convert	Into	Multiply by
gallons	cu cms	3,785.0
gallons	cu feet	0.1337
gallons	cu inches	231.0
gallons	cu meters	3.785×10^{-3}
gallons	cu yards	4.951×10^{-3}
gallons	liters	3.785
gallons (liq. British imp.)	gallons (U.S. liq.)	1.20095
gallons (U.S.)	gallons (imp.)	0.83267
gallons of water	pounds of water	8.3453
gallons/min	cu ft/sec	2.228×10^{-3}
gallons/min	liters/sec	0.06308
gallons/min	cu ft/hr	8.0208
gausses	lines/sq in	6.452
gausses	webers/sq cm	1×10^{-8}
gausses	webers/sq in	6.452×10^{-8}
gausses	webers/sq meter	1×10^{-4}
gilberts	ampere-turns	0.7958
gilberts/cm	amp-turns/cm	0.7958
gilberts/cm	amp-turns/in	2.021
gilberts/cm	amp-turns/meter	79.5810
gills (British)	cubic cm	142.07
gills	liters	0.1183
gills	pints (liq.)	0.25
grains	drams (avoirdupois)	0.03657143
grains (troy)	grains (avoirdupois)	1.0
grains (troy)	grams	0.06480
grains (troy)	ounces (avoirdupois)	2.0833×10^{-3}
grains (troy)	pennyweight (troy)	0.04167
grains/U.S. gal	parts/million	17.118
grains/U.S. gal	pounds/million gal	142.86
grains/imp gal	parts/million	14.286
grams	dynes	980.7
grams	grains	15.43
grams	joules/cm	9.807×10^{-5}
grams	joules/meter (newtons)	9.807×10^{-3}
grams	kilograms	0.001
grams	milligrams	1,000.0
grams	ounces (avoirdupois)	0.03527
grams	ounces (troy)	0.03215
grams	poundals	0.07093
grams	pounds	2.205×10^{-3}
grams/cm	pounds/inch	5.600×10^{-3}
grams/cu cm	pounds/cu ft	62.43
grams/cu cm	pounds/cu in	0.03613
grams/cu cm	pounds/mil-foot	3.405×10^{-7}
grams/liter	grains/gal	58.417
grams/liter	pounds/1,000 gal	8.345
grams/liter	pounds/cu ft	0.062427
grams/liter	parts/million	1,000.0
grams/sq cm	pounds/sq ft	2.0481
gram-calories	Btu	3.9683×10^{-3}
gram-calories	ergs	4.1868×10^{7}
gram-calories	foot-pounds	3.0880
gram-calories	horsepower-hrs	1.5596×10^{-6}
gram-calories	kilowatt-hrs	1.1630×10^{-6}
gram-calories	watt-hrs	1.1630×10^{-3}
gram-calories/sec	Btu/hr	14.286
gram-centimeters	Btu	9.297×10^{-8}
gram-centimeters	ergs	980.7
gram-centimeters	joules	9.807×10^{-5}
gram-centimeters	kg-cal	2.343×10^{-8}
gram-centimeters	kg-meters	1×10^{-5}

H

To Convert	Into	Multiply by
hand	cm	10.16
hectares	acres	2.471
hectares	sq feet	1.076×10^{5}
hectograms	grams	100.0
hectoliters	liters	100.0
hectometers	meters	100.0
hectowatts	watts	100.0
henries	millihenries	1,000.0
hogsheads (British)	cubic ft	10.114
hogsheads (U.S.)	cubic ft	8.42184
hogsheads (U.S.)	gallons (U.S.)	63.0
horsepower	Btu/min	42.44
horsepower	foot-lbs/min	33,000.0
horsepower	foot-lbs/sec	550.0
horsepower (metric) (542.5 ft lb/sec)	horsepower (550 ft lb/sec)	0.9863
horsepower (550 ft lb/sec)	horsepower (metric) (542.5 ft lb/sec)	1.014
horsepower	kg-calories/min	10.68
horsepower	kilowatts	0.7457
horsepower	watts	745.7
horsepower (boiler)	Btu/hr	33,479.0
horsepower (boiler)	kilowatts	9.803
horsepower-hrs	Btu	2,547.0
horsepower-hrs	ergs	2.6845×10^{13}
horsepower-hrs	foot-lbs	1.98×10^{6}
horsepower-hrs	gram-calories	641,190.0
horsepower-hrs	joules	2.684×10^{6}
horsepower-hrs	kg-calories	641.1
horsepower-hrs	kg-meters	2.737×10^{5}
horsepower-hrs	kilowatt-hrs	0.7457
hours	days	4.167×10^{2}
hours	weeks	5.952×10^{3}
hundredweights (long)	pounds	112.0
hundredweights (long)	tons (long)	0.05
hundredweights (short)	ounces (avoirdupois)	1,600.0
hundredweights (short)	pounds	100.0
hundredweights (short)	tons (metric)	0.0453592
hundredweights (short)	tons (long)	0.0446429

I

To Convert	Into	Multiply by
inches	centimeters	2.540
inches	meters	2.540×10^{2}
inches	miles	1.578×10^{5}
inches	millimeters	25.40
inches	mils	1,000.0
inches	yards	2.778×10^{2}
inches of mercury	atmospheres	0.03342
inches of mercury	feet of water	1.133
inches of mercury	kgs/sq cm	0.03453
inches of mercury	kgs/sq meter	345.3
inches of mercury	pounds/sq ft	70.73
inches of mercury	pounds/sq in	0.4912
inches of water (at 4° C)	atmospheres	2.458×10^{3}
inches of water (at 4° C)	inches of mercury	0.07355
inches of water (at 4° C)	kgs/sq cm	2.540×10^{3}
inches of water (at 4° C)	ounces/sq in	0.5781
inches of water (at 4° C)	pounds/sq ft	5.204
inches of water (at 4° C)	pounds/sq in	0.03613
international ampere	ampere (absolute)	0.9998
international volt	volts (absolute)	1.0003
international volt	joules (absolute)	1.593×10^{19}
international volt	joules	9.654×10^{4}

J

To Convert	Into	Multiply by
joules	Btu	9.480×10^{4}
joules	ergs	1×10^{7}
joules	foot-pounds	0.7376
joules	kg-calories	2.389×10^{4}
joules	kg-meters	0.1020
joules	watt-hrs	2.778×10^{4}
joules/cm	grams	1.020×10^{4}
joules/cm	dynes	1×10^{7}
joules/cm	joules/meter (newtons)	100.0
joules/cm	poundals	723.3
joules/cm	pounds	22.48

K

To Convert	Into	Multiply by
kilograms	dynes	980,665.0
kilograms	grams	1,000.0
kilograms	joules/cm	0.09807
kilograms	joules/meter (newtons)	9.807
kilograms	poundals	70.93
kilograms	pounds	2.205
kilograms	tons (long)	9.842×10^{-4}
kilograms	tons (short)	1.102×10^{-3}
kilograms/cu meter	grams/cu cm	0.001
kilograms/cu meter	pounds/cu ft	0.06243
kilograms/cu meter	pounds/cu in	3.613×10^{-5}
kilograms/cu meter	pounds/mil-foot	3.405×10^{-10}
kilograms/meter	pounds/ft	0.6720
kilograms/sq cm	dynes	980,665.0
kilograms/sq cm	atmospheres	0.9678
kilograms/sq cm	feet of water	32.81
kilograms/sq cm	inches of mercury	28.96
kilograms/sq cm	pounds/sq ft	2,048.0
kilograms/sq cm	pounds/sq in	14.22
kilograms/sq meter	atmospheres	9.678×10^{-5}
kilograms/sq meter	bars	98.07×10^{-6}
kilograms/sq meter	feet of water	3.281×10^{-3}
kilograms/sq meter	inches of mercury	2.896×10^{-3}
kilograms/sq meter	pounds/sq ft	0.2048
kilograms/sq meter	pounds/sq in	1.422×10^{-3}
kilograms/sq mm	kgs/sq meter	1×10^{6}
kilogram-calories	Btu	3.968
kilogram-calories	foot-pounds	3,088.0
kilogram-calories	hp-hrs	1.560×10^{-3}
kilogram-calories	joules	4,186.0
kilogram-calories	kg-meters	426.9
kilogram-calories	kilojoules	4.186
kilogram-calories	kilowatt-hrs	1.163×10^{-3}
kilogram-meters	Btu	9.294×10^{-3}
kilogram-meters	ergs	9.804×10^{7}
kilogram-meters	foot-pounds	7.233
kilogram-meters	joules	9.804
kilogram-meters	kg-calories	2.342×10^{-3}
kilogram-meters	kilowatt-hrs	2.723×10^{-6}
kilolines	maxwells	1,000.0
kiloliters	liters	1,000.0
kilometers	centimeters	1×10^{5}
kilometers	feet	3,281.0
kilometers	inches	3.937×10^{4}
kilometers	meters	1,000.0
kilometers	miles	0.6214
kilometers	millimeters	1×10^{6}
kilometers	yards	1,094.0
kilometers/hr	cms/sec	27.78
kilometers/hr	feet/min	54.68
kilometers/hr	feet/sec	0.9113
kilometers/hr	knots	0.5396
kilometers/hr	meters/min	16.67
kilometers/hr	miles/hr	0.6214
kilometers/hr/sec	cms/sec/sec	27.78
kilometers/hr/sec	ft/sec/sec	0.9113
kilometers/hr/sec	meters/sec/sec	0.2778
kilometers/hr/sec	miles/hr/sec	0.6214
kilowatts	Btu/min	56.92
kilowatts	foot-lbs/min	4.426×10^{4}
kilowatts	foot-lbs/sec	737.6
kilowatts	horsepower	1.341
kilowatts	kg-calories/min	14.34
kilowatts	watts	1,000.0
kilowatt-hrs	Btu	3,413.0
kilowatt-hrs	ergs	3.600×10^{13}
kilowatt-hrs	foot-lbs	2.655×10^{6}
kilowatt-hrs	gram-calories	859,850.0
kilowatt-hrs	horsepower-hrs	1.341
kilowatt-hrs	joules	3.6×10^{6}
kilowatt-hrs	kg-calories	860.5
kilowatt-hrs	kg-meters	3.671×10^{5}
kilowatt-hrs	pounds of water evaporated from and at 212° F	3.53
kilowatt-hrs	pounds of water raised from 62° to 212° F	22.75
knots	feet/hr	6,080.0
knots	kilometers/hr	1.8532
knots	nautical miles/hr	1.0
knots	statute miles/hr	1.151
knots	yards/hr	2,027.0
knots	feet/sec	1.689

L

To Convert	Into	Multiply by
league	miles (approx)	3.0
light-year	miles	5.9×10^{12}
light-year	kilometers	9.46091×10^{12}
lines/sq cm	gausses	1.0
lines/sq in	gausses	0.1550
lines/sq in	webers/sq cm	1.550×10^{-9}
lines/sq in	webers/sq in	1×10^{-8}
lines/sq in	webers/sq meter	1.550×10^{-5}
links (engineer's)	inches	12.0
links (surveyor's)	inches	7.92
liters	bushels (U.S. dry)	0.02838
liters	cu cm	1,000.0
liters	cu feet	0.03531
liters	cu inches	61.02
liters	cu meters	0.001
liters	cu yards	1.308×10^{-3}
liters	gallons (U.S. liq.)	0.2642
liters	pints (U.S. liq.)	2.113
liters	quarts (U.S. liq.)	1.057
liters/min	cu ft/sec	5.886×10^{-4}
liters/min	gals/sec	4.403×10^{-3}
lumen	spherical candle power	0.07958
lumen	watt	0.001496
lumens/sq ft	foot-candles	1.0
lumens/sq ft	lumen/sq meter	10.76
lux	foot-candles	0.0929

M

To Convert	Into	Multiply by
maxwells	kilolines	0.001
maxwells	webers	1×10^{-8}
megalines	maxwells	1×10^{6}
megohms	microhms	1×10^{12}
megohms	ohms	1×10^{6}
meters	centimeters	100.0
meters	feet	3.281
meters	inches	39.37
meters	kilometers	0.001
meters	miles (nautical)	5.396×10^{-4}
meters	miles (statute)	6.214×10^{-4}
meters	millimeters	1,000.0
meters	yards	1.094
meters/min	cms/sec	1.667
meters/min	feet/min	3.281
meters/min	feet/sec	0.05468
meters/min	kms/hr	0.06
meters/min	knots	0.03238
meters/min	miles/hr	0.03728
meters/sec	feet/min	196.8
meters/sec	feet/sec	3.281
meters/sec	kilometers/hr	3.6
meters/sec	kilometers/min	0.06
meters/sec	miles/hr	2.237
meters/sec	miles/min	0.03728
meters/sec/sec	cms/sec/sec	100.0
meters/sec/sec	ft/sec/sec	3.281
meters/sec/sec	kms/hr/sec	3.6
meters/sec/sec	miles/hr/sec	2.237
meter-kilograms	cm-dynes	9.807×10^{7}
meter-kilograms	cm-grams	1×10^{5}
meter-kilograms	pound-feet	7.233
microfarad	farads	1×10^{-6}
micrograms	grams	1×10^{-6}
microhms	megohms	1×10^{-12}
microhms	ohms	1×10^{-6}
microliters	liters	1×10^{-6}
microns	meters	1×10^{-6}
miles (nautical)	feet	6,080.27
miles (nautical)	kilometers	1.853
miles (nautical)	meters	1,853.0
miles (nautical)	miles (statute)	1.1516
miles (nautical)	yards	2,027.0
miles (statute)	centimeters	1.609×10^{5}
miles (statute)	feet	5,280.0
miles (statute)	inches	6.336×10^{4}
miles (statute)	kilometers	1.609
miles (statute)	meters	1,609.0
miles (statute)	miles (nautical)	0.8684
miles (statute)	yards	1,760.0
miles/hr	cms/sec	44.70
miles/hr	feet/min	88.0
miles/hr	feet/sec	1.467
miles/hr	kms/hr	1.609
miles/hr	kms/min	0.02682

To Convert	Into	Multiply by
miles/hr	knots	0.8684
miles/hr	meters/min	26.82
miles/hr	miles/min	0.1667
miles/hr/sec	cms/sec/sec	44.70
miles/hr/sec	feet/sec/sec	1.467
miles/hr/sec	kms/hr/sec	1.609
miles/hr/sec	meters/sec/sec	0.4470
miles/min	cms/sec	2,682.0
miles/min	feet/sec	88.0
miles/min	kms/min	1.609
miles/min	knots/min	0.8684
miles/min	miles/hr	60.0
mil-feet	cu inches	9.425×10^{-6}
milliers	kilograms	1,000.0
millimicrons	meters	1×10^{-9}
milligrams	grains	0.01543236
milligrams	grams	0.001
milligrams/liter	parts/million	1.0
millihenries	henries	0.001
milliliters	liters	0.001
millimeters	centimeters	0.1
millimeters	feet	3.281×10^{-3}
millimeters	inches	0.03937
millimeters	kilometers	1×10^{-6}
millimeters	meters	0.001
millimeters	miles	6.214×10^{-7}
millimeters	mils	39.37
millimeters	yards	1.094×10^{-3}
million gals/day	cu ft/sec	1.54723
mils	centimeters	2.540×10^{-3}
mils	feet	8.333×10^{-5}
mils	inches	0.001
mils	kilometers	2.540×10^{-3}
mils	yards	2.778×10^{-5}
minims (British)	cubic cm	0.059192
minims (U.S., fluid)	cubic cm	0.061612
minutes (angles)	degrees	0.01667
minutes (angles)	quadrants	1.852×10^{-4}
minutes (angles)	radians	2.909×10^{-4}
minutes (angles)	seconds	60.0

N

To Convert	Into	Multiply by
nepers	decibals	8.686
newton	dynes	1×10^{5}

O

To Convert	Into	Multiply by
ohm (international)	ohm (absolute)	1.0005
ohms	megohms	1×10^{-6}
ohms	microhms	1×10^{6}
ounces	drams	16.0
ounces	grains	437.5
ounces	grams	28.349527
ounces	pounds	0.0625
ounces	ounces (troy)	0.9115
ounces	tons (long)	2.790×10^{-5}
ounces	tons (metric)	2.835×10^{-5}
ounces (fluid)	cu inches	1.805
ounces (fluid)	liters	0.02957
ounces (troy)	grains	480.0
ounces (troy)	grams	31.103481
ounces (troy)	ounces (avoirdupois)	1.09714
ounces (troy)	pennyweights (troy)	20.0
ounces (troy)	pounds (troy)	0.08333
ounce/sq inch	dynes/sq cm	4,309.0
ounces/sq inch	pounds/sq in	0.0625

P

To Convert	Into	Multiply by
parsec	miles	19×10^{12}
parsec	kilometers	3.084×10^{13}
parts/million	grains/U.S. gal	0.0584
parts/million	grains/imperial gal	0.07016
parts/million	pounds/million gal	8.345
pecks (British)	cubic inches	554.6
pecks (British)	liters	9.091901
pecks (U.S.)	bushels	0.25
pecks (U.S)	cubic inches	537.605
pecks (U.S.)	liters	8.809582
pecks (U.S.)	quarts (dry)	8.0
pennyweights (troy)	grains	24.0
pennyweights (troy)	ounces (troy)	0.05
pennyweights (troy)	grams	1.55517
pennyweights (troy)	pounds (troy)	4.1667×10^{-3}
pints (dry)	cu inches	33.60

To Convert	Into	Multiply by
pints (liquid)	cu cm	473.2
pints (liquid)	cu feet	0.01671
pints (liquid)	cu inches	28.87
pints (liquid)	cu meters	4.732×10^{-4}
pints (liquid)	cu yards	6.189×10^{-4}
pints (liquid)	gallons	0.125
pints (liquid)	liters	0.4732
pints (liquid)	quarts (liquid)	0.5
Planck's quantum	erg-second	6.624×10^{-27}
poise	gram/cm sec	1.00
pounds (avoirdupois)	ounces (troy)	14.5833
poundals	dynes	13,826.0
poundals	grams	14.10
poundals	joules/cm	1.383×10^{3}
poundals	joules/meter (newtons)	0.1383
poundals	kilograms	0.01410
poundals	pounds	0.03108
pounds	drams	256.0
pounds	dynes	44.4823×10^{4}
pounds	grains	7,000.0
pounds	grams	453.5924
pounds	joules/cm	0.04448
pounds	joules/meter (newtons)	4.448
pounds	kilograms	0.4536
pounds	ounces	16.0
pounds	ounces (troy)	14.5833
pounds	poundals	32.17
pounds	pounds (troy)	1.21528
pounds	tons (short)	0.0005
pounds (troy)	grains	5,760.0
pounds (troy)	grams	373.24177
pounds (troy)	ounces (avoirdupois)	13.1657
pounds (troy)	ounces (troy)	12.0
pounds (troy)	pennyweights (troy)	240.0
pounds (troy)	pounds (avoirdupois)	0.822857
pounds (troy)	tons (long)	3.6735×10^{-4}
pounds (troy)	tons (metric)	3.7324×10^{-4}
pounds (troy)	tons (short)	4.1143×10^{-4}
pounds of water	cu feet	0.01602
pounds of water	cu inches	27.68
pounds of water	gallons	0.1198
pounds of water/min	cu ft/sec	2.670×10^{-4}
pound-feet	cm-dynes	1.356×10^{7}
pound-feet	cm-grams	13,825.0
pound-feet	meter-kgs	0.1383
pounds/cu ft	grams/cu cm	0.01602
pounds/cu ft	kgs/cu meter	16.02
pounds/cu ft	pounds/cu in	5.787×10^{-4}
pounds/cu ft	pounds/mil-foot	5.456×10^{-9}
pounds/cu in	gms/cu cm	27.68
pounds/cu in	kgs/cu meter	2.768×10^{4}
pounds/cu in	pounds/cu ft	1,728.0
pounds/cu in	pounds/mil-foot	9.425×10^{-6}
pounds/ft	kgs/meter	1.488
pounds/in	gms/cm	178.6
pounds/mil-foot	gms/cu cm	2.306×10^{6}
pounds/sq ft	atmospheres	4.725×10^{-4}
pounds/sq ft	feet of water	0.01602
pounds/sq ft	inches of mercury	0.01414
pounds/sq ft	kgs/sq meter	4.882
pounds/sq ft	pounds/sq in	6.944×10^{-3}
pounds/sq in	atmospheres	0.06804
pounds/sq in	feet of water	2.307
pounds/sq in	inches of mercury	2.036
pounds/sq in	kgs/sq meter	703.1
pounds/sq in	pounds/sq ft	144.0

Q

To Convert	Into	Multiply by
quadrants (angle)	degrees	90.0
quadrants (angle)	minutes	5,400.0
quadrants (angle)	radians	1.571
quadrants (angle)	seconds	3.24×10^{5}
quarts (dry)	cu inches	67.20
quarts (liquid)	cu cms	946.4
quarts (liquid)	cu feet	0.03342
quarts (liquid)	cu inches	57.75
quarts (liquid)	cu meters	9.464×10^{-4}
quarts (liquid)	cu yards	1.238×10^{-3}
quarts (liquid)	gallons	0.25
quarts (liquid)	liters	0.9463

R

To Convert	Into	Multiply by
radians	degrees	57.30

To Convert	Into	Multiply by
radians	minutes	3,438.0
radians	quadrants	0.6366
radians	seconds	2.063×10^5
radians/sec	degrees/sec	57.30
radians/sec	revolutions/min	9.549
radians/sec	revolutions/sec	0.1592
radians/sec/sec	revs/min/min	573.0
radians/sec/sec	revs/min/sec	9.549
radians/sec/sec	revs/sec/sec	0.1592
revolutions	degrees	360.0
revolutions	quadrants	4.0
revolutions	radians	6.283
revolutions/min	degrees/sec	6.0
revolutions/min	radians/sec	0.1047
revolutions/min	revs/sec	0.01667
revolutions/min/min	radians/sec/sec	1.745×10^{-3}
revolutions/min/min	revs/min/sec	0.01667
revolutions/min/min	revs/sec/sec	2.778×10^{-4}
revolutions/sec	degrees/sec	360.0
revolutions/sec	radians/sec	6.283
revolutions/sec	revs/min	60.0
revolutions/sec/sec	radians/sec/sec	6.283
revolutions/sec/sec	revs/min/min	3,600.0
revolutions/sec/sec	revs/min/sec	60.0
rod	chain (Gunter's)	0.25
rod	meters	5.029
rods (surveyor's meas.)	yards	5.5
rods	feet	16.5

S

To Convert	Into	Multiply by
scruples	grains	20.0
seconds (angle)	degrees	2.778×10^{-4}
seconds (angle)	minutes	0.01667
seconds (angle)	quadrants	3.087×10^{-6}
seconds (angle)	radians	4.848×10^{-6}
slug	kilogram	14.59
slug	pounds	32.17
sphere	steradians	12.57
square centimeters	circular mils	1.973×10^5
square centimeters	square feet	1.076×10^{-3}
square centimeters	square inches	0.1550
square centimeters	square meters	0.0001
square centimeters	sq miles	3.861×10^{-11}
square centimeters	sq millimeters	100.0
square centimeters	sq yards	1.196×10^{-4}
square feet	acres	2.296×10^{-5}
square feet	circular mils	1.833×10^8
square feet	sq cms	929.0
square feet	sq inches	144.0
square feet	sq meters	0.09290
square feet	sq miles	3.587×10^{-8}
square feet	sq millimeters	9.290×10^4
square feet	sq yards	0.1111
square inches	circular mils	1.273×10^6
square inches	sq cms	6.452
square inches	sq feet	6.944×10^{-3}
square inches	sq millimeters	645.2
square inches	sq mils	1×10^6
square inches	sq yards	7.716×10^{-4}
square kilometers	acres	247.1
square kilometers	sq cms	1×10^{10}
square kilometers	sq ft	10.76×10^6
square kilometers	sq inches	1.550×10^9
square kilometers	sq meters	1×10^6
square kilometers	sq miles	0.3861
square kilometers	sq yards	1.196×10^6
square meters	acres	2.471×10^{-4}
square meters	sq cms	1×10^4
square meters	sq feet	10.76
square meters	sq inches	1,550.0
square meters	sq miles	3.861×10^{-7}
square meters	sq millimeters	1×10^6
square meters	sq yards	1.196
square miles	acres	640.0
square miles	sq feet	27.88×10^6
square miles	sq kms	2.590
square miles	sq meters	2.590×10^6
square miles	sq yards	3.098×10^6
square millimeters	circular mils	1,973.0
square millimeters	sq cms	0.01
square millimeters	sq feet	1.076×10^{-5}
square millimeters	sq inches	1.550×10^{-3}
square mils	circular mils	1.273
square mils	sq cms	6.452×10^{-6}

To Convert	Into	Multiply by
square mils	sq inches	1×10^{-6}
square yards	acres	2.066×10^{-4}
square yards	sq cms	8,361.0
square yards	sq feet	9.0
square yards	sq inches	1,296.0
square yards	sq meters	0.8361
square yards	sq miles	3.228×10^{-7}
square yards	sq millimeters	8.361×10^5

T

To Convert	Into	Multiply by
temperature (°C) + 273	absolute temperature (°C)	1.0
temperature (°C) + 17.78	temperature (°F)	1.8
temperature (°F) + 460	absolute temperature (°F)	1.0
temperature (°F) − 32	temperature (°C)	5/9
tons (long)	kilograms	1,016.0
tons (long)	pounds	2,240.0
tons (long)	tons (short)	1.120
tons (metric)	kilograms	1,000.0
tons (metric)	pounds	2,205.0
tons (short)	kilograms	907.1848
tons (short)	ounces	32,000.0
tons (short)	ounces (troy)	29,166.66
tons (short)	pounds	2,000.0
tons (short)	pounds (troy)	2,430.56
tons (short)	tons (long)	0.89287
tons (short)	tons (metric)	0.9078
tons (short)/sq ft	kgs/sq meter	9,765.0
tons (short)/sq ft	pounds/sq in	2,000.0
tons of water/24 hrs	pounds of water/hr	83.333
tons of water/24 hrs	gallons/min	0.16643
tons of water/24 hrs	cu ft/hr	1.3349

V

To Convert	Into	Multiply by
volt inch	volt/cm	0.39370
volt (absolute)	statvolts	0.003336

W

To Convert	Into	Multiply by
watts	Btu/hr	3.4129
watts	Btu/min	0.05688
watts	ergs/sec	107.0
watts	foot-lbs/min	44.27
watts	foot-lbs/sec	0.7378
watts	horsepower	1.341×10^{-3}
watts	horsepower (metric)	1.360×10^{-3}
watts	kg-calories/min	0.01433
watts	kilowatts	0.001
watts (absolute)	Btu (mean)/min	0.056884
watts (absolute)	joules/sec	1.0
watt-hours	Btu	3.413
watt-hours	ergs	3.60×10^{10}
watt-hours	foot-pounds	2,656.0
watt-hours	gram-calories	859.85
watt-hours	horsepower-hrs	1.341×10^{-3}
watt-hours	kilogram-calories	0.8605
watt-hours	kilogram-meters	367.2
watt-hours	kilowatt-hrs	0.001
watt (international)	watt (absolute)	1.0002
webers	maxwells	1×10^8
webers	kilolines	1×10^5
webers/sq in	gausses	1.550×10^7
webers/sq in	lines/sq in	1×10^8
webers/sq in	webers/sq cm	0.1550
webers/sq in	webers/sq meter	1,550.0
webers/sq meter	gausses	1×10^4
webers/sq meter	lines/sq in	6.452×10^4
webers/sq meter	webers/sq cm	1×10^{-4}
webers/sq meter	webers/sq in	6.452×10^{-4}

Y

To Convert	Into	Multiply by
yards	centimeters	91.44
yards	kilometers	9.144×10^{-4}
yards	meters	0.9144
yards	miles (nautical)	4.934×10^{-4}
yards	miles (statute)	5.682×10^{-4}
yards	millimeters	914.4

OCCUPATIONAL GUIDE

This guide lists 95 occupations or occupational categories. The entries appear alphabetically, with each entry containing a description of the nature of work, the training required, desirable personal qualifications, and the work environment for the category or occupation described. The name and address of an organization that can furnish additional information for each occupation is also included.

ACCOUNTANT

NATURE OF WORK: Preparation of cost studies, tax returns, and other financial reports.

TRAINING: Bachelor's or master's degree; also available through correspondence courses and business schools. High school diploma essential.

PERSONAL QUALIFICATIONS: Aptitude for mathematical work.

WORK ENVIRONMENT: Office; regular hours.

FURTHER INFORMATION: American Institute of Certified Public Accountants
1211 Avenue of the Americas
New York, NY 10036

INTERNATIONAL HARVESTER *WORLD*

Qualified accountants can specialize within the major fields of accounting—public, management (industrial), and government.

ADVERTISING COPYWRITER

NATURE OF WORK: Creation of advertising slogans, headlines, and copy for all media.

TRAINING: Bachelor's or master's degree in journalism, advertising, or business.

PERSONAL QUALIFICATIONS: Creativity and facility with language; sense of competition.

WORK ENVIRONMENT: Office; regular hours.

FURTHER INFORMATION: American Advertising Federation
1225 Connecticut Avenue, N.W.
Washington, DC 20036

ADVERTISING EXECUTIVE

NATURE OF WORK: Planning and management of accounts for advertising agency.

TRAINING: Bachelor's or master's degree in management or marketing.

PERSONAL QUALIFICATIONS: Organizational ability and aggressiveness.

WORK ENVIRONMENT: Office; regular hours.

FURTHER INFORMATION: American Advertising Federation
1225 Connecticut Avenue, N.W.
Washington, DC 20036

AERONAUTIC TECHNICIAN

NATURE OF WORK: Assist engineers in designing aircraft and missile systems.

TRAINING: Vocational schooling or on-job preparation; high school diploma recommended.

PERSONAL QUALIFICATIONS: Exactness; mechanical ability; aptitude for mathematics.

WORK ENVIRONMENT: Research labs, assembly plants, missile bases, and airports; generally regular hours.

FURTHER INFORMATION: National Technical Association
1425 H Street, N.W., Suite 715
Washington, DC 20005

AIRLINE-RELATED OCCUPATIONS

NATURE OF WORK: Perform engineering, dispatch, mechanical, and air traffic control duties to assist in operations of travel.

TRAINING: High school diploma required; further training varies according to job; usually offered by company. Aircraft experience in Armed Forces often accepted as training.

PERSONAL QUALIFICATIONS: Between 20 and 40 years of age; other qualifications vary. Manual dexterity needed for technical positions.

WORK ENVIRONMENT: Highly favorable; reduced rate for travel by employees and their families; union benefits; some night and weekend work.

FURTHER INFORMATION: Information Retrieval Branch
Federal Aviation Administration
Library, HQ 630
Federal Aviation Administration
Washington, DC 20553
or
Local employment office of desired airline.

APPLIANCE SERVICEMAN

NATURE OF WORK: Diagnosing problems of household appliances and replacing parts.

TRAINING: One to three years of on-job training as helper; occasional company-sponsored courses when new products are introduced.

PERSONAL QUALIFICATIONS: Mechanical aptitude; ability to work without constant supervision.

WORK ENVIRONMENT: Location varies from homes to laundromats. Often involves driving small truck or van; generally regular hours except in emergencies.

FURTHER INFORMATION: Association of Home Appliance Manufacturers
20 North Wacker Drive
Chicago, IL 60606

ARCHITECT

NATURE OF WORK: Design construction and remodeling of buildings.

TRAINING: Five-year course at accredited school of architecture; three years internship (with full pay) and successful completion of state exam.

PERSONAL QUALIFICATION: Creativity; interest in people and their living habits and needs; facility with math; artistic ability.

WORK ENVIRONMENT: Office and drafting with workshop. Construction site supervision. Regular hours.

FURTHER INFORMATION: American Institute of Architects
1735 New York Avenue, N.W.
Washington, DC 20006

ARMED SERVICES OFFICER

NATURE OF WORK: Wide variety of jobs organizing and admistering programs of Army, Navy, Air Force, and Marine Corps.

TRAINING: Reserve officers training programs on college campuses, military academies, or officer candidate schools run by a particular branch of the service. Women's programs also available. High school recommended.

PERSONAL QUALIFICATIONS: Ability to give and take orders; neatness; punctuality; an aptitude for organization.

WORK ENVIRONMENT: Office, field, and combat locations; hours vary with duty assigned. Overseas assignments almost certain.

FURTHER INFORMATION: Recruiting stations at post offices; information also available in public libraries and counseling offices.

AUTO DEALER

NATURE OF WORK: Management of franchised automobile dealership.

TRAINING: High school diploma recommended; experience as sales or service representative for dealer. Formal or informal business education.

PERSONAL QUALIFICATIONS: Judgment; aggressiveness; business ability; tact and good grooming.

WORK ENVIRONMENT: Office and occasional car lot location; regular hours.

FURTHER INFORMATION: National Automobile Dealers Association
8400 Westpark Drive
McLean, VA 22102

BAKER

NATURE OF WORK: Specialized (as operation of machine in an industrial bakery) or general baking duties (as in small neighborhood bakery).

TRAINING: Varies from on-job, short term to college courses of various lengths.

PERSONAL QUALIFICATIONS: Good health; sense of precision in measuring; sense of hygiene.

WORK ENVIRONMENT: Irregular hours, often on night shifts; large factory or small shop. Many positions available in restaurants and hotels.

FURTHER INFORMATION: American Bakers Association
2020 K Street, N.W.
Washington, DC 20006

or

American Institute of Baking
P.O. Box 1448
Manhattan, KS 66502

AMERICAN BAKERS ASSOCIATION

Industrial bakeries depend upon complex equipment to assure uniformity of size, shape, and quality.

BANKER

NATURE OF WORK: Business executive, loan officer, or accountant bookkeeper.

TRAINING: Bachelor's degree in math, economics, business, or liberal arts.

PERSONAL QUALIFICATIONS: Business acumen; personableness; aggressiveness; good grooming.

WORK ENVIRONMENT: Office; regular hours.

FURTHER INFORMATION: American Bankers Association
1120 Connecticut Avenue, N.W.
Washington, DC 20036

BRICKLAYER

NATURE OF WORK: Heavy physical labor in construction of walls and foundations for new or remodeled buildings; placing and adjusting of scaffolding.

TRAINING: Apprenticeship of three to four years, including on-job training and 144 hours of classroom work per year.

PERSONAL QUALIFICATIONS: Good health; physical strength and endurance.

WORK ENVIRONMENT: Outdoor locations; much seasonal employment; regular hours.

FURTHER INFORMATION: Bricklayers, Masons, and Plasterers International Union
815 15th Street, N.W.
Washington, DC 20005

INTERNATIONAL HARVESTER *WORLD*

The skilled bricklayer needs an accurate eye and a deft touch.

BUTCHER

NATURE OF WORK: Cutting and displaying of meat in supermarkets or small shops. Some positions available in large restaurants.

TRAINING: On-job apprenticeship of two to three years generally required. High school diploma recommended but not essential.

PERSONAL QUALIFICATIONS: Good health; physical stamina; sense of hygiene.

WORK ENVIRONMENT: Regular hours, some evening work; small shop, large supermarket, or restaurant.

FURTHER INFORMATION: Amalgamated Meat Cutters
Suffridge Building
1775 K Street, N.W.
Washington, DC 20006

CARPENTER

NATURE OF WORK: Physical labor involved in the construction of frameworks, forms, floors, and roofs using both hand and power tools.

TRAINING: A four-year apprenticeship and high school diploma are desirable; 144 hours of classroom training per year during apprenticeship, plus on-job training.

PERSONAL QUALIFICATIONS: Physical strength; good balance; no fear of heights.

WORK ENVIRONMENT: Outdoor and indoor work; seasonal.

FURTHER INFORMATION: Union Brotherhood of Carpenters and Joiners of America.
101 Constitution Avenue, N.W.
Washington, DC 20001

CHEF

NATURE OF WORK: Preparation of meals in restaurants, schools, and institutions.

TRAINING: On-job training most common; courses offered by some schools and some union apprentice programs also available.

PERSONAL QUALIFICATIONS: Good health; stamina; a keen sense of taste and smell.

WORK ENVIRONMENT: Variable, from large restaurant or hotel kitchens to those of smaller establishments. Hours often irregular; often split shifts. Salary relates to experience and previous training.

FURTHER INFORMATION: Educational Director
National Restaurant Association
One IBM Plaza, Suite 2600
Chicago, IL 60611

CHEMIST

NATURE OF WORK: Highly specialized work on research projects for government, private industry, and universities.

TRAINING: Bachelor's degree essential; master's and doctoral degree applicants begin at higher salaries and are responsible for more advanced research. Ph.D. necessary for university positions.

PERSONAL QUALIFICATIONS: Facility with mathematics; patience; aptitude for abstract thinking.

WORK ENVIRONMENT: Chemical laboratories and small office or classroom; regular hours.

FURTHER INFORMATION: American Chemical Society
1155 16th Street, N.W.
Washington, DC 20036

ALLIED CHEMICAL CORPORATION

Chemists regularly perform intricate experiments to see if they validate their theories.

CLERICAL OCCUPATIONS

NATURE OF WORK: Keep records, handle communications by phone, mail, and messenger; attend to other office duties such as shipping and receiving merchandise, operating simple office machines.

TRAINING: High school diploma required; business courses advisable. Further training provided on-job.

PERSONAL QUALIFICATIONS: Knowledge of spelling and grammar; sense of organization and responsibility; good grooming.

WORK ENVIRONMENT: Regular hours; paid vacations and sick leave. Physical conditions vary with size, location, and purpose of business. Retirement benefits often available.

FURTHER INFORMATION: Pamphlet: "Clerical Occupations for Women Today and Tomorrow" Women's Bureau Bulletin #289, 1964
Superintendent of Documents
Washington, DC 20402

or

United Business Schools Association
1730 M Street, N.W., Suite 401
Washington, DC 20036

COMMERCIAL ARTIST

NATURE OF WORK: Illustrating and arranging layouts and lettering for magazines, newspapers, and books.

TRAINING: High school diploma together with two to three years training at art school; bachelor's degree recommended for rapid advancement.

PERSONAL QUALIFICATIONS: Artistic sense, draftsmanship, and creativity; good business sense necessary for free-lance artists and art directors.

WORK ENVIRONMENT: Agency, newspaper, or magazine art department; regular hours working largely with easel and drafting board.

FURTHER INFORMATION: National Association of Schools of Art
11250 Roger Bacon Drive, No. Five
Reston, VA 22090

COMPUTER PROGRAMMER

NATURE OF WORK: Writing and adjusting computer programs.

TRAINING: Bachelor's degree in engineering, math, or related field, or comparable on-job experience; two-year course or background in accounting and clerical work sufficient for some positions.

PERSONAL QUALIFICATIONS: Ability to think logically; facility with mathematics; sense of perfection, and creative imagination.

WORK ENVIRONMENT: New, large, well-organized office; regular hours.

FURTHER INFORMATION: Data-Processing Management Association
505 Busse Highway
Park Ridge, IL 60068

IBM CORPORATION
Computer programing requires constant checking and verification.

CONSTRUCTION INDUSTRY OCCUPATIONS

NATURE OF WORK: Wide variety of work in the building trades, including that of carpenter, painter, and electrician, involved in the remodeling or construction of buildings.

TRAINING: Apprenticeship program for particular trade or attendance at a trade school.

PERSONAL QUALIFICATIONS: Age 18 to 25 for apprentice; good physical condition. Age limits waived for veterans and others with experience.

WORK ENVIRONMENT: Often outdoors, on-site work; variable according to weather, season, and market demand for construction. Generally regular hours; very high union benefits and wages.

FURTHER INFORMATION: AFL-CIO: Building and Construction Trades Department
815 16th Street, N.W.
Washington, DC 20006
or
Associated General Contractors of America
1957 E Street, N.W.
Washington, DC 20006

CONTRACTOR

NATURE OF WORK: Handling administrative duties of the construction industry.

TRAINING: Practical experience in construction trade helpful; business ability acquired through formal courses in high school or college or on-job.

PERSONAL QUALIFICATIONS: Ability for mathematics; personableness, business sense, ambition.

WORK ENVIRONMENT: Largely in office; some on-site supervision. Regular hours.

FURTHER INFORMATION: Associated General Contractors of America
1957 East Street, N.W.
Washington, DC 20006

COSMETOLOGISTS

NATURE OF WORK: Specialize in hair care, such as shampooing, setting and tinting; also involves duties relating to make-up and manicure treatments.

TRAINING: Six- to twelve-month course from state-approved school. State exam upon completion determines license to practice.

PERSONAL QUALIFICATIONS: Good health; personableness; sense of hygiene; good grooming.

WORK ENVIRONMENT: Large or small beauty shop; regular hours. Salary supplemented by tips from customers.

FURTHER INFORMATION: National Hairdressers and Cosmetologists Association
3510 Olive Street
St. Louis, MO 63103

COUNSELOR

NATURE OF WORK: Work in assisting persons to develop and adjust to goals and anxieties of their lives, jobs, or handicap.

TRAINING: Bachelor's degree in psychology, education, social science, or related field. Most states require both counseling and teaching certificates from their departments of education.

PERSONAL QUALIFICATIONS: Outgoing personality; emotional stability; aptitude for coping with psychological dynamics of individuals and groups.

WORK ENVIRONMENT: Regular hours in office, clinic, or school; usually long vacations and limited union benefits.

FURTHER INFORMATION: American Personnel and Guidance Association, Inc.
Two Skyline Place, Suite 400
5203 Leesburg Pike
Falls Church, VA 22041

DENTAL HYGIENIST

NATURE OF WORK: Assist dentist with cleaning, x-raying, and other dental work.

TRAINING: High school diploma followed by a two-, three-, or four-year dental hygiene program at an accredited school.

Taking x-rays is a routine task of dental hygienists.

PERSONAL QUALIFICATIONS: Good health; manual dexterity; ability to relate well to public; excellent personal grooming.

WORK ENVIRONMENT: Regular hours; well-lit, clean office.

FURTHER INFORMATION: American Dental Hygenists' Association
444 N. Michigan Avenue
Chicago, IL 60611

DENTIST

NATURE OF WORK: Caring for teeth and total dental health, usually in a private practice.

TRAINING: Two to four years of college undergraduate work required by most dental schools; more than half of current dental candidates have received bachelor's degree. Four-year dental school program and licensing after satisfactory grade on state exam.

PERSONAL QUALIFICATIONS: Good health; scientific ability; manual dexterity; keen sensitivity to hygiene.

WORK ENVIRONMENT: Hours may be set in private practice by doctor; work in clean, well-lit office.

FURTHER INFORMATION: American Dental Association
Council on Dental Education
211 East Chicago Avenue
Chicago, IL 60611

INTERNATIONAL HARVESTER *WORLD*
Draftsmen use precision instruments to assure accuracy.

DRAFTSMAN

NATURE OF WORK: Translating designer's ideas and rough sketches into finished plans for manufactured products.

TRAINING: Some jobs available to well-prepared high school graduates; post-high school courses offered by technical institutes, community colleges, and on-job apprenticeships.

PERSONAL QUALIFICATIONS: Ability to visualize three-dimensional objects and do freehand drawing; sense of exact precision.

WORK ENVIRONMENT: Drafting table, usually in large, well-lit office; regular hours.

FURTHER INFORMATION: American Federation of Technical Engineers
1126 16th Street, N.W.
Washington, DC 20036

DRIVER: BUS, TRUCK, TAXI

NATURE OF WORK: Driving a passenger bus or long distance freight truck, or smaller local vehicles. Transporting city passengers in a cab.

TRAINING: On-job experience. Most states require applicants to pass special exam for operator's license.

PERSONAL QUALIFICATIONS: Sense of responsibility and direction; good physical strength and motor coordination. Precise knowledge of city for taxi drivers.

WORK ENVIRONMENT: Variable, day or night shifts. Seasonal demands for labor force; much time spent unsupervised while driving. Very high union wages and benefits.

FURTHER INFORMATION: American Trucking Associations
1616 P Street, N.W.
Washington, DC 20036

ELECTRICIAN

NATURE OF WORK: Design and wiring of electrical circuits and equipment in buildings.

TRAINING: Usually a four-year apprenticeship required; includes 144 hours of classroom work per year; most states license electricians by examination.

PERSONAL QUALIFICATIONS: Mechanical aptitude.

WORK ENVIRONMENT: Indoor and outdoor; somewhat seasonal.

FURTHER INFORMATION: International Brotherhood of Electrical Workers
1125 15th Street, N.W.
Washington, DC 20005

ENGINEER, CHEMICAL

NATURE OF WORK: Design of factories which produce chemicals; translate chemical discoveries to design for commercial production of goods.

TRAINING: Bachelor's degree for all engineering jobs; master's degree is often helpful in advancement or for research positions.

PERSONAL QUALIFICATIONS: Aptitude for figures; good problem-solving capabilities.

WORK ENVIRONMENT: Lab and desk work; site inspection; regular hours.

FURTHER INFORMATION: American Institute of Chemical Engineers
345 East 47th Street
New York, NY 10017

ENGINEER, CIVIL

NATURE OF WORK: Design and supervise the construction of roads, bridges, and other civil projects, such as transportation routes in cities.

TRAINING: Bachelor's degree in civil engineering.

PERSONAL QUALIFICATIONS: Aptitude for figures; some aesthetic sense.

WORK ENVIRONMENT: Both office and outdoor site inspection; regular hours.

AMERICAN SOCIETY OF CIVIL ENGINEERS
The civil engineer must inspect his project frequently.

FURTHER INFORMATION: American Society of Civil Engineers
345 East 47th Street
New York, NY 10017

ENGINEER, ELECTRICAL

NATURE OF WORK: Design of electrical apparatus ranging from power-generating stations to small appliances.

TRAINING: Bachelor's degree in electrical engineering.

PERSONAL QUALIFICATIONS: Aptitude for figures.

WORK ENVIRONMENT: Paper work; regular hours.

FURTHER INFORMATION: Institute of Electrical and Electronic Engineers
345 East 47th Street
New York, NY 10017

ENGINEER, MECHANICAL

NATURE OF WORK: Research and design projects on machinery, tools, and other mechanical systems.

TRAINING: Bachelor's degree in mechanical engineering.

PERSONAL QUALIFICATIONS: Aptitude for figures.

WORK ENVIRONMENT: Paper work; regular hours; sometimes extensive lab and computer work.

FURTHER INFORMATION: American Society of Mechanical Engineers
345 East 47th Street
New York, NY 10017

ENGINEER, OPERATING

NATURE OF WORK: Repair and operation of heavy construction machinery such as power shovels, derricks, hoists, bulldozers, and cranes.

TRAINING: A three-year apprenticeship to qualify for journeyman status. Possibility of job after work for several years as helper. Schools neither guarantee employment (despite claims to the contrary) nor provide thorough training. High school diploma necessary.

PERSONAL QUALIFICATIONS: Physical strength and stamina; must be age 18 to 25 for apprenticeship.

WORK ENVIRONMENT: Outdoor work; seasonal; often requiring travel to remote areas.

FURTHER INFORMATION: International Union of Operating Engineers
1125 17th Street, N.W.
Washington, DC 20036

FARMER

NATURE OF WORK: Combination of physical labor and business practice.

TRAINING: Study of agriculture and business practices in high school and college; personal experience on farm.

PERSONAL QUALIFICATIONS: Physical strength and stamina; love of the outdoors and animals; good business judgment.

WORK ENVIRONMENT: Long hours; work is strenuous, but very "independent."

FURTHER INFORMATION: United States Department of Agriculture
Washington, DC 20250

FIREMAN

NATURE OF WORK: Fire fighting, inspection, and educational activities.

TRAINING: Qualifying exam; training at state or city institution.

PERSONAL QUALIFICATIONS: Courage; physical strength and endurance; the ability to give and receive orders in dangerous situations.

WORK ENVIRONMENT: Work week of 50 to 60 hours is common; dull periods alternate with periods of great activity and danger.

FURTHER INFORMATION: International Association of Firefighters
1750 New York Avenue, N.W.
Washington, DC 20006

FLORIST

NATURE OF WORK: Growing, wholesaling, or retailing flowers, floral arrangements, and small plants.

TRAINING: On-job training and experience in the business are of paramount importance; high school and college courses in floriculture, accounting, and business are helpful.

PERSONAL QUALIFICATIONS: Love for plants; artistic ability; business acumen.

WORK ENVIRONMENT: For growers: much outdoor work in fields and large greenhouses; for wholesalers: office work and warehouse supervision; for retailers: typical self-employed small business atmosphere.

FURTHER INFORMATION: Society of American Florists
901 N. Washington Street
Alexandria, VA 22314

FORESTER

NATURE OF WORK: Land management including public land maintenance and control of timber and erosion.

TRAINING: Four-year college education from a forestry school.

PERSONAL QUALIFICATIONS: Physical strength; stamina; good health; love of the outdoors.

WORK ENVIRONMENT: Outdoor work, often unsupervised.

FURTHER INFORMATION: Society of American Foresters
5400 Grosvenor Lane
Washington, DC 20014

USDA

Special measuring tools are used by foresters to estimate the amount of salable wood each log will yield.

GOVERNMENT OCCUPATIONS

NATURE OF WORK: Wide variety of occupations available. Largely involved in administrative functions of the executive branch of government—international relations, conservation, care and treatment of war veterans and dependents, mail processing, administrating laws for general health, education, and welfare of nation's citizens.

TRAINING: High school diploma usually required; college degree usually necessary for managerial positions. Wages and responsibility depend on grade given on preemployment Civil Service exam, offered each month at government locations.

PERSONAL QUALIFICATIONS: Vary according to positions; general sense of responsibility and organization.

WORK ENVIRONMENT: Regular hours; sick leave; paid vacations; physical conditions vary from outdoors for mail carriers to large offices. Regular performance rating by supervisor. Regular opportunities for advancement.

FURTHER INFORMATION: Local post office. For state government positions, contact may be made by applying directly to specific branch desired under listings in telephone directory.

GROCER

NATURE OF WORK: Managing a retail grocery store, as an employee of a large chain or as owner of a small or medium sized store or chain of stores.

TRAINING: Although there are no minimum educational requirements, a high school diploma is nearly indispensable and post-high school courses, especially in business, are helpful; extensive experience in the industry is necessary before becoming a manager or owner.

PERSONAL QUALIFICATIONS: Organizational and managerial talent; aggressiveness; self-reliance; self-confidence.

WORK ENVIRONMENT: Long hours; evening and weekend work often required; some light physical labor required occasionally.

FURTHER INFORMATION: National Association of Retail Grocers
P.O. Box 17208
Washington, DC 20041

HOME ECONOMIST

NATURE OF WORK: Filling research and education positions dealing with family problems, especially those concerned with food and clothing.

TRAINING: Bachelor's degree with a major in home economics.

PERSONAL QUALIFICATIONS: Ability to meet and organize people from diverse socioeconomic backgrounds; neatness and good grooming.

WORK ENVIRONMENT: Teaching in secondary schools; positions are also available in industry and government programs.

FURTHER INFORMATION: American Home Economics Association
2010 Massachusetts Avenue, N.W.
Washington, DC 20036

HOSPITAL ORDERLY: SEE LICENSED PRACTICAL NURSE

HOTEL OCCUPATIONS

NATURE OF WORK: Organizing and implementing operations for service and maintenance of commercial, residential, and resort hotels and motels. Managerial positions, clerks, doormen, porters, and housekeeping staff available.

TRAINING: Varies according to occupation; managerial positions generally require specialized college courses. Other attendants and staff usually hired without high school diploma; on-job training received.

PERSONAL QUALIFICATIONS: Sense of responsibility; aptitude for dealing graciously with guests; sense of hygiene. Other qualities relate to positions.

WORK ENVIRONMENT: Generally pleasant; staff usually receive free meals. Irregular hours; sometimes seasonal work; union benefits.

FURTHER INFORMATION: American Hotel and Motel Association
888 Seventh Avenue
New York, NY 10019

INSURANCE AGENT

NATURE OF WORK: Selling life or casualty insurance to clients on a commission basis.

TRAINING: Although a college degree is not necessary, over half the agents hired in recent years have some college training; many have a degree. All states require insurance agents to be licensed.

PERSONAL QUALIFICATIONS: Personality for good salesman; good business sense.

WORK ENVIRONMENT: Hours are often over 40 hours per week; much evening and weekend work.

FURTHER INFORMATION: American Council of Life Insurance
1850 K Street, N.W.
Washington, DC 20006

INTERIOR DESIGNER

NATURE OF WORK: Planning arrangement of furniture and selection of paint, rugs, and fabric in home or professional locations.

TRAINING: Formal training has not been absolutely necessary in the past; completion of a two-or three-year course at an art school or of a four-year college program increasingly necessary.

PERSONAL QUALIFICATIONS: Aesthetic sense; salesmanship; business ability.

WORK ENVIRONMENT: Work in a large department store, for furniture company, or similar industry; regular hours; many part-time jobs.

FURTHER INFORMATION: National Society of Interior Designers
730 Fifth Avenue
New York, NY 10019

INTERNATIONAL OCCUPATIONS

NATURE OF WORK: Design and develop programs within or between foreign countries for purposes of national improvement and/or international relations. Both summer and semipermanent positions are increasingly available.

TRAINING: High school diploma minimum requirement; most positions require bachelor's degree. Graduate study necessary for management positions.

PERSONAL QUALIFICATIONS: Sense of responsibility; sensitivity to and deep respect for values, customs, and persons of different cultures. Foreign language proficiency helpful. Availability for overseas assignment essential.

WORK ENVIRONMENT: Varies greatly with company and country in which one is employed. Generally favorable, though long hours may result from pressing need, especially in less developed nations.

FURTHER INFORMATION: Jobs International Handbook
Box 475
Lodi, CA 95240

JEWELER

NATURE OF WORK: The preparation of dies, molds, and finished jewelry; stonecutting and setting; jewelry repair.

TRAINING: High school education recommended, followed by a three-or four-year apprenticeship or on-job informal training.

PERSONAL QUALIFICATIONS: Good eyesight; manual dexterity; exactness; business sense, and salesmanship if working in retail jewelry store.

WORK ENVIRONMENT: Either in a trade shop or in retail outlet; regular business hours.

FURTHER INFORMATION: Manufacturing Jewelers and Silversmiths of America, Inc.
340 Howard Building
155 Westminster Street
Providence, RI 02903

JOURNALIST

NATURE OF WORK: Writing and editorial work for newspapers, magazines, and trade publications.

TRAINING: Bachelor's degree, preferably in journalism; history and political science are also excellent backgrounds.

PERSONAL QUALIFICATIONS: The ability to write well and to meet people; creativity.

WORK ENVIRONMENT: On-the-spot reporting; office editing or organizing; often irregular hours.

FURTHER INFORMATION: The Newspaper Fund
P.O. Box 300
Princeton, NJ 08540

LAWYER

NATURE OF WORK: Providing counsel, drafting laws, and arguing cases for clients in State or Federal Courts.

TRAINING: Minimum of three years college is required to enter law school (which is three years), after which state bar exams must be passed. Some law schools require a bachelor's degree.

PERSONAL QUALIFICATIONS: Ability to use words accurately and clearly, to readily grasp abstractions; aptitude for keen, precise reasoning.

WORK ENVIRONMENT: Paper work; long office hours; some lawyers appear in court often, depending on number of clients and difficulty of cases.

FURTHER INFORMATION: American Bar Association
1155 East 60th Street
Chicago, IL 60637

LIBRARIAN

NATURE OF WORK: Administration of a school or public library; some positions similar to that of a teacher.

TRAINING: One year of graduate work in library science after obtaining bachelor's degree; many states require school librarians to have a teaching certificate.

PERSONAL QUALIFICATIONS: Interest in education, research, people, and books.

WORK ENVIRONMENT: Regular school or library hours; may be only a nine-month job annually.

FURTHER INFORMATION: American Library Association
50 East Huron Street
Chicago, IL 60611

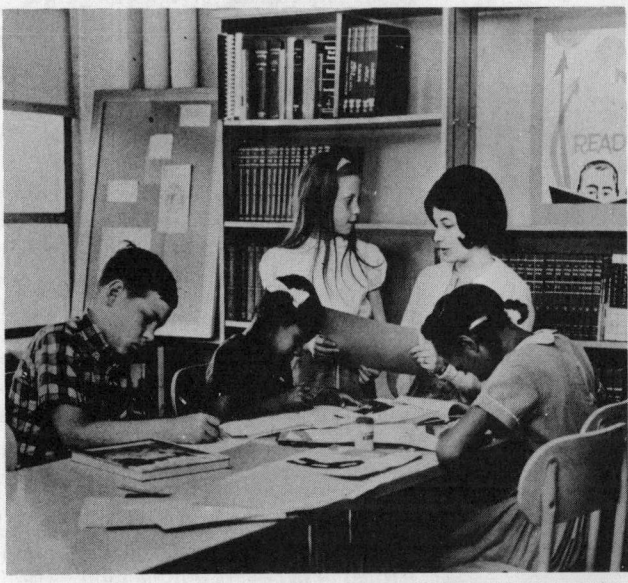

AMERICAN LIBRARY ASSOCIATION

Many school librarians help teachers plan the school curriculum.

LICENSED PRACTICAL NURSE
OR
HOSPITAL ORDERLY

NATURE OF WORK: Assist doctors and nurses in care of ill, handicapped, or convalescent in hospitals, nursing homes, or private residences. Provide most of bedside service given today. Orderlies and hospital attendants are responsible for transporting and positioning of patients and equipment.

TRAINING: Licensed by state after passing exam, preceded by course of instruction approved by state board of nursing. Minimum requirements: two years of high school, 17 years of age.

PERSONAL QUALIFICATIONS: Sensitivity to human suffering; responsibility; manual dexterity; ability to deal pleasantly and competently with the elderly, infirm, or handicapped.

WORK ENVIRONMENT: Shift hours; often night and weekend. Part-time positions available. Physical conditions vary with employer. Paid vacations and sick benefits.

FURTHER INFORMATION: ANA-NLN Nursing Careers Program
American Nurses Association
2420 Pershing Road
Kansas City, MO 64108

or

National Association for Practical
Nurse Education & Service
122 E. 42nd Street
New York, NY 10017

MACHINIST

NATURE OF WORK: Skilled metalwork; making parts for tools and machinery from blueprints and detailed specifications.

TRAINING: High school education followed by four years of apprenticeship.

PERSONAL QUALIFICATIONS: Physical strength and endurance; ability to concentrate on detailed work.

WORK ENVIRONMENT: Regular full-time job; usually daylight hours.

FURTHER INFORMATION: National Machine Tool Builders' Association
7901 Westpark Drive
McLean, VA 22102

or

International Association of Machinists and Aerospace Workers
Machinists Building
1300 Connecticut Avenue
Washington, DC 20036

MECHANIC

NATURE OF WORK: Maintain and repair appliances, equipment, automobiles, and machinery.

TRAINING: On-job or apprenticeship; courses at trade or vocational schools or in Armed Forces recommended. High school diploma not always required.

PERSONAL QUALIFICATIONS: Manual dexterity; aptitude for precision with tools; good health; at least 18 years of age.

WORK ENVIRONMENT: On site of malfunctioning machine—office, home, factory, service station. Some irregular hours and seasonal variations in demand; high union benefits and wages.

FURTHER INFORMATION: National Appliance and Radio-TV Dealers
Two N. Riverside Plaza
Chicago, IL 60606

or

Automotive Service Industry Association
444 North Michigan Avenue
Chicago, IL 60611

or

Local state employment office

MEDICAL LABORATORY ASSISTANT

NATURE OF WORK: Assist with routine laboratory work under supervision of medical technologists and doctors; perform tests using microscopes, centrifuges, and other instruments. Prepare slides of blood and body tissue for study. Be responsible for conditions and records of lab.

TRAINING: Generally on-job; some courses conducted in the hospital. Limited training available in vocational schools and junior colleges.

PERSONAL QUALIFICATIONS: Good vision; manual dexterity; ability to work well with others and remain calm under pressure.

WORK ENVIRONMENT: Clean, modern laboratory; 40 hour week; some night and weekend duty; vacation and sick leave benefits.

FURTHER INFORMATION: American Society for Medical Technologists
5555 West Loop S., Suite 200
Bellaire, TX 77401

A microscope is an important tool for the medical lab assistant.

MEDICAL RECORDS LIBRARIAN

NATURE OF WORK: Plan, prepare, maintain, and analyze records and reports on patients' illnesses and treatments in hospital or

AMERICAN MEDICAL RECORD ASSOCIATION

Medical records librarians store patient-care information.

nursing care center. Assist medical staff in research design and recording.

TRAINING: Some courses available in colleges and hospitals; two to four years of college work generally required to enroll. Certificate granted at completion of course.

PERSONAL QUALIFICATIONS: Accuracy; interest in detail; discretion with confidential information; ability to work under pressure.

WORK ENVIRONMENT: Regular hours; 40-hour week; paid vacations; sick leaves; other benefits.

FURTHER INFORMATION: American Medical Record Association
875 North Michigan Avenue
Suite 1850
Chicago, IL 60611

MEDICAL TECHNOLOGIST

NATURE OF WORK: Identifying and testing fluid and tissue samples for hospital or clinic.

TRAINING: Sixteen semester hours of training and laboratory experience beyond a bachelor's degree. Many schools have programs in which students can finish technologist training during senior year of college.

PERSONAL QUALIFICATIONS: Ability to work under pressure; scientific aptitude and sense of exactness. Good grooming and sensitivity to hygiene.

WORK ENVIRONMENT: Clean, bright, and usually well-equipped laboratories; day or night shift.

FURTHER INFORMATION: American Society for Medical Technologists
5555 West Loop S., Suite 200
Bellaire, TX 77401

MORTICIAN

NATURE OF WORK: Preparing corpses for funerals and wakes; making other arrangements for transporting body and family to cemetery and burial services.

TRAINING: One-year professional course, followed by apprenticeship. High school diploma required. In some states, one or two years of college also essential.

PERSONAL QUALIFICATIONS: Sense of tact and ability to deal maturely with bereaved persons; objectivity and sense of hygiene necessary for embalming processes.

WORK ENVIRONMENT: Usually self-employed, unless working for large firm; long and irregular hours.

FURTHER INFORMATION: National Funeral Directors Association
135 W. Wells Street
Milwaukee, WI 53203

MUSICIAN/MUSIC TEACHER

NATURE OF WORK: Similar to other teaching positions. Union musician plays in band, combo, or orchestra; does recording studio work, and may give private lessons.

TRAINING: Bachelor's degree with preparation for teaching certificate necessary for classroom position; musicians may be self-taught or attend professional school.

PERSONAL QUALIFICATIONS: Native talent; willingness to practice and undergo intensive training; perseverance; self-discipline; intensive love of rhythm and sound.

WORK ENVIRONMENT: Teaching involves regular school hours and calendar. Musician has wide variety in schedules and locations; often works at night.

FURTHER INFORMATION: American Federation of Musicians
1500 Broadway
New York, NY 10036

NURSE

NATURE OF WORK: Administration of physicians' prescriptions and treatment of patients; rehabilitation of patients.

TRAINING: Post-high school may consist of two years training, leading to an associate degree; three years, leading to a diploma; or four or five years, leading to a bachelor's degree in nursing.

PERSONAL QUALIFICATIONS: Good health; dependability; patience; accuracy.

WORK ENVIRONMENT: Day or night shifts; work with doctors in clinic, office, or hospital.

FURTHER INFORMATION: ANA-NLN Nursing Careers Program
American Nurses' Association
2420 Pershing Road
Kansas City, MO 64108

AMERICAN MEDICAL ASSOCIATION

Opportunities for professional nurses include hospital, private duty, office, public health, and industrial nursing.

OCCUPATIONAL THERAPIST

NATURE OF WORK: Helping mentally and physically disabled patients gain skills.

TRAINING: Four-year college program, followed by six to nine months of clinical experience and successful completion of registration examination.

PERSONAL QUALIFICATIONS: Emotional stability; desire to help others; patience.

WORK ENVIRONMENT: Work with a medical team composed of physicians, nurses, and physical therapists; work with the handicapped or elderly.

FURTHER INFORMATION: American Occupational Therapy Association
6000 Executive Blvd., Suite 200
Rockville, MD 20852

OCEANOGRAPHER

NATURE OF WORK: Conducting research concerned with conditions in oceans and large bodies of water; primarily employed by universities and governments.

TRAINING: Bachelor's degree in oceanography or other physical science or engineering; graduate work recommended if high level research is desired.

PERSONAL QUALIFICATIONS: Ability to work in confined atmosphere of diving gear or structures; physical strength; manual dexterity; ability in science and mathematics.

WORK ENVIRONMENT: Long voyages of weeks and months; some laboratory duties. Work as member of team of researchers.

FURTHER INFORMATION: Marine Technology Society
1730 M Street, N.W.
Washington, DC 20036

PUBLIC INFORMATION OFFICE, WOODS HOLE OCEANOGRAPHIC INSTITUTION

Oceanographers use sophisticated instruments to study the ocean.

PAINTER

NATURE OF WORK: Light physical labor involving painting, sanding, paperhanging, and maneuvering of equipment needed.

TRAINING: Apprenticeship through unions, in conjunction with employers, under contracts regulating pay, hours, and amount of education. High school diploma required.

PERSONAL QUALIFICATIONS: Manual dexterity, strength, and endurance; good eyesight; sense of color and balance.

WORK ENVIRONMENT: Generally regular hours; somewhat seasonal demands. No night work unless emergency deadline; indoor and outdoor locations.

FURTHER INFORMATION: Brotherhood of Painters and Allied Trades
1750 New York Avenue, N.W.
Washington, DC 20006

MONSANTO CHEMICAL COMPANY

A painter treats wood siding to protect its natural beauty.

PERFORMING ARTIST

NATURE OF WORK: Entertain public through individual or group performance on stage, screen, radio, record, or television.

TRAINING: Experience in high school recommended; other professionally related experience advisable. Training in professional school or academy increasingly demanded.

PERSONAL QUALIFICATIONS: Talent; physical stamina; ability to persevere under conditions of severe pressure; aptitude for intense communication of personal emotions to others.

WORK ENVIRONMENT: Theater or studio locations; highly irregular hours and great seasonal variations in positions available. Keen competition for limited opportunities; long, arduous hours of practice; few union benefits, little job security.

FURTHER INFORMATION: Actors Equity Association
1500 Broadway
New York, NY 10036

PERSONNEL MANAGER

NATURE OF WORK: Interviewing applicants for job openings; classifying and redesigning jobs based on counseling and negotiation with employees.

TRAINING: Bachelor's degree highly desirable; possibility of promotion to this position after long and successful experience in other areas of business.

PERSONAL QUALIFICATIONS: Persuasiveness; ability to deal creatively with people; aptitude for speaking and writing clearly.

WORK ENVIRONMENT: Office; regular 40-hour week.

FURTHER INFORMATION: American Personnel and Guidance Association, Inc.
Two Skyline Place, Suite 400
5203 Leesburg Pike
Falls Church, VA 22041

PHARMACIST

NATURE OF WORK: Combining and dispensing drugs; often includes managing drugstore and related responsibilities.

TRAINING: Five years of post-high school training in pharmacology leading to bachelor's degree.

PERSONAL QUALIFICATIONS: Scientific and mathematical ability; good business sense.

WORK ENVIRONMENT: Hospital or drugstore; generally regular hours.

FURTHER INFORMATION: American Pharmaceutical Association
2215 Constitution Avenue, N.W.
Washington, DC 20037

PHOTOGRAPHER

NATURE OF WORK: Taking, developing, and printing pictures for industry, publishing companies, magazines, newspapers, and individuals.

TRAINING: On-job training and apprenticeship are adequate training for some jobs; others require varying degrees of professional and technical education.

PERSONAL QUALIFICATIONS: Aesthetic sense and judgment; precision; manual dexterity.

WORK ENVIRONMENT: May either be regular hours (as in industrial photography) or irregular hours (as in free-lance and news photography).

FURTHER INFORMATIN: Professional Photographers of America
1090 Executive Way
Des Plaines, IL 60018

PHYSICAL THERAPIST

NATURE OF WORK: Helping patients with physical injuries overcome and adjust to their disabilities.

TRAINING: Most schools of physical therapy offer four-year bachelor degree programs, some have shorter courses (two years); 48 of the states require licenses.

PERSONAL QUALIFICATIONS: Stamina; patience; emotional stability; emotional sensitivity to needs of others.

WORK ENVIRONMENT: Regular hours; many part-time positions; work in hospitals and convalescent homes.

FURTHER INFORMATION: American Physical Therapy Association
593 Franklin Avenue
Garden City, NY 11530

AMERICAN PHYSICAL THERAPY ASSOCIATION

Physical therapists use mechanical equipment to help patients.

PHYSICIAN

NATURE OF WORK: Diagnosis, treatment, and prevention of diseases and accidents.

TRAINING: Four-year bachelor's degree program prior to four years of medical school; license by examination and one-year internship are required in most states.

PERSONAL QUALIFICATIONS: Above average intelligence; dedication; scientific ability; sensitivity to suffering.

WORK ENVIRONMENT: Long hours; irregular workweek filled with emergencies; many physicians specialize in one specific form of treatment.

FURTHER INFORMATION: Council on Medical Education
American Medical Association
535 North Dearborn Street
Chicago, IL 60610

PHYSICIST

NATURE OF WORK: Conduct research analyzing energy, matter, and their interrelationships; teach in colleges and universities, or research for government or industry.

TRAINING: Bachelor's degree is required; most research positions are open only to those with a master's or Ph.D. degree; doctorate required for faculty positions at universities.

PERSONAL QUALIFICATIONS: The ability to work with abstractions and a strong mathematical and scientific aptitude.

WORK ENVIRONMENT: Regular hours; laboratory and paper work.

FURTHER INFORMATION: American Institute of Physics
335 East 45th Street
New York, NY 10017

PILOT

NATURE OF WORK: Flying large aircraft for a commercial passenger or freight carrier company; some jobs as private pilots in industry or local taxi services.

TRAINING: Training may be gained either in the military, in a professional school, or as a major in aviation at some colleges and universities.

PERSONAL QUALIFICATIONS: Excellent health; ability to make decisions under pressure; good motor coordination; ability in math and sciences.

WORK ENVIRONMENT: Extremely high pay; most pilots work 100 hours a month or less; work often involves much time away from home and irregular hours.

FURTHER INFORMATION: International Air Line Pilots Association
1625 Massachusetts Avenue, N.W.
Washington, DC 20036

AMERICAN AIRLINES
A large instrument panel is checked by the captain and his crew.

PLASTERER

NATURE OF WORK: Applying plaster and stucco to interior and exterior surfaces.

TRAINING: Three-or four-year apprenticeship program, including 144 hours annually of classroom work and a total of 6,000 to 8,000 hours of on-job training.

PERSONAL QUALIFICATIONS: Physical strength; endurance; manual dexterity.

WORK ENVIRONMENT: Regular hours; outdoor environment generally.

FURTHER INFORMATION: Bricklayers, Masons, and Plasterers' International
Union of America
815 15th Street, N.W.
Washington, DC 20005

PLUMBER

NATURE OF WORK: Cutting, welding, soldering, and fitting pipes and fixtures in residential, commercial, and industrial occupation jobs.

TRAINING: Five-year apprenticeship includes classroom, shop, and on-job training. High school diploma required.

PERSONAL QUALIFICATIONS: Physical strength and good health.

WORK ENVIRONMENT: Outdoor and indoor work; seasonal, but less than other construction jobs due to volume of repair and maintenance; 40 hours per week.

FURTHER INFORMATION: National Association of Plumbing - Heating - Cooling
Contractors
1016 20th Street, N.W.
Washington, DC 20036

POLICE OFFICER

NATURE OF WORK: Enforce laws; arrest violators; conduct investigations and testify in court; educate and protect public from dangers.

TRAINING: Each community establishes its own criteria; generally, a candidate must be 21, have a high school diploma, and have successfully completed a civil service type of examination before attending a police-training institution.

PERSONAL QUALIFICATIONS: Physical strength; good health; good judgment; ability to deal with people; aptitude for acting with reason and calmness in emotionally tense situations.

WORK ENVIRONMENT: Work is often hazardous; hours are irregular, including much night work.

FURTHER INFORMATION: International Association of Chiefs of Police
11 Firstfield Road
Gaithersburg, MD 20760

POST OFFICE EMPLOYEE

NATURE OF WORK: Sorting and delivering mail; various related jobs.

TRAINING: Admission by competitive civil service examination, followed by on-job training.

PERSONAL QUALIFICATIONS: Sense of responsibility; good health; personableness; sense of organization.

WORK ENVIRONMENT: Office or outdoor work; regular hours, often including Saturdays.

FURTHER INFORMATION: Local post office

PRACTICAL NURSE: SEE LICENSED PRACTICAL NURSE

PRESSMAN, PRINTER

NATURE OF WORK: Operating and servicing a printing press.

TRAINING: Four- or five-year apprenticeship required; high school education helpful; some junior colleges and technical schools offer special courses.

PERSONAL QUALIFICATIONS: Normal color perception; average physical strength.

WORK ENVIRONMENT: 40-hour week, overtime often available; print rooms are often noisy; night work common on some jobs (such as morning newspapers).

FURTHER INFORMATION: International Printing and Graphics Communications Union
1730 Rhode Island Avenue, N.W.
Washington, DC 20036

PSYCHIATRIST

NATURE OF WORK: Analysis and treatment of mental disorders and illnesses.

TRAINING: Same as that for medical doctor, followed by four-year specialist residence at a hospital and a licensing examination.

PERSONAL QUALIFICATIONS: Mental stability; dedication and studiousness; keen sensitivity to human psychic forces, such as anxiety.

WORK ENVIRONMENT: Work either in private practice or on hospital or clinic staff; long hours.

FURTHER INFORMATION: Council on Medical Education
American Medical Association
535 North Dearborn Street
Chicago, IL 60610

PSYCHOLOGIST

NATURE OF WORK: Laboratory research work or clinical and counseling work with patients; involves study of human and animal behavior.

TRAINING: Most states require a master's or Ph.D. degree in psychology; some require a licensing examination; a degree in medicine is not required.

PERSONAL QUALIFICATIONS: Aptitude in sciences; ability to perceive behavior patterns and draw conclusions from massive data collections.

WORK ENVIRONMENT: Work for university, clinic, or business; regular hours and continuous reading in new research.

FURTHER INFORMATION: American Psychological Association
1200 17th Street, N.W.
Washington, DC 20036

PUBLIC RELATIONS OCCUPATIONS

NATURE OF WORK: Writing news releases and pamphlets; conducting plant tours; organizing trade fairs and exhibits of company's goods and services. Arrange for luncheons, dinners, seminars, etc., which have to do with improving company image and profit.

TRAINING: Bachelor's degree in liberal arts; several years experience in journalism or related fields recommended.

PERSONAL QUALIFICATIONS: Unusual facility with language and psychology; excellent grooming; good sense of organization, salesmanship, clear communication between individuals and groups.

WORK ENVIRONMENT: Generally regular hours; demands of market likely to be sporadic. Office in location central to metropolitan area business district.

FURTHER INFORMATION: Public Relations Society of America
845 Third Avenue
New York, NY 10022

RADIO-TV OCCUPATIONS

NATURE OF WORK: Prepare and produce programs; direct productions or operate equipment used; sell broadcast time to advertisers.

TRAINING: High school diploma required; college training or courses in specialized school increasingly demanded.

PERSONAL QUALIFICATIONS: Vary with jobs; manual dexterity and physical strength for engineering positions. Outgoing, attractive personality for performance personnel.

WORK ENVIRONMENT: Usually very pleasant. Clean, attractive environment in studio or practice area. Regular 40-hour week, though schedule variation depends on programming. Union wages and benefits for technicians.

FURTHER INFORMATION: National Association of Broadcast Employees
111 W. 50th Street
New York, NY 10020

CBC

A large staff works hard to create a relaxed atmosphere for a broadcast.

RADIOLOGIC TECHNOLOGIST, X-RAY TECHNOLOGIST

NATURE OF WORK: Operating x-ray equipment for hospital, government, and industrial health programs; conduct industrial research.

TRAINING: Two-year post-high school course, including work with patients, from approved school.

PERSONAL QUALIFICATIONS: Good health; willingness to work with sick and disabled persons; physical strength to maneuver large machines.

WORK ENVIRONMENT: Generally, regular 40-hour week; union benefits. Company plant, hospital, clinic, or health center.

FURTHER INFORMATION: American Society of Radiologic Technologists
55 E. Jackson Blvd., Suite 1820
Chicago, IL 60604

RAILROAD-RELATED OCCUPATIONS

NATURE OF WORK: Operate trains, maintain equipment, care for passenger's needs, and various related activities.

TRAINING: Almost all training received on-job. High school diploma not essential. Assigned to position after gaining seniority and experience.

PERSONAL QUALIFICATIONS: Good physical condition; excellent hearing and eyesight. Manual dexterity required for technicians; ability to deal with the public.

WORK ENVIRONMENT: In transit between cities or regular office. Hours vary; some night and weekend work. Good union benefits; free transportation for self and family.

FURTHER INFORMATION: Association of American Railroads
American Railroad Building
1920 L Street, N.W.
Washington, DC 20036

SANTA FE RAILROAD PHOTO

The alert traffic operator directs action in the freight yard.

REAL ESTATE AGENT

NATURE OF WORK: Appraising, selling, and financing property transactions and construction projects.

TRAINING: Liberal arts bachelor's degree, including real estate and business courses. State exams necessary to qualify for license.

PERSONAL QUALIFICATIONS: Good business sense; salesmanship; ability in mathematics and economics; aptitude for dealing graciously with customers.

WORK ENVIRONMENT: Long, irregular hours if self-employed. Duties involve combination of administrative, legal, and sales responsibilities.

FURTHER INFORMATION: National Association of Realtors
430 N. Michigan Avenue
Chicago, IL 60611

RECREATION WORKER

NATURE OF WORK: Administer, organize, and direct activities of individuals and groups at public or private agency centers. Administer physical, social, and cultural programs at camps, playgrounds, community centers, hospitals, or industries.

TRAINING: Bachelor's degree in physical education or recreation recommended; one-half of those presently employed, however, have not had formal training.

PERSONAL QUALIFICATIONS: Good health; emotional maturity; physical stamina; warm, lively personality; aptitude for dealing with groups.

WORK ENVIRONMENT: Some irregular hours; generally pleasant, often outdoor locations. Sick leave and paid vacations common; other benefits vary according to position and qualifications.

FURTHER INFORMATION: National Recreation and Park Association
1601 N. Kent Street
Arlington, VA 22209

RESTAURANT OWNER

NATURE OF WORK: Administrative duties concerned with owning and/or managing a restaurant; responsibilities may include serving as host or cook if establishment is small.

TRAINING: No technical training required; thorough knowledge of business practices and restaurant industry gained through practical experience sufficient. Some colleges offer degrees and training in hotel and restaurant management.

PERSONAL QUALIFICATIONS: Good business sense; good health. Ability to deal graciously with public.

WORK ENVIRONMENT: Some irregularity of hours because of varying shifts with some night and weekend work; main responsibilities include office work, hiring of personnel, contact with customers, and dealings with waitresses, cooks, and other employees.

FURTHER INFORMATION: Educational Director
National Restaurant Association
One IBM Plaza, Suite 2600
Chicago, IL 60611

SALES-RELATED OCCUPATIONS

NATURE OF WORK: Selling products or services for manufacturers, chain stores, or wholesale dealers.

TRAINING: High school diploma usually required; other qualifications vary with position. On-job training usually provided; college degree essential for more complex, specialized work.

PERSONAL QUALIFICATIONS: Creative ability to persuade others to purchase article or service; good grooming; average intelligence.

WORK ENVIRONMENT: Average 40-hour week, though many part-time positions available. Irregular hours for service salesmen, such as insurance; often work on commission basis. Large firms provide paid vacations, sick leave, and other benefits. Physical conditions variable.

FURTHER INFORMATION: United Food and Commercial Workers International Union
Suffridge Building
1775 K Street, N.W.
Washington, DC 20006

SECRETARY, STENOGRAPHER, TYPIST

NATURE OF WORK: Operating typewriter and other office machines; handling correspondence; often serving as bookkeeper and receptionist.

TRAINING: High school graduates who have taken commercial courses are preferred; many night school training programs available.

PERSONAL QUALIFICATIONS: Good grammar and spelling; accuracy; efficiency; reliability; excellent personal grooming.

WORK ENVIRONMENT: Regular hours; generally closely supervised. Physical conditions vary with employing firm.

FURTHER INFORMATION: Association of Independent Colleges and Schools
1730 M Street, N.W., Suite 401
Washington, DC 20036

SERVICE STATION OPERATOR

NATURE OF WORK: Managing a gasoline service station leased from a major oil company; tending to needs of motorists.

TRAINING: High school education desirable; oil companies sponsor two- to eight-week programs to train men who have experience in the business and want to advance to manager.

PERSONAL QUALIFICATIONS: Good business sense; ability to deal courteously and competently with motorist; mechanical aptitude; salesmanship.

WORK ENVIRONMENT: Outdoor work in all weather; some physical labor involved, some office work; often long and irregular hours.

FURTHER INFORMATION: American Petroleum Institute
Marketing Division
156 William Street
New York, NY 10038

SOCIAL SCIENTIST

NATURE OF WORK: Research and record developments in major fields of human behavior, psychology, history, economics, anthropology, political science, and sociology.

TRAINING: Bachelor's degree from accredited college. Master's degree or Ph.D. required for major positions in education, business, industry, and government.

PERSONAL QUALIFICATIONS: Ability to sustain concentration during long hours of research; aptitude for precision with statistics. Ability to reason abstractly from large amounts of data. Facility to communicate findings in clear, coherent manner.

WORK ENVIRONMENT: Varies with position; often more than 40-hour week, due to long hours of study. Little supervision in major positions; often work alone.

FURTHER INFORMATION: American Historical Society
400 A Street, S.E.
Washington, DC 20003

or

American Political Science Association
1527 New Hampshire Avenue, N.W.
Washington, DC 20036

or

Agency for International Development
Washington, DC 20523

or

Local state employment office

SOCIAL WORKER

NATURE OF WORK: Administration of government welfare and social service programs, including casework, group work, therapy, and counseling, often in cooperation with correctional or social security agencies.

TRAINING: Bachelor's degree, preferably with a major in social work or social service; many jobs require a graduate degree from one of the accredited schools of social work.

NATIONAL ASSOCIATION OF SOCIAL WORKERS, INC.

With physicians and therapists, the social worker helps patients during illness, recovery, and rehabilitation.

PERSONAL QUALIFICATIONS: Ability to work with people; emotional maturity and sensitivity. Concern for others and a keen sense of responsibility are essential.

WORK ENVIRONMENT: Field and office work, often visiting homes of the poor or handicapped. Contacts with a variety of community resources, including schools, hospitals, and government agencies.

FURTHER INFORMATION: Social Workers Vocational Bureau
386 Park Avenue South
New York, NY 10016

SPEECH THERAPIST

NATURE OF WORK: Diagnose and provide treatment for adults and children with impaired speech or hearing. Conduct research for improvement of treatment methods.

TRAINING: Bachelor's degree minimum required; master's degree advisable.

PERSONAL QUALIFICATIONS: Patience; sensitivity to personalities and to the possibilities of development of the handicapped.

WORK ENVIRONMENT: Forty-hour week; paid vacations and retirement benefits. Those engaged in research have less regular schedule.

FURTHER INFORMATION: American Speech and Hearing Association
10801 Rockville Pike
Rockville, MD 20852

STATE AND MUNICIPAL GOVERNMENT OCCUPATIONS

NATURE OF WORK: Teaching in school system or assisting in administering of programs in departments of health, highway, fire, police, water, transportation, electricity, gas, care of parks and recreation facilities, natural resource development, public housing, and urban renewal. Positions available also include sanitation services, clerical, and maintenance work with connected the above.

TRAINING: Variable according to position; high school diploma recommended. Exam similar to civil service given prior to hiring.

PERSONAL QUALIFICATIONS: Sense of responsibility; other qualifications vary with positions.

WORK ENVIRONMENT: Good wages; generally regular hours; often sick leave and retirement benefits; favorable physical environment.

FURTHER INFORMATION: American Society for Public Administration
1225 Connecticut Avenue, N.W.
Washington, DC 20036

STATISTICIAN

NATURE OF WORK: Compile and analyze data in specialized field; design and improve statistical methods.

TRAINING: Bachelor's degree with major in mathematics or statistics or in specialized field in which one wishes to work.

Mathematical statisticians must have a graduate degree.

PERSONAL QUALIFICATIONS: Ability to reason abstractly and use numbers; sense of precision.

WORK ENVIRONMENT: Work for industry, government, or university; regular office hours. Generally favorable location.

FURTHER INFORMATION: American Statistical Association
806 15th Street, N.W.
Washington, DC 20005

STEWARDESS

NATURE OF WORK: Attending passengers on domestic and international flights; duties include serving drinks and meals and maintaining cabin cleanliness.

TRAINING: Some college or business background recommended; high school diploma essential. Most airlines operate their own five-week training programs.

PERSONAL QUALIFICATIONS: Attractiveness; excellent grooming; friendliness; ability to speak foreign language required for international flights.

WORK ENVIRONMENT: Hours very irregular, including night work. May receive as much as a two-week vacation every month with limited free transportation for self and family.

FURTHER INFORMATION: Local airline office of desired airline.

AMERICAN AIRLINES

Stewardesses are specially trained to provide for the comfort and safety of their passengers.

TEACHER—ELEMENTARY AND SECONDARY

NATURE OF WORK: Instructing and disciplining young people; lesson preparation and presentation; informal counseling and guidance.

TRAINING: Bachelor's degree required for public school systems; also state certificate for teaching.

PERSONAL QUALIFICATIONS: Patience; love of learning and the young; ability to develop internal discipline, integrity, and sound reasoning in others.

WORK ENVIRONMENT: Constant interaction with students; most teachers receive two-month summer vacations; location determines physical conditions; long hours of preparation.

FURTHER INFORMATION: National Education Association
1201 16th Street, N.W.
Washington, DC 20036

IOWA STATE TEACHERS COLLEGE

The kindergarten teacher helps a child develop his curiosity, creativity, desire for learning, and ability to think.

TEACHER'S AIDE

NATURE OF WORK: Assist teachers and administrators in supervision, education, and disciplining of students, primarily on playground, in lunchroom, and recessed classroom.

TRAINING: Formal training seldom required; experience as wife or mother in similar situations accepted as qualifications in many school systems.

PERSONAL QUALIFICATIONS: Patience, ability to organize, utilize, and creatively direct the energies of the young; tolerance for noise and spontaneity.

WORK ENVIRONMENT: Usually part-time, in school surroundings; hours correspond to those of school day and calendar. Salaries and benefits vary with position.

FURTHER INFORMATION: Local office or district superintendent or principal of local school.

TELEPHONE OCCUPATIONS

NATURE OF WORK: Operate switchboards or perform clerical duties involved in billing, shipping equipment, etc; male positions include installers, repairmen, technicians.

TRAINING: High school diploma required; preemployment aptitude test given by company as well as classroom and on-job training for all positions.

PERSONAL QUALIFICATIONS: Vary with position; sense of responsibility and aptitude for dealing graciously with the public required for all.

WORK ENVIRONMENT: Generally favorable; large central office or small local branch. Irregular hour shifts distributed among entire staff. Good union wages and benefits.

FURTHER INFORMATION: Local telephone office

TELEVISION OCCUPATIONS:
SEE RADIO-TV OCCUPATIONS

VETERINARIAN

NATURE OF WORK: Prevention and treatment of disease and injury in animals; research into animal diseases.

TRAINING: Two years of college and four years of veterinary school required for license.

PERSONAL QUALIFICATIONS: Love of and competence in working with animals; good scientific ability, perseverance, physical strength.

WORK ENVIRONMENT: Work in private practice, clinic, or public agency; hours and salary vary with type of practice.

FURTHER INFORMATION: American Veterinary Medical Association
930 N. Meacham Road
Schaumburg, IL 60196

X-RAY TECHNICIAN:
SEE RADIOLOGIC TECHNOLOGIST

DICTIONARY OF MYTHOLOGY

The influence of classical mythology is seen in works ranging from Homer's *Iliad* to James Joyce's *Ulysses*. Mythology is both a field of scholarship and a tool necessary for understanding all literature. Because many of the classical myths developed in different eras and in two separate cultures, the Greek and the Roman, the stories are often similar but not identical. This dictionary lists each classical entry under the Greek name; the Roman name is indicated in the entry. To help you locate those Roman deities and characters for whom you do not know the Greek name, a cross-reference index is listed below, The *Dictionary of Mythology* also includes some names from Norse and Arthurian legend.

ROMAN	GREEK	ROMAN	GREEK	ROMAN	GREEK
Aesculapius	Asklepios	Furiae (Furies)	Eumenides (Erinyes)	Pax	Eirene
Aguilo	Boreas	Gratiae (Graces)	Charites	Pluto (Dis)	Hades (Plouton)
Ajax	Aias	Hercules	Heracles	Pollux	Polydeuces
Amor (Cupid)	Eros	Juno	Hera	Proserpina (Libera)	Persephone (Kore)
Apollo	Apollo	Jupiter	Zeus	Saturn	Cronos
Aurora	Eos	Latona	Leto	Sol (Sun)	Helios
Caelus (Sky)	Ouranos	Liber (Bacchus)	Dionysus	Terra (Earth)	Gaea
Ceres	Demeter	Mars	Ares	Trivia	Hecate
Diana	Artemis	Mercury	Hermes	Ulysses	Odysseus
Faunus	Pan	Minerva	Athena	Vesta	Hestia
Favonius	Zephyrus	Neptune	Poseidon	Venus	Aphrodite
Flora	Chloris	Parcae (Fates)	Moirai	Vulcan (Mulciber)	Hephaistos

Abderos, son of Hermes and armor bearer for Heracles. He was torn to pieces by the mares of Diomedes.

Acamas, son of Theseus and Phaedra; he entered Troy in the Trojan Horse.

Acarnan and **Amphoteros,** sons of Alcmaeon and Kallirhoe.

Acestes, a Trojan king of Drepanum, who lived in Sicily. He assisted Priam at Troy and later entertained Aeneas at Drepanum.

Acetes, a Lydian helmsman who, realizing that a youth captured by his crew was actually Dionysus in disguise, protected the god and became his follower.

Achates, a friend of Aeneas, known for his fidelity; hence the term "fidus Achates" —faithful companion.

Acheloides, the Sirens, daughters of the river Achelous. *See* **Sirens.**

Achelous, a river god, the son of Oceanus and Tethys. During a battle with Heracles for Deianira, Achelous changed himself first into a serpent and then into a bull. Heracles broke one of his horns (*see* **Cornucopia**), defeated him, and won Deianira.

Acheron, a son of Gaea; he was changed into a river in Hades for supplying the Titans with water during their struggle with the Olympian gods.

Achilles, son of Peleus and Thetis and most famous of the Greek heroes who fought in the Trojan War. As an infant, his mother plunged him into the river Styx making him invulnerable except in the heel by which she held him. During the Trojan War he quarreled with Agamemnon and refused to fight for the Greeks. When his friend Patroclus was killed, he rejoined his comrades and slew Hector, the Trojan leader, at the Scaean Gate. Ultimately, he was killed when Paris shot an arrow which pierced his vulner- able heel.

Acis, a Sicilian youth, son of Faunus and Simaethis. He fell in love with the sea nymph Galatea. The Cyclops Polyphemus, a jealous rival for Galatea's love, crushed Acis to death with a rock. The nymph then changed Acis into a river on Mount Aetna.

Aconteus, a hunter, changed into stone at the sight of Medusa's head during the nuptials of his friend Perseus and Andromeda.

Acrisius, son of Abas and Ocalea, and father of Danaë; a king of Argos who was killed by a discus thrown by his grandson, Perseus.

Actaeon, son of Aristaeus and Autonoë; he was changed into a stag and devoured by his own dogs because he had watched Artemis bathing.

Admete (or **Admeta**), daughter of Eurystheus, king of Mycenae; priestess of Hera's temple at Argos. The ninth labor imposed upon Heracles by Eurystheus was to obtain the girdle of Hippolyte, queen of the Amazons, for Admete.

Admetus, king of Pherai in Thessaly. Admetus was to die, but Apollo persuaded the Moirai to spare his life if Admetus found someone willing to die for him. (*See* **Moirai**.) His wife, Alcestis, offered herself as a substitute, died, but was revived by Heracles.

Adonis, son of Myrrha, born from the myrrh tree and loved by Aphrodite. While hunting, he was killed by a wild boar. Aphrodite transformed his blood into the anemone.

Adrastus, a king of Argos and leader of the Seven against Thebes, of whom he alone survived because of his swift horse Arion. Ten years later he led the Epigoni, the sons of the Seven, in the successful destruction of Thebes.

Aeacus (or **Aiakos**), a son of Zeus and grandfather of Achilles. After the inhabitants of Aegina were destroyed by pestilence, Zeus transformed ants into human beings, whom Aeacus called "Myrmidons." Aeacus, along with Minos and Rhadamanthus, became a judge in Hades.

Aeëtes, king of Colchis, brother of Circe, and father of Medea, Absyrtus, and Chalciope. Phrixus and Helle fled from their stepmother to Aeëtes' court on the back of a golden-fleeced ram. After the ram had been sacrificed, the Golden Fleece was given to Aeëtes.

Aegeus, king of Athens and father of Theseus. He married Aethra, daughter of Pittheus, king of Troezen. Aegeus departed for Athens before the birth of his son, Theseus, but told Aethra to send the boy to him as soon as he could lift the stone under which a sword and a pair of sandals lay concealed. Years later, when the young man arrived in Athens, his life was threatened by Medea, who had taken refuge with his father. Theseus later sailed to Crete where he destroyed the Minotaur. On his return voyage he forgot to hoist white sails—the prearranged signal of success—and Aegeus, concluding that his son was dead, threw himself from a high rock into the Aegean sea, which was named after him.

Aegina, a sea nymph carried off by Zeus to an island later named after her. There she gave birth to Aeacus.

Aegis, the shield of Zeus, which was fashioned by Hephaistos. It later became associated with Athena. After Perseus slew the Gorgon Medusa, he gave the head to Athena, who affixed it to the center of her aegis.

Aegisthus, king of Argos and son of Thyestes and the latter's daughter,

Pelopia. The lover of Clytemnestra, he helped her murder her husband, Agamemnon, when he returned from the Trojan War. Agamemnon's son, Orestes, then killed Clytemnestra and Aegisthus. *See* **Atreus.**

Aegyptus, king of Egypt whose fifty sons were married and murdered by the daughters of Danaus.

Aeneas, a Trojan prince, son of Aphrodite and Anchises. He appears in the *Iliad* and is the hero of Virgil's *Aeneid* which chronicles his adventures after the fall of Troy until he settled on the Tiber and killed Turnus, his rival for Lavinia. Aeneas then married Lavinia, and governed Lavinium—the town founded in her name. The Caesars traced their origin to him and all Romans worshiped him as their ancestral hero.

Aeolus, son of Poseidon and Arne, appointed by Zeus as keeper of the winds. He presented Odysseus, during his return voyage to Ithaca, with all the adverse winds tied in a leather bag, but Odysseus' companions opened it out of curiosity and so drove the ship from its course. In Roman mythology, Aeolus was the god of wind.

Aërope, wife of Atreus and mother of Agamemnon, Menelaus, and Anaxibia. Also beloved of Ares, she died giving birth to Aeropus.

Aesculapius, *see* **Asklepios.**

Aeson, father of Jason; he succeeded his father as king in Iolchus but was deposed by Pelias. Medea restored Aeson's youth and killed Pelias.

Agamemnon, king of Mycenae and Argos; son of Atreus; father of Electra, Orestes, Iphigeneia, and Chrysothemis; brother of Menelaus and Anaxibia. Forced to flee Argos when Atreus died, Agamemnon married Clytemnestra, daughter of the king of Sparta. When Paris abducted Menelaus' wife, Helen, Agamemnon led the Achaeans in the Trojan War. At Aulis, when the fleet was hampered by unfavorable winds, Agamemnon had to sacrifice Iphigeneia to appease Artemis, but the goddess intervened and replaced Iphigeneia with a bear. Upon his return home, Agamemnon was murdered by his wife's lover, Aegisthus.

Agenor, a king of Phoenicia; son of Poseidon and Libya; ancestor of Dido, queen of Carthage; father of Europa and Cadmus. *See* **Europa, Cadmus.**

Aglaia, daughter of Zeus and Eurynome; one of the three Graces. Her epithet was "the shining one."

Aias, (1.) the greater Aias was the son of Telamon and second only to Achilles as the most famous Greek warrior. Unable to possess Achilles' armor after his death, Aias slaughtered sheep and then stabbed himself. (2.) the lesser Aias was leader of the Lokrians who drowned while returning home because he either violated Cassandra in the temple of Athena or defied Poseidon. The Romans identify both as Ajax.

Alcathous, son of Pelops and king of Megara. He slew a lion that had killed King Megaraus' son, Euhippos, and then succeeded to the throne. In a variant story, Alcathous killed his brother Chrysippus,

escaped to Mergana, and then killed the lion.

Alcestis, daughter of Pelias and wife of Admetus. She willingly sacrificed her life to save Admetus from death. Heracles brought her back from the lower world and returned her to Admetus. *See* **Admetus.**

Alcinoüs, son of Nausithoüs and Periboea, king of the Phaiakes. He married his niece, Arete, by whom he had a daughter, Nausicaä.

Alcithoë, daughter of Minyas, king of Thessaly. Her spindle was changed into a vine, her yarn into ivy, and she herself was driven mad and changed into a bat because she had scorned Dionysus.

Alcmene (or **Alcmena**), daughter of Electryon, and wife of Amphitryon. Amphitryon accidently killed Electryon, and as penance, avenged the death of Alcmene's brothers. However, during his absence, Zeus assumed his form and sired Alcmene's son, Heracles.

Alcmeon, son of Amphiaraus who helped the Epigoni destroy Thebes. He slew his mother, Eriphyle, at his father's command, fled to Arcadia where he married Arsinoë, and gave her Harmonia's necklace. He moved to an island on the river Achelous, married Kallirhoe, daughter of the king of Calydon, and obtained the necklace from Phegeus under false pretense at her request. Pheqeus discovered the trick, and, with his sons, killed Alcmeon, but was killed in turn by Alcmeon's sons. The necklace was dedicated to Apollo at Delphi.

Alecto, one of the three Furies.

Alfadur, the supreme being of Norse mythology. His name literally means "all-father." After the Twilight of the Gods he will create a new, good world for men and gods.

Alpheus, a river god, son of Oceanus and Tethys. He became the river Alpheus in order to pursue the nymph Arethusa whom Artemis had transformed into a fountain in Sicily.

Althaea, wife of Oeneus, king of Calydon, and mother of Meleager. Althaea killed her son to avenge the deaths of her brothers, whom Meleager slew when they attempted to take the spoils of a dead boar away from Atalanta.

Amaltheia, the goat who suckled the infant Zeus in a cave at Lyktos on Crete. In another version, Amaltheia is a nymph who feeds Zeus with goat's milk. In some legends, Amaltheia had a bull's or goat's horn which would fill itself with whatever its owner wished and became known as the Cornucopia, or horn of plenty. (*See* **Cornucopia.**) She is also referred to as the Cumaean Sibyl, the prophetess of the Sibylline oracles of Rome.

Amata, in the *Aeneid*, wife of King Latinus, she promised her daughter Lavinia to Turnus before Aeneas' arrival. She opposed her husband's plans to betrothe Lavinia to Aeneas.

Amazons, a race of warlike women dwelling in Asia Minor, who, led by their queen Penthesilea, aided Troy during the Trojan War.

Ambrosia, the food of the gods, which, with nectar, preserved their immortality.

Ammon (also **Amen, Amon, Amun**), an ancient revered Egyptian divinity who was originally the patron of Thebes. He is identified with Ra under the name of Amen-Ra, and is represented as a human wearing a flat crown with two tall plumes affixed. The Egyptians accredited him with all their military victories. He, his consort Mut, and their son Khonsu, became the divine triad of Thebes.

Amphiaraus, son of Oicles and Hypermnestra. He took part in the hunt of the Calydonian boar and in the expedition of the Argonauts. A great prophet, he foresaw the fatal end of the expedition of Adrastus against Thebes, but his wife, Eriphyle, was able to persuade him to join. Before he left, his children promised to avenge his death by killing Eriphyle and marching against Thebes again. As he had predicted, the earth swallowed him up at Thebes before his enemies could kill him. (*See* **Adrastus, Alcmeon.**) A shrine was erected to him near Oropus, where prophesies were given through dreams.

Amphion, a famous musician and twin brother of Zethus; son of Zeus and Antiope, born at Sicyon where Antiope fled to avoid the wrath of Dirce, her sister-in-law. A shepherd raised the infants, who, upon reaching manhood, revenged their mother's torture when they besieged and murdered Lycus, their uncle, in Thebes, and tied his wife, Dirce, to a wild bull which dragged her to her death. (*See* **Antiope.**) Amphion, now king of Thebes, built a wall around the city by playing on his lyre. The stones, charmed by the music, moved into position by themselves. He married Niobe, daughter of Tantalus.

Amphitrite, daughter of Nereus and Doris, and mother of Triton by Poseidon.

Amphitryon, king of Thebes, who, because he avenged the deaths of Electryon's sons, was appointed his successor and given his daughter Alcmene in marriage. *See* **Alcmene.**

Amycus, son of Poseidon by Melia, an ash tree nymph; king of the Bebryces. A skillful boxer, Polydeuces, challenged him to a match and knocked him out. The Bebryces broke into the ring to avenge Amycus, but were routed by the Argonauts.

Amymone, one of the fifty daughters of Danaus and Erupa, and mother of Nauplius by Poseidon. Pursued by a satyr, she was saved by Poseidon, who made and named a spring in her honor.

Anaxibia, a nymph, loved by Helion, who escaped him.

Ancaeus, an Argonaut and son of Poseidon, who, because of his pride, was killed at the Calydonian boar hunt.

Anchises, lover of Aphrodite and by her, father of Aeneas. For boasting of his affair with the goddess, Zeus blinded him with a thunderbolt. When Troy fell, Aeneas carried his aged father from the city on his shoulders.

Androcles, a slave who, when thrown to the wild animals in the Roman arena, was spared by a lion from whose foot he had once extracted a thorn.

Andromache, wife of Hector and mother of Astyanax. After her husband's death in the Trojan War, she became the prize of Neoptolemus. Upon his death, she married Helenus, Hector's brother.

Andromeda, daughter of Cepheus, king of Ethiopia. When her mother, Cassiopeia, boasted that she was more beautiful then the Nereids, Poseidon took revenge by flooding the land and sending a sea monster to ravage the shore. To appease Poseidon, Cepheus was commanded by the oracle of Ammon to chain his daughter to a rock in the sea. Perseus came to her rescue, however, and turned the monster to stone with the magic head of Medusa. He then killed Phineus, a former suitor, and married Andromeda.

Antaeus, a Libyan giant and wrestler, son of Gaea and Poseidon, who was vanquished by Heracles. Realizing that Antaeus' strength depended upon contact with his mother Earth, Heracles lifted him from the ground and choked him to death.

Antigone, daughter of Oedipus by Jocasta. She defied the order of Creon, king of Thebes, that the body of her brother Polynices remain unburied. Condemned to be buried alive, Antigone killed herself. She became the Greek ideal of filial and sisterly devotion.

Antilochus, son of Nestor and Eurydice, he was chosen to tell Achilles of Patroclus' death. He was later killed at Troy by Memnon. Antilochus and his two friends, Achilles and Patroclus, were buried in the same spot.

Antiope, loved by Zeus and daughter of Nycteus, king of Thebes. To escape her father's anger, she fled to Sicyon where she bore twin sons, Amphion and Zethos. After her father committed suicide, her uncle, Lycus, imprisoned and punished her. She escaped, and later her sons avenged her torture. (*See* **Amphion.**) In another legend, Antiope is Queen of the Amazons, sister of Hippolyte, mistress of Theseus, and mother of Hippolytus.

Anubis (Inpu Hermanubis), son of the Egyptian god, Osiris, he took the souls of the dead before the Erynes of Hades. He is similar but not identical to the Greek god Hermes.

Aphrodite, Greek goddess of love, beauty, and sensual desire whom the Romans identified with Venus. Legend says that she landed either at Paphos in Cyprus or at Cythera, hence her epithets "Kypris" and "Cythera" which also indicate her connection with the goddesses Ishtar and Astarte. Homer calls her the daughter of Zeus and Dione. A more popular myth, according to Hesiod, is that she arose from the sea's foam which gathered around Ouranos' severed member following his castration by his son, Cronos. She was Hephaistos' wife, but had amorous adventures with both other gods and mortals. (*See* **Adonis, Anchises, Ares.**) She was worshipped as Aphrodite Urania (goddess of the sky and, later, goddess of higher intellectual love), and Aphrodite Pandemos (goddess of the folk, of marriage and family life). The Romans honored her as the mother of Aeneas. *See* **Aeneas.**

Apollo, god of light and prophecy, and patron of medicine, music, the lyre, and archery. He was the father of the god of medicine. (*See* **Asklepios.**) The son of Zeus and Leto, he was born on Delos with his twin sister, Artemis. His prophecies were heard at Delphi. His epithets were Lykeious, (wolf-god, patron of shepherds), Phoebus (the shining one), Namois (he of the pastures), and the "far-darter," the dealer of death. (*See* **Niobe.**) His legends include the slaying of the python, and his service to Admetus as penance for the killing of the Cyclops who had forged the thunderbolt which killed Asklepios. For other myths *see* **Cassandra, Hyacinthos, Midas, Sibyl.**

Arachne, daughter of Idmon of Colophon. She was so expert in weaving that she challenged Athena. For designs she chose scenes which depicted the foibles of the gods. Angered by such insults, Athena tore up the web. Arachne hanged herself in despair, but Athena saved her life and transformed her into a spider—which hangs by the thread it spins.

Ares, Greek god of war, son of Zeus and Hera, and identified as the Roman Mars. Attended by his sister Eris (Discord), his sons Deimos (Fear) and Phobos (Fright), and Enyo, an ancient war goddess, he personifies blind, bloodthirsty rage. Homer tells of Ares' love affair with Aphrodite.

Arethusa, a nymph who was pursued by the river god Alpheus and changed by Artemis into a fountain to escape him. This is also the name of one of the Hesperides.

Argo, the ship used by Jason and his companions in their search for the Golden Fleece.

Argonauts, the companions of Jason on the ship *Argo,* who set out to find the Golden Fleece; among whom were Heracles, Theseus, Nestor, Orpheus, Castor, and Polydeuces.

Argus, a giant with a hundred eyes, of which only two were asleep at one time. He was ordered by Hera to keep watch on Io, but Zeus sent Hermes to kill him. Afterward his eyes were put on the tail of Hera's sacred peacock.

Ariadne, the daughter of Minos of Crete. Having fallen in love with Theseus, she gave him some thread with which he was able to find his way out of the labyrinth. After Theseus had killed the Minotaur, he escaped, taking Ariadne with him, but he later deserted her at Naxos. Dionysus then married her and gave her a crown of seven stars which is identified with the constellation Corona.

Arion, a famous Greek poet and musician, who, when returning to Corinth from a music contest in Sicily, was threatened with death by sailors who wanted his prize. He leaped into the sea and a dolphin carried him safely to land. There is also a horse, Arion, the offspring of Poseidon and Demeter, who saved the life of Adrastus. *See* **Adrastus.**

Aristaeus, protector of flocks and agriculture, son of Apollo and Cyrene. He was reared by Gaea and the Seasons who nourished him with nectar and ambrosia and transformed him into Zeus and Apollo. According to legend, the centaur Chiron taught him medicine and soothsaying. He married Autonoë and fathered Actaeon. He was indirectly responsible for the death of Eurydice, for, in fleeing from his advances, she stepped on a snake and died from its bite. He was the first to teach men the art of beekeeping.

Arne, mother of Aeolus, wooed by Poseidon. *See* **Aeolus.**

Artemis, Greek goddess, daughter of Leto and Zeus, and twin of Apollo; born at Delos. She was the guardian of forests and wild animals and goddess of the moon and of birth. She was worshipped at her temples at Ephesus and Taurus under the titles of Parthenos (Virgin), Kalliste (Fairest), and Selene. For her mythology, see **Actaeon, Orion, Niobe, Iphigeneia.** Her Roman counterpart, Diana, was worshipped at Nemi.

Arthur (King Arthur), a semimythical British figure of the sixth century; at the age of fifteen succeeded his father, Uther Pendragon, to the throne by drawing the legendary sword, Excalibur, from the stone. He married Guinevere, daughter of King Laodegan of Carmalide, and brought peace to his kingdom for 20 years. He was fatally wounded in the battle of Camlan and was buried at Glastonbury.

Ascalaphos, son of Acheron, who was appointed by Hades to guard the abducted Persephone in the Elysian Fields. Because he said that the goddess had eaten pomegranate seeds, she could not be completely released from the lower world. For his spying, Persephone changed him into a screech owl.

Asgard, the abode of the Scandinavian gods, which was reached by crossing the Bifrost, the bridge of the rainbow. Its most beautiful palace was Odin's residence, Valhalla.

Asklepios, son of Koronis and Apollo; the god of medicine and healing worshipped at Epidaurus. Zeus killed him with a thunderbolt for restoring Hippolytus to life at Artemis' request. Identified by Romans as Aesculapius.

Astarte, an ancient Semitic goddess of fertility and reproduction; her epithets are Baalat (the lady) or Kedeshet (the holy one).

Asteria, daughter of Coeus, the Titan, wife of Perses, and mother of Hekate. Courted by Zeus in the form of a quail, she threw herself into the sea where she was changed into the island called Delos.

Astraea, the "Starry Maid," daughter of Zeus and Themis, and goddess of justice during the Golden Age. As the wickedness of mortals increased, she returned to heaven and was transformed into the constellation Virgo. She is represented as holding a pair of scales in one hand and a sword in the other.

Astyanax, son of Hector and Andromache, whom the victorious Greeks threw from the walls of Troy to destroy the city's heir.

Atalanta, (1.) the daughter of Clymene by Iasus of Arcadia. She was a huntress who participated in the Calydonian boar hunt and shared the spoils of victory with Meleager. (*See* **Althaia.**) (2.) the daughter of Schoineus of Boitia, and an expert in the foot race. She refused to marry anyone who could not outrun her and imposed the death penalty upon defeated suitors. At last, Hippomenes (or Meilanion according to some sources), acting upon Aphrodite's advice, threw three apples of the Hesperides at specified intervals in the running Atalanta's path. Unable to resist them, she stopped to pick them up; Hippomenes gained the lead, and won the race and a bride.

Atë, goddess of infatuation, rash actions, and mischief, and daughter of either Zeus or Eris (Strife). When Zeus evicted her from heaven, she took refuge among men and led them to impulsive actions. The Litai (prayers) followed her around, redressing the evil.

Athamas, A Greek king and son of Aeolus. He had three wives: Nephele, who bore him Phrixus and Helle; Ino, who bore him Learchos and Melicertes; and Themisto who gave birth to two children. Myths concerning Ino and Themisto involve their jealousy towards their stepchildren. Ino bribed messengers to bring back a false report from the Delphic oracle that a pestilence could only be stopped by sacrificing Nephele's children. During Helle's and Phrixus' flight to Colchis on the ram with the Golden Fleece, Helle fell into the sea since called the Hellespont. Hera drove Athamas and Ino mad; Athamas accidently killed Learchos, and Ino, running away with Melicertes, jumped over a cliff into the sea. Themisto, plotting to kill her stepchildren, ordered that her children be dressed in white and Ino's in black. However, Ino reversed this, and Themisto killed her own children and then herself.

Athena (Pallas Athene), the grey-eyed Greek goddess of war, wisdom, and handicrafts, and patroness of Athens. Zeus fearing that Metis would bear a son stronger than himself, swallowed her, but her child, Athena, sprang from his head fully armed with helmet, shield, and spear. Athena won the contest with Poseidon for Athens by producing the olive tree which the Athenians judged more useful than Poseidon's salt spring. She was worshipped as Polias (Goddess of the City), Bulaia (She of the Council), and Parthenos (Virgin); the Parthenon was her temple. The owl is her bird and she is keeper of the Aegis. She is credited with the taming of horses and the use of chariots. She is identified in Roman mythology as Minerva.

Atlantis, once a rich and powerful continent in the Atlantic, west of Gibraltar. Because its inhabitants became increasingly wicked, it sank into the ocean.

Atlas, son of Iapetus and Clymene; brother of Prometheus; and father of the Hesperides, Hyades, Pleiades, and Calypso. A Titan who warred against the gods, he was condemned to carry the heavens on his shoulders.

Atreidae, sons of Atreus: Agamemnon and Menelaus.

Atreus, son of Pelops and father of Agamemnon, Menelaus, and Anaxibia. When his wife, Aethra, and his brother, Thyestes, committed adultery, Atreus murdered Thyestes' children and served their flesh to their father at a banquet. Aegisthus, son of Thyestes and the latter's daughter, Pelopia, avenged the crime by killing Atreus and later murdering Agamemnon. *See* **Agamemnon, Pelops.**

Atropos, one of the three Moirai—the Inflexible—the goddess who cuts the thread of life.

Attis (Atys), Phrygian vegetation god represented as a young shepherd from Celaenae, and a priest who was loved by Cybele. When Attis broke his vow of chastity and married the daughter of the river Sangarius, Cybele drove him insane and he castrated himself and died. Violets grew from his blood and Cybele resurrected him in the form of a fir tree. Five days of orgiastic rites were observed in celebration. *See* **Galli.**

Augeas, king of Elis, owner of numerous oxen, whose enormous stables had not been cleaned for thirty years. Cleaning out the stalls was one of the twelve labors imposed upon Heracles; for this work Augeas promised him a tenth of his herd. When Heracles diverted the rivers Alpheus and Peneius from their courses to flow through the stables, Augeas refused to comply with the agreement with the excuse that Heracles was merely following Eurystheus' orders. As a result, Heracles conquered Elis and killed Augeas.

Aurora, Roman equivalent of Eos, Greek goddess of the dawn. *See* **Eos.**

Auster, the southwest wind, bringing rain and fog in winter and hot, dry air in summer.

Autolycus, son of Hermes, an Argonaut, and a notorious cattle thief. He was able to deceive the owners by changing the marks on the cattle, but Sisyphus, son of Aeolus, got the better of him by marking the feet of his oxen.

Avernus, a lake between Cumae and Naples, thought to be one of the entrances of Tartarus.

Bacchanalia, a Roman festival in honor of Bacchus, marked by wild orgies.

Bacchantes, devotees of Bacchus, who danced and threw themselves about with barbaric abandon at the Bacchanalia. Also called the Maenads.

Bacchus, Roman equivalent for the Greek god Dionysus. *See* **Dionysus.**

Baldur (also **Balder**), the Scandinavian god of light and son of Odin and Frigg. Invulnerable to everything except the mistletoe, Baldur was killed when the god Loki directed a blind god, Hodur, to throw a mistletoe branch at him.

Ban, a legendary king of Brittany and father of Launcelot.

Baucis, the wife of Philemon, who lived with her husband in a small cottage in Phrygia, where they were visited by Zeus and Hermes in disguise. As a reward for the hospitality extended to them, Zeus transformed the cottage into a splendid temple and promised them they would die together. As they died, Philemon became an oak and Baucis a linden tree.

Bellerophon, son of Glaucus. When he refused the advances of Antea, wife of Proteus, she accused him of attempting to seduce her. When Proteus told his father-in-law, King Iobates of Lycia, the king sent Bellerophon off to attack the Chimaera, a fire-breathing monster, hoping that Bellerophon would die. Aided by Athena, he destroyed the beast, but when he later tried to fly to heaven on the winged horse, Pegasus, Zeus sent a gadfly to sting the horse and Bellerophon was thrown to earth where he wandered, lame and blind, for the rest of his life.

Bellona, Roman goddess of war, daughter of Phorcys and Geto, and companion or sister of Mars. She is identified with the Greek Enyo. Her priests, called Bellonarii, inflicted wounds on themselves when offering sacrifices.

Boreas, the north wind personified, son of the Titan, Astraeus, and Eos, who carried away from the Ilissus the nymph Oreithyia. In Latin, he is called Aguilo.

Brahma, the major member of the Hindu triad, along with Vishnu and Siva. He is the creator.

Briareos, son of Ouranos and Gaea, a giant with a hundred arms and fifty heads, who helped the Olympians against the Titans.

Briseis, slave girl of Achilles whom Agamemnon surrendered to Apollo as a substitute for Chryseis in order to stop a plague. Achilles, angered, withdrew from the Trojan War, but rejoined it after the death of Patroclus.

Brunhild, one of the most famous Valkyries, she was deprived of her power and enclosed, by Odin, in a ring of flame. From there she was rescued and married by the great Siegfried.

Bucephalus, favorite horse of Alexander, after which the city Bucephala is named.

Busiris, king of Egypt and son of Poseidon. He attempted to sacrifice Heracles to avoid a drought, but the latter broke loose and slew him.

Cacus, a giant, son of Hephaistos and Medusa, who lived in a cave on the Aventine Hill. He stole some of the cattle of Geryon which Heracles was driving home and dragged them by the tails into his cave. Heracles heard them, however, and strangled Cacus.

Cadmus, son of Agenor. Unwilling to return home after losing his sister, Europa, he consulted the Delphic oracle who advised him to follow a certain cow and to found a city where the cow lay down. Once there, he killed a dragon, and armed men, who formed the original population of Thebes, sprang up where he sowed the dragon's teeth. Cadmus married Harmonia, daughter of Ares and Aphrodite, and begat Semele, Ino, Autonoë, and Agave. Legend credits him with teaching the Boitians the Greek alphabet.

Caduceus, the magic wand of Hermes, with which he conducted the souls of mortals across the river Styx and raised the dead to life.

Calchas, the Greek soothsayer and high priest who accompanied the Greeks to

Troy. He declared that the fleet could not sail until Iphigeneia was sacrificed, that the plague could not be stopped until Chryseis was restored to her father, and that Troy could only be taken after ten years and with Achilles' aid.

Calliope, the Muse of epic poetry, daughter of Zeus and Mnemosyne, and the mother of Orpheus by Apollo.

Callisto, attendant of Artemis, she loved Zeus and mothered Arcas, the ancestor of the Arcadians. Artemis changed her into a bear. She would have been killed by her son who was hunting one day had not Zeus changed her into the constellation Ursa Major and Arcas into Ursa Minor.

Calydon, a city of Aetolia, which was devastated by a boar sent by Artemis in revenge for the neglect of her rites. This disaster gave rise to the famous hunt for the Calydonian boar, in which many heroes took part. Meleager succeeded in slaying the animal and presented its head to Atalanta.

Calypso, daughter of Atlas, a sea nymph and queen of Ogygia. She offered Odysseus hospitality when he was shipwrecked, fell in love with him, and detained him for seven years.

Camelot, legendary seat of King Arthur's palace and court, thought to have been near Monmouthsire, England, on the river Usk.

Camenae, fountain nymphs and goddesses of prophecy in Roman mythology, who were identified with the Greek Muses.

Camilla, a warlike Volscian heroine; she was killed by Aruns in the war between Aeneas and Turnus.

Capaneus, one of the Seven against Thebes, son of Hipponous and Astinome, and husband of Evadne. Having boasted that not even Zeus could stop him from taking Thebes, he was killed by a bolt of lightning. His wife, Evadne, committed suicide by throwing herself on her husband's burning body.

Cassandra, daughter of Priam and Hecuba, to whom Apollo granted the gift of prophecy. When she resisted him, however, Apollo, who could not retract gifts, ordered that no one should believe her. After the fall of Troy, she became the captive of Agamemnon, who took her to Mycenae, where Clytemnestra slew her.

Cassiopeia, in Greek mythology, mother of Andromeda and wife of Cepheus, king of Ethiopia. She was transformed into a constellation.

Castalia, a fountain on Mount Parnassus, sacred to Apollo and the Muses.

Castor, twin brother of Polydeuces (Lat. *Pollux*), and noted for his skill in taming horses. The twins, called the Dioscuri, offspring of Leda and Zeus, accompanied the Argonauts and became patron deities of seamen and voyagers. Castor was slain in a battle which was the consequence of the kidnapping of Phoebe and Hilaeira, but the brothers were rejoined in the heavens in the constellation Gemini. In Roman mythology, the twins led the Roman army in the fifth century B.C. and announced the capture of Perseus.

Cecrops, founder and first king of Athens, often represented as serpentlike below the waist.

Celaeno, daughter of Atlas; also one of the Harpies.

Centaurs, a race of creatures half-horse, half-human, descendants of Ixion and Nephele, who inhabited Mount Pelion in Thesally. They tried to abduct the wife of Pirithous, king of the Lapithae, and lost the ensuing battle. Later, many were killed by Heracles, and the rest driven to Mount Pindus.

Cerberus, *see* **Kerberos.**

Ceres, Roman equivalent for the Greek goddess Demeter. *See* **Demeter.**

Chaos, the vast deep and confusion out of which proceeded the earth and the gods and all other things.

Charites, three goddesses, daughters of Zeus and Eurynome embodying grace and loveliness. They are associated with the goddess Aphrodite, and are identified in Roman mythology as the Gratiae (Graces).

Charon, son of Erebus, he ferries the souls of the dead over the waters of the rivers Styx and Acheron to Hades. He received payment for each passenger, hence the ancient Roman custom of putting a coin into the mouth of a corpse before burial.

Charybdis, a whirlpool in the Straights of Messina, exceedingly perilous to ships, which in avoiding it, often ran aground on Scylla. *See* **Scylla.**

Chimaera, a fire-breathing monster shaped like a lion in front, a dragon behind, and a goat in the middle, which devastated Lycia until it was killed by Bellerophon. *See* **Bellerophon.**

Chiron, the wisest of the centaurs, and the son of the Oceanid, Philyra, and Cronos. He instructed many Grecian heroes such as Jason and Achilles, and taught Asklepios the art of healing. Though immortal, he was accidentally killed by one of Heracles' poisoned arrows because he could not bear the pain. He relinquished his immortality to Prometheus and was transformed into the constellation Sagittarius.

Chloris, Greek personification of Spring, wife of Zephyrus and often identified with the Roman goddess Flora.

Chryseis, daughter of a priest of Apollo, taken prisoner by the Greeks and given to Agamemnon. When Agamemnon denied her father's plea for her freedom, Apollo sent a plague upon the Greeks which could only be placated by her release. Agamemnon, instead, substituted a slave girl and thus earned the enmity of Achilles. *See* **Briseis.**

Circe, daughter of Helios and Oceanid, sister of Aeëtes, and famous as a sorceress. After murdering her husband, she was banished to the island of Aeaea where Odysseus' companions were turned into swine when they landed there. Odysseus, who was saved by eating the herb moly, which Hermes had given him, forced Circe to turn his companions back into men. Odysseus stayed with Circe a year and sired Telegonus.

Clio, the Muse of history.

Clotho, one of the three Moirai—the Spinner—the goddess who spins the thread of life.

Clymene, in Greek mythology, mother of Phaethon and daughter of Minyas. She is also known as the daughter of Oceanus and Tethys, and mother of Atlas, Epimetheus, and Prometheus by Iapetus.

Clytemnestra, daughter of Tyndareus and Leda, or, according to legend, of Zeus who visited Leda in the form of a swan. She was the sister of Castor, Polydeuces, and Helen, the wife of Agamemnon and the mother of Orestes, Iphigeneia, and Electra. She became the lover of Aegisthus while her husband was in Troy and killed her spouse upon his return. Orestes, aided by Electra, avenged the murder by killing them both.

Clytie, a water nymph, who fell in love with Apollo. She was transformed by him into a sunflower so that she would always face him in his daily journey across the sky.

Cornucopia, the horn of plenty. Under the secret care of the nymphs, the infant Zeus was suckled by the goat Amaltheia, whose horn he gave to the nymphs, endowing it with the power to be filled with whatever its possessor wished. According to another tradition, the cornucopia is Achelous' broken horn which was filled with fruits and flowers by the Naiads. *See* **Achelous.**

Creon, king of Thebes who forbade burial of Polynices' dead body following the expedition of the Seven against Thebes. Antigone was caught disobeying the order and was entombed alive despite her betrothal to Creon's son, Haemon. She hanged herself in the tomb, and Haemon killed himself when he heard of her death.

Cronus, a Titan; son of Ouranos and Gaea; and father, by Rhea, of Zeus, Poseidon, Hades, Hestia, Demeter, and Hera; identified by the Romans as Saturn. Encouraged by his mother, he overthrew and castrated his father. His rule was the "Golden Age" when there was no evil or suffering in the world. But, to prevent his sons from overthrowing him, he swallowed all his offspring. His wife, however, hid the youngest, Zeus, from him. When he was older, Zeus rebelled and started the war of the Olympians against the Titans. *See* **Zeus.**

Cupid, Roman god of love. *See* **Eros.**

Curetes, *see* **Kuretes.**

Cybele, a Phrygian fertility goddess, worshipped as mother of the gods. She was identified with the Greek goddess Rhea and the Roman Magna Mater. Her priests castrated themselves observing her rites as did her beloved.(*See* **Attis.**) She was the mother of King Midas by Gordius, king of Phrygia.

Cyclopes, a race of shepherds of gigantic stature each with only one eye, which was in the middle of the forehead. They lived near Mount Aetna and assisted Hephaistos at his forges.

Daedalus, the cunning craftsman who built the labyrinth in which the Minotaur was placed. He flew from Crete to Italy with his son Icarus by means of wings fastened to their shoulders with wax. Daedalus arrived safely, but Icarus flew too near the sun, which melted the wax in his wings, and fell into the sea.

Daidale, literally, the "Cunningly Wrought." Hera, in one of her fits of jealousy, left Zeus. To get her back, Zeus announced that he was going to remarry. He had a wooden statue, called the Daidale, made and then had it driven around for all to see. Hera went after it, found that it was only a joke and happily went back to Zeus.

Danaë, daughter of Acrisius the king of Argos, and mother of Perseus. An oracle predicted that some day her son would kill his grandfather, Acrisius. To prevent such a calamity, the king had his daughter imprisoned in a dungeon so that no one would marry her. But she was visited by Zeus, who distilled himself into a shower of gold. After the birth of Perseus, she and the child were put in a chest and thrown into the sea, but they drifted to the shore of Seriphus and were saved. The oracle's prediction came true, for Acrisius was accidentally killed by a discus thrown by Perseus.

Danaids, the 50 daughters of Danaus, 49 of whom slew their bridegrooms on their wedding night. The Danaids' punishment in Hades was to forever try to fill water vessels which had holes in the bottom.

Danaus, son of Belus and twin brother of Aegyptus. Aegyptus had 50 sons and Danaus had 50 daughters. To escape his brother and his nephews, Danaus fled with his daughters to Argos and there became king. Hearing of their uncle's success, the sons of Aegyptus betook themselves to Argos and demanded his daughters for wives. On the wedding night each wife killed her husband with a dagger provided by Danaus. Only one escaped, Lynceus, who killed Danaus.

Daphne, a nymph who was loved by Apollo but did not return his love. Pursued by the god she fled and was changed into a laurel. Thereafter the laurel was Apollo's favorite tree.

Daphnis, a Sicilian shepherd, famous as a flutist and regarded by the Greeks as the originator of pastoral poetry. In one story, he was struck blind for faithlessness to a Naiad.

Dardanus, son of Electra, he was the founder of Troy and the ancestor of the Trojans.

Deianira, wife of Heracles and sister of Meleager, for whose love Achelous fought a fierce battle with Heracles and lost. Later, jealous of Heracles' attentions to Iole, Deianira put the blood of Nessus on Heracles' coat, since Nessus had told her the blood would gain his undying love. The blood proved poisonous, however, and killed Heracles. In grief, Deianira killed herself.

Deimos, god of fear who accompanied Ares.

Delphi, a city in central Greece at the foot of Mt. Parnassus, famous for the temple and oracle of Apollo.

Demeter, Greek goddess of agriculture and vegetation, and protectress of marriage, identified by the Romans as Ceres. Demeter was the daughter of Cronos and Rhea, and the mother of Persephone. After Hades abducted Persephone, the earth became barren during Demeter's search for her throughout the

world. *See* **Persephone.**

Deucalion, son of Prometheus and husband of Pyrrha. Deucalion and Pyrrha alone survived the deluge sent by Zeus to destroy the inhabitants of the earth. Prometheus had warned his son and instructed him to build a chest large enough to hold Deucalion and Pyrrha. The chest landed on the only dry place—the peak of Mt. Parnassus. In order to repopulate the earth, they were ordered to throw behind them the bones of their mother, which they interpreted as meaning the earth. They picked up some stones and flung them over their shoulders—those cast by Deucalion were transformed into men, and those by Pyrrha into women.

Diana, Roman equivalent for Greek goddess of hunting and the moon, Artemis. See **Artemis.**

Dido, queen of Carthage, who fled from Tyre with a large number of friends and followers and established a colony on the coast of Africa opposite Sicily. She assisted Aeneas after he had been shipwrecked, and fell in love with him. When he left her to sail on to Italy, she killed herself.

Dike, the personified goddess of justice, one of the three Horae.

Diomedes, son of Tydeus and king of Argos, he was a prominent Greek chieftain in the Trojan War. He fought with Ares (Lat. *Mars*) and wounded him so severely that the god of war retired from the battle. *See* **Ares.**

Dione, probably the first consort of Zeus and, according to one tradition, the mother of Aphrodite. Her name is the feminine form of Zeus.

Dionysus, Greek god of vegetation and wine, and son of Semele and Zeus (*see* **Semele.**) He was the father of Oenopion, Euanthes, and Staphylus by his wife, Ariadne. Dionysus traveled throughout Greece, Asia Minor, Syria, and Egypt introducing his rites attended by satyrs, nymphs, and maenads. The bull, goat, and serpent were sacred to him. He is depicted either as a bearded man or a youth with ivy leaves and grapes around his forehead, wearing a "nebris" (a fawn skin), and carrying a thyrsus (a pole with a pine cone or vine leaves decorating the top). Dionysus is identified by the Romans as Bacchus.

Dioscuri, name applied to Castor and Polydeuces, twin sons of Leda and Tyndareus or Zeus. *See* **Castor.**

Dirce, wife of Lycus, who herself suffered the torture which she planned to inflict upon Antiope: to be tied to the horns of a wild bull and dragged to her death.

Dryads, wood nymphs; the spirits or souls of trees. They are not immortal; each dryad comes to life and dies with her tree.

Echo, a mountain nymph who diverted the attention of Hera while Zeus made love to other nymphs. When Hera discovered the deception, she deprived Echo of the power of speaking except when spoken to, and then only the last syllable. Another legend has it that Echo was in love with Narcissus and pined away until only her voice remained.

Eirene, the Greek goddess of peace. Equivalent to Roman Pax.

Elaine, (1.) the daughter of King Pelles. She was magically given the appearance of Queen Guinevere and thereby became the mother of Sir Galahad by Launcelot du Lac. (2.) known as the "lily maid of Astolat," and realizing the hopelessness of her love for Launcelot, she requested that in death her body be placed on a barge, with a letter avowing her love, and floated down the river to the castle. Hearing of her tale, Arthur ordered her body buried with royal honors.

Electra, daughter of Agamemnon, she sent her brother Orestes to King Strophius in Phocis in order to protect him from Clytemnestra, her mother. After Orestes had avenged his father's death (*see* **Orestes**) by killing his mother, Electra married her brother's friend Pylades.

Elysion, the abode of the spirits of the blessed. Also called Elysian fields.

Endymion, a shepherd on Mount Latmos, a beautiful youth loved by Selene, who chose perpetual sleep in return for immorality. He sleeps in Caria, where Selene, the moon goddess, visits him by night.

Eos, Greek goddess of the dawn, daughter of Hyperion and Theia, sister of Selene (Moon) and Helios (Sun). She rose from the couch of her husband Tithonus to bring the first rays of daylight to mortals. She is portrayed as saffon-robed, driving a purple chariot drawn by two horses; as riding the horse Pegasus and carrying a torch; or as a winged goddess sprinkling dew from an urn. Eos was the mother of the four winds (Boreas, Zephyrus, Eurus, and Notus), Phosphorus, and Hesperus by Astraeus, and Memnon and Emathion, kings of Arabia and Ethiopia respectively, by Tithonus. She is identified by Romans as Aurora.

Epigoni, the sequel to the war of the Seven against Thebes. The sons of the Seven, with some help, attacked Thebes and were successful.

Erato, the Muse of erotic poetry.

Erebus, son of Chaos. He is one of the deities of the lower world. He is a personification of that dread darkness through which departing souls pass to Hades.

Eris, sister of Ares and goddess of discord and strife. She threw the apple to the guests at the wedding of Peleus and Thetis and thereby indirectly caused the Trojan War. *See* **Paris.**

Eros, the Greek god of love, son of Aphrodite. He pierced the hearts of gods and men with arrows of desire. The Romans identified him as Cupid.

Eteocles, a son of Oedipus and Jocasta. After his father's death, he and his brother Polynices agreed to reign in alternate years, Eteocles taking the first turn. At the end of his year, however, he refused to relinquish the throne. Polynices, therefore, appealed to Adrastus, king of Argos, whose daughter he had married. Adrastus sent an army and seven of his bravest generals (the Seven against Thebes) to his son-in-law's aid, and a severe conflict ensued. In the end the two brothers agreed to settle their differences in combat, and each fell by the other's hands.

Eumenides, a name meaning "good-tempered ones," given to placate the avenging spirits, the Furiae (Furies).

Eunomia, the personified goddess of law and order, one of the three Horae.

Euphrosyne, meaning joy, one of the three Graces, daughter of Zeus and Eurynome.

Europa, daughter of Agenor, king of Phoenicia. She was loved by Zeus, who assumed the form of a white bull and carried her off to Crete, where she became the mother of Minos, Sarpedon, and Rhadamanthus.

Eurus, the East Wind.

Eurydice, wife of Orpheus, who, after dying on her wedding day, was granted permission to leave Hades and accompany her husband to the world above on condition that he should not turn around to look at her until they had reached the upper world. But Orpheus, in a moment of forgetfulness, turned around and Eurydice fell back into Hades.

Eurytheus, ruler of Greece and cousin of Heracles. At the urging of Hera, he imposed the twelve labors on Heracles after Heracles had killed his own wife and children.

Euterpe, the Muse of lyric poetry.

Evadne, *see* **Capaneus.**

Evander, son of Hermes. He was leader of a group of Arcadian colonists that settled in Italy. He joined Aeneas in the war against Turnus.

Excalibur, King Arthur's sword which was magically fixed in a stone. Because he was the only one who could pull it out, Arthur proved his right to the throne. As he lay dying, Arthur requested one of his knights to throw the sword into the lake from which it was said to have come. It had been the gift of Vivien, the Lady of the Lake.

Fates, *see* **Moirai.**

Faunus, an Italian divinity, protector of agriculture and shepherds. He was identified with the Greek Pan. *See* **Pan.**

Flora, *see* **Chloris.**

Freki, *see* **Geri.**

Frigg, wife of Odin and most revered of the Norse goddesses.

Furies, three hideous winged females, Alecto, Tisiphone, and Magaera, who sprang from the blood of mutilated Ouranos. They were avenging deities who pursued and punished the guilty, especially murderers.

Gaea, the first being that sprang from Chaos. She is the personification of the Earth. She gave birth to Ouranos (Sky) and with him gave birth to the Titans who preceeded the gods. She is identified by the Romans as Terra.

(Sir) Galahad, son of Launcelot and Elaine and the purest and noblest knight of the Round Table. He was said to be the last person ever to have seen the Holy Grail.

Galatea, (1.) a sea nymph, the daughter of Nereus and Doris, who fell in love with Acis. (2.) the girl brought to life by Aphrodite when she transformed Pygmalion's statue of a maiden into a living form.

Galli, fraternity of priests of Cybele who celebrated orgiastic rites with frenzied dances to flutes, drums, and cymbals. They hit their shields with swords and castrated themselves.

Ganymede, cupbearer to the gods, a mortal youth of such grace and beauty that Zeus had him carried off to Olympus on the back of an eagle.

(Sir) Gawain, nephew of King Arthur and a Knight of the Round Table, known for his courtesy and chivalry. He was probably the original hero of the Quest for the Holy Grail.

Ge, *see* **Gaea.**

Genius, a special divinity assigned to every person and place. An individual's tutelary spirit which accompanies him through life.

Geri, one of the two wolves (the other being Freki) who lie at the feet of the Norse god Odin when he is on his throne.

Glaucus, (1.) a commander of the Lycians in the War of Troy and friend of Diomedes. (2.) a Boeotian fisherman who was changed by Oceanus into a divinity of the sea and granted the gift of prophecy by Apollo. His oracles are highly prized by fishermen.

Golden Fleece, the hide of the golden ram, entrusted by Phryxus to Aeëtes and guarded by Argus, the hundred-eyed monster. It was for the purpose of obtaining this fleece that Jason embarked on the Argonautic expedition.

Gorgons, three hideous wenches whose heads were covered with snakes instead of hair; anyone who looked into their eyes would turn to stone. The best known is Medusa; her sisters are Stheno and Eurydale.

Graces, three daughters of Zeus—Euphrosyne, Aglaia and Thalia—who represented the perfection of grace in body and mind. They are known by the Greeks as Charites and are usually shown as Aphrodite's attendants.

Guinevere, daughter of Laodegan, king of Carmalide, and wife of King Arthur of Camelot. According to Arthurian legend, she was secretly in love with Launcelot du Lac, but was seduced by Arthur's nephew Modred, causing the battle in which both Arthur and Modred died.

Hades, Greek name for the ruler and then the region of the Kingdom of the Underworld; known by the Romans as Pluto. He was the son of Cronus and the brother of Zeus and Poseidon. Hades was not represented as being evil. The Kingdom of the Underworld was given to him as an inheritance. The region, Hades, is not a Hell. All the dead, both good and bad, go there but can never leave.

Haemon, son of Creon and lover of Antigone. On hearing that his beloved had committed suicide, he too killed himself. *See* **Antigone.**

Hamadryads, tree nymphs, usually called dryads. *See* **Dryads.**

Harpies, greedy monsters with female heads, long claws, and wings. They snatched away bodies and food and devoured them. Harpies are responsible for all people who disappear without a trace.

Hebe, daughter of Zeus and Hera and wife of Heracles. She was cupbearer to the gods before being replaced by Ganymede. The Romans worshipped her as Juventas, the goddess of youth.

Hecate, goddess of sorcery and witchcraft, often represented with three heads. She personified the darkness and terror of night. She was the only Titan to retain her power under Zeus. Her domain extended over heaven, earth, and hell. She particularly haunted crossroads and was associated with the howling of dogs. She is identified by the Romans as Trivia.

Hector, son of Priam and Hecuba, and husband of Andromache. He was the leader of the Trojan forces and the most valiant of them. After killing Patroclus, the friend of Achilles, Achilles was provoked to return to the battle. There he killed Hector, whose body was dragged in triumph three times around the walls of Troy. Zeus interposed and ordered the body to be given up to Priam for burial.

Hecuba, wife of Priam and queen of Troy, who saw her husband and her sons killed by the Greeks. After the capture of Troy, she was captured by Odysseus and taken by the conquerors back to Greece. There, after avenging the murder of her son Polydorus, she was turned into a dog.

Helen, the most beautiful woman in the world, daughter of Zeus and Leda. In her youth, she was carried off by Theseus but was rescued by her brothers, Castor and Polydeuces. She became the wife of Menelaus, king of Sparta, but Paris later persuaded her to forsake her husband and accompany him to Troy. This started the Trojan War. When Paris was killed, in the ninth year of the war, Helen returned to Menelaus and lived with him until his death.

Helenus, son of Priam and Hecuba, famous for his prophetic powers. He was the only son of Priam to survive the Trojan War.

Helicon, a mountain in Greece, residence of Apollo and the Muses.

Helios, the god of the sun, who daily drove his four-horsed chariot across the sky. He is identified by the Romans as Sol.

Helle, daughter of Nephele and Athamas, who during her flight on the Golden Ram fell into the strait separating Europe from Asia, which was then named the Hellespont in her honor.

Hephaistos, the Greek god of Craftmanship and worker with fire in general, and husband of Aphrodite, identified with, but not the same as, the Roman Vulcan. *See* **Vulcan.**

Hera, sister and wife of Zeus, and queen of heaven. She was an exacting and jealous wife who took severe vengeance upon the numerous mortal maidens of whom Zeus became enamored, as well as upon their offspring. She was the mother of Ares, Hephaistos, and Hebe. In the Trojan War she was on the side of the Greeks. She is identified with the Roman Juno.

Heracles, son of Zeus and Alcmene, renowned for his strength; identified by the Romans as Hercules. While still in his cradle he strangled two serpents which Hera had sent to destroy him. Before reaching manhood he killed the lion of Mount Cithaeron. Afterward, having been driven mad by Hera, he killed his own children and his wife, Megara, daughter of Creon. On recovering he was so stricken with grief that he exiled himself and went to consult the oracle of Apollo at Delphi. He was commanded to serve Eurystheus for twelve years. During that period he performed twelve labors. The gods assisted him in his tasks, and he carried them out successfully. His first labor was to kill the lion of Nemea; the second, to destroy the nine-headed Lernaean hydra; the third was to capture the Arcadian stag; the fourth, to kill the wild boar of Erymanthus; the fifth to clean the Augean stables; the sixth, to kill the carnivorous birds of Stympalis; the seventh, to capture the wild bull of Crete; the eighth, to capture the mares of Diomedes; the ninth, to obtain the girdle of Hippolyte, queen of the Amazons; the tenth, to capture the oxen of Geryon; the eleventh, to obtain the golden apples from the garden of the Hesperides; and the twelfth, to bring Kerberos, the three-headed dog of Hades, to the upper world. After performing the twelve labors Heracles was free from service to Eurystheus and returned to Thebes. He married Deianira, daughter of Oeneus of Calydon. When Nessus, a centaur, tried to abduct her, Heracles shot him with a poisoned arrow. The dying Nessus told Deianira to keep his blood since it would always preserve her husband's love. Later, fearing that she was being supplanted by Iole, Deianira sent Heracles a garment soaked in the blood of Nessus, which poisoned him. After his death he was taken to Olympus, endowed with immortality, and married to Hera's daughter, Hebe.

Hercules, see **Heracles.**

Hermes, Greek messenger of the gods; called Mercury by the Romans. He was the son of Zeus and Maia, god of commerce, and patron of travelers, shepherds, traders, and robbers. Many of his exploits turn upon thievery or mischief. He wore a winged cap and had wings attached to his ankles, enabling him to travel from place to place with the speed of the wind.

Hero, the lover of Leander. *See* **Leander.**

Hesperides, the three daughters of Atlas and Hesperis, appointed to guard the golden apples which Gaea gave Hera at her marriage to Zeus. The dragon, Ladon, which was always on guard at the foot of the tree, was slain by Heracles when he seized the apples.

Hestia, the evening star, king of the Western lands, and identified by the Romans as Vesta.

Hippocrene, a fountain at the foot of Mount Helicon, dedicated to the Muses. It began to flow when the ground was struck by the hoofs of the winged horse, Pegasus.

Hippolyte, queen of the Amazons and daughter of Ares. She was slain by Heracles when he tried to get her girdle as one of his twelve labors.

Hodur, the blind Scandinavian god of darkness, who is said to have killed Baldur with an arrow made of mistletoe.

Holy Grail (also **Sangreal**), the chalice from which Jesus drank at the Last Supper. According to one legend, Joseph of Arimathea brought the Grail to England where it disappeared. In another, it is said to be kept by knights atop a mountain where it can be seen only by those of perfect purity. Most of the adventures of the Knights of the Round Table occur during the Quest for the Holy Grail.

Horae, the Greek goddesses of the seasons. They were the daughters of Zeus and Themis, and are Eunomia, Dike, and Eirene.

Hormonia, daughter of Aphrodite and Ares. She received a necklace made by Hephaistos for her wedding to Cadmus. The necklace proved fatal to all its owners.

Horus, one of the principle Egyptian deities, the son of Osiris and Isis. The living king is always regarded as Horus incarnate.

Hours, see **Horae.**

Hyacinthos, a beautiful youth, loved by Apollo and Zephyrus, accidentally killed when Zephyrus blew Apollo's discus from its course. From his blood sprang the hyacinth.

Hydra, a many-headed monster. The Lernaean hydra, which Heracles slew, was a water serpent with nine heads, one of which was immortal. For each head cut off, two would grow in its place unless the wound was cauterized. Heracles succeeded in burning away eight of its heads and buried the ninth under a rock.

Hygeia, goddess of health, daughter of Aesculapius.

Hylas, a beautiful youth loved by Heracles, who accompanied him on board the *Argo.* While Hylas was drawing water at a spring, a nymph drew him into the water and drowned him.

Hymen (or **Hymenaeus**), the god of marriage, represented as a youth bearing a bridal torch.

Hyperion, one of the Titans, son of Ouranos and Gaea. He was the father of the following: Helios, the sun god; Selene, the moon goddess; and Eos, goddess of the dawn.

Hypermnestra, one of the daughters of Danaus; the only one to spare her husband. *See* **Danaids.**

Icarus, see **Daedalus.**

Incubus, a supernatural being neither wholly good nor wholly evil. An incubus fathered Merlin, Arthur's counselor.

Io, princess of Argos and daughter of Inachus. She was loved by Zeus, who, to allay the suspicions of Hera, transformed her into a heifer. Hera was aware of the change and had the hundred-eyed Argus watch her. When Zeus had Argus killed by Hermes, Hera tormented Io with a gadfly, which drove her from place to place until she reached the Nile, where she recovered her human form and bore a son to Zeus.

Iphigeneia, daughter of Agamemnon and Clytemnestra. She was offered as a sacrifice to appease Artemis at the outbreak of the Trojan War. However, Artemis substituted her with a bear and carried Iphigeneia off to Tauris. She later became a priestess and saved the life of her brother Orestes when he was about to be sacrificed.

Iris, goddess of the rainbow, daughter of Thaumas and Electra, sister to the Harpies. She is also the Messengers of the gods, particularly Hera, and the rainbow is her path.

Isis, wife and sister of Osiris, and mother of Horus. Isis, Osiris, and Horus formed the powerful Egyptian trinity. She was the principle goddess of ancient Egypt, and identified with the moon. Cows were sacred to her and she is often depicted with cow's horns.

Ixion, king of Thessaly, who had promised his father-in-law, Deioneus, a valuable gift. When Ixion was unable to obtain the gift, he put Deioneus to death in order to be released from his promise. After a long period of expiation, he was summoned by Zeus to Mount Olympus and placed at the table of the gods. But Ixion, unappreciative of his host's hospitality, began to make love to Hera. As a punishment Ixion was sent to Hades and there tied to a fiery wheel which never ceases to revolve.

Janus, an old Roman divinity, represented with two faces turned in opposite directions. He was the god of beginnings and entrances; therefore, the first month of the year was named after him, and gates and doorways were under his protection. His temple at Rome was open in time of war and closed in time of peace. It was closed three times in Rome's first 700 years.

Jason, son of Aeson and leader of the Argonautic expedition. When his father was driven from the throne by Pelias, Jason was rescued and brought up by the centaur Chiron. Grown to manhood, he demanded the restitution of his father's Kingdom, a request which Pelias promised to satisfy if Jason would bring him the Golden Fleece, kept by King Aeëtes in the custody of a dragon. Accordingly, Jason had a ship built, which he named the *Argo.* He assembled a crew and set out for Colchis. King Aeëtes agreed to part with the fleece if Jason would perform several seemingly impossible deeds, such as yoking the fire-breathing oxen and sowing the dragon's teeth. He accomplished these tasks with the help of Medea, Aeëtes' daughter, who had fallen in love with him. Shortly thereafter Jason returned home with the fleece, taking Medea with him. After several years he deserted her for another woman. Medea was driven mad by jealousy and in revenge killed her children by Jason. Years later Jason was killed by a beam that fell from his ship.

Jocasta, wife of Laius, and mother and later wife of Oedipus. When she found out that she had married her son, she hanged herself. *See* **Oedipus.**

Juno, see **Hera.**

Jupiter, see **Zeus.**

Kassandra, see **Cassandra.**

Kerberos (or **Cerberus**), an offspring of Echidna and Typhon; a three-headed dog with a voice of bronze, who was the watchdog of Hades. Stationed at the gates, Kerberos allowed people to enter, but devoured them if they tried to leave. One of the labors of Heracles was to bring Kerberos from the underworld.

Klotho, *see* **Clotho.**

Kore, *see* **Persephone.**

Kuretes, dancers who muffled the wailings of the infant Zeus on Mt. Ida (or Mt. Dikte) by clashing their spears against their shields. They taught the Cretaus the arts of agriculture and metalworking.

Kyrene, daughter of Hypseus, a huntress who was loved by Apollo and who became the mother of Aristaios, a rustic deity.

Labyrinth, the underground maze in which Minos, the king of Crete, confined the Minotaur who found and ate all humans forced into it.

Lachesis, one of the Moirai, the goddess that measured and apportioned the thread of human life and determined its destiny.

Laertes, king of Ithaca, and father of Odysseus.

Laius, king of Thebes. *See* **Oedipus.**

Laocoön, brother of Anchises, priest of Apollo and later of Poseidon, who tried to warn the Trojans against bringing the wooden horse into Troy. While the people hesitated whether to accept or reject his advice, two giant serpents sent by Athena emerged from the sea and attacked his sons. Rushing to their rescue, Laocoön himself was attacked and all three were strangled.

Laodamia, wife of Protesilaus. In answer to her prayers her husband was restored to life for three hours. When he died a second time, Laodamia died with him.

Laomedon, father of Priam and king of Troy, for whom Poseidon and Apollo built the walls of Troy. When Laomedon refused to give the promised reward, Poseidon sent a monster to plague the city. The king was prepared to sacrifice his daughter to the beast, but Heracles appeared, rescued her, and slew the monster. Because Laomedon again broke his promise, Heracles attacked the city and killed him.

Lapithae, a people of Thessaly, who engaged in battle with the centaurs at the marriage feast of Hippodamia and Pirithous, their king.

Lares, ancient Roman divinities, the deified spirits of ancestors, who shielded their descendants against harm.

Latona, *see* **Leto.**

(Sir) Launcelot (Launcelot du Lac; Lancelot of the Lake), the son of King Ban of Brittany, and the most famous of Arthur's knights. While still an infant he was stolen by Vivien (the Lady of the Lake) and raised by her until she presented him to Arthur. Although said to have been a model of chivalry and gallantry, most legends portray him as the secret lover of Queen Guinevere, and hence the cause of the war which ended the Round Table and resulted in Arthur's death. The father of Sir Galahad by Lady Elaine, he died a repentant hermit.

Leander, a youth of Abydos, who swam nightly across the Hellespont to visit his lover, Hero, living in Sestos. He was guided by a lamp which she hung out from a tower, but one stormy night the light was blown out, and Leander, losing his way, was drowned. On seeing his body washed up by the waves, Hero threw herself into the sea.

Leda, wife of Tyndareus, king of Sparta. Zeus, in the form of a swan, approached and raped her. She brought forth two eggs, from one of which sprang Helen and Polydeuces and from the other Castor and Clytemnestra.

Leto, daughter of Coeus and Phoebe, and mother by Zeus of Apollo and Artemis. Persecuted by Hera, she wandered from place to place until Zeus gave her a refuge on Delos, where she gave birth to her children. She is identified by the Romans as Latona.

Loki, first conceived as a fire demon, he became the god of strife and the spirit of evil. He was finally chained to a rock, where he remains until the Twilight of the Gods.

Maenads, the female followers of Dionysus. He inspired them to ecstatic frenzy and they carried out his orgiastic rites.

Mars, primarily the Roman god of war, also god of agriculture, god of Spring, and patron of husbandmen. He was the son of Juno and a mystical flower, lover of Venus and legendary father of Romulus and Remus through Rhea Silvia. Bellona the warrior goddess accompanied him. He was derived from the Greek god Ares, but unlike his counterpart, was extremely popular.

Medea, a sorceress who helped Jason steal the Golden Fleece from her father, Aeëtes, king of Colchis. She then married Jason, but when he left her for the Corinthian princess Creusa, she killed her children by him in revenge. *See* **Jason.**

Medusa, one of the Gorgons, a terrible monster with hissing serpents for hair, whose face turned the beholder into stone. She was killed by Perseus who, while observing her image in a mirror, cut off her head with his sword.

Megaera, one of the three Furies.

Meleager, son of Oeneus and Althaea. He took part in the Argonautic expedition and led the chase for the Calydonian boar. It was decreed by the Moirai that he should live only as long as a certain firebrand remained unconsumed. His mother Althaea snatched the brand from the fire and jealously guarded it. When she heard of Meleager's slaying of the boar, she went to the temple to return thanks. On the way, however, she came upon the bodies of her brothers, who had been slain by Meleager because they had protested the skin's being given to Atalanta. This so incensed Althaea that she cast the fatal brand into the fire, and when the brand was consumed, Meleager was dead.

Melpomene, the Muse of tragedy.

Menelaus, son of Atreus, brother of Agamemnon, and king of Sparta. He was one of the prominent Greek generals in the Trojan War. The abduction of his wife, Helen, was the cause of the war.

Mentor, friend of Odysseus, to whom the care and education of Odysseus' and Penelope's only son, Telemachus, was entrusted during Odysseus' absence from home. The word "mentor" has come to mean a wise and faithful counselor.

Mercury, *see* **Hermes.**

Merlin, a sorcerer, friend, and teacher of King Arthur. He was said to have been the son of a damsel seduced by an incubus who was saved from Satan's power by being baptized. He was seduced and imprisoned by the enchantress Nimue, and ultimately enchanted by the spells of Vivien, the Lady of the Lake, who entangled him in a thornbush, where he still sleeps.

Midas, king of Phrygia, who, having done Dionysus a service, was permitted to choose his reward. He asked that whatever he touched be turned into gold. When the food he touched, the clothes he wore, and the water he washed in turned into gold he soon asked that the gift be revoked. On another occasion, because Midas ventured to remark that Pan made better music than Apollo, he was given ass's ears.

Midgard, literally the middle yard. This was the abode of man, one of the nine worlds of Norse mythology, fashioned from the body of a giant slain by Odin, Vili, and Ve.

Minerva, the Roman equivalent of the Greek goddess Athena. She was patroness of the arts and crafts. *See* **Athena.**

Minos, (1.) the son of Zeus and Europa, a famous lawgiver who became a judge in the lower world. (2.) grandson of the first Minos. Poseidon caused his wife, Pasiphae, to fall in love with a bull which Minos had refused to sacrifice to him. When Pasiphae gave birth to a monster, the Minotaur, Minos had a labyrinth built by Daedalus to imprison it and exacted tribute from the Athenians until Theseus intervened and slew the monster.

Minotaur, the half bull, half human creature, offspring of Pasiphae and a bull. Confined in the Cretan labyrinth by Minos, the monster annually devoured seven youths and seven maidens sent as tribute by the Athenians. Finally, with Ariadne's help, the Minotaur was slain by Theseus.

Mnemosyne, Greek goddess of memory, daughter of Ouranos and Gaea, and mother, by Zeus, of the Muses, goddesses of the arts.

Modred (or **Mordred**), son of Arthur's half sister Morgause—some Arthurian legends allege him to be Arthur's son. Either his seduction of Queen Guinevere or his hatred of Launcelot, which led him to expose the knight's secret love affair with Guinevere, led to Modred's revolt against Arthur and the war which led to the end of the Round Table, and in which Modred was slain at Camlan.

Moirai, Clotho, Lachesis, and Atropos; three daughters of Zeus and Themis. They controlled the actions and destinies of man. The Romans called them the Fates.

Morpheus, son of Somnus and the god of sleep and dreams. He is generally represented as a chubby, winged child, holding poppies in his hand.

Mors, the Roman personification of death.

Muses, daughters of Zeus and Mnemosyne

(Memory), nine divinities who presided over the arts. Their names and the arts assigned to them were: Clio, history; Euterpe, lyric poetry; Thalia, comedy; Melpomene, tragedy; Terpsichore, choral dance and song; Erato, erotic poetry; Polyhymnia, religious poetry and song; Urania, astronomy; Calliope, epic poetry.

Naiads, fresh-water nymphs, the daughters of Zeus.

Nanna, wife of Baldur. She threw herself upon his funeral pyre after he had been accidentally killed by Hodur.

Narcissus, a beautiful youth, son of the river god, Cephisus. To avenge Narcissus' rebuff of the nymph Echo's love, Aphrodite, who regarded the incident as a rebuke to herself, caused Narcissus to become enamored of his own reflection in the waters of a stream. Unable to embrace or kiss the image, he pined away until he was changed into a flower, the narcissus.

Nausicaä, daughter of the king of the Phaeacians, who took Odysseus to her father when he was shipwrecked on the coast.

Nemesis, goddess of retributive justice and daughter of Night, who relentlessly meted out just punishment to evildoers, lawbreakers, and the proud and haughty.

Neoptolemus (or Pyrrhus), son of Achilles, who slew Priam in the Trojan War and later settled in Epirus, where he was killed by Orestes.

Nephele, wife of Athamas and mother of Phryxus and Helle.

Neptune, *see* **Poseidon.**

Nereids, nymphs of the sea and ocean.

Nereus, a sea divinity, son of Oceanus and Gaea, and husband of Doris, by whom he had fifty daughters, called the Nereids. He was gifted with prophecy and lived in the Aegean Sea.

Nessus, a centaur slain by Heracles. *See* **Heracles.**

Nestor, king of Pylos, the oldest of the Greek commanders in the Trojan War, who was known for his wise counsel.

Niebelungs, a race of dwarfs in Teutonic mythology, who were conquered by Siegfried.

Niobe, daughter of Tantalus and wife of Amphion. Her intense pride in her children was the cause of their destruction. Because she had seven sons and seven daughters, she boasted of her superiority to the goddess Leto who had only two children: Apollo and Artemis. To punish her arrogance, Apollo killed all of Niobe's sons, while Artemis killed all her daughters. Niobe wept until she was transformed into a stone from which streamed incessant tears.

Nisus, king of Megara, whose lock of purple hair (on which his life and fortune depended) was snipped off by his daughter Scylla and presented to King Minos, with whom she had fallen deeply in love. Nisus was transformed into a sea eagle, and his daughter into a sea bird.

Notus, a personification of the south wind, also called Auster.

Nox, the Greek personification of Night, who was born out of the primordial Chaos.

Nymphs, female divinities that inhabited certain objects or places in nature. There are (1) Oceanids and Nereids, who were sea nymphs; (2) Naiads, fresh-water nymphs; (3) Dryads and Hamadryads, tree nymphs; and (4) Oreads, mountain nymphs.

Nyx, *see* **Nox.**

Oceanids, nymphs of the sea and ocean.

Oceanus, one of the Titans, son of Ouranos and Gaea, brother of Cronus, and husband of Tethys. He was god of the sea and father of all river gods and water nymphs until in old age he was replaced by Poseidon.

Odin, the Scandinavian god of wisdom, agriculture, poetry, and war. His brothers were named Vili and Ve. Odin created the progenitors of the human race and all other living things.

Odysseus, son of Laertes, husband of Penelope, and king of Ithaca. The wiliest of the Greek leaders at Troy, he was the inventor of the wooden horse. His wanderings on the way home from Troy, which form the subject of Homer's *Odyssey,* lasted twenty years. Finally he reached home and killed the suitors by whom Penelope had been surrounded during his absence. He is identified by the Romans as Ulysses.

Oedipus, king of Thebes, son of Laius and Jocasta, who, fulfilling a prophesy of the oracle at Delphi, unwittingly killed his father and married his mother. Laius, attempting to thwart Fate, ordered his infant son to be killed, but Jocasta had the child carried to Mount Cithaeron where he was raised by a shepherd. Unaware of his lineage, he killed his father on the road to Thebes years later and was rewarded with the hand of his mother, the queen of Thebes, for ridding the city of the dangerous Sphinx by guessing its riddle. Discovering her son's identity, Jocasta committed suicide and Oedipus blinded himself. He left Thebes with his daughter Antigone, and died at Colonus near Athens.

Oenomaus, a son of Ares by Harpina, the daughter of the river god, Asopus. He was the king of Elis and father of Hippodamia. Pelops, his son-in-law, defeated him in a chariot race which, in fulfillment of a prophesy, led him to his death. *See* **Pelops.**

Oenone, a nymph whom Paris married and later abandoned for Helen. Because of this indignity, Oenone refused to heal the wound received by Paris in the battle before Troy. When his injury proved fatal, she was overcome with remorse and hanged herself.

Oenopion, king of Chios. He put out Orion's eyes when Orion tried to abduct his daughter, Merope.

Olympus, a lofty mountain on the border between Macedonia and Thessaly, which was the abode of the gods.

Omphale, daughter of Jardanus and queen of Lydia, whom Heracles was forced to serve as slave for having murdered his friend Iphitus. Omphale fell in love with Heracles and freed him from slavery.

Oreads, the nymphs that inhabited the mountains and caves.

Orestes, son of Agamemnon and Clytemnestra, who killed his mother and her lover, Aegisthus, to avenge their murder of his father. Thereafter, he was haunted by the Furies and fled from country to country. When, by Apollo's command, he submitted to trial before the Areopagus at Athens, he was acquitted and returned to Argos to ascend the throne.

Orion, a famous giant and hunter, who asked for the hand of Merope, daughter of Oenopion, king of Chios. As the price of betrothal Oenopion set the task, which he quickly accomplished, of clearing the island of wild beasts. Instead of receiving his reward, however, he was made drunk and had his eyes put out by the king. After having recovered his eyesight by facing the rising sun, he took revenge on the king. After Orion's death, he was placed in the sky, where a constellation bears his name. According to some legends, Orion was killed because he challenged Artemis to a discus-throwing contest.

Orpheus, a famous lyrist, son of Apollo and Calliope, and husband of Eurydice. He received his lyre from Apollo and played upon it so exquisitely that all things, inanimate as well as animate, were charmed. He was one of the heroes of the Argonautic expedition and on his return married Eurydice. When Eurydice died from the sting of a serpent, Orpheus followed her to Hades and begged Pluto to allow her to accompany him back to earth. His request would be granted, he was told, if he would not look at Eurydice until the borders of Hades had been passed. The temptation was too great however. He looked—and lost her forever. In grief for her he spurned the Thracian women, who became incensed and tore him to pieces during the celebration of Dionysus.

Osiris, one of the chief Egyptian gods; god of the Nile, fertility, ghosts, and the afterworld; and first king of Egypt. He was killed by his brother, Set, out of jealousy and consequently became god of the afterworld by whom all are judged. Afterwards, the deceased Egyptian king always became Osiris and his successor, Horus, the son of Osiris and Isis.

Ossa, a mountain in Thessaly, upon which the Giants piled Mount Pelion in order to climb to the heavens.

Ouranos, god of the heavens, son and husband of Gaea (the Earth). He is identified by the Romans as Caelus. Ouranos was dethroned by his son, Cronus.

Palamedes, the ambassador sent by Greek chieftains to urge Odysseus to join the expedition against Troy. Odysseus, pretending to be insane, yoked an ass and an ox to the plow and began to sow his land with salt. In order to test him, Palamedes placed Odysseus' son in the furrow before the plow. He was convinced that Odysseus was sane when he turned it aside to avoid striking his son.

Palladium, an image of Pallas Athene at Troy, on which the safety of the city depended. It was stolen by Odysseus and Diomedes.

Pallas (or Pallas Athene), the Greek goddess identified with Minerva. *See* **Athena.**

Pan, the god of woods, fields, and shepherds; son of Hermes and a wood nymph. He is represented as having two small horns, a flat nose, and the lower limbs of a goat. He was very fond of music, enjoyed dancing with the nymphs, and mischievously frightened people who walked through forests at night. He is identified by the Romans as Faunus.

Pandora, the first woman ever created, whom Zeus intended as a curse for mankind. Entrusted with a box containing all the evils to which flesh is heir, Pandora could not contain her curiosity about its contents and opened it. Every human ill and plague escaped into the world, leaving only "hope" in the box. "Pandora's Box," therefore, has come to mean something which appears valuable but is, in truth, a curse.

Parcae, Roman name for the Fates. *See* **Moirai.**

Paris, son of Priam, whose abduction of Helen, wife of Menelaus, was the cause of the Trojan War. Brought up as a shepherd, he married Oenone, a nymph of Mt. Ida. At the marriage of Peleus and Thetis the goddess of discord, Eris, threw a golden apple inscribed "For the fairest," among the assembled guests. When Hera, Athena, and Aphrodite each claimed the apple, Zeus thought it best to let Paris pass judgement. His choice was to be based on the bribes each offered. He decided in favor of Aphrodite, who had promised him the most beautiful woman for a wife. The fairest of women proved to be Helen, whom Paris fell in love with and took to Troy, thus causing the war wherein he killed Achilles. After Paris was wounded, he returned to Oenone, but she refused to heal the wound and he died.

Parnassus, a mountain in Phocis, dedicated to the Muses, Apollo, and Dionysus.

Pasiphae, daughter of Helios, wife of Minos, and mother of Ariadne and the Minotaur. *See* **Minos.**

Pasithea (or **Aglaia**), one of the Graces.

Patroclus, friend of Achilles who was killed in battle by Hector. When Achilles refused to fight, Patroclus, wearing the armor of his friend, led the Greeks into battle. He fought bravely but was slain. The desire to avenge his death brought Achilles back into the field at Troy.

Peleus, husband of Thetis. Zeus wanted to be Thetis' lover but heard the prophesy that the son of Thetis would be more illustrious than his father, so he gave her to Peleus. The son was Achilles. *See* **Paris.**

Pelias, son of Poseidon and uncle of Jason, who, having seized the crown from his brother during the minority of Jason, refused later to surrender it. To prevent Jason from seizing the throne, he sent him in search of the Golden Fleece. When Pelias had grown old, his daughters requested Medea to rejuvenate their father. Medea consented, realizing that this would be the means of getting revenge. As a preliminary act of rejuvenation, she persuaded them that it was necessary for them to kill their father. But instead of restoring the old man to youth, she fled the country.

Pelion, a mountain of Thessaly. In their wars against the gods, the Giants placed Pelion on Mount Ossa in order to scale the heavens with greater ease.

Pelops, son of Tantalus. He was slaughtered by his father and served to the gods at a banquet. Demeter ate part of his shoulder, but the other gods realized what they were eating. Later, he was restored to life, his shoulder was replaced with ivory, and Tantalus was sent to Tartarus in Hades (*see* **Tantalus**). Pelops won Hippodamia as his bride by defeating her father, Oenomaus, in a chariot race, in which death awaited the loser. To win the race, Pelops bribed Myrtilos to replace the linchpin on Oenomaus' chariot wheel with wax. He drowned Myrtilos following his victory, however, thus bringing a curse on his house. *See* **Atreus.**

Penelope, wife of Odysseus. She was besieged by more than a hundred suitors during her husband's absence at Troy. She firmly believed that Odysseus would return and therefore delayed a decision as long as possible. Finally she promised to make a choice when she had completed a certain robe which she was then weaving. By undoing at night what she had woven during the day, she was able to put off the suitors until Odysseus returned.

Peneus, god of a river in Thessaly and father of the nymph Daphne, who was pursued by Apollo.

Penthesilea, queen of the Amazons, killed at Troy by Achilles.

Pentheus, king of Thebes, whom his mother, Agave, and her sisters mistook for a wild boar and tore to pieces when he tried to stop a Bacchic festival.

Persephone, daughter of Demeter and Zeus, commonly referred to as Kore. Hades carried her off and married her in the lower world. (*See* **Demeter.**) When Demeter found her, Persephone could not leave Hades permanently since she had eaten in the lower world. They struck a compromise by which Persephone would spend one-third of the year with Hades and two-thirds with Demeter. Now when Persephone is in Hades, the earth is barren; when she is with Demeter, the earth blossoms. She is identified by the Romans as Proserpina.

Perseus, son of Zeus and Danae, and husband of Andromeda. He was sent by Polydectes to kill the monster Medusa. Obtaining winged shoes and Pluto's helmet which rendered him invisible, he flew to the land of the Gorgons. He found them asleep, cut off Medusa's head, and flew away with it to Seriphus, rescuing Andromeda on the way. By means of the magic Gorgon's head, he turned Polydectes and his court into stone.

Phaedra, daughter of Minos who married Theseus after he had deserted her sister Ariadne. She fell in love with her stepson, Hippolytus, but when he spurned her advances, she aroused her jealous husband to murder him. Later when the truth was learned, she committed suicide.

Phaeton, son of Helios (the Sun). He was killed by Zeus when he drove his father's chariot too near the earth and almost set the world on fire.

Philemon, husband of Baucis, who was changed into a tree. *See* **Baucis.**

Phoebus, epithet of Apollo. *See* **Apollo.**

Phrixus, son of Athamas and Nephele, who with his sister, Helle, escaped on the back of the golden ram from their father to Colchis. *See* **Athamas.**

Pleiades, the seven daughters of Atlas, who being pursued by Orion, appealed to the gods for help. Zeus transformed them into doves and placed them among the stars.

Pluto, Roman equivalent of Hades. *See* **Hades.**

Pollux, *see* **Polydeuces.**

Polydeuces, famous warrior brother of Castor known to the Romans as Pollux. *See* **Castor.**

Polyhymnia, the Muse of sacred poetry and songs.

Polynices, *see* **Eteocles.**

Polyphemus, son of Poseidon and most renowned of the Cyclopes, who rivaled Acis for the affections of Galatea. He was blinded by Odysseus and 12 members of his crew whom he had taken as prisoners.

Poseidon, Greek god of the sea, the son of Cronus and Rhea, and brother of Zeus and Hades. He was swallowed at birth by his father, but later freed by Zeus. The three gods drew lots and Poseidon received the sea as his domain. He also created the horse and is the patron of horse racing. He is usually represented as seated in a chariot drawn across the sea by horses, holding a trident in his hand. The Romans called him Neptune.

Priam, king of Troy during the Trojan War, husband of Hecuba, and father of fifty sons including Hector and Paris. In the fighting before Troy, he was killed by Neoptolemus.

Priapus, a Greek god of fertility, son of Aphrodite and Dionysus.

Prometheus, a Titan, who stole fire from heaven and gave it to man. For his crime he was chained by Zeus to a rock on Mount Caucasus, where an eagle kept tearing at his liver until he was rescued by Heracles.

Proserpina, Roman equivalent of the Greek goddess Persephone. *See* **Demeter, Persephone.**

Proteus, a sea god and soothsayer who lived in a cave on the island of Pharos. He could be made to utter his prophecies only while asleep, since at other times he could escape by changing his shape so that he could not be recognized.

Psyche, a nymph who personifies the human soul and immortality. Eros married her and visited her nightly, concealing his features from her and leaving before dawn. Contriving to see him, she lighted her lamp one night and was enraptured by his beauty. When he was awakened by a drop of oil which fell on his face from the lamp, he fled, and she wandered in search of him, incurring the jealousy of Aphrodite, who tried to thwart the lovers. Eros' prayers were answered, however, and Psyche ultimately joined him on Olympus.

Pygmalion, a sculptor who carved an ivory

statue of a woman and, falling in love with it, appealed to Aphrodite to breathe life into it. The statue came to life, and the woman, who was named Galatea, loved and married Pygmalion.

Pylades, friend of Orestes, and husband of Electra.

Pyramus, *see* **Thisbe.**

Pyrrha, wife of Deucalion, who built an ark to escape the deluge sent by Zeus to destroy the human race. They both survived and the human race was saved from extinction.

Pyrrhus, *see* **Neoptolemus.**

Python, the famous serpent of the cave of Mount Parnassus, slain by Apollo.

Ra (also **Re**), ancient Egyptian sun god and lord of the sky. He brought himself into being out of the waters, and then created all the other gods and all things in the world.

Ragnarok, *see* **Twilight of the Gods.**

Re, *see* **Ra.**

Remus, twin brother of Romulus, son of Mars and the vestal virgin Sylvia. Their mother was condemned to be buried alive. The children, set adrift on the Tiber, were rescued and suckled by a she-wolf. Later Romulus killed Remus and founded a city which he named after himself (Rome), and became its first king.

Rhadamanthus, son of Zeus and Europa, who at his death was appointed one of the three judges in Hades—Minos and Aeacus being the other two.

Rhea, goddess of the earth. Known as "Mother of the Gods", she was the wife and sister of Cronus, and mother of Zeus, Poseidon, Hades, and other gods.

Romulus, *see* **Remus.**

Round Table, originally made by Merlin, the table was the gift of King Laodegan to Arthur when Arthur married Guinevere. Its shape allowed it to seat 150 knights without giving any one a favored position. Those seated at it were known as the Knights of the Round Table.

Sangreal, *see* **Holy Grail.**

Sarpedon, son of Zeus and Europa, and one of the favorites of the gods. He fought for Troy and was slain by Patroclus.

Saturn, *see* **Cronus.**

Satyrs, woodland deities addicted to sensual pleasure and associated with the worship of Dionysus.

Scylla, a female monster which barked like a dog and had twelve feet, six necks and six heads each with three rows of teeth. She and Charybdis (*see* **Charybdis**) harassed sailors in the Straits of Messina; it was impossible to avoid the danger of one without encountering the other.

Semele, loved by Zeus, and mother of Dionysus. The jealous Hera appeared to her in the form of an old woman and persuaded Semele to ask Zeus to appear to her in all the splendor of his divinity. Semele, unable to endure the lightning of Zeus was burnt to ashes, but he rescued her unborn child, Dionysus, and sewed him into his thigh from which he was later born. Later, Dionysus went to Hades and brought Semele out to Olympus where she became immortal.

Set, brother of Osiris, and Egyptian god of storm and turmoil. Out of jealousy he murdered his brother by locking him in a wooden chest and sinking it in the Nile.

Seven Against Thebes, the seven Argive heroes—Adrastus, Polynices, Tydeus, Amphiaraus, Hippomedon, Parthenopaeus, and Capaneus—who led an expedition against Thebes to restore Polynices to the throne usurped by his brother Eteocles. Of the seven, only Adrastus survived this ill-fated expedition.

Shiva, *see* **Siva.**

Sibyl, prophetess who, when Apollo asked her what she wanted, asked to live as many years as the number of grains of sand she held in her hand. But she forgot to ask for youth and consequently shrivelled to a tiny size. When children asked her, "Sibyl, what do you want?" she could only answer with the words "I want to die."

Sibyls, women with the gift of prophecy who interceded with the gods on behalf of human supplicants.

Siegfried, a king of the Netherlands who stole the treasure of the Niebelungs. He loved Brunhild, but forgot about her and married Gudrun after having been given a magic potion. He was later killed by the brothers of Gudrun.

Silenus, a jovial old Satyr, companion and teacher of Dionysus, with a gift for prophecy.

Sirens, sea nymphs who, by their song, lured all who heard them to their death.

Sisyphus, son of Aeolus and king of Corinth who, for his avarice and trickery, was condemned in the underworld to roll a huge rock uphill which, upon reaching the top, always rolled to the bottom.

Siva (also **Shiva**), third member of the divine Hindu trinity which includes Brahma and Vishnu; he is the destroyer, but also represents aspects of regeneration. He bears the title of prince of demons.

Sol, Roman god of the sun, identified with the Greek god, Helios. See **Helios.**

Somnus, Roman god of sleep, the son of night (Nox), brother of Death (Mors) and father of Morpheus.

Sphinx, a winged monster with the body of a lion and the head and breasts of a woman. She guarded the road on the way to Thebes and asked all those who passed to solve a riddle. She killed those that failed. When Oedipus finally solved her riddle, she killed herself.

Styx, the chief river of the underworld, which flows seven times around the realm of Hades. Charon ferries the souls of the dead across it.

Tantalus, a son of Zeus and father of Pelops. For revealing his father's secrets, he was punished in Tartarus with a raging thirst. Standing under a loaded fruit tree in water up to his chin, Tantalus could never quite either grasp the fruit or drink from the water. *See* **Pelops**

Tartarus, the very lowest depths of Hades where the rebellious Titans and other heinous offenders are punished.

Telegonus, son of Odysseus and Circe. He killed Odysseus without knowing who he was. Later, he married Penelope.

Telemachus, son of Odysseus and Penelope, who went in search of his father after he failed to return from Troy.

Tereus, according to different legends, Tereus either cut out his wife Procne's tongue and married her sister, Philomela, or he dishonored Philomela and cut out her tongue so that she might not reveal his misdeed. In any case, the sisters communicated with each other and Procne killed her son Itys and served up his flesh to Tereus out of revenge. When the sisters fled, pursued by Tereus, the gods changed all three into birds: Procne, a swallow; Philomela, a nightingale; and Tereus, a hawk.

Terpsichore, the Muse of choral song and dance.

Tethys, daughter of Ouranos and wife of Oceanus.

Thalia, the Muse of comedy; also the name of one of the Graces.

Thantos, Greek personification of death, son of Nox.

Themis, one of the Titans, goddess of law and justice, who was mother by Zeus of the Moirai and the Horae. She is also the original goddess of prophecy who received the oracle of Delphi.

Theseus, son of Aegus, king of Athens, and legendary hero of Attica. His most famous exploit was the slaying of the Minotaur. He went to Crete as one of the youths whom the Athenians sent annually to Minos. Ariadne, daughter of Minos, fell in love with him, and with her help he slew the Minotaur and escaped from the Labyrinth. He took Ariadne away with him but later deserted her on the island of Naxos. Among his other adventures were the battle with the Amazons, whose queen he seized, and the abduction of Helen from Sparta to Athens, whence she was rescued by Castor and Polydeuces.

Thetis, a Nereid, wife of Peleus and mother of Achilles. *See* **Peleus.**

Thisbe, the sweetheart of Pyramus. Her parents objected to her love affair, so the lovers arranged to meet secretly one day at the tomb of Ninus. As Thisbe reached the place, she saw a lion and fled, letting her cloak fall. When Pyramus arrived and found the torn garment, he thought she had been murdered and therefore killed himself. Thisbe returned and, at the sight of her dead lover, stabbed herself.

Thor, eldest of Odin's sons, and the strongest of all men or gods. He is the Norse god of Thunder and possesses a magic hammer, a belt of strength, and a pair of iron gloves.

Thyestes, son of Pelops and brother of Atreus. See **Atreus.**

Tiresias, a Theban whom the gods blinded. In compensation for the loss of his sight, they gave him the power of prophecy.

Tisiphone, one of the three Furies.

Titans, a race of giants who preceded the Olympian gods, and waged a ten year war with Zeus in which they were ultimately conquered and imprisoned in a cavern near Tartarus.

Tithonus, son of Laomedon and brother of Priam, for whom his wife, Eos, secured immortality. Because he forgot to ask also for eternal youth, he continued to grow older until Eos changed him into a grasshopper.

Tityos, a giant punished in Hades for trying to rape Leto.

Tristram and Isolde, the subject of many medieval romances which tell of the doomed love affair between Sir Tristram, one of King Arthur's knights, and Isolde, who was the daughter of the King of Ireland and was betrothed to Tristram's uncle, King Mark of Cornwall. According to one version, Tristram is slain by Mark when he is found with his uncle's wife, and according to another, Isolde is prevented from saving Tristram's life by his jealous wife.

Triton, a divinity of the sea, a son of Poseidon, who makes the roaring of the ocean by blowing through his shell.

Trojan War, see **Troy, Paris, Helen.**

Troy, the city ruled by Priam, to which Paris brought Helen, an act which resulted in the Trojan War. It fell after the Greeks tricked the Trojans into taking a giant wooden horse, in which many soldiers were hidden, into the city.

Turnus, an Italian prince who rivaled Aeneas for the love of Lavinia and was killed by him in battle.

Twilight of the Gods (Ragnarok), according to Norse myth, the day when Loki and his followers will break their bonds and meet the gods for their final battle. All will be killed, and there will be total destruction followed by regeneration. A new earth will arise, peopled by sons of Odin, Thor, Baldur, and Hodur who will live in harmony with man in the new world created by Alfadur.

Tyndareus, husband of Leda and father of Clytemnestra and Castor; also king of Sparta.

Ulysses, see **Odysseus.**

Uranie, the Muse of astronomy.

Uranus, see **Ouranos.**

Uther, a legendary king of the Britons, who, as the result of an adulterous affair with the wife of a Duke of Cornwall, became the father of King Arthur.

Valhalla, a great hall, the beautiful dwelling place of Odin and the other Scandinavian gods. Odin feasted there daily on wine and boar's meat with all his chosen warriors who had fallen in battle.

Valkyrie, Odin's messengers; warlike virgins, armed and mounted on horses, who enlisted warriors to fight with Odin when he faced his enemy in the final battle. They took all warriors who died in battle to Valhalla.

Ve, brother of Odin and Vili; he helped create the first man and woman and gave them expression, and speech.

Venus, Roman goddess of love, and daughter of Jupiter and Dione. See **Aphrodite.**

Vesta, the Roman goddess of the hearth, identified with the Greek Hestia. See **Hestia.**

Vili, brother of Odin and Ve. He helped create the first man and woman and gave them reason and motion.

Vishnu, second member of the divine Hindu trinity, which includes Brahma and Siva. He is a popular, benevolent god; his function is preservation.

Vivien, an enchantress who, because she lived in the middle of a magic lake, was called the Lady of the Lake. She stole the infant Launcelot from his father, the King of Brittany, and is also said to have given King Arthur the gift of his sword, Excalibur, which he asked to be returned to her at his death. Merlin's mistress, she eventually trapped him in a thornbush where she keeps him asleep.

Vulcan, Roman god of fire, and son of Jupiter and Juno, who made the armor of the gods and had his workshops in volcanic mountains. See **Hephaistos.**

Wotan, the Old High German form of Odin. See **Odin.**

Zephyrus, the west wind of Spring, identified by the Romans as Favonius.

Zethus, twin brother of Amphion. He married the nymph Thebe after whom the city of Thebes was named. See **Amphion, Antiope.**

Zeus, father of gods and men, and lord of Olympus. He was brought up in a cave on Mount Ida to be safe from his father, who had swallowed all his other children. With the help of the Cyclopes he defeated Cronus and the other Titans and thus became master of the world. He gave the sea to Poseidon and the underworld to Hades, reserving heaven for himself. He is usually depicted as seated on a throne, with thunderbolts in one hand and a sceptor of cypress in the other, wearing a wreath of olive or myrtle. He was called Jupiter by the Romans.

SECRETARIES' GUIDE
AND MANUAL OF INFORMATION

THE SUCCESSFUL SECRETARY

The Secretarial Position

The secretary acts as a personal representative, responsible for accurately conveying information to her employer and accurately issuing his communications and instructions. The activities of the secretary may vary greatly from employer to employer, sometimes involving only intelligent execution of instructions and in other instances demanding considerable initiative and judgment, but the elements of tact and mediation are always apparent. This is inevitable in the modern world, where the interrelationships between business and public, and between business and business are constantly developing new ramifications. The present-day secretary plays an important role, and upon her efficiency depends much of the smooth functioning of the executive.

This does not imply that the secretary has superseded the executive, notwithstanding fictional or actual instances to the contrary. Most employers consider themselves competent to do their own thinking, and often resent any but the most subtly phrased of unsolicited or solicited suggestions, although they are quick to appreciate all assistance that lightens their tasks without challenging their authority. Secretaries who think for their employers, functioning as a kind of master mind behind a screen, are largely a product of twentieth-century fiction. The competent executive's appetite for argument and advice is usually well satisfied by conference with his colleagues and clients.

One of the most important qualifications of a proficient secretary is accuracy. It insures the employer against having to check and recheck small items in search of possible errors. It gives him a comfortable feeling of security. If he has someone he can trust, he need not clog his mind with detail.

Accuracy is more a matter of self-discipline than education. A person widely read and highly educated may frequently be guilty of inaccuracies in his thinking and in the oral or written expression of his thoughts, particularly if he makes a point of glibly rattling off answers to all questions in order to create an impression of brilliance and encyclopedic knowledge. The really accurate individual makes a very clear distinction between facts of which he is certain and notions about which he is vague or doubtful. He has schooled himself to trust and employ the former, and not to waste time trying to puzzle out the latter, especially when consultation of some recognized authority would quickly resolve his doubts.

Accuracy, however, need not and should not involve constant recourse to authorities, whether they be books, persons, or information agencies. Such recourse can become a pernicious habit, subtly undermining the individual's confidence in his every belief and assertion, until the spelling of the simplest word or the recalling of the most familiar telephone number awakens overwhelming doubts. The competent secretary does not let such unreasonable worries get the upper hand. She not only knows, but she knows that she knows. Moreover, in consulting authorities, she seeks not only to find an answer for the immediate problem,

but also, time permitting, to imprint on her own mind the information so gained, provided it seems likely to be useful a second time and is of such a nature as to be readily learned. Such intelligent use of authorities is in itself an education, rapidly building up a skeleton framework of key facts, into which further information can easily be inserted. Knowledge, if so organized, begets knowledge, since interrelated facts provide clues to each other, and are much more easily recalled than isolated facts.

It is difficult to exaggerate the importance for the secretary of such a skeleton framework, including such fields as spelling, grammar, and usage; frequently-used addresses and telephone numbers; recognized form of letters; proper methods of indexing and filing; regulations on mailing and shipping; the names and faces of individuals and their personality, occupation, and degree of importance; office procedure both general and specific; and arrangement of interviews and appointments. The executive, specialist, or scholar can and very often should forget matters of detail in order to devote his mind more completely and effectively to larger issues. Indeed, it is for this very reason that he employs a secretary. He desires to be left with as free a hand as possible and depends on his secretary to handle all minor matters with intelligence, decision, and discretion. This division of labor, when properly carried out by both parties, is a very effective one.

The secretary should never, unless it is absolutely unavoidable, question the employer on matters of detail. Such questioning amounts to a confession that she doesn't know her job, and is especially irritating to the employer because it forces him to think about the very problems of which he wishes to be relieved.

In matters of knowledge and accuracy the requirements of the stenographer are similar to those of the secretary, except that the activities of the former are necessarily limited to a narrower field. Shorthand and typing are usually the sole occupations of the stenographer. To the secretary they are a type of equipment that she is able to use with great facility to accomplish her wider and more varied duties.

The duties of the secretary are not only more complicated and numerous than those of the stenographer; they involve greater responsibility and flexibility, and a significant personal element. The stenographer works with words; the secretary with people. In this connection the quality of restraint or unobtrusiveness, though not preeminent, is especially characteristic and undeniably important.

The successful secretary does not obviously impose her personality on her surroundings, but has a way of shading into the background. She cultivates a soft but distinct voice, a quiet but capable manner. Her style of dressing is pleasing to the eye but usually simple and neat, and, above all, suited to the type of establishment in which she is working. Tact and discretion are habitual to her. She is self-effacing —but never hesitant or shy, for she knows that such tactics are out of place in the office, immediately making her a bother rather than a help. At conferences and interviews she maintains a thoroughly impersonal attitude, which facilitates matters and avoids embarrassment. She manages to do this without appearing bored or aloof.

The nature of the secretarial function puts an unusually great premium on discretion and restraint. Inevitably the secretary comes to know a great many matters—many of which are confidential—concerning the firm and employer for whom she is working. Her position as a personal representative makes it dangerously easy for her to pass on private information about her immediate employer to the staff, and about members of the staff to her employer. Both of these activities can easily become unethical and damaging. The accomplished secretary avoids them; by establishing a reputation for discretion, she gains the cooperation of her colleagues. She also makes it possible for her employer to think, talk, plan, and thrash matters out freely, without feeling a need for caution in her presence and a fear of subsequent ridicule. She becomes a kind of business confidant. In so doing, she advances her status greatly and is better able to play the role of trusted assistant, leaving her employer free to consider major problems.

Ease and Efficiency

The personal qualities of a successful secretary cannot be singled out of her personality, for actually they are all interdependent. For example, accuracy, knowledge, self-discipline, and confidence go hand in hand; one cannot exist without at least something of the others. In the successful personality all qualities are well integrated.

The same is true of ease and efficiency. It is difficult to do things easily without doing them efficiently, and it is difficult to be truly efficient if nervous and tense. Naturally, a person cannot relax while learning a new job. At such times the mind is constantly active—learning, experimenting, testing, watching itself for errors. Even at such a time too much tenseness represents energy wasted. Once the groundwork of the job is learned, it is possible to devote more time to doing it smoothly. Matters of routine become a habit, and the mind is free for other considerations.

In the swiftly changing world of business, surprises are the rule. The secretary, whose tasks are usually so numerous that her work is never done, must be ready to meet all kinds of demands on her time. Correspondence to be read, letters to be typed, incoming and outgoing telephone calls, dictation, arranging of appointments and conferences, inquiries and instructions—all may descend upon her at once. She is expected to handle them all dexterously and without losing her poise.

The proficient secretary is busy but never preoccupied. She shifts smoothly from one job to another without hesitation because she knows which action takes precedence. When the telephone rings, she does not desperately attempt to finish several lines of typing before answering it —nor does she necessarily break off nervously in the middle of a word. By rigorous self-discipline she learns to leave a piece of work in the middle and come back to it with a minimum loss of time. If she is called upon to do so many things at once that she begins to forget some of them—and that can happen to the most skillful secretary—she takes care of the most pressing matters first and then turns her attention to the others.

Such efficiency is largely a matter of following a routine, and an effective and time-saving routine comprises two chief elements: good habits and the ability to make plans. Habit is what enables an individual to perform a task with a minimum of conscious thought. Any action that is repeated sufficiently becomes a habit: walking is a habit; dancing or typing may become habits. Saying "Good morning" to certain individuals and walking down one side of a street rather than another are matters of habit. But not all habits are desirable ones. In learning to use the typewriter,

for example, the "hunt and peck" system can become just as habitual as the touch system. A stenographer may learn to consult the dictionary automatically when confronted by an unfamiliar word, but she may also learn to become so dependent on the dictionary as to seriously limit her ability; both are habits. Saying "Hello" when answering the telephone may become a habit, although the word "Hello" is usually a waste of time, since it tells nothing and must be immediately followed by an explanation as to who is saying "Hello." In short, habit alone is not enough. Before allowing any action to become habitual, one should ask, "Is it an efficient and smooth-flowing action, performed in the fewest number of moves? Will it be an asset to my personality, or just an unnecessary burden? Is it a shortcut, or the long way around?" Thoughts, too, can become as habitual as actions: the mind develops its stereotyped patterns, which may be either helps or hindrances. In these matters, every person must be his own efficiency expert. Business and secretarial schools, of course, inculcate into the individual a groundwork of efficient habits, but the work does not end there. Every time a new routine is learned or an old routine is changed, careful thought must be devoted to habit-building. Question each procedure thoroughly as to its advantages and disadvantages.

The ability to make plans—the other element of an effective routine—demands clear thinking. Every executive has some method of arranging his day's work and that of his secretary. The first hour of the morning may be devoted to reading and answering correspondence; then interviews may be held with members of the staff, followed by interviews with salesmen and other outsiders, each task being handled at a definite time. But there is no such thing as a foolproof and unalterable routine. Interruptions are always coming up. Pressing matters must be given a special time allotment or shoved ahead. The day's routine must be rearranged again and again. Much of the responsibility for such tasks as postponing interviews without hurting feelings, or seeing that essential business is handled by an employer deep in conference, falls on the secretary. To plan a routine calls only for careful deliberation, but to break a routine and replace it with a new one on short notice demands ingenuity and quick thinking.

Dealing with People

The good secretary is well liked. Visitors to the office recall her courteous, cheerful manner, her intelligent considerateness, and her smile. Fellow employees value her helpful cooperation. As for her employer, he depends on her in a number of ways, not only in business dealings but sometimes in social matters as well. It is part of her job to create a good impression, and to establish and maintain friendly relations.

The business world moves at high speed. The office building hums with activity. Executives are drawn together by a complex web of letters, telephone calls, conversations, and agreements. Transactions are set underway whose success depends on the swift and efficient functioning of each employee, from the highest to the most subordinate. In this fast-moving world, confusions, misunderstandings, delays, and other manifestations of poor cooperation prove costly. Yet it is all too easy for an individual to develop a hurried, nervous tempo of working, no more efficient than a burst of speed by a high-powered auto in heavy traffic. Obviously, greater smoothness in personal relations and functioning is very important.

The secretary is a vital part of this swiftly moving scene and her position enables her to obtain a perspective of the entire picture. Since she is, among other things, a mediator, she is in a good position to help the office function smoothly.

She can make it easier for people to cooperate. She can help to keep those with whom she comes in contact in good humor, soften their disappointments, increase their enthusiasm. She can do her best to smooth over difficulties, lessen intraoffice jealousies, and avoid gaining the reputation of gossip and office spy.

The good secretary has developed the qualities of ease and efficiency and is therefore able to relax to a certain degree during her work; by doing this she makes it easier for others to relax. She does not "fight against" her job, wasting time in worry and bitterness, but makes her work a part of her life. She promotes a similarly healthy attitude in others.

To be able to do all this, the secretary must be an expert at personal relations. A great deal has been written about the art of handling people. Psychologists, authors, homespun philosophers, and "business experts" of varying intelligence and ability have told the world how to make "friends," conciliate enemies, and develop an irresistible personality. Their copious advice can usually be reduced to one central principle: that any human being is somewhat egotistical and likes to feel important. Therefore, he likes the sound of his own name; he likes to be reminded of his success and good points; he likes to be remembered and to feel that people have affection for him; he likes compliments, provided they are not too obviously flattering; he likes to think that his ideas and suggestions receive serious attention. He does not like to remember his failures and failings; he does not like to admit he's wrong or give up an untenable position in an argument, unless there is a graceful "out"; he fears sarcasm; he is jealous of success; and he does not like to be forgotten. All this is, of course, very true, as the secretary who understands anything of human nature is well aware; and she must also know how to make use of this knowledge. However, a human being is more than a self-centered, jealous child, and there is a limit to the use that can be made of methods for handling people by flattery, facile enthusiasm, and general heartiness. Sincerity, courtesy, and unforced human interest—natural rather than artificial qualities—are more important.

Another important consideration is that all individuals are different. Each has his own quirks and idiosyncracies. The methods that work with one will not necessarily work with another. The good secretary is a student of individual human nature, and learns more than names and faces and occupations. She discovers the things that please and displease the people with whom she comes in contact; she comes to know their strong and weak points. Above all, she studies the personality of her employer with a concentrated interest. His habits in giving dictation; his attitude toward salesmen; his tendencies to hurry through certain matters and linger over others, are all matters of importance to her. She discovers the extent to which he wishes her to make changes in the form of his letters, or rearrange materials on his desk. This study is for the most part a silent one, conducted by observation rather than questions, yet it is of vital importance. It enables the secretary to handle her work in the way her employer would like to see it handled, and, by adjusting her personality to his, to serve her employer most satisfactorily.

OFFICE ROUTINE

An effective office routine is based on common sense. It is no different from the routine used by a clear thinking and efficient individual in his personal affairs, except that it has greater scope and is adapted to the needs of a business and the workers who compose it. An orderly individual makes memoranda of approaching tasks and appointments; keeps a careful watch on bills, checks, and bank statements; files away important letters, documents, and receipts in such a fashion that he can find them again easily; makes careful plans before traveling; and in general tries to dispatch the business of life with a minimum of bother and error. The same is true of an efficient office. Time is a precious commodity, and hours saved can be devoted effectually to more important efforts.

This does not mean that all office routines are perfect. In some there is the hampering red tape and "system for system's sake." In others carelessness and laxity are conspicuous. It *does* mean, however, that an effective routine is intelligible to anyone who has common sense and is acquainted with the business in question. If things are done in a certain way, there is usually a sound reason. If certain rules are enforced and precautions taken, they are usually necessary. If a person wishes to understand any phase of office routine, he should try to determine the reason for it. A new worker may have to follow some routines blindly until he gets a chance to think them out, but, in the long run, common sense understanding proves more valuable than automatic, unreasoned obedience. This is especially true for the secretary, from whom a large degree of initiative is frequently expected.

There is, of course, some variation in method from office to office. Each business has its own individual problems, and each executive his own ideas about efficiency. Nevertheless, business organizations have many general principles of operation in common. They are all part of the same economic order, and the laws of common sense hold true for all of them.

The Secretary's Work

The secretary is an important figure in a business office. She performs a variety of duties, many of them demanding independent thought and decision. Her treatment of callers and handling of business letters help to establish the tone of a firm. She is largely responsible for the smooth functioning of the executive or executives to whom she may be specially assigned. Her position is that of an important minor hub, around which the wheels of office routine revolve.

The secretary, although she must usually be a good stenographer, is much more than that. The stenographer takes dictation and transcribes it on the typewriter. She is judged by her reliability, accuracy, and speed. Her work, though essential, is decidedly limited when compared with that of the secretary.

The term secretary is a flexible one. It is applied to the general clerical, stenographic assistant and receptionist of the individual executive or professional man. Such a secretary may sometimes be shared between two or more executives, performing similar services for each. In committees, institutions, clubs, and other nonbusiness organizations the term secretary is frequently applied to an important individual who performs all the actual work necessary to execute orders and decrees. This is somewhat similar to the secretary in the small office, who may be responsible for all office routine, or to the general secretary of a large office, who may have some of the duties of an office manager.

There are certain types of work which the business office secretary will almost certainly be called upon to perform. These are: (1) opening and sorting incoming mail; (2) taking dictation; (3) transcribing shorthand or machine dictation;

(4) dispatching outgoing mail; (5) filing letters and other materials; (6) making appointments; (7) handling callers and telephone calls; and (8) running errands. There are many other types of work, however, that the secretary may also be called upon to learn and execute, among them the following: (1) the arrangement, in part, of her employer's schedule; (2) reading mail and drafting replies to routine letters; (3) organizing and managing one or more filing systems and indexes; (4) reviewing and clipping articles from periodicals and newspapers; (5) interviewing callers; (6) planning itineraries; (7) ordering office supplies; (8) handling petty cash, stamps, etc.; (9) making bank deposits; (10) writing checks and paying bills; and (11) checking bank statements.

The secretary may also be responsible for holding the petty cash box and keeping the petty cash account.

Few secretaries have to perform all these duties. Some, on the other hand, may be expected to handle these and more. One cannot list all possible duties, since each business may have special ones attached to it. The secretary attempting to master her job and improve her efficiency has three reliable guides: the instructions of her employer, her experience, and her common sense. This section is intended as an introduction to those secretarial duties which are common to many offices.

Adjusting to a New Job

When the secretary is acquainting herself with the routine of a new position, it is a good idea for her to make a list of all tasks required, with memoranda of detailed procedures involved in the more important work. Her employer has a daily schedule, which it may become her duty to arrange, and she ought to keep a similar daily schedule for herself, with reminders of future work. She should also make a list of essential telephone numbers, and of the names of individuals and firms with which her employer comes in contact. Many of these things will soon become a part of her memory, but lists are always very helpful.

Good work cannot be done in unpleasant or uncomfortable surroundings. The responsibility for such matters lies chiefly with the employer. Nevertheless, the new secretary should keep her desk neat and clean, adjust her chair to the most comfortable height, and do whatever else she can to improve her working conditions. Her employer will appreciate this, since it increases her efficiency.

The following outline of the duties of the secretary is arranged for convenience in the order in which the tasks might ordinarily occur during the day.

The Executive's Schedule

The working hours of the modern executive must be apportioned carefully if he is to discharge his duties efficiently and advance the interests of his firm. For this purpose a series of written memoranda, entered on a desk pad or file cards, is much more reliable than memory. Many secretaries are responsible for such memoranda, and all secretaries should become familiar with the system their employers use.

The executive's schedule contains two types of entries: (1) reminders of daily appointments and other important nonroutine business; (2) "ticklers" or reminders that preparations should be made for matters that are coming up shortly, such as taxes or bills requiring payment, conferences at which a report or set of suggestions will have to be produced, or interviews necessitating special preparation. A "tickler"—so-called because it is intended to jog or "tickle" the memory—is entered on the schedule a suitable number of days before the coming event to which it refers.

If it is taken care of, it is crossed off the schedule. If not, a similar entry is made for the following day, and so on until it is taken care of. Naturally reminders and ticklers are usually both entered on the same schedule, since they are closely related.

Whether such entries are made on desk pads, index cards, or in folders depends on their number and complexity. In any case the executive almost always keeps a desk pad, frequently divided into sections for each hour of the working day, on which both he and the secretary enter his daily appointments. Such a pad is handy to use, since appointments may be entered at the moment they are made. Tickler entries may also be made on the desk pad, but are usually kept on a separate pad or set of cards.

Too often the sheets of desk pads are torn off and discarded. As these sheets are a valuable record, some form of desk pad should be used which allows the sheets to be turned under or to one side from day to day.

The secretary often finds it advisable to keep a desk pad of her own, on which are entered those things that she has been delegated to do and the things of which she is to remind her employer. The competent secretary has the knack of writing entries in a form that is clear and concise. It is unnecessary, for example, to preface each entry with the phrase "Remember to . . ." But no entry should be so brief as to be puzzling when referred to again after a few hours or days.

A tickler file consists of a set of cards, usually about thirty in number, one for each day of the month. At the end of each day, the card for that day is taken out and filed elsewhere. Before this is done, however, the entries are either crossed off or transferred to the card for the following day. At the same time a new card is added at the end of the file, thus keeping the number of cards in the file constant.

Another type of tickler file consists of a set of folders, again one for each day. Each folder contains notations of coming events and the papers, such as tax bills, inventory forms, and letters, which bear on them. This is a convenient system for the executive, permitting him to lay his hands on the pertinent documents without delay.

Handling Incoming Mail

In a small organization one person may open and sort all the mail. In a large organization mail for executives may be handled only by their secretaries. In either case, it is essential the mail be opened in such a way that there is little chance of tearing the contents or of throwing away enclosures with the envelopes. When the contents have been shaken away from the end to be opened, the envelope is slit with a paper knife. After the contents have been removed, the envelope may be cut on three sides and the interior examined to prevent the loss of enclosures, which should be clipped to the covering letter.

An entire delivery of mail should be opened at one time. After the letters have been opened, they should be sorted according to the nature of their contents. The custom of the office will determine the precise method of sorting, just as it will decide whether the secretary is to open letters marked "personal" or "confidential." As a rule advertisements and circulars are grouped together, orders are collected into another group, and routine correspondence is placed in a category by itself. Personal mail and letters requiring special handling are separated from all other groups.

In a small office the secretary who opens the mail usually distributes it among the individuals concerned. In a large office where the secretary is serving one executive, all the mail is placed on his desk, arranged according to the order of its importance, with the most urgent business at the top. Ordinarily the circulars and advertisements, being least important, would be placed at the bottom.

Some secretaries may be required to read incoming mail carefully, underline important matters to bring them to the executive's attention, and answer routine letters.

Taking Dictation

Success in taking dictation depends primarily on a thorough knowledge of shorthand and English, but the ability of the stenographer and the person giving dictation to work together smoothly is also of vital importance. The stenographer—or secretary doing stenographic work— should behave in a manner that is tactful, thoughtful, courteous, and businesslike. She should sit facing the person giving dictation, her notebook supported on the desk or some other firm surface. Most businessmen do not like to dictate to a person whose attention seems to be concentrated elsewhere. Neither do they like to have their flow of thought interrupted by a person who habitually anticipates words or constantly interrupts. The competent stenographer shows an intelligent interest in the executive's words.

The secretary prepares to take dictation as soon as she has finished opening and sorting the mail. Notebooks and sharpened pencils should always be kept in the same, readily accessible place, so that there will be no delay in reporting for dictation. Several pencils should be taken into the executive's office, so that the breaking of a pencil point will not cause loss of time. Filled pages in the notebook should be fastened together with a rubber band, which makes it easier to find the proper beginning page. Notes and notebooks should always be conspicuously dated, in case the executive wishes to make a quick reference to past dictation. Most offices require all stenographers to keep a file of their filled notebooks for at least one year. Even when this is not an office rule, it is a good practice, since stenographers' notebooks are a valuable record of past business transactions.

If, when taking dictation, the stenographer misses words or finds them confused, she may call attention to the matter by repeating the last word or phrase spoken. Or she may mark uncertain portions of her notes, and ask questions about them when the piece of dictation is finished. Pauses during dictation may be utilized in adding to and completing notes, and in reading through those which have been taken. Such readings help to fix the meaning of the notes and make the task of transcription easier. If a visitor enters the room and the executive breaks off dictating, it is customary for the stenographer to leave, unless specifically requested to remain.

Special attention should be given during dictation to dates, numbers, and unfamiliar names. Since accuracy is essential, the person giving dictation should allow the stenographer time to write these out in full.

If the dictation is too rapid, it is perfectly permissible for the secretary to request a more moderate pace. Most executives prefer such requests and questions about wording rather than spoiled stationary and time wasted through enforced retyping.

Transcribing Shorthand

No system of shorthand is infallible in practice. Therefore shorthand notes cannot be transcribed automatically. Constant exercise of thought and judgment is necessary. It is a good idea to read each letter quickly before beginning to type it, in order to get a general idea of the contents. Then each sentence should be read for meaning and consistency before being typed out. This avoids erasures. It is wise

to check dates and names against either enclosures or previous correspondence. Meaningless or ridiculous sentences should be questioned; otherwise retyping will obviously be necessary. Doubtful material should be questioned, or at least indicated by a lightly penciled question mark in the margin. The extent to which the stenographer may correct or improve wording depends entirely on the office and executive. In any case, she should watch out for excessive verbiage and words awkwardly repeated, since many dictators, when groping for words, tend to throw in unnecessary phrases.

In doing transcription, immediate attention should be given to telegrams and special instructions. Such notes should be prominently marked to distinguish them from the others. Telegrams should be transcribed and sent before letters are transcribed.

The transcriber should not hesitate to consult the dictionary and other authoritative works when in doubt. It is essential that the letter be cast in a proper form and effectively arranged on the page, and that the rules of proper spelling and good English be followed. For information on the form, arrangement, style, and content of business letters, the reader is referred to the section LETTER WRITING.

Unless otherwise instructed, the transcriber should always make at least one carbon copy of each letter, usually for filing with correspondence. Sometimes additional carbon copies will be needed, especially in the case of orders and instructions. If more than four carbon copies are to be made on a manual typewriter, a hard platen should be used; otherwise the lower carbons will not be legible.

Before submitting letters for signature, the transcriber should assure herself that they make sense, and that the typing is mechanically correct. The work of a good typist differs radically from that of an amateur. In addition to speed, it shows accuracy, uniformity of impression (all the characters being struck with equal force, so that they are alike in degree of density), and a pleasing arrangement of lines and margins.

Copy Typing

It is always possible to make mistakes when transcribing shorthand notes or in interpreting the words of a person giving dictation, but in copying materials already typed or printed the secretary is expected to do a perfect job. There is no excuse for mistaking definite words and characters.

Since such copies are usually of documents, contracts, and letters received, absolute accuracy is essential. Copies should always be headed by the word "Copy" in parentheses, and any signatures should be preceded by "signed," also in parentheses. Unless the secretary is instructed otherwise, all apparent errors in the original should be copied faithfully. It is a common practice, however, to place an asterisk (*) after such errors and, at the bottom of the page, another asterisk, followed by a footnote explaining that the error occurs in the original. In the most strict variety of this work, such as that performed in legal offices, it may be necessary to copy line for line and page for page. All copy typing should be proofread against the original for errors.

Typing clean copies of rough drafts made by someone in the firm is quite a different matter, and the secretary is usually permitted to make corrections in spelling and grammar. If the meaning of some phrase cannot be determined, she should not hesitate to consult the writer.

Drafting Letters

In some offices it is part of the secretary's job to prepare replies to routine letters. She should learn to decide quickly which letters are routine and which are not. Her answers should be clearly reasoned and to the point. The general instructions contained in the section LETTER WRITING should be followed. According to the common procedure, she submits her replies to her employer for reading or signature at the same time that she shows him the incoming letters. This arrangement saves time.

Handling Outgoing Mail

Presuming that the letter has been typed and read, and the envelope typed, there are still certain precautions that the secretary should automatically take. She should make sure that the address on the envelope is identical with that given in the letter. She should assure herself that the letter has been signed. Finally, she should glance through the letter to ascertain what enclosures should be included, and then check the enclosures accordingly.

The letter should be neatly folded so that it occupies most of the envelope but leaves ample space for opening the letter without danger of tearing the contents. Small supplementary folds made at the last minute have an ugly and untidy appearance. There is no excuse for them. The secretary should determine beforehand the best way of folding the different sizes of paper used in her office. Enclosures should usually be clipped to the letter, in order to avoid being lost. If pressure must be applied in sealing an envelope, it is advisable to place a sheet of paper over the flap, in order to avoid smudges. Postage should be affixed securely, after it has been checked for correct value.

To expedite business transactions, it is important that letters be mailed promptly. The accomplished secretary knows the times at which letters are collected from the box used by her office, and plans the mailing of batches of letters accordingly. If speed is essential, letters may be sent straight to the main postoffice, and letters or packages may be sent direct to local destinations by messenger.

Detailed information on postal regulations, classes of mail, and services is contained in the section POSTAL INFORMATION to which the reader is referred.

Filing Systems

In an efficient office, all materials pertaining to business transactions are made readily available for reference by a suitable filing system. The backbone of the system is almost always a correspondence file, consisting of folders, one for each separate firm or individual with whom there are business dealings—customers, creditors, manufacturers, and advertising agencies. Each folder contains letters received from the firm in question, carbon copies of letters sent in reply, and other pertinent documents, such as advertising matter and reports on interviews and conferences. The contents of each folder are arranged in the order of their dates, and therefore tell a complete, coherent story of vital importance to a businessman wishing to review for one purpose or another the stages in a set of transactions.

The secretary may be responsible for keeping such a file in order and up to date. She should file carbon copies of the letters which she has written for her employer. She may frequently be called upon to find material in the files.

The arrangement of items (folders, in the case of the correspondence file) is almost always alphabetical. There is a detailed discussion of this method in the section FILING BY ALPHABET. Other arrangements include the geographical, in which firms are grouped by regions, a method convenient for sales campaigns and distributions; the numerical; and the Dewey Decimal Classification, familiar in libraries. The latter method is seldom used in business offices.

Cardboard guides are used to separate the folders in a file. These guides bear identification tabs, which facilitate locating the material.

A large file is generally accompanied by a card index, in which each folder is represented by a corresponding card bearing the name of the firm or individual. If a firm is known by several different names, or different forms of the same name, there are cross reference cards; as, for example, "Corrugated Box and Fiberboard, Inc. Look under: Midwestern Corrugated Box and Fiberboard." Or "Antiquarian Society of America. See American Antiquarian Society." Similar cross reference cards would be used if the correspondence for two related firms happened to be filed in the same folder. Use of an index eliminates time wasted in long searches through the bulkier files. For a small file, however, an index is seldom worth the time necessary to maintain it.

There are many supplementary files and indexes used in business offices. These may include mailing lists, lists of customers and prospective customers, files of newspaper and magazine clippings, legal documents, receipts, orders, employee records, and indexes of references to books. In large offices each executive maintains an individual file of matters pertaining to his special province, and this file is usually kept in order by his private secretary.

A mailing list of any size is best kept on a series of cards, one for each firm or individual, rather than on typewritten sheets. Names can then be added to or dropped from the list without the need for a lengthy retyping and without disturbing the convenient alphabetical order. For similar reasons, card indexes of the names of customers and "prospects" are advisable. These may also be classified according to the item in which the customer is most interested, cards of a different color being used for this purpose; for example, a firm dealing in hardware might list purchasers of kitchen utensils on green cards, purchasers of tools on yellow cards, and general purchasers on white cards. Then if a special sales campaign for one type of product were undertaken, the appropriate cards could quickly be removed from the file.

There are certain general suggestions to follow for efficient filing:

1. A file or index is only valuable if kept up to date. Otherwise it is a source of error and confusion. When a firm changes its name or address, a new card should be made out immediately, and correspondence transferred to a new folder.

2. Care should be taken to list firms according to their complete, official name.

3. If there is doubt as to where an item should most properly be filed, the quickest thing to do is to file it arbitrarily in one place and then make out a number of cross reference cards.

4. Prior to being filed, material may be kept in a general "suspense folder." However, the contents of the suspense folder should be filed as soon as possible; otherwise it will quickly become larger than the file itself. Instead of a single suspense folder, several may be used, one for each type of material, thus allowing for a certain amount of preliminary filing.

5. It is advisable to have a definite charge-out procedure, to guard against the loss of materials and to facilitate location of materials temporarily out of the files. Out guides, out folders, and substitution cards are the most familiar aids in charge-out systems. When materials or folders are removed from the files, one of these aids is used to replace it. On it is noted a record of by whom the material was borrowed and when. If the entire contents of a folder must be borrowed, the original folder should be kept in the file and the materials should be given to the borrower in a

new, properly labeled folder. Any material received subsequent to the loan may then be filed in the original folder, eliminating the risk of misplacement of new materials before the borrowed ones are returned to the file.

6. Letters and other related papers are less bulky if stapled rather than clipped together.

7. Bulky material, such as catalogs, samples, and pamphlets, should be kept in a separate file or case, with cross reference cards indicating the location.

8. The drawers of a filing cabinet should be kept closed when not in immediate use, and locked when the office is empty.

9. The materials most frequently referred to should be kept where most easily reached, usually in the upper file drawers rather than in those next to the floor.

10. If several different folder files are in use in an office, it is well to mark the folders constituting each file with tabs of the same color, thus preventing folders from being returned to the wrong file.

The Treatment of Callers

If a caller does not have an appointment, it is the secretary's duty to learn the nature of his business. This she does in a polite and cordial manner. Although in many cases she may have to consult with her employer, usually she must decide, on the basis of her experience, whether the caller's business is such as to require her employer's attention or might better be handled by someone else. If the business should be handled by her employer and he is busy at the time, she may arrange for a later appointment. The secretary should do her best to lighten the visitor's disappointment and send him away in a good humor if he cannot be granted an interview.

Many employers wish their secretaries to act as buffers between them and callers they are unable or unwilling to see. Secretaries in this rather uncomfortable position are required to exercise a good deal of tact and patience. A secretary who can perform such a difficult task well, and who, in addition, can transact business with routine callers without referring them to her employer at all, is a very great asset to a business.

Many offices keep a daily list of callers, each entry ordinarily including the name of the caller, his business connection, and the errand on which he called. The lists are usually filed and retained as a semipermanent record.

The handling of telephone calls is essentially the same as the handling of callers. In both cases the secretary's duty is to learn the caller's business in as brief and courteous a way as possible, and then to refer the call in the manner determined by her experience. A cheerful voice creates a good impression. If a call must be kept waiting for some time before being answered by the person to whom it is referred, it is a good idea for the secretary to make occasional reassuring remarks so that the caller will not feel he has been forgotten or slighted. It is a good practice to keep a list of telephone calls similar to the list of those who call in person.

Appointments and Itineraries

In addition to scheduling her employer's day at the office, the secretary may be required to make arrangements for his time spent outside the office—such as visits to other firms or extended trips for sales and conferences. For this purpose it is desirable that she have a good working knowledge of local transportation facilities, general traveling conditions, and her employer's personal preferences in such matters. Naturally she should consult him when in doubt, but if she performs her task sensibly and efficiently, he will come to rely greatly on her judgment.

In making appointments, courtesy and the dignity of her firm are important considerations. Where possible, appointments should be definite rather than tentative, and arranged by one phone call rather than several.

An appointment broken or delayed often results in upsetting important plans. If an appointment must be broken, notification should be given at the earliest possible moment, with an explanation. An immediate attempt should be made to set up a new appointment.

There are certain hours of the working day during which an executive can best afford to be absent from the office. Such hours, often those of the afternoon, are most suitable for outside appointments. It is often expedient to combine business and social engagements by having a meeting during luncheon.

Before leaving for his appointment, the employer will usually want to refresh his mind by going over recent notes and correspondence concerning the person he is going to meet. Therefore, the appropriate folder should be brought to his attention, with notes on plans or proposals that he may wish to discuss.

Preparing an itinerary for an extended trip is a more complicated task, and usually involves the purchase of airline tickets, making hotel reservations, and making appointments in advance by letter or telephone. Very often the secretary will rely, to an extent, on the advice of a travel agent, but she must be careful to adopt an arrangement suited to her employer's preferences and convenience. It is wise for her to have timetables on hand, though great care should be taken to renew these whenever there is a change of schedules.

All arrangements should be confirmed by telephone or letter. Hotel reservations may be made by letter or through the local reservation service provided by many hotel systems, but written confirmation should always be requested. The accomplished secretary familiarizes herself with the travel and hotel facilities in those regions to which her employer's business interests are likely to carry him.

Economy of time and movement are essential points to be considered in planning itineraries. If several cities are to be visited, appointments should be made in such an order as to involve the least amount of traveling.

After the itinerary has been arranged, it should be drawn up on paper. A brief itinerary may indicate only the hours of arrival and departure, including, of course, the name of the airline and the flight number. A more complete itinerary indicates hotel reservations, time and place of appointments, names of individuals to be met, notes on matters to be discussed, plans and suggestions, subsidiary matters to be taken up if there is time available, and local transportation arrangements. Such an itinerary is chiefly for the convenience of the traveler, but copies should always be kept at the office. Then it will be possible to get in touch with the traveler if any important instructions or periodic reports are to be forwarded to him.

The secretary may pack for the traveler a special folder containing such office supplies as blank letterhead paper, plain paper, notebooks and pencils if there will be occasion to use them.

Care of Office Equipment

Secretaries are not usually mechanics, and they are not expected to repair their own typewriters. They are, however, supposed to clean and oil them in accordance with the manufacturer's instructions. The ability of the secretary to turn out good work depends largely on remembering to change the ribbon of her machine and cleaning its type whenever necessary. The care of office equipment involves covering typewriters, adding machines, and other office machines at the end of the working day, and dusting desks and office equipment at regular intervals. The interior portions of typewriters may be dusted effectively with a narrow, long-handled brush.

The secretary is often her employer's business housekeeper. In many offices the appearance of his desk is as much her responsibility as is the taking of his dictation. However, she should never rearrange his desk without determining whether that is agreeable to him.

Ordering Supplies

It may also be part of the secretary's duties to order office supplies. These usually include: letterheads; carbon paper; second sheets for carbon copies; envelopes, both blank and with the firm's name and address; postage; stenographic notebooks; memorandum pads; index cards; file folders; labels; tabs; bank deposit slips; pencils; pens; erasers for pencil, ink, and typewriter; clips; staples; pins; typewriter ribbons; oil for typewriter; paste; and transparent mending tape. In a large office she is more often required to requisition supplies from another department of the firm. In either case, it is her business to see that the quantities on hand are always adequate. Supplies should never be ordered in such quantities, however, that they deteriorate before use.

Bank Accounts

The handling of a bank account involves three chief operations: (1) making deposits; (2) writing checks and paying bills, (3) checking bank statements.

Checks issued and deposits made should always be entered in the stub portion of the check book, with the subtractions and additions made immediately so that the exact balance may be ascertained at a glance.

If possible, bills should be paid by check. When this is impossible, a receipt should be obtained for the cash disbursed. All offices have a procedure for verifying bills before paying them. These procedures always include verification of quantity, quality, and specifications; the checking of credit allowances and discounts; and the checking of the arithmetic of the bill.

When the bank statement and cancelled checks for the previous period are received from the bank, the secretary should go over them carefully. Checking a bank statement involves these processes:

1. The cancelled checks should be checked against the stubs in the check book and the withdrawal items on the bank statement.

2. The deposit items on the bank statement should be checked against the deposits recorded in the check book.

3. The total of deposits should be added to the balance on hand when the bank statement covering the preceding period was reconciled; from this figure the total of the checks issued during the period should be deducted. The amount then arrived at should equal the balance shown on the bank statement and that in the check book, provided there were no deposits in transit and no outstanding checks at the date of the bank statement. Any deposits in transit should be added to, and any outstanding checks should be deducted from, the balance given on the bank statement; the result should equal the balance in the check book less any bank charges.

The Large Office

The routine of a large office has certain special characteristics setting it off from that of a small office. As a result of the difference in size, the number of tasks are multiplied. The proper execution of such a complex routine is far beyond the powers of one secretary of general ability, or even several. Specialization is essential, each employee concentrating on a few steps in a highly complicated process. Even the work of the private secretary is usually limited to that entailed in serving one executive or a small group in a specialized field.

This specialization, though inescapable, brings up certain difficulties seldom found in small offices. Greater dependence must be placed on a carefully planned routine. Yet the specialized office worker performing only one task has difficulty in understanding the function of his work and seeing it in the proper perspective, and when tasks are performed by many individuals instead of one or two, there is a correspondingly greater chance for misunderstanding, error, and confusion.

To offset this disadvantage, many large offices make a practice of shifting workers from one task to another, so that they will gain a greater understanding of the whole routine and be better able to detect errors. Some workers resent being assigned to new tasks. They dislike the added mental effort involved and think it merely a matter of whim. Actually they should welcome such opportunities and look upon them as training for promotion. This is even more true when individuals are shifted from department to department, spending a certain amount of time in production work, advertising, merchandising, sales work, and distribution. Such varied training is a frequent preliminary to advancement. The wider your knowledge, the better are your chances for promotion.

It must always be remembered that the large general office should be an adjusting mechanism between the other departments, which have a less flexible sort of work and must struggle with external factors—the production department with machines and materials, the distribution department with transportation facilities, the sales department with general business conditions and consumers' demands. Unfortunately some office administrators consider that their job is to exercise authority and direct the activities of all other departments. This mistaken authoritarianism is largely an inheritance from the days of smaller businesses, when one or a few individuals personally supervised all activities. Proper office administration coordinates activities, smooths out difficulties, avoids interdepartmental difficulties, and in all ways acts as an adjusting mechanism. Therefore the more flexible the individual worker is and the better he is acquainted with other jobs besides his own, the better he will be able to serve his employer and himself.

LETTER WRITING

The Importance of Good Business Letters

For many secretaries, few tasks are as important or consume as much time as the writing of business letters. Some secretaries are expected merely to transcribe the letters dictated to them, with due attention to correctness and appearance; others have the additional responsibility of determining the wording of letters. Since secretaries are judged largely by the quality of their letters, they should become thoroughly familiar both with the effective use of English, and with correct business letter usage in the arrangement of parts, spelling, punctuation, and related subjects treated in this office manual.

Secretaries will sense the importance of this phase of their work when they realize that every letter reveals the character and personality of the organization which sends it. If the letter is intelligently composed and carefully typewritten, it adds to the recipient's respect for the organization, and in the long run to the esteem upon which a company's reputation and good will are based. The business letter thus has a role much like that of a firm's personal representative, who may impart either very favorable or extremely unfavorable impressions of his organization. The successful representative takes pains both to dress well and to approach his clients in a correctly trained manner. It rests with the secretary to see that the letter produces the proper effect by being suitably worded and neatly typed.

The importance of excellent business letters is increased by the permanence of the impression they produce, since all correspondence is kept on file, at least until it becomes certain that it will no longer be needed. In this way a letter may serve for a long time as a point of contact between organizations and individuals. Every time the executive reviews a file of correspondence, he experiences again the pleasant or unpleasant impressions that the letters produced when first received. Time expended in the careful preparation of letters is therefore time well invested.

Of course, the duties of the secretary in the writing of letters vary widely according to the individual situation. Some executives make a practice of indicating the essentials of the letter in a few general sentences, and require the secretary to express their ideas in appropriate words. The secretary should have a practical knowledge of writing methods to perform such a task successfully; and the person who has this ability is an indispensable and highly valued assistant. Other executives dictate the letter in full. Some resent the change of a word or a punctuation mark as unwarranted presumption, and expect the secretary only to typewrite the letter exactly as dictated, putting the parts in proper order and spacing the materials correctly on the page. But with either method of work the secretary who is perfectly informed in letter-writing usages will achieve the most satisfactory results.

The Language of Business Letters

Letters are of two main kinds: business letters and social letters. The letters that a secretary in a business office prepares are usually of the first kind. In social correspondence between friends a good deal of latitude is permitted in the choice of words and the arrangements of parts, but in the business letter it is necessary to follow conventional usage with greater strictness. The body of the business letter offers scope for individuality of treatment, but business letters may not use slang and the freedom of treatment that are acceptable in letters between friends. Both business and social letters require the observance of correct grammar, punctuation, and spelling at all times.

In general terms, the most effective business letters are those which combine cordiality with dignity. Such letters convey to the reader a sense of the sincerity and friendliness of the writer, and promote the objectives with which the letter is sent. Cordiality in business letters, however, degenerates into effusiveness if used to excess, sounding hollow and defeating its purpose of making the recipient wish to cooperate with the writer.

Courtesy and correctness are essential in all business correspondence, but the general tone will vary somewhat with the type of letter, depending upon whether an order for merchandise, a recommendation, a letter of information, an adjustment, or a sales letter is being written. An application for employment or a communication to an important government official is necessarily more formal and respectful than the ordinary business letter. Each sort of letter has a particular objective, and each should use the language and arrangement best suited for its attainment. Correspondence between people who have had a long business association in which an element of friendship may have entered usually is not as dignified and formal as correspondence between people who are communicating for the first time.

TRITE EXPRESSIONS—The message of the letter should be expressed in simple and natural terms. There are dozens of conventional phrases that have become so hackneyed that they have ceased to have any meaning, while others are unduly brief. Both types should be avoided entirely, since they destroy the clarity of the letter and make it seem old-fashioned. A business letter should resemble neither a telegram nor an engraved invitation to tea. Hence it should not contain telescoped expressions like "as per" and "in re," or effusions of pretended gratitude such as "your esteemed favor" and "thanking you in advance." Instead, brevity should be the result of clear thinking and avoidance of repetition. Courtesy should be present throughout the message, rather than being injected here and there by the use of a trite phrase.

Some of the trite and objectionable phrases that should be avoided in the interest of concise and unaffected expression follow. Besides the ones listed, there are many others which the alert person will learn to detect and avoid.

ADVISE. Should not be used in the sense of *tell* or *inform*.

AFOREMENTIONED. Appropriate in legal writing, but in business correspondence *mentioned previously* or *referred to above* would be acceptable.

AS PER. A correct phrase is *according to*.

ATTACHED FIND. If it is attached, it will be found. It is better to say *attached is*.

ATTACHED HERETO. *Hereto* is superfluous.

AT YOUR CONVENIFNCE; AT ANY EARLY DATE. Better be more specific. It may never be convenient; what is early to your reader may be late to you.

BEG TO ACKNOWLEDGE, ADVISE, INFORM, STATE. To *beg* means to beseech or implore, or to ask for charity. None of these fits the intention of the writer. Omit the expression and simply say or do something.

CONSIDERED OPINION. Opinions customarily are reached through consideration. Omit *considered*.

CONTENTS CAREFULLY NOTED. One is expected to notice the contents of letters carefully. It is a waste of time to tell the correspondent that this has been done.

DICTATED BUT NOT READ. The letter of a correspondent who uses this expression ought to be returned with the notation "Received but not read."

EAGERLY AWAIT. Not to be used unless one means to indicate either great enthusiasm or impatience.

HEREIN, HERETO, HEREWITH. All superfluous; just *enclose, attach,* or *send*.

HOPING TO HEAR FROM YOU. This is usually taken for granted.

IN DUE COURSE. This is too indefinite.

IN RE. A Latin term meaning "concerning," or "in the matter of." Should not be used except in legal writing.

KINDLY. This is an adverb meaning, generally, in a kind manner or spirit. Asking a correspondent to "Kindly fill out the enclosed form" might be presumptuous. Just say *please*.

PERMIT ME TO SAY. Since it is your letter, you need not request permission to make a comment. Omit the expression.

PLEASE BE ADVISED. Unnecessary introduction to a statement. Go right into whatever it is you intend to tell your reader.

RECENT DATE. A letter should be referred to either by the exact date or the subject, or by both.

REGRET TO STATE. Very stilted; better to say *sorry that.*

SAME. Should not be used as a pronoun except in legal documents.

THANKING YOU IN ADVANCE. It is presumptuous to assume that a request will be granted.

THE WRITER; THE UNDERSIGNED. The former is affected; the latter is appropriate in legal writing only. The pronoun *I* is correct.

THIS IS IN REPLY TO. Perfectly obvious from the contents of the letter.

TRUST YOU WILL. To be avoided unless you are quite confident. It generally is safer to say *hope you will.*

WISH TO ACKNOWLEDGE, INFORM, SAY. Just *acknowledge, inform, or say.*

Five Essentials of Business Letter English

The language used in every business letter, regardless of type, must contain five qualities that are indispensable in effective correspondence. These are:

1. Clearness
2. Conciseness
3. Completeness
4. Courtesy
5. Correctness

The writer who keeps these "Five C's" constantly in mind while composing the letter will find his task greatly simplified. Also, in reviewing the letter after it is drafted, he can estimate the value of his work according to the presence or absence of these qualities. The "Five C's" are the characteristics of good correspondence.

CLEARNESS—A letter is first of all a message to a reader. If the reader does not grasp this message easily and thoroughly, the letter has failed in its purpose, no matter how correct its form or how attractive its appearance may be. Consequently the writer must make sure that the letter conveys a message in unmistakable terms.

Clarity in letters can be achieved by following a very simple but important procedure. Before beginning the composition of the letter the writer must determine definitely what he wishes to say—whether or not he will order the materials, supply the information, give the recommendation, or do whatever else the reader has requested. If one waits until the actual writing of the letter to make these decisions, ambiguity and indecisiveness are almost certain to result. Although such a caution may appear obvious and needless, many letters are begun before the writers know what they are going to say.

After this first step, which is a matter of individual consideration for each case, the writer must find the best words for expressing the message decided upon. Clearness in the actual writing is attained by care in the selection of words; in the punctuation, the length, and arrangement of sentences; and the paragraphing. It is important to avoid vague words or those subject to misinterpretation. Sentences should be as direct as possible, not weighed down by parenthetical expressions, subordinate clauses, or participial phrases. In addition, sentences in a business letter should be reasonably brief, though too many very short sentences in succession give an undesirable staccato effect. Both vocabulary and sentence structure must be adapted to the intelligence and education of the reader. The principles of good paragraphing must also be observed, so that each topic or group of related topics occupies a paragraph by itself.

CONCISENESS—The businessman has so many claims on his limited time that he welcomes methods that conserve his working hours and energy. The best business letters, therefore, are those which enable him to grasp their message with the greatest ease and rapidity. Therefore, clearness in words and grammatical structure are necessities; another is conciseness. Conciseness in writing includes the omission of unessential matter, and the avoidance of repetition and of unduly long forms of expression. It should be noted, however, that concise writing need not be incomplete nor discourteous writing. Essential facts must not be overlooked, and the brusqueness which would result from the deletion of all expressions of cordiality and good will is undesirable.

The letter writer can find no better way to train himself in conciseness than to review his completed letters and note the number of phrases, words, and even whole sentences that could be left out without impairing the meaning of the whole.

COMPLETENESS—The completeness of the message should never be sacrificed in an exaggerated effort to achieve brevity of expression. Every item that is essential must be included in the letter, for omission of important details is likely to cause confusion. The writer's best way of avoiding this difficulty is to check over the items he intends to mention before the letter is begun, making sure that he has in mind all the necessary details and no more. The letter should be read through after it has been written, to see whether it complies with the requirements of completeness. If something has been forgotten, the letter should probably be rewritten, since details tacked on in a postscript are an admission that the letter was inexpertly drafted in the first place.

COURTESY—Every successful business organization shows great courtesy in personal contacts with individuals and other companies, for much of its success depends on the esteem of its clients and associates. Courtesy in business letters is no less essential, especially in view of the permanence of correspondence.

There is a great difference, however, between true courtesy, which consistently takes into account the problems, needs, and feelings of the reader, and sham courtesy. The latter expresses itself in resounding phrases which do not truly represent the sentiments of the writer. Furthermore, exaggerated expressions of thanks and esteem are in poor taste, even when they are sincere.

Courtesy depends in part on a properly chosen salutation and complimentary close, but to a much greater degree on the language in the body of the letter. True consideration rests in the acts of the individual or company, but whether these favor or disfavor the reader's interests, they must be communicated in courteous terms. With skill, even collection letters or refusals to grant charge accounts can be stated with a minimum of vexation to the reader. Business letters of this type should show respect for the dignity and character of the recipient, and should avoid imputing bad faith to him. Sarcasm and abuse should never appear in business letters of any kind, since they brand the writer as ill-bred, and antagonize the reader.

CORRECTNESS—Correctness in the business letter is a requirement so absolute that without it the time spent in drafting a clear, well-phrased, and courteous message is hardly worthwhile, for a letter that contains errors in formal details furnishes a sorry impression of the intelligence and character of the individual or firm that sent it. A carefully worded but carelessly transcribed letter is as ineffectual as a well-informed speaker with a severe stammer: neither the letter nor the speaker wins the favorable attention deserved by the quality of the message.

After the letter is composed, but before it is typewritten,

it should be checked for correctness in the following particulars: (1) grammar, (2) spelling, (3) capitalization, (4) punctuation, (5) the form of numerical expressions, and (6) abbreviations. When it is ascertained that the letter is correct in these usages, it should be typewritten with care, so that errors of fact do not creep in, and in accordance with the recommendations for spacing and the order of parts found in the following pages.

The Form of Business Letters

The letter's neat and pleasing appearance, like its correctness in details, enhances the value of skillful phrasing. Furthermore, clear-cut paragraph separations and proper spacing of the materials on the page permit quicker comprehension of the contents. Also, paper of good quality and a well-designed letterhead reflect credit on the writer.

A black typewriter ribbon is commonly used, although colors such as deep brown or very dark blue, to match the imprint on the letterhead, are not uncommon. Whatever the color, if the ribbon is made of cloth it should be fresh enough to provide a clear imprint. Carbon ribbons are, of course, made for single usage and therefore always produce clear, even copy. They are usable, however, only on typewriters that are made or adapted for them.

Carelessness in making corrections may produce smudges on the page. Such smudges can be avoided by using a celluloid or plastic cutout which exposes only the letter or word to be erased. Other aids are correction fluid (painted over the error) and correction paper (which obliterates the error with a white coating when the error is retyped over a piece of correction paper placed between the ribbon and the copy). Typographical errors should not be struck over with the correct letter; instead, the error should be carefully eradicated and the proper symbol typed in its place. Since it is difficult to insert the correction in exactly the right spot after the page has been removed from the typewriter and then replaced, it is best to read the letter over for errors before taking it out of the machine.

Few business letters run longer than one page. When they do, however, the bottom of the first sheet must not be crowded. Nor should the first page be crowded to avoid using a second. The second page should be headed with the name of the addressee, the page number, and the date, thus:

Mr. Ralph C. Roberts   2.   June 30, 1971

or, the same information may be placed in the upper left-hand corner of the second page, as follows:

Mr. Ralph C. Roberts
June 30, 1971
Page 2

Letterhead stationery is not used for any page after the first. If specially imprinted sheets are not available (usually just the firm's name in small type), plain paper of the same stock as the letterhead should be used.

Carbon copies of all letters should be made and promptly filed. This practice makes the review of correspondence an easy matter, and is essential for a smoothly running office. Equally essential is the permanent record that carbon copies provide.

SPACING—Proper spacing of the materials on the page has a great effect on the letter's legibility and attractiveness. The letter should be approximately centered on the page, but with the upper and left-hand margins slightly wider than the lower and the right-hand margins. If the letter occupies a full page or more, the upper and left-hand margins should be not less than 1¼ inches wide, and the lower and right-hand margins not less than 1 inch wide. A shorter letter will require wider margins, but these should

maintain the same proportions. The length of the lines also varies according to the length of the letter. A letter of 100 words or less presents the best appearance if the lines are about 40 characters long (counting both letters and the spaces between words). A letter containing from 100 to 150 words should have 50-character lines; one of more than 150 words should have 60-character lines. If the typewriter used has "elite" type (that is, type which measures 12 characters to the inch), letters exceeding 200 words in length should have 70-character lines; but if the typewriter has larger type than this, a line of 70 characters will be too long for the minimum margins of 1¼ inch and 1 inch. Before the transcription of the letter is begun the typist should make an approximate estimate of its length and set the typewriter's margin guides accordingly.

The length of the letter determines not only the preferable width of the lines, but also the vertical spacing. If the letter is a very brief one, it is likely to appear lost in a sea of white paper. This may be avoided by increasing the number of blank lines between the various parts of the letter, in order to expand it vertically on the page. The area which the letter covers on the page may also be increased by double-spacing.

LAYOUT—The most commonly used styles of layout are block, full-block, and semi-block. The simplified style is also frequently used, while the once popular indented style is now rarely seen. Punctuation styles, too, have changed. The formerly common closed punctuation required suitable marks after the date line, each line of the address, the salutation, the complimentary close, and each line of the signature. At the opposite extreme is open punctuation, which eliminates all marks unless a line happens to end in an abbreviation. Standard punctuation, the most generally used form, calls only for a colon after the salutation and a comma after the complimentary close (plus, of course, a period when a line ends in an abbreviation).

Block Style. The inside address, the attention line, the salutation, the identification line, and the paragraphs begin flush with the left-hand margin; the date ends flush with the right-hand margin or is centered under the letterhead imprint; and the complimentary close and signature lines begin slightly to the right of center. Standard or open punctuation may be used, but standard is the more common.

Full-Block Style. All components begin at the left-hand margin. Standard or open punctuation may be used. The dictator's initials are not included in the identification line.

Semi-Block Style. The same as block style, except that the paragraphs are indented five or ten spaces, or to the colon after a short salutation. Standard punctuation is usual.

Simplified Style. The same as full-block style but with no salutation or complimentary close. Usually a subject line (concocted if necessary) is placed between the address and the body of the letter. Open punctuation is used, and the dictator's initials are not included in the identification line.

The Parts of Business Letters

The business letter consists of seven main parts, found in the following order: (1) heading, (2) date, (3) address, (4) salutation, (5) body, (6) complimentary close, and (7) signature.

HEADING—The heading consists of the name and address of the sender, imprinted or engraved at the top of the sheet. The term *letterhead* applies to the heading as well as to the imprinted sheet as a whole.

DATE—Placement of the date varies according to the style of layout used, as explained in the preceding section.

Neither abbreviations nor figures should be used for the month; not should "st," "nd," "rd," or "th" follow the day of the month. The year should not be represented by an apostrophe followed by two digits. Correct and incorrect forms of the date line are illustrated below:

INCORRECT	CORRECT
Nov. 23, 1971	November 23, 1971
12/11/71	December 11, 1971
January 6th, 1971	January 6, 1971
April 17, '71	April 17, 1971

ADDRESS—The address in the letter follows the same form as that on the envelope. It should contain the name, street address, city, state, and zip code of the addressee. The name of a well-known office building sometimes supplements or replaces the street address. If a company name appears in the address, it should be the full, official name.

When a letter is addressed to an individual within a company, the business title always follows the name, on the same line or, if it is a long title, on the line below. The title should never be abbreviated. The only words that precede the name of an individual are courtesy titles ("Mr.," "Mrs.," and "Miss") and titles showing professional standing, like "Dr.," "Professor," and "The Reverend." These titles should always be used, even when a business or official title follows the name. But when initials indicating a degree follow the name, no title precedes it. Exceptions to these practices occur in addressing people of high position, as listed under FORMS OF ADDRESS FOR GOVERNMENT AND ECCLESIASTICAL OFFICIALS.

The following examples illustrate correct and incorrect forms for the name line of the address:

INCORRECT	CORRECT
Treasurer Richard J. Wilts	Mr. Richard J. Wilts, Treasurer
Dr. Harold Coombs, M.D.	Dr. Harold Coombs or Harold Coombs, M.D.
Professor Samuel Slaughter, PhD	Professor Samuel Slaughter or Samuel Slaughter, Ph.D.

The address is usually placed two or more lines below the date line, but in government correspondence and some very formal letters it is frequently found below the signature, at the lower left-hand corner of the page.

A variety of correct complete addresses follows:

Mr. John J. Creighton, President
General Machining Company, Inc.
630 Fifth Avenue
New York, New York 10020

Mr. Albert M. Browning
Executive Vice President
Pacific Coast Furniture Enterprises
209 Post Street
San Francisco, California 94108

Dr. William J. Moore
Winous-Point Building
1250 Euclid Avenue
Cleveland, Ohio 44115

Charles F. Morton, Ph.D.
Institute of Geological Studies
1201 Portland Place
Boulder, Colorado 80302

Miss Rosemary Bellingham
Assistant to the President
Plymouth Electric Industries, Inc.
1168 Commonwealth Avenue
Boston, Massachusetts 02134

The Reverend Ralph C. Roberts
Executive Director
Universal Gospel Society
2611 West End Avenue
Nashville, Tennessee 37203

Mrs. George C. Hambleton
309 South Fremont Street
Tampa, Florida 33606

Joseph C. Embry, D.D.S.
2855 Sky Harbor Boulevard
Phoenix, Arizona 85034

SALUTATION —The salutation marks the formal opening of the letter. It begins at the left-hand margin, usually two spaces below the inside address. In standard punctuation it is followed by a colon. Users of the open punctuation system use no punctuation mark after the salutation.

The choice of the salutation depends on the relationship between the writer and the reader of the letter. In ordinary business correspondence, moderately dignified salutations are desirable, unless the relationship has developed into a warmly personal one, when considerable informality is permissible. Special forms of address are used in writing to government officials; these are listed in FORMS OF ADDRESS FOR GOVERNMENT AND ECCLESIASTICAL OFFICIALS.

The salutations suitable for various situations are as follows:

For addressing a company or a group of men:

Gentlemen: (formal or informal)

For addressing a group of women:

Ladies: (formal or informal)
Mesdames: (formal)

For addressing an individual:

My dear Mr. O'Hara: (formal)
My dear Miss Foster: (formal)
Dear Sir: (moderately informal)
Dear Madam: (moderately informal)
Dear Mr. O'Hara: (moderately informal)
Dear Miss Foster: (moderately informal)

For addressing a close business acquaintance:

Dear Tom: (very informal)

The word "dear" in a salutation is capitalized only if it is the first word in the phrase. The only abbreviations used in salutations are "Mr.," "Mrs.," "Messrs.," "Mmes.," and "Dr."

A letter addressed directly to an organization should use the salutation "Gentlemen." However, if the writer wishes the letter to receive the attention of a particular individual in the firm, this is accomplished by inserting the phrase "Attention: Mr. _____" between the last line of the address and the salutation. In this event, either "Gentlemen" or "Dear Mr._____" would be an acceptable salutation. The layout would be as follows:

Simmons and Tate, Inc.
20 East 82nd Street
New York, New York 10028

Attention: Mr. John W. Harris

Gentlemen: (or Dear Mr. Harris:)

BODY—The body of the letter is the portion that contains the message. It begins two lines below the salutation. Unless the letter is very brief, it should be single-spaced, with a double space between paragraphs. If double-spacing is used, the paragraphs must be indented. Regardless of whether standard or open punctuation is used in the other parts of the letter, the body must be punctuated in accordance with conventional usage.

Following are four examples of the different ways the body of the letter may be spaced on the letterhead:

Double-spaced indented paragraphs with no blank lines between them:

Double-spaced indented paragraphs with blank line between them:

Single-spaced indented paragraphs with blank line between them:

Single-spaced paragraphs in block style, with blank line between them:

If the body of the letter contains an address for the information of the reader, it is helpful to make this stand out prominently for convenience in reference. This may be accomplished by centering it on the page, as in this example:

> For additional details we advise you to communicate with America's foremost authority in this field:
>
> Dr. Franz A. Heiden
> Hamm Building
> St. Paul, Minnesota 55102
>
> We feel confident that he will be glad to furnish the information you require.

COMPLIMENTARY CLOSE—The complimentary close is a formal expression of regard with which the writer takes leave of the reader. It follows the body of the letter, occupying a line by itself, two or more lines below the last line of the body. In the block and semi-block styles of layout, the complimentary close begins slightly to the right of center, while in the full-block and simplified styles it is placed flush with the left-hand margin.

The use of a particular phrase for the complimentary close, like the salutation, depends on the relationship between the sender and the receiver. The complimentary close should be consistent with the salutation in the degree of its formality.

The most frequently used complimentary closes for business correspondence are as follows:

> Respectfully yours, (very formal, and used principally for government officials and people in superior positions)
> Very truly yours, (moderately formal)
> Yours very truly, (moderately formal)
> Yours truly, (moderately formal)
> Sincerely yours, (informal)
> Cordially yours, (informal; most used in business correspondence between persons who know each other well)

The complimentary close should have only its first letter capitalized, and should contain no abbreviations. It should not be attached to the preceding sentence or follow such stereotyped expressions as "Hoping for a prompt reply I am ... " It is usually followed by a comma, except when open punctuation is used.

SIGNATURE—The signature is typewritten beneath the space allowed for the handwritten signature, three or four lines below the complimentary close, depending upon the need for compressing or expanding the materials on the page. It should contain the name of the writer and his position, which may be typed on one line or two. If this information is imprinted on the letterhead, no typewritten signature is necessary.

Business titles and degree or professional letters follow the typewritten signature. Neither the handwritten nor the typewritten portions of the signature should contain personal titles, such as "Mr.," "Rev.," "Dr.," or "Professor." The only exception to this rule is the use in parentheses of "Miss" or "Mrs." when a woman chooses to so identify herself.

Illustrations of typewritten signatures follow:

Russell J. Blair, Registrar

Mary J. Valentine, Ph.D.

Charles B. Harrison, Manager
Advertising Department

John C. Worth, C.P.A.

(Mrs.) Alice C. White, Secretary

ADDITIONAL PARTS—Although they do not appear in all business letters, three additional letter parts that require attention are the identification letters, the notice of enclosure, and the postscript.

Identification Letters. The identification letters are the initials of the writer of the letter and those of the secretary who transcribed it. The initials of the writer always come first. Identification letters are placed at the left margin, a few lines below the last line of the signature, in any of the following forms:

RJMcM/EMP   RJMcM:EMP   JMcM/emp
JMcM:emp

Notice of Enclosure. The notice of enclosure reminds the reader that something has been enclosed with the letter. The word "Enclosure" or the abbreviation "Enc." is written just below the identification letters. If there is more than one enclosure, the number should be stated, and if the enclosure is of special importance it should be identified, as:

RJMcM/emp   RJMcM:emp
Enclosures (3)   Enc. Check, $3,024.50

Postscript. Postscripts usually are avoided, since their use may be taken as evidence of confused thinking on the part of the writer who only remembered to include an essential detail after the letter was typewritten. There are times, however, when they are deliberately used, to create emphasis. When there is a postscript it should be placed at least two lines below the identification letters, or notice of enclosure if there is one, preceded by the letters "P.S."

Envelope. The envelope should be carefully typed and well-spaced. Both the sender's and the receiver's addresses should appear on the face. The address to which the letter is being sent should begin slightly more than halfway down the envelope and slightly to the left of the center. It should, of course, be identical to the address used in the letter.

The zip code should be the last notation of any kind on the envelope, to ensure expeditious handling in the mails. Should anything appear after the line on which the zip code is written, the automatic sorting machine will reject the piece of mail, throwing it aside for later manual handling. For this reason, the attention line should be placed just above and to the left of the address. The same positioning applies to notations regarding handling of the mail after it has reached its destination, such as "Personal," "Hold for Arrival," and "Please Forward." Notations concerning type of postal service (special delivery, air mail, registered mail) should be typed above and to the right of the address, directly below the place at which the postage will be affixed.

SKELETON ENVELOPE FORM

_____   (Printed
_____   Return
_____   Address)

(Type of Postal Service)

(Attention Line)

Dateline

Address

Salutation

**SKELETON BUSINESS
LETTER FORM**

Body

(Block style, standard punctuation)

Complimentary Close

Signature

Identification Initials
Enclosure Note

Dateline

Address

Salutation

**SKELETON BUSINESS
LETTER FORM**

Body

(Full-block style, open punctuation)

Complimentary Close

Signature

Typist's Initials
Enclosure Note

Dateline

Address

Salutation

SKELETON BUSINESS
LETTER FORM

(Semi-block style, standard punctuation)

Body

Complimentary Close

Signature

Identification Initials
Enclosure Note

Dateline

Address

Subject Line

SKELETON BUSINESS
LETTER FORM

(Simplified Style)

Body

Signature

Typist's Initials
Enclosure Note

Forms of Address for Government and Ecclesiastical Officials

Letters addressed to people in high positions in governmental or religious organizations require the use of special forms for the address, the salutation, and the complimentary close. Various expressions with differing degrees of formality are possible in some cases, those listed hereafter being the most formal.

The inside address in a letter to a government official may be placed either before the salutation, as in most business letters, or in the lower left-hand corner of the page below the level of the signature.

Two terms which should be used with special care are "the Honorable" and "the Reverend." Since they are adjectives rather than titles, they must be followed by the first name, the initials, or the appropriate title, rather than by the surname alone. They are usually abbreviated to "Hon." and "Rev." if the word "the" is omitted. Examples:

The Honorable Henry Robinson
The Honorable H. F. Robinson
The Honorable Mr. Robinson
   not
The Honorable Robinson

Hon. H. F. Robinson
   not
Hon. Robinson

The Reverend Matthew Watts
The Reverend M. Z. Watts
The Reverend Dr. Watts
   not
The Reverend Watts

Rev. Matthew Watts
   not
Rev. Watts

When a clergyman holds a doctoral degree, the initials of the degree should follow a comma after his name on the address line, or he may be addressed as "Rev. Dr. John F. Smith," with no initials after his name. The title "Doctor" may then be used in the salutation.

In closing a formal letter to a high governmental or ecclesiastical official, the most formally correct form for the complimentary close is "Respectfully yours," while "Very truly yours," is appropriately formal for a person of lower rank. The most common informal complimentary close is "Sincerely yours."

UNITED STATES OFFICIALS

THE PRESIDENT
Address:
   The President
   The White House
   Washington, D.C.   20500
      or
   The President of the United States
   The White House
   Washington, D.C.   20500
Salutation:
   Mr. President:
      or
   My dear Mr. President:
Complimentary Close:
   Respectfully yours,

THE VICE PRESIDENT
Address:
   The Vice President
   The United States Senate
   Washington, D.C.   20510
      or
   The Honorable (FULL NAME)
   Vice President of the United States
   Washington, D.C.
Salutation:
   Mr. Vice President:
      or
   My dear Mr. Vice President:
Complimentary Close:
   Respectfully yours,

CABINET MEMBERS
Address:
   The Honorable (FULL NAME)
   Secretary of (DEPARTMENT)
   Washington, D.C.
Salutation:
   Sir:
      or
   My dear Mr. Secretary:
Complimentary Close:
   Very truly yours,

ASSISTANT CABINET MEMBERS
Address:
   The Honorable (FULL NAME)
   Assistant Secretary of (DEPARTMENT)
   Washington, D.C.
Salutation:
   Sir:
      or
   My dear Mr. (SURNAME):
Complimentary Close:
   Very truly yours,

CHIEF JUSTICE OF THE SUPREME COURT
Address:
   The Chief Justice
   The Supreme Court
   Washington, D.C.   20543
Salutation:
   Sir:
      or
   My dear Mr. Chief Justice:
Complimentary Close:
   Very truly yours,

ASSOCIATE JUSTICE OF THE SUPREME COURT
Address:
   Mr. Justice (SURNAME)
   The Supreme Court
   Washington, D.C.   20543
Salutation:
   My dear Mr. Justice:
      or
   Dear Justice (SURNAME):
Complimentary Close:
   Very truly yours,

UNITED STATES SENATOR
Address:
   The Honorable (FULL NAME)
   United States Senate
   Washington, D.C.   20510
Salutation:
   Dear Sir:
      or
   My dear Senator (SURNAME):
Complimentary Close:
   Very truly yours,

UNITED STATES CONGRESSMAN
Address:
    The Honorable (FULL NAME)
    House of Representatives
    Washington, D.C.   20515
Salutation:
    Dear Sir:
        or
    My dear Mr. (SURNAME):
Complimentary Close:
    Very truly yours,

STATE AND LOCAL GOVERNMENT OFFICIALS

GOVERNOR OF A STATE
Address:
    The Honorable (FULL NAME)
    Governor of (STATE)
    (State Capitol, State)
Salutation:
    Dear Sir:
        or
    My dear Governor (SURNAME):
Complimentary Close:
    Respectfully yours,
        or
    Very truly yours,

STATE SENATOR
Address:
    The Honorable (FULL NAME)
    The State Senate
    (State Capitol, State)
Salutation:
    Dear Sir:
        or
    My dear Senator (SURNAME):
Complimentary Close:
    Very truly yours,

STATE ASSEMBLYMAN (OR REPRESENTATIVE)
Address:
    The Honorable (FULL NAME)
    Member of the Assembly
    (*or*, House of Representatives)
    (State Capitol, State)
Salutation:
    Dear Sir:
        or
    My dear Mr. (SURNAME):
Complimentary Close:
    Very truly yours,

MAYOR
Address:
    The Honorable (FULL NAME)
    Mayor of (CITY)
    (City, State)
Salutation:
    My dear Mr. Mayor:
        or
    My dear Mayor (SURNAME):
Complimentary Close:
    Very truly yours,

DIPLOMATIC OFFICIALS

UNITED STATES AMBASSADOR
Address:
    The Honorable (FULL NAME)
    American Ambassador
    (City and Country where stationed)
Salutation:
    Sir:
        or
    My dear Mr. Ambassador:
Complimentary Close:
    Very truly yours,

UNITED STATES CONSUL
Address:
    (FULL NAME), Esquire
    American Consul at (LOCATION)
    (City and Country where stationed)
Salutation:
    Dear Sir:
        or
    My dear Mr. (SURNAME):
Complimentary Close:
    Very truly yours,

ROMAN CATHOLIC CHURCH OFFICIALS

POPE
Address:
    His Holiness Pope (NAME)
    Vatican City
    Rome, Italy
Salutation:
    Most Holy Father:
        or
    Your Holiness:
Complimentary Close:
    Respectfully yours,

CARDINAL
Address:
    His Eminence (GIVEN NAME) Cardinal (SURNAME)
Salutation:
    Your Eminence:
Complimentary Close:
    Respectfully yours,

ARCHBISHOP
Address:
    The Most Reverend (FULL NAME)
    Archbishop of (LOCATION)
Salutation:
    Your Excellency:
Complimentary Close:
    Respectfully yours,

BISHOP
Address:
    The Most Reverend (FULL NAME)
    Bishop of (LOCATION)
Salutation:
    Your Excellency:
Complimentary Close:
    Respectfully yours,

PROTONOTARIES APOSTOLIC, DOMESTIC PRELATES, AND VICARS GENERAL
Address:
    Right Reverend Monsignor (FULL NAME)
Salutation:
    Right Reverend Monsignor:
Complimentary Close:
    Respectfully yours,

PAPAL CHAMBERLAINS
Address:
    Very Reverend Monsignor (FULL NAME)
Salutation:
    Very Reverend Monsignor:
Complimentary Close:
    Respectfully yours,

PRIEST
   Address:
      Reverend (FULL NAME) (followed by letters
        designating his order, if any)
   Salutation:
      Dear Father (SURNAME):
   Complimentary Close:
      Very truly yours,

PROTESTANT AND JEWISH ECCLESIASTICAL OFFICIALS

PROTESTANT EPISCOPAL BISHOP
   Address:
      The Right Reverend (FULL NAME)
      Bishop of (LOCATION)
   Salutation:
      Right Reverend:
         or
      Dear Sir:
   Complimentary Close:
      Respectfully yours,

PROTESTANT CLERGYMAN
   Address:
      The Reverend (FULL NAME) (followed by initials
        of degree, if any)
        or, if a Doctor of Divinity,
      The Reverend Doctor (FULL NAME)
   Salutation:
      Reverend Sir:
         or
      Dear Doctor (SURNAME):
   Complimentary Close:
      Very truly yours,

RABBI
   Address:
      Rabbi (FULL NAME)
   Salutation:
      Reverend Sir:
         or
      Dear Rabbi (SURNAME):
   Complimentary Close:
      Very truly yours,

POST OFFICE INFORMATION

Intelligent and economical use of the United States mails requires that the proficient secretary have a good working knowledge of the official classification system and rate structure. To avoid unnecessary delays and losses, the following recommendations should be kept in mind:

1. Be sure to give the name and address in full, with street and number, post office box, or R.F.D. address.

2. Always include zip code numbers, placing them at the end of the city and state line, two spaces after the name of the state.

3. If the name of the state must be abbreviated, use the official Post Office two-letter abbreviation.

4. "General Delivery" should be written above the address on matter for persons not permanently located in the city addressed.

5. Be certain that all letters are properly sealed, and all parcels securely wrapped.

6. Make sure that address labels and postage are firmly affixed.

7. Show a return address on envelopes and packages.

CLASSES OF MAIL

A general description of the four classes of mail follows.

In unusual situations or when there is doubt, specific information should be obtained from a post office.

First Class

This classification includes post and postal cards; all matter wholly or partially in writing, whether handwritten or typewritten, sealed or unsealed; matter specifically labeled as closed against postal inspection, as explained in the descriptions of third- and fourth-class mail; and bills and statements of accounts, except invoices accompanying third-or fourth-class mail.

Second Class

Newspapers, periodicals, publications issued by and in the interests of certain nonprofit organizations and associations, classroom publications, and certain agricultural science publications are considered second-class mail.

Third Class

Third-class mail consists of matter weighing less than sixteen ounces not mailed or required to be mailed as first-class and not permissible as second-class mail. It includes circulars, books, catalogs and other printed matter, merchandise, seeds, bulbs, and plants. An invoice may be sent with the package. Sealed pieces mailed at the single-piece rate must be marked "Third Class"; there are special provisions for marking bulk third-class mail.

Mailing of sealed articles at third-class rates of postage implies the sender's consent to postal inspection of the contents. If the sender does not wish the package to be opened for inspection, it should be plainly marked "First Class" and sent at that rate of postage.

Fourth Class (Parcel Post)

Merchandise, printed matter, mailable live animals, and all other matter not considered first-, second-, or third-class mail may be sent by parcel post. The weight and size limits vary, depending upon the contents and upon the class of the post office at or to which they are mailed. An invoice may be enclosed.

There are special fourth-class rates of postage for:

1. catalogues;

2. books, 16mm or narrower film, printed music, printed objective test materials, sound recordings, and numerous other items; the address side of each such package must be marked in a manner that identifies its contents, as "Special Fourth-Class Rate—Books," or "Special Fourth-Class Rate—16mm or Narrower Film."

3. certain articles mailed by a school, college, university, public library, or nonprofit organization; the address side of each such package must bear the statement "Library Rate."

Mailing of sealed packages at fourth-class rates of postage implies the sender's consent to postal inspection of the contents. If the sender does not wish the package to be opened for inspection, it should be plainly marked "First Class" and sent at that rate of postage.

SPECIAL TYPES OF SERVICE
Air Mail

Any matter that is accepted for surface mail may be sent by air mail, provided it is not subject to damage or harm by changes in temperature or atmospheric pressures. It is carried by air and by the fastest connecting surface carriers. Postage is charged by weight and also, in the case of items weighing more than seven ounces, by zone, regardless of the class of mail.

Special Delivery

This type of service provides immediate delivery at the office of address during reasonable hours. Special-delivery mail is handled and transported in the same manner as first-class mail, regardless of the class of mail. The fee for special delivery must be prepaid in addition to the regular postage for the class of mail used.

Special Handling

This service is available only for third- and fourth-class mail. It offers the most expedient handling, dispatch, and transportation but does not include special delivery.

Insurance

Third- and fourth-class mail may be insured against loss or damage by payment of a fee in addition to the regular postage, provided the articles are sufficiently well-packaged to withstand handling in the mail.

Registered Mail

This service provides evidence of mailing and added protection for valuable and important mail as well as—with payment of an additional fee—evidence of delivery and restricted delivery (to the addressee in person). It is available for matter with postage prepaid at regular first-class or air-mail rates. Registered mail is the proper type of service to use when mailing negotiable and non-negotiable instruments: money, valuable papers, jewelry, and other articles of unusual value. The basic fee for registry varies according to the full value of the contents, which must be declared when the matter is presented at the post office for registration.

Certified Mail

This service also is available for matter with postage prepaid at the regular first-class or air-mail rates. Certified mail is handled in the ordinary channels, and no indemnity is provided. The service is intended for matter of no intrinsic value on which a receipt for the sender and record of delivery at the office of address is desired. Evidence of delivery and restricted delivery are available upon payment of the respective required fees. The basic fee for certified mail is a fixed charge, less than the minimum fee for registered mail.

C.O.D.

Collect-on-delivery service is provided for those who wish the price of an article to be collected from the addressee, with the amount collected remitted to the sender by the Post Office. The fee, which includes insurance against loss or damage to the article, is based upon the amount to be collected, and is in addition to regular postage. Both the fee and the postage must be prepaid, but the mailer may include these charges in the amount to be collected from the addressee.

International Mail

There are two general categories of international mail: postal union mail and parcel post. Because of the wide variations in requirements regarding size, weight, sealing or not sealing, customs forms, and preparation for mailing, details should be obtained from a post office. A brief description of the two categories follows.

POSTAL UNION MAIL—This is divided into two groups, LC mail and AO mail. Letters, letter packages, air letters and post cards are considered LC mail. AO mail includes printed matter, samples of merchandise, matter for the blind, and small packets. Both groups may be sent by air or surface mail, at postage rates that vary according to the country of destination. Registration, return receipt, and special-delivery services are available to many countries.

PARCEL POST—Included in this category are all items that do not fit into one of the groups of postal union mail. Both air and surface parcel post are available to many countries, as is insurance, but registration is limited to only a few countries.

Official Post Office Abbreviations

State	Abbr.	State	Abbr.
Alabama	AL	Montana	MT
Alaska	AK	Nebraska	NE
Arizona	AZ	Nevada	NV
Arkansas	AR	New Hampshire	NH
California	CA	New Jersey	NJ
Colorado	CO	New Mexico	NM
Connecticut	CT	New York	NY
Delaware	DE	North Carolina	NC
District of Columbia	DC	North Dakota	ND
Florida	FL	Ohio	OH
Georgia	GA	Oklahoma	OK
Guam	GU	Oregon	OR
Hawaii	HI	Pennsylvania	PA
Idaho	ID	Puerto Rico	PR
Illinois	IL	Rhode Island	RI
Indiana	IN	South Carolina	SC
Iowa	IA	South Dakota	SD
Kansas	KS	Tennessee	TN
Kentucky	KY	Texas	TX
Louisiana	LA	Utah	UT
Maine	ME	Vermont	VT
Maryland	MD	Virginia	VA
Massachusetts	MA	Virgin Islands	VI
Michigan	MI	Washington	WA
Minnesota	MN	West Virginia	WV
Mississippi	MS	Wisconsin	WI
Missouri	MO	Wyoming	WY

FILING BY ALPHABET

Alphabetizing is the basis of the filing systems used in most business offices. Although the systems in ordinary use differ in details, all are based upon the same general rules. These rules are given below. It is important to remember that occasionally offices have developed systems which depart from standard practice in some respects.

Alphabetical Arrangement

Arrange words or proper names according to the order of their first, second, third letters, carrying the process far enough to place the words in correct alphabetical order. For example:

NOT ALPHABETICALLY ARRANGED	ALPHABETICALLY ARRANGED
Smithers	Smith
Smythe	Smithers
Smith	Smythe

NOT ALPHABETICALLY ARRANGED	ALPHABETICALLY ARRANGED
Abrams	Abarbanell
Abrahams	Abrahams
Abarbanell	Abrams
Bankhead	Bangs
Bangs	Bankhead
Davisson	Davidson
Davidson	Davisson
Slotkowsky	Schmidt
Slotkowski	Schultz
Schultz	Schulze
Schulze	Slotkowski
Schmidt	Slotkowsky
Winters	Stone
Witherspoon	Wallace
Wallace	Winters
Stone	Witherspoon

File the names of persons according to (1) surname, (2) given name or first initial, (3) middle name or middle initial. Initials are always filed before names beginning with the same letter. For example:

NOT ALPHABETICALLY ARRANGED	ALPHABETICALLY ARRANGED
Edward H. Bangs	Bangs, E. H.
E. H. Bangs	Bangs, E. Henry
Edward Howard Bangs	Bangs, Edward H.
Ernest H. Bangs	Bangs, Edward Henry
E. Henry Bangs	Bangs, Edward Howard
Edward Henry Bangs	Bangs, Ernest H.

When names are pronounced similarly but spelled differently, enter each in the file and make a cross reference to its alternatives:

Miller; *see also* Mueller, Muller.
Mueller; *see also* Miller, Muller.
Muller; *see also* Miller, Mueller.

Prefixes, with or without capital letters, such as *de*, *Mac*, *Mc*, *O'*, *van*, or *von* are treated as the first syllable of the surname, and apostrophes are disregarded:

NOT ALPHABETICALLY ARRANGED	ALPHABETICALLY ARRANGED
Robert LaChance	D'Artagnan, Raoul
Alfred von Tirpitz	De Forest, Lee
Jan van Rebeck	De Grey, John
John O'Hara	de Seversky, Alexander
Charles MacArthur	LaChance, Robert
Raoul D'Artagnan	MacArthur, Charles
Lee De Forest	O'Hara, John
John De Grey	van Rebeck, Jan
Alexander de Seversky	von Tirpitz, Alfred

Classify compound or hyphenated names by the first part of the compound·

NOT ALPHABETICALLY ARRANGED	ALPHABETICALLY ARRANGED
Michael Forbes-Robertson	Byng-Enfield, Stephen
Ernestine Schumann-Heink	Forbes-Robertson, Michael
Stephen Byng-Enfield	Rimsky-Korsakov, Nikolai
Nikolai Rimsky-Korsakov	Schumann-Heink, Ernestine

Titles, degrees, and abbreviated designations are placed last, in parentheses, and are not considered in alphabetizing except for arranging identical names:

NOT ALPHABETICALLY ARRANGED	ALPHABETICALLY ARRANGED
Col. John Quincy Jefferson	Astor, Nancy (Lady)
Rev. Edward Holmes	Edwards, Anthony (Prof.)
Lady Nancy Astor	Holmes, Edward (Rev.)
John W. Smith, Jr.	Jefferson, John Quincy (Col.)
Prof. Anthony Edwards	McGuire, C. Arnold (Ph.D.)
C. Arnold McGuire, Ph.D.	Murphy, John B. (M.D.)
John W. Smith, Sr.	Nordenskjold, Nils (Baron)
Baron Nils Nordenskjold	Smith, John W. (Jr.)
John B. Murphy, M.D.	Smith, John W. (Sr.)

When the title of nobility differs from the person's name, it is usually necessary to cross-refer to a listing by titles:

Buchan, John; *see* Tweedsmuir, Baron.
Disraeli, Benjamin; *see* Beaconsfield, Earl of.
Wellesley, Arthur; *see* Wellington, Duke of.

Names of Organizations

In general, the names of businesses, societies, and other organizations are alphabetized as printed. Be sure the correct, full name is used. There are many exceptions to the rule for institutional names, the most important of which are given below. If confusion is likely to arise, cross references should be used:

NOT ALPHABETICALLY ARRANGED	ALPHABETICALLY ARRANGED
General Cigar Company, Inc.	American Can Company
Ingersoll-Rand Company	Crown Zellerbach Corporation
American Can Company	General Cigar Company, Inc.
North American Van Lines, Inc.	Ingersoll-Rand Company
Crown Zellerbach Corporation	Merck & Co., Inc.
TRW, Inc.	North American Van Lines, Inc.
Swift and Company	Northwest Airlines, Inc.
Merck & Co., Inc.	Swift and Company
Northwest Airlines, Inc.	TRW, Inc.

An ampersand (the symbol "&"), when correctly a part of the name, should not be written out. *Brown & Jones* should not be written as *Brown and Jones*.

When *and* is spelled out in the name, the ampersand should not be used. *Jones and Brown* should not be written as *Jones & Brown*.

When the name of an institution contains the name of an individual, the individual's name determines the alphabetical classification for filing purposes:

NOT ALPHABETICALLY ARRANGED	ALPHABETICALLY ARRANGED
A. O. Smith Corporation	Davies, George E., Foundation
Arthur G. McKee & Co.	Goodrich, B. F., Company
B. F. Goodrich Company	McKee, Arthur G., & Co.
George E. Davies Foundation	Penney, J. C., Company, Inc.
J. C. Penney Company, Inc.	Smith, A. O., Corporation

The, when it occurs at the beginning of a corporate or institutional name, is placed in parentheses at the end of the name. *The Procter & Gamble Company* should be classified as *Procter & Gamble Company (The)*.

Articles ("a," "an," and "the"), prepositions ("for," "in," "of," etc.), and the word "and" or the ampersand "&" within the name are disregarded in filing.

Compounds, whether formed of the names of persons or otherwise, are treated as one word:

NOT ALPHABETICALLY ARRANGED	ALPHABETICALLY ARRANGED
Smart and Daniels	Adams-Millis Corporation
While-U-Wait Pressers	Dow Chemical Company (The)
Eat-and-Drink, Inc.	Eat-and-Drink, Inc.
Whitman and Kane	Smart-Cut Clothiers, Inc.
Adams-Millis Corporation	Smart and Daniels
The Dow Chemical Company	While-U-Wait Pressers
Smart-Cut Clothiers, Inc.	Whitman and Kane

Names containing words ending in "s," with or without an apostrophe, are alphabetized as written:

NOT ALPHABETICALLY ARRANGED	ALPHABETICALLY ARRANGED
Foster's American Shoe Company	Foster, Lee and Company
Foster, Lee and Company	Foster, Mark L., Corporation
Foster's Tailor Shop	Foster Hardware Store
Mark L. Foster Corporation	Foster and Young, Inc.
Foster Hardware Store	Foster's American Shoe Company
Foster and Young, Inc.	Foster's Tailor Shop

The numbers in a name should be treated as though they were spelled out:

NOT ALPHABETICALLY ARRANGED	ALPHABETICALLY ARRANGED
4-Deuces Club	18th National Bank
2222 Elm Street Building Corp.	4-Deuces Club
18th National Bank	2222 Elm Street Building Corp.

When several organizations have the same name, arrange them alphabetically by their locations, considering the town first:

Economy Chevrolet Company,
Fostoria, Ohio

Economy Chevrolet Company,
Newmarket, Indiana

Economy Chevrolet Company,
Newmarket, Wyoming

Names of Government Agencies

The names of government agencies and subdivisions, and officials thereof, are detailed in descending order:

The *Chief of the Bureau of Public Roads of the U.S. Department of Agriculture* should be filed as:

United States Government
Agriculture, Department of,
Public Roads, Bureau of,
.........., Chief.

United States Government is the customary heading for agencies of the U.S. Government. Other examples:

U.S. Agricultural Marketing Service should be filed as:
United States Government
Agriculture, Department of,
Agricultural Marketing Service.

U.S. Employment Service should be filed as:
United States Government
Commerce, Department of,
Employment Service.

The *Canadian Bureau of Parks and Forests* should be filed as:
Dominion of Canada
Mines and Resources, Department of,
Parks and Forests, Bureau of.

The *Bureau of Air Pollution Control of the State of Illinois* should be filed as:
Illinois, State of,
Public Health, Department of,
Air Pollution Control, Bureau of.

The *Bureau of Forestry and Parkways of the City of Chicago* should be filed as:
Chicago, City of,
Public Works, Department of,
Forestry and Parkways, Bureau of.

MULTIPLICATION TABLE

To multiply two numbers, each of 30 or less, find one of the numbers along the side of the table and follow this row to the column headed at the top by the other number. Thus: 14 × 19 = 266.

×	2	3	4	5	6	7	8	9	10	11	12	13	14	15	16	17	18	19	20	21	22	23	24	25	26	27	28	29	30
2	4	6	8	10	12	14	16	18	20	22	24	26	28	30	32	34	36	38	40	42	44	46	48	50	52	54	56	58	60
3	6	9	12	15	18	21	24	27	30	33	36	39	42	45	48	51	54	57	60	63	66	69	72	75	78	81	84	87	90
4	8	12	16	20	24	28	32	36	40	44	48	52	56	60	64	68	72	76	80	84	88	92	96	100	104	108	112	116	120
5	10	15	20	25	30	35	40	45	50	55	60	65	70	75	80	85	90	95	100	105	110	115	120	125	130	135	140	145	150
6	12	18	24	30	36	42	48	54	60	66	72	78	84	90	96	102	108	114	120	126	132	138	144	150	156	162	168	174	180
7	14	21	28	35	42	49	56	63	70	77	84	91	98	105	112	119	126	133	140	147	154	161	168	175	182	189	196	203	210
8	16	24	32	40	48	56	64	72	80	88	96	104	112	120	128	136	144	152	160	168	176	184	192	200	208	216	224	232	240
9	18	27	36	45	54	63	72	81	90	99	108	117	126	135	144	153	162	171	180	189	198	207	216	225	234	243	252	261	270
10	20	30	40	50	60	70	80	90	100	110	120	130	140	150	160	170	180	190	200	210	220	230	240	250	260	270	280	290	300
11	22	33	44	55	66	77	88	99	110	121	132	143	154	165	176	187	198	209	220	231	242	253	264	275	286	297	308	319	330
12	24	36	48	60	72	84	96	108	120	132	144	156	168	180	192	204	216	228	240	252	264	276	288	300	312	324	336	348	360
13	26	39	52	65	78	91	104	117	130	143	156	169	182	195	208	221	234	247	260	273	286	299	312	325	338	351	364	377	390
14	28	42	56	70	84	98	112	126	140	154	168	182	196	210	224	238	252	266	280	294	308	322	336	350	364	378	392	406	420
15	30	45	60	75	90	105	120	135	150	165	180	195	210	225	240	255	270	285	300	315	330	345	360	375	390	405	420	435	450
16	32	48	64	80	96	112	128	144	160	176	192	208	224	240	256	272	288	304	320	336	352	368	384	400	416	432	448	464	480
17	34	51	68	85	102	119	136	153	170	187	204	221	238	255	272	289	306	323	340	357	374	391	408	425	442	459	476	493	510
18	36	54	72	90	108	126	144	162	180	198	216	234	252	270	288	306	324	342	360	378	396	414	432	450	468	486	504	522	540
19	38	57	76	95	114	133	152	171	190	209	228	247	266	285	304	323	342	361	380	399	418	437	456	475	494	513	532	551	570
20	40	60	80	100	120	140	160	180	200	220	240	260	280	300	320	340	360	380	400	420	440	460	480	500	520	540	560	580	600
21	42	63	84	105	126	147	168	189	210	231	252	273	294	315	336	357	378	399	420	441	462	483	504	525	546	567	588	609	630
22	44	66	88	110	132	154	176	198	220	242	264	286	308	330	352	374	396	418	440	462	484	506	528	550	572	594	616	638	660
23	46	69	92	115	138	161	184	207	230	253	276	299	322	345	368	391	414	437	460	483	506	529	552	575	598	621	644	667	690
24	48	72	96	120	144	168	192	216	240	264	288	312	336	360	384	408	432	456	480	504	528	552	576	600	624	648	672	696	720
25	50	75	100	125	150	175	200	225	250	275	300	325	350	375	400	425	450	475	500	525	550	575	600	625	650	675	700	725	750
26	52	78	104	130	156	182	208	234	260	286	312	338	364	390	416	442	468	494	520	546	572	598	624	650	676	702	728	754	780
27	54	81	108	135	162	189	216	243	270	297	324	351	378	405	432	459	486	513	540	567	594	621	648	675	702	729	756	783	810
28	56	84	112	140	168	196	224	252	280	308	336	364	392	420	448	476	504	532	560	588	616	644	672	700	728	756	784	812	840
29	58	87	116	145	174	203	232	261	290	319	348	377	406	435	464	493	522	551	580	609	638	667	696	725	754	783	812	841	870
30	60	90	120	150	180	210	240	270	300	330	360	390	420	450	480	510	540	570	600	630	660	690	720	750	780	810	840	870	900

DISTANCES BETWEEN MAJOR WORLD CITIES

	BANGKOK THAILAND	BERLIN GERMANY	CAIRO EGYPT	CAPETOWN SOUTH AFRICA	CARACAS VENEZUELA	CHICAGO ILLINOIS	HONG KONG	HONOLULU HAWAII	ISTANBUL TURKEY	LIMA PERU	LONDON ENGLAND	MADRID SPAIN	MELBOURNE AUSTRALIA	MEXICO CITY MEXICO	MONTREAL CANADA	MOSCOW U.S.S.R.
ACCRA GHANA	6850	3330	2672	2974	4576	5837	7615	10052	3039	5421	3169	2412	9325	6677	5146	4038
AMSTERDAM NETHERLANDS	5707	360	2015	5997	4883	4118	5772	7254	1372	6538	222	921	10286	5735	3426	1337
ANCHORAGE ALASKA	6022	4545	6116	10478	5353	2858	5073	2778	5388	6385	4491	5181	7729	3776	3133	4364
ATHENS GREECE	4930	1121	671	4957	5815	5447	5316	8353	352	7312	1488	1474	9297	7021	4737	1387
AUCKLAND NEW ZEALAND	4645	9995	8825	6574	9620	9507	4625	5346	9203	7989	10570	10884	160	8274	10231	9018
BAGHDAD IRAQ	3756	2029	798	4924	7020	6430	4260	8399	1006	8487	2547	2675	8105	8082	5768	1583
BANGKOK THAILAND		5351	4521	6301	10558	8569	1050	6610	4648	12241	5929	6334	4579	9793	8337	4394
BEIRUT LEBANON	4272	1689	341	4794	6520	6097	4756	8536	614	7972	2151	2190	8579	7707	5405	1514
BELGRADE YUGOSLAVIA	5073	623	1147	5419	5587	5000	5327	7882	500	7169	1053	1263	9578	6610	4305	1066
BERLIN GERMANY	5351		1768	5958	5242	4415	5442	7323	1075	6893	580	1162	9929	6054	3740	1001
BOMBAY INDIA	1870	3915	2717	5103	9034	8066	2679	8036	3000	10389	4478	4689	6101	9739	7524	3132
BUENOS AIRES ARGENTINA	10490	7395	7360	4285	3155	5582	11478	7554	7608	1945	6907	6236	7219	4580	5597	8369
CAIRO EGYPT	4521	1768		4510	6337	6116	5057	8818	741	7725	2158	2069	8700	7677	5403	1770
CAPETOWN SOUTH AFRICA	6301	5958	4510		6361	8489	7377	11534	5204	6074	5988	5306	6428	8516	7920	6277
CARACAS VENEZUELA	10558	5242	6337	6361		2500	10171	6024	6050	1699	4662	4351	9703	2234	2443	6176
CHICAGO ILLINOIS	8569	4415	6116	8489	2500		7797	4256	5485	3772	3960	4192	9667	1688	746	4984
COPENHAGEN DENMARK	5361	222	1964	6179	5215	4263	5392	7101	1252	6886	595	1289	9936	5918	3605	971
DENVER COLORADO	8409	5092	6846	9331	3078	920	7476	3346	6164	3986	4701	5028	8755	1438	1639	5501
FRANKFURT EAST GERMANY	5305	50	1730	5944	5290	4460	5403	7341	1032	6940	628	1193	9882	6101	3787	961
FRANKFURT WEST GERMANY	5579	266	1789	5814	5029	4340	5699	7448	1157	6664	396	898	10148	5949	3643	1259
HELSINKI FINLAND	4903	689	2069	6490	5658	4442	4867	6818	1330	7349	1135	1835	9448	6127	3845	554
HONG KONG	1076	5443	5057	7377	10171	7797		5557	4989	11415	5986	6556	4605	8789	7736	4443
HONOLULU HAWAII	6610	7323	8818	11534	6024	4256	5557		8118	5944	7241	7874	5501	3791	4919	7049
HOUSTON TEXAS	9261	5337	7005	8608	2262	942	8349	3902	6400	3123	4860	5014	8979	749	1605	5925
ISTANBUL TURKEY	4648	1075	741	5204	6050	5485	4989	8118		7593	1551	1701	9100	7106	4798	1087
KARACHI PAKISTAN	2305	3365	2222	5153	8502	7564	2977	8059	2457	9943	3928	4152	6646	9249	6997	2600
KEFLAVIK ICELAND	6300	1505	3267	7107	4269	2942	6044	6085	2578	5965	1188	1802	10552	4614	2317	2083
KINSHASA ZAIRE	5974	3916	2618	2047	5752	7085	6904	11178	3241	6322	3951	3305	8112	7915	6378	4328
LENINGRAD U.S.S.R.	4718	826	2034	6500	5843	4589	4687	6816	1306	7534	1307	1985	9263	6276	4005	396
LIMA PERU	12241	6893	7725	6074	1699	3772	11415	5944	7593		6316	5907	8052	2635	3967	7855

ALL FIGURES ARE U.S. STATUTE MILES

	NAIROBI KENYA	NEW DELHI INDIA	NEW YORK NEW YORK	PARIS FRANCE	PEKING CHINA	RIO DE JANEIRO BRAZIL	ROME ITALY	SAN FRANCISCO CALIFORNIA	SINGAPORE SINGAPORE	STOCKHOLM SWEDEN	TEHERAN IRAN	TOKYO JAPAN	VIENNA AUSTRIA	WASHINGTON DISTRICT OF COLUMBIA
ACCRA GHANA	2603	5279	5126	2988	7359	3501	2624	7688	7183	3835	3874	8594	3100	5274
AMSTERDAM NETHERLANDS	4136	3958	3654	271	4890	5938	807	5465	6526	701	2533	5788	581	3856
ANCHORAGE ALASKA	8287	5709	3373	4697	3997	8145	5263	2005	6678	4102	5654	3463	4856	3373
ATHENS GREECE	2827	3120	4938	1305	4757	6030	654	6792	5629	1498	1539	5924	801	5140
AUCKLAND NEW ZEALAND	7315	6420	10194	10519	5626	8259	10048	7692	3848	9732	7935	5017	9886	10017
BAGHDAD IRAQ	2431	1966	6007	2405	3925	6938	1836	7466	4427	2164	431	5199	1781	6209
BANGKOK THAILAND	4481	1812	8669	5877	2027	9987	5493	7930	887	5141	3392	2865	5252	8807
BEIRUT LEBANON	2420	2479	5622	1987	4352	6478	1368	7302	4935	1931	913	5598	1401	5825
BELGRADE YUGOSLAVIA	3328	3270	4526	902	4634	6145	449	6296	5833	1010	1741	5720	309	4728
BERLIN GERMANY	3947	3598	3980	549	4600	6207	735	5673	6167	505	2184	5557	323	4182
BOMBAY INDIA	2811	722	7811	4367	2953	8334	3846	8406	2427	3880	1743	4196	3725	8003
BUENOS AIRES ARGENTINA	6479	9823	5279	6857	11994	1231	6925	6455	9870	7799	8565	11411	7334	5197
CAIRO EGYPT	2217	2752	5598	1973	4687	6153	1305	7436	5143	2084	1220	5937	1455	5800
CAPETOWN SOUTH AFRICA	2543	5769	7801	5782	8034	3773	5231	10248	6007	6422	5240	9155	5656	7892
CARACAS VENEZUELA	7179	8837	2124	4735	8978	2805	5198	3908	11408	5422	7322	8813	5374	2051
CHICAGO ILLINOIS	8012	7486	714	4145	6625	5288	4823	1860	9376	4288	6502	6313	4696	598
COPENHAGEN DENMARK	4156	3640	3857	642	4503	6321	953	5473	6195	325	2287	5415	540	4057
DENVER COLORADO	8867	7730	1631	4900	6385	5866	5587	953	9079	4879	7033	5815	5395	1494
FRANKFURT EAST GERMANY	3915	3550	4028	589	4567	6237	729	5709	6119	502	2135	5533	296	4229
FRANKFURT WEST GERMANY	3912	3809	3865	299	4865	5942	596	5691	6382	740	2348	5817	371	4068
HELSINKI FINLAND	4282	3247	4126	1192	3956	6872	1370	5435	5759	248	2062	4872	895	4319
HONG KONG	5447	2339	8061	5992	1195	11002	5773	6904	1608	5115	3844	1792	5432	8157
HONOLULU HAWAII	10740	7413	4969	7452	5084	8295	8040	2397	6728	6873	8072	3860	7632	4839
HOUSTON TEXAS	8746	8388	1419	5035	7244	5015	5702	1648	9954	5227	7442	6685	5609	1221
ISTANBUL TURKEY	2957	2837	5022	1400	4407	6378	853	6711	5379	1347	1274	5574	791	5225
KARACHI PAKISTAN	2708	678	7277	3817	3020	8082	3306	8078	2942	3340	1194	4313	3175	7472
KEFLAVIK ICELAND	5404	4749	2597	1402	4951	6090	2068	4196	7181	1352	3568	5497	1813	2790
KINSHASA ZAIRE	1505	4692	6378	3742	7002	4105	3186	8920	6132	4388	3612	8307	3619	6532
LENINGRAD U.S.S.R.	4234	3069	4291	1350	3789	7028	1460	5523	5575	431	1926	4733	986	4483
LIMA PERU	7821	10430	3635	6367	10365	2351	6748	4516	11689	7109	8850	9628	6990	3504

ALL FIGURES ARE U.S. STATUTE MILES

	BANGKOK THAILAND	BERLIN GERMANY	CAIRO EGYPT	CAPETOWN SOUTH AFRICA	CARACAS VENEZUELA	CHICAGO ILLINOIS	HONG KONG	HONOLULU HAWAII	ISTANBUL TURKEY	LIMA PERU	LONDON ENGLAND	MADRID SPAIN	MELBOURNE AUSTRALIA	MEXICO CITY MEXICO	MONTREAL CANADA	MOSCOW U.S.S.R.
LISBON PORTUGAL	6651	1442	2352	5301	4040	4001	6862	7835	2015	5591	989	317	11049	5396	3255	2433
LONDON ENGLAND	5929	580	2158	5988	4662	3960	5986	7241	1551	6316		786	10508	5558	3256	1556
MADRID SPAIN	6334	1162	2069	5306	4351	4192	6556	7874	1701	5907	786		10766	5642	3449	2140
MELBOURNE AUSTRALIA	4579	9929	8700	6428	9703	9667	4605	5501	9100	8052	10508	10766		8420	10390	8965
MEXICO CITY MEXICO	9793	6054	7677	8516	2234	1688	8789	3791	7106	2635	5558	5642	8420		2315	6671
MONTREAL CANADA	8337	3740	5403	7920	2443	746	7736	4919	4798	3967	3256	3449	10390	2315		4397
MOSCOW U.S.S.R.	4394	1001	1770	6277	6176	4984	4443	7049	1087	7855	1556	2140	8965	6671	4397	
NAIROBI KENYA	4481	3947	2217	2543	7179	8012	5447	10740	2957	7821	4229	3840	7159	9218	7267	3928
NEW DELHI INDIA	1812	3598	2752	5769	8837	7486	2339	7413	2837	10430	4178	4528	6340	9119	7012	2703
NEW YORK NEW YORK	8669	3980	5598	7801	2124	714	8061	4969	5022	3635	3473	3596	10352	2086	333	4680
OSLO NORWAY	5395	523	2243	6477	5167	4050	5342	6801	1518	6857	718	1485	9934	5722	3418	1024
PANAMA CITY PANAMA	10871	5856	7118	7021	867	2321	10089	5254	6756	1454	5285	5081	9027	1496	2542	6720
PARIS FRANCE	5877	549	1973	5782	4735	4145	5992	7452	1400	6367	215	652	10442	5723	3432	1550
PEKING CHINA	2027	4600	4687	8034	8978	6625	1195	5084	4407	10365	5089	5759	5632	7772	6541	3627
RABAT MOROCCO	6652	1623	2230	4954	4111	4282	6954	8177	2008	5590	1254	474	10856	5612	3537	2579
RIO DE JANEIRO BRAZIL	9987	6207	6153	3773	2805	5288	11002	8295	6378	2351	5751	5045	8218	4769	5082	7162
ROME ITALY	5493	735	1305	5231	5198	4823	5773	8040	853	6748	892	849	9940	6374	4102	1477
SAIGON SOUTH VIETNAM	467	5771	4987	6534	10905	8695	938	6302	5102	12180	6345	6779	4168	9718	8558	4798
SAN FRANCISCO CALIFORNIA	7930	5673	7436	10248	3908	1860	6904	2397	6711	4516	5369	5806	7850	1889	2544	5884
SANTIAGO CHILE	10967	7772	7967	4947	3033	5295	11615	6861	8135	1528	7241	6639	7017	4094	5436	8770
SEATTLE WASHINGTON	7455	5060	6809	10205	4096	1737	6481	2681	6077	4961	4799	5303	8176	2340	2289	5217
SHANGHAI CHINA	1797	5231	5188	8062	9508	7071	760	4947	4975	10665	5728	6386	4991	8033	7067	4248
SHANNON IRELAND	6256	940	2534	6188	4320	3583	6246	7006	1938	5992	387	884	10826	5172	2873	1863
SINGAPORE SINGAPORE	887	6167	5143	6007	11408	9376	1608	6728	5379	11689	6747	7079	3767	10331	9207	5236
ST. LOUIS MISSOURI	8763	4676	6370	8549	2414	265	7949	4134	5744	3589	4215	4426	9476	1425	978	5248
STOCKHOLM SWEDEN	5141	505	2084	6422	5422	4288	5115	6873	1347	7109	892	1613	9693	5965	3667	764
TEHERAN IRAN	3392	2184	1220	5240	7322	6502	3844	8072	1274	8850	2739	2974	7838	8182	5879	1534
TOKYO JAPAN	2865	5557	5937	9155	8813	6313	1792	3860	5574	9628	5956	6704	5070	7036	6470	4663
VIENNA AUSTRIA	5252	323	1455	5656	5374	4696	5432	7632	791	6990	767	1124	9802	6316	4007	1039
WARSAW POLAND	5032	322	1588	5934	5563	4679	5147	7368	858	7212	901	1425	9609	6335	4021	716

ALL FIGURES ARE U.S. STATUTE MILES

	NAIROBI KENYA	NEW DELHI INDIA	NEW YORK NEW YORK	PARIS FRANCE	PEKING CHINA	RIO DE JANEIRO BRAZIL	ROME ITALY	SAN FRANCISCO CALIFORNIA	SINGAPORE SINGAPORE	STOCKHOLM SWEDEN	TEHERAN IRAN	TOKYO JAPAN	VIENNA AUSTRIA	WASHINGTON DISTRICT OF COLUMBIA
LISBON PORTUGAL	4013	4844	3377	904	6040	4777	1163	5679	7393	1862	3288	6943	1432	3572
LONDON ENGLAND	4229	4178	3473	215	5089	5751	892	5369	6747	892	2739	5956	767	3676
MADRID SPAIN	3840	4528	3596	652	5759	5045	849	5806	7079	1613	2974	6704	1124	3794
MELBOURNE AUSTRALIA	7159	6340	10352	10442	5632	8218	9940	7850	3767	9693	7838	5070	9802	10174
MEXICO CITY MEXICO	9218	9119	2086	5723	7772	4769	6374	1889	10331	5965	8182	7036	6316	1883
MONTREAL CANADA	7267	7012	333	3432	6541	5082	4102	2544	9207	3667	5879	6470	4007	490
MOSCOW U.S.S.R.	3928	2703	4680	1550	3627	7162	1477	5884	5236	764	1534	4663	1039	4873
NAIROBI KENYA		3371	7365	4020	5720	5556	3340	9598	4636	4299	2709	6996	3625	7550
NEW DELHI INDIA	3371		7319	4103	2350	8747	3684	7691	2574	3466	1584	3638	3467	7500
NEW YORK NEW YORK	7365	7319		3638	6867	4805	4293	2574	9539	3939	6141	6757	4233	203
OSLO NORWAY	4446	3726	3686	838	4395	6462	1248	5196	6249	260	2462	5238	839	3883
PANAMA CITY PANAMA	8043	9422	2213	5388	8939	3296	5916	3326	11692	5956	8011	8441	6031	2067
PARIS FRANCE	4020	4103	3638		5138	5681	688	5579	6676	964	2624	6054	643	3841
PEKING CHINA	5720	2350	6867	5138		10778	5076	5934	2754	4197	3496	1305	4664	6965
RABAT MOROCCO	3733	4841	3636	1125	6206	4589	1184	5995	7348	2084	3263	7174	1546	3826
RIO DE JANEIRO BRAZIL	5556	8747	4805	5681	10778		5704	6621	9776	6638	7368	11535	6124	4783
ROME ITALY	3340	3684	4293	688	5076	5704		6259	6231	1229	2126	6140	476	4496
SAIGON SOUTH VIETNAM	4874	2268	8889	6303	2072	10290	5943	7829	682	5534	3851	2689	5687	9006
SAN FRANCISCO CALIFORNIA	9598	7691	2574	5579	5934	6621	6259		8449	5372	7362	5148	5992	2444
SANTIAGO CHILE	7180	10518	5106	7224	11859	1820	7391	5926	10190	8120	9185	10711	7760	4993
SEATTLE WASHINGTON	9006	7046	2409	5012	5432	6890	5680	679	8074	4731	6686	4793	5381	2330
SHANGHAI CHINA	5951	2646	7384	5772	645	11339	5679	6150	2363	4837	3974	1097	5281	7463
SHANNON IRELAND	4563	4529	3086	563	5288	5597	1247	5040	7089	1135	3117	6064	1153	3289
SINGAPORE SINGAPORE	4636	2574	9539	6676	2754	9776	6231	8449		5993	4106	3304	6039	9667
ST. LOUIS MISSOURI	8231	7736	878	4398	6792	5218	5073	1744	9544	4552	6766	6407	4955	716
STOCKHOLM SWEDEN	4299	3466	3939	964	4197	6638	1229	5372	5993		2217	5091	771	4135
TEHERAN IRAN	2709	1584	6141	2624	3496	7368	2126	7362	4106	2217		4775	1983	6340
TOKYO JAPAN	6996	3638	6757	6054	1305	11535	6140	5148	3304	5091	4775		5689	6792
VIENNA AUSTRIA	3625	3467	4233	643	4664	6124	476	5992	6039	771	1983	5689		4436
WARSAW POLAND	3800	3277	4271	853	4340	6453	819	5854	5846	504	1878	5346	347	4471

ALL FIGURES ARE U.S. STATUTE MILES

COMPOUND INTEREST TABLE

This table provides factors for computing the amount accumulated from, and the compound interest paid on, any principal at various interest rates over *n* years. These factors are defined by the *Annual Rate of Compound Interest* (given in a row along the top) and the *Years of Interest* (given in columns along the sides). To find the amount accumulated, multiply the original principal by the appropriate factor from the table. To find only the interest paid on the principal, subtract the original principal from the accumulated amount after *n* years.

For example: To find the amount accumulated from an original principal of $100 at 3½% annual interest after 20 years, multiply $100 by the appropriate factor from the table (1.9898). $100 × 1.9898 = $198.98. The amount accumulated after 20 years is the product, or $198.98. To find only the interest paid, subtract the original principal ($100) from the accumulated amount ($198.98). $198.98 − $100 = $98.98. The total interest paid over 20 years is the difference, or $98.98.

Annual Rate of Compound Interest

n	1%	1½%	2%	2½%	3%	3½%	4%	4½%	5%	5½%	6%	6½%	7%	7½%	8%	8½%	9%	n
1	1.0100	1.0150	1.0200	1.0250	1.0300	1.0350	1.0400	1.0450	1.0500	1.0550	1.0600	1.0650	1.0700	1.0750	1.0800	1.0850	1.0900	1
2	1.0201	1.0302	1.0404	1.0506	1.0609	1.0712	1.0816	1.0920	1.1025	1.1130	1.1236	1.1342	1.1449	1.1556	1.1664	1.1772	1.1881	2
3	1.0303	1.0457	1.0612	1.0769	1.0927	1.1087	1.1249	1.1412	1.1576	1.1742	1.1910	1.2079	1.2250	1.2423	1.2597	1.2773	1.2951	3
4	1.0406	1.0614	1.0824	1.1038	1.1255	1.1475	1.1699	1.1925	1.2155	1.2388	1.2625	1.2865	1.3108	1.3355	1.3605	1.3859	1.4116	4
5	1.0510	1.0773	1.1041	1.1314	1.1593	1.1877	1.2167	1.2462	1.2763	1.3070	1.3382	1.3701	1.4026	1.4356	1.4693	1.5037	1.5387	5
6	1.0615	1.0934	1.1262	1.1597	1.1941	1.2293	1.2653	1.3023	1.3401	1.3788	1.4185	1.4591	1.5007	1.5433	1.5869	1.6315	1.6772	6
7	1.0721	1.1098	1.1487	1.1887	1.2299	1.2723	1.3159	1.3609	1.4071	1.4547	1.5036	1.5540	1.6058	1.6590	1.7138	1.7701	1.8281	7
8	1.0829	1.1265	1.1717	1.2184	1.2668	1.3168	1.3686	1.4221	1.4775	1.5347	1.5938	1.6550	1.7182	1.7835	1.8509	1.9206	1.9927	8
9	1.0937	1.1434	1.1951	1.2489	1.3048	1.3629	1.4233	1.4861	1.5513	1.6191	1.6895	1.7626	1.8385	1.9172	1.9990	2.0839	2.1721	9
10	1.1046	1.1605	1.2190	1.2801	1.3439	1.4106	1.4802	1.5530	1.6289	1.7081	1.7908	1.8771	1.9672	2.0610	2.1589	2.2610	2.3676	10
11	1.1156	1.1779	1.2434	1.3121	1.3842	1.4600	1.5395	1.6229	1.7103	1.8021	1.8983	1.9992	2.1049	2.2156	2.3316	2.4532	2.5806	11
12	1.1268	1.1956	1.2682	1.3449	1.4258	1.5111	1.6010	1.6959	1.7959	1.9012	2.0122	2.1291	2.2522	2.3818	2.5182	2.6617	2.8129	12
13	1.1381	1.2136	1.2936	1.3785	1.4685	1.5640	1.6651	1.7722	1.8856	2.0058	2.1329	2.2675	2.4098	2.5604	2.7196	2.8879	3.0661	13
14	1.1494	1.2318	1.3195	1.4130	1.5126	1.6187	1.7317	1.8519	1.9799	2.1161	2.2609	2.4149	2.5785	2.7524	2.9372	3.1334	3.3421	14
15	1.1609	1.2502	1.3459	1.4483	1.5580	1.6753	1.8009	1.9353	2.0789	2.2325	2.3966	2.5718	2.7590	2.9589	3.1722	3.3997	3.6429	15
16	1.1725	1.2690	1.3728	1.4845	1.6047	1.7340	1.8730	2.0224	2.1829	2.3553	2.5404	2.7390	2.9522	3.1808	3.4259	3.6887	3.9708	16
17	1.1842	1.2880	1.4002	1.5216	1.6528	1.7947	1.9479	2.1134	2.2920	2.4848	2.6928	2.9170	3.1588	3.4194	3.7000	4.0023	4.3282	17
18	1.1961	1.3073	1.4282	1.5597	1.7024	1.8575	2.0258	2.2085	2.4066	2.6215	2.8543	3.1067	3.3799	3.6758	3.9960	4.3425	4.7178	18
19	1.2081	1.3270	1.4568	1.5987	1.7535	1.9225	2.1068	2.3079	2.5270	2.7656	3.0256	3.3086	3.6165	3.9515	4.3157	4.7116	5.1424	19
20	1.2202	1.3469	1.4859	1.6386	1.8061	1.9898	2.1911	2.4117	2.6533	2.9178	3.2071	3.5236	3.8697	4.2479	4.6610	5.1120	5.6053	20
25	1.2824	1.4509	1.6406	1.8539	2.0938	2.3632	2.6658	3.0054	3.3864	3.8134	4.2919	4.8277	5.4274	6.0983	6.8485	7.6868	8.6248	25
30	1.3478	1.5631	1.8114	2.0976	2.4273	2.8068	3.2434	3.7453	4.3219	4.9840	5.7435	6.6144	7.6123	8.7550	10.0627	11.5583	13.2709	30
35	1.4165	1.6839	1.9999	2.3732	2.8139	3.3336	3.9461	4.6673	5.5160	6.5138	7.6861	9.0623	10.6766	12.5689	14.7853	17.3796	20.4195	35
40	1.4887	1.8140	2.2080	2.6851	3.2620	3.9593	4.8010	5.8164	7.0400	8.5133	10.2857	12.4161	14.9745	18.0442	21.7245	26.1330	31.4193	40
45	1.5646	1.9542	2.4379	3.0379	3.7816	4.7024	5.8412	7.2482	8.9850	11.1266	13.7646	17.0111	21.0025	25.9048	31.9204	39.2951	48.3444	45
50	1.6444	2.1052	2.6916	3.4371	4.3839	5.5849	7.1067	9.0326	11.4674	14.5420	18.4202	23.3067	29.4570	37.1897	46.9016	59.0863	74.3980	50

Years of Interest

MONTHLY SALARY TABLE
40 Hours a Week — 5 Days of 8 Hours

MONTHLY RATE	ANNUAL	QUARTERLY	WEEKLY	DAILY	HOURLY	¼ HOURLY
$ 225	$ 2,700	$ 675	$ 51.92	$10.38	$1.30	$0.32
250	3,000	750	57.69	11.54	1.44	0.36
275	3,300	825	63.46	12.69	1.59	0.40
300	3,600	900	69.23	13.85	1.73	0.43
325	3,900	975	75.00	15.00	1.87	0.47
350	4,200	1,050	80.77	16.15	2.02	0.51
375	4,500	1,125	86.54	17.31	2.16	0.54
400	4,800	1,200	92.31	18.46	2.31	0.58
425	5,100	1,275	98.08	19.62	2.45	0.61
450	5,400	1,350	103.84	20.77	2.60	0.65
475	5,700	1,425	109.61	21.92	2.74	0.69
500	6,000	1,500	115.38	23.08	2.88	0.72
550	6,600	1,650	126.92	25.38	3.17	0.79
600	7,200	1,800	138.46	27.69	3.46	0.87
650	7,800	1,950	150.00	30.00	3.75	0.94
700	8,400	2,100	161.54	32.31	4.04	1.01
750	9,000	2,250	173.08	34.62	4.33	1.08
800	9,600	2,400	184.61	36.92	4.62	1.16
850	10,200	2,550	196.15	39.23	4.91	1.23
900	10,800	2,700	207.69	41.54	5.19	1.30
950	11,400	2,850	219.23	43.85	5.48	1.37
1,000	12,000	3,000	230.77	46.15	5.77	1.44
1,100	13,200	3,300	253.85	50.77	6.35	1.58
1,200	14,400	3,600	276.93	55.38	6.93	1.73
1,300	15,600	3,900	300.00	60.00	7.50	1.88
1,400	16,800	4,200	323.08	64.61	8.08	2.02
1,500	18,000	4,500	346.15	69.23	8.65	2.16

ANNUAL SALARY TABLE
40 Hours a Week — 5 Days of 8 Hours

ANNUAL RATE	QUARTERLY	MONTHLY	WEEKLY	DAILY	HOURLY	¼ HOURLY
$ 5,000	$1,250	$ 416.67	$ 96.15	$19.23	$2.40	$0.60
5,500	1,375	458.33	105.77	21.15	2.64	0.66
6,000	1,500	500.00	115.38	23.08	2.88	0.72
6,500	1,625	541.67	125.00	25.00	3.13	0.78
7,000	1,750	583.33	134.62	26.92	3.37	0.84
7,500	1,875	625.00	144.23	28.85	3.60	0.90
8,000	2,000	666.67	153.85	30.76	3.84	0.96
8,500	2,125	708.33	163.47	32.72	4.09	1.02
9,000	2,250	750.00	173.08	34.62	4.33	1.08
9,500	2,375	791.67	182.70	36.54	4.57	1.14
10,000	2,500	833.33	192.31	38.46	4.81	1.20
11,000	2,750	916.67	211.54	42.31	5.29	1.32
12,000	3,000	1,000.00	230.77	46.15	5.77	1.44
13,000	3,250	1,083.33	250.00	50.00	6.25	1.56
14,000	3,500	1,166.67	269.23	53.84	6.73	1.68
15,000	3,750	1,250.00	288.46	57.69	7.21	1.80
16,000	4,000	1,333.33	307.69	61.53	7.69	1.92
17,000	4,250	1,416.67	326.92	65.38	8.17	2.04
18,000	4,500	1,500.00	346.15	69.23	8.65	2.16
19,000	4,750	1,583.33	365.38	73.07	9.13	2.28
20,000	5,000	1,666.67	384.61	76.92	9.61	2.40

TIME ZONES OF THE WORLD

The globe is divided into twenty-four time zones — each 15° wide. The zone in which Greenwich, England, is located has been chosen as the "zero" point and is used as the point against which the times of the cities in the world are compared. The time in that zone is called Greenwich Mean Time (abbreviated GMT). Because the earth rotates to the east, zones to the west of Greenwich are behind GMT; zones to the east of Greenwich are ahead of GMT.

This time chart shows how far ahead or behind GMT the principal cities in the world are. If we assume it is twelve noon in Greenwich and begin traveling either east or west, we will reach a point on the other side of the world where it is midnight. Continuing past this point (approximately the 180th meridian, located in the 12th time zone and called the International Date Line) we will gain a day if traveling west, and lose a day if traveling east.

If the local time is known in any city of the world, then the local time can be found for any other city by comparing them both to GMT. If both cities are ahead of GMT or if both are behind GMT, then the smaller number (from the fourth or fifth column in the chart) is subtracted from the larger number (from the same column) to find the hours difference between the two cities. If one city is ahead of GMT and the other behind, then their differences from GMT are added; that is, the figure from column four and the figure from column five are added, to obtain the difference in hours between the two cities.

When the difference in time between the two cities is known, then that difference is added to the local time in the more westerly city to obtain the local time in the other. Or the difference can be subtracted from the local time in the more easterly city to obtain the local time in the other.

STANDARD TIME ZONES

In the standard time zone system, the world is divided into 24 longitudinal zones of 15° each. The Greenwich meridian has been designated as the starting point and is the center of the "zero" time zone. Each subsequent 15° zone represents a difference in time of one hour from the previous zone. Since the earth rotates from west to east, the zones west of Greenwich are later in time and the zones east are earlier in time than Greenwich.

The twelfth time zone is numbered both +12 and —12 and is divided, with some variation, by the 180th meridian which has been designated as the International Date Line. Moving across this line to the west, the traveler adds one day to the calendar date, and crossing this line to the east the traveler subtracts one day from the calendar date. The position of the International Data Line, fixed by international agreement, is indicated by a heavy dotted line on this map.

The zones on this map are identified by a number which represents the difference in hours between that zone and Greenwich time. At the border of the map, each zone is shaded. Those regions within the zone whose times conform with the zone time are shaded with the same tone as the border. Those regions within a zone whose times differ from the standard zone time are shaded with a different tone and display a number indicating the difference in that region's time from Greenwich time.

Map Source: UNITED STATES NAVAL OCEANOGRAPHIC OFFICE.

MERCATOR PROJECTION

Country	City	Time at 12:00 noon GMT	Hrs. ahead of GMT	Hrs. behind GMT
*Afghanistan	Kabul	4.30 P.M.	4½	—
*Algeria	Algiers	1.00 P.M.	1	—
*Argentina	Buenos Aires	8.00 A.M.	—	4
Australia	Adelaide	9.30 P.M.	9½	—
	Brisbane	10.00 P.M.	10	—
	Canberra	10.00 P.M.	10	—
	Melbourne	10.00 P.M.	10	—
	Perth	8.00 P.M.	8	—
	Sydney	10.00 P.M.	10	—
*Austria	Vienna	1.00 P.M.	1	—
*Barbados	Bridgetown	8.00 A.M.	—	4
*Belgium	Brussels	1.00 P.M.	1	—
*Bolivia	La Paz	8.00 A.M.	—	4
*Botswana	Gaborone	2.00 P.M.	2	—

*Denotes that it is the same time at all places in this country.

Country	City	Time at 12:00 noon GMT	Hrs. ahead of GMT	Hrs. behind GMT
Brazil	Belo Horizonte	9.00 A.M.	—	3
	Brasilia	9.00 A.M.	—	3
	Recife	9.00 A.M.	—	3
	Pôrto Velho	8.00 A.M.	—	4
	Rio de Janeiro	9.00 A.M.	—	3
	Sao Paulo	9.00 A.M.	—	3
*Bulgaria	Sofia	2.00 P.M.	2	—
*Burma	Rangoon	6.30 P.M.	6½	—
*Burundi	Bujumbura	2.00 P.M.	2	—
*Cameroon	Yaoundé	1.00 P.M.	1	—
Canada	Montreal	7.00 A.M.	—	5
	Ottawa	7.00 A.M.	—	5
	Toronto	7.00 A.M.	—	5
	Vancouver	4.00 A.M.	—	8
	Winnipeg	6.00 P.M.	—	6
*Central African Republic	Bangui	1.00 P.M.	1	—
*Chad	Fort-Lamy	1.00 P.M.	1	—
*Chile	Santiago	8.00 A.M.	—	4
*China	Peking	8.00 P.M.	8	—
*Colombia	Bogota	7.00 A.M.	—	5
*Congo, Rep. of	Brazzaville	1.00 P.M.	1	—
*Costa Rica	San Jose	6.00 A.M.	—	6
*Cuba	Havana	7.00 A.M.	—	5
*Cyprus	Nicosia	1.00 P.M.	1	—
*Czechoslovakia	Prague	1.00 P.M.	1	—
*Dahomey	Cotonou	1.00 P.M.	1	—
*Denmark	Copenhagen	1.00 P.M.	1	—
*Dominican Rep.	Santo Domingo	7.00 A.M.	—	5
*Ecuador	Quito	7.00 A.M.	—	5
*Egypt	Cairo	2.00 P.M.	2	—
*El Salvador	San Salvador	6.00 A.M.	—	6
*Equatorial Guinea	Santa Isabel	1.00 P.M.	1	—
*Ethiopia	Addis Ababa	3.00 P.M.	3	—
*Finland	Helsinki	2.00 P.M.	2	—
*France	Paris	1.00 P.M.	1	—
*Gabon	Libreville	1.00 P.M.	1	—
*Gambia	Banjul	12.00 noon	0	0
*Germany, East	Berlin	1.00 P.M.	1	—
*Germany, West	Bonn	1.00 P.M.	1	—
*Ghana	Accra	12.00 noon	0	0
*Greece	Athens	2.00 P.M.	2	—
*Guatemala	Guatemala City	6.00 A.M.	—	6
*Guinea	Conakry	12.00 noon	0	0
*Guyana	Georgetown	8.15 A.M.	—	3
*Haiti	Port-au-Prince	7.00 A.M.	—	5
*Honduras	Tegucigalpa	6.00 A.M.	—	6
*Hong Kong	Hong Kong	8.00 P.M.	8	—
*Hungary	Budapest	1.00 P.M.	1	—
*Iceland	Reykjavik	11.00 A.M.	—	1
*India	New Delhi	5.30 P.M.	5½	—
Indonesia	Bandung	7.00 P.M.	7	—
	Jakarta	7.00 P.M.	7	—
	Semarang	7.00 P.M.	7	—
	Surabaya	7.00 P.M.	7	—
	West Irian	9.00 P.M.	9	—
*Iran	Tehran	3.30 P.M.	3½	—
*Iraq	Baghdad	3.00 P.M.	3	—
*Ireland	Dublin	1.00 P.M.	1	—
*Italy	Rome	1.00 P.M.	1	—
*Ivory Coast	Abidjan	12.00 noon	0	0
*Jamaica	Kingston	7.00 A.M.	—	5
*Japan	Tokyo	9.00 P.M.	9	—
*Jordan	Amman	2.00 P.M.	2	—
*Kenya	Nairobi	3.00 P.M.	3	—
*Khmer Rep.	Phnom-Penh	7.00 P.M.	7	—
*Korea, North	Pyongyang	9.00 P.M.	9	—
*Korea, South	Seoul	9.00 P.M.	9	—
*Kuwait	Kuwait	3.00 P.M.	3	—
*Laos	Vientiane	7.00 P.M.	7	—
*Lebanon	Beirut	2.00 P.M.	2	—
*Lesotho	Maseru	2.00 P.M.	2	—
*Liberia	Monrovia	12.45 P.M.	¾	—

Country	City	Time at 12:00 noon GMT	Hrs. ahead of GMT	Hrs. behind GMT
*Libya	Tripoli	2.00 P.M.	2	—
*Luxembourg	Luxembourg	1.00 P.M.	1	—
*Malagasy Rep.	Tananarive	3.00 P.M.	3	—
*Malawi	Blantyre-Limbe	2.00 P.M.	2	—
*Malaysia	Kuala Lumpur	7.30 P.M.	7½	—
*Maldive Islands	Male	5.00 P.M.	5	—
*Mali	Bamako	12.00 noon	0	0
*Malta	Valletta	1.00 P.M.	1	—
*Mauretania	Nouakchott	12.00 noon	0	0
*Mauritius	Port Louis	4.00 P.M.	4	—
Mexico	Guadalajara	6.00 A.M.	—	6
	Mexico City	6.00 A.M.	—	6
	Monterey	6.00 A.M.	—	6
	Mazatlán	5.00 A.M.	—	7
*Mongolian Republic	Ulan Bator	8.00 P.M.	8	—
*Morocco	Rabat	12.00 noon	0	0
*Nepal	Katmandu	5.30 P.M.	5½	—
*Netherlands	Amsterdam	1.00 P.M.	1	—
*New Zealand	Wellington	12.00 midnight	12	—
*Nicaragua	Managua	6.00 A.M.	—	6
*Niger	Niamey	1.00 P.M.	1	—
*Nigeria	Lagos	1.00 P.M.	1	—
*Norway	Oslo	1.00 P.M.	1	—
*Pakistan (East)	Dacca	6.00 P.M.	6	—
*Pakistan (West)	Karachi	5.00 P.M.	5	—
*Panama	Panama City	7.00 A.M.	—	5
*Paraguay	Asunción	8.00 A.M.	—	4
*Peru	Lima	7.00 A.M.	—	5
*Philippines	Manila	8.00 P.M.	8	—
*Poland	Warsaw	1.00 P.M.	1	—
*Portugal	Lisbon	1.00 P.M.	1	0
*Rhodesia	Salisbury	2.00 P.M.	2	—
*Rumania	Bucharest	2.00 P.M.	2	—
*Samoa, Western	Apia	1.00 A.M.	—	11
*Saudi Arabia	Riyadh	4.00 P.M.	4	—
*Senegal	Dakar	12.00 noon	0	0
*Singapore	Singapore	7.30 P.M.	7½	—
*Somalia	Mogadishu	3.00 P.M.	3	—
*South Africa	Cape Town	2.00 P.M.	2	—
*Spain	Madrid	1.00 P.M.	1	—
*Sudan	Khartoum	2.00 P.M.	2	—
*Sweden	Stockholm	1.00 P.M.	1	—
*Switzerland	Berne	1.00 P.M.	1	—
*Syria	Damascus	2.00 P.M.	2	—
*Taiwan	Taipei	8.00 P.M.	8	—
*Tanzania	Dar es Salaam	3.00 P.M.	3	—
*Thailand	Bangkok	7.00 P.M.	7	—
*Togo Republic	Lome	12.00 noon	0	0
*Trinidad & Tobago	Port-of-Spain	8.00 A.M.	—	4
*Tunisia	Tunis	1.00 P.M.	1	—
*Turkey	Ankara	2.00 P.M.	2	—
*Uganda	Kampala	3.00 P.M.	3	—
Union of Soviet Socialist Republics	Alma-Ata	6.00 P.M.	6	—
	Baku	4.00 P.M.	4	—
	Gorky	4.00 P.M.	4	—
	Kharkov	3.00 P.M.	3	—
	Kiev	3.00 P.M.	3	—
	Kuibyshev	4.00 P.M.	4	—
	Leningrad	3.00 P.M.	3	—
	Minsk	3.00 P.M.	3	—
	Moscow	3.00 P.M.	3	—
	Novosibirsk	7.00 P.M.	7	—
	Odessa	3.00 P.M.	3	—
	Omsk	7.00 P.M.	7	—
	Perm	5.00 P.M.	5	—
	Rostov	4.00 P.M.	4	—
	Tashkent	6.00 P.M.	6	—
	Vladivostok	10.00 P.M.	10	—
	Volgograd	4.00 P.M.	4	—

Country	City	Time at 12:00 noon GMT	Hrs. ahead of GMT	Hrs. behind GMT
*United Kingdom	London	1.00 P.M.	1	—
United States of America	E.S.T.	Eastern Standard Time		
	C.S.T.	Central Standard Time		
	M.S.T.	Mountain Standard Time		
	P.S.T.	Pacific Standard Time		
	A.S.T.	Alaska Standard Time		
	Anchorage, Alaska, (A.S.T.)	2.00 A.M.	—	10
	Atlanta, Ga. (E.S.T.)	7.00 A.M.	—	5
	Baltimore, Md. (E.S.T.)	7.00 A.M.	—	5
	Boston, Mass. (E.S.T.)	7.00 A.M.	—	5
	Buffalo, N.Y. (E.S.T.)	7.00 A.M.	—	5
	Chicago, Ill. (C.S.T.)	6.00 A.M.	—	6
	Cincinnati, Ohio (E.S.T.)	7.00 A.M.	—	5
	Cleveland, Ohio (E.S.T.)	7.00 A.M.	—	5
	Columbus, Ohio (E.S.T.)	7.00 A.M.	—	5
	Denver, Colo. (M.S.T.)	5.00 A.M.	—	7
	Detroit, Mich. (E.S.T.)	7.00 A.M.	—	5
	Honolulu, Hawaii (A.S.T.)	2.00 A.M.	—	10
	Houston, Tex. (C.S.T.)	6.00 A.M.	—	6
	Indianapolis, Ind. (C.S.T.)	6.00 A.M.	—	6
	Kansas City, Mo. (C.S.T.)	6.00 A.M.	—	6
	Memphis, Tenn. (C.S.T.)	6.00 A.M.	—	6
	Minneapolis, Minn. (C.S.T.)	6.00 A.M.	—	6
	New York, N.Y. (E.S.T.)	7.00 A.M.	—	5
	Los Angeles, Calif. (P.S.T.)	4.00 A.M.	—	8
	Milwaukee, Wisc. (C.S.T.)	6.00 A.M.	—	6
	New Orleans, La. (C.S.T.)	6.00 A.M.	—	6
	Phoenix, Ariz. (M.S.T.)	5.00 A.M.	—	7
	Pittsburgh, Pa. (E.S.T.)	7.00 A.M.	—	5
	Philadelphia, Pa. (E.S.T.)	7.00 A.M.	—	5
	St. Louis, Mo. (C.S.T.)	6.00 A.M.	—	6
	San Antonio, Tex. (C.S.T.)	6.00 A.M.	—	6
	San Francisco, Calif. (P.S.T.)	4.00 A.M.	—	8
	Seattle, Wash. (P.S.T.)	4.00 A.M.	—	8
	Washington, D.C. (E.S.T.)	7.00 A.M.	—	5
*Upper Volta	Ouagadougou	12.00 noon	0	0
*Uruguay	Montivedeo	9.00 A.M.	—	3
*Venezuela	Caracas	8.00 A.M.	—	4
*Vietnam, North	Hanoi	8.00 P.M.	8	—
*Vietnam, South	Saigon	8.00 P.M.	8	—
*Yemen	Sana	3.00 P.M.	3	—
*Yugoslavia	Belgrade	1.00 P.M.	1	—
Zaire	Kinshasa	1.00 P.M.	1	—
	Lumbumbashi	2.00 P.M.	2	—
*Zambia	Lusaka	2.00 P.M.	2	—

Modern
SCIENCE DICTIONARY

astronomy • geology

biology • meteorology

chemistry • physics

compiled by A. HECHTLINGER, *Bronx High School of Science*

A

a. (1) Abbreviation for ampere; (2) abbreviation for acceleration.

A. (1) Chemical symbol for the element argon; (2) abbreviation for area; (3) abbreviation for absolute temperature.

Å. Abbreviation for ångstrom unit.

abacterial. Bacterium-free.

abaxial. Said of a leaf surface facing away from the stem.

Abbé condenser. A microscope attachment which gives strong light by means of a mirror and a series of wide-angled achromatic lenses placed beneath the stage.

Abbé refractometer. An instrument for measuring the refractive index of liquids; a prism combination devised by Abbé.

Abbé theory of the resolution of a microscope. A theory which relates the resolution of the microscope to the wave length of the light and the aperture of the surface.

abdomen. (1) The body region farthest from the head of an insect; (2) that portion of the animal's body cavity which is posterior to the thorax.

abdominal cavity. The cavity in man and other animals which is in the lower part of the trunk, below the diaphragm.

abducens nerve. The sixth cranial nerve of vertebrates which supplies the external rectus eye muscle.

abductor. A muscle that draws a part away from the center or median line.

aberration. (1) An apparent periodical change in the position of a star caused by the motion of light, as well as the motion of the earth in its orbit; (2) wandering or nonfocusing.

aberration, chromatic. The formation of colored fringes on lens images due to failure of the lens to focus light of all wave lengths at an equal distance from the lens.

aberration, light. A displacement of starlight owing to the earth's orbital motion.

aberration, spherical. A defect of lenses which causes light near the edge of the lens to focus closer to the lens than that falling near the center.

abiogenesis. Spontaneous generation; an old theory, now discredited, that living things may arise from nonliving objects.

abnormal reflections. Reflections of radio waves from the ionosphere at frequencies that are higher than the critical frequency of the layer.

abomasum. The digestive stomach of a ruminant.

aboral. Opposite the mouth.

abrasion. (1) A wound produced by rubbing or scraping off the skin or a mucous membrane; (2) a form of wind erosion in which the wind carries the sand to abrade solid rock.

abrasive. A hard substance used for grinding or polishing other substances; example, silicon carbide.

abscess. A disintegration of tissues that forms a localized collection of pus in a cavity.

abscission layer. Two rows of cells near the base of the petiole which disintegrate in cold weather and allow the leaves to fall.

absolute altimeter. An aircraft instrument for measuring altitude by means of radio-wave reflections from the ground.

absolute expansion. The true expansion of a liquid, not relative to the containing vessel. The coefficient of absolute expansion is equal to the sum of the coefficient of relative or apparent expansion of the liquid and the coefficient of volume expansion of the containing vessel.

absolute humidity. The actual quantity of water vapor per unit volume of air.

absolute magnitude. The apparent magnitude of a star at a distance of 10 parsecs.

absolute pressure. The actual pressure, not reduced by atmospheric pressure; the gage reading plus the atmospheric pressure.

absolute temperature. The temperature measured on a scale whose zero point is 273° below zero on the centigrade scale. To convert centigrade to absolute, add 273°.

absolute temperature scale. From centigrade add 273°; to centigrade subtract 273°.

absolute unit of force. The force which will give one pound of mass an acceleration of one foot per second per second, or one kilogram of mass an acceleration of one meter per second per second.

absolute units. Any set of units which are defined in terms of the fundamental units of mass, length, and time.

absolute zero. The zero point on the absolute temperature scale; it is the point of total absence of heat; 459°F below zero; −273°C.

absorbent. A substance that is able to absorb liquids or gases and is used for removing them from a given medium or region.

absorptiometer. A device for measuring the concentration of substances by their absorption of nearly monochromatic radiation at selected wave lengths; it is used for determining the solubility of gases in liquids.

absorption. (1) The taking up of one substance by another substance; (2) the conversion of radiant energy into energy of a different form; (3) the movement of water, digested food, and other soluble substances into the blood or cells of animals; (4) the diffusion of soil water into the roots of plants.

absorption band. A characteristic dark band in the absorption spectrum of a selectively absorbing substance.

absorption cell. A glass vessel which is used for holding liquids while determining their absorption spectra.

absorption dynamometer. A dynamometer in which the measured energy is absorbed and dissipated.

absorption edge. The wave length or frequency corresponding to an abrupt discontinuity in the intensity of an x-ray absorption spectrum, which has the appearance of a sharp edge in the photograph of such a spectrum.

absorption hygrometer. (1) A hygrometer which is operated by the elongation or shrinking of a hair or similar organic structure with a change in humidity; (2) an instrument for measuring the humidity of air by letting it pass through a drying agent and determining the increase in weight.

absorption loss, acoustic. A transmission loss due to the conversion of sound energy into other forms of energy or its dissipation, either within the medium or after reflection.

absorption of gases. The solution of gases in liquids.

absorption spectrophotometry. The measurement of the absorption of incident radiation, as a function of wave length, after passage through a given medium.

absorption spectrum. Dark lines or bands characteristic of a selectively absorbing substance.

absorptive air roots. Roots which absorb moisture directly from the air.

absorptivity. The fraction of the radiant energy incident on a surface, which is absorbed by that surface.

abyssal. Referring to the greatest depths of the ocean.

abyssal fauna. Animals found in the depths of the ocean below 600 fathoms.

abyssal rocks. Deep-seated igneous rocks or those which have crystallized from magmas far below the surface of the earth very slowly and under great pressure.

Ac. Chemical symbol for the element actinium.

A-C (a-c). Abbreviation for alternating current.

Acanthodii. A group of fossil fish having a row of paired fins with spines between pectoral and pelvic fins; they lived in the Devonian era.

Acarina. An order of Arachnida, including mites and ticks; some are parasites, cause of scabies.

accelerated motion. A motion whose velocity is not constant but increasing or decreasing; it is also called negative accelerated or decelerated motion when the velocity is decreasing.

accelerating chamber. An evacuated envelope in which charged particles are accelerated.

accelerating pump. A pump connected to the carburetor for increasing the richness of the mixture when the engine is accelerated.

acceleration. The rate of change of velocity expressed as centimeters or feet per second per second.

acceleration, gravitational. The gain in the velocity of a body falling freely in a vacuum.

accelerator. (1) A substance which increases the rate of vulcanization of rubber; (2) a substance that speeds up any chemical reaction acting as a positive catalyst; (3) an apparatus for speeding up small particles for bombarding the nuclei of atoms; (4) a mechanical device for regulating the amount of gas mixture fed to the engine, usually operated by foot.

accelerator tube. A vacuum tube in which ions can be accelerated to high energies by applying a very large potential difference between its electrodes.

accelerometer. An aircraft instrument that determines the acceleration of the system with which it moves; a transducer which gives a voltage proportional to the acceleration to which it is subjected; it records, measures, indicates acceleration.

accessory buds. Extra buds in the leaf axil.

accessory flower parts. Sepals and petals.

accessory fruit. An enlarged stem receptacle bearing numerous hard scattered fruits.

accessory nerve. The eleventh cranial nerve of tetrapod vertebrates; it is separate from the vagus only in mammals.

accommodation. The ability of the eye to adjust its focusing power to the distance of the object viewed.

accommodation coefficient. The degree to which reflected or reevaporated molecules, on the average, accommodate their energy to that of the surface they strike; it is measured by the ratio of the observed heat loss from a surface to the theoretical heat loss which would occur if all the gas molecules came to thermal equilibrium with the surface.

accumulation coefficient. The rate of increase in the concentration of molecules adsorbed on a surface, compared to the concentration of the same type of molecules in the phase in contact with the surface.

accumulation time. The time necessary for the accumulation of a quantum of radiant energy before it can be released.

accumulator. A device for storing electric energy which may be discharged when needed; it consists of two plates which are immersed in a liquid.

acetabulum. The cup-shaped socket of the hip into which the femur fits.

acetal. A colorless organic liquid of pleasant odor; obtained by oxidation of alcohols or by heating aldehydes or ketones; used in cosmetics and medicine.

acetaldehyde. CH_3CHO; a colorless liquid with a pungent fruity smell, formed by oxidation of ethyl alcohol; further oxidation gives acetic acid; used in manufacturing plastics and dyes.

acetamide. CH_3CONH_2; colorless crystals, odorless when pure, used as a solvent.

acetanilide. $CH_3CONHC_6H_5$; a white, crystalline solid obtained from acetic acid and aniline; used in the alleviation or checking of fever.

acetate. A salt of acetic acid.

acetate plastics. Plastics made from cellulose acetate.

acetate rayon. Cellulose acetate rayon.

acetic acid. CH_3COOH; the acid contained in vinegar (3 to 6%); a colorless, corrosive liquid with a pungent smell; at low temperature, it solidifies to glacial acetic acid; used in the chemical industries.

acetic acid bacteria. Microorganisms that transform alcohol into acetic acid.

acetobacter. An aerobic bacillus which uses the oxidation of alcohol to acetic acid to secure its energy.

acetone. CH_3COCH_3; dimethyl ketone; a colorless inflammable liquid with a pleasant smell; used as a solvent.

acetylcholine. $C_7H_{17}O_3N$; a substance, released at the end of a motor nerve, which causes muscles to contract.

acetylene. $CH:CH$; a colorless inflammable gas; used in explosives, dyes.

achene. An indehiscent one-seeded fruit, with the seed attached to the ovary wall at one point only.

Acheson process. The use of an electric furnace for the conversion of coke to graphite or for the manufacture of carborundum.

achlamydeous. Said of flowers that lack sepals and petals; example, willow.

achromat. A compound lens so corrected as to have the same focal length for two or more different wave lengths.

achromatic. Free from color; a term applied to lenses.

achromatic stimulus. A visual stimulus that is able to excite a color sensation of no hue.

acid. A substance that turns blue litmus paper red and generally tastes sour; a compound of hydrogen which yields hydrogen ions in water.

acid anhydride. (1) The oxide of a nonmetal which combines with water to form an acid; (2) a compound derived from an acid by the removal of water.

acid number. The degree of acidity of a substance; same as acid value.

acid radical. The negative part of an acid; examples, SO_4^{--}, Cl^-.

acid salt. A salt in which only part of the hydrogen from its corresponding acid has been replaced by a metal; example, $NaHSO_3$.

acid soil. A soil containing an excess of acid.

acid, strong. An acid which, when dissolved in water, is ionized to a large extent.

acid value. A measure of the free fatty acids present in a fat or oil; the number of milligrams of KOH required to neutralize the free fatty acids in one gram of a substance.

acid, weak. An acid which, when dissolved in water, is dissociated only to a slight extent.

acid-fast. Resistant to acids; applied to bacteria, not readily decolorized by acid or other means when stained.

acidic hydrogen. The hydrogen atoms in an acid which can be replaced by metals to form salts.

acidimeter. A special hydrometer for measuring the concentration of acids.

acidimetry. The determination of the amount of acid present in a solution by titration.

acidolysis. Hydrolysis by means of an acid.

Acoelomata. Animals that do not have a coelom or body cavity; examples, Coelenterata, Platyhelminthes, Nemertinea, Nematoda.

acontia. Filaments bearing stinging cells in sea anemones.

acoustic absorptivity. The ratio of the sound energy absorbed by a surface to that incident on it.

acoustic center. A sensory area.

acoustic center, effective. An acoustic generator; the point from which the spherically divergent sound waves, noticeable at distant points, appear to diverge.

acoustic feedback. The return of a small part of the output of an acoustical device to the input of the same device.

acoustical mirage. The distortion of a wave front by a strong temperature gradient in such a way that part of the wave length overlaps another so that the illusion of two sound sources is created, even though only a single source exists.

acoustics. The study of sound and hearing; the factors that determine how well an auditorium permits hearing a program.

acquired characteristics. Characteristics developed by an organism because of the special conditions under which it lives. These properties are not inherited.

acquired immunity. Immunity to a disease which is acquired by artificial means, such as having the disease or by inoculation.

Acrania. A subphylum of Chordata, containing only species of Amphioxus; they have no brain, skull, or cartilaginous or bony skeleton; but they have a tubular nerve cord, notochord, and gill slits.

acriflavine. A reddish-yellow dye which is also used as a germicide and antiseptic.

acrolein. $CH_2:CH\cdot CHO$; a colorless inflammable liquid with an irritating smell; used as a disinfectant, in plastics.

acromegaly. A condition in man and other mammals, caused by excessive secretion of the pituitary gland, in which there is an enlargement of certain bones, such as those of the hands, feet, and parts of the face.

acromion. The prolongation of the spine of the scapula forming the point of the shoulder.

acropetal succession. The development of organs in succession toward an apex; the oldest at the base, the youngest at the tip; leaves on a shoot.

acrosome. A part of the head in an animal sperm, usually forming a cap over the nucleus.

acrylic acid. $CH_2:CH\cdot COOH$; a corrosive liquid; used in making acrylic resins.

acrylic resins. Polymers of acrylic, substituted acrylic, and methacrylic acids, their salts, esters, and other derivatives.

acrylonitrile. CH_2:$CH\cdot CN$; vinyl cyanide; a colorless liquid; used in the manufacture of plastics and synthetic rubber.

ACTH (adrenocorticotropic hormone). A hormone of the pituitary gland that controls the function of the adrenal cortex.

actinic. Said of radiation capable of producing chemical changes, such as the photographic effect of light.

actinic rays. The portion of the sunlight, rich in ultraviolet rays, which has a strong effect on a photographic plate.

actinide elements. Elements in the natural radioactive series that begins with actinium (atomic number 89) and ends with lawrencium (atomic number 103).

actinium. A radioactive element; chemical symbol Ac; atomic number 89.

actinometer. An instrument for measuring the actinic value of light or other radiation.

actinometry. The determination of the photochemical intensity of light.

actinomorphic. Having flowers of a regular or star pattern, capable of bisection in two or more planes into similar halves.

Actinomyces. Parasitic fungi with radiating arrangement of the mycelium.

actinomycete. A member of the genus Actinomyces; a group of filamentous bacteria, parasitic in mammals.

Actinopteri. A class of fish which includes all common fish except sharks and skates.

Actinozoa. Sea anemones, corals, sea pens; a class of Coelenterata; they have no medusa stage, just a more complex polyp.

actinula. A larval stage of a hydroid, resembling a polyp with a short stalk.

action potential. A potential variation during the activity of living tissue; a change of electric potential between the inside and outside of a nerve fiber, which marks the position of an impulse as it travels along the fiber.

activated. Made more reactive; said of an adsorbent, whose surface has been freed of adsorbed gases.

activated adsorption. Adsorption, involving chemical forces, in which the activation energy is relatively high.

activated carbon. A carbon having a large specific surface for adsorption of gases or liquids; used for decolorizing, in gas masks.

activated charcoal. A specially treated and finely divided charcoal of high adsorptivity; prepared from sawdust by heating

in a limited supply of air or steam.

activated deposit. Solid radioactive layer deposited on surfaces exposed to radioactive emanations.

activated water. Water treated by ionizing radiation.

activation analysis. An analytical method in which a very small quantity of an element is detected by bombarding with neutrons in a reactor.

activation energy. Energy required to start a reaction; the excess energy over the ground state which must be acquired by an atomic system in order that a particular process may occur.

active acquired immunity. Same as active immunity.

active deposit. Any radioactive substance deposited on a surface.

active gas. Gas that combines easily with other substances.

active mass. Mass per unit volume, usually expressed in moles per liter.

active transport. Substance transfer from a region of low to a region of high concentration, accomplished by energy expenditure from the metabolism.

activity and success learning. A form of behavior in which an animal learns after many repetitions; also called trial and error learning.

activity series. A table of metals or nonmetals arranged in the order of their descending activity.

actomyosin. A complex of two proteins, actin and myosin, which is the major constituent of muscle; contraction of muscles due to actomyosin fibrils.

adaptation. Same as adaption.

adapter. A device by means of which objects of different size are connected or made interchangeable.

adaptation. A structure, part, or characteristic which aids in the survival of plants or animals under certain environmental conditions.

adaptive radiation. Evolution, from a primitive type of organism, of several divergent forms adapted to different modes of life.

adaptive response. Capacity of an organism to react favorably to changed external conditions.

adaxial. Said of a leaf surface facing the stem.

addition compound. An organic compound formed by opening of double or triple bonds and adding new atoms or groups to the molecule.

additive color process. Color photography in which the color build-up is obtained by the addition of colors one to another in the form of light rather than as colorants.

additives. Substances added to compounds to obtain a desired quality.

additivity. The numerical value of the whole is the sum of its constituent parts; example, the molecular weight is the sum of the weights of constituent atoms.

adductor. A muscle which draws a part or limb toward the median line.

adenoid. A mass of spongy tissue near the place where the nose opens into the throat, sometimes interfering with speech or breathing; glandlike.

adhesion. The molecular attraction of layers of unlike matter.

adhesion discs. Device used to measure and compare the adhesion between glass and water and other liquids.

adhesive. Substance used to bond or stick together two or more layers or units of other materials.

adiabat. Line on a chart showing the adiabatic lapse rate, wet or dry.

adiabatic. Occurring without gain or loss of heat.

adiabatic processes. Changes which take place without transfer of heat.

adiactinic. Occurring without transmission of photochemically active rays.

adion. An ion that is free to move on the surface on which it is adsorbed but not away from it.

adipose fin. A fleshy fin without supporting spines, occurring behind the dorsal fin in some fishes.

adipose tissue. Fatty tissue.

adjustable-pitch propeller. One whose blades are so attached to the hub that they may be set to any desired pitch when stationary.

admittance. The reciprocal of impedance of an electric circuit.

admittance, electronic. The admittance of a vacuum tube which is caused by the action of electron beams within the tube.

adnation. Growing together of two or more whorls in flowers.

ADP (adenosine diphosphate. A nucleotide produced by the hydrolysis of ATP; its interaction with ATP is important to the transfer of energy through the cell.

adrenal gland. A ductless gland located near each kidney in vertebrates.

adrenalin. A hormone secreted by the adrenal glands.

adrenergic. Said of a motor nerve fiber; secreting at its end a substance, noradrenalin, when nerve impulses arrive there. This substance stimulates the effector innervated by the nerve fiber.

adsorbate. A substance adsorbed on the surface of another.

adsorbent. A substance on whose surface adsorption occurs.

adsorption. A process in which molecules or ions of one substance cling to the surface of another substance.

adsorption equilibrium. Equilibrium between a substance that is adsorbed on a surface and the same substance in a solution or other medium that is in contact with the surface.

adsorption potential. The energy change a molecule or ion undergoes in passing from the gas or solution phase to the surface of the adsorbent.

adsorption space. The thickness of an adsorbed layer.

advection. The transfer of air and air characteristics by horizontal motion.

advection fog. Fog formed when warm moist air comes in contact with colder surfaces.

adventitious. Arising in abnormal position.

adventitious bud. One which grows anywhere on the plant except in the axils of the leaves.

adventitious roots. Roots that develop in unusual places on plants.

aeciospore. Yellow, one-celled spore of rust fungi formed in special clusters called aecia.

aecium. In rust, a cluster cup which produces aeciospores.

aeolian deposits. Sediments and sedimentary rocks on deserts which are largely composed of wind-blown material.

aeolotropic. Having different properties in different directions as in certain crystals; not isotropic.

aeration. The process of combining a substance with air or some other gas; purifying water by spraying it into the air or passing air through it.

aerator. An apparatus for mixing air with other fluids; grain fumigator.

aerenchyma. Loose porous secondary respiratory tissue found in stems, especially of aquatic or marsh plants; thin-walled cells with large, air-filled intercellular spaces.

aerial roots. Roots of plants living on trees, which may also function as leaves.

aerial stems. Stems that are grown above the ground.

aerobic. Being able to thrive only where oxygen is present.

aerobic respiration. Respiration in presence of free oxygen.

aerodynamic volume. The total volume of an aircraft, including its projecting parts.

aerodynamics. Study of gases in motion and of the forces that act on bodies moving in air; study of the effect of air on moving surfaces, such as the wing, propeller, or rudder of an airplane.

aerodyne. Aircraft which derives

its lift in flight chiefly from aerodynamic forces.

aerolites. Meteorites; especially those consisting of stony material rather than iron.

aerology. A branch of meteorology which treats the atmosphere at high altitudes, that is, not affected by surface conditions.

aerometeorograph. An instrument in an airplane for investigating the atmospheric conditions at various levels.

aerometer. An instrument used to measure the density of gases.

aeronautics. The science of design, manufacture, maintenance, testing, and use of aircraft.

aeropause. The dividing line between outer space and areas in which man and aircraft can function.

aerophase. An air-navigation radio beacon.

aerophysics. The study of airflow, heat transfer, and similar problems as related to the design, construction, and engineering of high-speed, rocket-type aircraft.

aerosol. A suspensoid in which gas is the dispersing medium.

aerospace. In astronautics, the total expanse beyond the earth's surface.

aerostat. Any lighter-than-air aircraft.

aerostatics. The science of gases at rest; it treats the equilibrium between gaseous fluids and solid objects immersed in them.

aerovane. An instrument that measures and records both the direction and speed of the wind.

afferent. Said of (1) nerve fibers carrying impulses toward the central nervous system; (2) arteries leading to vertebrate gills.

afferent fibers. Those which convey impulses to the sense organs, brain, or spinal cord.

affinity. Chemical attraction; force binding atoms together.

afterburner. Sometimes called tailpipe burner, a device fitted to a turbojet for extra thrust; it injects additional fuel into hot exhaust gases.

afterdamp. Gas, consisting primarily of carbon dioxide and nitrogen, that remains in a coal mine after an explosion.

afterflow. Plastic flow in a solid after the external stresses responsible for it have ceased.

afterglow. Phosphorescence; persistence of luminosity from a gas-discharge tube after the source of excitation has been removed.

afterimage. The image *"seen"* after the retina has been fatigued by a continued fixed stimulus; an impression which remains of a visual object after the direct stimulation has

ceased.

Ag. Chemical symbol for silver.

agamont. A single-celled animal which reproduces asexually.

agamospermy. All types of apomixis in which embryo and seeds are formed by asexual means; it excludes vegetative reproduction.

agar-agar. A gelatinlike substance obtained from seaweed; used in bacteriological culture media and in some foods and drugs.

agate. Multicolored striped chalcedony; silicon dioxide, SiO_2; used for ornamental purposes.

age hardening. Hardening an alloy at relatively low temperature.

agglomerate. Rock composed of water-worn fragments of volcanic origin.

agglomeration. The gathering of particles into a mass; large clump formation by parasites on the host.

agglutination. Cementing together; clumping of the blood or of bacteria.

agglutinin. Antibody which causes blood corpuscles or bacteria to clump together.

agglutinogen. An antigen which helps form agglutinins.

agglutinoid. An agglutinin which has lost its property of causing agglutination because of heat.

aggradation. Making the earth's surface more uniform by depositing material in depressions, such as river beds.

aggregate. The solid particles which form the major constituent of concrete.

aggregate fruit. Fleshy fruits which develop from several ovaries of a single flower, each single ovary is called a fruitlet; example, strawberry.

aggregate glands. Silk glands of spiders which produce the viscid spiral lines of the web.

aggressive coloration. Resemblance to the environment to conceal an animal as it lies in wait for prey.

aging of magnet. Increasing the magnetic permanency of a magnet.

Agnatha. Class of vertebrates; aquatic, fishlike, but without jaws and the two pairs of fins; example, lampreys and hagfish.

agonic line. An imaginary line on the earth's surface passing through points where the magnetic declination is 0°.

aileron. Hinged flap on an airplane wing which is used to turn the plane.

aileron angle. The angular displacement of an aileron from its neutral position. It is positive when the trailing edge is below the neutral position.

aileron roll. Rolling motion of an aircraft due to displacement of the ailerons.

aimless drainage. Drainage or stream pattern which occurs in

low swampy lands.

air. A colorless, odorless mixture of nitrogen and oxygen, with traces of other gases, water vapor, and some impurities.

air bladder. A membranous sac filled with air which helps fish control their movements by its buoyancy; it may also have respiratory or auditory functions.

air compressor. Pump used to increase air pressure above normal; air is then used as motive power.

air condenser. A condenser in which air spaces between disks serve to insulate the charges from one another.

air conduction. Conducting sound to the inner ear by an air path, that is, through the outer ear canal.

air control. Means operating the control surfaces of an aircraft.

air gap. (1) Spark gap, comprising two conducting electrodes, separated by air; (2) discontinuity in the material of magnetic circuits.

air lock. Airtight compartment in which the air pressure can be increased to the desired value; used in civil engineering.

air mass. The volume of air extending many miles over the earth's surface and up to several thousand feet in height; it moves as a unit and has the same temperature, pressure, and moisture content.

air mass analysis. Means of weather forecasting.

air monitor. Device for detecting and measuring air-borne radioactivity; used for warning and control purposes.

air pressure. The force exerted by air on a unit surface, measured, e.g., in pounds per square inch.

air propeller. Power-driven screw converting rotation into thrust.

air sacs. (1) In mammals and insects, very tiny, thin-walled chambers where new air and used air are exchanged and which make flying easier; (2) in water plants, small air-filled chambers which help the plants to float.

air space. (1) In leaves, large intercellular space; (2) space left between adjacent windings of an inductance coil to reduce dielectric loss.

air speed. The speed of an aircraft related to that of the air in which it moves.

air speed indicator. An instrument for the measurement of air speed.

air thermometer. An instrument for measuring temperature by the variations of air volume and pressure with temperature.

air-cushion vehicle, or **ground-effect machine** (GEM). A vehicle that flies close to land or water on a cushion of air created by a lifting propeller or

ducted fan.

airfoil. Any surface, such as airplane wing, aileron, or rudder, which is designed to obtain useful reaction, especially lift, from the air through which it moves.

airfoil profile. The outline of an airfoil.

airplane. Any heavier-than-air craft that depends on the relative motion of air for its support in flight; it has fixed wings and is power driven.

airship. A lighter-than-air craft provided with a power and control system, such as a dirigible. It may be rigid, semirigid, or flexible.

air-slaked lime. Powdered lime; quicklime exposed to the air for a long period of time.

airy points. The best points for supporting a shaft horizontally with the danger of bending at a minimum.

akene. Same as achene.

Al. Chemical symbol for aluminum.

alabaster. Natural massive form of hydrated calcium sulfate, $CaSO_4 \cdot 2H_2O$; with marble-like design; used for carving ornamental objects.

alastrim. A contagious virus disease; a mild form of smallpox.

albedo. In nuclear physics, the ratio of the neutron current density out of a medium to the neutron current density into it; ratio of light falling on a planet or satellite to that reflected.

albino. Man, animal, or plant lacking natural coloring matter.

albumin. Water-soluble simple proteins found in egg, meat, and vegetable tissues.

alcohol. Organic compound which contains one or more hydroxyl, OH, groups, such as ethyl alcohol.

alcohol, grain. Ethanol or ethyl alcohol, used as a solvent or in beverages; C_2H_5OH.

alcohol, wood. Methanol or methyl alcohol, CH_3OH; used for denaturing ethyl alcohol, as a solvent or antifreeze.

alcoholometer. Special hydrometer for measuring the percentage of alcohol in mixtures of alcohol and water.

alcoholometry. Determination of the ethyl alcohol content of spirits and other solutions.

Alcyonaria. Soft corals, coelenterates, which have eight tentacles and eight mesenteries.

Aldebaran. Leading star of the asterism known as the Hyades which follow the Pleiades in their nightly journey across the sky.

aldehyde. Organic compound containing the –CHO group; example, acetaldehyde, CH_3-CHO.

aldol. $CH_3CH(OH)CH_2CHO$; thick oily liquid formed by the condensation of acetaldehyde.

aldol condensation. Union of two molecules of aldehyde or ketone to form an aldol.

aleurone grains. Granules of protein occurring in storage regions of plants; common in seeds.

Alexanderson alternator. High-frequency inductor in which the rapid rotation of a slotted rotor induces current in the stator coils.

alexandrite. Variety of chrysoberyl; it appears emerald green by daylight but columbine red in artificial light.

algae. Simple chlorophyll-containing plants without roots, stems, or leaves.

algicide. Chemical used to kill algae.

alginic acid. Complex organic compound, related to carbohydrates, found in certain seaweeds; used for preparing emulsions and as a thickening agent in the food industry.

alidade. Instrument for measuring heights and distances.

alimentary canal. The digestive tract.

alizarin. Dihydroxyanthraquinone; red crystalline dye.

alkadiene. Straight- or branched-chain hydrocarbon with two double bonds between carbon atoms.

alkali. Substance that gives a basic reaction in water, that is, turns litmus paper blue; example, sodium hydroxide.

alkali metal. Monovalent metal whose hydroxide is a strong base; example, sodium.

alkalimetry. The determination by titration with standard acid of the amount of alkali present in a solution.

alkaline. Term applied to an alkali; opposite of acidic.

alkaline earth metals. Group of bivalent metals consisting of beryllium, magnesium, calcium, strontium, barium, and radium.

alkaline soils. Soils with an excess of alkali.

alkaline water. Water that contains compounds of calcium, sodium, and magnesium and is unfit for human consumption.

alkaloid. Complex nitrogenous organic compound of alkaline reaction, found in plants; example, nicotine.

alkane. A straight- or branched-chain hydrocarbon in which the carbon atoms are connected by a single covalent bond; a member of the paraffin series.

alkene. A straight- or branched-chain hydrocarbon in which two carbon atoms are connected by a double covalent bond; a member of the olefin series.

alkyd resins. Reaction products of plyhydric alcohols and polybasic acids; used in lacquers and varnishes.

alkyl radicals. Univalent hydrocarbon radicals, especially those derived from hydrocarbons of the paraffin series and having the general formula $C_nH_{2n+1}^-$.

alkylation. Refining gasoline to improve its quality by the addition of side chains to the hydrocarbon molecules; introducing an alkyl group into a hydrocarbon by heat, pressure, and in the presence of a catalyst.

alkyne. Straight- or branched-chain hydrocarbon in which two carbon atoms are linked by a triple covalent bond; member of the acetylene series.

allantois. Saclike organ that grows out of the abdomen of a vertebrate embryo; it contains blood vessels and assists in obtaining oxygen and eliminating carbon dioxide in some forms of animals.

alleles. Opposite characteristics carried by the same gene.

allelomorph. (1) Same as alleles, in biology; (2) in chemistry, one of two or more isomorphic substances which consist of the same atoms having the same valences, but differing in their linkage; the first of two or more isomers to be recovered or separated from a system.

allochromatic. Said of a crystal which has photoconductivity due to inclusions of microscopic impurities or as a result of exposure to certain forms of radiation.

allochromy. Any radiation of light or fluorescence in which the wave length or color of the emitted light is different from that of the absorbed light.

allochthonous. Extraneous; said of sedimentary rocks whose constituents have been transported and deposited some distance from the place of origin.

allogamy. Cross fertilization.

allomorphism. Property of substances of the same chemical composition but of different crystal forms.

allopatric. Having different geographical areas of distribution for different species.

allopolyploid. A polyploid in which one or more of the chromosomes come from one species, the rest from another.

allotetraploid. An allopolyploid which is created when an ordinary hybrid between two different species, containing a set of chromosomes from each parent, doubles its chromosome number.

allotriomorphic. Said of minerals in igneous rocks which are not bounded by their typical crystal faces.

allotropes. Two or more forms of the same element; example, ozone and oxygen.

allowed band. The possible energy range of electrons in a solid.

alloy. A special metal formed when two or more metals are melted together.

alloy, antifriction. An alloy which reduces friction.

alloy, fusible. A low-melting alloy.

alloy, nonferrous. An alloy not based on iron.

alluvial fans. Broad, fan-shaped accumulations of sediment deposited when the velocity of rivers, streams, or floods is reduced and cannot keep the particles in suspension.

alluvial soils. Soils, whose parent material, aluvium, has been transported and deposited by water.

alluvium. Deposit of sediment left by a stream.

alpha. (1) First letter of the Greek alphabet; (2) the brightest star in a constellation.

alpha iron. Soft, magnetic form of iron.

alpha particles. High-speed, positively charged helium nuclei.

alpha rays. Alpha particles emitted by radioactive elements.

alpha tocopherol. Vitamin E; it prevents sterility in rats, but probably not in man.

alpha-ray spectrum. Spectrum obtained by separation of alpha particles of different speeds, usually by a magnetic field alone or by both magnetic and electric fields.

alphyl. Univalent hydrocarbon radical.

altazimuth. An instrument for measuring the azimuth difference between some celestial object and a fixed azimuth mark on the surface of the earth.

alternate arrangement. Leaves or branches arranged singly on the stem of a plant.

alternate host parasites. Parasites which must live on two hosts during their life cycle.

alternating current. Electric current that reverses the direction of flow many times a second.

alternating-current component. Direct current which acts like an alternating current. The current strength increases and decreases, making the wave picture look like that of an alternating current, yet electrons flow in one direction only.

alternation of generation. Form of reproduction in which sexual and asexual generations alternate with each other; example, mosses.

alternator. A generator that is operated at constant speed and transforms mechanical energy into electrical energy of the required frequency.

altigraph. An altimeter equipped with a recording mechanism.

altimeter. An aneroid barometer in an airplane which measures the altitude by the decrease of air pressure with height.

altitude. (1) Height above sea level, or above the level of the ocean surface; (2) number of degrees (from 0 to 90) of a heavenly body above the horizon.

alto-cumulus. High (about two miles) widespread cotton-ball cloud, indicating fair weather.

alto-stratus. Heavy cloud formation, about three miles up; it may result in rain.

altricial. Said of birds which are born naked and usually blind and are raised in nests; example, robin.

alum. Potassium aluminum sulfate; used as an astringent.

alumina. Aluminum oxide; used as an abrasive.

aluminothermy. A thermit or similar process; reduction of metallic oxides by fine aluminum powder.

aluminum. Light metal, chemical symbol Al; atomic number 13.

aluminum brass. Brass containing small amounts of aluminum; used for condenser tubes.

aluminum bronze. Alloy containing 90% copper and 10% aluminum; used for ornamental articles and imitation gold.

aluminum chloride. $AlCl_3$; colorless crystals; used in synthesis.

aluminum oxide. Al_2O_3; colorless crystals.

aluminum sulfate. $Al_2(SO_4)_3$; colorless crystals; used for purifying water.

alum-stone. Same as alunite.

alunite. Mineral consisting of potassium and aluminum sulfate and hydroxide; used as a fertilizer.

alveolus. (1) Small cavity, such as the tiny air sacs in the mammalian lung; (2) the secreting portion of an alveolar gland; (3) socket of a tooth.

Am. Chemical symbol for americium.

Amagat units. System of units in which the unit of pressure is the atmosphere and the unit of volume is the gram-molecular volume (22.4 liters at standard conditions).

Amagat-Leduc rule. The volume occupied by a mixture of gases is equal to the total of the volumes they would occupy individually at the temperature and pressure of the mixture.

amalgam. Alloy of mercury with another metal; used for dental fillings and making mirrors.

amalgamation. Extraction of precious metals from their ores; covering with an amalgam.

amatol. Explosive mixture of 80% ammonium nitrate and 20% TNT.

amber. A yellowish resin found as fossil in alluvial soils.

ambergris. A fragrant waxy substance found in the intestine of the sperm whale and used in the manufacture of perfumes.

ambient temperature. Temperature of the surrounding medium, such as a gas or liquid.

ambipolar. Said of the current in an electrolytic cell, in which there are ions moving in both directions.

amboceptor. Antibody that joins the antigen with the complement.

ambulacral grooves. Grooves in the arms of the starfish which contain rows of openings through which the tube feet are extended; found also in other echinoderms.

americium. Artificially produced metallic element; chemical symbol Am; atomic number 95.

ametabolous. The young being images of their parents; property of certain insects.

amethyst. Purple or violet quartz; the color is believed to be due to the admixture of a small amount of manganese compounds.

Amici prism. Prism combination by which a beam of light is dispersed intraspectrum without mean deviation; used in spectroscopy.

amides. Organic compounds containing a —$CONH_2$ group and being derived from organic acids.

amidol. $C_6H_3OH(NH_2)_2 \cdot 2HCl$; grayish-white crystals; used as a developer in photography.

amines. Organic derivatives of ammonia obtained by substituting hydrocarbon radicals for one or more hydrogen atoms; organic bases related to proteins; RNH_2, R_2NH, or R_3N; example, methylamine CH_3-NH_2.

amino acids. Organic compounds that contain a carboxyl group and one or more amino or imino groups, thus having a dual character of acids and bases; constituents of proteins, forming giant molecules.

amino group. The univalent group, —NH_2.

aminoplast resins. Synthetic resins prepared from amino compounds; example, urea-formaldehyde.

amitosis. Cell division in which there is a simple cleavage of the nucleus without change in structure, followed by a division of the cytoplasm.

ammeter. A low-resistance instrument for the measurement of current. A galvanometer may be converted to an ammeter by placing a low-resistance shunt in parallel with the movable coil.

ammonia. NH_3; pungent-smelling gas, very soluble in water to give an alkaline solution, ammonium hydroxide, NH_4OH; used in refrigeration and in the manufacture of explosives and fertilizers.

ammonification. Decomposition of amino acids by bacteria, resulting in the production of ammonia.

ammonite. Extinct mollusk of the Mesozoic era whose shell resembled a coiled spring.

ammonium. Univalent radical, —NH_4, which in compounds behaves like an alkali metal, giving ammonium salts.

ammonium chloride. Sal ammoniac; NH_4Cl; white crystals; used in dry batteries.

ammonium hydroxide. NH_4OH; aqueous solution of ammonia.

ammonium nitrate. NH_4NO_3; colorless crystals; used in explosives and fertilizers.

ammonium sulfamate. NH_4SO_3-NH_2; colorless plates; used for fireproofing wood.

ammonium sulfate. $(NH_4)_2SO_4$; colorless soluble crystals; a byproduct of coal-gas manufacture; used in fireproofing and as a fertilizer.

amnion. A thin sac surrounding an embryo and containing a watery fluid.

Amniota. A group of vertebrates that develop an amnion and allantois; examples, reptiles, birds, and mammals.

amoeba. A microscopic shapeless one-celled animal that reproduces by division.

amoebocyte. Cell with active amoeboid movement found in the blood and other body fluids of invertebrates.

amoeboid movement. Streaming of protoplasm into one or more pseudopods.

amoebulae. Spores of amoeboid form which are produced by some one-celled animals.

amorphous. Noncrystalline; example, rubber.

amperage. The current, either alternating or direct, flowing through a wire.

ampere. A unit of electric current; 1,000,000 microamperes; 1,000 milliamperes; the current that will deposit 0.001118 gram of silver per second from an aqueous solution of silver nitrate; also called international ampere.

ampere turn. Unit of magnetomotive force, corresponding to the effect of a current of one ampere traversing one turn or winding; thus the total force is calculated by multiplying the amperes by the number of turns of an electromagnet.

ampere-hour. The quantity of electricity equivalent to a current of one ampere flowing in a conductor for one hour.

Ampère's rule. The magnetic flux generated by a current in a wire encircles the current counterclockwise, if the current is approaching the observer.

Ampère's theory of magnetism. The magnetic property is due to a current flowing in the molecules of the magnet.

Amperian current. An electric current in a resistanceless circuit in an atom or a molecule, accounting for its magnetic moment.

amperometric titration. Titration in which the equivalence point is determined by measuring the diffusion current which flows through the system as a result of imposing a constant voltage across two electrodes in the solution.

amphiaster. The figures produced by two asters and the spindle in the dividing cell.

amphibians. (1) Animals which may live both on land and in water; they have gills when young and develop lungs when they are adult; example, frog; (2) airplanes built to arise from and alight on either water or land.

amphibious. Capable of living either in water or on land; example, toad.

amphiboles. Large group of rock-forming silicates.

amphibolite. Crystalline rock of metamorphic character, containing amphibole.

amphicoelous. Concave at both ends; said of some vertebrae.

amphicribral. Said of vascular bundles in which xylem is surrounded by phloem.

amphidiploid. Same as allotetraploid.

amphimixis. True sexual reproduction.

Amphineura. Class of Mollusca, including Chitons; small group of marine animals with primitive features.

amphioxus. A small, burrowing, spindle-shaped marine animal; a possible ancestor of vertebrates.

Amphipoda. Order of Crustacea, including fresh-water shrimps.

amphiprotic. Capable of acting either as an acid or as a base.

amphitrichous. Having at each end a single flagellum or a tuft of flagella.

amphivasal. Arranged in vascular bundles, the strand of phloem being completely surrounded by xylem.

amphoteric. Acting as either an acid or a base; example, Al_2O_3.

amplidyne. A direct-current generator which yields a large power output from a small power input; used in servomechanisms.

amplifier. A device, usually a radio tube, for increasing the energy of a circuit.

amplitron. A high-efficiency microwave tube; with a battery of such tubes microwave energy is beamed to antennas on a platform at an altitude of 30,000 feet and converted into heat so that a stream of compressed air can power a turbine.

amplitude. The peak value of a wave; the amount of displacement in any oscillatory motion; usually applied to the motion of an air particle displaced by a sound wave, or to the motion of a vibrating string or pendulum.

amplitude modulation (AM). Variation of the amplitude of the carrier wave in accordance with the sound waves to be transmitted.

ampulla. A small bladder-shaped enlargement; water sacs attached to the tube feet of echinoderms.

ampulliform gland. Silk gland of spiders which produces the radial lines of the web.

amygdaloid. A vesicular rock, commonly lava, whose cavities have been filled with a secondary deposit of minerals; almond-shaped.

amyl. The univalent radical —C_5H_{11}.

amyl acetate. $C_5H_{11}COCH_3$; colorless liquid; used as a solvent in perfumes, lacquers.

amylase. Enzyme in plants and the pancreatic juice which effects digestion of starch to maltose.

anabatic wind. A wind which blows uphill by the convection of warm air.

anaerobic. Being able to thrive best in places where there is little or no free oxygen. Anaerobic organisms secure their oxygen by breaking down foods or other substances in which they live.

anaerobic respiration. Respiration without using oxygen from the air.

anal fin. Fin along the low midline of the body near the tail fin of fish.

analog computer. One of the two basic types of computers; usually built for special purposes, analog computers translate numbers into varying physical quantities; in electronic computers of this type a series of numbers is represented by initial voltages; the resulting voltage is the answer.

analogues. Structures that are not homologous but have a functional resemblance.

analytical balance. A sensitive instrument for weighing small amounts of substances very accurately.

analyzer. A Nicol prism in a polarimeter for determining the properties of polarized light.

Anamnia. Vertebrates which do not develop an amnion during embryonic life; examples, fish, amphibia.

anamorphism. Constructive metamorphism by which new minerals are formed from existing simpler minerals.

anandrous. Said of flowers which

lack stamens.

anaphase. The third phase of mitosis; one chromosome from each pair is moved to opposite sides of the cell.

anaphylactic shock. Violent symptoms caused in a sensitive animal by the second injection of a protein.

anaphylactogen. A substance which can cause anaphylaxis.

anaphylaxis. Same as anaphylactic shock.

anastomosis. Communication between two or more blood vessels, nerves, or other parts of the body.

anatase. Crystalline forms of natural titanium dioxide, TiO_2.

anatomy. The study of the structure of living organisms.

anatoxin. Detoxicated diphtheria toxin which can still stimulate formation of antitoxin.

anatropous. The ovule being reversed, with the micropyle close to the side of the hilum and the chalaza at the opposite end.

anchor ice. Spongy ice formed in stream beds which tends to reduce the velocity of the water and freezing takes place.

anchoring air roots. Very short nonabsorptive roots growing out horizontally from the stem and fastening the plant to a support, such as a wall or tree trunk.

Andrade's indicator. A solution of red acid fuchsin which is turned yellow by sodium hydroxide.

androdioecious. Having male and hermaphrodite flowers on separate plants.

androecium. Stamens of a flower collectively.

androgenesis. The development of an egg after the entry of the male germ cell without the participation of the egg nucleus; the embryo contains only paternal chromosomes.

androgens. Hormones made by the sex glands, which induce male characteristics.

androgynous. Having both male and female organs.

Andromede. Bielid meteor showers which were observed in the latter part of November; they are very rare now.

andromonoecious. Having male and hermaphrodite flowers on the same plant.

androsporangia. Sporangia which produce zoospores that develop into dwarf males.

androsterone. Male sex hormone.

-ane. Suffix for paraffin hydrocarbons.

anechoic room. A room in which sound reflections from the boundary surfaces have been reduced to a neglible amount.

anemograph. Instrument used for recording wind velocity.

anemometer. A device for measuring the velocity of wind.

anemoscope. An instrument actuated by a wind vane, and showing wind direction on a calibrated scale.

aneroid barometer. Barometer indicating atmospheric pressure by the expansion and contraction of a metallic capsule connected to an indicator needle on the dial; it also indicates altitude.

aneuploid. Having more or less than an integral multiple of the haploid number of chromosomes; unbalanced genetically.

aneurysm. A pathological sac formation by dilatation of the walls of an artery which communicates with the interior of the artery and is, therefore, filled with blood.

angiosperms. A large group of flowering plants which produce their seeds inside a ripening ovary or fruit.

angle of attack. The angle between the relative wind and the chord of an airfoil.

angle of bank. Same as angle of roll.

angle of contact. The angle which a liquid surface forms with the submerged part of the solid surface with which it is in contact.

angle of departure. The angle between the line of propagation of a radio wave and the earth's surface at the point of transmission.

angle of deviation. The angular change in the direction of a ray of light or other electromagnetic radiation, after entering another medium.

angle of friction. The angle of a plane surface, inclined relatively to the horizon, on which a body will, under specific conditions, just begin to slide. It varies with the nature of the materials in contact.

angle of incidence. The angle formed by an incident ray of light and a line drawn perpendicularly to the reflecting surface.

angle of lag. The phase angle by which the current lags behind the voltage.

angle of lead. The angle through which the commutator brushes are moved out of the normal plane to avoid sparking; the phase angle by which the current is ahead of the voltage.

angle of pitch. The angle between the longitudinal axis of an aircraft and the direction of the relative wind.

angle of reflection. The angle between the normal and the reflected ray of light from a mirror or surface; it is equal to the angle of incidence.

angle of repose. The maximum angle with the horizontal at which an object on an inclined plane will retain its position without tending to slide; angle

of friction.

angle of roll. The acute angle through which an aircraft must be rotated about its longitudinal axis in order to bring its lateral axis into a horizontal plane; if the right wing is lower than the left, this angle is positive.

angle of separation. The angle between an outward-drawn radius to any point of the line of separation and the direction of advance of the body in a sphere or a cylinder moving transversely through a fluid.

angle of slip. The angle between surfaces of slip or shear and the direction of stress during flow or during the plastic deformation of a solid.

angle of stabilizer setting. The angle between the line of thrust of an aircraft and the chord of the stabilizer.

angle of wing setting. The angle between the plane of the wing chord and the line of thrust.

angle of yaw. (1) The acute angle between the direction of the relative wind and the plane of symmetry of an aircraft; (2) the angle made by the direction of fluid flow with the direction displayed by a velocity-measuring instrument immersed in the flowing fluid.

anglesite. Naturally occurring lead sulfate.

ångström (angstrom). A small unit of length; 10,000,000 angstroms equal 39.37 inches; 1×10^{-8} centimeter.

angular acceleration. The rate of change of angular velocity; generally measured in radians per second per second.

angular distance. In astronomy, the distance between two stars, measured by the arc passing through them, with the observer being in the center.

angular impulse. The time integral of a torque; measured by the change in angular momentum which it would impart to a free mass if acting about a principal axis.

angular magnification. The ratio of the angle which is made by the optic axis with a ray emerging from an optical instrument to the angle of the corresponding incident ray.

angular momentum. The product of the moment of inertia and the angular velocity.

angular rate of the earth's rotation. Fifteen degrees per hour.

angular unconformity. An angle between the new horizontal sediment and the old rocks when the first covers the second due to submergence.

angular velocity. The rate of change of angular displacement; measured, as a rule, in radians per second.

anhydride (acid anhydride). A chemical compound obtained

from an acid by the elimination of water or a compound which reacts with water to yield an acid.

anhydrite. Naturally occurring anhydrous calcium sulfate, $CaSO_4$.

anhydrous. Without water; applied especially to a substance from which the water of crystallization has been removed.

anhysteretic. Taking place without hysteresis.

aniline. $C_6H_5NH_2$; phenyl amine; a coal-tar compound used in the manufacture of dyes and drugs.

animal charcoal. An adsorptive charcoal obtained by charring bones and other animal substances; used as a decolorizing agent.

animal hemisphere. That part of the egg which is composed of active cells.

animal pole. The apex of the upper hemisphere of the developing ovum, which contains little or no yolk.

animalcule. A very tiny animal, visible only under the microscope; example, Infusoria.

anion. An ion which moves toward the anode during electrolysis; a negative ion.

anionic current. The portion of the electric current carried by the anions.

anisogamete. A gamete that differs from the other conjugant either in size or in form.

anisogamy. Union of unlike gametes.

anisotropic. (1) Having different optical or other physical properties in different directions; (2) in botany, assuming different positions in response to external stimuli; (3) in zoology, displaying polarity with respect to the primary axis extending from the animal to the vegetable pole.

anisotropic medium. Any medium whose properties are different in different directions.

ankylosis (anchylosis). A union or knitting together of two or more bones or parts of bones.

annealing. Slow cooling after heating of metals to remove internal stress, to improve physical properties and workability; used in metallurgy and glass manufacture.

Annelida. A group of worms, having an elongated segmented body, a digestive tube, and a vascular system containing red blood; some have appendages without joints; examples, leech and earthworm.

annihilation radiation. Radiation induced by the collision and mutual annihilation of an electron and a positron moving in opposite directions.

annual. A plant which sprouts from seeds, grows to maturity, produces seeds, and dies in one growing season; one-year plant.

annual parallax. Yearly apparent change in the position of stars due to the annual motion of the earth around the sun.

annual range of temperature. The difference between the average temperatures of the warmest and coldest months.

annual ring. The ringlike band in the cross section of a woody tissue corresponding to one year's growth.

annual variation. The very small regular variation of the magnetic declination during a year in a given location.

annular eclipse. An eclipse of the sun in which the moon does not cover the sun completely, but leaves a ring of the sun exposed.

annulus. (1) A group of special cells in the capsule of ferns which facilitates the opening of the dry capsule; (2) in mosses, thick-walled cells along the rim of the capsule to which the peristome is attached.

anode. The positive electrode of an electrochemical apparatus.

anode drop. The voltage drop between the anode and the arc stream.

anode fall. In a gas-discharge tube, the component of the potential difference between the anode and cathode which is independent of the anode current.

anode mud. The insoluble residue remaining on the anode after electrolytic refining.

anode rays. Positively charged particles emitted by the heated anode of a vacuum tube.

anodizing. Producing a resistant oxide coating on a metal surface by making the anode in an electrolytic bath.

anolyte. The liquid surrounding the anode during electrolysis.

anomalous dispersion. An inversion of the usual change of refractive index with the wave length in the vicinity of an absorption band.

Anopheles. Tropical mosquitoes which are secondary hosts of malaria parasites.

Anoplura. Sucking lice; parasitic on mammals, whose blood they suck.

anotron. A cold-cathode, glow-discharge diode.

Anseriformes. Gooselike aquatic birds; examples, duck, swan, goose.

antagonism. (1) Interference with, or inhibition of, the growth of parasitic microorganisms by other microorganisms through the creation of unfavorable conditions; (2) opposing action of two muscles; example, the contraction of one muscle is accompanied by relaxation of the other; (3) the property of one toxic compound of neu-

tralizing another.

Antarctic Circle. 66½ ° south latitude; the circle bounding the South Pole.

Antares. One of the largest stars known; the "Red Giant" in the Scorpio constellation, estimated at over 300,000,000 miles in diameter.

antecedent river. River that antedated the present topography.

antecedent stream. A stream whose course or valley is not adapted to the existing structure and topography of the region.

antenna. (1) A conductor system for transmitting and receiving radio waves; (2) one of the feelers on the head of an insect.

antennules. Many jointed feelers found on some arthropods and located near the antennae.

anterior. (1) Situated near the head of an animal's body, or which is foremost in normal locomotion; (2) facing away from the main axis.

anthelminthics. Drugs used to remove parasitic worms from their hosts.

anther. A small knob at the end of the stamen of a flower, which contains pollen grains.

antheridium. The mother cell containing the male sexual cells found in algae and ferns.

anthesis. The opening of flower buds; also the life span of a flower from the opening of the bud to the starting of fruit.

anthocyan (anthocyanin). Coloring material found in the cell sap of plants; it is red in the presence of acids, but otherwise blue or violet.

anthoxanthin. Water-soluble yellow pigment occurring in plants.

anthozoa. Same as actinozoa.

anthracene. $C_{14}H_{10}$; colorless crystals showing bluish fluorescence, obtained from coal tar; used in the manufacture of dyes.

anthropoid. Similar to man.

Anthropoidea. A suborder of Primates, including monkeys, anthropoid apes, and man.

anthropology. The study of the natural history of man.

antibiosis. Antagonism between microorganisms, usually eliminating one of them.

antibiotic. An antibacterial substance produced by a living microorganism, such as a bacterium or fungus; example, penicillin.

antibody. Any substance in the blood which kills, or prevents the growth or reproduction of, disease bacteria, or neutralizes their poisons.

anticathode. (1) In an x-ray tube, the plate or block of metal on which the electron beam is focused and from which the x-rays are radiated; (2) the anode in a vacuum tube.

antichlor. A compound for neutralizing free chlorine; example, sodium bisulfite used in the bleaching industry.

anticlinal. (1) Having a division of cells situated approximately at right angles to the apex; (2) in geology, a fold in which the sides dip from a common crest.

anticline. An upward opening fold of rocks underlying the earth's crust, which was formed under enormous pressure.

anticlinorium. An arching group of anticlines.

anticryptic colors. The resemblance of animals to their environment to facilitate survival.

anticyclogenesis. Development of a new anticyclone.

anticyclone. An atmospheric condition in which wind direction and pressure distribution are opposite to those of a cyclone; the clockwise movement of cool air away from the area of high pressure; the high between two lows.

anticyclonic storm. High winds with freezing temperature and snow; example, blizzard.

antidiuretic hormone. A hormone secreted by the posterior lobe of the pituitary gland; it stimulates water reabsorption by the urinary tubule so that the volume of urine decreases; diabetes insipidus is caused by its deficiency.

antidrag wire. A wire usually built into the wing of a plane to resist forces acting parallel to the chord of the wing and in the direction of flight.

antifriction alloys. Friction-reducing alloys especially of lead, tin, zinc, and antimony used in bearings.

antigen. A plant, animal, or chemical substance, which produces an antibody when introduced into the body.

antiknock agent. Chemical which, when added in small amounts to gasoline, raises its octane number and thus reduces its tendency to detonate; example, tetraethyl lead.

antimatter (antiparticles). Matter composed of particles with charges opposite to those of known matter; atoms of antimatter have negative nuclei and positive electrons.

antimony. Bluish-white, lustrous, brittle metal; chemical symbol Sb; atomic number 51; used in alloying.

antineutron. The antiparticle of the neutron.

antinode. (1) The point of largest amplitude in stationary waves; (2) in acoustics, the place of maximum disturbance in interference between waves of the same frequency.

antioxidant. A negative catalyst which slows down the oxidation of rubber; example, phenyl-beta-naphthylamine.

antiozonants. Materials which impart to natural and synthetic rubber compounds various degrees of resistance to atmospheric ozone.

anitpodals. Three small wall-less cells in the embryo sac at the opposite end to the egg apparatus; each has a nucleus and a cytoplasm.

antiproton. An elementary particle having a mass essentially equal to that of the proton, but differing from the proton in the sign of its charge which is negative.

antitrade winds. Winds opposite in direction to and above the northeast and southwest trade winds.

Antonoff's rule. At the interface between two saturated liquid layers which are in equilibrium, the tension is equal to the difference between the individual surface tensions against air or vapor of the two saturated solutions.

antrum. A body cavity or chamber; example, a sinus.

Anura. An order of tailless amphibians; example, frog.

anus. Terminal opening of the alimentary canal through which solid wastes are eliminated from the body.

anvil. (1) The middle one of the three small bones in the mammalian ear; (2) the characteristic spreading top of a cumulonimbus cloud in full development; (3) the iron block used for supporting objects while forging.

aorta. The great artery which carries the blood from the heart to the body.

aortic arches. Bilateral branches of the aorta which, in fish, amphibia, and the early stages of vertebrates, branch out from the vicinity of the heart and unite again in the dorsal aorta.

aortic loops. In the earthworm, branches of the dorsal blood vessels looping around the esophagus and communicating with the ventral blood vessels; also called "hearts."

apatite. A mineral occurring in igneous rocks; calcium phosphate with calcium fluoride or calcium chloride.

ape. A long-armed, tailless, semi-erect primate that resembles man.

aperiodic. (1) Having no periodicity or rhythm; (2) not vibrating or oscillating under the effect of an impulse, due to satisfactory damping.

apertometer. An instrument for measuring the numerical aperture of microscope objectives.

aperture. (1) An orifice or opening; (2) the diameter of light path through a lens.

aperture angle. The ratio of the active diameter of a lens to its focal length.

apetalous. Said of flowers having a calyx but no corolla.

apex. The tip, point, or summit of a curve or surface.

aphanite. Fine-grained dark-colored igneous rock whose constituents cannot be distinguished with the naked eye.

aphelion. The point of the orbit of a planet or comet which is farthest from the sun.

aphid. A small sucking insect, belonging to the order Homoptera; plant louse.

aphyllous. Leafless.

apical. Referring to or located at the apex or top.

apical cell. (1) The starting point of longitudinal plant growth; (2) the rounded end cell of the Oscillatoria filament.

apical growth. Growth restricted to the apex of an organ; example, fungi.

apical meristem. Growing point at the tip of the root and stem in vascular plants, having its origin in a single cell.

apiculture. Bee keeping.

aplanatic. Having no spherical aberration; said of optical instruments.

aplanospore. A nonmotile fungus spore formed within a sporangium.

aplite. A fine-grained igneous rock of light hue.

apocarpous. Having several separate carpels.

apochromatic. Achromatized for more than two wave lengths.

Apoda. An order of tropical, burrowing, limbless, wormlike Amphibia which have scales buried in the skin.

apodeme. An inward projection of the exoskeleton of arthropods; it supports the internal organs and serves for muscle attachment.

apogee. The remotest point from the earth on the orbit of the moon.

apolar adsorption. Adsorption of nonpolar substances in nonpolar media.

apomict. A plant produced by apomixis.

apomixis. Reproduction that has the appearance of ordinary sexual cycle, but occurs without fertilization or meiosis.

aponeurosis. A broad fibrous sheet of tissue or fascia attaching a muscle.

apophysis. (1) In a moss capsule, the swelling at the base; (2) on the hypha of fungi, a swelling under the reproductive organ; (3) in vertebrates, a muscle attachment; (4) a tonguelike offshoot from an igneous layer.

apopyle. An opening for evacuating water from the flagellated chambers of sponges.

apothecium. A cup-shaped or saucer-shaped open ascocarp.

apparent candle power. An extended light source; it is the same as the candle power of a point source which would produce the same illumination at the same distance as the extended source.

apparent diameter. The angle opposite the diameter of a star at the eye of the observer, given in angular units.

apparent expansion coefficient. The difference between the true coefficient of expansion of a liquid and the coefficient of the cubic expansion of the dilatometer used for its measurement.

apparent power. The product of the effective emf and the effective current in an a-c circuit.

apparent solar time. Time of one's own meridian as measured by a sundial.

appendage. An elongated structure that projects from the body of an animal, usually movable, as legs, wings, antennae.

appendicular. Referring or attached to an appendage.

appendix. A small fingerlike organ at the place where the small and large intestines join in certain mammals.

apterous. Wingless.

aq. Symbol for water.

aqua fortis. Concentrated nitric acid; HNO_3.

aqua regia. A mixture of four volumes of hydrochloric and one volume of nitric acid (HNO_3 + 3 HCl), which dissolves gold and platinum.

aquamarine. Bluish form of beryl; used as a gem.

aquameter. A pulsometer; a steam pump for raising water.

aquarium. A glass tank used as a miniature habitat for aquatic plants and animals.

Aquarius. A constellation; the eleventh sign of the Zodiac, which is in the path of the sun and planets.

aquatic roots. Roots that are in water; they are small and lack root hairs.

aqueduct. (1) A pipe or conduit used to carry public-supply water; (2) in animals, a fluid-conveying channel.

aqueous humor. A transparent, jellylike fluid between the cornea and the lens of the eye.

aquifer. A porous rock which traps water between impervious layers above and below.

Aquila. A constellation lying in the milky way, which can be viewed with a low-powered telescope.

Ar. Chemical symbol for argon; an abbreviation for aryl radical.

Arachnida. A class of joint-legged animals with eight legs; examples, spiders and scorpions.

arachnoid. (1) Cobweblike; made of entangled fibers; (2) resembling Arachnida.

Arago. A large constellation in the Southern Hemisphere.

aragonite. Calcium carbonate; an unstable mineral which is often converted into calcite.

arboreal. (1) Pertaining to or living in trees; (2) treelike.

arborescent. Branching out or growing like a tree.

arc. (1) The luminous discharge between two electrodes; (2) any flashing between the terminals of an electric circuit when it has been interrupted; (3) a part of a circle, ellipse, parabola or hyperbola.

arc converter. An oscillator which makes use of an electric arc as the generator of alternating or pulsating current.

arc, electric. Highly luminous discharge, accompanied by a temperature of over 3000° C; used in arc furnaces.

arc furnace. An electric furnace heated by arc discharges between carbon electrodes.

arc lamp. An electric lamp whose source of illumination is an electric arc between two carbon electrodes.

arc process. The manufacture of nitric acid by the direct combination of nitrogen and oxygen in an electric arc and dissolving the nitric oxide in water.

arc spectrum. The spectrum from the nonionized atoms of a substance produced under the effect of an electric arc.

archaeopteryx. A reptilelike bird which lived during the Mesozoic era; it had a long, slim tail with feathers on both sides.

Archaeornithes. Extinct birdlike animals which had teeth and a long lizardlike tail.

Archegoniata. A main division of plants whose female sex organ is an archegonium; examples, Bryophyta and Pteridophyta.

archegonium. A female flask-shaped sessile organ located on the underside of the prothallus of ferns and mosses; it contains a single egg.

archenteron. The primitive digestive tract of a metazoan embryo, formed during gastrulation.

archeocytes. Ameboid cells of the sponges which inject and digest food, carry the products to other parts of the body, and form reproductive cells.

archeology. The scientific study of prehistoric and ancient human life.

Archeozoic era. The earliest period of geological history.

archesporium. Spore-producing tissue in ferns.

archetype. A primitive general pattern deduced from the characteristics of the members of a group of animals and assumed to be characteristic of the group.

Archiannelida. A class of Annelida, marine worms of simple structure.

Archichlamydeae. A subclass of Dicotyledones in which individual members of the corolla are entirely separate from each other or the perianth is incomplete.

Archimedes' principle. The loss of weight of a body immersed in a fluid—caused by the buoyant force of that fluid— is equal to the weight of the fluid displaced by the body.

arcing. Forming an arc, as at the brushes of a dynamo or in a broken circuit.

Arctic Circle. The parallel of latitude 66⅓° N., 23⅔° from the North Pole; the boundary of north-polar region.

Arcturus. A giant star of the constellation Boötes.

are. A metric unit of area; 100 square meters; 119.6 square yards.

area of high pressure. An anticyclone area.

area of low pressure. The center portion of a cyclonic storm.

areolar tissue. A connective tissue in which the cells are separated by mucin containing white and yellow fiber bundles.

areometer. A hydrometer.

argentiferous. Silver bearing.

argentite. A silver ore consisting of silver sulfide, Ag_2S; silver glance.

argillacious rock. Sedimentary rock composed of fine colloidal particles and crystal fragments of clay and quartz.

argillite. A dense, fine-grained, hard, nonfissile, sedimentary rock of slatelike cleavage, composed of minute grains of quartz; usually white, gray, or red.

arginine. An amino acid; a protein constituent.

argol. A reddish-brown crystalline deposit, consisting mainly of potassium hydrogen tartrate, in wine vats during fermentation.

argon. An inert gas found in air, used in light bulbs to prolong the life of the filament; chemical symbol Ar; atomic number 18.

aril. A brightly colored, succulent investment of the seed in a few plants; developed from the stalk, the base, or the ovule.

arista. Same as awn.

arm. (1) The curved part of the microscope from below the focusing adjustment, which is used for carrying; (2) an appendage of humans.

armature. The moving part of a magnetic circuit; example, the iron placed across the poles of a horseshoe magnet; it is an iron core wound with a large number of coils of insulated wire.

armature core. Assembled steel sheets forming the magnetic circuit of an armature.

armature reaction. The magnetomotive force of the armature current in the magnetic circuit of an electrical apparatus.

aromatic compound. An organic compound containing one or more benzene rings.

Arrhenius' theory of electrolytic dissociation. Spontaneous dissociation into positive and negative ions of a substance dissolved in a suitable solvent.

arroyo. Dry stream channels with nearly vertical walls and flat bottoms found in semiarid regions, which may become filled with torrential water after heavy rains.

arsenates. Metal salts in which the negative group is $AsO_4{}^{---}$.

arsenic. A steel-gray, crystalline semimetal; chemical symbol As; atomic number 33; used in alloys.

arsenious oxide. White arsenic; As_2O_3; used as a weed killer.

arsine. Hydrogen arsenide, AsH_3; very poisonous colorless gas.

arterioles. The smallest arteries which branch into capillaries; they have thin, muscular walls.

artery. One of the larger blood vessels, which carries blood away from the heart.

artesian well. A well from which water flows spontaneously due to water pressure from a source beneath the earth's surface but higher than the well.

Arthropoda. Invertebrate animals with jointed appendages; examples, insects and crabs.

articulation. (1) The junction of two or more bones; (2) the measure of the audibility of speech; (3) connecting two mechanical parts so that they can move relative to each other.

artifact. (1) A structure that does not appear in the living organism, but resulted from a faulty method of preparation of the specimen; (2) a stone tool made by prehistoric men.

artificial element. An element, not found in nature, that is made by bombarding natural elements with atomic particles.

artificial horizon. (1) A device which indicates the altitude of an aircraft with respect to the true horizon; (2) a substitute for a natural horizon consisting of a mercury-filled open container, a pendulum, or a gyroscope, incorporated in a navigating instrument.

artificial parthenogenesis. Artificial activation of an egg without contact by sperms; used in eggs that are usually not parthenogenic.

artificial pollination. Controlled pollination to produce a hybrid plant from selected plants.

artificial radioactivity. (1) Property of elements to radiate waves and/or particles after bombarding them in "atom smashers" or in atomic piles;

(2) radioactivity of artificially produced isotopes.

artificial selection. In man-controlled breeding, modifying organs by selection.

Artiodactyla. Even-toed ungulates, which walk on hooved toes; examples, pigs, camels, deer, sheep.

Arum. A family of European and Asiatic plants, such as calla lily and jack-in-the-pulpit.

aryl. Univalent aromatic hydrocarbon radical; example, phenyl, $C_6H_5{}^-$.

arytenoid. One of a pair of laryngeal cartilages that lie posterior to the thyroid cartilage.

As. Chemical symbol for arsenic.

asbestos. Fibrous silicate mineral; used for heat insulation and fireproofing.

Ascaris. A slender whitish roundworm that lives in pigs, horses, and other mammals; it is parasitic in the human intestine.

ascending colon. A part of the colon which extends upward at the right side of the abdomen.

ascending hyphae. Special hyphae of bread mold which have the sporangium at the tip.

ascending node. A point where a heavenly body crosses the ecliptic from south to north.

Ascidiacea. Tailless and sedentary members of Urochordata; example, sea squirt.

ascocarp. Fruiting body in Ascomycetes in which asci and ascospores are produced.

ascogonium. Female gametangium of Ascomycetes.

Ascomycetes. Large group of fungi which produce asci and ascospores.

ascorbic acid. The chemical name for vitamin C, the antiscurvy vitamin.

ascospore. Spore produced by an ascus.

ascus. A spore sac, within which usually eight ascospores are produced.

-ase. Suffix for an enzyme; example, protease.

asepsis. Excluding microorganisms and septic matter, usually by sterilization.

aseptic. Free from bacteria.

asexual. Without sex.

asexual reproduction. Reproduction in which there is only one parent and there is no union of special reproductive cells or sex cells; example, budding or binary fission.

ash soil. A fertile soil made from volcanic ashes.

aspect ratio. The ratio of the span of an aircraft wing to its mean chord; it gives a general idea of the shape of the aircraft.

Aspergillus. A genus of fungi which has round swollen conidiophores; example, common mold.

aspheric surface. A surface of a lens or mirror which has been changed slightly from a spheri-

cal form in order to produce aberrations.

aspirator. An apparatus for drawing a current of air or other gas through a liquid.

aspirator bottles. Bottles used to dispense liquids from an elevated position to permit gravity flow.

asporogenous. Not spore producing.

assay. Analysis for only a certain constituent or constituents of a mixture, the others being generally neglected.

assimilation. Changing of food into useful substances for a living organism; the metabolic process.

association. (1) Formation of polymeric compounds by addition of monomers; (2) the ability of the brain to link the memory of past experiences with present behavior; (3) stable plant community dominated by a particular species and named after it; example, heath association; (4) adherence of individuals without nuclear fusion.

assortive mating. Sexual reproduction in which the pairing of male and female is not at random, but in which a male of a particular kind tends to breed with a female of a partciular kind.

astatic. (1) Without orientation or directional characteristics; (2) not static.

astatic galvanometer. A very sensitive galvanometer which neutralizes the effect of the earth's magnetism by the use of astatic needles.

astatic system. Two or more magnetic needles suspended in such a manner that the earth's magnetic field does not affect them.

astatine. An unstable element obtained by bombarding bismuth with helium nuclei; chemical symbol At; atomic number 85.

aster. A starlike body found in the prophase of an animal cell as a result of centrosome dividing.

asterism. (1) A small group of stars; (2) a starlike pattern which may be seen in an x-ray spectrogram, when the x-rays pass through a thin crystal plate placed over the photographic plate.

asteroid. A small planet, also called "minor planet"; it moves around the sun as a planet; the great majority is found between Mars and Jupiter.

asthenosphere. An assumed zone beneath the lithosphere, or about 60 miles below the surface of the earth; it is believed to be the place where magmas originate.

astigmatic difference. The distance between the primary and secondary focus of an astigmatic optical system.

astigmatic focus. The meeting line of some of the rays from an off-axis point in an astigmatic system, which is perpendicular to a plane containing the point and the optical axis.

astigmatic spectral line. The image of the entrance slit at the primary focus of an astigmatic grating.

Aston dark space. In a glow-discharge tube, a narrow dark region between the cathode glow and the cathode itself in which the emitted electrons do not have sufficient energy to ionize the gas.

Aston whole number rule. The atomic weights of isotopes are whole numbers when expressed in atomic weight units, and the deviations from these whole numbers are due to the presence of several isotopes.

astral. (1) Referring or belonging to the stars; starlike; (2) resembling or referring to an aster.

astrocompass. A nonmagnetic instrument for determining direction relative to the stars.

astrodynamics. The science of adapting celestial mechanics to space flight.

astrolabe. An old instrument used for determining the altitudes of heavenly bodies from which time and latitude are deducible graphically.

astronaut. A person who travels through interplanetary space.

astronomer. A scientist who studies the earth's relation to the sun, moon, stars, and other heavenly bodies.

astronomical unit. A unit for measuring interstellar distances; it is the mean distance of the earth from the sun, that is, 92,900,000 miles.

astronomy. The science of the heavenly bodies, their size, motions, composition, and relation to one another.

astrophysics. The physics of heavenly bodies.

asymmetrical carbon atom. A carbon atom each valence of which holds a different atom or group, resulting in optical isomerism.

asymmetry. (1) Lack of symmetry; (2) the condition of an animal body in which there is no plane which would divide the body into two similar halves; example, a snail.

At. Chemical symbol for astatine.

atavism. Resemblance to a remote ancestor; the skipping of one or more generations by a character of an offspring.

ataxic. (1) Lacking system; (2) afflicted with ataxy.

ataxy. Incoordination of muscles.

athermancy. Inability to absorb heat radiations.

athermanous. Impervious to radiant heat.

atlas. The first cervical vertebra

which supports the skull.

atmolysis. Separation of a mixture of gases through a porous partition by means of their different diffusibility.

atmometer. An instrument for measuring evaporation, generally that of water, into the atmosphere.

atmosphere. The whole mass of fluid surrounding the earth, including some water vapor, dust, smoke, and other impurities.

atmospheric acoustics. The study of sound propagation and attenuation in the atmosphere, including such problems as sound ranging and signaling, and aircraft noise.

atmospheric duct. An atmospheric layer which conducts radio-frequency waves in the same manner as a true wave guide under certain conditions of temperature and humidity.

atmospheric interference. Same as atmospherics.

atmospheric inversion. Increase in the temperature of the atmosphere with height, which is contrary to the usual condition.

atmospheric pressure. The pressure exerted by the atmosphere not only downward but in all directions; the pressure exerted on a body by the atmosphere at sea level is about 14.7 pounds per square inch.

atmospheric refraction. The deflection of light rays by the atmosphere.

atmospherics. Statics; natural disturbances interfering with good radio and television reception.

atoll. A coral island consisting of a belt of coral reef surrounding a central lagoon.

atom. The smallest particle of an element that can enter into a chemical reaction.

atomic bomb. A missile of tremendous explosive power that utilizes the energy liberated by atomic fission.

atomic charge. The electrical charge of an ion which is equal to the number of electrons the atom has gained or lost in ionization, multiplied by the charge of one electron.

atomic clock. A device that uses the natural vibration frequencies of atoms to measure time; the most exact measurement of time yet devised; the atomic clock in the U.S. Naval Observatory is based on the natural oscillations of the cesium atom.

atomic core. An atom stripped of its valence-electron shells about the nucleus.

atomic distance. The average distance separating the centers of two atoms.

atomic energy. Energy released by splitting the nucleus of an element.

atomic frequency. The oscillation frequency of an atom.

atomic heat. The product of the atomic weight and the specific heat of an element which is approximately 6 calories per gram atom per degree according to Dulong and Petit; the heat quantity needed to raise the temperature of one gram atom by 1°C.

atomic kernel. Same as atomic core.

atomic mass. The mass of a neutral atom or a nuclide; in nuclear physics, the atomic mass unit is 1.660×10^{-24} g, which is one sixteenth of the mass of the oxygen isotope O^{16}.

atomic number. The number of protons in the nucleus of an atom or the number of electrons in the orbits of an atom.

atomic orbital. The wave function of an electron in an atom, that is, the possible motion of an individual electron in an atom.

atomic parameters. The distances between the various atoms in a crystal structure, as determined by x-ray analysis.

atomic pile. In nucleonics, a device containing fissionable material, a moderator, control and shielding means, and in which atomic fission takes place with the controlled release of energy.

atomic properties. Properties of substances which are due to the nature of the constituent atoms alone, as distinguished from those properties which are due to the arrangement of atoms in the molecules.

atomic species. A distinctive type of atom.

atomic spectrum. A spectrum emitted by an excited atom, due to changes within the atom.

atomic structure. The atom consists of a nucleus, which is the site of the atomic mass and carries positive charges corresponding to the atomic number, and negatively charged electrons also corresponding to the atomic number, which are in orbits surrounding the nucleus at relatively large distances; the chemical properties of an element depend generally on the electrons in the outermost orbit.

atomic theory. A theory that all matter is made up of small units, a different kind for each element, called atoms.

atomic transmutation. The changing of an atom into an atom of a different element with a different atomic weight.

atomic volume. The volume of one gram atom of an element.

atomic weight. The weight of an atom of an element compared with the weight of an atom of carbon, which is 12.

atomization. The breaking-up of a liquid into small droplets, usually in a high-speed jet or film by spraying through a nozzle.

ATP complex. The breakdown of adenine triphosphate which releases the energy needed for muscular contraction.

atrichous. Having no flagella.

atrium. An outer cavity in animals into which, depending on the species, various ducts open.

atropous. Orthotropous; said of an ovule with a straight axis, the chalaza being at the insertion and the micropyle at the opposite end, farthest from the hilum.

attachment constriction. Spindle attachment to a constricted part of a chromosome.

attenuation. (1) Weakening of microorganism virulence in a culture; (2) reduction in concentration, density, effectiveness; (3) a loss of current or power in a circuit measured in decibels; (4) the measure of the transparency of a layer.

attitude. The inclination of the three principal airplane axes to three fixed axes on the earth.

attraction. A force that tends to pull objects toward one another; examples, gravitation, magnetic and electrical attraction.

attrition test. Determination of the wear resistance of road-surfacing materials.

Atwood's machine. A device for demonstrating the laws of gravity.

Au. Chemical symbol for gold.

audio. Pertaining to sound or hearing.

audio amplifier. A tube circuit used to amplify the audio-frequency output of the detector circuit.

audio signal. Any information received by a radio set.

audio-frequency. Frequency of sound to which the ear responds; any frequency between about 10 and 10,000 cycles per second.

audio-frequency current. Current whose frequency is within the the audible range.

audiogram. Chart showing the least intensity of different sound frequency ranges which is audible to the human ear.

audiometer. (1) An instrument for measuring the power of hearing; (2) an instrument for measuring the minimum sound intensities audible to the human ear for given frequencies.

audion. The original three-element vacuum tube invented by de Forrest.

audio-oscillator. A generator of alternating currents within the audible frequency range.

auditory canal. The acoustic meatus; two passages of the ear; one leading auditory nerves from the cranial cavity and the other, from the outer opening of the tympanic membrane.

auditory capsule. The part of the skull of vertebrates in which the auditory organ develops.

auditory localization. The ability of the ear to locate the apparent direction of sound sources.

auditory nerve. The nerve that carries impulses from the cochlea to the brain.

auditory organ. A sense organ for detecting sound.

auditory sensation area. (1) The part of the brain which is responsive to auditory stimuli; the temporal lobe of the cortex; (2) a diagram showing the hearing capacity of the normal ear from the minimum perceivable to the maximum tolerable intensities.

Auer metal. A pyrophoric alloy of 35% iron and 65% mischmetal which is a mixture of cerium and other rare-earth metals.

Auger effect. The liberation of two electrons from different levels of an atom by a single x-ray quantum without radiation.

Auger's electron. An electron ejected from an excited atom in the Auger effect.

Auger's shower. A shower of Auger's electrons.

Aughey spark chamber. A device in which spectrum can be observed when traces of contamination in a gas have been excited.

aureole. A halo; (1) the contact metamorphic zone of varying width that often surrounds an igneous intrusion; (2) a corona; a less bright outer portion encircling a luminous body, such as the sun, when seen in fog or through a thin cloud.

auricle. Any earlike structure; (1) an ear-shaped projection of grass and leaves; (2) one of the two upper chambers of the heart where blood is received from the main veins.

Aurora Borealis. Northern lights; phenomenon seen only at night and best in the region of the North Pole; a large fan of bright—sometimes colored—light rays appearing above the horizon; it is assumed to be of electrical origin.

Aurora Polaris. Same as Aurora Borealis.

auroral line. A green line in the spectrum of the Aurora Borealis.

austenite. Solid solution of carbon or iron carbide in the gamma form of iron which is normally stable only at high temperatures, but may be preserved at normal temperatures by certain alloying elements or by rapid cooling.

Australopithecus. An extinct primate of South Africa; the limbs and teeth were human, but the skull was apelike; it probably walked upright; late Pliocene.

autecology. Division of ecology which treats single factors or species.

autoclave. (1) In medicine, an apparatus for sterilizing by means of superheated steam under pressure; (2) in chemistry, a strong-walled hermetically closed metal container—equipped with a thermometer, safety valve, and pressure gage; used for carrying out chemical reactions at high pressures and temperatures.

autocollimator. A self-adjusting collimator used in optical demonstrations.

autoelectronic effect. The emission of electrons from a cold cathode when an electric field of high intensity is applied to its surface.

autogamy. Self-fertilization; in Protozoa, a process in which the nucleus divides, each half undergoes maturation and the two persisting functional nuclei reunite.

autogenous. Self-generated, originating within the body.

autohemorrhage. Ejection of poisonous blood by some insects as a protection in attack.

autoionization. Automatic dissociation of a molecule, which occurs when the sum of its vibrations and electronic energies exceeds the energy necessary for dissociation.

autokinesis. Voluntary movement.

autolysin. A substance found in an organism which is capable of causing self-digestion.

autolysis. Disintegration of a cell or of an organism by its own enzymes.

automatic control system. Any operable combination of one or more automatic controls connected in closed loops with one or more processes.

automatic controller. A device which measures the value of a variable quantity or condition and operates to correct or limit deviation of this measured value from a selected reference.

automatic frequency control. An arrangement in some receivers by which the frequency of an oscillator is automatically maintained within specified limits after tuning.

automatic gain control. In radio receivers, elimination or reduction of the variations in signal strength by making the gain of the receiver inversely dependent on the demodulated carrier.

automatic pilot. An automatic control mechanism for keeping an aircraft level in flight and on a set course.

automatic propeller. A propeller whose blades are attached to a mechanism that automatically sets them at their optimum pitch for various flight conditions.

autonomic nervous system. A network of motor nerve fibers which controls gland activities, involuntary muscles, the heart, and alimentary tract; it consists of two chains or rows of ganglia, one on each side of the spinal cord.

autophotoelectric theory. A hypothesis of Richardson that thermionic emission is a form of photoelectric effect, in which the radiation comes from the hot substance itself.

autophyte. A plant which can make its own food.

autopolyploid. A polyploid in which all the chromosomes come from the same species.

autopulse magnetic fuel pump. An electrically operated device for maintaining the gasoline level in the carburetor.

autoradiograph. Radioautograph; a photographic record of treated specimens under the effect of a radioactive tracer.

autorotation. (1) Another name for the tailspin of a plane; (2) rotorcraft flight without power; example, flight of helicopter without operation of the engine.

autosome. Any chromosome except a sex chromosome.

autostylic jaw suspension. Attachment of the upper jaw of a vertebrate directly to the neurocranium; example, primitive fish.

autotomy. Self-mutilation; the automatic "voluntary" breaking off of a part of the body of an animal; example, lizards.

autotransformer. (1) A transformer in which the primary and secondary are connected together in one winding. It is usually more efficient, and has a lower first cost than ordinary transformers of the same capacity; (2) a variable compensator in which a choking coil is introduced across the alternating-current supply circuits so that varying currents can be obtained from different points on its windings.

autotrophic. Self-nourishing.

autoxidation. Spontaneous oxidation which takes place slowly with molecular oxygen or air at moderate temperatures without visible combustion.

autozooid. Member of polyp colonies whose function is to feed the colony.

auxanometer. A device for measuring the growth of plants.

auxesis. Cell division induced by a chemical.

auxin. A growth-producing hormone of plants.

auxochrome. A chemical group that can transfer the color of a dye to another substance; examples, SO_3H^-; NO_2^-, Cl^-, OH^-.

auxometer. An apparatus for measuring the magnifying power of a lens or any optical system.

auxospore. A special spore in diatoms, which seems to rejuvenate the cells.

avalanche. A great body of snow and ice sliding down a mountain.

Aves. Birds.

aviation. The art and science of aircraft operation.

Avogadro constant. The number of molecules contained in one gram molecule, 6.06×10^{23}.

Avogadro's hypothesis. Same as Avogadro's law.

Avogadro's law. Equal volumes of gases, measured under the same conditions of temperature and pressure, contain the same number of molecules.

Avogadro's number. Same as Avogadro's constant.

awn. Slender projection found on the lemmas of many grasses.

axenic. A term used in biological sciences to describe isolation from all other living things (e.g., from parasites, commensals, and symbionts).

axial. Referring to the axis; in vertebrates, pertaining to the skull, neck, and backbone.

axial gradient. Gradation of the rate of metabolism along the principal axis of an animal.

axial magnification. The ratio of the interval between two adjacent image points on the axis of an optical instrument to the interval between the conjugate object points.

axial organ. An organ of peculiar structure and unknown function found near the axis of the body of all echinoderms except the sea cucumber.

axial ratio. The ratio between the unequal axes of a crystal and the angles they form if these are not right angles.

axial sinus. A vertical portion of the body cavity in echinoderms into which the madreporite opens.

axial skeleton. That part of the vertebrate skeleton which consists of the skull, vertebrae and ribs.

axiation. Development of polarity in an embryo.

axil. The space between a leafstalk and the stem of the plant.

axile placentation. Arrangement in which the placentae are on the axis of the ovary.

axilla. The armpit.

axillary bud. Bud in the axil of a leaf.

axiotron. A high-vacuum thermionic diode in which the magnetic field produced by the filament current controls the anode current.

axis. (1) The second cervical vertebra; (2) an imaginary line around which parts of the body are symmetrically arranged; (3) the line about which a body turns.

axis cylinder. The rodlike excitable central portion of a medullated nerve fiber.

axis of the earth. An imaginary straight line passing through the earth's center about which it rotates.

axon. A nerve process which carries an impulse away from the cell body of the nerve.

axonometry. Measurement by means of the axes, especially in crystals.

Ayrton galvanometer shunt. A shunt in which the coils are so arranged that their relative multiplying power is always the same; the universal shunt.

azeotrope. One of two or more substances which, when mixed in certain proportions, have a constant boiling point.

azeotropic mixture. A constant-boiling mixture of two or more liquids which distills at a given temperature and the distillate has the same composition as the original mixture; example, isopropyl alcohol and water.

azimuth. The angular distance measured clockwise between a fixed point and the point at which a vertical circle through it intersects the horizon; example, the azimuth of a star.

azimuth angle. The angle between the plane of vibration and the normal to the plane of incidence when plane-polarized light is incident on the surface of a dielectric.

azo dyes. Mostly red or yellow organic dyestuffs derived from azobenzene, $C_6H_5N{:}NC_6H_5$.

azo group. The bivalent chromophore group, —N:N—.

azoic era. The lifeless period in the history of the earth.

azotobacter. A bacterium that is able to fix free nitrogen.

azurite. Natural basic copper carbonate; a blue mineral; $2\,CuCO_3{\cdot}Cu(OH)_2$.

azygos. An unpaired anatomical structure; example, the azygos vein of mammals.

B

B. Chemical symbol for boron.

B battery. The battery used to supply plate voltage to a vacuum tube.

Ba. Chemical symbol for barium.

Babbitt metal. A bearing alloy containing a high percentage of tin, with some copper, antimony, and lead.

babble. The aggregate simultaneous cross talk from a large number of disturbing channels.

Babes-Ernst bodies. Metachromatic granules.

Babinet's absorption rule. Two complimentary screens give similar diffraction patterns; the transparent portion of one screen corresponds to the opaque portion of the other.

Babo's law. The vapor pressure of a solution containing a nonvolatile solute is lower than that of the solvent by a quantity which is proportional to the concentration of the solute.

Bacillariophyta. Diatoms; class of algae; they occur singly or in colonies and have chloroplasts containing a brown pigment as well as chlorophyll.

bacillus (plural, bacilli). A rod-shaped bacterium.

Bacillus typhosus. The germ that causes typhoid fever.

back emf of a cell. The electromotive force of a cell connected in a circuit, which opposes the normal flow of current in that circuit.

back focal length. The distance from the back surface of a lens to the second focal point.

back scattering. The deflection of particles or of radiation with respect to the original direction of motion through angles greater than 90°.

backcross. The crossing of a first-generation hybrid with one of its parents.

backheating. An increase in cathode temperature in magnetrons, when high-velocity electrons are returned to the cathode surface.

backing wind shift. Succession of winds from northeast, north, and finally northwest.

backlash. The imperfect rectification of an alternating current by a thermionic valve, due to the presence of positive ions produced in the gas by the impact of thermoelectrons; striking back of a defective machine.

back-to-back connection. Connecting the cathode of one tube to the anode of the other, and vice versa.

bacteria. Microscopic, one-celled or threadlike organisms that do not have chlorophyll.

bacterial episome. A genetic element that can reproduce itself either as an integral part of a bacterial host or as a free-living particle in the cytoplasm; bacterial behavior in conjugation is determined by episomes known as fertility factors.

bacterial synergism. Reactions by two or more species of bacteria growing together, which are not produced by any of the organisms growing alone.

bacteriology. The study of bacteria.

bacteriolysin. An antibody capable of destroying or dissolving specific bacterial cells which stimulated its formation.

bacteriophage. An ultramicroscopic bacteria-destroying agent which is present in the intestinal tract and is regarded by some as an enzyme.

bacteriostasis. Prevention of the growth of bacteria, such as results from the addition of certain dyes to culture media.

bacteriostatic. Inhibiting the growth of bacteria but not killing them.

Baily's beads. Beadlike lights around the dark edge of the moon which last only for an instant immediately before and after a total eclipse of the sun.

Baird densitometer. A direct-reading instrument for measuring the density of a photographic plate.

baking powder. Mixture of sodium bicarbonate, cream of tartar, and an inert filler; used in baking as a yeast substitute.

baking soda. Sodium bicarbonate, $NaHCO_3$.

balance. (1) In aeronautics, a condition of steady flight in which the resultant force and moment on the airplane are zero; (2) a condition of partial or complete equilibrium; (3) an instrument used for weighing; (4) adjustment of a network in which an emf in one branch produces no current in another branch; (5) the vibrating part of a clock or watch.

balance coil. A coil for supplying a three-wire circuit from a two-wire circuit.

balance method. A method of measurement in which the quantity to be measured is by adjustment so related to the known quantity with which it is compared that the scale reading of the indicating instrument becomes zero.

balance of nature. A natural condition in which the type and number of plants and animals in a region remain substantially unaltered through a long period of time; the interdependence of living things and their environment.

balanced aquarium. An aquarium in which, under proper conditions of light and temperature, the plant and animal organisms produce substances necessary to each other in quantities that enable both kinds to live.

balanced currents. Currents flowing in the two conductors of a balanced line which, at every point along the line, are equal in magnitude but opposite in direction.

balanced line. A transmission line which has two conductors in the presence of ground, operated in such a way that the currents in both conductors are equal but of opposite phase.

balanced surface. In aeronautics, a control surface on both sides of the axis of the hinge or pivot which reduces the moment of air force about the hinge or pivot.

balanced terminations. A load presenting the same impedance to ground for each of the output terminals in a system or network that has two output terminals.

balancing organ. Semicircular canals of the ear that help the body keep its balance.

Balanoglossida. Wormlike, burrowing animals belonging to the Hemichorda.

baleen. Whalebone; transverse plate of keratin projecting on each side of the upper jaw of whales and serving as a food strainer.

ball and ring. A device which illustrates the expansion of metals with the application of heat; a device for determining the melting point of waxes.

ball and socket joint. A joint in which the enlarged end of one bone fits into a depression in another, allowing free motion; a joint between two rods, which permits angular displacement of the rods relative to each other in any plane.

ball bearing. A bearing for shafts that contains numerous steel balls to reduce friction.

ballast. Heavy material placed in a ship to increase its stability when it is floating without cargo or with light cargo.

ballast tanks. Airtight compartments in a submarine which may be pumped full or drained of water.

ballistic. (1) Pertaining to projectiles; (2) said of an instrument which indicates the effect of an impact or a sudden rush of energy.

ballistic galvanometer. A device for measuring the quantity of electricity passing through a circuit due to a momentary current.

ballistic pendulum. An instrument swinging in one plane used for measuring the horizontal velocity component of a projectile.

Balmer series. The visible and near-ultraviolet spectrum of hydrogen.

Balopticon projector. A projector used on opaque objects.

Baly tube. A tube or cell of variable length used to hold the solutions in absorption spectrographic determinations.

band edge. The frequency toward which the lines in any band of a band spectrum appear to be concentrated.

band igniter tube. A glow-discharge tube in which conduction is started when a high potential is applied.

band pass. The property of a wave filter of transmitting only a certain band or range of frequencies.

band pressure level. The effective sound-pressure level for the sound energy contained within a specific frequency band of a given sound.

band spectrum. Molecular absorption spectrum which consists of a number of fluted wide bands, each having one sharp edge.

band width. The number of cycles per second which expresses the difference between the limiting frequencies of a frequency band.

band-elimination filter. A wave filter that blocks frequencies of a given range while it freely transmits frequencies outside this range.

bank. In aeronautics, to cause an airplane to incline laterally to avoid skidding when making a turn.

bank winding. A mode of winding high-frequency coils to reduce their capacity, in which single turns are staggered.

banking. (1) The rotation of an airplane about its longitudinal axis; (2) in a mining shaft, replacing loaded wagons with empty ones.

banks. Shallow water of coastal margins.

banner. Large, broad, and conspicuous petal of legume type of flower.

bar. A unit of pressure; one bar is equivalent to a pressure of one million dynes per square centimeter or 750 mm of mercury.

bar magnet. A straight permanent magnet with poles at the two ends.

baraboo. Hill, mountain, or other eminence which was once buried by deposition of sedimentary material around it and has since become exposed by the erosion of the younger beds.

barb. (1) A tiny ray in the vane of a feather; (2) hooked, bristlelike hair.

barbel. A slender tactile projection near the mouth of a fish.

Barbula. A family of tufted slender mosses.

barbule. One of the divisions of the barb of a feather.

barchane. Crescent-shaped dune.

Barff process. Prevention of the rusting of iron and steel by oxidation with superheated steam.

barite. A mineral; $BaSO_4$.

barium. Silvery alkaline earth metal; chemical symbol Ba; atomic number 56.

barium sulfate. $BaSO_4$; white powder; used in chemical analysis, in paints.

bark. Thick layer of cork on tree trunks which protects the tissues beneath from mechanical injury and entrance of insects and fungus parasites.

Barkhausen effect. Abrupt discontinuities in the magnetization curve of ferromagnetic substances assumed to be due to atomic reorientation.

Barlow's rule. The spaces occupied by the various atoms in a given molecule are approximately proportional to the valences of the atoms.

Barlow's wheel. A primitive electric motor and generator of historic significance.

Barnett effect. The magnetization of a body by rotation.

baroclinic. Said of the atmosphere when isobaric surfaces and equal-density surfaces do not coincide.

barograph. A recording barometer.

barometer. A device that measures atmospheric pressure.

barometric slope. The slope of an isobaric surface; the fall of atmospheric pressure between two stations.

barometric tendency. The change of barometric pressure usually three hours before regular observation.

barophoresis. Diffusion of solid particles suspended in a liquid whose speed depends on external forces.

baroscope. An instrument indicating the changes in atmospheric pressure.

barostat. A pressure regulator.

barothermograph. An instrument which records both atmospheric pressure and temperature.

barotropic. Said of the atmosphere when isobaric surfaces and equal-density surfaces coincide.

barotropic fluid. A compressible fluid whose temperature is the same throughout.

Barratt method. An optical method of determining the concentration of solutions.

barrier. Any obstruction, physical, chemical, or biological, that prevents the migration of animals.

barrier beach. A gravel ridge that separates a bay from a larger body of water.

barrier reef. Coral reef that is separated from the shore by a lagoon.

bartz. Dark-colored, poorly shaped diamonds; used for polishing other diamonds.

barycenter. Center of gravity.

barycentric parallax. The slight oscillatory motion of the earth.

barysphere. The unknown interior of the earth which is heavier than the surface rock materials.

baryta. BaO; white powder; used in glass manufacture.

barytes. Heavy spar; natural barium sulfate, $BaSO_4$; colorless or varied-colored crystals.

basal conglomerate. A conglomerate that occurs just above a plane of erosion and forms the bottom layer of a sedimentary series.

basal metabolism. Rate of energy expenditure by an individual who has not eaten any food for 12 hours and who is lying still and relaxed but awake.

basal plane. A plane in a crystal parallel to the principal plane of symmetry.

basalt. A fine-grained, sometimes porphyritic, intrusive-extrusive igneous rock of black or greenish-black color.

base. (1) An alkali; a proton acceptor; a substance that turns litmus paper blue; (2) a compound which yields hydroxyl ions in a water solution; (3) the part of the petiole by which the leaf is attached to the stem; (4) a part of the framework of a microscope on which it rests.

base level. The lowest level to which a stream can cut.

base metal. Not precious metal; a metal that is oxidized by exposure to air or moisture.

base prongs. Small brass prongs set in the vacuum-tube base in such a way that they will fit into the tube socket only in the correct way.

basement membrane. A delicate connective tissue between the epithelium and tissues near it.

basic anhydride. A metal oxide which can combine with water to yield a base.

basic dyes. Salts of color bases and hydrochloric acid; used for dyeing cotton with a tannin mordant; dyes staining certain nuclei.

basic load. (1) In aeronautics, the load on an aircraft when it is at rest or in unaccelerated rectilinear flight; (2) the greatest mechanical load per unit length of an overhead conductor line.

basic rock. Igneous rock whose silica content is less than about 52%.

basic salt. A salt that is intermediate between a normal salt and the corresponding hydroxide; example, $Mg(OH)Cl$.

basic slag. An impure mixture of tetracalcium phosphate, calcium silicate, lime, and ferric oxide; a by-product of steel manufacture; used as a fertilizer.

basic steel. Steel produced by the Bessemer process or open-hearth process, in which a substantial part of the phosphorus is removed.

basic tissue. A group of plant cells with large vacuoles for the storage of foods and gases.

Basidiomycetes. A group of fungi characterized by the production of spores on a special structure, the basidium.

basidiospore. Special asexual type of spore on the basidium in Basidiomycetes.

basidium. Special club-shaped cell carrier of basidiospores in Basidiomycetes.

basilar membrane. In mammals, a membranous partition in the cochlea of the inner ear, containing auditory nerves which carry sound impulses to the brain.

basin. A geological formation in which the strata dip toward a central point from all directions.

basipetal. Developing toward the base; oldest at the apex, youngest at the base; said of plant organs.

basophilic. Stained strongly by basic dyes.

bast. Fibrous material in the phloem area of plant stems.

bast fibers. Tough, thick-walled fibers which give resistance to the bark.

bathochrome. A chromophore which displaces the spectrum of a compound toward the red end.

batholith. A very large igneous rock intrusion which has no visible bottom, but extends deeply toward the center of the earth.

bathymetric. Referring to the vertical spatial distribution of animals.

bathymetry. Measurement of depth, especially of the sea.

bathyscaph. An underwater craft used in oceanography at depths of over 12,000 feet; uses a light fluid such as gasoline for buoyancy and lead pellets for ballast control; observations are made from a pressure-resistant cabin.

bathysphere. An airtight chamber for two observers and instruments, to be lowered at the end of a cable to great depths of water; used in oceanography.

Batrachia. Amphibia; animals adapted for living on land or in water.

battery. Two or more electric cells connected so as to supply an electric current.

battery acid. The electrolyte of a storage battery; usually sulfuric acid.

battery capacity. The number of ampere-hours that can be obtained from a storage battery.

battery charger. An electrical device for charging a battery; it usually converts alternating current to direct current.

baud. A unit of telegraph signaling speed.

Baumé scale. A hydrometer scale for measuring the specific gravity of liquids.

bauxite. An aluminum ore; $Al_2O_3 \cdot 2H_2O$.

Bayer process. Extraction of aluminum from bauxite.

Be. Chemical symbol for beryllium.

bead test. A procedure for identifying certain metals by fusing with transparent borax or similar beads, usually in a blowpipe; the molten metallic oxides yield characteristic colors.

beak. (1) Point protuberance; (2) the snout of an animal; (3) horn-covered jaws of turtles and birds; (4) jaws of cephalopod molluscs.

beaker. A straight-sided lipped glass cup used in the laboratory.

beam candle power. Candle power of a searchlight.

beam interferometer. A device to measure the apparent diameters of stars.

beam power tube. A thermionic vacuum tube in which a space charge suppresses secondary emission and guides the electrons from the cathode in beams to the plate.

beam transmission. Point-to-point radio transmission, using highly directional beam antennas.

bearing. (1) A support for guiding and restraining moving elements; (2) a support which holds a rotating shaft in correct position.

bearing metals. Antifriction metals used for bearings.

beats. Rhythmic changes in loudness of the combined sounds from two sources of slightly differing frequencies.

Beaufort scale. A scale for measuring wind velocity ranging from 0 for calm weather to 12 indicating a hurricane.

Beckmann thermometer. A sensitive mercury thermometer of narrow range having a very large bulb and a very fine bore; used for precision measurements of small temperature changes.

Becquerel effect. The flow of current in a circuit having two identical electrodes immersed in an electrolyte, observed when one of the electrodes is illuminated.

Becquerel rays. Radiation by radioactive substances; alpha, beta, and gamma rays.

bedding. (1) Natural layering or stratification characteristic of sedimentary rocks; (2) impregnated jute layer used as a protective sheath on cables.

bedrock. The solid rock that lies under the soil; bottom rock.

beet sugar. Sucrose; $C_{12}H_{22}O_{11}$; sugar extracted from beets.

beetle. (1) An insect having two pairs of wings of which the outer ones are stiff cases that cover the other pair when folded; (2) a textile-finishing machine.

bel. The unit of power-level difference in electrical communication; 10 decibels; a logarithmic expression of the ratio of two quantities; example, the loudness of two sounds.

Belfil's bridge. A resonance bridge used to ascertain the harmonic purity of an electric wave train.

bell metal. Copper-base alloy containing 15 to 40% tin; used for bells and chimes.

bell-in-vacuo. A device to demonstrate that sound is not transmitted through a vacuum.

bell-ringing transformer. A small transformer which steps down the voltage of the ordinary house circuit to supply current for bell ringing.

bench photometer. A photometer whose parts are arranged on an optical bench.

bend test. (1) Determination of the ductility of a metal; (2) determination of the deflection of a beam under load.

bending moment. The torque which exists at any point in a bent elastic rod and to which the bending is due.

Benedict's reagent. A bluish solution used in testing for the presence of sugars.

benefication. Any process, physical or chemical, which makes an ore more suitable for reduction.

Bennettitales. Order of extinct plants that flourished during the Mesozoic era and resembled Cycas.

benthos. The plant and animal life on the bottom of the sea or lakes.

bentonite. Fine-grained clay formed by the decomposition under water of glass of volcanic origin.

benzene. C_6H_6; colorless inflammable liquid from coal tar; used as a solvent, motor fuel, and in organic synthesis.

benzol. Same as benzene.

benzyl. The univalent radical $C_6H_5CH_2-$.

Bergius process. Manufacture of liquid fuels from coal by hydrogenation at very high temperature and pressure and in the presence of a catalyst.

berkelium. Radioactive element obtained from americium; chemical symbol Bk; atomic number 97.

Bernoulli's theorem. If the speed of a liquid passing through a tube increases at any point, the pressure of the liquid decreases at that point, so that the total energy per unit mass will remain constant.

berry. A simple fleshy fruit with seeds in a juicy pulp; example, grape.

Berthollide compounds. Compounds whose chemical composition does not conform to a simple ratio of atoms in the molecule.

beryl. Natural beryllium aluminum silicate; $3BeO\cdot Al_2O_3\cdot 6SiO_2$; colorful hexagonal crystals.

beryllium. A magnesiumlike metallic element; chemical symbol Be; atomic number 4; used in corrosion-resistant alloys.

Bessemer converter. An egg-shaped steel furnace in which iron is converted into steel by burning out impurities with a blast of air.

Bessemer process. Making steel from pig iron by oxidizing the impurities with the aid of air blown into the Bessemer converter.

beta. Greek letter; among others, used to denote the second brightest star in a constellation.

beta disintegration. A radioactive transformation in which the atomic nucleus loses or gains an electron and the mass number is unchanged.

beta emitter. A radionuclide that undergoes disintegration by emission of a beta particle.

beta particle. An electron emitted from a nucleus undergoing beta disintegration.

beta rays. Negatively charged electrons emanating from radium and other radioactive substances.

betatron. Doughnut-shaped vacuum tube arranged between the poles of an electromagnet; an electron accelerator capable of producing electron beams of high energy as well as x-rays of extremely high penetrating power; used in nuclear research.

Betelgeuse. A red giant star in the Orion constellation; one of the largest stars known; its diameter is said to vary from 250 million to 400 million miles.

bev. Billion electron volts; a unit of energy.

bevatron. A more than ten billion electron volt accelerator of protons and other atomic particles; used in nucleonics.

bevel gear. A pair of toothed wheels for connecting shafts whose axes are in the same plane but at an angle to each other.

Bi. Chemical symbol for bismuth.

bi-. (1) A prefix meaning two; (2) in chemistry, acid salt of a dibasic acid; example, sodium bisulfate, $NaHSO_4$.

bias. The mean potential of the grid of a vacuum tube referred to the cathode.

bias cell. A small electric cell which is capable of supplying an open-circuit voltage of 1½ or 1¾ volts indefinitely.

bias lighting. A means of increasing iconoscope sensitivity by illuminating the mosaic from the rear with a constant light source.

biaxial. Said of crystals having two different optic axes.

bicarbonates. Acid salts of carbonic acid; example, $NaHCO_3$, sodium bicarbonate.

biceps. The large two-headed flexor muscle on the front of the upper arm.

bichloride of mercury. Mercuric chloride; $HgCl_2$.

bichromate of potash. Potassium dichromate, $K_2Cr_2O_7$.

bicollateral bundle. A vascular bundle consisting of one strand of xylem between two strands of phloem.

bicuspid valve. Valve which prevents blood from flowing back into the left auricle from the left ventricle.

bicuspids. Teeth with two points, lying between the canines and molars in mammals; also known as premolars.

Bielids. Late November meteors; they have not been seen since 1852.

biennials. Two-year plants; plants which grow vigorously during their first season, store food over the winter, produce seeds in and die at the end of the second season.

bifacial. Having distinctly different upper and lower surfaces.

Big Dipper. The seven principal stars of the constellation Ursa Major, in the form of a dipper, in the northern sky. It is called "big" to distinguish it from a similar but smaller constellation.

big-bang hypothesis. The assumption that all matter was once condensed in a single, giant, atomic nucleus that exploded and evolved into the universe we now observe.

bilateral cleavage. Cleavage which yields a bilaterally symmetrical arrangement of blastomeres.

bilateral symmetry. Divisibility of an organism into similar halves by one plane only.

bile. A yellowish-green secretion of the liver, which passes into the small intestine and aids in fat digestion.

bile acids. Monocarboxylic acids of the steroid group which occur in the bile of all vertebrates; example, glycocholic acid.

bile salts. Sodium salts of taurocholic and glycocholic acids secreted in the bile.

Bilharzia. Schistosomidae; trematode worms that are parasitic in blood.

bimetal. A composite of two unlike metal strips fastened together; their unequal expansion resulting in curling is used for measuring or controlling temperature.

bimorph cell. A combination of two piezoelectric plates cemented together in such a way that they make the cell bend when a potential causes one of the plates to expand and the other to contract.

binary. Consisting of two components; example, binary alloys are alloys of two metals.

binary fission. Division of a one-celled organism into two halves; a form of asexual reproduction.

binary stars. Double stars; two stars are gravitationally attracted to each other and revolve around their common center of gravity.

binding energy. (1) Energy required to separate the positively and negatively charged portions of a molecule or atom; (2) energy required to overcome the forces of cohesion and disperse a solid.

binding energy of an alpha particle. The energy required to remove an alpha particle from a nucleus.

binding energy of an electron. The energy necessary to remove an electron from an atom; identical with the ionization potential.

binding post. Threaded bolt and nut on a voltaic cell to which conductors may be attached.

binocular vision. Each eye gets a view from a slightly different angle so that slightly differing images are produced on the retinas of the two eyes, which are blended together in the brain to a spatial image.

binomial system of nomenclature. The classification of organisms introduced by Carl Linnaeus; every plant or animal is scientifically distinguished from every other plant or animal by two names, a generic (indicating the genus) and a specific (indicating the species).

bio-assay. Measuring the effectiveness of biologically active substances by testing them on standard animals.

bioastronautics. The application of space medicine and the life sciences to civil aeronautics and space travel.

biocatalyst. A substance that promotes biological reactions; example, insulin.

biocenology. A division of ecology which considers the factors associating animals and plants in a special area.

biochemistry. The chemistry of living things.

biocolloid. A lyophilic colloidal system within plant and animal organisms.

bioecology. Study of the relationships of animals and plants to their environment.

biogenesis. The doctrine that all living things spring from previously existing living things.

biogenetic law. All animals repeat, in a compact form, during the embryonic and larval period of their development, the evolutionary history of the race.

biogeography. Study of the geographical distribution of animals and plants.

bioherm. Bed or rock formation of gregarious marine fossils consisting predominantly of calcareous shells or skeletons.

biological control. Control of pests and parasites by the use of living organisms; example, control of mosquitoes by fish.

biological drive. Motivation arising from a need to stabilize the organism; example, hunger.

biological factor. The influence of one organism on another.

biology. The science of life, including a study of the development, structure, and behavior of living organisms.

bioluminescence. Light production by living organisms, such as bacteria, glow worms, fireflies, and luminous fish.

biometry. Application of mathematics to the study of living things, particularly the statistical study of resemblances and differences between groups of related organisms.

biophysics. Study of the physical processes taking place in living organisms.

biosphere. Those parts of the earth and its atmosphere which are inhabited or penetrated by living things.

biotherm. A life zone of North America which is marked off on the basis of the total heat above 43°F.

biotic area. A geographical zone characterized by similar plant and animal life.

biotin. A vitamin of the B complex group.

biotite. Silicate mineral also called black or iron mica.

Biot's hemisphere. A device which shows that an electrostatic charge is on the outer surface of a conductor.

Biot's law. When plane-polarized light is rotated by an optically active substance, the angle of rotation varies inversely with the wave length.

biotype. A group of individuals of similar hereditary traits.

biparria. Ciliated planktonic larva of starfish.

bipolar electrode. A secondary electrode; an electrode in an electroplating bath one surface of which acts as an anode and the other as a cathode.

biprism. An obtuse-angled prism used for beam splitting and thus obtaining two images of the same source.

bipropellant. A liquid rocket propellant consisting of fuel and oxidant stored in separate tanks until they are pumped into the combustion chamber.

biquartz. A quartz plate consisting of a dextrogyrate and a levogyrate semicircular portion, both of equal thickness and cemented together along the diameter; used to demonstrate polarization tints.

biramous appendage. The primitive two-branch appendage of Arthropoda, still found in various forms in the crusteaceans.

birefringence. Double refraction or splitting the incident light into two components by some crystalline minerals; in an extreme case, two images of the object viewed can be seen through such a crystal.

Birkeland and Eyde process. Process for the fixation of atmospheric nitrogen. Nitrogen and oxygen from the atmosphere are combined by an electric arc to form nitric oxide.

bisexual. Having both male and female sex organs in the same individual.

bismuth. Grayish-white metallic element; chemical symbol Bi; atomic number 83.

bismuth spiral. A coil of bismuth wire used for measuring magnetic fluxes.

bistable. A circuit with two stable states.

bittern. Mother liquor remaining after the crystallization of sodium chloride from sea water; source of magnesium, bromine, and iodine compounds.

bitumen. A flammable mixture of hydrocarbons, including hard asphalt and tars.

bituminous coal. Soft coal that serves both as a fuel and as a source of useful chemicals.

biuret reaction. Test for proteins; they show pink or purple coloration in the presence of biuret and some other chemicals.

bivalent. (1) Said of two homologous chromosomes while they are pairing during meiosis; (2) having a valence of two.

bivalve mollusk. A mollusk having a two-valved shell connected by a hinge; example, clam.

Bk. Chemical symbol for berkelium.

black ash. Impure sodium carbonate obtained in the Leblanc process.

black body. A theoretical body which, heated to incandescence, would emit a continuous light-ray spectrum; a body having one unit of absorptivity and no reflectivity; tungsten and carbon come closest to this ideal.

black damp. Carbon dioxide in coal mines which accumulated because of combustion or explosion; it causes suffocation.

black lead. Graphite or plumbago.

black-body radiation. The radiation from a black body at a given temperature.

black-body temperature. The temperature of a radiating body as indicated by a radiation pyrometer which has been calibrated with the use of a black body.

Blackburn pendulum. An apparatus used in studying harmonic motions which consists of a pendulum which may swing with different periods in two directions at right angles.

blacker-than-black region. The region where the synchronizing and blanking voltages are found in the video signal of television.

black-out effect. A temporary loss of sensitivity of a vacuum tube after a strong short pulse.

bladder. A bag or sac which stores body fluids; examples, gall bladder, urinary bladder, and air bladder.

blade. The flat and usually expanded portion of a leaf, sepal, or petal.

Blagden's law. In a dilute solution, the depression of the freezing point is proportional to the concentration of the dissolved substance.

blast gate. In aeronautics, a device for controlling the pressure in the nozzle box of a turbosupercharger by discharging into the free atmosphere a portion of the exhaust gases that would otherwise pass through the turbine wheel.

blastema. Tissue of undifferentiated cells which in emergency may develop into an organ to replace a lost part of the animal.

blasting gelatin. Jellylike mixture of guncotton with nitroglycerin; a very powerful explosive.

blastocoele. The first body cavity formed in the blastula during the embryonic development of animals.

blastocyst. The germinal vesicle; a thin-walled hollow sphere with an inner cell mass formed by cleavage of the ovum.

blastoderm. A sheet of cells at the top of the yolk which forms as a result of cleavage in a yolk-rich egg.

blastomere. A cleavage cell formed in the early stages of division of the fertilized ovum.

blastopore. The porelike opening allowing communication of the gastrula cavity with the exterior.

blastostyle. A zooid without mouth and tentacles which produces medusa buds.

blastula. A hollow ball whose wall consists of a single cell layer, resulting from cleavage of the ovum.

bleeder resistance. In electrical communication, response-curve controlling resistance connected across the secondary coil of a transformer.

bleeding of plants. Flowing of sap from the broken ends of branches, from fresh stumps, and from cracks.

blende. Natural zinc sulfide, ZnS.

blended inheritance. Inheritance in which there is no dominant or recessive character but a mixture of the two.

blepharoplast. The basal body of cilium or flagellum.

blight. A decay of plants, resulting in withering without rotting which may be caused by insect pests, fungi, weather or soil conditions.

blind flight. Piloting an aircraft by instruments only because of at-

mospheric conditions which reduce visibility to practically zero.

blind spot. An area of the retina of the eye where the optic nerve enters and which is insensitive to light.

block mountain. A mountain formed by faulting and uplifting.

blocking. The interruption of plate currents in a vacuum tube due to the application of a high negative voltage.

blocking layer. Contact surface between a conductor and a semiconductor, which acts as a rectifier.

blood. The circulating body fluid which delivers food and oxygen to all parts of the body and carries away wastes.

blood corpuscle. A cell suspended in the blood.

blood count. A count of the number of red and white blood cells found in a cubic millimeter of blood, made on a special slide.

blood film. Thin smear of blood, made on a slide, fixed, and stained, and used in microscopic examination.

blood grouping. Division of the blood into four groups or types; essential aid in blood transfusions, as the recipient and donor must belong to the same blood group.

blood plasma. Blood from which all corpuscles have been removed; the fluid portion of the blood.

blood platelet. A thrombocyte; a tiny grayish body found in very large numbers in the blood of higher vertebrates; essential in clotting.

blood pressure. The pressure exerted by the blood on the elastic walls of the blood vessels which varies with age and physical condition.

blood serum. A yellowish fluid squeezed out from clotted blood.

blood sugar. Glucose circulating in the blood; the normal sugar content is greatly increased in diabetes.

blood typing. Determining to which blood group a person belongs, according to the agglutination of his blood.

blood vessel. An enclosure bounded by walls through which the blood flows in an animal's body.

bloodstone. Heliotrope; a semiprecious chalcedony; dark-green quartz with small spots of red jasper.

blooming. Mushrooming and defocussing of the electron beam when the brightness control in a cathode-ray tube is set too high.

blowhole. Small irregular hole in a casting caused by trapping of gas bubbles, which developed during solidification.

blubber. In aquatic mammals, thick layer of fatty tissue of the dermis which serves as an insulation against heat loss.

blue glow. (1) Thermoluminescence of certain metallic oxides when heated; (2) the bluish luminosity of the gas near the cathode in a Geissler tube.

blue mud. A typical fine-grained deep-sea sediment, containing much calcium carbonate, whose bluish color is due to finely divided iron sulfide.

blue vitriol. Hydrated copper sulfate, $CuSO_4 \cdot 5H_2O$; used for copper plating.

bluestone. Cupric sulfate, $CuSO_4$.

body. In aeronautics, the fuselage of an airplane with its cowling, covering, and the nacelle, and nacelle mounting.

body capacitance. The capacitance produced when the operator's hand approaches a vacuum-tube circuit.

body cavity. Internal cavity of most three-layered animals, enclosing the viscera.

body-centered structure. A crystal structure in which the atoms are located at the corners and center of a cubic or rectangular lattice.

bog iron ore. Limonite; hydrated iron oxide, $xFe_2O_3 \cdot yH_2O$, found in marshes and bogs.

Bohr orbit. The theoretical path of the electrons around the nucleus of the atom as conceived by Bohr.

Bohr theory. Explanation of the structure and behavior of atoms, representing them as consisting of a positively charged nucleus surrounded by planetary negative electrons revolving in definite orbits; when an electron jumps to a smaller orbit, monochromatic radiation is emitted.

boiler efficiency. The ratio of the calorie output of a boiler to the calorie content of the fuel used for heating.

boiler feed water. The water pumped into a boiler for conversion into steam.

boiler scale. Insoluble calcium and magnesium salts deposited on the surface of boiler parts in contact with the water.

boiling. Rapid conversion from liquid to vapor, with violent bubble formation.

boiling point. The temperature at which the vapor pressure of a liquid equals the external pressure.

boiling-point elevation. The boiling point of a solvent is elevated by the addition of a nonvolatile solute in proportion to the molar concentration of the solute.

bole. A fine-grained, sticky, bright-red clay; the decomposition product of basic igneous rocks, such as basalt.

bolide. A large meteor which explodes in the air and breaks up into fragments.

bolograph. A recording bolometer.

bolometer. A very sensitive instrument for the measurement of feeble radiation; it operates on the principle that the resistance of a fine wire changes when it is exposed to radiation.

bolson. Extensive deposits of sediments forming desert valleys.

Boltzmann constant (k). The ratio of the mean energy of a molecule to the absolute temperature; 1.371×10^{-16} erg per degree.

Boltzmann factor. A correction for thermal excitation to be made in calculating spectral-line intensities.

bomb calorimeter. Instrument for determining the heating value of fuels, by burning them in compressed oxygen in a bomb-shaped steel container and measuring the temperature rise of a known volume of water into which the hot bomb is immersed.

bombardment. Subjecting to the impact of fast-moving particles or radiation; used in the production of other particles or radiation, or in the transmutation of atoms.

bond. An attachment between two atoms by sharing two electrons; often indicated by use of a dot or dash, each of which indicates a pair of shared electrons and a valence of one.

bond, atomic. A valence linkage between atoms consisting of a pair of electrons, one of which has been contributed by each of the bonded atoms.

bond, covalent. A linkage in which each atom contributes one electron to a shared pair that constitutes an ordinary chemical bond.

bond, dative. A semipolar bond; a covalent bond in which both electrons forming the bonding pair are supplied by one atom.

bond, electrostatic. A valence linkage in which two atoms are held together by electrostatic forces as a result of the transfer of one or more electrons from the outer shell of one atom to that of the other.

bond energy. Energy characterizing a chemical bond between atoms, as measured by the energy required to disrupt it.

bond force constant. The Hooke's law force constant for infinitesimal extension or compression of a chemical bond in a molecule.

bond, heteropolar. A valence linkage between two atoms, consisting of a pair of electrons which are not held equally by both atoms.

bond, homopolar. A valence linkage between two atoms con-

sisting of a pair of electrons that are held equally by both atoms, so that there is no difference in polarity of the atoms.

bond, metallic. A special type of bond existing in metals, in which the valence electrons of the constituent atoms are free to move in the periodic lattice and thus account for metallic properties.

bond moment. The dipole moment associated with a chemical bond in a polar molecule.

bond strength. The energy required to break apart a given valence bond in a given molecule.

bonding power. A measure of the effect, positive or negative, contributed by a shared electron in a molecule to the attraction or repulsion between atoms in the molecule.

bone. A connective tissue in vertebrates containing calcium phosphate and carbonate.

bone ash. Impure calcium phosphate, $Ca_3(PO_4)_2$, from calcination of bones in air; used as a fertilizer.

bone black. A finely divided animal charcoal; used as a pigment, for filtration and decolorization of liquids.

bone conduction. Conducting sound to the inner ear through the cranial bones.

Bonne's projection. A map on which the parallels are concentric circles, but the meridians are curved lines.

bony layer. The hard region of a bone between the periosteum and the marrow.

book lungs. Leaflike membranes with blood capillaries forming an air-filled cavity; respiratory organs of some Arachnida; example, spider.

boost. (1) To increase or amplify; (2) in aeronautics, to supply an engine with more air or mixture than it would normally induct at sea level.

boost control, automatic. In aeronautics, an automatic regulator of boost pressure.

booster. A device inserted in series in an electric circuit to increase or decrease the voltage of that circuit.

boracic acid. Boric acid.

borax. Sodium tetraborate; $Na_2B_4O_7 \cdot 10H_2O$; used as a water softener.

borax bead test. Analytical method of identifying certain substances; a borax bead is dipped into the substance and then heated to incandescence to produce a characteristic color.

Borda's mouthpiece. A tube extending inward from a discharge orifice, which modifies the conditions of flow; its theoretical discharge coefficient is one half.

Bordeaux mixture. Plant fungicide consisting of copper sulfate, slaked lime, and water.

Bordet-Gengou test. Complement fixation.

bore. (1) The interior diameter of a tube; (2) wall of water that is a result of a tidal wave rising very rapidly in the estuary of a river.

boric acid. H_3BO_3; white soluble crystals; it occurs in volcanic regions; used as an antiseptic and eye wash.

boron. Yellow crystals or brown amorphous powder; chemical symbol B; atomic number 5.

boron carbide. A fine, black, crystalline powder nearly as hard as diamond; used as an abrasive.

bort. Impure or discolored diamond; useless as a gem but as hard as pure diamond; used in drills and cutting tools.

Bosch process. The manufacture of water gas by passing steam over heated coke.

boss. A cross-cutting mass of igneous rock which has ascended into the crust of the earth and may represent the roots of volcanic conduits.

botany. The science of plant life.

boulder. A large fragment of at least eight-inch diameter of sedimentary rock, which has been moved from its place of origin by a natural agency or has been formed *in situ* by weathering.

boulder clay. Glacial deposit of clay with rock fragments of different sizes.

Bourdon gage. Pressure gage; a curved flat tube which tends to straighten under pressure, indicating the value of fluid pressure applied to it by means of a needle moving over a circular scale.

Bowman's capsule. The cup-shaped end of a kidney tubule that forms around a glomerulus.

Boyle's law. The volume of a confined gas varies inversely with the pressure at constant temperature.

Br. Chemical symbol for bromine.

brace root. Prop root; plant-supporting root growing from the stem above ground; example, corn.

brachial. Pertaining to an arm or armlike organ.

brachial plexus. Complex nerve network to the shoulders, arms, and chest.

Brachiopoda. Lamp shells; phylum of animals with a two-valve shell.

brachistochrone. The shortest curved path of a particle moving under a given force from one given point to another given point.

brachyblast. A short lateral branch especially in Gymnospermae which helps leaves reach the light.

brachycephalic. Short- or broad-headed; having a cephalic index of 80 or more.

brachydactyly. Abnormal shortness of fingers or toes.

Brackett series. A series of lines in the infrared of the hydrogen spectrum whose frequencies are multiples of $1/4^2 - 1/n^2$, where n is 5, 6, 7, etc.

bract. A small leaf found at the base of a flower stalk.

bracteole. A very small bract.

Bragg angle. The glancing angle for x-rays at the reflecting planes of a crystal.

Bragg reflection. The reinforced reflection of x-rays from the successive atomic planes of a crystal, or of electrons from the grating-line structure of its surface; used for crystal-structure study.

brain. The main ganglionic mass of the central nervous system, composed of the cerebrum, cerebellum, and medulla oblongata.

brain stem. Vertebrate brain conforming to the spinal cord without the cerebral cortex, cerebellum, or cerebral hemispheres.

brake. A device which absorbs mechanical energy by transforming it into heat through frictional resistance; used for slowing down the motion of a body.

brake horsepower. The useful horsepower of an engine measured by means of a brake applied to the driving shaft.

brake thermal efficiency. Engine efficiency calculated in brake horsepower; the ratio of the heat equivalent of brake output to the heat input to the engine by fuel.

braking, dynamic. Braking an electrically driven vehicle in which the motor acts as a generator dissipating the braking energy or returning it to the supply.

branch. (1) Lines forming a single band in a band spectrum; (2) a conductor joining any two given points of an electric network; (3) in biology, the offshoot of a main stem, blood vessel, etc.

branch transmission. The transmission of sound in a tube or conduit containing one or more branches.

branchia. Gills.

branchial. Said of gills.

branchial arch. A visceral arch lying between adjacent gill slits of fish and preventing them from collapsing.

branchial arteries. Blood vessels which lead both to and from the gills in fish.

branchial heart. A muscular expansion of the branchial veins in squid which pumps blood through the gills.

branchial veins. Branches of the vena cava of mollusks which carry the blood to the gills on its way back to the heart from the anterior part of the body.

branching. In radioactivity, the occurrence of more than one radioactive disintegration of a radionuclide.

branching ratio. The ratio of the number of atoms of a radioactive element, which undergoes two different types of transformation, emitting alpha particles to the number of those emitting beta particles.

Branchiopoda. A subclass of Crustacea; aquatic animals whose lobed swimming feet serve also as respiratory organs; example, brine shrimp.

branchiostegite. A lateral fold of the body cavity which covers the gills in some Crustacea.

brass. An alloy series containing about twice as much copper as zinc; used for plumbing and in electrical apparatus.

brazing. The joining of two pieces of metal by fusing spelter or brass between the surfaces to be joined.

breakdown voltage. The voltage needed for passing current through an insulating material.

breaker. Breakwater; natural or man-made barrier which breaks the force of waves and thus protects the harbor.

break-in operation. A communication system in which the receiving operator is able to break in or interrupt the transmission at any time.

breast wheel. Obsolete water wheel in which buckets are fastened on the wheel rim, into which the water enters in line with the wheel center.

breed. A group of related animals or plants; a group of domestic animals developed by man.

breed count. A microscopic method of counting bacteria on a dried milk film.

breeder reactor. An atomic pile or similar device in which nonfissionable material is converted into fissionable material during the operation of the pile.

breeding ratio. In a breeder reactor, a comparison between the amount of the new nuclear fuel produced and the amount consumed during fission.

Brewster's law. The polarization angle at the surface of a medium is equal to the angle whose tangent is the refractive index of that medium.

bridge grafting. Inserting cions above and below a wound in the bark of a tree.

bridging. The shunting of one electrical circuit by another.

bright-line spectrum. A spectrum composed of several brilliantly colored lines, separated by a wide dark space.

brightness. Intrinsic brilliancy; the quotient arrived at by dividing the light intensity from a given direction by the surface area normal to that direction; measured in candle power or lumens per square inch.

brightness control. The manual bias control of a cathode-ray tube.

brightness temperature. The temperature of a black body which has the same surface brightness as a source of radiant energy.

Brillouin effect. In a radiation from a liquid, two spectral satellites appearing one on each side of the unmodified line at a distance of about 0.04 angström.

Brillouin zone. A continuous ensemble of all energies and wave functions which may be obtained from one atomic energy level in a metallic crystal lattice.

brine. Concentrated aqueous sodium chloride solution; used for pickling.

Brinell hardness test. Determining the hardness of a metal by indenting its surface with a hard steel ball under standard load; the diameter of the indentation is measured and the value of Brinell hardness is read from a chart.

Britannia metal. Tin-base alloy hardened with antimony and other metals.

bromides. Salts of hydrobromic acid, HBr; used in photography and medicine.

bromine. Dark-red liquid; chemical symbol Br; atomic number 35.

bronchi. Cartilage-ringed tubes which branch from the trachea into the lungs.

bronchiole. A tiny bronchial tube.

Bronson's resistance. The resistance formed between two electrodes in a gas which is exposed to constant ionization.

bronze. A copper-base alloy containing about 88% copper, 8 to 10% tin, and the rest zinc; used for making statues, lamps.

brown body. In Bryozoa, a compact mass formed by the degenerating internal organs; it is assumed to have excretory function.

Brown converter. A relay used as an audio-frequency amplifier.

Brownian movement. In a colloidal solution, continuous agitation of the suspended particles.

browse. The tender shoots, twigs, and leaves of trees and shrubs used as animal food.

Brunswick green. Cupric oxychloride; used as a pigment.

brush. A conductor, usually made of carbon, which is used for making electrical contact between a stationary and moving surface.

brush discharge. (1) Electricity discharged from a conductor when the potential difference between the conductor and the surrounding medium is not sufficiently high to yield an arc or spark; (2) an electrical discharge in a gas, intermediate between a glow discharge and a spark and composed of minute sparks.

Bryophyta. A group of plants, including the true mosses and the liverworts; they are small, rootless, and have no organized vascular tissue.

Bryozoa. Polyzoa; aquatic animals which reproduce by budding.

Btu. The abbreviation for British thermal unit; it is the amount of heat required to raise the temperature of one pound of water 1°F; 252 calories; 778 foot-pounds of work.

bubble chamber. Similar to a cloud chamber.

bubble gage. Instrument for measuring the rate of gas flow by counting the gas bubbles, as they move through the liquid content of a small trap installed in the gas line.

Buchner funnel. A porcelain funnel having a flat circular perforated base; used for filtering by suction.

bucking coil. A coil so connected as to provide a demagnetizing effect in another coil.

Buckley gage. Pressure gage which is based on measurement of the ionization produced in the gas by a given current.

bud. A compact shoot consisting of a short stem bearing crowded, overlapping immature leaves.

bud mutation. Deviation from the normal shoot formation from a bud; example, a purple-flowered branch on a shrub having white flowers.

bud scales. Leaves covering the outside of a bud for protection.

Budde effect. The increase in the volume of halogens, especially chlorine and bromine vapor, on exposure to light which is due to the heat from recombination of atoms.

budding. (1) Asexual reproduction in which a small swelling or bud develops on the surface of the parent cell, increases in size, and forms a new organism resembling the parent; it may remain attached or separated; example, yeast; (2) artificial propagation by inserting a bud of one plant into an incision in the bark of another plant.

bud-scale scars. Rings around a twig, marking the place where the bud scales of the terminal buds were fastened.

buffer. (1) A substance which, when added to a solution, causes a resistance to any change in pH; (2) a mechanism which controls the recoil after firing a gun.

buffer solution. A solution whose pH is only slightly changed by the addition of acids and bases.

bulb. A special stem structure in which food is stored by a plant to start the growth the following season.

bulbil. A small reproductive body in some plants which is able to produce a new plant when it is removed from the parent.

bulbus arteriosus. A muscular expansion of the ventral aorta in front of the heart of bony fish.

bulk modulus. The ratio of the stress acting on an elastic substance to the decrease in volume per unit volume.

bulla. A hollow, round growth, such as the tympanic bulla.

Buna S. Trade name for a synthetic rubber; a copolymer of butadiene and styrene.

Bunsen burner. A gas burner in which the air content of the gas-air mixture can be mechanically controlled.

Bunsen cell. A primary cell with two fluids; a zinc anode is immersed in dilute sulfuric acid and a carbon cathode is immersed in concentrated nitric acid.

Bunsen coefficient. The solubility of a gas in a liquid at standard pressure and temperature expressed as volumes of gas absorbed by a unit volume of the liquid.

Bunsen photometer. Grease-spot photometer; an instrument for comparing the intensities of two light sources.

Bunsen screen. A photometer screen consisting of a sheet of paper or parchment with a central area made translucent by a grease spot.

buoyancy. (1) The weight loss of a body immersed in a fluid caused by the upward pressure of the fluid exerted on the body; (2) in aeronautics, the vertical thrust on an aircraft due to its immersion in a fluid.

burble point. The angle of attack at which the value of lift of an aircraft in flight decreases either with the increase or with the decrease of the angle; it is due to turbulence in the air current.

buret. A graduated long glass tube with a tap for measuring the volume of liquid run out from it; used in volumetric analysis.

burned bearing. A black rough surface of a bearing usually caused by poor lubrication.

burnout. The point at which rocket propellant is exhausted or ceases to flow, resulting in the end of fuel combustion.

burnt alum. Alum dried at 200°C and powdered; used for removing dead tissue.

burrowing. Said of animals digging underground hollows and living in them; example, mole.

bursa. A sac of connective tissue which serves as a cushion between the skin and bones or between muscles and bones.

burst. A sudden, intense ionization of a gas due to the effect of cosmic rays; it is observed in cloud chambers.

bus. A bus bar; a central electrical conductor to which secondary conductors are connected.

bushing. Insulation between a live conductor and an earthed wall or tank.

butadiene. $CH_2:CH\cdot CH:CH_2$; a four-carbon straight-chain hydrocarbon containing two carbon-to-carbon double bonds; used in the manufacture of synthetic rubbers and plastics.

butane. C_4H_{10}; colorless gas; used as a fuel, solvent, refrigerant.

butte. Similar to a mesa but smaller.

butter of antimony. Antimony trichloride; $SbCl_3$.

button. The container of carbon granules in a carbon microphone.

butyl. Univalent alkyl radical; $C_4H_9^-$.

butyl rubber. A copolymer of isobutylene with a small amount of isoprene; a synthetic rubber.

Buys-Ballot's law. Due to the earth's rotation, standing with the back to the wind, the low pressure is to the left and the high pressure is to the right of the observer in the Northern Hemisphere, with the reverse being true in the Southern Hemisphere.

bypass capacitor. A capacitor used to provide a comparatively low shunting impedance for the current at some point in a circuit.

bypass condenser. A condenser for removing high-frequency carrier components, offering a very low impedance to high-frequency currents, but a high impedance to low-frequency currents.

bysmalith. A pluglike igneous intrusion with a domed top and bounded laterally by circular faults; due to upward pushing of the magma as it forced its way into stratified rock.

byssus. Strong filaments used for attachment formed by a gland in the foot of bivalve mollusks.

C

C. Chemical symbol for carbon.

°C. Centigrade degrees.

Ca. Chemical symbol for calcium.

cabane. In aeronautics, the usually pyramidal supporting framework of the wings at the fuselage.

cadmium. A white ductile metallic element; chemical symbol Cd; atomic number 48; used in electroplating and to control the flow of neutrons in an atomic pile.

cadmium yellow. Cadmium sulfide; CdS; a yellow pigment.

caducous. Said of parts of a plant that fall off as other parts of the plant open; example, the sepals of a poppy fall off as the flower unfolds.

caecum. (1) The blind end of the large intestine below the point of junction of the small and large intestines; (2) a projection from the embryo sac into the endosperm.

caffeine. $C_8H_{10}N_4O_2$; the alkaloid in coffee and tea; used in medicine.

Cairngorm stone. Smoky brown variety of quartz; used as a semiprecious stone.

caking coal. Coal that forms coke when heated without air.

cal. Abbreviation for gram calories.

Cal. Abbreviation for kilogram calories.

calcareous. Chalky; composed of or containing calcium carbonate.

calcareous tufa. Travertine; light-colored porous deposit on plants growing near springs with holes through which grasses may grow.

calcicole. Said of plants that grow best on calcareous soils.

calciferol. $C_{28}H_{43}OH$; vitamin D; it prevents rickets.

calciferous glands. Glands in the esophagus of earthworms that produce calcareous particles.

calcifuge. Said of plants that do not grow on limy soil.

calcination. Subjecting a substance to a high temperature below its fusion point, usually to make it friable.

calcine. A partially roasted ore which is prepared for smelting.

calciphile. Same as calcicole.

calciphobe. Same as calcifuge.

calcite. Calcium carbonate; $CaCO_3$; one of the most widely distributed minerals.

calcium. A silver-white soft alkaline-earth metal; chemical symbol Ca; atomic number 20; it occurs in nature combined with other elements; used in metallurgy.

calcium carbonate. White insoluble solid; $CaCO_3$; it occurs in nature as chalk, marble, and limestone.

calcium chloride. Deliquescent crystals; $CaCl_2\cdot H_2O$; used as a dying agent and coagulant.

calcium hydroxide. Colorless crystals; $Ca(OH)_2$; used in medicine.

calcium hypochlorite. Bleaching powder; $CaOCl_2$.

calcium oxide. Lime; quicklime; CaO; used in leather manufacture.

caldera. A large crater believed to be the result of the sinking in of the top of the cone due to withdrawal of lava from beneath.

calibration. The graduation of an instrument so that accurate measurements in definite units can be made.

californium. Radioactive element obtained by bombarding curium 242 with helium nuclei; chemical symbol Cf; atomic number 98.

calipers. An instrument for measuring internal and external dimensions; a graduated rule with one fixed and one sliding jaw.

callose. A carbohydrate deposited on the sieve plates of degenerated or nonfunctioning sieve tubes.

callus. (1) A superficial tissue which develops in woody plants to protect the injured surface; (2) bony tissue effecting reunion of a broken bone; (3) horny mass formed in the outer layer of skin as a result of continued pressure or friction; (4) calcareous substance near the umbilicus in shells of certain snails; (5) glistening pads of callose which close the sieve plates of aged sieve tubes.

calms. In meteorology, very weak winds or absence of winds and very small pressure differences over extensive areas; the smoke rises vertically in calms.

calms of Cancer. The high-pressure belts north of the northeast trade winds.

calms of Capricorn. The high-pressure belts south of the southwest trade winds.

calorie. (1) A unit of heat in the metric system; the amount of heat required to raise the temperature of 1 gram of water 1°C; (2) a unit used in dietetics.

calorific intensity. The maximum temperature reached through combustion of a given fuel with atmospheric oxygen under atmospheric pressure.

calorific value. The number of units of heat obtained from the complete combustion of a unit mass of a fuel or other substance.

calorimeter. An instrument used for calorific measurements.

calorimeter, adiabatic. A well-insulated calorimeter in which there is no appreciable heat exchange with the environment.

calorimeter, differential. A device which measures a quantity of heat by comparing it with a known quantity of heat at the same temperature.

calorimeter, gas. An apparatus used in the analysis of combustible gases.

calorimeter, Nernst. A calorimeter in which the substance whose specific heat is to be measured is suspended in a glass or metal envelope which can be evacuated.

calorimeter, oxygen-bomb. A calorimeter in which a weighed sample of solid or liquid fuel is ignited by an electrically heated wire and burned in oxygen under pressure in a strong-walled steel container.

calorimetry. The quantitative determination of heat content.

Calosoma. Large predaceous ground beetles which feed on caterpillars.

calutron. An electromagnetic device constructed on the principle of the mass spectrograph which is used for separating the isotopes of uranium.

calyptra. A hoodlike covering of the capsule of mosses and liverworts which develops from the archegonial wall.

calyptrogen. Actively dividing cells found in a layer which forms over the apex of a growing plant or over the roots in many plants.

calyx. All the sepals of a flower collectively.

cam. An eccentric projection on a revolving shaft for changing rotary motion into linear motion or vice versa.

camber. The curve of an airfoil from its chord.

cambium. The growth or growing layer of a woody or other plant; example, dicotyledonous stems.

Cambrian period. An early period of the Paleozoic era in which Trilobites and many other aquatic animals flourished.

camera lucida. A device for use in drawing the image observed through the ocular of a microscope.

camera obscura. A darkened chamber in which an image of objects may be projected by a lens on a screen.

camouflage. (1) The blending of the coloration of an animal with its surroundings; (2) disguising to make something invisible or unrecognizable; technique used in war.

camptonite. A dark basaltic dike rock of similar composition to that of diorite.

campylotropous. Said of a curved ovule, one side of which has grown faster than the other, so as to bring its micropyle near the hilum.

camshaft. Shaft for operating the valves of an internal-combustion engine, on which cams are mounted.

Canada balsam. A yellow liquid derived from a fir tree; its refractive index is about the same as that of optical glass; used for mounting microscope slides, as an adhesive for optical instruments, in varnish manufacture.

canal. A tubular structure or passage serving special purposes in many groups of animals.

canaliculus. Tiny intercellular passage which connects bone and other cells.

Cancer. The fourth sign of the Zodiac.

candle. The unit of luminous intensity; one candle is the luminous intensity of 1/60 square centimeter of a black body radiation at the temperature of the solidification of platinum.

candle power. The illuminating power of a standard candle used as a measure of the illumination of electric filaments.

candle, standard. The candle designated by the United States Bureau of Standards as the one whose light emission is one candle power; used as a unit in photometric measurements.

candoluminescence. The excessive luminescence of an incandescent body, as distinguished from the visible radiation due to temperature alone.

cane sugar. Sucrose; a carbohydrate, $C_{12}H_{22}O_{11}$, extracted from sugar cane and used as a food.

cannel coal. A bituminous or soft coal which ignites easily and burns with a hot, bright, candlelike flame due to its high percentage of volatile matter.

canyon. A deep, narrow valley made by stream erosion.

caoutchouc. Raw rubber.

cap. (1) The spore-bearing part of a mushroom; (2) the highest portion of a cloud gathering at a mountain top.

capacitance. The characteristic quantity of electricity required by a substance to make its potential higher than that of its environment; the unit of capacitance is the farad.

capacitance altimeter. An instrument for the determination of the altitude of an aircraft in terms of its capacitance to earth.

capacitance, stray. Undesired and unintentional capacitance in a circuit; example, capacitance in a connecting wire of a radio circuit.

capacitive load. A load in an a-c circuit in which the current has a slight lead over the voltage.

capacitor. A condenser; a device for storing electricity consisting of two metal plates separated by air or some other insulating material.

capacitor, bypass. A capacitor offering a high impedance to low-frequency currents and low impedance to high-frequency currents.

capacity, electrical. (1) The output of an electrical apparatus; (2) same as capacitance.

capacity, heat. The amount of heat needed to raise the temperature of a body by a given amount; the product of the specific heat of that body and its mass.

capacity reactance. The measure in ohms of the effect of introducing a capacitance into an oscillating circuit.

capacity, thermal. Same as capacity, heat.

Capella. A large, bright binary star; one of its two members has a very similar spectrum to that of our sun.

capillarity. The rise of fluids in capillary tubes and fine spaces due to surface tension.

capillary. Thin-walled, very small vessels in the body which assist in the circulation of body fluids.

capillary action. The rising of water through porous soils.

capillary electrometer. An instrument for the measurement of small currents, whose operation depends on the movement of mercury in a capillary tube.

capillary fringe. A zone of moisture higher than the true water table; capillary pores above the zone of saturation are filled with water.

capillary pressure. The pressure developed through capillary action.

capillary water. Water held by the capillarity of soil particles.

capillitium. (1) Protoplasmic threads in tubular form found in fruit bodies of slime molds; changes in humidity cause them to move and discharge spores; (2) sterile hyphae in the fruit bodies of certain fungi; example, puffballs.

capitulum. An inflorescence in which the flowers are crowded around a flat enlarged apex and look like a single flower; example, daisy.

Capricornus. The tenth sign of the Zodiac.

capsule. (1) A pod that develops from a compound pistil and thus has more than one carpel; (2) spore case of mosses; (3) a simple, dry, dehiscent fruit; (4) a broad, colorless, mucoid or gelatinous layer which surrounds some bacteria; (5) a membrane covering a viscus; example, that of the kidney.

capture. A process by which an atomic or nuclear system gets another particle, for example, a neutron.

capture, radiative. The capture of a neutron by a nucleus, with the emission of a gamma ray.

carapace. The shell covering the cephalothorax of Crustacea; example, the upper shell of a turtle.

carat. (1) The unit of weight for precious stones, 1/5 gram; (2) a unit for stating the fineness of gold, pure gold being 24 carats.

carbide. A binary compound of carbon and a metal.

carbocyclic compounds. Organic ring compounds.

carbohydrate. A compound containing carbon with hydrogen and oxygen in the same proportions as in water; examples, starches and sugars.

carbolic acid. Phenol; C_6H_5OH; used as a disinfectant, in synthetic resins.

carbon. A nonmetallic element occurring in three dissimilar forms: amorphous carbon, diamond, and graphite; chemical symbol C; atomic number 6.

carbon arc. Light arc produced between two carbon electrodes.

carbon black. Finely divided black pigment, composed essentially of pure carbon; it is prepared by incomplete combustion of natural gas; used in inks, rubber, polishes.

carbon cycle. A series of thermonuclear reactions which release large quantities of energy; they are believed to furnish the energy radiated by the sun and stars.

carbon cycle, organic. Same as carbon dioxide cycle.

carbon dioxide. Colorless gas; CO_2; used by plants to make food; solidified, it is called "dry ice" and used as a refrigerant and in carbonated beverages.

carbon dioxide cycle. The circulation of carbon dioxide from air to plants and animals, and back to air.

carbon disulfide. Colorless liquid; CS_2; used as a solvent, in rayon manufacture and in pest killing.

carbon filament. An incandescent-lamp filament composed of a thread or fiber which has been reduced to carbon by heating in the absence of air.

carbon monoxide. A colorless, odorless, poisonous gas; a product of incomplete combustion; used in metallurgy.

carbon rheostat. An assembly of carbon blocks whose electrical resistance can be varied by compressing them by means of a screw.

carbon steel. A tool steel other than high-speed or alloy steels; its properties depend on its carbon content.

carbon tetrachloride. A colorless nonflammable liquid; CCl_4; used as a solvent and in dry cleaning.

carbonado. Black diamond; hard, dark carbon variety found in Brazil; used for drilling rocks.

carbonation. (1) The action of carbon dioxide on rocks to crumble and decay them; (2) saturating a liquid with carbon dioxide.

carbonic acid. A solution of carbon dioxide in water; H_2CO_3.

carbonic acid gas. Same as carbon dioxide.

Carboniferous period. A late period in the Paleozoic era in which the coal beds were formed.

carbonization. Destructive distillation; heating organic or carbon-containing matter in the absence of air to expel volatile products; it leaves a residue rich in carbon; example, the manufacture of coke from coal.

carbonized filament. A thoriated tungsten filament which has been treated with carbon to obtain a coating of tungsten carbide.

carbonyl. A compound of a metal with carbon monoxide; example, iron carbonyl, $Fe(CO)_4$.

carbonyl group. The divalent group $=CO$.

Carborundum (a trade-mark). Silicon carbide; SiC; used as an abrasive.

Carboxydomonas. An autotrophic genus of bacteria that obtain their energy through the oxidation of carbon monoxide to carbon dioxide.

carboxyl group. The $—COOH$ group, characteristic of organic acids.

carburizing. Hardening the surface of iron-base alloys by heating them below the melting point in contact with a carbonaceous substance.

cardinal points. (1) The two focal points, the two principal points, and the two nodal points of a lens or of a symmetrical optical instrument; (2) north, south, east, and west.

cardinal teeth. In the shell of some bivalve mollusks, the interlocking prominences of the two valves just below the umba.

cardinal vein or sinus. The main longitudinal vein in fish and tetrapod embryos, one on each side of the vertebral column, returning blood from most of the body to Cuvier's ducts and then to the heart.

cardioid condenser. An optical system for concentrating light on an object for a compound microscope; it gives an illumination which approximates that of an ultramicroscope.

cardo. The basal segment of an insect maxilla by which it is attached to the head.

Carey-Foster bridge. A type of Wheatstone bridge for measuring the difference between two nearly equal resistances, in which the two ratio arms are coils connected by a slide wire.

carina. Keel-like bone; example, the breast bone of birds.

Carinatae. All existing and most extinct birds other than Ratitae.

carnallite. Reddish, crystalline mineral; $MgCl_2 \cdot KCl \cdot 6H_2O$; used as a fertilizer.

carnassial teeth. Large molar or premolar teeth modified for shearing flesh.

carnelian. Red or reddish brown chalcedony; a quartz mineral.

Carnivora. An order of carnivorous or omnivorous mammals with well developed canines.

carnivorous. Meat eating.

carnotite. A yellow mineral; $K_2O \cdot 2U_2O_3 \cdot U_2O_5 \cdot 3H_2O$; a source of radium.

Carnot's cycle. The sequence of operations of a highest-efficiency, ideal heat engine. The four steps in the cycle are (1) isothermal expansion, (2) adiabatic expansion, (3) isothermal compression, and (4) adiabatic compression.

Carnot's principle. The amount of work done by a heat engine is dependent on its limiting temperatures alone and is independent of the stroke or the intermediary agent used.

carotene. Yellow substance found in some plants and animals; it can change to vitamin A.

carotenoids. Red, orange, or yellow coloring matter of bacterial origin and wide distribution in both plants and animals; they are insoluble in water but soluble in alcohol, ether or chloroform.

carotid artery. A main artery which supplies blood from the heart to the head of vertebrates.

carpal. One of the bones of the carpus; a wrist bone.

carpel. An ovule-bearing leaf, the ovule being generally attached to the margin.

carpogonium. The female sex organ of red algae; it has a swollen basal portion containing the egg and an elongated terminal projection which received the male gamete.

carpospore. A globular, nonmotile spore produced after sexual reproduction in red algae; it contains carposporangia, each of which yields a carpospore.

carpus. The wrist; the bones of the wrist.

carrier catalyst. A catalytic agent which forms an intermediate compound with one of the reactants and thus helps transfer an atom or group from one compound to another.

carrier current. A relatively high-frequency a-c current superimposed on the ordinary circuit frequencies in order to increase the usefulness of a given transmission line.

carrier frequency. The constant frequency which is modulated by signals without changing except for taking on side frequencies.

carrier suppression. Signal transmission in which the carrier wave is not transmitted.

carrier wave. The steady wave component from a radio or television transmitter which is not affected by modulation.

carrier-frequency range of a transmitter. The continuous range of frequencies within which the transmitter may be adjusted for normal operation at all times.

carrying capacity. The amount of current in amperes which a cable may carry safely, that is, without overheating.

Cartesian diver. A device which illustrates many laws and principles of physics, such as Archimedes' principle, Boyle's law, and Pascal's law; it consists of a hollow glass figure in a container of water; by varying the pressure on the cover of the container, the figure will float or sink.

cartilage. A tough, flexible, rubbery connective tissue, part of the skeleton of vertebrates.

cartilage bone. A bone which replaces embryonic cartilage.

cartridge fuse. A fuse enclosed in an insulating tube in order to confine the arc when the fuse blows.

caruncle. (1) A spongy outgrowth of the seed coat, especially prominent in the castor-bean seed; (2) a small fleshy growth in animals.

caryopsis. Simple, dry, one-seeded, indehiscent fruit, with the pericarp firmly united all around to the seed coat; example, wheat grain.

cascade. (1) An arrangement of condensers, analogous to the series arrangement of battery cells, in which the high-potential plate of each is connected to the lower of the next; (2) a series of electrical devices in which each member operates the next in order.

cascade liquefier. A device used to liquefy air, oxygen, etc.; the critical temperature of the gas to be liquefied is reached step by step, by using the expansion of gases having successively lower boiling points for condensing.

cascade shower. A cosmic-ray shower which occurs when a high-energy electron, passing through matter, produces one or more photons of energies of the order of magnitude of its own; these become electrons and positrons and the process continues until the energy level of the produced particles falls to a point where photon emission and pair production is no longer possible.

case hardening. Hardening steel by heating it in contact with carbon and nitrogen.

casein. A yellow protein of milk; used in fibers, plastics, adhesives.

Cassegrain mirror. A convex second mirror placed in front of the concave objective in a reflecting telescope. The rays are reflected through a tube inserted at the center of the objective mirror and produce an image beyond it.

Cassiopeia. A constellation forming a "W" in the northern sky.

cassiterite. Gray, reddish, or yellow mineral; the principal ore of tin; SnO_2.

caste. In social insects, a type of structurally and functionally specialized individual; each caste has its own job to do.

casting. (1) Earth voided by an earthworm; (2) pouring molten metal into molds of the required form where it is allowed to solidify.

catabolism. The breaking down process in a living organism; a part of the metabolism.

cataclastic. Said of rocks which underwent deformation and granulation during dynamic metamorphosis.

catacoustics. The science of reflected sound and echo.

catadioptric. Referring to or involving both the reflection and refraction of light.

catalase. An enzyme which decomposes hydrogen peroxide, freeing oxygen.

catalysis. (1) The use of a catalyst to alter the rate of a chemical reaction; (2) a reaction in which a catalyst participates.

catalyst. A substance which changes the speed of a chemical reaction without itself being changed.

catalyst, carrier. A catalytic agent which influences the speed of a reaction by forming an intermediate compound with one of the reactants.

catalyst, contact. A catalytic agent which influences the speed of a reaction by altering the contact efficiency between the molecules of the reactants; examples, platinum and palladium.

catalyst, negative. A catalyst which decreases the rate of a chemical reaction.

catalyst, positive. A catalyst which increases the rate of a chemical reaction.

catalytic cracking. The breaking up of large molecules into smaller ones by using a catalyst at high temperature and high pressure; used in gasoline manufacture.

catalytic poison. A chemical that reduces or destroys the efficiency of a catalyst; a substance which, when preferentially adsorbed on the surface of a contact catalyst, retards or stops its catalytic action.

catalyzer. Same as catalyst.

cataphoresis. The migration of colloidal particles toward an electrode under the influence of an electromotive force.

catapult. In aeronautics, a device by which an airplane can be launched at flying speed from the deck of an airplane carrier.

catenary. Curve formed under the effect of gravity by a chain or string hanging from two fixed points.

caterpillar. (1) A larva of certain insects, such as butterflies and moths; it has a soft body, with pairs of jointed legs on the thorax and short unjointed prolegs on the abdomen; (2) chain wheels used on tractors and other vehicles to increase their moving efficiency.

cathamplifier. A high-input impedance amplifier circuit which permits push-pull operation from an unbalanced source.

cathetometer. A device to measure vertical distances or displacements.

cathode. The electrode in a cell (voltaic or primary) that attracts the positive ions and repels the negative ions; the negative pole.

cathode, cold. A thermionic electrode which emits at room temperature.

cathode dark space. The space near the cathode in a Crookes tube that remains dark during discharge.

cathode disintegration. The destruction of the active area of a cathode by positive-ion bombardment.

cathode drop. (1) An abrupt fall of electric potential at the cathode of an electrolytic cell or a vacuum tube; (2) in arc welding, a voltage drop between the arc and the cathode.

cathode glow. A luminosity which immediately surrounds the cathode in a gas-discharbe tube when operating at moderately low pressure, and which increases with further reduction of the pressure.

cathode heating time. The time it takes for the cathode to reach operating temperature if normal voltage is applied to the heating element.

cathode, indirectly heated. The cathode of a thermionic tube to which heat is supplied by an independent heater element.

cathode, ionic-heated. A hot cathode that is heated primarily by ionic bombardment of the emitting surface.

cathode rays. An emission from the cathode of a discharge tube, consisting of electrons supplied by the cathode itself and projected at right angles to its surface.

cathode sheath. The region between the cathode and plasma of a gas-discharge tube across which the cathode fall appears.

cathode sputtering. A means of depositing very thin layers of a metal on a surface; the disintegrated cathode material is deposited on the anode or the walls of the discharge tube.

cathode, thermionic. A cathode which emits electrons on heating.

cathode-ray furnace. A very high temperature furnace which heats small objects in a vacuum by bombardment with intense electron beams.

cathode-ray lamp. An intense light source of small area in which a small block of refracting material is heated to incandescence by cathode rays.

cathode-ray oscilloscope. An oscilloscope in which the moving element is a cathode-ray pencil.

cathode-ray tube. A tube for producing cathode rays; used in oscilloscopes for television and radar.

cathode-ray tube deflecting coils. A pair of coils used to provide the magnetic field for electromagnetic deflection of the electron beam.

cathodoluminescence. Luminescence excited by cathode rays.

cathodophosphorescence. Phosphorescence excited by cathode rays.

catholyte (catolyte). The electrolyte in the immediate neighborhood of the cathode during electrolysis.

cation. A positive ion, which migrates toward the cathode.

cationic agent. A compound in which, when dissolved, the positive ion is a long hydrocarbon chain; used as a detergent.

cationic current. That portion of the total current which is carried by cations.

catkin. A deciduous, scaly spike of unisexual apetalous flowers; example, pussywillow.

cat's eye. (1) An opalescent mineral species; used as gems; (2) the surface appearance of molten crucible steel.

Caucasoid stock. One of the three main stocks of living men; it includes the natives of Caucasus and immigrants to those regions.

caudal. Relating to the tail.

caudal filament. A median, jointed sensory appendage resembling an antenna in some of the primitive insects.

caudal fin. The tail fin of fish.

cauline. Belonging to the stem or arising from it.

caustic. (1) Corrosive to animal tissues; (2) a curve or surface of revolution formed by parallel rays reflected by a concave mirror; its apex is at the focus of the mirror.

caustic potash. Potassium hydroxide; KOH; used in making soft soap.

caustic soda. Sodium hydroxide, NaOH; used in soap manufacture, tanning, textiles.

Cavendish experiment. The measurement of the gravitation constant by means of a torsion balance, originally carried out by Cavendish.

cavern. Underground natural rock chamber that originated partly by the dissolving effect of water on calcareous matter.

cavitation. (1) The formation of a partial vacuum around a part revolving at higher than its critical speed, causing slowdown; (2) the formation of gas-filled spaces and bubbles in the sepa-

ration of gas dissolved in a flowing liquid; (3) a cavity formed in the lungs due to tuberculosis.

cc. Abbreviation for cubic centimeter.

Cd. Chemical symbol for cadmium.

Ce. Chemical symbol for cerium.

cecum. The appendix; blind pocket of the large intestine at the junction of the small and large intestines, at the lower right side of the abdomen; a projection from the embryo sac of some plants.

ceiling. The maximum altitude at which existing meteorological conditions allow visibility of the ground sufficient for practical piloting operations.

ceiling balloon. A small free balloon, whose rate of ascent is known; used to determine the ceiling.

ceiling projector. A projector that produces an illuminated region on the underside of a cloud for determining the height of that part of the cloud above the indicator.

ceiling, zero. Fog, dust, or other obstruction to vision so that the ceiling is less than 50 feet above the ground.

ceiling-height indicator. A device that measures the height from the horizontal to the illuminated spot produced by a ceiling projector as seen from a fixed position.

celestial mechanics. Gravitational astronomy; a study of and research on the motions of celestial bodies under the influence of their mutual gravitational attraction.

celestial meridian. A large circle passing through the north and south celestial poles and the zenith.

celestial navigation. Navigation by reference to celestial bodies; sometimes called celestial guidance.

celestial sphere. The imaginary sphere to the inner surface of which the celestial bodies appear to be attached; the observer is at the center of the sphere.

cell. (1) In electricity, a producer of electromotive force as the result of chemical action, light, or heat; (2) in biology, the unit of life, consisting of a mass of protoplasm and nucleus.

cell aggregate. A cell organization in which the cell members are completely identical, carry on the same function, and are entirely independent of one another; example, protococcus.

cell, concentration. An electric cell in which the electrical energy comes from the transfer of a substance from a system of high concentration to one of low concentration.

cell differentiation. Modifications

in the nature of cells which enables them to perform specific functions.

cell, displacement. An electric cell in which the essential chemical reaction is the ionization and entry into solution of atoms of one element, and the discharge and deposition from solution of the ions of another; example, Daniell cell.

cell division. Division of a cell into two daughter cells by mitosis.

cell, dry. An electric cell in which the electrolyte is a damp paste.

cell, electric. A device used to transform chemical into electrical energy or the reverse.

cell, gravity. An electrolytic cell in which the difference in the specific gravities of two electrolytes maintains them separated in two layers.

cell membrane. A semipermeable membrane surrounding the plasma.

cell organism. A one-celled animal or plant.

cell plate. A membranous disk in the equator of the spindle in the late stages of mitosis in plant cells.

cell, primary. An electric cell in which an irreversible chemical reaction or reactions yield electrical energy.

cell, reversible. An electric cell in which the rate of chemical reaction varies continuously and reversibly with the applied external electromotive force; chemical and electrical energies can be reversibly interconverted.

cell sap. (1) A watery fluid found in vacuoles of plant cells; (2) the gell-like basic substance of animal cells.

cell, secondary. An electric cell in which the interacting substances may be restored to their original chemical form by sending a direct current of electricity through the cell in reverse direction to that of the discharge.

cell theory. All living things are made up of cells which have been formed by division of previously existing cells.

cell wall. The boundary membrane of cells.

cellobiose. A disaccharide obtained by incomplete hydrolysis of cellulose.

cellular. Pertaining to or consisting of cells.

cellular respiration. Internal respiration; diffusion of gases in plants between the cells and the air in the intercellular spaces.

cellulose. The fibrous material of plant-cell walls; $(C_6H_{10}O_5)_x$; used in making paper, rayon, lacquers.

cellulose acetate. Acetyl cellulose; an ester of cellulose and acetic acid; a yellowish, amorphous solid; used in the manufacture of rayon, plastics, film.

cellulose nitrate. Nitrocellulose; an ester of cellulose and nitric acid; a white amorphous solid; used in the manufacture of plastics, lacquers, and explosives.

Celsius scale. The centigrade thermometer scale.

cement (1) Laminated bone that covers the roots of teeth; (2) a finely powdered substance which becomes adhesive when combined with water.

cementation. (1) Aggregation of loose sediment into coherent rocks by a cement; (2) association of hyphae of fungi with the help of an excreted adhesive; (3) heating steel in contact with carbonaceous matter to increase its carbon content.

cementite. Iron carbide, Fe_3C; it is present in steel and causes its brittleness.

cenogenesis. The development of individual characters which do not repeat the racial characters of the group.

Cenozoic era. A geological period which began about 60 million years ago; it is characterized by the development of a great variety of mammals and the appearance of shrubs and flowering plants.

Centaurus. A large and brilliant constellation in the southern sky.

center, nerve. A region of the central nervous system with a restricted special function; example, the respiratory center in the medulla of vertebrates which controls the respiratory movements.

center of buoyancy. The point through which the resultant of the buoyancy forces on a submerged body act; it coincides with the center of gravity of the displaced fluid.

center of displacement. That point of a submerged or partially submerged body which coincides with the center of mass of the displaced fluid.

center of gravity. That point of a body in which all its weight seems to be concentrated and at which the body can be supported in equilibrium.

center of inertia. Same as center of mass.

center of mass. A point coinciding with the center of gravity; the point in a body in which its inertia resisting acceleration is concentrated.

center of moments. (1) The point about which a lever in equilibrium is free to move; (2) the reference axis used in calculating the moments of forces.

center of oscillation. The point in a compound pendulum which, when the pendulum is at rest, is below the suspension point on a vertical line and at a distance which corresponds to the length of a simple pendulum of the same period as the compound pendulum.

center of pressure. In a surface immersed in a fluid, the point at which the resultant pressure over the entire surface may be assumed to act; in aeronautics, the point in which the chord of an airfoil section and the resultant of air forces intersect each other.

center of symmetry. A point inside a crystal so located that all lines passing through it contact opposite faces of the crystal in corresponding points at equal distances.

center tap. A connection made to the center of a transformer winding or to the center of a resistor.

centering control. In cathode-ray-tube devices, a potentiometer which enables the viewer to move the image back and forth or up and down on the screen.

centigrade scale. A thermometer scale of one hundred equal divisions, between 0° as the freezing point and 100° as the boiling point of water. To convert centigrade into Fahrenheit degrees, multiply by 9/5 (1.8) and add 32.

centigram (cg). A metric unit of weight; 0.01 gram.

centimeter (cm). A metric unit of length; 10 millimeters; 0.01 meter; 0.4 inch.

centipoise. A cgs unit of viscosity, equal to 0.01 poise; water at 20°C has a viscosity of about 1 centipoise.

central cylinder. A stele; the central portion of the root or stem of a plant which contains vascular tissue.

central force. A force which acts along the line joining two centers.

central free placentation. An arrangement in which the placenta is not attached to the wall of the ovary.

central nervous system. The brain and the spinal chord; the main ganglia of the nervous system with their nerve cords.

central orbit. The orbit of a body or particle on which it moves under the influence of a central force.

central power station. A place where electrical energy is produced from an original source, such as fuel or water power, and sent out over a network of transmission lines to the region served.

centrifugal force. The force tending to draw a body away from the center about which it is revolving.

centrifugal hoops. A device which shows why the earth's polar diameter is 26° shorter than that of the equator.

centrifuge. A high-speed rotary machine for separating solids from liquids or liquids of different specific gravities from each other; example, separation of rubber from rubber latex.

centriole. Minute granules in resting cells, found just outside the nuclear membrane.

centripetal force. The force tending to draw a body toward the center about which it is rotating; it is equal but opposite in direction to the centrifugal force.

centrobaric. Having a true center of gravity.

centrode. The curve traced by the instantaneous center of rotation of a plane rolling on another plane.

centromere. In mitosis, the place of attachment of the spindle fiber to the chromosome.

centrosome. A tiny protoplasmic body connected to the nucleus, mostly in animal cells; it seems to play some part in mitosis.

centrosphere. A small body near the nucleus of an animal cell which contains the centrosome.

centrum. (1) The basal portion of a vertebra from which spring the spinous and transverse processes; (2) an association of asci and nutritive cells; (3) the point of origin of an earthquake at varying distances beneath the surface of the earth.

cephalic. Pertaining to or situated near the head.

cephalic gland. A structure lying in the anterior end of nemertine worms.

cephalic index. The ratio of the width to the length of the head.

cephalization. The centralization of important parts, such as the sense organs, in the head or head region.

cephalocone. Tentaclelike organ projecting from the head.

Cephalopoda. Mollusks that have tentacles, eyes and internal shells; example, octopus.

cephalothorax. A region of the skeleton of the crayfish which includes the head and thorax.

cerargyrite. Horn silver; a grayish mineral; silver chloride, AgCl.

ceraunograph. An electronic instrument for recording the occurrence of lightning and thunder in chronological order.

cercopod. A slender projection at the posterior end of the body in certain Crustacea.

cercus. An appendage attached to the abdomen of May flies.

cere. A fleshy growth at the base of the bill of some birds.

cereal. Any plant that has flour-yielding grains used for food; examples, wheat, rye, and corn.

cerebellum. The hind portion of the brain of vertebrates, which controls muscular coordination and balance.

cerebral aqueduct. Aqueduct of Sylvius; the canal between the third and fourth ventricle of the brain.

cerebral cortex. The outer layer of the brain; assumedly the site of subconscious and involuntary processes.

cerebral hemispheres. In man, the two portions of the brain that fill the upper part of the skull; assumedly the site of conscious and voluntary mental functions.

cerebral hemorrhage. The rupture of a blood vessel in the cerebrum of the brain or on its surface.

cerebral tube. A ciliated tube associated with the brain in certain marine worms.

cerebrospinal. Referring or belonging to the brain and spinal cord of vertebrates.

cerebrospinal fluid. A colorless fluid which fills the cavity inside the vertebrate brain and spinal cord; it is slightly alkaline and contains some inorganic salts, proteins, and dextrose.

cerebrum. The largest part of human brain, occupying the upper part of the skull; the two cerebral hemispheres.

Cerenkov radiation A visible radiation emitted by a high-energy particle moving in a medium having an index of refraction considerably greater than unity.

cerium. A soft, lustrous gray metal; chemical symbol Ce; atomic number 58; its compounds are used for coating carbon electrodes.

cerumen. (1) Earwax; secretion of the glands of external-ear passages in mammals; (2) dark wax made by some bees.

cerussite. A white or gray mineral; lead carbonate, $PbCO_3$.

cervical. Pertaining to the neck region.

cervical groove. A groove marking the boundary between head and thorax in Crustacea.

cervix. (1) The cylindrical posterior part of the uterus of mammals which leads into the vagina; (2) any narrow or necklike portion of an organ.

cesium. A silver-white ductile alkali metal; chemical symbol Cs; atomic number 55.

Cestoda. Tapeworms; Platyhelminthes; parasites.

Cetacea. Large aquatic carnivorous mammals with fishlike bodies and forelimbs modified into flippers.

cetane number. A means of comparing the ignition quality of diesel fuels.

Cf. Chemical symbol for californium.

cg. Abbreviation for centigram; 0.01 gram.

cgs system. The metric system of measurement in which the three fundamental units are the centimeter, gram, and second.

chaeta. A slender, pointed structure secreted by the cells of the integument in many invertebrates, such as the Annelida.

Chaetognatha. Arrow worms; marine animals abundant in plankton.

Chaetopoda. A class of Annelida, including bristle worms and earthworms.

chain reaction. A reaction which, once "triggered," continues to supply enough energy or particles to continue the reaction until the entire amount of available reactive material is used up.

chalaza. (1) The point at which the nucleus and envelope of an ovule are joined; (2) a treadle; twisted cords of albumen that keep the yolk of an egg in place.

chalcedony. A variety of quartz, SiO_2; gray or brown mineral.

chalcocite. Grayish-black copper ore; copper sulfide, Cu_2S.

chalcopyrite. A yellow ore of copper and iron; $CuFeS_2$.

chalk. A soft, porous limestone; calcium carbonate, $CaCO_3$; used as an antacid and alkalizer.

chalk soil. A soil mixed with limestone particles made of tiny marine shells.

chalybeate water. Natural water containing a small percentage of iron carbonate.

chamaephyte. A woody or herbaceous plant with perennating buds above soil level.

chamber process. Making sulfuric acid in large lead chambers from sulfur dioxide and air in the presence of nitrogen oxides as catalysts.

chandelle. An abrupt climbing turn of an airplane.

change of state. The conversion of a substance from one of the physical states of matter (solid, liquid, and gaseous) into another.

channel capacity. The number of signals per second which may be transmitted through a given channel.

channel frequency. The band of frequencies which is found associated with a single unit of intelligence in a communication system.

channeled spectrum. A molecular band spectrum.

channeling. The extra transmission of particles through a medium containing voids.

character. (1) A trait passed on from parent to offspring; (2) a feature that helps distinguish one species from another.

characteristic equation. An equation connecting the variables used to define the physical state of a body; example, volume, pressure, and temperature.

charactron. A cathode-ray tube.

Charadriiformes. An order of shore birds; examples, plover, gull, and sandpiper.

charcoal. A form of carbon obtained from wood, bones, and other organic matter by destructive distillation.

charge. (1) In metallurgy, the raw materials that go into a furnace; (2) the amount of electricity on a body, which is produced by adding or removing electrons from a neutral body.

charge, bound. An electric charge which is not free but bound by a charge of opposite sign that induced it.

charge density. Surface-charge density; the charge per unit area.

charge, free. Electric charge on the surface of a conductor or a dielectric, which is not bound, that is, it may escape to the earth when the conductor is grounded.

charge-mass ratio. The ratio of the electric charge carried by an electrified particle or ion to the mass of the particle or ion.

charging. Restoring the plates and electrolyte of a storage cell or battery by passing through direct current in a direction opposite to that of discharge.

charging by induction. Developing a charge on an uncharged body by bringing it in the vicinity of a charged body.

charging rate. The rate of flow, in amperes, of electric current through a storage battery while it is being charged.

Charles' law. Gay-Lussac's law; at constant pressure, the volume of a given mass of gas is directly proportional to the absolute temperature.

Chattock gage. A manometer using the difference in pressure of two columns of liquid of nearly equal density.

check experiment. An experiment repeated for verifying the results of the same experiment performed earlier.

cheek. Lateral wall of the oral cavity.

chela. A pincerlike grasping appendage found in Arthropoda.

chelation. Formation of a heterocyclic ring by attachment of compounds or radicals to a central metal or other ion by secondary or primary valence forces.

chelicerae. The first pair of appendages in spiders and related animals that are sometimes connected to a poison gland.

cheliped. The first walking leg of the crayfish and other Crustacea having a well-developed pincer.

Chelonia. An order of shell-covered reptiles; examples, the tortoise and turtle.

chemical. (1) Having to do with chemistry; (2) a substance produced by a chemical process.

chemical affinity. The force that holds atoms together in the molecule.

chemical analysis. Determination of the composition of a substance by splitting it up into its components.

chemical balance. A precision instrument used in chemistry for weighing small quantities with great accuracy.

chemical bond. The linkage between two atoms; as a rule, it consists of a pair of shared electrons.

chemical change. The change of a substance into another different substance; a chemical reaction.

chemical energy. The energy set free in a chemical reaction.

chemical engineering. Design, equipment, and operation of chemical plants.

chemical equation. The mathematical representation of a chemical reaction; there should be the same number of atoms on both sides of the equal sign.

chemical equilibrium. A condition of balance in a reversible chemical reaction so that the rate of reaction in one direction equals the rate of reaction in the reverse direction.

chemical equivalent. The combining weight; the atomic weight divided by the valence.

chemical formula. The composition or structure of a substance as represented by chemical symbols; examples, H_2SO_4, C_6H_5OH.

chemical property. The ability to undergo or induce a chemical change; examples, flammability, explosiveness.

chemical reaction. The interaction of two or more substances which results in a chemical change.

chemical symbol. A single capital letter, or a capital letter and a small letter used as an abbreviation for an atom of an element or a gram atom of an element.

chemical weathering. Changes in the composition, color, and texture of exposed materials.

chemically pure (cp). Containing no foreign substance or impurity.

chemiluminescence. Light without heat produced in a chemical reaction.

chemisorption. Irreversible adsorption in which the adsorbed substance is held by chemical forces.

chemistry. A science that treats the composition of substances, their structure, behavior, their reactions, analyses and syntheses.

chemoautotrophic nutrition. Assimilation of simple inorganic substances into food by plants; example, utilization of carbon dioxide by bacteria.

chemoreceptor. A sensory nerve ending for the reception of chemical stimuli.

chemosphere. The region of the atmosphere from 20 to 50 miles above the earth where ultraviolet rays are filtered out.

chemosynthesis. In physiology, the production of organic compounds by use of energy, secured from a chemical reaction.

chemotaxis. Chemotropism; the movement of an organism in which the diffusion of chemical substances is the stimulus.

chemotropism. A reflex response to a chemical stimulus.

chernozem. Very rich, black grassland soil in central Russia.

chert. A natural silica, SiO_2, resembling flint.

chest cavity. The upper division of the body cavity, containing the heart and lungs.

chiasma. (1) Optic chiasma; crossing of the optic nerves from the retina of the eye; (2) an interchange of material at corresponding points between homologous chromosomes during nuclear division.

chilaria. A pair of rudimentary appendages on the first abdominal or pregenital segment in the king crab.

Chile saltpeter. Sodium nitrate, $NaNO_3$; a source of nitrates.

Chilopoda. Centipedes; an order of Arthropoda.

chimaera. A plant having two or more genetically different tissues as a result of mutation or abnormal distribution of chromosomes.

chi-meson. Subatomic particle.

chimney rocks. Isolated columns of cliffs resulting from the effect of waves which widen joints and wash away blocks.

China clay. Kaolin; a relatively pure hydrated aluminum silicate, $Al_2O_3 \cdot 2SiO_2 \cdot 2H_2O$; used for the manufacture of porcelain and ceramics.

chinook. An American warm wind in the Rockies which causes melting of snow fields and avalanches.

Chiroptera. "Hand-winged" nocturnal mammals; example, bats.

chitin. The tough horny substance that forms most of the "shell" of insects, lobsters, spiders, etc.

Chladni's plates. A device which shows the nature of vibration.

chlamydospore. A large fungal spore with tough walls, formed inside a hypha by collection of protoplasm in the filament.

chloragogen cells. Cells surrounding the digestive tract and dorsal blood vessel of Annelida; they synthesize urea.

chloral. $CCl_3 \cdot CHO$; a pungent-smelling, colorless, oily liquid; used as a hypnotic.

chloral hydrate. $CCl_3 \cdot CH(OH)_2$; colorless crystals; a powerful sedative.

chlorates. Salts of chloric acid, $HClO_3$; used primarily in explosives, fireworks, and matches, because it readily decomposes into chlorine and free oxygen.

chlorenchyma. A tissue containing chloroplasts.

chloride. A salt of hydrochloric acid, HCl; example, table salt, NaCl.

chlorinated hydrocarbons. Hydrocarbons in which one or more of the hydrogen atoms have been replaced by chlorine; nonflammable solvents.

chlorination. (1) The purification of drinking water by the addition of chlorine; (2) addition of chlorine to organic compounds; (3) sewage treatment with chlorine.

chlorine. Yellowish-green poisonous gas; chemical symbol Cl; atomic number 17; used for bleaching and as a disinfectant.

chlorocruorin. A respiratory green pigment in the blood of certain Polychaeta; iron containing protein, closely-related to hemoglobin.

chloroform. Trichloromethane; $CHCl_3$; colorless liquid; used as an anesthetic and solvent.

chlorohydrin. $CH_2ClCHOHCH_2$-OH; yellow liquid; used in the manufacture of dye intermediates.

Chlorophyceae. Green algae.

chlorophyll. A green coloring matter in plant cells consisting of two yellow and two green pigments; it produces carbohydrates from carbon dioxide and water by photosynthesis.

chloroplast. Green plastid in plant cells, which contains chlorophyll.

chloroprene. CH_2:CHCCl:CH_2; colorless liquid; the monomer of a synthetic rubber.

choana. A funnel-like opening of the nasal cavity into the mouth of vertebrates.

choanocyte. Collar cells of sponges, bearing a high ridge surrounding a flagellum at the free end; they are in cavities and produce water currents through the passages in the body wall.

choke. A valve in the carburator of an internal-combustion engine which regulates the proportion of air and gasoline vapors entering the cylinders.

choke coil. A coil of low ohmic resistance and comparatively high impedance to alternating current.

choke damp. Black damp; carbon dioxide, CO_2; dangerous gas in mines.

cholesterol. $C_{27}H_{45}OH$; a sterol alcohol; white waxy substance present in human tissues; it performs vital functions; it is changed into vitamin D by ultraviolet rays.

choline. An organic base combined with fatty acids in the bile and egg yolk; it controls

the fat formation in the liver.

cholinergic. Said of a nerve fiber which secretes acetylcholine at its end under the effect of nerve impulses.

cholinesterase. An enzyme that splits and thus inactivates acetylcholine.

Chondrichthyes. Cartilaginous fish; almost exclusively marine with no true bone; examples, sharks, skates, rays, dogfish.

chondriosome. Small, rod-shaped or filamentlike structure found in the cytoplasm of cells; mitochondria.

chondrocranium. The cartilaginous cover of the brain of the embryo of vertebrates which also covers the inner ear.

chopper. (1) A mechanical device which gives a pulsating characteristic to a current or beam of light by regular and frequent interruptions; a ticker; (2) a device to modulate a signal by opening and closing contacts periodically.

chord. In aeronautics, a straight line drawn from the leading edge to the trailing edge of the wing.

Chordata. Animals with notochord and gill slits in the embryo stage, having a hollow nerve tube dorsal to the digestive tract.

chordate. Having a backbonelike notochord.

chordotonal organ. An auditory organ found in the insects singly or in bundles.

chorioid plexus. A projection into ventricles of the brain, which consists of tufts of blood vessels; it secretes cerebrospinal fluid.

chorion. (1) An accessory membrane during embryonic development in mammals which provides the connection with the mother for interchange of materials before birth; (2) shell of an insect egg.

choripetalous flower. Flower in which the corolla consists of separate, distinct petals.

choroid. The middle coat of the eye between the retina and the sclera.

chorology. Zoogeography; the study of the distribution of animals.

Christiansen filter. A wave filter for one specific wave length.

chroma. Chromaticity; color, characterized by hue and saturation but without reference to brilliance; example, green and red have chroma, white and black have none.

chromate. A salt of chromic acid, H_2CrO_4.

chromatic aberration. A defect in lenses resulting from failure to bring all wave lengths of light to the same focus, so that the component color images do not coincide.

chromaticity,   complementary.

The property of two light samples of producing an achromatic visual stimulus when combined in suitable proportions.

chromatics. The study of colors.

chromatid. A half chromosome; one of the four half chromosomes that unite to form a tetrad.

chromatin. Tiny bits of granular protoplasm within a cell nucleus which form the chromosomes.

chromatographic analysis. The application of the selective adsorption of colored solutes on an adsorbent to the determination of the composition of a dye solution.

chromatography. (1) Same as chromatographic analysis; (2) the study of colors.

chromatophore. (1) A chromoplast; a plastid containing one or more pigments; (2) in zoology, a cell with pigment in its cytoplasm, responsible for color markings on many animals; example, frogs.

chrome alum. Potassium chromium sulfate; $K_2SO_4·Cr_2$-$(SO_4)_3·24H_2O$; dark purple crystalline soluble salt; used in dyeing, tanning.

chrome red. Basic lead chromate; $PbO·PbCrO_4$; used as a pigment.

chrome steel. Tough, strong steel of varying chromium content; used for high-speed tools, gears.

chrome yellow. Lead chromate, $PbCrO_4$; yellow crystals; used as a paint pigment.

chrome-nickel steel. Stainless steel, in which chromium and nickel are the chief alloying components.

chrome-vanadium steel. An iron alloy containing up to 1.2% chromium and 0.15% vanadium; used for making automobile and other springs.

chromidia. Granules of chromatin in the cytoplasm of cells which stain deeply with basic stains and are derived from the nucleus.

chrominance. The colorimetric difference between any color and a reference color of equal brilliance with the reference color of a given chroma.

chromite. Brownish-black, crystalline mineral; $Cr_2O_3·FeO$; used as a source of chromium, in refractories.

chromium. Steel-gray, hard metal; chemical symbol Cr; atomic number 24; used in alloys and electroplating.

chromium plating. Depositing a thin, resistant film of chromium metal by electrolysis, with a solution of chromic anhydride, CrO_3, as the electrolyte.

chromogenic. Color-producing.

chromomere. A beadlike granule

present in the chromosomes; a constituent of chromatin.

chromonema. A slender thread of the nuclear network.

chromophore. An atom or group of atoms in a molecule which is believed to be responsible for the color of organic dyes; examples, C:N, N:N, N:O.

chromophoric electron. Electron in the double bond of the chromophore groups.

chromoplast. Chromatophore; a colored plastid which contains one or more pigments.

chromoscope. (1) An apparatus for measuring color values and intensities; (2) an optical instrument for combining color images.

chromosome. A rodlike body, consisting of chromatin granules, in the nucleus of cells; chromosomes are known to carry hereditary traits.

chromosome map. A diagram showing the position of the genes in a chromosome.

chromosphere. A deep layer of incandescent gas outside the photosphere around the sun.

chronaxie. The shortest time required for the excitation of a nerve by electricity.

chronograph. (1) A precision stop watch; (2) a time-recording mechanism.

chronometer. A very accurate clock used to determine the longitude of a ship.

chronoscope. A precision instrument for measuring very short time intervals.

chronotron. A device which measures the position of the superimposed loci of a pair of pulses on a transmission line to determine the time between the events which initiated the pulses.

chrysalis. Hard-covered pupa of some insects; example, the pupa of butterflies.

chrysotile. A serpentine mineral of fibrous structure; asbestos; used for fireproofing and insulation.

chyle. A milky lymph containing the products of digestion.

chyme. Partially digested food of the stomach which goes into the small intestine.

cicatrix. The scarring of connective tissue, which occurs after shedding of leaves or healing of wounds.

cilia. (1) Short, hairlike projections of plant and animal cells that are used as organs of locomotion in some forms; (2) the eyelashes.

ciliary body. The thickened rim of the choroid of the vertebrate eye, at the border of the cornea, which contains ciliary muscles as the means of accommodation.

ciliary feeding. Feeding by filtering minute organisms from a current of water drawn through or toward the animal by cilia; example, in amphioxus.

Ciliata. A group of ciliated unicellular organisms.

Ciliophora. A class of Protozoa, having cilia and a double nucleus.

cinnabar. A reddish mineral; mercuric sulfide, HgS; a mercury ore.

cion. A part, usually young stem with buds, of a tree or shrub which is grafted into another plant; a scion.

circinate venation. Unfolding from the bud; the leaf uncoils from the base toward the apex and grows until it reaches full size; example, ferns.

circle of least confusion. The small round spot that, on account of aberration effects, constitutes the smallest image of a point source through an uncorrected lens; its diameter is the measure of the limit of sharp definition.

circuit. The complete path, consisting of conductors, over which an electric current can flow from the source of electrical energy and back again.

circuit, balanced. A circuit in which the voltage of the two wires it consists of is equal but of opposite phase relative to the earth.

circuit breaker. A device, for example, an electromagnet, used for the interruption of a circuit under normal or abnormal conditions.

circuit, clipping. (1) A circuit to prevent the peak amplitude of an electrical signal from exceeding a predetermined level; (2) a circuit for eliminating the tail of an electrical pulse after a predetermined time; (3) a circuit element in a pulse amplifier for reducing the amplification at frequencies below a predetermined value.

circuit driver. A source of high frequency, especially a controlled vacuum tube, which provides electromotive force for experimental use.

circuit, integrating. A circuit whose output current or voltage is proportional to the time integral of its input current or voltage.

circuital field. A vector field resembling a circuit.

circular mil. A unit for expressing the cross section area of a wire; an area equal to that of a circle of 0.001 inch diameter.

circular polarization. Passing plane-polarized light through a quarter-wave plate whose principal plane makes a 45° angle with the plane of polarization.

circulating signal. A transmitted signal which travels one or more times around the earth.

circulation. (1) Movement on a path which returns to its starting point; example, air circula-

tion in a room; (2) the movement of blood throughout the body; (3) the rotary movement of the protoplasm in a cell.

circulator. A fluid-circulating mechanism.

circulatory system. The system of tubes or other structures through which a fluid carries food to the cells of the animal body.

circumpolar whirl. Winds that move counterclockwise on the Arctic Ocean and clockwise on the Antarctic Ocean.

circumscissile dehiscence. Spontaneous splitting open of fruit along a circular line.

cirque. An amphitheater-shaped basin, gouged out of a mountain by glacial erosion.

cirque lake. Mountain lake; tarn; a cirque filled with water.

Cirripedia. Barnacles; aquatic, sessile Crustacea, which feed by drawing a current of water toward the mouth with their whiplike appendage.

cirrocumulus. Mackerel sky; flaky mass of small round clouds containing tiny ice crystals, 4 miles up; it indicates a change from calm to windy weather.

cirrostratus. High milky veil clouds of tiny ice crystals.

cirrus. A tendril; a slender projection used by plants for climbing.

cirrus clouds. Fair-weather clouds of minute ice crystals which may be forerunners of an approaching storm; they occur at an altitude of 5 to 9 miles.

cisterna magna. A large cavity between the dorsal part of cerebellum and the medulla oblongata, in which the kidneys are located.

cis-trans isomerism. Geometrical isomerism of an unsaturated organic compound; in one isomer, two identical groups are on the same side of the plane of the double bond, whereas in the other isomer, two identical groups are on opposite sides.

citric acid. $C_6H_8O_7$; colorless, crystalline, soluble tribasic organic acid; it has a sour taste and occurs free in citrus fruits; used as a flavor.

Cl. Chemical symbol for chlorine.

Cladocera. Water fleas; freshwater Crustacea; a bivalve shield covers the body, but leaves the head free.

cladode. Modified stem having the appearance and function of

Cladophora. A genus of green algae having a thallus of firmbranched filaments.

clarification. The separation of suspended or colloidal solids from liquids; used in water purification and sewage treatment.

Clark cell. Standard primary cell in which a zinc anode and a mercurous-sulfate-coated mer-

cury cathode are immersed in a saturated zinc sulfate solution.

class. One of the main divisions of phylum; a large group of organisms which resemble one another in a few very important characters; example, birds.

classification. (1) Separation of particles of various sizes by mechanical means; examples, screening and settling; (2) the arrangement of organisms in selected groups according to their important characters.

clathrate compound. Chemical compound not held together by valency forces but through molecular imprisonment, the combined molecules forming a unit due to their configuration in space.

Clausius' law. The specific heat of an ideal gas at constant volume is independent of the temperature.

clavicle. The collar bone.

clay. A very-fine-grained, unconsolidated rock material which is plastic when wet, but becomes hard and strong when heated to redness; used for bricks and pottery.

clay soil. A soil which contains a high proportion of colloidal clay.

cleanup. The gradual decrease in the gas content of a discharge tube due to absorption of gases by the glass wall.

clearing. A step in the preparation of tissues for microscopical examination; they are soaked in benzene, xylene, etc., to make them transparent to transmitted light.

cleavage. (1) A series of cell divisions that a zygote undergoes in the first stage of its development; (2) tendency of a crystal to break according to definite planes; (3) splitting up a complex molecule into simpler ones.

cleavage cavity. A blastocoele; a segmentation cavity.

cleistocarp. Fruit body of certain Ascomycetes which is completely closed and from which spores are liberated by decay or rupture of its wall.

cleistogamy. Self-fertilization within an unopened flower; example, violet.

click gage. A device for the measurement of moderate pressures employing a thin diaphragm which has two stable positions.

climate. The average weather conditions in an area.

climatic factors. The effects of the climate on the plant life of an area.

climatic zones. The eight zones of typical climate on the surface of the earth: a tropical, two subtropical, two temperate, a boreal, and two polar zones.

climatology. A study of the various climates and their govern-

ing factors.

climax community. The established vegetation in a given location.

climax species. The dominating plant species in a climax community.

climbing root. A cluster of roots along the stem that clings to some support.

climbing stem. A slender and long aerial stem that clings to some support.

cline. Gradation of differences in the form or physiological properties found in the population of a species, attributed to geographical or ecological distribution.

clinometer. An instrument for measuring the angle of inclination; used in geology and surveying.

clinostat. A device, consisting of a clockwork-controlled rotating disk, which demonstrates geotropism and heliotropism in plants.

clipper. In communications, a circuit which does not allow the positive or negative level to exceed a certain value.

clisere. The succession of organism communities in an area caused by climatic changes.

clitellum. A bulge or bandlike enlargement formed by fusion of six segments of the earthworm, found thirty-one segments behind the anterior end; it secretes a cocoon and a protein to protect and feed the embryo.

clitoris. A homologue of the male's penis in a female mammal.

cloaca. A chamber in vertebrates, into which the alimentary canal, ureters, bladder, and reproductive organs empty.

clone. (1) The offspring produced by asexual reproduction of a single animal; (2) a stock of plants obtained from one original plant by grafting; example, a family of high-yielding rubber trees.

close coupling. Tight coupling; coupling between two circuits by which current changes in one have a strong effect on the current of the other, resulting in high energy transfer.

closed circuit. A complete path for current flow; example, the two plates of a voltaic cell connected by a conductor.

closed circulatory system. The system of blood circulation in vertebrates; blood pumped by the heart through the arteries, which branch into capillaries, and from the capillaries, into veins leading back to the heart.

closed system. A system which may reach a state of thermodynamic equilibrium since it is isolated from its surroundings.

close-packed hexagonal structure. An arrangement of the atoms in a hexagonal space lattice; crystal structure common in metals.

clostridium. Spindle-shaped anaerobic pathogenic bacterium; example, tetanus bacillus.

clot. Coagulated semisolid blood.

cloud. A mass of water droplets formed when air above the surface of the earth is cooled below the dew point.

cloud ceiling. In aeronautics, the limit of visibility; the number of feet from the ground to the cloud base.

cloud chamber. A high-pressure chamber; a device in which the paths of rapidly moving particles can be observed and photographed.

cloud chamber, diffusion. A cloud chamber in which the diffusion of vapor under the influence of a high temperature gradient is used to produce supersaturation.

cloud point. The temperature at which a solution becomes cloudy because a wax or other solid begins to separate or crystallize from it.

cloud track. A row or streak of droplets formed in a cloud chamber by the passage through it of a charged particle, whose path is thus revealed.

club mosses. Members of a small subdivision of Pteridophytes; creeping plants with erect stems bearing spores in conelike structures.

Clusius column. A device for the separation of isotopes by thermal diffusion.

cluster. (1) An aggregation of stars which move together; (2) atoms held together in permanent chemical union by the electrical attraction of a charged ion; (3) closely crowded small flowers.

cluster, globular. An aggregate of vast numbers of stars, in more or less spherical form.

cluster, open. A loose group of stars moving through space in open formation.

Cm. Chemical symbol for curium.

cm. Abbreviation for centimeter.

cm². Abbreviation for square centimeter.

cm³. Abbreviation for cubic centimeter.

Cnidaria. Hydroids with stinging cells; examples, jellyfish, sea anemones, corals, and polyps.

cnidoblast. A stinging cell or thread cell containing a nematocyst.

cnidocil. A hairlike process projecting from the cnidoblast, near the outer end of the nematocyst, which is discharged when the cnidocil is stimulated.

Co. Chemical symbol for cobalt.

coacervation. Separation of a lyophilic colloid into two nonmiscible liquids of different con-

centration; used in sewage disposal.

coagel. A gel formed by coagulation.

coagulant. An agent which causes coagulation or clotting.

coagulase. An enzyme that causes coagulation of a liquid protein.

coagulation. (1) Precipitation of a solid from a colloidal solution; (2) irreversible hardening of the protoplasm; clotting of blood by enzymes.

coagulum. A precipitated mass; the product of coagulation.

coal. Mineral carbon used as a fuel; formed by decomposition of vegetable matter over many years under heat and pressure.

coal age. A part of the Paleozoic era during which beds of coal were formed in the eastern half of North America.

coal ball. Calciferous agglomerate composed of mineralized plant fragments preserved by petrification.

coal gas. A fuel gas obtained by the destructive distillation of soft coal.

coal gas by-products. Substances obtained in or residues of the manufacture of coal gas; examples, coke, coal tar, ammonia, sulfuric acid, and pitch.

coal tar. The black pitch distilled from bituminous coal in the manufacture of coal gas; it contains hydrocarbons, phenols, and organic bases.

coal tar dyes. Organic dyestuffs derived from coal tar.

coalescence. Growing together of the walls of plant or animal parts.

coastal plain. A continental shelf that has been uplifted.

coated lens. A bloomed lens; a lens coated with a low-reflectance film, for example, with magnesium fluoride, to increase its light transmission.

coaxial cable. A central conductor surrounded by a cylindrical conductive envelope, with air as insulating medium.

cobalt. A silver-gray, magnetic metal; chemical symbol Co; atomic number 27; used in alloys and coloring glass and porcelain.

cobalt steel. A steel which contains 5 to 20% cobalt; used for high-speed cutting tools.

coccus. (1) A ball-shaped bacterium; (2) one-seeded portion of a dry fruit.

coccyx. Tailbones of the vertebral column in tailless primates.

cochineal. Natural red dyestuff obtained from the dried bodies of the Coccus cacti insects.

cochlea. A coiled tube that is part of the inner ear of mammals; its lining sends sensations of sound over the auditory nerve to the brain.

Cockcroft-Walton accelerator. A device in which rectified a-c voltage is used to charge a se-

ries of condensers to a high d-c potential, which is then applied to the acceleration of charged nuclear particles, especially protons.

cocoon. A protective case constructed of silk threads and containing eggs or young, or a developing animal in the inert stage; used for silk manufacture.

CODAN. Abbreviation for carrier operated device, antinoise.

coefficient of expansion. The increase in unit length, area, or volume for one degree rise in temperature.

coefficient of friction. The ratio of the force needed to move a body on a surface to the force opposing this motion.

Coelacanthidae. Order of fossil fresh-water fish, Crossopterygii.

Coelenterata. A phylum of animals made up of two layers of cells surrounding a large digestive cavity; their mouth is surrounded by tentacles and they have no anal opening; examples, hydra, jellyfish, polyps.

coelenteron. The single cavity in the body of Coelenterata.

coelom. (1) The secondary body cavity of animals in which the organs lie; (2) the true body cavity of earthworm between the alimentary canal and thick outer tube.

coelomoduct. A tubule opening at one end into the coelom and at the other end on the surface of the body; evolutionary forerunner of the excretory organs of vertebrates.

coenenchyma. Hard filling between individual polyps in a compound coral.

coengamete. A multinucleate gamete, with no walls separating the many nuclei.

coenobium. A cell colony in algae; a definite number of cells are arranged in a specific manner and behave as one unit; example, the hollow sphere of volvox.

coenocyte. A plant filament whose protoplasm is continuous and multinucleate and without any division by walls into separate protoplasts; example, algae.

coenosarc. The common stem joining the members of a hydroid colony.

coenospecies. A group of closely related species of plants or animals; a member of one group is infertile if it is crossed with a member of another group.

coenzyme. An organic compound which plays an essential part in a reaction catalyzed by some enzyme, usually acting as a temporary carrier of an intermediate product of the process.

coercimeter. An instrument for measuring the coercive force of magnetic materials.

coercive force. The magnetic intensity required to reduce the magnetic induction in a previously magnetized material to zero. If the material has been magnetized to saturation, this quantity is called the coercivity.

Coffey still. Apparatus for industrial-scale distillation of ethyl alcohol from grain mash.

coherer. A tube containing granules of a conducting material between two electrodes; it becomes highly conductive when subject to radio waves.

cohesion. (1) The force of attraction between like molecules; (2) the union of similar parts of a plant; example, a corolla of united petals.

coil, induction. An open-core transformer used to boost the voltage of low-voltage d-c sources; a high voltage in the secondary is produced when the current flow in the primary is interrupted.

coincidence method. A method of timing a periodic phenomenon by observing coincidences between the occurrences of the phenomenon in question and phenomena of a known period; example, the vibrations of a pendulum.

coir. The fibrous outer husk of coconut; the fibers are used for making cordage and door mats.

coke. The solid residue from the destructive distillation of bituminous coal; used as a fuel and in metallurgy.

col. A relatively small area about midway between two cyclones and two anticyclones where the pressure gradient is very weak and winds are usually light and variable; it is the area of intersection between a trough line and a wedge line.

colchicine. A yellow crystalline alkaloid extracted from autumn crocus, which, when applied to plant tissues, doubles or triples the number of chromosomes in the cell by interfering with normal cell division.

colcothar. Rouge; red iron oxide; ferric oxide, Fe_2O_3; used as a pigment and for polishing.

cold blooded. Without ability to regulate the body temperature, which is approximately that of the environment.

cold cathode. An electrode that emits electrons at normal temperature due to its high surface potential.

cold dome. A moving mass of cold, dense air.

cold front. The boundary along which a mass of cool air is flowing; it usually brings showers and high winds.

cold wave. Rapid drop in temperature, as much as 20°F in 24 hours, following a depression.

Coleoptera. Biting and chewing insects with thickened front wings which meet in a straight line along the back; example, beetles.

coleoptile. In grasses, a sheath which surrounds the plumules (young seedlings).

coleorhiza. A protective sheath surrounding the radicle of grass seedlings.

collagen. Ossein; a fibrous protein in the bones, cartilages and connective tissues; on boiling with water, it yields gelatin.

collar. A fold, ridge, or tissue more or less completely encircling the body of mollusks.

collar cell. A choanocyte; cell of one-celled animals bearing a flagellum at one end, surrounded by a collarlike membrane.

collateral bundle. A vascular bundle, having the xylem and phloem outside and on the same radius.

collector. (1) An exploring electrode, especially in a vacuum tube; (2) an apparatus for measuring the vertical potential gradient of the atmosphere.

Collembola. Spring tails; small, wingless insects.

collenchyma. A stem tissue composed of cells which fit rather closely together and the wall is thickened at the angle of the cells.

colleterial gland. In the reproductive system of female insects, glands which secrete an adhesive for cementing the eggs together or to form a protective covering over them.

colligative properties. Those properties of a solution which depend only on the concentration of molecules and ions present and not on their nature.

collimation. Aligning the constituents of an optical system.

collimator. A device for producing a beam of parallel rays, as in a spectroscope.

collision. Any encounter between free bodies in which they come near enough to exert a mutual influence, generally with an exchange of energy.

collision damping. An effect on the amplitude or phase of the radiation from an atom due to collision with other atoms, which results in a typical broadening of the spectrum lines.

collision density. The number of neutron collisions with matter per unit volume in unit time.

collision diameter of molecules. The distance of closest approach between the centers of any two molecules in a collision.

collision, elastic. A collision during which no change occurs in the internal energy of the participating system.

colloblast. A lasso cell; an adhesive cell used by the comb bearers in catching their prey.

colloid. A substance which is so finely divided that it remains permanently suspended in some fluid.

colloid mill. A device consisting of a rotor and a stator, between which coarse particles are broken up to the desired colloidal size.

colloidal metal. Colloidal dispersion of a metal, prepared by striking an electric arc between poles made of the metal under water, or by the reduction of a solution of the salt of the metal; used in medicine.

colloidal solution. Solution with the solute in colloidal state.

colloidal state. A state of subdivision of matter, the particle size ranging from that of the solute in a true solution to that of a suspension.

colloidal suspension. A two phase system having microscopically visible dispersed particles distributed throughout a dispersing medium.

colloidal system. A multiphase system in which there is at least one finely divided dispersed phase more or less uniformly distributed through the dispersing medium.

collum. A necklike or collarlike part or structure.

colon. The longest part of the large intestine in vertebrates, divided into ascending, transverse, and descending sections.

colonial animal. An animal organized as colonies of incompletely separate individuals; example, hydrozoa.

colonial organization. Groups of cells that herd together with a matrix; each cell can exist independently, but by banding together, they have more protection and better locomotion; example, volvox.

colony. (1) A group of animals or plants of the same kind living together, usually descendants of the same parents; (2) a group of bacteria on a solid medium usually derived by the multiplication of a single organism and visible to the naked eye.

color. A visual sensation which depends on the wave length of the radiation received by the eye.

color filter. A partially-transparent layer, film, or plate that absorbs or reflects certain frequencies of light and thus alters the spectral distribution of the light passing through it.

color index. (1) The amount of hemoglobin in the average red cell of a person compared with the normal amount; (2) the difference between the visual and photographic magnitude of a star; (3) the percentage of the dark-colored heavy silicate content of igneous rocks, which is a measure of their geological character.

color, nonspectral. Color not present in the spectrum of white light.

color sensation. The primary conscious response to stimulation of the eye by radiant energy in the visible region.

coloration. The combination and arrangement of colors in animals and plants.

colorimeter. A device for measuring the relative intensity of the color of solutions by comparison with standard solutions.

colorimetric analysis. Determination of the amounts of substances by comparing the intensity of color produced by them with specific reagents with the intensity of color produced by a standard solution with the same reagents; it is based on the fact that the color intensity of a solution is proportional to the concentration of the solute.

colorimetry. Same as colorimetric analysis.

colostrum. The milk secreted by the mammary gland a few days before and after partuition.

Columbidae. The family of pigeons and doves.

columella. (1) The axis of the spiral shell of a snail; (2) a bone in the middle ear of amphibians, reptiles, and birds; (3) in liverworts, a core of sterile tissue forming the axis of the sporophyte; (4) in mosses, mass of parenchyma-like, nonsporogenous cells in the capsule of the sporophyte; (5) in bread molds, a dome-shaped central structure in the sporangium.

columnar structure. Prismatic columns in igneous rocks of basic composition, due to the stress-strain relationships set up by rapid cooling.

colutron. An electromagnetic separator of isotopes that works on the principle of the mass spectrograph.

coma. (1) Spherical aberration of a lens, which results in pear-shaped elongation of point images at the periphery of the field; (2) bright, starlike nucleus surrounded by faintly luminous matter in the center of the head of a comet; (3) a group of hair hanging from a seed; (4) complete unconsciousness.

comb. A structure which is composed of six-sided wax cells in two layers; used for storage of honey and beebread, and for the rearing of young bees.

combination colors. A combination of pigments and structural modifications; most animal colors are of this type.

combination line. An atomic spectral line produced by a transition between two multiplet energy levels.

combination principle. Ritz's principle; an application of the quantum theory to spectral lines; addition or subtraction of the wave numbers of two lines of a spectrum will give the wave number of a third line of the same spectrum.

combination series. A series of spectral lines formed in accordance with the combination principle.

combining weight. Equivalent weight; the atomic weight of an element divided by its valence.

combustion. A chemical reaction in which heat and light are produced.

combustion chamber. In a furnace or engine, the space in which the fuel mixture is burned.

combustion-tube furnace. Laboratory apparatus used for the approximate determination of the carbon content in steel; it is equipped with electrically or gas heated horizontal tubes.

comet. A "long-haired" star; a heavenly body having a bright nucleus surrounded by a foggy coma and a long cloudlike tail; its orbit is an elipse, a hyperbola, or a parabola; it points away from the sun.

commensalism. A partnership of two different organisms, in which one (the commensal) lives in or on the other (the host) and shares its foods, but does not harm it.

commissure. (1) A bundle of nerve fibers connecting the right and left sides of the brain or spinal cord in vertebrates; (2) the joining surface of carpels.

common bundle. A vascular bundle which belongs to both the stem and the leaf.

common salt. Sodium chloride, NaCl.

common-ion effect. The shift in equilibrium which occurs when a substance is added to a solution of a second substance with which it has a common ion, the volume being kept constant.

community. In biology, a group of plants or animals that live together and depend on one another.

commutating pole. An electromagnetic bar inserted between the pole pieces of a dynamo to offset the crossmagnetization of the armature current.

commutator. That part of the armature of a dynamo which converts an alternating current into a direct current.

companion cells. Small cells, with dense cytoplasm and prominent nucleus, lying side by side with sieve-tube cells in the phloem of flowering plants.

comparator. (1) An instrument for the accurate measurement of moderately small lengths or distances; (2) a colorimeter.

comparator block. A simple colorimeter, consisting of a block of wood with holes in which the test tubes are placed which are to be compared and transverse holes through which one can view the colors.

comparison bridge. An electric bridge used to determine the difference in impedance between two nearly equal and essentially similar circuit elements.

compass. (1) A direction-indicating instrument; a magnetic needle free to swing above a dial with the directions marked on it; (2) an instrument for the measurement of angles.

compass, earth-inductor. An induction compass; a direction indicator used in aircraft which depends on the rate at which the earth's magnetic field is cut by a revolving coil carried by the aircraft.

compass, gyroscopic. A gyro compass; a direction indicator, depending on the tendency of the axis of a wheel rotating in antifriction bearings to point north-south.

compass, inductor. Same as compass, earth-inductor.

compass, magnetic. A pivoted magnet used with suitable charts to determine direction.

compass plant. A plant whose leaves extend in a north-south direction, regardless of the position in which the leaves are borne on the stem.

compensation sac. A reservoir opening to the exterior in some Bryozoa which fills with water when the tentacles are extruded and empties when they are retracted.

compensator. (1) An autotransformer; (2) an instrument for measuring the phase difference between the two components of elliptically polarized light.

compensatory hypertrophy. Increase in the size of the residual part of a tissue or organ whose other part has been removed or put out of action.

competitive inhibition. Inhibition of one process by diversion of available supplies of raw material to another.

complement. (1) A substance normally present in blood which takes essential part in the cytolysis produced by certain antibodies in bacteria or other cells; (2) an angle that makes 90° with another angle; (3) chromosomes derived from one nucleus.

complement fixation. Binding of complement by the union of an antigen and antibody, which is an indication of the presence of the antibody that is specific for the antigen; used as a test in immunology.

complemental air. The amount of air (about 100 cubic inches) the average adult inhales in addition to the tidal air by the deepest breath he can take.

complemental males. (1) In normally hermaphrodite barnacles, individuals that have no female organs; (2) in white-ant colonies, sexually mature males which do not carry on reproduction.

complementary colors. Two colors which combine to form a neutral color or gray; example, blue and orange.

complementoid. A complement which, through heating, has lost its activity but still retains its binding property with amboceptors.

complete double circulation. Flowing of the blood in two distinct circles; found in all warm-blooded animals.

complete flower. A flower which has both a floral envelope and the essential organs.

complete metamorphosis. The development from egg to adult in several stages, none of which resembles another.

complete radiator. A black body; an ideal body that absorbs all wave lengths of radiation; if heated to incandescence, it emits a continuous spectrum of light; example, tungsten.

complex ion. The combination of an ion by coordinate linkages with uncharged atoms or molecules.

complex spectrum. A spectrum containing multiplet lines.

complex tissue. A tissue consisting of two or more different kinds of cells that usually cooperate in the performance of a common activity.

compole. Same as commutating pole.

component. The smallest number of substances needed for equilibrium in a system; example, the system ice, water, and water vapor in equilibrium is composed of one component, H_2O.

component force. A part of a resultant force.

Compositae. Members of a family of flowering plants having two kinds of flowers gathered together into one head; examples, asters and daisies.

composition of forces. A method of finding a single resultant force that will replace two or more component forces.

compound. (1) In biology, made up of several parts; examples, compound eyes and compound leaves; (2) in chemistry, a substance composed of several elements joined together in definite proportions.

compound bar. A bimetal; a bar made of two metal strips of unequal coefficients of expansion which adhere to each other face to face; used in temperature measurement and control.

compound, covalent. A compound formed by the sharing of electrons between atoms.

compound engine. (1) An engine in which steam is successively expanded in two cylinders; (2) an airplane engine equipped with an exhaust-driven turbo supercharger.

compound eye. An eye made up of numerous simple minute eyes; example, the eyes of crayfish.

compound, intermetallic. In alloys, a compound made up of different metallic atoms, which are joined in definite proportions; example, CuZn.

compound, interstitial. A compound of a metal or metals and certain metalloids, in which the metalloid atoms occupy the interstices between the atoms of the metal lattice; examples, compounds of carbon, nitrogen, boron, and hydrogen with a metal.

compound leaf. A leaf whose blade is divided into three or more parts, which may fall off independently of one another.

compound machine. A machine composed of two or more simple machines.

compound microscope. A microscope consisting of two short-focus convex lenses. An eyepiece, and an objective.

compound, molecular. A compound formed by the union of two or more independent molecules; example, double salts.

compound, organometallic. A compound in which one or more alkyl radicals are attached to a metal atom; example, tetraethyl lead, Pb-$(C_2H_5)_4$.

compound pistil. A pistil composed of two or more carpels.

compound, saturated. A compound in which the valence of all the atoms is completely satisfied; having no double or triple bonds.

compound, stable. A chemical compound that does not decompose easily.

compound turbine. A turbine which has a high-pressure and a low-pressure casing.

compound, unstable. A chemical compound that decomposes easily.

compound-wound generator. A d-c generator whose field magnet is excited by both a shunt coil and a series coil.

compressed-air condenser. An electric condenser in which high-pressure air is the dielectric.

compression molding. Manufacture of various shapes from plastics by very high pressure at elevated temperature.

compression stroke. The engine stroke during which the charge is compressed.

Compton effect. A slight increase in the wave length of scattered x-rays due to collision of an electron with a photon.

Compton electron. An electron having momentum due to the impact of a high-energy radiation quantum.

Compton meter. An ionization chamber used for cosmic-ray measurements.

Compton shift. The change in the wave length of an x-ray quantum on scattering by impact with an electron.

compulsory parasite. An obligate parasite, which cannot exist without its host.

concatenation. (1) Linking in a chain of similar members; (2) a cascade connection in which each member of an electric circuit supplies and/or amplifies the power of the next member.

concave grating. An optical grating ruled on a concave, spherical, reflecting surface, which collimates and focuses the light without lenses.

concave lens. A divergent lens; a lens thinner in the middle than at the edges, which diminishes the convergence of the light beam passing through it.

concave mirror. A mirror whose reflecting surface curves away from the observer.

concavo-convex. Said of a lens whose concave surface is of smaller curvature than its convex surface.

concealing color. Camouflage; color or color patterns which resemble all or part of the background and thus help in the self-preservation of animals.

concentrated solution. A solution with a high solute content.

concentration. (1) The quantity of solute in a given volume or weight of solvent; (2) a process of increasing the concentration; example, evaporation of the solvent of a solution.

concentration, absolute. The quantity of a substance, or energy, or other entity found in a unit volume, expressed in mass per unit volume (ergs per cubic centimeter), or number of particles (as of atoms, hydrogen ions, etc.) per unit volume.

concentration cell. An electrolytic cell whose electromotive force is due to a difference in concentration between different parts of the electrolyte.

conceptacle. A flask-shaped pit or chamber in which sperms and eggs are formed; example, fucus.

conchiolin. A horny material which forms the outer layer of shell mollusks.

conchoidal fracture. An irregular break with a curved face exhibiting concentric rings similar to one half of a bivalve shell.

conchology. The study of mollusk shells.

concrete. In botany, grown together, forming a solid body.

concretion. (1) An irregular but rounded mass, which is usually built up of concentric layers around some sort of a nucleus, found in sedimentary rocks; (2) collection of organic matter in human organs.

condensation. (1) That part of a sound wave in which the medium (usually air) is compressed; (2) changing of vapors into a liquid; (3) formation of a large molecule from small ones with the elimination of water or some other simple compound.

condensation coefficient. The ratio of the total volume of the molecules of a gas to the volume of the gas.

condensed system. A system in which there is no vapor phase.

condenser. (1) A part of an optical projecting system which directs the light of a source on an object; (2) a device for liquefying hot vapors obtained during distillation; it consists of a tube which is cooled by water or air; the vapors enter the tube at one end and the liquid drips out at the other; (3) same as capacitor.

condenser electrolyte. The solution used in an electrolytic condenser.

condenser microphone. A microphone made up of a condenser, one plate of which is fixed and the other plate forms the diaphragm which receives the sound waves.

conditional reflex. A reflex response to a stimulus which depends on an earlier experience of the individual.

conditioned air. Air that has been freed from dust and in which the desired moisture content and temperature are maintained.

conditioned reflex. A modified reflex, the response being caused by some stimulus other than the one which originally would bring it about.

conductance. The reciprocal of electrical resistance; conducting power; the property of a material that a current may flow through it under the influence of a potential difference.

conductimeter. An apparatus for measuring the electrical conductivity of substances, especially liquids.

conductimetric analysis. Volumetric analysis in which the end point is determined by the increase in the conductance of the solution.

conduction. (1) Passage of nerve impulse through a cell or tissue as a result of stimulation at one point; (2) passing of heat energy from molecule to molecule through a substance; (3) passing of an electric current through a substance, such as metal.

conduction, thermal. Same as conduction (2).

conductivity cell. A cell which consists of a chamber containing two electrodes for determining the conductivity of a solution or fused solid.

conductivity, electrical. The reciprocal of the resistivity or specific resistance of a conductor; it is measured in reciprocal ohms, or mhos, per centimeter cube.

conductivity, thermal. Rate of transfer of heat along a body by conduction; measured in calories flowing per second across a centimeter cube of the substance, having a temperature difference of 1°C on opposite faces.

conductometer. An instrument for measuring conductivity, especially thermal conductivity.

conductometric titration. Titration in which the end-point determination depends on a change in conductivity of the solution being titrated.

conductor. A solid, liquid, or gas of low resistance through which an electric current flows; a metal rod or wire that transmits electricity efficiently.

conductor, thermal. A body, through which heat flows by conduction.

condyle. An ellipsoid knob on a bone, fitting into a socket in another bone; they form a joint allowing movement in one or two planes but no rotation; example, the condyle of the jaw.

Condy's fluid. A solution of potassium or calcium permanganate, $KMnO_4$ or $Ca(MnO_4)_2$; used as a disinfectant.

cone cell. A photosensitive cell of the retina.

cone-in-cone structure. Concentric cones observed in the structure of limestones and shales.

configuration, atomic. The spatial arrangement of the atoms in a molecule.

conformal wire grating. A wave filter made of wires bent to conform to the lines of the electronic feeler that are characteristics of the wave to be reflected.

conglomerate. A rock formed from cemented pebbles and gravel.

conical refraction. The transformation of a ray of light into a hollow cone by refraction at a suitable angle of incidence, in a biaxial crystal.

conidiophore. A hypha which bears one or a group of conidia.

conidiospore. Spore formed by abstriction.

conidium. An asexual-reproduction spore in certain fungi formed at the end of the hypha

and not surrounded by a sporangium.

Coniferae. Woody plants, chiefly large evergreen trees, which bear their seeds in cones; example, pine.

coniferous. Cone-bearing.

conjugate branches. Two branches of an electric network, so related that an electromotive force in one produces no current in the other.

conjugate foci. Two points, each being the focus for light rays diverging from the other.

conjugate points. Two points of an optical system, each being the image of the other.

conjugated double bonds. In unsaturated organic compounds, two double bonds separated by a single bond; example, butadiene, $CH_2{=}CH{-}CH{=}CH_2$.

conjugation. A fusion of similar or like gametes to form a zygote; example, spirogyra.

conjunction. Relation of two or more celestial bodies which are seen in the same part of the sky or have the same right ascension; example, Venus and Jupiter.

conjunction, inferior. Conjunction of a planet between the earth and the sun.

conjunction, superior. Conjunction of a planet when the sun is between the earth and that planet.

conjunctiva. A covering membrane over the cornea of the eye, which connects it with the inner covering of the eyelid.

connate water. Underground water which is preserved as the water, fresh or saline, in which the sediments were originally deposited.

connective tissue. An animal tissue which is tough, fibrous, and noncontractile; it joins other tissues together or forms part of the skeleton; examples, bone, cartilage.

connector. Any device for holding in electrical contact the ends of a conducting wire in such a manner that they may be readily released when it is desired to disconnect them.

consanguinity. A term designating a related group of igneous rocks which have been derived from a common magma and thus have a similar chemical composition and texture.

consequent pole. A third magnetic pole on a magnetized body which is at a distance from the usual two poles.

consequent stream. A stream valley which developed parallel to the cuesta.

conservation of energy, law of. (1) Energy can neither be created nor destroyed; (2) the total energy of an isolated system is constant.

conservation of mass. Same as conservation of matter.

conservation of matter, law of. (1) Matter can neither be created nor destroyed; (2) in any chemical reaction, the sum of the weights of the reactants equals the sum of the weights of the products.

conservation of momentum, law of. (1) Momentum, like energy and matter, can neither be created nor destroyed but can only be transferred from one body to another; (2) the sum of momentums in a closed system is constant and independent of changes within the system; (3) for a perfectly elastic collision, the total momentum of two bodies before impact is equal to their total momentum after impact.

conservative field. A field of force in which the work done by a particle moving from one point to another depends only on the initial and final position of the particle and is independent of its path.

conservative system. A mechanical system in which the work accomplished is zero if in a cycle of operations the arrangement of the system is the same at the end as it was at the outset.

consistency. (1) The ratio of the shearing stress to the rate of shear; (2) a quality which depends on the viscosity, plasticity, and resistance to deformation of a substance.

consistometer. An apparatus which measures hardness or consistency.

consociation. A unit of natural vegetation dominated by one particular species.

consolute. (1) Miscible or mutually soluble in all proportions; (2) soluble in both of two immiscible liquids which are in contact with each other.

consolute temperature. The critical temperature above which two partially miscible liquids become miscible in all proportions.

constant. (1) A magnitude whose value does not change; (2) an experimentally determined mathematical factor.

constant composition, law of. Same as law of definite proportions.

constant current. A current whose amperage is not variable.

constant deviation prism. A triangular prism so designed that the deviation of a ray of light entering it by one face and leaving it by another, after internal reflection at the third face, is always equal to the angle between the two refracting faces.

constant heat summation, law of. Hess' law; the energy change involved in a chemical reaction or series of reactions going from the same beginning to the same end is always the same and is independent of the intermediate course the reaction takes.

constant, ionization. (1) The equilibrium constant of a reversible reaction by which ions are produced from molecules; (2) the ratio of the product of the concentrations of the ions of a substance to the concentration of the undissociated molecules of the same substance.

constant of universal gravitation. 6.664×10^{-8} cgs units.

constant pressure cycle. A Diesel cycle; a four- or two-stroke cycle, in which air is compressed and fuel is injected at constant pressure into the heated charge, followed by expansion and exhaust of gases.

constant, velocity. The speed of a chemical reaction, at constant temperature, in which the concentration of each reactant is one mole per liter.

constant-resistance network. A network whose image impedances are constant and resistant at all frequencies to eliminate interaction and reflection losses.

constellation. Grouping of stars based on imagination rather than scientific facts; example, the big dipper.

constituent. A component of an alloy or a chemical compound.

constrain. To limit to a predetermined position or path; example, a body has constrained motion when restricted by material barriers to a given path.

contact. The touching of two or more specially arranged ends of electrical conductors to complete an electrical circuit or circuits.

contact angle. (1) At a solid-liquid interface, the angle formed on the surface of the solid measured as the dihedral angle in the liquid; (2) the angle formed by the interface between two fluids with the wall of the container.

contact breaker. An electromagnetic device for quickly and automatically breaking or making an electric circuit; example, an electric bell.

contact potential difference. A potential difference set up and maintained by two different metals when brought into contact with each other.

contact process. A process for making sulfuric acid in which sulfur dioxide and oxygen come in contact in the presence of a catalyst to form sulfur trioxide.

contactor. Electromagnetically or mechanically operated switch for repeatedly making and breaking a circuit.

continental air mass. An air mass that originated on land surfaces.

continental climate. Climatic conditions found in large areas away from the ocean.

continental glacier. An ice layer that covers a great area of a continent.

continental plateau. A wide platform that projects, with some abruptness, from bordering lowlands or from the sea.

continental shelf. An ocean floor that slopes gently away from the land for a distance; it is covered with deposits of gravel, sand, and mud.

continuity of germplasm. Neo-Darwinism; a theory evolved by August Weissman according to which the somatoplasm dies with the individual, but the germplasm passes on from one generation to the next and thus exists as long as the race does.

continuous beam. A beam which has more than two supports.

continuous oscillations. Undamped oscillations; alternating-current or radio waves of constant amplitude which are not separated into singly decaying groups.

continuous spectrum. Seven colors in one unbroken band; it is produced by incandescent solids, liquids, and high-pressure gases.

contour. (1) The outline of a surface or body; (2) the wavelength intensity curve for a particular line or band of the spectrum.

contour feathers. Plumes; top feathers with barbules, which form the smooth surface of the plumage and determine the body contours of birds.

contour interval. The vertical distance between two adjacent contour lines.

contour line. (1) An imaginary line which connects points of the same elevation; (2) an imaginary line of intersection between a given level surface and the ground surface.

contractile vacuole. A bubblelike structure in a one-celled animal; it fills up with waste, then collapses and thus evacuates the waste from the cell.

contractility. (1) That property of the protoplasm which enables it to change its shape; (2) the ability of some cells and tissues to contract and expand; example, muscle.

control. (1) An experiment or test made to confirm or to rule out error in clinical or experimental observations; (2) a system or device which exerts a restraining, governing, or directing influence.

control cable. In aeronautics, a line of wire or stranded cable leading from the control levers to the control surfaces, or interconnecting the control surfaces.

control column. A lever having a rotary wheel mounted at its upper end for operating the longitudinal and lateral control surfaces of an airplane.

control current. The current whose magnitude determines the magnitude of output in an amplifier.

control grid. The grid within a vacuum tube to which the signal voltage is applied that controls the magnitude of the current flowing from the cathode to the plate.

control plate. Culture in a petri dish which is not inoculated.

control rods. Rods of cadmium or boron steel used in a nuclear reactor to absorb neutrons so as to control fission.

control stick. The vertical lever which operates the lateral and longitudinal controls of an airplane; pitching is controlled by a fore-and-aft movement of the stick and rolling by its side-to-side movement.

control surface. A movable airfoil, the position of which may be altered by the pilot in order to change the altitude of an aircraft.

controllable-pitch propeller. A variable-pitch propeller; an airplane propeller whose blades are mounted to rotate on their own axes, so that the pitch may be changed while the propeller is rotating.

controlled atmosphere. The use of an inert gas instead of air in an apparatus or process to avoid possible reaction with atmospheric oxygen.

controlled breeding. Interbreeding of plants or animals so as to secure various combinations of their characteristics in their offsprings.

controller. A magnetic device for the automatic regulation of an electric current.

controls. The mechanisms used for the control of power, speed, direction, and altitude of an aircraft.

conus arteriosus. (1) A part of the heart of amphibians and certain fish from which the blood flows to the aorta; (2) in vertebrates, the conical projection of the right ventricle from which the pulmonary artery starts out.

convection. (1) The transmission of heat from one place to another, by fluid circulation between the spots of different temperature; (2) the flow of electricity by the motion of charged particles.

convection current. The movement of warm air upward and of colder air downward, which promotes the uniformity of temperature.

converge. Come to a point; example, light rays passing through a convex lens converge.

convergence. (1) An evolutionary development of resemblances between organisms whose ancestors were different, because of their simple and uniform surroundings; (2) coming to a point.

convergent evolution. Same as convergence (1).

convergent lens. A lens which brings to a point a beam of light passing through it; a convex lens.

conversion factor. A numerical constant used for calculating a quantity in other units than in which it is given; example, the conversion factor for pounds per square inch into kilograms per square centimeter is 0.070307.

conversion of energy. Changing one form of energy into another; example, conversion of chemical energy into electrical energy and vice versa.

conversion of temperature scales. $F = 9/5\ C + 32$; $C = 5/9\ F - 32$.

converter. A transformer; a machine used for changing electrical energy from one form to another.

converter reactor. A reactor that changes by capture of neutrons one type of fissionable substance into another type of fissionable substance.

converter, rotary. A synchronous converter; an electrical machine having a commutator at one end and slip rings at the other end of the armature; used for the conversion of a multiphase alternating current to a direct current.

converter tube. A vacuum tube that performs the functions of local oscillator and mixer tubes in a superheterodyne circuit; its input is a signal frequency and its output a fixed intermediate frequency.

convex lens. A lens thicker in the middle than at its edges.

convex mirror. A mirror whose reflecting surface curves toward the observer.

convexo-concave. A lens having two curved surfaces of which the convex one has greater curvature than the other, which is concave.

convolutions. Irregular folds of gray matter on the outer surface of the cerebrum.

Coolidge tube. An x-ray tube in which the electrons are emitted from a heated filament.

coordinate. (1) One of the two or more values required for defining the position in space of a point, plane or body; (2) a set of variables used to express the condition or behavior of a physical system; example, pressure, volume, and temperature of a gas.

coordinate bond. The sharing of two electrons supplied by one atom with another atom with the formation of a dipole.

coordinates, equatorial. The right ascension and declination.

coordinates, horizon. The altitude and azimuth.

coordination. The cooperation of parts of an organism for the benefit of the whole; example, coordination of muscular activities.

coordination lattice. A crystal lattice in which each ion bears the same relation to the adjacent ions in all three coordinate directions, so that the identity of the molecule becomes ambiguous.

coordination number. The number of attachments of a given atom in a crystal structure; for most covalent crystals the number is usually 4; for metals the coordination number may rise to 12.

coordination rule. The magnetic sublevels of a spectral line in weak fields are coordinated with the magnetic levels of the component vectors in strong fields; as the fields change, the coordinated levels merge.

Copepoda. A subclass of Crustacea; minute, often parasitic, marine species in the plankton; they serve as food for fish.

copolymer. A synthetic compound, the product of copolymerization, which consists of two or more different monomers; example, Butyl Rubber, which is a copolymer of isoprene and isobutylene.

copolymerization. The process of combining the molecules of two or more different relatively simple substances to form one giant molecule which is chemically different from its constituents.

copper. A reddish metal; chemical symbol Cu; atomic number 29; used in plumbing, wires, and alloys.

copper matte. A copper of about 35% sulfur content; an intermediate product in copper smelting.

copper sulfate. Blue vitriol; $CuSO_4 \cdot 5H_2O$; used to control the growth of algae in swimming pools, lakes and ponds, and in sprays to control fungus and insect pests.

copulation. (1) The act of sexual union by which the seminal fluid, containing the reproductive cells of the male, is transferred to the genital passages of the female; (2) in Protozoa, complete fusion of the gametes.

coquina. A coarse and highly porous limestone, made up of loosely cemented shells and shell fragments.

Coraciiformes. Short-legged birds; examples, the owl and woodpecker.

coracoid. One of the bones of the pectoral girdle of vertebrates.

coracoid bone. A cartilagenous bone which projects from the shoulder to the breast bone.

coral. Small colonial forms of Coelenterata which live in the ocean and build calcareous walls around themselves; this is also a name for the reefs formed by coral animals.

Corallina. A genus of red algae growing in deep-sea water, containing lime deposits in the cell walls and having branches that resemble corals.

Corbino effect. A form of the Hall effect in which, when a current is sent from the center to the circumference of a metal disk through a magnetic field normal to the disk, there is also a current flowing circumferentially.

Cordaitales. Extinct Paleozoic Gymnospermae which flourished during the Carboniferous era.

cordilla. A large regional grouping of a mountain system.

core. (1) A soft-iron center on which the coils of electromagnets and transformers are wound; radio-frequency transformers have air cores; (2) in a nuclear reactor, the region containing the fissionable material; (3) in an atom, the aggregate consisting of the nucleus and all electrons in closed shells; (4) the conductor in a cable and its insulation, without the protective coating.

core loss. The electric loss occurring in the core of an armature or transformer due to eddy currents, hysteresis, and like influences.

Coriolis force. A force which deflects the winds, airplanes, projectiles, etc., from their straight course to the left in the southern hemisphere and to the right in the northern hemisphere.

corium. The inner region of the skin of vertebrates.

cork cambium. Phellogen; a special layer of cells inside the stem or root which produce cork.

Corliss valve. A valve used in large steam engines which opens and closes by rocking or turning slightly in the valve seat.

corm. A thick rhizome or short, stout underground stem with a single bud which can grow into a new plant; a natural vegetative propagation; example, crocus.

cormidium. A group of individuals of various forms budded from the parent stalk of certain floating marine Coelenterata.

cornea. The transparent outer layer of the front of the eyeball.

corneagen cell. A cell found in the compound eyes of some insects which produces the transparent lenticular cornea at the outer surface of the eye.

corner reflector. A reflector made up of two or three mutually intersecting, conducting surfaces.

cornification. A conversion of epidermic cells into horn.

Cornu prism. A 60° quartz prism divided into halves, of right-and left-handed quartz to eliminate double refraction.

Cornu spiral. The limiting curve approached by a succession of vector lines whose lengths and directions represent the amplitudes and phases of the light vibration reaching any point from successively more remote areas of a wave front; used for the graphical solution of diffraction problems.

corolla. The whole group of petals of a flower; the inner circle of leaflike flower parts, usually of some color other than green.

corona. (1) In zoology, the shell of the sea urchin; (2) in geology, a radial stripe of a mineral encircling another mineral; (3) in astronomy, a halo around the sun; (4) in meteorology, colored rings observed around the moon or sun due to light diffraction by water droplets.

corona discharge. An ionization of gas around a conductor when the potential gradient is not sufficient to cause sparking.

corona tube. Same as corona voltmeter.

corona voltmeter. An apparatus for the measurement of high voltages by the corona discharge in a special wire.

coronary. (1) Crownlike; (2) a small bone of the lower jaw of reptiles.

coronary artery. An artery lying on the surface of the heart and carrying blood to the tissues of the heart.

coronary circulation. The blood circulation of the heart; at the root of the aorta, the coronary artery branches off to carry blood to tissues of the heart; the impure blood flows into the coronary vein which empties into the right auricle.

coronary embolism. An obstructive foreign particle or clot in a blood vessel in some part of the body which travels around to lodge in the coronary artery.

coronary occlusion. Same as coronary thrombosis.

coronary thrombosis. A clot formation in a coronary artery.

corpora allata. Small glandular organs in the head of insects; they produce hormones in some species.

corpus callosum. A broad band of nerve fibers in the brain of vertebrates, connecting the two cerebral hemispheres.

corpus luteum. An internal secretion of the hormone progesterone; formed in mammals in the interior of a ruptured Graafian follicle after ovulation.

corpuscle. (1) A cell of protoplasm floating in the blood; (2) a particle.

corpuscular theory of light. Newton's theory that light consists of minute particles in rapid motion.

correlation. (1) A quantitative relationship between two variables; (2) the balance among the organs of a plant; (3) joining together of separate strata of the same age.

correspondence principle. The frequency of radiation is the same whether calculated from the quantum theory or by classical methods for electron orbits away from the nucleus of an atom.

corrosion. A gradual change of metals due to chemical action; usually oxidation.

corrosive sublimate. Mercuric chloride, $HgCl_2$; white crystalline very poisonous soluble salt; used as a germicide.

cortex. (1) In plants, the cells between the conducting tubes and the epidermis; (2) in animals, the outer layer of an organ; example, the gray matter of the brain.

cortex of adrenal gland. A covering layer of the adrenal or suprarenal gland; it secretes cortin which prevents Addison's disease and cortisone which alleviates the symptoms of rheumatoid arthritis.

Corti's organ. A center of nerve terminals located in the inner ear, adjacent to the basilar membrane.

corundum. Aluminum oxide, AlO_3; a mineral occurring in different colors and crystal forms; used as an abrasive.

corymb. A flat-topped inflorescence, whose main axis is elongated, but the pedicels of the older flowers are longer than those of younger flowers, so that all flowers are approximately in one plane.

Corynebacterium. A slender Gram-positive, aerobic, nonmotile, rod-shaped organism; example, the bacillus of diphtheria.

cosine emission law. Lambert's law; the rate of emission or diffuse reflection of a radiant energy in a given direction from any element of area of a perfectly diffusing surface is proportional to the cosine of the angle of emission measured between the emitted ray and the normal to the surface; the illumination of a surface is proportional to the cosine of the angle the incident ray forms with the normal to the surface.

cosine photometer. A photometer in which the illumination of one surface to be compared is varied, in accordance with the cosine emission law, by varying its orientation.

cosmic dust. Small particles of matter distributed in space in sizes ranging from one-hundredth to one ten-thousandth of a millimeter; it is probably of meteoric origin.

cosmic rays. Strongly penetrating rays, discovered by Miliken in 1925, coming from beyond the earth's atmosphere and containing particles that move at extremely high speed.

cosmic-ray decay electrons. Electrons in the soft component of cosmic rays which resulted from the decay of mesons.

cosmic-ray showers. Same as cascade showers.

cosmic-ray tracks, heavy. Tracks found in cloud chambers and emulsions which are exposed to cosmic radiations at a very high altitude.

cosmic-space vehicle. Soviet term for a space vehicle.

cosmin. A hard calcareous substance found in fish scales.

cosmoid scale. A fish scale of three layers; a loose, vascular, bony sheet between the outer cosmin and inner isopedin layer.

cosmonaut. Soviet term for an astronaut.

cosmos. Another name for the universe; the corresponding Greek word (*kosmos*) means order or harmony.

cosmotron. A proton accelerator, about ten times more effective than the cyclotron; it contains a giant ring-shaped electromagnet.

costal cartilage. A cartilage that attaches the ribs to the sternum.

Cottrell precipitator. An electrical device to precipitate dispersed dust particles which carry an electrical charge.

cotyledon. The part of a seed which contains the food needed to start the new plant.

coulee lake. A lake formed when the lava from a volcano dams a river.

coulomb. The unit of static electricity; the quantity of electricity transferred by one ampere in one second.

coulombmeter. A voltmeter; an electrolytic cell used for the measurement of the quantity of electricity passing through a circuit by the quantity of metal deposited, or gas set free, from the electrolyte by the current in a given time.

Coulomb's law. The attraction or repulsion between two charged bodies or magnetic poles is proportional to the magnitude of their charges or pole strengths and inversely proportional to the square of their distance from each other.

counter emf. A counter electromotive force or back electromotive force; an emf, induced in a coil or an armature by self-induction, that opposes the applied voltage.

counter, gas. A radiation counter in which the sample is in the form of a gas and is introduced into the counter tube itself.

counter, gas-filled. A gas tube, in a radiation counter, used for the detection of radiation by means of gas ionization.

counter tube. A tube which indicates the passage of a cosmic ray or ionizing particle through it.

counterbalance. A counterweight; a weight that balances another.

counterbalancing. The application of a counterweight to a system in order to produce balance for the system as a whole and to offset the unbalance arising from some particular part.

counterpoise. An underground wire connected to the towers of an overhead electric line to offset the possible striking of lightning through the insulation.

countershading. A form of protective coloration in which darker colors on the upper side fade into lighter colors on the lower side, taking into account the natural distribution of light and shadow on the object to be camouflaged.

country rock. A main mass of valueless rock in which occur the veins, dikes, or ore bodies.

couple. Two parallel forces of equal magnitude but of opposite direction.

coupling. (1) A juxtaposition of two electric circuits in such a manner that variations of current in one circuit will affect the emf in the other; used in electrical communication; (2) an interaction between one of the electrons of an atom and the other parts of the atomic system; (3) a driving connection between two coaxial shafts or two railroad coaches.

coupling, direct. A coupling method for an electronic amplifier in which the frequency response is extended down to zero frequency or direct current.

coupling loop. A device for coupling an external circuit to a wave guide or resonator.

courtship colors. Colors that serve as means of attraction in males or in certain flowers to insure fertilization.

covalence. A chemical bond in which one or more pairs of electrons are shared by the combining atoms, each atom contributing one of the electrons of the pair.

covalence, dative. A semipolar bond; a covalent bond in which both electrons of the pair are furnished by one of the combining atoms.

covalent bond. Same as covalence.

covellite. A dark-blue mineral;

cupric sulfide, CuS.

cover crop. A catch crop; a crop planted to bind the soil or fix its nitrogen content; example, clover.

cover slip. A cover glass; a thin glass plate which covers a mounted object to be studied microscopically.

covibration. A natural vibration of the same frequency as the stimulating or exciting impulses.

covolume. The actual volume of the molecules of a gas.

Cowan's apparatus. A device for measuring the linear expansion of solids.

Cowper's gland. A pair of glands of the male reproductive ducts of mammals, located on both sides of the urinogenital canal, whose secretion is part of the seminal fluid.

coxa. The segment by which the leg of an arthropod is joined to the body.

coxal gland. An excretory gland opening in the fifth segment of the body in the king crab and scorpions.

coxopodite. That part of an arthropod limb which lies next to the body.

cp. Abbreviation for candlepower.

cP. Abbreviation for continental polar air mass.

cps. Abbreviation for cycles per second.

Cr. Chemical symbol for chromium.

cracking. Thermal or catalytic decomposition of organic compounds, especially of the hydrocarbons of petroleum, to break down the high-boiling constituents into lower-boiling fractions, such as gasoline.

cranial cavity. The cavity in the skull which contains the brain.

cranial nerve. Peripheral nerve emerging from the brain or the top end of the spinal cord of vertebrates.

Craniata. Vertebrata.

cranium. Same as cranial cavity.

crater. Usually inverted-cone-shaped central opening of a volcano through which the volcanic products erupt.

crater lake. A lake formed in the crater of an extinct volcano.

crater lamp. A glow-discharge tube with a solid cylindrical cathode and a conical or crater-shaped depression in one end.

crateriform. Depressed or hollowed; used to describe liquefaction of gelatin by certain bacteria.

creep. (1) A slow upward movement of the floor of a coal mine caused by pressure; (2) a movement of the deep polar waters toward the equator; (3) the plastic flow of metals under constant stress.

creep point. The temperature

above which additional stress causes creep in a metal.

creeping stem. An aerial stem that remains close to the ground and turns at the nodes.

Cretaceous period. Mesozoic era; it began about 120 million years ago; flowering plants, birds, mammals appear, but reptiles prevail; the dinosaurs disappear.

crevasse. Huge crack in the ice caused by unbalanced stresses in a glacier.

cribellum. A perforated plate associated with the spinnerets of some spiders.

cribriform. Sievelike; perforated.

Crinoidea. Simple sedentary and stalked flowerlike marine animals with long, branched feathery arms; example, sea lilies of the class of Echinodermata.

crit. The mass of fissionable material, which is critical under a given set of conditions.

crith. A unit suggested for the measurement of the mass of gases; it is equal to the weight in grams of one liter of hydrogen at standard temperature and pressure, 0.0906 gram.

critical altitude. The maximum altitude at which a supercharger can maintain a pressure in the intake manifold of an engine equal to that existing during normal operation at rated power and speed at sea level.

critical angle. In aeronautics, that angle of attack which is about to produce an abrupt change in lift and drag.

critical angle of a medium. The smallest angle of incidence of a light ray at which total internal reflection occurs.

critical coefficient. The ratio of the critical temperature of a substance to its critical pressure.

critical concentration. The concentration of the solute at the critical solution temperature.

critical damping. Damping out the oscillations of a mechanical instrument about the equilibrium position which the instrument takes up in the shortest possible time.

critical density. The density of a substance measured at its critical point.

critical frequency. The threshold frequency of an intermittent illumination which is just sufficient to prevent a sensation of flicker.

critical humidity. The water content of the atmosphere at which the partial pressure of water vapor is equal to the vapor pressure at the surface of a solid.

critical mass. The mass of a radioactive material that is sufficient for a self-sustaining chain reaction.

critical opalescence. A bluish haze formed just before the meniscus of a liquid becomes distinguishable when its vapors are lowered to the critical temperature.

critical point. The point at which the boundary line between the liquid and gaseous phases disappears and the physical properties of liquid and gas become identical.

critical potential. The minimum amount of energy needed for ionization or for excitation of an electron.

critical pressure. (1) The pressure required to liquefy a gas at its critical temperature; (2) the pressure at which the liquid and gaseous phases of a substance may exist in equilibrium with each other.

critical range. The range of temperature in which structural changes occur in a metal; example, the change of austenite to pearlite.

critical size. The size of core and reflector needed for a nuclear reactor to sustain a chain reaction.

critical solution temperature. The temperature below which two liquids are only partially soluble in each other, but above which they are miscible.

critical speed. The speed at which a rotating shaft becomes dynamically unstable because some periodic disturbing force coincides with its natural period of vibration.

critical temperature. (1) The highest temperature at which a substance can exist as a liquid; the temperature above which a gas cannot be liquefied by any amount of pressure; (2) the temperature at which internal changes occur in a metal; (3) the temperature at which a magnetic material becomes demagnetized.

critical velocity. The velocity at which the flow of a liquid reversibly changes from viscous to turbulent.

critical volume. The volume occupied by one mole of a gas at its critical temperature and critical pressure.

critical wave length. The wave length corresponding to the critical or threshold frequency in a quantum process brought about by radiation.

crocoite. Crocoisite; a red, crystalline mineral; lead chromate, $PbCrO_4$.

Cro-Magnon man. A man living in middle Europe about 50,000 years ago; large-headed, tall, erect species; an ancestor of European races.

Crookes' tube. An evacuated device for demonstrating the behavior of a cathode beam.

crop. (1) An organ of the alimentary canal of the earth-

worm, bird, and certain other animals which serves for food storage; (2) plants or plant products cultivated for use by man.

crop milk. A secretion of crop epithelium of the male and female pigeon on which nestlings are fed.

cross. The act or product of cross-fertilization.

cross bedding. An oblique lamination of certain beds in aeolian or water-laid sediments, caused by current action.

cross breeding. Hybridization; uniting the male of one species with the female of another.

cross fertilization. A union of a sperm and an egg of two individuals.

cross linkage. The joining of polymer molecules by valence bridges; example, the sulfur bonds in the molecules of vulcanized rubber.

cross matching. A test to make certain that certain persons are of the same blood group.

cross modulation. The modulation of a desired signal by an undesired signal caused by nonlinearity of the transmitting medium.

cross polarization The component of the electric field vector which is normal to the desired polarization component.

cross pollination. The transfer of pollen from one flower to the pistil of another; it may occur on two individual plants of the same species or on one and the same plant.

cross section. (1) A section perpendicular to the length of a body; (2) the effective area which an atom presents to an incident beam of elementary particles (neutrons, protons, etc.), which is a measure of successful collision resulting in electron capture or ionization.

cross wind force. The component of the total air force perpendicular to the lift and drag, acting on the aircraft as a whole or on any part of it.

crossed prisms. Two Nicol prisms or other polarizing systems set with their axes at right angles; they will not transmit light.

crosshead. A reciprocating part of a pump or engine which connects the piston rod and connecting rod.

crossing over. During synapsis, an exchange of the genes between a pair of chromosomes.

Crossopterygii. Fresh-water fish; only a few species exist in African waters; the rest are fossils.

Crova's disk. A device to illustrate longitudinal wave motion.

crucible. A vessel made of heat-resistant material and used at high temperatures for melting metals, fusing, igniting precipitates, etc.

crucible steel. A specially hardened steel made by alloying wrought iron with carbon and other metals in a crucible.

crude oil. Petroleum in its natural state as it comes from the earth.

Crustacea. Arthropoda with fused head and thorax; they live in water, have gills, two long antennae, jointed legs, and claws; examples, crab and lobster.

cryogenics. Low-temperature physics which is concerned with phenomena that occur at extremely low temperatures.

cryohydrate. A crystalline solid of constant composition and melting point obtained by freezing an aqueous solution.

cryohydric point. The eutectic point in cases in which the system contains water.

cryolite. Greenland spar; sodium aluminum fluoride, Na_3AlF_6; used for the electrolytic production of aluminum.

cryometer. A low-temperature thermometer.

cryophorus. An apparatus used to demonstrate the cooling effect of evaporation.

Cryophytes. Microplants which grow in ice and snow; mainly algae and a few mosses, fungi, bacteria, etc.

cryoplankton. Algae living in the polar region.

cryoscope. An instrument for measuring freezing or solidification points.

cryoscopic method. Determination of the molecular weight of a dissolved substance by measuring the depression of freezing point of the solvent it causes.

cryoscopy. Determination of the freezing point of solutions or of the molecular weight by the depression of the freezing point.

cryostat. A low-temperature thermostat.

crypt. A tubular small gland.

cryptic coloration. A coloration of animals which conceals and protects by resemblance to the surroundings or to another animal.

cryptocrystalline. So finely crystalline texture of an igneous rock that the individual crystals can only be distinguished in a thin section by transmitted polarized light.

cryptozoic. Said of animals which live in crevices, under stones and leaves.

crystal. (1) A piezo-electric crystal, usually a quartz crystal, used for controlling the frequency of a transmitter and other purposes in radio; (2) a solid in which the particles (molecules, atoms, ions) are arranged in a definite pattern in a crystal lattice; the crystal form reflects the regularity of internal structure; (3) the pro-

tective glass over the dial of a watch.

crystal analysis. The study of the arrangement of atoms, ions, or molecules in crystals, chiefly by x-ray methods.

crystal angles. The characteristic constant angles between the faces of a crystal form.

crystal, biaxial. A doubly refracting crystal which has two optic axes.

crystal counter. A device for detecting high-energy particles, containing a crystal which becomes temporarily conductive under the effect of an ionizing radiation.

crystal detector. A crystal rectifier that offers more resistance to the flow of electricity in one direction than in the other; examples, galena and silicon.

crystal diamagnetism. Abnormal and anistropic diamagnetism observed in crystals of a few substances; example, bismuth.

crystal field. The electrostatic field which acts locally inside a crystal as a result of the microscopic arrangement of atoms and ions in the lattice.

crystal grating. A crystal arranged in such a manner that it acts as a diffraction grating.

crystal habit. The external shape of a crystal, which depends on the relative development of the different faces and the interfacial angles characteristic of the crystal.

crystal, hemihedral. A crystal that has only one half of its faces developed.

crystal, holohedral. A crystal that has all of its faces developed.

crystal, ionic. A crystal consisting of ions arranged in a systematic order in its lattice.

crystal, isomorphous. One of two or more crystals which are similar in crystal form and in chemical properties.

crystal lattice. A three-dimensional regular structural pattern of crystals.

crystal, liquid. A liquid having the optical properties of a crystal.

crystal, macromolecular. A crystal consisting of molecular aggregates arranged in its lattice.

crystal, mixed. A crystal in which atoms of one element are substituted for atoms of another element.

crystal, molecular. A crystal consisting of molecules arranged in systematic order.

crystal oscillator. A source of electrical oscillation of constant frequency, including a piezoelectric crystal in its circuit.

crystal spectrograph. An instrument for photographing spectra formed by using a crystal, such as that of calcite, as the diffracting medium.

crystal system. Classification of

crystals according to the number and type of their planes of symmetry.

crystal, twin. Two crystals of the same substance having one common face.

crystal, uniaxial. A doubly refracting crystal which has but one optic axis and one direction of single refraction; example, Iceland spar.

crystalline. (1) Possessing a definite geometric shape; (2) consisting of crystals.

crystalline cone. A glassy body between the cornea and the sensory portion of each component of the compound eye in some species of insects.

crystalline solid. A solid whose particles are crystals; a solid in which the atoms or molecules are arranged systematically in a crystal lattice.

crystalline style. A rodlike, transparent protein mass, containing starch-digesting enzymes, secreted within a pouch of the gut of some mollusks.

crystallite. (1) One of the grains or small, imperfect crystals that make up a polycrystalline substance; (2) partly developed crystals in a glasslike igneous rock.

crystallization. Process of forming crystals of a substance by evaporating the solvent in which it is dissolved.

crystallography. The study of the external shape and internal structure of crystals.

crystalloid. (1) A substance that forms a true solution; opposite of colloid; (2) a protein crystal occurring in seeds.

crystalloluminescence. The emission of light after precipitation of crystals from a solution.

Cs. Chemical symbol for cesium.

ctenidial filaments. Slender processes of the ctenidia of mollusks.

ctenidium. A comblike projection of the body wall of mollusks, lying in the mantle cavity and usually serving as a gill.

Ctenophora. A subphylum of Coelenterata; they have no thread cells; their body is neither polyp nor medusa; their movement is due to cilia fused in rows; examples, comb jellies and sea gooseberries.

Cu. Chemical symbol for copper.

cu. cm. Abbreviation for cubic centimeters.

cu. ft. Abbreviation of cubic foot.

cu. in. Abbreviation for cubic inches.

cu. yd. Abbreviation of cubic yard.

cube photometer. An integrating photometer which contains a cubical cavity.

cubic centimeter (cc). A unit of volume in the metric system which is approximately equal to a milliliter; 1/1000 liter.

cubic foot. 1728 cubic inches; 28.3 liters.

cubic foot of air. At 0°C and 760 mm pressure, it weighs 0.0807 pound.

cubic foot of pure water. It weighs 62.4 pounds.

cubic yard. 27 cubic feet.

cud. The food brought back into the mouth from the first stomach of a ruminant, such as the cow.

cuesta. An erosion ridge with one face steep and the other tilting at a gentle angle.

cultigen. A cultivated plant that does not grow wild.

culture. A large number of bacteria growing on a medium; used for experiments.

culture medium. A preparation suitable and used for the growth and cultivation of microorganisms.

cumulonimbus. Thunderhead; large cloud masses, having a flat bottom and lofty top with majestic towers or anvils; they may bring thunderstorms.

cumulus. A dense cloud having a dome-shaped upper surface with protuberances and a horizontal base.

cupel. A porous shallow, thick-walled dish of bone ash used in cupellation and assaying.

cupellation. A separation of silver, gold, and other noble metals from lead, which is oxidized by hot air.

cuprammonium process. The manufacture of rayon from cotton, which is dissolved in a mixture of cupric sulfate solution and ammonia water; the viscous solution is forced through a spinnerette into a coagulating bath of dilute acid.

cupric. Compound of bivalent copper.

cuprite. Red, cubic mineral; copper oxide, Cu_2O.

cuprous. Compound of univalent copper.

curie. The unit of radioactivity; 3.7×10^{10} disintegrations per second.

Curie balance. A torsion balance used to measure the force on a nonferromagnetic body in a nonuniform magnetic field.

Curie constant. The product of the atomic or molar magnetic susceptibility of a paramagnetic substance and the absolute temperature.

Curie law. The magnetic susceptibility of a paramagnetic substance varies inversely as the absolute temperature.

Curie point. The temperature at which a ferromagnetic substance becomes paramagnetic.

curium. A chemical element obtained by bombarding plutonium with helium ions; chemical symbol Cm; atomic number 96.

current. The flow of electrical energy along a conductor from the higher to the lower of two points having different potentials.

current balance. An instrument for the determination of a current in absolute electromagnetic units.

current density. (1) The current per unit area of electrodes in electrolysis; (2) the current flowing through the unit cross section of a conductor.

current, eddy. The current which flows in a conductor as a result of a varying magnetic field.

current, instantaneous. The momentary value of a current which varies with time.

current refraction. A change in the direction of an electric current at an interface between two conductors of different conductivity.

curvilinear distortion. A photographic error, in which the straight lines of the object are not linear in the camera image.

cuspid. A canine tooth.

cut bank. A vertical wall on the outside of a river curve.

cutaneous. Pertaining to the skin.

cuticle. The thin, noncellular dead outermost covering layer of the epidermis.

cutin. An impermeable waxy substance on or in the pores of cell walls.

cutinization. Impregnation of the cell wall with waxy cutin.

cutis. The corium; the deeper layer of the skin.

cutoff. (1) A short canal formed by a stream when it cuts through a river bend; (2) a point in a cycle at which a mechanism cuts off the flow of certain frequencies to or from the cycle.

cutoff bias. The negative voltage which must be applied to the grid of a thermionic tube in order to stop the flow of anode or plate current.

cutoff voltage. Same as cutoff bias.

cutout. An electromagnetic or thermal device for opening a circuit when the current rise is beyond the safety limit.

cutting. Any cut portion (leaf, stem, or root) of a plant that is used for asexual reproduction.

Cuvierian organ. Defensive organ found in some sea cucumbers; sticky threads projecting from the body wall for entangling the attacker.

cyanamide. NH_2CN; colorless crystals.

cyanamide process. The manufacture of ammonia by the fixation of atmospheric nitrogen; calcium carbide is heated in a nitrogen atmosphere and the resulting calcium cyanide is changed into ammonia by treatment with steam under pressure.

cyanide. Salt of hydrocyanic acid, HCN; example, sodium cyanide, $NaCN$.

cyanide hardening. Surface hardening of iron or steel by heating in a cyanide bath followed by quenching.

cyanide process. Extracting gold from its ores by treatment with a dilute sodium cyanide solution.

cyaniding. Same as cyanide process and cyanide hardening.

cyanocobalamine. Vitamine B_{12}, found in liver; the antianemic factor.

cyanogen. Colorless poison gas of characteristic bitter-almond odor; C_2N_2.

Cyanophyceae. Myxophyceae; blue-green algae; aquatic or occurring in damp places; they are abundant in fresh-water plankton and soil; they are unicellular, filamentous and reproduce asexually.

cyanosis. Bluish discoloration of the skin caused by insufficient oxygenation of the blood.

cybernetics. The study of communication and control mechanisms in living beings and machines.

cybotaxis. A regular arrangement of the molecules in a liquid, as seen by x-ray examination, resembling that of crystals.

Cycas. A palmlike plant that lives in tropical countries.

cycle. (1) A repeated series of events or operations; (2) in a-c circuits, the periodic changes in voltage; (3) a standard unit of frequency, 0.000,001 megacycle, 0.001 kilocycle.

cycle of erosion. The stages of the development of a landscape by erosion.

cyclic arrangement. Growing of two or more leaves from one node.

cyclic compounds. Ring compounds; example, benzene, C_6H_6.

cyclone. (1) Local name for a tornado; (2) whirling motion of air masses that results when cold air rushes toward a low-pressure area and forces up warm air masses; it may have hurricane force.

cyclosis. The rotary streaming movement of the protoplasm in a cell.

Cyclostomata. Eel-like aquatic animals, with a jawless, sucking mouth, no bones, scales, or paired fins; they suck the blood of fish to which they attach themselves; examples, lampreys and hagfish.

cyclostrophic wind. A gradient wind; a wind which blows to balance a pressure gradient and as a result of centrifugal force.

cyclotron. A device by which atoms may be bombarded by electrically charged particles; two dees in a powerful magnetic field, whose high potential difference forces the charged particles to follow a spiral path at very high speed and with constant acceleration.

cyclotron frequency. The frequency at which an electron traverses an orbit in a steady, uniform magnetic field and zero electric field.

cyme. An inflorescence in which the flowers at the apex are the first to mature and open.

cyst. (1) A capsule or covering which forms around some tiny animals and which furnishes protection during a period of inactivity or of unfavorable conditions in the environment; (2) a small morbid fluid-containing lump or growth.

cysticercoid. The larva of certain tapeworms.

cystocarp. A structure found in red algae after fertilization.

cystolith. A stalked body in the epidermal cells of certain plants; it contains calcium carbonate.

cytochemistry. The chemistry of the cells.

cytochrome. A respiratory pigment, widely distributed in plant and animal cells; it is easily oxidized and reduced.

cytogenesis. Cell formation.

cytogenetics. The science which integrates the methods and findings of cytology and genetics.

cytokinesis. The division of cells.

cytology. The study of cells, their structure, function, and development.

cytolysin. An antibody which causes dissolution of cells.

cytolysis. The dissolution of cells, particularly through destruction of their surface membranes.

cyton. The cell body of a neuron.

cytopharynx. The pharynx or gullet of a protozoon; example, paramecium.

cytoplasm. The protoplasm in a cell outside the nucleus.

cytoplasmic inheritance. Non-Mendelian inheritance by self-propagating cytoplasmic particles as distinct from gene inheritance.

cytotaxonomy. Classification based on characters of somatic chromosomes.

D

D. Symbol for deuterium, heavy hydrogen, ^2H.

D region. D layer; the ionospheric region 25 to 50 miles above the surface of the earth; it absorbs radio waves which are reflected by higher regions.

dacite. An extrusive igneous rock of variable composition.

dactyl. A finger or toe.

daily march of temperature. Hourly changes in the thermometer readings during 24 hours.

daily range of temperature. The difference between the highest and lowest temperatures of the day.

daily variations of the earth's magnetic field. Small variations of the horizontal intensity, magnetic declination, and dip, recurring over a period of a day.

Dalton's law of partial pressure. The pressure of a gas mixture is equal to the sum of the pressures which would be exerted by the individual gases occupying the same volume.

damped balance. A balance equipped with means for damping the to-and-fro movements of the suspended system, so that the pointer comes to rest more rapidly.

damped oscillation. A mechanical or electrical oscillation whose amplitude is sharply reduced in successive cycles, so that they gradually die out to zero amplitude.

damping. (1) A decrease in the amplitude of an oscillation or wave motion with time; (2) the checking of a motion due to friction or similar cause.

damping off. A disease of young seedlings crowded together in wet soil caused by a primitive fungus.

damping tube, A cathode-ray tube used with magnetic-deflection coils to prevent any transient oscillation in the tube or its associated circuits.

Daniell cell. A primary cell having a zinc anode in a zinc sulfate solution and a copper cathode in a copper sulfate solution.

daraf. The unit of elastance of a condenser; the reciprocal of a farad.

Darcy's law. The velocity of fluid flow in a porous medium, due to inequality of pressure, is proportional to the pressure gradient.

dark adaptation. The property of the retina of improving the vision in reduced light.

dark current. A residual current flowing in a photocell when it is not illuminated.

dark discharge. An electrical discharge in a gas which has no visible luminosity.

dark-ground illumination. A device used in microscopy to make transparent or unstained objects appear as bright spots against a black background.

dark-line spectrum. A spectrum with dark or Fraunhofer lines, as that revealed by the solar spectroscope.

D'Arsonval galvanometer. A galvanometer whose moving element is a coil suspended or pivoted between the poles of a magnet; the ancestor of modern electric meters.

dart sac. A sacklike gland opening into the female genital duct of snails, which secretes a calcareous dart shot by muscular contraction into the body of another snail when the two approach each other prior to mating.

Darwinism. A theory of evolution through natural selection.

dashpot. A mechanical damping device; it consists of a piston connected to the part to be damped and arranged in a cylinder filled with oil; the vibration is absorbed by the viscosity of the oil.

date line, international. A line imagined on the earth's surface about along the meridian of longitude 180°; it indicates the change of date to travelers.

daughter cells. Two cells resulting from primary division.

day, astronomical. Mean solar day; 24 hours beginning at noon.

day, civil. The period recognized by the courts as a day; it begins at midnight.

day, lunar. Interval between two successive passages of the moon across the meridian.

day, mean solar. Average of a solar day.

day, sideral. Interval between two successive passages of the vernal equinox across the meridian.

day, solar. Interval between two successive passages of the sun across the meridian.

db. Abbreviation for decibel.

d-c. Abbreviation for direct current.

De Broglie wave. Electron waves in the ether.

dead band. In a magnetic amplifier, a region of input-signal change which causes no change in the output.

dead beat. Property of an instrument which comes to rest without oscillation; example, the indicator of a highly damped galvanometer.

dead center. The position of the crank of an engine when it is in a straight line with the connecting rod.

dead load. Dead weight; the weight of a structure and the permanent loading carried by it.

dead room. An enclosure in which there is a large amount of sound absorption.

dead spot. In radio reception, a location where the intensity of sound waves is low because of interference or focusing by a curved surface.

deaeration. Removal of dissolved air from boiler feed water by heating in a vessel under reduced pressure.

deamination. The removal of amino groups from a compound.

debunching. The dispersion of an electron beam caused by mutual repulsion between electrons.

Debye-Hükel theory. Strong electrolytes are completely dissociated; any deviation from this behavior is due to interionic attraction.

decade resistance box. A simple form of resistance box containing two sets of ten coils; in one set each coil has one ohm resistance and in the other, ten ohms resistance.

decalage. The acute angle between the wing chords of an airplane.

decalescence. The heat absorption of iron and steel above their critical point.

decantation. Separating substances having different specific gravities by allowing the denser to settle to the bottom of a container and pouring off the less dense substance; pouring off the supernatant liquid carefully so as not to disturb the precipitate.

decarburization. The removal of carbon from the surface of iron or steel, usually by heating in a reducing or oxidizing atmosphere.

decay. (1) A decomposition of timber by fungi or other agencies; (2) a decrease of luminescence with time.

decay constant. The ratio of the disintegration rate of a radioactive substance to the amount of unchanged substance.

decay product. A nuclide, radioactive or stable, resulting from the radioactive disintegration of a radionuclide directly or as a result of successive transformations in a radioactive series.

decay, radioactive. (1) Radioactive disintegration; (2) decrease with time of the number of radioactive atoms in a sample because of their spontaneous transformation.

deceleration. Speed reduction; measured in feet per second per second.

decibel. The unit of power-level difference; a measure of the response in electrical communication.

decidua. The mucous membrane lining the uterus during pregnancy in many mammals; it is ejected with the placenta at birth.

deciduous. Said of trees and shrubs shedding their leaves every year.

deciduous teeth. The temporary teeth of childhood; milk teeth.

decigram. In the metric system, one tenth of a gram.

deciliter. In the metric system, one tenth of a liter.

decimal rheostat. Same as decade resistance box.

decimeter. One tenth of a meter; 10 centimeters.

decimetric waves. Electromagnetic waves which have a wave length of the order of 10 centimeters.

decinormal solution. A standard solution used in titration which contains one tenth of a gram equivalent per liter.

declination. The angular distance of a celestial body from the celestial equator.

declinometer. An instrument for measuring magnetic declination.

decomposition. (1) The breaking down of organic substances by bacteria, fungi, or by chemical action; (2) the separation of compounds into their elements or into simpler compounds by heat.

decomposition voltage. The minimum electromotive force which will cause continuous electrolysis in an electrolytic cell.

decremeter. An instrument for measuring the damping of electric waves.

decrepitation. Cracking of crystals on heating, due to the expansion of water within the crystals.

deficiency. Dropping out of a gene from a chromosome.

definite proportions, law of. Every pure compound contains the same elements in the same weight proportion.

deflation. Removal of loose fine-grained sediment from the surface of rocks by the wind.

deflection yoke. A device consisting of one or more coils whose magnetic field deflects an electron beam.

deflocculation. Converting into very fine flakes.

deformation. Changes in the shape of a body caused by stress.

deformation bands. Regions in a metal crystal which have assumed different orientations as a result of slip.

deformation potential. The electric potential acting on a free electron in a metal or semiconductor as a result of a local deformation of the crystal lattice.

degassing. Removal of occluded gas from wires to be used in vacuum tubes or from metals to be plated.

degaussing. Demagnetization of a magnetized substance by surrounding it with a wire carrying an alternating current of ever-decreasing magnitude; applied to ships.

degenerate states. Different states of motion corresponding to the same energy level.

degeneration. Evolutionary retrogression.

deglutition. Swallowing; a complex reflex set off by stimulation of the pharynx.

degradation. (1) The conversion of a complex molecule into simpler molecules; (2) the process of energy becoming de-

creasingly less available for mechanical work; for example, by conversion into heat; (3) loss of energy by collision; (4) wearing away of rock by erosion.

degree. The unit of temperature difference; one three-hundred and sixtieth part (1/360) of a circle; a unit of measure of angles.

degree of dissociation. The fraction of the total number of molecules that is dissociated.

degree of freedom. The number of variables defining the state of a system which may be changed at will.

dehiscence. The property of a ripe fruit to open spontaneously.

dehumidification. Artificial drying of air or other gases.

dehydrating agent. A water-removing (hydrophilic or hygroscopic) substance.

dehydration. (1) Removal of water from a substance by heat or a dehydrating agent; (2) excessive loss of water from a body tissue.

dehydrogenase. A reducing plant enzyme.

dehydrogenation. The chemical reaction of removing hydrogen from a compound.

deionization potential. The potential at which conduction in a gas-discharge tube stops, when ionization ceases.

deionization time. The time needed for the grid of a gas-discharge tube to regain control after anode-current interruption.

deionizing. Water purification by passing through a hydrogen exchanger to convert the salts into acids which are removed by an adsorbent, e.g., synthetic resins.

dekagram. Metric unit, 10 grams.

dekaliter. Metric unit, 10 liters.

dekameter. Metric unit, 10 meters.

delay circuit. A circuit used in electrical communication to delay the starting of a wave form for a certain period of time to allow time for that wave form to operate the relays.

deliquescence. The property of certain substances to take up water from the air and thus form a solution.

deliquescent branching. Growing of ramified branches from older branches and not from the trunk.

delta. An extensive accumulation of sediment at the mouth of a stream where the velocity of the stream is checked as it enters a lake or sea.

Delta. A term used to denote the fourth brightest star in a constellation.

delta rays. Relatively slow-moving electrons emitted in large numbers by surfaces exposed to alpha rays.

demagnetization. Depriving a body of its magnetic properties or reducing the magnetization of a body.

demagnetizing ampere-turns. Back ampere-turns; a portion of the armature ampere-turns which has a direct demagnetizing effect on the poles.

demal solution. A solution which contains one gram-equivalent of solute per cubic decimeter of solution.

demineralizer. A water-purification apparatus for producing mineral-free deionized water.

demountable tube. An electron tube which may be taken apart for inspection or repair.

denatured alcohol. Ethyl alcohol for industrial use which has been made unfit for human consumption by the addition of evil-smelling or poisonous substances.

dendrites. (1) Thickly branched projections from the body of a nerve cell which carry impulses into the cell body; (2) a tree-like crystal formation.

denitrification. Breaking down nitrogenous compounds with evolution of free nitrogen.

denitrifying bacteria. Soil bacteria which, in the absence of oxygen, break down nitrates and nitrites in the soil, with evolution of free nitrogen.

densichron. A device which measures optical density.

densimeter. An instrument for the determination of density.

densitometer. An instrument for determining the blackening, or photographic density, of a developed photographic plate or film.

density. The mass of a body per unit volume; example, the density of water is 1 gram per cubic centimeter or 62.4 pounds per cubic foot.

density altitude. In aeronautics, the altitude corresponding to a given density in a standard atmosphere.

density, luminous. The luminous energy found in a unit volume of space.

density, radiant. The radiant energy found in a unit volume of space.

density, relative. The ratio of the mass of a given volume of a substance to that of the same volume of another substance chosen as a standard.

dentary. The upper bone of the lower jaw.

denticles. Toothlike scales on many fish.

dentine. The calcium-containing, bonelike hard substance of teeth and placoid scales.

dentition. The form and arrangement of the teeth in vertebrates.

deoxygenated blood. Blood from which the oxygen has been removed by the tissue cells.

dependent differentiation. Differ-

entiation in an embryonic tissue which is dependent on a stimulus coming from some other tissue.

dependent organism. Every animal, and any plant that lacks chlorophyll, and thus every organism that cannot make its own food.

depleted soil. Nonfertile soil that has lost minerals needed by plants for growth.

depolarization. Preserving the activity of a voltaic cell by preventing polarization which is the source of back emf.

depolarizer. An oxidizing agent used for fixing the hydrogen evolving from the decomposition of the acid in primary cells.

deposit. (1) A sediment; (2) a metal coating produced by electrolysis.

deposition. The process by which agents of erosion drop sediment or other eroded materials that they are carrying along.

deposition, electrical. Coating one metal with another by making them the electrodes in a cell with the salt of the metal to be deposited as electrolyte. One faraday is required for the deposition of one gram equivalent of any substance.

deposition potential. The minimum potential difference between an electrode and the surrounding electrolyte required to deposit ions of a given kind.

depression. A region over which atmospheric pressure is lower than that of surrounding regions; a depression brings cyclonic winds.

depression of freezing point. Lowering the freezing point of a solvent by dissolving a solid in it. The freezing-point depression of a solution is proportional to its concentration and is used in molecular-weight determinations.

depression slide. A glass slide with depression in it for holding liquids to be examined under the microscope.

derivative. (1) A substance derived or prepared from some other substance, usually retaining the general structure of the parent substance; example, nitrobenzene is a derivative of benzene; (2) a substance that was not actually prepared from another substance, but it is structurally so related to it that it may be thought of as its derivative; example, phenyl amine, $C_6H_5NH_2$, is regarded as a derivative of ammonia, NH_3, in which one H atom has been replaced by a phenyl group.

derived units. Units derived from the fundamental units of length, mass and time; example, the unit for velocity is derived from the units of length and time and is expressed as feet per second.

dermal. Pertaining to the skin.

dermal bone. A bone arising near the surface of an embryo from concentration of mesenchyme cells, with no cartilage precursor; it occurs in the skull and shoulder-girdle of most vertebrates.

dermis. The portion of skin below the epidermis; a highly sensitive layer, thicker than the epidermis, which contains fibrous connective tissue, sweat and oil glands, hair follicles, nerve endings, and blood vessels.

Dermoptera. Flying lemurs; a small order of mammals with hairy membranes stretching along the side of the body, between the wrist, ankle, and the tip of the tail.

descending colon. The part of the colon which extends down the left side of the abdomen.

descending nodes. Two points at which a satellite crosses the orbit of its primary from north to south.

desert type climate. Dry, windy climate with meager rainfall.

desiccate. To remove the moisture from; to dry thoroughly; to become dry.

desiccator. A laboratory apparatus for drying substances and keeping them free from moisture; it usually contains a dehydrating agent, such as calcium chloride or concentrated sulfuric acid.

desmogen strands. Elongated cells which develop into vascular tissues.

desorption. The opposite of absorption or adsorption; the release of a substance held in concentrated form on a surface or inside another substance.

desquamation. Shedding of the superficial cells of the skin in scales or large pieces.

destruction limit. The shearing stress at which a crystal begins to lose its lattice structure.

destructive distillation. The process of decomposing a solid by heating in a closed vessel; example, coal will yield coke, coal tar products, and gases by destructive distillation.

detailed balancing. (1) Imparting the energy of an ionized atom to a free electron or other particle; as a result, the atom is neutralized and the particle is sent off with additional velocity; (2) a principle of statistical mechanics which shows that the steady state at equilibrium is maintained by a direct balance between the instantaneous rates of opposing processes.

detection. (1) The qualitative identification of an element or a compound in a mixture; (2) the demodulation of an incoming electrical signal of a radio receiver.

detector. (1) A device, usually a triode, for rectifying current oscillations so that they can affect a speaker; (2) a simple galvanometer which will indicate the mere presence of a current in a circuit.

detector, traveling. A device for measuring electric field intensity in a wave guide as a function of distance along the guide.

determinate inflorescence. A cymose inflorescence; a flower developing at the end of the primary and each secondary axis.

detinning. Removing the tin from scrap or tinplate by the action of chlorine, which combines with the tin to form stannic chloride, $SnCl_4$.

detonating gas. A gaseous mixture that explodes on exposure to light or if sparked; examples, hydrogen and chlorine in the volume ratio of 1:1 and hydrogen and oxygen in the volume ratio of 2:1.

detonation. (1) An explosive reaction which takes place within a high-velocity shock wave known as the "detonation wave" or "reaction shock"; (2) a knock which is caused in the cylinders of an internal-combustion engine by spontaneous combustion of part of the charge.

detonator. A substance used to set off an explosion; example, mercury fulminate.

detritus. (1) Organic debris from decomposing plants and animals; (2) unconsolidated sediment derived from pre-existing rocks by natural agencies.

deuterium. Heavy hydrogen; the isotope of hydrogen, having an atomic weight of 2.

deuteron. The nucleus of deuterium, containing one proton and one neutron.

deutoplasm. Nonprotoplasmic substance in the cell body; example, the yolk of egg.

developer. An organic compound which reduces the silver salts exposed to light to metallic silver, thus forming the image; example, hydroquinone, $C_6H_4(OH)_2$.

developing, photographic. The action of certain chemicals, usually organic reducing agents, on an exposed photographic plate or film to bring out the latent image. A developer reduces to metallic silver those areas of the silver salts which have been exposed to light.

development. (1) The stages in the growth of a plant or an animal; (2) the growth and differentiation of a crystal.

deviation. The angle through which a light ray is bent by refraction or diffraction.

deviation of a compass. An error

in compass indication due to local conditions, such as the iron of a ship; the angle between the position of the compass needle and the true north-south direction.

deviation of complement. The Neisser-Wechsburg phenomenon of the failure of lysis to occur when a considerable excess of cytolysin is added to normal serum (complement) and antigen; the complement unites with the unbound cytolysin rather than with the cytolysin which has united with antigen.

devitrification. Natural conversion of rock glasses, such as obsidian, into cryptocrystalline rocks of dull appearance, which contain minute grains of minerals, usually quartz and feldspar.

devitrification of glass. Crystallization of glass, which is normally an amphorous mixture; as a result, the glass loses its characteristic clear transparency and becomes brittle; this is a difficulty to be overcome in glass manufacture.

Devonian period. A Paleozoic era; the age of fishes; the first plants appeared, especially ferns and conifers; there were also amphibians and insects.

dew. Droplets of water which appear on surfaces cooler than the air that is in contact with them.

dew point. The temperature to which the air must be cooled in order to cause dew, that is, moisture to condense, or precipitate.

Dewar flask. A double-walled glass flask used for storing liquid air; the space between the two walls is exhausted to a very high vacuum to minimize transfer of heat by convection and conduction and the inner surface of the walls is silvered to reduce transfer of heat by radiation.

dextrin. A water-miscible substance formed by heating starch; used as an adhesive and stiffener.

dextrogyrate. Same as dextrorotatory.

dextrorotatory. Rotating or deviating the plane of vibration of polarized light to the right when viewed in the direction in which the light travels.

dextrose. D-Glucose; $C_6H_{12}O_6$; used as a sweetening agent.

dg. Abbreviation for decigrams.

di-. A prefix meaning two identical atoms or groups in a molecule.

diacaustic. In optics, a caustic curve or surface produced by refraction.

diactinism. The property of transmitting actinic, that is, chemically active radiation.

diadelphous. Said of stamens

united by their filaments to form two bundles, or having one solitary and the other united.

diagenesis. (1) The formation of new products by rearrangement or recombination; (2) gradual and successive chemical or physical change which takes place in sediments prior to or during their consolidation.

diageotropism. The orientation of a plant part by growth in response to the stimulus of gravity in such a manner that its axis is at right angles to the direction of the gravitational force.

diakinesis. In meiosis, the chromosomes lying near or on the nuclear membrane.

dial bridge. A resistance bridge having its coils arranged in dials, the contacts being made by a movable arm instead of by the insertion of plugs.

dialysis. The separation of crystalloids from colloids by their different diffusibility through a semipermeable membrane.

dialyzed iron. A colloidal solution of ferric hydroxide, $Fe(OH)_3$; deep-red liquid used in medicine.

dialyzer. A semipermeable membrane by which colloids can be separated from true solutions.

diamagnetic. Being repelled by a magnet in air.

diamagnetic substance. A substance having a magnetic permeability less than 1; example, bismuth.

diamond. Pure crystalline carbon; the hardest mineral; used as a precious stone, in cutting tools and abrasives.

diapause. Exhibernation; a period of suspended development or growth, accompanied by greatly decreased metabolism, in some species of insects.

diaphanometer. An instrument used to measure the degree of transparency of solids, liquids, or gases.

diaphragm. (1) A thin muscular partition separating the chest from the abdomen and used in breathing; (2) a sound-producing vibrating metal disk; (3) a part of the illumination system of the microscope just beneath the condenser which adjusts the intensity of the light; (4) a porous plate between the electrodes of an accumulator; (5) a transverse cell layer at the node of plant stems.

diaphysis. The shaft of a long limb bone, or the central portion of a vertebra, in mammals.

diastase. An enzyme which effects the hydrolysis of starch with the formation of sugar.

diastema. (1) The plane of division of a cell during mitosis; (2) a gap between the teeth.

diastole. A part of the heart beat

in which the ventricles dilate and receive blood from the auricles.

diastolic blood pressure. The arterial blood pressure maintained between heart beats.

diathermancy. An ability to transmit heat radiations; similar to transparency with respect to light.

diathermanous. Highly transparent to infrared.

diatom. A one-celled form of green algae living in fresh water and forming a glasslike wall about the protoplasm; their skeletons are the source of diatomaceous earth which is used as an adsorbent and filter aid.

diatomaceous earth. Infusorial earth; porous fossil, containing skeletons of diatoms; used for clarifying liquids, in heat insulation.

diatomic. Said of an element whose molecule consists of two atoms; example, hydrogen, H_2.

diatreme. Volcanic pipes and circular vents, the result of the explosive action of magmatic gases.

diatropism. The orientation of organisms perpendicularly to the direction of a stimulus.

diazo compounds. Organic compounds of the general formula RN:NR′; many are important in the manufacture of dyes.

diazotization. A reaction of a primary aromatic amine with nitrous acid in the presence of excess mineral acid to produce a diazo compound.

dibasic acid. An acid that has two replaceable hydrogen atoms; example, sulfuric acid, H_2SO_4.

dibasic salt. A salt in which two of the hydrogen atoms in a tribasic acid have been replaced; example, Na_2HPO_4 from H_3PO_4.

dichasium. A branched inflorescence, in which each branch has two lateral branches of about the same size.

dichlamydeous. Said of flowers which have calyx and corolla.

dichogamy. Maturing of stamens and pistils of a flower at different times.

dichotomous. In biology, growing of two equal branches from the apical cell.

dichotomous venation. Forking of veins one or more times.

dichroism. The property, exhibited by certain crystals, of showing different colors of transmitted light, depending on the direction of incident light due to a difference in the absorption of different light rays.

dichromatic cell. A primary cell which has a positive pole of carbon and a negative pole of zinc in an electrolyte consisting of a solution of sulfuric acid and potassium dichromate, $K_2Cr_2O_7$, the second acting as a depolarizing agent by its oxi-

dizing action.

dichromatism. Color blindness in which only two colors of the spectrum can be distinguished.

dichroscope. An instrument used in studying the dichroism of crystals.

dichroscopic eyepiece. An eyepiece for a polariscope or polarizing microscope which gives a comparison view of the same object or field under illumination by the two complementary rays of polarized light.

diclinous. Unisexual, having the stamens in one flower and the pistils in another.

Dicotyledones. Dicots; plants which have seeds with two cotyledons, netted-vein leaves, a ring of cambium cells in their stem, and rings of food and water tubes.

dictyostele. Hollow vascular cylinder which is broken up into separate strands that remain distinct; separate bundles are scattered irregularly.

didynamous. Having two pairs of stamens of different lengths.

dielectric. The insulating material between the plates of a capacitor; a material through which electrical attraction or repulsion can be sustained.

dielectric absorption. The persistence of electric polarization in some dielectrics after the removal of the polarizing electric fields.

dielectric cohesion. The force with which the molecules of a dielectric oppose an electric field tending to ionize them.

dielectric constant. The ratio of the electric flux density produced by an electric force in a dielectric to the flux density produced by the same force in vacuum.

dielectric heating. The rapid and uniform heating of a dielectric material by a high-frequency alternating electric field due to molecular friction as a result of periodic reversal of molecular polarization.

dielectric hysteresis. An effect in a dielectric due to absorption, which is analogous to the hysteresis of magnetic materials.

dielectric, isotropic. A dielectric whose permittivity is independent of the direction of the applied field.

dielectric loss. The energy dissipated as heat when an electric current acts on a dielectric.

dielectric strength. The maximum potential gradient that a material can withstand without rupture.

diencephalon. A region of the vertebrate brain, just behind the cerebrum.

dienes. Unsaturated organic compounds which contain two carbon-to-carbon double bonds; example, butadiene, CH_2:CH·CH:CH_2, which is used for

making synthetic rubber.

difference amplifier. An amplifier which has two inputs and whose output is a function of their difference.

difference band. A spectral band arising in the transition from an excited state, rather than from the ground state.

difference tone. A combination tone whose pitch corresponds to a frequency equal to the difference in the frequencies of its two components.

differential. Gears in an automobile that distribute the driving force of the main shaft between the two rear wheels and at different speeds when moving on a curve.

differential galvanometer. A galvanometer having two identical coils, which gives a zero reading under the effect of two equal but opposite currents, which neutralize each other.

differential permeability. A property of a substance which allows only certain fluids to diffuse through them.

differential thermometer. A thermometer that indicates differences of temperature between two neighboring positions by the movement of a colored liquid in a U-shaped tube.

differential weathering. Differences in the rate of weathering in different rocks and even different parts of the same rock.

differentiation. (1) The development in embryonic cells of the shapes and structures of specialized cells, such as muscle and nerve cells; (2) separation of a homogeneous magma, while solidifying, into rocks of different compositions; (3) in microscopical specimens, removing the excess stain from certain parts to emphasize the differences in structure.

diffraction. (1) Appearance of fringes or dark or colored bands when light is deflected by passing through a small slit or is reflected by a ruled surface; (2) change in the propagation direction of sound waves due to differences in air density or wind velocity; (3) a property of radio waves of propagating around a curved barrier in their way.

diffraction grating. A ruled plate of 15,000 to 30,000 lines to an inch; used for producing diffraction spectra.

diffraction spectroscope. A spectroscope in which a diffraction grating replaces the prism.

diffuse reflection. The reflection of light from rough surfaces in all directions.

diffuse root system. Spreading out of slender roots.

diffuse series. Characteristic spectral lines in arc spectra.

diffused lighting. Even light distribution without glare.

diffuser. (1) A passage in a compressor or centrifugal pump so shaped that it will increase the pressure and reduce the velocity of fluid flow; (2) in photography, a silk sheet used for softening the light or for avoiding harsh lines; (3) a conical piece used in loudspeakers to promote the uniform distribution of sound waves of different frequencies.

diffusion. Homogenization of a gas, liquid, or solution due to the motion of its molecules.

diffusion analysis. The determination of the relative size or molecular weight by comparing their diffusion rates of particles, or by separating them by differential diffusion methods.

diffusion barrier. A porous partition for the separation of gases, especially of isotopes, which contains submicroscopic holes through which material transfer takes place by diffusion rather than by ordinary hydrodynamic flow.

diffusion column. A vertical tube, within which a radial temperature gradient is maintained; the relative concentrations of heavy and light molecules are different at the upper and lower ends of the column because of convection; used in the separation of isotopes.

diffusion current. The limiting current which is reached by electrolytic migration of the ions in a solution when a potential difference is applied to the electrodes.

diffusion of light. Scattering or alteration of direction of light rays by transmission through frosted glass, fog, etc., or by reflection from irregular surfaces.

diffusion pump. A device for producing a high vacuum in small systems.

diffusion time. Average lifetime; the average time that elapses between the moment of formation and the moment of absorption of a diffusing particle.

diffusive substances. Substances that readily dialyze through semipermeable partitions, such as crystalloids.

digestion. The changing of insoluble food to soluble forms by the actions of enzymes.

digestive gland. A hairlike gland in carnivorous plants that produces enzymes for digesting the prey.

digestive system. Special organs which make food suitable for assimilation by the body tissues.

digit. (1) A point; one-twelfth of the diameter of the sun or moon; used to denote the extent of an eclipse; (2) a finger or toe.

digital computer. One of two basic types of computer; it uses digits to represent physical quantities; problems to be solved are coded in a set of instructions called a program and are fed into the machine, which processes and solves the problems by a system of signals representing digits.

digitate drainage. The fingerlike pattern of stream valleys.

digitigrade. Walking on the toes; example, cat.

dihedral. A measure of the amount of tilt of the wings of an airplane upward or downward (negative dihedral) from a horizontal axis.

dihedral angle. An angle formed by two intersecting planes, measured in a plane that is normal to their intersection line.

dihybrid. The offspring of two parents which are unlike for two contrasting characteristics.

dikaryon. A fungus hypha or mycelium composed of cells containing two haploid nuclei which undergo simultaneous division during formation of each new cell.

dike. An igneous intrusion that cuts across layers of bedrock.

dilatancy. An increase in volume with a change in shape due to an increase in the distance of molecules from one another.

dilatation. The increase of volume per unit volume of continuous material.

dilation number. The ratio of the volume of a liquid to the volume of a solid of the same composition at the same temperature.

dilatometer. An apparatus used for determining the transition point of crystals.

diluent. A thinner; a liquid, usually a petroleum hydrocarbon, which is blended with an active solvent in a varnish or lacquer, generally to increase the bulk or reduce the cost.

dilute solution. A weak solution; a relatively small quantity of solute in a large amount of solvent.

diluting pipette. A special pipette for blood collection where dilution of the blood is necessary.

dilution. (1) The addition of a liquid, such as water, to a solution to make it more dilute; (2) sewage disposal by dilution with a large amount of water having oxygen dissolved in it.

dimorphism. (1) The existence of two types of individuals of the same species which differ in shape, size, structure, etc.; (2) two forms of flowers which occur in the same species but on different plants.

dimorphous. Existing in two different crystalline forms; example, rhombic and monoclinic sulfur.

dineric. Said of a solution in which there are two immiscible solvents with a single solute

soluble in both.

Dinosauria. A group of enormous extinct reptiles which lived in prehistoric times.

diode. A two-electrode vacuum tube which serves as a reflector of alternating current.

dioecious. (1) Having unisexual flowers on separate plants; (2) producing male and female gametes in separate animals.

diopter. The unit of the power of a lens; the power of a lens in diopters is the reciprocal of its focal length in meters, the value being positive for a converging and negative for a diverging lens.

dioptric system. A refractive system; an optical system in which lenses do the focusing; used in lighthouses.

diorite. A dark-colored, granitoid rock which does not contain quartz.

dip circle. A device used for determining the earth's magnetic field; it consists of a magnetic needle pivoted on a horizontal axis.

dip needle. A suspended magnetic needle for measuring the magnetic dip.

dipleura. A bilaterally symmetrical larva of the echinoderms, formed from the gastrula.

dipleurula. A planktonic organism developed by bilateral cleavage.

diploblastic. Derived from two embryonic germ layers, ectoderm and endoderm.

diploid number. The number of chromosomes found in body cells, which is characteristic of the species.

diplont. The diploid stage of an organism ending with meiosis.

diplophase. A phase of the reproductive cycle after fertilization and before meiosis, when the nuclei are diploid.

Diplopoda. Millipeds; order of Arthropoda.

diplosome. A centrosome with two centrioles.

Dipnoi. A group of fresh-water fish which have both gills and one or two lungs; they are mostly extinct; example, Lepidosiren, an eel-like fish living in the swamps of the Amazon.

dipole. (1) A television receiving antenna which is one-half wave length long; (2) a polar molecule, one region of which is positive and another region is negative.

dipole moment. The product of the ionic charges of a dipole and the distance between them.

dipole orientation. Hindering the free rotation of the molecules in a solid so that their dipole moments may only take on certain orientations.

dipping needle. Same as dip needle.

diprotic. Referring to an acid with two replaceable hydrogen

atoms.

Diptera. Flies having one pair of wings and caterpillarlike or grublike larvae; the adult has mouth parts for sucking.

direct combination. The formation of a compound by the direct union of its elements; example, $Zn + S \rightarrow ZnS$.

direct current (dc). The flow of electrons in one direction only along a conductor.

direct dye. Dye which is effective without the use of a mordant.

direct illumination. A system in which at least 90% of the light is directed downward.

directional gyro. A free gyroscope operated by air which holds its position in azimuth and thus indicates angular deviation from the course.

directional stability. The stability of an aircraft with reference to rotations about the normal axis.

direct-vision prism. A prism cemented together from two pieces of different dispersion; it disperses but does not deviate the light passing through it.

direct-vision spectroscope. A spectroscope containing a direct-vision prism; it is suitable only for approximate observation.

disaccharide. A double sugar which gives two simple sugars by hydrolysis; example, sucrose.

discharge. (1) The removal of charge from a capacitor; (2) the passage of electric current through a gas; (3) the volume of fluid flowing through a given cross section in unit time; (4) a substance ejected from the body.

discharge key. A device for suddenly switching from the connections of a condenser to the charging circuit to a circuit through which it is discharged.

discharge, submerged. A discharge of a liquid below the free surface of a container as opposed to surface discharge.

discontinuous spectrum. A spectrum consisting of separate lines that correspond to different wave lengths.

discriminator. (1) A circuit which changes a frequency-modulated signal into an amplitude-modulated signal; (2) an automatic mechanism in the metering apparatus of electrical supply which disconnects one meter and connects another, according to the demand.

disintegration. (1) The emission of an alpha or beta particle by a radioactive atom; (2) pulverization; (3) a breakdown of the filament in an electric bulb due to ejection of particles which causes the blackening of the inner surface of the bulb.

disk flower. The inner cluster of florets in a composite flower head, each floret having very

small petals or none; each disk flower develops a small dry fruit.

dislocation. (1) A displacement of units in the perfect configuration of a crystal lattice; (2) an abnormal displacement of one bone from a joint.

disperse system. A colloidal solution having two phases separated by a relatively large surface.

dispersed phase. The dispersed or suspended substance in a colloidal solution or suspension; it corresponds to the solute of a solution.

dispersing agent. A chemical which promotes the formation of a colloidal solution.

dispersing medium. The medium in which a colloid is dispersed; it corresponds to the solvent of a solution.

dispersing system. A system used to separate various wave lengths of radiant energy.

dispersion. (1) The separation of colors (different wave lengths) when white light is refracted by a lens or prism; (2) solid particles suspended in a liquid.

dispersion, electrical. The preparation of colloidal solutions by means of an electric current.

dispersion of light. The splitting of light of mixed wave-lengths into a spectrum.

dispersivity. Differential refractivity; the difference in refractivity of a medium for various wave lengths of radiant energy.

dispersoid. A highly dispersed colloidal suspension; example, an emulsion.

displacement. (1) The weight of water displaced by a ship when floating; (2) the mass of air displaced by a gas in a balloon; (3) the volume swept out by the piston face in a piston-and-cylinder mechanism; (4) a chemical change by which an element takes the place of another element in a compound.

displacement adsorption. Displacement from a surface of one adsorbed substance by another.

displacement current. Maxwell's name for a current in a dielectric due to variation of the electric flux through it; it is not connected with motion of charges in the dielectric.

displacement law. The emission of an α particle causes shifting two places to the left and the emission of a β particle causes shifting one place to the right in the periodic table.

dissected plateau. A plateau divided into hills and ridges by gorges or valleys.

dissecting pan. A wax-lined pan to hold the specimen while dissecting it.

dissimilation. Catabolism; destructive metabolism; a disintegration principally by oxidation.

dissipation of energy. The transformation of energy into unavailable forms, such as low-grade heat.

dissipative force. A force which opposes motion and whose action converts mechanical into thermal energy.

dissociation. (1) The separation of an electrovalent compound into its ions; example, sodium chloride when fused or dissolved in water separates into Na^+ and Cl^-; (2) reversible splitting of a molecule into simpler molecules; example, $NH_4Cl \rightleftarrows NH_3 + HCl$.

dissociation constant. The ratio of the product of the active masses of·molecules resulting from a dissociation to the active mass of the undissociated molecules at equilibrium.

dissociation continuum. A continuous absorption spectrum corresponding to a dissociation.

dissolve. To prepare a homogeneous solution of a solid in a liquid; example, sugar or salt dissolved in water.

dissonance. (1) Musical discord; (2) formation of maxima and minima by the superposition of two sets of interference fringes from light of two different wave lengths.

distal. Situated away from; farthest from the attachment point; example, a blood vessel away from the heart.

distance, geocentric. Distance from the earth's center.

distance, heliocentric. Distance from the sun.

distance receptor. Exteroceptor responding to distant stimuli; it permits the orientation of animals and the perception of distant objects.

distillate. The substances collected by condensing the vapors in a distillation process.

distillation. Evaporating a liquid and then condensing the vapors in order to obtain a pure substance; example, fresh water from salt water.

distillation, fractional. Separation of a mixture of liquids by distillation, according to their boiling points.

distilled water. A water from which the dissolved substances have been removed by distillation; used in the laboratory; not suitable for human consumption.

distilling flask. A round flask with a long neck and a side arm, just below the top of the neck; used in the laboratory.

distortion. (1) A change in the wave form in the transmission of a composite wave over a communication line, in which different component frequencies are transmitted at different speeds, or with unequal attenu-

ation; (2) imperfection in an optical image, due to spherical aberration or similar defects of the optical system.

distributary. An additional outlet as the delta becomes large and the main stream overflows; a branch flowing away from the main stream.

distributed capacitance. The capacitance of a radio coil which is the sum of the small capacitances distributed among its parts.

distribution. (1) The tendency of a solute to distribute in equilibrium concentration between the two phases of a mixture of immiscible or partially miscible solvents at a constant temperature; (2) geographical arrangement of living things on the earth's surface, which is determined by the relations of environmental conditions to inherited adaptation.

distribution coefficient. Partition coefficient; the constant ratio of the equilibrium concentrations of a solute dissolved in two immiscible liquids which are in contact in the same container.

distribution law. In a dineric solution, the ratio of the concentrations of the solute in the two solvents is independent of the quantity of solute.

distributor. (1) A device in the ignition system of an engine, which distributes with correct timing the high-tension current to the spark plugs; (2) a rotary electrical switch used to distribute electric current from one source to a number of separate circuits.

disturbance. (1) A local departure from the normal or average wind conditions; (2) signals coming from an unwanted source; example, statics.

diurnal variation. Atmospheric changes occurring during an average day.

divalent. Having the valency of 2.

divergence. Continuous departure of a body from its original state of motion, after having been disturbed from equilibrium.

divergent. Spreading in different directions from a common path or point.

divergent lens. A concave lens; a lens which causes a parallel beam of light passing through it to spread out.

diverticulum. (1) A blind-end tubular or saclike extension of a body cavity; (2) a protrusion of the mucous membrane of the colon through the muscular wall.

divide. A watershed; a region of high land that separates one drainage system from another; example, Great Divide.

dividing engine. A mechanism operated by a long micrometer screw for graduating instru-

mental scales.

dizygotic twins. Twins developed from two zygotes.

dkm. Abbreviation for dekameter.

dm. Abbreviation for decimeter.

DNA (deoxyribonucleic acid). A nucleic acid found only in the chromosomes; metabolically stable, once synthesized it is not easily broken down; thought to be the primary substance involved in heredity.

doldrum belt. An equatorial region of the ocean where calms prevail.

doldrums. The zone of greatest heat and light winds near the equator; a belt of calms.

dolerite. A basaltic rock occurring as dikes or sills.

dolichocephalic. Long-headed; having a cephalic index less than 70.

dolomite. Light-colored pearly, crystalline mineral; calcium magnesium carbonate, $CaCO_3·MgCO_3$; it resembles calcite; used in refractories.

doma. A primitive crystalline form consisting of two plane surfaces forming a dihedral angle, which is bisected by a third plane surface.

domain theory. A theory of magnetism, according to which ferromagnetic materials are composed of many tiny magnets or domains.

dome. (1) A dome-shaped anticline; example, Ozark dome; in oil-rich regions, a dome points to the presence of oil; (2) roof-like crystal form, in which two inclined faces meet in an edge.

dominance. The prevalence of a certain species in a plant community.

dominant. (1) Said of the most characteristic species in a plant community; (2) an inheritable condition or trait which prevails in the offspring over its opposite or recessive trait.

dominant wave length. The wave length of monochromatic light, which matches a color when combined in suitable proportions with a reference standard light.

donor. (1) An animal from which a graft is taken; (2) an individual who provides blood for transfusion; (3) the atom that furnishes the two electrons for a semipolar bond.

Doppler effect. The change in the pitch of sound or the color of light due to the rapid change in the distance between the source and the observer.

Doppler's principle. To an observer approaching the source of any wave motion, the frequency appears greater than to an observer moving away from it.

dormancy. The state of quiescence characteristic of seeds before germination.

dormant. Quiet or resting; examples, the pupa stage of an insect and the overwintering of trees.

dormant volcano. An inactive volcano which still shows some signs of activity, such as escaping steam.

dorsal fin. A fin or fins along the top mid-line of the body of a fish or other aquatic vertebrate; it may be spiny, with hard rays ending in sharp spines, or soft and lacking spines.

dorsal lamina. In the tunicates, a ciliated ridge along the middle line of the dorsal wall of the pharynx.

dorsal lip. A part of the rim of plastospore, corresponding to the future dorsal side, in amphibian embryo.

dorsal root. A nerve root of vertebrates containing sensory fibers.

dorsal suture. The line of a carpel corresponding to the midrib of the floral leaf.

dorsiventral leaf. A leaf showing differences in the structure of the upper and lower sides.

dot map. A map used in statistics on which each dot represents a definite number or quantity.

double bond. Two valency bonds linking two atoms in a chemical compound; characteristic of an unsaturated compound; two pairs of electrons are shared; example, ethylene, $CH=CH$.

double decomposition. A chemical reaction in which atoms or groups of two different compounds exchange places forming two new compounds.

double fertilization. The union of one sperm nucleus with the true egg to form a zygote and of the other sperm nucleus with the double nucleated cell of the embryo sac to form the endosperm nucleus.

double radial engine. An engine having two rows of cylinders arranged radially around a common crankshaft. The corresponding front and rear cylinders may or may not be in line.

double recessive. An individual which is homozygous for a particular recessive gene.

double refraction. Forming two refracted rays of light from a single incident ray; a property of most crystals; example, calcite.

double salt. (1) A compound with two different positive ions; example, Rochelle salt, $NaKC_4H_4O_6$; (2) a salt formed by molecular combination of two different salts.

double star. Two stars so close together that to the unaided eye they look like one.

double-contact lamp. A lamp whose base has two bottom terminals which make contact when the lamp is inserted in the socket.

double-filament lamp. A lamp which has two filaments, only one of which is lighted at a time. The filaments may be of the same or of different resistances, giving the same or different candle power.

double-image prism. A prism which consists of two wedges of doubly refracting crystals fitted together to form a rectangular block or prism and which divides the beam coming from the object into two parts plane-polarized at right angles; example, Wollaston prism.

doublet. (1) Two electrons which are shared by two atoms so as to form a nonpolar valence bond; (2) two associated spectrum lines characteristic of alkali metals.

Dow process. The preparation of magnesium metal by electrolysis of dehydrated, fused magnesium chloride.

down feathers. Feathers which insulate the body of a bird against rapid loss of heat; it is the plumage of newly hatched birds.

down-draft carburetor. A carburetor in which the air enters at the top and travels downward past the spray nozzle.

downwash. The air deflected perpendicularly to the direction of motion of an airfoil.

downwash angle. The angle through which the lifting surface of an airplane deflects the airstream.

draft. The depth of water a ship draws.

drag. (1) The resistance offered by a fluid to the motion of a body; (2) the resultant of the air force measured along the longitudinal axis of an airplane; (3) the lower half of a foundry casting mold.

drag axis. An imaginary line through the center of gravity of an airplane parallel to the relative wind.

drag effect. The reduced freedom of an ion to move in an electrical field, because of interionic attraction by ions of opposite charge surrounding a given ion.

drag strut. A fore-and-aft compression member of the internal bracing structure of an aircraft wing.

drainage area. Catchment area; the land drained by a river system.

Dreikanter. A three-faced pebble.

drier. A catalyst added to paint to speed up the oxidation of drying oils and thus the drying of the paint; examples, lead naphthenate and cobalt oleate.

drift. (1) The side speed or departure laterally from the normal course of an aircraft due to air currents; (2) deposits transported by a glacier; (3) a copper bar used as a punch.

drift angle. The horizontal angle between the longitudinal axis of an aircraft and its path over the ground; the angular deviation of an airplane from its normal course due to cross winds.

drift currents. Same as drifts.

drift meter. An instrument which measures the drift angle, that is, the angle between the longitudinal axis of an aircraft and its path over the ground.

drift plain. A plain where glacial deposition predominated.

drift speed. The mean speed with which electrons or ions move through a medium where they are continually colliding.

drifts. Currents that spread out and lose their velocity as they move to the margins of polar oceans and then eastward to the eastern shore of the ocean in which they have their origin; slow movement of surface water at about two miles per hour.

drizzle. A light rain of very small liquid droplets whose diameter is less than 0.5 mm.

drone. The male of social bees.

dropping bottle. A flask used for dispensing small quantities of liquids in the laboratory, which is so constructed that a liquid can be poured out from it drop by drop.

drop-weight method. Measuring the surface tension of a liquid by determining the weight of a drop that falls from a small tube of known cross section.

dross. The scum, consisting of metallic oxides, that floats on top of a molten metal.

droughts. Prolonged periods of dry weather.

drum armature. A dynamo or motor armature having a drum winding.

drum winding. Winding of the conductor under the outer surface of the armature of an electrical machine.

drumlin. An oval-shaped hill that looks like an inverted canoe which was formed by the clumping of the ground moraine under the ice.

drupe. A fleshy fruit with a stone which contains the seed; example, peach.

druse. (1) A cavity, usually in a sedimentary rock, whose walls are encrusted with minerals which have been derived, through underground solution, from the rocks in which the cavities are formed; (2) in some plant cells, a globular aggregate of calcium oxalate crystals around living matter.

dry battery. An electric battery made up of a number of dry voltaic cells.

dry cell. A primary electric cell, having a pasty rather than a liquid electrolyte; example, the

flash-light battery.

dry steam. A supersaturated steam which contains no entrained moisture.

drying agent. A hygroscopic substance which absorbs the moisture content of the substance to be dried; examples, calcium chloride and concentrated sulfuric acid; used in desiccators.

drying tube. A tube filled with a hygroscopic substance, such as calcium chloride; used to dry and purify gases.

dual ignition. (1) An ignition system which has two sources of current, such as a battery and a magneto, and uses the same set of spark plugs; (2) an ignition system which has two spark plugs which fire simultaneously for each cylinder.

duct. A tubelike passageway within a plant or animal.

ductile. Capable of being drawn out into a wire.

ductless gland. A gland that has no duct or tube and from which the secretion diffuses directly into the blood stream.

ductus Cuvieri. Cuvierian duct; one of two large veins leading to the heart in lower vertebrates.

Dulong and Petit's law. For a solid element, the product of the atomic weight and the specific heat is a constant and approximately equal to 6.4 calories.

Dumas' bulb. An apparatus, built on the principle of the pycnometer, for measuring the densities of vapors and thus, indirectly, their molecular weights.

dune. A mound or ridge of loose sand heaped up by the wind, especially in deserts.

duodenum. That part of the small intestine which is nearest the stomach.

duolateral coil. A honeycomb coil; a coil which has its conductors wound in a crisscrossed fashion so as to reduce winding capacitance.

duotriode. Two triodes in a single envelope.

duplet. A pair of electrons that is shared by two atoms and that corresponds to a covalent bond.

duplex carburetor. A carburetor which has a double venturi for mixture distribution; used in automobiles.

duplex pump. A direct-acting pump which has two working cylinders arranged side by side.

duplication. The union of a chromosome fragment with a whole chromosome of the same type.

dura mater. A firm connective tissue covering the brain and spinal cord of vertebrates and containing blood vessels; one of the meninges.

duration of vision. Persistence of vision; the persistence of the

image of an object formed on the retina of the eye for 1/20th to 1/16th of a second after the removal of the object; this makes motion pictures possible.

dust core. A powder core; a magnetic core composed of metal, especially molybdenum, powder bound together by a suitable binder; the small size of particles allows the cores to be used at much higher frequencies than otherwise possible.

dust devil. A whirlwind over sandy areas which picks up dust and sand, swirling them upward to a height of 3000 feet.

dust explosion. An explosion resulting from the ignition of flammable dust suspended in the air, particularly within a confined space; example, coal-dust explosion.

dust mulch. A layer of dry dust maintained over the soil surface during the dry season by cultivation to prevent evaporation of water.

dust or sand storm. Strong winds which have picked up considerable dust or sand over dusty, dry, or desert areas and carried it to considerable heights; they are usually preceded by a dust wall which may reach a height of several thousand feet.

dust-cloud theory. One of the theories to explain the origin of the solar system.

Dutch process. The stack process for making white lead in which lead plates or scrap are placed in vessels containing dilute acetic acid, and the stacked vessels are left in fermenting tanbark or manure for two or three months.

dwarf star. Star of low luminosity.

Dy. Chemical symbol for dysprosium.

dyad. An element having a valency of two; one half of a tetrad group of chromosomes which go to one pole at meiosis.

dye. A dyestuff; an aromatic staining or coloring matter with chromophore and auxochrome groups; used for dyeing fibers and fabrics.

dynamic allotropy. A reversible transition from one form into another with no definite transition temperature.

dynamic cooling. Lowering of the temperature of the air caused by its expansion in moving to a higher altitude or another region of lower pressure.

dynamic equilibrium. An equilibrium in a system in which two opposing processes are proceeding at the same rate; example, the equilibrium in a reversible chemical reaction.

dynamic factor. The ratio between the load carried by an aircraft when accelerating and the corresponding basic load.

dynamic load. A load due to the acceleration of an aircraft; it is proportional to the mass of the aircraft.

dynamic microphone. A moving-coil microphone; a microphone operating by electromagnetic induction.

dynamic pressure. (1) The product: $\frac{1}{2}\rho V^2$ where ρ is the density of the air, and V is its relative speed; (2) the pressure that a moving fluid would attain if it were brought to rest by an isentropic flow up a pressure gradient.

dynamic speaker. An electrodynamic loudspeaker or moving-coil loudspeaker in which a movable voice coil carrying the audio-frequency current is attached to a diaphragm.

dynamic stability. Tendency of an airplane to return to its steady motion after it has been disturbed during flight.

dynamics. A branch of mechanics that deals with forces and the motion they produce.

dynamo. A device used to convert mechanical energy into electrical energy.

dynamometer. An instrument for measuring force, such as the muscular power of men or animals, which consists of a spring or a weight combined with a scale on which the effort is indicated; example, a spring balance.

dynamotor. A rotary transformer; a double-armature rotating electrical machine.

dynatron. A triode or tetrode in which the grid and plate potentials are so chosen that the plate current decreases as the plate potential increases.

dyne. The cgs unit of force, defined as the force which, acting on a free mass of one gram, imparts to it an acceleration of one centimeter per second per second; it is equal to 1/980 gram.

dynetric balancing. An electronic method of balancing rotating parts.

dysprosium. A very magnetic rare-earth metal; chemical symbol Dy; atomic number 66.

dystectic mixture. A mixture of two or more solids that has a constant maximum melting point.

E

E. Symbol for electromotive force.

ear. (1) The sense organ of hearing; it consists of the outer, middle, and inner ear; (2) a projection on a wire, metal pipe, or structural member; used for support or attachment.

ear, inner. The labyrinth, which is connected by the auditory nerve to the brain.

ear, middle. The cavity between the eardrum and the auditory capsule, which is connected to the pharynx by the Eustachian tube and is filled with air.

ear ossicle. One of the three small bones in the middle ear which connect the eardrum with the inner ear.

eardrum. The tympanic membrane lying between the middle ear and the canal of the outer ear; it transmits vibrations to the small bones of the middle ear.

early prophase. A stage in mitosis in which chromatin ribbons begin to form.

Earnshaw theorem. It states that an electric charge cannot be in a stable equilibrium in an electric field unless acted on by forces other than those due to the field.

earth. The third planet from the sun in the solar system; its mass is 5.98×10^{27} grams; its polar diameter is 7900 miles.

earth indicator. A large coil, whose sudden rotation in the earth's magnetic field causes a surge of electricity and thus is a means of measuring the intensity of the field.

earth science. The study of weather, climate, local rock formations, mineral resources, soils, natural vegetation and animal life, and the presence and absence of water bodies.

earthquake. Shaking of a portion of the earth's crust, probably due to slipping of rock strata.

earth's crust. The lithosphere; the outer layer of surface soil lying on top of a mass of hard rock, several miles thick.

earth's gravity. Terrestrial gravitation; gravitational acceleration toward the center of the earth.

earthshine. The sunlight reflected from the earth which lights up slightly the dark portion of the moon so that at new moon, the entire disk of the moon is faintly visible.

ebb. Low tide; the return of the tidal wave to the ocean.

ebullioscope. An instrument for determining the molecular weight of a substance from the boiling-point elevation of its solution.

ecad. A plant showing nonheritable characteristics imposed by habitat conditions.

eccentric. A wheel that rotates about a point which is not its center; it is used to change circular motion into reciprocating motion or vice versa.

eccentricity. Throw; the deviation of the center of a body from the axis about which it turns.

ecdysis. Shedding of the cuticle by Arthropoda.

ecesis. Adjustment to a new habitat of colonizing plants.

echelette. A coarse diffraction grating ruled on metal to resemble a reflecting echelon of very small steps.

echelon grating. A high-resolution interferometer, similar to a set of glass steps; used in spectroscopy.

Echinodermata. Radially symmetrical marine animals with spiny, skinned exoskeleton; examples, starfish and sea lillies.

Echinoidea. A class of Echinodermata; their body is globular or heart-shaped and spiny; they have a fully developed skeleton; example, sea urchins.

echo. (1) Sound waves which are reflected from a smooth surface; (2) a disturbance in radio caused by the reception of a signal in addition to and later than the expected signal.

echo depth sounding. Determination of the depth of the ocean underneath the bottom of a ship, based on the delay in the arrival of an echo as compared to a direct sound wave.

echo, flutter. A multiple echo between parallel surfaces which are so far from each other that the individual echoes can be distinguished.

echo ranging. Sonar; sound navigation ranging; a device for the detection of underwater objects, such as mines and submarines, through high-frequency vibrations reflected by them.

eclipse. Stepping of a nonluminous body in the shadow of another.

eclipse, annular. A partial eclipse of the sun, in which the apparent diameter of the sun is greater than that of the moon, so that a ring of the surface of the sun is visible at the moment of eclipse.

eclipse of the moon. Lunar eclipse; an eclipse occurring when the shadow of the earth falls on the moon.

eclipse of the sun. Solar eclipse; an eclipse occurring when the shadow of the moon falls on the earth.

eclipsing binary. A double star whose orbit plane lies so nearly in the line of sight of the observer that the components undergo mutual eclipse.

ecliptic. The apparent path of the sun in the sky relative to the stars; the circle described by the sun on the celestial sphere in the course of a year.

eclogite. A coarse, granular rock composed chiefly of garnet and pyroxene.

ecology. The science that deals with the relations between plants and animals and their environment.

economic botany. Applied botany; a study of the utilization of plants to cover human needs and of products of vegetable origin, such as fibers, wood, drugs, rubber, etc.

economic geology. A study of mineral resources and engineering applications of geology.

economic speed. The speed at which fuel consumption is at a minimum for a given distance covered in still air by an aircraft.

ecospecies. A group of plants comprising one or more ecotypes within a coenospecies that can reproduce among themselves and not lose any fertility in the offspring.

ecotype. A group of plants within a species that are adapted genetically to a particular habitat.

ectocommensal. An organism that lives on the external surface of another organism without injuring it.

ectoderm. The outer layer of the cells of the gastrula, from which the epidermis, hair, nails, enamel of teeth, nervous system, and sense organs develop.

ectoneural system. Part of the nervous system of echinoderms which forms a plexus under the ectoderm and a radial nerve along each arm.

ectoparasite. A parasite that lives on the outside of another organism; example, flea.

ectoplasm. The layer of grainless, clear cytoplasm nearest the surface of a cell.

Ectoprocta. A group of small, colonial aquatic animals having the anus outside the tentacles; it is considered as a class of Polyzoa; example, sea mats.

ectosarc. Ectoplast; the outer layer of protoplasm of a protozoan.

ectotrophic mycorrhiza. A higher plant associated with a fungus, in which the mycelium of the fungus forms the external covering of the root of the higher plant.

edaphic factors. The physical, chemical, and biological characteristics of the soil which affect plant growth.

eddy current. A current induced in a conductor, for example, in the core of an armature of a motor, dynamo, or transformer, by changes in the magnetic field.

eddy-current loss. The power loss in electrical apparatus which is caused by eddy currents.

Edentata. Primitive placental mammals without teeth or with underdeveloped teeth; examples, sloth and armadillo.

edge effect. The abnormal behavior of an electric field due to a charge on the sharp edge of a conductor.

Edison battery. A nickel-iron alkaline storage battery in which the positive plate consists of perforated tubes filled with nickel oxide and nickel flake, while the negative electrode is formed by perforated tubes filled with iron; potassium hydroxide is used as electrolyte.

Edison effect. The current that flows between one of the terminals of the filament and an electrode placed in the bulb of an incandescent lamp.

eff. Symbol for efficiency.

effective atomic radius. One half of the distance between the atoms in a valence bond.

effective conductance. The ratio of the energy component of a current to the total electromotive force in an alternating-current circuit.

effective helix angle. The angle of the helix described by a particular point on a propeller blade as the airplane moves forward through air otherwise undisturbed.

effective propeller thrust. The net driving force developed by a propeller when mounted on an aircraft.

effective resistance. The resistance of a conductor to a periodic, or alternating, current, measured by the ratio of the total dissipation to the square of the effective current.

effector. An organ or structure that responds to a stimulus; examples, a gland, a muscle.

efferent. Leading away from; said of arteries, nerves.

effervescence. The rapid escape of gas bubbles from a liquid as a result of supersaturation or a chemical reaction.

efficiency. (1) The ratio of useful work accomplished to the total work expended, which is the measure of the performance of a machine; (2) the ratio of the total light emitted by a source to the fuel or power consumed.

efflorescence. (1) The loss of water of crystallization when a crystalline substance is exposed to air; as a result the crystal changes partly or fully to an amorphous powder; (2) the flowering period of plants; (3) a fine crystalline deposit on mineral surfaces.

effort arm. The distance from the point where the effort is exerted to the fulcrum of a lever.

effusiometer. An instrument which measures the rate of effusion of gases from a small orifice to determine their comparative molecular weights.

effusion. The passage of gases through small apertures under pressures; the relative rates of effusion of different gases under the same conditions are inversely proportional to the square roots of their densities.

egg apparatus. Three cells, the egg cell and two sterile cells, at the micropylar end of the embryo sac.

egg cell. Ovum; a female gamete.

egg membrane. A protective membrane which surrounds an animal egg.

eigen energy. Proper energy; the quantity of energy corresponding to the actual atomic state; it is equal to the product of the mass and the square of the electromagnetic constant.

eikonometer. A scale, attached to the eyepiece of a microscope, used to measure the dimensions of the objects viewed, the scale being superimposed on the image.

Einstein shift. A slight shift toward the red in the spectral lines of the sun due to its strong gravitational field.

Einstein-De Haas method. Measuring the gyromagnetic effect by reversing the magnetization of a freely suspended specimen and observing the resulting rotation.

einsteinium. Chemical symbol Es; atomic number 99.

ejaculatory duct. Ductus ejaculatorius; the portion of the male genital duct which is between the duct of the seminal vesicle and the urethra.

elaioplast. A minute body in the cytoplasm of some cells; it is assumed to be a form of plastid about which fat is deposited.

Elasmobranchii. Fishlike vertebrates with true jaws, having a skeleton of cartilage and no scales; examples, rays and sharks.

elastance. The reciprocal of the capacitance of a condenser, measured in darafs.

elastic aftereffect. The persistence of a strain, though gradually diminishing, after the stress has been removed from an elastic body.

elastic collision. An encounter between moving bodies or particles under ideal conditions, so that their total kinetic energy is the same after the impact as it was before.

elastic curve. The curve assumed by the longitudinal axis of a structural member when subjected to loads which cause bending within its elastic limits.

elastic fatigue. Slow return to the original form after deformation.

elastic limit. The maximum value of deforming force that does not cause permanent set.

elastic modulus. Young's modulus; the ratio of the stress to the strain in a given material; the ratio of the stretching force per unit cross section to the elongation per unit length; it is expressed in dynes per square centimeter.

elastic scattering. Scattering by elastic impact, that is, without loss of kinetic energy.

elastic strength. The greatest stress a substance is capable of sustaining within its elastic limit.

elasticity. The property of a body to resist deformation and recover its original shape and size after removal of the deforming force.

elasticity of compression. Elasticity of bulk; elasticity of volume of a body under the effect of pressure; example, the behavior of a rubber ball when squeezed.

elasticity of extension. Elasticity of elongation; returning to the original length after the stretching force ceases; example, the behavior of a rubber band when stretched.

elasticity of flexure. A tendency to straighten out on bending; example, the behavior of a strip of steel on bending.

elasticity of torsion. The elasticity of a coiled spring.

elastin. Highly extensible and elastic protein fibers found in vertebrate connective tissues.

elastomer. A rubberlike substance that can be stretched to several times its length and that, on release of the stress, returns rapidly to almost its original length; example, a synthetic rubber.

elastometer. An instrument for the measurement of elasticity.

elater. (1) A rubberlike appendage found in Equisetum, which is attached to the mature asexual spore; (2) elongated, spindle-shaped, sterile, hygroscopic cells in the capsule of liverworts; sporophytes.

electret. A dielectric which has a permanent magnetic moment.

electric arc furnace. A furnace heated by an electric arc between two carbon electrodes or between a carbon electrode and the metallic charge of the furnace.

electric breakdown. The passage of current through an insulating material due to excessive voltage (breakdown voltage).

electric cell. A device for changing chemical energy to electrical energy; it consists of two metallic electrodes and an electrolyte, usually an acid.

electric charge. The quantity of electricity on a body; an excess or deficiency of electrons.

electric current. A constant flow of electrons through a conductor.

electric density. The quantity of electricity per unit volume in any part of a space charge, or the charge per unit area of a surface.

electric dipole. A pair of electric charges, equal in size but opposite in sign and very close together.

electric discharge. The flow of electricity through an ionized gas.

electric eye. A photoelectric or photovoltaic cell.

electric field. An electrostatic field; the region near an electric charge, in which a force is exerted on a charged particle.

electric induction. The effect of a charged body on a conductor placed next to it; the conductor becomes charged due to redistribution of the electricity.

electric intensity. The force acting on a positively charged particle when placed in an electric field; electric force per unit charge.

electric motor. A machine for transforming electrical energy into mechanical power.

electric oscillation. An alternating current having a natural frequency dependent on the nature of the resonant circuit.

electric osmosis. Electroosmosis; the movement of a liquid through a diaphragm between two electrodes.

electric polarization. (1) Reduction of the electromotive force of primary cells due to the deposition of products of the electrolysis on the electrodes; (2) the effect of an electric field on a dielectric, which consists in a slight movement of the positive charge of each atom toward the electric force.

electric potential. The work necessary at a point to bring a unit positive electrical charge from an infinite distance to that point.

electric power. The ability of doing work by electricity, measured in watts and kilowatts; watts = volts × amperes.

electric pyrometer. A sensitive pyrometer for exact temperature measurements; it utilizes the change in the electrical resistance of platinum when heated.

electric screening. Completely surrounding any object or region by a closed metallic shield or casing, in order to exclude all extraneous electrostatic influence.

electric spark. An electric discharge, accompanied by light and sound, through a dielectric or insulator.

electric strength. The maximum voltage that can be applied to a dielectric or insulating material without breakdown.

electric wave. An electromagnetic wave; a hertzian wave; the waves used in radio communication.

electrical attraction. The force between electric charges of opposite sign, having a magnitude given by Coulomb's law.

electrical axis. The axis of a crystal which offers minimum resistance to the passage of current.

electrical balance. The condition of a bridge circuit when so adjusted that an electromotive force in one branch produces no current in the conjugate branch; example, Wheatstone bridge.

electrical capacity altimeter. An altimeter whose indications depend on the variation of an electrical capacity with the distance from the earth's surface.

electrical conductivity. The relative power of different substances of carrying an electric current, the conducting power of pure copper being taken as a standard.

electrical image. A set of point charges on one side of a conducting surface which would produce a similar electric field on the other side of the surface.

electrical resonance. The maximum flow of current in a circuit resulting when an impressed frequency corresponds to the natural frequency of the circuit.

electricity. A form of energy which is due to the orientation and movement of electrons.

electricity, frictional. Electric charges which result from rubbing together different insulating materials; example, glass and fur.

electricity, static. Electricity at rest; it is generated by mechanical means, such as friction, impact, etc.

electrification. (1) Charging a body electrically; adding electrons to or removing electrons from a body; (2) providing with electricity or changing to electrical operation.

electrified body. A body that has a plus or minus charge of electricity.

electrocapillarity. The effect of an electric current on the equilibrium of the interface between two liquids in a capillary tube, consisting apparently of a modification of the surface tension.

electrochemical change. Chemical change caused by an electric current.

electrochemical equivalent. The weight in grams of a substance deposited during electrolysis by a current of one ampere in one second.

electrochemical series. Electromotive series; elements arranged in the order of their increasing electrode potentials.

electrochemistry. A study of the mutual relations between electrical energy and chemical change.

electrode. The terminal by which a current leaves or enters an electrolytic cell; the anode and cathode.

electrode, control. An electrode on which a voltage is impressed to vary the current flowing between two or more other electrodes.

electrode dissipation. The power dissipated in the form of heat by an electrode as a result of electron and/or ion bombardment.

electrode, gas. An electrode consisting of a gas adsorbed on a surface.

electrode, glass. A thin glass plate, separating a solution of known pH from another solution whose pH is to be determined.

electrode potential. The potential of a metal in equilibrium with a solution of its ions.

electrode, self. An electrode made of the same material as that being analyzed in emission spectroscopy.

electrode, supporting. An electrode in emission spectroscopy in which the sample is supported.

electrodeless discharge. A luminous discharge in a gas confined in a closed tube without electrodes, due to a rapidly alternating electric field outside the tube wall or to the inductive action of the current in a neighboring high-frequency circuit.

electrodeposition. Depositing one metal on another by making them the electrodes in a solution of a salt of the metal to be deposited.

electrodialysis. The separation of an electrolyte from a colloid by dialysis under the effect of an electric current.

electrodynamics. The study of electricity in motion, the effects of electric currents on each other, and the interaction between currents and magnets.

electrodynamometer. An instrument for measuring alternating current by the interaction between a stationary and a moving coil.

electroendosmosis. The flow of a liquid through a porous partition due to a potential difference on the two sides of the partition.

electroforming. The production of metallic articles by electrodeposition.

electrographic effect. The effect of cathode rays on a metal surface, making the metal less sensitive to corrosive vapors and suitable for the production of developable cathode-ray images.

electrokinetics. The science of electricity in motion.

electroluminescence. Luminescence produced by high-frequency electrical discharges.

electrolysis. The decomposition of a substance by means of an electric current; example, preparation of hydrogen and oxygen from water.

electrolysis, Faraday's laws of. (1) The chemical change effected by a current is proportional to the quantity of electricity which passes; (2) the weights of substances liberated or deposited by the same quantity of electricity are proportional to their chemical equivalents.

electrolyte. A compound which ionizes when melted or dissolved and thus becomes a conductor of electricity.

electrolytic capacitor. A capacitor in which the dielectric between the plates is an electrolyte.

electrolytic condenser. A condenser in which one electrode is an aluminum foil coated with a thin layer of aluminum oxide and the other electrode is a salt solution or paste; to prevent removal of the oxide film by the hydrogen set free, the aluminum foil is maintained positive.

electrolytic conduction. The passage of electricity accompanied by the transfer of matter, that is, the migration of ions.

electrolytic copper. High-purity copper refined by electrolysis.

electrolytic dissociation. The separation of a compound into positive and negative ions when dissolved in water or another suitable solvent.

electrolytic gas. Detonating gas; a mixture of hydrogen and oxygen, in a ratio of 2 to 1 by volume, produced by the electrolysis of water.

electrolytic refining. The refining of metals by electrolysis.

electromagnet. A magnet made by a current of electricity passing through a coil of wire wound on a soft-iron core.

electromagnetic balance. Ampere balance; a laboratory instrument which measures a current of two coils by balancing it against a weight sliding on an arm; example, Kelvin balance.

electromagnetic field. The magnetic field surrounding a wire carrying an electric current, whose lines of force are circles with the wire as their axis.

electromagnetic induction. The generation of an electromotive force in a conductor by changes in its magnetic field.

electromagnetic spectrum. A spectrum produced by waves of a few millimeters to several thousands of meters.

electromagnetic units (emu). Units of the cgs system based on the unit magnetic pole which repels a similar pole, placed 1 centimeter away, with a force of 1 dyne.

electromagnetic waves. Transverse waves radiated through space, which are caused by oscillations of electrons or groups of electrons; the collective name for radio, infrared, light, ultraviolet, and cosmic rays, x-rays, etc.

electromagnetics. A study of the mutual relationships existing between electricity and magnetism.

electromagnetism. Magnetic lines of force set up by a current flowing through the turns of a wire wound on an iron core.

electromechanics. The science of machines producing or operated by electricity; examples, generators and motors.

electrometallurgy. The science of the application of electrical processes in metallurgy; examples, electroplating, electroforming.

electrometer. An instrument for measuring potential differences by the attraction or repulsion of charged plates.

electrometer tube. A specially designed thermionic vacuum tube for measuring very small currents.

electromotive force (emf). The force, measured in volts, that causes electrons to flow in an electric circuit; energy derived from the flow of electricity from points of higher potential toward points of lower potential.

electromotive series. An arrangement of the elements in the order of their increasing electrode potentials.

electron. A negatively charged particle which is present in every atom; beta rays consist of free electrons; the mass of an electron at rest is 9.107×10^{-28} and its charge is 4.774×10^{-10} electrostatic unit.

electron affinity. The tendency of an atom or a molecule to attach free electrons and form negative ions.

electron band. A molecular spectrum band due to electron transitions within the molecule.

electron beam. A stream of electrons which move with the same velocity and in the same direction.

electron charge. A state of electrical unbalance, resulting from an excess or a deficiency of electrons, whose magnitude is measured in coulombs.

electron cloud. A large number of relatively stationary electrons in the space between the electrodes of an electron-discharge tube.

electron concentration. The ratio of the number of valence electrons to the number of atoms in a molecule.

electron distribution. The arrangement of electrons in orbits or shells around the nucleus of an atom or an ion.

electron duplet. A pair of electrons which are shared by two atoms, forming a single, nonpolar chemical bond.

electron, extranuclear. An electron moving in an orbit around the nucleus of an atom.

electron, free. An electron which does not remain in the immediate neighborhood of the nucleus of an atom, but moves freely as in beta rays.

electron gas. An aggregation of electrons to which the kinetic theory may be applied.

electron gun. A part of a cathode ray tube, such as the picture tube of a television receiver, that produces, accelerates, and focuses an electron beam.

electron image tube. A cathode-ray tube which increases the brightness or size of an image or produces a visible image from invisible radiation, such as infrared.

electron micrograph. A photograph of an object made under an electron microscope.

electron microscope. A microscope of extremely high power, using beams of electrons instead of rays of light and recording the image on a photographic plate or fluorescent screen.

electron multiplier. A photoelectric cell used for extensive amplification of a photo current; it contains a photo cathode and several auxiliary electrodes of increasing positive potentials, each of which emits more secondary electrons than the number of the incident electrons.

electron, nuclear. An electron emitted from the nucleus of an atom.

electron octet. An electron group or electron shell containing eight electrons.

electron optics. The study and application of those properties of electron beams which are analogous to the properties of light.

electron orbit. The path of an electron in its revolution around the nucleus of an atom.

electron pair. A duplet; two electrons which occupy the same orbit.

electron shell. A group of electrons in the atom, all having the same quantum number.

electron specific heat. That part of the specific heat of a metal which is due to free electrons.

electron tube. A vacuum tube usually containing three elements, a cathode, a grid, and a plate between which electron discharge occurs.

electron, valence. One of the electrons in an incomplete outer shell of an atom; these electrons have the highest principal quantum number and are predominantly responsible for the physical and chemical properties of the atom.

electron volt. The increase in the energy of or work done on an electron when passing through a potential rise of 1 volt; 1.6×10^{-12} erg.

electron wave length. The wave length of a moving electron;

$$\sqrt{\frac{150}{\mu}} \times 10^{-8} \text{ centimeter,}$$

where μ is the velocity of the electron.

electronegativity. The relative property of a given atom or radical to attract and hold valence electrons.

electronic band spectrum. A molecular spectrum in the ultraviolet or visible range; it results from electronic charges in the molecule.

electronic charge. Elementary charge; the natural unit of electric charges; 1.602×10^{-19} coulomb; 4.803×10^{-10} electrostatic unit.

electronic equation. An equation that shows the number of electrons gained or lost by a substance in a reaction.

electronics. The study of free electrons and their applications.

electroosmosis. The movement of liquids through a membrane under the influence of an electromotive force.

electrophonic effect. The sensation of hearing produced when an alternating current of suitable frequency and magnitude from an external source is passed through the body.

electrophoresis. Cataphoresis and anaphoresis; the migration of colloidal particles toward one of the electrodes under the effect of an external electromotive force.

electrophorus. An apparatus consisting of a hard-rubber plate, on which rests a metal plate provided with an insulating handle; used for demonstrating electrostatic phenomena.

electroplating. (1) Depositing one metal on another by electrolysis, a salt of the metal to be deposited being used as the electrolyte; (2) making a wax recording conductive by sputtering or brushing on graphite powder and then coating with copper electrolytically.

electropositive elements. Elements that give up outer electrons readily to form ions.

electroscope. An instrument used for the detection of an electric charge, based on the repulsion between bodies carrying charges of the same sign.

electrosol. A colloidal solution of a metal produced by an arc between electrodes immersed in water.

electrosome. A chondrisome which is assumed to elaborate special chemical compounds.

electrostatic analysis. Separation or sorting by an electric field.

electrostatic field. An electric field produced by stationary charges.

electrostatic generator. An induction machine; a machine for producing high potentials by electrostatic means; example, Wimhurst machine.

electrostatic lens. An arrange-

ment of electrodes whose electric fields produce a focussing effect on a beam of charged particles.

electrostatic units (e.s.u.). A system of electrical units based on the electrostatic unit of charge, that is, the quantity of electricity that exerts a force of one dyne on the same quantity of electricity at a distance of one centimeter.

electrostatics. The study of the phenomena of electricity at rest or of frictional electricity.

electrostriction. The change in the dimensions of a dielectric when placed in an electric field.

electrovalence. The union of atoms in a molecule by the transfer of electrons from one atom to another.

electrovalent compound. Ionic compound; a compound in which the atoms are held together by polar or electrovalent bonds.

electroviscous effect. The change in viscosity of a sol when placed in a strong electrostatic field.

element. A substance which cannot be decomposed into simpler substances by ordinary chemical means.

element, electronegative. An element having a relatively strong attraction for valence electrons; an element carrying a negative charge.

element, electropositive. An element having a relatively weak attraction for valence electrons; an element carrying a positive charge.

element, parent. The heaviest, most complex, naturally occurring element in a disintegration series of radioactive elements.

element, radioactive. A heavy element that disintegrates spontaneously with the emission of various rays and particles.

elementary bodies. Minute intracellular bodies found in lesions produced by some virus.

elements of weather. Temperature, pressure, moisture, clouds, and wind.

elements, rare-earth. A group of chemically very closely related metallic elements which differ in electronic configuration only in the number of electrons in the second from the outside shell; it includes the elements of the following atomic numbers: 21, 39 and 57 to 71.

elements, transition. Elements which differ in electronic configuration only in the number of electrons in an inner electron shell; they are very similar to one another in their chemical and physical properties; example, rare earths.

elevation of boiling point. A rise in the boiling point of a liquid when a nonvolatile substance is dissolved in it.

elevator. A movable auxiliary airfoil whose function is to impress a pitching moment on the aircraft; the elevator is usually hinged to the stabilizer.

elevator angle. The angular displacement of an aircraft elevator from its neutral position; it is positive when its trailing edge is below its neutral position.

ellipse. An oval curve, in which the sum of distances from any point on its circumference to two fixed points, called foci, is constant.

ellipse, eccentricity of. Smaller than 1.

ellipse, major axis of. The maximum diameter of an ellipse.

ellipsoid. A solid figure generated by an ellipse rotating about one of its axes.

elliptic polarization. Polarization in which the cycle is an ellipse.

elliptically polarized light. Light which can be resolved into two vibrations lying in planes at right angles and not in phase.

elongation. (1) An increase in length; (2) a strain which accompanies tension.

elongation, greatest. Maximum apparent angular distance east or west of the sun for a planet interior to the earth's orbit.

elutriation. The separation of particles of different weight by washing and decantation.

elytron. The front wing of an insect, modified to form a leathery or rigid wing cover which folds above the body and conceals the hind wings at rest; example, beetles.

emanation. Radioactive gases resulting from the disintegration of radioactive elements.

embrittlement. An increase in the susceptibility of a metal to fracture under stress caused by various factors, such as gas inclusion, internal oxidation, or corrosion.

embryo. (1) An immature organism formed by the union of a sperm and an egg; a fertilized egg, a zygote; (2) the young plants, alive but inactive in the seed; (3) an animal before birth.

embryo sac. (1) An enlarged megaspore of flowering plants in which fertilization and development of the embryo take place; (2) the inner protoplasm of an ovule which contains the egg or female cell.

embryogeny. The development of an organism; the study of embryonic development.

embryology. The study of the development of embryos.

embryonic region. The area near the tip of a root or stem in which cells are formed by division.

emery. A mixture of corundum, magnetite or hematite, and quartz; used as an abrasive.

emf. Abbreviation for electromotive force.

emission, field. Cold emission; an electron emission from solids or liquids as a result of a high potential gradient at their surface.

emission of radiation. The net rate at which a body radiates heat to its surroundings; it is dependent on the temperature of the body, the temperature of its surroundings, and the nature of the surface of the body.

emission, photoelectric. An electron emission from solids or liquids as a result of bombarding their surface with photons.

emission spectrum. The spectrum of light which comes directly from a source.

emissive power. The energy emitted from the unit area of a surface of a body per second; it is dependent on the temperature of the body and the nature of its surface.

emissivity. The ratio of the emissive power of a body to the emissive power of a perfect black body at the same temperature.

emmetropic eye. A normal eye in which light from a distant object is focused exactly at the retina when the accommodation is entirely relaxed.

empirical formula. A chemical formula which gives the simplest numerical ratio between the atoms in a molecule; example, the empirical formula of benzene is CH, whereas its molecular formula is C_6H_6.

emulsifying agent. Emulsifier; a substance which will help form and maintain an emulsion.

emulsion. A colloidal mixture of two immiscible liquids, one being suspended in the other; example, milk.

emulsoid. A colloidal system in which there is a strong attraction between the dispersed substance and the dispersing liquid.

enamel. (1) The covering layer of the crown of the tooth which is the hardest substance in the body; (2) a vitreous substance fixed on the surface of pottery by firing in a kiln; (3) an oil paint containing finely ground resin.

enantiomorphism. Occurrence of a substance in two crystalline forms, one being a mirror image of the other.

enantiomorphs. Crystals having neither a plane nor a center of symmetry and which cannot be brought into coincidence with their reflected image, that is, they are mirror images of each other.

enantiotropic substance. A substance existing in two different crystal forms, one being stable below the transition tempera-

ture and the other above it.

encysted. Surrounded by a sac.

encystment. The formation of an impermeable protective membrane around an animal.

end brush. End plate; branched endings of the axon through which a stimulus passes into the dendrite of another neuron or into an effector.

end moraine. Terminal moraine; the moraine formed as the front end of a glacier advances.

end organ. A small sensory or motor organ which is composed of peripheral nerve endings and is connected to the central nervous system; example, an end plate.

end point. The end of a titration indicated by color change or formation of a precipitate; the point of neutralization of an acid by a base and vice versa.

end product. (1) The final, nonradioactive element of a radioactive series; (2) in digestion, the simplest compounds into which food is broken down and then absorbed; (3) the final product of the weathering of rocks; examples, sand and clay.

end reaction. (1) A reaction between certain ions which runs to completion due to the removal of the ions from the solution; (2) the last stage in a chemical reaction; example, the appearance of the end point in a titration.

endoblast. Hypoblast; a germinal layer inside the embryo of Metazoa, which produces the endoderm.

endocarp. The usually woody inner layer of a fruit wall.

endocrine glands. Ductless glands which produce hormones.

endocrinology. The study of endocrine glands and of hormones, their production, nature and effects.

endoderm. Hypoblast; (1) the innermost layer of cells in the hollow cup stage of an animal embryo; it forms the lining of the digestive system, the liver, lungs, etc.; (2) the inner layer of cells of a simple animal body.

endodermis. The innermost layer of cortex surrounding the stele in plants.

endoenzyme. An intracellular enzyme retained in the cell and not excreted into the surrounding medium.

endogamy. The pollination between two flowers on the same plant.

endogenetic. Said of rocks formed by solidification of molten matter, sublimation, or coagulation from solution.

endogenic. Said of processes originating within the earth.

endogenous. (1) Said of a plant whose sporulation occurs

within a host; (2) referring to metabolism that builds new or repairs used tissue.

endogeric. Requiring an input of heat or energy.

endometrium. A glandular mucous membrane which lines the uterus of mammals.

endomitosis. Doubling of chromosomes without division of the nucleus, resulting in polyploidy.

endomixis. The reorganization of nuclear material, not involving conjugation, in Protozoa.

endomorphism. Contact metamorphism, involving morphological or chemical changes, which takes place in the intrusive magma rather than in the rock mass which it invades.

endoparasite. A parasite living within the body of its host.

endophragmal skeleton. An internal framework found in some Crustacea which is made up of apodemes derived from the exoskeleton.

endoplasm. The central portion of the cytoplasm of cells.

endopodite. The principal internal branch of a biramous appendage of Crustacea.

Endoprocta. A small group of sedentary aquatic animals, having the anus opening inside the tentacle circlet, which is regarded as a subclass of Polyzoa.

Endopterygota. A subclass of insects in which the adult develops by extensive metamorphosis of the young.

endosarc. The inner mass of protoplasm in a single-celled animal.

endoskeleton. The internal framework of vertebrates covered by flesh.

endosmosis. The inward flow of water into a cell containing an aqueous solution, through a semipermeable membrane, due to osmosis.

endosome. The central mass of the nucleus of some Protozoa, consisting largely of chromatin.

endosperm. A multicellular tissue in a growing seed which serves as food for the embryo; it may develop into the nutritive substance of the ripe seed; example, a corn grain which contains starch and proteins.

endospore. The inside layer of the spore wall.

endostyle. A groove lying in the median line of the ventral wall of the pharynx in the tunicates; it is ciliated and secretes mucus.

endothelium. A cellular membrane that lines the blood vessels, heart, and lymphatic vessels.

endothermic reaction. A chemical reaction in which heat is absorbed.

endotoxin. A toxin retained within the bacterial cell and liberated only after the death

or disintegration of the organism.

endotrophic. Fed from within; example, a mycorrhiza within the cell or root cortex.

-ene. A suffix which denotes an unsaturated hydrocarbon.

energy, activation. Energy required initially to start a reaction.

energy, binding. The energy which holds the protons and neutrons together in the nucleus of an atom.

energy density of sound. The vibration energy per unit volume in a given enclosure at stable distribution of vibrating particles.

energy, disgregation. The energy of a body due to the tendency of its particles to repel each other.

energy, free. The energy of a chemical system which can be converted to useful work outside the chemical reaction.

energy level. A shell; a group of electrons of the same principal quantum number.

energy, luminous. The radiant energy of light which makes objects visible to the eye.

energy, radiant. The energy which is transmitted by electromagnetic waves without a corresponding transfer of matter.

energy, surface. (1) Surface tension; (2) the energy per unit area needed to increase the surface of a solid or a liquid.

energy value of food. The heat energy made available to the body when a given weight of a food is completely oxidized; it is usually measured in calories per pound.

engine. A device which is used to convert heat energy into mechanical work; any energy converter.

engine altimeter. An altimeter for indicating the altitude corresponding to the pressure produced in the intake manifold of a supercharged engine.

engine displacement. The total volume swept by the pistons of all the cylinders during one complete stroke of each piston.

Engler distillation. A laboratory method for the determination of the boiling range of petroleum.

enhanced line. A spectral line, from a spark or other very hot source, whose intensity is out of proportion with that of other lines of an arc or flame spectrum.

enrichment. Natural processes by which the lower levels of a sulfide arc deposit are enriched by valuable metals at the expense of the upper levels, or the original protarc, due to sinking of metal-containing solutions and their reacting with the sulfides.

entelechy. An element which controls the responses to stimuli.

enterokinase. Substance secreted by the small intestine of vertebrates which converts trypsinogen into trypsin.

enterozoa. Animals which have a digestive cavity, the enteric cavity; all animals, but the Protozoa and sponges.

enthalpy. The heat content per unit mass.

entire margin. The continuous margin of a leaf.

entomogenous. Said of fungi parasitic on insects.

entomology. The study of insects.

entomophily. Pollination by insects.

entrenched meander. A river valley which has a distinctly meandering old-age pattern and a V-shaped or canyon-shaped youthful transverse profile.

entropy. The ratio of the amount of heat taken up to the absolute temperature at which the heat is absorbed; a concept used in thermodynamic calculations.

entropy of solution. The heat of solution minus the free energy of the solution.

entropy of vaporization. The increase in the entropy of a substance when it changes from the liquid to the vapor state.

environment. Surroundings; the external conditions which affect the development and existence of living organisms.

environmental variations. Differences in members of the same species due to differences in their environment.

enzyme. A catalyst produced by living cells which changes the rate of chemical reactions; enzymes are specific in their effect; example, protease which is a protein-splitting enzyme and invertase, an enzyme that causes hydrolysis of cane sugar.

Eocene. The oldest subdivision of the Tertiary system.

Eohippus. The ancestor of modern horse which appeared during the early part of the Cenozoic era; it was as large as a cat and had four toes on the front foot and three on the hind foot.

eolian soils. Soils transported and deposited by the wind.

eolith. A stone implement used by early men.

eosin. Tetrabromofluorescein; a red dye; used in dyeing natural textiles and making red ink.

eosinophil leucocyte. A polymorphonuclear leucocyte of vertebrates, which is readily stained by eosin.

epeirogeny. Broad and relatively widespread or continental geological uplift.

ephemeral. A plant with a short life cycle, having several generations in one year.

Ephemerida. An order of slender short-lived insects with large forewings, small hind wings,

and short antennae; example, May flies whose larvae may live a year or longer, but the adult's life span is only a few hours.

ephippium. The thickened covering of the carapace of certain Crustacea, which is thrown off as a case for winter eggs.

ephyra. A saucer-shaped jelly-fish larva with a deeply notched margin.

epiblast. A leaf of the plumule of grasses, a rudimentary second cotyledon.

epiboly. The posterior growth of a fold or the blastoderm over the surface of the embryo in the process of forming the enteron during gastrulation.

epicentrum. The point of the maximum shock of an earthquake which lies directly above its focus.

epicotyl. Plumule; the first true leaves of a plant embryo; they unfold as the seed sprouts.

epicyclic gear. A combination of gears in which one or several wheels move around the outside or inside of another wheel with a stationary axis.

epidermis. The outer layer of the skin made up of epithelial cells; the outermost sheet may consist of dead, horny material, such as nails and hoofs.

epididymis. A long convoluted tube which is attached to the testis of amniote vertebrates and carries sperm into the vas deferens.

epidiorite. Gabbros, dolorites, and diabases, whose augite has been partly converted to hornblende, thus approaching a diorite in mineral composition.

epigamic character. Character of an animal other than gonads which is concerned in sexual reproduction; example, bird song.

epigamic colors. Courtship colors; coloring which is attractive to the opposite sex.

epigeal. (1) The seed leaves appearing above the ground in seed germination; (2) said of animals inhabiting the land surface.

epigenesis. The generally accepted theory that all the differentiated parts of an organism arise from undifferentiated germ cells.

epigenetic. Said of physical and chemical changes in igneous and sedimentary rocks which occurred later than the formation of the original rock.

epiglottis. A flap that covers the entrance to the windpipe during swallowing so that food does not get into the lungs.

epigynum. A plate above the opening of the reproductive duct of the female spider.

epigyny. A condition in which the receptacle surrounds and fuses with the ovary so that other flower parts appear to arise

from the top of the ovary.

epinasty. The more rapid growth of the upper side than of the lower side of a plant organ.

epinephrine. Adrenalin; a hormone secreted by the suprarenal glands; used in medicine as a heart stimulant.

epipetaly. Stamens being borne on and being partly fused with the petals.

epipharynx. A fold on the inner surface of the labrum of the insect mouth.

epiphragm. A tough membrane of calcified mucus with which some snails close the aperture of the shell during periods of dormancy.

epiphysis. The separately ossified ends of growing bones which form a joint.

epiphyte. A plant attached to another plant, not as a parasite but merely using it for support; example, orchids, mosses.

episematic colors. Recognition colors for members of the same species.

epistasis. The masking of one hereditary character by another which is genetically independent.

epistome. A projection above the mouth of some Bryozoa.

epithelium. (1) A layer of long cells lining schizogenously formed secretory canals of plants; example, the resin canals of pine; (2) a sheet or tube of secretory cells with very little intercellular matter; it lines cavities and tubes and covers exposed surfaces of the body.

epitoke. The posterior sexual portion of the body in certain worms.

epizoite. (1) A nonparasitic sedentary animal living attached to another animal; (2) a plant whose seeds are dispersed by animals.

epizootic. An animal epidemic.

epoch. A division of time in the earth's history, smaller than a period.

epoxy resin. A thermosetting synthetic resin.

Epsilon. A designation of the fifth brightest star in a constellation.

equal-energy source. A light source for which the rate of emission of energy per unit wave length is constant throughout the spectrum.

equalizing bar. A low-resistance bar that joins the armature ends of the series field windings of several compound generators which are run in parallel.

equation, chemical. The statement of a chemical change, using symbols of the substances taking part; based on the principle that matter is neither created nor destroyed in the course of a chemical reaction.

equation of state. An equation which connects the pressure, volume, and temperature of a

substance; example, van der Waals' equation.

equation of time. The difference between solar time, as given by a clock, and apparent solar time (sundial time).

equator. (1) An imaginary line encircling the earth midway between the north and south poles; (2) the great circle of the celestial sphere that coincides with the plane of the earth's equator.

equatorial air mass. A tropical air mass which originated in the equator area.

equatorial countercurrent. An eastward moving current between north and south equatorial currents.

equatorial plate. A chromosome setup during the metaphase of mitosis or meiosis in which all chromosomes lie approximately in one plane, at the equator of the spindle.

equatorial telescope. A telescope so mounted that it may be moved parallel to the equatorial coordinates of hour angle and declination.

equilibrium. (1) The state of a body at rest or moving at uniform speed; (2) a state of coordination which maintains an animal in normal posture; (3) a dynamic state in which two opposing processes take place at the same time and at the same rate.

equilibrium, chemical. A state of balance in a reaction, in which the change in one direction is just equal to the change in the opposite direction.

equilibrium constant. The product of the active masses of the substances produced at equilibrium divided by the product of the active masses of the reactants.

equilibrium, heterogeneous. An equilibrium between two or more phases; examples, a solid and a gas; a liquid and its saturated vapor.

equilibrium, homogeneous. An equilibrium in a one-phase, homogeneous system.

equilibrium, ionic. The state of balance attained in a reversible ionization between nonionized molecules in solution and their ions.

equilibrium, isothermal. An equilibrium reached in a process of constant temperature.

equilibrium, metastable. An apparent equilibrium observed because of the extremely low rate of a reaction.

equilibrium point. The external conditions, such as temperature and pressure, at which a system is in equilibrium.

equilibrium potential. The potential difference between an electrolyte and an electrode immersed in it, when they have come to equilibrium.

equilibrium, stable. The equilibrium state of a body whose potential energy is noticeably increased by a small displacement and which will spontaneously return to its equilibrium position.

equilibrium, unstable. The equilibrium state of a body whose potential energy is decreased by a small displacement and which will move further away from its equilibrium position after the displacement.

equimolecular mixture. Mixture which contains substances in equal molecular proportions.

equimomental. Said of two or more bodies which have equal masses and equal moments of inertia about corresponding axes.

equinox. The two points where the sun's center crosses the equator.

equinox, autumnal. The point where the sun's center crosses the equator from north to south; September 23.

equinox, precession of. Slow motion toward the west of the equinoctial points (period: 25,-800 years).

equinox, vernal. The point where the sun's center crosses the equator from south to north; March 21.

equipartition of energy. In any physical system in thermal equilibrium, the average energy per degree of freedom is the same and equals $KT/2$ where K is Boltzmann's constant and T is the absolute temperature of the system.

equipotential. Having the same value of potential throughout.

Equisetum. Horsetails; perennial, herbaceous plants.

equivalent circuit. An electrical circuit which is electrically equivalent to another circuit, or to a mechanical device.

equivalent electrons. Electrons in the same orbital of an atom.

Er. Chemical symbol for erbium.

era. One of the six greatest divisions of the earth's history.

erbium. A rare-earth metal; dark-gray powder; chemical symbol Er; atomic number 68.

erecting prism. Right-angled prism used in optical instruments to make an inverted image become upright.

erepsin. An enzyme of the intestinal juice which breaks down proteins and the products of peptic digestion into polypeptides and amino acid.

erg. A metric unit of work or energy; the equivalent of the work done by one dyne of force acting through one centimeter of distance; 13,582,000 ergs equal 1 foot-pound; 1 erg is equal to $1/1/6 \times 10^{-12}$ electron volt.

ergometer. A dinamometer; an apparatus for measuring used-up energy or work accomplished.

ergosterol. $C_{28}H_{44}O$; a sterol found in plants, yeast, and molds; irradiated by ultraviolet light it is changed into vitamin D.

eriometer. An instrument for measuring the diameters of very small particles or threads by diffraction.

Erlenmeyer flask. A wide-bottomed flask which tapers into a short neck.

erosion. Gradual wearing away and removal of the surface of the earth by water and wind.

erosion unconformity. A discontinuity of geological strata caused by erosion.

erratics. Stones of varied sizes, from pebbles to boulders, whose structure differs from the bedrock on which they now rest; they were brought there by moving glaciers.

eruption. The ejection of molten lava and other materials from a volcano.

eruptive. Igneous.

erythrocyte. A disclike red blood corpuscle of vertebrates containing hemoglobin.

erythrocytometer. A device for counting red blood corpuscles by the diffractometric method.

Es. Chemical symbol for einsteinium.

escape. A cultivated plant which grows wild.

esker. A long winding mound of glacial drift deposited by subglacial streams when their velocity decreases.

esophagus. The food tube leading from the pharynx to the stomach.

essential oils. Natural odoriferous compounds occurring in plants; used mainly for imparting odor and flavor to consumers' goods; examples, rose oil, lavender oil.

essential organs. Parts of a plant or animal necessary for continued life, growth, or reproduction; examples, stamens and pistils of flowers.

ester. A compound formed by the replacement of the acidic hydrogen of an organic acid by a hydrocarbon radical; a compound of an organic acid and an alcohol formed with the elimination of water; example, ethyl benzoate, C_6H_5COO-C_2H_5, which is a condensation product of benzoic acid and ethyl alcohol. Esters are used as flavors, solvents, etc.

esterification. The process of producing an ester by reaction of an acid with an alcohol with the elimination of water.

estivation. A summer inactivity of some snails as opposed to the hibernation of some other animals.

estuary. A long, narrow bay formed by the sea entering a river mouth and filling the lower part of a river valley.

etalon. An interferometer for producing interference effects by means of multiple reflection between fixed parallel, half-silvered glass plates; used for the study of fine spectrum lines.

ethane. $CH_3 \cdot CH_3$; the second member of the paraffin hydrocarbon series; colorless and odorless gas.

ether. (1) The hypothetical medium which is assumed to fill all space; it is thought of as distinct and different from matter and capable of transmitting all types of electromagnetic waves; (2) an organic oxide formed by the dehydration of two alcohol molecules; example, ethyl ether, $C_2H_5OC_2H_5$; used as an anesthetic, solvent, for the denaturation of alcohol.

ethmoid. A small bone forming the upper wall of the nasal passageway.

ethology. A study of the behavior of an animal in its normal environment.

ethyl alcohol. C_2H_5OH; grain alcohol; a colorless liquid prepared by the alcoholic fermentation of sugar; used as a solvent, in beverages, perfumes.

ethyl gasoline. A gasoline which contains small quantities of tetraethyl lead and ethylene bromide to avoid knocking.

ethyl group. —C_2H_5; a monovalent alkyl radical.

ethylene. $CH_2 : CH_2$; the first member of the olefine hydrocarbon series; colorless, inflammable gas; used in medicine, chemical synthesis.

ethylene glycol. CH_2OHCH_2OH; a colorless liquid; used as an antifreeze in automobiles, a solvent, in explosives.

etiolation. A loss of chlorophyll and decay of green plants which do not receive sufficient light.

Eu. Chemical symbol for europium.

euchromatin. The genetically active part of chromatin which stains less intensely than heterochromatin.

eucolloid. A colloid made up of particles which exceed 0.25 micron in length.

eudiometer. A graduated tube in which gases are subjected to the effect of an electric spark, and the changes in volume determined; used for gas analysis.

eugenics. A science which seeks to improve the human race by the improvement of hereditary traits.

Euglena. A one-celled flagellate organism on the borderline between plant and animal; it contains chlorophyll, but behaves like an animal and is capable of euglenoid movement.

euglenoid movement. Special movement of Euglena performed when the flagellum is inactive; the posterior portion of the cell draws forward and the cell assumes a rounded form; then the anterior portion of the cell is extended and the cell pushes forward.

euphotic zone. A 100-meter depth below the surface of the sea into which sufficient light penetrates for active photosynthesis.

euploid. Said of polyploid organisms, in which each of the different chromosomes of the set is present in the same number that is the exact multiple of the haploid chromosome number.

europium. A gray rare-earth metal; chemical symbol Eu; atomic number 63.

euryhaline. Tolerating a wide variation in the salt content of the water they inhabit; example, some Crustacea.

Eurypterida. An extinct order of Arachnida which resembled scorpions but were aquatic and up to 6 feet long.

eurythermous. Able to tolerate wide variations in the temperature of the environment.

euscope. A projector of microscope images for better viewing.

Eustachian tube. A slender tube between the pharynx and the middle ear which equalizes the air pressure on the two sides of the eardrum.

eutaxite. A stratified volcanic rock.

eutectic. (1) The lowest-melting mixture of two or more constituents which melt at a definite temperature to form a uniform liquid; (2) a mixture of two or more minerals in definite proportions which have crystallized simultaneously.

eutectic alloys. Binary or ternary alloys in which two or three constituents crystallize simultaneously.

eutectic change. The solidification of eutectic alloys or minerals.

eutectic point. (1) The melting point of an eutectic mixture; (2) a point in the constitutional diagram of eutectic alloys which indicates their composition and solidification temperature.

eutectoid. Analogous to eutectic, but two or three constituents are simultaneously formed from a solid instead of a melt.

euthenics. An attempt at improving the human race by bettering the environmental conditions under which men live.

Eutheria. Placentalia; Monodelphia; all mammals whose young are born in an advanced stage of development.

ev. Abbreviation for electron volt.

evagination. Turning inside out a hollow growth; the development of an outgrowth.

evaporation. Conversion of a liquid into vapor.

evaporation of electrons. Surface cooling caused by loss of electrons from that surface.

evaporation pull. Rise of water through the vessels of a stem due to the evaporation of transpired water from the surface of leaves.

evaporimeter. An instrument for measuring the rate of evaporation of water into the atmosphere.

even-even nuclei. Nuclei which contain an even number of protons and an even number of neutrons.

even-odd nuclei. Nuclei which contain an even number of protons and an odd number of neutrons.

evocation. Inducing a specialized development in an embryonic tissue by a chemical substance diffusing from a nearby tissue.

evolution. (1) The succession of changes by which a germ passes from a simple to a complex condition; (2) the gradual development of complex organisms from simpler ones.

evolution, organic. The theory that the complex organisms on earth today developed from simple organisms of the past.

excess. A larger quantity of a reagent than is theoretically necessary to carry a reaction to completion.

excitation. (1) Bringing an atom or a molecule into a state in which the total energy of its interior mechanism is greater than it is in the normal state; (2) stimulation of a plant organ; (3) activation or acceleration of a metabolic process; (4) the flux-producing magnetimotive force.

excitation energy. The energy needed to change a system from its ground state to a more reactive or excited state.

excitation potential. The critical potential difference needed for the excitation of a given radiation.

excited. Said of a molecule, atom, or nucleus which has a higher energy than in the ground state.

excited electron. An electron which is occupying a shell higher than its normal energy level.

exciter. A small d-c generator used to supply electricity for starting a larger electrical machine.

excretion. (1) Passing out waste products from the cells or the body; (2) a substance excreted.

excretory system. The set of organs which remove wastes from the body.

excurrent branching. Branches growing out from the main stem which forms the central shaft.

exfoliation. (1) The flaking off of surface layers of rocks because of excessive temperature varia-

tions; (2) the scaling off of bark from trees.

exhalant pore. The central opening at the top of a sponge through which water is passed outward.

exhaust. (1) The passage through which the spent steam of an engine cylinder is carried to the outer air or to a condenser; (2) the gases discharged from the cylinder; (3) a period of the engine cycle.

exhaust collector ring. In an aircraft, a circular duct into which the exhaust gases from the cylinders of a radial engine are discharged.

exhaust manifold. The hollow casting through which the gases from the various cylinders of an aircraft engine are conducted on their way through the exhaust pipe and the muffler.

exhaust pump. An air pump; a device which exhausts the air from a vessel to produce a vacuum.

exhaust stroke. The stroke in which the piston of an engine forces the burned fuel gases out of the cylinder.

exhaust valve. The valve of an engine which provides an outlet for the spent gas or steam.

exine. The outer coat of a spore or pollen grain.

exocarp. Epicarp; the outermost layer of the fruit wall.

exoccipital. A bone at the posterior part of the skull, on either side of the foramen magnum.

exodermis. A layer of closely fitting cells in the cortex which serves as a temporary protective casing of roots.

exoergic. Same as exothermic, that is, developing heat.

exogenetic. Said of superficial, or near superficial, geologic processes; examples, erosion, deposition, secondary enrichment of ore bodies.

exogenous. (1) Increasing in size by adding successive concentric rings outside the previous growth; (2) developed from surface tissue; (3) metabolism producing energy for external activity.

exopodite. The external branch of the biramous crustacean appendage.

Exopterygota. A subclass of insects in which the adult form develops gradually by successive molts.

exoskeleton. A hard or resistant covering on the outside of an animal; examples, the shell of a turtle, lobster, or insect.

exosmosis. Outward osmotic flow.

exosphere. The region of the atmosphere from about 250 miles above the earth to the upper edge of the atmosphere.

exothermic reaction. A chemical reaction in which heat is given

off.

exotic stream. A large stream which is fed by the abundant precipitation of mountain regions and flows across desert areas where few tributaries exist.

exotoxin. A toxin which is excreted by a microorganism into the surrounding medium and may be separated by filtration.

expansion. A process which causes a substance of constant mass to increase in volume.

expansion, adiabatic. An expansion of a substance or system without gain or loss of heat.

expansion, coefficient of. The expansion of unit length, area, or volume as a result of $1\,°C$ rise in temperature; it is called linear, superficial, and cubal or volume expansion.

experiment. (1) A test under controlled conditions for the purpose of discovering new facts or relations; (2) a test carried out to prove or discredit a theory.

experiment chamber. The central portion of a wind tunnel, where aircraft models or other objects are tested.

expiration. The exhaling of air by a lung-breathing animal.

explantation. Tissue culture; the culture of a tissue or organ taken from a living individual in an artificial medium.

exploring coil. A search coil; a small coil which may be moved in a magnetic field in order to test the magnetic intensity at various points by electromagnetic induction.

explosion. A violent and rapid exothermic chemical reaction, usually accompanied by sound, in which large quantities of gases are produced at high temperature.

explosion spectrum. The spectrum of the flash of a chemical explosion or of a filament exploded by a heavy current.

explosive. A substance that, either pure or with admixture of other substances, can be detonated or exploded.

exposure, acute. Radiation exposure which lasts a very short time.

exposure meter. An instrument for measuring light intensity to determine the correct time of photographic exposure.

exposure plates. Inoculation of culture in a Petri dish by exposing to air.

expressivity. The ability of a gene to change the organism to which it belongs.

exsiccatae. Dried, preserved plant specimens.

exsiccation. The forced evaporation of moisture.

extensometer. A micrometer by which the expansion of metals is measured.

extensor. A muscle which con-

tracts and thus straightens out a joint or limb.

external aileron. A separate airfoil mounted clear of the wing surface of an airplane but usually attached to its hem and deflected for lateral control.

external fertilization. Laying eggs to be fertilized outside the body of the female; example, fish roes.

external parasites. Parasites that live on the external surface of their host; examples, lice and fleas.

external phase. The continuous dispersing medium of an emulsion.

external secretion. A secreted substance which is eliminated from the body.

external work. The work done by a system against external forces, or on the system by external forces; example, the expansion or compression of a gas.

external-combustion engine. An engine in which the fuel is burned outside the cylinders.

exteroceptor. A receptor which detects stimuli arising outside of the body, such as light, heat, and sound.

extinct volcano. An inactive volcano.

extinction. A decrease in the intensity of a radiation due to both absorption and scattering by the medium traversed; example, a star traversing the atmosphere.

extinction photometer. A photometer in which the luminous intensity of a source of light is judged by the thickness of a given absorbing material necessary to make it invisible.

extinction potential. The lowest anode voltage which will cause a self-sustained discharge in a gas-discharge tube.

extraction. The separation of a desired constituent from the other constituents of a mass; example, obtaining a pure metal from its ore.

extraembryonic. Derived from the zygote, but found outside the epidermis of the embryo proper; examples, yolk sac, allantois, amnion, and chorion.

extrathecal zone. A projection of tissue about the base of a coral polyp, from which the young polyp develops.

extrorse. In the dehiscence of an anther, away from the center of a flower.

extrusion. Forcing hot melted metal or plastic through a die to form continuous tubes, rods, and wires.

extrusive rock. A magma solidified on the surface of the earth.

exudation. A sap or resinous liquid dripping from the pores of or an incision made in the stem of a plant; examples, rubber latex from the rubber tree and turpentine from conifers.

exumbrella. The upper or convex surface of the body of a jellyfish or other medusa.

exuvium. The skin cast off in molting.

eye. (1) A sensory organ which is stimulated by light, particularly an organ whose stimulation results in the formation of a mental image of the objects from which the light is reflected or radiated; (2) the undisturbed, calm area in the center of a hurricane; (3) a loop at the end of a wire or bolt.

eye muscles. (1) The set of six muscles which move each eyeball, characteristic of all vertebrates with functional eyes; (2) groups of intrinsic (smooth) and extrinsic (striated) muscles which perform various functions in the eye.

eyepiece. The lens, or system of lenses, in an optical instrument, such as a microscope or telescope, which is closest to the eye of the observer.

eyepiece, micrometer. A scale of small divisions ruled or photographed on transparent glass and placed in the focal plane of the eyepiece of a microscope for measuring the dimensions of the objects viewed.

eyespot. A small mass of pigment sensitive to light in lower organisms.

F

f. Abbreviation for (1) frequency; (2) focal length.

F. Chemical symbol for fluorine.

°F. Abbreviation for Fahrenheit degrees.

F_1 generation. The first generation of hybrids.

F_2 generation. The offspring of hybrid parents.

fabric. (1) A woven textile material; (2) the shape and arrangement of small crystals in an igneous rock.

face. (1) The anterior and ventral part of the head, bearing the mouth, eyes, and, in vertebrates, the nose; (2) the upper part of a plant organ; (3) the working surface of a machine part.

face-centered cubic structure. A crystal structure in which atoms occupy the corners and centers of the face of a cube.

facet. The corneal end of a rodlike structure in the compound eye of insects.

faceted spurs. Projecting spurs of bedrock that are ground flat.

facial nerve. One of the seventh pair of cranial nerves of vertebrates; it leads to the superficial muscles of the face and the salivary glands.

facies. Parts of igneous rocks which have been differentiated

from a parent magma so that they have a texture and composition different from those of the mass of the rocks.

facilitation. Promotion of impulse transmission due to the earlier passage of another impulse which often comes from a different stimulus.

facsimile telegraphy or radio. Sending photographs, maps, and other printed matter by electrical means over wire or by radio.

fact. The lens of one eye in a compound eye.

factor of safety. The number of times the minimum strength of a construction is increased to allow for unusual needs.

faculae. Large bright areas of the photosphere of the sun, which are at higher temperature than other parts of the sun surface.

facultative aerobe. A microorganism which is fundamentally an anaerobe but can grow also in the presence of free oxygen.

facultative anaerobe. A microorganism which is fundamentally an aerobe but can grow also in the absence of free oxygen.

facultative parasite. A parasite that may live without a host at certain times.

fader. A device installed in a communication channel for the continuous variation of the modulation level from zero to a maximum and back.

fadometer. An instrument for testing the resistance of materials to fading when they are exposed to artificial sunlight or ultraviolet light under controlled conditions.

Fahrenheit scale. A thermometer scale on which the freezing point of water is 32° and its boiling point is 212°; to convert from Fahrenheit to centigrade, subtract 32° from the Fahrenheit reading and multiply by 5/9 (0.55).

fairing. An auxiliary streamlining structure whose primary function is to reduce head resistance or drag of the aircraft part to which it is fitted.

fall wind. Katabatic wind; gravity wind; a wind which blows down a mountainside or which has a strong downward component; examples, foehn, mistral, bora.

Fallopian tube. The oviduct; a tube on each side of the uterus, extending from its upper angle outward to the side of the pelvis, ending near the ovary; they discharge the ova into the uterus.

fall-out. Radioactive particles that fall to earth as a result of an atomic or hydrogen-bomb explosion.

fallowing. Letting soil rest by not growing crops for a period of time in order to improve its fertility.

false bedding plane. Stratification at an angle to the main bedding plane; it occurs in a sedimentation by water or wind.

false cirrus. Thunderstorm cirrus; the cirriform top of a cumulo-cirro-stratus, that is, the rain cloud of a thunderstorm.

false indusium. In ferns, a covering of sporangia formed by a folding-over of the margin of the frond.

family. The individuals in an order or suborder; among animals, the members of a family generally look alike.

family of elements. Elements with similar properties; the elements in a vertical row of the periodic table; examples, the alkali metals, the halogens.

family tree. A genealogical tree; a treelike diagram which shows how living things are related to one another.

fang. (1) A sharp, hollow, or grooved tooth through which venom is injected by poisonous snakes; (2) an air duct along the side of a mine shaft.

fanglomerate. Coarse, clastic sediments deposited at the head of alluvial fans.

far field. The acoustic radiation field at large distances from the source.

far point. That point on the axis of the eye which is at such a distance that it is distinctly visible when the accommodation is completely relaxed.

farad. A unit of electrostatic capacity; a capacity of one farad requires one coulomb of electricity to raise its potential one volt; one farad equals 9×10^{11} electrostatic units; 1,000,000 microfarads; 1,000,000,000,-000 micromicro farads.

faraday. Quantity of electricity required to liberate or deposit one gram-equivalent of an ion; 96,490 coulombs.

Faraday dark space. The nonluminous region separating the negative glow from the positive column in a Crookes tube at moderate pressure.

Faraday effect. The rotation of the plane of vibration of polarized light by an otherwise isotropic substance placed in a magnetic field that has a component in the direction of the light rays; for a given substance, the rotation is proportional to the thickness penetrated by the light and to the strength of the magnetic field.

Faraday's disk. A disk used for simple demonstrations of electromagnetism.

Faraday's electrolytic constant. The quantity of electricity which, in electrolysis, is required to liberate a gram atom of any univalent element.

Faraday's laws. (1) The amount of chemical action is proportional to the amount of

electricity which has passed through the electrolyte; (2) the quantities of substances deposited or liberated by the same quantity of electricity are proportional to their chemical equivalents.

fascia. A band of connective tissue that covers and supports or binds parts together.

fasciation. Coalescing of stems, branches, etc., to form abnormally thick growths.

fascicled root. The clustered, fleshy root of dahlia and other plants.

fascicular cambium. A strand of cambium in each vascular bundle between xylem and phloem.

fast neutron. A neutron that has an energy level higher than 100,000 electron volts.

fat. (1) An important element of human diet as a source of energy; (2) a naturally occurring mixture of glyceryl esters of certain organic acids; example, glyceryl stearate.

fat body. (1) A large mass of fatty tissue found in insects, which acts as a reservoir for nitrogenous wastes in the adult; (2) a mass of fatty tissue located near the gonads in Amphibia.

fathom. A unit of marine depth; 6 feet.

Fathometer (a trade-mark). A depth-sounding instrument; example, the depth of the ocean is measured by noting the length of time it takes an echo of sound to return from the sea bed.

fatigue. (1) The tendency of a metal to fracture under repeated stress considerably below its ultimate tensile strength; (2) slowed-down response of animal cells to stimulation due to exhaustion.

fatigue, elastic. A delay in recovering the original size and shape by an elastic solid after the release of the deforming stress.

fatigue limit. The maximum stress to which a metal can be subjected indefinitely without fracture.

fatigue of metals. The deterioration of metals due to repeated stresses above a certain critical value; it results in changes in the crystalline structure.

fatigue strength. Same as fatigue limit.

fatty acids. Saturated and unsaturated organic aliphatic open-chain acids of the general formula $C_nH_{2n}O_2$; examples, acetic acid, CH_3COOH, and palmitic acid, $CH_3(CH_2)_{14}$-$COOH$.

fault. (1) A break in a mass of rock on one side of which the rock moves up or down and no layer connects at the same level with the rock on the other side; (2) a defect in a mechanism that hinders its normal operation.

fault current. The current flowing in a transmitting system due to a defect in the circuit.

fault mountain. A mountain formed as a result of a break in the earth's crust and an upward tilting of blocks or rock strata.

fault scarp. A cliff formed when one side of a rock stands higher than another as a result of a fault.

fauna. The animal life of a given period or region.

Fe. Chemical symbol for iron.

feather. (1) The characteristic covering of birds which is growing from the epidermis; (2) a key inserted into a shaft to allow axial sliding of the wheel, but preventing relative rotation.

feathering. (1) The controlled motion of paddle wheels which enter and leave the water at right angles to its surface; (2) the automatic turning of propeller blades on their axes while the propeller is rotating to reach the maximum thrust.

feces. (1) Waste material discharged from the bowels; excrements; dregs; (2) the sediment of distillation.

Fechner's colors. Colors seen when a white edge moves over a dark background.

feedback. A back coupling; in radio, a coupling for the transfer of energy from the output circuit of an amplifier to its input circuit.

feeder. (1) The line which carries the current supply to the branch circuits; (2) the mechanism that conveys the ore to the crusher; (3) the connection between a radio antenna and a transmitter or receiver.

feldspar. A rock-forming crystalline mixed silicate which constitutes about 60% of the earth's surface; examples, orthoclase, labradorite, and anorthite.

felsite. Dense, fine-grained, light-colored igneous rock which is rich in silica.

femur. (1) The upper bone of the lower limb in vertebrates; (2) the third joint of the leg of insects.

Fermat's principle of least time. When a ray of light or other wave motion passes the distance between any two points, the time taken is a minimum.

ferment. An enzyme; a substance which causes fermentation.

fermentation. A chemical change brought about by bacteria and other organisms, usually with the liberation of heat and gases; example, the fermentation of sugar to alcohol.

fermentation tube. A special test tube with a closed straight branch used to study the production of gas by bacteria.

fermium. Chemical symbol Fm; atomic number 100.

ferns. Flowerless plants of many species belonging to the Pteridophyta, with true leaves, roots, and horizontal stems of conducting tissue much like that in higher plants; the spores are borne on leaves or modified leaves.

Ferrel's law. Because of the earth's rotation, winds are deflected to the right in the northern hemisphere and to the left in the southern hemisphere.

ferric. Containing trivalent iron.

ferric chloride. Yellowish deliquescent crystalline mass; $FeCl_3 \cdot 6H_2O$; used in pigments, medicine, catalysis.

ferric oxide. Hematite; reddish crystals; Fe_2O_3; the most important ore of iron.

ferrite. The pure iron in pig iron or steel.

ferro-. A prefix denoting iron.

ferroelectric. Said of a dielectric which shows spontaneous polarization and hysteresis; example, Rochelle salt.

ferromagnetic material. Paramagnetic material; a material that is strongly attracted by magnets; examples, iron and nickel.

ferroresonance. A resonance occurring in armored submarine cables due to a flux in the armoring steel wires.

ferrosilicon. An acid-resistant alloy of iron and silicon; used in steel, in magnesium manufacture.

ferrosilicon process. The manufacture of magnesium by reduction of magnesium oxide with an alloy of iron and silicon.

ferrous. Containing divalent iron.

ferrous alloys. Iron-base alloys.

fertile. Producing spores or seeds.

fertile material. In nucleonics, a nonfissionable substance which in a reactor may become fissionable through a nuclear transformation.

fertilization. The fusion of dissimilar gametes to form the fertilized egg or zygote.

fertilized egg. A zygote; an egg cell after it has united with a sperm cell.

fertilizer. A plant food containing compounds of elements needed by the plants for growth; examples, calcium phosphate, sodium nitrate.

Fessenden oscillator. A low-frequency, moving-coil, electromagnetic sound generator, used as an underwater sound source.

fetal membrane. An extraembryonic membrane of a mammal.

fetus. The embryo of a viviparous animal in its later stages.

Feulgen method. A test for chromatin in the nucleus of microorganisms.

fibrils. (1) Minute fibers that form the bundles of threadlike fibers

of voluntary muscles; (2) very small fiberlike branches of plants.

fibrin. An insoluble precipitate formed when thrombin unites with fibrinogen in the clotting of blood.

fibrinogen. A protein in the blood serum that coagulates and causes clotting when exposed to air.

fibroblast. An irregular branching cell, found in vertebrate connective tissues; it forms and maintains collagen.

fibrous root system. A system of many branching roots which are slender and may be matted together; example, the roots of corn.

fibrous tissue. A connective tissue made up of white fiber bundles.

fibrovascular bundles. Groups of food- and water-conducting tubes in higher plants.

fibula. The smaller of the two bones of the lower leg of man.

field. (1) The area visible through an optical instrument; (2) the region around a magnet or electric charge in which the magnet or the charge is capable of exerting its influence.

field, atomic. The region surrounding an atom in which there is considerable repulsion for other particles.

field coil. (1) The coil carrying the current to an electric machine; (2) a coil of many thousands of turns of wire used to produce a powerful magnetic field in a speaker.

field core. The core of the field winding of a generator or motor.

field current. The current in the field coil of an electric machine.

field, electric. The region in which electric forces act.

field emission. Cold emission; autoemission; emission of electrons under the effect of a high potential difference.

field lens. The lens in the eyepiece system of optical instruments farthest from the eye.

field magnet. The electromagnet by which the magnetomotive force is produced for starting the flux in an electric machine.

field of force. The region around the pole of a magnet or around an electric current.

field of view. The area or solid angle visible through an optical instrument; it is usually restricted by a field stop in the eyepiece.

field stop. A circular opening in an opaque screen, which determines the field of view of an optical instrument.

field strength. The strength of an electric field at a given point as measured by the force in dynes excited on a unit charge at that point.

filament. (1) The threadlike con-

ductor in an electric light bulb that glows when an electric current is passed through it; (2) an electron-emitting heated wire in a thermionic tube; (3) a slender stalklike part of a stamen; (4) any threadlike structure in animals; (5) the axis of a feather down.

filament transformer. A transformer used in radio to reduce the supply voltage for the filaments or heaters of radio tubes.

filamentous. Threadlike; composed of long threadlike parts.

filar micrometer. A micrometer, the screw of which moves a wire or filament across the focal plane of a microscope or a telescope and measures the object under examination.

Filicales. Ferns.

filiform. Threadlike; in streak or stab cultures, having a uniform growth along the line of inoculation.

filled band. An energy band in which every level is occupied by electrons.

film. (1) A flexible strip coated with a light-sensitive emulsion; (2) the monomolecular layer which is formed on the surface of a solution or at an interface between two immiscible liquids.

film, condensed. A surface film in which the molecules are closely packed and steeply oriented to the surface.

film, expanded. A film whose properties are intermediate between those of gaseous and condensed films.

film, gaseous. A film in which the molecules move about freely.

film, monomolecular. A layer of a substance on the surface of a liquid or solid, produced by adsorption or by other means, that is one molecule thick.

film water. A very thin layer of water on soil particles.

filter. (1) A device for separating solids from liquids; (2) a transparent plate which transmits only certain wave-length ranges for photographic purposes; (3) a device in a high-frequency circuit which suppresses certain frequencies in a complex electric wave; (4) a device which cuts out certain frequencies of sound.

filter, light. A means of modifying the spectral composition of radiant energy by selective absorption or reflection.

filtrate. A liquid from which suspended solids have been removed by passing through a filter.

filtration. A process of separating suspended particles from a liquid by passing the liquid through a porous medium; the porous medium is the filter, the liquid which passes through is the filtrate, and the solid matter that remains on the filter is the residue.

fin. (1) A fixed or adjustable airfoil attached to an aircraft approximately parallel to the plane of symmetry to afford directional stability; (2) a thin projecting edge on a metal or plastic casting; (3) a broad, thin appendage, primarily an organ of locomotion of fish.

fin rays. Supports for the fins of fish.

fiord. Fjord; a narrow sea inlet surrounded by mountains; it was formed when huge glaciers moved down river valleys, and gouged out deep V-shaped cavities extending far below sea level.

fire point. The lowest temperature of a liquid in an open container at which vapors are evolved fast enough to support continuous combustion.

fireball. A bolide; a large exploding meteor that appears to be brighter than a planet.

fireclay. A silicious clay which lies directly under coal beds; it softens only at high temperatures and is used in refractories.

firedamp. Natural gas contained in coal, predominantly methane, CH_4; it is the cause of mine explosions.

fire-tube boiler. A steam-engine boiler in which the combustion gases are drawn through long horizontal tubes surrounded by water before they reach the chimney.

first law of thermodynamics. Energy cannot be created or destroyed, but can be converted from one form into another.

first-class lever. A lever in which the fulcrum is between the force and the resistance.

Fischer-Tropsch process. The manufacture of hydrocarbon oils from coal, lignite, or natural gas by the hydrogenation of carbon monoxide in the presence of a catalyst.

fish. An aquatic vertebrate usually covered with scales, breathing oxygen from water by means of gills, and reproducing by means of eggs discharged into water.

fish ladder. A channel around a dam through which fish can travel upstream.

fishtail. The swinging of the tail of an airplane from side to side to reduce speed in approaching the ground for landing.

fission. (1) An asexual reproduction involving merely the division of a single-celled individual into two new single-celled individuals of equal size; this is also called binary fission; (2) the breakdown of a heavy atomic nucleus to produce nuclei of lighter elements, yielding also neutrons and gamma rays; it may start a chain reaction.

fission bomb. The atomic bomb.

fission chamber. A device for detecting slow neutrons; an ionization chamber whose walls are lined with a thin layer of uranium.

fission neutrons. Neutrons emitted as a result of nuclear fission.

fission neutrons, delayed. Neutrons emitted by the products of a nuclear fission by disintegration of finite half life.

fission neutrons, prompt. Neutrons emitted during a nuclear fission.

fission, nuclear. Same as fission (2).

fission, photo. Nuclear fission induced by photons.

fission products. The radioactive nuclei formed in a nuclear fission.

fission spectrum. The distribution of energy of the neutrons from nuclear fission.

fission, spontaneous. Nuclear fission taking place without particles or photons entering the nucleus from the outside.

fission, ternary. The division of a nucleus into three parts.

fission yield. The fraction of fissions, usually expressed as a percentage, that gives rise to a specific nuclide or a group of isobars.

fissionable. Capable of undergoing nuclear fission.

fissure. (1) A cleft in a rock, open or filled with deposit, which originated from a fault but was widened by erosion; (2) an ulceration of the anus caused by constipation.

fissure spring. Ground water coming to the surface through a fissure in the bedrock.

fissure vein. A valuable mineral contained in a fissure in the crust of the earth.

Fittig's synthesis. The formation of aromatic hydrocarbons from aryl and alkyl bromides by the use of metallic sodium.

fix. The exact geographical position of an aircraft, determined by observation.

fixation. (1) The act of orienting the eye so that a given point of the retinal image falls on that point of the retina at which it may be most distinctly seen; (2) in making slides of organisms or tissues for microscopic study, treating the specimen with a chemical which will preserve it in à lifelike state; (3) the attachment of a free-swimming organism to a substratum.

fixation of nitrogen. Making chemical compounds from atmospheric nitrogen.

fixed axis of rotation. The locus of points of a system along a straight line which remain stationary when the rest of the system is in rotation.

fixed beam. A beam whose ends are firmly connected to supports.

fixed condenser. A condenser whose capacitance is constant.

fixed oil. A vegetable oil which is not changed by heat; example, linseed oil.

fixed point. (1) A characteristic temperature that can be accurately reproduced; example, the boiling point of a liquid; (2) the two reference points of a thermometer scale, that is, the temperature of melting ice and that of boiling water.

fixed stars. Stars that do not appear to alter their relative positions in the celestial sphere.

fixing bath. A sodium thiosulfate solution which stops the development of an exposed film at the right point and dissolves out the emulsion of unused silver bromide.

flaccid. Said of plants which are limp due to lack of water in the cells.

Flagellata. Mastigophora; a group of organisms that move by means of threadlike flagella which they lash to and fro.

flagellum. A threadlike projection from a cell that lashes like a whip and enables an organism to move about.

flame arc. An electric arc produced between carbons which have been impregnated with metal salts to color the flame.

flame cell. Solonocyte; a hollow, cup-shaped excretory cell in invertebrates which has branched processes.

flame, luminous. A pale or bright-colored flame; examples, candle flame and a sodium light; the inner cone of a Bunsen flame.

flame, nonluminous. The outer part of a Bunsen flame.

flame, oxidizing. The outer cone of a nonluminous Bunsen flame.

flame, reducing. The luminous tip and inner core of a Bunsen flame.

flame test. Identifying substances by their coloration of the flame of a Bunsen burner.

flaming arc. An arc lamp using mineral-cored carbons, giving a greater arc flame and greater light.

flap. A hinged or pivoted airfoil forming the rear portion of an aircraft wing to vary the effective camber.

flapping angle. In a helicopter, the difference between the coning angle and the instantaneous angle of the span axis of a blade of a rotary wing system relative to the plane perpendicular to the axis of rotation.

flash arc. The sudden increase in emission of a thermionic cathode as a result of irregularities in the cathode surface.

flash method. Pasteurization of milk by heating to approximately 160°F for a few seconds and prompt cooling below room temperature.

flash point. The lowest temperature at which a substance or mixture heated in an open container will give off flammable vapors sufficient to yield a momentary flash when approached by a small flame.

flash spectrum. In a total solar eclipse, the reversing layer and the chromosphere of the sun flashing into view when the photosphere of the sun is covered.

flashback voltage. The peak inverse voltage at which ionization occurs in a gas tube.

flash-over voltage. The voltage at which sparking occurs between two parts of an electrical machine or one part and the earth.

flat bones. The bones of the skeleton that protect and support; examples, scapula, sternum.

flat spin. An aircraft spin in which the longitudinal axis is less than 45° from the horizontal.

flatworm. A member of Platyhelminthes; an unsegmented worm; often parasitic; examples, liver fluke and tapeworm.

flavones. Yellow plant pigments.

fledgling. Just hatched young bird.

fleshy fruit. A fruit with a fleshy ovary wall.

fleshy root. Large taproot which stores the food supply of a plant; example, carrot.

Fletcher's trolley. A mechanism for demonstrating the relation between force, mass and acceleration in horizontal motion.

flexors. Muscles which bend joints.

flexure. A strain in which points, normally in a straight line, are displaced in a plane curve.

flight indicator. A compact aircraft instrument; a combination of a lateral inclinometer, a fore-and-aft inclinometer, and a turn indicator.

flight path. The path traced by the center of gravity of an aircraft in flight.

flight-path angle. The angle between the flight path of an aircraft and the horizontal.

flint. A compound rock, a cryptocrystalline form of silica; it is dense, tough, breaking with a conchoidal fracture.

flint glass. A glass used in optical instruments and fine glassware; it contains lead silicate.

flipper. (1) An appendage of aquatic mammals whose digits are enveloped by a continuous tissue so that the entire structure forms a flat paddle for swimming; example, seals; (2) a steam-engine-operated lever used for moving lumber.

floating plant. An aquatic plant whose roots grow in water and whose flowers float on the water; example, water lily.

flocculation. The coagulation and rapid precipitation of finely divided particles which ordinarily would remain in suspension.

flocculent precipitate. A flaky wool-like precipitate.

floccus. (1) Hyphal filaments of fungi; (2) the hair tuft at the end of some mammalian tails.

floe. Floating ice.

flood. High tide; incoming tide.

flood plains. Level land next to a river which is covered with alluvium during a flood.

flood tide. Same as flood.

flora. Plants of a certain region.

Florence flask. Flat-bottomed round flask which tapers off into a long neck; the body of the flask is often covered with straw.

floret. A small flower in an inflorescence; one of the flowers forming the head of the plants of the Compositae.

floriculture. The culture of flowering plants.

flotation. Ore separation by frothing the finely ground ore with oil and water; the metallic particles float on top, while the rock particles settle to the bottom.

flow, streamline. Viscous flow; a fluid flow in which the particles move slowly, continuously and at a constant rate.

flow structure. Banding in effusive igneous rocks due to the alignment of minerals, inclusions, and gas cavities during the flow of the still molten but viscous magma.

flow, turbulent. Eddy flow; a fluid flow in which the fluid velocity at a fixed point fluctuates with time in a random manner.

flowage. Internal movement of clays and rocks when stressed beyond the elastic limit; example, granulation.

flower. A plant organ used in sexual reproduction.

flower head. A cluster of individual flowers which has the appearance of a single flower; examples, daisy, dandelion.

flowers of sulfur. Fine yellow powder; very small crystals of sulfur obtained by condensation of sulfur vapors from the sublimation of crude sulfur.

flowmeter. An instrument for measuring the pressure, flow velocity, and discharge rate of a fluid flowing from a conduit.

fluctuating variation. Temporary nonheritable morphological or physiological changes, usually caused by environmental conditions, which occur in individuals of the same species.

flue gas. The gaseous products of combustion of a boiler which contain carbon dioxide, carbon monoxide, oxygen, nitrogen, and water vapor; the analysis of flue gas is a measure of boiler efficiency.

fluid. A substance that is able to flow and yields to any force

tending to change its shape without changing its volume; examples, water and air.

fluid friction. Friction of the molecules of a lubricating film between the moving surfaces of a machine.

fluid, homogenous. A fluid whose properties are the same at all points.

fluid mechanics. The study of the mechanical properties of fluids including hydrostatics, hydraulics, hydrodynamics, and gas dynamics.

fluid, perfect. An ideal frictionless fluid which offers no resistance to deformation, is incompressible, and of uniform density.

fluid pressure. The pressure transmitted by fluids, which is equal at all points and in all directions.

fluke. (1) A parasitic flatworm; (2) a small flat fish.

fluorescein. $C_{20}H_{12}O_5$; a red crystalline organic compound; it dissolves in alkalis to form a red solution of green fluorescence; used as an indicator, for dyeing textiles.

fluorescence. The absorption of light of a definite wave length and instantaneous emission of radiation of a greater wave length; thus ultraviolet light may cause fluorescence in the visible spectrum.

fluorescent lamp. An electron tube filled with mercury vapors which is coated on the inside with a fluorescent substance; it converts an ultraviolet discharge into visible light.

fluoride. A poisonous salt of hydrofluoric acid; example, sodium fluoride, NaF.

flourine. A greenish gas; the most negative halogen; chemical symbol F; atomic number 9.

fluorite. Fluorspar; a cubical mineral of varied colors; CaF_2; used as a flux in steel making.

fluorogen. A substance which induces fluorescence of another substance when mixed with it.

fluorometer. An instrument for the measurement of the intensity of fluorescence.

fluoroscope. (1) A device for observing fluorescence; (2) a fluorescent screen which changes invisible radiation to visible light; used in x-ray examination.

fluorspar. Same as fluorite.

flutter. An oscillation of definite period but unstable character set up in any part of an aircraft by a momentary disturbance and maintained by a combination of the aerodynamic, inertial, and elastic characteristics of the member itself.

flux. (1) A substance added to metals, minerals, and other solids to promote their fusion; (2) a substance used to remove the oxide coating from a metallic surface prior to soldering or

welding; (3) the magnetic force that is assumed to flow from a theoretical north pole to a theoretical south pole, without loss.

flux density. The magnetic lines of force per square centimeter; measured in gausses.

flux, luminous. The amount of light emitted by a source in unit time; measured in lumens.

flux, magnetic. The total amount of magnetic induction on a surface; it is measured in maxwells.

flux, radiant. The time rate of transfer of radiant energy; it is measured in ergs per second or in watts.

flux refraction. A change in the direction of the magnetic induction at the interface between two media of different permeability, or of the electric displacement at the interface between two dielectrics of different dielectric constant.

fluxmeter. Instrument for the measurement of the total magnetic flux of a circuit; a moving-coil galvanometer.

flyby. A space vehicle that passes by a celestial body, such as a planet, and continues its prescribed course without returning to earth.

flywheel. A heavy wheel that rotates steadily and thus regulates the speed of machinery to which it is attached or stores energy for use at short intervals; example, operating a punch.

Fm. Chemical symbol for fermium.

FM. Frequency modulation; a broadcasting method almost free from statics, in which the frequency of the carrier wave is changed to correspond to an audiosignal.

foam. Froth; a fairly stable suspension of a gas in a liquid; produced by agitation or chemical means.

foam extinguisher. A fire extinguisher which excludes air by spraying a frothy substance; used especially to fight oil fires.

foaming. Formation of gas bubbles in a liquid.

focal length. The distance between the principal focus of a lens or mirror and its optical center.

focal spot. The small area of an x-ray tube target on which the cathode rays are concentrated and from which the x-rays proceed.

focometer. Focimeter; an instrument for measuring the focal length of a lens or of an optical system.

focus. (1) The point of intersection of converging rays (real focus) or the point from which rays appear to diverge (virtual focus); (2) the place of maximum displacement of an earth-

quake.

focusing. (1) Causing an electron beam to converge to a point by an electric or magnetic field or by positive ions in a cathode-ray tube; (2) proper adjustment of the optical system of a camera before taking a picture; (3) the concentration of sound waves from a diaphragm.

focusing coil. A d-c coil which produces a magnetic field for focusing an electron beam.

foehn. A warm, dry Alpine wind.

fog. Fine water droplets, dust, or smoke, or all three combined obscuring the vision on the surface of the earth.

fog track. Cloud track; the path of condensed moisture formed in a cloud chamber with the charged gas atoms acting as nuclei for vapor condensation.

fogging. Blooming of paint.

folding. Bending of rock layers due to pressure.

foliation. The formation of a mineral structure consisting of thin plates with their cleavage faces in parallel arrangement, due to high local pressure.

folic acid. A member of the vitamin B complex that aids the bone marrow in making red blood corpuscles; orange crystals; extracted from leaves or prepared by synthesis.

follicle. (1) A glandular cavity or sac; (2) a dry fruit formed from a single carpel; the seeds fall out when it splits open along a single line of dehiscence; (3) the little pit in the skin from which a hair grows.

follicle cell. One of the cells of the ovarian follicle which nourish the ovum during its development.

fontanelle. A discontinuity in an infant's skull.

food. A substance which, when taken into the body of a living plant or animal and oxidized within its cells, produces energy, aids in the building up and growth of protoplasm, and helps remove wastes from the cells.

food chain. The interdependence of organisms of an animal community in which one animal feeds on another which in turn feeds on a third, and so on, until the chain reaches a herbivorous animal that feeds on green plants, which in turn depend on the sun's energy.

food pyramid. A diagram of a food chain; it indicates the numbers of organisms in each link of the chain.

food vacuole. A tiny space found in one-celled animals which contains a food particle surrounded by a liquid in the process of digestion and absorption.

fool's gold. Pyrite; iron sulfide mineral; FeS_2.

foot. (1) The appendage of locomotion of animals; (2) in liverworts, an expanded base portion of the sporophyte which attaches it to the gametophyte; (3) an English unit of length, 12 inches, 30.48 centimeters.

foot-candle. A practical unit of illumination; the illumination of the surface of a sphere of one-foot radius by a source of one candle power placed in its center; it is equivalent to one lumen per square foot.

foot-pound. The English unit of work and energy; the work done in raising one pound avoirdupois against the force of gravity to a vertical height of one foot; 13,560,000 ergs.

foot-pound-second system. A system of measurement in which the three fundamental units are the foot, pound, and second.

forage fish. Fish that have no food value but are vital as food for the larger species of game fish.

foramen. (1) The micropyle in plants; (2) an opening in a cartilage or bone.

foramen magnum. A large opening at the base of the skull through which the spinal cord passes.

foramen ovale. An opening between the left and right auricle of the heart of embryonic mammal.

Foraminifera. A group of marine rhizopod Protozoa, whose shell usually consists of lime.

forbidden band. A range of energies which no electron in a solid may possess.

force. The cause of acceleration of a body; the unit force causes one unit acceleration of a unit mass.

force feed. An engine lubrication by forcing oil through the hollow crankshaft into the bearings.

force, impressed electromotive. The force applied to a circuit by the generator.

force of friction. The force required to overcome friction and maintain uniform motion of one surface sliding over another.

force pump. (1) A compression pump having a valveless piston, that forces a liquid through the valves; (2) an air pump used for forcing air through pipes to clean them out.

forced double refraction. Double refraction in an isotropic medium as a result of strain.

forced vibrations. Vibrations induced by the application of a periodic force to a body, which can be greatly amplified by resonance.

forebrain. (1) The anterior of the three divisions in the vertebrate embryonic brain; (2) the prosencephalon of the adult brain.

forepump. An auxiliary air pump used to create a partial vacuum, preliminary to the operation of another, more effective air pump.

form. The smallest of the groups used in classifying plants.

form factor. A means for describing the shape of an alternating-current wave.

formaldehyde. HCHO; a colorless gas; soluble in water; used as an antiseptic, in embalming, and the manufacture of synthetic resins.

formalin. A commercial 40% solution of formaldehyde in water; used as a preservative.

formation. (1) A mineral bed or group of beds which are similar in general composition and texture and which can be distinguished from the other rocks above and below them; (2) a cartographic unit; (3) a division of plants and animals in a climatic region.

formic acid. HCOOH; a colorless, corrosive liquid; used as a reducing agent and in tanning.

formula. A group of symbols which show the number, type, and relative weight of the atoms in a molecule; examples, H_2SO_4 (sulfuric acid), CO_2 (carbon dioxide), H_2O_2 (hydrogen peroxide).

formula, electronic. A formula that shows the electronic relationships between the atoms in a molecule; example, the electronic formula of water is

$$H:\overset{..}{O}:H,$$ where the dots represent the valence electrons.

formula, empirical. A chemical formula showing the simplest numerical ratio between the atoms of a compound; example, the empirical formula of hydrogen peroxide is HO, whereas its molecular formula is H_2O_2.

formula, molecular. Same as formula.

formula, structural. A chemical formula which shows the arrangement of the atoms in the molecule and the valences that join them; example, the molecular formula of methane is CH_4; its structural formula is

$$H-\overset{\displaystyle H}{\underset{\displaystyle H}{C}}-H,$$ indicating that four monovalent hydrogen atoms are joined with one tetravalent carbon atom.

formula weight. Same as molecular weight, but referring to ionic compounds.

Fortin's barometer. A mercury cup barometer with an adjustable cistern used, together with correction tables, for more accurate measurements of atmospheric pressure than obtained by an ordinary barometer.

fossa. A pit or depression in a bone.

fossil: Traces of an organism, embedded and preserved in the earth's crust.

Foucault gyroscope. A gyroscope that is used as a stabilizer on a ship or aircraft; it is the basic element of the gyrocompass.

Foucault pendulum. A heavy metal ball suspended by a very long fine wire; the slow apparent change of the plane of oscillation of this pendulum is a proof of the rotation of the earth about its axis.

four cycle. Four-stroke cycle; the four piston strokes that complete a cycle in the operation of an internal-combustion engine; suction, compression, expansion, and exhaust.

fovea. Fovea centralis; the yellow spot; a small, light-sensitive spot on the retina of the eye where cone cells are especially abundant and the day vision is the sharpest.

fps. Foot-pound system of measurement; the English system.

Fr. Chemical symbol for francium.

fraction of saturation. Relative humidity; the ratio of the actual vapor pressure of the air to the maximum, or saturated, vapor pressure at the same temperature.

fractional crystallization. (1) The separation of a mixture of dissolved solids by evaporation until the least soluble component crystallizes out of solution; (2) the separation of the components of a magma by stepwise crystallization corresponding to the successive temperatures in the gradual cooling down of the entire mass.

fractional distillation. The process of separating a mixture of two or more liquids by means of the difference in their boiling points.

fractionating column. A long, vertical column or tube filled with packing material, sieve plates or bubble caps; it is connected to a distillation still for the effective separation of the higher and lower-boiling fractions of a liquid mixture with the aid of reflux inside the column.

fractionation. The separation of a mixture into its ingredients by fractional distillation or fractional crystallization.

fracture. (1) A break of a bone or cartilage; (2) the surface of a mineral broken not following its cleavage; example, calcite has a conchoidal fracture, but rhombic cleavage.

francium. Chemical symbol Fr; atomic number 87.

franklinite. Black, cubic mineral; $(Fe, Mn, Zn)(F_2O_2)_2$.

Frasch process. Extraction of sulfur from deposits deep down under sand by forcing superheated steam down a series of concentric pipes and forcing the melted sulfur to the surface.

fraternal twins. Twins that developed from two distinct eggs, each egg fertilized by a separate sperm; they are not always of the same sex and may be quite dissimilar.

Fraunhofer lines. Dark lines in the sun's spectrum caused by selective absorption in the cooler gaseous layer enveloping the glowing photosphere and in the earth's atmosphere; the lines are marked [A], [B], [C], etc., according to their position in the spectrum.

free. Uncombined, applied to elements which occur as such.

free central placentation. Attachment of the ovules in a plant to a placenta that projects from the ovary base free, without connection by partitions with the ovary walls.

free electron. An electron within a substance but not permanently attached to any atom and not restricted by potential gradients within the substance.

free energy. The energy of a reaction which can be converted into useful work outside the reaction.

free fall. The motion of an unrestrained body traveling in a gravitational field.

free grid. The grid of an electron tube which is electrically not connected.

free living. Not parasitic or attached.

free nuclear division. The division of the nucleus without cell-wall formation.

free surface. A phase boundary between two fluids.

free vibrations. The vibrations of a body at its natural frequency, without the application of outside force.

free water. (1) The water free to move among soil particles; it varies with the amount of rain; (2) the water that separates easily from a water-oil mixture.

freewheel. (1) A power-transmission system in automobiles; (2) a clutch in the rear hub of a bicycle which permits the rear wheel to continue turning when the pedal is not operated.

freeze-drying. Drying materials while in the frozen state by high vacuum.

freezing. A change of state from liquid to solid; it takes place at a constant temperature for any given substance under a given pressure.

freezing mixture. A mixture of two or more substances which produces a temperature below 32°F; example, the mixture of ice and sodium chloride.

freezing point. The temperature at which the solid form and the liquid form of a substance are in equilibrium; it is equivalent to the melting point; example, the freezing point of water and melting point of ice both are 0°C or 32°F.

freezing point depression. The lowering of the freezing point below its normal value by the presence of a solute in a liquid, which is proportional to the concentration of the solute; the value of the depression is constant for molar solutions of all substances; it is used for the determination of molecular weight.

frenulum. (1) A bristlelike structure in the humeral angle of the hind wing of a moth which holds the wings together in flight; (2) a membranous fold.

frequency. (1) The number of vibrations per second; (2) the number of cycles of an alternating current per second; (3) the relative number of a species in a given location.

frequency changer. A device that changes the frequency of the power it receives.

frequency condition. The condition of an atom or a molecule in which it is capable of emitting radiation of a given frequency.

frequency departure. The amount of variation of a carrier frequency or center frequency from its assigned value.

frequency meter. An instrument for measuring the frequency of an alternating current or of an electric oscillator.

frequency, natural. The frequency of free oscillation of a body or system.

fresnel. A unit of frequency; 10^{12} cycles per second.

Fresnel mirrors. A pair of mirrors placed side by side at an obtuse angle of a little less than 180°, which produce two adjacent images of a point or line source of light from which interference bands may be formed.

friction. The resistance that has to be overcome to move a surface over another surface.

friction layer. A layer of air below the free atmosphere where friction with the earth's surface affects the flow of air.

friction loss. The power absorbed by the bearings and sliding contacts of an electric machine.

frictional electricity. The electricity produced by rubbing together two dissimilar insulating materials; example, glass and fur.

Friedel-Crafts reaction. The preparation of aromatic hydrocarbons by the condensation of alkyl halides with benzene and its derivatives, with anhydrous aluminum chloride as the catalyst.

frigid zones. Areas between the Arctic and Antarctic circles and the poles.

fringes. Dark lines produced by the interference of light waves.

fringing reef. A coral reef built on or very near the shore so that the shoreline is pushed seaward.

frond. (1) Leaflike structure; (2) a leaf of sporophyte generation of a fern; (3) an expanded, flat thallus of a seaweed.

front. In meteorology, the boundary between two air masses; usually a region of most rapid weather changes.

frontal bone. One of the pair of large dermal bones covering the front part of the brain in vertebrates; in man, they unite into one bone forming the forehead and the top part of the orbits.

frontal lobe. The anterior part of each cerebral hemisphere.

frontal surface. A surface of discontinuity between air masses.

frontal thunderstorms. Thunderstorms due to vertical displacement of warm, moist air by a cold air mass along the entire cold front.

frontogenesis. The formation or intensification of a frontal surface.

frontolysis. Disintegration or weakening of a frontal surface.

frontoparietal index. The ratio of the smallest width of the forehead to the maximum width of the head.

frost. The condensation of water vapor into minute ice crystals on or near the ground when it has cooled below 32°F.

froth. Foam; a gas-in-liquid dispersion.

froth floatation. The separation of finely divided minerals by agitation in a mixture of water and oil; some ingredients will float, others will sink.

fructose. Levulose; fruit sugar; $C_6H_{12}O_6$; it occurs in fruit juices together with glucose.

fruit. A ripened ovary usually containing seeds.

fruit sugar. Same as fructose.

fruiting body. The spore-producing stalk of mushrooms.

fry. (1) A young fish just able to take care of itself; (2) an extraneous noise that has been added accidentally to recorded sound.

ft. Abbreviation for foot or feet.

ft-c. Abbreviation for foot candle.

ft-lb. Abbreviation for foot pound.

ft-lb/sec. Abbreviation for foot-pounds per second.

fuchsine. Rosaniline hydrochloride; dark-green crystals that yield a dark-red aqueous solution; used for dyeing silk and wool.

fucoid beds. Limestone series in the Cambrian system.

fucoxanthin. Brownish-red pigment present with chlorophyll in brown algae.

fucus. Brown algae; rockweeds; the dried stems of *Fucus vesi-*

culosus, which contain algin, are used in medicine.

fuel. A substance whose burning with air or oxygen yields heat energy; example, coal, petroleum, natural gas.

fuel dope. A chemical added to aircraft fuel in small quantities to prevent detonation and improve engine performance.

fuel oil. A liquid petroleum product used as a source of heat energy.

fugacity. The tendency of a substance to escape or disappear by some chemical process from the phase in which it is.

fulcrum. (1) A pivot about which a lever rotates; (2) a ridgelike scale in some fish; (3) a projection from the zygospore of some molds.

fulgurator. An apparatus used in spectroscopy consisting of an atomizer that sprays salt solution into a flame.

fumarole. An opening in lava or in a volcanic area through which steam and other hot gases are escaping into the air.

fume. Fine particles (0.1 to 1.0 micron) of a solid or liquid suspended in a gas.

fumigant. Toxic agent applied in the vapor phase to combat vermin, rodents, insects, molds, and bacteria; example, cyanogen, developed by pouring acid over sodium cyanide.

fumigation. Applying smoke, gases, or fumes as a means of disinfecting or killing pests.

function. The activity of a living cell, tissue or organ.

fundamental. (1) The basic frequency of a current containing currents of several frequencies; (2) the lowest note a sounding body can produce.

fungi. A subdivision of Thallophytes whose members contain no chlorophyll and display alternation of generations; examples, mushrooms, molds, rusts, yeasts.

fungicide. A chemical used to destroy fungi.

fungus. Singular of fungi.

funicle. The stalk of an ovule which attaches it to the placenta.

funiculus. (1) A structure that attaches the alimentary tract to the body wall of Bryozoa; (2) a segment of the antenna of some insects just before its terminal segment; (3) a bundle of nerve fibers in its sheath; (4) tracts of nerve fibers in the central nervous system of vertebrates.

funnel. (1) A conic vessel with a long hollow stem that is used for pouring liquids and powders from one container into another; (2) the swimming siphon of mollusks.

furca. (1) A forked organ in animals; (2) a pair of divergent projections at the caudal end

of the body of some Crustacea; (3) divergent nerve fibers of vertebrates.

furfural. C_4H_3OCHO; a colorless liquid; used as a solvent, in the manufacture of synthetic resins.

furnace. An apparatus for chemical processing at high temperatures.

fuse. (1) A low-melting alloy used in an electric circuit to break the circuit when an excessive current flows through it; (2) a gun-powder-filled tube used in mining for starting an explosion.

fused electrolyte. An electrically conductive molten compound; used for the manufacture of pure metals.

fusel oil. A colorless oily liquid; amyl alcohol; a by-product of alcoholic fermentation; used as a solvent, in varnish making.

fuselage. The body of an airplane which holds the engine, passengers, cargo, etc., and to which are attached the wings, tail, and landing gear.

fusibility. The readiness of a metal to change from the solid into the liquid state.

fusible alloy. A low-melting alloy.

fusiform. Spindle-shaped.

fusion. (1) The changing from a solid into a liquid; (2) the combination of nuclei of lighter elements to form a heavier nucleus.

fusion bomb. Hydrogen bomb.

fusion, nuclear. The union of two or more light atoms to make an atom of a heavier element, accompanied by the release of enormous energy.

fusion nucleus. One of two nuclei that unite into one in a central cell of a megaspore.

G

g. Abbreviation for gram, gravity, or conductance.

Ga. Chemical symbol for gallium.

gadolinium. A rare-earth metal that has not been isolated; chemical symbol Gd; atomic number 64.

gage (gauge). (1) An instrument for measuring pressure, temperature, water level, dimensions, etc.; (2) the thickness of a wire; (3) the relative distance of two ships; (4) the amount of gypsum in plaster.

gage, gas-discharge. A gage in which the gas discharge indicates the pressure of the system.

gage, ionization. A triode in which the rate of accumulation of positive ions on one electrode is used as a measure of the residual gas pressure in the tube.

gage, membrane. A pressure gage which uses the rate of damping the vibrations of a very thin, light silica membrane as a measure of pressure.

Gaillardia. A group of flowering plants.

gain. (1) The amplification of an electric circuit; (2) an increase in radio-signal power in transmission from one point to another; it is expressed in decibels.

gal. Abbreviation for gallon.

galactose. $C_6H_{12}O_6$; a simple sugar, a stereoisomer of glucose.

galaxy. The Milky Way; an astronomical system consisting of a vast number of suns, stars, and nebulae.

galaxy noise. A noise similar to thermal-electronic noise which comes from the general direction of the Milky Way.

gale. A wind of 39 to 54 miles per hour velocity.

galena. Dark-gray, cubic, common lead ore; lead sulfide, PbS.

Galilean telescope. A telescope, with a concave lens for ocular, in which no real image is formed; example, the opera glass.

gall. (1) Bile; a secretion of the liver of vertebrates; (2) an abnormal growth in plants caused by a parasite attack; (3) an injury of animal skin caused by a tight harness.

gall bladder. A pear-shaped organ on the underside of the liver which serves as a reservoir for bile.

gallery forests. Fringing forests that grow along a watercourse where there is a good supply of underground water.

Galliformes. Fowllike game birds; examples, pheasants, guinea hens, and quails.

gallium. Gray, crystalline, hard rare metal; chemical symbol Ga; atomic number 31; used in high-temperature thermometers.

gallon. An English unit of volume; 4 quarts; 231 cubic inches.

gallon of water. It weighs about 8 pounds.

Galton's whistle. A very-high-pitch whistle; used for determining the limit of audibility.

galvanic cell. The original naming of primary cells after Galvani.

galvanized iron. Iron covered with a protective coating of zinc.

galvanizing. The deposition of a zinc coating on iron or steel for corrosionproofing.

galvanoluminescence. A weak glow of the anode of some electrolytic cells in operation.

galvanometer. An instrument for measuring small electric currents.

galvanometer, astatic. A moving-magnet galvanometer which gives readings that are independent of the earth's magnetic field.

galvanometer, ballistic. A long-swing galvanometer used to measure the total quantity of electricity in a transient current.

galvanometer, D'Arsonval. A moving-coil galvanometer in which the fixed magnet is of the horseshoe type.

galvanometer, mirror. Reflecting galvanometer; a galvanometer in which the deflection is measured by the motion of a light beam reflected from a mirror attached to the moving part of the galvanometer.

galvanometer, moving-coil. A galvanometer in which a current-carrying coil is deflected by a fixed magnetic field.

galvanometer, tangent. A galvanometer in which a small magnetic needle is pivoted at the center of a large circular coil; the variations in the current are directly proportional to the tangent of the angle of deflection.

galvanometer, vibration. A galvanometer in which a straight, slender wire in the field of a magnet vibrates in synchronism with the frequency of the alternating current traversing it.

galvanoscope. An instrument for detecting the presence of an electric current.

galvanotropism. Galvanotaxis; the response of an organism to electrical stimulation.

gametangium. A plant organ in which the gametes are produced.

gamete. A male or female sex cell.

gametocyte. A mother cell which forms gametes after undergoing meiosis; example, oocyte.

gametogenesis. The formation of the mature gametes or sex cells by the gonads.

gametophyte. The plant or part of a plant which produces sex cells.

Gamma. (1) The third brightest star in a constellation; (2) a unit of magnetic field intensity; 10 oersteds.

gamma globulin. A protein in the blood plasma which does not build protoplasm, but contains antibodies as a protection against disease; it is used against measles and polio.

gamma iron. A nonmagnetic, allotropic form of iron which is the basic ingredient of austenite.

gamma rays. A highly penetrating emanation, which travels with the speed of light, from certain radioactive substances.

gamont. A sporont; an individual in the life cycle of certain one-celled animals whose subdivision produces gametes.

gamopetalous. Having united petals.

gamosepalous. Having united sepals.

ganglion. A group or mass of intimately connected nerve cells.

gangue. A worthless rock or vein in which valuable minerals occur.

ganoid scale. A rhomboidal fish scale consisting of an outer layer of ganoin over a layer of isopodin.

Ganoidei. An order of armored fish; examples, sturgeon and gar pike.

ganoin. A lime-containing substance secreted by the dermis, which forms the top layer of some fish scales.

gap. (1) A mountain pass opening through a ridge, connecting the valleys or lowlands on either side; (2) the space separating two electrodes between which a spark or arc is caused to pass; (3) an air gap separating two parts of a magnetic circuit.

gap arrester. A lightning arrester, based on the insertion of an air gap between the earth and the circuit to be protected.

gapeworm. A parasitic nematode roundworm that lives in the trachea and bronchi of fowls and other birds, causing the disease called gapes.

garnet. A group of red, cubic silicate minerals which show no cleavage; some species are used as gems.

gas. A state of matter characterized by the lack of definite shape and definite volume.

gas analysis. The quantitative determination of the constituents of gaseous mixtures by means of absorption.

gas balance. A device which measures the density of a gas.

gas carbon. A hard deposit of fairly pure carbon on the walls of the retorts used for the destructive distillation of coal; it is a good conductor of electricity and is used for carbon electrodes and crucibles.

gas discharge tube. A tube in which an electric discharge occurs in a gas.

gas focusing. Concentrating an electron beam through the action of ionized gas in a cathode-ray tube.

gas manometer. A pressure gage used for gases.

gas noise. A noise caused by the random production of ions in gas tubes and partially evacuated vacuum tubes.

gas oil. The residual oil left after the distillation of gasoline and kerosene from crude petroleum; yellow to brown oil; used as a Diesel fuel, for enriching water gas.

gas, permanent. A gas of very low temperature of liquefaction; examples, oxygen, hydrogen, nitrogen.

gas pressure. The pressure exerted by a gas on the walls of the containing vessel, caused by the molecules impinging on the walls.

gas producer. A machine for the manufacture of fuel gas from coal, steam, and air.

gas ratio. Gas factor; the ratio of the ion current in a vacuum tube to the electron current that produces it.

gas scrubbing. Removing the impurities from a gas by bubbling it through a liquid purifying agent.

gas thermometer. Air thermometer; a device for measuring temperature by the application of the gas laws concerning the variation of the volume and pressure of gases with the temperature.

gas tube. An electron tube in which the pressure of the contained gas or vapor affects the electrical characteristics of the tube.

gas, two-dimensional. A layer of adsorbed gas of monomolecular thickness.

gaseous tube generator. A power source made up of a gas-filled electron-tube oscillator, a power supply, and control equipment.

gas-filled lamp. A lamp which is filled with an inert gas at about atmospheric pressure.

gasoline. A low-boiling inflammable, volatile liquid obtained in the fractional distillation of petroleum; used as a fuel and as a solvent.

gasoline engine. An internal-combustion engine which uses the heat energy of gasoline for its operation.

gastric caeca. Enteric caeca; pouchlike processes on the front of the stomach, which secrete digestive fluid into the stomach of insects.

gastric filament. Slender projections on the floor of the stomach of a jellyfish which contain stinging cells to kill the living prey taken into the stomach.

gastric juice. A digestive juice secreted into the stomach where it acts on foods; about 99.5% of the human gastric juice is water which contains fractional percentages of free hydrochloric acid, sodium, potassium, and calcium chlorides, calcium, magnesium and iron phosphates, organic matter and enzymes.

gastric shield. A hard plate in the stomach of bivalve mollusks against which the crystalline style is worn away.

gastrocnemius. The large muscle on the posterior side of the lower leg of land vertebrates.

Gastropoda. Asymmetrical mollusks that have one shell, which is generally curved or coiled; examples, snails and limpets.

gastrovascular. Performing the functions of both digestion and circulation.

gastrovascular cavity. The central cavity of Porifera and Coelenterata.

gastrozooid. An individual in a hydrozoan colony whose function is to digest food for the colony.

gastrula. A stage in embryonic development in which the blastula folds in and forms a two-layered, cup-shaped mass.

gastrulation. Cell movements which occur in almost all animals at the end of the cleavage period; the cells move to their positions in the gastrula.

gate. (1) A circuit used in computers which has one output and a multiplicity of inputs in such a way that the output is energized when a certain definite set of input conditions is met; (2) the channel through which the molten metal flows into a mold; (3) a valve regulating the water supply in a conduit.

gauss. The metric unit of magnetic flux density; one maxwell per square centimeter; one line of induction per square centimeter.

Gaussian unit. An absolute unit of force, such as the dyne or poundal, defined in terms of its accelerating effect on a given mass.

Gay-Lussac's law of combining volumes. The volume of gases used and produced in a chemical reaction can always be represented by the ratio of small whole numbers.

GCA. Ground-Control Approach; an aircraft landing guided by radio; landing directions are given to the pilot by radio by a ground operator who uses a radarscope for observing the position of the landing aircraft.

Gd. Chemical symbol for gadolinium.

Ge. Chemical symbol for germanium.

Gegenschein. Faint, oval patch of light seen diametrically opposite the sun in the sky; it is analogous to the zodiacal light.

Geiger counter. A gas-filled metal tube with a needle electrode which indicates every ionizing particle entering the tube by the ionization of its gas content.

Geiger-Müller counter. A device for detecting and measuring radioactivity by the ionization it produces.

Geissler tube. A gas-discharge tube of moderate exhaustion, which exhibits bright glow discharges and sometimes fluorescence effects interrupted by dark spots.

gel. A colloidal sol which has set to a jellylike consistency.

gelatin. A protein found in animal cartilage and bones; it is a yellowish, transparent solid, soluble in water; used in food, photography, as an adhesive and protective colloid.

Gelignite (a trade-mark). An explosive consisting of a mixture of nitroglycerin, nitrocellulose, saltpeter, and wood pulp.

gelling point. The temperature at which a colloidal solution or other semiliquids become solid.

GEM (ground-effect machine). An air-cushion vehicle.

Gemini. A constellation which marks the third sign of the Zodiac.

gemma. (1) The organ of vegetative reproduction in mosses and liverworts, which becomes detached from the parent and develops into a new plant; (2) an asexual, nonmotile spore of some algae; (3) a bud which yields a new individual.

gemmation. Asexual reproduction by formation of a group of cells which develops into a new individual.

gemmule. Reproductive bodies of fresh-water sponges enclosed in protective capsules which enable them to withstand severe conditions of temperature and draught.

gene. According to the theory of chromosomes, a hypothetical unit in a cell nucleus which determines a hereditary character.

gene frequency. The frequency of occurrence of a gene in a population in relation to the frequency of its allelomorphs.

general circulation. Atmospheric circulation; the grand wind system of the entire earth.

general radiation. Continuous radiation; examples, white light and the background of an x-ray spectrum.

generation. The collective name for all living beings existing in a certain period of time; a geneological rank.

generation time. The average time between successive generations of thermal fissions in a nuclear reactor.

generative nucleus. A cell in a pollen grain which divides to form two sperms.

generator. (1) A device that converts mechanical energy into electrical energy; (2) a gas-producing chemical apparatus.

generator, acoustic. A transducer which changes electric, mechanical, or other forms of energy into sound.

generic. Pertaining to the genus.

genetics. The scientific study of heredity.

genital. Pertaining to the reproductive organ of either sex.

genital bursa. Bursa copulatrix; a female copulatory organ in certain animals; a cavity lined with ciliated ectoderm at the base of each arm of the brittle stars into which the reproductive glands discharge.

genital operculum. A small plate formed of the united vestiges of a pair of appendages, which cover the openings of the genital ducts of scorpions.

genital pore. An external opening on the ventral surface of a flatworm communicating with the genital atrium into which the reproductive duct discharges.

genital rachis. A ring of tissue in Echinodermata, whose branches bear the reproductive organs.

genital stolon. A mass of genital cells associated with the axial organ of Echinodermata.

genitalia. The organs of reproduction.

genome. The sum of all different chromosomes found in each nucleus of a given species.

genotype. The genetic constitution as contrasted with the characteristics manifested by the organism.

genu. A kneelike structure.

genus (plural, genera). A class between the family and species in the classification of plants and animals; a group of related species.

geobenthos. All organisms that live on the land surface.

geocentric coordinates. A system of coordinates on the celestial sphere which uses the center of the earth for its origin or reference point.

geocentric theory. Geocentrism; the ancient theory that the earth is the center of the universe.

geochemistry. Chemistry which deals with the chemical composition of and the past and present chemical changes in the earth's crust.

geode. A cavity in a stone nodule whose inside walls are lined with crystals.

geodesic line. The shortest distance between two points on a spherical surface; an arc of a great circle.

geodesy. Surveying in which allowance is made for the curvature of the earth.

geography. The science of the earth's surface and the life on it.

geology. The study of the composition and formation of the earth's crust.

geometrical optics. The study of light as if it were actually composed of rays diverging in various directions from the source and bent by refraction or turned back by reflection into paths determined by well-known laws.

geomorphology. The description and interpretation of the surface features or topographical pattern of the earth.

geophysics. The study of the physical properties of the earth, including its atmosphere and hydrosphere.

geosyncline. A long and narrow fold in sedimentary rocks, which has the greatest thickness in the center.

geotaxis. The movement of organisms in response to the gravitational force.

geothermal. Referring or pertaining to the internal heat from the earth.

geotropism. (1) Geotaxis; (2) a tendency of a plant to bring its parts in the direction of the gravitational force, resulting in one side growing faster than the other or bending of stems.

germ. (1) A small living mass from which a plant or animal may develop; (2) a virus; (3) the embryo in its early stages.

germ cell. A sexual reproductive cell.

germ layer. One of the three primary cell layers in an embryo, ectoderm, endoderm, or mesoderm.

germ plasm. The contents of germ cells, by which hereditary characters are transmitted.

German silver. Nickel silver; a silver-gray, lustrous, corrosion-resistant copper-base alloy, containing zinc and nickel; used for ornaments.

germanium. A grayish-white metallic element of the silicon group; chemical symbol Ge; atomic number 32; used in transistors.

germicide. A chemical which kills germs or microorganisms.

germinal epithelium. The epithelium that lines the seminiferous tubules of the vertebrate testis.

germinal vesicle. The nucleus of the animal oocyte during the period of cytoplasmic growth.

germination. The start of growth in a seed or spore.

gestation. The time which elapses between fertilization and birth; the development of the embryo in the uterus.

getter. An easily oxidizable substance, usually a metal, used to remove the final traces of gas from the inside of vacuum tubes or electric lamps.

geyser. Hot water and steam erupting violently into the air at more or less regular intervals; the eruption is caused by the volume expansion of boiling water turning into steam.

geyserite. A form of silica deposited in and about the craters of geysers or around hot springs which rise through volcanic rocks.

G-force. The gravitational pull needed to move a body 32 feet per second.

ghosts. False lines found in a line spectrum due to imperfections in the ruling of the diffraction grating used.

giant fiber. Nerve fiber of unusually large diameter occurring in many invertebrates and some vertebrates, providing for very rapid conduction of impulses for sudden locomotion in emergency.

giant star. A star of higher total luminosity than that of the other members of the same spectral class.

gianticlines. Anticlines of large dimensions.

gibbous. Said of the moon or a planet when more than one half of it is illuminated, but it is not fully luminous.

Gibbs' adsorption theory. A solute that lowers the surface tension of a solvent is usually adsorbed at the interface.

gilbert. The metric unit of magnetomotive force; it is equal to the magnetomotive force that would establish one line of force in a magnetic circuit of unit reluctance; $4\pi/10$ ampere-turns.

gilding. Depositing a layer of gold by electroplating, or coating with gold leaf or powder by hand.

gill. (1) The radiating gill-shaped plates on the lower side of the mushroom cap; around each gill, there is a spore-producing structure; (2) the respiratory organ of some aquatic animals; (3) the fleshy flap below the beak of a fowl.

gill arch. The support of the gill filaments and rakers.

gill bar. Gill rod; a tissue which contains blood vessels, nerves, and skeletal support and which separates adjacent gill slits in lancelets.

gill book. A series of many thin respiratory plates associated with the jointed appendages of the horseshoe crab.

gill chamber. A partially enclosed space containing gills.

gill cleft. Same as gill slit.

gill filament. A threadlike part of gills filled with capillaries which absorbs oxygen and excretes carbon dioxide as water flows past it.

gill fungi. Agarics; mushrooms which have a stalk and a cap, on the under surface of which are radially arranged gills bearing the hymenium.

gill plate. The respiratory organ of some bivalve mollusks.

gill pouch. (1) A sac in the chordate embryo, projecting from the side wall of the pharynx toward the epidermis; (2) a saclike gill slit in Cyclostomata.

gill rakers. Comblike projections, attached to the gill arch, which act as filters, sifting out food and other particles, thus keeping them away from the gill filaments.

gill slit. A branchial cleft; an opening between two branchial arches of vertebrates breathing by gills, through which water passes from the mouth to the

gills on the exterior; a perforation of the body wall of vertebrates, opening into the pharynx.

Ginkgoales. An order of Gymnospermae that flourished during the Mesozoic era; the only living member is the ginkgo of China, a tree having fan-shaped deciduous leaves and yellow drupelike fruit.

girdle. (1) A part of the mantle of a chiton which surrounds the shell plate; (2) the skeletal structure of vertebrates by which the appendages are associated with the trunk.

gizzard. Proventriculus; (1) a thick-walled, muscular chamber of the gut of earthworms, situated after the crop, which grinds the food; (2) an organ of the digestive system of birds modified for grinding food.

glacial acetic acid. Pure concentrated acetic acid of low melting point, so that it crystallizes readily, yielding icelike crystals; used in chemical synthesis.

glacial drift. Deposits laid down by glaciers.

glacial soil. Soil deposited by a glacier.

glacial striae. Grooves in the bedrock made by the grinding action of pebbles and rock fragments in the glacial moraine that passed over it; the direction of the striae is parallel to the motion of the glacier.

glacier. A large mass of ice formed from snow on high ground where winter snowfall exceeds summer melting.

Gladstone-Dale law. The refractivity of a medium is proportional to its density as it varies with the pressure or temperature.

gland. (1) A plant cell or group of cells which secretes a substance that is frequently resinous or oily or contains enzymes; (2) an epithelial cell or cell aggregate which is specialized in excreting some substance which is useful to the animal organism or is evacuated from it.

glands, sweat. Glands in all parts of the skin which secrete perspiration.

glass. An amorphous brittle, usually transparent, solid consisting ordinarily of a mixture of fused silicates.

glaze. (1) Sleet; an ice coating on road surfaces, etc., resulting from freezing rain; (2) a glossy, glasslike, colorless or pigmented coating applied to pottery or porcelain after the first firing.

glenoid cavity. A cuplike hollow on either side of the pectoral girdle into which the head of the humerus fits, forming the shoulder-joint in tetrapod vertebrates.

glia. Neuroglia; the supporting

tissue of the vertebrate central nervous system; cells with long fibrous processes.

gliadin. Prolamin; a protein found in wheat and other cereal grains.

glide. The descent of an aircraft at a normal angle without sufficient power for level flight.

glide landing. Same as glide.

glide plane. The common plane of two axes of a twin crystal.

glider. An aircraft similar in appearance to an airplane but without a power plant.

gliding. (1) The formation of twin crystals; (2) glide landing.

gliding angle. The angle between the flight path of a gliding aircraft and the horizontal.

gliding joint. A movable joint which provides flexibility and movement in any direction; example, the joint between the wrist bones.

gliding plane. A plane within a crystal along which a displacement without cleavage of the crystal lattice occurs under a shearing stress.

Globigerina. One-celled animals with shells near the surface of the ocean; chalk is made of the shells of these animals.

Globigerina ooze. Calcareous mud, covering about one third of the ocean floor, derived from shells of Globigerina, a genus of the order of Foraminifera.

globular clusters. An immense number of stars condensed in a roughly spherical form.

globulin. A group of heat-coagulable proteins, which are soluble in dilute salt solution, but not in water; the chief proteins of plant seeds and antibodies.

globulite. A microscopic crystal of globular shape, without definite plane faces, due to strong surface-tension effects at the time of formation of the crystal; they are found in natural glasses.

Gloeocapsa. A genus of blue-green algae appearing in colonies on damp tree trunks, rocks, and walls and occurring both in fresh and salt water.

glomerulus. (1) A minute rounded body in the cortex of a kidney; a knot of blood vessels; a Malpighian body which acts as a filter for the blood in the kidney; (2) an inflorescence consisting of a head of crowded small flowers.

glossmeter. A photometer which measures the ratio of the light regularly or specularly reflected from a surface to the total light reflected.

glossopharyngeal nerve. One of the ninth cranial-nerve pair of vertebrates; in mammals, it is concerned with both the sensory and motor aspect of the swallowing reflex and the taste buds at the back of the tongue.

glottis. The narrow opening between the vocal cords.

glow discharge. A luminous, silent electrical discharge in a gas-filled tube at low pressure and with low voltage.

glow potential. The value of voltage at which a glow discharge begins in a vacuum tube as the voltage gradually increases.

glucose. $C_6H_{12}O_6$; grape sugar; dextrose; it may be obtained by the hydrolysis of starch.

glucoside. An organic substance found in plants that, by hydrolysis, yields sugar.

glume. An empty bract which occurs at the base of the spikelet in grasses; usually two to each spikelet.

gluten. The protein substance in cereals which makes them sticky when wet and crushed.

glyceride. An ester of glycerol with organic acids; example, glyceryl monooleate.

glycerin. $CH_2OH \cdot CHOH \cdot CH_2OH$; a colorless, syrupy trihydric alcohol obtained from the hydrolysis of fats and as a by-product of soap making; used in cosmetics, explosives, as a solvent.

glycogen. An animal starch; a complex carbohydrate formed from glucose and starch in the liver and other organs of animals, serving as a sugar reserve.

glycol. Ethylene glycol; $CH_2OH \cdot CH_2OH$; a colorless liquid; used as an antifreeze, solvent, in explosives.

glycols. Dihydric alcohols derived from aliphatic hydrocarbons by substituting hydroxyl groups for two of the hydrogen atoms.

glycolysis. The hydrolysis of sugars.

glyptolith. A wind-faceted pebble.

Gnathostomata. Vertebrates with jaws.

gneiss. A coarse-grained rock derived by metamorphic processes from existing igneous or sedimentary formations; the light-colored bands are laminated, whereas the dark bands display a granular structure.

Gnetales. The order of Gymnospermae which resemble members of Angiospermae in that they have true vessels in the secondary wood.

gnomonic map. A map on which all great circles appear as straight lines.

goblet cell. A pear-shaped epithelial cell; the part near the free surface of the epithelium contains mucin which is secreted to the surface.

goethite. A reddish-brown mineral; hydrated iron oxide; it is the chief constituent of rust.

Golay pneumatic cell. A small transparent gas-filled cell which is used to ward and detect radiation.

gold. A corrosionproof noble metal that dissolves only in *aqua regia* (a mixture of four parts of concentrated hydrochloric acid and one part of concentrated nitric acid); chemical symbol Au; atomic number 79.

Goldschmidt process. Thermit process; the preparation of metals from the oxides by reduction with finely divided aluminum powder.

Golgi apparatus. A protoplasmic cell inclusion which is active in the metabolism of cells.

Golgi bodies. Cytoplasmic particles in a cell.

gonadotrophic hormones. Hormones secreted by the anterior lobe of the pituitary gland of vertebrates, which control the activity of the gonads.

gonads. Reproductive organs which are specialized for the production of mature gametes or sex cells.

gonangium. Gonotheca; a sheath enclosing the blastostyle and gonophores of certain hydroids.

gonidium. A minute intracellular body which serves as a means of asexual reproduction.

goniometer. An instrument for measuring the angles between the surfaces of a crystal or prism.

Gonium. A very small animal which consists of a colonial group of sixteen cells, each practically independent.

gonosome. The sexual stage of the hydrozoan-medusoid.

gonozooid. (1) An attached medusoid as borne by the blastostyle of some Hydrozoa; (2) sexual individuals in the salpian colony.

Goode's homolosine projection. A map representing the land areas of the world with a minimum distortion.

gorge. A narrow, steep river valley or canyon cut into bedrock.

gossan. The decomposed upper parts of sulfide mineral veins and ore deposits.

gr. Abbreviation for grain.

Graafian follicle. A spherical fluid-filled vesicle enveloped by a layer of epithelial tissue found in a mammalian ovary containing an ovum attached to its wall.

graben. A broad valley flanked on each side by fault scarps; it was formed when the earth dropped between parallel faults of great length.

gradation. In geology, bringing the land surface to a nearly uniform grade; the formation of plains by streams.

grade. (1) Gradient; the degree of slope; (2) a slope of the bed of a stream such that the water has just velocity enough to carry its load within either erosion or deposition; (3) the ratio of the height of an incline to its length.

graded bedding. A stratification characterized by a cyclic or rhythmic deposition of coarse to fine sediments.

gradient. (1) A deviation from a level surface to an inclined plane, measured in feet per mile; (2) unit rise in height per number of units covered along a slope; (3) the rate of change with distance; example, temperature gradient in a metal bar.

gradient wind. A flow of air necessary to balance a pressure gradient; its direction is along the isobars and its velocity is adjusted to yield an equilibrium of the gradient force and centrifugal force.

gradiometer. An instrument for measuring slopes or grades.

graduated cylinder. A calibrated vessel used to measure liquids.

graduation. Making the scale of an instrument.

grafting. (1) Inserting a part of a living plant into another so that it will continue to grow as a part of the second plant; (2) transferring by surgery a piece of tissue or bone from one part of the body to another.

Graham's law of gaseous diffusion. The velocity of diffusion of a gas is inversely proportional to the square root of its density.

grain. (1) A unit of weight; 64.8 milligrams; 1/7000 pound; (2) cereals in general; (3) the markings on wood due to annual rings, medullary rays and the size, shape, arrangement, and structure of the cells; (4) crystal in the metallic structure.

grain alcohol. Ethyl alcohol, C_2H_5OH; obtained by the fermentation of cereal grains.

gram. A unit of weight in the metric system; the weight of one cubic centimeter of water at 4°C; 100 centigrams; 1000 milligrams; 1/1000 kilogram; 0.035 ounce; 0.0022 pound; 15.4 grains.

gram atom. The atomic weight of an element expressed in grams.

gram calorie. Small calorie; the unit of heat in the metric system; the amount of heat required to raise the temperature of one gram of water 1°C.

gram ion. The sum of the atomic weights in an ion expressed in grams.

gram molecule. The molecular weight in grams.

gram-centimeter. A metric unit of work and energy; the work accomplished in exerting a force of one gram through a distance of one centimeter.

gram-equivalent weight. The weight of a substance in grams which will combine with or replace one gram of hydrogen.

Gramme ring. An electromagnet whose core is a continuous iron ring; used as an armature in electric machines.

gram-molecular volume. Molar volume; the volume of one gram-molecular weight of a gas at normal pressure and temperature; for an ideal gas, it is 22.4 liters.

Gram-negative bacteria. Bacteria that are decolorized by alcohol or acetone after staining with an aniline dye, such as methyl violet.

Gram-positive bacteria. Bacteria which are not decolorized by a decolorizing agent after staining with certain aniline dyes.

Gram's method. The differentiation of Gram-positive and Gram-negative bacteria by staining with gentian violet and treating with Gram's solution; the Gram-positive bacteria retain the stain, while the Gram-negative bacteria are decolorized.

grand period of growth. The total growth cycle of a cell, or organ of a plant under standard external conditions; the growth is slow at first, then reaches a peak, and finally falls off to zero at maturity.

granite. A very hard, crystalline, granular rock, consisting mainly of quartz, feldspar, and horneblende; used in building and road construction.

granitoid texture. The relatively uniform and coarse interlocking grain of batholithic rocks.

granules. Small particles found in cells; they are believed to consist of stored food or wastes.

granulite. Nonbanded granular rock that developed by metamorphic processes from quartz-feldspar rock.

grape sugar. D-Glucose; $C_6H_{12}O_6$; used for food.

graph. A diagram, generally plotted between axes at right angles to each other, showing the relation of one variable quantity to another.

graphic granite. Runite; a coarsely crystalline variety of granite composed almost entirely of quartz and feldspar which have intergrown in such a manner as to simulate semitic or cuneiform characters.

graphite. Naturally occurring allotropic form of carbon; used as a lubricant, in refractories, pencils, nuclear reactors.

graptolites. Fossilized skeletons of extinct colonial animals, which help geologists in classifying geological strata.

grassland. An area where there is a water supply insufficient for forests but enough for a heavy growth of grasses.

grating. A means of dispersing light or other wave emission by interference between wave trains issuing from fine, parallel slits in an opaque plate or from very narrow, parallel reflecting surfaces made by ruling grooves on polished metal.

grating constant. The distance between successive rulings of a diffraction grating.

gravel. (1) Pebbles mixed with sand; (2) small stones in the uterus or urinary bladder of animals.

gravimetric analysis. Quantitative chemical analysis by weight.

gravitation. The mutual attraction between masses which is directly proportional to the product of the masses and inversely proportional to their distance; specifically, the attraction exerted by the earth on an object on its surface.

gravitational water. Water that moves downward into the zone of ground water.

graviton. In quantum physics, the elemental unit of the gravitational field; its rest mass and charge are zero.

gravity. The force that pulls all bodies on or near the earth's surface toward the center of the earth.

gravity cell. A two-fluid voltaic cell in which the fluids are kept separate by the difference in their specific gravities.

gravity pressure. Pressure caused by the weight of liquids.

gravity tank. Fuel tank arranged above the engine of an aircraft so that it supplies the fuel without a pump, by gravity.

gravity water system. A water system in which the pressure is obtained by gravity due to a high location of the source of water.

gray. An achromatic color.

gray body. A body whose spectral emissivity is smaller than, but of the same distribution as, that of a black body at the same temperature.

gray iron. Pig or cast iron which contains graphitic carbon.

gray matter. A tissue made up mainly of nerve cells and nerve fibers; it forms the outer part of the brain and the inner part of the spinal cord.

gray scale. A series of achromatic tones ranging from black to white, usually divided into ten divisions; used in photography.

great circle. Any circle drawn on a sphere that divides the sphere into two equal halves.

Great Plains. A treeless area of gently rolling land, covered for the most part by short grass; it extends from the Mississippi to the Rocky Mountains.

great year. Platonic year; the time required for a complete revolution of the equinoctial points; 26,000 years.

great-circle chart. Gnomonic-projection chart; a chart prepared by projecting the surface of a sphere on a plane that is tangent to the sphere.

great-circle course. The shortest distance between any two points on the surface of a sphere; the great circle that passes through the points.

green glands. Glands in the head of crayfish; they remove wastes from the blood stream and excrete them through excretory pores at the base of the antenna.

green plant. An independent plant; one that contains chlorophyll and thus is able to make its own food.

green vitriol. Copperas; melanterite; ferrous sulfate, $FeSO_4 \cdot 7H_2O$.

greenockite. A yellow crystalline mineral; cadmium sulfide, CdS; used as a pigment in rubber and paper.

Greenwich mean time. The mean solar time; it begins at midnight and is the same as the universal time.

Greenwich meridian. The prime meridian from whose intersection with the equator the longitude is counted; located in Greenwich, England.

Gregorian telescope. A reflecting telescope with a concave secondary mirror to reflect the light through an opening in the primary mirror, and form a real image in the eyepiece.

grid. A coil, screen, or mesh of fine wires supported between the cathode and anode of a vacuum tube; it controls the flow of electrons from the cathode to the anode.

grid base. The region of grid voltage between the point where the plate current is cut off and that at which the grid current begins to flow; the positive grid region.

grid battery. C battery; a battery in the grid circuit of a vacuum tube, which controls the plate current.

grid bias. A steady voltage applied between the grid and cathode of a vacuum tube.

grid circuit. The input circuit of a vacuum tube; the circuit connected between the grid and the cathode.

grid condenser. The condenser placed between the grid and one filament terminal.

grid control. Controlling the anode current in a vacuum tube by means of the grid potential.

grid current. The current that flows from the grid to the cathode when the control grid becomes positive.

grid leak. A very high resistance placed in parallel with the grid condenser to avoid charge accumulation on the grid.

grid, radio. The electrode in a radio tube which controls the flow of electrons.

grid resistance. A starting resistance for very large d-c motors which consists of grids mounted next to each other in an iron frame.

grid resistor. A high resistance used in the grid circuit of a radio tube.

grid return. A wire connecting the end of the grid coil to the filament circuit.

grid swing. The amount by which the voltage on the control grid shifts up and down from its mean value, increasing and decreasing in step with and as a result of the signal voltage.

grid voltage, critical. The instantaneous value of grid voltage at which the anode current begins to flow in a gas tube.

grid-glow tube. A cold-cathode, glow-discharge tube with at least one starting grid for initiating the discharge between anode and cathode.

Grignard reagent. A reagent important in organic synthesis; it is a solution in ether of an organomagnesium halide; example, ethyl magnesium iodide, C_2H_5MgI.

grit. Coarse-grained sandstone whose components are angular.

gross structure. The general multiplet structure of an atomic spectrum.

Grotthuss-Draper law. The first law of fluorochemistry; light is photochemcially active only when it is absorbed by the substance affected.

ground. An electrical connection to the earth; usually a pipe driven into the earth, or metal plates buried in the earth.

ground form. The basic form of any crystal system which is bounded by natural faces, all of which intersect the crystal axis.

ground ice. Anchor ice; a porous ice layer that forms under the surface of flowing or still water.

ground gear. The equipment necessary for the landing and handling of an aircraft on the ground.

ground loop. An uncontrollable, sharp turn of an airplane while taxiing, or during the landing or take-off run.

ground meristem. A primary meristem which gives rise to the cortex, pericycle, pith rays, and pith.

ground moraine. A mantle of unassorted drift deposited underneath glacial ice.

ground speed. The velocity of an aircraft relative to the earth, measured horizontally.

ground state. The most stable state of an atom; the normal state of an atom when the movement of its circumnuclear electrons in orbits yields a minimum of energy.

ground swell. Wide and deep ocean waves that oscillate back and forth but have no average forward movement; they are caused by earthquake or lasting gale-force winds.

ground water. The water that collects in the subsoil.

ground wave. Direct ray; a radio wave that travels directly, without reflection, from the sender to the receiver.

ground-speed meter. An instrument for measuring the speed of an aircraft in relation to the ground.

ground-water level. (1) the water table; the top surface of the zone of the earth's crust that is saturated with water; (2) the position of ground water as compared to sea level.

group. A vertical column of elements in the periodic table.

group phenomena. Properties of the crystalline state which arise from the agglomeration of a definite number of atoms into groups.

growth. (1) A collective name for the processes by which an organism develops and increases in size; (2) a volume increase of cast iron due to repeated heating and cooling.

growth ring. Annual ring; a ring in the cross section of a tree trunk which corresponds to a yearly growth.

grub. The soft wormlike larva of certain beetles.

Grüneisen's law. The ratio of the coefficient of expansion of a metal to its specific heat at constant pressure is a constant at all temperatures.

guano. Large deposits formed from the excrement and bodies of seabirds in the coastal regions of South America and Africa; it is a fertilizer rich in nitrogen and phosphorus.

guard cells. A pair of crescent-shaped cells which regulate the size of each stoma.

Guarnieri bodies. Cytoplasmic inclusions found in an epithelial cell lesion in smallpox.

guide fossils. Fossils which are found only in rocks of a certain age.

guided missile. A self-steering missile, often driven by a rocket engine, steered toward the target by means of built-in radio or radar; it carries no pilot.

gullet. The food pipe or esophagus in multicelled animals; in Protozoa, the food tube leading into the cell.

gully. A gorge excavated by running water.

gum. A water-soluble substance exuded from plants.

gum arabic. Yellow powder obtained from the juice of acacia species; used as an adhesive, in food products.

gun metal. An alloy consisting of 88% copper, 10% tin, and 2% zinc; used for castings.

guncotton. Nitrocellulose; cellulose hexanitrate; a powerful explosive.

gunpowder. An explosive mixture of potassium nitrate, powdered charcoal, and sulfur.

gusher. (1) A geyser; (2) an oil well with a powerful natural flow.

gust. A squall; a sudden, violent, brief wind.

guttation. The exudation of a fluid from plant surfaces.

Gymnospermae. A group of plants, mostly conifers, which produce uncovered seeds, usually in conelike structures; commonly called evergreens.

gynandromorph. An animal having both female and male characteristics; due to a disturbance of the genetic sex-determination mechanism during embryonic cleavage.

gynodioecious. Having female and hermaphrodite flowers on separate plants.

gynoecium. The carpels of a flower; a collective name of pistils.

gynomonoecious. Having female and hermaphrodite flowers on the same plant.

gypsum. Mineral calcium sulfate, $CaSO_4 \cdot 2H_2O$; used for making plaster of Paris and Portland cement.

gyration. Whirling around a fixed axis or center.

gyro. Short for gyroscope.

gyro horizon. An artificial horizon used in aircraft indicated by a spinning gyroscope which maintains its position when set spinning in a horizontal plane.

gyrocompass. A gyroscope that is used for indicating direction; it depends for its action on the conservation of the angular momentum of a spinning body.

gyrodynamics. The dynamics of rotating bodies.

gyromagnetic. Pertaining to the magnetic properties of a rotating electric charge, especially of an electron moving within an atom.

gyroscope. A heavy wheel or disk rotated at high speed, which maintains a fixed axis of rotation; it is used as a compass and a stabilizer in ships and aircraft.

gyrostabilizer. An aircraft or ship stabilizer that contains a Foucault gyroscope which is restricted to a back-and-forth movement in a vertical plane.

gyrostat. Same as gyroscope.

H

H. Chemical symbol for hydrogen.

Haber process. The production of ammonia from atmospheric nitrogen and from hydrogen at 200 to 300 atmospheres pressure and about 500°C with the aid of catalysts.

habit. (1) An act which has to be learned at first but becomes an automatic act after frequent repetition; (2) the general mode of growth in a plant; (3) the usual behavior of an animal species; (4) the property of minerals of crystallizing in varying forms.

habitat. The place where a plant or animal naturally lives.

hachures. Lines drawn on a map to indicate slopes of ground.

hafnium. A metallic element; chemical symbol Hf; atomic number 72; used in tungsten filaments.

hail. Hailstones; ice globules built up of ice layers deposited on a frozen raindrop; they usually fall from thunderstorms.

hair. (1) A trichome; an outgrowth from an epidermal plant cell; (2) keratinous, slender projections from the Malpighian layer of the epidermis of mammals.

hair follicle. A slender pit in the skin which contains the root of a hair.

hair hygrometer. An instrument for measuring the relative humidity of the air based on the variations in the length of human hair with the changes in humidity.

half cell. A single-electrode system; an electrode immersed in an electrolyte, operating by reversible ionization between the electrode and the electrolyte.

half life. The length of time it takes for the disintegration rate of a radioactive substance to decrease by half.

half life, biological. The amount of time in which a living tissue, organ, or individual, eliminates, through biological processes, one-half of a given amount of a radioactive substance which has been introduced into it.

half life, effective. The half life of a radioactive isotope in a biological organism, resulting from the combination of radioactive decay and biological elimination.

half-period zone. Huyghens' division of the optical wave front into concentric zones in such a manner that the waves which reach a specific point ahead of the wave from adjacent zones differ in phase by half a period.

half-shade analyzer. A polarimeter in which one half of the field of vision is generally in shadow, but at the neutral point both halves have the same illumination and the angle of rotation can be read on a scale.

half-silvered. Said of a surface coated with a metallic film of such thickness that it transmits almost half of the light falling on it at normal incidence and reflects almost half.

half-value layer. In the absorption of radiation by any given substance, the thickness of that substance which will reduce the intensity to one half its initial value.

half-wave plate. A plate of double-refracting material cut parallel to the optic axes and of such thickness that there is a phase difference of one-half period between the ordinary and extraordinary waves, if light falls normally on it; used to change the plane of vibration of plane-polarized light.

half-wave rectification. Single-wave rectification; the change from alternating to direct current, in which a pulse of direct current flows for each positive half cycle of alternating current.

halide. A binary compound of one of the halogen elements; examples, sodium chloride, NaCl; hydrogen bromide, HBr.

haliplankton. A plankton found in salt water.

halite. Rock salt; the naturally occurring sodium chloride, NaCl.

Hall effect. The development of a transverse electric potential-gradient in a current-carrying conductor when a magnetic field is applied.

Hall process. The manufacture of aluminum by the electrolysis of fused aluminum oxide.

Hall tellurian globe. A device used for illustrating the motions of the earth and their effects, that is, the alternation of day and night, the seasons being dependent on the declination of the sun, etc.

halleflinta. A hard, dense, metamorphic rock composed chiefly of microscopic crystals of quartz and feldspar.

Hallen's law. A law that indicates the relative frequency of the birth of twins, triplets, quadruplets, and quintuplets in the total number of births.

hallux. The big toe of a pentadactyl hind-limb; often shorter than other digits.

Hallwachs effect. The discharge of a negatively charged body in a vacuum due to the incidence of ultraviolet light.

halo. (1) A colored ring or rings which encircle the sun or moon as a result of the dispersion of light by ice crystals in the cirrus clouds; (2) a ring surrounding a photographic image of a light source due to light being scattered.

halogenation. The introduction of a halogen into an organic molecule by addition or substitution.

halogens. The family of the negative elements: fluorine, chlorine, bromine, and iodine.

halophyte. A plant able to grow in salt marshes or on alkali soils.

haltere. The modified hind wing of the dipteran fly; it has sensory function.

hammer. Malleus; the outermost of the three small bones in the ear of mammals.

hammering. The sharp pounding of a liquid, such as water or mercury, often observed when the tube containing it is devoid of air, which would act as a cushion.

hamuli. A row of hooks on the costal margin of the hind wings of four-winged insects which hold the wings together in flight.

hand. The terminal portion of the pectoral appendage of mammals, developed for grasping and often not used for locomotion; true hands appear in primates.

hanging valley. (1) A valley carved out by glacial erosion; (2) a valley formed where a tributary joins the main stream and is left hanging above the main stream; it is separated from the main valley by rapids or waterfalls.

haploid number. The number of chromosomes found in mature sex cells; one half of the number of those of body cells.

haplont. The haploid stage of an organism which ends when fertilization occurs.

haplophase. A phase of the reproductive cycle after meiosis and before fertilization in which the nuclei are haploid.

hapten. Haptene; a substance which unites with a protein when it is injected into the body and forms a specific antigen.

haptotropism. Thigmotropism; the one-sided, curved growth of a plant due to touch or local pressure.

Harcourt pentane lamp. A pentane-burning lamp which is used as a standard source of light.

hard glass. A borosilicate glass, resistant to chemicals and heat.

hard landing. The deliberate destruction of a space probe upon impact with a predetermined target.

hard palate. The bony structure which forms the roof of the mouth.

hard water. A water containing calcium and magnesium salts which combine with soap and retard the formation of suds.

hardening. Quenching; treating steel by sudden cooling from above its critical temperature by dipping in oil or some other fluid, which results in increased hardness.

hardness, permanent. The hardness of water due to the presence of dissolved salts, such as chlorides and sulfates of calcium and magnesium, that cannot be removed by boiling.

hardness, temporary. The hardness of water due to the presence of dissolved salts, such as calcium and magnesium bicarbonate, that can be removed by boiling.

hardpan. A till or boulder clay which has been cemented by limonite.

harmonic motion. The vibration of elastic bodies; the acceleration is always toward the origin and directly proportional to the distance from it.

harmonic series of sounds. A series of sounds in which each basic frequency is an integral multiple of a fundamental frequency.

harmonics of a wave motion. Waves superimposed on a fundamental wave, having a frequency which is a whole multiple of the fundamental frequency.

harmotome. A zeolite; a varied-colored mineral consisting of complex silicates.

Harris flow. An electron flow in a cylindrical beam in which the space-charge divergence is overcome by the use of a radial electric field.

haustorium. A short suckerlike process which penetrates cells of the host and absorbs nourishment for parasitic fungi.

Haversian canals. Small tubes in the bone which contain blood vessels and nerves.

haze. Very small particles of dust dispersed in the air which lower the visibility and cause the atmosphere to appear off-color.

He. Chemical symbol for helium.

head. (1) The energy of a unit weight of a fluid due to its elevation as compared to the base of a column or to its pressure, or to its velocity; (2) the region of a bilaterally symmetrical animal body lying at the front end and, in bipedal vertebrates, at the highest level; (3) a crowded inflorescence, typical of Compositae, in which the flowers are grouped on a receptacle; (4) the edge of a spectral band or series.

head, kinetic-energy. Velocity head; the kinetic energy of fluid flow per unit volume.

head, total. The head measured by a Pitot tube; the sum of the hydrostatic pressure and the kinetic-energy head.

headwater erosion. Growing of a gully in length by erosion at the point where surface water pours in at its upper end.

heart. A muscular organ which forces blood through the body by its periodic contractions.

heartwood. The inner portion of tree stems which is darker than the outer layer and is not active in the transportation of water.

heat. A form of energy which consists of waves from 1 inch to 81/1,000,000 inch; it is closely related to light energy.

heat, atomic. The product of the gram-atomic weight of an element and its specific heat; the heat quantity required to raise the temperature of one gram atom of an element by 1°C.

heat balance. Accounting for all heat units in a process or for changes during which heat is transferred.

heat capacity. The quantity of heat which a definite quantity of a given substance absorbs before its temperature is raised one degree.

heat content. Enthalpy; the internal energy of a substance.

heat death. The final state of thermodynamic equilibrium which the material universe appears to be approaching, in accordance with the laws of dissipation of energy and increase of entropy.

heat equator. Thermal equator; the regions within the yearly 80° isotherms; the belt embraces large areas of Africa and India and the northern regions of South America.

heat, latent. The quantity of heat needed to change one gram of a substance from solid to liquid or from liquid to vapor without change in temperature.

heat, mechanical equivalent of. The conversion factor of any unit commonly used to express mechanical energy to a unit commonly used to express thermal energy; 4.1840 joules/calorie.

heat, molecular. The product of the gram-molecular weight of a compound and its specific heat; the quantity of heat required to raise the temperature of the gram molecular weight of a compound 1°C.

heat of activation. The increase of heat content which accompanies the transformation of a substance from a less active to a more reactive form.

heat of adsorption. The heat developed when a given amount of a substance is adsorbed; it is expressed in calories per gram or per mol, or, for gases, sometimes in calories per cubic centimeter.

heat of aggregation. The increase of heat content which accompanies the formation of aggregates of matter, such as crystals.

heat of combustion. The amount of heat set free when one gram molecule of a substance is burned in oxygen.

heat of compression. The heat generated per unit mass per unit change of pressure or of volume in the compression of

a substance, such as a gas.

heat of condensation. The number of calories of heat given off when one gram of a vapor condenses to a liquid without any change in temperature; numerically it is the same as the heat of vaporization.

heat of crystallization. The heat set free or absorbed when a unit weight of a substance crystallizes from its saturated solution.

heat of decomposition. The heat in calories absorbed or developed when one gram molecule of a substance is decomposed.

heat of dilution. The quantity of heat absorbed or evolved per gram or per mol of a solute when a solution of given concentration is infinitely diluted.

heat of dissociation. The heat required to break a gram molecular weight of a substance into its elements or into simpler molecules.

heat of emission. The additional heat energy that must be supplied to a surface, which is emitting electrons, in order to maintain it at a constant temperature.

heat of formation. The number of calories of heat absorbed or given off when one gram-molecular weight of a compound is formed from its elements.

heat of fusion. The amount of heat, in calories, required to melt one gram of a substance.

heat of hydration. The increase or decrease of heat content as a result of the formation of one mol of a hydrate from the anhydrous form of a compound in the presence of water; it is equal to the difference between the heats of solution of the anhydrous and hydrated compound.

heat of ionization. The heat quantity necessary to separate a mol of a compound into its ions.

heat of linkage. The energy required to break a chemical bond.

heat of mixing. The heat evolved or absorbed when two liquids are mixed, not due to chemical reaction between them.

heat of neutralization. The heat given off when hydrogen and hydroxyl ions combine to form water in a neutralization reaction.

heat of percussion. The heat produced by a blow.

heat of radioactivity. The heat generated per unit time by the radioactive disintegration in a unit mass of a radioactive substance.

heat of solidification. The increase in heat content when one mol of a solid is formed from a liquid.

heat of solution. The quantity of heat evolved or absorbed when

one gram molecule of a substance is dissolved in a large volume of solvent.

heat of sublimation. The heat liberated or absorbed per unit mass during the sublimation of a substance.

heat of transition. The increase in heat content when one mol of a substance changes to an allotropic form at the transition temperature.

heat of vaporization. The heat absorbed when the unit weight of a liquid is changed into vapors at its boiling point and 760 mm pressure.

heat of wetting. The quantity of heat evolved or absorbed per unit weight of dry material when thoroughly moistened by immersion in a liquid.

heat pump. An apparatus which extracts heat from flowing water in a continuous process.

heat radiation. Electromagnetic waves of wave lengths intermediate between those of visible red light and the shortest radio waves.

heat, specific. The number of calories required to raise the temperature of the unit mass of a substance 1°C.

heat transfer. Transmitting heat from one body to another by convection, radiation, and/or conduction.

heat treatment. (1) The carefully controlled heating and cooling of steel to improve its properties; (2) thermal treatment of metals for modifying their physical properties.

heater. The coil within a vacuum tube that carries current for heating the cathode.

heating value. Calorific value; the quantity of heat produced by the combustion, under specified conditions, of a unit weight or volume of a fuel.

Heaviside layer. Same as Heaviside-Kennelly layer.

Heaviside-Kennelly layer. Ionosphere; an ionized region of the upper atmosphere which reflects radio waves so that they travel parallel to the curved surface of the earth; there are at least two such layers.

heavy hydrogen. Deuterium; isotope of mass 2 of hydrogen.

heavy water. Deuterium oxide; ^2H_2O; its chemical properties are the same as those of water, but its physical properties are different.

hectare. A metric unit of area; 10,000 square meters; 2.47 acres.

hectocotylus arm. A tentacle of the male of certain cephalopod mollusks which is specialized for the insemination of the female.

hectoliter. In the metric system, 100 liters.

hectometer. In the metric system, 100 meters; 10 dekameters.

heel. (1) The prominence at the posterior end of the foot; (2) leaving edge; the edge of the brush of an electric machine which is contacted as the last by the commutator ring.

Heiligenschein. A diffraction effect resembling a halo, seen around the head of one's shadow due to reflection of sunlight from dew drops on the surrounding vegetation.

helical gear. A cogwheel whose teeth are cut in spiral form.

helicopter. A power-operated airplane whose large horizontal propeller rotating about a vertical axis makes it capable of vertical take-off and landing and which is supported by the air stream forced downward by its propeller.

heliocentric theory. Heliocentricism; the theory that the sun is the center of the universe.

heliostat. An arrangement of mirrors driven by a clockwork, which is used to reflect a beam of sunlight in a fixed direction as the sun moves across the sky.

heliotropism. Heliotaxis or phototropism; the response of living organisms to sunlight; example, sunflower.

helium. An inert rare gas found in the air; chemical symbol He; atomic number 2; it is obtained commercially from natural gas; used for filling the balloons of lighter-than-air craft.

helix. (1) A wire wound into a spiral coil; (2) a spirally coiled animal structure.

Helmholtz double layer. The surface of a metal in contact with an electrolyte which contains a layer of positively charged metallic ions in the electrolyte and an adjacent layer of negatively charged metal.

Helmholtz galvanometer. A galvanometer consisting of two equal circular coils placed coaxially at a distance equal to their radius and traversed by the same current; they produce a practically uniform field.

Helmholtz pendulum. A device which can charge a condenser for a definite short time, varied at will, or to impart varying amounts of magnetization to a specimen of iron.

Helmholtz resonator. A series of hollow spheres, each of which will produce resonance with a note of a certain pitch.

Helminthes. A group of parasitic worms.

helminthology. The biological science dealing with worms.

hemagglutinin. A substance in the blood serum which causes agglutination of red blood corpuscles.

hematite. A grayish-black mineral; ferric oxide, Fe_2O_3; an important iron ore.

hematocrit tube. A calibrated tube used for measuring the volume of packed red cells and their sedimentation rate.

hemicellulose. An intermediate product between simple sugars and cellulose, which is a polysaccharide; a condensation product of hexose sugars.

Hemichorda. A small group of marine animals; they have gill sets and a nerve cord.

hemicolloid. A colloid composed of very small particles, ranging from 0.005 to 0.0025 micron in length.

hemihedral. Said of a crystal that has only one half the number of faces necessary to complete a given type of symmetry.

hemimetabolous. Having incomplete metamorphosis.

hemimorphic. Said of crystals whose two ends are dissimilar as a result of polar symmetry.

Hemiptera. Insects having sucking mouth parts, two pairs of wings, and a beak attached to the tip of the head and back and down between the front legs; some feed on plant sap, others are ectoparasitic; examples, leaf hoppers, chinch bug.

hemisphere. (1) One half of a sphere as divided by a plane passing through its center; (2) one of the two cerebral hemispheres.

hemocoele. A primary body cavity; a cavity in which blood or hemolymph circulates.

hemocyanin. A copper-containing proteinous blue pigment, which combines readily with oxygen but forms unstable compounds and serves as a respiratory medium in arthropods and mollusks.

hemocytometer. A device for measuring the hemoglobin content of blood.

hemoglobin. The red respiratory coloring matter in the blood that carries the oxygen; a conjugated protein that reacts easily with oxygen and carbon dioxide.

hemoglobinometer. A device for measuring the percentage of hemoglobin in the blood.

hemolymph. The blood of higher invertebrates, consisting of a clear plasma, containing white corpuscles but no red corpuscles.

hemolysin. An antibody which causes the dissolution of foreign red blood corpuscles so that their hemoglobin is liberated.

hemolysis. Hemocytolysis; the dissolution or destruction of red blood corpuscles with liberation of the hemoglobin.

hemotoxin. A cytotoxin capable of destroying blood cells.

henry. The practical unit of inductance; 10^9 electromagnetic units; 1,000 millihenrys; 1,-000,000 microhenrys.

Henry's law. The solubility of a gas in a liquid at constant temperature is directly proportional to the pressure of the gas.

heparin. A substance which prevents blood clotting; it occurs in the liver and muscles.

hepatic. Pertaining to the liver.

hepatic portal system. Portal system; a group of veins carrying blood from the capillaries of the digestive organs of vertebrates to the liver.

hepatic vein. A large vein that carries blood from the liver to the inferior vena cava.

Hepaticae. Liverworts; a division of the Bryophyta; mosslike moisture-loving plants; they show an alternation of generations.

heptode. A seven-electrode electron tube containing an anode, a cathode, a control electrode, and four additional electrodes that are ordinarily grids; used as a frequency changer.

herb. A seed plant with a stem above ground which does not become woody; it may be annual, biennial, or perennial.

herbicide. A weed killer; a chemical for inhibiting the growth of undesirable plants.

Herbivora. Plant-eating animals.

Hercules. A constellation between Lyra and Corona Borealis.

heredity. An evolutionary factor that causes characteristics to pass from parent to offspring.

hermaphrodite. A plant or animal which has both male and female reproductive organs on one individual.

Hero's engine. A device to illustrate the earliest form of steam engines.

Hero's fountain. A device which demonstrates the raising of water by the elastic force of air.

herpetology. The study of reptiles and amphibians.

Herschel effect. A decrease in developable density on a photographic plate produced by a second exposure to the radiation of a longer wave length.

Herschel-Quincke tube. A branched caustic tube, resembling a divided or shunted electric conductor; used in studying acoustic interference phenomena.

hertz. A unit of frequency; one cycle per second.

hertzian waves. Electromagnetic waves covering a range of frequency from above 3×10^{10} cycles per second to below 1.5×10^5 cycle per second.

hesperidium. A fleshy fruit, with a firm rind; example, grapefruit.

Hess's law. If a chemical reaction is carried out in stages, the algebraic sum of the amounts of heat evolved in the separate stages is equal to the total amount of heat evolved when the reaction occurs directly.

heterochlamydeous. Said of a flower which has two kinds of perianth segments in distinct whorls.

heterochromatic. Having several, complex colors.

heterochromatin. A chromosome material which shows its greatest staining in the resting nucleus or in prophase and often a less dense staining during metaphase.

heterocyclic compound. An organic closed-chain or ring compound which contains in the ring an atom or atoms other than carbon; example, piperidine, $(CH_2)_5NH$.

heterocyst. A large, transparent cell in the colony of nostoc (blue-green algae) that occurs singly and differs from the other cells.

heterodont. Having teeth of different kinds; example, mammals.

heterodyne circuit. A radio reception, in which the interaction of the signal frequency and a local frequency generated within the receiver gives a constant difference frequency which is called intermediate frequency and is made audible.

heterodyne effect. A beat effect which is caused when two waves of different frequencies are superimposed.

heterodyne frequency meter. A device which compares the unknown frequency with a calibrated frequency standard in a beat-note detector circuit.

heterodyne oscillator. The oscillator in a superheterodyne receiver which provides the frequency required to beat with the signal frequency and thus produce the correct intermediate frequency.

heterodyne wave meter. A calibrated oscillator of variable frequency, which is set at the same frequency as that of the signal to be measured, so that the difference frequency falls to zero value.

heteroecious. Said of parasitic fungi which form one or more kind of spores on one host and one or more different spores on another host of different species; example, rust fungi.

heteroecism. A property of fungi which need two different host species for their complete life cycle.

heterogametes. Anisogametes; conjugant gametes dissimilar in size and behavior.

heterogamy. Metagenesis; the production of gametes of different types.

heterogeneous. Nonuniform in composition or in physical or chemical properties.

heterograft. A tissue or organ transplanted from one individual to another, which may belong to a different species.

heteroion. A complex ion consisting of a simple ion adsorbed on a molecule; the term is generally used when the adsorbing molecule is large, such as a protein molecule.

heterokaryosis. The association in somatic cells of nuclei of unlike genetical constitution; found in many fungi.

heterologous serum. A serum derived from another species than the one it is used for.

heteromorphic. (1) Said of algae in which there is alternation of generation, that is, vegetatively dissimilar generations; (2) occurring in two or more different crystal forms; (3) said of chromosome pairs which differ in shape and/or size.

heteromorphosis. Deviation from the normal form due to slightly different conditions in the animal or its environment.

heteronomous. Said of an animal, in which the metameres are not similar.

heterophyte. A parasite or saprophite; a plant which must secure its food ready made.

heterosis. Hybrid vigor; increased vigor of growth, fertility, etc., in a cross between two genetically different lines.

heterosphere. A layer of the atmosphere; it stretches about 22,000 miles.

heterospory. The formation of two kinds of spores in higher plants, which give rise to male and female gametophyte generations; example, certain Spermatophyta.

heterostyly. Difference in the length of style in flowers of different plants of a species; it insures cross-pollination.

heterothallic. Having plus and minus strains, that is, physiologically different mycelia; a property of some fungi and algae.

heterotrichous thallus. A thallus found in many filamentous algae in which there is a prostrate creeping system with projecting branched filaments.

heterotrophic. Unable to use simple inorganic substances for food, but requiring organic food from its environment.

heterozygote. An individual having both the dominant and the recessive allelomorphs for a given trait.

Heusler alloy. A ferromagnetic alloy of nonmagnetic metals; example, an alloy of copper, manganese, and aluminum.

hexacanth. Having six hooks; example, certain tapeworms.

hexagonal system. A crystal system in which three axes of equal length and in the same plane intersect at an angle of 60° and a fourth axis of different length is at right angles to all three.

hexapod. An animal with six legs; example, insects.

hexode. A six-electrode electron tube containing an anode, a cathode, a control electrode, and three additional electrodes that are ordinarily grids.

hexose. A monosaccharide sugar of six carbon atoms; example, glucose, $C_6H_{12}O_6$.

h-f. Abbreviation for high frequency.

Hf. Chemical symbol for hafnium.

Hg. Chemical symbol for mercury.

hibernation. Spending the winter in an inactive condition; the body processes of the animal slow down; example, bear.

high. An anticyclone; a whirlpool of air at high pressure, generally bringing fair weather.

high frequency. A frequency above the audible range; radio frequency.

high polymers. Polymerization products that have giant molecules.

high potential. A voltage above 650 volts.

high tension. A high voltage.

high-pass filter. An electric wave filter which transmits all frequencies above a certain limit and suppresses those below it.

high-speed steel. A hard steel which contains tungsten, chromium, vanadium, and molybdenum; used for cutting tools.

Hildebrand's rule. The ratio of the heat of vaporization to the temperature at which vaporization occurs is a constant for many substances if it is determined at the same molal concentration of vapor for each substance.

hilum. (1) A scar left on the side of a seed where the seed stalk was fastened; (2) a small particle in the center of a starch grain; (3) a small depression in the surface of an animal organ where a blood vessel enters or leaves.

hindbrain. The hindmost of the three divisions marked out by constrictions in the embryonic vertebrate brain; it develops into the medulla oblongata and the cerebellum.

hinge. (1) A flexible joint which permits back and forth movement; examples, a door hinge, an elbow; (2) the articulated joint of a bivalve shell.

hinge ligament. A tough, elastic connection between the dorsal margins of the two valves of the shell of bivalve mollusks.

hip girdle. Pelvic girdle; a skeletal support, situated in the body wall, for attachment of the hind fins or limbs of Vertebrata.

Hirudinea. Leeches; a class of Annelida; they have suckers at the anterior and posterior ends and are ectoparasitic hermaphrodites, with internal fertilization.

histamine. $C_5H_9N_3$; colorless crystals; it occurs in ergot and animal tissues; it raises the blood pressure and stimulates HCl secretion in the stomach.

histiocyte. Macrophage; a large phagocyte that destroys harmful substances and bacteria in the cells.

histoblast. A group of cells in the immature stages of insects, from which some organ of the adult will develop.

histochemistry. A study of the chemical composition of animal and vegetable tissues.

histogenesis. The origin, development, and differentiation of organic tissues.

histogens. Distinct zones of tissue differentiation recognizable in apical meristems of many plants, especially in roots.

histology. The study of the structure of plant and animal tissues.

histolysis. Dissolution or breakdown of tissues.

historical geology. Stratigraphy; the study of the fossils of plants and animals that are preserved in the rocks.

hock. The tarsal joint of the hind limb of quadrupeds which walk on the toes; it corresponds to the ankle of man.

hodectron. A mercury-vapor tube in which the discharge is initiated by means of a magnetic pulse.

hodoscope. An apparatus for tracing the paths of cosmic rays by means of an array of Geiger counters, each of which is connected with a neon lamp that flashes as the counter is set off by the cosmic particle.

Hofmeister series. Simple anions arranged in the order of their ability to coagulate hydrophilic colloids.

hogback. A ridgelike topographic feature which is the result of differential erosion of highly tilted hard and soft strata; a ridge with a sharp summit line and steep sides.

holdfast. A suckerlike disk by which the thallus of a plant is anchored to its support.

hole. An electron missing from the crystal lattice of a semiconductor which will conduct current when electrons from other lattice points fill the holes and thus leave new holes; example, silica.

hollow-cathode tube. Inert gas discharge tube in which radiation is emitted from the cathode glow inside a hollow electrode closed at one end.

holmium. One of the yttrium group of rare metals; symbol, Ho; atomic number, 67.

holoblastic. Said of an ovum that undergoes total cleavage.

Holocene. A recent geological period in which man developed from his Neolithic stage.

Holocephali. A group of fish which have only four gill clefts and no spiracle; example, chimera.

holocrystalline rock. An igneous rock composed entirely of crystals.

hologamy. (1) The fusion of two mature plant cells each of which has been fully changed by its gametangium; (2) a property of animals having gametes which are of the same shape and size as the ordinary cells of the same species.

holohedral. Having the full number of crystal faces, corresponding to the maximum possible symmetry.

holometabolous. Exhibiting complete metamorphosis.

holomorphic. Said of a crystal whose two ends are symmetrical with each other.

holophytic. Manufacturing its own food from simple substances by photosynthesis; example, green plants containing chlorophyll.

Holothuroidea. A class of the Echinodermata; its members have soft cylindrical bodies with small bones embedded and tube feet; example, sea cucumbers.

holotype. The type specimen.

holozoic. Said of the nutrition of most animals that involves ingestion and digestion of organic material.

Holtz tube. A vacuum tube which has funnel-shaped constrictions pointing in one direction; it transmits high-frequency discharges much more readily in one direction than in the other.

homeostasis. The maintenance of constancy and balance in one's internal environment.

hominidae. A family of the order of primates, of which man is the only living member.

homo sapiens. The scientific name for man.

homocentric rays. Stigmatic rays; light rays which pass through a common point.

homochlamydeous. Said of flowers which have perianth segments of one kind in two whorls.

homochromatic. Having the same color or a uniformity of color.

homochromy. Accommodation of animals in color to their environment.

homocline. A part of a geological structure in which the strata dip in one direction.

homocyclic compound. A ring compound containing only carbon atoms in the ring; example, benzene, C_6H_6.

homodont. Said of animals having teeth all of the same kind; example, vertebrates other than mammals.

homogametic. Having all gametes of the same type.

homogamy. (1) Interbreeding of segregated individuals of the same species; (2) maturation of the stamens and pistils at the same time.

homogeneous. Having similar properties throughout.

homogeneous reactor. A reactor in which the fuel, a uranium salt, is uniformly distributed in the moderator, water.

homogenization. Stabilization of an emulsion by reducing the size of the dispersed droplets by mechanical means.

homogenizer. A colloid mill that will produce uniform suspensions or homogeneous emulsions.

homograft. Graft originating from an animal of the same species as the recipient, but not from the recipient itself.

homoiotherm. Warm-blooded; maintaining a constant body temperature in spite of external fluctuations.

homokaryon. Fungus hypha composed of cells whose nuclei are of identical genetical constitution.

homologous. (1) Said of plants or animals that belong to different species but have certain parts or organs of corresponding structures; (2) of a series of organic compounds in which the formulas of adjacent members differ in one and the same group.

homologous chromosomes. The pair of chromosomes that unite in synapsis; they both affect the same character.

homologous field. A field of force in which the lines of force in a given plane all pass through one point.

homologous series. A series of related chemical compounds arranged in the order of their increasing molecular weights, the difference between adjacent members being CH_2; they display a regular gradation in physical properties and can be represented by a general formula; example, the paraffin series, C_nH_{2n+2}.

homologue. A member of a homologous series.

homology. The correspondence between structures of different organisms due to their inheritance of these structures from the same ancestry.

homometric pairs. Two crystal structures having the same x-ray diffraction pattern.

homomorphic. Said of chromosomes that have the same size and shape.

homonomous. Having homologous parts in one line; example, segments of an earthworm.

homoplasty. Similarity of anatomical features which do not result from a common ancestry; the similarity is due to convergent evolution.

homopolar. Electrically symmetrical; example, a compound which contains only covalent bonds.

homopolar bond. A covalent bond which has no resultant dipole moment.

Homoptera. An insect order whose members are characterized by two pairs of similar wings which slant upward to meet along the middle of the back when not in use; they have piercing and sucking mouth parts and incomplete metamorphosis.

homosphere. A layer of the atmosphere, about 55 miles above the earth's surface.

homospory. Production of but one kind of spore, in contrast to heterospory.

homostyly. A property of flowers of a species which have styles of the same length.

homothallic. Referring to fungi in which male gametangia and female gametangia are produced in the same filament or by the same individual.

homothermic. Warm-blooded.

homozygote. An individual produced by the union of two gametes that contain like genes for a given trait.

hoodoo. A columnar or pillarlike erosion remnant which has been carved and sculptured from relatively horizontal formation by the abrasion of wind-driven grains of sand.

hoof. A horny modified epidermis protecting the toes of some animals.

hook. (1) A spit which curves toward the shore as a result of the inward movement of waves and currents passing the point; (2) an appendage on the head of a tapeworm for attaching itself to the host.

Hooke's law. The strain is directly proportional to the stress up to the elastic limit.

hop. The path taken by a radio wave which arrives at the point of reception after one or more reflections from the ionosphere.

hopcalite. A mixture of copper and manganese oxides and some silver and cobalt oxides used as a catalyst in the oxidation of carbon monoxide at room temperature in gas masks and ventilating systems.

horizon. The line in which the earth and sky appear to meet.

horizontal. Perpendicular to the direction of gravity.

hormogone. A short section of filament activated by cells known as heterocysts in certain blue-green algae; they can break off and develop into a new filament.

hormone. (1) A stimulator; the

secretion of a ductless gland; example, insulin; (2) in plants, a chemical regulator of certain cell activities; example, auxin that regulates the rate of growth.

horn. (1) A hard translucent material formed from epidermal cells containing keratin; (2) a pointed and/or branched projection on the head of some mammals.

horn silver. Cerargyrite; silver chloride; AgCl; a cubic, varied-color mineral.

hornblende. An important rock-forming complex silicate mineral containing calcium, iron, magnesium, and aluminum; black monoclinic crystals.

hornblendite. A coarse-grained igneous rock which consists almost wholly of hornblende.

horopter. The locus of those points in the field of binocular vision which are seen as one point.

horse latitudes. Two areas of calms in the region of 35° north and 35° south latitude.

horsepower. A unit of power; 33,000 pounds lifted one foot in one minute, or 550 foot pounds per second; 746 watts; ¾ kilowatt; 42.42 British thermal units per minute.

horsetail. Scouring rush; a perennial, herbaceous, pteridophytic plant of the genus Equisetum; it has hollow, pointed stems.

host. An organism used as a source of food by a parasite which may live on the surface or within the organism.

hot spring. A thermal spring whose temperature is higher than 98°F.

hot wave. A high-temperature period, caused by southerly winds preceding a cyclone or by a stagnant anticyclone.

hot-wire ammeter. An instrument for measuring current on the basis of the expansion or changes in the resistance of a wire when an electric current flows through it.

hot-wire anemometer. An instrument for measuring wind velocity by means of its cooling effect on an electrically heated wire.

hot-wire gage. A pressure gage which depends on the cooling effect of the gas on a hot filament.

hot-wire voltmeter. A voltmeter operating on the same principle as the hot-wire ammeter.

hour angle. The angle that the observer's meridian makes with the declination circle of a heavenly body at the celestial pole; it is measured positively westward from the meridian, in hours, minutes, and seconds.

hp. Abbreviation for horsepower.

hr. Abbreviation for hour.

hub dynamometer. A device built into a propeller hub for meas-

uring the engine thrust and for torque.

Hübner's rhomb. A rhombic glass prism used for the comparison of two illuminated surfaces in photometry.

humerus. The larger bone of the upper arm.

humidification. Increasing the water content of air or other gases.

humidigraph. A device which records relative humidity.

humidity, absolute. The water vapor content of the air, given in grams per cubic centimeter.

humidity, relative. The ratio of the actual pressure of the water vapor in the atmosphere at a given temperature, to the maximum or saturated vapor pressure at the same temperature.

humification. Changing organic matter into humus.

humor. A fluid; the transparent liquid of the eyeball.

humus. A finely divided, blackish colloidal matter in the soil formed by the decay of vegetable and animal matter.

hunting. (1) The alternate lag and advance of a synchronous motor with respect to the current, or of one of two coupled alternators with respect to the other; (2) an instability in a control device, such as a thermostat, resulting in large fluctuations in the quantity which the device is intended to keep constant; (3) the tendency of a rotating mechanism which normally operates at constant speed to pulsate above and below the normal speed; (4) periodic variation in the speed of an aircraft during flight.

hurricane. A rain storm that originates near the equator and is accompanied by violent winds of 75 to over 130 miles per hour velocity.

Huygens' eyepiece. A telescope eyepiece consisting of a plano-convex field lens and a plano-convex eye lens placed behind the field lens, with a stop halfway between them.

Huygens' principle. Each point of an advancing wave is the source of a new train of waves, so that the advancing wave as a whole may be regarded as the resultant of the secondary waves arising from points in the medium already traversed.

Huygens' principle of superposition. The resultant displacement at any point due to the superposition of any system of waves is equal to the sum of the displacement of the individual waves at that point.

Huygen's wave surface. The wave front of light traversing a doubly refracting medium whose position is determined by Huygens' principle.

Hyades. An open V-shaped visible cluster of stars in the con-

stellation of Taurus.

hyaline. Glassy or semitransparent; example, a property of the clear substance of protoplasm.

hyaline cartilage. The transparent, nonfibrous homogeneous substance that covers the ends of bones at the joints; it contains small cavities including protoplasmic cartilage cells.

hybrid. The offspring that results from the mating of individuals of different races or species.

hybrid swarm. A continuous series of forms resulting from hybridization of two species followed by crossing and back-crossing of subsequent generations.

hybrid vigor. A natural vigor of a new hybrid that neither parent had.

hybridization. The crossing or mating of two different varieties of plants or animals to combine the desirable traits of each variety.

hydathode. A special structure (sometimes modified stomata) in leaves through which water of guttation can easily escape.

hydatid. (1) The bladderworm; (2) a large, fluid-filled cyst in the liver or other organs of the hoofed animals and man caused by the bladderworm; (3) a fluid-filled vesicle.

hydatid cyst. A cyst formed by the larva of certain tapeworms; a fluid-filled sac that contains larval heads which, when swallowed by a dog, produces tapeworms.

hydatogenesis. The crystallization of rock-forming minerals from aqueous solutions.

hydra. A fresh-water polyp of the phylum Coelenterata found attached to submerged objects; it has stinging cells, especially on its tentacles, with which it captures and kills its prey.

hydranth. An individual which receives and digests food for colonies of hydrozoan Coelenterata; it is a polyp attached to the remainder of the colony at its base and has a mouth surrounded by a circlet of tentacles at the free end.

hydrate. A chemical compound that contains water of crystallization; example, copper sulfate, $CuSO_4 \cdot 5H_2O$.

hydrated. Containing chemically combined water; said of a salt containing water of crystallization; opposite of anhydrous.

hydrated ion. An ion combined with one or more water molecules by coordinate bonds; example, $H^+(H_2O)$ or H_3O^+.

hydration. (1) Absorption of water by anhydrous minerals; (2) converting cellulose fibers into paper pulp by increasing their hygroscopicity by beating.

hydratuba. An attached polyplike form, which develops from the first larval stage of some jelly-fish.

hydraulic. Operated, moved, or effected by means of water power.

hydraulic gradient. The rate of fall of pressure head along a conduit in which a liquid is flowing.

hydraulic mining. The use of a stream of water to wash away dirt and rock particles, exposing valuable ore.

hydraulic press. A press exerting large forces by a plunger working in a cylinder containing high-pressure water; the work is pressed between a stationary surface and a platform attached to the plunger.

hydraulic slope. The slope of the hydraulic grade line at any point; it is numerically equal to the hydraulic gradient.

hydraulic turbine. A turbine operated by flowing water.

hydraulics. The science of flowing fluids and their applications in engineering.

hydrazine. $NH_2 \cdot H_2N$; a colorless liquid or white crystals; a powerful reducing agent.

hydride. A binary compound of hydrogen with any other element.

hydrobarometer. An instrument for determining the depth of sea water by its pressure.

hydrocarbon. A compound of hydrogen and carbon; it may be aliphatic or aromatic; saturated or unsaturated.

hydrocaulis. Coenosarc; the common tubular stalk bearing the individuals of a colony in the hydrozoan coelenterates.

hydrochloric acid. The aqueous solution of hydrogen chloride gas, HCl; an important acid of a great many chemical uses; it is secreted in the stomach and enables pepsin to digest meat.

hydrocyanic acid. Prussic acid; an aqueous solution of hydrogen cyanide gas, HCN; a powerful poison.

hydrodynamics. That branch of mechanics which deals with the laws of motion and action of water and other liquids.

hydroelectric. Relating to the production of electricity by water power.

hydrofluoric acid. An aqueous solution of hydrogen fluoride gas; it is formed by the decomposition of metallic fluorides by surfuric acid; very corrosive acid; used for glass etching, metal cleaning.

hydroforming. The preparation of ring compounds by heating straight-chain hydrocarbons with hydrogen in the presence of a catalyst.

hydrogel. A colloidal gel in which water is the liquid phase.

hydrogen. The lightest gas; chemical symbol H; atomic number 1; used as a reducing agent, for high-temperature flames, filling balloons.

hydrogen bomb. A projectile for releasing large quantities of energy through the fusion of nuclei.

hydrogen bond. A weak chemical bond between a hydrogen atom in one polar molecule and the negative atom in a second polar molecule of the same substance.

hydrogen bromide. A colorless gas or yellowish liquid; HBr; a strong acid.

hydrogen chloride. A colorless gas soluble in water, yielding hydrochloric acid; HCl.

hydrogen cyanide. Very poisonous gas; HCN, used as a fumigant.

hydrogen electrode. A platinum electrode coated with fine platinum powder, halfway immersed in water, and arranged in a circulating hydrogen atmosphere; used for the measurement of pH.

hydrogen fluoride. Fuming, corrosive liquid; HF.

hydrogen iodide. Colorless gas or yellowish liquid; hydroiodic acid; HI.

hydrogen ion. A positively charged hydrogen atom; a proton; the properties of acids in solution are due to the presence of hydrogen ions.

hydrogen peroxide. A colorless liquid, which is a strong oxidizing and bleaching agent and antiseptic; H_2O_2.

hydrogen scale. A system of electrode potentials based on the potential of hydrogen gas at 1 atmosphere pressure against hydrogen ions at unit activity.

hydrogen sulfide. A colorless, poisonous gas smelling like rotten eggs; H_2S; used in chemical analysis.

hydrogenation. The chemical combination of hydrogen gas with another substance in the presence of a catalyst; example, hydrogenation of coal to form liquid fuels.

hydrogenation of oils. Hardening of liquid animal and vegetable oils by the action of hydrogen.

hydrogen-ion concentration. The measure of the acidity of a solution; expressed as pH.

hydroid. The polyp form of Coelenterata; a tubular or saclike individual whose body wall is composed of two cellular layers separated by a thin mesogloea; it is attached to the stalk of a colony or directly to a supporting surface.

hydrokinetics. The study of liquids in motion.

hydrology. The study of water, its properties and occurrence on the earth's surface, underground, and in the atmosphere.

hydrolysis. (1) The reaction of a salt with water, yielding an acid and a base; (2) the decomposi-tion of organic compounds under the effect of water at room temperature or by heating, in the presence or absence of acids or alkalis.

hydromechanics. The science of the motion and equilibrium laws of liquids.

hydrometallurgy. The reduction of an ore to a metal with the help of an aqueous solution.

hydrometeor. A generic term for weather phenomena, such as rain, hail, snow, fog, which depend on the relative humidity of the atmosphere.

hydrometer. An instrument for measuring the specific gravity of liquids.

hydrone theory. An assumption that water consists of associated molecules.

hydronium. A hydrated hydrogen ion, H_3O^+.

hydrophilic. Having an affinity for water.

hydrophilic colloid. A colloid that forms stable aqueous solutions.

hydrophobic. Having no affinity for water.

hydrophobic colloid. A colloid which is readily coagulated from its aqueous solutions.

hydrophone. An instrument used for detecting underwater sounds; example, for spotting submarines.

hydrophyte. A plant adapted for living on or in water.

hydroplane. (1) A seaplane that may start from or land on water; (2) a hydrofoil, that is, a winglike structure that helps a seaplane or motorboat to move on water; (3) a motorboat that glides on water by means of its hydrofoils.

hydropolymer. A hydrogenated polymer.

hydroponics. Soilless gardening; the science and practice of growing plants in nutrient solutions.

hydrorhiza. A rootlike process by which colonies of hydrozoan coelenterates are attached to a supporting surface.

hydrosere. A sere which arises in water.

hydrosol. A colloidal solution in water.

hydrosphere. The water on the surface of the earth; its oceans, lakes, etc.

hydrostatic pressure. A uniform pressure exerted perpendicularly on a surface by a homogeneous liquid.

hydrostatics. The science of fluids at rest or in equilibrium.

hydrotropism. Hydrotaxis; the response of an organism to the stimulation of water.

hydroxide. A compound containing one or more hydroxyl, OH, radicals.

hydroxonium ion. A hydrated hydrogen ion, H_3O^+.

hydroxyl group. The —OH group.

hydroxyl ion. A negative ion, OH^-; the cause of alkaline behavior.

Hydrozoa. A class of Coelenterata showing typical alternation of generations; the hydroid phase is colonial; example, stinging corals, Portuguese man-of-war.

hyetograph. A device that measures and records rainfall.

hygrodeik. A wet-and-dry-bulb hygrometer which indicates relative humidity.

hygrograph. A clockwork-operated device which records continuously the humidity of the atmosphere.

hygrometer. An instrument used to measure the humidity in the air.

hygrometer, dew-point. An instrument which measures the temperature at which the air is saturated with moisture.

hygrometer, hair. A hygrometer in which the humidity of air is measured by means of a strand of human hair that expands with increasing humidity and contracts with decreasing humidity; one end of the hair operates a lever which moves a pointer over an experimentally calibrated scale.

hygrometer, wet-and-dry-bulb. A hygrometer consisting of two thermometers; the bulb of one is surrounded by damp cotton partly immersed in water; the evaporation of water from the cotton and the temperature drop shown by the thermometer are dependent on the relative humidity of the air; comparing the readings of the two thermometers with experimental tables will give the relative humidity.

hygroscope. An instrument for showing variations of the relative humidity of the air.

hygroscopic. Absorbing and retaining moisture from the atmosphere.

hygroscopic moisture. A thin film of water which surrounds soil particles.

hygrothermograph. A weather instrument which records temperature and humidity on the same chart.

hygrotropism. The response of an organism to the stimulation of the humidity in the air.

Hyla. A genus of amphibians, including the tree frog.

hymenium. A layer of parallelly arranged spore-producing structures found in fruit bodies of many ascomycetes and basidiomycetes.

Hymenoptera. Insects with four membranous wings, chewing, sucking, or lapping mouth parts, and complete metamorphosis; examples, bees and ants.

hyoid. A group of bones and cartilage at the base of the tongue of higher vertebrates.

hyoid arch. A visceral arch behind the jaws of vertebrates.

hyomandibular cartilage. The dorsal bone or cartilage of the hyoid arch of fish.

hyperfine structure. A set of very closely spaced lines (multiplets) making up a spectral line, or paramagnetic resonance line.

hypermetamorphosis. The development of a larva in two or more different instars.

hyperparasite. An organism which lives parasitically in or on another parasite.

hyperplasia. The excessive growth of a tissue by increase in the number of cells.

hypertonic. Said of a solution which has higher than normal osmotic pressure.

hypertrophy. An abnormal enlargement of an animal or plant cell or organ.

hypha. A simple or branched filament which extends like a root from a fungus or seaweed.

hypo. A common name for sodium thiosulfate, a photographic fixing solution; $Na_2S_2O_3 \cdot 5H_2O$.

hypobyssal. Referring to igneous rocks, such as sills and dikes, which have congealed under less pressure than the plutonic or deep-seated rocks, but under greater pressure than the effusive rocks, such as lava.

hypochlorite. A salt of hypochlorous acid, $HClO$; used as a disinfectant or bleach.

hypocotyl. A slender, fingerlike projection of a seedling, attached to the cotyledon, which develops into the lower portion of the stem.

hypodermis. (1) The layer of cells immediately beneath the epidermis of leaves of certain plants which form a reinforcement or a water-storage tissue; (2) in some invertebrates, the cuticle-secreting layer of cells underneath the cuticle.

hypogastric plexus. A sympathetic nerve plexus situated in front of the sacrum and supplying the organs of the abdomen.

hypogeal. (1) Having the cotyledon underground when the seed germinates; example, corn; (2) living beneath the surface of the ground.

hypoglossal nerve. The twelfth cranial nerve of vertebrates which supplies the muscles of the tongue.

hypogynous. Said of flowers in which sepals, petals, and stamens are attached below the ovary.

hyponasty. The more extensive growth of the lower side of a plant organ.

hypopharynx. A protuberance on the floor of the mouth of insects; it is similar to the tongue of vertebrates.

hypophysis. (1) A median ecto-dermal pit of an embryonic vertebrate head, just in front of the mouth, which fuses with infundibulum, forming the pituitary body; (2) a swelling below the sporangium.

hypopus. The larval form of certain mites having eight legs and no mouth but suckers enabling it to attach itself to another animal for transportation; it develops under unfavorable conditions to make possible a change in the environment.

hypopygium. (1) A protruding male genital organ of some flies; (2) the last visible ventral segment of an insect.

hypostome. The raised conical mouth region in Coelenterata.

hypothalamus. The floor and sides of the vertebrate brain, just behind the attachment of the cerebral hemispheres; it is derived from the forebrain of the embryo.

hypotonic. Said of a solution which has a lower osmotic pressure than the normal value.

hysometer. An instrument for the determination of the boiling point of water for estimating the altitude above sea level from its known variation with atmospheric pressure.

hysteresis. A lagging of an effect behind its expected value due to internal friction.

hysteresis cycle. Same as hysteresis loop.

hysteresis distortion. The distortion of voltage and/or current wave forms in circuits containing magnetic components, which is caused by the nonlinear hysteresis effect.

hysteresis, elastic. The internal friction of an elastic solid subjected to varying stress; the measure of the reversibility of elastic deformation; the difference between the elongation and retraction curve.

hysteresis energy. The energy used per cycle of operation to overcome hysteresis.

hysteresis graph. An instrument to trace hysteresis loops automatically for any specimen of magnetic material.

hysteresis heater. An induction device in which a charge or a muffler about the charge is heated by the hysteresis losses which are caused by a magnetic flux produced in it.

hysteresis loop. A closed figure obtained when the magnetizing force is plotted against the flux density through a cycle of magnetization and demagnetization.

hysteresis loss. The power lost in magnetizable metals by a cycle of repeated magnetizations and demagnetizations; its value is proportional to the area of the hysteresis loop.

hysteresis, magnetic. A lagging of the magnetic field intensity behind its magnetizing force.

hysteresis tester. Ewing's instrument for the direct measurement of magnetic hysteresis.

I

I. Chemical symbol for iodine.

-ic. A suffix indicating the higher of two possible valences of an element in its compound; example, ferric chloride, $FeCl_3$, as opposed to ferrous chloride, $FeCl_2$.

ICBM (intercontinental ballistic missile). A ballistic missile designed to strike targets from one continent to another; minimum range, 5,000 miles.

ice. The solid state of water formed by cooling water to $32°F$ or $0°C$; it is less dense than water; water expands on freezing and ice floats on water.

ice bomb. A device for demonstrating the extreme force exerted by water when it freezes.

ice calorimeter. A calorimeter in which the specific heat of a specimen is measured by the quantity of ice it melts.

ice pack. A large surface of floating ice pieces jammed together.

ice sheet. A glacier covering a large part of a continent; example, Greenland ice sheet.

iceberg. A fragment of a glacier floating in the sea; about one tenth of the iceberg is projecting above the surface of the ocean.

iceland spar. Calcite; it is used in Nicol prisms because of its double refraction of light.

ichneumon fly. An insect that deposits its eggs on, near, or beneath the skin of larvae of other insects; its larvae are internal parasites that destroy their host.

ichthyology. The study of fish.

Ichthyosauria. A fossil order of Mesozoic Reptilia; up to 40 feet long, fishlike marine animals with paddle limbs.

iconoscope. An electron tube which changes optical images into electric impulses for the purposes of television; it includes a photoemissive mosaic which receives the optical image to be scanned by a cathode-ray beam.

icterus index. A measurement of the intensity of the color of blood; in jaundice the index is higher than 15.

ideal gas. Perfect gas; a theoretical gas which obeys exactly the gas laws.

identical twins. Twins that result from a single fertilized egg that splits into two parts at an early stage of development; they are of the same sex and similar both in mental and physical traits.

idioblast. (1) A pseudo-idiomorphic crystal which occurs in metamorphic rocks; (2) a nonchlorophyllous plant cell whose wall thickness and shape are different from those of neighboring cells.

idiochromatic. Having photoelectric properties.

idiomorphic. Well crystallized and displaying a perfect crystal form.

igneous intrusions. A lava mass that does not reach the surface of the earth, but enters forcibly between other rock formations.

igneous rock. A rock formed by the hardening of magma.

ignis fatuus. Will-o'-the-wisp; a pale flame sometimes seen over marshy ground, probably caused by the spontaneous combustion of methane or other inflammable gases.

ignition coil. An induction coil in automobiles for changing the low-voltage current of the battery into the high-voltage current needed by the spark plug.

ignition temperature. The lowest temperature which will cause combustion to start and spread through a combustible mixture.

ignitron. A special metal-enveloped tube that uses a pool of mercury as a cathode to convert alternating current to hundred thousandths of amperes of direct current.

ileum. The posterior and longest part of the small intestine of vertebrates.

ilium. Hip bone; the dorsal bone of the pelvic girdle of vertebrates.

illumination. The ratio of the luminous flux incident on a surface element to the area of the element.

illumination, direct. (1) Direct lighting; lighting in which at least 90% of the light is directed downward; (2) the light which falls directly on the stage of the microscope from above without being reflected by the mirror.

illumination, indirect. Indirect lighting; lighting in which at least 90% of the light is directed upward.

illumination meter. A photometer for measuring light intensities.

illumination photometer. Same as illumination meter.

ilmenite. Igneous mineral consisting of iron and titanium oxides.

image force. The attraction between a charge concentrated on a small body and its electric image in a neighboring conductor.

image orthicon. A television camera tube, which is an improved modification of the iconoscope.

image, real. An image formed by a mirror or lens at a point through which the rays of light actually pass, and which can be projected to a screen or photographic plate.

image, virtual. An image that cannot be photographed or projected on a screen; an image from which the light rays appear to diverge.

imaginal disc. Imaginal bud; thickening of the epidermis in the pupa of a homometabolous insect which gives rise to the external organs of an adult during metamorphosis.

imago stage. Final instar; the adult stage of insects.

imbibition. (1) The absorption or adsorption of a liquid by a solid or gel and its resulting swelling; (2) a mechanical method for printing color pictures.

imbricate. Having overlapping leaves, petals or scales.

imfing. Seeding a liquid with a small crystal in order to induce crystallization.

immature soil. A soil whose formation has been interrupted or hindered by natural conditions.

immersion objective. Oil-immersion lens; an objective used in high-power microscopes, in which a drop of oil or water is placed between the front lens and the slide to be examined.

immiscibility. The property of some liquids that they cannot be mixed, but separate into layers; example, oil and water.

impact. (1) The mutual effect of two bodies in collision, which will change the velocity of one or both; (2) the force of a blow, such as that of a hammer against a nail, or of a baseball against a bat.

impact, elastic. A collision between two objects which may be deformed in the collision but immediately regain their original size and shape.

impact fluorescence. Fluorescence produced when one excited atom collides with another.

impact parameter. The distance of the initial line of motion of a scattered particle from the center of the scattering field.

impedance. The ratio of the root mean square value of the voltage applied to a circuit to the current that flows in it.

impedance coupling. Transferring energy between circuits through a condenser-choke coil circuit.

impedometer. An impedance-measuring device for very-high-frequency bands.

impeller. (1) A turbine with fanlike blades in jet propulsion; (2) the rotating member of a centrifugal pump.

impenetrability. The inability of two objects to occupy the same space at the same time.

imperfect flower. A flower that has either stamens or carpels but not both.

impermeable. Preventing the passage of a liquid or gas.

impervious layer. A layer through which water cannot pass.

impetus. Momentum; the force a moving body can exert due to its mass and velocity.

implant. A tissue or other material, which has been artificially introduced into an embryo or adult.

implantation. The embryo embedding itself into the uterine wall.

implosion. The opposite of explosion; the violent inward shattering of a glass vessel or container when the external pressure is greater than the internal pressure.

impounding. Damming up water in artificial lakes and ponds to raise the water table.

impulse. (1) The product of the average magnitude of a force and the time it acts; (2) a wave of energy change that travels along a nerve or muscle from the point of stimulation and causes physiological activity or inhibition.

impulse excitation. A means of producing an oscillator current in a circuit in which the duration of the impressed voltage is relatively short as compared with the duration of the current produced.

impulse generator. Surge generator; a device for producing short pulses of high voltage by charging capacitors in parallel and discharging them in series.

impulse radiation. A radiation that results from the impacts of rapidly moving particles on a body of matter.

In. Chemical symbol for indium.

in vitro. In a test tube; outside of the animal body; said of experiments.

in vivo. In the living body; said of experiments.

inactive gas. A rare gas; a gas that does not enter into reaction with other substances; examples, helium, neon, argon.

inactive substance. (1) Nonreactive substance; (2) an optically neutral substance.

inarch grafting. Inarching; uniting a rooted cion with a rooted stock.

inbreeding. Endogamy; mating closely related individuals to breed out desirable and undesirable traits.

incandescence. The emission of visible light by a substance due to its high temperature.

incandescent lamp. An electric bulb containing a thin wire or filament of an infusible conductor, which is heated to incandescence by the current.

incidence, angle of. The angle between a ray of light falling on a surface and the normal to the surface at that point.

incisor. The front teeth in both jaws of mammals used for cutting; they are particularly well developed in rodents.

inclination. (1) The tipping of the earth's axis toward the plane of its orbit; (2) the number of degrees of dip that a magnetic compass deviates from the horizontal when free to swing in a vertical plane.

inclination joint. A hinge on the base of the microscope which permits its upper portion to be tilted.

inclination of the earth's axis. The eccentricity of the ecliptic; the obliquity of the ecliptic; the angle formed by the earth's orbital plane with the celestial equator; its value is about 23°26′40″ and it is diminishing 0.47″ per year.

inclined plane. A simple machine consisting of a sloping surface on which heavy weights can be raised.

inclinometer. (1) An instrument for indicating the altitude of an aircraft by showing the inclination of its longitudinal axis to the horizontal; (2) a dip circle; a device for determining the direction of the earth's magnetic field relative to the plane of the horizon.

inclusion. (1) A foreign rock or mineral in an igneous rock; (2) a gas or liquid occluded in a mineral crystal; (3) nonliving matter in a living cell.

inclusion bodies. Round, oval, or irregular shaped bodies occurring in the cytoplasm of the nucleus of body cells infected with certain bacteria.

incompatibility. (1) Failure to set seed after pollination has taken place; (2) differences in the physiological properties of the host and parasite that prevent the development of the parasite; (3) not suitable or dangerous to use together; examples, certain drugs, different blood types.

incomplete dominance. Blending inheritance; the blending of the parents' characters in the offspring.

incomplete flower. A flower that lacks the floral envelope or some essential organ.

incomplete metamorphosis. Gradual change from the immature to the adult, without definite stages; example, the direct metamorphosis of insects.

incompressible volume. Covolume; a small fraction of the total volume of a gas which corresponds to the actual bulk of the gas molecules without the spaces between them.

incubation. (1) Causing eggs to hatch by natural or artificial heat; (2) the period that elapses between a parasitic infection and the first symptoms of disease.

incubator. (1) An apparatus for maintaining a constant temperature suitable for the growth and development of a bacterial culture; (2) an apparatus for the artificial hatching of eggs.

incurrent siphon. The tube through which water enters the gill chamber of clams.

incus. The anvil-shaped small bone of the middle ear.

indefinite growth. Indeterminate growth; elongation of a plant axis which is not limited by a terminal bud.

indehiscent fruit. A fruit that does not split open when ripe.

independent assortment. Mendelian segregation; law of unit characters; the segregation of genes in different pairs of chromosomes independently of one another.

independent organism. A green plant, which can make its own food with the help of its chlorophyll content.

indeterminate inflorescence. Racemose inflorescence; an inflorescence in which the oldest flowers are at the base or on the outside of the cluster and the flowers develop successively inwardly and toward the tip.

index of refraction. Refractive index; (1) the ratio of velocity of light in vacuum to its velocity in a given medium; (2) the ratio of the sine of the angle of incidence to the sine of the angle of refraction of a light ray traversing the interface between two media.

indicator. (1) An instrument used for the determination of the pressure-volume or pressure-time changes in an engine cylinder; (2) a substance, usually a weak organic acid or base, which indicates acidity or alkalinity, or the completion of a reaction by a change in its color; example, purple litmus, which turns red in acid and blue in alkaline solutions.

indigo. $C_{16}H_{10}N_2O_2$; a blue vat dye formerly extracted from plants; now manufactured synthetically on a large scale.

indirect stain. A stain which does not dye the organism itself but colors the background so that the organism becomes visible by contrast.

indium. A noncorrosive, ductile rare metal; chemical symbol In; atomic number 49; used in electroplating.

indole. C_8H_7N, benzopyrrole; colorless plates; indole derivatives are formed by the decomposition of albumins.

indraft. (1) The inward flow of a fluid; (2) the flow of air onto the blades from in front of the propeller of an aircraft.

induced drag. A fraction of the total air drag on an airfoil which is induced by its lift.

induced magnetism. The magnetism generated temporarily in a piece of iron when it touches or is brought near a magnet.

induced polarization. The polarization caused by an electric field acting on a dielectric that does not have a permanent dipole.

induced radioactivity. The radioactivity produced artificially, by corpuscular bombardment.

induced voltage. A voltage set up by a varying magnetic field linked with a wire, coil, or circuit.

inductance. (1) The property of an electric circuit that its variations induce an electromotive force in that circuit or a near-by circuit; (2) the ratio of the total induction in a circuit to the current producing it.

induction. (1) The differentiation of an embryonic tissue directed from the outside; (2) magnetizing iron and steel by bringing them near a magnet or touching a magnet; (3) producing an electric current in a conductor by moving the conductor across magnetic lines of force.

induction, charging by. Producing an electric charge by the presence of a body carrying an opposite charge.

induction coil. An arrangement of two coils so that an interrupted current in the first produces voltage in the second.

induction compass. Earth inductor compass; a compass, whose indications depend on the current generated in a coil revolving in and influenced by the earth's magnetic field; used as a course indicator in aircraft.

induction, electromagnetic. An electromotive force induced in the circuit when the magnetic flux through the circuit changes.

induction heating. Induction furnace; heating by inducing a current in the metallic charge of a furnace.

induction motor. Asynchronous motor; an alternating-current motor which does not run exactly in step with the current changes; the primary winding connected to the supply sets up a magnetic flux which induces a current in the rotor.

inductive load. Lagging load; the reactive load in an alternating-current circuit, which consists of the resistance and inductance of coils, solenoids, windings, etc.

inductive reactance. The resistance to the flow of electricity in a circuit which consists of turns of wire; the resistance is greater if the turns are wound on an iron core.

inductivity. The capacity or power for induction; inductive capacity.

inductometer. A variable inductance calibrated to indicate

the inductance in henrys or millihenrys.

inductor. (1) A coil having inductance; (2) a positive catalyst that speeds up a chemical reaction by reacting rapidly with one of the reactants.

induration. Hardening; a hardened spot.

indusium. An outgrowth of a fern leaf which covers and protects the sorus in many species.

inert gases. Rare gases; helium, neon, argon, krypton, xenon, and radon that are nonreactive.

inert substance. A chemical substance that does not react with other substances under the ordinary conditions of chemical reactions.

inertia. The tendency of matter to stay in one place until it is moved by force, and once it began to move, to keep moving in the same direction and at the same rate.

inexhaustible resources. Natural resources which cannot be exhausted; example, air.

infection. (1) The invasion of the body tissues by pathogenic organisms which multiply and cause disease; (2) the communication or spreading of disease.

infestation. Being attacked by parasites other than bacteria.

inflation. Gassing; expanding by filling with air or gas.

inflorescence. The flower-bearing part of a plant.

infrared rays. Heat rays; a wide range of invisible radiation; frequencies adjoining the visible red and merging into Hertzian waves.

infrared spectroscopy. The study of absorption spectra.

infrasonic. Below the range of human hearing.

infundibuliform. Funnel-shaped or inverted cone-shaped; example, the liquefaction of gelatin.

infundibulum. A funnel-shaped ventral projection of the brain of an embryo which will give rise to the pituitary gland in the adult.

infusible. Impossible or hard to melt.

infusorial earth. Diatomite; kieselguhr; a fine powder of the silicon-containing skeletons of diatoms; used as an adsorbent, insulator, in polishes.

ingestion. The reception of food into the body; swallowing.

inhalant pores. The mouths of tubes which conduct water inward through the walls of a simple sponge.

inherent stability. The stability of an aircraft due solely to the structure and arrangement of its fixed parts.

inheritance. The passing of characters on from parents to their offsprings.

inheritance of acquired character-

istics. Lamarckism; a theory of organic evolution suggested by the French naturalist, Jean Baptiste Lamarck; characteristics acquired by an organism during its lifetime are inherited by its offspring; effects of use and disuse are handed down through succeeding generations.

inhibition. (1) Deactivating an effector by the influence of nerve impulses; (2) stoppage or slowdown of a metabolic process.

inhibitor. (1) A substance that prevents or slows down the activity of an enzyme; (2) a negative catalyst used to slow down a reaction; example, corrosion inhibitor, which slows down the oxidation of iron.

initial permeability. The magnetic permeability corresponding to a very small, normal magnetic induction.

ink sac. A glandular sac opening into the alimentary canal of squids which secretes a dark fluid.

inner field. (1) The electric field immediately surrounding any individual molecule in the interior of a polarized dielectric; (2) the magnetic field surrounding a molecule of a magnetized substance.

innervation. The nerve supply to a particular organ.

innominate. Having no name; examples, the innominate artery in mammals; the innominate vein in primates; the innominate bone of the pelvic girdle.

inoculation. (1) Immunization against a certain type of pathogenic bacteria by injection of a vaccine containing the bacteria; (2) the introduction of the germ tube of a parasitic fungus into the host; (3) placing spores of bacteria or fungi in a culture medium; (4) starting crystallization by introducing a small crystal into a supersaturated solution.

inorganic chemistry. The study of the chemical elements and their compounds, including carbon, its oxides and sulfides, but excluding all other carbon compounds, which belong to organic chemistry.

inphase. The condition when like surges join at the same instant.

input. The power introduced into a machine or circuit for operating it.

insect. A six-legged, usually winged animal with segmented body and jointed legs.

insect pests. Insects of such habits and occurring in such abundance that they are harmful to man.

insecticide. A substance used for killing insects.

Insectivora. Insect-eating mammals; example, mole.

insectivorous plant. A plant

which obtains part of its nitrogen supply from bodies of small insects which are trapped by the plant; examples, sundew, bladderwort.

insemination. The introduction of the seminal fluid, bearing the reproductive cells of the male, into the genital passages of the female.

insertion. (1) The place of attachment of a muscle or other organ; (2) the attachment of one part of a plant to another.

insolation. (1) Weathering of rocks caused by extreme daily changes in the temperature which cause cracking and disintegration; (2) radiant energy that comes from the sun; (3) sunstroke.

insoluble. Said of a substance that cannot be dissolved; no substance is absolutely insoluble.

inspiration. Inhaling of air by a lung-breathing animal.

instantaneous sound pressure. The actual pressure at any point of a medium traversed by sound waves, at any instant, minus the normal static pressure.

instar. A period of growth of insect larvae, ending with a molt.

instinct. The tendency to act according to a fixed pattern without previous training.

instinctive behavior. Complicated inherited behavior in which there is a series of reflexes, each reflex serving as a stimulus to the next; examples, web spinning by spiders or nest building by birds.

instrument flying. Blind flying; controlling an aircraft solely by the use of instruments, that is, without visual observation of the terrain.

insulating strength. A measure of the ability of an electric insulator to withstand electric stress without breakdown.

insulation. (1) Preventing the flow of electric current; (2) inhibiting the transfer of heat; (3) reducing the propagation of sound; (4) covering an electric wire or cable with a nonconductor.

insulation resistance. The resistance between two conductors of a circuit or between a conductor and the earth when they are separated by an insulator.

insulator. A material that prevents the passage of electricity, heat, or sound; a nonconductor.

insulin. A proteinlike hormone in the pancreas which regulates the use of sugar by the body and prevents excessive blood sugar; used in diabetes.

intake stroke. Suction stroke; the stroke in which the piston of a gasoline engine draws a mixture of fuel and air into the cylinder.

integrating meter. An instrument that sums up or integrates the values measured over a period of time.

integument. (1) Covering of the body of a multicellular animal, composed of tissues adapted to meet the external conditions that prevail in the normal environment of the species; example, the skin; (2) a cell layer covering the ovule of plants; (3) the seed coat.

intensitometer. A device for determining the relative x-ray intensities during radiography, so that the exposure time may be controlled.

intensity. The quantity of electric current, or charge, or light, or magnetic flux, or magnetic field, or sound waves.

intensity level. The relation of one sound intensity to another, as expressed in bels or decibels.

intensity modulation. Controlling the luminosity of the television screen by variation of the beam current.

intensity of light. The radiation falling on or absorbed by a unit surface.

intensity of pressure. The fluid pressure per unit area.

intensity of radiation. The energy, or the number of photons or particles, flowing through unit area per unit time.

intensity of radioactivity. The number of atoms disintegrating in unit time.

intensity, radiant. The rate of transfer of radiant energy per unit solid angle in any direction from the source.

interaction space. The space between the electrodes in an electronic device, where energy is transferred to or from electrons.

intercalary growth. A plant growth that is not restricted to the apex of an organ.

intercalary meristem. A meristem located between regions of permanent tissue in the length of a plant, inducing intercalary growth.

intercellular. Said of the space or substance located between cells of a plant or animal tissue.

intercellular matter. Material secreted by certain tissue cells and piled up in the intercellular spaces.

interelectrode capacitance. The capacitance of a vacuum-tube circuit due to the condenser action of two of the electrodes, such as the plate and the grid.

interface. The area of contact between two phases of a chemical system.

interfacial angle. The dihedral angle between two adjacent faces of a crystal.

interfacial tension. The surface tension at the interface between two immiscible fluids; example, water and oil.

interfascicular cambium. A cambium layer lying between two vascular bundles and forming secondary xylem and phloem.

interference. (1) Any signal received by a radio receiver that was not intended for reception and which interferes with good reception; examples, atmospherics, operation of an elevator in the building; (2) superimposing one wave on another; (3) the aerodynamic influence of two or more bodies on one another.

interference fringes. Alternating light and dark bands obtained by illuminating the same part of a screen by two homogeneous light beams of constant phase relation.

interference guard bands. Two bands of frequencies on either side of the communication band and frequency tolerance which may be provided to minimize the possibility of interference.

interfence of light. Production of alternating dark and light lines or fringes when light waves of equal amplitude meet.

interferometer, acoustic. A device which measures the velocity and absorption of sonic or ultrasonic waves in a gas or liquid.

interferometer, optical. An instrument for comparing unknown wave lengths with a standard wave length of light with the aid of interference fringes; used for the analysis of a narrow spectrum region.

intermediate frequency. The frequency of the carrier wave coming from the frequency changer, which is the resultant of the mixing of two radio frequencies.

intermediate neurons. Associative neurons; they connect the afferent and efferent neurons.

intermontane plateau. A high surface surrounded by mountains.

internal energy. (1) The energy in a given state of a system which is determined by the state itself; (2) the sum of the potential and kinetic energy of the molecules of a body due exclusively to the position of the molecules and their constituents, and their motion inside the body.

internal fertilization. Fertilization which takes place within the body of a female; example, mammals.

internal friction. The resistance to relative motion between parts of the same body; example, the gradual damping of the vibrations of a tuning fork.

internal phase. Discontinuous phase; the dispersed phase of a colloidal suspension or emulsion.

internal potential. The average electric potential of the free electrons inside a metal.

internal reflection. The reflection of light incident on the surface of a body from the inside, or at an interface, the medium beyond having a lower refractive index than that in which the reflection occurs.

internal work. The work done by a system against forces operating within it or between its parts; or the work done on the system by such forces.

internal-combustion engine. An engine in which power is generated within one or more cylinders by the burning of a mixture of air and liquid fuel, which is converted into mechanical work by means of a piston.

international date line. An imaginary line set up by international agreement as being located in the Pacific Ocean halfway around the earth and coinciding with the 180° meridian from Greenwich, England; this is the place where each calendar day first begins; in reckoning time on crossing the date line westward, go forward one day on the calendar; eastward, go back one day.

internode. (1) The part of a plant stem between two adjacent leaf nodes; (2) the part of a nerve between two constrictions in the medulary sheath.

interoceptor. A sensory nerve ending which detects stimuli arising inside the body.

interphase. (1) Intermitosis; the resting stage of mitosis; (2) same as interface, that is, the boundary surface between two phases.

interphase cell. A cell that is not undergoing mitotic division.

interplanetary space. The space between or in the region of the planets.

interpole. Compole; a small field pole placed between the main field poles and electrically connected in series with the armature.

interrupter. A device for the automatic making and breaking of an electric circuit.

intersex. An abnormal individual whose cells are all of identical genetic composition; it is intermediate between two sexes in characteristics.

interstice. A small space within a phase or between particles.

interstitial atom. An atom squeezed in between the regular lattice sites in a crystal.

interstitial cells. (1) Small undifferentiated cells in the outer layer of polyps which develop into cnidoblasts and reproductive cells; (2) cells between the reproductive structure of the ovary and testis of vertebrates.

interstitial compound. A semimetallic compound formed in the crystal lattice of a transition metal through the penetration of an atom of small diameter.

interstitial position. A position that is not at the proper lattice sites in a crystal.

intertentacular organ. A temporary duct leading from the coelom to the exterior in Bryozoa, through which germ cells escape.

intertraction. Barophoresis; an increase in the density of a colloidal solution as a result of loss of solute by diffusion into a salt solution in contact with the colloidal solution.

intestine. (1) A food or waste tube leading from the stomach to the anus of vertebrates; (2) the part of the alimentary canal of invertebrates that corresponds or appears to correspond to the vertebrate intestine.

intine. The innermost coat of a pollen grain.

intracellular. Within the cell.

intraperitoneal inoculation. An injection administered through the abdominal wall.

intrathecal. Within the spinal membranes.

intrinsic energy. (1) The energy stored in a compound which is equivalent to its heat of formation; (2) the energy of a material system which is dependent only on its initial and final state.

introgressive hybridization. Infiltration of genes of one species into the genotype of another when hybrids backcross with the more abundant species.

intromittent organ. A protuberance or protusible organ of the male for introduction of the seminal fluid into the genital passage of the female during copulation.

introrse. (1) Said of an anther that opens toward the center of a flower; (2) bent inward.

intrusive rock. A molten rock which intruded into crevices or cavities of existing rocks and solidified there, forming an intrusion.

intussusception. A growth of living cells accomplished by introducing submicroscopic particles into the protoplasm.

invagination. Pushing inward part of a sheath of cells to form a pocket; common in embryonic development of animals.

invasion. The moving of plants or animals into a community to replace other organisms.

inverse photoelectric effect. The transformation of the kinetic energy of a moving electron into radiant energy.

inverse piezoelectric effect. The contraction or expansion of a piezoelectric crystal along an electric axis when subjected to the effect of an electric field in that direction.

inverse proportion. Two quantities are inversely proportional when an increase in one of them produces a corresponding decrease in the other.

inverse square law. The illumination of a surface of given area by a given light source is inversely proportional to the square of the distance of the light source.

inversion. (1) Reversal of the usual temperature gradient of the atmosphere; example, the increase of temperature with altitude; (2) the change of an optically active substance into one having the opposite rotatory effect; (3) a partial reversal of the gene sequence in a chromosome; (4) the splitting of a complex sugar into simpler sugars; example, the hydrolysis of cane sugar into a mixture of glucose and fructose.

invert sugar. A 1 to 1 mixture of glucose and fructose.

invertase. Sucrase; an enzyme contained in yeast; it converts cane sugar into glucose and fructose.

invertebrates. Animals without backbone.

inverter. An inverted rectifier; a device which converts direct current into alternating current; example, a gas-filled electron tube performing this function.

involucre. The protective cover of the reproductive organs of many plants.

involuntary behavior. A behavior that is not controlled consciously; examples, the contraction of plain muscles, the heart beat.

involuntary muscles. Muscles that work ordinarily without control; example, breathing muscles.

involution. (1) Backward evolution; degeneration; (2) the decrease in the size of an organ; example, thymus after puberty.

iodide. A binary compound of iodine; a salt of hydroiodic acid, HI.

iodine. A shiny blackish-gray nonmetallic element; chemical symbol I; atomic number 53; solutions of iodine are used as germ killers and in testing for the presence of starch.

ion. An electrically charged atom or radical which carries electricity through an electrolyte.

ion, amphoteric. An ion which has both a positive and a negative charge, at the opposite ends of a long chain; example, ions of amino-acids.

ion, aquo. A complex particle made up of an ion combined with one or more molecules of water; example, hydronium, $H^+(H_2O)$ or H_3O^+.

ion beam. A beam of charged particles other than electrons, all moving at the same speed in the same direction.

ion, complex. An ion that consists of and may dissociate into simpler ions.

ion exchange. The reversible interchange of ions between a solid and a liquid without a substantial change in the structure of the solid; example, water softening with a zeolite.

ion, hydrated. An ion of a solute to which molecules of water are adhering.

ion lattice. The space lattice of an ionic crystal.

ion, negative. An ion carrying a negative charge; an anion.

ion pair. A positive ion and a negative ion or electron, having charges of the same magnitude, and formed from a neutral atom or molecule by the action of radiation or by any other agency that supplies energy.

ion pair, primary. An ion pair produced directly by the causative radiation.

ion, positive. An ion carrying a positive charge; a cation.

ion-exchange resin. A synthetic resin which can exchange ions with a liquid; used in water purification.

ionic bond. Electrostatic bond; a linkage of atoms or radicals by the electrostatic attraction of oppositely charged ions.

ionic charge. Either the total charge carried by an ion or the charge carried by an ion which has unit charge.

ionic crystal. A crystal having charged ions, rather than neutral atoms or molecules at its lattice points; example, sodium chloride.

ionic equation. An equation which shows the number and type of ions which take part in a chemical reaction.

ionic micelle. A colloidal aggregate of ions.

ionic migration. The movement of charged particles of an electrolyte toward the electrodes under the influence of an electric current.

ionic potential. The ratio of the charge on an ion to its radius.

ionium. A naturally occurring radioactive nuclide; an isotope of thorium; chemical symbol Io; atomic number 90; atomic weight 230.

ionization. (1) An electrically neutral atom or molecule acquiring a charge; (2) electrolytic dissociation.

ionization by collision. Ionization produced in gas discharge tubes by the collisions of gas molecules.

ionization chamber. An enclosure used for the study of ionized gases; an instrument for the measurement of the radioactivity of a substance by measur-

ing the current resulting from ionization of its emanating vapor.

ionization condenser. An apparatus for testing the electrical properties of an ionized gas, consisting of two parallel metal plates, placed in the ionized gas and supplied with a high-frequency alternating-current voltage.

ionization constant. The equilibrium constant of a reversible reaction by which ions are produced from molecules.

ionization current. A current produced by an electric field in an ionized gas.

ionization of gases. The separation of gas atoms into charged particles, usually as the result of forcible collision with other particles.

ionization potential. The work, measured in electron-volts, which must be done to remove an electron from an atom.

ionization pressure. An increase in the pressure within a gas-discharge tube, due to ionization of the gas.

ionized. (1) Converted into an ion by losing an electron; (2) electrolytically dissociated.

ionizing energy. The average energy given up by an ionizing particle in producing an ion pair in a specified gas.

ionizing particle. A particle producing ion pairs directly in its passage through a substance.

ionogenic. Forming or furnishing ions; example, electrolytes.

ionometer. An ionization chamber used for measuring the intensity of an ionizing emission.

ionosphere. A region of ionized air beginning about 65 miles above the earth; it reflects radio waves.

Ir. Chemical symbol for iridium.

iridescence. The exhibition of the colors of the rainbow, caused by the interference of light of various wavelengths as reflected from thin superficial layers of a substance; example, mother of pearl.

iridium. A steel-gray brittle noble metal; chemical symbol Ir; atomic number 77; used in platinum alloys.

iris. (1) The colored part of the eye which surrounds the pupil; (2) a flowering plant commonly called a flag.

iron. The most important and abundant of all metals; chemical symbol Fe; atomic number 26.

iron filings. Finely divided iron; used for demonstrating magnetism.

iron, galvanized. Zinc-coated iron sheet or wire.

iron pyrite. Fool's gold; iron disulfide, FeS_2; a yellow cubic mineral; an important iron ore.

irradiation. The exposure to some form of radiation for therapeu-

tic purposes or for effecting desirable chemical changes.

irreversible reaction. A chemical reaction which proceeds to completion.

irrigation. (1) The artificial watering of land by means of ditches, sprinkling pipes, etc.; (2) the land treatment of sewage by filtration achieved by irrigating a plot of land with the liquid sewage.

irritability. The ability of living matter to respond to external stimuli.

irrotational. Free from rotatory motion; said of a moving fluid.

ischium. The posterior ventral bone of the pelvic girdle.

isentropic. Taking place without change of entropy.

islands of Langerhans. Langerhans' islets; irregular masses of endocrine tissue in the pancrease which secrete insulin.

isoallobars. Lines on a weather map joining points which have had equal changes of atmospheric pressure in a given period of time.

isobar. (1) A line drawn on a weather map through places having the same atmospheric pressure at a given time; (2) isotopes of different chemical elements, which have different atomic numbers but equal atomic masses.

isobar surface. A surface of equal atmospheric pressure; an altimeter will record constant height when moving along such a surface.

isobaric. Taking place without change of pressure.

isochore. A line which graphically represents the relationship between the pressure and temperature of a constant-volume liquid or gas.

isochromatic. Of the same color; said of lines of the same tint in the interference figures of biaxial crystals.

isochrone. A line connecting points having the same time values; example, points of the same gelation time for colloidal solutions.

isochronous. Said of a vibration that has a period independent of the amplitude.

isocline. The vertical duplication of geological formations by close folding.

isoclinic line. An imaginary line drawn through points on the earth's surface where the magnetic inclination is the same.

isocosm. A line of equal cosmic-ray intensity on the earth's surface.

isocyclic. Said of a flower having whorls with equal number of parts.

isodiaphere. One of two or more nuclides which have the same difference between the number of neutrons and protons in their nuclei.

isodimorphic. Said of a dimorphous substance which is isomorphous with another dimorphous substance in both its forms.

isodynamic line. A line passing through points of equal horizontal intensity of the earth's magnetic field.

isodynamostacy. A condition of kinetic equilibrium.

isoelectric point. (1) The hydrogen ion concentration in solutions of proteins and related compounds at which the dipolar ions are at a maximum; (2) the pH value at which the migration of ions in an amphoteric electrolyte is at a minimum.

isoelectronic. Having the same number of electrons outside the nucleus.

isoenergic. Taking place with the internal energy remaining constant.

isogam. A line of equal acceleration by gravity on the earth's surface.

isogametes. Gametes similar in size and shape.

isogamy. A sexual reproduction in which male and female germ cells are similar in size and form.

isogeotherm. Geoisotherm; depths of equal temperature below the earth's surface.

isogon. Isogonic line; an imaginary line drawn through the points on the earth's surface where the magnetic deviation is always the same.

isogonism. The property of some hydroids belonging to different genera that they have similar medusae.

isohemagglutinin. A specific substance in the blood serum which agglutinates the blood cells of other members of the same species.

isolation. Any factor or process that keeps organisms from breeding with their relatives.

isolux. A curve or surface of equal light intensity.

isomagnetic line. A line connecting points at which the magnetic force is equal.

isomer. A chemical compound that has the same molecular formula and molecular weight as another, but a different molecular structure and thus different properties; example, butane and methyl propane (also called isobutane) are isomers

isomerization. The transformation of one isomer into another by changing the configuration of atoms in the molecule.

isometric crystal system. Cubic system; a system in which the crystals have three equal and mutually perpendicular axes.

isomorph. One of two or more substances that crystallize in the same form.

isomorphic alternation of generations. Homologous alternation of generations; the theory that one phase of an organism developed from the previous phase; example, the sporophyte developed from the gametophyte.

isomorphism. The similarity or identity of crystalline form.

isomorphous crystals. Mixed crystals; crystals in which atoms of one element are substituted for those of another.

isopedin. The bonelike inner layer of some fish scales.

isophane. A line plotted on a map through regions presenting uniform association of biological and climatic factors.

isophote. A curve or surface of equal light intensity.

isoplanatic. An optical system free from coma.

Isopoda. An order of Crustacea, small bugs of seven free segments and seven pairs of equal legs; examples, wood lice, water skaters, pill bugs.

isoprene. $CH_2:C(CH_3)\cdot CH:CH_2$; a diolefine; the monomer of natural rubber, which is a high polymer; used in synthesis.

Isoptera. Insects having biting mouth parts that are used for boring into wood; they show incomplete metamorphosis; examples, termites, white ants.

isosmotic solutions. Two solutions of equal osmotic pressure.

isostasy. State of balance or equal pressure that is maintained in the earth's crust between basaltic layers below and the eroded material above.

isostatic adjustment. Establishing floating equilibrium between a basaltic layer below and the eroded material above.

isosterism. Having similar electronic structure and similar physical properties.

isoteniscope. An instrument for measuring vapor pressure by determining the change in liquid level in a U tube.

isotherm. A line on a weather map connecting places of the same temperature at a given time.

isothermal. Of constant temperature.

isothermal atmosphere. A region of the atmosphere in which the temperature does not vary with altitude; the stratosphere.

isothermal change. A change which takes place at constant temperature.

isotonic. Having the same osmotic pressure.

isotopes. Atoms of the same element which have the same atomic numbers and chemical properties, but different atomic masses and molecular weights; example, uranium-235 and uranium-238.

isotopic abundance. The relative amount of a particular isotope in a sample of an element; expressed as the number of atoms.

isotopic weight. The atomic weight of an individual isotope expressed on a scale in which the most abundant isotope of oxygen has a weight exactly equal to 16.

isotron. An electromagnetic device for separating isotopes by electrical sorting of their ions.

isotropic. Exhibiting uniform physical properties throughout in all directions.

ivory. The dentine of teeth, similar to bone but harder and of different minute structure; the material of elephant tusks.

ivory black. A carbon black obtained from animal charcoal by dissolving out the inorganic compounds with hydrochloric acid.

J

Jamin effect. A capillary tube containing a column of air bubbles separated by a liquid can withstand a substantial pressure difference between its ends without continued flow.

jarosite. A yellow mineral; hydrated potassium and iron silicate.

jasper. A bright-colored chalcedony; an impure form of natural silica, SiO_2; used as a gem.

Java man. *Pithecanthropus erectus;* a primitive apelike ancestor of man, who lived about half a million years ago in Java.

jaw. The assemblage of bones before and behind, or above and below, the mouth of a vertebrate, which helps opening and closing the mouth.

jejunum. A portion of the small intestine that extends from the end of the duodenum to the beginning of the ileum; it is eight feet long; it occupies the upper and left part of the abdomen.

jellyfish. A soft, jellylike marine animal related to the Hydra.

jet. (1) A hard and compact coal-black variety of lignite; (2) a rapidly moving fluid stream spouting from a nozzle.

jet engine. A reaction engine having one or more combustion chambers and one or more exhaust nozzles, and driven by jet propulsion, that is, by the forward-acting reaction forces derived from the rearward discharge of a high-speed stream of hot gases resulting from the burning of a mixture of air and jet fuel.

jet stream. A narrow stream of air at a high altitude which moves at speeds of 200 to 300 miles per hour.

joint. (1) Dividing planes in a rock with no apparent relative displacement; produced by tension; (2) mechanical connection of two or more parts; (3) the point at which two separate bones are joined by ligaments.

Jolly balance. A device used for the determination of the specific gravity of a substance by weighing it in air and in water; it verifies Hooke's Law.

Joly screen. A photometric screen which consists of two slightly separated parallel plates of a translucent substance, such as paraffin; the interface disappears when the plates are equally illuminated.

Joshi effect. An electric current running through a gas or vapor is increased or decreased by irradiating the gas or vapor with light.

joule. A unit of work or energy, equalling 10^7 ergs; (1) in electrical systems, it is equivalent to moving one coulomb through a potential difference of one volt; (2) in mechanical systems, it is the work done by a force of one newton acting through a distance of one meter; (3) it is liberated by one ampere flowing for one second through a resistance of one ohm.

Joule effect. (1) An extension accompanying a change of magnetization; (2) the heat generated by an electric current flowing through a resistance.

Joule's law. The internal energy of a gas at constant temperature is independent of the pressure and volume; this applies to an ideal gas only.

Joule-Thomson effect. When a gas expands through a porous plug, a fall in temperature occurs which is proportional to the pressure difference across the plug.

jugum. A slender, fingerlike structure on the forewing of a moth to hold the wings together during flight.

junction. In a wave guide, a point or region at which provision is made for the flow of energy into two or more paths.

Jupiter. The largest planet; fifth in order of distance from the sun; it has nine satellites.

Jurassic period. It began about 150 million years ago; the middle of the Mesozoic era; dinosaurs, toothed birds, insects, cycads, and conifers were dominant.

K

K. (1) Chemical symbol for potassium; (2) following an air-mass symbol, it means cold.

°K. Kelvin or absolute temperature.

kainite. A varied-colored mineral;

$MgSO_4 \cdot KCl \cdot 3H_2O$.

kalium. Latin name for potassium.

kames. Conical mounds of partially stratified drift deposited in and along the edges of the ice by temporary glacial streams.

kampometer. An instrument for measuring radiant energy, especially in the thermal region.

kaolin. Aluminum silicate, $Al_2O_3 \cdot 2SiO_2 \cdot 2H_2O$; used in making porcelain and ceramics.

kapnometer. An apparatus for the determination of the concentration of solid or liquid particles dispersed in a gas, such as the density of smoke or fog.

Karl Fischer reagent (KFR). A special solution for titrimetric moisture determination; it is a mixture of iodine, sulfur dioxide, pyridine, and methanol.

Karst plains. Small plains resulting from the solution of rocks by underground water.

Karst topography. A land surface dotted with depressions where the rain tends to disappear into underground channels.

karyokinesis. Mitosis; cell division.

karyotype. The appearance (size, shape, and number) of somatic chromosomes.

katabatic wind. The cold air moving downhill toward lower terrain; in desert ravines, katabatic winds locally reach high velocities.

katamorphism. Breaking down; surface alteration of rocks due to weathering.

Kater's pendulum. A pendulum for comparing the accelerations of gravity at different places on the earth.

katharometer. An instrument for the determination of the composition of a gas mixture by measuring variations in the thermal conductivity.

kc. Abbreviation for kilocycles per second.

Keber's organ. A paired glandular organ of bivalve mollusks which serves as an accessory organ of excretion.

keel. A projection on the breast bone of birds for the attachment of muscles for moving the wings.

keeper. An armature; a soft-iron bar placed across the poles of a permanent horseshoe magnet to prevent loss of magnetism.

keil. A legume type of flower made up of two petals loosely united along their edges.

kelp. Seaweeds; brown algae living in the ocean and often growing to a very large size; ashes of seaweed used as a source of iodine.

Kelvin balance. A laboratory instrument for measuring an electric current.

Kelvin bridge. A double bridge for the measurement of very low resistances.

Kelvin scale of temperature. See absolute temperature.

Kelvin's electrodynamics law. If a number of electric circuits carrying currents are displaced with respect to one another, the work appears as a change in the total electromagnetic energy of the circuits; or when a system of rigid circuits does mechanical work under constant current conditions, the energy of the circuits increases at the same rate as the work done.

Kennelly-Heaviside layer. Ionosphere; a layer of ions in the upper atmosphere, which reflects the waves coming from a transmitter on the ground.

Kennelly's law of magnetization. The reluctivity in magnetizing a specimen of iron is a linear function of the magnetizing force.

kenotron. A high-voltage diode rectifier tube which contains a hot cathode, either of filament or indirectly heated type, and an anode.

Kepler telescope. A telescope in which the objective and the ocular are both convergent lenses, the objective forming a real image to be viewed by the ocular in whose first focal plane it lies.

Kepler's laws. (1) Planets move about the sun in ellipses, with the sun at one focus; (2) the radius vector joining each planet with the sun describes equal areas in equal times; (3) the ratio of the square of the planet's year to the cube of the planet's mean distance from the sun is the same for all planets.

keratins. Natural insoluble scleroproteins which occur usually as protective covering in vertebrates; examples, hair, nails, hoofs, wool.

keratophyre. An igneous rock of fine-grained structure, containing anorthoclase.

kerosene. A petroleum distillate boiling between 150 and 300°C; used for heating and lighting.

Kerr cell. A device used in television which, in its simplest form, consists of a small glass cell into which two metal electrodes are sealed; the cell is filled with pure nitrobenzene, a transparent liquid which exhibits double refraction when a high potential difference is applied across the electrodes.

ketenes. Unsaturated organic compounds which contain both an ethylenic double bond and a carbonyl group; example, ethenone, $CH_2CH=CO$.

ketones. Organic compounds of the general formula $R—CO—R'$, in which R and R' may be identical or different alkyl or aryl groups; example, acetone, CH_3COCH_3.

kettle holes. Hollows formed when blocks of ice buried under glacial moraine melted, causing the earth above to sink in.

kev. Symbol for 1000 electron volts; a unit of energy.

keyword balance. A balance in which all small weights are handled by a series of keys mounted on the outside of the case.

kg. Abbreviation for kilogram.

kg-m. Abbreviation for kilogram-meter.

kidney. A gland near the spine which eliminates nitrogenous and other metabolic wastes from the body of vertebrates.

kieselguhr. Infusorial earth; a finely powdered hydrated silica from skeletons of diatoms; used for filtering, clarifying, as an absorbent, in the manufacture of explosives.

Kikuchi lines. Spectral lines obtained by directing an electron stream against the surface of a crystal; they are due to the scattering of electrons by atom layers in the crystal structure.

kilocycle. A unit of frequency; 1000 cycles.

kilogram. The weight of one liter of water at 4°C; 1000 g; 2.2 lb.

kilogram calorie. The quantity of heat needed to raise the temperature of one kilogram of water by 1°C; 1000 gram calories; 3.968 Btu.

kiloliter. A measure of volume in the metric system; 1000 liters.

kilometer. A measure of distance in the metric system; 0.62 mile; 1000 meters; 10 hectometers; 3280 feet and 10 inches.

kilovolt. A unit of electromotive force (emf); 1000 volts.

kilowatt. A unit of electrical power, equivalent to 44,000 foot-pounds per minute; 1000 watts; 4/3 horsepower.

kilowatt-hour. A unit of electrical energy; 2.25 MEV $\times 10^{19}$.

kimberlite. A mica in South Africa in which diamonds are found.

kinaesthetic. Refers to sense organs of vertebrate muscles, tendons, and joints; having muscle sense.

kinematics. The study of the laws of motion.

kinescope. A cathode-ray tube used in television receivers to reproduce images.

kinesis. The locomotion of an organism or cell in response to a stimulus; the speed, or frequency of turning, depends on the strength of the stimulus, but the stimulus does not control the direction of movement.

kinetic. Referring to, or caused by, motion.

kinetic energy. The ability of a moving body to perform work.

kinetic reaction. The reaction of inertia in an accelerated body.

kinetic theory of gases. Explanation of the behavior of gases by the concept that their molecules are elastic spheres in constant thermal agitation; gas pressure is due to the impact of the molecules against the walls of the containing vessel.

kinetic theory of matter. The theory which assumes that the molecules of all matter are in constant motion.

kinetics, chemical. The study of the velocities of chemical reactions.

kinetics, general. A branch of dynamics which deals with forces and the motions caused by them.

kinetochore. A kinetic constriction, connecting a portion of the chromosome to the spindle fiber.

kingdom. All natural objects are classified into the animal, the vegetable, and the mineral kingdoms.

Kingston valve. A valve in a submarine that allows water to rush into the ballast tanks when it is opened; the same valve supplies the circulating pumps in ships.

Kipp's generator. A device used for the continuous generation of certain gases, especially hydrogen sulfide in the laboratory.

Kirchhoff's bridge. A resistance bridge in which the potential differences through the known and the unknown resistances are balanced in a differential galvanometer.

Kirchhoff's laws. (1) In any network, the sum of the electric currents which meet at a point is zero; (2) the sum of the electromotive forces in any closed circuit or loop is equal to the sum of the potential differences in that circuit or loop.

kish. A graphite occasionally formed in iron-smelting furnaces.

Kjeldahl flask. A long-necked, round-bottomed flask used in nitrogen determination.

kl. Kiloliter.

klystron. A velocity-modulated electron tube used in ultra-high-frequency circuits.

km. Kilometer.

knob and basis topography. A region of undulating appearance, because of uneven morainal deposits.

knocked-on-atom. An atom of a solid which, after collision with an energized particle, such as a neutron, fission fragment, ion, or atom moving through the solid, recoils; it may have sufficient energy to displace other atoms or be displaced from its position in the lattice.

knot. The speed of one nautical mile (6080 feet) per hour.

Knudsen flow. A diffusion flow of

free molecules of a gas through a long tube at such pressures that the mean free path is greater than the radius of the tube.

Knudsen gage. A gage for measuring extremely low gas pressures which operates on the principle of unequal bombardment of a surface by molecules of different energies.

Koch's bacillus. The tuberculosis germ.

Kohlrausch's law. The conductivity of an electrolyte is equal to the sum of the conductivities of the ions of its dissociated substance, if ionization is complete.

Kopp's law. The molecular heat of a solid compound is approximately equal to the sum of the atomic heats of its constituents.

Kr. Chemical symbol for krypton.

Krebs cycle. A cycle of enzyme-controlled stepwise oxidation of carbohydrates and fats which explains also the synthesis of some amino acids.

Kroll's process. A method of extracting titanium from its ore.

krypton. A rare gas; chemical symbol Kr; atomic number 36.

Kundt's apparatus. A device for determining the velocity of sound in a metal rod by measuring the wave length of the sound produced by the vibrating rod in the air.

Kundt's effect. The rotation of the plane of polarized light by certain liquids and gases when they are placed in a magnetic field.

Kundt's rule. When the refractive index of a solution increases, its optical absorption bands are displaced toward the red, as a result of changes in composition, etc.

kva. Kilovolt-ampere.

kw. Kilowatt.

kw-hr. Kilowatt-hour.

kyanite. A bluish mineral; aluminum silicate, Al_2SiO_5.

kymograph. An instrument for recording the rotary motion of the propeller of an aircraft in flight.

L

l. Symbol for (1) length; (2) liter; (3) wave length.

L. Symbol for (1) inductance; (2) relative heat constant; (3) lambert.

ʟ. Symbol for levorotatory.

La. Chemical symbol for lanthanum.

labeled atom. A tracer element which can be detected in extremely small quantities, usually by either isotopic or radioactive means; often introduced to follow the pattern of biochemical reactions.

labile. Unstable; readily shifting, as in a spontaneous rearrangement of atoms within certain organic molecules.

labile oscillator. A local oscillator whose frequency is controlled from a remote location.

labium. A lip; in invertebrates, the lower lip as distinguished from the upper lip, or labrum; one of the folds of the female external genital organs.

Labrador Current. Water flowing southward from the Arctic Ocean between the northeast coast of Canada and the southwest of Greenland.

labradorite. A dark feldspar, usually of radiant blue sheen.

labrum. In invertebrates, the upper lip, as distinguished from the lower, or labium.

Labyrinthodonta. A division of extinct, large salamanderlike amphibians; late Devonian to Triassic.

lac. A dark-red resinous substance deposited by scale insects on the twigs of trees; used in making shellac.

laccolith. An intrusive igneous rock which has been injected along the bedding planes of sedimentary formations in such a way as to form a dome of the overlying strata.

LACE (liquid-air-cycle engine). A bipropellant rocket engine that produces its own oxidizer.

Lacertilia. A division of reptiles, of which lizards form the major group; closely allied structurally to the snake, though typical members have pentadactyl limbs.

lacrimal gland. In mammals, the tear gland, lying beneath the upper eyelid at the outer angle of the eye; normally, it secretes small amounts of saline fluid, which moistens the eye and facilitates its motion.

lactase. An enzyme, present in the intestinal juices of some animals, which changes milk sugar (lactose) into glucose and galactose.

lactation. The formation of milk by the mammary glands.

lacteal. One of the lymphatic vessels of the small intestine that carry absorbed food to the circulatory system.

lactic acid. A colorless organic acid formed in sour milk by the action of bacteria and formed in animals as a result of muscle contraction; synthetically it is prepared by fermentation of sugar or cornstarch; used in medicine as well as in dyeing and tanning.

lactogenic hormone. Prolactin; a secretion of the anterior lobe of the pituitary, which stimulates milk production in the mammalian breast.

lactometer. An instrument used to determine the richness of milk by the measurement of its specific gravity.

lactones. Inner esters of carboxylic acids.

lactose. Milk sugar, $C_{12}H_{22}O_{11}$; a hard, crystalline sugar, less sweet than cane sugar.

lacuna. A small cavity or intercellular space; in the bone, it contains bone cells.

lacustrine plain. A nonfertile plain formed as a result of lake destruction.

lag. The number of degrees an alternating current lags behind the voltage.

lag phase. The early period of slow multiplication following a bacterial inoculation into a culture medium.

lagging current. An alternating current which attains its highest value at a later moment in the cycle than the voltage which generates it.

lagoon. A body of water between the coast line and offshore bars.

lake plain. A flat plain that formerly was covered by marginal lakes.

Lamarckism. A belief that acquired characteristics are inherited; no longer generally accepted.

lambert. A unit of brightness used for describing a perfectly diffusing surface; one lambert is the equivalent of one lumen per square centimeter.

Lambert projection. An aeronautical map on which meridians are straight lines converging toward the north and parallels are arcs of concentric circles, equally spaced.

lamella. (1) The membrane or primary septum between any two cells; (2) a thin layer of bone deposited during one period of osteogenic activity; (3) in botany, a compound layer composed of the primary walls and a cementlike intercellular substance between the primary walls of two cells; (4) a flat plate formed by the fusion of ctenidial filaments in bivalve mollusks.

Lamellibranchia. Pelecypoda; bivalves including mussels, clams, oysters; they feed by ciliary currents.

lamina. A thin plate or layer; the blade or flattened part of a leaf.

laminated. Built up in layers.

laminated core. An armature core built up of layers of insulated iron plates in order to prevent the formation of eddy currents in the metal.

laminations. In geology, fine stratifications exhibited typically by shales and sandstones.

lamp, arc. A source of light which consists primarily of two carbon electrodes between which an electric arc is maintained; its high brilliance makes it useful for searchlights and spot-lights.

lamp, electric. A device, having a filament or arc which, when heated to incandescence, gives off light.

lamp, filament. A device for producing light by means of an electrically heated wire in a glass bulb that is either evacuated or partially filled with an inert gas.

lamp, mercury-vapor. A lamp containing mercury in a previously-evacuated bulb or tube, giving a blue-green light as the electricity is conducted by the mercury vapor between the electrodes.

lamp, quartz. A lamp which has a quartz bulb to transmit ultraviolet radiation; used as a light source rich in ultraviolet radiations; it is often of the mercury vapor type.

lamp shells. Brachiopod shells.

lamp, spectrum. A lamp which gives a nonluminous flame; used in the spectroscopic examination of radiation from solids or liquids introduced into the flame.

lampblack. The fine black soot, almost pure carbon, obtained by burning oils, fats, or tars in an atmosphere deficient in oxygen.

land breeze. A breeze moving from the land toward the water; usually caused by convection at night when the land is cooling faster than the sea.

land bridge. A strip of land which connected one land area with another at some earlier time, as between Asia and North America or Australia.

landing angle. The acute angle between the line of thrust of an airplane and the horizontal when the airplane is resting on level ground in its natural position.

landing speed. The minimum speed of an airplane at the instant of contact with the landing area in a normal landing.

Landolt band. A dark band which sometimes appears in the field of crossed Nicols when an intense source of light, such as the sun, is used; it is due to light being not strictly parallel.

landslide. The movement of a mass of earth or rock which has been delicately balanced.

Langmuir dark space. A nonluminous region surrounding a negatively charged probe inserted into the positive column of a glow or arc discharge.

lanthanides. A group of rare-earth elements, beginning with lanthanum.

lanthanum. Chemical symbol La; atomic number 57; discovered in 1839 by C. G. Mosander; a tin-white metal; malleable but not ductile; a rare-earth element.

lanugo. Very fine hair covering

the human fetus about the fifth month of gestation.

lapilli. Pieces of lava, about the size of walnuts, erupted from a volcano.

lapis lazuli. Sodium aluminum silicate containing sulfur; a rare blue mineral; probably the sapphire of the ancients.

lapse rate. The rate at which temperature decreases or lapses with altitude.

large calorie. Kilogram calorie; equal to 1000 gram calories. The gram calorie (or small calorie) is the quantity of heat required to raise the temperature of 1 gram of water from 15° to 16°C.

large intestine. In some higher invertebrates and in most vertebrates, that portion of the intestine which is posterior to the small intestine.

larva. An immature form or stage of an animal, following the egg; in insects, it is a wormlike or grublike stage of the complete metamorphosis.

larynx. The organ of the voice, located between the trachea and the base of the tongue; it is constructed of a series of cartilage.

laser (light amplification by stimulated emission of radiation). A microwave amplifier that operates in the visible spectrum. *See* MASER.

late prophase. The latter part of the first phase of mitosis; the nuclear membrane begins to fade out, spindles appear, chromosomes begin to form.

late telophase. The latter part of the final phase of mitosis; a period of reconstruction of nuclei; chromosomes begin to fade out, spindles disappear, the cell plate enlarges, and the nuclear membrane begins to form.

latent heat. The heat which changes the physical state of a substance without changing its temperature; example, the heat required to melt ice at 32°F to water at 32°F.

latent heat of condensation. The heat released by the condensation of water vapor, especially in the formation of clouds.

latent heat of vaporization. The heat energy of vapor, equivalent to the heat energy required to change a given quantity of liquid to vapor without any temperature change.

latent period. The time between the application of a stimulus and the first detectable response in a tissue.

latent photographic image. The invisible image which can be developed on exposure of a light-sensitive emulsion to light.

lateral bud. A bud which develops at a point other than the end of a stem.

lateral inversion. The inversion

produced by a plane mirror, seen when the image of anything printed is observed in a mirror; a television-image defect, the picture being reversed.

lateral line. A row of scales, neuromast organs, along each side of the fish; it marks the position of a sensory-type organ.

lateral moraine. An accumulation of matter picked up by a glacier and carried along the sides.

lateral plate. The unsegmented mesoderm on the lateral and ventral sides of vertebrate embryos; the perivisceral celom arises in it.

lateral stability. A stability with reference to disturbances in which the position of the plane symmetry of the aircraft is affected; examples, rolling or sideslipping.

laterite. An iron-containing red soil; a tropical aeolian iron- and aluminum-containing clay, resulting from the weathering of basic igneous rocks.

latex. A milky fluid found in many plants consisting of a white complex emulsion in which many substances, such as proteins, alkaloids, starches, sugars, oils, tannins, resins, and gums are found; a viscous fluid from the rubber trees, which yields rubber on coagulation.

Latimeria. Crossopterygii; the only known living representative of the great group of fossil fish; a coelacanth.

latitude. A distance north and south of the equator, measured in degrees.

latitude, lines of. Parallels of latitude; circles parallel to the equator, joining points of equal latitude; the equator is 0°, while the poles are 90° latitude.

lattice. An arrangement of points in space, representing the relative positions of corresponding atomic, molecular, or ionic centers in the elementary cells or structure units of a crystal.

lattice dynamics. A branch of the theory of the solid state, dealing with the properties of the thermal vibrations of crystal lattices.

lattice energy. The energy which depends on the configuration of the atoms in a crystal lattice, and which changes when any change is made in that configuration through mechanical stress, electric forces, or otherwise.

lava. A molten material which pours out on the surface of the earth through eruption from volcanoes or from fissures.

law of axes. The opposite ends of any one of the axes of a crystal are cut by the same number of similar faces which are similarly arranged.

law of conservation of energy.

Energy can be neither created nor destroyed; the total energy of a closed system is constant.

law of conservation of matter. Matter can neither be created nor destroyed.

law of corresponding states. If two of the three reduced variables of state are equal for two different bodies of gas, the third will also be equal for these bodies.

law of definite proportions. Elements combine in definite proportions to form a certain compound; therefore, the composition of a compound is independent of its method of preparation.

law of electric charges. Like charges repel each other while unlike charges attract each other.

law of equal areas. An application of Kepler's second law; a particle in motion under the influence of any central force moves in such a way that the radius vector sweeps out equal areas in equal intervals of time.

law of equilibrium. If a body is in equilibrium (at rest), the sum of the forces acting on it in one direction must balance the sum of the forces acting on it in the opposite direction.

law of gravitation. Every body attracts every other body with a force that is directly proportional to the product of their masses and inversely proportional to the square of the distance between their centers.

law of heat exchange. The total number of heat units lost by a warm substance equals the total number of heat units gained by a cooler substance when the two substances are in contact with each other.

law of inverse squares. If any physical quantity varies with the distance from a source, this variation is inversely proportional to the square of that distance; example, the intensity of illumination of a surface is inversely proportional to the square of its distance from the light source.

law of magnetic poles. Like poles of a magnet repel each other, unlike poles attract each other.

law of mass action. The velocity of a homogeneous chemical reaction is proportional to the product of the concentrations of the reactants.

law of moments. When a body is in equilibrium, the sum of the clockwise moments is equal to the sum of the counterclockwise moments.

law of multiple proportions. When two elements combine to form more than one compound, the different weights of one element which combine with fixed weights of the other are in a ratio of small whole

numbers.

law of octaves. In an arrangement of the elements according to their atomic weights, every eighth element has similar properties.

law of properties. Under constant conditions, a substance always has a definite and characteristic set of properties by which it can be described.

law of rebound. For a perfectly elastic ball, the angle of rebound equals the angle of impact.

law of stages. In crystallization from the liquid state, the atoms arrive at their final, permanent configuration through successive, temporary arrangements of varying stability.

law of work. The work output and work input are equal in an ideal machine.

lawrencium. Element 103; the last of the actinide series of elements; discovered in 1961; symbol, Lw.

layering. A form of vegetative reproduction in which a twig still attached to the main plant touches the ground and takes root.

lb. Abbreviation for pound.

Le Chatelier's law. If a stress is placed on a system in equilibrium, the reaction tends to go in the direction which relieves the stress.

leaching. Separating a soluble substance from an insoluble substance by washing with some solvent, such as water.

lead. (1) A bluish-gray metal; the heaviest and softest of common metals; chemical symbol Pb; atomic number 82; used in paints, storage batteries, bearing metals, etc.; (2) an electrical conductor which projects from an electrical device and to which an electrical connection is made.

lead acetate. Sugar of lead, $(CH_3COO)_2Pb \cdot 3H_2O$; a white, crystalline, soluble salt of sweet taste; used as a local astringent.

lead dioxide. Lead peroxide, PbO_2; dark-brown powder; used in storage batteries, as an oxidizing agent, etc.

lead oxide. Lead monoxide, PbO; a yellow to brownish-red compound; used as a pigment, in making flint glass, glazes, etc.

lead storage cell. A box containing plates of lead peroxide and spongy lead in an electrolyte of sulfuric acid; used for storing chemical energy which on the closing of a circuit will deliver an electrical current.

lead sulfide. Galena, PbS; blue cubic crystals; used in ceramics.

lead-chamber process. The manufacture of sulfuric acid by the action of nitrogen dioxide on sulfuric dioxide to give nitric oxide, NO, and sulfur trioxide,

SO_3; the NO combines with air to give NO_2; the SO_3 combines with water to give H_2SO_4.

leading current. An alternating current reaching its minimum and maximum value in advance of the electromotive force causing the current.

leaf. A thin, flat structure that arises as a lateral outgrowth from a stem; it provides food for the plant by photosynthesis.

leaf axile. The angle formed by the leaf stalk and the stem.

leaf cuttings. An artificial vegetative propagation; a new plant will develop from certain areas on the margin of the leaf when placed on moist soil or a moist blotter; example, Bryophyllum.

leaf gap. An interruption of the vascular cylinder of the stem caused by emergence of a leaf trace; characteristic of all vascular plants.

leaf mosaic. Any arrangement of leaves to expose the greatest possible leaf surface to the light.

leaf primordia. A minute lateral outgrowth just behind the tip of a stem which develops into a leaf.

leaf scar. A scar on the bark where leaves have fallen off.

leaf sheath. The base of a leaf modified to form a sheath around the stem.

leaf trace. Vascular supply from stem to leaf consisting of one or more vascular bundles.

leaflet. One of the parts of a compound leaf.

leak, grid. A high resistance placed in the grid circuit with the grid condenser.

leakage current. A current flow through an insulator.

leakage, neutron. The loss of neutrons of a specified energy range from a given region of a nuclear reactor due to their motion.

least circle of aberration. The smallest cross section of a bundle of rays from an optical system with spherical aberration.

least-energy principle. If a system is in a stable equilibrium, any slight change in its condition which requires work will put it out of equilibrium, so that, the system will return to its former state if left to itself and in so doing will give up the energy imparted when it was disturbed.

leavening agent. A substance which releases carbon dioxide in a dough or batter, that lightens it while baking.

Leblanc process. Salt cake process; the manufacture of sodium carbonate (Na_2CO_3) by using common salt (NaCl) and sulfuric acid (H_2SO_4).

Lecher oscillator. A device for producing a system of standing waves in two parallel wires.

Lecher wires. A special type of transmission line used primarily for the measurement of frequencies in the high radio-frequency range.

lecithin. A phosphatide which acts as a protective colloid; an emulsifying agent made from soybean oil; also used as a coating for candies.

Leclanché cell. An open-circuit primary cell using carbon and zinc electrodes, sal ammoniac electrolyte, and manganese dioxide depolarizer.

leeward. The direction of the wind.

left-hand rule for the direction of the magnetic lines of force. Grasp the wire with the left hand so that the extended thumb points in the direction of the electron flow. The curled fingers will then go around the wire in the same direction as the lines of force.

left-hand rule to determine which end of an electromagnet is the north pole. Grasp the coil with the left hand so that the fingers curl about the coil in the direction in which the electrons are flowing; the extended thumb will then point in the direction of the north pole of the electromagnet.

leg. (1) A jointed appendage, used for locomotion on a solid supported surface by walking, running, or jumping; (2) either side of a triangle other than the base.

legume. A dry fruit which splits its walls along two lines when ripe; it is a nitrogen-gathering plant; example, pea.

legumin. The protein substance found in seeds of the pea family.

lehr. An annealing oven used in glass factories in which glass is allowed to cool slowly so that the strain is reduced.

Leishman-Donovan bodies. Small round or oval bodies found in the spleen and liver of patients suffering from kalaazar.

Lemberg's solution. A solution of logwood digested in aqueous aluminum chloride which is used as a standard reagent for distinguishing between calcite or argonite and dolomite.

lemma. The lower one of the two bracts which immediately subtend the floret in the spikelet of grasses.

lens. (1) A transparent piece of glass or other substance with two opposite regular surfaces, of which at least one is curved to refract light; (2) a part of the eye which focuses light rays on the retina.

lens, achromatic. A compound lens consisting of at least two kinds of glass, which have the same focal length and same magnification for light of two different wave lengths.

lens, apochromat. A compound lens constructed in such a way that the focal length for three different wave lengths will be identical.

lens, converging. A lens which causes light parallel to its axis to converge to a real focus.

lens, cylindrical. A lens, one surface of which is a portion of the surface of a cylinder; used to correct astigmatism.

lens, diverging. A lens which causes light parallel to its axis to diverge, as if coming from a point which is the vertical focus of the lens.

lens, electric electron. A device which employs only electric fields to focus an electron beam.

lens, field. An auxiliary lens used to focus light which has passed through one or more stages of a long optical system, before it passes to later stages.

lens, magnetic. A system of coils, electromagnets, or magnets so arranged that the resulting magnetic fields exert a focusing force on a beam of charged particles.

lens, meniscus. A lens whose two surfaces have curvatures of the same sign: convexocave or concavoconvex.

lens, weak. A lens in which the focal lengths are too long compared with the extent of the lens field.

lensometer. An instrument designed for the measurement of the optical characteristics of spectacle lenses.

lenticel. A small, raised pit in the outer surface of younger woody stems, where gases may be exchanged with the atmosphere.

Lenz's law. Whenever a current is induced in an electric circuit, it flows in such a direction as to produce a magnetic field opposing the charge or motion that induced the current.

Leo. A constellation containing the bright star Regulus.

Leonids. A meteor shower observed about the 12th of November.

lepidolite. A mica group of minerals consisting of silicates of potassium, lithium, and aluminum; it is of pink or purple color.

Lepidoptera. The second largest group of insects; they have four wings; the mouth parts of larvae are of the true chewing type whereas those of adults are sucking; they have complete metamorphosis; example, butterflies.

leptocephalus. The larvae of the European eel which is found in Atlantic Ocean breeding grounds.

lepton. A particle of small mass in the same class as the electron, positron, neutrino, and antineutrino.

leptotene. The first stage in meiosis; the chromatin thread acquiring definite polarity.

lethal gene. A gene which bears a characteristic which is usually fatal to an organism.

leucocyte. A white blood corpuscle.

leucoplast. A colorless plastid in plant cells which stores starch.

leucoplastid. A colorless plastid.

levee. (1) A sediment deposited along the banks of a river; (2) a man-made embankment for controlling the flow and preventing inundation of a river.

level indicator. (1) A device which indicates level height, as in a tank; (2) a device which indicates the amount of radiation present in the vicinity of an instrument.

lever. A simple machine; a bar that is pivoted at a fixed point (fulcrum); the load is applied at one point of the bar and the effort to balance the load at another.

levigation. Grinding to a fine powder with water.

levogyrate. Same as levorotatory.

levorotatory. Rotating or deviating the plane of polarized light to the left.

lewisite. Chlorovinyl dichloroarsine; $ClCH:CHAsCl_2$; a pale-yellow liquid vesicant, used as a war gas; it is destroyed by oxidizing agents.

Leyden jar. A glass jar coated on its inner and outer surfaces with a conducting material; it is used as a capacitor for storing electricity.

Leyden temperature scale. A low-temperature range of the centigrade scale, based on the boiling point of hydrogen, $-252.74°C$, and that of oxygen, $-182.95°C$.

Li. Chemical symbol for lithium.

liana. A climbing plant which entwines itself around trunks and branches.

Lias. A thick layer of marine strata of the Jurassic system.

Libra. A small constellation which is the seventh sign of the Zodiac.

librations. Periodical oscillations of the moon which enable observers on the earth to see somewhat more than 50% of the moon's surface.

Lichenes. Composite plants, consisting of algae and fungi, associated as hosts and parasites.

lid. A temperature inversion in the atmosphere which prevents the air below and above the layer involved from mixing.

Liebig condenser. Two concentric glass tubes, between which cooling water is circulated; used in distillation.

Liesegang rings. A banded precipitate formed by ions which react by diffusion through certain gels.

life cycle. The complete series of

changes taking place during the entire life of an individual plant or animal.

life expectancy. The duration of life, after any specific age, to be expected from the average shown in mortality tables based on past experience.

life history. All stages in the life cycle of an organism from egg to adult or from egg to natural death.

life layer. The part of the earth in which organisms can live; its total thickness is 12 to 13 miles.

life, mean. The average time during which an atom remains activated.

life span. Period of existence of an organism.

life zone. A geographical area characterized by approximately uniform temperature conditions.

lifetime. The average time between the appearance and disappearance of a particle, in nucleonics.

lift. The perpendicular component of the force of the air against an airplane; the force opposed to gravity.

lift pump. A pump that lifts and discharges liquids and operates with the aid of air pressure.

lifting power. The difference between the weights of a given volume of air and of the same volume of a gas that is less dense than air.

ligament. (1) The connection between two parts of the shell of bivalve mollusks; (2) a fibrous band between the ends of two bones in vertebrates.

ligasoid. A colloidal system, in which the dispersed particles are liquid and the dispersion medium is gaseous.

light. A form of radiant energy received from the sun or other sources, which can act on the eye to induce a visual sensation.

light filter. A homogeneous optical medium that absorbs rays in certain regions of the spectrum.

light flux. The flow of radiant energy through a given area, measured in lumens.

light modulation. Controlling light intensity by electrical means to make it suitable for the purposes of television.

light, monochromatic. Light which consists of only one wavelength; example, the sodium flame.

light, quantity of. A measure of the time integral of luminous flux; commonly expressed in lumen-hours.

light quantum. A single train of light waves emitted by an atom or molecule without sudden changes in phase.

light valve. A device, either mechanical or electro-optical, for controlling the intensity of a beam of light.

light, velocity of. 2.9978×10^{10} cm/sec equals 186,326 miles/second.

light year. The distance which light can travel in 362.25636 days at the rate of 186.326 miles a second; about 11 million miles a minute, or almost 5 trillion, 880 million miles; used to express the distance of stars.

lightning. A discharge of electricity between two or more clouds or between clouds and the earth.

lightning arrester. A device that causes lightning to pass off to the earth thus serving to protect electrical machinery.

lightning conductor. Lightning rod; a conductor of electricity ending in one or more sharp points which is connected to earth and to the high part of a building to protect the building and its vicinity from lightning stroke.

lignification. The impregnation of a cell wall with lignin.

lignin. A celluloselike substance found in woody parts of plants.

lignite. A poor grade of brownish coal, which shows much of the structure of wood from which it is derived; used as a fuel.

ligroin. A mixture of petroleum hydrocarbons having a boiling range of 70° to 120°C.

ligule. An outgrowth from the upper and inner side of a grass blade where it joins the sheath.

lime. Calcium oxide, CaO; prepared by heating limestone to over 800°C; used in mortar and whitewash.

lime, hydrated. Same as slaked lime.

lime, slaked. Calcium hydroxide, $Ca(OH)_2$; used in agriculture.

lime sulfur. A mixture of calcium sulfide and sulfate; a contact insecticide; also used in leather treatment and in luminous paints.

limestone. A sedimentary rock containing calcium carbonate, $CaCO_3$; used as a basic flux.

limewater. An aqueous solution of calcium hydroxide; used as an antacid and in chemical analysis.

limiter. An electron tube used in frequency-modulation radio receivers to limit the amplitude of radio waves.

limiting density. The value which the density of a gas approaches as its pressure approaches zero at constant temperature.

limits of audibility. The thresholds of hearing; the minimum effective sound pressure that can be heard at a specified frequency forms the lower limit, while the minimum effective pressure that causes a feeling of pain in the ear forms the upper limit.

limnobiology. The study of the organisms, both plant and animal, living in fresh water.

limnology. A study of the physical, chemical, meteorological, and biological conditions in bodies of fresh water.

line breeding. The selection of closely related individuals as parents in order to keep a strain pure; the opposite of hybridization.

line density. The mass per unit length, as of a wire or a slender rod.

line of flow. The path followed by any one particle of a fluid when flowing.

line of force. A line representing an electric or magnetic field, whose direction at any point corresponds to the direction of the electric force or magnetic field at that point.

line of nodes. A straight line connecting the two points of intersection of an orbit with the ecliptic.

line of stress. An imaginary line extending through a stressed elastic substance in the direction of principal tension, compression, or shear.

line spectrum. Bright-line spectrum; a spectrum consisting of sharp irregular lines; example, the spectrum of an activated gas molecule.

line squall. Extremely turbulent, dark, roll-type squall clouds usually found at the leading edge of squall lines which bring cold temperature and hail or heavy rain.

linear accelerator. An electronic device consisting of a number of coaxial ring electrodes, through which electrons travel in a straight line at gradually increasing speed.

linear distortion. A distortion which is independent of the amplitude of the signal.

linear oscillator. A system composed of two parts so connected that they are capable of oscillating with respect to each other along the line joining them.

lingering period. The length of time it takes for an electron to remain in its orbit of highest energy level before it jumps to a lower orbit and radiates the difference in energy.

linin. Fine threads in a cell nucleus which participate in cell division.

linkage. (1) The passing of two or more nonallelomorphic genes from generation to generation as a unit; (2) a chemical bond; (3) the product of the magnetic flux and the number of turns in a closed electric circuit.

linkage, catenary. The linking of molecules to one another, end to end; example, aminoacids uniting to form polypeptides.

linkage, singlet. A valence bond between two atoms which consist of a single electron.

lip. A fleshy fold at the external orifice of a cavity, especially those which bound the mouth of vertebrates.

lipase. An enzyme of the pancreatic juice which digests fats and oils, changing them to glycerol and fatty acids.

lipides. Fats, fat derivatives, and substances related to them either chemically or metabolically, in plants and animals.

lipoclastic. Lipolytic; fat-splitting; said of enzymes which hydrolyze fats into fatty acids and glycerin; example, lipase.

lipoid. A fatlike substance.

liquation. (1) The separation or purification of metals based on differences in the melting points of the constituents; (2) a process of magnetic differentiation believed to take place as a result of the separation of two immiscible liquids from the parent magma.

liquefaction. Converting a gas or a solid into a liquid.

liquid. One of the three states of matter; a practically incompressible fluid whose shape depends on its container; examples, water, alcohol.

liquid air. Air that has been liquefied by cooling to —312°F.

liquid crystal. A liquid that has optical anisotrophy and other properties similar to those of a crystal.

liquid, polar. A liquid whose molecules have dipole moments.

lisaloid. A colloidal system consisting of a liquid phase surrounded by a solid phase; example, a jelly.

liter. A unit of volume in the metric system; the volume of 1 kilogram of water at 4°C; 1 cubic decimeter; 1000 cubic centimeters; 1000 milliliters; 1.06 quarts; 2.12 pints; 33.82 fluid ounces.

lithification. Turning to stone; consolidation and hardening of lava or aggregation of loose sediment to form rocks.

lithium. The lightest metal; a silver-white alkali metal; chemical symbol Li; atomic number 3; used in bearing alloys.

lithocyst. (1) A small hollow organ containing solid particles, found at the base of a tentacle on the margin of certain hydrozoan medusae; it is assumed to serve as an organ of hearing; (2) a plant cell containing compacted calcium carbonate.

lithology. The descriptive macroscopic study of rocks, including their structure, grain size, stratification, and mineral composition.

lithophysae. Concentric shells of fragile crystalline material occurring in lavas.

lithospermous. Having stonelike seeds.

lithosphere. The outer solid rock layer of the earth; the earth's crust.

litmus. An organic indicator used for detecting acids and alkalis; its purplish color turns red in acid and blue in alkali.

litter. The number of animals born at the same time.

littoral. Living along the shore line of the ocean in shallow waters and in the tidal zone which is periodically exposed to air.

liver. The largest gland in the body, between the stomach and diaphragm; it secretes bile and stores excess glucose.

liver fluke. A tiny, flattened, leaf-like parasitic worm that infests the livers of cattle, swine, and even of men, but is especially destructive to sheep.

liverwort. A bryophyte with flattened, leaflike body attached to the ground by rhizoids; it is similar to mosses and is limited to a moist habitat; example, Marchantia.

lixiviation. Leaching; extraction of the soluble ingredients from a mixture by repeated washing with a solvent and then precipitating from the solution.

Lloyd's mirror. A device for producing interference fringes between the direct light of a source and the light reflected by a mirror.

load. (1) The power output of an engine; (2) the power supplied by a source of electric current; (3) the resistance to be overcome by a prime mover.

loading coil. A coil of four equal windings and adjusted inductance inserted at uniform intervals in transmission lines to reduce the attenuation with frequency.

loam. A soil which contains clay, silt, fine sand, and humus.

local action. The corrosion of a metal due to the formation of galvanic cells between different parts of the metal piece.

local heat thunderstorms. Storms which may occur without warning as a result of local convection.

local time. The mean solar time, apparent solar, or sidereal time for a given longitude in contrast to standard time.

loculicidal dehiscence. Splitting open of the capsule of a fruit along the middle of each carpel.

loculus. (1) A chamber of the ovary in a compound pistil; (2) a small cavity or shell of animals.

locus. (1) A similar position along the length of all homologous chromosomes where always the same kind of gene is located; (2) a small particle in the center of a starch grain.

lodestone. A magnetic iron ore.

lodicules. Two scalelike structures which lie at the base of the ovary of a grass flower.

loess. Buff-colored, wind-blown deposit of fine silt, usually unstratified, which is often exposed in bluffs with steep to vertical faces.

log. Abbreviation for logarithm.

London dipole theory. A theory that accounts for the attractive forces between molecules by the interaction of their instantaneous dipole moments.

long ton. An English unit of weight; 2240 pounds.

longitude. The distance in degrees of any point on the earth's surface east or west from the prime meridian; the prime meridian is at Greenwich, England.

longitudinal. (1) Lengthwise; (2) a rigid support of the frame of an airship which connects the transverse frame members.

longitudinal stability. The steady flight of an aircraft without variations in pitching, and in the longitudinal and normal velocities.

longitudinal wave. A wave motion in which the particles vibrate to and fro along the path which the wave travels; example, sound waves.

looming. A mirage in which images of objects below the horizon appear in enlarged, distorted form, especially at sea.

loop antenna. Frame antenna; a closed-circuit antenna that consists of one or more conductor windings on a frame, for picking up or emitting radio waves.

loose coupling. A weak coupling; a coupling consisting of coils placed apart so that the magnetic transfer is weak.

lophophore. A ridge surrounding the mouth of Bryozoa which bears the tentacles.

lophotrichous. Having a tuft of flagellae at one end.

lopolith. An igneous intrusion in which the center is depressed, so that the upper surface, together with the overlying strata, forms a basis instead of a dome.

loran. Long-range navigation; a means of determining the position at sea or in the air from signals sent by a pair of radio stations working together.

Lorentz electromotive force. A force acting on an electric particle by reason of its motion relative to a magnetic field.

lorica. A structure formed of thickened integument which encloses the body of many Rotifera.

loss. The decrease in signal power in transmission from one point to another; expressed in decibels.

loudness. A characteristic of sound; the subjective measure of sound intensity; it depends primarily on the amplitude of the sound wave.

lovibond tintometer. A colorimeter in which the color of a solution or object is measured by comparison with glass slides of three colors.

low. A cyclone; an air mass of low pressure, generally bringing stormy weather.

low frequency. The range of 30 to 300 kilocycles.

lowland fog. Ground fog; a fog not higher than the average height of man.

low-melting alloy. Fusible alloy; an alloy melting under 450°F; used in fuses, solders.

low-pass filter. A wave filter that transmits all frequencies below a certain limit and suppresses those above it.

Lu. Chemical symbol for lutetium.

lubricant. A substance used to make surfaces smooth and slippery to reduce friction, especially in bearings; examples, oil, graphite.

lubrication. Separating two rubbing solid surfaces by a layer of a lubricant.

lumbar. Located at the region just posterior to the ribs of vertebrates.

lumbar vertebrae. Ribless vertebrae of the waist region, located between the rib-bearing thoracic and the sacral vertebrae.

lumen. (1) A unit of luminous flux; the light emitted by a source of one international candle intensity per unit space angle in a second; (2) the internal cavity of a hollow organ, such as a blood vessel.

lumen-hour. A unit quantity of luminous energy, equal to the emission of one lumen for one hour.

lumeter. An illumination photometer, depending on the comparison of the illuminated test area with an annular area illuminated by a lamp through a revolving, adjustable diaphragm.

luminescence. The emission of light not caused by high temperature.

luminophore. (1) A group of atoms which gives luminescence to a compound; (2) a substance that emits light at room temperature.

luminosity of a star. The brightness of a star compared with the brightness of the sun as a unity; it can also be expressed as the quantity of light emitted by the star.

luminous flux. The total visible energy emitted by a source of light.

luminous gas flame. Heating by breaking down hydrocarbons into carbon and hydrogen and heating the carbon to incandescence.

luminous intensity. Candle power; the amount of light emitted per unit solid angle by a point source in a given direction.

lunar cycle. (1) The Metonic cycle; 19 years, in which the new and full moon will be on the same days of the year; (2) the Callippic cycle, 27,759 days.

lunar eclipse. An eclipse that occurs when the earth passes directly across the path of the light from the sun to the moon, cutting it off and casting a shadow on the moon.

lunar month. Synodic month; the period of a complete revolution of the moon around the earth accomplished in 29 days, 12 hours, 44 minutes, and 27 seconds.

lunar probe. Any space vehicle designed to collect data on the moon and its surroundings.

lung. The respiratory organ of vertebrates, consisting of bronchi, bronchicles, alveoli, blood vessels, and connective tissue.

lunule. (1) A crescent-shaped mark on animals; example, the light area at the base of a finger nail; (2) a depression in front of the umbo or beak on the shell of some bivalve mollusks.

luteal tissue. Corpus luteum; yellow nodules which fill the cavity of a ruptured Graafian follicle.

luteinizing hormone. A hormone secreted by the anterior lobe of the pituitary in mammals which stimulates ovulation and formation of corpora lutea in females and secretion of androgen in males.

lutetium. A rare-earth metal; chemical symbol Lu; atomic number 71.

lux. Meter candle; a unit of illumination; one lumen per square meter.

luxmeter. A variable-aperture photometer for the measurement of light intensity.

luzerite. Mineral lapis lazuli used for ornaments; it contains sodium, calcium, and aluminum silicates.

Lycopodiales. Fern allies; club mosses.

Lycopodium. An erect creeping evergreen club moss related to ferns; example, ground fir.

lyddite. A shell explosive consisting of picric acid, mixed with 10% nitrobenzene and 3% petrolatum.

lye. Sodium hydroxide, NaOH; used as a household cleaner and in laundering.

lymph. Tissue fluid; a colorless, watery liquid which contains white blood cells; it acts as a medium of exchange between the cells and the blood.

lymph gland. Same as lymph node.

lymph node. Lymph gland; a

round, spongy mass of connective tissue containing lymphocites, with special cells located at intervals along the lymphatic vessel; it filters bacteria from the lmyph, preventing them from entering the blood.

lymphatic system. A tubular system supplementing the blood vascular system of vertebrates; it collects lymph from the tissue spaces and returns it to the venous circulation.

lymphocyte. A white blood cell in the lymph; it has a large round deeply staining nucleus.

lymphoid tissue. A tissue in vertebrates which produces lymphocytes by division of some of its cells; it is found in the spleen, lymph nodes, thymus, tonsils.

lyophilic colloid. A reversible colloid that is easy to disperse and difficult to precipitate.

lyophobic colloid. An irreversible colloid that is hard to disperse and yields an unstable colloidal solution.

Lyra. A small constellation which contains Vega, the brightest star in the northern sky.

Lyraid. A meteor shower which is observed about April 20th of each year.

lyrebird. An Australian bird, the male having very long tail feathers, resembling a lyre when spread.

lyriform organ. A sensory organ found on most segments of the legs and under the surface of the body of a spider; it contains a series of slits with special nerve endings.

lysigenous. Said of secretory cavities in plants which originated by dissolution of secreting cells.

lysin. An antibody in the blood stream which dissolves cells.

lysine. Diamino caproic acid found in albuminous substances; it promotes animal growth.

M

m. Abbreviation for meter and mass.

Macbeth illuminator. A device which matches optically the brightness of a surface with a known, variable surface brightness.

machine. Any device consisting of two or more rigid and resistant parts, used to transmit or transform motion or force; the six elementary machines are the lever, the wheel and axle, the wedge, the screw, the pulley, and the inclined plane.

mackerel sky. Altocumulus and cirrocumulum clouds which consist of uniform bands similar in appearance to a mackerel's back.

macrogamete. The larger, usually female, member of a pair of conjugating gametes.

macrogametocyte. A phase in Protozoa which will develop into female gametes.

macrogamy. Fusion of the gametes of two fully developed individuals of Protozoa.

macromere. A large, yolk-laden blastomere that is produced by unequal cleavage.

macromolecule. A very large molecule, usually of a polymer.

macronucleus. The larger nucleus in the paramecium; it is divided by amitosis.

macrophage. Macrocyte; a mobile phagocytic cell widely distributed in the vertebrate body.

macrophagus. Same as macrophage.

macrospore. Megaspore; a large spore in certain ferns and seed plants; it grows into the female prothallus or, in seed plants, into the embryo sac.

madreporite. A wartlike, perforated organ of the starfish that admits water and serves as a sieve to keep out sand.

Magdeburg hemispheres. Two hollow hemispheres which fit together to form a cavity from which the air can be evacuated; used for demonstrating the effects of air pressure.

magenta. Fuchsin; green crystals yielding a red dye solution in water; used for silk, wool, leather.

maggot. The headless and footless wormlike stage or larva of certain insects, especially flies.

magma. Molten igneous rock.

magnalium. An aluminum-base alloy containing some magnesium and other metals; used for aircraft parts.

magnesia. Magnesium oxide, MgO; used in medicine, refractories, rubber compounding.

magnesite. Magnesium carbonate mineral, $MgCO_3$; a basic refractory.

magnesium. A silver-white, light metal; chemical symbol Mg; atomic number 12; used in alloying, photography.

magnesium chloride. Colorless crystals; $MgCl_2$; used in ceramics.

magnet. A body or substance which attracts particles of iron and affects an electric current.

magnet core. The soft-iron center on which the wire of an electromagnet is wound.

magnetic analysis. The separation of a stream of electrified particles by a magnetic field according to their mass, charge, or speed.

magnetic circuit. The path of the magnetic flux in a magnetic substance or in a magnetic or electric apparatus.

magnetic coil. The winding of an electromagnet; a coil of wire wound in one direction on a soft-iron core, producing a dense magnetic field capable of attracting iron or steel when carrying a current of electricity.

magnetic compass. A compass consisting of a suspended magnetic needle which occupies a position corresponding to the earth's magnetic field.

magnetic cycle. A cycle of changes in the magnetic induction or the magnetization of a ferromagnetic substance due to an alternating magnetic density.

magnetic damping. Damping the vibrations of a mechanism by means of the eddy currents generated by its motion in a magnetic field.

magnetic declination. The angle between the true north and the north indicated by a compass needle.

magnetic dip. Angle of dip; the angle formed by the earth's magnetic field with the horizontal at any point on the earth's surface.

magnetic elements. The three quantities which define completely the earth's magnetic field at any point: magnetic declination, angle of dip, and horizontal intensity.

magnetic equator. A line drawn through those places on the earth's surface where the dip angle is zero.

magnetic field. The space in the vicinity of a magnet through which magnetic forces act.

magnetic field of electric current. The magnetic field surrounding a wire or coil which carries electric current.

magnetic flux. The magnetic lines of force set up by an electromagnet, permanent magnet, or solenoid; the surface integral of the magnetic field intensity perpendicular to the surface.

magnetic force. The force of attraction and repulsion exerted at the poles of a magnet.

magnetic inclination. Dip; the angle between the equilibrium position of a compass needle mounted on a horizontal axis and the horizon.

magnetic intensity. The strength of a magnetic field at a point; the force exerted on a unit north magnetic pole situated at that point, measured in oersteds.

magnetic iron ore. Magnetite.

magnetic lag. A delay, not due to eddy currents, in the establishment of the magnetic induction which corresponds to the magnetizing force.

magnetic latitude. The latitude reckoned from the magnetic, instead of the geographic, equator.

magnetic lens. An apparatus used for focusing beams of rapidly moving electrons or ions by means of a nonuniform magnetic field.

magnetic line of force. Line of magnetic force; a line, whose direction at any point is the same as that of the magnetic field at that point; the path along which a free north magnetic pole would travel.

magnetic meridian. An imaginary horizontal line on the earth's surface coinciding with the direction of the earth's magnetic field at that point.

magnetic moment. The torque exerted on a magnet at right angles to a uniform field of unit intensity.

magnetic pendulum. A bar magnet suspended in a magnetic field having a horizontal component.

magnetic permeability. The magnetic flux density produced in a permeable body divided by the magnetic flux density in air.

magnetic pickup. A phonographic pickup in which the electrical impulses to be amplified and changed into sound are produced by the movements of a magnet.

magnetic polarization. Producing optical activity in an inactive substance by placing it in a magnetic field.

magnetic pole. The region of a magnet where the magnetic force appears to be concentrated.

magnetic pole strength. The strength of a magnetic pole measured in terms of the unit magnetic pole.

magnetic pole, unit. The magnetic pole that will exert unit force on an equal magnetic pole in vacuum at unit distance.

magnetic potential. The work required to move a unit magnetic pole from the boundary of the field to the point at which the potential is measured.

magnetic potentiometer. A slender solenoid used for measuring the magnetomotive forces between points in a magnetic field.

magnetic screen. A soft-iron screen enveloping delicate electrical instruments to protect them from stray magnetic fields.

magnetic shell. A hypothetical double layer of magnetic charge, analogous to an electric double layer.

magnetic spectrograph. A magnetic mass or velocity spectrograph.

magnetic spectrum. A spectrum produced by cathode rays on a screen after traversing a magnetic field.

magnetic storms. Disturbances in the earth's magnetic field usually caused by solar flare; they may generate earth currents which interfere with electrical communication.

magnetic susceptibility. The ratio of the intensity of magnetization produced in a substance to the intensity of the magnetic field which acts on it.

magnetic transparency. The property of offering no resistance to the passage of a magnetic flux.

magnetism. (1) The property of iron, steel, and some other metals to exert forces of attraction and repulsion on each other or other substances; (2) the science of magnets and magnetic force.

magnetism, terrestrial. The earth's magnetic field, whose intensity varies with time and location.

magnetite. An important iron ore; ferrosoferric oxide, Fe_3O_4; it is a natural magnet.

magnetization. The act of acquiring or communicating magnetism.

magnetization, intensity of. The magnetic moment per unit volume of a magnetized body.

magnetization, spontaneous. The magnetic saturation of the domains of a ferromagnetic material without an applied magnetizing force.

magnetizing by induction. Developing magnetism in an unmagnetized body by placing it in the field of force around a second magnetized body.

magnetizing force. The magnetic intensity effective in producing the magnetization of a substance.

magneto. A device consisting of permanent magnets and an armature, for generating electricity by electromagnetic induction; used in the ignition of internal-combustion engines.

magnetocaloric effect. The reversible cooling of a ferromagnetic body, magnetized to saturation in a strong magnetic field, when the field is removed.

magnetochemistry. A study of the magnetic phenomena that accompany chemical reactions.

magnetocompass. An aircraft compass based on the inductive effect of the earth's magnetic field which excites the field magnet of a small magneto or dynamo.

magnetoelastic. Showing magnetostriction effects associated with elastic vibration.

magnetoelectric induction. The production of an electromotive force by the cutting of a magnetic flux.

magnetogenerator. Same as magneto.

magnetometer. (1) A pivoted magnetic needle which indicates the strength of magnetic fields; used in oil prospecting; (2) an instrument used for the determination of the elements of the earth's magnetic field.

magnetomotive force. The force responsible for the magnetic flux in a magnetic circuit; the line integral of the magnetizing force around the circuit.

magneton. A unit of magnetic moment; Bohr's magneton is equal to 5584 gauss-centimeter per mol.

magnetooptical analysis. A chemical analysis based on differences in the lag of the Faraday effect behind the magnetic intensity for different substances.

magnetoresistance. An increase in the electrical resistance of a conductor due to the effect of a constant magnetic field; it is dependent on the orientation of the conductor in the field.

magnetoscope. An instrument for detecting a magnetic force.

magnetosphere. A belt of highly charged particles trapped in the earth's magnetic field; extends to an altitude of over 40,000 miles at the Equator.

magnetostatics. The study of magnetic fields that do not vary with time.

magnetostriction. A change in the dimensions of a ferromagnetic substance on magnetization.

magnetostriction oscillator. An electrical oscillating system containing as one of its elements a magnetostriction resonator, which controls the frequency.

magnetostriction resonator. A bar magnet which lengthens and shortens periodically under the effect of a magnetic field.

magnetron. A thermionic vacuum tube, generator of very short radio waves by the deflecting effect of a transverse magnetic field on the electron beam.

magnification. The ratio of the size of an image formed by an optical system to the size of the object.

magnifying glass. A convex lens.

magnifying power. The ratio of the apparent size of an object as seen through an instrument to the apparent size of the same object as seen without the instrument.

magnitude. The degrees of brightness of a star or other heavenly body.

Magnus effect. A lateral thrust exerted by wind on a rotating cylinder whose axis is perpendicular to the wind direction; used in ship propulsion.

main supporting surface. The surface of the aircraft wings which are from tip to tip on the same level.

malachite. A green mineral; basic copper carbonate; a common ore of copper.

male. An individual producing sperms.

malleability. A deformability by mechanical treatment, such as hammering, extrusion, rolling; examples, gold, silver, tin, and zinc are malleable metals.

malleus. The hammer-shaped small bone of the middle ear.

Mallophaga. Biting lice, bird lice; wingless insects that live on birds as scavengers; they cannot pierce or suck.

Malpighian body. A structure in the vertebrate kidney composed of Bowman's capsule and the glomerulus.

Malpighian layer. A layer of the epidermis next to the dermis, consisting of active cells which replace the outer cells of the epidermis by division.

Malpighian tubules. Tubular excretory glands which open into the anterior part of the hind gut of insects; example, Arachnida and Myriapoda.

maltase. An enzyme of the intestinal juice which changes malt sugar into glucose.

maltose. Malt sugar; $C_{12}H_{22}O_{11} \cdot H_2O$; colorless crystals; less sweet than cane sugar; used as a nutrient.

mamma. Mammary gland; the milk gland of female mammals.

Mammalia. Vertebrate warm-blooded animals that feed their young on milk secreted by the mammary glands; their skin is hairy, they use lungs for breathing and a double heart for blood circulation; their young develop within the body of the female; examples, man, cat, dog, cow.

mammalogy. The study of mammals.

mammary gland. Same as mamma.

mammoth. A prehistoric huge elephant with long, upward-curving tusks and a long, thick, hairy coat.

mandible. (1) The lower jaw of vertebrates; (2) an appendage of Arthropoda used for mastication.

manganese. A hard, brittle metal; chemical symbol Mn; atomic number 25; used in alloying.

manganese bronze. A corrosion-resistant copper-zinc alloy containing up to 4% manganese.

manganese dioxide. A heavy black powder; MnO_2; used as an oxidizing agent.

manganese steel. A wear-resistant carbon steel that contains over 7% manganese; used for safes, railway crossings.

manganin. A copper-base alloy of high electrical resistance; used for electrical instruments.

manganite. Gray manganese ore; $Mn_2O_3 \cdot H_2O$.

manocryometer. An instrument for determining the variation of the freezing point with pressure.

manometer. An instrument for the measurement of gas pressure; it usually consists of a liquid-containing U tube, in which the change in the liquid level in the tube is indicative of the pressure.

manometer, differential. A manometer for measuring differences in pressure.

manometer, hot-wire. A device for the measurement of pressure by the heat loss of an electrically heated wire.

manometric balance. An apparatus for the comparison of the magnetic susceptibilities of liquids.

manometric flame. A small gas flame that vibrates due to the variation in pressure caused by sound waves.

mantle. (1) A fold of the dorsal body wall of mollusks which secretes the shell and forms a respiratory chamber; (2) body walls of tunicates, beneath and enclosing the tunic; (3) a gas mantle.

mantle-rock. Regolith; a loose rock layer which covers the solid rock of the earth's crust.

manubrium. (1) A handlelike process or part of animals; (2) a cylindrical cell protruding from each wall shield of stoneworts.

many-body force. An interaction between two particles modified by the presence of a third particle.

marble. A granular metamorphic rock formed from limestone; calcium carbonate, $CaCO_3$; it can be polished to a high luster; used for decorative purposes.

Marchantia. A genus of liverworts with a forked, ribbonlike thallus.

margin. (1) The edge of a leaf; (2) the edge of a fungal mycellium.

marginal lakes. Temporary glacial lakes which were formed when a glacial front retreated by melting down a gentle slope.

marginals. Shields on the outer row of carapace of a turtle.

marine biology. The study of all living organisms found in the ocean and their interrelation.

Mariotte's bottle. A device for demonstrating the differences in pressure and velocity of an efflux at different levels.

maritime polar air. An air mass that originates in the arctic or subarctic and moves over the North Pacific Ocean.

maritime tropical air. An air mass which originates over the Caribbean Sea.

marl. (1) A very-fine-grained rock; (2) calcareous clay, suitable for brick manufacture.

marrow. A soft tissue in the hollow bones of vertebrates, where red blood corpuscles are made.

Mars. The fourth planet in order of distance from the sun; its reddish color and rapid motion makes it conspicuous among the stars; it has two small satellites.

marsh gas. Fire damp; methane, CH_4.

Marsupialia. Pouched mammals;

in most cases, the young are born in an immature state and live in the pouch, which contains teats, for a long time after birth.

marsupium. A pouch formed of a fold of skin on the abdomen of the female marsupial; the young, born in early stage of development, are transferred to it and get their nourishment from the teats that open into the pouch.

Martens wedge. A quartz-wedge rotator for polarized light.

maser (microwave amplification by stimulated emission of radiation). A device that produces highly stable electromagnetic waves by harnessing the natural oscillations of an atomic or molecular system. Gas masers rely on the atoms of ammonia gas stimulated by high-frequency microwave energy; solid-state masers use ruby crystals, the atoms of which can be excited at will by microwave generators. Masers operating in the invisible and visible portions of the spectrum are called optical masers. The term *laser* is reserved for devices operating only in the visible portion of the spectrum. Devices operating in the infrared region are often called irasers.

mass. The quantity of matter contained in a body.

mass action, law of. The speed of a homogeneous reaction is proportional to the product of the reacting substances.

mass, atomic. The mass of an atom expressed in atomic mass units of 1.660×10^{-24} g; the mass of a neutron is 1.00893 and that of a proton 1.00758 atomic mass units.

mass, center of. The point in a body, coinciding with the center of gravity, which acts as if the total mass and inertia of the body were concentrated there.

mass culture. Breeding from a selected group of individuals.

mass defect. The difference between the isotopic weight of any atom and its mass number.

mass formula. An equation for the atomic mass of a nuclide as a function of its atomic number and mass number.

mass number. The number of protons and neutrons in a nuclide, assuming that each has unit mass; the mass of an isotope based on the most abundant oxygen isotope taken for 16.

mass of electron. The mass of an electron is a variable depending on its velocity according to the kinetic theory of masses.

mass radiator. A source of electromagnetic radiation which covers a broad band, extending to extremely high frequencies; it consists of metal particles

suspended in a liquid dielectric.

mass selection. The selection of ideal plants or animals from a large number to serve as parents for further breeding.

mass spectrograph. An apparatus in which electrical and magnetic fields are applied to rapidly moving particles so as to (1) determine the nature of the particles by the deflection produced and (2) to separate the particles according to their masses.

mass unit. The mass of a proton within the atom; 1.66×10^{-24} g.

mastication. (1) Chewing food with the teeth; (2) breaking down rubber by working between heated toothed cylinders.

Mastigophora. Flagellata; a class of small Protozoa which have one or more flagella in their principal phase.

mastodon. An extinct giant animal resembling an elephant but having different teeth.

mastoid process. An outgrowth of the human skull just behind the ear, containing air spaces which communicate with the middle ear.

material-testing reactor. A reactor used for studying the behavior of materials under very high radioactivity.

maternal. Pertaining to a mother.

mating. Insemination; the entry of the spermatozoon into the ovary, followed by fusion of male and female nuclei.

matrix. (1) A jellylike substance which holds the cells together in a colonial organization; (2) the outer layer of a chromozome that can be stained.

matte. A crude mixture of sulfides produced in a partially refined ore.

matter. All substances that occupy space and have weight.

matter, annihilation of. (1) The transformation of matter into energy; (2) the radiation of photons by the union of two particles.

Matthiessen rule. The total electrical or thermal resistivity of a metal is the sum of the separate resistivities due to scattering of the electrons by the thermal vibrations of the lattice, by impurities, or by imperfections.

maturation. The last stages in the development of gametes as the result of which the chromosomes are reduced to one half.

maturation of germ cells. The development of mature sperm and ova; it occurs in the testis and ovary and includes reduction division.

maturation region. The region of a root or stem where embryonic cells mature into tissues.

mature river. A river that has a broad valley, slow stream, and many tributaries.

mature soil. A soil that has been permitted to develop without interruption for long periods of time.

mauve. A purple aniline dye which was the first aniline dye prepared synthetically.

maxilla. (1) The upper jaw of vertebrates; (2) an appendage of insects, behind the mandibles, that helps cut and hold the food.

maxillary gland. An excretory organ of Crustacea, whose duct opens at the base of the maxilla.

maxilliped. A jointed appendage of the body region of Arthropoda, modified to serve as an accessory mouth part.

maximum and minimum thermometer. A thermometer that registers the highest and lowest temperature that occur in a 24-hour period.

maximum range. The maximum distance a given aircraft can cover under given conditions by flying at the economical speed and altitude at all stages of the flight.

maximum thermometer. A thermometer in which the mercury rises to the highest temperature of the day and remains there.

maximum voltage. The highest voltage reached in each alternation of an alternating electromotive force.

maxwell. One line of magnetic force; the metric unit of magnetic flux.

Maxwell bridge. An alternating-current bridge used for the determination of self-inductance.

Maxwell top. A gyroscope in the form of an adjustable top, whose point of support may be set below, at, or above the center of mass.

maxwell turn. A unit of magnetic linkage, corresponding to one line of force, surrounded by one turn of the circuit.

Maxwell's wheel. A swinging wheel, with a thin horizontally suspended axle, for demonstrating the laws of inertia and the conservation of energy.

mc. Abbreviation for megacycles per second.

mean free path. (1) The average distance traveled by a molecule of a gas before it collides with another; (2) the average distance traveled by a sound wave in a room between two successive reflections.

mean free time. The average time between two collisions of an atom.

mean horizontal candle power. The average candle power of a light source, as viewed from all directions in the horizontal plane containing it.

mean solar day. The constant interval between two crossings of the mean sun across the meridian.

mean solar time. The hour angle west of the fictitious sun; by international agreement, it is counted from midnight.

mean spherical candle power. The average candle power of a light source, as viewed from all directions.

mean sun. A fictitious sun which covers the celestial equator in the same time as the real sun does the ecliptic, but at a uniform rate, so that all mean solar days of the year are of equal length.

meander. A broad curve in a river caused by the erosion of the bank at points where the water has been deflected.

meatus. A body passage; example, the auditory meatus.

mechanical advantage. The ratio of the load or resistance of a machine to the applied force.

mechanical efficiency. The ratio of the useful horsepower to the total horsepower.

mechanical equivalent of heat. Joule's equivalent; the amount of work required to produce a unit quantity of heat; 778 ft-lb = 1 Btu; 4.18 joules = 1 calorie.

mechanical weathering. Physical processes by which a solid rock is broken into fragments, but is chemically unchanged.

mechanics. The study of the effects of forces on matter, and of motion.

mechanistic theory. Mechanism; all biological phenomena can be explained in physical, and chemical terms.

Meckel's cartilage. A strip of cartilage, one forming each side of the lower jaw of some fish.

meconium. The contents of the intestine of a mammalian fetus.

medial moraine. The union of lateral moraines to form trains of debris on the surface of a glacier at or near the center.

median. The midline that divides a bilaterally symmetrical organism or organ into right and left halves.

mediastinum. The space in the chest between the lungs, around and above the heart; it contains the heart and all the organs of the chest except the lungs.

medium (plural media). (1) A nutritive substance for growing microorganisms; (2) a substance through which a force acts or an effect is transmitted.

medulla. (1) A pith; an axial structure found in some hairs; (2) the central portion of a gland or tissue; (3) the marrow of bones.

medulla oblongata. The posterior portion of the vertebrate brain; it controls certain reflexes, involuntary muscular actions, and conducts impulses from the spinal cord to the brain.

medulla of adrenal gland. The inner mass of the suprarenal (or adrenal) gland which produces adrenalin, a powerful body stimulant.

medullary ray. Vascular ray; a thin bundle of woody cells extending from the pith to or toward the cambium and from the cambium to or toward the center in the stem and roots of plants.

medusa. A bell- or umbrella-shaped free-swimming form of Coelenterata; it is reproduced sexually, its fertilized eggs giving rise to polyps.

medusa bud. A formation in the polyp stage of a hydroid, whose function is asexual reproduction, resulting in the development of a gonophore or medusa.

medusoid. (1) Medusalike; an imperfectly developed sexual individual of Coelenterata that remains attached to the hydroid colony.

megacycle. One million cycles.

megadyne. One million dynes.

megaerg. One million ergs.

megaparsec. One million parsecs; the longest unit of measurement; 19,155,830,550,000,-000,000 miles; used by astronomers for the measurement of interstellar distances.

megasporangium. A sporangium which bears megaspores.

megaspore. A cell that originates in the pistil and will develop into a female gametophyte.

megasporophyll. A leaflike structure bearing megasporangia.

megohm. One million ohms.

meiosis. A cell division in which chromosomes are reduced from the diploid number to the haploid number during oogenesis and spermatogenesis.

Meker burner. A high-temperature gas burner.

melanin. Black, brown, orange, and red pigments of the hair and skin; insoluble in almost all solvents; produced by certain bacteria.

melanophore. A chromatophore containing melanin as pigment.

melting point. The temperature at which a solid changes to a liquid.

melting range. The temperature range in which an alloy melts.

membrane. A thin sheet of tissue composed of cells.

membrane bone. Dermal bone; a bone formed by the direct ossification of connective tissue.

membranelle. A thin vibrating projection adjacent to the mouth of most ciliate Protozoa, consisting of fused cilia.

mendelevium. Chemical symbol Mv; atomic number 101.

mendelism. The Mendelian laws of heredity; every character of an individual is either dominant or recessive; if a character is dominant in one of the parents and recessive in the

other, the offspring will inherit the dominant character; in the third generation, 25% of the offspring will resemble the dominant grandparent, 25% the recessive grandparent and 50% the hybrid parents of the second generation.

meninges. Three membranes covering the brain and spinal cord of vertebrates.

meniscus. (1) The concave or convex free surface of a liquid in a tube due to capillary action; (2) a crescent-shaped piece of cartilage in an animal joint.

meniscus lens. A lens which has a convex and a concave surface; a concavo-convex lens.

mensuration. The measurment of lengths, areas, and volumes.

menthol. $C_{10}H_{20}O$; an organic compound of the camphor group, which occurs in peppermint oil; used in medicine, as a flavor.

Mercator's map. A map on which parallels and meridians are straight lines; it is valuable in navigation.

mercerizing. The treatment of stretched cotton fibers or fabrics with concentrated sodium hydroxide to increase their luster.

mercurial barometer. Mercury barometer; a barometer in which a column of mercury is used to measure air pressure.

mercuric. Indicating a compound of bivalent mercury.

mercuric chloride. Corrosive sublimate, $HgCl_2$; white powder; used as an antiseptic, photographic intensifier.

mercurous. Indicating a compound of univalent mercury.

mercurous chloride. Calomel, HgCl; used in medicine, pyrotechnics.

mercury. Quicksilver; a heavy, silvery, metallic element that is liquid at ordinary temperatures; chemical symbol Hg; atomic number 80.

Mercury. The smallest planet; it is nearest to the sun.

mercury arc. The electric discharge through mercury vapor in a vacuum tube; used in photography, for sterilization.

mercury barometer. Same as mercurial barometer.

mercury-vapor lamp. Mercury discharge lamp; a lamp in which chiefly ultraviolet light is produced by passing a current through mercury vapor; used in therapy.

meridian. Any great imaginary circle about the earth which passes through both poles.

meridian, celestial. The great circle of the celestial sphere.

meridian circle. A telescope mounted on a horizontal axis, whose collimation plane is in the plane of the local meridian.

meristem. Embryonic or undif-

ferentiated tissue which is capable of division and forms the various kinds of permanent tissue.

meroblastic. Said of an egg, rich in yolk, that is undergoing only partial cleavage.

merogamete. A gamete formed by multiple division and smaller than the ordinary gametes; found in Protozoa.

merogony. (1) The development of an egg deprived of its nucleus; (2) the development of a cytoplasmic fragment of an egg after fertilization by a normal sperm.

mesa. A large, angular, flat-topped area with nearly vertical sides; it is the remains of old plateaus.

mesarch. The youngest wood occupying a central position in the vascular bundle, surrounded on all sides by the later wood.

mesencephalon. The midbrain of vertebrates, which is concerned with sight and hearing.

mesenchyme. A loose embryonic connective tissue derived chiefly from mesoderm.

mesentery. One of several folds of the thin membranes attached to the wall of the abdomen of a vertebrate; it holds the organs in place.

mesocarp. The middle layer of the fruit wall.

mesocephalic. (1) Having a cephalic index between 70 and 80; (2) said of the middle portion of the head.

mesocolloid. A colloid composed of particles of intermediate size: 250 to 2500 angstroms.

mesoderm. Mesoblast; a layer of cells which is located between the ectoderm and endoderm of an embryo.

mesogloea. A noncellular, jelly-like substance lying between the ectoderm and endoderm in Coelenterata and sponges.

mesomorphic. Having an intermediate form or state; example, semicrystalline.

meson. A subatomic particle of matter having a positive, negative, or zero charge and a mass of 210 to 1000 times that of the electron; it is assumed to contribute to the binding energy of the nucleus; its life is a few millionths of a second and it is found in cosmic radiation.

mesonephric duct. A duct leading from the mesonephric kidney to the cloaca.

mesonephros. The central part of vertebrate kidney which arises in embryonic development later than and replaces the pronephros.

mesophilic bacteria. Bacteria that grow best at moderate temperature.

mesophyll. A leaf tissue between the two epidermal layers.

mesophyte. A plant that likes

moderate water supply.

mesothelium. A layer of flattened cells which lines coelomic cavities of vertebrates.

mesothorax. The middle segment of the thorax of an insect; it bears a pair of legs and the first pair of wings.

Mesozoic era. The age of reptiles which lasted 150 million years, until about 60 million years ago; dinosaurs flourished and became extinct; insects, flowering plants, and the first mammals arose.

metabolism. A collective name for all the physical and chemical changes that take place in a living organism.

metabolism, basal. The rate of energy expenditure of an organ or animal at rest.

metabolite. A substance which takes part in a process of metabolism; it may be made by the organism or be taken from the environment during metabolism.

metacarpals. (1) Hand bones; (2) bones of the forelimb of an animal.

metacarpus. The palm region of man and the region of the fore-foot of tetrapods containing metacarpal bones.

metacenter. That point, always above the center of mass, of a rigid body floating in equilibrium, through which the buoyant force may be considered to act when the body is slightly tipped.

metacentric height. The distance between the metacenter and the center of gravity of a floating body.

metachemistry. A study of the atom and atomic changes.

metachromatic. Having a color different from the usual, when stained.

metachromatic granules. Deeply staining, irregular particles in the protoplasm of various bacteria.

metachronal rhythm. A pattern of the beating of cilia or multiple limbs.

metacrystalline state. An arrangement of molecules, due to strain or other influences, which, while it does not involve a true crystal structure, yields x-ray diffraction patterns analogous to those produced by crystals; example, a stretched strip of rubber.

metadyne. Amplidyne; a special, rotating control generator.

metagalaxy. The known universe, including all the galaxies except our own.

metagenesis. Alternation of sexual and asexual reproduction in the life cycle of some organisms.

metal filament. The thin wire which glows when heated in an incandescent lamp.

metaldehyde. A white, volatile,

inflammable, poisonous solid polymer of acetaldehyde, CH_3-CHO; used as a fuel.

metallic thermometer. A thermometer that indicates the temperature by the expansion and contraction of a metal strip.

metallography. The study of the structure of metals and alloys, especially by microscopic examination.

metalloid. An element that has certain properties characteristic of a metal, but which is generally classed as a nonmetal; examples, phosphorus, arsenic.

metallurgy. (1) The art and science of separating metals from their ores, their refining, alloying, and utilization; (2) the study of the properties and structure of metals and alloys.

metals. Elements characterized by their luster, ductility, malleability, conductance of heat and electricity; they form positive ions and their oxides unite with water to yield bases.

metamagnetic. Being either paramagnetic or diamagnetic, according to conditions, such as the intensity or direction of the applied field.

metamere. Merome; a somite; one of a series of homologous segments in a body.

metamerism. The body of an animal being made up of a series of homologous parts.

metamorphic rocks. Rocks derived from existing rocks by changes occurring in the earth's crust, such as pressure, heat, and the cementing action of underground water.

metamorphism. A collective name for the mineralogical, textural, and structural changes within the original mass of a rock.

metamorphosis. The development of an adult by passing through a series of stages; example, grasshopper.

metanephros. A part of the kidney in amniote vertebrates which arises in embryonic development later than, and posterior to, the mesonephros, one on each side.

metaphase. The second phase of mitosis in which the chromosomes line up at the center or equator of the cell; they divide in the length and the daughter chromosomes move to the poles of the mitotic spindle.

metaplasia. The transformation of one adult tissue into another; example, ossification of a cartilage.

metasoma. A structure behind the mandible in some Crustacea, which has no appendages.

metastable state. A relatively stable state; example, a supersaturated solution remains stable if it is left undisturbed,

but will crystallize if it is shaken or seeded with a crystal.

metastasic electron. An electron that moves from one atom to another, or from one shell to another in a given atom, or to the nucleus of the atom.

metatarsals. Foot bones.

metatarsus. (1) The region of the hind foot of tetrapods, containing metatarsal bones; (2) the first enlarged joint of an insect leg.

Metatheria. Marsupialia; mammals that carry and feed their young in an abdominal pouch.

metathesis. Double decomposition.

metathorax. The final segment of the thorax of certain insects which bears the leaping legs and the last pair of wings; example, grasshopper.

metaxenia. The influence of pollen on the maternal tissues of a plant.

metaxylem. A primary xylem that is differentiated from the procambium after the protoxylem; it has wider vessels, with thicker, more lignified walls.

Metazoa. Group of animals whose body consists of more than one cell which are highly coordinated; they usually have a nervous system and an enteric cavity.

meteor. A shooting star; a small mass which comes from interplanetary space and becomes incandescent on impact with the atmosphere.

meteoric shower. The appearance of a large number of meteors in August and November.

meteorite. A meteor that has fallen to the earth.

meteorograph. A recording device sent up into the upper atmosphere fastened to a balloon or kite for obtaining meteorological information; it contains instruments for recording temperature, pressure, and humidity.

meteorology. The study of the earth's atmosphere, types of weather, and principles of weather forecasting.

metepipodite. A process of the proximal limb of an arthropod.

meter. The basic unit of the metric system; a unit of length; 39.37 inches; 1.09 yards; 3.28 feet; 10 decimeters; 100 centimeters; 1000 millimeters; 1/1000 kilometer.

meter-candle. A unit of illumination; the same as the lux.

meter-candle-second. A unit of photographic exposure which corresponds to an illumination of one lux acting for one second.

methacrylic acid. $CH_2:C(CH_3)$-$COOH$; a corrosive liquid; used in the preparation of thermoplastic resins.

methane. Marsh gas, CH_4; an inflammable natural gas, which forms explosive mixtures with air; example, firedamp.

methanol. Wood alcohol; methyl alcohol, CH_3OH; it is prepared by the destructive distillation of wood; it is an important solvent, antifreeze, denaturant for ethyl alcohol.

methyl carbinol. Ethyl alcohol.

methyl group. The univalent organic radical —CH_3.

methylated spirits. A liquid fuel and solvent; 90% ethyl alcohol, 9.5% methyl alcohol, 0.5% pyridine.

methylene blue. $C_{16}H_{18}N_3SCl$-$3H_2O$; a water-soluble, intense-blue dye; used for dyeing cotton, in medicine, and as a stain in biology.

Metonic cycle. The period of 19 years between repetitions of lunar phases on the same day of the year.

metrechon. A form of electrostatic storage tube.

metric system. A decimal system of weights and measures.

metric ton. 1000 kilograms.

metrology. The study of weights and measures and of the methods of measurement.

mev. Abbreviation for million electron volts.

mg. Abbreviation for milligram.

Mg. Chemical symbol for magnesium.

mho. The unit of electrical conductance; the reciprocal of the ohm.

mica. Hydrogen potassium aluminum silicate; a mineral which cleaves into elastic sheets; it is an excellent electrical insulator.

micelle. A colloidal particle in a disperse system, consisting of a charged nucleus surrounded by a diffuse ionic atmosphere.

microaerophilic bacteria. Bacteria which grow at a low oxygen concentration.

microampere. One millionth of an ampere; 0.000,001 ampere.

microanalysis. Special analytical methods using very small samples.

microbalance. A device for weighing small masses very accurately.

microbar. A unit of pressure used in acoustics; one microbar is equal to one dyne per square centimeter.

microbe. A microscopic organism.

microbiology. The study of microorganisms.

microchemistry. The chemical study of very small quantities of substances.

microchronograph. An instrument for recording very small time intervals, such as the period of a sound vibration.

microclimate. The climate of a relatively small section of a region that is uniform, but

quite different from the general climate of the region.

microcrystalline. Said of substances or igneous rocks in which the individual crystals can only be seen with the aid of a microscope.

microcurie. One millionth of a curie.

microdensitometer. A microphotometer for the measurement of the density of photographic images.

microdissection. A dissection technique for cells and tissues on a minute scale under the microscope, by mechanically operated instruments.

microelectrophoresis. A technique for the investigation of the surface-charge characteristics of particles of microscopic size.

microfarad. One millionth of a farad.

microfelsite. The anisotropic groundmass of an igneous rock which became microcrystalline by devitrification.

microgamete. The male element of a conjugating pair of gametes.

microgametocyte. The male form of the malarial parasite which is transferred from man to the mosquito.

microgram. One millionth of a gram.

microhenry. One millionth of a henry.

microincineration. Examining the distribution of minerals in sections of tissues, or whole microorganisms, by placing them on a slide, burning away all organic constituents in a high-temperature furnace, and determining the nature and position of the ash microscopically.

microliter. One millionth of a liter.

microlites. Microscopic prismatic crystals.

micromanipulator. A device, controlled by compressed air or otherwise, for handling microscopic objects in any desired manner while under observation.

micromanometer. An instrument for observing and measuring very small pressure differences or fluctuations.

micromechanics. The dynamics of very minute bodies, such as the component parts of an atom or of a molecule.

micrometer. A device for measuring angles or linear quantities with great accuracy.

micrometer caliper. A caliper with a graduated micrometer screw for very accurate measurement of minute lengths.

micromicrofarad. A unit of electrical capacity; 10^{-12} farad.

micromicron ($\mu\mu$). One millionth of a micron; 10^{-6} micron = 10^{-12} meter.

micromillimeter. One millionth of a millimeter.

micron (μ). A linear unit for very small particles; one thousandth of a millimeter.

micronucleus. The smaller nucleus in the paramecium.

microorganism. A living plant or animal that is so small that it can be seen only through a microscope.

microphage. A small, active, motile, polynuclear phagocyte in the blood or lymph.

microphagous. Feeding on microorganisms.

microphotogram. Photomicrogram; a greatly enlarged photograph of a microscopic object.

microphotograph. Same as microphotogram.

microphotometer. A densitometer for measuring density variations over a very small area of a photographic image.

microprojector. An optical arrangement, consisting of a microscope lens system and an illuminator, for projecting on a screen the greatly enlarged images of microscopic objects.

micropyle. (1) A tiny hole through the testa of a dicot seed which provides entrance for the pollen tube during fertilization; a corresponding hole in the integument at the tip of the ovule; (2) an opening in the egg of an insect through which the spermatozoon may enter.

micropyrometer. (1) An apparatus for measuring the melting points of small specimens of refractory substances; (2) an instrument for the measurement by optical means of the temperature and emissivity of microscopic incandescent particles.

microradiometer. An instrument for the measurement of very feeble radiation.

microscope. An optical instrument that greatly magnifies minute objects.

microscope, compound. A microscope that contains two short-focus convex lenses, the objective and the eyepiece.

microscope, polarizing. The combination of a microscope with a polariscope.

microscope, simple. A short-focus convex lens which is used to produce a virtual image larger than the viewed object.

microscope, ultraviolet. A microscope in which ultraviolet light is used to illuminate the object or field under examination; the lenses are made of quartz or other material that transmits ultraviolet rays and the enlarged image is recorded photographically.

microscopic. Very small; visible only under the microscope; example, bacteria.

microscopy. The science of enlarging or magnifying small objects, so that they may be more readily seen and studied.

microsomes. Very small nucleoprotein and fat particles, which can be separated from the cytoplasm by centrifuging; they may contain enzymes.

microspectroscope. The combination of a microscope and a spectroscope.

microsporangium. A sporangium which bears microspores.

microspore. A small spore in certain ferns, developing into the male prothallus; in seed plants, it grows into the pollen tube.

Microsporidia. An order of Protozoa which are parasitic both in vertebrates and invertebrates.

microsporophyll. A modified leaf-like organ bearing microsporangia.

microtome. An instrument for cutting extremely thin slices of tissue for microscopic examination.

microvolt. One millionth of a volt.

microwatt. One millionth of a watt.

microwave region. The portion of the electromagnetic spectrum between the far infrared and the conventional radiofrequency.

microwaves. Radio waves of short wave length and thus comparatively high frequency; used in radar and communications.

middle lamella. A primary layer of the wall of a plant cell on which secondary layers are later deposited; it is composed of pectic substances.

midrib. The main vein or rib of a leaf running in the length through its center.

migration. (1) The movement of some animals to warm regions when winter comes; (2) the relatively slow movment of ions in electrolysis, due to the applied electric field, or any similar movement of minute particles under the effect of a force; (3) the dispersal of seed or spores followed by their germination and the successful development of the new individuals as part of the flora of the new territory; (4) the passage of a parasite from one part of the body to another.

migration, atomic. A change in the position of an atom or atoms within a molecule.

migration potential. The potential difference due to the settling or centrifuging of charged colloid particles; the reverse of electrophoresis.

mil. One thousandth of an inch; used in calculating the resistance of a wire.

mildew. (1) A whitish surface layer caused by fungal growth on moist organic materials, such as cloth, leather, and paper; (2) a fungus disease which affects leaves and flowers of plants.

mile. An English measure of distance equivalent to 320 rods, 1760 yards, 5280 feet, 63,360 inches, and 1.6094 kilometers.

mil-foot. A round wire of one foot length and one mil diameter.

milk sugar. Lactose; $C_{12}H_{22}O_{11}\cdot H_2O$; used as a nutrient and in bacteriology.

milk teeth. The deciduous first teeth of mammals which are later replaced with permanent teeth.

milkwort. Polygala; flowering herbs and shrubs in southern United States.

Milky Way. Galaxy; a luminous band encircling the heavens, composed of many stars so distant that they are separately invisible to the naked eye; the galaxy to which our solar system belongs.

milliammeter. An instrument that measures electric currents in milliamperes; generally used for the measurement of plate current.

milliampere. One thousandth of an ampere.

millibar. A unit of pressure; one thousand dynes per square centimeter; one thousandth of a bar.

millicurie. One thousandth of a curie; that quantity of a radioactive isotope which decays at the rate of 3.7×10 disintegrations per second.

milligram. One thousandth of a gram; 0.0154 grain.

millihenry. One thousandth of a henry.

millilambert. A unit of luminance, equal to 1/1000 lambert.

milliliter. A metric unit of volume; it is equal to one thousandth of a liter; for all practical purposes, it is equal to one cubic centimeter, 1 cc.

millimass unit. One thousandth of an atomic mass unit.

millimeter. One thousandth of a meter; 0.03937 inch; 1000 microns.

millimho. One thousandth of a mho.

millimicron (mμ). One thousandth of a micron; one millionth of a millimeter; there are 25,400,-000 millimicrons to the inch.

millivolt. One thousandth of a volt.

millivoltmeter. A voltmeter calibrated in thousandths of a volt.

milliwatt. One thousandth of a watt.

Millon's test. A test for proteins; a red precipitate is formed in the presence of proteins on addition of mecuric nitrate acidified with mercurous acid.

milt. (1) The sperms of a fish; (2) the spleen.

mimetic. Imitating another species for concealment or protection.

mimicry. The adaptation of one species to another species in color and shape as a protection against enemies.

Mindanao deep. The greatest ocean depth recorded, near the Philippines; 35,400 feet; also called Emden deep.

mineral. An inorganic substance which forms part of the soil and rocks; it has usually a definite composition and crystal form; plants use many minerals as food; example, table salt.

mineral acids. Strong inorganic acids; example, hydrochloric acid, HCl.

mineralizers. Magmatic gases, such as water vapor, hydrogen, fluorine, and other volatile substances, which are retained in solution under varying pressure and temperature and promote the crystallization of the minerals contained in the molten magma.

minim. (1) The smallest liquid measure; one sixtieth of a fluid dram; 0.06161 milliliter; (2) a small working ant.

minimum thermometer. A thermometer that records the lowest temperature of the day.

minor planet. Asteroid; a small planetary body revolving in space between Mars and Jupiter.

minute. (1) A unit of time; 60 seconds; there are 1440 minutes or 86,400 seconds in one 24-hour day; (2) a unit of angular measurement; the 60th part of a degree.

Miocene period. A geological era which began 25 million years ago; modern birds and trees, horses and elephants developed in this period.

miracidium. The ciliated larva of fluke; it emerges from an egg, which is released from the vertebrate host in excreta, and parasitizes a snail, in which it reproduces asexually.

mirage. An optical illusion caused by refraction of light through air layers of different densities.

mirror. (1) A highly polished surface which can be used to form images by the reflection of light; (2) a reflecting surface fastened to a microscope base and used to direct the light through the lenses.

mirror image. The true image of an object in a mirror which is reversed in such a way that the right side is seen on the left and vice versa.

miscegenation. An interbreeding of different races.

misch metal. A pyrophoric alloy of cerium with small amounts of other rare-earth metals; used for flints in lighters.

miscibility. The ability of two or

more substances to mix and to form a single, homogeneous phase; example, alcohol and water are miscible.

Mississippian period. The lowest of the three main divisions of the Carboniferous period in North America.

missourite. A basic, intrusive igneous rock of granite texture, containing an abundance of pyroxene, olivine, and leucite.

mist. (1) Ground fog; the condensation of water vapor in the air near the earth's surface, when warm, moist air is sufficiently cooled; (2) the suspension of a liquid in a gas.

mistral. A cold dry northerly wind that cools the coast of southern France.

mites. Members of the order of Acarina; small insects with saclike body and piercing mandibles; some are free-living and some parasitic.

mitochondria. Small, granular or rodlike cytoplasmic structures, possibly associated with certain metabolic reactions in the cell.

mitosis. A cell division in which the chromosomes split, doubling the number and leaving each new cell with the same number of chromosomes as the parent cell.

mitral valve. The bicuspid valve of the heart guarding the opening between the left auricle and the left ventricle and preventing the return of blood to the left auricle.

mixed bud. A bud containing both rudimentary leaves and flowers.

mixed crystal. A crystal composed of two or more different chemical substances, both of whose molecules or ions occupy positions in the same crystal lattice.

mixed culture. A large number of bacteria of different kinds growing in one medium.

mixed tides. Tides in which each alternate high tide is much lower than the preceding one.

mixer tube. A vacuum tube used in superheterodyne radio receivers to generate the intermediate frequency by mixing the signal frequency with the local oscillator frequency.

mixture. A combination of two or more substances which can be separated by physical means.

Mizar. A star of the big dipper; the first double star ever observed.

mks system. A system of measurement whose fundamental units are the meter, kilogram, and second.

ml. Abbreviation for milliliter.

mm. Abbreviation for millimeter.

Mn. Chemical symbol of manganese.

Mo. Chemical symbol of molybdenum.

mobility. Fluidity; low viscosity of a liquid, or of a plastic solid beyond its yield point.

moderation. Slowing down neutrons in a nuclear reactor by collisions with nuclei.

moderator. A substance, such as graphite, paraffin, or heavy water, used in a nuclear reactor to slow down neutrons.

modified leaves. Leaves that have special functions other than food making, etc.; example, the climbing tendril of grape vines.

modulated current. An alternating current that has been given the pattern of sound waves by causing variations either in its amplitude (AM) or in its frequency (FM).

modulation. Changing the phase, frequency, or magnitude of a high-frequency current by an impressed current.

module. A set of components combined on a common mounting so that they can be readily inserted into, or removed from, a specific place in a larger system.

modulus of elasticity. Young's modulus; the ratio of stress per unit area to the corresponding strain per unit length, the distortion or strain being within the elastic limit.

Mohs' scale of hardness. A scale in which each mineral listed is softer than all those following it; 1-talc; 2-gypsum; 3-calcite; 4-fluorite; 5-apatite; 6-orthoclase; 7-quartz; 8-topaz; 9-corundum; 10-diamond.

mol. Mole; one gram-molecular weight of a substance.

molal. Containing one gram molecule in 1000 grams of a solvent.

molar. (1) Molecular; (2) pertaining to a mol or measured in mols; (3) containing one gram molecule in one liter of a solution.

molar concentration. The number of mols of a substance per unit volume of a solution.

molar conductivity. The electrical conductivity of an electrolyte containing one mol of the solute.

molar free volume. The molar volume of a substance at any temperature in the liquid state, less its molar volume at the freezing point.

molar heat. The product of the molecular weight of a substance and its specific heat.

molar latent heat of vaporization. The quantity of heat needed to convert one mol of a substance into vapor at its boiling point under atmospheric pressure.

molar refraction. The product of the molecular weight of a substance and its specific refractive power.

molar solution. A solution containing one mol of solute in a liter of the solution.

molar surface. The surface of a sphere whose mass is one mol.

molar surface energy. The energy needed to form a sphere from one mol of any liquid.

molar volume. The volume, in liters, of one mol of a gas at standard temperature and pressure; 22.44 liters for an ideal gas.

molarity. Molality; the concentration of a solution expressed in mols of solute per liter of solution.

molars. Teeth with cusps on broad crowns which are used for crushing and grinding food.

mold. (1) A fungal growth chiefly on damp, decaying organic matter, but also on some living organisms; (2) a die for casting metal or plastic products or various shapes.

molecular. Same as molar.

molecular beam. A stream of neutral molecules in one direction passing through a vacuum, generally with thermal velocity.

molecular collision. A collision between molecules, which may be perfectly elastic or inelastic, resulting in chemical reaction, radiation, etc.

molecular compound. A compound formed by the chemical combination of two or more complete molecules.

molecular distillation. Evaporating molecules from a surface at extremely low pressure and condensing them before undergoing collisions; used for isotope separation and for the distillation of heat-sensitive substances, such as essential oils.

molecular formula. A chemical formula which shows the number of atoms of each constituent in the molecule.

molecular free path. The average free path or distance traveled by a molecule between collisions in a gas or in a solution.

molecular moment. The electric moment of a polar molecule.

molecular number. The sum of the atomic numbers of the atoms in a molecule.

molecular pump. An air pump in which the molecules of the gas to be exhausted are carried away by the friction of a rapidly revolving disk or cylinder.

molecular rays. Molecules that emerge from a succession of similar, parallel slits in plates set one in front of the other; only those molecules pass through the slits whose direction of motion is nearly parallel with the common axis of the slits.

molecular solution. A solution in which there are no associated molecules.

molecular spectrum. A band spectrum produced by energy changes within a molecule.

molecular volume. Same as molar volume.

molecular weight. The sum of the weights of the atoms in a molecule.

molecule. The smallest particle of a substance that can exist independently, retaining the chemical properties of the substance.

molecule, activated. A molecule containing one or more excited atoms.

molecule, homonuclear. A molecule composed of atoms whose nuclei are identical in charge and mass.

molecule, polar. A molecule in which there is a separation of charge caused by a nonuniform electron distribution.

Mollusca. Mollusks; soft-bodied limbless animals; some are protected by shells; examples, octopus, snail, and clam.

Mollweide projection. An equal-area projection of the earth's surface in which the equator is represented twice as long as the earth's axis; the meridians are equally spaced ellipses and the parallels are equally spaced straight parallel lines.

molting. The shedding of feathers, fur, skin, or exoskeleton by animals.

molts. Changes while developing from young to adult.

molybdenite. A grayish molybdenum ore; molybdenum sulfide, MoS_2.

molybdenum. A silver-white metal; chemical symbol Mo; atomic number 42; used as electrical wire, in alloying.

molybdenum steel. An alloy containing up to 10% molybdenum; used for high-speed tools.

moment of force. Torque; the effectiveness of a force in causing rotation; the product of the magnitude of the force and the perpendicular distance of the axis from the line of action of the force.

moment of inertia. The measure of the resistance of a body to angular acceleration; the sum of the products of each particle of a moving body multiplied by the squares of the distances of the particles from their neutral axis.

moment of momentum. The angular momentum.

momentum. The product of the mass of a body and its velocity.

monad. Flagellispore; a zoospore whose locomotive organ is a flagella.

monadelphous. Having all stamens united by their filaments to form a tube surrounding the style; example, lupin.

monadnock. A rounded remnant of an old mountain region; the rock structure is tilted or folded and rises from the surrounding peneplane.

monatomic molecule. A molecule made up of one atom.

monazite. A rare-earth mineral; it contains cerium and thorium phosphate; an important source of thorium.

Mongolian race. The greatest of the five divisions of the human race; it includes almost all the population of Asia and some of Europe; they have yellowish skin, coarse straight dark hair, broad flat face with prominent cheek bones, small nose, and dark slanted eyes.

Monilia. Parasitic fungi.

monitor. (1) A device for detecting and measuring radiation levels; (2) a mechanism for checking the quality of sound-wave transmission without interrupting or disturbing the transmission.

monobasic acid. An acid having only one replaceable hydrogen atom; example, hydrochloric acid, HCl.

monobasic salt. A salt in which only one of the hydrogen atoms in a polybasic acid has been replaced; example, NaH_2PO_4 from H_3PO_4.

monocarpic. (1) Flowering once during its life; (2) bringing a single fruit and then dying; (3) having one flagellum.

monochasium. A branching inflorescence in which each branch bears another branch.

monochlamydeous. Said of a flower having only one whorl of perianth segments.

monochromatic filter. A filter that transmits one wave length or a very narrow band of wave lengths only.

monochromatic illuminator. An instrument used for supplying a beam of light having some desired narrow range of wave lengths.

monochromatic light. A one-color light consisting of one wave length; example, a sodium flame.

monocline. A slightly inclined bed or stratified formation which changes its dip by increasing its steepness of inclination and then flattens out or resumes its normal, gentle dip.

monoclinic. Said of crystals which have three unequal crystal axes, one being perpendicular to the other two.

monocotyledonous. Said of a plant that has a seed which contains an embryo plant with one leaf; the adult plant bears parallel-veined leaves; examples, corn and grass.

monocyte. The largest type of white blood cell of the vertebrate blood.

monoecious. Said of plants which bear both terminal and pistillate flowers.

monohybrid. The offspring of two parents that are unlike for one character only.

monohydric. Containing one hydroxyl group in the molecule.

monokaryon. A nucleus containing only one central granule.

monomer. The initial molecule in a polymerization reaction.

monomolecular layer. Monolayer; a film or layer having the thickness of one molecule of the adsorbed substance.

monomorphic. Having one form only.

monophyletic. Descending from a single common parent form.

monoploid. Haploid; having half the number of chromosomes as compared to diploid.

monopodium. A plant axis produced and increasing in length through apical growth.

monosaccharide. A simple sugar of the formula $C_6H_{12}O_6$; examples, glucose and fructose.

Monotremata. Egg-laying primitive mammals; the young are nourished by nippleless mammary glands in a pouch developed during lactation; example, duckbill.

monotrichous. Having a single polar flagellum.

monotrophic. Monoghagous; (1) eating only one kind of food; (2) attacking one host only.

monotropic. Having only one stable crystal form.

monovalent. Univalent; having the valence of one.

monozygotic twins. Identical twins of the same sex; they result from fission into two, at some stage of its development, of the embryo derived from a single fertilized egg.

monsoon. A continental wind that reverses its usual direction in some season of the year.

moon. The earth's satellite; it is 2,163 miles in diameter and at a distance of 238,857 miles from the earth.

moraine. Stones, boulders, clay, and other matter deposited by melting glaciers.

mordant. An agent, usually a weak base, which is applied to cloth to fix a dye on it; example, ferric hydroxide.

morphogenesis. The creation of pattern and shape as a result of the foldings and mass movements of cell groups as the embryo develops.

morphogenetic movements. The displacement of masses of cells in the embryonic development of animals, especially during gastrulation.

morphogenetic phase. A stage during embryonic development during which the main outlines of the adult pattern are established in the multicellular embryo.

morphology. The study of the form and structure of organisms.

morphotropy. The change in the crystal form due to substituting other atoms or groups for certain atoms or groups of the original crystal.

morula. A globular mass of cells formed during the cleavage of an egg.

mosaic. (1) A virus disease of plants recognizable by the mottling of the leaves; (2) said of hybrids of mixed genetic composition; (3) development when the determination is complete but before the functional differentiation starts; (4) partly overlapping leaf arrangement or pattern in which all the leaves receive light; (5) the screen in an iconoscope containing numerous photoelectric cells.

mosaic vision. The vision of the compound eye of an insect; each visual unit of the eye forms an image of a part of the object and the total image is supposed to be a composite of all the units.

mosses. Musci; small plants that have rhizoids instead of roots and a stem with spirally arranged small, simple leaves; example, sphagnum.

mother cell. A cell which divides to yield daughter cells.

mother liquor. The solution remaining after the crystals have separated from a solution, or after precipitation of a solid from a solution.

moths. Noctural insects resembling butterflies; small lepidopterous insects which infest wool, cloth, fur, etc.

motility. The capability of moving about.

motion. A continuous change of place or position.

motive power. A source of energy which is used for activating a prime mover or a machine; examples, steam, water, wind.

motivity. Available energy.

motometer. Speedometer; a speed counter.

motor. (1) A machine that changes some other form of energy into mechanical energy; (2) the engine of an automobile or aircraft; (3) initiating motion in plants and animals.

motor effect. The repulsion force exerted by adjacent conductors carrying currents in opposite directions.

motor end plate. The terminus of the processes of a motor nerve in a muscle.

motor generator. An electric motor mechanically connected to a generator for changing an alternating current to a direct current, or the reverse.

motor neurons. Efferent neurons; nerve cells that carry impulses outward from the spinal cord or brain to the muscles or glands.

Mount Palomar. A mountain in southern California on which is located the Hale telescope, the world's largest reflecting telescope with the famous 200-inch mirror; 6138 feet high.

mountain. A lofty, upward projecting mass of rock which rises pronouncedly above the valleys and plains around it.

mountain lake. Cirque lake; a semicircular lake filling a hollow excavated among mountains by glacial effects.

mountain range. A ridge or group of parallel ridges.

mouth parts. Feeding structures which surround the mouth of Arthropoda.

moving clusters. A group of stars which move through space together in parallel paths.

mP. Abbreviation for maritime polar air mass.

mT. Abbreviation for maritime tropical air mass.

mu. (1) The amplification factor of a vacuum tube; (2) an abbreviation for micron.

mucin. Mucoprotein; a glucoprotein occurring in saliva and mucus.

mucoproteins. Compounds of certain carbohydrates with protein; found in mucin.

mucopurulent. Containing both mucus and pus.

mucosa. Mucous membrane.

mucous gland. A gland, located in mucous membranes, which secretes mucus.

mucous membrane. A moist tissue, containing mucus-secreting glands, that lines various cavities of the body.

mucus. A slimy fluid secreted by the mucous glands.

mud torrents. Rains that fall after an explosive eruption and that carry along volcanic dust and ash.

Müllerian ducts. A pair of ducts in vertebrate embryos from which the oviducts are formed; in mammals, they develop into the uterus and vagina of the female and become a vestigal structure in the male adult.

Müller's law. The difference between sensations is in the portion of the brain to which the impulses travel.

multicellular. Consisting of many cells.

multiciliate. Said of a spore or sperm which has many cilia.

multinucleate. Containing many nuclei in a cell.

multiple allelomorphs. A set of more than two genes, all allelomorphs, which originate from each other by mutation.

multiple fission. Multiplication of Protozoa by repeated division of the nucleus without corresponding division of the cytoplasm.

multiple fruit. Collective fruit; a compound fruit formed from several flowers in a cluster; example, pineapple.

multiple ionization. The extraction of more than one electron from an atom by the impact of an electron of sufficient speed.

multiple series. The parallel connection of two or more series circuits.

multiple star. Three or more stars revolving around a common center of gravity.

multiplet. (1) A group of lines in an atomic spectrum arising from transitions between the different components of two multiple spectral terms and thus exhibiting the characteristic frequency differences of these terms; (2) one of the individuals resulting from the segmentation of an ovum.

multiplier. Additional external resistances used to extend the range of a direct-current voltmeter.

multiplier phototube. A sensitive device for the detection of radioactivity.

multipolar. (1) Having more than two poles; (2) said of nerve cells that have several axons.

multivibrator. An electric oscillating system so designed that the energy is chiefly distributed among the harmonic partial frequencies rather than in the fundamental frequency.

muriatic acid. Hydrochloric acid, HCl.

Musci. Mosses; a division of Bryophyta, characterized by alternation of generations.

muscle. A tissue which produces motion by contracting.

muscle spindle. A sensory organ found at the end of muscles of vertebrates which is assumed to be stimulated by the variations of pressure resulting from the contraction of a muscle.

muscular coordination. The combined action of muscles to produce a movement.

muscular foot. A means of locomotion on the ventral surface of mollusks having shells.

muscular system. The entire assemblage of contractile structures by which movement is produced in complex animals.

muscular tissue. Long slender cells which contract when stimulated.

mushrooms. Fleshy edible fungi; example, field mushrooms which have pink gills.

mutarotation. A change with time in the optical rotation of a freshly prepared solution of an optically active substance; example, sugar solutions.

mutation. A change in the structure or composition of a gene which is heritable.

mutation theory. A theory of evolution formulated by Hugo de Vries: Favorable mutations are naturally selected for survival in the struggle for existence, and evolution occurs as a result of a series of mutations.

mutual inductance. The inductive effect of a moving magnetic field in one circuit on a second circuit and vice versa.

mutual induction. The induction

of an electromotive force in a circuit due to a changing current in a separate circuit with which it is magnetically linked.

mutualism. A relationship between two organisms in which neither species can survive without the other.

Mv. Chemical symbol for Mendelevium.

mv. Abbreviation for millivolts.

mw. Abbreviation for milliwatts.

mycelium. A network or mass of branched hypha found in molds.

Mycetozoa. (1) Myxomycetes; (2) semiterrestrial Protozoa; they have many pseudopods, but no skeleton or shell; they form cysts and spores.

mycology. The study of fungi.

mycoplasma. The smallest known organism capable of reproducing itself in a cell-free medium.

mycorrhiza. Fungus root; the association of a fungus with the root of a higher plant.

mycotrophic. Said of a plant having mycorrhizas.

mydriatic. A substance that makes the pupil of the eye dilate.

myelin. The fatlike substance that surrounds the axis cylinder of a medullated nerve.

myelocyte. A large ameboid marrow cell occurring in the bones of higher vertebrates.

myeloid tissue. A tissue producing polymorphs and red blood cells of the vertebrate blood.

myocardium. The muscular layer which constitutes the greater part of the wall of the vertebrate heart.

myofibrils. Small fibers in the protoplasm of the muscle cell or fiber.

myoneme. A fine contractile filament in the cytoplasm of one-celled animals.

myosin. An insoluble muscle protein; its formation causes the rigor mortis.

myotome. That part of the somatic mesoderm which forms striped muscles.

Myriapoda. A class of Arthropoda; they have long segmented bodies with many identical legs and a distinct head; example, centipedes.

myrrh. A brown, bitter, aromatic resin obtained from the stem of an East African tree.

myxamoeba. A naked cell, capable of amoeboid movement, characteristic of the vegetative phase of Myxomycetes and certain simply organized fungi.

myxomycetes. Slime fungi having both plant and animal properties; they live in decaying wood and in the soil.

myxophyceae. Sexless blue-green algae; they are one-celled or filamentous; they live in fresh or salt water and propagate by vegetative means.

N

N. Chemical symbol of nitrogen.

Na. Chemical symbol of sodium.

nadir. The point on the celestial sphere directly below the observer, diametrically opposite the zenith, that is, 180° from the zenith.

naked bud. A bud not protected by bud scales.

naked bulb. A bulb consisting of scales and having no protective casing; example, lily bulb.

naked flower. A flower having no perianth; example, willow.

nanoplankton. A microscopic plankton which passes through ordinary nets and must be secured by centrifuging.

nape. The back of the neck.

naphtha. A petroleum or coal-tar distillation product; a liquid fuel and solvent, more volatile than kerosene, but less than gasoline.

naphthalene. $C_{10}H_8$; a cyclic hydrocarbon occurring in coal tar; a white, shiny, crystalline solid of penetrating odor; used in the manufacture of organic dyes, as a moth repellent, in organic synthesis.

nappe. A mountain-chain structure; a great overfold of the earth's crust which includes formations that represent one or more geologic periods of the earth's history; they may have produced horizontal translocation of the earth's crust.

nares. The nasal passages of vertebrates.

nasal bone. One of a pair of small bones forming the bridge of the human nose and the corresponding portion of the skull in other vertebrates.

nasal capsule. The structure of the vertebrate nose which includes the nasal cavities.

nasal cavity. Nasal fossa; two cavities of the head containing olfactory organs and communicating with the mouth and the exterior through nares; they are lined with mucous membrane.

nascent. Referring to an element in the atomic form as it is just liberated in a chemical reaction; it is very reactive.

nasolabral groove. A groove extending from the nostril to the mouth in some fish and amphibians.

nastic movement. Curved growth of a plant in response to a stimulus of varying intensity.

native metal. A metal occurring uncombined in nature; example, native gold.

native protein. A protein in the naturally occurring state.

natrium. The latin name for sodium; used in the chemical terminology of some European countries.

natrolite. A zeolite mineral; a hydrated sodium aluminum silicate.

natron. A natural sodium sesquicarbonate, $Na_2CO_3 \cdot NaHCO_3 \cdot 2H_2O$; a plant nutrient.

natural fibers. Fibers of animal, vegetable, or mineral origin; examples, wool, cotton, and asbestos.

natural gas. A mixture of light hydrocarbon gases, sometimes also containing nitrogen, carbon dioxide, and/or helium, which occurs in pockets in the earth's crust; often found together with petroleum; methane, CH_4, is usually predominant.

natural magnet. Magnetite.

natural radioactivity. The spontaneous radiation of some substances in their natural states.

natural resources. The supply of water, minerals, oils, forests, grasslands, plants, and wildlife found in nature.

natural selection. Darwinism; the theory of evolution; survival of organisms with the best adaptive characters, which will be inherited by the next generation with slight, uncontrolled variations.

natural vegetative propagation. Propagation of plants by means of leaves, stems, and roots.

nauplius. A larval form of some Crustacea; it is the first unsegmented stage with three pairs of appendages and a single central eye.

nautical mile. One minute of the great circle of the earth; it has several different values in different countries; the international nautical mile now official in the United States and several other countries is 6,076.103 feet or 1852 meters.

navel. (1) The scar left where the umbilical cord of a mammal is cut off or broken at birth; (2) a navellike scar on the peel of a seedless orange.

Nb. Chemical symbol of niobium.

Nd. Chemical symbol of neodymium.

Ne. Chemical symbol of neon.

Neanderthal man. A now extinct Paleolithic man, who lived 60,000 to 100,000 years ago; he had an apelike flat receding forehead, a very low cephalic index, but a brain capacity similar to that of modern man.

neap tides. The lowest high tide and the highest low tide among the spring tides; they occur when the tidal influences of the sun and moon are acting at right angles with relation to the earth.

near field. The acoustic radiation field close to the source.

near point. The nearest point at which objects can be seen clearly, using the highest power of accommodation of the eye.

nebula. A faintly luminous spot in interstellar space; it is a gaseous cloud.

nebular hypothesis. Laplace's

theory on the origin of the solar system, stating that it was originally a mass of hot gases rotating in space; it gradually cooled, shrank, and cast off rings which were molded into planets in millions of years.

neck. (1) The region between the head and trunk of many vertebrates; (2) the lower part of the capsule of a moss; (3) a vertical volcanic conduit, consisting of lava and other volcanic products, which has been exposed to erosion.

neck of tooth. The part of the tooth between the crown and the root, surrounded by the gum.

necrosis. The death of a cell or of a portion of tissue in a living organism.

nectar. The sweet liquid secretion of flowers which attracts insects that are instrumental in pollination.

nectary. A gland located at the base of flower petals, which secretes nectar.

negative acceleration. Slowing down of a moving body.

negative adsorption. A phenomenon exhibited by certain solutions in which the solute concentration is lower at the surface than in the interior of the solution.

negative carbon. The carbon in a continuous-current arc lamp which is connected to the negative terminal of the supply.

negative catalysis. A reduction in the reaction speed due to a catalyst.

negative charge. The electrical charge carried by a body which has acquired an excess of electrons.

negative crystal. (1) A crystal which has negative double refraction; (2) a crystal-shaped cavity in a mineral.

negative electron. A name applied to an electron to distinguish it from a positron.

negative glow. A luminous region in a Crookes tube at moderate pressure, which is located between the Crookes dark space and the Faraday dark space.

negative plate. A plate in a voltaic cell to which the current flows during discharge.

negative pole. The south-seeking pole of a magnet.

negative tropism. Negative response; the movement of an organism away from the source of a stimulus.

negatively charged body. A body that has an excess of electrons.

negatron. A negative-resistance four-element vacuum tube which has an anode on one side of the cathode and an anode and a grid on the other.

Negri bodies. Cytoplasmic bodies found in the affected nerve cells in rabies.

Neisser-Wechsberg phenomenon.

Deviation of complement; the complement combines with the excess amboceptor so that it cannot affect the amboceptor combined with the antigen.

nekton. An aquatic organism that is capable of directive locomotion in water.

Nemathelminthes. A phylum including the roundworms, whose body is a three-layered, long, and threadlike tube with an anus and a body cavity; some are parasitic; example, hookworm.

nematic phase. A fluid phase of the mesomorphic state, with random orientation of the molecules; it yields a diffuse x-ray pattern.

nematocyst. A minute stinging organ filled with a poisonous fluid, found especially on the tentacles of the Hydra and used for paralyzing tiny animals.

Nematoda. Tubular, elongated, nonmetameric worms which have muscular, excretory, and reproductive systems; examples, roundworms, thread worms, and eel worms.

Nemertea. Ribbon worms; they have a long, flat body, with a mouth and anus, and a dorsal proboscis.

neodymium. A yellowish rare-earth metal; chemical symbol Nd; atomic number 60.

Neolithic age. The period that followed the Old Stone Age; men built shelters and boats, made polished stone implements, cultivated plants, and domesticated animals; it ended about 6,000 years ago.

neon. An inert rare gas; chemical symbol Ne; atomic number 10; minute quantities occur in the atmosphere; it is used in neon signs.

neopallium. The dorsal part of the cerebral cortex of vertebrates which is very highly developed in man and receives the impressions of the senses, except those of the olfactory organs.

neoprene. An oil-resistant synthetic rubber, the polymerization product of chloroprene.

neoteny. The retention of characteristics of immature stages during adult life.

neotype. A specimen chosen as a replacement of a destroyed proterotype.

nephelinite. A dense fine-grained igneous rock made up almost wholly of nephelite and augite.

nephelite. Sodium aluminum silicate; a hexagonal mineral occurring in igneous rocks.

nephelometer. A photometer used for the measurement of light transmitted or light scattered by translucent substances, or for the determination of the turbidity of liquids, from which the quantity of suspended matter can be calculated.

nephelometry. Quantitative analysis of a suspension by means of a nephelometer.

nephoscope. An instrument for determining the direction and speed of clouds.

nephridiopore. The opening of the excretory tube of segmented worms.

nephridium. A primitive kidney-like excretory organ in many invertebrates.

nephromixium. A compound excretory organ of segmented worms.

nephron. Kidney tubule; a functional unit of the vertebrate kidney, consisting of a Malpighian corpuscle, a secretory portion, and an excretory portion.

nephrostome. The ciliated funnel-shaped opening at the inner end of the nephridium through which the liquid wastes enter the tubule.

Neptune. The eighth planet from the sun; it is not visible to the naked eye; it has two satellites.

neptunium. A synthetic radioactive element; chemical symbol Np; atomic number 93.

neritic. Inhabiting the shallow water along the sea coast.

Nernst bridge. A four-arm bridge which has condensers instead of resistances and is used to measure capacitances at high frequencies.

Nernst effect. A potential difference between the two edges of a heated metal strip, which is placed in a magnetic field perpendicularly to its plane.

Nernst heat theorem. In the neighborhood of absolute zero, all physical and chemical processes are isentropic.

nerve. A group of nerve cells bound together and protected by a sheath.

nerve cell. Same as neuron.

nerve cord. A solid strand of nervous tissue, which is part of the central nervous system of invertebrates.

nerve ending. The structure at the peripheral end of a fiber of the peripheral nervous system, in which impulses start or finish.

nerve fiber. The axon of the nerve cell, with the special membranes which may surround it.

nerve gases. Poison gases that fatally affect the nerves.

nerve net. The network of nerve cells, distributed throughout the tissues; the primitive nervous system of Coelenterata.

nerve pathway. A series of nerve cells through which an impulse travels.

nerve root. The two roots from which each spinal nerve arises from the spinal cord of vertebrates; they join to form the spinal nerve as they pass through the wall of the vertebral column.

nervous system. A system made up of nerves or nerve cells; the nervous system of vertebrates consists of the brain, spinal cord, ganglia, and nerves.

nervous tissue. Nerve cells and/or their nerve fibers, together with the accessory cells which loosely surround them.

Nessler's solution. A solution of potassium mercuric iodide in potassium iodide, containing some sodium or potassium hydroxide; used in water analysis as a test for ammonia with which it gives a yellow coloration.

net transport. The difference between the total rate at which the desired isotopes are carried toward the production end of a separation plant through any section and the rate at which they would be carried in the same flow by a material of natural abundance.

nettle hair. A hairlike scale on some caterpillars which causes an irritation of human skin resembling that caused by nettles.

net-veined leaf. A leaf in which the veins branch again and again, forming a network.

network. A combination of network elements serving a special purpose.

network arm. A portion of a network consisting of one or more two-terminal elements in series.

network branch. Same as network arm.

network element. Any electrical device (such as inductor, resistor, capacitor, generator, electron tube) whose terminals may be directly connected to other electrical devices.

network mesh. A system of conductors which form a closed path in a network; if any one branch is omitted, the remaining branches do not form a closed path.

network node. A terminal of any branch of a network or a terminal that is common to two or more branches of a network.

network, star. A set of three or more branches of a network, each having one terminal connected at a common node.

Neufeld reaction. A method of typing pneumococci based on the fact that their capsule swells in the presence of a type-specific immune serum.

Neumann principle. The physical properties of a crystal cannot be of lower symmetry than the symmetry of the external form of the crystal.

neural. Pertaining to the nervous system.

neural arch. A bony arch resting on the center of each vertebra.

neural canal. Spinal canal; a canal formed by a set of neural arches that encloses the spinal cord.

neural crest. A strip of tissue between the outer layer of the neural fold and the neural tube of the embryo of vertebrates which later forms into ganglia of the dorsal roots of the spinal nerves, the sympathetic ganglia, and the nerve sheath cells.

neural fold. Medullary fold; a raised ridge of the neural plate and the epidermis along the edge of the neural plate, from which the neural tube of a vertebrate will develop.

neural plate. Medullary plate; a phase in the development of the central nervous system of vertebrates.

neural spine. The dorsal projection of a vertebra.

neural tube. An embryonic structure from which the entire central nervous system of vertebrates and much of the peripheral system are developed.

neurilemma. Neurolemma; the outermost sheath of a nerve fiber.

neurocoele. (1) Same as neural canal; (2) a cavity of the central nervous system; example, a ventricle of the brain.

neurocranium. The part of the skull which surrounds the brain and internal ear.

neurofibrils. A strand of protoplasm in the paramecium which connects the cilia with the nucleus.

neuroglia. Supporting cells of the central nervous system derived from the ectoderm.

neurohumoral theory. Nerve impulses are transmitted from a nerve fiber to an end organ or across a synapse by the secretion of minute amounts of chemical substances from the nerve fiber.

neuron. A nerve cell which consists of a cell body and its fibers.

Neuroptera. Insects with two similar pairs of mebranous wings which, when at rest, are held over the body; they have predaceous larvae and biting mouth parts; examples, lacewings, butterfly hawks, and scorpion flies.

neurotropic. Having an affinity for nervous tissues; example, a neurotropic virus.

neurula. A stage of vertebrate-embryo development, in which the nerve tissues begin their differentiation in an elongated gastrula.

neuter. Sexless; without or with imperfect reproductive organs.

neutral. Neither acid nor basic in reaction, containing an equal number of H^+ and OH^- ions; having a pH of 7.

neutral axis. A line in a beam that is being bent along which there is no stress.

neutral buoyancy. The buoyancy of a body that is only slightly lighter than water.

neutral curve. A pressure–temperature curve, at all points of which the specific volumes. of the solid and liquid phase are equal.

neutral density filter. A light filter which reduces the intensity of the light without changing the relative spectral distribution of the energy.

neutral equilibrium. An equilibrium state, in which a small displacement does not change the potential energy of a body.

neutral layer. That longitudinal layer in a rod or beam, perpendicular to the plane of flexure, which is neither lengthened nor shortened when the rod is bent.

neutral point. (1) In meteorology, any point at which the axis of a wedge of high pressure intersects the axis of a trough of low pressure; (2) in chemical analysis, the point where acidity and alkalinity are balanced; (3) in electrical engineering, the center of the neutral zone of a direct-current circuit.

neutral temperature. The temperature of the hot junction of a thermocouple at which the electromotive force of the circuit is at a maximum and its rate of change with temperature is at a minimum.

neutral zone. In an operating direct-current circuit, the commutator zone in which the voltage between adjacent bars is about zero.

neutralization. (1) The use of a balancing capacitance for neutralizing the objectionable effects of the anode-grid capacitance in a triode amplifying circuit; (2) the reaction between the hydrogen ions of an acid and the hydroxyl ions of a base to the point water.

neutrino. A particle which is smaller than an atom, has no charge, and has a mass which is close to zero.

neutron. A neutral particle found in the nucleus of an atom, which has about the same mass as a proton.

neutron current density. The number of neutrons which cross a unit surface per unit time in a direction normal to the surface.

neutron cycle. The life history of the neutrons in a nuclear reactor which begins with the fission process and ends when all the neutrons have been absorbed or have leaked out.

neutron density. The number of neutrons per unit volume in a reactor.

neutron excess. The difference between the number of neutrons and the number of protons in the nucleus.

neutron producer. A nuclear reactor which is used as a source of neutrons for isotope pro-

duction.

névé. Firn; a granular ice formed by the pressure of successive snowfalls.

New Stone Age. Same as Neolithic age.

newton. A unit of force in the metric system; it is equal to 100,000 dynes; the force that will produce an acceleration of 1 meter/second/second of a mass of 1 kilogram.

Newton emission theory. The theory advanced by Sir Isaac Newton that light was due to an emission of luminous corpuscles from a source.

Newtonian telescope. A reflecting telescope with a 45° mirror, so that the primary image is observed through a hole in the side of the tube.

Newton's first law. Law of inertia: A body at rest, tends to remain at rest, while a body in motion tends to continue its motion at constant speed in the same straight line unless acted on by an outside force.

Newton's law of cooling. The rate of cooling by radiation and convection is proportional to the difference between the temperature of the cooling body and the surrounding medium.

Newton's law of universal gravitation. The force of attraction between two bodies is proportional to each of their masses, and inversely proportional to the square of the distance between them.

Newton's rings. The circular interference bands formed by light reflected from the glass-air interface between a convex glass surface and a plane glass surface in contact with it, the center of the ring system being the point of contact.

Newton's second law. Law of momentum: When a force acts on a body, it changes the momentum of the body; this change is proportional to the applied force and to the time during which it acts on the body.

Newton's third law. Law of reaction: Every action is accompanied by an equal and opposite reaction.

Ni. Chemical symbol of nickel.

niacin. A member of the vitamin B complex, C_5H_4NCOOH; it prevents pellegra.

niccolite. Nickel arsenide, $NiAs$; a copper-red mineral; an important ore of nickel.

niche. The biotic and trophic relationship of an animal to its environment.

Nichols radiometer. An instrument for demonstrating the pressure of light and measuring the intensity of radiation in the visible and infrared.

nickel. Silver-white, corrosion-resistant metal; chemical sym-

bol Ni; atomic number 28; used for coins, in alloying.

nickel plating. Depositing a thin layer of metallic nickel by electrolysis.

nickel steel. A high-strength steel containing 4 to 6% nickel.

Nicol prism. A prism, cemented together from two calcite crystals; used for obtaining plane-polarized light.

nicotine. $C_{10}H_{14}N_2$; a very poisonous alkaloid, occurring in the leaves of the tobacco plant.

nicotine sulfate. A tobacco extract that is a strong contact spray or dust for killing insects.

nicotinic acid. Same as niacin.

nictitating membrane. The third eyelid of vertebrates which keeps the eyeball moist on land and serves as a protective covering when under water.

nidamental gland. Á gland of the female reproductive system of cephalopod mollusks which secretes an elastic membrane about the egg.

nidicolous bird. A bird which hatches in a relatively undeveloped state and remains in the nest for some time after hatching.

nidifugous bird. A bird that hatches well developed and leaves the nest immediately.

nimbostratus. A low layer of clouds heavy with moisture which gives them a dark color; they are the source of continuous rain or snow.

nimbus. A dark, shapeless cloud with irregular edges from which rain or snow is falling.

niobium. Same as columbium; a very rare metal; chemical symbol Nb; atomic number 41.

nipple. (1) The normally protruding outlet of the breast of mammals which is composed of erectile tissue; (2) a short piece of connecting pipe with screw threads on the outside.

Nissl bodies. Deeply staining granules in the body of nerve cells which disappear when the cell has been subjected to frequent and prolonged stimulation.

nit. The egg of a parasitic insect.

niter. Potassium nitrate, KNO_3; an oxidizing agent.

nitrates. Salts of nitric acid; they are important plant nutrients.

nitration. (1) The introduction of a nitro group, NO_2, into an organic compound; (2) the last stage of nitrification.

nitrobacter. A rod-shaped, nonmotile soil bacterium that oxidizes nitrites to nitrates.

nitrogen. A colorless, gaseous element found in free air; the principal constituent of the atmosphere; chemical symbol, N; atomic number, 7.

nitrogen fixation. (1) Converting atmospheric nitrogen into nitrogen compounds; examples, arc process and cyanamide process; (2) the formation of nitrogen compounds from elementary nitrogen by soil bacteria.

nitrogen monoxide. Laughing gas, N_2O; colorless gas, used in anesthesis.

nitrogen-fixing bacteria. Bacteria that absorb free nitrogen from the air and convert it into soluble nitrates usable by plants for making proteins; they live in nodulelike swellings in the roots of leguminous plants.

nitroglycerin. Glyceryl trinitrate, $C_3H_5(ONO_2)_3$; a colorless oil which is a powerful explosive.

Nitrosomonas. Rod-shaped soil bacteria that secure their energy by oxidizing ammonia to nitrites.

No. Chemical symbol of nobelium.

nobelium. Chemical symbol No; atomic number 102.

noble metals. Nonreactive metals which do not corrode or tarnish in air or water and are not easily attacked by acids; examples, silver, gold, and platinum.

Noctiluca. Complex bioluminescent flagellates; millions of these organisms group together and make the ocean look phosphorescent.

nodal points. Two points on the axis of a lens or lens system, such that if the incident ray passes through one, traveling in a given direction, the emergent ray passes through the other in a parallel direction.

nodal slide. A small optical bench on which a lens system may be mounted and which may be rotated about a vertical axis; used for the determination of the cardinal points of a compound lens.

node. (1) A point of no vibration, as in a string; (2) a slightly enlarged portion of the stem where leaves and buds arise and where branches are attached; (3) one of the two points where the orbit of the moon, or of a planet intersects the ecliptic.

nodes, line of. A straight line connecting two opposite nodes of a celestial orbit.

nodule. A small knoblike growth on a plant; example, the swelling on the roots of legume plants, containing nitrogen-fixing bacteria.

nomograph. An alignment chart from which the value of a dependent variable can be determined if the value of the independent variable is given.

noncombustible. Not burning in air.

nonconductor. An insulator; a substance that prevents to a considerable extent the transfer of heat, electricity, sound,

etc.; example, porcelain is a nonconductor of electricity.

nonelectrolyte. A nonionizing substance whose water solution does not conduct electricity; example, sugar.

nonferrous alloy. An alloy whose base is a metal other than iron.

nongreen plant. A plant that does not contain chlorophyll and thus cannot make its own food.

noninductive resistance. A resistance free from self-induction.

nonmetal. An element whose atoms borrow electrons; they are usually poor conductors; examples, chlorine, nitrogen, and oxygen.

nonpolar bond. A covalent bond.

nonpolar compound. A compound in whose molecules the atoms are arranged symmetrically so that the electric charges are uniformly distributed; they do not form electrolytes in the liquid state and do not ionize substantially in solution.

nonpolarizing cell. A voltaic cell in which the hydrogen cannot reach the positive plate.

nonprotein nitrogen. The nitrogen-containing waste products of cell activity which are taken up by the blood.

nonrenewable resources. Natural resources which cannot be renewed as they are used; example, coal.

nonshatterable glass. A sheet of tough, transparent plastic between two sheets of thin plate glass compressed into a single sheet under heat.

nonviable. Unable to survive.

noon. The instant the sun reaches the highest altitude in its daily path.

noon, apparent. The instant when the sun's center is on the meridian.

normal. A line drawn perpendicular to a surface.

normal atom. An atom which has no over-all electric charge and in which all the electrons surrounding the nucleus are at their lowest energy levels.

normal cathode potential drop. The constant value of the potential difference between the cathode and the negative glow in a discharge tube in which the cathode is not entirely covered by cathode glow.

normal electrode. A metal electrode immersed in a normal solution of an electrolyte having that metal as one of its ions.

normal gas. A gas whose molecules are of one kind and not polymerized.

normal lapse rate. The temperature decrease of about 3.5°F per 1000 feet encountered when flying upward through the air.

normal salt. A salt in which re-

placeable hydrogen or hydroxyl ions are not present; normal salts are formed by the complete neutralization of an acid by a base; example, NaCl.

normal solution. A solution containing one gram-equivalent weight of a substance for each liter of solution.

normal temperature and pressure. N.T.P.; 0°C and 760 mm of mercury.

normal vapor. A vapor whose molecules are all of one kind, and not polymerized.

normality. The number of gram equivalents of reagent per liter of a solution.

normalizing. Treating steel by heating above the critical temperature and then allowing to cool in air; it releaves internal stresses and results in a finer structure.

North Equatorial Current. Westward equatorial ocean current under the northeast trade winds.

north pole. The north end of the axis of the earth.

North Star. Pole star, Cynosure, Polaris; the star seen in the northern hemisphere to which the earth's axis approximately points.

norther. Norte; a dry cold wind of the southwestern United States; the temperature may drop 50° in two hours.

nose-down. Depressing the nose of an airplane in flight.

nose-heavy. The tendency of the nose of an airplane to drop in normal flight.

nose-up. Elevating the nose of an airplane in flight.

Nostoc. A one-celled green water plant which lives in chains; many chains may cover themselves with jelly, forming a dark lump floating on the water.

nostril. The opening in the nose through which air passes.

notochord. A rod of cartilage running longitudinally along the dorsal side of lower chordates and always present in the early embryonic stages of vertebrates.

novae. Temporary stars that flash out brilliantly in the sky for a few days or weeks and then rapidly fade away.

Np. Chemical symbol of neptunium.

N.T.P. Normal temperature and pressure; a temperature of 0°C and a pressure of 760 mm of mercury; standard conditions under which the volumes of gases are compared.

nucellus. Megasporangium; the central tissue of the young ovule, in which the embryo sac develops.

nuclear atom. An atomic nucleus without surrounding electrons.

nuclear breeder. A nuclear reactor in which more fissionable

material is formed in each generation than is used up in fission.

nuclear chain reaction. A self-propagating atom-splitting process.

nuclear change. A change which involves changes in the identity of the atoms themselves.

nuclear charge. The positive electric charge on the nucleus of an atom.

nuclear chemistry. The study of reactions which yield new elements.

nuclear disintegration. The emission of a proton or neutron from a nucleus as a result of bombarding the nucleus with alpha particles, protons, deuterons, or neutrons.

nuclear emulsion. A photographic emulsion which is used to register the track of a charged particle as a series of dark grains, visible under the microscope.

nuclear energy. Atomic energy; the energy released or absorbed in the spontaneously or artificially produced fission, fusion, or disintegration of the nuclei of atoms.

nuclear energy levels. Differences in the energy of atomic nuclei.

nuclear equation. An equation representing changes in the nuclei of atoms.

nuclear fission. Splitting the nucleus of an atom into two other nuclei by bombardment with neutrons, with the release of enormous quantities of energy.

nuclear forces. Forces that are not electromagnetic and that act between and are peculiar to nucleons.

nuclear fuel. A substance that is consumed during nuclear fission or nuclear fusion.

nuclear fusion. A union of the nuclei of the atoms of a light element, such as hydrogen, to form nuclei of a heavier element, such as helium; example, hydrogen bomb (H bomb).

nuclear induction. A magnetic induction in a solid, liquid, or gaseous substance originating in the magnetic moments of the constituent nuclei.

nuclear isomers. Atoms of an element of the same mass and charge, but having different rates of radioactive decay.

nuclear magnetic moment. The magnetlike behavior of an electrically charged particle possessing angular momentum.

nuclear membrane. A thin membrane surrounding the nucleus of an ovule.

nuclear number. Mass number; the mass of an isotope based on the mass of the most abundant oxygen isotope as 16; it gives the number of nucleons present in the nucleus.

nuclear paramagnetism. The paramagnetism associated with

nuclear magnetic moments.

nuclear physics. The study of the physical properties and effects of the atomic nucleus and of subatomic particles.

nuclear polarization. An alignment of the spin magnetic moments of atomic nuclei in the same direction, thus giving a net macroscopic magnetic moment.

nuclear power. The usable power released in an exothermic nuclear reaction.

nuclear reactions. Reactions in which the nuclei of atoms are changed, yielding either atoms of a different element or isotopes of the original element.

nuclear reactor. A device in which the controlled fission of a radioactive element produces new radioactive substances and energy.

nuclear transmutation. Changing atoms of one element into those of another by a suitable nuclear reaction.

nucleic acids. High-molecular-weight complex organic acids which occur in nucleoproteins; they probably participate in protein synthesis.

nucleogenesis. The formation of nuclei in nature on a large scale.

nucleolus. A rounded body within the cell nucleus that takes stain like chromatin, but is different from chromatin.

nucleon. A constituent of the nucleus of the atom.

nucleonics. Nuclear science and technology; a study of the changes in the atomic nucleus and of atomic energy and its applications.

nucleoplasm. A compact protoplasm in the cell nucleus.

nucleoprotein. A compound composed of a protein and a nucleic acid; germs and viruses are believed to consist of nucleoproteins.

nucleus. (1) The small, bright and dense part of the head of a comet; the umbra of a sunspot; (2) the center of development of a living cell; the gray matter in the vertebrate brain; (3) the central core of an atom, containing protons and neutrons.

nucleus, recoil. An atomic nucleus that recoils because (1) of a collision with a nuclear particle, or (2) of the emission of a particle from it.

nuclide. Nucleide; a species of atom characterized by the constitution of, and particularly the numbers of protons and neutrons in, its nucleus; examples U 235 and Co 60.

NULACE (nuclear-heated liquid-air-cycle engine). A rocket engine that uses a nuclear reactor for additional heating of hydrogen before combustion to in-crease specific impulse without an additional expenditure of propellant.

null method of measurement. Zero method; a measuring method in which adjustments are made until a detector occupies the zero position; example, Wheatstone bridge.

numerical density. The number of particles or points per unit space, area, or volume in any region.

nut. A hard, dry, one-seeded indehiscent fruit; example, chestnut.

nutation. (1) A spiral course pursued by the apex of a plant organ during growth due to continuous change in the position of its most rapidly growing region; (2) the oscillation of the poles of the earth about the mean position.

nutrient. Nourishing food.

nutrition. Feeding; the digestion and assimilation of food.

nyctinasty. The response of plants to the periodic alternation of day and night.

nymph. The immature stage of certain insects between egg and adult; the nymph resembles the adult, but has no wings and is sexually not mature.

O

O. Chemical symbol of oxygen.

obdiplostemonous. Having stamens in two whorls, the outer whorl being opposite to the petals and the inner, opposite to the sepals.

Obelia. A changeable sea animal that looks like a polyp in one generation and like a jellyfish in the next.

objective. The lens or set of microscope lenses nearest the object whose image is visible in the eyepiece.

objective prism. A prism placed in front of the objective of a spectroscope, which draws the starlight into the spectrum.

oblateness. Ellipticity; being flattened at the poles.

obligate anaerobe. An organism which can live and grow only in an environment with no or a minimum amount of free oxygen.

obligate parasite. An organism which is not capable of free existence.

obligate saprophyte. An organism which can live on dead organic matter exclusively.

occipital bone. A median unpaired bone of the vertebrate skull located at the posterior end of its dorsal wall.

occipital condyle. A bony knob at the back of the skull which articulates with the first vertebra.

occipital lobe. A lobe of the brain which is in the lower back region of the cerebrum.

occiput. (1) The back of the head or skull of vertebrates; (2) a plate of exoskeleton between the neck and the vertex of insects.

occlusion. (1) A warm front surrounded by a cold front and lifted off the earth's surface; (2) the absorption and retention of a gas or liquid by a solid, especially by a metal; (3) the blocking of an opening in a plant or animal.

occultation. The cutting off of the light of one celestial body by another; example, a star becoming invisible because of the passage of the moon between it and the observer.

ocean current. A more rapidly moving surface water of the ocean than the body of water; about 6 miles per hour.

oceanography. A study of oceans, their shorelines, tides, and currents.

ocellus. (1) A simple eye or eye spot in invertebrates; (2) a discolored large cell in a leaf.

ochre. A yellow clay; a natural pigment.

octane. C_8H_{18}; a hydrocarbon of the paraffin series which occurs in petroleum.

octane rating. Octane number; antiknock value; a measure of the knocking tendency of gasoline obtained by comparison with a test fuel of a rating of 100.

octant. An angle-measuring instrument similar to the sextant.

octant division. The division of an embryo cell into eight cells.

octet. A stable symmetrical electron shell containing four electron pairs.

octode. An eight-electrode vacuum tube, which contains an anode, a cathode, a control electrode, and five additional electrodes that are ordinarily grids.

octopod. Having eight feet, tentacles, or arms.

Octopoda. Mollusks having a head foot divided into eight tentacles, with suckers to hold the prey; example, octopus.

octuple circuit. A telephone system consisting of two equal quadruples in parallel, but with their corresponding charges reversed.

ocular. (1) Referring or belonging to the eye; (2) an eyepiece; the lens in an optical instrument which is closest to the user's eye.

ocular micrometer. A micrometer used with a telescope or microscope for measuring minute distances.

oculomotor. Causing eye movement.

oculomotor nerve. The third cranial nerve of vertebrates which moves the eye muscles.

odd-even nuclei. Nuclei which contain an odd number of protons and an even number of neutrons.

odd-odd nuclei. Nuclei which contain an odd number of protons and an odd number of neutrons.

Odonata. Insects with four membranous net-veined wings of about the same size, two compound eyes, and biting mouth parts; the larvae are aquatic; they have incomplete metamorphosis; example, dragonflies.

odontoblast. A cell in the pulp cavity of a vertebrate tooth which forms dentine.

Oedogonium. Chainlike freshwater algae that produce spores in the spring but sperms and eggs in autumn.

oenocyte. A large cell found in clusters associated with the trachea and fat bodies of insects.

oersted. The metric unit of magnetic field strength or magnetic intensity.

oesophageal glands. Esophageal glands; branching glands in the walls of the esophagus which secrete a fluid to lubricate the food.

oesophagus. Esophagus; a narrow portion of the alimentary tract behind the mouth which leads to the stomach.

oestrogen. Estrogen; the female sex hormone which sensitizes the lining of the uterus.

oestrus cycle. The build-up and drop in hormone concentration, ripening of follicles, release of eggs, and changes in the uterus.

ohm. A unit of electrical resistance; the resistance through which a potential difference of one volt can produce a current of one ampère.

ohm-centimeter. A unit of electric resistivity.

ohmmeter. An instrument for measuring ohms directly.

Ohm's law. The intensity of a steady current is directly proportional to the electromotive force and inversely proportional to the resistance of the circuit.

oil. A combustible substance, characteristically liquid or liquefiable on warming, that is soluble in ether, but not in water.

oil of bitter almonds. An essential oil obtained from bitter almonds; its chief ingredient is benzaldehyde; C_6H_5CHO; used as a flavor, in cosmetics.

oil of vitriol. Concentrated sulfuric acid, H_2SO_4.

oil of wintergreen. Methyl salicylate, $CH_3COOC_6H_4OH$; used as a flavor, in medicine.

oil shale. A laminated sedimentary rock containing bituminous material which will yield mineral oils by distillation.

oil-immersion objective. Immersion objective; a microscope objective which has a drop of oil of the same refractive index as that of glass between its front lens and the cover glass.

Old Stone Age. Paleolithic age; the first period in the history of civilization which is characterized by the use of crude stone implements; it ended about 10,000 years ago.

oleates. Salts and ester of oleic acid.

olecranon process. A bony process on the ulna of mammals which extends beyond the elbow joint; it is used for attaching muscles which straighten the forelimb.

olefin. Alkene; an unsaturated hydrocarbon of the series C_nH_{2n}; example, ethylene, $CH_2:CH_2$.

oleic acid. $C_{17}H_{33}COOH$; an unsaturated organic acid; it occurs in the form of glycerides in many fats and oils; used in making soap, waterproofing textiles, paint driers, etc.

oleorefractometer. An instrument for comparing the refractive indices of liquids, especially oils, with that of a standard liquid.

olfactory. Pertaining to the sense of smell.

olfactory lobe. A part of the vertebrate brain in which the olfactory nerves terminate and which receives their messages.

olfactory nerve. A nerve of the sense of smell that leads from the nose to the brain.

olfactory receptors. Receptors located in the mucous membrane of the upper part of the nose, which are stimulated by odors.

Oligocene period. A Cenozoic era; it began about 35 million years ago; it is characterized by elephants, mammals, and primates.

Oligochaeta. A class of Annelida; some live in fresh water, others are terrestrial; they are hermaphrodites with internal fertilization; example, earthworms.

olivenite. A complex basic arsenate of copper; it is a rare mineral.

olivine. A magnesium and iron orthosilicate; a rhombic mineral; the transparent green variety is used as a gem; other varieties serve as refractories.

ommatidium. An element of the compound eye of insects.

omnirange. Omnidirectional range; visual-aural range (VAR); a radio navigational system by which an aircraft determines its position and course by reference to radio beams received from many stations.

omnivorous. (1) Eating both plants and animals; (2) para-

sitic on many types of host.

onchosphere. The larva of tapeworm which has six hooks; it develops into a bladder worm or another intermediate stage.

ondoscope. An electric wave detector consisting of a glow-discharge tube.

ontogeny. The entire developmental history of an organism.

Onychophora. Protracheata; a small group of terrestrial Arthropoda; its members are wormlike with many short unjointed legs; they are found in Africa and Australia.

oocyst. An encysted oospore.

oocyte. A cell which undergoes meiosis to form an ovum.

ooecium. A brood pouch in which the embryo develops in Bryozoa and is nourished by specialized cells in the walls of the pouch.

oogamy. The fertilization of a large, nonmotile egg by a small male gamete.

oogenesis. A maturation process by which the ovaries produce female cells.

oogonium. A female gametangium, or egg-bearing organ, characteristic of the thallophyte.

oolith. A rounded, sandlike calcium carbonate particle; a common constituent of limestone.

Oomycetes. Fungi which reproduce sexually by antheridia and oogonia, forming oospores.

oosphere. A large, spherical nonmotile unfertilized female gamete.

oospore. The result of the fertilization of an egg cell by a sperm cell in a plant.

ootheca. An egg case of some mollusks and insects.

ootid. An egg cell that underwent meiosis.

ootype. (1) The part of the oviduct in which the egg shell is secreted; (2) a region of the genital passages of flatworms at the junction of the oviducts and vitelline ducts into which the shell glands open.

ooze. Muds on the ocean bottom of abysmal depths, which are composed of calcareous and silicified shells of plankton.

opacimeter. An instrument for measuring the opacity of substances.

opalescent. Reflecting irridescent light.

opaque. Light-absorbing.

open circuit. A circuit which is not electrically complete and in which there is no current.

open system. A system allowing interchange of heat and matter with its surroundings.

open-chain compounds. Aliphatic compounds; organic compounds whose atoms do not form a ring.

open-hearth furnace. A large reverbatory furnace in which

steel is made in a shallow pool.

open-hearth process. A process for making steel from pig iron and scrap, by melting and oxidizing in a large, shallow furnace.

operculum. (1) A flap covering an opening; (2) an enlarged branch of a tentacle in some marine Annelida; (3) the margin of zooecium of Bryozoa; (4) a horny plate which closes the aperture of the shells of some mollusks; (5) the cover of external apertures of the genital ducts of scorpions; (6) the gill covering of fish; (7) the cap of the capsule of mosses.

Ophidia. Limbless snakes with wide jaws and immovable eyelids; they have no eardrum.

Ophiuroidea. A class of Echinodermata; they are star-shaped, long arms radiating from the central disk; they easily break up by autotomy; example, brittle stars.

ophthalmoscope. An instrument used for eye examination by light reflected from a mirror.

opposite. Referring to a bud or leaf arrangement in which there are two buds or two leaves at a node facing each other.

opposition. (1) A phase difference of one-half cycle; (2) the position of a planet or of the moon in line with the earth and the sun.

opsonic index. The phagocytic power of the blood of an individual against any particular microorganism as compared with the phagocytic power of a normal blood.

opsonin. An antibody in the blood which makes microorganisms or red blood cells more phagocytic.

optic. Optical; pertaining to the eye or to sight.

optic axis. A line through a doubly refracting crystal along which no double refraction occurs.

optic lobes. In lower vertebrates, two distinct portions of the brain behind the cerebrum, which contain the centers of sight; in mammals, the optic lobes are small and inconspicuous.

optic nerve. A nerve that conducts messages of sight from the eye to the brain.

optical aberration. A defect of a lens or mirror which makes light rays coming from one point converge in different foci or deviate from a single focus.

optical activity. Optical rotation; the ability of some substances and their solutions to rotate the plane of vibration of polarized light; it is attributed to asymmetrical molecular structure.

optical altimeter. An altimeter whose indications depend on the manipulation of an optical

system.

optical anomaly. (1) The behavior of certain organic compounds, such as those containing conjugated double bonds, for which the observed values of molar refraction are not in accord with the calculated values; (2) an apparent contradiction between the optical properties and the crystal form of a mineral.

optical antipodes. Two compounds which are the same as to atoms and atomic linkages, but which differ in their structural formulas so that one is the mirror image of the other.

optical axis. Same as optic axis.

optical bench. A horizontal stand for mounting movable clamps designed to hold lenses, mirrors, and diffraction gratings, while performing various experiments.

optical center. The point in a lens through which the light rays pass without bending.

optical constants. A set of numerical values used to describe the optical properties of a substance; examples, refractive index, reflectivity, and absorption coefficient.

optical disk. A device for illustrating the fundamental laws of optics.

optical illusion. A visual perception which is different from the real character of the object perceived.

optical isomers. Two organic compounds containing an asymmetric carbon atom and differing in their optical activity.

optical lever. A lever equipped with a mirror and a fixed telescope and scale for measuring small lengths.

optical path. The path followed by the luminous energy through an optical system.

optical pyrometer. A device used for measuring high temperature by the comparison of the color brought about by intense heat with the color of a wire heated to a known temperature by means of an electric current.

optical recorder. A device which uses light to reproduce sound waves on film.

optical rotation. The rotation of the plane of polarized light to the right or left when passing through certain substances.

optically active. Capable of rotating the plane of polarized light.

optically void. Free from suspended solids and thus not exhibiting the Tyndall effect.

optics. The study of light.

optics, geometric. The study of the formation of images by mirrors and lenses, without consideration of the physical aspects of light.

orbit. (1) A bony depression of the vertebrate skull in which the eye is seated; (2) the path which a celestial body follows in its motion through space under the effects of gravitation; (3) the path of an electron around the nucleus of an atom.

orbital. (1) Referring to an orbit; (2) same as orbit (3).

Orchidaceae. Highly developed monocotyledons having stamens and pistils joined with the floral axis; they are highly adapted to cross pollination and have over 7,000 species, usually with colorful, conspicuous flowers; many varieties flourish in tropical climates and are cultivated in greenhouses.

order. One of the main divisions of a botanical or zoological class.

ordinary ray. The one of the two components into which plane-polarized light is split when going through a doubly refracting crystal whose refractive index is constant for all angles of incidence.

Ordovician period. The middle period of the lower Paleozoic era which began about 430 million years ago; invertebrates were dominant, the first vertebrates, corals, and fresh-water fish emerged.

ore. A mineral from which a useful material, such as a metal, may be extracted; example, hematite, an iron ore.

ore dressing. A physical processing of ores to yield a concentrate of the mineral values for further treatment.

organ. A unified structure or a part of the body that functions as a whole; usually composed of more than one kind of tissue.

organ system. A group of organs that perform a definite function; example, digestive system.

organelle. A specialized cell organ; a protoplasmic cell inclusion in Protozoa which performs a definite function and is comparable to an organ of multicellular animals; example, Golgi apparatus.

organic. (1) A part of a living organism or produced by a living organism; (2) said of a compound of carbon.

organic acid. A carbon compound that contains one or more carboxyl (COOH) groups; example, acetic acid, CH_3COOH.

organic ash. The mineral matter left after the complete burning of plant or animal substances.

organic chemistry. The study of carbon and its compounds.

organic compounds. Chemical compounds which contain carbon and hydrogen, and often oxygen, nitrogen, and other elements.

organic halides. Hydrocarbons whose hydrogen atoms, all or in part, are substituted by halogen atoms; example, carbon tetrachloride, CCl_4.

organic synthesis. The formation of organic compounds by a chemical reaction between simpler compounds or between chemical elements.

organism. A living plant or animal.

organization. The association of specialized parts in an organism for the coordinated performance of various functions for the welfare of the entire individual.

organizer. A part in an embryo that has an organizing influence on other parts.

organogenesis. Organ differentiation during embryonic development.

organogeny. The study of the formation of specialized tissues and organ systems during embryonic development.

organometallic compound. A compound in which one or more organic radicals are attached to a metallic atom; example, a Grignard reagent, such as methyl magnesium chloride, CH_3MgCl.

organosol. A suspensoid in which an organic liquid is the dispersing medium.

orientation. (1) The change in the position of an organ relative to the whole organism; (2) locomotion due to a stimulus; (3) directional arrangement of atoms, groups, or molecules in a crystal, or atoms or groups in the molecules of a compound.

orientation effect. A means of determining the attractive forces between molecules, or a component of such forces, from the interaction of molecular dipoles which is due to their relative orientation.

oriented adsorption. The arrangement of the adsorbed molecules in a definite pattern on the surface of the adsorbent.

orifice. (1) A small opening into a cavity; (2) an opening through which a fluid can be discharged.

orifice meter. A diaphragm inserted into a pipe in which a fluid is flowing; the difference in pressure on the two sides of the diaphragm is a measure of the speed of flow.

origin. (1) That part of a muscle which remains relatively fixed during contraction of the muscle; (2) the zero line in a band spectrum; (3) the point of intersection of two axes.

Orion. The most impressive of the constellations; Betelgeuse is one of its stars.

Ornithischia. A fossil order of herbivorous reptiles; they lived in the Mesozoic era.

ornithologist. A scientist who is engaged in the study of birds.

ornithology. The study of birds.

ornithorhynchus. Duck-billed platypus; an oviparous small aquatic mammal living in Australia.

orogenesis. Mountain building by compression of accumulated sediment, thus forming faults and folds.

orographic rain. A precipitation caused by the impact of humid air against hill and mountain sides.

orometer. An aneroid barometer which records elevation above sea level.

orthicon. An improved iconoscope; a television pickup in which electrons of low impact velocity are used for scanning.

orthochromatic film. A photographic film sensitive to all colors but red, which gives a more accurate representation of visual luminosities than an ordinary film.

orthoclase. Natural potassium aluminum silicate, $K_2O \cdot Al_2O_3 \cdot 6SiO_2$; a mineral constituent of granite.

orthogenesis. A theory of organic evolution which assumes the occurrence of progressive changes in living organisms along definite lines of development under the effect of environment.

orthographic projection. A projection in which the projecting lines are perpendicular to the plane of projection.

Orthoptera. Insects whose outer wings meet in a straight line in the middle of the back; they have biting mouth parts and are herbivorous or carnivorous; examples, crickets and grasshoppers.

orthorhombic system. Crystals that have three mutually rectangular axes, each different in length; examples, baryte and topaz.

orthoscopic. Free from optical distortion.

orthotomic. Said of a system of light rays which can all be cut at right angles by a suitable surface.

orthotropous. (1) Said of a straight ovule, in which the funicle is in a straight line with the micropyle, pointing away from the placenta; (2) said of organs which respond to a certain stimulus by a definite positive or negative tropism.

Os. Chemical symbol of osmium.

oscillating current. Alternating current; a high-frequency current.

oscillation. (1) The to and fro motions of a pendulum; (2) the back and forth motions of electrons in a circuit.

oscillation, forced. An alternating current whose frequency is dependent on an external periodic force.

oscillation, free. (1) An alternating current whose frequency depends solely on the constants of the circuit in which it is flowing; (2) an oscillatory motion caused by displacement from an equilibrium position.

oscillator. A device or circuit that emits sonic, supersonic, or electromagnetic waves.

oscillator, coherent. An oscillator which has a fixed phase relationship to some other oscillator.

oscillator, crystal. A stable-frequency electron-tube oscillator in which a piezoelectric crystal replaces one of the resonant circuits.

Oscillatoria. Blue-green algae forming long vibrating filaments.

oscillograph. An apparatus for recording electrical oscillations.

oscilloscope. A device in which a controlled beam of electrons from a cathode-ray tube traces a wave form on a fluorescent screen.

osculum. An opening of the central cavity of sponges through which water is evacuated.

osmeterium. A scent gland in some insects.

osmium. A hard, brittle, inert metal of the platinum group; the heaviest element; chemical symbol Os; atomic number 76; used in alloying and as a catalyst.

osmium tetroxide. OsO_4; yellow crystals; used as a stain in microscopy.

osmometer. An instrument for the measurement of osmotic pressure.

osmoregulation. The control of osmotic pressure.

osmosis. The diffusion of solvent molecules through a semipermeable membrane placed between two solutions of different concentration to the side of higher concentration until the two concentrations are equalized.

osmotic pressure. A pressure exerted by a solute as a result of the diffusion of its molecules through a membrane; it is measured by the counterpressure which will just prevent osmosis.

osphradium. A sensory organ of some mollusks.

osseous. Bony or bonelike.

ossicle. (1) A calcareous skeletal plate of Echinodermata; (2) a small bone, such as those in the middle ear.

ossification. The formation of a bone or the conversion of a tissue into bone or a bonelike substance.

Osteichthyes. Bony fish; example, lungfish.

osteoblast. A bone-forming cell.

osteoclast. A multinucleate cell which causes the breakdown of the calcified intercellular substance of bone.

osteocyte. A bone cell.

osteology. The study of the skeletal system.

ostiole. A pore in the fruit body of certain fungi and in conceptacles of brown algae through which spores and gametes are discharged.

ostium. The terminal opening or mouth of an animal duct or an opening in a body wall.

Ostwald process. The catalytic oxidation of ammonia to nitric acid.

otic. Concerning the ear or the auditory capsule.

otocyst. The auditory organ of some invertebrates.

otolith. A calcareous particle in the inner ear of vertebrates and in the otocyst of invertebrates.

Otto cycle. The four-stroke cycle in an internal-combustion engine: (1) suction; (2) compression; (3) expansion; (4) exhaust.

ounce. An English unit of weight; one twelfth of a pound; 28.35 grams.

outbreeding. Exogamy; a crossing of organisms of different parental stock.

outcrop. An exposed part of a bedrock.

outer ear. External ear; it consists of the funnel-shaped pinna and the external auditory canal, a membrane-lined tube connected to the pinna and ending in the ear drum.

outgassing. The removal of adsorbed gases by heating; used in the manufacture of vacuum tubes.

output. The useful energy obtained from a machine.

output impedance. The impedance presented by the transducer to the load.

output meter. An instrument for measuring the output of audio-amplifiers.

output transformer. A small transformer connected between the power tube and the speaker.

outwash plains. Stratified deposits formed by streams issuing from continental glaciers; nearly level areas; example, the southern part of Long Island.

oval window. An opening in the wall separating the inner ear from the middle ear, into which the stirrup bone fits.

ovarian follicle. The developing ovum surrounded by modified cells of the ovary.

ovary. (1) The female sex organ of animals which produces egg cells, or ova; (2) the enlarged base of the pistil of a flower which contains the ovules.

overcultivation. The cultivation of too much land rather than

increasing yields from land already cultivated.

overgrowth. The growth of a crystal of one substance over the surface of a crystal of another substance.

overheating. In the heat treatment of metals, heating above the temperature which yields the correct grain size.

overlap. Younger geological strata burying older ones.

overload. A larger than normal amount of current flowing through an electrical device.

overpotential. Overvoltage; the difference between the potential at which a gas is liberated from an electrolyte and the potential of an electrode of the same gas in the same electrolyte.

overshot wheel. A water wheel which is turned by the weight of the water running over its top and filling buckets which cover its circumference.

overthrust. A low thrust or compressional fault frequently resulting in the translocation of a mass of rocks several miles.

overvoltage, bubble. The overvoltage associated with the visible evolution of gas; example, oxygen bubbles at the anode.

oviduct. A small tube discharging the eggs from the ovary to the exterior.

oviparous. Egg-laying.

ovipositor. (1) Egg laying appendages of female insects consisting of three processes made of chitin; (2) an extension of the genital opening of some female fish.

ovogenesis. Same as oogenesis.

ovotestis. The genital organ of some hermaphrodite animals, such as the snail, which produces both ova and spermatozoa.

ovoviviparous. Producing eggs which hatch in the uterus of the mother; the nourishment for the development of the young is contained in the egg.

ovulation. The release of eggs from the ovary.

ovule. The megasporangium of a seed plant.

ovum (plural ova). A nonmotile female gamete.

oxalate. A salt of oxalic acid.

oxalic acid. $(COOH)_2 \cdot 2H_2O$; a white, crystalline, poisonous solid; it occurs in wood sorrel and other plants; used in dyeing, bleaching, ink manufacture, removing ink stains, and metal polishes.

oxbow lake. A crescent-shaped lake formed by a river breaking through the narrow neck of its oxbow bend.

oxidant. Same as oxidizing agent.

oxidase. An enzyme that catalizes, and thus promotes, oxidation in plant and animal cells.

oxidation. (1) The combination

of a substance with oxygen; examples, the burning of coal, $C + O_2 = CO_2$; the rusting of iron, $2Fe + 3O = Fe_2O_3$; (2) a reaction in which there is a loss of electrons; example, the change of a ferrous ion to a ferric ion, $Fe^{++} - e \rightarrow Fe^{+++}$

oxidation-reduction reaction. Any chemical reaction in which there is a partial or complete transfer of electrons.

oxide. A compound of oxygen with another element.

oxidizing agent. (1) A substance that supplies the oxygen necessary to the oxidation of another substance; example, hydrogen peroxide, H_2O_2; (2) a substance that loses electrons easily in a chemical reaction; example, chlorine gas, Cl_2.

oximes. Compounds containing an =NOH group and obtained by condensation of an aqueous or alcoholic solution of an aldehyde or ketone with hydroxylamine.

oxyacetylene burner. A burner which burns oxygenated acetylene to give a very-high-temperature flame.

oxygen. A colorless gas which constitutes one fifth of the atmosphere; chemical symbol O; atomic number 8; it supports combustion and is indispensable for respiration.

oxygen point. The equilibrium temperature between liquid and gaseous oxygen at 760 mm pressure.

oxygenating plants. Plants that grow completely under water and oxygenate water.

oxygenation. Supplying the blood with oxygen from the lungs.

oxygen-carbon dioxide cycle. The cycle in which plants take in carbon dioxide and give off oxygen in photosynthesis and animals take in oxygen and give off carbon dioxide in respiration.

oxyhemoglobin. A loose combination of oxygen with hemoglobin.

oxy-hydrogen blowpipe. A welding device which produces a high-temperature flame by burning a mixture of hydrogen and oxygen.

oxytocin. A hormone secreted by the posterior lobe of the pituitary which produces strong contraction of the uterine muscle.

oz. Abbreviation for ounce.

ozokerite. Mineral wax; a brownish or grayish natural mixture of solid hydrocarbons, resembling paraffin wax; used as a substitute for other waxes.

ozone. An allotropic form of oxygen; O_3; it is produced by silent electric discharges in air or oxygen or by ultraviolet rays; it is a powerful oxidizing agent.

ozonosphere. An ozone-rich layer of atmosphere above the stratosphere.

P

P. Chemical symbol for phosphorus.

Pa. Chemical symbol for protactinium.

pachymeter. An instrument for measuring thickness.

pachytene. A stage of meiosis in which the condensation of chromosomes begins.

package reactor. A relatively small, portable nuclear reactor.

packing, nuclear. The concentration of particles within the nucleus of an atom.

paedogamy. An autogamy in which both the nucleus and cytoplasm of Protozoa divide and reunite after the nuclear transformation is completed.

paedogenesis. (1) A reproduction by immature individuals or larvae; (2) much too early flowering of a plant.

paint. A colloidal dispersion of a pigment in a drying oil containing also thinners and driers; used as a protective and/or decorative surface coating.

pair production. The conversion of a photon into an electron and a positron when it crosses a strong electric field, usually that surrounding a nucleus or an electron.

pairing of chromosomes. Synapsis; syndesis; side-by-side association of homologous chromosomes in meiosis.

palate. (1) The roof of the mouth; a partition between the oral cavity and the nasal passages; (2) the projecting lower lip of a two-lipped corolla which closes its opening.

palea. A small, usually thin, bract or scale borne on the axis of a grass flower, just above the lemma.

paleobotany. The history of plant life as revealed by a study of fossil remains.

Paleocene. A Cenozoic era; it began about 55 million years ago and was characterized by flowering plants and the first primates.

paleochronology. A timetable of geological periods correlated with the succession of animal forms that have existed in the past, as determined by the study of fossil remains.

paleoclimatology. The study of climates during prehistoric periods as indicated by rocks and fossils.

Paleolithic era. Old Stone Age; pointed tools made of horn, bone, and ivory, animal pits and traps, and cave art are characteristic of this era, which embraces one to one and a half million years.

paleontology. The science which deals with the ancient life on earth as revealed by fossils, impressions, and other remains found in the strata of the earth's surface.

Paleozoic. The fourth era of the earth's history, in which animals first left abundant fossils; it began after the Proterozoic era and lasted about 325 million years; the first land plants and land-dwelling animals, primitive fish, woody plants, amphibians, insects, and reptiles appeared.

palisade layer. A layer of elongated, compactly arranged cells just beneath the upper epidermis of a leaf; it contains chloroplasts and participates in photosynthesis.

palladium. A metal of the platinum family; chemical symbol Pd; atomic number 46; used in alloying.

pallium. (1) The entire cortex of the cerebrum with its underlying white substance; (2) the mantle of mollusks and birds.

palm glass. A device for demonstrating the increase in vapor pressure with temperature.

palmate feet. Webbed feet.

palmate veining. Several equally prominent veins of a leaf which begin at the base of the leaf and branch out in a fanlike manner; example, linden.

palmitates. Metallic salts, or soaps, and esters of palmitic acid.

palmitic acid. $C_{15}H_{31}COOH$; a fatty acid; its glycerides occur in vegetable oils and fats.

palp. Palpus; a small fingerlike structure on the side of the lower lip of insects which aids in guiding food into the mouth.

palynology. The study of pollen grains and plant spores.

panchromatic. Sensitive to all colors.

pancreas. A large gland between the stomach and the first fold of the small intestine of vertebrates, which secretes digestive juice into the small intestine.

pancreatic duct. Canal of Wirsung; a tube which carries pancreatic fluid to the small intestine.

pancreatic enzymes. Amylopsin, erepsin, invertase, lactase, maltase, rennin, steapsin, and trypsin.

pancreatic juice. A secretion of the pancreas containing powerful enzymes which digest starch, protein, and fats.

pancreatin. A pancreas extract which contains digestive enzymes.

panicle. A complex branched inflorescence.

pantograph. (1) An instrument for copying drawings on an enlarged or reduced scale; (2) a sliding current collector.

pantothenic acid. A vitamin of the B complex; a growth stimulating vitamin; used as a drug in anemia.

papain. An enzyme, extracted from the fruit and leaves of the papaya tree, which splits proteins in neutral solution; used as a digestive aid.

paper condenser. A condenser having a dielectric of impregnated paper.

papilla. (1) A tiny projection on the surface of the tongue, which contains taste buds; (2) a vascular tissue nourishing the root of a hair, feather, or growing tooth; (3) an epidermal plant cell with a tiny hairlike projection; it gives a velvetlike appearance to flowers.

pappus. (1) The tuft of down or hair on the fruits of certain plants for distribution by the wind; example, dandelion; (2) scales or bristles representing a reduced calyx in composite flowers.

papulae. Small outer projections from the body wall of some marine animals, used for respiration; example, papulae of the starfish.

parabasal body. A structure associated with the nucleus of some of the flagellate Protozoa.

parabolic mirror. A mirror which yields an aberration-free point focus for a beam of light incident parallel to its axis; it consists of a curved reflector whose section is a parabola.

parabolic velocity. The speed which a particle at any point in the field of a gravitational-attraction center must have in order to attain a parabolic orbit of motion.

parachor. The actual molecular volume of a substance when its surface tension is of unit value.

paracrystalline state. The arrangement of the molecules of a substance as it approaches the crystallization point; an incipient crystallization.

paraffin oil. Kerosene; a mixture of hydrocarbons obtained in the distillation of petroleum at 150° to 300°C; used as a fuel and lamp oil.

paraffin sections. Sections of organic tissues cut by a microtome after embedding in paraffin wax; used for microscopic studies.

paraffin series. Alkanes; saturated aliphatic hydrocarbons of the general formula C_nH_{2n+2}.

paraffin wax. A white, translucent solid melting to a colorless liquid; it consists of refined petroleum hydrocarbons; used for candles, waxed paper, cosmetics, polishes.

paraform. Paraformaldehyde; a solid polymer of formaldehyde; used for fumigation.

paragaster. The large central cav-ity of sponges; it is not a digestive cavity, but water passes into it through the canal system of the body wall and flows out through the osculum.

paragenesis. (1) The order of development of the minerals in an igneous or metamorphic rock; (2) the formation of minerals in contact with and affecting each other.

paragnatha. (1) Two zones into which the lower lip of some Crustacea is divided; (2) lobes or appendages borne by the hypopharynx of the insect mouth.

parallax. (1) the difference in the direction of a planet or satellite as seen by an observer on the surface of the earth, and when observed from the earth's center; (2) a shift in the apparent position of a body, due to a change in the position of the observer.

parallel. A method of connecting electrical equipment so that all positive electrodes or terminals are connected to one conductor and all negative electrodes or terminals to another conductor.

parallel circuits. Two circuits connected in parallel, that is, in such a manner that the current is divided between them.

parallel forces. Forces acting in the same or opposite directions but along parallel lines.

parallel veining. Parallel leaf veins running side by side with no conspicuous branches; example, monocotyledons.

parallelepiped. Parallelepipedon; a prism with parallelograms as faces.

parallelism. The development of unrelated plants following similar lines.

parallelogram of forces. A diagrammatic representation of nonparallel or concurrent forces, following the rule that if two forces acting at a point are represented as two adjacent sides of a parallelogram their resultant will be the diagonal going through the common point.

parallels. The east and west lines of latitude that run parallel to the equator, which is taken as the starting point from which the parallels are numbered consecutively from 0 to 90° toward either pole.

paramagnetic substances. Substances that have a magnetic permeability greater than unity.

paramecium. Slipper-shaped Protozoa; they have a funnellike mouth cavity and use cilia for locomotion and getting food.

parameter. The intercept of a plane with the axes of a crystal; the position of the plane is determined by the ratio of its intercepts.

paramorphism. The ability of a mineral to change its molecu-lar structure without a chemical change.

paraphysis. A slender, multicellular hair; sterile branches of hyphae associated with asci in the fruiting body of certain fungi.

parapodium. A lobed appendage projecting from the lateral body wall in some of the segmented worms; it is used for locomotion.

parasite. (1) An organism that lives at the expense of another organism; (2) a current in a circuit due to some unintentional cause, such as inequalities of temperature or of composition.

parasite drag. A drag of an aircraft other than the induced drag of the wings.

parasitic capture. The absorption of a neutron which does not result in fission or in the production of a desired element.

parasitism. An association of two organisms which is to the disadvantage of one and to the advantage of the other; the first is called a host and the second, a parasite.

parasitology. The study of parasites.

parasphenoid. A dermal bone supporting the roof of the mouth in fish and amphibians.

parasympathetic system. A part of the autonomic nervous system of vertebrates; it supplies the smooth muscles and the glands.

parathormone. A secretion of the parathyroid glands which controls the calcium concentration in the blood.

parathyroid glands. A pair of ductless glands located in each lobe of the thyroid; they regulate the concentration of calcium in the blood.

paratonic. Said of plant movements induced by external stimuli.

paraxial. Said of light rays traversing an optical system nearly parallel to the axis.

Parazoa. Multicellular animals which have only two layers of tissue, no nervous system, and no enteric cavity; example, Porifera, that is, sponges.

parenchyma. (1) A plant tissue that consists of thin-walled cellulosic cells with large vacuoles; it may or may not have chloroplasts; (2) a soft cellular animal tissue whose spaces are filled with a fluid or a gelatinous mass.

parent. (1) The first or primordial element of a radioactive series; (2) a radioactive element whose disintegration yields another radioactive element.

parfocal. Having the lower focal points all in the same plane; a property of sets of eyepieces which are so mounted that they may be interchanged without varying the focus of the optical instrument in which they are used.

parhelion. One of the bright, colored spots which appear in cold weather on either side of and above and below the sun; they are due to the refraction of the sunlight by minute crystals of ice suspended in the air.

parietal. (1) Attached to or located near a plant wall; (2) one of the pair of bones which form the sides and roof of the vertebrate skull between the auditory capsules.

parietal bones. Same as parietal (2).

parietal lobe. The middle portion of each cerebral hemisphere.

parietal placentation. The attachment of the placenta to the united edges of carpel leaves.

parity. A concept of physics concerned with the mirror image of objects; the laws of physics are said to be independent of left-hand or right-hand properties, but this concept has been modified by the discovery that neutrinos and mesons possess handedness as an intrinsic property.

Parkes process. The separation of gold and silver from impure lead by melting with a small amount of zinc and then cooling; most of the silver and gold will be in the crust forming on the surface of the molten metal.

Parkinje phenomenon. When illumination is reduced to the level of twilight vision, the brightness produced by the longer-wave stimuli, such as red and orange, decreases more rapidly than the brightness produced by the shorter-wave stimuli, such as blue or violet.

parotid. One of the pair of salivary glands near the ear of mammals.

parsec. A unit used for measuring the distance of celestial bodies; 206,000 astronomical units; 3.26 light years.

parthenocarpic. Said of fruits that are seedless.

parthenocarpy. The development of fruit without fertilization.

parthenogenesis. A form of reproduction where a female sex cell develops into a new organism without fertilization; example, bees.

parthenogonidium. A cell that produces a miniature colony by asexual methods of multiplication; example, volvox.

partial eclipse. The incomplete hiding or darkening of one heavenly body by another; example, only part of the sun's disk is covered by the moon's shadow.

partial node. A region in a stationary wave system, similar to a node, but at which the amplitude is a minimum without being reduced to zero.

partial parasite. A plant that secures some of the nutrients it needs from a host, but is also capable of some photosynthesis.

partial pressures, Dalton's law of. The total pressure of a mixture of two or more gases or vapors is equal to the sum of the pressures that each component would exert if it were present alone and occupied the same volume as the whole mixture.

partial vacuum. A space within which the pressure is lower than that of the surrounding air.

particle accelerator. A device in which atomic particles are speeded up by the application of electric and magnetic fields; examples, cyclotron and cosmotron.

partition coefficient. Distribution ratio; the ratio of the equilibrium concentrations of a solute in two liquid phases.

Pascal's law. A force applied to any area of a confined fluid is transmitted with equal intensity to every other equal area of the fluid.

Paschen series. A series of lines in the infrared region of the emission spectrum of atomic hydrogen.

Paschen's law. The breakdown voltage for a pair of parallel electrodes in a gas at constant temperature is a function only of the product of the gas pressure and the distance between the electrodes.

pass. The lowest point of a divide.

passage cell. Unsuberized thin-walled root cells of endodermis in which fluids can diffuse in a transverse direction.

Passeriformes. The largest order of birds, mostly singing and perching birds; examples, robin, blue jay, wren, sparrow.

passive metal. A metal which has a thin corrosion-resistant oxide film on its surface.

passive resistance. The resistance of a system in unstable equilibrium which cannot release energy and become stable until slightly disturbed.

passivity. A lower than normal activity of a metal after dipping into a solution of an oxidizing agent or after anodic polarization.

pasteurization. Sterilization of milk by heating at 145°F for 30 minutes.

patella. (1) The kneecap and elbow joint of man and the corresponding bones of other vertebrates; (2) a short segment of the jointed legs of spiders and related forms between the femur and tibia.

path-reversal principle. If light follows a given course through any optical system, it will, if reversed, traverse the same course in the opposite direc-

tion, so that a point and its real image are interchangeable.

paurometabolous. Having incomplete metamorphosis, the young being similar to the adult both in form and behavior.

paxilla. A thick process, bearing small spines at the end; a modified spine of a starfish.

payload. Any useful cargo in a missile; the term covers passengers, guidance and communication devices, and, in military rockets, the warhead.

Pb. Chemical symbol for lead.

Pd. Chemical symbol for palladium.

peak. (1) The highest point of a mountain range; (2) the highest value of a quantity.

pearlite. A microstructure of iron and steel.

peat. A partly decomposed vegetable matter found in marshy regions; an early stage of coal; used as a fuel after drying.

pectinate bodies. Comblike structures formed by some fungi.

pectins. A group of complex, high-molecular-weight, water-soluble polysaccharides; they occur in plants and fruits; they form gels in the presence of the proper concentrations of acid and sugar.

pectoral. Belonging, attached, or referring to the chest.

pectoral fin. The paired fins nearest the head of fish, corresponding to the front legs or arms of mammals.

pectoral girdle. A group of bones and cartilage connecting the forelimbs to the axial skeleton.

pedicel. A stalk or stem of the individual flowers of an inflorescence, or which bears a single fruit.

pedicellaria. Minute pincers on the surface of starfish; modified spines formed with two or more opposed jaws.

pedicle. The narrow band between the cephalothorax and the abdomen of spiders.

pedigree. The line of ancestors of a person or some other organism; a record of family history.

pedipalp. A sensory organ of spiders in the shape of appendages on the fourth segment.

peduncle. (1) The principal stalk of an inflorescence; (2) the stalks by which sessile animals are attached to supporting surfaces.

peg of hypocotyl. The hard portion on the top of the arch of the hypocotyl which protects it from injury and helps in piercing the soil; example, cucumbers.

pegmatite. A coarse-grained igneous rock occurring as a vein in a large intrusive rock body.

Peking man. A primitive man superior to Java man but still with apelike features; recon-

structed from fourteen fragmentary skulls and skeletons found in China.

pelagic. (1) Inhabiting the open sea; (2) said of sediment accumulated under deep water.

Pelecypoda. Clams, oysters, and other mollusks with two externally similar shells.

Pélé's hair. Natural glass fibers consisting of congealed liquid lava blown out of volcanoes.

pelite. Fine-grained volcanic ash or rock particles.

pellicle. (1) A nonliving elastic membrane secreted by the protoplasm; (2) a thin membranous film on the surface of a liquid formed as a result of a bacterial growth; (3) a thin dry film of photographic emulsion.

Peltier coefficient. The quantity of heat developed or absorbed per second per ampere of current at a given thermojunction due to the Peltier effect.

Peltier effect. When an electric current flows across the junction between two different metals, a quantity of heat is evolved or absorbed, which is proportional to the total charge crossing the junction and depends on the direction of the current.

Pelton water wheel. An impulse turbine in which a stream of water is directed from a nozzle at a high speed against cuplike blades attached to the circumference of a wheel.

pelvic. Having to do with the pelvis or bones of the skeleton to which the hind legs are attached.

pelvic fins. The paired fins nearest the tail of fish, corresponding to the hind legs of terrestrial animals.

pelvic girdle. The part of the skeleton to which the bones of the hind limbs are attached.

pelvis. (1) A cavity in the vertebrate skeleton formed by the pelvic arch, the sacrum, and some vertebrae; (2) the dilated superior end of the ureter; (3) the pelvic girdle which consists of two bones attached to the sacrum in the human adult and of the ilium, ischium, and pubis in the embryo.

pencil of light. A narrow beam of rays proceeding from a point toward a point with the minimum of convergence or divergence.

pendulum. A body suspended so that it can swing to and fro about a horizontal axis.

peneplane. A plain formed by the erosion of a plateau or mountain down to almost base level.

penetrance. The power of a gene to assert itself; example, the penetrance is complete if a dominant gene is effective in all cases and a recessive gene is always effective when it is homozygous.

penetrance coefficient. A measure of the tendency of a liquid to penetrate a given solid which it wets; it is defined as half the product of the surface tension and the fluidity coefficient.

penetrating agent. A substance that promotes the penetration of a liquid into the pores of a solid.

penetration. The passage of particles or radiation through solids.

penetrometer. (1) An instrument for testing the hardness of plastic solids; (2) an instrument for indicating the quality or hardness of x-rays.

Penicillium. A green or blue mold; a fungus that secretes pencillin.

penis. A projecting, protrusible, or erectile organ of the male animal, used in the act of copulation to introduce the seminal fluid into the genital passages of the female.

Pennsylvanian period. Paleozoic era; it began about 260 million years ago; trees and scale ferns were abundant; insects were numerous and large; the first reptiles appeared.

pennyweight. One twentieth of a Troy ounce; 24 grains; about 1.56 grams.

penta prism. A five-sided optical prism, of which one angle is 90° and the other four are 112° 30′; a ray entering at one of the faces adjacent to the 90° edge emerges from the other, after two internal reflections, at right angles to its original direction.

pentadactyl appendage. The fundamental terrestrial vertebrate limb, from which all the specialized appendages of animals above the fishes have been derived; two pairs of vertebrate limbs, pectoral and pelvic, similar in structure and each pair attached to the girdle of the corresponding name.

pentane. C_5H_{12}; the fifth member of the paraffin series; a colorless flammable liquid.

pentane candle. International candle; a unit of light intensity.

pentatron. A common-cathode double triode in a single envelope.

pentode. An electron tube containing a filament, a plate, and three grids.

pentose. A monosaccharide sugar with five carbon and five oxygen atoms; it is found in nucleic acids and plant polysaccharides.

penumbra. The space of partial illumination, or partial shadow, between the umbra, or perfect shadow, and the full light.

pepsin. An enzyme of the gastric juice which digests proteins.

peptidase. An enzyme decomposing peptones or peptides by attacking terminal peptide linkages and splitting off amino acids.

peptide. A combination of two or more amino acids joined by peptide linkages.

peptization. Preparing colloidal suspensions by the addition of a substance which reduces the suspended particles to colloidal dimensions; making a sol from a gel.

peptizing agent. A substance which, when added to a suspension, causes peptization.

peptone. A water-soluble product of protein hydrolysis.

percentage composition. The percentage of each element in a compound.

perched rock. A boulder found on a mountain top whose structure differs from that of the bedrock because it was deposited there by glaciers or erosion.

perchlorates. Salts of perchloric acid, $HClO_4$; they are more stable than the corresponding chlorates.

percrystallization. The crystallization of a dissolved substance from a solution during or after dialysis.

pereiopods. The walking legs of Crustacea.

perennation. The survival of plants from year to year through vegetative means.

perennials. Plants which live more than two years, producing seeds each year, but sprouting again year after year from the old roots or stems.

perfect flower. A flower having both stamens and pistils; a hermaphrodite.

perfect fluid. An ideal fluid which has no viscosity.

perfect gas. An ideal gas which obeys the gas laws exactly.

perfusion. Forcing fluid into an animal organ or tissue through the blood vessels; example, perfusion of the liver with salt solution.

perianth. The petals and sepals of a flower taken together.

pericardial cavity. Same as pericardium.

pericardial sinus. Same as pericardium.

pericardium. (1) The cavity surrounding the heart of invertebrates; (2) the membranous sac containing the heart of vertebrates.

pericarp. The fruit wall that developed from the ovary wall.

perichaetium. The whorl of leaves surrounding the sex organs of mosses.

periclase. A natural magnesium oxide, MgO; a cubic mineral.

periclinal. Said of the plane of division of plant cells which is running parallel to the surface of a plant part.

pericycle. (1) A layer of thin-walled cells lying at the outer edge of the central cylinder and just inside the endodermis of the root; it is the source of secondary roots; (2) a tissue of stem or root bounded externally by the cortex and internally by xylem and phloem.

periderm. The cork cambium and its products.

peridium. (1) The covering of the hymenium of certain fungi, especially puffballs; (2) the hardened envelope which covers the sporangium of Myxomycetes.

peridotite. A coarse-grained igneous rock, related to gabbro, which consists of olivine and pyroxene in varying proportions; it can be commercially exploited.

perigee. The point nearest to the earth on the orbit of the moon.

perigynous. Said of flowers in which the sepals, petals, and stamens arise around the ovary.

perihelion. The point on the orbit of a planet or a comet which is nearest to the sun.

perikaryon. Cell body.

perineum. The wall between the urinogenital ducts and the rectum in mammals.

perinium. Epispore; a layer outside of exine and intine of an asexual spore of Equisetum.

period. A division of time in the earth's history smaller than an era.

period, natural. The period of a free oscillation of a body or system.

period of decay. Half life; the time period in which the activity of a radioactive element decreases to one half of its original value.

period of elements. The horizontal row of elements in the periodic table.

period of the pendulum. The time of one complete vibration.

periodic law. The properties of elements are periodic functions of their atomic weights or atomic numbers.

periodic motion. A motion repeated in equal time intervals.

periodic system. Same as periodic table.

periodic table. An arrangement of the elements in the order of their increasing atomic numbers, forming nine basic groups; the members of each group show similar physical and chemical properties.

periodism. The tendency for changes in a population or community to recur.

periodometer. A harmonic analyzer for the study of solar radiation and meteorological data.

periopod. A thoracic appendage of Crustacea, behind those which are associated with the mouth.

periosteum. The outer covering of bones.

periostracum. The hornlike outer layer of the shell of Brachiopoda and Molluska.

peripheral. Belonging to, or situated at, the surface or the edge.

peripheral electron. One of the outer electrons of the atom, to whose activity the spectral lines of visible light and thermal radiation are attributed and which are assumed to be responsible for chemical combination.

peripheral nerves. The cranial and spinal nerves.

peripheral nervous system. All nerve tissue that is not included in the central nervous system; the means of communication between various parts of the body and the central nervous system.

periproct. The area surrounding the anus.

perisarc. A sheath of chitin which surrounds the stalks and branches of the colony in hydrozoan coelenterates.

periscope. An optical instrument consisting of a tube containing a lens system and equipped with a reflecting surface at each end, placed at a 45° angle to each other so that the observer looking through an eyepiece at one mirror can see the objects reflected by the other mirror, which would be otherwise not visible to him; used in submarines.

perisperm. A nutritive tissue derived from the nucellus and surrounding the embryo in some seeds.

perisphere. The sphere around the centrosphere in a nerve cell.

Perissodactyla. Odd-toed Ungulata; a group of nonruminant, hoofed mammals whose third toe is larger than the others; examples, horse and rhinoceros.

peristalsis. Wavelike muscular contractions of the stomach and intestines which move the contents along the canal.

peristome. The region around the mouth or an opening of a plant or animal body.

peristomium. A modified segment behind the mouth in some segmented worms which bears tentacles and other sensory organs.

peritectic. Occurring between the liquid and solid phase of a solidifying melt.

perithecium. A spherical closed ascocarp.

peritoneal cavity. The abdominal cavity.

peritoneum. The thin membrane lining the body cavity and covering the viscera.

peritrichous. Having flagella surrounding the entire bacterium.

perivisceral cavity. Coelom; the body cavity of Metazoa.

perlite. Pearlite; (1) siliceous lava composed of concentric spheroidal layers; (2) a lamellar structure in steel from the transformation of austenite.

permanent gas. A gas which has a very low critical temperature and thus is difficult to liquefy; example, helium.

permanent hardness. The hardness of water that persists after prolonged boiling; it is due to calcium and magnesium sulfates and chlorides.

permanent magnet. A steel alloy, which is difficult to magnetize but retains its magetism after magnetization.

permanent parasites. Parasites that do not have a free-living stage.

permanent set. A deformation which persists after the sample has been released from stress.

permanent teeth. The second set of teeth of most mammals.

permatron. A hot-cathode gas-discharge diode in which the start of conduction is controlled by an external magnetic field.

permeability. (1) The ratio of the density of a magnetic flux generated in a substance to the magnetizing force; (2) the rate of diffusion of a gas under pressure through a porous substance.

permeameter. An instrument for measuring the average magnetic permeability of a ferromagnetic sample.

Permian. A Paleozoic period which lasted from about 200 to about 180 million years ago; it is characterized by the extinction of trilobites, rise of seed flora, and development of reptiles.

peroneus. The outer muscle on the dorsal part of the lower leg.

peronium. An ectodermal thickening at the base of a tentacle in some jellyfish.

peroxidase. A plant enzyme which catalyzes the oxidation of a substrate by the removal of hydrogen which combines with hydrogen peroxide.

peroxide. (1) An oxygen compound in which two oxygen atoms are linked to each other or which yield hydrogen peroxide with an acid; example, sodium peroxide, Na_2O_2; (2) the popular name of hydrogen peroxide, H_2O_2.

perpetual motion. The idea of a mechanism which, once started, would operate indefinitely; it is mechanically impossible as friction would always dissipate some mechanical energy and the mechanism would finally stop.

Perseids. Meteor showers that appear every year during August.

Perseus. A brilliant constellation of the northern sky.

persistence of vision. The ability of the retina to retain an image at least 1/16th of a second after cessation of the stimulus; the continuity of motion in motion pictures is due to this property.

personal equation. The correction necessary in reading a measuring instrument due to a consistent error made by an observer; the correction is usually constant for the same instrument and the same observer.

persorption. An absorption in which the absorbed molecules occupy vacant spaces in the lattice of the absorbing material, thus forming almost a molecular mixture of the two substances.

perspiration. A saline waste liquid excreted by the sweat glands of the skin.

perturbation. (1) An irregularity in the spacing of the lines of a band spectrum; (2) a disturbance in the regular motion of a heavenly body.

pes (plural pedes). The foot of the hind leg of quadrupeds.

petal. One of the colored leaves of the corolla.

petalite. A monoclinic lithium aluminum silicate; lithium was first discovered in this mineral.

petaloid area. A flowerlike arrangement of pores on the upper surface of some of the sea urchins.

petiole. A stalk extending from the blade to the base of the leaf.

petri dish. A shallow glass dish with a loose cover, used for growing bacteria or mold cultures.

petrification. Turning to stone of living organisms or parts.

petrified moss. Calcareous tufa; a porous rock deposited by streams.

petrified wood. Trees in which a deposit of calcium carbonate or silica replaced the woody material cell by cell, so that its original structural features have been preserved.

petrochemical. A chemical which is obtained from petroleum or natural gas or is a derivative of a petroleum product.

petrogenesis. The origin of rocks.

petrographic microscope. A microscope especially adapted for use by a petrologist and a mineralogist.

petrography. A study and systematic description, both macroscopic and microscopic, of the mineral composition, texture, and structure of rocks.

petrolatum. Petroleum jelly; a refined mixture of semisolid hydrocarbons; used in medicine, cosmetics, polishes.

petroleum. Crude mineral oil; a complex mixture of gaseous liquid and solid hydrocarbons as obtained from oil wells.

petroleum ether. Benzine; a mixture of the lower hydrocarbons of the paraffin series, consisting mainly of pentanes and hexanes.

petrology. A study of the origin, alterations, and composition of the lithosphere.

pewter. A tin-base alloy containing lead and some bismuth; used for ornaments.

Pfund series. A series of lines in the infrared region of the emission spectrum of atomic hydrogen.

pH. A value, based on the hydrogen-ion concentration, for expressing acidity or alkalinity on a scale running from one to fourteen; 7.0 is the neutral point; values under 7.0 indicate acidity, the strength increasing with decreasing values; values above 7.0 indicate alkalinity, the strength increasing with increasing values.

pH meter. An instrument for determining the hydrogen-ion concentration.

phacolith. A lens-shaped mass of igneous rock found either in the trough or in the crest of a folded structure.

Phaeophyceae. A group of algae characterized by a brown pigment; some members of the group are the largest algae known; they may measure several feet in length.

phage. Bacteriophage; a bacteria-destroying agent.

phagocyte. A white blood cell that captures and destroys bacteria and other foreign particles by ameboid movement.

phagocytosis. The destruction of microorganisms and other cells and substances by phagocytes.

phalanx (plural phalanges). One of the small bones of the toes and fingers of vertebrates.

phanatron. Phanotron; a gas-filled hot-cathode rectifier diode.

phanerocrystalline. Said of an igneous rock whose essential mineral constituents are distinguishable by the unaided eye.

phantastron. A one-tube relaxation oscillator.

phantom circuit. A third circuit obtained by using repeating or impedance coils in two communication circuits.

phantom loading. Testing and calibrating wattmeters by supplying the voltage and current connections from independent adjustable sources, rather than using actual loads.

pharmacophore. The portion of a molecule of a substance which is assumed to determine the special physiological action of the substance.

pharyngeal cleft. Gill slit; a branchial cleft; the outer opening of the gill cavity of fish.

pharynx. (1) The muscular portion of the digestive system of invertebrates between the mouth and the esophagus; (2) the part of the vertebrate alimentary canal which extends from the mouth to the esophagus and serves both for feeding and respiration.

phase. (1) A homogeneous, physically distinct, and mechanically separable portion of a chemical system; example, water has three phases, liquid water, water vapor, and ice; (2) a quantity which denotes the stage of progress of any cyclic operation, such as a vibration; (3) the instant when the maximum, zero, or other relative value is attained by an electric wave.

phase angle. The angle enclosed by two vectors which represent two periodically varying quantities of equal frequency; the phase difference between the primary voltage and the reversed secondary voltage of a transformer.

phase, continuous. External phase; dispersion medium; the enveloping phase in a colloidal system which contains one or more disperse phases.

phase control. The control of the output current of thyratrons, ignitrons, and similar devices by controlling the time or phase angle of the supply cycle.

phase, disperse. The colloidal particles dispersed in the continuous phase.

phase distortion. A distortion in the wave form of a transmitted signal which is the result of the lack of direct proportionality of phase shift to frequency over the frequency range required for transmission.

phase equilibrium. An equilibrium between two or more interconvertible phases of a substance, such as between ice, water, and water vapor.

phase meter. Power-factor indicator; an instrument for measuring the phase angle between the current and the voltage of a circuit.

phase microscope. A compound microscope which has an annular diaphragm and a phase plate that translates the phase differences of the transmitted light into image contrast.

phase reversal. (1) A change of phase of one-half cycle; (2) the inversion of the continuous and disperse phase of a colloidal system; example, changing an oil-in-water emulsion into a water-in-oil emulsion.

phase space. An ideal, multidimensional space in which the coordinates represent the variables required to specify the state of a substance or of a system.

phases of the moon. The changes in the shape of the bright portion of the moon as it revolves around the earth: new moon, first quarter, full moon, last quarter.

phasitron. A frequency-modulator vacuum tube with split concentric electrodes operating with a fan-shaped electron beam and three-phase voltage.

phellem. Cork.

phelloderm. The innermost layer of the periderm; a secondary cortex tissue formed by cork cambium.

phellogen. Cork cambium; a cambium giving rise to cork and phelloderm.

phenol. Carbolic acid; C_6H_5OH; colorless crystals obtained from a coal-tar fraction; a powerful disinfectant; used also in synthetic resins, dyestuffs, and pharmaceuticals.

phenol-formaldehyde resins. Thermosetting resins; polymerization products of phenol and formaldehyde; used for molding various products.

phenology. The study of the relation of climate to periodic biological phenomena, such as the flowering of plants, ripening of fruits, and migration of birds.

phenolphthalein. An indicator which is colorless in acid solutions, but turns red in alkaline solutions; used in chemical analysis and laxatives.

phenols. A class of aromatic compounds containing one or more hydroxyl groups; they correspond to the aliphatic alcohols.

phenotype. A type determined by visible characteristics which are common to a group, without taking into consideration the genetical characters.

phenyl. The univalent radical, $C_6H_5—$.

phillipsite. A fibrous zeolite mineral; a hydrous silicate of potassium, calcium, and aluminum.

phloem. A plant tissue made up of bast cells and sieve tubes which transport liquid food downward in the stem.

phlogiston. The name given to an imaginary substance assumed to escape during burning before the discovery of the mechanism of oxidation.

phlogopite. A natural magnesium mica containing a small amount of iron; used as an insulator.

phon. A unit of loudness or of the sound-level scale; used in measuring the intensity of sounds.

phonic wheel. A synchronous motor geared to a revolution counter, which can be used to measure the frequency of the alternating or interrupted current driving it.

phonodeik. A device for recording by photographic means on a moving film the wave forms of various musical instruments or of the human voice.

phonometer. An instrument for the measurement of the intensity and frequency of sound vibrations.

phonon. A hypothetical particle which represents a quantum of sound energy similarly to a photon which is a quantum of light energy.

Phoronidea. Wormlike sedentary marine animals; they have a ring of ciliated tentacles with which they feed; they resemble certain Polyzoa.

phosgene. Carbonyl chloride, $COCl_2$; a colorless, poisonous gas; used in the manufacture of dye intermediates and as a war gas.

phosphatase. An enzyme which hydrolyzes the phosphonic acid esters of carbohydrates.

phosphate. A salt of phosphoric acid, H_3PO_4; used as fertilizer.

phosphatide. A phosphorus-containing lipide; it occurs in living cells.

phosphine. Hydrogen phosphide, PH_3; colorless, inflammable, poisonous gas with a garliclike unpleasant smell.

phospholipide. Same as phosphatide.

phosphor. A phosphorescent inorganic sulfide used for coating the screens of cathode-ray tubes.

phosphor bronze. A fine-grain, tough copper-base alloy, containing some tin; used for ship propellers.

phosphorescence. (1) The emission of greenish light after illumination by visible or ultraviolet rays; (2) the luminosity of some animals; example, glow worms.

phosphoric acid. Ortho-phosphoric acid, H_3PO_4; colorless, deliquescent crystals; used in carbonated beverages, rustproofing.

phosphorite. Rock phosphate; an accumulation of calcium phosphate in compact masses occurring together with limestone; used in the manufacture of fertilizers.

phosphorogen. A substance which induces phosphorescence in another substance.

phosphoroscope. An instrument for measuring the time of phosphorescence.

phosphorus. A nonmetal that occurs in four allotropic forms; chemical symbol P; atomic number 15; it is found in minute quantities in protein.

phosphorus pentoxide. Deliquescent, colorless crystals; P_2O_5; used as a drying agent.

phosphorylation. The combination of sugar with phosphoric acid.

phot. A unit of illumination; one lumen per square centimeter.

photoanistropy. The property of some crystals of having different optical constants in different directions.

photocathode. A cathode that emits electrons on illumination.

photochemical. Having chemical activity brought about by the absorption of radiant energy.

photochemical reactions. Chemical reactions brought about by the absorption of light; examples, the photosynthesis of plants and the reduction of silver bromide by light on a photographic film.

photochemistry. A study of the chemical changes brought about by radiation and vice versa.

photoconductive detector. An apparatus used for detecting or measuring radiant energy by a change in the electrical resistance.

photoconductivity. An increase in the electric conductivity of some substances when illuminated; example, selenium.

photocurrent. A photoelectric or photovoltaic current; the current induced by the illumination of a sensitized surface.

photocyanin. A blue pigment, occurring in blue-green algae.

photodisintegration. (1) The disintegration of an atomic nucleus by radiant energy; (2) the dissociation of a chemical compound under the effect of radiant energy.

photodynamic sensitization. Increasing the toxicity to bacteria of ultraviolet rays of low intensity and of visible light by addition of certain dyes.

photoelasticity. Changes in the optical properties of isotropic transparent dielectrics when subjected to stresses.

photoelectric absorption. The conversion of radiant energy into the energy of photoelectric emission.

photoelectric cell. Photocell; a device in which electrons are released under the effect of light.

photoelectric effect. (1) A transfer of energy from light incident on a substance to electrons in the substance; (2) photoemission.

photoelectric effect, atomic. The ejection of a bound electron from one of the inner orbits of an atom of a gas, by an incident photon whose entire energy is absorbed for each electron ejected.

photoelectric effect, inverse. Transfer of energy from electrons to radiation.

photoelectric emission. Photoemission; the emission of electrons by certain substances on exposure to radiation.

photoelectric limiting potential. The stopping potential for the fastest electrons in a given photoelectric emission.

photoelectric multiplier. A phototube in which the initial photoemission current is multiplied many times by secondary emissions before being extracted at the anode.

photoelectric work function. The energy required to release electrons from a given surface by photoelectric emission.

photoelectricity. Electricity produced by light.

photoelectron. An electron emitted from a substance under the effect of light.

photoemission. The emission of electrons from a surface under the effect of light.

photoemissive detector. An apparatus for detecting and measuring radiant energy by emission of electrons from a photocathode.

photogenic. Light-producing; a protein, lucigerin, is oxidized in the production of light inside or outside the cell.

photogens. (1) Bacteria which are phosphorescent or luminous; (2) light-producing substances.

photoglow tube. A gas-filled glow-discharge tube in which the gas is ionized by photoelectric effect.

photogoniometer. An apparatus for studying the x-ray diffraction and x-ray spectra of crystals.

photographic film. A thin, transparent strip of cellulose acetate or cellulose nitrate covered with a thin layer of light-sensitive emulsion, on which photographs can be taken.

photography. The science, and art of forming permanent pictures by means of the action of light on light-sensitive layers of certain chemicals.

photoionization. The ionization of a gas by radiation quanta.

photoluminescence. Luminescence caused by exposure to visible or ultraviolet light.

photolysis. (1) The arrangement of the chloroplasts in a plant according to the light it receives; (2) the decomposition of a chemical compound caused by light absorption.

photomagnetic effect. The effect of light on the magnetic susceptibility of certain substances.

photomeson. A meson ejected from a nucleus by an impinging photon.

photometer. An instrument for comparing the intensities of two light sources.

photometric analysis. A method of volumetric analysis in which the end point is determined through measurement of turbidity by a photoelectric cell.

photometric standard. One sixtieth of the luminance of a complete radiator at the freezing point of platinum.

photometry. The measurement of light intensity for securing proper illumination.

photomicrography. Making pictures of normal size and visible details from microscopic slides.

photon. A light quantum; a unit of light or other radiant energy; the energy emitted when an electron is transferred from an inner orbit of the atom to the next.

photonasty. A response of a living organism to a general, nondirectional illumination stimulus; example, closing or opening of flowers at night time.

photonegative. Having negative phototropism.

photoneutron. A neutron emitted as a result of photodisintegration.

photonuclear reaction. A nuclear reaction induced by a photon.

photoperiodism. The response of plants to the relative lengths of day and night.

photophoresis. The migration of suspended particles under the effect of light.

photopositive. Exhibiting positive phototaxis.

photoproton. A proton emitted from a nucleus in a photonuclear reaction.

photoreceptor. A sensory nerve ending which responds to the stimulus of light waves.

photosensitivity. A sensitivity to visible or invisible light.

photosphere. The intensely bright surface of the sun which is visible to the unaided eye; a layer of heavy incandescent vapor around the sun which is believed to contain a large percentage of metals.

photosynthesis. The process by which green plants exposed to sunlight manufacture carbohydrates from carbon dioxide and water taken from the atmosphere; chlorophyll acts as a catalyst and oxygen is set free in the process.

phototaxis. The movement of organisms under the influence of light.

phototropism. Same as phototaxis.

phototropy. A reversible isomeric change of color of a solid substance according to the wave length of the light that falls on it.

phototube. A vacuum tube which emits electrons due to the effect of electromagnetic waves incident on a photoelectric surface.

phototube, multiplier. A phototube with one or more dynodes between its photocathode and the output electrode.

photovoltaic cell. Photochemical cell; a photoelectric cell which consists of two electrodes of the same metal immersed in an electrolyte; the illumination of one of the electrodes gives rise to a potential difference.

photovoltaic effect. Generation of an electric current as a result of a photochemical reaction.

phreatic. Said of underground waters that can be brought to the surface by well drilling.

phrenic nerves. The nerves that control the diaphragm.

phycocolloids. Colloidal polysaccharides found in certain sea plants or seaweeds; example, agar.

phycocyanin. Photosynthetic blue pigment linked with a protein occurring with chlorophyll in blue-green and in red algae.

phycoerythrin. A red pigment occurring in red algae.

Phycomycetes. A group of lower fungi which are similar to algae in some characters.

phyllite. A metamorphic rock, intermediate between slate and schist.

phylloclade. A modified stem having the appearance and function of a leaf; example, cladode.

phyllode. A leaf reduced to a flattened petiole.

phyllopodium. A biramous broad thin appendage of Crustacea; often used for feeding, respiration, and sometimes swimming.

phyllotaxis. The arrangement of leaves on the stems, such as opposite, whorled, and alternate.

phylogeny. The ancestral or evolutionary history of a species or higher group.

phylum (plural phyla). A large division of the plant or animal kingdom.

physical change. Any change in which the composition of a substance is not altered; example, dissolving sugar in water.

physical chemistry. The study of the physical changes associated with chemical reactions and of the interrelation of physical properties with chemical structure.

physical factors. Nonliving conditions which influence living organisms; examples, temperature and light.

physical geography. The study of the earth's surface, its natural divisions, its climate, and the effects of these on life.

physical properties. Characteristics of substances that are not observed in the course of a chemical reaction; examples, color, odor, state, density, solubility, etc.

physicist. A scientist who is engaged in the theoretical or practical problems of physics.

physics. A natural science covering matter, energy and their mutual relations.

physiography. (1) Same as physical geography; (2) the description of nature and natural phenomena.

physiological acoustics. The study of the production and detection of sound by living organs.

physiological chemistry. Biochemistry; the chemistry of life functions.

physiological oxidation. Slow combustion without flame or smoke but with the production of heat, carbon dioxide, and water; it is an important part of the metabolism of living organisms.

physiological saline. A sterile isotonic salt solution in distilled water in which cells will remain alive for some time.

physiological specialization. Differences in physiological, biochemical, or pathogenic character between groups or forms of a species, which cannot be distinguished structurally.

physiology. The study of the life activities of plants and animals.

phytobenthon. A collective name for attached aquatic plants.

phytochemistry. The study of chemical products of vegetable origin.

phytochrome. A plant pigment that resembles a protein; it plays an important role in the growth and development of plants.

phytophagous. Phytophilous; plant-eating.

phytoplankton. A collective name for free-floating plants.

pia mater. The innermost covering of the brain and spinal cord.

pia-arachnoid. The covering membrane of the brain and spinal cord, consisting of the pia mater and arachnoid.

pickling. (1) Protecting perishable foods from the undesirable action of enzymes and microorganisms by immersion in brine; (2) removing oxides, scale, and other impurities from metal surfaces by dipping in dilute acid; (3) preparing the dehaired hides for tanning by soaking in a weakly acid salt solution.

picric acid. Trinitrophenol, $C_6H_2(NO_2)_3(OH)$; a yellow dye for silk and wool; used also as an antiseptic and in explosives.

Piedmont alluvial plain. The union of a number of neighboring alluvial fans to form one continuous plain.

piezoelectric crystal. A crystal that expands along one axis and contracts along another under the effect of an electric current; examples, quartz and Rochelle salt.

piezoelectric effect. The conversion of strain in certain crystals into electrical impulses and vice versa.

piezoelectric generator. Same as piezoelectric oscillator.

piezoelectric oscillator. An electric oscillating system containing as one of its elements a piezoelectric resonator by which the frequency is controlled.

piezoelectric resonator. A plate or rod of piezoelectric crystal which may be excited electrically into resonant vibrations at one or more frequencies.

piezoelectricity. Same as piezoelectric effect.

piezometer. An instrument for measuring the compressibility of liquids.

pig iron. A crude iron reduced in a blast furnace and cast into ingots.

pigeon's milk. Crop milk; a milky fluid resulting from the breakdown of the crop lining of pigeons; it is discharged and used for feeding the young.

pigment. A coloring matter.

pigmental coloration. The characteristic color of some animals due to the presence of pigments in their structure.

pile, atomic. An assembly of graphite blocks in which uranium is transformed into plutonium.

pileus. The umbrella-shaped cap of fleshy fungi.

pilidium. A ciliated larval form of the nemertine worms.

piliferous layer. That part of the epidermis of a root which bears root hairs.

pillow lava. An effusive volcanic rock of basic composition which has a pillowlike structure due to the simultaneous movement and congelation of the lava.

pilot balloon. A small rubber balloon released for studying the movements of the air at high altitudes.

pilot plant. A small manufacturing plant built to help scientists and engineers work out the practical production problems of substances synthesized in the laboratory.

pinacocyte. A flattened cell of the outer layer of the body wall of sponges which is able to change its shape.

pineal eye. Parapineal eye; an outgrowth of some fish and lizards, which is similar to an eye in structure; it develops from the roof of the brain, and may have a lens and serve as a third eye.

pineal gland. A ductless gland located between the cerebral hemispheres and near the pituitary gland of vertebrates.

pinfeather. A young, not fully developed, slender, hairlike feather.

pinhole image. The inverted image formed by light passing from the source directly through a small opening and falling on a screen.

pinna. (1) The outer ear, supported by cartilage; (2) the fin of fish; (3) a leaflet of a fern leaf.

pinnate veining. Featherlike veining; example, willow.

Pinnipedia. Carnivorous placental aquatic mammals, having webbed paddle feet; examples, seals and walruses.

pinnule. (1) A small lateral branch of the arm of a feather star, giving the arm a featherlike shape; (2) one segment of the leaflet of a pinnate leaf.

pint. An English measure of capacity; ½ quart; 0.47 liter.

pipet. Pipette; a calibrated glass tube for measuring small quantities of a liquid; the liquid is taken up by suction.

Pisces. (1) Fish; they have a bony skeleton, gills, a two-chambered heart, and a body covered with scales; examples, trout, tuna; (2) a constellation, the twelfth sign of Zodiac.

pisciculture. Breeding of fish and maintaining their supply in heavily fished waters.

piscivorous. Fish-eating.

pistil. (1) Each separate carpel of an apocarpous gynaecium; (2) the gynaecium as a whole, whether apocarpous or syncarpous.

pistillate flower. A flower that has pistils but no stamens.

piston. A solid gastight cylindrical metal piece that reciprocates in the cylinder of an engine or a similar chamber of another machine.

piston ring. A steel ring that seals the space between the piston and the cylinder walls of an engine.

piston rod. The rod which moves the piston and is connected to the crosshead or crankshaft.

pit. (1) A small, sharply defined area in the wall of plant cells that remains thin while the rest of the wall becomes thickened; it coincides with a pit in the wall of an adjacent cell and facilitates communication between them; (2) a mine shaft.

pitch. (1) A residue of coal-tar distillation; a dark substance which melts to a viscous, tarry liquid; it contains bitumen and resins; (2) the distance between the threads of a screw; (3) the number of vibrations of a sound per second.

pitchblende. A dark, earthy ore of uranium.

pitching. (1) The angular movement of an airplane or ship around a lateral axis in a vertical plane; (2) adding a yeast culture to a fermentation mash; (3) soap fitting.

pitchstone. A volcanic glass of a dull pitchy luster; it contains about 5% water.

pith. Soft, thin-walled cells near or at the center of a plant stem; useful mostly for water storage; to destroy the brain of an animal such as a frog.

Pithecanthropus. A hypothetical extinct primate which would represent an intermediate species between the anthropoid apes and man.

pitocin. A hormone secretion of the posterior lobe of the pituitary gland which stimulates smooth muscles.

pitometer. An instrument for making a continuous record of the variations in velocity of flowing water; it consists of two Pitot tubes, one directed upstream and the other downstream.

Pitot tube. A narrow tube inserted in a fluid stream with its open end facing the current and communicating at the other end with a manometer; used for measuring the speed of flow.

pitressin. A hormone secretion of the posterior lobe of the pituitary gland which regulates the water content of blood and the blood pressure.

pitting. (1) A corrosion of a metal surface; (2) the formation of pinholes in a varnished surface.

pituitary gland. Pituitary body; hypophysis; a ductless endocrine gland located at the base of the brain to which it is attached by a stalk; it is a regulator of body activities by various hormones it secretes.

pituitrin. An extract of the posterior lobe of the pituitary gland which contains hormones.

pivot joint. A joint that allows only rotation.

placenta. (1) That part of the wall of the uterus of mammals to which the embryo is attached and through which it is nourished; (2) the fleshy spot of attachment of the ovules to the carpel wall.

Placentalia. Eutheria; a subclass of Mammalia whose embryo develops in the maternal uterus, attached to the maternal tissues by a highly organized placenta; the young are born in an advanced stage of development.

placentation. (1) The manner in which the placenta is distributed in the ovary; (2) the method of union of embryonic and maternal tissues.

placentation, axile. The inward folding and fusion of the margins of carpels in the center of the ovary to form a single, central placenta; example, lily.

placentation, free central. The arrangement of the ovules on a placenta which arises as a central growth from the ovary base; example, primrose.

placentation, parietal. The fusion of carpels only by their margins and the placenta appearing as an internal ridge on the ovary wall.

placoid scale. Denticle; small toothlike scales; example, the scales of sharks and skates.

plagiosere. The succession of plants deflected into a new course by a biotic factor or factors.

plain. A broad rather smooth land that is nearly level with the adjoining land or water.

plan position indicator (ppi). An oscilloscope which indicates the type and size of the objects a radar sees; for example, airplanes, ships, a bridge, a cliff.

Planaria. A family of nonparasitic fresh-water flatworms with soft thin bodies.

Planckian color. The color, or the wave-length intensity distribution, of the light emitted by a black body at a given temperature.

Planck's constant. The universal constant relating the frequency of a radiation to its quantum; 6.547×10^{-27} erg/second.

plane of symmetry. An imaginary plane by which a body is divided into two parts, each of which is the exact mirror image of the other in the plane of symmetry.

plane of the earth's orbit. An imaginary flat surface passing through the center of the earth and the center of the sun in the revolution of the earth around the sun.

plane of the ecliptic. The plane of the earth's orbit extended to the celestial sphere.

plane of union. The plane at which the two components of a twin crystal are united.

plane polarization. A polarization in which the cycle is a straight line, corresponding to a rectilinear vibration.

planet. One of the nine known heavenly bodies of the solar system which revolve around the sun: Mercury, Venus, Earth, Mars, Jupiter, Saturn, Uranus, Neptune, and Pluto.

planetarium. A device or structure for illustrating the position and motions of the heavenly bodies; example, Zeiss planetarium.

planetary gear. A gear wheel whose axis moves on a circular path around the axis of another gear wheel; example, the bevel wheels of a differential.

planetary nebulae. Gaseous clouds in interstellar space seen by telescope as oval disks.

planetesimal hypothesis. Chamberlin and Moulton's theory on the origin of the solar system; they suggested that the planets were formed by the aggregation of small secondary bodies they named planetesimals.

planetoid. (1) Asteroid; small planets, mostly between Mars and Jupiter, that travel around the sun; (2) planetlike.

planimeter. An instrument for measuring the area of any plane figure by guiding a tracer around its outline.

plankton. An aquatic fauna composed of animals and plants which float and drift near the water surface and whose active locomotion is not directional; they are usually small or minute organisms.

plano-concave. Having one plane and one concave surface.

plano-convex. Having one plane and one convex surface.

plant ecology. The study of the relations of plants to their environment.

plant geography. Phytogeography; a study of the distribution of plants over the surface of the earth and of the factors responsible for it.

plant society. A group of plants living together under similar environmental conditions.

plant succession. The replacement of one plant society by another as the environment changes.

plantigrade. Walking on the whole sole of the foot; example, man.

planula. The ciliated free-swimming flat larval form of certain invertebrates; example, Coelenterata.

plasma. (1) An amber-colored, somewhat sticky liquid found in blood; about 90% water, containing many dissolved substances; (2) that part of an electric discharge in a rarified gas which contains electrons and positive ions in such numbers that their charges nearly neutralize one another; (3) a translucent green semiprecious silica mineral.

plasma membrane. A thin membrane formed by the cytoplasm which surrounds each cell.

plasma propulsion. A method of providing rocket propulsion that uses electricity to ionize a gaseous propellant, that is, convert it into plasma.

plasma protein. Dissolved proteins of the vertebrate blood plasma.

plasmagene. A hypothetical particle in cytoplasm which has the properties of a gene, such as self-reproduction; it is assumed to affect the hereditary and physiological characters of the cytoplasm.

plasmatron. A continuously controllable gas-discharge tube which uses an independently generated gas-discharge plasma as a conductor between a hot cathode and an anode.

plasmochin. A synthetic quinoline compound used in malaria therapy.

plasmodesm. A fine protoplasmic thread passing through the wall which separates two protoplasts.

Plasmodia. A species of Protozoa that causes malaria.

plasmodium. (1) A slimy mass of protoplasm in Myxomycetes, with no surrounding wall and with numerous free nuclei distributed throughout; it is capable of ameboid movement and taking in solid food; (2) an animal tissue complex formed by the union of many uninuclear individuals, without the fusion of their nuclei.

plasmoid. Said of luminous bodies of various shapes which appear in highly exhausted tubes under excitation of very high frequency.

plasmolysis. The loss of water from a cell by osmosis, accompanied by shrinkage of the protoplasm.

plasmoptysis. The bursting of protoplasm through a cell wall as a result of water intake by osmotic action.

plasmotomy. The reproduction of certain one-celled animals; a multinucleate form divides into two or more parts, each with several nuclei.

plaster of Paris. Partially dehydrated gypsum; calcium sulfate, $(CaSO_4)_2 \cdot H_2O$; used for casts.

plastic deformation. A permanent deformation of a plastic substance under stress.

plasticity. A continuous shear or flow of certain solids when subjected to shearing stress.

plasticizer. (1) An organic liquid of high boiling point added to lacquers to prevent the resulting film from becoming brittle; example, tricresyl phosphate; (2) a substance added to plastics or other solids to make them more workable.

plastics. Synthetic resins or their mixtures, which can be formed into various shapes by heat and pressure and retain these shapes after the heat and pressure have been removed.

plastid. A pigmented cytoplasmic body in plant cells.

plastogamy. The union by which the plasmodium of the slime molds is formed; the cytoplasm becomes confluent, but the nuclei remain distinct.

plastogene. A hypothetical submicroscopic factor present in plant plastids which affects their physiological and hereditary functions.

plastometer. An apparatus for measuring the plasticity of a substance by forcing it through a small tube by standard pressure and measuring the time required.

plastron. The lower shell of a turtle.

plate. (1) The electrode of an accumulator cell; (2) the conducting surface of a condenser; (3) an anode.

plate circuit. A circuit consisting of the anode of an electron tube, associated tuning circuits, transformers, headphones or speaker, the B battery or other power supply, and a return to the cathode.

plate current. The current, generally of a few milliamperes, flowing in the plate circuit.

plate dissipation. The power loss which occurs at the anode of an electronic tube.

plate efficiency. The ratio of load circuit power (a-c) to the plate power input (d-c).

plate load impedance. The total impedance between the anode and cathode, exclusive of the electron stream.

plate power input. The direct-current power delivered to the anode of an electron tube by the source of supply.

plate return. The wire connecting the anode circuit to the tube filament.

plate voltage. The potential difference or voltage drop between the anode and cathode of a vacuum tube.

plateau. A broad and relatively smooth land surface which is distinctly higher than nearby land or water, at least on one side.

platelets. Tiny particles of cytoplasm in blood, derived from red bone marrow; there are about 250,000 platelets in one cubic centimeter of blood; they set free a chemical that starts clotting.

platform balance. Platform scale; a weighing apparatus which has a flat platform for holding the objects to be weighed.

platinite. An iron-nickel alloy; used for sealing wires into electric light bulbs.

platinized asbestos. An asbestos in the fibers of which a black deposit of finely divided platinum has been formed; used as a catalyst.

platinum. An inert rare noble metal; chemical symbol Pt; atomic number 78; used for jewelry, as a catalyst, for chemical apparatus.

platinum needle. A platinum wire for the transfer of bacteria from one culture to another.

Platyhelminthes. Soft-bodied bilaterally symmetrical flattened, often unsegmented, worms that have no true body cavity; they are mostly parasitic; examples, tapeworms and Planaria.

Platyrrhina. New world monkeys; they have a broad nasal septum, usually thirty-six teeth, and often a prehensile tail.

playa. A salt pan; a shallow lake that appears in arid and semiarid regions after each rain, but disappears before the next rain, leaving a salt layer on evaporation.

Plecoptera. Insects with four membraneous wings, the front pair being narrower than the hind pair; they have long antennae, biting mouth parts, and aquatic immature stages; example, stoneflies.

Pleiades. A group of bright stars in the constellation of Taurus.

Pleistocene period. Great Ice Age; a part of the Cenozoic era; it began one to two million years ago; the major part of northern Europe and North America was ice-covered; man made his appearance in this period.

pleochroic halos. Dark halolike zones surrounding radioactive mineral inclusions in some crystals; they are attributed to radioactive emanation; examples, zircon and biotite.

pleochromatism. A selective absorption of light by certain crystals along different crystal axes and thus exhibiting different colors in these directions.

pleomorphism. Polymorphism; (1) the assumption of various distinct forms by an individual organism of a species during its life cycle; (2) the occurrence of morphologically different types within the same species; (3) the property of some chemical compounds of occurring as minerals of different crystal forms of different geological origin; example, magnesium carbonate occurs in nature as magnesite, nesquehonite, and lansfordite.

pleopod. Swimmeret; a form of the biramous appendage of Crustacea which is used for swimming.

plerocercoid. A larva of tapeworms, especially fish tapeworms.

Plesiosauria. A fossil order of marine Reptilia which lived during the Jurassic period; they had a long neck and short tail, and were up to 50 feet long.

pleura. The lining of the chest cavity containing the lungs.

pleural cavity. A coelomic chamber surrounding each lung in mammals; it is separated from the rest of perivisceral coelom by a diaphragm.

Pleurococcus. Protococcus; one of the most numerous organisms on earth; one-celled green algae.

pleuropodite. A basal joint of the biramous appendage of certain Crustacea.

plexus. (1) The network of ganglia and nerves lying near or within the walls of some of the internal organs in the autonomic nervous system of the higher vertebrates; (2) a network of nerve fibers in the central nervous system; (3) a network of blood vessels.

Pliocene period. A Cenozoic era which began 10 to 12 million years ago; it is characterized by the appearance of manlike apes and primitive cats and dogs.

pliotron. A high-vacuum tube which has one or more grids; examples, triode and tetrode.

plugging. A system of dynamic braking for electric motors by making them tend to turn in the opposite direction.

plumb line. A string to which a weight is attached; it is used for determining the true vertical direction.

plumbago. Graphite; used in lead pencils and for making refractory crucibles.

plumule. (1) The primary bud of a germinating seed plant; (2) a down feather.

plumule sheath. The upper part of a plant embryo.

pluteus. A larval form of brittle stars and sea urchins; it is bilateral with a tubular alimentary tract; its locomotion is accomplished by cilia arranged in a band.

Pluto. The ninth major planet farthest from the sun.

plutonic intrusion. Deep-seated igneous rocks as distinguished from volcanic lavas which cool and solidify in air or under water.

plutonium. A radioactive element formed by the loss of an electron from the nucleus of neptunium; chemical symbol Pu; atomic number 94; it was developed in connection with the atomic-bomb research; it has two isotopes, 238 and 239.

Pm. Chemical symbol for promethium.

pneumatic. Operated by air pressure or filled with compressed air.

pneumatic trough. A laboratory apparatus by which gas is collected under water.

pneumatics. The study of the mechanical properties of gases.

pneumatolysis. The alteration of existing rocks and mineral deposits, or the formation of new ones by gases or vapors emanating from the partially consolidated magma.

pneumococcus. A Gram-positive bacterium which causes pneumonia.

pneumogastric nerve. The tenth cranial or vagus nerve of vertebrates whose branches lead to the lungs and the stomach.

pneumostome. An opening which leads to the chamber containing the respiratory organs of scorpions and spiders.

Po. Chemical symbol for polonium.

pod. The fruit of a legume plant formed from a single carpel; it opens on two sides as the seeds are discharged.

podical plate. One of a pair of triangular plates flanking the anus in certain insects.

podium. (1) The third limb of

land vertebrates; (2) the tube foot of Echinodermata.

podzol (podsol). Typical ashlike soils of regions having subarctic climates.

poikilothermy. Cold-bloodedness; fluctuation of the temperature of the animal body according to that of its surroundings.

Poinsot motion. The motion of a rigid body having one fixed point under the effect of forces whose resultant is zero.

point pole. A pointed magnetic pole, from which the field radiates almost as if from a point.

point source of light. A theoretical concept of a source of light in which all the light is emitted from a single point.

Pointers. Two stars of the Big Dipper that are in line with the North Star.

poise. A metric unit of viscosity; the viscosity of a fluid at which one gram force will maintain a unit rate of shear in a film of unit thickness between two surfaces of unit area.

poison. (1) A substance which absorbs neutrons without fission in a nuclear reactor; (2) a substance which reduces the emission of an electrode; (3) a substance which, introduced into the body, may cause death; (4) a substance that reduces or destroys the effectiveness of a catalyst.

poison claw. A jointed appendage of the first body segment of centipedes which bears poison glands to capture and kill prey.

polar. (1) Situated at the end or pole of a cell; (2) having positive and negative ends; (3) said of chemical compounds formed by the complete transfer of an electron; (4) belonging or referring to a pole.

polar adsorption. The adsorption of electrically unequal amounts of ions, so that the adsorbed film has an over-all electrical charge.

polar body. A small nonfunctional cell thrown off during the meiosis or maturation in a single nucleus.

polar bond. Electrovalence; a chemical bond resulting from the unequal sharing of a valence electron between atoms of intermediate difference in electronegativity.

polar caps. (1) Groups of delicate fibers at the opposite poles of the nucleus during mitosis; (2) two white regions seen in the telescope around the poles of Mars; they are assumed to be snow-covered fields.

polar compound. A compound whose atoms are held together by electrostatic forces; the electric charges are not uniformly distributed and the molecule has a plus end and a minus end; ionic compounds are highly polar; examples, hydro-

gen chloride and water.

polar covalent compound. A compound in which the shared electrons are closer to one of the atoms than to the other, forming a molecule with a positive and negative end.

polar front. The windshift line of a polar cyclone; the boundary between the cold polar air mass and the warmer air of lower regions.

polar molecule. A molecule which has an electric moment due to a nonuniform electron distribution.

polar projection. A circular map with the station point in the center and the plane of projection passing through one of the polar circles; valuable in aeronautics.

polar regions. The regions near the north and south poles.

polarimeter. An instrument for measuring the rotation of the plane of polarized light by optically active substances.

polarimetry. The investigation of optical phenomena in which polarized light is involved.

Polaris. The North Star of the Little Dipper.

polariscope. A device consisting of a polarizer and an analyzer; used for the demonstration of polarization phenomena by placing transparent specimens between its two parts and examining them by transmitted polarized light.

polaristor. The resistance formed when fine particles of a dielectric material, suspended in a highly dielectric fluid, such as oil, are subjected to a strong electrostatic field.

polarity. The property of having two opposite poles; example, a magnet has polarity.

polarization. (1) A gas accumulation on the electrodes of primary cells, which reduces the voltage and current; (2) changing ordinary light to waves whose vibrations are in one plane only; (3) the separation of the positive and negative charges in the molecule.

polarization, angle of. The angle of reflection from a dielectric medium at which the reflected ray is completely polarized, the plane of vibration being at right angles to the plane of incidence.

polarization photometer. A photometer in which the intensity of the light from one or both sources is varied by the use of a polarizing apparatus.

polarization, plane of. The plane perpendicular to the polarized light waves.

polarization potential. Polarization voltage; the counterelectromotive force, arising in many electrolytic processes which increases with the progress of polarization.

polarization tint. A coloration of the field of a polariscope analyzer when using a white-light source, due to the emergence of the different wave lengths from the analyzer with altered relative intensities.

polarized light. A light whose vibrations are in one plane only.

polarizer. A Nicol prism or other device for polarizing light.

polarogram. The record of variations in a current or current-voltage ratio which is obtained by means of a polarograph.

polarograph. A device used for registering the current-voltage relationship, particularly of polarized microelectrodes; used for the electroanalysis of solutions with a dropping mercury cathode.

polarography. Microanalysis with the use of a polarograph.

polder. A small area of swampland rescued by the construction of dikes or artificial levees.

pole. (1) One of the ends of a magnet where its magnetism appears to be concentrated; (2) either end of the earth's axis; (3) one of the terminals, electrodes, or binding posts of an electric cell; (4) either of the two opposite ends of an organism or cell.

pole effect. A discrepancy observed in the wave lengths and character of spectral lines when the light comes from the vicinity of the electrodes of a metallic arc.

Pole Star. Same as North Star or Polaris.

poles, celestial. The intersections of the earth's extended axis with the celestial sphere.

poling. Immersing wooden poles into molten copper; the reducing gases developing by the burning of the pole bind the excess oxygen and thus prevent the oxidation of the copper.

pollen. Tiny yellow bodies produced by the anthers of seed-bearing plants that contain the male sex cells.

pollen grain. An individual pollen particle; a spore usually consisting of a single cell.

pollen sac. A sac in the anther containing pollen grains.

pollen tube. A threadlike projection which grows downward through the stigma and style from the pollen grain and conveys the male nuclei to the egg nucleus.

pollex. Thumb; the first digit of a pentadactyl forelimb; it is shorter than other digits.

pollination. The transfer of pollen from the male to the female part of plants.

pollinium. A coherent mass of pollen grains which is transported as a whole in pollination; example, orchid.

polliwog. A young frog or toad

soon after hatching from the egg.

Pollux. The brighter of the Twin Stars, Castor and Pollux.

polocyte. A polar body.

polonium. A radioactive rare metal; chemical symbol Po; atomic number 84.

polyadelphous. Said of stamens united by their filaments into several groups.

polybasic acid. An acid which has more than one replaceable hydrogen atom; example, H_2SO_4.

Polychaeta. Marine Annelida with numerous bristles borne on projections of the body; they have external fertilization and development by metamorphosis; example, tube worms.

polychromatic. Polychromic; multicolored.

polycrystal. A crystalline substance consisting of a number of small crystals in a mass.

polydactyly. The condition of having more than the normal number of fingers or toes.

polydisperse. Said of a disperse system having particles of different sizes.

polyembryony. The development of more than one individual from a single fertilized egg cell.

polyester resin. An alkyd resin which may be cured or hardened at room temperature under little or no pressure.

polyethylene. Polythene; a thermoplastic high polymer of ethylene; a transparent plastic used for wrapping and electrical purposes.

polygamous. Having perfect pistillate, staminate, and hermaphrodite flowers on the same individual or on different individuals.

polygene. Said of a volcano built up by several eruptions following one another.

polygon of forces. Forces acting on a particle will be in equilibrium if they can be represented in magnitude and direction by the sides of a polygon.

polymer. A substance composed of large molecules made by joining many small molecules of one or several monomers; examples, rubber is a polymer of isoprene; phenolics are polymers of phenol and formaldehyde.

polymer gasoline. A gasoline made by polymerization of gaseous hydrocarbons, such as methane.

polymerization. The union of two or more molecules to form a larger molecule, a polymer, of the same percentage composition.

polymorph. (1) Polymorphonuclear leucocyte; a white blood cell whose nucleus is divided into lobes connected by chromatin strands and surrounded by granular cytoplasm; granu-locyte; it is active in phago-cytosis; (2) an organ that oc-curs in several forms; (3) a substance which has two or more crystalline forms.

polymorphic. Heteromorphic; ex-isting in two or more crystal-line forms.

polymorphism. (1) The natural occurrence of two or more sharply distinct forms of ani-mals in a single species; (2) the occurrence of several dif-ferent structural forms in the cycle of development of one individual.

polyp. The attached form of Coelenterata; a simple tube-shaped water animal with ten-tacles at the tip of its body.

polypeptide. A condensation product of amino acids united by peptide linkages.

polypetalous. Said of a corolla consisting of free petals; ex-ample, buttercup.

polyphase. Consisting of two or more phases or electrical cir-cuits.

polyphyletic. Descendant of sev-eral different ancestors and displaying their characters.

polyphyly. An evolutionary hy-pothesis which assumes that animals have originated by several lines of descent from many ancestral forms, rather than from a single primordial form by gradual divergence.

polypide. The member of a col-ony of Polyzoa.

polyploidy. The possession of more than double the haploid number of chromosomes re-sulting in new characters; this condition can be induced by chemicals and has a great im-portance in successful hybridi-zation.

polypterus. A primitive actinop-terygian fish of tropical Africa, with well developed lungs and ganoid scales.

polysaccharides. A class of nat-ural carbohydrates having the general formula $(C_6H_{10}O_5)_x$; example, cellulose.

polysepalous. Said of a calyx consisting of free sepals; ex-ample, buttercup.

polyspermy. The penetration of numerous sperms into one ovum at fertilization; but only one sperm nucleus fuses with the egg nucleus.

polystyrene. An important ther-moplastic material; a polymer of styrene, $C_6H_5CH{:}CH_2$; it has good electrical properties and is used for radio and tele-vision parts.

polyvalent. (1) Having a valence greater than one; (2) having antibodies specific for more than one species of bacteria.

Polyzoa. Fixed and colonial aquatic animals, resembling hy-droid Coelenterata, but more complex; examples, sea-mats

and coralline.

pome. Simple, fleshy fruit derived from several carpels; the inner pericarp is papery; examples, apple, pear.

pons. (1) A nerve-fiber group be-neath the cerebrum; (2) a bridge; a connecting body part.

pool tube. A gas-discharge tube with a cold cathode which con-sists of a pool of mercury.

porcellanite. Metamorphosed marls and shales which look like porcelain.

Porifera. Many-celled sessile and aquatic animals; they have one tubular body cavity consisting of two layers with pores through which water may en-ter; example, sponges.

porocyte. A conical cell of sponges that carries water from the surface to the paragaster, that is, the internal cavity.

porosimeter. An instrument for the determination of the po-rosity of solids, that is, their permeability by fluids.

porosity. (1) The occurrence of small pores throughout the mass of a substance; (2) the volume percentage of pores in a solid; (3) the ease with which a fluid can pass through an electrical insulator.

porous rock. A rock through which water can seep.

porphyry. An igneous rock con-taining large crystals set in a background of small crystals.

Porro prism. A triangular optical prism having one 90° and two 45° angles; it inverts and re-verses the image viewed by totally reflecting twice the light passing through it; it allows shortening the telescope tube and thus to build two of them into a binocular.

portal circulation. Portal system; blood circulation through the loop of blood vessels which bring blood from the digestive organs through the liver into the vein going to the heart.

portal vein. The large vein that carries blood from the diges-tive organs and spleen to the liver.

position angle. The angle between the great circle, joining any two celestial objects, and the hour circle through one of the objects.

position effect. The influence of the change of position of a gene in the chromosome rela-tive to other genes on the char-acter it produces.

positive. (1) Said of an electrode which has a higher potential than another electrode; (2) a photographic image whose contrasts of light and shade correspond to the original ob-ject.

positive column. A striated, lu-minous region adjacent to the anode in a Crookes tube at moderate pressure.

positive crystal. A uniaxial, bire-fringent crystal in which the extraordinary wave has the lower speed.

positive ion. An ion that carries a positive charge due to the loss of one or more electrons.

positive lens system. A con-vergent lens system.

positive loops. Loops drawn above the time line.

positive magnetic pole. The north-seeking pole of a mag-net.

positive nucleus. The nucleus of an atom which always has a positive charge whose magni-tude depends on the atomic species.

positive rays. Canal rays; streams of positively charged ions in a rarified-gas discharge.

positive response. The movement or growth of an organism to-ward the source of stimula-tion.

positive tropism. Same as positive response.

positive valence. A valence result-ing from the loss of one or more electrons by an atom or group.

positive-ion emission. A thermi-onic emission of positive par-ticles; the ions may be those of the metal, but are commonly due to some impurity.

positive-ion vacancy. A site in the lattice of an ionic crystal from which a positive ion is absent.

positive-ray analysis. The sepa-ration and measurement of atomic masses by subjecting their positive ions to deflection by electric or magnetic fields.

positron. A particle similar to an electron but having a positive charge.

post central. A pair of shields of the carapace of the turtle at the posterior end above the base of the tail.

postcaval vein. Inferior vena cava; a vein carrying blood from the rear of the vertebrate body to the heart.

posterior. (1) Nearest the main axis of a flower; situated on the back of another plant or-gan; (2) arranged near the hind end of an animal.

posterior root. Dorsal root; a nerve root of the spine that consists of sensory fibers.

potash. Potassium carbonate, K_2CO_3; colorless deliquescent crystals; used in tanning, ferti-lizers, soft-soap manufacture.

potash mica. Muscovite; alumi-num and potassium orthosili-cate; a fibrous mineral used as an insulator and filler.

potassium. A soft, waxlike, sil-very alkali metal which oxi-dizes rapidly in moist air; chemical symbol K; atomic number 19.

potassium bicarbonate. White soluble crystals; $KHCO_3$; used

in medicine.

potassium bromide. A white, crystalline salt; KBr; used in medicine and photography.

potassium carbonate. Same as potash.

potassium chlorate. Colorless crystals; $KClO_3$; used as an oxidizing agent, in pyrotech-nics, explosives.

potassium chloride. Colorless sol-uble crystals; KCl; used in medicine.

potassium cyanate. Colorless needles; KCNO; used for the control of crab grass.

potassium dichromate. Red crys-tals; $K_2Cr_2O_7$; used as an oxi-dizing agent, in the paint and dye industries, explosives, med-icine.

potassium hydroxide. Caustic potash; KOH; a white deli-quescent crystalline solid; used as a mordant, in soap manu-facture, medicine.

potassium iodide. White granules; KI; used in photography.

potassium nitrate. Niter; KNO_3; a white, soluble, crystalline salt; used in medicine, pickling meat, gunpowder.

potassium oxide. Soluble, color-less crystals; K_2O.

potassium permanganate. Deep-purple soluble crystalline salt; $KMnO_4$; used as a disinfectant, in volumetric analysis.

potassium sulfate. Colorless crys-tals; K_2SO_4; used in fertilizers, chemical analysis.

potential. The potential difference between a given point and the earth.

potential barrier. A region in which the electric potential is such that moving electric charges attempting to traverse it encounter opposition and may be turned back.

potential, contact. The difference in the affinities for electrons of the material of the cathode and those of other electrodes in a cathode-ray tube.

potential difference. A difference in the electrical states of two points which results in the flow of a current between them; it is measured by the work neces-sary for the transfer of a unit charge from one point to the other.

potential energy. The energy of a body due to its position or condition; stored energy.

potential energy, nuclear. The av-erage total potential energy of all of the nucleons in a nucleus which is due to the specific nuclear forces between them, but excluding the electrostatic potential energy.

potential galvanometer. A gal-vanometer of such high re-sistance that it can be used as a voltmeter.

potential hole. A region toward which the electric potential drops abruptly and throughout which its value is distinctly lower than on either side.

potential of a field of force. The potential energy per unit mass for a gravitational field of force.

potential, sparking. The potential difference necessary to cause an electrical spark to pass between two given points in a given insulating medium at a given temperature.

potential, stopping. The potential difference needed to bring an emitted electron to rest.

potential, striking. (1) The potential needed to initiate an arc; (2) starter-anode potential for a cold-cathode gas triode which will start anode-current flow.

potential temperature. The temperature that a compressible fluid would have if it were compressed or expanded adiabatically from its existing state to standard pressure.

potentiometer. An instrument used for comparing a voltage with a constant standard.

potentiometer, direct-reading. A potentiometer with the slide-wire calibrated in volts.

pothole. A circular depression gouged out of the bedrock of a stream by sharp rocks and stones spinning about in a whirlpool of water.

potometer. An instrument for measuring the water absorbed by a cut shoot.

pound. (1) A unit of weight or mass in the English system; 16 ounces; 0.456 kilogram; 454.0 grams; (2) the unit of force in the foot-pound-second system; it gives a mass of one slug an acceleration of one foot per second per second.

powder pattern. (1) Diffraction effects of amorphous substances; (2) the pattern of parallel lines or bands of ferromagnetic powder deposited on the surface of a magnetized crystal.

power. (1) The rate of doing work; (2) the degree of magnification of an optical instrument.

power amplifier. An arrangement in electrical communication which is designed to yield a definite power output with a given nonlinear distortion.

power factor. The ratio of the true power (watts read by a wattmeter) to the apparent power (volt-amperes as read by a voltmeter and ammeter).

power plant. (1) The assembly of the engine, carburetion, ignition, cooling, and lubrication systems of an automotive vehicle; (2) a power-generating industrial plant.

power stroke. The expansion stroke of an internal-combustion engine.

power supply. The sources of

electric power in an electron tube.

power transformer. A transformer specially designed for power circuits and usually enclosed in an iron box.

power venturi. A short tube with a widened end and narrow connecting part which is placed parallel to the air current for operating the gyroscopic turn indicator and other instruments in an aircraft.

pozzuolana. (1) A finely ground hydraulic cement; (2) a loosely agglomerated silica-containing rock of volcanic origin.

Pr. Chemical symbol for praseodymium.

prairie. A grassy land with scattered groves of trees; most prairies are flat or rolling.

praseodymium. A rare-earth metal; chemical symbol Pr; atomic number 59.

precaval vein. Vena cava superior; a vein carrying blood from the head and neck to the heart.

precession. (1) A slow revolution of the earth's axis on a small circle about the pole of the ecliptic which causes a slight backward shift of the equinoctial points; the period of revolution is 25,800 years; (2) the slow motion of the axis of a symmetrical revolving body which generates a cone; (3) the passing of the miotic spindle by chromosomes ahead of the autosomes.

precipitate. An insoluble product formed by a chemical action between solutions of two substances.

precipitation. (1) Moisture falling from the clouds or separating from the air, such as rain, snow, sleet, hail, fog, frost, dew; (2) separating solids from their solutions by chemical means.

precipitin. An antibody formed in response to the injection of soluble antigens, which can cause a precipitation or flocculation of the antigen when mixed with it.

precipitinogen. A substance which stimulates the formation of precipitin in the bloodstream.

precocial. Said of birds whose young are born with down and are able to walk after hatching; examples, turkey and duck.

preconduction current. The small electrode current in a gas-discharge tube that is present before a self-maintained discharge is started.

predacious animals. Animals that prey and eat other animals.

predator. An organism that preys or feeds on other organisms.

predissociation. The tendency of a diatomic or polyatomic molecule after the absorption of light to dissociate spontaneously usually into two un-

charged parts.

preformation. (1) The theory that every germ cell contains the adult individual complete in all details and development consists only in enlargement from the microscopic to the final proportions; (2) compacting molding powder without heat to the approximate shape of the product to be molded.

pregnancy. The period during which young develop in a female mammal.

prehensile. Adapted for seizing or holding; example, the tail of the opossum.

prehension. The flexion of an appendage to grasp an object by folding around it.

prehistoric. Existing before the time of recorded history or referring to that time.

prehnite. A greenish fibrous mineral; an acid orthosilicate of calcium and aluminum.

preischiopodite. A segment of the biramous appendage of Crustacea.

premaxilla. One of the two anterior membrane bones of the upper jaw.

premolars. Teeth with cusps on broad crowns which are used for crushing and grinding food; they lie between the canines and molars in mammals; man has two in each jaw, called bicuspids; in contrast to true molars they are preceded by milk molars.

preservatives. (1) Liquids used for preserving specimens; examples, alcohol, formaldehyde; (2) a substance added to food products, which retards or stops the growth of bacteria and thus prevents decay and spoiling; example, sodium benzoate.

pressure. (1) An electromotive force or voltage; (2) the thrust exerted on the unit area of a surface by a gas or liquid in contact with it.

pressure altitude. The altitude corresponding to a given pressure in a standard atmosphere.

pressure, atmospheric. The pressure exerted by the atmosphere on objects on the earth's surface; 1.013×10^6 dynes per square centimeter; 14.7 pounds per square inch; 760 millimeters of mercury at 0°C.

pressure broadening. An often asymmetrical increase in the half width of a line in the spectrum of a gas, when the source is under high pressure.

pressure, critical. The pressure required to liquefy a gas at its critical temperature.

pressure, gage. The pressure measured by a gage, that is, the pressure above the atmospheric pressure.

pressure gradient. The rate of change of pressure between two places.

pressure head. (1) the energy of a fluid per unit weight, due to its pressure; (2) an aircraft instrument containing a Pitot tube, which indicates the velocity of air currents.

pressure, impact. The pressure exerted by a moving fluid on a plane perpendicular to its direction of flow; it is measured in the direction of flow.

pressure, partial. The pressure exerted by a single gaseous component of a mixture of gases.

pressure shift. A change in the wave length of spectral lines when the source is under high pressure.

pressure, standard. The pressure exerted by a 760-millimeter column of mercury at 0°C.

pressure, vapor. (1) The pressure exerted by the vapors of a confined liquid or solid; (2) the pressure of a vapor alone or in a gaseous mixture.

pressurized cabin. A cabin in an aircraft in which the pressure is kept near its value at the surface of the earth by means of a supercharger.

presumptive region. The part of an embryo that includes all the cells which will, in normal development, become a particular organ or tissue.

prevailing westerlies. The normal winds that blow from the southwest between latitudes 30 and 60 of the Northern Hemisphere, and from the northwest in the same latitudes of the Southern Hemisphere.

prevailing wind. A wind which blows almost always from one direction.

Prevost's law of heat exchange. The total number of heat units lost by the warmer substance equals the total number of heat units gained by the cooler substance.

prickles. Superficial outgrowths from the bark which are neither specialized stems nor leaves.

primaries. The largest quill feathers of a bird's wing.

primary bow. A rainbow that shows the entire range of rainbow colors; the inner and brighter of the two rainbows sometimes seen.

primary cell. A voltaic cell in which chemical energy is transformed into electricity; it usually consists of an electrolyte in which two electrodes of different metals are immersed; the chemical reaction is irreversible and thus a primary cell cannot be recharged electrically.

primary coil. The coil of an electrical apparatus into which the current is introduced and which sets up the magnetic flux required to the operation of the apparatus.

primary colors. The fundamental colors from which all others are made; (1) for pigments, red, yellow, and blue; (2) in photography, red, green, and blue.

primary dark space. Aston dark space; a narrow nonluminous region which appears between the cathode and the cathode glow in certain gases.

primary egg cell. The cell in the ovary from which a mature egg develops after two divisions.

primary electron. (1) An electron from a primary emission; (2) that electron which, after a collision of two electrons, has the greater energy.

primary embryo. An individual formed in the ovicell of some Bryozoa; it is nourished by the parent through the wall of the ovicell and produces other individuals by budding.

primary emission. The incident emission which may excite a secondary emission from the irradiated matter.

primary germ layers. The group of cells in a developing embryo from which the tissues and organs of the adult develop; examples, ectoderm, mesoderm, and endoderm.

primary host. The host that contains the adult stage of a parasite.

primary meristem. A region of active cell division that has persisted from the time of its origin in the embryo or young plants.

primary root. The main central root of a plant that develops first from the radicle.

primary sperm cell. Primary spermatocyte; the cell in the testes from which mature sperm cells or spermatozoa develop after two divisions.

Primates. The class of erect mammals with highly developed brain; it includes man.

prime meridian. The Greenwich meridian; the meridian from which the numbering of the meridians of longitude begins, both east and west.

priming illumination. A small steady illumination applied to a photoelectric cell to make it more sensitive to the variations in illumination which the cell is being used to measure or record.

primitive streak. A longitudinal thickening in the disklike early embryo of birds or mammals during gastrulation; its source is an accumulation of mesoderm which moves inside the embryo.

primordial meristem. Promeristem; the apex of growing points of vascular plants; the earliest meristem.

principal axis. A line so chosen with reference to a rigid body that the body may rotate about it without developing a cen-

trifugal torque in any plane containing that line.

principal axis of a lens. A straight line passing through the centers of curvature.

principal axis of a mirror. A line through the center of curvature and the mid point (vertex) of a curved mirror.

principal focus. The point to which the parallel rays of light are brought by a lens or mirror.

principal line. The first and strongest line of a spectral series.

principal moment of inertia. The moment of inertia of a body with respect to one of its principal axes.

principal plane. A plane containing the optical axis and either the ordinary ray or the extraordinary ray of a crystal exhibiting double refraction.

principal section. The plane passing through the optic axis of a crystal and at right angles to one of the crystal faces.

principal strain. The component of strain, and the corresponding component of stress, that is in the direction of one of the strain axes at any point of an elastic solid under deformation.

printing-out paper. A photographic paper on which a visible image is produced by exposure to light, without development.

prionotron. A velocity-modulation tube.

prisere. Primary sere; a complete natural succession of plants from bare habitat to climax.

prism. A triangular glass piece used in optical instruments to separate rays of light into colors.

prism binocular. A binocular having a pair of right-angled, total-reflection Porro prisms in each telescope tube.

prismatic. (1) In the shape of a prism; (2) consisting of prisms.

Proboscidea. An order of mammals with a trunk; example, elephant.

proboscis. (1) The long and flexible snout of an animal; example, the trunk of an elephant; (2) a long, trunklike organ of various insects which is situated near the mouth.

procambium. A primary meristem which gives rise to vascular bundles.

process. (1) A series of steps leading to a certain end; (2) a projecting part of plants or animals.

Prochordata. Same as Protochordata.

proctodeum. A hollow structure, formed by the invagination of the outer layer of the embryonic body, which will constitute the caudal end of the alimentary tract.

Procyon. A large star of the Canis

Minor constellation.

producer gas. A relatively low-cost gas mixture obtained by burning coal or coke in a limited supply of air; used as an industrial fuel.

proembryo. A group of cells arising from the division of the fertilized egg cell, some of which are so-called suspensor cells and others are embryo cells.

profile drag. The difference between the total wing drag and the induced drag of an aircraft; the sum of surface-friction and form drag.

progesterone. A hormone secreted by the corpus luteum of the mammalian ovary; it prepares the reproductive organs for pregnancy and provides for the nourishment and protection of the embryo during pregnancy.

proglottis. Proglottid; one of the sections of a tapeworm; each proglottis has its own excretory system, nervous system, and both male and female reproductive organs.

projectile. A body ejected by force and continuing in motion by its own inertia; example, a missile from a firearm.

projection. (1) Representing an enlarged image on a screen from a photographic film or plate; (2) a method of representing the earth's surface on a map.

projection lantern. An optical system containing two lenses for projecting magnified images from a lantern slide.

projector. An optical instrument for transferring pictures to a screen and reproducing sound from sound tracks.

prolactin. A pituitary hormone necessary for the production of milk by the mammary glands.

prolate. Elongated in the direction of a line joining the poles.

prolegs. Paired projections at the end of the abdomen of caterpillars; they support the hind part of the wormlike body; they have small hooklets called crochets.

proliferation. (1) A growth by active cell division; (2) the production of shoots which may be cut off and used for starting a new plant; (3) the growth of an organ after a period of inactivity.

promeristem. A round cone of meristemic tissue at the growing points and in the embryo.

prometacenter. The center of a curve of buoyancy at any point.

promethium. A rare-earth metal, fission product of uranium; chemical symbol Pm; atomic number 61.

prominences. Regions of the solar chromosphere which extend to a considerable height as glowing projections from the nor-

mal upper surface of the solar atmosphere.

promoter. A substance that activates a catalyst.

pronephros. The first kidney formed in the vertebrate embryo; it is often missing in the adult.

Pronuba. A genus of moths; example, yucca moth, a small silvery moth which carries pollen to the flowers of yucca plants; its larvae feed on the seed pods of the plants.

pronucleus. (1) The sperm nucleus after its entry into the ovum at fertilization, but before fusion with the ovum nucleus; (2) the ovum nucleus after completion of meiosis but before fusion with the sperm nucleus.

Prony brake. An absorption dynamometer which consists of two friction blocks, bearing against a brake drum; the absorbed torque is balanced by weights at the end of an arm connected to the blocks.

proof spirit. A standard mixture of alcohol and water; in the United States, it consists of equal volumes of the two liquids.

prop root. A root above the ground that gives support to the stem from which it arises.

propagation. (1) The continuance of a species from generation to generation through reproduction; (2) the multiplication of plants by vegetative means.

propane. C_3H_8; the third hydrocarbon of the paraffin series; an inflammable gas; used as a refrigerant.

propeller. Airscrew; a helical structure having two, three, or four blades; used for the propulsion of aircraft and vessels.

propeller disk area. The total area swept by a propeller.

propeller efficiency. The ratio of the thrust to the power input of a propeller.

propeller shaft. Drive shaft; the shaft which transfers the power from the transmission to the rear axle of an automobile.

propeller thrust. The component parallel to the propeller axis of the total air force on the propeller.

proper motion. The component of the motion of a star relative to the other stars which is perpendicular to the line of sight.

property, additive. A property of a system that is equal to the sum of the values of that property for the constituents of the system; example, a property of a molecule that is the sum of the properties of its individual atoms.

property, colligative. A property of a substance that depends on the number of molecules involved and not on their nature.

property, constitutive. A property

of a substance that depends on the arrangement of the atoms in the molecule.

prophase. The first stage in mitosis when chromatin granules form spireme and then break up into chromosomes; the chromosome then divides lengthwise in half.

propolis. Bee glue; a brown waxy substance gathered by bees from the buds of some trees; it is used as a cement in building the hive.

proprioceptor. A receptor of internal stimuli; example, the balancing organs of the internal ear.

propyl alcohol. C_3H_7OH; a colorless liquid; used as a solvent of waxes and resins.

prosencephalon. Forebrain; that part of the vertebrate brain that comprises the cerebral hemispheres and the olfactory lobes.

prosopyle. A minute pore connecting the inhalant and radical canals of sponges.

prostate gland. A gland surrounding the neck of the bladder and urethra in the male.

prosthetic group. A nonprotein group in a protein; example, the nucleic acid group in a nucleoprotein.

prostrate stem. A stem that creeps on the ground.

prostomium. The anterior portion of the first segment of annelids, overhanging the mouth region.

protactinium. Same as protoactinium.

protandrous. (1) Said of flowers whose anthers mature before the carpels; example, dandelions; (2) said of animals which produce first sperms and then eggs; example, roundworm.

proteases. Protein-splitting enzymes.

protective colloid. A colloid used for the stabilization of a colloidal solution by preventing coagulation.

protective coloration. Assuming a coloration and markings similar to those of the surroundings by animals to mislead their enemies.

protective resemblance. (1) A resemblance to the environment; (2) the resemblance of a harmless organism to a harmful or distasteful one; example, viceroy butterfly and monarch butterfly.

protein. A complex nitrogenous organic compound of high molecular weight; it consists of amino acids joined by peptide linkages; proteins are necessary for the growth and repair of living tissues.

protein synthesis. The process by which amino acids form proteins.

proteinase. A proteolytic enzyme.

proteolysis. The hydrolysis of proteins by proteolytic enzymes.

proteolytic enzymes. Enzymes that break down proteins by hydrolysis; examples, pepsin, trypsin, and rennin.

proteoses. Soluble protein derivatives formed by digestion with gastric and pancreatic juices.

Proterozoic era. A geological era that began about one billion years ago; the few fossils from this period indicate the existence of simple marine life, such as algae, and annelid worms.

prothallus. A tiny flat green plant that grows out of a spore of ferns and their relatives; it produces in time eggs and sperm, and dies when the plant matures; a sexual phase in the life history of ferns.

prothorax. The first segment of an insect thorax to which the head and first pair of legs are attached.

prothrombin. Thrombogen; serozyme; a proteinlike substance in the blood plasma which is assumed to react with cephalin and calcium ions.

Protista. A collective name for all one-celled organisms; the plantlike members belong to Protophyta; the animallike members are classed as Protozoa; they are the most primitive form of life.

protium. A hydrogen isotope with no neutron in the nucleus.

protoactinium. A rare radioactive element; chemical symbol Pa; atomic number 91.

protocerebrum. The first of the three principal parts of the arthropod brain derived from the pair of ganglia in the first segment of the head and innervating the simple or compound eyes.

Protochordata. A heterogeneous group of Chordata; they have no brain or sense organs; they have gill slits, notochord, and dorsal hollow nerve cord; examples, amphioxis, sea squirt.

Protococcus. Pleurococcus; one-celled green algae that live on the shady side of trees, rocks, and walls.

protoderm. Dermatogen; a primary meristem which gives rise to epidermis.

protogynous. The female sex cells maturing earlier than the male sex cells.

proton. A positively charged particle in the nucleus of an atom; its charge is equal but opposite to that of an electron; its mass is 1.672×10^{-24} gram.

proton acceptor. A base according to the Brönsted concept.

proton donor. An acid according to the Brönsted concept.

protonema. (1) A tiny green branching filament that grows out of a spore of mosses and their relatives; it will grow into a plant by giving rise to lateral buds; (2) an early stage of some algae which is different from the adult.

protonephridium. The excretory organ of Platyhelminthes, Nemertea, and Rotifera; it has one or more flame cells.

protoplasm. The living matter of cells; a grayish gelatinous substance in which chemical and physical changes occur.

protoplast. (1) Energid; the contents of a protoplasmic cell; the cell nucleus and cytoplasm; (2) a plastid; (3) a one-celled animal.

protostele. A vascular cylinder found in almost all roots, the central xylem being surrounded by phloem.

prototype. (1) An accurate copy of a primary standard unit; (2) the original ancestral type.

protoxylem. The first wood which forms in the younger portion of a root; it consists of small loose vessels.

Protozoa. Single-celled animals; some form colonies; they have no true organs or tissues; examples, ameba, paramecium and volvox.

protozoology. The study of Protozoa.

protractor. (1) A muscle that draws some part of the body forward; (2) a drafting instrument for measuring or drawing angles.

proustite. A silver-bearing arsenical mineral.

proventriculus. The anterior part of the stomach in certain animals; example, in birds.

Proxima Centauri. The nearest star to the earth aside from the sun; it is 24,600,000,000,-000 miles away.

proximal. Nearer to the point of attachment of an organ.

proximate analysis. (1) The determination of moisture, volatile matter, fixed carbon, and ash in coal; (2) the determination of a group of related ingredients; example, total protein content.

proximity effect. The increased high-frequency resistance of a conductor when brought near another conductor; it is due to eddy currents; it is observed in a coil with closely adjacent turns.

Prussian blue. Ferricferrocyanide; $Fe_4[Fe(CN)_6]_3$; dark-blue crystals; used as a pigment.

prussic acid. Hydrocyanic acid, HCN; a very poisonous colorless liquid or gas; used as a fumigant.

pseudaposematic colors. Colors that help mimicry, that is, the imitation of one species by another.

pseudoadiabatic process. The cooling of rising air in which water-vapor condensation and precipitation occur.

pseudobranchia. A small supplementary gill on the inner surface of the operculum in certain fish.

pseudocoele. The so-called fifth ventricle of the brain.

pseudogamy. The development of an ovum into a new individual as a result of stimulation by a male gamete, whose nucleus does not fuse with the ovum and contributes nothing to the hereditary constitution of the embryo.

pseudomorph. A mineral that has the crystal form of one species and the chemical composition of another.

pseudopod. A footlike projection of the body wall; used for locomotion and for ingestion of food; examples, certain amebae and larvae.

pseudopodiospore. Amebula; a reproductive body or spore produced by some of the one-celled animals; it can form pseudopods.

pseudoscolex. The anterior end of a tapeworm which lacks a true scolex.

pseudostigmatic organ. A bristle, often clubbed at the tip, which occurs in some of the mites.

pseudovelum. A narrow rim of tissue near the margin of the body of jellyfish which has no muscles and nerve ring.

Psilophytales. An order of extinct Pteridophytes that flourished in the Devonian era; the oldest land plants.

Psocoptera. Wingless insects that live in damp rooms and feed on fungi; examples, book lice and deathwatches.

psychrometer. An instrument for measuring relative humidity; example, wet-and-dry-bulb hygrometer.

psychrophilic bacteria. Cold-loving bacteria whose optimum temperature for growth is 15 to 20°C, or below.

pt. Abbreviation for pint.

Pt. Chemical symbol for platinum.

Pteridophyta. Plants that have true roots, stems, and leaves, but are not as well developed as seed-bearing plants; they show alternation of generations; examples, ferns, club mosses, and horsetails.

pterodactyl. An extinct flying reptile that lived during the lower Jurassic era.

Pteropoda. Sea butterflies; hermaphroditic gastropod mollusks with winglike swimming organs and with or without a shell.

pterygoid. One of a pair of cartilage bones of the skull bracing the posterior part of the jaws.

Ptilota. A genus of the red algae noted for their graceful featherlike form and beautiful color.

ptyalin. An enzyme in saliva which digests starch to sugar.

Pu. Chemical symbol for plutonium.

puberty. Sexual maturity.

pubic symphysis. A joint formed mid-ventrally between the pubic bones of the two halves of the pelvic girdle in most mammals.

pubis. The anterior part of the hip or pelvic girdle.

puddling. The preparation of wrought iron from pig iron, which contains a high percentage of carbon, by heating in an oxidizing atmosphere with constant agitation.

pulley. A wheel having a grooved rim to hold an endless belt, rope or chain; used as a simple machine.

pulmonary. Belonging or referring to the lung.

pulmonary circulation. An independent circulation of deoxygenated blood from the heart to the lungs where it is oxygenated and then returned to the heart.

Pulmonata. An order of gastropod fresh-water or terrestrial mollusks which have a lung; examples, snails and slugs.

pulp. (1) A crude fibrous material obtained from wood and formed into paper sheets; (2) a spongy soft tissue in the interior of an animal organ; example, dental pulp.

pulp, tooth. Dental pulp; a spongy mass that fills the central part of a tooth; it contains blood vessels and nerves which enter the tooth through an opening in the root.

pulsating direct current. A direct current flowing in one direction and regularly changing its magnitude.

pulsation. (1) The throbbing of the heart or of an artery; (2) a periodically returning impulse; (3) the surge of electrons in one direction during an alternation of an alternating current.

pulsation theory. The Cepheid variable stars expand and contract periodically, and are the brightest in the final stage of contraction.

pulse. (1) A regular periodic expansion of the artery walls following each contraction of the heart; (2) changes in the strength of a direct current; (3) a very short radio signal.

pulverizing. Grinding a substance to a powder.

pulvillus. The last segment of the foot of an insect; it has a claw on either side of a pad.

pulvinus. An enlargement at the point of attachment of a leaf or leaflet.

pumice. An igneous rock formed when molten lava was hurled into the air, cooled, and solidified while the steam and other gases were still coming forth from the lava; used as an abrasive.

pump. A machine for raising fluids from a deeper to a higher level.

punctate. Marked with dots or small depressions.

punctiform colonies. Pin-point colonies measuring less than one millimeter in diameter.

Punnett square. A diagram which facilitates the study of crossings or matings.

pupa. An inactive stage in the life of an insect between the larval and adult stages; the pupa is covered with a horny case and cannot move about.

pupil. The central opening in the iris of the eye which admits light.

pure culture. A bacterial culture which develops only one species.

pure line. (1) A group of organisms which have the same kind of genes for special characters; (2) a community of individuals that are descendants of one ancestor.

pure spectrum. A spectrum each point of which corresponds to only one wave length of frequency of the dispersed radiation.

purebred. An animal from a breed that was kept pure for many generations.

purine. $C_5H_4N_4$; a pyrimidine derivative found mainly in plants and to a lesser degree in animals.

Purkinje effect. An increased sensitivity of the normal eye in poor illumination to blue light and in good illumination to yellow light.

purple of Cassius. A purple pigment, consisting of a mixture of colloidal gold, and stannic and stannous chlorides; used in the manufacture of ruby glass.

pus. A yellowish-white viscous fluid that may form in an infected body part, consisting of white blood cells, dead and living germs, and some plasma.

push-pull amplifier. Two vacuum tubes which are so connected that when the grid of one is positively charged that of the other is negatively charged and vice versa.

pustule. (1) A mass of spores of fungi and their hyphae; (2) a small pus-containing swelling.

pusule. A small vacuole opening to the exterior by a canal in some one-celled animals, such as mastigophores.

putrefaction. The decomposition of animal or vegetable matter in the absence of oxygen by microbes, characterized by the formation of amino acids, mercaptans, indol, skatol, and hydrogen sulfide and accompanied by an unpleasant odor.

putty powder. Impure tin oxide, SnO_2.

pycnidium. A minute, globose, or flask-shaped fungus body with apical ostiole, lined internally with conidiophores.

pycnometer. Pyknometer; a small graduated glass container for measuring the specific gravity of liquids.

pycnosis. The contraction of a nucleus into a compact deeply-staining mass; it occurs as the cell dies.

pygidium. A caudal portion of the body of some scale insects.

pyloric caeca. Tubular cavities in fish where the stomach and intestine join.

pyloric sphincter. A circular band of muscle at the pylorus, the opening between the stomach and small intestine; when relaxed, food can go into the intestine.

pyloric valve. Same as pyloric sphincter.

pylorus. An opening of the vertebrate stomach that leads into the small intestine.

pyranometer. An instrument which measures the intensity of the radiation received from any portion of the sky by comparison with the heating effect of an electric current of known intensity.

pyrene. $C_{16}H_{10}$; a tetracyclic hydrocarbon obtained by the distillation of coal tar; yellowish crystals.

pyrenoids. Rounded bodies of stored food or chloroplast in some algae.

pyrethrum. A strong insect poison extracted from the flowers of the pyrethrum plant, Anacyclus pyrethrum.

pyrgeometer. An instrument measuring radiation from the earth's surface into space.

pyrheliometer. An instrument for measuring the radiation from the sun.

pyribole. Pyroxene and/or amphibole containing dark minerals.

pyridine. C_5H_5N; a heterocyclic compound; a colorless liquid coal-tar fraction with an unpleasant smell; used as a solvent, in medicine.

pyridoxin. $C_8H_{11}NO_3$; vitamin B_6; its lack causes dermatitis in rats.

pyriform gland. The pear-shaped gland of spiders that secretes silk for the formation of the disks to which the threads are anchored.

pyrite. Fool's gold; a yellow mineral; iron sulfide, FeS_2; the most common source of sulfur.

pyro-. A prefix meaning (1) fire, and thus high temperature; (2) an acid or its salts containing less water than the normal acid and obtained by heating the normal acid.

pyroelectricity. The simultaneous development of positive and negative charges on different parts of the same crystal by heating; example, tourmaline.

pyrogallol. Pyrogallic acid, $C_6H_3(OH)_3$; soluble white powder; used in photographic developers and in gas analysis for the determination of oxygen.

pyrogenic. (1) Causing or caused by fever; (2) of igneous origin; (3) heat generating.

pyroligneous acid. An aqueous solution obtained by the destructive disillation of wood; it contains acetic acid, methyl alcohol, acetone, and small amounts of other organic compounds.

pyrolusite. A gray mineral; manganese dioxide, MnO_2; used as a source of manganese.

pyrolysis. Decomposition by heat.

pyrometallurgy. The reduction of ores to metals with the help of high temperatures; examples, roasting, smelting.

pyrometer. An instrument for measuring high temperatures.

pyrometric cones. Seger cones; small cones that differ in the temperature at which they soften on heating; they consist of a mixture of oxides and are used for the measurement of temperatures in the range of 1100° to 3700°F.

pyrometry. The science of the measurement of high temperatures.

pyron detector. A crystal detector employing iron pyrite.

pyrophoric alloys. Cerium-base alloys which emit sparks when scraped or struck; used in cigaret lighters; example, misch metal.

pyrophyllite. A yellowish mineral; hydrous aluminum silicate; it is used as a paper filler.

pyroscope. An optical pyrometer which compares the color of the heated substance with that of the flame of a kerosene burner.

pyrotechnics. The study and manufacture of fireworks.

pyroxylin. Soluble cellulose nitrates; used in explosives, lacquers.

pyrrhotite. Magnetic pyrite; an iron sulfide with variable amounts of dissolved sulfur.

pyrrole. A five-membered ring compound, containing one nitrogen and four carbon atoms; a fundamental building block of many natural coloring matters.

Q

qt. Abbreviation for quart.

quadrant. (1) A quarter of a circle; an arc of 90°; (2) a sextant-type instrument for measuring altitude; (3) a section of the segmenting ovum from a primary blastomere.

quadrant electrometer. Kelvin electrometer; an electrometer consisting of a light metallic needle suspended horizontally in a flat metal cylinder divided into quadrants.

quadrate bone. One of two roughly quadrangular cartilage bones in the vertebrate skull to which the lower jaw is attached, except that of mammals.

quadratojugal. One of a pair of posterior bones of the upper jaw in some vertebrates.

quadratron. A high-vacuum tetrode.

quadrature. (1) A phase difference of one-quarter cycle; (2) the position of the moon when lines drawn to it and to the sun from the earth are at right angles.

quadruped. A four-footed animal; examples, horse, dog.

quadruple line. A spectral line found in the spectra of nebulae and the aurora.

quadruple point. The temperature at which four phases are in equilibrium.

quadrupole. A system consisting of two equal dipoles parallel to each other, but with their corresponding charges reversed.

qualitative analysis. The identification of the constituents of a substance without the determination of their amounts.

quantitative analysis. The determination of the quantities of the various constituents of a substance.

quantity of radiation. The time integral of the intensity of radiation; it is the total energy which has passed through a unit area perpendicularly to the beam and is expressed in ergs per square centimeter or watt-seconds per square centimeter.

quantization. Expressing a variable as a multiple of a definite quantity.

quantized. Said of particles that have energies of certain definite values.

quantum. The basic unit of certain quantities, according to the quantum theory; example, a photon is the quantum of electromagnetic radiation.

quantum efficiency. The number of photoelectrons emitted from a metal per quantum of incident radiation.

quantum equivalence principle. When, in a photoelectric or photovoltaic process, a quantum of radiation is absorbed, its entire energy reappears in some other definite form.

quantum mechanics. The mechanics of phenomena for which the quantum theory holds true; example, atomic and molecular changes.

quantum number. An integral number which is characteristic of the state of an atomic system.

quantum state. Energy level; one

of the states in which an atom or a molecule may exist permanently or momentarily; transitions between these states are accompanied by the emission or absorption of radiation quanta, corresponding to lines of the spectrum.

quantum theory. Planck's concept of energy consisting of minimum indivisible "particles" called quanta; radiant energy is emitted or absorbed only in quanta or photons, each with an energy in ergs of 6.6624×10^{-27} times the frequency of the radiation in cycles per second.

quantum theory of heat capacity. A theory which explains the decrease of specific heat at low temperatures to a value below its classical values on the basis of energy quantization.

quantum transition. Quantum jump; atomic rearrangement which is accompanied by the emission or absorption of a quantum of radiant energy.

quantum yield. The number of photon-induced reactions of a specified type per photon absorbed.

quart. An English measure of capacity; 2 pints; ¼ gallon; 0.946 liter.

quarter-sawing. Rift sawing; sawing timber lengthwise into quarters and cutting the boards, etc., from the quarters to show the medullary wood rays obliquely and to minimize warping.

quarter-wave plate. A plate of double-refracting material cut parallel to the optic axis of the crystal in such a thickness that there is a quarter of a period delay between the ordinary and secondary rays falling on the plate at right angles; used for analysis of polarized light.

quartz. A transparent, usually colorless, hard mineral; silicon dioxide, SiO_2; used for making special laboratory ware and in electrical apparatus.

quartz clock. A clock which is regulated by a quartz crystal vibrating with a definite constant frequency under the effect of an alternating electric field tuned to the resonance frequency of the crystal; used for precision work.

quartz-fiber manometer. A manometer which measures gas pressure by the damping which it offers to the vibrations of a quartz fiber.

quartzite. A hard compact metamorphic rock composed almost entirely of quartz.

quaternary ammonium compound. A compound of the general formula R_4NOH derived from ammonium hydroxide by replacement of the hydrogen atoms with organic radicals; example, tetra-

ethyl ammonium hydroxide, $(C_2H_5)_4NOH$.

queen bee. A fully developed female bee, the mother of a community of bees, whose only duty is to lay eggs in cells prepared by the workers; (2) a radio-controlled pilotless aircraft used as a target in anti-aircraft practice.

quenching. (1) Hardening steel or other alloys by dipping into water, oil, or another cold bath after heating above the critical temperature; (2) ending a discharge in a radiation counter tube by preventing reignition.

quicklime. Burnt lime; a white infusible solid; calcium oxide, CaO; used in mortar, leather manufacture.

quicksilver. Mercury, Hg; used in thermometers.

quiet volcano. A volcano that discharges liquid lava with little gas and no solids.

quill. (1) Calamus; the hollow end of the rachis of a feather; (2) the hollow shaft of a spindle.

quill feathers. Wing and tail feathers of birds which are used for flying and steering.

Quincke tube. A sound-transmission tube having two parallel branches; used for sound filtration.

quinones. Unsaturated cyclic diketones; they are widely distributed in plants and can be prepared from benzene and its homologues; used in photography, dye manufacture.

quinquevalent. Pentavalent; having a valency of five.

quintaplane. A plane with five wings.

quintuple point. The temperature at which five phases are in equilibrium.

R

R meter. An ionization measuring instrument calibrated in roentgens.

Ra. Chemical symbol for radium.

rabbit. Shuttle; a small container pneumatically or hydraulically propelled through a tube in a nuclear reactor, so that samples containing atoms with very short half lives can be removed.

Rabi field. A nonuniform magnetic field between parallel flat rectangular poles that is used for deflecting particles having an intrinsic magnetic movement.

race track. Several calutrons, assembled in the shape of a race track, which have a common magnetic field.

raceme. An inflorescence in which the flowers are arranged spirally around a central axis; example, lily of the valley.

racemic compound. An equimolecular optically inactive mixture of the levo- and dextrorotatory isomers of an optically active compound.

racemization. The conversion of an optically active compound into its racemic, or optically inactive, form.

rachilla. The central axis of a spikelet of grass.

rachis. (1) The main axis of an inflorescence; (2) the extension of the petiole corresponding to the midrib of the entire compound leaf; (3) the vertebral column; (4) the shaft of a feather.

racon. A radar beacon used for directing aircraft.

rad. A unit of absorbed radiation dose; 100 ergs per gram of the tissue.

radar. Short for "radio detection and ranging"; a device that determines the location and distance of objects by ultra-high-frequency radio waves.

radar echo. Radio-frequency energy reflected from objects around the transmitter.

radar indicator. A cathode-ray oscilloscope on which the returned signal is recorded for visual observation.

radar target. Any reflecting surface in the beam of the radar antenna which causes a signal to be returned to the receiver.

radial engine. An engine which has stationary cylinders arranged radially around a common crankshaft; aircraft engines are usually of this type.

radial symmetry. The arrangement of parts of an animal in such a way that they radiate from a central point; example, the arms of a starfish.

radial velocity. Line-of-sight velocity; the speed at which a heavenly body is approaching or moving away from the observer; it is determined spectroscopically and expressed in kilometers per second.

radiance. The luminous flux radiated per unit area of a surface.

radiant intensity. The radiant flux emitted by a point source per unit solid angle in a specified direction.

radiating atom. An atom which is emitting radiation during the transition of one or more of its electrons from higher to lower energy levels.

radiation. (1) The transfer of energy by electromagnetic waves; (2) the emission of particles and/or waves by radioactive bodies; (3) the emission of light rays.

radiation damping. A decrease in the amplitude of an electric oscillation due to the emission of energy by radiation.

radiation, heterogeneous. Radiation at several different frequencies and/or energies.

radiation, homogeneous. Radiation with a narrow band of frequencies, and/or having identical particles with the same energy.

radiation, monochromatic. Radiation having only one frequency or wave length.

radiation potential. Resonance potential; the energy, expressed in electron volts, needed to transfer an electron from its normal position in an atom to some other possible position.

radiation potentiometer. An instrument for studying the spectral-energy distribution of thermal radiation.

radiation pressure. A very small pressure exerted on a surface exposed to light or another electromagnetic radiation; its value is proportional to the radiant-energy density in the medium.

radiation pyrometer. A pyrometer which indicates the temperature of the heated body by measuring the total intensity or the spectral-energy distribution of the thermal radiation emitted by it.

radiation, recoil. A radiation emitted during nuclear disintegration which is attended by an observable recoil of the nucleus emitting the radiation.

radiation resistance. That part of the apparent or measured resistance of an oscillating circuit which is due to the loss of energy by radiation.

radiation, stray. All radiation that reaches the detector at wave lengths that do not correspond to the spectral position under consideration.

radiation temperature. The temperature to which an ideal black body must be heated to have the same emissive power as the source of thermal radiation in question.

radiation, visible. A radiation within the visible spectrum.

radiative equilibrium. The maintenance of a constant temperature by the absorption and emission of radiant energy at the same rate.

radical. (1) A group of atoms of different elements which behaves like a single atom in chemical reactions; examples, —OH, =SO₄, —NO₃; (2) arising from the root or crown of a plant.

radicle. (1) A small projection of a dicot seed which is a rudimentary root and develops into a root; (2) any very small root.

radio. A general term covering all the forms of transmission of audible signals or programs by electromagnetic waves, without wires.

radio altimeter. A terrain-clearance indicator operating on the radar principle; used in aviation.

radio astronomy. A branch of astronomy that uses radio telescopes instead of optical telescopes to study the radiation emitted by celestial bodies.

radio beacon. A radio transmitting station maintained and operated for the determination of radio bearings.

radio bearing. The direction from which a radio signal is received.

radio channel. A frequency band wide enough to permit its use for radio communication.

radio compass. A position finder in navigation which employs the directional characteristics of the loop antenna.

radio fix. A radio bearing or bearings which help determine a geographical position.

radio frequency. The frequency of the electromagnetic waves used in the transmission of radio signals, which are just beyond the audible frequencies.

radio horizon. The locus of points at which direct rays from a transmitter are tangential to the earth's surface.

radio interference. Any noise which interferes with the reception of a desired signal.

radio proximity fuze. Variable-time fuze; VT fuze; an electronic fuse which is triggered by microwaves sent out by a transmitter in the shell after reception of waves reflected back from the target; it detonates the projectile.

radio receiver. An apparatus which receives signals sent out by a transmitter and demodulates these signals so that they may be heard as speech, music, or code signals.

radio wave. An electromagnetic wave caused by the oscillation of electric charges, and converted into sound by receiving sets.

radioactive decomposition. A radioactive change in which a nucleus emits corpuscular rays forming a lighter, more stable nucleus.

radioactive deposit. A film of radioactive matter formed on an object from the disintegration of a radioactive emanation.

radioactive displacement law. when a nucleus emits an alpha particle, the new nucleus formed has an atomic number two less than the parent and a mass number, four less; the loss of an electron means no change in mass, but an increase by one of the atomic number; the loss of a positron means no change in mass but the decrease by one of the atomic number; the emission of gamma rays causes no change of mass or atomic number.

radioactive elements. Elements that radiate waves and/or particles either spontaneously or after bombardment with high-velocity particles.

radioactive emanations. Radioactive gases given off by certain radioactive elements.

radioactive fall-out. The showering down of radioactive particles which were originally carried high into the air by a nuclear explosion.

radioactive heat. Radiogenic heat; the heat produced by radioactivity.

radioactive isotope. Radioisotope; an isotope that has been made radioactive by radiation; used in tracer work.

radioactive product. A substance resulting from the radioactive disintegration of a parent substance.

radioactive series. A succession of radioactive elements, each of which is derived from the disintegration of the one preceding it.

radioactive standard. A sample of radioactive substance with a long half life and of known properties; it is used as a radiation source for calibrating radiation-measurment equipment.

radioactive tracer. A radioactive element introduced in small quantities to determine the behavior of chemically similar nonradioactive atoms in various physical or chemical changes; it owes its name to the fact that it can be traced by its radioactivity in any phase of a reaction.

radioactivity. The spontaneous uncontrollable disintegration of the nucleus of an atom with the emission of α, β and/or γ rays.

radioactivity, artificial. Radioactivity induced in an element by bombarding it with particles and/or radiation.

radioactivity, induced. Same as artificial radioactivity.

radioautograph. Autoradiograph; a photographic record obtained when a thin biological or other specimen, containing a radioactive isotope, is placed in contact with a photographic plate, exposed for a suitable period, and then developed; the distribution of the radioactive element in the specimen is seen in the image.

radio-communication circuit. A system which transmits one communication at a time in either direction between two points by electromagnetic waves.

radioelement. A product of radioactivity.

radio-field strength. The electric or magnetic field intensity at a given location when radio waves pass through it.

radio-frequency amplifier. An amplifier of radio oscillations inserted in the receiver circuit before the detecting tube or frequency changer.

radiogenetics. The study of the effects of radiation on heredity.

radiogenic. Resulting from radioactivity.

radiogram. (1) A radiograph; (2) an x-ray pattern produced by crystal diffraction; (3) a wireless telegraph message.

radiograph. An x-ray or radium photograph, showing the non-uniform density of the structure through which the rays pass.

radiography. The formation of images on fluorescent screens or photographic film by short-wave-length radiation, such as x-rays.

radioisotope. Same as radioactive isotope.

Radiolaria. A group of marine planktonic rhizopod Protozoa; their skeleton of silica is important in forming flint and oozes of the ocean bottom.

radioluminescence. A luminescence from radioactive emission or x-rays.

radiometeorograph. Radiosonde; a meteorograph which, when sent up on a balloon, automatically reports atmospheric conditions, that is, pressure, temperature, and humidity, by radio to the receiving apparatus at the ground station.

radiometer. An instrument for measuring the intensity of radiant energy.

radiometric gage. A low-pressure gas manometer whose operation depends on the inequality of pressure due to molecular bombardment on opposite sides of a suspended vane.

radiometry. The measurement of radiant energy by converting it into mechanical energy.

radiomicrometer. An instrument which is sensitive to very feeble thermal radiation and thus suitable for its measurement; it consists of a short-circuited bismuth-silver thermocouple suspended in a strong magnetic field and connected in series with a galvanometer.

radionavigation. The use of radio aids to navigation for checking the dead-reckoning position of a ship.

radionuclide. A natural or artificial nuclide which exhibits radioactivity.

radiopaque. Impermeable to x-rays or other radiation.

radiophotoluminescence. A luminescence exhibited by certain minerals when irradiated with beta and gamma rays, followed by exposure to light.

radioscope. An instrument for detecting radioactivity in water, soil, ore, or gas by the scintillation method.

radiosensitive. Sensitive to radiation; capable of being destroyed by radiation.

radiosonde. A radio transmitter

attached to a balloon which carries weather instruments to high altitudes, records weather conditions, and sends them to earth by radio signals; used in weather forecasting.

radiothermoluminescence. A luminescence exhibited by certain vitreous and crystalline substances when irradiated with beta and gamma rays, followed by heat.

radioulna. The fused radius and ulna bones of an amphibian forearm; example, in frog.

radio-wave propagation. The transfer of energy by electromagnetic radiation at frequencies lower than about 3×10^{12} cycles per second.

radium. A radioactive metal found in nature; chemical symbol Ra; atomic number 88.

radium emanation. Same as radon.

radius. (1) The bone on the thumb side of the lower arm extending from the elbow to the wrist; (2) a primary radiating division of the body of Echinodermata; (3) a straight line drawn from the center of a circle to its circumference, or from the center of a sphere to its surface.

radius of gyration. The square root of the quotient of the moment of inertia divided by the mass.

radome. A dome-shaped dielectric housing for radar equipment.

radon. Radium emanation; the heaviest inert gas liberated by the disintegration of radium; chemical symbol Rn; atomic number 86; used in the treatment of cancer.

radula. A horny strip on the floor of a snail's mouth with many rows of minute teeth; it is used for scraping food.

rain. Drops of water falling from the clouds as a result of the condensation of excess water vapor when humid air is cooled below the dew point; to be able to fall down, the weight of the rain drops must overcome the frictional resistance of the atmosphere.

rain forest. A tropical lush forest developing under the most favorable climatic conditions, with an abundant and continuous water supply and a long growing season.

rain gage. An instrument for measuring precipitation over a given period of time; it usually consists of a funnel and a graduated collecting vessel.

rain shadow. The phenomenon that the leeward sides of the mountain are drier than the windward side.

rainbow. A curved band of colored light in the sky, caused by drops of water acting as prisms refracting and internally reflecting the sunlight.

Raman effect. The appearance of extra spectrum lines in the vicinity of each prominent line of the spectrum of gases, liquids, and solids when they are illuminated by monochromatic light; they result from the frequency changes due to the light quanta losing energy to or gaining energy from the vibrating molecules.

ramenta. Brown chaffy scaly epidermal hairs which cover the young leaves and stems of ferns.

ramet. An independent individual of a clone.

ramjet. A jet engine which, after being set in motion, gets the air needed for combustion through a funnel-shaped opening at the front of the engine.

Ramsauer effect. (1) The absorption of slow-moving electrons by interposed matter; (2) the low collision probability of slow-moving electrons traversing an inert gas.

Ramsden eyepiece. An eyepiece consisting of two similar planoconvex lenses with their convex faces facing each other and at a distance equal to two thirds the focal length of either; used in optical instruments for crosswire measurements.

ramus. (1) A branch or branching part; (2) the barb of a feather.

Raney nickel. A hydrogenation catalyst consisting of nickel hydride.

range. (1) A continuous arrangement of peaks, ridges, and valleys; (2) the entire area where a wild plant or animal lives; (3) the depth to which a corpuscular emission will penetrate a given substance; (4) the distance an aircraft can travel without refueling; (5) the horizontal distance a projectile can reach.

range of stability. The angle through which a floating body may be rotated from its equilibrium position without capsizing.

Rankine temperature scale. A temperature scale which corresponds to the Kelvin scale, but is based on the absolute zero of the Fahrenheit system, so that 0° Rankine is equal to −459.69°F.

Raoult's law. The vapor pressure of a substance in solution is proportional to its mol fraction.

raphe. (1) A ridge, formed by the stalk of the ovule, on seeds in which the funiculus is sharply bent at the base of the ovule; (2) the junction between the two halves of the vertebrate brain.

raphide. A bundle of fine sharp needlelike crystals occurring in plant cells.

rapids. Sloping segments of swift streams; where the course is broken by some obstruction, but there is no waterfall or cascade.

Raptores. Birds of prey; an order of birds having sharp hooked beaks, strong sharp curved claws, powerful flight, and keen vision; examples, eagle and vulture.

rare earths. The group of fourteen metallic elements between lanthanium and hafnium; they differ in electronic configuration from their neighbors only in the number of electrons in the second from the outside shell.

rarefaction, acoustic. A local decrease in air pressure caused by a passing sound wave.

raster. Parallel lines on a fluorescent television screen; the image is formed by changing the brightness of different parts of the raster.

rate of decay of sound. The time rate at which sound decreases at a given point and at a given time; its practical unit is the decibel, the loss of power in a mile of standard cable at 800 cycles.

ratio of transformation. The ratio of the number of turns on the primary coil to the number of turns on the secondary coil of a transformer, affecting both voltage and current.

Ratitae. Flightless birds; the wings are reduced in size and have no barbules on the feathers or keel on the sternum; examples, emu, ostrich, and rhea.

ray. (1) A thin beam of light; (2) an imaginary line representing the direction of heat or light energy; (3) a structure of Echinodermata supporting the tube feet.

ray flowers. The outer ring of flowers in a composite flower head.

ray, ordinary. The ray which is deviated at an angle of refraction independent of the angle of incidence when light is incident obliquely to an anistropic crystal or other double-refracting medium.

Rayleigh disk. An acoustic radiometer which consists of a suspended small disk that is placed at an angle in the path of a sound wave; it is used for measuring particle velocity.

Rayleigh law. At very low values of the maximum magnetic induction, the hysteresis loss in a magnetic cycle is proportional to the cube of the induction.

Rayleigh line. That component of a spectrum line, in scattered radiation, which has the same frequency as the corresponding incident radiation that arises from ordinary or Rayleigh scattering.

Rayleigh scattering. The selective scattering of light by very small particles suspended in the air, such as dust or even the molecules of the air itself.

rays, parallel. A bundle of rays which are parallel to each other and to the optic axis of an optical system.

rays, skein. Rays that are not confined to a meridian plane, do not intersect the optic axis, and are difficult to trace.

Rb. Chemical symbol for rubidium

Re. Chemical symbol for rhenium

reactance. The opposition of an alternating-current circuit to the flow of an electric current because of the inductance or capacitance of the circuit; the reactance due to inductance is called inductive reactance and that due to capacitance, capacity reactance.

reactance tube. A vacuum tube which operates in such a manner that it presents the characteristics of a reactance to the rest of the circuit.

reactant. A substance participating in a chemical reaction; it appears on the left-hand side of a chemical equation.

reaction. (1) To every action there is an equal and opposite reaction; (2) regeneration feedback; (3) a chemical change; (4) the change in the behavior of an organism in response to a stimulus.

reaction, reversible. A reaction in which the products formed react with each other yielding the original substances at such a rate that equilibrium finally results between the two opposing chemical changes; example, the ionic dissociation of an electrolyte.

reaction time. (1) The time it takes for an organism to act in response to a stimulus; (2) the time required to the completion of a chemical reaction.

reactive. Entering easily into chemical reaction; chemically active.

reactor. Nuclear reactor; pile; a device in which controlled chain reactions take place to produce nuclear energy; it contains a fuel which undergoes fission when bombarded by neutrons and which then produces more neutrons to maintain the chain reaction.

reactor, bare homogeneous thermal. A nuclear reactor in which the thermal neutrons induce fission, the fuel being homogeneously distributed throughout the moderator, with no reflector.

reactor, heterogeneous. A nuclear reactor in which the fuel is distributed in the moderator in the form of discrete lumps.

reactor, homogeneous. A nuclear reactor in which the fissionable material and moderator are combined in a homogeneous mixture.

reactor, intermediate. A nuclear reactor which has neutrons with energies greater than thermal but less than those of fission neutrons.

reactor, power. A nuclear reactor used principally to produce power economically.

reactor, production. A nuclear reactor which produces fissionable material, usually Pu 239.

reactor, simple. A linear reactor.

reactor system, critical state of. The state in which there are as many neutrons being produced by fission as are lost by absorption and leakage.

reagent. A chemical used in chemical analysis for producing a characteristic effect.

real image. An image formed by the convergence of light rays, which can be projected on a screen.

realgar. Red arsenic; AsS; a reddish-brown mineral.

realm. A group of neighboring regions cut off from other regions by impassable barriers which prevent the migration of life forms.

rearrangement. A reaction in organic chemistry which involves the transfer of an atom or group from one part of the molecule to another.

Réaumur scale. A temperature scale in which the melting point of ice is 0°R and the boiling point of water is 80°R.

recalescence. Heat evolution by iron or steel while allowing it to cool through the critical range; this heat is sufficient to halt the cooling and even produce a momentary heating.

recapitulation theory. The theory that the individual in its development passes through the ancestral history of the race; ontogeny repeats phylogeny.

receiver. (1) That part of the telephone that converts the electric currents it receives into sound waves; (2) a radio set which receives the signals sent out by a transmitter and changes them so that they may be heard as music, speech, or code signals.

receiver, superheterodyne. A radio receiver in which all incoming radiofrequency signals are changed to a common intermediate carrier frequency before conversion to the original modulation.

recent period. Holocene; the last Cenozoic era; about 25,000 years; man dominates the scene.

receptacle. (1) The enlarged or flattened end of a flower stalk which holds the parts of the flower; (2) the shortened axis of an inflorescence; (3) the widened end of a branch in algae, that holds the reproductive organs; (4) the tissue mass carrying the sporangia of ferns.

receptaculum seminis. A sac of the female in which the seminal fluid received from the male during coitus is stored.

receptor. (1) A sense organ or sensory nerve ending of an animal which receives stimuli from outside or inside the body; (2) in Ehrlich's side-chain theory of immunity, that part of a cell molecule which can combine with the haptophore group of toxins or other antigens.

recessional moraine. New terminal moraine formed whenever a glacier pauses for a time in its retreat.

recessive. Recessive character; the character which is masked or hidden by the dominant character in the hybrid generation.

reciprocal cross. A cross between two plants in which each plant receives pollen from the other.

reciprocating engine. An engine in which the piston is repeatedly driven from one end of the cylinder to the other.

reciprocating motion. A back-and-forth or up-and-down motion.

reclamation. Making arid land fertile by supplying water for irrigation; projects under the Reclamation Act of 1902.

recoil atom. An atom which undergoes a sudden change or reversal of its direction of motion as a result of its emission of a particle or radiation.

recoil particle. A particle that begins to move because of a collision or a process involving the ejection of another particle.

recombination. (1) Regrouping of chromosomes and their genes during gamete production, followed by random union of different sorts of gamete at fertilization; (2) the reunion of ions in an ionized gas due to various causes.

recombination spectrum. A faint continuous spectrum ascribed to the recombination of ions in an ionized gas.

recovery. (1) The percentage of mineral obtained in ore processing; (2) a return to the original state or condition.

recovery of metals. Removing the effects of work hardening without changing the microstructure.

recrystallization. (1) Purification of a substance by dissolving it repeatedly and evaporating the solvent to form crystals while the impurities remain in the solvent; (2) heating a cold-worked metal to its recrystallization temperature which results in a new, more desirable grain structure.

rectification. (1) The purification of a liquid by distillation; (2) the conversion of an alternating current into a direct current.

rectifier. A device for changing alternating current into direct current.

rectifier, half-wave. Single-wave rectifier; a rectifier which uses only half of the input alternating wave form, either the positive or the negative half cycles.

rectifier, linear. A rectifier, whose output current or voltage contains a wave identical in form with that of the envelope of an impressed signal wave.

rectifier, magnetron. A cold-cathode gas-diode rectifier controlled by an external field.

rectifier, radio. A device for converting alternating-current waves into impulses in one direction.

rectifying valve. A diode used for rectification; it will pass current only when the anode is at a positive potential with respect to the cathode.

rectigon. A high-pressure thermionic-cathode gas diode used for battery charging.

rectilinear. (1) Along a straight line; (2) said of a lens that forms images without distortion.

rectum. The terminal portion of the alimentary tract in which the feces accumulate, pending their periodic discharge through the anus.

rectus muscle. (1) A straight muscle; (2) one of the four muscles of the eye.

red blood corpuscle. Erythrocyte; a flat disklike cell having no nucleus; it contains hemoglobin.

red clay. The most common of deep-sea sediments; insoluble substances settled down from the surface waters.

red lead. Minium; lead tetroxide, Pb_3O_4; used as a paint pigment, for rustproofing iron, in rubber compounding.

red marrow. The tissue in some of the bones of mammals that gives rise to red and white blood corpuscles.

red mud. A reddish-brown deep-sea mud which is deposited off the seaward end of a large delta.

red rust. (1) A parasitic fungus which has two hosts, wheat and barberry, during its life history; it is also called black rust from its mature stage in wheat; (2) the plant disease caused by the red rust.

red shift. (1) A general shift of the lines of a spectrum in the direction of longer wave length; (2) an increase in the wave length observed in the spectra of distant spiral nebulae or galaxies, which appears to become greater with greater distance.

redia. One of the last stages of larval development of flukes; it is parasitic in snails; it reproduces asexually.

redox reactions. Reactions involving oxidation and reduction.

reducer. (1) A solution that reduces the contrast in photographic images; (2) a thinner of paints or other viscous liquids.

reducing agent. (1) A substance which takes oxygen from another compound; (2) a substance that gives electrons to another substance; examples, hydrogen and stannous chloride.

reducing flame. A flame with insufficient oxygen for complete combustion; the tip of the Bunsen flame.

reducing glass. A double concave lens for viewing objects in reduced sizes.

reductases. Enzymes which cause reduction of organic compounds.

reduction. (1) The removal of oxygen from a compound; (2) a gain of electrons resulting in a reduced valence; (3) diminishing the density of a photographic negative or print.

reduction division. Meiosis; a cell division in which the number of chromosomes in each of the daughter cells is reduced to one half the number in the parent cell.

reef. A ridge of rock at or near the surface of the water.

reflectance. Radiant reflectance; the fraction of light reflected from a surface.

reflectance, spectral. Spectral reflection factor; the ratio of the reflected radiant energy to the homogeneous radiant energy incident on a surface.

reflecting telescope. Newtonian telescope; a telescope that eliminates chromatic aberration by the use of a large mirror to reflect the light rays, and the image is then inverted, reversed, and magnified by an eyepiece.

reflection. The return of waves after they impinge on a surface.

reflection, angle of. The angle between a ray of light reflected from a surface, and the normal to the surface at that point.

reflection grating. A grating ruled on a reflecting surface, such as a speculum metal or a glass-chromium-aluminum surface.

reflection of light, laws of. (1) The incident ray, the reflected ray, and the normal to the reflecting surface at the point of incidence lie in the same plane; (2) the angle between the incident ray and the normal is equal to the angle between the reflected ray and the normal.

reflectivity. Reflection coefficient; reflection factor; the ratio of reflected light to the total incident light.

reflectometer. A photometer for

measuring the reflection factor of reflecting surfaces.

reflector. (1) A scattering substance surrounding the core of a nuclear reactor, used for reducing the loss of neutrons due to leakage, and thus making the dimensions of the reactor smaller; (2) a polished metal surface of suitable shape for reflecting in the desired direction the light or heat rays falling on it.

reflex. An automatic and involuntary nervous response to a stimulus; it is inborn and unlearned.

reflex arc. The pathway taken by a simple reflex; sensory neuron → associative neuron → motor neuron.

reflux condenser. A condenser which returns the condensed vapor continuously to the still.

refracting telescope. The telescope first invented; it consisted of a convergent objective and an eyepiece.

refraction. The change in the direction of a light ray or radio wave when it passes from one medium into another.

refraction, atomic. The product of the specific refraction of an element and its atomic weight.

refraction index. Refractive index; the ratio of the speed of a refracted radiation before refraction to its speed after refraction.

refraction, laws of. (1) The refracted ray, the incident ray, and the normal to the surface of separation of the two media at the point of incidence all lie in the same plane; (2) Snell's law; the ratio of the sine of the angle of incidence to the sine of the angle of refraction is a constant for any surface separating two media.

refraction, molar. Molecular refraction; the product of the specific refraction and the molecular weight.

refraction of light. (1) The bending or changing of the direction of a ray of white light passing through a prism of glass or other medium denser or less dense than air; (2) the bending of light in its passage through the earth's atmosphere.

refraction of sound, convective. The refraction of sound in a single medium, such as the atmosphere, by the effect of wind on the sound velocity.

refraction of sound, temperature. The refraction of sound, in a single medium, such as the atmosphere, by the effect of point-to-point temperature variations.

refraction sound loss. The part of the transmission loss which is due to refraction because of nonuniformity of the medium.

refraction, specific. Specific refractivity; refractive index

minus 1 divided by the density.

refraction, standard. The refraction which would occur in an ideal atmosphere where the index of refraction decreases uniformly with height at the rate of 39×10^{-6} per kilometer.

refractive index. Same as refraction index.

refractivity. Same as specific refraction.

refractometer. An instrument for measuring the refractive index of substances; special types are used for solids, liquids, and gases.

refractory. A substance that withstands high temperatures without changes in its shape, weight, or physical properties; used as a lining for furnaces; examples, fireclay, silica, kaolin, and alumina.

refrangible. Refractible; can be bent by passing from one medium into another.

refrigerant. A substance that is suitable for use in electrical refrigerators or cold-storage plants; commonly, a liquid which evaporates readily with the absorption of heat; examples, ammonia and methyl chloride.

regelation. Melting ice by pressure and freezing the water again by discontinuing the pressure.

regenerated cellulose. A cellulose which was dissolved and then precipitated into fibers again; used in viscose-rayon manufacture.

regeneration. (1) Feed-back; feeding some energy from the anode circuit back into the grid circuit to increase amplification; (2) replacement of a lost body part or the growth of a new individual from a small piece of the organism; examples, hydra, starfish, and earthworm.

regenerative circuit. A radio circuit in which the current in the grid circuit is increased by the inductive action of the anode circuit.

regenerative heating. Utilizing hot waste gases from a furnace in heating a checkerwork over which ores and fuel gases, which burn in the furnace, pass and are heated.

region. A primary geographic division which is based on similar flora and fauna and includes several life zones.

regolith. Mantle rock; loose sediment and fragments covering the solid rock.

regular flower. Actinomorphic flower; perfect flower; a flower which has all its petals and sepals of the same size and shape; example, rose.

regular reflection. (1) Specular reflection; the reflection of an undistorted light beam from a reflecting surface at the same

angle as the angle of incidence and in such a manner that the reflected beam appears to come from the image of the source on the reflecting surface; (2) the reflection of sound waves which results in echoes.

reinforcing agent. A finely divided solid that imparts improved mechanical properties to another solid in which it is dispersed; example, carbon black in rubber.

rejuvenation. (1) The restoration of the vigor of a tree by pruning, soil treatment, etc.; (2) restoring the youthful vigor of an animal; (3) renewed erosive activity of a stream.

relative humidity. The ratio of the water vapor in the air at a given temperature to the maximum amount of water vapor air can hold at that temperature.

relative inclinometer. An instrument which indicates the altitude of an aircraft with reference to apparent gravity, that is, to the resultant of the acceleration of the aircraft and that due to gravity.

relative luminosity. The ratio of the value of the luminosity at a particular wave length to the value at the wave length of maximum luminosity.

relative weight. The atomic weight which is based on the weight of an atom of oxygen set at 16.

relative wind. The movement of the air in relation to the wing of an airplane.

relativity. A modern system of natural philosophy, largely developed by Albert Einstein, based on the principles that: the observed value of light velocity is constant and independent of the relative motion of the observer and light source; if two systems are moving with uniform linear velocity relative to each other, an observer in one system cannot determine the values of the motion in the other system by observation and/or measurement.

relaxation. Any phenomenon in which a system requires an observable length of time for responding to sudden changes in conditions, forces, or effects which are applied to the system.

relay. An electrically operated switch for the closing and opening of a circuit.

reluctance. The resistance offered by a magnetizable material to a magnetic flux.

REM (roentgen-equivalent-man). A unit used to measure the biological effect produced by the absorption of nuclear radiation.

remanence. Retentivity; the residual magnetization of a ferromagnetic substance when the

magnetizing field is reduced to zero.

renal. Referring or pertaining to the kidneys.

renal circulation. A short branch of the systemic circulation through the kidneys.

renal corpuscle. Malpighian body; a structural unit of the vertebrate kidney; it consists of Bowman's capsule and the glomerulus.

renal papilla. (1) A projection extending into the mantle cavity of cephalopod mollusks, which contains the opening of the excretory duct; (2) a renal pyramid, that is, a conical body formed by the urine-collecting ducts of the mammalian kidney.

rennet. Abomasum; the contents or lining of the fourth stomach of ruminants, especially of the calf, which contains rennin.

rennin. An enzyme of the gastric juice which causes the coagulation of milk.

renopericardial canal. A passage connecting the pericardial cavity of mollusks with the kidney.

repeater. A vacuum-tube amplifier that is inserted at intervals in a telephone or telegraph circuit for amplifying the message and delivering it to the line.

replacement. (1) Substitution; a chemical reaction in which one element takes the place of another in a compound; (2) one atom taking the place of another in a crystal lattice without changing the crystal form.

replacement series. An arrangement of elements in the order of their ability to replace hydrogen or comparable elements.

representative observation. A record of the true or typical meteorological conditions prevailing in an air mass.

reproduction. Perpetuation of the species by the production of new organisms similar to the parents.

reproductive system. Genitalia; the male and female organs of reproduction.

Reptilia. Vertebrates covered by scales, having a three-chambered heart, cold blood, and lungs; the young hatch from soft-shelled eggs; examples, snakes and turtles.

repulsion. (1) The force by which two bodies tend to repel each other; (2) the tendency of genes or characters to be independent rather than linked.

reradiation. A radiation emitted by a body as a result of an earlier absorption of radiation; example, the reradiation of the heat waves absorbed by the earth.

reselection. A method of breeding in which the best hybrids from a previous crossing are chosen and bred to get a pure strain.

residual air. About 100 cubic inches of air which remains in the lungs no matter how forcibly one exhales.

residual blue. The blue coloration of white light scattered by small particles in suspension as viewed through a Nicol prism.

residual charge. The feeble charge on the plates of a condenser, which remains temporarily bound, after an initial discharge, by that part of the polarization of its imperfect dielectric which is due to electron migration.

residual induction. The magnetic induction in a sample after the saturating magnetizing force is removed.

residual ionization. An ionization of air or another gas in a closed vessel, attributed to cosmic rays.

residual magnetism. Magnetism remaining in a magnetic core after the magnetizing force ceased to act.

residual radiation. A nearly monochromatic infrared radiation isolated from the output of a white-hot solid by successive reflections from surfaces of a given crystalline substance, such as quartz, or rock salt.

residual resistance. That part of the electrical resistance of a metal which is independent of the temperature and thus remains when the resistance due to scattering of the electrons by lattice vibrations becomes small at low temperatures.

residual soil. A soil resulting from the decay of rock where it was formed.

residual stress. A stress remaining in a solid after mechanical and/or heat treatment, due not to external forces but apparently to the fact that certain portions have been stressed beyond the elastic limit while others have not.

residue. The solid left after evaporation or distillation of a liquid.

resilience. (1) The capability of a strained body to recover its size and shape after deformation; (2) the work performed per unit volume of an elastic body by a bending or shear force while producing strain.

resin. A natural or synthetic gumlike solid or semisolid substance used in the manufacture of paints, varnishes, and similar products.

resistance. (1) That property of a substance that opposes the flow of an electric current through it; (2) the ability of an organism to ward off infection, parasites, and disease.

resistance box. A box containing known resistances, from which the required amount can be inserted into the circuit by means of plugs or dials.

resistance coupling. A coupling between the electron tubes of an amplifier which will transfer, through a resistance, the anode current of one tube as changes of potential to the grid of the next tube.

resistance, electrical. The resistance offered by an electrical conductor to the flow of current through it; the ratio of volts to amperes in a conductor.

resistance furnace. A furnace in which heat is produced by electrical resistance.

resistance, negative. A decrease in voltage with the increase in current, found in some electron tubes used for maintaining continuous oscillations in a resonant circuit.

resistance neutralization. The effect of a triode associated with a circuit in such a way as to lower the effective resistance of certain branches.

resistance thermometer. Resistance pyrometer; a thermometer operating on the principle that the electrical resistance of a conductor varies with temperature; usually a platinum wire is used as the conductor.

resistivity. Specific resistivity; volume resistivity; the resistance of a unit volume of a material.

resistor. A device designed to provide resistance; it may consist of carbon or metal wire and may have a fixed resistance of a specified number of ohms, or it may be variable.

resolution. (1) Resolving a force into two component forces acting in specific directions; (2) separating a racemic compound into its optically active components.

resolution of mass spectrometer. The separation of adjacent peaks of a mass spectrum by a mass spectrometer.

resolving power. (1) The ability of an optical system to produce separate images of objects very close together; (2) the power of a spectroscope to distinguish between similar wave lengths.

resonance. (1) The conditions under which the capacitive reactance and inductance in a tuned circuit are equal; (2) the property of an atom or molecule of shifting its electronic structure between two or more different patterns; example, benzene; (3) an increase in sound intensity due to secondary vibrations.

resonance absorption. The absorption of neutrons in a nuclear reactor, that have energies corresponding to a nuclear resonance level of the absorber.

resonance bridge. An alternating-current bridge in one arm of which an inductance and a capacitance are adjusted to such values that the bridge is in resonance.

resonance circuit. A circuit in which the inductive and capacitive reactances are equal.

resonance fluorescence. A radiation emitted by an excited atom, which is of the same frequency as the exciting radiation.

resonance hybrid. A molecule whose properties show that its structure resonates among several possible covalent bonding arrangements.

resonance penetration. The penetration of an atomic nucleus by a charged particle whose energy corresponds to one of the energy levels of the nucleus.

resonance radiation. A radiation from a gas or a vapor in a state of excitation brought about by a radiation of the same frequency.

resonance state. A state of excitation which gives rise to resonance radiation.

resonant frequency. (1) A frequency at which a diaphragm vibrates most easily; (2) the frequency of a resonant circuit, which is so adjusted that its inductive reactance equals its capacitive reactance.

resonator. (1) An apparatus designed to resonate, or respond to a given frequency; example, a piezoelectric crystal; (2) an enclosure that has sharp acoustic resonance.

resorption. Redissolving of earlier formed crystals by the molten magma followed by recrystallization, usually in a different form.

respiration. The interchange of oxygen and carbon dioxide in katabolic processes of living organisms.

respiration calorimeter. An instrument for measuring the oxygen consumed and carbon dioxide eliminated by man and animals and also the work done and heat produced as compared to the food consumed.

respiratory enzyme. An enzyme which catalyzes oxidation-reduction reactions; examples, oxidase and dehydrogenase.

respiratory movements. The movement of animal muscles connected with the intake of air or water for respiration.

respiratory organ. A specialized organ that assists in securing the necessary oxygen; examples, lung and gill.

respiratory pigment. A colored substance in the blood which combines reversibly with oxygen, carrying it to the tissues or storing it; example, hemoglobin.

respiratory system. A system of respiratory organs.

response. The reaction of an organism to stimulation.

rest mass. The mass of a body at rest relative to the observer, that is, without the additional mass acquired by motion, according to the relativity theory.

rest potential. A residual potential difference between an electrode and the electrolyte, which remains after the electrode has become polarized.

resting cell. A cell that is not undergoing mitotic division.

resting egg. Winter egg; a thick-shelled egg of some fresh-water invertebrates which is able to resist all types of adverse conditions during the dormant period.

resting stage. A period during which a plant does not show signs of growth.

restitution coefficient. The ratio of the relative velocity of two elastic balls after and before a direct impact.

restocking. (1) Bringing wild animals from other regions to a place where they once lived but died out or became scarce; (2) populating a stream depleted of fish.

restricted internal rotation. Restriction of the free rotation of the molecules or parts of molecules in some substances, at certain temperatures, leading to anomalies in the specific heat.

resultant. A single force that can be substituted for two or more forces without altering the effect.

retardation. Negative catalysis; slowing down a chemical reaction by the addition of a negative catalyst.

retentivity. Remanence; the density of the magnetic flux remaining in a substance after removal of the magnetizing force.

reticle. A set of two or more fine lines or wires placed at the principal focus of a telescope lens; when the object appears at the intersection of the wires, the telescope is pointing directly at it; used also in telescopic gun sights.

reticular density. The number of points per unit area in a network, for example, a plane of a crystal lattice.

reticular tissue. A connective tissue containing a network of collagenous fibers.

reticulate. (1) Similar to a net; (2) having netlike ridges.

reticulin fibers. Very fine intercellular fibers forming a network around the cells in many vertebrate tissues to hold them together.

reticulo-endothelial system. Phagocytic cells of vertebrates in contact with blood or lymph to free them from suspended foreign particles.

retina. The light-sensitive layer of the eye.

retinula. The visual element of

the eyes of Arthropoda; a group of cells containing a pigment and a central rod (rhabdom); in the compound eye, each ommatidium contains a single retinula.

retort. A distillation vessel.

retractor. A contractile muscle which pulls a part back to its normal resting position in or near the body.

retrograde rays. Corpuscular rays of atomic dimensions which move away from the cathode instead of toward it.

retrorocket. An accessory rocket used to retard vehicle motion with an impulse counter to the direction of flight; retrorockets may be used in projected manned lunar missions to decelerate the landing vehicle.

retting. Rotting; soaking the stalks of flax in water, which contains bacteria, to loosen the fibers from the woody tissue.

reverberation. Echo; a sound that persists because of repeated reflections after the original source of sound has been cut off.

reverberation chamber. An enclosure in which all the surfaces have been made as sound-reflective as possible; used for acoustic measurements.

reverberation time. The length of time a sound can be heard after it has been made.

reverberatory furnace. A furnace in which the charge is heated both directly and by the heat reflected from the low roof of the furnace.

reverse-rocket approach. The use of rocket motors to allow a spaceship to come down tail first, to a more or less gentle landing.

reversible colloid. A colloid that can be readily dispersed in a medium and can be dispersed again after coagulation.

reversible engine. An ideal heat engine of maximum efficiency working in a reversible thermodynamic cycle; example Carnot cycle.

reversible path. A path at any point of which the direction of a moving system can be reversed by an infinitesimal change in the thermodynamical coordinates of the system.

reversible process. A theoretical thermodynamic process which can be performed fully in the reverse direction, the system being in complete equilibrium at each phase of the process.

reversible reaction. A chemical reaction which can proceed in both directions and is thus normally incomplete.

reversing layer. The lower part of the sun's atmosphere in which Fraunhofer lines are found.

reversion. Atavism; the appearance in an organism of hereditary characters which were not present in its parents but occurred in previous generations.

revolution. (1) Orbital motion; the moving of one body in a circular path around another body or a center; example, the motion of the earth around the sun; (2) a drastic change in the surface structure of the earth or in the distribution of land and sea.

revolving-field alternator. An alternating-current generator which has stationary conductors and rotating field magnets.

Rh. Chemical symbol for rhodium.

Rh factor. Rhesus factor; an agglutinogen present in the red blood cells of most humans; its determination is important in selecting the donors for blood transfusion and it affects the health of an infant if one parent has the factor (Rh-positive) and the other does not (Rh-negative).

rhabdom. A rodlike structure formed of the united sensory borders of the adjacent retina cells of the compound eye of Arthropoda.

rhabdomere. The receptive area of a retinal cell which is one of the components of the rhabdom.

rhenium. A hard, malleable metal; chemical symbol Re; atomic number 75; used in thermocouples.

rheology. The study of the deformation and flow of matter, including viscosity, plasticity, and elasticity.

rheometer. An instrument for measuring and controlling currents.

rheopexy. An accelerated setting of sols containing rodlike or platelike particles to the gel form brought about by any mechanical means that will facilitate the orientation of the particles.

rheostat. A device that is used to vary the flow of current by means of a variable resistance.

rheotrol. A device that controls the temperature of electric furnaces, ovens, and heaters.

rheotron. Betatron; a proton-accelerating device.

rheotropism. Rheotaxis; the response of an organism to air or water currents; example, fish at rest in moving water have their heads pointed upstream.

rhinencephalon. The olfactory lobes of the vertebrate brain.

rhinophore. A posterior tentacle of olfactory function in some of the marine mollusks.

Rhizobium. A rod-shaped nitrobacterium that lives symbiotically on the roots of leguminous plants and fixes free nitrogen.

rhizoids. Rootlike hyphae of molds which penetrate the substratum and serve as absorbing and attaching structures.

rhizome. A rootlike underground stem which has scale leaves and buds; roots grow from its undersurface and branches from the upper surface to form new plants by natural vegetative reproduction; example, lily of the valley.

rhizomorph. A compact strand of fungus hyphae which grows apically and transports food from one part of the thallus to another; it also keeps the fungus spread over or through the substratum.

rhizophore. A leafless branch which grows downward from the leafy stems of certain club mosses and gives rise to roots when it comes in contact with the soil.

Rhizopoda. Sarcodina; Protozoa that have rootlike pseudopodia; example, ameba.

rhizosphere. The area of the soil which surrounds the roots where there is greater microbiological activity.

rhodium. A silver-white metallic element of the platinum group; chemical symbol Rh; atomic number 45; used as a catalyst, in thermocouples, plating silver for tarnishproofing.

rhodonite. A pink mineral; manganese metasilicate, $MnO \cdot SiO_2$; used as an ornamental stone.

Rhodophyceae. Red seaweeds; a group of algae characterized by a red pigment; they have no motile reproductive organs.

rhodopsin. Visual purple; a complex organic compound in the retina of the eye; it makes the eye sensitive to very dim light; its lack causes night blindness; it contains vitamin A.

rhombic crystal. A crystal having three unequal axes at right angles to one another.

rhombohedron. A prism with six similar sides, all of which are parallelograms.

Rhynchocephalia. A small order of reptiles having abdominal ribs and a pineal eye; it includes the tuatara of New Zealand and a number of extinct forms.

rhynchodaeum. The part of the proboscis of nemertine worms which lies in front of the brain; it is an eversible structure.

rib. (1) One of the several pairs of bones protecting the chest and attached to the spine; (2) a large vein of the leaf; (3) a structural member of an airfoil.

ribbon microphone. A microphone operated by electromagnetic induction through the motion of a metal strip arranged in the gap of a magnet.

riboflavin. The chemical name of vitamin B_2; it promotes growth.

ridge. A range of hills or mountains.

riffle. A strip laid crosswise in a sluice for retaining gold particles or other minerals.

rift valley. Graben; a long valley between two faults.

Righi-Leduc effect. A temperature difference developing between the two edges of a strip of metal when it is heated at one end while in a magnetic field perpendicular to its plane.

right ascension. The angular distance along the celestial equator from the vernal equinox to the hour circle of the body whose location is to be determined.

rigidity modulus. The ratio of the shearing stress to the shearing strain.

Riker mount. A container for mounting botanical or zoological specimens.

rind. (1) The outer covering of the monocot stem, composed of thick-walled hard cells; (2) the outer layer of a fruit.

ring. A cut made completely around the stem and just through the bark of a woody plant, without removal of any of the bark or other parts.

ring canal. (1) A part of the body cavity of Bryozoa which is only partly separated from the principal chamber and prolonged into the tentacles; (2) a canal of the water vascular system of starfish which forms a complete circle in the disk.

ring compound. A cyclic compound; an organic compound in which the carbon atoms are joined into a closed ring rather than an open chain; the ring may also contain atoms other than carbon.

ring porous wood. A wood whose spring wood contains many large vessels and whose summer wood consists mainly of fibers; example, elm and ash.

ripple marks. (1) A series of little ridges and valleys made in sand and mud by wave action near the shore; (2) similar ridges found in sedimentary rocks; they are caused by water or air currents before the solidification of the rock.

ripple voltage. The alternating component of a direct-current voltage from a direct-current rectifier or generator.

ripples. (1) Surface waves on a liquid, whose wave length is so short that the motion can be controlled by surface tension; (2) the alternating-current component from a direct-current power supply, arising from sources within the power supply.

Ritchie wedge. A photometer with a movable wedge.

Ritz principle. Every wave number occurring in the spectrum of a substance may be expressed as a difference between two of a much smaller group of terms characteristic of the substance.

river flat. A level land along the banks of a river which is occasionally flooded.

river soil. A soil formed by the action of streams.

Rn. Chemical symbol for radon.

RNA (ribonucleic acid). A nucleic acid found chiefly in the cytoplasm; it is directly involved in protein synthesis.

roasting. Heating sulfide ores with an excess of air, for producing the oxide of the metal with sulfur dioxide as a by-product.

Robin's law. When a system is in chemical or physical equilibrium, an increase in pressure favors the system formed with a decrease in volume.

roche moutonée. A rock that was smoothed and polished to a round shape by glaciers.

Rochelle salt. Potassium sodium tartrate, $KNaC_4H_4O_6$; used in medicine, for piezoelectric crystals.

Rochon prism. A doubly refracting prism used for obtaining plane-polarized light.

rock. A solid massive part of the earth's crust, different samples of which are usually composed of several minerals in varying proportions.

rock, cleavage. A rock that splits very easily along the planes of shearing; example, slate.

rock crystal. Pure colorless crystalline natural silica.

rock flour. The finely ground rock that is found in the water when a glacier melts.

rock glacier. Stone run; loose boulders and stone blocks in streamlike formation at the bottom of some valleys.

rock mantle. Loose fragments and sediment that covers a rock.

rock phosphate. Phosphorite; fibrous tricalcium phosphate, $Ca_3(PO_4)_2$; used in fertilizers.

rock salt. Halite; sodium chloride mineral, $NaCl$.

rock wool. A fibrous mineral; used as an insulator and for fireproofing.

rocket. A tubular device consisting of a combustion chamber supplied with fuel and the oxygen necessary for combustion and an exhaust nozzle; it is projected into the air by the escape of the combustion gases.

rocket booster. A rocket used to increase the speed or altitude of a space vehicle.

rocket engine. A reaction engine in which the oxygen necessary to burn fuel is carried in pressure tanks and blended with the fuel; used in aircraft.

rocking stone. A perched boulder; a large stone, left in a balanced position by melting ice or weathering, that can be moved back and forth with a relatively small force.

Rockwell hardness test. Measur-

ing the hardness of metals by the depth of penetration of a steel ball or diamond cone under a given load.

rodent. A small mammal with chisel-like front teeth.

Rodentia. An order of gnawing mammals; they are mostly terrestrial, but some are aquatic; examples, hare, beaver, rat, and squirrel.

rods and cones. Light-sensitive receptor cells of the retina.

roentgen. The unit of x-ray intensity.

Roentgen rays. X-rays.

roentgenization. (1) A discoloration which develops in some transparent substances, such as glass, after prolonged irradiation with x-rays; (2) a therapeutic treatment with x-rays.

roentgenometer. An instrument of the ionization-chamber type for measuring the intensity of x-rays or gamma rays.

Roget's spiral. A helical wire that contracts when current passes through it; it is used to demonstrate the magnetic attraction between adjacent wires carrying current in the same direction.

rogue. Sport; an individual differing distinctly from a standard type due to genetical factors.

roll. An aircraft maneuver in which a complete revolution about the longitudinal axis is made, the horizontal direction of flight being approximately maintained.

rolling friction. The friction between two surfaces which are separated by rollers or balls.

root. The part of vascular plants that grows downward into the soil, anchors the plant, and absorbs water containing nutrients.

root cap. A cone of loosely packed cells at the tip of the root which protect the root as it grows.

root grafting. Inserting a cion in the root of the stock.

root hair. A fine tubular projection from the epidermis cells of young roots; it increases the amount of surface area available for absorption of water and dissolved minerals from the soil.

root nodule. A small swelling on the root of a plant which is produced by nitrogen-fixing bacteria.

root of tooth. That part of a tooth which is in a socket and which attaches the tooth firmly to the jawbone.

root pressure. The pressure by which water rises into the stem of plants from the roots.

rootstock. Same as rhizome.

rosette. A leaf arrangement in which the leaves are close together on a short stem; example, dandelion.

rosin. Colophony; a yellow, amorphous substance; a residue of the distillation of turpentine; used in varnish, soap, lubricants.

rostellum. (1) A projection at the end of the scolex of a tapeworm which bears the hooks and serves as an organ of attachment; (2) a beaklike projection from an orchid.

rostrum. (1) The beak of birds; (2) a protective beak projecting from the carapace of Arthropoda; (3) a snout of certain fishes and of the labium of bugs.

rotameter. An instrument for measuring the rate of flow of gases and liquids.

rotary condenser. Synchronous condenser; a lightly loaded synchronous motor which is the source of a leading current for power-factor correction.

rotary engine. An early model of aircraft engine in which the radial cylinders and crankcase rotate about a stationary crank.

rotary field. A magnetic field whose direction rotates about a perpendicular axis.

rotary pump. A large-delivery, low-pressure pump in which the fluid is forced by matching vanes on parallel rotating shafts.

rotation. (1) The whirling or spinning of a body on its axis; example, the turning of the earth on its axis; (2) the movement of the protoplasm in a cell in one direction.

rotation axis. A line within the structure of a unit crystal cell about which atoms are arranged in regular plane polygons centered on the axis.

rotation diagram. The photographic record of diffracted beams produced when a slender beam of homogeneous x-rays impinges on a rotating single crystal.

rotation, molar. The product of the specific rotation and the molecular weight, divided by 100.

rotation of the plane of polarization. The ability of optically active substances to rotate the plane of polarization of polarized light passing through them when placed in a strong magnetic field.

rotation photograph. A photograph of the diffraction pattern obtained by rotation of a single crystal in the beam of impinging x-rays; used in crystal analysis.

rotation, specific. The angular rotation of the plane of polarization as it passes through an optically active substance, divided by the length of the path and the density of the substance.

rotation spectrum. (1) A molecular spectrum in the far infrared; (2) an x-ray spectrum or dif-

fraction pattern produced by a crystal which is rotated while being traversed by an x-ray beam.

rotational entropy. That part of the entropy of a body which is due to molecular rotation.

rotational state. One of the energy levels of molecular rotation, changes in which are responsible for molecular-rotation spectral lines.

rotational structure. (1) The fine structure of an atomic spectrum; (2) the structure of a molecular-rotation spectrum.

rotational temperature. The temperature of an excited vapor as indicated by the radiation-energy distribution in the rotational spectrum.

rotator. (1) A voluntary muscle which rotates a body part or organism about its axis; (2) an optical apparatus which rotates the polarization plane of light traversing it; (3) a small electric motor for rotating color disks, Geissler tubes, etc.

rotatory. Optically active; capable of rotating the plane of polarized light; dextrorotatory or levorotatory.

rotatory dispersion. The dispersion of light arising from the fact that the polarization plane of polarized light of different wave lengths is rotated at different rates by optically active substances.

rotatory power. Specific rotation; the number of degrees by which the plane of polarization of polarized light is rotated by a solution containing one gram per cubic centimeter of an optically active substance.

rotenone. A strong contact insecticide extracted from the root of the derris plant.

Rotifera. Minute Metazoa which swim and feed by means of a ciliated hand.

rotor. The rotating part of a machine.

round window. An opening from the cavity of the inner ear to the middle ear; it is covered by an elastic membrane and is sometimes called the secondary eardrum.

roundworm. A slender nematode worm with a tubular body which is not divided into segments; example, pinworm.

row lines. Lines formed by the diffraction spots on a rotation photograph of a crystal which is rotated in a beam of x-rays.

Rowland circle. A circle whose diameter is the radius of a diffraction grating; by placing the slit anywhere on the circumference of the circle, the spectra of different orders are formed in exact focus around the circle.

Rowland mounting. A method of mounting a diffraction grating and plate holder at the ends of a rigid bar.

royal jelly. A thick, white liquid formed in the stomach of worker honey bees by partial digestion of honey and pollen, which is fed to the young larvae during the first three days of their existence and to the larvae of the queen bee until they are fully developed.

rpm. Abbreviation for revolutions per minute.

Ru. Chemical symbol for ruthenium.

rubber. A natural elastomer obtained by coagulation from the latex of the rubber tree and other plants; it is the raw material of tires and hundreds of important products.

rubidium. A soft alkali metal; chemical symbol Rb; atomic number 37.

ruby. A red variety of the mineral, corundum; aluminum oxide, Al_2O_3; used as a precious stone.

rudder. (1) A flat piece of fabric-covered wood or a piece of metal hinged to the vertical fin of an airplane to control its direction to the right or left; (2) a wide flat structure hinged to the stern post of a ship which serves to change the course of the ship when it moves out of line with the keel.

rudder angle. The acute angle between the rudder and the plane of symmetry of an aircraft.

ruderal. A plant found in waste places near habitations.

rudimentary. Early or primitive; not fully developed.

rugae (singular ruga). Ridges or folds, as in the lining of the stomach.

ruling engine. A mechanism operated by a long micrometer screw for ruling the equally spaced lines on optical gratings.

rumen. A part of the stomach of a ruminant in which the unchewed food is stored until it can be chewed; first stomach.

Ruminantia. Hoofed mammals some of which chew their own cud; the stomach consists of four chambers: rumen, reticulum, omasum and abomasum.

runner. (1) A slender stem growing along the ground, taking root at intervals, and producing new plants; example, strawberry; (2) a vertical passage inside of a casting mold through which the metal is poured in.

runoff. (1) The rain water which runs off the surface of the ground and enters the drainage system; (2) the syrup that is removed from the sugar crystals in sugar manufacture.

Rupert's drop. A globule of glass which has been suddenly congealed by allowing the fused drop to fall into water; it contains residual stresses which·

are fairly balanced, but will cause it to explode violently by shock or by cutting off its tail.

rupture. (1) The forcible breaking or collapse of some structure due to pressure or strain; (2) hernia; the projecting of a viscus through a defective spot of its cavity.

rupture, modulus of. A measure of the ultimate strength or the breaking load per unit area of a specimen as determined by a torsion or, more commonly, by a bending test.

Russell effect. The formation of latent developable images on a photographic film or plate by agents other than radiant energy; examples, by resins, metals, printing inks, volatile liquids, fumes, etc.

rust. (1) Hydrated iron oxide, mainly $Fe_2O_3 \cdot H_2O$, formed on exposure of iron to moisture and air; (2) a plant disease caused by parasitic fungi; example, red rust (black rust) of wheat.

ruthenium. A silvery hard and brittle metal of the platinum group; chemical symbol Ru; atomic number 44.

rutherford. (1) A unit of radioactivity; 106 disintegrations per second; (2) the quantity of a nuclide that has an activity of one rutherford.

rutile. Brown prisms; a titanium dioxide mineral, TiO_2; it is a source of titanium.

rye. A hardy annual plant, which has a tendency to become a perennial; its grains are used for flour and whiskey.

S

S. Chemical symbol for sulfur.

sabin. An acoustic unit of absorption; it represents the absorption of one square foot of a perfectly absorbing surface.

sac. A pouchlike structure in a living body.

saccharimeter. A special polarimeter designed for use in the analysis of sugar solutions.

saccharin. $C_6H_4SO_2CONH$; a white crystalline soluble solid; it has no food value, but is three hundred times sweeter than sugar; used as a sweetening agent in diabetes, etc.

saccharolytic enzyme. An enzyme that attacks sugars, producing a gas, an acid, or an alcohol; example, lactase.

saccharometer. A hydrometer used for determining the concentration of sugar solutions by measuring their density.

Saccharomyces. Yeasts; a genus of Ascomycetes; fungi causing the fermentation of sugars; used in the manufacture of bread and alcoholic beverages.

sacral vertebra. A vertebra of

tetrapods which articulates with the ilium of the hip girdle.

sacrum. The portion of the spinal column of vertebrates, usually formed of several fused vertebrae, with which the pelvis is articulated.

safety factor. The ratio of the strength of a construction material or structural part to the maximum load which it will have to support.

safranine. A reddish-brown dye; used as a microscopic stain.

sagittal. The plane extending longitudinally and dorsoventrally in the mid-line of an animal body; it divides a bilaterally symmetrical animal into two similar halves.

sagittal ray. Any one of a narrow bundle of rays in a symmetrical optical instrument which lies in the longitudinal section of the bundle made by the plane containing the chief ray and perpendicular to the meridian section.

Sagittarius. Archer; a large constellation; the ninth sign of the Zodiac.

Saint Elmo's fire. An electrical discharge between the mast of a ship and a thunder cloud; a glow seen above the ship on a stormy night.

sal. The Latin term for salt; used in naming pharmaceuticals; example, sal ammoniac (ammonium chloride).

sal ammoniac. Ammonium chloride, NH_4Cl; it is obtained as a by-product of natural gas manufacture; used as a flux in soldering, in manufacture of dyestuffs, as an electrolyte in dry cells, in medicine.

sal soda. Sodium carbonate decahydrate, $Na_2CO_3 \cdot 10H_2O$; used as washing soda.

salinometer. A hydrometer used for measuring the density of sea water and the concentration of salt solutions; it is calibrated in empirical units.

saliva. A secretion of the salivary glands, which moistens, softens, and lubricates the food to make it easier to swallow; it contains mucin and ptyalin.

salivary glands. Glands opening into the mouth cavity, which produce saliva.

salivary-gland chromosomes. Giant chromosomes occurring in the salivary glands of dipterous insects such as Drosophila; they facilitated genetic and cytological research.

salivate. To produce a large amount of saliva.

salt. A compound of a metal with a nonmetal or a nonmetal radical; the reaction product of the neutralization of an acid by a base.

salt bridge. A liquid junction connecting two electrolytic solutions.

salt cake. Sodium sulfate, Na_2-

$SO_4 \cdot 10H_2O$; a by-product of hydrochloric acid manufacture.

salt, common. Sodium chloride, NaCl; used as a flavor, for making sodium compounds and chlorine.

saltation. A sudden biological change that occurs as a result of mutation.

salting out. The precipitation of a colloidal dispersion by the addition of a salt.

saltpeter. Potassium nitrate, KNO_3; soluble colorless crystals; used in the manufacture of matches, pyrotechnics.

samara. A simple, dry, one- or two-seeded indehiscent fruit with the pericarp bearing a winglike outgrowth; examples, ash, maple, and elm keys.

samarium. A rare-earth metal; chemical symbol Sm; atomic number 62.

sand. (1) A loose sediment, especially round quartz particles; (2) molding sand; clay-containing siliceous sand used for making molds for metals.

sand collar. A thin collar-shaped plate consisting of sand glued together with mucus; it is formed by some marine snails in depositing their eggs.

sand dunes. Mounds of sand piled up in desert regions by the winds at points where rocks or trees break the force of the wind.

sandbar. A bar or ridge of silt and sand, formed in rivers, lakes, and oceans near the surface.

sandstone. Sedimentary rocks which have been cemented together by some substance that was dissolved in the water around the sand grains; it may contain variable amounts of other minerals.

sandy soil. A soil containing a large proportion of sand, with little or no humus; it has good drainage.

sap. The watery liquid in the xylem of plants that supplies dissolved minerals and organic substances to all the living cells and carries away waste.

saponification. (1) A reaction between a fat and an alkali to yield a soap and glycerin; (2) the hydrolysis of fatty esters to acids and alcohols.

saponification number. A number characteristic of a fat or oil; the milligrams of potassium hydroxide needed for the complete saponification of 1 gram of a fat or oil.

saprophyte. An organism that obtains its food from the dead body, or the nonliving products, of another plant or animal.

saprozoic. Said of an animal that lives on decaying organic matter.

sapwood. The outer porous portion of a tree trunk between the heartwood and the bark; it is lighter in color than the heartwood and active in conducting water.

Sarcina. A genus of micrococcal bacteria, characterized by cell division in three planes; they are mostly harmless; some produce a yellow pigment.

sarcode. Name given by Dujardin to the protoplasm of one-celled animals.

sarcolemma. A thin membrane surrounding a skeletal, or striated, muscle cell.

sarcoplasm. The fluid protoplasmic substance of skeletal muscle fibers.

Sargasso Sea. A quiet strip of water near the center of the North Atlantic Ocean; the movement of the water is negligible and a seaweed, Sargassum, grows there.

Sargassum. Gulfweed; a form of ocean algae found commonly in the Gulfstream and parts of the Atlantic Ocean; it has a branching thallus and leafy segments.

saros. The interval between two similar solar eclipses (18 years and 10 to 11 days).

satellite. A heavenly body that revolves around a larger heavenly body; example, the moon is a satellite of the earth.

satellite, artificial. A manmade space object launched into space so that it moves in orbit about the earth or any other celestial body.

satellite, earth. A manmade body in orbit around the earth.

satellite electrons. The electrons in an orbit outside the nucleus of an atom.

satellite, synchronous. A satellite in orbit parallel to and 22,000 miles over the Equator, at which altitude the satellite is in a period identical with that of the earth and appears to be stationary; such satellites are used as communications relay stations.

saturated air. Air that contains the maximum amount of water vapor.

saturated compound. A compound in which all valences are satisfied and thus it cannot attach atoms by addition; an organic compound which has no double or triple bonds; example, ethane, $H_3C—CH_3$.

saturated hydrocarbons. Hydrocarbons which do not contain double or triple bonds and thus cannot form compounds by addition.

saturated magnet. A magnet having all its molecules aligned in the same direction.

saturated solution. A solution which contains all the solute it can hold at a given temperature.

saturated steam. Water vapor at the temperature of the boiling point corresponding to a given pressure.

saturated vapor. A vapor which can exist in equilibrium with the liquid from which it originated.

saturated vapor pressure. The pressure exerted by a saturated vapor; its value is dependent on the temperature.

saturation. (1) The condition of air when it has all the water vapor it can hold; (2) the condition of a magnetic material when it reached its highest flux density; (3) the state of purity and maximum brilliance of a color; (4) a condition in a vacuum tube when all the electrons emitted from the cathode have been taken up by the anode and/or other electrodes; (5) dissolving the largest possible amount of a substance in a solvent to obtain a saturated solution.

saturation current. Total emission; the limit which the current through an ionized gas, the thermionic current or the photoelectric current, approaches with increasing voltage.

saturation point. Dew point.

Saturn. The sixth planet from the sun; it is surrounded by three rings and has ten satellites.

Saturn's rings. Three concentric rings seen around the planet Saturn; they consist of densely crowded small solid bodies.

Sauria. Lizards; a suborder of Squamata.

Saurischia. An order of extremely large fossil reptiles; they lived during the Mesozoic era; example, dinosaur.

savanna. (1) A tropical or subtropical grassland, with some widely scattered trees; (2) a treeless southern plain.

Savart's plate. A quartz plate cut in two halves; used for the study of polarized light.

Sb. Chemical symbol for antimony.

Sc. Chemical symbol for scandium.

scalar quantity. A quantity which has only magnitude and no direction.

scalariform thickening. An internal thickening of the wall of a xylem vessel or tracheid in the form of transverse bars which look like ladder rungs.

scale. (1) A small platelike horny outgrowth which covers the body of fish and reptiles, the legs of birds, and the body of some insects; (2) a balance used for weighing; (3) a series of markings at regular intervals which are used for measurement or computation; (4) a defined set of values in terms of which quantities of the same nature as those defined may be measured; example, a temperature scale.

scale of eight. A vacuum-tube circuit for counting pulses, in groups of eight, from ion or photon counters.

scale scars. Marks left on a stem after the bud opened and the scales dropped off.

scaler. An electronic device that produces an output pulse whenever a set number of input pulses has been received.

scalp. A soft tissue which covers the human head and normally bears hair.

scalpel. A knifelike instrument with a narrow sharp blade; used for dissection.

scandium. A rare-earth metal; chemical symbol Sc; atomic number 21.

scanning. Transmitting or reproducing a television image by covering or sweeping it, point by point, with a beam of light.

scape. (1) A leafless peduncle; (2) the bottom joint of the antenna of an insect.

Scaphopoda. Bilaterally symmetrical mollusks; they have a shell which is open at both ends; example, tusk shells.

scapula. The shoulder blade of vertebrates.

scarp. Escarpment; a short steep clifflike ridge that resulted from erosion or faulting.

scattering. The diffuse reflection of wave energy when a ray encounters a body or passes through a heterogeneously ionized region.

scattering angle. The angle between the original direction of an emission and its direction after scattering.

scattering, coherent. Scattering of particles or photons so that there is a definite phase relation between incoming and scattered waves.

scattering, Compton. When x-rays are scattered by light particles their wave length is slightly increased by the collision of photons with electrons.

scattering, Delbrück. The scattering of light by a Coulomb field.

scattering, incoherent. Scattering of particles or photons so that the scattering elements act independently and there is no definite phase relation between different parts of the scattered beam.

scattering loss. The transmission loss due to the scattering of electromagnetic waves.

scattering, multiple. Repeated scattering of a particle or photon so that the final displacement is the sum of many displacements.

scattering power. The ratio of the total energy of scattered radiation per unit length of path in a scattering medium to the energy of the incident beam.

scattering, Rutherford. The scattering of charged particles occurs at various angles because of interaction with atoms of a solid.

scattering, single. The deflection of a particle from its original path when it encounters a single scattering center in the medium traversed.

scavengers. Organisms that feed on waste material.

scavenging. (1) The use of an unspecific precipitate to remove from solution through adsorption or coprecipitation a fair amount of undesirable radionuclides; (2) returning used oil to the tank from the crankcase of an engine; (3) adding a reagent to metals to remove undesirable constituents.

scheelite. Calcium tungstate, $CaWO_4$; a varied-colored ore of tungsten.

schist. Metamorphic foliated rocks formed under heat and pressure; they usually contain mica or talc.

Schistosoma. Bilharzia; a genus of blood flukes, including human parasites of very great medical importance in parts of China, South America, and Africa.

schizocarp. A dry fruit with two or more united carpels, which split apart at maturity.

schizogenous. Said of secretory cavities in plants which are formed by separation of cells.

schizogony. The vegetative reproduction of Protozoa by fission.

Schizomycetes. The plant class to which all bacteria belong.

schlieren. Streaky local segregations which occur in coarse-grained intrusive igneous rocks, usually near the contact of the intrusion with the main rock.

Schmidt objective. An objective for reflecting telescopes, designed to correct the aberration of the spherical mirror.

Schottky effect. The ionic current in a vacuum tube increases with the increase of potential difference between anode and cathode.

Schottky noise. A noise occurring in the anode current of an electron tube due to irregular variations in the surface conditions of the cathode.

Schüffner's dots. Coarse red granules in parasitized erythrocytes in tertian malaria on staining with polychrome methylene blue.

Schüler tube. A vacuum tube having a hollow cathode; used for the production of ionized-gas or vapor spectra.

Schumann plate. A photographic plate, containing very little or no gelatin, for use in the extreme ultraviolet and in positive-ray analysis, in which regions gelatin is very absorbent.

Schumann region. A range of very short ultraviolet waves.

Schwann's sheath. Neurilemma; a thin sheet enclosing each nerve fiber.

Schweitzer's reagent. An ammoniacal copper hydroxide solution, a solvent for cellulose; used in the manufacture of cuprammonium rayon.

scientific notation. A simplified system of expressing values as the powers of 10 multiplied by the significant number; example, the charge of an electron is 1.59×10^{-20} electromagnetic units.

scintillation. (1) The twinkling of stars due to the deflection of the light rays by the earth's atmosphere; (2) a momentary luminescence of a high-energy particle.

scion. A twig or part of the stem of a plant used for grafting.

sclerenchyma. (1) A plant tissue composed of thick-walled cells of various forms; the mature cells are dead and contain no protoplasm; it is used for protection mainly of fruits and seeds; (2) the hard skeletal tissue of corals.

sclerite. A hard calcareous plate.

scleroblast. Cells in the mesogloea of sponges which secrete the spicules.

sclerometer. An instrument for determining the hardness of a substance, especially metals, by measuring the pressure needed for scratching it.

scleroproteins. Insoluble fibrous proteins forming skeletal tissues; examples, keratin, chondrin, and elastin.

scleroscope. An instrument for determining the hardness of metals by the measurement of the rebound of a standard ball dropped on their surface from a fixed height.

sclerosis. (1) The hardening of plant tissues by lignification; (2) the hardening of vertebrate tissues by increase in the concentration of collagen; example, hardening of the arteries.

sclerotic coat. The outer coat of the wall of the eyeball.

sclerotium. A compact mass of fungus hyphae with a thickened rind which can remain dormant for long periods; example, ergot.

scolex. A portion of the adult tapeworm which is attached to the tissues of the host; a small rounded organ at the end of the slender neck, which bears hooks and/or suckers.

scolophore. A spindle-shaped organ formed of sensory cells grouped about a nerve ending; it is the fundamental auditory organ of insects.

scopometer. An instrument used for turbidimetric or nephelometric measurements by contrasting a field of constant brightness and an illuminated line placed behind the solution under test.

scoria. A lava that was hurled into the air, solidified, and large holes formed in it because of expanding gas bubbles.

Scorpion. The eighth sign of the Zodiac; too far south to be seen in Europe and North America.

scotopic vision. Scotopia; a vision in dim light, using the rods of the retina.

scouring. (1) The corroding effect of slag on furnace linings; (2) removing the natural gums from silk threads before dyeing; removing grease and dirt from wool yarns or fabrics before dyeing.

screen grid. A grid placed between the control grid and the anode of a vacuum tube to overcome a grid-to-anode capacitance.

screen process. Color photography in which color analysis and synthesis are carried out additively by the use of a mosaic screen of minute primary color filters.

screening. (1) The effect of the inner orbital electrons of an atom on the attraction of the nucleus for the outer electrons; (2) the effect of the outer layer of atoms in a crystal which prevents a radiation or a field of force from reaching the inner layers; (3) the protection of a magnetic field from the surroundings by a metal envelope.

screw. (1) A simple machine consisting of an inclined plane wound around a cylinder; (2) an amphipod crustacean.

scrotum. A muscular pouch containing the two testicles situated behind and below the penis; it is divided into two compartments by a septum in the middle.

scrubbing. (1) A mechanical process by which a dispersoid, usually a solid, is removed from a gas stream by washing the gas stream with a liquid; (2) cleaning metals after pickling with running water between revolving brushes.

scute. One of the large scales on the abdomen of a snake.

scutellum. (1) The shield-shaped cotyledon lying under the embryo in corn and other grains; (2) a shield-shaped structure in insects and birds.

scutum. The central subdivision of the exoskeleton of an insect.

scyphistoma. The larval stage of some jellyfish which undergoes transverse segmentation to form other individuals, each of which develops into an adult jellyfish.

Scyphomedusae. Same as Scyphozoa.

Scyphozoa. A class of Coelenterata; jellyfish whose polyps are small or absent; the medusae are large and more complex.

Se. Chemical symbol for selenium.

sea anemone. A sea polyp of the phylum Coelenterata; it is beautifully colored and grows singly.

sea cliff. A steep cliff formed by the erosive effect of sea waves.

sea water. Salt water, containing sodium, potassium, and magnesium chloride and magnesium and calcium sulfate.

sea weeds. Marine plants, especially red, brown, or green algae, living in or by the sea.

seaplane. Hydroplane; a plane that can take off from and land on water.

season. One of the four three-month periods of the year, during which the vertical rays of the sun are moving north and/or southward toward or from the Equator.

sebaceous gland. A gland of the skin of mammals which secretes an oily substance called sebum; it is usually associated with hair follicles.

sebum. The fatty secretion of the sebaceous glands.

sec. Abbreviation for second.

second. (1) A unit of time, one sixtieth of a minute; (2) an angular unit; one sixtieth of a minute of arc.

secondaries. (1) Feathers of a wing which cover the primaries; (2) the hind wings of an insect.

secondary. Usually the output coil of a transformer.

secondary bow. A less distinct rainbow above the primary rainbow which shows the colors in reverse order to those of the primary bow.

secondary cell. A voltaic cell which operates by reversible chemical action, so that it can be recharged.

secondary circuit. A circuit in which an electromotive force is induced by the variation of the current in another, primary, circuit.

secondary coil. A coil in which current is induced by that flowing in a primary coil.

secondary color. A color obtained by mixing two or more primary colors; examples, red and yellow make orange; yellow and blue make green.

secondary cosmic rays. The radiation of particles in the earth's atmosphere when primary cosmic rays meet with nuclei and electrons.

secondary electron. (1) An electron resulting from a secondary emission; (2) that electron which, after a collision of two electrons, has the less energy.

secondary embryo. An individual formed by budding from another that has not yet completed its development; example, in Bryozoa.

secondary emission. (1) An emission of electrons from a surface as a result of bombardment with electrons from a primary emission; (2) fluorescence.

secondary flagellum. A small branch of the antenna of Crustacea.

secondary host. A host which is infested by eating eggs, a larva, or an asexual parasite.

secondary meristem. A region of actively dividing cells that has arisen from permanent tissue; example, cork cambium.

secondary metal. A metal reclaimed from scrap.

secondary of transformer. A transformer winding connected to a load; the primary is an energized winding.

secondary radiation. Photons absorbed and reradiated by electrons, delta rays, etc.

secondary root. (1) A branch of the primary root of a plant; (2) an adventitious root.

secondary sexual characters. Characters, other than the sex organs, in which the male and female of a species differ; examples, the breast of a woman, the comb of a cock.

secondary spectrum. (1) The spectrum of the hydrogen molecule as distinct from that of the atom; (2) the residual chromatic aberration of a corrected lens.

secondary thickening. An additional vascular tissue formed after the differentiation of primary tissues by the activity of the cambium so that the stem and roots increase in diameter.

second-class lever. A lever in which the resistance is between the fulcrum and the force.

secretin. A hormone produced by the small intestine which stimulates the pancreas to secrete its digestive juice.

secreting tissue. A plant tissue that produces such substances as latex or chicle.

secretion. A substance secreted by a gland, which aids in some body function; example, saliva.

sector, warm. An area of warm, usually tropical, air in the early stages of a cyclone.

sedentary. Said of animals that are permanently attached to a substratum; example, barnacle.

sediment. (1) Materials deposited by a stream; (2) substances that settle from a liquid at the bottom of the container.

sedimentary rock. A layered rock formed from sediment.

sedimentation. The separation of solids and liquids, causing the solid to settle by gravity or centrifuging.

sedimentation potential. A potential difference set up by the falling of a particle through a liquid.

sedimentation test. The measurement of the speed of settling of blood cells which is increased if the patient is pregnant or ill.

Seebeck effect. The current flowing in a circuit when two wires of different metals are joined at their ends to form a circuit and the two junctions are maintained at different temperatures.

seed. A ripened ovule which will produce a new plant if placed under suitable conditions; it consists of the embryo, food, and a protective covering.

seed dispersal. The scattering or distribution of seeds from the fruit.

seed germinating box. A device used for the observation of seed germination and root growth.

seedling. A young plant from the time it emerges from the seed until it becomes capable to manufacture its own food.

Seger cones. Pyrometric cones; fusion cones; small conical pieces consisting of a mixture of clay with certain oxides placed in a furnace to indicate the approximate temperature.

segment. (1) One of the insulated sections of a commutator; (2) a section of the body of a metameric animal; example, earthworms; (3) one joint of an appendage; example, insects; (4) a portion of the lamina of a segmented leaf.

segmentation. (1) Metamerism; the repetition of a pattern of elements, belonging to each of the main organ systems of the body, along the anteroposterior axis of the body; example, earthworms; (2) cleavage of a fertilized egg.

segregation. The separation, first into different gametes and then into different offsprings, of the two members of any pair of allelomorphs of an individual.

seism. An earthquake.

seismic detector. A microphone connected to a recording oscillograph and located in a strategic position on the earth's surface to detect sound waves transmitted through the earth.

seismograph. An extremely sensitive instrument used to record vibrations of the earth's crust and to detect the location of earthquakes.

seismonasty. The response of a plant to a nondirectional shock stimulus; example, the rapid folding of leaflets and drooping of leaves in mimosa when lightly struck or shaken.

Selachii. Aquatic animals having gills, paired fins, and sharp teeth; the upper jaw is not fused to the skull; examples, shark, dogfish, skate, and carp.

selectance. The numerical value of selectivity.

selection. A method of breeding in which suitable parents are first selected so that desirable

traits are combined in the offspring.

selective absorption. The ability of a root to absorb certain dissolved minerals and exclude others.

selective cutting. Cutting timber trees from a managed forest only when they are mature.

selective membrane. Semipermeable membrane; a membrane which allows some substances to go through while rejecting others.

selective radiator. An emitter which gives off radiation of different spectral-energy distribution from that of a black body at the same temperature.

selective reflection. The reflection of one color or wave length more than another.

selectivity. The ability of a set or circuit to tune to only the frequency wanted.

selector. A mechanism in the automatic telephone circuit that is operated by the dialing impulses to make the desired connection.

selenium. A metalloid; chemical symbol Se; atomic number 34; used in photoelectric cells, glass manufacture.

selenium cell. A photoelectric cell which depends on photoconductive or photovoltaic effect for its operation.

self-capacitance. The distributed capacitance of an electric circuit due to its containing closely wound coils of insulated wire, the adjacent turns of which have a condenser effect.

self-differentiation. The differentiation of a region, tissue, or feature of an embryo which is independent of the influence of other parts of the embryo.

self-excitation. The operation of a machine which generates the current for supplying its field.

self-fertilization. The union of sperm and egg both of which have been produced by the same hermaphrodite organism.

self-inductance. The back voltage caused by the first rush of current through the turns of a coil.

self-induction. The phenomenon that the magnetic field of one turn of a coiled conductor induces an electromotive force in an adjacent turn.

self-pollination. The transfer of pollen from an anther to the stigma of the same flower or flowers of the same plant.

self-preservation. A basic instinct of living organisms to protect themselves.

self-protective metal. A metal which corrodes somewhat on its exposed surface to form a thin continuous and closely adhering film which prevents further oxidation.

self-shielding. (1) The absorption of radiation by the source of radiation; (2) the shielding of

one part of a region in a nuclear reactor from particles or radiation arising in another part.

self-sterility. The property of some hermaphrodites which are unable to form viable offsprings by self-fertilization.

semen. The thick grayish-white secretion of the male testicles that contains the spermatozoa or fertilizing male cells; it is stored in the seminal vesicles and ejaculated through the penis.

semiaquatic. Said of plants and animals living both in water and on land.

semicircular canals. The three curved passages of the inner ear that are associated with balance.

semiconductor. An electrical conductor whose resistance decreases with a rise in temperature and the presence of impurities; example, graphite.

semilunar valves. Crescent-shaped valves which prevent blood from flowing back from the pulmonary artery to the right ventricle.

seminal. Referring to or containing seed or semen; example, seminal fluid.

seminal receptacles. Vesicula seminalis; a saclike organ in many animals in which sperms are stored while they are developing.

seminal vesicle. An expanded portion of the genital duct of the male, or a pouchlike derivative of the duct, either for the storage of spermatozoa or for the secretion of accessory substances.

seminiferous tubule. A tube in the testis whose lining produces spermatozoa.

semipermeable membrane. A membrane that is permeable to the solvent but impermeable to the solute.

semisolid media (singular, medium). Media prepared from a mixture of agar and gelatin.

semitransparent. Translucent.

semitransparent photocathode. A photocathode in which a radiant flux incident to one side produces photoelectric emission from the opposite side.

sensation unit. An obsolete name of decibel, a unit of sound intensity.

sense organ. A receptor of stimuli.

sensible heat. The heat which is measured by a thermometer, as opposed to latent heat.

sensible temperature. The sensation of temperature by the body; substantially the temperature indicated by the wet-bulb thermometer.

sensilla. The sense organs of insects, including integumentary sense organs, scolophore (organs of hearing), and the om-

matidia and retinulae of the eyes.

sensitive volume. That part of a counter tube or ionization chamber which responds to a specific radiation.

sensitivity. (1) The ability to respond to a stimulus, irritability; (2) the extent of response of a radio receiver to the waves received.

sensitized fluorescence. The emission of radiation by one atom due to energy received in collision with another atom which has been excited by radiation.

sensitometry. The measurement of the response of photographic emulsions to light or other forms of radiant energy.

sensory. Referring or belonging to receptors.

sensory neuron. Afferent neuron; a nerve cell that carries impulses from outside the body to the spinal cord or brain.

sepal. One of the outer leaflike parts at the base of a flower; it protects the other flower parts before the bud opens.

separate excitation. Supplying the current needed for the field of an electric machine from some outside source.

separation energy. The binding energy of a proton, neutron, or alpha particle within a nucleus.

separator. A thin perforated insulator sheet between the plates of a battery.

separator tube. A device for separating isotopes by thermal diffusion.

septate. Divided by cross walls into cells or compartments.

septicidal dehiscence. The opening of fruit along the line of union of the carpels.

septum (plural septa). (1) A thin-walled partition between two plant cells; (2) a cross wall in plant filaments, spores, or hyphae; (3) a wall between two cavities; example, the septum of the nose.

sequestering agent. Chelating agent; a chemical that forms a very soluble complex with metal ions; used to remove boiler scale.

sere. A unit of a plant succession.

serial homology. The homology of different segments of the same individual.

series. A method of connecting electrical equipment so that the current will flow through each device in turn.

series limit. The convergence frequency of a series of spectral lines; no line occurs at this point, but a related continuous spectrum may begin just beyond it.

series motor. An electric motor having a series field winding.

series winding. A field coil connected in series with the armature of a motor or generator.

serosa. (1) Serous membrane; the

chorion; a thin membrane enveloping the developing embryo of terrestrial vertebrates and all the other extraembryonic membranes; it contributes to the formation of the placenta; (2) the lining membrane of lymph cavities in the vertebrate body.

serous. Referring to, producing, containing, or resembling serum.

serous coat. The outer peritoneal-membrane covering of the viscera.

serous gland. A gland that produces a watery secretion; example, the salivary glands.

serous membrane. Same as serosa.

Serpek process. A process for the fixation of atmospheric nitrogen by reacting aluminum with nitrogen to form aluminum nitride, which is then decomposed by steam to give ammonia.

serrate. Finely toothed; example, the edge of a cherry leaf.

serum. A fluid containing antibodies; a secretion of the serous membranes; the liquid part of the blood after coagulation, as distinguished from the circulating plasma of the blood.

serum albumin. A mixture of two or more albuminous compounds contained in the blood plasma, blood serum, and other body fluids.

serum globulin. A protein mixture in the plasma and serous fluids.

servo control. A control device to reinforce the pilot's effort by an aerodynamic or mechanical relay.

servomotor. A mechanism used for enlarging a small effort by hydraulic means.

sesamoid bone. A bone developed within a tendon of vertebrates, especially in mammals where the tendon works over a ridge of underlying bone; example, the knee cap.

sessile. Attached by the base without a stalk or stem; stationary.

seta. (1) A bristle on every segment of the ventral surface of earthworms; they aid in locomotion; (2) a short stalk of the sporophyte of liverworts which connects the foot and the capsule; (3) an elongated cell or group of cells in some algae.

settling. Sedimentation; removing heavy solid particles from a liquid by allowing it to stand undisturbed for some time.

sex. The distinction between male and female; the ability to produce sperm or eggs.

sex chromosome. A chromosome of which there is a homologous pair in the nuclei of one sex, and a dissimilar pair or unpaired chromosome in the other sex.

sex limitation. The conditioning

of the expression of a hereditary character in the individual according to sex.

sex linkage. Characters linked to the sex chromosomes.

sex ratio. The relative proportion of the numbers of males and females in a population.

sex-limited character or gene. A gene developing in only one of the two sexes; example, the gene for milk production.

sextant. A reflecting instrument used for measuring the angle of elevation of a celestial body above the horizon.

sexual dimorphism. The differences in the structure and appearance of the males and females of the same species.

sexual reproduction. A reproduction by the union of sperm and egg.

shading of band. The gradual decrease in intensity of a spectral band on the side opposite to the band head.

shadow zone. A region in the atmosphere or under water which cannot be penetrated by sound waves.

shaft. (1) The slender middle portion of a long bone; (2) the rachis of a feather; (3) a vertical passage into a mine; (4) a rod or bar that supports a rotating machine part.

shale. A fine-grained sedimentary laminated rock, consisting of clay and sometimes containing oil.

shatter oscillation. An oscillation in a liquid of such frequency and amplitude that it will break the continuity of the liquid.

shear. A stress applied to a body in the plane of one of its faces.

shearing stress. The stress which accompanies shear in an elastic body.

sheath. (1) That part of a leaf which surrounds the stem; example, grasses; (2) a protective structure in animals; (3) a space-charge region in a gas-discharge tube, due to an excess of either positive or negative charges.

sheet erosion. An erosion that removes an even layer of fertile top soil exposing the subsoil beneath.

sheet lightning. A lightning flash occurring behind a cloud, which illuminates the cloud fully or partly.

shell. (1) A region about the nucleus of an atom in which electrons move; each electron shell corresponds to a definite energy level; (2) a hard external covering secreted by folds of the body wall of many animals.

shell filler. An explosive that requires a severe shock to explode.

shell gland. (1) A specialized region of the ducts of the female reproductive system of some vertebrates which secretes a

more or less rigid covering surrounding the egg; (2) a gland of some invertebrates that secretes the materials which form the shell.

shellac. Lac; a resinous substance formed by insects on tree bark; used in varnishes, gramaphone records.

shellfish. Shelled mollusks and crustaceans; example, lobster.

shelter belt. Rows of trees planted to protect land areas against damage by wind.

shelter chain. A series of organisms which provide shelter for one another.

Shenstone effect. An increase in the photoelectric emission of certain metals immediately after having been traversed by an electric current.

shield. (1) A radiation-averting structure; (2) an electrode for controlling the intensity of a cathode-ray beam.

shielding. A metallic covering around an electric apparatus as a protection against outside magnetic or electrostatic fields.

shock absorber. A frictional or hydraulic damping device.

shock wave. An extremely narrow region in which the air flow changes from subsonic to supersonic; it is connected with a sudden and extensive rise in pressure and temperature.

shooting star. Meteor; a small incandescent interplanetary body flashing through the earth's atmosphere and then falling to the earth's surface.

shoran. Short-range navigation; a navigation system in which an aircraft sends out two radar signals that are received and returned by two ground stations of known locations; from the time necessary for these operations, the range of the aircraft relative to the stations can be calculated.

shore dunes. Sand hills formed by the wind along a low coast.

shore effect. An electromagnetic wave changes its characteristics as it passes along a land-sea boundary, because each region has its own propagation characteristics.

short circuit. An additional and unwanted path that develops in an electric circuit, through which part of the current leaves the desired circuit, is wasted, and may do damage.

short ton. 2,000 pounds.

short wave. Waves of a maximum wave length of 60 meters.

shot. A lead containing small amounts of arsenic, formed into small balls by dripping the molten metal into cold water.

shot effect. A sputtering or popping noise in radio and amplifier apparatus due to variations in the number of thermions emitted per second from the

tube filament.

shoulder girdle. Pectoral girdle; that part of the vertebrate skeleton to which the arms or forefeet are connected.

shrub. A woody, perennial seed plant, with side stems branching just above the ground; they have no main trunk and are usually smaller than trees.

shunt. A parallel connection of two circuits, in which the same electromotive force is applied to both.

shunt circuit. A circuit in which the electric current is divided between two paths.

shunt generator. A machine for generating an electric current in which the winding for producing the magnetic field is connected in shunt, or parallel with the armature or rotating part.

shunt motor. A motor with a shunt winding which is able to maintain an even speed for all loads.

shunt winding. A field winding which is connected in shunt across the armature of a motor.

Si. Chemical symbol for silicon.

Siamese twins. Twins that result from a single fertilized egg that does not completely split into two parts at an early stage of development; the twins are identical but their bodies are joined at certain points because of incomplete splitting.

siblings. Brothers and/or sisters; offsprings of the same parents.

side band. A frequency band on both sides of the carrier frequency of a modulated radio wave; it is as wide as the highest modulating frequency.

side chain. An aliphatic radical attached to benzene or another cyclic organic molecule; example, the methyl group, CH_3, is a side chain in toluene, $C_6H_5 \cdot CH_3$.

sidereal. Relating or belonging to the stars.

sidereal day. The time that elapses between the passage of a given star across a particular meridian and the next passage of the same star across the same meridian; 23 hours, 56 minutes and 4.09 seconds.

sidereal period. Time required for a heavenly body to return to the same position as compared to the fixed stars.

sidereal year. The time that elapses between two passages of the sun through the ecliptic meridian of the same star; 365 days, 6 hours, 9 minutes, and 9.54 seconds.

siderite. A gray mineral; iron carbonate, $FeCO_3$; an iron ore.

Siegbahn unit. The wave length of 10^{-11} centimeter; used for measuring x-rays.

sieve cells. Large cells with perforated ends which are a part of the phloem of a fibrovascular bundle.

sieve plates. Cell walls with holes which form at the top and bottom or side of a sieve tube.

sieve tube. A tubular element in the phloem consisting of living cells through which manufactured food is conveyed.

signal colors. Recognition colors; distinctive coloration of members of the same species.

signal generator. A wide-range radio-frequency oscillator; used for testing radio receivers.

signal voltage. (1) The voltage induced by the electromagnetic waves intercepted by the antenna; (2) the voltage supplied to the control grid of a vacuum tube.

silanes. Silicon hydrides; a homologous series analogous to the hydrocarbons, the difference between adjacent members being SiH_2; examples, silane, SiH_4; disilane, Si_2H_6.

silica. Silicon dioxide, SiO_2; it occurs as various minerals; used in glass, refractories.

silicates. Salts of silicic acid; they occur widely distributed in nature; examples, mica and feldspar.

silicon. A brown amorphous powder; chemical symbol Si; atomic number 14; used in metallurgy.

silicon carbide. Carborundum, SiC; a very hard substance; used as an abrasive.

silicon dioxide. Same as silica.

silicon steel. A low-carbon steel containing 1 to 5% silicon; used for transformer cores, automobile springs.

silicone. A high-polymeric synthetic resin, consisting of a chain of alternate silicon and oxygen atoms, with organic groups attached to the silicon atoms; it is highly resistant to heat; used as an insulator.

silique. A multiseeded fruit, characteristic of mustard; it consists of valves splitting from the bottom and leaving the placentae with the false partition stretched between.

silk. (1) A fabric made from threads produced by the silkworm; (2) a liquid produced by many insects and spiders; it contains fibroin and sericin; it hardens to a fibrous material in air and is used by the insects for making cocoons, or cases in which pupation takes place or eggs are deposited, and webs for the capture of prey.

silk gland. A gland secreting a viscous fluid from which silk is produced by insects and spiders; the silk glands of most insects are modified salivary glands.

sill. A small igneous intrusion in which lava spreads horizontally between two layers of rock.

silt. Very small particles of sediment that settle out of still water.

Silurian period. A Paleozoic era; it began about 370 million years ago; it is characterized by the appearance of the first land animals, reef corals, and first lava plants.

silver. A soft white lustrous metal; chemical symbol Ag; atomic number 47; used for coins, tableware, jewelry.

silver bromide. Yellowish crystals; AgBr; used in photography.

silver chloride. White crystals; AgCl; used in photography.

silver cyanide. White crystals; AgCN; used for silverplating.

silver fineness. A measure of the amount of silver in an alloy; sterling silver is 925 fine and contains 92.5 percent pure silver.

silver nitrate. White soluble crystals; $AgNO_3$; used in marking inks, medicine, chemical analysis.

silver plating. Depositing a layer of metallic silver on the surface of a metallic object which is made the cathode in a silver-salt solution as electrolyte.

silver sulfide. Black crystals; Ag_2S.

silver thaw. A glazelike ice coat formed on trees and other exposed objects when, after prolonged severe cold weather, a warm air mass is passing over a region.

simoon. A hot, dry, sand-laden wind of the Arabian Desert; a whirlwind which lasts a few minutes and forms sand spouts.

simple decomposition. The breakdown of a compound into two or more simpler substances.

simple eye. Ocellus; (1) a single organ of sight or a light-sensitive spot of insects; (2) a discolored large cell in a leaf; (3) a light-sensitive swelling in some fungi.

simple harmonic motion. The oscillation of a point along a line about a central point so that its acceleration is proportional to its displacement from the position of rest.

simple leaf. A leaf whose blade is in one piece.

simple machine. A simple device for the transfer of energy to facilitate the performance of work; the six elementary machines: lever, pulley, inclined plane, wheel and axle, wedge, and screw.

simple pendulum. Mathematical pendulum; a theoretical pendulum consisting of a material point, suspended on a weightless string, and oscillating without friction.

simple pistil. A pistil composed of one carpel.

simple tissue. A tissue consisting of cells essentially alike in structure.

Sinanthropus pekinensis. Peking man; an extinct species from the lower Pleistocene; it is similar to Pithecanthropus; it has been reconstructed based on fourteen fragmentary skulls.

sine galvanometer. A galvanometer which is more sensitive than the tangent galvanometer; the coil and scale are turned and the needle is kept at zero; the sine of the deflection is then proportional to the current.

sine wave. The wave form of transverse simple harmonic vibrations.

sinew. A tendon.

singing arc. A direct-current arc which generates oscillations of audio frequency when an inductance and a condenser are connected in parallel with it.

single circulation. A circulation in which the heart has two chambers; the auricle receives blood from the veins and the ventricle pumps blood through the arteries to all tissues; example, the circulatory system of fish.

single crystal. A solid mass in which all parts have the same crystallographic orientation; it results from slow crystallization from a liquid.

single phase. A single, independent alternating-current circuit or winding consisting of two conductors.

single-pole switch. A switch that opens and closes only one of the two leads of a circuit.

single-stage rocket. A rocket that makes a flight in one step.

singular point or line. A point or line in a field of force at which or along which the field intensity or the potential gradient is zero.

singular temperature. A temperature at which some property of a substance becomes discontinuous.

sintering. Compacting metal powder into a continuous mass by compressing and then heating below the fusion temperature; the particles are held together by cohesive forces.

sinuauricular node. A small mass of tissue on top of the heart in which the heart beat starts.

sinus. (1) An irregular cavity or depression in a bone, blood vessel, or among the cells of a tissue; (2) clefts in the leaf blade.

sinus venosus. (1) A sac on top of the fish's heart into which the cardinal vein empties; (2) the back chamber of the heart of a vertebrate embryo in the early stages of its development.

sinusoids. Large irregular blood spaces which are comparable to capillaries as their walls consist of an endothelial tube, but they differ from capillaries in that their lumina are larger than those of capillaries.

siphon. Syphon; (1) a tube or pipe bent in the shape of an inverted U, through which a liquid flows to a lower level after first rising to a higher level; (2) a passage between the mantle folds of bivalve mollusks through which water enters or leaves the mantle cavity; (3) a slender tube associated with the alimentary tract of sea urchins; (4) a long cell that extends to the full length of a joint of some red algae.

Siphonaptera. Wingless insects with piercing and sucking mouth parts and legs adapted for leaping; they have complete metamorphosis; example, flea.

Siphonophora. Floating, colonial animals with extreme specialization of members for feeding and protection; they have no skeleton; their medusae remain attached; example, Portuguese man-of-war.

Siphonopoda. Cephalopoda; mollusks which have sucker arms around their head; examples, octopus and cuttlefish.

siphonstele. A continuous vascular cylinder which encloses the pith in the stem of woody Dicotyledones.

siphuncle. A slender tube extending from the visceral hump of the nautilus through perforations in the septa of the shell along the entire spiral; it contains blood vessels and is assumed to maintain the gas content of the enclosed chambers of the shell.

Siphunculata. Anoplura; insects with sucking mouths, that are parasitic on mammals and man; example, louse.

Sirenia. Placental aquatic herbivorous mammals with an expanded tail and a very short neck; examples, sea cows and manatees.

Sirius. The brightest star in the sky; a star of the constellation Canis Major.

sirocco. A warm moist southern wind around the Mediterranean.

sizing agent. An adhesive or glue used for improving the strength, smoothness and sheen of textiles and paper.

skeletal muscle. Striped muscle; striated muscle; a transversely striated multinucleate contractile tissue.

skeleton. The framework which supports the animal body and protects the internal organs; the human skeleton consists of bones and cartilages; the skeleton of some animals consists of shells, hardened skin, etc.

skiagraph. A shadowlike x-ray picture taken on a sensitized plate.

skiascope. Retinoscope; an instrument for studying the optical refraction of the eye, which contains a mirror that reflects light on the retina and makes possible the observation of the movement of the shadow across the pupil.

skiatron. A cathode-ray tube in which the opacity of the screen is varied as a function of beam intensity.

skidding. A sidewise movement of an airplane upward or outward from the center of a turn.

skin. (1) The outer protective covering of the animal body; (2) the epidermis of a plant.

skin effect. A concentration of current density toward the surface of an alternating-current conductor, due to a self-induced counter electromotive force which results in an increase in the effective resistance.

skip distance. The distance between adjacent regions of good radio reception.

skipping. The audibility of a radio signal at relatively large distances, but not at some near-by areas because of the reflecting effect of the Heaviside layer.

skull. The bone structure of the head of vertebrates.

sky condition. The state of the sky; (1) clear sky: less than one-tenth cover of clouds; (2) scattered clouds: one-tenth to five-tenths cover; (3) broken clouds: five-tenths to nine-tenths cover; (4) overcast: more than nine-tenths cover.

sky wave. Indirect wave; ionospheric ray; a radio wave which is reflected by the Heaviside layer on its way from transmitter to receiver.

slag. A waste material formed in a furnace by the reaction of a flux with the impurities of an ore.

slaked lime. Calcium hydroxide, $Ca(OH)_2$; formed by dissolving calcium oxide in water; used in mortar, for whitewashing.

slant. A culture medium allowed to harden in a test tube set at a slant to increase the surface for the growth of colonies; example, agar slant.

slate. A fine-grained homogeneous sedimentary rock composed of clay or volcanic ash that has been metamorphosed so as to develop a high degree of fissility or slaty cleavage which is usually at a large angle to the plane of stratification; used as a roofing material and for blackboards.

sleet. Frozen rain.

slide. (1) A glass plate used in a projecting lantern for throwing a picture on a screen; (2) a small glass plate on which specimens are placed for microscopic examination; (3) a preparation made on a small glass plate.

slide rule. An instrument used for rapid calculations; it consists of two rules, one sliding in the other and both marked with logarithmic scales.

slide-wire. A resistance-measuring device used with a Wheatstone bridge; it is a wire equipped with a sliding contact whose position can be adjusted along the wire according to a linear scale.

sliding friction. The friction between two solid surfaces.

slime layer. A carbohydrate jelly layer believed to surround the cell wall of bacteria.

slime molds. Myxomycetes; saprophytic simple organisms representing the borderline between plants and animals; they are growing on wood, rocks, or grass, or wherever there is sufficient moisture.

sling psychrometer. An instrument for measuring the humidity in the atmosphere; it consists of two thermometers fastened to a handle so that they can be whirled in a circle by hand until the reading remains unchanged.

slip. (1) The difference between the actual speed of a ship and the speed it would have if its propeller acted on a solid; (2) the difference in speed between a rotor field and the stator field; (3) the plastic deformation of metal crystals due to shear displacement.

slip bands. Steps formed on the surface of plastically deformed single crystals which show the planes along which shear displacement has taken place.

slip rings. Metallic rings by which the armature of an alternating-current dynamo is connected to the brushes.

slip surface. A surface along which a solid under severe stress tends to crack or shear.

slipping. Sideslipping; a sidewise movement of an airplane downward or toward the center of a turn.

slipstream. The air current generated by the propeller.

slit. A long narrow opening through which radiation enters or leaves an optical instrument.

slit, double. Two long narrow parallel openings used in some diffraction and interference experiments.

slough. The cast-off skin of a snake.

slow neutron. A neutron that travels at the rate of a mile a second.

slow oxidation. (1) The oxidation of food in the cells; (2) the combination of substances with oxygen without burning; example, the rusting of iron.

sludge. (1) The impurities formed at the anode in the electrolytic refining of a metal; (2) the sediment from sewage treatment.

slug. An English unit of mass; the mass of a body which is accelerated at the rate of 1 foot per second when 1 pound of force acts on it; 32.174 pounds.

slurry. A suspension in water of insoluble matter, such as clay or cement.

Sm. Chemical symbol for samarium.

small circles. Parallels on the earth's surface which grow smaller as the poles are approached.

small intestine. A portion of the alimentary canal of an amphibian, reptile, or a mammal in which the digestion is practically completed; in humans, it consists of the duodenum, jejunum, and ileum; through its walls the digested food is absorbed into the blood.

smaltite. Smaltine; a gray cubic mineral; cobalt diarsenide, $CoAs_2$; an ore of cobalt; it is almost always associated with chloanthite, nickel diarsenide.

smectic phase. A transition between the liquid and solid states.

smelting. Extracting a metal from its ore by fusing with a flux at high temperatures; the resulting melt consists of two layers, the slag is on top and the separated impure metal at the bottom.

smithsonite. Calamine; a yellowish mineral; zinc carbonate, $ZnCO_3$.

smog. A heavy dark city fog containing dust, pollen, bacteria, smoke, and chemical waste gases.

smoke. A suspension of very small solid particles in a gas, usually air; its chief source is the incomplete burning of fuels.

smoke chamber. A device used to observe the Brownian movement of fine smoke particles under a microscope.

smokeless powder. A nitrocellulose explosive.

smooth muscle. An involuntary muscle, that is, one which is not under the control of the will; it consists of spindle-shaped cells and is located in the wall of internal organs.

smut. (1) Ustilaginales; fungus parasites that cause plant diseases by living inside the host and destroying its flowers; they cause much damage in cereals; (2) the plant disease caused by these parasites.

Sn. Chemical symbol for tin.

Snell's law. The angles of incidence and of refraction of a light refracted at a surface between two media have sines in a constant ratio to each other (called the "refractive index") and lie in the same plane.

snorkel. The breathing tube of a submarine through which fresh air can be pumped in and foul air can be pumped out.

snow. (1) Ice crystals formed from frozen water vapor; they fall down singly or as flakes, which are random accumula-

tions of ice crystals; (2) a colloquial term for the random pattern of white dots on a television screen under a weak or zero signal condition.

snow line. The lower limit of altitude of the region of perpetual snow; it varies with the mountain and is dependent, to some extent, on the summer temperature of the region; example, in the Himalayas it is 15,000 feet.

soap. (1) The metallic salt of a higher fatty acid; (2) the product of saponification or neutralization with alkalis of fats, oils, and resins.

soapless soap. A synthetic detergent.

soaps, soluble. Salts of the alkali metals and one or more of the higher fatty acids.

social insects. Insects which live together in colonies, sharing the duties of the group; examples, a hive of bees and a termite nest.

society. (1) A group of individuals of the same species, living together for mutual benefit, with some division of labor; (2) a minor plant community within a consociation, arising from some local variation in conditions and dominated by species other than that dominant in the consociation.

soda ash. Anhydrous sodium carbonate, Na_2CO_3; a white hygroscopic powder; used in glass and soap manufacture.

soda water. A water containing carbon dioxide, CO_2, under pressure; when the pressure is released, the solubility of the gas is lowered and effervescence occurs.

sodium. A silver-white very reactive alkali metal; chemical symbol Na; atomic number 11; it occurs in nature only in compounds; used in the manufacture of chemicals.

sodium bicarbonate. Baking soda, $NaHCO_3$; a white soluble salt; used in baking powder and medicine.

sodium chlorate. Colorless crystals; $NaClO_3$; used as an oxidizing agent.

sodium chloride. Common salt; $NaCl$.

sodium hydroxide. Caustic soda, $NaOH$; a white deliquescent solid; it dissolves in water to give an alkaline solution; used in leather and textile treatment, soap manufacture.

sodium nitrate. A white soluble crystalline salt; $NaNO_3$; used as a fertilizer, in the manufacture of nitric acid and explosives.

sodium peroxide. A yellow powder; Na_2O_2; used as an oxidizing agent, bleach, germicide.

sodium silicate. White soluble crystals; Na_2SiO_3; its concentrated aqueous solution is called water glass, which is used as an adhesive and preservative.

sodium sulfate. Glauber's salt, $Na_2SO_4 \cdot 10H_2O$; efflorescent colorless crystals; used in textile printing, medicine.

sodium thiosulfate. Hypo, $Na_2S_2O_3 \cdot 5H_2O$; white efflorescent crystals; used in photography, as a mordant, in leather manufacture.

soft coal. A bituminous coal that yields illuminating gas, coal tar, and coke on heating without air.

soft iron. An iron containing very little carbon; it is not a permanent magnet.

soft landing. An approach to the moon or any other celestial body at a speed of less than 500 feet per second in order to avoid destruction of the landing vehicle.

soft palate. Velum; a folded membrane in the rear of the mouth cavity; a continuation of the hard palate.

soft water. Water that is relatively free from mineral salts.

softener. Plasticizer; a substance added to synthetic resins, rubbers, and plastics to modify their properties, especially to preserve their flexibility; examples, tricresyl phosphate and glycol esters.

softening temperature. A temperature at which viscous flow changes to plastic flow.

sogasoid. A dispersion of a solid in a gas.

soil. The loose surface layer of the earth from which plants obtain the substances essential for their growth.

soil binders. Plants whose roots hold the soil particles and prevent wind and water erosion; example, grasses.

soil chemistry. The study of the soil as a chemical system.

soil conservation. Wise use of the soil.

soil depletion. The gradual using up of the minerals and organic matter in the soil.

soil profile. A series of distinct layers visible in a vertical section through the soil.

soil technician. Agronomist; an expert in soil management.

soil texture. The size of soil particles.

soil-building crops. Crops that build up minerals in the soil; example, legumes.

soil-depleting crop. A crop that uses up all nitrates; example, corn.

soilless culture. Hydroponics; growing plants without soil; the roots of the plants are usually immersed in a solution of plant nutrients.

sol. A colloidal solution; a liquid which contains colloidal particles in permanent suspension.

solar constant. The rate at which the earth is receiving energy from the sun corrected for loss through absorption by the atmosphere; about 1.8 horsepower falls on each square meter of the earth each second; approximately 1.34×10^6 ergs per square centimeter per second.

solar day. The time that elapses between two successive crossings of a given meridian by the sun.

solar eclipse. An eclipse that occurs when the moon passes between the sun and the earth and casts a shadow on the sun.

solar flare. Bright eruptions that occur on the sun's surface, emitting intense radiations; the occasional giant solar flares could be hazardous to a manned lunar mission.

solar plexus. The large nerve ganglion of the sympathetic nervous system located in the abdomen.

solar radiation. The radiation from the sun which covers a wide range of wave lengths from the long infrared rays to the short ultraviolet rays.

solar spectrum. The spectrum of the sun with Fraunhofer and telluric absorption lines resulting from absorption by the sun's and the earth's atmosphere.

solar system. The sun, nine major planets, and a great many asteroids, meteors, and comets.

solar time. A time measured by reference to the sun; the hour angle of the sun at a given location.

solarimeter. A pyrheliometer for direct reading of solar radiation.

solarization. (1) The effect of sunlight or of artificial ultraviolet light on glass, which results in a reduction of its transparency to ultraviolet and causes a permanent discoloration; (2) a reversal of the gradation sequence in a dense photographic image when the normal development is applied after overexposure; (3) the temporary stoppage of photosynthesis in a plant after a lengthy exposure to bright light.

solation. The change of a gel to a sol.

solder. A low-melting alloy used for joining metals; soft solders are lead-base alloys; hard solders are copper-base alloys.

soldiers. Male or female termites that have undeveloped sex organs; they are defenders of the colony.

solenocyte. An excretory cell in annelid worms and in amphioxus from which cilia extend into the associated excretory tubule.

solenoid. Superimposed layers of an insulated electrical conductor wound on a nonmagnetic or soft-iron core; if direct current flows through it, it behaves like a bar magnet.

solid. A state of matter which has a definite volume and a definite shape; the molecules of a solid vibrate about a fixed mean position, but they do not have translational motion.

solid medium. A culture medium consisting essentially of agar, gelatin, or albumin.

solid of revolution. A solid generated by the revolution of a plane area about a line, the axis of revolution.

solid solution. A solid homogeneous mixture of two or more substances; example, an alloy; a mixed crystal of two or more isomorphous substances.

solid state. Same as solid.

solidification point. The freezing point of liquids.

solidification range. The temperature range in which the solidification of an alloy takes place.

solid-state physics. A branch of physics which deals with the structure and properties of solids.

soliquid. A dispersion of a solid in a liquid.

solitary. (1) A single flower which grows at the end of its stalk; (2) occurring singly; (3) nonsocial.

solstices. The two time periods when the sun's vertical rays reach their northern and southern limits: in summer, June 21; in winter, December 22.

solubility. The amount of a substance that can be dissolved in a given amount of a solvent.

solubility product. The product of the concentrations of the ions of a dissolved electrolyte when it is in equilibrium with an undissolved substance.

solute. Any substance which is dissolved in a solution.

solution. A liquid or solid which contains the uniformly scattered molecules of one or more liquids or solids; an intimate mixture of two or more substances one of which is usually a liquid and which can be separated by physical methods.

solution, buffered. A solution containing a relatively high concentration of a buffer salt which tends to maintain a constant pH.

solution, colloidal. Sol; a solution consisting of two phases; the solvent is the continuous phase, and the suspended matter the disperse phase.

solution equilibrium. An equilibrium between the dissolving and crystallizing of solute in a solution.

solution, molal. A solution containing one mol of solute per 1000 grams of solvent.

solution, molar. A solution containing one mol of solute per liter of solution.

solution, normal. A solution containing one gram equivalent of solute in one liter of solution.

solution pressure. The tendency of a substance to go into solution; the concentration of a solution becomes constant when the solution pressure and osmotic pressure are equal.

solution, saturated. A solution in which the concentration of solute cannot be changed by the addition of more solute.

solution, standard. A solution of known definite concentration.

solution, supersaturated. A solution in metastable equilibrium which contains more of the solute than corresponds to saturation at the given temperature; the excess solute separates out when the solution is jarred or stirred.

solvation. The combination of the molecules or ions of a solute with a definite proportion of solvent molecules.

Solvay process. The ammonia-soda process for making sodium carbonate from sodium chloride.

solvent. The dissolving medium in a solution.

solvent extraction. Removing one or several ingredients of a mixture by its or their preferential solubility in a definite solvent.

solvolysis. Lyolysis; the opposite of neutralization; the formation of an acid and a base from a salt by the effect of a solvent; example, hydrolysis.

soma. The entire body of an animal, exclusive of the reproductive cells.

somatic. Pertaining or referring to the body.

somatic cell. A nonreproductive cell of the animal body.

somatic mesoderm. Mesodermal somite; two longitudinal strips of tissue developed by the mesodermal cells on either side of the developing neural canal of the vertebrate embryo.

somatic mutation. A mutation in cells other than reproductive cells; in organisms that reproduce negatively, this mutation may be passed on.

somatotropic hormone. A hormone secreted by the anterior lobe of the pituitary gland which regulates the growth of the skeleton.

somite. (1) One of the longitudinal segments into which the body of earthworms is divided; (2) a segment of the spinal column of man.

sonar. Sound navigation ranging; asdic; an apparatus for detecting submarines, mines, and other submerged objects by reflected high-frequency oscillations.

sonics. The analysis and testing of materials and products by the use of mechanical vibratory effects.

sonometer. Monochord; an instrument used to test the vibration rate of strings and show how they vibrate.

soot. A finely divided carbon deposited by the smoke of a flame.

soredium. A special reproductive body of lichens, consisting of a few algal cells surrounded by fungal hyphae.

Soret effect. Thermal diffusion; the differences in the concentration of a solute in different parts of a solution which are at different temperatures.

sorus. (1) A cluster of spore cases on the underside of the frond of a fern; (2) a powder on the thallus of lichens, consisting of soredia.

sosoloid. A dispersed system of a solid phase in a solid phase.

sound. (1) The sensation of hearing; the impression which a vibrating object makes on the hearing center of the brain; (2) the energy that produces the stimulus of hearing.

sound absorption coefficient. The percentage of sound energy not reflected by a large plane surface when a sound wave falls on it at a specific angle.

sound barrier. Sonic barrier; the shock waves caused by the sudden increase of aerodynamic drag when an aircraft attains the speed of sound; in earlier times it was considered an impossibility to pass the sound barrier.

sound field. A region containing detectable sound waves.

sound source, simple. A source which radiates sound uniformly in all directions under free field conditions.

sound track. A narrow strip along the left-hand edge of a motion picture film; it is a photograph of the vibrations of a beam of light which has been set in motion by a source of sound.

sound, velocity of. The velocity of propagation of sound waves in any medium; in dry air at 0°C (32°F), it is approximately 760 miles per hour or 1120 feet per second.

sounding balloon. A small balloon without men sent into the air with a meteorograph and other instruments for recording weather conditions.

sound-level meter. An instrument, consisting of a microphone, amplifier, output meter, and networks, for the measurement of noise and sound levels.

soundproofing. Using acoustically absorbent materials in walls and partitions to make them impervious to sound or to reduce the transmission of sound.

sound-ranging altimeter. An altimeter, whose indications depend on the measurement of the time required for a sound wave to travel from the aircraft to the earth and back.

sound-recording system. A combination of transducing devices and associated equipment to store sound in such a way that it can be reproduced.

sound-reproducing system. A combination of transducing devices and associated equipment for reproducing recorded sound.

south pole. The south end of the axis of the earth.

south-seeking pole. The pole of a freely moving magnet which points to south in its position of rest.

Soxhlet extraction apparatus. A laboratory device for extracting the soluble portion of a substance by the continuous circulation of a boiling solvent through it; it consists of a distillation flask, a reflux condenser, and a cylindrical container with a siphon.

sp. gr. Abbreviation for specific gravity.

space biology. The study of man's survival in space.

space charge. The negative charge in the space inside a vacuum tube due to the presence of electrons emitted by the cathode.

space group. A group of points in the lattice of a crystal which exhibit the same type of symmetry.

space lattice. A regular three-dimensional arrangement of points in a crystal, at each of which there is an atom, ion, or group of atoms.

space probe. Any vehicle launched into space to collect information through the instruments it carries.

space time. A four-dimensional continuum, having four coordinates, three spatial and one temporal.

space velocity. The speed and direction of the motion of celestial bodies in three-dimensional space.

spadix. (1) An inflorescence consisting of a fleshy axis on which flowers are crowded together; (2) a conical structure of a male nautilus, consisting of four modified tentacles.

spall. A piece or fragment split off from a target, surface, nucleus, etc., by bombardment.

spark. A short and sudden discharge of electricity in air or another insulating medium.

spark coil. An induction coil which is a high-voltage source in a spark transmitter.

spark lag. The time interval between the attainment of the sparking voltage and the passage of a spark.

spark plug. A plug fitting into the cylinder head of a gasoline engine which produces the electric spark that ignites the explosive mixture in the cylinder.

spark spectrum. The spectrum of a substance produced with light from a spark between terminals composed of that substance, or in an atmosphere of that substance; it contains lines attributed to ions, which are not present in the arc spectrum.

sparking potential. Sparking voltage; the potential difference required for an electric spark to pass across a given gap of insulating material.

spathe. A large bract that encloses a large, highly branched inflorescence before it expands.

spawn. (1) The eggs of aquatic animals, especially when laid in masses; (2) the mycelium of a mushroom.

spawning. The laying of eggs by aquatic animals during the breeding season.

specialization. (1) The formation of special cells and organs in the body to perform specific jobs; (2) the tendency of a parasite to live on one special type of host.

speciation. The evolutionary process of species formation; the splitting of one species into two as a result of changes by mutation or saltation.

species. A group of plants or animals that have the same or nearly the same characters; a division of a genus.

specific. (1) Specially adapted for preventing or curing a disease; example, quinine in the treatment of malaria; (2) peculiar to a species; (3) referring to the second name in a binomial nomenclature of plants or animals; examples, Streptococcus pyogenes and Arachis hypogaea (peanut).

specific activity. (1) The activity per unit weight of any sample of radioactive material; (2) the activity of a radioisotope of an element per unit weight of the element present in the sample; (3) the activity per unit mass of a pure radionuclide.

specific adsorption. (1) The quantity of an adsorbed substance held per unit area of the adsorbent; (2) the preferential adsorption of one substance over another.

specific energy. The internal energy per unit mass of a body.

specific entropy. The entropy per unit mass of a body.

specific gravity. The ratio of the mass of a given volume of a substance to that of an equal volume of water at 4°C.

specific heat. The heat quantity needed to raise the temperature of the unit mass of a substance by 1°C.

specific humidity. The number of grams of water vapor per kilogram of moist air.

specific impulse. A way of measuring the efficiency of rocket propellants; specific impulse is the number of pounds of thrust produced by a pound of propellant in a second.

specific inductive capacity. The dielectric constant or permittivity of a substance.

specific resistance. Resistivity; the resistance in ohms of a conductor that is one centimeter long and has a cross section of one centimeter.

specific soluble substance. A complex, highly type-specific polysaccharide extracted from the capsular material of various bacteria.

specific surface. The surface per unit mass of a very finely divided powder.

specific volume. The reciprocal of specific gravity; the volume of a unit mass.

specific weight. (1) Same as specific gravity; (2) the weight per horsepower of an aircraft engine.

specific-gravity bottle. Pycnometer; density bottle; an accurately calibrated glass bottle for the determination of the specific gravity of liquids.

spectral color. The color sensation produced by a narrow frequency range of stimulating radiation, or the color sensation produced by monochromatic light.

spectral density. The relative distribution of radiant energy throughout the spectrum.

spectral selectivity. The variation of some property of a substance or a surface with the wave length or frequency of incident radiation.

spectral sensitivity. (1) The sensitivity of a detector measured for various spectral bands throughout the spectrum; (2) the sensitivity of a photoelectric device to a wave length; (3) the relative response of a photographic emulsion to lights of different wave lengths.

spectral series. A system of spectral lines which is different for different wave lengths.

spectral transmission. The relative opacity of a filter for lights of different wave lengths.

spectrobolometer. An infrared spectrometer using a bolometer as the receiving instrument.

spectrochemical analysis. An analysis of mixtures based on the emission spectra of its elements when excited in an arc or high-voltage spark.

spectrocomparator. A stereoscopic instrument used for the measurement of line spectra.

spectrogram. A photograph of a spectrum.

spectrograph. (1) An instrument by which spectra may be photographed; (2) same as spectrogram.

spectroheliograph. An instrument for photographing the sun by monochromatic light; it consists of a spectroscope which has a second slit that can be set in such a manner that it lets pass only light of the desired wave length.

spectrohelioscope. An instrument for observing an image of the entire sun by light of one wave length.

spectrometer. An instrument for the measurement of refractive indices.

spectrometry. The relative measurement of radiant energy as a function of wave length or frequency of light.

spectrophotoelectric. Pertaining to the dependence of photoelectric or photovoltaic phenomena on the wave length of the incident radiation.

spectrophotometer. An instrument for analyzing the spectral-energy distributions of sources of light; the combination of a spectroscope and a photometer.

spectrophotometric analysis. A quantitative analysis based on the spectral-energy distribution in the absorption spectrum of a substance in solution.

spectropyrheliometer. An instrument used to determine the spectral distribution of the total solar radiation.

spectroradiometer. A combination of a spectroscope and a radiometer used for measuring the spectral-energy distribution in any type of radiation and for analyzing the wave-length-intensity characteristic of the output from a radio transmitter.

spectroscope. An optical instrument consisting of a collimator tube, a glass prism, and a telescope; it is used for producing and studying spectra.

spectroscopy. The production and study of spectra, including the measurement of the wave lengths of radiant energy.

spectrothermograph. A spectrograph for the study of thermal radiation.

spectrum. The arrangement of the colors constituting white light in the order of their frequencies.

spectrum analysis. The determination of the composition of substances by observation of their spectra; it is especially suitable for the detection of metallic impurities.

spectrum, arc. A spectrum produced at the temperature of the electric arc; it is the spectrum of a nonionized atom.

spectrum, atomic. Line spectrum; the spectrum of an excited atom, consisting of well-defined lines.

spectrum, band. A molecular spectrum, consisting of groups or bands of closely spaced lines.

spectrum colors. Pure colors; red, orange, yellow, green, blue, in-

digo, and violet.

spectrum, comparison. A spectrum, containing many lines of known wave lengths, used as a standard for comparison with other spectra in spectrographic work; example, the arc spectrum of iron.

spectrum, dark-line. Fraunhofer lines; dark lines in the spectrum of the sun, resulting from the selective light absorption by the cooler gases surrounding the photosphere.

spectrum, diffraction. The spectrum produced by a diffraction grating.

spectrum, discontinuous. Combined band and line spectrum; it contains isolated lines that correspond to definite wave lengths.

spectrum, emission. The spectrum produced by radiation from an emitting source.

spectrum, explosion. A spectrum emitted by a solid or liquid while exploding.

spectrum, flame. The spectrum of a substance which is evaporated in a nonluminous flame.

spectrum, infrared. That region of the electromagnetic spectrum which comprises radiations having wave lengths extending from the end of the visible red, at about 7.5×10^{-5} centimeter, to about 3×10^{-2} centimeter.

spectrum, infrared absorption. A spectrum produced by molecular absorption of a radiation having wave lengths in the infared region.

spectrum, line. A spectrum consisting of more or less sharp lines; it is the spectrum of excited gas atoms.

spectrum, mass. A positive-ray spectrum which shows the distribution in mass or in mass-to-charge ratio of ionized atoms, molecules, or molecular fragments; used especially for the study of isotopes.

spectrum, microwave. A spectrum of wave lengths lying in the region between the far infrared and the conventional radio-frequency region.

spectrum, primary. The first-order spectrum produced by a diffraction grating.

spectrum, reversal. A spectrum which contains some lines darker than others, or than a continuous spectrum background.

spectrum, spark. A spectrum emitted by a metal when a spark passes from it to another metal.

spectrum tubes. Tubes which show the characteristic spectral lines of various substances.

specular reflection. Perfect or regular reflection; a light reflection in which the angle of reflection is equal to the angle of incidence and the reflected

light appears to come from the image of the source in the reflecting surface.

speculum metal. A copper-base alloy; used for mirrors and reflectors.

speed. (1) The ratio of the distance covered by a moving point or body to the time, without reference to direction; (2) a measure of the sensitiveness of a photographic emulsion to light; example, low speed means that long exposure is necessary.

speed of lenses. The speed with which a photograph can be taken.

speed of light. Approximately 186,300 miles a second.

spelter. An impure, commercial form of zinc.

sperm. A male gamete or reproductive cell.

sperm nuclei. Two nuclei in a pollen tube which are considered male sex cells.

sperm vesicle. A dilation of the terminal portion of the vas deferens of arrowworms which opens directly to the exterior.

spermaceti. A white waxy solid, consisting mainly of cetyl palmitate; it is obtained from the head of the sperm whale; used in candles, soaps, and cosmetics.

spermagonium. Spermogonium; a flask-shaped structure of some ascocarpous fungi and lichens which bears spermatia.

spermary. The organ which produces sperms; the testis.

spermatheca. Receptaculum semenis; a pouch or cavity of invertebrates used for storing spermatozoa.

spermatic duct. A tube that conveys sperm.

spermatid. A male germ cell immediately before assuming the form of a sperm; it is formed from a secondary spermatocyte by division.

spermatium. (1) A cell borne at the tip of the hyphae of rust fungi, which lines the interior of spermagonia; (2) the nonmotile male gamete of red algae.

spermatocyte. (1) A plant cell which becomes a spermatozoid without cell division; (2) an animal cell which undergoes meiosis and forms spermatids.

spermatogenesis. The maturation process by which male gonads produce male gametes.

spermatogonium. A basic cell of the animal gonad which undergoes repeated mitosis and eventually forms spermatocytes.

spermatophore. A small packet of sperm, produced by some animal species which have internal fertilization; example, newt.

Spermatophyta. Seed plants.

spermatozoa (singular, spermatozoon). Male gametes.

spermatozoid. A small motile male gamete with flagella.

sphalerite. Blende; a zinc sulfide mineral, ZnS; a source of zinc.

sphenethmoid. A bone of the skull of amphibians.

Sphenodon. Hatteria; a genus of animals containing the tuatara; a lizardlike New Zealand primitive reptile; the only surviving member of Rhynchocephalia; it has a well-developed pineal body which served as an eye in past ages.

sphenoid. (1) Wedge-shaped; (2) a bone of the vertebrate skull; (3) a crystal form having four triangular faces.

Sphenophyllales. Extinct Pteriophytes which attained their maximum development in the Carboniferous and Permian periods; they were similar to club mosses and horsetails.

sphere. (1) A round body, every part of the surface of which is equally distant from a point within, called its center; (2) the apparent surface of the sky.

sphere gap. A spark gap between two spherical knobs of equal diameter; it serves as a protection against excess voltage.

sphere of exclusion. The spherical surface drawn about any molecule, from which the center of any other molecule is excluded.

sphere of influence. The region surrounding a gas molecule, within which its van der Waals force of attraction exerts an appreciable effect on other molecules.

spherical aberration. The nonfocusing of parallel rays at the principal focus; a defect of spherical mirrors and lenses.

spheroid. Elipsoid; a solid figure generated by an ellipse rotating about its minor or major axis.

spheroidal state. The condition of a liquid in apparent contact with a hot solid, but with a layer of vapor between them; example, water drops on a hot horizontal iron plate are surrounded by a water-vapor envelope and roll about on the plate until they evaporate.

spherometer. A device to measure lens curvature and other spherical surfaces.

sphincter. (1) A muscle in the lower end of the rectum for opening and closing its orifice and thus controlling the elimination of intestinal waste; (2) other muscles of similar function.

sphygmograph. An instrument for tracing the movements of the arterial pulse.

sphygmomanometer. An apparatus for measuring blood pressure.

sphygmus. Pulse; the beat of the arteries corresponding to that of the heart.

spicules. Pointed mineral rods which form the supporting skeleton of sponges.

spider. A device used to adjust and to center the nail coil in the gap between the cores of the dynamic-speaker field magnet of a radio.

spiegeleisen. Pig iron; an alloy of iron, carbon, and manganese that is added to steel in the Bessemer process as a deoxidizing agent.

spike. An inflorescence consisting of a flower cluster with numerous sessile flowers arranged closely on an elongated common axis.

spikelet. Several flowers borne together; the unit of the inflorescence of grasses; a small group of grass flowers.

spin. (1) In nuclear physics, the spinning of a particle about an axis within itself which results in energy release; (2) a continuous spiral dive of an aircraft.

spin coupling. The interaction between two or more fields due to electron spin.

spin moment. The rotational momentum of an electron spinning on its own axis.

spin, nuclear. The total angular momentum of the atomic nucleus, when it is considered as a single particle.

spinal column. Vertebral column.

spinal cord. The cord, consisting of nerve cells and fibers, that connects the brain with all parts of the nervous system; it is located in and protected by the spinal column (backbone).

spinal fluid. Cerebrospinal fluid; a lymphlike fluid in the neural canal, filling the spaces between the meninges of the brain and the spinal cord.

spinal nerves. Nerves extending from the spinal cord and transmitting impulses to the voluntary muscles; man has thirty-one pairs of such nerves.

spindle. A structure made up of many fine threads on which the chromosomes move during mitosis.

spindle attachment. The region of a chromosome which is attached to the spindle at mitosis or meiosis.

spinel. Mineral combinations of bivalent and trivalent oxides of magnesium, zinc, iron, manganese, aluminum, and chromium; used as gems.

spinneret. A tubelike appendage for producing fine silken threads from the secretion of glands; example, the spinneret of the female spider.

spinthariscope. A device for observing the scintillations caused by alpha rays.

spiracle. (1) A respiratory opening on segments of an insect, through which air enters the trachea; (2) the first visceral cleft of fish.

spiral. Terminal coils on the hypha of some species of molds.

spiral arrangement. One leaf at each node.

spiral cleavage. A cleavage in which clockwise and anticlockwise divisions alternate.

spiral nebula. A large spiral-shaped galaxy, similar to ours.

spiral thickening. An internal thickening of the wall of xylem or tracheid in the form of a spiral band.

spiral valve. A spiral fold of mucous membrane which extends into the intestine of certain fish to increase the absorption surface; example, Lampreys.

spireme. A continuous coiled structure of chromatin granules, formed in prophase.

spirillum (plural, spirilla). A corkscrew-shaped bacterium, which may be motile and equipped with flagella.

spirochetes. Spiral-shaped one-celled organisms, resembling both bacteria and protozoa, which cause diseases in animals and man.

Spirogyra. Pond scum; green algae occurring in masses of fine filaments.

spirometer. An instrument for measuring the capacity of the lungs.

spit. An underwater narrow strip of land formed by sediments dropped by a current passing a headland and hitting the quieter water of a bay.

splanchnic. Referring to the viscera; visceral.

splanchnocranium. A part of the skull consisting of the jaws and their attachments.

spleen. A ductless organ which is closely associated with the circulatory system; its functions are: the formation of blood cells, destruction of old red blood corpuscles, removal of other debris from the blood stream, and to serve as a reservoir for blood; it is located in the left upper part of the human abdomen, behind the stomach, just below the diaphragm.

split flap. A hinged plate forming the rear upper or lower portion of an airfoil; used for lateral control or increased lift.

spodumene. A lithium aluminum silicate; a crystalline mineral; a source of lithium compounds.

sponges. Porifera; aquatic animals which have one large body cavity that receives water through the porous body walls.

spongin. The horny fibrous material of the skeleton of certain sponges.

spongoblast. The spongin-producing cell of sponges.

spongy. (1) Consisting of loosely constructed tissue with many irregular pores; (2) having many irregular pores.

spongy layer. A layer of irregular, loosely arranged cells between the palisade layer and lower epidermis of plants; it contains a network of fine veins to transport water and dissolved minerals.

spontaneous. Occurring by nature of inherent properties or energy as distinguished from processes carried out by deliberate application of an external agency; examples, spontaneous evaporation, combustion, oxidation.

spontaneous combustion. Fire caused by heat developing as a result of slow oxidation of a substance of low kindling temperature, stored where most of the heat of oxidation cannot escape.

spontaneous generation. The theory, now discarded, which postulated that living organisms originated from nonliving matter.

sporangiophore. A spore-bearing filament or hypha.

sporangium (plural, sporangia). A case or capsule in which asexual spores are formed.

spore. An asexual reproductive cell.

spore case. Same as sporangium.

spore mother cell. (1) A diploid plant cell that gives rise to four haploid spores by meiosis; (2) a stage of Protozoa in which spores are formed.

sporidium. The basidiospore of smut fungi.

sporoblast. The mother cell of certain Protozoa which divides into sporozoites.

sporocarp. (1) A multicellular mass of red algae that produces asexual carpospores; (2) the spore-producing body of fungi; (3) the sporangium of mosses.

sporocyst. A heavy protecting wall enclosing the spores of Protozoa.

sporogonium. A spore-producing structure of liverworts and mosses that develops after sexual reproduction.

sporogony. A sexual reproduction with the formation of spores.

sporont. A stage in the reproductive cycle of one-celled parasites, the Sporozoa, that forms, by subdivision, active sporozoites, which in turn begin a new life cycle.

sporophore. The fruiting body of fleshy and woody fungi which produces spores.

sporophyll. A modified leaf that bears a sporangium.

sporophyte. The asexual generation in those plants which show alternation of generations; a spore-producing plant or part of a plant.

sporosac. A degenerate gonophore of some hydroids that remains attached to the parent colony; it produces reproductive cells.

sporozoite. A stage in the reproductive cycle of one-celled Sporozoa, which is the active individual formed by the subdivision of the zygote or sporont.

sport. A mutant; a sudden variation from normal characteristics, the change being inheritable.

sporulation. A subdivision of the parent cell to form smaller active cells which begin a new life cycle; it is common in plants and occurs also in some one-celled animals.

spot. The area instantaneously affected by the impact of an electron beam in a cathode-ray tube.

spot test. A sensitive chemical test for the rapid identification of a compound or element.

Sprengel pump. A mercury air pump whose operation is dependent on the dropping of mercury down a tube.

spring. (1) Underground water streaming to the surface; (2) an elastic body which will deflect or elongate under the action of an externally applied force and return to its original shape after removal of the force.

spring balance. A weighing device in which the object to be weighed is suspended by a spring, calibrated so that a pointer attached to the spring indicates the weight directly by its position relative to a graduated scale.

spring tides. Higher flood tides and lower ebb tides, occurring when the earth, sun, and moon are almost in a straight line.

springwood. A sapwood containing many large vessels that develops in spring; it is generally of lighter color and softer than summerwood.

spur. (1) Calcar; a short, stiff, sharp spine; example, on a rooster's leg; (2) a projection from a sepal or petal of a flower.

spur gear. Gear wheels used for connecting two parallel shafts.

spurious oscillation. Parasitic oscillation; an undesirable oscillation of an amplifier.

sputtering. A disintegration of the cathode of a vacuum tube in which the ejected particles are deposited on other electrodes and the walls of the tube, and the surface of the cathode becomes uneven.

sputum. Spittle; saliva; a thick discharge from the lungs and throat in diseases of the respiratory tract.

squall. A sudden, strong wind which may or may not be accompanied by a wind shift; rain and snow squalls are showers accompanied by strong gusts.

squall line. Wind-shift line; the

succession of thunderstorms and gusty winds developing along the lines of an advancing cold front.

Squamata. An order of reptiles whose body is covered with horny epidermal scales; examples, lizards and snakes.

squamosal. A T-shaped membrane bone of the vertebrate skull.

squamous epithelium. Pavement epithelium; a sheet of epithelium consisting of one or more layers of flat scalelike cells.

square foot. A unit of area; 144 square inches; 929 square centimeters.

square yard. A unit of area; 9 square feet; 0.8361 square meter.

Sr. Chemical symbol for strontium.

stab culture. A culture in which the organisms are inoculated far down into the solidified medium to allow for possible anaerobic growth.

stability. A tendency of an object or system to return to its equilibrium position after it has been moved away by an external force.

stabilization. The prevention of the chemical decomposition of a substance by the addition of a stabilizer or a negative catalyst.

stabilizer. (1) A fixed, horizontal part of the tail of an airplane that maintains its level flight; a gyroscopic or pendulum mechanism for stabilizing the motion of an aircraft; (2) a device used in cathode-ray tubes for securing a constant current flow under a wide range of variable conditions; (3) an emulsifier that prevents or retards the precipitation of colloids; (4) a negative catalyst.

Stabilovolt (a trade-mark). A special type of gas-discharge tube used as a voltage stabilizer or regulator.

stable compound. A chemical compound that is not easily decomposed.

stable equilibrium. The state of equilibrium of a body in which the center of gravity will rise if the body is displaced and it will return to its original position.

stable oscillation. The oscillation of a body or system that does not increase without the application of an external force.

stage. (1) That part of the framework of a microscope on which the specimen is mounted; (2) a part of a geological series consisting of rocks which were deposited during a geological age.

stage efficiency. The fraction of adiabatic heat drop in a steam turbine stage that is transferred to the rotor as mechanical energy.

stain. A coloring matter or chemical used for coloring tissues or organisms for microscopic study.

stainless steel. A corrosion-resistant steel, containing high percentages of chromium; used for tableware, appliances, tools.

stalactite. Icicles of calcium carbonate hanging from the roofs of limestone caves.

stalagmite. Columns of calcium carbonate deposited on the floors of limestone caves.

stalagmometer. An instrument for the determination of the surface tension of liquids by the drop method.

stalagmometry. The measurement of surface tension by determining the weight or volume of a drop of the liquid hanging from the end of a tube.

stalling angle. The angle corresponding to the maximum lift of an aircraft.

stamen. The organ of a flower which produces pollen; it consists of a stalk or filament and an anther.

staminate. Said of flowers that have stamens but no carpels.

staminode. A sterile stamen that does not produce pollen; an imperfect or vestigial stamen.

standard. (1) A reference unit or substance; (2) a banner; a large petal serving as a background for a flower.

standard atmosphere. A standard relationship of temperature, pressure, and altitude, chosen to represent conditions in calculating the performance of an aircraft.

standard cell. Weston cell; a cadmium cell whose stable electromotive force is 1.0182 volts at 20°C.

standard conditions. The temperature and pressure arbitrarily agreed on as *standard;* 0°C and 760 millimeters of mercury.

standard pressure. The pressure of a column of mercury of 760 millimeters.

standard solution. A solution in which the concentration of the solute is known precisely; examples, normal solution and molar solution.

standard state. The stable form of a substance at 1 atmosphere pressure and 18°C temperature.

standard temperature. The temperature of melting ice, 0°C.

standard temperature and pressure. STP; 0°C and 760 millimeters of mercury.

standard volume. The volume of one mol of a gas at 0°C and one atmosphere pressure.

standing waves. Radio waves which are apparently standing still as a result of two sets of similar waves traveling in opposite directions.

stannic. A compound of quadri-valent tin.

stannite. A gray mineral; a sulfostannate of copper and iron, sometimes with some zinc.

stannous. A compound of bivalent tin.

stannum. Latin name for tin.

stapes. The stirrup-shaped small bone of the middle ear.

star catalogue. A listing of stars, usually arranged in the order of increasing right ascension, giving their size and some other data.

star, nuclear. A radiating group of tracks due to ionizing particles originating at a common point either in a nuclear emission or in a cloud chamber.

starch. Amylum; $(C_6H_{10}O_5)_x$; a white amorphous hygroscopic powder that yields dextrin by hydrolysis; it is widely distributed throughout the plant world and is stored principally in seeds, fruits, tubers, roots, and stem pith; used for the preparation of dextrin, glucose, in laundering.

Stark effect. The effect of a strong transverse electric field on the spectrum lines of a gas.

Stark-Einstein law. Every molecule which takes part in a chemical reaction caused by exposure to light absorbs one quantum of the radiation causing the reaction.

Stark-Luneland effect. The polarization of light given off by a beam of moving atoms in the absence of a field.

stars. Other suns like ours which produce their own light.

starter. (1) A mechanism in an internal-combustion engine whlich supplies the initial effort from an external source of power for the engine to start; (2) a culture of microorganisms used for inoculating milk in making sour cream, butter, cheese, etc.

Stassfurt deposits. Several-strata-thick natural salt deposits in Germany; about 25,000 feet; they are the source of potassium and magnesium chloride, and rock salt.

state of aggregation. The physical condition of matter: solid, liquid, or gaseous.

state of matter. Same as state of aggregation.

static balance. Standing balance; the balance of a rotating body or system in which the center of gravity and the axis of rotation coincide.

static charge. An electric charge that remains on a substance and does not flow; example, the electric charge produced by rubbing glass with silk.

static electricity. Stationary electric charges located on insulators.

static equilibrium. An equilibrium in which the resultant of the forces acting on a body is zero.

static hysteresis. A permanent deformation or elastic lag in a stressed solid, which is independent of the rate of loading.

static machine. A frictional electric machine for storing electricity of relatively high voltage; example, Wimhurst machine.

static pressure. The pressure exerted perpendicularly to the surface of a body moving freely through a fluid.

static state. A state in meteorology in which the position or properties of an air mass or frontal zone are not changing or moving.

statics. A branch of mechanics which deals with forces in equilibrium.

station model. A system of recording on a weather map by symbols the observations made at the various weather stations.

stationary front. The meeting of two air masses so that the resulting front does not move.

stationary line. An absorption line in the spectrum of a star which does not exhibit the Doppler shift observed in the other lines.

stationary phase. The stage in the growth of a bacterial culture at which the multiplication of organisms gradually decreases, so that as many bacteria are formed as die.

stationary waves. An interference between sound waves of the same frequency resulting in a variation of the intensity between maxima and minima.

statoblast. An asexual reproductive body of fresh-water Bryozoa; when the colony dies in winter, the statoblasts remain alive and inactive, but they produce new colonies in the spring.

statocyst. (1) A cell containing one or more statoliths; (2) an organ of balance and orientation.

statolith. (1) A calcareous secretion within a statocyst of an animal; (2) a solid inclusion of a plant cell; example, a starch granule.

stator. The stationary part or coil of an electric machine, such as a motor or generator.

statoscope. An instrument that indicates slight changes in the altitude of an aircraft.

staurolite. A reddish-brown mineral; a complex silicate of iron and aluminum; it often has twin crystals in the shape of a cross; its transparent varieties are used as gems.

steady flow. Viscous flow; a fluid flow in which the velocity of a fixed point remains unchanged, while the particles of the fluid are in continuous steady motion.

steady-state theory. The assumption that the universe is in a state of equilibrium; matter is assumed to be continually changing, and the formation of elements is thought to have taken place in the stars.

steam chest. The steam compartment of a steam engine connected to the steam pipe and equipped with a steam valve.

steam distillation. A distillation method for liquids, which are not soluble in water, by bubbling steam through them.

steam engine. A machine which produces power available for various purposes by the expansion of high-pressure steam in its cylinder or cylinders.

steam rate. The rate at which a steam engine or turbine consumes steam per unit power output.

steam turbine. A turbine in which a high-velocity steam jet rotates a bladed disc or drum.

steapsin. Lipase; an enzyme of the pancreatic juice that changes fats into fatty acids and glycerin.

stearates. Metallic salts or soaps and esters of stearic acid; major constituents of animal fats.

stearic acid. $C_{17}H_{35}COOH$; a white solid fatty acid; used in cosmetics, candles.

steatite. Soapstone; a soft talc of granular structure; used for carving ornaments, as an insulator.

steel. A carbon-containing iron alloy to which varying amounts of other metals have been added; it has better mechanical properties and corrosion resistance than iron.

Stefan-Boltzman law. The total emissive power of a black body is proportional to the fourth power of its absolute temperature.

Stegocephalia. Fossil salamander-like large amphibia with a tail, well-developed limbs and a bony covering extending to the head.

stele. The center of plant root and stem which consists of xylem and phloem; a vascular cylinder.

stellar interferometer, An attachment for an astronomical telescope which is used to measure the angular diameters of celestial bodies which cannot be resolved by the telescope.

stellar magnitude. The apparent brightness of the stars.

stellar parallax. Heliocentric parallax; a means of expressing the distance of a given star; it is the angle that would be subtended by the mean distance of the earth from the sun at the distance of the star from the sun.

stellar photometry. The comparison of the brightness of one star with the brightness of a star of standard magnitude.

stem. (1) The glass portion of a vacuum tube that supports the lead-in wires to which the electrodes are connected; (2) the aerial part or axis of a plant with leaves, buds, and flowers; (3) scapus; the stiff axial part of a feather.

stem correction. A correction made in the reading of a thermometer which is only partly immersed in the fluid whose temperature is measured.

Stender dish. A vessel used to prepare and store pathological and zoological specimens, for staining, paraffin embedding, etc.

stenohaline. Unable to tolerate wide variations in the saline concentration of its environment.

stenopodium. The biramous appendage of Crustacea with slender branches.

stenothermous. Unable to tolerate wide variations in the temperature of the environment.

step-down transformer. A transformer which changes the line voltage to a lower value; it has fewer turns in the secondary than in the primary.

stephanite. A black mineral; silver antimony sulfide; an important silver ore.

steppe. Steppeland; a vast semi-arid desert region, with drought-resistant vegetation, without forests; steppes occur especially in Asia and in the southeastern parts of Europe.

steptoe. A hill or mountain whose top projects above a lava flow which has surrounded its lower flanks.

step-up transformer. A transformer with more turns in the secondary than in the primary; it raises the voltage.

stere. A metric unit of volume; 1 cubic meter.

stereochemistry. The study of the spatial arrangement of the atoms and groups within a molecule and its effect on the physical and chemical properties.

stereoisomerism. An isomerism resulting from the possibility of different spatial arrangements of the atoms within a molecule; the isomers are mirror images of each other.

stereomicroscope. A microscope that magnifies and gives depth to the microscopic specimen at the same time.

stereophone. An acoustical system in which microphones, transmission channels and reproducers are arranged so as to provide the sensation of the spatial distribution of the original sound sources.

stereophonic. Combining sound and perspective.

stereophony. The art of using, designing, or manufacturing stereophonic equipment.

stereophotometer. A photometer in which light from two sources falls simultaneously on the same moving object.

stereopticon. An early device for projecting pictures, which made one projected image fade into another.

stereoscope. Three-dimensional viewer.

stereoscopic. Having a three-dimensional character.

stereoscopic microscope. Same as stereomicroscope.

stereoscopic radius. The greatest distance at which the stereoscopic effect can be perceived.

steric hindrance. A resistance to chemical action attributed to the arrangement of the atoms in the molecule.

sterigma (plural, sterigmata). A short hypha which bears a spore of a fungus.

sterile. (1) Containing no living bacteria; (2) unable to reproduce sexually.

sterility. (1) Inability to reproduce; barrenness; (2) the state of being free from bacteria.

sterilization. (1) Complete elimination of microbial life by heat and/or chemicals; (2) any procedure by which an individual is made incapable of reproduction.

sterilizer. A device which sterilizes with boiling water, steam, or dry heat.

Stern multiplier. A device for converging a number of narrow beams of molecular rays at one point.

Stern-Gerlach field. A special, nonhomogeneous magnetic field used for studying molecular rays.

sternum. (1) The breast bone; (2) a cuticle on the ventral side of each segment of an insect.

steroids. Organic compounds of plant or animal origin with a tetracyclic hydroaromatic ring system; example, bile acids, vitamin D.

sterol. A solid alcohol; a complex compound of biological importance containing 27 to 30 carbon atoms; example, cholesterol.

stibine. Antimony hydride, SbH_3; a poisonous gas.

stibnite; A gray mineral; antimony trisulfide, Sb_2S_3; it is the chief ore of antimony.

stigma. (1) A distinctive sexual mark on the wings of butterflies; (2) an external opening of the trachea of Arthropoda; (3) a light-sensitive pigment, or eyespot, in certain Protozoa; (4) the top part of the pistil of a flower which receives the pollen.

stigmatic. (1) Homocentric; converging into a single point; (2) said of a lens that has been corrected for astigmatism.

stilb. A unit of surface brightness;

1 candle per square centimeter.

stilbite. A zeolite mineral, occurring in a great variety of colors.

still. An apparatus used for the distillation of liquids.

stimulus. Any environmental change or force that will cause a response in an organism; an agency which will generate a nerve impulse and cause its propagation in a nerve fiber.

sting. (1) A pointed poison-containing organ of offense or defense in animals; example, the sting of bees; (2) stinging hair; a hollow hair of plants filled with a caustic liquid secreted by the plant; its tip breaks off and penetrates into the skin of an animal; example, nettle.

stipe. (1) The stalk of the fruit body of mushrooms; (2) the thalus of sea weeds.

stipule. One member of a pair of small leaflike structures usually found at the base of the petiole.

stirrup bone. Stapes; the innermost ossicle of the middle ear.

stock. (1) A rooted part on the stalk of a woody plant into which a scion is grafted; (2) a breed or group of animals; example, livestock; (3) a supply of materials or apparatus; example, a stock of chemicals; (4) a mass of igneous rock of circular or elliptical cross section, which intruded vertically into previously existing formations.

stoichiometry. The mathematics of chemical reactions and processes.

STOL (short takeoff and landing). Airplanes that resemble VTOL aircraft but do not have the lifting force needed for vertical takeoff.

stolon. (1) A connective hypha; a filament of bread mold which spreads across the bread and give rise to new mats of fibers; (2) a horizontal stem growing from the main stem, bearing scale leaves and adventitious roots; (3) a rootlike part of a colony of hydroids which fixes it to the substrate and which may give rise to new individuals or colonies.

stoma (plural stomata). A small pore in the epidermis of the stem or leaves for the exchange of gases between the atmosphere and the active tissues within.

stomach. A pouchlike organ of the digestive system between the esophagus and the intestine.

stomium. A part of the wall of fern sporangium where splitting occurs at maturity, releasing the spores.

stomodaeum. The anterior part of the alimentary tract, formed in the embryo by invagination of the external body wall, lined with ectoderm.

stone. An English measure of

weight; 14 pounds.

stone cell. A lignified cell of the hard shield of nuts and pits of cherries and peaches.

stop. An opening in a diaphragm which limits the cross section of the beam of light that passes through an optical system.

stopping condenser. A condenser in a circuit which permits the flow of alternating current, but prevents the flow of direct current.

stopping potential. A potential difference which is sufficient to stop the outward movement of photoelectrons or thermins; used to determine the speed of emission.

stopping power. A measure of the effect of a substance on the kinetic energy of a charged particle passing through it.

storage battery. A group of secondary cells connected in series for generating the necessary amount of electric energy by chemical action, in which the cells after having been discharged may be recharged by passing a direct current through them in a direction opposite to the flow of the current of discharge.

storage cell. A secondary cell for generating electric current; a unit of a storage battery.

storm cloud. A dark-gray rain- or snow-bearing cloud.

stormy westerlies. Winds that blow from subtropical highs toward the poles.

S.T.P. The abbreviation for "standard temperature and pressure," 0°C and 760 millimeters of mercury.

straight-chain compound. An organic chain compound which has no side chains or branches.

strain. (1) A tension or stress; (2) a deformation due to stress; (3) a variety of a plant or animal species that has distinctive shape and structure.

strain axes. Three mutually perpendicular lines through any point of an elastic solid, which remain mutually perpendicular when the solid is subjected to strain.

strain ellipsoid. The ellipsoid resulting from a small sphere under strain.

strain gage, electrical. A grid of fine resistance wire supported on a paper base for measuring strains of the order of 10^{-4} to 10^{-2}.

strain, nonuniform. A strain which varies from point to point under the same stress.

strata (singular, stratum). Layers of rock formed by sediment.

stratification. (1) Layer formation in sedimentary rocks due to periodical interruption of the sedimentary process, or the differences in the nature of the deposit or the speed of deposition; (2) layer formation in cell walls.

stratified rock. Rock laid down in layers.

stratiform. Formed in layers.

stratiform cloud. Stratus; a cloud spread out into nearly unbroken horizontal layers or sheets at relatively low altitude.

stratigraphy. The study of the origin and chronological successions of the rocks of the lithosphere, including its structure and composition.

strato-cumulus. Large dark circular clouds covering the entire sky and forming a wavy layer; they do not bring rain.

stratosphere. The layer of the atmosphere, about six miles from the earth's surface, which has even low temperature, no convection, and substantially no vertical temperature gradient.

stratum compactum. The dense surface layer of the decidua vera of the skin.

stratum corneum. Outer keratinic cell layer of the skin.

stratum germinativum. The mitotic innermost cell layer in the epidermis of the skin.

stratum spongiosum. The inside layer of the decidua vera of the skin.

stratus clouds. Low-lying clouds that form a dull gray sky.

stray flux. A current leakage of an electric machine.

streak. (1) The inoculation of slants or plates with a streak or a direct line movement across the surface of the culture medium; (2) the color of a mineral powder obtained by rubbing the mineral against paper or scratching it with a knife; (3) a strip of plant tissue that differs in color or structure from the adjacent tissues.

stream capture. Stream piracy; the natural diversion of a stream into the channel of another.

streaming potential. A potential difference produced by the flow, under pressure, of a liquid through a capillary tube or a membrane.

streamline. The path of a small portion of a fluid relative to a solid body with respect to which the fluid is moving.

streamline flow. Viscous flow; a steady fluid flow in which there is a constant relation between the particles of the fluid.

streamline form. The shape of a body that produces approximately streamline flow.

streamlined. Having a shape that offers the least possible resistance to air or water.

strength of current. The number of amperes flowing through a circuit.

streptococcus. A Gram-positive bacterium which occurs in chains; there are several pathogenic types.

stress. The deforming force acting on a body.

stress, compressive. The force per unit area directed so as to produce a change in density in the region where it is applied.

stress, shearing. The force per unit area directed tangentially to a set of parallel planes so as to produce relative motion of the planes parallel to themselves.

stress, tensile. The force per unit area directed perpendicularly to one surface.

stress, torsional. The shearing stress which occurs at any point in a body when a torque or torsional load is applied.

striated discharge. The presence of alternate light and dark bands in the positive column of a gas discharge, generally due to a mixture of gases.

striated muscle. Skeletal striped or voluntary muscle, which is under direct control of the will.

striation. Stria; (1) the striped appearance of the positive column in a Crookes tube at suitable pressures, consisting of transverse, alternate bright and dark bands; (2) parallel ridges or marks; examples, parallel lines on the face of a crystal; narrow parallel grooves in glacial rock surfaces.

striation technique. Making sound waves visible by using their individual ability to refract light waves.

stridulation. Producing sounds by rubbing together parts of the animal body; example, the noise made by a grasshopper by rubbing the hind leg against part of the forewing.

strike. (1) An initial thin deposit in electroplating; (2) the electrolyte used for making a preliminary deposit.

striking potential. The potential difference necessary to start an electric arc.

stripped atom. An atomic nucleus without surrounding electrons.

stripping. (1) A bombardment with deuterons or heavier nuclei, when only part of the incident particle merges with the target nucleus and the remainder proceeds in its original direction with its original momentum; (2) the removal of electrodeposits from a metal by chemical or electrical means; (3) removing dyes from textile fabrics; (4) the removal of the light fractions from an oil.

strobila. (1) A string of proglottids of tapeworms; (2) a segment of the medusoid stage of jellyfish, produced by transverse fission.

strobilization. (1) An asexual reproduction by terminal buding; example, the proglottids of tapeworms are formed by this process; (2) the transverse fission which yields medusoids in the development of jellyfish.

strobilus. A group of sporophylls, or spore-bearing leaves, aggregated to form a compact cone-like structure.

stroboscope. An instrument for studying motion by means of a rapidly flashing, that is, periodically interrupted, light; it measures the frequency of motion.

strobotron. A special cold-cathode gas tube for supplying a short-duration high-intensity arc for a stroboscope.

stroke. The distance traveled by the piston of an engine or pump.

stroma. (1) A tissuelike mass of fungal hyphae in or from which fruit-bodies are produced; (2) the dense colorless part of a chloroplast; (3) a framework of an animal organ; example, the framework of mammalian ovary or testis, that consists of connective tissue.

strontianite. A green or gray mineral; strontium carbonate, $SrCO_3$; found in limestone.

strontium. A silver-white ductile alkaline-earth metal; chemical symbol Sr; atomic number 38.

strontium-90. A strontium isotope, the mass number of which is 90; it is an important fission product and an element in fallout.

structural balance. An equilibrium state in which the outer electron shells of an atom are complete.

structural color. (1) A color due to the scattering of white light by colloidally suspended particles; (2) a color produced by the modification of the exposed surface structure of animals, such as minute striations, punctuations, and sculptured areas; example, the irridescent color of some beetles.

structural formula. Constitutional formula; a formula which shows the arrangement of the atoms in a molecule.

structural geology. Geotectonic geology; the study of the arrangement or rearrangement, form, and internal structure of constituents of the lithosphere, or outer rocky portion of the earth.

structure, atomic. The internal structure of the atom, which is made up of the nucleus and the electrons surrounding it; the nucleus has a mass which corresponds to that of the atom and a positive charge which corresponds to the atomic number; the number of electrons is equal to the atomic number; they are in orbits; the chemical and physical properties of a substance are largely due to the electrons in the outermost orbit.

structure, molecular. The arrangement of the atoms in the molecule and the valence bonds that hold them together.

structure, nuclear. The internal structure of the atomic nucleus.

structureless lamella. Mesogloea; an amorphous gelatinlike matter between the ectoderm and endoderm.

strychnine. $C_{21}H_{22}N_2O_2$; a poisonous alkaloid used in small quantities as a body stimulant and in larger quantities as a poison to kill rodents.

style. The stalklike part of a pistil just above the ovary.

styrene. Phenylethylene, C_6H_5-$CH{:}CH_2$; a colorless liquid used in the manufacture of synthetic rubbers and plastics.

subatomic. Smaller than, or forming a part of, the atom.

subclavian. Located under the clavicle, or collarbone; example, a subclavian artery or vein.

subcooling. Cooling below the normal freezing point without solidification.

subcutaneous. Located beneath the skin.

subcuticular. (1) Beneath the cuticle; (2) not quite cuticular.

suberin. A waxy substance in the walls of cork cells in the outer tissues of stems, roots, and other plant parts; it is impervious to water, thus preventing the loss of water from the living cells and a decay of the plant.

suberization. The impregnation of cell walls with suberin, thus forming cork cells.

sublevel. The energy level or quantum state of the electrons in an atomic subshell.

sublimation. The change from the solid to the vapor state or from the vapor to the solid state without formation of a liquid.

sublimation pressure. The solid-vapor equilibrium pressure of a volatile solid at a given temperature.

sublingual glands. Saliva-secreting glands situated under the tongue.

submarine canyons. Canyons on the face of the continental slope which cut back into the shelf.

submaxillary glands. Saliva-secreting glands situated inside of and near the edge of the lower jaw.

submerged valley harbor. A harbor formed by stream erosion.

submersed plants. Plants that grow completely under water.

submicron. A particle whose diameter is between 5×10^{-7} and 2×10^{-5} centimeter.

submucosa. (1) The second principal layer of the wall of the digestive tract; (2) a tissue layer beneath a mucous membrane.

subneural gland. A gland below the brain in the ascidians; it leads to a supposedly sensory ciliated funnel.

subphylum. A large group of plants or animals ranking next to a phylum.

subscript. A number written below and to the side of a symbol; if it is at the left of a chemical symbol, it represents the atomic number, if at the right, it represents the number of atoms in the molecule.

subshell. A subdivision of an electron shell, all the electrons of which have the same azimuthal quantum number.

subsidence. Settling or slow descending of air to the earth's surface at the center of an anticyclone.

subsoil. A soil which lies below the topsoil and which is usually poor in inorganic substances that are necessary for plant life.

subspecies. A subdivision of a species; a group whose members resemble one another in certain characteristics and differ from other members of the species.

substitution. The replacement of one or more hydrogen atoms in a compound with other atoms.

substitutional alloy. A metallic alloy in which atoms of one element have been replaced by atoms of another, without changing the basic crystal structure.

substratum (plural, substrata). substrate; (1) a surface to which an animal is attached or on which it moves; (2) the material in which a plant grows and draws nutrients.

subterminal. Situated near but not at the very end, or extremity.

subtractive color. A color produced by the removal of some part of white light; for example, by passage through one or more filters.

succession. (1) The transition from one type of fauna to another within a given area; the major phases are herbaceous vegetation, shrubs, and finally forest, with minor transitions in each phase; (2) changes in the population of an area, as a result of the response of competing organisms to the environment.

succinic acid. $(CH_2COOH)_2$; a white crystalline organic dibasic acid; used in the manufacture of dyes, lacquers, etc.

succinite. Amber; a fossil resin that yields succinic acid; used in lacquers and varnishes.

succulent. A fleshy xerophytic plant with the stems or leaves greatly enlarged to serve as storage organs; example, cactus.

succus entericus. The digestive juice secreted by the walls of the small intestine of vertebrates; it contains many enzymes.

sucker. (1) A disk-shaped organ by which certain animals attach themselves to other animals or to objects; example, a structure on the head of tapeworms; (2) the sucking mouth of an animal; example, the mouth of leeches; (3) a shoot developing fast from the root or base of a plant.

sucrase. Invertase or saccharase; an enzyme of the intestinal juice which hydrolyzes sucrose into glucose and fructose.

sucroclastic. Sugar-splitting; a term applied to enzymes that hydrolyze complex carbohydrates; example, invertase.

sucrose. $C_{12}H_{22}O_{11}$; cane sugar; white sugar obtained from sugar cane or sugar beets.

suction. An external force that raises a fluid or solid as a result of the difference between the atmospheric pressure and the partial vacuum that prevails over part of its surface.

Suctoria. An order of insects which have sucking mouths; example, fleas.

sugar. A carbohydrate; examples sucrose and glucose.

sugar of lead. Lead acetate; $Pb(C_2H_3O_2)_2 \cdot 3H_2O$; colorless crystals; used as a mordant and astringent.

sulcus. A shallow fissure or groove in an animal body; example, sulcus of the brain.

sulfate. A salt of sulfuric acid; example, calcium sulfate, $CaSO_4$.

sulfation. An accumulation of lead sulfate on the plates of a storage cell, which lowers the efficiency of the cell.

sulfide. A binary compound of sulfur and a metal; example, lead sulfide, PbS.

sulfite. A salt of sulfurous acid, H_2SO_3; example, sodium sulfite, Na_2SO_3.

sulfite process. A method of converting wood chips into pulp in the manufacture of paper, by cooking with sulfite liquor.

sulfonation. The introduction of the $—SO_3H$ group into an organic compound.

sulfonic acid. An organic acid containing one or more sulfonic groups, $—SO_3H$.

sulfur. A nonmetallic element which occurs in three different forms; chemical symbol S; atomic number 16; used in medicine, as a parasiticide.

sulfur bacteria. Bacteria which obtain their energy from the reduction of sulfur compounds; example, Thiobacteriales.

sulfur dioxide. A colorless gas with a penetrating smell; SO_2; used in refrigeration, bleaching.

sulfur trioxide. A white crystalline solid; SO_3; it combines with water to form sulfuric acid.

sulfuric acid. Vitriol; a colorless corrosive oily liquid; H_2SO_4; it dissolves in water with the evolution of heat; it is used as a drying agent, in the manufacture of chemicals, explosives, etc.

summer egg. A thin-shelled egg laid by some Crustacea during the summer; they develop rapidly by parthenogenesis.

Sumptner principle. Each part of the interior of a sphere is equally illuminated if the sphere has perfectly diffusing walls and a light source is set at any point inside it.

sun. The center and dominating body of the solar system; it gives the light and heat without which life on the earth would soon become extinct; it is a sphere of incandescent gases; its diameter is about 864,000 miles; it is 333,400 times heavier than the earth.

sun compass. A compass which makes use of the direction of the sun instead of the direction of the magnetic north or south pole; used in aeronautics.

sun facula. Same as sunspot.

sun time. The time of one's own meridian.

sundew. An insectivorous herb of the genus Drosera, growing in bogs and secreting a sticky substance on the leaves.

sunlight recorder. A device used in meteorology which records the time integral of the sun's visible radiation.

sunspots. Dark spots on the photosphere; the umbra is the darkest central part, surrounded by the less dark penumbra; they have strong magnetic fields.

supercharged engine. An engine equipped with a supercharger for increasing the air or charge mixture taken into the cylinder beyond that induced normally at the existing atmospheric pressure.

supercharger. A mechanical device for supplying an internal-combustion engine with a greater weight of charge than would normally be drawn in by the pumping action of the pistons at the prevailing atmospheric pressure and temperature; used in aircraft engines.

superconductivity. A property of some metals that they lose all electrical resistance and become a perfect conductor below characteristic transition temperatures.

supercooled. Cooled below the freezing point without solidification.

supercooled water. Water particles well below the freezing point (down to 5°F) occurring in clouds.

supergiant stars. Stars of very high luminosity; example, Betelgeuse.

superheated steam. A steam heated at constant pressure without contact with water, so that its temperature is higher than the boiling point.

superheater. An apparatus for superheating steam.

superheterodyne receiver. A receiver in which the frequency of the carrier wave is changed to a given value above the audible limit; then it is amplified, and finally rectified.

superimposed river valley. Antecedent river valley; a river valley which is independent of the present geological structure of the area.

superior air mass. A very warm and dry air mass that probably comes from the higher levels of the subtropical belt of high pressure over the North Pacific.

superlattice. Superstructure; an arrangement of atoms in a multicomponent solid system, in which the atoms of an element occupy certain regular positions in the atomic lattice of another element.

superrefraction. The transmission of microwave frequencies far beyond the line of sight because of an atmospheric duct.

supersaturated solution. An unstable solution which holds more of the solute than it normally could at that temperature.

supersaturation. A metastable state in which the concentration of a solution or vapor is greater than would correspond to saturation.

superscript. A number written above and to the side of a symbol; if at the right of a chemical symbol, it represents the approximate atomic weight.

supersonic. Ultrasonic; said of waves whose frequencies are greater than those which are audible to the human ear.

supersonic plane. An airplane that can travel faster than the speed of sound.

supersonic speed. A speed faster than the speed of sound in air, which is about 738 miles per hour.

supersonic waves. Short waves of a frequency above the limit of audibility.

superstructure. Same as superlattice.

supplemental air. The amount of air the average adult inhales, in addition to the tidal and complemental air, when exercising; it provides for the extra oxidation needed in the cells.

supporting tissue. A woody plant tissue that gives form and strength to the trunks of trees and other plant organs.

suppression. (1) Elimination of any component of an emission; (2) nonappearance of a normally occurring natural face on a crystal; (3) the missing of a plant member which is normally present; (4) the stoppage of a secretion or absence of an organ which is normally pres-

ent in an animal.

suppressor grid. A grid having about the same negative potential as the cathode and located next to the anode for preventing a secondary emission from the anode from reaching the other electrodes.

suprarenal gland. Adrenal gland; an endocrine gland near the kidney, which secretes substances important for the metabolism.

surf. The breaking and rushing forward of foamy waves on a beach.

surface balance. An apparatus used to measure the surface pressure and surface area of monomolecular films on water.

surface cold front. The front edge of the cool or cold polar air mass which is advancing toward the south and east.

surface color. The color determined as the reflection from a surface.

surface duct. Ground-based duct; an atmospheric radio duct for which the lower boundary is the surface of the earth.

surface energy. The product of the area of a surface and its surface tension in ergs.

surface film. A film formed spontaneously by the action of intermolecular and chemical forces at an interface between two immiscible bulk phases.

surface lattice. The structural pattern at a natural cleavage surface of a crystal.

surface orientation. The arrangement of certain molecules in the surface of a liquid in which always the same part of the molecule is turned toward the liquid.

surface tension. Interfacial tension; the tendency of the surface of a liquid to occupy the smallest possible area; it is caused by unbalanced molecular cohesive forces near the surface; the force in dynes acting along one centimeter in the surface of the liquid.

surface waves. (1) Distortion waves on the free surface separating two fluid phases; (2) ground waves; an electromognetic wave component trailing parallel to the earth's surface.

surface-active agent. Surfactant; a substance that is capable of changing the surface tension or interfacial energy; examples, wetting, dispersing, and foaming agents, detergents, and penetrants.

surge. (1) A general change of atmospheric pressure distinct from local cyclonic and diurnal changes; (2) a sudden variation in a current or voltage.

survey instrument. An instrument used to detect and measure radiation under varied physical conditions.

survival. Living of a race to ma-

turity and reproducing.

survival of the fittest. According to Darwin's theory of natural selection, the survival in the struggle for existence of the best adapted organisms, which thus become the parents of the next generation.

survival value. The usefulness of a character of an organism in the struggle for survival.

susceptibility. (1) A lack of immunity to a disease; (2) the ratio of magnetization in a substance to the magnetizing force; (3) the ratio of the polarization in a dielectric to the electric intensity responsible for it.

suspension. (1) A very finely divided insoluble solid, stirred through a liquid and slow in settling; (2) the device or mechanism by which an element of a machine or instrument is suspended; examples, the wire holding the coil of a galvanometer; the springs supporting the vehicle body on the axles.

suspensoid. Lyophobic colloid; an irreversible colloidal suspension in which there is little attraction between the dispersed substance and the dispersing liquid.

suspensor. (1) A row or group of cells that pushes the developing embryo down into the embryo sac; (2) a hypha which serves as the stalk of a gametangium of Zygomycetes.

suture. (1) The line of union between the adjacent flat bones making up the skull; (2) the surgical sewing up of a wound or incision; (3) the line of fusion of the edges of the carpel of a flowering plant; (4) a junction between plates of the hardened cuticle of the exoskeleton of insects.

suture line. The junction line between two animal structures; example, the suture line of the shell of nautilus.

swarm spore. Zoospore; an asexual reproductive cell which has flagella for swimming.

swarming. The departure from the hive of a queen bee and most of the workers to form a new colony.

sweat glands. Small coiled glandular tubes with openings through the surface of the skin, which secrete perspiration.

sweep. The tendency toward a thermal equilibrium.

swelling. The expansion of a solid in contact with certain liquids; example, the swelling of rubber in gasoline.

swim bladder. Air bladder; a thin-walled elliptical sac which allows the fish to maintain a level in the water; it may also serve as respiratory organ.

swimmeret. An abdominal appendage of Arthropoda; used for swimming and to carry the

eggs of the female.

switch. A mechanical device for making, breaking, or changing the connections of an electric circuit.

syconium. The multiple fruit of the fig, in which the receptacle is hollow and succulent, and lined on the inside with numerous seeds.

syenite. A coarse-grained intrusive igneous rock of the same general composition as granite except that quartz is absent or present only in very small amounts.

sylvanite. A gray mineral; telluride of gold and silver, found associated with pyrite; used as a source of gold.

sylvite. A white or colored crystalline mineral, potassium chloride, KCl; a source of potash salts, which are used as fertilizers.

symbionts. Organisms living together in symbiosis.

symbiosis. A relationship between two organisms living together, by which each benefits in some way.

symbol. (1) The abbreviation that stands for an element or one atom of an element; examples, C = carbon, Fe = iron (Latin, ferrum), Na = sodium (Latin, natrium), Au = gold (Latin, aurum; (2) an arbitrary or conventional sign that indicates a value, position, operation, direction, etc.

symmetry. The correspondence of parts of a figure with reference to a plane, line, or point of symmetry; examples, the arrangement of the faces of a crystal which reflects its internal structure; the arrangement of the parts and organs of the animal body.

symmetry, center of. A point in the interior of a crystal; any line through this point will intersect the crystal at equal distances on opposite sides.

symmetry elements. Rotation axes, reflection planes, inversion centers, and rotation-reflection axes of crystals.

symmetry number. The number of different symmetry planes of a body or a group of atoms.

symmetry, plane of. A plane through a body that divides it into two halves which are mirror images of each other.

sympathetic nervous system. (1) A part of the autonomic nervous system of vertebrates consisting of a series of ganglia and nerves which supply the glands and smooth muscles; (2) a part of the visceral nervous system of invertebrates which supplies the alimentary canal.

sympathetic vibration. The vibrations of a body which are of the same frequency as the vibrations of the body that induced it.

sympatric. Said of different species or subspecies that have areas of distribution that coincide or overlap.

Sympetalae. A subclass of Angiospermae in which the petals are united into a sympetalous corolla.

sympetalous flower. A flower whose petals are united into a more or less tubular corolla.

symphysis. A joint of bones which permits slight movement, the surfaces of the articulating bones being closely tied together by collagen fibers; example, pubic symphysis.

sympodium. A branch system that expands by successive development of lateral branches when the main axis or basic branch stops growing in length.

synandrium. A group of united anthers.

synandrous. Having united anthers.

synangium. A compound structure formed by lateral union of sporangia; example, in certain ferns.

synapse. The connection between branches of two nerve cells so that impulses can pass from one cell to the other.

synapsis. Syndesis; a temporary union of two members of each pair of chromosomes in meiotic nuclear division.

syncarpous. Having united carpels.

synchro. An electrical system for remote control or indication.

synchro-cyclotron. A cyclotron which yields greater energies by compensating for the mass variations with increasing velocity.

synchronograph. An automatic telegraph.

synchronous. (1) Having the same period; (2) having the same period and phase.

synchronous motor. A motor whose speed is an exact multiple of the frequency of the alternating current operating it.

synchroscope. A form of oscillograph used to test the phase difference of two alternating currents or electric oscillations.

synchrotron. A combination of a cyclotron and betatron, in which charged particles move in a circular path due to a high-frequency electric field and a low-frequency magnetic field.

syncline. A troughlike downward fold of rocks underlying the earth's crust; it formed under enormous pressure.

synclinorium. A composite fold of the earth's crust.

syncytium. An undivided mass of protoplasm containing many nuclei.

synecology. The ecology of communities as opposed to individual species.

syneresis. The spontaneous separation of an initially homogeneous colloid system into two phases, a coherent gel and a liquid; it is a reversible change.

synergidae (singular, synergida). Synergids; two nuclei at the upper end of the embryo sac which, together with the egg, constitute the egg apparatus.

synergism. A positive interaction between components of a mixture with a total effect higher than the sum of individual effects.

syngamy. Conjugation; the union of gametes in fertilization.

syngenesious. Said of stamens united by their anthers; example, dandelion.

synodic period. The time required by a celestial body to move from some particular position relative to the sun as seen from the earth back to the same position again.

synoptic chart. A weather map which gives a general view or synopsis of the weather conditions which are the basis of weather forecasting.

synovia. A transparent sticky fluid contained in a joint cavity, or tendon sheath; it is secreted by the synovial membrane and serves as a lubricant for the joint or tendon.

synovial membrane. The shiny smooth lining membrane of a joint or tendon sheath, which secretes the synovia.

synsepalous. Having united sepals.

synthetic resins. Resinous compounds obtained by the polymerization of suitable simpler compounds, called monomers; example, urea-formaldehyde resins, that are polymerization products of the monomers, urea and formaldehyde.

synthetic rubber. A man-made elastomer that closely resembles natural rubber; example, Neoprene, a polymer of chloroprene.

synthetic sapphire. A man-made gem that has all the physical and chemical properties of natural sapphire; it is obtained by fusing pure aluminum oxide with pigments.

syrinx (plural syringes). (1) The vocal organ of birds; (2) a fistula.

system. (1) A particular portion of matter which contains a definite amount of a substance or substances, arranged in one or more phases; (2) a group of organs whose functions are related to one another; examples, digestive system, circulatory system; (3) a group of mountains which were formed during the same geological period; example, Jurassic system; (4) the purposeful arrangement and connection of mechanical parts to perform special functions; ex-

ample, telephone system.

system, condensed. A system in which there is no vapor phase or it may be disregarded since it has very little effect on the processes under consideration.

system, heterogeneous. A system which consists of more than one phase.

system, homogeneous. A system which consists of only one phase.

system, stable. A system that can undergo considerable variations in external conditions, such as temperature, pressure, etc., without a fundamental change.

systematics. The study of the classification and nomenclature of living organisms, with an emphasis on their evolutionary relationship.

systemic. (1) Distributed throughout an organism; example, a systemic insecticide that is absorbed by all parts of a plant; (2) referring to the body as a whole.

systemic arch. One of the large arteries leading away from the heart in some vertebrates.

systemic circulation. The general circulation of the blood as distinct from the pulmonary circulation.

systemic heart. (1) The principal heart of the cephalopod mollusk; it includes two or four auricles which receive blood from the gills; (2) the left-side auricle and ventricle of the heart of mammals and birds which delivers blood to the body as a whole.

systole. (1) The heart beat in which the ventricles contract and force blood into the arteries; (2) the dissolution of the nuclear membrane and ejection of the nuclear content into the cytoplasm during mitosis.

systolic pressure. The blood pressure at the moment when the ventricles of the heart contract; the point of maximum pressure beyond which the pulse can no longer be felt; it is indicated by a manometer on a mercury scale.

T

Ta. Chemical symbol for tantalum.

TA. Symbol for tropical Atlantic air.

tab. An auxiliary airfoil attached to a control surface for reducing the control force or trimming the aircraft.

tachometer. An instrument for measuring the revolutions per minute of a rotating shaft.

tachylite. A natural basic black glass which may form along the chilled margins of dikes or

sills.

taconite. A flintlike rock containing iron oxide; a commercial ore of iron.

tactile. Referring or belonging to the sense of touch.

tactile organs. Organs of touch; sensory organs located at the surface of the body and stimulated by pressure.

tadpole. The aquatic form in the life history of frogs, toads, etc.; it hatches from the egg.

tagged atoms. Tracers; radioactive isotopes which, when introduced into a reaction or the body, can be traced and thus help in explaining the use of various elements in body processes and the mechanism of chemical reactions.

tagma (plural, tagmata). A body region of Arthropoda formed by the fusion of cells.

taiga. Subarctic lands of Eurasia with large swamps and coniferous forests; long bitter-cold winters and very short cool summers are the rule.

tail. (1) Cauda; a solid prolongation of the axis of the vertebrate body at the end opposite the head; it contains a portion of the spinal column, together with blood vessels, nerves, and muscles, but is posterior to the body cavity which is confined to the trunk; (2) the horizontal back portion of an airplane.

tail feathers. A fan-shaped group of large stiff feathers of the tail of birds.

tail unit. The stabilizing and control surfaces at the rear end of an aircraft.

Talbot bands. Interference bands appearing in a prism spectrum when half of the aperture is covered by a thin glass plate whose edge is parallel to the edge of the prism.

talc. A hydrated magnesium silicate, $3MgO \cdot 4SiO_2 \cdot H_2O$; used in cosmetics, as a filler in paper manufacture, as a lubricant.

tallow. The rendered fat of animals, particularly ox and sheep; it is a white waxlike substance that consists of various glycerides; it is used in soap and candle making.

Tallquist scale. A standard scale used for determining the hemoglobin content of blood; a drop of blood is absorbed in a special filter paper and its color compared with the colors on this empirical scale.

talon. A sharp claw, especially of a bird of prey.

talus. Scree; large and small blocks of rock which have been broken off from a cliff by frost action; they are found at the foot of the cliff.

talus slope. Rock blocks at the foot of a cliff, which rolled down by gravity.

tangent. A straight line touching a curved line at only one point and drawn perpendicular to the radius of the curvature at that point.

tangent galvanometer. A galvanometer in which a small magnet needle is mounted in the center of a fixed coil; the current in the coil is proportional to the angle of deflection of the needle.

tannin. Tannic acid; $C_{76}H_{52}O_{46}$; it is found in many plants; dissolved in water, it yields an astringent solution which is used in leather tanning and ink manufacture.

tantalum. A very ductile and malleable corrosion-resistant metal; chemical symbol Ta; atomic number 73; used in electrolytic and chemical equipment.

tap. (1) An electrical connection made to some point in a coil or transformer winding other than at the ends; (2) a connection made to some intermediate point on a resistor.

tapetum. (1) A reflecting structure in the eye of nocturnal insects; (2) a nutritive tissue in the sporangium of plants.

tapeworm. A parasitic flatworm; the adult lives in the intestine of vertebrates; its body is long and ribbonlike and consists of a chain of proglottids; it has no mouth, but absorbs the digested food of the host through the surface of the body.

tapping. Running the molten metal from the crucible of a furnace into a ladle.

taproot. A long and often thickened vertical primary root with a few branches; example, the taproot of dandelion.

tar. Coal tar; a mixture of hydrocarbons and organic bases resulting from the carbonization of coal.

Tardigrada. Bear animalcules; minute animals found in moss and ditches; they have sucking mouth parts and four legs with claws.

target. Anticathode; a metal plate against which the electrons impinge at high speed and which becomes a source of secondary electrons.

tarn. A cirque filled with water; a steep-sided small mountain lake.

tarnish. The formation of a thin oxide or sulfide film on the exposed surface of a metal; it becomes dull as a result.

tarsal. One of the ankle bones.

tarsus. (1) The end of the leg of some insects that has five joints; (2) the shank of the leg of a bird; (3) the proximal portion of the foot of vertebrates, containing tarsal bones; example, the ankle; (4) a framework of connective tissue which supports the eyelid of vertebrates.

tartaric acid. COOH(CHOH)$_2$-COOH; a white soluble crystalline solid occurring in many plants and fruits; used in dyeing, tanning, baking powder, and effervescent health salts.

tartrates. Salts and esters of tartaric acid; used in medicine.

taste bud. A sensory organ of vertebrates serving to indicate the taste of foods to the brain; it consists of spindle-shaped gustory cells enveloped by other cells like leaves of a bud; in man and higher vertebrates, taste buds are usually on the tongue and soft palate; there are four basic taste sensations: sweet, sour or acid, salty, and bitter.

Taurus. Bull; the second sign of the Zodiac; a constellation containing the two clusters of the Pleiades, and the Hyades.

tautomerism. The existence of a substance as an equilibrium mixture of two forms which can be converted into each other; example, the keto and enol forms of acetone.

taxidermy. The art of mounting and stuffing animal skins in their natural appearance for display or sale.

taxis. A locomotory movement of an organism in response to a stimulus.

taxon. A taxonomic group, whatever its rank.

taxonomy. The science of classifying and naming living organisms.

Tb. Chemical symbol for terbium.

Tc. Chemical symbol for technetium.

TC. Symbol for tropical continental air mass.

Te. Chemical symbol for tellurium.

technetium. A metallic element resulting from the bombardment of molybdenum with neutrons; chemical symbol Tc; atomic number 43.

tectonic. Said of geological structures that are due to the movements of the earth.

tegmen (plural, tegmina). (1) A coat within the testa of a dicot seed which protects the seed contents; (2) the thickened forewing of an insect; example, grasshopper; (3) the leathery top of the calyx of sea lilies.

tektite. An obsidianlike green or black glass ball; a meteorite which some scientists believe may have been dislodged from the moon's surface by the impact of another meteorite.

telecamera. A vacuum tube which converts an optical image into an electric current; examples, image dissector, orthicon, and iconoscope.

telecentric stop. A stop used in optical measurements to avoid parallax between image and scale.

telemeter. An instrument for measuring various quantities at a distance.

telemicroscope. A device which can be used both as a telescope and a low-power microscope.

Teleostei. A subclass of Actinopteri containing the great majority of existing fish.

Teleostomi. A group of fish in a now obsolete classification.

telephase. The terminal stage of mitosis or meiosis during which nuclei revert to a retiring stage; the chromosomes reach the poles of the cell and the cell plate begins to form.

telephony. The art of transmitting speech over a distance by means of an electric current; the basic requirements are: (1) a transmitter that will produce a current which is a replica of the sound wave; (2) a transmission system to carry the current to the receiving point; (3) a receiver to convert the electric current into sound again.

telephoto lens. A combination of a convex and a concave lens which replaces the ordinary lens of a camera in order to magnify the image.

telephotography. The art of taking enlarged photographs of distant objects by a camera equipped with a telephoto lens.

telescope. An optical instrument used for magnifying distant objects and making them more visible; it consists of a system of lenses and mirrors.

telethermometer. An apparatus by which distant temperature effects are electrically communicated to a measuring or recording instrument; example, a thermoelectric circuit connected to a galvanometer.

teliospore. A two-celled black winter spore in the life cycle of the black stem rust.

telium. A group of teliospores with their hyphae.

tellurium. A white metallic element; chemical symbol Te; atomic number 52; a byproduct of copper refining.

telson. The posterior segment of the abdomen of certain Crustaceae, such as the crayfish; a flat triangular part which constitutes the seventh segment.

temperature. The intensity of heat, as measured by a thermometer.

temperature, absolute. The temperature measured from the absolute zero point, which is −273°C.

temperature, color. The temperature at which the light from a body with complete radiation matches in chromaticity the light from the given source.

temperature, critical. That temperature above which a gas cannot be liquefied by pressure, no matter how great.

temperature wave. A progressing variation of temperature; example, a wave started by strongly heating one end of a long bar of cold metal.

tempering. The heating and subsequent quick cooling of a metal to obtain the desired degree of hardness; example, tempering of steel.

temporal. A cartilage bone of the vertebrate skull; it forms the posterior part of the cheek bone with the articulation of the lower jaw, and bears the mastoid process behind the ear.

temporal lobe. A large lobe of the brain below the frontal and parietal lobes along the side of each cerebral hemisphere.

temporary hardness. The hardness of water caused by the bicarbonates of calcium and magnesium, which can be removed by boiling the water.

temporary magnetism. Induced magnetism; the magnetism which a body displays while in a magnetic field and which disappears when the body is removed from the field.

temporary parasites. Organisms that are parasitic only during a portion of their lives.

tenaculum. (1) A surgical instrument consisting of a fine pointed metal hook fastened in a handle that is used for holding severed arteries and blood vessels; (2) a pair of partly fused appendages on the third segment of some insects.

tendon. A fibrous tissue connecting a muscle to a bone or to another muscle.

tendril. A modified leaf or stem that is used for twining and climbing.

tensile strength. The breaking strength of a material under the effect of a stretching force; it is expressed in pounds per square inch.

tensimeter. An apparatus for the determination of the transition point by measuring the temperature at which the vapor pressures of the two modifications become equal.

tensiometer. An apparatus for measuring the surface tension of a liquid by recording the force necessary to detach a metal ring from the surface.

tension. A pulling force; the opposite of compression.

tensor. A muscle that stretches a part of the body.

tentacle. (1) A slender extension of the body of an animal used for feeling or grasping; examples, in jellyfish, marine worms, and the octopus; (2) a hair of a plant which serves to capture small insects; example, on the leaf of sundew.

tentaculocyst. A sense organ of jellyfish and of a few allied forms; a reduced tentacle at the margin of the body that bears a pigment spot which may be a light-sensitive organ and is flanked by two pits regarded as olfactory organs.

tepal. An individual member of a perianth, particularly of a perianth that is not clearly differentiated into corolla and calyx.

terbium. A rare-earth metal; chemical symbol Tb; atomic number 65.

tergum. A thickened plate of cuticle on the dorsal side of a segment of Arthropoda.

terminal. (1) The connection point of electrodes or other parts of a circuit; (2) the end branch of the veins of a leaf; (3) a secondary wood parenchyma that develops at the end of the growing season; (4) the atoms or groups at the two ends of a polymeric molecule.

terminal branches. End brush; end plate; fine branches at the end of an axon.

terminal bud. A main bud at the end of a branch or stem of a plant.

terminal bud scars. Ringlike markings around the bark of a twig showing the position of the terminal buds of previous years.

terminal moraine. A mass of assorted rocks left at the end of a glacier.

terminal velocity. The constant velocity of a particle falling under the effect of the force of gravity in air or water, when the gravitational pull is in equilibrium with the friction.

termitary. Termitarium; the nest or home of a termite colony, which consists of a complicated system of rooms and passages.

termite. White ant; a soft-bodied social insect.

termitophile. An insect of another species living in the nest of termites as a scavenger or in commensal relationship; examples, flies and larvae of moths.

ternary compound. A compound composed of three elements; example, calcium carbonate, $CaCO_3$.

terpene. An unsaturated hydrocarbon occurring in plant oils and resins.

terra rossa. A red ferruginous residue resulting from the surface alteration of limestones.

terrace. (1) A level area between two slopes, usually at the bank of a river; (2) a steplike embankment built of soil to prevent slipping or erosion of soil during heavy rainfall.

terracing. A method of soil conservation in which a long slope is broken up into shorter slopes or terraces to prevent water from being washed away.

terrain. A plot of ground under observation or attention.

terrain clearance indicator. Radio altimeter; an instrument for indicating the distance of an airplane above ground, based on the time required for a radio wave sent out from the airplane to be reflected from the ground.

terrarium. A small indoor garden similar to a glasshouse for keeping live land plants and animals.

terrella. Magnetic globe; a device for the demonstration of the earth's magnetism.

terrestrial. Living on the ground; said of land plants and animals.

terrestrial telescope. A telescope with a third convex lens in its eyepiece for reinverting the image.

Tertiary. A geological period which lasted from about 60 million to 1 million years ago.

tertiary color. A color obtained by mixing two or more secondary colors.

Tesla coil. A high-frequency coil; an induction coil which has a high-frequency spark gap; its secondary gives a strong frequency discharge.

test chamber. A space in which experiments are carried out.

test tube. A thin-walled glass tube closed at one end; used in the laboratory.

testa. (1) The outer coat of a dicotyledonous seed which protects the embryo, stores food, and absorbs moisture and air when germination begins; (2) an exoskeleton or shell.

testicle. One of two egg-shaped glandular organs in the male; it produces spermatozoa and a hormone which controls sex development and personality factors interacting with hormones of other glands, particularly the pituitary gland.

testis (plural, testes). Same as testicle.

testosterone. A male hormone secreted by the testes; $C_{19}H_{28}O_2$; a hydroxyketone; it controls sex tendencies.

tetrad. (1) A group of four spores formed by meiosis with a spore mother cell; (2) paired chromosomes of meiosis, after each chromosome has duplicated itself and the pair is visibly four-stranded; (3) an element having a valence of four.

tetradynamous. Said of a flower with six stamens, of which four are longer than the other two.

tetragonal crystal. A crystal having three mutually rectangular axes, two of which are equal.

tetrahedral atom. A configuration of a tetravalent atom, in which the valence bonds are directed from the nucleus to the four corners of a tetrahedron.

tetrahedrite. A gray mineral; copper antimony sulfide; an ore of copper.

tetraploid. Having four times the haploid number of chromsomes

in a nucleus.

tetrapoda. Four-footed animals.

tetraspore. The first cell of the gametophyte generation in many brown and red algae; the spores are formed in fours in a tetrasporangium following meiosis.

tetrode. Screened-grid tube; a vacuum tube containing a cathode, anode, grid, and screen grid; used as a high-frequency amplifier.

texture. The sizes of mineral parts and their arrangement in a rock.

Th. Chemical symbol for thorium.

thalamus. (1) The nerve center of the brain; communication between the centers of the cerebral cortex and the outlying parts of the body are established by nerve impulses traveling through the thalamus; (2) the receptacle of a flower.

thallium. A gray metal; chemical symbol Tl; atomic number 81.

Thallophyta. A division of plants whose body is a thallus having no differentiation into roots, stems, and leaves; they produce no flowers or seeds; examples, fungi, algae, and bacteria.

thallus. A one-celled or multicellular plant body which has no root, stem or leaf.

Thalofide cell. A photoelectric cell whose photosensitive element is thallium oxysulfide.

theca. (1) The outer ridge surrounding the depression in the hard deposit of a coral in which the polyp lives; (2) an anther; (3) a pollen sac; (4) the capsule of a moss.

theodolite. An optical instrument which can be used to measure the height and speed of clouds; a special form of telescope used by surveyors for measuring vertical and horizontal angles.

theory, atomic. Dalton's atomic theory; a theory which explains the definite composition of substances and the proportions in which substances react with one another in terms of the indivisible atoms of which substances are composed.

Therapsida. Mammal-like upright walking reptiles that lived from the Permian to the Triassic period, until the appearance of dinosaurs.

therm. A unit of heat; 100,000 ergs; 1,000 large calories.

thermal. (1) Referring or pertaining to heat; (2) an upward current of warm air.

thermal agitation. A random movement of the molecules of a substance, which is believed to give rise to the phenomena associated with heat and kinetic energy.

thermal analysis. The use of heating and cooling curves for investigating the equilibrium conditions and phase relations in metals.

thermal capacity. Water equivalent; the quantity of heat required to increase the temperature of a body by unity; it is equivalent to the mass of water that requires the same amount of heat to raise its temperature by one degree.

thermal conduction. The transmission of heat from one part of a medium to another by the transfer of heat energy from molecule to molecule.

thermal convection. The transfer of heat by the automatic circulation of a fluid, either liquid or gas, due to differences in temperature and density.

thermal cracking. The breaking up of large molecules into smaller ones by the use of high temperature and high pressure.

thermal death point. The temperature at which bacteria are killed or viruses are inactivated.

thermal efficiency. The output in heat units divided by the heat supplied to a machine.

thermal energy. The energy of a body that can be transmitted in the form of heat.

thermal equation. A balanced chemical equation which states also the number of calories of heat given off or absorbed in a chemical reaction.

thermal equilibrium. That condition of a system in which the net rate of heat exchange among the parts is zero.

thermal ionization. An ionization due to high temperature.

thermal neutrons. Neutrons of a very low speed and energy; their energy is of the same order as that of the substance through which they are passing; they are responsible for various nuclear actions.

thermal radiation. The transmission of heat in the form of heat waves.

thermal value of a chemical reaction. The quantity of heat emitted or absorbed in a chemical reaction, usually per gram equivalent of the reacting substances.

thermion. An electron emitted from a hot cathode.

thermionic emission. The emission of electrons from a heated electrode.

thermionic tube. Thermionic valve; a tube containing a hot cathode emitting electrons, an anode receiving the electrons, and usually additional electrodes for controlling the flow of electrons.

thermionics. The study of the electron emission from substances under the effect of heat.

thermistor. A semiconductor, whose resistance decreases rapidly with temperature increase; used as a sensitive temperature-measuring device.

thermite process. The preparation of a metal from its oxide by reduction with aluminum.

thermochemistry. The measurement and interpretation of heat changes which accompany changes of state and chemical reactions.

thermocouple. A pair of different metals which produce an electric current when their junction is heated.

thermodynamic cycle. A cyclic change of state of a body or a system which involves changes of temperature or the transmission of heat to or from the body or system.

thermodynamic equilibrium. The condition of a system whose members have conformed to the principle of equipartition of energy; a state in which no spontaneous change can occur as the temperature and pressure are equal throughout the system.

thermodynamic temperature scale. A temperature scale which is independent of the physical properties of any substance and is derived from the thermodynamical considerations of the heat exchange in an ideal Carnot cycle.

thermodynamic transformation. A change in the state of a body or system which involves changes of temperature or the emission or absorption of heat.

thermodynamics. The study of the general laws that govern the processes which involve heat changes.

thermodynamics, laws of. (1) Heat and mechanical work are mutually convertible and in any process involving such conversion one calorie of heat is equivalent to 4.18×10^7 ergs of mechanical work. (2) Heat cannot be transferred by any continuous, self-sustaining process from a colder to a hotter body. (3) The absolute zero temperature cannot be reached.

thermoelectric effect. An electric current produced by junction of dissimilar metals at different temperatures.

thermoelectric inversion. A reduction in the electromotive force of a thermocouple when the temperature is raised beyond a certain neutral point.

thermoelectric power. The rate of change of the thermoelectric electromotive force of a thermocouple circuit with the temperature of the hot junction.

thermoelectricity. Electricity produced by the direct conversion of heat energy into electrical energy; the electromotive force produced by heating the junction of two different metals.

thermoelectromotive force. The electromotive force generated when the junction of a thermo-

couple is heated.

thermoelectron. A negative thermion.

thermoelement. A combination of a thermocouple with a heating filament; used for measuring small currents.

thermogalvanometer. A galvanometer for the measurement of feeble high-frequency alternating currents by their heating effect, as detected by a sensitive thermocouple.

thermograph. An instrument for recording temperature.

thermolabile. Easily altered or decomposed by heat.

thermoluminescence. The luminescence exhibited by certain substances when heated below incandescence.

thermolysis. The dissociation of a molecule by the effect of heat.

thermomagnetic effects. (1) The effects of a magnetic field on the flow of heat or the temperature distribution in a conductor; (2) the effects of temperature on the magnetic properties of a substance.

thermomagnetic potential difference. A change in the electromotive force of a thermojunction, due to placing it in a magnetic field.

thermometer. An instrument for measuring changes in temperature.

thermometer, clinical. A mercury thermometer for the measurement of the temperature of the human body; it is calibrated to cover a range of a few degrees on either side of the normal body temperature, subdivided into one tenths of a degree.

thermometer, maximum and minimum. A thermometer which records the highest and lowest temperatures reached during a given period of time.

thermometry. The measurement of temperature and of changes in temperature.

thermomilliammeter. An instrument for measuring small alternating currents.

thermonasty. The response of a plant to a general nondirectional temperature stimulus.

thermonuclear reaction. A nuclear reaction which requires very high temperatures (millions of degrees) to start; example, the fusion of hydrogen to helium.

thermophilic bacteria. Bacteria which grow best at a temperature of about 55°C.

thermophosphorescence. A phosphorescence induced by heating after excitation.

thermopile. A group of dissimilar materials arranged alternately in such a manner that the junctions can be heated to produce an electric current.

thermoplastic. A plastic which can be melted by heat for molding and be remelted re-

peatedly after solidification without a substantial change in its physical and chemical properties; examples, cellulose acetate, polystyrenes, and vinyl resins.

thermoregulator. A device which controls the temperature of a bath by regulating its heat supply.

thermorelay. A device for amplifying small galvanometric deflections.

thermosetting plastic. An irreversible plastic that cannot be softened by heat after it has once set; examples, phenol-formaldehyde and urea-formaldehyde resins.

thermostable. Not affected by moderate heat.

themostat. A temperature-regulating device which cuts off the heat supply when the temperature rises to a higher than the set value.

thermotaxis. Same as thermotropism.

thermotropism. The response of an organism to a heat stimulus.

thiamine. Vitamin B_1; it is important for carbohydrate metabolism; its lack causes beriberi.

thigmotropism. Thigmotaxis; the response of an organism to the stimulus of touch.

thinner. A solvent added to paint to reduce its viscosity and thus make it easier to apply; examples, turpentine and mineral oil.

thio-. A prefix denoting sulfur as an ingredient, in naming a chemical compound.

thiobacillus. Small rod-shaped bacteria which obtain their energy from the oxidation of sulfides, thiosulfates, or sulfur, forming sulfur dioxide, persulfates, sulfuric acid, and sulfates.

third-class lever. A lever in which the force is between the fulcrum and the resistance.

thixotropy. Rate of change of viscosity of gels with time.

Thomas precession. The precession of the spin axis of an electron due to the acceleration given to it by the electric field of its nucleus.

Thomson effect. Kelvin effect; a temperature gradient along a conducting wire gives rise to an electric potential gradient along the wire and vice versa.

Thomson electromotive force. The electromotive force resulting from the potential difference between two points of different temperature on a metallic conductor.

thoracic. Pertaining to the thorax or chest.

thoracic duct. A lymphatic duct through which the lymph returns to the blood stream.

thorax. (1) A division of the body of Arthropoda and Crustacea

between the head and abdomen; (2) the region of the trunk of vertebrates just behind the head and neck; it is supported by ribs and contains the thoracic cavity; (3) one of the main segments of the body of insects, between the head and abdomen, bearing three pairs of legs and the wings if there are any.

thoriated filament. A filament of tungsten to which some thorium has been added to reduce the temperature of electronic emission in cathode-ray tubes.

thorite. A radioactive mineral; the silicate of thorium, containing some helium.

thorium. A corrosion-resistant, ductile dark-gray radioactive metal; chemical symbol Th; atomic number 90; used in alloying.

thorn. A specialized stem or leaf that terminates in a sharp point.

thread cell. Cnidoblast; nematocyst; a cell that develops threadlike appendages.

threadworms. Nematoda; worms having an unsegmented cylindrical body; their coelom is not lined with epithelium; examples, trichina and pinworm.

three-phase equilibrium. The equilibrium which may exist, at a given temperature and pressure, among all three phases of a pure substance: solid, liquid, and vapor.

threshold. (1) The measure of the sensitivity of an organ; (2) the intensity of stimulus below which there is no response; a limiting value of any quantity.

threshold current. The current at which a gas discharge changes from an induced to a self-sustained discharge.

threshold of absolute luminence. The smallest amount of luminence which can be discriminated by the fully dark-adapted eye.

threshold of color. Any measure of the degree of color discrimination; the measurement can be absolute or differential.

threshold wave length. The maximum wave length of radiation for the emission of electrons from a given surface.

throat. (1) The passage through the neck to the stomach and lungs; the cavity behind the mouth into which the nasal passages open and from which the esophagus and trachea lead; (2) the opening of a gamopetalous corolla.

thrombin. A substance formed in blood clotting as a result of the reaction of prothrombin, thromboplastin, and calcium.

thrombocyte. Blood platelet; a spindle-shaped nucleated cell in the vertebrate blood which plays an important part in blood clotting.

thrombokinase. A substance that promotes blood clotting by changing thrombogen into thrombin.

thromboplastic. Said of a substance that accelerates blood clotting; example, thrombokinase.

thrust. The forward motion given to an airplane by its propeller or jet engine.

thulium. A rare-earth metal; chemical symbol Tm; atomic number 69.

thunder. The rumbling or explosionlike sound following a flash of lightning due to the sudden expansion of air in the path of discharge.

thunder cloud. Cumulo-nimbus; a dark, mountainlike cloud which gives rise to thunderstorms.

thunderstorm. An intense local cyclonic whirl after an excessive heat wave; torrential rain with thunder and lightning.

thymol. $C_{10}H_{14}O$; a phenol derivative; white crystals; used as a mild antiseptic.

thymonucleic acid. A nucleic acid of the desoxyribose type; it was first extracted from thymus which is rich in nuclei.

thymus gland. A ductless gland of vertebrates that may have growth functions.

thyratron. An arc-discharge triode containing inert gas or vapor at low pressure, in which a grid controls the starting of the discharge.

thyroglobulin. A thyroxin-containing protein in the thyroid gland.

thyroid gland. A ductless gland located in the neck across the trachea, below the larynx; it secretes thyroxin, controls the use of energy by all tissues, and stimulates growth, development, and maintenance of mental capacity in youth.

thyrotropic hormone. A hormone secreted by the anterior lobe of pituitary, which stimulates the secretory activity of the thyroid gland.

thyroxine. A hormone secreted by the thyroid gland, which controls the oxidation rate in the body.

Thysanoptera. Insects with rasping mouth parts and two pairs of narrow wings; example, thrips.

Thysanura. Insects having ten or eleven body segments, many antennae, and bristles on the end of the abdomen; example, silverfish.

Ti. Chemical symbol for titanium.

tibia. (1) The larger of the two bones of the leg; (2) the fourth joint of the leg of some insects.

tidal air. The amount of air the average adult inhales in a normal quiet breathing; it is about 30 cubic inches.

tidal bore. A tidal flood that advances up many rivers that empty into the sea, at very high speed; it is dangerous for shipping.

tidal inlets. Narrow openings in the offshore bars through which sea water flows landward with the coming of tide and seaward as it ebbs.

tidal marsh. A marsh formed when vegetation creeps into a lagoon from the landward side.

tidal range. The difference between the levels of low and high tide.

tidal scout. An erosion caused by tidal waves; it keeps the inlets in the offshore bars open.

tidal wave. A great wave in the ocean caused by an earthquake or strong wind; tidal waves should not be confused with the tides caused by the attraction of the sun and moon.

tide. The rise and fall of the ocean about every twelve hours, caused by the gravitational attraction of the moon and the sun.

till. A boulder clay laid down by glaciers.

tiller. A side shoot from the base of the stem of grasses and corn.

tiltometer. An instrument for measuring inclination to the horizontal.

timber line. A line along a mountainside above which there are no trees or only small ones.

time belt. A geographical area in which the same time standard is used.

time, standard. The time system based on a selected meridian.

time zone. Same as time belt.

time-delay relay. An electromagnetic device that operates only after a definite time has elapsed from the variation in the circuit.

tin. A silvery ductile corrosion-resistant metal; chemical symbol Sn; atomic number 50; used in alloying, as a coating on steel.

tin pest. The disintegration of tin metal to a gray powder which is an allotropic form of tin.

tincture. An alcoholic extract or alcoholic solution.

tinplate. A thin steel sheet covered with a layer of tin; used for tin cans and other food containers.

tint. (1) A chromatic color of relatively low saturation; (2) the mixture of a color with white.

tintometer. A colorimeter for measuring color intensity by comparison with standard colored solutions or glass slides.

tissue. A group of like cells which form a continuous layer and perform similar functions.

tissue culture. Separating minute pieces of tissue from a growing mass and placing them under aseptic conditions in a nutrient medium where they can be observed microscopically.

tissue fluid. The extracellular fluid which constitutes the environment of body cells.

titanium. A gray cubic corrosion-resistant metal; chemical symbol Ti; atomic number 22; used as a stabilizer in stainless steel, as an alloying ingredient.

titration. The volumetric measurement of the amount of a substance in a solution by adding a reagent solution of known strength (standard solution) from a graduated tube (burette) until the reaction is just completed, which is indicated by the formation of a slight precipitate or a color change (if necessary a so-called indicator is added to the unknown sample).

Tl. Chemical symbol for thallium.

Tm. Chemical symbol for thulium.

TNT. Trinitrotoluene; $C_6H_2(CH_3)(NO_2)_3$; used as an explosive.

tocopherol. Vitamin E; its lack causes sterility.

tolerance. (1) The maximum error, or variation from a standard, permissible in a measuring instrument or machine part; (2) the ability of a plant to withstand adverse conditions of environment.

toluene. Toluol; $C_6H_5CH_3$; a hydrocarbon of the benzene series; used as a solvent, for preparing many important derivatives.

toluidines. $CH_3C_6H_4NH_2$; ortho-, meta-, and para-methyl derivatives of aniline; used in the manufacture of dyes.

tombolo. A reef of gravel that connects the mainland with an island.

ton. A unit of weight; 2,000 pounds.

tongue. The movable, muscular organ attached to the floor of the oral cavity; it is usually projecting or protrusible; it is used by higher vertebrates for the manipulation of food, in chewing and sometimes as an aid in capturing smaller animals; example, Amphibia; in man, it is also an important instrument of speech.

tonoplast. An inner plasma membrane surrounding a vacuole of a plant cell.

tonsil. One of the two masses of lymphatic tissue on either side of the throat near the base of the tongue.

tonus. Tone; a constant state of contraction of certain muscles, so that parts of the body can be kept in the proper position for good posture; a state of persistent excitation in both involuntary and voluntary muscles.

tooth. (1) An irregularity on the margin of a leaf; (2) a hard horny or calcareous projecting element used by vertebrates and invertebrates for cutting and masticating food; (3) a projection on the circumference of a toothed wheel.

toothed margin. The notched margin of a leaf.

topaz. Aluminum fluorosilicate; a yellow, colorless, or light-blue mineral; used as a gem.

topographical. Showing the details of the surface features of a region.

topographical map. A fairly large-scale map that shows the details of a locality or region, giving contours representing the elevations and noting the various other physical features by conventional signs.

topography. The description or representation of the natural and artificial surface features of an area, including hills, swamps, streams, etc.

topsoil. The topmost fertile layer of the soil; it is generally spongy and contains much decayed plant material; it is suitable for growing crops.

tornado. One of the most violent windstorms, noted for its funnel-shaped clouds, high-speed winds, and great destruction over a short path and a small area.

tornaria. The ciliated planktonic larva of Balanoglassida (Hemichordata).

torque. (1) The moment of a tangential force tending to produce rotation around a point; (2) the turning effort of the rotor of an electric motor; (3) the product of the force and the length of the arm on which it acts; (4) the total air force acting on the propeller blade of an airplane.

Torricellian vacuum. A space evacuated by filling a tube with mercury, then inverting it and placing its open end into a vessel of mercury; the mercury column will sink to a level corresponding to the atmospheric pressure, leaving a vacuum between the closed end of the tube and the surface of the mercury.

Torrid Zone. Tropical Zone; the part of the earth between the Tropics of Cancer and Capricorn.

torsiometer. An instrument for studying the elastic behavior of solids under torsion.

torsion. The strain produced by twisting.

torsion balance. An instrument for measuring very weak forces of attraction or repulsion by the twisting of a vertical thread; it demonstrates Coulomb's law.

torsion head. A rotary cap, graduated in degrees, atop the vertical tube supporting a torsion suspension.

torsion pendulum. A pendulum whose bob rotates in a plane perpendicular to the line of suspension by the twisting and untwisting of the suspending fiber; used where long oscillation is required.

tortoise shell. The mottled horny plates of the shell of a marine turtle, the hawksbill or tortoise; it is thermoplastic; used for molding ornaments, combs and spectacle frames.

torus. (1) The receptacle of a flower; (2) the thickened portion of the closing membrane of bordered pits; (3) a ridge or fold of an animal body.

total eclipse. The complete hiding of the sun by the shadow of the moon.

total reflection. The reflection of light from a polished surface, at the interface between two media, into the more refractive medium, at an angle of incidence exceeding the critical angle.

total relief of the earth. The vertical distance from the top of the highest mountain to the greatest depth of the ocean; it is more than 12 miles.

touch. The tactile sense; a stimulus received through the tactile nerves.

tourmaline. A multicolored mineral; a complex silicate of aluminum and boron with small admixtures of other elements; some varieties are used for jewelry.

toxin. A poisonous substance of bacterial origin; injected into animals it induces the formation of a specific antitoxin.

trace element. An element required in a very small amount for growth or health; examples, manganese and iron.

tracer. (1) A radioactive substance added to other substances so that the course of a reaction or their path through a living organism can be followed; (2) a smoke- or flame-producing attachment of a projectile which makes the path observable.

tracer chemistry. The use of radioisotopes in the study of chemical reactions, especially biochemical reactions in plants and animals.

trachea. (1) Windpipe; a wide tube whose opening is in the pharynx; (2) a conducting element of the xylem; (3) one of the branched breathing tubes of an insect.

tracheal gill. An organ of aquatic larvae containing many tracheae whose thin walls in contact with water allow the interchange of respiratory gases.

tracheid. A thick-walled conducting tube of wood which helps carry sap up the stem.

tracheole. The terminal branch of insect trachea that is pervading the tissues in very large numbers.

tract. (1) A bundle of nerve fibers in the vertebrate central nervous system; they connect certain nuclei with each other and with the peripheral nervous system; example, optic tract; (2) a long passage of the animal body; example, digestive tract.

traction. The motive force of a self-propelled vehicle.

trade winds. Prevailing winds in the belts 10 to 25° north and south of the equator; in the northern hemisphere they blow toward the equator from the northeast, and in the southern hemisphere, from the southeast.

trailing edge. (1) The rear end of an airfoil or the rear edge of a propeller; (2) that edge of the brush of an electric device which is the last in contact with the commutator ring during revolution.

trait. A characteristic or peculiarity of an organism which is passed on from one generation to another by the genes.

trajectory. The curve which a body, such as a missile, describes as it moves through space.

transceiver. A portable device which can be used both as a transmitter and as a receiver of radio communications.

transducer. (1) A device inserted between electrical, acoustical, and mechanical elements of a communication system for power transformation; (2) a device that can be actuated by waves from one or more transmission systems and will supply related waves to one or more other transmission systems.

transducer, electric. A transducer in which all of the waves are electric.

transducer, electroacoustic. A transducer for receiving waves from an electric system and delivering waves to an acoustic system, or vice versa.

transducer, electromechanical. A transducer for receiving waves from an electric system and delivering waves to a mechanical system, or vice versa.

transect. The line or belt of vegetation selected for charting plants; used for the study of changes in the composition of the vegetation of a particular area.

transfer of cultures. Transplanting viable bacteria from an old medium into a fresh new one.

transference number. Transport number; that portion of the total current which is carried by any species of ions present in the electrolyte.

transformation of energy. Changing of one form of energy into another; example, changing mechanical energy into electrical energy.

transformation period. The half life of a radioactive substance.

transformer. An apparatus used for increasing or decreasing voltage by magnetic induction.

transformer coupling. Transferring energy from one circuit to another by means of a transformer.

transfusion tissue. Tissue of empty cells with pitted internally hardened walls, accompanying vascular tissues in the leaves of most gymnosperms; they convey substances to and from the vascular tissues.

transient. (1) A momentary current due to a surge of voltage; (2) a noncyclic change in an electrical communication system; (3) an irregular sound wave of short duration.

transistor. A miniature electronic device, usually consisting of a germanium crystal, so connected in a circuit as to perform most of the functions of an electron tube.

transit. (1) The passage of some heavenly body, such as Venus or Mercury, between the earth and the sun; (2) the apparent passage of a heavenly body through a local meridian due to the earth's rotation about its own axis.

transit instrument. An astronomical instrument used for observing the exact time of the passage of a celestial body across the meridian.

transit time. (1) The time needed by an electron to pass between a given pair of electrodes; (2) the time of transit of a celestial body across the meridian.

transition cell. An electrolytic cell with an electrolyte in which the valence of one of the ions changes, with a corresponding change in the electromotive force; (2) the terminal phloem cell of the vein of a leaf.

transition element. An element which differs in electronic configuration from the element of the next lower or higher atomic number only in the number of electrons in an inner shell; example, a rare-earth element.

transition point. The temperature at which the two crystalline forms of a dimorphic substance are in equilibrium.

transition region. (1) The region, between two homogeneous semiconductors in which the impurity concentration changes; (2) that part of a young plant axis where the root gives rise to a shoot.

transition temperature. Same as transition point.

translation. A change in the position of an animal organ.

translatory motion. The motion along a line.

translocation. (1) Same as translation; (2) the movement of foods through the veins of a leaf or in some other part of a plant; (3) a change in the chromosome setup when a chromosome exchanges parts with one belonging to another pair and not its own mate.

translucent. Transmitting light only partially, so that distinct vision through a translucent medium is not possible.

transmission limit. A limiting wave length or frequency, above or below which a given type of radiation is almost entirely absorbed by a given medium.

transmission line. The conducting system for electrical energy between two or more points; it consists of overhead wires and underground cable.

transmission of light. The ratio of the light flux leaving a medium to the light flux incident on it.

transmission plane. The plane of vibration of polarized light which will pass through a given polarizer.

transmission system, acoustic. An assembly of elements adapted for the transmission of sound.

transmission system, mechanical. An assembly of elements adapted for the transmission of mechanical power.

transmissometer. A photometer for measuring the transmission factor of semitransparent bodies.

transmitter. A device in communication which sends out signals intended for a distant receiver.

transmutation. Changing one substance into another; example, converting a base metal into gold; the dream of alchemists.

transparent. Transmitting light so that objects can be distinctly seen through it; pervious to light.

transpiration. (1) The diffusion of water vapor from the stomates of a plant into the atmosphere; (2) the passage of a gas or a vapor through a capillary, or its exhalation from the pores of an absorbing substance.

transpirometer. An instrument for measuring the water loss in plants.

transplantation. Artificial removal of part of an organism from its normal position to an abnormal position in the same or to any position in another organism.

transported soil. The soil carried by wind, rivers, or glaciers.

transuranic elements. Elements which have a higher atomic number than uranium; they are all radioactive; example, plutonium.

transverse. Crosswise; extending in a direction which is at right angles to the length of the body.

transverse colon. That part of the colon which extends from right to left.

transverse process. One of the lateral projections of a vertebra.

transverse waves. A wave motion in which the vibrations are at right angles to the direction of propagation; example, electromagnetic waves.

trap. (1) A dense dark-colored igneous rock; (2) an absorption filter used to trap or remove an undesired signal from a receiver; (3) a device which reduces the effect of vapor pressure of mercury or oil in a diffusion pump on the high-vacuum side of the system; (4) a bend in a drainage tube that prevents its clogging and sewer gases from escaping into the house.

travertine. Calcareous tufa; used as a decorative stone under the name of onyx marble.

tree line. Same as timber line.

tree of life. Phylogenetic tree; a diagrammatic scheme for showing the probable evolutionary relationship of all existing and extinct animals.

trellis drainage. Drainage pattern which is similar to a trellis or fireman's ladder; it is characteristic of the canoe-shaped valleys of the Appalachians.

Trematoda. A class of Platyhelminthes; parasites with a tough cuticle, two suckers, and a forked gut; example, fluke.

tremolite. A white or gray mineral; calcium-magnesium-silicate.

triad. (1) A group of three elements, the middle one having an atomic weight which is approximately the same as the average of the atomic weights of the other two; (2) a trivalent element.

triangle of forces. If three forces acting at the same point can be represented in magnitude and direction by the sides of a triangle, taken in order, they will be in equilibrium.

triangle of velocities. If a body has tree component velocities which can be represented in magnitude and direction by the sides of a triangle, taken in order, the body will remain at rest.

Triassic period. A Mesozoic era; it began about 180 million years ago; reptiles, cycads, and conifers were dominant.

tribasic acid. An acid whose molecule has three replaceable hydrogen atoms; example, phosphoric acid, H_3PO_4.

tribe. A family; a minor group in classifying plants; the name of tribes ends in -eae; example, Malpighiaceae.

triboelectric. Electrified by friction.

triboluminescence. Frictional luminescence; the emission of light when certain crystals, such as cane sugar, are crushed.

tribophosphorescence. Phosphorescence caused by friction.

tributary. A stream flowing into a larger stream.

triceps. A large muscle on the arms and legs of vertebrates; it has three heads or origins.

Trichina. Trichinella; a small roundworm sometimes occurring in underdone meat, especially pork; its larvae are parasitic and the cause of trichinosis in man.

trichocyst. A tiny structure inside the plasma membrane of paramecium which discharges fine hairs as a defense against enemies.

trichogyne. (1) A filament at the free end of the carpogonium of red algae which receives the sperm; (2) the long tubular outgrowth of the ascogonium of ascomycetes.

trichome. A plant filament consisting of a uniseriate or multiseriate chain of cells; example, in blue-green algae.

Trichophyton. A genus of ringworm fungi which are parasitic in man and animals.

Trichoptera. An order of Endopterygota, with hairy bodies and wings; the aquatic larvae have biting mouth parts and live in silky cases which they make from wood, sand, leaves, etc.; example, caddis fly.

trichroism. The property of showing three different colors when viewed from as many different directions.

triclinic crystal. A crystal structure, having three unequal axes which intersect at angles other than right angles.

tricuspid valve. The valve between the right auricle and right ventricle of the heart of mammals, which prevents blood from flowing back to the auricle.

tridymite. A quartz mineral; a high-temperature variety of silicon dioxide.

trigeminus. The fifth cranial nerve of vertebrates which has three branches.

Trilobita. A group of extinct Arthropoda that lived in great abundance in the seas during the Paleozoic era; the head was covered by a circular shield that contained two compound eyes.

trinitrotoluene. Same as TNT.

triode. A vacuum tube containing a cathode, a grid, and an anode; the grid controls the electron flow from the cathode to the anode.

triple aplanat. A compound lens made of two negative lenses of flint glass, with a double-convex lens of crown glass cemented between them.

triple bond. A chemical bond in which three pairs of electrons are shared; it is an indication of a highly unsaturated compound; example, acetylene, $HC{\equiv}CH$.

triple point. The temperature and pressure at which the gaseous, liquid, and solid phases of a substance are in equilibrium.

triple-fusion nucleus. A nucleus formed by the union of two polar nuclei of the embryo sac and one sperm nucleus; it is developing into an endosperm.

triplet. (1) Same as triple bond; (2) three individuals resulting from the division of an ovum into three parts.

triploblastic. Derived from the three primary germ layers: ectoderm, mesoderm, and endoderm.

triploid. Having three times the haploid number of chromosomes in a nucleus; a form of polyploidy.

triprotic. Having three replaceable hydrogen atoms; example, phosphoric acid, H_3PO_4.

trisomic. Diploid, but with one extra chromosome, homologous with one of the existing pairs, so that one kind of chromosome is represented three times.

tritium. A hydrogen isotope of mass 3; chemical symbol T.

tritocerebrum. The third posterior division of the brain of Arthropoda; it is derived from the pair of ganglia of one segment of the head.

triton. The nucleus of tritium, containing one proton and two neutrons; symbol H_3; used for nuclear bombardment.

trivalent. (1) Having a valency of 3; (2) said of threefold chromosomes.

trochanter. The second joint of an insect's leg.

trochlear nerve. The fourth cranial nerve of vertebrates; it is a motor nerve, supplying the eye muscle.

trochophore. Trochosphere; an invertebrate larva with a bent or curved tubular alimentary canal; it is free swimming before undergoing transformation to become an adult; examples, in Bryozoa, Brachiopoda, Annelida, and Mollusca.

trochus. The ciliated disk at the end of the body of Rotifera.

Trojan group. Eleven asteroids which are named after the various heroes of the Trojan Wars; their periods and mean distances are nearly identical with those of the planet Jupiter.

trophallaxis. Interchange of nourishment between the various members of an insect colony; the insects exude secretions at the surface of the body which are licked off by others.

trophoblast. An embryonic epithelium which encloses the embryonic structure of a placental mammal, forming the outer layer of the chorion and establishing close contact with the maternal tissue.

trophosome. An individual that takes in and digests food in colonial animals; the polyp stage of Hydrozoa.

tropic hormone. A hormone that stimulates an endocrine gland to secrete its hormone.

tropical red soils. Soils that are low in most of the minerals needed by plants.

tropical year. Solar year; 20 minutes and 23½ seconds shorter than the sideral year.

tropism. The movement of an entire organism in response to an external stimulus.

tropopause. The boundary between the troposphere and the stratosphere.

troposphere. The lowest portion of the atmosphere that is located between the earth and the stratosphere.

tropotron. A form of magnetron, that is, a vacuum tube in which the electron flow from the cathode is regulated by an external magnetic field.

trough. The lowest point of a wave.

trough line. A line drawn in a pressure field along which the isobars are symmetrical and curved cyclonically; a V-shaped trough contains a front; a U-shaped trough has no front or has a very weak one.

Trouton's rule. The ratio of the latent heat of vaporization per gram molecule to the boiling point in absolute degrees is approximately the same for all liquids; its value is 21 at asmospheric pressure.

true hybrid. A hybrid resulting from crossing two different species.

truncus arteriosus. The great arterial vessel leading from the heart of vertebrates in the primitive unpaired condition and in the embryo.

trunk. (1) The body of a vertebrate, bearing the neck and head at one end and the tail at the other, with the two pairs of appendages attached laterally or ventrolaterally near the two ends; (2) the proboscis of the elephant; (3) the main stem or stock of a tree.

trunnion. One of a pair of opposite protruding pivots that provide a means of turning a heavy vessel.

truss. A combination of beams, rods, and bars bolted together to form the rigid steel framework of a bridge.

Trypanisoma. Flagellate elongated Protozoa, tapering at both ends; an undulating membrane along the margin is attached to the flagellum; there are three species which are pathogenic to humans.

trypsin. An enzyme of the pancreatic juice which converts proteins into proteases and peptones.

trypsinogen. The inactive form in which trypsin is secreted by the pancreas; it is changed to trypsin by enterokinase.

tsunami. Tidal waves that result from earthquakes or volcanic eruptions which occur under the ocean.

tube. (1) A hollow cylinder which forms the body of a microscope; the upper portion contains the eyepiece; (2) an electron tube; (3) the cylindrical lower part of a corolla.

tube counter. A tubular ion counter.

tube, discharge. A tube containing gas or vapor at low pressure and two or more electrodes through which energy is supplied to maintain an electric discharge.

tube foot. Podium; a characteristic tubular appendage of Echinodermata, associated with the water-vascular system; it is an organ of locomotion which grips the surface by adhesion and suction.

tube nucleus. One of three nongametic nuclei in a pollen tube which controls the growth of the tube.

tube, soft. A tube which has not been completely evacuated, or a vacuum tube which has lost part of its vacuum because gas was released from the electrodes and envelope.

tube voltmeter. A vacuum tube used for the measurement of small alternating-current voltages.

tuber. An enlarged and modified underground stem containing considerable amounts of starch as stored food and having buds, called eyes; when a tuber or eye is planted, a new plant is formed; example, potato.

tubule. (1) A very small tube in the animal body; example, the filtering tubules of the kidneys; (2) the neck of a plant perithecium.

tubuliform glands. Silk glands; glands in the abdomen of female spiders whose secretion is used for forming the cocoon to contain the eggs.

tufa. A variety of limestone deposited by the water of hot springs.

tundra. Arctic plains which, while growing mosses and lichens in profusion and locally various flowering shrubs, are treeless; the top is usually a black muck; the subsoil is frozen.

tungsten. Wolfram; a corrosion-resistant ductile metal; chemical symbol W; atomic number

74; it has an extremely high melting point; used for filaments in bulbs and tubes, for alloying, in cemented-carbide tools.

tungsten steel. A steel alloy containing up to 20% tungsten and some chromium and vanadium; used for cutting tools.

Tunicata. Urochorda; marine chordate animals; example, sea squirts.

tuning circuits. Circuits used for blacking out undesired carrier signals in a radio receiver.

tuning transformer. An air-core radio-frequency transformer used in receiving circuits.

Turbellaria. A class of Platyhelminthes; mostly aquatic, free-living flatworms; their epidermis is ciliated; their gut is a simple or branched sac.

turbidimeter. An instrument for measuring the turbidity of a liquid by light absorption; used, e.g., in water-purification plants.

turbidity. The cloudiness of a liquid due to the presence of finely divided particles in suspension.

turbinate bones. Conchae; three bony layers in the nasal passages.

turbine. A rotary engine consisting of a wheel with curved blades driven by water, steam, or gas.

turbojet. A jet engine having an air compressor run by a gas turbine to provide the air needed for burning the fuel.

turbulence. Eddies or disturbances produced in a fluid, generally by the passage of a solid body or particle through it.

turbulent air. Rising and sinking air currents.

turbulent flow. (1) The opposite of smooth flow of a fluid; (2) a fluid flow in which the velocity at a given point varies more or less rapidly in magnitude and direction with time.

turgid. (1) Distended with air or liquid; (2) swollen.

turgor. The balance between the elasticity of cell walls and the osmotic pressure exerted by the sap on the walls.

turgor pressure. The pressure within the cell resulting from the absorption of water into the vacuole.

turion. A detached food-storing winter bud by means of which many water plants survive the winter.

turpentine. Oil of turpentine; a mixture of hydrocarbons extracted by distillation from the rosin of pine trees; used as a solvent in paints, lacquers, polishes.

twig. A small terminal branch or shoot.

twilight zone. The intermediate area of the ocean between the photic zone and the abyssal

zone.

twin axis. The line perpendicular to both crystal axes of a twin crystal.

twin crystal. A crystal resulting from the symmetrical growing together of two crystals, which are mirror images of each other.

twins. Two mammalian individuals born at the same birth.

two phase. Quarter phase; two windings or circuits with a phase displacement of 90 electrical degrees.

tylose. A balloonlike outgrowth which develops from the living parenchyma cells in the woody tissues of stems; it pushes through the pits in the cell wall and gradually fills the lumen or tube of the cell until it is completely clogged.

tympanic membrane. Eardrum; a thin membrane separating the outer ear from the middle ear.

tympanum. (1) Same as tympanic membrane; (2) a vibrating membrane in some insects; example, grasshopper.

Tyndall effect. The visibility of the path of a beam of light in a colloidal dispersion, when viewed at right angles to its direction.

type specimen. Holotype, an individual that serves as the basis of the description of a species.

typhlosole. A median dorsal infolding along the whole length of the intestines of the earthworm; it increases the absorbing surface.

typhoon. A tornadolike storm which develops in the Pacific Ocean near China.

U

U. Chemical symbol for uranium.

U valley. A river valley whose transverse profile has been changed from a V to a U shape by glacial erosion; it has a flat floor and nearly vertical sides.

udder. The organ that includes the mammary glands of some animals; example, cow.

udell. An earthenware container for condensing iodine vapor; it is shaped like a short pipe with a constricted end by which it fits into another similar container.

udometer. A rain gage.

Ulbricht globe photometer. A device for the direct measurement of the mean spherical candle power of a lamp; it consists of a hollow sphere with a reflecting internal surface.

ulna. The long bone in the vertebrate forearm that forms the elbow.

Ulothrix. A pond scum consisting of green algae fastened together in a chain.

ultimate analysis. The determination of the chemical elements present in a compound and their proportions.

ultimate tensile stress. Tenacity; the maximum load divided by the original cross section.

ultracentrifuge. A high-speed centrifuge for separating ultramicroscopic particles.

ultrafiltration. A special method of suction or pressure filtration for separating highly dispersed substances in colloidal solution from the dispersing medium by means of a semipermeable membrane or colloidal filter.

ultrahigh frequency. UHF; transmission at frequencies of 300 to 3000 megacycles in radio and television.

ultramarine. An artificial lapis lazuli made by heating together clay, sodium sulfate, carbon, and sulfur; used as a coloring matter.

ultramicrometer. A sensitive electrical instrument for the measurement of very small displacements, in the range of one millionth of an inch.

ultramicroscope. An instrument for making visible light reflected from particles too small to be seen by an ordinary microscope; it contains an electric arc, a combination of lenses, and a compound microscope.

ultraphotic rays. Rays beyond the visible region of the spectrum.

ultrashort waves. Electromagnetic waves that are shorter than 10 yards and longer than about 1 inch.

ultrasonic. Above the range of human hearing.

ultrasonic coagulation. The bonding of small particles into larger aggregates by ultrasonic waves.

ultrasonic cross grating. A space grating resulting from the crossing of beams of ultrasonic waves having different directions of propagation.

ultrasonic delay line. A contained medium, usually a liquid like mercury, which makes use of the propagation time of sound to obtain a time delay of an ultrasonic signal.

ultrasonic detector. A mechanical, electrical, thermal, or optical device for the detection and measurement of ultrasonic waves.

ultrasonic dispersion. A suspension or emulsion of one substance in another produced by the action of high-intensity ultrasonic waves.

ultrasonic frequency. Supersonic frequency; a frequency which lies above the audio-frequency range.

ultrasonic generator. A device for producing sound waves of ultrasonic frequency.

ultrasonic light diffraction. An

optical diffraction spectrum formed when a beam of light is passed through a longitudinal ultrasonic-wave field.

ultrasonic space grating. A periodic spatial variation of the index of refraction caused by the presence of ultrasonic waves within the medium.

ultrasonic stroboscope. A device for interrupting light through the modulation of a light beam by an ultrasonic field.

ultrasonic thermal action. The temperature rise in the ultrasonic field in a liquid caused by the dissipation of the waves by absorption.

ultrasonics. The science of vibrations that are above the audible range.

ultraviolet radiation. A range of invisible radiation of frequencies next higher to those of the visible violet; their approximate wave length is 4×10^{-5} to 5×10^{-7} centimeter.

umbel. An inflorescence whose axis is short and whose pedicels are of nearly equal length; they are called rays because they appear to radiate from one point; example, carrot.

umbilical cord. A tubelike structure extending from the navel of the fetus to the placenta of the mother; it contains two arteries and one vein and serves as an excretory, digestive, and respiratory mechanism for the fetus.

umbilicus (plural, umbilici). Navel; the scar on the ventral surface of placental mammals where the umbilical cord is severed at birth.

umbo. A rounded prominence near the hinged edge of a bivalve shell.

umbra. The darkest middle portion of the shadow of a celestial body, for example, the moon.

uncertainty principle. Principle of indeterminateness; a statement of the quantum mechanics of Heisenberg according to which it is not possible to obtain simultaneously accurate measurements of the position and velocity of a particle of electronic size.

unconformity. A discontinuity in stratified geological layers caused by interlacing of rocks corresponding to different periods.

underground stems. Stems that grow underground.

undershot wheel. A water wheel which receives its power from the impact of water against the vanes; example, the Poncelet wheel, that has curved vanes.

undertow. A current beneath the water surface that moves in an opposite direction to the current of the surface; especially the current at the seashore that drags against the force of the

incoming waves.

undulating membrane. Vibratile membrane; a form of organelle found in some of the one-celled animals; it vibrates in an undulating movement as an organ of locomotion.

undulatory. Consisting of or resembling waves.

Ungulata. Grass-eating, terrestrial hoofed mammals; examples, sheep, horse, and cow.

unguligrade. Walking on hoofs; example, horse.

uniaxial crystal. A double-refracting crystal having only one optic axis; that is, only one direction of single refraction; example, a tetragonal crystal.

unicellular. Consisting of one cell only.

unidirectional current. Direct current; a current that flows in one direction only.

unified field theory. A phase of the Einsteinian relativity theory which seeks to treat gravitational, electric, and magnetic fields as aspects of a single entity.

uniform acceleration. An acceleration in which the speed is increased by the same amount each second.

uniform flow. A flow in which the cross section of every stream tube remains constant, each particle moving along its streamline with constant speed.

unimolecular layer. Monomolecular layer; monolayer; a layer which has the thickness of a single molecule; examples, fatty acids and oils poured on water; used to study surface-tension phenomena.

uniovular twins. Monozygotic twins; twins developed from a single fertilized egg.

unipolar induction. The generation of an electromotive force by one pole of a magnet.

uniramous limb. A crustacean appendage consisting of a single unbranching series of segments.

unisexual. (1) Having the stamens and carpels on separate flowers; (2) producing either male or female gametes.

unit, absolute. A unit that can be defined in terms of the fundamental units, without the introduction of other arbitrary standards.

unit cell. The simplest geometric figure which includes all the characteristics of, and is repeated indefinitely to form, the lattice structure of a crystal.

unit character. A characteristic that is inherited as a whole.

unit, concrete. A unit applied to or associated with a particular magnitude; example, 1 gram.

unit, derived. A unit that is derived from the three fundamental units: those of length, mass and time; examples, units of area and density.

unit, fundamental. The units of

length, mass, and time which form the basis of a system; example, the fundamental units of the cgs system are the centimeter, gram, and second.

unit magnetic pole. A magnetic pole which will repel an equal and like pole with a force of one dyne at a distance of one centimeter.

univalent. Monovalent; having a valence of one.

univalve. Said of a shell consisting of one piece; example, the shell of the snail.

univariant. Having one degree of freedom; example, the system of liquid water and water vapor.

universal attraction. The gravitational attraction which is proportional to the masses and inversely proportional to the square of the distance.

universal gravitation. Each particle of matter attracts every other particle.

universal joint. A joint that allows movement in all directions.

universal motor. A motor connected in series, which operates on both alternating and direct current.

universal shunt. Several different shunts in a resistance box for use with galvanometers of different resistance to increase their range.

universe. An aggregate of all created and existing things known to man; it includes everything comprised in comprehensible space, together with its forces and laws.

unlimited ceiling. A description of visibility for aircraft when less than half the sky is overcast or when the lowest clouds are more than 10,000 feet high.

unquantized state. A state of an atom in which there are electrons whose motion is not subject to quantum conditions and which give rise to continuous spectral bands rather than lines.

unsaturated compound. A carbon compound which contains one or more double or triple bonds and is thus capable of forming association products; examples, ethylene and styrene.

unsaturated solution. A solution that can dissolve more of the solute at a certain temperature.

unstable compound. A compound that decomposes easily.

unstable equilibrium. A state of a body in which the potential energy is reduced by any small displacement and the body has the tendency to move away from its equilibrium position.

unstriated muscle. Smooth muscle; involuntary muscle; a contractile tissue, consisting of spindle-shaped uninucleate cells, which lines the cavity of hollow organs.

uralite. Hornblende; a mineral metamorphosed from pyroxene; it is fibrous and retains the original form of the pyroxene.

uraninite. Pitchblende; a black crystalline mineral; it consists principally of uranium, but contains also lead, thorium, yttrium, helium, and argon.

uranium. A radioactive metal; chemical symbol U; atomic number 92; half life 4.5 $\times$ 10^9.

uranium oxide. A green mineral; U_3O_8; used in ceramics, pigments.

Uranus. The seventh planet revolving around the sun; it is not visible to the naked eye; it is about fourteen times larger than the earth and has four small satellites.

urea. Carbamide; NH_2CONH_2; colorless crystals; a waste substance found chiefly in the urine of mammals, but formed in the liver from broken-down proteins; it was the first organic compound produced synthetically by Wöhler from ammonium isocyanate.

urea-formaldehyde resins. Urea resins; oil-resistant condensation products of urea and formaldehyde; one of the most important classes of thermosetting resins.

urease. An enzyme which splits urea into ammonia and water.

uredinium. A source of urediospores.

urediospore. A reddish-brown one-celled summer spore in the life cycle of rust fungi.

uredosorus. Same as uredinium.

uredospore. Same as urediospore.

urestelic. Excreting urea as the main breakdown product of amino acids.

ureter. A tube that connects each kidney with the bladder and through which the urine secreted by the kidney is conveyed.

urethra. A narrow canal from the bladder to the exterior for the passage of urine and also for the passage of the semen of the vertebrate male.

uric acid. $C_5H_4N_4O_3$; a white crystalline powder; a complex organic compound, which is only slightly soluble in water; it is the main excretory product of the breakdown of proteins and nucleic acid; its accumulation causes rheumatism.

uricotelic. Excreting uric acid as the main breakdown product of amino acids.

urinary bladder. A muscular sac lined with transitional epithelium where urine is stored before it leaves the body.

urine. A transparent amber fluid of slightly acid reaction elaborated by the vertebrate kidneys; the medium by which the body gets rid of large portions of the toxic matter that accumulates in the system and of the end products of food metabolism; it contains urea, ammonia, purine bodies, salt, and uric acid.

uriniferous tubule. A narrow coiled glandular urine-secreting tube in the kidney of vertebrates leading from Bowman's capsule to the collecting ducts which carry the urine to the ureter.

urinogenital tract. The combined urinary and reproductive canals.

Urochorda. A group of marine Chordata; the adult is sedentary, feeding by ciliary currents; it has gill slits and a reduced nervous system; it has no notochord; it is commonly covered with a gelatinous layer containing tunicin; example, sea squirts.

Urodela. Caudata; scaleless Amphibia; they have an elongated body with a tail and normal limbs; examples, newts and salamanders.

urogenital system. The group of organs that are concerned with excretion and reproduction; they are closely associated in vertebrates.

uropod. An appendage of certain Crustacea modified as an expanded swimming organ; it sculls the animal rapidly backward through the water.

urostyle. (1) The unsegmented caudal region of the vertebral column of Anura; (2) a bone in the tail fin of some fish.

Ursa Major. Great Bear; Big Dipper; a northern constellation containing the two Pointers that point toward the North Star.

Ursa Minor. Little Bear; Little Dipper; a constellation which includes the North Star.

use and disuse. The concept in Lamarck's theory of how organisms change through the ages.

uterine tubes. Fallopian tubes; oviducts; about four-inch long passages between the uterus and the lateral pelvic walls; they receive the ova liberated by the ovary and propel them toward the uterus.

uterus. A portion of the female reproductive passages in which the eggs or young are retained during all or part of the embryonic development.

uviol glass. A glass which is highly transparent to ultraviolet light.

uvula. A soft mass of tissue that hangs from the posterior of the soft palate above the base of the tongue.

V

V. (1) Chemical symbol for vanadium; (2) symbol for volt.

vacuolar membrane. A protoplasmic membrane surrounding a vacuole, which regulates the movement of stored substances into and from the cytoplasm.

vacuole. A small cavity within the cytoplasm which contains water, gases, food being digested, enzymes, and wastes.

vacuum. A space from which most of the air or other gas has been removed; the highest vacuum obtained so far is 10^{-6} millimeter of mercury.

vacuum pump. An air pump used for reducing the pressure in a closed container.

vacuum spectrograph. A spectrograph which operates in a vacuum, so as to introduce no air absorption of the emission under examination.

vacuum thermocouple. A thermocouple for measuring very feeble alternating or direct currents by means of their heating effect.

vacuum tube. Thermionic tube; an evacuated tube containing a heated electron-emitting cathode, an anode that receives the electrons, and additional electrodes that control the flow of electrons from the cathode to the anode.

vacuum weight. The weight corrected for the buoyancy of the air.

vadose water. The water above the level of ground water in the earth's crust.

vagina. A sheath; (1) the passage from the uterus of female mammals to the outside of the body, through which the embryo passes; (2) the sheathlike base of a leaf.

vagus. The tenth cranial nerve of vertebrates; the principal nerve of the parasympathetic system.

valence. Valency; (1) the ability of an atom or radical to combine with other atoms or radicals in definite proportions; (2) a number indicating the proportion in which a given atom or radical combines in terms of hydrogen atoms.

valence angle. The angle formed by two hypothetical lines connecting two adjacent atoms to a central atom.

valence band. The range of energy states in the spectrum of a solid crystal that represents the energies of the valence electrons which bind the crystal together.

valence crystal. A crystal which is bound together by covalent bonds.

valence, dative. A covalence in which one of the two atoms joined by the valence bond furnishes both of the shared elec-

trons.

valence electrons. The electrons in the outermost shell of the atom.

valence, free. A valence that does not appear to be satisfied; example, the valence of a free radical.

valence, maximum. The highest valence shown by an element in any of its compounds.

valence, negative. (1) The number of electrons an atom can accept; example, chlorine has a negative valence of one; (2) the valence of a negatively charged ion.

valence, normal. The valence that an element normally exhibits in a majority of its compounds.

valence, null. The lack of valence in an element since it normally has a complete outer electronic shell; example, neon.

valence number. The number of electrons an atom loses, or acquires, or shares during combination.

valence, positive. (1) The number of electrons an atom can liberate; example, hydrogen has a positive valence of one; (2) the valence of a positively charged ion.

valence shell. The outermost electron shell of an atom.

valence, supplementary. A residual valence which connects atoms, groups, or molecules in which the ordinary valences are already satisfied.

valency. Same as valence.

valency bond. Valence bond; the force that holds atoms together in a molecule.

valley. A low area among hills or mountains, usually traversed by streams or rivers.

valley breeze. An uphill air current; an anabatic wind that dies at sunset; it occurs on hot days and is due to an uneven terrain.

valley glaciers. Glaciers which move along river valleys.

valley train. The sand and gravel that is carried down the valley as a valley glacier melts.

value. (1) The quality of brightness or darkness of the shades in a photographic image; (2) the magnitude of a quantity or property.

valve. (1) Each half of a fruit pod; (2) one half of the cell wall of a diatom; (3) each half of the bivalve shell of mollusks; (4) one or more folds in the lining tissue of a blood vessel or other organ that prevents or checks the flow of a liquid in the opposite direction; (5) a device, usually in a tube or pipe, that serves to open and close a passage.

valve overlap. The number of degrees of rotation of the crankshaft near the center when both the intake and exhaust valves are open

Van Allen radiation. Belts of high-

ly charged particles trapped in the earth's magnetic field; they are probably subdivisions of a larger complex of particles; the outer belt, the magnetosphere, extends to an altitude of 40,000 miles at the Equator.

van der Graaf generator. An electrostatic machine for producing artificial lightning and high voltages; used in x-ray machines and atomic research.

van der Waals' equation. An equation of state which covers intermolecular attraction at high densities and the effective volume as reduced by the actual volume of the molecules.

van der Waals' force. The force of attraction which exists among the molecules of all substances; this force arises from the movement of electrons in neighboring atoms or molecules.

vanadinite. A red crystalline mineral composed of lead chloride and lead vandate; used mainly as an ore of vanadium.

vanadium. A gray mineral; chemical symbol V; atomic number 23; used as an alloying ingredient in steel.

vanadium steel. An iron alloy containing small percentages of vanadium which serves as a deoxidizing agent; used for axles and gears.

vane. (1) A weathercock for indicating the direction of the wind; (2) a blade of a turbine; (3) the barb or barbule of a feather which extends from the central axis.

van't Hoff factor. A factor by which the molecular weight of an electrolyte, as calculated from the freezing-point depression, must be multiplied to give its true molecular weight; the ratio of the number of ions and undissociated particles in a solution to the number of particles that would be present if the molecules of the solute were not dissociated.

van't Hoff's law. The osmotic pressure of a dilute solution is the same as that the solute would exert in the gaseous state occupying the same volume as the solution, at the same temperature.

van't Hoff's law of equilibrium. When the temperature of a system in equilibrium is raised, the reaction tends to go in the direction which absorbs heat.

vapor. The gaseous form of a substance that is a liquid or a solid at ordinary temperatures.

vapor density. The weight of a vapor per unit volume at standard temperature and pressure.

vapor lamp. An electric discharge lamp, emitting from ionized sodium, mercury, etc.

vapor pressure. The pressure exerted at any temperature by the vapors of a substance alone or in a mixture with other gases.

vapor, saturated. A vapor which, at a given temperature, is in equilibrium with its liquid.

vapor tension. The tendency of a liquid to enter the vapor state balanced by, and numerically equal to, the vapor pressure.

vaporimeter. An instrument for measuring the volatility of essential oils by heating them in an air current.

vaporization. Changing a liquid or solid to a gas.

vaporization, heat of. The amount of heat needed to change a unit mass of a substance into its vapor at the boiling point and atmospheric pressure.

vaporization, molar latent heat of. The amount of heat needed to change one gram molecule of a substance into its vapor at the boiling point and one atmosphere pressure.

vapor-pressure thermometer. A thermometer whose indications are based on the maximum vapor pressure of a liquid.

variable condenser. A condenser whose capacity can be varied by moving one group of plates relative to the other.

variable of state. A variable, such as pressure, volume, temperature, or entropy, which determines the physical state of a body and in terms of which its thermodynamic transformations are expressed.

variable resistance. Rheostat; a resistance that can be adjusted or changed to different values.

variable star. Same as variables (1).

variable-pitch propeller. A propeller whose blades are so mounted that they may be turned about their axis to any desired pitch while the propeller is in rotation.

variables. (1) Stars of variable apparent magnitude; there are long-period, short-period, and irregular variables; (2) a quantity, as distinguished from a constant, to which any number of values can be assigned in a given set.

variance. Variability; the number of degrees of freedom of a system; the number of variables that determine the state of a substance.

variant. An organism that differs from the normal characters of the species.

variation. (1) Declination; the angular deflection of the compass needle from true north; (2) the differences of structure or function between individuals of the same species.

variegations. Irregular variations in the color of plant organs, such as leaves and flowers, due to suppression of pigment development in certain areas.

variety. Subdivision within a spe-

cies based on some hereditary difference which is considered too small to serve as a basis for a new species.

variolite. A fine-grained basic rock that contains spherical varioles consisting of feldspar fibers in radial development.

variometer. (1) A device for measuring or recording variations in terrestrial magnetism; (2) a rate-of-climb indicator; an aircraft instrument indicating the rate of climb or descent.

varves. Lake deposits of glacial origin that show alternate coarse and fine bands.

varying-speed motor. Variable-speed motor; a motor whose speed varies with the load, ordinarily decreasing as the load increases.

vas deferens. An excretory duct which carries sperm away from the testes.

vasa efferentia. Small ducts which carry semen from the testes to the vas deferens.

vascular. Referring or belonging to tubes or passages which convey fluids in plants and animals; examples, vascular bundle and vascular system.

vascular bundle. A longitudinal strand of vascular tissue consisting essentially of xylem and phloem.

vascular cylinder. Stele; the central part of the plant stem or root.

vascular elements. The conductive cells of plants, especially those of the xylem and phloem.

vascular plant. A plant that has a vascular system; example, ferns.

vascular system. (1) A circulatory system in plants consisting of ducts and tubes which carry water and dissolved minerals upward, and dissolved food and oxygen downward; (2) the organs of blood circulation.

vascular tissue. Xylem and phloem.

vasculum. (1) A box used on field trips to collect insects or plants; (2) ascidium; a pitcher-shaped leaf or leaf part.

vasoconstriction. The narrowing of blood vessels when the smooth muscles in their walls contract.

vasodilation. An expansion of blood vessels usually by the relaxation of muscles.

vasomotor nerves. Nerves of the autonomic nervous system which control the contraction and expansion of blood vessels.

vat dyes. Direct dyes; insoluble dyes which are applied to fibers or fabrics in the form of their water-soluble leuco compounds which are oxidized to the dyes directly on the fibers or fabrics.

vector. (1) A carrier of viruses, bacteria, or Protozoa; it usually refers to the animal host

that carries the pathogenic organism from one human host to another; (2) a straight line that represents both the magnitude of the force and the direction in which it acts.

vector field. A region of space each point of which is described by a vector.

vector quantity. A quantity which has magnitude and direction.

vectors, parallelogram law of. If two like vector quantities are represented by the two sides of a parallelogram drawn from a point, the resultant of the two vectors is represented in magnitude and direction by the diagonal of the parallelogram drawn through the point.

vectors, triangle law of. If two vector quantities are represented by two sides of a triangle taken in order, the resultant vector is represented by the third side of the triangle.

veering wind shift. The changing of wind clockwise.

Vega. The second brightest star visible in northern latitudes; it is the brightest member of the constellation Lyra.

Vegard-Kaplan bands. Spectral bands due to metastable nitrogen molecules.

vegetable oil. An oil, consisting mainly of triglycerides, extracted from plants, especially seeds.

vegetation. The plant life of an area.

vegetative multiplication. The formation of new plants by the breaking off and rooting of parts of a parent plant.

vegetative organs. The plant organs which are concerned directly or indirectly with the nutrition of the plant body, providing for its growth and continued existence; examples, root, stem, and leaves.

vegetative pole. Animal pole; the upper part of the developing egg which contains little or no yolk and in which rapid segmentation takes place.

vegetative reproduction. Asexual reproduction; development of a new plant from pieces of roots, stems, and other parts of a parent plant.

veil. Velum; a membrane covering the gills of mushrooms in early stages of their development.

vein. (1) A blood vessel through which blood moves toward the heart; (2) a small bundle of connective tissue in a leaf; (3) a small irregular intrusion in a rock.

velamen. The outside layer of an aerial root of certain orchids; it is adapted to gather water.

velarium. A flange of thin tissue projecting from the margin of a jellyfish over the concave surface of the body.

veliger. A larval form of some mollusks; the shell becomes coiled.

velocity. The rate of movement of a body; it is a vector quantity having both magnitude and direction.

velocity, escape. The speed that a rocket must attain to escape completely from a planet's gravitational field; a vehicle launched from the earth needs an escape velocity of about 6.9 miles per second.

velocity of light. 3×10^{10} centimeters per second in vacuum; about 186,300 miles per second.

velocity of modulation. The variation of the velocity of a beam of electrons as a periodic function of time.

velocity, orbital. The speed required at a given location for a space vehicle to establish a closed orbit around the earth; for a vehicle launched from the earth, orbital velocity is between 4.9 and 6.9 miles per second.

velocity ratio of a machine. The ratio of the distance through which the point of application of the force moves, to the corresponding distance for the resistance; for an ideal machine, the velocity ratio is equal to the mechanical advantage.

velocity spectrograph. An apparatus for separating an emission of electrically charged particles into distinct streams according to their speeds, by means of magnetic or electric deflection.

velocity, spin. A system of velocities of many points, resulting from a given angular velocity about a given axis.

velum. (1) A thin flange of tissue projecting from the margin of the body of a hydrozoan medusa over the concave surface; it contains a nerve ring and muscles, and aids in locomotion; (2) a ciliated organ adjacent to the mouth of the veliger larva of mollusks; (3) a double ciliated ring surrounding the oral end of the body of a rotifer.

vena cava. One of the three main mammalian veins that carry blood to the right auricle of the heart.

vena contracta. That part of the free jet of a liquid issuing from a container through an orifice, which is contracted to its smallest size.

venation. (1) The arrangement of the veins of a leaf; (2) the arrangement of nervures.

venom. A poison produced by such animals as spiders and snakes; often used as a means of protection or while attacking their prey.

venomous. Having poison-secreting glands.

venter. (1) The enlarged basal portion of an archegonium in which the egg cell is borne; (2) the ventral surface of the abdomen.

ventral. (1) Front or uppermost, if referring to a plant surface; (2) downward or abdominal, if referring to an animal.

ventral canal cell. The cell above the egg cell in the archegonium.

ventral root. A vertebrate nerve root which contains motor fibers.

ventricle. (1) A chamber in the heart from which blood is sent to the arteries; (2) a brain cavity filled with cerebrospinal fluid.

Venturi meter. A device for measuring the rate of flow of fluids through pipes, usually of fairly large diameter.

venule. The smallest branch of a vein that carries blood away from the capillaries; example, veins in insect wings.

Venus. Evening star; morning star; the second planet from the sun; the brightest star in the sky; it has no satellites.

verdigris. A green deposit formed on copper exposed to the atmosphere; it consists of basic copper carbonate of variable composition.

vergency. Either divergence or convergence of rays from a lens or a mirror, expressed as the reciprocal of the distance from the lens or mirror to the focus of the rays.

vermiform appendix. Vermiform process; a slender, tubelike pouch projecting from the cecum of the large intestine.

vermilion. Mercuric sulfide, HgS; a red paint pigment.

vernalization. The freezing of winter seed after the beginning of germination to promote the development of a hormone that is necessary to flower formation.

vernation. The manner in which the leaves are folded or rolled up in the bud.

vernier. An auxiliary scale, sliding along a main scale, which permits the reading of the smallest main-scale subdivision with greater accuracy.

vernier caliper. A slide caliper for measuring inside and outside diameters and wall thicknesses, equipped with a vernier scale for measuring fractions of a unit.

versatile. (1) Said of an anther attached to the tip of the filament in such a manner that it can swing freely and thus disperse the pollen; (2) said of a freely moving organ of an animal; example, the toes of some birds which can be moved back and forth.

vertebra (plural, vertebrae). One of the thirty-three bones which make up the spinal column; there are seven cervical, twelve thoracic, five lumbar, five sacral, and four coccygeal vertebrae.

vertebral column. The backbone; the spinal column.

Vertebrata. Craniata; a subclass of Chordata; animals having a skull, spine, brain, and sense organs.

vertebrate paleontology. The study, description, and uses of vertebrate fossils in solving paleobiological and stratigraphic problems.

vertex. (1) The point of a refracting or a reflecting surface at which it is intersected by the axis of the optical system; (2) the top of the skull of vertebrates; (3) the zenith.

vertical. (1) Lying in the direction of gravity; (2) perpendicular to the plane of the horizon.

vertical circle. A great circle on the celestial sphere which passes through the zenith and nadir; it is perpendicular to the horizon, as the zenith and nadir are the poles of the horizon.

vertical intensity. The intensity of the vertical component of the earth's magnetic field at any point.

vertical rays. Those rays of the sun which strike the earth perpendicular to its surface.

vesicle. A small sac or blister in an animal or plant containing a liquid.

vesicula seminalis. Seminal vesicle; a sac in which spermatozoa are stored while they are developing.

vessel. A linear series of water-conducting cells formed in the xylem of angiosperms by the dissolution of the end walls of the cells in the linear row; the lateral walls are thickened and pitted, and there is no cytoplasm in the vessel.

vestige. A useless trace of an organ whose presence in the body indicates possible use in the past.

vestigial. Small or degenerate, but a structure that was better developed or functional at one time.

vestigial organs. Organs that are inadequate in one animal and yet well developed in one of its relatives.

vesuvianite. A multicolored mineral; a complex silicate of calcium and aluminum with fluorine and also varying amounts of boron, iron, lithium, magnesium, manganese, potassium, sodium, and titanium.

viability. The ability to live and grow.

viable. Capable of living and development.

vibraculum. A modified form of individual in the bryozoan colony which protects the entire group against lodging of sessile animals; it is a bristle or filament that moves back and forth, sweeping across the surface of the colony.

vibrating contacter. A device used to make and break contact in cycles; used for converting direct-current signals to alternating-current signals.

vibration. The periodic motion in alternately opposite directions of the particles of an elastic body when its equilibrium has been disturbed; example, the motion of a stretched cord when it is plucked.

vibration, fundamental mode of. The mode of oscillation of a system which has the lowest frequency.

vibration galvanometer. An undamped alternating-current galvanometer in which the natural oscillation frequency of the moving element is equal to the frequency of the alternating current applied to it.

vibration meter. An instrument for measuring the displacement velocity or acceleration of a vibrating body.

vibration, normal mode of. A characteristic distribution of vibration amplitude among the parts of a system, each part of which is vibrating freely at the same frequency.

vibration rotation spectrum. A molecular spectrum in the infrared indicating the vibrational and rotational transitions within a molecule.

vibrational analysis. Separating a molecular spectrum into bands, with the assignment of a definite pair of vibrational quantum numbers to each band and the determination of these two quantum numbers for all bands.

vibrational quantum number. A quantum number, associated with the vibration of the atoms about their mean positions in a molecule; it must be an integer for any permissible stationary state of the vibration.

vibrational specific heat. That part of the specific heat of a substance which results from the energy of internal vibration of the molecules, as distinct from translational motion and rotation.

vibrograph. A device for recording vibrations graphically.

vibrometer. Same as vibration meter.

vibroscope. Same as vibrograph.

vibrotron. A movable-anode triode.

villus (plural, villi). (1) A fingerlike projection on the inner surface of the vertebrate intestine, whose function is absorption; (2) a thin branch projecting from the stem of mosses.

vine. A plant whose stem requires support; it climbs by tendrils or some other means, or creeps on the ground.

vinegar. A dilute (4 to 6%) acetic acid, CH_3COOH; it is obtained by fermentation of fruit juices or destructive distillation of wood; used for salad dressings, pickling, flavoring.

vinyl group. $CH_2{:}CH{-}$.

vinyl resins. Thermoplastic resins obtained by polymerization of a vinyl compound or copolymerization of several monomers, containing vinyl groups; used for plastic tiles, records, protective coatings.

Viperidae. Thick-bodied poisonous mostly viviparous snakes; examples, rattlesnake, copperhead, and water moccasin.

virgin neutrons. Neutrons, from any source, before they collide.

Virgo. Virgin; the sixth sign of the Zodiac; one of the first-named constellations; it contains many nebulae.

virial. The product of the distance between two particles and of the stress resulting from their mutual attraction or repulsion, divided by 2.

virology. The study of viruses.

virtual displacement. The projection, on the original line of action of a force, of the path followed by the point of application of the force during an infinitely small displacement.

virtual entropy. The entropy of a system which is generally a factor independent of temperature and does not contribute to the heat capacity.

virtual height. The apparent height of an ionized layer determined from the time interval between the transmitted signal and the ionospheric echo at vertical incidence.

virtual image. An image from which the light rays appear to diverge; it cannot be photographed or projected.

virtual oscillator. An ideal electric oscillator, consisting of a charged point in harmonic motion.

virtual temperature. The temperature required to maintain the density of the air constant if its water-vapor content is removed.

virtual velocity. That component of the velocity of a particle which is in the direction of a given force in any assumed displacement through the position of equilibrium.

virtual work. The quantity of work done during an infinitely small displacement under the action of either a constant or a variable force.

virus. A submicroscopic agent, the cause of many diseases in plants and animals; its nature is not well known; it may be a living organism or a complex protein molecule.

viscera (singular, viscus). Organs lying more or less freely in the cavities of the body; examples, stomach, intestine, spleen, and liver.

visceral arch. Gill arch; (1) tissue rings between adjacent gill slits in the wall of the pharynx of fish; (2) the gills supported by these arches.

visceral mass. A compact mass of tissue containing some of the internal organs of mollusks; it forms the main part of their body.

visceral skeleton. The portion of the vertebrate skeleton that supports the walls of the pharynx and forms the jaws and hyoid apparatus.

viscerotropic. Having a selective action on the visceral organs, including the liver and spleen; said of certain viruses.

viscidity. A combination of cohesion and viscosity in a liquid which results in its being sticky and capable of being drawn out into fine threads; examples, glue and viscose.

viscometer. Viscosimeter; an instrument for the measurement of viscosity.

viscose process. A method of rayon manufacture; wood pulp or splinters are converted into alkali cellulose by treatment with caustic soda and then changed to cellulose xanthate by the treatment with carbon disulfide; the cellulose xanthate solution is forced through the fine holes of a spinnerette into a bath of dilute sulfuric acid, which coagulates the rayon fibers.

viscosimeter. Same as viscometer.

viscosity. The resistance offered by a fluid to flow; it is due to the combined effect of cohesive and adhesive forces.

viscosity, kinematic. Viscosity divided by density.

viscosity, relative. (1) The ratio of the viscosity of a solution to the viscosity of the solvent; (2) the ratio of the viscosity of a liquid to that of another liquid taken as a standard.

viscosity, specific. The ratio of the difference between the viscosities of the solution and of pure solvent to the viscosity of the pure solvent.

viscosity, unit of. The poise is the metric unit of viscosity; it is equal to 1 dyne-second per square centimeter.

viscous flow. A continuous motion of fluid particles which is always constant at a given point.

visibility. The clearness of the atmosphere; it varies from 0 to 9, that is, from dense fog to excellent visibility which extends to about 30 miles.

visibility factor. For a radiation of a given wave length, the

ratio of the luminous flux of that wave length to the corresponding radiant flux.

visibility meter. An instrument for measuring the clearness of definition with which an object can be seen under given circumstances.

visible spectrum. The array of colors obtained by the dispersion of white light.

vision, persistence of. The ability of the retina to retain the visual sensation for a short period after the stimulus has ceased.

visual acuity. The keenness of sight; the ability to distinguish details; the average individual is able to see two lines that are at an angle of 1' apart.

visual angle. The angle formed by the two lines drawn from the extremities of an object to the center of the eye.

visual axis. The line of vision; the line joining the fixation point of the ocular field of view with the first nodal point.

visual binary. A double star for which the angular separation between the two components is great enough to permit them to be observed separately in a telescope.

visual purple. Rhodopsin; a light-sensitive purple pigment in the retina; it is associated with night vision.

vital functions. Life functions which must continue at all times or the organism will die; examples, circulation and respiration.

vital staining. Staining living organisms without killing them; used for the determination of morphogenetic movements in the embryo.

vitalistic theory. Vitalism; the theory that life and all biological phenomena are due to a vital force, which is distinct from chemical and physical forces.

vitalometer. An instrument which determines the maximum volume of gas that can be expelled from the lungs by a forceful effort following a maximal inspiration.

vitamin. A complex organic nutrient necessary in minute quantities for normal metabolism, regulation of many protoplasmic activities, and prevention of deficiency diseases.

vitamin A. Axerophthol; a very complex unsaturated alcohol; it is necessary for body growth and tissue repair; it occurs in cod-liver oil and other fish-liver oils, milk, eggs, and vegetables; it cures night blindness.

vitamin B₁. Thiamin; a water-soluble vitamin that is essential for the proper functioning of the brain and the nervous system; it prevents or cures beriberi.

vitamin B₂ complex. A mixture containing riboflavin, important for growth; niacin, the antipellagra vitamin; pyridoxin, its deficiency causing a special skin disease; pantothenic acid, used against anemia; folic acid, used for the treatment of pernicious anemia; and vitamin B_{12}, whose absence appears to be the cause of pernicious anemia; this complex occurs in milk, eggs, vegetables, and yeast.

vitamin C. Ascorbic acid; a lactone that prevents scurvy, aids in the growth of teeth, and maintains healthy gums; among its sources are fruits, green vegetables, and potatoes.

vitamin D. A mixture of antirachitic compounds; it helps in teeth and bone building and prevents rickets; it occurs in animal fats, especially fish-liver oils.

vitamin E. Tocopherol; antisterility factor; its sources are cereals and vegetable oils.

vitamin F. Unsaturated fatty acids; needed for the digestion of fats.

vitamin K. A fat-soluble vitamin that aids blood clotting and helps prevent hemorrhages; it occurs in the leaves of green plants.

vitellarium. A yolk-forming organ in flatworms; it is associated with the oviducts.

vitellin. A phosphoprotein in egg yolk.

vitelline. Referring or belonging to the yolk of an egg.

vitelline membrane. A membrane enclosing the fertilized egg and preventing the penetration of additional sperm.

vitrella. A crystal cell between the cornea and the retinula in the compound eye of Arthropoda.

vitreous humor. A transparent, jellylike substance which fills the ball of the eye; it gives shape to the eyeball and supports the retina.

vitrification. The fusion to a glasslike substance.

vitrophyre. A porphyritic glass; a volcanic glass containing distinct crystals of feldspar and other minerals.

vivarium. A glass tank that can be used as an aquarium or a terrarium for raising animals or plants indoors.

vivianite. Hydrous iron phosphate, $Fe_3(PO_4)_2 \cdot 8H_2O$; a blue iron ore.

viviparous. (1) Said of animals whose young are born alive; (2) said of seeds that germinate before they are separated from the plant; (3) producing bulbs instead of flowers.

vocal cord. Folds in the lining of the vertebrate larynx whose vibration produces the voice.

vocal sacs. A pair of air-filled sacs

in the mouth of some frogs, which add resonance and volume to their croak.

Voigt effect. A double refraction occurs when a strong magnetic field is applied to a vapor through which light is passing perpendicularly to the direction of lines.

volatile. Easily changed to a gas or vapor; example, ether.

volatile liquid. A liquid which vaporizes readily.

volatile oil. Essential oil; an odoriferous oil extracted from a flower or fruit.

volatility product. The product of the equilibrium pressure of two or more gases that resulted from the dissociation of a liquid or solid.

volcanic ash. Small fragments of rock and lava, products of a volcanic eruption.

volcanic cone. A hill or mountain consisting of the products of volcanic eruption.

volcanic neck. A part of a volcanic cone that remains after complete erosion has taken place.

volcanism. The formation and effects of volcanoes.

volcano. An opening in the earth's crust from which molten rock, steam, etc., are poured or thrown out; it is usually a cone-shaped hill or mountain, with a crater in the middle; it may be active, dormant or extinct.

volt. A unit of electromotive force; 1,000,000 microvolts; 1,000 millivolts.

volt box. Voltage divider; a series arrangement of fixed resistances; used for the determination of the value of a voltage by measuring a fraction of it.

Volta law. The contact potential difference of two conductors is the same, whether in direct contact or joined by intermediate conductors.

voltage. An electromotive force resulting from a difference in potential between two points; it is measured in volts.

voltage drop. A potential difference.

voltage multiplier. A series arrangement of a condenser charged by rapidly rotating brushes, resulting in a high direct-current voltage.

voltage regulator. A device that varies the output voltage of a generator.

voltaic cell. A device for transforming chemical energy into electrical energy; it consists of a cathode, an anode, and an electrolyte.

voltaic couple. A pair of dissimilar metals in contact, which produce a potential difference.

voltameter. A device for measuring the magnitude of a current by the quantity of metal deposited or a gas set free from an electrolyte by the current in a definite time period.

voltammeter. A combination instrument that can be used as a voltmeter or as an ammeter.

volt-ampere. The practical unit of apparent power in a variable-current circuit; effective volts × effective amperes.

voltmeter. An instrument used for measuring the potential difference in volts between any two points in a circuit diagram.

voltmeter, vacuum-tube. A very-high-input impedance voltmeter, using the power gain of a vacuum tube to operate a suitable meter movement without loading the source of the voltage to be measured.

volt-second. The practical unit of magnetic flux; 10^8 maxwells.

volume. (1) The product of three dimensions: length, width, and height; it is expressed in cubic units; (2) the loudness of a sound.

volume, critical. The volume occupied by a unit mass of a liquid or gas at its critical temperature and critical pressure.

volume, molecular. The volume occupied by a gram molecule of a substance at standard temperature and pressure; the product of the specific volume and molecular weight.

volume, standard. The volume occupied by one gram molecular weight of a gas at 0°C and a pressure of one atmosphere.

volumetric analysis. A method of quantitative chemical analysis, involving the measurement of the volumes of the reacting substances, one of the reactants being a standard solution of known concentration.

voluntary muscles. Striated or striped muscles; muscles that respond to the will.

volva. A hypha sheath surrounding the body of some mushrooms; it breaks open when ripe and may form a cup at the base of the mushroom umbrella.

Volvox. A minute pale-green globular flagellate borderline organism; it occurs in colonies made up of a single layer of hundreds of individual cells grouped into a hollow ball.

vomer. One of a pair of bones of the vertebrate skull; in mammals, it is a thin vertical plate in the posterior part of the nasal septum.

vomerine teeth. Teeth projecting from the bones of the roof of the mouth of the frog; they are used for holding the prey.

vortex. A whirlpool; a portion of a fluid which rotates about an axis, with resulting centrifugal force and reduced pressure at the axis, and which is surrounded by a relatively sta-

tionary portion of the same fluid; it forms a cavity in the center which attracts bodies being in the fluid with great force.

vorticity. A measure of the extent to which the motion of a fluid is rotational.

VTOL (vertical takeoff and landing). Aircraft that combine the speed and range of conventional aircraft with features of the helicopter, being able to take off and land vertically.

V-type engine. An internal-combustion engine in which two rows of cylinders are arranged at an angle, thus forming a V.

vug. A rock cavity lined, but not filled, with mineral matter.

vulcanite. (1) A fine-grained igneous rock; (2) hard rubber; a rubber vulcanized with 25% or more sulfur.

vulcanization. Heating rubber with sulfur or a sulfur compound to improve its physical and chemical properties.

vulcanized fiber. An insulating material obtained by the treatment of paper pulp with zinc chloride; it is also used as an artificial leather.

vulcanized rubber. Cured rubber; a crude rubber whose physical properties have been improved by reaction with sulfur.

W

W. Chemical symbol for tungsten.

Wadsworth mirror. A plane mirror used in certain forms of prism spectrometer.

Wadsworth mounting. A device which operates as a constant-déviation prism.

Wagner ground. Wagner earth; a device for preventing false indications of the detector in alternating-current bridge measurements, due to capacitance effects between the bridge and the ground.

wake. (1) The track of a boat in the water; (2) the track left by a moving body in a fluid; example, the region of the atmosphere behind an aircraft.

Walden law. The limiting equivalent conductance of a solution is inversely proportional to the viscosity coefficient of the solvent, the constant being the same for all solvents.

wall energy. The energy per unit area of the boundary between oppositely oriented ferromagnetic domains.

wandering cells. Cells of blood and connective tissue which actively migrate in vivo; example, macrophages.

warm blooded. Idiothermous; said of animals whose body temperature remains almost constant, regardless of the external temperature and is usually higher than that of the

surroundings.

warm front. A front where warmer air is displacing colder air; it usually brings rain.

warning coloration. Aposematic color; marks or colors which make an insect or other animal conspicuous to its enemies; examples, bee and skunk.

warping. (1) The permanent deformation of wood by humidity and heat; (2) the distortion of a gramophone record during storage; (3) broad bends in the earth's crust which are not as intense as folding.

wash bottle. A laboratory water dispenser, equipped with a two-holed stopper through which two glass tubes are inserted; by blowing air through one of the tubes the water is forced out in a thin uniform stream from the other tube.

washing soda. Sodium carbonate, $Na_2CO_3 \cdot 10H_2O$; used as a water softener.

water. A compound of hydrogen and oxygen, H_2O; one cubic foot of water at 4°C weighs 62.5 pounds; it covers a large portion of the earth's surface; water of 4°C has the highest density and sinks below the surface; that is why only the surface layer of rivers and lakes freezes in winter.

water bath. A metal container with removable concentric rings serving as its cover; it is filled with water and used for heating substances when the temperature may not exceed 212°F.

water calorimeter. A calorimeter which measures the quantity of heat by the change in the temperature of a known volume of water.

water conditioning. All processes used in treating water to remove undesirable impurities or to reduce them to specific tolerances.

water, conductivity. Water, prepared by repeated distillations, which is pure and can be used in electrical-conductivity measurements of aqueous solutions.

water cycle. The never-ending round trip of water: evaporating from the surface of the oceans, lakes, streams, etc., as water vapor into the atmosphere, forming clouds and condensing to rain, and returning into lakes, oceans, etc.

water dip net. A net used for aquatic collecting.

water, distilled. Pure water obtained by distillation; used in the laboratory; it is not suitable for drinking.

water equivalent. The mass of water which would have the same thermal capacity as a given body; the product of the mass of a body and its specific heat.

water erosion. The dissolving of

substances by water from the soil and rocks as well as the transportation of soil and rock particles by water.

water gap. A notch formed in the ridges of hills as a river cuts across at right angles; example, Delaware Water Gap.

water gas. A mixture of hydrogen and carbon monoxide made by passing steam over hot coke.

water glass. A dense solution of sodium silicate in water; used as an adhesive and filler.

water head. A measure of water pressure; the vertical distance between the level of the water at the place in question and the highest level of the water in the system.

water of constitution. The portion of water of crystallization, which cannot be removed without disrupting the molecules.

water of crystallization. A definite number of water molecules that combined with a salt to form a hydrate; examples, hydrated potassium carbonate, $K_2CO_3 \cdot 2H_2O$ and blue vitriol, $CuSO_4 \cdot 5H_2O$.

water of hydration. The chemically combined water that forms a hydrate.

water, permanently hard. A water that remains hard after boiling; it contains calcium and magnesium chloride and sulfate.

water pressure. (1) The force of water due to its weight; (2) the pressure of water caused by mechanical means.

water softener. A chemical used for removing the hardness from water; examples, borax and sodium carbonate.

water still. A water-distillation apparatus.

water table. The level below which a porous mantle rock is saturated with water.

water, temporarily hard. A water that can be softened by boiling; it contains calcium and magnesium bicarbonate.

water turbine. A device for changing the potential energy of water into the kinetic energy of a rotating shaft; it consists of curved vanes on the circumference of a wheel against which the water current impinges.

water vapor. The gaseous state of water.

water vascular system. A tubular system of Echinodermata through which the sea water is circulated; it is formed from the coelom and is associated chiefly with locomotion, respiration, and the securing of food.

waterfall. The plunge of a stream over a high steep ridge of rock.

water-in-oil emulsion. An emulsion in which oil is the external phase and water the internal phase.

watershed. A drainage area; the

region or area contributing to the supply of a river or lake.

waterspout. A tornado moving over a body of water.

watt. The unit of power, 10^7 ergs per second; one volt-ampere; one joule work per second; about 10,200 gram-centimeters per second; 1/746 horsepower.

wattage. The amount of electrical power, measured in watts.

watt-hour. A unit of electrical energy; one watt of power acting for one hour; 3.6×10^{10} ergs.

watt-hour meter. Energy meter; an instrument for measuring the energy of an electric circuit in kilowatt-hours.

wattmeter. An instrument for measuring electric power in watts; a combination of a volt-meter and an ammeter.

wattmeter, astatic. An electro-dynamic wattmeter designed to be insensitive to uniform external magnetic fields.

wattmeter, electrodynamic. An electrodynameter whose fixed or current coil is in series with the load and its movable or voltage coil connected across the load.

wattmeter, thermocouple. A matched-pair double thermocouple wattmeter, one junction being heated by the load voltage and the other by the load current.

wave. (1) A set of disturbances which repeat themselves regularly and advance at a regular rate; (2) a row of vibrating particles.

wave, compressional. A wave in an elastic medium which causes a decrease in volume.

wave, continuous. (1) A wave whose successive oscillations are identical under steady-state conditions; (2) an undamped radio wave which is received without changes in its amplitude or intensity.

wave crest. The position of maximum positive disturbance of a progressive wave.

wave, damped. An electric wave which decreases in amplitude with time, due to absorption of energy by the medium.

wave, direct. A wave which travels on a straight path from the transmission source to the point of reception, without reflection or refraction.

wave distortion. Changes in the form of the sky wave in passing through the twilight zone.

wave, elastic. A mechanical wave which propagates in an elastic medium.

wave frequency. The rate of vibration of a wave.

wave front. The locus of all points in the path of a wave motion which have the same phase; the direction of propagation is perpendicular to the wave front.

wave group. The resultant of two or more wave trains of different

frequency traversing the same path.

wave guide. A hollow metal conductor through which very short waves are transmitted; used in radar.

wave length. The distance from the crest of one wave to the crest of the next.

wave meter. A calibrated electric resonator of variable frequency; used for measuring electric oscillation or wave frequencies.

wave motion. The propagation of a periodic disturbance carrying energy.

wave number. The number of waves in unit length.

wave packet. A wave disturbance which is confined to a limited volume of space.

wave period. The time interval between two successive maximum disturbances of a harmonic wave.

wave, refracted. That part of an incident wave which travels from one medium into another.

wave, spherical. A wave whose equiphase surfaces form a family of concentric spheres.

wave, standing. A wave disturbance which does not progress since there is a superposition of two waves traveling in opposite directions, having identical amplitudes and frequencies.

wave, surface. (1) A wave of distortion on the free surface separating two fluid phases; (2) ground wave; an electromagnetic wave component traveling parallel to the earth's surface.

wave, tidal. A wave in the sea or the atmosphere induced by gravitational or thermal effects of the moon or sun.

wave train. The series of waves produced by a vibrating body.

wave, transverse. A wave in which the vibration of the particles is perpendicular to the direction of propagation.

wave trough. A point of minimum value of the disturbance in a progressive wave; the opposite of wave crest.

waveband. A group of frequencies set aside by law for a specific purpose or service; examples, police band, broadcast band, and amateur band.

wave-cut bench. A tablelike surface of rock formed by the errosive effect of waves.

wave-form picture. A diagram showing the changes in direct and alternating current flow.

wax. An amorphous plastic mass of mineral, vegetable, animal or synthetic origin; commonly, it is a fatty acid ester of a higher fatty alcohol or a mixture of such esters.

waxing. An increase in area; example, waxing of the moon.

weak acid. An acid that ionizes

only to a slight degree in water; example, oxalic acid, COOH·COOH.

weak base. A base that ionizes only slightly in an aqueous solution.

weather. The meteorological condition of the atmosphere.

weather factors. The conditions which make up the weather, such as precipitation, temperature, humidity, wind velocity and direction, conditions of the sky, and atmospheric pressure.

weather map. Synoptic chart; a map indicating the weather factors observed at weather stations for a given hour of the day; weather forecasts are based on weather maps.

weather vane. A weathercock; a device that indicates the direction from which the wind is blowing.

weather zone. A layer of rock which has decayed and broken up into pieces.

weathering. The decomposition or disintegration of parts of the lithosphere due to exposure to the atmosphere, heat, wind, frost, snow and rain.

weathering of glass. A chemical attack, due to exposure to the atmosphere, which changes the surface of glass.

weber. A unit of magnetic flux; 10^8 maxwells.

wedge. A simple machine that consists of two inclined planes, placed back to back, in which the effort exerted on the head overcomes the resistance at the sides.

wedge photometer. A photometer in which the intensity of the light from one source or both sources to be compared is varied by means of a wedge of absorbing material pushed into the beam until the requisite thickness has been interposed.

weed. (1) A plant growing where it is not wanted; (2) an undesirable plant growing among cultivated crop plants.

weight. A measure of the gravitational force exerted by the earth on a body on its surface; its value varies at different points of the earth, wheras that of the mass remains constant.

weight, atomic. The average relative weight of the atoms of the naturally occuring mixture of isotopes of an element, based on the average weight of the atoms of the naturally occurring mixture of oxygen isotopes as 16.000.

weight, combining. Same as equivalent weight.

weight, equivalent. That weight of an element which combines with or replaces 1 part of hydrogen or 8 parts of oxygen; the atomic weight of an element divided by its valence.

weight, formula. The sum of the atomic weights in the formula of an ionic compound; example, Na^+Cl^-.

weight, gram-atomic. The atomic weight of an element expressed in grams.

weight, gram-equivalent. The equivalent weight of a substance expressed in grams.

weight, gram-molecular. The molecular weight of a substance expressed in grams.

weight, molecular. The weight of a molecule of a substance, based on the atomic weight of oxygen taken for 16.000.

weightlessness. The absence of gravitational pull on an object; absolute weightlessness occurs when an object, deprived of support, falls freely in a vacuum or when a body moves at a speed capable of counteracting the gravitational attraction of any other body upon it.

weir. A dam or bulkhead over which water flows or a bulkhead containing a notch through which water flows.

Welsbach mantle. A gaslight mantle, consisting of a gauze of thorium and cerium oxides; the heat derived from the combustion of the gas makes the mantle incandescent and is thus converted into light energy.

wernerite. Scapolite; a tetragonal mineral; a silicate of calcium and aluminum which contains some soda and chlorine.

Weston cell. A cadmium cell; a primary cell used as a standard of electromotive force.

Westphal balance. A balance for determining the density of liquids by comparing the loss in weight of a bob immersed in the liquid and in water at the same temperature.

wet-and-dry-bulb hygrometer. An instrument for determining the relative humidity of the atmosphere; it consists of two identical thermometers, the bulb of one of which is kept wet with water supplied by a wick surrounding it; the lowering of the temperature by evaporation depends on the relative humidity of the air.

wetting agent. A substance that lowers the surface tension of a liquid, causing it to spread out better and to wet the substance with which it is in contact; example, soap.

Wheatstone bridge. A two-branched circuit, each containing two resistances in series; used for the measurement of resistance.

wheel and axle. A simple machine consisting of a wheel or crank mounted on an axle, both of which move around the same axis; used for changing the direction of and/or multiplying the force.

wheel animalcules. Rotifera; microscopic multicellular aquatic animals; the front end of their body is a retractable disc with one or two rows of cilia and the rear end is a tail.

wheel control. The wheel of a control column; a device used for controlling the movements of an aircraft.

whip. The first-year growth of a tree from a bud or graft.

whip grafting. Making a slit in the direction of grain in both the scion and the stock and inserting one of the two sections thus formed on each into the slit of the other.

whirlwind. A small cyclonic whirl of air, usually not more than a few hundred feet high and tens of feet in diameter.

white blood corpuscles. Leucocytes; colorless irregularly-shaped nucleated ameboid cells in the blood serum.

white fibrous tissue. Strong, pliable white fibers arranged in wavy bundles.

white gold. A gold-base alloy containing some palladium, nickel and zinc; used for jewelry.

white lead. Basic lead carbonate, $Pb(OH)_2 \cdot 2PbCO_3$; a white powder; used as a pigment in paint.

white light. A light consisting of all colors of the visible spectrum in proper proportions.

white matter. The fibers of nerve cells in the brain and spinal cord which are surrounded by a fatty sheath.

white object. An object which reflects all wave lengths of light with equal intensity so that it appears colorless.

white radiation. General radiation; any radiation which produces a continuous spectrum.

whole mount. An entire organism or part of an organism, prepared by fixation, staining, dehydration, and clearing, but not cut into sections by a microtome; used for microscopic examination.

whorl. (1) A circle of flower parts or of leaves; (2) a turn of a spiral shell.

whorled. Referring to a bud or leaf arrangement in which there are three or more buds or leaves at a node.

Wiedemann law. The molar susceptibility of a substance in solution is independent of its concentration.

Wiedemann-Franz law. The ratio of the thermal conductivity to the electrical conductivity is the same at a given temperature for all metals and is proportional to the absolute temperature.

wiggler. The larva of a mosquito.

wild type. A phenotype which is characteristic of the majority of individuals of a species in natural conditions.

wildlife. The wild animals of a

region.

willemite. White or colored mineral; zinc orthosilicate, Zn_2SiO_4; an ore of zinc.

Wilson cloud chamber. An apparatus for making visible the path of nuclear particles.

wilting. A condition of plants in which the cells lose their turgidity, and leaves, young stems, etc., droop; it is due to excessive water loss over water absorption.

Wimhurst static machine. A device consisting of two discs of insulating material rotated in opposite direction and contact brushes made of metal; it generates electricity by friction and stores it at fairly high potentials.

wind. A natural air current resulting from pressure differences.

wind erosion. The wearing away and transportation of soil and rock fragments by wind.

wind gap. A gap in a mountain ridge in which no stream flows.

wind indicator. A device that indicates the direction and velocity of surface wind; erected at airfields.

wind pollination. Anemophily; the transfer of pollen from one plant to another by the wind.

wind tunnel. An aircraft testing apparatus, producing an artificial wind or air stream, in which models are placed for investigating the air flow about them and the aerodynamic forces exerted on them.

wind vane. A device which shows the direction of the wind.

windpipe. Trachea; a passage from the larynx to the lungs in the respiratory system of air-breathing vertebrates.

wind-shift line. Squall line; cold front; the boundary between cold and warm winds.

windward. In the direction of the wind.

wing. (1) A broad thin appendage used to support an animal in the air, either through its resistance to air currents or by muscular movement against the air; (2) a lateral petal of a legume type of flower; (3) a wing-shaped structural unit; example, an airplane wing.

wing top. A winglike metal piece placed on top of a Bunsen burner to broaden and flatten the flame for glass bending.

winter egg. A thick-shelled egg produced by some invertebrates, usually in the fall; it passes through winter before hatching; similar eggs may be produced at the beginning of other unfavorable periods, such as a period of drought.

winter monsoons. Cold surface winds moving out from Asia toward the surrounding sea.

winterizing. Making a fatty oil resistant to solidification at low

temperatures by removing some of its higher-melting glycerides.

witches' broom. Broomlike malformations on woody plants caused by ascomycetes and rusts.

Wolffian duct. A vertebrate kidney duct; there is one on each side.

wolfram. Tungsten; a corrosion-resistant metal; chemical symbol W; atomic number 74; used as a filament in light bulbs, for alloying and tools.

wolframite. A dark-gray mineral; a tungstate of iron and manganese, $Fe \cdot Mn \cdot WO_4$; an ore of tungsten.

Wollaston prism. Two equal right-angled prisms united along their long faces; one of them transmits light along the optic axis and the other, perpendicularly to the optic axis; it produces plane-polarized light and is used in ultraviolet spectroscopy.

wood. The solid part of a woody stem between the pith and the cambium; it consists of xylem.

wood alcohol. Methyl alcohol, CH_3OH; a colorless toxic liquid; used as a solvent, antifreeze, denaturant.

wood charcoal. A coal prepared from wood by destructive distillation, that is, heating without air.

word equation. A brief statement which identifies the reactants entering into a chemical reaction and the products formed.

work. The product of a force and the distance the force moves a body; work is done whenever a body is moved, or its motion stopped by a force; it is usually measured in foot-pounds or ergs.

workers. (1) Sterile female bees who do all the work of the hive except reproduction; (2) similar individuals among any social insects.

working substance. The fluid under pressure that operates some movable part in thermodynamic processes.

worm. An invertebrate having a flat or cylindrical body which in some cases is composed of segments; commonly, it has no appendages; examples, roundworm and flatworm.

worm gear. A combination of a screw and a helical gear; used for connecting shafts. plane.

Wright's stain. A stain used for routine blood films.

wrist. The attachment of the forearm to the hand; it contains a group of small carpal bones between the radius and ulna of the arm and the metacarpals of the hand.

X

X and Y chromosomes. Chromosomes whose principal function is the determination of sex.

X chromosomes. Chromosomes that play a part in determining sex and in the inheritance of sex-linked traits, such as hemophilia.

x unit. A unit of wave length; 10^{-11} centimeter; it is used mainly for expressing the wave lengths of x-rays.

xanthates. Salts of xanthic acid of the general formula ROCSSH; used in the manufacture of viscose rayon.

xanthophyll. A carotene derivative; a yellow pigment found in chloroplasts and in some autumn leaves.

Xe. Chemical symbol for xenon.

xenia. The direct effect of pollen on the seed in cross pollination, hybrid characteristics appearing in the same generation.

xenoblast. A crystal in a metamorphic rock which is not bounded by its own crystal faces, but adjacent crystals impressed their shape on it.

xenocryst. A crystal, usually corroded, which is foreign to the magma from which the igneous rock in which it occurs has crystallized.

xenolith. A fragment or a foreign rock included in an igneous mass.

xenon. A colorless, inert gas; chemical symbol Xe; atomic number 54.

xeromorphy. The protection of a plant against an excessive loss of water by hair, cuticles, etc.; example, xerophytes.

xerophytes. Plants adapted to survive in a very dry environment; example, cactus.

xerosere. A sere that begins on dry land.

x-ray analysis. A method of determining the crystal structure by x-ray diffraction patterns.

x-ray hardness. The penetrating power of x-rays which is an inverse function of the wave length.

x-ray spectrograph. An apparatus for recording x-ray diffraction patterns.

x-ray spectrometer. An instrument for measuring the wave lengths of x-rays by means of their reflection by crystals.

x-ray spectrum. A spectrum obtained by bombarding the chemical elements with cathode rays; they emit x-rays of a characteristic frequency which depends on the atomic number.

x-ray structure. The atomic crystal structure of substances as determined by x-ray diffraction patterns.

x-ray tube. A vacuum tube for producing x-rays by shooting a stream of high-speed electrons at a target or anticathode in their path.

x-rays. A radiation of very short wave lengths which has the power of penetrating matter which is opaque to ordinary light.

x-rays, characteristic. Secondary x-rays characteristic of the element from which they are scattered.

x-rays, heterogeneous. X-rays which have a considerable number of frequencies.

x-rays, homogeneous. X-rays which have a single frequency or a narrow band of frequencies.

xylan. A complex polysaccharide which occurs closely associated with cellulose in plants.

xylem. A woody supporting tissue of plants containing tubes that transport liquid to and up the stem.

xylene. Dimethylbenzene, C_6H_4-$(CH_3)_2$; a liquid resembling toluene; it occurs in coal tar; used as a solvent.

Y

Y. Chemical symbol for yttrium.

Y chromosome. A chromosome that plays a part in determining the sex of an individual; the male chromosome.

Yarkovsky effect. A force acting on a body rotating around the sun, produced by uneven radiation due to a phase lag in the surface temperature; the body spirals outward when the spin and orbital angular momentum are parallel.

yaw. The deviation of an airplane by angular motion around its vertical axis.

Yb. Chemical symbol for ytterbium.

yd. Abbreviation of yard.

year. The longest natural unit of time.

yeasts. One-celled microorganisms which reproduce by budding; fungi which cause alcoholic fermentation.

yellow fibers. Elastic fibers which make the connective tissues flexible.

yellow marrow. A marrow containing 95% fat, found in long bones.

yield point. The stress at which there is a sudden substantial plastic deformation at constant load; it is characteristic of iron and annealed steels.

ylem. A hypothetical primordial substance which is assumed to be the source of chemical elements.

yolk. The food stored in an egg or sac to be used by a developing embryo.

yolk gland. Vitellarium; a yolk-secreting gland.

yolk sac. An accessory embryonic

membrane found in vertebrates as an envelope around the yolk of the egg; it is connected with the mid-gut of the embryo and is used for absorption of nourishment.

Young-Helmholtz color-vision theory. The theory that the retina of the eye is provided with three sets of nerves, each of which is sensitive to one of the three primary colors.

Young's construction. A graphical method of tracing a ray of light through a spherical boundary between media of different refractive indices.

Young's modulus. The ratio of the tensile stress per unit cross section in a stretched elastic solid to the change in length per unit length.

ytterbium. A rare metallic element; chemical symbol Yb; atomic number 70.

yttrium. A rare-earth metal; chemical symbol Y; atomic number 39.

yucca. A member of the lily family, having stiff pointed leaves and a tall thickened flower stalk.

Z

Zeeman effect. When a substance which emits a line spectrum is placed in a strong magnetic field, the single lines are split up into groups of closely spaced lines; deductions concerning the atomic structure can be made from the separation of the lines in these groups.

Zener current. The current induced in a semiconductor in a very strong electric field, which is sufficient to excite an electron directly from the valence band to the conduction band.

Zener voltage. The electric field needed to excite the Zener current; of the order of 1 volt per unit cell, or 10^7 volts per centimeter.

zenith. The point on the celestial sphere directly overhead; one of the poles of the horizon.

zenith distance. The angular distance of a heavenly body from the zenith (90° minus altitude).

zeolite. A natural hydrated silicate of aluminum and sodium, potassium, barium, and calcium; used for softening hard water by the base-exchange method.

zeolite process. A method of softening water by passing it through a zeolite filter.

zero beat. A point where an oscillating receiver is adjusted to resonance with an incoming signal; at this point no carrier whistle is heard.

zero branch. A series of lines in an absorption band of a molecular spectrum, in the formation

of any one of which there is no change in the rotational quantum number.

zero line. A wave length in an absorption band of a molecular spectrum, which corresponds to a gap in the sequence of absorption lines and which marks an origin or axis of the band as a whole.

zero-field emission. The thermionic emission from a hot conductor surrounded by a region of uniform electric potential.

zero-point energy. The energy an atom or molecule of a substance would have at 0°K, that is, 0° absolute temperature; this temperature has not been attained.

zero-point entropy. According to the third law of thermodynamics, the entropy of a system in equilibrium at absolute zero must be zero.

zero-valent. Not entering into reaction with other elements; example, inert gases.

zinc. A bluish-white corrosion-resistant metal; chemical symbol Zn; atomic number 30; used for rustproofing iron.

zinc blende. Sphalerite; zinc sulfide, ZnS; a yellowish-brown mineral; an ore of zinc.

zinc chloride. White deliquescent crystals; $ZnCl_2$; used as a mordant, in electroplating.

zinc oxide. White amorphous powder; ZnO; used as a pigment.

zinc sulfide. White granules; ZnS; used as a filler and accelerator in rubber, as a pigment.

zinc-copper couple. Metallic zinc coated with a thin film of copper by immersing it in a copper sulfate solution; used as a reducing agent.

zincite. Red zinc ore; zinc oxide, ZnO; an important source of zinc.

zircon. A colorless or yellow to brown mineral; zirconium silicate, $ZnSiO_4$; used as a gem.

zirconium. A silver-gray metal; chemical symbol Zr; atomic number 40; used in alloys as a deoxidizer.

Zn. Chemical symbol for zinc.

Zodiac. An about 18° wide imaginary celestial belt, with the ecliptic as its median line, which includes the paths of the sun, moon, and principal planets.

Zodiac, signs of. The twelve original divisions of the Zodiac named Aries, Taurus, Gemini, Cancer, Leo, Virgo, Libra, Scorpio, Sagittarius, Capricornus, Aquarius, and Pisces.

zodiacal light. A faint glow which appears extending along the ecliptic or Zodiac from the vicinity of the sun; it is best observed in the western sky in the spring after the sunset twilight completely disappears, or in the eastern sky in the fall

just before the morning twilight appears.

zona pellucida. A transparent elastic membrane around the mammalian egg, which disappears before implantation.

zonal aberration. The spherical or monochromatic aberration of a lens of wide aperture due to the fact that the refracting power is different for different zones concentric to the axis.

zone. (1) A given area; example, a life zone; (2) a belt of crystal faces extending around a crystal, the planes of which form a prismatic surface; (3) a portion of the surface of a sphere included between two parallel circles or bounded by one circle.

zone axis. A straight line through the origin or center of a crystal which is parallel to all faces of a definite zone.

zone, interfacial. The boundary area between two phases, consisting of the boundary particles of each phase.

zone leveling. The passage of one or more molten zones along a semiconductor for the purpose of uniformly distributing impurities throughout a material.

zone of a crystal. A set of faces of a crystal which meet in a series of edges, all of which are parallel to the zone axis, a line passing through the center of the crystal.

zone of fracture. The region of the earth's crust in which deformation may occur by fracture.

zone plate. A transparent screen having photographed on it a series of concentric opaque rings corresponding to alternate half-period elements of light waves; placed in a beam of light, it shows similar effects to those of a converging lens.

Zoochlorelia. Green algae that live in the tissues of various animals, such as flatworms, coelenterates, sponges, and one-celled species, in symbiosis.

zooecium. The body wall of the individual in a colony of Bryozoa; it acts as a sheath into which the polypide can retract when it is disturbed.

zoogeography. Chorology; the distribution of animals on the surface of the earth.

zooid. One member of a colony of animals; example, polyp.

zoologist. A biologist who specializes in the study of animals.

zoology. The study of animals, their genetics and biology.

zooplankton. Animals floating in the waters on the earth's surface.

zoosporangium. A cell in which zoospores are formed.

zoospore. (1) A motile spore or reproductive cell which can swim; it is asexual and is formed from the protoplast of the cell; (2) a germ of Protozoa resulting from sporulation.

Zr. Chemical symbol for zirconium.

zwitterion. An ion carrying both positive and negative charges, which thus constitutes an electrically neutral molecule with a dipole moment and can react with both acids and bases.

zygomatic arch. Zygoma; a narrow bridge of bone extending, in the mammalian skull, from in front of the ear to the cheekbone, below the temple.

zygospore. A thick-walled resting cell which forms around the zygote after conjugation.

zygote. A single cell resulting from the fusion of gametes; a fertilized egg.

zygotene. A stage in meiosis.

zymase. An enzyme secreted by yeast; it changes sugar to alcohol.

zymogen. The inactive form of an enzyme.

WIND CHILL TABLE

The chilling effect of low temperatures on exposed flesh increases in ratio to wind velocity. A temperature in conjunction with wind feels colder than that same temperature with no wind. For example, a temperature of 10° F with a 20 mph wind has a cooling effect equal to −25° F with no wind; or the chill factor of 0° F with a 35 mph wind would be that of −51° minus wind. Wind speeds greater than 40 mph have little additional chilling effect. The following table gives temperature equivalents of specific degrees of cold plus wind.

Equivalent Temperature

(degrees Fahrenheit)

Wind Speed (mph)																
0	40	35	30	25	20	15	10	5	0	−5	−10	−15	−20	−25	−30	−35	−40
5	38	32	28	21	16	12	6	1	−6	−10	−15	−20	−26	−31	−36	−41	−47
10	27	21	16	10	3	−3	−9	−12	−21	−27	−32	−39	−46	−52	−58	−64	−70
15	22	15	10	2	−5	−11	−18	−26	−34	−40	−45	−51	−59	−65	−71	−78	−85
20	18	11	4	−3	−10	−17	−25	−32	−40	−46	−52	−60	−68	−75	−81	−88	−96
25	15	7	0	−7	−15	−22	−29	−37	−44	−51	−59	−67	−74	−81	−87	−95	−104
30	12	5	−2	−11	−18	−26	−33	−40	−48	−56	−63	−70	−78	−86	−94	−101	−109
35	10	3	−4	−13	−20	−28	−35	−43	−51	−59	−66	−73	−82	−90	−98	−105	−113
40	9	2	−5	−14	−21	−29	−37	−45	−53	−61	−69	−76	−86	−93	−101	−109	−116

TABLE OF SQUARES, CUBES, SQUARE ROOTS, AND CUBE ROOTS

No.	Square	Cube	Square Root	Cube Root	No.	Square	Cube	Square Root	Cube Root
1	1	1	1.000	1.000	51	2,601	132,651	7.141	3.708
2	4	8	1.414	1.260	52	2,704	140,608	7.211	3.732
3	9	27	1.732	1.442	53	2,809	148,877	7.280	3.756
4	16	64	2.000	1.587	54	2,916	157,464	7.348	3.780
5	25	125	2.236	1.710	55	3,025	166,375	7.416	3.803
6	36	216	2.449	1.817	56	3,136	175,616	7.483	3.826
7	49	343	2.646	1.913	57	3,249	185,193	7.550	3.848
8	64	512	2.828	2.000	58	3,364	195,112	7.616	3.871
9	81	729	3.000	2.080	59	3,481	205,379	7.681	3.893
10	100	1,000	3.162	2.154	60	3,600	216,000	7.746	3.915
11	121	1,331	3.317	2.224	61	3,721	226,981	7.810	3.936
12	144	1,728	3.464	2.289	62	3,844	238,328	7.874	3.958
13	169	2,197	3.606	2.351	63	3,969	250,047	7.937	3.979
14	196	2,744	3.742	2.410	64	4,096	262,144	8.000	4.000
15	225	3,375	3.873	2.466	65	4,225	274,625	8.062	4.021
16	256	4,096	4.000	2.520	66	4,356	287,496	8.124	4.041
17	289	4,913	4.123	2.571	67	4,489	300,763	8.185	4.061
18	324	5,832	4.243	2.621	68	4,624	314,432	8.246	4.082
19	361	6,859	4.359	2.668	69	4,761	328,509	8.307	4.101
20	400	8,000	4.472	2.714	70	4,900	343,000	8.367	4.121
21	441	9,261	4.583	2.759	71	5,041	357,911	8.426	4.141
22	484	10,648	4.690	2.802	72	5,184	373,248	8.485	4.160
23	529	12,167	4.796	2.844	73	5,329	389,017	8.544	4.179
24	576	13,824	4.899	2.884	74	5,476	405,224	8.602	4.198
25	625	15,625	5.000	2.924	75	5,625	421,875	8.660	4.217
26	676	17,576	5.099	2.962	76	5,776	438,976	8.718	4.236
27	729	19,683	5.196	3.000	77	5,929	456,533	8.775	4.254
28	784	21,952	5.292	3.037	78	6,084	474,552	8.832	4.273
29	841	24,389	5.385	3.072	79	6,241	493,039	8.888	4.291
30	900	27,000	5.477	3.107	80	6,400	512,000	8.944	4.309
31	961	29,791	5.568	3.141	81	6,561	531,441	9.000	4.327
32	1,024	32,768	5.657	3.175	82	6,724	551,368	9.055	4.344
33	1,089	35,937	5.745	3.208	83	6,889	571,787	9.110	4.362
34	1,156	39,304	5.831	3.240	84	7,056	592,704	9.165	4.379
35	1,225	42,875	5.916	3.271	85	7,225	614,125	9.219	4.397
36	1,296	46,656	6.000	3.302	86	7,396	636,056	9.274	4.414
37	1,369	50,653	6.083	3.332	87	7,569	658,503	9.327	4.431
38	1,444	54,872	6.164	3.362	88	7,744	681,472	9.381	4.448
39	1,521	59,319	6.245	3.391	89	7,921	704,969	9.434	4.465
40	1,600	64,000	6.325	3.420	90	8,100	729,000	9.487	4.481
41	1,681	68,921	6.403	3.448	91	8,281	753,571	9.539	4.498
42	1,764	74,088	6.481	3.476	92	8,464	778,688	9.592	4.514
43	1,849	79,507	6.557	3.503	93	8,649	804,357	9.644	4.531
44	1,936	85,184	6.633	3.530	94	8,836	830,584	9.695	4.547
45	2,025	91,125	6.708	3.557	95	9,025	857,375	9.747	4.563
46	2,116	97,336	6.782	3.583	96	9,216	884,736	9.798	4.579
47	2,209	103,823	6.856	3.609	97	9,409	912,673	9.849	4.595
48	2,304	110,592	6.928	3.634	98	9,604	941,192	9.899	4.610
49	2,401	117,649	7.000	3.659	99	9,801	970,299	9.950	4.626
50	2,500	125,000	7.071	3.684	100	10,000	1,000,000	10.000	4.642

AN ENVIRONMENTAL GLOSSARY

by ROBERT F. KUNZ

The following glossary is intended as a guide to some of the more common terms appearing in our news media, related to the current crisis concerning the quality of our environment.

Airshed: A common air supply demarcated by arbitrary or convenient borders, such as an urban area.

Allowable release levels: Levels of nuclear radiation that are officially accepted as harmless to humans. Some scientists claim there is no radiation level below which genetic damage, cancer, or shortening of life does not occur.

Aquifers: Underground water-bearing rock strata that supply most of our well water.

Biodegraduable: Organic substance that is quickly broken down by normal environmental processes.

Biological magnification: The process whereby an organism can build up and store quantities of a substance vastly in excess of the average concentration in its' environment. For example, oysters can extract pesticides to 80,000 times the amount in the water around them.

Biosphere: That envelope made up of the Earth's waters, land crust, and atmosphere where all organisms, including man, live.

Biota: All living organisms, both plant and animal, of a region or period.

BOD: The biological oxygen demand of aquatic organisms for survival.

Carcinogen: A substance capable of provoking cancer.

Chlorinated hydrocarbons: Insecticides that last for years or decades, travel around the globe in the air and water, and accumulate in hazardous concentrations in the tissues of non-target animals. Examples are: DDT, DDD, Endrin, TDE, Aldrin, Dieldrin, Toxaphene, Heptachlor, and Lindane (BH-C).

Coliform bacteria: Microscopic one-celled organisms that are always but not exclusively present in human intestines.

Compost: A mixing of garbage and degradable trash with soil in a pile. Bacteria in the soil cause decomposition and thereby return desirable organic material back to nature.

Decibel: The unit of measuring the intensity of sound. Zero on the decibel scale is the slightest sound that can be heard by humans—rustling leaves, breathing. The scale: EARDRUM RUPTURES (140 decibels—jet taking off); DEAFENING (100 decibels—thunder, car horn at three feet, loud motorcycle, loud power lawn mower); VERY LOUD (eighty decibels—portable sander, food blender; continued exposure brings about loss of hearing, impossible to use phone); LOUD (sixty decibels—city playground, average restaurant or living room); FAINT (twenty decibels—courtroom or classroom, private office, a whisper at five feet).

Decomposers: Living plants and animals, chiefly fungi and bacteria, that live by extracting energy from the tissues of dead plants and animals.

Demography: The study of populations—births, deaths, marriages, etc.—by means of statistics.

Ecocide: A substance which enters, permeates, and kills an entire system, be that system an insect pest, a lake, or a man-environment community.

Ecosystem: An integrated unit or "system" in nature, sufficient unto itself, to be studied as a separate entity—e.g., a rotting log in the forest, a coral atoll, a continent, or the Earth with all its biota.

Effluent: A discharge from an exit that is relatively self-contained, such as an industrial smokestack, nuclear power plant thermal plume, or a sewage treatment plant; generally carrying pollutants.

Energy cycle: The process by which the energy of the sun is passed from one living organism to another or is stored, as in coal or oil.

Environment: All that surrounds a designated ecosystem.

Estuary: A coastal area of high marine productivity where fresh and salt waters mingle, including the associated tidal rivers, marshes, flats, lagoons, bays, and shallow sounds.

Eutrophication: An aging process that occurs to aquatic ecosystems naturally over a long period of time. Nutrients entering the water support an increasingly dense growth of aquatic life, which depletes the oxygen supply. In time, the body of water progresses from lake or pond to swamp, marsh, and meadow. Eutrophication can be accelerated by excessive nutrient enrichment resulting from man-made fertilizers, detergents, and human and animal wastes.

Green revolution: The hoped-for arithmetical increase in agricultural production that would provide food for the geometrically increasing human population.

Greenhouse effect: The effect of pollution in the air that absorb infrared or heat rays and so prevent the radiation back into space of a certain fraction of the energy Earth receives from the sun.

Herbicide: A kind of chemical that injures or kills plant life by interfering with normal growth.

Hydrology: The study of water in all its forms and manifestations in the biosphere.

Inversion: An atmospheric condition occurring when a layer of cool air sits on a layer of hot air and prevents the warmer air from rising. If the stagnant hot air is heavily polluted, it becomes increasingly harmful to life.

Nitrogen fixation: The process whereby bacteria and other soil microorganisms convert atmospheric nitrogen into nitrates, which become available to growing plants.

Non-renewable resources: Resources that once used (or misused) cannot renew themselves. For example: coal, oil.

Particulates: Dust and soot in the air.

Phosphates: Salts and esters of phosphoric acid, containing phosphorus.

Photosynthesis: The photochemical process by which the energy in light, acting in presence of a catalyst—such as the pigment chlorophyll—converts atmospheric carbon dioxide, water, and inorganic salts into tissue. The fundamental food-making process in green plants on which all life on Earth directly or indirectly depends.

Plankton: The microscopic floating plant and animal organisms of lakes, rivers, and oceans. Basic organisms in the food chains leading to the large fishes and aquatic mammals. A critical source of oxygen for the entire world.

Pollution: The condition of any system unable to recleanse itself.

Producers: Green plants upon which all other living things ultimately depend.

Pumped storage power plant: A technological device designed to supply extra electric power during peak-load periods. At those hours (late evening, early morning) when extra power is available, water is pumped from a lower to an upper reservoir. During the periods of peak-load demand (beginning and end of the workday), the stored water is is dropped through turbines to produce the needed power.

Recycling: The reutilization of natural resources and man-made products.

Renewable resources: Those biological resources which renew themselves by growth and reproduction.

Smog: As originally defined in England, smoke plus fog equals smog. It has come to mean air that is heavily contaminated with particulates, nitrogen oxides, and waste hydrocarbons.

Sonic boom: Shock wave produced by movement of objects through the atmosphere at speeds faster than the speed of sound.

Symbiosis: The association of two or more organisms for mutual benefit.

Thermal pollution: The ejection of heated water into the environment, usually aquatic ecosystems, raising the temperature above normal limits.

Trophic level: The energy level at which an organism sustains itself.

Wetland: Inland—any area that is more or less regularly wet or flooded, where the water table stands at or above the land surface for at least part of the year. Coastal—land types such as salt marshes, tidal marshes, and brackish marshes subject to saline and/or tidal influences.

ROBERT F. KUNZ, Executive Vice-President, Connecticut Conservation Association, Mystic, Connecticut. Reprinted from January 2, 1971 *Saturday Review.* Copyright © 1970 Saturday Review, Inc.

DECLARATION OF INDEPENDENCE
In Congress, July 4, 1776

THE UNANIMOUS DECLARATION OF THE

THIRTEEN UNITED STATES OF AMERICA,

When in the Course of human events, it becomes necessary for one people to dissolve the political bands which have connected them with another, and to assume among the Powers of the earth, the separate and equal station to which the Laws of Nature and of Nature's God entitle them, a decent respect to the opinions of mankind requires that they should declare the causes which impel them to the separation.

We hold these truths to be self-evident, that all men are created equal, that they are endowed by their Creator with certain unalienable Rights, that among these are Life, Liberty and the pursuit of Happiness. That to secure these rights, Governments are instituted among Men, deriving their just powers from the consent of the governed, That whenever any Form of Government becomes destructive of these ends, it is the Right of the People to alter or to abolish it, and to institute new Government, laying its foundation on such principles and organizing its powers in such form, as to them shall seem most likely to effect their Safety and Happiness. Prudence, indeed, will dictate that Governments long established should not be changed for light and transient causes; and accordingly all experience hath shown, that mankind are more disposed to suffer, while evils are sufferable, than to right themselves by abolishing the forms to which they are accustomed. But when a long train of abuses and usurpations, pursuing invariably the same Object evinces a design to reduce them under absolute Despotism, it is their right, it is their duty, to throw off such Government, and to provide new Guards for their future security.—Such has been the patient sufferance of these Colonies; and such is now the necessity which constrains them to alter their former Systems of Government. The history of the present King of Great Britain is a history of repeated injuries and usurpations, all having in direct object the establishment of an absolute Tyranny over these States. To prove this, let Facts be submitted to a candid world.

He has refused his Assent to Laws, the most wholesome and necessary for the public good.

He has forbidden his Governors to pass Laws of immediate and pressing importance, unless suspended in their operation till his Assent should be obtained; and when so suspended, he has utterly neglected to attend to them.

He has refused to pass other Laws for the accommodation of large districts of people, unless those people would relinquish the right of Representation in the Legislature, a right inestimable to them and formidable to tyrants only.

He has called together legislative bodies at places unusual, uncomfortable, and distant from the depository of their Public Records, for the sole purpose of fatiguing them into compliance with his measures.

He has dissolved Representative Houses repeatedly, for opposing with manly firmness his invasions on the rights of the people.

He has refused for a long time, after such dissolutions, to cause others to be elected; whereby the Legislative Powers, incapable of Annihilation, have returned to the People at large for their exercise; the State remaining in the mean time exposed to all the dangers of invasion from without, and convulsions within.

He has endeavoured to prevent the population of these States; for that purpose obstructing the Laws of Naturalization of Foreigners; refusing to pass others to encourage their migration hither, and raising the conditions of new Appropriations of Lands.

He has obstructed the Administration of Justice, by refusing his Assent to Laws for establishing Judiciary Powers.

He has made Judges dependent on his Will alone, for the tenure of their offices, and the amount and payment of their salaries.

He has erected a multitude of New Offices, and sent hither swarms of Officers to harass our People, and eat out their substance.

He has kept among us, in times of peace, Standing Armies without the Consent of our legislature.

He has affected to render the Military independent of and superior to the Civil Power.

He has combined with others to subject us to a jurisdiction foreign to our constitution, and unacknowledged by our laws; giving his Assent to their acts of pretended legislation:

For quartering large bodies of armed troops among us:

For protecting them, by a mock Trial, from Punishment for any Murders which they should commit on the Inhabitants of these States:

For cutting off our Trade with all parts of the world:

For imposing taxes on us without our Consent:

For depriving us in many cases, of the benefits of Trial by Jury:

For transporting us beyond Seas to be tried for pretended offences:

For abolishing the free System of English Laws in a neighbouring Province, establishing therein an Arbitrary government, and enlarging its Boundaries so as to render it at once an example and fit instrument for introducing the same absolute rule into these Colonies:

For taking away our Charters, abolishing our most valuable Laws, and altering fundamentally the Forms of our Governments:

For suspending our own Legislature, and declaring themselves invested with Power to legislate for us in all cases whatsoever.

He has abdicated Government here, by declaring us out of his Protection and waging War against us.

He has plundered our seas, ravaged our Coasts, burnt our towns, and destroyed the lives of our people.

He is at this time transporting large armies of foreign mercenaries to complete the works of death, desolation and tyranny, already begun with circumstances of Cruelty & perfidy scarcely paralleled in the most barbarous ages, and totally unworthy the Head of a civilized nation.

He has constrained our fellow Citizens taken Captive on the high Seas to bear Arms against their Country, to become the executioners of their friends and Brethren, or to fall themselves by their Hands.

He has excited domestic insurrections amongst us, and has endeavoured to bring on the inhabitants of our frontiers, the merciless Indian Savages, whose known rule of warfare, is an undistinguished destruction of all ages, sexes and conditions.

In every stage of these Oppressions We have Petitioned for Redress in the most humble terms: Our repeated Petitions have been answered only by repeated injury. A Prince, whose character is thus marked by every act which may define a Tyrant, is unfit to be the ruler of a free People.

Nor have We been wanting in attention to our British brethren. We have warned them from time to time of attempts by their legislature to extend an unwarrantable jurisdiction over us. We have reminded them of the circumstances of our emigration and settlement here. We have appealed to their native justice and magnanimity, and we have conjured them by the ties of our common kindred to disavow these usurpations, which, would inevitably interrupt our connections and correspondence. They too have been deaf to the voice of justice and of consanguinity. We must, therefore, acquiesce in the necessity, which denounces our Separation, and hold them, as we hold the rest of mankind, Enemies in War, in Peace Friends.

We, therefore, the Representatives of the united States of America, in General Congress, Assembled, appealing to the Supreme Judge of the world for the rectitude of our intentions, do, in the Name, and by Authority of the good People of these Colonies, solemnly publish and declare, That these United Colonies are, and of Right ought to be Free and Independent States; that they are Absolved from all Allegiance to the British Crown, and that all political connection between them and the State of Great Britain, is and ought to be totally dissolved; and that as Free and Independent States, they have full Power to levy War, conclude Peace, contract Alliances, establish Commerce, and to do all other Acts and Things which Independent States may of right do. And for the support of this Declaration, with a firm reliance on the Protection of Divine Providence, we mutually pledge to each other our Lives, our Fortunes and our sacred Honor.

New Hampshire—Josiah Bartlett, Wm. Whipple, Matthew Thornton. *Massachusetts-Bay*—John Hancock, Saml. Adams, John Adams, Robt. Treat Paine, Elbridge Gerry. *Rhode Island*—Step. Hopkins, William Ellery. *Connecticut*—Roger Sherman, Sam. Huntington, Wm. Williams, Oliver Wolcott, Matthew Thornton. *New York*—Wm. Floyd, Phil. Livingston, Frans. Lewis, Lewis Morris. *New Jersey*—Richd. Stockton, Jno. Witherspoon, Fras. Hopkinson, John Hart, Abra. Clark. *Pennsylvania*—Robt. Morris, Benjamin Rush, Benj. Franklin, John Morton, Geo. Clymer, Jas. Smith, Geo. Taylor, James Wilson, Geo. Ross. *Delaware*—Caesar Rodney, Geo. Read, Tho. M'Kean. *Maryland*—Samuel Chase, Wm. Paca, Thos. Stone, Charles Carroll of Carrollton. *Virginia*—George Wythe, Richard Henry Lee, Th. Jefferson, Benj. Harrison, Ths. Nelson, j., Francis Lightfoot Lee, Carter Braxton. *North Carolina*—Wm. Hooper, Joseph Hewes, John Penn. *South Carolina*—Edward Rutledge, Thos. Heyward, Junr., Thomas Lynch, Junr., Arthur Middleton. *Georgia*—Button Gwinnett, Lyman Hall, Geo. Walton.

THE CONSTITUTION OF THE UNITED STATES

We the People of the United States, in Order to form a more perfect Union, establish Justice, insure domestic Tranquility, provide for the common defence, promote the general Welfare, and secure the Blessings of Liberty to ourselves and our Posterity, do ordain and establish this Constitution for the United States of America.

ARTICLE I

Section 1. All legislative Powers herein granted shall be vested in a Congress of the United States, which shall consist of a Senate and House of Representatives.

Section 2. The House of Representatives shall be composed of Members chosen every second Year by the People of the several States, and the Electors in each State shall have the Qualifications requisite for Electors of the most numerous Branch of the State Legislature.

No Person shall be a Representative who shall not have attained to the Age of twenty five Years, and been seven Years a Citizen of the United States, and who shall not, when elected, be an Inhabitant of that State in which he shall be chosen.

[Representatives and direct Taxes shall be apportioned among the several States which may be included within this Union, according to their respective Numbers, which shall be determined by adding to the whole Number of free Persons, including those bound to Service for a Term of Years, and excluding Indians not taxed, three fifths of all other Persons.][1] The actual Enumeration shall be made within three Years after the first Meeting of the Congress of the United States, and within every subsequent Term of ten Years, in such Manner as they shall by Law direct. The Number of Representatives shall not exceed one for every thirty Thousand, but each State shall have at Least one Representative; and until such enumeration shall be made, the State of New Hampshire shall be entitled to chuse three, Massachusetts eight, Rhode-Island and Providence Plantations one, Connecticut five, New-York six, New Jersey four, Pennsylvania eight, Delaware one, Maryland six, Virginia ten, North Carolina five, South Carolina five, and Georgia three.

When vacancies happen in the Representation from any State, the Executive Authority thereof shall issue Writs of Election to fill such Vacancies.

The House of Representatives shall chuse their Speaker and other Officers; and shall have the sole Power of Impeachment.

Section 3. The Senate of the United States shall be composed of two Senators from each State, [chosen by the Legislature thereof,][2] for six Years; and each Senator shall have one Vote.

Immediately after they shall be assembled in Consequence of the first Election, they shall be divided as equally as may be into three Classes. The Seats of the Senators of the first Class shall be vacated at the Expiration of the second Year, of the second Class at the Expiration of the fourth Year, and of the third Class at the Expiration of the sixth Year, so that one third may be chosen every second Year; [and if Vacancies happen by Resignation, or otherwise, during the Recess of the Legislature of any State, the Executive thereof may make temporary Appointments until the next Meeting of the Legislature, which shall then fill such Vacancies.][3]

No Person shall be a Senator who shall not have attained to the Age of thirty Years, and been nine Years a Citizens of the United States, and who shall not, when elected, be an Inhabitant of that State for which he shall be chosen.

The Vice President of the United States shall be President of the Senate, but shall have no Vote, unless they be equally divided.

The Senate shall chuse their other Officers, and also a President pro tempore, in the Absence of the Vice President, or when he shall exercise the Office of President of the United States.

The Senate shall have the sole Power to try all Impeachments. When sitting for that Purpose, they shall be on Oath or Affirmation. When the President of the United States is tried, the Chief Justice shall preside: And no Person shall be convicted without the Concurrence of two thirds of the Members present.

Judgment in Cases of Impeachment shall not extend further than to removal from Office, and disqualification to hold and enjoy any Office of honor, Trust or Profit under the United States: but the Party convicted shall nevertheless be liable and subject to Indictment, Trial, Judgment and Punishment, according to Law.

Section 4. The Times, Places and Manner of holding Elections for Senators and Representatives, shall be prescribed in each State by the Legislature thereof; but the Congress may at any time by Law make or alter such Regulations, except as to the Places of chusing Senators.

The Congress shall assemble at least once in every Year, and such Meeting shall [be on the first Monday in December,][4] unless they shall by Law appoint a different Day.

Section 5. Each House shall be the Judge of the Elections, Returns and Qualifications of its own Members, and a Majority of each shall constitute a Quorum to do Business; but a smaller Number may adjourn from day to day, and may be authorized to compel the Attendance of absent Members, in such Manner, and under such Penalties as each House may provide.

Each House may determine the Rules of its Proceedings, punish its Members for disorderly Behaviour, and, with the Concurrence of two thirds, expel a Member.

Each House shall keep a Journal of its

---

[1]The clause included in brackets is amended by the 14th Amendment, Section 2.
[2]The qualification in brackets is amended by the 17th Amendment.
[3]The clause in brackets is amended by the 17th Amendment.
[4]The part in brackets is amended by the 20th Amendment, Section 2.

Proceedings, and from time to time publish the same, excepting such Parts as may in their Judgment require Secrecy; and the Yeas and Nays of the Members of either House on any question shall, at the Desire of one fifth of those Present, be entered on the Journal.

Neither House, during the Session of Congress, shall, without the Consent of the other, adjourn for more than three days, nor to any other Place than that in which the two Houses shall be sitting.

SECTION 6. The Senators and Representatives shall receive a Compensation for their Services, to be ascertained by Law, and paid out of the Treasury of the United States. They shall in all Cases, except Treason, Felony and Breach of the Peace, be privileged from Arrest during their Attendance at the Session of their respective Houses, and in going to and returning from the same; and for any Speech or Debate in either House, they shall not be questioned in any other Place.

No Senator or Representative shall, during the Time for which he was elected, be appointed to any civil Office under the Authority of the United States, which shall have been created, or the Emoluments whereof shall have been encreased during such time; and no Person holding any Office under the United States, shall be a Member of either House during his Continuance in Office.

SECTION 7. All Bills for raising Revenue shall originate in the House of Representatives; but the Senate may propose or concur with Amendments as on other Bills.

Every Bill which shall have passed the House of Representatives and the Senate, shall, before it become a Law, be presented to the President of the United States; If he approve he shall sign it, but if not he shall return it, with his Objections to that House in which it shall have originated, who shall enter the Objections at large on their Journal, and proceed to reconsider it. If after such Reconsideration two thirds of that House shall agree to pass the Bill, it shall be sent, together with the Objections, to the other House, by which it shall likewise be reconsidered, and if approved by two thirds of that House, it shall become a Law. But in all such Cases the Votes of both Houses shall be determined by yeas and Nays, and the Names of the Persons voting for and against the Bill shall be entered on the Journal of each House respectively. If any Bill shall not be returned by the President within ten Days (Sundays excepted) after it shall have been presented to him, the Same shall be a Law, in like Manner as if he had signed it, unless the Congress by their Adjournment prevent its Return, in which Case it shall not be a Law.

Every Order, Resolution, or Vote to which the Concurrence of the Senate and House of Representatives may be necessary (except on a question of Adjournment) shall be presented to the President of the United States; and before the Same shall take Effect, shall be approved by him, or being disapproved by him, shall be repassed by two thirds of the Senate and House of Representatives, according to the Rules and Limitations prescribed in the

Case of a Bill.

SECTION 8. The Congress shall have Power To lay and collect Taxes, Duties, Imposts and Excises, to pay the Debts and provide for the common Defence and general Welfare of the United States; but all Duties, Imposts and Excises shall be uniform throughout the United States;

To borrow Money on the credit of the United States;

To regulate Commerce with foreign Nations, and among the several States, and with the Indian Tribes;

To establish an uniform Rule of Naturalization, and uniform Laws on the subject of Bankruptcies throughout the United States;

To coin Money, regulate the Value thereof, and of foreign Coin, and fix the Standard of Weights and Measures;

To provide for the Punishment of counterfeiting the Securities and current Coin of the United States;

To establish Post Offices and post Roads;

To promote the Progress of Science and useful Arts, by securing for limited Times to Authors and Inventors the exclusive Right to their respective Writings and Discoveries;

To constitute Tribunals inferior to the supreme Court;

To define and punish Piracies and Felonies committed on the high Seas, and Offences against the Law of the Nations;

To declare War, grant Letters of Marque and Reprisal, and make Rules concerning Captures on Land and Water;

To raise and support Armies, but no Appropriation of Money to that Use shall be for a longer Term than two Years;

To provide and maintain a Navy;

To make Rules for the Government and Regulation of the land and naval Forces;

To provide for calling forth the Militia to execute the Laws of the Union, suppress Insurrections and repel Invasions;

To provide for organizing, arming, and disciplining, the Militia, and for governing such Part of them as may be employed in the Service of the United States, reserving to the States respectively, the Appointment of the Officers, and the Authority of training the Militia according to the discipline prescribed by Congress;

To exercise exclusive Legislation in all Cases whatsoever, over such District (not exceeding ten Miles square) as may, by Cession of particular States, and the Acceptance of Congress, become the Seat of the Government of the United States, and to exercise like Authority over all Places purchased by the Consent of the Legislature of the State in which the Same shall be, for the Erection of Forts, Magazines, Arsenals, dock-Yards, and other needful Buildings; — And

To make all Laws which shall be necessary and proper for carrying into Execution the foregoing Powers, and all other Powers vested by this Constitution in the Government of the United States, or in any Department or Officer thereof.

SECTION 9. The Migration or Importation of such Persons as any of the States now existing shall think proper to admit, shall not be prohibited by the Congress prior to the Year one thousand eight

hundred and eight, but a Tax or duty may be imposed on such Importation, not exceeding ten dollars for each Person.

The Privilege of the Writ of Habeas Corpus shall not be suspended, unless when in Cases of Rebellion or Invasion the public Safety may require it.

No Bill of Attainder or ex post facto Law shall be passed.

No Capitation, or other direct, Tax shall be laid, unless in Proportion to the Census or Enumeration herein before directed to be taken.

No Tax or Duty shall be laid on Articles exported from any State.

No Preference shall be given by any Regulation of Commerce or Revenue to the Ports of one State over those of another: nor shall Vessels bound to, or from, one State, be obliged to enter, clear, or pay Duties in another.

No Money shall be drawn from the Treasury, but in Consequence of Appropriations made by Law; and a regular Statement and Account of the Receipts and Expenditures of all public Money shall be published from time to time.

No Title of Nobility shall be granted by the United States: And no Person holding any Office of Profit or Trust under them, shall, without the Consent of the Congress, accept of any present, Emolument, Office, or Title, of any kind whatever, from any King, Prince or foreign State.

SECTION 10. No State shall enter into any Treaty, Alliance, or Confederation; grant Letters of Marque and Reprisal; coin Money; emit Bills of Credit; make any Thing but gold and silver Coin a Tender in Payment of Debts; pass any Bill of Attainder, ex post facto Law, or Law impairing the Obligation of Contracts, or grant any Title of Nobility.

No State shall, without the Consent of the Congress, lay any Imposts or Duties on Imports or Exports, except what may be absolutely necessary for executing it's inspection Laws; and the net Produce of all Duties and Imposts, laid by any State on Imports or Exports, shall be for the Use of the Treasury of the United States; and all such Laws shall be subject to the Revision and Controul of the Congress.

No State shall, without the Consent of Congress, lay any Duty of Tonnage, keep Troops, or Ships of War in time of Peace, enter into any Agreement or Compact with another State, or with a foreign Power, or engage in War, unless actually invaded, or in such imminent Danger as will not admit of delay.

ARTICLE II

SECTION 1. The executive Power shall be vested in a President of the United States of America. He shall hold his Office during the Term of four Years, and, together with the Vice President, chosen for the same Term, be elected, as follows

Each State shall appoint, in such Manner as the Legislature thereof may direct, a Number of Electors, equal to the whole Number of Senators and Representatives to which the State may be entitled in the Congress: but no Senator or Representative, or Person holding an Office of Trust or Profit under the United States, shall be appointed an Elector.

[The Electors shall meet in their respective States, and vote by Ballot for two Persons, of whom one at least shall not be an Inhabitant of the same State with themselves. And they shall make a List of all the Persons voted for, and of the Number of Votes for each; which List they shall sign and certify, and transmit sealed to the Seat of the Government of the United States, directed to the President of the Senate. The President of the Senate shall, in the Presence of the Senate and House of Representatives, open all the Certificates, and the Votes shall then be counted. The Person having the greatest Number of Votes shall be the President, if such Number be a Majority of the whole Number of Electors appointed; and if there be more than one who have such Majority, and have an equal Number of Votes, then the House of Representatives shall immediately chuse by Ballot one of them for President; and if no person have a Majority, then from the five highest on the List the said House shall in like Manner chuse the President. But in chusing the President, the Votes shall be taken by States, the Representation from each State having one Vote; A quorum for this Purpose shall consist of a Member or Members from two thirds of the States, and a Majority of all the States shall be necessary to a Choice. In every Case, after the Choice of the President, the Person having the greatest Number of Votes of the Electors shall be the Vice President. But if there should remain two or more who have equal Votes, the Senate shall chuse from them by Ballot the Vice President.]⁵

The Congress may determine the Time of chusing the Electors, and the Day on which they shall give their Votes; which Day shall be the same throughout the United States.

No Person except a natural born Citizen, or a Citizen of the United States, at the time of the Adoption of this Constitution, shall be eligible to the Office of President; neither shall any Person be eligible to that Office who shall not have attained to the Age of thirty five Years, and been fourteen Years a Resident within the United States.

[In Case of the Removal of the President from Office, or of his Death, Resignation, or Inability to discharge the Powers and Duties of the said Office, the Same shall devolve on the Vice President, and the Congress may by Law provide for the Case of Removal, Death, Resignation or Inability, both of the President and Vice President, declaring what Officer shall then act as President, and such Officer shall act accordingly, until the Disability be removed, or a President shall be elected.]⁶

The President shall, at stated Times, receive for his Services, a Compensation, which shall neither be encreased nor diminished during the Period for which he shall have been elected, and he shall not receive within that Period any other Emolument from the United States, or any of them.

Before he enter on the Execution of his Office, he shall take the following Oath or Affirmation:—"I do solemnly swear (or affirm) that I will faithfully execute the Office of President of the United States, and will to the best of my Ability, preserve, protect and defend the Constitution of the United States."

SECTION 2. The President shall be Commander in Chief of the Army and Navy of the United States, and of the Militia of the several States, when called into the actual Service of the United States; he may require the Opinion, in writing, of the principal Officer in each of the executive Departments, upon any Subject relating to the Duties of their respective Offices, and he shall have Power to grant Reprieves and Pardons for Offences against the United States, except in Cases of Impeachment.

He shall have Power, by and with the Advice and Consent of the Senate, to make Treaties, provided two thirds of the Senators present concur; and he shall nominate, and by and with the Advice and Consent of the Senate, shall appoint Ambassadors, other public Ministers and Consuls, Judges of the supreme Court, and all other Officers of the United States, whose Appointments are not herein otherwise provided for, and which shall be established by Law: but the Congress may by Law vest the Appointment of such inferior Officers, as they think proper, in the President alone, in the Courts of Law, or in the Heads of Departments.

The President shall have Power to fill up all Vacancies that may happen during the Recess of the Senate, by granting Commissions which shall expire at the End of their next Session.

SECTION 3. He shall from time to time give to the Congress Information of the State of the Union, and recommend to their Consideration such Measures as he shall judge necessary and expedient; he may, on extraordinary Occasions, convene both Houses, or either of them, and in Case of Disagreement between them, with Respect to the Time of Adjournment, he may adjourn them to such Time as he shall think proper; he shall receive Ambassadors and other public Ministers; he shall take Care that the Laws be faithfully executed, and shall Commission all the Officers of the United States.

SECTION 4. The President, Vice President and all civil Officers of the United States, shall be removed from Office on Impeachment for, and Conviction of, Treason, Bribery, or other high Crimes and Misdemeanors.

ARTICLE III

SECTION 1. The judicial Power of the United States, shall be vested in one supreme Court, and in such inferior Courts as the Congress may from time to time ordain and establish. The Judges, both of the supreme and inferior Courts, shall hold their Offices during good Behaviour, and shall, at stated Times, receive for their Services, a Compensation, which shall not be diminished during their Continuance in Office.

SECTION 2. The judicial Power shall extend to all Cases, in Law and Equity, arising under this Constitution, the Laws of the United States, and Treaties made, or which shall be made, under their Authority;—to all Cases affecting Ambassadors, other public Ministers and Consuls;—to all Cases of admiralty and maritime Jurisdiction;—to Controversies to which the United States shall be a Party;—to Controversies between two or more States;—[between a State and Citizens of another State;]⁷—between Citizens of different States,—between Citizens of the same State claiming Lands under Grants of different States, and between a State, or the Citizens thereof, and foreign States, Citizens or Subjects.

In all Cases affecting Ambassadors, other public Ministers and Consuls, and those in which a State shall be Party, the supreme Court shall have original Jurisdiction. In all the other Cases before mentioned, the supreme Court shall have appellate Jurisdiction, both as to Law and Fact, with such Exceptions, and under such Regulations as the Congress shall make.

The Trial of all Crimes, except in Cases of Impeachment, shall be by Jury; and such Trial shall be held in the State where the said Crimes shall have been committed; but when not committed within any State, the Trial shall be at such Place or Places as the Congress may by Law have directed.

SECTION 3. Treason against the United States, shall consist only in levying War against them, or in adhering to their Enemies, giving them Aid and Comfort. No Person shall be convicted of Treason unless on the Testimony of two Witnesses to the same overt Act, or on Confession in open Court.

The Congress shall have Power to declare the Punishment of Treason, but no Attainder of Treason shall work Corruption of Blood, or Forfeiture except during the Life of the Person attainted.

ARTICLE IV

SECTION 1. Full Faith and Credit shall be given in each State to the Public Acts, Records, and judicial Proceedings of every other State. And the Congress may by general Laws prescribe the Manner in which such Acts, Records and Proceedings shall be proved, and the Effect thereof.

SECTION 2. The Citizens of each State shall be entitled to all Privileges and Immunities of Citizens in the several States.

A Person charged in any State with Treason, Felony, or other Crime, who shall flee from Justice, and be found in another State, shall on Demand of the executive Authority of the State from which he fled, be delivered up, to be removed to the State having Jurisdiction of the Crime.

[No Person held to Service or Labour in one State, under the Laws thereof, escaping into another, shall, in Consequence of any Law or Regulation therein, be discharged from such Service or Labour, but

---

⁵The clause in brackets has been superseded by the 12th Amendment.
⁶The clause in brackets is affected by the 25th Amendment.

⁷The part in brackets is limited by the 11th Amendment.

shall be delivered up on Claim of the Party to whom such Service or Labour may be due.]⁸

Section 3. New States may be admitted by the Congress into this Union; but no new States shall be formed or erected within the Jurisdiction of any other State; nor any State be formed by the Junction of two or more States, or Parts of States, without the Consent of the Legislatures of the States concerned as well as of the Congress.

The Congress shall have Power to dispose of and make all needful Rules and Regulations respecting the Territory or other Property belonging to the United States; and nothing in this Constitution shall be so construed as to Prejudice any Claims of the United States, or of any particular State.

Section 4. The United States shall guarantee to every State in this Union a Republican Form of Government, and shall protect each of them against Invasion; and on Application of the Legislature, or of the Executive (when the Legislature cannot be convened) against domestic Violence.

ARTICLE V

The Congress, whenever two thirds of both Houses shall deem it necessary, shall propose Amendments to this Constitution, or, on the Application of the Legislatures of two thirds of the several States, shall call a Convention for proposing Amendments, which, in either Case, shall be valid to all Intents and Purposes, as Part of this Constitution, when ratified by the Legislatures of three fourths of the several States, or by Conventions in three fourths thereof, as the one or the other Mode of Ratification may be proposed by the Congress; Provided that no Amendment which may be made prior to the Year One thousand eight hundred and eight shall in any Manner affect the first and fourth Clauses in the Ninth Section of the first Article; and that no State, without its Consent, shall be deprived of it's equal Suffrage in the Senate.

ARTICLE VI

All Debts contracted and Engagements entered into, before the Adoption of this Constitution, shall be as valid against the United States under this Constitution, as under the Confederation.

This Constitution, and the Laws of the United States which shall be made in Pursuance thereof; and all Treaties made, or which shall be made, under the Authority of the United States, shall be the supreme Law of the Land; and the Judges in every State shall be bound thereby, any Thing in the Constitution or Laws of any State to the Contrary notwithstanding.

The Senators and Representatives before mentioned, and the Members of the several State Legislatures, and all executive and judicial Officers, both of the United States and of the several States, shall be bound by Oath or Affirmation, to support this Constitution; but no religious Test shall ever be required as a Qualification to any Office or public Trust under the United States.

ARTICLE VII

The Ratification of the Conventions of nine States, shall be sufficient for the Establishment of this Constitution between the States so ratifying the Same.

Done in Convention by the Unanimous Consent of the States present the Seventeenth Day of September in the Year of our Lord one thousand seven hundred and Eighty seven and of the Independence of the United States of America the Twelfth. In witness whereof We have hereunto subscribed our Names,

⁸The clause in brackets is superseded by the 13th Amendment.

New Hampshire—John Langdon, Nicholas Gilman. *Massachusetts*—Nathaniel Gorham, Rufus King. *Connecticut*—Wm. Saml. Johnson, Roger Sherman. *New York*—Alexander Hamilton. *New Jersey*—Wil. Livingston, David Brearley, Wm. Paterson, Jona. Dayton. *Pennsylvania*—B. Franklin, Thomas Mifflin, Robt. Morris, Geo. Clymer, Thos. FitzSimons, Jared Ingersoll, James Wilson, Gouv. Morris. *Delaware*—Geo. Read, Gunning Bedford, jun., John Dickinson, Richard Bassett, Jaco. Broom. *Maryland*—James McHenry, Dan. of St. Thos. Jenifer, Danl. Carroll. *Virginia*—Go. Washington, John Blair, James Madison, Jr. *North Carolina*—Wm. Blount, Richd. Dobbs Spaight, Hu. Williamson. *South Carolina*—J. Rutledge, Charles Cotesworth Pinckney, Charles Pinckney, Pierce Butler. *Georgia*—William Few, Abr. Baldwin.

AMENDMENTS TO THE CONSTITUTION

Articles in addition to, and Amendment of the Constitution of the United States of America, proposed by Congress, and ratified by the Legislatures of the several States, pursuant to the fifth Article of the original Constitution. [The first ten amendments went into effect November 3, 1791.]

AMENDMENT I

Congress shall make no law respecting an establishment of religion, or prohibiting the free exercise thereof; or abridging the freedom of speech, or of the press; or the right of the people peaceably to assemble, and to petition the government for a redress of grievances.

AMENDMENT II

A well regulated Militia, being necessary to the security of a free State, the right of the people to keep and bear Arms, shall not be infringed.

AMENDMENT III

No Soldier shall, in time of peace be quartered in any house, without the consent of the Owner, nor in time of war, but in a manner to be prescribed by law.

AMENDMENT IV

The right of the people to be secure in their persons, houses, papers, and effects, against unreasonable searches and seizures, shall not be violated, and no Warrants shall issue, but upon probable cause, supported by Oath or affirmation, and particularly describing the place to be searched, and the persons or things to be seized.

AMENDMENT V

No person shall be held to answer for a capital, or otherwise infamous crime, unless on a presentment or indictment of a Grand Jury, except in cases arising in the land or naval forces, or in the Militia, when in actual service in time of War or public danger; nor shall any person be subject for the same offence to be twice put in jeopardy of life or limb; nor shall be compelled in any criminal case to be a witness against himself, nor be deprived of life, liberty, or property, without due process of law; nor shall private property be taken for public use, without just compensation.

AMENDMENT VI

In all criminal prosecutions, the accused shall enjoy the right to a speedy and public trial, by an impartial jury of the State and district wherein the crime shall have been committed, which district shall have been previously ascertained by law, and to be informed of the nature and cause of the accusation; to be confronted with the witnesses against him; to have compulsory process for obtaining witnesses in his favor, and to have the Assistance of Counsel for his defence.

AMENDMENT VII

In Suits at common law, where the value in controversy shall exceed twenty dollars, the right of trial by jury shall be preserved, and no fact tried by a jury, shall be otherwise re-examined in any Court of the United States, than according to the rules of the common law.

AMENDMENT VIII

Excessive bail shall not be required, nor excessive fines imposed, nor cruel and unusual punishments inflicted.

AMENDMENT IX

The enumeration in the Constitution, of certain rights, shall not be construed to deny or disparage others retained by the people.

AMENDMENT X

The powers not delegated to the United States by the Constitution, nor prohibited by it to the States, are reserved to the States respectively, or to the people.

AMENDMENT XI[9]
January 8, 1798

The Judicial power of the United States shall not be construed to extend to any suit in law or equity, commenced or prosecuted against one of the United States by Citizens of another State, or by Citizens or Subjects of any Foreign State.

AMENDMENT XII[10]
September 25, 1804

The Electors shall meet in their respective states, and vote by ballot for President and Vice-President, one of whom, at least, shall not be an inhabitant of the same state with themselves; they shall name in their ballots the person voted for as President, and in distinct ballots the person voted for as Vice-President, and they shall make distinct lists of all persons voted for as President, and of all persons voted for as Vice-President, and of the number of votes for each, which lists they shall sign and certify, and transmit sealed to the seat of the government of the United States, directed to the President of the Senate;—The President of the Senate shall, in the presence of the Senate and House of Representatives, open all the certificates and the votes shall then be counted;—The person having the greatest number of votes for President, shall be the President, if such number be a majority of the whole number of Electors appointed; and if no person have such majority, then from the persons having the highest numbers not exceeding three on the list of those voted for as President, the House of Representatives shall choose immediately, by ballot, the President. But in choosing the President, the votes shall be taken by states, the representation from each state having one vote; a quorum for this purpose shall consist of a member or members from two-thirds of the states, and a majority of all the states shall be necessary to a choice. [And if the House of Representatives shall not choose a President whenever the right of choice shall devolve upon them, before the fourth day of March next following, then the Vice-President shall act as President, as in the case of the death or other constitutional disability of the President.][11]—The person having the greatest number of votes as Vice-President, shall be the Vice-President, if such number be a majority of the whole number of Electors appointed, and if no person have a majority, then from the two highest numbers on the list, the Senate shall choose the Vice-President; a quorum for the purpose shall consist of two-thirds of the whole number of Senators,

and a majority of the whole number shall be necessary to a choice. But no person constitutionally ineligible to the office of President shall be eligible to that of Vice-President of the United States.

AMENDMENT XIII
December 18, 1865

SECTION 1. Neither slavery nor involuntary servitude, except as a punishment for crime whereof the party shall have been duly convicted, shall exist within the United States, or any place subject to their jurisdiction.

SECTION 2. Congress shall have power to enforce this article by appropriate legislation.

AMENDMENT XIV
July 28, 1868

SECTION 1. All persons born or naturalized in the United States, and subject to the jurisdiction thereof, are citizens of the United States and of the State wherein they reside. No State shall make or enforce any law which shall abridge the privileges or immunities of citizens of the United States; nor shall any State deprive any person of life, liberty, or property, without due process of law; nor deny to any person within its jurisdiction the equal protection of the laws.

SECTION 2. Representatives shall be apportioned among the several States according to their respective numbers, counting the whole number of persons in each State, excluding Indians not taxed. But when the right to vote at any election for the choice of electors for President and Vice President of the United States, Representatives in Congress, the Executive and Judicial officers of a State, or the members of the Legislature thereof, is denied to any of the male inhabitants of such State, being twenty-one years of age, and citizens of the United States, or in any way abridged, except for participation in rebellion, or other crime, the basis of representation therein shall be reduced in the proportion which the number of such male citizens shall bear to the whole number of male citizens twenty-one years of age in such State.

SECTION 3. No person shall be a Senator or Representative in Congress, or elector of President and Vice President, or hold any office, civil or military, under the United States, or under any State, who, having previously taken an oath, as a member of Congress, or as an officer of the United States, or as a member of any State legislature, or as an executive or judicial officer of any State, to support the Constitution of the United States, shall have engaged in insurrection or rebellion against the same, or given aid or comfort to the enemies thereof. But Congress may by a vote of two-thirds of each House, remove such disability.

SECTION 4. The validity of the public debt of the United States, authorized by law, including debts incurred for payment of pensions and bounties for services in suppressing insurrection or rebellion, shall

not be questioned. But neither the United States nor any State shall assume or pay any debt or obligation incurred in aid of insurrection or rebellion against the United States, or any claim for the loss or emancipation of any slave; but all such debts, obligations and claims shall be held illegal and void.

SECTION 5. The Congress shall have power to enforce, by appropriate legislation, the provisions of this article.

AMENDMENT XV
March 30, 1870

SECTION 1. The right of citizens of the United States to vote shall not be denied or abridged by the United States or by any State on account of race, color, or previous condition of servitude—

SECTION 2. The Congress shall have power to enforce this article by appropriate legislation—

AMENDMENT XVI
February 25, 1913

The Congress shall have power to lay and collect taxes on incomes, from whatever source derived, without apportionment among the several States, and without regard to any census or enumeration.

AMENDMENT XVII
May 31, 1913

The Senate of the United States shall be composed of two senators from each State, elected by the people thereof, for six years; and each Senator shall have one vote. The electors in each State shall have the qualifications requisite for electors of the most numerous branch of the State legislature.

When vacancies happen in the representation of any State in the Senate, the executive authority of such State shall issue writs of election to fill such vacancies: *Provided*, That the legislature of any State may empower the executive thereof to make temporary appointments until the people fill the vacancies by election as the legislature may direct.

This amendment shall not be so construed as to affect the election or term of any senator chosen before it becomes valid as part of the Constitution.

AMENDMENT XVIII
January 29, 1919

After one year from the ratification of this article, the manufacture, sale, or transportation of intoxicating liquors within, the importation thereof into, or the exportation thereof from the United States and all territory subject to the jurisdiction thereof for beverage purposes is hereby prohibited.

The Congress and the several States shall have concurrent power to enforce this article by appropriate legislation.

This article shall be inoperative unless it shall have been ratified as an amendment to the Constitution by the legislatures of the several States, as provided in the Constitution, within seven years from the date of the submission hereof to the States by Congress.

---

[9]Amendment XI qualifies Article III, Section 2.
[10]This amendment replaces Clause 3 in Article II, Section I, and annuls it.

[11]The clause in brackets is superseded by the 20th Amendment, Section 3.

AMENDMENT XIX
August 26, 1920

The right of citizens of the United States to vote shall not be denied or abridged by the United States or by any States on account of sex.

Congress shall have power by appropriate legislation to enforce the provisions of this article.

AMENDMENT XX
February 6, 1933

SECTION 1. The terms of the President and Vice-President shall end at noon on the twentieth day of January, and the terms of Senators and Representatives at noon on the third day of January, of the years in which such terms would have ended if this article had not been ratified; and the terms of their successors shall then begin.

SECTION 2. The Congress shall assemble at least once in every year, and such meeting shall begin at noon on the third day of January, unless they shall by law appoint a different day.

SECTION 3. If, at the time fixed for the beginning of the term of the President, the President-elect shall have died, the Vice-President-elect shall become President. If a President shall not have been chosen before the time fixed for the beginning of his term, or if the President-elect shall have failed to qualify, then the Vice-President-elect shall act as President until a President shall have qualified; and the Congress may by law provide for the case wherein neither a President-elect nor a Vice-President-elect shall have qualified, declaring who shall then act as President, or the manner in which one who is to act shall be selected, and such person shall act accordingly until a President or Vice-President shall have qualified.

SECTION 4. The Congress may by law provide for the case of the death of any of the persons from whom the House of Representatives may choose a President whenever the right of choice shall have devolved upon them, and for the case of the death of any of the persons from whom the Senate may choose a Vice-President whenever the right of choice shall have devolved upon them.

SECTION 5. Sections 1 and 2 shall take effect on the 15th day of October following the ratification of this article.

SECTION 6. This article shall be inoperative unless it shall have been ratified as an amendment to the Constitution by the legislatures of three-fourths of the several States within seven years from the date of its submission.

AMENDMENT XXI
December 5, 1933

SECTION 1. The eighteenth article of amendment to the Constitution of the United States is hereby repealed.

SECTION 2. The transportation or importation into any State, Territory, or possession of the United States for delivery or use therein of intoxicating liquors, in violation of the laws thereof, is hereby prohibited.

SECTION 3. This article shall be inoperative unless it shall have been ratified as an amendment to the Constitution by conventions in the several States, as provided in the Constitution, within seven years from the date of the submission hereof to the States by the Congress.

AMENDMENT XXII
February 26, 1951

SECTION 1. No person shall be elected to the office of the President more than twice, and no person who has held the office of President, or acted as President, for more than two years of a term to which some other person was elected President shall be elected to the office of the President more than once. But this Article shall not apply to any person holding the office of President when this Article was proposed by the Congress, and shall not prevent any person who may be holding the office of President, or acting as President, during the term within which this Article becomes operative from holding the office of President or acting as President during the remainder of such term.

SECTION 2. This article shall be inoperative unless it shall have been ratified as an amendment to the Constitution by the legislatures of three-fourths of the several States within seven years from the date of its submission to the States by the Congress.

AMENDMENT XXIII
April 3, 1961

SECTION 1. The District constituting the seat of Government of the United States shall appoint in such manner as the Congress may direct:

A number of electors of President and Vice President equal to the whole number of Senators and Representatives in Congress to which the District would be entitled if it were a State, but in no event more than the least populous State; they shall be in addition to those appointed by the States, but they shall be considered, for the purposes of the election of President and Vice President, to be electors appointed by a State; and they shall meet in the District and perform such duties as provided by the twelfth article of amendment.

SECTION 2. The Congress shall have power to enforce this article by appropriate legislation.

AMENDMENT XXIV
February 4, 1964

SECTION 1. The right of citizens of the United States to vote in any primary or other election for President or Vice President, for electors for President or Vice President, or for Senator or Representative in Congress, shall not be denied or abridged by the United States or any State by reason of failure to pay any poll tax or other tax.

SECTION 2. The Congress shall have power to enforce this article by appropriate legislation.

AMENDMENT XXV
February 10, 1967

SECTION 1. In case of removal of the President from office or of his death or resignation, the Vice President shall become President.

SECTION 2. Whenever there is a vacancy in the office of the Vice President, the President shall nominate a Vice President who shall take the office upon confirmation by a majority vote of both Houses of Congress.

SECTION 3. Whenever the President transmits to the President pro tempore of the Senate and the Speaker of the House of Representatives his written declaration that he is unable to discharge the powers and duties of his office, and until he transmits to them a written declaration to the contrary, such powers and duties shall be discharged by the Vice President as Acting President.

SECTION 4. Whenever the Vice President and a majority of either the principal officers of the executive departments or of such other body as Congress may by law provide, transmit to the President pro tempore of the Senate and the Speaker of the House of Representatives their written declaration that the President is unable to discharge the powers and duties of his office, the Vice President shall immediately assume the powers and duties of the office as Acting President.

Thereafter, when the President transmits to the President pro tempore of the Senate and the Speaker of the House of Representatives his written declaration that no inability exists, he shall resume the powers and duties of his office unless the Vice President and a majority of either the principal officers of the executive department or of such other body as Congress may by law provide, transmit within four days to the President pro tempore of the Senate and the Speaker of the House of Representatives their written declaration that the President is unable to discharge the powers and duties of his office. Thereupon Congress shall decide the issue, assembling within forty-eight hours for that purpose if not in session. If the Congress, within twenty-one days after receipt of the latter written declaration, or, if Congress is not in session, within twenty-one days after Congress is required to assemble, determines by two-thirds vote of both Houses that the President is unable to discharge the powers and duties of his office, the Vice President shall continue to discharge the same as Acting President; otherwise, the President shall resume the powers and duties of his office.

AMENDMENT XXVI
June 30, 1971

SECTION 1. The right of citizens of the United States, who are eighteen years of age or older, to vote shall not be denied or abridged by the United States or by any State on account of age.

SECTION 2. The Congress shall have power to enforce this article by appropriate legislation.

Quest
for the
Stars

IMPORTANT DATES IN SPACE HISTORY

October 4, 1957
The USSR launched the first successful artificial satellite, Sputnik 1. This was followed by Sputnik 2, a space capsule, launched on **November 3, 1957,** carrying a dog, "Laika."

February 1, 1958
The first U.S. satellite, Explorer 1, was launched with a lifetime expectancy of from 4 to 10 years. It discovered the inner (Van Allen) radiation belt.

1959
The USSR launched three separate spacecrafts. Luna 1 was launched on **January 2** and became the first luna probe. The second launching took place on **September 12** making Luna 2 the first spacecraft to make contact with the surface of the moon. Luna 3, launced on **October 4,** supplied the first pictures of the moon's far side.

April 1, 1960
TIROS, an acronym for Television and Infrared Observation Satellite, was launched and the U.S. successfully established the first weather satellite, which sent back 22,952 photographs of global cloud conditions, enabling meteorologists to follow, predict and analyze storms.

August 12, 1960
Echo 1 was launched by the U.S. This inflated 100-foot diameter, aluminum-coated sphere, became the first passive communication satellite in orbit. Voices and pictures were transmitted by reflection from the satellite.

May 24, 1960
The first missle launch detection satellite, Midas 2, was equipped with infrared sensors capable of picking up the exhaust heat from a ballistic missle as it left the ground.

April 12, 1961
The USSR successfully launched Vostok 1, carrying Yuri A. Gagarin, the first man in space. Spacecraft weight at liftoff was 10,417 pounds. The flight time was 1 hour, 48 minutes, in altitudes from 112 to 203 miles.

May 5, 1961
Alan B. Shephard Jr., first American in space, completed a suborbital flight in 15 minutes in the spacecraft, Mercury-Redstone 3. The weight at liftoff was 4,040 pounds.

June 29, 1961
The first nuclear power supply in space and triple launching was achieved by the U.S. when Transit 4A, Injun 1 and Solrad 3 satellites entered space.

July 21, 1961
Mercury-Redstone 4, manned by Virgil Grissom of the U.S., made a suborbital flight lasting 16 minutes.

August 6, 1961
Vostok 2, manned by Gherman S. Titov, launched by the USSR, was the first manned flight to exceed 24 hours and made 17 orbits.

February 20, 1962
The first U.S. astronaut to orbit the earth was John H. Glenn, Jr., manning Mercury-Atlas 6. He made three orbits of the earth in 4 hours, 55 minutes.

May 24, 1962
The second U.S. manned flight, by M. Scott Carpenter, was carried out in the spacecraft, Mercury-Atlas 7. Carpenter made three orbits in 4 hours, 56 minutes, and landed 250 miles away from target.

Right. One of the chimpanzees, specially trained for the Mercury-Redstone 2 flight, is shown in the couch in which the monkey rode during the 16-minute ballistic flight from Cape Canaveral, Florida. The MR-2 launch was one of a series of launches scheduled by NASA in its manned orbital flight program, Project Mercury.

Below. Astronaut John Glenn photographed in space by an automatic sequence motion picture camera. Glenn was in a state of weightlessness traveling at 17,500 mph as these pictures were taken.

July 10, 1962
Telstar 1, a U.S. satellite, was the first commercially financed comsat. It made possible transmissions of TV, voice, and photographs between U.S., U.K., and France.

August 11, 1962
Vostok 3 and 4, USSR satellites manned by Andrian Nikolayev and Pavel Popovich, made the first group flight. On the first orbit Vostok 4 came within three miles of Vostok 3. Flight time for Vostok 3 was 94 hours, 22 minutes and it made 64 orbits; for Vostok 4 the flight time was 70 hours, 57 minutes and it orbited 48 times.

October 3, 1962
Mercury-Atlas 8, a U.S. satellite manned by Walter Schirra, made 6 orbits in 9 hours and 13 minutes and landed 45 miles from target.

December 14, 1962
Mariner 2, U.S. Venus Probe, passed within 22,000 miles of Venus. The probe provided measurements of surface and atmospheric temperatures, magnetic field and communications to 54 million miles.

Left and below. Astronaut Edward H. White II is shown performing his spectacular space feat during the third orbit of the Gemini-Titan 4 flight. White floats into space, secured to the Gemini-4 spacecraft by a 25-ft. umbilical line and a 23-ft. tether line, both wrapped together with gold tape to form one cord. White became the first American astronaut to leave his spacecraft for a total of 21 minutes.

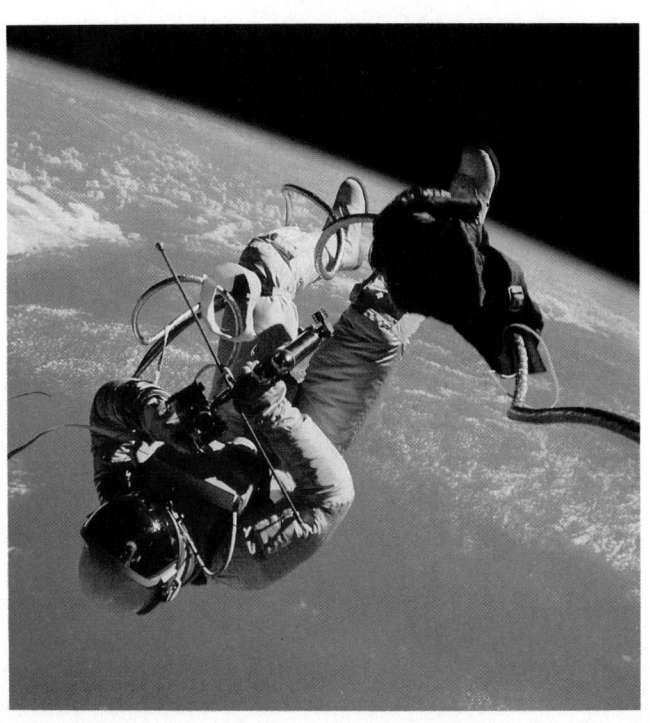

May 15, 1963
First long U.S. flight, by L. Gordon Cooper, in spacecraft Mercury-Atlas 9, made 22 orbits in 34 hours, 20 minutes. It provided the U.S. with its first evaluation of the effects on man of one day in space.

June 14, 1963 and June 16, 1963
Second dual mission for USSR of Vostok 5, manned by Valeri F. Bykovsky, and Vostok 6, manned by the first woman cosmonaut in space, Valentina V. Tereshkova. Vostok 5 made 81 orbits in 119 hours, 6 minutes and Vostok 6 made 48 orbits in 70 hours, 50 minutes.

July 28, 1964
The U.S. moon probe Ranger 7 transmitted over 4,000 TV photos of the moon's surface before impact.

September 5, 1964
The U.S. launched OGO 1, an orbiting geophysical observatory carrying 20 coordinated geophysical experiments.

October 12, 1964
First flight of a three-man crew was USSR's Voskhod 1 satellite manned by Konstantin Feoktistov, Vladimir Komorov, and Boris Yegorov. Spacecraft made 16 orbits in 24 hours, 17 minutes.

March 18, 1965
Voskhod 2 was launched by the USSR, manned by Aleksei A. Leonov and Pavell Belyayev. During the flight, Leonov made the first walk in space for ten minutes. The flight lasted 26 hours, 2 minutes.

March 23, 1965
Gemini 3 was the first U.S. two-man flight and first manned spacecraft to change its orbital path. Virgil I. Grissom and John W. Young were the astronauts who made the three-orbit flight in 4 hours, 53 minutes.

April 6, 1965
Intelsat 1, also known as Early Bird, was the first U.S. commercial communications satellite in synchronous orbit. It was launched by NASA for the Comsat Corp.

November 16, 1965
The first spacecraft, launched this date, to impact another planet was the USSR Venera 3, which struck Venus.

June 3, 1965
Astronauts James McDivitt and Edward White manned the Gemini 4, a U.S. satellite. The first U.S. walk in space, lasting 21 minutes, was made by White; the spacecraft made 66 orbits in a total flight time of 17 hours, 59 minutes.

Left. The Agena Target Docking Vehicle as seen from the command pilot's hatch window on board the Gemini X spacecraft. Crew members for the National Aeronautics and Space Administration's Gemini X mission were Astronauts John Young and Michael Collins.

Below, center. The Agena Target Docking Vehicle at a distance of approximately 100 feet from the National Aeronautics and Space Administration's Gemini XII spacecraft. This view was taken after disconnection of the tether between the two space vehicles. Crew members for the Gemini XII mission were astronauts James A. Lovell and Edwin E. Aldrin Jr.

Below, right. The Apollo 9 Command/Service Module is photographed from the Lunar Module "Spider" on the fifth day of the Apollo 9 earth-orbital mission. Inside the Lunar Module were Astronauts James A. McKivitt and Russell L. Schweickart. Astronaut David R. Scott remained at the controls in the Command Module.

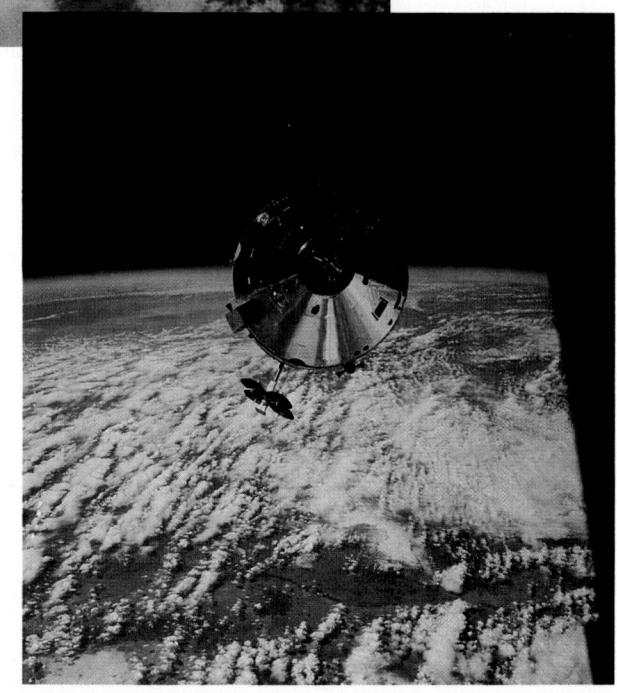

August 21, 1965

U.S. Gemini 5 satellite, manned by L. Gordon Cooper and Charles Conrad, Jr., was launched. The flight lasted 190 hours, 55 minutes and made 120 orbits. It was the first use of fuel cells for electric power; also evaluated the navigation and guidance system.

December 4, 1965

Frank Borman and James Lovell, manning the U.S. Gemini 7, made the longest Gemini flight of 330 hours, 35 minutes and 220 orbits. The weight at lift-off was 8,069 pounds.

December 15, 1965

U.S. satellite Gemini 6-A, manned by Walter Schirra and Thomas Stafford, completed first space rendezvous, moving within a foot of Gemini 7. Its flight time was 25 hours, 51 minutes; 17 orbits.

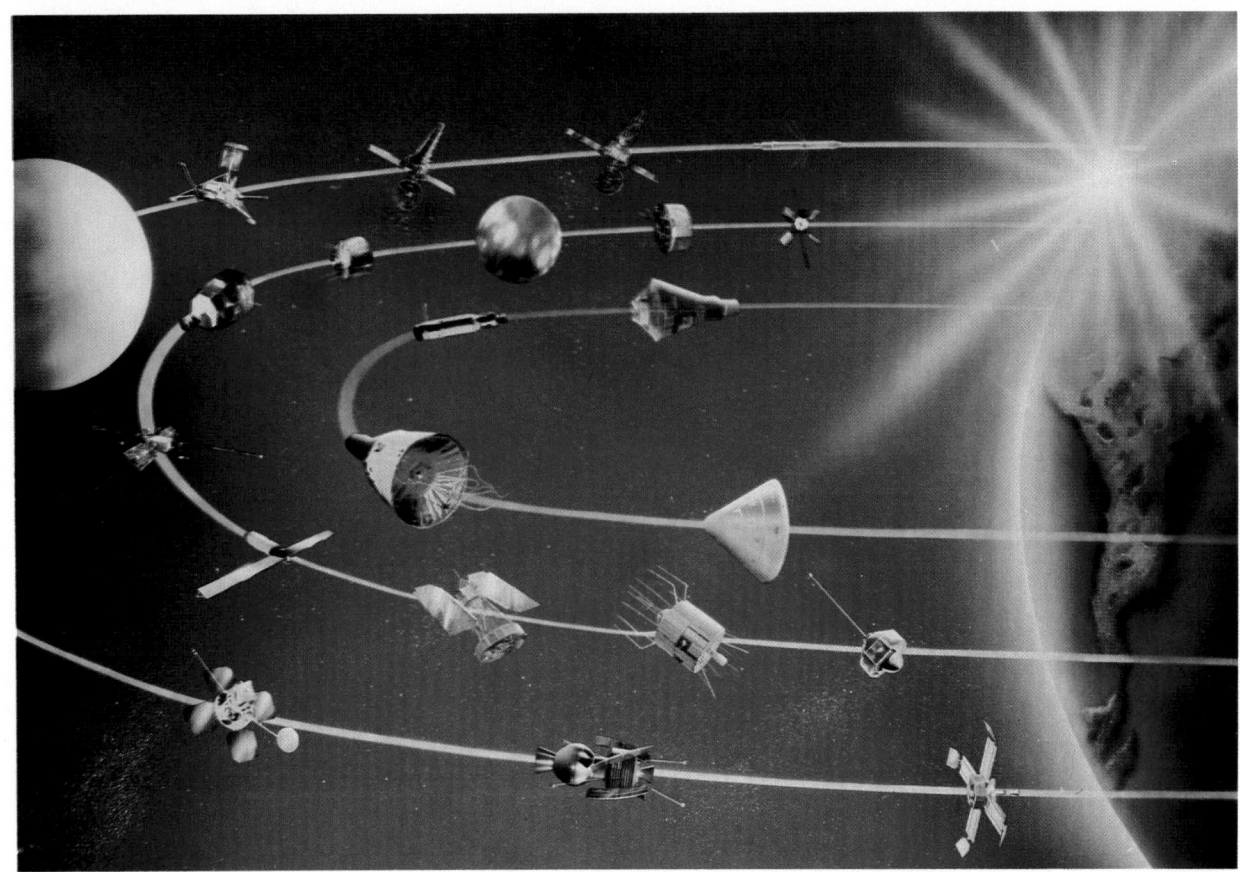

Representative spacecraft, shown in this artist's conception, are symbolic of the National Aeronautics and Space Administration's first 10 years of space exploration from its establishment on Oct. 1, 1958. In that time, NASA successfully launched hundreds of spacecraft, broadening our knowledge of space, other planets and even earth itself.

March 16, 1966
U.S. spacecraft Gemini 8, was launched, manned by Neil Armstrong and David Scott. It completed first docking in space of two orbiting spacecrafts. Flight time, 10 hours, 18 minutes; 6.5 orbits.

May 30, 1966
Lunar probe Surveyor 1, in the first U.S. soft landing on the moon, made 11,150 televised photos of itself and the lunar surface.

July 18, 1966
U.S. Gemini 10 spacecraft was launched, manned by John Young and Michael Collins. It made the first dual rendezvous and first retrieval of a space object in the target vehicle by Collins' extravehicular activity. It made 46 orbits in 70 hours, 47 minutes.

August 10, 1966
U.S. Lunar Orbiter 1, a lunar probe, the first of five successful missions, made photographs of the lunar surface and studied possible Apollo landing sites.

September 12, 1966
U.S. Gemini 11, manned by Charles Conrad, Jr. and Richard F. Gordon, Jr., began the highest earth-orbit altitude of 739.2 miles, in a flight time of 71 hours, 17 minutes.

November 11, 1966
U.S. Gemini 12, launched on this date and transporting James Lovell, Jr. and Edwin E. Aldrin, Jr., had the distinction of carrying out the longest extravehicular activity to date of 5 hours, 37 minutes. The flight lasted 94 hours, 35 minutes and made 59 orbits.

April 24, 1967
Vladimir Komarov, cosmonaut piloting the USSR Souz 1, was killed in the recovery phase after orbiting 18 times and flying 26 hours, 35 minutes.

October 11, 1968
The first U.S. three-man mission with astronauts Walter Schirra, Donn Eisele, and Walter Cunn-

Man on the moon. On this lunar mission (July 26, 1971), astronauts David Scott and James Irwin made the first deep space walk and used the Lunar Roving Vehicle. They stayed on the moon 66 hours and 55 minutes.

Above, left. Artist's concept of the Apollo-Soyuz Test Project docking. The major objective of the program was the inflight testing of the jointly designed international docking mechanism. *Above, right.* Taken from the window of the Apollo spacecraft, this photo shows the Soviet spacecraft against a black sky with a heavily cloud-covered Earth below. The three major components of the Soyuz are the spherical Orbital Module, the bell-shaped Descent Vehi-

cle, and the cylindrical Instrument Assembly Module. The docking mechanism on the Orbital Module was designed to interface with the docking mechanism on the Apollo's Docking Module. *Below.* The aft end of Soyuz taken through the window of the Apollo spacecraft. Two solar panels protrude out from the spacecraft's Instrument Assembly Module. Astronauts and cosmonauts visited each other's spacecraft while Soyuz and Apollo were docked.

ingham was undertaken on the lunar spacecraft, Apollo 7. Weight at liftoff was 45,989 pounds. It made orbital tests at altitudes ranging from 141 to 176 miles. The flight time was 260 hours, 8 minutes and it made 163 orbits.

October 26, 1968
USSR Soyuz 3 satellite, manned by cosmonaut Georgi Beregovoy, maneuvered near the unmanned Soyuz 2, totalled 64 orbits in 94 hours, 51 minutes.

December 21, 1968
U.S. Apollo 8, spacecraft manned by Frank Borman, James A. Lovell, Jr., and William A. Anders, made the first manned orbits of the moon, the first departure from the earth's sphere of influence and the highest speed ever reached in manned flight. Flight time was 147 hours, and it made 10 orbits of the moon.

January 14, 1969
USSR Soyuz 4, manned spacecraft by Vladimir Shatalov, docked with Soyuz 5, another USSR manned spacecraft, carrying Boris Volynov, Aleksei Yeliseyev and Yevgeny Khrunov. Two cosmonauts transferred to Soyuz 4. Soyuz 4 had a flight time of 71 hours, 14 minutes and made 45 orbits; Soyuz 5 had a flight time of 72 hours, 46 minutes and made 46 orbits.

March 3, 1969
The first manned flight of lunar module by Apollo 9, was launched this date, carrying James McDivitt, David Scott, and Russell Schweickart, made 151 orbits in 241 hours.

May 18, 1969
The manned lunar mission of U.S. Apollo 10 took flight, carrying Thomas Stafford, Eugene Cernan, and John Young. Their objective was to test the lunar excursion module in lunar orbit and they successfully achieved descent to 14,300 miles above the lunar surface. Apollo 10 made 31 orbits of the moon in 192 hours, 3 minutes.

July 16, 1969
U.S. Apollo 11 took Neil A. Armstrong, Edwin E. Aldrin, Jr., and Michael Collins on the first lunar landing mission. Armstrong and Aldrin were the first men to walk on the lunar surface **(July 20th)**. They brought back to earth the first collection of 55 pounds of rock and soil samples. Weight at liftoff was 95,000 pounds. Flight time was 195 hours, 18 minutes.

July 31, 1969
U.S. Mariner 6, Mars probe, launched **February 24, 1969,** passed Mars at 2,200 miles, taking photos of the Martian surface.

October 11, 12, 13, 1969
The Soviets launched three manned satellites. They did not dock but operated as a group flight, each conducting certain experiments among which the first welding of metals took place. The first satellite launched was Soyuz 6, manned by Georgi Shonin and Valery Kubasov; the second satellite was Soyuz 7, manned by Anatoly Filipchenko, Vladislov Volkov and Victor Garbatko and the third one was Soyuz 8, manned by Vladimir Shatalov and Aleksei Yeliseyev. Each satellite orbited 79 times and the flight time was approximately 118 hours.

November 14, 1969
U.S. Apollo 12, the second lunar landing mission, took Charles Conrad, Jr., Alan L. Bean and Richard F. Gordon, Jr., to the moon. On **November 19,** Conrad and Bean landed on the moon and became the third and fourth men to walk on the lunar surface. They retrieved parts of the Surveyor 3 probe. The total flight time was 244 hours, 36 minutes.

This color picture of Mars was made from three frames shuttered nine seconds apart by the Viking 1 Orbiter on June 18, 1976. Just below center of picture and near the morning terminator is the large impact basin, Argyre. Interior of the basin is bright, suggesting ground frost or a ground haze. Bright area south of Argyre probably is an area of discontinuous frost cover near the south pole. The pole itself is in the dark at lower left. North of Argyre, the "Grand Canyon" of Mars, called Vallis Merineris, can be seen near the terminator. Markings elsewhere on the planet are mostly due to differences in brightness; however, color differences are present, suggesting compositional differences. Area at top is the eastern side of the Tharsis volcanic region and is bright because of cloud activity.

April 11, 1970
U.S. Apollo 13 began its lunar mission, carrying James Lovell, Jr., Fred Haise, Jr., and John Swigart, Jr. However, the mission was aborted when the oxygen tank exploded in the Service Module. The spacecraft circled the moon and the Lunar Module was used as the means of return to Earth on **April 17.** The flight time was 142 hours, 55 minutes. The recovery was made 600 miles south of Pago Pago.

This color picture of Mars was taken July 21, 1976—the day following Viking 1's successful landing on the planet. The local time on Mars is approximately noon. The view is southeast from the Viking. Orange-red surface materials cover most of the surface, apparently forming a thin veneer over darker bedrock exposed in patches, as in the lower right. The reddish surface materials may be limonite (hydrated ferric oxide). Such weathering products form on Earth in the presence of water and an oxidizing atmosphere. The sky has a reddish cast, probably due to scattering and reflection from reddish sediment suspended in the lower atmosphere. The scene was scanned three times by the spacecraft's camera #2, through a different color filter each time.

February 11, 1970
The Japanese launched their first satellite, the Rising Sun 1, becoming the fourth nation to achieve a space launch.

April 24, 1970
Communist China became the fifth nation to launch a satellite.

January 31, 1971
Apollo 14 began the third lunar landing mission with astronauts Alan Shephard, Edgar Mitchell and Stuart Roosa. Shephard and Mitchell landed on the lunar surface **February 5** and remained for 33 hours, 31 minutes. They collected 96 pounds of lunar samples. Their flight time was 216 hours, 2 minutes.

April 19, 1971
USSR Salyut 1, was launched. It was an orbiting laboratory to be used by Soyuz flights.

April 22, 1971
USSR Soyuz 10, manned by Vladimir Shatalov,

Aleksei Yeliseyev, and Nikolai Rukavishnikov, docked with Salyut for 5½ hours.

June 6, 1971
USSR Soyuz 11, manned by Georgi T. Dobrovoisky, Vladislav N. Volkov, and Viktor I. Patsayev, was launched into space to dock with Salyut. The cosmonauts orbited in Salyut for 23 days; however, they died in the re-entry phase from loss of pressurization.

July 26, 1971
U.S. Apollo 15, the fourth lunar landing mission, was launched, carrying David Scott, James Irwin and Alfred Worden. Scott and Irwin made the first deep space walk and the first use of the Lunar Roving Vehicle. They stayed on the moon for 66 hours, 55 minutes. They carried back 170 pounds of samples.

November 13, 1971
Mariner 9, a U.S. Mars probe, launched **May 30, 1971,** entered Mars' orbit and transmitted photos and extensive data.

March 2, 1972
The U.S. launched Pioneer 10, Jupiter probe, the first spacecraft to explore the asteroid belt and to pass Jupiter at a distance of 81,000 miles on **December 3, 1973.** Pioneer 10 continued its flight out of the solar system, carrying a plaque containing a symbolic message to other possible civilizations.

March 7, 1972
USSR launched Venera 8, a satellite which reached Venus on **July 22** and landed instruments on the planet.

April 16, 1972
The U.S. launched Apollo 16, the fifth lunar landing mission with John Young, Charles Duke, and Thomas Mattingly. Young and Duke landed on the moon **April 20** and remained on the lunar surface 71 hours, 2 minutes. They collected 213 pounds of samples.

December 7, 1972
Apollo 17, launched this date, was the sixth U.S. manned lunar mission, with Eugene A. Cernan, Ronald E. Evans and Harrison H. Schmitt on board. Cernan and Schmitt landed on the lunar surface **December 11,** made three lunar excursions, collected 243 pounds of samples and made a record lunar stay of 75 hours.

Viking 1 obtained this color picture of the Martian surface and sky on July 24, 1976. Camera #1 facing southeast, captured part of the spacecraft's gray structure in the foreground. A bright orange cable leads to one of the descent rocket engines. Orange-red surface materials cover most of the surface, apparently forming a thin veneer over darker bedrock. A zone of large dark boulders is present in the far-field.

January 8, 1973
The USSR lunar probe, Luna 21, was launched and after landing on **January 16,** unloaded Lunokhod 2, a vehicle which travelled 23 miles on the lunar surface over a period of four months, conducting many experiments.

April 5, 1973
Pioneer 11, a U.S. Saturn probe, was launched. On **December 2, 1974,** it flew within 26,600 miles of Jupiter, transmitting many pictures of the planet. It then continued on to become the first Saturn probe.

May 25, 1973
Skylab 2, a U.S. Apollo spacecraft, launched this date, with Charles Conrad, Jr., Joseph Kerwin, and Paul Weitz, docked with the Skylab space station. It was the first U.S. manned orbiting space station in which the crew lived for 28 days, repairing the damage caused during boost, and making long flight tests.

July 28, 1973
Skylab 3, another U.S. Apollo spacecraft, was launched, transporting Alan L. Bean, Jack R. Lousma and Owen K. Garriott. Spacecraft docked with the Skylab space station and remained almost 60 days. The crew, systems and operational tests went beyond the plans for scientific activities.

November 16, 1973
U.S. Apollo spacecraft was launched with Gerald P. Carr, Edward G. Gibson and William Pogue to dock with Skylab. This fourth Skylab mission holds the record for space walks of 7 hours, 1 minute. The crew set a record of 84 days in a weightless environment.

July 15, 1975
The first cooperative international space flight was begun on this date. The U.S. Apollo 18 with Vance Brand, Tomas P. Stafford and Donald K. Slayton linked up with the USSR Soyuz 19, carrying Aleksei Leonov and Valery Kubasov. The spacecrafts were launched from their respective sites. The two docked on **July 17,** and then they proceeded to conduct experiments together, share their meals and hold a news conference. The Apollo 18 made 136 orbits in 217 hours, 30 minutes; the Soyuz 19 made 96 orbits in 143 hours, 31 minutes.

August 20, 1975
The U.S. Mars probe, Viking 1, softlanded on Mars and transmitted the first photographs from the planet's surface and scientific data on soil and atmospheric conditions.

March 12, 1981
Two cosmonauts, Vladimir Kovalyonok and Viktor Savinykh, were launched aboard the Soyuz T-4. They linked with the orbiting Salyut 6 space station and remained in space for 75 days. During their stay, they were visited by Vladimir Dzhanibekov and Jugderdemidiyn Gurrageha who were aboard the Soyuz 39, which was launched on March 22 and returned to earth on March 30. They were also visited, between May 14 and May 22, by Leonid Popov and Dumitru Prunariu aboard the Soyuz 40.

April 12, 1981
U.S. Columbia opened the era of the space shuttle. It

Photo courtesy of Rockwell International's Space Systems Group

The future. Space Shuttle capabilities will permit delivery of both materials and machinery required to build large space structures, such as this satellite solar power station. After being fabricated and assembled in low earth orbit, a power station would be transferred to its permanent place in orbit (about 22,000 miles out in space). There it would beam a continuous stream of microwave energy to earth receivers, which would convert the energy to electricity.

was manned by John W. Young and Capt. Robert L. Crippen. The world's first re-usable spaceship with a life expectancy of 100 missions glided to a landing April 14 after 54 hours, 21 minutes.

November 12, 1981
The U.S. launched Columbia for the second time. It was manned by Col. Joe Engle and Capt. Richard Truly. The flight lasted 54 hours and 36 orbits and landed at Edwards Air Force Base in California.

March 1, 1982
Venera 13, an unmanned Soviet probe, landed on Venus and survived long enough (127 minutes) to radio back eight photographs and information from soil-sampling experiments. On March 5, Venera 14 landed and provided additional data in the hour before the planet's intense heat put it out of commission.

March 22, 1982
The U.S. launched the space shuttle Columbia for the third time. It was manned by Col. Jack Lousma and Col. C. Gordon Fullerton. The flight lasted 8 days and landed at White Sands Missile Range in New Mexico.

June 27, 1982
The U.S. launched Columbia for its fourth and final

test, manned by Capt. Thomas K. Mattingly and Henry W. Hartsfield. It carried on board military as well as scientific equipment. Landing was as scheduled at Edwards Air Force Base on July 4.

August 19, 1982
Svetlana Savitskaya became the second woman cosmonaut in space, aboard the Soyuz T-7 with Col. Leonid Popov and Aleksandr Serebrov. They linked with the orbiting Salyut 7 on August 20 and returned to earth on August 26 aboard the Soyuz T-5.

November 11, 1982
The U.S. launched Columbia on its first operational flight. It was manned by Vance Brand, Col. Robert Overmyer, William Lenoir, and Joseph Allen. It successfully delivered two satellites into orbit for commercial customers, and landed safely at Edwards Air Force Base in California on November 16.

November 14, 1982
A new record for time in space was set by Soviet cosmonauts Lt. Col. Anatoly Berezovnoy and Valentin Lebedev when they entered day 186 of their mission, aboard the Salyut 7 space station. They returned to earth in the Soyuz T-7 on December 10, having spent a total of 211 days in space.

A DICTIONARY OF SPACE ENGLISH

A-1 *n.* First French satellite, launched November 26, 1965. The capsule carried no scientific equipment other than radio and radar transmitters for tracking purposes. The satellite proved the efficacy of the **Diamant** launch vehicle.

A-2 *n.* Projected Federal Republic of Germany upper-atmospheric research satellite. The spacecraft is scheduled for launch in 1972 by a U.S. **Scout** rocket under provisions of an agreement with NASA.

A-4 *n.* Projected Federal Republic of Germany upper-atmospheric research satellite. Scheduled for launch in 1973 by a U.S. **Scout** rocket, the main task of the spacecraft will be the investigation of cosmic gamma-ray activity.

AACB *(ac.) n.c.* "Aeronautics and Astronautics Coordinating Board," branch of U.S. Department of Defense (**DOD**) which coordinates NASA/DOD efforts in space.

ablating material /ǽbleytiŋ mətìriyəl/ *n.c.* Silicate and plastic spacecraft coating substance; absorbs initial **reentry** heat, melts, and falls away from the vehicle, thereby preventing critical thermal damage. See **ablation; ablation cooling.**

ablation /əbléyšən/ *n.* Melting of the surface material on a spacecraft's heat shield during reentry; prevents dangerous overheating of the craft and its contents. See **ablating material; ablation cooling.**

ablation cooling /əbléyšən kùwliŋ/ *n.c.* Method of protecting a spacecraft from the extreme heat encountered during **reentry** by the shedding of material on the craft's heat shield. See **ablating material; ablation.**

abort /əbórt/ **1.** *v. tr.* To cancel a launch,

mission, or phase of a mission before its completion. Cf. **scrub.**

2. *n.* Cancellation of a launch, mission, or phase of a mission before its completion.

3. *attr.* Of or pertaining to the cancellation of a launch, mission, or any aspect of a mission.

abort guidance subsystem /əbórt gàydəns səbsistəm/ See **AGS.**

abort mode /əbórt mòwd/ *n.c.* Preplanned series of maneuvers required to **abort** a mission at any given moment. Measures vary depending on spacecraft position and time at which abort is initiated. See **LES.**

abort sequence /əbórt sìykwens/ See **abort mode.**

absolute magnitude /ǽbsəluwt mǽgnətuwd/ *n.c.* Magnitude a **stellar** body would seem to have if seen by a human at a distance of ten **parsecs** or 32.6 **light years.**

absolute zero /ǽbsəluwt zíyrow/ *n.c.* Lowest possible temperature: −273.16° Centigrade, −459.69° Farenheit, 0° Kelvin.

acceleration /æksseləéyšən/ *n.* Rate of increase in speed. In the U.S. manned space program, it is usually measured as feet per second.

accelerometer /æksseləámətər/ *n.* Device used to record spacecraft velocity changes.

acceptance checkout equipment /ækséptəns čèkawt iykwìpmənt/ See **ACE.**

acceptance checkout equipment for spacecraft /ækséptəns čèkawt iykwìpmənt for spéyskræft/ See **ACE.**

ACCESS /ǽkses/ *(ac.) n.c.* "Automated Clearinghouse for Collection and Exchange of Sighting Statistics." See **NICAP.**

access arm /ǽkses àrm/ *n.c. Apollo.* Gang-

plank linking the CM and the **umbilical tower.** Kept in position until five minutes prior to **liftoff** as an astronaut emergency escape route.

accumulator /əkyúwmyəleytər/ *n.* Any device which provides storage for either tangible or intangible items such as fluids, computer programs, or figures.

ACE *(ac.) n.c. Apollo.* "Acceptance checkout equipment," computer apparatus used to determine the flight readiness of spacecraft before launch; housed in the Manned Spaceflight Operations Building (**MSOB**).

ACE/SC *(ac.) n.c. Apollo.* "Acceptance checkout equipment for spacecraft." See **ACE.**

acquisition /ækwəzíšən/ *n.* **1.** Locating a satellite's orbit or space probe's trajectory in order to gather spacecraft data.

2. Process of properly orienting a spacecraft antenna or telescope so that data can be gathered.

acquisition and tracking radar /ækwəzíšən ænd trǽkin rèydar/ *n.c.* **Radar** system, either ground based or spaceborne, which finds and tracks spacecraft or other objects.

acquisition lights /ækwəzíšən làyts/ *n.c.* Intense lights attached to the passive vehicle in a **rendezvous** maneuver which make it readily visible to the approaching spacecraft.

acquisition of signal /ækwəzíšən əv sígnəl/ See **AOS.**

activated charcoal /ǽktəveytəd čárkowl/ *n.c.* Odor-absorbing material used to keep the air fresh in a spacecraft carrying living creatures.

active communications satellite /ǽktiv kəmyuwnəkéyšənz sǽtəlayt/ *n.c.* **Comsat** carrying equipment enabling it to transmit either received or stored messages. Cf. **passive communications satellite.**

active repeater /ǽktiv riypíytər/ *attr.* Of or pertaining to a **comsat** capable of receiving and storing messages from one ground station and, later, sending them on command to another station.

active seismic experiment /ǽktiv sâyzmik ekspérəmənt/ See **ASE.**

actuator /ǽkčuweytər/ *n.* Device capable of converting electrical signals into mechanical movement using pneumatic or hydraulic power.

adapter skirt /ədǽptər skə̀rt/ *n.c.* Rocket-stage or section extension that serves as a collar for the addition of another stage.

advanced vidicon camera system /ædvǽnst vîdikàn kǽmrə sìstəm/ See **AVCS.**

AE *(ac.) n.c. Apollo.* "Ascent engine," 3,500-lb. thrust engine of the ascent or upper stage of the LM which is used for liftoff from the lunar surface or in case of prelanding abort.

AE *(ac.) n.c.* "Atmosphere Explorer," U.S. geophysical satellites, numbers 17 and 32 of the **Explorer** series, launched in April 1963 and May 1966. The two satellites investigated the earth's upper atmosphere and took direct measurements of its temperature, density, and other related phenomena.

All Apollo aborts implemented below 295,000 feet use the launch escape subsystem and are called Mode 1 aborts. Aborts above this altitude are effected after the jettison of the launch escape tower. Illustrated below are the specific Mode 1 abort procedures.

NORTH AMERICAN ROCKWELL

Three-advanced AEs are planned for launch beginning in 1973. These will study the transitional region of the atmosphere (75 to 95 miles up) and have eccentric orbits requiring the firing of small rocket engines at **perigee** to keep the satellites from decaying. The satellites' inclinations will vary to allow total coverage of the transition region.

AEC *(ac.) n.c.* "Atomic Energy Commission," U.S. government agency that manages the national atomic-energy program. Joint NASA/AEC efforts have been directed toward producing nuclear power sources for space applications (see **NERVA; SNAP**).

aeroballistics /erowbəlístiks/ *n.* Branch of science dealing with the motion of bodies whose flight path is determined by principles of **aerodynamics** and **ballistics**.

aerodynamic heating /erowdaynǽmik híytiŋ/ *n.c.* Heating of a spacecraft due to air friction. This is especially significant during **reentry**.

aerodynamics /erowdaynǽmiks/ *n.* Branch of physics dealing with the motion of air and the forces acting on bodies moving in air.

aeronautics /erənɔ́tiks/ *n.* Science that deals with all aspects of designing, making, and operating airborne vehicles.

Aeronautics and Astronautics Coordinating Board /erənɔ́tiks ænd æstrənɔ́tiks kowɔ́rdəneytiŋ bɔ̀rd/ See **AACB**.

Aeronautics and Space Engineering Board /erənɔ́tiks ænd spêys enjəníriŋ bôrd/ See **ASEB**.

aeronomy /eránəmiy/ *n.* Branch of science dealing with the atmosphere of any **celestial** body.

aeropause /êrowpɔ́z/ *n.* Point in space at which Earth's atmosphere no longer affects men or spacecraft.

aerospace /êrowspéys/ *n.* Earth's atmosphere and space.

2. *attr.* Of or pertaining to Earth's atmosphere and space.

aerospace glider /êrowspêys gláydə/ See **ASP**.

aerospace plane /êrowspêys pléyn/ See **ASP**.

aerothermodynamic border /êrowθɔ̂mowdaynǽmik bórdə/ *n.c.* Point at an altitude of about 100 miles, below which **aerodynamic heating** is a factor in flight.

aerothermodynamics /êrowθɔ̂mowdaynǽmiks/ *n.* Science dealing with **aerodynamic heating**.

AFETR *(ac.) n.c.* "Air Force Eastern Test Range," 10,000-mile instrumented U.S. test range extending from Florida to the Indian Ocean, which includes the shorter Atlantic Missile Range (AMR). AFETR employs stations, aircraft, and ships to test and track both military and civilian rockets or spacecraft. Cf. **AFWTR**.

afflight /ǽflayt/ *n.* Lunar approach **trajectory** that does not encircle the moon, although it allows the spacecraft involved to "see" the entire hidden side prior to Earth return.

AFP *(ac.) n.c.* "Alternative flight plan," emergency procedure outlined in detail prior to any mission and updated through-

out that mission which provides for safest return in case of mishap.

AFSC *(ac.) n.c.* "Air Force Systems Command," U.S. Air Force agency established in 1961 to fulfill Department of Defense (**DOD**) space responsibilities. AFSC supports specified NASA projects under NASA/DOD agreements.

aft /ǽft/ **1.** *adv.* Rear or underside of an aerospace vehicle; originally naval jargon.

2. *attr.* Of the pertaining to the bottom or back of a vehicle.

aft equipment bay /ǽft iykwípmənt bèy/ See **equipment bay**.

afterbody /ǽftəbàdiy/ *n.* Jettisoned material or debris which drifts with an orbiting craft.

afterburning /ǽftəbɔ̀niŋ/ *n.* Irregular burning of excess fuel after termination of main **burn**.

aft-firing thruster /ǽft fáyəiŋ θrǿstə/ *n.c.* Any maneuvering rocket located in the tail of a spacecraft.

aft interstage /ǽft íntəstèyj/ *n.c.* Protective covering that encloses the rocket **nozzles** of the **Saturn** launch vehicle's second and third stages during launch.

AFWTR *(ac.) n.c.* "Air Force Western Test Range," instrumented U.S. test range extending into the Pacific Ocean over 1,500 miles in a west-to-south arc from its headquarters at Vandenberg Air Force Base, California. AFWTR incorporated the former Pacific Missile Range (PMR) and became fully operational in early 1965 with tracking, testing, and launch facilities. Vandenberg, one of three U.S. launch sites, is ideally situated for launching spacecraft into polar orbit, since it can boost them southward over open water. Cf. **AFETR; KSC; Wallops Station**.

Agate /agát/ *n.* "Agate," French single-stage rocket, used primarily as the first stage of the **Rubis** sounding rocket.

Agate stands 28 ft. high, weighs 7,500 lbs., and develops 50,000 lbs. of thrust.

Agena /əjíynə/ *n.* U.S. single-stage rocket used primarily as an upper stage for **Atlas, Thor**, and **Titan** launch vehicles. Agenas were the first space vehicles to achieve three-axis control in flight and restart capability, and the first to put satellites in circular and polar orbits.

Used since 1959, this multipurpose booster is capable of inserting a spacecraft into earth orbit, as with project **Discoverer**; of becoming an orbiting satellite itself, as in March 1966, when, modified into the *Gemini Agena Target Vehicle (GATV)*, it took part in the first manned space docking (see **Gemini**); and of reigniting in earth orbit and injecting payloads into deep space, as with projects **Mariner** and **Surveyor**.

The standard Agena stands 26 ft. high, weighs 15,000 lbs. fueled, and has a thrust potential of 16,000 lbs.

AGS /ǽgs/ *(ac.) n.c. Apollo.* "Abort guidance subsystem," that part of the guidance, navigation, and control system (**GNCS**) whose instruments serve as a back-up to the primary guidance and navigation system (**PGNS**) in case of abort.

AIAA *(ac.) n.c.* "American Institute of

Aeronautics and Astronautics," U.S. organization formed in 1963 by the consolidation of the **American Rocket Society** and the Institute of the Aerospace Sciences. The more than 30,000 AIAA members are committed to advancing all phases of aeronautical and astronautical development.

AIMP *(ac.) n.c.* "Anchored Interplanetary Monitoring Platform." See **IMP**.

air-breathing /ér brìyðiŋ/ *attr.* Of or pertaining to an engine which requires air for the combustion of its fuel. Cf. **anaerobic**.

Air Density Explorer /ér dènsitiy eksplórə/ *n.c.* U.S. geophysical satellites, numbers 9, 19, 24, and 39 of the **Explorer** series, launched between 1961 and 1968. Air Density Explorers are large balloons used to investigate upper-atmospheric density over various regions of the earth. *Explorer 24* was launched in November 1964 along with an **Injun** satellite (*Explorer 25*) in NASA's first double launch. *Explorer 39* was also launched in tandem with an Injun (*Explorer 40*) in August 1968.

Air Force Eastern Test Range /ér fors íystən tést rèynj/ See **AFETR**.

Air Force Systems Command /êr fors sístəmz kəmǽnd/ See **AFSC**.

Air Force Western Test Range /êr fors wêstən tést rèynj/ See **AFWTR**.

airglow /érglow/ *n.* Steady brightness of the night sky caused by the effects of the sun's radiation on the upper atmosphere.

airlock /érlak/ *n.* Interim area between two compartments of unequal pressure. Airtight doors allow access from one compartment to the other after a repressurization period during which the pressure of the connecting compartment is equalized to that of the area about to be entered.

Airlock Module /érlak màdyul/ See **AM**.

AK *(ac.) n.c.* "Apogee kick," rocket **burn** initiated by a spacecraft in an elliptical orbit at the farthest point from the **central body** of that orbit. It places the craft in a circular orbit.

albedo /ælbíydow/ *n.* Reflective power of planets or satellites; usually measured as the ratio of light reflected by a body to the amount falling on it.

Algol /ǽlgɔl/ *n.* **1.** U.S. rocket which serves as the first stage in the **Scout** launch vehicle. Basic version of the Algol stands 30 ft. high, weighs 20,000 lbs. fueled, and produces 88,000 lbs. of thrust.

2. Second-**magnitude** star in our **galaxy**.

3. A computer language.

all balls /ɔl bɔ́lz/ See **balls**.

all systems go /ɔl sístəmz gów/ *i.s.* Everything functioning as planned.

ALOS *(ac.) n.c. Apollo.* "Apollo Lunar Orbital Science," program of experiments conducted aboard or by the **CSM** while in orbit around the moon. In July 1971 as part of ALOS the **Apollo Lunar Particles and Fields Subsatellite** was released from the CSM of *Apollo 15*.

Alouette /æluwét/ *n.* Either of two Canadian upper-atmospheric research satellites launched in 1962 and 1965 by NASA launch vehicles from the Air Force West-

---

/a/ *father;* /aw/ *wow;* /ay/ *buy;* /b/ *boy;* /č/ *witch;* /d/ *doll;* /e/ *bet;* /ey/ *say;* /f/ *few;* /g/ *bag;* /h/ *hole;* /i/ *it;* /iy/ *be;* /j/ *gin;* /k/ *cat;* /l/ *lamb;*
/m/ *man;* /n/ *now;* /o/ *orbit;* /ow/ *tow;* /oy/ *boy;* /p/ *pat;* /r/ *run;* /s/ *send;* /š/ *shoe;* /t/ *toy;* /u/ *put;* /uw/ *do;* /v/ *eve;* /w/ *way;* /y/ *yes;*

DEPARTMENT OF COMMUNICATIONS (CANADA)

The *Alouette*, a Canadian satellite, is 42 inches in diameter and weighs 320 pounds.

American Institute of Aeronautics and Astronautics /əmêrəkən înstìtuwt əv erənɔ́tiks ænd æstrənɔ́tiks/ See **AIAA**.

American Rocket Society /əmêrəkən rákət səsàyetiy/ *n.c.* U.S. organization formed in 1934 to study all aspects of rockets and space travel. See also **AIAA**.

Ames Research Center /êymz ríysɚč sèntɚ/ *n.c.* **NASA** research facility at Moffet Field, California.

ammonium /əmówniyəm/ *n.* Common **oxidizer** in solid propellants.

AMR *(ac.) n.c.* "Atlantic Missile Range." See **AFETR**.

AMU *(ac.) n.c. Gemini.* "Astronaut maneuvering unit," powered, chairlike backpack intended to control an astronaut's movements while on EVA. During *Gemini 9A* (see **Gemini**), first test of the AMU under extended weightlessness, Eugene A. Cernan experienced difficulty in attaching the backpack. Further use of the AMU was canceled.

anacoustic zone /ǽnəkûwstik zówn/ *n.c.* Silent region of space beginning about 100 miles above the earth's surface. No sound waves can be propagated above this altitude because of the scarcity of air molecules.

anaerobic /ǽnerówbik/ *attr.* Of or pertaining to an engine which can function in a vacuum. Both rocket engines and nuclear-powered engines are anaerobic. Cf. **air-breathing**.

Anchored Interplanetary Monitoring Platform /ǽŋkɚd întɚplǽnəteriy mánitɚiŋ plǽtform/ See **IMP**.

Anechoic Chamber Test Facility /ǽnekowik čêymbɚ tést fəsìlətiy/ *n.c.* Major installation at **NASA**'s Manned Spacecraft Center (**MSC**) consisting primarily of an echo-free chamber used for testing space-vehicle communications equipment.

angel /éynjəl/ *n.* Indication on a radar device of a flying object which cannot be verified by visual sighting or otherwise be accounted for. An angel may be caused by unusual atmospheric conditions, particularly in summer; by birds and other flying objects; by smoke and debris in the air; by the aurora borealis, lightning, or solar flares; or by reflections from the moon or meteors.

Since radar functions primarily to detect a presence and not to draw a picture of what has been detected, a problem of identification arises when angels appear on the scope. These may be particularly serious in security measures such as early warning systems designed to give notice of intercontinental ballistics. In 1960 a signal indicating an attack on the U.S. was underway was found to be caused by radar beams reflected from the moon.

In a specialized sense, an angel is a slow-moving target appearing on the radar scope, as opposed to a vague and sporadic return probably caused by meteorological effects, or to a sharp, persistent return similar to that coming from a moving aircraft. Slow-moving angels, never suitably explained, have been associated with theories concerning UFO's.

angel hair /éynjəl hèr/ *n.c.* Any cobweblike

ern Test Range (**AFWTR**). *Alouette 1*, launched September 28, 1962, was Canada's first satellite. The Alouettes' primary mission was ionospheric study.

ALSD *(ac.) n.c. Apollo.* "Apollo lunar surface drill," battery-powered instrument carried by Apollo lunar landing crews to make the lined borehole in the moon's surface needed for soil-analysis probes. Consisting of fiberglass sections reinforced with boron, the drill may be extended as penetration increases.

ALSEP /ɔ́lsep/ *(ac.) n.c. Apollo.* "Apollo Lunar Surface Experiments Package," any lunar-research equipment connected to a central atomic power station; various configurations of ALSEP were carried from *Apollo 12* on, in the descent stage of the LM. Included among ALSEP apparatus have been the passive seismic experiment (**PSE**), heat-flow experiment (**HFE**), lunar-dust detector (**LDD**), lunar-surface magnetometer (**LSM**), solar-wind spectrometer (**SWS**), cold cathode ion gauge (**CCIG**), active seismic experiment (**ASE**), suprathermal ion detector experiment (**SIDE**), and charged-particle lunar environment experiment (**CPLEE**). By the end of Project Apollo, ALSEPs will form a series of scientific observatories in widely scattered sites on the moon. A simpler, lighter experimental package, the Early Apollo Scientific Experiments Package (**EASEP**), was carried on *Apollo 11*.

Altair /ɔltér/ *n.* 1. U.S. rocket which serves as the fourth stage of the **Scout**, and the third stage of the **Delta** launch vehicles. Basic version of the 5-ft. high, spin-stabilized booster weighs 600 lbs., fueled, and

produces 6,000 lbs. of thrust.
  2. Star in the constellation *Eagle.*

alternative flight plan /ɔltɚ́nətiv fláyt plæn/ See **AFP**.

altimeter /ǽltímətɚ/ *n.* Calibrated device which measures the distance between an **aerospace** vehicle and the surface of a **celestial** body.

aluminum /əlúwmənəm/ *n.* Metal which, when finely ground, is mixed with certain spacecraft propellants to increase their exhaust velocity.

AM *(ac.) n.c.* "Airlock Module," one of four major components of the proposed U.S. **Skylab** space station; the portion of Skylab used for EVA egress. A pressurized, 17-foot passage between Orbital Workshop (**OWS**) and Multiple Docking Adapter (**MDA**), the AM will consist of three parts: *structural transition section (STS), tunnel assembly,* and *flexible tunnel extension.* The funnel-shaped STS will be rigidly attached to the MDA; it will have four windows and contain displays and controls for environmental, electric, and communications systems. The central tunnel assembly will contain an airlock compartment which can be depressurized and repressurized without affecting the rest of Skylab. From this section, two astronauts will egress for EVA. The flexible tunnel extension will be a bellowslike tube connecting the AM to the OWS. Several truss support assemblies and the Apollo Telescope Mount (**ATM**) deployment assembly are also associated with the AM.

ambient /ǽmbiyənt/ *n.* Standard conditions for any given environment; LM ambient is 4.5 pounds per square inch at 70°F.

/z/ zero; /ž/ azure; /θ/ thin; /ð/ then; /ŋ/ song; /æ/ bat; /ɔ/ law; /ə/ sun; /ɚ/ bird. Foreign symbols: [(n)] nasalization of some French vowels followed by /n/; [R] French uvular rolled /r/ sound; [ü] high front lip-rounded vowel; [x] Russian voiceless laryngeal fricative.

substance which appears to fall from the sky, especially strange material which might have been deposited by **UFO's.** In many cases, angel hair is undoubtedly an extraordinary quantity of gossamers from ballooning spiders. In some cases, various artificial materials such as aluminum foil used in escaping radar detection, silver dioxide used in seeding clouds, and debris from textile mills have been reported as angel hair. Instances are on record, however, of falls of a threadlike substance which dissipated and therefore escaped analysis in the laboratory. A complete understanding of this phenomenon is not available.

Anik /éynik/ *n.* Projected Canadian comsat series to be owned and operated by the Canadian government. First launch is scheduled for late 1972.

ANNA /ǽnə/ *(ac.) n.c.* "Army, Navy, NASA, Air Force," U.S. geodetic satellite launched in October 1962. It was the first satellite to carry an optical beacon — used for some earth-measuring experiments — into orbit.

annular space /ǽnyələ spéys/ *n.c.* Near-vacuum region, used as insulation, between the double walls of spacecraft fuel and storage tanks.

anomalistic period /ənâməlîstik píriyəd/ *n.c.* Time span between the **perigees** of two consecutive orbits.

ANS *(ac.) n.c.* "Astronomical Netherlands Satellite," Dutch scientific research satellite projected for launch in 1974 by a U.S. **Scout** rocket at the Air Force Western Test Range (**AFWTR**). Basic objectives of the spacecraft will be the study of ultraviolet and x-ray emissions in deep space.

The *ANS* satellite will be launched into a sun-synchronous orbit and align itself for experiments using the sun, stars, and horizon.

Antares /ǽntériyz/ *n.* **1.** U.S. rocket which serves as the third stage in the **Scout** launch vehicle. Basic version of the Antares stands 11 ft. high, weighs 2,100 lbs. fueled, and produces 21,000 lbs. of thrust.

2. Name of *Apollo 14* LM (see **Apollo**).

3. Major star in our **galaxy** in the constellation *Scorpio*.

antenna /ænténə/ *n.* **1.** Any conductor used to transmit or receive radio or television

signals. The largest ground-based antennas are the 210-ft. **dish reflectors** used by NASA for tracking and telemetry, and the 1000-ft. diameter, fixed-position radar-radio telescope antennas used in astronomical research. Spacecraft antennas vary in form and size from the 31-in. diameter S-band antennas used in Apollo missions to the 146-ft. expandable antenna of **Alouette** research satellites. Sometimes the metallic outer surface of a satellite itself acts as an antenna.

2. *Apollo.* That part of the telecommunications (**T/C**) system which transmits and receives radio and television signals.

antigravity /ǽntaygrǽvətiy/ *n.* Imaginary energy field which would be able to neutralize a gravitational force.

antipode /ǽntipòwd/ *n.* Hypothetical line that runs from the center of the moon through the center of the earth, emerging on the opposite surface of the moon. In **Apollo** it is the point of **splashdown** at the end of a lunar mission.

A.O.K. *n. sl.* Working properly.

AOS *(ac.) n.c.* "Acquisiton of signal," establishment or reestablishment of radio contact with a spacecraft. In **Apollo**, contact has to be reacquired with the CSM after communications are blocked by its pass behind the moon. Cf. **LOS.**

aphelion /əfíyliyən/ *n.* Point in a solar orbit at which an orbiting body is farthest from the sun. Cf. **perihelion.**

apocynthion /ǽpowsínθiyən/ *n.* Point in a lunar orbit where an orbiting body launched from another **celestial** body is farthest from the moon. Cf. **pericynthion.**

apogee /ǽpəjiy/ *n.* Point in an Earth orbit where an orbiting body is farthest from the earth. Cf. **perigee.**

apogee engine /ǽpəjiy ènjən/ *n.c.* Small rocket motor which is fired to induce apogee kick (**AK**). Also called *apogee kick rocket.*

apogee kick /ǽpəjiy kìk/ See **AK.**

apogee kick rocket /ǽpəjiy kík ràkət/ *n.c.* **Apogee engine.**

Apollo /əpálow/ *n.c.* **1.** Third and current American manned spaceflight project; the program in which the first men were landed on the moon. The program and its objectives, as announced in July 1960 by NASA, included sending a three-man spacecraft into orbit around the moon; landing two men on the lunar surface while the third remained in orbit; returning the lunar expeditionary force, after as many as 70 hours on the moon, to the orbiting spacecraft; and returning all three men safely to Earth. President John F. Kennedy made the landing of a man on the moon a national goal in May 1961.

Preceded by three successful unmanned test flights during 1966, a manned flight was scheduled for launch in February 1967. On January 27, 1967, during a dress rehearsal for this mission, astronauts Virgil I. Grissom, Edward H. White II, and Roger B. Chaffee were trapped in their spacecraft as a fatal flash fire swept through the sealed compartment. The trag-

edy resulted in complete reevaluation of the program and a delay of more than a year.

The first manned Apollo flight followed three more unmanned experimental launches. Designated *Apollo 7*, it tested spacecraft, crew, and support elements in earth orbit. The next three missions continued testing of various spacecraft components in earth or lunar environments. The first landing on the moon was achieved at 4:18 p.m. (EST) July 20, 1969, when *Apollo 11*'s lunar module *Eagle* touched down on the southwestern edge of a plain called the Sea of Tranquility. At 10:56 p.m. (EST), Mission Commander Neil A. Armstrong became the first man to set foot on the moon.

Except for *Apollo 13*, which was aborted due to a tank explosion during lunar approach, all missions subsequent to *Apollo 11* have landed successfully on the moon. Science stations have been deployed by each of the missions which have landed, thus establishing a network of equipment for lunar experiments. One more flight (*Apollo 17*) is projected for 1972 to complete the program. The next step in the manned U.S. space program, an Earth-orbital space station, is titled **Skylab.**

The sections of the Apollo spacecraft include the *command module* (**CM**) and *service module* (**SM**), referred to jointly as the **CSM**; as well as the *lunar module* (**LM**). The conical CM is control center and living quarters for most of the mission and the only section that returns to Earth; the unmanned SM contains the main spacecraft propulsion system and most of the consumables (oxygen, water, and propellant). The spiderlike LM carries men from the orbiting CM to the moon and back; it is then jettisoned. The LM, situated between the SM and the launch vehicle during launch, is covered by a *spacecraft-lunar module adapter* (**SLA**) until the craft has been injected into lunar trajectory.

Launch vehicle for lunar Apollo missions is the *Saturn 5* (see **Saturn**), which uses its 8.7 million pounds of thrust to orbit the spacecraft and then inject it into lunar trajectory. The SM provides sufficient thrust for the remainder of the mission.

2. Greek god of music and prophecy.

Apollo Lunar Orbital Science /əpálow lùwnɚ órbətəl sàyəns/ See **ALOS.**

Apollo Lunar Particles and Fields Subsatellite /əpálow lùwnər pàrtikəlz ænd fìyldz sɜ̀bsǽtəlayt/ *n.c.* U.S. astrophysical satellite; first satellite to be orbited from a manned spacecraft. The satellite was inserted into lunar orbit on August 4, 1971 from the CSM of *Apollo 15*. It was used for gathering data on the lunar environment and cislunar space. Another **subsatellite** was inserted into lunar orbit from the CSM of *Apollo 16* in April, 1972.

Apollo lunar surface drill /əpálow lùwnɚ sɚfəs drìl/ See **ALSD.**

Apollo Lunar Surface Experiments Package /əpálow lùwnɚ sɚfəs ekspérəmənts pæ̀kij/ See **ALSEP.**

/a/ *father;* /aw/ *wow;* /ay/ b*uy;* /b/ *boy;* /č/ wit*ch;* /d/ *doll;* /e/ b*et;* /ey/ *say;* /f/ *few;* /g/ *bag;* /h/ *hole;* /i/ *it;* /iy/ *be;* /ǰ/ *gin;* /k/ *cat;* /l/ *lamb;* /m/ *man;* /n/ *now;* /o/ *orbit;* /ow/ *tow;* /oy/ *boy;* /p/ *pat;* /r/ *run;* /s/ *send;* /š/ *shoe;* /t/ *toy;* /u/ *put;* /uw/ *do;* /v/ *eve;* /w/ *way;* /y/ *yes;* /z/ *zero;* /ž/ *azure;* /θ/ *thin;* /ð/ *then;* /ŋ/ so*ng;* /æ/ b*at;* /ɔ/ *law;* /ə/ *sun;* /ɚ/ b*ird.* Foreign symbols: [(n)] nasalization of some French vowels followed by /n/; [R] French uvular rolled /r/ sound; [ü] high front lip-rounded vowel; [x] Russian voiceless laryngeal fricative.

MANNED APOLLO FLIGHTS

Mission	Crew	Dates	Remarks
Apollo 7	Walter M. Schirra, Jr. (Capt., USN) Mission Commander R. Walter Cunningham (Civilian) Pilot, LM Donn F. Eisele (Maj., USAF) Pilot, CM	Oct. 11–22, 1968 (260 hrs. 09 min.)	Demonstrated spacecraft, crew, and support elements. Launched by *Saturn 1B* rocket. 163 Earth orbits.
Apollo 8	Frank Borman (Col., USAF) Mission Commander William A. Anders, Jr. (Maj., USAF) Pilot, LM James A. Lovell, Jr. (Cmdr., USN) Pilot, CM	Dec. 21–27, 1968 (147 hrs. 00 min.)	First manned flight to the vicinity of another celestial body. First manned flight of *Saturn 5* rocket. 10 lunar orbits.
Apollo 9	James A. McDivitt (Col., USAF) Mission Commander Russell L. Schweickart (Civilian) Pilot, *Spider* (LM) David R. Scott (Col., USAF) Pilot, *Gumdrop* (CM)	Mar. 3–13, 1969 (241 hrs. 01 min.)	Earth-orbital test of all spacecraft components. First trial of LM in space; first Apollo EVA, by Schweickart (40 min.); first CSM/LM docking. 151 Earth orbits.
Apollo 10	Thomas P. Stafford (Col., USAF) Mission Commander Eugene A. Cernan (Cmdr., USN) Pilot, *Snoopy* (LM) John W. Young (Cmdr., USN) Pilot, *Charlie Brown* (CM)	May 18–26, 1969 (192 hrs. 03 min.)	Dress rehearsal for lunar touchdown. LM descended to within 9 miles of lunar surface before rejoining CSM. 31 lunar orbits.
Apollo 11	Neil A. Armstrong (Civilian) Mission Commander Edwin E. Aldrin, Jr. (Col., USAF) Pilot, *Eagle* (LM) Michael Collins (Lt. Col., USAF) Pilot, *Columbia* (CM)	July 16–24, 1969 (195 hrs. 18 min.)	First landing of a man on the moon. Total stay on lunar surface 21 hrs. 36 min.; total lunar EVA 2 hrs. 15 min.; 30 lunar orbits.
Apollo 12	Charles Conrad, Jr. (Cmdr., USN) Mission Commander Alan L. Bean (Cmdr., USN) Pilot, *Intrepid* (LM) Richard F. Gordon, Jr. (Cmdr., USN) Pilot, *Yankee Clipper* (CM)	Nov. 14–24, 1969 (244 hrs. 36 min.)	Total stay on lunar surface 31 hrs. 31 min.; total lunar EVA 7 hrs. 45 min.; 45 lunar orbits.
Apollo 13	James A. Lovell, Jr. (Capt., USN) Mission Commander Fred W. Haise, Jr. (Civilian) Pilot, *Aquarius* (LM) John L. Swigert, Jr. (Civilian) Pilot, *Odyssey* (CM)	Apr. 11–17, 1970 (142 hrs. 55 min.)	Mission aborted due to failure of SM oxygen tank 205,000 miles from Earth.
Apollo 14	Alan B. Shepard, Jr. (Capt., USN) Mission Commander Edgar D. Mitchell (Cmdr., USN) Pilot, *Antares* (LM) Stuart A. Roosa (Maj., USAF) Pilot, *Kitty Hawk* (CM)	Jan. 31–Feb. 9, 1971 (216 hrs. 02 min.)	Exploration of lunar highlands. Total stay on lunar surface 33 hrs. 31 min.; total lunar EVA 9 hrs. 25 min.; 34 lunar orbits.
Apollo 15	David R. Scott (Col., USAF) Mission Commander James B. Irwin (Lt. Col., USAF) Pilot, *Falcon* (LM) Alfred M. Worden (Maj., USAF) Pilot, *Endeavor* (CM)	July 26–Aug. 7, 1971 (295 hrs. 12 min.)	Lunar Roving Vehicle (*LRV*) provided motorized transportation on lunar surface. Lunar satellite launched from CM. Worden made first EVA in deep space (16 min.) on return trip. Total stay on lunar surface 67 hrs.; total lunar EVA 18 hrs. 37 min.; 74 lunar orbits.
Apollo 16	John W. Young (Capt., USN) Mission Commander Charles M. Duke, Jr. (Lieut. Col., USAF) Pilot, *Orion* (LM) Thomas K. Mattingly, II (Lieut. Comdr., USN) Pilot, *Casper* (CM)	April 16–April 27, 1972 (265 hrs. 51 min.)	Exploration of Descartes highlands, using second LRV. 1 hr. 02 min. deep space EVA by Mattingly on return trip. Total stay on lunar surface 71 hrs. 12 min.; total lunar EVA 20 hrs. 14 min.; 65 lunar orbits.
Apollo 17	Eugene A. Cernan (Capt. USN) Mission Commander Harrison H. Schmitt (Civilian) Pilot, *Challenger* (LM) Ronald E. Evans (Cmdr. USN) Pilot, *America* (CM)	Dec. 7–Dec. 19, 1972 (301 hrs. 52 min.)	Exploration of Taurus-Littrow valley using LRV. 47 min. EVA by Evans on return trip. Total stay on lunar surface 74 hrs. 59 min.; total lunar EVA 22 hrs. 05 min.; 75 lunar orbits.

1.

2.

THE VOYAGES OF APOLLO

On July 16, 1969, *Apollo 11, 1,* lifted off for the moon with astronauts Edwin Aldrin, Neil Armstrong, and Michael Collins. Four days later on July 20, Neil Armstrong, *2,* became the first man to set foot on lunar soil, calling his action "a small step for a man, a giant leap for mankind." In November 1969, *Apollo 12* continued *Apollo 11's* historic feat, and astronaut Alan Bean, *3,* collected a valuable sample of lunar soil on the mission. On the *Apollo 14* mission in February 1971, astronauts Alan Shepard, Stuart Roosa, and Edgar Mitchell caught a magnificent view of the crescent Earth, *4.* Shepard, *5,* even struck a pose for a photograph of himself, with the U.S. flag firmly implanted in the lunar soil, while his companion, Edgar Mitchell, *6,* took a lunar stroll involved with setting up some of the scientific experiments. In August of the same year, the *Apollo 15* mission was able to obtain a close-up view of a "relatively fresh" crater, *7,* with the Apennine Front and the Hadley Delta in the left and right backgrounds, respectively. One of the most successful lunar missions was *Apollo 16, 8,* which blasted off from Cape Kennedy on April 16, 1972. For a period of nearly three full days, astronauts John Young and Charles Duke explored the moon's Descartes highlands in the Lunar Rover Vehicle. One of the first extravehicular activities of the mission included a leaping salute to the U.S. flag by Young, *9,* while his fellow astronaut Duke stood by watching the patriotic display. *Apollo 17* was the final manned mission to the moon. It produced a fantastic view of the planet Earth, *10,* which clearly delineates the Mediterranean Sea, the African continent, and the Arabian peninsula. During the mission, Eugene Cernan took a picture of Harrison Schmitt near a huge lunar boulder, *11,* which made Schmitt appear dwarflike. The Lunar Roving Vehicle, *12,* was given a test drive by Cernan as part of the first Apollo 17 extravehicular activity. The wheels of this "moonmobile," *inset,* were especially built for the lunar surface. After a successful mission, the Apollo 17 spacecraft glided to splashdown, *13,* on December 19, 1972, thus completing the entire Apollo Project.

5.   3.

4.

6.

7.

11.

9.

ALL PHOTOS
COURTESY OF NASA

2.

13.

Apollo Range Instrumentation Aircraft /əpâlow rèynj instrəmentéyšən èrkræft/ See **ARIA**.

Apollo Telescope Mount. /əpâlow téləskowp màwnt/ See **ATM**.

apolune /ǽpəlùwn/ n. Point at which an object launched from the moon into lunar orbit is farthest from the moon's surface. Cf. **perilune**.

apparent magnitude /əpêrənt mǽgnətuwd/ n.c. Measure of luminosity from any **celestial** body as observed from Earth.

apparition /æpəríšən/ n. Period during which a comet is in an ideal position for observation from Earth.

Applications Technology Satellite /æpləkêyšənz teknáləjiy sǽtəlayt/ See **ATS**.

APS /æps/ (ac.) n.c. Apollo. "Ascent propulsion system," LM equipment complex which provides, through a liquid-fueled rocket engine, the thrust needed to lift off from the lunar surface and rendezvous with the CSM. A **pressurization subsystem** and **propellant feed subsystem** supply the engine.

apsis /ǽpsis/ n. Either end of the major axis of an orbital path; corresponds to the highest and lowest points of an orbit in reference to the **central body**.

APT /æpt/ (ac.) n.c. "Automatic picture transmission," camera system used on some U.S. weather satellites; relays daylight photographs immediately by converting them to electrical signals. APT photos are advantageous because they can be received by simple, relatively inexpensive ground equipment, thereby enabling remoter local areas to use satellite weather services. Cf. **AVCS**.

Aquarius /əkwériyəs/ n. 1. Name of Apollo 13 LM (see **Apollo**).

2. Eleventh constellation of the Zodiac, "The Water Bearer."

3. Due to the precession of the equinoxes, the constellation in which the sun is located on the first day of spring changes about every 2,200 years. These periods are sometimes called Ages. Astronomers compute that we are now in the Age of Pisces and will enter the Age of Aquarius about A.D. 2300.

arc-jet engine /ârkjet énjən/ n.c. Experimental spacecraft motor in which power for rocket propulsion is provided by heating a propellant gas by means of an electric arc.

areography /êriyágrəfiy/ n. Study of Martian topography.

ARIA /áriyə/ (ac.) n.c. Apollo. "Apollo Range Instrumentation Aircraft," fleet of eight U.S. Air Force Boeing 707 airplanes used to fill ground tracking system communications gaps during flights of Project **Apollo**.

Ariel /ériyəl/ n. British upper-atmospheric research satellite series consisting of three craft orbited by U.S. launch vehicles from 1962 to 1967. The primary mission of the satellites, also called UK-1, -2, and -3, was the investigation of phenomena in the ionosphere.

Ariel 1 (UK-1), Great Britain's first satellite, was launched on April 26, 1962 by a Thor-Delta from Kennedy Space Center (KSC). Although the spacecraft's casing was provided by the U.S., all internal components were British designed and built. Ariel 2 (UK-2) was launched in March 1964; Ariel 3 (UK-3) in May 1967.

Army, Navy, NASA, Air Force /ârmiy nêyviy nǽsə ér fòrs/ See **ANNA**.

ARS (ac.) n.c. Apollo. "Atmosphere revitalization subsystem," that part of the LM environmental control system (**ECS**) whose equipment cleans and conditions oxygen for use in the crew compartment and space suits. The subsystem also provides water for space-suit cooling.

artificial gravity /artəfîšəl grǽvitiy/ n.c. Gravity created within spacecraft to prevent the ill effects of **weightlessness**.

artificial horizon /artəfîšəl həráyzən/ n.c. Device that monitors spacecraft **attitude** in flight.

artificial satellite /artəfîšəl sǽtəlayt/ n.c. Man-made orbiting body; **satellite**.

ascent engine /ǽsent ènjən/ See **AE**.

ascent propulsion system /əsênt prəpə́lšən sìstəm/ See **APS**.

ascent stage /ǽsent stèyj/ n.c. Apollo. Manned upper section of the LM; section which carries astronauts from the lunar surface back to the orbiting CSM. The ascent stage houses crew, controls, and ascent engine (**AE**).

ascent trajectory /əsént trəjèktəiy/ n.c. Flight path a spacecraft follows from **launch** to **apogee**.

ASE (ac.) n.c. Apollo. "Active seismic experiment," scientific device carried to the moon as part of the Apollo Lunar Surface Experiments Package (**ALSEP**). The ASE measures lunar tremors caused by charges deliberately set off on the moon. Shotgun-type and grenade-type explosives are used to cause the vibrations.

ASEB (ac.) n.c. "Aeronautics and Space Engineering Board," branch of the U.S. National Academy of Engineering which serves as government advisor on engineering aspects of space and aeronautics.

ASP (ac.) n.c. "Aerospace plane," experimental gliderlike space vehicle able to follow a given **trajectory** to achieve a horizontal landing.

asteroid /ǽstəoyd/ n. Any of thousands of minor planets in **heliocentric** orbit principally between the orbits of Mars and Jupiter. The asteroids are expected to be a major hazard on journeys beyond Mars.

astrionics /æstriyániks/ n. Science which deals with the application of electronics to aerospace flight.

Astris /ǽstrəs/ n. Federal Republic of Germany single-stage rocket series used primarily as the uppermost stage in the ELDO international launch vehicle, the **Europa**. Other stages are the **Blue Streak** and the **Coralie**.

Astris stands 12 ft. high, weighs 9,800 lbs. fueled, and develops 4,500 lbs. of thrust.

astro /ǽstrow/ (ac.) n. "Astronaut;" "astronautics."

astroballistics /æstrowbəlístiks/ n. Science dealing with the study of bodies entering the atmosphere at high speeds.

astrobiology /æstrowbayáləjiy/ n. Branch of science dealing with life, or the search for life, on **celestial** bodies other than the earth.

astrodynamics /æstrowdaynǽmiks/ n. Plotting and directing trajectories of craft through space.

astrogation /æstrəgéyšən/ n. Navigation in space.

astrogeology /æstrowjiyáləjiy/ n. Extraterrestrial geology.

astrograph /ǽstrowgrǽf/ n. Photographic telescope.

astronaut /ǽstrənɔt/ n. Crewman of a U.S. spacecraft.

astronautics /æstrənɔ́tiks/ n. Science dealing with the technology of space flight.

astronaut maneuvering unit /ǽstrənɔt mənúwvəiŋ yùwnət/ See **AMU**.

astronomical /æstrənámikəl/ attr. Of or pertaining to the properties of **celestial** bodies.

Astronomical Netherlands Satellite /æstrənâmikəl nêðəɭəndz sǽtəlayt/ See **ANS**.

astronomical satellite /æstrənâmikəl sǽtəlayt/ n.c. Any orbiting craft developed for the purpose of studying the properties and movements of **celestial** bodies. U.S. astronomical satellites include the **OAO**, **OSO**, and **SAS** series.

astronomical unit (æstrənâmikəl yúwnət/ See **AU**.

astronomy /əstránəmiy/ n. Scientific study of the universe and the **celestial** bodies and phenomena in it.

astrophysical /æstrowfízikəl/ attr. Of or pertaining to the physics of **celestial** bodies.

astrophysics /æstrowfíziks/ n. Physics of **celestial** bodies.

The Atlas has been used as the launch vehicle in several major U.S. projects. In 1962, it was the first stage of the Ranger 3 spacecraft.

NASA

/a/ father; /aw/ wow; /ay/ buy; /b/ boy; /č/ witch; /d/ doll; /e/ bet; /ey/ say; /f/ few; /g/ bag; /h/ hole; /i/ it; /iy/ be; /j/ gin; /k/ cat; /l/ lamb; /m/ man; /n/ now; /o/ orbit; /ow/ tow; /oy/ boy; /p/ pat; /r/ run; /s/ send; /š/ shoe; /t/ toy; /u/ put; /uw/ do; /v/ eve; /w/ way; /y/ yes;

SE–8

ATDA *(ac.) n.c. Gemini.* "Augmented Target Docking Adapter." See **TDA**.

Atlantic Missile Range /ætlǽntik mísəl rèynj/ See **AFETR**.

Atlas /ǽtləs/ *n.* **1.** U.S. single-stage rocket used as a launch vehicle. Developed from America's first intercontinental ballistic missile (**ICBM**), Atlas usually serves as a first stage in combination with other rockets.

Without additional stages, Atlas launched the four manned orbital flights of the **Mercury** program and was used to insert **Agena** Target Vehicles into Earth orbit for docking exercises during Project **Gemini**. *Atlas-Agena* and *Atlas-Centaur*, combinations of Atlas first stages with **Agena** and **Centaur** upper stages, were employed as launch vehicles in projects **Ranger, Mariner,** and **Surveyor**.

The standard Atlas stands 66 ft. high, weighs 238,000 lbs. fueled, and has a thrust potential of between 360,000 and 380,000 lbs. Atlas-Agena is 91 ft. high, weighs 275,000 lbs. fueled, and develops 388,000 lbs. of thrust; Atlas-Centaur is 100 ft. high, weighs 300,000 lbs. fueled, and is also capable of producing 388,000 lbs. of thrust.

2. In Greek mythology, a Titan who bore the heavens on his shoulders.

ATM *(ac.) n.c.* "Apollo Telescope Mount," one of four principal sections of the proposed U.S. **Skylab** space station, and one of Skylab's two main experiment packages (the other being the **EREP**). The ATM will be used to study the sun, and will have a clearer view of it than is available through the earth's atmosphere.

After launch, the ATM's television cameras, telescopes, and other external instruments will swing out at a 90° angle from the Multiple Docking Adapter (**MDA**). Various sun shields will protect the workings of the instruments without blocking their views. Four extendable solar panels will generate power.

The astronauts aboard Skylab will monitor the experiments and, using a console located in the MDA, point the instruments towards regions of interest on the sun. Astronauts will change the film packs of ATM cameras during EVA.

atmosphere /ǽtməsfir/ *n.* Gaseous shell that surrounds some planets, stars, and natural satellites.

Atmosphere Explorer /ǽtməsfir eksplòrə/ See **AE**.

atmosphere revitalization subsystem /ǽtməsfir riyvaytəlizêyšən səbsistəm/ See **ARS**.

atmospheric braking /ǽtməsfîrik bréykiŋ/ *n.c.* Maneuver which uses the resistance of an atmosphere to aid in spacecraft deceleration before soft-landing (see **softland**).

atomic energy /ətâmik énəjiy/ *n.c.* Power created by the alteration of the nucleus of an atom.

Atomic Energy Commission /ətâmik énəjiy kəmišən/ See **AEC**.

ATS *(ac.) n.c.* "Applications Technology Satellite," U.S. multipurpose, synchronous satellite series consisting of five spacecraft

APPLICATIONS TECHNOLOGY SATELLITE (ATS-B)

Applications Technology Satellites will study techniques for cloud-cover photography.

launched between 1966 and 1969, and two craft planned for launch in 1973 and 1975. The ATS was designed to test technology and equipment for future satellite application. Among its more important tests have been those regarding gravity gradient stabilization (**GGS**). Satellites in the ATS series have also carried out experiments in the fields of communications, meteorology, navigation, radiation detection, and radio propagation.

ATS-F, projected for launch in 1973, will conduct educational television experiments with India (see **broadcast satellite**). Both ATS-F and *ATS-G* (projected for 1975 launch) will test the possibility of deploying collapsible **dish reflectors** in space.

A *Small Applications Technology Satellite (SATS)* is also proposed for the 1970s for Earth science projects that may arise.

attitude /ǽtətuwd/ *n.* Position of a craft in space; determined by the inclination of its axis to a fixed reference point.

attitude control /ǽtituwd kəntròwl/ *n.c. Apollo.* That part of the stabilization and control system (**SCS**) which either retains or changes the vehicle's orientation.

attitude control jets /ǽtətuwd kəntrówl jèts/ See **attitude jets**.

attitude jets /ǽtətuwd jèts/ *n.c.* Gas nozzles on a spacecraft which are fired to correct or maintain proper orientation. Also referred to as *steering jets, attitude control jets,* and *pitch, roll,* and *yaw jets*.

attitude reference /ǽtətuwd rèfəns/ *n.c. Apollo.* That part of the stabilization and

control system (**SCS**) which indicates the orientation of the vehicle as well as any discrepancy between actual and desired positions.

AU *(ac.) n.c.* "Astronomical unit," unit of measurement equal to the average Earth-sun distance (92,957,000 miles). It is used in discussing distance in the **solar system**.

Augmented Target Docking Adapter /ɔ́gmentəd târgət dákiŋ ədǽptə/ See **TDA**.

aurora /ərórə/ *n.* Airglow caused by solar particles, predominantly protons, interacting with the earth's atmosphere; commonly called the *northern* or *southern lights*.

Aurora 1 /ərôrə wə́n/ *n.* U.S. geophysical satellite launched in June 1967 for investigation of the aurora borealis and the aurora australis (see **aurora**).

Aurora 7 /ərôrə sévən/ *n.* **1.** Alternate name for the *Mercury 7* spacecraft (see **Mercury**).

2. Latin for "dawn"; hence, "a beginning."

aurora australis /ərôrə ɔstréylis/ *n.c.* "Southern lights." See **aurora**.

aurora borealis /ərôrə boriyǽelis/ *n.c.* "Northern lights." See **aurora**.

Aurorae /əróray/ See **ESRO**.

AUSTRALIA

Australia's first active participation in a space program came during International Geophysical Year (**IGY**) activities in 1957 when the U.S. asked for and received permission to establish a satellite tracking facility at **Woomera**. Since that time, additional tracking facilities have been es-

---

/z/ *zero;* /ž/ *azure;* /θ/ *thin;* /ð/ *then;* /ŋ/ *song;* /æ/ *bat;* /ɔ/ *law;* /ə/ *sun;* /ɚ/ *bird.* Foreign symbols: [(n)] nasalization of some French vowels followed by /n/; [R] French uvular rolled /r/ sound; [ü] high front lip-rounded vowel; [x] Russian voiceless laryngeal fricative.

AUSTRALIAN NEWS AND INFORMATION BUREAU

The 210-foot revolving radio telescope in Parkes, Australia, was developed by Dr. Edward Bowen. When put into operation, it doubled in size the area of the observable universe.

tablished at Carnarvon, Tidbinbilla, Cooby Creek, Orroral Valley, and Honeysuckle Creek. Woomera has been expanded into an international launch facility serving **ELDO** and the U.S. as well as Australia and Great Britain.

Australia has no launch vehicles of its own; the U.S. provides launchers for Australian satellites.

Weapons Research Establishment Satellite (**WRESAT**), Australia's first satellite, was launched in November 1967 by a U.S. **Redstone** launcher from the Woomera space center. *OSCAR 5* (see **OSCAR**), a small private comsat built by Australian students, was launched aboard a U.S. rocket in January 1970.

Australia's space program is one of cooperation, primarily with Great Britain, U.S., ELDO, and **ESRO**. Responsibility for Australian space efforts lies with the Weapons Research Establishment.

autocorrector /ɔ́towkəˈréktər/ *n.* Device capable of correcting the trajectory or velocity of a spacecraft by means of small, strategically placed, rockets.

Automated Clearinghouse for Collection and Exchange of Sighting Statistics /ɔ́təmeytəd klíriŋhaws for kəlékšən ænd eksčéynj əv sáytiŋ stətístiks/ See **NICAP**.

automatic countdown sequencer /ɔ́təmǽtik káwntdòwn sìykwənsər/ *n.c.* **Blockhouse** computer which monitors all phases of a mission until **liftoff**. It is capable of aborting a mission (see **abort**).

automatic picture transmission /ɔ́təmǽtik píkčər trænzmìšən/ See **APT**.

AVCS *(ac.) n.c.* "Advanced vidicon camera system," television camera system used on some U.S. weather satellites. AVCS takes daylight photographs and holds them for delayed transmission on command. The high-speed scanning technique of AVCS is combined with an ability to detect one-half-mile features at an altitude of 575 miles. Cf. **APT**.

axis /ǽksəs/ *n.* **1.** Hypothetical straight line about which a body rotates.

2. One of three fixed imaginary lines in reference to which a spacecraft holds its **orientation:** the **X-axis** (longitudinal) is the center of **roll** movement; the **Y-axis** (lateral) is the center for **pitch;** and the **Z-axis** (vertical) is the **yaw** center.

azimuth /ǽziməθ/ *n.* Horizontal bearing from a fixed point; measured in degrees.

Azur /atsúr/ *n.* First Federal Republic of Germany satellite, launched November 7, 1969 by a U.S. **Scout** rocket from the Air Force Western Test Range (**AFWTR**). Its basic mission was the study of cosmic radiation and the magnetosphere.

B

back contamination (bǽk kəntæmənèyšən/ *n.c.* Hypothetical contamination brought back by crewmen returning from interplanetary or lunar missions. Preventive measures in the way of biological isolation were instituted during the early **Apollo** program, but proved unnecessary. See **BIG; LRL; MQF.**

backout /bǽkawt/ *n.* Reversing the **countdown** for a **hold,** either due to technical or weather problems.

backpack /bǽkpæk/ *n. sl. Apollo.* **PLSS.**

backup /bǽkəp/ *n.* Replacement available in case any part of a mission fails: instrument, system, or astronaut.

ballistic missile /bəlîstik mísəl/ *n.c.* Unmanned armed military vehicle whose launch is controlled, but whose trajectory

and follow through are dictated by the laws of gravity.

Ballistic Research Laboratory /bəlîstik ríysərč læbrətoriy/ See **France.**

ballistics /bəlístiks/ *n.* Science dealing with the properties and behavior of propelled bodies.

ballistic trajectory /bəlîstik trəjéktəiy/ *n.c.* Flight path of a propelled vehicle when its rockets are shut down and the force of gravity takes over.

ball lightning /bɔ́l láytniŋ/ *n.c.* A form of lightning which maintains a roughly spherical shape up to several feet in diameter for a short time, during which it behaves erratically, sometimes scarcely moving, sometimes following wires. It may evaporate suddenly or explode violently. Called *Kugelblitz* in German, ball lightning was described as early as 60 B.C. by the Roman poet Lucretius. Mechanics of the electrical field forming ball lightning are not understood, although they have been partially duplicated in the laboratory. Some authorities hold ball lightning is merely an optical illusion following a flash of lightning striking nearby. It is sometimes offered as the explanation for **UFO** sightings.

balls /bɔ́lz/ *n. sl. Apollo.* Zeros on a computer **console.** *All balls,* meaning all zeros, was in use for a short time but proved offensive to the public and was dropped.

ballute /bəlúwt/ *n.* Combination balloon and parachute used to break an object's fall.

barbeque mode /bárbiykyuw mòwd/ *n.c. sl.* **PTC.**

barber chair /bárbər čèr/ *n.c. sl. Apollo.* **Couch.**

barber's pole /bárbəz pòwl/ *n.c. sl. Apollo.* Black and white diagonally striped indicator found in both CM and LM; shows, by turning, that a system is operating.

Barker /bárkər/ See **Laika.**

barrier reef /bériyər rìyf/ *n.c. sl. Apollo.* Hazardous area.

The Federal Republic of Germany's Azur satellites are tested in chambers that are baffled to absorb reverberation (anechoic chambers).

MESSERSCHMITT-BÖLKOW-BLOHM

/a/ *father;* /aw/ *wow;* /ay/ *buy;* /b/ *boy;* /č/ *witch;* /d/ *doll;* /e/ *bet;* /ey/ *say;* /f/ *few;* /g/ *bag;* /h/ *hole;* /i/ *it;* /iy/ *be;* /j/ *gin;* /k/ *cat;* /l/ *lamb;*
/m/ *man;* /n/ *now;* /o/ *orbit;* /ow/ *tow;* /oy/ *boy;* /p/ *pat;* /r/ *run;* /s/ *send;* /š/ *shoe;* /t/ *toy;* /u/ *put;* /uw/ *do;* /v/ *eve;* /w/ *way;* /y/ *yes;*

SE – 10

barycentric orbit /bêrisèntrik órbət/ *n.c.* Flight path encircling two bodies and having as its center the center of mass of the two bodies considered as a unit; a barycentric orbit of the earth and moon would have its center somewhere between the two, though nearer the earth.

bay /béy/ *n.* 1. Equipment bay.
2. Unevenness of the lunar surface caused by planes juxtaposed to borders of depressions.

Beacon /bíykən/ *n.* 1. U.S. geophysical satellites, numbers 22 and 27 of the **Explorer** series, launched in October 1964 and April 1965. *Beacon B (Explorer 22)* studied the ionosphere and was the first satellite to reflect laser beams for tracking and geodetic purposes. *Beacon C (Explorer 27)* continued these studies.
2. *l.c.* See **transponder**.

BECO /bíykow/ *(ac.) n.c.* "Booster engine cutoff."

beeper /bíypə/ *n. sl.* Man who guides a mission by remote control.

BEF *(ac.) n.c.* "Blunt end forward," spacecraft **attitude** in which the aft end of the craft is facing the direction of flight.

beryllium /bəíliyəm/ *n.* Light metal finely ground and mixed with certain propellants; used to increase thrust.

Beta Lyrae /bêytə líray/ See **OAO**.

BIG *(ac.) n.c. Apollo.* "Biological isolation garment," lightweight suit which completely covered the wearer, worn by astronauts and **pararescuemen** during **recovery** phase of *Apollo 11* and *12*. Use of the BIG, a precaution against the occurrence of **back contamination** between the CM and mobile quarantine facility (**MQF**), was discontinued when no danger of contamination was discovered.

billy que net /bíliy kyùw nèt/ *n.c. Apollo.* Rescue seat, similar in appearance to half of a birdcage, used in lifting crew members from spacecraft to helicopter after **splashdown**.

binary digit /báynəiy díjət/ See **bit**.

binary notation /bâynəiy nowtéyšən/ *n.c.* Digital computer method of transmitting spacecraft information. Only two numbers, one and zero, are used in groups of short and long signals. See **bit**.

bingo /bíŋgow/ *n. cd. Apollo.* Warning to be transmitted to the LM crew when they have reached the stage in descent to the lunar surface where they must land within 20 seconds or **abort**.

bioastronautics /bâyowæstrənótiks/ *n.* Science dealing with the effect of space travel on life.

bioinstrumentation harness /bâyowinstrəmentéyšən hàrnəs/ *n.c. Apollo.* Instrumented belt worn next to the skin; biosensors (see **sensors**) are attached to it and to the astronaut's body to monitor his condition during a mission.

biological barrier /bayəlâjikəl bériyə/ *n.c.* Quarantine procedure which prevents **back contamination**.

biological isolation garment /bayəlâjikəl aysəléyšən gàrmənt/ See **BIG**.

biomedical inflight monitoring /bâyowmêdikəl înflâyt mánətəiŋ/ *n.c.* System whereby sensors attached to astronauts constantly transmit various metabolic rates to ground-based surgeons. Generally used to determine how much activity the crew may safely perform.

biomedicine /bâyowmédəsin/ *n.* Science combining medicine and biology and concerned with gauging and analyzing human stress tolerances.

bionics /bayániks/ *n.* Technical discipline which studies various living systems for application to mechanical systems; e.g., studying the eye for development of a lens.

Biosatellite /bâyowsǽtəlayt/ *n.* U.S. biological research satellite series; three craft were launched between 1966 and 1969 and one more mission is planned. Biosatellites are used for investigating the effects of weightlessness, radiation, and lack of Earth rotation on various life forms. Mission duration varies and recovery of the satellite is considered essential.

biosensor /bâyowsénsə/ See **sensor**.

bioshield /bâyowšìyld/ *n.* Special covering used to insure the sterility of a spacecraft during its use or until ready for use. Bioshields are of vital importance when an object of the mission is to detect life; scientists must be sure no Earth organisms traveling on the craft are mistakenly "discovered." *Can* is the slang term for bioshield.

biosphere /báyowsfìr/ *n.* Region of the earth and atmosphere where the major portion of life exists.

bipropellant /bâyprəpélənt/ *n.* Rocket propellant consisting of a liquid fuel and a liquid oxidizer which are maintained separately until injected into the combustion chamber.

bird /bəd/ *n. sl.* **Missile; rocket**.

birdwatcher /bə́dwàcə/ *n. sl.* Habitual viewer of rocket launches.

birdworks /bə́dwəks/ *n. sl.* Company that produces rockets or missiles.

bit /bít/ *(ac.) n.c.* "Binary digit," smallest unit of digital computer data; one number in **binary notation**.

Black Arrow /blǽk érow/ *n.c.* Primary British launch vehicle; a three-stage rocket developed from the successful two-stage test vehicle *Black Knight*. The Black Arrow, on October 28, 1971, launched the experimental **Prospero** satellite making Great Britain the sixth nation to launch its own satellite with an internally developed launch vehicle. The vehicle stands 38 ft. high, weighs 40,000 lbs., and has a maximum thrust potential of 65,000 lbs.

black box /blǽk báks/ *n.c. sl.* Small electronic unit which can be easily replaced without disturbing the rest of a major **system**.

Black Knight /blǽk náyt/ See **Great Britain**.

blackout /blǽkàwt/ *n.* 1. Loss of radio communications because of ionospheric disturbances.
2. Period of time when communications between **ground stations** and spacecraft are lost during **reentry**.

blanketing /blǽŋkətiŋ/ *n.* Reception distortion or **blackout** caused by the intrusion of an unwanted signal.

blank tape /blǽŋk téyp/ *n.c.* Data recording tape that did not copy any information on a space mission.

blast area /blǽst èriyə/ *n.c.* Hazardous region surrounding a **launch pad**.

blastoff /blǽstɔ̀f/ *n.* **Liftoff**.

blockhouse /blákhaws/ *n.* Reinforced concrete building in the immediate area of a **launch pad**; serves as a control center.

blockhouse measurements /blákhàws mêžəmənts/ *n.c.* Data transmitted from a spacecraft to the **blockhouse** during **countdown**.

Block 1 /blák wə́n/ *n.c. cd. Apollo.* Designation of Apollo Spacecraft for trial flights.

Block 2 /blák túw/ *n.c. cd. Apollo.* Designation of Apollo spacecraft for lunar missions.

blowoff /blówɔ̀f/ *n.* Deliberate explosion which separates one section of a rocket from the remainder.

blue phone line /blúw fówn làyn/ *n.c.* Telephone system which connects all important personnel during a **countdown**; conversations are recorded.

Blue Streak /blúw stríyk/ *n.c.* British single-stage rocket series, developed from the Blue Streak **IRBM**, used primarily as the first stage in the **ELDO** international launch vehicle, the **Europa**. Other stages are the **Coralie** and the **Astris**.
Blue Streak stands 60 ft. high, weighs 180,000 lbs. fueled, and develops 172,000 lbs of thrust.

blunt end forward /blə̂nt ênd fórwəd/ See **BEF**.

body sensor /bádiy sènsə/ *n.c.* Biosensor (see **sensor**).

boilerplate /bóyləplèyt/ *n.* Full-size model of a spacecraft used for experimental purposes in early stages of a program.

boiloff /bóylɔ̀f/ *n. sl.* Vaporization of liquid oxygen from a liquid-fueled rocket awaiting launch; seen as a white cloud.

boost /búwst/ 1. *v. tr.* To apply rocket propulsion.
2. *n.* Rocket propulsion.

booster /búwstə/ *n.* 1. That stage of a **launch vehicle** which produces the main propulsion.
2. An entire **launch vehicle** which carries a payload.

booster engine /búwstə ènjən/ *n.c.* Rocket motor capable of providing the largest or initial **thrust** in a launch vehicle.

boost-glide vehicle /búwst gláyd vìyhikəl/ See **skip-glide bomber**.

boost protective cover /búwst prətêktiv kə́və/ See **BPC**.

booties /búwtiyz/ See **flight coverall**.

bootstrap photography /búwtstræp fətàgrəfiy/ *n.c. sl. Apollo.* Taking pictures on one mission for use in future missions.

bootstrapping /búwtstræpiŋ/ *n. sl.* Method which allows a device to be self-sustaining.

Boreas /boréyəs/ See **ESRO**.

boundary layer /báwndriy lèyə/ *n.c.* Thin, almost motionless air layer around a vehicle flying in the atmosphere.

bow wave /bów wèyv/ *n.c.* 1. Curved temporary **shock wave** created when a spacecraft reenters Earth's atmosphere.
2. Curved permanent shock wave created where the **solar wind** meets Earth's **magnetosphere**.

/z/ *z*ero; /ž/ a*z*ure; /θ/ *th*in; /ð/ *th*en; /ŋ/ so*ng*; /æ/ b*a*t; /ɔ/ l*a*w; /ə/ s*u*n; /ə/ b*ir*d. Foreign symbols: [(n)] nasalization of some French vowels followed by /n/; [R] French uvular rolled /r/ sound; [ü] high front lip-rounded vowel; [x] Russian voiceless laryngeal fricative.

BPC (ac.) n.c. Apollo. "Boost protective cover," launch escape system (**LES**) equipment; a cone-shaped **shroud** which prevents damage to the CM during launch. Permanently attached to the launch escape tower (**LET**), it is eventually jettisoned with other escape equipment.

braking ellipses /bréykiŋ iylìpsiyz/ n.c. **Reentry** process utilizing a series of elliptical orbits, decreasing in altitude, to decrease speed before final **touchdown.**

broadcast satellite /brɔ́dkæst sǽtəlayt/ n.c. Any Earth-orbiting satellite which would be capable of sending its signals directly to local or home-based receivers instead of to large terminals which would rebroadcast on a large scale. ATS-F (see **ATS**), projected for launch by the U.S. in 1973, will conduct feasibility experiments from a **geostationary orbit** in a cooperative program with India whereby educational television will be beamed to villages in rural areas.

BSLSS (ac.) n.c. Apollo. "Buddy secondary life support system," connecting hose, carried after Apollo 13, which allows an astronaut with a malfunctioning portable life support system (**PLSS**) to share the water supply of another PLSS. The oxygen purge system (**OPS**) would supply emergency oxygen in case of PLSS failure.

buddy secondary life support system /bâdiy sêkənderiy láyf səpòrt sìstəm/ See **BSLSS.**

buffeting /bʌ́fətiŋ/ n. Violent vibration that can occur in a launch vehicle during the high speeds required to escape the atmosphere.

built-in hold /bîlt in hówld/ n.c. Period during **countdown** during which problems may be corrected without delaying the entire procedure. See **hold.**

bulkhead /bʌ́lkhed/ n. Domed partition that covers the end of a rocket propellant tank.

burn /bən/ 1. n. Firing of a vehicle's rocket in space.

2. v. tr. To start a rocket engine in flight.

burnout /bə́nawt/ n. Point in time at which a rocket engine ceases functioning, usually due to exhaustion of fuel.

burnout velocity /bə́nawt vəlàsitiy/ n.c. Speed of a vehicle traveling along a **ballistic trajectory** when its fuel has been consumed.

burn time /bə́n tàym/ n.c. Period during which rocket engines are fired in space.

C

cabin /kǽbən/ n. Living quarters of a manned spacecraft.

California Institute of Technology /kæləfɔ̀rnyə ìnstituwt əv teknálǝjiy/ See **JPL.**

can /kæn/ n. sl. **Bioshield.**

CANADA

Canada's first active participation in a space program came during International Geophysical Year (**IGY**) activities in 1957 when a firing range for upper atmospheric research rockets was established at Fort Churchill in the province of Manitoba. During IGY, all the rockets fired were U.S. vehicles; however, the impetus was provided for the development of Canadian vehicles.

Research satellite Alouette 1 (see **Alouette**), Canada's first spacecraft, was launched in September 1962, under a cooperative program with the U.S. from the Air Force Western Test Range (**AFWTR**). ISIS 1 (see **ISIS**) was launched in January 1969 from the AFWTR by the U.S. It was the first satellite of Canada's second series of craft.

Future Canadian space projects include **Anik,** a domestic comsat series. The first launch is scheduled for late 1972. Canada's space program is basically a cooperative effort with the U.S. which provides launch vehicles and support. Coordination of Canadian space activities is the responsibility of the Interdepartmental Committee on Space.

canard /kənárd/ n. 1. Short, thick wing on an airplane or spacecraft for improved stability.

2. Apollo. Winglike structure of the launch escape system (**LES**); would place the CM into a blunt end forward (**BEF**) position in case of **abort.**

Canopus /kǽnəpəs/ n. Brightest star in the Southern Hemisphere; used by both manned and unmanned spacecraft as a fixed reference point.

CapCom /kǽpkàm/ (ac.) n.c. "Capsule communicator," Mission Control Center (**MCC**) official, usually an astronaut, who maintains constant dialogue with a spacecraft crew.

Cape Canaveral /kêyp kənǽvərəl/ See **KSC.**

Cape Kennedy /kêyp kénədiy/ See **KSC.**

CapSep /kǽpsèp/ (ac.) n.c. "Capsule separation." 1. Point in a mission when the spacecraft detaches from the launch vehicle.

2. Detaching of the spacecraft from its launch vehicle.

capsule /kǽpsəl/ n. Manned portion of spacecraft, called **module** since Project Apollo. It provided for crew health and safety from **launch** to **splashdown.** Capsule and module are often used interchangeably for the manned portion of a spacecraft.

capsule communicator /kǽpsəl kəmyúwnəkeytɚ/ See **CapCom.**

capsule separation /kǽpsəl sepɚéyšən/ See **CapSep.**

captive firing /kǽptiv fáyɚiŋ/ n.c. **Static testing.**

capture /kǽpčɚ/ n. 1. Moment during interplanetary space travel when the gravity of another planet replaces the pull of a previous one on a spacecraft.

2. During docking, the moment when the two spacecraft are locked together.

capture latches /kǽpčɚ lǽčəz/ See **probe assembly.**

Casper /kǽspɚ/ n. Name of Apollo 16 CM (see **Apollo**).

Castor /kǽstɚ/ n. 1. U.S. rocket which serves as the second stage of the **Scout** launch vehicle and as the strap-on booster for the Thrust-Augmented Delta (see **Delta**). Basic version of the Castor is 20 ft.

high, weighs 23,000 lbs. fueled, and produces 60,000 lbs. of thrust.

2. One of the stars in the constellation **Gemini.** The other is Pollux.

3. In Greek mythology, Castor, the twin of Pollux, was renowned for his athletic ability and horsemanship.

CAT (ac.) n.c. "Clear Air Turbulence," atmospheric disturbance occurring at high altitudes, not associated with clouds that are visible or detectable by radar. CAT is normally involved with jet streams, inversion layers, or mountains. Jet planes striking such turbulence without warning may be subjected to violent movements or be thrown completely out of control. It has been found that a temperature inversion is always present with CAT, and a system of detecting such inversions by infrared scanning is under development. Means of confirming presence and severity of CAT have not been developed yet. CAT is thought to be one cause of radar **angels.**

catch nets /kǽč nèts/ n.c. Stiff nets attached to the **umbilical tower;** they protect the **umbilicals** as they drop away from a launch vehicle.

catch-up orbit /kǽčəp ɔ̀rbət/ n.c. Apollo. Orbit which brings the LM within range of redocking with the CSM after a lunar expedition has been completed. The catch-up orbit results from concentric sequence initiation (**CSI**).

catch-up rate /kǽčəp rèyt/ n.c. Apollo. Velocity LM must attain in **catch-up orbit** to close with the **CSM.**

caution and warning system /kɔ́šən ænd wɔ́rniŋ sìstəm/ n.c. Apollo. System that maintains a watch over the various vital spacecraft systems and reports any failures or problems. The master alarm consists of a red indicator light on the **console** and an audio signal transmitted directly to the crew through headphones.

cavitation /kævitéyšən/ n. Formation of bubbles in liquids flowing under low pressure; can cause serious damage to rocket parts through vibration.

CCIG (ac.) n.c. Apollo. "Cold cathode ion guage," scientific device carried to the moon as part of the Apollo Lunar Surface Experiments Package (**ALSEP**). CCIG, mounted on the suprathermal ion detector experiment (**SIDE**), studies the number and kinds of lunar ions and gauges lunar atmospheric pressure.

CDDT (ac.) n.c. "Countdown demonstration test," dress rehearsal for actual **countdown;** both simulated and actual loading of propellants takes place. Astronauts are involved only during the former stage.

CDH (ac.) n.c. Apollo. "Constant delta height," LM maneuver which brings the LM, after liftoff from the moon, into an orbit parallel to and fifteen miles from that of the CSM. The second phase of CDH, lunar orbit rendezvous (**LOR**), is followed by terminal phase initiation (**TPI**).

CDR (ac.) n. "**Commander.**"

celestial /səlésčəl/ attr. Of or pertaining to the stars or planets.

celestial guidance /səlêsčəl gáydəns/ n.c. Spacecraft navigation using celestial bodies as reference points.

/a/ father; /aw/ wow; /ay/ buy; /b/ boy; /č/ witch; /d/ doll; /e/ bet; /ey/ say; /f/ few; /g/ bag; /h/ hole; /i/ it; /iy/ be; /j/ gin; /k/ cat; /l/ lamb;
/m/ man; /n/ now; /o/ orbit; /ow/ tow; /oy/ boy; /p/ pat; /r/ run; /s/ send; /š/ shoe; /t/ toy; /u/ put; /uw/ do; /v/ eve; /w/ way; /y/ yes;

celestial mechanics /sǝlêščǝl mǝkǽniks/ *n.c.* Science concerned with the movement of celestial bodies, especially those of the **solar system.** Its laws influence all of man's endeavors in space.

celestial sphere /sǝlésčǝl sfír/ *n.c.* Hypothetical sphere of infinite size with the earth as its center.

Centaur /séntòr/ *n.* U.S. single-stage rocket used primarily as the upper stage on **Atlas** launch vehicles. Centaur was the first rocket to use liquid hydrogen and oxygen as propellant.

The standard Centaur stands 46 ft. high, weighs 37,000 lbs. fueled, and has a thrust potential of 30,000 lbs.

Center for Aerospace Research /sêntǝ for èrowspêys riysɔ̀č/ See **CRA.**

center of gravity /sêntǝ ǝv grǽvǝtiy/ *n.c.* Mid-point of mass or weight distribution. See **gravity.**

central body /sêntrǝl bádiy/ *n.c.* Celestial body which a **satellite** orbits.

Centre National d'Études Spatiales /sɔ(n)tR nasyonâl detued spasyál/ See **CNES.**

centrifugal force /sentrîfǝgǝl fórs/ *n.c.* Force which tends to draw an orbiting body away from its center of rotation.

centrifuge /séntrǝfyùwǰ/ *n.* **Simulator** composed of a rotating arm with a compartment at the end; used to duplicate and study the effects of increased gravitational pull on men, animals, or objects.

centripetal force /sentrîpǝtǝl fórs/ *n.c.* Force that tends to draw an orbiting body toward the center of its rotation. Satellites maintain orbit by balancing **centrifugal force** and centripetal force.

Centro Ricerche Aerospaziale /čêntro rìčêrke aerospatsiále/ See **CRA.**

CES *(ac.) n.c. Apollo.* "Control electronics subsystem," that part of the LM guidance, navigation, and control system (**GNCS**) which maintains attitude control by firing the thrusters of the reaction control system (**RCS**). In the CSM, this firing is a function of the stabilization and control system (**SCS**).

CETI *(ac.) n.c.* "Communication with Extraterrestrial Intelligence," a proposed project which would determine whether other civilizations in space may be sending radio, laser, or other signals to Earth in an effort to establish communication. The project was the subject of an international conference in September 1971, sponsored by the U.S. and U.S.S.R. academies of science and hosted by an academy in Soviet Armenia. Cf. **Cyclops, Project; Ozma, Project.**

chaff /čǽf/ *n.* Metallic chips released by reentering spacecraft to aid trackers.

chamber pressure /čéymbǝ prèšǝ/ *n.c.* Pressure maintained in a rocket engine's **thrust chamber.**

characteristic velocity /kèrǝktɔ̀ìstik vǝlásǝtiy/ *n.c.* Sum total of all the speeds that must be overcome in order for a spacecraft to brake at any given point.

charged particle lunar environmental experiment /čárǰd pârtikǝl lùwnɔ envayɔnméntǝl ekspèrǝmǝnt/ See **CPLEE.**

Charlie Brown /čârliy bráwn/ *n.c.*
1. Name of *Apollo 10* CM (see **Apollo**).

2. Famous American cartoon character loved by children and adults alike.

checkout /čékawt/ *n.* Sequential operational testing performed on a particular system or a complete craft.

cherry picker /čériy pìkɔ/ *n.c. sl.* Crane whose cab is next to a spacecraft on the **launch pad** in order to provide an astronaut escape route.

chicken switch /číkǝn swìč/ *n.c. sl.* Control lever situated beside an astronaut's knee; in an emergency it can be used to separate the **capsule** from the **launch vehicle.**

chilldown /číldàwn/ *n.* Cooling down launch vehicle fuel system and tanks prior to loading supercold propellants.

CHINA, PEOPLE'S REPUBLIC OF

Fifth nation to orbit satellites using internally developed launch vehicles, under a program whose specifics were still secret at the end of 1971.

Chinese launch vehicle development had begun by 1965, when U.S. intelligence photos showed construction of an **ICBM** missile center several hundred miles east of Lop Nor, in northwestern Sin Kiang province. Some U.S. analysts predicted the Chinese would be able to launch their first satellite before the end of 1967.

It was not until April 24, 1970, however, that the first successful Chinese spaceshot occurred. The satellite was sent into an orbit that passed over both the U.S. and the U.S.S.R., and was said to weigh 381 lbs.—about twice as much as the first **Sputnik.** Its transmitter alternately broadcast telemetric signals and "Dong Fang Hong" ("The East is Red"), a popular Chinese song in praise of Chairman Mao Tse-Tung.

A second satellite, launched in March 1971, is estimated to weigh 486 lbs. Hsinhua, the Chinese press agency, reported at the time that the satellite "successfully sent back scientific data on various experiments . . . and is now continuing the planned work of scientific experiments."

chromosphere /krówmǝsfir/ *n.* Rose-colored lower layer of gases in the sun's atmosphere.

chuffing /čǝ́fiŋ/ *n.* Noise sometimes made by rockets whose fuel burns irregularly.

cinetheodolite /sìnǝθiyádǝlayt/ *n.* Tracking instrument which combines a telescope and camera to determine and record the position-and-time chart of an object in flight.

circadian rhythm /sǝkêydiǝn ríðm/ *n.c.* Biological cycle with a period of about 24 hours.

circular velocity /sɔ̀kyǝlɔ vǝlásitiy/ *n.c.* Speed required for a body to maintain circular orbit.

circumflight /sɔ̀kǝmfláyt/ *n.* Orbital flight.

circumlunar /sɔ̀kǝmlúwnɔ/ *attr.* Of or pertaining to lunar orbit.

circumlunar rocket /sɔ̀kǝmlûwnɔ rákǝt/ *n.c.* Spacecraft designed to reach the moon, orbit it, and return to Earth under rocket propulsion.

circumlunar trajectory /sɔ̀kǝmlûwnɔ trǝĵéktɔiy/ *n.c.* Flight path around the moon and back to Earth.

The Apollo command module is the control center and living quarters for astronauts for most of each lunar mission. It contains all necessary subsystems for survival in space and return to the Earth: launch escape, communications, environmental control, guidance and navigation, electrical power, thermal protection, service propulsion, stabilization and reaction control, and earth landing.

NASA

DOCKING TUNNEL
EARTH LANDING EQUIPMENT
FORWARD COMPARTMENT BULKHEAD
REACTION CONTROL PITCH ENGINES
STRINGER
MAIN DISPLAY CONSOLE
INSULATION SPACE
CREW ACCESS HATCH
ABLATIVE MATERIAL
RENDEZVOUS WINDOW
STAINLESS STEEL HONEYCOMB
MAINTENANCE PANELS
ALUMINUM HONEYCOMB
REACTION CONTROL ROLL ENGINES
COMPARTMENT EQUIPMENT
WIRE BUNDLE
REACTION CONTROL PITCH ENGINES
REACTION CONTROL YAW ENGINES
REACTION CONTROL ROLL ENGINES
POTABLE WATER TANK

/z/ zero; /ž/ azure; /θ/ *thin*; /ð/ *then*; /ŋ/ *song*; /æ/ bat; /ɔ/ law; /ǝ/ sun; /ɔ/ bird. Foreign symbols: [(n)] nasalization of some French vowels followed by /n/; [R] French uvular rolled /r/ sound; [ü] high front lip-rounded vowel; [x] Russian voiceless laryngeal fricative.

circumterrestrial /sə̀kəmteréstriyəl/ *attr.* Around the earth.

cislunar /sìslûwnə/ *attr.* Of or pertaining to the area between the earth and the moon.

cislunar space /sìslúwnə spéys/ *n.c.* Region between Earth and moon.

Clear Air Turbulence /klîr êr tə́byələns/ See **CAT.**

closed ecological system /klôwzd iykəlâjikəl sístəm/ *n.c.* System which will provide, through chemistry or photosynthesis, for all waste matter to be converted into life-supporting oxygen and food on space voyages.

closed loop /klôwzd lúwp/ *n.c.* Control units linked in circular fashion, allowing for self-correction. Cf. **open loop.**

close-out /klôwzàwt/ *n.* Sealing of the spacecraft hatch prior to **liftoff.** Accomplished by a crew of four (on **Apollo** missions), close-out completes the **ingress** procedure.

cluster /klə́stə/ *n.* **1.** Two or more rocket engines which operate together.

2. Grouped components of the **Skylab** space station.

CM *(ac.) n.c. Apollo.* "Command module," one of the three main sections of the basic **Apollo** spacecraft. The six-ton, cone-shaped unit contains forward, crew, and aft compartments, two **hatches,** five windows, **equipment bays,** protection panels, **impact attenuators,** and is covered by **heat shields.** Fifteen miles of wiring facilitate its operations.

The unpressurized forward compartment, at the top of the cone, is dominated by the earth landing system (**ELS**) and the CM components of the **docking system.** The crew compartment, in the center of the CM, maintains a 210 cu. ft. **shirtsleeve environment** except during **launch, reentry, docking,** and crew transfer to the **LM.** Crew accomodations and supplies, spacecraft controls and displays, protection panels, equipment bays, windows, and the majority of spacecraft systems are located in this section. The inaccessible, unpressurized aft compartment contains **reaction control engines,** consumables, and impact attenuators.

From **liftoff** to **reentry,** the CM and service module (**SM**) are attached and referred to jointly as the command and service module (**CSM**).

CMG *(ac.) n.c.* "Control moment gyros," stabilizing system for the proposed U.S. **Skylab** space station. The Apollo Telescope Mount (**ATM**) will house this system, whose sensing components include gyroscopes and sun sensors.

CMP *(ac.) n.c. Apollo.* "Command module pilot," second in command on a U.S. **Apollo** mission. The CMP is the expert on CSM systems and is the primary navigator. He occupies the center couch in the CM and remains in lunar orbit while his two fellow crew members carry out their mission on the lunar surface. See **commander; LMP.**

CNES *(ac.) n.c.* "Centre National d'Études Spatiales" (National Center of Space Studies), French department in charge of France's national space program. Officially created in 1962, CNES controls development and deployment of French space hardware, tracking facilities, and the **Guiana Space Center** located at Kourou, French Guiana, in South America. Prior to the establishment of CNES, rocketry in France was under the control of the department of defense.

COAS /kówæz/ *(ac.) n.c. Apollo.* "Crewman optical alignment sight," CM and LM component of the **docking system;** used in the maneuvering craft to aid astronauts in docking. The COAS seems to project an image on the **docking target** of the passive craft.

coasting flight /kówstiŋ flàyt/ *n.c.* Flight of a rocket at **staging** when no engines are burning.

cold cathode ion gauge /kôwld kǽθowd áyan gèyj/ See **CCIG.**

cold-flow test /kôwld flów tèst/ *n.c.* Check-out of the pressurization and fuel flow of a liquid-propelled rocket which is accomplished without actually firing the engines.

coldplate /kówldplèyt/ *n.* One of two metal sheets held together by thousands of little posts; **water-glycol** passes between the sheets, absorbing heat and cooling electronic equipment attached to the outside of them. Part of the environmental control system (**ECS**) equipment.

cold welding /kôwld wéldiŋ/ *n.c.* Surface adhesion of two materials coming into contact under deep-vacuum conditions; common problem in deep space.

collar /kálə/ *n.* Mechanical fitting.

Columbia /kələ́mbiyə/ *n.* **1.** Name of *Apollo 11* CM (see **Apollo**).

2. Poetic title for the United States derived from the name of Christopher Columbus, who discovered America in 1492.

comet /kámət/ *n.* Sometimes visible celestial body which orbits the sun. Some comets have a sweeping trail of gases, called a *tail,* which may extend for millions of miles.

command /kəmǽnd/ *n.* Signal transmitted to a spacecraft instrument in order to initiate a sequence of events.

command and service module /kəmǽnd ænd sə́vəs màdyul/ See **CSM.**

command destruct /kəmǽnd distrə́kt/ *n.c.* Launch vehicle explosive system. It is utilized to safely destroy vehicles which are dangerously off-course. See **EGADS** button.

commander /kəmǽndə/ *n. Apollo.* Top-ranking member of the three-man U.S. **Apollo** spacecraft crew. The commander is cross-trained as both command module pilot (**CMP**) and lunar module pilot (**LMP**). Occupying the left couch of the CM, he runs the mission, performs most of the engine burns, and is one of the crewmen to descend to the lunar surface.

command module /kəmǽnd màdyul/ See **CM.**

command module pilot /kəmǽnd màdyul pâylət/ See **CMP.**

Committee on Space Research /kəmîtiy an spéys rìysəč/ See **COSPAR.**

communications carrier /kəmyuwnəkéyšənz kèriyə/ *n.c. Apollo.* Close-fitting cap worn during spaceflight for voice and telemetric communications; contains earphones, microphones, and a **dosimeter.**

communications satellite /kəmyuwnəkéyšənz sǽtəlayt/ See **Comsat.**

Communications Satellite Corporation /kəmyuwnəkéyšənz sǽtəlayt korpəèyšən/ See **Comsat.**

communications satellite ship /kəmyuwnəkéyšənz sǽtəlayt šip/ *n.c.* Ocean-going vessel that can communicate with orbiting satellites. Such ships are part of the overall tracking system employed during major space missions.

Communication with Extraterrestrial Intelligence /kəmyuwnəkéyšən wiθ êkstrətəèstriyəl intéləjəns/ See **CETI.**

companion body /kəmpǽnyən bàdiy/ *n.c.* **Afterbody.**

comparator /kəmpérətə/ *n.* Device that analyzes two sets of supposedly identical data.

Complex 39 /kâmpleks θ̀ətiy náyn/ See **KSC.**

composite /kâmpázət/ *n.* Solid propellant in which fuel and oxidizer are mixed together into a **grain.**

compressors /kəmprésəz/ See **ECU.**

computer /kəmpyúwtə/ *n.* Vital spacecraft component primarily considered part of the **guidance system** (see **GNCS; PGNS**) but important to aspects of spaceflight other than directional control. Controlled through the display and keyboard (**DSKY**), the computer contains information on star references, routines, programs, etc., and can also be used for direct control of equipment such as the main rocket engine.

computer subsystem /kəmpyûwtə sə́bsistəm/ *n.c. Apollo.* A digital spacecraft computer which, as part of the guidance, navigation, and control system (**GNCS**), determines and initiates course corrections.

Comsat /kámsæt/ *(ac.) n.c.* **1.** "Communications Satellite Corporation," U.S. company formed in 1963 as the first private enterprise devoted to space communications. Proposer of the International Telecommunications Satellite Consortium (**Intelsat**) and chief investor and manager of that organization's communications satellite system. Comsat employs NASA to launch Intelsat satellites. The first of these, **Early Bird,** was launched in April 1965.

2. *l.c.* "Communications satellite," any Earth-orbiting craft developed to relay radio signals between ground stations. It is either *active* (actually receiving, regenerating, and transmitting signals) or *passive* (merely reflecting signals). Since its operation is not limited by the curvature of the earth, it makes global communications possible. The first comsat was **SCORE,** launched by the U.S. in December 1958.

concentric sequence initiation /kənsêntrik síykwens inišiyèyšən/ See **CSI.**

condensation trail /kândenséyšən trèyl/ See **contrail.**

configuration /kənfigyəéyšən/ *n.* Size and shape formed by the relative positioning of components.

conic /kánik/ *attr.* Of or pertaining to the curve obtained by cutting a cone with a plane without passing through its apex. All trajectories and orbits are conic.

/a/ father; /aw/ wow; /ay/ buy; /b/ boy; /č/ witch; /d/ doll; /e/ bet; /ey/ say; /f/ few; /g/ bag; /h/ hole; /i/ it; /iy/ be; /j/ gin; /k/ cat; /l/ lamb; /m/ man; /n/ now; /o/ orbit; /ow/ tow; /oy/ boy; /p/ pat; /r/ run; /s/ send; /š/ shoe; /t/ toy; /u/ put; /uw/ do; /v/ eve; /w/ way; /y/ yes;

console /kánsòwl/ *n.* Instrument panel; on **Apollo,** the CM console covers 21 square feet and each of the three crewman are trained to handle all of its controls.

constant delta height /kânstənt délta hàyt/ See **CDH.**

constant wear garment /kânstənt wér gàrmənt/ *n.c. Apollo.* One-piece astronaut undergarment worn during spaceflight beneath the **flight coverall** or the pressure garment assembly (**PGA**). Replaced by the **liquid cooling garment** during **EVA.**

consumables /kənsúwməbəlz/ *n.* Supplies carried on a space mission.

contingency ascent staging /kəntínjənsiy əsént stèyjiŋ/ *n.c. Apollo.* Emergency separation of the ascent stage of the **LM** from the descent section either immediately before or after lunar **touchdown.**

contingency sample /kəntínjənsiy sæmpəl/ *n.c. Apollo.* Example of lunar surface material picked up as soon as an astronaut sets foot on the moon. This ensures the mission of having at least one sample should an emergency **liftoff** be required before completion of mission.

contrail /kántrèyl/ *(ac.) n.c.* "Condensation trail," vapor which appears behind aircraft and spacecraft passing through the atmosphere, caused by the sudden compression and expansion of the air.

control /kəntrówl/ 1. *v. tr.* To direct a spacecraft using global ground stations.

2. *n.* **Attitude control; GNCS; SCS.**

control center /kəntrówl sèntər/ *n.c.* Location either on the ground or in a spacecraft from which various aspects of a mission can be directed. See **LCC.**

control electronics subsystem /kəntrówl əlektrâniks səbsistəm/ See **CES.**

control jet /kəntrówl jèt/ *n.c.* **Thruster** which can change a spacecraft's speed or direction.

Control Moment Gyros /kəntrówl mòwmənt jâyrowz/ See **CMG.**

control rocket /kəntrówl ràkət/ *n.c.* **Control jet.**

controls and displays /kəntrówlz ənd displéyz/ *n.c. Apollo.* That part of the stabilization and control system (**SCS**) which indicates spacecraft position or keeps the craft on a desired course. This subsystem is shared by the other four SCS subsystems: **attitude reference, attitude control, thrust vector control,** and the **entry monitor subsystem.**

converter /kənvə́tər/ *n.* Device that changes information from one form into another.

cookbook /kúkbuk/ *n. sl. Apollo.* **Flight plan.**

coordinate /kowordinət/ *n.* Measurement used to determine a point's position on a plane or in space.

copy /kápiy/ 1. *n.* Rehearsal of the sequence of operations involved in a manual **reentry.**

2. *v. tr.* To receive and comprehend radio information; popular alternative to **roger.**

Coralie /koRalí/ *n.* French single-stage rocket series used primarily as the second stage in the **ELDO** international launch vehicle, the **Europa.** Other stages are the **Blue Streak** and the **Astris.**

Coralie stands 17 ft. high, weighs 23,000

lbs. fueled, and develops 56,000 lbs. of thrust.

coriolis effect /koryówləs iyfèkt/ *n.c.* Nausea and dizziness experienced by an astronaut turning his head in the opposite direction of a spacecraft's spin.

coriolis force /koriyówləs fòrs/ *n.c.* Force caused by the rotation of the earth; objects in the northern hemisphere move to the right, those in the southern hemisphere move to the left. Such forces can be duplicated in spinning spacecraft, causing **coriolis effect.**

corona /korównə/ *n.* 1. Outer layer of gases on the sun, generally seen only during total eclipse.

2. Type of electrical discharge enveloping the surface of a high voltage terminal. It results from ionization of the air around the terminal. Such ionization is caused by the high voltage, and it may appear as a blue glow. Coronas have sometimes been offered as explanations of **UFO** sightings.

coronal /korównəl/ *attr.* Of or pertaining to the outer layer of gases on the sun called the **corona.**

corposant /korpówsənt/ See **St. Elmo's fire.**

CORSA /kórsə/ *(ac.) n.c.* "Cosmic Radiation Satellite," Japanese scientific research satellite projected for launch in 1972–73. The spin-stabilized satellite's primary mission will involve extensive study of cosmic radiation.

cosmic dust /kâzmik də́st/ *n.c.* **Micrometeoroids** that appear to be dust.

cosmic noise /kâzmik nóyz/ *n.c.* Radio signals coming naturally from deep space.

Cosmic Radiation Satellite /kâzmik reydiyéyšən sètəlayt/ See **CORSA.**

cosmic rays /kâzmik réyz/ *n.c.* High-energy nuclear particles which continually strike the earth. They are thought to originate directly in the sun and in space beyond the **solar system.**

Cosmic Rocket /kâzmik rákət/ *n.c.* Early U.S.S.R. designation for three of its **Luna** probes. The three were later renamed *Luna 1, Luna 2,* and *Luna 3.*

cosmic speed /kâzmik spíyd/ *n.c. U.S.S.R.* 1. Five miles per second, the velocity required to put a satellite in Earth orbit; called *first cosmic speed.*

2. Seven miles per second, the velocity required to escape Earth's gravitational pull; called *second cosmic speed.*

cosmodrome /kázmədròwm/ *n. U.S.S.R.* Spaceflight center.

cosmogony /kazmájəniy/ *n.* Science that studies the creation of celestial bodies.

cosmology /kazmáləjiy/ *n.* Science concerning the laws governing the universe and its evolution.

cosmonaut /kázmənɔt/ *n. U.S.S.R.* **Astronaut.**

cosmonautics /kâzmənɔ́tiks/ *n. U.S.S.R.* **Astronautics.**

cosmonette /kâzmənét/ *n. U.S.S.R.* Woman astronaut.

Cosmos /kázmɔs/ See **Kosmos.**

cosmovision /kázməvìžən/ *n. U.S.S.R.* Television, as broadcast from space by a **cosmonaut.**

COSPAR /kówspàr/ *(ac.) n.c.* "Committee

on Space Research," group within the International Council of Scientific Unions (**ICSU**). Formed in 1958, COSPAR continues the international space cooperation of the International Geophysical Year (**IGY**) 1957–1958 by encouraging progress in scientific research which utilizes rockets. It is not, however, concerned with rocket technology itself.

couch /káwč/ *n.* Adjustable spacecraft chair.

countdown /káwntdàwn/ *n.* 1. Step-by-step process which leads to the launching of a missile or rocket.

2. Process of counting inversely during the acts leading to launch; zero is **liftoff.** *Countup* (see **GET**) is the process of keeping time after launch. See also **T-time.**

countdown demonstration test /káwntdawn demənstréyšən tèst/ See **CDDT.**

countup /káwntəp/ See **GET.**

Courier 1-B /kə́iyə wə̀n bíy/ *n.* First active-repeater comsat, launched by the U.S. in October 1960 and used experimentally for both real-time and delayed-message transmission.

CPLEE /síypliy/ *(ac.) n.c. Apollo.* "Charged particle lunar environment experiment," scientific device carried to the moon as part of the Apollo Lunar Surface Experiments Package (**ALSEP**). CPLEE measures the energy of electrons and protons that reach the moon from the sun.

CRA *(ac.) n.c.* "Centro Ricerche Aerospaziale" (Center for Aerospace Research), Italian government agency responsible for that country's national space program. The organization was formed by an agreement between the University of Rome and the Italian Air Force. Its responsibility covers aerospace projects from conceptual design to fulfillment and launch. The joint Italian-U.S. **San Marco** project is administered by CRA in conjunction with NASA.

craft /kræft/ *n.* **Spacecraft.**

crater /kréytə/ *n.* Huge depression on the surface of a celestial body. Theories as to the source of lunar craters vary from volcanic activity to meteor bombardment. Some are over 200 miles wide and 3 miles deep.

crawler /krɔ́lə/ *n. sl. Apollo.* **Transporter.**

crawlerway /krɔ́ləwèy/ *n. sl. Apollo.* Special road built for the **transporter.**

creep /kríyp/ *n.* Metal distortion caused by extreme stress.

crew compartment /krúw kəmpàrtmənt/ *n.c.* Astronauts' living quarters in a spacecraft.

crewman optical alignment sight /krúwmən òptikəl əláynmənt sàyt/ See **COAS.**

cross-range /krɔ́srèyŋj/ *n.* Gliding factor in the **reentry of Space Shuttle.**

cross the trough /krɔ́s ðə trɔ́f/ *idiomatic complex verb.* To pass from the gravitational influence of the earth to that of the moon.

cryogenic /kràyowjénik/ *attr.* 1. Of or pertaining to temperatures below −50° C. or approaching **absolute zero** (−273.16°C.).

2. Of or pertaining to rocket fuel which remains liquid only at extremely low temperatures.

/z/ *zero;* /ž/ *azure;* /θ/ *thin;* /ð/ *then;* /ŋ/ *song;* /æ/ *bat;* /ɔ/ *law;* /ə/ *sun;* /ə/ *bird.* Foreign symbols: [(n)] nasalization of some French vowels followed by /n/; [R] French uvular rolled /r/ sound; [ü] high front lip-rounded vowel; [x] Russian voiceless laryngeal fricative.

NASA

The CSM-LM docking maneuver is executed twice on each Apollo mission. The first docking, *A*, precedes the journey of the CSM-LM to the moon, and the second when the LM, after lunar liftoff, rejoins the CSM in lunar orbit, *B*.

cryogenics /krayowjéniks/ *n.* Branch of physics dealing with the production and effects of extremely low temperatures.

CSI *(ac.) n.c. Apollo.* "Concentric sequence initiation," LM maneuver which establishes a **catch-up orbit** for it; first phase of lunar orbit rendezvous (**LOR**). CSI is followed by the constant delta height (**CDH**) maneuver.

CSM *(ac.) n.c. Apollo.* "Command and service module," U.S. manned spacecraft made up of a joined CM and SM. The CSM functions as a unit from **liftoff** to **reentry**. On Apollo lunar missions, the CSM, also called the *mother ship*, remains in lunar orbit while the LM completes its moon landing mission. During the **Skylab** program, slightly modified CSMs will carry three-man crews to and from an orbiting space station.

CSM circularization /síy es em səkyuləizéyšən/ *n.c. Apollo.* CSM maneuver which gives it a nearly circular lunar orbit. The operation simplifies rendezvous of CSM and LM once the LM has completed its mission on the moon and lifted off. On *Apollo 11* and *12* this maneuver preceeded CSM/LM separation and descent orbit insertion (**DOI**); from *Apollo 14* it succeeded DOI.

cutoff /kə́təf/ *n.* Exact moment at which a spacecraft, having reached its desired predetermined velocity, automatically stops its engines.

cut off /kə̂t ə́f/ *v. tr.* To stop a rocket engine.

cyclic testing /sâyklik téstiŋ/ *n.c.* Repeated regular testing for maximum reliability.

Cyclops, Project /sáyklaps prâjekt/ *n.c.* A proposed experiment similar to Project Ozma (see **Ozma, Project**) but conceived on a much vaster scale. It envisions a connected arrangement of 1000 to 10,000 **dish reflectors** in an area 10 miles wide. It would detect beamed signals from any civilization within 1000 light years, and might "eavesdrop" on regular transmission of civilizations within 100 light years distance. It might also be aimed at a target galaxy in the hope that signals generated anywhere in the galaxy might be detected. Under consideration at NASA's **Ames Research Center**, there is no timetable for realization of this project. Cf. **CETI**.

D

D-1A *n.* French technological research satellite launched from **Hammaguir Space Center** in February 1966. The satellite, also called *Diapason*, further tested the **Diamant** launch vehicle and conducted geodetic studies.

D-2A *n.* French scientific research satellite, also called *Tournesol* ("Sunflower"), launched April 1971 from the **Guiana Space Center** by a *Diamant B* (see **Diamant**) launch vehicle. The primary mission of the D-2A was solar radiation study, particularly hydrogen distribution.

data /déytə/ *n. Apollo.* That part of the telecommunications (**T/C**) system which gathers and processes information from spacecraft, astronaut biosensors, or the ground.

data deduction /déytə diydə̀kšən/ *n.c.* Transfer of information from code into understandable language.

data dump /déytə də̀mp/ *n.c.* Playback, on command, of **telemetry** temporarily stored on a spacecraft's tape recorder.

data files /déytə fàylz/ *n.c. Apollo.* Twenty-volume compendium of all the information required on a mission; stored in the CM.

data link /déytə lìŋk/ *n.c.* Communications circuit which feeds tape-recorded information into a computer for analysis.

DE *(ac.) n.c. Apollo.* "Descent engine," LM descent or lower-stage engine which allows **soft landing** on the lunar surface. It is the only **Apollo** engine which has a throttle, operable either automatically or manually.

deadband /dédbænd/ *n.* Range of flexibility in a control system within which variations will cause only a negligible effect.

deadface /dédfèys/ *v. tr. Apollo.* To cut off electrical power between the **CM** and **SM** just prior to **reentry**.

deboost /dìybúwst/ *n.* Retrograde maneuver which lowers either the **perigee** or **apogee** of craft.

debriefing /dìybríyfiŋ/ *n.* Postmission question and answer session between Mission Control Center (**MCC**) personnel and astronauts.

debug /dìybə́g/ *v. tr.* To remove faults from a device or spacecraft.

decay /diykéy/ 1. *n.* The slowing down and falling of a satellite toward the body which it orbits.
2. *v. intr.* Of a satellite, to slow down and fall toward the body which it orbits.

decay orbit /diykéy òrbət/ *n.c.* Flight path of a decaying satellite (see **decay**).

deceleration /diyseləéyšən/ *n.* Act of slowing down.

decomposition /diykampəzíšən/ *n.* Thermal-chemical reaction releasing hot gases for rocket propulsion.

decompression /dìykəmpréšən/ *n.* Lowering of the pressure of a man-made atmosphere.

deep space /dìyp spéys/ *n.c.* All of space far beyond the earth's atmosphere.

Deep Space Network /dìyp spéys nètwərk/ See **DSN**.

Defense Satellite Communications System /diyfêns sætəlayt kəmyuwnəkéyšənz sìstəm/ See **DSCS**.

Delta /déltə/ *n.* 1. U.S. three-stage launch vehicle developed from the **Thor** rocket. In use since 1960, the Delta is comprised of a Thor first stage and two **Vanguard** upper stages. The *Thrust-Augmented Delta (TAD)*, developed in 1964, is essentially the same vehicle with the addition of three **Castor** rockets strapped onto the first stage. The *Long Tank Delta (LTD)*, introduced in 1968, has an enlarged first stage capable of supporting up to nine strap-on rockets.

The basic Delta launched the majority of U.S. scientific and communications satellites, including **TIROS, Telstar, Explorer,** and **Relay.** The more powerful TAD was employed in the launches of Syncom C (see **Syncom**) and **Early Bird.** The LTD is used for launching heavy payloads into near-Earth and lunar orbits as well as deep space. **ESSA 7** (see **ESSA**) was the first satellite launched by an LTD.

The standard Delta is 90 ft. high, weighs 114,000 lbs. fueled, and develops 185,000 lbs. of thrust. The TAD is the same height; however, it weighs 149,500 lbs. fueled, and develops 346,000 lbs. of thrust. The LTD

/a/ f*a*ther; /aw/ w*ow*; /ay/ b*uy*; /b/ *b*oy; /č/ wit*ch*; /d/ *d*oll; /e/ b*e*t; /ey/ s*ay*; /f/ *f*ew; /g/ *b*ag; /h/ *h*ole; /i/ *i*t; /iy/ b*e*; /j/ *g*in; /k/ *c*at; /l/ *l*amb; /m/ *m*an; /n/ *n*ow; /o/ *o*rbit; /ow/ t*ow*; /oy/ b*oy*; /p/ *p*at; /r/ *r*un; /s/ *s*end; /š/ *sh*oe; /t/ *t*oy; /u/ p*u*t; /uw/ d*o*; /v/ *e*ve; /w/ *w*ay; /y/ *y*es;

SE – 16

stands 106 ft. high, weighs 200,000 lbs. fueled, and has a thrust potential of 348,-000 lbs.

2. *l.c. cd.* Change or differential.

deorbit /dìyórbət/ *v. intr.* Of a spacecraft, to gradually stop orbiting as the result of a programmed or other deliberate command.

Department of Defense /diypârtmənt əv diyféns/ See **DOD.**

deploy /diyplóy/ 1. *v. tr.* To set up, unfold, or assemble for use, as of experiment apparatus used on the moon.

2. *v. intr.* Of spacecraft equipment, to become unfolded so as to be ready for use.

deployment /diyplóymənt/ *n.* The unfolding or assembling of spacecraft equipment.

deployment ring /diyplóymənt rìŋ/ See **D-ring.**

deployment tape /diyplóymənt tèyp/ *n.c.* Special band which, while being unwound, causes equipment to **deploy.** See **SSE.**

depressurization /dìyprèṣʌrəzéyšən/ *n.* Creation of vacuum conditions within a spacecraft prior to opening the hatch in deep space, i.e., equalizing spacecraft pressure to surrounding outside pressure.

depressurize /dìypréṣʌrayz/ 1. *v. tr.* To create a vacuum in an enclosed space.

2. *v. intr.* Of a closed chamber, to become a vacuum.

descent engine /díysent ènĵən/ See **DE.**

descent orbit /diysént òrbət/ *n.c.* Flight path a spacecraft may follow in order to approach a celestial body for observation or landing.

descent orbit insertion /diysènt òrbət insʌ́šən/ See **DOI.**

descent propulsion system /diysènt prəpʌ́lšən sìstəm/ See **DPS.**

descent stage /díysent stèyĵ/ *n.c. Apollo.* Lower section of the **LM;** section which slows the fall of the LM during lunar landing and which serves as launch pad for the **ascent stage's** return to lunar orbit. The descent stage contains descent engine **(DE),** fuel tanks, landing gear, and storage sections.

descent transfer orbit /diysènt trǽnsfʌ òrbit/ *n.c. Apollo.* **Equiperiod transfer orbit.**

destruct button /distrʌ́kt bətən/ See **EGADS button.**

destruct device *n.c.* /distrʌ́kt divàys/ *n.c.* **Destruct package.**

destructive readout /distrʌ́ktiv ríydàwt/ *n.c.* Transmission of computer memory bank data resulting in the intentional erasure of the information from the computer.

destruct package /distrʌ́kt pǽkəĵ/ *n.c.* Explosive device placed aboard a missile or launch vehicle for intentional detonation in case of emergency. Also called *destruct device, destruct system.*

destruct system /distrʌ́kt sìstəm/ *n.c.* **Destruct package.**

Diadème /diadém/ *n.* French scientific research satellite series consisting of two craft launched in February 1967 by **Diamant** launch vehicles from **Hammaguir Space Center.** The principal mission of the vehicles, to determine the shape and area of land masses and the curvature and dimensions of Earth, was not achieved.

Dial /diál/ *n.* Second Federal Republic of Germany satellite, launched in March 1970 by a French **Diamant** rocket from the **Guiana Space Center** in French Guiana, as part of a continuing German/French cooperative program. The spacecraft's basic mission was investigation of atmospheric radiation.

Diamant /diamɔ́(n)/ *n.* "Diamond," French series of multistage launch vehicles based on designs evolving from the National Basic Studies Program of 1960. The series consists of three models: *Diamant A, Diamant B,* and *Diamant B-C.* The former two are three-stage vehicles; the latter has four stages.

The Diamant A, basic model of the series, was first launched November 26, 1965, carrying France's first satellite, **A-1,** into orbit. Its first stage is an **Emeraude** rocket; the second stage is a **Topaze** rocket (the combination of the two is referred to as the **Saphir).** The upper stage is a small solid-propellant booster. Diamant A launched three other scientific satellites in addition to the A-1. The Diamant B model has an uprated first stage, a Topaze second stage, and a third stage which also serves on the **ELDO** *Europa II* (see **Europa)** launcher. It has launched three scientific satellites including the Federal Republic of Germany's **Dial.** The Diamant B-C has the same upper stage as the Diamant B; a small second stage, the **Rita,** originally developed for a ballistic missile; a small booster third stage; and a spin-stabilized upper stage. Still in the experimental phase, it has not been involved in any actual launches.

The Diamant A stands 63 ft. high, weighs 40,000 lbs. fueled, and is capable of developing 105,000 lbs. of thrust. The B model is 77 ft. high and weighs 55,000 lbs. fueled. The Diamant B-C stands 74 ft. high, weighs 60,000 lbs. fueled, and has a thrust potential of 137,300 lbs.

Diamond /dáymənd/ See **Diamant.**

Diapason /dáyəpeysən/ See **D-1A.**

digital computer /dìĵitəl kəmpyúwtʌ/ *n.c.* Computer based on counting; its counterpart is an *analog computer,* which is based on measuring.

digital windows /dìĵitəl wíndowz/ *n.c.* Squares on the display and keyboard **(DSKY)** where lighted numbers appear. These numbers show what information is being put into or requested from the computer and the information or answers the computer gives in return. In effect, the digital windows are the "voice" of the computer.

diplexer /dáypleksʌ/ *n.* Mechanism which allows two transmitters to use one antenna simultaneously.

direct ascent /dʌêkt əsént/ *n.c.* Interplanetary or lunar flight without the use of earth parking orbit **(EPO).**

direct flight /dʌêkt fláyt/ *n.c.* Point to point space voyage without any maneuvers, such as rendezvousing, during the journey.

direct movement /dʌêkt múwvmənt/ *n.c.* Counterclockwise movement of a celestial body on its own axis or about another body. Cf. **retrograde.**

disconnect tower /diskənékt tàwʌ/ *n.c.* **Umbilical tower.**

Discoverer /diskʌ́vʌʌ/ *n.* Largest U.S. military multipurpose satellite series, with launches beginning in February 1959; includes *Discoverer 13,* launched in August 1960, the first U.S. manmade item to be recovered from space. The project was classified after *Discoverer 38,* and neither the number nor objectives of subsequent launchings is available.

Discoverers were first launched to test methods of recovering spacecraft at sea or in mid-air, and gain information on propulsion, communication, radiation, and the atmosphere. *Discoverer 1,* launched in February 1959, was the first U.S. satellite to be sent into polar orbit. *Discoverer 14,* launched in August 1960, was the first satellite to be recovered in mid-air, a technique now in common use. *Discoverer 21,* launched in February 1961, achieved the first starting of an engine in space.

dish antenna /díš æntènə/ *n.c.* **dish reflector.**

dish reflector /díš riyflèktʌ/ *n.c.* Shallow bowl-shaped **antenna;** may range from several inches to several hundred feet in diameter.

display /displéy/ *n.* Indicators, often lighted, which give information on the functioning of spacecraft components.

display and keyboard /displêy ænd kíybord/ See **DSKY.**

divergent nozzle /divʌ́ĵənt názəl/ *n.c.* Conical exhaust pipe which expands in the direction of the outflow of gases. It increases speed in a rocket if the outflow is **supersonic** in nature.

dock /dák/ *v. tr.* To link one spacecraft to another during flight.

docking /dákiŋ/ *n.* Linking or joining two in-flight spacecraft; follows **rendezvous.**

docking latches /dákiŋ lǽčəz/ See **docking ring.**

docking ports /dákiŋ pòrts/ *n.c.* Specially equipped places on a spacecraft where

The steerable dish antenna in Cornwall, England, is 85 feet wide and weighs 800 tons.

A.T. & T.

/z/ zero; /ž/ azure; /θ/ thin; /ð/ then; /ŋ/ song; /æ/ bat; /ɔ/ law; /ə/ sun; /ʌ/ bird. Foreign symbols: [(n)] nasalization of some French vowels followed by /n/; [R] French uvular rolled /r/ sound; [ü] high front lip-rounded vowel; [x] Russian voiceless laryngeal fricative.

SE – 17

DROGUE ASSEMBLY · PROBE ASSEMBLY · DOCKING RING (CM) · LATCH ASSEMBLIES

The Apollo docking system allows the CM to dock with the LM. During the maneuver, the probe on the CM engages the drogue on the LM and the LM and CM are pulled together by a pressure system in the probe. On contact, 12 latches on the CM docking ring lock the modules together. In orbit around the moon, the drogue and probe assemblies are removed and two astronauts transfer from the CM to the LM through the docking-ring passage. The unit is then replaced in preparation for the return of the astronauts from the moon.

properly outfitted craft can **dock.** See **MDA.**

docking ring /dákiŋ rìŋ/ *n.c. Apollo.* CM component of the **docking system;** contains the *docking latches* (twelve pivoting locks) and the *docking seals* used to provide an airtight connection between the LM and CSM.

docking seals /dákiŋ sìylz/ See **docking ring.**

docking system /dákiŋ sìstəm/ *n.c.* U.S. manned spacecraft equipment complex which enables the CSM and another properly outfitted vehicle to join in space with an airtight seal. In **Apollo,** the CSM docked with the LM; in **Skylab,** the CSM will join the rest of the cluster in flight to become one unit.

docking target /dákiŋ tàrgət/ *n.c. Apollo.* CM and LM component of the **docking system;** mounted on the passive craft to aid the maneuvering craft in docking. See **COAS.**

docking tunnel /dákiŋ tənəl/ *n.c. Apollo.* Crew passageway between a docked CSM and LM.

DOD *(ac.) n.c.* "Department of Defense," U.S. government executive division primarily responsible for national defense but also involved in space efforts, especially in the areas of satellites for reconnaissance, navigation, and communications. DOD space responsibilities are carried out by the Air Force Systems Command (**AFSC**); cooperation with NASA is maintained through the Aeronautics and Astronautics Coordinating Board (**AACB**).

doghouse /dóghàws/ *n. sl.* Protuberance that serves as an instrument housing on the outside of a spacecraft.

DOI *(ac.) n.c. Apollo.* "Descent orbit inser-

tion," maneuver which places the LM in an elliptical lunar orbit so that the LM will have a minimal distance to travel during descent to the surface. During *Apollo 11* and *12,* DOI was a descent-engine (**DE**) maneuver that put the LM **pericynthion** at 9.2 miles, just uprange of the lunar landing site; the CSM remained in the circular orbit resulting from lunar orbit insertion (**LOI**). The LM orbit formed by DOI was an **equiperiod transfer orbit,** and the LM was positioned for powered descent initiation (**PDI**) at pericynthion.

From *Apollo 14,* in order to save DE fuel for lunar landing, DOI took place while the CSM and LM were still linked, and used CSM power. After **separation,** the LM was ready for PDI and the CSM then circularized its own orbit (see **CSM circularization**).

Doppler curve /dâplə kóv/ *n.c.* Graph line showing the apparent frequency of a satellite signal.

Doppler effect /dâplə əfèkt/ *n.c.* Apparent frequency change of waves which results when the source and recipient of the waves move toward, and then away, from each other.

Doppler shift /dâplə šíft/ *n.c.* **Doppler effect.**

dosimeter /dəsímətə/ *n.* Radiation-measuring unit worn by astronauts.

double star /dâbəl stár/ *n.c.* Two stellar bodies revolving about their common center of mass, i.e., around each other.

downlink data /dáwnliŋk dèytə/ *n.c.* Information transmitted from a spacecraft to Earth.

downrange /dáwnrèynǰ/ *adv.* Along a course away from a launch site.

down the slot /dâwn ðə slát/ *phr. adv. sl.*

Along the planned **trajectory.**

downtime /dáwntàym/ *n.* Period during which equipment is inoperable.

DPS /díps/ *(ac.) n.c. Apollo.* "Descent propulsion system," LM equipment complex which provides, through a liquid-fueled rocket engine, the power needed to deorbit the craft and land on the moon. A **pressurization subsystem** and **propellant feed subsystem** supply the engine.

drag /dráeg/ *n.* Air resistance to a body in flight.

drain rate /dréyn rèyt/ *n.c.* Speed at which energy in a system is used.

Dream /dríym/ See **Mechta.**

drifting flight /dríftiŋ flàyt/ *n.c.* Orbiting without the use of any controls for **stabilization** or **orientation.**

D-ring /díyrìŋ/ *(ac.) n.c.* "Deployment" ring, device which, when pulled, starts the **deployment** of some spacecraft equipment.

drogue /drówg/ *n.* 1. Part of the **docking system** into which the **probe** is inserted; located on the LM.

2. Small stability parachute deployed at an altitude of 20,000 ft. by reentering spacecraft; part of the earth landing system (**ELS**).

droppable /drápəbəl/ *n.* Equipment that may be jettisoned during a launch vehicle's ascent.

dry /dráy/ See **dry workshop.**

dry weight /dráy wéyt/ *n.c.* Mass of a spacecraft without its fuel, crew, or consumables.

dry workshop /dráy wókšap/ *n.c.* A rocket converted on Earth into a habitable workshop and launched *dry,* i.e., empty of its usual fuel. **Skylab** space station's **OWS** will be a dry workshop. Cf. **wet workshop.**

/a/ *father;* /aw/ *wow;* /ay/ *buy;* /b/ *boy;* /č/ *witch;* /d/ *doll;* /e/ *bet;* /ey/ *say;* /f/ *few;* /g/ *bag;* /h/ *hole;* /i/ *it;* /iy/ *be;* /ǰ/ *gin;* /k/ *cat;* /l/ *lamb;* /m/ *man;* /n/ *now;* /o/ *orbit;* /ow/ *tow;* /oy/ *boy;* /p/ *pat;* /r/ *run;* /s/ *send;* /š/ *shoe;* /t/ *toy;* /u/ *put;* /uw/ *do;* /v/ *eve;* /w/ *way;* /y/ *yes;*

SE – 18

DSCS *(ac.) n.c.* "Defense Satellite Communications System," U.S. military comsat program, originally known as the Initial Defense Communications Satellite Program (**IDCSP**), consisting of two phases: The Initial Defense Satellite Communications System (**IDSCS**), and an unnamed, improved second phase yet to be implemented. DSCS is intended to provide enemy-safe communications for a variety of

The *DSCS-2* satellite

special requirements including intelligence, warning, and presidential needs.

DSKY /dískiy/ *(ac.) n.c. Apollo.* "Display and keyboard," 19-button panel, considered part of the **guidance system** (see **GNCS** or **PGNS**), used to instruct or question the spacecraft **computer**. Both digital and word buttons are available and lighted digital windows or displays relay information to the crewman.

DSN *(ac.) n.c.* "Deep Space Network," **NASA** global tracking and communications system linking ground controllers and unmanned interplanetary and lunar probes; part of **NASCOM**. DSN stations are located at Canberra and Woomera, Australia; Madrid, Spain; Johannesburg, South Africa; and in the U.S., at Goldstone, California. An auxiliary station is located at Kennedy Space Center (**KSC**). Jet Propulsion Laboratory (**JPL**) controls the DSN for NASA.

dump /dómp/ *v. tr.* 1. **Jettison.** 2. Transmit, as in **data dump.**

duplexer /dúwpleksɚ/ *n.* Device which allows a single antenna to receive as well as transmit.

dynamic geodesy /daynǽmǝk jiyádǝsiy/ *n.c.* **Gravimetric geodesy.**

dynamic pressure /daynǽmik préšɚ/ *n.c.* Pressure exerted on a spacecraft during its passage through the atmosphere.

E

Eagle /íygǝl/ *n.* Name of *Apollo 11* LM (see **Apollo**).

Early Apollo Scientific Experiments Package /ɚ́liy ǝpâlow sayentífik ekspérǝmǝnts pǽkij/ See **EASEP.**

Early Bird /ɚ́liy bɚ́d/ *n.c.* First international communications satellite, used in the International Telecommunications Satellite Consortium (**Intelsat**) global communications network; launched into synchronous orbit April 6, 1965. Also called *Intelsat 1.*

early warning satellite /ɚ́liy wɚ́rniŋ sǽtǝlàyt/ *n.c.* Earth-orbiting vehicles of a military nature designed to detect enemy missile launchings for purposes of defense. These satellites employ both cameras and infrared sensors to note launchings. Most of these satellites are classified.

Earth /ɚ́θ/ *n.* Fifth largest planet in the solar system. The diameter of Earth is 8,000 miles. It is the third planet from the sun; its orbit lies at an average of 93 million miles from the sun. Earth has one natural satellite, the **moon.**

earth landing system /ɚ́θ lǽndiŋ sìstǝm/ See **ELS.**

earth orbit rendezvous /ɚ́θ orbǝt rándeyvuw/ *n.c.* Meeting of two spacecraft in earth orbit.

earth parking orbit /ɚ́θ párkiŋ òrbǝt/ See **EPO.**

Earth Resources Experiments Package /ɚ́θ rìysorsǝz ekspérǝmǝnts pǽkǝj/ See **EREP.**

Earth Resources Technology Satellite /ɚ́θ rìysorsǝs teknálǝjiy sǽtǝlayt/ See **ERTS.**

earthrise /ɚ́θràyz/ *n.* As seen from the lunar surface, the appearance of the earth over the horizon.

earth sensor /ɚ́θ sènsɚ/ *n.c.* Device that uses the earth for an **attitude** reference.

EASEP /íysep/ *(ac.) n.c. Apollo.* "Early Apollo Scientific Experiments Package," lunar research equipment carried on *Apollo 11.* Forerunner to the Apollo Lunar Surface Experiments Package (**ALSEP**), EASEP consisted of only two experiments: the passive seismic experiment (**PSE**) and laser ranging retro-reflector (**LRRR**). Since it was carried in a storage bay of the descent stage of the LM, the lighter EASEP was chosen for use on *Apollo 11* instead of the heavier ALSEP.

East /íyst/ See **Vostok.**

Eastern Standard Time /íystɚn stǽndɚd táym/ See **EST.**

Eastern Test Range /íystɚn tést rèynj/ See **AFETR.**

East is Red, The /ðiy íyst iz réd/ See **China, People's Republic of.**

EBW *(ac.) n.c.* "Exploding bridgewire," metal which melts at the high temperatures produced by large electrical impulses; initiates such acts as **retrorocket** firings and stage **separations.**

Eccentric Geophysical Observatory /eksêntrik jiyowfízikǝl ǝbzɚ́vǝtoriy/ See **OGO.**

eccentricity /èksentrísǝtiy/ *n.* Amount a spacecraft deviates from a circular orbit.

eccentric orbit /eksêntrik órbǝt/ *n.c.* Noncircular or elliptical orbit.

Echo /ékow/ *n.* First passive comsat series; either of two metalized balloons launched by the U.S. in August 1960 and January 1964. These experimental satellites served simply to bounce radio signals from one point to another on Earth. The program showed the feasibility of passive communications satellites, improved ground testing techniques for radio wave reflectivity measurements, and provided an opportunity for joint scientific research with the U.S.S.R., which observed the Echos when they were out of U.S. tracking range.

COURTESY OF A.T. & T. CO.

The *Echo* is packed in a 28-inch sphere at launch. Its diameter after inflation is 100 feet.

ecliptic /iyklíptik/ *n.* Plane of the earth's orbit around the sun; the apparent annual path of the sun in the heavens.

ECS *(ac.) n.c. Apollo.* "Environmental control system," equipment complex which provides breathable air and fresh water and which regulates temperature either in the craft or in the space suits of the astronauts during the mission and after splashdown.

In **Apollo**, four CSM and one CM subsystem are responsible for the aims of the overall system: **oxygen subsystem, pressure suit circuit, water subsystem, water-glycol subsystem,** and **post-landing ventilation.** The LM ECS has four subsystems: atmosphere revitalization subsystem (**ARS**), oxygen supply and cabin pressure control subsystem (**OSCPCS**), water management subsystem (**WMS**), and heat transport subsystem (**HTS**).

ECU *(ac.) n.c. Apollo.* "Environmental control unit," center of the environmental control system (**ECS**) of the CSM. Contains a *water chiller,* **water-glycol** *evaporators,* **lithium hydroxide** *canisters, suit heat exchanger* (cools air in **space suits** and controls suit humidity), and *compressors* (circulate air in space suits).

EDS *(ac.) n.c. Apollo.* "Emergency detection system," U.S. spacecraft equipment complex, associated with the launch escape system (**LES**), which monitors conditions

/z/ zero; /ž/ azure; /θ/ thin; /ð/ then; /ŋ/ song; /æ/ bat; /ɔ/ law; /ǝ/ sun; /ɚ/ bird. Foreign symbols: [(n)] nasalization of some French vowels followed by /n/; [R] French uvular rolled /r/ sound; [ü] high front lip-rounded vowel; [x] Russian voiceless laryngeal fricative.

SE – 19

during launch; capable of relaying warnings of trouble to the crew and initiating **abort**. It operates from **umbilical** separation until 100 seconds after **liftoff**.

effector /iyféktɚ/ *n.* Any instrument used to maneuver a vehicle during flight.

EGADS /îygǽdz/ *(ac.) n.c.* "Electronic ground automatic destruct sequencer." See **EGADS button**.

EGADS button /îygǽdz bòtən/ *(ac.) n.c.* "Electronic ground automatic destruct sequencer" button, ground console switch which can activate the self-destruct mechanism of a missile or launch vehicle in flight.

EGO /íygow/ *(ac.) n.c.* "Eccentric Geophysical Observatory." See **OGO**.

egress /íygres/ 1. *v. tr.* To exit a spacecraft.

2. *n.* Entire procedure involved in exiting a spacecraft.

3. *attr.* Of or pertaining to the exiting of a spacecraft.

egress tube /íygres tùwb/ *n.c. Apollo.* Tunnellike **EVA** exit located in the forward compartment of the CM. The egress tube also provides access to the **docking tunnel**.

EI *(ac.) n.c.* "Entry interface," 400,000-ft. point at which a spacecraft **re-enters** the earth's atmosphere. On **Apollo** missions EI follows transearth coast (**TEC**).

eight ball /éytbɔl/ *n.c. sl.* **Artificial horizon**.

ejecta /iyjéktə/ *n.* Material scattered when meteors impact on the lunar surface.

ejection /iyjékšən/ 1. *n.* Expulsion of gases produced in a rocket engine.

2. See **TD&E**.

ejection seats /iyjékšən sìyts/ *n.c. Gemini.* Escape mode for astronauts in a malfunctioning craft. **Abort** during launch could be initiated manually, hurling the crew from the spacecraft to safety. Cf. **LES**.

ejection velocity /iyjékšən vəlàsətiy/ *n.c.* Speed required to take a spacecraft from **orbit** into **trajectory**.

elasticizer /iylǽstəsàyzɚ/ *n.* Substance employed in a solid propellant that prevents it from cracking and adheres it to the combustion chamber walls.

ELDO /éldow/ *(ac.) n.c.* "European Launcher Development Organization," an intergovernmental coalition set up under an agreement signed in February 1964 to provide Europe with an independent source of launchers for spacecraft intended for peaceful purposes. The member states are Australia, Belgium, Federal Republic of Germany, France, Great Britain, Italy and the Netherlands. Denmark and Switzerland participate as observers. Organization headquarters are maintained at Neuilly, a suburb of Paris.

The organization had two initial goals. First, the development of an experimental prototype three-stage launch vehicle, the *Europa I* (see **Europa**), which was completed with a final test launch from Woomera in June 1970. The second goal was the development of *Europa II* and *III*, second generation rockets which will carry actual telecommunications satellites into orbit. Though these launches are through the development phase, budgetary cutbacks by member nations have postponed their use until 1973.

The organization's future plans call for increased relations with the U.S.S.R., U.S., and UN. Current endeavors include consultation with NASA regarding U.S. post-Apollo **Space Shuttle** and space station programs.

electrical power system /əlêktrikəl páwɚsìstəm/ See **EPS**.

electric engine /iylêktrik énjən/ *n.c.* **Ion engine**.

electric rocket /iylêktrik rákət/ *n.c.* **Ion rocket**.

Electrodynamic Explorer /iylêktrowdaynǽmik eksplórɚ/ See **Explorer**.

electromagnetic /iylêktrowmægnétik/ *attr.* Of or pertaining to magnetism produced by electric current.

electromagnetic radiation /iylêktrowmægnêtik reydiyéyšən/ *n.c.* Radiation that carries an electrical charge; included in this category are potentially dangerous **x-rays, gamma rays,** and **ultraviolet rays**.

electronic ground automatic destruct sequencer /əlektrânik gràwnd ɔtəmǽtik diystrɔ́kt sìykwensɚ/ See **EGADS button**.

electronic ground automatic destruct sequencer button /əlektrânik gràwnd ɔtəmǽtik diystrɔ́kt síykwensɚ bòtən/ See **EGADS button**.

Electronics Research Center /əlektrâniks ríysɚč sèntɚ/ *n.c.* **NASA** research facility at Cambridge, Massachusetts.

Elektron /əléktran/ *n.* U.S.S.R. series of four scientific research satellites. Goal of the Elektrons was investigation of cislunar space, particularly the **Van Allen Radiation Belts**. The spacecraft were launched in pairs, two satellites per launch vehicle, in January and July of 1964. The dual launches were accomplished using the powerful **Vostok** carrier rocket, equipped with a special system which released one of the satellites from the launcher's last stage while its engines were still firing.

elephant ear /éləfənt ìr/ *n.c. sl. Apollo.* Thick reinforcement plate on a spacecraft **hatch**.

ellipse /iylíps/ *n.* Plane closed curve in which the sum of the distances from any point on the curve to two fixed points, called foci, is constant. The shape of an ellipse is oval.

ELS *(ac.) n.c. Apollo.* "Earth landing subsystem," spacecraft equipment complex designed to provide safe **splashdown** and **recovery** of astronauts and their capsule.

ELSS *(ac.) n.c. Gemini.* "Extravehicular life support system," shoebox-sized chestpack used in conjunction with an extravehicular suit; an **umbilical** which provides atmosphere, ventilation, and communication during **EVA**.

Emerald /émrəld/ See **Emeraude**.

Emeraude /eməRód/ *n.* "Emerald," French single-stage rocket, used primarily as a component of the **Diamant** launch vehicle.

Emeraude stands 32 ft. high and has a thrust potential of 66,000 lbs.

emergency detection system /iymɚ́jənsiy diytékšən sìstəm/ See **EDS**.

emissivity /iymisívətiy/ *n.* Thermal-radiation emission capacity of a surface.

emplace /empléys/ *v. tr.* To put instruments manually on the lunar surface.

EMU *(ac.) n.c. Apollo.* "Extravehicular mobility unit," combination of extravehicular **PGA** and **PLSS** worn during inflight or lunar-surface **EVA**.

encounter /enkáwntɚ/ See **near encounter**.

Endeavor /endévɚ/ *n.* Name of *Apollo 15* CM (see **Apollo**).

Energetic Particles Explorer. /enɚjêtik pártikəlz eksplòrɚ/ See **EPE**.

enslavement /ensléyvmənt/ *n.* Putting one device under the regulatory control of another.

entry corridor /éntriy kòrədɚ/ *n.c.* **Reentry corridor**.

entry interface /éntriy íntɚfeys/ See **EI**.

entry monitor subsystem /êntriy manətɚ sə̀bsistəm/ *n.c. Apollo.* That part of the **CM** stabilization and control system (**SCS**) and guidance, navigation, and control system (**GNCS**) which indicates changes in velocity to the crew. The entry monitor subsystem also contains controls by which thrust may be altered manually.

environmental control system /envâyənmentəl kəntrówl sìstəm/ See **ECS**.

environmental control unit /envâyənmentəl kəntrówl yùwnət/ See **ECU**.

Environmental Science Services Administration /envâyənmentəl sâyəns sɚ́visəs ædminəstrèyšən/ See **ESSA**.

environmental space chamber /envâyənmêntəl spéys čèymbɚ/ See **simulator**.

Environmental Survey Satellite /envayənmêntəl sɚ́vey sætələyt/ See **ESSA**.

Eole /eól/ *n.* French experimental meteorological satellite launched August 1971 by a NASA **Scout** launch vehicle. The satellite's mission is the establishment of a constant meteorological survey of atmospheric conditions: wind, pressure, and temperature. Using a series of balloons equipped with measurement devices, the Eole gleans information collected by these balloons and retransmits it to ground stations.

The French meteorological satellite *Eole*

CNES

/a/ *father*; /aw/ *wow*; /ay/ *buy*; /b/ *boy*; /č/ *witch*; /d/ *doll*; /e/ *bet*; /ey/ *say*; /f/ *few*; /g/ *bag*; /h/ *hole*; /i/ *it*; /iy/ *be*; /ĵ/ *gin*; /k/ *cat*; /l/ *lamb*; /m/ *man*; /n/ *now*; /o/ *orbit*; /ow/ *tow*; /oy/ *boy*; /p/ *pat*; /r/ *run*; /s/ *send*; /š/ *shoe*; /t/ *toy*; /u/ *put*; /uw/ *do*; /v/ *eve*; /w/ *way*; /y/ *yes*;

SE–20

EPE *(ac.) n.c.* "Energetic Particles Explorer," U.S. physical research satellites, launched between 1961 and 1964 as numbers 12, 14, 15, and 26 of the **Explorer** series. EPE investigated the radiation belt, magnetosphere, solar wind, and cosmic rays.

ephemeris /əfémərəs/ *n.* Table indicating the computed positions of celestial bodies from day to day or at regular intervals throughout the year.

EPO *(ac.) n.c.* "Earth parking orbit," temporary flight path around Earth during which spacecraft systems are checked prior to **injection** into deep space. For lunar missions, the next major maneuver is translunar injection (**TLI**).

EPS *(ac.) n.c. Apollo.* "Electrical power system," equipment complex which provides, controls, and distributes electricity throughout a space vehicle. **Fuel cells**, which produce the power, provide water as a by-product.

Epsilon Eridani /êpsilan eridǽni/ *n.* Star no. 5 in the constellation Eridanus. Its apparent visual magnitude is 3.8 (see **Ozma, Project**).

equatorial orbit /iykwətôriyəl órbət/ *n.c.* Earth orbit with a plane near or identical to that of the equator.

equatorial plane /iykwətôriyəl pléyn/ *n.c.* Imaginary plane which slices through the earth at the equator.

equiperiod transfer orbit /ekwipîriəd trǽnsfɚ òrbit/ *n.c. Apollo.* On *Apollo 11* and *12*. Highly elliptical LM orbit following **separation** from the CSM and resulting from descent orbit insertion (**DOI**). Its time span equaled that of the circular orbit of the CSM in case emergency redocking was required.

equipment bay /iykwípmənt bèy/ *n.c.* Storage compartment.

equipment section /iykwípmənt sèkšən/ See **Gemini**.

erector /əréktɚ/ *n.* Cranelike tower used to place a rocket on its transport vehicle or to raise a rocket to firing position on a **launch pad**.

EREP /írep/ *(ac.) n.c.* "Earth Resources Experiments Package," one of the principal experiment packages to be carried on the proposed U.S. **Skylab** space station. Housed in Skylab's Multiple Docking Adapter (**MDA**), the EREP will include among its instruments six cameras and an infrared spectrometer. These components should correlate data from Skylab with data from the proposed Earth Resources Technology Satellite (**ERTS**) to be launched in 1972.

ERTS /ɚts/ *(ac.) n.c.* "Earth Resources Technology Satellite," proposed U.S. geophysical experimental satellite series, with the first launch projected for 1972. Transmitting television pictures and data from near-polar orbits, the satellites will study food sources, natural resources, extant air and water pollution, and other man-oriented Earth problems.

escape rocket /əskéyp ràkət/ See **LEM**.

escape tower /əskéyp tàwɚ/ See **LES**.

escape velocity /əskéyp vəlàsitiy/ *n.c.* Speed necessary, discounting air resistance, for a spacecraft to escape a celestial body's gravitational pull.

ESOC /íysak/ *(ac.) n.c.* "European Space Operations Center," branch of **ESRO** responsible for operational activities and data gathering and storage. It is based at Darmstadt, Federal Republic of Germany.

ESRANGE /ésrèynj/ *(ac.) n.c.* "European Sounding Rocket Launching Range," branch of **ESRO** responsible for the launching of sounding rockets. The range and its associated support elements are located at Kiruna, Sweden.

ESRIN /ésrin/ *(ac.) n.c.* "European Space Research Institute," branch of **ESRO** responsible for advanced physical research. It is based at Frascati, Italy.

ESRO /ésrow/ *(ac.) n.c.* "European Space Research Organization." 1. An international organization studying peaceful applications of space technology, established in June 1962 by Belgium, Denmark, Federal Republic of Germany, France, Great Britain, Italy, the Netherlands, Spain,

EUROPEAN SPACE RESEARCH ORGANIZATION
ESRO-2, launched in 1968, studies solar and galactic cosmic rays and particles.

Sweden, and Switzerland. Major programs include development of sounding rockets and the ESRO and **HEOS** satellites. ESRO maintains headquarters in Paris, with research centers in the Netherlands (**ESTEC**) and Italy (**ESRIN**), administrative and data processing facilities (**ESOC**) in Germany, a sounding rocket launching range (**ESRANGE**) in Sweden, and a network of telemetry stations (**ESOC**) in Belgium, Federal Republic of Germany, Great Britain, Norway, and the U.S. The initial ESRO charter expired at the end of 1971 and Denmark withdrew. Austria, Ireland, and Norway participate in ESRO as official observers, and cooperative links have been established with India, Japan, the U.S. and the U.S.S.R.

2. Any of several multiple-experiment satellites developed by ESRO. *ESRO-2* (also called *Iris*) was launched in May 1968 for studies of solar astronomy and cosmic rays. *ESRO-1* (also called *Aurorae*) and *ESRO-1B* (also called *Boreas*), launched October 1968 and October 1969 respectively, studied polar ionospheric and auroral

phenomena. *ESRO-4*, scheduled for launch late in 1972, will investigate atomic particles in the upper atmosphere. The first three ESRO satellites were launched by **NASA**.

ESSA /ésə/ *(ac.) n.c.* 1. "Environmental Science Services Administration," former U.S. government agency under the Department of Commerce, absorbed into the National Oceanic and Atmospheric Administration (**NOAA**) in October 1970; sponsor of the ESSA satellites.

2. "Environmental Survey Satellite," first U.S. operational meteorological satellite series, developed Television and Infrared Observation Satellites (**TIROS**) and early **Nimbus** technology for utilization in the TIROS Operational System (**TOS**). Nine ESSA's were launched from 1966 to 1969. Each could view the whole earth at least once a day from its sun-synchronous orbit. Beginning with *ESSA 3*, odd-numbered ESSA's carried the advanced vidicon camera system (**AVCS**) which stored photos for relay over special locations; the other ESSA's carried automatic picture transmission (**APT**) cameras which simultaneously recorded and transmitted photographic images directly to earth stations.

EST *(ac.) n.c.* "Eastern Standard Time," used along the eastern coast of the U.S. Kennedy Space Center (**KSC**) is located in the EST zone.

ESTEC /éztek/ *(ac.) n.c.* "European Space Research and Technology Center," branch of **ESRO** responsible for the design and construction of space vehicles and the promotion of pure and applied research in space-oriented sciences. The organization is based at Noordwijk, the Netherlands.

ethylene glycol /èθəliyn glǽykɔl/ See **water-glycol**.

ETR *(ac.) n.c.* "Eastern Test Range." See **AFETR**.

Europa /yurówpə/ *n.* 1. .**ELDO** multistage satellite launch vehicle series developed for joint European space efforts. The series consists of *Europa I*, a three-stage rocket first launched in November 1968, and *Europa II* and *III*, four-stage vehicles scheduled to launch large telecommunications satellites beginning in 1973. The basic model, Europa I, consists of a British **Blue Streak** first stage, a French **Coralie** second stage, and an **Astris** upper stage built by the Federal Republic of Germany. It was developed as an experimental prototype for the Europa II and III. The Europa II is the basic model with additional engines in a fourth stage allowing its projected payload, a comsat, to achieve geostationary orbit. The Europa III is the basic model with an additional thrust increasing transstage.

The Europa I stands 89 ft. high, weighs 212,800 lbs. fueled, and has a thrust potential of 332,000 lbs. Europa II and III stand 105 ft. and 135 ft. high, respectively.

2. In Greek mythology, a Phoenician princess abducted by Zeus, who carried her off to Crete.

European Launcher Development Organization /yurəpîyən lɔ́nčɚ diyvéləpmənt orgənəzèyšən/ See **ELDO**.

/z/ *zero;* /ž/ *azure;* /θ/ *thin;* /ð/ *then;* /ŋ/ *song;* /æ/ *bat;* /ɔ/ *law;* /ə/ *sun;* /ɚ/ *bird.* Foreign symbols: [(n)] nasalization of some French vowels followed by /n/; [R] French uvular rolled /r/ sound; [ü] high front lip-rounded vowel; [x] Russian voiceless laryngeal fricative.

NASA

During an umbilical EVA, the astronaut is connected to his spacecraft with an umbilical line and a 25-foot tether. He carries an emergency oxygen supply and a self-maneuvering unit.

confirmed the existence of the Van Allen Radiation Belt, one of the most significant findings of the Space Age. By the beginning of 1972, forty-five Explorers had been launched successfully. Further launches, tentatively titled *Electrodynamic Explorer*, *Neutral Point Explorer*, *Plasmopause Explorer*, and *Synchronous Explorer*, are planned throughout the 1970s.

Originally a U.S. Army project, the Explorer program has been carried out under NASA auspices since *Explorer 5*, launched in July 1959. Explorers handle a variety of jobs in the geophysical and astrophysical fields and use numerous spacecraft, from simple cylinders and balloons to complex vehicles having an array of extendible arms and panels.

Satellites with specific goals, such as **Air Density Explorer**, Atmosphere Explorer (**AE**), **Beacon**, Energetic Particles Explorer (**EPE**), Geodetic Earth Orbiting Satellite (**GEOS**), Interplanetary Monitoring Platform (**IMP**), **Injun**, **Micrometeoroid Explorer**, Radio Astronomy Explorer (**RAE**), and Small Astronomy Satellite (**SAS**) belong to Explorer subseries.

NASA

Explorer 1, launched in 1958

European Sounding Rocket Launching Range /yurəpîyən sâwndiŋ ràkət lónčiŋ rèynǰ/ See **ESRANGE**.

European Space Operations Center /yurəpîyən spéys apə`èyšənz sèntə/ See **ESOC**.

European Space Research and Technology Center /yurəpîyən spéys ænd teknáləǰiy sèntə/ See **ESTEC**.

European Space Research Institute /yurəpîyən spéys rìysəč ìnstətuwt/ See **ESRIN**.

European Space Research Organization /yurəpîyən spéys rìysəč orgənəzèyšən/ See **ESRO**.

EVA (*ac.*) *n.c.* "Extravehicular activity," any work performed by an astronaut on a mission while outside his craft. There are three types of EVA: *umbilical* (also called a *space walk*), in which the astronaut remains attached to the craft by an **umbilical tether**; *standup* (*SEVA*), in which the astronaut stands in the spacecraft hatch with only half of his body outside the craft; and *lunar*, in which an astronaut walks or rides, as in the lunar roving vehicle (**LRV**), on the moon's surface. Cf. **IVA**.

For all forms of EVA, astronauts wear special protective garments (see **PGA**).

evasive maneuver /iyvêysiv mənúwvə/ *n.c.* *Apollo.* CSM maneuver, following transposition, docking, and ejection (**TD&E**), in which a short retrograde-rocket burn moves the docked CSM/LM out of the

immediate range of the jettisoned third stage of the launch vehicle. Translunar coast (**TLC**) is the period in which the evasive maneuver takes place.

exhaust velocity /egzɔ́st vəlàsitiy/ *n.c.* Rate at which gases are forced from the nozzles of a **rocket engine**.

exobiology /êksowbayáləǰiy/ *n.* Search for and study of **extraterrestrial** life.

exosphere /éksowsfìr/ *n.* Outermost shell of Earth's atmosphere.

exothermic /êksow θ´ɔmik/ *attr.* Of or pertaining to that which gives off heat.

exotic fuel /egzâtik fyúwl/ *n.c.* Unusual fuel mixture.

expansion rate /ekspǽnšən rèyt/ *n.c.* Rate at which gas expands upon leaving the nozzle of the thrust chamber. It is determined by dividing the pressure of gas in a rocket's **thrust chamber** by the pressure under which the gas leaves the nozzle.

experiment package /ekspérəmənt pǽkiǰ/ *n.c.* Scientific apparatus, other than that used to run the craft itself, carried on a manned spacecraft as part of its **payload**. Experiment packages usually require manned tending, at least in the **deployment** of the components.

exploding bridgewire /eksplôwdiŋ briǰwáyə/ See **EBW**.

Explorer /eksplórə/ *n.* Largest U.S. multipurpose satellite series, and which includes America's first satellite, *Explorer 1*. Launched January 31, 1958, *Explorer 1*

explosive bolts /eksplôwsiv bówlts/ *n.c.* Couplings equipped with small detonating devices which, when exploded, insure release.

extraterrestrial /ekstrəteréstriyəl/ *attr.* Of or pertaining to anything beyond or away from the earth.

extravehicular /ekstrəviyhíkyələ/ *attr.* Of or pertaining to the area outside a spacecraft.

extravehicular activity /ekstrəviyhíkyələ æktívətiy/ See **EVA**.

extravehicular gloves /èkstrəviyhíkyələ glǽvz/ See **PGA**.

/a/ *father*; /aw/ *wow*; /ay/ *buy*; /b/ *boy*; /č/ *witch*; /d/ *doll*; /e/ *bet*; /ey/ *say*; /f/ *few*; /g/ *bag*; /h/ *hole*; /i/ *it*; /iy/ *be*; /ǰ/ *gin*; /k/ *cat*; /l/ *lamb*; /m/ *man*; /n/ *now*; /o/ *orbit*; /ow/ *tow*; /oy/ *boy*; /p/ *pat*; /r/ *run*; /s/ *send*; /š/ *shoe*; /t/ *toy*; /u/ *put*; /uw/ *do*; /v/ *eve*; /w/ *way*; /y/ *yes*;

extravehicular life support system /èkstrəviyhîkyələ láyf səpòrt sìstəm/ See **ELSS**.

extravehicular mobility unit /èkstrəviyhîkyələ mowbílətiy yùwnət/ See **EMU**.

extravehicular visor /èkstrəviyhîkyələ váyzə/ See **PGA**.

eyeballs down /âybɔlz dáwn/ *n.c. sl.* Head-downward stress experienced during extreme acceleration upward; felt most in the eyes, hence the expression.

eyeballs in /âybɔlz ín/ *n.c. sl.* Acceleration force experienced from the chest toward the back; felt most in the eyes, hence the expression.

eyeballs out /âybɔlz áwt/ *n.c. sl.* Deceleration force experienced from the back toward the chest; felt most in the eyes, hence the expression.

eyeballs up /âybɔlz ə́p/ *n.c. sl.* Acceleration force experienced upward from the feet during downward acceleration; felt most in the eyes, hence the expression.

F–G

fail-safe /féyl sèyf/ *attr.* Of or pertaining to equipment or design which has built-in safety devices to anticipate and prevent accidents.

fairing /fériŋ/ *n.* Cover designed to reduce **drag** which encases nonstreamlined items.

Faith 7 /fèyθ sévən/ *n.c.* Nickname for *Mercury 9* spacecraft (see **Mercury**).

Falcon /fǽlkən/ *n.* Name of *Apollo 15* LM (see **Apollo**).

fall-out /fɔ́làwt/ *n. sl.* Side benefits resulting from the space program.

filament /fíləmənt/ *n.* Fibers used in structural elements to increase strength and decrease weight.

fire /fáyə/ *v. tr.* To start a rocket engine.

fireball /fáyəbɔl/ *n.* **1.** Reentry condition during which the heat shield of the spacecraft becomes incandescent and air particles around the craft ionize.

2. Spherically shaped, airborne, burning or glowing substance.

fire deluge system /fáyə dèlyuwj sìstəm/ *n.c.* Remotely controlled sprinklers located throughout a launch pad area for use in case of fire or explosion.

fire detection system /fáyə diytékšən sìstəm/ *n.c. Apollo.* **Sensors** in the first stage of the **Saturn** launch vehicle capable of transmitting an automatic signal to **ground controllers** in case of fire before **ignition**.

fire in the hole /fáyə in ðə hówl/ See **FITH**.

firing room /fáyəiŋ rùwm/ *n.c.* Location at a launch site from which ground controllers start the rocket engines of a launch vehicle.

first cosmic speed /fə́st kâzmik spíyd/ See **cosmic speed**.

first motion /fə́st mówšən/ *n.c.* **Liftoff**.

FITH /fíθ/ *(ac.) n.c. Apollo.* "Fire in the hole," LM maneuver during lunar-surface liftoff, descent, or inflight abort in which the ascent engine (**AE**) fires while the ascent and descent stages are mated but not bound together. Lunar orbit rendezvous (**LOR**) follows.

five by five /fàyv bay fáyv/ *attr.* Of or pertaining to radio transmissions which are loud and clear; decreasing numbers indicate a loss of either element.

flag /flǽg/ *n.* Warning signal.

flame bucket /fléym bə̀kət/ *n.c. sl.* **Flame deflector**.

flame deflector /fléym diyflèktə/ *n.c.* Structure at the base of a **launch pad** which diverts rocket exhaust horizontally.

flashback /flǽšbæk/ *n.* Sudden reversal of **rocket engine** flame.

flashing beacon /flǽšiŋ bíykən/ *n.c. Apollo.* Light on the **reentry** capsule which is activated about eight seconds after the **main parachutes** are deployed; designed to facilitate rescue in total darkness. The flashing beacon is part of the earth landing system (**ELS**) equipment.

flashpoint /flǽšpòynt/ *n.* Temperature at which fuel vapor ignites momentarily.

flexible tunnel extension /flêksəbəl tə́nəl ekstènšən/ See **AM**.

flight /fláyt/ **1.** *n. sl.* Flight director at the Mission Control Center (**MCC**).

2. *u.c.* See **Polyot**.

Flight Acceleration Facility /flâyt əkseləréyšən fəsìlətiy/ *n.c.* Major installation at **NASA**'s Manned Spacecraft Center (**MSC**) housing a centrifuge and related equipment.

flight control system /fláyt kəntrowl sìstəm/ *n.c.* Spacecraft equipment complex which commands attitude, control, and stability. Cf. **SCS**.

flight coverall /fláyt kə̀vərɔl/ *n.c. Apollo.* Two-piece astronaut garment with accompanying foot gear called *booties;* worn over the **constant wear garment** while a shirt-sleeve environment is maintained during spaceflight. **Velcro** on the booties provides a restraint in the weightless environment of space; an astronaut can stand on similar material in front of the CM console.

flight path /fláyt pæ̀θ/ *n.* **Trajectory**.

flight plan /fláyt plæ̀n/ *n.c.* Prearranged syllabus for any space mission.

flight profile /fláyt prò̀wfayl/ *n.c.* Plotted graph which indicates a spacecraft's various altitudes along its trajectory.

flight-readiness firing /flâyt rédiynəs fàyəiŋ/ *n.c.* **Static firing**.

Flight Research Center /flâyt ríysə̀č sèntə/ *n.c.* **NASA** research facility at Edwards Air Force Base, California.

flotation collar /flowtéyšən kàlə/ *n.c.* Air-filled device used at splashdown to maintain buoyancy and stability of a spacecraft, thus allowing the crew safe **egress**. Attached by naval recovery teams so as to encircle the base of the capsule.

fly-away disconnects /flâyəwey diskənékts/ *n.c.* Power and air **umbilicals** which are swung away prior to **liftoff**.

Among the safety procedures instituted after spacecraft splashdown are the inflation of three bags to right the craft and attachment of a flotation collar to keep it afloat.

/z/ *zero;* /ž/ *azure;* /θ/ *thin;* /ð/ *then;* /ŋ/ *song;* /æ/ *bat;* /ɔ/ *law;* /ə/ *sun;* /ə̀/ *bird.* Foreign symbols: [(n)] nasalization of some French vowels followed by /n/; [R] French uvular rolled /r/ sound; [ü] high front lip-rounded vowel; [x] Russian voiceless laryngeal fricative.

flyby /fláybay/ *n.* Flight of a spacecraft past a celestial object for scientific study.

fly-by /fláybay/ *attr.* Of or pertaining to a spacecraft or a mission concerned with studying an object while passing by it. Sometimes this enables the observation of several celestial items (see **Outer Planets Mission**).

fly-by-wire /fláybay wàyə/ *n.c.* Semiautomatic flight mode employed by spacecraft pilot.

FOBS /fábz/ *(ac.) n.c.* "Fractional-Orbit Bombardment System," U.S.S.R. experimental military satellite series with the potential of delivering nuclear warheads from orbit to targets on Earth. Such vehicles would have the capability of rendering radar useless. Since the test flights conducted so far, 1967–1970, did not complete full orbits (i.e., had fractional-orbits) and were in all probability unarmed, they were not in violation of the UN treaty banning the use of nuclear weapons in outer space, a treaty to which the Soviet Union subscribes.

Foo Fighter /fûw fáytə/ *n.c.* Apparent **fireball**, first thought to be a newly discovered weapon, which followed military aircraft during World War II. It is theorized that jet planes create an electrical field conducive to formation of fireballs and these fireballs then follow them in flight. Foo Fighters are sometimes offered as explanations of **UFO** sightings.

footpad /fútpæd/ See **landing gear assembly**.

footprint /fútprìnt/ *n. sl.* Foot-shaped ocean area which encompasses the possible **recovery** region of a reentering spacecraft.

Fort Churchill /fòrt čə́čəl/ See **Canada**.

forward /fórwəd/ **1.** *adv.* Top or front of an aerospace vehicle; originally naval jargon.

2. *attr.* Of or pertaining to the top or front of a vehicle.

forward heat shield /fòrwəd híyt šìyld/ See **forward; heat shield**.

FPS *(ac.) attr.* "Feet per second," of or pertaining to the speed achieved during space flight.

FR-1A *n.* French satellite, launched in December 1965 by a NASA **Scout** launch vehicle from the Air Force Western Test Range (**AFWTR**) under a Franco-American cooperative agreement. The satellite, also called *Fria*, studied radio-wave propagation in the upper atmosphere.

Fractional-Orbit Bombardment System /frǽkšənəl ôrbət bambárdmənt sìstəm/ See **FOBS**.

FRANCE

Third nation to orbit satellites using internally developed launch vehicles.

Rocket development in France began officially in 1950 when the French department of national defense ordered the Ballistic Research Laboratory to begin design studies. The result was the single-stage **Véronique**, a scaled down **V-2**, first launched in 1953. This success led to the development of more than four rocket families. The third generation of French rockets was the "precious stones" launch-vehicle series: **Topaze, Emeraude, Saphir,**

Rubis, Agate, and **Diamant.** The Diamant, in its three versions, serves as the basic launch vehicle for the French space program.

France's first satellite, **A-1,** was launched November 26, 1965, by a three-stage Diamant launch vehicle. It was followed in December by the **FR-1A,** launched by a NASA **Scout** launcher. Both satellites carried only radio transmitters and receivers for tracking purposes. The **D-1A,** launched in February 1966, was a geodetic research vehicle. It was orbited by a Diamant, as all French satellites have been since then. Two **Diadème** satellites were launched in February 1967. In 1970, Diamants launched **Dial,** a research satellite developed and built by the Federal Republic of Germany, and **Péole.** The **D-2A** and the **Eole** were launched in 1971 with NASA cooperation. Future satellites include the **Symphonie** (a telecommunications satellite), an air traffic control satellite, and a meteorological satellite. These programs are projected through 1974.

France's role in international space development includes membership in **ELDO** and **ESRO,** and joint efforts with the U.S. and U.S.S.R. The **Europa** rockets, internationally developed by ELDO, include a second stage of French origin, the **Coralie.** Other projects, like Symphonie, are conducted with fellow ELDO-ESRO member nations. French-made equipment has been used in several Soviet launches, specifically *Luna 17* (see **Luna**), which carried a French laser. In addition to launches employing the U.S. Scout rocket, the French are actively participating in **Space Shuttle** and other U.S. post-Apollo projects.

The overall responsibility for the French space program falls under the Centre National d'Etudes Spatiales (National Center of Space Studies) [**CNES**]. Primary French launch site, until Algeria gained its independence in 1967, was **Hammaguir Space Center** in the Sahara. It has since been relocated to the **Guiana Space Center,** Kourou, French Guiana, in South America.

Freedom 7 /frîydəm sévən/ *n.c.* Nickname for *Mercury 3* spacecraft (see **Mercury**).

free fall /frîy fól/ *n.c,* Unrestricted, unpowered motion of an object in a field of gravity.

free flight /frîy fláyt/ *n.c.* Unpowered flight, as in orbiting and gliding.

free-flyer /frîyfláyə/ See **RAM**.

free-flying module /frîyflàyin mádyul/ See **RAM**.

free gyros /frîy jáyrowz/ *n.c.* Spacecraft gyroscopes that maintain attitude based on stellar rather than Earth references.

free return trajectory /frîy riytə́n trəjèktəiy/ *n.c. Apollo.* Flight path designed to allow a moonbound spacecraft to go around the far side of the moon and return to Earth without expending fuel (see **free flight**). Used as a safety measure before *Apollo 12* in order to insure Earth return in case of rocket malfunction prior to lunar orbit insertion (**LOI**).

Fria /frîyə/ See **FR-1A**.

friction /fríkšən/ *n.c.* **Drag**.

Friendship 7 /frêndšip sévən/ *n.c.* Nickname for *Mercury 6* spacecraft (see **Mercury**).

front porch /frânt pórč/ *n.c. sl.* **LM** egress platform.

FSTV *(ac.) n.c.* "Full scale test vehicle." See **boilerplate**.

fuel /fyúwl/ *n.* Substance which when ignited in combination with oxygen releases heat and energy; employed as a **propellant**.

fuel cell /fyúwl sèl/ *n.c.* Electrochemical generator which converts the energy produced by the reaction of fuel and oxygen directly into electricity; part of the electrical power system (**EPS**). Fuel cells were first used by the U.S. in the Gemini program.

fuel sloshing /fyúwl slàšiŋ/ *n.c.* Movement of fuel away from tank outlets during **weightlessness**.

full scale test vehicle /fûl skêyl tést vìyhikəl/ See **boilerplate**.

g *n.* **1.** The acceleration caused by the force resulting from gravity. On earth this acceleration is 32.2 feet per second per second.

2. *ac.* Gravity.

galaxy /gǽləksiy/ *n.* A system of stars, nebulae, etc., held together by gravitation and considered as a discrete unit. The Earth and the Sun are in the Milky Way galaxy.

gamma rays /gǽmə rèyz/ *n.c.* Penetrating electromagnetic rays emanating from the nuclei of radioactive atoms or from deep space.

gantry /gǽntriy/ *n.c.* **Service tower**.

garbage /gárbəj/ *n. sl.* Anything jettisoned from a manned spacecraft, either in space or on an **extraterrestrial** body.

gas cap /gǽs kæp/ *n.c. sl.* Body of compressed air directly in front of a spacecraft as it passes through an atmosphere.

gas chromatograph /gǽs krowmǽtəgræf/ *n.c.* Gas analysis device carried on the CM.

GATV *(ac.) n.c.* "Gemini Agena Target Vehicle." See **Agena; Gemini**.

GCTA *(ac.) n.c. Apollo.* "Ground command television assembly," **LRV**-mounted television system which can be controlled either directly by the LRV crew or remotely by the Mission Control Center (**MCC**).

Gemini /jéməniy/ *n.* **1.** Second American manned spaceflight project, a transitional stage between projects **Mercury** and **Apollo;** program in which the first spacecraft docking was accomplished. Project Gemini was conceived before the first Mercury orbital shot and publicly announced in December 1961. Its primary objectives were the testing and perfecting of techniques that would be employed in Project Apollo.

The first two Gemini flights, in April 1964 and January 1965, were unmanned tests of the spacecraft and systems; *Gemini 3* was not only the first manned Gemini flight but also the first American mission to send more than one man into space. On the first day of the *Gemini 4* mission, Edward H. White II became the first American to spacewalk, undertaking an **EVA** of 21 minutes. America's first rendezvous of manned orbiting vehicles occurred when

/a/ *father;* /aw/ *wow;* /ay/ *buy;* /b/ *boy;* /č/ *witch;* /d/ *doll;* /e/ *bet;* /ey/ *say;* /f/ *few;* /g/ *bag;* /h/ *hole;* /i/ *it;* /iy/ *be;* /j/ *gin;* /k/ *cat;* /l/ *lamb;* /m/ *man;* /n/ *now;* /o/ *orbit;* /ow/ *tow;* /oy/ *boy;* /p/ *pat;* /r/ *run;* /s/ *send;* /š/ *shoe;* /t/ *toy;* /u/ *put;* /uw/ *do;* /v/ *eve;* /w/ *way;* /y/ *yes;*

SE–24

MANNED GEMINI FLIGHTS

Mission	Crew	Date(s)	Remarks
Gemini 3	Virgil I. Grissom (Maj., USAF) John W. Young (Lt. Cmdr., USN)	March 23, 1965 (04 hrs. 53 min.)	America's first two-man flight. 3 orbits.
Gemini 4	James A. McDivitt (Maj., USAF) Edward H. White II (Maj., USAF)	June 3–7, 1965 (97 hrs. 56 min.)	First EVA by an American astronaut performed by White (21 min.). Extensive maneuver of spacecraft by pilot. 62 orbits.
Gemini 5	L. Gordon Cooper, Jr. (Lt. Col., USAF) Charles Conrad, Jr. (Lt. Cmdr., USN)	August 21–29, 1965 (190 hrs. 55 min.)	Extended time in space environment. 120 orbits.
Gemini 7	Frank Borman (Lt. Col., USAF) James A. Lovell, Jr. (Cmdr., USN)	December 4–18, 1965 (330 hrs. 35 min.)	Served as target vehicle for *Gemini 6*. 206 orbits.
Gemini 6A*	Walter M. Schirra, Jr. (Cmdr., USN) Thomas P. Stafford (Maj., USAF)	December 15–16, 1965 (25 hrs. 51 min.)	First American space rendezvous. 16 orbits.
Gemini 8	Neil A. Armstrong (Civilian) David R. Scott (Maj., USAF)	March 16, 1966 (10 hrs. 41 min.)	First docking of a manned spacecraft with an unmanned vehicle. 6½ orbits.
Gemini 9A*	Thomas P. Stafford (Lt. Col., USAF) Eugene A. Cernan (Lt. Cmdr., USN)	June 3–6, 1966 (72 hrs. 21 min.)	Three rendezvous of spacecraft and target vehicle. EVA by Cernan (2 hrs. 7 min.). 44 orbits.
Gemini 10	John W. Young (Cmdr., USN) Michael Collins (Maj., USAF)	July 18–21, 1966 (70 hrs. 47 min.)	First use of target vehicle as source of propellant power after docking. 43 orbits.
Gemini 11	Charles Conrad, Jr. (Cmdr., USN) Richard F. Gordon, Jr. (Lt. Cmdr., USN)	September 12–15, 1966 (71 hrs. 17 min.)	Rendezvous and docking in initial orbit. Multiple docking in space. Formation flight of two space vehicles joined by a tether. 44 orbits.
Gemini 12	James A. Lovell, Jr. (Cmdr., USN) Edwin E. Aldrin, Jr. (Maj., USAF)	November 11–15, 1966 (94 hrs. 35 min.)	EVA by Aldrin (5 hr. 30 min.). Photo of a solar eclipse from space. 59 orbits.

*Missions 6 and 9 were postponed because their target vehicles, launched prior to
manned liftoff, failed to achieve orbit. They were rescheduled and subsequently
launched with new target vehicles as missions 6A and 9A.*

**Gemini 7 was photographed through the hatch
window of Gemini 6 when the two modules met
160 miles above the Earth for rendezvous and
station-keeping maneuvers on Dec. 15, 1965.**

NASA

the *Gemini 6A* craft maneuvered to within
three feet of the previously orbited *Gemini
7*. World's first rendezvous of a manned
craft with an unmanned object took place
when the *Gemini 8* craft made a controlled
approach to a separately orbited *Gemini
Agena Target Vehicle (GATV)*. First docking of spacecraft was also achieved during
Gemini 8, on March 16, 1966, less than half
an hour after rendezvous with the GATV.
The last four Gemini missions refined rendezvous and docking procedures with
Agena Target Vehicles and extended prov-
en capabilities for sustained spaceflight.
Gemini experiments validated life support
techniques, equipment, and concepts for
future space missions: Project Apollo and
lunar exploration could follow.

The two-man Gemini spacecraft followed
basic Project Mercury design, a cone shape;
however, the vehicle was 19 feet long, 10
feet wide, and contained 50 percent more
cabin area. It was designed to be manually
operated by its crew after launch. The
spacecraft consisted of three sections: the
reentry module, the *retrograde section*, and
the *equipment section*. The reentry module

contained crew living quarters and was the
only section that returned to earth. Its forward portion included rendezvous and
docking equipment. The retrograde section, between the reentry module and
equipment, included the retrorockets used
for speed reduction and the thrusters used
to increase velocity during rendezvous and
docking maneuvers. The equipment section consisted of the fuel cells, attitude controls, part of the environmental system,
electrical components, and various mechanical devices.

The GATV was a specially outfitted
Agena rocket orbited separately from the
Gemini spacecraft. After being launched
by an **Atlas** launch vehicle, the unmanned
Agena turned around and went backwards,
thus bringing its front end into docking
position. The forward end of the GATV was
fitted with a cylindrical collar which contained mechanisms that locked onto the
inserted nose of the Gemini and moored
the two vehicles.

The **Titan** launch vehicle was used to
orbit all the Gemini spacecraft. Official
designations for the missions were given

/z/ *zero*; /ž/ *azure*; /θ/ *thin*; /ð/ *then*; /ŋ/ *song*; /æ/ *bat*; /ɔ/ *law*; /ə/ *sun*; /ɚ/ *bird*. Foreign symbols: [(n)] nasalization of some French
vowels followed by /n/; [R] French uvular rolled /r/ sound; [ü] high front lip-rounded vowel; [x] Russian voiceless laryngeal fricative.

accordingly, with *GT* standing for *Gemini-Titan*.

   2. Constellation in the Milky Way galaxy (see **Castor**).

Gemini Agena Target Vehicle /jêməniy əĵíynə tárgət vìyhikəl/ *See* **Agena; Gemini.**

Gemini Launch Vehicle /jêməniy lɔ̀nč vìyhikəl/ *n.c.* **Titan.**

Gemini Titan /jêməniy táytən/ *See* **Gemini; Titan.**

geocentric /jîyowséntrik/ *attr.* Of or pertaining to the center of the earth as frame of reference.

geocorona /jîyowkərównə/ *n.* Gaseous hydrogen belt encircling the earth and extending some 40,000 miles out.

geocosmic flight /jîyowkâzmik fláyt/ *n.c.* Journey through space from one part of Earth to another.

geodesy /jiyówdəsiy/ *n.* Science dealing with the shape and area of large tracts of land, the exact position of geographical points, and the curvature, shape, and dimensions of Earth.

geodetic /jiyədétik/ *attr.* Of or pertaining to the science of **geodesy**.

Geodetic Earth Orbiting Satellite /jiyədêtik ɔ́θ ɔ̀rbətiŋ sǽtəlayt/ *See* **GEOS.**

geodetic satellite /jiyədêtik sǽtəlayt/ *n.c.* Any Earth-orbiting craft developed for geodetic studies. Important U.S. geodetic satellites are **ANNA, Beacon, GEOS,** and **PAGEOS.**

geoid /jíyoyd/ *n.* Mean sea-level surface of Earth; projected under the continents.

Geophysical Satellite /jiyowfízikəl sǽtəlayt/ *n.c.* **1.** Projected Federal Republic of Germany geodetic satellite, scheduled for launch in 1974 by a U.S. **Scout** rocket. The spacecraft's main mission will be cloud-cover photography, the measurement of atmospheric temperature, and the study of geophysical structure.

   2. *l.c.* Any orbiting spacecraft designed and developed to investigate the properties and composition of the earth including the atmosphere, magnetosphere, and the radiation belts. Satellites better categorized as meteorological or geodetic because of their specific tasks are technically geophysical in type. Notable U.S. geophysical satellites are the **OGO** series, **Pegasus** and most of the **Explorers.**

GEOS /jíyows/ *(ac.) n.c.* **1.** "Geodetic Earth Orbiting Satellite," U.S. geodetic satellites, numbers 29 and 36 of the **Explorer** series, launched in November 1965 and January 1968 respectively. Both were used to survey land masses in order to improve mapping accuracy. Another satellite of the subseries, able to measure sea level with great accuracy, may be launched in 1973.

   2. "Geostationary Satellite," ESRO satellite planned for launch in 1976. The craft will be in a geosynchronous orbit and will investigate particle fluxes and electromagnetic radiation.

geostationary /jiyowstéyšəneriy/ *attr.* Of a satellite, appearing stationary when viewed from the earth. Such satellites must be **synchronous**; they must also lie in the equatorial plane and travel in the direction of the earth's rotation. The first

Three-dimensional, deep-space navigation is a complex problem which Apollo crews solve by first establishing their position, using a telescope and sextant, and then feeding this information into the guidance–navigation system and stabilization–control system computers.

      NASA

geostationary satellite was *Syncom 3* (see **Syncom**).

Geostationary Operational Environmental Satellite /jiyowstêyšəneriy apəêyšənəl envayənmêntəl sǽtəlayt/ *See* **GOES.**

Geostationary Satellite /jîyowstêyšəneriy sǽtəlayt/ *See* **GEOS.**

geosynchronous /jiyowsíŋkrənəs/ *attr.* Of a satellite, completing an orbit in the same amount of time that it takes the earth to rotate about its axis. If the satellite lies in the equatorial plane and travels in the direction of the earth's rotation, it is **geostationary** as well.

GERMANY, FEDERAL REPUBLIC OF

   During World War II, an unpartitioned Germany developed and launched the first ballistic missiles, the V-1 and **V-2**; however, at the conclusion of the war, rocket technology was lost to the Allies. The postwar Federal Republic of Germany entered space activity in 1963 with the launch of its first sounding rocket. Today, although it has not developed full launch capacity, it contributes **Astris**, the third stage of the **ELDO Europa** launch vehicle.

   Azur, Germany's first satellite, was orbited November 1969 under a cooperative agreement with NASA. It was launched by a U.S. **Scout** rocket from the Air Force Western Test Range (**AFWTR**). **Dial**, Germany's second satellite, was launched in March 1970 by a French **Diamant** launcher from the **Guiana Space Center** in French Guiana. Dial was the result of a continuing German-French cooperative space program. Future German satellites include: A-2, A-4, Geophysical Satellite, **Symphonie,** and **Helios;** all are projected for launch between 1972 and 1974.

   The Federal Republic of Germany's space program is built on a number of agreements with France, the U.S., **ELDO,** and **ESRO;** all German ventures into space are joint projects.

   Responsibility for German space research is shared by the ministries of Transportation and Research, and the Post Office (telegraphy and radio communications).

GET *(ac.) n.c.* "Ground elapsed time," exact amount of time elapsed at any point in a mission beginning with **liftoff** and ending with **splashdown.** The process of accumulating this time is called the *countup.* See also **T-time.** Cf. **countdown.**

g force /jíy fòrs/ *n.c.* **g.**

GGS *(ac.) n.c.* "Gravity gradient stabilization," orientation of a spacecraft by equalizing **centrifugal force** and Earth's **gravity.** Experiments in this technique were carried out in the Applications Technology Satellite (**ATS**) series.

giant planets /jâyənt plǽnəts/ *See* **outer planets.**

gimbal /gímbəl/ *n.* Instrument which allows movement on two axes.

gimbaled motor /gîmbəld mówtə/ *n.c.* **Rocket engine** so mounted that movement in two directions is permitted.

gimbal lock /gîmbəl lák/ *n.c.* Condition of a **gyroscope** that has reached a point beyond its intended limit and is frozen. It must be reset to be useful again.

GIRD /gíRd/ *(ac.) n.c.* "Group for the Study of Reactive Propulsion." See **Union of Soviet Socialist Republics.**

Glenn effect /glén əfèkt/ *n.c.* Unexplained phenomenon of brief flashes of light first

---

/a/ father; /aw/ wow; /ay/ buy; /b/ boy; /č/ witch; /d/ doll; /e/ bet; /ey/ say; /f/ few; /g/ bag; /h/ hole; /i/ it; /iy/ be; /ĵ/ gin; /k/ cat; /l/ lamb; /m/ man; /n/ now; /o/ orbit; /ow/ tow; /oy/ boy; /p/ pat; /r/ run; /s/ send; /š/ shoe; /t/ toy; /u/ put; /uw/ do; /v/ eve; /w/ way; /y/ yes;

seen by John Glenn during his **Mercury** flight and subsequently reported by other astronauts.

glitch /glič/ *n. sl.* Small problem or mistake.

GLV *(ac.) n.c.* "Gemini Launch Vehicle," **Titan**.

glycol /gláykɔl/ *n.* Ethylene glycol, usually used with water (see **water-glycol**).

gnat's hair /næts hèr/ *n.c. sl. Apollo.* Exact second of lunar **touchdown**.

GNCS *(ac.) n.c. Apollo.* "Guidance, navigation, and control system," U.S. spacecraft equipment complex which determines the location and direction of the vehicle in flight and sends commands for changes to the proper rocket engines. The system interlocks with the stabilization and control system (**SCS**) and utilizes the reaction control system (**RCS**) and the service propulsion system (**SPS**).

The CSM has three GNCS subsystems: **inertial subsystem, optical subsystem,** and **computer subsystem**. The LM has five GNCS subsystems: primary guidance and navigation subsystem (**PGNS**), abort guidance subsystem (**AGS**), control electronics subsystem (**CES**), **landing radar,** and **rendezvous radar**.

gnomon /nówmɔn/ *n. Apollo.* Instrument used for lunar photography; provides angle reference, for perspective, and color verification.

go /ɡów/ *attr. (pred. adj.)* Functioning properly.

Goddard, Robert H. /gádəd râbət êyč/ See **United States of America**.

Goddard Space Flight Center /gâdəd spéys flàyt sèntə/ See **GSFC**.

GOES /ɡówz/ *(ac.) n.c.* "Geostationary Operational Environmental Satellite," proposed U.S. meteorological satellite still in the development stage. It will be preceded by the prototype Synchronous Meteorological Satellite (**SMS**) scheduled for launch in 1972 or 1973.

golden slippers /ɡôwldən slípəz/ *n.c. sl. Apollo.* Gold-plated footholds for astronauts egressing the LM.

Goldstone /ɡówldstòwn/ *n.* NASA **tracking station** located in the Mojave Desert in California. Goldstone operates a 210 ft. **dish reflector,** the largest such **antenna** in the world. See also **DSN; maser; STADAN**.

go/no-go /ɡôw nów gòw/ *attr.* Of or pertaining to a decision, or point in time or space when the decision is made, regarding the continuation or cancellation of any aspect of a mission.

grain /ɡréyn/ *n.* Solid rocket propellant the shape of which corresponds to the type of burn required. Maximum burn surface produces greatest thrust and least burntime; minimum surface produces least thrust and greatest burntime.

Grand Tour /ɡrǽnd túr/ *n.c.* Possible U.S. mission on which four of the giant outer planets (Jupiter, Saturn, Uranus, and Neptune) could be visited by a single fly-by spacecraft. **Launch window** for such a mission will occur in 1977-1978, but not again for 179 years, when a rare alignment of the four planets will again make it possible for a probe to use the gravitational field

of each successive body to swing on to the next. In 1972 plans for Grand Tour were scrapped in favor of less complex three-planet fly-bys (see **Outer Planets Mission**).

grapefruit /ɡréypfrùwt/ *n. sl.* Nickname given the **Vanguard** satellite because of its shape and dimensions.

grass /ɡrǽs/ *n. sl.* Interference, as seen on a **radar** screen.

gravimetric geodesy /ɡrǽvəmetrik jiyádəsiy/ *n.c.* Branch of **geodesy** that measures variations in the earth's **gravity**. Also called *dynamic geodesy*.

gravipause /ɡrǽvəpɔz/ *n.* Point between two heavenly bodies where the **gravity** of one is equal to that of the other. Also called *neutral point.*

gravisphere /ɡrǽvəsfìr/ *n.* That section of space wherein the gravitational influence of a particular celestial body is predominant.

gravitation /ɡrǽvətéyšən/ *n.* Universal attraction or pull that exists between all particles of matter.

gravitational /ɡrǽvətéyšənəl/ *attr.* Of or pertaining to the forces that exist between all particles of matter.

gravity /ɡrǽvətiy/ *n.* The force exerted by a physical object that attracts other objects towards the center of its mass. Abbr.: *g.*

gravity anomaly /ɡrǽvətiy ənàməliy/ *n.c.* Deviation between theoretically predicted **gravity** and actual **gravity**. See **mascon; minicon**.

gravity gradient stabilization /ɡrǽvətiy grèydiyənt steybələzéyšən/ See **GGS**.

gravity simulation /ɡrǽvətiy simyəléyšən/ *n.c.* Use of **centrifugal force** to duplicate actual conditions of **gravity** exerted during **takeoff** and **reentry**.

gravity well /ɡrǽvətiy wèl/ *n.c.* Analogy in which a gravitational field is represented as a deep hole from which a spacecraft must ascend in order to escape the attraction of a planetary body.

GREAT BRITAIN

Sixth nation to orbit satellites using internally developed launch vehicles.

Great Britain's initial thrust toward the development of a space program came shortly after World War II. Having been exposed to the effects of tactical rocketry by German **V-2** rockets, research scientists proposed the development of intermediate and intercontinental range missiles. By an agreement with Australia in 1946, the British established a test range at **Woomera** in Australia. Little else came of this early proposal.

From 1946 through 1960, rocket development in Great Britain was basically of a small-scale, military nature. By the time the first **Sputnik** was launched, general interest in a space program became very evident. However, government sources revealed that no plans were being drawn for planetary probes, or the orbiting of animals or men. The official British stance on a space program consisted of developing large rockets for upper atmospheric sounding and for use as possible launch vehicles for scientific satel-

lites. The results of this position were a sounding rocket, a two-stage test vehicle (the *Black Knight*), and the single-stage **Blue Streak IRBM**. The success of the Black Knight resulted in the development of the **Black Arrow**, Great Britain's first successful launch vehicle. The Blue Streak was cancelled in 1960 as a tactical missile and subsequently modified to become the first stage of the international **ELDO** Europa launcher.

Great Britain's first satellite was the *Ariel 1* (see **Ariel**) launched April 26, 1962, by a U.S. Thor-Delta from Kennedy Space Center (**KSC**) as the product of a joint British/U.S. program. Two similar Ariel satellites were launched by U.S. launch vehicles in 1964 and 1967. Two British **Skynet** military comsats were launched by U.S. vehicles in 1969 and 1970. The satellites provide communications between London and the Far East.

On October 28, 1971, Great Britain became the sixth nation to orbit a satellite using its own launch vehicle when it orbited **Prospero** by means of a Black Arrow three-stage rocket. The satellite was a purely experimental spacecraft used to test techniques and equipment for future launches. Future British satellite programs include **X-4,** projected for launch in early 1974, and **MetSat,** scheduled for 1973.

Cooperative programs have been established with Australia, **ELDO,** and the U.S. British participation in ELDO has been all but completely withdrawn due to Great Britain's fiscal cut-back in space-related spending. Future cooperative activities will be mainly with the U.S.

Responsibility for the British space program is divided among the Ministries of Defense, Education and Science, Technology, and Posts and Telecommunications.

GREB /gréb/ *(ac.) n.c.* "Galactic Radiation Energy Background," early name for craft used in the Solar Radiation Monitoring Satellite Program (**SOLRAD**).

green /ɡríyn/ *attr. (pred. adj.)* **Go**.

greenhouse /ɡríynhàws/ *n.* Steril glass enclosure that is a part of the **service tower** and surrounds a spacecraft prior to **liftoff**.

ground command television assembly /gråwnd kəmǽnd téləvižən əsèmbliy/ See **GCTA**.

ground-control /gráwnd kəntròwl/ *attr.* Of or pertaining to directing a craft or a mission from the ground.

ground control /gráwnd kəntròwl/ *n.c.* Direction of a spacecraft or a mission from some Earth-based location.

ground controller /gráwnd kəntròwlə/ *n.c.* Person who directs a spacecraft or mission from an Earth-based location.

ground elapsed time /gråwnd iylǽpst táym/ See **GET**.

ground start /gráwnd stàrt/ *n.c.* Rocket ignition and thrust buildup using propellant from a source other than the rocket itself, preserving onboard fuel for actual flight.

ground station /gráwnd stèyšən/ *n.c.* Loca-

/z/ zero; /ž/ azure; /θ/ thin; /ð/ then; /ŋ/ song; /æ/ bat; /ɔ/ law; /ə/ sun; /ɚ/ bird. Foreign symbols: [(n)] nasalization of some French vowels followed by /n/; [R] French uvular rolled /r/ sound; [ü] high front lip-rounded vowel; [x] Russian voiceless laryngeal fricative.

SE–27

tion on Earth from which tracking equipment monitors a space mission.

ground support equipment /grâwnd səpórt iykwìpmənt/ See **GSE.**

ground trace /grâwnd trèys/ *n.c.* Line drawn on a map or ·globe that represents the **trajectory** of an airborne vehicle.

ground-tracking /grâwnd trǽkiŋ/ *attr.* Of or pertaining to the monitoring of a mission from an Earth-based location.

ground tracking /grâwnd trǽkiŋ/ *n.c.* Monitoring a mission from an Earth-based location.

Group for the Study of Reactive Propulsion /grùwp for ðə stə̀diy əv riyǽktiv prəpálšən/ See **Union of Soviet Socialist Republics.**

GSE *(ac.) n.c.* "Ground support equipment," equipment connected with a space flight that remains on the ground at **liftoff.**

GSFC *(ac.) n.c.* "Goddard Space Flight Center," **NASA** research facility, named for Robert H. Goddard, a pioneer in rocketry, and located at Greenbelt, Maryland. GSFC is responsible for the development of spacecraft, and for tracking, communications, and data analysis.

GT *(ac.) n.c.* "Gemini Titan." See **Gemini; Titan.**

Guiana Space Center /giyǽnə spéys sèntɚ/ *n.c.* Primary French space-vehicle launch site located near Kourou in French Guiana, South America. Being located near the equator, the base provides an excellent position for placing satellites into both polar and equatorial orbits. The Guiana facilities are open to **ELDO** for **Europa** launches as part of French participation in that international organization.

guidance /gáydəns/ *n.* Act of directing a space vehicle along a given path.

guidance, navigation, and control system /gâydəns nævəgêyšən ænd kəntrówl sìstəm/ See **GNCS.**

guidance system /gáydəns sìstəm/ *n.c.* System which measures and evaluates flight information, correlates it with projected data, converts the results into instructions for maintaining a desired flight path, and then transmits this data to the flight control system in the form of commands; in **Apollo,** the **GNCS.**

guido /gáydow/ *n. sl.* Guidance officer at the Mission Control Center (**MCC**).

gyroscope /jáyrowskowp/ *n.* Gimbal-mounted wheel which, when set into rotation, maintains a constant direction despite absence of a true reference point.

H–I–J

hack /hǽk/ *n.* Time hack.

Hammaguir Space Center /hǽməgwayɚ [*Fr.* amagíR] spéys sèntɚ/ *n.c.* First French space-vehicle launch site; located near Colombe-Bechar in the Algerian Sahara. Following Algerian independence in 1967, the base was replaced by the **Guiana Space Center** in South America.

hand-held maneuvering unit /hǽnd hèld mənúwvəɨŋ yùwnət/ See **HHMU.**

handover /hǽndowvɚ/ *n.* Point in time when responsibility for tracking a spacecraft is shifted from one **ground station** to another.

hard base /hárd bèys/ *n.c.* Launch installation, usually military, protected against nuclear attack by either natural or man-made protective cover. Cf. **soft base.**

hard landing /hárd lǽndiŋ/ *n.c.* Uncontrolled, high-speed impact of a space vehicle on a celestial body.

hardware /hárdwer/ *n.* Manufactured equipment; physical, tangible items. Cf. **software.**

hatch /hǽč/ *n.* Door or cover for an external spacecraft opening; sometimes completely removable, like the CM forward hatch.

heat flow experiment /híyt flòw ekspèrəmənt/ See **HFE.**

heat shield /híyt šìyld/ *n.c.* Insulating material which coats the blunt end of a spacecraft to prevent overheating and fire during **reentry.** See **ablation.**

NORTH AMERICAN ROCKWELL SPACE DIVISION

Apollo 15 carried a hitchhiker satellite in its SM and launched it into orbit around the moon.

heat sink /híyt sìŋk/ *n.c.* Heat-absorbing material, or the location of such material, on a spacecraft; used to protect vital components or crew. A heat sink is a type of **heat shield.**

heat transport subsystem /híyt trænsport səbsìstəm/ See **HTS.**

heliocentric /hìyliyowséntrik/ *attr.* Sun-centered.

Helios /híyliyɔs/ *n.* Projected Federal Republic of Germany solar-research satellite. Scheduled for launch in 1974 by a U.S. **Atlas** rocket, the main mission of the spacecraft will be investigation of solar phenomena and their effects on interplanetary space.

HEOS /híyows/ *(ac.) n.c.* "Highly Eccentric Orbiting Satellite," **ESRO** scientific-research satellites series. The basic objective of the spacecraft is the investigation of solar phenomena and their effects on interplanetary space. *HEOS A* was launched in December 1968 by a U.S. rocket. *HEOS A2* is scheduled for launch in 1972; it will study interplanetary space and solar emissions.

HFE *(ac.) n.c. Apollo.* "Heat flow experiment," scientific device carried to the moon as part of the Apollo Lunar Surface Experiments Package (**ALSEP**). The HFE is used to measure any release of heat from the interior of the moon.

HGA *(ac.) n.c. Apollo.* "High-gain antenna," principal CSM **deep space antenna,** consisting of four separate 31-inch-diameter **dish reflectors;** used in conjunction with the unified S-band equipment (**USBE**). The HGA is part of the telecommunications (T/C) system.

HHMU *(ac.) n.c.* "Hand-held maneuvering unit," propulsion mechanism carried by an astronaut on inflight **EVA** enabling him to direct his motions under **weightless** conditions.

high bit rate data /hây bít rèyt dèytə/ *n.c.* Information transmitted from spacecraft to ground receiving stations at rates of thousands of **bits** per second.

high-gain antenna /hây gêyn ænténə/ See **HGA.**

high gate /hây gèyt/ See **PDI.**

Highly Eccentric Orbiting Satellite /hâyliy eksêntrik òrbətiŋ sǽtəlayt/ See **HEOS.**

hitchhiker /híčhaykɚ/ *n.* Small experimental satellite launched with a major spacecraft by the same **booster.**

Heat shields covering Apollo capsules must withstand the temperatures of boost (1,200° F), deep space (280° F), and reentry (5,000° F).

FORWARD HEAT SHIELD

CREW COMPARTMENT HEAT SHIELD

AFT HEAT SHIELD

/a/ *father;* /aw/ *wow;* /ay/ *buy;* /b/ *boy;* /č/ *witch;* /d/ *doll;* /e/ *bet;* /ey/ *say;* /f/ *few;* /g/ *bag;* /h/ *hole;* /i/ *it;* /iy/ *be;* /j/ *gin;* /k/ *cat;* /l/ *lamb;* /m/ *man;* /n/ *now;* /o/ *orbit;* /ow/ *tow;* /oy/ *boy;* /p/ *pat;* /r/ *run;* /s/ *send;* /š/ *shoe;* /t/ *toy;* /u/ *put;* /uw/ *do;* /v/ *eve;* /w/ *way;* /y/ *yes;*

Hohmann transfer /hôwnən trǽnsfɚ/ *n.c.* Flight path which takes a spacecraft from Earth orbit to the moon with the minimum expenditure of energy. Based on a theoretical trajectory worked out in 1925 by Dr. Walter Hohmann, head architect of Essen, Germany.

hold /hówld/ *n.* Unscheduled delay in a launch sequence of a missile or spacecraft. Cf. **built-in hold.**

hold-down arm /hówld dàwn àrm/ *n.c.*. Any of several mechanisms attached to spacecraft to restrain the launch vehicle prior to **liftoff.** They prevent liftoff until the rocket engines have reached 95 per cent **thrust.**

horse collar /hórs kàlɚ/ *n.c.* Sling lowered from rescue helicopter for retrieval of a spacecraft's crew following **splashdown.**

housekeeping /háwskiypiŋ/ *n. sl.* Regular period set aside during spaceflight for capsule upkeep chores: waste management, consumables checks, etc.

hover time /hávɚ tàym/ *n.c. Apollo.* Period just prior to **touchdown** during which the LM remains in stationary attitude above the moon's surface.

HTS *(ac.) n.c. Apollo.* "Heat transport subsystem," that part of the LM environmental control system (**ECS**) which provides thermal control for spacecraft parts and for the oxygen and water circulating through the space suits.

hybrid trajectory /hâybrid trəjéktɚiy/ *n.c. Apollo.* Modified **free return trajectory** requiring a rocket burn while the spacecraft is on the far side of the moon. If the burn does not take place, the spacecraft will be unable to return to Earth. Used from *Apollo 12* on because it allows a more direct lunar approach.

hydrogen peroxide /hâydrəjən pɚáksayd/ *n.c.* Fuel which, when turned into steam, activates small jets which control a spacecraft's attitude in space.

hydrosphere /háydrowsfìr/ *n.* A planet's envelope of surface and atmospheric water.

hydrostatic pressure /hâydrowstǽtik préšɚ/ *n.c.* Pressure developed by an enclosed body of fluid under the force of **gravity** or acceleration G's.

hyperbolic reentry /hâypɚbâlik riyéntriy/ *n.c.* **Reentry** into the earth's atmosphere at speeds greater than 37,000 feet per second.

hypergol /háypɚgal/ *n.* **Propellant** which does not require an ignition system. Elements of these propellants ignite on contact.

hypergolic /hàypɚgálik/ *attr.* **1.** Of or pertaining to a **hypergol.**
2. Self-igniting.

hypersonic /hàypɚsánik/ *attr.* Of or pertaining to speeds in excess of Mach 5 (see **Mach number**). See also **supersonic; ultrasonic.**

ICBM *(ac.) n.c.* "Intercontinental ballistic missile," ground-to-ground missile of a military nature capable of traveling at least 5,000 miles. In the U.S., a majority of these missiles have been modified for use in the U.S. space program as **launch vehicles.**

ICSU *(ac.) n.c.* "International Council of Scientific Unions," global organization which strives for increased international cooperation in space. ICSU sponsored the International Geophysical Year (**IGY**) of 1957 to 1958 which began the **Space Age.**

IDCSP *(ac.) n.c.* "Initial Defense Communications Satellite Program." **1.** U.S. military comsat series, noted for its high-resolution photographs, which consists of 31 craft launched into nearly synchronous orbits from 1966 to 1968. Used in the Initial Defense Satellite Communications System (**IDSCS**), 23 of the satellites remained operational as of January 1971.
2. Former name of U.S. military comsat program Defense Satellite Communications System (**DSCS**).

IDSCS *(ac.) n.c.* "Initial Defense Satellite Communications System," U.S. military comsat program, the first phase of the Defense Satellite Communications System (**DSCS**). At the beginning of 1972, IDSCS consisted of 23 operational Initial Defense Communications Satellite Program (**IDCSP**) satellites operating in near-synchronous orbits.

igniter /ignáytɚ/ *n.* Sparkpluglike device used to ignite solid fuels in a rocket engine's combustion chamber.

ignition /igníšən/ *n.* Moment of combustion in a **rocket engine.** Due to the enormous amount of **thrust** necessary to launch larger vehicles, there is usually an interim of five to ten seconds between ignition and **liftoff.**

IGY *(ac.) n.c.* "International Geophysical Year," period from July 1, 1957 to December 31, 1958 during which concentrated scientific study of the universe took place. Over 50 nations participated in the program, which marked the beginning of the Space Age with the launch of the first artificial satellite *Sputnik 1* (see **Sputnik**) on October 3, 1957.

IMP /ímp/ *(ac.) n.c.* "Interplanetary Monitoring Platform," U.S. astrophysical satellite series launched beginning in 1963; subseries of the **Explorer** satellites consisting, at the beginning of 1972, of *Explorer 18, 21, 28, 33, 34, 34, 41* and *43.* The first seven IMP's, *IMP A* through *IMP G,* charted the earth's magnetosphere and cislunar space, gauged cosmic rays, and studied the bow wave or shock front created by the Earth's magnetosphere meeting the solar wind. Except for *IMP E (Explorer 35),* launched in July 1967, all the craft have traveled in highly eccentric Earth orbits. *IMP E,* in lunar orbit, is designated an *Anchored Interplanetary Monitoring Platform (AIMP).* With *IMP I,* the last craft in the series at the beginning of 1972, a new experimental concept for the IMP series was instituted: instead of merely noting space phenomena, IMP's would investigate the sources of various phenomena. Further launches are scheduled for 1972 and 1973.

impact /ímpækt/ *n.* Time and point at which a spacecraft touches down.

impact attenuator /ímpækt ətènyuweytɚ/ *n.c.* Collapsible spacecraft structural part which absorbs the shock of landings and other impacts; used to prevent damage to vital spacecraft systems.

impeller /impélɚ/ *n.* Device that pushes fuel in a desired direction.

Improved TIROS Operational Satellite /imprûwyd tâyrows apɚéyšənəl sǽtəlayt/ See **ITOS.**

Improved TIROS Operational System /imprûwyd tâyrows apɚéyšənəl sìstəm/ See **ITOS.**

IMU *(ac.) n.c.* "Inertial measuring unit," central component of U.S. spacecraft **guidance systems** (see **GNCS, PGNS**); serves as an inertial reference for attitude control and also contains **accelerometers** as well as **gimbals** and **gyroscopes.** The IMU is mounted on the navigation base (**NB**).

incidence angle /ínsədəns ǽngəl/ *n.c.* Angle between a spacecraft's **trajectory** and the Earth.

inclination /iŋklənéyšən/ *n.* **1.** Angle between the **orbital plane** of a satellite and the **equatorial plane** of its central body.
2. Angle between the **orbital plane** of another planet of the solar system and the orbital plane of the earth (ecliptic).

inclined synchronous orbit /inklâynd sîŋkrənəs órbət/ *n.c.* Orbital plane of a synchronous satellite which intersects the **equatorial plane** of reference.

inertia /inɚ̂šə/ *n.* Property of an object which, if the object is motionless, causes it to remain so, or, if it is moving, causes it to continue its movement in a constant direction at a constant speed.

inertial measuring unit /inɚ̂šəl mézɚiŋ yùwnət/ See **IMU.**

inertial orbit /inɚ̂šəl òrbət/ *n.c.* Orbit of a spacecraft not under propulsion; **free flight** orbit.

inertial space /inɚ̂šəl spéys/ *n.c.* Arbitrarily established set of stationary coordinates in space which serve as a frame of reference for the calculation of a spacecraft's **trajectory.**

inertial subsystem /inɚ̂šəl sə́bsistəm/ *n.c. Apollo.* That part of the guidance, navigation, and control system (**GNCS**) which senses attitude and velocity changes.

inferior planet /infîryɚ plǽnət/ *n.c.* Mercury or Venus; the orbits of these planets lie closer to the sun than Earth's orbit. Cf. **superior planet.**

infrared /înfrəréd/ *attr.* Of or pertaining to low-frequency radiation extending from the red limit of the visible spectrum to the microwaves used in radar.

ingress /iŋgrés/ **1.** *v. tr.* To enter a spacecraft.
2. *n.* /íŋgres/ All the procedures involved in entering a spacecraft.

inhibitor /inhíbətɚ/ *n.* Substance injected into rocket propellant in order to control direction of combustion and thereby control **thrust.**

Initial Defense Communication Satellite Program /iníšəl diyfêns kəmyuwnəkéyšən sǽtəlayt prôwgræm/ See **IDCSP.**

Initial Defense Satellite Communications System /iníšəl diyfêns sǽtəlayt kəmyuwnəkéyšənz sìstəm/ See **IDSCS.**

inject /injékt/ *v. tr.* To place a craft on a trajectory from an orbit.

injection /injékšən/ *n.* Transferral of a spacecraft from an orbit to a calculated flight path. Cf. **insertion.**

/z/ *zero;* /ž/ *azure;* /θ/ *thin;* /ð/ *then;* /ŋ/ *song;* /æ/ *bat;* /ɔ/ *law;* /ə/ *sun;* /ɚ/ *bird.* Foreign symbols: [(n)] nasalization of some French vowels followed by /n/; [R] French uvular rolled /r/ sound; [ü] high front lip-rounded vowel; [x] Russian voiceless laryngeal fricative.

MEMBER NATIONS IN INTELSAT
March 1972

Algeria	Ethiopia	Japan	Nicaragua	Switzerland
Argentina	France	Jordan	Nigeria	Syrian Arab Republic
Australia	Gabon	Kenya	Norway	Tanzania
Austria	Germany, Federal	Korea, Republic of	Pakistan	Thailand
Barbados	Republic of	Kuwait	Panama	Trinidad and Tobago
Belgium	Ghana	Lebanon	Peru	Tunisia
Brazil	Greece	Libyan Arab Republic	Philippines, The	Turkey
Cameroon	Guatemala	Liechtenstein	Portugal	Uganda
Canada	India	Luxembourg	Saudi Arabia	United Kingdom
Chile	Indonesia	Malagasy Republic	Senegal	United States
China, Republic of	Iran	Malaysia	Singapore	Vatican City
Colombia	Iraq	Mauritania	South Africa,	Venezuela
Costa Rica	Ireland	Mexico	Republic of	Vietnam, Republic of
Denmark	Israel	Monaco	Spain	Yemen
Dominican Republic	Italy	Morocco	Sri Lanka	Yugoslavia
Ecuador	Ivory Coast	Netherlands, The	Sudan	Zaire
Egypt	Jamaica	New Zealand	Sweden	Zambia

Injun /ínjən/ *n.* U.S. geophysical satellite series; four successful launches were made between 1961 and 1968. Injuns, used to investigate radiation in space, are usually launched with other craft on dual launches or as **hitchhikers.** *Injun 4*, launched in November 1964, also bore the designation *Explorer 25*. It was part of the first dual-launch effort by NASA.

Injuns are designed and built by State University of Iowa staff members and students. Another Injun is projected for launch at an unspecified future date.

Injun Explorer /ínjən eksplórə/ See **Injun.**

insert /insə́t/ *v. tr.* To place a spacecraft into an orbit from a celestial body by means of a rocket.

insertion /insə́shən/ *n.* **1.** The placing of a spacecraft into an orbit around the earth or other celestial bodies by means of booster or auxiliary rockets.

2. The precise moment at which a spacecraft enters orbit. Cf. **injection.**

instantaneous readout /instəntêyniyəs rídawt/ *n.c.* Computer display of information received and processed so rapidly that there is no apparent time lapse between reception and display.

Institute of the Aerospace Sciences /ínstətuwt əv ðiy êrowspêys sáyənsəs/ See **AIAA.**

instrumented range /ínstrəmentəd réynj/ See **test range.**

instrument unit /ínstrəmənt yùwnət/ See **IU.**

integral tank /íntəgrəl tǽŋk/ *n.c.* Storage tank which employs the outer wall of a rocket as its wall.

integrated thermal micrometeoroid garment /íntəgreytəd θə́məl maykrowmíytiyəroyd gàrmənt/ See **PGA.**

Intelsat /intélsæt/ *(ac.) n.c.* "International Telecommunications Satellite Consortium." **1.** Organization formed in 1964 to establish a worldwide comsat network; responsible for the Intelsat satellite. Members, as of March 1972, included government agencies and private companies from 83 nations. Controlling interest is owned by the U.S. Communications Satellite Corporation (**Comsat**).

2. Any of a series of synchronous communications satellites developed by the Intelsat organization. The Intelsats are used for global transmission of telephone calls, telegrams, data, facsimiles, and television broadcasts. Fourteen privately built satellites were launched by NASA from 1965 to 1971, in four subseries. **Early Bird,** launched in April 1965, was the first Intelsat.

intercommunications /intəkəmyuwnəkéyshənz/ *n. Apollo.* That part of the telecommunications (**T/C**) system which, using radio frequency equipment, routes voice information between ground and craft or between astronauts.

intercontinental ballistic missile /intəkantənêntəl bəlistik mísəl/ See **ICBM.**

intergalactic /ìntəgəlǽktik/ *attr.* Of or pertaining to phenomena between galaxies.

Interkosmos /íntəkázmows/ *n.* International multipurpose-satellite series launched by the U.S.S.R. under a cooperative program among East European socialist countries. Initial launch of the series, in October 1969, was attended by representatives of Bulgaria, Czechoslovakia, the German Democratic Republic, Hungary, Poland, and Rumania. Four of the satellites had been orbited at the beginning of 1972.

Interkosmos 1 was orbited to study ultraviolet and X-ray radiation effects on the earth's upper atmosphere. *Interkosmos 2*, launched in December 1969 for ionospheric study, carried a computer-operated transmitter developed by the German Democratic Republic, and a high-frequency sounding instrument of Czech design and construction. *Interkosmos 3* was launched in August 1970 to investigate the earth's radiation belts and solar activity. *Interkosmos 4*, launched in October 1970, continued the mission of Interkosmos 1.

intermediate-range ballistic missile /intəmîydyət rèynj bəlîstik mísəl/ See **IRBM.**

International Communications System Using Artificial Earth Satellites /intənǽšənəl kəmyuwnəkéyšənz sìstəm yùwzing artəfìšəl ə́θ sǽtəlayts/ See **Intersputnik.**

International Council of Scientific Unions /intənǽšənəl kâwnsəl əv sayəntîfik yúwnyənz/ See **ICSU.**

International Geophysical Year /intənǽšənəl jiyowfîzikəl yír/ See **IGY.**

International Satellite for Ionospheric Studies /intənǽšənəl sǽtəlayt for ayanəsfîrik stádiyz/ See **ISIS.**

International Telecommunications Satellite Consortium /intənǽšənəl telekəmyuwnəkêyšənz sǽtəlayt kənsórtiyəm/ See **Intelsat.**

interplanetary /intəplǽnəteriy/ *attr.* Between planets.

Interplanetary Monitoring Platform /intəplǽnəteriy mánətəiŋ plǽtform/ See **IMP.**

Intersputnik /íntəspùtnik/ *n.* "International Communications System Using Artificial Earth Satellites," Eastern bloc organization formed in November 1971 for the development of a worldwide **comsat** network. Charter members are the U.S.S.R., Bulgaria, Cuba, Czechoslovakia, German Democratic Republic, Hungary, Mongolia, Poland, and Rumania; membership is open to all countries, including non-Communist powers. The organization's governing body is composed of one voting representative from each of the member states.

interstage /íntəsteyj/ *n.* Connecting section between stages of spacecraft.

interstellar /intəstélə/ *attr.* Between stars.

in the blind /in ðə bláynd/ *phr. attr.* Without certainty of signal reception, such as "broadcasting in the blind."

in the mud /in ðe mə́d/ *adv. phr.* Without signal clarity, such as "receiving a message down in the mud."

intravehicular /intrəviyhîkyələ/ *attr.* Within a spacecraft.

intravehicular activity /intrəviyhîkyələ ǽktívətiy/ See **IVA.**

intravehicular cover /intrəviyhîkyələ kə́və/ See **PGA.**

/a/ father; /aw/ wow; /ay/ buy; /b/ boy; /č/ witch; /d/ doll; /e/ bet; /ey/ say; /f/ few; /g/ bag; /h/ hole; /i/ it; /iy/ be; /j/ gin; /k/ cat; /l/ lamb; /m/ man; /n/ now; /o/ orbit; /ow/ tow; /oy/ boy; /p/ pat; /r/ run; /s/ send; /š/ shoe; /t/ toy; /u/ put; /uw/ do; /v/ eve; /w/ way; /y/ yes;

HUGHES AIRCRAFT COMPANY

Intelsat 4 went through extensive tests in an anechoic chamber before its launch in 1971. It is a communications satellite connecting the U.S. and Europe and can carry 9,000 two-way telephone calls, 12 color television programs, or various combinations of voice, video, or data transmissions.

DEPARTMENT OF COMMUNICATIONS (CANADA)
The Canadian satellite, *ISIS-2*

Intrepid /intrépəd/ *n.* Name of *Apollo 12* LM (see **Apollo**).

ion /áyan/ *n.* Electrically charged particle.

ion engine /áyan ènjən/ *n.c.* Spacecraft powerplant that employs **ion propulsion**.

ionization /àyənəzéyšən/ *n.* Transforming electrically neutral atoms into charged particles (ions) by adding or removing electrons.

ionization layer /ayənəzéyšən lèyər/ *n.c.* Envelope of superheated air that surrounds a spacecraft reentering the atmosphere with electrically charged particles, temporarily blocking all **telemetry**.

ionized layer /àyənayzd léyər/ *n.c.* Area of increased ionization within the **atmosphere**, hypothetically the result of solar radiation.

ionizing radiation /àyənayziŋ reydiyéyšən/ *n.c.* Radiation with the capacity to remove electrons from atoms.

ionosphere /ayánəsfir/ *n.* Highly electri-cally charged layer of the earth's atmosphere located between the **exosphere** and the **stratosphere**. It extends from 50 miles to 250 miles above the earth's surface.

Ionospheric Sounding Satellite /ayan-əsfîrik sáwndiŋ sǽtəlayt/ *n.c.* Projected Japanese upper-atmospheric research satellite currently in the development stage.

ion propulsion /áyan prəpə́lšən/ *n.c.* **Rocket engine thrust** produced by the acceleration of electrically charged particles.

ion rocket /áyan ràkət/ *n.c.* Rocket powered by an **ion engine**.

IRBM *(ac.) n.c.* "Intermediate range ballistic missile," military guided missile designed to travel between 1,000 and 3,000 miles. In the U.S. a few of these missiles (**Jupiter, Thor**) have been modified for use in the U.S. space program.

Iris /áyrəs/ See **ESRO**.

ISIS /áysis/ *(ac.) n.c.* "International Satel-lite for Ionospheric Studies," either of two Canadian upper-atmospheric research satellites. The craft were launched in January 1969 and April 1971 by U.S. launch vehicles from the Air Force Western Test Range (**AFWTR**).

ITALY

The Italian space program can be dated from September 1962 when the **San Marco** project was officially formed by an agreement signed between the U.S. and Italy.

Following several nonorbital test firings in 1963, *San Marco 1*, Italy's first satellite, was launched December 15, 1964, by a U.S. **Scout** rocket from **Wallops Station** in the U.S. An all-Italian crew of technicians and scientists manned the launch facility and was responsible for all phases of the launch. Subsequent Italian launches have been made from the San Marco Range off the east coast of equatorial Africa. San Marco project launches are scheduled through 1973. In December 1970, the San Marco team launched the U.S. satellite *Explorer 42* (see **SAS**) aboard a Scout; it was the first launch of a U.S. spacecraft by another nation.

A cooperative program, besides the basic one with NASA, has been established with **ELDO**, of which Italy is a member. The Italian space program is under the direction of Centro Ricerche Aerospaziale (Center for Aerospace Research [**CRA**]) an official government agency composed of representatives of the Italian Air Force and the University of Rome.

ITOS /áytows/ *(ac.) n.c.* 1. "Improved TI-ROS Operational System," U.S. meteorological satellite system providing global, day-and-night weather observation. The system replaces the TIROS Operation System (**TOS**), which required two satellites to do the work done by one ITOS satellite. At the beginning of 1972, satellites in the

/z/ zero; /ž/ azure; /θ/ thin; /ð/ then; /ŋ/ song; /æ/ bat; /ɔ/ law; /ə/ sun; /ɚ/ bird. Foreign symbols: [(n)] nasalization of some French vowels followed by /n/; [R] French uvular rolled /r/ sound; [ü] high front lip-rounded vowel; [x] Russian voiceless laryngeal fricative.

SE – 31

system included *ITOS-1* and *NOAA-1* (see **NOAA**).

2. "Improved TIROS Operational Satellite," *ITOS-1*, the first satellite in the Improved TIROS Operational System. Launched in January 1970, it was the prototype for other satellites in the system.

IU *(ac.) n.c. Apollo.* "Instrument unit," nonpropulsive **Saturn** stage which houses the **launch vehicle's** major technical systems, such as electronics and guidance. Because it joins the rest of the launch vehicle to the CSM, it is sometimes called the *wedding ring.*

IVA *(ac.) n.c.* "Intravehicular activity," any function taking place inside a spacecraft that requires the use of a **space suit.** Cf. **EVA.**

JAPAN

Fourth nation to orbit satellites using internally developed launch vehicles and first nation to control orbital attitude using unguided gravity turn.

Space research began in 1955; development of the one-stage, solid-fueled *Kappa* rocket led to three-stage sounding rockets, and eventually to the **Lambda 4-S** and **M-4S** four-stage launch vehicles.

By the end of 1971, three satellites had been orbited successfully using these vehicles. **Oshumi** (February 1970) and **Tansei** (February 1971) were developmental satellites used to test launch procedures on the Lambda 4-S and M-4S vehicles, respectively. **Shinsei** (September 1971), orbited by a M-4S for measurement of solar radio emission, ionospheric plasma, and cosmic rays, was Japan's first scientific satellite.

Programs under development include Radio Exploration Satellite (**REXS**), Solar Radiation and Thermospheric Structure Satellite (**SRATS**), Cosmic Radiation Satellite (**CORSA**), and **Ionospheric Sounding Satellite.** The aims of these projects will be to measure radiation and particle densities in the upper atmosphere.

Cooperative programs have been initiated with India, the U.S., **ELDO, ESRO,** and **Intelsat.** Initial satellite and launcher development was primarily the responsibility of the Institute of Space and Aeronautical Science of the University of Tokyo. A National Space Development Agency, partially government supported, was set up in 1969 to unify Japanese space efforts.

Jet Propulsion Laboratory /jêt prəpálšən læbrətoriy/ See **JPL.**

jet steering /jêt stíriŋ/ *n.c.* **Attitude** control using gas jets for small corrective thrusts.

jettison /jétəsən/ *v. tr.* To eject and discard anything from a spacecraft during a mission.

jet vane /jét vèyn/ *n.c.* Heat-resistant material placed in a rocket's exhaust stream to influence the rocket's course.

J Mission /jéy mìšən/ *n.c. cd. Apollo.* Scientific mission to the moon. *Apollo 15, 16* and *17* are in this category.

JPL *(ac.) n.c.* "Jet Propulsion Laboratory," U.S. government-owned facility at Pasadena, California; operated by the California Institute of Technology for NASA. JPL

has been responsible for research and development of such deep-space probes as **Mariner, Ranger, Surveyor,** and the **Viking** craft due for launch in 1975. JPL also manages the Deep Space Network (**DSN**).

Juno /júwʀow/ *n.* 1. U.S. four-stage launch vehicle, now obsolete. The rocket was developed from the Jupiter intermediate range ballistic missile (**IRBM**) and was employed in unmanned spacecraft launches. There were two models. *Juno 1* (also called *Jupiter C*) became America's earliest successful launch vehicle when it placed the first U.S. satellite, *Explorer 1,* into Earth orbit in 1958 (see **Explorer**). *Juno 2,* an uprated version, launched the first successful U.S. lunar fly-by, *Pioneer 4,* in 1959 (see **Pioneer**).

Juno 1 was 70 ft. high, weighed 64,000 lbs. fueled, and produced 126,700 lbs. of thrust. The Juno 2 stood 77 ft. high, weighed 121,000 lbs. fueled, and had a thrust potential of 173,000 lbs.

2. Wife of Jupiter, and the Roman goddess of marriage.

Jupiter /júwpitəʀ/ *n.* 1. Largest planet in the solar system: the diameter of Jupiter is 89,000 miles. Its orbit lies 484 million miles from the sun. With its twelve moons, Jupiter has more natural satellites than any other planet in the solar system. In order to learn more about the planet, NASA sent a fly-by craft (see **Pioneer**) to Jupiter in 1972. Jupiter is also included in the **Outer Planets Missions.**

2. Supreme god in the Roman pantheon.

Jupiter C /jûwpitəʀ síy/ See **Juno.**

K–L

Kappa /kǽpə/ See **Japan.**

kapton /kǽptən/ *n. Apollo.* Silver-or gold-colored plastic material used as insulation on the outside of the LM.

Kennedy Space Center /kênədiy spéys sèntəʀ/ See **KSC.**

Kitty Hawk /kítiy hɔ̀k/ *n.c.* 1. Name of **Apollo** 14 CM (see **Apollo**).

2. Place in North Carolina near where the first successful American airplane flight was made by Orville and Wilbur Wright in 1903.

known site /nôwn sáyt/ *n.c.* Earth location whose exact geographical position has been pinpointed. Cf. **unknown site.**

Kosmos /kósmos/ *n.* "Cosmos," 1. U.S.S.R. multipurpose, Earth-orbital satellite series; the world's largest satellite series. At the beginning of 1972, more than 470 Kosmos satellites had been announced since first launch in March 1962. The series includes the Soviet Union's first meteorological satellite (*Kosmos 23,* launched in December 1963), the first global magnetic-survey vehicle (*Kosmos 26,* launched in March 1964), and the first totally automatic vehicles to dock in space (*Kosmos 186* and *Kosmos 188,* both launched in October 1967). Official Soviet sources report that the Kosmos satellites are all scientific research vehicles; however, U.S. intelligence speculates that many of the craft are of used for surveillance.

The investigative program of the Kos-

mos series, as defined by the Soviet government, includes upper-atmospheric and ionospheric exploration, meteorological studies, radiation-belt and ionospheric-particle registration, cosmic-ray and magnetic-field effects analysis, and meteorite-matter influence. Extensions of the program, such as the automatic docking maneuvers between Kosmos 186 and 188, and the 22-day flight of *Kosmos 110* with an experimental animal payload, have been concerned with scientific applications toward manned spaceflight.

Some Kosmos satellites have relatively brief flights, but others maintain active performance of extended duration. The satellites may be powered by solar or chemical energy. Some, such as those carrying animal payloads, may be recovered; some gradually decay. Physical appearance of the satellites varies from small, compact spheres to huge cylinders. As many as eight separate satellites have been orbited by a single launch vehicle.

2. Basic launch vehicle for the U.S.S.R. Kosmos and other artificial Earth satellites. The standard model is a liquid-fueled, two-stage rocket which stands approximately 29 ft. high and has a thrust potential of 24,200 lbs. It can be modified into more powerful three- or four-stage configurations for heavier payloads.

Kourou [*Fr.* kuRú] See **Guiana Space Center.**

KSC *(ac.) n.c.* "Kennedy Space Center," **NASA** facility named for U.S. President John F. Kennedy; located at Cape Kennedy, Florida (formerly Cape Canaveral) by the Atlantic Ocean. One of three U.S. launch sites, KSC handles the assembling, checking, and launching of many U.S. space vehicles and has been the only location of U.S. manned spaceflight launchings (cf. **AFWTR; Wallops station**). Launch Complex 39, on KSC's Merritt Island, became famous as the site of **Apollo** launchings. Installations at Launch Complex 39 include the Manned Spaceflight Operations Building (**MSOB**), Vehicle Assembly Building (**VAB**), and Launch Control Center (**LCC**).

Kugelblitz [*Ger.* kúgəlblits] See **ball lightning.**

LAD *(ac.) n.c. Apollo.* "Lunar atmosphere detector." See **CCIG; SIDE.**

Laika /láykə/ *n.* "Barker," U.S.S.R. dog, the first living creature to survive an orbital space flight. Laika was launched in *Sputnik 2* (see **Sputnik**) in November 1957.

Lambda 4-S /lǽmdə fôr és/ *n.c.* Japanese four-stage launch vehicle series; used to launch Japan's first satellite, **Ohsumi,** in February 1970. The rocket stands 55 ft. high, weighs 17,000 lbs. fueled, and has a thrust potential of 80,000 lbs.

landing gear assembly /lǽndiŋ gìr əsèmbliy/ *n.c. Apollo.* Four cantilevered LM legs and associated structures; included are **impact attenuators,** footpads (round, flat feet on which the LM rests), and the **LM egress platform** on the forward landing gear.

landing platform helicopter /lǽndiŋ plǽtform héləkaptəʀ/ See **LPH.**

/a/ *father;* /aw/ *wow;* /ay/ *buy;* /b/ *boy;* /č/ *witch;* /d/ *doll;* /e/ *bet;* /ey/ *say;* /f/ *few;* /g/ *bag;* /h/ *hole;* /i/ *it;* /iy/ *be;* /j/ *gin;* /k/ *cat;* /l/ *lamb;* /m/ *man;* /n/ *now;* /o/ *orbit;* /ow/ *tow;* /oy/ *boy;* /p/ *pat;* /r/ *run;* /s/ *send;* /š/ *shoe;* /t/ *toy;* /u/ *put;* /uw/ *do;* /v/ *eve;* /w/ *way;* /y/ *yes;*

SE–32

landing radar /lǽndiŋ rèydar/ *n.c. Apollo.* That part of the LM guidance, navigation, and control system (**GNCS**) which provides lunar approach and touchdown data for the primary guidance and navigation system (**PGNS**).

Langley Research Center /lǽŋliy rísɚč sèntɚ/ *n.c.* **NASA** research facility at Hampton, Virginia.

Large Space Telescope /lârj spêys téləskowp/ See **LST**.

laser /léyzɚ/ *(ac.) n.c.* "Light amplification by stimulated emission of radiation," a type of **maser** which uses light waves. The laser sends out a highly concentrated one-way (coherent) beam of light by heating for a short time materials which release steady light-wave energy while cooling. The laser is currently under study as a communications medium in future space efforts.

laser altimeter /lêyzɚ æltìmətɚ/ *n.c. Apollo.* A highly accurate altitude-monitoring device which employs a **laser**.

laser ranging retro-reflector /lêyzɚ rêynjiŋ rétrow riyflèktɚ/ See **LRRR**.

launch /lɔ́nč/ 1. *v. tr.* Of a rocket, to send forth under its own power.

    2. *n.* **Liftoff**.

    3. *n.* **Takeoff**.

launch complex /lɔ́nč kàmpleks/ *n.c.* Site equipped for **launch** of space vehicles.

Launch Complex 39 /lɔ́nč kàmpleks θɚ̀tiy náyn/ See **KSC**.

Launch Control Center /lɔ́nč kəntrówl sèntɚ/ See **LCC**.

launch escape motor /lɔ́nč əskéyp mòwtɚ/ See **LEM**.

launch escape system /lɔ́nč əskéyp sìstəm/ See **LES**.

launch escape tower /lɔ́nč əskéyp tàwɚ/ See **LET**.

launch pad /lɔ́nč pæ̀d/ *n.c.* Concrete base from which a rocket is launched. An **umbilical tower** and portable **service tower** are essential equipment used on the launch pad.

launch vehicle /lɔ́nč vìyhikəl/ *n.c.* Rocket used to carry a **payload** into space. Launch vehicles come in an array of sizes and configurations (one or more stages, transstages, etc.); the size and shape of the vehicle is dependent on the specific task and size of its payload.

    Multistage launch vehicles undergo **separation** in flight; after a preplanned period of time, the first or main stage falls away and the next stage fires to carry the lighter vehicle and payload even higher. This process repeats until the final stage of the launch vehicle boosts the payload into the desired orbit. This last stage usually either drifts as orbital debris or is sent onto a trajectory into **deep space**.

launch window /lɔ́nč wìndow/ *n.c.* Period during which ideal conditions are in effect for the launching of a **payload** to accomplish a specific goal. These periods vary with the seasons and are less frequent regarding interplanetary space shots.

LCC *(ac.) n.c. Apollo.* "Launch Control Center," **blockhouse** at Launch Complex 39 of **NASA**'s Kennedy Space Center (**KSC**). LCC has four firing rooms and four com-

puters. Its overall facilities enable checkout and coordination of activities both at the adjacent **VAB** and at the launch pad.

LCRU *(ac.) n.c. Apollo.* "Lunar communications relay unit," self-contained, suitcase-sized portable station for relaying voice, television, and telemetry directly between the **LRV** crew and Mission Control during lunar EVA. It is mounted on the LRV or hand carried, and eliminates having to use the LM communications and extends the LRV range of operation on the lunar surface.

LDD *(ac.) n.c. Apollo.* "Lunar dust detector," scientific device carried to the moon as part of the Apollo Lunar Surface Experiments Package (**ALSEP**); used to investigate interaction between solar radiation and lunar dust.

LEC *(ac.) n.c. Apollo.* "Lunar equipment conveyor," pulley device used to load and

unload the ascent stage of the LM; eliminates numerous trips up and down the ladder.

LEM *(ac.) n.c.* **1.** "Launch escape motor," in U.S. **Mercury** and **Apollo** programs, a solid fuel rocket engine which, in emergency, would pull the manned portion of the craft away from a malfunctioning launch vehicle. In Apollo, part of the launch escape system (**LES**) and capable of more than 147,000 lbs. of thrust. LEM would operate from ground level to an altitude of 285,000 ft.

    2. *obs. Apollo.* "Lunar excursion module." **LM**.

LES *(ac.) n.c.* **1.** *Apollo.* "Launch escape system," equipment complex designed to pull the manned portion of a craft away from a malfunctioning launch vehicle at any time from umbilical separation to LES jettison at about 285,000 ft. With the CSM,

The LCRU, mounted on the LRV, consists of a color television camera and a communications relay unit. The camera can be controlled from earth by the box-shaped unit under the camera housing.   RCA

/z/ zero; /ž/ azure; /θ/ thin; /ð/ then; /ŋ/ song; /æ/ bat; /ɔ/ law; /ə/ sun; /ɚ/ bird. Foreign symbols: [(n)] nasalization of some French vowels followed by /n/; [R] French uvular rolled /r/ sound; [ü] high front lip-rounded vowel; [x] Russian voiceless laryngeal fricative.

LM, and spacecraft-LM adapter (SLA), the LES is considered part of the total Apollo spacecraft.

2. "Lincoln Experimental Satellite," U.S. military experimental comsat series used in the Tactical Satellite Communications (TacSatCom) system. The series consists of six satellites, the first of which was launched in 1965. *LES 6* is in synchronous orbit.

NORTH AMERICAN ROCKWELL SPACE DIVISION

The Apollo launch escape tower and associated launch escape equipment

LET /lét/ *(ac.) n.c. Apollo.* "Launch escape tower," launch escape system (**LES**) equipment, a latticelike connector between the rocketed section of the escape system and the boost protective cover (**BPC**).
LEV *(ac.) n.c. obs. Apollo.* "Lunar excursion vehicle." **LM.**
Lewis Research Center /lúwəs ríysэrč sèntэr/ *n.c.* **NASA** research facility at Cleveland, Ohio.
LGE *(ac.) n.c. Apollo.* "Lunar geology experiment," scientific examination of lunar surface materials by astronauts on lunar **EVA.** The LGE consists of taking pictures, and collecting samples, and testing lunar surface material qualities such as hardness, color, and composition.
LH₂ *(abbr.) n.c.* "**Liquid hydrogen.**"
Liberty Bell 7 /líbэtiy bèl sévэn/ *n.c.*
1. Nickname for *Mercury 4* spacecraft (see **Mercury**).
libration /libréyšэn/ *n.* Real or apparent oscillatory motion, especially of the moon.
lifeboat /láyfbowt/ *n.* Any vehicle that could be stored on a manned spacecraft for use as emergency shelter in the event that the spacecraft were to become uninhabitable. Some U.S. models would provide a breathable atmosphere but necessitate rescue from orbit; others would have full **reentry** capability. Proposed lifeboats vary in passenger capacity.
life raft /láyf ræft/ *n.c.* **Lifeboat.**
life support system /láyf sэpórt sìstэm/ *n.c.* An equipment complex designed to sup-

ply drinking water and control the temperature, pressure, and makeup of an astronaut's air supply; in **Apollo**, the environmental control system (**ECS**).
lift-drag ratio /lìft drǽg rèyšyow/ *n.c.* Upward force on a vehicle computed by dividing the area of its lifting surfaces by the atmospheric **drag** encountered.
lifting body /líftiŋ bàdiy/ *n.c.* Wedge-shaped, wingless aircraft that is dependent entirely on its aerodynamic design to achieve lift and stability.
lifting reentry /líftiŋ riyéntriy/ *n.c. Apollo.* Method of slowing down a reentering **Apollo** spacecraft employing the use of its aerodynamic shape. Cf. **skip reentry.**
liftoff /líftòf/ *n.* **1.** Vertical ascent of an aerospace vehicle from a resting place such as a launch pad or the surface of the moon.
2. Initial moment of vertical ascent of an aerospace vehicle; distinguished from **takeoff,** which may occur at any angle.
lift off /lìft óf/ *phr. v. intr.* Of an aerospace vehicle, to ascend vertically from a resting place such as a launch pad or the moon. Lift off is distinguished from **take off,** which implies no specific angle of ascent.
light amplification by stimulated emission of radiation /làỳt æmplэfэkèyšэn bay stîmyэleytэd iymìšэn эv reydiyéyšэn/ See **laser.**
Light Blue /làỳt blúw/ *See* **Tansei.**
Lightning /láytniŋ/ *See* **Molniya.**
light year /láyt yìr/ *n.c.* Distance covered in one year by light, which travels at a veloc-

ity of 186,284 miles per second; equivalent to approximately six trillion miles.
Lincoln Experimental Satellite /lîŋkэn eksperэmêntэl sǽtэlayt/ See **LES.**
liquid cooling garment /lîkwэd kúwliŋ gàrmэnt/ *n.c. Apollo.* Astronaut undergarment, heat controlled by water circulation; worn during **EVA** only beneath the extravehicular **PGA.** Cf. **constant wear garment.**
liquid hydrogen /lîkwэd háydrэjэn/ *n.c.* Unstable rocket fuel created by cooling hydrogen gas to −423° F.; usually combined with liquid oxygen (**LOX**).
liquid oxygen /lîkwэd áksijэn/ See **LOX.**
liquid propellant /lîkwid prэpélэnt/ *n.c.* Rocket fuel in liquid form.
lithergol /líθэgal/ *n.* Rocket propellant formed by a mixture of solid and liquid fuels.
lithium hydroxide /líθiyэm haydráksayd/ *n.c.* Substance employed in a **life support system** to purify the atmosphere in space capsules and space suits.
LLRV *(ac.) n.c. Apollo.* "Lunar landing research vehicle," NASA **simulator** used to give astronauts actual practice on Earth flying a vehicle similar in function and design to the moon-landing craft, the LM. Cf. **LOLA simulator.**
LM /lém/ *(ac.) n.c. Apollo.* "Lunar module," one of the three main sections of the basic **Apollo** spacecraft. It was originally designated the lunar excursion vehicle (**LEV**) and later the lunar excursion module (**LEM**). The LM, an ungainly 18-ton, two-stage vehicle, is designed to carry two astronauts from a lunar orbiting **CSM** to the surface of the moon and back.

The lower half of the LM, the unmanned, unpressurized **descent stage,** contains a descent engine (**DE**), used to deorbit the craft and soft-land it on the moon; propellant and supply tanks; a landing gear assembly; scientific equipment housing; and the lunar roving vehicle (**LRV**). After lunar exploration, the descent stage serves as a launch pad for the ascent stage.

The manned ascent stage consists of

/a/ *father*; /aw/ *wow*; /ay/ *buy*; /b/ *boy*; /č/ *witch*; /d/ *doll*; /e/ *bet*; /ey/ *say*; /f/ *few*; /g/ *bag*; /h/ *hole*; /i/ *it*; /iy/ *be*; /j/ *gin*; /k/ *cat*; /l/ *lamb*; /m/ *man*; /n/ *now*; /o/ *orbit*; /ow/ *tow*; /oy/ *boy*; /p/ *pat*; /r/ *run*; /s/ *send*; /š/ *shoe*; /t/ *toy*; /u/ *put*; /uw/ *do*; /v/ *eve*; /w/ *way*; /y/ *yes*;

Labels on figure: NOSE CONE & Q BALL; BALLAST; PITCH CONTROL MOTOR; TOWER JETTISON MOTOR; LAUNCH ESCAPE MOTOR; STRUCTURAL SKIRT; LAUNCH ESCAPE MOTOR THRUST ALIGNMENT FITTING; STUDS & FRANGIBLE NUTS; CANARD; CANARD ACTUATOR; SOLID PROPELLANT; POWER SYSTEMS & INSTRUMENTATION WIRE HARNESS; LAUNCH ESCAPE TOWER; ELECTRICAL DISCONNECT FITTINGS; BOOST PROTECTIVE COVER (APEX SECTION)

INERTIAL MEASUREMENT UNIT
S-BAND STEERABLE ANTENNA
VHF ANTENNA (2)
DOCKING HATCH
DOCKING TARGET RECESS
GASEOUS OXYGEN TANK (2)
AFT EQUIPMENT BAY
REPLACEABLE ELECTRONIC ASSEMBLY
FUEL TANK (REACTION CONTROL)
LIQUID OXYGEN TANK
HELIUM TANK (2)
HELIUM TANK (REACTION CONTROL
RENDEZVOUS RADAR ANTENNA
ASCENT ENGINE COVER
S-BAND INFLIGHT ANTENNA (2)
REACTION CONTROL ASSEMBLY (4 PLACES)
OXIDIZER TANK
WINDOW (2 PLACES)
INGRESS/EGRESS HATCH
CREW COMPARTMENT
WATER TANK (2)
FUEL TANK
OXIDIZER TANK (REACTION CONTROL

The Apollo lunar module is composed of two parts which are joined together for moon landing: the ascent stage, *above*, and the descent stage, *below*. The descent stage contains a rocket engine, fuel and water tanks, scientific equipment storage bays, and the landing gear.

The ascent stage is a pressurized vehicle in which the astronauts ride on the trip from the orbiting command-service module to the moon and back. When the ascent stage of the LM blasts off from the surface of the moon, it leaves the descent stage behind.

FUEL TANK
THERMAL SHIELD
DESCENT ENGINE
OXIDIZER TANK
FUEL TANK
WATER TANK
OXIDIZER TANK
SCIENTIFIC EQUIPMENT BAY
LM-ADAPTER ATTACHMENT POINT (4 PLACES)
BACKPACK BATTERIES, S-BAND ANTENNA STORAGE
LANDING GEAR
HELIUM TANK
DESCENT ENGINE SKIRT
OXYGEN TANK
GIMBAL RING

/z/ zero; /ž/ azure; /θ/ thin; /ð/ then; /ŋ/ song; /æ/ bat; /ɔ/ law; /ə/ sun; /ɚ/ bird. Foreign symbols: [(n)] nasalization of some French vowels followed by /n/; [R] French uvular rolled /r/ sound; [ü] high front lip-rounded vowel; [x] Russian voiceless laryngeal fricative.

SE-35

Lunar samples from *Apollo 11* and *12* were taken to the Lunar Receiving Laboratory. Here, in the Bioprep Laboratory, the samples underwent biological tests.

crew compartment, midsection, aft equipment bay, tank section, and ascent engine (**AE**). The pressurized crew compartment contains living quarters, LM controls, windows, and a side hatch for **EVA** or lunar **egress**. The midsection, partly pressurized, contains the AE used for returning to the CSM, propellant and helium tanks, LM components of the **docking system,** and several LM systems. The inaccessible aft equipment bay houses remaining LM systems and supplies.

LM egress platform /lêm íygres plǽtform/ *n.c. Apollo.* Porchlike structure on the LM; equipped with a ladder for crew descent to the lunar surface.

LMP *(ac.) n.c. Apollo.* "Lunar module pilot," third in command on U.S. **Apollo** missions. He is the expert on LM systems and handles electronics and communications during translunar and transearth coast (**TLC; TEC**). The LMP occupies the right couch in the CM and is one of the two men who descend to the lunar surface. Cf. **CMP; commander.**

LM pad /lém pæd/ See **landing gear assembly.**

lock /lák/ 1. *v. tr.* To tune in on and hold a radio frequency.
   2. *n.* Hold on a radio frequency.

LOI *(ac.) n.c. Apollo.* "Lunar orbit insertion," maneuver which places a spacecraft into lunar orbit following translunar coast (**TLC**) or following lunar liftoff (see **FITH**). On journeys toward the moon, LOI is followed by descent orbit insertion (**DOI**); on return trips, by lunar orbit rendezvous (**LOR**).

LOLA simulator /lówlə sìmyəleytə/ *(ac.) n.c. Apollo.* "Lunar orbit and landing approach" **simulator,** NASA device which enables a pilot, via closed-circuit television and three-dimensional maps, to practice flying the LM (though on the ground) from a simulated height of 100 miles to 200 feet above the moon. Cf. **LLRV.**

Long Tank Delta /lɔ́ŋ tæŋk dêltə/ See **Delta.**

LOR *(ac.) n.c. Apollo.* "Lunar orbit rendezvous," four-maneuver operation whereby the LM and CSM meet for redocking after completion of the lunar landing mission, liftoff, and lunar orbit insertion (**LOI**). The maneuvers of LOR are: concentric sequence initiation (**CSI**), constant delta height (**CDH**), terminal phase initiation (**TPI**), and terminal phase finalization (**TPF**). The entire process from lunar liftoff to TPF takes about three-and-one-half hours.

LOS *(ac.) n.c.* "Loss of signal," communications blackout. In **Apollo,** it occurs when the CSM is passing behind the moon and again during **reentry.** Cf. **AOS.**

loss of signal /lɔ́s əv sígnəl/ See **LOS.**

low gate /lów gèyt/ See **PDI.**

LOX /láks/ *(ac.) n.c.* "Liquid oxygen," supercooled pressurized oxygen gas that serves as an **oxidizer** in some liquid-fueled rockets; oxygen becomes a liquid at −297°F.

LPH *(ac.) n.c. Apollo.* "Landing platform helicopter," prime recovery vehicle; used to recover the CM and astronauts after **splashdown.**

LPM *(ac.) n.c. Apollo.* "Lunar portable magnetometer," scientific device carried to the moon during Project **Apollo** as an independent experiment. Since the LPM can be toted around with the astronauts, it is used to gauge the lunar magnetic field over distance. Cf. **LSM.**

LPO *(ac.) n.c.* "Lunar parking orbit," any temporary flight path around the moon. In **Apollo,** the CSM stays in LPO while the LM descends to the lunar surface.

LR³ See **LRRR.**

LRL *(ac.) n.c. Apollo.* "Lunar Receiving Laboratory," major installation at **NASA's** Manned Spacecraft Center (**MSC**); quarantine facility in which astronauts and lunar samples from *Apollo 11* and *12* were studied upon return to Earth. The total isolation guaranteed protection of terrestrial life from **back contamination** and avoided exposing lunar samples to terrestrial organisms. The LRL is no longer used for quarantine purposes since no danger of any contamination was discovered.

LRRR *(ac.) n.c. Apollo.* "Laser ranging retro-reflector," scientific device carried to the moon as part of the Early Apollo Scientific Experiments Package (**EASEP**) and

The lunar roving vehicle has been used on three Apollo missions. It transports the astronauts, and carries two antennas, four cameras, a radio, tools, and test equipment.

/a/ *father;* /aw/ *wow;* /ay/ *buy;* /b/ *boy;* /č/ *witch;* /d/ *doll;* /e/ *bet;* /ey/ *say;* /f/ *few;* /g/ *bag;* /h/ *hole;* /i/ *it;* /iy/ *be;* /j/ *gin;* /k/ *cat;* /l/ *lamb;*
/m/ *man;* /n/ *now;* /o/ *orbit;* /ow/ *tow;* /oy/ *boy;* /p/ *pat;* /r/ *run;* /s/ *send;* /š/ *shoe;* /t/ *toy;* /u/ *put;* /uw/ *do;* /v/ *eve;* /w/ *way;* /y/ *yes;*

NVOSTI PRESS AGENCY

Luna 2, built by the U.S.S.R., was the first man-made object to reach the moon.

later as an independent experiment. The shiny LRRR serves as a passive target for returning **laser** beams directed to the moon from various earth observatories and is used to measure the exact Earth-moon distance.

LRV *(ac.) n.c. Apollo.* "Lunar roving vehicle," first manned transportation system designed for operation on the moon; used initially on *Apollo 15.* The LRV is 10 ft. long and weighs 460 lbs. Each wheel is powered by an electric engine which draws its power from two batteries. Front and rear wheels have separate steering systems, in case of failure in either. The LRV can carry a payload 2.5 times its own weight. Five major systems—mobility, navigation, power, thermal control, and crew station—provide for LRV operations. The LRV is carried folded within one quadrant of the LM's descent stage storage area, and is deployed by the astronauts upon landing. See **SSE.**

LSM *(ac.) n.c. Apollo.* "Lunar surface magnetometer," scientific device carried to the moon as part of the Apollo Lunar Surface Experiments Package (**ALSEP**). LSM is used to gauge the magnetic field at the surface of the moon over a period of time.

LST *(ac.) n.c.* "Large Space Telescope," proposed U.S. scientific instrument projected for launch into Earth orbit in the 1980's for astronomical observations unobscured by the earth's atmosphere. Development of the mirror for such a telescope is planned for the 1970's.

LTD *(ac.) n.c.* "Long Tank Delta." See **Delta.**

Luna *[Rus. lúna] n.* "Moon," U.S.S.R. moonprobe series which included the first object launched into deep space, the first artificial moon satellite, the first man-made artifact landed on the moon, and the first vehicle to photograph the dark side of the moon.

Twenty craft were announced from 1959 to 1972.

The first three probes, originally called *Cosmic Rocket 1, 2,* and *3,* were later redesignated *Luna 1, 2,* and *3.* Luna 1, launched January 2, 1959, became the first man-made object to go into heliocentric orbit. Luna 2, the first man-made object to hit another celestial body, impacted on the moon in September 1959. Luna 3, launched in October 1959, swung around the moon and relayed the first photos of its dark side.

Luna 9 made the first soft landing on the moon in February 1966 and transmitted the first photographs taken from the surface. *Luna 10* became the first satellite of the moon on April 3, 1966. *Luna 13,* launched in December 1966, landed on the moon and conducted extensive soil-density gauging experiments. *Luna 16* soft-landed on the lunar surface in September 1970, collected soil samples, and returned them to Earth, the first automated return from the surface of another celestial body. *Luna 17,* launched in November 1970, carried *Lunakhod 1,* the first unmanned, automatic lunar rover (see **Lunakhod**).

Lunakhod *[Rus.* lunaxót] *n.* "Moon Rover," any of several remote-controlled vehicles presumably planned by the U.S.S.R. for use on the moon. *Lunakhod 1,* the first mobile lunar payload, was an eight-wheeled, solar-powered, driverless car deposited on the moon in November 1970 by *Luna 17* (see **Luna**). The vehicle, operated from Earth, was equipped with a French built **laser** reflector for tracking purposes, four television cameras for Earth guidance, a digging apparatus for taking soil samples, and an x-ray spectrometer for soil analysis. The vehicle was shut down and reactivated several times during its life span, which ended in October 1971 after nuclear heater fuel was exhausted. The laser reflector

The U.S.S.R. has explored the moon's surface with Lunakhods controlled from earth.

NVOSTI PRESS AGENCY

/z/ zero; /ž/ azure; /θ/ thin; /ð/ then; /ŋ/ song; /æ/ bat; /ɔ/ law; /ə/ sun; /ɚ/ bird. Foreign symbols: [(n)] nasalization of some French vowels followed by /n/; [R] French uvular rolled /r/ sound; [ü] high front lip-rounded vowel; [x] Russian voiceless laryngeal fricative.

SE – 37

remained serviceable. Lunakhod 1 produced 500 lunar panoramas, 20,000 television pictures, and carried out over 25 chemical analyses of lunar-surface samples.

lunar /lúwnɚ/ *attr.* Of or pertaining to the moon.

lunar atmosphere detector /lûwnɚ ǽtməsfir diytèktɚ/ See **CCIG; SIDE**.

lunar boot /lûwnɚ búwt/ See **PGA**.

lunar communications relay unit /lûwnɚr kəmyuwnəkêyšɚnz ríyley yùwnət/ See **LCRU**.

lunar dust detector /lûwnɚ dɚst diytèktɚ/ See **LDD**.

lunar equipment conveyor /lûnɚ iykwípmənt kɚnvèyɚ/ See **LEC**.

lunar EVA /lûwnɚ íy vìy éy/ See **EVA**.

lunar excursion module /lûwnɚ ekskɚ́žən màjəl/ See **LM**.

lunar excursion vehicle /lûwnɚ ekskɚ́žən vìyhikəl/ See **LM**.

lunar geology experiment /lûwnɚ jiyáləjiy ekspèrəmənt/ See **LGE**.

lunar gravity /lûwnɚ grǽvətiy/ *n.c.* Force of gravity of the moon; equal to one-sixth that of gravity on Earth.

lunar highlands /lûwnɚ háyləndz/ *n.c.* Mountainous or hilly regions on the moon.

lunar landing research vehicle /lûwnɚ lǽndiŋ ríysɚč vìyhikəl/ See **LLRV**.

lunar module /lûwnɚ májəl/ See **LM**.

lunar module pilot /lûwnɚ májəl pàylət/ See **LMP**.

lunar orbit and landing approach /lûwnɚ ôrbət ænd lǽndiŋ əprówč/ See **LOLA simulator**.

lunar orbit and landing approach simulator /lûwnɚ ôrbət ænd lǽndiŋ əprówč sìmyəleytɚ/ See **LOLA simulator**.

Lunar Orbiter /lûwnɚ órbitɚ/ *n.c.* U.S. lunar satellite series, consisting of five craft launched in 1966 and 1967. Lunar Orbiters were the first U.S. craft to go into orbit around the moon. They photographed the entire lunar surface, making possible the first atlas of the moon and allowing a survey of possible landing sites for manned missions. The series succeeded Project **Ranger** and was itself superceded by Project **Surveyor**.

lunar orbit insertion /lûwnɚ ôrbət insɚ́šən/ See **LOI**.

lunar orbit rendezvous /lûwnɚ ôrbət rándeyvuw/ See **LOR**.

lunar parking orbit /lûwnɚ párkiŋ òrbət/ See **LPO**.

lunar probe /lûwnɚ prówb/ *n.c.* Unmanned spacecraft which is used to survey the moon. Notable lunar probes include the U.S. **Ranger** and **Surveyor** series and the U.S.S.R. **Luna** series.

lunar rays /lûwnɚ réyz/ *n.c.* Light-colored material radiating in trails from certain craters on the moon; one **Apollo** objective is the study of these rays.

Lunar Receiving Laboratory /lûwnɚ riysíyviŋ lǽbrətoriy/ See **LRL**.

lunar rover /lûwnɚ rówvɚ/ See **LRV**.

lunar roving vehicle /lûwnɚ rôwviŋ víyhikəl/ See **LRV**.

lunar samples /lûwnɚ sǽmpəlz/ *n.c.* Rocks and soil collected on the moon and returned to Earth for examination.

lunar sphere of influence /lûwnɚ sfîr əv ínfluwəns/ See **MSI**.

lunar surface magnetometer /lûwnɚ sɚ́fəs mægnətámətɚ/ See **LSM**.

lunar trajectory /lûwnɚ trɚjéktɚiy/ *n.c.* Flight path to the moon.

Lunik /luník/ *n. sl.* Misnomer originally applied to the Soviet **Luna** program by the American press; blend of "lunar" and "sputnik."

M–N

M-4S *n.c.* Japanese four-stage launch vehicle series. The *M-4S-2* launched Japan's second satellite, **Tansei**, February 16, 1971. It stands 138 ft. high, weighs 131,000 lbs. fueled, and develops 535,000 lbs. of thrust.

MA (ac.) *n.c.* "Mercury Atlas." See **Atlas; Mercury**.

Mach /mǽk/ See **Mach number**.

Mach number /mǽk nɚ̀mbɚ/ *n.c.* Ratio between the velocity of a moving object and the speed of sound traveling through the same medium; expressed in units called *Machs* with *Mach 1* being the speed of sound in a given medium.

magnetic field /mægnêtik fíyld/ *n.c.* Any area in space under the magnetic influence of a celestial body. See **magnetosphere**.

magnetohydrodynamics /mægnêtowhây-drowdaynǽmiks/ *n.* Study of ionized gases acted upon by electric and magnetic fields.

magnetometer /mægnetámətɚ/ *n.* Scientific device used to locate and measure magnetic fields in interplanetary space.

magnetosphere /mægnétowsfir/ *n.* Area beyond the earth's atmosphere under the influence of Earth's magnetism. It consists of highly charged electrical particles in motion along magnetic lines of force.

The influence of the **solar wind** forces compression of the magnetosphere on the sun side of the earth and on the other side sweeps it into a cometlike tail of undetermined length.

magnetospheric substorm /mægnêtowsfîrik sɚ́bstorm/ *n.c.* Spasmodic disturbance in the **magnetosphere** caused by energy released by the **solar wind**.

magnitude /mǽgnətuwd/ *n.* Measurement of relative stellar light intensity; first magnitude is the apparent brightness of a candle flame viewed from a distance of 1,300 ft. In the original system, first-magnitude stars were the brightest, and sixth-magnitude stars were the faintest objects visable to the unaided eye. Magnitude is computed on the basis that each unit is 2.512 times brighter than the next unit following it, e.g., a first-magnitude star is 2.512 times brighter than a second-magnitude star and 100 times brighter than a sixth-magnitude star. New observational techniques, including the use of photography and telescopes, have necessitated extending the magnitude numbers into negative integers for objects brighter than first-magnitude stars and into integers higher than six for objects dimmer than sixth-magnitude stars.

main parachute /mêyn pérəšuwt/ *n.c.* Largest parachute of the earth landing system (**ELS**); during **Apollo** missions,

three are deployed at 10,000 ft. by three **pilot parachutes**.

main stage /mêyn stéyj/ *n.c.* That time in the thrust build-up of a rocket or launch vehicle at which maximum thrust is achieved.

majority rule circuit /mɚjóritiy rúwl sɚ̀kit/ *n.c.* Triplicated critical circuit in a spacecraft computer; identical signals from two units will overrule a different one from the third. See **redundant**.

malfunction /mǽlfɚŋkšən/ 1. *v. intr.* To operate incorrectly.

2. *n.* Abnormality.

malfunction detection system /mǽlfɚ̀ŋkšən diytékšən sìstem/ See **MDS**.

maneuver controller /mənúwvɚ kɚntròwlɚ/ *n.c. Gemini.* Control device for directional changes of spacecraft while in Earth orbit.

manned /mǽnd/ *attr.* Of or pertaining to full-time crew operation of a spacecraft. Cf. **man-tended**.

Manned Orbital Platform /mǽnd ôrbətəl plǽtform/ See **MOP**.

Manned Orbiting Laboratory /mǽnd ôrbətiŋ lǽbrətoriy/ See **MOL**.

Manned Spacecraft Center /mǽnd spéyskræft sèntɚ/ See **MSC**.

Manned Space Flight Network /mǽnd spéys flàyt nêtwɚk/ See **MSFN**.

Manned Spaceflight Operations Building /mǽnd spêysflayt apɚéyšənz bìldiŋ/ See **MSOB**.

man-rated /mǽn réytəd/ *attr.* Of or pertaining to any spacecraft or spacecraft system which has been found safe for use in a manned effort.

man-tended /mǽn téndəd/ *attr.* Of or pertaining to a spacecraft not normally manned, but visited by men occasionally for maintenance.

manual control /mǽnyuwəl kɚntrówl/ *n.c.* Flight **mode** in which a crew member pilots a vehicle without the use of an automatic control system.

manual data insertion unit /mǽnyuwəl dêytə insɚ́šən yùwnət/ See **MDIU**.

mare /márey/ *n.* "Sea," Latin name given by early astronomers to the dark areas, which they thought were waterfilled, on the moon. Although it is now known that there is no water on the lunar surface, the name has been retained and is used in lunar cartography. The plural is *maria.*

maria /máriyə/ See **mare**.

Mariner /mérinɚ/ *n.* U.S. interplanetary probe series, successfully launched since 1962, consisting at the end of 1971 of six craft, including the first to orbit another planet. Mariners studied atmospheric and surface conditions of the planets Venus (*Mariner 2* and *5*) and Mars (*Mariner 4, 6, 7,* and *9*) relaying the information back to Earth. Mariner 4, launched in November 1964, took the first close-range pictures of another planet from space. All of the missions were fly-bys except Mariner 9, launched in May 1971 which on November 13, 1971, became the first satellite to go into orbit around another planet. Using information from the Mars Mariners, landing sites will be chosen for the 1975 unmanned **Viking** missions to Mars.

/a/ *father;* /aw/ *wow;* /ay/ *buy;* /b/ *boy;* /č/ *witch;* /d/ *doll;* /e/ *bet;* /ey/ *say;* /f/ *few;* /g/ *bag;* /h/ *hole;* /i/ *it;* /iy/ *be;* /j/ *gin;* /k/ *cat;* /l/ *lamb;* /m/ *man;* /n/ *now;* /o/ *orbit;* /ow/ *tow;* /oy/ *boy;* /p/ *pat;* /r/ *run;* /s/ *send;* /š/ *shoe;* /t/ *toy;* /u/ *put;* /uw/ *do;* /v/ *eve;* /w/ *way;* /y/ *yes;*

Mariner-Venus/Mercury is a proposed fly-by mission to Mercury by way of Venus, scheduled for launch in 1973. The gravity of Venus will help swing the Mariner toward Mercury. As the probe reaches the vicinity of Mercury—the nearest planet to the sun—it will encounter increasing solar radiation. This will create both an advantage in power generation (since fewer solar panels will be required than on previous Mariner missions) and a problem in heat control. Seven experiments, including two that involve television cameras, will be attempted.

Mars [*Rus.* márs] *n.* 1. U.S.S.R. Martian probe series. Three craft had been launched by December 1971, with two more flights tentatively scheduled for 1973 and 1975.

Mars 1 was launched in November 1962. Although it flew past Mars, before radio communications failed it transmitted information on the existence of a previously undetected third radiation belt surrounding the earth. The probe also relayed data on the earth's magnetic field, the solar wind, and meteoric particle distribution.

Mars 2 and *3* were launched in May 1971; they successfully entered Martian orbits in November and December 1971, respectively. Shortly after achieving orbit, Mars 2 deposited on Mars a capsule, the first manmade object on that planet, containing a pennant bearing the Soviet coat of arms. Mars 3 soft-landed a television-camera equipped capsule on the surface December 2, 1971. It stopped transmitting about 20 seconds after touchdown, apparently due to interference from a 300 m.p.h. dust storm that enveloped most of Mars at the time the probe landed.

2. /márz/ Fourth planet in the solar system; 141 million miles from the sun. The planet is about one-half the size of the earth; its diameter is 4,219 miles. Its distance from the earth ranges from a maximum of 248 million miles to a minimum of 34 million miles. The force of gravity is 38 percent that of Earth's; a Martian day lasts 24 hrs. 37 min. Mars has 2 moons. Long imagined to support extraterrestrial life and constantly observed by telescopes and probes, the planet seems a likely target for future manned spaceflight.

3. Roman god of war.

Mars excursion module /márz ekskə́žən mə̀dyul/ See **MEM**.

Marshall Space Flight Center /mâršəl spéys flàyt sêntə/ See **MSFC**.

Mars orbit insertion /márz ôrbət insə́šən/ See **MOI**.

Mars rover vehicle /márz rówvə vìyhikəl/ See **MRV**.

mascon /mǽskan/ *(ac.) n.c.* "Mass concentration," one of innumerable areas on the moon which produce variations in gravitational pull. Their origin has been theorized as the result of vast, localized bombardment. Cf. **minicon**.

maser /méyzə/ *(ac.) n.c.* "Microwave amplification by stimulated emission of radiation," instrument used to produce or strengthen electromagnetic waves; its main function regarding space is the amplification of signals from spacecraft. A maser used in the antenna at Goldstone, a station of the Deep Space Network (**DSN**), strengthens a signal before it is blurred by the electronic noise inherent in the receiving system. Since heat can be a source of noise, the maser at Goldstone is kept in liquid helium at −452°F.

mass concentration /mǽs kansəntréyšən/ See **mascon**.

mass ratio /mǽs rèyšyow/ *n.c.* Relationship between a rocket and the amount of **propellant** it can carry; figure is obtained by dividing total takeoff mass by mass remaining after fuel consumption.

master alarm /mǽstə əlárm/ See **caution and warning system**.

mate /méyt/ *v. tr.* To fit parts of a spacecraft together before launch.

maxifootball /mǽksiyfútbɔl/ *n. sl. Apollo.* **Equiperiod transfer orbit**.

max-Q /mǽks kyúw/ *n. cd.* Maximum **dynamic pressure**.

MCC *(ac.) n.c.* 1. "Mission Control Center," major installation at **NASA**'s Manned Spacecraft Center (**MSC**). MCC has been in operation since June 1965 as central ground-control location for all U.S. manned flights. Through the use of over 170 consoles, 130 televisions, and 550 receivers, ground-control teams can monitor a flight constantly. Computers provide vital information and updates.

2. "Midcourse correction," directional change made on a space mission, usually during a long gliding period like **TEC** or **TLC**.

MDA *(ac.) n.c.* "Multiple Docking Adapter," one of four main elements of the proposed U.S. **Skylab** space station. Externally, the MDA will feature two docking ports for CSM's; internally, it will provide space for technological experiments in a 1,140 cubic-foot laboratory with two windows. The MDA will contain the Earth Resources Experiments Package (**EREP**), controls for the Apollo Telescope Mount (**ATM**), Skylab's heating-control system, and storage facilities.

At launch the MDA will be stacked between Airlock Module (**AM**) and ATM. In orbit, however, the ATM will swing to a 90° angle from the MDA, thereby exposing one of the MDA's docking ports.

MDIU *(ac.) n.c. Gemini.* "Manual data insertion unit," small digital keyboard used to command the on-board spacecraft **computer**.

MDS *(ac.) n.c. Gemini.* "Malfunction detection system," spacecraft equipment complex capable of determining emergency conditions during launch and signaling them to the crew so abort may be manually initiated. Cf. **EDS**.

mechanical border /mekǽnəkəl bórdə/ *n.c.* Atmospheric layer at an altitude between 120 and 140 miles where air **drag** becomes negligible.

Mechta [*Rus.* méčta] *n.* "Dream," Russian name given to the first **Luna** moon probe; also called *Cosmic Rocket 1*.

MECO /míykow/ *(ac.) n.c.* "Main engine cutoff."

MEM /mém/ *(ac.) n.c.* "Mars excursion module," proposed U.S. vehicle which would be used for manned Mars landings. Functionally comparable to the **LM** of lunar missions.

memory /mémə̀iy/ *n.* Information-storage section of a computer.

Mercury /mə́kyə̀iy/ *n.* 1. First U.S. manned spaceflight project; program in which the first Americans were put into space. Project Mercury was given official status in October 1958 with the basic objectives of putting a man into orbit, testing his ability to function in space, and returning him safely to earth.

Suborbital flights began in July 1960 and tested spacecraft and systems. Of seven such flights, only the last two were manned, although the third, in January 1961, carried a chimpanzee named Ham. The sixth suborbital flight, *Freedom 7*, carried Alan B. Shepard, Jr. to an altitude of 116 miles, making him the first American to enter space. *Freedom 7* and the following craft *Liberty Bell 7* were flown to test human reactions to spaceflight in addition to mechanical considerations.

Orbital flights began in September 1961. The first two orbital flights were un-

The Mercury capsule *Freedom 7* was the first American craft to enter space.

MCDONNELL AIRCRAFT CORP.

/z/ zero; /ž/ azure; /θ/ *thin*; /ð/ *then*; /ŋ/ *song*; /æ/ *bat*; /ɔ/ *law*; /ə/ *sun*; /ə/ *bird*. Foreign symbols: [(n)] nasalization of some French vowels followed by /n/; [R] French uvular rolled /r/ sound; [ü] high front lip-rounded vowel; [x] Russian voiceless laryngeal fricative.

SE–39

MANNED MERCURY FLIGHTS

Mission	Pilot	Date(s)	Remarks
MR-3 (*Freedom 7*)	Alan B. Shepard, Jr. (Cmdr., USN)	May 5, 1961 (00 hrs. 15 min.)	America's first manned space flight. Sub-orbital.
MR-4 (*Liberty Bell 7*)	Virgil I. Grissom (Capt., USAF)	July 21, 1961 (00 hrs. 16 min.)	Evaluated spacecraft functions. Sub-orbital.
MA-6 (*Friendship 7*)	John H. Glenn, Jr. (Lt. Col., USMC)	February 20, 1962 (04 hrs. 55 min.)	America's first manned orbital flight. 3 orbits.
MA-7 (*Aurora 7*)	M. Scott Carpenter (Lt. Cmdr., USN)	May 24, 1962 (04 hrs. 56 min.)	Initiated research experiments for future missions. 3 orbits.
MA-8 (*Sigma 7*)	Walter M. Schirra, Jr. (Cmdr., USN)	October 3, 1962 (09 hrs. 13 min.)	Developed techniques and procedures applicable to extended time in space. 6 orbits.
MA-9 (*Faith 7*)	L. Gordon Cooper, Jr. (Maj., USAF)	May 15 – 16, 1963 (34 hrs. 20 min.)	Met final objective of Mercury program—one day in space. 22 orbits.

manned, the first carrying a "mechanical man" and the second, a chimpanzee named Enos. In February 1962, John H. Glenn, Jr., piloting *Friendship 7*, became the first American to orbit the earth. Three more manned orbital missions, each longer and more complex in objectives than the previous one, closed out the program.

Project Mercury established the feasibility of American manned spaceflight and established precedents of design and procedure for future manned endeavors. A global communications network was established, recovery capabilities were successfully tried, and a basic conical spacecraft design was adopted. When initiated, the Mercury missions were to be succeeded by Project **Apollo**; however, prior to Mercury's first orbital shot, Project **Gemini** was instituted as a transitional program.

The Mercury spacecraft was shaped somewhat like a bell, 74.5 inches wide across the bottom and about 9 feet tall. An escape tower, attached at launch but jettisoned shortly thereafter, added another 17 feet for an overall length of approximately 26 feet at launch.

Two launch vehicles were used in the program: the **Redstone** (limited to suborbital flights) and the **Atlas**. Official designations for missions were given according to the launch vehicle used, with *MR* standing for *Mercury Redstone* and *MA*, for *Mercury-Atlas*.

2. Planet whose orbit is nearest the sun and the smallest planet in the solar system. The diameter of Mercury is 3,000 miles. Its orbit lies about 36 million miles from the sun. **Mariner** craft are scheduled to study Mercury in 1973.

3. Roman messenger god.

Mercury Atlas /mə́kyəiy ǽtləs/ See **Atlas**; **Mercury**.

Mercury Redstone /mə́kyəiy rédstown/ See **Mercury**; Redstone.

Merritt Island Launch Area /mèrit áylənd lɔ́nč èriyə/ See **KSC**.

MESA /méysə/ *(ac.) n.c. Apollo*. "Modular equipment stowage assembly," storage area located in the descent stage of the LM; among its contents are a television, a camera, lunar tools, and two sample-return containers (**SRC**).

mesosphere /mésowsfir/ *n.* Layer of Earth's **atmosphere** from 37 to 56 miles up.

MET /mét/ *(ac.) n.c. Apollo*. "Modular equipment transporter," two-wheeled, handpulled, rickshaw-type cart used to carry equipment and act as a portable workbench during lunar EVA on *Apollo 14*.

Meteor /míytiyə/ *n.* **1.** Meteorological system within the U.S.S.R. Kosmos series of research satellites. The first satellite of the Meteor variety was launched in March 1967 under the designation *Kosmos 144*. Weather satellites within the Kosmos series had been launched as early as August 1964, but with the introduction of the Meteor system, they were standardized.

The conical Kosmos weather satellites of the Meteor system are equipped with two television cameras, infrared sensors, and an attitude stabilization system. Each vehicle's cameras and sensors are constantly directed toward Earth; its solar panels are always sun-oriented. Both day and night photographic capability is maintained from the satellite's nearly polar retrograde orbit.

Satellites currently operating in the Meteor system include *Kosmos 144, 156,* and *206*. Reports and photos from the Meteor system are sent to a number of international weather centers, including Washington, D. C.

2. *l.c.* Free-floating solid space matter which occasionally enters Earth's atmosphere and ignites; also called *shooting star*. Cf. **meteorite**; **meteoroid**; **micrometeoroid**.

meteorite /míytiyəayt/ *n.* Portion of a **meteor** that survives its trip through the earth's atmosphere and strikes the surface. Cf. **meteoroid**; **micrometeoroid**.

meteoroid /míytiyəoyd/ *n.* Solid object traveling through space. Cf. **meteor**; **meteorite**; **micrometeoroid**.

meteoroid bumper /míytiyəoyd bə̀mpə/ *n.c. sl.* See **Meteoroid shield**.

meteoroid shield /míytiyəoyd šìyld/ *n.c.* Protective cover over a spacecraft for the prevention of **meteoroid** penetration.

meteorological satellite /mìytiyəəlâĵikəl sǽtəlayt/ *n.c.* Any earth-orbiting spacecraft developed for the purpose of supplementing and improving conventional weather forecasts. Most provide photographs of cloud cover and measure infrared radiation. U.S. meteorological satellites include the **TIROS, ESSA,** and **Nimbus** series.

Meteorological Satellite /mìytiyəəlâĵikəl sæ̀təlayt/ See **MetSat**.

MetSat /métsæt/ *(ac.) n.c.* "Meteorological Satellite," proposed British meteorological satellite scheduled for launch in 1973.

microatmosphere /mâykrowǽtməsfir/ *n.* Artificial atmosphere within a spacecraft.

micrometeoroid /mâykrowmíytiyəoyd/ *n.* Tiny particle of matter in space. Cf. **meteor**; **meteorite**; **meteoroid**.

Micrometeoroid Explorer /mâykrowmìytiyəroid eksplórə/ *n.c.* U.S. geophysical satellites, numbers 13, 16 and 23 of the **Explorer** series; launched from 1961 to 1964. These satellites investigated micrometeoroid encounters in NEO-space (see **NEO**) and their effect on various materials. The fourth stage of a **Scout** houses the instruments of Micrometeoroid Explorers.

microwave /máykrowwèyv/ *n.* High energy **electromagnetic** wave.

microwave amplification by stimulated emission of radiation /máykrowwèyv æ̀mpləfəkèyšən bay stìmyəleytəd iymîšən əv reydiyéyšən/ See **maser**.

MIDAS /máydəs/ *(ac.) n.c.* "Missile Defense Alarm System" or "Missile Detection and

/a/ father; /aw/ wow; /ay/ buy; /b/ boy; /č/ witch; /d/ doll; /e/ bet; /ey/ say; /f/ few; /g/ bag; /h/ hole; /i/ it; /iy/ be; /ĵ/ gin; /k/ cat; /l/ lamb; /m/ man; /n/ now; /o/ orbit; /ow/ tow; /oy/ boy; /p/ pat; /r/ run; /s/ send; /š/ shoe; /t/ toy; /u/ put; /uw/ do; /v/ eve; /w/ way; /y/ yes;

Surveillance," U.S. military satellite series first launched in 1961; used for detection of non-U.S. **ICBM** launchings. The satellites have been classified since late 1961, leaving the information on exact dates and number of launches unavailable.

midcourse correction /mîdkòrs kəékšən/ See **MCC**.

MILA /máylə/ *(ac.)* *n.c.* "Merritt Island Launch Area," location of Launch Complex 39 (see **KSC**).

mild detonating fuse /mâyld détəneytiŋ fyùwz/ *n.c.* Metal-sheathed explosive used to separate rocket stages.

minicon /mínikan/ *n.* Hypothetical lunar area where less than standard gravitational pull is evident. Cf. **mascon**.

Minimum Weight Tracking /mînəməm wêyt trǽkiŋ/ See **STADAN**.

Minitrack /míniytræk/ *(ac.)* *n.c.* "Minimum Weight Tracking." See **STADAN**.

mirror-image maneuver /mîrəimíj mənùwvə/ See **TPF**.

missile /mísəl/ *n.* Rocket, usually military in nature, which flies a predetermined suborbital flight path to a predetermined objective.

Missile Defense Alarm System /mîsəl diyfèns əlárm sìstəm/ See **MIDAS**.

Missile Detection and Surveillance /mîsəl diytêkšən ænd səvéyləns/ See **MIDAS**.

missile range /mísəl rèynj/ See **test range**.

mission /míšən/ *n.* 1. Space journey.
2. Objective of any space flight.

mission area /míšən èriyə/ *n.c.* One of four general types of spacecraft objectives: sounding, deep-space probe, manned flight, and earth satellite.

mission commentary /mîšən kámənteriy/ *n.c.* Transmissions between the Mission Control Center (**MCC**) and a spaceflight crew, usually interspersed with explanatory dialogue.

Mission Control Center /míšən kəntrówl sèntə/ See **MCC**.

mission profile /míšən prówfayl/ *n.c.* **Flight plan**.

mobile launcher /mówbəl lɔ́nčə/ *n.c.* Portable **launch pad** with **umbilical tower** located at Kennedy Space Center (**KSC**); on the mobile launcher, **Saturn** spacecraft **stacks** are constructed at the Vehicle Assembly Building (**VAB**), hauled to the **launch complex** by a **transporter**, and used as a launch pad. The base has an area of 18,000 sq. ft.; the tower stands 380 ft. high. The entire structure weights over 5,000 tons.

Mobile Quarantine Facility /mówbəl kwórəntiyn fəsìlətiy/ See **MQF**.

mobile service structure /mówbəl sə́vəs strə̀kčə/ See **MSS**.

mode /mówd/ *n.* Preplanned series of steps for the purpose of carrying out a task or coping with a situation.

modular equipment stowage assembly /mâjələ iykwîpmənt stówij əsèmbliy/ See **MESA**.

modular equipment transporter /mâjələ iykwîpmənt trænzpòrtə/ See **MET**.

module /mâjəl/ *n.* Self-contained space-craft unit which serves as a section of the overall structure, but also has the capacity to perform individually (see **CM**; **LM**; **SM**). Module and **capsule**, a term in use before Project **Apollo**, are often used interchangeably when referring to the manned portion of a craft.

MOI *(ac.)* *n.c.* "Mars orbit insertion," any maneuver which places a spacecraft in orbit around the planet Mars. It is used particularly with the U.S. **Viking** missions, during which a probe will descend to the planet's surface from orbit rather than attempting a landing directly from Earth-Mars trajectory.

MOL /mówl/ *(ac.)* *n.c.* "Manned Orbiting Laboratory," now defunct U.S. military program, a counterpart to **Skylab**. As proposed in 1963, a pressurized cylinder and a modified **Gemini** capsule were to be launched together. Once in orbit, the crew would enter the lab section (the cylinder) from the capsule. The entire program was canceled in 1969 for economic reasons.

Molniya /mólniya/ *n.* "Lightning," U.S.S.R. active-repeater comsat series; *Molniya 1,* launched in April 1965, was the first Soviet comsat. The Molniyas, 20 of which had been launched as of December 1971, make up the Soviet **Orbita** communications system. Launched into highly elliptical twelve-hour orbits, the satellites spend eight hours over the U.S.S.R. The spacecraft recharge over the North American continent saving downtime and providing the Soviet Union with maximum coverage.

monopropellant /mânowprəpélənt/ *n.* Premixed combination of fuel and **oxidizer**.

moon /múwn/ *n.* 1. Earth's only natural **satellite**; first extraterrestrial body to be reached by man (see **Apollo**). It is about one-fourth the size of Earth with a diameter of 2,160 miles. The mean distance from the earth is 233,000 miles. The moon circles the earth every 27 days; the same side always faces the Earth. Inhospitable to life as we know it, the moon has almost no atmosphere and surface temperatures range from −250°F. to +250°F. Gravity is

one-sixth that of Earth. Returned lunar samples show parts of the surface to be very similar to volcanic rock on Earth. It is hoped that further investigation of the specimens will uncover some of the mysteries of the moon, especially its origin.
2. Any planet's natural satellite.
3. *U.C.* see **Luna**.

moonglow /múwnglow/ *n.* Glow of the essentially unreflective lunar surface; scientists speculate its source to be the **solar wind**.

moonquake /múwnkweỳk/ *n.* Seismic disturbance on the moon; may indicate internal activity.

moonrock /múwnrak/ *n.* Lunar surface samples.

Moon Rover /múwn ròwvə/ See **Lunakhod**.

moonshot /múwnsat/ *n.* Any mission to the moon.

moon's sphere of influence /mûwnz sfîr əv ínfluwəns/ See **MSI**.

mother ship /mə́ðə šìp/ *n.c.* Principal or base craft of several manned vehicles working together in space. In **Apollo**, the **CSM** was the mother ship—in it the men went from and returned to Earth.

MQF *(ac.)* *n.c. Apollo.* "Mobile Quarantine Facility," **NASA**'s portable pressurized isolation trailer; shelter used to temporarily quarantine astronauts and lunar samples from *Apollo 11* and *12* from time of recovery to transfer into the Lunar Receiving Laboratory (**LRL**). The MQF was used to prevent cross contamination of lunar travelers and samples with terrestrial life.

MR *(ac.)* *n.c.* "Mercury Redstone." See **Mercury**; **Redstone**.

MRV *(ac.)* *n.c.* "Mars rover vehicle," proposed U.S. vehicle to be used for traveling short distances on Mars. Comparable to the **LRV** of lunar missions.

MSC *(ac.)* *n.c.* "Manned Spacecraft Center," **NASA** facility at Houston, Texas, responsible for technology of present and future manned craft, management of design and manufacture of spacecraft, selection and training of astronauts, ground control of

The mobile quarantine facility, used to isolate returning *Apollo 11* and *12* astronauts, contained bunks, chairs, tables, a lavatory, sink, and other items for the astronauts' comfort.

NASA

/z/ zero; /ž/ azure; /θ/ *th*in; /ð/ *th*en; /ŋ/ so*ng*; /æ/ bat; /ɔ/ law; /ə/ sun; /ə/ bird. Foreign symbols: [(n)] nasalization of some French vowels followed by /n/; [R] French uvular rolled /r/ sound; [ü] high front lip-rounded vowel; [x] Russian voiceless laryngeal fricative.

SE−41

manned flights from liftoff to recovery, and management of experiments conducted on manned flights. Major installations at MSC include Mission Control Center (MCC), **Space Environment Simulation Laboratory, Flight Acceleration Facility, Anechoic Chamber Test Facility,** and Lunar Receiving Laboratory (**LRL**).

MSFC (ac.) n.c. "Marshall Space Flight Center," **NASA** research facility, named for General George C. Marshall and located at Redstone Arsenal near Huntsville, Alabama. MSFC develops large rockets and numbers among its successes the **Saturn** launch vehicle.

MSFN /mísfin/ (ac.) n.c. "Manned Space Flight Network," **NASA** global tracking and communications system linking ground controllers and manned spacecraft; part of NASA Communications Network (**NASCOM**). MSFN stations are at Antigua Island; Ascension Island; Canton Island; Carnavon, Australia; Bermuda; Grand Bahama Island; Grand Canary Island; Grand Turk Island; Tananarive, Malagasy; Kano, Nigeria; Pretoria, South Africa; and in the United States, at Point Arguello, California; Eglin and Kennedy Space Center, Florida; Kauai, Hawaii; White Sands, New Mexico; and Corpus Christi, Texas. Three ships, the *Rose Knot, Coastal Sentry,* and *Range Tracker,* are also used as part of MSFN. For Project **Apollo** additional ships and airplanes were used (see **ARIA**).

MSI (ac.) n.c. "Moon's sphere of influence," region, beginning about 30,000 miles from the moon, where a spacecraft is under the force of **gravity** of the moon rather than that of the Earth. In this region, the position of a spacecraft is given with regard to the moon instead of Earth.

MSOB (ac.) n.c. Apollo. "Manned Spaceflight Operations Building," installation at **NASA**'s Kennedy Space Center (**KSC**) where **Apollo** spacecraft are tested prior to being mated to launch vehicles (see **VAB**).

MSS (ac.) n.c. "Mobile service structure," gigantic movable **service tower** used in conjunction with the **mobile launcher** for **Saturn** launchings at Kennedy Space Center (**KSC**). The tower has five maintenance platforms which surround the space vehicle until about seven hours before launch when the tower is moved away.

M storm /ém stòrm/ n.c. Magnetic storm produced in the earth's **magnetosphere** by disturbances on the sun.

multidisciplinary research facility /mə̀ltiydîsəplə̀neriy ríysə̀č fəsìlətiy/ n.c. **Space base.**

multi-engine-out-capability /mòltiy énĵən àwt keypəbîlətiy/ n.c. Ability of the **Saturn** launch vehicle to maintain flight even if one or more of its five first-stage engines malfunctions after the first ten seconds of flight.

multi-impulse orbit /môltiyímpəls orbət/ n.c. Multiburn lunar orbit necessary for **touchdown** in regions away from the moon's equator.

Multiple Docking Adapter /môltipəl dákiŋ ədǽptə/ See **MDA**.

NASA

The 415-foot mobile service structure, *left*, facilitates preparation of Saturn launch vehicles. When in position, it surrounds the 365-foot Saturn, thereby providing access to the rocket for prelaunch service. The tower can be moved to and from the launch site by crawler transporter.

NACA /nǽkə/ (ac.) n.c. "National Advisory Committee for Aeronautics," organization formed in 1915; its structure and facilities were absorbed into **NASA** upon that agency's creation in 1958.

narrow angle target of opportunity /nérow ǽŋgəl târgət əv apə̀túwnətiy/ See **NATO**.

NASA /nǽsə/ (ac.) n.c. "National Aeronautics and Space Administration," U.S. government agency formed October 1, 1958; responsible for all U.S. civilian aerospace activities and for international civilian cooperation in space. Four departments reflect NASA's areas of interest: Office of Manned Space Flight (**OMSF**), Office of Space Science and Applications (**OSSA**), Office of Advanced Research and Technology (**OART**), and Office of Tracking and Data Acquisition (**OTDA**). NASA, headquartered in Washington, D. C., spends some five billion dollars a year and employs from about 30,000 to 150,000 people depending on its schedule and programs.

NASA Communications Network /nǽsə kəmyuwnəkéyšənz nètwək/ See **NASCOM**.

NASCOM /nǽskam/ (ac.) n.c. "NASA Communications Network," organization which provides global linkage of all **NASA** ground stations with each other in order to provide nearly instantaneous contact between ground controllers and spacecraft. Controlled from Goddard Space Flight Center (**GSFC**), NASCOM is organized into several specialized networks: Satellite Tracking and Data Acquisition Network (**STADAN**), Manned Space Flight Network (**MSFN**). and Deep Space Network (**DSN**). **SCAMA** is the voice division of NASCOM.

National Advisory Committee for Aeronautics /nǽšənəl ədváyzə̀iy kəmìtiy for erənɔ́tiks/ See **NACA**.

/a/ *father;* /aw/ *wow;* /ay/ *buy;* /b/ *boy;* /č/ wit*ch;* /d/ *doll;* /e/ *bet;* /ey/ *say;* /f/ *few;* /g/ *bag;* /h/ *hole;* /i/ *it;* /iy/ *be;* /ĵ/ *gin;* /k/ *cat;* /l/ *lamb;*
/m/ *man;* /n/ *now;* /o/ *orbit;* /ow/ *tow;* /oy/ *boy;* /p/ *pat;* /r/ *run;* /s/ *send;* /š/ *shoe;* /t/ *toy;* /u/ *put;* /uw/ *do;* /v/ *eve;* /w/ *way;* /y/ *yes;*

National Aeronautics and Space Administration /næšənəl erənὁtiks ænd spéys ədminəstrèyšən/ See **NASA**.

National Aeronautics and Space Council /næšənəl ərənὁtiks ænd spéys kàwnsəl/ *n.c.* U.S. advisory body which assists the president on all national aerospace matters. The vice-president serves as chairman. Headquarters of the council are located in Washington, D.C.

National Center of Space Studies /næšənəl sèntɚ əv spéys stὲdiyz/ See **CNES**.

National Environmental Satellite Service /næšənəl envayənmêntəl sǽtəlayt sὸvəs/ See **NESS**.

National Investigations Committee on Aerial Phenomena /næšənəl investəgéyšənz kəmὶtiy an êriyəl fənámənə/ See **NICAP**.

National Oceanic and Atmospheric Administration /næšənəl owšiyǽnik ænd ætməsfírik ædminəstrèyšən/ See **NOAA**.

NATO /néytow/ *(ac.) n.c.*1. "North Atlantic Treaty Organization," alliance formed by various Western nations in 1948 for the purpose of mutual defense. The member states are Belgium, Canada, Denmark, Federal Republic of Germany, France, Great Britain, Greece, Iceland, Italy, Luxembourg, Netherlands, Norway, Portugal, Turkey, and the U.S. In the field of space, Nato's program is confined to communications satellites. Its first comsat, *NATO SAT 1* (see **NATO SAT**), was launched March 20, 1970, from Kennedy Space Center (**KSC**).

Original plans for a NATO-sponsored satellite communications system were approved by the organization's Working Group in 1963. The U.S., in 1966, offered its assistance with technical and monetary aid. NATO is currently involved in cooperative programs with **ELDO** and **ESRO** as well as the U.S. Tactical Satellite Communications (**TacSatCom**) is a joint NATO/U.S. project begun in 1967. Future NATO plans for satellite activity were not available at the end of 1971.

2. *Apollo.* "Narrow angle target of opportunity," zoom-in camera close-up.

NATO SAT /néytow sǽt/ *(ac.) n.c.* "NATO Satellite," North Atlantic Treaty Organization (**NATO**) comsat series consisting of two craft orbited in 1970 and 1971. *NATO SAT 1* was launched March 20, 1970 from Kennedy Space Center (**KSC**). The spacecraft is in geostationary orbit, positioned over the eastern Atlantic Ocean. It links NATO's national capitals and command stations on both sides of the ocean. *NATO SAT 2*, NATO's second and only other satellite, was launched February 2, 1971. Its basic function is to serve as a back-up should the first satellite fail. NATO's communications system is equipped to handle one satellite only.

NATO Satellite /néytow sǽtəlayt/ See **NATO SAT**.

nautical mile /nὁtikəl máyl/ See **NM**.

navigation /nævəgéyšən/ *n.* Determination of the position and velocity of a space vehicle.

navigation base /nævəgéyšən bèys/ See **NB**.

Navigation Satellite /nævəgéyšən sǽtəlayt/ 1. See **NavSat**.

2. *l.c.* See **NavSat**.

NavSat /nǽvsæt/ *(ac.) n.c.*1. "Navigation Satellite," name used for satellites in the U.S. **Transit** series since 1963.

2. *l.c.* "Navigation satellite," Earth-orbiting spacecraft designed to provide all-weather location determination for surface vehicles. U.S. navsats operate by sending two types of signals—one which provides orbital-path data and one producing a **Doppler effect**. *Transit 1-B* (see **Transit**), launched by the U.S. in 1960, was the first navsat.

NB *(ac.) n.c.* "Navigation base," platform which supports the inertial measuring unit (**IMU**) and the sextant and telescope used on space flights; part of the **guidance system** (see **GNCS**; **PGNS**).

NDS *(ac.) n.c.* "Nuclear Detection Satellite." See **Vela**.

near-earth orbit /nîr ɔ̀θ ὁrbət/ See **NEO**.

near-earth orbit-space /nîr ɔ̀θ ὁrbət spèys/ See **NEO**.

near encounter /nîr enkáwntɚ/ *n.* Flyby between 6,000 and 2,000 miles from the surface of a celestial body; flybys at higher altitudes are referred to as *encounters*.

nebula /nébyulə/ *n.* Huge cloud of celestial matter outside the solar system.

negative G /nêgətiv jíy/ *n.c.* Gravitational pull experienced during descent; also referred to as **eyeballs up.**

negative pressure /nêgətiv préšɚ/ *n.c.* Pressure within an object that is lower than pressure on the outside.

NEO *(ac.) n.c.* "Near-earth orbit," any flight path around Earth whose **apogee** and **perigee** fall within the area between 100 and 22,000 miles from Earth. This region is *near-earth orbit-space (NEO-space)*. **Synchronous** satellites occupy a place at the outer edge of NEO-space.

NEO-space /ên iy ów spèys/ See **NEO**.

Neptune /néptuwn/ *n.* 1. Fourth largest planet in the solar system and the eighth planet from the sun. The diameter of Neptune is 31,200 miles and its orbit lies at a mean distance of 2,793 million miles from the sun. Neptune is scheduled for investigation by a probe from the **Outer Planets Missions.**

2. Roman god of the sea.

NERVA /nɚvə/ *(ac.) n.c.* "Nuclear Engine for Rocket Vehicle Application," U.S. project for a nuclear-powered rocket engine, canceled in 1972. A smaller unit in the 15,000–20,000 lb. thrust range will be developed instead. NERVA would have developed 75,000 lbs. of thrust.

NESS /nés/ *(ac.) n.c.* "National Environmental Satellite Service," branch of the National Oceanic and Atmospheric Administration (**NOAA**) which operates environmental satellite systems and gathers and analyzes their data. Provisions have been made for NESS to expand to handle such satellites as the Earth Resources Technology Satellite (**ERTS**).

NETHERLANDS, THE

The first Dutch space project, Astronomical Netherlands Satellite (**ANS**), was ap-

proved in December 1969 as a joint effort with NASA. The satellite, the Netherland's first, is scheduled for launch in 1974. A U.S. **Scout** rocket will be employed; the launch site will be the Air Force Western Test Range (**AFWTR**).

The Netherlands is also involved in cooperative programs with **ELDO**, **ESRO**, and **CNES**. The space program of the Netherlands is administered by the Ministries of Economic Affairs, and Education and Sciences.

neutral point /nûwtrəl poynt/ *n.c.* Point in space between two neighboring celestial bodies where the gravitational attraction of one is equal to that of the other. Also called *gravipause*.

Neutral Point Explorer /nûwtrəl póynt eksplὸrɚ/ See **Explorer**.

NICAP /náykæp/ *(ac.) n.c.* "National Investigations Committee on Aerial Phenomena," a nonprofit corporation based in Washington, D.C., formed in 1956 for the purpose of investigating **UFOs**. It has maintained that some UFO reports cannot be explained away as natural phenomena, and that the only reasonable explanation for UFOs is that they are spacecraft under the control of beings of superior technology. NICAP has recently instituted the Automated Clearinghouse for Collection and Exchange of Sighting Statistics (**ACCESS**) to store data on all available sightings of UFO's in a computer and has made that information available to the public.

Nimbus /nímbəs/ *n.* Advanced U.S. experimental meteorological satellite series, based on the **TIROS** project. At the end of 1971, four Nimbus satellites had been orbited, each moving in sun-synchronous orbit with its instruments always facing Earth. Two additional missions are planned to complete the series.

Nimbus 1, launched in August 1964, introduced use of the advanced vidicon camera system (**AVCS**) to increase photographic resolution of cloud pictures; the satellite also was the first to be able to take pictures on the dark side of the earth. *Nimbus 3*, launched in April 1969, was the first satellite to measure the earth's heat balance globally and the first weather sat-

The *Nimbus* satellite is positioned so that its instruments always face the earth.

RCA

/z/ zero; /ž/ azure; /θ/ *th*in; /ð/ *th*en; /ŋ/ so*ng*; /æ/ *ba*t; /ɔ/ *la*w; /ə/ *su*n; /ɚ/ *bi*rd. Foreign symbols: [(n)] nasalization of some French vowels followed by /n/; [R] French uvular rolled /r/ sound; [ü] high front lip-rounded vowel; [x] Russian voiceless laryngeal fricative.

SE–43

ellite with two nuclear power sources; it also carried apparatus for receiving and relaying signals from small radio transmitters on bouys, balloons, and migratory animals.

nitrogen /náytrəJən/ *n.* Gas which makes up 70 percent of the earth's atmosphere.

NM *(ac.) n.c.* "Nautical mile," distance measurement unit used in space; 1.15 statute miles.

NOAA /nówə/ *(ac.) n.c.* **1.** "National Oceanic and Atmospheric Administration." U.S. Department of Commerce agency, created October 3, 1970, replacing the Environmental Science Services Administration (**ESSA**) and several other groups. Its prime concern is scientific study of the atmosphere, land masses, oceans, and the sun.

2. Operational meteorological satellite, the second Improved TIROS Operational System (**ITOS**) satellite and the most sophisticated U.S. weather satellite at the beginning of 1972. Launched in December 1970 into sun-synchronous orbit, *NOAA-1* scans the entire globe twice daily. It can also be shut down in orbit for use as a standby for *ITOS-1*.

nodal crossing /nôwdəl krɔ́siŋ/ *n.c.* Point of intersection of two orbits. See **node**.

node /nówd/ *n.* Either of two points where the orbital plane of a satellite intersects the orbital plane of its central body.

no-go /nów gòw/ *attr.* **1.** Of or pertaining to a condition when things are not functioning properly.
2. *n.c.* A condition in which things are not functioning properly.

noise /noyz/ *n. sl.* Radio or radar static.

no joy /nôw Jóy/ *phr. attr. sl.* Without success.

nominal /námənəl/ *attr.* Of or pertaining to anything that is within a preset range of norms.

nominal descent trajectory /nâmənəl diysént trəJèktəriy/ *n.c. Apollo.* LM flight path during powered descent initiation (**PDI**), beginning at the pericynthion of the descent orbit (see **DOI**).

nonfree return trajectory /nânfriy riytər̃n trəJèktə̀iy/ *n.c.* Flight path back to Earth from another celestial body which requires one or more rocket **burns** to assure that the craft will reach Earth. Cf. **free return trajectory; hybrid trajectory.**

North Atlantic Treaty Organization /nôrθ ətlǽntik tríytiy orgənəzèyšən/ See **NATO.**

North Atlantic Treaty Organization Satellite /nórθ ətlǽntik tríytiy ɔrgənəzèyšən sǽtəlayt/ See **NATO Sat.**

northern lights /nɔ́rðərn láyts/ See **aurora.**

nose cone /nówz kòwn/ *n.c.* Aerodynamically pointed tip of a rocket in which a **payload** can be carried.

nova /nówvə/ *n.* Star which exhibits a brief (days, weeks, or months), dramatic increase in brightness and then returns to its original luminosity. The phenomenon, which may temporarily increase the brightness of a star 100,000 times, is evidently caused by the rapid expansion of the outer layers of the star's atmosphere and is not accompanied by an increase in the star's surface temperature. It is conjectured that the nova period is a normal stage in the evolution of a variable star.

nozzle /názəl/ *n.* Gimbal-mounted, flared end of a rocket exhaust system.

Nuclear Detection Satellite /nûwkliyər diytékšən sǽtəlayt/ See **Vela.**

Nuclear Engine for Rocket Vehicle Application /nûwkliyər énJən for rákət vìyhikəl æpləkèyšən/ See **NERVA.**

nuclear pulse jet /nûwkliyər pôls jét/ *n.c.* Proposed small nuclear device which would be detonated to provide thrust for spacecraft on interplanetary flights.

O–P

OAMS /ówmz/ *(ac.) n.c. Gemini.* "Orbit attitude and maneuvering system," spacecraft equipment complex which provided and controlled the craft's rocket power for all major maneuvers. It combined various functions of the launch escape system (**LES**), reaction control system (**RCS**), stabilization and control system (**SCS**), and service propulsion system (**SPS**).

OAO *(ac.) n.c.* "Orbiting Astronomical Observatory," U.S. astronomical satellite series, so far consisting of two craft, launched in 1966 and 1968. OAO is designed to gather data by locking instruments on specific stars upon command. Its relatively few experiments operate on solar power. *OAO 2*, launched in December 1968, discovered a huge hydrogen cloud around the comet Tago-Sato-Kosaka and also investigated the twin star group Beta Lyrae.

OART *(ac.) n.c.* "Office of Advanced Research and Technology," NASA department which handles technological research for future space flights. Its facilities include **Ames Research Center, Flight Research Center, Langley Research Center, Lewis Research Center,** and **Electronics Research Center.**

occultation /akəltéyšən/ *n.* Passage of a smaller body, such as a satellite, behind a larger one, such as the moon or other celestial body.

Odyssey /ádəsiy/ *n.* **1.** Name of *Apollo 13* CM (see **Apollo**).

2. Homer's poem in which the hero Odysseus spends ten years trying to reach his home on Ithaca; hence, "a long journey filled with vicissitudes."

Office of Advanced Research and Technology /ɔ́fəs əv ədvǽnst rîysər̃č ænd teknálǝJiy/ See **OART.**

Office of Manned Space Flight /ɔ́fəs əv mǽnd spéys flàyt/ See **OMSF.**

Office of Space Science and Applications /ɔ́fəs əv spéys sàyəns ænd æpləkéyšənz/ See **OSSA.**

Office of Tracking and Data Acquisition /ɔ́fəs əv trǽkiŋ ænd déytə ækwəzìšən/ See **OTDA.**

OFO /ówfow/ *(ac.) n.c.* "Orbiting Frog Otolith," U.S. biological satellite launched in November 1970 to study the effects of weightlessness on the balance mechanism of the inner ear, of which the otolith is a part. Bullfrogs, which have inner ears that are structurally similar to those of man, were used as experimental animals. Two frogs were orbited for seven days. Preliminary data indicated that adaptability to prolonged weightlessness is possible.

ogive /ówJayv/ *n.* **Nose cone.**

OGO /ówgow/ *(ac.) n.c.* "Orbiting Geophysical Observatory," U.S. geophysical satellite series consisting of six spacecraft launched between 1964 and 1969. Each was equipped with 20 or more experimental packages for the simultaneous monitoring of phenomena both in and outside the earth's atmosphere. Alternating OGO's had widely differing orbits.

OGO 1, launched in September 1964; *OGO 3*, launched in June 1966; and *OGO 5*, launched in March 1968 were each given the designation *EGO* for *Eccentric Geophysical Observatory*. They were able to study the **Van Allen Radiation Belts,** solar phenomena, and aspects of particle and electromagnetic radiation.

OGO 2, launched in October 1965; *OGO 4*, launched in July 1967; and *OGO 6*, launched in June 1969 were each called *POGO* for *Polar Orbiting Geophysical Observatory*. They studied the effects of variations in solar activity on the earth's atmosphere.

omnidirectional antenna /àmniydəˈk-šənəl ænténə/ *n.c.* Spacecraft antenna which is capable of vertical movement only.

OMSF *(ac.) n.c.* "Office of Manned Space Flight," NASA department concerned with research and development of all vehicles and technology required for manned space travel. Its facilities include Marshall Space Flight Center (**MSFC**), the Manned Spacecraft Center (**MSC**), and Kennedy Space Center (**KSC**).

on-board guidance computer /ânbòrd gáydəns kəmpyúwtər/ *n.c.* Compact spacecraft computer for directional calculations.

on-board stored data /ânbòrd stɔ́rd déytə/ *n.c.* Information recorded on a spaceflight and held for future transmission to Earth.

open ended mission /ówpən êndəd míšən/ *n.c.* Spaceflight designed to continue as long as equipment functions or until all goals are met.

open loop /ówpən lúwp/ *n.c.* Control system which has no provisions for self-correction. Cf. **closed loop.**

opposition /apəzíšən/ *n.* Situation in which Earth is between one of the **superior planets** and the Sun.

OPS /áps/ *(ac.) n.c. Apollo.* "Oxygen purge system," thirty-minute emergency oxygen supply for **EVA** in case of portable life support system (**PLSS**) failure. Shoe-box sized, the 40-lb. package is generally mounted on top of the PLSS. See also **BSLSS.**

optical navigation /âptikəl nævəgéyšən/ *n.c.* Guidance based on visual sighting rather than mathematical or mechanical means.

optical subsystem /âptikəl sə́bsistəm/ *n.c. Apollo.* That part of the guidance, navigation, and control system (**GNCS**) which uses spatial landmarks to determine the spacecraft's location.

orbit /órbət/ **1.** *n.* Closed loop path, beginning and ending at a fixed point, which is followed by a gravitationally held body

---

/a/ *father;* /aw/ *wow;* /ay/ *buy;* /b/ *boy;* /č/ *witch;* /d/ *doll;* /e/ *bet;* /ey/ *say;* /f/ *few;* /g/ *bag;* /h/ *hole;* /i/ *it;* /iy/ *be;* /J/ *gin;* /k/ *cat;* /l/ *lamb;*
/m/ *man;* /n/ *now;* /o/ *orbit;* /ow/ *tow;* /oy/ *boy;* /p/ *pat;* /r/ *run;* /s/ *send;* /š/ *shoe;* /t/ *toy;* /u/ *put;* /uw/ *do;* /v/ *eve;* /w/ *way;* /y/ *yes;*

around a body which is the source of the gravity. Usually elliptical rather than circular in shape, orbits are described in terms of **orbital period, inclination, perigee,** and **apogee.** Different types of orbits include **eccentric, geostationary, polar, sun-synchronous,** and **synchronous.**

2. *v. tr.* To place an object into a closed loop path.

3. *v. tr.* To follow a closed loop path around a **central body.**

Orbita [*Rus.* órbita] *n.* "Orbiter," U.S.S.R. communications network based on the **Molniya** comsat series. First operational in November 1967, the system now has increased to include other Communist bloc countries.

orbital confirmation /ôrbətəl kanfəméyšən/ *n.c.* Mathematical proof of a spacecraft's orbital stability based on computer- and tracking-data analysis.

orbital curve /ôrbətəl kə́əv/ *n.c.* Satellite's track across the surface of its **central body.**

orbital period /ôrbətəl píriyəd/ *n.c.* Duration of one full orbit.

orbital plane /ôrbətəl pléyn/ *n.c.* Imaginary flat circle whose edges are formed by an **orbit**; bisects the **central body.**

orbital velocity /ôrbətəl vəlásətiy/ *n.c.* Speed required to keep a spacecraft in orbit.

Orbital Workshop /ôrbətəl wə́əkšap/ See **OWS.**

orbit attitude and maneuvering system /ôrbət ǽtətuwd ænd mənúwvəiŋ sìstəm/ See **OAMS.**

Orbiter /ôrbətə/ See **Orbita.**

Orbiting Astronomical Observatory /ôrbətiŋ æstrənâmikəl əbzə́vətôriy/ See **OAO.**

Orbiting Frog Otolith /ôrbətiŋ fróg àtəliθ/ See **OFO.**

Orbiting Geophysical Observatory /ôrbətiŋ jiyowfîzikəl əbzə́vətôriy/ See **OGO.**

Orbiting Satellite Carrying Amateur Radio /ôrbətiŋ sǽtəlayt kêriyiŋ ǽməčə réydiyow/ See **OSCAR.**

Orbiting Solar Observatory /ôrbətiŋ sôwlə əbzə́vətôriy/ See **OSO.**

orbit node /ôrbət nòwd/ *n.c.* Point at which an orbiting body crosses some point of reference.

ordnance device /órdnəns divàys/ *n.c.* Any of several explosive units used in a spacecraft to separate or discharge coverings, etc.

ordnance tower /órdnəns tàwə/ *n.c.* Safety-insured isolated structure where **ordnance devices** are installed in a rocket and checked.

Orion /oráyən/ *n.* 1. Name of *Apollo 16* LM (see **Apollo**).

2. Constellation in our **galaxy.**

3. Greek hunter loved by Diana. She unwittingly killed him and then set him in the heavens as a constellation.

OSCAR /áskə/ *(ac.) n.c.* "Orbiting Satellite Carrying Amateur Radio," international comsats; six craft launched between 1961 and 1970. Developed by amateurs for amateur radio testing, OSCAR's are launched by the U.S. as hitchhikers on major missions. Australian students were responsible for *OSCAR* 5, launched in January 1970.

OSCPCS *(ac.) n.c. Apollo.* "Oxygen supply and cabin pressure control subsystem," that part of the LM environmental control system (**ECS**) which maintains oxygen pressure in the crew compartment and pressure suits.

Oshumi [*Jap.* ošúmi] *n.* First Japanese satellite, also called *Rising Sun Satellite 1,* was launched February 11, 1970 by a Lambda 4-S launch vehicle. Oshumi was equipped with a radio transmitter for tracking purposes, but no other scientific equipment was aboard.

OSO /ówsow/ *(ac.) n.c.* "Orbiting Solar Observatory," U.S. astronomical satellite series used to investigate the sun. Seven OSO's were launched between 1962 and 1971. Solar cells power the craft after launch. The cells are mounted, along with various other instruments, on an upright projection which always faces the sun. The satellite is stabilized by its base, a spinning drum. *OSO* 7, launched in September 1971, is an advanced version of the earlier models; additional improved OSO models are being planned.

OSSA /ásə/ *(ac.) n.c.* "Office of Space Science and Applications," **NASA** department concerned with the scientific investigation of space and with the practical application of space technology to everyday life. Its facilities include Goddard Space Flight Center (**GSFC**), Jet Propulsion Laboratory (**JPL**), and **Wallops Station.**

OTDA *(ac.) n.c.* "Office of Tracking and Data Acquisition," **NASA** department responsible for development and management of world-wide spacecraft tracking networks and equipment; department which operates NASA Communications Network (**NASCOM**). OTDA's central offices are at NASA headquarters in Washington, D. C., where data is processed. Cf. **DSN; MSFN; STADAN.**

otolith /átəliθ/ *n.* Sensitive section of the inner ear partially responsible for man's balance and orientation. Space authorities fear it may be disturbed by establishment of artificial gravity for long periods in space. See **OFO.**

outer planets /âwtə plǽnəts/ *n.c.* Jupiter, Saturn, Uranus, Neptune, Pluto. The first four of these planets are the largest in the solar system and sometimes called the *giant planets.*

Outer Planets Mission /âwtə plǽnets mìsən/ *n.c.* Any of several U.S. interplanetary fly-by missions proposed for the late 1970s. Each would inject a spacecraft into a trajectory past three of the solar system's outer planets for information gathering purposes.

The missions would be confined to launch windows in which the gravitational fields of the planets could help pull the craft along their trajectories. Jupiter-Saturn-Pluto launches are possible in 1976 and 1977, and Jupiter-Uranus-Neptune launches, in 1979. A four-planet mission called **Grand Tour** had been projected for 1977–1979, but was canceled in 1972.

Missions would use Thermoelectric Outer Planets Spacecraft (**TOPS**), specially designed for long-life reliability. Missions to Jupiter, Saturn, and Pluto could take eight and one-half years; missions to Jupiter, Uranus, and Neptune, nine years.

outer space /âwtə spéys/ *n.c.* **Space.**

outgas /áwtgæs/ *v. intr.* To produce gas in a vacuum.

out mission /áwt mìsən/ *n.c. sl.* Space journey along a **heliocentric** orbit which lies wholly outside Earth's orbit of the sun.

Orbiting solar observatories have been circling the earth since 1962. More advanced models may contain a telescope, a spectrometer, an x-ray monitor, and a gamma-ray detector. These instruments can be aimed with great precision at any spot on the sun's surface.

NASA

/z/ zero; /ž/ azure; /θ/ *th*in; /ð/ *th*en; /ŋ/ so*ng*; /æ/ bat; /ɔ/ *la*w; /ə/ s*u*n; /ə/ b*i*rd. Foreign symbols: [(n)] nasalization of some French vowels followed by /n/; [R] French uvular rolled /r/ sound; [ü] high front lip-rounded vowel; [x] Russian voiceless laryngeal fricative.

overburn /ówvəbən/ *n*. Firing of a rocket engine beyond established cut-off point; results in a velocity increase and incorrect position.

OWS *(ac.) n.c.* **1.** "Orbital Workshop," largest of the four components of the proposed U.S. **Skylab** space station; living quarters and laboratory for Skylab's three-man crew. The OWS will be fitted out on Earth within an empty *Saturn 4B* (see **Saturn**). The rocket's 10,000 cubic foot liquid hydrogen fuel tank will be divided into two floors. One will be crew quarters, featuring a sealed wardroom with a window on Earth, a sealed waste compartment, a sleep compartment, and a work area; the other floor will be a laboratory whose major experiments will be of a medical nature. The rocket's smaller liquid oxygen tank will serve as a waste receptacle.

Like the *Saturn 4B* from which it is made, the OWS will be located just over the second stage of the *Saturn 5* at launch. Once in orbit, the OWS will be pressurized with a two-gas atmosphere (nitrogen and oxygen) kept at a temperature of 60° to 90° F. A meteoroid shield will stand out about five inches from the sides of the OWS and two huge solar panels will deploy to provide, along with those of the Apollo Telescope Mount (**ATM**), power for the whole space station.

2. Early name for the **Skylab** Program.

oxidizer /áksədayzə/ *n*. Substance in a rocket propellant which provides the oxygen required for efficient combustion.

oxygen /áksijən/ *n*. Gas which constitutes approximately 20 percent of the earth's atmosphere.

oxygen purge system /áksijən pə́j sìstəm/ See **OPS**.

oxygen subsystem /âksijən sə́bsistəm/ *n.c. Apollo*. That part of the environmental control system (**ECS**) which controls the flow and pressure of oxygen in crew compartment and space suits. Oxygen reserves are also maintained by this subsystem.

oxygen supply and cabin pressure control subsystem /áksijən səplày ənd kǽbin prèšə kəntrôwl sə́bsistəm/ See **OSCPCS**.

Ozma, Project /ázmə prâjekt/ *n.c.* The first human effort to receive communications from other civilizations in space. The experiment consisted in aiming the 85-foot **dish reflector** of the radio telescope at the National Radio Astronomy Observatory, Green Bank, West Virginia, at the stars Tau Ceti and Epsilon Eridani for 150 hours in May, June, and July 1960. The theory had been advanced by several scientists that other intelligent beings in the universe might be seeking to communicate by broadcasting radio signals. The two stars selected were chosen for relative nearness to our solar system, comparative lack of radio interference in their portion of the sky, and similarity to our own sun. No unusual signals were detected. See also **Cyclops, Project**.

ozone /ówzown/ *n*. **Oxygen** which contains three oxygen atoms per molecule; pure oxygen contains only two.

ozone layer /ówzown lèyə/ *n.c.* **Ozonosphere**.

ozonosphere /owzánəsfir/ *n*. Layer of

The methods used to recover *Apollo 11* astronauts after splashdown established procedural precedents for subsequent Apollo missions. The pararescueman shown here is sealing the *Apollo 11* hatch while the three astronauts await helicopter pickup.

NASA

/a/ *father*; /aw/ *wow*; /ay/ *buy*; /b/ *boy*; /č/ *witch*; /d/ *doll*; /e/ *bet*; /ey/ *say*; /f/ *few*; /g/ *bag*; /h/ *hole*; /i/ *it*; /iy/ *be*; /j/ *gin*; /k/ *cat*; /l/ *lamb*; /m/ *man*; /n/ *now*; /o/ *orbit*; /ow/ *tow*; /oy/ *boy*; /p/ *pat*; /r/ *run*; /s/ *send*; /š/ *shoe*; /t/ *toy*; /u/ *put*; /uw/ *do*; /v/ *eve*; /w/ *way*; /y/ *yes*;

SE – 46

Earth's **atmosphere** approximately 20 miles above sea level which serves to absorb solar **ultraviolet rays.** Oxygen in this layer is converted into **ozone** by this absorption.

Pacific Missile Range /pəsîfik mísəl rèynǰ/ See **AFWTR.**

pad /pǽd/ *n.* **Launch pad.**

pad abort /pǽd əbòrt/ *n.c.* Cancellation of a mission just before or during **liftoff.**

pad chief /pǽd čìyf/ *n.c.* Coordinator of **launch pad** activities.

pad deluge /pǽd dèlyuwǰ/ *n.c.* Pre- and post-launch dousing of launch pad area with water; counter-measure to the intense heat created by liftoff. As many as 350,000 gallons may be used during an **Apollo** launch.

paddlewheel satellite /pǽdlhwiyl sǽtələyt/ *n.c. sl.* Satellite equipped with extendible **solar panels.**

PAGEOS /péyǰiyows/ *(ac.) n.c.* "Passive Geodetic Earth Orbiting Satellite," a 100-ft. metallic balloon launched into polar orbit by the U.S. in June 1966. The shiny surface of PAGEOS served as a light source which was photographed against the stars. The resulting pictures were used in determining the exact locations of points on Earth.

pallet /pǽlət/ See **RAM.**

PAO *(ac.) n.c.* "Public Affairs Officer," NASA press official responsible for information flow to news media and other interested parties.

parachute /pérəšuwts/ See **drogue; main parachute; pilot parachute.**

parallel redundancy /pêrəlel riydéndənsiy/ *n.c.* Action of two systems or devices working simultaneously to achieve a single desired goal which either one could actually achieve alone.

parameter /pərǽmətər/ *n.* Given constant or norm.

pararescueman /pêrəréskyuwmæn/ *n.* Frogman who jumps from a rescue helicopter into the ocean after a spacecraft **splashdown** to assist in recovery of the spacecraft and crew.

parking orbit /párkiŋ òrbət/ *n.c.* Temporary orbit which serves as a preliminary to another maneuver in a mission. See **EPO; LPO.**

parsec /parsék/ *n.* Unit of measure equal to 3.26 **light years** or about 19 trillion miles. It is the distance of a star whose parallax is one second of arc.

passive communications satellite /pǽsiv kəmyuwnəkéyšənz sǽtələyt/ *n.c.* Uninstrumented **comsat** which operates by simply reflecting signals transmitted to it. Cf. **active communications satellite.**

passive environmental control /pǽsiv envayənmêntəl kəntrówl/ *n.c.* Thermal regulation in spacecraft based strictly on insulation.

Passive Geodetic Earth Orbiting Satellite /pǽsiv ǰiyədêtik ə̂θ òrbətiŋ sǽtələyt/ See **PAGEOS.**

passive satellite /pǽsiv sǽtələyt/ *n.c.* Earth-orbiting craft without any instrumentation. See **Echo; PAGEOS.**

passive seismic experiment /pǽsiv sâyzmik ekspérəmənt/ See **PSE.**

passive tension tie /pǽsiv ténšən tày/ *n.c. Apollo.* **CM docking system** component used to connect the boost protective cover (**BPC**) and the **probe assembly;** the tie is released in normal flight to permit later docking. During **abort,** the **docking ring** is released and the whole probe assembly is removed when the BPC comes off to permit parachute deployment.

passive thermal control /pǽsiv θə̂məl kəntrówl/ See **PTC.**

payload /péylowd/ *n.* Spacecraft's essential cargo; does not include what is needed for propulsion.

PDI *(ac.) n.c. Apollo.* "Powered descent initiation," twelve-minute, three-phase LM landing maneuver beginning at an altitude of 50,000 ft. above the moon's surface and culminating in lunar touchdown. Phase I consists of firing the descent engine (**DE**) to reduce the 3,600 m.p.h. forward speed to a 2 m.p.h. vertical descent rate. The LM is turned face up as instruments check the distance to the moon and maintain attitude control. Phase II, also called *high gate,* begins vertical descent from 7,600 ft. Visual contact with the lunar surface is restored and a go/no go decision is made regarding landing site. Phase III, also called *low gate,* stops all descent speed at 500 ft. and brings the LM to touchdown at 2 m.p.h.

Pegasus /pégəsəs/ *n.* 1. U.S. geophysical satellite series consisting of three craft launched in 1965. The satellites investigated meteorite activity in NEO-space (see **NEO**), using 96-ft. panels that recorded micrometeoroid penetration. Information obtained was used in designing future spacecraft. Each Pegasus was a modified upper stage of a *Saturn 1* (see **Saturn**) and was orbited as a byproduct of a Saturn 1 test.

2. In Greek mythology, a winged horse created from the blood of Medusa.

penumbra /penə́mbrə/ *n.* Twilight part of a shadow; often along a **terminator.** Cf. **umbra.**

Péole [*Fr.* peól] *n.* French geodetic research satellite launched December 1970 from the **Guiana Space Center** by a *Diamant B* (see **Diamant**) launch vehicle. The satellite's primary mission was geodetic. The launch also served as a dry run for the **Eole** launch which followed in 1971.

pericynthion /pèrisínθiyən/ *n.* Point in a lunar orbit where an orbiting body launched from another celestial body is closest to the moon. Cf. **apocynthion.**

perigee /pérəǰiy/ *n.* Point in an Earth orbit where the orbiting body is closest to Earth.

perihelion /pèrihíyliyən/ *n.* Point in a **heliocentric** orbit where an orbiting body is closest to the sun.

perilune /pérəluwn/ *n.* Point in a lunar orbit where an orbiting body launched from the moon is closest to it.

period /píriyəd/ *n.* Duration of one complete orbit.

personal preference kit /pə́sənəl préfərəns kìt/ See **pilot's preference kit.**

perturbation /pə̀tərbéyšən/ *n.* Orbital disturbance caused by variations in gravitational attraction.

PGA *(ac.) n.c. Apollo.* "Pressure garment assembly," U.S. space suit worn during Project **Apollo** in either of two configurations for intravehicular activity or EVA. For operations within the spacecraft requiring the use of a space suit for safety (launch, docking, crew transfer to LM or CM, reentry) the PGA consists of an individually fitted *torso limb suit,* which covers the entire body except for the head and hands; *pressure helmet;* individually molded, touch-retaining, mitten-like *pressure gloves;* various *controls and instruments;* and an *intravehicular cover* which provides protection for the torso limb suit from abrasion and fire.

The pressure garment assembly must provide astronauts with protection from the extremely hot or cold vacuum environment of deep space. An important part of the assembly is the portable life support system which holds oxygen, water, and power supplies.

GRUMMAN AEROSPACE CORPORATION

OXYGEN PURGE SYSTEM — ANTENNA — LEVA — PLSS RCU — POCKET — COMMUNICATIONS UMBILICAL — OPS O₂ IN — PLSS O₂ IN — PLSS LIQUID COOLING UMBILICAL — PRESSURE GAGE — CUFF CHECKLIST — UTILITY POCKET — PENLIGHT POCKET — PENCIL POCKET — BIOMEDICAL INJECTION DISK — DATA LIST POCKET — IV USE ONLY — PLSS — POCKET — OPS ACTUATOR — PLSS O₂ OUT — PURGE VALVE — BSLSS — PLSS LOWER SUPPORT — LOWER PLSS BRACKET — EV GLOVE — PRESSURE RELIEF VALVE — UCTA CONNECTOR — SCISSORS POCKET — CHECKLIST POCKET — LUNAR BOOTS

/z/ *zero;* /ž/ *azure;* /θ/ *thin;* /ð/ *then;* /ŋ/ *song;* /æ/ *bat;* /ɔ/ *law;* /ə/ *sun;* /ɚ/ *bird.* Foreign symbols: [(n)] nasalization of some French vowels followed by /n/; [R] French uvular rolled /r/ sound; [ü] high front lip-rounded vowel; [x] Russian voiceless laryngeal fricative.

For EVA the above PGA equipment is used with the substitution of the *integrated thermal micrometeoroid garment* (TMG) for the intravehicular cover. The TMG provides heat control as well as fire, abrasion, micrometeoroid impact, and ultraviolet ray protection. Supplemental gear includes the *extravehicular visor*, worn over the pressure helmet and providing protection from light, heat, and micrometeoroids to the astronaut and the helmet; the *extravehicular gloves*, for added thermal control; and the *lunar boot*, worn over both the boot of the torso limb suit and that of the TMG and providing thermal control and abrasion protection. See also **PLSS** and **EMU**.

Other basic items worn with either of the PGA's include a **constant wear garment** (or a **liquid cooling garment** for EVA), **bioinstrumentation harness, communications carrier,** and equipment from the waste management system (**WMS**).

PGNS *(ac.) n.c. Apollo.* "Primary guidance and navigation system," that part of the LM guidance, navigation, and control system (**GNCS**) whose equipment provides automatic control for all major LM maneuvers including **abort.**

phase procurement /féyz prowkyùrmənt/ *n.c.* NASA method of future program planning based on gradual economic development: feasibility studies, specification studies, research and development, and construction.

phasing /féyziŋ/ *n.* Synchronizing maneuver between two spacecraft before **rendezvous.**

photo cell /fówtow sèl/ *n.c.* **Solar cell.**

photometry /fətámətriy/ *n.* Measuring of light intensity.

photon /fówtan/ *n.* Theoretically, particles of electromagnetic radiation.

photon engine /fówtan ènʲən/ *n.c.* Projected spacecraft engine in which **thrust** would be developed from light rays.

photosphere /fówtəsfir/ *n.* Outer layer of the sun's surface.

pigtail /pígteyl/ *n. sl.* Coiled wire used as igniter connection.

pilot parachute /páylət pèrəšuwt/ *n.c.* Small parachute of the earth landing system (**ELS**); used to deploy the **main parachutes.**

pilot's preference kit /páyləts préfʳəns kìt/ *n.c. Apollo.* Small cloth bag for any personal possessions an astronaut may wish to carry on a mission.

Pioneer /payənír/ *n.* U.S. astrophysical probe series for study of near, deep-space, and solar phenomena. Consisting, in early 1972, of ten craft, the series includes the first NASA spacecraft and the first object intended to escape our solar system.

The first five Pioneers, launched between 1958 and 1960, were designed to travel past the moon for study of the sun and extraterrestrial radiation. *Pioneer 1,* launched October 11, 1958, was NASA's first craft and the first deep-space probe launched by the U.S. *Pioneer 4,* launched in March 1959, was the first U.S. vehicle to go into heliocentric orbit. *Pioneer 5,* launched in 1960, confirmed the existence of interplanetary magnetic fields.

PIONEER VI SPACECRAFT

SPACE ENVIRONMENT EXPERIMENT

MIDCOURSE AND TERMINAL CORRECTION ROCKETS

COSMIC RAY DETECTOR PORTS

MICROMETEORITE DIAPHRAGM

ACTIVE TEMPERATURE CONTROL

SOLAR CELL PADDLE

SEARCH COIL MAGNETOMETER

SPIN AXIS

NASA

Pioneer 4 measured the energetic radiation of the outer Van Allen zone.

Four Pioneers were launched between 1965 and 1968 to study interplanetary space from widely separated positions. All four were in heliocentric orbits at the end of 1971.

Pioneer 10, launched March 2, 1972, is the first of two *Pioneer-Jupiter* missions. The craft will fly by Jupiter, taking photographs and measuring such phenomena as radiation belts, magnetic fields, and cloud

The plaque attached to *Pioneer 10* contains symbols representing a hydrogen atom, *upper left,* the positions and frequencies of 14 pulsars, *center left,* the solar system, *bottom,* the pioneer satellite, *background right,* and two human beings. By recognizing the hydrogen atom and knowing its wavelength, intelligent beings of other solar systems could determine the following facts about the satellite: the solar system from which it came, the time of its launching, and the size of the human beings that made it.

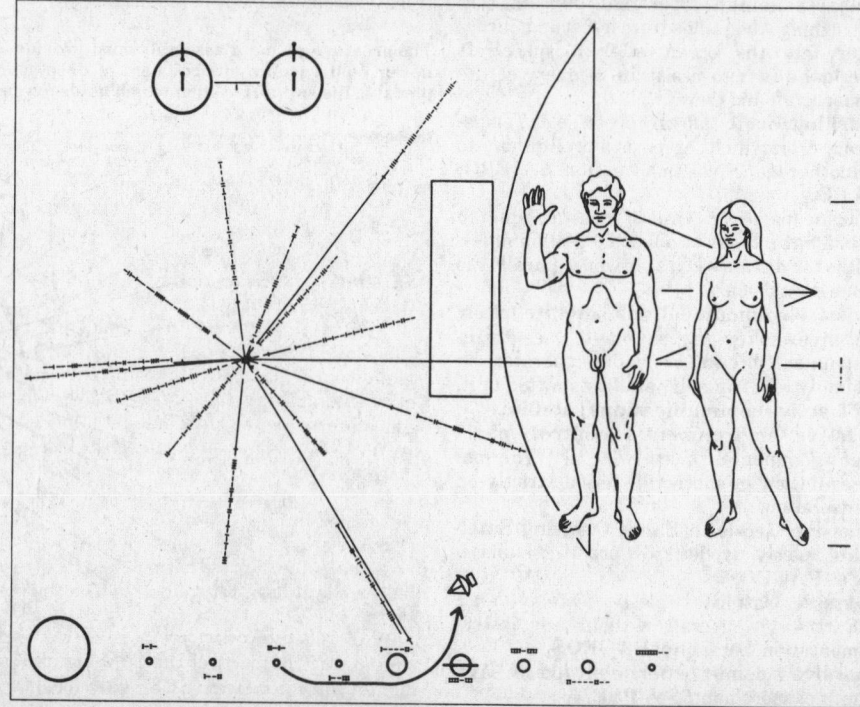

/a/ father; /aw/ wow; /ay/ buy; /b/ boy; /č/ witch; /d/ doll; /e/ bet; /ey/ say; /f/ few; /g/ bag; /h/ hole; /i/ it; /iy/ be; /j/ gin; /k/ cat; /l/ lamb; /m/ man; /n/ now; /o/ orbit; /ow/ tow; /oy/ boy; /p/ pat; /r/ run; /s/ send; /š/ shoe; /t/ toy; /u/ put; /uw/ do; /v/ eve; /w/ way; /y/ yes;

SE–48

structures. Jupiter's field of gravity will cause the craft to escape the solar system and become the first interstellar probe. On the chance that it might be captured in space by other intelligent beings, the craft carries a plaque showing in scientific symbols where, when, and by what kind of creatures it was launched. A second Pioneer-Jupiter mission is scheduled for launch in 1973.

PIP *(ac.) n.c.* "Predicted impact point," estimated place where **splashdown** will occur.

pitch /píč/ *n.* Vertical movement of a spacecraft around its lateral axis (**Y-axis**). Cf. **roll; yaw.**

pitch control motor /píč kəntròwl mòwtɚ/ *n.c. Apollo.* Launch escape system (**LES**) rocket which ensures **pitchover** for the escape system and manned capsule in case of **pad abort** or abort at low altitude.

pitch jets /píč jèts/ See **attitude jets.**

pitchover /píčowvɚ/ *n.* Post-launch maneuver that moves a vehicle from a vertical path onto a slight horizontal inclination.

planet /plǽnət/ *n.* Celestial body (excluding **comets** and **meteoroids**) which orbits the sun in a **solar system.**

planetary entry parachute /plǽnəteriy éntriy pèrəšuwt/ *n.c.* Parachute system for soft-landing interplanetary probes on celestial bodies with atmospheres.

planetary motions /plǽnəteriy mówšənz/ *n.c.* Laws defining orbital behavior of planets.

planetology /plǽnətáləjiy/ *n.* Science dealing with the topology of planets.

plasma /plǽzmə/ *n.* Ionized-gas envelope which encircles reentering spacecraft causing temporary communications blackout.

Plasmopause Explorer /plǽzməpɔz eksplórɚ/ See **Explorer.**

plasticiser /plǽstəsayzɚ/ *n.* Solidifying element in solid propellants.

PLSS /plís/ *(ac.) n.c. Apollo.* "Portable life support system," 68-lb. backpack unit containing oxygen, water, and power supplies and communications equipment. The PLSS enables an astronaut on **EVA** to operate independently of his craft for up to seven hours. See **EMU.**

plus count /plʌ́s kàwnt/ *n.c.* Countup (see **GET**). Cf. **countdown.**

Pluto /plúwtòw/ *n.* **1.** Outermost and second smallest planet in the solar system. It has a diameter of 3,700 miles and its orbit lies at a mean distance of 3.6 billion miles from the sun. Pluto has the most eccentric orbit, and its orbit's inclination to the plane of the **ecliptic** (17.1°) is by far the greatest of any known planet. Discovered only in 1930, Pluto remains for the most part uninvestigated because of its distance from Earth. It is scheduled for study on an **Outer Planets Mission.**

2. Roman god of Hades.

PMR *(ac.) n.c.* "Pacific Missile Range." See **AFWTR.**

POGO /pówgow/ *(ac.) n.c.* "Polar Orbiting Geophysical Observatory." See **OGO.**

pogo effect /pówgow əfὰkt/ *n.c.* Vertical vibrations in a rocket, usually beginning just after **liftoff**; main cause has been established as the sloshing, back-and-forth

movement of fuel in the various stages.

point mass /póynt mæs/ *n.c.* Center of mass and **gravity.**

polar orbit /pówlɚ órbət/ *n.c.* Flight path which passes over both poles. Because the axis of rotation of the earth is close to being perpendicular to the orbital plane, a satellite in polar orbit is capable of providing total global coverage.

Polar Orbiting Geophysical Observatory /pówlɚ òrbətiŋ jiyowfízìkəl əbzɚ́vətoriy/ See **OGO.**

poll the room /pówl ðə rúwm/ *phr. id.* To let the majority of concerned personnel determine the course of action on a manned mission.

Pollux /páləks/ See **Castor.**

Polyot [*Rus.* pəlyót] *n.* "Flight," one of two U.S.S.R. experimental satellites launched in November 1963 and April 1964. The first spacecraft to carry out extensive maneuvering in outer space, Polyots made numerous orbital changes. Their basic objective was the study and practical application of approach and docking techniques.

porch /pórč/ *n. sl.* **LM egress platform.**

portable life support system /pôrtəbəl láyf səpòrt sìstəm/ See **PLSS.**

posigrade /pázəgreyd/ *attr.* Of or pertaining to an increase in velocity.

posigrade rocket /pázəgreyd ràkət/ *n.c.* Any of a number of small rockets used to speed a space capsule away from its final booster stage after **separation.**

positive G /pàsətiv jiy/ *n.c.* Acceleration upward; also known as **eyeballs down.**

post-landing ventilation /pòwst lǽndiŋ ventəléyšən/ *n.c. Apollo.* That part of the CSM environmental control system (**ECS**) which admits outside air to the crew compartment for breathing and thermal control after **splashdown.**

postpass /pòwstpæs/ *attr.* Of or pertaining to that period following a spacecraft's overhead pass.

potable water /pòwtəbəl wótɚ/ *n.c.* Drinkable water produced by U.S. spacecraft fuel cells.

powered descent initiation /pâwɚd diysént ənišiyèyšən/ See **PDI.**

PPS *(ac.) attr.* "Pounds per second," pertains to **weight flow rate.**

precession /priyséšən/ *n.* Change of the orbital plane or of the direction of the axis of rotation of a celestial body caused by the action of an outside force.

predicted impact point /prədíktəd ímpækt pòynt/ See **PIP.**

preretro update /prìyrètrow ə́pdeyt/ *n.c.* Information relayed to a spacecraft about its position before a **reentry** maneuver.

press kit /prés kìt/ *n.c.* Mission syllabus and other relevant information provided by NASA to media representatives prior to space missions.

pressure garment assembly /préšɚ gàrmənt əsèmbliy/ See **PGA.**

pressure gloves /préšɚ glə̀vz/ See **PGA.**

pressure helmet /préšɚ hèlmət/ See **PGA.**

pressure suit /préšɚ sùwt/ *n.c.* **PGA; space suit.**

pressure suit circuit /préšɚ suwt sɚ̀kət/ *n.c. Apollo.* That part of the CSM environmental control system (**ECS**) which cleans

and conditions the atmosphere of the crew compartment and **space suits.**

pressurization subsystem /preššizêyšən sə́bsistəm/ *n.c. Apollo.* In the service propulsion system (**SPS**), descent propulsion system (**DPS**), or ascent propulsion system (**APS**), the system which maintains fuel and oxidizer tank pressure so that propellants will feed into the engine more easily during thrust.

pressurized /préšɚayzd/ *attr.* Of or pertaining to a closed compartment, instrument or system which maintains an artificial pressure.

pressurized general purpose laboratory /prêšɚayzd jènɚəl pɚ́pəs læbrətoriy/ See **RAM.**

prestage /príystèyj/ *n.* Sequence in which introduction of propellant prior to ignition is begun.

primary /práymeriy/ *n.* **Central body.**

primary crater /práymeriy kréytɚ/ *n.c.* Lunar surface depression created by **meteorite** impact.

primary guidance and navigation subsystem /práymeriy gáydəns ænd nævəgêyšən sə́bsistəm/ See **PGNS.**

primary voice link /práymeriy vóys lìŋk/ *n.c.* Most efficient radio frequency for voice communications between a manned spacecraft and **ground control** at any given time.

prime crew /práym krúw/ *n.c.* Astronaut team scheduled to man a flight; should any reason prevent their participation in a mission, a **back-up** crew is always standing by.

probe /prówb/ See **probe assembly.**

probe /prówb/ *n.* **1.** Unmanned vehicle other than an Earth satellite; usually a **fly-by** craft.

2. See **Zond.**

probe assembly /prówb əsèmbliy/ *n.c. Apollo.* CM component of the **docking system**; consists mainly of a *probe*, which makes the initial contact with the LM **drogue** during docking; *capture latches*, which are located on the probe head and make the initial lock between the two docking craft; a *ratchet assembly*, which is used to fold and remove or install the whole probe assembly; and *probe umbilicals*, which provide power for the probe assembly.

probe umbilicals /prówb əmbílikəlz/ See **probe assembly.**

programmed roll /prôwgræmd rówl/ *n.c.* Automatic **roll** maneuver initiated before **pitchover.**

programmed turn /prôwgræmd tɚ́n/ *n.c.* **Pitchover.**

propagation /prapəgéyšən/ *n.* Manner in which a signal travels from one point to another.

propellant /prəpélənt/ *n.* Mixture of fuel and **oxidizer** which, when burned, provides **thrust.** The sophisticated Space-Age propellants may be either solid or liquid.

propellant feed subsystem /prəpélənt fiyd sə́bsistəm/ *n.c. Apollo.* In the descent propulsion system (**DPS**) or ascent propulsion system (**APS**), the equipment which delivers fuel and oxidizer to the engine thrust chamber.

/z/ *z*ero; /ž/ a*z*ure; /θ/ *th*in; /ð/ *th*en; /ŋ/ so*ng*; /æ/ b*a*t; /ɔ/ l*a*w; /ə/ s*u*n; /ɚ/ b*ir*d. Foreign symbols: [(n)] nasalization of some French vowels followed by /n/; [R] French uvular rolled /r/ sound; [ü] high front lip-rounded vowel; [x] Russian voiceless laryngeal fricative.

propellant subsystem /prəpêlənt səbsìstəm/ n.c. Apollo. That part of the service propulsion system (**SPS**) which feeds fuel and oxidizer into the main engine's thrust chamber.

propellant tanks /prəpélənt tǽŋks/ See **tanks, propellant.**

propellant utilization and gauging subsystem /prəpêlənt yuwtəlǝzèyšən ænd gêyǰiŋ səbsìstəm/ See **PUGS.**

propulsion system /prəpʌ́lšən sìstəm/ n.c. All onboard equipment necessary to propel a rocket: engines, fuel lines, nozzles, etc.

propulsive vent /prəpʌ́lsiv vènt/ n.c. **Jettison** of unconsumed propellant into space.

Prospero /práspərow/ n. British experimental satellite, also called X-3, launched in October 1971 by a **Black Arrow** rocket from the Australian rocket range at **Woomera.** With Prospero, Great Britain became the sixth nation in the world to orbit a satellite using an internally developed launcher.

The satellite's basic task was the testing of procedures and equipment for future satellite projects.

Proton [Rus. protón] n. U.S.S.R. electric-particle research satellite series consisting of four spacecraft launched from 1965 to 1968. The largest satellites ever launched, the vehicles weighed between 13 and 18 tons each. Protons were fundamentally concerned with investigation of cosmic rays and other high-energy matter.

PSE (ac.) n.c. Apollo. "Passive seismic experiment," scientific device carried to the moon as part of the Early Apollo Scientific Experiments Package (**EASEP**) and the Apollo Lunar Surface Experiments Package (**ALSEP**). PSE gauges the source and intensity of lunar tremors.

pseudo-random noise /súwdow rǽndəm nóyz/ n.c. Apollo. Ground signals transmitted to the LM to aid in tracking the craft.

PSI (ac.) n.c. "Pounds per square inch," describing pressure.

PTC (ac.) n.c. "Passive thermal control," **mode** maintaining the thermal balance of a spacecraft by slow rotation during prolonged solar exposure. Also called barbecue mode.

Public Affairs Officer /pʌ́blik əférz ɔ́fəsə/ See **PAO.**

PUGS /pʌ́gz/ (ac) n.c. Apollo. "Propellant utilization and gauging subsystem," that part of the service propulsion system (**SPS**) which monitors and rectifies any imbalance in the propellant mixture and measures the amount of fuel and oxidizer remaining in the tanks as the mission progresses.

pulse /pʌ́ls/ n. Ultra-short radio signal emitted by a spacecraft or missile for range-gauging purposes.

purge /pɔ́ʒ/ **1.** v. tr. To clean out a system; usually the waste water or fuel complexes.

2. n. Cleaning out of a system.

pushbutton indicator /pʊ́šbətən ìndikeytə/ n.c. Dual-purpose device which lights up to indicate a problem and is pushed to alleviate the problem.

pyrotechnic /pâyrətéknik/ attr. Explosive.

pyrotechnic battery /pâyrətéknik bǽtəriy/ n.c. Apollo. One of several small batteries used in both the **LM** and **CSM** to detonate various explosive devices; part of the electrical power system (**EPS**).

Q–R

Q n. cd. Dynamic pressure.

Q-ball /kyúw bɔ̀l/ n.c Apollo. Launch escape system (**LES**) nose-cone device which gauges the flight angle of the escape equipment and attached manned capsule.

QD (ac.) attr. "Quick-disconnect," pertains to objects designed to separate immediately in case of emergency.

quad /kwɔ́d/ n. Any set of four **thrusters** in the reaction control system (**RCS**).

qualify /kwɔ́ləfay/ v. tr. To prove performance capability by an actual flight test which is usually unmanned.

quarantine facility /kwɔ́rəntiyn fəsìlətiy/ See **LRL.**

quick-disconnect /kwîk diskənékt/ See **QD.**

radar /réydar/ (ac.) "Radio detection and ranging." **1.** n.c. System which uses microwave reflectivity to locate aerospace objects.

2. attr. Of or pertaining to a radar system.

radial velocity /rêydiyəl vəlásitiy/ n.c. Rate at which two objects approach or recede from each other.

radiation /reydiyéyšən/ n. Energy transmitted as particles waves through either a vacuum or a medium; usually refers to **electromagnetic radiation.**

radiation belt /reydiyéyšən bêlt/ n.c. Electrically charged particles held around a spatial body by its magnetic field. See **Van Allen Radiation Belt.**

radiation pressure /reydiyéyšən prêšə/ n.c. Slight force exerted by **electromagnetic** radiation on any surface it strikes.

radiation survey meter /reydiyêyšən sɔ́vey mìytə/ n.c. Apollo. Flashlight-sized instrument which is used to measure radiation quantities. It is clipped in a CM bracket and is taken with the astronauts when they transfer to the LM.

radio-altimeter /rêydiyow ǽltímətə/ n. Instrument which measures space vehicle altitude; operates on **radar** principles.

radio astronomy /rêydiyow əstránəmiy/ n.c. Branch of astronomy which uses **radio telescopes,** instead of optical ones, to study celestial bodies.

Radio Astronomy Explorer /rêydiyow əstrάnəmiy eksplòrə/ See **RAE.**

Radio Exploration Satellite /rèydiyow eksplɔ́yšən sǽtəlayt/ See **REXS.**

radio frequency equipment /rêydiyow fríykwənsiy əkwìpmənt/ n.c. Apollo. That part of the telecommunications (**T/C**) system which consists of all radio equipment except antennas needed to transmit and receive voices, data, telemetry, and tracking and ranging information from the ground, a craft, or an astronaut.

Radioisotope thermoelectric generator /rèydiyowâysətowp θɔ́mowiylêktrik jénɔeytə/ See **RTG.**

radio-ranging /rêydiyow réynǰiŋ/ attr. Of or pertaining to the use of radio signals for giving directions.

radio source /réydiyow sòrs/ n.c. Area or object in space which emits radio waves; **radio telescopes** are used to study such phenomena.

radio telescope /rêydiyow télǝskowp/ n.c. Instrument utilizing a large antenna to pick up **microwaves** emanating from sources deep in space. See **radio astronomy.**

RAE (ac.) n.c. "Radio Astronomy Explorer," U.S. astronomical satellite, number 38 of the **Explorer** series, launched in July 1968 to investigate low-frequency radio waves in space. Another model is planned for lunar orbit to study radio-wave sources on the earth, sun, and Jupiter.

RAM /rǽm/ (ac.) n.c. "Research and Applications Module," any of four types of manned or man-tended spacecraft under development by the U.S. RAMs would provide versatile and economical laboratory facilities for scientific research and applications. According to preliminary studies begun in 1969, RAMs would be used in conjunction with the **Space Shuttle,** and later, with a U.S. space station. In an effort to avoid major developmental costs, NASA intends to use, whenever possible, equipment already designed.

Four types of RAM are projected: support module, pressurized general laboratory, pallet, and free-flying module. The support module houses scientific and operational crews as well as data and experiment control equipment and power sources. It would be limited in its own experimental apparatus, but would be the servicing and data-collecting element for the other three types of RAM.

The pressurized general purpose laboratory will house experiments which do not require vacuum conditions, but do require manned support, such as biological work or material research. It will normally be launched attached to the support module.

The pallet will be a simple framework to which scientific equipment can be attached for operation in the vacuum of space. It will always be attached to another module, usually the RAM support module.

The free-flying module will be an automated, unmanned satellite which will be serviced periodically by a RAM support module. The free-flyer could operate for three or four months between maintenance revisits. It could be in orbit for a year or more before being recaptured by a Space Shuttle and returned to Earth for renovation and reoutfitting.

Size of the RAMs will be limited by the cargo-bay capacity of the Space Shuttle launch vehicle. RAMs may be 14 feet in diameter and up to 58 feet long, although they could be much shorter. More than one RAM could be launched at a time, as long as their total length did not exceed the capacity of the Space Shuttle cargo bay.

RAM support module /rǽm səpórt màjəl/ See **RAM.**

range /réynǰ/ See **test range.**

range and range rate /réynǰ ænd rêynǰ réyt/ n.c. Tracking system based on the reception of signals from a spacecraft by three separate ground stations. These sta-

---

/a/ father; /aw/ wow; /ay/ buy; /b/ boy; /č/ witch; /d/ doll; /e/ bet; /ey/ say; /f/ few; /g/ bag; /h/ hole; /i/ it; /iy/ be; /ǰ/ gin; /k/ cat; /l/ lamb; /m/ man; /n/ now; /o/ orbit; /ow/ tow; /oy/ boy; /p/ pat; /r/ run; /s/ send; /š/ shoe; /t/ toy; /u/ put; /uw/ do; /v/ eve; /w/ way; /y/ yes;

NASA

Research applications modules will be launched from Earth in Space Shuttles. Once in orbit, the Shuttle will open its cargo bay doors and the RAM will be placed in orbit. When finished with its experiments, the RAM returns to the Shuttle for the trip back to Earth.

tions measure the vehicle's **radial velocity** and the distance from each station. Computers, which correlate data from the stations, are then able to locate the position of the craft within an area of 50 feet.

Ranger /réynjɚ/ *n.* Initial U.S. lunar probe series; spacecraft series that provided the first closeup pictures of the moon. Nine craft were launched from 1961 to 1965. *Ranger 4*, launched in April 1962, became the first U.S. vehicle to hit the moon. No photographs were transmitted back to Earth until July 1964 when *Ranger 7* and

The *Ranger* vehicle contained deployable solar panels which provided power for the satellite's observational and attitude-control equipment.

NASA

the two that followed it provided more than 17,000 pictures of the lunar surface. The Ranger program was superceded by **Lunar Orbiter.**

Range Safety Officer /rêynĵ séyftiy ɔ́fəsɚ/ *n.c.* The person responsible for the destruction of rockets which go off course. The officer aborts such vehicles to prevent them from causing damage by crashing.

range safety system /rêynĵ séyftiy sìstəm/ *n.c.* Spacecraft instrumentation which enables the **Range Safety Officer** to destroy malfunctioning launch vehicles after liftoff.

ranging /réynjiŋ/ *n.* Finding the distance between spacecraft and ground station.

ratchet assembly /ráčət əsèmbliy/ See **probe assembly.**

RCS *(ac.) n.c. Apollo.* "Reaction control system," spacecraft thruster complex which maintains stability and attitude during ascent and descent burns, docking maneuvers, and reentry. The RCS may be operated manually or automatically by the stabilization and control system (**SCS**).

reaction control engine /riyǽkšən kəntrówl ènĵən/ *n.c.* Small **rocket engine** used in groups on the Apollo modules to maintain **attitude** while preserving the main fuel supply for major maneuvers.

reaction control system /riyǽkšən kəntrówl sìstəm/ See **RCS.**

reaction engine /riyǽkšən ènĵən/ *n.c.* Rocket engine.

read /ríyd/ *v. tr.* To receive and understand voice transmissions from manned spacecraft.

readout /ríydàwt/ *n.* **1.** Transmission of spacecraft data.
  2. The data itself.

real time /ríyl táym/ *attr.* **1.** Of or pertain-

ing to things processed almost simultaneously with their occurence.
  2. Of or pertaining to devices able to process data while receiving it.

Real Time Computer Complex /ríyl tâym kəmpyúwtɚ kàmpleks/ See **RTCC.**

reconnaissance satellites /riykánəsəns sæ̀tələyt/ *n.c.* Any spacecraft used primarily to investigate the military installations and equipment of another nation. Some reconnaissance satellites have low perigees and operate by taking photographs of areas of interest. Other reconnaissance satellites can record signals (*ferret satellites*) or detect missile launchings. Most of the satellites, launched under secret programs, are orbited for short periods and then recovered.

recoverable /riykɚ́vɚəbəl/ *attr.* Of or pertaining to any spacecraft which can be made to return to Earth with its contents in good condition; not applied to manned craft.

recovery /riykɚ́vɚiy/ *n.* Act of retrieving a spacecraft and its **payload** after reentry; U.S. craft are recovered in midair or at sea.

recovery forces /riykɚ́vriy fòrsəz/ *n.c.* Personnel stationed around the world in readiness for the **splashdown** of a manned U.S. craft.

recycle /rîysáykəl/ *v. tr.* To return to an earlier place in a **countdown** and then continue on from there.

red /réd/ *attr.* **No-go.**

red-line values /rêd láyn vèlyuwz/ *n.c.* Temperature and pressure tolerances in spacecraft systems.

redout /rédàwt/ *n.* Visual condition in which things appear red; occurs under **negative G.**

Redstone /rédstòwn/ *n.* U.S. single-stage

/z/ zero; /ž/ azure; /θ/ thin; /ð/ then; /ŋ/ song; /æ/ bat; /ɔ/ law; /ə/ sun; /ɚ/ bird. Foreign symbols: [(n)] nasalization of some French vowels followed by /n/; [R] French uvular rolled /r/ sound; [ü] high front lip-rounded vowel; [x] Russian voiceless laryngeal fricative.

SE – 51

rocket used as a launch vehicle in the sub-orbital portion of Project **Mercury.** Developed as the first U.S. intermediate-range ballistic missile (**IRBM**), the Redstone was a direct descendant of the German **V-2.** Despite attempted modifications, the Redstone could not be converted from a tactical vehicle to a launch vehicle that could place a man into orbit.

The Redstone, as used in Project Mercury, stood 83 ft. high, weighed over 60,000 lbs., and was capable of developing 110,000 lbs. of thrust.

redundancy /riydéndənsiy/ n. Condition in which two identical instruments or systems are carried on spacecraft in case one fails; helps to ensure mission fulfillment.

redundant /riydéndənt/ attr. Duplicate.

reentry /riyéntriy/ n. Space vehicle's return to the earth's atmosphere.

reentry corridor /riyéntriy kòrədə/ n.c. Space-Earth **trajectory** which allows a spacecraft to be recovered safely. Unless this path is followed accurately, the craft will either burn up on reentry or be deflected away from Earth.

reentry module /riyéntriy màjəl/ See **Gemini.**

regenerative cooling /rìyjénəətiv kúwliŋ/ n.c. Method by which rocket engines are cooled by the circulation of their own fuel.

Relay /ríyley/ n. U.S. experimental active-repeater comsat series used in intercontinental transmission of television, telephone, data, and facsimile. Relay 1 and Relay 2, both featuring redundant major parts, were launched in 1962 and 1964. Relay 2, an improved model, also carried equipment to monitor its own systems and to study the **Van Allen Radiation Belts.**

rendezvous /rándeyvuw/ 1. n. Prescheduled meeting of spacecraft in orbit.
2. v. tr. To meet other spacecraft while in orbit.

rendezvous evaluation pod /rándeyvuw iyvælyuwéyšən pàd/ See **REP.**

rendezvous radar /rándeyvuw rèydar/ n.c. Apollo. The part of the LM guidance, navigation, and control system (**GNCS**), which in association with the CSM equipment, supplies the primary guidance and naviga-

tion system (**PGNS**) with tracking data on the CSM during both descent to and ascent from the moon.

REP (ac.) n.c. Gemini. "Rendezvous evaluation pod," small electronic satellite released by Gemini 5 for rendezvous exercises that subsequently were never carried out.

Research and Applications Module /rìysəč ænd æpləkéyšənz màjəl/ See **RAM.**

residual /rəzíjuwəl/ attr. Leftover.

residuals /rəzíjuwəlz/ n. Supplies remaining at the end of a space mission; usually water or fuel.

resin /rézən/ n. Synthetic used as a component in solid propellants.

retro /rétrow/ (ac.) n. See **Retrorocket.**

retrofit /rétrofìt/ v. tr. To alter a spacecraft or component after its construction.

retrograde /rétrowgreyd/ attr. Reverse.

retrograde section /rétrowgreyd sèkšən/ See **Gemini.**

retrorocket /rétrowràkət/ n. Small rocket that fires opposite the flight direction of a spacecraft for braking.

reusable vehicle /rìyyûwzəbəl víyhikəl/ See **Space Shuttle.**

revolution /rèvəlúwšən/ n. One complete orbit.

REXS /réks/ (ac.) n.c. "Radio Exploration Satellite," Japanese upper atmospheric research satellite projected for launch in 1972–73. The satellite's mission is to conduct electromagnetic measurements and studies in the upper ionosphere and lower magnetosphere.

rill /ríl/ n. Crevasselike lunar surface feature superimposed over all others; scheduled for exploration during the **Apollo** program.

Rising Sun Satellite 1 /râyziŋ sên sætəlayt wέn/ See **Oshumi.**

Rita [Fr. Ritá] n. French single-stage rocket used as a ballistic missile and **Diamant** launch-vehicle component. The rocket weighs 8,900 lbs. fueled, stands 6 ft. high, and develops 45,000 lbs. of thrust.

rock box /rák bàks/ n.c. sl. Apollo. **SRC.**

rocket /rákət/ n. 1. Vehicle propelled by one or more rocket engines. Rockets are

often stacked on each other in **stages** for special purposes (see **launch vehicle**).
2. **Rocket engine.**

rocket engine /rákət ènjən/ n.c. Motor which produces hot gases for propulsion.

rocketry /rákətriy/ n. Branch of science that deals with the technology and development of the **rocket.**

roger /rájə/ sl. "I understand."

roll /rówl/ 1. v. intr. To move about the longitudinal axis (**X-axis**).
2. n. Movement of a spacecraft around the longitudinal axis (**X-axis**).

roll jets /rówl jets/ See **attitude jets.**

rollout /rówlawt/ n. Transfer of a spacecraft from the **VAB** to the launch area.

rotation /rowtéyšən/ n. Movement of a body about its axis.

RP-1 n. cd. Hydrocarbon similar to kerosene fuel used in the **Saturn.**

RTCC (ac.) n.c. "Real Time Computer Complex," five computers and storage units which provide data to NASA's Mission Control Center (**MCC**) for flight decisions.

RTG (ac.) n.c. "Radioisotope thermoelectric generator," atomic power source used for the Apollo Lunar Surface Experiments Package (**ALSEP**), for Pioneer 10 (see **Pioneer**), and projected for use in **Viking** and Thermoelectric Outer Planets Spacecraft (**TOPS**) missions. The RTG utilizes heat from isotopes such as plutonium-238.

Rubis [Fr. Rübi] n. "Ruby," French two-stage sounding rocket; a combination of the **Agate** and the small third-stage component of the **Diamant** series.

S

St. Elmo's fire /seynt êlmowz fáyə/ n.c. A corona discharge of atmospheric electricity which sometimes occurs at the tips of high objects—church spires, treetops, ships' masts, and parts of aircraft in flight—during stormy weather. It appears as a bluish glow and usually is accompanied by a crackling sound. Also called corposant, St. Elmo's fire is sometimes offered as an explanation for **UFOs.**

Salute /səlúwt/ See **Salyut.**

Salyut [Rus. salyút] n. "Salute," first space station, launched by the U.S.S.R. into

The *Salyut* scientific orbital station, *right*, can dock with a *Soyuz* spacecraft, *left*, for the transfer of materials and crew.

/a/ father; /aw/ wow; /ay/ buy; /b/ boy; /č/ witch; /d/ doll; /e/ bet; /ey/ say; /f/ few; /g/ bag; /h/ hole; /i/ it; /iy/ be; /j/ giṇ; /k/ cat; /l/ lamb; /m/ man; /n/ now; /o/ orbit; /ow/ tow; /oy/ boy; /p/ pat; /r/ run; /s/ send; /š/ shoe; /t/ toy; /u/ put; /uw/ do; /v/ eve; /w/ way; /y/ yes;

Earth orbit on April 19, 1971. Operations involving Salyut were undertaken by two different **Soyuz** missions before the space station's decay in October of the same year.

Soyuz 10 became the first spacecraft to dock with the space station on April 24, 1971; its crew then boarded Salyut and spent some 5½ hours checking the station before returning to Earth. The crew of *Soyuz 11* spent 22 days on board the space station, breaking all previous records for time spent in space.

Salyut was 66 ft. long, including a built-in booster. It had a volume of 2700 cubic feet and weighed over 25 tons. It was basically cylindrical, with four winglike extensions holding panels of solar cells. The craft was equipped with extensive scientific research apparatus, consumables, life-support systems, and vehicular controls.

Its orbit was almost circular, the craft varying between a maximum of 138 miles and a minimum of 124 miles distance from Earth. Its orbital period was 89.3 minutes.

SAMOS /séymows/ *(ac.) n.c.* "Satellite and Missile Observation System," U.S. military satellite series used for photo reconnaissance. Launching of *SAMOS 2* was announced in early 1961. The series has since been classified.

sample return container /sæmpəl riytə̀n kəntèynə̀/ See **SRC.**

San Marco [*It.* sæn márkow] *n.* **1.** Continuing Italian/U.S. space project formally initiated September 5, 1962, between Italy's Centro Ricerche Aerospaziali (**CRA**) and NASA. The basic objective of the project is the investigation of upper-air density and associated ionospheric phenomena. Realization of this goal involves using U.S. **Scout** rockets to launch Italian-designed

The *San Marco 3* satellite
CENTRO RICERCHE AEROSPAZIALI

and Italian-built scientific research satellites. Technicians and launch crews are Italians trained by NASA. Italy, as part of its role in the project, established a space center, the San Marco Range, in Formosa Bay off the east coast of equatorial Africa. The center consists of two floating platforms three miles out; one serves as a launch pad, the other as control center. Since its construction in 1965, the Range has successfully orbited three Italian satellites (*San Marco 1, 2,* and *3*) and one U.S. spacecraft (see **SAS**).

2. Any of several Italian satellites launched by U.S. vehicles under the auspices of the Italian/U.S. San Marco project. *San Marco 1*, Italy's first satellite, was launched December 15, 1964 from **Wallops Station** in Virginia. Both San *Marco 2* and *3* were launched from the San Marco Range in April 1967 and April 1971, respectively.

San Marco Range /sæn márkow rèynj/ See **San Marco.**

SAO/Optical Tracking Network /ês ey ów âptikəl trǽkiŋ nètwə̀k/ *(ac.) n.c.* "Smithsonian Astrophysical Observatory" Optical Tracking Network, that branch of NASA's Satellite Tracking and Data Acquisition Network (**STADAN**) which locates Earth satellites photographically. Stations are located at Villa Delores, Argentina; Woomera, Australia; Curaçao; Naini Tal, India; Shiraz, Iran; Tokyo, Japan; Aeroquipa, Peru; Olifantsfontein, South Africa; San Fernando, Spain; and in the U.S., at Jupiter, Florida; Maui, Hawaii; and Organ Pass, New Mexico.

Saphir [*Fr.* safîR] *n.* "Sapphire," French two-stage rocket; a combination of the **Topaze** and **Emeraude.** First launched in 1965 as an experimental launch vehicle.

Sapphire /sǽfayə̀/ See **Saphir.**

SARAH /sérə/ *(ac.) n.c.* "Search and Range Homing," British-made flashing light used as a recovery aid in Mercury and Gemini; part of the earth landing system (**ELS**). Cf. **flashing beacon.**

SAS /sæs/ *(ac.) n.c.* "Small Astronomy Satellite," U.S. astronomical satellite series first launched in 1970 and used to locate x-ray and gamma ray sources. Spacecraft attitude is maintained by the reaction of a magnetic coil to the earth's magnetosphere. *SAS-A* or *X-ray Explorer* (number 42 of the **Explorer** series) was launched into an equatorial orbit in December 1970 from Italy's San Marco Range. It was the first U.S. satellite to be launched by a foreign nation. Two more SASs, one for gamma ray and one for x-ray investigation, will complete the series.

satellite /sǽtəlayt/ *n.* **1.** Natural celestial body which revolves around a planet; called a *moon.*

2. Man-made body which orbits a celestial body; the first artificial satellite was *Sputnik 1* (see **Sputnik**), launched by the U.S.S.R. on October 3, 1957.

3. See **Sputnik.**

Satellite and Missile Observation System /sǽtəlayt ænd mîsəl abzə̀véyšən sìstəm/ See **SAMOS.**

Satellite Tracking and Data Acquisition

Network /sǽtəlayt trǽkiŋ ænd dêytə əkwəzíšən nètwə̀k/ See **STADAN.**

SATS /sæts/ *(ac.) n.c.* "Small Applications Technology Satellite." See **ATS.**

Saturn /sǽtə̀n/ *n.* **1.** U.S. launch vehicle series developed specifically to place the **Apollo** spacecraft in orbit and insert it into lunar trajectory. Three basic vehicles have been produced: *Saturn 1, Uprated Saturn 1* (also called *Saturn 1B*), and *Saturn 5.*

Saturn 1, a two-stage model, was employed as a test launcher during early unmanned flights of Project Apollo; it also launched several satellites of the **Pegasus** series. The three-stage Uprated Saturn 1 served as the launch vehicle for unmanned Apollo earth-orbital test flights and for the manned *Apollo 7.* The massive Saturn 5, also a three-stage vehicle, has launched all of the subsequent Apollo flights.

Saturn 1 stands 122 ft. high, weighs 1,165,000 lbs. fueled, and develops 1,590,000 lbs. of thrust. Uprated Saturn 1 is 142 ft. high, weighs 1,300,000 lbs. fueled, and produces 1,800,000 lbs. of thrust. Saturn 5, the most powerful U.S. launcher, stands 281 ft. high, weighs 6,100,000 lbs. fueled, and has a thrust potential of 8,950,000 lbs.

2. Second largest planet in the solar system. The diameter of Saturn is 75,000 miles. It is the sixth planet from the sun and its orbital radius is 886 million miles. It is circled by three gaseous rings and ten moons. Little is known about it, compared with nearer planets. Fly-by probes of the planet are included in the **Outer Planets Missions.**

3. Roman god of agriculture.

Saturn Workshop /sǽtə̀n wə̀kšap/ See **Skylab.**

S-band /és bænd/ *n.* Radio frequency in the range from 1550 to 5200 megacycles per second.

SCAMA /skǽmə/ *(ac.) n.c.* "Station Conferencing and Monitoring Arrangement," the section of the NASA Communications Network (**NASCOM**) which makes possible multiline conference communications between ground controllers and manned spacecraft.

scientific instrument module /sayəntîfik ínstrəmənt màjəl/ See **SIM bay.**

scientific instrument module bay /sayəntîfik ínstrəmənt màjəl bêy/ See **SIM bay.**

scintillation /sintəléyšən/ *n.* Apparent twinkling of **star** light caused by the atmosphere.

SCORE /skór/ *(ac.) n.c.* "Signal Communications by Orbiting Relay Equipment," first comsat, launched by the U.S. in December 1958. It demonstrated the feasibility of using satellites for communications purposes. It transmitted a prerecorded Christmas message from President Dwight D. Eisenhower.

Scorpio /skórpiyow/ See **Antares.**

Scout /skáwt/ *n.* U.S. four-stage rocket used as a launch vehicle for lightweight unmanned spacecraft. First launched in 1960, Scout has carried American experimental and classified spacecraft, as well as satellites of other nations. The boosters which

/z/ zero; /ž/ azure; /θ/ *th*in; /ð/ *th*en; /ŋ/ so*ng*; /æ/ bat; /ɔ/ law; /ə/ sun; /ə̀/ bird. Foreign symbols: [(n)] nasalization of some French vowels followed by /n/; [R] French uvular rolled /r/ sound; [ü] high front lip-rounded vowel; [x] Russian voiceless laryngeal fricative.

The Scout 6 satellite S-55 was used to measure micrometeoroids in deep space.

NASA

comprise the Scout are called **Algol, Castor, Antares,** and **Altair.**

The standard Scout stands 72 ft. high, weighs 40,000 lbs., and has a thrust potential of 192,000 lbs.

scrub /skrə́b/ *v. tr. sl.* To cancel a scheduled mission before **launch.** Cf. **abort.**

SCS *(ac.) n.c. Apollo.* "Stabilization and control system," spacecraft equipment complex which monitors the position of the spacecraft and utilizes the reaction control system (**RCS**) and service propulsion system (**SPS**) to maintain a position and direct thrust of the rocket engines. The system is closely tied to the guidance, navigation, and control system (**GNCS**). Five subsystems handle the various aspects of the overall SCS: **controls and displays, attitude reference, attitude control, thrust vector control,** and the **entry monitor subsystem.**

SDL *(ac.) n.c.* "Space Disturbances Laboratory," research facility which investigates solar terrestrial physics. Solar activity is of special interest to SDL because of its effects on Earth. A related SDL activity is

operation of the Solar Proton Alert Network (**SPAN**).

sea /síy/ See **mare.**

sea marker /síy màrkə/ *n.c.* Yellow-green dye used as a recovery aid after **splashdown;** part of earth landing system (**ELS**).

Sea of Tranquility /síy əv trǽŋkwílətiy/ See **Apollo.**

Search and Range Homing /sə́č ənd réynj hòwmiŋ/ See **SARAH.**

SEC *(ac.) n.c. Apollo.* "Special environmental container," airtight cylinder used to hold a lunar sample, taken from a preselected site, in its original environment until personnel at the Lunar Receiving Laboratory (**LRL**) can examine it.

SECO /síykow/ *(ac.) n.c.* **"Sustainer engine cutoff."**

secondary crater /sêkənderiy kréytə/ *n.c.* Lunar surface hole or depression caused by flying debris resulting from a meteoroid impact. See **primary crater.**

second cosmic speed /sêkənd kâzmik spíyd/ See **cosmic speed.**

SECS *(ac.) n.c. Apollo.* "Sequential events control system," electronic instruments

which maintain proper sequence and control of maneuvers during such flight phases as **abort, ascent,** and **reentry.**

seismograph /sáyzməgræf/ *n.* Instrument which registers movement of the earth's crust. Cf. **seismometer.**

seismometer /sayzmámətə/ *n.* Instrument which measures the intensity of lunar tremors. Cf. **seismograph.**

selenocentric /sèlənowséntrik/ *attr.* Moon-centered.

selenodesy /selənádəsiy/ *n.* Science that deals with the size and shape of the moon and its field of **gravity.** Cf. **geodesy.**

selenographic /sèlənowgrǽfik/ *attr.* Of or pertaining to the surface of the moon.

selenography /selənógrəfiy/ *n.* Science which deals with the surface features of the moon.

selenology /sèlənáləjiy/ *n.* Science that deals with the nature and origin of the surface features of the moon.

self-propelled /sêlf prəpéld/ *attr.* Of or pertaining to unmanned projectiles equipped with engines for propulsion.

self test and repair /sêlf têst ænd riypér/ See **STAR.**

sensible atmosphere /sênsibəl ǽtməsfir/ *n.c.* Layer of Earth's atmosphere, from sea level to 100,000 ft., which presents resistance to ascending bodies.

sensor /sénsə/ *n.* **1.** Spacecraft device which locates celestial objects for study or for use as reference points (see **sunseeker**). **2.** Device which monitors an instrument and signals errors. Special sensors designed for use on humans to monitor bodily conditions are called *biosensors.*

separation /sepəréyšən/ *n.* **1.** Prescheduled point in time in a mission when the sections of a spacecraft divide, the upper portion continuing the flight and the lower portion usually dropping back to Earth. **2.** Preplanned dividing of a spacecraft which results in only the upper portion going into orbit (see **launch vehicle**).

separation rocket /sepəréyšən ràkət/ *n.c.* Small optional **strap-on** rocket which aids the upper stage of a launch vehicle in pulling away from its jettisoned lower portion.

sequential events control system /siykwênčəl iyvênts kəntrówl sìstəm/ See **SECS.**

SERT /sə́t/ *(ac.) n.c.* "Space Electric Rocket Test," U.S. nonorbital spacecraft series; first craft successfully launched in February 1970. The basic mission of SERT craft is the investigation of two types of **ion engines.**

service module /sə́vəs májəl/ See **SM.**

service propulsion system /sə́vəs prəpélšən sìstəm/ See **SPS.**

service tower /sə́vəs tàwə/ *n.c.* Scaffolding with platforms on various levels used to support equipment needed for maintaining a rocket on the **launch pad.** Unlike the **umbilical tower,** the service tower is moved away from the rocket before launch.

SEVA /síyvə/ *(ac.) n.c.* "Standup EVA." See **EVA.**

sextant /sékstənt/ *n.* Navigational instrument used to measure angular distances between celestial bodies.

SHE *(ac.) n.c.* "Supercritical helium," chem-

/a/ *father;* /aw/ *wow;* /ay/ *buy;* /b/ *boy;* /č/ *witch;* /d/ *doll;* /e/ *bet;* /ey/ *say;* /f/ *few;* /g/ *bag;* /h/ *hole;* /i/ *it;* /iy/ *be;* /j/ *gin;* /k/ *cat;* /l/ *lamb;* /m/ *man;* /n/ *now;* /o/ *orbit;* /ow/ *tow;* /oy/ *boy;* /p/ *pat;* /r/ *run;* /s/ *send;* /š/ *shoe;* /t/ *toy;* /u/ *put;* /uw/ *do;* /v/ *eve;* /w/ *way;* /y/ *yes;*

SE−54

ical used to pressurize spacecraft liquid fuel tanks.

Shinsei [*Jap.* šinséi] *n.* First Japanese scientific research satellite, launched in September 1971 by an **M-4S** launch vehicle. The satellite's basic mission is the measurement of solar radio emission, ionospheric plasma, and cosmic rays.

shirtsleeve environment /šə́tsliyv envày-ənmənt/ *n.c.* Interior of a spacecraft so conditioned that the crew does not need **space suits.** Although weightless conditions may exist, air pressure and composition are much like that of Earth.

shock diamond /šák dàymənd/ *n.c.* Triangular exhaust fume pattern caused by the **shock waves** of a rocket lifting off.

shock wave /šák wèyv/ *n.c.* Pulsating band of compaction formed when fast moving energy or material travels through a medium.

shoebox computer /šúwbaks kəmpyùwtə/ *n.c. sl. Gemini.* Small spacecraft computer used for rendezvous and docking maneuvers with the *Gemini Agena Target Vehicle (GATV)* (see **Gemini**).

shooting star /šúwtiŋ stár/ See **meteor.**

shot /šát/ *n.* Flight; launching; mission.

shroud /šráwd/ *n.* Conical shield used to protect a **payload** during **launch;** it is jettisoned in space.

shutdown /šə́tdàwn/ *n.* Stopping of a **rocket engine;** always deliberate, usually preplanned.

shut down /šə́t dáwn/ *v. tr.* To stop a **rocket engine.**

SIDE *(ac.) n.c. Apollo.* "Suprathermal ion detector experiment," scientific device carried to the moon as part of the Apollo Lunar Surface Experiments Package (**ALSEP**). SIDE investigates all ionic phenomena near the moon's surface.

side arm controller /sáyd àrm kəntrôwlə/ *n.c.* 'Steering wheel' of a manned spacecraft.

sidereal /saydíriyəl/ *attr.* Of or pertaining to time in relation to the stars instead of the sun. A *sidereal day* on Earth, for instance, is four minutes shorter than the day measured with reference to the sun.

sidereal day /saydíriyəl déy/ See **sidereal.**

Sigma 7 /sîgmə sévən/ *n.c.* Nickname for *Mercury 8* spacecraft (see **Mercury**).

Signal Communications by Orbiting Relay Equipment /sígnəl kəmyuwnəkêyšənz bay ôrbətiŋ ríyley iykwìpmənt/ See **SCORE.**

silo /sáylow/ *n.* Underground **launch pad;** usually for **missiles.**

SIM /sím/ *(ac.) n.c. Apollo.* "Scientific instrument module." See **SIM bay.**

SIM bay /sím bèy/ *(ac.) n.c. Apollo.* "Scientific instrument module" bay, empty section of the SM used, since *Apollo 15,* to house equipment and cameras used for research while the CSM is in lunar parking orbit (**LPO**) or on transearth or translunar coast (**TEC; TLC**).

simulation /simyəléyšən/ *n.* Duplication on Earth of conditions an astronaut will encounter in space.

simulator /símyəleytə/ *n.* 1. Device used to imitate conditions that an astronaut will meet in space.

2. Duplicate space-mission equipment in which or with which an astronaut can practice on Earth.

skin tracking /skín trǽkiŋ/ *n.c.* Following an object through space with **radar** alone and disregarding any signals being sent by the object.

skip-glide bomber /skîp glàyd bámə/ *n.c.* Winged vehicle launched by rocket power into space; it glances off the upper atmosphere as it circles the globe.

skip reentry /skíp riyèntriy/ *n.c.* Hypothetical return to the earth's atmosphere in which the spacecraft would glance off into space again before descending; rejected for **Apollo** missions for fear that too great a skip might render the craft unrecoverable.

skirt /skə́t/ *n.* **Adapter skirt.**

Skylab /skáylæb/ *(ac.) n.c.* "Sky Laboratory." 1. Program under which the U.S. will orbit and man its first space station. Given official status in 1969, the program's objectives include probing man's adaptability to space over extended periods of time, affirming man's value in monitoring experiments and instruments in space, studying the durability of space hardware, and investigating both the sun and the earth.

The space station will be launched and readied for occupancy in 1973 under the designation *First Skylab Mission.* The station will consist of four elements: an *Orbital Workshop* (**OWS**), also referred to as the *Saturn Workshop (SWS);* an *Airlock Module* (**AM**); a *Multiple Docking Adapter* (**MDA**); and an *Apollo Telescope Mount* (**ATM**). The OWS will be an empty *Saturn 4B* rocket with its liquid hydrogen tank modified into laboratory and living quarters for a crew of three (see **Saturn**). The tubular AM will be fitted at one end of the OWS, providing an area for EVA egress

and a systems control center. Attached to the AM, the MDA will provide two possible places for docking with manned spacecraft; it will also contain an *Earth Resources Experiments Package* (**EREP**). The ATM will be the final component, serving as a solar observatory.

Part one (*SL-1*) of the First Skylab Mission will launch the unmanned elements into a nearly circular orbit 235 miles high. The orbital plane will be inclined 50 degrees from the equatorial plane, thus allowing a view of the majority of the inhabited portions of the earth.

Once in orbit, the station will prepare itself for occupants. The ATM will automatically swing to a 90 degree angle from its launch position, thereby exposing one of the two docking mechanisms of the MDA. Solar panels will fold out from the ATM and the OWS to provide electrical power, and a metal sheath will expand a few inches away from the hull of the OWS to protect it against meteoroids. The interior of the craft will pressurize, and its attitude will stabilize.

Part two (*SL-2*) of the First Skylab Mission will occur one day after the launch of the space station. A three-man crew will enter space aboard a modified Apollo *CSM* and, after rendezvous and docking, board the space station. The crew will live in the station for 28 days before returning to earth.

The *Second Skylab Mission* (*SL-3*) and *Third Skylab Mission* (*SL-4*) will both be similar to SL-2, but will entail 56-day stays aboard the station. Over 50 scientific experiments will be conducted during the three visits. All Skylab EVA's will involve two astronauts in space simultaneously.

Launch vehicle for SL-1 will be a modified two-stage version of the Saturn 5.

One of Skylab's experiment packages, the Apollo telescope mount, will give man his first chance to study the sun with telescopes free from the interference of Earth's atmosphere.

NASA

SKYLAB CLUSTER

GENERAL CHARACTERISTICS
CONDITIONED WORK VOLUME 12,700 CU FT
OVERALL LENGTH 117 FT
WEIGHT·INCLUDING CSM·199,000
WIDTH·OWS, INCLUDING SOLAR ARRAY· 90 FT

SOLAR PANELS
EXPERIMENTS
MICROMETEOROID SHIELD
WARD ROOM
WASTE COMPARTMENT
SLEEP COMPARTMENT
SATURN WORKSHOP
APOLLO TELESCOPE MOUNT
MULTIPLE DOCKING ADAPTER
COMMAND & SERVICE MODULE
AIRLOCK MODULE

/z/ zero; /ž/ azure; /θ/ *th*in; /ð/ *th*en; /ŋ/ so*ng*; /æ/ bat; /ɔ/ law; /ə/ sun; /ɚ/ bird. Foreign symbols: [(n)] nasalization of some French vowels followed by /n/; [R] French uvular rolled /r/ sound; [ü] high front lip-rounded vowel; [x] Russian voiceless laryngeal fricative.

During liftoff and stage separation in Apollo missions, the CSM and LM are protected by the SLA. In deep space the SLA is no longer needed, so its four doors swing open and the unit is jettisoned.

NORTH AMERICAN ROCKWELL

Remaining Skylab flights will use the much smaller *Saturn 1B*, since their payloads will be considerably lighter.

2. Space station to be orbited during the Skylab Program, considered apart from the **Apollo** CSM which docks with it.

Sky Laboratory /skáy læbrətoriy/ See **Skylab.**

Skynet /skáynet/ *n.* British military synchronous comsat series consisting of two craft launched in November 1969 and August 1970, respectively, by U.S. launch vehicles. Part of a cooperative program between Great Britain, NATO, and the U.S., the satellites provide communications between London and the Far East. Future satellites are planned for a Skynet II series.

SLA *(ac.) n.c. Apollo.* "Spacecraft-LM adapter," truncated cone which houses the LM from **liftoff** through translunar injection (**TLI**); serves also to join the **CSM** and the third stage of the *Saturn 5* (see **Saturn**). The SLA is jettisoned when the CSM and LM separate from it for CSM-LM docking; nevertheless, the SLA is sometimes considered part of the Apollo spacecraft.

slant range /slǽnt rèynj/ *n.c.* Line of sight distance between an aerospace vehicle and a **ground station** or landing site.

slidewire /sláydwayər/ *n. Apollo.* Steel cable extending 2,200 ft. from near the manned capsule, mounted on its launch vehicle, to the ground. In the event of emergency before launch, astronauts may evacuate their craft in a cable car on the slidewire.

slingshot /slíŋšat/ *attr.* Pertaining to the fact that a vehicle in a flight path behind the moon will be forced by lunar **gravity** into a **heliocentric** orbit.

sloshing /slóšiŋ/ *n.c.* Movement of liquid fuel in rocket tanks after launch; causes **pogo effect.**

slush point /slə́š pòynt/ *n.c.* Freezing point of **water-glycol.**

SLV *(ac.) n.c.* "Standard launch vehicle," type of rocket usually used for a given mission; the SLV for **Apollo** was **Saturn.**

SM *(ac.) n.c. Apollo.* "Service module," one of the three main sections of the basic Apollo spacecraft. The cylindrical 26-ton SM houses the main rocket engine, propellant tanks, and several **reaction control engines.** From a central tunnel, radial beams divide the unit into six sectors, five of which contain consumables, fuel cells, and service propulsion system (**SPS**) equipment. The last sector, called the Scientific Instruments Module (see **SIM bay**), contains experimental equipment. **Bulkheads** close the top and bottom of the SM and an aft heat shield protects the unit from the heat of the main rocket engine. A **fairing** joins the SM and the command module (**CM**), forming the command and service module (**CSM**).

Small Applications Technology Satellite /smɔl æpləkêyšənz teknálәjiy sǽtәlayt/ See **ATS.**

Small Astronomy Satellite /smɔl əstránəmiy sǽtәlayt/ See **SAS.**

Smithsonian Astrophysical Observatory Optical Tracking Network /smiθsówniyən æstrowfîzikəl əbzȧ̀vətoriy áptikəl trǽkiŋ nètwɚk/ See **SAO/Optical Tracking Network.**

SMS *(ac.) n.c.* "Synchronous Meteorological Satellite," proposed U.S. meteorlogical satellite projected for launch in late 1972 or early 1973. This geostationary satellite will be the prototype for the Geostationary Operational Environmental Satellite (**GOES**). Not only will the SMS provide weather coverage for the same location on a continuous basis, but it will also be able to collect information from various ground stations and relay it to a central data bank. The high resolution visible-infrared spin-scan radiometer (**VISSR**), a camera, may be used on the SMS.

SNAP /snæp/ *(ac.) n.c.* "System for Nuclear Auxiliary Power," radioisotope thermoelectric generator (**RTG**) developed jointly by NASA, AEC, and DOD for spacecraft use. First use of nuclear generators in space was in 1961 when a **Transit** satellite carried a SNAP into orbit. Since *Apollo 12*, SNAP units have powered **ALSEP** equipment.

Snoopy /snúwpiy/ *n.* Name of *Apollo 10* LM (see **Apollo**).

2. The dog in the popular comic strip of which **Charlie Brown** is the hero.

SOFAR /sówfar/ *(ac.) attr. Mercury.* "Sound fixing and ranging," pertains to a tracking system used in Mercury spacecraft recovery; part of the earth landing system (**ELS**).

soft base /sɔ́ft béys/ *n.c.* Launching site unprotected against enemy **missile** attack. Cf. **hard base.**

soft-land /sɔ́ft lǽnd/ *v. tr.* To deliberately touch down a craft on a celestial body in a manner which avoids damage to the craft, its contents, and crew.

soft landing /sɔ́ft lǽndiŋ/ *n.c.* Touching down a spacecraft on a celestial body in a manner which avoids damage to the craft, its contents, and crew. Cf. **hard landing.**

soft undocking /sɔ́ft əndákiŋ/ *n.c.* Separation of two craft in space in such a manner that neither loses its original orbit; in the case of the **separation** of the LM and the CSM in the vicinity of the moon, only the CSM maneuvers.

software /sɔ́ftwèr/ *n.* Computer programs, concepts, and other intangibles that go into any space mission. Cf. **hardware.**

soil mechanics experiment /sôyl məkǽniks eksperəmənt/ *n.c. Apollo.* Astronaut investigation of the lunar surface as a whole; consists of noting quantity of dust raised by various activities and gauging the bearing strength of the soil.

solar cell /sówlɚ sèl/ *n.c.* Silicon-treated instrument which converts sunlight into energy; used for power on many spacecraft. Rows of solar cells are usually found on large structures called **solar panels.**

solar corona /sôwlɚ kəównə/ *n.c.* **Corona.**

solar cycle /sôwlɚ sáykəl/ *n.c.* Eleven year time period during which solar activity intensifies, diminishes, and intensifies again.

solar flare /sôwlɚ flér/ *n.c.* Sudden disturbance on the surface of the sun which produces high-energy radiation emissions. Solar flares are of concern because the resulting radiation causes radio-reception problems on Earth and constitutes a possible threat to space travelers.

solar noise /sôwlɚ nóyz/ *n.c.* Radiation from the sun detectable with radio equipment.

solar panel /sôwlɚ pǽnəl/ *n.c.* Structure which supports banks of **solar cells.** Solar

/a/ father; /aw/ wow; /ay/ buy; /b/ boy; /č/ witch; /d/ doll; /e/ bet; /ey/ say; /f/ few; /g/ bag; /h/ hole; /i/ it; /iy/ be; /j/ gin; /k/ cat; /l/ lamb; /m/ man; /n/ now; /o/ orbit; /ow/ tow; /oy/ boy; /p/ pat; /r/ run; /s/ send; /š/ shoe; /t/ toy; /u/ put; /uw/ do; /v/ eve; /w/ way; /y/ yes;

panels are often extended after launch and are movable so that they always face the sun.

solar plasma /sôwlɚ plǽzmə/ *n.c.* **Solar wind.**

Solar Proton Alert Network /sôwlɚ prówtan ələt nètwɚk/ See **SPAN.**

Solar Radiation and Thermospheric Structure Satellite /sôwlɚ reydiyêyšən ænd θɚməsfîrik strɅ́kčɚ sǽtəlayt/ See **SRATS.**

Solar Radiation Monitoring Satellite Program /sôwlɚ reydiyêyšən mànitɚiŋ sǽtəlayt prɂwgræm/ See **SOLRAD.**

solar sail /sôwlɚ séyl/ *n.c.* Large lightweight structure on a spacecraft designed to provide thrust by harnessing the force of solar **radiation pressure.**

solar system /sówlɚ sìstəm/ *n.c.* Group of celestial bodies held around a star by its gravitation. Our solar system consists of the **sun** and its nine planets (**Mercury, Venus, Earth, Mars, Jupiter, Saturn, Uranus, Neptune,** and **Pluto**), as well as meteoroids, asteroids, comets, and interplanetary gases.

solar wind /sôwlɚ wínd/ *n.c.* Hot, electrified gas particles that radiate in streams from the sun. The solar wind produces the interplanetary magnetic fields by pulling along with it the magnetic field of the sun itself.

solar wind composition /sôwlɚ wínd kampəzìšən/ See **SWC.**

solar wind spectrometer /sôwlɚ wind spektrómetɚ/ See **SWS.**

solid fuel /sáləd fyúwl/ *n.c.* Rocket propellant of varying materials mixed with an **oxidizer** and shaped into a **grain.**

SOLRAD /sówlræd/ *(ac.) n.c.* "Solar Radiation Monitoring Satellite Program," U.S. astronomical satellite series developed to study solar phenomena, especially the mechanisms of solar emissions. Ten craft were launched between 1960 and 1971, some as **hitchhikers.** *SOLRAD 10,* launched in July 1971, was used to monitor radiation for the *Apollo 15* mission.

sound fixing and ranging /sáwnd fìksiŋ ænd réynjiŋ/ See **SOFAR.**

sounding /sáwndiŋ/ *attr.* Of or pertaining to atmospheric studies.

sounding rocket /sáwndiŋ ràkət/ *n.c.* Upper-atmosphere research vehicle consisting of one or more stages; usually solid-

fueled and comparatively inexpensive. Many are launched each year by the U.S. as supplements to the extensive satellite program.

southern lights /sɅ̂ðɚn láyts/ See **aurora.**

Soyuz [*Rus.* sayús] *n.* "Union," current, third U.S.S.R. manned spaceflight program. It is the first program in which men were able to return to earth in a different craft from that in which they were launched. It also accomplished the first rendezvous involving three spacecraft and the first dockings with a space station. The purpose of the program is increased investigation of circumterrestrial space and the establishment of temporary earth-orbiting space stations.

After an undisclosed number of unmanned test flights, *Soyuz 1* carried Vladimir M. Kamarov into orbit on April 22, 1967. His flight ended in tragedy when the craft's parachute failed during reentry, causing a fatal crash after a four-mile free fall.

Soyuz 4 and *5,* launched on consecutive days in January 1969, achieved Russia's first docking of manned vehicles; two of the

---

MANNED SOYUZ FLIGHTS

Mission	Crew	Dates	Remarks
Soyuz 1	Vladimir M. Komarov (Col., AF)	April 23–24, 1967 (26 hrs. 40 min.)	Initial test flight of the *Soyuz* spacecraft; pilot killed due to capsule parachute failure. 18 orbits.
Soyuz 3	Georgy T. Beregovoi (Col., AF)	October 26–30, 1968 (94 hrs. 51 min.)	Three successful rendezvous with unmanned *Soyuz 2.* 61 orbits.
Soyuz 4	Vladimir A. Shatalov (Lt. Col., AF)	January 14–17, 1969 (71 hrs. 14 min.)	Acted as target vehicle for rendezvous and docking with *Soyuz 5;* carried members of the *Soyuz 5* crew back to Earth. 48 orbits.
Soyuz 5	Boris V. Volynov (Lt. Col., AF) Aleksei S. Yeliseyev (Civilian) Evegny V. Khrunov (Lt. Col., AF)	January 15–17, 1969 (72 hrs. 46 min.)	First crew transfer in space: Yeliseyev and Khrunov boarded *Soyuz 4,* while Volynov returned to Earth alone in *Soyuz 5.* 49 orbits.
Soyuz 6	Georgy S. Shonin (Lt. Col., AF) Valery N. Kubasov (Civilian)	October 11–16, 1969 (118 hrs. 42 min.)	Successful rendezvous and formation maneuvers with *Soyuz 7* and *Soyuz 8.* Welding experiments carried out successfully. Over 30 various maneuvers and course changes. 75 orbits.
Soyuz 7	Anatoly V. Filipchenko (Lt. Col., AF) Viktor V. Gorbatke (Lt. Col., AF) Vladislav N. Volkov (Civilian)	October 12–17, 1969 (118 hrs. 41 min.)	Extensive rendezvous and maneuvering with *Soyuz 6* and *Soyuz 8.* 75 orbits.
Soyuz 8	Vladimir A. Shatalov (Col., AF) Aleksei S. Yeliseyev (Civilian)	October 13–18, 1969 (118 hrs. 41 min.)	Extensive rendezvous and maneuvering with *Soyuz 6* and *Soyuz 7.* 75 orbits.
Soyuz 9	Adriyan G. Nikolayev (Col., AF) Vitaly I. Sevastyanov (Civilian)	June 1–19, 1970 (424 hrs. 52 min.)	Extensive manual and automatic systems tests. Tests of crew compatibility and effects of weightlessness during prolonged spaceflight. 287 orbits.
Soyuz 10	Vladimir A. Shatalov (Col., AF) Aleksei S. Yeliseyev (Civilian) Nikolai N. Rukavishnikov (Civilian)	April 23–25, 1971 (48 hrs. 14 min.)	First docking and boarding of a space station; on board *Salyut* 5½ hrs. 32 orbits.
Soyuz 11	Georgy T. Dobrovolsky (Lt. Col., AF) Vladislav N. Volkov (Civilian) Viktor I. Patsayev (Civilian)	June 6–30, 1971 (ca. 569 hrs. 40 min.)	Crew spent 22 days inside *Salyut* space station. Undocking and reentry outwardly successful; but crew died due to depressurization of reentry capsule. 360 orbits.

/z/ zero; /ž/ azure; /θ/ thin; /ð/ then; /ŋ/ song; /æ/ bat; /ɔ/ law; /ə/ sun; /ɚ/ bird. Foreign symbols: [(n)] nasalization of some French vowels followed by /n/; [R] French uvular rolled /r/ sound; [ü] high front lip-rounded vowel; [x] Russian voiceless laryngeal fricative.

NVOSTI PRESS AGENCY

Soyuz 11 before launch

Soyuz 5 crew then transferred to and landed in *Soyuz 4*.

Soyuz 6, 7, and *8,* launched on three successive days in October 1969, were the first missions involving more than two spacecraft. The three maneuvered to within yards of each other, set up and tested intervehicular communications, and flew in formation.

The missions of *Soyuz 10* and *Soyuz 11* involved docking with Salyut, the first experimental space station. The three-man crew of *Soyuz 11* spent 23 productive days in space; but after a seemingly successful reentry, the cosmonauts were found dead, victims of a life-support system failure in the reentry capsule.

The Soyuz spacecraft is designed to accommodate a crew of up to five. Like earlier Soviet space vehicles, it has two separate crew and instrumentation sections. Only the crew module returns to Earth.

All flights in the Soyuz program have been launched by uprated versions of the **Vostok** launch vehicle.

space /spéys/ *n.* Region in which all spatial bodies move; generally considered to begin beyond the atmosphere of the earth; also called *outer space*.

Space Age /spéys èyj/ *n.c. popular.* Historical era beginning in 1957 with the launch of *Sputnik 1* (see **Sputnik**).

space base /spéys bèys/ *n.c.* Large space station envisioned as base for launching missions to higher orbits, to the moon, and into deep space. The first U.S. space base has been proposed as a group of separately launched space stations assembled into a single unit once in orbit.

spaceborne /spéysbòrn/ *attr.* Of or pertaining to items in the area beyond the earth's atmosphere.

spacecraft /spéyskràft/ *n.* Any extraterrestrial vehicle, manned or unmanned.

spacecraft-LM adapter /spêyskræft lêm adǽptæ/ See SLA.

spacecraft lunar module adapter /spêyskræft lúwnæ mâjəl ədǽptæ/ See SLA.

Space Disturbances Laboratory /spéys distɔ̀bənsəz lǽbrətoriy/ See SDL.

Space Electric Rocket Test /spéys iylêktrik rákət tèst/ See SERT.

Space Environmental Simulation Laboratory /spéys envayənmêntəl simyəléyšən lǽbrətoriy/ *n.c.* Major installation at NASA's Manned Spacecraft Center (**MSC**) used to test spacecraft under space conditions duplicated in either of two chambers.

spaceflight /spéysflàyt/ *attr.* Of or pertaining to a journey through space.

space medicine /spéys mèdəsən/ *n.c.* Branch of science that deals with the health of humans in space; still largely in experimental stages.

space platform /spéys plǽtform/ *n.c.* Space station.

space power tool /spêys páwæ tùwl/ *n.c.* Instrument which can tighten a nut or do other small maintenance jobs under **weightless** conditions without its reactions affecting the astronaut.

space radiator /spéys rèydiyeytæ/ *n.c.* Equipment which dissipates excess spacecraft heat in space using **water-glycol** as the medium.

Space Science Board /spéys sàyəns bòrd/ *n.c.* Branch of the U.S. National Academy of Sciences; acts as that agency's advisor on scientific applications of space efforts.

spaceship /spéysšìp/ *n.* Popular term for a manned spacecraft.

Space Shuttle /spéys šâtəl/ *n.c.* U.S. project under which a reusable manned spacecraft will be launched as early as 1978. Official plans announced in January 1972 call for the upper stage of a two-stage rocket to land like an airplane after orbiting in space, allowing it to be reserviced and flown again as many as 100 times.

Booster and orbiter stages will be launched vertically as one vehicle. The piggy-back orbiter will separate at about 250,000 ft. altitude and continue into Earth orbit under its own power, while the booster will fall into the ocean. Upon completion of its mission, the winged orbiter could land horizontally at any large airport. Plans to make the booster similarly reusable have been dropped due to cost limitations.

The orbiter portion of the Space Shuttle is expected to be about 120 ft. long. In addition to its crew of two, it will be able to carry as many as 14 additional men as part of its payload of up to 65,000 pounds. Satellites may be released, or manned modules (see **RAM**) operated from a cargo bay 15 feet in diameter and 60 feet long. The orbiter will be capable of servicing or retrieving satellites. It could be used, if necessary, in space rescues, and is planned for use in conjunction with space stations.

space simulator /spéys sìmyəleytæ/ *n.c.* Simulator.

space station /spéys stèyšən/ *n.c.* Orbiting vehicle designed as a stopping place for manned missions. The first space station was the U.S.S.R. **Salyut,** launched April 19, 1971. The first U.S. space station will be called **Skylab**.

The Space Shuttle, which is still being developed, may have to incorporate several different types of power systems so that it can operate in different environments. Among these are air-breathing engines for atmospheric use and rocket engines for operation in the vacuum of deep space.

NORTH AMERICAN ROCKWELL

/a/ *father;* /aw/ *wow;* /ay/ *buy;* /b/ *boy;* /č/ *witch;* /d/ *doll;* /e/ *bet;* /ey/ *say;* /f/ *few;* /g/ *bag;* /h/ *hole;* /i/ *it;* /iy/ *be;* /j/ *gin;* /k/ *cat;* /l/ *lamb;* /m/ *man;* /n/ *now;* /o/ *orbit;* /ow/ *tow;* /oy/ *boy;* /p/ *pat;* /r/ *run;* /s/ *send;* /š/ *shoe;* /t/ *toy;* /u/ *put;* /uw/ *do;* /v/ *eve;* /w/ *way;* /y/ *yes;*

SE – 58

space suit /spéys sùwt/ *n.c.* **1.** Durable, pressurized, multilayered life-support outer garment; it supplies, when supported by auxiliary systems, all that an astronaut needs in order to survive a short period in a vacuum either within or outside his spacecraft.

2. *Apollo.* **PGA.**

space support equipment /spéys səpòrt, iykwìpmənt/ See **SSE.**

space telescope /spéys tèləskowp/ See **ATM; LST.**

space tug /spéys tə̀g/ *n.c.* Proposed U.S. manned spacecraft intended for taxiing between points in space. The tug would move from orbit to orbit to reposition or otherwise service manned and unmanned satellites. It would also ferry personnel and equipment between Moon bases and Moon-orbiting craft and help assemble space bases and large Mars-bound craft which would be assembled in Earth orbit from sections delivered from the ground.

space treaty /spéys trìytiy/ See **UN.**

space walk /spéys wɔ̀k/ See **EVA.**

SPAN /spǽn/ *(ac.) n.c.* "Solar Proton Alert Network," global observation system which watches the sun for **solar flares** during manned missions in **deep space.** SPAN warnings enable astronauts on **EVA** to take refuge in their craft during such solar activity. SPAN is operated by the Space Disturbances Laboratory (**SDL**).

spatiography /spèyšágrəfiy/ *n.* Science that deals with the mapping of fields and areas in space.

special environmental container /spêšəl envayənmêntəl kəntéynə/ See **SEC.**

specific impulse /spəsîfik ímpəls/ *n.c.* Measure of rocket performance expressed in seconds; pounds of thrust is divided by the **weight flow rate.**

spectrometer /spektrámətə/ *n.* Device used to study a given type of light wave.

spectrum /spéktrəm/ *n.* Range of energies; usually that of visible light produced by a prism.

speed of light /spîyd əv láyt/ See **light year.**

sphere of influence /sfîr əv ínfluwəns/ *n.c.* Area over which a given celestial body exerts more gravitational influence than any other spatial body. See **MSI.**

sphereographical navigation /sfîrowgrǽfikəl nævigéyšən/ *n.c.* Celestial guidance based on two successive detections of a satellite rather than a star.

Spider /spáydə/ *n.* Name of *Apollo 9* LM (see **Apollo**).

spin /spín/ **1.** *v. intr.* Of a spacecraft, to move about one of its axes.

2. *n.* Movement of a spacecraft about one of its axes.

spin-off /spín ɔ̀f/ *n.c.* **Fall-out.**

spin stabilized /spîn stéybəlayzd/ *attr.* Of or pertaining to a spacecraft which is deliberately whirled to maintain its **orientation.**

splashdown /splǽšdawn/ *n.* Point in time when a spacecraft falls into the ocean for **recovery.**

splash down /splǽš dáwn/ *v. intr.* Of a spacecraft, to fall into the ocean after reentry.

NOVOSTI PRESS AGENCY

A view of the details of *Sputnik 1*, the first artificial Earth satellite

SPS *(ac.) n.c. Apollo.* "Service propulsion system," U.S. spacecraft equipment complex which provides, through one liquid-fueled rocket engine, most of the thrust for an **Apollo** mission. Three subsystems facilitate power production: **pressurization subsystem, propellant subsystem,** and propellant utilization and gauging subsystem (**PUGS**).

Sputnik [*Rus.* spútnyik] *n.* "Satellite," name applied to the first ten satellites launched by the U.S.S.R. Sputniks included the first artificial satellite launched (*Sputnik 1,* October 4, 1957); the first vehicle to carry a living organism into outer space, the dog Laika (*Sputnik 2,* November 1957); and the first spacecraft retrieved from outer space (*Sputnik 5,* August 1960). The basic task of the initial Sputnik launches was the study of systems applicable to manned spaceflight. Sputnik 1 was orbited as part of the Soviet Union's activities during the International Geophysical Year (**IGY**). It opened the Space Age, and gave the U.S.S.R. a five month head start over the U.S. The general class of Soviet satellites following *Sputnik 10* has been officially designated **Kosmos.**

spy satellite /spáy sǽtəlayt/ *n.c.* **Reconnaissance satellite.**

squawk box /skwɔ́k bàks/ *n.c. sl.* Public-address system speaker.

squib /skwíb/ *n.* Device used to produce **ignition.**

SRATS /srǽts/ *(ac.) n.c* "Solar Radiation and Thermospheric Structure Satellite," Japanese upper atmospheric research satellite projected for launch in 1972–73. The satellite's mission will include extensive investigation of ionspheric electron activity.

SRC *(ac.) n.c. Apollo.* "Sample return container," airtight receptacle in which lunar samples are carried back to Earth; two are carried for each Apollo lunar landing mission. Each SRC, cut from a solid aluminum block, weighs 14 lbs. and can hold 65 lbs. An SRC is sometimes called a *rock box.*

SSE *(ac.) n.c. Apollo.* "Space support equipment," system which keeps the **LRV** in stowage and can later deploy it on the lunar surface. The SSE can be activated manually, although the normal method is by unreeling a **deployment tape.**

stability /stəbílətiy/ *n.* Quality of steady spacecraft orientation with regard to direction or some celestial body.

stabilization and control system /steybələzêyšən ænd kəntrówl sìstəm/ See **SCS.**

stabilize /stéybəlayz/ *v. tr.* To keep a spacecraft in constant orientation with regard to either its direction or some celestial body. Cf. **tumbling.**

stabilizer /stéybəlayzə/ *n.* Chemical added to some solid fuels to retard their combustion.

stable 1 /stêybəl wə́n/ *n.* Upright position of a spacecraft after **splashdown;** readily allows crew **egress.** Cf. **stable 2.**

stable 2 /stêbəl túw/ *n.* Upside-down position of a spacecraft after **splashdown;** craft must be righted to **stable 1** position before crew can **egress.**

stack /stǽk/ *n.* Assembled rocket with **payload** in position.

STADAN /stéydæn/ *(ac.) n.c.* "Satellite Tracking and Data Acquisition Network," **NASA** global tracking and communications system linking ground controllers and Earth satellites; part of NASA Communications Network (**NASCOM**). STADAN stations are situated in a north-south belt and an east-west belt. They include: Canberra and Woomera, Australia; St. Johns, Canada; Santiago, Chile; Quito, Ecuador; Winkfield, England; Tananarive, Malagasy; Lima, Peru; Johannesburg, South Africa; and in the United States, Anchorage and Gilmore Creek, Alaska; Goldstone, California; Fort Meyers, Florida; Blossom Point, Maryland; East Grand Forks, Minnesota; and Rosman, North Carolina. Either of two types of facilities are employed by STADAN stations: movable dish reflectors or Minitrack ("Minimum Weight Tracking"), which uses rail-like antennas laid on the ground. A branch of STADAN is the **SAO/Optical Tracking Network.**

stage /stéyj/ **1.** *n.* Independent rocket-powered unit, several of which are used to form most **launch vehicles.**

2. *v. intr.* To disengage a rocket unit from the remainder of a launch vehicle as part of a preplanned maneuver.

/z/ zero; /ž/ azure; /θ/ thin; /ð/ then; /ŋ/ song; /æ/ bat; /ɔ/ law; /ə/ sun; /ə/ bird. Foreign symbols: [(n)] nasalization of some French vowels followed by /n/; [R] French uvular rolled /r/ sound; [ü] high front lip-rounded vowel; [x] Russian voiceless laryngeal fricative.

stage-and-a-half /stêyj ænd ə hǽf/ *n.c.* Unit of liquid-fueled rocket whose **strap-on** boosters fall away before the main section is burned out.

staging /stéyjiŋ/ *n.* Prescheduled division of the rocket units of a **launch vehicle** after **liftoff.**

standard atmosphere /stǽndəd ǽtməsfir/ *n.c.* Theoretical set of conditions for layers of the earth's atmosphere.

standardized satellite /stǽndədayzd sǽtəlayt/ *n.c.* Craft which is suitable for a number of different missions depending on which items are 'plugged in' to its sections.

standard launch vehicle /stǽndəd lɔ́nč viyhikəl/ See **SLV.**

standby redundancy /stǽndbay riydə́ndənsiy/ *n.c.* Condition of duplication where a **back-up** system is not used until the first one fails. Cf. **parallel redundancy; redundancy.**

standup EVA /stǽndəp iy viy éy/ See **EVA.**

standup extravehicular activity /stǽndəp ekstrəviyhîkyələ æktívətiy/ See **EVA.**

STAR /stár/ **1.** *(ac.) attr.* "Self test and repair," of an instrument, especially a computer, able to detect and eliminate or repair its own malfunctions. A STAR computer is being developed for the U.S. **TOPS** flyby.

2. *l.c. n.* Self-luminous celestial body, distinct from a **comet** or **nebula.**

star check /stár ček/ *n.c.* Celestial navigational sighting.

star tracker /stár trækə/ *n.c.* Instrument which sights on a star for use as a reference point in navigation.

state vector /stéyt vèktə/ *n.c.* Ground-computed information on a spacecraft's location, velocity, etc., relayed to the craft for crew use.

static firing /stǽtik fáyəiŋ/ *n.c.* Testing of **rocket engines** not yet installed in a vehicle or without allowing the vehicle to **lift off.**

Station Conferencing and Monitoring Arrangement /stêyšən kànfəənsiŋ ænd mânitəiŋ əréynjmənt/ See **SCAMA.**

stationkeeping /stéyšənkìypiŋ/ *n.c.* Orbiting exactly and at a steady speed, usually in formation with some other craft.

stay/no-stay /stéy nów stèy/ *attr. Apollo.* Of or pertaining to the decision, or point in time when the decision is made, on whether to remain on the moon after the LM has landed.

steering jets /stíriŋ jèts/ See **attitude jets.**

stellar /stélə/ *attr.* Of or pertaining to a **star.**

step rocket /stép ràkət/ *n.c.* Multistaged space vehicle.

strap-on rocket /strǽp ɔn ràkət/ *n.c.* Small rocket which provides added propulsion for a **launch vehicle;** several are usually placed around the base of the **stage** which needs the additional boost.

stratosphere /strǽtəsfìr/ *n.* Layer of Earth's atmosphere extending from 7 to 37 miles up.

streetcar satellite /stríytkar sætəlayt/ *n.c. sl.* **Standardized satellite.**

structural transition section /strȃkčəl trænzíšən sèkšən/ See **AM.**

STS *(ac.) n.c.* "Structural transition section." See **AM.**

sublimation /səbləméyšən/ *n.* Transformation of ice directly to steam.

sublimator /səbləmeytə/ *n.* Instrument which removes heat from **water-glycol** in a spacecraft; it can also produce **sublimation.**

suborbital /səbórbətəl/ *attr.* Of or pertaining to a space shot which does not complete a full orbit.

subsatellite /səbsætəlayt/ *n.* Craft launched into orbit from a vehicle already in orbit. The first U.S. subsatellite was launched from the CSM of *Apollo 15* in July, 1971.

subsystem /səbsistəm/ *n.* Small or lower level **system.** Subsystems are usually grouped to form an actual system with a major overall function. The distinction between subsystem and system is rather arbitrary.

subweight /səbwèyt/ *n.* Any weight between a normal and a **weightless** condition.

suit heat exchanger /sûwt híyt eksčèynjə/ See **ECU.**

sun /sən/ *n.***1.** Star situated at the center of our **solar system.** It is 865,000 miles in diameter and is completely gaseous. Surface temperature is estimated at over 10,000°F. Although 93 million miles from Earth, the sun is essential to life processes on Earth. Solar activity waxes and wanes in cycles (see **solar cycle**), but the sun always emits constant intense radiation and is the source of a magnetic field so powerful and broad that it forms the interplanetary magnetic fields of the solar system.

2. Any star.

Sunflower /sə́nflàwə/ See **D-2A.**

Sunrise /sə́nràyz/ See **Voskhod.**

sunseeker /sə́nsiykə/ *n.* Device used to keep spacecraft solar-oriented equipment locked on the sun.

sunspot cycle /sə́nspat sàykəl/ See **solar cycle.**

sun-synchronous /sə́n sìŋkrənəs/ *attr.* **1.** Of an orbital plane fixed in an angle with the sun's rays. Sun-synchronous orbits are nearly polar and shift slightly each day so as to keep the sunlight/orbital plane angle constant as the earth moves about the sun.

2. Of a satellite moving in a sun-synchronous orbit. Such satellites are ideal for Earth photography, since illumination of a given latitude remains the same during every orbit. This allows repeated examination of any location, always under the same lighting conditions. The first sun-synchronous satellite was *TIROS 9* (see **TIROS**).

sun tracker /sə́n trækə/ *n.c.* **Sunseeker.** Cf. **star tracker.**

supercritical helium /sûwpəkrîtikəl híyliyəm/ See **SHE.**

superior planet /supîryə plǽnət/ *n.c.* Planet or satellite whose **heliocentric** orbit is larger than Earth's. Cf. **inferior planet.**

supersonic /sûwpəsánik/ *attr.* Of or pertaining to speeds faster than that of sound (approximately 767 m.p.h.). See **hypersonic; Mach number.**

support crew /səpórt krùw/ *n.c.* Personnel at a launch site who aid in the preparations for **liftoff.**

support module /səpórt màjəl/ See **RAM.**

suprathermal ion detector experiment /sûwprəθ ə́məl áyan diytèktə ekspèrimənt/ See **SIDE.**

surge tank /sə́j tæŋk/ *n.c.* CM oxygen container used from **reentry** to **recovery.**

Surveyor /səvéyə/ *n.* U.S. lunar probe series consisting of seven craft launched between 1966 and 1968. Surveyor was designed to soft-land on the moon to directly investigate possible manned landing sites. *Surveyor 1,* launched in May 1966, was equipped only for picture taking, but later probes tested the surface and soil as well. Parts from *Surveyor 3,* launched in April 1967, were brought back to Earth by the crew of *Apollo 12.* Surveyor was the final NASA lunar probe series; it followed

The *Symphonie* satellite will be launched by a vehicle composed of British, French, and German rockets.

CNES

/a/ *father;* /aw/ *wow;* /ay/ b*uy;* /b/ *boy;* /č/ *witch;* /d/ *doll;* /e/ *bet;* /ey/ *say;* /f/ *few;* /g/ *bag;* /h/ *hole;* /i/ *it;* /iy/ *be;* /j/ *gin;* /k/ *cat;* /l/ *lamb;*
/m/ *man;* /n/ *now;* /o/ *orbit;* /ow/ *tow;* /oy/ *boy;* /p/ *pat;* /r/ *run;* /s/ *send;* /š/ *shoe;* /t/ *toy;* /u/ *put;* /uw/ *do;* /v/ *eve;* /w/ *way;* /y/ *yes;*

SE – 60

Ranger and **Lunar Orbiter.**

survival kit /sɚváyvəl kìt/ *n.c. Apollo.* Two sacks of basic supplies for astronauts in case the **CM** does not touch down on Earth in a preplanned area. Food, water, medical supplies, and a three-man life raft are included.

sustainer engine /səstéynɚ ènjən/ *n.c.* Rocket motor used to maintain the initial velocity of a craft. It is usually burned at **perigee** if the orbit touches Earth's atmosphere, since the atmosphere causes **drag.**

SV-5 *n. cd.* NASA/USAF experimental wingless rocket-powered vehicle. Unmanned test flights ended in 1967 and manned flights testing maneuverability during deceleration were scheduled.

SWC *(ac.) n.c. Apollo.* "Solar wind composition," scientific device carried to the moon during Project **Apollo** as an independent experiment. The instrument is a four-square-foot sheet of aluminum foil deployed perpendicularly to the lunar surface. The SWC experiment traps particles of the solar wind; it is returned to earth for examination.

sweat cooling /swét kùwliŋ/ *n.c.* **Reentry** heat abatement process which employs heat absorbing liquids in surfaces subjected to high reentry temperatures.

swimmer's umbilical /swîmɚz əmbílikəl/ *n.c.* Cord released from a manned craft after splashdown. It holds a **sea marker** and a radio allowing conversation with astronauts inside the capsule. It is part of the earth landing system (**ELS**).

swing-around trajectory /swíŋ əràwnd trəjèktɚiy/ *n.c.* Flight path which utilizes a target planet's gravity to either return to the planet of origin or go on to another target.

swing-by trajectory /swíŋ bày trəjèktɚiy/ See **swing-around trajectory.**

SWS *(ac.) n.c.* **1.** *Apollo.* "Solar wind spectrometer," scientific device carried to the moon as part of the Apollo Lunar Surface Experiments Package (**ALSEP**). SWS studies the solar wind and its relationship to the moon; the tail of the earth's magnetosphere is also studied by this instrument.

2. "Saturn Workshop." See **Skylab.**

Symphonie [*Fr.* se(n)foné] *n.* "Symphony," proposed geostationary telecommunications satellite being developed under a joint venture by Belgium, Federal Republic of Germany, and France. Two such satellites are scheduled to be launched in 1974. Symphonies will provide communications coverage for Europe, Africa, South America, and the eastern seaboard of the U.S. Plans call for launch using **Europa** launch vehicles.

sync hack /síŋk hæk/ *n.c.* **Time hack.**

synchronous /síŋkrənəs/ *attr.* **1.** Of or pertaining to recurring events, such as orbits, completing cycles in the same amount of time.

2. Of or pertaining to a satellite possessing a period of the same duration as that of its central body. Especially applied to **geostationary** satellites.

Synchronous Communications Satellite /síŋkrənəs kəmyuwnəkéyšənz sætələyt/ See **Syncom.**

Synchronous Meteorological Satellite /síŋkrənəs miytiyɚələjikəl sætələyt/ See **SMS.**

Syncom /síŋkam/ *(ac.) n.c.* "Synchronous Communications Satellite." **1.** First synchronous comsat series; any of three experimental active-repeater type satellites launched by the U.S. between 1963 and 1964. *Syncom 3*, orbited in August 1964, became the world's first geostationary satellite. Its performance proved the value of such satellites for communications purposes; only three would be needed for nearly global coverage.

2. *l.c.* Any comsat in synchronous orbit.

synergic curve /sinɚ̀jik kɚv/ *n.c.* Planned trajectory which aims at the highest speeds with the lowest fuel consumption.

system /sístəm/ *n.* Hardware within spacecraft which is arranged into sets to perform its function (see **ECS; GNCS; LES; RCS**).

System for Nuclear Auxiliary Power /sîstəm for nûwkliyɚ ɔgzîlyɚiy páwɚ/ See **SNAP.**

T

Tacsat /tæksæt/ *(ac.) n.c.* "Tactical Communications Satellite," U.S. military experimental comsat series used in the Tactical Satellite Communications (**TacSatCom**) system. *Tacsat 1*, launched into synchronous orbit in February 1969, showed that

HUGHS AIRCRAFT COMPANY

Syncom 1, foreground, the world's first synchronous satellite, was launched in 1963 and weighed only 80 pounds. Its successor, *Tacsat 1, background,* launched in 1969, weighted 1,600 pounds.

/z/ zero; /ž/ azure; /θ/ *thin;* /ð/ *then;* /ŋ/ *song;* /æ/ *bat;* /ɔ/ *law;* /ə/ *sun;* /ɚ/ *bird.* Foreign symbols: [(n)] nasalization of some French vowels followed by /n/; [R] French uvular rolled /r/ sound; [ü] high front lip-rounded vowel; [x] Russian voiceless laryngeal fricative.

comsats could be used for military purposes.

TacSatCom /tǽksætkám/ *(ac.) n.c.* "Tactical Satellite Communications," joint U.S./NATO experimental military comsat system begun in 1967 to allow mobile forces to use synchronous satellites in communications. U.S. **LES** and **Tacsat** vehicles were the first craft involved in the system.

Tactical Communications Satellite /tǽktikəl kəmyuwnəkéyšənz sǽtəlayt/ See **Tacsat.**

Tactical Satellite Communications /tǽktikəl sǽtəlayt kəmyuwnəkéyšənz/ See **TacSatCom.**

TAD *(ac.) n.c.* "Thrust-Augmented Delta." See **Delta.**

Tago-Sato-Kosaka [*Jap.* tago sato kosáka] See **OAO.**

takeoff /téykɔ̀f/ *n.* The action of an aerospace vehicle as it leaves the ground or other resting place. Cf. **liftoff.**

take off /tèyk ɔ́f/ *phr. v. intr.* Of an aerospace vehicle, to leave the surface of the ground or other resting place at any angle. Cf. **lift off.**

talkback /tɔ́kbæk/ *n. sl.* **Barber's pole.**

tangential ellipse /tænjênšəl iylíps/ *n.c.* **Transfer ellipse.**

tanks, propellant /prəpélənt tǽŋks/ *n.c.* Rocket fuel containers; they run most of a rocket's length.

Tansei [*Jap.* tanséi] *n.* "Light Blue," Japanese satellite launched February 1971 by an **M-4S** launch vehicle. The satellite's primary mission was testing the capabilities of the launcher. No scientific equipment other than radio and telemetric devices were included in Tansei's payload.

tape dump /téyp dəmp/ *n.c.* **Data dump.**

target /tárgət/ *n.* Nonmaneuvering craft in a **rendezvous** and **docking** procedure.

Target Docking Adapter /tárgət dákiŋ ədǽptə/ See **TDA.**

Target Launch Vehicle /tárgət lɔ́nč vìyhikəl/ See **TLV.**

TAT *(ac.) n.c.* "Thrust-Augmented Thor." See **Thor.**

Tau Ceti /tâw síytay/ or /tâw kéti/ *n.c.* Star no. 19 in the constellation Cetus. Its apparent visual magnitude is 3.6 (see **Ozma, Project**).

T/C *(ac.) n.c. Apollo.* "Telecommunications," U.S. equipment system which provides for the processing and transmission of voice, television, telemetry, and tracking and ranging information between the ground and a craft, and between astronauts within a craft. The instruments of four subsystems, **intercommunications, data, radio frequency equipment,** and **antenna,** handle various aspects of the T/C system.

TDA *(ac.) n.c. Gemini.* "Target Docking Adapter," apparatus on the *Gemini Agena Target Vehicle (GATV)* (see **Gemini**) with which the spacecraft docked. The TDA consisted of a cone-shaped opening, and lights and signals used for aligning the nose of the Gemini properly.

The *Augmented Target Docking Adapter (ATDA)*, an improved system with more sophisticated electronics, replaced the TDA in 1966.

TD&E *(ac.) n.c. Apollo.* "Transposition, docking, and ejection," three-phase maneuver following translunar injection (**TLI**). During transposition, the CSM turns toward the LM; during docking, CSM and LM join and lock together; during ejection, the CSM/LM combination pulls away from the SLA. **Evasive maneuver** follows TD&E.

TEC *(ac.) n.c. Apollo.* "Transearth coast," the long glide from transearth injection (**TEI**) to entry interface (**EI**); midcourse corrections (**MCC**) may be made during this period.

TEI *(ac.) n.c. Apollo.* "Transearth injection," CSM maneuver in which a rocket burn boosts the craft from lunar parking orbit (**LPO**) into a trajectory toward the earth. Transearth coast (**TEC**) follows.

tektites /téktayts/ *n.c.* Glass particles on Earth believed to have originated on the moon; generally found in southeast Asia.

telecommunication /teləkəmyuwnəkéyšən/ *n.* Transmission of information by **electromagnetic** means.

telecommunications /teləkəmyuwnəkéyšənz/ See **T/C.**

telecommunications system /tèləkəmyuwnəkéyšənz sìstəm/ See **T/C.**

Telecommunications via the Stars /teləkəmyuwnəkéyšənz vàyə ðə stárz/ See **Telstar.**

telemetric /tèləmétrik/ *attr.* Of or pertaining to **telemetry.**

telemetry /təlémətriy/ *n.* 1. Process by which spacecraft data is transmitted between two points.

   2. Spacecraft information.

Television and Infrared Observation Satellite /tèləvižən ænd ìnfrərêd abzɚvéyšen sǽtəlayt/ See **TIROS.**

Telstar /télstàr/ *(ac.) n.c.* "Telecommunications via the Stars," first commercial comsat series launched between 1962 and 1963 by NASA for American Telephone and Telegraph. The series' two experimental

The *Telstar 2* communications satellite

A.T. & T.

active-repeater type satellites were able to send television and telephone signals, and facsimile and data. *Telstar 1* made the first trans-Atlantic satellite TV transmission in July 1962. The International Telecommunications Satellite Consortium (**Intelsat**) series superceded Telstar.

terebenthene, essence of /tɔ́əbenθiyn/ *n.c.* Distilled conifer resins used as rocket fuel in France.

terminal count /tɔ́mənəl káwnt/ *n.c.* Final 28 hour period of a **countdown.**

terminal guidance /tɔ́mənəl gáydəns/ *n.c.* Navigation of a craft in the final stages of **rendezvous.**

terminal phase finalization /tɔ́mənəl féyz faynəlizèyšən/ See **TPF.**

terminal phase initiation /tɔ́mənəl féyz inišiyèyšən/ See **TPI.**

terminal velocity /tɔ́mənəl vəlásətiy/ *n.c.* Maximum speed a spacecraft could reach under any specific set of conditions.

terminator /tɔ́məneytɚ/ *n.* Line dividing darkness and light on nonradiant **celestial** bodies.

terrestrial /tɚéstriyəl/ *attr.* Of or pertaining to Earth.

tertiary crater /tɔ́šiyeriy kréytɚ/ *n.c.* Impression in the surface of the moon resulting from the impact of material thrown off when **secondary craters** were formed.

test range /tést rèynj/ *n.* Closely monitored, marked-off area used for testing missiles or rockets. Regular launch sites are also associated with some test ranges (see **AFETR; AFWTR**).

test stand /tést stænd/ *n.c.* Device which holds a **rocket engine** for **static testing.**

theodolite /θiyádəlayt/ *n.* Device for visual **tracking.**

thermal heating /θɔ́məl híytiŋ/ *n.c.* Heating produced by high-speed travel through an atmosphere.

thermal meteoroid garment /θɔ́məl míytiyəroyd gàrmənt/ See **PGA.**

thermal micrometeoroid garment /θɔ́məl maykrowmíytiyəoyd gàrmənt/ See **PGA.**

thermal shock /θɔ́məl šák/ *n.c.* Reaction of bodies that are poor conductors of heat to a sudden increase in temperature.

thermocouple /θɔ́məkəpəl/ *n.* Device which when heated produces electricity.

Thermoelectric Outer Planets Spacecraft /θɔ́mowiylêktrik âwtɚ plǽnəts spèyskræft/ See **TOPS.**

thermosphere /θɔ́məsfir/ *n.* Layer of Earth's atmosphere from 56 to 373 miles up.

Thor /θór/ *n.* U.S. single-stage rocket developed from the Thor intercontinental ballistic missile (ICBM). Thor is used as a first stage with other rockets to form more than 25 different multirocket launch vehicles. Notable among these are the *Thor-Agena D*, a combination with an **Agena** second stage, and the *Thrust-Augmented Thor (TAT)*, an Agena combination with strap-on boosters added to the Thor. Both the Thor-Agena D and the TAT have been used primarily for launching heavy scientific satellites, including those of the Orbiting Geophysical Observatory (**OGO**) and **Nimbus** series.

/a/ *father*; /aw/ *wow*; /ay/ *buy*; /b/ *boy*; /č/ *witch*; /d/ *doll*; /e/ *bet*; /ey/ *say*; /f/ *few*; /g/ *bag*; /h/ *hole*; /i/ *it*; /iy/ *be*; /j/ *gin*; /k/ *cat*; /l/ *lamb*; /m/ *man*; /n/ *now*; /o/ *orbit*; /ow/ *tow*; /oy/ *boy*; /p/ *pat*; /r/ *run*; /s/ *send*; /š/ *shoe*; /t/ *toy*; /u/ *put*; /uw/ *do*; /v/ *eve*; /w/ *way*; /y/ *yes*;

On April 1, 1960, a Thor-Able vehicle launched *Tiros 1*, an experimental weather-prediction satellite. The Tiros program was eventually superseded by the ESSA program.

time dilation /táym daylèyšən/ *n.c.* According to Einstein's special theory of relativity, time, as we measure it on Earth, elapses more slowly for objects moving at extremely high velocities than it does for stationary objects. Hence, time can be said to be *dilated* ("expanded"). For example, if two identical clocks were run for a year but one was kept stationary while the other was continually moved at nearly the speed of light, a comparison of the two clocks at the end of the year would show that significantly less time had elapsed on the moving clock. This phenomenon may eventually enable a single spacecraft crew to make a journey that would last for several lifetimes measured in Earth time.

time hack /táym hæk/ *n.c.* The synchronizing of ground-control and spacecraft clocks.

time of ignition /tâym əv igníšən/ See **TIG.**

TIROS /táyrows/ *(ac.) n.c.* "Television and Infrared Observation Satellite," U.S. ex-

NASA

Tiros satellites became more complex as the program developed. The *Tiros 3* has two wide-angle cameras and an infrared experiment.

The average Thor is 65 ft. high, weighs around 100,000 lbs. fueled, and produces 150,000 lbs. thrust. Thor-Agena D stands 76 ft. high, weighs 125,000 lbs. fueled, and produces 186,000 lbs. of thrust. The TAT is also 76 ft. high, but weighs 136,000 lbs. fueled; the addition of first stage strap-on boosters increases its thrust potential to 348,000 lbs.

2. Norse god of thunder and rain.

Thor-Agena D /ôr əĵîynə díy/ See **Thor.**

thrust /θrást/ *n.* Lifting force produced by a rocket engine; measured in pounds.

Thrust-Augmented Delta /θrást əgmèntəd déltə/ See **Delta.**

Thrust-Augmented Thor /θrást əgmèntəd θór/ See **Thor.**

thrust buildup /θrást bíldəp/ *n.c.* Progressive increase in rocket power from ignition to full **thrust** which occurs just before **lift-off.**

thrust chamber /θrást čèymbə/ *n.c.* Rock-et-engine compartment where fuel components are burned producing lifting power.

thruster /θrástə/ *n.* Small rocket engine used in addition to the main engine on a spacecraft; usually **reaction control engine.**

thrust-to-weight ratio /θrást tuw wéyt rèyšiyow/ *n.c.* Comparison of the rocket power with the total mass of the empty rocket.

thrust vector /θrást vèktə/ *n.c.* Direction of power of a **rocket engine.**

thrust vector control /θrást vèktə kəntròwl/ *n.c. Apollo.* That part of the stabilization and control system (**SCS**) which determines the firing direction of the service propulsion engine (**SPS**).

TIG *(ac.) n.c.* "Time of ignition," ground elapsed time (**GET**), calculated to the tenth of the second, at which any preplanned rocket **burn** is initiated for a course correction.

perimental meteorological satellite series which, by providing the first successful cloud-cover photography, allowed more accurate weather prediction than ever before. Ten drum-shaped satellites, launched between 1960 and 1965, used television cameras to take cloud pictures and infrared sensors to measure the earth's heat radiation. *TIROS 8,* launched in December 1963, was the first satellite to transmit weather pictures directly to ground stations (see **APT**). *TIROS 9* was the first satellite to be launched into sun-synchronous orbit (January 1965) and was thus able to take better-lighted photos than previous satellites. The TIROS satellites led to those in the Environmental Science Services Administration (**ESSA**) series; *ESSA 1* was also called *TIROS 11.* The designation *TIROS M* was given to the satellite *ITOS-1* (see **ITOS**), launched in 1970.

TIROS Operational Satellite /tâyrows apəéyšənəl sætəlayt/ See **TOS.**

TIROS Operational System /tâyrows apəéyšənəl sìstəm/ See **TOS.**

/z/ zero; /ž/ azure; /θ/ *th*in; /ð/ *th*en; /ŋ/ so*ng*; /æ/ b*a*t; /ɔ/ l*a*w; /ə/ s*u*n; /ɚ/ b*i*rd. Foreign symbols: [(n)] nasalization of some French vowels followed by /n/; [R] French uvular rolled /r/ sound; [ü] high front lip-rounded vowel; [x] Russian voiceless laryngeal fricative.

SE – 63

Titan /táytən/ *n.* U.S. multistage launch vehicle series, developed from the *Titan 2* intercontinental ballistic missile (**ICBM**).

The *Titan 2*, a two-stage rocket, is the basic model of the series. It was used to launch the **Gemini** manned missions. The *Titan 3*, a three-stage model, is the heavy-duty standard military launch vehicle. Spacecraft launched by Titan 3 have included those of the Lincoln Experimental Satellite (**LES**) and Tactical Communications Satellite (**Tacsat**) series. The *Titan 3/Centaur*, a basic Titan 2 with strap-on rockets plus a **Centaur** upper stage, has been projected to launch the Viking/Mars probe in 1975 (see **Viking**).

The standard Titan 2 stands 90 ft. high, weighs 300,000 lbs. fueled, and develops 530,000 lbs. of thrust. The Titan 3 is 130 ft. high, weighs 1,400,000 lbs. fueled, and is capable of producing 2,400,000 lbs. of thrust. The Titan 3/Centaur stands 184 ft. high, weighs 2,600,000 lbs. fueled, and has a thrust potential of 3,000,000 lbs.

TJM *(ac.) n.c. Apollo.* "Tower jettison motor," launch escape system (**LES**) rocket which pulls the escape equipment away from the combined launch vehicle/manned spacecraft during normal flight or which, during **abort,** separates the escape equipment from the capsule, thereby enabling its parachutes to deploy.

TLC *(ac.) n.c.* "Translunar coast," on lunar missions, the long glide from translunar injection (**TLI**) to lunar orbit insertion (**LOI**) or a swing around the moon; some midcourse corrections (**MCC**) are made during this period. On Apollo, the **evasive maneuver** also takes place early in TLC.

TLI *(ac.) n.c.* "Translunar injection," spacecraft maneuver, for lunar missions, in which a rocket burn boosts the craft from earth parking orbit (**EPO**) into a trajectory toward the moon. For Apollo, the third stage of the Saturn launch vehicle provides the necessary thrust and is then jettisoned. The next major Apollo maneuver after TLI is transposition, docking, and ejection (**TD&E**).

TLV *(ac.) n.c. Gemini.* "Target Launch Vehicle," **Atlas** rocket used to launch the **Agenas** for Gemini rendezvous and docking maneuvers.

TMG *(ac.) n.c. Apollo.* "Thermal meteoroid (or micrometeoroid) garment." See **PGA**.

Topaz /tówpæz/ See **Topaze**.

Topaze [*Fr.* topáz] *n.* "Topaz," French single-stage rocket, used primarily as the first stage in the **Diamant** launch vehicle.

Topaze stands 15 ft. high and develops 33,000 lbs. of thrust.

topping-off /tâpiŋ óf/ *n.c. sl.* Replacing propellant components which are lost because of **boil-off,** just before launch.

TOPS /táps/ *(ac.) n.c.* "Thermoelectric Outer Planets Spacecraft," U.S. multipurpose spacecraft series planned for use as probe in the **Outer Planets Missions.** Since the missions will last up to nine years each, TOPS is specially designed for a long lifetime.

Special features of the craft include a radioisotope thermoelectric generator (**RTG**) and a self-test and repair (**STAR**) computer. The RTG will be used for power instead of today's standard solar panels, since available solar energy decreases in intensity as the probe recedes from the sun. The STAR computer will increase the craft's reliability and thus its chances of performing properly for the duration of the mission.

torque /tórk/ *n.* A twisting force.

torquing command /tórkiŋ kəmænd/ *n.c.* Order directed to a vehicle's **gyroscopes** to maintain **attitude** of the craft.

torso limb suit /tôrsow lím sùwt/ See **PGA**.

TOS *(ac.) n.c.* **1.** "TIROS Operational System," U.S. operational meteorological satellite system, the first to provide global weather data. Nine Environmental Science Services Administration (**ESSA**) satellites, launched between February 1966 and February 1969, comprised the system. Used in pairs, they provided both instantaneous and delayed photos. TOS was superceded by the Improved TIROS Operational System (**ITOS**).

2. "TIROS Operational Satellite," any satellite used in the TIROS Operational System, including all the ESSAs.

total impulse /tôwtəl ímpəls/ *n.c.* **Specific impulse.**

touchdown /tóčdàwn/ **1.** *n.* Point in time in a mission when a craft makes full contact with the surface of a celestial body in a soft landing (see **soft-land**).

2. *attr.* Of or pertaining to the **soft landing** of a craft.

touch down /tóč dáwn/ *v. tr.* To set a craft down on a celestial body by vertical descent. See also **soft-land.**

Tournesol [*Fr.* tuRnasó] See **D-2A.**

tower jettison motor /táwə jètisən mòwtə/ See **TJM.**

TPF *(ac.) n.c. Apollo.* "Terminal phase finalization," LM maneuver which brings the LM and CSM close enough for docking; fourth and final phase of lunar orbit rendezvous (**LOR**). The CSM duplicates TPF in mirror-image maneuver so that if LM engines fail, docking can still be accomplished. After jettison of the ascent stage, docking, and crew and equipment transfer, the transearth injection (**TEI**) is initiated.

TPI *(ac.) n.c. Apollo.* "Terminal phase initiation," LM maneuver which uses rocket thrust to decrease the fifteen-mile distance between the LM and CSM which remains after the constant delta height (**CDH**) maneuver. The third phase of lunar orbit rendezvous (**LOR**), TPI is followed by terminal phase finalization (**TPF**).

tracking /trǽkiŋ/ *n.* Following of a body in flight; **radar** is the most common system used.

tracking station /trǽkiŋ stèyšən/ *n.c.* Ground- or sea-based post containing all the complex equipment needed to monitor a spacecraft's flight path. See also **ground station.**

trajectory /trəjéktəiy/ *n.* Flight path.

transceiver /trænsíyvə/ *n.* Instrument which can both transmit and receive.

transducer /trænzdúwsə/ *n.* Instrument capable of changing energy from one form into another.

transearth /trænzə́θ/ *attr.* Of or pertaining to the area between another celestial body and Earth. See **TEC.**

transearth coast /trænzə́θ kówst/ See **TEC.**

transearth injection /trænzə́θ injékšən/ See **TEI.**

transfer ellipse /trǽnsfə iylìps/ *n.c.* Trajectory followed by a spacecraft going from one elliptical orbit to another. A *tangential transfer ellipse* produces a small angle between the orbits and uses less energy to effect the change over.

transfer orbit /trǽnsfə òrbət/ *n.c.* Orbit used to change from one orbit to another.

transfer tunnel /trǽnsfə tənəl/ See **docking tunnel.**

transient event /trǽnziənt iyvént/ *n.c.* Short-lived phenomena seen on an **extraterrestrial** body.

Transit /trǽnzit/ *(ac.) n.c.* **1.** USN navsat system, fully operational since 1968, involving ground stations, four satellites, and shipboard equipment. The system allows military secrecy because it does not require a ship to send out a signal while fixing position. At present, the complexity and expense of the system precludes commercial application.

2. USN series of navsats, launched from April 1960. *Transit 1-B*, the first of the series, was the first navsat and proved the feasibility of the program. *Transit 2-A*, launched in June 1960, was part of the first U.S. two-payload launch. *Transit 4-A*, launched in 1961, was the first spacecraft to carry a nuclear generator. Satellites in this series have been called *NavSat* since 1963.

APPLIED PHYSICS LAB, JOHNS HOPKINS UNIVERSITY
The *Transit* satellites *1B, 2A,* and *4A.* The small sphere on *4A, left,* contained plutonium 238.

translation /trænzléyšən/ *n.* Moving of a spacecraft to a new position.

translunar /trænzlúwnə/ *attr.* Of or pertaining to the area beyond the moon's path around Earth; sometimes used to mean **cislunar.**

translunar coast /trænzlûwnə kówst/ See **TLC.**

translunar injection /trænzlûwnə injékšən/ See **TLI.**

translunar injection point /trænzlûwnə injékšən pòynt/ *n.c.* Point in Earth orbit where a moon-bound trajectory is entered by a spacecraft.

transmitter /trænzmítə/ *n.* Instrument used to relay signals.

transpiration cooling /trænspəêyšən kúwliŋ/ *n.c.* Method of abating heat in a reen-

/a/ father; /aw/ wow; /ay/ buy; /b/ boy; /č/ witch; /d/ doll; /e/ bet; /ey/ say; /f/ few; /g/ bag; /h/ hole; /i/ it; /iy/ be; /j/ gin; /k/ cat; /l/ lamb; /m/ man; /n/ now; /o/ orbit; /ow/ tow; /oy/ boy; /p/ pat; /r/ run; /s/ send; /š/ shoe; /t/ toy; /u/ put; /uw/ do; /v/ eve; /w/ way; /y/ yes;

SE–64

tering spacecraft by using heat-absorbent gas or vapor to remove heat from **reentry** surfaces.

transponder /trænspándɚ/ *n*. Instrument which employs a **transceiver** and is capable of automatic signal transmission on variable wave lengths.

transporter /trænspórtɚ/ *n*. Vehicle used to bring a loaded or unloaded **mobile launcher** from the **VAB** to the launch site; also used to move the **mobile service structure**. The six-million-pound vehicle has a platform measuring 131 ft. by 114 ft.

transposition /trænzpəsíšən/ See **TD&E.**

transposition, docking, and ejection /trænspəzîšən dâkiŋ ænd iyjékšən/ See **TD&E.**

transstage /trǽnsstéyǰ/ *n*. Top stage of a *Titan 3* (see **Titan**); equipped with restart capability.

troposphere /trówpəsfir/ *n*. Lowest layer of the Earth's atmosphere; extends from sea level up to 7 miles.

Tsiolkovsky, Konstantin E. [*Rus.* cyolkófskiy konstantyín] See **Union of Soviet Socialist Republics.**

T-time /tíy tàym/ *n*. Amount of time remaining before **liftoff**, or the amount of time since liftoff (see **GET**); expressed in minus or plus values with *T* the code for liftoff. See also **countdown.**

tumbling /támbliŋ/ *n*. Uncontrolled end-over-end movement of a spacecraft in flight; highly undesirable. Cf. **stabilization.**

tunnel assembly /tánəl əsèmbliy/ See **AM.**

turbopump /tɚbowpəmp/ *n*. Device which feeds liquid fuel from propellant tanks into the **thrust chamber** of a rocket.

two-gas system /tûw gæs sístəm/ *n.c.* Spacecraft atmosphere in which oxygen is combined with some inert gas, usually nitrogen. Use of pure oxygen is considered both unsafe and unhealthy.

U–V

UFO *(ac.) n.c.* "Unidentified Flying Object." 1. Any object or effect observed in Earth's atmosphere which cannot be recognized as a conventional aircraft, weather balloon, celestial or meteorological body, or other normal phenomenon.

2. Any of a large number of unexplained objects or phenomena which are sometimes purported to be extraterrestrial spacecraft because they have no complete scientific or logical explanation. The synonym *flying saucer* was coined in 1947 following the sighting of nine disc-shaped objects near Mt. Ranier, Washington, by a civilian pilot. Similar sightings have occurred throughout history, and their exact nature has been a cause of extensive controversy and investigation.

A typical flying saucer is luminous, reddish-orange or bluish-white, sometimes with green lights showing; most often round or oval but sometimes cigar-shaped; usually noiseless but sometimes giving off a hissing sound. It is capable of hovering or shooting off at great velocity.

Various naturalistic explanations of UFO sightings have been advanced: they are electromagnetic phenomena similar to **ball lightning;** they are little-understood electrical phenomena similar to **St. Elmo's fire,** to radar **angels,** or to the **Foo Fighters** observed by World War II pilots; or they are attributable to pollution, clear air turbulence (see **CAT**), temperature inversions, electrical fields generated by thunderstorms, or tornadoes. Scientific experiments to verify such theories are lacking or in their infancy.

Advocates of the theory that UFOs are spaceships point to their apparent extreme mobility and maneuverability and to "curiosity" and other intelligent behavior, such as flying in formation, and the ability of these craft to perform seemingly impossible feats of flight as evidence that those in control possess superior knowledge.

Several reports of occupant cases have been made, in which sighters claimed to have seen extraterrestrial visitors, or even to have ridden in their vehicles. Such sighters are often accused of hyper-excitement, self-hypnosis, hallucination, illusion, or outright fabrication. Photographs of UFOs have been taken, but the possibilities of mishaps in development of film must be weighed; some hoaxes have occurred.

The large number of reported sightings following the 1947 incident prompted an official investigation conducted under U.S. Air Force auspices. During and after Air Force investigations, various civilian groups alleged that vital facts were concealed, and that some of the scientists conducting the study were prejudiced. The study was terminated in 1969 after 22 years, with results that were described as inconclusive. Some maintain the ultimate answer to the problem of presently unexplained UFOs will require either the examination of a space ship which has crashed or landed, or the reproduction of unusual UFO behavior in experiments proving the existence of phenomena not now understood.

According to the National Investigations Committee on Aerial Phenomena (**NICAP**), UFO reports usually run in a five-year cycle, with new cycles beginning in 1972 and 1977. The Air Force maintains UFOs pose no threat to national security.

UHF *(ac.) attr.* "Ultra-high frequency," pertains to radio waves.

UK *(ac.) n.c.* "United Kingdom." See **Ariel.**

ullage /áləǰ/ *n*. Volume of air above a partially full fuel tank.

ullage maneuver /áləǰ mənùwvɚ/ *n.c. Apollo.* Firing of four small ullage rockets following the *Saturn 5*'s first stage burn-out (see **Saturn**). Resulting thrust forces fuel to the rear of the second stage tanks for proper feeding.

ullage rocket /áləǰ ràkət/ *n.c.* Small rocket which is occasionally fired in order to keep propellant correctly situated for burning.

ultrasonic /əltrəsánik/ *attr.* Of or pertaining to speeds between Mach 1 and Mach 5. See **hypersonic; Mach number; supersonic.**

ultraviolet ray /əltrəvâyələt réy/ *n.c.* High-energy electromagnetic waves with a wavelength shorter than light rays and longer than **x-rays.**

umbilical /əmbílikəl/ *n*. Connecting power, fuel, or life-support line used in numerous instances in spaceflight.

umbilical boom /əmbílikəl bùwm/ *n.c.* **Umbilical tower.**

umbilical connector /əmbílikəl kənèktɚ/ *n.c.* **Umbilical.**

umbilical EVA /əmbílikəl îy vìy éy/ See **EVA.**

umbilical tower /əmbílikəl tàwɚ/ *n.c.* Scaffolding on a **launch pad** from which **umbilicals** extend to a rocket until **liftoff.** Cf. **service tower.**

umbra /ámbrə/ *n*. Portion of a shadow where there is total absence of light. Cf. **penumbra.**

UN *(ac.) n.c.* "United Nations," global organization formed in 1945 as a forum for discussion and solution of world problems. In the field of space, the UN has been responsible for the formulation of a treaty banning the use of weapons in outer space, encouraging care to avoid contaminating Earth's environment (1967), and an agreement concerning the rescue and return of astronauts or space equipment to the launching nation (1967). The UN also has encouraged exploration and scientific research in space.

unguided gravity turn /əngâydəd grǽvətiy tɚn/ *n.c.* Satellite **attitude** control system employed by the Japanese in their space program. The system involves the inclusion of a control device in the last stage of a launch vehicle. The device serves as a gyroscope prior to the stage's insertion into orbit. It is adjusted to place a payload on a course parallel to the earth's surface; if the actual course deviates from the planned course upward or downward by more than five degrees, the payload will not go into orbit. The system was successfully employed in **Oshumi,** Japan's first satellite.

Unidentified Flying Object ·/ənaydêntəfayd flâyiŋ ábjekt/ See **UFO.**

unified S-band equipment /yûwnifayd és bænd iykwìpmənt/ See **USBE.**

Union /yúwnyən/ See **Soyuz.**

UNION OF SOVIET SOCIALIST REPUBLICS

First nation to orbit satellites, animals, and men; achievements in these basic categories include the first rendezvous in space, the first EVA, the first soft landings on other celestial bodies, and innovations in the use of automated vehicles.

Rocketry, as a practical science, had its beginnings in czarist Russia. As early as 1897, Konstantin E. Tsiolkovsky (1857–1935) established a theory of rocket propulsion still used today. His theories were applied by individual rocket study groups in the 1920s and 1930s. One of these, the Group for the Study of Reactive Propulsion (GIRD), developed and successfully launched the first Soviet liquid-fueled rocket in 1933.

The present day Soviet space program can trace its beginnings to the post-war acquisition of German **V-2** rockets and scientists in 1945; an uprated V-2 was used in

/z/ zero; /ž/ azure; /θ/ thin; /ð/ then; /ŋ/ song; /æ/ bat; /ɔ/ law; /ə/ sun; /ɚ/ bird. Foreign symbols: [(n)] nasalization of some French vowels followed by /n/; [R] French uvular rolled /r/ sound; [ü] high front lip-rounded vowel; [x] Russian voiceless laryngeal fricative.

SE – 65

the U.S.S.R. as a sounding rocket in the 1950s. Soviet launch vehicles, like those in the U.S., were developed by the military as a result of the Cold War ballistic missile build-up. The **Kosmos** and **Vostok** launch vehicles, used for satellite and manned missions respectively, are based on **ICBMs**. Modification, by the addition of strap-on rockets and extra stages, makes these basic vehicles adaptable to the largest payloads. The International Geophysical Year (**IGY**) of 1957 and 1958 saw the beginning of the so-called space race since the U.S.S.R. undertook and met the challenge of launching the first artificial satellite; *Sputnik 1* (see **Sputnik**) was orbited October 3, 1957, nearly four months ahead of the first U.S. success.

The Soviets were first again when Yuri A. Gagarin was orbited in *Vostok 1* on April 12, 1961, becoming the first man ever to travel in space. The first rendezvous in space was made between two Vostok craft in 1962, and the final flight of the series, *Vostok 6*, was piloted by Valentina V. Tereshkova, the first woman in space. The **Voskhod** program, which followed, produced other innovations: the first multimanned craft and the first instance of EVA, performed by Aleksei A. Leonov in March 1965. The objectives of the **Soyuz** project, the third generation of Soviet manned flight, were to gather information on the manning of orbital space stations. The most recent Soyuz flights, *Soyuz 10* and *11*, have involved docking with and working in a **Salyut** prototype space station. No further flights had been scheduled as of December 1971.

Unmanned Soviet projects have included many diverse craft. Sputnik 1 was the forerunner of literally hundreds of satellites. The largest single group is the Kosmos series. Since 1962, more than 400 Kosmos satellites have been launched for the announced purpose of scientific research, although U.S. intelligence feels that many have been of a military or surveillance nature. Among other Soviet satellites, those of the **Proton** series, launched between 1965 and 1968, were notable for being the heaviest ever orbited. Meteorological and communications satellites are also part of the U.S.S.R. space program.

Soviet interplanetary probes include four series: **Luna, Venera, Mars,** and **Zond.** Craft of the Luna series took the first photographs of the dark side of the moon (1959); made the first lunar soft landing (1966); landed on the moon, collected samples, and returned to Earth—the first such automated mission (1970); and, landed the first unmanned, remotely controlled vehicle (**Lunakhod**) on the moon (1970). Venera and Mars craft made the first soft landings on Venus and Mars in 1967 and 1971 respectively. *Zond 5* was the first interplanetary probe to be recovered (1968).

Military satellites, most of which are operated secretly, include the Fractional-Orbit Bombardment System (**FOBS**), experimental satellites capable of nuclear attack from orbit.

Salyut represents the present stage of development of the Soviet future project, Manned Orbital Platform (**MOP**). This space station, as projected by U.S.S.R. scientists, would consist of a series of interlocking, welded laboratories with launch facilities for interplanetary missions. Future endeavors also include a cooperative program with the U.S., agreed to in 1972, involving docking of craft from both nations and work in space.

Other cooperative efforts include **Interkosmos** and **Intersputnik** as well as individual agreements with various other countries. Responsibility for the space program in the U.S.S.R. is handled exclusively by the national government.

United Kingdom /yuwnâytəd kíŋdəm/ See **Ariel; Great Britain.**

United Nations /yuwnâytəd néyšənz/ See **UN.**

UNITED STATES OF AMERICA

Second nation to orbit satellites and send men into space using internally developed launch vehicles; first nation to land men on the moon.

The work of Robert H. Goddard (1882–1945) is the foundation of American space technology. Goddard proved, through experiments, that rockets would work in the vacuum of space. He launched the first liquid-fueled rocket in March 1926, and in 1929 he sent up the first scientific payload: a barometer, thermometer, and camera.

Present-day American interest in space flight did not develop fully until the postwar acquisition of German **V-2** rockets and scientists in 1945. In the early 1950s, captured V-2s were fired as sounding rockets, but when the supply ran low, internal development of a rocket for scientific purposes became necessary. The Cold War with the U.S.S.R. during the 1950s led to competition in the development of another type of rocket, the ballistic missile. As a result of this competition, the first American, as well as Soviet, launch vehicles were developed by military organizations. The first American launch vehicle was the **Juno,** developed from the **Jupiter ICBM.** Technology has since developed several types of launch vehicles including **Atlas, Thor, Delta, Titan, Scout,** and **Saturn.** The latter was developed especially for the Apollo program.

In 1955 the **Vanguard** satellite program was begun by the U.S. Navy in preparation for a launch during the International Geophysical Year (**IGY**) 1957–1958. The U.S.S.R. also decided to answer the challenge for a launching of an artificial satellite during the IGY; their *Sputnik 1* (see **Sputnik**) was launched October 3, 1957, preceding the first U.S. satellite by nearly four months. The failure of the U.S. to produce a "first" resulted in what became popularly known as the "space race." The feeling that the U.S. needed to accelerate its space program led to the creation of the National Aeronautics and Space Administration (**NASA**) in late 1958.

The manned program of the United States was initiated in 1958, but again the U.S.S.R. produced a space first when in April 1961 Yuri A. Gagarin was sent into space. A frustrated U.S. thereupon declared that its space goal for the 1960s was the landing of men on the moon in Project **Apollo. Mercury,** the first American manned program, began one-man missions with the suborbital flight of Alan B. Shepard, Jr. on May 5, 1961, in the *Freedom 7* or *Mercury 3*. Transitional two-man **Gemini** flights followed in 1965–1966. The culmination of manned efforts in the 1960s was reached when the Apollo program landed the first men on the moon; Neil A. Armstrong and Edwin E. Aldrin, Jr., on July 20, 1969.

Unmanned U.S. space ventures have included both satellites and probes. Satellites, beginning with the launch of the first American satellite, *Explorer 1* (see **Explorer**), on January 31, 1958, were developed technology improved and fields of interest grew. Size and sophistication have continuously increased as various series of craft have been launched. Flights of over fifteen series of craft have been initiated. The extensive U.S. satellite program has produced several firsts. The U.S. produced the first utilitarian satellite by launching the first comsat, *Score*, in 1958. The first commercial comsat, **Telstar** (1962) was an American spacecraft. Synchronous satellites, which should prove to be of considerable value in the study of earth sciences, were first launched by the U.S. with the flight of *Syncom I* (see **Syncom**) in 1963. The first meteorological satellite, *TIROS 1* (see **TIROS**), was launched by the U.S. in 1960.

U.S. probes form five distinct families: **Ranger, Surveyor,** and **Lunar Orbiter** investigated the moon; **Pioneer** surveyed interplanetary space; and **Mariner** went to Venus and Mars.

Military satellites, most of which are operated under secret programs, have also contributed to space technology; *Transit 1-B* (see **Transit**), launched in 1960, was the first navsat. Communications satellites, surveillance satellites, and those which detect nuclear explosions or missile launchings are among the other types of U.S. military satellites.

Future missions of the U.S. include the manned **Skylab** and **Space Shuttle** as well as the satellites **ERTS, HEAO,** and **SMS** and the probes Mariner-Venus/Mercury (see **Mariner**), Pioneer-Jupiter (see **Pioneer**), **Viking,** and **TOPS.**

Cooperative programs with other nations have been a part of the U.S. space program since the first international satellite, *Ariel 1* (see **Ariel**), was launched for the British in 1962. All U.S. cooperative agreements are made with civilian NASA-like agencies on the basis of a scientific or technical decision. Australia, Canada, Federal Republic of Germany, France, Great Britain, and Italy have been among the nations cooperating in space ventures with the U.S. International organizations cooperating with NASA include **ELDO** and **ESRO.** The American company **Comsat** is also a member of **Intelsat,** a type of

/a/ father; /aw/ wow; /ay/ buy; /b/ boy; /č/ witch; /d/ doll; /e/ bet; /ey/ say; /f/ few; /g/ bag; /h/ hole; /i/ it; /iy/ be; /j/ gin; /k/ cat; /l/ lamb; /m/ man; /n/ now; /o/ orbit; /ow/ tow; /oy/ boy; /p/ pat; /r/ run; /s/ send; /š/ shoe; /t/ toy; /u/ put; /uw/ do; /v/ eve; /w/ way; /y/ yes;

SE–66

commercial cooperative organization responsible for a comsat system. Information from utilitarian U.S. programs, like TIROS, is made available world wide. Scientific returns like lunar samples have also been shared with all nations. In 1970 *SAS-A* (see **SAS**) was the first U.S. payload to be launched by another nation (Italy). Future programs involve an educational television experiment with India (**ATS**) and a project, agreed to in 1972, with the U.S.S.R. involving work in space between astronauts from both nations while their craft are docked.

NASA is the government agency responsible for the civilian U.S. space program. It was formed to consolidate all nonmilitary space efforts (formerly under the auspices of competing military branches), and it was based on the National Advisory Committee for Aeronautics (**NACA**) formed in 1915. The **DOD, AEC,** and Department of Commerce are other government agencies primarily involved with NASA's efforts. However, since the development of space technology's practical application, additional government agencies have begun cooperating with NASA.

unknown site /ənnôwn sáyt/ *n.c.* Earth location whose exact geographical position has not been determined. Cf. **known site.**

update /ə́pdeyt/ 1. *n.* Current spacecraft situation data. See **update pad.**

2. /ə́pdeyt/ *v. intr.* To provide with new or recently acquired knowledge.

update pad /ə́pdeyt pǽd/ *n.c.* Spacecraft situation data regularly transmitted from the ground to astronauts for their **flight plan.**

uplink data /ə́pliŋk dèytə/ *n.c.* Computer information transmitted to a spacecraft from ground controllers.

uprighting system /ə́praytiŋ sìstəm/ *n.c.* Inflatable bags deployed to right a spacecraft which lands upside down at **splashdown**; part of the earth landing system (**ELS**).

Uranus /yuréynəs/ *n.* 1. Third largest planet, with a diameter of 29,300 miles. The seventh planet from the sun, its orbital radius is 1,783 million miles. Uranus has five moons, but little else is known about it. It is scheduled for study on the **Outer Planets Missions.**

2. Greek god who was the personification of the heavens and ruler of the world.

USBE *(ac.) n.c. Apollo.* "Unified S-band equipment," CM instrument package which provides the usual telecommunications link between spacecraft and Earth; part of the telecommunications system (**T/C**). The equipment is used in conjunction with the **high-gain antenna.**

v *n. ac.* **Velocity.**

V-1 See **Germany, Federal Republic of.**

V-2 *cd. n.* First large tactical ballistic missile, developed and employed by Germany during World War II. First fired in 1942, more than 1,500 of the missiles were launched, primarily against Great Britain, before the war's end. A number of V-2s were captured by both the U.S. and U.S.S.R., becoming the basis of both countries' missile and space programs.

NASA

NASA's 525-foot vehicle assembly building is, in terms of volume, the largest building in the world. It easily holds the 415-foot mobile service structure used to transport the Saturn.

The vehicle stood 46 ft. high, weighed 27,000 lbs., and had a thrust potential of 60,000 lbs. Its operational range was nearly 200 miles.

VAB *(ac.) n.c. Apollo.* "Vehicle Assembly Building," structure at Launch Complex 39 of **NASA's** Kennedy Space Center (**KSC**); installation which houses **Saturn** rocket stages and **Apollo** spacecraft while being mated for launch. One of the world's largest buildings, it contains eight acres of working space in which four Saturns can be assembled simultaneously.

Van Allen Radiation Belts /væn ǽlən reydiyéyšən bèlts/ *n.c.* Layers of magnetically trapped, electrically charged particles surrounding Earth from an altitude of 600 miles. They were discovered by an experiment which was designed by James A. Van Allen of the State-University of Iowa and carried aboard *Explorer 1* (see **Explorer**).

Vandenberg AFB /vǽndənbəg êy èf bíy/ See **AFWTR.**

Vandenberg Air Force Base /vǽndənbəg ér fòrs bêys/ See **AFWTR.**

Vanguard /vǽŋgard/ *n.* U.S. three-stage rocket; the first developed specifically to serve as a satellite launch vehicle. Actually a modified Viking, it was initially fired in 1957 and subsequently inserted the Vanguard satellites into Earth orbit. The Vanguard stood 72 ft. high and produced 38,000 lbs. of thrust.

2. Second U.S. multipurpose satellite series, with three craft orbited from 1958 to 1959. *Vanguard 1*, launched in March 1958, determined that the Earth is pear shaped. *Vanguard 2*, launched in February 1959, took the first cloud-cover photographs. *Vanguard 3*, launched in September 1959, was a geophysical satellite. All

Vanguards were still in orbit at the beginning of 1972.

VECO /víykow/ *(ac.) n.c.* "Vernier engine cutoff." See **thruster.**

vector /véktə/ *n. sl.* **Velocity vector.**

Vehicle Assembly Building /víyhikəl əsémbliy bìldiŋ/ See **VAB.**

Vela /vélə/ *n.* "Watchman," U.S. military satellite series, originally called *Vela Hotel*, consisting of six pairs of spacecraft launched from 1963 to 1970, and used for the detection of nuclear radiation in space.

The *Vanguard* launch vehicle placed the first U.S. satellite in orbit on March 17, 1958.

NASA

/z/ zero; /ž/ azure; /θ/ *thin*; /ð/ *then*; /ŋ/ so*ng*; /æ/ b*a*t; /ɔ/ l*a*w; /ə/ s*u*n; /ɚ/ b*ir*d. Foreign symbols: [(n)] nasalization of some French vowels followed by /n/; [R] French uvular rolled /r/ sound; [ü] high front lip-rounded vowel; [x] Russian voiceless lâryngeal fricative.

SE – 67

The satellites can detect violations of the nuclear test ban treaty, as well as monitor dangerous radiation which might hinder manned space flights.

Vela Hotel /vîylə howtél/ See **Vela.**

Velcro /vélkrow/ *n.* Either of two integrated types of cloth which, when sewed or glued onto other items, is used to hold two items together. Half of a Velcro closing is hook material and half is a pile to which the hooks bond.

velocity /vəlásətiy/ *n.* Rate of speed.

velocity vector /vəlásətiy vèktə/ *n.c.* Amount of speed, plus direction, of a space vehicle.

Venera [*Rus.* vyenyéra] "Venus," U.S.S.R. Venusian probe series which included the first manmade object placed on another planet. Basic objectives of the series were a soft landing on Venus, investigation of the planet's atmospheric and surface conditions, and general investigation of the interplanetary space between Venus and Earth.

Venera 1, the first probe ever sent toward another planet, was launched from Earth orbit in February 1961 but suffered loss of radio contact shortly thereafter.

Both *Venera 2* and *3* were launched in November 1965. Venera 2 flew past the planet and into heliocentric orbit in February 1966. Venera 3, containing a pennant bearing the Soviet coat of arms, crashed into the surface of Venus on March 1, 1966, the first manmade object to reach another planet.

Venera 4, launched in June 1967, soft-landed on Venus the following October. It transmitted the information that the planet's atmospheric temperature, pressure, and makeup are hostile to human life. *Venera 5* and *6*, each launched in January 1969, descended to the planet's surface in May and substantiated Venera 4's earlier analysis.

Venera 7, launched in August 1970, successfully soft-landed in December. It transmitted both while descending and for 23 minutes after landing, showing surface temperatures to be over 840°F. and atmospheric pressure at "sea level" to be 90 times that of Earth.

vent /vént/ **1.** *v. tr.* To flush out a spacecraft system.

2. *n.* Opening through which wastes are ejected.

Venus /víynəs/ *n.* **1.** Fourth smallest planet, Venus has a diameter of 7,600 miles. Second planet from the sun, its orbital radius is 67 million miles. The sidereal period of Venus is about 225 days and its axial rotation period is 243 days so its "day" is longer than its "year." Venus is covered by an extremely dense and cloudy atmosphere, and it is the only planet in the solar system with retrograde rotation. **Venera** and **Mariner** craft have flown to or past Venus several times (see **Venera**).

2. Roman goddess of love and beauty.

vernier engine /və̀nyey énjən/ *n.c.* **Thruster.**

Véronique [*Fr.* veRonik] *n.* French single-stage rocket; first such vehicle developed by the French. It was used as a sounding

NORTH AMERICAN ROCKWELL SPACE DIVISION

The *Viking* Mars probe is one of the most ambitious spacecrafts planned by the U.S. It consists of two parts: the orbiter, which will guide the craft through space and position it in orbit around Mars; and the biologically pure lander.

rocket throughout the 1950s and early 1960s.

The standard vehicle stood 24 ft. high and weighed 1,500 lbs. at takeoff.

VHF *(ac.) attr.* "Very high frequency," frequencies between 30 and 300 megacycles; pertains to radio waves.

VHF multiplexer /vîy èyč êf mə́ltipleksə/ *n.c.* Device which makes possible simultaneous transmission and reception of VHF signals with a single **antenna.**

Viking /váykiŋ/ *n.* **1.** Either of two planned U.S. probes projected for launch toward Mars in 1975. The Vikings will build on information gained from the **Mariner** series, and will conduct experiments to determine whether life exists on Mars.

Each craft will consist of two joined parts, an orbiter and a lander. The orbiter portion will navigate during the flight to Mars, maneuver the spacecraft into orbit, and conduct independent research. It will also support the operations of the lander,

relaying signals from the lander to Earth after the lander separates from it.

The lander portion will take photographs, analyze soil and atmosphere, and search for signs of life on the Martian surface. It will be kept almost dormant during the flight to Mars, during Mars orbit insertion (**MOI**), and during the search for a landing site. It will then separate from the orbiter and descend to the Martian surface. It will be kept sterile until it lands so that it will not contaminate the Martian surface and also so that scientists will know that any life it records is of Martian origin.

2. Early U.S. sounding rocket series developed from the German **V-2.** Vikings varied in height from 42 to 48 ft. A modified version was employed as the first stage of the **Vanguard** launch vehicle.

visible-infrared spin-scan radiometer /vîzəbəl ìnfrərêd spînskǽn reydiyámətər/ See **VISSR.**

VISSR *(ac.) n.c.* "Visible-infrared spin-scan

/a/ *father*; /aw/ *wow*; /ay/ *buy*; /b/ *boy*; /č/ *witch*; /d/ *doll*; /e/ *bet*; /ey/ *say*; /f/ *few*; /g/ *bag*; /h/ *hole*; /i/ *it*; /iy/ *be*; /j/ *gin*; /k/ *cat*; /l/ *lamb*; /m/ *man*; /n/ *now*; /o/ *orbit*; /ow/ *tow*; /oy/ *boy*; /p/ *pat*; /r/ *run*; /s/ *send*; /š/ *shoe*; /t/ *toy*; /u/ *put*; /uw/ *do*; /v/ *eve*; /w/ *way*; /y/ *yes*;

S-Band Antenna (Low Gain)

UHF Antenna (Relay to Earth)

S-Band Antenna (Direct to Earth)

Meteorology Sensors

Cameras

Power Generators (SNAP-19 Radioisotopic Thermoelectric Generator)

Soil Sample Processor Assembly

Soil Sampler and Magnetic Array Unit

Weight: lander & aeroshell - 2,365 lb   lander - 1,198 lb
Size (less instruments):   height - 40 in.   width - 9 ft, 4 in.

NORTH AMERICAN ROCKWELL SPACE DIVISION

The *Viking* lander will test for life on Mars by gathering soil samples with telescoping 10-foot arms. The samples will be processed in a miniature laboratory inside the craft and all information will be conveyed to Earth via the section of the *Viking* orbiting Mars.

radiometer," special camera projected for use on the proposed U.S. Synchronous Meteorological Satellite (**SMS**). The VISSR is capable of taking pictures on several channels or wavelengths of the visible to infrared spectrum simultaneously. This camera will allow for high resolution in photographs.

voice-operated relay /vôys âpəeytəd ríyley/ *n.c. Apollo.* Communications device which automatically transmits at the sound of an astronaut's voice and receives when he is not speaking.

Voskhod [*Rus.* vəsxót] *n.* "Sunrise," second U.S.S.R. manned spaceflight program; program in which the first multimanned craft was launched and in which the first EVA was accomplished. Purposes of the project were the developmental testing of spacecraft technology as well as testing of capacities for work and interaction of a crew.

A series of unmanned Voskhod flights,

chiefly for testing reentry soft-landing procedures, was conducted before completion of the **Vostok** program. *Voskhod 1* was launched in October 1964 with a crew that included the first civilians to enter space. During the flight of *Voskhod 2*, on March 18, 1965, Aleksei A. Leonov took the first "walk in space" maintaining **EVA** for twelve minutes. A two-year manned spaceflight moratorium ensued between the flight of *Voskhod 2* and that of *Soyuz 1* in 1967 (see **Soyuz**).

The Voskhod spacecraft was designed to maintain a crew of three in a shirtsleeve environment. Like the Vostok craft that preceded it, Voskhod consisted of a spherical crew section and a cylindrical instrumentation section. The crew section was designed to soft-land on solid ground by means of retrorockets and parachutes.

All the Voskhod missions were launched by uprated Vostok launch vehicles capable

of 1.5 million pounds of thrust.

Vostok [*Rus.* vəstók] *n.* "East." **1.** First U.S.S.R. manned spaceflight program; program in which both the first man and the first woman were put into space, and program in which the first spacecraft rendezvous was accomplished. Comparable to the American **Mercury** project, Vostok's immediate goal was to orbit a one-man spacecraft and safely recover the vehicle following reentry.

Five experimental unmanned flights carrying test animals, mannequins, and life-support metering equipment preceded the first manned space shot. At 9:07 AM (Moscow Time) on April 12, 1961, Yuri A. Gagarin became the first human being to be launched into space. His spacecraft *Vostok 1* completed one orbit of the earth in a flight that lasted 108 minutes; by *Vostok 5* duration capability was extended to almost 120 hours. On August 12, 1962, *Vostok 4* was placed in an orbit almost identical to that of the previously launched *Vostok 3*, achieving the first rendezvous in space. On June 16, 1963, Valentina V. Tereshkova became the first woman in space when she orbited in *Vostok 6*, the last of the series. The six Vostok flights enabled Soviet scientists to answer many questions concerning the feasibility of manned spaceflight, in terms of both spacecraft structure and systems, and man's ability to function under extraterrestrial conditions. In 1964 the Vostok program was superseded by **Voskhod**.

The Vostok spacecraft was cylindrically shaped and consisted of two basic sections: a pilot's compartment and an instrument section. The spherically shaped pilot's compartment was equipped with controls, life support systems, and landing equipment; it served as the reentry capsule and was designed to touch down on solid earth (rather than splash down in water, as with American capsules). The instrument section contained inflight instrumentation and a retrorocket system; it was jettisoned soon after the spacecraft began its return to earth.

2. Principal launch vehicle for all Soviet manned spaceflight missions. The basic model, used as launcher for the Vostok project, is a three-stage, liquid-fueled rocket. It weighs 720,000 lbs. at takeoff and stands 187 ft. high. Its thrust potential is 1.1 million lbs. Modifed versions of the rocket were used to launch Voskhod spacecraft, and, with an additional stage, **Soyuz** and **Salyut**. The first stage core of the Vostok

MANNED VOSKHOD FLIGHTS

Mission	Crew	Dates	Remarks
Voskhod 1	Vladimir M. Komarov (Col., AF) Boris B. Yegorov (Civilian) Konstantin P. Feoktistov (Civilian)	October 12–13, 1964 (24 hrs. 17 min.)	First flight of a multimanned spacecraft. Successful test of spacecraft systems and reentry procedures; crew compatibility. 16 orbits.
Voskhod 2	Aleksei A. Leonov (Lt. Col., AF) Pavel I. Belyayev (Col., AF)	March 18–19, 1965 (26 hrs. 02 min.)	First EVA, performed by Leonov for 12 min. 17 orbits.

/z/ zero; /ž/ azure; /θ/ thin; /ð/ then; /ŋ/ song; /æ/ bat; /ɔ/ law; /ə/ sun; /ɚ/ bird. Foreign symbols: [(n)] nasalization of some French vowels followed by /n/; [R] French uvular rolled /r/ sound; [ü] high front lip-rounded vowel; [x] Russian voiceless laryngeal fricative.

MANNED VOSTOK FLIGHTS

Mission	Pilot	Date(s)	Remarks
Vostok 1	Yuri A. Gagarin (Maj., AF)	April 12, 1961 (01 hr. 48 min.)	First man in space. 1 orbit.
Vostok 2	Gherman S. Titov (Maj., AF)	August 6–7, 1961 (25 hrs. 18 min.)	Test of day-long spaceflight. 17 orbits.
Vostok 3	Andriyan G. Nikolayev (Maj., AF)	August 11–15, 1962 (94 hrs. 22 min.)	First space rendezvous; acted as target vehicle for *Vostok 4*. 64 orbits.
Vostok 4	Pavel R. Popovich (Col., AF)	August 12–15, 1962 (70 hrs. 57 min.)	First space rendezvous; approached within 3 mi. of *Vostok 3*. 64 orbits.
Vostok 5	Valery F. Bykovsky (Lt. Col., AF)	June 14–19, 1963 (119 hrs. 06 min.)	Acted as target vehicle for *Vostok 6*. Left orbit via aerodynamic braking; retrorockets not fired. 81 orbits.
Vostok 6	Valentina V. Tereshkova (Lt., AF)	June 16–19, 1963 (70 hrs. 50 min.)	First woman in space. Rendezvoused within 3 mi. of *Vostok 5*. 48 orbits.

NVOSTI PRESS AGENCY

A *Vostok* spacecraft at assembly plant.

launch vehicle is based on the Soviet *S-66* ICBM.

W–X–Y–Z

Wallops Island /wâləps áylənd/ See **Wallops Station.**

Wallops Station /wâləps stéyšən/ *n.c.* U.S. space-research facility and rocket-launching site located at Wallops Island, Virginia. Foreign satellites are also frequently launched from Wallops Station. It is one of three U.S. launch sites (cf. **AFWTR; KSC**).

WAP *(ac.) n.c. Apollo.* "Wide-angle panorama," specific camera shot.

warning streamer /wórniŋ strìymæ/ *n.c.* Colored ribbon or piece of cloth attached to a cover on a fragile spacecraft part reminding technicians to remove the cover before **launch.**

waste management system /wéyst mænəjmənt sìstəm/ See **WMS.**

Watchman /wáčmən/ See **Vela.**

water chiller /wôtæ čìlæ/ See **ECU.**

water deluge /wôtæ dèlyuwj/ See **pad deluge.**

water-glycol /wôtæ gláykɔl/ *n.c.* Water and ethylene glycol mixture used as a coolant in the spacecraft environmental control system (**ECS**); after absorbing heat, it is recooled by passage through a **sublimator** or **space radiator.**

water-glycol subsystem /wôtæ gláykɔl səbsistəm/ *n.c. Apollo.* That part of the CSM environmental control system (**ECS**) which distributes water-glycol coolant for thermal control in pressure suits, crew compartment, potable water, and vehicle components.

water management subsystem /wôtæ mænəjmənt səbsistəm/ See **WMS.**

water subsystem /wôtæ səbsistəm/ *n.c. Apollo.* That part of the CSM environmental control system (**ECS**) which accumulates potable and waste water. Both hot and cold fresh water are available to the crew through this subsystem.

Weapons Research Establishment /wépənz ríysæč əstæblišmənt/ See **Australia.**

Weapons Research Establishment Satellite /wépənz ríysæč əstæblišmənt sætəlayt/ See **WRESAT.**

wedding ring /wédiŋ rìŋ/ *n.c. sl. Apollo.* **IU.**

weight /wéyt/ *n.* Mass of a body under the influence of **gravity.**

weight-disposal /wéyt dispòwzəl/ *n.c.* Dropping off of empty tanks or used engines to lighten the load still to be orbited by remaining spacecraft engines.

weight-shedding /wéyt šèdiŋ/ See **weight-disposal.**

weight flow rate /wéyt flòw rèyt/ *n.c.* Speed at which liquid fuel runs into a **thrust chamber;** given in pounds per second.

weightless /wéytləs/ *attr.* Of or pertaining to **weightlessness.**

weightlessness /wéytləsnəs/ *n.* State of a body without any gravitational influence working on it.

Western Test Range /wêstæn tést rèynj/ See **AFWTR.**

wet /wét/ See **wet workshop.**

wet workshop /wêt wækšap/ *n.c.* A rocket launched "wet," i.e., fully fueled, and converted into habitable working quarters once fuel is consumed. The Skylab space station's **OWS** was originally planned as a wet workshop. Cf. **dry workshop.**

white noise /hwâyt nóyz/ *n.c.* Radio static.

white room /hwáyt rùwm/ *n.c.* Ultraclean room used for dealing with sensitive spacecraft components and for astronaut preparation prior to **launch** of a craft.

wide-angle panorama /wâyd æŋgəl pænəræmə/ See **WAP.**

wilco /wílkow/ *(ac.) i.s., sl.* "Will comply."

window /wíndow/ *n.* **Launch window.**

windows down /wìndowz dáwn/ *n.c.* Upside-down position of a spacecraft (see **windows up**).

windows up /wìndowz əp/ *n.c.* Right-side-up position of a spacecraft (see **windows down**).

winged /wíŋd/ *attr.* Of or pertaining to spacecraft with small lifting surfaces used for a gliding **reentry** or landing.

WMS *(ac.) n.c.* 1. "Waste management system," U.S. spacecraft equipment complex used to remove both human and spacecraft wastes from either the **space suit** or the vehicle; even a vacuum cleaner is employed to clean surfaces in the craft and to pick up the food particles which drift in a zero-gravity cabin. There is some overlap between the function of this system and that of the **water subsystem.**

2. *Apollo.* "Water management subsystem," that part of the LM environmental control system (**ECS**) which supplies all spacecraft water requirements.

Woomera /wúwmææ/ *n.* Australian rocket launch center located in South Australia. Originally established as a satellite tracking facility during International Geophys-

/a/ *father;* /aw/ *wow;* /ay/ *buy;* /b/ *boy;* /č/ *witch;* /d/ *doll;* /e/ *bet;* /ey/ *say;* /f/ *few;* /g/ *bag;* /h/ *hole;* /i/ *it;* /iy/ *be;* /j/ *gin;* /k/ *cat;* /l/ *lamb;* /m/ *man;* /n/ *now;* /o/ *orbit;* /ow/ *tow;* /oy/ *boy;* /p/ *pat;* /r/ *run;* /s/ *send;* /š/ *shoe;* /t/ *toy;* /u/ *put;* /uw/ *do;* /v/ *eve;* /w/ *way;* /y/ *yes;*

AUSTRALIAN NEWS AND INFORMATION SERVICE

Various ELDO space vehicles have been launched from the facilities at Woomera, Australia. Woomera is operated jointly with Great Britain and is one of the world's foremost launching sites.

satellite scheduled for an early 1974 launch.

X-15 *n. cd.* NASA/USAF experimental winged rocket-powered vehicle. The X-15, which has been flown since 1959, is launched from the wing of an airplane high above Earth. Powered flight is followed by a coasting period and then landing. Record speeds have been reached on X-15 flights.

X-axis /éks ǽksəs/ *n.c.* Imaginary longitudinal axis of a spacecraft. See **roll**.

x-ray /éks rèy/ *n.* Potentially dangerous high-energy **electromagnetic radiation** found naturally in space.

X-ray Explorer /êks rèy eksplórə/ See **SAS**.

Yankee Clipper /yǽŋkiy klípə/ *n.c.* Name of *Apollo 12* CM (See **Apollo**).

yaw /yɔ́/ *n.* Spacecraft movement around its vertical axis (**Z-axis**).

yaw jets /yɔ́ jèts/ See **attitude jets**.

Y-axis /wáy ǽksəs/ *n.* Imaginary lateral axis of a spacecraft. See **pitch**.

zap /zǽp/ *v. tr. sl.* Damage; break.

Z-axis /zíy ǽksəs/ *n.* Imaginary vertical axis of a spacecraft. See **yaw**.

zero /zíyrow/ *n.* Point in time, at the end of a **countdown**, when **liftoff** occurs.

zero G /zîrow jíy/ *n.c.* See **zero gravity**.

zero gravity /zîrow grǽvətiy/ *n.c.* Condition of complete **weightlessness**. Also called *zero G*.

zero stage /zìyrow stéyj/ *n.c.* See **strap-on rocket**.

zilch /zílč/ *n. sl.* Zero; nothing.

zip /zíp/ *n. sl.* Numeric zero; indicates perfect maneuver.

Zond [*Rus.* zónt] *n.* "Probe," U.S.S.R. interplanetary and lunar probe series which included the first extraterrestrial probe to be recovered. Eight Zonds were announced from 1964 to 1970.

Zond 1 and 2, launched toward Venus and Mars respectively, were less than fully successful. *Zond 3*, launched in heliocentric orbit in July 1965, transmitted pictures of previously unphotographed parts of the moon. *Zond 4* failed to leave Earth orbit.

Remaining missions have been concerned with recovery of a probe after it has made a circuit of the moon: *Zond 5*, launched in September 1968, became the first probe to reenter the earth's atmosphere for recovery after such a trip. Turtles and other organisms carried by *Zond 6*, launched in November 1968, were recovered in the Indian Ocean after a week in space. *Zond 7*, launched in August 1969, achieved guided reentry and a soft landing at a preselected site.

ical Year (**IGY**) activities in 1957, the facility was improved and developed into a modern space center. It is used by Australia, Great Britain, the U.S., **ELDO**, and **ESRO**.

working fluid /wɔ́kiŋ flùwəd/ *n.c.* Fuel of a nonchemical **rocket engine** like a radioisotope thermoelectric generator (**RTG**).

WRESAT /ríysæt/ *(ac.) n.c.* "Weapons Research Establishment Satellite," first Aus-

tralian satellite, launched November 29, 1967, by a U.S. **Redstone** from the **Woomera** space center. The main objective of the spacecraft was upper atmospheric research.

WTR *(ac.) n.c.* "Western Test Range." See **AFWTR**.

X *attr. cd.* Experimental.

X-3 See **Prospero**.

X-4 *n.* Proposed British scientific research

/z/ zero; /ž/ azure; /θ/ thin; /ð/ then; /ŋ/ song; /æ/ bat; /ɔ/ law; /ə/ sun; /ɚ/ bird. Foreign symbols: [(n)] nasalization of some French vowels followed by /n/; [R] French uvular rolled /r/ sound; [ü] high front lip-rounded vowel; [x] Russian voiceless laryngeal fricative.

NUTRITIVE VALUES OF FOODS

(Dashes in the columns for nutrients show that no suitable value could be found although there is reason to believe that a measurable amount of the nutrient may be present. The abbreviations used are g for gram(s), mg for milligram(s), cal for calories, and IU for International Units.)

Food	Measure	Weight g	Water %	Cal	Protein g	Fat g	Carbo-hydrate g	Cal-cium mg	Iron mg	Vita-min A IU	Thia-mine mg	Ribo-flavin mg	Niacin mg	Vita-min C mg
Milk Group														
Cheese														
Cheddar	1 oz	28	37	115	7	9	1	213	.3	370	.01	.13	trace	0
cottage, creamed	12 oz	340	78	360	46	14	10	320	1.0	580	.10	.85	.3	0
cream	3 oz	85	51	320	7	32	2	53	.2	1,310	.02	.20	.1	0
Milk														
buttermilk	1 cup	245	90	90	9	trace	12	296	.1	10	.10	.44	.2	2
dry, nonfat, instant	1 cup	68	4	245	24	trace	35	879	.1	20	.24	1.21	.6	5
evaporated, undiluted	1 cup	252	74	345	18	20	24	635	.3	810	.10	.86	.5	3
skim (unfortified)	1 cup	245	90	90	9	trace	12	296	.1	10	.09	.44	.2	2
sweetened condensed, undiluted	1 cup	306	27	980	25	27	166	802	.3	1,100	.24	1.16	.6	3
whole	1 cup	244	87	160	9	9	12	288	.1	350	.07	.41	.2	2
Milk beverage														
cocoa, homemade	1 cup	250	79	245	10	12	27	295	1.0	400	.10	.45	.5	3
Milk desserts														
baked custard	1 cup	265	77	305	14	15	29	297	1.1	930	.11	.50	.3	1
ice cream	1 cup	133	63	255	6	14	28	194	.1	590	.05	.28	.1	1
Yogurt														
made from partially skimmed milk	1 cup	245	89	125	8	4	13	294	.1	170	.10	.44	.2	2
made from whole milk	1 cup	245	88	150	7	8	12	272	.1	340	.07	.39	.2	2
Meat Group														
Fish and Shellfish														
crabmeat, canned	3 oz	85	77	85	15	2	1	38	.7	—	.07	.07	1.6	—
fish sticks, breaded	8 oz pkg.	227	66	400	38	20	15	25	.9	—	.09	.16	3.6	—
flounder, cooked	3.5 oz	100	58	202	30	8	0	23	1.4	—	.07	.08	2.5	2
halibut, cooked	3.5 oz	100	67	171	25	7	0	16	.8	680	.05	.07	8.3	—
salmon, canned	3 oz	85	71	120	17	5	0	167	.7	60	.03	.16	6.8	—
shrimp, canned	3 oz	85	70	100	21	1	1	98	2.6	50	.01	.03	1.5	—
tuna, canned, drained	3 oz	85	61	170	24	7	0	7	1.6	70	.04	.10	10.1	—
Meat														
bacon, broiled or fried crisp	2 slices	15	8	90	5	8	1	2	.5	0	.08	.05	.8	—
beef														
ground, regular, broiled	3 oz	85	54	245	21	17	0	9	2.7	30	.07	.18	4.6	—
pot roast, lean	2.5 oz	72	62	140	22	5	0	10	2.7	10	.04	.16	3.3	—
steak, sirloin, lean only	2 oz	56	59	115	18	4	0	7	2.2	10	.05	.14	3.6	—
ham, roasted, lean and fat	3 oz	85	54	245	18	19	0	8	2.2	0	.40	.16	3.1	—
lamb														
chop, broiled, lean only	2.6 oz	74	62	140	21	6	0	9	1.5	—	.11	.20	4.5	—
leg, roasted, lean only	2.5 oz	71	62	130	20	5	0	9	1.4	—	.12	.21	4.4	—
liver, beef, fried	2 oz	57	57	130	15	6	3	6	5.0	30,280	.15	2.37	9.4	15
pork														
chop, cooked, lean only	1.7 oz	48	53	130	15	7	0	7	1.9	0	.54	.16	3.3	—
roast, lean only	2.4 oz	68	55	175	20	10	0	9	2.6	0	.73	.21	4.4	—
sausage														
bologna	(3x⅛ inch) 2 slices	26	56	80	3	7	trace	2	.5	—	.04	.06	.7	—
Braunschweiger	(2x¼ inch) 2 slices	20	53	65	3	5	trace	2	1.2	1,310	.03	.29	1.6	—
frankfurter, heated	1	56	57	170	7	15	1	3	.8	—	.08	.11	1.4	—
veal, roast	3 oz	85	55	230	23	14	0	10	2.9	—	.11	.26	6.6	—
Meat Alternates														
beans														
Great Northern, cooked	1 cup	180	69	210	14	1	38	90	4.9	0	.25	.13	1.3	0

Food	Measure	Weight g	Water %	Cal	Protein g	Fat g	Carbo-hydrate g	Cal-cium mg	Iron mg	Vita-min A IU	Thia-mine mg	Ribo-flavin mg	Niacin mg	Vita-min C mg
red kidney, canned	1 cup	255	76	230	15	1	42	74	4.6	10	.13	.10	1.5	—
peanuts, roasted, salted	1 cup	144	2	840	37	72	27	107	3.0	—	.46	.19	24.7	0
peanut butter	1 tbsp	16	2	95	4	8	3	9	.3	—	.02	.02	2.4	0
peas, split dry, cooked	1 cup	250	70	290	20	1	52	28	4.2	100	.37	.22	2.2	—

Poultry and Eggs
chicken

Food	Measure	Weight g	Water %	Cal	Protein g	Fat g	Carbo-hydrate g	Cal-cium mg	Iron mg	Vita-min A IU	Thia-mine mg	Ribo-flavin mg	Niacin mg	Vita-min C mg
broiled, boneless	3 oz	85	71	115	20	3	0	8	1.4	80	.05	.16	7.4	—
drumstick, fried, flesh and skin	1.3 oz	38	55	90	12	4	trace	6	.9	50	.03	.15	2.7	—
eggs, whole	1 egg	50	74	80	6	6	trace	27	1.1	590	.05	.15	trace	—

Fruit and Vegetable Group
Fruits

Food	Measure	Weight g	Water %	Cal	Protein g	Fat g	Carbo-hydrate g	Cal-cium mg	Iron mg	Vita-min A IU	Thia-mine mg	Ribo-flavin mg	Niacin mg	Vita-min C mg
apple, raw	1	150	85	70	trace	trace	18	8	.4	50	.04	.02	.1	3
apricots, raw	3	114	85	55	1	trace	14	18	.5	2,890	.03	.04	.7	10
avocado, raw	1 medium	284	74	370	5	37	13	22	1.3	630	.24	.43	3.5	30
banana, raw	1 medium	175	76	100	1	trace	26	10	.8	230	.06	.07	.8	12
blueberries, raw	1 cup	140	83	85	1	1	21	21	1.4	140	.04	.08	.6	20
cantaloupe	½ medium	385	91	60	1	trace	14	27	.8	6,540	.08	.06	1.2	63
dates, pitted, cut	1 cup	178	22	490	4	1	130	105	5.3	90	.16	.17	3.9	0
grapefruit, white	½ medium	241	89	45	1	trace	12	19	.5	10	.05	.02	.2	44
grapes, raw	1 cup	160	81	95	1	trace	25	17	.6	140	.07	.04	.4	6
orange, raw	1 medium	180	86	65	1	trace	16	54	.5	260	.13	.05	.5	66
orange juice, reconstituted from frozen concentrated	1 cup	249	87	120	2	trace	29	25	.2	550	.22	.02	1.0	120
peach, raw	1 medium	114	89	35	1	trace	10	9	.5	1,320	.02	.05	1.0	7
pear, raw	1 medium	182	83	100	1	1	25	13	.5	30	.04	.07	.2	7
pineapple, raw, diced	1 cup	140	85	75	1	trace	19	24	.7	100	.12	.04	.3	24
plum, raw	1 medium	60	87	25	trace	trace	7	7	.3	140	.02	.02	.3	3
prunes, uncooked	4 medium	32	28	70	1	trace	18	14	1.1	440	.02	.04	.4	1
raisins	(½ oz) 1 pkg.	14	18	40	trace	trace	11	9	.5	trace	.02	.01	.1	trace
raspberries, red, raw	1 cup	123	84	70	1	1	17	27	1.1	160	.04	.11	1.1	31
rhubarb, cooked, sugar added	1 cup	272	63	385	1	trace	98	212	1.6	220	.06	.15	.7	17
strawberries, raw, hulled	1 cup	149	90	55	1	1	13	31	1.5	90	.04	.10	1.0	88
tangerine, raw	1 medium	116	87	40	1	trace	10	34	.3	360	.05	.02	.1	27
watermelon, raw	(4x8 inches) 1 wedge	925	93	115	2	1	27	30	2.1	2,510	.13	.13	.7	30

Vegetables

Food	Measure	Weight g	Water %	Cal	Protein g	Fat g	Carbo-hydrate g	Cal-cium mg	Iron mg	Vita-min A IU	Thia-mine mg	Ribo-flavin mg	Niacin mg	Vita-min C mg
asparagus, cooked	4 spears	60	94	10	1	trace	2	13	.4	540	.10	.11	.8	16
beans green, cooked, drained	1 cup	125	92	30	2	trace	7	63	.8	680	.09	.11	.6	15
lima, cooked, drained	1 cup	170	71	190	13	1	34	80	4.3	480	.31	.17	2.2	29
bean sprouts, mung, cooked, drained	1 cup	125	91	35	4	trace	7	21	1.1	30	.11	.13	.9	8
beets, cooked, drained, sliced	1 cup	170	91	55	2	trace	12	24	.9	30	.05	.07	.5	10
broccoli, chopped, cooked, drained	1 cup	155	91	40	5	1	7	136	1.2	3,880	.14	.31	1.2	140
Brussels sprouts, cooked	7-8 per cup	155	88	55	7	1	10	50	1.7	810	.12	.22	1.2	135
cabbage, coarsely shredded	1 cup	70	92	15	1	trace	4	34	.3	90	.04	.04	.2	33
carrots, cooked, diced	1 cup	145	91	45	1	trace	10	48	.9	15,220	.08	.07	.7	9
cauliflower, cooked	1 cup	120	93	25	3	trace	5	25	.8	70	.11	.10	.7	66
celery, raw	1 stalk	40	94	5	trace	trace	2	16	.1	100	.01	.01	.1	4
collard greens, cooked	1 cup	190	91	55	5	1	9	289	1.1	10,260	.27	.37	2.4	87
corn, sweet	1 ear	140	74	70	3	1	16	2	.5	310	.09	.08	1.0	7
cucumber, raw, peeled	6 slices	50	96	5	trace	trace	2	8	.2	trace	.02	.02	.1	6
lettuce, iceberg	1 head	454	96	60	4	trace	13	91	2.3	1,500	.29	.27	1.3	29

Food	Measure	Weight g	Water %	Cal	Protein g	Fat g	Carbo-hydrate g	Cal-cium mg	Iron mg	Vita-min A IU	Thia-mine mg	Ribo-flavin mg	Niacin mg	Vita-min C mg
onions, cooked	1 cup	210	92	60	3	trace	14	50	.8	80	.06	.06	.4	14
peas, green, cooked	1 cup	160	82	115	9	1	19	37	2.9	860	.44	.17	3.7	33
peppers, green	1 medium	74	93	15	1	trace	4	7	.5	310	.06	.06	.4	94
potato, baked in peel	1 medium	99	75	90	3	trace	21	9	.7	trace	.10	.04	1.7	20
potatoes, french-fried (frozen), heated	10 pieces	57	53	125	2	5	19	5	1.0	trace	.08	.01	1.5	12
spinach, cooked	1 cup	180	92	40	5	1	6	167	4.0	14,580	.13	.25	1.0	50
squash, summer, diced	1 cup	210	96	30	2	trace	7	52	.8	820	.10	.16	1.6	21
squash, winter, baked, mashed	1 cup	205	81	130	4	1	32	57	1.6	8,610	.10	.27	1.4	27
sweet potato, baked in peel	1	110	64	155	2	1	36	44	1.0	8,910	.10	.07	.7	24
tomato, raw	1 medium	200	94	40	2	trace	9	24	.9	1,640	.11	.07	1.3	42
turnips, cooked, diced	1 cup	155	94	35	1	trace	8	54	.6	trace	.06	.08	.5	34
turnip greens, cooked	1 cup	145	94	30	3	trace	5	252	1.5	8,270	.15	.33	.7	68

Bread and Cereal Group

Biscuit, homemade

Food	Measure	Weight g	Water %	Cal	Protein g	Fat g	Carbo-hydrate g	Cal-cium mg	Iron mg	Vita-min A IU	Thia-mine mg	Ribo-flavin mg	Niacin mg	Vita-min C mg
(enriched flour)	1	28	27	105	2	5	13	34	.4	trace	.06	.06	.1	trace
Bread														
cracked wheat	1 slice	25	35	65	2	1	13	22	.3	trace	.03	.02	.3	trace
raisin	1 slice	25	35	65	2	1	13	18	.3	trace	.01	.02	.2	trace
rye, light	1 slice	25	36	60	2	trace	13	19	.4	0	.05	.02	.4	0
white	1 slice	20	36	55	2	1	10	17	.5	trace	.05	.04	.5	trace
whole wheat	1 slice	28	36	65	3	1	14	24	.8	trace	.09	.03	.8	trace
Farina, quick-cooking, enriched, cooked	1 cup	245	89	105	3	trace	22	147	.7	0	.12	.07	1.0	0
Macaroni, enriched, cooked	1 cup	130	64	190	6	1	39	14	1.4	0	.23	.14	1.8	0
Noodles, enriched, cooked	1 cup	160	70	200	7	2	37	16	1.4	110	.22	.13	1.9	0
Oatmeal, cooked	1 cup	240	87	130	5	2	23	22	1.4	0	.19	.05	.2	0
Rice, enriched, cooked	1 cup	205	73	225	4	trace	50	21	1.8	0	.23	.02	2.1	0
Spaghetti, enriched, cooked	1 cup	140	72	155	5	1	32	11	1.3	0	.20	.11	1.5	0

Source: Adapted from *Nutritive Value of Foods* (Home and Garden Bulletin No. 72).

English—Spanish Dictionary

A

a, *prep.* to; at
a·ba·ce·rí·a, *f.* grocery
a·ba·ce·ro, *m.* grocer
á·ba·co, *m.* abacus
a·ba·dí·a, *f.* abbey
a·ba·jo, *adv.* below; down; beneath. *prep.* down
a·ban·do·na·do, *a.* forlorn; derelict
a·ban·do·nar, *v.* abandon; desert; maroon; forsake
a·ban·do·no, *m.* abandonment; dereliction
a·ba·ni·car, *v.* fan
a·ba·ni·co, *m.* fan
a·ba·ra·tar, *v.* make cheaper; lower
a·bar·car, *v.* encompass; embrace; comprise
a·bas·te·ce·dor, *m.* caterer
a·ba·ti·do, *a.* dejected; downcast; glum
a·ba·ti·mien·to, *m.* dejection
a·ba·tir(se), *v.* depress; knock down; fall
ab·di·car, *v.* abdicate
ab·do·men, *m.* abdomen
a·be·dul, *m.* birch
a·be·ja, *f.* bee
a·be·jo·rro, *m.* bumblebee
a·be·rra·ción, *f.* aberration
a·ber·tu·ra, *f.* opening; aperture; breach; gap
a·be·to, *m.* fir
a·bier·ta·men·te, *adv.* outright
a·bier·to, *a.* open
a·bi·ga·rra·do, *a.* motley; many-colored
a·bis·mo, *m.* abyss
ab·ju·rar, *v.* abjure
a·blan·dar(se), *v.* soften
a·bo·fe·te·ar, *v.* cuff; slap
a·bo·ga·do, *m.* lawyer; attorney; advocate; counsel
a·bo·gar, *v.* advocate; plead
a·bo·len·go, *m.* ancestry
a·bo·lir, *v.* abolish
a·bo·lla·du·ra, *f.* dent
a·bo·mi·nar, *v.* loathe; abominate
a·bo·nar, *v.* fertilize; credit
a·bo·no, *m.* fertilizer; pass
a·bo·rí·ge·nes, *m. pl.* aborigines
a·bo·rre·cer, *v.* abhor; hate
a·bo·rre·ci·mien·to, *m.* hatred
a·bor·to, *m.* abortion
a·bo·to·nar, *v.* button up
a·bo·za·lar, *v.* muzzle
a·bra·sión, *f.* abrasion
a·bra·za·de·ra, *f.* brace; clamp
a·bra·zar(se), *v.* embrace; hug; cuddle
a·bra·zo, *m.* embrace; hug
a·bre·via·ción, *f.* abbreviation
a·bre·viar, *v.* abbreviate; abridge; condense; curtail
a·bri·gar(se), *v.* harbor; shelter
a·bri·go, *m.* overcoat; coat; shelter
a·bril, *m.* April
a·bri·llan·tar, *v.* brighten; cut into facets
a·brir(se), *v.* open; open up; spread out
a·bro·char, *v.* fasten; button up
a·bro·gar, *v.* repeal; abrogate
a·brup·to, *a.* blunt; steep; abrupt
abs·ce·so, *m.* abscess
ab·so·lu·to, *a.* absolute; complete
ab·sol·ver, *v.* absolve; acquit; clear
ab·sor·ber, *v.* absorb; soak up; engross
ab·sor·to, *a.* intent; absorbed
abs·te·mio, *a.* abstemious
abs·te·ner·se, *v.* refrain; abstain
abs·trac·to, *a.* abstract
abs·tra·er, *v.* abstract
ab·sur·do, *a.* absurd; silly; preposterous
a·bue·la, *f.* grandmother
a·bue·lo, *m.* grandfather; grandparent
a·bun·dan·cia, *f.* abundance; amplitude
a·bun·dan·te, *a.* abundant; plentiful; ample; bounteous
a·bun·dar, *v.* abound
a·bu·rri·mien·to, *m.* boredom
a·bu·rrir, *v.* bore
a·bu·sar, *v.* abuse; misuse; maltreat
a·bu·so, *m.* abuse; encroachment
ab·yec·to, *a.* abject
a·cá, *adv.* here; hither
a·ca·ba·do, *m.* finish; end; conclusion. *a.* finished
a·ca·bar, *v.* finish; end; accomplish; achieve; fail
a·ca·de·mia, *f.* academy
a·ca·dé·mi·co, *a.* academic
a·ca·li·zar, *v.* alkalize
a·cam·par, *v.* camp
a·ca·ri·ciar, *v.* fondle; pet; pat
a·ca·rre·ar, *v.* cart
a·ca·rreo, *m.* cartage
ac·ce·der, *v.* accede
ac·ce·si·ble, *a.* accessible
ac·ce·so, *m.* access; approach; fit
ac·ce·so·rio, *m.* accessory; subordinate; *pl.* accessories
ac·ci·den·ta·do, *a.* broken; uneven; eventful
ac·ci·den·te, *m.* accident; casualty
ac·ción, *f.* action; movement; share of stock
a·ce·bo, *m.* holly
a·ce·char, *v.* lurk; spy on
a·cei·te, *m.* oil
a·cei·to·so, *a.* oily
a·cei·tu·na, *f.* olive

a·ce·le·rar(se), *v.* accelerate; speed up; expedite
a·cen·to, *m.* accent; stress; emphasis
a·cen·tuar(se), *v.* accent; stress; emphasize
a·cep·tar, *v.* accept; adopt; agree to; allow
a·ce·ra, *f.* sidewalk
a·cer·car(se), *v.* approach; near
a·ce·ri·co, *m.* pincushion
a·ce·ro, *m.* steel
a·cer·ti·jo, *m.* riddle
a·cé·ti·co, *a.* acetic
a·ce·to·na, *f.* acetone
á·ci·do, *m.* acid
á·ci·do bó·ri·co, *m.* boric acid
á·ci·do cí·tri·co, *m.* citric acid
á·ci·do sul·fú·ri·co, *m.* sulphuric acid
a·cla·ma·ción, *f.* acclaim
a·cla·mar, *v.* acclaim
a·cla·ra·ción, *f.* clarification
a·cla·rar, *v.* clarify; clear; rinse
a·cli·ma·tar, *v.* acclimate
ac·né, *m.* acne
a·co·bar·dar(se), *v.* cringe; flinch; quail; unnerve
a·co·gi·da, *f.* welcome; reception
a·co·la·da, *f.* accolade
a·col·char, *v.* pad
a·có·li·to, *m.* acolyte; altar boy
a·co·me·ter, *v.* assail; attempt
a·co·mo·da·di·zo, *a.* obliging; easygoing
a·co·mo·da·dor, *m.* usher
a·co·mo·dar, *v.* accommodate; suit; fit; adjust; usher
a·com·pa·ñan·te, *m.* escort; (*mus.*) accompanist
a·com·pa·ñar, *v.* accompany; escort; go with; attend
a·con·di·cio·na·dor de ai·re, *m.* air conditioner
a·con·se·jar(se), *v.* advise; take advice
a·con·te·cer, *v.* happen; chance
a·con·te·ci·mien·to, *m.* happening; occasion
a·cor·dar(se), *v.* agree; agree on; harmonize; remember
a·cor·de, *m.* chord
a·cor·deón, *m.* accordion
a·cor·near, *v.* gore
a·co·rra·lar, *v.* corral; corner
a·cor·tar(se), *v.* clip; shorten
a·co·sar, *v.* pursue; harass; beset
a·cos·tar(se), *v.* lie down; go to bed
a·cos·tum·brar(se), *v.* habituate; accustom oneself to
a·cre, *m.* acre. *a.* acrid; sour
a·cre·cen·tar, *v.* increase
a·cree·dor, *m.*, a·cree·do·ra, *f.* creditor
a·cri·mo·nia, *f.* acrimony; bitterness
a·cró·ba·ta, *m., f.* acrobat
ac·ti·tud, *f.* attitude; pose; position
ac·ti·var, *v.* activate
ac·ti·vi·dad, *f.* activity; movement; briskness
ac·ti·vo, *a.* active; alive; brisk. *adv.* astir. *m. pl.* assets
ac·to, *m.* act
ac·tor, *m.* actor
ac·triz, *f.* actress
ac·tual, *a.* actual; instant
ac·tual·men·te, *adv.* actually; now
ac·tuar, *v.* act; perform
a·cua·rio, *m.* aquarium
a·cuá·ti·co, *a.* aquatic
a·cu·chi·llar, *v.* knife; slash; hack
a·cue·duc·to, *m.* aqueduct
á·cueo, *a.* aqueous; watery
a·cuer·do, *m.* agreement; accord; resolution. es·tar de a·cuer·do, concur
a·cu·mu·lar, *v.* accumulate; cumulate; amass; stockpile; congest; fund
a·cu·ña·ción, *f.* coinage
a·cu·ñar, *v.* mint; coin
a·cu·sar, *v.* accuse; charge; impeach; indict
a·cús·ti·ca, *f.* acoustics
a·chi·car, *v.* bail; humble; diminish
a·chi·co·ria, *f.* chicory
a·chis·pa·do, *a.* tipsy
a·da·gio, *m.* adage; proverb; (*mus.*) adagio
a·dap·ta·ble, *a.* versatile; adaptable
a·dap·tar, *v.* adapt; adapt oneself to; adjust
a·de·cua·do, *a.* adequate; fit; suitable
a·de·ha·la, *f.* bonus; tip
a·de·lan·ta·do, *a.* advanced; fast
a·de·lan·tar(se), *v.* proceed; further; go ahead; advance; gain upon
a·de·lan·te, *adv.* forward, forwards; forth; onward
a·de·lan·to, *m.* advance; progress
a·del·ga·zar(se), *v.* slim down; lose weight; taper
a·de·mán, *m.* gesture; attitude
a·de·más, *adv.* moreover; besides; furthermore; also. *prep.* besides
a·de·re·zar, *v.* garnish; adorn; dress
a·de·re·zo, *m.* adornment
a·dhe·rir(se), *v.* cling; adhere; cohere; cleave to; espouse
ad·he·si·vo, *a.* adhesive. *m.* adhesive
a·di·ción, *f.* addition; increment; annex
a·di·cio·nal, *a.* additional; more; extra
a·dies·trar(se), *v.* train; exercise
a·diós, *m.* farewell. *int.* farewell; goodby, goodbye
a·di·vi·nar, *v.* guess; divine; foretell
ad·je·ti·vo, *a.* adjective

ad·ju·di·ca·ción, *m.* adjudment; award
ad·ju·di·car(se), *v.* award; allot
ad·jun·tar, *v.* annex
ad·mi·nis·tra·ción, *f.* administration; management
ad·mi·nis·tra·dor, *m.*, ad·mi·nis·tra·do·ra, *f.* administrator; manager; steward
ad·mi·nis·trar, *v.* administer; manage; dispense
ad·mi·ra·ble, *a.* admirable; fine; excellent
ad·mi·rar(se), *v.* admire; wonder
ad·mi·si·ble, *a.* admissible; acceptable
ad·mi·tir, *v.* admit; receive; permit
a·do·be, *m.* adobe
a·do·les·cen·cia, *f.* adolescence
a·dop·tar, *v.* adopt; embrace
a·do·rar, *v.* adore; worship
a·dor·me·cer(se), *v.* drowse; fall asleep
a·dor·mi·de·ra, *f.* poppy
a·dor·nar, *v.* decorate; adorn; deck; bedeck; grace
a·dor·no, *m.* ornament; adornment; array; *pl.* finery
ad·qui·rir, *v.* acquire; secure; obtain
a·dre·na·li·na, *f.* adrenaline
ads·cri·bir, *v.* ascribe; assign
a·dua·na, *f.* custom-house; *pl.* customs
a·du·la·ción, *f.* adulation; flattery; blarney
a·du·la·dor, *m.*, a·du·la·do·ra, *f.* sycophant; flatterer
a·du·lar, *v.* flatter
a·dul·te·rio, *m.* adultery
a·dul·to, *m.* adult; grownup. *a.* grown-up
ad·ver·bio, *m.* adverb
ad·ver·sa·rio, *m.* adversary; opponent
ad·ver·si·dad, *f.* adversity
ad·ver·so, *a.* adverse; averse; unfavorable
ad·ver·tir, *v.* caution; notify; take notice of
ad·ya·cen·te, *a.* adjacent
aé·reo, *a.* aerial
ae·ro·náu·ti·ca, *f.* aeronautics
ae·ro·puer·to, *m.* airport
a·fa·ble, *a.* affable; kind; genial
a·fán, *m.* travail; anxiety
a·fec·ción, *f.* affection; fondness
a·fec·ta·ción, *f.* affectation; pretense
a·fec·tar, *v.* affect
a·fec·to, *m.* affection. *a.* affectionate
a·fec·tuo·sa·men·te, *adv.* affectionately; fondly
a·fei·ta·do, *m.*, a·fei·ta·da, *f.* shave. *a.* shaven
a·fe·rrar(se), *v.* furl; grasp
a·fian·zar, *v.* guaranty; bail; clinch
a·fi·cio·na·do, *m.*, a·fi·cio·na·da, *f.* amateur; fancier; fan
a·fi·jo, *m.* affix
a·fi·lar(se), *v.* hone; sharpen
a·fi·liar(se), *v.* affiliate; join
a·fín, *a.* related
a·fi·na·ción, *f.* refining; (*mus.*) tuning
a·fi·nar, *v.* tune; polish
a·fi·ni·dad, *f.* affinity
a·fir·mar(se), *v.* affirm; assert; contend; aver; make fast
a·fir·ma·ti·vo, *a.* affirmative
a·flic·ción, *f.* affliction; anxiety; bereavement
a·fli·gi·do, *a.* stricken
a·fli·gir(se), *v.* afflict; grieve
a·flo·jar(se), *v.* slacken; loosen; weaken
a·fluen·cia, *f.* affluence
a·fo·ris·mo, *m.* aphorism
a·for·tu·na·do, *a.* fortunate; prosperous; lucky
a·fren·ta, *f.* affront; insult
a·fren·tar(se), *v.* affront; insult; be affronted
a·fro·di·sía·co, *a.* aphrodisiac
a·fue·ra, *adv.* out; outside. *f. pl.* suburbs
a·ga·char(se), *v.* crouch; bow down; squat
a·ga·lla, *f.* gill
a·ga·rrar(se), *v.* seize; grasp; grapple; clinch; clutch
a·ga·rro, *m.* grab; clutch; grip
a·gen·cia, *f.* agency; bureau
a·gen·te, *m.* agent; officer. a·gen·te de po·li·cía, cop
á·gil, *a.* agile; nimble; active; lithe; lithesome
a·gi·li·dad, *f.* agility
a·gi·ta·ción, *f.* agitation; excitement; stir; flutter; flurry
a·gi·tar(se), *v.* agitate; stir up; churn; shake; flutter
a·glo·me·ra·do, *a.* agglomerate
a·glo·me·rar, *v.* agglomerate
ag·nós·ti·co, *m.*, ag·nós·ti·ca, *f.* agnostic
a·go·nía, *f.* agony; pain
a·gos·to, *m.* August
a·go·ta·mien·to, *m.* depletion; exhaustion
a·go·tar(se), *v.* exhaust; drain; deplete; give out; tire
a·gra·da·ble, *a.* agreeable; pleasant; delightful; gracious; nice; goodly
a·gra·de·cer(se), *v.* acknowledge; thank; appreciate
a·gra·de·ci·do, *a.* grateful; thankful
a·gra·rio, *a.* agrarian
a·gra·var, *v.* aggravate; get or

make worse; burden
a·gra·vio, *m.* grievance
a·gre·gar(se), *v.* aggregate; join together
a·gre·miar(se), *v.* unionize
a·gre·sión, *f.* aggression
a·gre·si·vo, *a.* aggressive
a·griar(se), *v.* sour; acetify
a·gri·cul·tor, *m.* farmer
a·gri·cul·tu·ra, *f.* agriculture; farming
a·grie·tar(se), *v.* chap
a·gri·men·sor, *m.* surveyor
a·grio, *a.* sour; acid; acrid; bitter; surly
a·gro·no·mía, *f.* agronomy
a·gru·par(se), *v.* group; bunch; cluster
a·gua·ca·te, *m.* avocado; avocado tree
a·gua·fuer·te, *f.* etching
a·gua·ma·nil, *m.* ewer
a·gua·nie·ve, *f.* sleet
a·guan·tar(se), *v.* endure; put up with; support
a·gu·de·za, *f.* acuity; acumen; keenness; brightness; witticism
a·gu·do, *a.* keen; sharp; acute; quick-witted; exquisite
a·güe·ro, *m.* omen; augury
a·gui·ja·da, *f.* goad
a·gui·la, *f.* eagle
a·gui·le·ño, *a.* aquiline
a·gui·lón, *m.* gable
a·gui·lu·cho, *m.* eaglet
a·gu·ja, *f.* needle; pin; spire
a·gu·je·ro, *m.* hole
ah, *int.* ha, hah
a·he·cha·du·ra, *f.* chaff; winnowing
a·he·rrum·brar(se), *v.* rust
a·hí, *adv.* there
a·hi·ja·da, *f.* goddaughter
a·hi·ja·do, *m.* godson; godchild
a·ho·gar(se), *v.* suffocate; choke; drown; smother; stifle
a·ho·ra, *adv.* now. has·ta a·ho·ra, heretofore
a·hor·car, *v.* hang
a·ho·rrar, *v.* save; economize
a·ho·rros, *m. pl.* savings
ai·re, *m.* air; manner; aspect; tune. al ai·re li·bre, outdoors
ai·rear(se), *v.* aerate; air; cool oneself
ai·ro·so, *a.* airy; jaunty
ais·la·mien·to, *m.* isolation; insulation
ais·lar, *v.* isolate; seclude; sequester; insulate
a·jar, *v.* crumple; rumple
a·je·drez, *m.* chess
a·je·no, *a.* alien
a·jo, *m.* garlic
a·jus·ta·do, *a.* snug; tight-fitting
a·jus·tar, *v.* adjust; settle; bargain
a·jus·te, *m.* settlement; fitting; fit; accommodation
a·la·ban·za, *f.* praise
a·la·bar, *v.* praise; extol; commend
a·la·bas·tro, *m.* alabaster
a·la·cri·dad, *f.* alacrity
a·lam·bre, *m.* wire. a·lam·bre de púas (de espino), barbed wire, barb wire
a·lar·de, *m.* boast; review
a·lar·gar(se), *v.* elongate; extend; prolong; reach; hand
a·lar·ma, *f.* alarm; alert
a·lar·mar, *v.* alarm; startle
a·lar·mis·ta, *m.* alarmist
a·lba, *f.* dawn
a·lba·cea, *m., f.* executor
a·lba·ha·ca, *f.* basil
a·lba·ñal, *m.* sewer
a·lba·ñil, *m.* mason
a·lba·ñi·le·ría, *f.* masonry; brick work
a·lba·ri·co·que, *m.* apricot
a·lba·tros, *m.* albatross
a·lber·gar(se), *v.* lodge; shelter
a·lbi·no, *m.* albino. *a.* albino
a·lbón·di·gas, *f.* meatballs
a·lbo·ro·tar, *v.* brawl; riot
a·lbo·ro·to, *m.* brawl; uproar; disturbance; turmoil; *inf.* ruckus
á·lbum, *m.* album
a·lbu·men, *m.* albumen
a·lbú·mi·na, *f.* albumin
a·lca·hue·ta, *f.* bawd; procuress
a·lca·hue·te, *m.* pimp
a·lca·hue·tear, *v.* procure
a·lcal·de, *m.* mayor
á·lca·li, *m.* alkali
a·lcan·ce, *m.* scope; range; reach; extent
a·lcan·cear, *v.* spear
a·lcan·ta·ri·lla, *f.* culvert; sewer
a·lcan·zar(se), *v.* overtake; gain; reach; attain; achieve
a·lca·ra·vea, *f.* caraway
a·lce, *m.* moose; elk
a·lco·ba, *f.* bedroom; alcove
a·lco·hol, *m.* alcohol
Al·co·rán, Co·rán, *m.* Koran
a·ldea, *f.* village
a·lde·hue·la, *f.* hamlet
a·lea·ción, *f.* alloy
a·le·ga·ción, *f.* allegation
a·le·ga·do, *a.* alleged
a·le·gar, *v.* argue
a·le·go·ría, *f.* allegory
a·le·grar(se), *v.* cheer; rejoice; exhilarate
a·le·gre, *a.* happy; joyous; glad; cheerful; gay; convivial; jolly; hilarious; jocund; light-hearted; blithe; airy
a·le·gre·men·te, *adv.* happily; gaily
a·le·gría, *f.* joy; gladness; cheer; gaiety; mirth; hilarity
a·le·jar(se), *v.* recede; move away; separate
a·le·lu·ya, *int.* hallelujah
a·len·ta·dor, *a.* encouraging
a·len·tar, *v.* hearten; animate; raise (the spirits of); get well
a·ler·gia, *f.* allergy
a·le·ro, *m.* overhang; *pl.* eaves
a·ler·ta, *a.* alert. *f.* watchword
a·ler·tar, *v.* alert; put on guard
a·le·ta, *f.* fin
a·le·teo, *m.* flutter of wings
a·lfa·be·to, *m.* alphabet
a·lfal·fa, *f.* alfalfa
a·lfa·re·ría, *f.* pottery
a·lfé·rez, *m.* ensign; subaltern
a·lfi·ler, *m.* pin. a·lfi·ler de pe·cho, broach
a·lfom·bra, *f.* rug; carpet
a·lfom·brar, *v.* carpet
a·lfor·fón, *m.* buckwheat
a·lga, *f.* alga. a·lga ma·ri·na, seaweed
á·lge·bra, *f.* algebra
a·lgo, *m.* aught; something. *pron.* anything. *adv.* somewhat
a·lgo·dón, *m.* cotton. dril de al·go·dón, denim
a·lgua·cil, *m.* bailiff; constable; marshal
a·lguien, *pron.* somebody; someone; anybody; anyone
a·lgu·no, al·gún, *pron.* any; anybody; anyone; *pl.* some. *a.* any; some
a·lia·do, *m.*, a·lia·da, *f.* ally
a·lian·za, *f.* alliance; coalition; covenant
a·liar(se), *v.* align; ally
a·lias, *m.* alias. *adv.* alias
a·li·ca·tes, *m.* pliers
a·lien·to, *m.* breath; respiration. sin a·lien·to, breathless
a·li·ge·ra·mien·to, *m.* alleviation
a·li·ge·rar(se), *v.* lighten; relieve; alleviate
a·li·men·tar(se), *v.* nourish; feed
a·li·men·ti·cio, *a.* alimentary; nutritious
a·li·men·to, *m.* aliment; food; *pl.* alimony
a·li·near(se), *v.* range; line; align
a·lis·ta·mien·to, *m.* enlistment
a·lis·tar(se), *v.* enlist; join up
a·li·viar, *v.* relieve; alleviate; ease; allay
a·li·vio, *m.* relief; alleviation
a·lma, *f.* soul; spirit
a·lma·cén, *m.* store; storehouse; warehouse
a·lma·na·que, *m.* almanac
a·lme·ja, *f.* clam
a·lme·na·ra, *f.* beacon
a·lmen·dra, *f.* almond; kernel
a·lmiar, *m.* haystack
a·lmí·bar, *m.* syrup
a·lmi·dón, *m.* starch
a·lmo·ha·da, *f.* pillow; cushion
a·lmo·ha·di·lla, *f.* pad; pin cushion
a·lmol·dar, *v.* mold, mould
a·lmor·zar, *v.* lunch
a·lmuer·zo, *m.* lunch; luncheon
a·lo·ja·mien·to, *m.* lodging; housing; billet; quarters
a·lo·jar(se), *v.* lodge; house; billet; room
a·lque·ría, *f.* farmhouse
a·lqui·lar(se), *v.* rent; hire; charter
a·lqui·ler, *m.* rent; wages
a·lqui·mia, *f.* alchemy
a·lqui·trán, *m.* tar
a·lre·de·dor, *adv.* around; round. *prep.* about; round. *m. pl.* outskirts; surroundings
a·lta·ne·ro, *a.* haughty; proud; disdainful
a·ltar, *m.* altar
a·lta·voz, *m.* loudspeaker
a·lte·ra·ción, *f.* alteration; change; pervert
a·lter·ca·ción, *f.* altercation; quarrel
á·lter e·go, *m.* alter ego
a·lter·nar, *v.* alternate; rotate; take turns
a·lter·na·ti·va, *f.* alternative
a·lter·no, *a.* alternate
a·lti·me·tro, *m.* altimeter
a·lti·tud, *f.* altitude
a·lto, *a.* high; tall; upper; loud. *adv.* aloud; high. *m.* height; half; (*mus.*) alto
a·ltruis·mo, *m.* altruism
a·ltu·ra, *f.* height; elevation; altitude
a·lu·ci·na·ción, *f.* hallucination
a·lud, *m.* avalanche
a·lu·dir, *v.* allude; hint at; refer to
a·lu·mi·nio, *m.* aluminum
a·lum·no, *m.*, a·lum·na, *f.* scholar; student; pupil; alumnus
a·lu·sión, *f.* allusion; reference
a·lza·mien·to, *m.* lift; insurrection
a·lzar(se), *v.* lift; hoist; raise; arise; rebel
a·llá, *adv.* there; in or to that place; thither. más a·llá, beyond
a·lla·nar, *v.* level; even; smooth
a·llí, *adv.* there; in or to that place
a·ma, *f.* owner; mistress
a·ma·ble, *a.* amiable; nice; kindly; goodhearted; lovable; likeable
a·ma·do, *m.*, a·ma·da, *f.* dear; sweetheart. *a.* beloved; darling
a·ma·dri·gar(se), *v.* burrow
a·mal·ga·ma, *f.* amalgam
a·mal·ga·mar(se), *v.* amalgamate
a·ma·ne·cer, *v.* dawn; daybreak
a·man·te, *m., f.* lover

a·mar, *v.* love
a·mar·go, *a.* bitter; tart; acrid
a·mar·gu·ra, *f.* bitterness; sharpness
a·ma·ri·llo, *a.* yellow. *m.* yellow
a·ma·rrar, *v.* moor; fasten; tie up
a·mar·ti·llar, *v.* cock a gun; hammer
a·ma·sar, *v.* mash; knead; mix
a·ma·tis·ta, *f.* amethyst
a·ma·to·rio, *a.* amatory
a·ma·zo·na, *f.* amazon; horse-woman
ám·bar, *m.* amber
am·bi·ción, *f.* ambition
am·bi·cio·so, *a.* ambitious
am·bi·dex·tro, *a.* ambidextrous
am·bien·te, *m.* atmosphere; environment
am·bi·güe·dad, *f.* ambiguity
am·bi·guo, *a.* ambiguous; equivocal; uncertain
am·bi·va·len·cia, *f.* ambivalence
ám·bi·to, *m.* amble
am·bos, *a.* both. *pron.* both
am·bri·no, *a.* amber
am·bu·lan·te, *a.* ambulatory; mobile; traveling
a·mén, *int.* amen
a·me·na·za, *f.* threat; menace
a·me·na·zar, *v.* threaten; menace; loom
a·me·ni·dad, *f.* amenity; pleasantness
a·me·ri·ca·na, *f.* jacket
a·me·ri·ca·no, *a.* American
a·mi·ba, *f.* amoeba, ameba
a·mi·ga, *f.* friend; girl friend
a·míg·da·la, *f.* tonsil
a·mig·da·li·tis, *f.* tonsillitis
a·mi·go, *m.* friend, boyfriend; *pl. archaic.* kith
a·mis·tad, *f.* friendship
a·mis·tar(se), *v.* befriend; become friends
a·mis·to·so, *a.* friendly; amicable
am·ne·sia, *f.* amnesia
am·nis·tía, *f.* amnesty
a·mo, *m.* employer; boss; master; owner
a·mo·nes·tar, *v.* caution; warn; admonish
a·mo·nía·co, *m.* ammonia
a·mon·to·nar(se), *v.* heap; amass; mound; hoard; bank up; drift; huddle
a·mor, *m.* love; lover. a·mor pro·pio, conceit
a·mo·ral, *a.* amoral
a·mor·da·zar, *v.* gag; muzzle
a·mor·fo, *a.* amorphous
a·mo·río, *m.* romance; love affair
a·mo·ro·so, *a.* amorous
a·mor·ti·guar, *v.* deaden; cushion; buff
a·mor·ti·za·ción, *f.* amortization; redemption
a·mor·ti·zar, *v.* amortize
a·mo·ti·nar(se), *v.* mutiny; riot; incite to revolt
am·pe·rio, *m.* ampere
am·plia·ción, *f.* enlargement
am·pli·fi·car, *v.* amplify
am·plio, *a.* ample; extensive; broad
am·pli·tud, *f.* amplitude; fullness
am·po·lla, *f.* blister
am·pu·lo·si·dad, *f.* bombast; verbosity
am·pu·ta·ción, *f.* amputation
am·pu·tar, *v.* amputate
a·mu·le·to, *m.* amulet; charm
a·na·car·do, *m.* cashew
a·na·con·da, *f.* anaconda
a·na·cro·nis·mo, *m.* anachronism
a·na·gra·ma, *m.* anagram
a·nal, *a.* anal
a·nal·fa·be·tis·mo, *m.* illiteracy
a·nal·fa·be·to, *m.*, a·nal·fa·be·ta, *f.* illiterate. *a.* illiterate
a·nal·gé·si·co, *m.* analgesic. *a.* analgesic
a·ná·li·sis, *m.* analysis; review; breakdown
a·na·li·za·dor, *m.* analyst
a·na·li·zar, *v.* analyze
a·na·lo·gía, *f.* analogy
a·na·quel, *m.* ledge; shelf
a·na·ran·ja·do, *a.* orange
a·nar·quía, *f.* anarchy
a·nar·quis·mo, *m.* anarchism
a·nar·quis·ta, *m., f.* anarchist
a·na·te·ma, *m.* anathema
a·na·to·mía, *f.* anatomy
an·ca, *f.* haunch; rump
an·cia·no, *a.* old; aged. *m.* old man
an·cla, *f.* anchor
an·co·ra, *m.* anchor
an·cho, *a.* broad; wide; roomy; loose
an·choa, *f.* anchovy
an·chu·ra, *f.* width; breadth; fullness
an·da·mio, *m.* scaffold; stage
an·dar, *v.* walk; ambulate; go; work, as machines. *m.* gait
an·dén, *m.* platform; sidewalk
an·dor·rear, *v.* gad about; wander about
an·dra·jos, *m. pl.* tatters
a·néc·do·ta, *f.* anecdote
a·nea, *f.* bulrush
a·ne·gar(se), *v.* drown; flood
a·ne·mia, *f.* anemia, anaemia
a·ne·mó·me·tro, *m.* anemometer
a·nes·te·sia, *f.* anesthesia
a·nes·té·si·co, *a.* anesthetic. *m.* anesthetic
a·ne·xar, *v.* annex; append
a·ne·xión, *f.* annexation
an·fi·bio, *a.* amphibious. *m.* am-

phibian
an.fi.tea.tro, m. amphitheater
an.fi.trión, m. host
án.gel, m. angel
an.gé.li.co, a. angelic
an.glo.sa.jón, m., an.glo.sa.jo.na, f. Anglo-Saxon. a. Anglo-Saxon
an.go.ra, f. angora
an.gos.to, a. narrow
an.gui.la, f. eel
an.gu.lar, a. angular
án.gu.lo, m. angle; corner
an.gu.lo.so, a. angular
an.gus.tia, f. agony; anguish; woe; heart break; heartache
an.gus.tio.so, a. harrowing; anguished
an.he.lar, v. long for; crave; hanker
an.he.lo, m. longing; hankering; aspiration
an.hí.dro, a. anhydrous
a.ni.dar, v. nest; shelter
a.ni.llo, m. ring
a.ni.ma.ción, f. animation; life; vivacity
a.ni.ma.do, a. animated; lively; sprightly; animate
a.ni.mad.ver.sión, f. animadversion
a.ni.mal, m. animal. a. animal. a.ni.mal do.més.ti.co, pet
a.ni.mar(se), v. animate; liven; rouse; encourage
á.ni.mo, m. spirit; courage; resolution
a.ni.mo.si.dad, f. animosity
a.ni.ña.do, a. childish
a.ni.qui.la.ción, f. annihilation
a.ni.qui.lar(se), v. annihilate; destroy; decline; waste away
a.nís, m. anise
a.ni.ver.sa.rio, m. anniversary
a.no, m. anus
a.no.che, adv. last night
a.no.che.cer, v. get dark. m. nightfall; evening
á.no.do, m. anode
a.no.ma.lía, f. anomaly
a.nó.ma.lo, a. anomalous
a.nó.ni.mo, a. anonymous. m. anonymity
a.nor.mal, a. abnormal; unnatural; subnormal
a.no.tar, v. annotate; note down; enter
an.sia, f. anxiety; anguish; worry; eagerness; thirst; longing
an.sio.so, a. anxious; eager
an.ta.go.nis.ta, m., f. antagonist
an.tár.ti.co, a. antarctic
ante, prep. before. m. suede; buckskin; buff
an.te.bra.zo, m. forearm
an.te.cá.ma.ra, f. anteroom
an.te.ce.den.te, m. antecedent; pl. background. a. previous
an.te.ce.der, v. antecede; precede
an.te.da.tar, v. antedate
an.te.di.lu.via.no, a. antediluvian
an.te.ma.no, de an.te.ma.no, a. beforehand. de an.te.ma.no, in advance
an.te.me.ri.dia.no, a. antemeridian. Abbr. a.m.
an.te.na, f. antenna; aerial; feeler
an.te.o.jo, m. eyeglass; pl. goggles
an.te.pa.sa.do, m. forefather; ancestor
an.te.ra, f. anther
an.te.rior, a. anterior; former; prior; above; preceding; fore
an.tes, adv. before; heretofore. an.tes de, before. an.tes de que, before; ere
an.ti, prefix. anti
an.ti.á.ci.do, m. antacid
an.ti.bió.ti.co, m. antibiotic. a. antibiotic
an.ti.ci.pa.ción, f. anticipation
an.ti.ci.par(se), v. advance; anticipate
an.ti.cli.max, m. anticlimax
an.ti.con.cep.cio.nal, a. contraceptive
an.ti.con.cep.ción, m. contraception; birth control
an.ti.cua.do, a. antiquated; old-fashioned; obsolete; inf. square
an.ti.cuar, v. antiquate
an.ti.cuer.po, m. antibody
an.tí.do.to, m. antidote
an.tí.fo.na, f. anthem; antiphony
an.ti.gua.men.te, adv. formerly; in old times
an.ti.güe.dad, f. antiquity; antique
an.ti.guo, a. antique; old; ancient; erstwhile
an.tí.lo.pe, m. antelope
an.ti.pa.tía, f. antipathy; dislike
an.tí.po.das, m. pl. antipodes
an.ti.se.mi.tis.mo, m. anti-Semitism
an.ti.sép.ti.co, a. antiseptic. m. antiseptic
an.ti.so.cial, a. antisocial
an.tí.te.sis, f. antithesis
an.ti.to.xi.na, f. antitoxin
an.to.lo.gía, f. anthology
an.tó.ni.mo, m. antonym
an.tor.cha, f. torch
an.tra.ci.ta, f. anthracite
án.trax, m. anthrax
an.tro.poi.de, a. anthropoid
an.tro.po.lo.gía, f. anthropology
an.tro.po.ló.go, m. anthropologist
a.nual, m. annual. a. annual
a.nu.blar(se), v. cloud; blight; get dark
a.nu.dar, v. knot
a.nu.la.ción, f. annulment; repeal

a.nu.lar, v. annul; cancel; undo
a.nun.cia.ción, f. annunciation; announcement
a.nun.ciar, v. advertise; announce; annunciate; forbode
a.nun.cio, m. announcement; notice; bulletin
a.ña.di.du.ra, f. addition
a.ña.dir, v. add; increase; affix
a.ñil, m. indigo; bluing
a.ño, m. year. a.ño bi.sies.to, leap year. a.ño de luz, light year
a.ño.ran.za, f. yearning; hankering
aor.ta, f. aorta
a.pa.ci.ble, a. gentle
a.pa.ci.guar(se), v. placate; appease; calm down
a.pa.ga.do, a. out; dull; spiritless
a.pa.gar(se), v. quench; muffle; put out; go out
a.pa.la.brar, v. bespeak; engage; agree
a.pa.lear, v. batter; beat
a.pa.ra.dor, m. dresser; buffet
a.pa.ra.to, m. apparatus; device; gadget
a.pa.rear(se), v. mate; pair
a.pa.re.cer(se), v. appear; show up; come; haunt
a.pa.re.jar(se), v. prepare; rig out; get ready
a.pa.ren.te, a. apparent; ostensible
a.pa.ri.ción, f. appearance
a.pa.rien.cia, f. appearance; guise; pl. looks
a.par.ta.men.to, m. apartment
a.par.tar(se), v. separate; divide; avert; remove; estrange
a.par.te, adv. apart; asunder. m. aside. a.par.te de, apart from
a.pa.sio.na.do, a. passionate; ardent; fiery; vehement
a.pa.tía, f. apathy
a.pe.la.ción, f. appeal
a.pe.lan.te, m., f. appellant
a.pe.lar, v. appeal
a.pe.lli.do, m. name; surname
a.pe.nar(se), v. pain; grieve
a.pe.nas, adv. hardly; barely; just
a.pen.dec.to.mía, f. appendectomy
a.pén.di.ce, m. appendix; appendage
a.pen.di.ci.tis, f. appendicitis
a.peo, m. survey
a.pe.ten.cia, f. appetite; relish
a.pe.ti.to, m. appetite
a.pe.ti.to.so, a. appetizing
á.pi.ce, m. apex; top; vertex
a.pi.ñar(se), v. jam; crowd together
a.pio, m. celery
a.pi.so.na.do.ra, f. steamroller
a.plas.tan.te, a. crushing
a.plas.tar(se), v. crush; flatten
a.plau.dir, v. applaud; clap; cheer
a.plau.so, m. applause; cheer
a.pla.za.mien.to, m. deferment; adjournment
a.pla.zar, v. postpone; procrastinate; delay; defer
a.pli.ca.ción, f. application
a.pli.car(se), v. apply; devote to
a.plo.mo, m. poise; aplomb
a.po.ca.lip.sis, m. apocalypse
a.po.dar, v. nickname
a.po.de.ra.do, m. proxy; commissioner
a.po.de.rar(se), v. seize; empower; grant power of attorney
a.po.do, m. nickname
a.po.geo, m. apogee; inf. heyday; heydey
a.po.lo.gía, f. apology; defense
a.po.ple.jía, f. apoplexy
a.po.plé.ti.co, a. apoplectic
a.po.rrear(se), v. club; cudgel; beat; toil
a.po.si.ción, f. apposition
a.pos.tar, v. bet; station
a.pós.ta.ta, m., f. apostate
a.pós.tol, m. apostle
a.pos.tó.li.co, a. apostolic
a.pós.tro.fo, m. apostrophe
a.po.yar(se), v. prop; support; rest on; bolster; back; second
a.po.yo, m. support; prop
a.pre.ciar, v. appreciate; value; regard
a.pre.cio, m. estimation; appraisal; appreciation
a.pre.hen.sión, f. apprehension
a.pren.der, v. learn. a.pren.der de me.mo.ria, memorize
a.pren.diz, m. a.pren.di.za, f. apprentice. po.ner de a.pren.diz, apprentice
a.pre.sa.dor, m., a.pre.sa.do.ra, f. captor
a.pre.sar, v. capture; seize
a.pre.su.ra.do, a. hasty
a.pre.su.rar(se), v. hurry; quicken; bustle
a.pre.tar, v. push; press; crowd; clench; clutch
a.pre.tón, m. grip; squeeze; tighten. a.pre.tón de ma.nos, handshake
a.prie.to, m. fix
a.pro.ba.ción, f. approbation; approval
a.pro.ba.do, a. approved; inf. O.K.
a.pro.bar, v. approve; pass. no a.pro.bar, flunk
a.pro.pia.do, a. appropriate; proper; suitable
a.pro.piar(se), v. appropriate; fit; borrow
a.pro.ve.char(se), v. avail; utilize; take advantage of; benefit; profit
a.pro.xi.ma.ción, f. approximation;

approach
a.pro.xi.ma.do, a. approximate
a.pro.xi.mar(se), v. approximate; approach
ap.ti.tud, f. aptitude; ability
ap.to, a. apt; suitable
a.pues.ta, f. bet
a.pun.tar(se), v. point; aim; note; jot down
a.pun.te, m. cue; memorandum; pl. notes
a.pu.ña.lar, v. stab; thrust
a.pu.rar(se), v. fret; worry; refine; verify
a.pu.ro, m. hardship; predicament; plight; pl. straits; inf. jam
a.quel, a.que.lla, a. a.quél; pl. a.que.llos, a.que.llas, f. those
a.quél, pron. m., a.qué.lla, pron. f. that one; pl. a.qué.llos, a.qué.llas, f. those
a.quí, adv. here. de a.quí en a.de.lan.te, henceforth; henceforward
a.quie.tar, v. lull; quiet; tranquilize; still; allay
á.ra.be, a. Arab; Arabian. m., f. Arab
a.ra.do, m. plow
a.rán.da.no, m. cranberry
a.ra.ña, f. spider. a.ra.ña de lu.ces, chandelier
ar.bi.tra.je, m. arbitration
ar.bi.trar(se), v. arbitrate; umpire; manage
ar.bi.tra.rio, a. arbitrary
ár.bi.tro, m. referee; umpire; arbiter
ár.bol, m. tree
ar.bo.le.da, f. grove
ar.bó.reo, a. arboreal
ar.bus.to, m. bush; shrub; pl. shrubbery
ar.ca, f. ark; box; chest
ar.ca.da, f. arcade
ar.cai.co, a. archaic
ar.cán.gel, m. archangel
ar.ce, m. maple
ar.ci.lla, f. clay
ar.ci.pres.te, m. archpriest
ar.co, m. arc; arch; bow. ar.co í.ris, rainbow
ar.chi.du.que, m. archduke
ar.chi.du.que.sa, f. archduchess
ar.chi.pié.la.go, m. archipelago
ar.chi.var, v. file
ar.chi.vo, m. archive(s); file; pl. records
ar.der(se), v. blaze; burn; burn up. ar.der sin lla.mas, smolder
ar.did, m. ruse
ar.dien.do, a. afire. adv. afire
ar.dien.te, a. ardent; aglow; burning; fiery
ar.dor, m. ardor; fire; heat
ar.duo, a. arduous
á.rea, f. area
a.re.na, f. sand; grit. a.re.na mo.ve.di.za, quicksand
a.ren.ga, f. harangue
a.ren.gar, v. harangue
a.re.nis.ca, f. sandstone
a.re.no.so, a. sandy; gritty
ar.ga.ma.sa, f. plaster
ar.go, m. argon
ar.go.lla, f. ring
ar.got, m. slang
ar.gu.men.ta.dor, a. argumentative
ar.gu.men.to, m. argument
a.ria, f. aria
a.ri.dez, f. aridity; dryness
á.ri.do, a. arid; dry
a.ris.to.cra.cia, f. aristocracy
a.ris.tó.cra.ta, m., f. aristocrat
a.ris.to.crá.ti.co, a. aristocratic
a.rit.mé.ti.ca, f. arithmetic
a.rit.mé.ti.co, a. arithmetician. arithmetic
ar.ma, f. arm; weapon. ar.ma de fue.go, firearm; gun
ar.ma.da, f. armada
ar.ma.di.llo, m. armadillo
ar.ma.du.ra, f. armor; frame
ar.ma.men.to, m. armament
ar.mar(se), v. arm; get ready
ar.ma.rio, m. armoire; buffet; cupboard; closet
ar.ma.zón, f. bedstead; skeleton
ar.me.ría, f. armory; gunsmith
ar.mi.ño, m. ermine
ar.mis.ti.cio, m. armistice
ar.mo.nía, f. harmony; accord
ar.mó.ni.ca, f. harmonica
ar.mo.nio.so, a. harmonious
ar.mo.ni.zar, v. harmonize
a.ro, m. rim; ring; hoop
a.ro.ma, m. aroma; bouquet; fragrance
a.ro.má.ti.co, a. aromatic
ar.pa, f. harp
ar.pe.o, m. grapple; grappling iron
ar.pía, f. shrew; vixen
ar.pi.lle.ra, f. burlap; sackcloth
ar.pis.ta, m., f. harpist
ar.pón, m. harpoon; grapple; gaff
ar.po.near, v. harpoon
ar.quear(se), v. arch; retch
ar.queo.lo.gía, f. archaeology; archeology
ar.que.ro, m. archer
ar.que.ti.po, m. archetype
ar.qui.tec.to, m. architect
ar.qui.tec.tó.ni.co, a. architectural
ar.qui.tec.tu.ra, f. architecture
a.rran.car, v. rip out; pull up; wrest; start
a.rras.trar(se), v. draw; pull; drag; trail; creep; crawl
a.rre.ba.tar(se), v. grab; snatch; get carried away

a.rre.ba.ti.ña, f. scrimmage
a.rre.glar(se), v. arrange; order; fix; set; settle; marshal
a.rre.glo, m. arrangement; compromise
a.rre.mo.li.nar(se), v. swirl; crowd
a.rren.da.jo, m. jay
a.rren.dar, v. lease; rent
a.rre.os, m. pl. paraphernalia; trappings; harness
a.rre.pen.ti.do, a. sorry; contrite
a.rre.pen.ti.mien.to, m. contrition; repentance
a.rre.pen.tir.se, v. repent; regret
a.rri.ba, adv. up; above; upstairs. de a.rri.ba a.ba.jo, upside down
a.rrien.do, m. lease
a.rries.ga.do, a. venturesome; daring; dangerous; hazardous; desperate
a.rries.gar(se), v. risk; venture; dare; hazard; jeopardize
a.rri.mar(se), v. stow; bring close; snuggle; nestle
a.rrin.co.nar(se), v. corner; lay aside; retire
a.rro.di.llar(se), v. kneel; kneel down
a.rro.gan.cia, f. arrogance; hauteur; haughtiness
a.rro.gan.te, a. arrogant; supercilious; haughty; proud
a.rro.jar(se), v. throw; fling; hurl; pelt; emit; expel
a.rro.llar(se), v. curl; coil; roll up
a.rro.yo, m. stream; brook; gutter
a.rroz, m. rice
a.rru.gar(se), v. pucker; rumple; crinkle; wrinkle
a.rrui.nar(se), v. ruin; destroy; spoil; wreck
a.rru.llar(se), v. coo; rock to sleep
ar.se.nal, m. arsenal
ar.sé.ni.co, m. arsenic
ar.te, m., f. art; craft; skill. be.llas ar.tes, fine arts
ar.te.ria, f. artery
ar.te.rial, a. arterial
ar.te.sa.nía, f. handicraft; craftsmanship
ar.te.sa.no, m. craftsman
ár.ti.co, a. arctic
ar.ti.cu.la.ción, f. articulation
ar.ti.cu.la.do, a. articulate
ar.ti.cu.lar, v. articulate
ar.tí.cu.lo, m. article; item. ar.tí.cu.lo de fon.do, editorial
ar.ti.fi.cial, a. artificial
ar.ti.lle.ría, f. artillery
ar.tis.ta, m., f. artist
ar.tís.ti.co, a. artistic
ar.trí.ti.co, a. arthritic
ar.tri.tis, f. arthritis
ar.zo.bis.po, m. archbishop
as, m. ace
a.sal.ta.dor, m. assailant
a.sal.tar, v. attack; molest; inf. mug
a.sal.to, m. assault; attack
a.sam.blea, f. assembly; meeting
a.sar(se), v. roast. a.sar en.te.ro, barbecue. a.sar a la pa.rri.lla, broil; grill
as.bes.to, m. asbestos; asbestus
as.cen.der, v. ascend; advance; promote
as.cen.sión, f. ascension; ascent
as.cen.sor, m. elevator
as.ce.ta, m., f. ascetic
as.cé.ti.co, a. ascetic
as.ce.tis.mo, m. asceticism
as.co, m. disgust; revulsion
as.cua, f. ember
a.sea.do, a. cleanly
a.se.diar, v. besiege
a.se.gu.rar(se), v. secure; fasten; insure; assure; anchor
a.se.me.jar(se), v. resemble; make similar
a.sen.tar(se), v. sit down; seat
a.sen.ti.mien.to, m. assent
a.sen.tir, v. assent
a.se.si.nar, v. assassinate; murder
a.se.si.na.to, m. assassination; murder
a.se.si.no, m. assassin; cutthroat
a.se.ve.rar, v. asseverate
a.se.xual, a. asexual
as.fal.to, m. asphalt
as.fi.xia, f. asphyxiation
as.fi.xiar(se), v. asphyxiate; suffocate
a.sí, adv. so; thus. a.sí a.sí, so-so
a.si.dua.men.te, adv. assiduously
a.sí.duo, a. assiduous; diligent
a.sien.to, m. seat
a.sig.na.ción, f. assignment
a.sig.nar, v. assign; allocate; allot
a.si.lo, m. sanctuary; asylum; haven; fluster; muddle
a.si.mien.to, m. seizure; grasp
a.si.mi.la.ción, f. assimilation
a.si.mi.lar(se), v. assimilate
a.si.mis.mo, adv. likewise
a.sir(se), v. grab; grip; take hold of
a.sis.ten.te, m. assistant; helper; orderly
a.sis.tir, v. attend
as.ma, f. asthma
as.má.ti.co, a. asthmatic
a.si.nal, a. asinine
a.so.cia.ción, f. association; society; combine
a.so.cia.do, a. associate; fellow. m. associate
a.so.ciar(se), v. associate; consort with; pool
a.so.mar(se), v. loom; show
a.som.brar(se), v. astonish; amaze; astound
a.som.bro, m. amazement; astonish-

ment
a.so.nan.cia, f. assonance
as.pec.to, m. aspect; configuration; usu. pl. looks
as.pe.re.za, f. asperity; severity
ás.pe.ro, a. harsh; rough; sour; brusque, brusk; surly
ás.pid, m. asp
as.pi.ra.ción, f. aspiration; breath
as.pi.ra.dor de pol.vo, m. vacuum cleaner
as.pi.ran.te, m. candidate; applicant
as.pi.rar, v. inhale; breathe; aspire to
as.pi.ri.na, f. aspirin
as.que.ro.so, a. nasty; disgusting
as.ta, f. antler; flagstaff
ás.ta.co, m. crayfish
as.ter, m. aster
as.te.ris.co, m. asterisk
as.ti.lla, f. splinter; chip
as.ti.llar, v. chip
as.tro.lo.gía, f. astrology
as.tró.lo.go, m. astrologer
as.tro.nau.ta, m., f. astronaut; spaceman; spacewoman
as.tro.na.ve, f. spaceship
as.tró.no.mo, m. astronomer
as.tro.no.mía, f. astronomy
as.tu.cia, f. craftiness; cunning; guile
as.tu.to, a. astute; sly; artful; crafty; foxy; canny; knowing; subtle; cunning
a.su.mir, v. assume; don
a.sun.ción, f. assumption
a.sun.to, m. matter; affair; issue; business; concern
a.sus.tar(se), v. scare; frighten; be startled
a.ta.car, v. attack; assault; sic; strike; charge
a.ta.jo, m. shortcut
a.ta.que, m. attack; seizure. a.ta.que aé.reo, airraid. a.ta.que ful.mi.nan.te, stroke
a.tar(se), v. bind; tie; rope; lash; lace; brace
a.tar.de.cer, v. get dark. m. dusk
a.tas.car(se), v. clog; stop up; stall
a.taúd, m. coffin; casket
a.ta.viar(se), v. array
a.teís.mo, m. atheism
a.te.mo.ri.za.do, a. afraid
a.ten.ción, f. attention; notice; kindness
a.ten.der, v. attend to; heed; cater
a.ten.to, a. attentive; intent; considerate
a.teo, m., a.tea, f. atheist
a.te.rrar(se), v. terrify; appall; appal; land
a.te.rri.za.je, m. touchdown; landing
a.te.rri.zar, v. land
a.te.rro.ri.zar, v. terrorize; terrify
a.tes.tar(se), v. clutter; stuff
a.tes.ti.guar, v. testify; attest
a.te.za.do, a. swarthy
a.tie.sar(se), v. stiffen; tighten
a.tí.pi.co, a. atypical
a.ti.zar, v. poke; stoke
at.las, m. atlas
at.le.ta, m., f. athlete
at.lé.ti.co, a. athletic
at.mós.fe.ra, f. atmosphere
at.mos.fé.ri.co, a. atmospheric
a.to.lón, m. atoll
a.to.lon.dra.do, a. reckless; stunned
a.tó.mi.co, a. atomic
a.to.mi.zar, v. atomize
á.to.mo, m. atom
a.tor.men.tar, v. harass; torment; anguish; tantalize; bait
a.tor.ni.llar, v. screw on
a.trac.ción, f. attraction
a.trac.ti.vo, a. attractive; fetching; engaging
a.traer, v. attract; engage; draw; lure; appeal to; allure
a.trás, adv. back; aback; backward; behind
a.tra.sa.do, a. late; behind hand; backward(s)
a.tra.ve.sar, v. traverse; cross; go through
a.tre.ver.se, v. dare
a.tre.vi.do, a. daring; forward
a.tre.vi.mien.to, m. daring; audacity
a.tri.bu.ción, f. attribution
a.tri.buir, v. attribute to; ascribe
a.trin.che.rar(se), v. entrench
a.tro.ci.dad, f. atrocity; outrage; cruelty; enormity
a.tro.fia, f. atrophy
a.troz, a. atrocious; heinous
a.tún, m. tuna
a.tur.dir(se), v. stun; daze; bewilder; fluster; muddle
au.daz, a. audacious
au.daz.men.te, adv. boldly
au.di.ción, f. audition; concert
au.dien.cia, f. audience
au.di.to.rio, m. auditorium
au.gus.to, a. grand; august
au.llar, v. howl; bay
au.lli.do, m. howl; bay
au.men.tar(se), v. increase; augment; grow; magnify; enhance
au.men.to, m. increase; raise; enlargement
aun, adv. even
aún, adv. yet; still
aun.que, conj. though; although; albeit
áu.reo, a. aureate
au.re.o.la, f. halo
au.rí.cu.la, f. auricle
au.ri.ga, m. charioteer
au.ro.ra, f. aurora; dawn

au.sen.te, a. absent; missing. m., f. absentee
aus.pi.cio, m. auspice
aus.te.ri.dad, f. austerity
aus.te.ro, a. austere; stern; dour
au.ten.ti.car, v. authenticate
au.ten.ti.ci.dad, f. authenticity
au.tén.ti.co, a. authentic; genuine
au.to.bio.gra.fía, f. autobiography
au.to.bió.gra.fo, m. autobiographer
au.to.bús, m. bus; omnibus
au.to.cra.cia, f. autocracy
au.tó.cra.ta, m., f. autocrat
au.tó.gra.fo, m. autograph
au.tó.ma.ta, m. robot; automaton
au.to.má.ti.co, a. automatic
au.to.ma.ti.za.ción, f. automation
au.to.mó.vil, m. automobile; car; inf. auto
au.to.no.mía, f. autonomy; self-government
au.tó.no.mo, a. autonomous
au.to.pis.ta, f. freeway; highway. au.to.pis.ta de pea.je, turnpike; tollroad
au.top.sia, f. autopsy; post-mortem
au.tor, m. au.to.ra, f. author; writer
au.to.ri.dad, f. authority
au.to.ri.za.ción, f. authorization
au.to.ri.zar, v. authorize; sanction; empower
au.xi.liar, a. auxiliary. m., f. assistant. v. help
a.val.ú.o, m. aid
a.van.ce, m. advance
a.van.za.do, a. advanced; early
a.van.zar(se), v. advance; promote
a.va.ri.cia, f. avarice; greed; cupidity
a.va.ro, m. miser. a. greedy; avaricious
a.ve, f. bird; fowl. a.ves de co.rral, poultry
a.ve.lla.no, m. hazel
a.ve.na, f. oats
a.ve.ni.da, f. avenue; boulevard
a.ven.ta.jar(se), v. excel; surpass
a.ven.tu.ra, f. adventure; escapade. a.ven.tu.ra a.mo.ro.sa, affair
a.ven.tu.rar(se), v. adventuresome
a.ven.tu.rar(se), v. venture; dare; stake
a.ven.tu.re.ro, a. venturesome
a.ver.gon.za.do, a. ashamed
a.ver.gon.zar(se), v. shame; abash; be embarrassed
a.ve.ría, f. damage; breakdown
a.ve.ri.guar, v. ascertain; find out
a.ver.sión, f. aversion; distaste
a.ves.truz, m. ostrich
a.via.ción, f. aviation
a.via.dor, m. aviator; flyer, flier
á.vi.do, a. avid
a.vión, m. airplane; plane; aircraft. a.vión a reac.ción, jet
a.víos, m. pl. kit
a.vi.sar, v. advise; inform; counsel
a.vi.so, m. notice; announcement; warning; tip
a.vi.var(se), v. enliven; brighten
a.xio.ma, m. axiom
a.xio.má.ti.co, a. axiomatic
a.xis, m. axis
a.yu.da, f. help; assistance; aid
a.yu.dan.te, m., f. adjutant; assistant
a.yu.dar, v. help; aid; assist; abet
a.yu.nar, v. fast
a.yu.no, m. fast
a.za.ba.che, m. jet
a.za.dón, m. hoe
a.za.do.nar, v. hoe
a.za.fa.ta, f. stewardess
a.za.frán, m. crocus
a.zar, m. chance; luck; hazard. al a.zar, at random
a.za.ro.so, a. risky; eventful
a.zo.ga.do, a. fidgety
a.zo.tar, v. flog; lash
a.zú.car, m. sugar
a.zu.ca.rar, v. sweeten; add sugar to
a.zue.la, f. adz; adze
a.zu.fre, m. brimstone
a.zul, a. blue. m. blue. a.zul ma.ri.no o de mar, navy; also navy blue
a.zu.lar, v. color blue

B

ba.bear, v. slobber; drool
ba.bel, m. babel; confusion. Also Babel
ba.be.ro, m. bib
ba.bor, m. port
ba.bo.sear, v. slobber
ba.ca.lao, m. codfish; cod
ba.ca.nal, a. bacchanalian; f. bacchanalia
ba.ci.lo, m. bacillus
bac.te.ria, f. bacterium
bac.te.rio.lo.gía, f. bacteriology
bac.te.rió.lo.go, m. bacteriologist
ba.chi.lle.ra.to, m. baccalaureate
ba.ga.je, m. baggage; luggage
ba.ga.te.la, f. trifle; trinket
ba.hía, f. bay
bai.la.dor, m., bai.la.do.ra, f. dancer
bai.lar, v. dance
bai.la.ri.na, f. ballerina
bai.le, m. dance; ball
ba.ja, f. casualty; drop
ba.jar(se), v. lower; subside; fall; descend; alight
ba.jo, adv. lowly; below. a. small; short; low; deep; bass. prep. underneath; under. m. bass
ba.jón, m. (mus.) bassoon; decline;

slump
ba·la, f. bullet; bale
ba·la·da, f. ballad
ba·la·dro·na·da, f. boast
ba·lan·cear(se), v. teeter; swing balance
ba·lan·za, f. balance; scale
ba·lar, v. baa; bleat
ba·laus·tra·da, f. balustrade
bal·bu·cear, v. stutter; babble
bal·cón, m. balcony
bal·da·quín, m. canopy
ba·li·do, m. baa; bleat
ba·lís·ti·ca, f. ballistics
ba·lís·ti·co, a. ballistic
bal·nea·rio, m. spa
ba·lon·ces·to, m. basketball
ba·lo·ta, f. ballot
bal·sa, f. raft; balsa
bal·sá·mi·co, a. balmy
bál·sa·mo, m. balsam; balm
ba·luar·te, m. bulwark; bastion
ba·lle·na, f. whale
ba·lles·te·ría, f. archery
ba·llet, m. ballet
bam·bo·lear(se), v. sway; wobble
bam·bú, m. bamboo
ba·na·na, f. banana
ban·ca, f. banking
ban·ca·rro·ta, f. bankruptcy
ban·co, m. bank; bench; stripe; strip; band; pew
ban·da·da, f. bevy; flock
ban·de·ra, f. flag; ensign; colors
ban·di·do, m. bandit
ban·jo, m. banjo
ban·que·ta, f. stool
ban·que·te, m. banquet; feast
ban·que·tear, v. feast; banquet
ba·ñar(se), v. bathe; suffuse
ba·ñis·ta, m., f. bather
ba·ño, m. bath; bathtub
bar, m. bar
ba·ra·ja, f. deck of cards
ba·ra·jar, v. shuffle (cards)
ba·ra·to, a. cheap; inexpensive. adv. cheap; cheaply
bar·ba, f. chin; beard; stubble; pl. whiskers
bar·ba·coa, f. barbecue
bar·ba·do, a. bearded
bar·ba·ri·dad, f. barbarity; outrage
bár·ba·ro, n., bár·ba·ra, f. barbarian; savage. a. barbaric
bar·bear, v. shave
bar·be·ro, m. barber
bar·bi·tu·ra·to, m. barbituate
bar·co, m. boat; vessel; ship
bar·dar, v. thatch
bar·do, m. bard
ba·rio, m. barium
ba·rí·to·no, m. baritone
bar·niz, m. glaze; varnish
bar·ni·zar, v. glaze; varnish
ba·ro·mé·tri·co, a. barometric
ba·ró·me·tro, m. barometer
ba·rón, m. baron
ba·ro·ne·sa, f. baroness
ba·rra, f. bar
ba·rra·ca, f. hut; booth
ba·rran·ca, f. gully; ravine
ba·rrer, v. sweep
ba·rre·ra, f. barrier; barricade; barrage
ba·rri·ca·da, f. barricade
ba·rri·ga, f. belly
ba·rril, m. cask; barrel
ba·rrio, m. neighborhood; quarter
ba·rro, m. mud; clay; pimple
ba·rro·co, a. baroque
ba·sal·to, m. basalt
ba·sar, v. base
ba·se, f. base; foundation; basis
bá·si·co, a. basic; basal
ba·sí·li·ca, f. basilica
bás·quet·bol, m. basketball
bas·tan·te a. enough; sufficient. adv. enough
bas·tar, v. suffice; be enough
bas·tar·dear, v. bastardize; debase
bas·tar·do, m., bas·tar·da, f. bastard. a. bastard
bas·tar·di·lla, f. italics
bas·ti·dor, m. wing of a theater; frame
bas·to, a. coarse; rough
bas·tón, m. cane; stick; baton
bas·tos, m. pl. clubs
ba·su·ra, f. garbage; rubbish
ba·su·re·ro, m. dump; garbage man
ba·ta, f. bathrobe; negligee; smock
ba·ta·lla, f. battle
ba·ta·llar, v. battle; struggle
ba·ta·llón, m. battalion
ba·ta·ta, f. sweet potato
ba·te·ría, f. battery
ba·ti·do, m. batter. a. beaten
ba·tir(se), v. beat; churn; clash; fight
ba·tu·ta, f. baton
baúl, m. trunk
bau·tis·mo, m. baptism; christening
bau·ti·zar, v. christen; baptize
bau·ti·zo, m. baptism; christening
ba·ya, f. berry
ba·yo, a. bay
ba·yo·ne·ta, f. bayonet
ba·zar, m. bazaar
ba·zo, m. spleen
ba·zo·fia, f. swill
ba·zu·ca, f. bazooka
bea·ti·fi·car, v. beatify
bea·tí·fi·co, a. beatific
bea·ti·tud, f. beatitude
be·bé, m. baby
be·ber, v. drink
be·bi·da, f. drink; beverage. be·bi·da al·co·hó·li·ca, liquor; inf. booze
be·ca, f. scholarship

be·ce·rro, m. calf
be·far, v. jeer; taunt
bei·ge, m. beige. a. beige
béis·bol, m. baseball
be·li·cis·ta, m., f. warmonger. a. warmongering
be·li·co·so, a. bellicose; warlike
be·li·ge·ran·cia, f. belligerency
be·li·ge·ran·te, a. belligerent. m., f. belligerent
be·lle·za, f. beauty
be·llo, a. beauteous; beautiful
be·mol, m. (mus.) flat
ben·de·cir, v. bless
ben·di·ción, f. benediction; blessing. ben·di·ción de la me·sa, grace
ben·di·to, a. blessed; holy
be·ne·fi·ciar(se), v. benefit
be·ne·fi·cia·rio, m., be·ne·fi·cia·ria, f. beneficiary
be·ne·fi·cio, m. benefaction; benefit; profit; interest; behalf
be·ne·fi·cio·so, a. beneficial
be·né·fi·co, a. beneficent; charitable
be·ne·vo·len·cia, f. benevolence; kindness
be·né·vo·lo, a. benevolent
ben·ga·la, f. flare
be·nig·ni·dad, f. benignity; kindness
be·nig·no, a. benign; kind; mild
be·ren·je·na, f. eggplant
ber·ga·mo·ta, f. bergamot
be·rrin·che, m. tantrum
be·sar(se), v. kiss; inf. smooch
be·so, m. kiss
bes·tia, f. beast; animal
bes·tial, a. bestial
bes·tia·li·dad, f. beastliness; bestiality
Bi·blia, f. Bible
bí·bli·co, a. Biblical
bi·blio·gra·fía, f. bibliography
bi·blió·gra·fo, m. bibliographer
bi·blio·te·ca, f. library
bi·blio·te·ca·rio, m., bi·blio·te·ca·ria, f. librarian
bí·ceps, m. pl. biceps
bi·ci·cle·ta, f. bicycle; inf. bike
bi·ci·clis·ta, m., f. bicyclist
bi·cho, m. bug
bien, m. good; advantage; pl. goods. adv. well; quite; fully; gladly
bie·nal, a. biennial
bie·na·ven·tu·ra·do, a. blissful; happy; blessed
bien·he·chor, m. benefactor. a. beneficial
bien·ve·ni·da, f. welcome; greeting
bien·ve·ni·do, a. welcome
bi·fur·car·se, v. fork
bi·ga·mia, f. bigamy
bí·ga·mo, m., bí·ga·ma, f. bigamist
bi·go·te, m. mustache
bi·la·te·ral, a. bilateral
bi·lio·so, a. bilious
bi·lis, f. gall; bile
bi·llar, m. billiards
bi·lle·te, m. ticket; bill
bi·llón, m. trillion (Br. billion)
bi·men·sual(mente), adv. bimonthly
bi·mes·tral(mente), adv. bimonthly
bi·na·rio, a. binary
bio·gra·fía, f. biography
bio·grá·fi·co, a. biographic
bió·gra·fo, m. biographer
bio·lo·gía, f. biology
bio·ló·gi·co, a. biological
bió·lo·go, m. biologist
biop·sia, f. biopsy
bió·xi·do, m. dioxide, bió·xi·do de car·bo·no, carbon dioxide
bí·pe·do, m. biped
bi·sa·bue·la, f. great-grandmother
bi·sa·bue·lo, m. great-grandfather; pl. great-grandparents
bi·sec·tar, v. bisect
bi·sec·ción, f. bisection
bi·se·xual, a. bisexual
bis·mu·to, m. bismuth
bi·son·te, m. bison
bi·tu·mi·no·so, a. bituminous
biz·quear, v. squint
blan·co, a. white; blank. m. white; blank; target; aim; mark. cen·tro del blan·co, bull's-eye
blan·dir, v. brandish; flourish
blan·do, a. soft; supple; bland; mild
blan·quear, v. bleach; whiten; blanch
blas·fe·mar, v. blaspheme; swear; curse
blas·fe·mia, f. blasphemy; profanity; oath
blin·da·do, a. armored
blo·que, m. block; bloc
blo·quear, v. blockade; block
blo·queo, m. blockade
blu·sa, f. blouse; smock
bo·bo, a. silly; stupid. m. ninny; fool; clown
bo·ca, f. mouth; muzzle; opening. bo·ca de rie·go, hydrant
bo·ca·ca·lle, f. intersection
bo·ca·di·llo, m. sandwich
bo·ca·do, m. morsel; bite
bo·char·no·so, a. sultry
bo·da, f. wedding; marriage
bo·de·ga, f. bar; wine cellar
bo·fe·ta·da, f. slap; buffet
boi·co·tear, v. boycott
boi·co·teo, m. boycott
boi·na, f. beret
bo·la, f. ball; fib. bo·la de me·sa, dumpling
bo·le·tín, m. bulletin
bo·li·che, m. bowling
bo·li·ta, f. pellet

bol·sa, f. pouch; bag; pocket
bol·si·llo, m. pocket
bol·sis·ta, m. stockbroker
bol·so, m. purse; handbag; bag
bo·llo, m. bun; bump; dent
bom·ba, f. bomb; pump. bom·ba de in·cen·dios, fire engine
bom·bar·dear, v. bomb; shell; bombard
bom·bar·deo, m. bombardment
bom·bar·de·ro, m. bomber; bombardier
bom·bear, v. pump; pad; shell
bom·bi·lla, f. bulb
bom·bón, m. sweet; pl. sweets. bom·bón de me·ren·gue, marshmallow
bon·dad, f. goodness; kindness
bon·da·do·so, a. good; kindly; kindhearted
bo·ni·to, a. pretty
bo·quea·da, f. gasp
bo·quear, v. gasp
bo·quia·bier·to, a. agape
bo·qui·lla, f. nozzle; mouthpiece
bó·rax, m. borax
bor·da·do, m. embroidery
bor·de, m. border; edge; lip; brim; brink; verge
bor·di·llo, m. curb
bor·la, f. tassel
bo·rra·cha, f. spree
bo·rra·cho, a. drunk; drunken. m. drunkard
bo·rra·dor, m. draft; eraser
bo·rra·du·ra, f. deletion
bo·rrar, v. erase; rub out; blur
bo·rras·co·so, a. boisterous; stormy
bo·rrón, m. blot; blur
bos·que, m. forest; woods
bos·que·jar, v. outline; sketch
bos·que·jo, m. outline; sketch; delineation
bos·te·zar, v. yawn
bo·ta, f. boot; wine bag
bo·tá·ni·co, m., bo·tá·ni·ca, f. botanist. a. botanical. jar·dín bo·tá·ni·co, arboretum
bo·te, m. canister; jackpot; kitty; bounce; boat. bo·te sal·va·vi·das, life boat
bo·te·lla, f. bottle
bo·ti·ca·rio, m. apothecary; druggist
bo·tín, m. plunder; loot; booty; pl. spoils
bo·tón, m. button; stud
bo·to·nes, m. bellboy, bellhop
bó·ve·da, f. vault
bo·vi·no, a. bovine
bo·xea·dor, m. boxer
bo·xear, v. box
bo·xeo, m. boxing
bo·ya, f. buoy
bo·yan·te, a. buoyant
bo·zal, m. muzzle
bra·man·te, m. string; twine
bra·mar, v. bellow; bluster
bra·mi·do, m. bellow
bra·va·ta, f. bravado; brag
bra·vo, a. brave; stormy; wild. int. bravo
bra·za, f. fathom
bra·za·do, m. armful
bra·zo, m. arm
brea, f. tar
bré·col, m. broccoli
bre·cha, f. breach
bre·ve, a. brief; short; terse
bre·ve·dad, f. brevity; conciseness
bre·zal, m. heath
bri·bón, a. lazy. m. knave; rogue; rascal
bri·da, f. bridle
bri·ga·da, f. brigade
bri·llan·te, a. brilliant; shiny; bright. m. diamond
bri·llan·tez, f. brilliance
bri·llar, v. shine; glow; gleam; beam; blaze; flare
bri·llo, m. shine; glow; glare; burnish
brin·car, v. leap; jump; caper about; gambol
brin·dar, v. toast
brin·dis, m. toast
brío, m. spirit; jauntiness; vitality; verve
brio·so, a. spirited
bri·sa, f. breeze
briz·na, f. blade; thread
bro·ca·do, m. brocade
bro·cha, f. brush
bro·che, m. clasp; brooch
bro·ma, f. joke; prank
bro·mear(se), v. joke
bro·mis·ta, m., f. joker
bro·mu·ro, m. bromide
bron·ce, m. bronze
bron·cea·do, m. suntan. a. bronze; tanned
bron·cear, v. bronze; tan
bron·quial, a. bronchial
bro·que·ta, f. skewer
bro·tar, v. sprout; bud; spring up
bro·te, m. bud; outbreak
bru·ja, f. witch; hag; harridan
bru·mo·so, a. hazy; foggy
bru·ñir, v. burnish
brus·co, a. brusque, brusk; sudden; curt
bru·se·las, f. pl. tweezers
bru·tal, a. brutal. m. brute
bru·ta·li·dad, f. brutality
bru·to, a. brute; gross; rough; raw. m. brute; beast
bu·ca·ne·ro, m. buccaneer
bu·cle, m. lock; curl
bu·dín, m. pudding
bue·no, a. good; sound; fine; kind

buey, m. ox
bu·fan·da, f. muffler; scarf
bu·fi·do, m. snort
bu·fón, m. buffoon; clown. a. comical
bú·ho, m. owl
bu·ho·ne·ro, m. peddler, pedler, pedlar
bui·tre, m. vulture
bu·jía, f. taper; candle
bul·bo, m. bulb
bu·le·var, m. boulevard
bul·to, m. bulk; mass; lump; heft; parcel; ticket
bu·lla, f. fuss; uproar; crowd; brawl
bu·lli·cio, m. bustle; riot; racket
bu·me·rang, m. boomerang
bu·ñue·lo, m. fritter
bu·que, m. ship. bu·que de car·ga, freighter
bur·bu·ja, f. bubble
bur·bu·jear, v. bubble
bur·del, m. brothel; bagnio
bur·gués, m., bur·gue·sa, f. bourgeois. a. bourgeois
bur·gue·sía, f. bourgeoisie
bur·la, f. banter; taunt; ridicule; joke
bur·lar(se), v. hoax; gibe; jibe; joke; mock; inf. roast
bur·lón, m., bur·lo·na, f. joker. a. mocking; quizzical
bu·ro·cra·cia, f. bureaucracy
bu·ró·cra·ta, m., f. bureaucrat
bu·rro, m. burro; donkey; ass; jackass
bur·sa, f. rubbish
bus·ca, f. pursuit; search
bus·car, v. look for; seek
bús·que·da, f. quest; search
bus·to, m. bust
bu·zo, m. diver
bu·zón, m. mailbox

C

cá·ba·la, f. cabal
ca·bal·ga·ta, f. parade; cavalcade
ca·ba·lle·ro, m. gentleman; cavalier; knight
ca·ba·lle·ro·si·dad, f. chivalry
ca·ba·lle·ro·so, a. chivalrous
ca·ba·lle·te, m. easel
ca·ba·llo, m. horse. ca·ba·llo de fuer·za, horsepower
ca·ba·llón, m. ridge
ca·ba·ña, f. cabin
ca·ba·ret, m. cabaret; bistro
ca·be·cear, v. nod the head
ca·be·ci·lla, m. ringleader
ca·be·llo, m. hair
ca·ber, v. fit
ca·bes·tri·llo, m. sling
ca·bes·tro, m. halter
ca·be·za, f. head. do·lor de ca·be·za, headache
ca·be·zu·do, a. heady
ca·bil·dear, v. lobby
ca·ble, m. cable
ca·ble·gra·fiar, v. cable
ca·ble·gra·ma, m. cable; cablegram
ca·bo, m. cape; corporal; end; butt; stub
ca·bra, f. goat
ca·bria, f. hoist
ca·brío, m. rafter. ma·cho ca·brío, m. billy goat
ca·brio·la, f. caper; antic
ca·bri·to, m. kid
ca·ca·hue·te, m. peanut
ca·cao, m. cocoa; cacao
ca·ca·rear, v. cackle; crow
ca·ca·túa, f. cockatoo
ca·ce·ro·la, f. pan; casserole
ca·ci·que, m. chief; party boss
ca·co·fo·nía, f. cacophony
cac·to, m. cactus
ca·cha·lo·te, m. sperm whale
ca·chi·po·rra, f. bludgeon; blackjack
ca·cho·rro, m. cub; puppy
ca·da, a. each; every. ca·da u·no, each one
ca·dá·ver, m. corpse; body; cadaver. inf. stiff
ca·da·vé·ri·co, a. cadaverous
ca·de·na, f. chain
ca·den·cia, f. cadence; rhythm
ca·de·ra, f. hip
ca·de·te, m. cadet
caer(se), v. fall; tumble down. caer en·fer·mo, sicken; fall ill
ca·fé, m. coffee; cafe, café
ca·feí·na, f. caffeine
ca·fe·te·ría, f. cafeteria
caí·da, f. fall; tumble; downfall
cai·mán, m. alligator
ca·ja, f. box. ca·ja de car·tón, carton. ca·ja de cau·da·les, safe. ca·ja de em·ba·la·je, crate
ca·je·ro, m., ca·je·ra, f. teller; cashier
ca·jón, m. case; drawer; till
cal, f. lime
ca·la, f. cove
ca·la·ba·za, f. pumpkin; gourd
ca·la·bo·zo, m. jail
ca·la·fa·tear, v. caulk, calk
ca·la·mar, m. squid
ca·lam·bre, m. cramp
ca·la·mi·dad, f. calamity
ca·la·mi·to·so, a. calamitous; baleful
ca·lar, v. swoop; soak; penetrate
cal·ce·te·ría, f. hosiery
cal·ce·tín, m. sock
cal·ci·fi·ca·ción, f. calcification
cal·ci·fi·car(se), v. calcify
cal·cio, m. calcium

cal·cu·lar, v. calculate; estimate; reckon
cál·cu·lo, m. calculus; calculation
cal·de·ra, f. boiler; cauldron, caldron
cal·do, m. soup; stock; broth; bouillon
ca·le·fac·ción, f. heating
ca·len·da·rio, m. calendar
ca·len·ta·dor, m. heater
ca·len·tar(se), v. warm; heat up
ca·le·ta, f. bight
ca·li·bra·ción, f. calibration
ca·li·brar, v. calibrate
ca·li·bre, m. caliber, calibre
ca·li·có, m. calico
ca·li·dad, f. quality; importance
cá·li·do, a. warm; hot
ca·li·dos·co·pio, m. kaleidoscope
ca·lien·te, a. hot; warm
ca·li·fa, m. caliph, calif
ca·li·fa·to, m. caliphate, califate
ca·lor, m. heat; warmth
ca·lo·ría, f. calorie
ca·ló·ri·co, a. caloric
ca·lum·nia, f. calumny; slander
ca·lum·niar, v. slander; libel; slur; traduce
ca·lu·ro·so, a. warm
cal·vi·cie, f. baldness
cal·vo, a. bald
cal·za·da, f. drive; causeway
cal·za·dor, m. shoehorn
cal·zo·nes, m. pl. trousers; breeches. cal·zo·nes cor·tos, shorts
ca·lla·do, a. quiet; silent
ca·llar(se), v. hush; stop talking; keep quiet
ca·lle, f. street. ca·lle sin sa·li·da, dead-end
ca·lle·jue·la, f. alley
ca·llo, m. corn; callus
ca·ma, f. bed. ro·pa de ca·ma, bedding; bedclothes
ca·ma·da, f. brood; litter
ca·ma·feo, m. cameo
ca·ma·león, m. chameleon
cá·ma·ra, f. chamber; room; camera
ca·ma·ra·da, m., f. comrade
ca·ma·re·ra, f. waitress; barmaid; chambermaid
ca·ma·re·ro, m. waiter; steward
ca·ma·rón, m. shrimp
ca·ma·ro·te, m. cabin
cam·biar(se), v. change; shift; alter; switch; vary; exchange
cam·bio, m. change; shift; alteration; switch; exchange
ca·me·llo, m. camel
ca·mi·lla, f. stretcher
ca·mi·nar, v. walk; trek
ca·mi·na·ta, f. hike
ca·mi·no, m. road; route; way. a me·dio ca·mi·no, halfway
ca·mión, m. truck. ca·mión de mu·dan·zas, van
ca·mio·ne·ro, m. truckdriver; teamster
ca·mio·nis·ta, m. truckdriver; teamster
ca·mi·sa, f. shirt
ca·mi·se·ta, f. T-shirt, tee-shirt; undershirt
cam·pa·men·to, m. camp
cam·pa·na, f. bell
cam·pa·na·rio, m. steeple; belfry
cam·pa·ña, f. campaign; expedition
cam·pe·si·no, a. peasant; country. m. peasant
cam·pis·ta, m., f. camper
cam·po, m. country; field; camp
ca·mu·fla·je, m. camouflage
ca·mu·flar, v. camouflage
ca·nal, m. canal; channel; pipe
ca·na·le·te, m. paddle
ca·na·lla, m. f. scoundrel; swine
ca·na·rio, m. canary
ca·nas·ta, f. basket; hamper
can·ce·la·ción, f. cancellation
can·ce·lar, v. cancel
cán·cer, m. cancer
can·ci·ller, m. chancellor
can·ción, f. song. can·ción de cu·na, lullaby
can·de·la, f. candle
can·de·la·bro, m. candelabrum
can·di·da·to, m. candidate; candidacy
cán·di·do, a. unsophisticated; naive
ca·ne·la, f. cinnamon
can·gre·jo, m. crab
can·gu·ro, m. kangaroo
ca·ní·bal, m. cannibal. a. cannibal
ca·ni·ba·lis·mo, m. cannibalism
ca·ni·ca, f. marble
ca·ni·no, a. canine
can·je, m. exchange
ca·noa, f. canoe
ca·non, m. canon
ca·no·ni·za·ción, f. canonization
ca·no·ni·zar, v. canonize
can·sa·do, a. tired; weary; tiresome; rundown
can·sar(se), v. tire; weary; jade
can·ta·lu·po, m. cantaloup, cantaloupe, cantalope

can·tan·te, m., f. singer
can·tar, v. sing; chant. m. song
can·te·ra, f. quarry
can·ti·dad, f. quantity; sum; amount; deal
can·tim·plo·ra, f. canteen
can·ti·na, f. canteen; barroom
can·to, m. rim; singing; croak
ca·tu·rrear, v. hum; croon
ca·ña, f. reed; cane. ca·ña de pes·car, fishing rod
cá·ña·mo, m. hemp
ca·ño, m. spout; pipe
ca·ñón, m. cannon; canyon; barrel; pipe
cao·ba, f. mahogany
caos, m. chaos
caó·ti·co, a. chaotic
ca·pa, f. layer; stratum; cloak; cape; coating
ca·pa·ci·dad, f. capacity; competence; capability
ca·pa·taz, m. taskmaster; foreman
ca·paz, a. capable; roomy
ca·pe·llán, m. chaplain
ca·pi·lla, f. chapel
ca·pi·tal, m. capital. a. capital
ca·pi·ta·lis·mo, m. capitalism
ca·pi·ta·lis·ta, m., f. capitalist. a. capitalistic
ca·pi·ta·li·zar, v. capitalize
ca·pi·tán, m. captain
ca·pi·to·lio, m. capitol
ca·pi·tu·lar, v. capitulate
ca·pí·tu·lo, m. chapter
ca·pri·cho, m. caprice; whim; fancy; quirk; vagary
ca·pri·cho·so, a. capricious; temperamental
cáp·su·la, f. capsule
cap·tu·ra, f. catch; capture
cap·tu·rar, v. capture
ca·pu·cha, f. hood
ca·pu·llo, m. cocoon
ca·qui, m. khaki
ca·ra, f. face; countenance. ca·ra i fe·rior, underside
ca·ra·bi·na, f. carbine
ca·ra·col, m. snail
ca·rác·ter, m. character; nature
ca·rac·te·rís·ti·ca, f. characteristic; trait
ca·rac·te·rís·ti·co, a. characteristic; typical
ca·rac·te·ri·zar, v. characterize
cá·rám·ba·no, m. icicle
ca·ra·me·lo, m. caramel; taffy; toffee
ca·ra·va·na, f. caravan
car·bón, m. coal. pa·pel car·bón, carbon paper. car·bón ve·ge·tal, charcoal
car·bo·na·to, m. carbonate
car·bo·ni·llo, m. cinder
car·bo·no, m. carbon
car·bun·co, m. carbuncle
car·bu·ra·dor, m. carburetor
car·ca·ja·da, f. guffaw
cár·cel, f. jail; prison; inf. calaboose
cár·cel mi·li·tar, guardhouse
car·ci·no·ma, m. carcinoma
car·de·nal, m. cardinal
car·día·co, a. cardiac
car·di·nal, a. cardinal
car·do, m. thistle
ca·re·cer, v. lack
ca·ren·cia, f. need
ca·res·tía, f. dearness; shortage
car·ga, f. load; burden; tax; charge
car·ga·men·to, m. cargo
car·gar(se), v. load; burden; charge
car·go, m. burden; office; charge; care
ca·riar·se, v. decay
ca·ri·bú, m. caribou
ca·ri·ca·tu·ra, f. caricature
ca·ri·dad, f. charity
ca·ri·llón, m. carillon
ca·ri·ño, m. love; affection
ca·ri·ño·so, a. loving; affectionate; fond
ca·ri·ta·ti·vo, a. charitable
car·me·sí, a. crimson. m. crimson
car·nal, a. carnal
car·na·li·dad, f. carnality
car·na·val, m. carnival
car·ne, f. meat; pulp; flesh. car·ne de va·ca, beef
car·ne·ro, m. ram
car·ni·ce·ría, f. butcher shop; carnage; bloodshed; slaughter
car·ni·ce·ro, m. butcher
car·ní·vo·ro, a. carnivorous. m. carnivore
car·o, a. dear; expensive
car·pa, f. carp
car·pe·ta, f. folder
car·pin·te·ría, f. carpentry
car·pin·te·ro, m. carpenter
ca·rre·ra, f. race; career
ca·rre·ro, m. carrier
car·te·ra, f. cartage
ca·rre·te, m. spool; reel; coil
ca·rre·te·ra, f. highway; road
ca·rri·llo, m. jowl
ca·rro, m. cart; chariot
ca·rro·ña, f. carrion
ca·rro·za, f. chariot; coach; float
ca·rrua·je, m. carriage
car·ta, f. letter; card. car·ta ad·jun·ta, enclosure. car·ta de na·ve·gar, chart
car·tel, m. poster; placard
car·te·le·ra, f. billboard
car·te·ra, f. wallet; billfold; portfolio
car·te·ro, m. mailman; postman
car·ti·la·go, m. cartilage; gristle
car·to·gra·fía, f. cartography
car·tó·gra·fo, m. cartographer

car·tón, *m.* cardboard
car·tu·cho, *m.* cartridge
ca·sa, *f.* house; home
ca·sa·men·te·ro, *m.*, **ca·sa·men·te·ra**, *f.* matchmaker
ca·sar(se), *v.* marry; wed; mate
cas·ca·bel, *m.* bell
cas·ca·da, *f.* cascade
cas·ca·jo, *m.* gravel
cás·ca·ra, *f.* shell; hull; husk
cas·co, *m.* helmet; skull; hoof
cas·co·te, *m.* rubble
ca·si, *adv.* almost
ca·si·mir, *m.* cashmere
ca·si·no, *m.* casino
ca·so, *m.* case; happening. **ha·cer ca·so de**, heed
cas·pa, *f.* dandruff
cas·ta, *f.* caste; breed; cast
cas·ta·men·te, *adv.* chastely
cas·ta·ñe·tear, *v.* chatter; snap
cas·ta·ñue·las, *f. pl.* castanets
cas·ti·dad, *f.* chastity
cas·ti·gar, *v.* castigate; punish; chastise
cas·ti·go, *m.* castigation; discipline; penalty
cas·ti·llo, *m.* castle
cas·to, *a.* chaste
cas·tor, *m.* beaver
cas·tra·ción, *f.* castration
cas·trar, *v.* castrate; geld
ca·sual, *a.* accidental; incidental
ca·sua·li·dad, *f.* chance; coincidence
ca·ta·clis·mo, *m.* cataclysm; upheaval
ca·ta·cum·bas, *f. usu. pl.* catacomb
ca·ta·le·jo, *m.* spyglass
ca·ta·li·za·dor, *m.* catalyst
ca·ta·lo·gar, *v.* catalog, catalogue
ca·tá·lo·go, *m.* catalog, catalogue
ca·ta·pul·ta, *f.* catapult
ca·ta·ra·ta, *f.* cataract; waterfall
ca·ta·rro, *m.* catarrh; cold
ca·tar·sis, *f.* catharsis
ca·tás·tro·fe, *f.* catastrophe
ca·tas·tró·fi·co, *a.* catastrophic
ca·te·dral, *f.* cathedral
ca·te·drá·ti·co, *m.*, **ca·te·drá·ti·ca**, *f.* professor
ca·te·go·ría, *f.* category; standing
ca·te·gó·ri·co, *a.* categorical
ca·te·quis·mo, *m.* catechism
Ca·to·li·cis·mo, *m.* Catholicism
Ca·tó·li·co, *m.*, **Ca·tó·li·ca**, *f.* Catholic. *a.* catholic
ca·tor·ce, *a.* fourteen
ca·tre, *m.* cot
cau·ce, *m.* channel
cau·ción, *f.* bail
cau·cho, *m.* rubber
cau·di·llo, *m.* leader; head of state
cau·sa, *f.* cause. **a·cau·sa de**, because of
cau·sar, *v.* cause; produce; make
cáus·ti·co, *a.* caustic
cau·te·la, *f.* caution; stealth
cau·te·lo·so, *a.* cautious; wary
cau·te·ri·zar, *v.* cauterize
cau·ti·var, *v.* captivate; capture
cau·ti·ve·rio, *m.* captivity
cau·ti·vo, *a.* captive
ca·var, *v.* dig; delve
ca·ver·na, *f.* cavern
ca·ver·no·so, *a.* cavernous
ca·viar, *m.* caviar, caviare
ca·vi·dad, *f.* cavity
ca·za, *f.* hunt; hunting; game
ca·za·dor, *m.*, **ca·za·do·ra**, *f.* hunter
ca·zar, *v.* hunt; bag
ca·zue·la, *f.* pan
ce·ba·da, *f.* barley
ce·bar, *v.* prime; feed; bait
ce·bo, *m.* bait
ce·bo·lla, *f.* onion
ce·bra, *f.* zebra
ce·cear, *v.* lisp
ce·der, *v.* give in; relent; cede
ce·dro, *m.* cedar
cé·du·la, *f.* warrant, certificate; charter
ce·gar, *v.* blind
ce·gue·ra, *f.* blindness
ce·ja, *f.* eyebrow
cel·da, *f.* cell
ce·le·bra·ción, *f.* celebration
ce·le·brar(se), *v.* celebrate; solemnize
cé·le·bre, *a.* celebrated; famous
ce·le·bri·dad, *f.* celebrity
ce·les·tial, *a.* celestial; heavenly
ce·li·ba·to, *m.* celibate. *m.* celibacy
ce·lo·fán, *m.* cellophane
ce·los, *m.* jealousy
ce·lo·sía, *f.* jalousie; jealousy
ce·lo·so, *a.* jealous; zealous
cé·lu·la, *f.* cell
ce·lu·lar, *a.* cellular
ce·lu·lo·sa, *f.* cellulose
ce·men·tar, *v.* cement
ce·men·te·rio, *m.* cemetery; graveyard
ce·men·to, *m.* cement
ce·na, *f.* dinner; supper
ce·nar, *v.* dine; eat dinner; sup
ce·ni·za, *f.* ash; *pl.* cinders
cen·so, *m.* census
cen·sor, *m.* censor
cen·su·ra, *f.* censure; blame; stricture; censorship
cen·su·ra·ble, *a.* censurable
cen·su·rar, *v.* censure; blame; censor
cen·tau·ro, *m.* centaur
cen·ta·vo, *m.* penny; cent
cen·te·llear, *v.* twinkle; sparkle
cen·te·lleo, *m.* twinkle
cen·te·na·rio, *a.* centennial. *m.* centenary
cen·te·no, *m.* rye

cen·té·si·mo, *a.* hundredth
cen·tí·gra·do, *a.* centigrade; Celsius
cen·tí·me·tro, *m.* centimeter
cen·ti·ne·la, *m., f.* sentry; sentinel
cen·tral, *a.* central
cen·tra·li·zar, *v.* centralize
cen·trar, *v.* center
cén·tri·co, *a.* central
cen·tro, *m.* center; middle; core
cen·tu·rión, *m.* centurion
ce·ñir(se), *v.* encircle; gird
ce·ño, *m.* frown; scowl
ce·pi·llo, *m.* brush. **ce·pi·llo de dientes**, toothbrush
ce·ra, *f.* wax
ce·rá·mi·ca, *f.* ceramics
ce·rá·mi·co, *a.* ceramic
cer·ca, *adv.* close; near; nearby; by. *prep.* beside; near; toward
cer·ca, *f.* fence
cer·ca·no, *a.* close; near
cer·car, *v.* surround; enclose; fence; encompass
cer·co, *m.* siege
cer·da, *f.* bristle; pig
cer·do, *m.* pig
cer·do·so, *a.* bristly
ce·real, *m.* cereal. *a.* cereal
ce·re·bral, *a.* cerebral
ce·re·bro, *m.* brain
ce·re·mo·nia, *f.* ceremony; formality; *pl.* solemnities
ce·re·mo·nial, *m.* ceremonial. *a.* ceremonial
ce·re·za, *f.* cherry
ce·ri·lla, *f.* match
ce·ro, *m.* zero; naught; cipher
ce·rra·do, *a.* a shut; closed
ce·rra·du·ra, *f.* lock
ce·rrar(se), *v.* close; shut; turn off; seal
ce·rro·jo, *m.* bolt
cer·te·za, *f.* certitude
cer·ti·dum·bre, *f.* certitude; certainty
cer·ti·fi·ca·do, *m.* certificate; *a.* certified
cer·ti·fi·car, *v.* certify
cer·va·to, *m.* fawn
cer·ve·ce·ría, *f.* brewery
cer·ve·za, *f.* beer; ale. **cer·ve·za de jen·gi·bre**, gingerale
ce·sa·ción, *f.* cessation; stoppage
ce·sar, *v.* cease
ce·se, *m.* cessation
ce·sión, *f.* cession; grant
cés·ped, *m.* lawn; grass; sod; turf
ces·ta, *f.* basket
ce·tri·no, *a.* sallow
cia·nu·ro, *m.* cyanide
ci·cla·mi·no, *m.* cyclamen
cí·cli·co, *a.* cyclic
ci·clis·ta, *m., f.* cyclist
ci·clo, *m.* cycle; circle
ci·clón, *m.* cyclone
ci·clo·trón, *m.* cyclotron
ci·cu·ta, *f.* hemlock
cie·go, *a.* blind; sightless
cie·lo, *m.* sky; heaven; *usu. pl.* heavens
cien (cien·to), *a.* a hundred
cié·na·ga, *f.* swamp
cien·cia, *f.* science
cien·tí·fi·co, *m.* scientist. *a.* scientific
cien·to (cien), *a.* hundred. *m.* hundred
cie·rre, *m.* snap
cier·ta·men·te, *adv.* certainly
cier·to, *a.* a sure; certain
cier·vo, *m.* stag; hart
ci·fra, *f.* cipher; figure; code
ci·frar, *v.* code; cipher
ci·ga·rri·llo, *m.* cigarette, cigaret
ci·güe·ña, *f.* stork
ci·lín·dri·co, *a.* cylindric(al)
ci·lin·dro, *m.* cylinder
ci·ma, *f.* top; crest; summit; acme
ci·mi·ta·rra, *f.* scimitar, simitar, scimiter
cin·cel, *m.* chisel
cin·co, *a.* five. *m.* five
cin·cuen·ta, *a.* fifty. *m.* fifty
cin·cha, *f.* cinch; girth
ci·ne, *m.* cinema; movies
cí·ni·co, *a.* cynical. *m.* cynic
ci·nis·mo, *m.* cynicism
cin·ta, *f.* ribbon; reel; tape. **gra·bar en cin·ta**, tape
cin·to, *m.* girdle
cin·tu·rón, *m.* belt
ci·prés, *m.* cypress
cir·co, *m.* circus
cir·cui·to, *m.* circuit. **cor·to cir·cui·to**, short-circuit
cir·cu·la·ción, *f.* circulation; currency
cir·cu·lar, *a.* circular. *v.* circulate
cír·cu·lo, *m.* circle
cir·cun·ci·dar, *v.* circumcise
cir·cun·ci·sión, *f.* circumcision
cir·cun·fe·ren·cia, *f.* circumference
cir·cun·lo·cu·ción, *f.* circumlocution
cir·cun·na·ve·gar, *v.* circumnavigate
cir·cuns·cri·bir, *v.* circumscribe
cir·cuns·pec·to, *a.* circumspect
cir·cuns·tan·cia, *f.* circumstance
ci·rio, *m.* taper; candle
ci·rro, *m.* cirrus
ci·rro·sis, *f.* cirrhosis
ci·rue·la, *f.* plum. **ci·rue·la pa·sa**, prune
ci·ru·gía, *f.* surgery
ci·ru·ja·no, *m.* surgeon
cis·ma, *m.* schism
cis·ne, *m.* swan
cis·ter·na, *f.* cistern
ci·ta, *f.* assignation; meeting; appointment; date; tryst; quotation;

extract; citation
ci·ta·ción, *f.* citation; subpoena, subpena; summons
ci·tar(se), *v.* summon; quote; cite
ciu·dad, *f.* city; town
ciu·da·da·no, *m.*, **ciu·da·da·na**, *f.* citizen; citizenry
ciu·da·de·la, *f.* citadel
cí·vi·co, *a.* civic
ci·vil, *a.* civilian; civil. *m.* civilian
ci·vi·li·dad, *f.* civility
ci·vi·li·za·ción, *f.* civilization
ci·vi·li·zar(se), *v.* civilize; become civilized
cla·mor, *m.* noise; clamor; outcry
cla·mo·ro·so, *a.* clamorous
clan, *m.* clan
clan·des·ti·no, *a.* clandestine
cla·ra·men·te, *adv.* clearly
cla·re·te, *m.* claret
cla·ri·dad, *f.* clarity; clearness
cla·ri·fi·ca·ción, *f.* clarification
cla·ri·fi·car, *v.* clarify; light up
cla·rín, *m.* bugle
cla·ri·ne·te, *m.* clarinet
cla·ri·vi·den·cia, *f.* clairvoyance
cla·ro, *a.* bright; light; clear; transparent; articulate; lucid; apparent. *m.* clearing; glade
cla·se, *f.* class; grade; sort; order. **de pri·me·ra cla·se**, first-rate
clá·si·co, *a.* classic, classical; vintage. *m.* classic
cla·si·fi·ca·ción, *f.* classification
cla·si·fi·car(se), *v.* classify; class; categorize; sort; grade
claus·tro, *m.* cloister
cla·var(se), *v.* stick; nail; thrust
cla·ve, *a.* key. *f.* key; gist; clef
cla·vel, *m.* carnation
cla·vi·ja, *f.* peg
cla·vo, *m.* nail; spike
cle·men·cia, *f.* clemency; mercy
cle·men·te, *a.* clement
cle·ri·cal, *a.* clerical
clé·ri·go, *m.* parson; priest
cle·ro, *m.* clergy; ministry
clien·te, *m.* client; customer; patron
cli·ma, *m.* climate
clí·max, *m.* climax
clí·ni·ca, *f.* clinic
clí·ni·co, *a.* clinical
clo·quear, *v.* cluck
clo·ro, *m.* chlorine
clo·ro·fi·la, *f.* chlorophyll, chlorophyl
coac·ción, *f.* compulsion; constraint
coac·ti·vo, *a.* coercive
coa·gu·la·ción, *f.* coagulation
coa·gu·lar(se), *v.* coagulate; clot
coa·li·ción, *f.* coalition
coar·ta·da, *f.* alibi
co·bal·to, *m.* cobalt
co·bar·de, *a.* cowardly. *m.* coward; dastard
co·bar·día, *f.* cowardice
co·bra, *f.* cobra
co·bra·dor, *m.*, **co·bra·do·ra**, *f.* conductor
co·brar(se), *v.* cash; charge; receive; recover
co·bre, *m.* copper
co·bro, *m.* collection; recovery
co·ca·ína, *f.* cocaine
co·cer, *v.* cook; bake. **co·cer en hor·no**, bake
co·cien·te, *m.* quotient
co·ci·na, *f.* kitchen; stove
co·ci·nar, *v.* cook
co·ci·ne·ro, *m.*, **co·ci·ne·ra**, *f.* cook; chef
co·co, *m.* coconut, cocoanut
co·co·dri·lo, *m.* crocodile
coc·tel, *m.* cocktail
co·che, *m.* car; automobile; coach. **co·che·co·me·dor**, diner. **co·che fú·ne·bre**, hearse
co·di·cia, *f.* greed; covetousness; cupidity
co·di·ciar, *v.* covet
co·di·cio·so, *a.* greedy; covetous
co·di·fi·car, *v.* codify
có·di·go, *m.* code
co·do, *m.* elbow
co·dor·niz, *f.* quail
co·e·du·ca·ción, *f.* coeducation
coer·cer, *v.* coerce
coer·ción, *f.* coercion
coe·tá·neo, *m.* contemporary. *a.* contemporary
co·fra·día, *f.* fraternity; gang
co·fre, *m.* chest
co·ger, *v.* take; get; pick; choose; cull; pluck; catch; net; *inf.* nab; cop
co·gi·da, *f.* catch; toss
co·gu·lla, *f.* cowl
co·he·char, *v.* bribe
co·he·cho, *m.* bribery
co·he·ren·cia, *f.* coherence
co·he·ren·te, *a.* coherent
co·he·si·vo, *a.* cohesive
co·he·te, *m.* rocket; skyrocket
co·hor·te, *f.* cohort
coin·ci·den·cia, *f.* coincidence
coin·ci·den·te, *a.* coincidental
coin·ci·dir, *v.* coincide; agree
coi·to, *m.* coitus; intercourse
co·jear, *v.* limp; hobble
co·je·ra, *f.* limp
co·jín, *m.* cushion
co·jo, *a.* lame
col, *f.* cabbage. **en·sa·la·da de col**, coleslaw
co·la, *f.* tail; queue; line; glue
co·la·bo·ra·ción, *f.* collaboration
co·la·bo·rar, *v.* collaborate
co·la·de·ra, *f.* sieve

co·la·dor, *m.* strainer
co·lap·so, *m.* collapse
co·la·te·ral, *a.* collateral
col·cha, *f.* quilt; comforter; spread
col·chón, *m.* mattress
co·lec·ción, *f.* collection; batch
co·lec·cio·nar, *v.* collect
co·lec·ti·vo, *a.* collective
co·le·ga, *m.* colleague
co·le·gio, *m.* academy; high school; college
có·le·ra, *f.* choler; anger; cholera
co·lé·ri·co, *a.* choleric; irate; angry
co·le·ta, *f.* pigtail
col·ga·du·ra, *f.* drape; hangings
col·gar, *v.* hang; suspend; dangle
co·li·brí, *m.* hummingbird
có·li·co, *m.* colic
co·li·flor, *f.* cauliflower
co·li·na, *f.* hill
co·li·seo, *m.* coliseum
col·me·na, *f.* beehive; hive
col·me·nar, *m.* apiary
col·mi·llo, *m.* tusk; fang; eyetooth
col·mo, *m.* climax; height; culmination
co·lo·ca·ción, *f.* location; placing; situation
co·lo·car(se), *v.* put; place; locate; lay; settle; pose; range; array
co·lon, *m.* colon
co·lo·nia, *f.* colony
co·lo·nial, *a.* colonial
co·lo·ni·za·ción, *f.* colonization; settlement
co·lo·ni·za·dor, *m.* colonist
co·lo·no, *m.* settler
co·lor, *m.* color; hue
co·lo·re·te, *m.* rouge
co·lo·sal, *a.* colossal; gargantuan. *m.* colossus
co·lum·na, *f.* column; pillar
co·lum·na·ta, *f.* colonnade
co·lum·nis·ta, *m.* columnist
co·lum·piar(se), *v.* swing
co·lum·pio, *m.* swing
co·lu·sión, *f.* collusion
co·ma, *f.* comma; coma
co·ma·dre, *f.* gossip
co·man·dan·te, *m.* commander; major
co·man·do, *m.* command
co·ma·to·so, *a.* comatose
com·ba, *f.* bend; warp; sag
com·bar(se), *v.* sag; bend
com·ba·te, *m.* combat; fight
com·ba·tien·te, *m.* combatant
com·ba·tir(se), *v.* combat; fight; struggle
com·bi·na·ción, *f.* combination; blend; slip
com·bi·na·do, *a.* joint; combined
com·bi·nar(se), *v.* combine; blend; unite
com·bus·ti·ble, *a.* combustible. *m.* fuel
com·bus·tión, *f.* combustion
co·me·dia, *f.* comedy
co·me·jén, *m.* termite
co·men·ta·dor, *m.* commentator
co·men·tar, *v.* comment on
co·men·ta·rio, *m.* commentary; observation
co·men·zar, *v.* start; begin; commence
co·mer(se), *v.* eat; consume; eat up
co·mer·cial, *a.* commercial
co·mer·cian·te, *m.* merchant
co·mer·ciar, *v.* trade
co·mer·cio, *m.* trade; commerce; business; intercourse
co·mes·ti·ble, *a.* edible; eatable. *m. pl.* groceries
co·me·ta, *m.* comet. *f.* kite
co·me·ter, *v.* commit; make
co·me·dian·te, *f.* comedienne
có·mi·co, *a.* comical; funny; burlesque. *m.* comic; comedian
co·mi·da, *f.* meal; fare; keep
co·mien·zo, *m.* start; beginning; commencement
co·mi·llas, *f. pl.* quotation marks
co·mi·sa·rio, *m.* commissioner; commissary
co·mi·sión, *f.* commission
co·mi·té, *m.* committee
co·mi·ti·va, *f.* train; retinue
co·mo, *adv.* as; like. *conj.* as
có·mo, *adv.* how? what? why?
co·mo·di·dad, *f.* comfort; coziness; convenience
co·mo·dín, *m.* (cards) joker
có·mo·do, *a.* comfortable; snug; cozy; convenient; *inf.* comfy; homey, homy
com·pac·to, *a.* dense; compact
com·pa·de·cer, *v.* pity
com·pa·dre, *m.* friend; godfather
com·pa·ñe·ris·mo, *m.* fellowship
com·pa·ñe·ro, *m.* companion; associate; mate; buddy; *inf.* side-kick
com·pa·ñía, *f.* company; troupe
com·pa·ra·ble, *a.* comparable
com·pa·ra·ción, *f.* comparison
com·pa·rar, *v.* compare; contrast; liken; equate
com·pa·ren·do, *m.* subpoena, subpena
com·par·sa, *m., f.* supernumerary
com·par·ti·mien·to, *m.* compartment; division
com·par·tir, *v.* share
com·pás, *m.* compass; measure
com·pa·sión, *f.* compassion; sympathy
com·pa·si·vo, *a.* compassionate; sympathetic
com·pa·ti·ble, *a.* compatible
com·pa·trio·ta, *m., f.* compatriot

com·pe·ler, *v.* compel
com·pen·sa·ción, *f.* compensation; *pl.* amends
com·pen·sar, *v.* compensate
com·pe·ten·cia, *f.* competence; competition
com·pe·ten·te, *a.* competent; able
com·pe·ti·dor, *m.*, **com·pe·ti·do·ra**, *f.* rival; competitor
com·pe·tir, *v.* compete; vie
com·pi·la·ción, *f.* compilation
com·pi·lar, *v.* compile
com·ple·ji·dad, *f.* intricacy; complexity
com·ple·men·to, *m.* complement
com·ple·ta·men·te, *adv.* completely; fully; quite
com·ple·tar, *v.* complete
com·ple·to, *a.* complete; thorough; absolute; full
com·pli·ca·ción, *f.* complication
com·pli·car(se), *v.* complicate; involve
cóm·pli·ce, *m.* accessory; accomplice
com·po·ner(se), *v.* compose; make; constitute; compound
com·por·ta·mien·to, *m.* behavior; deportment
com·por·tar(se), *v.* behave
com·po·si·ción, *f.* composition
com·pra, *f.* purchase; buy. **ir de com·pras**, to shop
com·pra·dor, *m.*, **com·pra·do·ra**, *f.* buyer; shopper
com·prar, *v.* buy; purchase; trade
com·pren·sión, *f.* comprehension
com·pren·der, *v.* understand; comprehend; grasp; see; comprise
com·pren·si·vo, *a.* comprehensive; broad
com·pre·sión, *f.* compression
com·pri·mir, *v.* compress
com·pro·ba·ción, *f.* proof; substantiation
com·pro·bar, *v.* verify; substantiate
com·pro·me·ter(se), *v.* compromise; involve
com·pro·mi·so, *m.* predicament; obligation
com·pues·to, *m.* compound. *a.* compound; composite
com·pul·sión, *f.* compulsion; stress; coercion
com·pu·ta·dor, *m.* computer
com·pu·tar, *v.* compute
co·mún, *a.* common
co·mu·ni·ca·ción, *f.* communication; message
co·mu·ni·car(se), *v.* impart; communicate
con, *prep.* with; towards. *adv.* along
con·ca·vi·dad, *f.* hollow
con·ce·bi·ble, *a.* conceivable
con·ce·bir, *v.* conceive
con·ce·der, *v.* concede; allow; accord; grant; give
con·ce·jo, *m.* council
con·cen·tra·ción, *f.* concentration
con·cen·trar(se), *v.* concentrate
con·cep·ción, *f.* conception
con·cep·to, *m.* concept; notion
con·ce·sión, *f.* concession; allowance
con·cien·cia, *f.* conscience
con·cien·zu·do, *a.* thorough; conscientious
con·cier·to, *m.* concert
con·ci·liar(se), *v.* conciliate; reconcile
con·ci·so, *a.* concise; terse
con·cluir(se), *v.* conclude; end
con·clu·sión, *f.* conclusion; end
con·cor·dar, *v.* agree; tally
con·cor·dia, *f.* concord
con·cre·to, *a.* concrete
con·cu·bi·na, *f.* concubine
con·cu·rren·cia, *f.* turnout; concurrence
con·cu·rrir, *v.* concur; meet
con·cur·san·te, *m., f.* participant
con·cur·so, *m.* contest
con·da·do, *m.* county
con·de, *m.* count; earl
con·de·co·rar, *v.* decorate
con·de·na, *f.* sentence
con·de·na·ción, *f.* condemnation
con·de·nar(se), *v.* condemn; convict; doom; damn
con·den·sa·ción, *f.* condensation
con·de·sa, *f.* countess
con·di·ción, *f.* condition; state
con·di·cio·nal, *a.* conditional
con·di·men·tar, *v.* condition
con·di·men·to, *m.* condiment; flavoring; seasoning
con·do·len·cia, *f.* condolence
con·du·cir(se), *v.* drive; steer; lead; conduct
con·duc·ta, *f.* behavior
con·duc·to, *m.* conduit; duct
co·nec·tar, *v.* connect; (*elec.*) switch on
co·ne·je·ra, *f.* warren
co·ne·ji·to, *m.* bunny
co·ne·jo, *m.* rabbit
co·ne·xión, *f.* connection
con·fec·ción, *f.* confection
con·fec·cio·nar, *v.* concoct; make up
con·fe·de·ra·ción, *f.* confederacy; confederation
con·fe·de·ra·do, *a.* confederate. *m.* confederate; ally
con·fe·ren·cia, *f.* conference; lecture
con·fe·rir, *v.* bestow; grant

con·fe·sar(se), *v.* confess; acknowledge; admit
con·fe·sión, *f.* confession; admission; avowal
con·fe·sio·na·rio, *m.* confessional
con·fe·so, *m.* confessor
con·fe·ti, *m.* confetti
con·fia·ble, *a.* reliable
con·fian·za, *f.* trust; dependence, dependance; confidence
con·fiar, *v.* entrust; trust; rely; confide
con·fi·den·cial, *a.* confidential; private
con·fi·gu·ra·ción, *f.* configuration
con·fín, *m. usu. pl.* bound; confines
con·fir·ma·ción, *f.* confirmation; corroboration
con·fir·mar, *v.* confirm; ratify
con·fis·ca·ción, *f.* confiscation
con·fis·car, *v.* confiscate
con·fla·gra·ción, *f.* conflagration
con·flic·to, *m.* conflict; clash
con·for·mar(se), *v.* conform; adjust
con·for·me, *a.* agreeable; similar
con·for·mi·dad, *f.* conformity
con·for·tar, *v.* comfort
con·fron·ta·ción, *f.* confrontation
con·fron·tar, *v.* confront
con·fun·dir(se), *v.* confound; confuse; perplex; puzzle; baffle; bemuse; mix
con·fu·sión, *f.* confusion; mess; jumble
con·fu·tar, *v.* confute; disprove
con·ge·la·ción, *f.* frostbite
con·ge·lar(se), *v.* freeze; congeal
con·gé·ni·to, *a.* congenital
con·ges·tión, *f.* congestion
con·glo·me·ra·ción, *f.* conglomeration
con·glo·me·ra·do, *m.* conglomerate
con·gre·gar(se), *v.* congregate; assemble; flock
con·gre·so, *m.* congress; convention
co·ní·fe·ra, *f.* conifer
con·je·tu·ra, *f.* conjecture; guess; surmise
con·je·tu·rar, *v.* conjecture; surmise
con·ju·gar(se), *v.* conjugate
con·jun·ción, *f.* conjunction
con·jun·to, *m.* ensemble; whole
con·ju·rar, *v.* conjure
con·me·mo·rar, *v.* commemorate
con·me·mo·ra·ti·vo, *a.* memorial
con·mo·ción, *f.* commotion; stir; concussion
con·mo·ve·dor, *a.* stirring
con·mo·ver(se), *v.* move; thrill; shake
con·no·tar, *v.* connote
co·no, *m.* cone
co·no·cer(se), *v.* know; recognize
co·no·ci·do, *m.*, **co·no·ci·da**, *f.* acquaintance. *a.* familiar; known
co·no·ci·mien·to, *m.* knowledge; *pl.* ken; lore
con·quis·ta, *f.* conquest
con·quis·ta·dor, *m.* conqueror
con·quis·tar, *v.* conquer; vanquish
con·sa·gra·ción, *f.* consecration
con·sa·grar, *v.* consecrate
con·san·guí·neo, *a.* akin
cons·cien·te, *a.* conscious
con·se·cuen·cia, *f.* consequence; result; consistency
con·se·cuen·te, *a.* consistent
con·se·cu·ti·vo, *a.* consecutive
con·se·je·ro, *m.*, **con·se·je·ra**, *f.* counselor
con·se·jo, *m.* counsel; advice; board. **con·se·jo de gue·rra**, court-martial
con·sen·so, *m.* consensus
con·sen·ti·mien·to, *m.* consent
con·sen·tir, *v.* consent; accede; acquiesce; indulge
con·ser·va, *f. usu. pl.* preserve
con·ser·va·ción, *f.* conservation
con·ser·var(se), *v.* conserve; save; preserve
con·ser·va·to·rio, *m.* conservatory
con·si·de·ra·ble, *a.* considerable; goodly
con·si·de·ra·ción, *f.* consideration; regard; sake; account; thought
con·si·de·rar, *v.* consider; entertain; regard; take into account
con·sig·na·ción, *f.* consignment
con·sig·nar, *v.* consign
con·si·go, *pron.* with him, her, you, etc.
con·si·guien·te, *a.* consequent
con·sis·ten·cia, *f.* consistency
con·sis·tir, *v.* consist of
con·so·lar(se), *v.* comfort; console; solace
con·so·li·da·ción, *f.* consolidation
con·so·li·dar, *v.* consolidate; fund
con·sor·te, *m., f.* consort
cons·pi·cuo, *a.* visible
cons·pi·ra·ción, *f.* conspiracy; plot
cons·pi·ra·dor, *m.*, **cons·pi·ra·do·ra**, *f.* conspirator
cons·pi·rar, *v.* conspire
cons·tan·cia, *f.* constancy
cons·tan·te, *a.* constant; steady; uniform
cons·tan·te·men·te, *adv.* constantly
cons·te·la·ción, *f.* constellation
cons·ter·na·ción, *f.* consternation
cons·ter·nar(se), *v.* dismay
cons·ti·tuir(se), *v.* constitute; form
cons·truc·ción, *f.* construction; structure

cons·truc·ti·vo, *a.* constructive
cons·truir, *v.* construct; build; structure
con·sue·lo, *m.* consolation
cón·sul, *m.* consul
con·su·la·do, *m.* consulate
con·sul·ta, *f.* consultation
con·sul·tar, *v.* consult
con·su·mar, *v.* consummate; carry out
con·su·mi·dor, *m.*, con·su·mi·do·ra, *f.* consumer
con·su·mir(se), *v.* consume; waste away
con·su·mo, *m.* consumption
con·sun·ción, *f.* consumption
con·tac·to, *m.* contact
con·ta·giar(se), *v.* infect; catch
con·ta·gio, *m.* contagion
con·ta·gio·so, *a.* contagious; catching
con·ta·mi·na·ción, *f.* contamination; pollution
con·ta·mi·nar(se), *v.* contaminate
con·tar(se), *v.* count; number; tell; relate. con·tar con, depend on; rely on
con·tem·pla·ción, *f.* contemplation
con·tem·plar, *v.* contemplate; meditate; view
con·tem·po·rá·neo, *a.* contemporary
con·ten·der, *v.* contend; strive; contest
con·ten·dien·te, *m.*, *f.* contestant
con·te·ner(se), *v.* contain; hold; include; suppress
con·te·ni·do, *a.* usu. pl. content
con·ten·to, *a.* contented; happy
con·tes·ta·ción, *f.* answer
con·tes·tar, *v.* answer; reply
con·tien·da, *f.* strife; struggle; contest
con·ti·guo, *a.* adjacent. *prep.* next
con·ti·nen·tal, *a.* continental
con·ti·nen·te, *a.* continent; mainland; container
con·tin·gen·cia, *f.* contingency
con·ti·nua·ción, *f.* continuation
con·ti·nuar, *v.* continue
con·ti·nuo, *a.* continuous; constant; perpetual
con·to·near(se), *v.* strut
con·tor·no, *m.* contour; outline
con·tra, *prep.* against; versus. *adv.* against
.n·tra·ba·jo, *m.* bass
con·tra·ban·dis·ta, *m.*, *f.* smuggler
con·tra·ban·do, *m.* contraband; smuggling
con·trac·ción, *f.* contraction
con·tra·de·cir, *v.* contradict; gainsay
con·tra·dic·ción, *f.* contradiction
con·tra·er(se), *v.* contract
con·tra·fuer·te, *m.* buttress
con·tra·ha·cer, *v.* counterfeit; *inf.* fudge
con·tral·to, *m.*, *f.* contralto; alto
con·tra·rie·dad, *f.* vexation; snag
con·tra·rio, *a.* contrary; adverse; opposite. lo con·tra·rio, reverse
con·tras·tar, *v.* contrast
con·tras·te, *m.* contrast
con·tra·tiem·po, *m.* mishap; upset
con·tra·to, *m.* agreement; contract
con·tra·ven·ta·na, *f.* shutter
con·tri·bu·ción, *f.* contribution; tax
con·tri·buir, *v.* contribute
con·trol, *m.* control
con·tro·lar, *v.* control
con·tro·ver·sia, *f.* controversy
con·tu·sión, *f.* contusion; bruise
con·va·le·cen·cia, *f.* convalescence
con·va·le·cer, *v.* convalesce
con·va·le·cien·te, *m.*, *f.* convalescent
con·ven·cer, *v.* convince; satisfy
con·ven·ción, *f.* convention
con·ven·cio·nal, *a.* conventional
con·ve·nien·cia, *f.* expediency; *pl.* amenities
con·ve·nien·te, *a.* convenient; handy; fitting; expedient
con·ve·nir(se), *v.* befit; agree; go with
con·ven·to, *m.* convent; abbey. con·ven·to de mon·jas, nunnery
con·ver·gir, *v.* converge
con·ver·sa·ción, *f.* conversation
con·ver·sar, *v.* converse
con·ver·sión, *f.* conversion
con·ver·so, *m.*, con·ver·sa, *f.* convert
con·ver·tir(se), *v.* convert; turn into
con·ve·xo, *a.* convex
con·vic·ción, *f.* conviction
con·vi·da·do, *m.*, con·vi·da·da, *f.* guest
con·vi·dar(se), *v.* invite; volunteer
con·vi·te, *m.* invitation
con·vo·ca·ción, *f.* convocation
con·vo·car, *v.* convene; summon
con·voy, *m.* convoy
con·vul·sión, *f.* convulsion
co·ñac, *m.* cognac; brandy
co·o·pe·ra·ción, *f.* cooperation; teamwork
co·o·pe·rar, *v.* cooperate
co·or·di·na·ción, *f.* coordination
co·or·di·nar, *v.* coordinate
co·pa, *f.* glass; goblet
co·pe·te, *m.* tuft
co·pia, *f.* copy; imitation; duplicate
co·piar, *v.* copy
co·pio·so, *a.* copious
co·pu·lar·se, *v.* copulate
co·que, *m.* coke
co·que·ta, *f.* flirt; coquette
co·que·tear, *v.* flirt
co·ral, *a.* choral. *m.* chorale; coral
Co·rán, *m.* Koran
co·ra·zón, *m.* heart; core

co·ra·zo·na·da, *f.* hunch
cor·ba·ta, *f.* tie; cravat
cor·cel, *m.* steed
cor·che·te, *m.* clasp; *pl.* brackets
cor·cho, *m.* cork
cor·del, *m.* string
cor·de·ro, *m.* lamb
cor·dial, *a.* cordial; hearty
cor·dia·li·dad, *f.* cordiality
cor·do·bán, *m.* cordovan
cor·dón, *m.* shoelace; cord
co·re·o·gra·fía, *f.* choreography
co·re·ó·gra·fo, *m.*, co·re·ó·gra·fa, *f.* choreographer
co·ris·ta, *m.*, *f.* chorister
cor·ne·ta, *m.* bugler
cor·ni·sa, *f.* cornice
cor·nu·co·pia, *f.* cornucopia
co·ro, *m.* choir; chorus
co·ro·la, *f.* corolla
co·ro·la·rio, *m.* corollary
co·ro·na, *f.* crown; corona
co·ro·na·ción, *f.* coronation
co·ro·nar, *v.* crown; top
co·ro·na·ria, *f.* coronary
co·ro·nel, *m.* colonel
cor·pi·ño, *m.* bodice
cor·po·ra·ción, *f.* corporation
cor·po·ral, *a.* corporal
cor·po·ra·ti·vo, *a.* corporate
cor·pó·reo, *a.* bodily
corps, *m.* *pl.* corps
cor·pu·len·to, *a.* stout
cor·pús·cu·lo, *m.* corpuscle
co·rral, *m.* corral; barnyard; pen
co·rrea, *f.* strap
co·rrec·ción, *f.* correction; propriety
co·rrec·to, *a.* correct; right; seemly
co·rrec·tor de prue·bas, *m.*, co·rrec·to·ra de prue·bas, *f.* proofreader
co·rre·dor, *m.* broker
co·rre·gir(se), *v.* correct; revise; amend
co·rre·la·ción, *f.* correlation
co·rreo, *m.* mail; post. co·rreo aé·reo, airmail
co·rre·o·so, *a.* tough
co·rrer(se), *v.* run; stream; move along
co·rre·ría, *f.* foray
co·rres·pon·den·cia, *f.* correspondence
co·rres·pon·der(se), *v.* correspond; concern
co·rre·ta·je, *m.* brokerage
co·rrien·te, *a.* running; current; regular; common; ordinary. *f.* current; flow; stream
co·rro·bo·rar, *v.* corroborate
co·rro·er(se), *v.* corrode; erode
co·rrom·per(se), *v.* corrupt; rot; taint
co·rro·sión, *f.* corrosion
co·rro·si·vo, *a.* corrosive
co·rrup·ción, *f.* corruption
cor·sé, *m.* corset
cor·ta·do, *a.* cut; abrupt
cor·ta·du·ra, *f.* cut; slit
cor·tan·te, *a.* sharp; edged
cor·tar(se), *v.* cut; chop; slit; clip; crop; sever; pare
cor·te, *m.* cut; court
cor·te·jar, *v.* court
cor·tés, *a.* polite; courteous; civil; courtly; gracious
cor·te·sía, *f.* courtesy; civility
cor·te·za, *f.* bark; rind; peel; crust
cor·ti·jo, *m.* grange
cor·ti·na, *f.* curtain. cor·ti·na de fue·go, barrage
cor·to, *a.* short; brief
co·sa, *f.* thing; affair
co·se·cha, *f.* harvest; crop
co·se·char, *v.* harvest
co·ser, *v.* sew; stitch
cos·mé·ti·co, *a.* cosmetic. *m.* cosmetic
cós·mi·co, *a.* cosmic
cos·mo·po·li·ta, *a.* cosmopolitan. *m.*, *f.* cosmopolitan
cos·mos, *m.* cosmos
cos·qui·llear, *v.* tickle
cos·qui·llo·so, *a.* ticklish
cos·ta, *f.* coast; cost
cos·tar, *v.* cost
cos·te, *m.* cost; price
cos·ti·lla, *f.* rib
cos·to·so, *a.* costly; expensive; valuable
cos·tra, *f.* scab
cos·tro·so, *a.* crusty
cos·tum·bre, *f.* custom; practice; habit; usage
cos·tu·ra, *f.* seam; joint
cos·tu·re·ra, *f.* seamstress
co·ti·dia·no, *a.* daily
co·ti·za·ción, *f.* quotation
co·yo·te, *m.* coyote
co·yun·tu·ra, *f.* juncture
crá·neo, *m.* skull
cra·so, *a.* crass; thick
crá·ter, *m.* crater
crea·ción, *f.* creation
crea·dor, *m.* creator
crear, *v.* create; make; launch; establish
cre·cer(se), *v.* grow; increase
cre·cien·te, *a.* crescent. *a.* increasing
cre·ci·mien·to, *m.* growth
cre·den·cial, *f.* credential; *pl.* credentials
cré·di·to, *m.* credit
cre·do, *m.* creed; credo
cré·du·lo, *a.* gullible; credulous
creen·cia, *f.* belief; faith
creer(se), *v.* believe; think; credit
cre·í·ble, *a.* believable; plausible
cre·ma, *f.* cream

cre·ma·lle·ra, *f.* zipper
cre·pús·cu·lo, *m.* twilight; dusk
cre·sa, *f.* maggot
cres·po, *a.* crisp
cres·ta, *f.* crest
cre·ta, *f.* chalk
cria·da, *f.* maid; handmaiden
crian·za, *f.* upbringing; breeding
criar(se), *v.* rear; raise; breed; nurse; nurture
cria·tu·ra, *f.* creature; infant
cri·men, *m.* crime; felony; offense
cri·mi·nal, *a.* criminal. *m.*, *f.* criminal; felon
crin, *f.* mane
crip·ta, *f.* crypt
cri·sá·li·da, *f.* chrysalis; pupa
cri·san·te·mo, *m.* chrysanthemum
cri·sis, *f.* crisis; breakdown; emergency
cri·sol, *m.* crucible
cris·par(se), *v.* twitch
cris·tal, *m.* glass; crystal; window pane
cris·ta·li·zar(se), *v.* crystallize
cris·tian·dad, *f.* Christendom
cris·tia·nis·mo, *m.* Christianity
cris·tia·no, *m.*, cris·tia·na, *f.* Christian. *a.* Christian
Cris·to, *m.* Christ
cri·te·rio, *m.* criterion
crí·ti·ca, *f.* criticism; censure; stricture
cri·ti·car, *v.* criticize; *inf.* knock
crí·ti·co, *a.* critical. *m.* critic
croar, *v.* croak
cro·má·ti·co, *a.* chromatic
cro·mo, *m.* chrome
cro·mo·so·ma, *m.* chromosome
cró·ni·ca, *f.* chronicle
cró·ni·co, *a.* chronic
cro·nis·ta, *m.*, *f.* chronicler; reporter
cro·no·lo·gía, *f.* chronology
cro·no·ló·gi·co, *a.* chronological
cro·nó·me·tra, *v.* time
cro·nó·me·tro, *m.* chronometer
cro·quet, *m.* croquet
cro·que·ta, *f.* croquette
cru·ce, *m.* crossing; intersection
cru·ce·ro, *m.* cruiser
cru·ci·fi·car, *v.* crucify
cru·ci·fi·jo, *m.* crucifix
cru·ci·fi·xión, *f.* crucifixion
cru·do, *a.* raw; crude
cruel, *a.* cruel; heartless; ruthless; inhuman
cruel·dad, *f.* cruelty
cru·ji·do, *m.* creak; crack
cru·jir, *v.* creak; crunch; swish
crus·tá·ceo, *m.* crustacean
cruz, *f.* cross
cru·za·da, *f.* crusade
cru·za·do, *m.* crusader. *a.* crossed
cru·zar(se), *v.* cross; intersect; bridge; span
cua·der·no, *m.* workbook
cua·dra, *f.* stable
cua·dra·do, *m.* square. *a.* square
cua·dra·gé·si·mo, *a.* fortieth
cua·dran·te, *m.* dial; quadrant
cua·drar(se), *v.* square; tally
cua·dri·lá·te·ro, *m.* quadrilateral
cua·dri·lon·go, *m.* oblong. *a.* oblong
cua·dro, *m.* picture; square; cheek
cua·drú·pe·do, *m.* quadruped
cua·dru·pli·car(se), *v.* quadruple
cua·ja·da, *f.* (*often pl.*) curd
cua·jar(se), *v.* curdle; jell; clot; set
cual, *adv.* as. *prep.* like. *a.* such as. *pron.* which
cuál, *pron.* which (one)? what?
cua·li·dad, *f.* quality
cual·quier(a), *a.* either; any; whichever. *pron.* any; anybody; anyone
cuán, *adv.* how
cuan·do, *adv.* when. *conj.* when; although. *prep.* when
cuán·do, *adv.* when? *conj.* when?
cuan·to, *a.* as much as. *pron.* all that; *pl.* as many as
cuán·to, *a.* how much? *pron.* how many? *adv.* how
cua·ren·ta, *a.* forty
cuar·ta, *f.* fourth. *m.* fourth; quarter; room; chamber
cuar·zo, *m.* quartz
cua·si, *a.* quasi
cua·tro, *a.* four. *m.* four
cu·ba, *f.* vat; barrel
cu·be·ta, *f.* tray
cu·bi·car, *v.* cube
cú·bi·co, *a.* cubic
cu·bier·ta, *f.* cover; casing; deck
cu·bil, *m.* lair
cu·bo, *m.* pail; pailful; bucket; cube
cu·brir(se), *v.* cover; conceal; bank
cu·ca·ra·cha, *f.* cockroach; roach
cu·co, *m.* cuckoo
cu·cha·ra, *f.* spoon; ladle
cu·cha·ra·da, *f.* spoonful; tablespoonful
cu·cha·ra·di·ta, *f.* teaspoonful
cu·cha·ri·lla, *f.* teaspoon
cu·cha·ri·ta, *f.* teaspoon
cu·cha·rón, *m.* ladle
cu·chi·lla·da, *f.* gash; slash
cu·chi·lle·ría, *f.* cutlery
cu·chi·llo, *m.* knife
cue·llo, *m.* neck; collar
cuen·ca, *f.* basin
cuen·ta, *f.* bill; check; count; tally; score; account. dar·se cuen·ta de, realize
cuen·ta·ki·ló·me·tros, *m.* speedometer
cuen·tis·ta, *m.*, *f.* storyteller
cuen·to, *m.* story; tale

cuer·da, *f.* rope; cord. cuer·da de tri·pa, catgut
cuer·do, *a.* sane
cuer·no, *m.* horn; antler
cue·ro, *m.* leather; hide. cue·ro ca·be·llu·do, scalp
cuer·po, *m.* body; force; corpse
cuer·vo, *m.* raven
cues·ta, *f.* ascent; slope
cues·tión, *f.* question
cues·tio·na·rio, *m.* questionnaire
cue·va, *f.* cave
cui·da·do, *m.* care; heed; keep
cui·da·do·so, *a.* careful
cui·dar(se), *v.* care for; look after; mind; conserve
cu·le·bra, *f.* snake
cu·li·na·rio, *a.* culinary
cul·mi·na·ción, *f.* culmination
cul·mi·nar, *v.* culminate
cul·pa, *f.* fault; guilt; *inf.* rap
cul·pa·bi·li·dad, *f.* guilt
cul·pa·ble, *a.* guilty; blameworthy
cul·par, *v.* blame; accuse; censure
cul·ti·va·ble, *a.* arable; cultivable
cul·ti·var, *v.* cultivate; farm; culture
cul·ti·vo, *m.* cultivation
cul·to, *m.* cult; worship
cul·tu·ra, *f.* culture
cul·tu·ral, *a.* cultural
cum·bre, *f.* top; peak; crown
cum·plea·ños, *m.* birthday
cum·pli·do, *m.* compliment. *a.* complete
cum·pli·men·tar, *v.* compliment
cum·pli·mien·to, *m.* fulfillment; fulfilment
cum·plir, *v.* comply with; accomplish; discharge; fulfill; serve; observe
cu·na, *f.* cradle; bassinet
cu·ña·da, *f.* sister-in-law
cu·ña·do, *m.* brother-in-law
cu·ñe·te, *m.* keg
cuo·ta, *f.* quota
cu·po, *m.* quota; allocation
cu·pón, *m.* coupon
cú·pu·la, *f.* dome
cu·ra, *m.* priest. *f.* cure
cu·ran·de·ro, *m.* quack
cu·rar(se), *v.* cure; heal; treat; recover
cu·rio·si·dad, *f.* curiosity
cu·rio·so, *a.* curious; inquisitive; *inf.* nosy
cur·si, *a.* cheap; vulgar
cur·si·llo, *m.* short course
cur·so, *m.* course
cur·tir(se), *v.* tan; coarsen
cur·va, *f.* curve; bend; crook
cus·to·dia, *f.* custody; keeping
cus·to·dio, *m.* custodian; caretaker
cu·tí·cu·la, *f.* cuticle
cu·tis, *m.*, *f.* skin
cu·yo, *a.* whose

CH

cha·cal, *m.* jackal
chal, *m.* shawl
cha·le·co, *m.* vest
cha·let, *m.* chalet
cham·pán, cham·pa·ña, *m.* champagne
cham·pi·ñón, *m.* mushroom
cham·pú, *m.* shampoo
cha·mus·car, *v.* singe; scorch
chan·clo, *m.* overshoe; *pl.* galoshes; rubbers
chan·ta·je, *m.* blackmail
chan·za, *f.* jest; joke
cha·pa, *f.* veneer; plate
cha·pi·tel, *m.* spire
cha·po·tear, *v.* splash
cha·pu·cear, *v.* bungle
cha·pu·ce·ro, *m.* bungler. *a.* shoddy
cha·pu·rreo, *m.* jabber
cha·pu·zar(se), *v.* duck
cha·que·ta, *f.* jacket
cha·ra·da, *f.* charade
char·ca, *f.* pond
char·co, *m.* puddle
char·la, *f.* chat; talk; gossip
char·lar, *v.* chat; talk; gossip; *inf.* jaw
char·la·tán, *m.* charlatan; quack
cha·rro, *a.* flashy; tawdry; ill-bred
cha·sis, *m.* chassis
chas·quear, *v.* snap; click
chas·to, *a.* snub-nosed; squat
che·que, *m.* check
chi·ca, *f.* girl; lass
chi·co, *m.* boy; lad. *a.* small
chi·fla·do, *a.* cranky. *m.* *inf.* crank
chi·le, *m.* chili, chilie, chile
chi·llar, *v.* shriek; screech; scream
chi·llón, *a.* gaudy; shrill
chi·me·nea, *f.* chimney
chim·pan·cé, *m.* chimpanzee; chimp
chi·na, *f.* china; (*cap.*) China
chin·chi·lla, *f.* chinchilla
chi·qui·tín, *a.* tiny
chi·ri·pa, *f.* fluke
chi·rriar, *v.* chirp; squeak
chi·rri·do, *m.* squeak
chis·me, *m.* gossip
chis·pa, *f.* spark; drop
chis·po·rro·tear, *v.* sizzle; hiss; sputter
chis·te·ra, *f.* top hat
chis·to·so, *a.* facetious; funny
cho·car, *v.* collide; hit; bump; knock; clash; conflict
cho·co·la·te, *m.* chocolate; cocoa
cho·chez, *f.* dotage

chó·fer, *m.* chauffeur
cho·que, *m.* collision; crash; clash; shock
cho·rrear, *v.* spout; jet; gush
cho·rro, *m.* spout; spurt; jet
cho·za, *f.* shack; shanty
chu·bas·co, *m.* shower
chu·che·ría, *f.* bauble; knickknack
chu·le·ta, *f.* cutlet; chop
chu·par(se), *v.* suck; sip
chu·pe·chup, *m.* *inf.* lolipop, lollypop
chus·ca·da, *f.* drollery

D

da·do, *m.* die; *pl.* dice
da·ma, *f.* lady. da·ma de ho·nor, bridesmaid
dan·za, *f.* dance
da·ñar(se), *v.* hurt (oneself); damage; harm
da·ño, *m.* injury; damage
dar(se), *v.* give; bestow; allow. dar·se cuen·ta de, realize. dar·se pri·sa, hurry
dá·til, *m.* date
de, *prep.* from; of; with; to. *conj.* than
de·ba·jo, *adv.* under; underneath
de·ba·tir, *v.* debate
de·be, *m.* debit
de·ber, *aux.* *v.* ought; must. *m.* duty
de·bi·do, *a.* due
dé·bil, *a.* weak; dim; feeble
de·bi·li·dad, *f.* weakness
de·bi·li·tar(se), *v.* weaken
de·bu·tan·te, *f.* debutante
de·ca·den·cia, *f.* decadence; decline
de·ca·den·te, *a.* decadent
de·caer, *v.* decay; ebb
de·ca·no, *m.* dean
de·ca·pi·tar, *v.* behead
de·cen·cia, *f.* decency
de·ce·nio, *m.* decade
de·cen·te, *a.* decent; proper
de·ci·da·men·te, *adv.* decidedly
de·ci·dir, *v.* decide; resolve
de·ci·mal, *a.* decimal. *m.* decimal
de·ci·mo·cuar·to, *a.* fourteenth
de·ci·mo·quin·to, *a.* fifteenth
de·cir, *v.* say; state; speak; tell; mean
de·ci·sión, *f.* decision
de·ci·si·vo, *a.* decisive; crucial
de·cla·ra·ción, *f.* declaration
de·cla·rar(se), *v.* declare; propose; allege; pronounce
de·cli·nar, *v.* decline
de·cli·ve, *m.* slope; drop
de·co·ra·ción, *f.* decoration
de·co·ra·dor, *m.*, de·co·ra·do·ra, *f.* decorator
de·co·ro, *m.* propriety
de·cré·pi·to, *a.* decrepit
de·cre·tar, *v.* decree; enact
de·cre·to, *m.* decree
de·dal, *m.* thimble
de·di·car(se), *v.* devote
de·do, *m.* finger; digit. de·do del pie, toe
de·du·cir, *v.* deduce
de·fa·mar, *v.* defame
de·fec·ción, *f.* defection
de·fec·to, *m.* defect; fault; shortcoming
de·fen·der, *v.* defend; uphold; plead; contest
de·fen·sa, *f.* defense, defence; plea
de·fen·si·vo, *a.* defensive
de·fen·so, *m.* advocate
de·fen·sor, *m.* supporter
de·fe·ren·cia, *f.* deference
de·fi·cien·cia, *f.* deficiency; shortage
de·fi·cien·te, *a.* wanting
dé·fi·cit, *m.* deficit
de·fi·ni·do, *a.* definite
de·fi·nir, *v.* define
de·fi·ni·ti·vo, *a.* definitive
de·for·mar(se), *v.* deform; loose shape
de·for·mi·dad, *f.* deformity
de·frau·dar, *v.* defraud; cheat
de·ge·ne·rar, *v.* degenerate
de·gra·da·ción, *f.* degradation
de·gra·dar(se), *v.* degrade; demean; evolve
dei·dad, *f.* deity
de·jar, *v.* let; quit; leave; lay. de·jar de, cease
de·lan·tal, *m.* apron
de·lan·te, *adv.* before; ahead. de·lan·te de, before
de·lan·te·ro, *a.* front; forward
de·le·ga·do, *m.* delegate
de·le·gar, *v.* delegate
de·lei·ta·ble, *a.* delectable
de·lei·tar(se), *v.* delight
de·lei·te, *m.* joy
de·le·trear, *v.* spell
del·ga·do, *a.* slender; slim; thin
de·li·be·rar, *v.* deliberate
de·li·ca·de·za, *f.* delicacy; sensitivity
de·li·ca·do, *a.* delicate; sensitive; dainty; ticklish
de·li·cio·so, *a.* delicious
de·lin·cuen·cia, *f.* delinquency
de·lin·cuen·te, *a.* delinquent. *m.*, *f.* delinquent
de·li·near, *v.* delineate
de·li·ran·te, *a.* delirious
de·li·rar, *v.* rave
de·li·rio, *m.* delirium
de·li·to, *m.* misdemeanor
del·ta, *f.* delta
de·ma·cra·ción, *f.* emaciation
de·ma·go·gis·mo, *m.* demagoguery
de·ma·go·go, *m.* demagogue, demagog

de·man·da, *f.* claim; challenge
de·man·dan·te, *m.*, *f.* claimant
de·man·dar, *v.* demand; sue
de·más, *a.* other. *adv.* too
de·men·te, *a.* demented
de·mé·ri·to, *m.* demerit
de·mo·cra·cia, *f.* democracy
de·mó·cra·ta, *m.*, *f.* democrat
de·mo·crá·ti·co, *a.* democratic
de·mo·ler, *v.* demolish
de·mo·nio, *m.* demon; devil; fiend
de·mo·rar(se), *v.* delay
de·mos·tra·ción, *f.* demonstration
de·mos·trar, *v.* demonstrate; display
de·no·mi·na·ción, *f.* denomination
de·no·mi·na·dor, *m.* denominator
de·no·tar, *v.* denote
den·si·dad, *f.* density
den·so, *a.* dense; thick; close
den·tis·ta·du·ra, *f.* dentist
den·tis·ta, *m.*, *f.* dentist
den·tro, *adv.* within; inside; within; in; indoors. den·tro de, inside
de·nun·cia, *f.* denunciation
de·nun·ciar, *v.* denounce
de·par·ta·men·to, *m.* department; office
de·pen·den·cia, *f.* dependence; dependency
de·pen·der, *v.* depend
de·pen·dien·te, *m.*, *f.* dependent, dependant. *a.* subordinate
de·plo·ra·ble, *a.* deplorable
de·po·ner, *v.* depose
de·por·ta·ción, *f.* deportation
de·por·tar, *v.* deport
de·por·te, *m.* sport
de·por·tis·ta, *m.*, *f.* sportsman; sportswoman
de·po·si·tar, *v.* deposit; bank
de·pó·si·to, *m.* deposit; depot; vat. de·pó·si·to de ca·dá·ve·res, morgue
de·pra·va·ción, *f.* depravity
de·pra·var, *v.* deprave
de·pre·cia·ción, *f.* depreciation
de·pre·sión, *f.* depression; slump
de·pri·mi·do, *a.* depressed
de·pri·mir, *v.* depress
de·re·cho, *a.* standing; straightforward; upright; right. m. law; due; right. de·re·cho de au·tor, royalty
de·ri·va·do, *a.* derivative. m. by-product
de·ri·var(se), *v.* derive; drift
de·rre·tir(se), *v.* melt
de·rri·bar(se), *v.* prostrate; fell; floor
de·rro·ta, *f.* defeat; checkmate
de·rro·tar(se), *v.* rout; ruin
de·rrum·ba·mien·to, *m.* collapse
des·a·co·piar, *v.* disconnect
des·a·cos·tum·bra·do, *a.* unaccustomed
des·a·cre·di·tar, *v.* discredit
des·a·cuer·do, *m.* disagreement; variance
des·a·fiar, *v.* defy; brave
des·a·fío, *m.* defiance; challenge
des·a·gra·da·ble, *a.* disagreeable; unpleasant
des·a·gra·dar, *v.* displease
des·a·gre·ga·ción, *f.* disintegration
des·a·güe, *m.* drain; drainage
des·a·hu·ciar, *v.* evict
des·ai·rar, *v.* snub
des·ai·re, *m.* snub; slight
des·a·len·tar, *v.* dishearten
des·a·lien·to, *m.* discouragement
des·a·li·ño, *a.* squalid
des·am·pa·ra·do, *a.* destitute; underprivileged
des·a·ni·mar(se), *v.* discourage; dismay
des·á·ni·mo, *m.* depression; *pl.* doldrums
des·a·pa·re·cer, *v.* disappear; vanish
des·a·pa·ri·ción, *f.* disappearance
des·a·pro·bar, *v.* disapprove
des·ar·mar, *v.* disarm
des·a·rrai·gar, *v.* uproot; eradicate
des·a·rre·glar(se), *v.* disarrange; derange
des·a·rre·glo, *m.* disorder
des·a·rro·llar(se), *v.* develop; unfold; evolve
des·a·rro·llo, *m.* development
des·a·so·sie·go, *m.* unrest
des·as·tre, *m.* disaster
des·as·tro·so, *a.* disastrous
des·a·tar(se), *v.* loosen; undo
des·a·ten·der, *v.* disregard
des·a·ten·to, *a.* unthinking
des·a·yu·no, *m.* blunder
des·a·yu·nar, *v.* breakfast
des·a·yu·no, *m.* breakfast
des·ba·ra·tar(se), *v.* thwart; spoil
des·ca·li·fi·car(se), *v.* disqualify
des·can·sar, *v.* rest
des·can·so, *m.* rest
des·ca·ra·do, *a.* bold; brazen; insolent; sassy
des·car·gar(se), *v.* discharge; unload; vent
des·ca·ro, *m.* gall; *inf.* nerve
des·car·tar, *v.* discard
des·cas·ca·rar, *v.* shell
des·cen·den·cia, *f.* offspring; origen
des·cen·den·te, *a.* downward
des·cen·der, *v.* descend
des·cen·dien·te, *m.*, *f.* descendant
des·cen·so, *m.* decline; descent
des·ci·frar, *v.* decipher
des·co·lo·rar(se), *v.* fade
des·com·po·ner(se), *v.* decompose; unsettle
des·com·po·si·ción, *f.* decomposition

des·con·cer·tar(se), v. disconcert; embarrass
des·con·fiar, v. distrust
des·co·no·cer, v. disown; disavow
des·co·no·ci·do, a. unknown; strange. m. stranger
des·con·ten·to, m. discontent
des·con·ti·nuar, v. discontinue
des·cor·tés, a. discourteous; impolite
des·co·ser(se), v. rip; come apart
des·cri·bir, v. describe
des·crip·ción, f. description
des·cu·bri·mien·to, m. discovery
des·cu·brir, v. discover; find
des·cuen·to, m. discount; deduction
des·cui·da·do, a. careless; remiss; reckless
des·cui·dar, v. neglect
des·de, prep. from; since. conj. since.
des·de lue·go, certainly
des·dén, m. scorn
des·de·ñar, v. disdain
des·de·ño·so, a. disdainful
des·di·cha, f. unhappiness
des·di·cha·do, a. unlucky; unhappy
des·e·a·ble, a. elegible
des·ear, v. desire; hope; wish; want
des·e·char, v. reject
des·em·bo·car, v. land
des·em·bol·sar, v. disburse
des·en·can·tar, v. disenchant
des·en·cor·var, v. unbend
des·en·chu·fa·do, a. off
des·en·fre·na·do, a. unbridled; rampant; wanton
des·en·la·ce, m. end; ending
des·en·mas·ca·rar, v. unmask
des·en·re·dar(se), v. unravel; unsnarl; extricate
des·en·ro·llar(se), v. unroll
des·eo, m. wish; craving; inf. yen
des·e·qui·li·bra·do, a. unbalanced
de·ser·tar, v. defect
de·ser·tor, m. deserter
des·es·pe·ra·ción, f. desperation
des·es·pe·rar, v. despair
des·fal·car, v. embezzle
des·fi·gu·rar, v. disfigure; blemish; deface
des·fi·lar, v. march
des·fi·le, m. parade
des·ga·rrar(se), v. tear
des·gas·tar(se), v. wear; weather
des·gas·te, m. wear; waste
des·gra·cia, f. trial; misfortune
des·gra·cia·do, a. unlucky; miserable. m. unfortunate
des·ha·cer(se), v. undo; unwrap
des·ha·rra·pa·do, a. seedy
des·he·lar(se), v. thaw
des·he·re·dar, v. disinherit
des·hi·dra·ta·ción, f. dehydration
des·hi·dra·tar, v. dehydrate
des·hi·la·char(se), v. fray
des·hi·lar(se), v. ravel
des·hon·ra, f. dishonor; disgrace
des·hon·rar, v. dishonor; disgrace; shame
de·sier·to, m. desert
des·i·gual, a. uneven; irregular
des·i·lu·sio·nar(se), v. disillusion
des·in·fec·tan·te, m. disinfectant
des·in·flar, v. deflate
des·in·te·rés, m. disinterest
de·sis·tir, v. desist
des·leal, a. disloyal
des·li·zar(se), v. slide; glide; slip
des·lo·car·se, v. dislocate
des·lu·ci·do, a. dingy
des·lum·bra·mien·to, m. daze
des·lum·brar, v. dazzle; blind
des·lus·trar(se), v. tarnish; dull
des·lus·tre, m. tarnish
des·ma·yar·se, v. faint; swoon
des·ma·yo, m. faint
des·mi·ga·jar(se), v. crumble
des·mon·tar(se), v. dismantle
des·mo·ra·li·zar, v. demoralize
des·mo·ro·na·do, a. dilapidated
des·na·tar, v. skim
des·nu·dez, f. nudity
des·nu·do, a. naked; nude; bare
des·nu·tri·ción, f. malnutrition
des·o·be·de·cer, v. disobey
des·o·be·dien·cia, f. disobedience
des·o·cu·pa·do, a. empty; free
des·o·do·ran·te, m. deodorant
des·o·do·ri·zar, v. deodorize
des·o·la·ción, f. desolation
des·or·den, m. disorder; mess
des·or·de·nar, v. mess up
des·or·ga·ni·zar, v. disrupt
des·pa·bi·la·do, a. wide-awake
des·pa·cio, adv. slowly
des·pa·char, v. dispatch; speed
des·pe·di·da, a. parting. f. farewell
des·pe·dir(se), v. say goodbye; discharge; fire
des·pe·gue, m. takeoff
des·pei·na·do, a. unkempt
des·pen·sa, f. pantry; larder
des·per·di·ciar, v. squander; waste; trifle
des·per·tar(se), v. wake up; awaken; arouse; rouse
des·pia·da·do, a. pitiless
des·pier·to, a. awake
des·pis·tar, v. mislead
des·plan·ta·dor, m. trowel
des·ple·gar(se), v. unfold
des·po·jar(se), v. despoil; strip
des·po·sar(se), v. get engaged; marry
dés·po·ta, m. despot
des·po·tis·mo, m. despotism
des·pre·cia·ble, a. despicable; vile; worthless
des·pre·ciar(se), v. despise; scorn

des·pro·vis·to, a. devoid of
des·pués, adv. later; after. prep. since
des·te·llar, v. sparkle; glint
des·te·rra·do, m. exile
des·te·rrar, v. exile; banish
des·te·tar(se), v. wean
des·ti·lar, v. distill
des·ti·le·ría, f. distillery
des·ti·no, m. destiny; fate; destination
des·tre·za, f. skill; dexterity; workmanship
des·tri·par, v. gut
des·truc·ción, f. destruction
des·truir, v. destroy
des·u·nir, v. disunite
des·va·lo·ri·zar, v. devaluate
des·ván, m. attic; loft
des·va·ne·cer(se), v. vanish
des·ven·ta·ja, f. disadvantage; drawback; handicap
des·ver·gon·za·do, a. shameless; unabashed
des·viar(se), v. deviate; divert; deflect; wander
de·ta·lla·do, a. detailed; elaborate
de·ta·llar, v. detail; itemize
de·ta·lle, m. detail
de·tec·ti·ve, m., f. detective; sleuth
de·te·ner(se), v. detain; arrest
de·ten·te, f. détente
de·ter·gen·te, a. detergent. m. detergent
de·te·rio·rar(se), v. deteriorate; decay
de·ter·mi·na·ción, f. determination
de·ter·mi·nar, v. determine; decide
de·tes·tar, v. detest; hate
de·trás, adv. behind; aback. de·trás de, after
deu·da, f. debt
deu·dor, m. deu·do·ra, f. debtor
de·va·lua·ción, f. devaluation
de·va·nar, v. wind
de·vas·ta·ción, f. devastation
de·vas·tar, v. devastate
de·vo·ción, f. devotion
de·vol·ver, v. return; refund; restore
de·vo·rar, v. devour
de·vo·to, a. devout
día, m. day; daytime. ca·da día, daily. día de fies·ta, holiday
dia·be·tes, f. diabetes
dia·bé·ti·co, a. diabetic
dia·blo, m. devil
dia·bó·li·co, a. diabolic(al); devilish
diá·co·no, m. deacon
dia·frag·ma, m. diaphragm
diag·nos·ti·car, v. diagnose
diag·nós·ti·co, m. diagnosis
dia·go·nal, a. diagonal. m. diagonal
dia·gra·ma, m. diagram
dia·lec·to, m. dialect
dia·man·te, m. diamond
diá·me·tro, m. diameter
dia·po·si·ti·va, f. slide
dia·rio, a. daily. m. daily; journal
dia·rrea, f. diarrhea
dia·tri·ba, f. tirade
di·bu·jan·te, m. designer; cartoonist
di·bu·jar, v. draw; sketch
di·bu·jo, m. drawing; cartoon
dic·cio·na·rio, m. dictionary. dic·cio·na·rio geo·grá·fi·co, gazetteer
di·ciem·bre, m. December
dic·ta·do, m. dictation
dic·ta·dor, m. dictator
dic·tar, v. dictate
di·cho, m. saying
die·ci·nue·ve, a. nineteen
die·cio·cho, a. eighteen
die·ci·séis, a. sixteen
die·ci·sie·te, a. seventeen
dien·te, m. tooth
dies·tro, a. dexterous; adroit
die·té·ti·co, a. dietary
diez, a. ten
diez·mo, m. tithe
di·fa·ma·ción, f. defamation; libel
di·fe·ren·cia, f. difference
di·fe·ren·ciar(se), v. differ
di·fe·ren·te, a. different
di·fe·rir, v. defer
di·fí·cil, a. difficult; hard; trying
di·fi·cul·tad, f. difficulty
dif·te·ria, f. diphtheria
di·fun·dir(se), v. diffuse
di·fun·to, a. deceased
di·fu·sión, f. diffusion
di·fu·so, a. diffuse; widespread
di·ge·rir, v. digest
di·ges·tión, f. digestion
di·ges·to, m. digest
dí·gi·to, m. digit
dig·nar·se, v. deign; condescend
dig·ni·dad, f. dignity
dig·no, a. worthy
di·gre·sión, f. digression
di·la·tar(se), v. dilate; procrastinate
di·le·ma, m. dilemma
di·li·gen·cia, f. diligence
di·li·gen·te, a. diligent
di·lu·ción, f. dilution
di·luir, v. dilute
di·lu·viar, v. pour
di·lu·vio, m. deluge; flood
di·men·sión, f. dimension
di·mi·nu·to, a. diminutive
di·na·mi·ta, f. dynamite
di·na·mo, m. di·na·mo, f. dynamo
di·nas·tía, f. dynasty
di·ne·ro, m. money. di·ne·ro con·tan·te, cash
di·no·sau·rio, m. dinosaur

dió·ce·sis, f. diocese
dios, m. god; (cap.) God; Lord
dio·sa, f. goddess
di·plo·ma, m. diploma
di·plo·ma·cia, f. diplomacy
di·plo·má·ti·co, a. diplomatic. m. diplomat
dip·ton·go, m. diphthong
di·pu·ta·ción, f. delegation
di·que, m. dike
di·rec·ción, f. direction; address; control
di·rec·ta·men·te, adv. directly; straight
di·rec·to, a. direct; straight
di·rec·tor, m. di·rec·to·ra, f. director; conductor
di·ri·gir(se), v. direct; lead; control; send; operate
dis·cer·ni·mien·to, m. discernment; discrimination
dis·cer·nir, v. discern
dis·ci·pli·na, f. discipline
dis·ci·pli·nar, v. discipline
dis·cí·pu·lo, m. disciple
dis·co, m. disc, disk; dial; record
dis·cor·dia, f. discord
dis·cre·ción, f. discretion
dis·cre·pan·cia, f. discrepancy
dis·cre·par, v. differ; disagree
dis·cre·to, a. discreet
dis·cri·mi·na·ción, f. discrimination
dis·cul·pa, f. apology; excuse
dis·cul·par, v. excuse
dis·cur·so, m. speech
dis·cu·sión, f. discussion
dis·cu·tir, v. discuss; argue
di·se·car, v. dissect
di·se·mi·nar, v. spread
di·sen·sión, f. dissension
di·sen·te·ría, f. dysentery
di·se·ñar, v. design
dis·fraz, m. disguise; costume; mask
dis·fra·zar, v. disguise
dis·fru·tar, v. enjoy
dis·gre·gar(se), v. disintegrate
dis·gus·tar(se), v. disgust; annoy
dis·gus·to, m. displeasure
di·si·den·cia, f. nonconformity
di·si·mu·la·do, a. sly
di·si·par(se), v. dissipate
dis·lo·ca·ción, f. dislocation
dis·mi·nuir(se), v. diminish; decrease; abate; dwindle
di·so·lu·to, a. loose
di·sol·ver(se), v. dissolve
di·so·nan·cia, f. dissonance
dis·pa·rar(se), v. fire; go off
dis·pa·ri·dad, f. disparity
dis·pen·sa, f. dispensation
dis·per·sar(se), v. disperse; dispel
dis·po·ner(se), v. dispose; prepare
dis·po·ni·ble, a. available
dis·po·si·ción, f. layout; temperament
dis·pues·to, a. ready; willing
dis·pu·ta, f. argument; dispute
dis·pu·tar, v. dispute; quarrel
dis·tan·cia, f. distance
dis·tan·te, a. distant
dis·tin·ción, f. distinction
dis·tin·gui·ble, a. distinguishable
dis·tin·guir, v. distinguish
dis·tin·to, a. distinct; separate
dis·trac·ción, f. distraction
dis·tra·er(se), v. distract; beguile
dis·traí·do, a. distracted
dis·tri·bu·ción, f. distribution
dis·tri·buir, v. distribute; issue
dis·tri·to, m. district
dis·tur·bio, m. disturbance; trouble
di·sua·dir, v. dissuade; deter
di·ver·gen·cia, f. divergence; deviation
di·ver·gir, v. diverge
di·ver·si·dad, f. diversity
di·ver·sión, f. diversion; amusement
di·ver·so, a. diverse; varied; pl. several; sundry
di·ver·ti·do, a. merry
di·ver·tir(se), v. amuse oneself
di·vi·den·do, m. dividend
di·vi·dir(se), v. divide; portion; split
di·vi·ni·dad, f. divinity
di·vi·no, a. divine
di·vi·sa, f. badge
di·vi·sar, v. espy
di·vi·sión, f. division; split; section
di·vor·ciar(se), v. divorce; get divorced
di·vor·cio, m. divorce
di·vul·gar(se), v. divulge; circulate; blab
do·bla·di·llar, v. hem
do·blar(se), v. double; fold; bend; crease. m. turn
do·ble, a. double. m. double
do·ce, a. twelve
do·ce·na, f. dozen
dó·cil, a. docile; meek
doc·to, a. learned
doc·tor, m. doc·to·ra, f. doctor
doc·tri·na, f. doctrine
doc·tri·nar, v. indoctrinate
dog·ma, m. dogma; tenet
dog·má·ti·co, a. dogmatic
dó·lar, m. dollar
do·len·cia, f. ailment
do·ler(se), v. hurt; pain; ache; grieve
do·lor, m. pain; ache; distress
do·lo·ri·do, a. sore
do·mes·ti·ca·do, a. tame
do·mes·ti·car(se), v. domesticate
do·més·ti·co, a. domestic
do·mi·ci·lio, m. abode
do·mi·na·ción, f. domination
do·mi·nar(se), v. dominate; master

do·min·go, m. Sunday
do·mi·nio, m. domain; dominion
don, m. gift
do·nan·te, m., f. donor
do·nar, v. donate
don·ce·lla, f. maiden; maid
don·de, adv. where
dón·de, adv. where?
don·de·quie·ra, adv. anywhere
do·rar, v. gild
dor·mir(se), v. sleep
dor·mi·tar, v. nap; doze; snooze
dor·mi·to·rio, m. dormitory
dos, a. two. m. two
do·sis, f. dose. do·sis ex·ce·si·va, overdose
do·tar, v. endow
dra·gar, v. dredge
dra·gón, m. dragon
dra·ma, m. drama
dra·má·ti·co, a. dramatic
dra·ma·ti·zar, v. dramatize
dra·ma·tur·go, m. playwright; dramatist
drás·ti·co, a. drastic
dre·na·je, m. drainage
dro·ga, f. drug
dual, a. dual
du·ca·do, m. dukedom
du·cha, f. shower
du·char·se, v. shower
du·da, f. doubt
du·dar, v. doubt; query
du·do·so, a. doubtful; dubious
due·lo, m. duel
duen·de, m. bogy, bogey; elf
due·ña, f. owner; duenna
due·ño, m. master; proprietor
duer·me·ve·la, f. catnap
dul·ce, a. sweet. m. candy; pl. sweets
du·na, f. dune
dúo, m. duet
duo·dé·ci·mo, a. twelfth
du·pli·ca·ción, f. duplication
du·pli·car(se), v. duplicate
du·pli·ci·dad, f. duplicity
du·que, m. duke
du·que·sa, f. duchess
du·ra·ción, f. duration; standing
du·ra·de·ro, a. lasting; durable
du·ran·te, prep. during; in
du·rar, v. endure; last
du·re·za, f. hardness
du·ro, a. hard; stern; stiff; severe; tough

E

é·ba·no, m. ebony
e·cle·siás·ti·co, a. ecclesiastic. m. ecclesiastic; minister
e·clip·se, m. eclipse
e·co, m. echo
e·co·lo·gía, f. ecology
e·co·ló·gi·co, a. ecologic
e·có·lo·go, m. ecologist
e·co·no·mía, f. economy; thrift; pl. economics
e·co·no·mis·ta, m., f. economist
e·co·no·mi·zar, v. economize
e·cua·ción, f. equation
e·cua·dor, m. equator
e·cua·ni·mi·dad, f. equanimity
e·cu·mé·ni·co, a. ecumenical
ec·ze·ma, ec·ce·ma, m. eczema
e·cha·da, f. throw; toss
e·char(se), v. toss; throw; eject; cast; lie
e·dad, f. age
e·di·ción, f. edition; issue
e·dic·to, m. edict
e·di·fi·ca·ción, f. edification
e·di·fi·car, v. edify
e·di·fi·cio, m. edifice
e·di·tar, v. edit
e·di·tor, m. editor; publisher
e·di·to·ria·lis·ta, m., f. editorialist
e·du·ca·ción, f. education
e·du·car, v. educate
e·fec·to, m. effect; pl. goods
e·fec·tuar, v. accomplish; contrive
e·fi·caz, a. effective
e·fi·me·ro, a. ephemeral
e·go·cén·tri·co, a. self-centered
e·goís·ta, m., f. egoist
e·je, m. axle; axis; shaft
e·je·cu·ción, f. execution
e·je·cu·tar, v. execute
e·je·cu·ti·vo, a. executive
e·jem·plar, a. exemplary
e·jem·plo, m. example; sample
e·jer·cer, v. exert; exercise; practice
e·jer·ci·cio, m. exercise; drill
e·jér·ci·to, m. army
el, def. art. m. pl. los. the
él, pron. m. he; (neuter) it
e·la·bo·ra·ción, f. elaboration
e·la·bo·rar, v. elaborate
e·lás·ti·co, a. elastic
e·lec·ción, f. election
e·lec·to, a. elect
e·lec·to·ral, m. precinct
e·lec·tri·ci·dad, f. electricity
e·lec·tri·cis·ta, m., f. electrician
e·lec·tro·cu·tar, v. electrocute
e·lec·tro·do, m. electrode
e·lec·trón, m. electron
e·lec·tró·ni·ca, f. electronics
e·le·fan·te, m. elephant
e·le·gan·cia, f. elegance; grace
e·le·gan·te, a. elegant; chic; smart
e·le·gía, f. elegy; lament
e·le·gi·ble, a. eligible
e·le·gi·do, a. elect; chosen
e·le·gir, v. pick; choose; select; elect
e·le·men·to, m. element
e·le·va·ción, f. elevation
e·le·va·do, a. high; lofty; overhead;
stately
e·le·var(se), v. raise; elevate; lift; heighten
e·li·mi·nar, v. eliminate
e·lip·se, f. ellipse
e·líp·ti·co, a. elliptical
e·li·xir, m. elixir
e·lo·cu·ción, f. elocution
e·lo·cuen·cia, f. eloquence
e·lo·giar, v. eulogize
e·lo·gio, m. eulogy
e·lu·ci·dar, v. elucidate
e·lu·di·ble, a. avoidable
e·lu·dir, v. elude
e·lla, pron. f. she; (neuter) it. e·lla mis·ma, herself
e·llas, pron. f. pl. they; them
e·llo, neuter pron. it
e·llos, pron. m. pl. they; them
e·ma·nar, v. emanate
e·man·ci·pa·ción, f. emancipation
e·man·ci·par(se), v. emancipate
em·ba·ja·da, f. embassy
em·ba·ja·dor, m. ambassador
em·ba·lar, v. bale
em·bal·sa·mar, v. embalm
em·ba·ra·za·da, a. pregnant
em·ba·ra·zo, m. pregnancy
em·bar·ca·de·ro, m. pier
em·bar·car(se), v. embark
em·bar·go, m. embargo. sin em·bar·go, nevertheless
em·bau·car, v. fool; dupe
em·be·lle·cer, v. embellish
em·ble·ma, m. emblem
em·bo·rra·char(se), v. get drunk
em·bos·ca·da, f. ambush
em·bo·ta·do, a. blunt; dull
em·bo·tar, v. blunt; dull
em·bo·te·lla·dor, m. bottler
em·bo·te·llar, v. bottle
em·bra·gue, m. clutch
em·brear, v. tar
em·bria·gar(se), v. intoxicate
em·bria·guez, f. drunkenness
em·brión, m. embryo
em·bro·llo, m. muddle
em·bru·te·cer(se), v. brutalize
em·bu·do, m. funnel
em·bus·te, m. lie; inf. story
em·bu·ti·do, m. sausage
e·mi·gran·te, m., f. emigrant
e·mi·grar, v. emigrate
e·mi·nen·cia, f. eminence
e·mi·nen·te, a. eminent
e·mi·sa·rio, m. emissary
e·mi·sión, f. emission; issue; broadcast
e·mi·tir, v. emit; issue
e·mo·ción, f. emotion; feeling; excitement
e·mo·cio·nar(se), v. thrill
em·pa·car, v. bale
em·pa·cho, m. surfeit
em·pa·la·gar, v. cloy
em·pa·ñar(se), v. film over; steam; swaddle
em·pa·pa·do, a. sodden; soggy
em·pa·par(se), v. soak; drench
em·pa·que·tar, v. package
em·pa·ren·ta·do, a. related; kindred
em·pas·te, m. filling
em·pa·tar, v. tie
em·pa·te, m. tie; draw
em·pe·drar, v. pave
em·pei·ne, m. instep
em·pe·ñar, v. pledge; pawn
em·peo·rar(se), v. worsen
em·pe·ra·dor, m. emperor
em·pe·ra·triz, f. empress
em·per·nar, v. bolt
em·pe·zar, v. begin; start
em·plea·do, m. employee
em·plear(se), v. employ; use
em·pleo, m. work; employment; use
em·po·bre·cer(se), v. impoverish
em·po·llar, v. hatch; brood
em·pren·der, v. undertake
em·pre·sa, f. business; enterprise; undertaking
em·prés·ti·to, m. loan
em·pu·jar, v. push; poke; shove; thrust
em·pu·je, m. push; thrust
e·mu·lar, v. emulate
e·mul·sión, f. emulsion
en, prep. in; into; within; at; on; onto
e·na·je·nar, v. alienate
e·na·mo·rar(se), v. enamor; fall in love
e·na·no, m. dwarf; midget
en·ca·be·za·mien·to, m. caption
en·ca·de·nar, v. chain; shackle
en·ca·jar(se), v. encase; foist
en·ca·jo·nar, v. box; case
en·can·ta·do, a. delighted; winning
en·can·ta·dor, a. enchanting; delightful
en·can·tar, v. enchant; charm; bewitch
en·can·to, m. enchantment; charm; captivation
en·ca·rar(se), v. face
en·car·ce·lar, v. jail
en·car·go, m. commission; order
en·car·go, m. task
en·car·na·ción, f. incarnation
en·cen·der(se), v. light; ignite; kindle
en·ce·rrar(se), v. enclose; confine; encase
en·cía, f. gum
en·ci·clo·pe·dia, f. encyclopedia
en·cie·rro, m. custody; constraint
en·ci·ma, adv. above; atop; overhead. en·ci·ma de, upon; over
en·cin·ta, a. pregnant
en·claus·trar, v. cloister
en·co·ger(se), v. shrink. en·co·ger·se

de hom·bros, shrug
en·co·lar, v. glue
en·co·le·ri·zar(se), v. incense; anger
en·co·men·dar(se), v. commend
en·co·mio, m. commendation
en·co·nar·se, v. fester
en·con·trar(se), v. encounter; meet; find; discover
en·cor·va·do, a. bent; crooked
en·cor·var(se), v. curve; bend
en·cru·ci·ja·da, f. crossroads
en·cua·der·nar, v. bind
en·cu·brir, v. cloak; hide; inf. whitewash
en·cuen·tro, m. encounter; meeting
en·cur·ti·do, m. pickle
en·chu·fe, m. plug; socket
en·de·cha, f. dirge
en·de·re·zar(se), v. straighten
en·dia·blar, v. bedevil
en·do·sar, v. endorse
en·do·so, m. endorsement
en·dul·zar, v. sweeten
en·du·re·cer(se), v. harden; toughen; cake
e·nel·do, m. drill
e·ne·mi·go, m. enemy; foe
e·ne·mis·tad, f. enmity
e·ner·gía, f. energy; spirit; drive
e·ne·ro, m. January
en·fa·da·do, a. angry; mad
én·fa·sis, m. emphasis; stress
en·fá·ti·co, a. emphatic
en·fer·me·dad, f. illness
en·fer·me·ra, f. nurse
en·fer·me·ría, f. infirmary
en·fer·mi·zo, a. unhealthy
en·fer·mo, a. sick; ill
en·fla·que·cer(se), v. emaciate
en·fo·car(se), v. focus
en·fre·nar, v. bridle
en·friar(se), v. chill; cool
en·fu·re·cer(se), v. enrage; anger
en·gan·char(se), v. catch; hook
en·ga·ñar(se), v. deceive; trick; fool; hoax
en·ga·ño, m. trick; deceit
en·gas·te, m. setting
en·ga·tu·sar, v. wheedle; blandish; coax
en·gen·drar, v. father; breed
en·go·mar, v. gum
en·gor·dar, v. fatten
en·gra·sar, v. grease
en·gu·llir, v. gobble; guzzle
en·he·brar, v. thread
e·nig·ma, m. enigma
e·nig·má·ti·co, a. enigmatic(al)
en·ja·bo·nar, v. soap
en·jam·brar, v. swarm
en·jau·lar, v. cage
en·jua·gar, v. rinse out
en·ju·gar, v. wipe dry
en·la·ce, m. liaison; link
en·la·zar(se), v. link
en·ne·gre·cer(se), v. blacken
en·no·ble·cer, v. ennoble
e·no·ja·do, a. inf. sore
e·no·jar(se), v. anger; vex
e·nor·me, a. enormous; huge
en·ra·ma·da, f. bower
en·re·dar(se), v. tangle; mesh; involve
en·re·do, m. intricacy; jam
en·re·ja·do, m. trellis
en·ri·que·cer(se), v. enrich; prosper
en·ros·car(se), v. twist; twine
en·sa·la·da, f. salad. en·sa·la·da de col, coleslaw
en·san·char(se), v. widen
en·san·gren·tar, v. bloody
en·sar·tar, v. string
en·sa·yar(se), v. rehearse
en·sa·yis·ta, m., f. essayist
en·sa·yo, m. essay; theme; test
en·se·na·da, f. inlet
en·se·ñan·za, f. teaching; tuition
en·se·ñar, v. teach; instruct; show
en·se·res, m. pl. chattel
en·si·llar, v. saddle
en·si·mis·ma·do, a. withdrawn
en·sor·de·cer, v. deafen
en·su·ciar(se), v. soil
en·sue·ño, m. daydream
en·ta·blar, v. upholster
en·ten·der(se), v. understand; interpret
en·ten·di·mien·to, m. understanding
en·te·ra·do, a. aware
en·te·ra·men·te, adv. entirely
en·te·rar(se), v. learn; acquaint
en·te·ro, a. entire; whole; long
en·te·rrar, v. bury
en·ti·dad, f. entity
en·tie·rro, m. funeral
en·ton·ces, adv. then
en·tra·da, f. entry; entrance; ticket; inlet
en·tram·par, v. trap
en·tra·ñas, f. pl. entrails
en·trar, v. enter. en·trar sin de·re·cho, trespass
en·tre, prep. between; among; amid
en·tre·a·bier·to, a. ajar
en·tre·ga, f. delivery; installment
en·tre·gar(se), v. entrust; give in; deliver
en·tre·pa·ño, m. panel
en·tre·puen·te, m. steerage
en·tre·sue·lo, m. mezzanine
en·tre·te·jer(se), v. intertwine
en·tre·te·ner(se), v. entertain; amuse; dally
en·tre·vis·ta, f. interview
en·tris·te·cer(se), v. sadden
en·tro·me·ter·se, v. meddle

en·tu·sias·mo, m. enthusiasm
e·nu·me·ra·ción, f. enumeration
e·nu·me·rar, v. enumerate
e·nun·ciar, v. enunciate
en·ve·je·cer(se), v. age
en·ve·ne·nar, v. poison
en·via·do, m. envoy
en·viar, v. send; dispatch
en·vi·dia, f. envy; jealousy
en·vi·diar, v. envy
en·vío, m. shipment
en·vol·ver(se), v. envelop; wrap
en·zi·ma, f. enzyme
é·pi·ca, f. epic
e·pi·de·mia, f. epidemic
e·pi·der·mis, f. epidermis
e·pi·lep·sia, f. epilepsy
e·pí·lo·go, m. epilogue, epilog
e·pis·co·pal, a. episcopal
e·pi·so·dio, m. episode
e·pís·to·la, f. epistle
e·pi·ta·fio, m. epitaph
e·pí·te·to, m. epithet
e·pi·to·mar, v. epitomize
é·po·ca, f. epoch; age; period
e·po·pe·ya, f. epic
e·qui·dad, f. equity
e·qui·li·brar(se), v. balance
e·qui·li·brio, a. equilibrium; poise
e·qui·noc·cio, m. equinox
e·qui·pa·je, m. luggage
e·qui·par, v. equip
e·qui·po, m. equipment; team
e·qui·ta·ti·vo, a. equitable
e·qui·va·len·te, a. equivalent
e·qui·vo·car(se), v. mistake; inf. slip-up
e·qui·vo·ca·do, a. wrong
e·qui·vo·car(se), v. mistake; err
e·ra, f. era
e·ri·gir, v. erect
er·mi·ta·ño, m. hermit
e·ro·sión, f. erosion
e·ró·ti·co, a. erotic
e·rran·te, a. errant
e·rrar(se), v. err; miss; wander
e·rrá·ti·co, a. erratic
e·rró·neo, a. wrong; erroneous
e·rror, m. error
e·ruc·tar, v. belch
e·ru·di·ción, f. erudition; scholar-ship
e·ru·di·to, a. erudite. m. scholar
e·rup·ción, f. eruption; rash; out-break
e·sa, a. that; pl. those
é·sa, pron. f. that; that one; pl. those
es·bel·to, a. svelte; slender
es·bo·zo, m. sketch
es·ca·be·char, v. marinate
es·ca·bel, m. hassock
es·ca·bro·so, a. rocky; rugged
es·ca·la, f. ladder; scale
es·ca·lar, v. scale
es·cal·dar(se), v. scald
es·ca·le·ra, f. steps; stairs; staircase; stairway; ladder. es·ca·le·ra de ti·je·ra, stepladder. es·ca·le·ra mó·vil, escalator
es·cal·far, v. poach
es·ca·lo·frío, m. chill
es·ca·lo·nar, v. stagger
es·cal·pe·lo, m. scalpel
es·ca·ma, f. flake; scale
es·can·da·li·zar(se), v. shock
es·ca·par(se), v. escape; flee; leak; slip
es·ca·pe, m. escape; leak
es·ca·ra·ba·jo, m. beetle
es·ca·ra·mu·za, f. skirmish
es·car·cha, f. frost
es·car·nio, m. taunt
es·car·pa·do, a. abrupt; sheer; crag-gy
es·ca·sez, f. shortage
es·ca·so, a. scarce; stingy
es·ca·ti·mar, v. spare; stint
es·ce·na, f. scene; stage; view
es·cép·ti·co, m. skeptic; unbeliever. a. skeptical
es·cla·vi·tud, f. slavery; bondage
es·cla·vi·zar, v. enslave
es·cla·vo, m. slave
es·co·ba, f. broom
es·co·ger, v. choose; pick; opt; select
es·co·gi·do, a. chosen
es·co·lar, a. scholastic
es·col·tar, v. escort
es·co·llo, m. reef
es·com·bro, m. mackerel; pl. debris
es·con·der(se), v. hide; screen
es·con·di·te, m. cache
es·co·pe·ta, f. shotgun
es·co·plear, v. chisel
es·co·ria, f. slag
es·cor·pión, m. scorpion
es·co·ti·lla, f. hatch; hatchway
es·co·ti·llón, m. trap door
es·cri·bir, v. write; correspond
es·cri·tor, m., es·cri·to·ra, f. writer
es·cri·to·rio, m. desk
es·cri·tu·ra, f. writing
es·crú·pu·lo, m. scruple; qualm
es·cru·ti·nio, m. scrutiny
es·cua·dra, f. squad
es·cua·dri·lla, f. squadron
es·cu·char, v. listen to; heed
es·cu·di·lla, f. bowl
es·cu·do, m. shield
es·cu·dri·ñar, v. scrutinize
es·cue·la, f. school
es·cul·pir, v. sculpture; carve
es·cul·tor, m., es·cul·to·ra, f. sculp-tor
es·cul·tu·ra, f. sculpture
es·cu·pir, v. spit
e·se, a. that; pl. e·sos. those

é·se, pron. that; that one; pl. é·sos. those
e·sen·cia, f. essence
e·sen·cial, a. essential; necessary. m. essential
es·fe·ra, f. sphere; field
es·for·zar(se), v. endeavor; strive
es·fuer·zo, m. effort; attempt; strug-gle; exertion
es·gri·ma, f. fencing
es·la·bón, m. link
es·mal·te, m. enamel
es·me·ral·da, f. emerald
es·me·ril, m. emery
es·nob, m. snob
e·so, neuter pron. that
e·só·fa·go, m. esophagus, oeso-phagus; gullet
e·so·té·ri·co, a. esoteric
es·pa·ciar(se), v. space; spread
es·pa·cio, m. space
es·pa·da, f. sword
es·pa·da·chín, m. swashbuckler; swordsman
es·pa·gue·ti, m. spaghetti
es·pal·da, f. back
es·pan·to·so, a. frightful
es·par·cir(se), v. scatter; litter
es·pá·rra·go, m. asparagus
es·pas·mo, m. spasm
es·pas·mó·di·co, a. spasmodic
es·pás·ti·co, a. spastic
es·pá·tu·la, f. spatula
es·pe·cia, f. spice
es·pe·cial, a. special; especial
es·pe·cia·li·dad, f. specialty
es·pe·cia·lis·ta, m. f. specialist
es·pe·cia·li·za·ción, f. specialization
es·pe·cia·li·zar(se), v. specialize; ma-jor in
es·pe·cie, f. spice
es·pe·cie, f. species, pl.; sort
es·pe·ci·fi·ca·ción, f. specification
es·pe·ci·fi·car, v. specify
es·pé·ci·men, m. specimen
es·pec·ta·cu·lar, a. spectacular
es·pec·tá·cu·lo, m. spectacle; pag-eant; show; sight
es·pec·ta·dor, m., es·pec·ta·do·ra, f. spectator; witness
es·pec·tro, m. ghost; specter; inf. spook; spectrum
es·pe·cu·lar, v. speculate
es·pe·jis·mo, m. mirage
es·pe·jo, m. mirror
es·pe·ra, f. wait
es·pe·ran·za, f. expectation; hope
es·pe·rar, v. wait; hope for; expect
es·pe·so, a. thick; bushy
es·pe·tar, v. spit; pierce
es·pía, m., f. spy
es·piar, v. spy; inf. snoop
es·pi·ga, f. spike; ear
es·pi·na, f. thorn; spine
es·pi·na·ca, f. spinach
es·pi·na·zo, m. spine; backbone
es·pi·ni·lla, f. shin
es·pio·na·je, m. espionage
es·pi·ral, f. spiral. a. spiral
es·pi·rar, v. exhale
es·pi·ri·tis·mo, m. spiritualism
es·pi·ri·tis·ta, m. f. spiritualist. se·sión de es·pi·ri·tis·tas, séance
es·pí·ri·tu, m. spirit
es·pi·ta, f. spigot
es·plén·di·do, a. splendid
es·plen·dor, m. splendor
es·plie·go, m. lavender
es·po·le·ta, f. fuse
es·pon·ja, f. sponge
es·pon·jo·so, a. spongy
es·pon·tá·neo, a. spontaneous
es·po·ra, f. spore
es·po·rá·di·co, a. sporadic
es·po·sa, f. wife; pl. handcuffs
es·po·so, m. husband; spouse
es·pue·la, f. spur
es·pu·ma, f. foam; lather; froth
es·que·le·to, m. skeleton; framework
es·quí, m. ski
es·quiar, v. ski
es·qui·na, f. corner
es·qui·var(se), v. shirk; dodge
es·qui·vo, a. elusive
es·qui·zo·fre·nia, f. schizophrenia
es·ta(s), a. f. this; pl. these
es·ta(s), pron. f. this; this one; pl. these
es·ta·bi·li·dad, f. stability
es·ta·ble·cer(se), v. establish; form; settle
es·ta·ble·ci·mien·to, m. establish-ment; recovery
es·ta·blo, m. stable; stall
es·ta·ca, f. stake; peg
es·ta·ca·da, f. stockade
es·ta·car, v. stake out
es·ta·ción, f. season; station; depot
es·ta·dio, m. stadium; furlong
es·ta·dis·ta, m. statesman
es·ta·dís·ti·ca, f. statistics, pl.
es·ta·dís·ti·co, m. statistic; statisti-cian
es·ta·do, m. state; status. es·ta·do de cuen·ta, statement
es·ta·fa, f. swindle; gyp
es·ta·far, v. swindle; defraud; inf. gyp
es·ta·fe·ta, f. courier
es·ta·lac·ti·ta, f. stalactite
es·ta·lag·mi·ta, f. stalagmite
es·ta·llar, v. explode
es·tam·bre, m. stamen; worsted
es·tam·par, v. impress; stamp
es·tam·pi·da, f. stampede
es·tam·pi·do, m. boom
es·tan·car(se), v. stagnate; stem
es·tan·cia, f. stay; stanza; farm

es·tan·co, a. watertight
es·tan·dar·te, m. standard
es·tan·que, m. pond; pool
es·tan·te, m. shelf
es·tar, v. be; lie; be present
es·tar·cir, v. stencil
es·ta·tua, f. statue
es·ta·tuir, v. charter; establish
es·ta·tu·ra, f. height; stature
es·ta·tu·to, m. statute
es·te, a. east. m. east; Orient
es·te(s), a. m. pl. es·tos. these
és·te, pron. this; this one; pl. és·tos, these
es·te·la, f. trail; wash
es·te·pa, f. steppe
es·te·ra, f. mat
es·te·reo·fó·ni·co, a. stereophonic
es·te·reo·ti·pa·do, a. stereotyped
es·té·ril, a. sterile
es·te·ri·li·dad, f. sterility
es·te·ri·li·za·ción, f. sterilization
es·te·ri·li·zar, v. sterilize
es·ter·li·na, a. sterling
es·ter·nón, m. sternum; breastbone
es·te·ta, m., f. aesthete
es·té·ti·co, a. esthetic, aesthetic
es·te·tos·co·pio, m. stethoscope
es·te·va·do, a. bandy-legged
es·ti·ba, f. stowage
es·ti·ba·dor, m. stevedore
es·ti·bar, v. stow
es·tiér·col, m. manure; dung
es·tig·ma, m. stigma
es·ti·le·te, m. stiletto
es·ti·lo, m. style; fashion
es·ti·ma, f. esteem
es·ti·ma·ble, a. estimable
es·ti·ma·ción, f. esteem; value
es·ti·mar(se), v. estimate; value; es-teem
es·ti·mu·lan·te, m. stimulant; stimu-lus
es·ti·mu·lar, v. stimulate; inspire
es·ti·mu·lo, m. stimulation; stimulus
es·ti·pen·dio, m. stipend
es·ti·pu·lar, v. stipulate
es·ti·rar, v. stretch; strain
es·to, neuter pron. this; pl. these
es·to·fa·do, m. stew
es·to·far, v. stew
es·toi·co, m. stoic. a. stoical
es·tó·ma·go, m. stomach
es·tor·bar, v. obstruct; impede; inter-rupt
es·tor·nu·dar, v. sneeze
es·tor·nu·do, m. sneeze
es·tra·bis·mo, m. squint
es·tra·do, m. podium
es·tra·go, m. havoc; ravage
es·tran·gu·la·dor, m. strangler
es·tran·gu·lar, v. strangle; choke
es·tra·ta·ge·ma, f. stratagem; device
es·tra·te·ga, m. strategist
es·tra·te·gia, f. strategy
es·tra·té·gi·co, a. strategic
es·tra·ti·fi·car(se), v. stratify
es·tra·to, m. stratum; layer; bed
es·tra·tos·fe·ra, f. stratosphere
es·tre·char(se), v. narrow; shake
es·tre·cho, a. narrow; parochial. m. strait
es·tre·lla, f. star. es·tre·lla de mar, starfish. es·tre·lla fu·gaz, shooting star
es·tre·llar(se), v. crash; smash
es·tre·me·cer(se), v. shudder; trem-ble; shake
es·tre·me·ci·mien·to, m. shiver
es·tre·no, m. premiere; debut
es·tre·ñi·mien·to, m. constipation
es·tre·ñir(se), v. constipate
es·tré·pi·to, m. racket
es·tría, f. groove
es·tri·bi·llo, m. refrain; chorus
es·tri·bo, m. stirrup
es·tri·bor, m. starboard
es·tric·ni·na, f. strychnine
es·tric·to, a. strict
es·tri·den·te, a. shrill; strident
es·tro·fa, f. stanza; stave
es·tro·pa·jo, m. mop
es·tro·pear(se), v. spoil; mar; ruin
es·truc·tu·ra, f. structure; frame
es·truen·do, m. thunder; roar
es·tru·jón, m. squeeze
es·tua·rio, m. estuary
es·tu·che, m. case
es·tu·dian·te, m., f. student
es·tu·diar, v. study
es·tu·dio, m. study; studio; den
es·tu·dio·so, a. studious
es·tu·fa, f. stove
es·tu·pe·fac·ción, f. stupefaction
es·tu·pen·do, a. stupendous; stun-ning
es·tu·pi·dez, f. stupidity
es·tú·pi·do, a. stupid
es·tu·por, m. stupor; lethargy
e·ta·pa, f. stage
et·cé·te·ra, etcetera
é·ter, m. ether
e·té·reo, a. ethereal
e·ter·ni·dad, f. eternity
e·ter·no, a. eternal; timeless
é·ti·ca, f. ethics
é·ti·co, a. ethical
e·ti·mo·lo·gía, f. etymology
e·ti·mo·lo·gis·ta, m., f. etymologist
e·ti·que·ta, f. tag; label; etiquette
ét·ni·co, a. ethnic(al)
et·no·lo·gía, f. ethnology
Eu·ca·ris·tía, f. Eucharist
eu·fe·mis·mo, m. euphemism
eu·fo·nía, f. euphony
eu·fo·ria, f. euphoria
eu·nu·co, m. eunuch

eu·ta·na·sia, f. euthanasia
e·va·cua·ción, f. evacuation
e·va·cuar, v. evacuate
e·va·dir, v. evade; dodge
e·va·lua·ción, f. evaluation
e·va·luar, v. evaluate
e·van·gé·li·co, a. evangelical
e·van·ge·lio, m. gospel
e·van·ge·lis·ta, m. evangelist
e·va·po·ra·ción, f. evaporation
e·va·po·rar(se), v. evaporate
e·va·sión, f. evasion
e·va·si·va, f. evasion
e·ven·tua·li·dad, f. eventuality
e·vi·den·cia, f. evidence
e·vi·den·te, a. evident; plain; obvious
e·vi·tar, v. avoid; shun
e·vo·car, v. evoke
e·vo·lu·ción, f. evolution
e·xac·ción, f. levy; extortion
e·xac·ta·men·te, adv. exactly; right
e·xac·to, a. exact; precise
e·xa·ge·ra·ción, f. exaggeration
e·xa·ge·rar, v. exaggerate
e·xal·tar, v. exalt; elevate
e·xa·men, m. examination; test
e·xa·mi·nar(se), v. examine; inspect; test
e·xas·pe·ra·ción, f. exasperation
e·xas·pe·rar(se), v. exasperate
e·xca·va·ción, f. excavation; dig
ex·ce·der(se), v. exceed; surpass
ex·ce·len·cia, f. excellence
ex·ce·len·te, a. excellent
ex·cen·tri·ci·dad, f. eccentricity
ex·cén·tri·co, a. eccentric. m. eccen-tric
ex·cep·to, prep. except; but; unless. conj. save
ex·ce·si·vo, a. excessive; undue
ex·ce·so, m. excess; surfeit
ex·ci·tar(se), v. excite; arouse
ex·cla·mar, v. exclaim
ex·cla·ma·ción, f. exclamation
ex·cluir, v. exclude; bar
ex·clu·sión, f. exclusion
ex·co·mu·nión, f. excommunication
ex·cre·men·to, m. excrement; pl. feces
ex·cur·sión, f. excursion; outing; tour
ex·cu·sa, f. excuse; alibi
ex·cu·sar, v. excuse
ex·ha·lar, v. exhale
ex·hor·ta·ción, f. exhortation
ex·hor·tar, v. exhort
e·xi·gen·te, a. exacting; exigent
e·xi·gir, v. demand; exact; require
e·xi·lio, m. exile
e·xis·ten·cia, f. existence; life
e·xis·tir, v. exist; live
é·xi·to, m. success; hit
é·xo·do, m. exodus
e·xó·ti·co, a. exotic
ex·pan·sión, f. expansion
ex·pec·ta·ción, f. expectation
ex·pe·di·ción, f. expedition
ex·pe·dir(se), v. stratify
ex·pen·der, v. expend
ex·pe·rien·cia, f. experience
ex·pe·ri·men·tal, a. experimental
ex·pe·ri·men·tar, v. experience; test
ex·pe·ri·men·to, m. experiment
ex·per·to, a. expert; adept. m. expert
ex·pia·ción, f. atonement
ex·piar, v. atone for
ex·pli·ca·ción, f. explanation
ex·pli·car(se), v. explain
ex·plí·ci·to, a. explicit
ex·plo·ra·ción, f. exploration
ex·plo·ra·dor, m. explorer; scout; pioneer
ex·plo·rar, v. explore
ex·plo·sión, f. explosion
ex·plo·ta·ción, f. exploitation
ex·por·ta·ción, f. export; exportation
ex·por·tar, v. export
ex·po·si·ción, f. exhibition; show; exposure
ex·po·si·tor, m. exhibitor
ex·pre·sar(se), v. express; voice
ex·pre·sión, f. expression
ex·pri·mir, v. wring; squeeze
ex·pul·sar, v. expel
ex·qui·si·to, a. exquisite
éx·ta·sis, f. ecstasy
ex·ten·der(se), v. extend; expand; en-large
ex·ten·sión, f. extension; range
ex·ten·so, a. extensive; wide
ex·te·rior, a. exterior. m. exterior; outside
ex·ter·mi·nar, v. exterminate
ex·ter·no, a. external
ex·tin·ción, f. extinction
ex·tin·guir(se), v. extinguish
ex·tin·to, a. extinct
ex·traer, v. extract; dig
ex·tran·je·ro, m., ex·tran·je·ra, f. foreigner; alien. a. foreign. en el ex·tran·je·ro, abroad; overseas
ex·tra·ño, a. strange; weird
ex·tra·or·di·na·rio, a. extraordinary
ex·tra·viar, v. mislay; stray
ex·tre·mi·da·des, m. pl. extremities
ex·tre·mo, a. extreme; radical. m. ex-treme; end
ex·ul·ta·ción, f. exultation

F

fá·bri·ca, f. factory; mill
fa·bri·ca·ción en se·rie, mass pro-duction
fa·bri·car, v. manufacture
fa·bu·lo·so, a. fabulous
fac·ción, f. faction; feature
fa·ce·ta, f. facet

fá·cil, a. easy; simple
fa·ci·li·dad, f. facility; ease
fa·ci·li·tar, v. facilitate; expedite
fac·sí·mi·le, m. facsimile
fac·tor, m. factor
fac·tó·tum, m. handyman
fac·tu·rar, v. bill; invoice
fa·cul·tad, f. faculty; power
fa·cha·da, f. facade
fa·chen·da, f. inf. splurge
fai·sán, m. pheasant
fa·ja, f. girdle; sash; band
fa·la·cia, f. fallacy
fal·da, f. skirt
fa·li·ble, a. fallible
fa·lo, m. phallus
fal·sear, v. forge
fal·se·dad, f. falsity; untruth
fal·si·fi·ca·ción, f. forgery; counter-feit
fal·si·fi·car, v. falsify; misrepresent
fal·so, a. false; dishonest; unsound
fal·ta, f. lack; deficiency; want; fault
fal·tar, v. lack; fail. fal·tar a, neglect
fa·lla, f. lacking
fa·llar, v. fail; (cards) trump
fa·lle·cer, v. decease; die
fa·lle·ci·mien·to, m. demise
fa·llo, m. verdict; failure
fa·ma, f. fame; name
fa·mi·lia, f. family
fa·mi·liar, a. familiar; family
fa·mi·lia·ri·dad, f. familiarity
fa·mo·so, a. famous; well-known
fa·ná·ti·co, a. fanatic(al). m. fanatic; zealot
fa·na·tis·mo, m. fanaticism; bigotry
fan·fa·rro·near, v. swagger
fan·ta·sía, f. fantasy
fan·tas·ma, m. phantom; ghost; ap-parition; spirit
fan·tás·ti·co, a. fantastic; fanciful; bizarre
fa·raón, m. pharaoh
far·do, m. pack
far·fu·llar, v. jabber
far·ma·céu·ti·co, m. druggist. a. pharmaceutical
far·ma·cia, f. pharmacy
fa·ro, m. headlight; beacon; light-house
far·sa, f. farce
fas·ci·nar, v. fascinate; intrigue
fas·cis·mo, m. fascism
fas·cis·ta, m., f. fascist
fa·se, f. phase
fas·ti·diar(se), v. pester; bother; hassle; inf. bug
fas·ti·dio, m. annoyance
fas·ti·dio·so, a. bothersome; weari-some
fa·tal, a. fatal; mortal
fa·ta·li·dad, f. fatality
fa·ta·lis·mo, m. fatalism
fa·ta·lis·ta, m., f. fatalist
fa·ti·ga, f. fatigue
fa·ti·gar(se), v. tire; fatigue; fag
faus·to, m. ostentation; pomp
fa·vor, m. favor
fa·vo·ra·ble, a. favorable
fa·vo·re·cer, v. favor; become
fa·vo·ri·tis·mo, m. favoritism
fa·vo·ri·to, a. favorite; pet. m., fa·vo·ri·ta, f. favorite
fe, f. faith; belief
fe·bre·ro, m. February
fe·bril, a. feverish; hectic
fé·cu·la, f. starch
fe·cun·di·dad, f. fertility
fe·cun·do, a. fertile; fecund
fe·cha, f. date
fe·char, v. date
fe·de·ra·ción, f. federation
fe·de·ral, a. federal
fe·li·ci·dad, f. felicity; bliss; good fortune
fe·li·ci·ta·ción, f. usu. pl. congratu-lation
fe·li·ci·tar, v. congratulate
fe·li·no, a. feline
fe·liz, a. happy; felicitous
fel·pu·do, m. mat
fe·me·ni·no, a. female; feminine
fe·mi·nis·mo, m. feminism
fé·mur, m. femur
fe·nó·me·no, m. phenomenon
feo, a. ugly; unslightly
fé·re·tro, m. bier
fe·ria, f. fair
fer·men·ta·ción, f. fermentation
fer·men·tar, v. ferment
fe·ro·ci·dad, f. ferocity
fe·roz, a. ferocious; fierce
fe·rre·te·ría, f. hardware
fe·rro·ca·rril, m. railroad
fe·rro·pru·sia·to, m. blueprint
fér·til, a. fertile; rich
fer·ti·li·zar, v. fertilize
fér·vi·do, a. fervid
fer·vor, m. fervor
fer·vo·ro·so, a. ardent; fervent
fes·te·jar, v. entertain; celebrate; fete
fes·ti·vo, a. festive; merry
fes·tón, m. festoon; scallop
fe·ti·che, m. fetish
fé·ti·do, a. fetid
fe·to, m. fetus
feu·dal, a. feudal
feu·da·lis·mo, m. feudalism
fia·dor, m. sponsor; guarantor
fian·za, f. security
fias·co, m. fiasco
fi·bro·so, a. fibrous; stringy
fic·ción, f. fiction
fic·ti·cio, a. fictitious
fi·cha, f. token

fi·de·dig·no, a. trustworthy
fi·dei·co·mi·sa·rio, m. trustee
fi·dei·co·mi·so, m. trust
fi·de·li·dad, f. fidelity; loyalty
fie·bre, f. fever; temperature. fie·bre ti·foi·dea, typhoid fever
fiel, a. faithful; loyal; true; devoted. m. pl. congregation
fiel·tro, m. felt
fie·ra, f. virago; wild beast
fie·ra·brás, m. spitfire
fies·ta, f. party; feast; celebration; festival
fi·gu·ra, f. figure
fi·gu·rar(se), v. figure
fi·gu·rín, m. figurine; model
fi·jar(se), v. fix; determine; assess; set
fi·jo, a. fixed; stated; confirmed; set; static
fi·la, f. file; row; rank; line; tier
fi·lan·tro·pía, f. philanthropy
fi·le·te, m. fillet; steak
fi·li·gra·na, f. filigree; watermark
fil·mar, v. film
fi·lo, m. edge
fi·lón, m. vein; lode
fi·lo·so·fía, f. philosophy
fi·ló·so·fo, m. philosopher
fil·trar(se), v. filter; strain
fil·tro, m. filter
fin, m. end; finish; purpose
fi·nal, a. final; last. m. end; finale
fi·na·li·dad, f. finality
fi·na·lis·ta, m., f. finalist
fi·nal·men·te, adv. finally; lastly
fi·nan·ciar, v. finance
fi·nan·cie·ro, a. financial. m. finan-cier
fi·nan·zas, f. pl. finance
fin·ca, f. estate
fin·gi·do, a. sham; feigned
fin·gir(se), v. feign; pretend; fake; sham
fi·ni·to, a. finite
fi·no, a. fine; delicate; acute; nice; po-lite
fir·ma, f. firm; signature
fir·ma·men·to, m. firmament
fir·mar, v. sign; autograph
fir·me, a. firm; hard; adamant; fast; steady; strong
fir·me·za, f. firmness; decision
fis·cal, a. fiscal
fis·gón, m. snoop
fis·go·near, v. pry
fí·si·ca, f. physics
fí·si·co, a. physical
fla·co, a. thin; skinny; lean; gaunt; spare
fla·mear, v. flame
flá·mu·la, f. streamer
fla·quear, v. weaken
flau·ta, f. flute
fle·cha, f. arrow. pun·ta de fle·cha, arrowhead
flem·a, f. phlegm
fle·xi·ble, a. flexible; pliant; supple
flir·tear, v. flirt
flo·jo, a. loose; slack; limp; weak
flor, f. flower; blossom
flo·re·cer, v. flower; blossom; bloom; flourish; prosper
flo·reo, m. flourish
flo·re·ro, m. vase; florist
flo·re·te, m. foil
flo·ri·do, a. florid
flo·ris·ta, m., f. florist
flo·ta, f. fleet
flo·tar, v. float
flo·ti·lla, f. flotilla
fluc·tua·ción, f. fluctuation; vacila-tion
fluc·tuar, v. fluctuate; bob
flui·dez, f. fluency
flúi·do, a. fluid. m. fluid
fluir, v. flow
flu·jo, m. flow; flux
fluo·res·cen·te, a. fluorescent
fluo·ri·za·ción, f. fluoridation
fo·bia, f. phobia
fo·ca, f. seal
fo·co, m. focus; spotlight; floodlight
fo·gón, m. galley; stove
fo·lí·cu·lo, m. follicle
folk·lo·re, m. folklore
fo·lla·je, m. foliage; leafage
fo·lle·to, m. booklet; brochure; pam-phlet
fo·men·tar, v. foment; promote; en-courage
fon·do, m. depth; bottom; back-ground; pl. funds
fon·ta·ne·ro, m. plumber
fo·ra·ji·do, m. outlaw
fo·ras·te·ro, m., fo·ras·te·ra, f. stranger; outsider
fór·ceps, m. forceps
for·ja·do, a. wrought
for·jar, v. forge
for·ma, f. form; shape; build; method
for·ma·ción, f. formation; array
for·ma·li·dad, f. formality
for·mar(se), v. form; make; shape; fashion
for·ma·to, m. format
for·mi·da·ble, a. formidable; tre-mendous
for·món, m. chisel
fór·mu·la, f. formula
for·ni·car, v. fornicate
fo·ro, m. forum
fo·rra·je, m. forage; fodder
for·ta·le·cer(se), v. strengthen; forti-fy
for·ta·le·za, f. fortress
for·ti·fi·ca·ción, f. fortification
for·tui·to, a. fortuitous; casual; hap-hazard

for·tu·na, f. fortune
for·zar, v. force; coerce; strain; violate
fo·sa, f. socket; cavity
fos·fa·to, m. phosphate
fos·fo·res·cen·cia, f. phosphorescence
fós·fo·ro, m. phosphorus
fó·sil, a. fossil. m. fossil
fo·so, m. moat; trench
fo·to, f. photograph; snapshot
fo·to·co·pia, f. photocopy
fo·to·gé·ni·co, a. photogenic
fo·to·gra·fía, f. photography; photograph
fo·tó·gra·fo, m., fo·tó·gra·fa, f. photographer
fra·ca·sar, v. fail; flop; break down
fra·ca·so, m. failure; debacle
frac·ción, f. fraction
frac·tu·ra, f. fracture; breakage
frac·tu·rar(se), v. fracture
fra·gan·cia, f. fragrance
frá·gil, a. fragile; frail; breakable
frag·men·to, m. fragment; shred
fra·gor, m. clash; uproar
fra·gua, f. forge
frai·le, m. friar
fram·bue·sa, f. raspberry
fran·ca·che·la, f. inf. jamboree
fran·ca·men·te, adv. frankly
fran·cés, a. French
fran·co, a. frank; candid; open; direct
fran·co·te, a. bluff; blunt
fran·quear, v. frank
fran·queo, m. postage
fran·que·za, f. frankness
fras·co, m. flask; flagon
fra·se, f. phrase; sentence
fra·seo·lo·gía, f. wording
fra·ter·nal, a. fraternal
fra·ter·ni·dad, f. fraternity; brotherhood
frau·de, m. fraud; deception
frau·du·len·to, a. fraudulent
fre·cuen·cia, f. frequency
fre·cuen·tar, v. frequent; haunt
fre·cuen·te, a. frequent
fre·ga·de·ro, m. sink
fre·gar, v. scour; scrub; wash
freír(se), v. fry
fre·nar, v. brake
fre·ne·sí, m. frenzy
fre·né·ti·co, a. frantic; frenetic
fre·no, m. brake; curb
fren·te, f. brow; forehead; front. al frente, ahead. in fren·te, opposite
fre·sa, f. strawberry
fres·ca·chón, a. buxom; healthy
fres·co, m. fresco. a. fresh; cool; smart
fres·cu·ra, f. coolness; nerve
fres·no, m. ash tree
fre·za, f. spawn
frial·dad, f. coldness; aloofness
fric·ción, f. friction
frío, a. cold; cool; chilly; frigid. m. cold
fri·so, m. frieze
frí·vo·lo, a. frivolous; trivial
fron·tal, a. frontal
fron·te·ra, f. frontier; border; boundary; limit
fro·tar(se), v. rub; chafe
fro·te, m. friction
fru·gal, a. thrifty; frugal
frun·ce, m. gather; tuck
frun·cir, v. gather; purse
frus·tra·ción, f. frustration
frus·trar(se), v. frustrate; defeat; foil; thwart
fue·go, m. fire. al·to el fue·go, ceasefire. ar·ma de fue·go, firearm; gun. cor·ti·na de fue·go, barrage. fue·gos ar·ti·fi·cia·les, fireworks
fue·lle, m. bellows
fuen·te, f. fountain; spring; source
fue·ra, adv. away; outside; off; abroad
fuer·te, m. fort. a. strong; sturdy; potent
fuer·za, f. force; power; might; strength
fu·ga, f. escape; elopement
fu·gar·se, v. flee; abscond
fu·gaz, a. fleeting
fu·gi·ti·vo, a. fugitive; runaway
ful·cro, m. fulcrum
ful·gu·rar, v. flare; gleam
fu·mar, v. smoke
fu·mi·gar, v. fumigate
fun·ción, f. function; show; performance
fun·cio·nar, v. function; work
fun·da·ción, f. foundation
fun·da·dor, m. founder
fun·da·men·tal, a. fundamental
fun·dar(se), v. found; establish
fun·di·ción, f. foundry
fun·dir(se), v. fuse; cast
fú·ne·bre, a. funeral
fu·nes·to, a. baneful
fur·gón, m. wagon. fur·gón de co·la, caboose
fu·ria, f. fury
fu·rio·so, a. furious
fu·ror, m. furor
fur·ti·vo, a. furtive
fu·rún·cu·lo, m. boil
fu·sión, f. coalescence; fusion
fút·bol, m. football; soccer
fu·tu·ro, a. future. m. future

G

ga·bar·di·na, f. gabardine
ga·ba·rra, f. barge
ga·bi·ne·te, m. cabinet; study
ga·ce·la, f. gazelle
ga·ce·ta, f. gazette
ga·fas, f. pl. glasses; spectacles. ga·fas de sol, sunglasses
ga·fe, m. jinx
gai·ta, f. usu. pl. bagpipe
ga·lan·te·ría, f. gallantry
ga·la·xia, f. galaxy
ga·le·ra, f. galley
ga·le·ría, f. gallery; arcade; veranda
ga·li·ma·tías, m. gibberish
ga·lón, m. gallon
ga·lo·par, v. gallop
gal·va·ni·zar, v. galvanize
ga·lle·ta, f. biscuit; cookie
ga·lli·na, f. chicken; hen
ga·lli·ne·ro, m. coop
ga·llo, m. rooster; cock
ga·ma, f. doe; gamut
gam·bi·to, m. gambit
ga·mu·za, f. chamois
ga·na, f. appetite; desire
ga·na·de·ro, m. cattleman; rancher
ga·na·do, m. cattle; livestock
ga·na·dor, m., ga·na·do·ra, f. winner
ga·nan·cia, f. gain; profit
ga·nar, v. win; gain; earn; profit
gan·cho, m. hook
gan·du·lear, v. lounge; loaf
gan·ga, f. bargain; inf. steal
gan·gre·na, f. gangrene
gángs·ter, m. gangster
gan·so, m. goose; gander
ga·ñir, v. yelp; yip
ga·ra·je, m. garage
ga·ran·te, m. surety
ga·ran·tía, f. guarantee; guaranty; surety; warrant; warranty
ga·ran·ti·zar, v. guarantee; vouch for; pledge
gar·a·pi·ña, f. icing
gar·ban·zo, m. chickpea
gar·gan·ta, f. throat; neck
gár·ga·ras, f. gargle
gar·ga·ri·zar, v. gargle
ga·rra, f. talon; claw
ga·rra·fa, f. decanter
ga·rra·pa·tear, v. scribble
ga·rro·te, m. cudgel; club
gá·rru·lo, a. garrulous
gar·za, f. heron
gas, m. gas
ga·sa, f. chiffon; gauze
ga·so·li·na, f. gasoline; gas
gas·ta·do, a. worn-out; trite
gas·tar(se), v. spend; use up; eat up; consume; wear out
gas·to, m. expense; expenditure
gás·tri·co, a. gastric
gas·tro·no·mía, f. gastronomy
gas·tró·no·mo, m. gourmet
ga·ti·llo, m. trigger
ga·ti·to, m. kitten; kitty; pussy
ga·to, m. cat; jack
ga·vio·ta, f. gull
ga·za, f. loop
gaz·mo·ño, m., gaz·mo·ña, f. prude; hypocrite
géi·ser, m. geyser
ge·la·ti·na, f. gelatin
ge·ma, f. gem
ge·me·lo, a. twin. m., ge·me·la, f. twin; m. usu. pl. binoculars
ge·mi·do, m. groan; wail
ge·mir, v. groan; moan; wail
gen, m. gene
ge·nea·lo·gía, f. genealogy
ge·ne·ra·ción, f. generation
ge·ne·ra·dor, m. generator
ge·ne·ral, a. general. a. general; common. por lo ge·ne·ral, usually
ge·ne·ra·li·dad, f. generality
ge·ne·ra·li·zar(se), v. generalize; become known
ge·ne·rar, v. generate
ge·né·ri·co, a. generic
gé·ne·ro, m. gender; genus; nature; kind; type; sort. gé·ne·ros di·ver·sos, sundries
ge·ne·ro·si·dad, f. generosity
ge·né·si·co, a. genetic
gé·ne·sis, f. genesis. m. (cap.) Genesis
ge·né·ti·ca, f. genetics
ge·nio, m. temper; nature; genius
ge·no·ci·dio, m. genocide
gen·te, f. people; folk; nation
gen·til, a. comely; graceful
gen·ti·le·za, f. gentility; gracefulness; courtesy
ge·nui·no, a. genuine; true; real
geo·fí·si·ca, f. geophysics
geo·gra·fía, f. geography
geo·grá·fi·co, a. geographic, geographical
geó·gra·fo, m. geographer
geo·lo·gía, f. geology
geo·ló·gi·co, a. geologic, geological
geó·lo·go, m. geologist
geo·me·tría, f. geometry
geo·mé·tri·co, a. geometric
ge·ren·te, m. manager
ge·ria·tría, f. geriatrics
ger·men, m. germ
ger·mi·na·ción, f. germination
ger·mi·nar, v. germinate
ge·run·dio, m. gerund
ges·ti·cu·lar, v. gesticulate
ges·tio·nar, v. negotiate; work towards
ges·to, m. gesture; face; expression
gi·ba, f. hump
gi·bón, m. gibbon
gi·gan·te, m. giant
gi·gan·tes·co, a. gigantic; giant
gim·na·sia, f. gymnastics
gim·na·sio, m. gymnasium; inf. gym
gim·nas·ta, m., f. gymnast
gi·mo·tear, v. whine
gin, m. gin
gi·ne·co·lo·gía, f. gynecology
gi·ra, f. circuit; tour
gi·rar, v. turn; rotate; revolve; gyrate; twirl; spin; swivel
gi·ra·sol, m. sunflower
gi·ro, m. turn; twirl; draft
gi·ros·co·pio, m. gyroscope
gi·ta·no, m., gi·ta·na, f. gipsy, gypsy
gla·cial, a. arctic; glacial; icy; wintry
gla·ciar, m. glacier
gla·dio·lo, gla·dio·lo, m. gladiolus, gladiola
glán·du·la, f. gland
glan·du·lar, a. glandular
glau·co·ma, m. glaucoma
glo·bo, m. globe; balloon
gló·bu·lo, m. corpuscle; globule
glo·ria, f. glory
glo·riar·se, v. glory
glo·ri·fi·car(se), v. glorify; glory in
glo·sa·rio, m. glossary
glo·tis, f. glottis
glo·tón, m. glutton
gno·mo, m. gnome
go·ber·na·dor, m. governor; ruler
go·ber·nar, v. govern; rule
go·bier·no, m. government; guidance
golf, m. golf
gol·fo, m. gulf
go·lon·dri·na, f. swallow
go·lo·si·na, f. dainty; tidbit; inf. goody
gol·pa·zo, m. inf. wallop
gol·pe, m. hit; blow; band; stroke; coup
gol·pear, v. hit; slug; strike; beat; knock; buffet; rap; jab
gol·pe·ci·to, m. pat; flick; dab
go·ma, f. gum; rubber band. go·ma la·ca, shellac, shellack
gón·do·la, f. gondola
gon·do·le·ro, m. gondolier
go·no·rrea, f. gonorrhea
gor·do, a. fat; corpulent; overweight
gor·go·tear, v. gurgle
gor·go·teo, m. gurgle
gor·jear, v. twitter
gor·jeo, m. twitter; chirp; warble
go·ta, f. drop; drip; bead; gout. caer go·ta a go·ta, dribble
go·tear, v. drip; trickle
go·te·ra, f. leak
go·zar(se), v. enjoy
goz·ne, m. hinge; hinge joint
gra·ba·do, m. engraving; print
gra·ba·dor, m. engraver
gra·ba·do·ra, f. stapler; recorder
gra·bar, v. engrave; record
gra·cia, f. grace; pl. thanks
gra·cio·so, a. graceful; funny; droll
gra·da, f. step; pl. bleachers
gra·da·ción, f. gradation
gra·do, m. grade; degree
gra·dua·ción, f. graduation; rank
gra·dua·do, m., gra·dua·da, f. graduate
gra·dual, a. gradual
gra·duar(se), v. graduate
grá·fi·ca, f. graph
grá·fi·co, m. chart; graph. a. graphic; vivid
gra·fi·to, m. graphite
gra·má·ti·ca, f. grammar
gra·ma·ti·cal, a. grammatical
gra·mo, m. gram
gra·na·da, f. shell; gra·na·da de ma·no, hand grenade
gra·na·te, m. garnet
gran·de (gran), a. great; big; large
gran·dio·so, a. grand; grandiose
gra·ne·ro, m. granary; barn
gra·ni·to, m. granite; pimple
gra·ni·zar, v. hail
gra·ni·zo, m. hail. pie·dra de gra·ni·zo, hailstone
gran·ja, f. farm
gra·no, m. grain; cereal; pimple
gra·nu·lar, v. granulate
grá·nu·lo, m. granule
gra·pa, f. staple; clamp
gra·sa, f. fat; grease
gra·sien·to, a. greasy; oily
gra·ti·fi·ca·ción, f. gratification
gra·tis, a. free; gratis. adv. gratis
gra·tui·to, a. gratuitous; complimentary; free
gra·var, v. encumber
gra·ve, a. grave; serious; grievous; dignified
gra·ve·dad, f. gravity
gra·vi·ta·ción, f. gravitation
graz·nar, v. squawk
graz·ni·do, m. squawk. graz·ni·do del pa·to, quack
gre·ga·rio, a. gregarious
gre·mio, m. guild; union
grie·ta, f. fissure; rift; crack
gri·fo, m. faucet; tap; griffin, griffon
gri·lle·te, m. shackle
gri·llo, m. cricket; pl. fetters
gri·pe, f. grippe; inf. flu
gris, a. gray; grizzled. m. gray
gri·tar, v. shout; cry; yell; inf. holler
gri·to, m. shout; yell; outcry; scream
gro·se·lla, f. currant
gro·se·ro, a. gross; vulgar; uncouth; coarse
gro·tes·co, a. grotesque
grúa, f. crane
grue·sa, f. gross
grue·so, a. gross; thick; heavy
gru·lla, f. crane
gru·mo, m. clot
gru·ñi·do, m. grunt
gru·ñir, v. grunt; growl
gru·ñón, a. grumpy
gru·po, m. group; bunch
gru·ta, f. grotto
gua·da·ña, f. scythe
guan·te, m. glove
guan·te·le·te, m. gauntlet
gua·po, a. good-looking
guar·da·es·pal·das, m. bodyguard
guar·da·fan·go, m. fender
guar·dar(se), v. guard; keep; watch; beware
guar·dia, f. guard. m. guard; sentry
guar·dián, m. guardian; caretaker; warden
guar·di·lla, f. garret
gua·ri·da, f. den
guar·ne·cer, v. man; adorn
guar·ni·ción, f. garrison; adornment; fittings
gua·són, m. tease
gu·bia, f. gouge
gue·rra, f. war; warfare. gue·rra ci·vil, civil war. gue·rra fría, cold war
gue·rre·ro, m. fighter; warrior
gue·rri·lle·ro, m. guerrilla
guía, f. guidebook; guide. m. guide
guiar, v. guide; lead; steer
gui·ja·rro, m. pebble
gui·llo·ti·na, f. guillotine
gui·ñar, v. wink
gui·ño, m. wink
guión, m. hyphen; dash
guir·nal·da, f. garland; wreath
gui·san·te, m. pea
gui·ta, f. twine
gui·ta·rra, f. guitar
gu·la, f. gluttony
gu·sa·no, m. worm. gu·sa·no de tie·rra, earthworm
gus·tar, v. like; please; relish
gus·to, m. taste; pleasure; gusto; zest. con mu·cho gus·to, gladly; with pleasure. dar gus·to, please
gu·tu·ral, a. guttural

H

ha·ba, f. bean
ha·ber, aux. v. used in compound tenses. m. pl. assets; goods
há·bil, a. dexterous; adroit; knowing
ha·bi·li·dad, f. skill; ability; craft; workmanship
ha·bi·li·tar, v. qualify
ha·bi·ta·ble, a. habitable
ha·bi·ta·ción, f. habitat; habitation; room; lodging
ha·bi·tan·te, m., f. inhabitant
ha·bi·tar, v. inhabit; dwell
há·bi·to, m. habit
ha·bi·tual, a. habitual; usual
ha·bi·tuar(se), v. inure; accustom to
ha·bla, f. speech
ha·bla·dor, a. talkative; voluble
ha·blar, v. speak; talk. ha·blar en·tre dien·tes, mumble
ha·ce, a. ago. adv. ago
ha·cer(se), v. do; make; act; perform; become
ha·cia, prep. to; towards; about. ha·cia a·de·lan·te, onward(s). ha·cia ca·sa, homeward(s). ha·cia den·tro, inward. ha·cia fue·ra, outward(s)
ha·cien·da, f. ranch
ha·cha, f. ax, axe
ha·da, f. fairy
ha·do, m. fate
ha·la·gar, v. cajole; allure
ha·la·go, m. cajolery
hal·cón, m. hawk; falcon
ha·lo, m. halo
ha·llar(se), v. find; locate; find oneself
ha·llaz·go, m. discovery
ha·ma·ca, f. hammock
ham·bre, f. hunger; famine
ham·brien·to, a. hungry; starving
ham·bur·gue·sa, f. hamburger
ha·ra·ga·near, v. loaf; idle
ha·ra·pien·to, a. tattered
ha·rén, m. harem
ha·ri·na, f. flour; meal
har·tar(se), v. sicken; satiate; glut; gorge
has·ta, adv. to. prep. till; as far as. conj. until
ha·ya, f. beech
haz, f. sickle. haz de le·ña, fagot
ha·za·ña, f. exploit; deed
he·bi·lla, f. buckle
he·bra, f. strand; thread
he·chi·ce·ra, f. witch; sorceress
he·chi·ce·ría, f. sorcery
he·chi·ce·ro, m. sorcerer; wizard; warlock
he·chi·zar, v. bewitch; entrance; charm
he·chi·zo, m. charm; spell
he·cho, a. done; ready-made. m. deed; fact; act
he·der, v. stink
he·dor, m. stench; stink
he·la·da, f. frost
he·la·do, m. ice cream. a. icy
he·lar(se), v. freeze; ice
hé·li·ce, f. propeller; helix; spiral
he·li·cóp·te·ro, m. helicopter
he·lio, m. helium
he·mis·fe·rio, m. hemisphere
he·mo·rra·gia, f. hemorrhage
he·mo·rroi·des, f. hemorrhoids
he·nal, m. loft
hen·der(se), v. split; crack; rend; gash
he·no, m. hay
he·rál·di·ca, f. heraldry
her·cú·leo, a. herculean
he·re·dad, f. domain; landed property
he·re·dar, v. inherit
he·re·de·ra, f. heiress
he·re·de·ro, m. heir
he·re·di·ta·rio, a. hereditary
he·re·je, m. heretic
he·re·jía, f. heresy
he·ren·cia, f. heredity; heritage; inheritance
he·ri·da, f. hurt; wound
he·ri·do, a. wounded; stricken
he·rir, v. wound; injure
her·ma·na, f. sister
her·ma·nas·tra, f. stepsister
her·ma·nas·tro, m. stepbrother
her·man·dad, f. brotherhood
her·ma·no, m. brother
her·mo·so, a. lovely; beautiful; handsome
her·nia, f. hernia; rupture
hé·roe, m. hero
he·roí·na, f. heroine; heroin
he·roís·mo, m. heroism
he·rra·du·ra, f. horseshoe
he·rra·mien·ta, f. tool; implement; pl. gear
he·rre·ro, m. blacksmith; smith, smithy
he·rrum·bro·so, a. rusty
her·vir, v. boil; seethe
he·te·ro·gé·neo, a. heterogeneous
he·xá·go·no, m. hexagon
hí·bri·do, m. hybrid
hi·dal·go, m. nobleman
hi·dráu·li·co, a. hydraulic
hi·dró·ge·no, m. hydrogen
hi·dro·pe·sía, f. dropsy
hie·dra, f. ivy
hie·lo, m. ice
hie·na, f. hyena
hier·ba, f. grass; herb. ma·la hier·ba, weed
hie·rro, m. iron; pl. irons. hie·rro fun·di·do, cast iron
hí·ga·do, m. liver
hi·gie·ne, f. hygiene
hi·go, m. fig
hi·ja, f. daughter
hi·jas·tra, f. stepdaughter
hi·jas·tro, m. stepson
hi·jo, m. son; pl. children
hi·la, f. lint; row
hi·la·za, f. yarn
hi·le·ra, f. row; file
hi·lo, m. thread
hil·va·nar, v. baste; tack
him·no, m. hymn. him·no na·cio·nal, anthem
hin·char(se), v. swell; bloat; stuff; billow
hin·cha·zón, f. bump
hip·no·sis, f. hypnosis
hip·nó·ti·co, a. hypnotic. es·ta·do hip·nó·ti·co, trance
hip·no·ti·zar, v. hypnotize
hi·po, m. hiccup, hiccough
hi·po·con·dría·co, a. hypochondriac
hi·po·cre·sía, f. hypocrisy
hi·pó·cri·ta, m., f. hypocrite
hi·po·dér·mi·co, a. hypodermic
hi·po·pó·ta·mo, m. hippopotamus
hi·po·te·ca, f. mortgage
hi·po·te·car, v. mortgage
hi·po·te·nu·sa, f. hypotenuse
hi·pó·te·sis, f. hypothesis
his·té·ri·co, a. hysteric(al)
his·to·ria, f. history; story; record
his·to·ria·dor, m., his·to·ria·do·ra, f. historian
his·tó·ri·co, a. historic(al)
his·trió·ni·co, a. histrionic(al)
ho·ci·co, m. snout; muzzle
ho·gar, m. home; hearth; fireplace
ho·gue·ra, f. bonfire
ho·ja, f. sheet; leaf; blade
ho·jear, v. browse; skim; leaf through
ho·jue·la, f. pancake; pl. flakes
ho·la, int. hello
ho·lo·caus·to, m. holocaust
ho·llar, v. tread on
ho·llín, m. soot
hom·bre, m. man
hom·bro, m. shoulder
ho·me·na·je, m. homage; tribute
ho·mi·ci·dio, m. homicide
ho·mi·lía, f. homily
ho·mo·gé·neo, a. homogeneous
ho·mó·ni·mo, m. homonym
hon·do, a. deep
hon·go, m. mushroom; toadstool; fungus
ho·nor, m. honor; credit; pl. laurels
ho·no·ra·rio, a. honorary. m. pl. fees
hon·ra, f. honor; virtue
hon·ra·dez, f. honesty
hon·ra·do, a. honest; upstanding
hon·rar, v. honor; exalt; dignify
ho·ra, f. hour; time. ho·ra de a·ta·que, zero hour
ho·ra·rio, m. schedule; timetable
hor·ca, f. gallows
hor·da, f. horde
ho·ri·zon·tal, a. horizontal
ho·ri·zon·te, m. horizon
hor·mi·ga, f. ant
hor·mi·gón, m. concrete
hor·mo·na, f. hormone
hor·na·da, f. batch
hor·no, m. oven; kiln; furnace
ho·rós·co·po, m. horoscope
hor·qui·lla, f. barrette; hairpin
ho·rren·do, a. dire
ho·rri·ble, a. horrible; hideous; gruesome; ghastly; awful
ho·rror, m. horror
ho·rro·ri·zar(se), v. horrify
hor·ti·cul·tu·ra, f. horticulture
hos·co, a. surly; gloomy
hos·pe·dar(se), v. lodge; harbor
hos·pi·tal, m. hospital
hos·pi·ta·la·rio, a. hospitable
hos·pi·ta·li·dad, f. hospitality
hos·tia, f. wafer; host
hos·ti·ga·mien·to, m. harassment
hos·ti·gar, v. harry; scourge
hos·til, a. hostile
hos·ti·li·dad, f. hostility
ho·tel, m. hotel
hoy, m. today; present time. adv. today, to-day
ho·yo, m. hole; pit; cavity
ho·yue·lo, m. dimple
hu·cha, f. bin
hue·co, m. gap; hollow
huel·ga, f. strike; walkout
hue·lla, f. footprint; trace. hue·lla dac·ti·lar, fingerprint
huér·fa·no, m. orphan
huer·ta, f. garden
huer·to, m. orchard
hue·so, m. bone; pit
hués·ped, m. host; guest; boarder
hués·pe·da, f. hostess; guest
hue·vo, m. egg
hui·da, f. flight
huir(se), v. escape; flee
hu·ma·ni·dad, f. humanity
hu·ma·ni·ta·rio, a. humanitarian. m. humanitarian
hu·ma·no, m. human. a. human
hu·mear, v. smoke; fume
hu·me·dad, f. humidity; moisture
hu·me·de·cer(se), v. humidify; moisten
hú·me·do, a. humid; damp; wet; moist
hu·mil·dad, f. humility
hu·mil·de, a. humble; low
hu·mi·lla·ción, f. humiliation
hu·mi·llar(se), v. humble; humiliate
hu·mo, m. smoke
hu·mor, m. humor; mood
hun·di·do, a. sunken
hun·dir(se), v. sink; slump; cave in; collapse
hu·ra·ca·na, f. hurricane
hu·rón, m. ferret
hur·tar(se), v. rob; steal; steal away
hus·mear, v. sniff; scent
hu·so, m. spindle

I

i·bis, f. ibis
ice·berg, m. iceberg
í·co·no, m. icon
i·co·no·clas·ta, m., f. iconoclast
ic·te·ri·cia, f. jaundice
i·da, f. going
i·dea, f. idea; thought; notion
i·deal, a. ideal. m. ideal
i·dea·li·zar, v. idealize
i·dear, v. design; invent
i·dén·ti·co, a. identical; same
i·den·ti·dad, f. identity
i·den·ti·fi·ca·ción, f. identification
i·deo·lo·gía, f. ideology
i·di·lio, m. idyll
i·dio·ma, m. tongue; language
i·dio·má·ti·co, a. idiomatic
i·dio·sin·cra·sia, f. idiosyncrasy
i·dio·ta, m., f. idiot
i·dio·tis·mo, m. idiom
i·do·la·trar, v. idolize
i·do·la·tría, f. idolatry
í·do·lo, m. idol
i·gle·sia, f. church
ig·no·ran·cia, f. ignorance
ig·no·ran·te, a. ignorant
i·gual, a. equal; even. m. equal; match
i·gua·lar(se), v. even; equal; match
i·gual·dad, f. equality
i·ja·da, f. loin; flank
i·le·gal, a. illegal; unlawful
i·le·gi·ble, a. illegible
i·le·gi·ti·mi·dad, f. illegitimacy
i·le·gí·ti·mo, a. illegitimate; bastard
i·le·so, a. unhurt; unscathed
i·lí·ci·to, a. illicit
i·lu·mi·nar, v. illuminate; light; enlighten
i·lu·sión, f. illusion
i·lu·sio·nis·ta, m., f. magician; conjurer, conjuror
i·lus·tra·ción, f. illustration; picture
i·lus·trar, v. illustrate
i·ma·gen, f. image
i·ma·gi·na·ción, f. imagination
i·ma·gi·nar(se), v. imagine; conceive; guess; fancy
i·mán, m. magnet
im·bé·cil, m., f. imbecile; half-wit. a. imbecile
i·mi·ta·ción, f. imitation
i·mi·tar, v. imitate; mimic
im·pa·cien·te, a. impatient; anxious; eager
im·pac·to, m. impact
im·par, a. odd
im·par·cial, a. impartial
im·pa·si·ble, a. stolid
im·pá·vi·do, a. dauntless
im·pe·ca·ble, a. impeccable
im·pe·di·men·to, m. impediment; check; obstacle
im·pe·dir, v. impede; hinder; prevent; deter
im·pe·ler, v. urge
im·pe·ne·tra·ble, a. impervious

im·per·di·ble, *m.* safety pin
im·per·fec·ción, *f.* flaw
im·pe·rio, *m.* empire
im·pe·rio·so, *a.* imperious; authoritative
im·per·mea·ble, *m.* waterproof; raincoat
im·per·so·nal, *a.* impersonal
im·per·ti·nen·te, *a.* impertinent
im·pe·tu, *m.* impetus; momentum
im·pe·tuo·so, *a.* impetuous; brash
im·plo·rar, *v.* implore; invoke
im·po·ner, *v.* impose; charge
im·por·tan·cia, *f.* importance; value
im·por·tan·te, *a.* important; prominent; weighty
im·por·tar, *v.* matter; care; import
im·por·tu·nar, *v.* solicit; pester
im·po·si·ble, *a.* impossible
im·pos·tor, *m.* im·pos·to·ra, *f.* impostor
im·pos·tu·ra, *f.* sham; fake
im·po·ten·te, *a.* impotent
im·pre·me·di·ta·do, *a.* impromptu; unpremeditated
im·pren·ta, *f.* press; printing
im·pres·cin·di·ble, *a.* indispensable
im·pre·sión, *f.* impression; print
im·pre·sio·nan·te, *a.* striking; stunning
im·pre·sio·nar(se), *v.* impress
im·pre·vis·to, *a.* sudden; unexpected; un-looked-for; extemporaneous
im·pri·mir, *v.* print; imprint; impress
im·pro·ba·ble, *a.* improbable
im·pro·pio, *a.* improper
im·pro·vi·sar, *v.* improvise
im·pru·den·te, *a.* rash
im·pú·di·co, *a.* immodest
im·pues·to, *m.* tax
im·pul·sar, *v.* impel
im·pul·so, *m.* impulse; urge
im·pu·re·za, *f.* impurity
in·a·bor·da·ble, *a.* unapproachable
in·ac·ti·vo, *a.* quiescent; inactive
in·a·de·cua·do, *a.* inadequate
in·a·ni·ma·do, *a.* inanimate
in·a·pli·ca·ble, *a.* irrelevant
in·a·pre·cia·ble, *a.* priceless
in·au·di·to, *a.* unheard-of
in·au·gu·rar, *v.* inaugurate
in·cal·cu·la·ble, *a.* untold
in·can·des·cen·te, *a.* incandescent
in·ca·pa·ci·dad, *f.* disability
in·ca·pa·ci·tar, *v.* incapacitate
in·ca·paz, *a.* incapable; unable; helpless
in·cau·to, *a.* unwary
in·cen·diar(se), *v.* burn; catch fire
in·cen·dio, *m.* fire. in·cen·dio pre·me·di·ta·do, arson
in·cen·ti·vo, *m.* incentive
in·cer·ti·dum·bre, *f.* uncertainty; suspense
in·ce·san·te, *a.* ceaseless; incessant
in·ces·to, *m.* incest
in·ci·den·tal, *a.* incidental
in·ci·den·te, *m.* incident
in·cien·so, *m.* incense
in·cier·to, *a.* uncertain; vague; treacherous
in·ci·ne·ra·ción, *f.* cremation
in·ci·ne·rar, *v.* incinerate; cremate
in·ci·sión, *f.* incision
in·ci·tar, *v.* incite; spur; urge; prompt
in·cle·men·to, *a.* inclement
in·cli·na·ción, *f.* inclination; propensity; slant; slope; tilt
in·cli·nar(se), *v.* incline; lean; slant; slope; sway; bow
in·cluir, *v.* include; enclose
in·co·mo·dar(se), *v.* inconvenience
in·co·mo·di·dad, *f.* discomfort; inconvenience
in·có·mo·do, *a.* uncomfortable
in·com·pe·ten·te, *a.* incompetent
in·com·ple·to, *a.* incomplete; unfinished
in·con·di·cio·nal, *a.* unconditional
in·con·gruo, *a.* incongruous
in·cons·cien·te, *a.* unconscious; unwitting
in·con·se·cuen·te, *a.* inconsequential
in·con·si·de·ra·do, *a.* thoughtless; wanton
in·cons·tan·te, *a.* fickle
in·con·ve·nien·te, *f.* inconvenience
in·co·rrec·to, *a.* incorrect
in·creí·ble, *a.* incredible
in·cri·mi·nar, *v.* incriminate
in·cu·ba·do·ra, *f.* incubator
in·cues·tio·na·ble, *a.* unquestionable
in·cul·to, *a.* crude
in·cu·rrir, *v.* incur; commit
in·da·ga·ción, *f.* inquiry
in·de·cen·cia, *f.* indecency
in·de·cen·te, *a.* indecent; unseemly
in·de·ci·sión, *f.* indecision; hesitation
in·de·ci·so, *a.* uncertain; undecided
in·de·co·ro·so, *a.* unseemly; unbecoming
in·dem·ni·za·ción, *f.* indemnity
in·dem·ni·zar, *v.* compensate
in·de·pen·den·cia, *f.* independence
in·de·pen·dien·te, *a.* independent; self-sufficient; strong-minded
in·des·truc·ti·ble, *a.* indestructable
in·di·ca·ción, *f.* indication; suggestion
in·di·ca·dor, *m.* gauge; register. *a.* telltale
in·di·car, *v.* indicate; show; suggest; insinuate
ín·di·ce, *m.* index
in·di·cio, *m.* symptom; trace; clue

in·di·fe·ren·te, *a.* indifferent; apathetic
in·dí·ge·na, *m., f.* native, *a.* indigenous
in·di·gen·cia, *f.* destitution
in·di·gen·te, *a.* indigent
in·di·ges·tión, *f.* indigestion
in·dig·ni·dad, *f.* indignity
in·dig·no, *a.* unworthy
in·di·rec·ta, *f.* hint
in·di·rec·to, *a.* indirect; oblique; round
in·dis·cre·ción, *f.* indiscretion
in·dis·pues·to, *a.* out of sorts; unwell
in·dis·tin·to, *a.* vague; obscure
in·di·vi·dual, *a.* individual
in·di·vi·duo, *m.* individual
in·do·len·te, *a.* indolent
in·du·cir, *v.* induce
in·dul·gen·te, *a.* lenient
in·dul·to, *m.* pardon
in·dus·tria, *f.* industry
in·e·fi·caz, *a.* weak; inefficient
in·fa·li·ble, *a.* foolproof
in·fan·te·ría, *f.* infantry
in·fan·til, *a.* infant; baby; childish
in·fec·ción, *f.* infection
in·fec·tar(se), *v.* infect
in·fe·liz, *a.* unhappy; unfortunate
in·fe·rior, *a.* inferior; worse; under. *m.* inferior
in·fe·rir, *v.* infer
in·fer·nal, *a.* infernal; hellish
in·fes·tar, *v.* infest
in·fi·de·li·dad, *f.* infidelity
in·fiel, *a.* unfaithful. *m.* infidel
in·fier·no, *m.* hell
in·fil·trar(se), *v.* infiltrate
in·fi·ni·ti·vo, *m.* infinitive
in·fi·ni·to, *a.* infinite. *m.* infinity
in·fla·ma·ble, *a.* flammable
in·flar(se), *v.* blow up; puff up
in·fle·xi·ble, *a.* inflexible; unyielding; grim
in·fluen·cia, *f.* influence; sway
in·for·ma·ción, *f.* information; intelligence
in·for·mal, *a.* informal; unceremonious
in·for·mar(se), *v.* inform; report
in·for·me, *m.* report
in·for·tu·nio, *m.* misfortune
in·fre·cuen·te, *a.* infrequent; seldom
in·frin·gir, *v.* trespass
in·fun·dir, *v.* infuse
in·fu·sión, *f.* infusion
in·ge·nie·ría, *f.* engineering
in·ge·nie·ro, *m.* engineer
in·ge·nio, *m.* device; wit
in·ge·nio·so, *a.* ingenious; clever; subtle; witty
in·ge·nuo, *a.* naive
in·gle, *f.* groin
in·glés, *m.*, in·gle·sa, *f.* English. *a.* English
in·gre·dien·te, *m.* ingredient
in·gre·sar, *v.* enter; deposit
in·gre·so, *m.* entry; *pl.* income; revenue
in·ha·bi·li·dad, *f.* inability
in·ha·lar, *v.* inhale
in·he·ren·te, *a.* inherent
in·hi·bi·ción, *f.* inhibition
in·hu·ma·no, *a.* inhuman
i·ni·cia·ción, *f.* initiation
i·ni·cial, *a.* initial. *f.* initial
i·ni·ciar, *v.* initiate
i·ni·cia·ti·va, *f.* initiative; enterprise
i·ni·qui·dad, *f.* iniquity
in·jer·tar, *v.* graft
in·ju·ria, *f.* injury; abuse
in·jus·ta·men·te, *adv.* unjustly; wrong
in·jus·ti·cia, *f.* injustice
in·jus·to, *a.* unjust
in·ma·du·ro, *a.* immature
in·me·dia·to, *a.* immediate; instant
in·men·so, *a.* immense; huge; vast
in·mer·sión, *f.* immersion
in·mi·gra·ción, *f.* immigration
in·mi·gran·te, *m., f.* immigrant
in·mi·grar, *v.* immigrate
in·mi·nen·te, *a.* imminent
in·mo·ral, *a.* immoral
in·mor·tal, *a.* immortal
in·mó·vil, *a.* immobile; still; stationary
in·mun·di·cia, *f.* filth
in·mu·ni·dad, *f.* immunity
in·na·to, *a.* inborn; innate
in·no·ble, *a.* ignoble
in·no·cuo, *a.* harmless
in·no·va·ción, *f.* innovation
in·nu·me·ra·ble, *a.* unnumbered; innumerable; countless
i·no·cen·cia, *f.* innocence
i·no·cen·te, *a.* innocent; clear
i·no·cu·la·ción, *f.* inoculation
in·o·por·tu·no, *a.* untimely; inopportune
in·quie·tar(se), *v.* worry; upset; trouble; harry; agitate
in·quie·to, *a.* anxious; concerned; fidgety
in·quie·tud, *f.* unrest; alarm; anxiety; *inf.* jitters
in·qui·si·ción, *f.* inquisition
in·sa·lu·bre, *a.* unhealthy; unwholesome
ins·cri·bir(se), *v.* inscribe; enroll
ins·crip·ción, *f.* inscription
in·sec·to, *m.* insect
in·se·gu·ro, *a.* insecure; unsteady
in·sen·sa·to, *a.* insane; senseless
in·ser·tar, *v.* insert
in·sig·nias, *f. pl.* insignia
in·sig·ni·fi·can·cia, *f.* insignificance

in·sig·ni·fi·can·te, *a.* insignificant; negligible
in·si·nua·ción, *f.* insinuation
in·si·nuar, *v.* insinuate; hint
in·sí·pi·do, *a.* insipid; vapid; flat
in·sis·tir, *v.* insist
in·so·la·ción, *f.* sunstroke
in·so·len·cia, *f.* insolence
in·sol·ven·te, *a.* bankrupt
in·som·nio, *m.* insomnia
ins·pec·ción, *f.* inspection; survey
ins·pec·cio·nar, *v.* inspect; survey
ins·pi·ra·ción, *f.* inspiration
ins·pi·rar, *v.* inspire
ins·ta·la·ción, *f.* fixture; wiring. ins·ta·la·ción de ca·ñe·rías, plumbing
ins·ta·lar, *v.* install
ins·tan·tá·neo, *a.* instantaneous
ins·tan·te, *m.* instant; *inf.* jiffy
ins·ti·gar, *v.* instigate; abet
ins·tin·to, *m.* instinct; flair
ins·ti·tu·ción, *f.* institution
ins·ti·tuir, *v.* institution; institute
ins·ti·tu·triz, *f.* governess
ins·truc·ción, *f.* instruction
ins·truir, *v.* instruct; teach; enlighten; learn
ins·tru·men·to, *m.* instrument; tool
in·su·fi·cien·te, *a.* insufficient; short; deficient
in·su·li·na, *f.* insulin
in·sul·tar, *v.* insult
in·su·rrec·ción, *f.* insurrection; uprising
in·tac·to, *a.* intact
in·ta·cha·ble, *a.* blameless
in·te·gra·ción, *f.* integration
in·te·grar(se), *v.* integrate
in·te·gri·dad, *f.* integrity
in·te·lec·to, *m.* intellect
in·te·li·gen·cia, *f.* intelligence; mind; intellect
in·te·li·gen·te, *a.* intelligent; brainy
in·ten·ción, *f.* intention; meaning
in·ten·si·dad, *f.* intensity
in·ten·si·fi·car, *v.* intensify; deepen
in·ten·so, *a.* intense; strong; vivid; violent. *m.* intent
in·ten·tar, *v.* try; endeavor; attempt; essay; mean
in·ter·ac·ción, *f.* interplay
in·ter·cam·biar, *v.* interchange
in·ter·cam·bio, *m.* interchange
in·ter·ce·der, *v.* intercede
in·ter·ce·sión, *f.* intercession
in·te·rés, *m.* interest; stir; cause
in·te·re·sar(se), *v.* interest; concern
in·ter·fe·ren·cia, *f.* interference
in·te·rin, *m.* interim; meantime
in·te·rior, *m.* interior; inside. *a.* interior; internal; inner; indoor
in·ter·jec·ción, *f.* interjection
in·ter·me·dio, *a.* intermediate. *m.* interlude; medium
in·ter·mi·sión, *f.* intermission
in·ter·na·cio·nal, *a.* international
in·ter·no, *a.* internal; inside; inward(s). *m.* intern
in·ter·po·ner(se), *v.* interpose; intervene
in·ter·pre·ta·ción, *f.* translation; interpretation
in·ter·pre·tar, *v.* interpret
in·te·rro·ga·ción, *f.* interrogation. sig·no de in·te·rro·ga·ción, question mark
in·te·rro·gar, *v.* interrogate; examine; quiz; *inf.* grill
in·te·rrum·pir, *v.* interrupt
in·te·rrup·ción, *f.* interruption
in·ter·sec·ción, *f.* intersection
in·ter·ven·ción, *f.* interference
in·ter·ve·nir, *v.* intervene; interfere; mediate; audit
in·ter·ven·tor, *m.* comptroller; auditor
in·tes·ti·no, *m.* intestine; gut; *pl.* bowels
in·ti·mar, *v.* intimate
in·ti·mi·dad, *f.* closeness
in·ti·mi·dar(se), *v.* intimidate; browbeat; bully; cow
ín·ti·mo, *a.* intimate
in·ti·tu·lar, *v.* title; style
in·to·le·ran·te, *a.* intolerant
in·tran·qui·lo, *a.* uneasy; restless
in·tran·si·ti·vo, *a.* intransitive
in·tra·ve·no·so, *a.* intravenous
in·tré·pi·do, *a.* intrepid; bold; fearless
in·tri·ga, *f.* intrigue
in·tri·gar, *v.* intrigue; scheme; plot
in·trín·se·co, *a.* intrinsic(al)
in·tro·duc·ción, *f.* introduction
in·tro·du·cir(se), *v.* introduce; broach; slip in
in·tui·ción, *f.* intuition
i·nun·da·ción, *f.* flood
i·nun·dar, *v.* deluge; flood; swamp
i·nú·til, *a.* useless; futile
in·va·dir, *v.* invade; overrun
in·vá·li·dar, *v.* void; invalidate
in·va·sión, *f.* invasion
in·ven·ci·ble, *a.* invincible
in·ven·ción, *f.* invention; contrivance; figment
in·ven·tar, *v.* invent; fabricate; devise; contrive
in·ver·nal, *a.* winter; wintry
in·ver·nar, *v.* winter
in·ver·sión, *f.* inversion
in·ver·so, *a.* reverse
in·ver·te·bra·do, *m.* invertebrate. *a.* invertebrate
in·ver·tir, *v.* reverse; invert; invest
in·ves·ti·ga·ción, *f.* investigation; probe; *pl.* research

in·ves·ti·gar, *v.* investigate
in·ves·tir, *v.* invest
in·vic·ti·va, *f.* tirade
in·vier·no, *m.* winter
in·vi·si·ble, *a.* invisible
in·vi·ta·ción, *f.* invitation
in·vi·tar, *v.* invite; treat
in·vo·car, *v.* invoke
in·vo·lun·ta·rio, *a.* involuntary
in·yec·ción, *f.* injection; *inf.* shot
in·yec·tar, *v.* inject
ion, *m.* ion
ir(se), *v.* go; leave; depart; quit; move; ride
i·ra, *f.* ire; rage; anger
i·ri·des·cen·te, *a.* iridescent
i·ris, *m.* iris. ar·co i·ris, rainbow
i·ro·nía, *f.* irony
i·ró·ni·co, *a.* ironic(al); wry
i·rra·cio·nal, *a.* irrational
i·rra·diar, *v.* irradiate
i·rre·gu·lar, *a.* irregular
i·rre·sis·ti·ble, *a.* irresistible
i·rres·pon·sa·ble, *a.* irresponsible
i·rre·ve·ren·cia, *f.* irreverence
i·rri·sión, *f.* derision
i·rri·ta·ble, *a.* irritable; touchy; crusty
i·rri·ta·ción, *f.* irritation
i·rri·tar(se), *v.* irritate; chafe; anger; pique
is·la, *f.* island; isle
i·sós·ce·les, *a.* isosceles
ist·mo, *m.* isthmus
i·ti·ne·ra·rio, *m.* itinerary
iz·quier·da, *f.* left
iz·quier·do, *a.* left

J

ja·ba·lí, *m.* wild boar
ja·ba·li·na, *f.* javelin
ja·bón, *m.* soap
ja·bo·na·du·ras, *f. pl.* suds
ja·ca, *f.* pony; cob; nag
ja·cin·to, *m.* hyacinth
jac·tan·cia, *f.* bluster; bragging
jac·tar·se, *v.* brag; boast
ja·de, *m.* jade
ja·dear, *v.* pant
ja·deo, *m.* pant
ja·guar, *m.* jaguar
jal·be·gue, *m.* whitewash
ja·lea, *f.* jelly
ja·leo, *m.* fuss; racket
ja·más, *adv.* never; ever
jam·ba, *f.* jamb
ja·món, *m.* ham
ja·que, *m.* check in chess. dar ja·que ma·te, checkmate
ja·ra·be, *m.* syrup
ja·ra·near, *v.* carouse
jar·dín, *m.* garden; park. jar·dín bo·tá·ni·co, arboretum. jar·dín de la in·fan·cia, kindergarten. jar·dín zoo·ló·gi·co, zoo
ja·rra, *f.* jug
ja·rro, *m.* jug; flagon
ja·rrón, *m.* vase
jau·la, *f.* cage; cell
jaz·mín, *m.* jasmine, jasmin
jazz, *m.* jazz
jeep, *m.* jeep
je·fe, *m.* boss; chief; head; leader
Je·ho·vá, *m.* Jehovah
jen·gi·bre, *m.* ginger. cer·ve·za de jen·gi·bre, gingerale. pan de jen·gi·bre, gingerbread
je·que, *m.* sheik, sheikh
je·rar·quía, *f.* hierarchy
jer·ga, *f.* slang; jargon; gibberish
je·rin·ga, *f.* syringe
je·ro·glí·fi·co, *a.* hieroglyphic. *m.* hieroglyphic; hieroglyph
jer·sey, *m.* sweater; jersey
ji·ga, *f.* jig
ji·ne·ta, *f.* equestrienne
ji·ne·te, *m.* horseman; equestrian
ji·ra, *f.* picnic
ji·ra·fa, *f.* giraffe
ji·ro·nes, *m. pl.* tatters
joc·key, *m.* jockey
jo·co·so, *a.* jocose; jocular
jo·fai·na, *f.* basin
jor·nal, *m.* often *pl.* wage
jo·ro·ba, *f.* hump
jo·ro·ba·do, *a.* hunchback
jo·ro·bar, *v.* tease; annoy
jo·ta, *f.* iota; jot
jo·ven, *a.* young; juvenile. *m., f.* youth; *inf.* youth
jo·ven·ci·to, *m.*, jo·ven·ci·ta, *f.* youngster
jo·vial, *a.* jovial
jo·ya, *f.* jewel; gem; *pl.* jewelry
jo·ye·ro, *m.* jeweler
jua·ne·te, *m.* bunion
ju·bi·lar(se), *v.* retire; pension
ju·bi·leo, *m.* jubilee
ju·bi·lo, *m.* jubilation; glee
ju·daís·mo, *m.* Judaism
ju·día, *f.* bean
ju·di·cial, *a.* judicial
ju·do, *m.* judo
jue·go, *m.* game; play; set; suite
jue·ga, *f.* spree
jue·ves, *m.* Thursday
juez, *m.* judge; justice
ju·ga·da, *f.* gamble; move
ju·gar, *v.* play; game; toy with; gamble
ju·go, *m.* juice
ju·gue·te, *m.* toy; plaything
ju·gue·tear, *v.* frolic; play
jui·cio, *m.* judgment; verdict; sense; wit. jui·cio sa·no, sanity

ju·lio, *m.* July
jun·co, *m.* junk; rush
ju·nio, *m.* June
jun·qui·llo, *m.* jonquil
jun·ta, *f.* union; board
jun·tar(se), *v.* join; connect; band; assemble
jun·to, *a.* joined. *adv.* together. jun·to a, near; against
jun·tu·ra, *f.* junction; joint; splice
ju·ra·do, *m.* juror; jury
ju·ra·men·to, *m.* oath
ju·rar, *v.* swear; vow
ju·ris·dic·ción, *f.* jurisdiction
ju·ris·pru·den·cia, *f.* law; jurisprudence
ju·ris·ta, *m., f.* jurist
jus·ta, *f.* joust
jus·ta·men·te, *adv.* fairly
jus·tar, *v.* joust
jus·ti·cia, *f.* justice
jus·ti·fi·ca·ción, *f.* justification; substantiation
jus·ti·fi·car, *v.* justify; warrant
jus·ti·llo, *m.* jerkin
jus·to, *a.* just; fair
ju·ve·nil, *a.* juvenile; youth
ju·ven·tud, *f.* youth
juz·gar, *v.* judge; try; deem

K

ki·lo, *m.* kilogram
ki·lo·ci·clo, *m.* kilocycle
ki·lo·gra·mo, *m.* kilogram
ki·lo·mé·tri·co, *a.* kilometric
ki·ló·me·tro, *m.* kilometer
ki·lo·va·tio, *m.* kilowatt

L

la(s), *def. art.* the; *pl.* them
la·be·rin·to, *m.* labyrinth; maze
la·bial, *a.* labial
la·bio, *m.* lip
la·bor, *f.* labor; work; task
la·bo·ra·to·rio, *m.* laboratory; *inf.* lab
la·bo·rio·so, *a.* laborious; painstaking
la·bra·dor, *m.* farmer
la·bran·tío, *a.* arable
la·brar, *v.* till
la·ca, *f.* lacquer
la·ca·yo, *m.* lackey
la·ce·rar, *v.* lacerate
la·cio, *a.* lank; limp
la·có·ni·co, *a.* laconic
lac·tar, *v.* suckle
lác·ti·co, *a.* lactic
la·dear(se), *v.* lean; skirt; tip; heel
la·do, *m.* side; flank
la·drar, *v.* bark
la·dri·do, *m.* bark
la·drón, *m.* thief; burglar; *inf.* crook
la·gar, *m.* winery
la·gar·to, *m.* alligator; lizard
lá·gri·ma, *f.* tear
la·gu·na, *f.* lagoon; lacuna
lai·ca·do, *m.* laity
la·ma, *f.* lama
la·mé, *m.* lamé
la·me·du·ra, *f.* lick
la·men·ta·ción, *f.* lamentation
la·men·tar(se), *v.* lament; mourn; regret; rue; wail
la·mer, *v.* lick; lap
lá·mi·na, *f.* sheet
la·mi·nar, *v.* laminate
lám·pa·ra, *f.* lamp; light
lam·prea, *f.* lamprey
la·na, *f.* wool
lan·ce, *m.* throw; stroke
lan·cha, *f.* launch
lan·gos·ta, *f.* lobster
lan·gui·de·cer, *v.* languish; pine
lán·gui·do, *a.* languid; listless
la·ni·lla, *f.* nap; bunting
la·no·li·na, *f.* lanolin
la·nu·do, *a.* fleecy
lan·za, *f.* spear; lance
lan·za·de·ra, *f.* shuttle
lan·zar(se), *v.* throw; hurl; launch
lá·pi·da, *f.* stone. lá·pi·da se·pul·cral, tombstone
lá·piz, *m.* pencil. lá·piz de co·lor, crayon
lap·so, *m.* lapse; span
lar·go, *a.* length. *a.* long. a lo lar·go, along
la·rin·ge, *f.* larynx
la·rin·gi·tis, *f.* laryngitis
lar·va, *f.* larva
las·ci·vo, *a.* lascivious; sensual; lewd; wanton
la·si·tud, *f.* lassitude
lás·ti·ma, *f.* pity
las·ti·mo·so, *a.* pitiful; sorry
las·tre, *m.* ballast
la·ta, *f.* can. con·ser·var en la·tas, can
la·ten·te, *a.* latent
la·te·ral, *a.* lateral; sidelong. *m.* side
la·te·ral·men·te, *adv.* sidelong
lá·tex, *m.* latex
la·ti·ga·zo, *m.* lash
la·ti·go, *m.* whip; lash. lá·ti·go mo·cho, crop
la·ti·tud, *f.* latitude
la·tón, *m.* brass
la·tro·ci·nio, *m.* larceny
laúd, *m.* lute
lau·rel, *m.* laurel; bay
la·va, *f.* lava
la·va·bo, *m.* washstand; washroom
la·va·de·ro, *m.* laundry
la·va·do, *a.* washed. *m.* wash
la·va·do·ra, *f.* washer

la·va·ma·nos, *m.* washstand
la·var(se), *v.* wash. la·var y plan·char, launder
la·xan·te, *a.* laxative. *m.* laxative
la·xo, *a.* lax
la·zar, *v.* lasso
la·zo, *m.* lasso; lariat; bow; band. la·zo co·rre·di·zo, noose
le(s), *pron.* him; *pl.* them
leal, *a.* loyal
leal·men·te, *adv.* faithfully
leal·tad, *f.* loyalty; devotion
lec·ción, *f.* lesson; reading
lec·tu·ra, *f.* reading; lecture
le·che, *f.* milk. le·che de man·te·ca, buttermilk
le·che·ría, *f.* dairy
le·cho, *m.* watercourse; bed
le·chu·ga, *f.* lettuce; frill
le·chu·za, *f.* owl
leer, *v.* read
le·ga·ción, *f.* legation
le·ga·do, *m.* legacy; bequest
le·gal, *a.* legal; lawful
le·ga·li·dad, *f.* legality
lé·ga·mo, *m.* slime
le·ga·ño·so, *a.* bleary
le·gar, *v.* will; bequeath
le·gen·da·rio, *a.* legendary
le·gi·ble, *a.* legible
le·gión, *f.* legion
le·gio·na·rio, *m.* legionnaire
le·gis·la·ción, *f.* legislation
le·gis·lar, *v.* legislate
le·gí·ti·mar, *v.* legitimate
le·gí·ti·mo, *a.* legitimate; rightful
le·go, *a.* lay. *m.* layman
le·gum·bre, *f.* vegetable; legume
le·ja·no, *a.* far; distant; far off
le·jía, *f.* lye; bleach
le·jos, *adv.* far; away; wide. prep. off. más le·jos, further
le·ma, *m.* motto
len·gua, *f.* tongue; language
len·gua·je, *m.* language
len·güe·ta, *f.* tongue; reed
le·ni·dad, *f.* lenience; leniency
len·te, *m.* lens. len·tes de con·tac·to, contact lenses
len·te·jue·la, *f.* sequin
len·to, *a.* slow; sluggish
le·ño, *m.* log; lumber; kindling
león, *m.* lion
leo·na·do, *a.* tawny
leo·par·do, *m.* leopard
le·pra, *f.* leprosy
le·pro·so, *m.*, le·pro·sa, *f.* leper
le·tar·go, *m.* lethargy
le·tra, *f.* letter. le·tra bas·tar·di·lla, italic. le·tra cur·si·va, script. le·tra de u·na can·ción, lyric
le·tre·ro, *m.* sign
leu·ce·mia, *f.* leukemia
le·va, *f.* levy
le·va·du·ra, *f.* yeast; leaven; leavening
le·van·tar(se), *v.* rise; raise; erect; lift
lé·xi·co, *m.* lexicon
ley, *f.* law; act
le·yen·da, *f.* legend
liar(se), *v.* tie; bind; bundle
li·be·ral, *a.* liberal. *m., f.* liberal
li·be·ra·li·dad, *f.* liberality; bounty
li·ber·tad, *f.* freedom; liberty; release
li·ber·tar, *v.* liberate; free
li·ber·ti·no, *a.* promiscuous. *m.* rake
li·bi·do, *m.* libido
li·bra, *f.* pound
li·brar(se), *v.* rid; free
li·bre, *a.* free; vacant
li·bre·to, *m.* libretto
li·bro, *m.* book
li·cen·cia, *f.* license; furlough
li·cen·cia·do, *m.*, li·cen·cia·da, *f.* graduate; bachelor
li·cen·ciar, *v.* license
li·ci·ta·dor, *m.* auctioneer
li·cor, *m.* liquor; liqueur; spirits
lí·der, *m.* leader
lie·bre, *f.* hare
lien·zo, *m.* canvas; linen
li·ga, *f.* league; garter
li·ga·do, *a.* bound
li·ga·du·ra, *f.* ligature
li·ga·men·to, *m.* ligament
li·gar(se), *v.* tie; band together; alloy
li·ge·ra·men·te, *adv.* lightly
li·ge·re·za, *f.* levity
li·ge·ro, *a.* airy; light; mild; flippant
li·la, *f.* lilac
li·ma, *f.* file; lime
li·ma·du·ras, *f. pl.* filings
li·mar, *v.* file
lim·bo, *m.* limbo
li·mi·ta·ción, *f.* limitation
li·mi·tar, *v.* limit; confine; restrict; bound
lí·mi·te, *m.* limit; *pl.* bounds
li·món, *m.* lemon
li·mo·na·da, *f.* lemonade
li·mo·ne·ro, *m.* lemon
li·mos·na, *f.* alms; dole; charity
lim·piar(se), *v.* clean; cleanse; polish
lim·pie·za, *f.* cleanliness
lim·pio, *a.* clean
li·mu·si·na, *f.* limousine
li·na·je, *m.* lineage; ancestry; birth
lin·ce, *m.* lynx; bobcat
lin·char, *v.* lynch
lin·dar, *v.* flank; adjoin
lí·nea, *f.* line. lí·nea aé·rea, airline
li·neal, *a.* linear
lin·fa, *f.* lymph
lin·go·te, *m.* ingot
lin·güís·ta, *m., f.* linguist
li·ni·men·to, *m.* liniment
li·no, *m.* linen; flax
li·nó·leo, *m.* linoleum

lin·ter·na, f. lantern. lin·ter·na e·
léc·tri·ca, flashlight
lío, m. bundle; liaison; row; inf. ruckus
li·quen, m. lichen
li·qui·dar(se), v. liquefy; liquidate
lí·qui·do, a. liquid. m. liquid
li·ra, f. lyre
lí·ri·co, a. lyric
li·rio, m. lily; iris
li·sia·do, m. cripple. a. lame
li·siar, v. lame; cripple
li·so, a. smooth; sleek
li·son·je·ro, a. complimentary
lis·ta, f. list; roll. lis·ta de pla·tos,
menu. lis·ta ro·mi·na, roster
lis·tar, v. streak; list
lis·to, a. ready; nimble; quick; smart;
clever
lis·tón, m. lath
li·te·ra, f. litter; berth
li·te·ral, a. literal
li·te·ra·rio, a. literary
li·te·ra·tu·ra, f. literature
li·to·ral, m. coastline
li·tur·gia, f. liturgy
lí·vi·do, a. livid
lo(s), neuter def. art. the; m. pl of el
loa·ble, a. laudable
lo·bo, m. wolf
ló·bre·go, a. gloomy
lo·cal, a. local. m. site
lo·ca·li·dad, f. locality
lo·ción, f. lotion
lo·co, a. insane; mad; crazy; wild. m.
madman; lunatic
lo·co·mo·tor, a. locomotive
lo·co·mo·to·ra, f. engine; locomotive
lo·cu·ra, f. insanity; lunacy; folly
lo·do, m. mud
lo·gia, f. lodge
ló·gi·ca, f. logic
ló·gi·co, a. logical; coherent
lo·grar, v. succeed; achieve; win; carry; get; attain
lo·gro, m. attainment; success
lom·briz, f. angleworm
lo·mo, m. loin; rib; ribs
lon·ge·vi·dad, f. longevity
lon·gi·tud, f. longitude
lo·ro, m. parrot
lo·sa, f. flagstone
lo·te·ría, f. lottery
lo·za, f. crockery. lo·za de ba·rro,
earthenware
lo·za·no, a. luxuriant
lu·bri·can·te, m. lubricant
lu·bri·car, v. lubricate
lu·bri·fi·car, v. oil; grease
lú·ci·do, a. lucid
lu·ciér·na·ga, f. firefly; glowworm
lu·cir(se), v. flaunt; show off; light up
lu·cra·ti·vo, a. lucrative
lu·cha, f. battle; fight; strife; struggle
lu·char, v. fight; battle; struggle
lue·go, adv. then
lu·gar, m. place; space; room
lu·jo, m. luxury. de lu·jo, deluxe;
fancy
lu·jo·so, a. luxurious
lu·ju·ria, f. lust
lu·ju·riar, v. lust
lu·mi·no·so, a. luminous; illuminated
lu·na, f. moon. lu·na de miel, honeymoon
lu·nar, a. lunar. m. mole
lu·nes, m. Monday
lus·tre, m. luster; shine; sheen; gloss;
brightness
lus·tro·so, a. glossy
lu·to, m. mourning
luz, f. light. luz del día, daylight. luz
de la lu·na, moonlight

LL

lla·ga, f. sore; ulcer
lla·ma, f. flame; blaze; llama
lla·ma·da, f. call; knock
lla·ma·do, a. so-called
lla·mar(se), v. be named; name; call;
ring; summon; rap
lla·ma·ti·vo, a. flamboyant; garish;
showy
lla·no, a. even; flat. m. plain
llan·to, m. cry
lla·ve, f. key
lle·ga·da, f. arrival
lle·gar(se), v. arrive; come; land; approach. lle·gar a ser, become
lle·nar(se), v. fill; stuff; pack; occupy
lle·no, a. full. lle·no de, full of;
fraught with
lle·var(se), v. carry; bear; convey;
tote; lead; wear
llo·rar, v. cry; weep; bawl; mourn
llo·ri·quear, v. whimper
llo·ver, v. rain; shower
llo·viz·nar, v. drizzle; sprinkle
llu·via, f. rain; rainfall
llu·vio·so, a. rainy; wet

M

ma·ca·bro, a. macabre
ma·ca·rrón, m. macaroon
ma·ca·rro·nes, m. pl. macaroni
ma·ci·zo, a. massive; solid
ma·cha·do, m. hatchet
ma·che·te, m. machete
ma·cho, a. male; masculine. m. male
ma·de·ra, f. wood; timber; lumber
Ma·do·na, f. Madonna
ma·dras·tra, f. stepmother
ma·dre, f. mother
ma·dri·gue·ra, f. burrow
ma·dri·na, f. godmother

ma·dru·ga·da, f. morning
ma·du·rar(se), v. mature; ripen
ma·du·rez, f. maturity
ma·du·ro, a. mature; ripe
maes·tro, m. teacher; master; maestro. a. skilled
ma·gen·ta, f. magenta
ma·gia, f. magic. ma·gia ne·gra,
black magic
má·gi·co, a. magic
ma·gis·tra·do, m. magistrate
mag·ná·ni·mo, a. magnanimous
mag·na·te, m. tycoon
mag·ne·sio, m. magnesium
mag·ne·tis·mo, m. magnetism
mag·ní·fi·co, a. magnificent; grand;
splendid
mag·ni·tud, f. magnitude
ma·go, m. magician
ma·gro, a. lean
ma·gu·llar, v. bruise
ma·ha·ra·ja, m. maharajah, maharaja
maíz, m. corn; maize
ma·jes·tad, f. majesty
ma·jes·tuo·so, a. stately
mal, a. bad; ill. adv. wrongly. m. evil;
mischief; harm
ma·la·men·te, adv. evil; badly
mal·dad, f. badness; evil; villainy
mal·de·cir, v. curse
mal·di·ción, f. curse
ma·lea·ble, a. malleable
ma·le·cón, m. jetty
ma·le·ta, f. suitcase; valise; bag
ma·lé·vo·lo, a. malignant
ma·le·za, f. underbrush; scrub
mal·gas·tar, v. waste; squander
mal·he·chor, m., mal·he·cho·ra, f.
evildoer; wrongdoer
mal·hu·mo·ra·do, a. cross; crabby;
cantankerous
ma·li·cia, f. malice
ma·li·cio·so, a. malicious; wicked;
mischievous
ma·lig·no, a. malignant
ma·lí·si·mo, a. wretched; very bad
ma·lo, a. bad; evil; wrong; poor;
naughty
ma·lo·gro, m. miscarriage
mal·par·to, m. miscarriage
mal·ta, f. malt
mal·tra·tar, v. mistreat; misuse
mal·va·do, m. villain
mal·ver·sa·dor, m. embezzler
ma·lla, f. mesh; mail
ma·lle·ja, f. gizzard
ma·má, f. mama, mamma; inf. mom;
ma
ma·mar, v. suck
ma·mí·fe·ro, m. mammal
ma·mut, m. mammoth
ma·ná, f. manna
man·co·mu·nar(se), v. pool; merge
man·cha, f. smudge; spot; soil; smear
man·char(se), v. blemish; soil; dirty;
spot
man·chi·ta, f. speck
man·da·mien·to, m. commandment
man·dar, v. send; command; order;
control; lead; tell
man·da·rín, m. mandarin
man·da·to, m. mandate; order
man·do, m. command; rule
man·do·li·na, f. mandolin
man·dril, m. baboon
ma·ne·jar(se), v. manage; handle;
drive
ma·ne·ra, f. manner; way
man·ga, f. sleeve; beam; hose
man·ga·ne·so, m. manganese
man·go, m. handle; mango
man·gos·ta, f. mongoose
man·gui·to, m. muff
ma·nía, f. mania; rage; fad
ma·nía·co, a. maniac. m., ma·nía·ca,
f. maniac
ma·ni·atar, v. handcuff
ma·ni·co·mio, m. asylum; madhouse
ma·ni·cu·ra, f. manicure
ma·ni·fes·ta·ción, f. manifestation;
demonstration
ma·ni·fes·tar(se), v. manifest; show
ma·ni·fies·to, a. manifest; evident.
m. manifest; manifesto
ma·nio·bra, f. maneuver; handling
ma·nio·brar, v. maneuver; handle
ma·ni·pu·la·ción, f. manipulation
ma·ni·pu·lar, v. manipulate; maneuver
ma·ni·quí, m. mannequin; dummy
ma·no, f. hand. he·cho a ma·no,
handmade. ma·no de o·bra, handicraft
ma·no·sear, v. handle; paw
ma·no·ta·da, f. smack
man·so, a. tame; mild
man·ta, f. blanket
man·te·ca, f. fat; butter. man·te·ca
de cer·do, lard
man·te·co·so, a. buttery
man·te·ner(se), v. maintain; support;
hold; service
man·te·ni·mien·to, m. maintenance
man·te·que·ra, f. churn
man·te·qui·lla, f. butter
man·to, m. mantel; cloak
ma·nual, a. manual. m. manual;
handbook
ma·nu·bri·o, m. crank; handle
ma·nu·fac·tu·ra, f. manufacture
ma·nus·cri·to, m. manuscript
ma·nu·ten·ción, f. upkeep
man·za·na, f. apple; block. man·za·
na sil·ves·tre, crab apple
ma·ña, f. knack
ma·ña·na, f. morning; tomorrow.
adv. tomorrow

ma·pa, m. map
ma·qui·lla·je, m. makeup
má·qui·na, f. machine
ma·qui·na·ria, f. machinery
mar, m. f. sea
ma·ra·vi·lla, f. wonder
ma·ra·vi·llar(se), v. marvel
mar·be·te, m. tag; label. mar·be·te
en·go·ma·do, sticker
mar·ca, f. mark; brand; check; print;
landmark. mar·ca re·gis·tra·da,
trademark
mar·ca·do, a. pronounced
mar·car(se), v. mark; brand; dial
mar·cial, a. martial
mar·co, m. frame; setting
mar·cha, f. march; run
mar·char(se), v. go; travel; march
mar·chi·tar(se), v. wilt; wither; sear
ma·rea, f. tide
ma·rear(se), v. get seasick; feel dizzy;
navigate
ma·reo, m. seasickness
mar·fil, m. ivory
mar·ga·ri·na, f. margarine
mar·gen, m. margin; fringe
ma·ri·cón, m. inf. queer
ma·ri·jua·na, f. marijuana; inf. pot
ma·ri·na, f. navigation. ma·ri·na de
gue·rra, navy
ma·ri·ne·ro, m. sailor; seaman
ma·ri·no, a. marine
ma·rio·ne·ta, f. marionette
ma·ri·po·sa, f. butterfly
ma·ris·cal, m. marshal
ma·ris·co, m. shellfish
ma·ri·tal, a. marital
ma·rí·ti·mo, a. maritime; naval
már·mol, m. marble
mar·qués, m. marquis
mar·que·sa, f. marquise
mar·so·pa, f. porpoise
mar·su·pial, a. marsupial. m. marsupial
mar·tes, m. Tuesday
mar·ti·llar, v. hammer
mar·ti·lleo, m. hammering; clatter
már·tir, m. f. martyr
mar·ti·ri·zar, v. martyr
mar·zo, m. March
mas, conj. but
más, a. more; most; plus. adv. more.
m. more. más de, over
ma·sa, f. mass; lump; dough. en ma·
sa, wholesale
mas·car, v. chew
más·ca·ra, f. mask
mas·ca·ra·da, f. masquerade;
masque; mask
mas·ca·rón de proa, figurehead
mas·co·ta, f. mascot
mas·cu·li·no, a. masculine; male. m.
masculine
ma·si·lla, f. putty
ma·so·quis·mo, m. masochism
ma·so·quis·ta, m., f. masochist
mas·ti·car, v. masticate
más·til, m. mast
mas·to·don·te, m. mastodon
mas·tur·ba·ción, f. masturbation
ma·tan·za, f. slaughter
ma·tar(se), v. kill (oneself); slaughter; slay
ma·ta·se·llos, m. postmark
ma·te, a. mat, matt, matte. m. checkmate
ma·te·má·ti·cas, f. mathematics; inf.
math
ma·te·ria, f. material; matter; substance; stuff
ma·te·rial, a. material. m. material
ma·ter·nal, a. maternal
ma·ter·ni·dad, f. motherhood;
maternity
ma·ter·no, a. mother
ma·tiz, f. shade; hue
ma·ti·zar, v. tinge
ma·tón, m. hoodlum; bully
ma·trí·cu·la, f. enrollment
ma·tri·cu·lar(se), v. enroll; matricu-
late
ma·tri·mo·nio, m. marriage; matrimony; wedlock
ma·triz, f. womb; matrix
ma·tro·na, f. matron
ma·tu·teo, m. smuggling; inf. dope
má·xi·ma, f. maxim
má·xi·mo, a. maximum; greatest
má·xi·mum, m. maximum
ma·yo, m. May
ma·yo·ne·sa, f. mayonnaise
ma·yor, a. adult; utmost; main; major. m. elder; (mus.) major. al por
ma·yor, wholesale
ma·yor·do·mo, m. butler
ma·yo·ría, f. majority
ma·yús·cu·la, f. capital letter
ma·za, f. wench; bat
maz·mo·rra, f. dungeon
ma·zo, m. mallet
me, pron. me
me·cá·ni·ca, f. mechanics
me·cá·ni·co, a. mechanical. m. mechanic
me·ca·nis·mo, m. mechanism
me·ca·nó·gra·fo, m., me·ca·nó·gra·
fa, f. typist
me·ce·nas, m. patron
me·cer, v. rock; cradle
me·cha, f. wick
me·da·lla, f. medal
me·da·llón, m. medallion
me·dia, f. stocking; pl. nylons; hose
me·dia·no, a. median; medium
me·dia·no·che, f. midnight
me·diar, v. mediate; intervene

me·di·ca·ción, f. medication
me·di·ca·men·to, m. medicine
me·di·ci·na, f. medicine
mé·di·co, a. medical. m. doctor;
physician
me·di·da, f. measure; measurement;
arrangement
me·die·val, a. medieval
me·dio, a. half; average; mean; middle. adv. mid; half. m. midst; middle; mean; medium; agency. en
me·dio, between. en me·dio de,
among
me·dio·día, m. noon; midday
me·dir, v. measure; gauge; span; survey
me·di·ta·ción, f. meditation
me·di·tar, v. meditate; ponder
mé·du·la, f. marrow
me·du·sa, f. jellyfish
me·ji·lla, f. cheek
me·jor, a. better; best. adv. better;
best
me·jo·ra, f. improvement
me·jo·ra·mien·to, m. betterment;
improvement
me·jo·rar(se), v. improve; better
me·lan·co·lía, f. dejection; melancholy; blues
me·lan·có·li·co, a. wistful; gloomy;
blue
me·la·za, f. molasses
me·lo·co·tón, m. peach
me·lo·día, f. melody
me·lo·dra·ma, m. melodrama
me·lón, m. melon
me·llar, v. indent; notch; dent
me·llo, m. indentation; notch
mem·bra·na, f. membrane; web
me·mo·ra·ble, a. memorable; eventful
me·mo·rán·dum, m. memorandum;
inf. memo
me·mo·ria, f. memory; memoir
me·mo·rial, m. memorial
me·na, f. ore
men·ción, f. mention
men·cio·nar, v. mention
men·di·gar, v. beg; inf. panhandle
men·di·go, m. beggar
me·near(se), v. wag; wiggle; flutter
men·guar, v. ebb; wane; lessen
me·no·pau·sia, f. menopause
me·nor, a. least; less; minor; junior.
m. junior. me·nor de e·dad, minor
me·nos, a. less. adv. least; less. prep.
less; minus. a me·nos que, except;
unless. sig·no me·nos, minus sign
me·nos·pre·ciar, v. disparage; despise; underrate
me·nos·pre·cio, m. contempt; scorn
men·sa·je·ro, m. messenger
mens·trua·ción, f. menstruation
men·sual, a. monthly
men·sual·men·te, adv. monthly
men·ta, f. mint; peppermint. men·ta
ver·de, spearmint
men·tal, a. mental
men·te, f. mind
men·tir, v. lie; fib
men·ti·ra, f. lie; falsehood
men·ti·ro·so, a. men·ti·ro·sa, f.
liar. a. untruthful
men·tol, m. menthol
me·nú, m. menu; bill of fare
me·nu·di·llos, m. pl. giblets
me·nu·do, a. minute; insignificant. a
me·nu·do, often
mer·ca·de·ría, f. commodity
mer·ca·do, m. market; mart
mer·can·cías, f. pl. wares; goods
mer·ced, f. mercy
mer·ce·na·rio, a. mercenary. m.
mercenary; hireling
mer·cu·rio, m. mercury
me·re·cer, v. merit; deserve; earn
me·ren·gue, m. meringue
me·ri·dia·no, m. meridian
me·ri·dio·nal, a. southern
me·rien·da, f. snack
mé·ri·to, m. merit; worth
mer·me·la·da, f. marmalade; jam
me·ro, a. mere; very
mes, m. month
me·sa, f. table; plateau
me·si·zo, m., mes·ti·za, f. half-
caste; mongrel. a. half-breed;
mongrel
me·ta, f. goal
me·ta·bo·lis·mo, m. metabolism
me·tá·fo·ra, f. metaphor
me·tal, m. metal
me·ta·mor·fo·sis, f. metamorphosis
me·teo·ri·to, m. meteorite
me·teo·ro·lo·gía, f. meteorology
me·ter(se), v. insert; put; interfere;
meddle
mé·to·do, m. method; system; way
me·tro, m. meter; metre; subway
me·tró·po·li, f. metropolis
me·tro·po·li·ta·no, a. metropolitan
mez·cla, f. mixture; mix; concoction
mez·clar(se), v. mix; blend; mingle;
jumble
mez·qui·no, a. petty
mi, a. my
mí, pron. me; myself
mía, f. pron. mine
mi·ca, f. mica
mi·cro·bio, m. microbe
mi·cro·cos·mo, m. microcosm
mi·cró·fo·no, m. microphone
mi·cros·co·pio, m. microscope
mie·do, m. fear. te·ner mie·do, fear;
be afraid
miel, f. honey
miem·bro, m. member; limb
mien·tras, conj. while. adv. mean-

while. mien·tras tan·to, meantime
miér·co·les, m. Wednesday
mi·ga, f. crumb
mi·gra·to·rio, a. migratory
mil, a. thousand. m. thousand
mi·la·gro, m. miracle; wonder
mi·la·gro·so, a. miraculous
mil·deu, m. mildew
mi·le·nio, m. millennium
mi·lé·si·mo, a. thousandth
mi·li·cia, f. militia
mi·lí·me·tro, m. millimeter
mi·li·tar, a. military. m. soldier; serviceman
mi·lla, f. mile
mi·llón, m. million
mi·llo·na·rio, m., mi·llo·na·ria, f.
millionaire
mi·mar, v. pamper; coddle
mi·me·ó·gra·fo, m. mimeograph
mi·mo, m. mime
mi·na, f. mine
mi·nar, v. mine
mi·ne·ral, a. mineral. m. mineral
mi·nia·tu·ra, f. miniature
mí·ni·mo, a. minimum; least. m.
minimum
mi·nis·te·rio, m. ministry
mi·nis·tro, m. minister; (cap.) Secretary
mi·no·ría, f. minority
mi·nu·cio·so, a. exhaustive; meticulous
mi·nu·to, m. minute
mío, m. pron. mine
mio·pe, a. near-sighted; myopic
mi·ra·da, f. look; gaze; expression
mi·rar(se), v. watch; look; glance;
gaze; regard
mi·ría·da, f. myriad
mir·lo, m. blackbird
mi·sa, f. mass
mi·sal, m. missal
mi·sán·tro·po, m. misanthrope
mi·se·ra·ble, a. miserable; wretched;
paltry. m. wretch
mi·se·ria, f. misery
mi·se·ri·cor·dia, f. mercy
mi·sión, f. mission
mi·sio·ne·ro, m., mi·sio·ne·ra, f.
missionary
mis·mo, a. same; self-same; very
mis·te·rio, m. mystery
mis·te·rio·so, a. mysterious; uncanny
mís·ti·ca, f. mysticism
mis·ti·cis·mo, m. mysticism
mís·ti·co, m., mís·ti·ca, f. mystic. a.
mystic
mi·tad, f. half
mí·ti·co, a. mythic(al)
mi·ti·gar, v. mitigate; alleviate; soft-
en
mi·to, m. myth
mi·to·lo·gía, f. mythology
mi·tón, m. mitten
mi·tra, f. miter, mitre
mo·bi·lia·rio, m. furniture; pl. furnishings
mo·ca·sín, m. moccasin
mo·ción, f. motion
mo·co, m. mucus
mo·co·so, m. brat
mo·da, f. mode; fashion; vogue. de
mo·da, fashionable
mo·de·lar, v. model; form
mo·de·lo, m. model; pattern; ideal;
norm; mannequin
mo·de·ra·ción, f. moderation
mo·de·ra·do, a. moderate. m. moderate
mo·de·rar(se), v. moderate; temper
mo·der·ni·zar(se), v. modernize; update
mo·der·no, a. modern; new
mo·des·to, a. modest
mo·di·fi·ca·ción, f. modification
mo·di·fi·car, v. modify; alter
mo·dis·ta, f. dressmaker
mo·do, m. mode; manner; guise; sort;
pl. means
mo·du·lar, v. modulate
mo·fa, f. mockery; taunt
mo·far(se), v. taunt; sneer; jeer; scoff;
gibe
mo·fe·ta, f. skunk
mo·hi·no, a. sulky
mo·ho, m. mold; mould; mildew
mo·ho·so, a. rusty
mo·ja·do, a. wet
mo·jar(se), v. wet; dampen; drench
mo·jón, m. landmark
mol·de, m. mold; mould; cast
mol·dear, v. mold; mould; shape
mo·lé·cu·la, f. molecule
mo·ler, v. grind; mill
mo·les·tar(se), v. trouble; molest;
pester; bother; annoy; vex
mo·les·tia, f. nuisance; bother; annoyance
mo·les·to, a. troublesome; tiresome;
unpleasant
mo·li·no, m. mill. mo·li·no de vien·
to, windmill
mo·lus·co, m. mollusk; mollusc
mo·lle·te, m. muffin
mo·men·tá·neo, a. momentary
mo·men·to, m. moment; minute;
momentum
mo·mia, f. mummy
mo·nar·ca, m. monarch; sovereign
mo·nar·quía, f. monarchy
mo·nas·te·rio, m. monastery
mo·ne·da, f. coin; currency; silver

mo·ni·tor, m. monitor
mon·ja, f. nun
mon·je, m. monk
mo·no, m. monkey; ape; simian. a.
pretty; cute
mo·no·ga·mia, f. monogamy
mo·no·gra·ma, m. monogram
mo·no·li·ta, f. monolith
mo·nó·lo·go, m. monologue, mono-
log
mo·no·po·lio, m. monopoly
mo·no·po·li·zar, v. monopolize; engross
mo·no·to·nía, f. monotony
mo·nó·to·no, a. monotonous
mo·nó·xi·do, m. monoxide. mo·nó·
xi·do de car·bo·no, carbon
monoxide
mons·truo, m. monster
mons·truo·si·dad, f. monstrosity;
freak
mon·ta·car·gas, m. hoist
mon·ta·je, m. erection; hookup;
montage
mon·ta·ña, f. mountain
mon·ta·ño·so, a. hilly; mountainous
mon·tar, v. ride; mount; put together
mon·te, m. woodland; mountain
mon·tón, m. mound; heap; pile; bank
mo·nu·men·to, m. monument
mo·ra·da, f. dwelling
mo·ra·dor, m., mo·ra·do·ra, f. tenant; inhabitant
mo·ral, a. moral. f. morale
mo·ra·le·ja, f. moral
mo·ra·li·dad, f. morality
mo·ra·li·zar, v. moralize
mo·rar, v. live; dwell; reside; sojourn
mo·ra·to·ria, f. moratorium
mór·bi·do, a. morbid
mor·daz, a. trenchant; biting
mor·da·za, f. gag
mor·de·du·ra, f. bite
mo·re·na, f. brunette
mo·re·no, a. brown; dark
mor·fi·na, f. morphine
mo·rir(se), v. die; kill
mor·sa, f. walrus
mor·ta·ja, f. shroud
mor·tal, a. mortal; deadly; lethal; fatal. m., f. mortal
mor·ta·li·dad, f. mortality
mor·tuo·rio, m. mortuary
mo·rue·co, m. ram
mo·sai·co, m. mosaic
mos·ca, f. fly
mos·que·te, m. musket
mos·qui·to, m. mosquito
mos·ta·za, f. mustard
mos·tra·dor, m. counter
mos·trar(se), v. show; exhibit; demonstrate; appear
mo·te, m. motto; slogan
mo·tín, m. mutiny; uprising; riot
mo·ti·vo, m. motive; sake; reason
mo·to·ci·cle·ta, f. motorcycle
mo·tor, m. motor; engine. a motor
mo·ver(se), v. move; shift; power
mó·vil, a. mobile
mo·vi·mien·to, m. movement; motion; traffic
mo·za, f. lass; girl
mo·zo, m. lad; chap. mo·zo de ca·ba·
llos, groom. mo·zo de es·ta·ción,
porter
mu·co·so, a. mucous
mu·cha·cha, f. girl; lass
mu·cha·cho, m. boy; lad
mu·che·dum·bre, f. crowd; throng
mu·cho, a. many. adv. much. m.
much; pl. many
mu·dar(se), v. move; change
mu·do, a. dumb; mute; silent
mue·ble, m. furniture
mue·la, f. tooth; molar; grindstone.
do·lor de mue·las, toothache
mue·lle, m. pier; jetty; spring
muer·te, f. death
muer·to, a. dead; lifeless
mues·ca, f. notch; nick
mues·tra, f. sample; specimen
mu·gre, f. dirt; grime
mu·jer, f. woman; wife
mu·le·ta, f. crutch
mu·lo, m. mule
mul·ta, f. ticket; fine
mul·tar, v. fine
múl·ti·ple, a. multiple
mul·ti·pli·ca·ción, f. multiplication
mul·ti·pli·car(se), v. multiply; increase
múl·ti·plo, m. multiple
mul·ti·tud, f. multitude; crowd;
army
mun·da·no, a. mundane; worldly
mun·dial, a. world; world-wide
mun·do, m. world
mu·ni·ción, f. ammunition; pl. munitions
mu·ni·ci·pal, a. municipal
mu·ñe·ca, f. doll; wrist
mu·ñón, m. stump
mu·ral, m. mural. a. mural
mu·ra·lla, f. wall; rampart
mur·cié·la·go, m. bat
mur·mu·llo, m. murmur; muttering
mur·mu·rar, v. murmur; mutter;
gossip
mu·ro, m. wall
mu·sa, f. muse
mús·cu·lo, m. muscle
mu·se·li·na, f. muslin
mu·seo, m. museum
mus·go, m. moss
mu·si·cal, a. musical
mú·si·co, a. musical. m. musician
mus·lo, m. thigh

mu·ti·lar, v. mutilate; maim; cripple
mu·tuo, a. mutual; joint
muy, adv. very; much; too; greatly

N

na·bo, m. turnip
na·cer(se), v. be born; give birth; spring from; sprout
na·ci·do, a. born
na·cien·te, a. infant; recent
na·ci·mien·to, m. birth; origin. de·re·chos de na·ci·mien·to, birthright
na·ción, f. nation
na·cio·nal, m., f. national. a. national; native
na·cio·na·li·dad, f. nationality
na·cio·na·lis·mo, m. nationalism
na·da, pron. none. adv. by no means. f. nothing; naught
na·da·dor, m. na·da·do·ra, f. swimmer
na·dar, v. swim
na·die, pron. no one; one; nobody; none
naf·ta, f. naphtha
nai·lon, m. nylon
nai·pe, m. playing card; pl. cards
nal·gas, f. pl. buttocks
na·ran·ja, f. orange. na·ran·ja man·da·ri·na or tan·ge·ri·na, tangerine
na·ran·ja·da, f. orangeade
nar·ci·sis·mo, m. narcissism
nar·ci·so, m. narcissus
nar·có·ti·co, a. narcotic. m. narcotic; drug; dope
nar·co·ti·zar, v. dope; drug
na·ri·ces, f. pl. nostrils
na·riz, f. nose
na·rra·ción, f. narration; story
na·rrar, v. narrate; tell
na·rra·ti·va, f. narrative
na·rra·ti·vo, a. narrative
na·sal, f. nasal
na·ta, f. cream. na·ta ba·ti·da, whipped cream
na·ta·ción, f. swim; swimming
na·tal, a. natal
na·ti·llas, f. pl. custard
na·ti·vi·dad, f. nativity
na·ti·vo, m., na·ti·va, f. native. a. native
na·tu·ral, a. natural; native
na·tu·ra·le·za, f. nature
na·tu·ra·li·zar(se), v. naturalize
na·tu·ral·men·te, adv. naturally; by all means
nau·fra·gar, v. be shipwrecked; sink
nau·fra·gio, m. wreck; shipwreck
náu·sea, f. nausea; qualm; repulsion
nau·sear, v. nauseate
náu·ti·ca, f. navigation
náu·ti·co, a. nautical
na·va·ja, f. pocketknife; jackknife
na·val, a. naval
na·ve, f. nave; ship. na·ve la·te·ral, aisle
na·ve·ga·ble, a. navigable
na·ve·ga·ción, f. navigation
na·ve·gar, v. navigate; cruise; sail
Na·vi·dad, f. Christmas; nativity; yule
ne·bli·na, f. mist
ne·bu·lo·sa, f. nebula
ne·ce·sa·rio, a. necessary
ne·ce·si·dad, f. necessity; need
ne·ce·si·tar, v. require; need; necessitate; want; lack
ne·cio, a. foolish; vacuous. m. dolt
ne·cro·lo·gía, f. obituary
néc·tar, m. nectar
ne·fa·rio, a. nefarious
ne·gar, v. deny; disclaim; refuse
ne·ga·ti·va, f. denial; negative
ne·ga·ti·vo, a. negative; minus. m. (photog.) negative
ne·gli·gen·te, a. negligent; slack
ne·go·cia·ción, f. negotiation
ne·go·ciar, v. negotiate; bargain
ne·go·cio, m. trade; transaction; business; affair
ne·gro, a. black
ne·na, f. baby; tot
ne·ne, m. baby; tot
ne·nú·far, m. water lily
neón, m. neon
ner·vio, m. nerve
ner·vio·so, a. nervous; edgy; highstrung
nes·ga, f. gore
ne·to, a. net; clean; pure
neu·má·ti·co, a. tire. neu·má·ti·co de re·pues·to, spare tire
neu·ral·gia, f. neuralgia
neu·ro·sis, f. neurosis
neu·ró·ti·co·a, m., neu·ró·ti·ca, f. neurotic. a. neurotic
neu·tral, a. neutral. m., f. neutral
neu·tra·li·dad, f. neutrality
neu·tra·li·zar, v. neutralize
neu·tro, a. neuter
neu·trón, m. neutron
ne·var, v. snow
ni, a. neither. conj. neither; nor
nin·ra, f. stack
ni·co·ti·na, f. nicotine
ni·cho, m. recess
ni·do, m. nest
nie·bla, f. fog
nie·ta, f. granddaughter
nie·to, m. grandson
nie·ve, f. snow. bo·la de nie·ve, snowball. co·po de nie·ve, snowflake. fi·gu·ra de nie·ve, snowman
ni·lón, m. nylon
nin·fa, f. nymph
nin·gu·no (nin·gún), pron. none; nei-

ther; nobody. a. none; no. en nin·gu·na par·te, nowhere
ni·ña, f. girl; child; baby
ni·ñe·ra, f. nurse
ni·ñez, f. childhood
ni·ño, m. boy; child; baby. ni·ño ex·pó·si·to, foundling
ní·quel, m. nickel
ni·tra·to, m. nitrate
ni·tró·ge·no, m. nitrogen
ni·tro·gli·ce·ri·na, f. nitroglycerin
ni·vel, m. standard; level
ni·ve·la·do, a. flush
no, adv. no; not; nay. m. no
no·ble, a. noble. m. noble; nobleman
no·ble·za, f. nobility
no·ción, f. notion
noc·tur·no, a. nightly; nocturnal; night
no·che, f. night; nighttime. es·ta no·che, tonight
no·gal, m. walnut
nó·ma·da, m., f. nomad
nom·bra·mien·to, m. nomination; appointment; designation
nom·brar, v. name; call; nominate; appoint
nom·bre, m. name; title; reputation
nó·mi·na, f. payroll; list
no·mi·na·ción, f. nomination
no·mi·nal, a. nominal
nor·des·te, m. northeast
nor·ma, f. norm; standard. nor·ma de me·di·das, gauge
nor·mal, a. normal; standard; regular
nor·mal·men·te, adv. normally
no·roes·te, m. northwest. a. northwest
nor·te, m. north. a. north; northern
nos, pron. us
no·so·tras, f. pron. we; us; ourselves
no·so·tros, m. pron. we; us; ourselves
nos·tal·gia, f. nostalgia
nos·tál·gi·co, a. homesick; nostalgic
no·ta, f. mark; footnote; often pl. note
no·ta·ble, a. notable. m., f. notable
no·ta·ción, f. notation
no·tar, v. note; notice; remark
no·ta·rio, m. notary; notary public
no·ti·cia, f. notice; information; pl. news; tidings
no·ti·fi·car, v. notify
no·to·rio, a. notorious; flagrant
no·ve·dad, f. novelty; fad
no·ve·la, f. novel
no·ve·les·co, a. fictional; romantic
no·ve·no, a. ninth
no·ven·ta, a. ninety
no·via, f. fiancée; girl friend; bride
no·viaz·go, m. courtship
no·vi·cio, m., no·vi·cia, f. novice
no·viem·bre, m. November

m. objective
ob·je·to, m. object; thing; article. ob·je·to ex·pues·to, exhibit
o·blea, f. wafer
o·bli·cua·men·te, adv. sideways; obliquely
o·bli·cuo, a. oblique
o·bli·ga·ción, f. obligation; liability; bond; trust
o·bli·ga·do, a. indebted; liable
o·bli·gar(se), v. obligate; make; compel; bind
o·bli·ga·to·rio, a. mandatory; compulsory
o·blon·go, a. oblong
o·boe, m. oboe
ob·ra, f. work; handiwork; opus. o·bras clá·si·cas, classics. o·bra dra·má·ti·ca, play. o·bra maes·tra, masterpiece
o·brar, v. work; operate; proceed
o·bre·ro, m. o·bre·ra, f. worker; workman. a. labor
obs·ce·ni·dad, f. obscenity
obs·ce·no, a. obscene; lewd
obs·cu·re·cer(se), v. obscure; shadow; darken
obs·cu·ri·dad, f. obscurity
obs·cu·ro, a. obscure; opaque; dark
ob·ser·va·ción, f. observation; remark; comment
ob·ser·van·cia, f. observance
ob·ser·var, v. observe; watch
ob·ser·va·to·rio, m. observatory
ob·se·sión, f. obsession
obs·tá·cu·lo, m. obstacle; hindrance; bar; clog; snag
obs·tan·te, adv. in the way. no obs·tan·te, notwithstanding; nevertheless
obs·ti·na·do, a. obstinate; stubborn
obs·truc·ción, f. obstruction; blockage
obs·truc·cio·nis·ta, m., f. obstructionist; filibuster
obs·truir, v. obstruct; block
ob·te·ner, v. obtain; get; procure
ob·vio, a. obvious; self-explanatory
o·ca·sión, f. occasion; cause
oc·ci·den·tal, a. western
oc·ci·den·te, m. west
o·céa·no, m. ocean
o·cio, m. leisure
o·cio·so, a. idle
oc·tá·go·no, m. octagon
oc·ta·va, f. octave
oc·ta·vo, a. eighth. m. eighth
oc·tu·bre, m. October
o·cu·lar, a. ocular. tes·ti·go o·cu·lar, eyewitness
o·cul·tar(se), v. hide; conceal; secrete; cache
o·cul·to, a. secret; occult
o·cu·pa·ción, f. occupation; profession; occupancy
o·cu·pa·do, a. busy; engaged; occupied
o·cu·par(se), v. occupy; fill; employ; busy
o·cu·rrir(se), v. occur; happen
o·chen·ta, a. eighty; fourscore
o·cho, a. eight. m. eight
o·da, f. ode
o·diar, v. hate
o·dio, m. hate. o·dio de san·gre, vendetta
o·dio·so, a. odious; hateful
oes·te, m. west. a. west; western
o·fen·der(se), v. offend; take offense; injure; insult
o·fen·sa, f. offense
o·fen·si·vo, a. offensive; obnoxious; repugnant
o·fer·ta, f. offer; bid
o·fi·cial, a. official. m. official; officer
o·fi·ci·na, f. office. de o·fi·ci·na, clerical
o·fi·ci·nes·co, a. white-collar
o·fi·ci·nis·ta, m., f. clerk
o·fi·cio, m. business; role; occupation
o·fre·cer(se), v. offer; present; extend; volunteer; bid
o·fre·ci·mien·to, m. offer; offering
o·gro, m. ogre
oí·ble, a. audible
oí·do, m. ear; hearing. al·can·ce del oí·do, earshot
oír, v. hear; listen. oír por ca·sua·li·dad, overhear
o·ja·lá, int. if only; if only it were so
o·jea·da, f. glance
o·jear, v. ogle; eye
o·je·te, m. eyelet
o·jo, m. eye
o·la, f. wave
o·lé, int. bravo
o·lea·da, f. billow; surge
o·lea·je, m. surf
o·ler, v. smell; sniff; reek
ol·fa·to, m. sense of smell
o·li·va, f. olive
ol·mo, m. elm
o·lor, m. odor; smell; scent
o·lo·ro·so, a. fragrant
ol·vi·da·di·zo, a. forgetful
ol·vi·dar(se), v. forget; omit
ol·vi·do, m. oversight; oblivion
o·lla, f. pot; stew
om·bli·go, m. navel
o·mi·sión, f. omission
o·mi·tir, v. omit; leave out
om·ni·po·ten·cia, f. omnipotence
om·ni·po·ten·te, a. omnipotent; almighty
om·ni·pre·sen·cia, f. omnipresence;

m. objective
ubiquity
om·nis·cien·cia, f. omniscience
om·ní·vo·ro, a. omnivorous
on·ce, a. eleven. m. eleven
on·da, f. wave
on·dear, v. wave; flap
on·du·la·ción, f. wave; undulation
on·du·la·do, a. wavy; undulating
on·du·lar(se), v. wave; undulate
ó·ni·ce, m. onyx
on·za, f. ounce
o·pa·ci·dad, f. opacity
o·pa·co, a. opaque
ó·pa·lo, m. opal
ó·pe·ra, f. opera
o·pe·ra·ción, f. operation; deal
o·pe·rar(se), v. operate; work; bring about
o·pe·re·ta, f. operetta
o·pi·nar, v. judge
o·pi·nión, f. opinion; view
o·pio, m. opium
o·po·ner(se), v. oppose; object; encounter
o·por·to, m. port
o·por·tu·ni·dad, f. opportunity; chance
o·por·tu·no, a. opportune; timely; due; happy
o·pri·mir, v. oppress; press; squeeze
óp·ti·co, a. optical
op·ti·mis·mo, m. optimism
o·pues·to, a. opposite
o·pu·len·to, a. opulent; affluent
o·ra·ción, f. oration; prayer
o·rá·cu·lo, m. oracle
o·ra·dor, m., o·ra·do·ra, f. speaker
o·ral, a. oral
o·rar, v. pray
or·be, m. orb
ór·bi·ta, f. orbit
or·den, m. order; arrangement; command. f. order; writ. or·den del día, agenda
or·de·na·do, a. tidy
or·de·nar(se), v. ordain; arrange; bid
or·de·ñar, v. milk
or·di·na·rio, a. ordinary; common; coarse
o·re·ja, f. ear; tab; lug
or·gan·dí, m. organdy; organdie
or·gá·ni·co, a. organic
or·ga·ni·llo, m. barrel organ
or·ga·nis·mo, m. organism
or·ga·ni·za·ción, f. organization
or·ga·ni·zar(se), v. organize
ór·ga·no, m. organ
or·gía, f. orgy
or·gu·llo, m. pride
or·gu·llo·so, a. proud; lofty; haughty
o·rien·tal, m., f. oriental. a. oriental; eastern
o·rien·tar(se), v. orient oneself; direct
o·rien·te, m. east; (cap.) the Orient
o·ri·fi·cio, m. vent; orifice
o·ri·gen, m. origin; source
o·ri·gi·nal, a. original; eccentric. m. original
o·ri·gi·nar(se), v. originate
o·ri·lla, f. bank; shore. o·ri·lla del mar, seashore
o·rín, m. rust
o·ri·na, f. urine
o·ri·nar(se), v. urinate
o·ri·nes, m. pl. urine
or·la, f. fringe; trimming
or·na·men·ta·ción, f. ornamentation
or·na·men·to, m. ornament
or·na·to, m. decoration
o·ro, m. gold; (cards) pl. diamonds
o·ro·pel, m. tinsel
or·ques·ta, f. orchestra
or·ques·tar, v. score; orchestrate
or·to·do·xia, f. orthodoxy
or·to·do·xo, a. orthodox
or·to·gra·fía, f. spelling; orthography
o·ru·ga, f. caterpillar
os·ci·la·ción, f. swing; oscillation
os·ci·lar, v. vibrate; waver; oscillate
os·cu·re·cer(se), v. darken; dim; overshadow
os·cu·ri·dad, f. darkness; gloom
os·cu·ro, a. dark; dim; dusky
os·mo·sis, f. osmosis
o·so, m. bear. o·so hor·mi·gue·ro, anteater
os·ten·ta·ción, f. ostentation; pomp
os·tra, f. oyster
os·tra·cis·mo, m. ostracism
o·te·ro, m. knoll
o·to·ño, m. autumn; fall
o·tor·gar, v. grant; confer; bestow; award
o·tro, a. other; another; else. pron. another. o·tra vez, again
o·va·ción, f. ovation
o·val, a. oval
ó·va·lo, m. oval
o·va·rio, m. ovary
o·ve·ja, f. sheep; ewe
ó·vu·lo, m. ovum
ox·i·dar(se), v. oxidize; rust
óx·i·do, m. oxide
ox·í·ge·no, m. oxygen
o·zo·no, m. ozone

P

pa·be·llón, m. pavilion
pa·cer, v. graze
pa·cien·cia, f. patience
pa·cien·te, a. patient
pa·ci·fi·car(se), v. pacify; calm
pa·cí·fi·co, a. pacific

pa·ci·fis·mo, m. pacifism
pac·to, m. pact; covenant; treaty; bargain
pa·de·cer, v. suffer
pa·dras·tro, m. stepfather
pa·dre, m. father; sire; parent
pa·dri·no, m. godfather; pl. godparents
pa·ga, f. pay; payment
pa·ga·no, m., pa·ga·na, f. pagan. a. pagan; heathen
pa·gar, v. pay; repay; defray
pá·gi·na, f. page
pa·gi·nar, v. page
pa·go·da, f. pagoda
país, m. country; land; landscape
pai·sa·je, m. landscape; scenery
pa·ja, f. straw
pá·ja·ro, m. bird
pa·ji·lla, f. straw
pa·la, f. shovel; spade
pa·la·bra, f. word; speech
pa·la·bro·ta, f. swearword
pa·la·cio, m. palace
pa·la·dar, m. palate
pa·la·dín, m. paladin; champion
pa·lan·ca, f. crowbar; lever
pa·lan·que·ta, f. jimmy
pa·le·on·to·lo·gía, f. paleontology
pa·le·ta, f. palette; scoop
pa·li·de·cer(se), v. pale; blanch
pa·li·dez, f. pallor
pá·li·do, a. pale; pallid; wan; waxen
pa·li·za·da, f. palisade; stockade
pal·ma, f. palm
pal·ma·da, f. clap; slap; pl. applause
pal·mo·teo, m. clap
pa·lo, m. pole; staff; (cards) suit
pa·lo·ma, f. pigeon
pal·pa·ble, a. palpable
pal·par, v. touch; feel
pal·pi·ta·ción, f. palpitation; throb
pal·pi·tar, v. throb; palpitate
pa·lu·dis·mo, m. malaria
pan, m. bread; loaf. pan tos·ta·do, toast
pa·na, f. corduroy
pa·na·cea, f. panacea
pa·na·de·ría, f. bakery
pa·na·de·ro, m. baker
pa·nal, m. honeycomb
pán·creas, m. pancreas
pan·de·re·ta, f. tambourine
pan·di·lla, f. clique; gang
pa·ne·ci·llo, m. roll
pa·nel, m. panel
pa·no·ra·ma, m. panorama; view
pan·ta·lo·nes, m. pl. pants; trousers; slacks
pan·ta·lla, f. screen
pan·ta·no, m. swamp; bog; marsh; morass
pan·teís·mo, m. pantheism
pan·te·ra, f. panther
pan·to·mi·ma, f. pantomime; mime
pan·to·que, m. bilge
pa·ñal, m. diaper
pa·ñe·ría, f. drapery
pa·ñi·to, m. cloth. pa·ñi·to de a·dor·no, doily
pa·ño, m. cloth. pa·ño pa·ra la·var·se, washcloth
pa·ñue·lo, m. handkerchief; kerchief; babushka
pa·pa, m. (cap.) Pope; potato
pa·pá, m. papa; pa; dad; daddy
pa·pa·do, m. papacy
pa·pa·ga·yo, m. parrot
pa·pel, m. paper; role. pa·pel pin·ta·do, wallpaper. pa·pel se·can·te, blotter
pa·pe·le·ría, f. stationery
pa·pe·ras, f. pl. mumps
pa·pi·ro, m. papyrus
pa·que·te, m. package; parcel
par, m. par; pair; couple; peer; even number. a. even
pa·ra, prep. for
pa·rá·bo·la, f. parable; parabola
pa·ra·bri·sas, m. windshield
pa·ra·caí·das, m. parachute
pa·ra·cai·dis·ta, m. paratrooper
pa·ra·cho·ques, m. bumper
pa·ra·da, f. stop; standstill; halt; breakdown; check; parade
pa·ra·de·ro, m. whereabouts; lodging
pa·ra·do·ja, f. paradox
pa·ra·fi·na, f. paraffin
pa·rá·fra·sis, f. paraphrase
pa·ra·guas, m. umbrella
pa·raí·so, m. paradise
pa·ra·le·lo, a. parallel. m. parallel
pa·rá·li·sis, f. paralysis
pa·ra·li·zar(se), v. paralyze
pa·rá·me·tro, m. parameter
pá·ra·mo, m. moor
pa·ra·noia, f. paranoia
pa·rar(se), v. stop; halt; stay; check; parry; end
pa·ra·rra·yos, m. lightning rod
pa·rá·si·to, m. parasite; pl. static
par·ce·la, f. plot
par·cial, a. partial; part
par·cia·li·dad, f. partiality; faction
pa·re·cer(se), v. resemble; appear; look like; seem
pa·re·ci·do, a. like; similar; such. m. semblance
pa·red, f. wall
pa·re·ja, f. pair; couple. sin pa·re·ja, odd
pa·ren·tes·co, m. kinship
pa·rén·te·sis, f. parenthesis
pa·ria, m., f. pariah
pa·rien·te, m. relation; kinsman; pl. kin; kindred
pa·rir, v. give birth

pa·ra·men·to, m. usu. cap. parliament; parley
pa·ro·dia, f. parody; skit; travesty
pa·ro·diar, v. caricature; burlesque
pa·ró·ti·das, f. mumps
pa·rox·is·mo, m. paroxysm
par·pa·dear, v. blink; wink
par·pa·deo, m. winking; blinking
par·que, m. park
pá·rra·fo, m. paragraph
pa·rri·lla, f. grill; grating
pa·rro·quia, f. parish; customers
pa·rro·quial, a. parochial
par·te, f. part; portion; lot; share. en to·das par·tes, anywhere; everywhere
par·te·ra, f. midwife
par·ti·ción, f. partition
par·ti·ci·pa·ción, f. participation; share; notice
par·ti·ci·par, v. participate; notify
par·ti·ci·pe, m., f. participant
par·ti·cu·la, f. speck; particle
par·ti·cu·lar, a. particular; private; special
par·ti·cu·la·ri·dad, f. particularity; peculiarity
par·ti·da, f. departure; party; group; item; certificate
par·ti·da·rio, m., par·ti·da·ria, f. partisan; follower; campaigner. a. partisan
par·ti·do, m. side; party; match; game. de dos par·ti·dos, bipartisan
par·tir(se), v. part; depart; cleave; share
par·to, m. labor
pa·sa, f. raisin
pa·sa·ble, a. respectable; passable
pa·sa·do, m. past. adv. ago. a. ago; past; bygone. pa·sa·do de mo·da, out-of-date
pa·sa·dor, m. bolt; pl. cufflinks
pa·sa·je, m. passage
pa·sa·je·ro, m., pa·sa·je·ra, f. passenger. a. transient
pa·sa·ma·no, m. bannister; banister
pa·sa·por·te, m. passport
pa·sar, v. happen; pass; spend; elapse; while; live; fade. pa·sar por al·to, miss
pa·sa·tiem·po, m. pastime; amusement; hobby
pa·sear, v. walk; stroll
pa·seo, m. walk; stroll; airing; run. pa·seo en co·che, drive
pa·si·llo, m. corridor; hallway; aisle; gangway
pa·sión, f. passion
pa·si·vo, a. passive
pas·mar(se), v. dumfound, dumbfound; amaze
pa·so, m. pace; step; footstep; tread; gateway. pa·so a ni·vel, crossing
pas·ta, f. paste; cardboard; pasta
pas·tel, m. cake; pie; pl. pastry
pas·te·li·llo, m. pat
pas·teu·ri·za·ción, f. pasteurization
pas·teu·ri·zar, v. pasteurize
pas·ti·lla, f. lozenge; cake
pas·to, m. pasture; grass
pas·tor, m. shepherd; herdsman; pastor; minister
pa·ta, f. leg of an animal; paw; foot. pa·tas a·rri·ba, topsy-turvy
pa·ta·da, f. kick
pa·tán, m. lout
pa·ta·ta, f. potato
pa·tear, v. stamp
pa·ten·te, f. patent. a. patent; self-evident
pa·ter·ni·dad, f. fatherhood; paternity
pa·ter·no, a. paternal
pa·té·ti·co, a. pathetic
pa·ti·llas, f. pl. sideburns
pa·tín, m. skate
pa·ti·nar, v. skate; skid
pa·ti·na·zo, m. skid
pa·tio, m. yard; patio. pa·tio de re·creo, playground
pa·to, m. duck
pa·to·lo·gía, f. pathology
pa·tria, f. fatherland; native land
pa·triar·ca·do, m. patriarchy
pa·tri·mo·nio, m. patrimony; inheritance
pa·trio·ta, m., f. patriot
pa·tro·ci·na·dor, m., pa·tro·ci·na·do·ra, f. sponsor
pa·tru·lla, f. patrol
pa·tru·llar, v. patrol
pau·sa, f. pause; interruption
pa·vi·men·tar, v. pave
pa·vi·men·to, m. pavement
pa·vo, m. turkey. pa·vo real, peacock
pa·vo·near(se), v. strut; swagger
pa·vor, m. dread
pa·ya·so, m. clown. ha·cer el pa·ya·so, clown
paz, f. peace; tranquility
pea·je, m. toll. au·to·pis·ta de pea·je, tollway; tollroad
pea·tón, m. pedestrian
pe·ca, f. freckle
pe·ca·di·llo, m. peccadillo
pe·ca·do, m. sin; transgression
pe·ca·dor, m., pe·ca·do·ra, f. sinner. a. sinful
pe·car, v. sin; transgress; trespass
pe·ce·ra, f. fishbowl
pe·cio, m. flotsam
pe·cu·liar, a. peculiar; characteristic
pe·cu·lia·ri·dad, f. peculiarity; kink
pe·cho, m. breast; bust; chest
pe·dal, m. pedal
pe·da·zo, m. piece; patch; bit; mor-

sel. ha·cer·se pe·da·zos, shatter
pe·der·nal, m. flint
pe·des·tal, m. pedestal
pe·des·tre, a. pedestrian; walking
pe·di·cu·ro, m. chiropodist
pe·dir, v. charge; order; ask; beg; request; bid
pe·dre·go·so, a. stony, stoney
pe·dre·jón, m. boulder
pe·ga·jo·so, a. adhesive; catching
pe·gar(se), v. slap; strike; glue; paste; cleave; adhere; attach; hang
pe·go·te, m. hanger-on; sticking plaster
pei·na·do, m. coiffure; hairdo
pei·nar, v. comb; arrange the hair
pei·ne, m. comb
pe·la·do, a. bare; hairless
pe·lar(se), v. peel; shear
pel·da·ño, m. rung; stair
pe·lea, f. fight; scuffle; inf. hassle
pe·lear(se), v. fight; scuffle
pe·le·jo, m. pelt
pe·lí·cu·la, f. movie; picture; motion picture; film. pe·lí·cu·la del oes·te, western
pe·li·gro, m. danger; peril; jeopardy. po·ner en pe·li·gro, endanger
pe·li·gro·sa·men·te, adv. dangerously
pe·li·gro·so, a. dangerous
pe·li·rro·jo, a. red-headed
pe·lo, m. hair; coat; fur
pe·lo·ta, f. ball
pe·lo·tón, m. squad; platoon; tangle
pel·tre, m. pewter
pe·lu·ca, f. wig
pe·lu·do, a. furry; hairy
pe·lu·que·ría, f. barber shop; beauty shop
pe·lu·que·ro, m. barber; hairdresser
pe·lu·sa, f. fuzz; fluff; down
pel·vis, f. pelvis
pe·lla, f. pellet
pe·lle·jo, m. hide; skin
pe·lliz·car, v. pinch; nip
pe·na, f. distress; anxiety; trouble; hardship; penalty
pe·na·do, m. convict
pe·nal, a. penal
pen·dien·te, m. pendant, pendent; earring; incline. a. pending; hanging
pén·du·lo, m. pendulum
pe·ne·tran·te, a. sharp; penetrating
pe·ne·trar(se), v. penetrate; pierce; fathom
pe·ni·ci·li·na, f. penicillin
pe·nín·su·la, f. peninsula
pe·ni·ten·te, a. penitent. m., f. penitent
pe·no·so, a. painful; grueling; wearing; laborious; grievous; trying; uphill
pen·sa·mien·to, m. thought; notion; pansy
pen·sar, v. think; ponder; think over; think up
pen·sa·ti·vo, a. pensive; wistful; thoughtful
pen·sión, f. pension; room and board; boarding house
pen·sio·nis·ta, m., f. boarder; pensioner
pen·tá·go·no, m. pentagon
pe·ñón, m. large rock; wall of rock
peón, m. laborer; peon
peo·nía, f. peony
peón·za, f. top
peor, a. worse; worst. adv. worse; worst
pe·pi·ni·llo, m. gherkin
pe·pi·no, m. cucumber
pe·que·ñi·to, a. wee; tiny
pe·que·ño, a. small; little; slight; short
pe·ra, f. pear
per·ca, f. perch
per·ce·be, m. barnacle
per·cep·ción, f. perception
per·cep·ti·ble, a. discernible; perceptible
per·cep·ti·vo, a. perceptive
per·ci·bir, v. see; perceive; espy
per·cha, f. roost; perch; rack; hanger
per·der(se), v. lose; forfeit; waste; miss; get lost. per·der su sa·bor, pall
per·di·ción, f. perdition
pér·di·da, f. loss; forfeiture
per·di·do, a. lost; missing; inveterate
per·di·gón, m. buckshot
per·diz, f. partridge
per·dón, m. pardon; forgiveness
per·do·nar, v. pardon; remit; spare; forgive; excuse
per·du·ra·ble, a. enduring
per·du·rar, v. endure; last
pe·re·cer, v. perish
pe·re·gri·na·ción, f. peregrination
pe·re·gri·no, m. pe·re·gri·na, f. pilgrim. a. traveling
pé·re·jil, m. parsley
pe·ren·ne, a. perennial
pe·re·zo·so, a. lazy; sluggish
per·fec·ción, f. perfection
per·fec·cio·nar, v. perfect
per·fec·cio·nis·ta, m., f. perfectionist
per·fec·to, a. perfect. m. perfect tense
per·fil, m. profile; outline
per·fo·ra·ción, f. perforation
per·fo·rar, v. perforate; puncture
per·fu·mar, v. perfume
per·fu·me, m. perfume; scent; essence

per·ga·mi·no, m. parchment. ro·llo de per·ga·mi·no, scroll
pe·ri·cia, f. expertise; proficiency; skill; inf. know-how
pe·ri·crá·neo, m. scalp
pe·ri·fe·ria, f. periphery
pe·rí·me·tro, m. perimeter
pe·rió·di·co, m. periodical; newspaper; journal
pe·rio·dis·mo, m. journalism
pe·rio·dis·ta, m., f. journalist
pe·rio·do, m. period
pe·ris·co·pio, m. periscope
per·ju·di·car, v. prejudice; handicap; damage
per·ju·di·cial, a. harmful
per·ju·rar(se), v. perjure
per·ju·rio, m. perjury
per·la, f. pearl
per·ma·ne·cer, v. remain
per·ma·nen·te, a. permanent
per·mi·si·vo, a. permissive
per·mi·so, m. permission; consent; permit; pass; leave
per·mi·tir(se), v. permit; let; admit; allow; tolerate; enable; give
per·mu·tar, v. barter; exchange
pe·ro, conj. but; yet
per·pen·di·cu·lar, a. perpendicular. f. perpendicular
per·pe·tra·ción, f. commission; perpetration
per·pe·trar, v. perpetrate
per·pe·tuo, a. perpetual
per·ple·jo, a. perplexed. m. puzzle
pe·rra, f. female dog; bitch; slut
pe·rre·ra, f. kennel
pe·rro, m. dog; canine
per·se·cu·ción, f. persecution; chase
per·se·gui·mien·to, m. pursuit
per·se·guir, v. pursue; follow; chase; hunt; hound; persecute
per·sis·tir, v. persist
per·so·na, f. person. por per·so·na, apiece
per·so·na·je, m. somebody; character; personality
per·so·nal, a. personal. m. personnel staff
per·so·na·li·dad, f. personality
pers·pec·ti·va, f. perspective; outlook; prospect; insight
pers·pi·ca·cia, f. foresight; perspicacity
pers·pi·caz, a. keen; discerning
per·sua·dir(se), v. persuade
per·sua·sión, f. persuasion
per·te·ne·cer, v. pertain; appertain; concern; belong
per·te·nen·cias, f. pl. belongings; possessions
per·ti·nen·cia, f. relevance; relevancy
per·ti·nen·te, a. pertinent; relevant
per·tur·ba·ción, f. perturbation; upset
per·tur·ba·do, a. upset
per·tur·bar, v. disturb; upset; faze; treat; gratification
per·ver·si·dad, f. perversity
per·ver·sión, f. perversion
per·ver·ti·do, a. perverted
per·ver·tir(se), v. pervert; warp
pe·sa·dez, f. heaviness; tediousness
pe·sa·di·lla, f. nightmare
pe·sa·do, a. heavy; weighty; tiresome; dull; boring; clumsy
pé·sa·me, m. condolence
pe·sar, v. weigh; sorrow; grieve; regret. a pe·sar de, in spite of; notwithstanding
pes·ca, f. fishing
pes·ca·do, m. fish. so·pa de pes·ca·do, chowder
pes·ca·dor, m. fisherman
pes·car, v. fish
pe·se·bre, m. manger; crib
pe·si·mis·mo, m. pessimism
pe·si·mis·ta, a. pessimistic; morbid. m., f. pessimist
pe·so, m. weight; load; burden
pes·que·ra, f. fishery
pes·qui·sa, f. investigation. pes·qui·sa ju·di·cial, inquest
pes·ta·ña, f. eyelash
pes·ta·ñear, v. wink
pes·te, f. plague
pes·ti·ci·da, m. pesticide
pé·ta·lo, m. petal
pe·tar·deo, m. backfire
pe·tar·dis·ta, m., f. cheat
pe·tar·do, m. firecracker
pe·ti·ción, f. petition; request; demand
pe·ti·me·tre, m. fop; dude
pe·ti·rro·jo, m. robin
pe·tró·leo, m. petroleum; oil
pez, m. fish. f. pitch
pe·zón, m. nipple; teat
pia·do·so, a. pious; clement; godly
pia·nis·ta, m., f. pianist
pia·no, m. piano
piar, v. chirp
pi·ca·di·llo, m. hash
pi·ca·do, a. choppy; minced
pi·ca·du·ra, f. sting
pi·ca·ma·de·ros, m. woodpecker
pi·car(se), v. stick; prick; sting; pink; pick; chop; chip; nibble; bite; itch
pí·ca·ra, f. hussy
pi·ca·res·co, a. picaresque
pí·ca·ro, m. rascal; rogue. a. naughty; villainous
pi·ca·zón, m. itch
pi·cea, f. spruce
pi·co, m. beak; bill; peak; pick
pi·chel, m. mug
pie, m. foot; bottom. a pie, on foot. de·do del pie, toe

pie·dad, f. pity; piety
pie·dra, f. stone. pie·dra ca·li·za, limestone. pie·dra cla·ve, keystone. pie·dra de a·fi·lar, hone. pie·dra de gra·ni·zo, hailstone. pie·dra pó·mez, pumice stone
piel, f. skin; rind; pelt; leather; fur. piel de o·so, bearskin
pier·na, f. leg
pie·za, f. piece; chessman
pig·men·to, m. pigment
pig·meo, m., pig·mea, f. pygmy; pigmy. a. pygmy; pigmy
pi·ja·ma, m. pyjamas
pi·la, f. battery; sink
pi·lar, m. pillar
píl·do·ra, f. pill
pi·lón, m. loaf; pylon
pi·lo·to, m. pilot
pi·llar, v. pillage; plunder
pi·llo, m. blackguard; rascal
pi·llue·lo, m. urchin
pi·men·tón, m. cayenne pepper
pi·mien·ta, f. pepper
pi·mien·to, m. pepper
pi·ná·cu·lo, m. pinnacle
pin·char(se), v. pierce; puncture; jab
pin·cha·zo, m. puncture; flat
pi·no, m. pine
pin·ta, f. pint; spot
pin·tar(se), v. paint; put on makeup
pin·ta·rra·jo, m. daub
pin·tor, m., pin·to·ra, f. painter
pin·tu·ra, f. paint; painting
pin·za, f. tongs; clothespin
pin·zón, m. finch
pio·jo, m. louse; pl. lice
pi·pa, f. pipe
pi·que, m. pique
pi·ra, f. pyre
pi·rá·mi·de, f. pyramid
pi·ra·ta, m. pirate; freebooter
pi·ro·po, m. compliment
pi·ro·tec·nia, f. pyrotechnics
pi·rue·tear, v. pirouette; twirl
pi·ru·lí, m. lollipop; lollypop
pi·sar, v. step; tread; walk on; trample
pis·ci·na, f. swimming pool; inf. pool
pi·so, m. floor; story; apartment; flat
pi·so·tear, v. trample on
pis·ta, f. track; court; rink; clue; trail; scent. pis·ta de a·te·rri·za·je, runway. pis·ta de ce·ni·za, speedway
pis·to·la, f. pistol
pis·to·le·ra, f. holster
pis·to·le·ro, m. gangster
pis·tón, m. piston
pi·ti·llo, m. cigarette, cigaret
pi·to, m. whistle; woodpecker
pi·tón, m. spout; python
pi·vo·te, m. pivot
pi·za·rra, f. blackboard; slate
piz·ca, f. particle; pinch
pla·cen·ta, f. placenta
pla·cer, v. pleasure; enjoyment; treat; gratification
plá·ci·do, a. placid
pla·ga, f. plague
pla·gar(se), v. infest; plague
pla·gio, m. plagiarism
plan, m. plan; layout; scheme; contrivance
plan·cha, f. iron; slab; gangplank
plan·char, v. iron; press. la·var y plan·char, launder
pla·near, v. plan
plá·neo, m. glide
pla·ne·ta, m. planet
pla·no, a. flat; level. m. plan; plane. pri·mer pla·no, foreground
plan·ta, f. plant; floor; story; sole of the foot
plan·ta·ción, f. plantation
plan·tar, v. plant
plan·tear, v. pose; create
plan·tel, m. nursery
pla·ñi·de·ra, f. paid mourner
plas·ma, m. plasma
plás·ti·co, m. plastic. a. plastic
pla·ta, f. silver; money
pla·ta·for·ma, f. platform
plá·ta·no, m. banana
pla·te·ro, m. silversmith
pla·ti·llo, m. saucer; cymbal
pla·ti·no, m. platinum
pla·to, m. plate; dish; course
pla·tó·ni·co, a. platonic
plau·si·ble, a. plausible
pla·ya, f. beach; shore
pla·za, f. public square
pla·zo, m. installment; term
ple·bis·ci·to, m. plebiscite
ple·gar(se), v. fold; pleat; crease
ple·ga·ria, f. prayer
plei·to, m. lawsuit; suit; controversy
ple·ni·po·ten·cia·rio, m. plenipotentiary
ple·no, a. full
plé·to·ra, f. plethora
plie·gue, m. pleat; fold; wrinkle; crease
plo·mo, m. lead
plu·ma, f. feather; pen. plu·ma de gan·so, quill
plu·ma·da, f. stroke of the pen
plu·ma·je, m. plumage
plu·món, m. down
plu·mo·so, a. feathery; fluffy
plu·ral, a. plural. m. plural
plus, m. bonus
plus·cuam·per·fec·to, m. pluperfect
plu·to·cra·cia, f. plutocracy
po·bla·ción, f. population
po·blar(se), v. people; populate; inhabit
po·bre, a. poor. m., f. indigent person; pauper

po·bre·za, f. poverty
po·ci·lgo, m. sty
po·ción, f. potion
po·co, adv. little; pl. few. a. little. m. little. po·co a po·co, gradually
po·dar, v. prune
po·den·co, m. hound
po·der, v. can; may; be able to. m. power; might; strength; proxy
po·de·ro·so, a. powerful; forceful
po·dio, m. podium
po·dri·do, a. rotten; putrid; bad
po·e·ma, m. poem. po·e·ma li·ri·co, lyric
po·e·sía, f. poem; poetry
po·e·ta, m. poet; bard
po·é·ti·co, a. poetic; poetical
po·e·ti·sa, f. poetess
pó·ker, m. poker
po·lar, a. polar
po·la·ri·dad, f. polarity
po·la·ri·zar(se), v. polarize
pol·ca, f. polka
po·lea, f. pulley
po·lé·mi·ca, f. polemic
po·le·mis·ta, m., f. debater
po·len, m. pollen
po·li·cía, f. police; constabulary; policeman; constable. a·gen·te de po·li·cía, policeman; cop
po·lie·ti·le·no, m. polyethylene
po·li·fa·cé·ti·co, a. versatile
po·li·ga·mia, f. polygamy
po·lí·go·no, m. polygon
po·li·lla, f. moth
pó·li·po, m. polyp
po·li·teís·mo, m. polytheism
po·lí·ti·ca, f. politics; policy
po·lí·ti·co, m. politician. a. political
pó·li·za, f. insurance policy
po·lo, m. polo; pole
po·lu·ción, f. pollution
pol·vo, m. dust; powder. qui·tar el pol·vo, dust
pól·vo·ra, f. gunpowder
pol·vo·rien·to, a. dusty
po·lla, f. (cards) kitty
po·llo, m. chicken; fowl
po·llue·lo, m. chick
pom·pa, f. pomp; ostentation
pom·po·so, a. pompous; grandiose; highfalutin, highfaluting
pon·che, m. punch
pon·de·rar, v. ponder; consider
pon·de·ro·so, a. ponderous
po·ner(se), v. put; place; lay; set; shelter; don. po·ner·se a ha·cer, set about. po·ner en bas·tar·di·lla, italicize. po·ner cua·ren·te·na, quarantine. po·ner en ca·mi·no, set out. po·ner en du·da, doubt. po·ner·se pol·vos, powder
pon·ti·fi·ca·do, m. papacy
pon·ti·fi·ce, m. pontiff; pope
pon·ti·fi·cial, a. pontifical
po·pa, f. stern. a po·pa, aft
po·pu·la·cho, m. populace
po·pu·lar, a. popular
po·pu·la·ri·dad, f. popularity
po·pu·la·ri·zar(se), v. popularize
pó·quer, m. poker
po·qui·tín, m. a little bit. a. very little
po·qui·to, a. very little
por, prep. for; by; from; per; along; through; thru; via. por cien·to, percent. es·tar por, feel like. por la no·che, nightly. por más que, notwithstanding; however much. por me·dio de, through; by means of. por su·pues·to, of course. por qué, why?
por·ce·la·na, f. porcelain; china
por·cen·ta·je, m. percentage
por·ción, f. portion; section; fraction; part
por·dio·se·ro, m. por·dio·se·ra, f. beggar
por·fía, f. stubbornness
por·fia·do, a. insistent; obstinate
por·no·gra·fía, f. pornography
por·no·grá·fi·co, a. pornographic
po·ro, m. pore
po·ro·si·dad, f. porosity
por·que, conj. because
por·qué, m. why; reason
por·que·ría, f. filth; nastiness
po·rra, f. club; cudgel
po·rrón, m. wine jar with a long spout
por·ta·dor, m. carrier
por·tae·qui·pa·je, m. trunk of a car
por·tal, m. entrance
por·tar·se, v. behave; comport oneself
por·tá·til, a. portable
por·ta·voz, m. spokesman
por·te, m. bearing; demeanor; carriage; postage
por·te·ro, m. porter; concierge; janitor
por·te·zue·la, f. hatch
pór·ti·co, m. porch; portico
por·ve·nir, m. future
po·sa·da, f. inn
po·sa·de·ro, m. landlord; innkeeper
po·sar(se), v. perch; sit upon; alight
po·si·ción, f. position; place; placement
po·se·er, v. own; possess; have
po·se·sión, f. possession; tenancy; dependency; dependancy; pl. possessions; lands
po·se·si·vo, a. possessive
po·si·bi·li·dad, f. possibility
po·si·bi·li·tar, v. facilitate
po·si·ble, a. possible
po·si·ble·men·te, adv. possibly
po·si·ti·vo, a. positive

ment; standing; status
po·si·ti·vo, a. positive; certain; absolute
pre·sa·gio, m. omen
po·so, m. deposit; sediment; pl. grounds
pos·ta, f. slug
pos·tal, f. postcard
pos·te, m. post
pos·te·ri·dad, f. posterity
pos·te·rior, a. posterior; later; after
pos·ti·zo, a. artificial. m. toupé
post·me·ri·dia·no, a. postmeridian. Abbr. p.m., P.M.
pos·tra·ción, f. prostration. pos·tra·ción ner·vio·sa, shock
pos·trar(se), v. prostrate; exhaust
pos·tre, m. dessert
pos·tu·ra, f. posture; attitude; wager
po·ta·sio, m. potassium
po·ten·cial, a. potential
po·ten·te, a. potent; powerful
po·tra, f. filly
po·tro, m. rack; foal; colt
po·zo, m. well; shaft. po·zo de pe·tró·leo, oilwell. po·zo de vi·si·ta, manhole
prác·ti·ca, f. practice; observance; custom
prac·ti·ca·ble, a. practicable
prac·ti·car, v. practice
prác·ti·co, a. practical
pra·de·ra, f. prairie; meadow; field; pasture
prag·má·ti·co, a. pragmatic
prag·ma·tis·mo, m. pragmatism
prag·ma·tis·ta, m., f. pragmatist
pre·ám·bu·lo, m. preamble
pre·ca·rio, a. insecure; precarious
pre·cau·ción, f. precaution
pre·ca·ver(se), v. beware; prevent
pre·ce·den·cia, f. precedence
pre·ce·den·te, m. precedent. a. precedent
pre·ce·der, v. precede; antedate; forego
pre·cep·to, m. precept; commandment
pre·cep·tor, m. teacher; tutor
pre·cio, m. price; cost; value; rate; fare. a pre·cio re·du·ci·do, cutrate
pre·cio·so, a. valuable; precious; rich
pre·ci·pi·cio, m. precipice
pre·ci·pi·ta·ción, f. precipitation
pre·ci·pi·ta·do, a. precipitate; hasty; headlong
pre·ci·pi·tar(se), v. rush; hasten; dash
pre·ci·sa·men·te, adv. precisely; just
pre·ci·sar, v. obligate; compel
pre·ci·sión, f. precision; obligation
pre·ci·so, a. precise; mandatory
pre·co·ci·dad, f. precocity; earliness
pre·coz, a. precocious
pre·cur·sor, m., f. precursor; forerunner; herald
pre·de·ce·sor, m., pre·de·ce·so·ra, f. predecessor
pre·de·cir, v. predict; foretell
pre·des·ti·na·ción, f. predestination
pre·de·ter·mi·na·do, a. foregone; predetermined
pre·di·ca·ción, f. sermon
pre·di·car, v. preach
pre·di·lec·ción, f. predilection
pre·dis·po·ner, v. prejudice; predispose
pre·do·mi·na·ción, f. predominance
pre·do·mi·nan·te, a. predominant
pre·do·mi·nar, v. prevail; predominate; compel
pre·fa·cio, m. preface; foreword
pre·fe·ren·cia, f. preference; choice
pre·fe·ri·ble, a. preferable
pre·fe·ri·do, a. chosen; preferred
pre·fe·rir, v. prefer
pre·fi·jo, m. prefix
pre·gun·ta, f. question; query; inquiry
pre·gun·tar, v. question; query; inquire; ask
pre·his·tó·ri·co, a. prehistoric
pre·jui·cio, m. prejudice; bias; detriment
pre·juz·gar, v. prejudge
pre·li·mi·nar, a. preliminary
pre·lu·dio, m. prelude
pre·me·di·ta·do, a. premeditated; deliberate; willful, wilful
pre·me·di·tar, v. premeditate
pre·miar, v. reward; prize
pre·mio, m. award; prize; premium; bounty
pren·da, f. pledge; token. pren·da de ves·tir, garment
pren·der, v. apprehend; catch; inf. nab
pren·sa, f. press
pre·o·cu·pa·ción, f. preoccupation; worry; concern
pre·o·cu·pa·do, a. preoccupied
pre·o·cu·par(se), v. preoccupy; absorb; worry; mind; fuss
pre·pa·ra·ción, f. preparation
pre·pa·ra·do, a. prepared
pre·pa·rar(se), v. prepare; ready; coach; fix
pre·pa·ra·ti·vo, m. preparation
pre·pon·de·ran·cia, f. preponderance
pre·po·si·ción, f. preposition
pre·pós·te·ro, a. preposterous
pre·pu·cio, m. foreskin
pre·rro·ga·ti·va, f. prerogative
pre·sa, f. prey; quarry; dam; booty

pre·sa·giar, v. forebode, forbode; presage; bode
pres·cri·bir, v. prescribe
pre·sen·cia, f. presence
pre·sen·ta·ción, f. presentation; debut, début
pre·sen·tar(se), v. present; introduce; exhibit; feature; submit
pre·sen·te, a. present; current. te·ner pre·sen·te, bear in mind
pre·sen·ti·mien·to, m. premonition; foreboding; often pl. misgiving
pre·ser·var, v. preserve; keep
pre·ser·va·ti·vo, a. preservative. m. preservative
pre·si·den·cia, f. presidency
pre·si·den·te, m. president (often cap.); chairman
pre·si·dio, m. penitentiary
pre·si·dir, v. preside
pre·sión, f. pressure
pre·so, m., pre·sa, f. prisoner
prés·ta·mo, m. loan
pres·tar, v. lend; loan; extend
pres·ti·di·gi·ta·ción, f. prestidigitation; sleight of hand
pres·ti·gio, m. prestige; status
pre·su·mir, v. presume
pre·sun·ción, f. presumption; conceit; self-importance
pre·su·po·ner, v. presuppose
pre·su·pues·to, m. pretext; budget
pre·ten·der, v. pretend; seek; attempt
pre·ten·dien·te, m., f. pretender; suitor
pre·té·ri·to, m. preterite. a. preterite; past
pre·tex·to, m. pretext; pretense
pre·va·le·cer, v. prevail
pre·ven·ción, f. prevention; preparation
pre·ve·nir(se), v. arrange; prepare; avert; prevent; bias
pre·ver, v. foresee
pre·vio, a. previous; prerequisite
pre·vi·sión, f. foresight; forecast
pri·ma, f. cousin; insurance premium
pri·ma·do, a. primary. m. primate
pri·mal, m. yearling
pri·ma·ria·men·te, adv. primarily; principally
pri·ma·rio, a. primarily; elementary
pri·ma·ve·ra, f. spring; springtime
pri·ma·zo, m. cousinship
pri·me·ra·men·te, adv. first; mainly
pri·me·ro (pri·mer, pri·me·ra), a. first; foremost; erstwhile; prime. adv. uppermost; first. de pri·me·ra ma·no, firsthand, first-hand. de pri·me·ra cla·se, first-class. pri·me·ra cu·ra, first aid
pri·mi·ti·vo, a. primitive; early; original
pri·mo, m. cousin
pri·mo·ge·ni·tu·ra, f. primogeniture
pri·mor·dial, a. primordial
pri·mo·ro·so, a. neat; fine; delicate
prin·ce·sa, f. princess
prin·ci·pa·do, m. principality
prin·ci·pal, a. principal; main; chief; leading; prime; head; master. adv. uppermost. m. principal; capital
prin·ci·pal·men·te, adv. mostly; principally
prín·ci·pe, m. prince
prin·ci·pian·te, m., f. novice; beginner
prin·ci·pio, m. principle; beginning; outset. al prin·ci·pio, at the beginning; at first
prin·gar, v. baste as meat
prior, a. prior. m. prior
prio·ra, f. prioress
prio·ra·to, m. priory
pri·sa, f. hurry; haste; promptness. dar·se pri·sa, hurry
pri·sión, f. confinement; imprisonment; prison
pri·sio·ne·ro, m. prisoner
pris·ma, m. prism
pris·má·ti·co, a. prismatic
pri·va·ción, f. hardship; privation; deprivation
pri·va·do, a. private; deprived
pri·var, v. deprive; prohibit
pri·vi·le·gio, m. privilege; concession
proa, f. prow; bow
pro·ba·bi·li·dad, f. probability; chance
pro·ba·ble, a. probable; likely
pro·ba·ble·men·te, adv. probably
pro·ba·do, a. tried
pro·ban·za, f. proof
pro·bar(se), v. try; taste; sample; fit; prove; give evidence; chance
pro·ble·ma, m. problem
pro·ble·má·ti·co, a. problematical
pro·ce·der, v. proceed; behave. pro·ce·der de, stem from
pro·ce·di·mien·to, m. procedure
pro·ce·sar, v. prosecute; indict
pro·ce·sión, f. procession; parade
pro·ce·so, m. process; trial; action
pro·cla·ma·ción, f. proclamation
pro·cla·mar, v. proclaim; announce; herald
pro·cli·vi·dad, f. proclivity
pro·cón·sul, m. proconsul
pro·cre·a·ción, f. procreation
pro·crear, v. procreate
pro·cu·rar, v. procure; obtain; endeavor
pró·di·ga·men·te, adv. richly; wastefully
pro·di·gar, v. lavish; waste; squander

pro·di·gio, m. prodigy
pro·di·gio·sa·men·te, adv. prodigiously
pro·di·gio·so, a. prodigious
pró·di·go, a. prodigal; lavish; extravagant; spendthrift. m. prodigal
pro·duc·ción, f. production; output; turnout; yield. **pro·duc·ción en se·rie,** mass production
pro·du·cir, v. produce; create; yield; bear; do; turn out
pro·duc·ti·vi·dad, f. productivity
pro·duc·ti·vo, a. productive
pro·duc·to, m. product; produce. **pro·duc·to se·cun·da·rio,** byproduct
proe·mio, m. preface
proe·za, f. feat; prowess
pro·fa·ni·dad, f. profanity
pro·fa·no, a. profane; irreligious
pro·fe·cía, f. prophecy
pro·fe·rir, v. utter
pro·fe·sar, v. profess; sustain
pro·fe·sión, f. profession; occupation; vocation; trade
pro·fe·sio·nal, a. professional. m., f. professional
pro·fe·sio·nal·men·te, adv. professionally
pro·fe·sor, m., **pro·fe·so·ra,** f. professor; teacher
pro·fe·ta, m. prophet; seer
pro·fé·ti·ca·men·te, adv. prophetically
pro·fé·ti·co, a. prophetic; prophetical
pro·fe·ti·za, f. prophetess
pro·fe·ti·zar, v. prophesy
pro·fi·cien·te, a. proficient
pro·fi·lác·ti·co, a. prophylactic. m. prophylactic
pro·fun·da·men·te, adv. profoundly
pro·fun·di·dad, f. depth; profundity
pro·fun·di·zar, v. deepen
pro·fun·do, a. profound; deep
pro·fu·sa·men·te, adv. profusely
pro·fu·sión, f. profusion
pro·fu·so, a. profuse
pro·ge·nie, f. progeny; offspring; brood
pro·ge·ni·tor, m. progenitor; ancestor
prog·no·sis, f. forecast
pro·gra·ma, m. program; plan; syllabus
pro·gre·sar, v. progress; advance
pro·gre·sión, f. progression; progress
pro·gre·si·va·men·te, adv. progressively
pro·gre·si·vo, a. progressive; onward
pro·gre·so, m. progress; headway; march
pro·hi·bi·ción, f. prohibition; ban
pro·hi·bi·do, a. prohibited; forbidden
pro·hi·bir, v. prohibit; forbid; debar; ban
pro·hi·bi·ti·vo, a. prohibitive
pro·hi·jar, v. adopt
pró·ji·mo, m. fellow man
pro·le·ta·rio, m., **pro·le·ta·ria,** f. proletarian. a. proletarian
pro·li·fe·ra·ción, f. proliferation
pro·li·fe·rar, v. proliferate
pro·lí·fi·co, a. prolific
pró·lo·go, m. prologue; preface
pro·lon·ga·ción, f. lengthening; extension
pro·lon·ga·do, a. prolonged; long
pro·lon·gar(se), v. prolong; lengthen; continue
pro·me·diar, v. find the average of
pro·me·dio, m. average; mean
pro·me·sa, f. promise; pledge; vow
pro·me·ter, v. promise; pledge
pro·me·ti·do, a. engaged. m. offer; promise
pro·mi·nen·cia, f. prominence; protuberance
pro·mi·nen·te, a. prominent
pro·mis·cuo, a. promiscuous
pro·mo·ción, f. promotion
pro·mon·to·rio, m. promontory; headland
pro·mo·ver, v. promote; advance; pioneer
pro·mul·ga·ción, f. promulgation
pro·mul·gar, v. promulgate; proclaim
pro·nom·bre, m. pronoun
pro·no·mial, a. pronominal
pro·nos·ti·ca·ción, f. prediction
pro·nos·ti·car, v. forecast; predict
pro·nós·ti·co, m. prognosis; prediction; forecast
pron·ta·men·te, adv. promptly
pron·ti·tud, f. swiftness; promptness
pron·to, a. ready; prompt. adv. soon. **de pron·to,** suddenly
pro·nun·cia·ción, f. pronunciation; utterance
pro·nun·cia·do, a. pronounced
pro·nun·ciar(se), v. pronounce; utter; enunciate; deliver
pro·pa·ga·ción, f. propagation
pro·pa·gan·da, f. propaganda
pro·pa·gan·dis·ta, m., f. propagandist
pro·pa·gar(se), v. spread; propagate
pro·pen·sión, f. propensity; bias; bent
pro·pen·so, a. subject to; inclined
pro·pia·men·te, adv. properly
pro·pi·ciar, v. propitiate
pro·pi·cia·ción, f. propitiation
pro·pi·cio, a. propitious; favorable
pro·pie·dad, f. property; estate;

copyright
pro·pie·ta·ria, f. proprietress; landlady
pro·pie·ta·rio, m. proprietor; landlord
pro·pi·na, f. tip; gratuity. **dar pro·pi·na a,** tip
pro·pi·nar, v. tip
pro·pio, a. own; proper; fitting; very
pro·po·ner(se), v. propose; intend; present
pro·por·ción, f. proportion
pro·por·cio·na·do, a. proportionate
pro·por·cio·nal, a. proportional
pro·por·cio·nal·men·te, adv. proportionally
pro·por·cio·nar, v. supply; provide; furnish
pro·po·si·ción, f. proposition
pro·pó·si·to, m. purpose; intention; aim; object. **a pro·pó·si·to,** pertinent. **a pro·pó·si·to de,** apropos of; about
pro·pues·ta, f. proposition; offer; proposal; view
pro·pul·sar, v. propel; push
pro·pul·sión, f. propulsion
pro·sa, f. prose
pro·sai·ca·men·te, adv. prosaically
pro·sai·co, a. prosaic
pros·cri·bir, v. proscribe; outlaw
pros·crip·ción, f. proscription
pros·cri·to, a. proscribed. m. outcast
pro·se·guir, v. prosecute; pursue
pro·sé·li·to, m. proselyte
pros·pec·to, m. prospectus
prós·pe·ra·men·te, adv. prosperously
pros·pe·rar, v. prosper; thrive
pros·pe·ri·dad, f. prosperity. **pros·pe·ri·dad re·pen·ti·na,** boom
prós·pe·ro, a. successful; prosperous
prós·ta·ta, f. prostate
pros·ti·tu·ción, f. prostitution; harlotry
pros·ti·tuir, v. prostitute oneself
pros·ti·tu·ta, f. prostitute; whore
pro·ta·go·nis·ta, m., f. protagonist
pro·tec·ción, f. protection; pl. auspices
pro·tec·tor, m., **pro·tec·to·ra,** f. patron. a. protective
pro·tec·to·ra·do, m. protectorate
pro·te·ger, v. protect; shield; defend
pro·teí·na, f. protein
pro·tes·ta, f. protest
pro·tes·ta·ción, f. solemn declaration; protestation
pro·tes·tan·te, m., f. Protestant. a. Protestant
pro·tes·tar, v. protest
pro·to·co·lo, m. protocol
pro·tón, m. proton
pro·to·plas·ma, m. protoplasm
pro·to·ti·po, m. prototype
pro·tu·be·ran·cia, f. protuberance
pro·ve·cho, m. usefulness; profit; advantage. **buen pro·ve·cho,** good appetite; enjoy your meal
pro·ve·cho·sa·men·te, adv. beneficially
pro·ve·cho·so, a. beneficial; profitable; fruitful
pro·veer, v. provide; furnish; supply; cater; equip; fit out; fill
pro·ver·bial, a. proverbial
pro·ver·bio, m. proverb
pro·vi·den·cia, f. providence; judgment
pro·vi·den·cial, a. providential
pro·vi·den·te, a. provident
pro·vin·cia, f. province
pro·vin·cial, m., **pro·vin·cia·la,** f. provincial. a. provincial
pro·vin·cia·nis·mo, m. provincialism
pro·vi·sión, f. provision; hoard; pl. supplies
pro·vi·sio·nal, a. temporary; tentative; provisional
pro·vi·sio·nal·men·te, adv. provisionally
pro·vo·ca·ción, f. provocation
pro·vo·ca·dor, a. provocative
pro·vo·car, v. provoke; excite; irritate; nettle; antagonize
pro·vo·ca·ti·vo, a. provocative; sexy; defiant
pro·xi·mi·dad, f. vicinity; proximity; closeness
pró·xi·mo, a. next; near; handy; forthcoming
pro·yec·ción, f. projection; slide
pro·yec·tar(se), v. project; map; contemplate; throw out
pro·yec·til, m. missile; projectile
pro·yec·to, m. project; plan
pru·den·cia, f. caution; prudence
pru·den·te, a. prudent; shrewd; canny
pru·den·te·men·te, adv. prudently; wisely
prue·ba, f. proof; evidence; test; trial
prú·ri·to, m. itch
psi·coa·ná·li·sis, m. psychoanalysis
psi·coa·na·li·zar, v. psychoanalyze
psi·co·lo·gía, f. psychology
psi·co·ló·gi·ca·men·te, adv. psychologically
psi·co·ló·gi·co, a. psychological
psi·có·lo·go, m. psychologist
psi·co·sis, f. psychosis
psi·co·te·ra·pia, f. psychotherapy
psi·có·ti·co, a. psychotic
psi·que·dé·li·co, a. psychedelic
psi·quia·tra, psi·quía·tra, m., f. psychiatrist
psi·quia·tría, f. psychiatry
psi·quiá·tri·co, a. psychiatric

pto·maí·na, f. ptomaine, ptomain
púa, f. barb; spine; tooth
pu·ber·tad, f. puberty
pu·bli·ca·ción, f. publication. **pu·bli·ca·ción pe·rió·di·ca,** periodical
pú·bli·ca·men·te, adv. publicly
pu·bli·car, v. publish; issue; advertise
pu·bli·ci·dad, f. publicity; advertising
pú·bli·co, a. public; overt. m. public; audience
pu·dín, m. pudding
pu·drir(se), v. rot; decay; putrefy
pue·blo, m. town; village; people; populace; nation
puen·te, m. bridge, **puen·te col·gan·te,** suspension bridge. **puen·te le·va·di·zo,** drawbridge
puer·co, a. foul; rude. m. hog; swine. **puer·co es·pín,** porcupine
puer·ta, f. door; entrance; gate. **de puer·ta en puer·ta,** from door to door. **de puer·ta a·den·tro,** indoor
puer·to, m. port; harbor; haven. **puer·to de en·tra·da,** port of entry
pues, conj. for; then; since. adv. well; exactly. int. well
pues·ta, f. (cards) bet; setting. **pues·ta del sol,** sunset
pues·to, m. position; post; station; booth; stall; stand
pues·to que, conj. inasmuch as; since
pug·na, f. conflict
pug·na·ci·dad, f. pugnacity
pug·nar, v. fight
pug·naz, a. pugnacious
pu·ja, f. bid; effort
pu·jar, v. push; bid
pul·cri·tud, f. pulchritude; neatness
pul·cro, a. sleek; graceful; neat
pul·ga, f. flea
pul·ga·da, f. inch
pul·gar, m. thumb
pu·li·do, a. polished; buffed; tidy
pu·li·mien·to, m. polish
pu·lir(se), v. polish; buff; shine
pul·món, m. lung
pul·mo·nar, a. pulmonary
pul·mo·nía, f. pneumonia
pul·pa, f. pulp; flesh
púl·pi·to, m. pulpit
pul·po, m. octopus
pul·po·so, a. pulpy
pul·que, m. pulque
pul·sa·ción, f. pulsation; beating
pul·sar, v. pulsate; beat
pul·se·ra, f. bracelet
pul·so, m. pulse; wrist
pu·lu·lar, v. swarm
pul·ve·ri·za·ción, f. pulverization
pul·ve·ri·zar, v. pulverize; grind; spray
pu·lla, f. wisecrack
pu·ni·ti·vo, a. punitive

pun·ta, f. tip; point. **pun·ta del pie,** toe
pun·ta·da, f. stitch
pun·ta·pié, m. kick. **dar un pun·ta·pié,** kick
pun·tea·do, a. dotted
pun·tear, v. dot; sew
pun·te·ría, f. aim
pun·tia·gu·do, a. sharp
pun·ti·lla, f. lace; tack
pun·ti·llo·so, a. punctilious
pun·to, m. point; period; state; spot; dot; stitch. **dos pun·tos,** colon. **ha·cer pun·to,** knit. **pun·to de vis·ta,** standpoint. **pun·to fi·no,** nicety. **pun·to y co·ma,** semicolon
pun·tua·ción, f. punctuation
pun·tual, a. punctual; prompt; reliable
pun·tua·li·dad, f. punctuality; promptness
pun·tual·men·te, adv. punctually; promptly
pun·tuar, v. punctuate
pun·za·da, f. pang; sharp pain; puncture
pun·zar, v. punch; prod; prick; puncture
pun·zón, m. punch
pu·ña·do, m. handful
pu·ñal, m. dagger
pu·ña·la·da, f. stab
pu·ñe·ta·zo, m. punch; pl. fisticuffs
pu·ño, m. fist; cuff; hilt of a sword
pu·pi·la, f. pupil of the eye
pu·pi·lo, m. ward
pu·pi·tre, m. desk
pu·ra·men·te, adv. purely; entirely
pu·ré, m. mash; purée
pu·re·za, f. purity; pureness
pur·gan·te, a. purgative; cathartic. m. purgative; cathartic
pur·gar(se), v. purge
pur·ga·ti·vo, a. purgative
pur·ga·to·rio, m. purgatory
pu·ri·fi·ca·ción, f. purification
pu·ri·fi·car(se), v. purify; cleanse
pu·ris·ta, m., f. purist
pu·ri·ta·nis·mo, m. puritanism
pu·ri·ta·no, m. puritan, **pu·ri·ta·na,** f. puritan. a. puritan
pu·ro, a. pure; genuine; simple; unblemished. m. cigar
púr·pu·ra, f. purple
pur·pú·reo, a. purple
pus, m. pus
pu·ta, f. whore; prostitute
pu·tre·fac·ción, f. rot; putrefaction
pu·tre·fac·to, a. rotten

Q

que, rel. pron. what; whom; which; when. conj. than; that

qué, interrog. pron. what?
que·bra·di·zo, a. brittle; easily broken
que·bra·do, a. broken; uneven; bankrupt
que·bra·du·ra, f. breaking; fissure; rupture
que·brar(se), v. break; fracture; hinder; bankrupt
que·che, m. ketch
que·da, f. curfew
que·dar(se), v. stay; remain; last. **que·dar mal,** come off badly
que·ha·cer, m. affairs; task
que·ja, f. complaint; resentment; groan
que·jar·se, v. complain; grumble; moan; inf. beef; bitch
que·ji·do, m. whine; moan
que·jo·so, a. complaining; querulous
que·ma, f. burn; conflagration; burning
que·ma·do, a. burnt; burned
que·ma·du·ra, f. burn
que·mar(se), v. burn; scald; scorch
que·re·lla, f. complaint
que·re·llar(se), v. lament; complain; scold
que·rer, v. want; desire; wish; love; like. m. desire; love. **co·mo quie·ra,** as you like. **que·rer de·cir,** mean
que·ri·da, a. dear; darling. f. dear; darling; beloved; inf. mistress
que·ri·do, a. dear; darling; beloved. m. dear; darling; beloved
que·ru·bín, m. cherub
que·se·ría, f. dairy
que·so, m. cheese
quie·bra, f. bankruptcy; fissure; break
quien, rel. pron. who. **a quien,** whom
quién, interrog. pron. who? **a quién,** to whom?
quien·quie·ra, pron. whoever. **a quien·quie·ra,** whomever
quie·ta·men·te, adv. quietly
quie·tar(se), v. quiet; quiet down; calm down
quie·to, a. quiet; quiescent; still
quie·tud, f. quiet; stillness; tranquility
qui·ja·da, f. jaw; chin; jowl
qui·jo·tes·co, a. quixotic
qui·la·te, m. carat; karet
qui·lla, f. keel
qui·me·ra, f. chimera, chimaera; fancy
qui·mé·ri·co, a. chimeric; chimerical
quí·mi·ca, f. chemistry
quí·mi·co, a. chemical. m. chemist
quin·ce, a. fifteen
quin·ce·na, f. fortnight
quin·cua·gé·si·mo, a. fiftieth
qui·nien·tos, a. five hundred
qui·ni·na, f. quinine
quin·taes·en·cia, f. quintessence
quin·to, a. fifth. m. fifth
quin·tu·pli·car(se), v. quintuple; quintuplet
quin·tu·plo, a. quintuple. m. quintuple
quios·co, m. kiosk
qui·ro·man·cia, f. palmistry
qui·ro·pe·dia, f. chiropody
qui·rúr·gi·co, a. surgical
quis·qui·llo·so, a. oversensitive
quis·te, m. cyst
qui·ta·es·mal·te, m. nail polish remover
qui·ta·man·chas, m. stain remover
qui·tar(se), v. shed; take off; remove; get rid of
qui·ta·sol, m. parasol
qui·te, m. removal
qui·za(s), adv. maybe; perhaps
quó·rum, m. quorum

R

rá·ba·no, m. radish. **rá·ba·no pi·can·te,** horseradish
ra·bi, m. rabbi
ra·bia, f. rabies; rage
ra·bie·ta, f. tantrum
ra·bi·no, m. rabbinical
ra·bi·no, m. rabbi
ra·bio·so, a. rabid; furious; violent
ra·bo, m. tail
ra·cial, a. racial
ra·ci·mo, m. cluster; bunch
ra·ción, f. ration; helping; allowance
ra·cio·nal, a. rational
ra·cio·na·lis·mo, m. rationalism
ra·cio·nal·men·te, adv. rationally
ra·cis·mo, m. racism
ra·dar, m. radar
ra·dia·ción, f. radiation
ra·diac·ti·vi·dad, f. radioactivity
ra·diac·ti·vo, a. radioactive
ra·dian·te, a. radiant; shining
ra·diar, v. radiate; broadcast
ra·di·cal, a. radical. m. radical; root
ra·di·cal·men·te, adv. radically
ra·dio, m. radium; radius. f. radio
ra·dio·gra·fía, f. X-ray
ra·dio·gra·fiar, v. X-ray
ra·dio·so, a. radiant
raer, v. scrape; remove the bark of
rá·fa·ga, f. squall; gust; blast; flurry
raí·do, a. shabby; worn; threadbare
raíz, f. pl. raí·ces. root; origin. **bie·nes raí·ces,** property
ra·ja, f. slit; sliver
ra·já, m. rajah
ra·jar(se), v. crack; split; sliver; slice

ra·ma, f. limb; branch; bough
ra·ma·da, f. branches
ra·mal, m. strand; branch
ra·me·ra, f. prostitute; harlot; strumpet
ra·mi·fi·ca·ción, f. ramification
ra·mi·fi·car·se, v. branch; ramify
ra·mi·ta, f. sprig; twig
ra·mo, m. bouquet; branch
ram·pa, f. ramp
ra·na, f. frog
ran·cio, a. rancid; mellow. m. rankness
ran·cho, m. ranch
ran·go, m. rank; degree; position
ra·nu·ra, f. slot; groove
ra·paz, a. rapacious. f. bird of prey
ra·pé, m. snuff
rá·pi·da·men·te, adv. rapidly; fast; zippy
ra·pi·dez, f. rapidity; speediness
rá·pi·do, a. rapid; fast; quick; express; cursory
ra·pi·ña, f. rapine. **a·ve de ra·pi·ña,** bird of prey
ra·pi·ñar, v. steal
ra·po·so, m. fox
rap·so·dia, f. rhapsody
rap·só·di·co, a. rhapsodic
rap·to, m. rapture; ravishment; rape
rap·tor, m. kidnapper
ra·que·ta, f. racket
ra·ra·men·te, adv. seldom; rarely
ra·re·fac·ción, f. rarefaction
ra·re·za, f. oddity; rarity; infrequency
ra·ri·dad, f. rarity
ra·ri·fi·car(se), v. dilute
ra·ro, a. odd; rare; strange; unusual; bizarre; queer
ras·ca·cie·los, m. skyscraper
ras·ca·du·ra, f. rasping; scraping
ras·ca·mo·ño, m. zinnia; hatpin
ras·car, v. scratch; scrape; rasp
ras·ga·du·ra, f. rip; rend; rip
ras·gar(se), v. tear; rend; rip
ras·go, m. trait; feature; flourish; stroke
ras·guear, v. strum a guitar
ras·gu·ñar, v. scratch
ras·gu·ño, m. scratch; outline drawing
ra·so, a. flat; clear. m. satin. **sol·da·do ra·so,** private
ras·pa, f. rasp
ras·pa·dor, m. scraper
ras·pa·du·ra, f. abrasion; rasping; scraping
ras·par, v. scrape; erase; scratch
ras·tra, f. dredge; sledge
ras·trear, v. track; trail; investigate
ras·tri·llar, v. rake
ras·tri·llo, m. rake
ras·tro, m. trace; trail; vestige; rake
ras·tro·jo, m. stubble
ra·su·ra, f. levelness; shaving
ra·su·rar(se), v. shave
ra·ta, f. rat. **ra·ta al·miz·cle·ra,** muskrat
ra·tear, v. filch; pilfer; creep
ra·te·ro, m. pickpocket
ra·ti·fi·ca·ción, f. ratification
ra·ti·fi·car, v. ratify
ra·ti·to, m. little while
ra·to, m. while; time. **pa·sar el ra·to,** pass the time
ra·tón, m. mouse
ra·to·ne·ra, f. mousetrap; mousehole
rau·do, a. rushing
ra·ya, f. line; stripe; streak; dash
ra·ya·do, a. striped; ruled; variegated
ra·yar(se), v. stripe; streak; rule; line; scratch
ra·yo, m. ray; beam; bolt; thunderbolt; spoke
ra·yón, m. rayon
ra·za, f. race; lineage; strain
ra·zón, f. reason; cause; sometimes pl. grounds; rate; ratio
ra·zo·na·ble, a. reasonable; rational; sensible
ra·zo·na·ble·men·te, adv. reasonably
ra·zo·na·mien·to, m. reasoning
ra·zo·nar, v. argue; reason
re, m. (mus.) re
rea·bas·te·cer, v. refuel
reac·ción, f. reaction; response; backlash
reac·cio·nar, v. react
reac·cio·na·rio, m., **reac·cio·na·ria,** f. reactionary. a. reactionary
reac·tor, m. reactor
rea·fir·ma·ción, f. reaffirmation
rea·gru·par(se), v. regroup
rea·jus·tar(se), v. readjust
rea·jus·te, m. readjustment
real, a. real; actual; true; veritable; royal; regal
rea·le·za, f. royalty
rea·li·dad, f. reality. **en rea·li·dad,** really
rea·lis·mo, m. realism
rea·lis·ta, f. realist. a. realistic
rea·li·za·ción, f. fruition; realization
rea·li·zar, v. realize; fulfill, fulfil; sell
real·men·te, adv. really; truly
real·zar, v. heighten; emboss
rea·ni·mar(se), v. reanimate; revive; rally
re·a·pa·re·cer, v. reappear
re·a·pa·ri·ción, f. reappearance
rea·ta, f. rope
re·ba·ja, f. reduction; discount
re·ba·jar(se), v. stoop; abase; reduce;

lessen; depress
re·bal·sar, v. dam up
re·ba·na·da, f. slice, as of bread
re·ba·nar, v. slice
re·ba·tir, v. ward off; refute
re·be·ca, f. cardigan
re·be·lar·se, v. revolt; rebel; balk
re·bel·de, a. rebel; rebellious. m., f. rebel
re·bel·día, f. default; disobedience
re·be·lión, f. rebellion; revolt
re·bel·lo, a. fractious; stubborn; restive
re·bor·de, m. border
re·bo·sar, v. overflow
re·bo·tar, v. bounce; glance off
re·bo·te, m. ricochet; rebound; bounce
re·bo·zo, m. muffler
re·bu·far, v. recoil
re·bus·car, v. search through
re·buz·nar, v. bray
re·buz·no, m. bray
re·ca·do, m. errand; message; pl. provisions
re·caer, v. relapse
re·caí·da, f. relapse
re·cal·car, v. emphasize; squeeze
re·cal·ci·tran·te, a. recalcitrant
re·ca·len·tar(se), v. reheat; overheat
re·ca·ma·do, m. embroidery
re·ca·mar, v. embroider
re·cá·ma·ra, f. chamber; small room; breech
re·ca·pi·tu·la·ción, f. recapitulation
re·ca·pi·tu·lar, v. recapitulate
re·car·gar, v. reload; overload
re·car·go, m. increase
re·ca·to, m. caution; modesty
re·cau·da·ción, f. collection
re·cau·dar, v. collect
re·cau·do, m. precaution; collection
re·ce·lar, v. apprehend; fear
re·ce·lo, m. mistrust; jealousy; distrust
re·ce·lo·so, a. mistrustful; suspicious
re·cep·ción, f. reception; welcome
re·cep·tá·cu·lo, m. receptacle
re·cep·ti·vi·dad, f. receptivity
re·cep·ti·vo, a. receptive
re·cep·tor, m. receiver
re·ce·sión, f. recession
re·ce·ta, f. recipe; prescription
re·ci·bi·mien·to, m. reception; receiving; lobby
re·ci·bir, v. receive; accept; welcome
re·ci·bo, m. usu. pl. receipt
re·cién, adv. recently. **re·cién ca·sa·dos,** newlyweds
re·cien·te, a. recent; new
re·cien·te·men·te, adv. lately; recently
re·cin·to, m. campus; precinct; enclosure
re·cio, a. strong
re·ci·pien·te, m. recipient
re·ci·pro·ca·ción, f. reciprocation
re·ci·pro·ca·men·te, adv. reciprocally
re·ci·pro·car(se), v. reciprocate
re·ci·pro·ci·dad, f. reciprocity
re·cí·pro·co, a. reciprocal
re·ci·ta·ción, f. recitation
re·ci·tar, v. recite
re·cla·ma·ción, f. reclamation; claim
re·cla·mar, v. claim; reclaim
re·cli·nar(se), v. recline
re·clu·so, m. recluse
re·clu·ta, m. recruit
re·clu·ta·mien·to, m. recruitment
re·clu·tar, v. recruit
re·co·brar(se), v. recover; regain; retrieve; recuperate
re·co·bro, m. recovery; recuperation
re·co·ger(se), v. gather; collect; harvest; shorten; shelter
re·co·gi·da, f. withdrawal
re·co·gi·mien·to, m. withdrawal; collection
re·co·men·da·ción, f. recommendation; testimonial
re·co·men·dar, v. recommend; advocate
re·com·pen·sa, f. recompense; reward
re·com·pen·sar, v. recompense; repay
re·con·ci·lia·ble, a. reconcilable
re·con·ci·lia·ción, f. reconciliation
re·con·ci·liar(se), v. reconcile
re·cón·di·to, a. concealed
re·con·for·tar, v. strengthen
re·co·no·cer, v. recognize; acknowledge; own up to; avow; reconnoiter
re·co·no·ci·ble, a. recognizable
re·co·no·ci·mien·to, m. recognition; gratitude; inspection; reconnaissance
re·con·quis·ta, f. reconquest
re·con·quis·tar, v. reconquest; recapture
re·con·si·de·rar, v. reconsider
re·cons·truc·ción, f. reconstruction
re·cons·truir, v. reconstruct
re·con·tar, v. retell; recount
re·con·ver·tir, v. reconvert
re·cor·dar(se), v. remind; remember; recall
re·co·rrer, v. scour; run over; travel; traverse
re·co·rri·do, m. round; course; reconnaissance
re·cor·tar, v. trim; shorten
re·cor·te, m. snip; cutting
re·co·si·do, m. darn
re·cos·tar(se), v. recline; lean back; lie down

re·crear(se), v. recreate; entertain
re·crea·ti·vo, a. recreational
re·creo, m. recreation
re·cri·mi·na·ción, f. recrimination
re·cri·mi·nar, v. recriminate
re·cru·de·cer, v. worsen
re·cru·des·cen·cia, f. recrudescence
rec·tal, a. rectal
rec·tan·gu·lar, a. rectangular
rec·tán·gu·lo, m. rectangle. a. rectangular
rec·ti·fi·car, v. rectify
rec·ti·tud, f. rectitude; rightness
rec·to, a. upright; right; straight. m. rectum
re·cuer·do, m. souvenir; remembrance; memento; memory; often pl. remembrances
re·cu·pe·ra·ción, f. recuperation; recovery
re·cu·pe·rar(se), v. recuperate; recover; retrieve
re·cu·rrir, v. resort to
re·cur·so, m. recourse; remedy; expedient; resource; resort
re·cu·sa·ción, f. challenge
re·cu·sar, v. challenge
re·cha·za·do, a. outcast; repulsed
re·cha·zar, v. rebuff; repel; reject; turn out; fend off
re·cha·zo, m. rejection
re·chi·na·mien·to, m. grating; gnashing
re·chi·nar, v. gnash; grate
re·chon·cho, a. squat; stocky; chubby
red, f. net; network; mesh; trap
re·dac·ción, f. editing; writing
re·dac·tar, v. compose; edit
re·dac·tor, m., re·dac·to·ra, f. editor; writer
re·da·da, f. catch, as of fish
re·den·ción, f. redemption
re·den·tor, m. redeemer. a. redeeming
re·di·mir, v. redeem; pay off
ré·di·to, m. yield; rent
re·don·do, a. round(ed); spherical
re·dro·jo, m. round
re·duc·ción, f. reduction; lessening
re·du·ci·do, a. reduced; narrow; low
re·du·cir(se), v. reduce; abate; shorten; condense; confine
re·dun·dan·te, a. redundant
re·e·di·fi·car, v. rebuild
re·e·lec·ción, f. re-election
re·e·le·gir, v. re-elect
re·em·bol·sar, v. repay; reimburse
re·em·bol·so, m. refund; repayment
re·em·pla·za·ble, a. replaceable
re·em·pla·zar, v. replace; substitute
re·em·pla·zo, m. replacement; substitution
re·en·car·na·ción, f. reincarnation
re·fe·ren·cia, f. reference
re·fe·ren·dum, m. referendum
re·fe·ren·te, a. referring
re·fe·rir(se), v. refer; recite; relate
re·fi·na·do, a. refined; polished
re·fi·na·mien·to, m. refinement
re·fi·nar, v. refine; polish
re·fi·ne·ría, f. refinery
re·fle·ja, f. reflection. a. reflected
re·fle·jar(se), v. reflect; consider
re·fle·jo, m. a reflex; reflexive
re·fle·xi·o·nar, v. reflect; speculate
re·fle·xi·va·men·te, adv. reflectively
re·fle·xi·vo, a. reflexive
re·flu·jo, m. ebb
re·for·ma, f. reform; (usu. cap.) Reformation
re·for·ma·ción, f. reformation
re·for·ma·do, a. reformed
re·for·mar(se), v. reform; mend; reconstruct
re·for·za·do, a. reinforced
re·for·zar, v. reinforce; brace; strengthen
re·frac·ción, f. refraction
re·frac·tar(se), v. refract
re·frán, m. proverb
re·fre·nar, v. refrain; restrain; curb
re·fren·dar, v. countersign
re·fres·ca·mien·to, m. refreshment
re·fres·car(se), v. refresh; freshen
re·fres·co, m. refreshment
re·fri·ge·ra·ción, f. refrigeration
re·fri·ge·rar, v. refrigerate; cool
re·fu·gia·do, m. re·fu·gia·da, f. refugee. a. refugee
re·fu·giar(se), v. take refuge
re·fu·gio, m. refuge; shelter; asylum
re·fun·fu·ñar, v. grumble; inf. grouch
re·fun·fu·ño, m. grumbling
re·fu·ta·ción, f. rebuttal; refutation
re·fu·tar, v. refute
re·ga·du·ra, f. irrigation
re·ga·la, f. gunwale, gunnel
re·ga·lar(se), v. make a present of; regale
re·ga·liz, m. licorice, liquorice
re·ga·lo, m. gift; present
re·ga·ñar, v. nag; scold; berate
re·gar, v. water; irrigate
re·ga·te·ar, v. bargain; dicker; haggle
re·ga·tón, m. tip
re·ga·zo, m. lap
re·ge·ne·ra·ción, f. regeneration
re·ge·ne·rar, v. regenerate
re·gen·te, m. regent
re·gi·ci·dio, m. regicide
ré·gi·men, m. regime; regimen; diet
re·gi·mien·to, m. regiment; administration

re·gión, f. region; district; area
re·gio·nal, a. regional
re·gio·na·lis·mo, m. regionalism
re·gir, v. govern; conduct; obtain
re·gis·trar(se), v. register; log; record; search
re·gis·tro, m. register; record; search
re·gla, f. law; rule; ruler
re·gla·men·ta·ción, f. regulations
re·gla·men·tar, v. regulate
re·gla·men·to, m. regulation; bylaw
re·glar, v. rule off
re·go·ci·ja·da·men·te, adv. merrily
re·go·ci·ja·do, a. merry; festive; joyous
re·go·ci·jar(se), v. rejoice; gladden; exult
re·go·ci·jo, m. joy; elation; festivity
re·gor·de·te, a. chubby
re·gre·sar, v. return
re·gre·si·vo, a. regressive
re·gu·la·ción, f. regulation
re·gu·la·dor, m. throttle. a. regulating
re·gu·lar, a. regular; common; tolerable. v. regulate
re·gu·la·ri·dad, f. regularity; custom
re·gu·lar·men·te, adv. regularly; generally
re·ha·bi·li·ta·ción, f. rehabilitation
re·ha·bi·li·tar, v. rehabilitate
re·ha·cer, v. redo; remake
re·hén, m. hostage
re·hi·lar, v. whiz, whizz; reel
re·huir, v. refuse
re·hu·sar, v. refuse; decline; deny
re·im·pri·mir, v. reprint
rei·na, f. queen
rei·na·do, m. reign
rei·nar, v. reign; command
re·in·ci·dir, v. backslide
rei·no, m. realm; kingdom
reír(se), v. laugh; scoff. reír en·tre dien·tes, chuckle; chortle
rei·te·ra·ción, f. reiteration
rei·te·rar, v. reiterate
re·ja, f. grating; grid
re·ju·ve·ne·cer(se), v. rejuvenate
re·la·ción, f. relation; recital; correspondence; bearing; account
re·la·cio·nar(se), v. relate; connect
re·la·ja·ción, f. relaxation
re·la·jar(se), v. relax; loosen; weaken
re·la·tar, v. relate; report; impart
re·la·ti·va·men·te, adv. relatively
re·la·ti·vi·dad, f. relativity
re·la·ti·vo, a. relative; comparative; germane
re·la·to, m. report; account; narration
re·le·ga·ción, f. relegation
re·le·gar, v. relegate
re·le·var, v. pardon; relieve
re·li·ca·rio, m. shrine
re·lie·ve, m. relief
re·li·gión, f. religion; creed; piety
re·li·gio·sa·men·te, adv. religiously
re·li·gio·so, a. religious; pious; godly
re·lin·char, v. whinny
re·lin·cho, m. whinny
re·li·quia, f. relic; vestige
re·loj, m. clock; watch; timepiece. re·loj des·per·ta·dor, alarm clock
re·lu·cien·te, a. glittering; shining
re·lu·cir, v. glitter; shine; glisten
re·lum·brar, v. glare; sparkle; glisten
re·lum·bre, m. luster
re·lle·nar(se), v. refill; stuff; cram
re·lle·no, m. filling; stuffing. a. stuffed
re·ma·che, m. rivet
re·mar, v. row
re·ma·te, m. conclusion; end; auction
re·me·da·dor, m., re·me·da·do·ra, f. mimic
re·me·dar, v. mimic
re·me·diar, v. remedy; cure; repair
re·me·dio, m. remedy; recourse; help
re·men·da·do, a. repaired
re·men·dar, v. repair; patch; mend; blotch
re·me·sa, f. remittance
re·mien·do, m. patch
re·mil·ga·do, a. squeamish; prudish
re·mil·gar·se, v. be squeamish
re·mil·go, m. squeamishness; prudery
re·mi·nis·cen·cia, f. reminiscence; memory
re·mi·sión, f. remission; remittance
re·mi·so, a. remiss
re·mi·tir, v. remit; refer to; defer; postpone
re·mo, m. oar
re·mo·de·lar, v. remodel
re·mo·jar, v. soak
re·mo·la·cha, f. beet
re·mol·ca·dor, m. tugboat
re·mol·car, v. tug; tow
re·mo·ler, v. grind up
re·mo·li·nar(se), v. swirl; whirl
re·mo·li·no, m. swirl; whirlpool; eddy
re·mol·que, m. tow; caravan; trailer
re·mon·tar(se), v. soar; remount; resole
re·mor·di·mien·to, m. remorse; regret; compunction
re·mo·ta·men·te, adv. remotely
re·mo·to, a. remote; faraway; unlikely
re·mo·ver, v. remove; transfer; shift
re·mo·zar(se), v. rejuvenate
re·mu·ne·ra·ción, f. remuneration
re·mu·ne·ra·dor, a. remunerative
re·mu·ne·rar, v. remunerate
re·na·cer, v. be reborn; grow again;

revive
re·na·ci·mien·to, m. rebirth; (usu. cap.) Renaissance
re·na·cua·jo, m. tadpole
ren·ci·lla, f. grudge; feud
ren·ci·llo·so, a. quarrelsome
ren·cor, m. rancor; grudge; spite; spleen; bitterness; venom
ren·co·ro·sa·men·te, adv. resentfully
ren·co·ro·so, a. rancorous; bitter; catty
ren·di·ción, f. surrender; yielding
ren·di·do, a. worn-out; submissive
ren·di·mien·to, m. submission; rent; exhaustion
ren·dir(se), v. surrender; yield; overcome
re·ne·ga·do, m. re·ne·ga·da, f. renegade. a. renegade
re·nom·bra·do, a. renowned
re·nom·bre, m. renown
re·no·va·ble, a. renewable
re·no·va·ción, f. renovation
re·no·va·do, a. renovated; renewed
re·no·var, v. renew; renovate; repair; reform
ren·ta, f. revenue; income; rent. ren·ta vi·ta·li·cia, annuity
re·nun·ciar, v. renounce; surrender; resign; waive; forego; abnegate
re·nun·cia·ción, f. renunciation; disclaimer; waiver
re·ñir, v. quarrel; argue; feud; bicker
reo, m., f. criminal; defendant
re·or·ga·ni·za·ción, f. reorganization
re·or·ga·ni·zar, v. reorganize
re·pa·ra·ción, f. repair; amends; reparation
re·pa·ra·dor, m. serviceman
re·pa·rar, v. repair; mend; make amends
re·pa·ro, m. recovery; repair; doubt
re·par·ti·dor, m. deliveryman
re·par·ti·mien·to, m. division; apportionment; distribution
re·par·tir(se), v. apportion; distribute; mete out; share; dole; cast
re·par·to, m. allocation; delivery; deal; theatrical cast
re·pa·sar, v. revise; review; glance over
re·pa·so, m. revision; review
re·pa·tria·ción, f. repatriation
re·pa·triar(se), v. repatriate
re·pe·ler, v. repel
re·pen·ti·na·men·te, adv. suddenly
re·pen·ti·no, a. sudden; abrupt; snap
re·per·cu·sión, f. repercussion
re·per·to·rio, m. repertory; repertoire
re·pe·ti·ción, f. repetition; recurrence; encore
re·pe·ti·da·men·te, adv. repeatedly
re·pe·tir(se), v. repeat; recur; rehearse
re·pi·car, v. peal; chime
re·pi·que, m. chime
re·ple·gar, v. refold
ré·pli·ca, f. reply; answer; rebuttal
re·pli·car, v. answer; respond
re·po·blar, v. repopulate
re·po·ner(se), v. replace; replenish; recuperate
re·por·ta·je, m. report; reporting
re·po·sa·da·men·te, adv. restfully
re·po·sa·do, a. restful; quiet
re·po·sar, v. repose; rest
re·po·si·ción, f. reposition
re·po·si·to·rio, m. repository
re·po·so, m. repose
re·pre·gun·tar, v. cross-examine
re·pren·der, v. reprimand; rebuke; berate; chide
re·pren·si·ble, a. reprehensible
re·pre·sar, v. dam; stem
re·pre·sen·ta·ción, f. representation; performance; authority
re·pre·sen·tan·te, m., f. representative; agent
re·pre·sen·ta·ti·vo, a. representative
re·pre·si·vo, a. repressive
re·pri·men·da, f. reprimand; rebuke
re·pri·mir, v. repress; quell; curb
re·pro·bar, v. chide; condemn
re·pro·char, v. reproach
re·pro·che, m. reproach; rebuke
re·pro·duc·ción, f. reproduction
re·pro·du·cir(se), v. reproduce; breed
rep·til, a. reptile. m. reptile
re·pú·bli·ca, f. republic
re·pu·dia·ción, f. repudiation
re·pu·diar, v. repudiate; disown; divorce
re·pues·to, m. store. de re·pues·to, spare
re·pug·nan·cia, f. repugnance; disgust
re·pug·nan·te, a. repugnant; revolting; ugly
re·pul·sa, f. repulse; snub; rebuff
re·pul·sar, v. repulse; reject; refuse
re·pul·si·vo, a. repulsive; unsightly
re·pu·ta·ción, f. reputation; credit
re·que·rir, v. require; need; want; investigate
re·qui·sar, v. commandeer; requisition
re·qui·si·ción, f. requisition
re·qui·si·to, m. prerequisite; requirement; necessity
res, m. beast. res muer·ta, carcass
re·sa·ca, f. hangover
re·sal·tar, v. stand out; stick out
re·sar·ci·mien·to, m. compensation

revive
re·sar·cir, v. compensate
res·ba·la·di·zo, a. slippery
res·ba·lar, v. slip; glide; slip up; err
res·ba·lón, m. slip
res·ca·tar, v. ransom; rescue; recover
res·ca·te, m. ransom; rescue; deliverance
re·sen·ti·do, a. resentful; sullen
re·sen·ti·mien·to, m. resentment; umbrage
re·sen·tir·se, v. resent
re·se·ña, f. review
re·ser·va, f. reserve; reservation; closeness. con re·ser·va, in confidence
re·ser·va·ción, f. reservation
re·ser·va·da·men·te, adv. privately
re·ser·va·do, a. reserved; shy; aloof
re·ser·var, v. reserve; set aside; bespeak; book
res·fria·do, m. cold
res·friar(se), v. catch cold; cool
res·guar·dar(se), v. shelter; protect
res·guar·do, m. shelter; guard; collateral
re·si·den·cia, f. residence
re·si·den·cial, a. residential
re·si·den·te, a. resident. m., f. resident
re·si·dir, v. reside; dwell; live
re·si·dual, a. residual
re·sig·na·ción, f. resignation; submission
re·sig·na·da·men·te, adv. resignedly
re·sig·nar(se), v. resign; give up
re·si·na, f. resin
re·sis·ten·cia, f. resistance; stamina; strength; endurance
re·sis·ten·te, a. tough; resistant
re·sis·tir(se), v. resist; withstand; oppose; contend
res·ma, f. ream
re·so·lu·ción, f. resolve; resolution; decision; purpose; steadfastness. con re·so·lu·ción, decisively
re·so·lu·to, a. resolute; determined
re·sol·ver(se), v. resolve; settle; determine; solve; figure out
re·so·llar, v. wheeze
re·so·nan·cia, f. resonance
re·so·nan·te, a. resonant
re·so·nar, v. echo; resound
res·pal·do, m. back
res·pec·ti·va·men·te, adv. respectively
res·pec·ti·vo, a. respective
res·pec·to, m. respect. res·pec·to a, re; with regard to
res·pe·ta·bi·li·dad, f. respectability
res·pe·ta·ble, a. respectable
res·pe·tar, v. respect
res·pe·to, m. respect; consideration
res·pe·tuo·sa·men·te, adv. respectfully
res·pe·tuo·so, a. respectful
res·pin·gar, v. wince; balk
res·pi·ra·ción, f. breathing; respiration
res·pi·rar, v. breathe; inhale. res·pi·rar as·má·ti·ca·men·te, wheeze
res·pi·ra·to·rio, a. respiratory
res·pi·ro, m. respite; breathing
res·plan·de·cer, v. glitter; glow; shine
res·plan·de·cien·te, adv. gleaming
res·plan·dor, m. glitter; blaze
res·pon·der, v. respond; answer; reply
res·pon·sa·bi·li·dad, f. responsibility
res·pon·sa·ble, a. responsible; accountable; amenable
res·pues·ta, f. reply; response; answer
res·ta, f. remainder; subtraction
res·ta·ble·cer(se), v. revive; re-establish
res·ta·ble·ci·mien·to, m. re-establishment; recovery
res·tan·te, a. remaining
res·ta·ñar, v. stanch, staunch
res·tar, v. deduct; subtract
res·tau·ra·ción, f. restoration
res·tau·ran·te, res·tau·rán, m. restaurant
res·tau·rar, v. restore; renew
res·ti·tu·ción, f. restitution
res·to, m. rest; remainder; balance; pl. wreckage
res·tric·ción, f. restriction
res·tric·ti·va·men·te, adv. restrictively
res·tric·ti·vo, a. restrictive
res·trin·gir, v. restrict; restrain; cramp
re·su·ci·ta·ción, f. resuscitation
re·su·ci·tar, v. resuscitate; resurrect; revive
re·suel·ta·men·te, adv. resolutely
re·suel·to, a. resolute; determined; unflinching; strong-minded; stout
re·sul·ta·do, m. result; outcome; product; issue; sequel; upshot
re·sul·tan·te, a. resultant
re·sul·tar, v. result; follow; prove to be
re·su·men, m. resume; résumé; syllabus; summary; abstract; rundown. en re·su·men, in short
re·su·mir, v. summarize; condense; abridge
re·sur·gi·mien·to, m. resurgence
re·su·rrec·ción, f. resurrection
re·ta·guar·dia, f. rearguard
re·tar·da·ción, f. retardation
re·tar·da·do, a. belated; held up; delayed
re·tar·dar, v. retard; slow down;

delay
re·ten·ción, f. retention
re·te·ner, v. retain; withhold; keep; detain
re·ti·na, f. retina
re·tin·tín, m. jingle; tinkling
re·ti·ñir, v. jingle; tinkle
re·ti·ra·da, f. retreat; withdrawal
re·ti·ra·do, a. retired; pensioned
re·ti·rar(se), v. retire; withdraw; recall
re·ti·ro, m. retreat; seclusion
re·to·ñar, v. sprout
re·to·ño, m. sprout
re·tor·cer(se), v. contort; twist; wring; writhe; squirm
re·tor·ci·do, a. twisted
re·tor·ci·mien·to, m. twisting; writhing
re·tó·ri·ca, f. rhetoric
re·tó·ri·ca·men·te, adv. rhetorically
re·tó·ri·co, a. rhetorical
re·tor·nar, v. restore; return
re·to·zar, v. frisk about; romp; frolic
re·to·zón, a. frolicsome
re·trac·ción, f. retraction
re·trac·tar(se), v. retract; take back; recant
re·tra·sa·do, a. late; delayed
re·tra·sar, v. delay
re·tra·to, m. picture; portrait; description
re·tre·te, m. toilet; water-closet
re·tri·bu·ción, f. payment; vengeance; retribution
re·tro·ac·ti·vo, a. retroactive
re·tro·ce·der, v. recede; fall back
re·tro·ce·so, m. recession; retrocession
re·tros·pec·ti·va·men·te, adv. retrospectively
re·tros·pec·ti·vo, a. retrospective
re·tum·bar, v. rumble; boom; clink
re·tum·bo, m. rumble; boom
reu·má·ti·co, a. rheumatic
reu·ma·tis·mo, m. rheumatism
reu·nión, f. reunion; assembly; rally; meeting
reu·nir(se), v. meet; gather; combine; collect; mass; rally; herd
re·ve·la·ción, f. revelation; exposure; disclosure
re·ve·la·dor, a. revealing
re·ve·lar, v. reveal; manifest; unbosom; betray; disclose
re·ven·tar, v. burst
re·ven·tón, m. burst; explosion; difficulty
re·ve·ren·cia, f. reverence; homage; bow; curtsy
re·ve·ren·cial, a. reverential
re·ve·ren·do, m. reverend. a. revered
re·ve·ren·te·men·te, adv. reverently
re·ver·so, m. reverse
re·ver·tir, v. revert to
re·vés, m. reverse; back side; setback. al re·vés, backward
re·ves·tir(se), v. put on
re·vi·sar, v. revise; review; go over; overhaul
re·vi·sión, f. revision; review; audit
re·vis·ta, f. magazine; journal; review
re·vi·vir, v. revive
re·vo·ca·ción, f. revocation; repeal
re·vo·car, v. revoke; annul; repeal
re·vol·car·se, v. welter; wallow in; knock over
re·vo·lo·tear, v. flutter; flit
re·vo·lu·ción, f. revolution; revolt
re·vo·lu·cio·na·rio, m., re·vo·lu·cio·na·ria, f. revolutionary. a. revolutionary
re·vól·ver, m. revolver; pistol
re·vol·ver(se), v. revolve; revert; scramble; rummage
re·vuel·to, a. scrambled; confused. hue·vos re·vuel·tos, scrambled eggs
rey, m. king
re·za·ga·do, m. straggler
re·za·gar(se), v. lag; straggle behind
re·zar, v. pray
re·zu·mar(se), v. exude; leak; seep
ria·chue·lo, m. creek
ri·bal·de·ría, f. ribaldry
ri·be·ra, f. shore
ri·be·te, m. trimming
ri·be·tear, v. edge; hem
ri·ca·men·te, adv. richly; lavishly
ri·co, a. rich; wealthy; affluent
ri·di·cu·la·men·te, adv. ridiculously
ri·di·cu·li·zar, v. ridicule; deride
ri·dí·cu·lo, m. ridicule. a. ridiculous; ludicrous; farcical
rie·go, m. irrigation. bo·ca de rie·go, hydrant
rie·lar, v. shimmer
rien·da, f. usu. pl. rein
ries·go, m. risk; chance; danger; hazard; liability
ri·fa, f. raffle
ri·fle, m. rifle
ri·gi·da·men·te, adv. rigidly; sternly
ri·gi·dez, f. rigidity
rí·gi·do, a. rigid; stiff; set; stern
ri·gor, m. rigor; strictness; severity; inflexibility
ri·go·ris·ta, m., f. stickler
ri·gu·ro·sa·men·te, adv. rigorously
ri·gu·ro·so, a. rigorous; strict; stringent; severe
ri·ma, f. rhyme
ri·mar, v. rhyme
ri·me·ro, m. stack; pile

rin·cón, m. corner
ri·no·ce·ron·te, m. rhinoceros
ri·ña, f. quarrel; dispute; fracas
ri·ñón, m. kidney
río, m. river
ri·pio, m. rubble
ri·que·za, f. wealth; affluence; riches
ri·sa, f. laugh; laughter. ri·sa so·fo·ca·da, giggle
ris·co, m. bluff; cliff; crag
ri·si·ta, f. chortle; titter
rít·mi·co, a. rhythmic; rhythmical
rit·mo, m. rhythm; cadence; beat
ri·to, m. rite
ri·tual, a. ritual. m. ritual
ri·tua·lis·mo, m. ritualism
ri·val, a. rival. m. rival
ri·va·li·dad, f. rivalry
ri·va·li·zar, v. rival; compete with
ri·za·do, a. curly
ri·zar(se), v. curl; ruffle
ri·zo, m. curl; ringlet
ro·ba·do, a. robbed
ró·ba·lo, m. bass
ro·bar, v. rob; steal; burglarize; inf. snitch; rustle
ro·ble, m. oak
ro·bo, m. theft; robbery
ro·bus·ta·men·te, adv. robustly
ro·bus·tez, f. robustness; hardiness
ro·bus·to, a. robust; strong; hale; hardy; lusty
ro·ca, f. rock
ro·cia·da, f. spray
ro·ciar, v. spray; sprinkle; scatter
ro·cín, m. hack; jade
ro·cío, m. dew
ro·da·do, a. dappled; rounded
ro·da·ja, f. castor
ro·dar, v. roll; wheel along
ro·dear, v. encircle; circle; surround; ring; loop
ro·deo, m. detour
ro·de·ra, f. rut
ro·di·lla, f. knee
ro·do·den·dro, m. rhododendron
roe·dor, m. rodent
roer, v. gnaw; gnaw at; eat away
ro·gar, v. pray; plead with; entreat; request; ask
ro·jear, v. turn red
ro·ji·zo, a. reddish
ro·jo, a. red. m. red
ro·llo, m. roll; coil; bolt
ro·man·ce, m. tale of chivalry. a. (cap.) Romance
ro·mán·ti·ca·men·te, adv. romantically
ro·man·ti·cis·mo, m. romanticism
ro·mán·ti·co, a. romantic
ro·me·ría, f. pilgrimage
rom·pe·ca·be·zas, m. jigsaw puzzle; puzzle
rom·peo·las, m. breakwater
rom·per(se), v. break; crush; smash; burst; dash; breach; tear
rom·pi·mien·to, m. break; rupture
ron, m. rum
ron·car, v. snore
ron·co, a. husky; hoarse
ron·da, f. round; patrol; beat, as of a policeman
ron·dar, v. do the rounds
ron·que·dad, f. hoarseness
ron·qui·do, m. snore
ron·ro·near, v. purr
ron·ro·neo, m. purr
ro·pa, f. clothes; clothing; dress; apparel; wear. ro·pa blan·ca, lingerie. ro·pa de ca·ma, bedclothes; bedding. ro·pa in·te·rior, underclothes; underwear. ro·pa la·va·da, laundry
ro·pe·ro, m. wardrobe
ro·sa, f. rose
ro·sa·do, a. pink; rosy
ro·sa·rio, m. rosary
ros·ca, f. thread, as of a screw; ring
ros·tro, m. face
ro·ta·ción, f. rotation
ro·to, a. broken; shattered; smashed
ro·tu·lar, v. label; ticket; letter
ró·tu·lo, m. label
ro·tun·da·men·te, adv. roundly
ro·tun·do, a. rotund; round
ro·tu·ra, f. breakage; rupture; crack
ro·za·mien·to, m. chafing
ro·zar(se), v. graze; rub; chafe; browse
ru·bí, m. ruby
ru·bia, f. blonde
ru·bio, a. blond, blonde; fair; red
ru·bor, m. flush
ru·bo·ri·za·do, a. flushed
ru·bo·ri·zar(se), v. make blush; flush
ru·di·men·tal, a. rudimentary
ru·di·men·to, m. rudiment
ru·do, a. rude; uncouth; churlish
rue·da, f. wheel. rue·da vo·lan·te, flywheel
rue·go, m. request; plea; entreaty
ru·fián, m. ruffian
ru·gi·do, m. roar; bellow
ru·gir, v. roar; bellow
rui·bar·bo, m. rhubarb
rui·do, m. noise; sound; clatter; noisiness; rattle; row; commotion
rui·do·sa·men·te, adv. noisily
rui·do·so, a. noisy; loud; blatant; rowdy; boisterous
ruin, a. mean; weak
rui·na, f. ruin; downfall; bane; wreck
rui·nar, v. ruin
rui·no·so, a. ruinous
rui·se·ñor, m. nightingale
ru·le·ta, f. roulette
rum·bo, m. route; direction; course; way

ru·mia, f. cud; rumination
ru·mi·nar, v. chew cud; brood over
ru·mor, m. murmur; rumor; hearsay
rup·tu·ra, f. break; rupture
ru·ral, a. rural
ru·ral·men·te, adv. rurally
rús·ti·co, m., rús·ti·ca, f. rustic. a. rustic; countrified
ru·ti·na, f. routine; route; rut
ru·ti·na·rio, a. routine

S

sá·ba·do, m. Saturday
sá·ba·na, f. sheet
sa·ban·di·jas, f. insect; bug; pl. vermin
sa·ba·ni·lla, f. small piece of cloth
sa·ba·ñón, f. chilblain
sa·ber, v. knowledge; ken; learning. v. know; learn; ken. a sa·ber, namely; that is to say
sa·bia·men·te, adv. wisely; sagely
sa·bi·du·ría, f. learning; wisdom
sa·bio, a. wise; sage; learned; sapient. m. sage
sa·bor, m. flavor; taste; savor
sa·bo·rear, v. taste; savor
sa·bo·ta·je, m. sabotage
sa·bo·tear, v. sabotage
sa·bro·sa·men·te, adv. deliciously
sa·bro·so, a. tasty; delicious
sa·bue·so, m. bloodhound; hound
sa·ca, f. extraction; export
sa·ca·cor·chos, m. corkscrew
sa·car, v. take out; elicit; extract; draw out; withdraw. sa·car u·na fo·to, photograph; take a picture
sa·ca·ri·na, f. saccharine
sa·cer·do·cio, f. priesthood
sa·cer·do·te, m. priest
sa·ciar, v. sate; satiate
sa·cie·dad, f. satiety
sa·co, m. sack; bagful. sa·co de ma·no, grip
sa·cra·men·tal, a. sacramental
sa·cra·men·to, m. sacrament
sa·cri·fi·car(se), v. sacrifice; sacrifice oneself
sa·cri·fi·cio, m. sacrifice; offering
sa·cri·le·gio, m. sacrilege
sa·crí·le·go, a. sacrilegious
sa·cris·tía, f. vestry; sacristy
sa·cro·san·to, a. sacrosanct
sa·cu·di·da, f. jolt; shaking
sa·cu·di·mien·to, m. shock
sa·cu·dir(se), v. shake; jar; jerk; jolt; thrash; flap
sa·dis·mo, m. sadism
sae·ta, f. dart; religious song
sa·fa·ri, m. safari
sa·ga, f. saga
sa·ga·ci·dad, f. sagacity
sa·gaz, a. wise; shrewd; discerning
sa·gra·do, a. holy; sacred. Sa·gra·da Es·cri·tu·ra, Holy Scriptures
sai·ne·te, m. farce
sal, f. salt (sodium chloride); wit
sa·la, f. hall. sa·la de es·tar, lounge; drawing room. sa·la de re·ci·bo, parlor, parlour
sa·la·do, a. salt; salty; witty
sa·la·man·dra, f. salamander
sa·lar, v. salt
sa·la·rio, m. salary; often pl. wage
sa·laz, a. salacious
sal·chi·cha, f. frankfurter; sausage
sal·do, m. balance
sa·li·da, f. departure; emergence; exit; outlet; vent; sally
sa·lien·te, a. projecting
sa·li·no, a. saline
sa·lir, v. emerge; come out; issue; leave; escape. sa·lir bien, succeed. sa·lir fue·ra, protrude
sa·li·va, f. saliva; spit; spittle
sa·li·va·ción, f. salivation
sal·mo, m. psalm
sal·món, m. salmon
sa·lo·bre, m. brackish
sa·lón, m. salon; assembly room. sa·lón de bai·le, ballroom
sal·pi·ca·du·ra, f. splash; splatter; spatter
sal·pi·car, v. splash; spatter; dabble
sal·sa, f. sauce; gravy. sal·sa pi·can·te de to·ma·te, ketchup, catsup
sal·ta·dor, m. jumper
sal·ta·mon·tes, m. grasshopper
sal·tar, v. jump; leap; hop; spring; skip; vault; bound
sal·tear, v. hold up
sal·te·rio, m. psalter
sal·to, m. jump; hop; leap; usu. pl. bound; dive. sal·to mor·tal, somersault
sa·lu·bre, a. healthy
sa·lu·bri·dad, f. salubrity
sa·lud, f. health
sa·lu·da·ble, a. salutary; healthy; wholesome
sa·lu·dar, v. greet; salute; hail
sa·lu·do, m. greeting; salutation; salute; hail
sa·lu·ta·ción, f. salutation
sal·va, f. salvo; salute
sal·va·ción, f. salvation
sal·va·do, m. bran
sal·va·dor, m. savior; (cap.) Savior, Saviour
sal·va·guar·dia, f. safeguard
sal·va·ja·da, f. savage act
sal·va·je, a. savage; wild. m., f. savage
sal·va·men·to, m. salvage; salvation
sal·var(se), v. save; rescue; escape from danger

sal·va·vi·das, m. life preserver
sal·ve, int. hail
sal·via, f. sage
sal·vo, prep. saving. a. safe; except
San (San·to), m. Saint
sa·na·ble, a. curable
sa·na·men·te, adv. sanely; wholesomely
sa·nar, v. heal; recover
sa·na·to·rio, m. sanatorium. Also sanitarium
san·ción, f. sanction
san·cio·nar, v. sanction
san·da·lia, f. sandal
san·día, f. watermelon
sa·nea·mien·to, m. indemnification; drainage
sa·near, v. indemnify; drain
san·grar, v. bleed; tap; drain; indent
san·gre, f. blood; gore. de san·gre fría, cold-blooded. in·yec·ta·do de san·gre, bloodshot. pu·ra san·gre, thoroughbred
san·gría, f. drink made of red wine and fruit; drainage
san·grien·ta·men·te, adv. bloodily
san·grien·to, a. bloody
san·gui·jue·la, f. leech
san·gui·na·rio, a. sanguinary; bloodthirsty
san·gui·neo, a. sanguine; of blood
sa·ni·dad, f. health
sa·ni·ta·rio, a. sanitary; healthy
sa·no, a. healthy; healthful; sane; sound; fit; hearty
san·ta, f. (female) saint
san·ti·dad, f. sanctity; holiness
san·ti·fi·ca·ción, f. sanctification
san·ti·fi·car, v. sanctify; consecrate
san·to, m. saint. a holy; saintly. san·to y se·ña, password; watchword
san·tua·rio, m. sanctuary
sa·ñu·da·men·te, adv. furiously
sa·po, m. toad
sa·quea·dor, m. ransacker; looter
sa·quear, v. loot; plunder; ransack; sack
sa·queo, m. plunder; ransacking
sa·ram·pión, m. measles
sa·ra·pe, m. blanket
sar·cas·mo, m. sarcasm; taunt
sar·cás·ti·ca·men·te, adv. sarcastically
sar·cás·ti·co, a. sarcastic
sar·có·fa·go, m. sarcophagus
sar·di·na, f. sardine
sar·dó·ni·ca·men·te, adv. sardonically
sar·dó·ni·co, a. sardonic
sar·gen·to, m. sergeant
sa·ri, m. sari, saree
sar·na, f. itch
sar·tén, m. skillet; frying pan
sas·tre, m. tailor
sas·tre·ría, f. tailoring
Sa·ta·nás, m. Satan
sa·tá·ni·ca·men·te, adv. satanically
sa·tá·ni·co, a. satanic. Also satanical
sa·té·li·te, m. satellite
sá·ti·ra, f. satire
sa·tí·ri·ca·men·te, adv. satirically
sa·tí·ri·co, a. satirical
sa·ti·ri·zar, v. satirize; lampoon
sá·ti·ro, m. satyr
sa·tis·fac·ción, f. satisfaction; content; amends; apology
sa·tis·fa·cer, v. satisfy; gratify; quench; indulge; sate
sa·tis·fac·to·ria·men·te, adv. satisfactorily
sa·tis·fac·to·rio, a. satisfactory
sa·tis·fe·cho, a. satisfied
sa·tu·ra·ción, f. saturation
sa·tu·rar, v. saturate; steep
sa·tur·ni·no, a. morose; saturnine
sau·ce, m. willow
sa·via, f. sap
sa·xo·fón, m. saxophone
sa·zón, f. ripeness; flavoring
sa·zo·na·do, a. seasoned
sa·zo·nar, v. flavor; season
se, pron., m., f. neuter. himself; herself; yourself; itself; pl. themselves; yourselves; one; one another
se·bo, m. suet; tallow
se·bo·so, a. greasy
se·ca·men·te, adv. drily
se·car(se), v. dry; wipe; blot; wither; shrivel; parch
sec·ción, f. section; segment; department; branch
se·ce·sión, f. secession; sequence
se·ce·sio·nis·ta, m., f. secessionist
se·ca·to, a. sensible; lucid
sen·si·bi·li·dad, f. sensibility
se·cre·ción, f. secretion
se·cre·ta·men·te, adv. secretly
se·cre·tar, v. secrete
se·cre·ta·rio, m., se·cre·ta·ria, f. secretary
se·cre·tear, v. whisper (secrets)
se·cre·to, a. secret; confidential; covert; cryptic; classified; undercover; underhanded. m. secret; secrecy
sec·ta, f. sect
sec·tor, m. sector
se·cues·tra·ción, f. sequestration; kidnapping
se·cues·tra·dor, m.. se·cues·tra·do·ra, f. kidnapper
se·cues·trar, v. kidnap; abduct; sequester
se·cues·tro, m. kidnapping
se·cu·lar, a. secular
se·cu·la·ri·za·ción, f. secularization
se·cu·la·ri·zar, v. secularize
se·cun·dar, v. second
se·cun·da·rio, a. secondary; circumstantial; subordinate; minor

se·cun·di·nas, f. pl. afterbirth
sed, f. thirst. te·ner sed, be thirsty
se·da, f. silk. se·da flo·ja, floss
se·da·ti·vo, m. sedative
se·de, f. see
se·den·ta·rio, a. sedentary
se·di·ción, f. sedition
se·di·cio·sa·men·te, adv. seditiously
se·di·cio·so, a. seditious
se·di·men·ta·ción, f. sedimentation
se·di·men·ta·rio, a. sedimentary
se·di·men·to, m. sediment; silt
se·do·so, a. silky
se·duc·ción, f. seduction; seducement; allure
se·du·cir, v. seduce; lead astray; captivate
se·duc·tor, m. seducer
se·ga·dor, m. harvester
se·gar, v. mow; reap; harvest
seg·lar, m. layman
seg·men·to, m. segment
se·gre·ga·ción, f. segregation
se·gre·gar, v. segregate
se·gui·da, f. continuation. en se·gui·da, at once; immediately
se·gui·da·men·te, adv. continuously
se·gui·do, a. continuous
se·gui·dor, m., se·gui·do·ra, f. follower
se·gui·mien·to, m. continuation; pursuit
se·guir, v. follow; continue; ensue; pursue; shadow
se·gún, prep. according to; by; as
se·gun·do, a. second. m. second
se·gu·ra·men·te, adv. surely; certainly
se·gu·ri·dad, f. security; certainty; safety
se·gu·ro, a. sure; certain; secure; safe; sound; confident; reliable; watertight; trusty. m. insurance
seis, a. six. m. six
seis·cien·tos, a. six hundred
seís·mo, m. earthquake
se·lec·ción, f. selection; choice
se·lec·cio·nar, v. select; choose
se·lec·ti·vi·dad, f. selectivity
se·lec·ti·vo, a. selective
se·lec·to, a. select; choice
sel·va, f. jungle; forest
sel·vá·ti·co, a. wild; rustic
sel·vo·so, a. wooded; of the jungle
se·lla·du·ra, f. sealing
se·llar, v. stamp; seal
se·llo, m. stamp; seal. se·llo de co·rreo, postage stamp
se·má·fo·ro, m. stoplight; semaphore
se·ma·na, f. week. Se·ma·na San·ta, Holy Week
se·ma·nal, a. weekly
se·mán·ti·ca, f. semantics
se·mán·ti·co, a. semantic
sem·blan·te, m. countenance; aspect
sem·brar, v. sow; seed; plant
se·me·jan·te, a. similar; alike; akin
se·me·jan·za, f. similarity; likeness; resemblance
se·men, m. semen
se·mes·tral, a. half-yearly
se·mes·tre, m. semester; six months
se·mi·cir·cu·lar, a. semicircular
se·mi·cír·cu·lo, m. semicircle
se·mi·con·so·nan·te, f. semiconsonant
se·mi·fi·nal, a. semifinal. m. usu. pl. semifinal
se·mi·fi·na·lis·ta, a. semifinalist. m., f. semifinalist
se·mi·lla, f. seed
se·mi·nal, a. seminal
se·mi·na·rio, m. seminar; seminary
se·mi·vi·vo, a. half-alive
se·na·do, m. senate; (cap.) Senate
se·na·dor, m. senator
se·na·to·rial, a. senatorial
sen·ci·lla, a. simple; plain; unassuming; naive; single
sen·ci·lla·men·te, adv. simply; plainly
sen·ci·llez, f. simplicity
sen·da, f. track; lane; footpath
se·nil, a. senile
se·no, m. breast; bosom; sinus
sen·sa·ción, f. sensation; sense; feeling
sen·sa·cio·nal, a. sensational; lurid
sen·sa·tez, f. sensibleness
sen·sa·to, a. sensible; lucid
sen·si·bi·li·dad, f. sensibility
sen·si·ble, a. sensitive; alive; lamentable
sen·si·ble·men·te, adv. sensitively; markedly
sen·si·ti·vo, a. sensitive
sen·so·rio, a. sensory. Also sensorial
sen·sual, a. sensual
sen·sua·li·dad, f. sensuality
sen·sual·men·te, adv. sensually
sen·ta·da, f. sitting
sen·tar(se), v. sit down; sit; seat
sen·ten·cia, f. sentence; judgment; conviction
sen·ten·ciar, v. adjudge; sentence
sen·ten·cio·sa·men·te, adv. sententiously
sen·ten·cio·so, a. sententious
sen·ti·do, m. meaning; sense; construction
sen·ti·men·tal, a. sentimental
sen·ti·men·tal·men·te, adv. sentimentally
sen·ti·mien·to, m. sentiment; regret
sen·tir(se), v. feel; sense; regret
se·ña, f. sign; mark. ha·cer se·ñas, motion; signal

se·ñal, f. signal; sign; token; (often pl.) note
se·ña·la·da·men·te, adv. signally; plainly
se·ña·la·do, a. signal; noted
se·ña·lar(se), v. mark; appoint; designate; distinguish
se·ñor, m. mister, abbr. Mr.; sir; gentleman; master; lord
se·ño·ra, f. lady; madam; mistress; Mrs.; wife; inf. ma'am
se·ño·rear, v. domineer; rule
se·ño·ril, a. lordly
se·ño·río, m. manor; lordliness; lordship
se·ño·ri·ta, f. miss; young lady
se·ñue·lo, m. bait; lure; decoy
sé·pa·lo, m. sepal
se·pa·ra·ción, f. separation; segregation; isolation
se·pa·ra·da·men·te, adv. separately
se·pa·ra·do, a. separate; detached; isolated
se·pa·rar(se), v. separate; part; detach; split; sever; sequester
se·pa·ra·tis·mo, m. separatism
sep·ten·trio·nal, a. northern
sép·ti·co, a. septic
sep·tiem·bre, m. September
sép·ti·mo, a. seventh. m. seventh
se·pul·cro, m. tomb; sepulcher
se·pul·tar, v. bury
se·pul·tu·ra, f. vault; grave; tomb
se·que·dad, f. dryness; gruffness
se·quía, f. drought
sé·qui·to, m. following; entourage
ser, v. be; belong. ser de, be of; be made of
ser, m. being; life. ser hu·ma·no, human being
se·rá·fi·co, a. seraphic
se·ra·fín, m. seraph
se·re·na·men·te, adv. serenely; quietly
se·re·na·ta, f. serenade
se·re·ni·dad, f. serenity; calmness; composure
se·re·no, a. serene; calm; fair; sober. m. night watchman
se·ria·men·te, adv. seriously
se·rie, f. series; sequence; string; run; suite; train. en se·rie, mass
se·rie·dad, f. seriousness; gravity. con se·rie·dad, earnestly
se·rio, a. serious; grave; sober; earnest
ser·món, m. sermon
ser·pen·tear, v. wind; meander
ser·pen·ti·no, a. snakelike; winding
ser·pien·te, f. serpent; snake. ser·pien·te de cas·ca·bel, rattlesnake
se·rra·nía, f. mountain range
se·rrar, v. saw
ser·vi·cio, m. service. ser·vi·cio do·més·ti·co, domestic service
ser·vi·dor, m., ser·vi·do·ra, f. servant
ser·vi·dum·bre, f. servitude; servants
ser·vil, a. servile; menial; subservient
ser·vi·lle·ta, f. napkin
ser·vir(se), v. serve; wait on; do; answer
se·sen·ta, a. sixty; threescore. m., f. sixty
ses·ga·da·men·te, adv. slanting; sloping
ses·ga·do, a. slanting; bias; awry
ses·gar(se), v. slant; slope
ses·go, m. slope; slant; bias. al ses·go, aslant
se·sión, f. session; meeting
se·so, m. brain; understanding
se·te·cien·tos, a. seven hundred
se·ten·ta, a. seventy. m., f. seventy
se·to, m. hedge; fence
seu·dó·ni·mo, m. pseudonym
se·ve·ra·men·te, adv. severely; harshly
se·ve·ri·dad, f. severity; sternness; harshness
se·ve·ro, a. severe; harsh; stern; strict; forbidding; grim; rough; rugged
sex·o, m. sex. sex·o fe·me·ni·no, womankind
sex·te·to, m. sextet
sex·to, a. sixth
sex·ual, a. sexual
sex·ua·li·dad, f. sexuality
sex·ual·men·te, adv. sexually
si, conj. if; whether
sí, reflexive pron. sí mis·mo, himself; yourself; itself; oneself; also one's self. sí mis·ma, herself; yourself; itself
sí, adv. yes. int. aye; ay; yea
si·co·mo·ro, m. sycamore
si·dra, f. cider
siem·pre, adv. always; forever; ever. siem·pre que, whenever
sien, f. temple
sie·rra, f. saw. sie·rra de vai·vén, jigsaw
sier·vo, m., sier·va, f. serf; slave
sies·ta, f. nap
sie·te, a. seven. m., f. seven
sí·fi·lis, f. syphilis
si·fón, m. siphon; syphon
si·gi·lo, m. secrecy; secret
si·gi·lo·sa·men·te, adv. secretly
si·glo, m. century
sig·ni·fi·ca·ción, f. significance
sig·ni·fi·ca·do, m. significance
sig·ni·fi·ca·ti·vo, a. significant
sig·ni·fi·car(se), v. signify; mean; imply; make known
sig·ni·fi·ca·ti·va·men·te, adv. significantly

sig·no, m. sign
si·guien·te, a. next; following
sí·la·ba, f. syllable
si·la·bear, v. syllabicate; syllabify
si·la·beo, m. syllabication; syllabification
sil·bar, v. whistle; hiss; whiz; whizz
sil·bi·do, m. whistle; hiss; whiz, whizz
si·len·cio, m. silence; hush; quiet
si·len·cio·sa·men·te, adv. silently
si·len·cio·so, a. silent; quiet
si·li·cio, m. silicon
si·lo, m. silo
si·lue·ta, f. silhouette
sil·ves·tre, a. wild; sylvan, silvan
sil·vi·cul·tu·ra, f. forestry
si·lla, f. chair. si·lla de mon·tar, saddle. si·lla de rue·das, wheelchair
si·ma, f. chasm
sim·bó·li·ca·men·te, adv. symbolically
sim·bó·li·co, a. symbolic; symbolical
sim·bo·lis·mo, m. symbolism
sim·bo·li·zar, v. symbolize; typify
sím·bo·lo, m. symbol
si·me·tría, f. symmetry
si·mé·tri·ca·men·te, adv. symmetrically
si·mé·tri·co, a. symmetrical
si·mio, a. simian
si·mien·te, f. seed
si·mi·lar, a. similar
sim·pa·tía, f. sympathy; friendliness
sim·pá·ti·co, a. nice; congenial; likeable; sympathetic
sim·ple, a. simple; plain
sim·ple·men·te, adv. simply; barely; plainly
sim·pli·ci·dad, f. simplicity
sim·pli·fi·ca·ción, f. simplification
sim·pli·fi·car, v. simplify
si·mu·lar, v. simulate
si·mul·tá·nea·men·te, adv. simultaneously; together
si·mul·tá·neo, a. simultaneous
sin, prep. without; wanting. sin em·bar·go, however; yet. sin ton ni son, without rhyme or reason. sin va·lor, worthless. sin vo·lun·tad, weak-minded
sin·ce·ra·men·te, adv. sincerely
sin·ce·ri·dad, f. sincerity; cordiality
sin·ce·ro, a. sincere; genuine; wholehearted; heartfelt
sin·cro·ni·zar(se), v. synchronize
sin·di·car, v. syndicate; unionize
sin·di·ca·to, m. union; trade union; syndicate
si·ne·cu·ra, f. sinecure
sin·fo·nía, f. symphony
sin·gu·lar, a. singular; quaint. m. singular
sin·gu·la·ri·dad, f. singularity; oddity
sin·gu·lar·men·te, adv. singularly
si·nies·tro, a. sinister; baleful
si·no, conj. but; except
si·no·do, m. synod
si·nó·ni·mo, m. synonym. a. synonymous
si·nop·sis, f. synopsis
sín·te·sis, f. synthesis
sin·té·ti·ca·men·te, adv. synthetically
sin·té·ti·co, a. synthetic
sín·to·ma, m. symptom
sin·to·ni·zar, v. tune
sin·ver·güen·za, m., f. person without shame
sio·nis·mo, m. Zionism
si·quie·ra, adv. although; at least. ni si·quie·ra, not even
si·re·na, f. mermaid; siren
sir·vien·te, m., sir·vien·ta, f. servant
sis·mó·gra·fo, m. seismograph
sis·te·ma, m. system
sis·te·má·ti·ca·men·te, adv. systematically
sis·te·ma·ti·zar, v. systematize
si·tiar, v. besiege; surround; beleaguer; beset; invest
si·tio, m. place; space; site; spot; room; siege
si·tua·ción, f. situation; location; plight. si·tua·ción e·co·nó·mi·ca, circumstances
si·tuar, v. situate; post; station
smo·king, m. tuxedo
so·ba·co, m. armpit
so·be·ra·nía, f. sovereignty
so·be·ra·no, m. sovereign. a. sovereign
so·ber·bia, f. haughtiness; anger
so·ber·bio, a. haughty
so·bor·nar, v. bribe
so·bor·no, m. bribe; graft
so·bra, f. surplus; pl. scraps
so·bran·te, a. spare; remaining; odd; waste. m. margin
so·brar, v. remain; surpass
so·bre, prep. on; upon; atop; onto; over; above; about. m. envelope
so·bre to·do, above all
so·bre·car·ga, f. surcharge; overload
so·bre·car·gar, v. overload
so·bre·co·ger(se), v. startle
so·bre·hu·ma·no, a. superhuman
so·bre·lle·var, v. buoy; float
so·bre·po·ner(se), v. superimpose; overcome
so·bre·sa·lien·te, a. outstanding. m., f. understudy
so·bre·sa·lir, v. project; jut; excel; transcend

so·bre·sal·tar(se), v. start; startle
so·bre·sal·to, m. scare; surprise
so·bres·cri·to, m. superscription
so·bre·to·do, m. topcoat
so·bre·vi·vien·te, m., f. survivor
so·bre·vi·vir, v. survive
so·brie·dad, f. sobriety; restraint
so·bri·na, f. niece
so·bri·no, m. nephew
so·brio, a. sober
so·ca·var, v. undermine
so·cia·bi·li·dad, f. sociability
so·cia·ble, a. sociable
so·cia·ble·men·te, adv. sociably
so·cial, a. social
so·cia·lis·mo, m. socialism
so·cia·li·zar, v. socialize; fraternize
so·cie·dad, f. society; company; corporation; league. so·cie·dad a·nó·ni·ma, incorporated company
so·cio, m. associate; partner
so·cio·lo·gía, f. sociology
so·cio·ló·gi·co, a. sociological
so·co·rrer, v. succor; help; aid
so·co·rro, m. help; succor. int. help!
so·dio, m. sodium
so·do·mía, f. sodomy
so·fá, m. sofa; couch
so·fis·ma, f. sophism; chicanery
so·fis·te·ría, f. sophistry; chicanery
so·fo·ca·ción, f. suffocation
so·fo·can·te, a. suffocating; stifling; close
so·fo·car(se), v. suffocate; smother; choke; swelter; quell
so·ga, f. rope
so·juz·ga·ción, f. subjugation
so·juz·gar, v. subjugate; conquer; subdue
sol, m. sun; sunlight. luz del sol, sunlight; sunshine. pues·ta del sol, sundown; sunset. sa·li·da del sol, sunrise. to·mar el sol, sun; sunbathe
so·la·men·te, adv. only; alone; solely
so·la·pa, f. lapel; flap
so·la·par, v. overlap
so·lar, a. solar. m. site; floor
so·laz, m. solace; relaxation
sol·da·do, m. soldier; GI, also G.I.; pl. military. sol·da·do de ca·ba·lle·ría, trooper; cavalryman. sol·da·do ra·so, private
sol·dar, v. soldar; weld
so·le·dad, f. privacy; solitude
so·lem·ne, a. solemn; impressive
so·lem·ne·men·te, adv. solemnly
so·lem·ni·dad, f. solemnity; ceremony
so·lem·ni·zar, v. celebrate
so·li·ci·ta·ción, f. solicitation
so·li·ci·tar, v. solicit; request; seek; apply for; canvass
so·li·ci·tud, f. care; application
só·li·da·men·te, adv. solidly
so·li·da·ri·dad, f. solidarity
so·li·di·fi·ca·ción, f. solidification
só·li·do, a. solid. m. solid
so·li·lo·quio, m. soliloquy
so·li·ta·ria·men·te, adv. solitarily
so·li·ta·rio, a. solitary; lonely; lone; lonesome. m. recluse
so·lo, a. sole; solitary; one; alone; lonely; lonesome. m. (mus.) solo
só·lo, adv. only; solely. conj. but
sol·tar(se), v. release; loose; undo
sol·te·ría, f. bachelorhood
sol·te·ro, a. unattached; single. m. bachelor
sol·te·ro·na, f. spinster
so·lu·ble, a. soluble
so·lu·ción, f. solution; answer
so·lu·cio·nar, v. solve
sol·ven·te, m. solvent
sol·lo·zar, v. sob; wail
sol·llo·zo, m. sob
som·bra, f. shadow; shade; suspicion
som·brea·do, a. shady
som·brear, v. shade
som·bre·ro, m. hat
som·brío, a. somber; dismal; overcast
so·me·ter(se), v. submit; subject; yield
so·me·ti·mien·to, m. submission
som·no·len·cia, f. drowsiness; sleepiness
som·no·len·te, a. drowsy; sleepy
so·mor·gu·jo, m. loon
son, m. sound. sin ton ni son, without rhyme or reason
so·na·je·ro, m. rattle
so·nar(se), v. sound; ring; rattle; chink; blow the nose
son·da, f. probe
son·deo, m. poll; canvass
so·ne·to, m. sonnet
so·ni·do, m. sound
so·no·ro, a. sonorous
son·reír(se), v. smile; grin
son·ri·sa, f. smile. son·ri·sa bur·lo·na, smirk
son·ro·jar·se, v. flush; blush
son·ro·jo, m. blush
so·ña·dor, m., so·ña·do·ra, f. dreamer. a. dreamy
so·ñar, v. dream
so·ño·lien·ta·men·te, adv. sleepily
so·ño·lien·to, a. sleepy; drowsy
so·pa, f. soup. so·pa de pes·ca·do, chowder
so·pe·ra, f. tureen
so·plar, v. blow; puff; inf. snitch
so·plo, m. blow; puff; blast; tip
so·por·ta·ble, a. bearable
so·por·tar, v. endure; bear; tolerate; abide; bracket; support

so·pra·no, *m., f.* soprano
sor·ber, *v.* sip; soak up
sor·be·te, *m.* sherbet
sor·bo, *m.* sip; swallow; taste
sor·de·ra, *f.* deafness
sór·di·do, *a.* sordid; dirty; nasty
sor·di·na, *f.* (*mus.*) mute
sor·do, *a.* deaf
sor·do·mu·do, *m.*, sor·do·mu·da, *f.* deaf-mute
sor·pren·den·te, *a.* surprising; astonishing; startling
sor·pren·der(se), *v.* surprise; amaze; startle
sor·pre·sa, *f.* surprise; amazement
sor·te·o, *m.* raffle
so·sa, *f.* soda
so·se·ga·da·men·te, *adv.* quietly
so·se·ga·do, *a.* quiet; sedate; gentle
so·se·gar(se), *v.* pacify; calm; rest
so·sie·go, *m.* peace; calmness
so·so, *a.* insipid; tame; shy
sos·pe·cha, *f.* suspicion; inkling
sos·pe·char, *v.* suspect; be suspicious of
sos·pe·cho·sa·men·te, *adv.* suspiciously
sos·pe·cho·so, *a.* suspect; suspicious; doubtful; fishy
sos·tén, *m.* support; stand; brassiere; *inf.* bra
sos·te·ner, *v.* support; sustain; maintain; uphold
sos·te·ni·do, *a.* sustained. *m.* (*mus.*) sharp
sos·te·ni·mien·to, *m.* maintenance
so·ta, *f.* (*cards*) jack
so·ta·na, *f.* cassock
só·ta·no, *m.* cellar; basement
so·ta·ven·to, *m.* lee
su, *a.* his; her; its; your; *pl.* your; their
sua·ve, *a.* soft; smooth; mild; bland; gentle; balmy; mellow
sua·ve·men·te, *adv.* gently; softly; mildly; smoothly
sua·vi·dad, *f.* gentleness; smoothness; softness
sua·vi·za·dor, *m.* strop
sua·vi·zar, *v.* soften; smooth; mellow; subdue
su·ba·rren·dar, *v.* sublease; sublet
su·bas·ta, *f.* sale; auction
su·bas·ta·dor, *m.* auctioneer
su·bas·tar, *v.* auction
sub·cons·cien·cia, *f.* subconscious
sub·cons·cien·te, *a.* subconscious
sub·cons·cien·te·men·te, *adv.* subconsciously
sub·cu·tá·neo, *a.* subcutaneous
súb·di·to, *m.* subject
sub·di·vi·dir, *v.* subdivide
sub·di·vi·sión, *f.* subdivision
su·bes·ti·mar, *v.* underestimate
su·bi·da, *f.* ascent; rise; increase
su·bir(se), *v.* raise; lift up; rise; ascend; increase; accede
sú·bi·ta·men·te, *adv.* suddenly
sú·bi·to, *a.* sudden
sub·je·ti·va·men·te, *adv.* subjectively
sub·je·ti·vi·dad, *f.* subjectivity
sub·je·ti·vo, *a.* subjective
sub·jun·ti·vo, *a.* subjunctive
su·ble·va·ción, *f.* uprising; revolt
su·ble·var, *v.* incite to rebellion
su·bli·ma·ción, *f.* sublimation
su·bli·mar, *v.* sublimate
su·bli·me, *a.* sublime; majestic
su·bli·me·men·te, *adv.* sublimely
su·bli·mi·dad, *f.* sublimity
sub·ma·ri·no, *m.* submarine; *inf.* sub
su·bor·di·na·ción, *f.* subordination
su·bor·di·na·do, *a.* subordinate. *m.* underling; minor
su·bor·di·nar, *v.* subordinate
sub·ra·yar, *v.* underscore; underline; emphasize
subs·cri·bir(se), *v.* subscribe to
subs·crip·ción, *f.* subscription
sub·si·dia·rio, *a.* a subsidiary
sub·si·dio, *m.* subsidy; benefit
sub·si·guien·te, *a.* a subsequent
sub·sis·ten·cia, *f.* subsistence
sub·sis·tir, *v.* subsist; live; endure
subs·tan·cia, *f.* substance; meaning
subs·tan·ciar, *v.* substantiate
subs·tan·cial, *a.* substantial; material
subs·tan·cial·men·te, *adv.* substantially
subs·tan·ti·vo, *m.* noun; substantive. *a.* substantive
subs·ti·tu·ción, *f.* substitution
subs·ti·tuir, *v.* substitute
subs·ti·tu·to, *m.* substitute; surrogate. *a.* substitute; vicarious
subs·trac·ción, *f.* subtraction
subs·traer, *v.* subtract
sub·ter·fu·gio, *m.* subterfuge
sub·te·rrá·neo, *a.* subterranean; underground
sub·ti·tu·lo, *m.* subheading; subtitle
su·bur·ba·no, *a.* suburban
su·bur·bio, *m.* suburb, *often pl.*
sub·ven·ción, *f.* subsidy
sub·ven·cio·nar, *v.* subsidize
sub·ver·sión, *f.* subversion
sub·ver·si·vo, *a.* subversive. *m.* subversive
sub·ver·tir, *v.* subvert
su·bu·ga·ción, *f.* subjugation
sub·yu·gar, *v.* subjugate; overcome
suc·ción, *f.* suction
su·ce·der, *v.* happen; occur; transpire; succeed; make out
su·ce·sión, *f.* succession; issue; estate
su·ce·si·vo, *a.* successive; consecutive
su·ce·so, *m.* event; incident; result
su·ce·sor, *m.*, su·ce·so·ra, *f.* successor

sor
su·cie·dad, *f.* dirtiness
su·cin·to, *a.* succinct; brief
su·cio, *a.* dirty; unclean; filthy; foul; nasty; grubby; dingy
su·cu·len·to, *a.* succulent
su·cum·bir, *v.* succumb
su·dar, *v.* perspire; sweat
sud·es·te, *m.* southeast
sud·oes·te, *m.* southwest
su·dor, *m.* perspiration; sweat
su·do·ro·so, *a.* sweaty
sue·gra, *f.* mother-in-law
sue·gro, *m.* father-in-law
sue·la, *f.* sole
suel·do, *m.* pay; salary
sue·lo, *m.* ground; land; floor
suel·to, *a.* unattached; loose; free
sue·ño, *m.* sleep; dream
sue·ro, *m.* serum
suer·te, *f.* luck; chance; fate; doom; fortune; lot
sué·ter, *m.* sweater
su·fi·cien·cia, *f.* sufficiency; complacency
su·fi·cien·te, *a.* sufficient; adequate
su·fi·cien·te·men·te, *adv.* sufficiently
su·fi·jo, *m.* suffix
su·fra·gio, *m.* suffrage; vote
su·fri·mien·to, *m.* suffering; misery; patience
su·frir, *v.* suffer; sustain; undergo
su·ge·rir, *v.* suggest; hint
su·ges·tión, *f.* suggestion; hint
su·ges·ti·vo, *a.* suggestive
sui·ci·da, *m., f.* suicide
sui·ci·dar·se, *v.* commit suicide
sui·ci·dio, *m.* suicide
su·je·ción, *f.* subjection; control
su·je·tar(se), *v.* attach; clamp; cramp; subject
su·je·to, *m.* subject; matter. *a.* subject; attached
sul·fa·to, *m.* sulphate
sul·fú·ri·co, *a.* sulphuric
sul·tán, *m.* sultan
sul·ta·na·to, *m.* length of a sultan's reign
sul·ta·ní·a, *f.* sultanate
su·ma, *f.* sum; amount; total
su·ma·men·te, *adv.* exceedingly; very
su·mar, *v.* add; sum up
su·ma·rio, *m.* a summary
su·mer·gi·mien·to, *m.* submergence
su·mer·gir(se), *v.* submerge; submerse; dive
su·mer·sión, *f.* submergence; submersion
su·mi·nis·trar, *v.* supply; provide
su·mi·sión, *f.* submission; compliance
su·mi·so, *a.* submissive; compliant; obedient
su·mo, *a.* utmost; highest; supreme. su·mo sa·cer·do·te, high priest
sun·tuo·sa·men·te, *adv.* sumptuously
sun·tuo·so, *a.* sumptuous
su·pe·rar, *v.* surmount; surpass; exceed; cap
su·pe·ren·ten·der, *v.* superintend; supervise
su·per·fi·cial, *a.* superficial
su·per·fi·cial·men·te, *adv.* superficially
su·per·fi·cie, *f.* surface
su·per·flua·men·te, *adv.* superfluously
su·per·flui·dad, *f.* superfluity
su·per·fluo, *a.* superfluous; needless
su·pe·rin·ten·den·cia, *f.* superintendence
su·pe·rin·ten·den·te, *m., f.* superintendent; supervisor
su·pe·rior, *a.* superior; better; senior; upper. *m. usu. pl.* superior; better
su·pe·rio·ri·dad, *f.* superiority
su·per·la·ti·vo, *a.* superlative
su·per·mer·ca·do, *m.* supermarket
su·per·nu·me·ra·rio, *m.*, su·per·nu·me·ra·ria, *f.* supernumerary. *a.* supernumerary
su·per·só·ni·co, *a.* supersonic
su·pers·ti·ción, *f.* superstition
su·pers·ti·cio·sa·men·te, *adv.* superstitiously
su·pers·ti·cio·so, *a.* superstitious
su·per·vi·sor, *m.*, su·per·vi·so·ra, *f.* supervisor
su·per·vi·ven·cia, *f.* survival
su·pi·no, *a.* supine
su·plan·tar, *v.* supplant; supersede
su·ple·men·ta·rio, *a.* supplementary
su·ple·men·to, *m.* supplement
sú·pli·ca, *f.* supplication; plea; appeal
su·pli·can·te, *m., f.* supplicant; applicant
su·pli·car, *v.* supplicate; plead; beseech; appeal; crave
su·plir, *v.* supplement
su·po·ner, *v.* suppose; presume; *inf.* reckon
su·po·si·ción, *f.* supposition; assumption
su·pre·ma·cia, *f.* supremacy
su·pre·ma·men·te, *adv.* supremely
su·pre·mo, *a.* supreme; final
su·pre·sión, *f.* suppression; deletion
su·pri·mir, *v.* suppress; remove
su·pues·to, *a.* alleged; so-called; would-be. por su·pues·to, of course
su·pu·ra·ción, *f.* suppuration
su·pu·rar, *v.* suppurate
sur, *m.* south
sur·car, *v.* furrow

sur·co, *m.* furrow
sur·gir, *v.* emerge; originate; arise
sur·ti·da, *f.* sally
sur·ti·do, *m.* stock; assortment
sur·ti·dor, *m.* jet of water
sur·tir, *v.* stock; supply
sus·cep·ti·bi·li·dad, *f.* susceptibility
sus·cep·ti·ble, *a.* susceptible
sus·pen·der, *v.* hang; sling; suspend; stop; cease; adjourn; knock off
sus·pen·sión, *f.* suspension; recess; reprieve
sus·pi·rar, *v.* sigh; yearn for
sus·pi·ro, *m.* sigh
sus·ten·tan·te, *a.* sustaining
sus·ten·tar, *v.* sustain; support
sus·ten·to, *m.* sustenance
sus·to, *m.* fright; shock; surprise
su·su·rrar, *v.* whisper; rustle
su·su·rro, *m.* whisper; rustle
su·til, *a.* subtle; keen; thin
su·ti·le·za, *f.* subtlety; finesse; cunning; fineness
su·ti·li·zar, *v.* refine
su·til·men·te, *adv.* subtly; finely
su·yo, *pron.* his; hers; yours; its; one's; *pl.* theirs; yours

T

ta·ba·co, *m.* tobacco
tá·ba·no, *m.* gadfly
ta·ber·na, *f.* tavern; barroom; *inf.* pub
ta·ber·ná·cu·lo, *m.* tabernacle
ta·bi·que, *m.* partition
ta·bla, *f.* board; slab
ta·ble·ro, *m.* panel; board. ta·ble·ro de ins·tru·men·tos, dashboard
ta·ble·ta, *f.* tablet
ta·bli·lla, *f.* slat; splint
ta·blón, *m.* plank
ta·bú, *a.* taboo. *m.* taboo, tabu
ta·bu·lar, *v.* tabulate. *a.* tabular
ta·bu·re·te, *m.* stool
ta·ca·ño, *a.* stingy; mean; parsimonious
tá·ci·ta·men·te, *adv.* tacitly
tá·ci·to, *a.* tacit
ta·ci·tur·no, *a.* taciturn; reserved; sullen
ta·co, *m.* tablet; wad; cue
ta·cón, *m.* heel
tác·ti·ca, *f.* tactics
tác·ti·co, *a.* tactical
tac·to, *m.* tact; feel; touch
ta·cha, *f.* blemish
ta·char, *v.* delete; find fault with
ta·chón, *m.* trimming
ta·chue·la, *f.* tack
ta·fe·tán, *m.* taffeta
ta·ja·da, *f.* slice
ta·jar, *v.* hew; chop; slice
tal, *a.* such. *adv.* so. *pron.* such; such a thing. tal vez, maybe; perhaps
ta·la·drar, *v.* bore; drill
ta·la·dro, *m.* bore; drill
ta·lar, *v.* fell
tal·co, *m.* talc. pol·vo de tal·co, talcum powder
ta·len·to, *m.* talent
ta·len·to·so, *a.* talented
ta·lis·mán, *m.* talisman
ta·lón, *m.* heel
ta·lla, *f.* size; sculpture
ta·llar, *v.* (*cards*) deal; carve
ta·lla·rín, *m.* noodle
ta·lle, *m.* shape; figure; waistline
ta·ller, *m.* studio; atelier; shop; workshop
ta·llo, *m.* stalk; stem
ta·ma·ño, *m.* bulk. de ta·ma·ño na·tu·ral, life size, also life-sized
tam·ba·lear, *a.* a rickety
tam·ba·lear·se, *v.* stagger; reel
tam·bién, *adv.* also; besides; too; likewise
tam·bor, *m.* drum
tam·bo·ri·lear, *v.* drum
ta·miz, *f.* sieve
ta·mi·zar, *v.* sift; sieve
tam·po·co, *adv.* neither
tan, *adv.* so; such
tan·da, *f.* shift; batch
tan·gen·te, *a.* tangent. *f.* tangent
tan·gi·ble, *a.* tangible
tan·go, *m.* tango
tan·que, *m.* tank; cistern
tan·tear, *v.* score; calculate; size up
tan·te·o, *m.* score
tan·to, *adv.* so much; as many. por lo tan·to, therefore. tan·to me·jor, so much the better
ta·ñer, *v.* toll; ring
ta·ñi·do, *m.* twang; ring
ta·pa, *f.* cap; lid; top
ta·pa·gu·je·ros, *m.* stopgap
ta·par, *v.* plug; stop up; cover up
ta·pi·ce·ria, *f.* tapestry; upholstery
ta·pio·ca, *f.* tapioca
ta·pir, *m.* tapir
ta·piz, *m., pl.* ta·pi·ces, tapestry
ta·pi·zar, *v.* upholster; hang with tapestries
ta·pón, *m.* stopper; plug
ta·qui·gra·fia, *f.* stenography; shorthand
ta·qui·gra·fo, *m.*, ta·quí·gra·fa, *f.* stenographer
ta·rán·tu·la, *f.* tarantula
tar·dan·za, *f.* delay
tar·dar, *v.* delay; tarry; linger
tar·de, *adv.* late. *f.* afternoon; evening. bue·nas tar·des, good afternoon; good evening
tar·dío, *a.* late; belated; tardy
ta·rea, *f.* task; job; homework
ta·ri·fa, *f.* tariff

ta·ri·ma, *f.* bunk; platform
tar·je·ta, *f.* card. tar·je·ta pos·tal, postcard
tar·ta, *f.* tart; cake
tar·ta·mu·dear, *v.* stammer; stutter
tar·ta·mu·deo, *m.* stammer; stutter
tar·tán, *m.* plaid; tartan
tár·ta·ro, *m.* tartar
ta·sa, *f.* estimate; price
ta·sa·ción, *f.* valuation
ta·sar, *v.* rate; appraise; assess; tax
ta·tua·je, *m.* tatoo
ta·tuar, *v.* tatoo
tax·i, *m.* taxi; taxicab; cab
tax·is·ta, *m.* cabdriver; *inf.* cabby
ta·za, *f.* cup. ta·za pa·ra té, teacup
ta·zón, *m.* basin
te, *pron.* you; thee
té, *m.* tea. mu·ñe·ca de té, teabag. so·bre de té, teabag. ta·za pa·ra té, teacup
tea·tral, *a.* theatrical
tea·tral·men·te, *adv.* theatrically
tea·tro, *m.* theater; drama
te·beo, *m.* comic strip
te·cla, *f.* key, as of a typewriter
te·cla·do, *m.* keyboard
téc·ni·ca, *f.* technique
téc·ni·ca·men·te, *adv.* technically
téc·ni·co, *a.* technical. *m.* technician
tec·no·lo·gía, *f.* technology
tec·no·ló·gi·co, *a.* technological
te·char, *v.* roof
te·cho, *m.* roof; ceiling
te·dio, *m.* tedium; tediousness
te·dio·so, *a.* tedious; wearisome; loathsome
te·ja, *f.* tile
te·ja·do, *m.* tiled roof
te·ja·ma·nil, *m.* shingle
te·je·dor, *m.*, te·je·do·ra, *f.* weaver
te·jer, *v.* weave; knit
te·ji·do, *m.* textile; weave; tissue; *pl.* yardgoods
te·jón, *m.* badger
te·jo, *m.* yew
te·la, *f.* material; fabric; cloth; web. te·la de a·ra·ña, spiderweb; cobweb
te·lar, *v.* loom
te·la·ra·ña, *f.* spiderweb; cobweb
te·le·co·mu·ni·ca·ción, *f.* telecommunication
te·le·fo·near, *v.* telephone; *inf.* phone
te·lé·fo·no, *m.* telephone; *inf.* phone
te·le·gra·fía, *f.* telegraphy
te·le·gra·fiar, *v.* telegraph; wire
te·lé·gra·fo, *m.* telegraph
te·le·gra·ma, *m.* telegram; *inf.* wire
te·le·pa·tía, *f.* telepathy
te·les·có·pi·co, *a.* telescopic
te·les·co·pio, *m.* telescope
te·le·vi·sar, *v.* televise
te·le·vi·sión, *f.* television. Abbr. T.V.
te·le·vi·sor, *m.* television. Abbr. T.V.
te·lón, *m.* curtain. te·lón de fo·ro, backdrop
te·ma, *m.* theme; text; topic
te·má·ti·co, *a.* thematic
tem·blar, *v.* tremble; shake; quiver; shiver
tem·blor, *m.* quiver; tremor; trembling
te·mer, *v.* dread; be afraid
te·me·ra·ria·men·te, *adv.* recklessly
te·me·ra·rio, *a.* foolhardy; reckless; rash
te·me·ri·dad, *f.* temerity; boldness
te·me·ro·so, *a.* fearful; timid
te·mi·ble, *a.* fearsome; awful
te·mor, *m.* fear
tém·pa·no, *m.* ice floe; kettledrum
tem·pe·ra·men·tal, *a.* temperamental
tem·pe·ra·men·to, *m.* temperament
tem·pe·ra·tu·ra, *f.* body or atmospheric temperature
tem·pes·tad, *f.* storm; tempest
tem·pes·tuo·sa·men·te, *adv.* tempestuously
tem·pes·tuo·so, *a.* stormy; tempestuous
tem·pla, *f. usu. pl.* temple
tem·pla·da·men·te, *adv.* temperately
tem·pla·do, *a.* temperate; lukewarm
tem·plan·za, *f.* temperance; mildness
tem·plar, *v.* temper; anneal; warm up
tem·plo, *m.* temple; church
tem·po·ra·da, *f.* spell; season
tem·po·ral, *a.* temporary; temporal
tem·po·rá·neo, *a.* temporary
tem·pra·no, *a.* early. *adv.* early (in the day)
te·naz, *a.* tenacious; dogged; tough
te·na·zas, *f. pl.* tongs
ten·den·cia, *f.* tendency; trend; tone
ten·der(se), *v.* tend; trend; stretch out
ten·de·ro, *m.* shopkeeper
ten·dón, *m.* tendon; sinew
te·ne·bro·so, *a.* dark; gloomy
te·ne·dor, *m.* fork. te·ne·dor de li·bros, bookkeeper
te·nen·cia, *f.* lieutenancy; tenure; holding; occupation
te·ner, *v.* have; possess; hold; keep; include. te·ner deu·das, owe. te·ner ham·bre, be hungry. te·ner mie·do, be afraid. te·ner que, ought; must. te·ner vein·te a·ños, be twenty years old
te·nia, *f.* tapeworm
te·nien·te, *m.* lieutenant
te·nis, *m.* tennis
te·nor, *m.* tenor
ten·sión, *f.* tension; stress; strain

ten·so, *a.* tense
ten·ta·ción, *f.* temptation; enticement
ten·tá·cu·lo, *m.* tentacle
ten·tar, *v.* attempt; try; tempt; lure; entice; allure
ten·ta·ti·va, *f.* try; attempt
te·ñir, *v.* dye; stain; tinge
teo·lo·gía, *f.* theology
teo·ló·gi·ca·men·te, *adv.* theologically
teo·ló·gi·co, *a.* theological
teó·lo·go, *m.* theologian
teo·re·ma, *m.* theorem
teo·ría, *f.* theory
teó·ri·ca·men·te, *adv.* theoretically
teó·ri·co, *a.* theoretical
teo·ri·zar, *v.* theorize
te·ra·péu·ti·ca, *f.* therapy
ter·ce·ro, *a.* third. *a.* third person. *a.* third
ter·cio, *m.* third
ter·cio·pe·lo, *m.* velvet
ter·co, *a.* unyielding; obstinate; headstrong; willful, wilful
ter·mal, *a.* thermal
ter·mi·nal, *a.* terminal; final. *m.* terminal
ter·mi·nar, *v.* terminate; end; finish; complete; stop; close; culminate; expire
tér·mi·no, *m.* end; term; terminus; territory; boundary
ter·mi·no·lo·gía, *f.* terminology
ter·mó·me·tro, *m.* thermometer
ter·mo·nu·clear, *a.* thermonuclear
ter·mos·ta·to, *m.* thermostat
ter·ne·ra, *f.* veal
ter·que·dad, *f.* stubbornness; self-will
te·rra·plén, *m.* mound; embankment
te·rra·za, *f.* terrace
te·rre·mo·to, *m.* earthquake; quake
te·rre·no, *m.* terrain; *sometimes pl.* ground. te·rre·no de pas·to, range.
te·rre·no ri·be·re·ño, waterfront
te·rres·tre, *a.* terrestrial; earthly
te·rri·ble, *a.* terrible; dreadful
te·rri·ble·men·te, *adv.* terribly
te·rri·fi·co, *a.* terrific
te·rri·to·ria·li·dad, *f.* territoriality
te·rri·to·rio, *m.* territory; region
te·rrón, *m.* lump
te·rror, *m.* terror; panic
te·rro·ris·mo, *m.* terrorism
te·rro·ris·ta, *m., f.* terrorist
te·rro·so, *a.* earthy
te·sau·ro, *m.* thesaurus
te·sis, *f.* thesis
te·so·re·ría, *f.* treasury
te·so·re·ro, *m.* treasurer
te·so·ro, *m.* treasure; treasury
tes·ta·men·to, *m.* testament; will
tes·ti·fi·car, *v.* testify; attest
tes·ti·go, *m.* witness. tes·ti·go de vis·ta, eyewitness
tes·ti·mo·nio, *m.* testimony; certificate; witness; evidence
te·ta, *f.* teat
te·te·ra, *f.* teakettle; teapot; kettle
tex·til, *a.* textile
tex·to, *m.* text; textbook
tex·tual, *a.* textual
tex·tu·ra, *f.* texture
ti, *pron.* you; thee
tía, *f.* aunt
ti·bia, *f.* tibia
ti·bio, *a.* tepid; lukewarm
ti·bu·rón, *m.* shark
tic, *m.* tic
tic·tac, *m.* tick
tiem·po, *m.* time; movement; tempo; weather. de tiem·po en tiem·po, from time to time. ha·ce mal tiem·po, the weather is bad. ha·ce mu·cho tiem·po, a long time ago. per·der el tiem·po, dawdle; dally
tien·da, *f.* store; shop. tien·da de cam·pa·ña, tent
tier·na·men·te, *adv.* tenderly; affectionately
tier·no, *a.* tender; soft; affectionate
tie·rra, *f.* earth; land; soil; *sometimes pl.* ground
tie·so, *a.* taut; rigid
ties·to, *m.* pot
tie·su·ra, *f.* tautness; rigidity
ti·fón, *m.* typhoon
ti·fus, *m.* typhus
ti·gre, *m.* tiger
ti·je·ras, *f. pl.* scissors. ti·je·ras gran·des, shears
ti·je·re·ta·da, *f.* clip; snip
ti·je·re·tear, *v.* snip
ti·mar, *v.* chisel; cheat; gull
tim·bre, *m.* timbre
tí·mi·da·men·te, *adv.* timidly; shyly
ti·mi·dez, *f.* timidity; bashfulness; coyness
tí·mi·do, *a.* timid; shy; coy; self-conscious; sheepish
ti·món, *m.* helm; rudder. ca·ña del ti·món, tiller
ti·mo·nel, *m.* helmsman
tím·pa·no, *m.* kettledrum. tím·pa·no del oí·do, eardrum
ti·na, *f.* tub; vat
ti·nie·bla, *f. usu. pl.* darkness
tin·ta, *f.* ink
tin·tar, *v.* dye; tinge
tin·te, *v.* dye; tinge
tin·tu·ra, *f.* tincture; dyeing
tío, *m.* uncle; chap; *inf.* guy
tio·vi·vo, *m.* merry-go-round
tí·pi·ca·men·te, *adv.* typically
tí·pi·co, *a.* typical; characteristic
ti·ple, *m.* (*mus.*) treble. *m., f.* so-

prano
ti·po, *m.* type; figure; pattern
ti·po·gra·fía, *f.* typography; printing
ti·ra, *f.* band; strip
ti·ra·dor, *m.* knob; shot; marksman
ti·ra·nía, *f.* tyranny; oppression
ti·rá·ni·ca·men·te, *adv.* tyrannically
ti·rá·ni·co, *a.* tyrannical; *inf.* bossy
ti·ra·ni·zar, *v.* tyrannize; domineer
ti·ra·no, *m., f.* tyrant
ti·ran·te, *a.* taut. *m.* strap
ti·rar, *v.* throw; cast; pitch; sling; pull; haul
ti·ro, *m.* shot
ti·roi·des, *m.* thyroid gland
ti·rón, *m.* pull; jerk; tug; haul
ti·tá·ni·co, *a.* titanic
ti·te·re, *m.* puppet
ti·tu·bear, *v.* falter; stagger
ti·tu·lar, *v.* title; entitle; name
tí·tu·lo, *m.* title; heading; caption
ti·za, *f.* chalk
tiz·nar, *v.* smudge; brand
ti·zón, *m.* brand; blight
toa·lla, *f.* towel
to·bi·llo, *m.* ankle
to·bo·gán, *m.* toboggan
to·ca·dis·cos, *m.* phonograph; record player
to·car(se), *v.* touch; handle; finger; (*mus.*) play
to·ca·yo, *m.* namesake
to·ci·no, *m.* bacon
to·cón, *m.* stump
to·da·vía, *adv.* yet; still
to·do, *a.* all; whole; every. *adv.* entirely. *m.* whole; all. a pe·sar de to·do, all the same. so·bre to·do, above all. to·do el dí·a, all day long. to·do lo po·si·ble, *inf.* the works. to·do lo que, whatever
to·do·po·de·ro·so, *a.* almighty
to·ga, *f.* toga
tol·do, *m.* awning
to·le·ra·ble, *a.* tolerable; bearable
to·le·ran·cia, *f.* tolerance; sufferance
to·le·ran·te, *a.* tolerant; broad-minded
to·le·rar, *v.* tolerate; permit; endure
tol·va, *f.* chute
to·ma, *f.* taking
to·mar, *v.* take; assume; accept; eat. to·mar el pa·pel de, portray. to·mar el pe·lo, tease; *inf.* kid. to·mar el sol, bask in the sun. to·mar par·te, partake in
to·ma·te, *m.* tomato
to·mo, *m.* volume
to·nel, *m.* cask
to·ne·la·da, *f.* ton
to·ne·la·je, *m.* tonnage
tó·ni·co, *a.* tonic. *m.* tonic; bracing
ton·si·la, *f.* tonsil
ton·ta·men·te, *adv.* foolishly; dumbly
ton·te·ría, *f.* nonsense; foolishness folly; balderdash
ton·to, *a.* silly; foolish; witless. *m.* fool; half-wit; idiot; chump
to·pa·cio, *m.* topaz
to·pe·tar, *v.* butt
tó·pi·co, *a.* topical
to·po, *m.* mole
to·po·gra·fía, *f.* topography
to·po·grá·fi·co, *a.* topographical
to·que, *m.* touch. to·que de trom·pe·tas, fanfare
tó·rax, *m.* thorax
tor·be·lli·no, *m.* whirlwind
tor·ce·du·ra, *f.* sprain; wrench
tor·cer(se), *v.* twist; distort; sprain; strain; swerve; wring; buckle; gnarl
tor·ci·do, *a.* twisted; wry
to·re·ar, *v.* fight bulls
to·re·ro, *m.* bullfighter
tor·men·ta, *f.* storm
tor·men·to, *m.* torment; affliction
tor·na·do, *m.* tornado
tor·na·pun·ta, *f.* strut
tor·neo, *m.* tournament
tor·ni·llo, *m.* vise; screw
tor·ni·que·te, *m.* tourniquet; turnstile
tor·no, *m.* lathe; winch
to·ro, *m.* bull
to·ron·ja, *f.* grapefruit
tor·pe, *a.* slow; dull; dumb; rusty; clumsy; awkward; gauche; crass
tor·pe·do, *m.* torpedo
tor·pe·men·te, *adv.* slowly; awkwardly
tor·pe·za, *f.* clumsiness; dullness; awkwardness
to·rre, *f.* tower; (*chess*) castel; rook
to·rre·ci·lla, *f.* turret
to·rren·cial, *a.* torrential
to·rren·te, *m.* torrent; stream
tó·rri·do, *a.* torrid
tor·sión, *f.* twist; torsion
tor·so, *m.* torso
tor·ta, *f.* tart
tor·te·ra, *f.* griddle
tor·ti·lla, *f.* omelet
tor·tu·ga, *f.* turtle; tortoise
tor·tuo·sa·men·te, *adv.* tortuously; winding; sinuous; devious
tor·tuo·so, *a.* tortuous; winding; sinuous; devious
tor·tu·ra, *f.* torture
tor·tu·rar, *v.* torture; worry
to·run·da, *f.* swab
tos, *f.* cough. tos se·ca, hack
tos·ca·men·te, *adv.* coarsely; roughly
tos·co, *a.* rough; coarse; rude
to·ser, *v.* cough

tos·ta·da, f. toast
tos·ta·do, a. crisp; toasted; tanned
tos·tar, v. toast; tan
to·tal, a. total; whole; utter; aggregate. m. total; count
to·ta·li·dad, f. whole; entirety; all
to·ta·li·ta·rio, a. totalitarian
to·ta·li·zar, v. total
to·tal·men·te, adv. totally; entirely
tóx·i·co, a. toxic. m. poison
tox·i·co·lo·gía, f. toxicology
tox·i·na, f. toxin
tra·ba, f. tether; bond
tra·ba·ja·dor, m., tra·ba·ja·do·ra, f. worker
tra·ba·jar, v. work; toil; labor. tra·ba·jar de ma·sía·do, overwork
tra·ba·jo, m. work; toil; labor; job; avocation; occupation. tra·ba·jo a des·ta·jo, piecework
tra·ba·jo·sa·men·te, adv. laboriously
tra·ba·jo·so, a. laborious
tra·bar, v. fetter; fasten; tie; join
trac·tor, m. tractor
tra·di·ción, f. tradition
tra·di·cio·nal, a. traditional
tra·di·cio·nal·men·te, adv. traditionally
tra·duc·ción, f. translation
tra·du·cir, v. translate
tra·duc·tor, m., tra·duc·to·ra, f. translator
traer, v. bring; carry
tra·fi·car, v. traffic in; trade
trá·fi·co, m. traffic; trade
tra·gar, v. swallow; gulp
tra·ge·dia, f. tragedy
trá·gi·ca·men·te, adv. tragically
trá·gi·co, a. tragic
tra·go, m. gulp; swallow; drink (usu. alcoholic)
trai·ción, f. treason; betrayal; treachery
trai·cio·nar, v. betray
trai·cio·ne·ro, a. treacherous
trai·dor, m., trai·do·ra, f. traitor; turncoat. a. treacherous
traí·lla, f. leash
tra·je, m. suit; dress; outfit; robe. tra·je de ba·ño, bathing suit. tra·je de no·che, evening dress
tra·mar, v. plot; concoct; cabal
trá·mi·te, m. stage; procedure
tra·mo, m. flight of stairs
tram·pa, f. trap; snare; catch; trick; cheat. tram·pa ca·mu·fla·da, booby trap
tran·qui·la·men·te, adv. tranquilly; quietly
tran·qui·li·dad, f. tranquility; calmness; ease. tran·qui·li·dad an·tes de u·na tor·men·ta, lull before the storm
tran·qui·li·zar, v. tranquilize; calm; quiet; reassure
tran·qui·lo, a. tranquil; still; quiet; calm; peaceful
tran·sac·ción, f. transaction
trans·at·lán·ti·co, a. transatlantic
trans·bor·da·dor, m. ferry
trans·bor·do, m. transfer
trans·cri·bir, v. transcribe; copy
trans·crip·ción, f. transcription; copy
tran·seún·te, m., f. transient
trans·fe·ren·cia, f. transference; transfer
trans·fe·rir, v. transfer
trans·for·ma·ción, f. transformation; change
trans·for·ma·dor, m. transformer
trans·for·mar(se), v. transform; change
trans·fu·sión, f. transfusion
trans·gre·sión, f. sin; transgression
tran·si·ción, f. transition
tran·si·gir, v. compromise
tran·sis·tor, m. transistor
tran·si·ti·vo, a. transitive
trán·si·to, m. transit; movement; transition
tran·si·to·rio, a. transitory; transient
trans·lu·ci·dez, f. translucence
trans·lú·ci·do, a. translucent
trans·mi·sión, f. transmission
trans·mi·sor, m. transmitter
trans·mi·tir, v. transmit; transfer
trans·mu·ta·ción, f. transmutation
trans·pa·ren·cia, f. transparency
trans·pa·ren·te, a. transparent; sheer; clear
trans·pi·rar, v. perspire; transpire
trans·po·ner, v. transpose; transfer
trans·por·ta·ción, f. transportation
trans·por·tar, v. transport; convey; ship; carry; (mus.) transpose
trans·por·te, m. transport; transportation; conveyance
trans·ver·sal, a. transverse
trans·ver·sal·men·te, adv. transversally
tran·vía, f. trolley; streetcar
tra·pe·cio, m. trapeze
tra·pe·zoi·de, m. trapezoid
tra·po, m. rag; tatter
trá·quea, f. trachea; windpipe
tras, prep. after; behind. u·no tras o·tro, one after the other
tra·se·ra, f. backside
tra·se·ro, a. back; hind. m. backside
tras·go, m. goblin
tras·la·dar(se), v. move; transfer; postpone
tras·la·par, v. overlap; lap
tras·pa·sar, v. transgress; cross; penetrate
tras·pié, m. stumble; trip
tras·plan·tar, v. transplant

tras·to, m. furniture. tras·tos vie·jos, junk
tras·tor·nar, v. upset; overturn; daze
tras·tor·no, m. upset; disturbance
tra·sun·to, m. transcript
tra·ta·ble, a. amenable; sociable
tra·ta·do, m. treaty; treatise; tract
tra·ta·mien·to, m. treatment
tra·tan·te, m. dealer
tra·tar(se), v. treat; discuss. tra·tar de, try to; deal with
tra·to, m. treatment; intercourse; deal
trau·ma, m. trauma
trau·má·ti·co, a. traumatic
tra·vés, m. slant; misfortune. a tra·vés de, aslant; across; through, thru. al tra·vés, crosswise. de tra·vés, across; crosswise; awry
tra·ve·sa·ño, m. transom; crosspiece
tra·ve·se·ro, m. bolster
tra·ve·sía, f. crossing; passage; voyage
tra·ve·su·ra, f. mischief; antic; prank; caper; frolic
tra·vie·so, a. naughty; wayward; mischievous
tra·yec·to·ria, f. trajectory
tra·za, f. appearance; design; sketch
tra·zar, v. trace; map; sketch
tré·bol, m. clover
tre·ce, a. thirteen. m. thirteen; baker's dozen
tre·gua, f. truce; cease-fire; respite
trein·ta, a. thirty
tre·me·dal, m. quagmire
tre·men·do, a. terrific; inf. tremendous
tre·men·ti·na, f. turpentine
tren, m. train. tren rá·pi·do, express train
tren·za, f. tress of hair; braid
tren·zar, v. braid
tre·par, v. climb; drill
tres, a. three. m. three
tre·ta, f. feint, as in swordplay
trian·gu·lar, a. triangular
trian·gu·lar·men·te, adv. triangularly
trián·gu·lo, m. triangle
tri·bu, f. tribe
tri·bu·la·ción, f. tribulation; affliction; persecution; adversity
tri·bu·na, f. rostrum
tri·bu·nal, m. court; tribunal
tri·bu·ta·rio, m. tributary. a. tributary
tri·bu·to, m. tribute
tri·ci·clo, m. tricycle
tri·go, m. wheat
tri·go·no·me·tría, f. trigonometry
tri·lo·gía, f. trilogy
tri·lla·do, a. hackneyed; beaten
tri·mes·tral, a. quarterly
tri·mes·tre, m. term
tri·nar, v. warble; trill
trin·char, v. carve
trin·che·ra, f. trench; entrenchment
tri·neo, m. sled; sleigh
tri·no, m. warble; trill
trío, m. trio
tri·pa, f. gut; intestine; tripe
tri·ple, a. triple; treble; threefold
tri·pli·car(se), v. triplicate; triple
trí·po·de, m. tripod
tri·pu·la·ción, f. crew
tris·te, a. sad; sorry; dreary; bleak; cheerless; dismal
tris·te·men·te, adv. sadly; sorrowfully; drearily; bleakly; dismally
tris·te·za, f. sadness; gloom; bleakness
triun·fal, a. triumphal; victorious
triun·fal·men·te, adv. triumphantly
triun·fan·te, a. triumphant; victorious
triun·far, v. triumph; win; be victorious
triun·fo, m. triumph; victory; win; (cards) trump. triun·fo fá·cil, inf. walkover
triun·vi·ra·to, m. triumvirate
tri·vial, a. trivial; common; of little importance
tri·via·li·dad, f. triviality; banality
tri·vial·men·te, adv. trivially; commonly
tri·za, f. shred; fragment
tro·car, v. change; trade; barter
tro·ci·to, m. snatch; little bit
tro·feo, m. trophy
trom·ba ma·ri·na, f. waterspout
trom·bón, m. trombone
trom·bo·sis, f. coronary thrombosis
trom·pa, f. elephant's trunk
trom·pe·ta, f. trumpet. m. bugler
tro·nar, v. boom; thunder; fulminate
tron·co, m. trunk of a tree; trunk line; team of horses
tro·no, m. throne
tro·pa, f. troop
tro·pel, m. throng; mob; confusion
tro·pe·zar, v. stumble; slip; trip; flounder. tro·pe·zar con, bump into; meet
tro·pe·zón, m. stumble
tro·pi·cal, a. tropical
tró·pi·co, m. tropic
tro·pie·zo, m. trip; difficulty; setback
tro·quel, m. die
tro·te, m. trot
tro·va·dor, m. troubadour
tro·zo, m. piece; bit
tru·co, m. trick; gimmick; pool
tru·cha, f. trout
true·no, m. thunder; thunderclap
trun·car, v. truncate; cut short

tu, poss. a. your; thy; pl. yours
tú, pron. you (familiar); thou. tú mis·mo, yourself
tu·ba, f. tuba
tu·ber·cu·lo·sis, f. tuberculosis
tu·ber·cu·lo·so, a. tuberculous
tu·bo, m. tube; pipe. tu·bo de en·sa·yo, test tube
tu·fo, m. stench; exhalation
tu·li·pán, m. tulip
tu·lli·do, m., tu·lli·da, f. cripple. a. paralyzed
tu·llir(se), v. cripple
tum·ba, f. tomb
tu·mor, m. tumor; growth
tu·mul·to, m. tumult; turmoil; riot
tu·mul·tua·rio, a. tumultuous; uproarious
tu·mul·tuo·sa·men·te, adv. tumultuously
tu·mul·tuo·so, a. tumultuous; uproarious
tun·dra, f. tundra
tú·nel, m. tunnel
tú·ni·ca, f. tunic
tur·ba, f. multitude; mob
tur·ba·ción, f. perturbation; embarrassment
tur·ba·do, a. distraught; embarrassed
tur·ban·te, m. turban
tur·bi·na, f. turbine
tur·bu·len·cia, f. turbulence; disorder
tur·bu·len·ta·men·te, adv. turbulently
tur·bu·len·to, a. turbulent; unsettled; muddy
tu·ris·mo, m. tourism
tu·ris·ta, m., f. tourist; sightseer
tur·no, m. turn; say
tur·que·sa, f. turquoise
tu·te·la, f. tutelage; protection
tu·yo, pron. yours; thine

U

u, conj. or (before a word beginning with o or ho)
u·bi·cui·dad, f. ubiquity
u·bi·cuo, a. ubiquitous. Also ubiquitary
u·bre, f. udder
úl·ce·ra, f. ulcer
ul·te·rior, a. ulterior; farther
ul·te·rior·men·te, adv. subsequently
úl·ti·ma·men·te, adv. finally; ultimately
ul·ti·má·tum, m. ultimatum
úl·ti·mo, a. ultimate; last; final
ul·tra, a. ultra; beyond
ul·tra·jar, v. insult
ul·tra·je, m. insult
ul·tra·jo·so, a. outrageous
ul·tra·só·ni·co, a. ultrasonic
ul·tra·vio·le·ta, a. ultraviolet
u·lu·lar, v. hoot
um·bi·li·cal, a. umbilical
um·bral, m. threshold
un, indef. art. a; an. a. one
u·na, indef. art. a; an. a. one. u·na vez, once
u·ná·ni·me, a. unanimous
u·ná·ni·me·men·te, adv. unanimously
un·ción, f. unction
un·dé·ci·mo, a. eleventh
un·gir, v. anoint
un·güen·to, m. ointment; salve; unguent
ú·ni·ca·men·te, adv. solely; only
ú·ni·co, a. only; sole; single; unique
u·ni·cor·nio, m. unicorn
u·ni·dad, f. unity; unit
u·ni·do, a. united
u·ni·fi·ca·ción, f. unification
u·ni·fi·car, v. unify
u·ni·for·mar, v. standardize; make uniform
u·ni·for·me, a. uniform; even; steady. m. uniform
u·ni·for·me·men·te, adv. uniformly
u·ni·for·mi·dad, f. uniformity
u·ni·la·te·ral, a. unilateral
u·ni·la·te·ral·men·te, adv. unilaterally
u·nión, f. union; unity; joint; connection
u·nir(se), v. join; unite; couple; attach; link
u·ní·so·no, a. sounding alike; in harmony. al u·ní·so·no, in unison
u·ni·ver·sal, a. universal; general; world-wide
u·ni·ver·sa·li·zar, v. universalize
u·ni·ver·sal·men·te, adv. universally
u·ni·ver·si·dad, f. university
u·ni·ver·si·ta·rio, a. university
u·no, indef. art. a; an. a. one. pron. one; pl. some. u·no a u·no, one by one. u·no u o·tro, either
un·tar, v. anoint; smear
un·tuo·so, a. greasy
u·ña, f. fingernail; nail; claw
u·ra·nio, m. uranium
U·ra·no, m. Uranus
ur·ba·ni·dad, f. urbanity; politeness
ur·ba·no, a. urban; urbane; courteous
ur·dir, v. plot; brew
ur·gen·cia, f. urgency; exigence; pressure
ur·gen·te, a. urgent
ur·gen·te·men·te, adv. urgently
ur·na, f. urn
ur·ti·ca·ria, f. hive
u·sa·do, a. used; worn; well-worn
u·san·za, f. usage

u·sar(se), v. use; make use of; wear
u·so, m. use; usage; wear; custom; mode
us·ted, pron. m., f., pl. us·te·des. you. Abbr. Vd., Ud. us·ted mis·mo, yourself
u·sual, a. usual; customary; general
u·sual·men·te, adv. usually; regularly
u·su·ra, f. usury
u·sur·pa·ción, f. usurpation; encroachment
u·sur·par, v. usurp; encroach
u·ten·si·lio, m. utensil; pl. tools
ú·te·ro, m. uterus; womb
ú·til, a. useful; helpful; serviceable
u·ti·li·dad, f. utility; usefulness; profit
u·ti·li·ta·rio, a. utilitarian
u·ti·li·za·ble, a. usable
u·ti·li·zar, v. utilize; use; make use of; profit from
u·to·pía, u·to·pí·a, f. utopia
u·va, f. grape. u·va es·pi·na, gooseberry. u·va pa·sa, raisin

V

va·ca, f. cow
va·ca·ción, f. usu. pl. vacation; holiday
va·can·te, f. vacancy. a. vacant; unoccupied
va·ciar(se), v. empty; void; hollow out
va·cie·dad, f. emptiness
va·ci·la·ción, f. vacillation; hesitation
va·ci·lan·te, a. vacillating; hesitant; waver
va·ci·lar, v. vacillate; hesitate; falter; waver
va·cío, a. void; vacant; empty; hollow. m. void; vacuum
va·cui·dad, f. vacuity; emptiness
va·cu·na, f. vaccine
va·cu·na·ción, f. vaccination
va·cu·nar, v. vaccinate
va·dear, v. wade; ford
va·do, m. ford
va·ga·bun·dear, v. rove; wander
va·ga·bun·do, a. vagabond; vagrant. m. vagabond; tramp; bum; hobo
va·ga·men·te, adv. vaguely
va·gan·cia, f. vagrancy
va·gar, v. wander; roam; rove; stray; stroll
va·gi·na, f. vagina
va·go, a. vague; indistinct; hazy; vacant; wandering
va·gón, m. wagon; coach; carriage
va·gue·dad, f. vagueness
va·ho, m. fume; vapor
vai·na, f. pod; sheath
vai·ni·lla, f. vanilla
va·ji·lla, f. service. va·ji·lla de pla·ta, silverware
va·le, m. IOU
va·le·de·ro, a. valid
va·len·tía, f. valor; bravery; courage; feat
va·ler, v. be worth; be valid; make use of. m. value
va·le·ro·sa·men·te, adv. valiantly
va·le·ro·so, a. valorous; valiant
va·li·dar, v. validate
va·li·dez, f. validity; soundness
vá·li·do, a. valid; good; sound; strong
va·lien·te, a. valiant; brave; courageous
va·lien·te·men·te, adv. valiantly; courageously
va·lio·so, a. valuable; wealthy
va·lor, m. bravery; valor; courage; value; worth; pl. securities; stocks
va·lo·ra·ción, f. appraisal; assessment
va·lo·rar, v. appraise; value; price
va·lua·ción, f. valuation
va·luar, v. price
vál·vu·la, f. valve. vál·vu·la de se·gu·ri·dad, safety valve
va·lla, f. hurdle; barricade
va·lle, m. valley; dale; vale
vam·pi·ro, m. vampire
va·na·glo·riar·se, v. boast
van·da·lis·mo, m. vandalism
ván·da·lo, m. vandal
van·guar·dia, f. vanguard; van
va·ni·dad, f. vanity; nonsense; shallowness
va·ni·do·so, a. vain; conceited; haughty
va·no, a. vain; useless; empty. en va·no, in vain
va·por, m. vapor; steam; steamship. bu·que de va·por, steamer; steamboat
va·po·ri·zar(se), v. vaporize
va·po·ro·so, a. vaporous; steamy; cloudy
va·que·ro, m. cowboy
va·qui·lla, f. heifer
va·ra, f. rod; wand. va·ra de me·dir, yardstick
va·ria·bi·li·dad, f. variability; variableness
va·ria·ble, a. variable
va·ria·ble·men·te, adv. variably
va·ria·ción, f. variation; variance; change
va·ria·do, a. varied; various; assorted
va·rian·te, a. variant. f. variant
va·riar, v. vary; change; alternate
va·rie·dad, f. variety
va·rio, a. various; variable; pl. several

eral
va·rón, a. male. m. male; man
va·ro·nil, a. manly; masculine
va·sa·llo, m. vassal
vas·cu·lar, a. vascular
va·se·li·na, f. vaseline
va·si·ja, f. vessel; receptacle
va·so, m. glass; tumbler; vessel. va·so ca·pi·lar, capillary. va·so de a·gua, glass of water
vas·ta·go, m. shout; offspring
vas·te·dad, f. vastness
vas·to, a. vast
va·ti·ci·nar, v. foretell; predict
va·ti·ci·nio, m. prediction
va·tio, m. watt
va·ya, int. well
ve·ci·nal, a. local; neighboring
ve·ci·na·men·te, adv. next
ve·cin·dad, f. vicinity; neighborhood
ve·cin·da·rio, m. neighborhood
ve·ci·no, m., f. ve·ci·na, f. neighbor. a. next; neighboring
vec·tor, m. vector
ve·dar, v. prohibit; impede; suspend
ve·ge·ta·ción, f. vegetation
ve·ge·tal, a. vegetable. m. vegetable
ve·ge·tar, v. vegetate
ve·ge·ta·ria·nis·mo, m. vegetarianism
ve·ge·ta·ria·no, m., ve·ge·ta·ria·na, f. vegetarian. a. vegetarian
ve·he·men·cia, f. vehemence; vehemency; impetuosity
ve·he·men·te, a. vehement; violent; impetuous
ve·he·men·te·men·te, adv. vehemently
ve·hí·cu·lo, m. vehicle
vein·te, a. twenty. m. twenty; score
vein·te·na, f. score
ve·ja·ción, f. vexation; oppression
ve·jar, v. vex; harass; persecute; condemn
ve·ja·to·rio, a. vexatious
ve·jez, f. old age
ve·ji·ga, f. bladder
ve·la, f. candle; sail; watchfulness; vigil
ve·la·da, f. social gathering
ve·la·dor, m. watchman
ve·lar, v. watch; guard; sit up at night watching a sick person
ve·lei·do·so, a. fickle
ve·le·ta, f. vane
ve·lo, m. veil; pretext
ve·lo·ci·dad, f. velocity; rate; speed. a to·da ve·lo·ci·dad, at full speed
ve·loz, a. swift; fleet; fast
ve·loz·men·te, adv. swiftly; rapidly
ve·llón, m. fleece
ve·llo·so, a. fuzzy
ve·llu·di·llo, m. velour
ve·llu·do, a. shaggy; fuzzy; downy
ve·na, f. vein; strain
ve·na·do, m. stag. car·ne de ve·na·do, venison
ve·nal, a. venal; commercial
ve·na·li·dad, f. venality
ven·ce·dor, m., ven·ce·do·ra, f. victor; conqueror
ven·cer, v. vanquish; conquer; defeat; beat
ven·ci·do, a. defeated; conquered
ven·da·je, m. bandaging
ven·dar, v. bandage; bind
ven·de·dor, m., ven·de·do·ra, f. vendor
ven·der(se), v. sell; market; trade. se ven·de, for sale
ven·di·ble, a. vendible; marketable
ven·di·mia, f. vintage; grape harvest
ven·di·miar, v. harvest grapes
ve·ne·no, m. venom; poison
ve·ne·no·si·dad, f. poisonousness
ve·ne·no·so, a. venomous; poisonous
ve·ne·ra, f. scallop
ve·ne·ra·ble, a. venerable
ve·ne·ra·ción, f. veneration
ve·ne·rar, v. venerate; worship; revere
ve·né·reo, a. venereal. m. venereal disease
ven·ga·dor, m., ven·ga·do·ra, f. avenger
ven·gan·za, f. vengeance; revenge
ven·gar(se), v. revenge; avenge
ven·ga·ti·vo, a. vindictive
ve·nia, f. forgiveness
ve·nial, a. venial
ve·nir, v. come; happen. el a·ño que vie·ne, next year. ve·nir·se a·ba·jo, topple
ven·ta, f. sale; market. de ven·ta, on sale. ven·ta a pla·zos, sell on credit
ven·ta·ja, f. advantage; blessing; vantage
ven·ta·jo·sa·men·te, adv. advantageously
ven·ta·jo·so, a. advantageous
ven·ta·na, f. window. ven·ta·na de la na·riz, nostril
ven·ta·rrón, m. gale; gust of wind
ven·ti·la·ción, f. ventilation; airing
ven·ti·la·dor, m. ventilator
ven·ti·lar, v. ventilate; air; discuss
ven·tis·ca, f. blizzard
ven·to·so, a. windy
ven·tral, a. ventral
ven·trí·cu·lo, m. ventricle
ven·trí·lo·cuo, m. ven·trí·lo·cua, f. ventriloquist
ven·tu·ro·quia, f. ventriloquy
ven·tu·ra, f. fortune; happiness

ven·tu·ro·so, a. lucky; fortunate
Ve·nus, m. Venus
ver(se), v. see; view; sight; meet. te·ner que ver con, pertain to; concern. va·mos a ver, let's see
ve·ra, f. border
ve·ra·ci·dad, f. veracity; truthfulness
ve·ra·nie·go, a. summer; summery
ve·ra·no, m. summer
ve·ras, f. pl. truth. de ve·ras, indeed; really
ve·raz, a. veracious; truthful
ver·bal, a. verbal; oral
ver·bal·men·te, adv. verbally
ver·bo, m. verb. e·char ver·bos, swear
ver·bo·si·dad, f. verbosity; verbiage
ver·bo·so, a. verbose; wordy
ver·dad, f. truth; veracity. ver·dad de Pe·ro Gru·llo, truism
ver·da·de·ra·men·te, adv. truly; indeed
ver·da·de·ro, a. veritable; true; real
ver·de, a. green; verdant; dirty; obscene. m. green
ver·du·go, m. lash
ver·du·gón, m. welt
ver·du·ra, f. greenery
ve·re·da, f. path
ve·re·dic·to, m. verdict
ver·gon·zan·te, a. shamefaced
ver·gon·zo·sa·men·te, adv. shamefully
ver·gon·zo·so, a. disgraceful; shameful; bashful
ver·güen·za, f. shame; disgrace; bashfulness
ve·ri·fi·ca·ción, f. verification; confirmation
ve·ri·fi·car(se), v. verify; confirm; carry out
ver·ja, f. grille; grill
ver·mi·no·so, a. full of vermin
ver·mut, m. vermouth
ver·ná·cu·lo, a. vernacular
ver·nal, a. vernal
ve·ro·sí·mil, a. probable
ve·ro·si·mi·li·tud, f. verisimilitude
ve·rru·co, m. boar
ve·rru·ga, f. wart
ver·sa·do, a. versed. ver·sa·do en, conversant with
ver·sal, f. capital letter
ver·sá·til, a. changeable
ver·sa·ti·li·dad, f. fickleness; versatility
ver·si·cu·lo, m. verse
ver·si·fi·ca·ción, f. versification
ver·si·fi·car, v. versify
ver·sión, f. version
ver·so, m. verse. ver·so suel·to, blank verse
vér·te·bra, f. vertebra
ver·te·bra·do, a. vertebrate. m. vertebrate
ver·ter(se), v. spill; slop; pour; shed
ver·ti·cal, a. vertical; upright. m. vertical
ver·ti·cal·men·te, adv. vertically
vér·ti·ce, m. vertex
ver·ti·gi·no·sa·men·te, adv. dizzily
ver·ti·gi·no·so, a. dizzy; vertiginous
vér·ti·go, m. vertigo; dizziness; giddiness
ves·tí·bu·lo, m. vestibule; hall; foyer
ves·ti·do, m. dress; frock; garb; clothing. a. clad; dressed
ves·ti·gio, m. vestige; pl. remains
ves·tir(se), v. dress; clothe; attire. ves·tir·se bien, dress well
ves·tua·rio, m. wardrobe; dressing room
ve·ta, f. vein; lode
ve·tar, v. veto
ve·tea·do, a. veined; striped
ve·te·ra·no, a. veteran. m. veteran
ve·te·ri·na·ria, f. veterinary science
ve·te·ri·na·rio, m. veterinarian; inf. vet. a. veterinary
vez, f. pl. ve·ces. time. a ve·ces, sometimes; at times. de vez en cuan·do, from time to time; off and on. en vez de, instead of. ha·bía u·na vez, once upon a time. tal vez, perhaps
vía, f. way; route; line; means. por vía aé·rea, by airmail. por vía de, by way of
via·bi·li·dad, f. viability; feasibility
via·ble, a. viable; feasible
via·duc·to, m. viaduct
via·jan·te, m., f. traveler. a. traveling
via·jar, v. travel; take a trip; voyage; journey. via·jar por, tour
via·je, m. trip; excursion; voyage; journey; ride; pl. travels
via·je·ro, m., via·je·ra, f. traveler; passenger; wayfarer
ví·bo·ra, f. viper
vi·bra·ción, f. vibration; shaking
vi·bran·te, a. vibrant
vi·brar, v. vibrate; quaver; shake
vi·ca·rio, m. vicar
vi·ce·pre·si·den·cia, f. vice-presidency
vi·ce·pre·si·den·te, m. vice-president
vi·ce·ver·sa, adv. vice versa
vi·ciar(se), v. vitiate; corrupt; invalidate
vi·cio, m. vice; bad habit; forwardness
vi·cio·sa·men·te, adv. viciously
vi·cio·so, a. vicious; defective
víc·ti·ma, m., f. victim; casualty
vic·to·ria, f. victory; win; triumph
vic·to·rio·sa·men·te, adv. victoriously

vic·to·rio·so, *a.* victorious; winning
vid, *f.* vine
vi·da, *f.* life; livelihood. **en mi vi·da,** never in my life
vi·den·te, *m., f.* seer; clairvoyant
vi·driar, *v.* glaze
vi·drio, *m.* glass. **ho·ja de vi·drio,** pane
vi·drio·so, *a.* glassy
vie·jo, *a.* old; aged; antiquated. *m.* old man
vien·to, *m.* wind. **ha·ce vien·to,** it's windy
vien·tre, *m.* abdomen; belly. **do·lor de vien·tre,** bellyache
vier·nes, *m.* Friday
vi·ga, *f.* beam; girder
vi·gen·te, *a.* in force; valid
vi·gía, *f.* lookout
vi·gi·lan·cia, *f.* vigilance; surveillance
vi·gi·lan·te, *a.* vigilant; watchful; alert; heedful. *m.* watchman; caretaker; guard
vi·gi·lan·te·men·te, *adv.* vigilantly
vi·gi·lar, *v.* watch; guard; oversee
vi·gi·lia, *f.* vigil; watchfulness
vi·gor, *m.* vigor; force; vim; strength
vi·go·ri·zar, *v.* invigorate; exhilarate
vi·go·ro·sa·men·te, *adv.* vigorously
vi·go·ro·so, *a.* vigorous; robust; forceful; strong
vil, *a.* vile; low; mean; miserable; sordid; sorry
vi·li·pen·dio·so, *a.* contemptible
vil·men·te, *adv.* vilely; meanly; sordidly
vi·lla, *f.* villa
vi·llan·ci·co, *m.* Christmas carol
vi·lla·nía, *f.* villainy
vi·na·gre, *m.* vinegar
vi·na·gro·so, *a.* vinegary
vin·cu·lar, *v.* entail
vin·di·ca·ción, *f.* vindication
vin·di·car, *v.* vindicate; avenge
vin·di·ca·ti·vo, *a.* vindictive
vi·no, *m.* wine **vi·no blan·co,** white wine. **vi·no se·co,** dry wine. **vi·no tin·to,** red wine
vi·ña, *f.* vineyard
vi·ñe·ta, *f.* vignette
vio·la, *f.* viol; viola
vio·la·do, *a.* violet
vio·la·ción, *f.* violation; rape
vio·lar, *v.* violate; rape; ravish
vio·len·cia, *f.* violence
vio·len·tar(se), *v.* force

vio·len·te·men·te, *adv.* violently
vio·len·to, *a.* violent
vio·le·ta, *f.* violet
vio·lín, *m.* violin; fiddle; violinist
vio·lon·ce·lis·ta, vio·lon·che·lis·ta, *m., f.* cellist; violoncellist
vio·lon·ce·lo, vio·lon·che·lo, *m.* violoncello
vi·ra·da, *f.* tack
vi·rar, *v.* veer; change direction
vir·gen, *a.* virgin; maiden. *f.* virgin
vir·gi·nal, *a.* virginal
vir·gi·ni·dad, *f.* virginity
vi·ril, *a.* virile
vi·ri·li·dad, *f.* virility; manhood
vi·rrey, *m.* viceroy
vir·tual, *a.* virtual
vir·tual·men·te, *adv.* virtually
vir·tud, *f.* virtue
vir·tuo·sa·men·te, *adv.* virtuously
vir·tuo·sis·mo, *m.* virtuosity
vir·tuo·so, *a.* virtuous. *m.* virtuoso
vi·rue·la, *f.* smallpox
vi·ru·len·cia, *f.* venom; virulence
vi·ru·len·to, *a.* virulent
vi·rus, *m.* virus
vi·sa·je, *m.* grimace
vi·sar, *v.* grant a visa; endorse
vis·co·si·dad, *f.* viscosity
vis·co·so, *a.* viscous; sticky
vi·se·ra, *f.* visor
vi·si·bi·li·dad, *f.* visibility
vi·si·ble, *a.* visible; conspicuous
vi·si·ble·men·te, *adv.* visibly; conspicuously
vi·sión, *f.* vision; sight; view
vi·sio·na·rio, vi·sio·na·ria, *f.* visionary
vi·si·ta, *f.* visit; call; visitor. **ha·cer u·na vi·si·ta,** pay a visit
vi·si·ta·ción, *f.* visitation
vi·si·tar, *v.* visit; see; call upon
vis·lum·brar, *v.* sight; catch sight of; glimpse
vis·lum·bre, *f.* glimpse; glimmer
vi·so, *m.* viewpoint; outlook; aspect
vís·pe·ra, *f.* eve; *pl.* vespers
vis·ta, *f.* view; vision; sight; scenery. **a vis·ta de,** in view of. **has·ta la vis·ta,** good-bye; so long; until we meet again. **pun·to de vis·ta,** viewpoint
vis·ta·zo, *m.* glance; *inf.* gander
vis·to·so, *a.* gorgeous; gay; showy
vi·sual, *a.* visual
vi·tal, *a.* vital; essential
vi·ta·li·dad, *f.* vitality

vi·ta·mi·na, *f.* vitamin
vi·te·la, *f.* vellum
ví·treo, *a.* vitreous; glassy
vi·tri·na, *f.* showcase; cabinet
vi·trio·lo, *m.* vitriol
vi·tu·pe·ra·ción, *f.* vituperation; censure
vi·tu·pe·rar, *v.* vituperate; censure
viu·da, *f.* widow
viu·dez, *f.* widowhood
viu·do, *m.* widower
vi·va·ci·dad, *f.* vivacity; liveliness
vi·va·men·te, *adv.* vividly; acutely; deeply
vi·va·que, *m.* bivouac
vi·va·quear, *v.* bivouac
vi·va·ra·cho, *a.* vivacious; sprightly
vi·vaz, *a.* vivacious; lively
ví·ve·res, *m. pl.* victuals; provisions
ví·vi·do, *a.* vivid
vi·vien·da, *f.* dwelling; place where one lives
vi·vien·te, *a.* living
vi·vir, *v.* live; have life; reside
vi·vo, *a.* live; lively; vivid; smart; sharp
viz·con·de, *m.* viscount
viz·con·de·sa, *f.* viscountess
vo·ca·blo, *m.* word
vo·ca·bu·la·rio, *m.* vocabulary
vo·ca·ción, *f.* vocation; calling; occupation
vo·cal, *a.* vocal. *f.* vowel
vo·ca·li·za·ción, *f.* vocalization
vo·ca·li·zar, *v.* vocalize
vo·ci·fe·ra·ción, *f.* vociferation
vo·ci·fe·rar, *v.* clamor; blare; shout
vod·ka, *f.* vodka
vo·lan·te, *a.* flying. *m.* flywheel
vo·lar, *v.* fly; explode; blast
vo·lá·til, *a.* volatile
vo·la·ti·li·dad, *f.* volatility
vo·la·ti·li·zar, *v.* vaporize
vol·cán, *m.* volcano
vol·cá·ni·co, *a.* volcanic
vol·car(se), *v.* upset; overturn; capsize
vo·lea, *f.* volley
vo·lear, *v.* volley
vo·leo, *m.* volley
vo·li·ción, *f.* volition
vol·ta·je, *m.* voltage
vol·tea·dor, *m.,* **vol·tea·do·ra,** *f.* tumbler
vol·tear, *v.* tumble; roll over; upset
vol·te·re·ta, *f.* somersault

vol·tio, *m.* volt
vo·lu·bi·li·dad, *f.* volubility; fickleness
vo·lu·ble, *a.* voluble; fickle
vo·lu·men, *m.* volume; bulkiness
vo·lu·mi·no·so, *a.* voluminous; bulky
vo·lun·tad, *f.* will; volition; determination. **a vo·lun·tad,** at will. **ma·la vo·lun·tad,** ill will
vo·lun·ta·ria·men·te, *adv.* voluntarily
vo·lun·ta·rio, *a.* voluntary; unconstrained. *m.* volunteer
vo·lun·ta·rio·sa·men·te, *adv.* willfully
vo·lun·ta·rio·so, *a.* willful, wilful; wayward
vo·lup·tuo·sa·men·te, *adv.* voluptuously
vo·lup·tuo·so, *a.* voluptuous. *m.* voluptuary
vol·ver(se), *v.* return; turn back; recur; revert; turn; render. **vol·ver en sí,** come to one's senses
vo·mi·tar, *v.* vomit; puke; spew, spue
vó·mi·to, *m.* vomit
vo·raz, *a.* voracious; greedy
vo·raz·men·te, *adv.* voraciously; greedily
vór·ti·ce, *m.* vortex; hurricane
vos, *pron. m., f.* you
vo·so·tras, *pron. f.* you; ye
vo·so·tros, *pron. m.* you; ye
vo·ta·ción, *f.* vote; ballot
vo·tan·te, *m., f.* voter
vo·tar, *v.* vote
vo·to, *m.* vote; vow
voz, *f.* voice; report. **en voz al·ta,** aloud; loudly. **dar vo·ces,** shout
vuel·co, *m.* spill
vue·lo, *m.* flight
vuel·ta, *f.* return; spin; turn. **dar u·na vuel·ta,** take a ride. **de i·da y vuel·ta,** round trip
vues·tra, *a.* your. *poss. pron. f.* yours
vues·tro, *a.* your. *poss. pron. m.* yours
vul·ca·ni·za·ción, *f.* vulcanization
vul·ca·ni·zar, *v.* vulcanize
vul·gar, *a.* vulgar; common; coarse
vul·ga·ri·dad, *f.* vulgarity
vul·ga·ri·zar, *v.* vulgarize; polularize
vul·gar·men·te, *adv.* vulgarly; commonly
vul·ne·ra·bi·li·dad, *f.* vulnerability
vul·ne·ra·ble, *a.* vulnerable
vul·va, *f.* vulva

W-X-Y

wá·ter, *m.* lavatory; toilet; water-closet
whis·key, *m.* whiskey, whisky
xe·no·fo·bia, *f.* xenophobia
xe·nón, *m.* xenon
xe·ro·co·pia, *f.* xerox copy
xe·ro·co·piar, *v.* xerox
xi·ló·fo·no, *m.* xylophone
xi·lo·gra·fía, *f.* xylography
y, *conj.* and; plus
ya, *adv.* already; now
yac, yak, *m.* yak
yan·qui, *m., f.* Yankee. *a.* Yankee
yar·da, *f.* yard
ya·te, *m.* yacht
ye·gua·da, *f.* stud
ye·gua, *f.* mare
ye·ma, *f.* yolk of an egg. **ye·ma del de·do,** fingertip
yer·mo, *m.* wilderness; wasteland; *often pl.* wilds
yer·no, *m.* son-in-law
yes·ca, *f.* tinder
ye·so, *m.* gypsum; plaster
yo, *pron.* I. *m.* ego. **yo mis·mo,** myself
yo·do, *m.* iodine
yo·ga, *m.* yoga
yo·gui, *m.* yogi
yo·gur, *m.* yogurt
yo·quéy, yo·qui, *m.* jockey
yu·ca, *f.* yucca
yu·go, *m.* yoke
yu·gu·lar, *a.* jugular
yun·que, *m.* anvil
yun·ta, *f.* yoke of oxen; team
yu·te, *m.* jute
yux·ta·po·ner, *v.* juxtapose
yux·ta·po·si·ción, *f.* juxtaposition

Z

za·far(se), *v.* run away; loosen; embellish
za·fi·ro, *m.* sapphire
za·gal, *m.* lad
za·ga·la, *f.* lass
za·ho·rí, *m.* seer; soothsayer
za·la·gar·da, *f.* ambush; ambuscade
za·la·me·ro, *a.* unctuous. *m.* flatterer
za·ma·rra, *f.* sheepskin jacket
za·ma·rro, *m.* sheepskin
zam·bu·lli·da, *f.* dive; submersion
zam·bu·llir, *v.* douse; plunge; dive
za·na·ho·ria, *f.* carrot

zan·ca·da, *f.* stride
zan·ca·jo, *m.* heel, as of a shoe or stocking
zan·co, *m.* stilt
zán·ga·no, *m.* drone
zan·ja, *f.* ditch; trench; conduit
zan·jar, *v.* dig ditches
zan·qui·va·no, *m.* spindlelegs. *a.* spindle-legged
za·par, *v.* sap
za·pa·te·ría, *f.* shoeshop
za·pa·te·ro, *m.* cobbler; shoemaker
za·pa·ti·lla, *f.* slipper
za·pa·to, *m.* shoe
zar, *m.* czar
za·ran·dear, *v.* sift
zar·ci·lla, *f.* tendril
za·ri·na, *f.* czarina
zar·par, *v.* weigh anchor
zar·za, *f.* bramble
zar·za·mo·ra, *f.* blackberry
zar·zo, *m.* hurdle
zig·zag, *m.* zigzag
zig·za·guear, *v.* zigzag
zo·co, *a.* left-handed
zo·dí·a·co, *m.* zodiac
zo·na, *f.* zone
zo·o·lo·gía, *f.* zoology
zoo·ló·gi·co, *a.* zoological. *m.* zoo. **jar·dín zoo·ló·gi·co,** zoo
zoó·lo·go, *m.* zoologist
zo·pen·co, *m.* dunce. *a.* stupid; doltish
zo·que·te, *m.* oaf; chunk of wood
zo·rra, *f.* fox; vixen
zo·rro, *m.* fox
zo·te, *m.* booby; dunce. *a.* dense
zo·zo·bra, *f.* foundering; overturning
zo·zo·brar, *v.* keel over; overturn; capsize
zue·co, *m.* wooden shoe; clog
zu·ma·que, *m.* sumac, sumach
zum·ba, *f.* banter; raillery
zum·ba·dor, *m.* electrical buzzer
zum·bar, *v.* buzz; whir, whirr; hum; drone; zoom; tease
zum·bi·do, *m.* buzz; hum; zoom; whir, whirr
zu·mo, *m.* juice
zu·mo·so, *a.* juicy
zur·ci·do, *m.* mending; darn; stitch
zur·cir, *v.* darn; mend; stitch
zu·rrar, *v.* spank; thrash; *inf.* wallop; dress leather
zu·rria·go, *m.* whip
zu·ta·no, *m.,* **zu·ta·na,** *f.* so-and-so

A

a, *indef. art.* un, una
a·back, *adv.* detrás; atrás
a·ba·cus, *n.* ábaco
a·ban·don, *v.* abandonar
a·base, *v.* humillar; rebajar
a·bash, *v.* avergonzar
a·bate, *v.* disminuir; reducir
ab·bey, *n. pl.* **-beys.** abadía; monasterio; convento
ab·bre·vi·a·tion, *n.* abreviación
ab·di·cate, *v.* abdicar
ab·do·men, *n.* abdomen; vientre
ab·duct, *v.* secuestrar
ab·er·ra·tion, *n.* aberración
a·bet, *v.* instigar; ayudar
ab·hor, *v.* aborrecer
a·bide, *v.* habitar; soportar
a·bil·i·ty, *n.* habilidad; aptitud
ab·ject, *a.* abyecto
ab·jure, *v.* abjurar
a·ble, *a.* capaz; competente
ab·ne·gate, *v.* renunciar; negar
ab·nor·mal, *a.* anormal
a·board, *adv., prep.* a bordo
a·bode, *n.* domicilio
a·bol·ish, *v.* abolir
a·bom·i·nate, *v.* abominar
ab·o·rig·i·nes, *n.* aborígenes
a·bor·tion, *n.* aborto
a·bound, *v.* abundar
a·bout, *prep.* alrededor de; sobre. *adv.* casi; cerca de
a·bove, *prep.* encima de; sobre. *a.* anterior. *adv.* encima; arriba
a·bra·sion, *n.* abrasión; raspadura
a·breast, *adv.* de frente; al lado
a·bridge, *v.* abreviar; resumir
a·broad, *adv.* fuera (de casa); en el extranjero
ab·ro·gate, *v.* abrogar
ab·rupt, *a.* repentino; brusco; escarpado
ab·scess, *n.* absceso
ab·scond, *v.* fugarse
ab·sent, *a.* ausente
ab·so·lute, *a.* absoluto; positivo; completo
ab·solve, *v.* absolver
ab·sorb, *v.* absorber; preocupar
ab·stain, *v.* abstenerse
ab·ste·mi·ous, *a.* abstemio
ab·stract, *v.* abstraer. *a.* abstracto. *n.* resumen
ab·surd, *a.* absurdo
a·bun·dant, *a.* abundante
a·buse, *v.* maltratar. *n.* abuso; injuria
a·but, *v.* confinar
a·byss, *n.* abismo
ac·a·dem·ic, *a.* académico
ac·ad·e·my, *n. pl.* **-mies.** academia; colegio
ac·cede, *v.* acceder; consentir; subir
ac·cel·er·ate, *v.* acelerar
ac·cent, *n.* acento. *v.* acentuar
ac·cept, *v.* aceptar; recibir
ac·cess, *n.* acceso
ac·ces·si·ble, *a.* accesible
ac·ces·so·ry, *n. pl.* **-ries.** accesorios; cómplice. *a.* accesorio
ac·ci·dent, *n.* accidente
ac·claim, *v.* aclamar. *n.* aclamación
ac·cli·mate, *v.* aclimatar
ac·co·lade, *n.* acolada
ac·com·mo·date, *v.* acomodar
ac·com·pa·ny, *v.* acompañar
ac·com·plice, *n.* cómplice
ac·com·plish, *v.* acabar; efectuar; cumplir
ac·cord, *n.* acuerdo; armonía. *v.* conceder; convenir
ac·cor·di·on, *n.* acordeón
ac·count, *v.* considerar; explicar. *n.* cuenta; relato; consideración
ac·count·a·ble, *a.* responsable
ac·cu·mu·late, *v.* acumular
ac·cu·ra·cy, *n.* exactitud
ac·cu·rate, *a.* exacto; fiel
ac·cuse, *v.* acusar; culpar
ac·cus·tom, *v.* acostumbrar
a·ce·tic, *a.* acético
ac·e·tone, *n.* acetona
ache, *n.* dolor. *v.* doler
a·chieve, *v.* lograr; acabar
ac·id, *a.* agrio. *n.* ácido
ac·knowl·edge, *v.* reconocer; confesar; agradecer
ac·me, *n.* cima
ac·ne, *n.* acné
ac·o·lyte, *n.* acólito
a·corn, *n.* bellota
a·cous·tics, *n.* acústica
ac·quaint, *v.* dar a conocer; informar; enterar
ac·quaint·ance, *n.* conocido
ac·qui·esce, *v.* consentir
ac·quire, *v.* adquirir
ac·quit, *v.* absolver
a·cre, *n.* acre
ac·rid, *a.* acre
ac·ri·mo·ny, *n.* acrimonia
ac·ro·bat, *n.* acróbata
a·cross, *adv.* de través. *prep.* a través de
act, *v.* hacer; actuar; representar; fingir. *n.* acto; hecho; obra; ley
ac·tion, *n.* acción; proceso
ac·ti·vate, *v.* activar
ac·tive, *a.* activo; ágil
ac·tor, *n.* actor
ac·tress, *n.* actriz
ac·tu·al, *a.* real; efectivo; actual
a·cu·i·ty, *n.* agudeza
a·cu·men, *n.* agudeza
a·cute, *a.* agudo; fino
ad·age, *n.* adagio
ad·a·mant, *a.* firme

a·dapt, *v.* adaptar
add, *v.* añadir; aumentar; sumar
ad·di·tion, *n.* adición; añadidura
ad·dress, *v.* dirigir(se a). *n.* dirección; discurso
a·dept, *n., a.* experto
ad·e·quate, *a.* adecuado; suficiente
ad·here, *v.* adherirse; pegarse; cumplir
ad·he·sive, *a., n.* adhesivo
ad·ja·cent, *a.* adyacente; contiguo
ad·jec·tive, *n.* adjetivo
ad·join, *v.* juntar; estar contiguo
ad·journ, *v.* suspender
ad·judge, *v.* juzgar; sentenciar
ad·just, *v.* ajustar; adaptar
ad·ju·tant, *n.* ayudante
ad·lib, *v.* improvisar
ad·min·is·ter, *v.* administrar
ad·min·is·tra·tion, *n.* administración
ad·mire, *v.* admirar
ad·mis·si·ble, *a.* admisible
ad·mis·sion, *n.* entrada; confesión
ad·mit, *v.* dar entrada; admitir; confesar; permitir
ad·mon·ish, *v.* amonestar
a·do·be, *n.* adobe
ad·o·les·cence, *n.* adolescencia
a·dopt, *v.* adoptar; aceptar
a·dore, *v.* adorar
a·dorn, *v.* adornar
a·dren·a·line, *n.* adrenalina
a·droit, *a.* hábil; diestro
ad·u·la·tion, *n.* adulación
a·dult, *a.* mayor. *n.* adulto
a·dul·ter·y, *n.* adulterio
ad·vance, *v.* avanzar; ascender. *a.* adelantado. *n.* avance; adelanto
ad·van·tage, *n.* ventaja
ad·ven·ture, *n.* aventura
ad·ven·ture·some, *a.* aventurado
ad·verb, *n.* adverbio
ad·ver·sar·y, *n. pl.* **-ies.** adversario
ad·verse, *a.* adverso; contrario
ad·ver·si·ty, *n. pl.* **-ties.** adversidad
ad·ver·tise, *v.* anunciar; publicar; poner un anuncio
ad·vice, *n.* consejo
ad·vise, *v.* aconsejar; avisar
ad·vo·cate, *v.* abogar; recomendar. *n.* abogado; defensa
adz, adze, *n.* azuela
ae·gis, *n.* égido
aer·ate, *v.* ventilar; airear
aer·i·al, *a.* aéreo. *n.* antena
aer·o·nau·tics, *n. pl.* aeronáutica
aes·thete, *n.* esteta, *m., f.*
aes·thet·ic, *a.* estético
a·far, *adv.* lejos
af·fa·ble, *a.* afable; cortés
af·fair, *n.* asunto; acción; aventura amorosa
af·fect, *v.* afectar
af·fec·ta·tion, *n.* afectación
af·fec·tion, *n.* afección; afecto
af·fec·tion·ate, *a.* cariñoso
af·fi·ance, *v.* desposarse
af·fi·da·vit, *n.* declaración jurada
af·fil·i·ate, *v.* afiliar
af·fin·i·ty, *n. pl.* **-ties.** afinidad
af·firm, *v.* afirmar
af·firm·a·tive, *n.* aserción. *a.* afirmativo
af·fix, *v.* añadir; fijar. *n.* afijo
af·flict, *v.* afligir
af·flic·tion, *n.* aflicción
af·flu·ence, *n.* afluencia; riqueza
af·flu·ent, *a.* rico; opulento
af·ford, *v.* tener medios para; dar
af·front, *v.* afrentar. *n.* afrenta
a·fire, *a., adv.* ardiendo
a·flame, *a., adv.* en llamas
a·float, *a., adv.* a flote
a·foul, *a., adv.* enredado
a·fraid, *a.* atemorizado
a·fresh, *adv.* de nuevo; otra vez
aft, *a., adv.* en (a) popa
af·ter, *a.* posterior. *adv.* después. *prep.* después de; detrás de
af·ter·birth, *n.* secundinas, *f. pl.*
af·ter·noon, *n.* tarde, *f.*
af·ter·ward, af·ter·wards, *adv.* después
a·gain, *adv.* otra vez; de nuevo
a·gainst, *prep.* contra; junto
a·gape, *a., adv.* boquiabierto
age, *n.* edad; época; vejez. *v.* envejecer
a·ged, *a.* viejo
a·gen·cy, *n. pl.* **-cies.** agencia; acción; medio
a·gen·da, *n. pl.* orden del día
a·gent, *n.* agente; representante
ag·glom·er·ate, *v.* aglomerar. *a.* aglomerado
ag·gran·dize, *v.* engrandecer
ag·gra·vate, *v.* agravar
ag·gre·gate, *v.* agregar; juntar. *n.* masa. *a.* total
ag·gres·sion, *n.* agresión
ag·gres·sive, *a.* agresivo
a·ghast, *a.* horrorizado
ag·ile, *a.* ágil
a·gil·i·ty, *n.* agilidad
ag·i·tate, *v.* agitar; inquietar
a·glow, *a.* ardiente
ag·nos·tic, *n.* agnóstico
a·go, *a., adv.* hace; pasado
ag·o·ny, *n. pl.* **-nies.** agonía; angustia
a·grar·i·an, *a.* agrario
a·gree, *v.* concordar; acordar; ponerse de acuerdo
a·gree·a·ble, *a.* agradable; conforme
a·gree·ment, *n.* acuerdo; contrato
ag·ri·cul·ture, *n.* agricultura
a·gron·o·my, *n.* agronomía

a·ground, *a., adv.* encallado
a·head, *adv.* delante; al frente
ail·ment, *n.* enfermedad; dolencia
aim, *v.* apuntar; aspirar. *n.* puntería; blanco; propósito
air, *n.* aire. *v.* airear; ventilar
air con·di·tion·er, *n.* acondicionador de aire
air·craft, *n. pl.* **air·craft.** avión
air·field, *n.* campo de aviación
air·ing, *n.* ventilación; paseo
air·lift, *n.* puente aéreo
air·line, *n.* línea aérea
air·mail, air·mail, *n.* correo aéreo
air·plane, *n.* avión
air·port, *n.* aeropuerto
air·raid, *n.* ataque aéreo
air·y, *a.* ligero; alegre
aisle, *n.* nave lateral; pasillo
a·jar, *a., adv.* entreabierto
a·kin, *a.* semejante; consanguíneo
al·a·bas·ter, *n.* alabastro
a·lac·ri·ty, *n.* alacridad
a·larm, *n.* alarma; inquietud. *v.* alarmar
a·larm·ist, *n.* alarmista, *m., f.*
al·ba·tross, *n.* albatros
al·be·it, *conj.* aunque
al·bi·no, *n. pl.* **-nos.** albino
al·bum, *n.* álbum
al·bu·men, *n.* albumen
al·bu·min, *n.* albúmina
al·che·my, *n.* alquimia
al·co·hol, *n.* alcohol
ale, *n.* cerveza
a·lee, *adv.* a sotavento
a·lert, *a.* alerta; vigilante. *n.* alarma. *v.* alertar
al·fal·fa, *n.* alfalfa
al·ga, *n. pl.* **al·gae.** alga
al·ge·bra, *n.* álgebra
a·li·as, *n. pl.* **a·li·as·es.** alias
al·i·bi, *n.* coartada; excusa
al·ien, *a.* ajeno. *n.* extranjero
al·ien·ate, *v.* enajenar
a·light, *v.* bajar; posarse
a·lign, *v.* alinear; aliar
a·like, *a.* semejante. *adv.* igualmente; del mismo modo
al·i·ment, *n.* alimento
al·i·men·tar·y, *a.* alimenticio
al·i·mo·ny, *n.* alimentos, *m. pl.*
a·live, *a.* vivo; activo; sensible
al·ka·li, *n. pl.* **-lies, -lis.** álcali
al·ka·lize, *v.* alcalizar
all, *a.* todo(s). *n.* totalidad. *adv.* completamente. **above all,** sobre todo.
all but, casi
al·lay, *v.* aliviar; aquietar
al·le·ga·tion, *n.* alegación
al·lege, *v.* alegar; declarar
al·leged, *a.* supuesto; alegado
al·le·giance, *n.* lealtad
al·le·go·ry, *n. pl.* **-ries.** alegoría
al·ler·gy, *n. pl.* **-gies.** alergia
al·le·vi·ate, *v.* aliviar; calmar; mitigar
al·le·vi·a·tion, *n.* aligeramiento
al·ley, *n. pl.* **-leys.** callejuela
al·li·ance, *n.* alianza
al·li·ga·tor, *n.* caimán; lagarto
al·lo·cate, *v.* asignar
al·lo·ca·tion, *n.* reparto; cupo
al·lot, *v.* asignar; distribuir; adjudicar
al·low, *v.* permitir; aceptar; dar; conceder
al·low·ance, *n.* permisión; concesión; ración
al·loy, *n.* aleación. *v.* ligar
al·lude, *v.* aludir
al·lure, *v.* atraer; tentar. *n.* encanto
al·lu·sion, *n.* alusión
al·lu·vi·um, *n. pl.* **-vi·ums, -vi·a.** derrubio
al·ly, *n. pl.* **-lies** aliado; confederado
al·ly, *v.* aliarse; hacer alianza
al·ma·nac, *n.* almanaque
al·might·y, *a.* omnipotente; todopoderoso
al·mond, *n.* almendra; almendro
al·most, *adv.* casi
alms, *n. pl.* **alms.** limosna
a·loft, *adv.* en alto
a·lone, *a.* solo. *adv.* sólo; solamente
a·long, *adv. con. prep.* por; a lo largo
a·loof, *adv.* lejos. *a.* reservado
a·loof·ness, *n.* frialdad
a·loud, *adv.* en voz alta; alto
al·pha·bet, *n.* alfabeto
al·read·y, *adv.* ya
al·so, *adv.* también; además
al·tar, *n.* altar
al·ter, *v.* cambiar; alterar; modificar
al·ter·a·tion, *n.* alteración; cambio
al·ter·ca·tion, *n.* altercación; altercado
al·ter e·go, *n.* álter ego
al·ter·nate, *v.* alternar; variar. *a.* alterno
al·ter·na·tive, *n.* alternativa
al·though, *conj.* aunque
al·tim·e·ter, *n.* altímetro
al·ti·tude, *n.* altura; altitud
al·to, *n.* alto; contralto
al·to·geth·er, *adv.* enteramente; en total
al·tru·ism, *n.* altruismo
a·lu·mi·num, *n.* aluminio
a·lum·na, *n. f. pl.* **-nae.** graduada
a·lum·nus, *n. pl.* **-ni.** graduado
al·ways, *adv.* siempre
a.m., antemeridiano
a·mal·gam, *n.* amalgama
a·mal·gam·ate, *v.* amalgamar
a·mass, *v.* acumular; amontonar
am·a·teur, *n.* aficionado

am·a·to·ry, *a.* amatorio
a·maze, *v.* asombrar
a·maze·ment, *n.* asombro; sorpresa
am·a·zon, *n.* amazona
am·bas·sa·dor, *n.* embajador
am·ber, *n.* ámbar. *a.* ambarino
am·bi·dex·trous, *a.* ambidextro
am·bi·gu·i·ty, *n.* ambigüedad; doble sentido
am·big·u·ous, *a.* ambiguo
am·bi·tion, *n.* ambición
am·bi·tious, *a.* ambicioso
am·biv·a·lence, *n.* ambivalencia
am·ble, *v.* amblar; andar lentamente. *n.* paso de andadura
am·bu·late, *v.* andar
am·bu·la·to·ry, *a.* ambulante. *n.* claustro
am·bus·cade, *n.* emboscada
am·bush, *n.* emboscada. *v.* emboscar
a·me·ba, *n.* amiba
a·mel·io·rate, *v.* mejorar
a·mel·io·ra·tion, *n.* mejora; mejoramiento
a·men, *int.* amén
a·me·na·ble, *a.* tratable; dócil; responsable
a·mend, *v.* enmendar; corregir
a·mends, *n. pl.* compensación
a·men·i·ty, *n. pl.* **-ties.** amenidad; *pl.* conveniencias
A·mer·i·can, *a.* americano
am·e·thyst, *n.* amatista
a·mi·a·ble, *a.* amable
am·i·ca·ble, *a.* amistoso
a·mid, *prep.* en medio de; entre. Also **a·midst**
a·mid·ships, *adv.* en medio del navío
a·miss, *adv., a.* impropiamente; mal
am·mo·nia, *n.* amoníaco
am·mu·ni·tion, *n.* munición
am·ne·sia, *n.* amnesia
am·nes·ty, *n. pl.* **-ties.** amnistía. *v.* amnistiar
a·moe·ba, *n. pl.* **-bae, -bas.** amiba
a·mong, *prep.* entre; en medio de. Also **a·mongst**
a·mor·al, *a.* amoral
am·o·rous, *a.* amoroso
a·mor·phous, *a.* amorfo
am·or·tize, *v.* amortizar
a·mount, *n.* cantidad; suma. *v.* importar; ascender
am·pere, *n.* amperio
am·phib·i·an, *a.* anfibio
am·phib·i·ous, *a.* anfibio
am·phi·the·a·ter, *n.* anfiteatro
am·ple, *a.* amplio; abundante
am·pli·fy, *v.* amplificar; extender
am·pli·tude, *n.* amplitud; abundancia
am·pu·tate, *v.* amputar
am·pu·ta·tion, *n.* amputación
a·muck, *adv.* furiosamente
am·u·let, *n.* amuleto
a·muse, *v.* divertir; entretener
a·muse·ment, *n.* diversión; pasatiempo
an, *indef. art.* un; uno; una
a·nach·ro·nism, *n.* anacronismo
an·a·con·da, *n.* anaconda
a·nae·mi·a, *n.* anemia
an·a·gram, *n.* anagrama, *m.*
a·nal, *a.* anal
an·al·ge·sic, *a., n.* analgésico
a·nal·o·gize, *v.* analogizar
a·nal·o·gy, *n. pl.* **-gies.** analogía
a·nal·y·sis, *n. pl.* **-ses.** análisis
an·a·lyst, *n.* analizador
an·a·lyze, *v.* analizar
an·ar·chism, *n.* anarquismo
an·ar·chist, *n.* anarquista, *m., f.*
an·ar·chy, *n.* anarquía
a·nath·e·ma, *n. pl.* **-mas.** anatema, *m.*
a·nat·o·my, *n. pl.* **-mies** anatomía
an·ces·tor, *n.* antepasado
an·ces·try, *n. pl.* **-tries.** linaje; abolengo
an·chor, *n.* ancla; áncora. *v.* asegurar
an·cho·vy, *n. pl.* **-vies.** anchoa
an·cient, *a.* antiguo
and, *conj.* y (e before i-, hi-)
an·ec·dote, *n.* anécdota
a·ne·mi·a, *n.* anemia
an·e·mom·e·ter, *n.* anemómetro
an·es·the·sia, *n.* anestesia
an·es·thet·ic, *n., a.* anestésico
a·new, *adv.* de nuevo; otra vez
an·gel, *n.* ángel
an·gel·ic, *a.* angélico
an·ger, *n.* ira; cólera. *v.* enojar
an·gle, *n.* ángulo. *v.* pescar con caña
an·gle·worm, *n.* lombriz, *f.*
An·gli·cize, *v.* inglesar
an·gling, *n.* pesca con caña
An·glo-Sax·on, *n., a.* anglosajón
an·go·ra, *n.* angora
an·gry, *a.* colérico; enfadado
an·guish, *n.* angustia; ansia. *v.* atormentar
an·gu·lar, *a.* angular; anguloso
an·hy·drous, *a.* anhidro
an·i·mad·ver·sion, *n.* animadversión
an·i·mad·vert, *v.* censurar
an·i·mal, *n.* animal; bestia. *a.* animal
an·i·mal·ize, *v.* animalizar
an·i·mate, *v.* animar; dar vida. *a.* vivo; animado
an·i·ma·tion, *n.* animación
an·i·mos·i·ty, *n.* animosidad
an·ise, *n.* anís, *m.*
an·kle, *n.* tobillo
an·nals, *n. pl.* anales, *m. pl.*
an·neal, *v.* templar
an·nex, *v.* anexar; adjuntar. *n.* adición
an·nex·a·tion, *n.* anexión

an·ni·hi·late, *v.* aniquilar
an·ni·hi·la·tion, *n.* aniquilación
an·ni·ver·sa·ry, *n. pl.* **-ries.** aniversario
an·no·tate, *v.* anotar
an·nounce, *v.* anunciar; proclamar
an·nounce·ment, *n.* anuncio; aviso
an·noy, *v.* molestar
an·noy·ance, *n.* molestia; fastidio
an·nu·al, *a.* anual. *n.* planta anual
an·nu·i·ty, *n. pl.* **-ties.** renta vitalicia
an·nul, *v.* anular
an·nul·ment, *n.* anulación
an·nun·ci·ate, *v.* anunciar
an·nun·ci·a·tion, *n.* anunciación
an·ode, *n.* ánodo
a·noint, *v.* untar; ungir
a·nom·a·lous, *a.* anómalo
a·nom·a·ly, *n.* anomalía
a·non·y·mous, *a.* anónimo
an·oth·er, *a., pron.* otro
an·swer, *v.* responder; contestar; servir. *n.* respuesta; contestación; solución
ant, *n.* hormiga
ant·ac·id, *n.* antiácido
an·tag·o·nist, *n.* antagonista, *m., f.*
an·tag·o·nize, *v.* provocar; contender
ant·arc·tic, *a.* antártico
ant·eat·er, *n.* oso hormiguero
an·te·cede, *v.* anteceder
an·te·ced·ent, *n.* antecedente
an·te·date, *v.* antedatar; preceder
an·te·di·lu·vi·an, *a.* antediluviano
an·te·lope, *n. pl.* **-lopes, -lope.** antílope
an·ten·na, *n. pl.* **-nae, -nas** antena
an·te·ri·or, *a.* anterior
an·te·room, *n.* antecámara
an·them, *n.* antífona. **na·tion·al anthem,** himno nacional
an·ther, *n.* antera
an·thol·o·gy, *n. pl.* **-gies.** antología
an·thra·cite, *n.* antracita
an·thrax, *n. pl.* **-thra·ces.** ántrax
an·thro·poid, *a.* antropoide
an·thro·pol·o·gist, *n.* antropólogo
an·thro·pol·o·gy, *n.* antropología
an·ti-, *prefix.* anti; contra
an·ti·bi·ot·ic, *n., a.* antibiótico
an·ti·bod·y, *n. pl.* **-ies.** anticuerpo
an·tic, *n.* travesura; cabriola
an·tic·i·pate, *v.* anticipar; esperar
an·tic·i·pa·tion, *n.* anticipación; expectación
an·ti·cli·max, *n.* anticlímax
an·ti·dote, *n.* antídoto
an·tip·a·thy, *n. pl.* **-thies.** antipatía
an·ti·po·des, *n. pl.* antípoda
an·ti·quate, *v.* antiquar
an·ti·quat·ed, *a.* viejo; anticuado
an·tique, *a.* antiguo. *n.* antigüedad
an·tiq·ui·ty, *n. pl.* **-ties.** antigüedad
an·ti-Sem·i·tism, *n.* antisemitismo
an·ti·sep·tic, *a., n.* antiséptico
an·ti·so·cial, *a.* antisocial
an·tith·e·sis, *n. pl.* **-ses.** antítesis, *f.*
an·ti·tox·in, *n.* antitoxina
ant·ler, *n.* cuerna; asta
an·to·nym, *n.* antónimo
a·nus, *n.* ano
an·vil, *n.* yunque
anx·i·e·ty, *n. pl.* **-ties.** inquietud; ansia
anx·ious, *a.* inquieto; impaciente
an·y, *a., pron.* algún; cualquier; alguno
an·y·bod·y, *pron.* alguno; alguien; cualquiera
an·y·how, *adv.* de cualquier modo; de todas formas
an·y·one, *pron.* alguno; alguien; cualquiera
an·y·thing, *pron.* algo; cualquier cosa
an·y·way, *adv.* de cualquier modo; de todas formas
an·y·where, *adv.* en todas partes; dondequiera
a·or·ta, *n. pl.* **-tas, -tae.** aorta
a·part, *adv.* aparte. **a·part from,** aparte de
a·part·ment, *n.* piso; apartamento
ap·a·thet·ic, *a.* indiferente
ap·a·thy, *n. pl.* **-thies.** apatía
ape, *n.* mono. *v.* imitar
ap·er·ture, *n.* abertura
a·pex, *n. pl.* **-pex·es, -pi·ces.** ápice, *m.*
aph·o·rism, *n.* aforismo
aph·ro·dis·i·ac, *n.* afrodisíaco
a·pi·a·rist, *n.* colmenero
a·pi·ar·y, *n. pl.* **-ies.** colmenar
a·piece, *adv.* cada uno; por persona
a·plomb, *n.* aplomo
a·poc·a·lypse, *n.* apocalipsis, *m.*
a·pol·o·gize, *v.* disculparse; excusar
a·pol·o·gy, *n. pl.* **-gies.** apología; disculpa
ap·o·plec·tic, *a.* apopléptico
ap·o·plex·y, *n.* apoplejía
a·port, *adv.* a babor
a·pos·tate, *n.* apóstata, *m., f.*
a·pos·ta·tize, *v.* apostatar
a·pos·tle, *n.* apóstol
a·pos·tol·ic, *a.* apostólico
a·pos·tro·phe, *n.* apóstrofo
a·poth·e·car·y, *n. pl.* **-ies.** boticario
ap·pall, ap·pal, *v.* aterrar
ap·pa·rat·us, *n. pl.* **-rat·us, -us·es.** aparato
ap·par·el, *n.* ropa *v.* vestir
ap·par·ent, *a.* claro; aparente
ap·pa·ri·tion, *n.* fantasma, *m.*
ap·peal, *v.* apelar; suplicar; atraer. *n.* súplica; apelación

ap·pear, *v.* aparecer; parecer
ap·pear·ance, *n.* aparición; apariencia
ap·pease, *v.* apaciguar
ap·pel·lant, *n.* apelante, *m., f.*
ap·pel·la·tion, *n.* nombre
ap·pend, *v.* anexar
ap·pend·age, *n.* apéndice
ap·pen·dec·to·my, *n. pl.* **-mies.** apendectomía
ap·pen·di·ci·tis, *n.* apendicitis, *f.*
ap·pen·dix, *n. pl.* **-dix·es, -di·ces.** apéndice
ap·per·tain, *v.* pertenecer
ap·pe·tite, *n.* apetito; gana
ap·pe·tiz·ing, *a.* apetitoso; apetitivo
ap·plaud, *v.* aplaudir
ap·plause, *n.* aplauso
ap·ple, *n.* manzana
ap·pli·cant, *n.* suplicante, *m., f.*
ap·pli·ca·tion, *n.* aplicación; solicitud
ap·ply, *v.* aplicar; solicitar
ap·point, *v.* señalar; nombrar
ap·point·ment, *n.* cita; nombramiento
ap·por·tion, *v.* repartir
ap·po·si·tion, *n.* aposición
ap·prais·al, *n.* valoración
ap·praise, *v.* valorar
ap·pre·ci·ate, *v.* apreciar; valorar; agradecer
ap·pre·ci·a·tion, *n.* aprecio; aumento en valor
ap·pre·hend, *v.* prender; entender; recelar
ap·pre·hen·sion, *n.* aprehensión
ap·pren·tice, *n.* aprendiz, *m. v.* poner de aprendiz
ap·prise, ap·prize, *v.* informar
ap·proach, *v.* acercarse; aproximarse. *n.* acceso; aproximación
ap·pro·ba·tion, *n.* aprobación
ap·pro·pri·ate, *v.* apropiarse; destinar. *a.* apropiado
ap·prov·al, *n.* aprobación
ap·prove, *v.* aprobar
ap·prox·i·mate, *v.* aproximar. *a.* aproximado
A·pril, *n.* abril
a·pron, *n.* delantal, *m.*
ap·ro·pos of, *prep.* a propósito de
apt, *a.* apto; listo
ap·ti·tude, *n.* aptitud
a·quar·i·um, *n. pl.* **-i·ums, -i·a.** acuario
a·quat·ic, *a.* acuático. *n. pl.* deportes acuáticos
aq·ue·duct, *n.* acueducto
a·que·ous, *a.* ácueo
aq·ui·line, *a.* aguileño
Ar·ab, *n., a.* árabe, *m., f.*
A·ra·bic nu·mer·als, *n.* números arábigos
ar·a·ble, *a.* labrantío; cultivable
ar·bi·ter, *n.* árbitro
ar·bi·trar·y, *a.* arbitrario
ar·bi·tra·tion, *n.* arbitraje
ar·bi·tra·tor, *n.* arbitrador
ar·bo·re·al, *a.* arbóreo
ar·bo·re·tum, *n. pl.* **-tums, -ta.** jardín botánico
arc, *n.* arco. *v.* formar un arco voltaico
ar·cade, *n.* arcada; galería
arch, *n.* arco. *v.* arquear
arch-, *prefix.* principal
ar·chae·ol·o·gy, ar·che·ol·o·gy, *n.* arqueología
ar·cha·ic, *a.* arcaico
arch·an·gel, *n.* arcángel
arch·bish·op, *n.* arzobispo
arch·duch·ess, *n.* archiduquesa
arch·duke, *n.* archiduque
arch·er, *n.* arquero
arch·er·y, *n.* ballestería
ar·che·type, *n.* arquetipo
ar·chi·pel·a·go, *n. pl.* **-goes, -gos.** archipiélago
ar·chi·tect, *n.* arquitecto
ar·chi·tec·tur·al, *a.* arquitectónico
ar·chi·tec·ture, *n.* arquitectura
ar·chive, *n.* archivo
arch·priest, *n.* arcipreste
arc·tic, *a.* ártico; glacial
ar·dent, *a.* ardiente; fervoroso
ar·dor, *n.* ardor
ar·du·ous, *a.* arduo; difícil
a·re·a, *n.* área; región
a·re·na, *n.* arena
ar·gon, *n.* argo
ar·got, *n.* jerga
ar·gue, *v.* discutir; razonar
ar·gu·ment, *n.* argumento; disputa
ar·gu·men·ta·tive, *a.* argumentador
a·ri·a, *n.* aria
ar·id, *a.* árido
a·rid·i·ty, *n.* aridez
a·rise, *v.* alzarse; surgir
ar·is·toc·ra·cy, *n. pl.* **-cies.** aristocracia
a·ris·to·crat, *n.* aristócrata, *m., f.*
a·ris·to·crat·ic, *a.* aristocrático
a·rith·me·tic, *n.* aritmética
a·rith·me·ti·cian, *n.* aritmético
ark, *n.* arca
arm, *n.* brazo; arma. *v.* armar
ar·ma·da, *n.* armada
ar·ma·dil·lo, *n. pl.* **-los.** armadillo
ar·ma·ment, *n.* armamento
arm·ful, *n. pl.* **-fuls.** brazado
ar·mi·stice, *n.* armisticio
ar·moire, *n.* armario
ar·mor, *n.* armadura
ar·mored, *a.* blindado
ar·mor·y, *n. pl.* **-ies.** armería
arm·pit, *n.* sobaco

ar·my, *n. pl.* **-mies**. ejército; multitud
a·ro·ma, *n.* aroma, *m.*
ar·o·mat·ic, *a.* aromático
a·round, *adv.* alrededor; a la vuelta. *prep.* alrededor de
a·rouse, *v.* despertar; excitar
ar·range, *v.* arreglar; prevenir
ar·range·ment, *n.* arreglo; orden; medida
ar·rant, *a.* consumado
ar·ray, *n.* orden; formación; adorno. *v.* colocar; ataviar
ar·rest, *v.* detener. *n.* detención
ar·ri·val, *n.* llegada
ar·rive, *v.* llegar
ar·ro·gance, *n.* arrogancia
ar·ro·gant, *a.* arrogante
ar·row, *n.* flecha
ar·row·head, *n.* punta de flecha
ar·se·nal, *n.* arsenal
ar·se·nic, *n.* arsénico
ar·son, *n.* incendio premeditado
art, *n.* arte, *m.;* destreza; *pl.* artes, *f.*
ar·te·ri·al, *a.* arterial
ar·ter·y, *n. pl.* **-ies**. arteria
art·ful, *a.* ingenioso; astuto
ar·thrit·ic, *a.* artrítico
ar·thri·tis, *n.* artritis, *f.*
ar·ti·cle, *n.* artículo; objeto
ar·tic·u·late, *a.* articulado; claro. *v.* articular
ar·tic·u·la·tion, *n.* articulación
ar·ti·fi·cial, *a.* artificial
ar·til·ler·y, *n.* artillería
art·ist, *n.* artista, *m., f.*
ar·tis·tic, *a.* artístico
as, *adv., conj., prep.* como
as·bes·tos, **as·bes·tus**, *n.* asbesto
as·cend, *v.* subir; ascender
as·cen·sion, *n.* ascensión
as·cent, *n.* subida; cuesta
as·cer·tain, *v.* averiguar
as·cet·ic, *a.* ascético; asceta, *m., f.*
as·cet·i·cism, *n.* ascetismo
as·cribe, *v.* adscribir; atribuir
a·sex·u·al, *a.* asexual
ash, *n.* ceniza; fresno
a·shamed, *a.* avergonzado
a·side, *adv.* a un lado. *n.* aparte
as·i·nine, *a.* asnal
ask, *v.* preguntar; pedir; rogar
a·skance, *adv.* con recelo. Also **a·skant**
a·slant, *adv.* al sesgo. *prep.* a través de
a·sleep, *a., adv.* dormido
asp, *n.* áspid, *m.*
as·par·a·gus, *n.* espárrago
as·pect, *n.* aspecto; aire
as·per·i·ty, *n. pl.* **-ties**. aspereza
as·per·sion, *n.* calumnia
as·phalt, *n.* asfalto
as·phyx·i·ate, *v.* asfixiar
as·phyx·i·a·tion, *n.* asfixia
as·pi·ra·tion, *n.* aspiración; anhelo
as·pire, *v.* aspirar
as·pi·rin, *n.* aspirina
ass, *n.* burro; tonto
as·sail, *v.* acometer
as·sail·ant, *n.* asaltador
as·sas·sin, *n.* asesino
as·sas·si·nate, *v.* asesinar
as·sas·si·na·tion, *n.* asesinato
as·sault, *n.* asalto. *v.* atacar
as·sem·ble, *v.* congregar; juntar
as·sem·bly, *n. pl.* **-blies**. reunión; asamblea
as·sent, *n.* asentimiento. *v.* asentir
as·sert, *v.* afirmar
as·sess, *v.* fijar; tasar
as·sess·ment, *n.* valoración; imposición
as·set, *n.* haber; *pl.* activo
as·sev·er·ate, *v.* aseverar
as·sid·u·ous, *a.* asiduo
as·sign, *v.* asignar
as·sig·na·tion, *n.* cita
as·sign·ment, *n.* asignación
as·sim·i·late, *v.* asimilar
as·sim·i·la·tion, *n.* asimilación
as·sist, *v.* ayudar
as·sist·ance, *n.* ayuda
as·sist·ant, *a.* auxiliar. *n.* asistente; ayudante
as·so·ci·ate, *v.* asociar(se). *a.* asociado. *n.* socio; compañero
as·so·ci·a·tion, *n.* asociación; sociedad
as·so·nance, *n.* asonancia
as·sort·ed, *a.* variado
as·sort·ment, *n.* surtido
as·suage, *v.* mitigar
as·sume, *v.* asumir; tomar
as·sump·tion, *n.* asunción; suposición
as·sure, *v.* asegurar
as·ter, *n.* aster, *m.*
as·ter·isk, *n.* asterisco
a·stern, *adv.* por la popa; a popa
asth·ma, *n.* asma
asth·mat·ic, *a.* asmático
a·stir, *adv.* activo
as·ton·ish, *v.* asombrar
as·ton·ish·ment, *n.* asombro
a·stound, *v.* asombrar
a·stray, *adv.* descarriado
a·stride, *adv., prep.* a horcajadas
as·trol·o·ger, *n.* astrólogo
as·trol·o·gy, *n.* astrología
as·tro·naut, *n.* astronauta, *m., f.*
as·tron·o·mer, *n.* astrónomo
as·tron·o·my, *n.* astronomía
as·tute, *a.* astuto
a·sun·der, *adv.* aparte
a·sy·lum, *n.* asilo; manicomio
at, *prep.* en; a
at·el·ier, *n.* taller

a·the·ism, *n.* ateísmo
a·the·ist, *n.* ateo
ath·lete, *n.* atleta, *m., f.*
ath·let·ic, *a.* atlético
a·thwart, *adv.* contrariamente. *prep.* al través
at·las, *n. pl.* **-las·es**. atlas
at·mos·phere, *n.* atmósfera; ambiente
at·mos·pher·ic, *a.* atmosférico
at·oll, *n.* atolón
at·om, *n.* átomo
a·tom·ic, *a.* atómico
at·om·ize, *v.* atomizar
a·tone, *v.* expiar
a·tone·ment, *n.* expiación
a·top, *adv.* encima. *prep.* sobre
a·tro·cious, *a.* atroz
a·troc·i·ty, *n. pl.* **-ties**. atrocidad
at·ro·phy, *n. pl.* **-phies**. atrofia
at·tach, *v.* sujetar; unir; pegar
at·tack, *v.* atacar. *n.* ataque
at·tain, *v.* lograr; alcanzar
at·tain·ment, *n.* logro
at·tempt, *v.* intentar. *n.* tentativa; esfuerzo
at·tend, *v.* acompañar; asistir
at·ten·tion, *n.* atención
at·test, *v.* atestiguar
at·tic, *n.* desván
at·tire, *v.* vestir
at·ti·tude, *n.* actitud; postura
at·tor·ney, *n. pl.* **-neys**. abogado
at·tract, *v.* atraer
at·trac·tion, *n.* atracción
at·trib·ute, *v.* atribuir
at·tri·bu·tion, *n.* atribución
a·typ·i·cal, *a.* atípico
auc·tion, *n.* subasta. *v.* subastar
auc·tion·eer, *n.* subastador; licitador
au·da·cious, *a.* audaz
au·dac·i·ty, *n.* atrevimiento
au·di·ble, *a.* oíble
au·di·ence, *n.* audiencia; público
au·dit, *n.* revisión. *v.* intervenir
au·di·tion, *n.* audición
au·di·tor, *n.* interventor
au·di·to·ri·um, *n.* auditorio
au·di·to·ry, *a.* auditivo
aught, *n.* algo
aug·ment, *v.* aumentar
Au·gust, *n.* agosto
aunt, *n.* tía
au·re·ate, *a.* áureo
au·ri·cle, *n.* aurícula
au·ro·ra, *n.* aurora
aus·pice, *n. pl.* **-pic·es**. auspicio; *usu. pl.* protección
aus·pi·cious, *a.* favorable
aus·tere, *a.* austero
aus·ter·i·ty, *n.* austeridad
au·then·tic, *a.* auténtico
au·then·ti·cate, *v.* autenticar
au·then·tic·i·ty, *n.* autenticidad
au·thor, *n.* autor
au·thor·i·ta·tive, *a.* autorizado; imperioso
au·thor·i·ty, *n. pl.* **-ties**. autoridad
au·thor·i·za·tion, *n.* autorización
au·thor·ize, *v.* autorizar
au·to, *n. inf.* automóvil
au·to·bi·og·ra·pher, *n.* autobiógrafo
au·to·bi·og·ra·phy, *n. pl.* **-phies**. autobiografía
au·toc·ra·cy, *n. pl.* **-cies**. autocracia
au·to·crat, *n.* autócrata, *m., f.*
au·to·graph, *n.* autógrafo. *v.* firmar
au·to·mat·ic, *a.* automático
au·to·ma·tion, *n.* automatización
au·tom·a·ton, *n. pl.* **-tons, -ta**. autómata
au·to·mo·bile, *n.* automóvil; coche
au·ton·o·mous, *a.* autónomo
au·ton·o·my, *n. pl.* **-mies**. autonomía
au·top·sy, *n. pl.* **-sies**. autopsia
au·tumn, *n.* otoño
aux·il·ia·ry, *a.* auxiliar
a·vail, *v.* aprovechar(se); ser útil. *n.* utilidad
a·vail·a·ble, *a.* disponible
av·a·lanche, *n.* alud, *m.*
av·a·rice, *n.* avaricia
av·a·ri·cious, *a.* avaro
a·venge, *v.* vengar
a·veng·er, *n.* vengador
av·e·nue, *n.* avenida
a·ver, *v.* afirmar
av·er·age, *n.* promedio. *a.* medio. *v.* calcular el término medio
a·verse, *a.* adverso
a·ver·sion, *n.* aversión
a·vert, *v.* desviar; apartar; prevenir
a·vi·a·tion, *n.* aviación
a·vi·a·tor, *n.* aviador
av·id, *a.* ávido
av·o·ca·do, *n. pl.* **-dos**. aguacate
av·o·ca·tion, *n.* diversión; trabajo
a·void, *v.* evitar
a·void·a·ble, *a.* evitable; eludible
a·vow, *v.* reconocer
a·vow·al, *n.* confesión
a·wait, *v.* esperar
a·wake, *a.* despierto. *v.* despertar(se)
a·wak·en, *v.* despertar(se)
a·ward, *v.* adjudicar; otorgar. *n.* adjudicación; premio
a·ware, *a.* enterado
a·way, *adv.* lejos. *a.* fuera
awe, *n.* temor reverencial. *v.* infundir miedo
aw·ful, *a.* imponente; horrible
a·while, *adv.* un rato
awk·ward, *a.* torpe; difícil; embarazoso
awn·ing, *n.* toldo
a·wry, *a.* sesgado. *adv.* de través
ax, **axe**, *n.* **ax·es**. hacha

ax·i·om, *n.* axioma, *m.*
ax·i·o·mat·ic, *a.* axiomático
ax·is, *n. pl.* **ax·es**. axis; eje
ax·le, *n.* eje
aye, **ay**, *int., n.* sí
az·ure, *a., n.* azul celeste

B

baa, *n.* balido. *v.* balar
bab·ble, *n.* murmullo. *v.* parlotear; balbucear
babe, *n.* criatura
ba·bel, *n.* babel. Also **Ba·bel**
ba·boon, *n.* mandril
ba·bush·ka, *n.* pañuelo
ba·by, *n. pl.* **-bies**. nene; niño. *a.* infantil. *v.* tratar como niño
bac·ca·lau·re·ate, *n.* bachillerato
bac·cha·na·li·an, *a.* bacanal
bach·e·lor, *n.* soltero
bach·e·lor·hood, *n.* soltería
ba·cil·lus, *n. pl.* **-li**. bacilo
back, *n.* espalda; fondo. *v.* apoyar; retroceder. *a.* trasero. *adv.* atrás
back·bone, *n.* espinazo; firmeza
back·drop, *n.* telón de foro
back·fire, *n.* petardeo. *v.* salir el tiro por la culata
back·gam·mon, *n.* juego de chaquete
back·ground, *n.* fondo; antecedentes
back·hand·ed, *a.* dado con el revés de la mano
back·lash, *n.* reacción
back·side, *n.* trasero
back·slide, *v.* apostatar; reincidir
back·ward, *adv.* atrás; al revés. *a.* atrasado. Also **back·wards**
ba·con, *n.* tocino
bac·te·ri·ol·o·gist, *n.* bacteriólogo
bac·te·ri·ol·o·gy, *n.* bacteriología
bac·te·ri·um, *n. pl.* **-i·a**. bacteria
bad, *a.* malo; podrido. *n.* lo malo
badge, *n.* divisa
badg·er, *n.* tejón. *v.* molestar
bad·min·ton, *n.* juego de volante
bad·ness, *n.* maldad
baf·fle, *v.* confundir; desconcertar
bag, *n.* saco; maleta; bolso. *v.* ensacar; cazar
bag·gage, *n.* equipaje
bag·nio, *n. pl.* **-los**. burdel
bag·pipe, *n. usu. pl.* gaita
bail, *v.* achicar; afianzar. *n.* caución
bail·iff, *n.* alguacil
bait, *n.* cebo. *v.* cebar; atormentar
bake, *v.* cocer en horno; endurecer
bak·er, *n.* panadero
bak·er's doz·en, *n.* trece
bak·er·y, *n. pl.* **-ies**. panadería
bal·ance, *n.* balanza; equilibrio; resto. *v.* equilibrar(se)
bal·co·ny, *n. pl.* **-nies**. balcón
bald, *a.* calvo
bal·der·dash, *n.* tonterías
bald·ness, *n.* calvicie, *f.*
bale, *n.* bala. *v.* embalar; empacar
ba·leen, *n.* ballena
bale·ful, *a.* calamitoso; siniestro
balk, *v.* viga; obstáculo. *v.* impedir; rebelarse
ball, *n.* bola; pelota; baile
bal·lad, *n.* balada
bal·last, *n.* lastre. *v.* lastrar
bal·le·ri·na, *n.* bailarina
bal·let, *n.* ballet
bal·lis·tic, *a.* balístico
bal·lis·tics, *n.* balística
bal·loon, *n.* globo
bal·lot, *n.* balota; votación
ball·room, *n.* salón de baile
balm, *n.* bálsamo
balm·y, *a.* balsámico; suave
ba·lo·ney, *n. inf.* disparates
bal·sa, *n.* balsa
bal·sam, *n.* bálsamo
bal·us·trade, *n.* balaustrada
bam·boo, *n.* bambú, *m.*
ban, *v.* prohibir. *n.* prohibición
ba·nal, *a.* vulgar
ba·nal·i·ty, *n.* trivialidad
ba·nan·a, *n.* plátano; banana
band, *n.* grupo; faja; banda. *v.* juntar
band·age, *n.* venda. *v.* vendar
ban·dit, *n. pl.* **-dits, -dit·ti**. bandido
ban·dy, *v.* cambiar. *a.* arqueado
ban·dy-leg·ged, *a.* estevado
bane, *n.* ruina; daño
bane·ful, *a.* funesto
bang, *v.* golpear; hacer estrépito. *n.* golpe
ban·ish, *v.* desterrar
ban·ish·ment, *n.* destierro
ban·is·ter, *n.* pasamano
ban·jo, *n.* banjo
bank, *n.* orilla; montón; banco. *v.* amontonar; cubrir; depositar
bank·er, *n.* banquero
bank·rupt, *a.* insolvente. *v.* quebrar
bank·rupt·cy, *n. pl.* **-cies**. bancarrota; quiebra
ban·nis·ter, *n.* pasamano
ban·quet, *n.* banquete. *v.* banquetear
ban·ter, *n.* zumba; burla. *v.* zumbar; chancearse con
bap·tism, *n.* bautismo; bautizo
bar, *n.* barra; obstáculo; bar. *v.* impedir; excluir
barb, *n.* púa
bar·bar·i·an, *n.* bárbaro
bar·bar·ic, *a.* bárbaro
bar·bar·i·ty, *n. pl.* **-ties**. barbaridad
bar·be·cue, *n.* barbacoa. *v.* asar
barbed wire, *n.* alambre de púas (de espino). Also **barb·wire**
bar·ber, *n.* peluquero; barbero
bar·ber·shop, *n.* peluquería

ax·i·om, *n.* axioma, *m.*
bar·bi·tu·rate, *n.* barbiturato
bard, *n.* poeta, *m.;* bardo
bare, *a.* desnudo; pelado. *v.* desnudar; descubrir
bare-faced, *a.* descarado
bare·ly, *adv.* simplemente; apenas
bar·gain, *n.* pacto; ganga. *v.* negociar; regatear
barge, *n.* gabarra
bar·i·tone, *n.* barítono
bar·i·um, *n.* bario
bark, *n.* corteza; ladrido. *v.* descortezar; raer; ladrar
bar·ley, *n. pl.* **-leys**. cebada
bar·maid, *n.* camarera
barn, *n.* granero
bar·na·cle, *n.* percebe
barn·yard, *n.* corral, *m.*
ba·rom·et·er, *n.* barómetro
bar·o·met·ric, *a.* barométrico
bar·on, *n.* barón
bar·on·ess, *n.* baronesa
ba·roque, *a.* barroco
bar·rack, *n. usu. pl.* cuartel, *m.*
bar·rage, *n.* cortina de fuego
bar·rel, *n.* barril, *m.;* cañón
bar·rel or·gan, *n.* organillo
bar·ren, *a.* estéril
bar·rette, *n.* horquilla
bar·ri·cade, *n.* barricada
bar·ri·er, *n.* barrera
bar·room, *n.* taberna; cantina
bar·ter, *v.* trocar; permutar
ba·sal, *a.* básico
ba·salt, *n.* basalto
base, *n.* base, *f. a.* bajo; vil
base·ball, *n.* béisbol
base-born, *a.* de nacimiento humilde
base·less, *a.* infundado
base·ment, *n.* sótano
bash, *v. inf.* golpear
bash·ful, *a.* vergonzoso
bash·ful·ness, *n.* timidez, *f.*
ba·sic, *a.* básico
ba·sil, *n.* albahaca
ba·sil·i·ca, *n.* basílica
ba·sin, *n.* tazón; jofaina; cuenca
ba·sis, *n. pl.* **-ses**. base, *f.*
bask, *v.* tomar el sol
bas·ket, *n.* cesta; canasta
bas·ket·ball, *n.* baloncesto; básquetbol
bass, *n.* bajo; contrabajo. *a.* bajo
bass, *n. pl.* **bass, bass·es**. róbalo
bas·si·net, *n.* cuna
bas·soon, *n.* bajón
bas·tard, *n.* bastardo. *a.* ilegítimo
bas·tard·ize, *v.* bastardear
baste, *v.* hilvanar; pringar
bas·tion, *n.* baluarte
bat, *n.* murciélago; maza. *v.* golpear
batch, *n.* hornada; colección
bath, *n. pl.* **baths**. baño
bathe, *v.* bañar(se)
bath·er, *n.* bañista, *m., f.*
bat·on, *n.* bastón; batuta
bat·tal·ion, *n.* batallón
bat·ter, *v.* apalear; desgastar. *n.* batido
bat·ter·y, *n. pl.* **-ies**. batería; pila
bat·tle, *n.* batalla; lucha. *v.* luchar
bat·ty, *a. inf.* loco
bau·ble, *n.* chuchería
bawd, *n.* alcahueta
bawd·y, *a.* obsceno
bawl, *v.* gritar; llorar
bay, *n.* bahía; laurel; aullido. *a.* bayo. *v.* aullar; encerrar
bay·o·net, *n.* bayoneta
ba·zaar, *n.* bazar, *m.*
ba·zoo·ka, *n.* bazuca
be, *v.* ser; estar
beach, *n.* playa
bea·con, *n.* faro; almenara
bead, *n.* cuenta; gota
beak, *n.* pico
beam, *n.* viga; manga; rayo. *v.* emitir; brillar
bean, *n.* judía; haba
bear, *v. pl.* **bears, bear**. oso. *v.* llevar; soportar; producir
bear·a·ble, *a.* soportable
beard, *n.* barba
beard·ed, *a.* barbado
bear·ing, *n.* cojinete; porte; relación
bear·skin, *n.* piel de oso
beast, *n.* bestia; bruto
beast·li·ness, *n.* bestialidad
beat, *v.* golpear; batir; vencer. *n.* ritmo; ronda
beat·en, *a.* batido; derrotado
be·at·i·fy, *v.* beatificar
be·at·i·tude, *n.* beatitud
beau, *n.* galán; bello
beau·ti·ful, *a.* hermoso
beau·ty, *n. pl.* **-ties**. belleza
bea·ver, *n.* castor
be·cause, *conj.* porque; a causa de
beck·on, *v.* llamar con señas
be·come, *v.* llegar a ser; hacerse; favorecer
be·com·ing, *a.* conveniente; que va bien
bed, *n.* cama; lecho; estrato
bed·clothes, *n. pl.* ropa de cama
bed·ding, *n.* ropa de cama
bed·deck, *v.* adornar
be·dev·il, *v.* endiablar
bed·lam, *n.* confusión; manicomio
be·drag·gle, *v.* ensuciar
bed·rid·den, *a.* postrado en cama
bed·room, *n.* alcoba
bed·stead, *n.* armazón
bee, *n.* abeja
beech, *n.* haya
beef, *n. pl.* **beefs, beeves**. carne de vaca; buey; *inf.* fuerza muscular. *v.*

inf. quejarse
bee·hive, *n.* colmena
beer, *n.* cerveza
bees·wax, *n.* cera de abejas
beet, *n.* remolacha
bee·tle, *n.* escarabajo
be·fit, *v.* convenir
be·fit·ting, *a.* conveniente
be·fore, *adv.* delante; antes. *prep.* delante de; antes de; ante. *conj.* antes que
be·fore·hand, *adv.* de antemano
be·friend, *v.* amistar; favorecer
beg, *v.* mendigar; pedir
beg·gar, *n.* mendigo
be·gin, *v.* empezar; comenzar; iniciar
be·gin·ning, *n.* comienzo; principio
be·guile, *v.* engañar; distraer
be·half, *n.* favor; beneficio
be·have, *v.* comportarse; portarse
be·hav·ior, *n.* conducta; comportamiento
be·head, *v.* decapitar
be·hind, *prep.* detrás de. *adv.* detrás; atrás; en retardo
be·hind·hand, *adv.* atrasada; con atraso
beige, *n.* beige
be·ing, *n.* existencia; ser
be·lat·ed, *a.* retardado; tardío
belch, *v.* eructar. *n.* eructo
bel·ea·guer, *v.* sitiar
bel·fry, *n. pl.* **-fries**. campanario
be·lief, *n.* creencia; fe, *f.*
be·liev·a·ble, *a.* creíble
be·lieve, *v.* creer
bell, *n.* campana; cascabel, *m.*
bell·boy, *n.* botones. Also **bell·hop**
bel·li·cose, *a.* belicoso
bel·lig·er·en·cy, *n.* beligerancia
bel·lig·er·ent, *a.* beligerante
bel·low, *n.* bramido. *v.* bramar; rugir
bel·lows, *n. pl.* fuelle
bel·ly·ache, *n.* dolor de vientre. *v. inf.* quejarse
be·long, *v.* pertenecer
be·long·ings, *n. pl.* pertenencias
be·loved, *a.* querido. *n.* amado
be·low, *prep.* debajo de. *adv.* abajo
belt, *n.* cinturón. *v. inf.* golpear
be·moan, *v.* lamentar
be·muse, *v.* confundir
bench, *n.* banco; tribunal de justicia
bend, *v.* doblar; encorvar; inclinar. *n.* comba; curva
be·neath, *adv.* abajo. *prep.* debajo de
ben·e·dic·tion, *n.* bendición
ben·e·fac·tion, *n.* beneficio
ben·e·fac·tor, *n.* bienhechor
be·nef·i·cent, *a.* benéfico
ben·e·fi·cial, *a.* provechoso; beneficioso
ben·e·fi·ci·ar·y, *n. pl.* **-ar·ies**. beneficiario
ben·e·fit, *n.* beneficio. *v.* beneficiar; aprovechar(se)
be·nev·o·lence, *n.* benevolencia
be·nev·o·lent, *a.* benévolo
be·nign, *a.* benigno
be·nig·nant, *a.* benigno
be·nig·ni·ty, *n. pl.* **-ties**. benignidad
bent, *a.* encorvado; determinado. *n.* inclinación
be·queath, *v.* legar
be·quest, *n.* legado
be·rate, *v.* reprender; regañar
be·reave·ment, *n.* aflicción
berth, *n.* amarradero; litera
be·seech, *v.* suplicar
be·set, *v.* sitiar; acosar
be·side, *prep.* cerca; junto a
be·sides, *adv.* además, *prep.* además de
be·siege, *v.* sitiar; asediar
be·smirch, *v.* manchar
be·speak, *v.* reservar; apalabrar
best, *a. irreg. superl. of good.* mejor. *adv.* mejor; más bien. *n.* lo mejor. *v.* vencer
bes·tial, *a.* bestial
bes·ti·al·i·ty, *n. pl.* **-ties**. bestialidad
be·stow, *v.* dar; otorgar; conferir
bet, *n.* apuesta. *v.* apostar
be·tray, *v.* traicionar; revelar
be·tray·al, *n.* traición
be·troth, *v.* prometer en matrimonio
bet·ter, *a. compar. of good.* mejor; superior. *adv. compar. of well.* mejor. *n. usu. pl.* superiores. *v.* mejorar
bet·ter·ment, *n.* mejoramiento
be·tween, *prep.* entre. *adv.* en medio
bev·er·age, *n.* bebida
bev·y, *n. pl.* **-ies**. bandada; grupo
be·ware, *v.* guardarse; precaverse
be·wil·der, *v.* aturdir
be·wil·der·ment, *n.* aturdimiento
be·witch, *v.* hechizar; encantar
be·yond, *adv.* más allá. *prep.* después de
bi·as, *n.* sesgo; propensión; prejuicio. *a.* sesgado. *v.* prevenir
bib, *n.* babero
Bi·ble, *n.* Biblia
bib·li·cal, *a.* bíblico
bib·li·og·ra·pher, *n.* bibliógrafo
bib·li·og·ra·phy, *n. pl.* **-phies**. bibliografía
bi·ceps, *n. pl.* biceps, *m.*
bick·er, *v.* reñir
bi·cy·cle, *n.* bicicleta. *v.* ir en bici-

inf. quejarse
bi·cy·clist, *n.* biciclista, *m., f.*
bid, *v.* pedir; ordenar; ofrecer. *n.* oferta; puja
bid·dy, *n. pl.* **-dies**. gallina
bide, *v.* esperar
bi·en·ni·al, *a.* bienal
bier, *n.* féretro
big, *a.* grande; importante
big·a·mist, *n.* bígamo
big·a·my, *n. pl.* **-mies**. bigamia
bight, *n.* caleta
big·ot, *n.* fanático
big·ot·ry, *n. pl.* **-ries**. fanatismo; intolerancia
bike, *n. inf.* bicicleta
bi·lat·er·al, *a.* bilateral
bile, *n.* bilis, *f.;* mal genio
bilge, *n.* pantoque
bil·ious, *a.* bilioso
bilk, *v.* defraudar
bill, *n.* cuenta; billete; propuesta de ley; pico. *v.* facturar
bill·board, *n.* cartelera
bil·let, *n.* alojamiento. *v.* alojar
bill·fold, *n.* cartera
bil·liards, *n. pl.* billar
bil·lion, *n.* billón
bill of fare, *n.* menú, *m.*
bil·low, *n.* oleada. *v.* hincharse
bil·low·y, *a.* hinchado
bil·ly goat, *n.* macho cabrío
bi·month·ly, *a., adv.* bimestral(mente); bimensual(mente)
bin, *n.* hucha
bi·na·ry, *a.* binario
bind, *v.* atar; vendar; encuadernar; obligar
bind·er, *n.* encuadernador
bind·er·y, *n. pl.* **-ies**. taller de encuadernador
bin·oc·u·lar, *n. usu. pl.* gemelos
bi·og·ra·pher, *n.* biógrafo
bi·o·graph·ic, *a.* biográfico
bi·og·ra·phy, *n. pl.* **-phies**. biografía
bi·o·log·i·cal, *a.* biológico
bi·ol·o·gist, *n.* biólogo
bi·ol·o·gy, *n.* biología
bi·op·sy, *n. pl.* **-sies**. biopsia
bi·par·ti·san, *a.* de dos partidos
bi·ped, *n.* bípedo
birch, *n.* abedul, *m.*
bird, *n.* ave, *f.;* pájaro
bird's-eye, *a.* vista de pájaro
birth, *n.* nacimiento; linaje
birth·day, *n.* cumpleaños
birth·mark, *n.* marca de nacimiento
birth·right, *n.* derechos de nacimiento
bis·cuit, *n.* galleta
bi·sect, *v.* bisecar
bi·sec·tion, *n.* bisección
bi·sex·u·al, *a.* bisexual
bish·op, *n.* obispo
bish·op·ric, *n.* obispado
bis·muth, *n.* bismuto
bi·son, *n.* bisonte
bis·tro, *n. pl.* **-tros**. cabaret, *m.*
bit, *n.* trozo; pedazo; bocado del freno
bitch, *n.* perra. *v. inf.* quejarse
bite, *v.* morder; picar. *n.* mordedura; bocado
bit·ter, *a.* amargo
bit·ter·ness, *n.* amargura; rencor
bi·tu·mi·nous, *a.* bituminoso
bi·valve, *n.* molusco bivalvo
biv·ou·ac, *n.* vivaque. *v.* vivaquear
bi·zarre, *a.* fantástico; raro
blab, *v.* divulgar; chismear
black, *a., n.* negro. *v.* ennegrecer
black·ber·ry, *n. pl.* **-ries**. zarzamora
black·bird, *n.* mirlo
black·board, *n.* pizarra
black·en, *v.* ennegrecer; difamar
black·guard, *n.* pillo
black·head, *n.* espinilla
black·heart·ed, *a.* malvado
black·jack, *n.* cachiporra; juego de naipes
black mag·ic, *n.* magia negra
black·mail, *n.* chantaje
black·smith, *n.* herrero
blad·der, *n.* vejiga
blade, *n.* brizna; hoja
blame, *v.* culpar; censurar. *n.* censura
blame·less, *a.* intachable
blame·wor·thy, *a.* culpable
blanch, *v.* blanquear; palidecer
bland, *a.* suave
blan·dish, *v.* engatusar
blank, *a.* blanco. *n.* blanco
blan·ket, *n.* manta. *a.* general
blare, *v.* vociferar
blar·ney, *n.* adulación
blas·pheme, *v.* blasfemar
blas·phem·y, *n. pl.* **-ies**. blasfemia
blast, *n.* ráfaga; explosión. *v.* destruir; volar
bla·tant, *a.* ruidoso; poco sutil
blaze, *n.* llama; resplandor. *v.* arder; brillar
bleach, *v.* blanquear. *n.* lejía
bleach·ers, *n. pl.* gradas
bleak, *a.* desierto; triste
blear·y, *a.* legañoso
bleat, *v.* balar. *n.* balido
bleed, *v.* sangrar
blem·ish, *v.* desfigurar; manchar. *n.* tacha
blend, *v.* mezclar. *n.* combinación
bless, *v.* bendecir
bless·ing, *n.* bendición; ventaja
blight, *n.* tizón. *v.* añublar
blind, *a.* ciego. *v.* cegar; deslumbrar
blind·fold, *n.* venda. *v.* vendar los ojos
blind·ness, *n.* ceguera

blink, v. parpadear. n. destello
bliss, n. felicidad
bliss·ful, a. bienaventurado
blis·ter, n. ampolla. v. ampollar(se)
blithe, a. alegre
bliz·zard, n. ventisca
bloat, v. hinchar
block, n. bloque; manzana; obstáculo. v. obstruir
block·ade, a. bloqueo. v. bloquear
block·age, n. obstrucción
blond, blonde, a. rubio
blood, n. sangre, f.
blood·hound, n. sabueso
blood·shed, n. efusión de sangre; carnicería
blood·shot, a. inyectado de sangre
blood·thirst·y, a. sanguinario
blood·y, a. sangriento; ensangrentado. v. ensangrentar
bloom, n. flor, f. v. florecer
bloom·ing, a. floreciente
blos·som, n. flor, f. v. florecer
blot, n. borrón. v. manchar; secar
blotch, n. erupción
blot·ter, n. papel secante
blouse, n. blusa
blow, v. soplar; sonar; inflar. n. soplo; golpe
blow·up, n. explosión
blub·ber, n. grasa de ballena. v. llorar a lágrima viva
bludg·eon, n. cachiporra
blue, a. azul; melancólico. n. azul. v. azular
blue·print, n. ferroprusiato
blues, n. pl. melancolía
bluff, a. escarpado; francote. n. risco. v. engañar; similar
blu·ing, n. añil, m.
blun·der, v. disparatar. n. desatino
blunt, a. embotado; abrupto. v. embotar
blur, v. borrar; hacer borroso. n. borrón
blurt, v. decir sin pensar
blush, v. ruborizarse. n. sonrojo
blus·ter, v. bramar. n. jactancia
blus·ter·ous, a. tempestuoso
boar, n. verraco
board, n. tabla; pensión; consejo. v. entablar; abordar
board·er, n. pensionista; huésped
boast, v. jactarse. n. baladronada; alarde
boast·ful, a. jactancioso
boat, n. barco; bote
boat·swain, n. contramaestre
bob, v. fluctuar; desmochar
bob·by pin, n. horquilla
bob·cat, n. lince
bob·white, n. codorniz, f.
bode, v. presagiar
bod·ice, n. corpiño
bod·i·ly, a. corpóreo. adv. enteramente
bod·y, n. pl. -ies. cuerpo; cadáver; grupo
bod·y·guard, n. guardaespaldas
bog, n. pantano
bog·gy, a. pantanoso
bo·gus, a. falso
bo·gy, bo·gey, bog·ie, n. duende
boil, v. hervir. n. furúnculo
boil·er, n. caldera
bois·ter·ous, a. borrascoso; ruidoso
bold, a. intrépido; descarado
bold·ly, adv. audazmente
bol·ster, n. travesaño. v. apoyar
bolt, v. rayo; cerrojo; rollo. v. empernar; engullir
bomb, n. bomba. v. bombardear
bom·bard, v. bombardear
bom·bar·dier, n. bombardero
bom·bard·ment, n. bombardeo
bom·bast, n. ampulosidad
bom·bas·tic, a. altisonante
bomb·er, n. bombardero
bond, n. lazo; obligación. v. dar fianza
bond·age, n. esclavitud
bone, n. hueso. v. deshuesar
bon·fire, n. hoguera
bon·net, n. gorra
bo·nus, n. pl. -nus·es. adehala; plus
bon·y, a. huesudo
boo·boo, n. inf. desatino
boo·by, n. pl. -bies. zote
boo·by trap, n. trampa camuflada
book, n. libro. v. reservar
book·bind·er, n. encuadernador de libros
book·keep·er, n. tenedor de libros
book·keep·ing, n. teneduría de libros
book·let, n. folleto
boom, n. estampido; prosperidad repentina. v. tronar; desarrollar rápidamente
boo·me·rang, n. bumerang, m.
boon, n. beneficio
boor, n. persona grosera
boost, v. empujar. n. empuje
boot, n. bota. v. a una patada en
booth, n. puesto
boo·ty, n. pl. -ties. botín
booze, n. bebida alcohólica. v. emborracharse
borax, n. bórax, m.
bor·der, n. borde; frontera
bore, v. taladrar; aburrir. n. pesado; taladro
bore·dom, n. aburrimiento
bo·ric ac·id, n. ácido bórico
born, a. nacido
bor·row, v. pedir prestado; apropiarse
bos·om, n. seno. a. íntimo
boss, n. jefe. v. dominar

boss·y, a. inf. tiránico
bo·sun, n. contramaestre. Also **bos'n, bo's'n, bo'sun**
bo·tan·ic, bo·tan·i·cal, a. botánico
bot·a·nist, n. botánico
bot·a·ny, n. botánica
botch, n. chapucería. v. remendar
both, a., pron. ambos; los dos. conj. a la vez
both·er, n. molestia. v. molestar
both·er·some, a. fastidioso
bot·tle, n. botella. v. embotellar
bot·tler, n. embotellador
bot·tom, n. fondo; pie. a. último
bough, n. rama
bought, pt. and pp. of **buy**
bouil·lon, n. caldo
boul·der, n. pedrejón
boul·e·vard, n. avenida; bulevar
bounce, v. rebotar. n. bote; rebote
bounc·ing, a. fuerte
bound, n. saltar; brincar. a. ligado; obligado
bound·a·ry, n. pl. -ries. término; frontera
boun·te·ous, a. abundante
boun·te·ous·ness, n. generosidad
boun·ty, n. pl. -ties. liberalidad; premio
bou·quet, n. ramo; aroma distinto
bour·geois, n., pl. -geois. burgués. a. burgués
bour·geoi·sie, n., pl. -sie. burguesía
bout, n. vez, f.; lucha
bo·vine, a. bovino
bow, n. arco; lazo. v. encorvar
bow, v. inclinar. n. reverencia; proa
bow·el, n. usu. pl. intestino
bow·er, n. enramada
bowl, n. escudilla. v. jugar a las bochas
bow·leg·ged, a. patiestevado
bowl·ing, n. juego de bolos
box, n. pl. box·es. caja. v. encajonar; boxear
box·er, n. boxeador
box·ing, n. boxeo
boy, n. niño; chico; muchacho
boy·cott, v. boicotear. n. boicoteo
boy·hood, n. muchachez, f.
boy·ish, a. juvenil
bra, n. inf. sostén
brace, n. abrazadera. v. atar; reforzar
brace·let, n. pulsera
brac·ing, a. tónico
brack·et, n. soporte; corchete. v. poner entre corchetes
brack·ish, a. salobre
brad, n. punta
brag, v. jactarse. n. bravata
brag·gart, n. jactancioso
braid, v. trenzar. n. trenza
brain, n. cerebro; pl. sesos
brain·less, a. estúpido
brain·y, a. listo; inteligente
braise, v. dorar (carne) y cocer a fuego lento
brake, n. freno. v. frenar
bram·ble, n. zarza
bran, n. salvado
branch, n. rama; sección. v. ramificar
brand, n. tizón; marca. v. marcar
bran·dish, v. blandir
bran·dy, n. pl. -dies. coñac
brash, a. impetuoso
brass, n. latón. a. de latón
bras·siere, n. sostén
brass·y, a. descarado
brat, n. mocoso
bra·va·do, n. bravata
brave, a. valiente. v. desafiar
brav·er·y, n. pl. -ies. valor
bra·vo, int. ¡bravo!
brawl, v. alborotar. n. alboroto
brawn, n. fuerza muscular
brawn·y, a. musculoso
bray, v. rebuznar. n. rebuzno
bra·zen, a. descarado
breach, n. brecha; abertura. v. romper
bread, n. pan
breadth, n. anchura
break, v. romper; quebrar; domar. n. rompimiento; ruptura; interrupción
break·a·ble, a. frágil
break·age, n. fractura; rotura
break·down, n. parada; avería; crisis, f.; análisis, m.
break·fast, n. desayuno. v. desayunar(se)
break·wa·ter, n. rompeolas
breast, n. pecho; seno
breast·bone, n. esternón
breath, n. aliento
breathe, v. respirar
breath·ing, n. respiración
breath·less, a. sin aliento
breech, n. trasero; recámara
breech·es, n. pl. calzones
breed, v. criar; engendrar. n. casta
breeze, n. brisa
breth·ren, n. pl. of **broth·er**
brev·i·ty, n. brevedad
brew, v. hacer; urdir
brew·er·y, n. pl. -ies. cervecería
bribe, v. sobornar. n. cohechar
brib·er·y, n. pl. -ies. cohecho
brick, n. ladrillo
brid·al, a. nupcial
bride, n. novia
bride·groom, n. novio
brides·maid, n. dama de honor
bridge, n. puente; juego de naipes. v. cruzar
bri·dle, n. brida. v. enfrenar

brief, a. breve. n. escrito. v. dar órdenes a
brief·ly, adv. en pocas palabras
bri·gade, n. brigada
bright, a. claro; brillante; listo
bright·en, v. abrillantar
bright·ness, n. lustre; agudeza
bril·liance, n. brillantez, f.
bril·liant, a. brillante
brim, n. borde
brim·stone, n. azufre
bring, v. traer
brink, n. borde; extremo
brisk, a. activo; vigoroso
bris·tle, n. cerda. v. erizar(se)
bris·tly, a. cerdoso
brit·tle, a. quebradizo
broach, v. introducir
broad, a. ancho; amplia; comprensivo
broad·cast, v. emitir. n. emisión
broad·mind·ed, a. tolerante
broad·side, n. andanada
bro·cade, n. brocado
broc·co·li, n. brécol, m.
bro·chure, n. folleto
broil, v. asar a la parrilla
bro·ken, a. quebrado; roto; accidentado
bro·ker, n. corredor
bro·ker·age, n. corretaje
bro·mide, n. bromuro
bron·chi·al, a. bronquial
bronze, n. bronce. v. broncear
brooch, n. broche; alfiler de pecho
brood, n. camada; progenie, f. v. empollar; ruminar
brook, n. arroyo
broom, n. escoba
broth, n. caldo
broth·el, n. burdel, m.
broth·er, n. pl. broth·ers, breth·ren. hermano
broth·er·hood, n. hermandad; fraternidad
broth·er·in·law, n. pl. broth·ers·in·law. cuñado
brow, n. ceja; frente, f.
brow·beat, v. intimidar
brown, a. moreno. n. color pardo
browse, v. rozar; hojear
bru·in, n. oso
bruise, v. magullar. n. contusión
bru·net, bru·nette, a. moreno. n. morena
brush, n. cepillo; brocha; maleza. v. (a)cepillar
brusque, brusk, a. áspero; brusco
bru·tal, a. brutal
bru·tal·i·ty, n. pl. -ties. brutalidad
bru·tal·ize, v. embrutecer(se)
brute, n. bruto
bub·ble, n. burbuja. v. burbujear
buc·ca·neer, n. bucanero
buck, n. macho de algunos animales. v. corcovear
buck·et, n. cubo
buck·le, n. hebilla. v. hebillar; torcer
buck·shot, n. perdigón
buck·skin, n. piel de ante
buck·wheat, n. alforfón
bud, n. brote. v. brotar
bud·dy, bud·die, n. pl. -dies. compañero
budge, v. mover(se)
budg·et, n. presupuesto. v. presupuestar
buff, n. ante. v. pulir
buf·fa·lo, n. pl. -loes, -los. búfalo
buf·fet, n. bofetada. v. golpear
buf·fet, n. armario; aparador
buf·foon, n. bufón
bug, n. bicho. v. inf. fastidiar
bug·gy, n. pl. -gies. calesín
bu·gle, n. clarín
bu·gler, n. corneta, m.
build, v. construir; hacer. n. forma
build·ing, n. construcción
bulb, n. bulbo; bombilla
bul·bous, a. bulboso
bulge, n. pandeo. v. pandearse
bulk, n. bulto
bulk·y, a. voluminoso
bull, n. toro
bul·let, n. bala
bul·le·tin, n. anuncio; boletín
bul·lion, n. oro o plata en barras
bull·ock, n. novillo
bull's-eye, n. centro del blanco
bul·ly, n. pl. -lies. matón. v. intimidar
bul·rush, n. anea
bul·wark, n. baluarte
bum, n. vagabundo. v. holgazanear
bum·ble·bee, n. abejorro
bump, v. chocar; tropezar con. n. hinchazón; bollo; choque
bump·er, n. parachoques
bun, n. bollo
bunch, n. grupo; racimo. v. agrupar
bun·dle, n. lío. v. liar
bun·ga·low, n. casa de un solo piso
bun·gle, v. chapucear
bun·gler, n. chapucero
bun·ion, n. juanete
bunk, n. tarima
bun·ny, n. pl. -nies. conejito
bun·ting, n. lanilla
buoy, n. boya. v. sobrenadar
buoy·ant, a. boyante
bur·den, n. carga; peso. v. cargar
bur·den·some, a. gravoso
bu·reau, n. pl. bu·reaus, bu·reaux. escritorio; agencia
bu·reauc·ra·cy, n., pl. -cies. burocracia
bu·reau·crat, n. burócrata, m., f.
bur·glar, n. ladrón

bur·glar·ize, v. robar
bur·gla·ry, n. pl. -ries. robo en una casa
bur·i·al, n. entierro
bur·lap, n. arpillera
bur·lesque, n. parodia. a. cómico. v. parodiar
bur·ly, a. membrudo
burn, v. quemar; incendiar. n. quemadura
burn·ing, a. ardiente
bur·nish, n. brillo. v. bruñir
burnt, a. quemado
bur·ro, n. pl. -ros. burro
bur·row, n. madriguera. v. amadrigar
burst, v. reventar; romper. n. reventón; estallido
bur·y, v. enterrar
bus, n. pl. bus·es, bus·ses. autobús
bush, n. arbusto
bush·el, n. medida de áridos
bush·y, a. espeso
busi·ness, n. comercio; oficio; asunto; empresa
bust, n. pecho; busto
bus·tle, v. apresurarse. n. bullicio; polizón
bus·y, a. ocupado; lleno de movimiento. v. ocupar(se)
but, conj. pero; sino; sólo. prep. excepto
butch·er, n. carnicero. v. matar
but·ler, n. mayordomo
butt, n. cabo; blanco. v. topetar
but·ter, n. mantequilla. v. untar con mantequilla
but·ter·fly, n. pl. -flies. mariposa
but·ter·milk, n. leche de manteca
but·ter·y, a. mantecoso
but·tocks, n. pl. nalgas
but·ton, n. botón. v. abotonar
but·tress, n. contrafuerte. v. apoyar
bux·om, a. frescachón
buy, v. comprar. n. compra
buy·er, n. comprador
buzz, v. zumbar; llamar. n. zumbido
buzz·er, n. zumbador
by, prep. por; cerca de; según. adv. cerca
by·gone, a. pasado. n. pl. lo pasado
by·law, n. reglamento
by·prod·uct, n. derivado; producto secundario
by·stand·er, n. espectador
by·way, n. camino apartado
by·word, n. dicho

C

cab, n. taxi, m.; casilla
ca·bal, n. cábala. v. tramar
cab·a·ret, n. cabaret, m.
cab·bage, n. col, f.
cab·by, n. pl. -bies. inf. taxista, m. f.
cab·in, n. cabaña; camarote
cab·i·net, n. vitrina; gabinete
ca·ble, n. cable; cablegrama, m. v. cablegrafiar
ca·ble·gram, n. cablegrama, m.
ca·boose, n. furgón de cola
cache, n. escondite. v. ocultar
cack·le, v. cacarear. n. cacareo
cack·ler, n. cacareador
ca·coph·o·ny, n. pl. -nies. cacofonía
cac·tus, n. pl. -tus·es, -ti. cacto
cad, n. persona mal educada
ca·dav·er, n. cadáver
ca·dav·er·ous, a. cadavérico
cad·dish, a. desvergonzado
ca·dence, n. cadencia; ritmo
ca·det, n. cadete
ca·fe, n. café
caf·e·te·ri·a, n. cafetería
caf·feine, n. cafeína
cage, n. jaula. v. enjaular
ca·jole, v. halagar
ca·jol·er·y, n. pl. -ries. halago
cake, n. tarta; pastel, m.; pastilla. v. endurecer
cal·a·boose, n. inf. cárcel, f.
ca·lam·i·tous, a. calamitoso
ca·lam·i·ty, n. pl. -ties. calamidad
cal·ci·fi·ca·tion, n. calcificación
cal·ci·fy, v. calcificar
cal·ci·um, n. calcio
cal·cu·late, v. calcular
cal·cu·lat·ed, a. calculado; intencionado
cal·cu·lat·ing, a. intrigante
cal·cu·la·tion, n. cálculo
cal·cu·lus, n. pl. -li, -lus·es. cálculo
cal·dron, n. caldera
cal·en·dar, n. calendario
calf, n. pl. calves. becerro; ternero; pantorrilla
cal·i·ber, cal·i·bre, n. calibre; capacidad
cal·i·brate, v. calibrar
cal·i·bra·tion, n. calibración
cal·i·co, n. pl., -coes, -cos. calicó
ca·liph, ca·lif, n. califa
cal·iph·ate, cal·if·ate, n. califato
cal·is·then·ics, n. calistenia
call, v. llamar; nombrar; dar voces. n. llamada; visita
call·ing, n. vocación
cal·lous, a. insensible
cal·low, a. inexperto
cal·lus, n. pl. -lus·es. callo
calm, n. calma. a. tranquilo. v. calmar(se)
ca·lor·ic, a. calórico
cal·o·rie, n. pl. -ries. caloría
ca·lum·ni·ate, v. calumniar
ca·lum·ny, n. pl. -nies. calumnia
ca·lyp·so, n. pl. -sos. calipso

ca·lyx, n. pl., ca·lyx·es, cal·y·ces. cáliz
cam, n. leva
cam·el, n. camello
ca·mel·lia, n. camelia
cam·e·o, n. camafeo
cam·er·a, n. máquina fotográfica; cámara
cam·ou·flage, n. camuflaje. v. camuflar
camp, n. campamento. v. acampar
cam·paign, n. campaña. v. servir en campaña
cam·paign·er, n. veterano; partidario
camp·er, n. campista, m., f.
cam·pus, n. pl., -pus·es. recinto
can, aux. v. could. poder
can, n. lata. v. conservar en latas
ca·nal, n. canal, m.
ca·nar·y, n. canario
can·cel, v. cancelar; anular
can·cel·la·tion, n. cancelación
can·cer, n. cáncer
can·de·la·brum, n. pl., -bra, -brums. candelabro
can·did, a. franco
can·di·da·cy, n. pl. -cies. candidatura
can·di·date, n. aspirante; candidato
can·dle, n. candela; vela
can·dor, n. franqueza
can·dy, n. pl., -dies. dulce; azúcar cande o candi. v. garapiñar
cane, n. caña; bastón
ca·nine, a. canino. n. perro
can·is·ter, n. bote
can·ker, n. llaga gangrenosa
can·na·bis, n. marijuana
can·ner·y, n. pl., -ies. fábrica de conservas
can·ni·bal, n. caníbal, m., f.
can·ni·bal·ism, n. canibalismo
can·non, n. pl., can·nons, can·non. cañón
can·ny, a. prudente; astuto
ca·noe, n. canoa. v. ir en canoa
can·on, n. canon
can·on·i·za·tion, n. canonización
can·on·ize, v. canonizar
can·o·py, n. pl., -pies. dosel; baldaquín
cant, n. hipocresía; jerga; sesgo
can·ta·loup, can·ta·loupe, can·ta·lope, n. cantalupo
can·tan·ker·ous, a. malhumorado
can·teen, n. cantina; cantimplora
can·ter, n. medio galope
can·vas, n. lona; tela; lienzo
can·vass, v. solicitar; discutir. n. sondeo
can·vass·er, n. solicitador
can·yon, n. cañón
cap, n. gorra; tapa. v. poner tapa; superar
ca·pa·bil·i·ty, n. pl., -ties. capacidad
ca·pa·ble, a. capaz
ca·pac·i·ty, n. pl., -ties. capacidad
cape, n. cabo; capa
ca·per, n. cabriola; travesura. v. brincar
cap·il·lar·y, n. pl., -ies. vaso capilar. a. capilar
cap·i·tal, n. capital; principal. n. capital, m.; f. mayúscula
cap·i·tal·ism, n. capitalismo
cap·i·tal·ist, n. capitalista, m., f.
cap·i·tal·is·tic, a. capitalista
cap·i·tal·ize, v. capitalizar
cap·i·tol, n. capitolio
ca·pit·u·late, v. capitular
ca·price, n. capricho
ca·pri·cious, a. caprichoso
cap·size, v. volcar
cap·sule, n. cápsula. v. capitanear
cap·tain, n. capitán. n. encabezamiento; título
cap·tion, n. cautivar
cap·ti·vate, v. encanto
cap·tive, a., n. cautivo
cap·tiv·i·ty, n. pl., -ties. cautiverio
cap·tor, n. apresador
cap·ture, v. apresar; capturar
car, n. automóvil; coche
car·a·mel, n. caramelo
car·at, n. quilate
car·a·van, n. caravana; remolque
car·a·way, n. alcaravea
car·bine, n. carabina. Also **car·a·bine**
car·bon, n. carbono
car·bon·ate, n. carbonato
car·bon di·ox·ide, n. bióxido de carbono
car·bon mon·ox·ide, n. monóxido de carbono
car·bon pa·per, n. papel carbón
car·bun·cle, n. carbunco
car·bu·re·tor, n. carburador
car·cass, car·case, n. res muerta
car·ci·no·ma, n. pl., -mas, -ma·ta. carcinoma, m.
card, n. tarjeta; carta; pl. naipes
card·board, n. cartón
car·di·ac, a. cardiaco; cardíaco
car·di·gan, n. jersey; rebeca
car·di·nal, a. cardinal. n. cardenal, m.; a. cardinal
care, v. cuidar; importar. n. cuidado; solicitud; cargo
ca·reer, n. carrera
care·free, a. despreocupado
care·ful, a. cuidadoso; vigilante
care·less, a. descuidado
care·tak·er, n. vigilante; guardián
car·go, n. pl., -goes, -gos. cargamento
car·i·bou, n. pl., -bous, -bou. caribú, m.
car·i·ca·ture, n. caricatura. v.

parodiar
car·il·lon, n. carillón
car·nage, n. carnicería
car·nal, a. carnal
car·nal·i·ty, n. carnalidad
car·na·tion, n. clavel, m.
car·ni·val, n. carnaval, m.
car·niv·o·rous, a. carnívoro
car·ol, n. villancico
ca·rouse, n. jarana. v. jaranear
ca·rous·er, n. jaranero
carp, n. pl., carp, carps. carpa. v. criticar
car·pen·ter, n. carpintero
car·pen·try, n. carpintería
car·pet, n. alfombra. v. alfombrar
car·riage, n. porte; carruaje; vagón
car·ri·er, n. portador; carrero
car·ri·on, n. carroña
car·rot, n. zanahoria
car·ry, v. llevar; tener consigo; transportar; lograr
cart, n. carro. v. acarrear
cart·age, n. carretaje; acarreo
car·ti·lage, n. cartílago
car·tog·ra·pher, n. cartógrafo
car·tog·ra·phy, n. cartografía
car·ton, n. caja de cartón
car·toon, n. dibujo cómico
car·toon·ist, n. dibujante, m., f.
car·tridge, n. cartucho
carve, v. esculpir; trinchar
cas·cade, n. cascada
case, n. caso; caja; estuche. v. encajonar
cash, n. dinero contante. v. cobrar
cash·ew, n. anacardo
cash·ier, n. cajero
cash·mere, n. casimir
cas·ing, n. cubierta; envoltura
ca·si·no, n. pl., -nos. casino
cask, n. barril, m.; tonel, m.
cas·ket, n. cajita; ataúd, m.
cas·se·role, n. cacerola
cas·sock, n. sotana
cast, v. echar; tirar; dar; repartir; fundir. n. reparto; molde; echada casta
cas·ta·nets, n. pl. castañuelas
caste, n. casta
cast·er, n. rodaja
cas·ti·gate, v. castigar
cas·ti·ga·tion, n. castigo
cas·ti·ga·tor, n. castigador
cast i·ron, n. hierro fundido
cast-i·ron, a. de hierro fundido; inflexible
cas·tle, n. castillo; (chess) torre, f.
cast·off, a. de desecho. n. cosa desechada
cas·tor, n. castóreo
cas·trate, v. castrar
cas·tra·tion, n. castración
cas·u·al, a. fortuito; despreocupado
cas·u·al·ly, adv. casualmente
cas·u·al·ty, n. pl., -ties. accidente; víctima; baja
cat, n. gato
cat·a·clysm, n. cataclismo
cat·a·comb, n. usu. pl. catacumbas
cat·a·log, cat·a·logue, n. catálogo. v. catalogar
cat·a·lyst, n. catalizador
cat·a·pult, n. catapulta. v. catapultar
cat·a·ract, n. catarata
ca·tarrh, n. catarro
ca·tas·tro·phe, n. catástrofe, f.
cat·a·stroph·ic, a. catastrófico
catch, v. coger; prender; enganchar. n. cogida; captura; trampa
catch·ing, a. contagioso
cat·e·chism, n. catequismo
cat·e·gor·i·cal, a. categórico
cat·e·gor·i·cal·ly, adv. categóricamente
cat·e·go·rize, v. clasificar
cat·e·go·ry, n. pl., -ries. categoría
ca·ter, v. atender; proveer
ca·ter·er, n. abastecedor
cat·er·pil·lar, n. oruga
cat·gut, n. cuerda de tripa
ca·thar·sis, n. pl., -ses. catarsis, f.
ca·thar·tic, a. n. catártico; purgante
ca·the·dral, n. catedral, f.
ca·thol·ic, a. católico. n. (cap.) católico
ca·thol·i·cism, n. catolicismo
cat·kin, n. amento
cat·nap, n. duermevela. v. dormitar
cat·sup, n. salsa picante de tomate
cat·tle, n. ganado
cat·tle·man, n. pl., -men. ganadero
cat·ty, a. rencoroso
cau·cus, n. pl., -cus·es. reunión de partido
caul·dron, cal·dron, n. caldera
cau·li·flow·er, n. coliflor, f.
caulk, calk, v. calafatear
cause, n. causa; razón; interés, m. v. causar
cause·way, n. calzada
caus·tic, a. n. cáustico
cau·ter·ize, v. cauterizar
cau·tion, n. cautela; prudencia. v. advertir; amonestar
cau·tious, a. cauteloso
cav·al·cade, n. cabalgata
cav·a·lier, n. caballero. a. desdeñoso
cav·al·ry, n. pl., -ries. caballería
cav·al·ry·man, n. pl., -men. soldado de caballería
cave, n. cueva. v. hundirse
cav·ern, n. caverna
cav·ern·ous, a. cavernoso
cav·i·ar, cav·i·are, n. caviar
cav·il, v. sutilizar
cav·i·ty, n. pl., -ties. cavidad; hoyo
ca·vort, v. inf. hacer cabriolas

cay·enne, *n.* pimentón
cease, *v.* cesar; dejar de; suspender
cease-fire, *n.* alto el fuego; tregua
cease·less, *a.* incesante
ce·dar, *n.* cedro
cede, *v.* ceder
ceil·ing, *n.* techo; límite
cel·e·brate, *v.* celebrar; solemnizar
cel·e·brat·ed, *a.* célebre
cel·e·bra·tion, *n.* celebración; fiesta
ce·leb·ri·ty, *n. pl.* **-ties**. celebridad
ce·ler·i·ty, *n.* celeridad
cel·er·y, *n.* apio
ce·les·tial, *a.* celestial
cel·i·ba·cy, *n.* celibato
cel·i·bate, *n., a.* celibato; célibe
cell, *n.* celda; célula
cel·lar, *n.* sótano
cel·list, *n.* violoncelista, violon-
   chelista, *m.; f.*
cel·lo, *n. pl.* **-los**. violoncelo,
   violonchelo
cel·lo·phane, *n.* celofán
cel·lu·lar, *a.* celular
cel·lu·lose, *n.* celulosa
ce·ment, *n.* cemento. *v.* cementar
cem·e·ter·y, *n. pl.* **-ies**. cementerio
cen·sor, *n.* censor. *v.* censurar
cen·sor·ship, *n.* censura
cen·sur·a·ble, *a.* censurable
cen·sure, *n.* censura; crítica. *v.* censurar; culpar
cen·sus, *n. pl.* **-sus·es**. censo
cent, *n.* centavo
cen·taur, *n.* centauro
cen·ten·ni·al, *a., n.* centenario
cen·ter, *n.* centro. *v.* centrar; concentrar
cen·ti·grade, *a.* centígrado. Also
   Cel·sius
cen·ti·me·ter, *n.* centímetro
cen·tral, *a.* central; céntrico
cen·tral·ize, *v.* centralizar
cen·tu·ri·on, *n.* centurión
cen·tu·ry, *n. pl.* **-ries**. siglo
ce·ram·ic, *a.* cerámico
ce·ram·ics, *n.* cerámica
ce·re·al, *n.* cereal, *m.;* grano
cer·e·bral, *a.* cerebral
cer·e·mo·ni·al, *n., a.* ceremonial
cer·e·mo·ni·ous, *a.* ceremonioso
cer·e·mo·ny, *n. pl.* **-nies**. ceremonia
ce·rise, *n., a.* color de cereza
cer·tain, *a.* cierto; seguro
cer·tain·ly, *adv.* ciertamente; desde
   luego
cer·tain·ty, *n. pl.* **-ties**. certidumbre,
   f.
cer·ti·fi·a·ble, *a.* certificable
cer·tif·i·cate, *n.* certificado; testimonio; partida
cer·ti·fy, *v.* certificar
cer·ti·tude, *n.* certidumbre, *f.;* cer-
   teza
ces·sa·tion, *n.* cesación; cese
ces·sion, *n.* cesión
chafe, *v.* frotar; rozar; irritar
chaff, *n.* ahechadura. *v.* tomar el pelo
   a
cha·grin, *n.* mortificación. *v.* disgustar
chain, *n.* cadena. *v.* encadenar
chair, *n.* silla
chair·man, *n. pl.* **-men**. presidente
chal·et, *n.* chalet, *m.*
chal·ice, *n.* cáliz, *m.*
chalk, *n.* tiza; creta
chal·lenge, *n.* desafío; demanda;
   recusación. *v.* desafiar; recusar
cham·ber, *n.* cuarto; cámara;
   recámara
cham·ber·maid, *n.* camarera
cha·me·le·on, *n.* camaleón
cham·ois, *n. pl.* **cham·ois**. gamuza
cham·pagne, *n.* champán, champaña
cham·pi·on, *n.* campeón; paladín
chance, *n.* suerte; casualidad; riesgo.
   v. acontecer; probar
chan·cel·lor, *n.* canciller
chan·de·lier, *n.* araña de luces
change, *v.* cambiar; trocar; transformar. *n.* cambio
chan·nel, *n.* canal, *m.;* cauce
chant, *v.* cantar. *n.* canto llano
chan·ti·cleer, *n.* gallo
cha·os, *n.* caos, *m.*
cha·ot·ic, *a.* caótico
chap, *v.* agrietar(se). *n.* grieta
chap, *n.* tío; mozo
chap·el, *n.* capilla
chap·e·ron, **chap·er·one**, *n.* carabina; dueña
chap·lain, *n.* capellán
chap·ter, *n.* capítulo
char, *v.* carbonizar
char·ac·ter, *n.* carácter; personaje
char·ac·ter·is·tic, *a.* característico.
   n. característica
char·ac·ter·i·za·tion, *n.* caracteriza-
   ción
char·ac·ter·ize, *v.* caracterizar
cha·rade, *n.* charada
char·coal, *n.* carbón vegetal
charge, *v.* cargar; imponer; acusar;
   pedir; atacar. *n.* carga; cargo;
   acusación
char·i·ot, *n.* carroza; carro
char·i·ot·eer, *n.* auriga, *m.*
char·i·ta·ble, *a.* caritativo
char·i·ty, *n. pl.* **-ties**. caridad
char·la·tan, *n.* charlatán
charm, *n.* encanto; hechizo; amuleto.
   v. encantar; hechizar
chart, *n.* gráfico; carta de navegar. *v.*
   poner en una carta
char·ter, *n.* cédula; carta. *v.* estatuir;
   alquilar
chase, *v.* cazar; perseguir. *n.* persecu-

chasm, *n.* sima
chas·sis, *n.* chasis
chaste, *a.* casto
chaste·ly, *adv.* castamente
chas·tise, *v.* castigar
chas·tise·ment, *n.* castigo
chas·ti·ty, *n.* castidad
chat, *v.* charlar. *n.* charla
chat·tel, *n.* enseres, *m.*
chat·ter, *v.* charlar; castañetear. *v.*
   cháchara
chauf·feur, *n.* chófer
cheap, *a.* barato; cursi. *adv.* barato
cheap·en, *v.* abaratar
cheap·ly, *adv.* barato
cheat, *v.* defraudar; engañar. *n.* trampa; petardista, *m., f.*
check, *n.* parada; impedimento;
   cheque; cuenta; marca; cuadro. *v.*
   parar; examinar
check·mate, *n.* mate; derrota. *v.* dar
   jaque mate
cheek, *n.* mejilla
cheek·y, *a.* descarado
cheer, *n.* alegría; aplauso. *v.* alegrar;
   aplaudir
cheer·ful, *a.* alegre
cheer·less, *a.* triste
cheese, *n.* queso
chef, *n.* cocinero
chem·i·cal, *a.* químico
chem·ist, *n.* químico
chem·is·try, *n.* química
cher·ish, *v.* querer; cuidar
cher·ry, *n. pl.* **-ries**. cereza; cerezo
cher·ub, *n. pl.* **-ubs**, **-u·bim**. queru-
   bín
chess, *n.* ajedrez, *m.*
chess·man, *n. pl.* **-men**. pieza
chest, *n.* pecho; cofre
chew, *v.* mascar
chic, *a.* elegante
chi·can·er·y, *n. pl.* **-ies**. sofistería;
   sofismas, *m. pl.*
chick, *n.* polluelo
chick·en, *n.* pollo; gallina
chic·o·ry, *n. pl.* **-ries**. achicoria
chide, *v.* reprobar; reprender
chief, *a.* principal. *n.* jefe; cacique
chief·tain, *n.* cacique
chif·fon, *n.* gasa
chil·blain, *n.* sabañón
child, *n. pl.* **chil·dren**. niño; hijo
child·hood, *n.* niñez
child·ish, *a.* infantil; aniñado
chil·i, **chil·li**, **chil·e**, *n. pl.* **-ies**, **-lies**,
   -es. chile
chill, *n.* frío; escalofrío. *v.* enfriar
chill·y, *a.* frío
chime, *n.* juego de campanas. *v.* repicar
chi·me·ra, **chi·mae·ra**, *n.* quimera
chi·mer·ic, *a.* quimérico
chim·ney, *n.* chimenea
chim·pan·zee, *n.* chimpancé. Also
   chimp
chin, *n.* barba
chi·na, *n.* porcelana; china
chin·chil·la, *n.* chinchilla
chink, *n.* grieta. *v.* hender(se); sonar
chintz·y, *a.* barato
chip, *v.* picar; astillar. *n.* astilla
chi·rop·o·dist, *n.* pedicuro
chirp, *n.* gorjeo. *v.* piar; chirriar
chis·el, *n.* cincel, *m.;* formón. *v.* esco-
   plear; timar
chiv·al·rous, *a.* caballeroso
chiv·al·ry, *n. pl.* **-ries**. caballe-
   rosidad
chlo·rine, *n.* cloro
chlo·ro·phyll, **chlo·ro·phyl**, *n.* clo-
   rofila
choc·o·late, *n.* chocolate
choice, *n.* selección; preferencia. *a.*
   selecto
choir, *n.* coro
choke, *v.* estrangular; sofocar; obstruir
chol·er, *n.* cólera
chol·er·a, *n.* cólera
chol·er·ic, *a.* colérico
choose, *v.* escoger; elegir
chop, *v.* cortar; picar. *n.* chuleta
chop·py, *a.* picado
cho·ral, *a.* coral
cho·rale, *n.* coral, *m.*
chord, *n.* acorde
cho·re·og·ra·pher, *n.* coreógrafo
cho·re·og·ra·phy, *n.* coreografía
chor·is·ter, *n.* corista, *m.*
chor·tle, *v.* reírse entre dientes. *n.*
   risita
cho·rus, *n. pl.* **-rus·es**. coro; estribillo
cho·sen, *a.* escogido; preferido
chow·der, *n.* sopa de pescado
Christ, *n.* Cristo
chris·ten, *v.* bautizar
Chris·ten·dom, *n.* cristiandad
chris·ten·ing, *n.* bautismo
Chris·tian, *n., a.* cristiano
Chris·ti·an·i·ty, *n. pl.* **-ties**. cris-
   tianismo
Christ·mas, *n.* Navidad
chro·mat·ic, *a.* cromático
chrome, *n.* cromo
chro·mo·some, *n.* cromosoma, *m.*
chron·ic, *a.* crónico
chron·i·cle, *n.* crónica. *v.* historiar
chron·i·cler, *n.* cronista, *m.*
chron·o·log·i·cal, *a.* cronológico
chro·nol·o·gy, *n. pl.* **-gies**. crono-
   logía
chro·nom·e·ter, *n.* cronómetro
chrys·a·lis, *n. pl.* **-lis·es**, **chry·sal·i·**
   des. crisálida
chry·san·the·mum, *n.* crisantemo

chub·by, *a.* regordete; rechoncho
chuck, *v.* dar la mamola; arrojar
chuck·le, *v.* reír entre dientes
chum, *n.* compinche
chum·my, *a.* íntimo
chump, *n.* tonto
chunk, *n.* pedazo grueso
church, *n.* iglesia
churl·ish, *a.* grosero; rudo
churn, *n.* mantequera. *v.* batir; agitar
chute, *n.* tolva
ci·der, *n.* sidra
ci·gar, *n.* puro
cig·a·rette, **cig·a·ret**, *n.* cigarrillo;
   pitillo
cinch, *n.* cincha
cin·der, *n.* carbonilla; *pl.* cenizas
cin·e·ma, *n. pl.* **-mas**. cine
cin·na·mon, *n.* canela
ci·pher, *n.* cero; cifra. *v.* cifrar
cir·cle, *n.* círculo; ciclo. *v.* rodear;
   dar vueltas
cir·cuit, *n.* gira; circuito
cir·cu·lar, *a., n.* circular
cir·cu·late, *v.* hacer circular; divulgar; esparcir; circular
cir·cu·la·tion, *n.* circulación
cir·cum·cise, *v.* circuncidar
cir·cum·ci·sion, *n.* circuncisión
cir·cum·fer·ence, *n.* circunferencia
cir·cum·lo·cu·tion, *n.* circunlocu-
   ción
cir·cum·nav·i·gate, *v.* circunnavegar
cir·cum·scribe, *v.* circunscribir; limitar
cir·cum·spect, *a.* circunspecto
cir·cum·stance, *n.* circunstancia; *pl.*
   situación económica
cir·cum·stan·tial, *a.* circunstan-
   ciado; secundario
cir·cus, *n. pl.* **-cus·es**. circo
cir·rho·sis, *n.* cirrosis, *f.*
cir·rus, *n. pl.* **cir·ri**. cirro
cis·tern, *n.* tanque; cisterna
cit·a·del, *n.* ciudadela
ci·ta·tion, *n.* cita; citación
cite, *v.* citar
cit·i·zen, *n.* ciudadano
cit·i·zen·ry, *n. pl.* **-ries**. ciudadanos
cit·ric ac·id, *n.* ácido cítrico
cit·y, *n. pl.* **-ies**. ciudad
civ·ic, *a.* cívico
civ·il, *a.* civil; cortés
ci·vil·ian, *a.* civil. *n.* civil, *m., f.*
ci·vil·i·ty, *n. pl.* **-ties**. cortesía;
   civilidad
civ·i·li·za·tion, *n.* civilización
civ·i·lize, *v.* civilizar
civ·il war, *n.* guerra civil
clad, *a.* vestido
claim, *v.* reclamar; demandar. *n.*
   demanda; reclamación
claim·ant, *n.* demandante, *m., f.*
clair·voy·ance, *n.* clarividencia
clair·voy·ant, *a.* vidente, *m., f.*
clam, *n.* almeja
clam·or, *n.* clamor. *v.* vociferar
clam·or·ous, *a.* clamoroso
clamp, *n.* abrazadera; grapa. *v.* sujetar; juntar
clan, *n.* clan
clan·des·tine, *a.* clandestino
clang, *n.* sonido metálico. *v.* hacer
   sonar
clap, *v.* aplaudir; batir. *n.* palmada;
   palmoteo
claret, *n.* clarete
clar·i·fi·ca·tion, *n.* clarificación;
   aclaración
clar·i·fy, *v.* clarificar; aclarar
clar·i·net, *n.* clarinete
clar·i·ty, *n.* claridad
clash, *v.* chocar; batir. *n.* fragor;
   choque; conflicto
clasp, *n.* broche; corchete; abrazo. *v.*
   abrochar; abrazar
class, *n.* clase, *f.* *v.* clasificar
clas·sic, *a.* clásico. *n.* autor clásico;
   pl. obras clásicas
clas·si·cal, *a.* clásico
clas·si·fi·ca·tion, *n.* clasificación
clas·si·fied, *a.* secreto
clas·si·fy, *v.* clasificar
clat·ter, *v.* hacer ruido. *n.* ruido;
   martilleo
clause, *n.* cláusula
claw, *n.* garra; uña. *v.* desgarrar
clay, *n.* arcilla; barro
clean, *a.* limpio; neto. *v.* limpiar
clean·li·ness, *n.* limpieza
clean·ly, *a.* aseado
cleanse, *v.* limpiar; purificar
clear, *a.* claro; transparente; inocente; despejado. *v.* aclarar; despe-
   jar; absolver
clear·ance, *n.* despacho de aduana;
   espacio muerto
clear·ing, *n.* claro
clear·ly, *adv.* claramente
clear·ness, *n.* claridad
cleave, *v.* hender; partir; pegarse; ad-
   herir
clef, *n.* clave, *f.*
cleft, *n.* hendedura
clem·en·cy, *n.* clemencia
clem·ent, *a.* clemente; piadoso
clench, *v.* apretar
cler·gy, *n. pl.* **-gies**. clero
cler·i·cal, *a.* clerical; de oficina
clerk, *n.* oficinista, *m., f.;* dependiente
clev·er, *a.* listo; ingenioso
clev·er·ness, *n.* destreza
click, *n.* golpe seco. *v.* chasquear
cli·ent, *n.* cliente, *m., f.*
cliff, *n.* risco
cli·mate, *n.* clima, *m.*
cli·max, *n.* clímax, *m.;* colmo

climb, *v.* trepar
clinch, *v.* afianzar; agarrar
cling, *v.* adherirse
clin·ic, *n.* clínica
clin·i·cal, *a.* clínico
clip, *v.* cortar; acortar. *n.* tijeretada;
   golpe
clique, *n.* pandilla
cloak, *n.* capa; manto. *v.* encapotar;
   encubrir
clock, *n.* reloj, *m.*
clock·wise, *adv., a.* en la dirección de
   las agujas o manecillas del reloj
clog, *v.* impedir; atascar. *n.* obstáculo; zueco
clois·ter, *n.* claustro. *v.* enclaustrar
close, *v.* cerrar; terminar. *n.* fin
close, *a.* sofocante; cercano; denso.
   adv. cerca
close·ness, *n.* proximidad; reserva;
   intimidad
clos·et, *n.* armario. *v.* estar encerrado
   con; deliberar en secreto
clot, *n.* grumo. *v.* cuajarse
cloth, *n. pl.* **cloths**. tela; paño
clothe, *v.* vestir
clothes, *n. pl.* ropa
cloth·ing, *n.* vestidos; ropa
cloud, *n.* nube, *f.* *v.* anublar(se); nu-
   blar
cloud·i·ness, *n.* nubosidad
cloud·y, *a.* nuboso
clove, *n.* clavo de especia; diente (de
   ajo)
clo·ver, *n.* trébol, *m.*
clown, *n.* payaso. *v.* hacer el payaso
cloy, *v.* empalagar
club, *n.* porra; club; *pl.* bastos. *v.*
   aporrear
cluck, *v.* cloquear
clue, *n.* pista; indicio
clum·si·ness, *n.* torpeza
clum·sy, *a.* torpe; pesado
clus·ter, *n.* racimo. *v.* agruparse
clutch, *v.* agarrar; apretar. *n.* agarro;
   embrague
clut·ter, *n.* desorden. *v.* atestar
coach, *n.* coche; carroza; vagón; en-
   trenador. *v.* preparar
co·ag·u·late, *v.* coagular(se)
co·ag·u·la·tion, *n.* coagulación
coal, *n.* carbón
co·a·lesce, *v.* unir(se)
co·a·les·cence, *n.* fusión
co·a·li·tion, *n.* coalición; alianza
coarse, *a.* basto; tosco; grosero
coars·en, *v.* curtir(se)
coast, *n.* costa. *v.* ir en punto muerto
coast·line, *n.* litoral, *m.*
coat, *n.* abrigo; pelo; mano, *f.* *v.* cubrir
coat·ing, *n.* capa
coax, *v.* engatusar
cob, *n.* mazorca de maíz; jaca
co·balt, *n.* cobalto
cob·ble, *v.* remendar
cob·bler, *n.* zapatero
co·bra, *n.* cobra
cob·web, *n.* telaraña
co·caine, *n.* cocaína
cock, *n.* gallo; grifo. *v.* amartillar
cock·a·too, *n. pl.* **-toos**. cacatúa
cock·roach, *n.* cucaracha
cock·tail, *n.* coctel, *m.*
cock·y, *a.* engreído
co·coa, *n.* cacao; chocolate
co·co·nut, **co·coa·nut**, *n.* coco
co·coon, *n.* capullo
cod, *n. pl.* **cod**, **cods**. bacalao
cod·dle, *v.* mimar
code, *n.* código; cifra. *v.* cifrar
cod·fish, *n.* bacalao
cod·i·fy, *v.* codificar
co·ed, *n.* alumna de una escuela co-
   educacional
co·ed·u·ca·tion, *n.* coeducación
co·erce, *v.* forzar; coercer
co·er·cion, *n.* coerción; compulsión
co·er·cive, *a.* coactivo
cof·fee, *n.* café
cof·fin, *n.* ataúd, *m.*
cog, *n.* diente de rueda
co·gen·cy, *n.* fuerza
co·gent, *a.* convincente
cog·i·tate, *v.* meditar
cog·nac, *n.* coñac, *m.*
cog·ni·zance, *n.* conocimiento
co·here, *v.* adherirse
co·her·ence, *n.* coherencia
co·her·ent, *a.* coherente; lógico
co·he·sive, *a.* cohesivo
coif·fure, *n.* peinado
coil, *v.* arrollar. *n.* carrete; rollo; adujada. *v.*
   arrollar
coin, *n.* moneda. *v.* acuñar
coin·age, *n.* acuñación; invención
co·in·cide, *v.* coincidir
co·in·ci·dence, *n.* coincidencia;
   casualidad
co·in·ci·den·tal, *a.* coincidente
co·i·tus, *n.* coito
coke, *n.* coque
cold, *a.* frío. *n.* frío; resfriado
cold-blood·ed, *a.* de sangre fría
cold·ness, *n.* frialdad
cole·slaw, *n.* ensalada de col
col·ic, *n.* cólico
col·i·se·um, *n.* coliseo
col·lab·o·rate, *v.* colaborar
col·lab·o·ra·tion, *n.* colaboración
col·lapse, *v.* hundirse. *n.* derrum-
   bamiento; colapso
col·lar, *n.* cuello
col·lat·er·al, *a.* colateral. *n.* resguardo
col·league, *n.* colega, *m., f.*
col·lect, *v.* recaudar; reunir; colec-

col·lec·tion, *n.* colección; cobro
col·lec·tive, *a.* colectivo
col·lege, *n.* colegio
col·le·gi·ate, *a.* colegiado
col·lide, *v.* chocar
col·li·sion, *n.* choque
col·lo·qui·al, *a.* familiar
col·lo·qui·al·ism, *n.* expresión familiar
col·lu·sion, *n.* colusión; confabula-
   ción
co·lon, *n. pl.* **-lons**, **-la**. colon; dos
   puntos
colo·nel, *n.* coronel
co·lo·ni·al, *a.* colonial
col·o·nist, *n.* colonizador
col·o·ni·za·tion, *n.* colonización
col·o·nade, *n.* columnata
col·o·ny, *n. pl.* **-nies**. colonia
col·or, *n.* color; *usu. pl.* bandera. *v.*
   colorear; teñir
col·or·ful, *a.* lleno de color
co·los·sal, *a.* colosal
co·los·sus, *n. pl.* **-si**, **-sus·es**. coloso
colt, *n.* potro
col·umn, *n.* columna
col·umn·ist, *n.* columnista, *m., f.*
co·ma, *n. pl.* **-mas**. coma, *m.*
co·ma·tose, *a.* comatoso
comb, *n.* peine. *v.* peinar
com·bat, *v.* combatir. *n.* combate
com·bat·ant, *a., n.* combatiente
com·bi·na·tion, *n.* combinación
com·bine, *v.* combinar; reunir. *n.*
   asociación
com·bus·ti·ble, *n.* combustible
com·bus·tion, *n.* combustión
come, *v.* venir; aparecer; llegar
co·me·di·an, *n.* cómico
co·me·di·enne, *n.* cómica
com·e·dy, *n. pl.* **-dies**. comedia
come·ly, *a.* gentil
com·et, *n.* cometa, *m.*
com·fort, *v.* confortar; consolar. *n.*
   consuelo
com·fort·a·ble, *a.* cómodo
com·fort·er, *n.* colcha
com·fy, *a. inf.* cómodo
com·ic, *a., n.* cómico
com·i·cal, *a.* cómico
com·ic strip, *n.* tebeo
com·ma, *n. pl.* **-mas**. coma
com·mand, *v.* mandar; comandar. *n.*
   mando; orden
com·man·deer, *v.* requisar
com·mand·er, *n.* comandante
com·mand·ment, *n.* mandamiento;
   mandato
com·mem·o·rate, *v.* conmemorar
com·mem·o·ra·tion, *n.* conmemora-
   ción
com·mence, *v.* comenzar
com·mence·ment, *n.* comienzo;
   graduación
com·mend, *v.* alabar; encomendar
com·men·da·tion, *n.* encomio
com·ment, *v.* comentar. *n.* observación
com·men·tar·y, *n. pl.* **-ies**. comen-
   tario
com·men·ta·tor, *n.* comentador
com·merce, *n.* comercio
com·mer·cial, *a.* comercial
com·mis·sar·y, *n. pl.* **-ies**. comisario
com·mis·sion, *n.* comisión; perpetra-
   ción; nombrar; encargar
com·mis·sion·er, *n.* comisario;
   apoderado
com·mit, *v.* cometer; entregar
com·mit·ment, *n.* compromiso
com·mit·tee, *n.* comité
com·mod·i·ty, *n. pl.* **-ties**. merca-
   dería
com·mon, *a.* común; corriente; vulgar
com·mon·place, *n.* lugar común. *a.*
   trivial
com·mon·wealth, *n.* república; estado
com·mo·tion, *n.* tumulto
com·mune, *v.* conversar
com·mu·ni·ca·ble, *a.* comunicable
com·mu·ni·cate, *v.* comunicar(se)
com·mu·ni·ca·tion, *n.* comunicación
com·mun·ion, *n.* comunión
com·mu·nism, *n.* comunismo
com·mu·nist, *n.* comunista, *m., f.*
com·mu·ni·ty, *n. pl.* **-ties**. comuni-
   dad
com·mute, *v.* conmutar
com·pact, *n.* pacto. *a.* compacto;
   breve
com·pan·ion, *n.* compañero
com·pa·ny, *n. pl.* **-nies**. compañía;
   sociedad
com·pa·ra·ble, *a.* comparable
com·par·a·tive, *a.* relativo
com·pare, *v.* comparar
com·par·i·son, *n.* comparación
com·part·ment, *n.* compartimiento
com·pass, *n.* brújula; compás, *m.;* extensión
com·pas·sion, *n.* compasión
com·pas·sion·ate, *a.* compasivo
com·pat·i·ble, *a.* compatible
com·pa·tri·ot, *n.* compatriota, *m., f.*
com·pel, *v.* obligar; forzar
com·pen·sate, *v.* compensar; indem-
   nizar
com·pen·sa·tion, *n.* compensación
com·pete, *v.* competir
com·pe·tence, *n.* competencia;
   capacidad
com·pe·tent, *a.* competente
com·pe·ti·tion, *n.* competencia
com·pet·i·tive, *a.* de competencia
com·pet·i·tor, *n.* competidor

com·pi·la·tion, *n.* compilación
com·pile, *v.* compilar
com·pla·cence, *n.* suficiencia. Also
   com·pla·cen·cy
com·plain, *v.* quejarse
com·plaint, *n.* queja
com·ple·ment, *n.* complemento
com·plete, *a.* completo; acabado. *v.*
   completar; terminar
com·ple·tion, *n.* terminación
com·plex, *n., a.* complejo
com·plex·ion, *n.* cutis, *m.*
com·plex·i·ty, *n. pl.* **-ties**. complejidad
com·pli·ance, *n.* sumisión
com·pli·ant, *a.* condescendiente
com·pli·cate, *v.* complicar
com·pli·cat·ed, *a.* complicado
com·pli·ca·tion, *n.* complicación
com·pli·ment, *n.* cumplido; piropo.
   v. cumplimentar
com·pli·men·ta·ry, *a.* lisonjero;
   gratuito
com·ply, *v.* cumplir; obedecer
com·po·nent, *a.* componente
com·pose, *v.* componer; redactar;
   calmar
com·pos·ite, *a., n.* compuesto
com·po·si·tion, *n.* composición
com·po·sure, *n.* serenidad
com·pound, *v.* componer. *a.* compuesto. *n.* compuesto; mezcla
com·pre·hend, *v.* comprender
com·pre·hen·sion, *n.* comprensión
com·pre·hen·sive, *a.* extenso
com·press, *v.* comprimir. *n.* com-
   presa
com·pres·sion, *n.* compresión
com·prise, *v.* comprender; abarcar
com·pro·mise, *n.* arreglo. *v.* comprometer; transigir
comp·trol·ler, *n.* interventor
com·pul·sion, *n.* fuerza; coacción
com·pul·so·ry, *a.* obligatorio
com·punc·tion, *n.* remordimiento
com·pu·ta·tion, *n.* cómputo
com·pute, *v.* computar
com·put·er, *n.* computador
com·rade, *n.* camarada, *m., f.*
con, *adv.* contra
con·cave, *a.* cóncavo
con·ceal, *v.* ocultar
con·cede, *v.* conceder
con·ceit, *n.* presunción; amor propio
con·ceit·ed, *a.* vanidoso
con·ceiv·a·ble, *a.* concebible
con·ceive, *v.* concebir; imaginar
con·cen·trate, *v.* concentrar(se)
con·cen·tra·tion, *n.* concentración
con·cept, *n.* concepto
con·cep·tion, *n.* concepción; idea
con·cep·tu·al, *a.* conceptual
con·cern, *v.* interesar; concernir. *n.*
   preocupación; asunto
con·cerned, *a.* inquieto
con·cern·ing, *prep.* acerca de
con·cert, *n.* concierto
con·ces·sion, *n.* concesión
con·cil·i·ate, *v.* conciliar
con·cil·i·a·tion, *n.* conciliación
con·cise, *a.* conciso
con·clude, *v.* concluir
con·clu·sion, *n.* conclusión
con·coct, *v.* tramar; confeccionar
con·coc·tion, *n.* mezcla
con·cord, *n.* concordia
con·course, *n.* concurso
con·crete, *a.* concreto; de hormigon.
   n. hormigón
con·cu·bine, *n.* concubina
con·cur, *v.* estar de acuerdo; concu-
   rrir
con·cur·rent, *a.* concurrente
con·cus·sion, *n.* conmoción
con·demn, *v.* condenar
con·dem·na·tion, *n.* condenación
con·dense, *v.* condensar; abreviar
con·den·sa·tion, *n.* condensación
con·de·scend, *v.* dignarse
con·di·ment, *n.* condimento
con·di·tion, *n.* condición. *v.* condi-
   cionar
con·di·tion·al, *a.* condicional
con·do·lence, *n.* pésame; con-
   dolencia
con·done, *v.* condonar
con·du·cive, *a.* conducente
con·duct, *v.* conducir; dirigir. *n.* conducta
con·duc·tor, *n.* director; cobrador
con·duit, *n.* conducto
cone, *n.* cono
con·fec·tion, *n.* dulce; confección
con·fed·er·a·cy, *n. pl.* **-cies**. confederación
con·fed·er·ate, *a., n.* confederado
con·fed·er·a·tion, *n.* confederación
con·fer, *v.* otorgar; conferenciar
con·fer·ence, *n.* conferencia
con·fess, *v.* confesar
con·fes·sion, *n.* confesión
con·fes·sion·al, *n.* confesonario
con·fes·sor, *n.* confesor
con·fet·ti, *n.* confeti, *m.*
con·fide, *v.* confiar
con·fi·dence, *n.* confianza
con·fi·dent, *a.* seguro
con·fi·den·tial, *a.* confidencial
con·fig·u·ra·tion, *n.* configuración;
   aspecto
con·fine, *n. usu. pl.* confín. *v.* limitar;
   encerrar
con·fine·ment, *n.* prisión
con·firm, *v.* confirmar; verificar
con·fir·ma·tion, *n.* confirmación
con·firmed, *a.* inveterado; fijo
con·fis·cate, *v.* confiscar
con·fis·ca·tion, *n.* confiscación

con·fla·gra·tion, n. conflagración
con·flict, n. conflicto. v. chocar
con·form, v. conformar(se)
con·form·i·ty, n. pl., -ties. conformidad
con·found, v. confundir
con·found·ed, a. inf. maldito; condenado
con·front, v. confrontar; hacer frente a
con·fron·ta·tion, n. confrontación
con·fuse, v. confundir
con·fu·sion, n. confusión
con·fute, v. confutar
con·geal, v. congelar
con·gen·ial, a. simpático
con·gen·i·tal, a. congénito
con·gest, v. acumular
con·ges·tion, n. congestión
con·glom·er·ate, n. conglomerado
con·glom·er·a·tion, n. conglomeración
con·grat·u·late, v. felicitar
con·grat·u·la·tion, n. usu. pl. felicitación
con·gre·gate, v. congregar(se)
con·gre·ga·tion, n. fieles
con·gress, n. congreso
con·gres·sion·al, a. del congreso
con·gress·man, n. pl., -men. diputado
con·ic, a. cónico
con·i·cal, a. cónico
co·ni·fer, n. conífera
con·jec·ture, n. conjetura. v. conjeturar
con·ju·gate, v. conjugar
con·junc·tion, n. conjunción
con·jure, v. conjurar; hacer juegos de manos
con·jur·er, con·jur·or, n. ilusionista, m., f.
con·nect, v. juntar; conectar
con·nec·tion, n. unión, f.; conexión
con·nive, v. hacer la vista gorda
con·no·ta·tion, n. connotación
con·note, v. connotar
con·quer, v. vencer; conquistar
con·quer·or, n. conquistador
con·quest, n. conquista
con·science, n. conciencia
con·sci·en·tious, a. concienzudo
con·scious, a. consciente; intencional
con·se·crate, v. consagrar
con·se·cra·tion, n. consagración
con·sec·u·tive, a. consecutivo; sucesivo
con·sen·sus, n. consenso
con·sent, v. consentir. n. consentimiento; permiso
con·se·quence, n. consecuencia
con·se·quent, a. consiguiente
con·ser·va·tion, n. conservación
con·serv·a·tive, a. moderado. n. conservador
con·serv·a·to·ry, n. pl., -ries. invernadero; conservatorio
con·serve, v. conservar; cuidar
con·sid·er, v. considerar; tomar en cuenta
con·sid·er·a·ble, a. considerable
con·sid·er·ate, a. considerado; atento
con·sid·er·a·tion, n. consideración
con·sid·er·ing, prep. en consideración a
con·sign, v. consignar
con·sign·ment, n. consignación; envío
con·sist, v. consistir; constar
con·sist·en·cy, n. pl., -cies. consistencia; consecuencia
con·sist·ent, a. consecuente
con·so·la·tion, n. consuelo
con·sole, v. consolar
con·sol·i·date, v. consolidar
con·sol·i·da·tion, n. consolidación
con·so·nant, n. consonante, f.
con·sort, n. consorte. v. asociarse
con·spic·u·ous, a. visible
con·spir·a·cy, n. pl., -cies. conspiración
con·spir·a·tor, n. conspirador
con·spire, v. conspirar
con·sta·ble, n. policía
con·stab·u·lar·y, n. pl., -ies. policía
con·stan·cy, n. constancia
con·stant, a. constante; continuo
con·stant·ly, adv. constantemente
con·stel·la·tion, n. constelación
con·ster·na·tion, n. consternación
con·sti·pate, v. estreñir
con·sti·pa·tion, n. estreñimiento
con·sti·tute, v. componer; constituir
con·sti·tu·tion, n. constitución
con·strain, v. obligar; forzar
con·straint, n. encierro; coacción
con·struct, v. construir
con·struc·tion, n. construcción; sentido
con·struc·tive, a. constructivo
con·strue, v. interpretar
con·sul, n. cónsul, m.
con·su·late, n. consulado
con·sult, v. consultar
con·sul·ta·tion, n. consulta
con·sume, v. consumir; comerse
con·sum·er, n. consumidor
con·sum·mate, v. consumar
con·sum·ma·tion, n. consumación
con·sump·tion, n. consumo; consunción
con·tact, n. contacto
con·ta·gion, n. contagio
con·ta·gious, a. contagioso
con·tain, v. contener
con·tain·er, n. continente
con·tam·i·nate, v. contaminar

con·tam·i·na·tion, n. contaminación
con·tem·plate, v. contemplar; proyectar
con·tem·pla·tion, n. contemplación
con·tem·po·rar·y, n. pl., -ies. coetáneo, a. contemporáneo
con·tempt, r. desprecio
con·tempt·i·ble, a. vil
con·temp·tu·ous, a. desdeñoso
con·tend, v. contender; disputar; afirmar
con·tent, a. contento. n. satisfacción; usu. pl. contenido
con·test, v. defender; contender. n. contienda; concurso
con·test·ant, n. contendiente, m., f.
con·ti·nent, n. continente
con·ti·nen·tal, a. continental
con·tin·gen·cy, n. pl., -cies. contingencia
con·tin·gent, a. contingente
con·tin·u·a·tion, n. continuación
con·tin·ue, v. continuar; prolongar; seguir
con·tin·u·ous, a. continuo
con·tort, v. retorcer
con·tour, n. contorno
con·tra·band, n. contrabando
con·tra·cep·tion, n. anticoncepcionismo
con·tra·cep·tive, a. anticoncepcional
con·tract, v. contraer. n. contrato
con·trac·tion, n. contracción
con·tra·dict, v. contradecir
con·tra·dic·tion, n. contradicción
con·tra·dic·to·ry, a. contradictorio
con·tral·to, n. pl., -tos, -ti. contralto
con·tra·ry, n. pl., -ries. contrario. a. contrario
con·trast, v. comparar; contrastar. n. contraste
con·trib·ute, v. contribuir
con·tri·bu·tion, n. contribución
con·trite, a. arrepentido
con·tri·tion, n. arrepentimiento
con·triv·ance, n. plan; invención
con·trive, v. inventar; efectuar
con·trol, v. controlar; mandar; dirigir. n. dirección; control
con·tro·ver·sy, n. pl., -sies. controversia
con·tu·sion, n. contusión
con·va·lesce, v. convalecer
con·va·les·cence, n. convalecencia
con·va·les·cent, a., n. convaleciente, m., f.
con·vene, v. convocar
con·ven·ience, n. comodidad
con·ven·ient, a. conveniente; cómodo
con·vent, n. convento
con·ven·tion, n. convención; congreso
con·ven·tion·al, a. convencional
con·verge, v. convergir
con·ver·gence, n. convergencia
con·ver·sant, a. familiar; versado en
con·ver·sa·tion, n. conversación; inversa
con·verse, v. conversar. n. conversación; inversa
con·ver·sion, n. conversión
con·vert, v. convertir. n. converso
con·vex, a. convexo
con·vey, v. transportar; llevar
con·vey·ance, n. transporte; vehículo
con·vict, v. condenar. n. penado
con·vic·tion, n. sentencia; convicción
con·vince, v. convencer
con·viv·i·al, a. alegre
con·vo·ca·tion, n. convocación
con·voy, v. convoyar. n. convoy, m.
con·vulse, v. convulsionar
con·vul·sion, n. convulsión
coo, v. arrullar
cook, v. cocer; cocinar. n. cocinero
cook·ie, cook·y, n. pl. cook·ies. galleta; dulce
cool, a. frío; fresco. v. enfriar
cool·ness, n. frescura; frío
coop, n. gallinero. v. encerrar
co·op·er·ate, v. cooperar
co·op·er·a·tion, n. cooperación
co·or·di·nate, v. coordinar
co·or·di·na·tion, n. coordinación
cop, v. inf. coger. n. agente de policía
cope, v. contender con
co·pi·ous, a. copioso
cop·per, n. cobre
cop·u·late, v. copularse
cop·u·la·tion, n. cópula
cop·y, n. pl., -ies. copia. v. copiar
cop·y·right, n. propiedad literaria
co·quette, n. coqueta
cor·al, n. coral, m.
cord, n. cuerda
cor·dial, a. cordial
cor·di·al·i·ty, n. cordialidad
cor·do·van, a. cordobán
cor·du·roy, n. pana
core, n. corazón; centro
cork, n. corcho. v. tapar con corcho
cork·screw, n. sacacorchos
corn, n. maíz, m.; callo
cor·ner, n. rincón; ángulo; esquina. v. arrinconar
cor·net, n. corneta
cor·nice, n. cornisa
cor·nu·co·pi·a, n. cornucopia
co·rol·la, n. corola
cor·ol·lar·y, n. pl., -ies. corolario
co·ro·na, n. pl., -nas, -nae. corona
cor·o·nar·y, n. trombosis coronaria
cor·o·na·tion, n. coronación
cor·po·ral, a. corporal. n. cabo
cor·po·rate, a. corporativo
cor·po·ra·tion, n. corporación; socie-

dad anónima
corps, n. pl., corps. cuerpo
corpse, n. cadáver
cor·pu·lence, cor·pu·len·cy, n. obesidad
cor·pu·lent, a. gordo
cor·pus·cle, n. corpúsculo; glóbulo
cor·pus·cu·lar, a. corpuscular
cor·ral, n. corral, m. v. acorralar
cor·rect, v. corregir, a. correcto
cor·rec·tion, n. corrección
cor·re·la·tion, n. correlación
cor·re·spond, v. corresponder; escribir
cor·re·spond·ence, n. correspondencia
cor·ri·dor, n. pasillo
cor·rob·o·rate, v. corroborar
cor·rob·o·ra·tion, n. confirmación
cor·rode, v. corroer
cor·ro·sion, n. corrosión
cor·ro·sive, a. corrosivo
cor·rupt, v. corromper. a. corrompido
cor·rup·tion, n. corrupción
cor·sage, n. corpiño
cor·set, n. corsé
cos·met·ic, a., n. cosmético
cos·mic, a. cósmico
cos·mo·pol·i·tan, a. cosmopolita. n. cosmopolita, m., f.
cos·mos, n. cosmos, m.
cost, n. precio; coste. v. costar
cost·ly, a. costoso
cos·tume, n. disfraz, m.
cot, n. catre
cot·tage, n. casita de campo
cot·ton, n. algodón. a. de algodón
couch, n. sofá, m.
cough, n. tos, f. v. toser
coun·cil, n. concejo
coun·cil·or, coun·cil·man, n. concejal
coun·sel, n. consejo; abogado. v. avisar
coun·se·lor, n. consejero
count, v. contar; considerar. n. cuenta; total; conde
coun·te·nance, n. cara; semblante
count·er, n. mostrador. a., adv. contrario. v. oponerse
coun·ter·feit, a. falso. n. falsificación; imitación. v. contrahacer
coun·ter·sign, v. refrendar
count·ess, n. condesa
count·less, a. innumerable
coun·tri·fied, a. rústico
coun·try, n. pl., -tries. país; campo. a. campesino
coun·ty, n. pl., -ties. condado
coup, n. pl., coups. golpe
cou·ple, n. par; pareja. v. unir
cou·pon, n. cupón
cour·age, n. valor
cou·ra·geous, a. valiente
cour·i·er, n. estafeta
course, n. curso; dirección; rumbo; plato
court, n. corte; tribunal, m.; pista. v. cortejar
cour·te·ous, a. cortés
cour·te·sy, n. pl., -sies. cortesía
court·ly, a. cortés
court·mar·tial, n. pl., courts·martial. consejo de guerra
court·ship, n. noviazgo
cous·in, n. primo
cove, n. cala
cov·e·nant, n. pacto; alianza
cov·er, v. cubrir; tapar. n. cubierta
cov·er·let, n. colcha
cov·ert, a. secreto
cov·et, v. codiciar
cov·et·ous, a. codicioso
cov·et·ous·ness, n. codicia
cow, n. pl., cows. vaca. v. intimidar
cow·ard, n. cobarde
cow·ard·ice, n. cobardía
cow·boy, n. vaquero
cowl, n. cogulla
coy, a. tímido
coy·ness, n. timidez, f.
coy·o·te, n. coyote
co·zi·ness, n. comodidad
co·zy, a. cómodo
crab, n. cangrejo. v. quejarse
crab ap·ple, n. manzana silvestre
crab·by, a. malhumorado
crack, v. hender; chasquear. n. crujido; grieta
crack·er, n. galleta
cra·dle, n. cuna. v. mecer
craft, n. arte, m.; habilidad; embarcación
craft·i·ness, n. astucia
crafts·man, n. pl. -men. artesano
craft·y, a. astuto
crag, n. risco
crag·gy, a. escarpado
cramp, v. restringir; sujetar. n. calambre
cran·ber·ry, n. pl., -ries. arándano
crane, n. grulla; grúa
crank, n_ manubrio; inf. chiflado
crank·y, a. chiflado
crash, v. estrellar; romperse. n. estrépito; estallido; choque
crass, a. craso; torpe
crate, n. caja de embalaje
cra·ter, n. cráter
cra·vat, n. corbata
crave, v. anhelar; suplicar
cra·ven, a. cobarde
crav·ing, n. deseo ardiente
crawl, v. arrastrar(se). n. arrastramiento
cray·fish, n. pl., -fish·es, -fish. ástaco
cray·on, n. lápiz de color

cra·zy, a. loco
creak, v. crujir. n. crujido
cream, n. nata; crema
crease, n. pliegue. v. doblar
cre·ate, v. crear; producir
cre·a·tion, n. creación
cre·a·tor, n. creador
crea·ture, n. criatura
cre·den·tial, n. credencial; pl. credenciales
cred·it, v. creer; abonar. n. crédito; honor
cred·i·tor, n. acreedor
cre·do, n. pl. -dos. credo
cred·u·lous, a. crédulo
creed, n. credo
creek, n. riachuelo
creep, v. arrastrar(se)
cre·mate, v. incinerar
cre·ma·tion, n. incineración
cres·cent, n. creciente
crest, n. cresta; cima
crew, n. tripulación
crib, n. pesebre
crick·et, n. grillo
crime, n. crimen
crim·i·nal, a., n. criminal
crim·son, a., n. carmesí
cringe, v. acobardarse
crin·kle, v. arrugar
crip·ple, n. tullido; lisiado. v. mutilar
cri·sis, n. pl., cri·ses. crisis, f.
crisp, a. tostado; crespo
cri·te·ri·on, n. pl., -ri·a, -ons. criterio
crit·ic, n. crítico
crit·i·cal, a. crítico
crit·i·cism, n. crítica
crit·i·cize, v. criticar
croak, v. croar. n. canto
cro·chet, n. hacer croché
crock·er·y, n. loza
croc·o·dile, n. cocodrilo
cro·cus, n. pl., -cus·es, -ci. azafrán
crook, n. curva; inf. ladrón
crook·ed, a. encorvado
croon, v. canturrear
crop, n. cosecha; látigo mocho. v. cortar
cro·quet, n. croquet, m.
cro·quette, n. croqueta
cross, n. cruz, f. a. malhumorado. v. cruzar
cross·ex·am·ine, v. repreguntar
cross·ing, n. cruce; paso a nivel
cross·roads, n. encrucijada
cross·wise, adv. de través; al través
crotch, n. horcajadura
crouch, v. agacharse
crow, n. cuervo; canto del gallo. v. cacarear
crow·bar, n. palanca
crowd, n. muchedumbre, f. v. apretar
crown, n. corona; cumbre, f. v. coronar
cru·cial, a. decisivo
cru·ci·ble, n. crisol, m.
cru·ci·fix, n. crucifijo
cru·ci·fix·ion, n. crucifixión
cru·ci·fy, v. crucificar
crude, a. crudo; inculto
cru·el, a. cruel
cru·el·ty, n. pl., -ties. crueldad; atrocidad
cruise, v. navegar
cruis·er, n. crucero
crumb, n. miga
crum·ble, v. desmigajar(se); desmenuzar(se)
crum·ple, v. ajar
crunch, v. crujir
cru·sade, n. cruzada. v. ir en una cruzada
cru·sad·er, n. cruzado
crush, v. aplastar
crush·ing, a. aplastante; abrumador
crust, n. corteza
crus·ta·cean, n. crustáceo
crust·y, a. costroso; irritable
crutch, n. muleta
cry, v. gritar; llorar. n. pl., cries. grito; llanto
crypt, n. cripta
cryp·tic, a. secreto
crys·tal, n. cristal, m. a. cristalino
crys·tal·li·za·tion, n. cristalización
crys·tal·lize, v. cristalizar(se)
cub, n. cachorro
cu·bic, a. cúbico
cuck·oo, n. pl., -oos. cuco
cu·cum·ber, n. pepino
cud, n. rumia
cud·dle, v. abrazarse
cudg·el, n. garrote; porra. v. aporrear
cue, n. apunte; taco
cuff, n. puño. v. abofetear
cu·li·nar·y, a. culinario
cull, v. coger
cul·mi·nate, v. culminar; terminar
cul·mi·na·tion, n. culminación; colmo
cul·prit, n. delincuente
cult, n. culto
cul·ti·vate, v. cultivar
cul·ti·va·tion, n. cultivo
cul·tur·al, a. cultural
cul·ture, n. cultura. v. cultivar
cul·vert, n. alcantarilla
cum·ber·some, a. incómodo
cu·mu·late, v. acumular
cun·ning, n. astucia; sutileza. a. astuto; artificioso
cup, n. taza
cup·ful, n. pl., -fuls. contenido de una taza
cu·pid·i·ty, n. codicia; avaricia
cur, n. perro de mala raza
curb, n. freno; bordillo. v. refrenar

curd, n. (often pl.) cuajada
cur·dle, v. cuajar(se)
cure, v. curar. n. cura
cur·few, n. queda
cu·ri·os·i·ty, n. pl., -ties. curiosidad
cu·ri·ous, a. curioso
curl, v. rizar(se); arrollar(se). n. rizo; bucle
curl·y, a. rizado
cur·rant, n. grosella
cur·ren·cy, n. pl., -cies. circulación; moneda
cur·rent, a. corriente. n. corriente, f.
cur·ric·u·lum, n. pl., -lums, -la. curso de estudios
curse, v. maldecir; blasfemar. n. maldición
cur·so·ry, a. rápido
curt, a. brusco
cur·tail, v. abreviar
cur·tain, n. cortina; telón
curt·sy, n. pl., -sies. reverencia. v. hacer una reverencia
curve, n. curva. v. encorvar(se)
cush·ion, n. cojín
cus·tard, n. natillas
cus·to·di·an, n. custodio
cus·to·dy, n. pl., -dies. custodia; encierro
cus·tom, n. costumbre, f.; pl. aduana
cus·tom·ar·y, a. usual
cus·tom·er, n. cliente
cut, v. cortar; dividir. n. corte; cortadura. a. cortado
cute, a. mono
cu·ti·cle, n. cutícula
cut·ler·y, n. cuchillería
cut·let, n. chuleta
cut·rate, a. a precio reducido
cut·throat, n. asesino. a. despiadado
cy·a·nide, n. cianuro
cy·cla·men, n. ciclamino
cy·cle, n. ciclo. v. ir en bicicleta
cy·clic, a. cíclico
cy·clist, n. ciclista, m., f.
cy·clone, n. ciclón
cy·clo·tron, n. ciclotrón
cyg·net, n. pollo del cisne
cyl·in·der, n. cilindro
cy·lin·dric, cy·lin·dri·cal, a. cilíndrico
cym·bal, n. platillo
cyn·ic, n. cínico
cyn·i·cal, a. cínico
cyn·i·cism, n. cinismo
cy·press, n. ciprés, m.
cyst, n. quiste
czar, n. zar
cza·ri·na, n. zarina

D

dab, v. tocar ligeramente. n. golpecito
dab·ble, v. salpicar
dad, n. inf. papá, m. Also dad·dy, pl. dad·dies
daft, a. loco
dag·ger, n. puñal, m.
dai·ly, a. diario; cotidiano. adv. cada día
dain·ti·ness, n. delicadeza
dain·ty, a. delicado. n. pl., -ties. golosina
dair·y, n. pl., -ies. lechería; quesería
dair·y·man, n. pl., -men. lechero
da·is, n. estrado
dale, n. valle
dal·li·ance, n. diversión
dal·ly, v. perder tiempo; entretenerse
dam, n. presa. v. represar
dam·age, n. daño; avería. v. perjudicar; dañar
damn, v. condenar. a. maldito
dam·na·ble, a. detestable
dam·na·tion, n. condenación
damned, a. condenado
damp, a. húmedo
damp·en, v. mojar
dance, v. bailar; danzar. n. baile; danza
dan·cer, n. bailador
dan·der, n. ira
dan·druff, n. caspa
dan·ger, n. peligro; riesgo
dan·ger·ous, a. peligroso
dan·gle, v. colgar
dank, a. liento
dap·pled, a. rodado
dare, v. atreverse; arriesgarse
dar·ing, n. atrevimiento
dark, a. oscuro; moreno. n. oscuridad
dark·en, v. oscurecer
dark·ness, n. oscuridad
dar·ling, n. querido
darn, v. zurcir
dash, v. romper; golpear; precipitarse. n. guión; raya
dash·board, n. tablero de instrumentos
das·tard, n. cobarde
das·tard·ly, a. vil
date, n. fecha; cita; dátil. v. fechar
daub, v. pintarrajar
daugh·ter, n. hija
daugh·ter-in-law, n. pl., daugh·ters-in-law. nuera
daunt·less, a. impávido
daw·dle, v. perder el tiempo
dawn, v. amanecer. n. alba
day, n. día, m.
day·break, n. amanecer
day·dream, n. ensueño
day·light, n. luz del día
day·time, n. día
daze, v. aturdir. n. deslumbramiento
daz·zle, v. deslumbrar

daz·zling, a. deslumbrante
dea·con, n. diácono
dea·con·ess, n. f. diaconisa
dea·con·ry, n. diaconía
dead, a. muerto
dead·en, v. amortiguar
dead-end, n. calle sin salida
dead end, n. callejón sin salida
dead·ly, a. mortal
deaf, a. sordo
deaf·en, v. ensordecer
deaf-mute, n. sordomudo
deaf·ness, n. sordera
deal, n. cantidad; trato; reparto. v. tratar de; dar
deal·er, n. tratante
dean, n. decano; deán
dear, a. querido; caro
dear·ness, n. carestía
death, n. muerte, f.
death·less, a. inmortal
death·ly, a. mortal
de·ba·cle, n. fracaso
de·bar, v. prohibir
de·bat·a·ble, a. discutible
de·bate, v. debatir. n. debate; discusión
de·bat·er, n. polemista, m., f.
de·bauch, v. corromper
de·bauch·er·y, n. pl., -ies. libertinaje
de·bil·i·tate, v. debilitar
de·bil·i·ta·tion, n. debilitación
de·bil·i·ty, n. pl., -ties. debilidad
deb·it, n. debe
deb·o·nair, a. cortés; elegante. Also deb·o·naire, deb·on·naire
de·bris, n. escombros, m.
debt, n. deuda
debt·or, n. deudor
de·but, dé·but, n. presentación; estreno
deb·u·tant, deb·u·tante, n. debutante
dec·ade, n. decenio
de·ca·dence, n. decadencia
dec·a·dent, a. decadente
de·cant·er, n. garrafa
de·cay, v. decaer; cariarse; deteriorar
de·cease, v. morir; fallecer
de·ceased, a. muerto; difunto
de·ceit, n. engaño
de·ceit·ful, a. engañoso
de·ceive, v. engañar
De·cem·ber, n. diciembre
de·cen·cy, n. pl., -cies. decencia
de·cent, a. decente
de·cep·tion, n. fraude
de·cep·tive, a. engañoso
de·cide, v. decidir
de·cid·ed, a. decidido
de·cid·ed·ly, adv. decididamente
dec·i·mal, a. decimal, f.
de·ci·pher, v. descifrar
de·ci·sion, n. decisión; firmeza
de·ci·sive, a. decisivo
de·ci·sive·ly, adv. con resolución
deck, v. adornar. n. cubierta; baraja
dec·la·ra·tion, n. declaración
de·clare, v. declarar
de·cline, v. declinar; rehusar. n. descenso
de·com·pose, v. descomponer(se)
de·com·po·si·tion, n. descomposición
dec·o·rate, v. adornar; condecorar
dec·o·ra·tion, n. decoración; ornato
dec·o·ra·tor, n. decorador
de·coy, n. señuelo
de·crease, v. disminuir(se)
de·creas·ing·ly, adv. en disminución
de·cree, n. decreto. v. decretar; mandar
de·crep·it, a. decrépito
de·cry, v. rebajar
de·duce, v. deducir
de·duct, v. restar
de·duc·tion, n. deducción; descuento
deed, n. hecho
deem, v. juzgar
deep, a. hondo; profundo
deep·en, v. profundizar; intensificar
de·face, v. desfigurar
def·a·ma·tion, n. difamación
de·fame, v. difamar
de·fault, n. a falta de
de·feat, n. derrota. v. vencer; frustrar
de·fect, n. defecto. v. desertar
de·fec·tion, n. defección
de·fec·tive, a. defectuoso
de·fend, v. defender
de·fend·ant, n. demandado
de·fense, de·fence, n. defensa
de·fen·sive, a. defensivo
de·fer, v. diferir; aplazar
def·er·ence, n. deferencia
de·fer·ment, n. aplazamiento
de·fi·ance, n. desafío
de·fi·ant, a. provocativo
de·fi·cien·cy, n. pl., -cies. deficiencia; falta
de·fi·cient, a. insuficiente
def·i·cit, m. déficit, m.
de·file, v. manchar
de·fine, v. definir
def·i·nite, a. concreto; definido
def·i·ni·tion, n. definición
de·fin·i·tive, a. definitivo
de·flate, v. desinflar
de·fla·tion, n. desinflación
de·flect, v. desviar
de·form, v. deformar; desfigurar
de·for·mi·ty, n. deformidad
de·fraud, v. defraudar; estafar
de·fray, v. pagar
deft, a. diestro
deft·ness, n. habilidad
de·funct, a. difunto
de·fy, v. desafiar; contravenir

de·gen·er·ate, v. degenerar
deg·ra·da·tion, n. degradación
de·grade, v. degradar
de·gree, n. grado; rango
de·hy·drate, v. deshidratar
de·hy·dra·tion, n. deshidratación
de·i·fy, v. deificar
deign, v. dignarse
de·i·ty, n. pl. -ties. deidad
de·ject·ed, a. abatido
de·jec·tion, n. melancolía; abatimiento
de·lay, v. aplazar; demorar
de·lec·ta·ble, a. deleitable
del·e·gate, v. delegar. n. delegado
del·e·ga·tion, n. diputación
de·lete, v. tachar
de·le·tion, n. supresión; borradura
de·lib·er·ate, v. deliberar. a. premeditado
del·i·ca·cy, n. pl. -cies. delicadeza
del·i·cate, a. delicado; fino
de·li·cious, a. delicioso
de·light, v. deleitar
de·light·ful, a. agradable; encantador
de·lin·e·ate, v. delinear
de·lin·e·a·tion, n. bosquejo
de·lin·quen·cy, n. pl. -cies. delincuencia
de·lin·quent, a., n. delincuente, m., f.
de·lir·i·ous, a. delirante
de·lir·i·um, n. pl. -iums, -i·a. delirio
de·liv·er, v. entregar; pronunciar
de·liv·er·ance, n. rescate
de·liv·er·y, n. entrega; reparto
del·ta, n. delta
de·lude, v. engañar
del·uge, n. diluvio. v. inundar
de·lu·sion, n. engaño; ilusión
de·luxe, a. de lujo
delve, v. cavar
dem·a·gogue, dem·a·gog, n. demagogo
dem·a·gog·er·y, n. demagogismo
de·mand, v. exigir; demandar. n. petición
Also **de·mar·ka·tion**
de·mar·ca·tion, n. demarcación.
de·mean, v. degradarse
de·mean·or, n. porte
de·ment·ed, a. demente
de·mer·it, n. demérito
de·mise, n. fallecimiento; cesión
de·moc·ra·cy, n. pl. -cies. democracia
dem·o·crat, n. demócrata, m., f.
dem·o·crat·ic, a. democrático
de·mol·ish, v. demoler
dem·o·li·tion, n. derribo
de·mon, n. demonio
dem·on·strate, v. demostrar
dem·on·stra·tion, n. demostración; manifestación
de·mor·al·ize, v. desmoralizar
de·mote, v. degradar
de·mo·tion, n. degradación
den, n. guarida; estudio
de·ni·al, n. negativa
den·im, n. dril de algodón
de·nom·i·na·tion, n. denominación
de·nom·i·na·tor, n. denominador
de·note, v. denotar
de·nounce, v. denunciar
dense, a. denso; compacto
den·si·ty, n. pl. -ties. densidad
dent, n. abolladura v. mellar
den·tal, a. dental
den·tist, n. dentista, m., f.
den·ture, n. dentadura
de·nude, v. desnudar
de·nun·ci·ate, v. denunciar
de·nun·ci·a·tion, n. denuncia
de·ny, v. negar; rehusar
de·o·dor·ant, n. desodorante
de·o·dor·ize, v. desodorizar
de·part, v. irse; partir
de·part·ment, n. departamento; sección
de·part·men·tal, a. departamental
de·par·ture, n. partida; salida
de·pend, v. depender; contar con
de·pend·ence, de·pend·ance, n. confianza
de·pend·en·cy, de·pend·an·cy, n. pl. -cies. dependencia; posesión
de·pend·ent, de·pend·ant, a. dependiente
de·pict, v. representar
de·plete, v. agotar
de·ple·tion, n. agotamiento
de·plor·a·ble, a. deplorable
de·plore, v. lamentar
de·port, v. deportar
de·por·ta·tion, n. deportación
de·port·ment, n. comportamiento
de·pose, v. deponer
de·pos·it, v. depositar. n. depósito; poso
de·pot, n. estación; depósito
de·prave, v. depravar
de·praved, a. depravado
de·prav·i·ty, n. pl. -ties. depravación
de·pre·ci·a·tion, n. depreciación
de·press, v. deprimir; rebajar
de·pressed, a. deprimido; desalentado
de·pres·sion, n. depresión; desaliento
dep·ri·va·tion, n. privación
de·prive, v. privar
depth, n. fondo; profundidad
dep·u·ty, n. pl. -ties. suplente
de·range, v. desarreglar
de·range·ment, n. desarreglo
der·e·lict, a. abandonado
der·e·lic·tion, n. abandono

de·ride, v. mofar
de·ri·sion, n. irrisión
der·i·va·tion, n. derivación
de·riv·a·tive, a. derivado
de·rive, v. derivar(se)
der·rick, n. grúa
de·scend, v. descender; bajar
de·scend·ant, n. descendiente, m., f.
de·scribe, v. describir
de·scrip·tion, n. descripción
de·scrip·tive, a. descriptivo
des·ert, n. desierto. v. abandonar
de·sert·er, n. desertor
de·serve, v. merecer
de·sign, v. idear; diseñar
des·ig·nate, v. señalar; nombrar
des·ig·na·tion, n. nombramiento
de·sign·er, n. diseñador; dibujante, m., f.
de·sire, v. desear
de·sist, v. desistir
desk, n. pupitre
des·o·la·tion, n. desolación
de·spair, v. desesperar
des·per·ate, a. desesperado; arriesgado
des·per·a·tion, n. desesperación
des·pi·ca·ble, a. despreciable
de·spise, v. despreciar
de·spite, prep. a pesar de
de·spoil, v. despojar
de·spond·en·cy, n. desaliento
des·pot, n. déspota, m.
des·pot·ism, n. despotismo
des·sert, n. postre
des·ti·na·tion, n. destino
des·tine, v. destinar
des·ti·ny, n. pl. -nies. destino
des·ti·tute, a. desamparado
des·ti·tu·tion, n. indigencia
de·stroy, v. destruir
de·struct·i·ble, a. destructible
de·struc·tion, n. destrucción
de·tach, v. separar
de·tached, a. separado; objetivo
de·tail, v. detallar. n. detalle
de·tain, v. detener; retener
de·tect, v. descubrir
de·tec·tive, n. detective
dé·tente, n. detente
de·ter, v. disuadir; impedir
de·ter·gent, n., a. detergente
de·te·ri·o·rate, v. deteriorar(se)
de·te·ri·o·ra·tion, n. empeoramiento
de·ter·mi·na·tion, n. determinación
de·ter·mine, v. determinar; fijar; resolver
de·ter·mined, a. resuelto
de·test, v. detestar
de·test·a·ble, a. detestable
de·tour, n. rodeo
det·ri·ment, n. perjuicio
de·val·u·ate, v. desvalorizar
de·val·u·a·tion, n. devaluación
dev·as·tate, v. devastar
dev·as·ta·tion, n. devastación
de·vel·op, v. desarrollar; desenvolver
de·vel·op·ment, n. desarrollo; explotación
de·vi·ate, v. desviarse
de·vi·a·tion, n. desviación; divergencia
de·vice, n. ingenio; estratagema
dev·il, n. diablo; demonio
dev·il·ish, a. diabólico
de·vi·ous, a. tortuoso
de·vise, v. inventar
de·void, a. desprovisto
de·vote, v. dedicar
de·vot·ed, a. fiel
dev·o·tee, n. devoto
de·vo·tion, n. devoción; lealtad
de·vour, v. devorar
de·vout, a. devoto
dew, n. rocío
dex·ter·i·ty, n. destreza
dex·ter·ous, a. diestro; hábil
di·a·be·tes, n. diabetes, f.
di·a·bet·ic, a. diabético
di·a·bol·ic, a. diabólico. Also **di·a·bol·i·cal**
di·a·dem, n. diadema
di·ag·nose, v. diagnosticar
di·ag·no·sis, n. pl. -ses. diagnóstico
di·ag·o·nal, a. diagonal, f.
di·a·gram, n. diagrama, m.
di·al, n. cuadrante; disco. v. marcar
di·a·lect, n. dialecto
di·a·logue, n. diálogo
di·am·e·ter, n. diámetro
di·a·met·ric, a. diametral. Also **di·a·met·ri·cal**
dia·mond, n. diamante; oros
di·a·per, n. pañal
di·a·phragm, n. diafragma, m.
di·ar·rhe·a, n. diarrea. Also **di·ar·rhoea**
di·a·ry, n. pl. -ries. diario
dice, n. pl.; sing. die. dados. v. jugar a los dados; cortar en cuadritos
dick·er, v. regatear
dic·tate, v. mandar; dictar. n. orden
dic·ta·tion, n. dictado
dic·ta·tor, n. dictador
dic·ta·to·ri·al, a. dictatorio
dic·ta·tor·ship, n. dictadura
dic·tion, n. dicción
dic·tion·ar·y, n. pl. -ies. diccionario
did, v. past tense of do
die, v. morir. n. dado; troquel, m.
di·et, n. régimen. v. estar a dieta
di·e·tar·y, a. dietético
dif·fer, v. diferenciarse; discrepar
dif·fer·ence, n. diferencia
dif·fer·ent, a. diferente
dif·fi·cult, a. difícil
dif·fi·cul·ty, n. pl. -ties. dificultad
dif·fuse, v. difundir. a. difuso

dif·fu·sion, n. difusión
dig, v. cavar; extraer. n. excavación
di·gest, v. digerir. n. digesto
di·ges·tion, n. digestión
dig·it, n. dígito; dedo
dig·ni·fied, a. grave
dig·ni·fy, v. dignificar; honrar
dig·ni·ty, n. pl. -ties. dignidad
di·gres·sion, n. digresión
dike, n. dique
di·lap·i·dat·ed, a. desmoronado
di·late, v. dilatar(se)
di·lem·ma, n. dilema, m.
dil·i·gence, n. diligencia
dil·i·gent, a. diligente; asiduo
dill, n. eneldo
di·lute, v. diluir
di·lu·tion, n. dilución
dim, a. débil; oscuro. v. oscurecer
dime, n. diez centavos
di·men·sion, n. dimensión
di·min·ish, v. disminuir(se)
di·min·u·tive, a. diminuto
dim·ple, n. hoyuelo
din, n. estruendo
dine, v. cenar
din·er, n. coche-comedor
din·gy, a. sucio; deslucido
din·ner, n. cena
di·no·saur, n. dinosaurio
dint, n. fuerza
di·oc·e·san, a. diocesano
di·o·cese, n. diócesis, f.
dip, v. mojar; meter
diph·the·ri·a, n. difteria
diph·thong, n. diptongo
di·plo·ma, n. diploma, m.
di·plo·ma·cy, n. pl. -cies. diplomacia
dip·lo·mat, n. diplomático
dip·lo·mat·ic, a. diplomático
dire, a. horrendo
di·rect, a. directo; franco. v. dirigir
di·rec·tion, n. dirección
di·rect·ly, adv. directamente
di·rec·tor, n. director
dirge, n. endecha
dirt, n. mugre, f.; tierra; porquería
dirt·y, a. sucio; verde. v. ensuciar
dis·a·bil·i·ty, n. pl. -ties. incapacidad
dis·a·ble, v. mutilar; inutilizar
dis·ad·van·tage, n. desventaja
dis·ad·van·ta·geous, a. desventajoso
dis·a·gree, v. discrepar
dis·a·gree·a·ble, a. desagradable
dis·a·gree·ment, n. desacuerdo
dis·ap·pear, v. desaparecer
dis·ap·pear·ance, n. desaparición
dis·ap·point, v. desilusionar
dis·ap·point·ment, n. contratiempo
dis·ap·prov·al, n. desaprobación
dis·ap·prove, v. desaprobar
dis·arm, v. desarmar
dis·ar·ray, n. desorden
dis·as·ter, n. desastre
dis·as·trous, a. desastroso
dis·a·vow, v. desconocer
dis·band, v. licenciar
dis·bar, v. expulsar
dis·burse, v. desembolsar
dis·burse·ment, n. desembolso
disc, disk, n. disco
dis·card, v. descartar
dis·cern, v. discernir
dis·cern·i·ble, a. perceptible
dis·cern·ing, a. perspicaz
dis·cern·ment, n. discernimiento
dis·charge, v. descargar; despedir; cumplir
dis·ci·ple, n. discípulo
dis·ci·pli·nar·y, a. disciplinario
dis·ci·pline, n. disciplina; castigo. v. disciplinar
dis·claim, v. negar
dis·claim·er, n. renuncia
dis·clo·sure, n. revelación
dis·com·fort, n. incomodidad
dis·con·cert, v. desconcertar
dis·con·nect, v. desacoplar; desconectar
dis·con·tent, n. descontento
dis·con·tin·ue, v. descontinuar
dis·con·tin·u·ous, a. discontinuo
dis·cord, n. discordia
dis·count, n. descuento
dis·cour·age, v. desanimar
dis·cour·age·ment, n. desaliento
dis·cour·te·ous, a. descortés
dis·cov·er, v. descubrir; encontrar
dis·cov·er·y, n. pl. -ies. descubrimiento; hallazgo
dis·cred·it, n. desacreditar
dis·creet, a. discreto
dis·crep·an·cy, n. pl. -cies. discrepancia
dis·cre·tion, n. discreción
dis·crim·i·nate, v. distinguir
dis·crim·i·na·tion, n. discriminación; discernimiento
dis·cuss, v. discutir
dis·cus·sion, n. discusión
dis·dain, v. desdeñar
dis·dain·ful, a. desdeñoso
dis·ease, n. enfermedad
dis·en·chant, v. desencantar
dis·en·chant·ment, n. desencanto
dis·fig·ure, v. desfigurar
dis·grace, n. deshonra; vergüenza. v. deshonrar
dis·grace·ful, a. vergonzoso
dis·guise, v. disfrazar. n. disfraz, m.
dis·gust, n. asco; repugnancia. v. disgustar
dis·gust·ing, a. asqueroso
dish, n. plato
dis·heart·en, v. desalentar; descorazonar

dis·hon·est, a. fraudulento; falso
dis·hon·es·ty, n. pl. -ties. fraude
dis·hon·or, n. deshonra. v. deshonrar
dis·hon·or·a·ble, a. deshonroso
dis·il·lu·sion, v. desilusionar
dis·in·fect·ant, n. desinfectante
dis·in·her·it, v. desheredar
dis·in·te·grate, v. disgregar(se)
dis·in·te·gra·tion, n. desagregación
dis·in·ter·est, n. desinterés
disk, disc, n. disco
dis·like, n. antipatía
dis·lo·cate, v. dislocar
dis·lo·ca·tion, n. dislocación
dis·loy·al, a. desleal
dis·loy·al·ty, n. deslealtad
dis·mal, a. triste; sombrío
dis·man·tle, v. desmontar
dis·may, v. consternar; desanimar
dis·mem·ber, v. desmembrar
dis·miss, v. despedir
dis·o·be·di·ence, n. desobediencia
dis·o·bey, v. desobedecer
dis·or·der, n. desorden, m.
dis·or·gan·i·za·tion, n. desorganización
dis·own, v. desconocer
dis·par·age, v. menospreciar
dis·par·i·ty, n. disparidad
dis·patch, n. enviar; despachar
dis·pel, v. dispersar
dis·pen·sa·tion, n. dispensa
dis·pense, v. dispensar
dis·perse, v. dispersar(se)
dis·play, v. exponer; demostrar
dis·please, v. desagradar
dis·pleas·ure, n. disgusto
dis·pose, v. disponer
dis·prove, v. confutar
dis·pute, v. disputar. n. disputa
dis·qual·i·fi·ca·tion, n. inhabilitación
dis·qual·i·fy, v. descalificar
dis·re·gard, n. descuido. v. desatender
dis·rep·u·ta·ble, a. de mala fama
dis·re·spect, n. desacato
dis·re·spect·ful, a. irrespetuoso
dis·rupt, v. desorganizar
dis·sat·is·fac·tion, n. descontento
dis·sect, v. disecar
dis·sen·sion, n. disensión
dis·sent, v. disentir
dis·si·pate, v. disipar
dis·solve, v. disolver(se)
dis·so·nance, n. disonancia
dis·suade, v. disuadir
dis·sua·sion, n. disuasión
dis·tance, n. distancia
dis·tant, a. lejano; distante
dis·taste, n. aversión
dis·till, v. destilar
dis·till·er·y, n. destilería
dis·tinct, a. distinto
dis·tinc·tion, n. distinción
dis·tin·guish, v. distinguir
dis·tin·guish·a·ble, a. distinguible
dis·tin·guished, a. distinguido
dis·tort, v. torcer
dis·tract, v. distraer
dis·tract·ed, a. distraído
dis·trac·tion, n. distracción; diversión
dis·traught, a. turbado
dis·tress, n. dolor; pena
dis·trib·ute, v. distribuir
dis·tri·bu·tion, n. distribución
dis·trict, n. distrito; región
dis·trust, v. desconfiar. n. recelo
dis·turb, v. perturbar
dis·turb·ance, n. alboroto; disturbio
dis·u·nite, v. desunir
ditch, n. zanja
dive, v. sumergirse. n. salto; zambullida
di·ver, n. buzo
di·verge, v. divergir
di·ver·gence, n. divergencia
di·verse, a. diverso
di·ver·sion, n. diversión
di·ver·si·ty, n. diversidad
di·vert, v. desviar; divertir
di·vide, v. dividir(se)
div·i·dend, n. dividendo
di·vine, a. divino. v. adivinar
di·vin·i·ty, n. pl. -ties. divinidad
di·vi·sion, n. división; repartimiento
di·vorce, n. divorcio. v. divorciarse
di·vulge, v. divulgar
diz·zi·ness, n. vértigo
diz·zy, a. mareado; vertiginoso
do, v., did, done, do·ing. hacer; producir; cumplir; representar; servir
doc·ile, a. dócil
dock, n. dársena; dique
doc·tor, n. médico; doctor
doc·trine, n. doctrina
doc·u·ment, n. documento. v. documentar
doc·u·men·ta·ry, a. documental
dodge, v. evadir
doe, n. pl., does, doe. gama
doff, v. quitar(se)
dog, n. perro
dog·ged, a. tenaz
dog·ma, n. pl. -mas. dogma, m.
dog·mat·ic, a. dogmático
dog·ma·tize, v. dogmatizar
doi·ly, n. pl., -lies. paño de adorno
dol·drums, n. pl. desánimo
dole, n. limosna. v. repartir
doll, n. muñeca
dol·lar, n. dólar
dol·or·ous, a. doloroso
dolt, n. imbécil; necio
do·main, n. dominio; heredad
dome, n. cúpula

do·mes·tic, a., n. doméstico
do·mes·ti·cate, v. domesticar
dom·i·nant, a. dominante
dom·i·nate, v. dominar
dom·i·na·tion, n. dominación
dom·i·neer, v. tiranizar
dom·i·neer·ing, a. dominante
do·min·ion, n. dominio
don, v. ponerse; asumir
do·nate, v. donar
done, a. hecho
do·nor, n. donante
doom, n. juicio; suerte, f. v. condenar
door, n. puerta; entrada
dope, n. narcótico. v. narcotizar
dor·mi·to·ry, n. pl., -ries. dormitorio
dor·sal, a. dorsal
dos·age, n. dosificación
dose, n. dosis, f.
dot, n. punto. v. puntear
dot·age, n. chochez, f.
dou·ble, a. doble. v. doblar(se)
doubt, v. dudar. n. duda
doubt·ful, a. dudoso; sospechoso
doubt·less, adv. sin duda
dough, n. masa
dough·nut, n. buñuelo
dour, a. austero
douse, v. mojar; zambullir
dow·a·ger, n. viuda de un titulado
dow·dy, a. desaliñado; poco elegante
down, adv. abajo; por tierra. prep. abajo. a. descendente. n. plumón
down·cast, a. abatido
down·fall, n. caída
down·heart·ed, a. desanimado
down·ward, adv. hacia abajo. Also **down·wards**
doze, v. dormitar
doz·en, n. pl., -ens. docena
drab, a. monótono
draft, n. destacamento; giro; borrador
drag, v. arrastrar
drag·on, n. dragón
drain, v. agotar; desaguar. n. desagüe; desaguadero
drain·age, n. desagüe; drenaje
dra·ma, n. drama, m.
dra·mat·ic, a. dramático
dram·a·tist, n. dramaturgo
dram·a·tize, v. dramatizar
drape, v. poner colgaduras. n. colgadura
dra·per·y, n. pl., -ies. pañería
dras·tic, a. drástico; enérgico
draw, v. arrastrar; girar; sacar; atraer; dibujar
draw·back, n. desventaja
draw·bridge, n. puente levadizo
draw·er, n. cajón
draw·ing, n. dibujo
drawl, v. arrastrar las palabras
drawn, a. ojeroso
dread, v. temer. n. pavor
dread·ful, a. terrible
dream, n. sueño. v. soñar
dream·er, n. soñador
dream·y, a. soñador
drear·y, a. triste
dredge, n. rastra. v. dragar
dreg, n. usu. pl. heces, f. pl.
drench, v. empapar
dress, v. vestir(se). n. ropa; vestido
dress·er, n. aparador
drib·ble, v. caer gota a gota
drift, n. impulso de la corriente; montón. v. amontonar(se); derivar
drift·wood, n. madera llevada por el agua
drill, v. taladrar. n. taladro; ejercicios
drink, v., drank, drunk, drink·ing. beber. n. bebida
drip, v. gotear. n. gota
drive, v. conducir; manejar; empujar. n. paseo en coche; energía; calzada
driz·zle, v. lloviznar
droll, a. gracioso
droll·er·y, n. pl., -ies. chuscada
drone, n. zángano. v. zumbar
drool, v. babear
droop, v. inclinar
drop, n. gota; declive. v. dejar caer
drop·sy, n. hidropesía
dross, n. escoria
drought, n. sequía
drown, v. ahogar; anegar
drowse, v. adormecer(se)
drow·si·ness, n. somnolencia
drow·sy, a. soñoliento
drudg·er·y, n. pl., -ies. faena penosa
drug, n. droga; narcótico. v. administrar drogas
drug·gist, n. farmacéutico; boticario
drum, n. tambor. v. tamborilear
drum·stick, n. baqueta
drunk, a. borracho; ebrio
drunk·ard, n. borracho
drunk·en, a. borracho
drunk·en·ness, n. embriaguez, f.
dry, a. seco; árido. v. secar(se)
dry·ness, n. sequedad
du·al, a. dual
du·al·i·ty, n. dualidad
dub, v. armar caballero
du·bi·ous, a. dudoso
duch·ess, n. duquesa
duck, v. chapuzar(se). n. pato
duct, n. conducto
dude, n. petimetre
due, a. debido; oportuno. n. derecho
du·el, n. duelo. v. batirse en duelo
du·et, n. dúo
duke, n. duque
duke·dom, n. ducado
dull, a. torpe; pesado; embotado. v. embotar; deslustrar

dull·ness, dul·ness, n. torpeza
du·ly, adv. debidamente
dumb, a. torpe; mudo
dum·found, v. pasmar. Also **dumb·found**
dum·my, n. pl., -mies. maniquí, m.; muerto
dump, v. descargar. n. basurero
dump·ling, n. bola de masa
dunce, n. zopenco
dune, n. duna
dung, n. estiércol, m.
dun·geon, n. mazmorra
dupe, v. embaucar
du·pli·cate, v. duplicar. a. duplicado. n. copia
du·pli·ca·tion, n. duplicación
du·plic·i·ty, n. pl., -ties. duplicidad
du·ra·ble, a. duradero
du·ra·tion, n. duración
du·ress, n. compulsión
dur·ing, prep. durante
dusk, n. crepúsculo
dusk·y, a. oscuro
dust, n. polvo. v. quitar el polvo
dust·y, a. polvoriento
du·ti·ful, a. obediente
du·ty, n. pl., -ties. deber; derechos
dwarf, n. enano
dwell, v. morar; habitar
dwell·ing, n. morada
dwin·dle, v. disminuir
dye, n. tinte. v. teñir
dye·ing, n. tintura
dy·nam·ic, a. dinámico
dy·nam·i·cal, a. dinámico
dy·na·mite, n. dinamita
dy·na·mo, n. pl., -mos. dinamo, dínamo, f.
dy·nas·ty, n. pl., -ties. dinastía
dys·en·ter·y, n. disentería

E

each, a. cada. pron. cada uno. adv. para cada uno
ea·ger, a. ansioso; impaciente
ea·ger·ly, adv. con ansia
ea·ger·ness, n. ansia
ea·gle, n. águila
ea·glet, n. aguilucho
ear, n. oreja; oído; espiga
ear·drum, n. tímpano del oído
earl, n. conde
earl·dom, n. condado
ear·li·ness, n. precocidad
ear·ly, adv. temprano. a. avanzado; temprano; primitivo
earn, v. ganar; merecer
ear·nest, a. fervoroso; serio
ear·nest·ly, adv. con seriedad
earn·ings, n. pl. ganancias; sueldo
ear·ring, n. pendiente
ear·shot, n. alcance del oído
earth, n. tierra; mundo
earth·en·ware, n. loza de barro
earth·ly, a. terrestre; mundano
earth·quake, n. terremoto
earth·y, a. terroso
ease, n. tranquilidad; facilidad. v. aliviar; facilitar
ea·sel, n. caballete
eas·i·ly, adv. fácilmente
eas·i·ness, n. facilidad
east, n. este; oriente. a. oriental. adv. al este
east·ern, a. del este
east·ward, adv. hacia el este. Also **east·wards**
eas·y, a. cómodo; fácil
eas·y-go·ing, a. acomodadizo; de manga ancha
eat, v. comer; gastar
eat·a·ble, a. comestible. n. pl. comestibles
eaves, n. pl. alero
eaves·drop, v. escuchar a escondidas; espiar
ebb, v. menguar; decaer. n. reflujo
eb·on·y, n. pl., -ies. ébano. a. de ébano
ec·cen·tric, a., n. excéntrico
ec·cen·tric·i·ty, n. pl., -ties. excentricidad
ec·cle·si·as·tic, a., n. eclesiástico
ec·cle·si·as·ti·cal, a. eclesiástico
ech·o, n. pl., -oes. eco. v. resonar
e·clipse, n. eclipse. v. eclipsar
e·clip·tic, a. eclíptico
ec·o·log·ic, a. ecológico
ec·o·log·i·cal, a. ecológico
e·col·o·gy, n. ecología
ec·o·nom·ic, a. económico
ec·o·nom·i·cal, a. económico
ec·o·nom·ics, n. pl. economía
e·con·o·mist, n. economista, m., f.
e·con·o·mize, v. economizar
e·con·o·my, n. pl., -ies. economía
ec·sta·sy, n. pl., -sies. éxtasis, m.
ec·stat·ic, a. extático
ec·u·men·i·cal, a. ecuménico
ec·ze·ma, n. eczema, eccema, m.
ed·dy, n. pl., -dies. remolino
e·den·tate, a. desdentado
edge, n. filo; agudeza; borde. v. ribetear
edged, a. cortante
edg·y, a. nervioso
ed·i·ble, a. comestible. n. usu. pl. comestibles
e·dict, n. edicto
ed·i·fi·ca·tion, n. edificación
ed·i·fice, n. edificio
ed·i·fy, v. edificar
ed·it, v. editar; dirigir
e·di·tion, n. edición
ed·i·tor, n. director; editor
ed·i·to·ri·al, a. editorial. n. artículo

de fondo
ed·i·to·ri·al·ist, *n.* editorialista, *m.,* *f.*
ed·u·cate, *v.* educar
ed·u·ca·tion, *n.* educación
eel, *n. pl.,* eels, eel. anguila
ee·rie, *a.* espantoso; fantástico
ef·face, *v.* borrar
ef·fect, *n.* efecto; resultado; *pl.* efectos. *v.* efectuar
ef·fec·tive, *a.* efectivo; eficaz
ef·fec·tu·al, *a.* eficaz
ef·fem·i·nate, *a.* afeminado
ef·fer·vesce, *v.* estar en efervescencia
ef·fer·ves·cence, *n.* efervescencia
ef·fer·ves·cent, *a.* efervescente
ef·fi·ca·cious, *a.* eficaz
ef·fi·cien·cy, *n. pl.,* -cies. eficiencia
ef·fi·cient, *a.* eficiente
ef·fi·gy, *n. pl.,* -gies. efigie, *f.*
ef·fort, *n.* esfuerzo
ef·fort·less, *a.* sin esfuerzo
ef·fuse, *v.* derramar
ef·fu·sion, *n.* efusión
ef·fu·sive, *a.* expansivo; efusivo
egg, *n.* huevo. *v.* incitar
e·go, *n. pl.,* -gos. el yo
e·go·tist, *n.* egotista, *m.,* *f.*
e·gress, *n.* salida
eight, *a.,* *n.* ocho
eight·een, *a.,* *n.* dieciocho
eight·eenth, *a.,* *n.* decimoctavo
eighth, *a.,* *n.* octavo
eight·i·eth, *a.,* *n.* octogésimo
eight·y, *a.,* *n. pl.,* -ies. ochenta
ei·ther, *a.* cualquier. *pron.* uno u otro. *adv.* también; tampoco
e·ject, *v.* echar; expulsar
e·jec·tion, *n.* expulsión
eke, *v.* aumentar. eke out, ganar a duras penas
e·lab·o·rate, *v.* elaborar. *a.* detallado
e·lab·o·ra·tion, *n.* elaboración
e·lapse, *v.* pasar
e·las·tic, *a.* elástico
e·las·tic·i·ty, *n.* elasticidad
e·late, *v.* exaltar; alegrar
e·la·tion, *n.* regocijo
el·bow, *n.* codo
eld·er, *a.* mayor. *n.* mayor; anciano
el·der·ly, *a.* de edad
eld·est, *a.* el mayor
e·lect, *v.* elegir. *a.* elegido; electo
e·lec·tion, *n.* elección
e·lec·tive, *a.* electivo
e·lec·tor, *n.* elector
e·lec·tor·ate, *n.* electorado
e·lec·tric, *a.* eléctrico; vivo. Also e·lec·tri·cal
e·lec·tri·cian, *n.* electricista, *m.,* *f.*
e·lec·tric·i·ty, *n.* electricidad
e·lec·tri·fy, *v.* electrizar
e·lec·tro·cute, *v.* electrocutar
e·lec·tro·cu·tion, *n.* electrocución
e·lec·trode, *n.* electrodo
e·lec·tron, *n.* electrón
e·lec·tron·ic, *a.* electrónico
e·lec·tron·ics, *n. pl.* electrónica
el·e·gance, el·e·gan·cy, *n.* elegancia
el·e·gant, *a.* elegante
el·e·gize, *v.* hacer una elegía
el·e·gy, *n. pl.,* -gies. elegía
el·e·ment, *n.* elemento
el·e·men·ta·ry, *a.* elemental; primario
el·e·phant, *n.* elefante
el·e·phan·tine, *a.* elefantino
el·e·vate, *v.* elevar; exaltar
el·e·va·tion, *n.* elevación; altura
el·e·va·tor, *n.* ascensor
el·e·ven, *a.,* *n.* once
el·e·venth, *a.,* *n.* undécimo
elf, *n. pl.,* elves. duende
elf·in, *a.* de elfo
e·lic·it, *v.* sacar
el·i·gi·bil·i·ty, *n.* elegibilidad
el·i·gi·ble, *a.* elegible; deseable
e·lim·i·nate, *v.* eliminar
e·lim·i·na·tion, *n.* eliminación
e·lite, *n.* lo mejor
e·lix·ir, *n.* elixir
elk, *n. pl.,* elks, elk. alce
el·lipse, *n.* elipse, *f.*
el·lip·ti·cal, *a.* elíptico
elm, *n.* olmo
el·o·cu·tion, *n.* elocución
el·on·gate, *v.* alargar
e·lope, *v.* fugarse con su amante para casarse
e·lope·ment, *n.* fuga
el·o·quence, *n.* elocuencia
el·o·quent, *a.* elocuente
else, *a.* otro; más. *adv.* en otro caso
else·where, *adv.* en (a) otra parte
e·lu·ci·date, *v.* elucidar
e·lude, *v.* eludir; escapar de
e·lu·sive, *a.* esquivo
e·ma·ci·ate, *v.* enflaquecer(se)
e·ma·ci·a·tion, *n.* demacración
em·a·nate, *v.* emanar
e·man·ci·pate, *v.* emancipar
e·man·ci·pa·tion, *n.* emancipación
em·balm, *v.* embalsamar
em·balm·er, *n.* embalsamador
em·bar·go, *n. pl.,* -goes. embargo
em·bark, *v.* embarcar(se)
em·bar·rass, *v.* desconcertar
em·bas·sy, *n. pl.,* -sies. embajada
em·bel·lish, *v.* embellecer
em·ber, *n.* ascua
em·bez·zle, *v.* desfalcar
em·bez·zler, *n.* malversador
em·blem, *n.* emblema, *m.*
em·boss, *v.* realzar
em·brace, *v.* abrazar; aceptar; abarcar. *n.* abrazo
em·broi·der, *v.* recamar
em·broi·der·y, *n. pl.,* -ies. bordado

em·bry·o, *n. pl.,* -os. embrión
em·er·ald, *n.* esmeralda. *a.* de color de esmeralda
e·merge, *v.* surgir; salir
e·mer·gence, *n.* salida
e·mer·gen·cy, *n. pl.,* -cies. crisis, *f.;* necesidad
em·er·y, *n.* esmeril, *m.*
em·i·grant, *n.* emigrante, *m.,* *f.*
em·i·grate, *v.* emigrar
em·i·gra·tion, *n.* emigración
em·i·nence, *n.* eminencia
em·i·nent, *a.* eminente
em·is·sar·y, *n. pl.,* -ies. emisario
e·mis·sion, *n.* emisión
e·mit, *v.* emitir; arrojar
e·mo·tion, *n.* emoción
em·per·or, *n.* emperador
em·pha·sis, *n. pl.,* -ses. énfasis, *m.*
em·pha·size, *v.* acentuar; recalcar
em·phat·ic, *a.* enfático
em·pire, *n.* imperio
em·ploy, *v.* emplear; ocupar
em·ploy·ee, em·ploy·e, *n.* empleado
em·ploy·er, *n.* amo; patrón
em·ploy·ment, *n.* empleo; colocación
em·pow·er, *v.* autorizar
em·press, *n. f.* emperatriz
emp·ti·ness, *n.* vacuidad; vacío
emp·ty, *a.* vacío; desocupado; vano. *v.* vaciar(se)
em·u·late, *v.* emular
e·mul·sion, *n.* emulsión
e·mul·sive, *a.* emulsivo
en·a·ble, *v.* hacer que; permitir
en·act, *v.* decretar; hacer el papel de
e·nam·el, *n.* esmalte. *v.* esmaltar
en·am·or, *v.* enamorar
en·case, *v.* encerrar; encajar
en·chant, *v.* encantar
en·chant·ing, *a.* encantador
en·chant·ment, *n.* encanto
en·cir·cle, *v.* ceñir; rodear
en·close, *v.* cercar; encerrar; incluir
en·clo·sure, *n.* cercamiento; carta adjunta
en·com·pass, *v.* cercar; abarcar
en·core, *n.* repetición
en·coun·ter, *n.* encuentro. *v.* encontrar; oponerse
en·cour·age, *v.* animar; fomentar
en·cour·ag·ing, *a.* alentador
en·croach, *v.* usurpar; pasar los límites
en·croach·ment, *n.* usurpación; abuso
en·cum·ber, *v.* estorbar; gravar
en·cy·clo·pe·di·a, *n.* enciclopedia. Also en·cy·clo·pae·di·a
end, *n.* fin; conclusión; extremo; final, *m.;* desenlace. *v.* terminar; acabar
en·dan·ger, *v.* poner en peligro
en·dear, *v.* hacer querer
en·deav·or, *n.* esfuerzo. *v.* esforzarse; intentar
end·ing, *n.* fin, *m.;* desenlace
en·dorse, *v.* endosar
en·dorse·ment, *n.* endoso
en·dow, *v.* dotar
en·dur·ance, *n.* resistencia
en·dure, *v.* soportar; aguantar; durar
en·dur·ing, *a.* perdurable
en·e·my, *n. pl.,* -mies. enemigo
en·er·get·ic, *a.* enérgico
en·er·gy, *n. pl.,* -gies. energía
en·force, *v.* hacer cumplir; exigir
en·gage, *v.* emplear; apalabrar; atraer; engranar
en·gaged, *a.* ocupado; prometido
en·gage·ment, *n.* compromiso; obligación
en·gag·ing, *a.* atractivo
en·gen·der, *v.* engendrar
en·gine, *n.* motor; locomotora
en·gi·neer, *n.* ingeniero
en·gi·neer·ing, *n.* ingeniería
English, *a.,* *n.* inglés
en·grave, *v.* grabar
en·grav·er, *n.* grabador
en·grav·ing, *n.* grabado
en·gross, *v.* absorber; monopolizar
en·hance, *v.* aumentar
e·nig·ma, *n.* enigma, *m.*
en·ig·mat·ic, en·ig·mat·i·cal, *a.* enigmático
en·join, *v.* imponer
en·joy, *v.* gozar de; disfrutar
en·joy·ment, *n.* placer; disfrute
en·large, *v.* extender(se)
en·large·ment, *n.* aumento; ampliación
en·light·en, *v.* iluminar; instruir
en·list, *v.* alistar(se)
en·list·ment, *n.* alistamiento
en·liv·en, *v.* avivar
en·mi·ty, *n. pl.,* -ties. enemistad
en·no·ble, *v.* ennoblecer
e·nor·mi·ty, *n. pl.,* -ties. enormidad; atrocidad
e·nor·mous, *a.* enorme
e·nough, *a.,* *adv.* bastante. *n.* lo suficiente
en·rage, *v.* enfurecer
en·rich, *v.* enriquecer
en·roll, *v.* matricular(se); inscribir(se)
en·roll·ment, *n.* matrícula
en·sem·ble, *n.* conjunto
en·sign, *n.* bandera. *milit.* alférez, *m.*
en·slave, *v.* esclavizar
en·sue, *v.* seguir
en·tail, *v.* vincular
en·tan·gle, *v.* enredar
en·ter, *v.* entrar (en); ingresar; anotar
en·ter·prise, *n.* empresa; iniciativa
en·ter·pris·ing, *a.* emprendedor
en·ter·tain, *v.* festejar; entretener;

considerar
en·ter·tain·ment, *n.* diversión; espectáculo
en·thrall, *v.* encantar. Also en·thral
en·thu·si·asm, *n.* entusiasmo
en·thu·si·ast, *n.* entusiasta, *m.,* *f.*
en·tice, *v.* tentar
en·tice·ment, *n.* tentación
en·tire, *a.* entero
en·tire·ly, *adv.* totalmente
en·tire·ty, *n.* totalidad
en·ti·tle, *v.* dar derecho; titular
en·ti·ty, *n. pl.,* -ties. entidad
en·trails, *n. pl.* entrañas
en·trance, *n.* entrada. Also en·trance·way
en·trance, *v.* hechizar
en·treat, *v.* rogar
en·treat·y, *n.* ruego
en·tree, *n.* entrada
en·trench, *v.* atrincherar
en·trench·ment, *n.* trinchera
en·trust, *v.* entregar; confiar
en·try, *n. pl.,* -tries. entrada; ingreso; partida
e·nu·mer·ate, *v.* enumerar
e·nu·mer·a·tion, *n.* enumeración
e·nun·ci·ate, *v.* enunciar; pronunciar
en·vel·op, *v.* envolver
en·ve·lope, *n.* sobre
en·vi·ous, *a.* envidioso
en·vi·ron·ment, *n.* ambiente
en·voy, *n. pl.,* -vies. envidia. *v.* envidiar
en·zyme, *n.* enzima
e·phem·er·al, *a.* efímero
ep·ic, *a.* épico. *n.* epopeya
ep·i·dem·ic, *a.* epidémico. *n.* epidemia
ep·i·der·mis, *n.* epidermis, *f.*
ep·i·lep·sy, *n.* epilepsia
ep·i·lep·tic, *a.,* *n.* epiléptico
ep·i·logue, ep·i·log, *n.* epílogo
e·pis·co·pal, *a.* episcopal
ep·i·sode, *n.* episodio
e·pis·tle, *n.* epístola
ep·i·taph, *n.* epitafio
ep·i·thet, *n.* epíteto
e·pit·o·me, *n.* resumen; epítome
e·pit·o·mize, *v.* epitomar
ep·och, *n.* época
e·qua·ble, *a.* uniforme
e·qual, *a.,* *n.* igual. *v.* igualar
e·qual·i·ty, *n. pl.,* -ties. igualdad
e·qual·ize, *v.* igualar
e·qual·ly, *adv.* igualmente
e·qua·nim·i·ty, *n.* ecuanimidad
e·quate, *v.* comparar
e·qua·tion, *n.* ecuación
e·qua·tor, *n.* ecuador
e·ques·tri·an, *a.* ecuestre. *n.* jinete
e·ques·tri·enne, *n. f.* jineta
e·qui·lib·ri·um, *n. pl.,* -ums, -a. equilibrio
e·qui·nox, *n.* equinoccio
e·quip, *v.* proveer; equipar
e·quip·ment, *n.* equipo
eq·ui·ta·ble, *a.* equitativo
eq·ui·ty, *n. pl.,* -ties. equidad
e·quiv·a·lent, *a.,* *n.* equivalente
e·quiv·o·cal, *a.* equívoco
e·ra, *n.* era
e·rad·i·cate, *v.* desarraigar
e·rad·i·ca·tion, *n.* extirpación
e·rase, *v.* borrar
e·ras·er, *n.* borrador
ere, *conj.* antes de que. *prep.* antes de
e·rect, *v.* levantar; erigir. *a.* erguido
e·rec·tion, *n.* erección; montaje
er·mine, *n. pl.,* -mine, -mines. armiño
e·rode, *v.* corroer
e·ro·sion, *n.* erosión
e·rot·ic, *a.* erótico
e·rot·i·cism, *n.* erotomanía
err, *v.* vagar; errar
er·rand, *n.* recado
er·rant, *a.* errante
er·rat·ic, *a.* errático; excéntrico
er·ro·ne·ous, *a.* erróneo
er·ror, *n.* error
erst·while, *a.* antiguo; primero
er·u·dite, *a.* erudito
er·u·di·tion, *n.* erudición
e·rupt, *v.* estar en erupción
e·rup·tion, *n.* erupción
es·ca·la·tor, *n.* escalera móvil
es·ca·pade, *n.* aventura
es·cape, *v.* escapar; huir. *n.* fuga; escape
es·chew, *v.* evitar
es·cort, *n.* acompañante; escolta. *v.* acompañar; escoltar
e·soph·a·gus, oe·soph·a·gus, *n. pl.,* -gi, -ji. esófago
es·o·ter·ic, *a.* esotérico
es·pe·cial, *a.* especial
es·pe·cial·ly, *adv.* especialmente
es·pi·o·nage, *n.* espionaje
es·pouse, *v.* adherirse a; casarse
es·py, *v.* divisar; percibir
es·say, *n.* ensayo. *v.* intentar
es·say·ist, *n.* ensayista, *m.,* *f.*
es·sence, *n.* esencia; perfume
es·sen·tial, *a.,* *n.* esencial
es·tab·lish, *v.* establecer; probar; fundar
es·tab·lish·ment, *n.* establecimiento
es·tate, *n.* finca; propiedad
es·teem, *v.* estimar. *n.* estima
es·thet·ic, *a.* estético
es·ti·ma·ble, *a.* estimable
es·ti·mate, *v.* calcular; estimar. *n.* tasa
es·ti·ma·tion, *n.* juicio; aprecio
es·trange, *v.* apartar
es·tu·ar·y, *n. pl.,* -ies. estuario

et cet·er·a, *n.* etcétera
etch, *v.* grabar al agua fuerte
etch·ing, *n.* aguafuerte, *f.*
e·ter·nal, *a.* eterno
e·ter·nal·ly, *adv.* eternamente
e·ter·ni·ty, *n. pl.,* -ties. eternidad
e·ther, *n.* éter
e·the·re·al, *a.* etéreo
eth·i·cal, *a.* ético
eth·ics, *n. pl.* ética
eth·nic, *a.* étnico. Also eth·ni·cal
eth·nol·o·gy, *n.* etnología
et·i·quette, *n.* etiqueta
é·tude, *n.* estudio
et·y·mol·o·gist, *n.* etimologista, *m.,* *f.*
et·y·mol·o·gy, *n. pl.,* -gies. etimología
eu·gen·ics, *n. pl.* eugenismo
eu·lo·gize, *v.* elogiar
eu·lo·gy, *n. pl.,* -gies. elogio
eu·nuch, *n.* eunuco
eu·phe·mism, *n.* eufemismo
eu·phon·ic, *a.* eufónico
eu·pho·ny, *n.* eufonía
eu·pho·ri·a, *n.* euforia
eu·phor·ic, *a.* eufórico
eu·tha·na·sia, *n.* eutanasia
e·vac·u·ate, *v.* evacuar
e·vac·u·a·tion, *n.* evacuación
e·vade, *v.* evadir
e·val·u·ate, *v.* evaluar
e·val·u·a·tion, *n.* evaluación
e·van·gel·i·cal, *a.* evangélico
e·van·ge·lism, *n.* evangelismo
e·van·ge·list, *n.* evangelista, *m.;* evangelizador
e·vap·o·rate, *v.* evaporar(se)
e·vap·o·ra·tion, *n.* evaporación
e·va·sion, *n.* evasión; evasiva
e·va·sive, *a.* evasivo
eve, *n.* víspera
e·ven, *a.* llano; uniforme; par. *adv.* aun. *v.* igualar; allanar
eve·ning, *n.* tarde, *f.* de noche
e·vent, *n.* suceso
e·vent·ful, *a.* memorable
e·ven·tu·al·i·ty, *n. pl.,* -ties. eventualidad
ev·er, *adv.* siempre; nunca; jamás
ev·er·y, *a.* cada; todo
e·vict, *v.* expulsar; desahuciar
e·vic·tion, *n.* desahucio
ev·i·dence, *n.* prueba; testimonio; evidencia. *v.* probar
ev·i·dent, *a.* evidente
e·vil, *a.* malo. *adv.* malamente. *n.* mal, *m.*
e·vil·do·er, *n.* malhechor
e·voke, *v.* evocar
ev·o·lu·tion, *n.* desarrollo; evolución
e·volve, *v.* desarrollar
ewe, *n.* oveja
ew·er, *n.* aguamanil, *m.*

ex·act, *v.* exigir. *a.* exacto
ex·act·ing, *a.* exigente
ex·ag·ger·ate, *v.* exagerar
ex·ag·ger·a·tion, *n.* exageración
ex·alt, *v.* exaltar; honrar
ex·al·ta·tion, *n.* exaltación
ex·am·i·na·tion, *n.* examen
ex·am·ine, *v.* examinar; interrogar
ex·am·in·er, *n.* examinador
ex·am·ple, *n.* ejemplo
ex·as·per·ate, *v.* exasperar
ex·as·per·a·tion, *n.* exasperación
ex·ca·vate, *v.* excavar
ex·ca·va·tion, *n.* excavación
ex·ceed, *v.* exceder; superar
ex·ceed·ing·ly, *adv.* sumamente
ex·cel, *v.* sobresalir; aventajar
ex·cel·lence, *n.* excelencia
ex·cel·lent, *a.* excelente
ex·cept, *v.* exceptuar. *prep.* excepto. *conj.* *a.* menos que
ex·cep·tion, *n.* excepción
ex·cep·tion·al, *a.* excepcional
ex·cerpt, *v.* citar un texto. *n.* extracto
ex·cess, *n.* exceso
ex·ces·sive, *a.* excesivo
ex·change, *v.* cambiar. *n.* cambio; canje
ex·cise, *n.* impuestos sobre ciertos artículos. Also ex·cise tax
ex·cit·a·ble, *a.* excitable
ex·cite, *v.* excitar; provocar
ex·cite·ment, *n.* agitación; emoción
ex·cit·ing, *a.* emocionante
ex·claim, *v.* exclamar
ex·cla·ma·tion, *n.* exclamación
ex·clude, *v.* excluir
ex·clu·sion, *n.* exclusión
ex·clu·sive, *a.* exclusivo
ex·com·mu·ni·cate, *v.* excomulgar
ex·com·mu·ni·ca·tion, *n.* excomunión
ex·cre·ment, *n.* excremento
ex·cur·sion, *n.* viaje; excursión
ex·cuse, *v.* perdonar; disculpar; excusar. *n.* excusa; disculpa
ex·e·cute, *v.* ejecutar; llevar a cabo
ex·e·cu·tion, *n.* ejecución
ex·ec·u·tive, *a.* ejecutivo. *n.* poder ejecutivo
ex·ec·u·tor, *n.* albacea, *m.*
ex·em·pla·ry, *a.* ejemplar
ex·em·pli·fy, *v.* chistoso
ex·empt, *v.* exentar. *a.* exento
ex·emp·tion, *n.* exención
ex·er·cise, *n.* ejercicio. *v.* ejercitar(se); ejercer
ex·ert, *v.* ejercer
ex·er·tion, *n.* esfuerzo
ex·hale, *v.* exhalar; espirar
ex·haust, *v.* agotar
ex·haus·tion, *n.* agotamiento
ex·haus·tive, *a.* minucioso
ex·hib·it, *v.* mostrar; presentar. *n.* objeto expuesto

ex·hi·bi·tion, *n.* exposición
ex·hib·i·tor, *n.* expositor
ex·hil·a·rate, *v.* vigorizar; alegrar
ex·hort, *v.* exhortar
ex·hor·ta·tion, *n.* exhortación
ex·i·gent, *a.* exigente
ex·ile, *n.* destierro; desterrado; exilado. *v.* desterrar
ex·ist, *v.* existir
ex·ist·ence, *n.* existencia
ex·it, *n.* salida
ex·o·dus, *n.* éxodo
ex·or·bi·tant, *a.* excesivo
ex·ot·ic, *a.* exótico
ex·pand, *v.* extender; ensanchar
ex·panse, *n.* extensión
ex·pan·sion, *n.* expansión
ex·pan·sive, *a.* expansivo
ex·pect, *v.* esperar; contar con
ex·pect·an·cy, *n. pl.,* -cies. expectación
ex·pect·ant, *a.* expectante
ex·pec·ta·tion, *n.* esperanza; expectación
ex·pe·di·en·cy, *n.* conveniencia
ex·pe·di·ent, *a.* conveniente. *n.* recurso
ex·pe·dite, *v.* facilitar; acelerar
ex·pe·di·tion, *n.* expedición
ex·pel, *v.* arrojar; expulsar
ex·pend, *v.* expender
ex·pend·i·ture, *n.* gasto; *pl.* gastos
ex·pense, *n.* gasto; *pl.* gastos
ex·pen·sive, *a.* caro
ex·pe·ri·ence, *n.* experiencia. *v.* experimentar
ex·per·i·ment, *n.* experimento
ex·per·i·men·tal, *a.* experimental
ex·pert, *a.,* *n.* experto
ex·pire, *v.* exhalar; morir; terminar
ex·plain, *v.* explicar
ex·pla·na·tion, *n.* explicación
ex·plic·it, *a.* explícito
ex·plic·it·ly, *adv.* explícitamente
ex·plode, *v.* estallar; volar
ex·ploit, *n.* hazaña. *v.* explotar
ex·ploi·ta·tion, *n.* explotación
ex·plo·ra·tion, *n.* exploración
ex·plore, *v.* explorar; examinar
ex·plor·er, *n.* explorador
ex·plo·sion, *n.* explosión
ex·po·nent, *n.* exponente
ex·port, *v.* exportar. *n.* exportación. *a.* de exportación
ex·por·ta·tion, *n.* exportación
ex·pose, *v.* exponer; desenmascarar
ex·po·si·tion, *n.* exposición
ex·po·sure, *n.* exposición; revelación
ex·pound, *v.* exponer
ex·press, *v.* expresar. *a.* explícito; rápido
ex·pres·sion, *n.* expresión; gesto
ex·pres·sive, *a.* expresivo
ex·pul·sion, *n.* expulsión
ex·pul·sive, *a.* expulsivo
ex·qui·site, *a.* exquisito; agudo
ex·tant, *a.* existente
ex·tem·po·ra·ne·ous, *a.* improviso
ex·tend, *v.* extender; ofrecer
ex·ten·sion, *n.* extensión; prolongación
ex·ten·sive, *a.* extenso
ex·tent, *n.* extensión; alcance
ex·te·ri·or, *a.,* *n.* exterior
ex·ter·mi·nate, *v.* exterminar
ex·ter·mi·na·tion, *n.* exterminación; exterminio
ex·ter·nal, *a.* externo
ex·tinct, *a.* extinto
ex·tinc·tion, *n.* extinción
ex·tin·guish, *v.* extinguir
ex·tol, *v.* alabar
ex·tort, *v.* obtener por fuerza
ex·tor·tion, *n.* exacción
ex·tra, *a.* adicional. *n.* extra. *adv.* extraordinariamente
ex·tract, *v.* extraer; sacar. *n.* cita
ex·trac·tion, *n.* extracción
ex·tra·or·di·nar·y, *a.* extraordinario
ex·trav·a·gance, *n.* exorbitancia
ex·trav·a·gant, *a.* pródigo
ex·treme, *a.,* *n.* extremo
ex·trem·i·ty, *n. pl.,* -ties. necesidad; *usu. pl.* extremidades
ex·tri·cate, *v.* desenredar
ex·tro·vert, *n.* extrovertido
ex·u·ber·ant, *a.* exuberante
ex·ude, *v.* rezumar
ex·ult, *v.* regocijarse
ex·ul·ta·tion, *n.* exultación
eye, *n.* ojo. *v.* ojear
eye·let, *n.* ojete
eye·tooth, *n. pl.,* -teeth. colmillo
eye·wit·ness, *n.* testigo ocular

F

fa·ble, *n.* fábula
fab·ric, *n.* tela
fab·ri·cate, *v.* inventar
fab·u·lous, *a.* fabuloso
fa·cade, *n.* fachada
face, *n.* cara; rostro. *v.* encararse
fac·et, *n.* faceta
fa·ce·tious, *a.* chistoso
fa·cial, *a.* facial
fac·ile, *a.* fácil
fa·cil·i·tate, *v.* facilitar
fa·cil·i·ty, *n. pl.,* -ties. facilidad; *often pl.* facilidades
fac·sim·i·le, *n.* facsímile
fact, *n.* hecho
fac·tion, *n.* facción
fac·tor, *n.* factor
fac·to·ry, *n. pl.,* -ries. fábrica
fac·tu·al, *a.* basado en datos
fac·ul·ty, *n.* facultad

fad, *n.* novedad
fade, *v.* descolorar(se)
fag, *v.* fatigar
fag·ot, *n.* haz de leña
Fahr·en·heit, *a.* de Fahrenheit
fail, *v.* faltar; acabar; fracasar
fail·ure, *n.* fracaso
faint, *v.* desmayarse. *n.* desmayo. *a.* débil
faint·ness, *n.* debilidad
fair, *a.* rubio; sereno; justo. *n.* feria
fair·ly, *adv.* justamente
fair·y, *n. pl.,* -ies. hada
faith, *n.* fe, *f.;* creencia; confianza
faith·ful, *a.* fiel
faith·ful·ly, *adv.* lealmente
faith·less, *a.* desleal
fake, *v.* fingir. *n.* impostura
fal·con, *n.* halcón
fall, *v.,* fell, fall·en, fall·ing. caer(se). *n.* caída; otoño; *usu. pl.* cascada. fall back, retroceder. fall off, disminuir. fall out, reñir. fall to, empezar
fal·la·cious, *a.* engañoso
fal·la·cy, *n.* error; falacia
fal·li·ble, *a.* falible
fal·low, *a.* en barbecho
false, *a.* falso
false·hood, *n.* mentira
false·ly, *adv.* falsamente
fal·si·fy, *v.* falsificar
fal·si·ty, *n.* falsedad
fal·ter, *v.* vacilar; titubear
fame, *n.* fama
fa·mil·iar, *a.* conocido; familiar
fa·mil·i·ar·i·ty, *n.* familiaridad
fam·i·ly, *n. pl.,* -lies. familia
fam·ine, *n.* hambre, *f.*
fam·ish, *v.* morirse de hambre
fa·mous, *a.* famoso
fan, *n.* abanico; aficionado. *v.* abanicar
fa·nat·ic, *a.,* *n.* fanático. Also fa·nat·i·cal
fa·nat·i·cism, *n.* fanatismo
fan·ci·er, *n.* aficionado
fan·ci·ful, *a.* fantástico
fan·cy, *n. pl.,* -cies. fantasía; capricho; inclinación. *a.* de lujo. *v.* imaginarse
fan·fare, *n.* toque de trompetas
fang, *n.* colmillo
fan·tas·tic, *a.* fantástico
fan·ta·sy, *n. pl.,* -sies. fantasía
far, *a.* lejano. *adv.* lejos
far·a·way, *a.* remoto
farce, *n.* farsa
far·ci·cal, *a.* ridículo
fare, *v.* pasarlo. *n.* precio; comida
fare·well, *int.* adiós. *n.* despedida
far·fetched, *a.* improbable
farm, *n.* granja; estancia. *v.* cultivar
farm·er, *n.* labrador; agricultor
farm·house, *n.* alquería
farm·ing, *n.* agricultura
far·off, *a.* lejano
fas·ci·nate, *v.* fascinar
fas·cism, *n.* fascismo
fas·cist, *a.,* *n.* fascista, *m.,* *f.*
fash·ion, *n.* estilo; moda; uso. *v.* formar
fash·ion·a·ble, *a.* de moda
fast, *a.* rápido; fijo; firme. *adv.* rápidamente. *v.* ayunar. *n.* ayuno
fas·ten, *v.* abrochar; asegurar
fas·tid·i·ous, *a.* fino; esquilimoso
fat, *a.* gordo; graso. *n.* grasa
fa·tal, *a.* fatal
fa·tal·ism, *n.* fatalismo
fa·tal·ist, *n.* fatalista, *m.,* *f.*
fa·tal·i·ty, *n. pl.,* -ties. fatalidad
fate, *n.* destino; hado; suerte, *f.*
fate·ful, *a.* fatal
fa·ther, *n.* padre. *v.* engendrar
fa·ther·hood, *n.* paternidad
fa·ther-in-law, *n. pl.,* fa·thers-in-law. suegro
fath·om, *n. pl.,* -oms, -om. braza. *v.* penetrar
fa·tigue, *n.* fatiga. *v.* fatigar
fat·ten, *v.* engordar
fau·cet, *n.* grifo
fault, *n.* defecto; falta; culpa. *v.* tachar
fault·y, *a.* defectuoso
fa·vor, *n.* favor. *v.* favorecer
fa·vor·a·ble, *a.* favorable
fa·vored, *a.* favorecido
fa·vor·ite, *a.,* *n.* favorito
fa·vor·it·ism, *n.* favoritismo
fawn, *n.* cervato
faze, *v.* perturbar
fear, *n.* miedo; temor. *v.* tener miedo
fear·ful, *a.* temeroso
fear·less, *a.* intrépido
fear·some, *a.* temible
fea·si·bil·i·ty, *n.* viabilidad
fea·si·ble, *a.* factible
feast, *n.* banquete; fiesta. *v.* banquetear
feat, *n.* proeza
feath·er, *n.* pluma
feath·er·y, *a.* plumoso
fea·ture, *n.* facción; rasgo. *v.* presentar
Feb·ru·ar·y, *n.* febrero
fe·ces, *n. pl.* excrementos
fe·cund, *a.* fecundo
fed·er·al, *a.* federal
fed·er·a·tion, *n.* federación
fee, *n.* honorario
fee·ble, *a.* débil
fee·bly, *adv.* flojamente
feed, *v.* dar de comer; alimentar
feel, *v.* sentir(se). *n.* tacto
feel·er, *n.* antena
feel·ing, *n.* sensación; emoción

feign, v. fingir
feint, n. treta
fe·lic·i·tate, v. felicitar
fe·lic·i·tous, a. oportuno; feliz
fe·lic·i·ty, n. felicidad
fe·line, a, n. felino
fell, v. derribar; talar
fel·low, n. compañero. a. asociado
fel·low·ship, n. compañerismo
fel·on, n. criminal, m., f.
fel·o·ny, n. crimen
felt, n. fieltro
fe·male, a. femenino. n. hembra
fem·i·nine, a. femenino
fem·i·nism, n. feminismo
fe·mur, n. fémur
fence, n. cerca. v. cercar; esgrimir
fenc·ing, n. esgrima
fend, v. rechazar
fend·er, n. guardafango
fer·ment, v. fermentar
fer·men·ta·tion, n. fermentación
fern, n. helecho
fe·ro·cious, a. feroz
fe·roc·i·ty, n. ferocidad
fer·ret, n. hurón
fer·ry, n. transbordador
fer·tile, c fértil; fecundo
fer·til·i·ty, n. fecundidad
fer·ti·lize, v. fertilizar; abonar
fer·ti·liz·er, n. abono
fer·vid, a. férvido
fer·vor, n. fervor
fes·ter, v. enconarse
fes·ti·val, n. fiesta
fes·tive, a. festivo
fes·tiv·i·ty, n. pl. -ties. regocijo; fiesta
fes·toon, n. festón
fetch, v. ir por
fetch·ing, a. atractivo
fete, fête, n. fiesta. v. festejar
fet·id, a. fétido
fet·ish, n. fetiche
fet·ter, n. grillos, pl. v. trabar
fet·tle, n. condición
fe·tus, n. feto
feud, n. enemistad. v. reñir
feu·dal, a. feudal
feu·dal·ism, n. feudalismo
fe·ver, n. fiebre, f.
fe·ver·ish, a. febril
few, a. pocos
fi·an·ce, n. novio
fi·an·cee, n. novia
fi·as·co, n. pl. -cos, -coes. fiasco
fi·at, n. fiat, m.
fib, n. bola. v. mentir
fi·ber, fi·bre, n. fibra
fi·brous, a. fibroso
fick·le, a. inconstante
fic·tion, n. ficción
fic·tion·al, a. novelesco
fic·ti·tious, a. ficticio

fid·dle, n. violín. v. tocar el violín
fi·del·i·ty, n. fidelidad
fidg·et, v. inquietar
fidg·et·y, a. inquieto; azogado
field, n. campo; esfera; prado
fiend, n. demonio
fiend·ish, a. diabólico
fierce, a. feroz
fier·y, a. ardiente; apasionado
fif·teen, a, n. quince
fif·teenth, a. decimoquinto
fifth, a. quinto. n. quinta
fif·ti·eth, a. quincuagésimo
fif·ty, a. n. cincuenta
fig, n. higo
fight, v. combate; lucha; pelea. v. luchar; pelear
fight·er, n. guerrero
fig·ment, n. invención
fig·ur·a·tive, a. figurado
fig·ure, n. figura; cifra; tipo. v. figurar(se). figure out, resolver
fig·ure·head, n. mascarón de proa
fig·ur·ine, n. figurín
fil·a·ment, n. filamento
filch, v. ratear
file, n. lima; archivo; fila. v. limar; archivar
fi·let, n. filete. Also fil·let
fil·i·bus·ter, n. obstruccionista
fil·i·gree, n. filigrana
fil·ings, n. pl. limaduras
fill, v. llenar; ocupar. fill out, llenar
fill·ing, n. empaste; relleno
fil·ly, n. pl. -lies. potra
film, n. película. v. filmar; empañarse
fil·ter, n. filtro. v. filtrar
filth, n. inmundicia
filth·y, a. sucio
fin, n. aleta
fi·nal, a. final; último
fi·na·le, n. final, m.
fi·nal·ist, n. finalista, m., f.
fi·nal·i·ty, n. finalidad
fi·nal·ly, adv. finalmente; por fin
fi·nance, n. finanzas; pl. fondos. v. financiar
fi·nan·cial, a. financiero
fin·an·cier, n. financiero
finch, n. pinzón
find, v. encontrar; descubrir; hallar
fine, a. fino; admirable; multa. v. multar
fin·er·y, n. adornos
fi·nesse, n. sutileza; diplomacia
fin·ger, n. dedo. v. tocar
fin·ger·nail, n. uña
fin·ger·print, n. huella dactilar
fin·ish, v. terminar; acabar. n. fin, m.; acabado
fi·nite, a. finito
fir, n. abeto
fire, n. fuego; ardor. v. encender; disparar; despedir

fire·arm, n. arma de fuego
fire·crack·er, n. petardo
fire en·gine, n. bomba de incendios
fire·fly, n. luciérnaga
fire·man, n. pl. -men. bombero
fire·place, n. hogar
fire·works, n. pl. fuegos artificiales
firm, n. firma. a. firme
fir·ma·ment, n. firmamento
firm·ly, adv. firmemente
firm·ness, n. firmeza
first, a., n. primero
first·class, a. de primera clase
first·hand, first·hand, a. de primera mano
first·rate, a. de primera clase
fis·cal, a. fiscal
fish, n. pl., fish, fish·es. pez, m.; pescado. v. pescar
fish·er·man, n. pl. -men. pescador
fish·er·y, n. pesquera
fish·y, a. sospechoso
fis·sion, n. fisión
fis·sure, n. grieta
fist, n. puño
fist·i·cuffs, n. pl. puñetazos
fit, n. acceso; ajuste. a. adecuado; sano. v. acomodar; proveer; probar
fit·ful, a. espasmódico
fit·ting, n. ajuste; pl. guarniciones. a. propio; conveniente
five, a., n. cinco
fix, v. fijar; preparar; arreglar. n. aprieto
fix·a·tion, n. fijación
fixed, a. fijo
fix·ture, n. cosa o instalación fija
flab·by, a. flojo; débil
flag, n. bandera. v. flaquear
flag·on, n. jarro; frasco
fla·grant, a. notorio
flag·stone, n. losa
flail, n. mayal, m. v. golpear
flair, n. instinto
flake, n. escama. v. formar hojuelas
flak·y, a. escamoso
flam·boy·ant, a. llamativo
flame, n. flamear. n. llama
flam·ma·ble, a. inflamable
flank, n. ijada; lado. v. lindar; flanquear
flap, v. sacudir; ondear. n. cartera; solapa
flare, n. brillar; fulgurar. n. bengala
flash, n. relámpago; ráfaga. v. lanzar
flash·light, n. linterna eléctrica
flash·y, a. charro
flask, n. frasco
flat, a. llano; plano; insípido. n. piso; pinchazo; bemol, m.
flat·ter, v. adular
flat·ter·y, n. adulación
flaunt, v. lucir
fla·vor, n. sabor. v. sazonar
fla·vor·ing, n. condimento
flaw, n. imperfección. v. estropear
flax, n. lino
flay, v. desollar
flea, n. pulga
fleck, n. mancha
flee, v. huir; fugarse; escapar de
fleece, n. vellón
fleec·y, a. lanudo
fleet, a. veloz. n. flota
fleet·ing, a. fugaz
flesh, n. carne, f.; pulpa
flex, v. doblar
flex·i·ble, a. flexible
flick, n. golpecito. v. dar un golpecito a
fli·er, n. aviador
flight, n. vuelo; huida; tramo
flim·sy, a. endeble
flinch, v. acobardarse
fling, v. arrojar
flint, n. pedernal, m.
flip, v. mover de un tirón
flip·pant, a. ligero
flirt, v. flirtear; coquetear. n. coqueta
flit, v. revolotear
float, v. flotar; hacer flotar. n. carroza
flock, n. rebaño. v. congregarse
floe, n. témpano
flog, v. azotar
flood, n. diluvio; inundación. v. inundar
floor, n. suelo; piso. v. solar; derribar
flop, v. caer pesadamente; fracasar
flo·ra, n. pl., -ras, -rae. flora
flo·ral, a. floral
flor·id, a. florido
flo·rist, n. florista, m., f.
floss, n. seda floja
flo·til·la, n. flotilla
flot·sam, n. pecio
flounce, v. moverse airadamente. n. volante
floun·der, v. tropezar
flour, n. harina
flour·ish, v. florecer; blandir. n. rasgo; floreo
flout, v. mofarse
flow, v. fluir; correr, f.; flujo
flow·er, n. flor, f. v. florecer
flu, n. infl. gripe, f.
fluc·tu·ate, v. fluctuar
flue, n. cañón de chimenea
flu·en·cy, n. fluidez, f.
flu·ent, a. facundo
fluff, n. plumosa
fluff·y, a. n. fluido
fluke, n. chiripa
flunk, v. inf. no aprobar
flu·o·res·cent, a. fluorescente
fluor·i·da·tion, n. fluorización
flur·ry, n. pl. -ries. ráfaga; agitación
flush, v. sonrojarse; brotar. n. rubor.

a. nivelado
flus·ter, v. aturdir
flute, n. flauta
flut·ter, v. menear; revolotear. n. agitación; aleteo
flux, n. mudanza; flujo. v. fundir
fly, v. pl., flies. mosca; bragueta. v. volar; ir en avión
fly·er, n. aviador
fly·wheel, n. rueda volante
foal, n. potro
foam, n. espuma
fo·cus, n. pl. -cus·es, fo·ci. foco. v. enfocar; concentrar
fod·der, n. forraje
foe, n. enemigo
fog, n. niebla
fo·gy, fo·gey, n. pl., -gies, -geys. persona de ideas anticuadas
foi·ble, n. flaco
foil, n. hoja; florete. n. frustrar
foist, v. encajar
fold, v doblar; plegar. n. pliegue
fold·er, n. carpeta
fo·li·age, n. follaje
folk, n. pl., folk, folks. gente, f.; pl. parientes
folk·lore, n. folklore
fol·li·cle, n. folículo
fol·low, v. seguir; resultar; perseguir
fol·low·er, n. seguidor; partidario
fol·low·ing, n. séquito. a. siguiente
fol·ly, n. pl., -lies. locura; tontería
fo·ment, v. fomentar
fond, a. cariñoso
fon·dle, v. acariciar
fond·ly, adv. afectuosamente
food, n. alimento
fool, n. tonto. v. embaucar; engañar
fool·har·dy, a. temerario
fool·ish, a. necio
fool·proof, a. infalible
foot, n. pl., feet. pie; pata
foot·ball, n. fútbol, m.
foot·note, n. nota
foot·print, n. huella
foot·step, n. paso
fop, n. petimetre
for, prep. por; para. conj. pues
for·age, n. forraje. v. forrajear
for·ay, n. correría
for·bear, v. contenerse
for·bid, v. prohibir
for·bid·den, a. prohibido
for·bid·ding, a. severo
force, n. fuerza; vigor; cuerpo. v. forzar
force·ful, a. vigoroso; poderoso
for·ceps, n. fórceps, m.
for·ci·ble, a. enérgico; eficaz
ford, n. vado. v. vadear
fore, a. anterior
fore·arm, n. antebrazo
fore·bode, for·bode, v. presagiar
fore·bod·ing, n. presentimiento
fore·cast, v. pronosticar. n. pronóstico
fore·fa·ther, n. antepasado
fore·fin·ger, n. dedo índice
fore·go, v. preceder; renunciar
fore·gone, a. predeterminado
fore·ground, n. primer plano
fore·head, n. frente, f.
for·eign, a. extranjero; exterior
for·eign·er, n. extranjero
fore·man, n. pl., -men. capataz, m.
fore·most, a. primero
fore·run·ner, n. precursor
fore·see, v. prever
fore·sight, n. previsión; perspicacia
fore·skin, n. prepucio
for·est, n. bosque
for·est·ry, n. silvicultura
fore·tell, v. predecir
for·ev·er, adv. siempre
fore·word, n. prefacio
for·feit, v. perder
for·fei·ture, n. pérdida; multa
forge, n. fragua. v. forjar; falsear
for·ger·y, n. falsificación
for·get, v. olvidar(se)
for·get·ful, a. olvidadizo
for·give, v. perdonar
for·give·ness, n. perdón
fork, n. tenedor. v. bifurcarse
for·lorn, a. abandonado
form, n. forma. v. formar; establecer
for·mal, a. ceremonioso
for·mal·i·ty, n. pl., -ties. formalidad; ceremonia
for·mat, n. formato
for·ma·tion, n. formación
for·mer, a. anterior
for·mer·ly, adv. antiguamente
for·mi·da·ble, a. formidable
for·mu·la, n. pl., -las, -lae. fórmula
for·ni·cate, v. fornicar
for·ni·ca·tion, n. fornicación
for·sake, v. abandonar
for·te, a. fuerte
forth, adv. en adelante
forth·com·ing, a. próximo
forth·right, a. directo
forth·with, adv. sin dilación
for·ti·eth, a. cuadragésimo
for·ti·fi·ca·tion, n. fortificación
for·ti·fy, v. fortalecer
for·ti·tude, n. fortaleza
for·tress, n. fortaleza
for·tu·i·tous, a. fortuito
for·tu·nate, a. afortunado
for·tune, n. fortuna; suerte, f.
for·ty, n. pl., -ties. cuarenta
fo·rum, n. foro
for·ward, adv. adelante. Also for·wards. a. delantero; atrevido. v. enviar
fos·sil, n. fósil, m.

foul, a. sucio; vil. n. falta. v. ensuciar
found, v.; pt. and pp. of find. fundar
foun·da·tion, n. fundación; base, f.
found·ling, n. niño expósito
found·ry, n. pl. -ries. fundición
fount, n. fuente, f.
foun·tain, n. fuente, f.
four, a., n. cuatro
four·score, a., n. ochenta
four·teen, a., n. catorce
four·teenth, a. decimocuarto
fourth, a., n. cuarto
fowl, n. ave, f.; pollo
fox, n. pl., fox·es. zorra. v. confundir
fox·y, a. astuto
foy·er, n. vestíbulo
fra·cas, n. riña
frac·tion, n. fracción; porción
frac·tious, a. rebelón
frac·ture, n. fractura. v. fracturar; quebrar
frag·ile, a. frágil
frag·ment, n. fragmento
fra·grance, n. fragancia
fra·grant, a. oloroso
frail, a. débil; frágil
frail·ty, n. pl., -ties. fragilidad
frame, n. estructura; marco. v. poner un marco a
frame·work, n. esqueleto
franc, n. franco
fran·chise, n. derecho de sufragio
frank, a. franco. v. franquear
frank·furt·er, n. salchicha
frank·in·cense, n. incienso
frank·ly, adv. francamente
frank·ness, n. franqueza
fran·tic, a. frenético
fra·ter·nal, a. fraternal
fra·ter·ni·ty, n. pl., -ties. fraternidad
fraud, n. fraude
fraud·u·lent, a. fraudulento
fraught, a. lleno de
fray, v. deshilacharse
freak, n. monstruosidad; fenómeno
freck·le, n. peca
free, a. libre; gratis. v. libertar
free·boot·er, n. pirata, m.
free·dom, n. libertad
free·way, n. autopista
freeze, v. helar(se); congelar
freight, n. flete
freight·er, n. buque de carga
French, a., n. francés
fre·net·ic, a. frenético
fren·zy, n. pl., -zies. frenesí, m.
fre·quen·cy, n. pl., -cies. frecuencia
fre·quent, a. frecuente. v. frecuentar
fres·co, n. pl., -cos, -coes. fresco
fresh, a. fresco; nuevo
fresh·en, v. refrescar(se)
fresh·man, n. pl., -men. estudiante de primer año
fret, v. apurarse
fret·ful, a. displicente
fri·ar, n. fraile
fric·tion, n. fricción; frote
Fri·day, n. viernes, m.
friend, n. amigo
friend·ly, a. amistoso
friend·ship, n. amistad
frieze, n. friso
fright, n. susto
fright·en, v. asustar
fright·ful, a. espantoso
frig·id, a. frío
frill, n. lechuga
fringe, n. orla; margen
frisk, v. retozar
frisk·y, a. juguetón
frit·ter, v. desperdiciar. n. buñuelo
friv·o·lous, a. frívolo
fro, adv. atrás
frock, n. vestido
frog, n. rana
frol·ic, n. travesura. v. juguetear
frol·ic·some, a. retozón
from, prep. de; desde; por
fron·tal, a. frontal
fron·tier, n. frontera
frost, n. helada; escarcha
frost·bit·ten, a. congelado
froth, n. espuma
fro·ward, a. indócil
frown, v. mirar con ceño. n. ceño
frow·zy, a. desaliñado
fru·gal, a. frugal
fruit, n. fruta
fruit·ful, a. provechoso
fru·i·tion, n. realización
fruit·less, a. infructuoso
frus·trate, v. frustrar
frus·tra·tion, n. frustración
fry, v. freír(se)
fudge, v. contrahacer. n. dulce
fu·gi·tive, a., n. fugitivo
fu·el, n. combustible
ful·crum, n. pl., -crums, -cra. fulcro
ful·fill, ful·fil, v. cumplir; realizar
ful·fill·ment, ful·fil·ment, n. cumplimiento
full, a. lleno; completo. adv. en pleno
full·blown, a. maduro
full·ness, n. amplitud
ful·ly, adv. completamente
ful·mi·nate, v. volar; tronar
ful·some, a. insincero
fum·ble, v. manosear
fume, n. vaho. v. humear; enojarse
fu·mi·gate, v. fumigar
fun, n. diversión
func·tion, n. función. v. funcionar
func·tion·al, a. funcional
fund, n. fondo; pl. fondos. v. acumular; consolidar

fun·da·men·tal, a. fundamental. n. esencial
fu·ner·al, n. entierro
fu·ne·re·al, a. fúnebre
fun·gus, n. pl., -gi, -gus·es. hongo
fun·nel, n. embudo
fun·ny, a. gracioso; cómico
fur, n. piel, f.
fu·ri·ous, a. furioso
furl, v. aferrar
fur·long, n. estadio
fur·lough, n. licencia
fur·nace, n. horno
fur·nish, v. proveer; proporcionar
fur·nish·ings, n. pl. mobiliario
fur·ni·ture, n. mueblaje
fu·ror, n. furor
fur·row, n. surco. v. surcar
fur·ry, a. peludo
fur·ther, adv. más lejos; además. a. más lejos; nuevo. v. adelantar
fur·ther·more, adv. además
fur·thest, a, adv. más lejos
fur·tive, a. furtivo
fu·ry, n. pl., -ries. furia
fuse, n. fusible; espoleta. v. fundir
fuss, n. bulla. v. preocuparse
fuss·y, a. exigente
fu·tile, a. inútil
fu·ture, a, n. futuro
fuzz, n. pelusa
fuzz·y, a. velloso

G

gab·ar·dine, n. gabardina
ga·ble, n. aguilón; faldón
gad, v. andorrear
gad·fly, n. tábano
gad·get, n. aparato
gaff, n. arpón
gag, v. amordazar. n. mordaza; inf. chiste
gai·e·ty, n. alegría
gai·ly, adv. alegremente
gain, v. ganar; alcanzar. n. ganancia
gain·say, v. contradecir
gait, n. modo de andar
ga·la, n. fiesta
gal·ax·y, n. pl., -ies. galaxia
gale, n. ventarrón
gall, n. bilis, f.; descaro. v. irritar
gal·lant, a. valeroso
gal·lant·ry, n. galantería
gal·ler·y, n. pl., -ies. galería
gal·ley, n. galera; fogón
gal·lon, n. galón
gal·lop, n. galope. v. galopar
gal·lows, n. horca
gal·va·nize, v. galvanizar
gam·bit, n. gambito
gam·ble, v. jugar. n. jugada
gam·bol, v. brincar
game, n. juego; partido; caza. a. cojo. v. jugar
gam·ut, n. gama
gan·der, n. ganso; inf. vistazo
gang, n. pandilla
gang·plank, n. plancha
gang·grene, n. gangrena
gang·ster, n. gángster; pistolero
gang·way, n. pasillo
gap, n. abertura; hueco
ga·rage, n. garaje
garb, n. vestido
gar·bage, n. basura
gar·ble, v. mutilar
gar·den, n. jardín
gar·gan·tu·an, a. colosal
gar·gle, v. gargarizar. n. gárgaras
gar·ish, a. llamativo
gar·land, n. guirnalda
gar·ment, n. prenda de vestir
gar·ner, n. granero. v. entrojar
gar·net, n. granate
gar·nish, v. aderezar; adornar. n. aderezo
gar·ret, n. guardilla
gar·ri·son, n. guarnición
gar·ru·lous, a. gárrulo
gar·ter, n. liga
gas, n. gas; gasolina. v. asfixiar con gas
gas·e·ous, a. gaseoso
gash, n. cuchillada. v. hender
gas·o·line, n. gasolina
gasp, v. boquear. n. boqueada
gas·tric, a. gástrico
gas·tron·o·my, n. gastronomía
gate, n. puerta
gate·way, n. paso
gath·er, v. reunir; recoger; fruncir. n. frunce
gauche, a. torpe
gaud·y, a. chillón
gauge, n. norma de medida; indicador, v. medir
gaunt, a. flaco
gaunt·let, n. guantelete
gauze, n. gasa
gauz·y, a. de gasa
gawk·y, a. desgarbado
gay, a. alegre; vistoso
gaze, v. mirar. n. mirada
ga·zelle, n. gacela
ga·zette, n. gaceta
gaz·et·teer, n. diccionario geográfico
gear, n. engranaje; herramientas. v. engranar
gel·a·tin, n. gelatina
ge·lat·i·nous, a. gelatinoso
geld, v. castrar
gem, n. joya; gema
gen·der, n. género
gene, n. gen
ge·ne·al·o·gy, n. genealogía
gen·er·al, a. general; usual. in gen·er·al, en general

gen·er·al·i·ty, n. generalidad
gen·er·al·ize, v. generalizar
gen·er·ate, v. generar
gen·er·a·tion, n. generación
gen·er·a·tor, n. generador
ge·ner·ic, a. genérico
gen·er·os·i·ty, n. generosidad
gen·er·ous, a. generoso
gen·e·sis, n. génesis, f.; (cap.) Génesis
ge·net·ic, a. genésico
ge·net·ics, n. pl. genética
gen·ial, a. afable
gen·i·tal, a. genital
gen·i·tals, n. pl. órganos genitales
gen·ius, n. genio
gen·o·cide, n. genocidio
gen·teel, a. elegante; bien criado
gen·til·i·ty, n. gentileza
gen·tle, a. suave; apacible
gen·tle·man, n. pl., -men. caballero; señor
gen·tly, adv. suavemente
gen·u·ine, a. genuino; sincero
ge·nus, n. género
ge·o·gra·pher, n. geógrafo
ge·o·graph·ic, ge·o·graph·i·cal, a. geográfico
ge·og·ra·phy, n. geografía
ge·o·log·ic, ge·o·log·i·cal, a. geológico
ge·ol·o·gist, n. geólogo
ge·ol·o·gy, n. geología
ge·o·met·ric, a. geométrico
ge·om·e·try, n. geometría
ge·o·phys·i·cal, a. geofísico
ge·o·phys·ics, n. pl. geofísica
ger·i·at·rics, n. pl. geriatría
germ, n. germen
ger·mane, a. relativo
ger·mi·nate, v. germinar
ger·mi·na·tion, n. germinación
ger·und, n. gerundio
ges·tic·u·late, v. gesticular
ges·ture, n. ademán; gesto. v. hacer gestos
get, v. got, got or got·ten, get·ting. obtener; lograr; comprender. get a·way, quitar. get at, llegar a. get e·ven with, desquitarse con. get o·ver, vencer. get up, levantarse
gey·ser, n. géiser
ghast·ly, a. horrible
gher·kin, n. pepinillo
ghost, n. fantasma, m.
ghost·ly, a. espectral
ghoul, n. demonio
GI, n. pl. GI's, GIs. soldado. Also G.I.
gi·ant, n. gigante. a. gigantesco
gib·ber·ish, n. galimatías; jerga
gib·bon, n. gibón
gib·let, n. usu. pl. menudillos
gid·di·ness, n. vértigo
gid·dy, a. mareado; ligero
gift, n. regalo; don
gi·gan·tic, a. gigantesco
gig·gle, n. risa sofocada
gild, v. dorar
gill, n. agalla
gilt, a. dorado
gim·mick, n. truco
gin, n. desmotadera de algodón; ginebra
gin·ger, n. jengibre
gin·ger ale, n. cerveza de jengibre
gin·ger·bread, n. pan de jengibre
gin·ger·ly, a. cauteloso
gip·sy, gyp·sy, n. pl., -sies. gitano
gi·raffe, n. jirafa
gird, v. ceñir
gird·er, n. viga
gir·dle, n. cinto; faja
girl, n. niña; chica; muchacha
girl·ish, a. de niña
girth, n. cincha
gist, n. esencial; clave, f.
give, v. gave, giv·en, giv·ing. dar; conceder; entregar; permitir; ceder. give in, ceder. give off, emitir. give out, estar agotado; distribuir. give up, entregar; renunciar
giv·en, a. citado
giz·zard, n. molleja
gla·cial, a. glacial
gla·cier, n. glaciar
glad, a. alegre
glad·den, v. regocijar
glade, n. claro
glad·ly, adv. con mucho gusto
glad·ness, n. alegría
glad·i·o·lus, n. gladíolo; gladiolo. Also glad·i·o·la
glam·our, glam·or, n. encanto
glam·our·ous, a. encantador
glance, v. mirar; lanzar miradas; rebotar. n. vistazo; ojeada
gland, n. glándula
glan·du·lar, a. glandular
glare, v. relumbrar. n. brillo; mirada feroz
glar·ing, a. evidente
glass, n. vidrio; vaso; pl. gafas
glass·y, a. vítreo
glau·co·ma, n. glaucoma, m.
glaze, v. vidriar. n. barniz, m.
gleam, n. destello. v. brillar
glean, v. espigar
glee, n. júbilo
glen, n. cañada
glide, v. deslizarse. n. planeo
glim·mer, v. brillar débilmente
glimpse, n. vislumbre, f.
glint, v. destellar
glis·ten, v. relucir
glit·ter, v. relucir. n. resplandor
gloat, v. manifestar satisfacción

maligna
globe, *n.* globo; esfera
glob·ule, *n.* glóbulo
gloom, *n.* oscuridad; tristeza
gloom·y, *a.* lóbrego; melancólico
glo·ri·fy, *v.* glorificar
glo·ri·ous, *a.* glorioso
glo·ry, *n.* gloria. *v.* gloriarse
gloss, *n.* lustre
glos·sa·ry, *n. pl.,* **-ries.** glosario
gloss·y, *a.* lustroso
glot·tis, *n.* glotis, *f.*
glove, *n.* guante
glow, *v.* brillar. *n.* calor vivo
glow·er, *v.* mirar con ceño
glow-worm, *n.* luciérnaga
glue, *v.* pegar; encolar. *n.* cola
glum, *a.* abatido
glut, *v.* hartar
glut·ton, *n.* glotón
glut·ton·y, *n.* gula
gnarl, *v.* torcer
gnash, *v.* rechinar
gnat, *n.* jején
gnaw, *v.* roer
gnome, *n.* gnomo
go, *v.* went, gone, go·ing. ir(se); marchar(se); convenir. *n.* energía. **go af·ter,** seguir. **go off,** dispararse. **go over,** revisar. **go with,** acompañar
goad, *n.* aguijada; incitar
goal, *n.* meta; gol, *m.*
goat, *n.* cabra
gob·ble, *v.* engullir
gob·let, *n.* copa
gob·lin, *n.* trasgo
God, *n.* Dios
god, *n.* dios
god·child, *n. pl.,* **-chil·dren.** ahijado
god-daugh·ter, *n.* ahijada
god·dess, *n.* diosa
god·fa·ther, *n.* padrino
god·ly, *a.* piadoso
god·moth·er, *n.* madrina
god·par·ent, *n.* padrino; madrina
god·send, *n.* buena suerte
god·son, *n.* ahijado
gog·gles, *n. pl.* anteojos
go·ing, *n.* ida; estado del camino
gold, *n.* oro; dinero. *a.* de oro
golf, *n.* golf, *m.*
gon·do·la, *n.* góndola
gon·do·lier, *n.* gondolero
gong, *n.* gong, *m.*
gon·or·rhe·a, *n.* gonorrea
good, *a.* bien; *pl.* mercancías; efectos. *a.* **bet·ter, best.** bueno; bondadoso; genuino; válido
good-by, **good-bye,** *int., n.* adiós
good-heart·ed, *a.* amable
good-look·ing, *a.* guapo
good·ly, *a.* agradable; considerable
good·ness, *n.* bondad
good·y, *n. pl.,* **-ies,** *inf.* golosina
goose, *n. pl.,* **geese.** ganso
goose·ber·ry, *n. pl.,* **-ries.** uva espina
gore, *n.* sangre, *f.;* nesga. *v.* acornear
gorge, *n.* barranco. *v.* hartarse
gor·geous, *a.* magnífico; vistoso
gos·pel, *n.* evangelio
gos·sa·mer, *n.* gasa sutil
gos·sip, *n.* chisme; comadre, *f. v.* charlar
gouge, *n.* gubia. *v.* excavar
gourd, *n.* calabaza
gour·met, *n.* gastrónomo
gout, *n.* gota
gov·ern, *v.* gobernar
gov·ern·ess, *n.* institutriz, *f.*
gov·ern·ment, *n.* gobierno
gov·er·nor, *n.* gobernador; director
gown, *n.* vestido
grab, *v.* asir; arrebatar. *n.* agarro
grace, *n.* elegancia; gracia; bendición de la mesa. *v.* adornar
grace·ful, *a.* gracioso
gra·cious, *a.* agradable; cortés
gra·da·tion, *n.* gradación
grade, *n.* grado; clase, *f. v.* clasificar
grad·u·al, *a.* gradual
grad·u·al·ly, *adv.* poco a poco
grad·u·ate, *v.* graduar(se). *n.* licenciado
grad·u·a·tion, *n.* graduación
graft, *n.* injerto; soborno. *v.* injertar
grain, *n.* grano; fibra
gram, *n.* gramo
gram·mar, *n.* gramática
gram·mat·i·cal, *a.* gramatical
gra·na·ry, *n. pl.,* **-ries.** granero
grand, *a.* grandioso; augusto; magnífico
grand·child, *n. pl.,* **-chil·dren.** nieto
grand-daugh·ter, *n.* nieta
grand·fa·ther, *n.* abuelo
gran·di·ose, *a.* grandioso; pomposo
grand·moth·er, *n.* abuela
grand·par·ent, *n.* abuelo
grand·son, *n.* nieto
grange, *n.* cortijo
gran·ite, *n.* granito
grant, *v.* otorgar; conceder; conferir. *n.* cesión; concesión
gran·u·late, *v.* granular
gran·ule, *n.* gránulo
grape, *n.* uva
grape·fruit, *n.* toronja
graph, *n.* gráfica
graph·ic, *a.* gráfico
graph·ite, *n.* grafito
grap·nel, *n.* arpeo
grap·ple, *n.* arpeo. *v.* agarrar
grasp, *v.* agarrar; comprender. *n.* asimiento; garras
grasp·ing, *a.* codicioso
grass, *n.* pasto; hierba; césped, *m.*
grass·hop·per, *n.* saltamontes

grass·y, *a.* herboso
grate, *n.* parrilla de hogar. *v.* rechinar
grate·ful, *a.* agradecido
grat·i·fi·ca·tion, *n.* gratificación; placer
grat·i·fy, *v.* complacer; satisfacer
grat·ing, *n.* reja
gra·tis, *a., adv.* gratis
grat·i·tude, *n.* reconocimiento
gra·tu·i·tous, *a.* gratuito; injustificado
gra·tu·i·ty, *n. pl.,* **-ties.** propina
grave, *n.* sepultura. *a.* grave
grav·el, *n.* cascajo
grav·en, *a.* grabado
grave·yard, *n.* cementerio
grav·i·tate, *v.* gravitar
grav·i·ta·tion, *n.* gravitación
grav·i·ty, *n. pl.,* **-ties.** seriedad; gravedad
gra·vy, *n.* salsa
gray, **grey,** *a., n.* gris
graze, *v.* pacer; rozar
grease, *n.* grasa. *v.* engrasar
greas·y, *a.* grasiento
great, *a.* grande; gran
greed, *n.* avaricia; codicia
greed·y, *a.* avaro; codicioso; goloso
green, *a., n.* verde
green·er·y, *n.* verdura
greet, *v.* saludar
greet·ing, *n.* saludo
gre·gar·i·ous, *a.* gregario
gre·nade, *n.* granada de mano
grid, *n.* reja; parrilla
grid·dle, *n.* tortera
grid·i·ron, *n.* campo de fútbol; parrilla
grief, *n.* pesar
griev·ance, *n.* agravio
grieve, *v.* afligirse
griev·ous, *a.* grave; penoso
grif·fin, grif·fon, *n.* grifo
grill, *v.* asar a la parrilla; *inf.* interrogar
grille, grill, *n.* verja
grim, *a.* inflexible; severo
gri·mace, *n.* visaje. *v.* hacer muecas
grime, *n.* mugre, *f.*
grim·y, *a.* mugriento
grin, *v.* sonreír. *n.* sonrisa burlona
grind, *v.* moler; pulverizar
grind·stone, *n.* muela
grip, *v.* agarro; apretón; saco de mano. *v.* asir
grippe, *n.* gripe, *f.*
gris·ly, *a.* horroroso
gris·tle, *n.* cartílago
grit, *n.* arena; firmeza
grit·ty, *a.* arenoso
griz·zled, *a.* gris
griz·zly, *a.* gris
groan, *v.* gemir. *n.* gemido
gro·cer, *n.* abacero
gro·cer·y, *n. pl.,* **-ies.** abacería; *pl.* comestibles
groin, *n.* ingle, *f.*
groom, *n.* novio; mozo de caballos. *v.* cuidar
groove, *n.* estría
grope, *v.* buscar a tientas
gross, *a.* bruto; grosero; grueso. *n.* gruesa
gro·tesque, *a.* grotesco
grot·to, *n. pl.,* **-toes, -tos.** gruta
grouch, *v. inf.* refunfuñar
ground, *n. sometimes pl.* tierra; terreno; razón; poso. *a.* molido
ground·work, *n.* fundamento
group, *n.* grupo. *v.* agrupar
grouse, *v.* quejarse
grove, *n.* arboleda
grov·el, *v.* arrastrarse
grow, *v.* grew, grown, grow·ing. crecer; cultivar; aumentar
growl, *v.* gruñir
grown-up, *a.* adulto
grown-up, *n.* adulto
growth, *n.* crecimiento; tumor
grub·by, *a.* sucio
grudge, *v.* dar de mala gana. *n.* rencor
gru·el·ing, *a.* penoso
grue·some, *a.* horrible
gruff, *a.* malhumorado
grum·ble, *v.* quejarse
grump·y, *a.* gruñón
grunt, *v.* gruñir. *n.* gruñido
guar·an·tee, *v.* garantizar. *n.* garantía. Also **guar·an·ty**
guard, *v.* guardar; vigilar. *n.* guardia
guard·house, *n.* cárcel militar
guard·i·an, *n.* guardián
gu·ber·na·to·ri·al, *a.* del gobernador
guer·ril·la, *n.* guerrillero
guess, *v.* adivinar; imaginar. *n.* conjetura
guest, *n.* huésped; convidado
guf·faw, *n.* carcajada
guid·ance, *n.* gobierno
guide, *v.* guiar. *n* guía, *m., f.*
guild, *n.* gremio
guile, *n.* astucia
guil·lo·tine, *n.* guillotina
guilt, *n.* culpabilidad
guilt·y, *a.* culpable
guise, *n.* modo; apariencia
gui·tar, *n.* guitarra
gulf, *n.* golfo
gull, *n.* gaviota. *v.* timar
gul·let, *n.* esófago
gul·li·ble, *a.* crédulo
gul·ly, *n. pl.,* **-lies.** barranca
gulp, *v.* tragar. *n.* trago
gum, *n.* encía; goma; chicle. *v.* engomar
gun, *n.* arma de fuego
gun·pow·der, *n.* pólvora

gun·wale, gun·nel, *n.* regala
gur·gle, *v.* gorgotear. *n.* gorgoteo
gush, *v.* chorrear
gust, *n.* ráfaga
gus·to, *n.* gusto; entusiasmo
gut, *n.* intestino; cuerda de tripa; *pl. inf.* valor. *v.* destripar
gut·ter, *n.* arroyo; gotera
gut·tur·al, *a.* gutural
guy, *n.* viento; *inf.* individuo; tío
guz·zle, *v.* engullir
gym, *n. inf.* gimnasio
gym·na·si·um, *n.* gimnasio
gym·nast, *n.* gimnasta, *m., f.*
gym·nas·tic, *a.* gimnástico
gym·nas·tics, *n.* gimnasia
gy·ne·col·o·gy, *n.* ginecología
gyp, *v. inf.* estafar. *n.* estafa
gyp·sum, *n.* yeso
gyp·sy, *n. pl.,* **-sies.** gitano
gy·rate, *v.* girar
gy·ro·scope, *n.* giroscopio

H

ha, hah, *int.* ah
hab·it, *n.* hábito; costumbre, *f.*
hab·it·a·ble, *a.* habitable
hab·i·tat, *n.* habitación
hab·i·ta·tion, *n.* habitación
ha·bit·u·al, *a.* habitual
ha·bit·u·ate, *v.* acostumbrarse
hack, *v.* acuchillar. *n.* tos seca; rocín
hack·neyed, *a.* trillado
had, *v. pt. and pp.* of **have**
hag, *n.* bruja
hag·gard, *a.* ojeroso
hag·gle, *v.* regatear
hail, *v.* saludar; granizar. *int.* salve. *n.* saludo; granizo
hail·stone, *n.* piedra de granizo
hair, *n.* pelo; cabello
hair·breadth, *n.* ancho de un pelo. Also **hair's-breadth, hairs·breadth**
hair·dress·er, *n.* peluquero
hair·pin, *n.* horquilla
hale, *a.* robusto
half, *n. pl.,* **halves.** mitad. *a.* medio. *adv.* medio
half-heart·ed, *a.* indiferente
half·way, *adv.* a medio camino
half-wit, *n.* imbécil; tonto
hall, *n.* sala; vestíbulo
hal·le·lu·jah, *int.* aleluya
hal·low, *v.* consagrar
hal·lu·ci·na·tion, *n.* alucinación
hall·way, *n.* pasillo
ha·lo, *n. pl.,* **-los, -loes.** halo; aureola
halt, *n.* parada. *v.* parar; hacer alto
hal·ter, *n.* cabestro
halt·ing, *a.* vacilante
halve, *v.* partir por mitad
ham, *n.* jamón
ham·burg·er, *n.* hamburguesa
ham·let, *n.* aldehuela
ham·mer, *n.* martillo. *v.* martillar
ham·mock, *n.* hamaca
ham·per, *v.* impedir. *n.* canasta
hand, *n.* mano, *f.;* obrero; aplauso. *v.* dar; alargar
hand·bag, *n.* bolso
hand·book, *n.* manual
hand·cuff, *n. usu. pl.* esposas. *v.* maniatar
hand·ful, *n. pl.,* **-fuls,** puñado
hand·i·cap, *n.* desventaja. *v.* perjudicar
hand·i·craft, *n.* mano de obra; artesanía
hand·i·ly, *adv.* con destreza
hand·i·work, *n.* obra
hand·ker·chief, *n.* pañuelo
han·dle, *n.* mango; manubrio. *v.* manosear; tocar; manejar
hand·maid·en, *n.* criada. Also **hand·maid**
hand·some, *a.* hermoso; generoso
hand·y, *a.* conveniente; próximo; hábil
hand·y-man, *n. pl.,* **-men.** factótum
hang, *v.* hung or hanged. colgar; ahorcar; pegar
hang·er-on, *n. pl.,* **-ers-on.** pegote
han·ker, *v.* anhelar
han·ker·ing, *n.* anhelo; añoranza
hap·haz·ard, *a.* fortuito
hap·less, *a.* desventurado
hap·pen, *v.* ocurrir; pasar; acontecer
hap·pen·ing, *n.* acontecimiento
hap·pi·ly, *adv.* alegremente
hap·pi·ness, *n.* felicidad; alegría
hap·py, *a.* feliz; oportuno
ha·rangue, *n.* arenga. *v.* arengar
ha·rass, *v.* atormentar; acosar
har·ass·ment, *n.* hostigamiento
har·bor, *n.* puerto. *v.* hospedar; abrigar
hard, *a.* duro; firme; difícil. *adv.* diligentemente; mucho
hard-core, *a.* inflexible
hard·en, *v.* endurecer
hard-heart·ed, *a.* cruel
har·di·ness, *n.* robustez, *f.*
hard·ly, *adv.* apenas; difícilmente
hard·ness, *n.* dureza
hard·ship, *n.* privación; pena
hard·ware, *n.* ferretería
har·dy, *a.* robusto
hare, *n. pl.,* **hares, hare.** liebre, *f.*
har·em, *n.* harén
hark, *v.* escuchar
har·lot, *n.* ramera
har·lot·ry, *n.* prostitución
harm, *n.* daño. *v.* dañar; hacer daño a
harm·ful, *a.* dañino; perjudicial
harm·less, *a.* innocuo
har·mon·i·ca, *n.* armónica

har·mo·ni·ous, *a.* armonioso
har·mo·nize, *v.* armonizar
har·mo·ny, *n. pl.,* **-nies.** armonía
har·ness, *n.* arreos. *v.* enjaezar; *fig.* utilizar
harp, *n.* arpa. *v. inf.* machacar
harp·ist, *n.* arpista, *m., f.*
har·poon, *n.* arpón. *v.* arponear
har·ri·dan, *n.* bruja
har·row·ing, *a.* angustioso
har·ry, *v.* hostigar; inquietar
harsh, *a.* áspero; severo
harsh·ness, *n.* severidad
hart, *n. pl.,* **harts, hart.** ciervo
har·vest, *n.* cosecha. *v.* cosechar
har·vest·er, *n.* segador
hash, *n.* picadillo
has·sle, *n. inf.* pelea. *v.* fastidiar
has·sock, *n.* escabel, *m.*
haste, *n.* prisa
has·ten, *v.* darse prisa
hast·y, *a.* apresurado; precipitado
hat, *n.* sombrero
hatch, *n.* escotilla; portezuela. *v.* empollar
hatch·et, *n.* machado
hatch·way, *n.* escotilla
hate, *v.* odiar; detestar. *n.* odio
hate·ful, *a.* odioso
ha·tred, *n.* aborrecimiento
haugh·ti·ness, *n.* arrogancia
haugh·ty, *a.* altanero
haul, *v.* tirar. *n.* tirón
haunch, *n.* anca
haunt, *v.* frecuentar; aparecer
hau·teur, *n.* arrogancia
have, *v.,* **have, has; had; hav·ing.** tener; poseer
ha·ven, *n.* puerto; asilo
hav·er·sack, *n.* mochila
hav·oc, *n.* estrago
hawk, *n.* halcón
hay, *n.* heno
hay·stack, *n.* almiar
haz·ard, *n.* riesgo; azar. *v.* arriesgar
haz·ard·ous, *a.* arriesgado
haze, *n.* calina
ha·zel, *n.* avellano
ha·zy, *a.* brumoso; vago
he, *pron.; sing. nom.* he; *poss.* **his;** *obj.* **him;** *intens. and refl.* **himself;** *pl. nom.* **they;** *poss.* **their or theirs;** *obj.* **them.** él
head, *n.* cabeza; jefe; crisis, *f. a.* principal
head·ache, *n.* dolor de cabeza
head·ing, *n.* título
head·land, *n.* promontorio
head·light, *n.* faro
head·long, *adv.* de cabeza. *a.* precipitado
head-quar·ters, *n. pl.* cuartel general
head·strong, *a.* terco
head·way, *n.* progreso
head·y, *a.* cabezudo
heal, *v.* sanar; curar
health, *n.* salud, *f.;* sanidad
health·ful, *a.* sano
health·y, *a.* salubre; sano
heap, *n.* montón. *v.* amontonar
hear, *v.,* **heard, hear·ing.** oír; hacer caso
hear·ing, *n.* oído
heark·en, *v.* escuchar
hear·say, *n.* rumor
hearse, *n.* coche fúnebre
heart, *n.* corazón; *(cards)* coros
heart·ache, *n.* angustia
heart·break, *n.* angustia
heart·en, *v.* alentar
heart·felt, *a.* sincero
hearth, *n.* hogar
heart·less, *a.* cruel
heart·sick, *a.* desconsolado
heart·y, *a.* cordial; sano
heat, *n.* calor. *v.* calentar(se)
heat·er, *n.* calentador
heath, *n.* brezal, *m.*
hea·then, *a., n.* pagano
heave, *v.* heaved or hove, heav·ing. levantar
heav·en, *n.* cielo; *usu. pl.* cielos
heav·en·ly, *a.* celestial
heav·i·ness, *n.* pesadez, *f.*
heav·y, *a.* pesado; fuerte
heck·le, *v.* interrumpir
hec·tic, *a.* febril
hedge, *n.* seto
heed, *v.* escuchar; hacer caso. *n.* cuidado
heel, *n.* ladearse; poner tacón. *n.* talón; tacón
heft, *n.* bulto
heft·y, *a.* fuerte
heif·er, *n.* vaquilla
height, *n.* estatura; altura
height·en, *v.* elevar; realzar
hei·nous, *a.* atroz
heir, *n.* heredero
heir·ess, *n.* heredera
heir·loom, *n.* herencia; reliquia de familia
hel·i·cop·ter, *n.* helicóptero
he·li·um, *n.* helio
he·lix, *n. pl.,* **hel·i·ces, he·lix·es.** hélice, *f.*
hell, *n.* infierno
hell·ish, *a.* infernal
hel·lo, *int.* hola
helm, *n.* timón
hel·met, *n.* casco
helms·man, *n. pl.,* **-men.** timonel, *m.*
help, *v.* ayudar; auxiliar. *n.* ayuda; criada
help·ful, *a.* útil
help·ing, *n.* ración
help·less, *a.* incapaz

hem, *n.* dobladillo. *v.* dobladillar; encerrar
hem·i·sphere, *n.* hemisferio
hem·i·spher·ic, hem·i·spher·i·cal, *a.* hemisférico
hem·lock, *n.* cicuta
hem·or·rhage, *n.* hemorragia
hem·or·rhoid, haem·or·rhoid, *n. usu. pl.* hemorroides, *f. pl.*
hemp, *n.* cáñamo
hen, *n.* gallina
hence, *adv.* de aquí; por lo tanto
hence·forth, *adv.* de aquí en adelante. Also **hence·for·ward**
her, *pron. obj. and poss. case of* **she**
her·ald, *n.* heraldo; precursor. *v.* proclamar
he·ral·dic, *a.* heráldico
her·ald·ry, *n. pl.,* **-ries.** heráldica
herb, *n.* hierba
her·ba·ceous, *a.* herbáceo
her·cu·le·an, *a.* herculeo
herd, *n.* rebaño. *v.* reunir
herds·man, *n. pl.,* **-men.** pastor
here, *adv.* aquí; acá
here·af·ter, *adv.* en el futuro
he·red·i·tar·y, *a.* hereditario
he·red·i·ty, *n. pl.,* **-ties.** herencia
here·in, *adv.* incluso
her·e·sy, *n. pl.,* **-sies.** herejía
he·ret·ic, *n.* hereje, *m., f.*
he·ret·i·cal, *a.* herético
here·to·fore, *adv.* hasta ahora
her·it·age, *n.* herencia
her·met·ic, *a.* hermético. Also **her·met·i·cal**
her·mit, *n.* ermitaño
her·mit·age, *n.* ermita
her·ni·a, *n.* hernia
he·ro, *n. pl.,* **-roes.** héroe
he·ro·ic, *a.* heroico
her·o·ine, *n.* heroína
her·o·ism, *n.* heroísmo
her·on, *n.* garza
hers, *pron. poss. case of* **she**
her·self, *pron.* ella misma; sí misma
hes·i·tan·cy, *n. pl.,* **-cies.** indecisión
hes·i·tant, *a.* vacilante
hes·i·tate, *v.* vacilar
hes·i·ta·tion, *n.* indecisión
het·er·o·ge·ne·ous, *a.* heterogéneo
hew, *v.,* **hewed, hewed or hewn.** tajar
hex·a·gon, *n.* hexágono
hex·ag·o·nal, *a.* hexagonal
hey·day, hey·dey, *n.* apogeo
hi·ber·nate, *v.* invernar
hic·cup, *n.* hipo. *v.* tener hipo. Also **hic·cough**
hide, *v.,* **hid, hid·den or hid, hid·ing.** esconder(se); ocultar(se). *n.* pellejo
hid·e·ous, *a.* horrible; feo
hi·er·ar·chy, *n. pl.,* **-chies.** jerarquía
hi·er·o·glyph·ic, *a., n.* jeroglífico. Also **hi·er·o·glyph**
high, *a.* alto; elevado. *adv.* arriba
high-fa·lu·tin, *a.* pomposo. Also **high-fa·lu·ting**
high·way, *n.* carretera
hike, *v.* ir a pie. *n.* caminata
hi·lar·i·ous, *a.* alegre
hi·lar·i·ty, *n.* alegría
hill, *n.* colina
hill·y, *a.* montañoso
hilt, *n.* puño
him, *pron. obj. case of* **he**
him·self, *pron.* él mismo; sí mismo
hind, *a.* trasero
hin·der, *v.* impedir
hind·most, *a.* postrero
hin·drance, *n.* obstáculo
hinge, *n.* gozne. Also **hinge joint.** *v.* engoznar
hint, *n.* indirecta. *v.* insinuar
hip, *n.* cadera
hip·po·pot·a·mus, *n. pl.,* **-mus·es, -mi.** hipopótamo
hire, *v.* alquilar
hire·ling, *n.* mercenario
his, *pron.* suyo; a su
hiss, *v.* silbar. *n.* silbido
his·to·ri·an, *n.* historiador
his·tor·ic, his·tor·i·cal, *a.* histórico
his·to·ry, *n. pl.,* **-ries.** historia
his·tri·on·ic, *a.* histriónico. Also **his·tri·on·i·cal**
hit, *v.* golpear; chocar. *n.* golpe; éxito
hitch, *v.* atar. *n.* obstáculo
hitch·hike, *v.* hacer autostop
hith·er, *adv.* acá
hith·er·to, *adv.* hasta ahora
hive, *n.* colmena; *pl.* urticaria
board, *n.* provisión. *v.* amontonar
hoarse, *a.* ronco
hoax, *n.* engaño. *v.* engañar
hob·ble, *v.* cojear
hob·by, *n. pl.,* **-bies.** pasatiempo
ho·bo, *n. pl.,* **-boes, -bos.** vagabundo
hoe, *n.* azadón. *v.* azadonar
hog, *n.* puerco
hoist, *v.* alzar. *n.* montacargas; cabria
hold, *v.,* **held, hold·ing.** tener; mantener; contener. *n.* bodega
hold·ing, *n.* tenencia
hole, *n.* hoyo; agujero
hol·i·day, *n.* día de fiesta; *pl.* vacaciones
ho·li·ness, *n.* santidad
hol·ler, *v. inf.* gritar
hol·low, *a.* hueco; vacío. *n.* concavidad
hol·ly, *n. pl.,* **-lies.** acebo
hol·o·caust, *n.* holocausto
hol·ster, *n.* pistolera
ho·ly, *a.* santo; sagrada
hom·age, *n.* homenaje
home, *n.* casa; hogar. *a.* doméstico.

adv. a casa
home·ly, *a.* feo
home·sick, *a.* nostálgico
home·ward, *adv.* hacia casa. Also **home·wards**
hom·ey, hom·y, *a. inf.* cómodo
hom·i·ly, *n. pl.,* **-lies.** homilía
ho·mo·gen·e·ous, *a.* homogéneo
hone, *n.* piedra de afilar. *v.* afilar
hon·est, *a.* honrado
hon·es·ty, *n. pl.,* **-ties.** honradez
hon·ey, *n. pl.,* **-eys.** miel, *f.*
hon·ey·comb, *n.* panal, *m.*
hon·ey·moon, *n.* luna de miel
hon·ey·suck·le, *n.* madreselva
hon·or, *n.* honor; honra. *v.* honrar
hon·or·a·ble, *a.* honorable
hon·or·ar·y, *a.* honorario
hood, *n.* capucha
hood·lum, *n.* matón
hood·wink, *v.* engañar
hoof, *n. pl.,* **hoofs, hooves.** casco
hook, *n.* gancho. *v.* enganchar; encorvar
hoop, *n.* aro
hoot, *v.* ulular. *n.* grito
hop, *v.* saltar. *n.* salto
hope, *n.* esperanza. *v.* esperar; desear
hope·less, *a.* desesperado
horde, *n.* horda
ho·ri·zon, *n.* horizonte
hor·i·zon·tal, *a.* horizontal
hor·mone, *n.* hormona
horn, *n.* cuerno
hor·o·scope, *n.* horóscopo
hor·ri·ble, *a.* horrible
hor·ri·fy, *v.* horrorizar
hor·ror, *n.* horror
horse, *n. pl.,* **hors·es, horse.** caballo
horse·man, *n. pl.,* **-men.** jinete
horse·pow·er, *n.* caballo de fuerza
horse·rad·ish, *n.* rábano picante
horse·shoe, *n.* herradura
hor·ti·cul·ture, *n.* horticultura
hose, *n. pl.,* **hose.** *pl.* medias
hose, *n. pl.,* **hos·es.** manga
ho·sier·y, *n.* calcetería
hos·pi·ta·ble, *a.* hospitalario
hos·pi·tal, *n.* hospital, *m.*
hos·pi·tal·i·ty, *n. pl.,* **-ties.** hospitalidad
host, *n.* anfitrión; patrón; multitud
hos·tage, *n.* rehén
host·ess, *n.* huéspeda
hos·tile, *a.* hostil; enemigo
hos·til·i·ty, *n. pl.,* **-ties.** hostilidad
hot, *a.* caliente; cálido
ho·tel, *n.* hotel, *m.*
hot·house, *n.* invernáculo
hound, *n.* podenco. *v.* perseguir
hour, *n.* hora
house, *n. pl.,* **hous·es.** casa; cámara
house·keep·er, *n.* ama de llaves
hous·ing, *n.* alojamiento
how, *adv.* cómo; hasta qué punto
how·ev·er, *adv.* en todo caso. *conj.* sin embargo
howl, *v.* aullar. *n.* aullido
hub, *n.* cubo
hud·dle, *v.* amontonar(se)
hue, *n.* color; matiz, *m.*
hug, *v.* abrazar. *n.* abrazo
huge, *a.* inmenso; enorme
hulk, *n.* casco
hull, *n.* cáscara; casco
hum, *v.* zumbar; canturrear. *n.* zumbido
hu·man, *a., n.* humano
hu·man·i·tar·i·an, *a., n.* humanitario
hu·man·i·ty, *n. pl.,* **-ties.** humanidad
hum·ble, *a.* humilde. *v.* humillar
hu·mid, *a.* húmedo
hu·mid·i·fy, *v.* humedecer
hu·mid·i·ty, *n.* humedad
hu·mil·i·ate, *v.* humillar
hu·mil·i·a·tion, *n.* humillación
hu·mil·i·ty, *n.* humildad
hum·ming·bird, *n.* colibrí, *m.*
hu·mor, *n.* humor. *v.* complacer
hump, *n.* giba; joroba
hunch, *v.* corazonada
hunch·back, *n.* jorobado
hun·dred, *a., n. pl.,* **-dred, -dreds.** ciento (cien)
hun·dredth, *a.* centésimo
hun·ger, *n.* hambre, *f.*
hun·gry, *a.* hambriento
hunt, *v.* cazar; perseguir. *n.* caza
hunt·er, *n.* cazador
hur·dle, *n.* valla; zarzo
hurl, *v.* lanzar
hur·ri·cane, *n.* huracán
hur·ry, *v.* apresurar; darse prisa. *n.* prisa
hurt, *v.* hacer daño; doler; dañar. *n.* herida
hus·band, *n.* marido; esposo
hush, *v.* callar. *n.* silencio
husk, *n.* cáscara
husk·y, *a.* ronco
hus·sy, *n. pl.,* **hus·ies.** pícara
hus·tle, *v.* empujar
hut, *n.* barraca
hy·a·cinth, *n.* jacinto
hy·brid, *n.* híbrido
hy·drant, *n.* boca de riego
hy·drau·lic, *a.* hidráulico
hy·dro·gen, *n.* hidrógeno
hy·e·na, *n.* hiena. Also **hy·ae·na**
hy·giene, *n.* higiene, *f.*
hymn, *n.* himno
hy·phen, *n.* guión
hyp·no·sis, *n. pl.,* **-ses.** hipnosis, *f.*
hyp·no·tize, *v.* hipnotizar
hy·po·chon·dri·ac, *n.* hipocondríaco
hy·poc·ri·sy, *n. pl.,* **-sies.** hipocresía

hyp·o·crite, n. hipócrita, m., f.
hy·po·der·mic, a. hipodérmico
hy·pot·e·nuse, n. hipotenusa
hy·poth·e·sis, n. pl., -ses. hipótesis, f.
hy·po·thet·i·cal, a. hipotético
hys·te·ri·a, n. histerismo
hys·ter·i·cal, hys·ter·i·cal, a. histérico
hys·ter·ics, n. pl histerismo

I

I, pron. yo
i·bis, n. pl., i·bis·es, i·bis. ibis, f.
ice, n. hielo. v. helar
ice·berg, n. iceberg, m.
ice cream, n. helado
i·ci·cle, n. carámbano
ic·ing, n. garapiña
i·con, n. icono
i·con·o·clast, n. iconoclasta, m., f.
i·cy, a. helado; glacial
i·de·a, n. idea
i·de·al, a. ideal. n. ideal; modelo
i·de·al·ize, v. idealizar
i·den·ti·cal, a. idéntico
i·den·ti·fi·ca·tion, n. identificación
i·den·ti·fy, v. identificar
i·den·ti·ty, n. pl., -ties. identidad
i·de·ol·o·gy, n. pl., -gies. ideología
id·i·om, n. gram. idiotismo
id·i·o·mat·ic, a. idiomático
id·i·o·syn·cra·sy, n. pl. -sies. idiosincrasia
id·i·ot, n. idiota, m., f.; tonto
i·dle, a. ocioso. v. haraganear
i·dol, n. ídolo
i·dol·a·trous, a. idólatra
i·dol·a·try, n. pl., -tries. idolatría
i·dol·ize, v. idolatrar
i·dyll, i·dyl, n. idilio
i·dyl·lic, a. idílico
if, conj. si
ig·nite, v. encender(se)
ig·no·ble, a. innoble
ig·no·min·y, n. pl., -ies. ignominia
ig·no·rance, n. ignorancia
ig·no·rant, a. ignorante
ig·nore, v. no hacer caso de
ill, n., worse, worst. enfermo; mal
il·le·gal, a. ilegal
il·leg·i·ble, a. ilegible
il·le·git·i·ma·cy, n. pl., -cies. ilegitimidad
il·le·git·i·mate, a. ilegítimo
il·lic·it, a. ilícito
il·lit·er·a·cy, n. pl., -cies. analfabetismo
il·lit·er·ate, a., a. analfabeto
ill·ness, n. enfermedad
il·lu·mi·nate, v. iluminar
il·lu·sion, n. ilusión
il·lus·trate, v. ilustrar
il·lus·tra·tion, n. ilustración; ejemplo
im·age, n. imagen, f.
i·mag·i·nar·y, a. imaginario
i·mag·i·na·tion, n. imaginación
i·mag·ine, v. imaginar(se)
im·be·cile, n. imbécil
im·i·tate, v. imitar
im·i·ta·tion, n. imitación; copia
im·ma·ture, a. inmaturo
im·meas·ur·a·ble, a. inmensurable
im·me·di·ate, a. inmediato
im·mense, a. inmenso
im·mer·sion, n. inmersión
im·mi·grant, n. inmigrante
im·mi·grate, v. inmigrar
im·mi·gra·tion, n. inmigración
im·mi·nent, a. inminente
im·mo·bile, a. inmóvil
im·mod·est, a. impúdico
im·mor·al, a. inmoral
im·mor·tal, a. inmortal
im·mune, a. inmune
im·mu·ni·ty, n. pl., -ties. inmunidad
imp, n. diablillo
im·pact, n. impacto
im·pair, v. deteriorar
im·part, v. comunicar; relatar; dar
im·par·tial, a. imparcial
im·pa·tient, a. impaciente
im·peach, v. acusar
im·pec·ca·ble, a. impecable
im·pede, v. impedir; estorbar
im·ped·i·ment, n. impedimento; estorbo
im·pel, v. impulsar
im·pe·ri·al, a. imperial
im·pe·ri·ous, a. imperioso
im·per·son·al, a. impersonal
im·per·ti·nent, a. impertinente
im·per·vi·ous, a. impenetrable
im·pet·u·ous, a. impetuoso
im·pe·tus, n. pl., -tus·es. impetu, m.
im·pi·e·ty, n. pl., -ties. impiedad
im·ple·ment, n. herramienta
im·pli·cate, v. enredar
im·plore, v. implorar
im·ply, v. dar a entender; significar
im·po·lite, a. descortés
im·port, v. importar
im·por·tance, n. importancia
im·por·tant, a. importante
im·pose, v. imponer
im·pos·si·bil·i·ty, n. pl., -ties. imposibilidad
im·pos·si·ble, a. imposible
im·pos·tor, n. impostor
im·po·tence, im·po·ten·cy, n. impotencia
im·po·tent, a. impotente
im·pov·er·ish, v. empobrecer
im·prac·ti·cal, a. impracticable
im·preg·na·ble, a. inexpugnable
im·press, v. estampar; imprimir; impresionar
im·pres·sion, n. impresión

im·print, v. imprimir
im·prob·a·ble, a. improbable
im·promp·tu, a. impremeditado. adv. de improviso
im·prop·er, a. impropio
im·prove, v. mejorar
im·prove·ment, n. mejora
im·prov·i·sa·tion, n. improvisación
im·pro·vise, v. improvisar
im·pulse, n. impulso; estímulo
im·pu·ri·ty, n. pl., -ties. impureza
in, prep. en; durante; dentro de. adv. dentro
in·a·bil·i·ty, n. inhabilidad
in·ad·e·quate, a. inadecuado
in·an·i·mate, a. inanimado
in·as·much as, conj. puesto que
in·au·gu·rate, v. inaugurar
in·born, a. innato
in·can·des·cent, a. incandescente
in·ca·pa·ble, a. incapaz
in·ca·pac·i·tate, v. incapacitar
in·car·na·tion, n. encarnación
in·cen·di·ar·y, a. incendiario
in·cense, n. incienso. v. encolerizar
in·cen·tive, n. incentivo
in·ces·sant, a. incesante
in·cest, n. incesto
in·ces·tu·ous, a. incestuoso
inch, n. pulgada
in·ci·dent, n. incidente; suceso
in·ci·den·tal, a. incidental; casual
in·cin·er·ate, v. incinerar
in·cip·i·ent, a. incipiente
in·ci·sion, n. incisión
in·cite, v. incitar
in·clem·ent, a. inclemente
in·cli·na·tion, n. inclinación
in·cline, v. inclinar(se)
in·clude, v. incluir; contener; tener
in·clu·sion, n. inclusión
in·cog·ni·to, a., adv. de incógnito
in·come, n. renta; ingresos
in·com·pa·ra·ble, a. incomparable
in·com·pe·tent, a. incompetente
in·com·plete, a. incompleto
in·com·pre·hen·si·ble, a. incomprensible
in·con·gru·ous, a. incongruo
in·con·se·quen·tial, a. inconsecuente
in·con·ven·ience, n. inconveniencia; incomodidad. v. incomodar
in·cor·rect, a. incorrecto
in·cor·ri·gi·ble, a. incorregible
in·crease, v. acrecentar; crecer; aumentar. n. aumento
in·cred·i·ble, a. increíble
in·crim·i·nate, v. incriminar
in·cu·ba·tor, n. incubadora
in·cur, v. incurrir
in·cur·a·ble, a. incurable
in·debt·ed, a. obligado
in·de·cen·cy, n. pl., -cies. indecencia
in·de·cent, a. indecente
in·deed, adv. de veras
in·def·i·nite, a. indefinido
in·dem·ni·ty, n. pl., -ties. indemnización
in·dent, v. sangrar; mellar
in·den·ta·tion, n. mella
in·de·pend·ence, n. independencia
in·de·pend·ent, a. independiente
in·de·struct·i·ble, a. indestructible
in·dex, n. pl., -dex·es, -di·ces. índice
in·di·cate, v. indicar
in·di·ca·tion, n. indicación
in·dict, v. acusar
in·dif·fer·ent, a. indiferente
in·dig·e·nous, a. indígena
in·di·gent, a. indigente; pobre
in·di·ges·tion, n. indigestión
in·dig·nant, a. indignado
in·dig·ni·ty, n. pl., -ties. indignidad
in·di·go, n. pl., -gos, -goes. añil, m.
in·di·rect, a. indirecto
in·dis·creet, a. indiscreto
in·dis·cre·tion, n. indiscreción
in·dis·pen·sa·ble, a. imprescindible
in·di·vid·u·al, a. individual. n. individuo
in·di·vid·u·al·i·ty, n. pl., -ties. individualidad
in·doc·tri·nate, v. doctrinar
in·do·lent, a. indolente
in·door, a. interior; de puertas adentro
in·doors, adv. dentro
in·duce, v. inducir
in·duct, v. iniciar
in·dulge, v. satisfacer; consentir
in·dus·tri·al, a. industrial
in·dus·tri·ous, a. laborioso
in·dus·try, n. pl., -tries. industria; diligencia
in·e·bri·ate, v. embriagar
in·el·i·gi·ble, a. inelegible
in·ept, a. inepto
in·ert, a. inerte
in·er·tia, n. inercia
in·ev·i·ta·ble, a. inevitable
in·ex·pli·ca·ble, a. inexplicable
in·fal·li·ble, a. infalible
in·fa·mous, a. infame
in·fa·my, n. pl., -mies. infamia
in·fan·cy, n. pl., -cies. infancia
in·fant, n. criatura. a. infantil; naciente
in·fan·try, n. pl., -tries. infantería
in·fect, v. infectar; contagiar
in·fec·tion, n. infección
in·fe·ri·or, a. n. inferior
in·fer·nal, a. infernal
in·fest, v. infestar
in·fi·del, n. infiel, m., f.
in·fi·del·i·ty, n. pl., -ties. infidelidad
in·fi·nite, a. infinito

in·fin·i·tive, n. infinitivo
in·fin·i·ty, n. pl., -ties. infinito; infinidad
in·fir·ma·ry, n. pl., -ries. enfermería
in·flame, v. inflamar; provocar
in·flam·ma·ble, a. inflamable
in·flate, v. hinchar; inflar
in·fla·tion, n. inflación
in·flec·tion, n. inflexión
in·flict, v. infligir; imponer
in·flu·ence, n. influencia. v. influir
in·flu·en·za, n. gripe, f.
in·form, v. informar; avisar
in·for·mal, a. sin ceremonia
in·for·ma·tion, n. información; conocimientos
in·for·ma·tive, a. instructivo
in·fre·quent, a. infrecuente
in·fu·ri·ate, v. enfurecer
in·fuse, v. infundir
in·fu·sion, n. infusión
in·gen·ious, a. ingenioso
in·ge·nu·i·ty, n. ingeniosidad
in·got, n. lingote
in·gre·di·ent, n. ingrediente
in·hab·it, v. habitar
in·hab·it·ant, n. habitante
in·hale, v. inhalar; aspirar
in·her·ent, a. immanente; inherente
in·her·it, v. heredar
in·her·it·ance, n. herencia
in·hib·it, v. inhibir
in·hi·bi·tion, n. inhibición
in·hu·man, a. inhumano; cruel
in·iq·ui·ty, n. pl., -ties. iniquidad
in·i·tial, a. inicial. n. inicial, f.
in·i·ti·ate, v. iniciar
in·i·ti·a·tion, n. iniciación
in·i·ti·a·tive, n. iniciativa
in·ject, v. inyectar; introducir
in·jec·tion, n. inyección
in·jure, v. hacer daño a; ofender
in·ju·ry, n. pl., -ries. daño; injuria
in·jus·tice, n. injusticia
ink, n. tinta
ink·ling, n. sospecha
in·let, n. entrada; ensenada
in·mate, n. inquilino
inn, n. posada
in·nate, a. innato
in·ner, a. interior
in·no·cence, n. inocencia
in·no·cent, a. inocente
in·no·va·tion, n. innovación
in·nu·en·do, n. pl., -dos, -does. indirecta
in·nu·mer·a·ble, a. innumerable
in·oc·u·late, v. inocular
in·oc·u·la·tion, n. inoculación
in·quest, n. pesquisa judicial
in·quire, v. preguntar
in·quir·y, n. pl., -ies. indagación; pregunta
in·qui·si·tion, n. inquisición
in·quis·i·tive, a. curioso
in·sane, a. insensato; loco
in·san·i·ty, n. pl., -ties. locura
in·scribe, v. inscribir
in·scrip·tion, n. inscripción
in·sect, n. insecto
in·se·cure, a. inseguro; precario
in·sert, v. insertar; meter
in·ser·tion, n. inserción
in·side, n. interior. a. interno. adv. dentro. prep. dentro de
in·sight, n. perspicacia
in·sig·ni·a, n. pl. insignias
in·sig·nif·i·cance, n. insignificancia
in·sig·nif·i·cant, a. insignificante
in·sin·u·ate, v. insinuar
in·sin·u·a·tion, n. insinuación; indirecta
in·sip·id, a. insípido
in·sist, v. insistir
in·sist·ent, a. insistente; porfiado
in·so·lence, n. insolencia
in·so·lent, a. insolente; descarado
in·som·ni·a, n. insomnio
in·spect, v. examinar; inspeccionar
in·spec·tion, n. inspección; reconocimiento
in·spi·ra·tion, n. inspiración
in·spire, v. inspirar; estimular
in·stall, v. instalar
in·stall·ment, n. plazo; entrega
in·stance, n. ejemplo
in·stant, a. inmediato. n. instante
in·stan·ta·ne·ous, a. instantáneo
in·stead, adv. en lugar; en vez de
in·step, n. empeine
in·sti·gate, v. instigar
in·stinct, n. instinto
in·stinc·tive, a. instintivo. Also in·stinc·tu·al
in·sti·tute, v. instituir; empezar. n. instituto
in·sti·tu·tion, n. instituto; institución
in·struct, v. instruir; enseñar
in·struc·tion, n. instrucción
in·stru·ment, n. instrumento
in·suf·fi·cient, a. insuficiente
in·su·late, v. aislar
in·su·la·tion, n. aislamiento
in·su·lin, n. insulina
in·sult, n. insulto; ultraje. v. insultar
in·sur·ance, n. seguro
in·sure, v. asegurar
in·sur·rec·tion, n. insurrección
in·tact, a. intacto
in·te·ger, n. número entero
in·te·grate, v. integrar(se)
in·te·gra·tion, n. integración
in·teg·ri·ty, n. integridad
in·tel·lect, n. intelecto; inteligencia
in·tel·lec·tu·al, a. intelectual
in·tel·li·gence, n. inteligencia; información

in·tel·li·gent, a. inteligente
in·tend, v. proponerse; querer decir
in·tense, a. intenso
in·ten·si·ty, n. pl., -ties. intensidad
in·tent, a. atento; absorto. n. intento
in·ten·tion, n. intención; propósito
in·ter, v. enterrar
in·ter·cede, v. interceder
in·ter·cept, v. interceptar
in·ter·ces·sion, n. intercesión
in·ter·change, n. intercambiar. n. intercambio
in·ter·course, n. comercio; trato; coito
in·ter·est, n. interés, m.; beneficio. v. interesar(se)
in·ter·fere, v. intervenir; meterse
in·ter·fer·ence, n. intervención; interferencia
in·ter·im, n. ínterin. a. interino
in·te·ri·or, a., n. interior
in·ter·jec·tion, n. interjección
in·ter·lude, n. intermedio; (mus.) interludio
in·ter·me·di·ate, a. intermedio. v. intervenir
in·ter·mis·sion, n. intermisión
in·tern, v. interno. v. encerrar
in·ter·nal, a. interno; interior
in·ter·na·tion·al, a. internacional
in·ter·play, n. interacción
in·ter·pose, v. interponer
in·ter·pret, v. explicar; interpretar; entender
in·ter·pre·ta·tion, n. interpretación
in·ter·ro·gate, v. interrogar
in·ter·ro·ga·tion, n. interrogación
in·ter·rupt, v. interrumpir; estorbar
in·ter·rup·tion, n. interrupción
in·ter·sect, v. cruzarse; intersecarse
in·ter·sec·tion, n. intersección; cruce
in·ter·twine, v. entretejer(se)
in·ter·val, n. intervalo
in·ter·vene, v. intervenir; interponerse
in·ter·view, n. entrevista. v. entrevistarse con
in·tes·tine, n. often pl. intestino
in·ti·mate, a. íntimo. v. intimar; dar a entender
in·tim·i·date, v. intimidar
in·to, prep. en; hacia el interior
in·tol·er·a·ble, a. intolerable
in·tol·er·ant, a. intolerante
in·to·na·tion, n. entonación
in·tox·i·cate, v. embriagar; excitar
in·tran·si·tive, a. intransitivo
in·tra·ve·nous, a. intravenoso
in·trep·id, a. intrépido
in·tri·ca·cy, n. pl., -cies. complejidad; enredo
in·tri·cate, a. intrincado
in·trigue, v. intrigar; fascinar. n. intriga
in·trin·sic, a. intrínseco. Also in·trin·si·cal
in·tro·duce, v. introducir; presentar
in·tro·duc·tion, n. introducción; prólogo
in·trude, v. entremeterse
in·tu·i·tion, n. intuición
in·ure, v. habituar
in·vade, v. invadir
in·val·id, a., n. inválido
in·var·i·a·ble, a. invariable
in·va·sion, n. invasión
in·vent, v. inventar
in·ven·tion, n. invención; inventiva
in·ven·to·ry, n. pl., -ries. inventario
in·ver·sion, n. inversión
in·vert, v. invertir
in·ver·te·brate, a., n. invertebrado
in·vest, v. vestir; sitiar; invertir; investir
in·ves·ti·gate, v. investigar
in·ves·ti·ga·tion, n. investigación; pesquisa
in·vig·or·ate, v. vigorizar
in·vin·ci·ble, a. invencible
in·vis·i·ble, a. invisible
in·vi·ta·tion, n. invitación; convite
in·vite, v. invitar; convidar
in·vo·ca·tion, n. invocación
in·voice, n. factura
in·voke, v. invocar; implorar
in·vol·un·tar·y, a. involuntario
in·volve, v. complicar; comprometer; enredar
in·ward, adv. hacia dentro. a. interno. Also in·wards
i·o·dine, n. yodo
i·on, n. ion
i·o·ta, n. jota
ir·e, n. ira
i·ri·des·cent, a. iridiscente
i·ris, n. pl., i·ris·es, ir·i·ses. iris; lirio
irk, v. molestar
i·ron, n. hierro; plancha; pl. hierros. a. de hierro. v. planchar
i·ron·ic, a. irónico. Also i·ron·i·cal
i·ro·ny, n. pl., -nies. ironía
ir·ra·di·ate, v. irradiar
ir·ra·tion·al, a. irracional
ir·rec·on·cil·a·ble, a. irreconciliable
ir·ref·u·ta·ble, a. irrefutable
ir·reg·u·lar, a. irregular; desigual
ir·rel·e·vant, a. inaplicable
ir·re·sist·i·ble, a. irresistible
ir·re·spon·si·ble, a. irresponsable
ir·rev·er·ence, n. irreverencia
ir·ri·gate, v. regar
ir·ri·ga·tion, n. riego
ir·ri·ta·ble, a. irritable
ir·ri·tate, v. irritar; provocar; molestar
ir·ri·ta·tion, n. irritación
is, v. third person pres. sing. of be
is·land, n. isla

isle, n. isla
i·so·late, v. aislar
i·so·la·tion, n. aislamiento; separación
i·sos·ce·les, a. isósceles
is·sue, n. emisión; sucesión; resultado; asunto; edición. v. emitir; salir; distribuir; publicar
isth·mus, n. pl., -mus·es, -mi. istmo
it, pron. third person sing. neuter. él, ella, ello, lo, la
i·tal·ic, n. usu. pl. letra bastardilla
i·tal·i·cize, v. poner en bastardilla
itch, v. picar. n. picazón; prurito
i·tem, n. artículo; partida
i·tem·ize, v. detallar
i·tin·er·ar·y, n. pl., -ies. itinerario
its, pron. a poss. case of it
it·self, pron. él, ella, ello o sí mismo
i·vo·ry, n. pl., -ries. marfil, m.; a. de marfil
i·vy, n. pl., -vies. hiedra

J

jab, v. golpear. n. pinchazo
jab·ber, v. farfullar. n. chapurreo; farfulla
jack, n. mozo; marinero; gato; sota
jack·al, n. chacal, m.
jack·ass, n. burro; tonto
jack·et, n. chaqueta
jack·knife, n. pl., -knives. navaja. v. doblar
jack·pot, n. bote
jade, n. jade; rocín. v. cansar
jag·uar, n. jaguar
jail, n. cárcel, f.; calabozo. v. encarcelar
jal·ou·sie, n. celosía
jam, v. apiñar; atascar. n. agolpamiento; mermelada; inf. apuro
jamb, n. jamba
jam·bo·ree, n. inf. francachela
jan·gle, n. sonido discordante
jan·i·tor, n. portero
Jan·u·ar·y, n. enero
jar, n. jarra. v. sacudir
jar·gon, n. jerga
jas·mine, jas·min, n. jazmín
jaun·dice, n. ictericia
jaunt, n. excursión
jaun·ty, a. airoso
jave·lin, n. jabalina
jaw, n. quijada. v. charlar
jay, n. arrendajo
jazz, n. jazz, m.
jeal·ous, a. celoso; envidioso
jeal·ous·y, n. pl., -ies. celos; recelo; envidia
Jeep, n. trademark. jeep
jeer, v. mofarse; befar
jeop·ard·ize, v. arriesgar
jeop·ard·y, n. peligro
jerk, v. arrojar; sacudir. n. tirón
jer·kin, n. justillo
jer·sey, n. jersey, m.
jest, n. chanza
jet, n. chorro; surtidor; avión a reacción; azabache. v. chorrear
jet·sam, n. echazón, f.
jet·ti·son, n. echazón, f. v. echar
jet·ty, n. pl., -ties. malecón; muelle
jew·el, n. joya
jew·el·er, n. joyero
jew·el·ry, n. joyas
jif·fy, n. pl., -fies. inf. instante
jig, n. giga
jig·saw, n. sierra de vaivén
jig·saw puz·zle, n. rompecabezas
jilt, v. dar calabazas
jim·my, n. pl., -mies. palanqueta
jin·gle, v. retiñir; tintinear. n. retintín
jinx, n. inf. gafe
jit·ters, n. pl. inf. inquietud
job, n. trabajo; tarea
jock·ey, n. pl., -eys. jockey, m.
jo·cose, a. jocoso
joc·u·lar, a. jocoso
jo·cund, a. jovial
jog, v. empujar; correr despacio
join, v. juntar(se); unir(se). n. costura
joint, n. juntura; unión, f. a. combinado. v. juntar
joist, n. viga
joke, n. chiste; broma. v. bromear
jok·er, n. bromista, m., f.; (cards) comodín
jol·ly, a. alegre
jolt, v. sacudir. n. sacudida
jon·quil, n. junquillo
jos·tle, v. empujar. n. empellón
jot, n. jota. v. apuntar
jour·nal, n. diario; periódico; revista
jour·nal·ism, n. periodismo
jour·nal·ist, n. periodista, m., f.
jour·ney, n. viaje. v. viajar
jour·ney·man, n. pl., -men. oficial, m.
joust, n. justa. v. justar
jo·vi·al, a. jovial
jowl, n. quijada; carrillo
joy, n. alegría; regocijo; deleite
joy·ous, a. alegre
ju·bi·la·tion, n. júbilo; jubileo
Ju·da·ism, n. judaísmo
judge, v. juzgar; opinar; considerar. n. juez, m.
judg·ment, n. juicio; sentencia; discernimiento
ju·di·cial, a. judicial
ju·di·cious, a. juicioso
jug, n. jarro

jug·gle, v. hacer juegos malabares
jug·u·lar, a. yugular
juice, n. zumo; jugo
Ju·ly, n. julio
jum·ble, v. mezclar. n. confusión
jump, v. saltar; brincar. n. salto. jump at, apresurarse a aceptar
jump·er, n. saltador
junc·tion, n. juntura; empalme
junc·ture, n. juntura; coyuntura
June, n. junio
jun·gle, n. selva
jun·ior, a. más joven; menor. n. menor
ju·ni·per, n. enebro
junk, n. trastos viejos; junco
ju·ris·dic·tion, n. jurisdicción
ju·ris·pru·dence, n. jurisprudencia
ju·rist, n. jurista, m., f.
ju·ror, n. jurado
ju·ry, n. pl., -ries. jurado
just, a. justo; imparcial. adv. precisamente; apenas
jus·tice, n. justicia; juez, m.
jus·ti·fi·ca·tion, n. justificación
jus·ti·fy, v. justificar
jut, v. sobresalir
ju·ve·nile, a. juvenil. n. joven

K

kale, n. col rizada
ka·lei·do·scope, n. calidoscopio
kan·ga·roo, n. pl., -roos, roo. canguro
kar·at, n. quilate
keel, n. quilla. keel o·ver, zozobrar; volcar
keen, a. agudo; perspicaz; entusiasta; afilado
keep, v. kept, keep·ing. tener; retener; cumplir; guardar; detener; mantener; continuar. n. comida; cuidado
keep·ing, n. custodia
keg, n. cuñete
ken, v. saber. n. conocimientos
ken·nel, n. perrera
ker·chief, n. pañuelo
ker·nel, n. almendra; núcleo
ker·o·sene, ker·o·sine, n. queroseno
ketch, n. queche
ketch·up, n. salsa picante de tomate
ket·tle, n. tetera
key, n. llave, f.; tecla; tono. a. clave. key up, excitar
key·board, n. teclado
key·stone, n. piedra clave
khak·i, n. caqui, m. a. de caqui
kick, v. dar patadas; dar un puntapié; inf. quejarse. n. patada
kid, n. cabrito; inf. niño. v. inf. tomar el pelo
kid·nap, v. secuestrar
kid·ney, n. riñón
kill, v. matar; destruir. n. matanza
kiln, n. horno
kil·o·cy·cle, n. kilociclo
kil·o·gram, n. kilo; kilogramo
kil·o·me·ter, n. kilómetro
kil·o·watt, n. kilovatio
kin, n. parientes
kind, n. género. a. bueno; benigno; afable
kin·der·gar·ten, n. jardín de la infancia
kind·heart·ed, a. bondadoso
kin·dle, v. encender
kind·ly, a. amable; bondadoso
kind·ness, n. benevolencia; atención
kin·dred, n. parientes. a. emparentado
king, n. rey, m.
king·dom, n. reino
kink, n. coca; peculiaridad
kin·ship, n. parentesco
kins·man, n. pl., -men. pariente
kiss, v. besar. n. beso
kit, n. equipo; avíos
kitch·en, n. cocina
kite, n. cometa
kith, n. archaic. amigos
kit·ten, n. gatito. Also kit·ty
knack, n. maña
knap·sack, n. mochila
knave, n. bribón
knead, v. amasar
knee, n. rodilla
kneel, v. knelt or kneeled, kneel·ing. arrodillarse
knell, n. doble
knick·knack, n. chuchería
knife, n. pl., knives. cuchillo. v. acuchillar
knight, n. caballero. v. armar caballero
knit, v. knit·ted or knit, knit·ting. hacer punto; juntar
knob, n. tirador; bulto
knock, v. chocar; golpear; dar golpes; inf. criticar. n. llamada; golpe. knock down, derribar. knock off, suspender
knoll, n. otero
knot, n. nudo. v. anudar
know, v. knew, known, know·ing. saber; conocer
know-how, n. inf. pericia
know·ing, a. astuto; hábil
knowl·edge, n. conocimiento; conocimientos
knowl·edge·a·ble, a. erudito
knuck·le, n. nudillo
Ko·ran, n. Alcorán, Corán
ko·sher, a. autorizado por la ley judía

L

lab, n. inf. laboratorio
la·bel, n. marbete; etiqueta. v. rotular
la·bi·al, a. labial
la·bor, n. trabajo; labor, f.; parto. v. trabajar
lab·o·ra·to·ry, n. pl., -ries. laboratorio
la·bor·er, n. peón
la·bo·ri·ous, a. laborioso; penoso
lab·y·rinth, n. laberinto
lace, n. cordón; puntilla. v. atar
lac·er·ate, v. lacerar
lack, n. falta. v. faltar; necesitar
lack·ey, n. lacayo
la·con·ic, a. lacónico
lac·quer, n. laca
lac·tic, a. láctico
la·cu·na, n. pl., -nas, -nae. laguna; hoyo
lac·y, a. de encaje
lad, n. mozo; chico; muchacho
lad·der, n. escala; escalera
la·dle, n. cucharón
la·dy, n. señora; dama
lag, v. rezagarse
la·goon, n. laguna. Also la·gune
lair, n. cubil, m.
la·i·ty, n. pl., -ties. laicado
lake, n. lago
la·ma, n. lama, m.
lamb, n. cordero
lame, a. cojo; débil. v. lisiar
la·ment, v. lamentar(se). n. elegía
lam·en·ta·tion, n. lamentación
lam·i·nate, v. laminar
lamp, n. lámpara
lam·poon, n. pasquín. v. satirizar
lam·prey, n. pl., -preys. lamprea
lance, n. lanza. v. abrir con lanceta
lan·cet, n. lanceta
land, n. tierra; suelo; país. v. desembocar; llegar; aterrizar
land·la·dy, n. pl., -dies. propietaria
land·locked, a. cercado de tierra
land·lord, n. propietario; posadero
land·mark, n. mojón; marca
land·scape, n. paisaje
land·slide, n. desprendimiento de tierras
lane, n. vereda; senda
lan·guage, n. lenguaje
lan·guid, a. lánguido; flojo
lank, a. flaco, alto y descarnado; lacio
lan·o·lin, n. lanolina
lan·tern, n. linterna
lap, v. doblar; traslapar; lamer. n. regazo
la·pel, n. solapa
lapse, n. lapso; error. v. caer en un desliz
lar·ce·ny, n. pl., -nies. latrocinio
lard, n. manteca de cerdo
lar·der, n. despensa
large, a. grande; extenso
lar·gess, lar·gesse, n. dadivosidad
lar·i·at, n. lazo
lar·va, n. pl. -vae. larva
lar·yn·gi·tis, n. laringitis, f.
lar·ynx, n. pl., lar·ynx·es, la·ryn·ges, laringe, f.
las·civ·i·ous, a. lascivo
lash, n. látigo; latigazo; injuria. v. azotar; atar
lass, n. moza; chica; muchacha
las·si·tude, n. lasitud
las·so, n. pl., -sos, -soes. lazo. v. lazar
last, a. último; final. adv. finalmente. v. durar
last·ing, a. duradero
last·ly, adv. finalmente
latch, n. picaporte
late, a. tardío; atrasado; difunto. adv. tarde
late·ly, adv. recientemente
la·tent, a. latente
lat·er, a. posterior. adv. después; más tarde
lat·er·al, a. lateral
la·tex, n. pl., la·tex·es, lat·i·ces. látex, m.
lath, n. listón
lathe, n. torno
lath·er, n. espuma. v. enjabonar
lat·i·tude, n. latitud
lat·ter, a. más reciente
laud·a·ble, a. loable
laugh, v. reír(se). n. risa
laugh·ter, n. risa
launch, v. lanzar; echar al agua; crear. n. lancha
laun·der, v. lavar; lavar y planchar
laun·dry, n. pl., -dries. lavadero; ropa lavada
lau·rel, n. laurel, m.; pl. honor
la·va, n. lava
lav·a·to·ry, n. pl., -ries. wáter, m.
lav·en·der, n. espliego
lav·ish, a. pródigo. v. prodigar
law, n. ley, f.; regla; derecho; jurisprudencia
law·ful, a. legal; lícito
law·less, a. desordenado
lawn, n. césped
law·suit, n. pleito
law·yer, n. abogado
lax, a. descuidado; laxo
lax·a·tive, a., n. laxante
lay, v., laid, lay·ing. poner; colocar; dejar. a. lego
lay·er, n. capa; estrato
lay·ette, n. canastilla
lay·man, n. pl., -men. lego
lay·out, n. plan; disposición
la·zy, a. perezoso
lead, n. plomo

lead, v., led, lead·ing. llevar; conducir; dirigir; mandar; guiar. n. delantera
lead·er, n. líder; jefe
lead·er·ship, n. dirección
lead·ing, a. principal
leaf, n. pl. leaves. hoja. v. hojear
leaf·age, n. follaje
leaf·let, n. folleto
league, n. liga; sociedad
leak, v. rezumar(se); escaparse. n. gotera; escape
lean, v., leaned or leant, lean·ing. ladearse; inclinar(se). a. flaco; magro
leap, v. leaped or leapt, leap·ing. saltar; brincar. n. salto
learn, v., learned or learnt, learn·ing. aprender; enterarse de
learn·ed, a. docto
lease, n. arriendo. v. arrendar
leash, n. traílla
least, a. menor. n. lo menos. adv. menos
leath·er, n. cuero; piel, f. a. de cuero
leave, v., left, leav·ing. irse; salir; dejar. n. permiso
leav·en, n. levadura. Also leav·en·ing
lec·ture, n. conferencia. v. dar una conferencia
ledge, n. anaquel, m.
ledg·er, n. libro mayor
lee, n. sotavento
leech, n. sanguijuela
leer, v. mirar con malicia. n. mirada maliciosa o impúdica
left, a. izquierdo. n. izquierda. adv. a la izquierda
leg, n. pierna; pata. v. inf. correr
leg·a·cy, n. pl., -cies. legado
le·gal, a. legal; lícito
le·gal·i·ty, n. pl., -ties. legalidad
le·ga·tion, n. legación
leg·end, n. leyenda
leg·end·ar·y, a. legendario
leg·i·ble, a. legible
le·gion, n. legión, f.; multitud
le·gion·naire, n. legionario
leg·is·late, v. legislar
leg·is·la·tion, n. legislación
leg·is·la·ture, n. cuerpo legislativo
le·git·i·mate, a. lícito; legítimo. v. legitimar
leg·ume, n. legumbre, f.
lei·sure, n. ocio
lem·on, n. limón. a. limonado
lem·on·ade, n. limonada
lend, v., lent, lend·ing. prestar
length, n. largo; duración
le·ni·ence, le·ni·en·cy, n. lenidad
le·ni·ent, a. indulgente
lens, n. pl., lens·es. lente, m., f.
leop·ard, n. leopardo
lep·er, n. leproso
lep·ro·sy, n. lepra
less, a. menos; menor. adv., prep. menos
less·en, v. disminuir(se); rebajar
les·son, n. lección
lest, conj. de miedo que
let, v., let, let·ting. permitir; dejar; alquilar
le·thal, a. mortal
leth·ar·gy, n. pl., -gies. letargo; estupor
let·ter, n. letra; carta; pl. letras. v. rotular
let·tuce, n. lechuga
leu·ke·mi·a, n. leucemia
lev·el, n. nivel, m.; llano. a. plano. v. nivelar
lev·er, n. palanca
lev·i·ty, n. ligereza
lev·y, n. pl., -ies. leva; exacción. v. exigir
lewd, a. lascivo; obsceno
lex·i·con, n. léxico
li·a·bil·i·ty, n. pl., -ties. responsabilidad; riesgo; obligación
li·a·ble, a. obligado; inclinado
li·ai·son, n. enlace; lío
li·ar, n. mentiroso
li·bel, n. difamación. v. calumniar
lib·er·al, a., n. liberal
lib·er·ate, v. libertar
lib·er·ty, n. pl., -ties. libertad
li·bi·do, n. libido
li·brar·i·an, n. bibliotecario
li·brar·y, n. pl., -ies. biblioteca
li·bret·to, n. pl., -tos, -ti. libreto
lice, n. pl. of louse. piojos
li·cense, n. licencia; desenfreno. v. licenciar
li·chen, n. liquen
lick, v. lamer; inf. vencer. n. lamedura
lic·o·rice, li·quo·rice, n. regaliz, m.
lid, n. tapa
lie, v., lay, lain, ly·ing. echarse; acostarse; estar tendido
lie, v., lied, ly·ing. mentir. n. mentira
lieu, n. archaic. lugar. in lieu of, en lugar de
lieu·ten·an·cy, n. pl., -cies. tenencia
lieu·ten·ant, n. teniente
life, n. pl., lives. vida; existencia; animación
life·boat, n. bote salvavidas
life·less, a. muerto; flojo
life·long, a. de toda la vida
life·size, a. de tamaño natural. Also life·sized
lift, v. alzar; elevar; levantar(se). n. alzamiento
lig·a·ment, n. ligamento
lig·a·ture, n. ligadura
light, n. luz, f.; lámpara. a. claro;

ligero. v. light·ed or lit, light·ing. encender(se); iluminar
light·en, v. iluminar; aligerar
light·er, n. encendedor
light·heart·ed, light·heart·ed, a. alegre
light·house, n. faro
light·ly, adv. ligeramente
light·ning, n. relámpago
light·ning rod, n. pararrayos
light-year, n. año de luz
like, a. parecido. prep. como. conj. nonstandard. igual que. v. gustar; querer. n. gusto
lik·en, v. comparar
like·ness, n. semejanza
like·wise, adv. asimismo; también
li·lac, n. lila. a. de color de lila
lil·y, n. pl., -ies. lirio
limb, n. miembro; rama
lim·ber, a. flexible
lim·bo, n. limbo
lime, n. cal, f.; lima
lime·stone, n. piedra caliza
lim·it, n. límite; frontera. v. limitar
lim·i·ta·tion, n. limitación
lim·ou·sine, n. limusina
limp, v. cojear. n. cojera. a. flojo
line, n. línea; raya; fila; vía. v. rayar; alinear; forrar
lin·e·age, n. linaje
lin·e·ar, a. lineal
lin·en, n. lino. a. de lino
lin·er, n. ropa blanca
lin·go, n. pl., -goes. inf. jerga
lin·guist, n. lingüista, m., f.
lin·guis·tics, n. pl. lingüística
lin·i·ment, n. linimento
link, n. eslabón. v. enlazar; unirse
li·no·le·um, n. linóleo
lint, n. hila
li·on, n. león
lip, n. labio; borde
liq·ue·fy, v. liquidar(se)
li·queur, n. licor
liq·uid, a., n. líquido
liq·ui·date, v. liquidar
liq·uor, n. licor; bebida alcohólica
lisp, v. cecear. n. ceceo
list, n. lista. v. poner en una lista; escorar
lis·ten, v. escuchar; oír
list·less, a. lánguido
lit·er·al, a. literal
lit·er·ar·y, a. literario
lit·er·a·ture, n. literatura
lithe, a. flexible; ágil. Also lithe·some
lit·ter, n. desorden; camada; litera. v. esparcir
lit·tle, a., lit·tler or less or less·er; lit·tlest or least. pequeño; poco. a. poco. adv., less, least. poco
lit·ur·gy, n. pl., -gies. liturgia

live, v. vivir; existir; pasar; morar
live, a. vivo; ardiente
live·li·hood, n. vida
live·ly, a. vivo; animado
liv·en, v. animar
liv·er, n. hígado
live·stock, n. ganado
liv·id, a. lívido
liz·ard, n. lagarto
lla·ma, n. llama
load, n. carga; peso. v. cargar
loaf, n. pl., loaves. pan; pilón. v. haraganear
loan, n. préstamo; empréstito. v. prestar
loath, loth, a. poco dispuesto
loathe, v. abominar
lob·by, n. pl., -bies. vestíbulo usado como una sala de espera; camarilla de cabilderos. v. cabildear
lob·ster, n. langosta
lo·cal, a. local; de la región; limitado
lo·cal·i·ty, n. pl., -ties. localidad
lo·cate, v. colocar; encontrar
lo·ca·tion, n. situación; colocación
lock, n. bucle; cerradura. v. cerrar(se) con llave; unirse
lo·co·mo·tive, a. locomotor. n. locomotora
lode, n. filón
lodge, v. alojar(se); albergar(se); hospedar(se); colocar. n. casa de guarda; logia
lodg·ing, n. habitación; alojamiento
loft, n. henil, m.; desván
loft·y, a. elevado; orgulloso
log, n. leño; diario de navegación. v. registrar
log·ic, n. lógica
log·i·cal, a. lógico
loin, n. usu. pl. ijada; lomo
loi·ter, v. holgazanear; perder el tiempo
lol·li·pop, lol·ly·pop, n. pirulí, m.; inf. chupechup
lone, a. solitario
lone·ly, a. solitario; solo
lone·some, a. solitario; solo
long, a. largo; prolongado. adv. mucho tiempo. v. anhelar
lon·gev·i·ty, n. longevidad
long·ing, n. anhelo
lon·gi·tude, n. longitud
long·shore·man, n. pl., -men. estibador
long·wise, adv. a lo largo. Also long·ways
look, v. mirar; buscar; parecer. n. mirada; usu. pl. aspecto; apariencia
look·ing glass, n. espejo
look·out, n. vigilancia; vigía
loom, n. telar. v. asomar; amenazar
loon, n. somorgujo

loop, n. gaza. v. hacer gazas; rodear
loop·hole, n. escapatoria
loose, a. suelto; flojo; disoluto; vago. v. soltar; desatar
loot, n. botín; inf. dinero. v. saquear
lop·sid·ed, a. desequilibrado
lord, n. señor; (cap.) Dios; (cap.) British lord. v. dominar
lore, n. conocimientos
lose, v., lost, los·ing. perder(se)
loss, n. pérdida
lost, a. perdido; extraviado
lot, n. suerte, f.; parte, f.
lo·tion, n. loción
lot·ter·y, n. pl., -ies. lotería
loud, a. ruidoso; alto
loud-speak·er, n. altavoz, m.
lounge, v. gandulear. n. sala de estar
louse, n. pl., lice. piojo
lout, n. patán
lov·a·ble, love·a·ble, a. amable
love, n. amor; cariño. v. querer; amar
love·ly, a. hermoso
lov·er, n. amante, f.
lov·ing, a. cariñoso
low, a. bajo; reducido; humilde; vil. adv. bajo; abajo
low·er, a. más bajo. v. bajar; rebajar
low·ly, a. humilde. adv. bajo
loy·al, a. leal; fiel
loy·al·ty, n. pl., -ties. lealtad; fidelidad
loz·enge, n. pastilla
lu·bri·cant, n. lubricante
lu·bri·cate, v. lubricar
lu·cid, a. lúcido; claro; sensato
luck, n. suerte, f.; azar
luck·y, a. afortunado; de buena sombra
lu·cra·tive, a. lucrativo
lu·di·crous, a. ridículo
lug, v. tirar de. n. oreja
lug·gage, n. equipaje
luke·warm, a. tibio; indiferente
lull, v. aquietar; calmar. n. tranquilidad antes o después de una tormenta
lull·a·by, n. pl., -bies. canción de cuna
lum·ber, v. andar pesadamente. n. maderas; leño
lu·mi·nous, a. luminoso
lump, n. masa; terrón; bulto. v. amontonar
lu·na·cy, n. pl., -cies. locura
lu·nar, a. lunar
lu·na·tic, n., a. loco
lunch, n. almuerzo. v. almorzar
lunch·eon, n. almuerzo
lung, n. pulmón
lure, n. señuelo. v. atraer; tentar
lu·rid, a. sensacional; cárdeno
lurk, v. acechar
lus·cious, a. delicioso

lust, n. lujuria. v. lujuriar
lus·ter, n. lustre
lus·ty, a. robusto
lute, n. laúd, m.
lux·u·ri·ant, a. lozano
lux·u·ri·ous, a. lujoso
lux·u·ry, n. pl., -ries. lujo
lye, n. lejía
lymph, n. linfa
lynch, v. linchar
lynx, n. pl., lynx, lynx·es. lince
lyre, n. lira
lyr·ic, a. lírico. n. poema lírico; usu. pl. letra de una canción

M

ma, n. inf. mamá
ma'am, n. inf. señora
ma·ca·bre, a. macabro
mac·a·ro·ni, n. macarrones
mac·a·roon, n. macarrón
ma·chet·e, n. machete
ma·chine, n. máquina
ma·chin·er·y, n. maquinaria
mack·er·el, n. escombro
mack·in·tosh, mac·in·tosh, n. impermeable
mad, a. loco; furioso; enfadado
mad·am, n. señora
made·moi·selle, n. señorita
mad·house, n. casa de locos; manicomio
mad·man, n. loco
Ma·don·na, n. Madona
maes·tro, n. maestro
mag·a·zine, n. revista
ma·gen·ta, n. magenta
mag·got, n. cresa
mag·ic, n. magia. a. mágico
ma·gi·cian, n. mago; ilusionista, m., f.
mag·is·trate, n. magistrado
mag·nan·i·mous, a. magnánimo
mag·ne·si·um, n. magnesio
mag·net, n. imán
mag·net·ism, n. magnetismo
mag·nif·i·cent, a. magnífico; grandioso
mag·ni·fy, v. magnificar; aumentar
mag·ni·tude, n. magnitud
ma·ha·ra·jah, ma·ha·ra·ja, n. maharajá
ma·hog·a·ny, n. caoba
maid, n. criada; doncella
maid·en, n. doncella. a. soltera; virgen
mail, n. correo; cota de malla. v. echar al correo
mail·man, n. pl., -men. cartero
maim, v. mutilar
main, a. principal. n. cañería maestra; océano
main·land, n. continente

main·tain, v. mantener; sostener
main·te·nance, n. mantenimiento
maize, n. maíz, m.
maj·es·ty, n. majestad
ma·jor, a. mayor; (mus.) mayor. n. especialización; comandante. v. especializarse
ma·jor·i·ty, n. pl., -ties. mayoría
make, v., made, mak·ing. hacer; formar; crear; causar; fabricar; ganar; obligar; cometer. n. marca; forma. make be·lieve, fingir. make out, suceder; entender. make sure, asegurarse. make up, componer; pintarse. make way, hacer lugar
make·up, n. maquillaje; modo de ser
ma·la·dy, n. pl., -dies. enfermedad
male, a., n. macho; masculino; varón
mal·e·dic·tion, n. malévolo
mal·fea·sance, n. conducta ilegal
ma·lig·nant, a. maligno; maligno
mal·le·a·ble, a. maleable
mal·nu·tri·tion, n. desnutrición
mal·prac·tice, n. tratamiento erróneo; mala conducta
malt, n. malta
mam·ma, ma·ma, n. mamá
mam·mal, n. mamífero
mam·moth, n. mamut, m. a. enorme
man, n. pl., men. hombre; el género humano. v. guarnecer
man·a·cle, n. often pl. esposas
man·age, v. manejar; dirigir
man·age·ment, n. administración; gerente
man·da·rin, n. mandarín
man·da·to·ry, a. obligatorio; preciso
man·do·lin, n. mandolina
mane, n. crin, f.
ma·neu·ver, n. maniobra. v. maniobrar; manipular
man·ga·nese, n. manganeso
man·ger, n. pesebre
man·go, n. mango
man·hole, n. pozo de visita
man·hood, n. virilidad
ma·ni·a, n. manía
ma·ni·ac, n., a. maníaco
man·i·cure, n. manicura
man·i·fest, a. manifiesto. v. manifestar; revelar. n. manifiesto
man·i·fes·to, n. manifiesto
man·i·fold, a. múltiple; vario
ma·nip·u·late, v. manipular
ma·nip·u·la·tion, n. manipulación
man·kind, n. el género humano
man·na, n. maná, m.
man·ne·quin, n. maniquí, m.; modelo
man·ner, n. manera; modo; aire; especie, f.; pl. modales
man·ner·ly, a., adv. bien criado
man·or, n. señorío; casa solariega
man·pow·er, n. mano de obra
man·sion, n. casa solariega
man·slaugh·ter, n. homicidio impremeditado
man·tel, n. manto
man·u·al, a., n. manual, m.
man·u·fac·ture, n. manufactura. v. fabricar
ma·nure, n. estiércol, m.
man·u·script, n. manuscrito
man·y, a., more, most. muchos. n., pron. gran número
map, n. mapa, m. v. trazar; proyectar
ma·ple, n. arce
mar, v. estropear
mar·ble, n. mármol, m.; canica. a. marmóreo

March, n. marzo
march, v. marchar; desfilar. v. marcha; progreso
mare, n. yegua
mar·ga·rine, n. margarina
mar·gin, n. margen; sobrante
ma·ri·jua·na, n. marijuana
mar·i·nate, v. escabechar
ma·rine, a. marino. n. soldado de marina
mar·i·o·nette, n. marioneta
mar·i·tal, a. marital
mar·i·time, a. marítimo
mark, n. marca; señal, f.; huella; nota; blanco. v. marcar; señalar
mar·ket, n. mercado; venta. v. vender
marks·man, n. pl., -men. tirador
mar·ma·lade, n. mermelada
ma·roon, v. abandonar
mar·quis, n. pl., -quis·es, -quis. marqués, m.
mar·quise, n. f., pl., -quis·es. marquesa
mar·riage, n. matrimonio; boda
mar·row, n. médula
mar·ry, v. casar(se)
marsh, n. pantano
mar·shal, n. mariscal, m.; alguacil, m. v. arreglar
marsh·mal·low, n. bombón de merengue
mar·su·pi·al, n., a. marsupial, m.
mart, n. mercado
mar·tial, a. marcial
mar·tyr, n. mártir. v. martirizar
mar·vel, n. maravilla. v. maravillar(se)
mas·cot, n. mascota
mas·cu·line, a. masculino
mash, v. amasar; mezcla; puré
mask, n. máscara; disfraz, m. v. enmascarar
mas·och·ism, n. masoquismo
mas·och·ist, n. masoquista, m., f.

ma·son, n. albañil, m.
ma·son·ry, n. albañilería
masque, mask, n. mascarada
mas·quer·ade, n. mascarada
mass, n. masa; bulto; montón; misa. a. en serie. v. reunir
mas·sa·cre, n. carnicería. v. hacer una carnicería
mas·sage, n. masaje
mas·sive, a. macizo
mass pro·duc·tion, n. fabricación en serie
mast, n. mástil, m.
mas·ter, n. dueño; señor; maestro. v. dominar. a. principal
mas·ter·piece, n. obra maestra
mas·ti·cate, v. masticar
mas·to·don, n. mastodonte
mas·tur·ba·tion, n. masturbación
mat, n. felpudo; estera. v. enredar
mat, matt, matte, a. mate
match, n. cerilla; partido; igual, m., f. v. igualar; hacer juego con
match·mak·er, n. casamentero
mate, n. compañero. v. casar; aparear
ma·te·ri·al, n. materia; material, m.; tela. a. material
ma·ter·nal, a. maternal
ma·ter·ni·ty, n. maternidad
math, n. inf. matemáticas
math·e·mat·ics, n., pl. matemáticas
mat·i·nee, n. función de tarde
ma·tric·u·late, v. matricular(se)
mat·ri·mo·ny, n. matrimonio
ma·trix, n. pl., -tri·ces, -trix·es. matriz, f.
ma·tron, n. matrona
mat·ter, n. materia; asunto. v. importar
mat·tress, n. colchón
ma·ture, a. maduro. v. madurar
ma·tu·ri·ty, n. madurez, f.
maul, maul, v. maltratar
mau·so·le·um, n. mausoleo
max·im, n. máxima
max·i·mum, n. máximum. a. máximo
May, n. mayo
may, v. pt., might. poder; ser posible
may·be, adv. quizá(s); tal vez
may·on·naise, n. mayonesa
may·or, n. alcalde
maze, n. laberinto
me, pron. me; mí
mead·ow, n. prado
mea·ger, a. exiguo
meal, n. comida; harina
mean, v., meant, mean·ing. intentar; querer decir; significar. a. inferior; tacaño; vil; medio. n. medio; pl. modo; medios. by all means, naturalmente. by no means, de ningún modo
mean·ing, n. intención; sentido
mean·time, n. ínterin. adv. mientras tanto
mea·sles, n. sarampión
meas·ure, n. medida; compás. v. medir
meas·ure·ment, n. medida
meat, n. carne, f.
me·chan·ic, n. mecánico
me·chan·i·cal, a. mecánico
me·chan·ics, n. mecánica
mech·an·ism, n. mecanismo
med·al, n. medalla
me·dal·lion, n. medallón
med·dle, v. entrometerse; meterse
me·di·an, a. mediano
med·i·ate, v. mediar; intervenir
med·i·cal, a. médico
med·i·ca·tion, n. medicación
med·i·cine, n. medicamento; medicina
me·di·e·val, a. medieval
me·di·o·cre, a. mediocre
med·i·tate, v. meditar; contemplar
med·i·ta·tion, n. meditación
me·di·um, n. pl., -di·a, -di·ums. medio; intermedio. a. mediano
meek, a. dócil
meet, v., met, meet·ing. encontrar(se); tropezar con; reunirse; honrar. n. reunión
meet·ing, n. reunión; encuentro; cita
mel·an·chol·y, n. melancolía
mel·low, v. suavizar. a. suave; maduro
mel·o·dra·ma, n. melodrama, m.
mel·o·dy, n. melodía
mel·on, n. melón
melt, v. derretir(se); fundir(se)
mem·ber, n. miembro
mem·brane, n. membrana
me·men·to, n. pl., -tos, -toes. recuerdo
mem·o, n. inf. memorándum, m.
mem·oir, n. memoria
mem·o·ra·ble, a. memorable
mem·o·ran·dum, n. pl., -dums, -da. apunte; memorándum, m.
me·mo·ri·al, n. memorial. a. conmemorativo
mem·o·rize, v. aprender de memoria
mem·o·ry, n. pl., -ries. memoria; recuerdo
men·ace, v. amenazar. n. amenaza
mend, v. reparar; reformar
me·ni·al, a. servil. n. doméstico
men·o·pause, n. menopausia
men·stru·a·tion, n. menstruación
men·tal, a. mental
men·thol, n. mentol, m.
men·tion, n. mención. v. mencionar
men·u, n. menú, m.; lista de platos
mer·ce·nar·y, a., n. mercenario
mer·chan·dise, n. mercancía
mer·chant, n. comerciante

mer·cu·ry, n. mercurio
mer·cy, n. misericordia; merced; clemencia
mere, a. mero
me·rid·i·an, n. meridiano
me·ringue, n. merengue
mer·it, n. mérito. v. merecer
mer·maid, n. sirena
mer·ry, a. regocijado; divertido; festivo
mer·ry-go-round, n. tiovivo
mesh, n. malla; pl. red. v. enredarse
mess, n. desorden; confusión. v. desordenar
mes·sage, n. comunicación; recado
mes·sen·ger, n. mensajero
me·tab·o·lism, n. metabolismo
met·al, n. metal
met·a·mor·pho·sis, n. pl., -ses. metamorfosis, f.
met·a·phor, n. metáfora
mete, v. repartir
me·te·or·ite, n. meteorito
me·te·or·ol·o·gy, n. meteorología
me·ter, me·tre, n. metro
meth·od, n. método
me·trop·o·lis, n. metrópoli, f.
met·ro·pol·i·tan, a. metropolitano
mez·za·nine, n. entresuelo
mi·ca, n. mica
mi·crobe, n. microbio
mi·cro·cosm, n. microcosmo
mi·cro·phone, n. micrófono
mi·cro·scope, n. microscopio
mid, a. medio. prep. entre
mid·day, n. mediodía
mid·dle, a. medio. n. medio; centro
midg·et, n. enano
mid·night, n. medianoche
mid·ship·man, n. pl. -men. guardia marina
midst, n. medio. prep. entre
mid·wife, n. pl. -wives. partera
might, n. fuerza; poder
mi·grate, v. emigrar
mi·gra·to·ry, a. migratorio
mild, a. suave; manso; ligero
mil·dew, n. mildeu, m.; maho
mile, n. milla
mi·lieu, n. pl., -lieus. medio ambiente
mil·i·tant, a. militante
mil·i·tar·y, a. militar. n. los militares; soldados
mi·li·tia, n. milicia
milk, n. leche, f. v. ordeñar
mill, n. molino; fábrica. v. moler
mil·len·ni·um, n. pl., -ni·a, -ni·ums. milenio
mil·li·me·ter, n. milímetro
mil·lion, n. millón
mil·lion·aire, n. millonario
mime, n. mimo; pantomima
mim·e·o·graph, n. mimeógrafo
mim·ic, v. imitar. n. remedador
mince, v. desmenuzar
mind, n. mente, f.; inteligencia. v. obedecer; cuidar; preocuparse
mine, pron. mío; mía. n. mina. v. minar
min·er·al, a. n. mineral, m.
min·gle, v. mezclar(se)
min·i·a·ture, n. miniatura. a. en miniatura
min·i·mum, a. mínimo. n. mínimo
min·is·ter, n. pastor; eclesiástico; ministro
min·is·try, n. ministerio; clero
mink, n. visón
mi·nor, a. menor; secundario; menor de edad. n. subordinado; menor de edad
mi·nor·i·ty, n. minoría
mint, n. casa de moneda; menta. v. acuñar
mi·nus, prep. menos; falto de. n. signo menos. a. negativo
min·ute, n. minuto; momento; pl. acta
mi·nute, a. menudo
mir·a·cle, n. milagro
mi·rac·u·lous, a. milagroso
mi·rage, n. espejismo
mir·ror, n. espejo
mirth, n. alegría
mis·an·thrope, n. misántropo
mis·ap·pre·hend, v. entender mal
mis·car·riage, n. malparto; malogro
mis·cel·la·ne·ous, a. misceláneo; diverso
mis·chief, n. travesura; mal, m.
mis·chie·vous, a. malicioso
mis·con·cep·tion, n. equivocación
mis·de·mean·or, n. delito
mi·ser, n. avaro
mis·er·a·ble, a. desgraciado; infeliz; vil
mis·er·y, n. sufrimiento; miseria
mis·for·tune, n. infortunio
mis·giv·ing, n. often pl. presentimiento
mis·hap, n. contratiempo
mis·lay, v., -laid, -lay·ing. extraviar
mis·lead, v., -led, -lead·ing. despistar; engañar
mis·print, n. error de imprenta
mis·rep·re·sent, v. falsificar
miss, v. errar; perder; no acertar; pasar por alto. n. error; señorita
mis·sal, n. misal, m.
mis·sile, n. proyectil, m.
miss·ing, a. ausente; perdido
mis·sion, n. misión
mis·sion·ar·y, n. misionero
mist, n. neblina
mis·take, v., -took, -tak·en, -tak·ing. equivocar(se)
mis·ter, n. señor. Abbr. Mr.
mis·tle·toe, n. muérdago

mis·treat, v. maltratar
mis·tress, n. señora; querida
mis·trust, n. recelo. v. desconfiar de
mis·un·der·stand, v., -stood, -stand·ing. entender mal
mis·use, v. maltratar; abusar
mi·ter, mi·tre, n. mitra; inglete
mit·i·gate, v. mitigar
mit·ten, n. mitón
mix, v. mezclar(se); confundir. n. mezcla
mix·ture, n. mezcla
moan, v. gemir; quejarse. n. quejido
moat, n. foso
mob, n. tropel, m.; turba. v. festejar tumultuosamente
mo·bile, a. móvil; ambulante
moc·ca·sin, n. mocasín
mock, v. burlarse de. a. falso
mock·er·y, n. mofa
mode, n. modo; moda
mod·el, n. modelo. v. modelar
mod·er·ate, a., a. moderado. v. moderar(se)
mod·ern, n. a. moderno
mod·est, a. modesto
mod·i·fi·ca·tion, n. modificación
mod·i·fy, v. modificar
mod·u·late, v. modular
moist, a. húmedo
mois·ten, v. humedecer
mois·ture, n. humedad
mo·lar, n. muela
mo·las·ses, n. melaza
mold, mould, n. molde; moho. v. moldear; amoldar
mold·ing, mould·ing, n. moldura
mole, n. lunar; topo
mol·e·cule, n. molécula
mo·lest, v. molestar; asaltar sexualmente
mol·lusk, mol·lusc, n. molusco
mol·ten, a. fundido
mom, n. inf. mamá
mo·ment, n. momento
mo·men·tar·y, a. momentáneo
mo·men·tum, n. ímpetu, m.
mon·arch, n. monarca, m.
mon·ar·chy, n. monarquía
mon·as·ter·y, n. pl., -ies. monasterio
Mon·day, n. lunes, m.
mon·e·tar·y, a. monetario
mon·ey, n. dinero
mon·goose, n. mangosta
mon·grel, n. a. mestizo
mon·i·tor, n. monitor
monk, n. monje
mon·key, n. pl., -keys. mono. v. imitar
mon·o·ga·my, n. monogamia
mon·o·gram, n. monograma, m.
mon·o·lith, n. monolito
mon·o·logue, mon·o·log, n. monólogo
mo·nop·o·lize, v. monopolizar
mo·nop·o·ly, n. monopolio
mon·o·tone, n. monotonía
mo·not·o·nous, a. monótono
mo·not·o·ny, n. monotonía
mon·ox·ide, n. monóxido
mon·sieur, n. pl. mes·sieurs. Fr. señor
mon·soon, n. monzón, m., f.
mon·ster, n. monstruo
mon·stros·i·ty, n. monstruosidad
month, n. mes, m.
month·ly, a. mensual. adv. mensualmente
mon·u·ment, n. monumento
mood, n. humor
moon, n. luna
moon·light, n. luz de la luna
moor, n. páramo. v. amarrar
moose, n. pl., moose. alce
mop, n. estropajo
mor·al, a. moral. n. moraleja; pl. moralidad
mo·rale, n. moral, f.
mor·al·ize, v. moralizar
mo·rass, n. pantano
mor·a·to·ri·um, n. pl., -ums, -a. moratoria
mor·bid, a. mórbido; pesimista
more, a. más; adicional. adv., n. más
more·o·ver, adv. además
morgue, n. depósito de cadáveres
morn·ing, n. mañana; madrugada
mo·rose, a. malhumorado; saturnino
mor·phine, n. morfina
mor·sel, n. pedazo; bocado
mor·tal, a. mortal; fatal. n. mortal, m., f.
mor·tal·i·ty, n. mortalidad
mort·gage, n. hipoteca. v. hipotecar
mor·tu·ar·y, n. mortuorio
mo·sa·ic, n. mosaico
mos·qui·to, n. pl., -toes, -tos. mosquito
moss, n. musgo
most, a. más; la mayor parte de. adv. lo más; muy
most·ly, adv. principalmente
moth, n. polilla
moth·er, n. madre. a. materno. v. servir de madre a
moth·er·hood, n. maternidad
moth·er-in-law, n. pl., moth·ers-in-law. suegra
mo·tion, n. movimiento; moción. v. hacer señas
mo·tion pic·ture, n. película
mo·tive, n. motivo
mot·ley, a. abigarrado
mo·tor, n., a. motor. v. ir en coche
mo·tor·cy·cle, n. motocicleta
mot·to, n. pl., -toes, -tos. mote; lema, m.
mound, n. terraplén; montón. v.

amontonar
moun·tain, n. montaña
mourn, v. lamentarse; llorar
mourn·ing, n. luto
mouse, n. pl. mice. ratón
mouth, n. boca; embocadero
move, v. mover(se); trasladar(se); ir(se); mudar(se); conmover. n. acción; jugada
move·ment, n. movimiento; actividad; tiempo
mov·ie, n. película
mow, v., mowed, mowed or mown, mow·ing. segar
Mr., n. pl., Messrs. señor
Mrs., n. pl., Mmes. señora
Ms., n. señorita; señora
much, adv., a. more, most. mucho; muy. n. mucho
mu·cous, a. mucoso
mu·cus, n. moco
mud, n. barro; lodo
mud·dle, v. aturdir. n. embrollo
muff, n. manguito
muf·fin, n. mollete
muf·fle, v. embozar; apagar
muf·fler, n. bufanda
mug, n. pichel, m.; inf. jeta. v. inf. asaltar
mule, n. mulo
mul·ti·ple, a. múltiple. n. múltiplo
mul·ti·pli·ca·tion, n. multiplicación
mul·ti·ply, v. multiplicar(se)
mul·ti·tude, n. multitud
mum·ble, v. hablar entre dientes
mum·my, n. momia
mumps, n. paperas; parótidas
mun·dane, a. mundano
mu·nic·i·pal, a. municipal
mu·ni·tion, n. usu. pl. municiones
mu·ral, n., a. mural, m.
mur·der, n. asesinar. n. asesinato
mur·mur, n. murmullo. v. murmurar
mus·cle, n. músculo
mus·cu·lar, a. muscular; musculoso
muse, v. meditar. n. musa
mu·se·um, n. museo
mush·room, n. champiñón; hongo
mu·sic, n. música
mu·si·cal, a. musical; músico
mu·si·cian, n. músico
mus·ket, n. mosquete
musk·rat, n., pl., -rat, -rats. rata almizclera
mus·lin, n. muselina
must, v. deber; tener que
mus·tache, n. bigote
mus·tard, n. mostaza
mute, a. mudo. n. mudo; (mus.) sordina
mu·ti·late, v. mutilar
mu·ti·ny, n. motín. v. amotinarse
mut·ter, v. murmurar. n. rumor
mu·tu·al, a. mutuo
muz·zle, n. hocico; boca; bozal. v. abozalar
my, a. mi
myr·i·ad, n. miríada
my·self, pron. pl., our·selves. yo mismo
mys·te·ri·ous, a. misterioso
mys·ter·y, n. pl., -ies. misterio
mys·tic, a. n. místico
mys·ti·cism, n. misticismo; mística
myth, n. mito
myth·i·cal, myth·i·cal, a. mítico
my·thol·o·gy, n. mitología

N

nab, v. inf. coger; prender
nag, v. regañar. n. jaca
nail, n. clavo; uña. v. clavar
na·ive, na·ïve, a. ingenuo; sencillo
na·ive·té, na·ïve·te, n. ingenuidad
na·ked, a. desnudo
name, n. nombre; apellido; fama. v. llamar; nombrar
name·sake, n. tocayo
nap, v. dormitar. n. siesta; lanilla
nape, n. nuca
naph·tha, n. nafta
nap·kin, n. servilleta
nar·cis·sism, n. narcisismo
nar·cis·sus, n. pl., -cis·sus·es, -cis·si. narciso
nar·cot·ic, n., a. narcótico
nar·rate, v. narrar
nar·ra·tion, n. narración; relato
nar·ra·tive, n. narrativa. a. narrativo
nar·row, a. estrecho; angosto; reducido. v. estrechar(se)
na·sal, a. nasal. (phon.) sonido nasal
nas·ty, a. sucio; asqueroso; rencoroso
na·tal, a. natal
na·tion, n. nación; pueblo
na·tion·al, a. nacional. n. nacional, m., f.
na·tion·al·ism, n. nacionalismo
na·tion·al·i·ty, n. pl., -ties. nacionalidad
na·tive, a. nativo; natural. n. nacional, m., f.; indígena, m., f.
na·tiv·i·ty, n. pl., -ties. natividad; (cap.) Navidad
nat·u·ral, a. natural; genuino
nat·u·ral·ize, v. naturalizar(se)
na·ture, n. naturaleza; carácter; género
naught, n. nada; (arith.) cero
naugh·ty, a. travieso; pícaro
nau·se·a, n. náusea
nau·se·ate, v. nausear; dar asco
nau·ti·cal, a. náutico
na·val, a. naval; marítimo
nave, n. nave, f.
na·vel, n. ombligo

nav·i·ga·ble, a. navegable
nav·i·gate, v. navegar; marear
nav·i·ga·tion, n. navegación; náutica
na·vy, n. pl., -vies. marina de guerra; azul marino o de mar. Also na·vy blue
nay, adv. no. n. voto negativo
near, a. cercano; próximo. adv. cerca. prep. cerca de; junto a. v. acercarse a
near·ly, adv. cerca
near·sight·ed, a. miope
neat, a. esmerado; primoroso
neb·u·la, n. pl., -las, -lae. nebulosa
nec·es·sar·y, a. necesario; esencial. n. pl., -ies. lo necesario
ne·ces·si·ty, n. pl., -ties. necesidad; requisito
neck, n. cuello
nec·tar, n. néctar
need, n. carencia; necesidad. v. necesitar; requerir
nee·dle, n. aguja
need·less, a. superfluo
ne·far·i·ous, a. nefario
neg·a·tive, a. negativo. n. negativa; (photog.) negativo. v. negar; poner veto a
ne·glect, v. descuidar; faltar a. n. descuido; dejadez, f.
neg·li·gee, n. bata
neg·li·gi·ble, a. insignificante; sin importancia
ne·go·ti·ate, v. negociar; gestionar
ne·go·ti·a·tion, n. negociación
neigh·bor, n., a. vecino. v. estar contiguo a
neigh·bor·hood, n. vecindad; barrio
nei·ther, a., conj. ni; tampoco. pron. ninguno
ne·on, n. neón
neph·ew, n. sobrino
nerve, n. nervio; valor; inf. descaro
nerv·ous, a. nervioso
nest, n. nido. v. anidar
nes·tle, v. arrimarse
net, n. red, f. v. coger. a. neto
net·work, n. red, f.
neu·ral·gia, n. neuralgia
neu·ro·sis, n. pl., -ses. neurosis, f.
neu·rot·ic, a. neurótico. n. neurótico
neu·ter, a. neutro
neu·tral, a. neutral. n. neutral, m., f.
neu·tral·i·ty, n. neutralidad
neu·tral·ize, v. neutralizar
neu·tron, n. neutrón
nev·er, adv. nunca; jamás
nev·er·the·less, adv. sin embargo; a pesar de todo
new, a. nuevo; reciente; moderno. adv. nuevamente
new·ly, adv. nuevamente
new·ly·wed, n. recién casados
news, n. pl. noticias; nuevas
next, a. próximo; siguiente. adv. inmediatamente después. prep. contiguo
nib·ble, v. picar; mordiscar
nice, a. simpático; amable; agradable; fino
ni·ce·ty, n. pl., -ties. usu. pl. punto fino
nick, n. muesca
nick·el, n. níquel, m.; moneda de cinco centavos
nick·name, n. apodo. v. apodar
nic·o·tine, n. nicotina. Also nic·o·tin
niece, n. sobrina
night, n. noche, f. a. nocturno
night·in·gale, n. ruiseñor
night·ly, a. nocturno. adv. por la noche
night·mare, n. pesadilla
night·time, n. noche, f.
nim·ble, a. ágil; listo
nine, n., a. nueve
nine·teen, n., a. diecinueve
nine·ty, a., n. pl., -ties. noventa
nin·ny, n. pl., -nies. bobo
ninth, a. noveno
nip, v. pellizcar; cortar
nip·ple, n. pezón
ni·trate, n. nitrato
ni·tro·gen, n. nitrógeno
ni·tro·glyc·er·in, n. nitroglicerina
no, adv. no. n. pl. noes, nos. no. a. ninguno
no·bil·i·ty, n. pl., -ties. nobleza
no·ble, a. noble. n. noble
no·ble·man, n. pl., -men. noble; hidalgo
no·bod·y, pron. nadie. n. pl., -ies. nadie
noc·tur·nal, a. nocturno
nod, v. cabecear; inclinar (la cabeza). n. señal hecha con la cabeza
noise, n. ruido; clamor
nois·y, a. ruidoso; estrepitoso
no·mad, n. nómada, m., f.
nom·i·nal, a. nominal
nom·i·nate, v. nombrar
nom·i·na·tion, n. nombramiento; nominación
non·cha·lant, a. indiferente
non·con·form·i·ty, n. disidencia
non·de·script, a. inclasificable; indefinible
none, pron. nadie; nada; ninguno. adv. de ninguna manera
non·pa·reil, n. persona o cosa sin par. a. sin igual
non·prof·it, a. no comercial
non·sense, n. tontería
noo·dle, n. tallarín
noon, n. mediodía, m.
no one, pron. nadie. Also no-one
noose, n. lazo corredizo

nor, conj. ni
norm, n. norma; modelo
nor·mal, a. normal
nor·mal·ly, adv. normalmente
north, n. del norte. adv. al norte. n. norte
north·east, n. nordeste
north·ern, a. del norte; al norte
north·ward, adv. hacia el norte
north·west, n. noroeste
nose, n. nariz, f.
nos·tal·gia, n. nostalgia
nos·tril, n. ventana de la nariz; pl. narices, f. pl.
nos·y, a. inf. curioso
not, adv. no; de ningún modo
no·ta·ble, a., n. notable
no·ta·ry, n. pl., -ries. notario. Also no·ta·ry pub·lic
no·ta·tion, n. notación
notch, n. mella; muesca. v. mellar
note, n. often pl. nota; apunte; señal, f. v. notar; apuntar
noth·ing, n. nada. adv. de ninguna manera
no·tice, n. aviso; anuncio; atención. v. notar; fijarse en
no·ti·fy, v. notificar
no·tion, n. noción; concepto; idea
no·to·ri·ous, a. notorio
not·with·stand·ing, prep. a pesar de. adv. no obstante. conj. por más que
noun, n. substantivo
nour·ish, v. nutrir; alimentar
nov·el, n. novela. a. nuevo
nov·el·ty, n. pl., -ties. novedad
No·vem·ber, n. noviembre
nov·ice, n. principiante, m., f.
now, adv. ahora; actualmente
no·where, adv. en ninguna parte
noz·zle, n. boquilla
nu·cle·ar, a. nuclear
nu·cle·us, n. pl., -us·es, -i. núcleo
nude, a. desnudo. n. desnudo
nu·di·ty, n. desnudez, f.
nui·sance, n. molestia; incomodidad
null, a. nulo
numb, a. entumecido; entorpecido. v. entumecer
num·ber, n. número. v. numerar; contar
nu·mer·a·tor, n. numerador
nu·mer·i·cal, a. numérico
nu·mer·ous, a. numeroso
nun, n. monja
nun·ner·y, n. pl., -ies. convento de monjas
nup·tial, a. nupcial. n. usu. pl. nupcias
nurse, n. enfermera; niñera. v. criar; cuidar
nurs·er·y, n. pl., -ies. cuarto de los niños; plantel, m.
nur·ture, v. nutrir; criar
nut, n. nuez, f.
nu·tri·tion, n. nutrición
nu·tri·tious, a. nutritivo
ny·lon, n. nailon; nilón; pl. medias
nymph, n. ninfa

O

oaf, n. zoquete
oak, n. roble. a. de roble
oar, n. remo
o·a·sis, n. pl., -ses. oasis, m.
oat, n. usu. pl. avena
oath, n. pl., oaths. juramento; blasfemia
o·be·di·ence, n. obediencia
o·bese, a. obeso
o·bey, v. obedecer; cumplir
o·bit·u·ar·y, n. pl., -ries. necrología
ob·ject, n. objeto; propósito; fin. v. oponerse; objetar
ob·jec·tion, n. objeción; inconveniente
ob·jec·tive, a. objetivo. n. objetivo
ob·li·gate, v. obligar; precisar
ob·li·ga·tion, n. obligación; compromiso
o·blige, v. obligar; hacer un favor a
ob·lique, a. oblicuo; indirecto
ob·long, a. oblongo. n. cuadrilongo
ob·nox·ious, a. detestable; ofensivo
o·boe, n. oboe
ob·scene, a. obsceno
ob·scen·i·ty, n. pl., -ties. obscenidad
ob·scure, a. oscuro; indistinto. v. oscurecer
ob·serv·ance, n. observancia; práctica
ob·ser·va·tion, n. observación
ob·ser·va·to·ry, n. pl., -ries. observatorio
ob·serve, v. observar; cumplir
ob·ses·sion, n. obsesión
ob·so·lete, a. anticuado
ob·sta·cle, n. obstáculo; impedimento
ob·sti·nate, a. obstinado; terco
ob·struct, v. obstruir; estorbar
ob·tain, v. obtener; adquirir; regir
ob·vi·ous, a. obvio; evidente
oc·ca·sion, n. ocasión; acontecimiento
oc·cult, a. oculto
oc·cu·pan·cy, n. pl., -cies. ocupación
oc·cu·pa·tion, n. empleo; tenencia; ocupación
oc·cu·py, v. ocupar
oc·cur, v., -curred, -cur·ring. ocurrir; suceder
o·cean, n. océano
oc·ta·gon, n. octágono
oc·tave, n. octava
Oc·to·ber, n. octubre

oc·to·pus, n. pulpo
odd, a. raro; sobrante; sin pareja; impar. n. pl. ventaja
odd·i·ty, n. pl., -ties. rareza
ode, n. oda
o·di·ous, a. odioso
o·dor, n. olor
of, prep. de; sobre
off, adv. fuera. a. desenchufado. prep. lejos. int. fuera de aquí. be off, irse; estar parado. off and on, de vez en cuando. turn off, cerrar; apagar
of·fend, v. ofender
of·fense, n. ofensa; crimen
of·fer, v. ofrecer(se); deparar. n. oferta; ofrecimiento
of·fice, n. oficina; cargo; departamento
of·fic·er, n. oficial, m.; agente
of·fi·cial, a. oficial. n. oficial, m.
off·spring, n. pl., -spring, -springs. descendiente; descendencia
of·ten, adv. a menudo; muchas veces
of·ten·times, adv. a menudo. Also oft·times
o·gle, v. ojear
o·gre, n. ogro
oil, n. aceite; petróleo. v. lubrificar
oil·y, a. aceitoso; grasiento
oint·ment, n. ungüento
O.K., a. muy bien; vale; aprobado. v., O.K.'d O.K.'ing. aprobar. Also O.K., o·kay
old, a. old·er or eld·er, old·est or eld·est. viejo; antique; anciano
old-fash·ioned, a. pasado de moda
ol·ive, n. aceituna; olivo
om·e·let, om·e·lette, n. tortilla
o·men, n. agüero; presagio
o·mis·sion, n. omisión; descuido
o·mit, v., o·mit·ted, o·mit·ting. omitir; olvidar
om·ni·bus, n. pl., -bus·es. autobús, m.
om·nip·o·tence, n. omnipotencia
om·nis·cience, n. omnisciencia
om·niv·or·ous, a. omnívoro
on, prep. sobre; en; sin cesar. on foot, a pie. on sale, de venta
once, adv. una vez; en otro tiempo. n. una vez
one, a. uno; un; una; solo. n., pron. uno
one·self, pron. sí mismo; sí. Also one's self
on·ion, n. cebolla
on·ly, adv. sólo; solamente. a. solo; único
on·slaught, n. ataque furioso
on·to, prep. en; sobre
on·ward, a. progresivo. adv. hacia adelante. Also on·wards
on·yx, n. ónice
o·pac·i·ty, n. pl., -ties. opacidad
o·pal, n. ópalo
o·paque, a. opaco; oscuro
o·pen, a. abierto; franco. v. abrir(se); empezar
o·pen-hand·ed, a. generoso
o·pen·ing, n. abertura; oportunidad
o·per·a, n. ópera
op·er·ate, v. hacer funcionar; obrar; operar; dirigir
op·er·a·tion, n. operación
op·er·et·ta, n. opereta
o·pin·ion, n. opinión; juicio
o·pi·um, n. opio
op·po·nent, n. adversario. a. opuesto
op·por·tune, a. oportuno
op·por·tu·ni·ty, n. pl., -ties. oportunidad
op·pose, v. oponerse; resistir
op·po·site, a. opuesto. n. lo contrario. adv. en frente. prep. en frente de
op·press, v. oprimir
opt, v. escoger
op·ti·cal, a. óptico
op·ti·mism, n. optimismo
op·tion, n. opción
op·u·lent, a. opulento
o·pus, n. pl. o·pe·ra, o·pus·es. obra
or, conj. o; u
or·a·cle, n. oráculo
o·ral, a. oral; verbal
or·ange, n. naranja. a. anaranjado
or·ange·ade, n. naranjada
o·ra·tion, n. oración
orb, n. orbe
or·bit, n. órbita. v. girar
or·chard, n. huerto
or·ches·tra, n. orquesta
or·dain, v. ordenar
or·der, n. orden, m., f.; clase, f.; mandato. v. arreglar; mandar; encargar
or·der·ly, a. ordenado, n., pl., -lies. asistente
or·di·nar·y, a. corriente; ordinario
ore, n. mena
or·gan, n. órgano
or·gan·dy, or·gan·die, n. organdí, m.
or·gan·ic, a. orgánico
or·gan·ism, n. organismo
or·gan·i·za·tion, n. organización
or·gan·ize, v. organizar(se)
or·gy, n. pl., -gies. orgia
o·ri·ent, n. este; (cap.) oriente. v. orientar
or·i·gin, n. origen
o·rig·i·nal, a., n. original, m.
o·rig·i·nate, v. originar(se); surgir
or·na·ment, n. ornamento; adorno
or·phan, n. huérfano
or·phan·age, n. orfanato
or·tho·dox, a. ortodoxo
or·tho·dox·y, n. pl., -ies. ortodoxia
os·mo·sis, n. ósmosis, osmosis, f.
os·ten·si·ble, a. aparente

os·ten·ta·tion, n. ostentación; fausto
os·tra·cism, n. ostracismo
os·trich, v. avestruz, m.
oth·er, a. otro. prep. el otro. adv. de otra manera
oth·er·wise, adv. de otra manera; si no
ought, aux. v. deber; tener que
ounce, n. onza
our, a. nuestro
ours, pron. el nuestro
our·selves, pron. pl. nosotros (mismos)
oust, v. expulsar
out, adv. fuera (de casa); afuera; apagado. prep. fuera de. a. sin sentido
out·break, n. erupción
out·cast, n. proscrito. a. rechazado
out·come, n. resultado
out·cry, v. pl., -cries. grito; clamor
out·dat·ed, a. fuera de moda
out·door, a. al aire libre
out·er, a. externo
out·fit, n. equipo; traje
out·grow, v., -grew, -grown, growing. ser ya viejo para
out·ing, n. excursión
out·law, v. forajido. v. proscribir
out·let, n. salida
out·line, n. contorno; bosquejo. v. bosquejar
out·live, v. sobrevivir a
out·look, n. perspectiva
out-of-date, a. pasado de moda
out·put, n. producción
out·rage, n. atrocidad
out·right, adv. completamente; abiertamente. a. entero
out·set, n. principio
out·side, n. exterior. a. externo. adv. fuera
out·sid·er, n. forastero
out·spo·ken, a. franco
out·stand·ing, a. sobresaliente
out·ward, a. exterior; óbvio. adv. hacia fuera. Also out·wards
out·wear, v., -wore, -worn, wear·ing. durar más tiempo que
out·wit, v. ser más listo que
o·val, a. oval. n. óvalo
o·va·ry, n. pl., -ries. ovario
o·va·tion, n. ovación
ov·en, n. horno
o·ver, prep. encima de; sobre; más de. adv. de arriba abajo. a. otra vez
o·ver·all, a. en total
o·ver·bear·ing, a. imperioso
o·ver·board, adv. al agua
o·ver·coat, n. abrigo
o·ver·come, v., -came, -come, -coming. superar
o·ver·dose, n. dosis excesiva
o·ver·due, a. vencido y no pagado
o·ver·flow, v., -flowed, -flown, -flowing. robasar; derramarse. n. inundación
o·ver·haul, v. revisar
o·ver·head, a. elevado. adv. encima
o·ver·hear, v., -heard, -hear·ing. oír por casualidad
o·ver·lap, v. traslapar; solapar. n. solape
o·ver·look, v. no hacer caso de; tener vista a
o·ver·night, adv. durante la noche. a. de noche
o·ver·pow·er, v. dominar
o·ver·run, v., -ran, -run, -run·ing. invadir
o·ver·seas, adv., a. en el extranjero. Also o·ver·sea
o·ver·see, v., -saw, -seen, -see·ing. vigilar
o·ver·shoe, n. chanclo
o·ver·sight, n. descuido; olvido
o·ver·sleep, v., -slept, -sleep·ing. dormir demasiado
o·vert, a. público
o·ver·take, v., -took, -ta·ken, tak·ing. alcanzar
o·ver·throw, v., -threw, -thrown, -throw·ing. echar abajo
o·ver·ture, n. (mus.) obertura; propuesta
o·ver·turn, v. volcar
o·ver·weight, n. exceso; gordo
o·ver·work, v. trabajar demasiado
o·vum, n. pl., o·va. óvulo
owe, v. tener deudas
owl, n. búho; lechuza
own, a. propio. v. poseer; reconocer
ox, n. pl., ox·en, buey, m.
ox·ide, n. óxido
ox·y·gen, n. oxígeno
oys·ter, n. ostra
o·zone, n. ozono

P

pa, n. inf. papá, m.
pace, n. paso. v. medir a pasos
pa·cif·ic, a. pacífico
pac·i·fism, n. pacifismo
pac·i·fy, v. pacificar; calmar
pack, n. fardo. v. llenar; empaquetar
pack·age, n. paquete
pact, n. pacto
pad, n. almohadilla. v. acolchar
pad·dle, n. canalete
pad·lock, n. candado
pa·gan, n. pagano
page, n. página. v. paginar
pag·eant, n. espectáculo
pa·go·da, n. pagoda
pail, n. cubo. Also pail·ful

pain, n. dolor. v. doler; apenar
pain·ful, a. doloroso; penoso
pains·tak·ing, a. laborioso; esmerado
paint, v. pintar. n. pintura
paint·ing, n. pintura; cuadro
pair, n. pl., pairs, pair. pareja; par. v. aparear
pa·jam·as, n. pl. pijama, m.
pal·ace, n. palacio
pal·ate, n. paladar
pale, a. pálido; claro. v. palidecer(se)
pa·le·on·tol·o·gy, n. paleontología
pal·ette, n. paleta
pal·i·sade, n. palizada
pall, v. perder su sabor
pal·lid, a. pálido
pal·lor, n. palidez, f.
palm, n. palma
palm·is·try, n. quiromancia
pal·pa·ble, a. palpable
pal·pi·ta·tion, n. palpitación
pal·try, a. miserable
pam·per, v. mimar
pam·phlet, n. folleto
pan, n. cacerola; cazuela. v. separar en una gamella
pan·a·ce·a, n. panacea
pan·cake, n. hojuela
pan·cre·as, n. páncreas, m.
pan·de·mo·ni·um, n. pandemónium
pane, n. hoja de vidrio
pan·el, n. panel, m.; entrepaño; tablero; jurado
pang, n. punzada; dolor
pan·han·dle, v. inf. mendigar
pan·ic, n. terror
pan·o·ram·a, n. panorama, m.
pan·sy, n. pl., -sies. pensamiento; inf. maricón
pant, v. jadear. n. jadeo; pl. pantalones
pan·the·ism, n. panteísmo
pan·ther, n. pantera
pan·to·mime, n. pantomima
pan·try, n. pl., -tries. despensa
pa·pa, n. papá, m.
pa·pa·cy, n. pl., -cies. papado; pontificado
pa·per, n. papel, m. v. empapelar
pa·pier-mâ·ché, n. cartón piedra
pa·poose, pap·poose, n. crío
pa·py·rus, n. pl., -rus·es, -ri. papiro
par, n. par
par·a·ble, n. parábola
par·a·chute, n. paracaídas, m.
pa·rade, n. cabalgata; desfile; parada. v. formar en parada
par·a·dise, n. paraíso
par·a·dox, n. paradoja
par·af·fin, n. parafina
par·a·graph, n. párrafo
par·al·lel, a. paralelo. n. paralelo
pa·ral·y·sis, n. pl., -ses. parálisis, f.
par·a·lyze, v. paralizar
pa·ram·e·ter, n. parámetro; límite
par·a·noi·a, n. paranoia
par·a·pher·nal·ia, n. pl., sing. or pl. in constr. arreos
par·a·phrase, n. paráfrasis, f.
par·a·site, n. parásito
par·a·troop·er, n. paracaidista, m.
parch, v. secar
parch·ment, n. pergamino
par·don, v. perdonar. n. perdón; indulto
pare, v. cortar
par·ent, n. padre; madre, f.
par·en·the·sis, n. pl., -ses, paréntesis, m.
pa·ri·ah, n. paria, m., f.
par·ish, n. parroquia
park, n. parque; jardín. v. estacionar; aparcar
par·ley, v. parlamentar. n. parlamento
par·lia·ment, n. (usu. cap.) parlamento
par·lor, par·lour, n. sala de recibo
pa·ro·chi·al, a. parroquial; estrecho
par·o·dy, n. pl., -dies. parodia
pa·role, n. libertad bajo palabra
par·ox·ysm, n. paroxismo
par·rot, n. papagayo; loro
par·ry, v. parar
pars·ley, n. perejil, m.
par·son, n. clérigo
part, n. parte, f.; porción. v. partir(se); separar(se). a. parcial
par·take, v., -took, -ta·ken, tak·ing. tomar parte
par·tial, a. parcial
par·ti·al·i·ty, n. pl., -ties. parcialidad
par·tic·i·pant, n. partícipe. n. concursante, m., f.
par·tic·i·pate, v. participar
par·tic·i·pa·tion, n. participación
par·ti·ci·ple, n. participio
par·ti·cle, n. partículo; pizca
par·tic·u·lar, a. particular; exigente. n. usu. pl. detalle
par·tic·u·lar·i·ty, n. pl., -ties. particularidad
part·ing, n. despedida
par·ti·san, n. partidario
par·ti·tion, n. partición; tabique
part·ner, n. socio
par·tridge, n. pl., -tridg·es, -tridge. perdiz, f.
par·ty, n. pl., -ties. partido; grupo; fiesta
pass, v. pasar; cruzar; aprobar. n. permiso
pas·sage, n. pasaje; travesía; pasadizo
pas·sen·ger, n. pasajero; viajero
pas·sion, n. pasión
pas·sion·ate, a. apasionado

pas·sive, a. pasivo
pass·port, n. pasaporte
pass·word, n. santo y seña
past, a. pasado. prep. después de. n. pasado
paste, n. enguido; pasta. v. pegar
paste·board, n. cartón
pas·teur·i·za·tion, n. pasteurización
pas·teur·ize, v. pasteurizar
pas·time, n. pasatiempo
pas·tor, n. pastor
pas·try, n. pl., -tries. pasteles, m. pl.
pas·ture, n. pasto. v. pastar
pat, v. golpecito; pastelillo. v. dar una palmadita; acariciar
patch, n. pedazo. v. remendar
pat·ent, n. patente, f. a. patente
pa·ter·nal, a. paternal; paterno
pa·ter·ni·ty, n. paternidad
path, n. senda
pa·thet·ic, a. patético
pa·thol·o·gy, n. pl., -gies. patología
pa·tience, n. paciencia
pa·tient, n. paciente. n. enfermo
pa·ti·o, n. pl., -os. patio
pa·tri·ar·chy, n. pl., -chies. patriarcado
pat·ri·mo·ny, n. pl., -nies. patrimonio
pa·tri·ot, n. patriota, m., f.
pa·trol, v. patrullar. n. patrulla
pa·tron, n. cliente, m.; f.; patrocinador
pat·tern, n. modelo; patrón
pau·per, n. pobre, m., f.
pause, n. pausa. v. detenerse
pave, v. empedrar; pavimentar
pave·ment, n. pavimento
pa·vil·ion, n. pabellón
paw, n. pata. v. manosear
pawn, v. empeñar
pay, v., paid, pay·ing. pagar; provechoso. n. paga; sueldo
pay·roll, n. nómina
pea, n. pl., peas, pease. guisante
peace, n. paz, f.; sosiego
peace·ful, a. tranquilo
peach, n. melocotón
pea·cock, n. pl., -cocks -cock. pavo real; pavón
peak, n. pico; cumbre, f.
peal, v. repicar
pea·nut, n. cacahuete
pear, n. pera
pearl, n. perla
peas·ant, n. campesino. a. campesino
peb·ble, n. guijarro
pec·ca·dil·lo, n. pl., -loes -los. pecadillo
pe·cu·liar, a. peculiar; raro
pe·cu·liar·i·ty, n. pl., -ties. particularidad; peculiaridad
ped·al, n. pedal, m.
ped·dle, v. vender por las calles
ped·dler, ped·ler, ped·lar, n. buhonero
ped·es·tal, n. pedestal, m.
pe·des·tri·an, n. peatón. a. pedestre
ped·i·gree, n. genealogía
peel, v. pelar. n. corteza
peer, n. par
peg, n. clavija; estaca
pel·let, n. bolita; pella
pelt, v. pellejo; piel, f. v. arrojar
pel·vis, n. pl., -vis·es, -ves. pelvis, f.
pen, n. pluma; corral, m.
pe·nal, a. penal
pe·nal·ty, n. pl., -ties. pena; castigo
pen·cil, n. lápiz, m.
pend·ant, pend·ent, n. pendiente
pend·ing, a. pendiente
pen·du·lum, n. péndulo
pen·e·trate, v. penetrar; comprender
pen·i·cil·lin, n. penicilina
pen·in·su·la, n. península
pen·i·tent, n. penitente, m., f. a. penitente
pen·i·ten·tia·ry, n. pl., -ries. presidio
pen·ny, n. pl., -nies. centavo
pen·sion, n. pensión. v. jubilar
pen·sive, a. pensativo
pen·ta·gon, n. pentágono
pe·on, n. peón
pe·o·ny, n. pl., -nies. peonía
peo·ple, n. pl., -ple, -ples. pueblo; gente, f. v. poblar
pep·per, n. pimienta; pimiento
pep·per·mint, n. menta
per, prep. por
per·ceive, v. percibir; darse cuenta de
per·cent, per·cent, n. pl., per·cent, per·cents. por ciento
per·cent·age, n. porcentaje
per·cep·tion, n. percepción
perch, n. percha; perca. v. posar(se)
per·di·tion, n. perdición
per·en·ni·al, a. perenne
per·fect, a. perfecto. v. perfeccionar
per·fec·tion, n. perfección
per·fo·rate, v. perforar
per·form, v. efectuar; hacer; representar
per·for·mance, n. representación; función
per·fume, n. perfume. v. perfumar
per·il, n. peligro
pe·rim·e·ter, n. perímetro
pe·ri·od, n. período; época; punto
pe·ri·od·i·cal, n. publicación periódica
pe·riph·er·y, n. pl., -ies. periferia
per·i·scope, n. periscopio
per·ish, v. perecer
per·jure, v. perjurar(se)
per·ju·ry, n. pl., -ries. perjurio
per·ma·nent, a. permanente
per·mis·sion, n. permiso
per·mit, v., -mit·ted, -mit·ting. per-

mitir; tolerar. n. permiso
per·pen·dic·u·lar, a. perpendicular
per·pet·u·al, a. perpetuo; continuo
per·plex, v. confundir
per·se·cute, v. perseguir; molestar
per·se·cu·tion, n. persecución
per·sist, v. persistir
per·son, n. persona
per·son·al·i·ty, n. pl., -ties. personalidad; personaje
per·son·nel, n. personal
per·spec·tive, n. perspectiva
per·spi·ra·tion, n. sudor
per·spire, v. sudar; transpirar
per·suade, v. persuadir
per·sua·sion, n. persuasión
per·tain, v. pertenecer; tener que ver con
per·ti·nent, a. pertinente; a propósito
per·ver·sion, n. perversión
per·vert, v. pervertir; estropear; alterar
pes·si·mism, n. pesimismo
pest, n. plaga
pes·ter, v. importunar; molestar; fastidiar
pet, n. animal doméstico; favorito. a. favorito. v. acariciar
pet·al, n. pétalo
pe·ti·tion, n. petición. v. solicitar
pe·tro·le·um, n. petróleo
pet·ty, a. mezquino
pew, n. banco
pew·ter, n. peltre
phal·lus, n. pl., -li, -lus·es. falo
phan·tom, n. fantasma, m.
phar·aoh, n. faraón
phar·ma·ceu·ti·cal, a. farmacéutico
phar·ma·cy, n. pl., -cies. farmacia
phase, n. fase, f.
pheas·ant, n. pl., -ant, -ants. faisán
phe·nom·e·non, n. pl., -na, -nons. fenómeno
phi·lan·thro·py, n. pl., -pies. filantropía
phi·los·o·pher, n. filósofo
phi·los·o·phy, n. pl., -phies. filosofía
phlegm, n. flema
pho·bi·a, n. fobia
phone, n. inf. teléfono
pho·no·graph, n. tocadiscos
phos·phate, n. fosfato
phos·pho·res·cence, n. fosforescencia
pho·to·pho·rus, n. fósforo
pho·to·cop·y, n. fotocopia
pho·to·gen·ic, a. fotogénico
pho·to·graph, n. fotografía; foto, f. v. sacar una foto
pho·tog·ra·phy, n. fotografía
phrase, n. frase, f.
phys·i·cal, a. físico
phy·si·cian, n. médico
phys·ics, n. física
pi·an·ist, n. pianista, m., f.
pi·an·o, n. piano
pic·a·resque, a. picaresco
pick, v. escoger; elegir; coger; picar. n. pico
pick·le, n. encurtido
pick·pock·et, n. ratero
pic·nic, n. excursión al campo; jira
pic·ture, n. cuadro; retrato; ilustración; película; foto, f.
pie, n. pastel, m.
piece, n. pieza; pedazo; trozo
piece·work, n. trabajo a destajo
pier, n. embarcadero; muelle
pierce, v. penetrar; agujerear; pinchar
pi·e·ty, n. piedad
pig, n. cerdo
pi·geon, n. paloma
pig·ment, n. pigmento
pig·tail, n. coleta
pile, n. montón; rimero
pil·grim, n. peregrino
pill, n. píldora
pil·lage, n. pillaje
pil·lar, n. pilar; columna
pil·low, n. almohada
pil·low·case, n. funda de almohada
pi·lot, n. piloto
pimp, n. alcahuete
pim·ple, n. grano
pin, n. n. alfiler
pinch, v. pellizcar; apretar
pin·cush·ion, n. acerico
pine, n. pino. v. languidecer
pink, n. picar. a. rosado
pin·na·cle, n. pináculo
pint, n. pinta
pi·o·neer, n. explorador. v. explorar; promover
pi·ous, a. piadoso
pipe, n. tubo; pipa
pique, n. pique. v. ofender; irritar
pi·rate, n. pirata, m.
pis·tol, n. pistola; revólver
pis·ton, n. pistón
pit, n. hoyo; hueso
pitch, n. pez, f.; tono. v. tirar
pitch·er, n. cántaro
pit·i·ful, a. lastimoso
pit·i·less, a. despiadado
pit·y, n. piedad; lástima. v. compadecer
piv·ot, n. pivote
pix·y, n. duende, f.
plac·ard, n. cartel, m.
pla·cate, v. apaciguar
place, n. sitio; lugar; posición. v. poner
pla·cen·ta, n. placenta
plac·id, a. plácido
pla·gia·rism, n. plagio
plague, n. peste, f.; plaga
plaid, n. tartán

plain, a. llano. a. llano; sencillo; evidente
plan, n. plan; plano; proyecto. v. planear
plane, n. cepillo; plano; inf. avión
plan·et, n. planeta, m.
plank, n. tablón
plant, n. planta. v. plantar; sembrar
plan·ta·tion, n. plantación
plas·ma, n. plasma, m.
plas·ter, n. argamasa
plas·tic, a. plástico. n. plástico
plate, n. plato
plat·form, n. plataforma; andén
plat·i·num, n. platino
pla·toon, n. pelotón
plau·si·ble, a. plausible; creíble
play, v. obra dramática; juego. v. jugar; (mus.) tocar
play·ful, a. juguetón
play·ground, n. patio de recreo
play·ing card, n. naipe
play·off, n. partido de desempate
play·thing, n. juguete
play·wright, n. dramaturgo
plea, n. súplica; defensa
plead, v. defender; suplicar; rogar
pleas·ant, a. agradable
please, v. dar gusto; contentar; gustar
pleas·ure, n. placer; gusto
pleat, n. pliegue. v. plegar
pleb·i·scite, n. plebiscito
pledge, n. prenda; promesa. v. empeñar; garantizar; prometer
plen·i·po·ten·ti·ar·y, n. plenipotenciario
plen·ti·ful, a. abundante
plen·ty, n. abundancia
pleth·o·ra, n. plétora
pli·ant, a. flexible
pli·ers, n. pl. alicates
plight, n. situación; apuro
plot, n. parcela; conspiración. v. intrigar
plow, v. arado
pluck, v. coger
plug, n. tapón; enchufe. v. tapar
plum, n. ciruela
plum·age, n. plumaje
plumb·er, n. fontanero
plumb·ing, n. instalación de cañerías
plun·der, v. saquear. n. saqueo; botín
plunge, v. hundir
plu·ral, a. plural. n. plural
plus, a. más; y
pneu·mo·nia, n. pulmonía
po·em, n. poema, m., poesía
po·et, n. poeta, m.
po·et·ic, po·et·i·cal, a. poético
po·et·ry, n. poesía
point, n. punto; punta; fin. v. apuntar
poise, n. equilibrio; aplomo
poi·son, n. veneno. v. envenenar
poke, v. atizar; empujar
pok·er, n. póquer
po·lar, a. polar
po·lar·i·ty, n. pl., -ties. polaridad
pole, n. palo; polo
po·lice, n. policía. v. mantener orden
pol·i·cy, n. pl., -cies. política; póliza
pol·ish, v. pulir; limpiar. n. bruñido; brillo; urbanidad
po·lite, a. cortés; fino
po·lit·i·cal, a. político
pol·i·ti·cian, n. político
pol·i·tics, n. pl., sing or pl. in constr. política
pol·ka, n. polca
poll, n. elección; sondeo
pol·len, n. polen
pol·lute, v. ensuciar
pol·lu·tion, n. polución; contaminación
po·lyg·a·my, n. poligamia
pol·y·gon, n. polígono
pol·yp, n. pólipo
pol·y·the·ism, n. politeísmo
pomp, n. pompa
pomp·ous, a. pomposo
pond, n. charca; estanque
pon·der, v. ponderar; pensar; meditar
pon·tiff, n. pontífice
po·ny, n. pl., -nies. jaca
pool, n. estanque; polla; truco; inf. piscina; v. mancomunar
poor, a. pobre; malo
pope, n. (often cap.) papa, m.
pop·py, n. pl., -pies. adormidera
pop·u·lace, n. pueblo; populacho
pop·u·lar, a. popular
pop·u·late, v. poblar
pop·u·la·tion, n. población
por·ce·lain, n. porcelana
porch, n. pórtico
por·cu·pine, n. puerco espín
pore, v. examinar. n. poro
pork, n. carne de cerdo
por·nog·ra·phy, n. pornografía
por·poise, n. pl., -pois·es, -poise. marsopa
port, n. puerto; babor; oporto
por·ta·ble, a. portátil
por·ter, n. portero; mozo de estación
port·fo·li·o, n. pl., -os. cartera
por·ti·co, n. pl., -coes, -cos. pórtico
por·tion, n. porción; parte, f. v. dividir
por·trait, n. retrato
por·tray, v. retratar; tomar el papel de

pose, v. colocarse; plantear. n. actitud
po·si·tion, n. posición; actitud; puesto
pos·i·tive, a. positivo; enfático
pos·sess, v. poseer
pos·ses·sion, n. posesión
pos·si·bil·i·ty, n. pl., -ties. posibilidad
pos·si·ble, a. posible
post, n. poste; puesto; correo. v. echar al correo; situar
post·age, n. porte; franqueo
post card, n. tarjeta (postal)
post·er, n. cartel, m.
pos·te·ri·or, a. posterior
post·man, n. pl., -men. cartero
post·mark, n. matasellos
post me·rid·i·em, a. postmeridiano. Abbr. p.m., P.M.
post·mor·tem, n. autopsia
post·pone, v. aplazar
post·script, n. posdata
pos·ture, n. postura
pot, n. olla; tiesto; inf. marijuana
po·tas·si·um, n. potasio
po·ta·to, n. pl., -toes. patata; papa
po·tent, a. potente; fuerte
po·ten·tial, a. potencial
po·tion, n. poción
pot·ter·y, n. pl., -ies. alfarería
pouch, n. bolsa
poul·try, n. aves de corral
pound, n. libra
pour, v. verter; diluviar
pout, v. hacer pucheros
pov·er·ty, n. pobreza
pow·der, n. polvo. v. ponerse polvos
pow·er, n. poder; fuerza; facultad
pow·er·ful, a. potente; poderoso
prac·ti·cal, a. práctico
prac·tice, v. practicar; ejercer. n. práctica; costumbre, f.
prag·mat·ic, a. pragmático
prai·rie, n. pradera
praise, n. alabanza. v. alabar
prank, n. travesura
pray, v. rezar; orar; rogar
prayer, n. oración
preach, v. predicar
pre·am·ble, n. preámbulo
pre·cau·tion, n. precaución
pre·cede, v. preceder
prec·e·dent, n. precedente
pre·cinct, n. recinto; distrito electoral
pre·cious, a. precioso; de gran valor
prec·i·pice, n. precipicio
pre·cip·i·ta·tion, n. precipitación
pre·cise, a. preciso; exacto
pre·co·cious, a. precoz
pre·cur·sor, n. precursor
pred·e·ces·sor, n. predecesor
pre·des·ti·na·tion, n. predestinación
pre·dic·a·ment, n. apuro
pre·dict, v. predecir; pronosticar
pre·dic·tion, n. pronóstico
pre·dom·i·nant, a. predominante
pref·ace, n. prólogo; prefacio
pre·fer, v., -ferred, -fer·ring. preferir
pref·er·ence, n. preferencia
pre·fix, n. prefijo
preg·nan·cy, n. pl., -cies. embarazo
preg·nant, a. encinta; embarazada
pre·his·tor·ic, a. prehistórico
prej·u·dice, n. prejuicio. v. perjudicar; predisponer
pre·lim·i·nar·y, n. pl., -ies. preliminar. a. preliminar
prel·ude, n. preludio
pre·med·i·tate, v. premeditar
pre·miere, n. estreno
pre·mi·um, n. premio; prima
pre·mo·ni·tion, n. presentimiento
pre·oc·cu·pied, a. preocupado
prep·a·ra·tion, n. preparación; preparativo
pre·pare, v. preparar(se); aparejar
prep·o·si·tion, n. preposición
pre·pos·ter·ous, a. absurdo
pre·req·ui·site, n. requisito previo
pre·rog·a·tive, n. prerrogativa
pre·scribe, v. prescribir; recetar
pre·scrip·tion, n. receta
pres·ence, n. presencia
pres·ent, v. presentar; ofrecer. n. regalo. a. presente
pres·en·ta·tion, n. presentación
pre·serv·a·tive, a. preservativo. n. preservativo
pre·serve, v. preservar; conservar. n. usu. pl. conserva
pre·side, v. presidir
pres·i·dent, n. (often cap.) presidente
press, n. prensa; imprenta. v. apretar; planchar
pres·sure, n. presión; urgencia
pres·ti·dig·i·ta·tion, n. prestidigitación
pres·tige, n. prestigio
pre·sume, v. presumir; suponer
pre·tend, v. fingir; pretender
pre·tense, n. pretexto
pret·ty, a. guapo; bonito; mono, adv. bastante
pre·vail, v. prevalecer; predominar
pre·vent, v. impedir
pre·vi·ous, a. previo
prey, n. presa
price, n. precio. v. valuar; fijar un precio
price·less, a. inapreciable
prick, v. punzar
pride, n. orgullo
priest, n. sacerdote; cura, m.
pri·ma·ry, a. primario
prime, a. primero; principal. v. cebar

prim·i·tive, *a.* primitivo
pri·mo·gen·i·ture, *n.* primogenitura
prince, *n.* príncipe
prin·cess, *n.* princesa
prin·ci·pal, *a.* principal. *n.* principal
prin·ci·pal·i·ty, *n. pl.,* **-ties.** principado
prin·ci·ple, *n.* principio
print, *n.* marca; impresión; grabado. *v.* imprimir
print·ing, *n.* tipografía; imprenta
pri·or, *a.* anterior
pri·or·i·ty, *n. pl.,* **-ties.** prioridad
pri·or·y, *n. pl.,* **-ries.** priorato
prism, *n.* prisma, *m.*
pris·on, *n.* cárcel, *f.;* prisión
pri·va·cy, *n.* soledad
pri·vate, *a.* privado; confidencial; particular. *n.* soldado raso
priv·i·lege, *n.* privilegio
prize, *n.* premio
prob·a·bil·i·ty, *n. pl.,* **-ties.** probabilidad
prob·a·ble, *a.* probable
probe, *n.* sonda; investigación. *v.* explorar
prob·lem, *n.* problema, *m.*
pro·ce·dure, *n.* procedimiento
pro·ceed, *v.* proceder; adelantar
proc·ess, *n.* proceso
pro·claim, *v.* proclamar
pro·cliv·i·ty, *n. pl.,* **-ties.** proclividad; inclinación
pro·cras·ti·nate, *v.* dilatar; aplazar
pro·cure, *v.* obtener; alcahuetear
prod, *v.* punzar
prod·i·gal, *a.* pródigo. *n.* pródigo
prod·i·gy, *n. pl.,* **-gies.** prodigio
pro·duce, *v.* producir; causar. *n.* producto
prod·uct, *n.* producto; resultado
pro·fane, *a.* profano
pro·fan·i·ty, *n. pl.,* **-ties.** profanidad; blasfemia
pro·fes·sion, *n.* profesión; ocupación
pro·fes·sor, *n.* profesor; profesora; catedrático
pro·fi·cien·cy, *n.* pericia
pro·file, *n.* perfil, *m.*
prof·it, *n.* ganancia; beneficio. *v.* ganar; aprovechar
pro·found, *a.* profundo
pro·fuse, *a.* profuso
pro·fu·sion, *n.* profusión
prog·e·ny, *n. pl.,* **-nies.** progenie, *f.*
prog·no·sis, *n. pl.,* **-ses.** pronóstico
pro·gram, *n.* programa, *m.*
prog·ress, *n.* progreso; desarrollo
pro·gres·sive, *a.* progresivo
pro·hib·it, *v.* prohibir
pro·hi·bi·tion, *n.* prohibición
pro·ject, *v.* proyectar; sobresalir. *n.* proyecto
pro·jec·tile, *n.* proyectil, *m.*
pro·lif·ic, *a.* prolífico
pro·logue, *n.* prólogo
pro·long, *v.* prolongar; alargar
prom·i·nent, *a.* prominente; importante
pro·mis·cu·ous, *a.* promiscuo; libertino
prom·ise, *n.* promesa. *v.* prometer
prom·on·to·ry, *n. pl.,* **-ries.** promontorio
pro·mote, *v.* promover; fomentar; ascender
pro·mo·tion, *n.* promoción
prompt, *a.* puntual; pronto. *v.* incitar
pro·noun, *n.* pronombre
pro·nounce, *v.* pronunciar(se); declarar
pro·nounced, *a.* marcado
pro·nun·ci·a·tion, *n.* pronunciación
proof, *n.* prueba
proof·read·er, *n.* corrector de pruebas
prop, *n.* apoyo. *v.* apoyar
prop·a·gan·da, *n.* propaganda
pro·pel, *v.,* **-pelled, -pel·ling.** propulsar
pro·pel·ler, *n.* hélice, *f.*
pro·pen·si·ty, *n. pl.,* **-ties.** propensión; inclinación
prop·er, *a.* propio; apropiado; decente
prop·er·ty, *n. pl.,* **-ties.** propiedad
proph·e·cy, *n. pl.,* **-cies.** profecía
proph·e·sy, *v.* profetizar
proph·et, *n.* profeta, *m.*
pro·phy·lac·tic, *a.* profiláctico. *n.* profiláctico
pro·pi·tious, *a.* propicio
pro·por·tion, *n.* proporción
pro·pose, *v.* proponer(se); declararse
prop·o·si·tion, *n.* proposición; propuesta
pro·pri·e·tor, *n.* propietario
pro·pri·e·ty, *n. pl.,* **-ties.** corrección; decoro
pro·scribe, *v.* proscribir
prose, *n.* prosa
pros·e·cute, *v.* proseguir; procesar
pros·pect, *n.* perspectiva
pros·per, *v.* prosperar; florecer
pros·per·i·ty, *n.* prosperidad
pros·ti·tute, *n.* prostituta; ramera
pros·trate, *v.* postrar(se); derribar
pro·tag·o·nist, *n.* protagonista, *m., f.*
pro·tect, *v.* proteger
pro·tein, *n.* proteína
pro·test, *v.* protestar. *n.* protesta
pro·to·col, *n.* protocolo
pro·ton, *n.* protón
pro·to·plasm, *n.* protoplasma, *m.*
pro·trude, *v.* salir fuera
proud, *a.* orgulloso; arrogante
prove, *v.,* **proved, proved or prov·en, prov·ing.** probar; comprobar

prov·erb, *n.* proverbio; refrán
pro·vide, *v.* proporcionar; proveer
prov·ince, *n.* provincia
pro·vi·sion, *n.* provisión; abastecimiento
pro·voc·a·tive, *a.* provocativa; provocador
pro·voke, *v.* provocar
prow, *n.* proa
prox·y, *n. pl.,* **-ies.** poder; apoderado
prude, *n.* gazmoña
prune, *n.* ciruela pasa. *v.* podar
pry, *v.,* **pried, pry·ing.** meterse; fisgonear
psalm, *n.* salmo
pseu·do·nym, *n.* seudónimo
psy·che·del·ic, *a.* psiquedélico
psy·chi·a·trist, *n.* psiquiatra, psiquiatra, *m., f.*
psy·chi·a·try, *n.* psiquiatría
psy·cho·a·nal·y·sis, *n.* psicoanálisis, *m.*
psy·cho·an·a·lyze, *v.* psicoanalizar
psy·cho·log·i·cal, *a.* psicológico
psy·chol·o·gy, *n.* psicología
psy·cho·sis, *n. pl.,* **-ses.** psicosis, *f.*
pto·maine, pto·main, *n.* ptomaína
pub, *n. inf.* taberna
pu·ber·ty, *n.* pubertad
pub·lic, *a.* público. *n.* público
pub·li·ca·tion, *n.* publicación
pub·li·ci·ty, *n.* publicidad
pub·lish, *v.* publicar
pub·lish·er, *n.* editor
puck·er, *v.* arrugar
pud·ding, *n.* pudín
pud·dle, *n.* charco
puff, *v.* soplar; inflar. *n.* soplo
pug·na·cious, *a.* pugnaz
puke, *v.* vomitar
pull, *v.* tirar; arrastrar. *n.* tirón; *inf.* influencia
pul·ley, *n.* polea
pul·mo·nar·y, *a.* pulmonar
pulp, *n.* pulpa; carne, *f.*
pul·pit, *n.* púlpito
pulse, *n.* pulso
pul·ver·ize, *v.* pulverizar
pum·ice, *n.* piedra pómez
pump, *n.* bomba. *v.* bombear; sacar por bomba
pump·kin, *n.* calabaza
pun, *n.* juego de palabras o vocablos
punch, *v.* punzar, punzón; puñetazo; ponche
punc·tu·al, *a.* puntual
punc·tu·a·tion, *n.* puntuación
punc·ture, *n.* pinchazo. *v.* pinchar; perforar
pun·ish, *v.* castigar
pu·ny, *a.* encanijado
pu·pa, *n. pl.,* **-pae, -pas.** crisálida
pu·pil, *n.* alumno; pupila; estudiante, *m., f.*
pup·pet, *n.* títere
pur·chase, *v.* comprar. *n.* compra
pure, *a.* puro
pur·ga·to·ry, *n. pl.,* **-ries.** purgatorio
pu·ri·fy, *v.* purificar; depurar
pu·ri·tan, *n.* puritano. *a.* puritano
pur·ple, *a.* purpúreo
pur·pose, *n.* fin; propósito; resolución
purr, pur, *n.* ronroneo
purse, *n.* bolso; bolsa. *v.* fruncir
pur·sue, *v.,* **-sued, -su·ing.** perseguir; seguir; acosar
pur·suit, *n.* perseguimiento; busca; ocupación
pus, *n.* pus, *m.*
push, *v.* empujar; apretar. *n.* empuje
puss·y, *n. pl.,* **-ies.** gatito
put, *v.,* **put, put·ting.** poner(se); colocar; meter
pu·tre·fy, *v.* pudrir
pu·trid, *a.* podrido
put·ty, *n.* masilla
puz·zle, *v.* confundir; estar perplejo. *n.* rompecabezas, *m.*
pyg·my, pig·my, *n., pl.,* **-mies.** pigmeo. *a.* pigmeo
pyr·a·mid, *n.* pirámide, *f.*
pyre, *n.* pira
py·ro·tech·nics, *n. pl., sing. or pl. in constr.* pirotecnia
py·thon, *n.* pitón

Q

quack, *n.* graznido del pato; charlatán
quad·ran·gle, *n.* cuadrángulo
quad·rant, *n.* cuadrante
quad·ri·lat·er·al, *a.* cuadrilátero. *n.* cuadrilátero
quad·ru·ped, *n.* cuadrúpedo
quad·ru·ple, *v.* cuadruplicar
quag·mire, *n.* tremedal, *m.*
quail, *n.* codorniz, *f. v.* acobardarse; desanimarse
quaint, *a.* singular
quake, *v.* estremecerse. *n.* terremoto
qual·i·fy, *v.* habilitar; modificar
qual·i·ty, *n. pl.,* **-ties.** cualidad; calidad
qualm, *n.* náusea; escrúpulo
quan·da·ry, *n. pl.,* **-ries.** apuro
quan·ti·ty, *n. pl.,* **-ties.** cantidad
quar·an·tine, *v.* poner en cuarentena
quar·rel, *n.* riña. *v.* reñir; disputar
quar·ry, *n. pl.,* **-ries.** presa; cantera
quart, *n.* cuarto de galón
quar·ter, *n.* cuarto; alojamiento
quartz, *n.* cuarzo
qua·si, *a.* cuasi
qua·ver, *v.* vibrar
queen, *n.* reina
queer, *a.* raro; *inf.* maricón

R

rab·bi, *n.,* **-bis.** rabino; rabí
rab·bit, *n.* conejo
ra·bies, *n.* rabia
race, *n.* carrera; raza. *v.* correr de prisa
ra·cial, *a.* racial
rac·ism, *n.* racismo
rack, *n.* percha; potro. *v.* atormentar
rack·et, *n.* raqueta; estrépito; *inf.* estafa
ra·dar, *n.* radar
ra·di·ant, *a.* radiante
ra·di·a·tion, *n.* radiación
rad·i·cal, *a.* radical; extremo. *n.* radical, *m., f.*
ra·di·o, *n. pl.,* **-os.** radio, *f.*
ra·di·o·ac·tiv·i·ty, *n.* radiactividad
rad·ish, *n.* rábano
ra·di·um, *n.* radio
ra·di·us, *n. pl., di·i, -us·es.** radio
raf·fle, *n.* rifa
raft, *n.* balsa
raft·er, *n.* cabrio
rag, *n.* trapo
rage, *n.* rabia; ira; manía. *v.* enfurecerse
rag·ged, *a.* harapiento; desigual
raid, *n.* incursión. *v.* invadir; atacar
rail, *n.* barandilla; carril, *m.*
rail·ing, *n.* baranda
rail·road, *n.* ferrocarril, *m.*
rain, *n.* lluvia. *v.* llover
rain·bow, *n.* arco iris
rain·coat, *n.* impermeable
rain·fall, *n.* cantidad de lluvia
raise, *v.* levantar; elevar; criar; subir. *n.* aumento
rai·sin, *n.* pasa
rake, *n.* rastro; libertino. *v.* rastrillar
ral·ly, *v.* reunir(se); reanimar. *n. pl.,* **-lies.** reunión
ram, *n.* morueco; carnero
ramp, *n.* rampa
ram·pant, *a.* desenfrenado
ram·shack·le, *a.* destartalado
ranch, *n.* rancho; hacienda
ran·cid, *a.* rancio
ran·cor, *n.* rencor
ran·dom, *a.* fortuito. **at ran·dom,** al azar
range, *v.* alinear; ordenar; colocar. *n.* terreno de pasto; alcance; extensión
rank, *n.* fila; rango; graduación
ran·sack, *v.* saquear
ran·som, *n.* rescate. *v.* rescatar
rant, *v.* vociferar
rap, *v.,* **rapped, rap·ping.** golpear; llamar; *inf.* discutir. *n.* golpe seco; *inf.* culpa
rape, *n.* violación. *v.* violar
rap·id, *a.* rápido
rapt, *a.* extático; absorto
rap·ture, *n.* rapto; éxtasis, *m.*
rare, *a.* raro; poco asado
rar·i·ty, *n. pl.,* **-ties.** rareza
ras·cal, *n.* pícaro; bribón
rash, *a.* imprudente. *n.* erupción
rasp·ber·ry, *n. pl.,* **-ries.** frambuesa
rat, *n.* rata
rate, *n.* razón, *f.;* precio; velocidad. *v.* tasar
rath·er, *adv.* más bien; un poco
rat·i·fy, *v.* ratificar; confirmar
ra·tion, *n. pl.,* **-tios.** razón
ra·tion, *n.* ración
ra·tion·al, *a.* racional; razonable
rat·tle, *v.* sonar; *inf.* confundir. *n.* ruido; sonajero
rat·tle·snake, *n.* serpiente de cascabel
rau·cous, *a.* ronco
rav·age, *n.* estrago. *v.* destruir
rave, *v.* delirar
rav·el, *v.* deshilar
ra·ven, *n.* cuervo

rav·en·ous, *a.* hambriento
ra·vine, *n.* barranca
rav·ish, *v.* violar; encantar
raw, *a.* crudo; bruto; *inf.* desnudo
ray, *n.* rayo
ray·on, *n.* rayón
ra·zor, *n.* navaja de afeitar
re, *n. (mus.)* re. *prep.* respecto a
reach, *v.* alargar; extenderse; alcanzar. *n.* alcance
re·act, *v.* reaccionar
re·ac·tion, *n.* reacción
re·ac·tion·ar·y, *n.* reaccionario
re·ac·tor, *n.* reactor
read, *v.,* **read, read·ing.** leer; interpretar; decir. *a.* instruido
read·ing, *n.* lectura; lección
re·ad·just, *v.* reajustar
read·y, *a.* listo; pronto; dispuesto
read·y-made, *a.* hecho
re·al, *a.* real; verdadero
re·al·i·ty, *n. pl.,* **-ties.** realidad
re·al·ize, *v.* darse cuenta de; realizar
re·al·ly, *adv.* en realidad; realmente
realm, *n.* reino
re·al·ty, *n.* bienes raíces
ream, *n.* resma
reap, *v.* segar
rear, *v.* criar. *n.* parte posterior
re·ar·range, *v.* arreglar de nuevo
rea·son, *n.* razón, *f. v.* razonar
rea·son·a·ble, *a.* razonable
re·as·sure, *v.* tranquilizar
reb·el, *n.* rebelde. *a.* rebelde
re·bel·lion, *n.* rebelión
re·buff, *n.* repulsa. *v.* rechazar
re·buke, *v.* reprender. *n.* reprimenda
re·but·tal, *n.* refutación
re·call, *v.* hacer volver; retirar
re·cant, *v.* retractar(se)
re·ca·pit·u·late, *v.* recapitular
re·cede, *v.* retroceder; alejarse
re·ceipt, *n. usu. pl.* recibo; *pl.* ingresos
re·ceive, *v.* recibir; cobrar; acoger
re·cent, *a.* reciente
re·cep·ta·cle, *n.* receptáculo
re·cep·tion, *n.* recepción; acogida
re·ces·sion, *n.* retroceso
re·ci·pe, *n.* receta
re·cip·ro·cal, *a.* recíproco
re·cit·al, *n.* relación; *(mus.)* recital, *m.*
rec·i·ta·tion, *n.* recitación
re·cite, *v.* referir; recitar
reck·less, *a.* temerario; descuidado; atolondrado
reck·on, *v.* calcular; considerar; *inf.* suponer
re·claim, *v.* reclamar
re·cline, *v.* reclinar(se); recostar(se)
rec·luse, *n.* recluso. *a.* solitario
rec·og·ni·tion, *n.* reconocimiento
rec·og·nize, *v.* reconocer
rec·om·mend, *v.* recomendar
rec·om·men·da·tion, *n.* recomendación
rec·om·pense, *v.* recompensar. *n.* recompensa
rec·on·cile, *v.* reconciliar
re·con·nais·sance, *n.* reconocimiento
re·con·noi·ter, *v.* reconocer
re·con·struct, *v.* reconstruir
re·cord, *v.* registrar; grabar. *n.* registro; historia; disco
re·course, *n.* recurso
re·cov·er, *v.* recuperar; recobrar
re·cov·er·y, *n. pl.,* **-ies.** restablecimiento
rec·re·a·tion, *n.* recreo
re·cruit, *n.* recluta. *v.* reclutar
rec·tan·gle, *n.* rectángulo
rec·ti·fy, *v.* rectificar
rec·tum, *n. pl.,* **-tums, -ta.** recto
re·cu·per·ate, *v.* recuperar; reponerse
re·cu·per·a·tion, *n.* recuperación
re·cur, *v.,* **-curred, -cur·ring.** repetirse; volver
re·cur·rence, *n.* repetición
red, *a.* rojo. *n.* color rojo
red·den, *v.* ponerse rojo
red·dish, *a.* rojizo
re·deem, *v.* redimir
re·demp·tion, *n.* amortización; redención
re·do, *v.,* **-did, -done, -do·ing.** rehacer
re·duce, *v.* reducir; rebajar; disminuir
re·duc·tion, *n.* reducción; rebaja
reed, *n.* caña; *(mus.)* lengüeta
reef, *n.* escollo
reek, *v.* oler. *n.* olor
reel, *n.* carrete. *v.* tambalear
re·fer, *v.,* **-ferred, -fer·ring.** referir(se); remitir
ref·er·ee, *n.* árbitro
ref·er·ence, *n.* referencia
ref·er·en·dum, *n. pl.,* **-dums, -da.** referéndum, *n.*
re·fill, *v.* rellenar
re·fine, *v.* refinar
re·fin·er·y, *n. pl.,* **-ies.** refinería
re·flect, *v.* reflejar; reflexionar
re·flec·tion, *n.* reflejo
re·flex, *a.* reflejo
re·flex·ive, *a.* reflexivo
re·form, *v.* reformarse. *n.* reforma
ref·or·ma·to·ry, *n. pl.,* **-ies.** reformatorio
re·fract, *v.* refractar
re·frain, *v.* abstenerse; refrenar. *n.* estribillo
re·fresh, *v.* refrescar
re·fresh·ment, *n. usu. pl.* refresco
re·frig·er·ate, *v.* refrigerar

ref·uge, *n.* refugio
ref·u·gee, *n.* refugiado
re·fund, *v.* devolver. *n.* reembolso
re·fuse, *v.* rehusar; negar
re·gain, *v.* recobrar
re·gal, *a.* real
re·gard, *v.* mirar; considerar; apreciar. *n.* consideración
re·gard·ing, *prep.* en cuanto a
re·gen·er·ate, *v.* regenerar
re·gent, *n.* regente
re·gime, *n.* régimen
reg·i·men, *n.* régimen
reg·i·ment, *n.* regimiento
re·gion, *n.* región
reg·is·ter, *n.* registro; indicador. *v.* registrar
re·gret, *v.* lamentar. *n.* pesar; sentimiento
reg·u·lar, *a.* regular; corriente
reg·u·la·tion, *n.* regulación; reglamento
re·ha·bil·i·tate, *v.* rehabilitar
re·ha·bil·i·ta·tion, *n.* rehabilitación
re·hearse, *v.* ensayar
reign, *n.* reinado. *v.* reinar
re·im·burse, *v.* reembolsar
rein, *n. usu. pl.* rienda
re·in·car·na·tion, *n.* reencarnación
re·in·force, *v.* reforzar
re·it·er·ate, *v.* reiterar
re·ject, *v.* rechazar; desechar
re·joice, *v.* regocijar(se)
re·lapse, *v.* reincidir. *n.* recaída
re·late, *v.* relatar; contar
re·lat·ed, *a.* emparentado; afín
re·la·tion, *n.* relación; pariente
re·lax, *v.* relajar
re·lay, *v.* transmitir
re·lease, *v.* soltar. *n.* libertad; descargo
re·lent, *v.* ceder
rel·e·vance, rel·e·van·cy, *n.* pertinencia
re·li·a·ble, *a.* seguro; confiable
rel·ic, *n.* reliquia
re·lief, *n.* alivio
re·lieve, *v.* aliviar
re·li·gion, *n.* religión
re·li·gious, *a.* religioso
rel·ish, *v.* gustar. *n.* apetencia; condimento
re·luc·tant, *a.* poco dispuesto
re·ly, *v.,* **-lied, -ly·ing.** confiar; contar con
re·main, *v.* quedar(se)
re·mark, *n.* observación. *v.* notar
rem·e·dy, *n. pl.,* **-dies.** remedio; recurso. *v.* remediar
re·mem·ber, *v.* recordar; acordarse de
re·mind, *v.* recordar
rem·i·nis·cence, *n.* reminiscencia
re·miss, *a.* descuidado
re·mit, *v.,* **-mit·ted, -mit·ting.** remitir; perdonar
re·mit·tance, *n.* remesa
re·morse, *n.* remordimiento
re·mote, *a.* remoto
re·move, *v.* quitar(se); suprimir; apartar(se)
re·nais·sance, *n.* renacimiento
rend, *v.,* **rent or rend·ed, rend·ing.** rasgar; hender
ren·der, *v.* devolver; dar
ren·dez·vous, *n. pl.,* **-vous.** cita. *v.* reunirse
ren·e·gade, *n.* renegado
re·new, *v.* renovar(se)
re·nounce, *v.* renunciar
re·nown, *n.* renombre
rent, *n.* alquiler. *v.* alquilar
re·pair, *v.* reparar; renovar; remendar. *n.* reparación
re·pay, *v.,* **-paid, -pay·ing.** reembolsar; recompensar; pagar
re·peal, *v.* abrogar. *n.* revocación
re·peat, *v.* repetir(se)
re·pel, *v.,* **-pelled, -pel·ling.** rechazar; repeler
re·pent, *v.* arrepentirse
re·per·cus·sion, *n.* repercusión
rep·er·toire, *n.* repertorio
rep·e·ti·tion, *n.* repetición
re·place, *v.* reponer; reemplazar
re·ply, *v.* contestar. *n. pl.,* **-plies.** respuesta
re·port, *n.* informar; relatar. *n.* informe; voz, *f.*
re·pose, *v.* poner confianza; reposar
rep·re·hen·si·ble, *a.* reprensible
rep·re·sent, *v.* representar; describir
rep·re·sen·ta·tion, *n.* representación
rep·re·sen·ta·tive, *a.* representativo. *n.* representante, *m., f.*
re·press, *v.* reprimir
re·prieve, *n.* suspensión
rep·ri·mand, *n.* reprimenda. *v.* reprender
re·proach, *v.* reprochar. *n.* reproche
re·pro·duce, *v.* reproducir
re·pro·duc·tion, *n.* reproducción
rep·tile, *n.* reptil, *m.*
re·pub·lic, *n.* república
re·pug·nant, *a.* repugnante; ofensivo
re·pulse, *v.* repulsar. *n.* repulsa
rep·u·ta·tion, *n.* reputación; nombre
re·quest, *n.* petición; ruego. *v.* rogar; solicitar
re·quire, *v.* exigir; requerir; necesitar
req·ui·si·tion, *n.* requisición
res·cue, *v.* rescatar; salvar. *n.* rescate
re·search, *n.* investigaciones, *f. pl. v.* investigar
re·sem·ble, *v.* parecerse a; asemejarse a
re·sent, *v.* resentirse de

va
re·serve, *v.* reservar. *n.* reserva
re·side, *v.* residir; morar; vivir
res·i·dent, *a.* residente. *n.* residente, *m., f.*
re·sign, *v.* renunciar; resignarse
res·ig·na·tion, *n.* resignación
res·in, *n.* resina
re·sist, *v.* resistir
re·sist·ance, *n.* resistencia
res·o·lu·tion, *n.* resolución
re·solve, *v.* resolver(se); decidir. *n.* resolución
res·o·nance, *n.* resonancia
re·sort, *v.* recurrir. *n.* recurso
re·source, *n.* recurso; *pl.* recursos
re·spect, *n.* respeto
re·spect·a·ble, *a.* respetable; pasable
res·pi·ra·tion, *n.* respiración
res·pite, *n.* respiro; tregua
re·spond, *v.* responder
re·sponse, *n.* respuesta; reacción
re·spon·si·bil·i·ty, *n. pl.,* **-ties.** responsabilidad
rest, *n.* descanso; resto. *v.* descansar; pararse
res·tau·rant, *n.* restaurante
rest·less, *a.* intranquilo
res·to·ra·tion, *n.* restauración
re·store, *v.* restaurar; devolver
re·strain, *v.* refrenar
re·strict, *v.* restringir
re·stric·tion, *n.* restricción
re·sult, *v.* resultar. *n.* resultado; consecuencia
re·sume, *v.* reanudar
ré·su·mé, re·su·me, *n.* resumen
res·ur·rect, *v.* resucitar
res·ur·rec·tion, *n.* resurrección
re·sus·ci·tate, *v.* resucitar
re·tail, *n.* venta al por menor
re·tain, *v.* retener
re·take, *v.,* **-took, -tak·en, -tak·ing.** volver a tomar
re·tal·i·ate, *v.* vengarse
re·tard, *v.* retardar
ret·i·na, *n. pl.,* **-nas, -nae.** retina
re·tire, *v.* retirarse; jubilarse
re·tract, *v.* retractar(se)
re·treat, *n.* retirada; retiro
ret·ri·bu·tion, *n.* justo castigo
re·trieve, *v.* recuperar; recobrar
ret·ro·ac·tive, *a.* retroactivo
re·turn, *v.* devolver; volver. *n.* vuelta
re·un·ion, *n.* reunión
re·veal, *v.* revelar
rev·e·la·tion, *n.* revelación
re·venge, *v.* vengar(se). *n.* venganza
rev·e·nue, *n.* renta; ingresos
re·vere, *v.* venerar
rev·er·ie, rev·er·y, *n. pl.,* **-ies.** ensueño
re·verse, *v.* volver al revés; invertir. *a.* inverso. *n.* lo contrario; revés, *m.*
re·vert, *v.* volver
re·view, *v.* examinar; pasar revista. *n.* revista; reseña
re·vise, *v.* revisar; corregir; repasar
re·vi·sion, *n.* revisión
re·vive, *v.* restablecer; resucitar; revivir
re·voke, *v.* revocar
re·volt, *v.* rebelar(se). *n.* sublevación
rev·o·lu·tion, *n.* revolución
rev·o·lu·tion·ar·y, *a.* revolucionario. *n.* revolucionario
re·volve, *v.* revolverse; girar
re·volv·er, *n.* revólver
re·ward, *v.* premiar. *n.* recompensa
rhap·so·dy, *n. pl.,* **-dies.** rapsodia
rhe·tor·i·cal, *a.* retórico
rheu·mat·ic, *a.* reumático
rheu·ma·tism, *n.* reumatismo
rhi·noc·er·os, *n. pl.,* **-os·es, -os.** rinocerote
rho·do·den·dron, *n.* rododendro
rhu·barb, *n.* ruibarbo
rhyme, *n.* rima. *v.* rimar
rhythm, *n.* ritmo
rib, *n.* costilla
rib·bon, *n.* cinta
rice, *n.* arroz, *m.*
rich, *a.* rico; precioso; fértil
rich·es, *n. pl.* riqueza
rick·et·y, *a.* tambaleante
ric·o·chet, *n.* rebote
rid, *v.,* **rid or rid·ded, rid·ding.** librar(se)
rid·dle, *n.* acertijo
ride, *v.,* **rode, rid·den, rid·ing.** montar; ir. *n.* viaje
ridge, *n.* caballón; cadena de colinas
rid·i·cule, *n.* burla; ridículo. *v.* ridiculizar
ri·dic·u·lous, *a.* ridículo
ri·fle, *n.* rifle
rift, *n.* grieta
rig, *v.* equipar; manipular
right, *a.* derecho; justo; correcto; exacto. *n.* derecho. *adv.* exactamente
right·ful, *a.* legítimo
rig·id, *a.* rígido; inflexible
rig·or·ous, *a.* riguroso
rile, *v. inf.* sulfurar
rim, *n.* aro; canto
rind, *n.* piel, *f.;* corteza
ring, *n.* anillo; argolla; repique de campana. *v.,* **rang, rung, ring·ing.** rodear; sonar; llamar
ring·lead·er, *n.* cabecilla, *m.*
rink, *n.* pista
rinse, *v.* aclarar; enjuagar
ri·ot, *n.* motín; tumulto
rip, *v.,* **ripped, rip·ping.** rasgar; descoser; arrancar. *n.* rasgadura
ripe, *a.* maduro
rise, *v.,* **rose, ris·en, ris·ing.** levan-

tarse; elevarse; subir. n. subida; desarrollo
risk, n. riesgo. v. arriesgar
rite, n. rito
rit·u·al, a. ritual. n. ritual, m.
ri·val, n. competidor. a. rival. v. rivalizar
ri·val·ry, n. pl., -ries. rivalidad
riv·er, n. río
riv·et, n. remache
roach, n. pl., roach, roach·es. cucaracha
road, n. camino; carretera
roam, v. vagar
roar, v. rugir. n. rugido; estruendo
roast, v. asar; inf. burlarse. n. carne asada
rob, v., robbed, rob·bing. robar; hurtar
robe, n. traje talar; bata
rob·in, n. petirrojo
ro·bot, n. autómata, m.
ro·bust, a. robusto; vigoroso
rock, n. roca; inf. joya. v. mecer
rock·et, n. cohete
rock·y, a. inestable; escabroso
rod, n. vara; caña de pescar
ro·dent, n. roedor
roe, n. corzo
rogue, n. pícaro; bribón
role, n. papel, m.
roll, v. hacer rodar; rodar. n. lista; rollo; panecillo
ro·mance, n. cuenta de aventuras; amorío
Ro·man nu·mer·als, n. números romanos
ro·man·tic, a. romántico
ro·man·ti·cism, n. romanticismo
romp, v. retozar
roof, n. tejado. v. techar
rook, n. torre, f. v. estafar
room, n. cuarto; habitación; sitio; lugar
room·mate, n. compañero de cuarto
room·y, a. espacioso
roost, n. percha
roost·er, n. gallo
root, n. raíz, f.; esencia. v. echar raíces
rope, n. cuerda; soga. v. atar
ro·sa·ry, n. pl., -ries. rosario
rose, n. rosa. a. de color de rosa
ros·ter, n. lista; nómina
ros·trum, n. pl., -tra, -trums. tribuna
ros·y, a. rosado
rot, v., rot·ted, rot·ting. pudrir(se). n. putrefacción
ro·tate, v. girar; alternar
rot·ten, a. podrido; malísimo
ro·tund, a. rotundo
rouge, n. colorete
rough, a. áspero; fragoso; tosco; severo
rou·lette, n. ruleta
round, a. redondo; esférico; de ida y vuelta. adv. alrededor. prep. alrededor de. n. ronda
round·a·bout, a. indirecto
rouse, v. despertar(se); animar
rout, v. derrotar
route, n. ruta; rumbo
rou·tine, n. rutina. a. de costumbre
rove, v. vagar
row, v. remar. n. fila; hilera; lío
row·dy, a. ruidoso
roy·al, a. real
roy·al·ty, n. pl., -ties. realeza; derecho de autor
rub, v., rubbed, rub·bing. frotar; fregar; borrar; rozar
rub·ber, n. caucho; goma; pl. chanclos
rub·bish, n. basura
rub·ble, n. cascote
ru·by, n. pl., -bies. rubí, m.
ruck·sack, n. mochila
ruck·us, n. inf. lío; alboroto
rud·der, n. timón
rud·dy, a. frescote
rude, a. rudo; descortés; tosco
ru·di·ment, n. rudimento; usu. pl. rudimentos
rue, v., rued, ru·ing. lamentar
ruf·fle, v. rizar(se); fruncir. n. volante fruncido
rug, n. alfombra
rug·ged, a. escabroso; severo
ru·in, n. ruina. v. derrotar; estropear; arruinar
rule, n. regla; mando. v. gobernar; rayar
rul·er, n. gobernador; regla
rum, n. ron
rum·ble, v. retumbar
rum·mage, v. revolver
ru·mor, n. rumor
rum·ple, v. arrugar
run, v., ran, run, run·ning. correr; dirigir; funcionar. n. paseo; marcha; serie, f.
run·a·way, n. fugitivo
run·down, n. resumen. a. cansado; en decadencia
rung, n. peldaño
run·ning, a. corriente
runt, n. redrojo
run·way, n. pista de aterrizaje
rup·ture, n. hernia; rompimiento
ru·ral, a. rural
ruse, n. ardid
rush, v. ir de prisa; precipitarse. n. ímpetu, m.; junco
russ·set, n. color bermejo
rust, n. orín. v. aherrumbrar(se)
rus·tic, a. rústico
rus·tle, v. susurrar; inf. robar
rust·y, a. herrumbroso; mohoso

torpe
rut, n. rodera; rutina
ruth·less, a. cruel; despiadado
rye, n. centeno

S

Sab·bath, n. (cristiano) domingo; (judío) sábado
sa·ber, n. sable
sa·ble, n. cebellina. a. negro
sab·o·tage, n. sabotaje. v. sabotear
sac·cha·rin, n. sacarina
sack, n. saco; costal, m.
sac·ra·ment, n. sacramento; (often cap.) Eucaristía
sa·cred, a. sagrado
sac·ri·fice, n. sacrificio. v. sacrificar
sac·ri·lege, n. sacrilegio
sad, a. triste
sad·den, v. entristecer
sad·dle, n. silla de montar. v. ensillar
sad·ism, n. sadismo
sa·fa·ri, n. pl., -ris. safari, m.
safe, a. seguro; salvo. n. caja de caudales
safe·ty, n. pl., -ties. seguridad
safe·ty pin, n. imperdible
sag, v., sagged, sag·ging. combar(se). n. comba
sa·ga, n. saga
sage, a. sabio. n. sabio; salvia
sail, n. vela. v. navegar
sail·or, n. marinero
saint, a. santo. n. santo
sake, n. motivo; consideración
sal·ad, n. ensalada
sal·a·man·der, n. salamandra
sal·a·ry, n. pl., -ries. sueldo; salario
sale, n. venta; subasta
sa·line, a. salino
sa·li·va, n. saliva
sal·low, a. cetrino
sal·ly, n. pl., -lies. salida
salm·on, n. pl., -ons, -on. salmón
sa·lon, n. salón
sa·loon, n. taberna; salón
salt, n. sal, f. a. salado
sa·lu·tar·y, a. saludable
sa·lu·ta·tion, n. saludo
sa·lute, v. saludar. n. saludo; salva
sal·vage, v. salvamento
sal·va·tion, n. salvación
salve, n. ungüento
sal·vo, n. pl., -vos, -voes. salva
same, a. idéntico; mismo
sam·ple, n. muestra. v. probar
san·a·to·ri·um, n. pl., -ums, -a. sanatorio. Also **san·i·tar·i·um**
sanc·ti·fy, v. santificar
sanc·tion, n. sanción. v. sancionar; autorizar
sanc·ti·ty, n. pl., -ties. santidad
sanc·tu·ar·y, n. pl., -ies. santuario; asilo
sand, n. arena. v. enarenar
san·dal, n. sandalia
sand·stone, n. arenisca
sand·wich, n. bocadillo
sand·y, a. arenoso
sane, a. cuerdo; sano
san·gui·nar·y, a. sanguinario
san·i·tar·i·um, n. pl., -ums, -a. sanatorio. Also **san·a·to·ri·um**
san·i·tar·y, a. sanitario
san·i·ta·tion, n. instalación sanitaria
san·i·ty, n. juicio sano
sap, n. savia. v. agotar
sa·pi·ent, a. sabio
sap·phire, n. zafiro
sar·casm, n. sarcasmo
sar·cas·tic, a. sarcástico
sar·coph·a·gus, n. pl., -gi, -gus·es. sarcófago
sar·dine, n. pl., -dines, -dine. sardina
sa·ri, sa·ree, n. pl., -ris, -rees. sari, m.
sash, n. faja; marco de una ventana
sas·sy, a. descarado
Sa·tan, n. Satanás
sa·tan·ic, a. satánico. Also **sa·tan·i·cal**
sate, v. saciar; satisfacer
sat·el·lite, n. satélite
sa·ti·ate, v. saciar; hartar
sat·in, n. raso
sat·ire, n. sátira
sat·is·fac·tion, n. satisfacción
sat·is·fy, v. satisfacer; convencer
sat·u·rate, v. saturar
Sat·ur·day, n. sábado
sa·tyr, n. sátiro
sauce, n. salsa
sau·cer, n. platillo
sau·sage, n. embutido; salchicha
sav·age, a. salvaje. n. salvaje; bárbaro
save, v. salvar; conservar; ahorrar. conj. prep. excepto
sav·ing, n. economía; pl. ahorros. prep. salvo. conj. excepto
sav·ior, n. salvador; (cap.) Salvador
sa·vor, n. sabor. v. saborear
saw, n. sierra. v., sawed, sawed or sawn, saw·ing. serrar
sax·o·phone, n. saxofón
say, v., said, say·ing. decir. n. turno
say·ing, n. dicho
scab, n. costra
scaf·fold, n. andamio
scald, v. escaldar
scale, n. balanza escama; escala. v. escamar; escalar
scal·lop, n. venera. v. festonear
scalp, n. pericráneo; cuero cabelludo
scal·pel, n. escalpelo
scan, v. escudriñar; mirar rápidamente

scan·dal, n. escándalo
scan·dal·ize, v. escandalizar
scant, a. escaso; corto
scant·y, a. escaso
scape·goat, n. cabeza de turco
scar, n. cicatriz, f. v. marcar con una cicatriz
scarce, a. escaso; poco común
scare, v. asustar. n. susto
scare·crow, n. espantajo; espantapájaros
scarf, n. pl., scarfs, scarves. bufanda
scar·let, n. escarlata
scat·ter, v. esparcir
scav·en·ger, n. basurero
scene, n. escena; vista; escándalo
scen·er·y, n. pl., -ies. paisaje; vista; decoraciones
scent, n. olor; perfume; pista
sched·ule, n. horario; inventario
scheme, v. proyectar; intrigar. n. plan
schism, n. cisma, m.; f.
schiz·o·phre·ni·a, n. esquizofrenia
schol·ar, n. erudito; alumno
schol·ar·ship, n. erudición; beca
scho·las·tic, a. escolar
school, n. escuela. v. enseñar
sci·ence, n. ciencia
sci·en·tist, n. científico
scim·i·tar, sim·i·tar, n. cimitarra. Also **scim·i·ter**
scis·sors, n. pl. tijeras
scoff, v. mofarse
scold, v. regañar
scoop, n. paleta. v. sacar con pala
scoot·er, n. patinete
scope, n. alcance
scorch, v. chamuscar
score, n. tanteo; cuenta; veinte. v. marcar; orquestar
scorn, n. desdén. v. despreciar
scor·pi·on, n. escorpión
scotch, v. frustrar
scoun·drel, n. canalla, m.; f.
scour, v. fregar; recorrer
scout, n. explorador
scowl, v. poner mal gesto. n. ceño
scrag·gy, a. escarnido
scram·ble, v. revolver
scrap, n. fragmento; sobras
scrape, v. raspar; raer
scratch, v. rayar; rasguñar; rascar. n. rasguño
scrawl, n. garrabatos, garrapatos
scream, v. chillar. n. grito
screen, n. biombo; pantalla. v. esconder
screw, n. tornillo. v. atornillar
scrib·ble, v. garrapatear
scrim·mage, n. arrebatiña
script, n. letra cursiva; guión
scrip·ture, n. (cap.) Sagrada Escritura
scroll, n. rollo de pergamino
scrub, v. fregar. n. maleza
scru·ple, n. escrúpulo
scru·ti·nize, v. escudriñar
scru·ti·ny, n. pl., -nies. escrutinio
scuf·fle, v. pelear. n. pelea
sculp·tor, n. escultor
sculp·ture, n. escultura. v. esculpir
scum, n. espuma
scur·ry, v. darse prisa
scur·vy, n. escorbuto
scut·tle, v. echar a pique
scythe, n. guadaña
sea, n. mar, m.; f.
seal, n. pl., seals, seal. foca
seal, n. sello. v. cerrar
seam, n. costura
sea·man, n. pl., -men. marinero
sea·stress, n. costurera
seam·y, a. asqueroso
sé·ance, n. sesión de espiritistas
sea·port, n. puerto de mar
sear, v. marchitar; chamuscar
search, v. buscar; registrar. n. registro
sea·shore, n. orilla del mar
sea·sick·ness, n. mareo
sea·son, n. estación. v. sazonar
sea·son·ing, n. condimento
seat, n. asiento. v. sentar
sea·weed, n. alga marina
se·clude, v. aislar
se·clu·sion, n. retiro
sec·ond, a. segundo. n. segundo. v. apoyar
sec·ond·ar·y, a. secundario
sec·ond·hand, a. de segunda mano
sec·ond-rate, a. inferior
se·cre·cy, n. pl., -cies. secreto
se·cret, a. secreto; oculto. n. secreto
sec·re·tar·y, n. pl., -ies. secretario; (cap.) Ministro
se·crete, v. secretar; ocultar
se·cre·tion, n. secreción
sect, n. secta
sec·tion, n. sección; porción; división
sec·tor, n. sector
sec·u·lar, a. secular
se·cure, a. seguro. v. asegurar; adquirir
se·cu·ri·ty, n. pl., -ties. seguridad; fianza; pl. valores
se·date, a. sosegado
sed·a·tive, a. calmante. n. sedativo
sed·en·tar·y, a. sedentario
sed·i·ment, n. sedimento
se·di·tion, n. sedición
se·duce, v. seducir
se·duc·tion, se·duce·ment, n. seducción
see, v., saw, seen, see·ing. ver; visitar; comprender; percebir. n. sede, f.
seed, n. pl., seeds, seed. semilla; simiente, f. v. sembrar
seed·y, a. desharrapado

seek, v., sought, seek·ing. buscar; solicitar
seem, v. parecer
seem·ly, a. decoroso; correcto
seep, v. rezumarse
se·er, n. profeta, m.
seg·ment, n. segmento; sección
seg·re·gate, v. segregar
seg·re·ga·tion, n. segregación; separación
seize, v. asir; agarrar; apoderarse de
sei·zure, n. asimiento; ataque
sel·dom, adv. raramente. a. infrecuente
se·lect, v. escoger; elegir. a. selecto
se·lec·tion, n. selección
self, n. pl. selves. See my·self, your·self, etc.
self-cen·tered, a. egocéntrico
self-com·mand, n. dominio de sí mismo
self-con·fi·dence, n. confianza en sí mismo
self-con·scious, a. tímido
self-con·trol, n. dominio de sí mismo
self-ev·i·dent, a. patente
self-ex·plan·a·to·ry, a. evidente; obvio
self-gov·ern·ment, n. autonomía
self-im·por·tance, n. presunción
self·ish, a. egoísta; interesado
self·less, a. desinteresado
self-re·li·ance, n. confianza en sí mismo
self·same, a. mismo
self-suf·fi·cient, a. independiente
self-will, n. terquedad
sell, v. sold, sell·ing. vender(se)
se·man·tics, n. pl. semántica
sem·blance, n. parecido; apariencia
se·men, n. semen
se·mes·ter, n. semestre
sem·i·cir·cle, n. semicírculo
sem·i·co·lon, n. punto y coma
sem·i·fi·nal, a. semifinal. n. usu. pl. semifinales, f. pl.
sem·i·nar, n. seminario
sem·i·nar·y, n. pl., -ies. seminario
sem·i·of·fi·cial, a. semioficial
sem·i·pre·cious, a. semiprecioso
sem·i·week·ly, a. bisemanal. n. pl., -lies. publicación bisemanal
sen·ate, n. senado; (cap.) Senado
sen·a·tor, n. senador
send, v., sent, send·ing. enviar; mandar; dirigir; lanzar
se·nile, a. senil
sen·ior, a. mayor de edad; superior. n. alumno del último año en una universidad or escuela secundaria
sen·ior·i·ty, n. antigüedad
sen·sa·tion, n. sensación
sense, n. sentido; sensación; juicio. v. percibir
sense·less, a. sin sentido; insensato
sen·si·bil·i·ty, n. pl., -ties. sensibilidad
sen·si·ble, a. razonable
sen·si·tive, a. impresionable; delicado
sen·si·tiv·i·ty, n. pl., -ties. delicadeza
sen·so·ry, a. sensorio. Also **sen·so·ri·al**
sen·su·al, a. sensual; lascivo
sen·su·ous, a. sensorio
sen·tence, n. frase, f.; condena. v. condenar
sen·ti·ment, n. sentimiento
sen·ti·nel, n. centinela, m.
sen·try, n. pl., -tries. centinela, m.; guardia, m.
se·pal, n. sépalo
sep·a·rate, v. separar(se). a. separado; distinto
se·a·ra·tion, n. separación
Sep·tem·ber, n. septiembre
sep·tic, a. séptico
se·pul·cher, n. sepulcro
se·quel, n. resultado
se·quence, n. sucesión; serie, f.
se·ques·ter, v. separar; aislar
se·quin, n. lentejuela
ser·aph, n. pl., -aphs, -a·phim. serafín
ser·e·nade, n. serenata
se·rene, n. sereno
se·ren·i·ty, n. pl., -ties. serenidad
serf, n. siervo
ser·geant, n. sargento
se·ri·al, a. en serie. n. novela por entregas
se·ries, n. serie, f.
se·ri·ous, a. serio; grave
ser·mon, n. sermón
ser·pent, n. serpiente, f.
se·rum, n. pl., se·rums, se·ra. suero
serv·ant, n. serviente; servidor
serve, v. servir; cumplir
serv·ice, n. servicio. v. mantener
serv·ice·man, n. pl., -men. militar; reparador
ser·vile, a. servil
ses·sion, n. sesión
set, v., set, set·ting. poner(se); fijar; arreglar; cuajarse. n. juego. a. fijo; rígido; establecido. set a·bout, ponerse a hacer. set on, atacar. set out, ponerse en camino
set·back, n. revés, m.
set·ting, n. marco; engaste
set·tle, v. resolver; ajustar; arreglar; colocar; establecer(se); calmar(se)
set·tle·ment, n. colonización; ajuste
set·tler, n. colono
sev·en, n. siete. a. siete
sev·en·teen, a. diecisiete
sev·enth, a. séptimo. n. séptimo
sev·en·ty, a. setenta. n. setenta

sev·er, v. separar; cortar
sev·er·al, a. varios; diversos
se·vere, a. severo; riguroso; duro
se·ver·i·ty, n. pl., -ties. severidad; aspereza
sew, v., sewed, sewn or sewed, sew·ing. coser
sew·er, n. albañal, m.
sex, n. sexo
sex·tet, n. sexteto
sex·u·al, a. sexual
sex·y, a. provocativo
shab·by, a. raído; en mal estado
shack, n. choza
shack·le, n. grillete. v. encadenar
shade, n. sombra; matiz, m. v. sombrear
shad·ow, n. sombra. v. oscurecer; sombrear; seguir
shad·y, a. sombreado
shaft, n. eje; pozo
shag·gy, a. velludo
shake, v., shook, shak·en, shak·ing. sacudir; temblar; agitar; estrechar
shak·y, a. poco firme; débil
shale, n. esquisto
shal·low, a. poco profundo. n. often pl. bajío
sham, n. impostura. a. fingido. v. fingir(se)
sham·bles, n. pl. desorden
shame, n. vergüenza. v. avergonzar; deshonrar
shame·less, a. desvergonzado
sham·poo, v. lavar. n. champú, m.
shan·ty, n. pl., -ties. choza
shape, n. forma; talle. v. formar
shape·ly, a. bien formado
share, n. parte, f.; acción. v. partir; repartir; compartir
shark, n. tiburón
sharp, a. cortante; agudo; penetrante; vivo. n. sostenido
sharp·en, v. afilar; sacar punta a
shat·ter, v. hacer(se) pedazos
shave, v., shaved, shaved or shav·en, shav·ing. afeitar(se). n. afeitado, afeitada
shav·er, n. máquina de afeitar
shawl, n. chal, m.
she, pron. ella
shears, n. tijeras grandes
shed, v., shed, shed·ding. quitarse; verter. n. barraca
sheen, n. lustre
sheep, n. pl., sheep. oveja
sheep·ish, a. tímido
sheer, a. transparente; completo; escarpado
sheet, n. sábana; hoja; lámina
sheik, sheikh, n. jeque
shelf, n. pl., shelves. estante
shell, n. cáscara; caparazón; granada. v. descascarar; bombardear
shel·lac, shel·lack, n. goma laca
shell·fish, n. pl., -fish, -fish·es. marisco
shel·ter, n. abrigo; resguardo; refugio. v. poner(se) al abrigo
shep·herd, n. pastor
sher·bet, n. sorbete
sher·iff, n. sheriff, m.
sher·ry, n. pl., -ries. jerez, m.
shield, n. escudo. v. proteger
shift, v. mover(se); cambiar. n. cambio; tanda
shil·ly-shal·ly, v. vacilar
shim·mer, v. rielar
shin, n. espinilla
shine, v., shone or shined, shin·ing. brillar; relucir; pulir. n. lustre
shin·gle, n. ripia; tejamanil, m.
shin·y, a. brillante
ship, n. buque; barco. v. transportar
ship·mate, n. camarada de a bordo
ship·ment, n. embarque; envío
ship·shape, a. en buen orden
ship·wreck, n. naufragio. v. naufragar
shirk, v. evitar; esquivar
shirt, n. camisa
shiv·er, v. temblar. n. estremecimiento
shock, n. susto; choque; postración nerviosa. v. escandalizar
shod·dy, a. de pacotilla; falso
shoe, n. pl., shoes. zapato. v. herrar
shoe·horn, n. calzador
shoe·lace, n. cordón
shoot, v., shot, shoot·ing. disparar; fusilar; lanzarse; espigar. n. retoño
shoot·ing, n. tiro; caza con escopeta
shoot·ing star, n. estrella fugaz
shop, n. tienda; taller. v. ir de compras
shop·keep·er, n. tendero
shore, n. playa
short, a. corto; bajo; breve; insuficiente. n. deficiencia; pl. calzones cortos. v. engañar. in short, en resumen
short·age, n. deficiencia; escasez, f.
short·com·ing, n. defecto
short·cut, n. atajo
short·en, v. acortar(se); reducir(se)
short·hand, n. taquigrafía
short-lived, a. de breve duración
short-tem·pered, a. de mal genio
shot, n. tiro; tirador; inf. inyección
shot·gun, n. escopeta
should, aux. v. past form of shall
shoul·der, n. hombro
shout, n. grito. v. gritar
shove, v. empujar
shov·el, n. pala
show, v., showed, shown or showed, show·ing. mostrar(se); indicar;

enseñar. n. exposición; función
show·case, n. vitrina
show·er, n. ducha; chubasco. v. llover; ducharse
show·man, n. pl., -men. director de espectáculos
shred, v., shred·ded or shred, shred·ding. hacer tiras. n. triza; fragmento
shrew, n. arpía
shrewd, a. sagaz; prudente
shriek, v. chillar
shrill, a. estridente
shrimp, n. pl., shrimps, shrimp. camarón
shrine, n. relicario
shrink, v., shrank or shrunk, shrunk·en, shrink·ing. encoger(se)
shriv·el, v. encoger(se); secar(se)
shroud, n. mortaja
shrub, n. arbusto
shrub·ber·y, n. pl., -ies. arbustos
shrug, v. encogerse de hombros
shud·der, v. estremecerse
shuf·fle, v. arrastrar los pies; (cards) barajar
shun, v. evitar; apartarse de
shut, v., shut, shut·ting. cerrar(se). a. cerrado. shut down, cerrar. shut out, excluir. shut up, encerrar; hacer callar
shut·ter, n. contraventana
shut·tle, n. lanzadera
shy, a. tímido; reservado
sic, v., sicked, sick·ing. atacar
sick, a. enfermo
sick·en, v. hartar; enfermar(se)
sick·le, n. hoz, f.
sick·ness, n. enfermedad
side, n. lado; partido; equipo. a. lateral
side·burns, n. pl. patillas
side·kick, n. inf. compañero
side·long, a. lateral. adv. lateralmente
side·track, v. desviar
side·walk, n. acera
side·ways, adv. oblicuamente
siege, n. sitio; cerco
sieve, n. coladera; tamiz, m. v. tamizar
sift, v. tamizar
sigh, v. suspirar. n. suspiro
sight, n. vista; visión; espectáculo. v. ver. catch sight of, vislumbrar
sight·less, a. ciego
sight·see·ing, n. visita de puntos de interés
sign, v. firmar. n. señal, f.; signo; letrero
sig·nal, n. señal, f. a. señalado. v. hacer señas
sig·na·ture, n. firma
sig·nif·i·cance, n. significación
sig·ni·fy, v. significar
si·lence, n. silencio. v. hacer callar
si·lent, a. silencioso; mudo
sil·hou·ette, n. silueta
sil·i·ca, n. sílice, f.
sil·i·con, n. silicio
silk, n. seda. a. de seda
silk·y, a. de seda; sedoso
sil·ly, a. tonto; absurdo; bobo
si·lo, n. pl., -los. silo
silt, n. sedimento
sil·ver, n. plata; moneda. a. de plata
sil·ver·smith, n. platero
sil·ver·ware, n. vajilla de plata
sim·i·an, a. símico. n. mono
sim·i·lar, a. parecido; similar
sim·i·lar·i·ty, n. pl., -ties. semejanza
sim·i·le, n. hervir a fuego lento
sim·per, v. sonreírse afectadamente
sim·ple, a. sencillo; fácil; simple
sim·pli·fy, v. simplificar
sim·ply, adv. sencillamente
sim·u·late, v. simular
si·mul·ta·ne·ous, a. simultáneo
sin, n. pecado; transgresión. v. pecar
since, adv. desde entonces; desde; después. conj. desde que; puesto que
sin·cere, a. sincero
sin·cer·i·ty, n. sinceridad
si·ne·cure, n. sinecura
sin·ew, n. tendón
sing, v., sang or sung, sung. cantar
singe, v. chamuscar
sing·er, n. cantante, m.; f.
sin·gle, a. soltero; único; sencillo
sin·gle-hand·ed, a. sin ayuda
sin·gu·lar, a. singular. n. singular
sin·is·ter, a. siniestro
sink, v., sank or sunk, sunk or sunk·en, sink·ing. hundir(se). n. fregadero
sin·ner, n. pecador
si·nus, n. seno
sip, v. sorber. n. sorbo
si·phon, sy·phon, n. sifón
sir, n. señor
sire, n. padre. v. engendrar
si·ren, n. sirena
sir·loin, n. solomillo
sis·ter, n. hermana
sis·ter-in-law, n. pl., sis·ters-in-law. cuñada
sit, v., sat, sit·ting. sentar(se); posarse
site, n. sitio; solar
sit·u·a·tion, n. situación; colocación
six, n. seis. a. seis
six·teen, n. dieciséis. a. dieciséis
sixth, a. sexto. n. sexto
six·ty, n. sesenta. a. sesenta
size, n. tamaño; talla
siz·zle, v. chisporrotear
skate, n. patín. v. patinar

skel·e·ton, n. esqueleto; armazón
skep·tic, scep·tic, n. escéptico
skep·ti·cal, scep·ti·cal, a. escéptico
sketch, n. esbozo; bosquejo. v. dibujar
skew·er, n. broqueta
ski, n. pl. **skis, ski.** esquí, m. v. esquiar
skid, n. patinazo. v. patinar
skill, n. habilidad; pericia; destreza
skil·let, n. sartén
skim, v. espumar; desnatar; hojear
skin, n. piel, f.; cutis, m. v. despellejar
skin·ny, a. flaco
skip, v. saltar; pasar por alto
skir·mish, n. escaramuza
skirt, n. falda. v. ladear
skit, n. parodia
skull, n. cráneo
skunk, n. mofeta
sky, n. pl. **skies.** cielo
sky·rock·et, n. cohete. v. subir rápidamente
sky·scrap·er, n. rascacielos
slab, n. tabla; plancha
slack, a. flojo; negligente
slack·en, v. aflojar
slacks, n. pl. pantalones
slag, n. escoria
slam, v. cerrarse de golpe
slan·der, n. calumnia. v. calumniar
slang, n. argot, m.; jerga
slant, v. inclinar(se); sesgar(se). n. inclinación
slap, n. bofetada; palmada. v. pegar
slash, v. acuchillar
slat, n. tablilla
slate, n. pizarra; lista de candidatos
slaugh·ter, n. matanza; carnicería. v. matar
slave, n. esclavo
slav·er·y, n. esclavitud
slaw, n. ensalada de col
slay, v. **slew, slain, slay·ing.** matar
sled, n. trineo
sleek, a. liso; pulcro
sleep, v., **slept, sleep·ing.** dormir. n. sueño
sleep·y, a. soñoliento
sleet, n. aguanieve, f.
sleeve, n. manga
sleigh, n. trineo
slen·der, a. delgado; limitado
sleuth, n. inf. detective
slice, n. rebanada; tajada. v. tajar
slide, v., **slid, slid** or **slid·den, slid·ing.** deslizarse. n. resbalón; diapositiva
slight, a. pequeño; de poco importancia. n. desaire
slim, a. delgado. v. adelgazar
slime, n. légamo
sling, v., **slung, sling·ing.** tirar; suspender. n. cabestrillo
slip, v. introducir; deslizar(se); resbalar; escaparse. n. error; combinación
slip·knot, n. nudo corredizo
slip·per, n. zapatilla
slip·per·y, a. resbaladizo
slip·up, n. inf. equivocación
slit, v., **slit, slit·ting.** cortar. n. raja
sliv·er, n. astilla
slob·ber, v. babear; babosear
slo·gan, n. mote
slop, v. verter
slope, n. declive; inclinación. v. inclinar(se)
slot, n. ranura
slov·en·ly, a. descuidado; desaseado
slow, a. lento; torpe. v. ir más despacio; retardar
slow·ly, adv. despacio
slug, n. posta. v. golpear
slug·gish, a. perezoso; lento
slum, n. often pl. barrio bajo
slump, v. hundirse. n. depresión; baja repentina
slur, v. comerse palabras; calumniar. n. mancha
slut, n. pazpuerca; perra
sly, a. astuto; disimulado
smack, n. manotada. v. pegar
small, a. pequeño; bajo; chico
small·pox, n. viruelas
smart, v. escocer. a. vivo; listo; elegante; fresco
smash, v. romper(se)
smear, v. manchar; untar
smell, v., **smelled** or **smelt, smell·ing.** oler. n. olfato; olor
smile, v. sonreír(se). n. sonrisa
smirk, n. sonrisa afectada
smith, n. herrero. Also **smith·y**
smock, n. blusa de labrador; bata
smog, n. niebla y humo mezclados
smoke, n. humo. v. humear; fumar
smol·der, smoul·der, v. arder sin llamas
smooch, v. inf. besar
smooth, a. liso; suave. v. allanar
smoth·er, v. ahogar(se); sofocar(se)
smudge, n. mancha. v. tiznar
smug, a. papado de sí mismo
smug·gle, v. pasar de (o hacer) contrabando
smug·gler, n. contrabandista, m., f.
snack, n. merienda
snag, n. obstáculo; rasgón
snail, n. caracol, m.
snake, n. culebra; serpiente, f.
snap, v. chasquear; romper(se); tratar de morder; sacar una foto. n. cierre. a. repentino
snap·shot, n. foto, f.
snare, n. trampa
snatch, n. pl., **snatch·es.** fragmento; trocito. v. agarrar; arrebatar

snaz·zy, a. inf. a la moda
sneak, v. moverse a hurtadillas
sneer, v. mofarse. n. mirada de desprecio
sneeze, v. estornudar. n. estornudo
sniff, v. husmear; oler
snip, v. tijeretear. n. recorte
snitch, v. inf. robar; soplarse
snob, n. esnob, m., f.
snoop, v. inf. espiar. n. fisgón
snooze, v. inf. dormitar
snore, v. roncar. n. ronquido
snort, n. bufido
snout, n. hocico
snow, n. nieve, f. v. nevar
snow·ball, n. bola de nieve
snow·flake, n. copo de nieve
snow·man, n. pl., **-men.** figura de nieve
snub, v. desairar. n. desaire; repulsa. a. chato
snuff, n. rapé
snug, a. cómodo; ajustado
snug·gle, v. arrimarse
so, adv. tan; así; de este modo. conj. por tanto. **so that,** de modo que
soak, v. absorber; remojar; empapar
soap, n. jabón. v. jabonar; enjabonar
soar, v. remontarse
sob, v. sollozar. n. sollozo
so·ber, a. sobrio; sereno; serio
so·bri·quet, sou·bri·quet, n. apodo
so·called, a. llamado; supuesto
soc·cer, n. fútbol, m.
so·cia·ble, a. sociable
so·cial, a. social. n. velada
so·cial·ism, n. socialismo
so·cial·ize, v. socializar
so·ci·e·ty, n., pl., **-ties.** sociedad; mundo elegante
so·ci·ol·o·gy, n. sociología
sock, n. pl., **socks, sox.** calcetín. v. inf. pegar
sock·et, n. enchufe; fosa
sod, n. césped
so·da, n. sosa; bebida no alcohólica
so·da wa·ter, n. agua de seltz
sod·den, a. empapado
so·di·um, n. sodio
so·di·um chlo·ride, n. sal, f.
sod·om·y, n. sodomía
so·fa, n. sofá, m.
soft, a. blando; suave; tierno
sof·ten, v. ablandar(se); suavizar(se); mitigar
sog·gy, a. empapado
soil, n. tierra. v. ensuciar; manchar
so·journ, v. morar
sol·ace, v. consolar. n. consuelo; solaz, m.
so·lar, a. solar
sol·der, v. soldar
sol·dier, n. soldado; militar
sole, n. planta; suela. a. solo; único
sole·ly, adv. solamente
sol·emn, a. solemne
so·lem·ni·ty, n. pl., **-ties.** solemnidad; usu. pl. ceremonia
so·lic·it, v. solicitar; importunar
sol·id, a. sólido; macizo. n. sólido
sol·i·dar·i·ty, n., pl., **-ties.** solidaridad
so·lil·o·quy, n., pl., **-quies.** soliloquio
sol·i·tar·y, a. solitario; solo
so·lo, n., pl., **-los, -li.** solo
sol·u·ble, a. soluble
so·lu·tion, n. solución
solve, v. resolver
sol·vent, a. solvente
som·ber, a. sombrío
some, a. alguno (algún); algo de. pron. algunos. adv. aproximadamente
some·bod·y, pron. alguien. n. pl., **-dies.** personaje
some·day, adv. algún día
some·how, adv. de algún modo
some·one, pron. alguien
som·er·sault, n. salto mortal
some·thing, n. algo
some·times, adv. a veces
some·what, adv. algún tanto
some·where, adv. en alguna parte
son, n. hijo
song, n. canción; cantar
son-in-law, n. pl., **sons-in-law.** yerno
son·net, n. soneto
soon, adv. pronto
soot, n. hollín m.
soothe, v. calmar
sop, v. empapar; absorber
soph·ist·ry, n. pl., **-ries.** sofistería
soph·o·more, n. estudiante de segundo año
so·pran·o, n., pl., **-os, -pran·i.** soprano; tiple
sor·cer·er, n. hechicero
sor·cer·ess, n. fem. hechicera
sor·cer·y, n. pl., **-ies.** hechicería
sor·did, a. avaricioso; vil
sore, a. dolorido; inf. enojado. n. llaga
sor·row, n. pesar; dolor; aflicción
sor·ry, a. arrepentido; triste; vil; lastimoso
sort, n. especie, f.; género; clase, f.; modo. v. clasificar. **out of sorts,** indispuesto
so-so, a. mediocre. adv. así así
soul, n. alma
sound, n. sonido; ruido. v. sonar. a. sano; seguro; bueno
soup, n. sopa; caldo
sour, a. agrio. v. agriar(se)
source, n. origen; fuente, f.
south, n. sur. a. del sur. adv. hacia el sur
south·east, n. sudeste. a. del sudeste

south·ern, a. del sur; meridional
south·west, n. sudoeste. a. del sudoeste
sou·ve·nir, n. recuerdo
sov·er·eign, a. soberano. n. soberano; monarca, m., f.
sov·er·eign·ty, n., pl., **-ties.** soberanía
sow, v., **sowed, sown** or **sowed, sow·ing.** sembrar
spa, n. balneario
space, n. espacio; sitio; lugar. v. espaciar
space·man, n. pl., **-men,** astronauta, m., f.
space·ship, n. astronave, f. Also **space·craft**
spa·cious, a. espacioso
spade, n. pala
spa·ghet·ti, n. espagueti, m.
span, n. lapso. v. medir; cruzar
spank, v. zurrar
spare, v. perdonar; escatimar; pasarse sin. a. sobrante; de repuesto; flaco
spark, n. chispa
spar·kle, v. destellar; centellear
spar·row, n. gorrión
sparse, a. poco denso
spasm, n. espasmo
spas·mod·ic, a. espasmódico
spas·tic, a. espástico
spat·ter, v. salpicar
spat·u·la, n. espátula
spawn, n. freza; huevas. v. desovar; frezar
speak, v., **spoke, spok·en, speak·ing.** hablar; decir
speak·er, n. el que habla; orador
spear, n. lanza. v. alancear
spear·mint, n. menta verde
spe·cial, a. especial; particular
spe·cial·ist, n. especialista, m., f.
spe·cial·ize, v. especializar(se)
spe·cial·ty, n., pl., **-ties.** especialidad
spe·cies, n., pl., **spe·cies.** especie, f.
spe·cif·ic, a. específico; explícito. n. específico
spec·i·fi·ca·tion, n. especificación
spec·i·fy, v. especificar
spec·i·men, n. espécimen, m.; muestra
spe·cious, a. especioso
speck, n. manchita; partícula
specs, n. pl. gafas. Abbr. for specifications
spec·ta·cle, n. espectáculo; pl. gafas
spec·tac·u·lar, a. espectacular
spec·ta·tor, n. espectador
spec·ter, n. espectro
spec·trum, n. pl., **-tra, -trums.** espectro
spec·u·late, v. especular; reflexionar
spec·u·la·tion, n. especulación
speech, n. palabra; discurso
speech·less, a. mudo
speed, v., **sped** or **speed·ed, speed·ing.** acelerar; despachar; apresurarse
speed·om·e·ter, n. cuentakilómetros
speed·way, n. pista de ceniza
spell, v., **spelled** or **spelt, spell·ing.** deletrear. n. hechizo; temporada
spell·bind, v., **-bound, -bind·ing.** encantar
spell·ing, n. ortografía
spend, v., **spent, spend·ing.** gastar (dinero); pasar
spend·thrift, n. pródigo
sperm, n., pl., **sperm, sperms.** esperma
sperm whale, n. cachalote
spew, v. vomitar. Also **spue**
sphere, n. esfera
spher·i·cal, a. esférico
spice, n. especia; picante. v. especiar
spic·y, a. picante
spi·der, n. araña
spike, n. clavo; espiga
spill, v., **spilled** or **spilt, spill·ing.** derramar(se); verter(se). n. vuelco
spin, v., **spun, spun, spin·ning.** hilar; girar. n. vuelta
spin·ach, n. espinaca
spi·nal, a. espinal
spin·dle, n. huso
spin·dle-legs, n. pl. zanquivano
spine, n. espinazo; púa
spin·ning wheel, n. torno de hilar
spin·ster, n. soltera; solterona
spi·ral, n. espiral, f.; hélice, f. a. espiral
spire, n. aguja; chapitel, m.
spir·it, n. espíritu, m.; alma; fantasma, m.; energía; pl. ánimo; often pl. licor
spir·it·u·al, a. espiritual
spir·it·u·al·ism, n. espiritismo
spir·it·u·al·ist, n. espiritista, m., f.
spit, v.t. **spit** or **spat, spit·ting.** escupir. v. t. **spit·ted, spit·ting.** espetar. n. saliva; espetón; asador
spite, n. despecho; rencor. v. causar pena o indignación. **in spite of,** a pesar de
spit·fire, n. fierabrás, m.
spit·tle, n. saliva
spit·toon, n. escupidera
splash, v. salpicar; chapotear. n. salpicadura
splat·ter, v. salpicar
spleen, n. bazo; rencor
splen·did, a. espléndido; grandioso; magnífico
splen·dor, n. esplendor
splice, v. empalmar. n. empalme; juntura
splint, n. tablilla

splin·ter, n. astilla. v. hacer(se) astillas
split, v., **split, split·ting.** separarse; hender(se); dividir. n. hendedura; división
splurge, v. inf. fachenda
spoil, v., **spoiled** or **spoilt, spoil·ing.** estropear(se); arruinar(se); echar(se) a perder. n. often pl. botín
spoke, n. rayo
spo·ken, a. hablado
spokes·man, n. pl., **-men.** portavoz, m.
sponge, n. esponja. v. limpiar con esponja
spon·gy, a. esponjoso
spon·sor, n. fiador; patrocinador
spon·ta·ne·i·ty, n., pl., **-ties.** espontaneidad
spon·ta·ne·ous, a. espontáneo
spook, n. inf. fantasma, m.; espectro
spool, n. carrete; canilla
spoon, n. cuchara
spoon·ful, n., pl., **-fuls.** cucharada
spo·rad·ic, a. esporádico
spore, n. espora
sport, n. deporte; diversión. v. divertirse
sports·man, n., pl., **-men.** deportista, m., f.; caballero
spot, n. punto; mancha; sitio. v. manchar. a. hecho al azar. **on the spot,** inf. en el acto
spot·light, n. foco
spot·ted, a. moteado
spot·ty, a. manchado
spouse, n. esposo; esposa
spout, n. pitón; chorro; caño. v. chorrear
sprain, v. torcer(se). n. torcedura
spray, n. rocío. v. rociar
spread, v., **spread, spread·ing.** extender(se); diseminar. n. extensión; colcha
spree, n. juerga; borrachera
sprig, n. ramita
spright·ly, a. animado
spring, v., **sprang** or **sprung, sprung, spring·ing.** saltar; nacer. n. muelle; fuente, f.; primavera. a. primaveral
spring·time, n. primavera
sprin·kle, v. rociar; lloviznar
sprout, v. brotar; retoñar. n. retoño
spruce, n. picea. a. apuesto
spry, a. ágil; vivo
spue, v. vomitar
spume, n. espuma
spunk, n. inf. valor
spur, n. espuela; estímulo. v. incitar
spu·ri·ous, a. falso; espurio
spurt, n. chorro; esfuerzo supremo
sput·ter, v. chisporrotear
spy, n., pl., **spies.** espía, m., f. v. spy·ing. espiar; observar
spy·glass, n. catalejo
squab·ble, v. disputar. n. riña
squad, n. escuadra; pelotón
squad·ron, n. escuadrilla; escuadrón
squal·id, a. desaliñado; asqueroso
squall, n. ráfaga
squal·or, n. miseria e inmundancia
squan·der, v. malgastar; desperdiciar
square, n. cuadrado. a. cuadrado; justo; inf. anticuado. v. cuadrar
squash, v. aplastar(se). n. pl., **squash·es.** calabaza
squash·y, a. blando
squat, v., **squat·ted** or **squat, squat·ting.** agacharse. a. rechoncho
squat·ter, n. intruso
squawk, v. graznar; inf. quejarse. n. graznido
squeak, v. chillar; chirriar. n. chirrido
squeal, n. grito agudo. v. chillar; inf. cantar
squeam·ish, a. delicado; remilgado
squeeze, v. exprimir; apretar. n. estrujón
squid, n. pl., **squids.** calamar
squint, v. bizquear; mirar de soslayo. n. estrabismo
squirm, v. retorcerse
stab, v. apuñalar. n. puñalada
sta·bil·i·ty, n. pl., **-ties.** estabilidad
sta·ble, n. establo; cuadra. a. estable
stack, n. rimero; niara; cañón de chimenea. v. amontonar
sta·di·um, n. pl., **-di·ums, -di·a.** estadio
staff, n., pl., **staves, staffs.** palo; asta; personal, m.
stag, n. ciervo; venado; inf. para hombres solos
stage, n. etapa; escena. v. representar
stage·coach, n. diligencia
stag·ger, v. tambalear; escalonar
stag·nant, a. estancado
stag·nate, v. estancarse
staid, a. serio
stain, v. manchar; teñir. n. mancha; deshonra
stair, n. escalón; peldaño; pl. escalera
stair·case, n. escalera
stair·way, n. escalera
stake, n. estaca; apuesta. v. estacar; aventurar
sta·lac·tite, n. estalactita
sta·lag·mite, n. estalagmita
stalk, n. tallo. v. cazar al acecho; andar con paso majestuoso
stall, n. casilla de establo; puesto. v. pararse
stal·lion, n. caballo padre
stal·wart, a. fornido; leal
sta·men, n. pl., **-mens, stam·i·na.** estambre

stam·i·na, n. resistencia; fuerza vital
stam·mer, v. tartamudear
stamp, v. estampar; sellar; patear. n. sello
stam·pede, n. estampida. Also **staunch**
stanch, v. restañar. Also **staunch**
stand, v., **stood, stand·ing.** estar de pie; colocar; resistir; tolerar. n. resistencia; puesto; sostén
stand·ard, n. norma; nivel, m.; estandarte. a. normal
stand·ard·ize, v. uniformar
stand·by, n. pl., **-bys.** persona o artículo digno de confianza
stand·ing, n. posición; duración. a. derecho
stand·point, n. punto de vista
stand·still, n. parada
stan·za, n. estancia; estrofa
sta·ple, n. grapa; producto principal. a. corriente
sta·pler, n. grabadora
star, v., **starred, star·ring.** presentar como estrella. n. estrella; astro
star·board, n. estribor. a. de estribor
starch, n. fécula; almidón
stare, v. clavar la vista; mirar fijamente. n. mirada fija
star·fish, n. pl., **-fish, -fish·es.** estrella de mar
star·gaze, v. fig. soñar despierto
stark, a. completo; rígido. adv. en cueros
star·less, a. sin estrellas
star·ry, a. estrellado
start, v. empezar; comenzar; poner(se) en marcha; sobresaltarse. n. sobresalto; comienzo
star·tle, v. asustar; alarmar
star·tling, a. alarmante
star·va·tion, n. hambre, f. a. de hambre
starve, v. morir de hambre; pasar hambre
stash, v. inf. ocultar
state, n. condición; estado. a. de estado. v. exponer; decir
state·craft, n. arte de gobernar
stat·ed, a. establecido; fijo
state·ly, a. majestuoso; elevado
state·ment, n. declaración; estado de cuenta
states·man, n. pl., **-men.** estadista, m.
stat·ic, a. fijo; estático. n. parásitos
sta·tion, n. puesto; estación. v. situar
sta·tion·ar·y, a. inmóvil
sta·tion·er·y, n. papelería
sta·tis·tic, n. estadístico
sta·tis·ti·cian, n. estadístico
sta·tis·tics, n. pl. estadística
stat·ue, n. estatua
stat·ure, n. estatura
sta·tus, n. estado; posición; prestigio
staunch, a. firme; fiel. v. restañar. Also **stanch**
stave, n. duela; estrofa. v., **staved** or **stove, stav·ing.** quebrar
stay, v., **stayed** or **staid, stay·ing.** quedar(se); sostener; parar. n. estancia
stead, n. lugar
stead·fast, sted·fast, a. firme; constante
stead·y, a. firme; constante; uniforme. v. sostener
steak, n. filete
steal, v., **stole, stol·en, steal·ing.** robar; hurtar. n. inf. ganga
stealth, n. cautela
steam, n. vapor. v. empañar
steam·boat, n. buque de vapor
steam·er, n. buque de vapor
steam·roll·er, n. apisonadora
steam·ship, n. vapor
steam·y, a. vaporoso
steed, n. corcel, m.
steel, n. acero. a. de acero; duro. v. acerar
steep, a. empinado; inf. excesivo. v. saturar
stee·ple, n. campanario
steer, v. guiar; gobernar; conducir. n. novillo
steer·age, n. entrepuente
stel·lar, a. estelar
stem, n. tallo; pie. v. proceder de; represar
stench, n. hedor; tufo
sten·cil, v. estarcido. v. estarcir
ste·nog·ra·pher, n. taquígrafo
ste·nog·ra·phy, n. taquigrafía
sten·to·ri·an, a. estentóreo
step, n. paso; escalera. v. pisar
step·broth·er, n. hermanastro
step·child, n. pl., **-child·ren.** hijastro; hijastra
step·daugh·ter, n. hijastra
step·fa·ther, n. padrastro
step·lad·der, n. escalera de tijera
step·moth·er, n. madrastra
step·par·ent, n. padrastro; madrastra
steppe, n. estepa
step·sis·ter, n. hermanastra
step·son, n. hijastro
ster·e·o·phon·ic, a. estereofónico
ster·e·o·typed, a. estereotipado
ster·ile, a. estéril
ster·il·i·ty, n. esterilidad
ster·il·i·za·tion, n. esterilización
ster·i·lize, v. esterilizar
ster·ling, a. esterlina
stern, a. austero; duro. n. popa
stern·ness, n. severidad
ster·num, n. pl., **-na, -nums.** esternón

steth·o·scope, n. estetoscopio
ste·ve·dore, n. estibador
stew, n. estofado. v. estofar
ste·ward, n. administrador; camarero
stew·ard·ess, n. f. azafata
stick, n. palo. v., **stuck, stick·ing.** picar; pegar; clavar
stick·er, n. marbete engomado
stick·ler, n. rigorista, m., f.
stick-up, stick·up, n. inf. atraco
stick·y, a. viscoso
stiff, a. duro; rígido; estirado. n. inf. cadáver
stif·fen, v. atiesar(se)
sti·fle, v. ahogar(se); ocultar
sti·fling, a. sofocante
stig·ma, n. pl., **-mas, -ma·ta.** estigma, m.
sti·let·to, n. pl., **-tos, -toes.** estilete
still, a. inmóvil; tranquilo. v. aquietar. n. alambique. adv. todavía; sin embargo
still·ness, n. quietud
stilt, n. zanco
stilt·ed, a. hinchado
stim·u·lant, n. estimulante
stim·u·late, v. estimular
stim·u·la·tion, n. estímulo
stim·u·lus, n., pl., **-li.** estímulo; estimulante
sting, v., **stung, sting·ing.** picar. n. picadura; aguijón
stin·gy, a. tacaño; escaso
stink, v., **stank** or **stunk, stunk, stink·ing.** heder. n. hedor
stint, v. limitar; restringir. n. tarea
sti·pend, n. estipendio
stip·u·late, v. estipular; especificar
stip·u·la·tion, n. estipulación
stir, v. agitar; excitar. n. conmoción; interés, m.
stir·ring, a. conmovedor
stir·rup, n. estribo
stitch, v. coser. n. puntada; punto
stock, n. valores; acciones; surtido; ganado; palo. v. surtir
stock·ade, n. estacada; palizada
stock·brok·er, n. bolsista, m.
stock·hold·er, n. accionista, m., f.
stock·ing, n. media
stock·pile, v. acumular
stock·y, a. rechoncho
stod·gy, a. pesado
sto·ic, n. estoico
sto·i·cal, a. estoico
stoke, v. echar carbón
stol·id, a. impasible
stom·ach, n. estómago. v. inf. aguantar
stone, n. piedra. v. apedrear; deshuesar
stone-deaf, a. completamente sordo
ston·y, ston·ey, a. pedregoso; empedernido
stool, n. banqueta
stoop, v. inclinarse; rebajarse. n. cargazón de espaldas
stop, v. parar(se); terminar; suspender; tapar. n. parada
stop·gap, n. tapagujeros
stop·light, n. semáforo
stop·page, n. cesación
stop·per, n. tapón
stor·age, n. almacenaje
store, n. tienda; almacén; repuesto. v. tener en reserva
store·house, n. almacén
sto·ried, sto·reyed, a. de (el número de) pisos
stork, n. cigüeña
storm, n. tormenta; tempestad. v. asaltar
storm·y, a. tempestuoso
sto·ry, n., pl., **-ries.** historia; cuento; piso; inf. embuste
sto·ry·tell·er, n. cuentista, m., f.; inf. embustero
stout, a. corpulento; resuelto
stove, n. cocina; estufa
stow, v. estibar; colocar
stow·age, n. estiba
stow·a·way, n. polizón
strad·dle, v. montar a horcajadas
strag·gle, v. extraviarse; rezagarse
strag·gler, n. rezagado
strag·gly, a. desordenado
straight, a. recto; directo; honrado. adv. directamente
straight·en, v. enderezar
straight·for·ward, a. honrado; derecho
straight·way, adv. en seguida
strain, n. linaje; vena; tensión. v. forzar; estirar; filtrar; torcer
strain·er, n. colador
strait, n. estrecho; often pl. apuro
strand, n. hebra; ramal, m. v. quedarse colgado
strange, a. desconocido; raro; extraño
stran·ger, n. forastero; desconocido
stran·gu·la·tion, n. estrangulación
stran·gle, v. estrangular
stran·gler, n. estrangulador
strap, n. correa; tirante
strap·less, a. sin tirantes
strap·ping, a. inf. robusto
strat·a·gem, n. estratagema
stra·te·gic, a. estratégico
strat·e·gist, n. estratega, m.
strat·e·gy, n., pl., **-gies.** estrategia
strat·i·fi·ca·tion, n. estratificación
strat·i·fy, v. estratificar
strat·o·sphere, n. estratosfera
stra·tum, n. pl., **-ta, -tums.** estrato; capa
straw, n. paja; pajilla. a. de paja

straw·ber·ry, n. pl., **-ries.** fresa
stray, v. vagar; extraviarse. a. extraviado
streak, n. raya. v. rayar; listar
stream, n. arroyo; corriente, f.; torrente. v. correr
stream·er, n. flámula
street, n. calle, f.
street·car, n. tranvía, m.
strength, n. fuerza; poder; resistencia; vigor
strength·en, v. fortalecer(se); hacer(se) más fuerte
stren·u·ous, a. enérgico; arduo
stress, n. tensión; compulsión; énfasis, m.; acento. v. dar énfasis
stretch, v. extender(se); estirar. n. extensión
stretch·er, n. camilla
strew, v. **strewed, strewed** or **strewn, strew·ing.** derramar
strick·en, a. afligido; herido
strict, a. estricto; severo; riguroso
strict·ness, n. rigor
stric·ture, n. crítica; censura
stride, v. **strode, strid·den, strid·ing.** andar a pasos largos. n. zancada
stri·dent, a. estridente
strife, n. contienda; lucha
strike, v. **struck, struck** or **strick·en, strik·ing.** golpear; pegar; atacar; encender; declararse en huelga. n. huelga
strik·ing, a. impresionante
string, n. cordel, m.; bramante; serie, f. v. **strung, strung** or **stringed, string·ing.** encordar; ensartar
strin·gent, a. riguroso
string·y, a. fibroso
strip, v. despojar(se); desnudar(se). n. tira
stripe, n. banda; raya. v. rayar
striped, a. rayado
strip·ling, n. mozuelo
strive, v. **strove, striv·en, striv·ing.** esforzarse; contender
stroke, n. golpe; ataque fulminante; plumada. v. acariciar
stroll, v. pasear(se); vagar. n. paseo
strong, a. fuerte; intenso; robusto; firme
strong·hold, n. plaza fuerte
strong-mind·ed, a. resuelto; independiente
strop, n. suavizador
struc·tur·al, a. estructural
struc·ture, n. estructura; construcción. v. construir
strug·gle, v. luchar. n. esfuerzo; contienda
strum, v. rasguear
strum·pet, n. ramera
strut, v. contonearse; pavonearse. n. tornapunta
strych·nine, n. estricnina
stub, n. cabo; fragmento. v. dar un tropezón
stub·ble, n. rastrojo; barba
stub·born, a. obstinado; inquebrantable
stub·born·ness, n. obstinación; porfía
stuc·co, n. pl., **-coes, -cos.** estuco
stud, n. yeguada; tachón; botón
stu·dent, n. estudiante; alumno
stud·ied, a. premeditado
stu·di·o, n. pl., **-os.** estudio; taller
stu·di·ous, a. estudioso
stud·y, n. pl., **-ies.** estudio. v. estudiar
stuff, n. material, m.; cosas. v. hinchar; rellenar; llenar
stuff·ing, n. relleno
stuff·y, a. mal ventilado
stum·ble, v. tropezar. n. traspié; tropezón
stump, n. muñón; tocón. v. inf. dejar perplejo
stun, v. aturdir
stun·ning, a. impresionante; estupendo
stunt, v. impedir el desarrollo. n. proeza
stu·pe·fac·tion, n. estupefacción; aturdimiento
stu·pe·fy, v. causar estupor
stu·pen·dous, a. estupendo
stu·pid, a. estúpido; tonto; necio
stu·pid·i·ty, n. estupidez, f.
stu·por, n. estupor
stur·dy, a. fuerte; firme; vigoroso
stur·geon, n. pl., **-geon, -geons.** esturión
stut·ter, v. balbucear; tartamudear. n. tartamudeo
sty, n. pl., **sties.** pocilgo; (med.) orzuelo
style, n. estilo; manera; modo. v. intitular
styl·ish, a. a la moda
sty·mie, v. dejar perplejo
styp·tic, a. estíptico
suave, a. cortés; urbano
sub, n. inf. submarino
sub·con·scious, a. subconsciente. n. subconsciencia
sub·cu·ta·ne·ous, a. subcutáneo
sub·di·vide, v. subdividir
sub·di·vi·sion, n. subdivisión
sub·due, v. sojuzgar; suavizar
sub·head·ing, n. subtítulo
sub·ject, n. sujeto; súbdito. a. sujeto; propenso. v. someter
sub·jec·tion, n. sujeción
sub·jec·tive, a. subjetivo
sub·jec·tiv·i·ty, n. subjetividad
sub·join, v. adjuntar
sub·ju·gate, v. subyugar, sojuzgar
sub·ju·ga·tion, n. subyugación; sojuzgación

sub·lease, v. subarrendar
sub·let, v. subarrendar
sub·li·mate, v. sublimar
sub·li·ma·tion, n. sublimación
sub·lime, a. sublime
sub·lim·i·ty, n. pl., **-ties.** sublimidad
sub·ma·rine, a. submarino
sub·merge, v. sumergir(se)
sub·mer·gence, n. sumersión
sub·merse, v. sumergir(se)
sub·mer·sion, n. sumersión
sub·mis·sion, n. sumisión; resignación
sub·mis·sive, a. sumiso
sub·mit, v. someter(se); presentar
sub·nor·mal, a. anormal
sub·or·di·nate, a. subordinado; secundario; dependiente. v. subordinar
sub·or·di·na·tion, n. subordinación
sub·poe·na, sub·pe·na, n. citación; comparendo
sub·scribe, v. subscribir(se); firmar
sub·scrip·tion, n. subscripción
sub·se·quent, a. subsiguiente
sub·ser·vi·ent, a. servil
sub·side, v. bajar; calmarse
sub·sid·i·ar·y, a. subsidiario
sub·si·dize, v. subvencionar
sub·si·dy, n. pl., **-dies.** subvención; subsidio
sub·sist, v. subsistir; existir
sub·sis·tence, n. subsistencia
sub·stance, n. substancia; materia; esencia
sub·stan·tial, a. substancial
sub·stan·ti·ate, v. comprobar
sub·stan·ti·a·tion, n. comprobación; justificación
sub·stan·tive, n. substantivo. a. substantivo
sub·sti·tute, v. substituir. n. substituto
sub·sti·tu·tion, n. substitución; reemplazo
sub·ter·fuge, n. subterfugio
sub·ter·ra·ne·an, a. subterráneo
sub·ti·tle, n. subtítulo
sub·tle, a. sutil; ingenioso; delicado; astuto
sub·tle·ty, n. sutileza
sub·tract, v. substraer
sub·trac·tion, n. substracción; resta
sub·urb, n. often pl. suburbio
sub·ur·ban, a. suburbano
sub·ver·sion, n. subversión
sub·ver·sive, a. subversivo
sub·vert, v. subvertir
sub·way, n. metro
suc·ceed, v. tener éxito; lograr; suceder
suc·cess, n. éxito
suc·cess·ful, a. próspero; afortunado
suc·ces·sion, n. sucesión
suc·ces·sor, n. sucesor
suc·cinct, a. sucinto
suc·cor, n. socorro; auxilio. v. socorrer
suc·cu·lent, a. suculento
suc·cumb, v. sucumbir; morir
such, a. tal; parecido. pron. tal; los que. adv. tan
suck, v. chupar; mamar
suck·le, v. lactar; amamantar
suc·tion, n. succión
sud·den, a. imprevisto; repentino; súbito
sud·den·ly, adv. de repente
suds, n. pl. jabonaduras
sue, v. demandar
suede, n. ante
su·et, n. sebo
suf·fer, v. sufrir; padecer; tolerar
suf·fer·ance, n. tolerancia
suf·fice, v. bastar
suf·fi·cien·cy, n. pl., **-cies.** suficiencia
suf·fi·cient, a. suficiente
suf·fix, n. sufijo
suf·fo·cate, v. sofocar; asfixiar
suf·fo·ca·tion, n. sofocación
suf·frage, n. sufragio
suf·fuse, v. extender; bañar
suf·fu·sion, n. difusión
sug·ar, n. azúcar
sug·ar·y, a. azucarado; almibarado
sug·gest, v. sugerir; indicar; insinuar
sug·ges·tion, n. indicación; sugestión
sug·ges·tive, a. sugestivo
su·i·cide, n. suicida, m., f.; suicidio
suit, n. traje; pleito; (cards) palo. v. acomodar; ir bien
suit·a·ble, a. apropiado
suit·case, n. maleta
suite, n. juego; serie, f.
suit·or, n. pretendiente
sul·fur, sul·phur, n. azufre
sul·fu·ric ac·id, n. ácido sulfúrico
sulk, v. estar de mal humor
sulk·y, a. mohíno
sul·len, a. hosco
sul·ly, v. manchar
sul·tan, n. sultán
sul·tan·ate, n. sultanato
sul·try, a. bochornoso
sum, n. suma; cantidad. v. sumar
su·mac, su·mach, n. zumaque
sum·ma·rize, v. resumir
sum·ma·ry, n. pl., **-ries.** resumen. a. sumario
sum·mer, n. verano. a. veraniego; de verano
sum·mit, n. cima; cumbre, f.
sum·mon, v. citar; llamar; convocar
sum·mons, n. pl., **sum·mons·es.** citación
sump·tu·ous, a. suntuoso
sun, n. sol, m. v. tomar el sol

sun·bathe, v. tomar el sol
sun·dae, n. helado con fruta, jarabe, nueces, etc.
Sun·day, n. domingo
sun·der, v. hender
sun·down, n. puesta del sol
sun·dries, n. pl. géneros diversos
sun·dry, a. diversos; varios
sun·flow·er, n. girasol, m.
sun·glass·es, n. pl. gafas de sol
sunk·en, a. hundido
sun·light, n. luz del sol
sun·ny, a. expuesto al sol; alegre
sun·rise, n. salida del sol
sun·set, n. ocaso; puesta del sol
sun·shine, n. luz del sol
sun·stroke, n. insolación
sup, v. cenar
su·per·an·nu·ate, v. jubilar
su·perb, a. magnífico; grandioso
su·per·cil·i·ous, a. desdeñoso; arrogante; imperioso
su·per·fi·cial, a. superficial
su·per·fi·ci·al·i·ty, n. pl., **-ties.** superfluidad
su·per·flu·ous, a. superfluo
su·per·high·way, n. autopista
su·per·hu·man, a. sobrehumano
su·per·im·pose, v. sobreponer
su·per·in·tend, v. dirigir; superentender
su·per·in·tend·ent, n. superintendente, m., f.
su·pe·ri·or, a. superior. n. superior
su·pe·ri·or·i·ty, n. superioridad
su·per·la·tive, a. superlativo. n. superlativo
su·per·mar·ket, n. supermercado
su·per·nat·u·ral, a. sobrenatural
su·per·nu·mer·ar·y, n. pl., **-ies.** supernumerario; comparsa, m., f.
su·per·scrip·tion, n. sobrescrito
su·per·sede, v. suplantar
su·per·son·ic, a. supersónico
su·per·sti·tion, n. superstición
su·per·sti·tious, a. supersticioso
su·per·vise, v. superentender; supervisar
su·per·vi·sor, n. superintendente, m., f.; supervisor, m., f.
su·pine, a. supino
sup·per, n. cena
sup·plant, v. suplantar
sup·ple, a. flexible; blando
sup·ple·ment, n. suplemento. v. suplir
sup·ple·men·ta·ry, a. suplementario
sup·pli·cant, n. suplicante, m., f.
sup·pli·cate, v. suplicar
sup·pli·ca·tion, n. súplica
sup·ply, v. proveer; suministrar; proporcionar. n. pl., **-plies.** provisión
sup·port, v. apoyar; sostener; aguantar; mantener. n. apoyo; sostén
sup·port·er, n. defensor
sup·pose, v. suponer; imaginar
sup·po·si·tion, n. suposición
sup·press, v. suprimir; contener
sup·pres·sion, n. supresión
sup·pu·rate, v. supurar
sup·pu·ra·tion, n. supuración
su·prem·a·cy, n. pl., **-cies.** supremacía
su·preme, a. supremo; sumo
sur·charge, n. sobrecarga
sure, a. seguro; cierto
sure·ly, adv. seguramente
sure·ty, n. pl., **-ties.** garantía; garante
surf, n. oleaje
sur·face, n. superficie, f. v. salir a la superficie
sur·feit, n. exceso; empacho. v. hartar(se)
surge, v. agitarse
sur·geon, n. cirujano
sur·ger·y, n. pl., **-ies.** cirugía
sur·gi·cal, a. quirúrgico
sur·ly, a. áspero; hosco; agrio
sur·mise, n. conjetura. v. conjeturar
sur·mount, v. superar
sur·name, n. apellido
sur·pass, v. exceder; superar
sur·plus, n. excedente
sur·prise, n. sorpresa. v. sorprender
sur·pris·ing, a. sorprendente
sur·ren·der, v. rendir(se); renunciar a. n. rendición
sur·ro·gate, n. substituto
sur·round, v. rodear; cercar; sitiar
sur·veil·lance, n. vigilancia
sur·vey, v. inspeccionar; medir. n. inspección; apeo
sur·vey·or, n. agrimensor
sur·viv·al, n. supervivencia
sur·vive, v. sobrevivir
sur·vi·vor, n. sobreviviente, m., f.
sus·cep·ti·bil·i·ty, n. pl., **-ties.** susceptibilidad
sus·cep·ti·ble, a. susceptible; impresionable
sus·pect, v. sospechar. n. sospechoso. a. sospechoso
sus·pend, v. colgar; suspender
sus·pense, n. incertidumbre, f.
sus·pen·sion, n. suspensión
sus·pi·cion, n. sospecha; sombra
sus·pi·cious, a. sospechoso
sus·tain, v. sostener; sufrir; sustentar
sus·te·nance, n. sustento
svelte, a. esbelto
swab, n. torunda. v. limpiar
swad·dle, v. empañar
swag·ger, v. pavonearse; fanfarronear
swal·low, n. golondrina. v. tragar
swamp, n. pantano; ciénaga. v. inundar
swamp·y, a. pantanoso

swan, n. cisne
swap, v. inf. cambiar
swarm, n. enjambre. v. enjambrar; pulular
swarth·y, a. atezado
swash·buck·ler, n. espadachín
swat, v. matar
sway, v. bambolearse; inclinar. n. influencia
swear, v. **swore, sworn, swear·ing.** jurar; blasfemar
swear·word, n. palabrota
sweat, v. **sweat** or **sweat·ed, sweat·ing.** sudar. n. sudor
sweat·er, n. jersey, m.; suéter
sweat·y, a. sudoroso
sweep, v. **swept, sweep·ing.** barrer. n. extensión
sweet, a. dulce. n. pl. dulces; bombones
sweet·en, v. azucarar; endulzar
sweet·heart, n. querida; novia
sweet·meat, n. often pl. dulce
swell, v. **swelled, swelled** or **swol·len, swell·ing.** hinchar(se)
swel·ter, v. sofocarse
swerve, v. torcer(se); desviar(se)
swift, a. veloz
swift·ness, n. prontitud
swig, v. beber a grandes tragos
swill, n. bazofia
swim, v. **swam, swum, swim·ming.** nadar. n. natación
swim·mer, n. nadador
swin·dle, v. estafar. n. estafa
swin·dler, n. estafador
swine, n. pl., **swine.** puerco
swing, v. **swung, swing·ing.** columpiar(se); balancear(se). n. oscilación; columpio
swirl, v. arremolinar(se). n. remolino
swish, v. crujir
switch, n. cambio; desviación. v. cambiar; (elect.) conectar
switch·board, n. cuadro de distribución
swiv·el, v. girar
swoon, v. desmayarse. n. desmayo
swoop, v. calarse
sword, n. espada
sword·play, n. maneja de la espada
swords·man, n. pl., **-men.** espadachín
syc·a·more, n. sicomoro
syc·o·phant, n. adulador
syl·la·ble, n. sílaba
syl·lab·i·cate, v. silabear
syl·lab·i·ca·tion, n. silabeo
syl·lab·i·fi·ca·tion, n. silabeo
syl·lab·i·fy, v. silabear
syl·la·bus, n. pl., **-bus·es, -bi.** resumen; programa, m.
syl·van, sil·van, a. silvestre
sym·bol, n. símbolo
sym·bol·ic, a. simbólico
sym·bol·ism, n. simbolismo
sym·bol·ize, v. simbolizar
sym·me·try, n. pl., **-tries.** simetría
sym·pa·thet·ic, a. compasivo; simpático
sym·pa·thy, n. pl., **-thies.** simpatía; compasión
sym·pho·ny, n. pl., **-nies.** sinfonía
symp·tom, n. síntoma, m.; indicio
syn·a·gogue, syn·a·gog, n. sinagoga
syn·chro·nize, v. sincronizar(se)
syn·di·cate, n. sindicato. v. sindicar
syn·od, n. sínodo
syn·o·nym, n. sinónimo
syn·on·y·mous, a. sinónimo
syn·op·sis, n. pl., **-ses.** sinopsis, f.
syn·the·sis, n. pl., **-ses.** síntesis, f.
syn·thet·ic, a. sintético
syph·i·lis, n. sífilis, f.
sy·ringe, n. jeringa
syr·up, sir·up, n. jarabe; almíbar
sys·tem, n. sistema, m.; método
sys·tem·at·ic, a. sistemático
sys·tem·a·tize, v. sistematizar

T

tab, n. oreja; cuenta
tab·er·nac·le, n. tabernáculo
ta·ble, n. mesa; tabla
ta·ble·spoon, n. cuchara grande o de sopa
ta·ble·spoon·ful, n. pl., **-fuls.** cucharada
tab·let, n. taco; tableta
ta·boo, ta·bu, a. tabú. n. tabú. v. prohibir
tab·u·lar, a. tabular
tab·u·late, v. tabular
tac·it, a. tácito
tac·i·turn, a. taciturno
tack, n. tachuela; virada. v. hilvanar; virar
tack·le, n. equipo; carga. v. abordar; agarrar
tact, n. tacto
tac·tics, n. pl. táctica
tad·pole, n. renacuajo
taf·fe·ta, n. tafetán
taf·fy, n. caramelo
tag, n. etiqueta; marbete
tail, n. cola; rabo; pl. inf. cruz de una moneda. v. inf. pisar los talones
tai·lor, n. sastre
taint, v. inficionar(se); corromper(se). n. mancha
take, v. **took, tak·en, tak·ing.** tomar; coger; aceptar; asumir; sacar. **take af·ter,** parecerse a. **take back,** retractar. **take in,** admitir; comprender. **take o·ver,** encargarse de. **take up,** acortar
talc, n. despegue
tal·cum pow·der, n. polvo de talco
tale, n. cuenta

genio; mal genio
tem·per·a·ment, n. temperamento; disposición
tem·per·a·men·tal, a. temperamental; caprichoso
tem·per·ance, n. templanza
tem·per·ate, a. templado
tem·per·a·ture, n. temperatura; fiebre, f.
tem·pest, n. tempestad
tem·pes·tu·ous, a. tempestuoso
tem·ple, n. templo; sien, f.
tem·po, n. pl., **-pos, -pi.** tiempo
tem·po·ral, a. temporal
tem·po·rar·y, a. temporáneo; interino; provisional
tempt, v. tentar
temp·ta·tion, n. tentación
ten, n. diez. a. diez
te·na·cious, a. tenaz
ten·ant, n. inquilino; arrendatario; morador
tend, v. tener tendencia; tender; atender
ten·den·cy, n. tendencia
ten·der, a. tierno; afectuoso; delicado. n. oferta. v. ofrecer
ten·der·ly, adv. tiernamente
ten·don, n. tendón
ten·dril, n. zarcillo
ten·e·ment, n. casa de vecindad
ten·et, n. dogma, m.
ten·nis, n. tenis, m.
ten·or, n. tenor
tense, a. tieso; tenso. v. tensar. n. tiempo
ten·sion, n. tensión
tent, n. tienda de campaña
ten·ta·cle, n. tentáculo
ten·ta·tive, a. provisional
ten·u·ous, a. tenue
ten·ure, n. tenencia
tep·id, a. tibio
term, n. término; plazo; trimestre; pl. condiciones
ter·mi·nal, n. terminal, f. a. terminal
ter·mi·nate, v. terminar
ter·mi·nol·o·gy, n. terminología
ter·mi·nus, n. pl., **-nus·es, -ni.** término
ter·mite, n. comején
ter·race, n. terraza
ter·rain, n. terreno
ter·res·tri·al, a. terrestre
ter·ri·ble, a. terrible; inf. malísimo
ter·ri·er, n. perro de busca
ter·rif·ic, a. terrífico; tremendo; inf. estupendo
ter·ri·fy, v. aterrar; aterrorizar
ter·ri·to·ry, n. pl., **-ries.** territorio; término
ter·ror, n. terror
ter·ror·ism, n. terrorismo
ter·ror·ist, n. terrorista, m., f.
ter·ror·ize, v. aterrorizar
terse, a. conciso
test, n. prueba; examen. v. examinar
tes·ta·ment, n. testamento; (cap.) Testamento
tes·ti·fy, v. atestiguar; testificar
tes·ti·mo·ni·al, n. recomendación
tes·ti·mo·ny, n. pl., **-nies.** testimonio
teth·er, n. traba. v. atar
text, n. texto; tema, m.
text·book, n. libro de texto
tex·tile, a. textil. n. textil, m.; tejido
tex·ture, n. textura
than, conj. que
thank, v. dar gracias a; agradecer
thank·ful, a. agradecido
thanks, n. pl. gracias
thanks·giv·ing, n. acción de gracias
that, pron. pl., **those.** ése; ésa; eso; aquél; aquélla; aquello; el cual; la cual. a. ese; esa; aquel; aquella. conj. que
thaw, v. deshelar(se). n. deshielo
the, def. art. el; la; lo; los; las
the·a·ter, n. teatro
the·at·ri·cal, a. teatral
thee, pron. te; ti (obj. and dat. of thou)
theft, n. robo
their, a. poss. of they. su(s)
them, pron. obj. of they. los; las; les; ellos; ellas
theme, n. tema, m.; ensayo
them·selves, pron. pl. ellos (sí) mismos; ellas (sí) mismas
then, adv. entonces; luego. conj. en tal caso
thence, adv. desde entonces. Also **thence·for·ward**
the·ol·o·gy, n. pl., **-gies.** teología
the·o·rem, n. teorema, m.
the·o·ret·i·cal, a. teórico
the·o·rize, v. teorizar
the·o·ry, n. pl., **-ries.** teoría
ther·a·py, n. pl., **-pies.** terapéutica
there·a·bout, adv. cerca de
there·af·ter, adv. después de eso
there·by, adv. de ese modo
there·fore, adv. por lo tanto; por esta razón
ther·mal, a. termal
ther·mom·e·ter, n. termómetro
ther·mo·nu·cle·ar, a. termonuclear
ther·mo·stat, n. termostato
the·sau·rus, n. tesoro
these, a. pl. estos; estas. pron. pl. éstos; éstas
the·sis, n. pl., **-ses.** tesis, f.
they, pron. ellos; ellas
thick, a. grueso; espeso; denso
thick·et, n. espesura
thief, n. pl., **thieves.** ladrón
thieve, v. robar; hurtar

thigh, n. muslo
thim·ble, n. dedal, m.
thin, a. delgado; flaco; ligero; escaso; tenue
thing, n. cosa; objeto; pl. efectos; trapos
think, v., thought, think·ing. pensar; meditar; creer; imaginar
third, n. tercio; tercera. a. tercero
thirst, n. sed, f.; ansia. v. tener sed
thir·teen, n., trece. n. trece
thir·ty, a. treinta. n. treinta
this, pron. pl., these. éste; ésta; esto. a. este; esta. adv. tan
this·tle, n. cardo
thith·er, adv. allá
tho·rax, n. tórax, m.
thorn, n. espina
thorn·y, a. espinoso
thor·ough, a. completo; concienzudo
thor·ough·bred, a. de pura sangre
thor·ough·fare, n. vía pública
thou, pron. (poetic, Biblical). tú
though, conj. aunque. adv. sin embargo; no obstante
thought, n. pensamiento; idea; consideración
thought·ful, a. pensativo; atento
thought·less, a. descuidado; inconsiderado
thou·sand, a. mil. n. mil
thou·sandth, a. milésimo. n. milésimo
thrash, v. zurrar; menear; sacudirse
thread, n. hilo; rosca. v. enhebrar
thread·bare, a. raído
threat, n. amenaza
threat·en, v. amenazar
three, a. tres. n. tres
three·score, a. sesenta
thresh·old, n. umbral, m.
thrice, adv. tres veces
thrift, n. economía; frugalidad
thrift·y, a. frugal
thrill, v. emocionar(se); conmover(se). n. emoción
thrive, v., thrived or throve, thrived or thriv·en. prosperar; crecer con vigor
throat, n. garganta
throb, v. palpitar
throne, n. trono
throng, n. tropel, m.; muchedumbre, f. v. venir en tropel
throt·tle, v. estrangular. n. regulador
through, thru, prep. a través de; por; por medio de. adv. de parte a parte. a. directo
through·out, prep. por todo. adv. en todas partes; durante todo
throw, v., threw, thrown. echar; arrojar; lanzar; tirar. n. tirada; echada; lance
thru, prep., adv. See through
thrust, v., thrust, thrust·ing. empujar; clavar. n. empuje; ataque
thud, n. ruido sordo
thumb, n. pulgar
thun·der, n. trueno; estruendo
thun·der·bolt, n. rayo
Thurs·day, n. jueves, m.
thus, adv. así; de este modo; en esta manera
thwart, v. frustrar; desbaratar
thy·roid gland, n. tiroides, m.
tib·i·a, n. tibia
tic, n. tic, m.
tick, n. golpecito; tictac, m.; garrapata
tick·et, n. billete; entrada; boleto; multa. v. rotular
tick·le, v. cosquillear; sentir cosquillas
tick·lish, a. cosquilloso; delicado
tid·bit, n. golosina
tide, n. marea
ti·dings, n. pl. noticias
ti·dy, a. ordenada; inf. considerable. v. poner en orden
tie, v., tied, ty·ing. atar; ligar; empatar. n. corbata; empate
tier, n. fila
ti·ger, n. tigre
tight, a. ajustado; apretado. adv. bien
tight·en, v. apretar; atiesar
tights, n. pl. traje de malla
tile, n. baldosa; teja
till, prep. hasta. conj. hasta que. v. labrar. n. cajón
till·er, n. caña del timón
tilt, v. inclinar(se). n. inclinación
tim·ber, n. madera; madero
tim·bre, n. timbre
time, n. tiempo; época; hora; vez, f. v. cronometrar
time·less, a. eterno
time·ly, a. oportuno
time·piece, n. reloj, m.
time·ta·ble, n. horario
tim·id, a. tímido
tim·id·i·ty, n. timidez, f.
tin, n. estaño; lata
tinc·ture, n. tintura
tin·der, n. yesca
tinge, v. teñir; matizar; tintar. n. tinte
tin·gle, v. sentir hormigueo
tink·er, v. tratar de remendar
tin·kle, v. tintinar
tin·sel, n. oropel, m.
tint, n. matiz, m. v. teñir; matizar
ti·ny, a. muy pequeño; chiquitín
tip, n. punta; regatón; propina; aviso; soplo. v. ladear; dar propina
tip·sy, a. achispado
tip·toe, v. andar de puntillas
ti·rade, n. invectiva; diatriba
tire, v. cansar(se); fatigar(se). n. neumático

tired, a. cansado
tire·some, a. molesto; pesado
tis·sue, n. tejido; tisú, m.
ti·tan·ic, a. titánico
tithe, n. diezmo
ti·tle, n. título; nombre. v. intitular; titular
tit·ter, v. reír a medias
tit·u·lar, a. titular
TNT, T.N.T., n. explosivo (trinitrotolueno)
to, prep. a; hacia; de; hasta. adv. hacia
toad, n. sapo
toad·stool, n. hongo; hongo venenoso
toast, v. tostar; brindar. n. pan tostado; brindis, m.
to·bac·co, n. tabaco
to·bog·gan, n. tobogán, m.
to·day, to-day, adv. hoy; hoy día. n. hoy
toe, n. dedo del pie; punta del pie
tof·fee, tof·fy, n. caramelo
to·ga, n. toga
to·geth·er, adv. juntos; juntamente; simultáneamente
toil, v. trabajar asiduamente; afanarse. n. trabajo
toi·let, n. retrete; wáter; tocado
toi·let·ry, n. artículo de tocador
to·ken, n. indicio; prenda; señal, f.; ficha. a. simbólico
tol·er·a·ble, a. tolerable; regular
tol·er·ance, n. tolerancia
tol·er·ant, a. tolerante
tol·er·ate, v. tolerar; soportar; permitir
toll, n. peaje. v. tañer
to·ma·to, n. pl., -toes. tomate
tomb, n. tumba; sepulcro
tomb·stone, n. lápida sepulcral
to·mor·row, to-mor·row, n. mañana. adv. mañana
ton, n. tonelada
tone, n. tono; tendencia
tongs, n. pl. tenazas
tongue, n. lengua; lengüeta; idioma, m.
ton·ic, n. tónico
to·night, to-night, adv. esta noche. n. esta noche
ton·nage, n. tonelaje
ton·sil, n. amígdala; tonsila
ton·sil·li·tis, n. amigdalitis, f.
too, adv. demasiado; también; además
tool, n. herramienta; instrumento
tooth, n. pl., teeth. diente; muela
tooth·ache, n. dolor de muelas
tooth·brush, n. cepillo de dientes
top, n. cumbre, f.; ápice; cima; tapa; peonza. a. más alto; primero. v. coronar
to·paz, n. topacio
top·coat, n. sobretodo
top hat, n. chistera
top·ic, n. tema, m.
top·i·cal, a. tópico; actual; del día
to·pog·ra·phy, n. topografía
top·ple, v. venirse abajo
top·sy·tur·vy, adv. patas arriba
torch, n. antorcha; hacha
tor·ment, n. atormentar. n. tormento
tor·na·do, n. pl., -does, -dos. tornado
tor·pe·do, n. pl., -does. torpedo. v. torpedear
tor·rent, n. torrente
tor·rid, a. tórrido
tor·so, n. torso
tor·tu·a, n. tortuga
tor·tu·ous, a. tortuoso
tor·ture, v. torturar; atormentar. n. tortura
toss, v. echar; agitarse. n. cogida; echada
tot, n. nene; nena
to·tal, a. total; entero. n. total, m.; suma. v. totalizar
to·tal·i·tar·i·an, a. totalitario
to·tal·ly, adv. totalmente
tote, v. inf. llevar
to·tem, n. tótem, m.
tot·ter, v. bambolearse
touch, v. tocar(se); palpar; conmover. n. toque; tacto
touch·y, a. irritable
tough, a. duro; resistente; difícil
tough·en, v. endurecer(se); hacer(se) correoso
tour, n. viaje; excursión. v. viajar por
tour·ism, n. turismo
tour·ist, n. turista, m., f.
tour·na·ment, n. torneo
tour·ni·quet, n. torniquete
tou·sle, v. despeinar
tow, v. llevar a remolque. n. remolque
to·ward, prep. hacia; cerca de; con respecto a. Also to·wards
tow·el, n. toalla
tow·er, n. torre, f.
town, n. ciudad; pueblo
tox·ic, a. tóxico
tox·in, n. toxina
toy, n. juguete. v. jugar (con)
trace, n. indicio; huella; rastro. v. seguir la pista de; trazar
tra·che·a, n. tráquea
track, n. vía; pista; senda. v. rastrear; seguir la pista de; manchar con huellas
tract, n. extensión; tratado
trac·tor, n. tractor
trade, n. comercio; negocio; profesión. v. comprar; vender; comerciar; trocar
trade·mark, n. marca de fábrica

marca registrada
trade un·ion, n. sindicato
tra·di·tion, n. tradición
tra·di·tion·al, a. tradicional
tra·duce, v. calumniar
traf·fic, n. tráfico; movimiento. v. traficar
trag·e·dy, n. pl., -dies. tragedia
trag·ic, a. trágico
trail, v. arrastrar(se); rastrear. n. pista; rastro; estela
trail·er, n. remolque
train, n. tren; hilo; serie, f.; comitiva. v. adiestrar; entrenar
trait, n. característica; rasgo
trai·tor, n. traidor
tra·jec·to·ry, n. pl., -ries. trayectoria
tramp, v. andar con pasos pesados. n. vagabundo
tram·ple, v. pisotear
trance, n. arrobamiento; estado hipnótico
tran·quil, a. tranquilo
tran·quil·li·ty, n. tranquilidad
tran·quil·ize, v. tranquilizar; aquietar
tran·quil·iz·er, n. tranquilizante
trans·act, v. despachar
trans·ac·tion, n. transacción; negocio
trans·scend, v. sobresalir; exceder
tran·scribe, v. transcribir
tran·script, n. trasunto
tran·scrip·tion, n. transcripción; copia
trans·fer, v. transferir; trasladar. n. transferencia; transbordo
trans·fer·ence, n. transferencia
trans·form, v. transformar
trans·for·ma·tion, n. transformación; metamorfosis, f.
trans·form·er, n. transformador
trans·fu·sion, n. transfusión
trans·gress, v. traspasar; pecar
trans·gres·sion, n. transgresión; pecado
tran·sient, a. transitorio; pasajero. n. transeúnte, m., f.
tran·sis·tor, n. transistor
trans·it, n. tránsito
tran·si·tion, n. transición
tran·si·tive, a. transitivo
tran·si·to·ry, a. transitorio; fugaz
trans·late, v. traducir
trans·la·tion, n. traducción; interpretación
trans·lu·cent, a. translúcido
trans·mis·sion, n. transmisión
trans·mit, v. transmitir
trans·mit·ter, n. transmisor
trans·om, n. travesaño
trans·par·ent, a. transparente; claro; obvio
tran·spire, v. transpirar; suceder; ocurrir
trans·plant, v. trasplantar
trans·port, v. transportar. n. transporte
trans·por·ta·tion, n. transportación; transporte
trans·pose, v. transponer; (mus.) transportar
trans·verse, a. transversal
trap, v. trampa. v. entrampar; atrapar
trap door, n. escotillón
tra·peze, n. trapecio
trap·e·zoid, n. trapezoide
trap·pings, n. pl. adornos; arreos
trash, n. hojarasca; basura
trau·ma, n. trauma, m.
trau·mat·ic, a. traumático
tra·vail, n. afán; dolores del parto
trav·el, v., -eled or -elled, -el·ing or -el·ling. viajar; recorrer. n. pl. viajes
trav·erse, v. atravesar; recorrer
trav·es·ty, n. pl., -ties. parodia
tray, n. bandeja; cubeta
treach·er·ous, a. traicionero; traidor; incierto
treach·er·y, n. traición
tread, v., trod, trod·den or trod, tread·ing. pisar; hollar. n. paso; huella
trea·son, n. traición
treas·ure, n. tesoro. v. atesorar; guardar
treas·ur·er, n. tesorero
treas·ur·y, n. pl., -ies. tesorería; tesoro
treat, v. tratar; curar; invitar. n. placer
trea·tise, n. tratado
treat·ment, n. tratamiento
trea·ty, n. pl., -ties. tratado; pacto
tre·ble, a. triple. n. (mus.) tiple, m., f. v. triplicar(se)
tree, n. árbol, m.
trek, v. caminar
trel·lis, n. enrejado; espaldera
trem·ble, v. temblar; estremecerse
tre·men·dous, a. inf. tremendo
trem·or, n. temblor
trench, n. foso; trinchera
trench·ant, a. mordaz
trend, n. dirección; tendencia. v. tender
tres·pass, v. infringir; pecar; entrar sin derecho
tress, n. trenza
tri·al, n. proceso; prueba; desgracia
tri·an·gle, n. triángulo
tri·an·gu·lar, a. triangular
tribe, n. tribu, f.
trib·u·la·tion, n. tribulación; aflicción
tri·bu·nal, n. tribunal, m.
trib·u·tar·y, n. pl., -ies. afluente. a.

tributario
trib·ute, n. homenaje; tributo
trick, n. truco; trampa; engaño; (cards.) baza. v. engañar
trick·le, v. gotear
tri·cy·cle, n. triciclo
tried, a. probado
tri·fle, n. bagatela. v. desperdiciar
tri·fling, a. sin importancia
trig·ger, n. gatillo
trig·o·nom·e·try, n. trigonometría
tril·lion, n. billón
trim, v. recortar; guarnecer. a. en buen estado
trin·ket, n. dije
tri·o, n. pl., -os. trío
trip, n. viaje; tropiezo; traspié; paso falso. v. tropezar; coger en falta
tri·ple, a. triple. v. triplicar(se)
trip·let, n. trillizo
trip·li·cate, v. triplicar. a. triplicado
tri·pod, n. trípode
trite, a. gastado
tri·umph, n. triunfar. n. triunfo
tri·um·phant, a. triunfante
triv·i·al, a. trivial; frívolo
triv·i·al·i·ty, n. pl., -ties. trivialidad
trol·ley, n. tranvía
trom·bone, n. trombón
troop, n. tropa; escuadrón
troop·er, n. soldado de caballería
tro·phy, n. pl., -phies. trofeo
trop·ic, n. trópico
trop·i·cal, a. tropical
trot, v. ir al trote; hacer trotar. n. trote
trou·ba·dour, n. trovador
trou·ble, v. molestar(se); inquietar(se); agitar. n. dificultad; pena; disturbio
trou·ble·some, a. molesto
trough, n. abrevadero
troupe, n. compañía
trou·sers, n. pl. pantalones
trous·seau, n. ajuar
trout, n. trucha
trow·el, n. paleta; desplantador
tru·ant, n. novillero
truce, n. tregua
truck, n. camión; carretilla. v. acarrear
true, a. fiel; verdadero; genuino
tru·ly, adv. verdaderamente; realmente
trump, n. triunfo. v. fallar
trum·pet, n. trompeta
trun·cate, v. truncar
trunk, n. tronco; baúl, m.; porta·equipaje(s); línea principal; trompa
truss, v. empaquetear
trust, n. confianza; obligación; fideicomiso. v. confiar en; esperar
trus·tee, n. fideicomisario
trust·wor·thy, a. fidedigno; confiable
trust·y, a. seguro
truth, n. verdad
truth·ful, a. veraz
try, v., tried, try·ing. intentar; probar; juzgar. n. tentativa
try·ing, a. difícil; penoso
tryst, n. cita
T-shirt, n. camiseta. Also tee shirt
tub, n. baño; tina
tu·ba, n. tuba
tube, n. tubo
tu·ber·cu·lo·sis, n. tuberculosis, f.
tuck, v. alforzar
Tues·day, n. martes, m.
tuft, n. copete
tug, v. tirar con fuerza; remolcar. n. tirón
tug·boat, n. remolcador
tu·i·tion, n. enseñanza
tu·lip, n. tulipán
tum·ble, v. voltear; caer(se). n. caída
tu·mor, n. tumor
tu·mult, n. tumulto
tu·mul·tu·ous, a. tumultuoso
tu·na, n. atún
tun·dra, n. tundra
tune, n. aire; afinación. v. afinar; sintonizar
tu·nic, n. túnica
tun·nel, n. túnel, m.
tur·ban, n. turbante
tur·bid, a. túrbido
tur·bine, n. turbina
tur·bu·lence, n. turbulencia; confusión
tur·bu·lent, a. turbulento
tu·reen, n. sopera
turf, n. césped
tur·key, n. pl., -keys. pavo
tur·moil, n. alboroto; tumulto
turn, v. girar; dar vueltas a; volver(se); convertirse. n. vuelta; turno. in turn, por turnos. turn down, doblar; rechazar. turn out, apagar; producir
turn·coat, n. traidor
tur·nip, n. nabo
turn·out, n. concurrencia; producción
turn·pike, n. autopista de peaje
turn·stile, n. torniquete
tur·pen·tine, n. trementina
tur·quoise, n. turquesa
tur·ret, n. torrecilla
tur·tle, n. tortuga
tusk, n. colmillo
tus·sle, n. agarrada
tu·te·lage, n. tutela
tu·tor, n. preceptor, tutor. v. enseñar
tux·e·do, n. pl., -dos. smoking, m.
TV, n. pl., TVs, TV's. televisión
twang, n. tañido; timbre nasal

tweed, n. mezcla de lana
tweez·ers, n. pl. bruselas
twelfth, a. duodécimo
twelve, n. doce. a. doce
twen·ty, n. veinte. a. veinte
twice, adv. dos veces
twig, n. ramita
twi·light, n. crepúsculo
twill, n. tela cruzada
twin, n. gemelo. a. gemelo
twine, n. guita; bramante. v. enroscarse
twinge, n. dolor agudo
twin·kle, v. centellear. n. centelleo
twirl, v. girar; piruetear. n. giro
twist, v. enroscar(se); torcer(se); retorcer(se). n. torsión
twitch, v. crisparse. n. contracción nerviosa
twit·ter, v. gorjear. n. gorjeo
two, n. dos. a. dos
two-faced, a. falso; hipócrita
ty·coon, n. (fin.) magnate
type, n. tipo; género. v. escribir a máquina
type·write, v., -wrote, -writ·ten, -writ·ing. escribir a máquina. Also type
type·writ·er, n. máquina de escribir
ty·phoid, n. fiebre tifoidea. Also ty·phoid fe·ver
ty·phoon, n. tifón
ty·phus, n. tifus, m.
typ·i·cal, a. típico; característico
typ·i·fy, v. simbolizar
typ·ist, n. mecanógrafo
ty·pog·ra·phy, n. tipografía
ty·ran·ni·cal, a. tiránico; despótico
tyr·an·nize, v. tiranizar
tyr·an·ny, n. tiranía
ty·rant, n. tirano
ty·ro, n. novicio

U

u·biq·ui·tous, a. ubicuo. Also u·biq·ui·tar·y
u·biq·ui·ty, n. ubicuidad; omni·presencia
ud·der, n. ubre, f.
ug·ly, a. feo; repugnante
ul·cer, n. úlcera
ul·te·ri·or, a. ulterior
ul·ti·mate, a. último; fundamental
ul·ti·ma·tum, n. pl., -tums, -ta. ul·timátum, m.
ul·tra, a. ultra
ul·tra·son·ic, a. ultrasónico
ul·tra·vi·o·let, a. ultravioleta
um·bil·i·cal, a. umbilical
um·brage, n. resentimiento
um·brel·la, n. paraguas, m.
um·laut, n. diéresis, f.
um·pire, n. árbitro
ump·teen, a. inf. muchos
un·a·bashed, a. desvergonzado; descarado
un·a·ble, a. incapaz
un·a·bridged, a. íntegro
un·ac·count·a·ble, a. inexplicable
un·ac·cus·tomed, a. desacostumbrado
un·af·fect·ed, a. sin afectación; sincero
un·af·fect·ed·ly, adv. sin afectación
u·nan·i·mous, a. unánime
un·ap·proach·a·ble, a. inabordable
un·armed, a. desarmado
un·as·sum·ing, a. modesto; sencillo; sin pretensión
un·at·tached, a. soltero; suelto; no embargado
un·a·void·a·ble, a. inevitable
un·a·wares, adv. de improviso
un·bal·anced, a. desequilibrado
un·be·com·ing, a. que sienta mal; indecoroso
un·be·liev·a·ble, a. increíble
un·be·liev·er, n. escéptico; descreído
un·bend, v., -bent or -bend·ed, -bend·ing. desencorvar; aflojar
un·bend·ing, a. inflexible
un·bi·ased, a. imparcial
un·blem·ished, a. sin tacha; puro
un·born, a. no nacido
un·bos·om, v. revelar
un·break·a·ble, a. irrompible
un·bri·dled, a. desenfrenado; ingobernable
un·called-for, a. inmerecido
un·ceas·ing, a. incesante
un·cer·e·mo·ni·ous, a. informal; descortés
un·cer·tain, a. incierto; indeciso
un·char·i·ta·ble, a. implacable; duro
un·cle, n. tío
un·clean, a. sucio
un·com·fort·a·ble, a. incómodo
un·com·mon, a. poco común; extraordinario
un·com·mu·ni·ca·tive, a. poco comunicativo
un·com·pro·mis·ing, a. inflexible; intransigente
un·con·cern, n. indiferencia
un·con·cerned, a. despreocupado
un·con·di·tion·al, a. incondicional
un·con·scion·a·ble, a. desrazonable; sin conciencia
un·con·scious, a. sin sentido; inconsciente
un·con·sti·tu·tion·al, a. inconstitucional
un·con·strained, a. voluntario
un·con·trol·la·ble, a. ingobernable
un·con·ven·tion·al, a. no convencional; original
un·couth, a. grosero; rudo
un·cov·er, v. descubrir; destapar

unc·tion, n. unción
unc·tu·ous, a. zalamero
un·de·cid·ed, a. indeciso
un·de·ni·a·ble, a. innegable
un·de·pend·a·ble, a. poco confiable
un·der, prep. debajo de; bajo. adv. debajo. a. inferior
un·der·brush, n. maleza
un·der·class·man, n. pl., -men. estudiante de primer o segundo año
un·der·clothes, n. pl. ropa interior
un·der·cov·er, a. secreto
un·der·cur·rent, n. corriente submarina
un·der·es·ti·mate, v. subestimar
un·der·go, v., -went -gone, -go·ing. sufrir
un·der·ground, adv. bajo tierra. a. subterráneo
un·der·hand·ed, a. secreto
un·der·line, v. subrayar
un·der·ling, n. subordinado
un·der·ly·ing, a. fundamental
un·der·mine, v. socavar
un·der·neath, prep. bajo. adv. debajo
un·der·priv·i·leged, a. desamparado
un·der·rate, v. menospreciar
un·der·score, v. subrayar
un·der·side, n. cara inferior
un·der·stand, v., -stood, -stand·ing. comprender; entender
un·der·stand·ing, n. entendimiento; acuerdo
un·der·stud·y, n. pl., -ies. sobresaliente, m., f.
un·der·take, v., -took, -tak·en, -tak·ing. emprender
un·der·tak·er, n. director de pompas fúnebres
un·der·tak·ing, n. empresa
un·der·wear, n. ropa interior
un·do, v., -did, -done, -do·ing. deshacer; anular; desatar
un·dress, v. desnudar(se)
un·due, a. excesivo
un·du·ly, adv. indebidamente
un·earth, v. desenterrar; descubrir
un·eas·y, a. incómodo; intranquilo
un·em·ployed, a. sin empleo; sin trabajo
un·e·ven, a. desigual
un·ex·pect·ed, a. imprevisto
un·faith·ful, a. infiel
un·fa·mil·iar, a. poco familiar
un·fin·ished, a. incompleto
un·flinch·ing, a. resuelto
un·fold, v. abrir; desplegar; extender; revelar
un·for·get·ta·ble, a. inolvidable
un·for·tu·nate, a. desgraciado; infeliz. n. desgraciado
un·furl, v. desplegar
un·gain·ly, a. desgarbado
un·guent, n. ungüento
un·hand, v. soltar
un·hap·pi·ness, n. desdicha; infelicidad
un·hap·py, a. desdichado; infeliz
un·health·y, a. enfermizo; insalubre
un·heard-of, a. inaudito
un·hurt, a. ileso
u·ni·corn, n. unicornio
u·ni·fi·ca·tion, n. unificación
u·ni·form, a. uniforme; constante. n. uniforme
u·ni·form·i·ty, n. pl., -ties. uniformidad
u·ni·fy, v. unificar
u·ni·lat·er·al, a. unilateral
un·in·ter·est·ed, a. desinteresado
un·ion, n. unión; junta; sindicato
un·ion·ize, v. agremiar(se)
u·nique, a. único; sin igual
u·ni·son, n. unisonancia. in u·ni·son, al unísono
u·nit, n. unidad
u·nite, v. unir(se); aliarse
u·nit·ed, a. unido
u·ni·ty, n. pl., -ties. unidad; unión
u·ni·ver·sal, a. universal
u·ni·ver·sal·ize, v. universalizar
u·ni·verse, n. universo
u·ni·ver·si·ty, n. pl., -ties. universidad
un·just, a. injusto
un·kempt, a. despeinado
un·known, a. desconocido
un·law·ful, a. ilegal
un·less, conj. a menos que. prep. excepto
un·like, a. distinto. prep. a diferencia de
un·like·ly, a. improbable
un·lim·it·ed, a. ilimitado
un·load, v. descargar
un·looked-for, a. imprevisto; inopinado
un·luck·y, a. desgraciado; desdichado
un·mask, v. desenmascarar
un·mer·ci·ful, a. despiadado
un·mis·tak·a·ble, a. inequívoco
un·mit·i·gat·ed, a. no mitigado
un·nat·u·ral, a. anormal; cruel; afectado
un·nec·es·sar·y, a. innecesario
un·num·bered, a. innumerable
un·pack, v. desempaquetar; deshacer
un·par·al·leled, a. sin par
un·pleas·ant, a. desagradable; molesto
un·pop·u·lar, a. impopular
un·prec·e·dent·ed, a. sin precedente
un·prin·ci·pled, a. sin principios
un·ques·tion·a·ble, a. incuestionable; indudable
un·ques·tioned, a. incontestable; indisputable
un·rav·el, v. desenredar(se); des-

marañar(se)
un·re·al, a. imaginario
un·rea·son·a·ble, a. irrazonable; inmoderado
un·re·lent·ing, a. inexorable
un·rest, n. desasosiego; inquietud
un·roll, v. desenrollar
un·ru·ly, a. ingobernable
un·sa·vor·y, a. desagradable
un·scathed, a. sano y salvo; ileso
un·scru·pu·lous, a. sin conciencia; sin escrúpulos
un·seem·ly, a. indecente; indecoroso
un·set·tle, v. descomponer; agitar
un·sight·ly, a. repulsivo; feo
un·skilled, a. inexperto
un·snarl, v. desenredar
un·so·phis·ti·cat·ed, a. ingenuo; cándido
un·sound, a. falso; defectuoso
un·sta·ble, a. inestable
un·stead·y, a. poco firme; inseguro
un·sung, a. celebrado
un·think·a·ble, a. inconcebible
un·think·ing, a. irreflexivo; desatento
un·til, conj. hasta que. prep. hasta
un·time·ly, a. inoportuno; intempestivo
un·to, prep. archaic. a
un·told, a. incalculable
un·truth, n. falsedad
un·truth·ful, a. mentiroso
un·u·su·al, a. poco común; raro
un·var·nished, a. sin adornos
un·veil, v. descubrir
un·war·y, a. incauto
un·whole·some, a. insalubre
un·will·ing, a. desinclinado; de mala gana
un·wit·ting, a. inconsciente
un·wor·thy, a. indigno
un·wrap, v. deshacer; desempapelar; desenvolver
un·yield·ing, a. inflexible; terco
up, adv. arriba; hacia arriba; acabado. a. ascendente; en pie. prep. en lo alto de; subiendo
up·braid, v. reprender
up·bring·ing, n. crianza
up·date, v. modernizar; poner al día
up·heav·al, n. cataclismo
up·hill, adv. cuesta arriba. a. ascendente; penoso
up·hold, v., -held, -hold·ing, sostener; defender
up·hol·ster, v. entapizar; tapizar
up·hol·ster·y, n. pl., -ies. tapicería
up·keep, n. manutención
up·on, prep. encima de; sobre
up·per, a. superior; alto. n. pala de zapato
up·per·most, a. (el) más alto. adv. principal; primero
up·pish, a. arrogante; engreído
up·raise, v. inf. levantar
up·right, a. vertical; recto; derecho
up·ris·ing, n. insurrección; sublevación
up·roar, n. alboroto
up·roar·i·ous, a. tumultuoso
up·root, v. desarraigar
up·set, v., -set, -set·ting. volcar; trastornar. n. contratiempo; trastorno. a. perturbado
up·shot, n. resultado
up·side down, adv. de arriba abajo; al revés
up·stairs, a. en pl. usu. sing. in constr. piso superior
up·stand·ing, a. honrado
up·to·date, a. moderno
up·turn, v. volver hacia arriba
up·ward, adv. hacia arriba. Also up·wards
u·ra·ni·um, n. uranio
U·ra·nus, n. Urano
ur·ban, a. urbano
ur·bane, a. urbano; fino
ur·chin, n. pilluelo
urge, v. impeler; instar; incitar. n. impulso
ur·gen·cy, n. pl., -cies. urgencia
ur·gent, a. urgente; apremiante
u·ri·nate, v. orinar(se)
u·rine, n. orina
urn, n. urna
us, pron. nos; nosotros, nosotras
us·a·ble, use·a·ble, a. utilizable
us·age, n. uso; usanza; costumbre, f.
use, v. usar; emplear; utilizar. n. uso; empleo. be of no use, no servir para nada. use up, agotar
used, a. usado
use·ful, a. útil
use·ful·ness, n. utilidad; provecho
use·less, a. inútil; inservible
ush·er, n. acomodador. v. acomodar
u·su·al, a. usual; habitual
u·su·al·ly, adv. por lo general; usualmente
u·surp, v. usurpar
u·su·ry, n. pl., -ries. usura
u·ten·sil, n. utensilio
u·ter·us, n. pl., u·ter·i. útero
u·ti·lize, v. utilizar; aprovechar
ut·most, a. sumo; mayor; más lejano. n. grado supremo
u·to·pi·a, n. utopía, utopia
ut·ter, a. absoluto; total. v. pronunciar
ut·ter·ance, n. pronunciación

V

va·can·cy, n. pl., -cies. vacante, f.
va·cant, a. vacío; libre; vago
va·cate, v. dejar vacante

va·ca·tion, n. vacación; vacaciones
vac·ci·nate, v. vacunar
vac·ci·na·tion, n. vacunación
vac·cine, n. vacuna
vac·il·late, v. vacilar
vac·il·la·tion, n. vacilación; fluctuación
va·cu·i·ty, n. pl., -ties. vacuidad
vac·u·ous, a. mentecato; necio
vac·u·um, n. pl., -ums. vacío. v. limpiar con un aspirador de polvo
vag·a·bond, a. vagabundo. n. vagabundo
va·gar·y, n. pl., -ies. capricho
va·gran·cy, n. vagancia
va·grant, n. vagabundo
vague, a. vago; indistinto; incierto
vain, a. vanidoso; vano. in vain, en vano
vale, n. valle
val·e·dic·to·ry, n. pl., -ries. discurso de despedida
val·en·tine, n. novia o novio en el día de San Valentín
val·id, a. válido; valedero
val·i·date, v. validar
va·lid·i·ty, n. pl., -ties. validez, f.
va·lise, n. maleta
val·ley, n. pl., -leys. valle; arroyada
val·or, n. valor; valentía
val·u·a·ble, a. valioso; costoso; precioso; n. usu. pl. objetos de valor
val·u·a·tion, n. valuación; tasación
val·ue, n. valor; precio; importancia; estimación. v. valorar; valuar; apreciar
val·ued, a. estimado
valve, n. válvula
vam·pire, n. vampiro
van, n. vanguardia; camión de mudanzas
van·dal, n. vándalo
van·dal·ism, n. vandalismo
vane, n. veleta
van·guard, n. vanguardia
va·nil·la, n. vainilla
van·ish, v. desvanecerse; desaparecer
van·i·ty, n. pl., -ties. vanidad
van·quish, v. vencer; conquistar
van·tage, n. ventaja; provecho
vap·id, a. insípido
va·por, n. vapor
va·por·ize, v. vaporizar(se)
va·por·ous, a. vaporoso
var·i·a·bil·i·ty, var·i·a·ble·ness, n. variabilidad
var·i·a·ble, a. variable; vario. n. variable
var·i·ance, n. variación; desacuerdo
var·i·ant, a. variante; diferente. n. variante, f.
var·i·a·tion, n. variación
var·i·cose, a. varicoso
var·ied, a. variado; diverso
var·i·e·gat·ed, a. abigarrado
va·ri·e·ty, n. pl., -ties. variedad
var·i·ous, a. vario; variado; diverso
var·nish, n. barniz, m. v. barnizar; paliar
var·si·ty, n. pl., -ties. equipo principal de una universidad
var·y, v. variar; desviarse; cambiar
vase, n. jarrón; florero
vas·sal, n. vasallo
vast, a. vasto; inmenso
vat, n. tina; cuba; depósito
vault, v. saltar. n. bóveda; sepultura; cámara acorazada
veal, n. ternera
vec·tor, n. vector; radio vector
veer, v. virar
veg·e·ta·ble, n. legumbre, f.; vegetal, m.
veg·e·tar·i·an, n. vegetariano
veg·e·tate, v. vegetar
veg·e·ta·tion, n. vegetación
ve·he·mence, ve·he·men·cy, n. vehemencia
ve·he·ment, a. vehemente; apasionado
ve·hi·cle, n. vehículo; medio
veil, n. velo
veined, a. veteado
vel·lum, n. vitela
ve·loc·i·ty, n. pl., -ties. velocidad
vel·ours, vel·our, n. pl., -lours. velludillo
vel·vet, n. terciopelo
vel·vet·y, a. aterciopelado
ve·nal, a. venal
ve·nal·i·ty, n. venalidad
vend, v. vender
ven·det·ta, n. odio de sangre
ven·di·ble, a. vendible. n. usu. pl. artículo de comercio
ve·neer, n. chapa
ven·er·a·ble, a. venerable
ven·er·ate, v. venerar
ven·er·a·tion, n. veneración
ve·ne·re·al, a. venéreo
ven·geance, n. venganza; retribución
ve·ni·al, a. venial
ven·i·son, n. carne de venado
ven·om, n. veneno; rencor; virulencia
ven·om·ous, a. venenoso
vent, n. salida; orificio. v. descargar
ven·ti·late, v. ventilar
ven·ti·la·tion, n. ventilación
ven·tral, a. ventral
ven·tri·cle, n. ventrículo
ven·tril·o·quism, n. ventriloquia
ven·tril·o·quist, n. ventrílocuo
ven·ture, n. empresa arriesgada. v. aventurar(se)
ven·ture·some, a. aventurero; arriesgado

Ve·nus, n. Venus, m., f.
ve·ra·cious, a. veraz
ve·rac·i·ty, n. veracidad
ve·ran·da, ve·ran·dah, n. galería
verb, n. verbo
ver·bal, a. verbal
ver·ba·tim, adv. palabra por palabra
ver·bi·age, n. verbosidad; palabrería
ver·bose, a. verboso
ver·bos·i·ty, n. verbosidad
ver·dant, a. verde
ver·dict, n. veredicto; juicio; fallo
verge, n. borde
ver·i·fi·ca·tion, n. verificación
ver·i·fy, v. verificar; comprobar
ver·i·si·mil·i·tude, n. verosimilitud
ver·i·ta·ble, a. verdadero; real
ver·i·ty, n. pl., -ties. verdad
ver·mil·ion, ver·mil·lion, n. bermellón. a. bermejo
ver·min, n. pl., ver·min. sabandijas
ver·mouth, n. vermut, m.
ver·nac·u·lar, a. vernáculo. n. lengua vulgar
ver·nal, a. vernal
ver·sa·tile, a. adaptable; polifacético
ver·sa·til·i·ty, n. adaptabilidad
verse, n. verso; versículo
ver·si·fy, v. versificar
ver·sion, n. versión
ver·sus, prep. contra
ver·te·bra, n. pl., -brae. vértebra
ver·te·brate, a. vertebrado
ver·tex, n. pl., -tex·es, -ti·ces. ápice; vértice
ver·ti·cal, a. vertical. n. vertical
ver·ti·go, n. pl., -ti·goes, -tig·i·nes. vértigo
verve, n. brío; vigor
ver·y, adv. muy; sumamente. a. mismo; mero
ves·pers, n. vísperas
ves·sel, n. embarcación; vasija; vaso
vest, n. chaleco
ves·ti·bule, n. vestíbulo
ves·tige, n. vestigio; rastro
ves·try, n. pl., -tries. sacristía
vet, n. inf. veterinario
vet·er·an, n. veterano. a. veterano
vet·er·i·nar·i·an, n. veterinario
vet·er·i·nar·y, n., pl., -ies. veterinario. a. veterinario
ve·to, n. veto. v. vetar
vex, v. molestar; enojar; vejar; irritar
vex·a·tion, n. contrariedad; molestia
vi·a, prep. por
vi·a·duct, n. viaducto
vi·al, n. frasco pequeño
vi·brant, a. vibrante
vi·brate, v. vibrar; oscilar
vi·bra·tion, n. vibración
vic·ar, n. vicario
vi·car·i·ous, a. substituto
vice, n. vicio
vice·pres·i·dent, n. vicepresidente
vice·roy, n. virrey, m.
vice ver·sa, adv. viceversa
vi·cin·i·ty, n. pl., -ties. vecindad; proximidad
vi·cious, a. depravado; vicioso; cruel
vic·tim, n. víctima
vic·tim·ize, v. hacer víctima; estafar
vic·tor, n. vencedor
vic·to·ri·ous, a. victorioso
vic·to·ry, n. pl., -ries. victoria; triunfo
vict·ual, n. usu. pl víveres, m. pl.
vie, v., vied, vy·ing. competir
view, n. vista; escena; panorama, m.; propuesta; opinión. v. ver; contemplar
view·point, n. punto de vista
vig·il, n. vigilia
vig·i·lance, n. vigilancia
vig·i·lant, a. vigilante; alerta
vi·gnette, n. viñeta
vig·or, n. vigor
vig·or·ous, a. vigoroso
vile, a. vil; despreciable; horrible
vil·la, n. casa de campo
vil·lage, n. aldea
vil·lain, n. malvado
vil·lain·y, n. pl., -ies. maldad
vim, n. vigor
vin·di·cate, v. vindicar
vin·dic·tive, a. vengativo
vine, n. vid, f.
vin·e·gar, n. vinagre
vine·yard, n. viña
vin·tage, n. vendimia. a. antiguo; clásico
vi·ol, n. viola
vi·o·la, n. viola
vi·o·late, v. violar; forzar
vi·o·la·tion, n. violación
vi·o·lence, n. violencia
vi·o·lent, a. violento; intenso; vehemente
vi·o·let, n. violeta. a. violado
vi·o·lin, n. violín
vi·o·lon·cel·lo, n. violonchelo, violoncelo
vi·per, n. víbora
vi·ra·go, n. pl., -goes, -gos. fiera
vir·gin, n. virgen. a. virgen
vir·gin·i·ty, n. virginidad
vir·ile, a. viril
vi·ril·i·ty, n. virilidad
vir·tu·al, a. virtual
vir·tu·al·ly, adv. virtualmente
vir·tue, n. virtud, f.
vir·tu·os·i·ty, n. pl., -ties. virtuosismo
vir·tu·o·so, n. pl., -sos, -si. virtuoso
vir·tu·ous, a. virtuoso
vir·u·lent, a. virulento
vi·rus, n. pl., -rus·es. virus, m.
vi·sa, n. visado

vis·cos·i·ty, n. viscosidad
vis·count, n. vizconde
vis·count·ess, n. vizcondesa
vise, n. tornillo
vis·i·bil·i·ty, n. visibilidad
vis·i·ble, a. visible; conspicuo
vi·sion, n. visión; vista
vi·sion·ar·y, n. pl., -ies. visionario. a. visionario
vis·it, v. visitar; ir a ver. n. visita
vis·it·a·tion, n. visitación
vi·sor, n. visera
vis·u·al, a. visual
vis·u·al·ize, v. representarse la mente
vi·tal, a. vital; de suma importancia
vi·tal·i·ty, n. pl., -ties. vitalidad; brío
vi·ta·min, n. vitamina
vit·re·ous, a. vítreo
vit·ri·ol, n. vitriolo
vi·tu·per·ate, v. vituperar
vi·va·cious, a. vivaz; animado; vivaroyo
vi·vac·i·ty, n. pl., -ties. vivacidad; animación
viv·id, a. vivo; intenso; gráfico
vix·en, n. arpía; zorra
vo·cab·u·lar·y, n. pl., -ies. vocabulario
vo·cal, a. vocal; de la voz
vo·cal·ist, n. cantante, m., f.
vo·cal·ize, v. vocalizar
vo·ca·tion, n. vocación; profesión
vod·ka, n. vodka
vogue, n. moda; boga
voice, n. voz, f. v. expresar
void, a. nulo; vacío. v. vaciar; invalidar. n. vacío
vol·a·tile, a. volátil
vol·can·ic, a. volcánico
vol·ca·no, n. pl., -noes, -nos. volcán
vo·li·tion, n. voluntad; volición
vol·ley, n. pl., -leys. descarga; voleo. v. volear
volt, n. voltio
volt·age, n. voltaje
vol·u·ble, a. hablador
vol·ume, n. volumen; tomo; cantidad; volumen sonoro
vo·lu·mi·nous, a. voluminoso; extenso
vol·un·tar·y, a. voluntario
vol·un·teer, n. voluntario. v. ofrecerse a
vo·lup·tu·ar·y, n. pl., -ies. voluptuoso
vo·lup·tu·ous, a. voluptuoso
vom·it, v. vomitar. n. vómito
vo·ra·cious, a. voraz
vor·tex, n. pl., -tex·es, -ti·ces. vórtice
vote, n. voto; votación; sufragio. v. votar
vot·er, n. votante, m., f.
vouch, v. confirmar; garantizar
vouch·er, n. comprobante
vow, n. promesa solemne; voto. v. jurar
vow·el, n. vocal, f.
voy·age, n. travesía; viaje. v. viajar
vul·can·ize, v. vulcanizar
vul·gar, a. vulgar; grosero
vul·gar·i·ty, n. pl., -ties. grosería; cursilería
vul·gar·ize, v. vulgarizar
vul·ner·a·bil·i·ty, n. vulnerabilidad
vul·ner·a·ble, a. vulnerable
vul·ture, n. buitre
vul·va, n. pl., -vae, -vas. vulva

W

wack·y, a. inf. loco; chiflado
wad, n. fajo; taco; rollo; bolita
wad·dle, v. anadear
wade, v. vadear; pasar con dificultad
wag, v. menear(se)
wage, n. often pl. salario; jornal, m. pl., sing. or pl in constr. salario. v. hacer
wa·ger, n. apuesta. v. apostar
wag·on, n. carro
waif, n. niño abandonado
wail, v. lamentarse; sollozar. n. gemido
waist, n. cintura
waist·coat, n. chiefly Brit. chaleco
waist·line, n. talle
wait, v. esperar; estar listo; servir. n. espera
wait·er, n. camarero
wait·ress, n. fem. camarera
waive, v. renunciar a; abandonar
waiv·er, n. renuncia
wake, v., waked or woke, waked, wak·ing. despertar(se). n. vela; estela
wake·ful, a. vigilante
wak·en, v. despertar(se)
walk, v. andar; caminar; ir a pie. n. paseo; caminata
walk·out, n. huelga
walk·o·ver, n. inf. triunfo fácil
wall, n. pared, f.; muro; muralla. v. emparedar
wall·board, n. cartón de yeso
wal·let, n. cartera
wal·lop, v. inf. zurrar. n. inf. golpazo
wal·low, v. revolcarse
wall·pa·per, n. papel pintado
wal·nut, n. nogal, m.
wal·rus, n. pl., -rus·es, -rus. morsa
waltz, n. vals, m. v. valsar
wan, a. pálido
wan·der, v. vagar; errar; desviarse
wan·der·lust, n. deseo de viajar
wane, v. disminuir; menguar
want, v. requerir; necesitar; desear;

querer. n. falta; carencia
want·ing, a. deficiente. prep. sin
wan·ton, a. lascivo; desenfrenado; inconsiderado
war, n. guerra. v. guerrear; hacer la guerra
war·ble, v. trinar. n. trino; gorjeo
war·bler, n. grito de guerra
ward, v. desviar. n. pupilo; distrito electoral; crujía
war·den, n. guardián; alcaide
ward·robe, n. guardarropa; vestuario
ware, n. usu. pl. mercancías
ware·house, n. almacén
war·fare, n. guerra
war·lock, n. hechicero
warm, a. caliente, cálido; caluroso. v. calentar(se)
warm·heart·ed, warm·heart·ed, a. afectuoso
war·mon·ger, n. belicista, m., f.
warmth, n. calor; entusiasmo
warn, v. advertir; avisar
warn·ing, n. advertencia; aviso; admonición
warp, v. alabearse; pervertir. n. comba
war·rant, n. autorización; garantía; orden; cédula. v. justificar
war·ran·ty, n. pl., -ties. garantía
war·ren, n. conejera
war·ri·or, n. guerrero
wart, n. verruga
war·y, a. cauteloso
was, pret. of be
wash, v. lavar(se); fregar. n. lavado; estela
wash·cloth, n. paño para lavarse
wash·er, n. lavadora; arandela
wash·ing, n. lavado
wash·out, n. derrumbe de aluvión; fracaso
wash·room, n. lavabo
wash·stand, n. lavamanos
wash·tub, n. tina o cuba de lavar
wasp, n. avispa
wast·age, n. desgaste; merma
waste, v. malgastar; desperdiciar. n. desgaste; pérdida; yermo; pl. excremento. a. sobrante
wast·rel, n. derrochador
watch, v. vigilar; guardar; observar; mirar. n. vigilia; reloj, m.
watch·ful, a. vigilante; desvelado
watch·man, n. pl., -men. vigilante
watch·word, n. santo y seña
wa·ter, n. agua. v. regar; aguar
wa·ter·col·or, n. acuarela
wa·ter·course, n. corriente, f.; lecho
wa·ter·fall, n. cascada
wa·ter·fowl, n. pl., -fowls, -fowl. ave acuática
wa·ter·front, n. terreno ribereño
wa·ter lil·y, n. pl. lil·ies. nenúfar
wa·ter·logged, a. anegado
wa·ter·mark, n. nivel de agua; filigrana
wa·ter·mel·on, n. sandía
wa·ter·proof, a. impermeable. n. impermeable
wa·ter·side, n. orilla del agua
wa·ter soft·en·er, n. ablandador químico de agua
wa·ter·spout, n. tromba marina; manga
wa·ter·tight, a. estanco; seguro
wa·ter·way, n. canal, m.
wa·ter·y, a. acuoso; insípido
watt, n. vatio
wave, n. ola; onda; ondulación. v. ondear; ondular; hacer ademanes
wa·ver, v. oscilar; vacilar
wav·y, a. ondulado
wax, n., pl. wax·es. cera. v. encerar; aumentarse; crecer
wax·en, a. de cera; pálido
wax·work, n. figura de cera
way, n. modo; manera; dirección; distancia; vía; camino; método. under way, en marcha
way·far·er, n. viajero
way·lay, v., -laid, -lay·ing. acechar; asaltar
way·side, n. borde del camino
way·ward, a. voluntarioso; travieso
we, pron. nosotros; nosotras
weak, a. débil; flojo; ineficaz
weak·en, v. debilitar(se)
weak·ling, n. alfeñique
weak·ly, a. achacoso. adv. débilmente
weak·mind·ed, a. sin voluntad; irresoluto
weak·ness, n. debilidad
wealth, n. riqueza
wealth·y, a. rico
wean, v. destetar
weap·on, n. arma
weap·on·ry, n. armas, f. pl.
wear, v., wore, worn, wear·ing. llevar; usar(se); desgastar(se). n. ropa; desgaste; uso
wear·ing, a. penoso
wear·i·some, a. fastidioso
wea·ry, a. fatigado; aburrido
wea·sel, n. pl., -sels, -sel. comadreja
weath·er, n. tiempo. v. desgastar(se); aguantar
weath·er·beat·en, a. curtido por la intemperie
weath·er·glass, n. barómetro
weath·er·man, n. pl., -men. pronosticador del tiempo
weave, v., wove or weaved, wov·en or wove, weav·ing. tejer. n. tejido
web, n. tela; membrana
web·bing, n. cincha
wed, v., wed·ded or wed, wed·ding.

wed·ding, n. boda
wedge, n. cuña. v. acuñar
wed·lock, n. matrimonio
Wednes·day, n. miércoles, m.
wee, a. pequeñito
weed, n. mala hierba. v. escardar
week, n. semana
week·day, n. día laborable o de trabajo
week·end, n. fin de semana
week·ly, a. semanal. adv. cada semana
weep, v., wept, weep·ing. llorar
wee·vil, n. gorgojo
weigh, v. pesar
weight, n. peso; pesa. v. cargar
weight·y, a. pesado; importante
weird, a. fantástico; extraño
wel·come, a. bienvenido; agradable. n. bienvenida. v. acoger
weld, v. soldar
wel·fare, n. bienestar
well, n. pozo; fuente, f. adv., bet·ter, best. bien; pues. a. bien de salud. int. vaya; pues
well·be·ing, n. bienestar
well·bred, a. bien criado
well·dis·posed, a. bien dispuesto
well·known, a. conocido; famoso
well·off, a. adinerado
well·read, a. leído
well·thought·of, a. bien mirado
well·timed, a. oportuno
well·to·do, a. acaudalado
welt, n. verdugón
wel·ter, v. revolcar(se). n. conmoción
wench, n. moza
were, pret. of be
were·wolf, wer·wolf, n. pl., -wolves. hombre que puede transformarse en lobo
west, n. oeste; occidente. a. del oeste. adv. al oeste
west·ern, a. occidental. n. película del oeste
west·ward, adv. hacia el oeste. Also west·wards
wet, a. mojado; húmedo; lluvioso. v., wet or wet·ted. mojar(se)
whack, v. inf. golpear. n. golpe ruidoso
whale, n. ballena
whale·bone, n. ballena
wharf, n. pl., wharves, wharfs. muelle
what, pron. pl., what. lo que; qué. a. que; qué; cuál. int. qué. what if, y si
what·ev·er, pron. todo lo que. a. cualquier
what·not, n. estante; juguetero
wheat, n. trigo
whee·dle, v. engatusar; halagar
wheel, n. rueda. v. dar una vuelta
wheel·bar·row, n. carretilla
wheel·chair, n. silla de ruedas
wheeze, v. respirar asmáticamente; resollar
when, adv. cuándo. conj. cuando
whence, adv. de dónde; de qué
when·ev·er, adv. siempre que; todas las veces que
where, adv. dónde; adónde. conj. donde
where·a·bouts, n. pl., sing. or pl in constr. paradero
where·as, conj. mientras que; visto que
where·up·on, adv. con lo cual
wher·ev·er, adv. dondequiera que
where·with·al, n. medios
whet, v. afilar; estimular
wheth·er, conj. si
whey, n. suero de la leche
which, pron. cuál; que; el, la, lo que; el, la, lo cual. a. cuál; qué
which·ev·er, a. cualquier. pron. cualquiera
whiff, n. olorcillo
while, n. rato. conj. mientras (que). v. pasar; entretener
whim, n. capricho; antojo
whim·per, v. lloriquear
whim·si·cal, a. caprichoso
whine, v. gimotear. n. quejido
whin·ny, n. pl., -nies. relincho. v. relinchar
whip, v. whipped or whipt, whip·ping. azotar; batir. n. azote; látigo
whir, whirr, v., whirred, whir·ring. zumbar; batir
whirl, v. girar rápidamente
whirl·pool, n. remolino
whirl·wind, n. torbellino
whisk·ers, n. pl. barbas; bigotes
whis·key, whis·ky, n. pl., -keys, -kies. whisky, m.
whis·per, v. cuchichear. n. cuchicheo; susurro
whis·tle, v. silbar. n. silbido; pito
white, a. blanco. n. blanco; clara de un huevo
white·col·lar, a. oficinesco
whit·en, v. blanquear
white·wash, n. jalbegue. v. enjalbegar; inf. encubrir
whith·er, adv. adónde. conj. adonde
whit·tle, v. cortar poco a poco
whiz, whizz, v. silbar; zumbar. n. whizzing, whiz·zing. silbar; rehilar. n. pl., -zes. silbido
who, pron. quien; quién; que; el, la, lo que
who·ev·er, pron. quienquiera que
whole, a. entero; todo. n. todo; totalidad
whole·heart·ed, a. sincero; incondicional

whole·sale, n. venta al por menor. a. al por mayor. adv. en masa
whole·some, a. saludable
whol·ly, adv. completamente
whom, pron. a quién; a quien; que
whom·ev·er, pron. a quienquiera
whoop, n. alarido. v. gritar
whore, n. puta; prostituta
whose, pron. de quién; cuyo
why, adv. por qué. n. pl., **whys.** causa; porqué
wick, n. mecha
wick·ed, a. malo; malicioso; inicuo
wick·er, a. de mimbre
wide, a. ancho; amplio; extenso. adv. lejos
wide·a·wake, a. despabilado
wid·en, v. ensanchar(se)
wide·spread, a. extendido; difuso
wid·ow, n. viuda
wid·ow·er, n. viudo
width, n. anchura
wield, v. ejercer; mandar; manejar
wife, n. pl., **wives.** esposa; mujer
wig, n. peluca
wig·gle, v. menear(se); cimbrearse
wild, a. salvaje; silvestre; descabellado; loco. n. often pl. yermo
wild boar, n. jabalí, m.
wil·der·ness, n. yermo; desierto
wile, n. ardid
will, aux. v., past **would.** aux. del futuro. querer
will, n. voluntad; albedrío; testamento. v. legar
will·ful, wil·ful, a. voluntarioso; terco; premeditado
will·ing, a. dispuesto; complaciente
wil·low, n. sauce
wil·low·y, a. esbelto
wil·ly-nil·ly, adv. de grado o por fuerza
wilt, v. marchitar(se)

win, v., **won, win·ning.** ganar; triunfar; lograr. n. victoria
wince, v. estremecerse; respingar. n. mueca de dolor
winch, n. torno
wind, n. viento
wind, v., **wound, wind·ing.** serpentear; arrollar(se); devanar
wind·fall, n. ganancia inesperada
wind·mill, n. molino de viento
win·dow, n. ventana
win·dow·pane, n. cristal, m.
wind·shield, n. parabrisas, m.
wind·y, a. ventoso; expuesto al aire
wine, n. vino
win·er·y, n. pl., **-ies.** lagar; candiotera
wing, n. ala
wink, v. guiñar; pestañear. n. guiño
win·ner, n. ganador
win·ning, n. usu. pl. ganancias. a. victorioso; encantador
win·now, v. aventar
win·some, a. atractivo; alegre
win·ter, n. invierno. a. invernal. v. invernar
win·try, a. glacial; invernal
wipe, v. enjugar; secar; borrar. n. limpión
wire, n. alambre; inf. telegrama, m. v. telegrafiar
wire·tap, v. intervenir
wir·ing, n. instalación de alambres
wir·y, a. nervudo
wis·dom, n. sabiduría
wise, a. sabio; sagaz; juicioso; acertado
wise·crack, n. cuchufleta; pulla
wish, v. desear. n. deseo
wish·ful, a. deseoso
wish·y-wash·y, a. soso
wist·ful, a. pensativo; melancólico
wit, n. sal, f.; ingenio; juicio

witch, n. pl., **witch·es.** bruja; hechicera
witch·craft, n. brujería
with, prep. con; de
with·draw, v., **-drew, -drawn, -draw·ing.** retirar(se); sacar
with·draw·al, n. retirada
with·drawn, a. ensimismado
with·er, v. marchitar(se); secarse
with·hold, v., **-held, -hold·ing.** retener
with·in, prep. dentro de; en. adv. dentro
with·out, prep. sin; a falta de. adv. por fuera
with·stand, v., **-stood, -stand·ing.** resistir
wit·less, a. tonto
wit·ness, n. espectador; espectadora; testigo; testimonio. v. ver
wit·ti·cism, n. dicho gracioso
wit·ty, a. salado; ingenioso
wiz·ard, n. hechicero
wob·ble, v. bambolear; bailar
woe, n. aflicción; infortunio. int. ay de mí
wolf, n. pl., **wolves.** lobo
wom·an, n. pl., **-en.** mujer
wom·an·kind, n. sexo femenino
womb, n. matriz, f.; útero
wom·en's rights, n. pl. derechos de la mujer. Also **wom·an's rights**
won·der, v. desear saber; asombrarse. n. maravilla; milagro
won·der·ful, a. maravilloso
woo, v., **wooed, woo·ing.** cortejar
wood, n. madera; pl. bosque
wood·en, a. de madera; sin expresión
wood·land, n. monte
wood·peck·er, n. picamaderos, m.; pito
wood·work, n. madraie
wood·y, a. leñoso

wool, n. lana
wool·en, wool·len, a. de lana
wool·ly, wool·y, a. lanudo
word, n. palabra; vocablo; recado. v. expresar
word·ing, n. fraseología
word·y, a. verboso
work, n. trabajo; labor, f.; empleo; obra. v. trabajar; operar; funcionar; obrar. **the works,** inf. todo lo posible
work·book, n. cuaderno
worked-up, a. emocionante
work·er, n. obrero; trabajador
work·man·ship, n. habilidad; destreza
work·shop, n. taller
world, n. mundo
world·ly, a. mundano
world-wide, a. mundial; universal
worm, n. gusano
worn, a. raído; usado
worn-out, a. gastado; rendido
wor·ri·some, a. aprensivo
wor·ry, v. preocupar(se); inquietar(se). n. pl., **-ries.** preocupación
worse, a., irreg. compar. of **bad** and **ill.** peor; inferior
wors·en, v. empeorar
wor·ship, n. culto; adoración. v. venerar; adorar
worst, a., irreg. superl. of **bad** and **ill.** peor. n. el, lo peor. adv. del peor modo posible
wor·sted, n. estambre
worth, n. valor; mérito. a. que vale; que merece
worth·less, a. sin valor; despreciable
worth·while, a. digno de atención
wor·thy, a. benemérito; digno de
would-be, a. supuesto
wound, n. herida. v. herir
wraith, n. fantasma, m.

wrap, v. envolver; arropar. n. pl. abrigo. **wrapped up in,** inf. absorto en. **keep un·der wraps,** inf. guardar el secreto
wrath, n. ira; furor
wreak, v. descargar
wreath, n. pl., **wreaths.** guirnalda
wreck, n. naufragio; desastre; ruina. v. destruir; naufragar
wreck·age, n. restos, m. pl.
wrench, n. torcedura; arranque; llave inglesa
wring, v., **wrung, wring·ing.** torcer(se); retorcer; exprimir
wrin·kle, n. arruga; pliegue. v. arrugar(se)
wrist, n. muñeca
write, v., **wrote, writ·ten, writ·ing.** escribir
writ·er, n. escritor; escritora
writ·ing, n. escritura; let. a; escrito
wrong, a. erróneo; equivocado; malo. n. mal, m.; agravio. adv. mal; injustamente. v. agraviar

X - Y - Z

x-ray, n. radiografía. v. radiografiar
Yan·kee, n. yanqui, m., f.
yank, v. sacar de un tirón
yard, n. yarda; patio
yard goods, n. tejidos
yard·stick, n. vara de medir
yarn, n. hilaza; inf. cuento
yar·row, n. milenrama
yawn, v. bostezar. n. bostezo
ye, pron. vosotros
yea, adv. sí
year, n. año
year·ling, n. primal, m.
year·ly, adj. anual. adv. anualmente
yearn, v. suspirar; anhelar
yearn·ing, n. anhelo

yeast, n. levadura
yell, v. gritar. n. grito
yel·low, a. amarillo; inf. cobarde. n. amarillo
yes, adv. sí
yes·ter·day, n. ayer
yet, adv. todavía; aún. conj. sin embargo
yew, n. tejo
yield, v. producir; rendir(se); someterse. n. rédito
yolk, n. yema
yon·der, adv. allí; allá
yore, n. antaño
you, pron. tú; vos; vosotros; vosotras; usted; ustedes
young, a. joven; nuevo. n. jóvenes; hijuelos
young·ster, n. jovencito
your, poss. a. tu(s); su(s); vuestro(s); vuestra(s)
yours, pron. de usted(es); el tuyo; el suyo
your·self, pron. pl., **-selves.** tú mismo; usted mismo; sí mismo
youth, n. pl., **youth, youths.** juventud; jóvenes
youth·ful, a. juvenil
zeal, n. celo; ardor
zeal·ous, a. celoso; entusiasta
ze·bra, n. pl., **-bras, -bra.** cebra
ze·nith, n. cenit, m.
ze·ro, n. pl., **-ros, -roes.** cero
ze·ro hour, n. hora de ataque
zest, n. entusiasmo; gusto
zone, n. zona
zoo, n. pl., **zoos.** jardín zoológico
zo·o·log·i·cal, a. zoológico
zuc·chi·ni, n. pl., **-ni, -nis.** cidracayote de verano
zy·gote, n. cigoto

Scenic Lake Louise, Banff National Park

PLACES OF INTEREST IN CANADA

ALBERTA

Although often referred to as a Prairie Province, Alberta is covered with trees over more than half of its area. The true prairie lies in the southern portion, covered with short prairie grass. In central Alberta the natural grass is longer, and bluffs of poplar and willow appear, merging finally into the northern timberlands. This northern region of great rivers, lakes, and forests comprises about half of the province. Some of the most exciting scenery in Canada's national parks is found in Alberta. Hunting and fishing are excellent. Abundant wild game inhabits the mountains, forests, marshes, and uplands. Fishing in the mountain streams and lakes is among the best. Fine tourist accommodations are provided by luxury hotels nestled in the Canadian Rockies, a region of superb scenic grandeur. Beautiful alpine valleys set with sparkling lakes or coursed by rushing streams lie amid the many peaks. Maligne Lake and Lake Louise are considered to be among the most delightful scenic settings in North America.

The Badlands. Alberta's badlands consist of a vast area of the Red Deer River valley from a point located near Three Hills almost to the Saskatchewan boundary. They present a fantastic conglomeration of coulees, red-shale hills, ravines, and flats. Remains of petrified forest, prehistoric oysterbeds, and mile after mile of spectacular vistas in canyon-like splendor are very colorful in the sun's rays. Although scores of skeletons and other remains of prehistoric life have been taken from these badlands to museums, none is visible in the valley.

Banff National Park. The second-largest Canadian park is a magnificent scenic recreational area and wildlife sanctuary in the central Rockies. Established in 1885, it was the first of the Canadian system of national parks maintained and administered by the Canadian

government at Ottawa. The resort town of **Banff** is known for its mineral hot springs, which have a year-round appeal to tourists for their recreational and therapeutic values. The Cascades Rock Garden, with its terraces and fountains, and the park museum, which has displays of the geology and natural history of the park, are located here. The Banff School of Fine Arts, an extension of the University of Alberta, offers summer courses here. Originally conceived in 1933 as a school in the arts related to the theater, it has a wide selection of fine-arts courses. The famous resort town of **Lake Louise,** northwest of Banff, is nestled in the majestic Rocky Mountains. The center for trips through the park, it has many fine recreational and sporting facilities. The area is also noted for its excellent fishing and mountaineering. Two miles southwest of the town, at the foot of Mt. Victoria, is the small, peaceful Lake Louise. Banff National Park contains many mountain peaks of the Rockies, with several over 10,000 feet. The highest, Mt. Assiniboine, located on the Alberta–British Columbia border at the southern end of the peak, reaches a height of 11,870 feet. This, like the other mountains, has been majestically carved by glaciers. Some of these mountain glaciers are still the sources of the great rivers that flow into the Hudson Bay and the Pacific Ocean. Northeast of Banff in a forested valley is **Lake Minnewanka,** one of the most beautiful lakes in the park. Banff is popular as a summer and winter resort, offering facilities for golfing, tennis, dancing, swimming, skiing, fishing, riding, and exploring. Some of the finest skiing areas in the world are found near Banff and Lake Louise. The famous Alberta sunshine and the comfort of the lodges combine for an incomparable skiing holiday. At the Mt. Norquay ski run, the chair lift, said to be the world's steepest, rises a vertical height of 1,300 feet through a distance of 3,240 feet to the top of the run. There is an annual winter carnival at Banff, which attracts spectators from the surrounding areas.

Calgary. One of Canada's highest cities, it lies in the foothills of the Rockies. The city's Memorial Park is noted for its beautiful gardens. Two tourist attractions are found on St. George's Island, which is in the Bow River. One is the zoo with its wide selection of birds and animals; the other point of interest is the dinosaur display, which consists of life-size models of prehistoric animals. A popular recreational area on the Bow River outside the city is Bowness Park. Among the various facilities offered here are swimming, boating, and dancing. One of the most active cultural centers in the city is Coste House. Located in a residential section, this art center is the scene of sculptural, painting, musical, and other artistic activities. One of the most popular events in Canada is the annual cattle stampede held in Calgary during the summer. Reminiscent of the early days when Calgary was a cowman's town, this well-known stampede and exhibition is a thrilling spectacle.

Edmonton. Capital of Alberta and one of Canada's fastest growing cities, with many new industries and a great petrochemical industry. The discovery of a vast new supply of oil at the nearby Leduc fields is a major reason for its tremendous expansion. A group of oil refineries, a petrochemical plant, and oil storage tanks east of the city are sometimes known as Refinery Row. One of the notable features of the city is the Parliament Building. It is on the site of Edmonton House, which was built by the Hudson's Bay Company on a bluff overlooking the river. The lookout tower in the dome affords an excellent view of the city and the surrounding country. The cruciform building has pavilions with huge Corinthian columns for the main entrance and the wings. The center of Alberta's higher learning is the University of Alberta, located in Edmonton. The fine-arts building contains a geological museum, and the library has a fine display of Indian material. The oldest building in Edmonton is the George McDougall Memorial

Assoc. Screen News, Ltd.
Parliament Building in Edmonton, Alberta

Can. Natl. Ry.
Churchill Range in Jasper National Park

Photo. Alta. Govt.
A dinosaur, St. George's Island, Calgary

Can. Govt. Trav. Bur.
Lake Beauvert, Jasper National Park

Photo, Chuck Ross, Alta. Govt.
Refineries and storage tanks in Edmonton

Shrine and Museum, which was the first structure to be erected outside the walls of the Hudson's Bay Company's Fort Edmonton. The church, which carries the inscription "Methodist Church, 1871," is now a museum. Borden Park is noted for its zoological gardens. Nearby are the exhibition grounds where the Edmonton exhibition is held annually in mid-July. In addition to the agricultural, livestock, and industrial displays, there are horseracing and other amusements.

Elk Island National Park. Known for its large herd of plains buffalo. About 30 miles east of Edmonton, the park has achieved outstanding popularity by virtue of its highly scenic setting and its large herds of wild animals. It enjoys the distinction of being the first national park in Canada to be set aside primarily as a wild-animal reserve; it was established in 1906 to preserve from extinction the wapiti, or elk, of the region. The park contains an area of about 75 square miles and is dotted with enchanting lakes and hills. The park is a natural range for big-game species, such as elk, moose, mule deer, and buffalo, and in summer its numerous small lakes and ponds form ideal resting places and breeding grounds for waterfowl of many kinds. It has become one of the more important bird sanctuaries in western Canada. The famous buffalo herd, the chief attraction in the park, was acquired in 1906 by the Canadian government when it was thought that the species had become almost extinct. Numerous lakes in the park provide an additional attraction for the visitors. **Astotin Lake,** the largest, is the site of the recreational park and park headquarters. It is studded with numerous islands, several of which are connected to the mainland by rustic bridges. Among these are Long Island, on the western side of the lake, and Elk Island, off the southern shore. Accommodations are provided at the lake, and attractions include camping, boating, swimming, golf, and nature study. On the eastern side of Astotin Lake a recreational center, known as Sandy Beach, has been developed as a bathing site. There are also facilities for children's amusements, picnicking, and boating.

Jasper National Park. Established in 1907, it is one of the largest national parks on the North American continent. A noted mountain playground and wildlife sanctuary, it has an area of 4,200 square miles extending along the eastern slopes of the Canadian Rockies. In grandeur and magnificence it is unsurpassed; it contains icefields, beautiful lakes, hot mineral springs, and majestic snow-capped peaks, which in contrast to the dark forests in the valleys and lower slopes offer a spectacular beauty. The park is unrivaled as a wildlife sanctuary; many mountain caribou, moose, black bears, brown bears, grizzly bears, and others may be seen from the trails and roads.

On the Banff-Jasper Highway, famous for its magnificent viewpoints is the **Columbia Icefield.** Located on the border of Banff and Jasper parks, it covers an area of about 100 square miles and is the source of many rivers. One of the glaciers extending from the icefield is the Athabaska Glacier. Snowmobiles take visitors far up the glacier on scenic rides. In the Athabaska River valley east of the Athabaska Falls is Maligne Lake. It is the largest fresh-water lake in the Rocky Mountain region and lies in a very picturesque setting surrounded by the Queen Elizabeth Ranges. Farther north on the Maligne River is Maligne Canyon. This chasm, 190 feet deep, has large potholes and "revolving boulders." The town of **Jasper,** the headquarters of the park, in contrast to Banff, lies in a wide, heavily timbered valley, which is remarkable for its numerous little lakes, all of which are easily accessible by road or by footpath. They afford excellent fishing and are kept well stocked with trout.

Some of the highest peaks of the Canadian Rockies are within the park. The principal mountain peaks are Chown, Kitchener, Edith Cavell, Fryatt, Alberta (in Winston Churchill Range), Columbia, Athabaska, Poboktan, Simon Peak, and The Twins. The park offers a variety of summer and winter sports. There is swimming in some of the lakes for those who like the cool lake water, and at Miette Hot Springs visitors may bathe in the mineral waters. The placid waters of the lakes in the Jasper region are excellent for boating, and there is also good fishing. Ample facilities are provided for campers. The mountains offer unlimited opportunities for climbers. There are trails for those interested in hiking, cycling, or riding, and there are also facilities for skiing.

Totem Pole, Jasper Park Lodge; the town of Jasper; main street, Banff; Lake Minnewanka, Banff National Park
Photos: Can. Natl. Ry., Alta. Govt., Can. Govt. Trav. Bur.

PLACES OF INTEREST IN CANADA

Medicine Hat. Located on the South Saskatchewan River, the city is the center of one of the world's largest natural-gas reserves. Set in an arid cattle-ranching country, its gardens and trees provide a decided contrast. Early expansion of the city came after the discovery of an abundant supply of natural gas, which gave the city the benefit of cheap fuel. This, along with municipally owned water and power utilities, brought many industries to Medicine Hat. The chief industry is the production of clay products, for which the great clay banks in the district supply the material. The city is also the distributing center for southeast Alberta. In the locality are geological formations known as petrified coulees and fossils of prehistoric trees and animals.

Waterton Lakes National Park. Established in 1895, it is situated in the extreme southwestern corner of Alberta. It covers 204 square miles along the eastern slope of the Rocky Mountains immediately north of the international boundary and is part of the Waterton-Glacier International Peace Park, most of which is in the United States. The park is one of the most colorful and charming of Alberta's mountain playgrounds. The mountains rise almost abruptly from the plains in ice-sharpened peaks, a result of the now departed glaciers. Their remarkable colorings of purple, green, and gold give to the peaks a warm and brilliant tone. The mountainous surface rises to a height of 9,600 feet. The larger lake of the Waterton Lakes straddles the Alberta-Montana border. An exhibition herd of plains buffalo occupies a fenced area on the northern boundary of the park. Waterton Park village is the headquarters of the park. There are also good recreational facilities here. Recreation includes swimming in Lake Linnet and boating on upper Waterton Lake. The lakes and streams of the park offer good fishing. A golf course is located on the slopes of Mt. Crandell. For those who like to explore the mountain scenery of the park there are excellent trails for hiking and riding. Among the most popular trails are those to Bertha Lake and Crypt Lake at the top of Hell Roaring Canyon. Mountain climbing is also a favorite sport. Accommodations in the park are provided by hotels, motels, chalets, and lodges, most of which are located in the townsite. There are also many suitable camping areas.

Wood Buffalo National Park. Situated partly in the province of Alberta and partly in the Northwest Territories, it is the largest big-game preserve on the North American continent. It is also the home of the largest remaining herd of bison on the continent. The park lies west of Lake Athabaska and is bounded on the east by the Athabaska and Slave rivers. It contains an area of 17,300 square miles of forest, open plains, and numerous lakes, 13,675 square miles of which

are in Alberta. Established primarily for the protection of a herd of wood bison, or buffalo, it now forms a vast unfenced preserve for many other species of big-game and fur-bearing animals. Other animals found in the park include bear, caribou, deer, moose, beaver, waterfowl, and fish, such as the popular goldeye. The park is not easily accessible to the general public, as it cannot be reached by automobile or rail. River-boat and air services provide access to the park. West of Lake Athabaska is the largest lake in the park, Lake Claire. It is about 40 miles long and 28 miles wide and contains a large number of goldeye. The Peace River is the largest river crossing the park.

BRITISH COLUMBIA

It is almost two centuries since Captain James Cook sailed the waters of Canada's west coast, but visitors are still discovering anew British Columbia's fish and game and its scenic splendor. Much of the province's charm lies in its diversity. Between the mountain ranges that arch their way up the province's length, British Columbia has wide plateaus and fertile valleys, tumbling rivers, broad lakes, and quiet streams. The multitude of islands and numerous large indentations of gulfs, inlets, and bays along the western side of the province are conspicuous features of the coastline, perhaps the most remarkable in that respect in the world. There are countless indentations, from the little bays and snug harbors to the long, deep sounds and inlets extending far inland. All the great rivers flowing into the Pacific, with the exception of the Colorado, have their sources within the boundaries of British Columbia. The climate is Canada's mildest, and roses bloom the year round at Victoria, the provincial capital.

Dawson Creek. The southern terminus of the Alaska Highway, which continues through the Yukon into Alaska. Situated near the Alberta border, this village has had a tremendous population growth since the construction of the Alaska Highway. It is an active distribution center; it serves as the terminus of railroad and highway with Edmonton and as a transfer point for goods destined for the Yukon and Alaska.

Douglas Channel. From a broad inlet on the coast, this channel leads into the mainland, passes a great fiord and Gribbell and Hawkesbury islands, and flows east to Kitimat, the head of the channel. A huge new aluminum plant, among the largest in the world, is located here. The power for this plant is supplied from the hydroelectric plant at **Kemano**, near the head of the fiord. The **Gardner Canal**, which joins the Douglas Channel at its mouth, is renowned for having some of the most spectacular scenery on the Pacific coast.

The mountains rise from the canal to sculptured, snow-capped peaks. Some glaciers descend from the mountains into hanging valleys that send their cascading waterfalls into the fiord below.

Fraser Canyon. An awesome canyon, which starts at the junction of the Thompson and Fraser rivers in southern British Columbia and extends to Hope at the mouth of the canyon. The reddish rocks near Lytton rise toward giant peaks, some over 7,000 feet. Near North Bend the canyon narrows somewhat and form's Hell's Gate. Farther south it becomes a whirlpool known as the Devil's Washbasin.

Glacier National Park. A superb alpine region in southeastern British Columbia on the summit of the Selkirk Mountains. It consists of 521 square miles of towering peaks, glaciers, and forests. The snowfall in these mountains has been higher than in the rest of the Rockies, causing more active glaciers and more frequent waterfalls, torrents, and avalanches. Forests of cedar, fir, spruce, and hemlock grow on the lower slopes. Mountain-climbing enthusiasts have unrivaled opportunities for difficult climbs, and the Alpine Club of Canada holds its annual camp here. There are also facilities for skiing and camping. The Canadian Pacific Railway enters the park from the north and goes down the scenic route of the Beaver River. Before reaching the town of Glacier, the train passes through **Connaught Tunnel,** one of the longest in North America. This tunnel, which is 5 miles long, was cut through one of the larger mountains and is a great engineering feat. One of the outstanding attractions of the park is the **Illecillewaet Glacier.** The snowfield is reached by a good trail involving very little climbing. In spite of the enormous snowfall for which the district is noted, this glacier, in common with other glaciers in the Canadian Rockies and Selkirks, is gradually retreating.

Kamloops. Located at the junction of the North and South Thompson rivers, this city, in addition to being an important rail junction and distribution point, is one of British Columbia's leading resorts. The surrounding district offers excellent fishing and hunting. The lake country surrounding the city, including such lakes as Nicola, Bonaparte, Shuswap, and dozens of others, is famous for its trout. There is big-game hunting for moose and mule deer. Grouse and other upland birds, as well as pheasants, ducks, and geese, are plentiful. A beautiful open space in the city, Riverside Park, offers swimming and various children's amusements. In and around the city, hiking, riding, boating, and swimming are available. Kamloops is also an ideal winter resort, with a rolling terrain that is ideal for skiing.

Mount Robson; Radium Hot Springs, Kootenay National Park; Takakkaw Falls, Yoho National Park; Thunderbird Park, Victoria

Photos: Can. Natl. Ry., B.C. Govt. Trav. Bur., Can. Govt. Trav. Bur., B.C. Govt.

Downtown Vancouver and its fine harbor

Mount Revelstoke National Park

Sullivan silver-lead-zinc mine, Kimberley

The Parliament Buildings in Victoria

Lions Gate Bridge in Vancouver

PLACES OF INTEREST IN CANADA

Kimberley. This city in southeast British Columbia is one of Canada's largest centers for the mining of zinc, silver, and lead. It is the site of the famous Sullivan Mine, one of the world's largest zinc mines. The city is also a winter sports center.

Kootenay National Park. This park, with an area of 543 square miles, was established in 1920 and is known for its scenic highway. The park extends approximately 5 miles on each side of the Vermilion-Sinclair section of the Banff-Windermere Highway for a distance of 60 miles. It includes the valleys of the Vermilion and Kootenay rivers, which form natural avenues for travel. Situated on the western slope of the Canadian Rockies and bordering Banff National Park in Alberta, it contains superb mountain scenery. Other remarkable features include broad valleys, deep canyons, spectacular waterfalls, an iceberg lake, and mineral hot springs. The lower slopes of its valleys are well forested, and it is a noted wildlife sanctuary. Moose, elk, bighorn sheep, and mule deer are among the most abundant wildlife. Four lakes, three rivers, and several small streams offer good fishing during certain seasons of the year. Hiking, mountain climbing, and swimming are some forms of recreation provided for visitors. **Marble Canyon,** one of the park's scenic attractions, is a rocky gorge that was cut to a depth of about 200 feet by Tokumm Creek. The canyon received its name from the layers of exposed marble. Other interesting features are a natural rock bridge and a waterfall. At the southwest edge of the park in the narrow valley of the Sinclair Creek is the site of **Radium Hot Springs,** the park headquarters. The chief attractions here are the swimming pools, which receive water from the hot mineral springs. Among the hottest in the Rockies, these pools are visited by many who believe that there are healing powers in the waters.

Mount Revelstoke National Park. The park is situated on the summit of Mt. Revelstoke and has an area of 100 square miles. It occupies a broad undulating plateau at a general elevation of about 7,000 feet above sea level. The park lies on the western slope of the Selkirk Mountains between the valleys of the Columbia River on the west and the Illecillewaet River on the south. Mount Revelstoke was established as a national park in 1914. The views from the lookout at the summit are spectacular. Three mountain ranges are visible from this location, with colorful alpine meadows for contrast. To the east is the picturesque Columbia Valley, and to the north is the Clachnacudainn Snowfield. Below the lookout at the junction of the Columbia and Illecillewaet rivers is the town of **Revelstoke.** The town is a popular winter-sports center. It is known as the pioneer championship ski-jumping center of Canada, and many of the earlier records were made on the southern slopes of Mt. Revelstoke. There is also an excellent downhill course. Wild animals, especially grizzly bears, and bird life are very abundant.

Mount Robson and Mount Waddington. These two peaks are among the highest in the province. Mount Robson is located on the western slope of the Rocky Mountains near the Alberta border and Jasper National Park. It is the highest elevation in the Canadian Rockies (12,972 feet), and the main attraction of Mount Robson Provincial Park. This region is very picturesque, with many glaciers, high peaks, and lakes. The highest mountain in the Coast Mountains in southwest British Columbia is Mt. Waddington. The peak, located about 170 miles northwest of Vancouver, reaches a height of 13,260 feet.

Tweedsmuir Provincial Park. An immense wilderness area (5,400 square miles), as yet undeveloped, on the eastern slope of the Coast Mountains in west-central British Columbia. Several peaks are over 7,000 feet high. The largest of the numerous lakes are Eutsuk, Whitesail, Tahtsa, and Tetachuck lakes. There are a few trails in the eastern and southern regions. An Indian village, Ulkatcho, is situated near the southeast border.

Vancouver. As an important rail and ocean connection, it is the chief city in the province. It is located on a peninsula that juts out into Burrard Inlet, and it has one of the finest natural harbors in the world. Because of its situation, it is the headquarters of the larger industrial interests of the province. Not far from the commercial center are natural parks, beaches, and mountain playgrounds in the city itself and in the surrounding communities. Stanley Park, with its giant trees, is a center of attraction in the city. Nearly surrounded by water, the park offers miles of trails and paths that pass through the largely natural grounds and the formal gardens, including the well-known rose gardens. Different views of the city may be had from various lookout points in the park. In addition to the zoological gardens, there are facilities for swimming, golf, and lawn bowling. Hastings Park is the site of the exhibition grounds where the Pacific National Exhibition is held every August. The Empire Stadium is here. The Lipsett Indian Museum, which has one of the most complete collections of the Indian life and art of British Columbia, is also in the park grounds. The University of British Columbia is located on the far western section of greater Vancouver. One attraction of the university is **Totem Grove,** a display of colorful Indian totem poles and handicraft. The Vancouver harbor covers about 100 miles of waterfront and provides excellent dock and grain-elevator facilities. There are many berths for ocean-going vessels. In contrast to the bustling commerce of the inner harbor, Vancouver's outer harbor provides many fine beaches and bays for yachting, swimming, and fishing. The Lions Gate Bridge crosses Burrard Inlet and connects Stanley Park with North Vancouver. It is one of the longest suspension bridges in Canada. Another well-known bridge is the Capilano Canyon suspension bridge in West and North Vancouver. It is a narrow bridge for hikers, 200 feet above a tumbling, glacier-fed river. Whytecliff Park offers excellent facilities for swimming, boating and fishing. Ski runs are not far from the city at Holleyburn, Grouse, and Seymour mountains.

Vancouver Island. The island, largest on the western coast of North America, is about 285 miles long and up to about 80 miles wide and has considerable economic importance. It is heavily wooded, and lumbering is an important occupation. The western coast of the island is deeply indented with numerous fiords, sounds, and sheer mountain cliffs. The highest mountains, in the center of the island, are over 7,000 feet in height. The eastern coast is generally even and is more populated. There are numerous lakes throughout the island. The scenic mountains, the canyons and waterfalls, the fine salmon fishing, and the

PLACES OF INTEREST IN CANADA

equable climate are some of many attractions. **Strathcona Provincial Park,** in the central part of the island, is in a heavily forested mountainous area. It contains the highest mountains on the island. The many streams and lakes provide excellent fishing. The area is also a game sanctuary.

Victoria. The capital of British Columbia rests on the most southerly point of Vancouver Island. Although it is the island's chief seaport and possesses some industries, it is essentially a residential and social center. Its beautiful scenery and its equable climate account for its popularity as a tourist resort. Colorful gardens surround many of the houses in the city. The Parliament Buildings, which overlook the head of the harbor, are very imposing. The main building has an impressive dome with a gilded statue on it of George Vancouver, a British captain who was the first person to circumnavigate the island that bears his name. A unique display of Indian totem poles is found in **Thunderbird Park.** A workshop is located on the grounds so that the native craftsmen may copy the decaying totem poles and replace them with new ones. One of the largest enclosed salt-water swimming pools in North America is located at Victoria's Crystal Gardens. From Beacon Hill Park a beautiful panorama of the sea and the surrounding mountains may be viewed. Located in the central part of the city, this 150-acre park offers, in addition to a scenic view and lakes enhanced by graceful swans, a Chinese bell imported from the sacred palace at Peking. At the Dominion Astrophysical Observatory the city has one of the world's largest telescopes. Also of interest is the Dominion Meteorological Observatory. As a city of gardens, Victoria has displays from the flower-bordered lawns of the Parliament Buildings and those that flank the two sides of the unique inner harbor to the decorative beds that bloom all year round in Beacon Hill Park. Victoria's harbor can handle large oceangoing vessels; its picturesque inner harbor can also accommodate sizable vessels. Not far away is Esquimalt Harbour, a naval base, where one of the largest drydocks in Canada is situated.

Wells Gray Provincial Park. A vast, undeveloped mountain and lake playground that is noted for its excellent hunting and fishing. The park is located in the Cariboo Mountains and has varied and beautiful scenery, ranging from majestic mountain peaks, lakes, and waterfalls to glaciers and icefields. The larger lakes are Hobson, Azure, Clearwater, and Murtle.

Yoho National Park. This large area of mountainous terrain lies along the western slope of the Canadian Rockies, its eastern boundary adjoining the Banff and Kootenay national parks along the Continental Divide. It is divided into two parts by the Kicking Horse River. The park derives its name from the Indian word *Yoho,* an exclamation meaning "It is wonderful." The splendor of its wild valleys, the lofty snow-capped peaks, the color of its alpine lakes, and its spectacular glaciers and waterfalls make the park a region of outstanding natural beauty. Several peaks (Goodsir, Stephen, Gordon, and Vaux) are over 10,000 feet high. The park is a very popular mountain-climbing center. In addition, there are ample facilities for fishing, hiking, and riding. At Kicking Horse Pass, the highest point (5,339 feet) on the Cana-

dian Pacific Railway, are spiral railroad tunnels that are necessary to negotiate the pass and are of interest to travelers. Glacier-fed Lake O'Hara, in its beautiful setting, is a favorite place for artists. The Yoho Valley is the setting for some magnificent waterfalls. The Takakkaw Falls are found in a deep, narrow canyon. The cascading water drops about 1,500 feet into the Yoho River. The headquarters of the park are located at Field.

MANITOBA

Although Manitoba has rich, rolling wheat country to the south, the northern part of the province consists of a forest-covered frontier wilderness. It is known to North American hunters not only for big game but also for waterfowl. Each autumn thousands of migrating ducks and geese pass through the marsh country on their way south from arctic breeding grounds. Often thought of as a flat, treeless prairie land, stretching mile after mile with little variety, Manitoba actually varies greatly. It is a combination of rolling stretches of open and wooded farmland, densely forested areas, three large fresh-water lakes and thousands of smaller lakes and waterways, a wide rock belt, and a great area of northern tundra. Only about a third of the province is prairie land. A large portion of the northern boundary is swept by the salt waters of Hudson Bay, with its important seaport at Churchill.

Churchill. Located at the Churchill River's entrance into Hudson Bay, this port is the terminus of the Hudson Bay Railway. A major grain-shipping port, it has a giant grain elevator, and visitors may watch wheat being loaded onto vessels for shipment to Europe. It is also a whaling headquarters, and whales may be seen frolicking in the bay. There is an interesting Eskimo museum in the rectory of the mission. On the other side of the river is **Fort Prince of Wales National Historic Park.** This contains the most northerly fortress on the North American continent; it was built in the years between 1733 and 1771 by the Hudson's Bay Company in order to secure control of Hudson Bay. It was surrendered to, and partly destroyed by, a French naval force in 1782. The ruins, which were among the most interesting military remains on the continent, are gradually being rebuilt. The park covers an area of 50 acres.

Flin Flon. Situated on the Saskatchewan border, Flin Flon is one of Canada's largest mining towns. The area produces not only gold, copper, and zinc ores but also silver, selenium, tellurium, and cadmium. Mines and smelters dominate the town, and they are its economic mainstay.

Lake Winnipeg. A remnant of the ancient glacial Lake Agassiz, Lake Winnipeg drains into Hudson Bay through the Nelson River. It receives the Red and Winnipeg rivers in the south and the Saskatchewan River in the north. On its shores are many pleasant summer resorts, with excellent swimming, boating, and fishing. These include Grand Beach, Hillside Beach, Victoria Beach, and Winnipeg Beach with its popular amusement park.

Lower Fort Garry National Historic Park. This stone-walled fort, built between 1831 and 1839 by the Hudson's Bay Company, stands on the west bank of the Red River, 20 miles north of Winnipeg. It was occupied by

Man. Trav. & Publicity Bur.
Rock cliffs in Whiteshell Forest Reserve

Man. Trav. & Publicity Bur.
The lily pond at Assiniboine Park, Winnipeg

Man. Trav. & Publicity Bur.
Engineering Building at University of Manitoba

Can. Govt. Trav. Bur.
Lake Audy in Riding Mountain National Park

Ruins in Fort Prince of Wales National Park
Can. Govt. Trav. Bur.

this company until 1911. There are five buildings in a good state of repair within the stone walls of the structure. The fort area, including the bastions, comprises nearly 13 acres.

Riding Mountain National Park. Situated in the southwestern part of Manitoba approximately 125 miles north of the U.S. border, this park occupies the broad undulating plateau that forms the summit of Riding Mountain, one of the highest points of the Manitoba escarpment. The heavily timbered uplands of Riding Mountain, which rise to a height of 2,200 feet above sea level, are in pleasing contrast to the surrounding fertile plains. The park was established in 1929 and contains an area of 1,148 square miles. Many of the small lakes with which the area is abundantly endowed nestle between ridges and hollows made by ancient glaciers. Clear Lake, the largest and most beautiful body of water in the park, lies just above the southern boundary. The lake is 9 miles long and more than 2 miles across at its widest point. Other lakes in the park include Audy, Katherine, Ministik, Moon, Edwards, and Whirlpool. The townsite of **Wasagaming,** an Indian name meaning "clear water," is situated on the southern shore of Clear Lake and is a summer resort and the administrative headquarters of the park. The log-and-stone museum building contains wildlife exhibits and Indian, geological, and other displays. In the park is a small exhibition herd of buffalo. There are also native elk, deer, moose, and bear, which present countless opportunities for camera studies. The numerous varieties of birds include migratory waterfowl. Besides natural attractions the park has picnic grounds and offers opportunities for fishing, riding, hiking, tennis, golf, and other recreational pursuits.

The Pas. Begun as a fur-trading post, this gateway to the North is today principally a lumbering town. Lumbermen, trappers, miners, prospectors, and fishermen are its residents. In February the **Trappers Festival** with its Dog Derby brings considerable excitement to The Pas. Other contests include rat skinning, ice fishing, square dancing, and jigging competitions.

Whiteshell Provincial Park. A forest reserve covering 1,088 square miles, it consists of a maze of lakes and streams that offer excellent fishing. Game and waterfowl are also plentiful. Among the most popular resort areas are West Hawk Lake, Falcon Lake, and Caddy Lake in the southern part and Brereton Lake in the central section. Whiteshell Provincial Park, lying on the Ontario border, is about a two-hour drive east from Winnipeg.

Winnipeg. Capital of Manitoba. It lies at the junction of the Red River and its largest tributary, the Assiniboine. As a result the city offers fine swimming, fishing, sailing, water skiing, and other aquatic amusements. Railroad, highway, and air routes converge upon the city, and because of its importance as a transportaton center between eastern and western Canada Winnipeg is sometimes called the "Chicago of Canada." Although it has important industries, it is primarily a commercial city and wheat-trading center. Among the imposing buildings on its wide streets are the Wheat Pool Building and the Grain Exchange. Other interesting structures include the City Hall, built in Edwardian style; the Parliament Building, a handsome Tyndall

Can. Natl. Ry.
A covered wooden bridge in New Brunswick

limestone building with four wings and a central tower; and the Dominion Public Building. Near the Parliament Building is the Winnipeg Auditorium, home of the symphony orchestra. The art gallery and a museum are also there. A few miles south of Winnipeg in a bend of the Red River lie the grounds of the University of Manitoba, with its distinctive white Arts Building and its modernistic glass library.

NEW BRUNSWICK

Once New Brunswick's timber provided masts for the sailing ships of the British fleet. Today its forests still cover 22,000 square miles of a province that, though small in area, has some remarkably large and important rivers. Notable among these is the 450-mile St. John River, which rises in the wooded areas of neighboring Maine. Nature's curiosities in New Brunswick include the Reversing Falls of the St. John River and the deceiving Magnetic Hill near Moncton. Good salmon fishing is available in New Brunswick, and the province's 600 miles of shoreline have many fine beaches. Game is plentiful. The greater part of the province consists of lowlands, nowhere more than 500 feet in height. There are only two highland areas, a narrow ridge in the south and a wider mountainous sector in the northwest where Mt. Carleton, the highest peak, reaches 2,700 feet. The remainder of the province is rolling countryside with varied and picturesque vistas and with many lakes and a network of rivers abounding in game fish.

Campobello Island. This summer resort and fishing region lies in the Bay of Fundy, opposite Eastport, Maine, at the entrance to Passamaquoddy Bay. At **Welshpool** in the center of the island is the Roosevelt summer home, where Franklin D. Roosevelt spent many vacations from his boyhood days on. A commemorative stone monument has been erected there.

Fort Beauséjour National Historic Park. Comprising an area of 81 acres, this park is situated about midway between Sackville, New Brunswick, and Amherst, Nova Scotia. Fort Beauséjour was constructed by the French between 1751 and 1755 in the course of their long struggle with the English for possession of Canada. It stood on a ridge overlooking an arm of Chignecto Bay and was erected as a counterdefense against Fort Law-

Can. Govt. Trav. Bur.
Museum, Fort Beauséjour National Park

rence, which was built by the English on a parallel ridge 1½ miles to the southeast. The fort was captured in 1755, before its actual completion, by the English under Robert Monckton. After the War of 1812 it gradually fell into ruins. In 1926 the site was established as a national historic park, and since that time considerable restoration work has been carried out. A spacious stone museum is near the entrance.

Fredericton. Capital of New Brunswick, on the right bank of the St. John River. Points of interest include the Legislative Assembly Building, topped by an elegant Georgian-style dome, and Christ Church Cathedral, a small Anglican church that is considered one of the finest examples of Gothic architecture in North America. Also of interest are the buildings and grounds of the University of New Brunswick and St. Thomas University.

Fundy National Park. Skirting the Bay of Fundy for a distance of 8 miles, the bold, irregular shoreline of the park is featured by numerous coves and inlets. The tides of the bay have worn and carved the sandstone cliffs into sculptured, rocky masses of rugged grandeur. Several swift rivers and streams add to the scenic beauty. The land rises in steps from the bay until, at an elevation of 1,000 feet, it becomes rolling tableland, richly covered with forest. From the top of Hastings Hill there is a commanding view of the head of Chignecto Bay and the coastal area. On the horizon the hills of Nova Scotia may be seen. Reaching inland from the park, the ridges are covered with maple groves, which in the autumn become a beautiful sea of crimson and gold. Fundy National Park covers an area of approximately 80 square miles. Besides the magnificent scenery, visitors to the park may enjoy numerous recreational activities, such as swimming, golfing, and tennis. There are picnic and camping grounds, and plays, motion pictures, and concerts are given in the amphitheater. Moose, deer, bear, beaver, fox, weasel, and lynx are among the wildlife found in the park. Numerous kinds of birds may also be seen. All wildlife is protected, and hunting is forbidden. The **Bay of Fundy** is noted for its high tides. As the tide rolls in from the Atlantic Ocean, it piles up in this funnel-shaped bay until, at the narrower points, there is a vertical rise of nearly 60 feet.

Grand Falls. Almost surrounded by a bend of the St. John River, this town is popular

New Brunswick Museum, Saint John
N.B. Govt. Inf. Bur.

Bennett Lake, Fundy National Park
Can. Govt. Trav. Bur.

Legislative Assembly Building, Fredericton

N.B. Govt. Inf. Bur.

with tourists for its nearby scenic waterfall with a vertical drop of about 75 feet. **Pulpit Rock** hangs over a narrow gorge, and farther downstream are the **Wells,** deep holes hollowed out by the falls when they were located here before they wore their way to the present location. The falls have been harnessed to provide electricity for much of northern and western New Brunswick.

Moncton. Commercial and industrial city on the land bridge to Nova Scotia. Because of its location it is a busy railroad, highway, and air center. In the old Free Meeting House services for worshipers of all denominations were held before they had constructed their own churches. At Moncton, situated on the Petitcodiac River, the famous **tidal bore** of this river can be observed. This phenomenon is a wall of water, sometimes 6 feet high, which rolls up the river twice each day, breaking on the wharves at Moncton. Irregularity of the river mouth and the pressure of the great tides of the Bay of Fundy combine to cause the bore, which is a continuing curiosity to visitors. A few miles north of Moncton is **Magnetic Hill,** where automobiles appear to be able to coast uphill. It was for a long time considered a result of magnetic attraction by the hill, but it is probably an optical illusion caused by the peculiar conformation of the terrain. South of Moncton, at Hopewell Cape, are grotesque rock formations called the **Sentinels.** They are enormous wave-sculptured columns of red sandstone that stand before caves that also have been carved by the sea.

Saint John. New Brunswick's largest city, located at the St. John River's entrance into the Bay of Fundy. Its deep, sheltered harbor is ice free the year round, and Saint John is

The Market Slip at Saint John

Can. Pac. Ry. Co.

one of eastern Canada's main ports. It has extensive wharf and grain-elevator facilities and many mills, factories, and machine shops. The city's center is King Square, around which are the old court house, the Old Burial Ground, and the City Market. In Market Square on the waterfront a large boulder marks the place where thousands of United Empire Loyalists, fleeing from New England, landed after the Revolutionary War to establish the town. The site of **Fort Howe,** built in 1778 for the protection of the little settlement below, rises north of the harbor and offers a fine view of the city. The New Brunswick Museum contains an important nautical collection, relics of the province's history, and a fine small-arms collection. The bridge across the St. John River is one of the longest single-span bridges in the world. This bridge offers an excellent view of the famous **Reversing Falls** at the river's mouth. For half the day the river tumbles through a gorge into the Bay of Fundy, but when the great tides come in, the cycle reverses itself, and the water runs uphill, over the falls, and into the river. The turbulent waters of Reversing Falls perform on a time schedule governed by the tides, and time tables for the tides are available to visitors. The old Martello Tower in West Saint John is a defensive work dating from the War of 1812. Near Saint John is the renowned summer resort of St. Andrews-by-the-sea, which offers numerous seaside recreations, including yachting and offshore deep-sea fishing.

NEWFOUNDLAND

Canada's easternmost province includes politically not only the island of Newfoundland but also Labrador on the mainland. The island was discovered by John Cabot, who landed at Cape Bonavista in 1497, though some claim the Norsemen found the ancient island 500 years before. It was settled by Devonshire fishermen in the 16th century and became a Canadian province in 1949, which makes it both the oldest and newest of the provinces. Newfoundland's coastline is deeply indented with many bays and fiordlike inlets. Numerous islands surround it. The highest elevation is in the northwest, where some peaks rise above 2,000 feet. The interior is a network of lakes and rivers set in undulating country with low, rocky hills. Here heavily forested areas and barrens alternate, and large herds of moose, caribou, and smaller game are found. Fishing is the chief occupation and is also a favorite form of recreation. Salmon and trout abound in the fresh waters, and giant tuna and cod off the coast offer a challenge to the fisherman.

Corner Brook. This town started as a small lumbering village and has expanded into one of Newfoundland's largest towns. It is situated on the south side of the Humber fiord. The first settlement came in 1864 with the opening of a sawmill, but the big growth occurred in the 1920's when the Bowater paper and pulp mills were built. At the Humber estuary, below Corner Brook, the scenery is picturesque, and the area is well suited for resort purposes. There are numerous salmon rivers near Corner Brook. A leader in the development of winter sports in Newfoundland, the town has an area for skiing.

Gander. The town is the site of a major transatlantic airport. It was selected as an air station for experimental transport flights in

Signal Hill, St. John's, Newfoundland

Photo, N.F.B.

1935, but the airport was not completed until 1939. During World War II it was expanded and became a vital Allied base. Gander is also a sports center. The surrounding country offers fine hunting and fishing.

Grand Banks. This submarine plateau off the southeast coast of Newfoundland extends about 420 miles from east to west and about 350 miles from north to south, with a depth ranging generally between 20 and 100 fathoms. This comparative shallowness allows penetration of sunlight, stimulating a profuse marine growth on which fish feed. As a result the Grand Banks are important fishing grounds. They are one of the world's greatest cod-fishing regions and for centuries have been visited by fishermen from Canada, Great Britain, the United States, France, and Scandinavia. The area is dangerous because of the fog and icebergs brought by the Labrador Current.

Grand Falls and Bishop's Falls. An important pulp and paper-milling center, Grand Falls was established by some English publishers in need of a large and steady supply of newsprint. They founded a company that built mills and established a thriving town. The town is the center for fishing in the Exploits River. There is also good hunting for moose and caribou in this wooded area. **Bishop's Falls** is another town known for its pulp milling. The manufactured pulp is pumped up the Exploits River to the paper mills at Grand Falls. The port for the paper and pulp mills at Grand Falls and Bishop's Falls is Botwood.

Heart's Content. A coast village on Trinity Bay where the first successful transatlantic

Placentia on Placentia Bay, Newfoundland

Photo, N.F.B.

Can. Natl. Ry.

Curling, a fishing port in Newfoundland

Photo, N.F.B.

The harbor at St. Anthony, Newfoundland

Can. Natl. Ry.

Old Clock Tower, Halifax, Nova Scotia

cable was landed in 1866. It is now the western terminus of several transatlantic cables. There is some cod fishing and canning, but after the closing of the railway that served the community the town declined somewhat.

Labrador. The mainland portion of the province of Newfoundland. Labrador has a bleak, rocky, and indented coastline swept by the cold Labrador Current. The region becomes mountainous to the north. Numerous lakes are found in the southwest. Settlement is mainly along the coast, where the chief occupations are lumbering and fishing for cod and salmon. A small proportion of the population are Eskimos who live along the coast north of Hamilton Inlet. There are some Indians who inhabit the interior, where they hunt and trap the fur-bearing animals. The spectacular **Grand Falls** are located on the upper Hamilton River. The river narrows to 200 feet southwest of Michikamau Lake, flows over rapids, and drops about 245 feet. The torrent passes McLean Canyon, where sheer and rocky walls rise several hundred feet on both sides, and then flows through the canyon over more rapids. The total fall from the beginning at the rapids above the main falls to the end of the rapids of the canyon is about 1,038 feet. A place of interest in Labrador is **Goose Bay**, where an important airport is located. During World War II it was used as a Canadian military and ferrying base. It is now used for commercial flights.

Placentia. The French made this town their first and most important settlement in Newfoundland when they built a fort here in 1662. From here they made repeated attacks on St. John's, the English capital. There are still remains of the French forts and a church from the 17th century. This small port, located on Placentia Bay, has excellent fishing grounds. On Aug. 14, 1941, Franklin D. Roosevelt and Winston Churchill signed the Atlantic Charter aboard the British battleship *Prince of Wales* in Placentia Bay.

St. John's. The capital and largest city in Newfoundland claims to be the oldest city in North America; it was first settled by the British in the latter part of the 16th century. It is a seaport with a fine landlocked harbor with cliffs rising on both sides. St. John's is also the commercial center of the island and has a great fishing fleet. Of historical importance is Signal Hill, where Marconi received the first wireless signal across the Atlantic in 1901. For many years forts on this hill guarded the entrance of the harbor. Cabot Tower, a monument to John Cabot, the discoverer of the island, offers fine views. Government House has been the residence of the governors of the island since 1828, and it is now the lieutenant governor's residence. Before 1850 the Newfoundland legislature met here. Now the legislature meets in the Colonial Building. This structure is distin-

guished by its huge Ionic portico of stone brought from Ireland. The Roman Catholic cathedral is situated on a hill overlooking the city. It has a richly decorated interior with paintings and statuary. An outstanding example of ecclesiastical Gothic architecture is the Anglican cathedral. The original stone cathedral was destroyed by fire, but the present one was built along the same lines. Along the coast not far from St. John's are picturesque resort towns. The coastal scenery is highlighted by the quaint fishing villages. A beautiful little village north of St. John's is Pouch Cove, a favorite of artists and photographers. Nearby is Cape St. Francis, where a lighthouse is located on a rock promontory. Holyrood is a resort at the head of Conception Bay. Its rugged mountain scenery and its excellent fishing appeal to the tourist.

Terra Nova National Park. Maritime area of 156 square miles on Bonavista Bay in eastern Newfoundland. A region of rocky headlands and forests, it contains abundant wildlife, including moose, caribou, bear, and waterfowl. As yet undeveloped, Terra Nova was established as a national park in 1957.

NOVA SCOTIA

Like the other Atlantic provinces, Nova Scotia has a maritime climate, and its summers are consequently cool and pleasant. The seacoast has a series of jutting cliffs, sheltered bays, and sandy beaches, with Cape Breton Highlands National Park a favored vacation place for recreation. There are numerous lakes and small rivers, many of them tidal rivers noted for a high tidal flow. The inland is covered with forests and some fine farming areas. In the fields near Grand Pré, oxen are still used for plowing, and there are other reminders of a storied past. The quaint fishing villages are a special attraction to artists and photographers. Colorful annual events like the Annapolis Valley Blossom Festival and the Gaelic Mod brighten the Nova Scotia scene for visitors. Halifax, ancient capital of the province, handles enormous tonnages of shipping. It was the western anchor of the North Atlantic defenses in both World Wars.

Cape Breton Island. The Canso Causeway, completed in 1955, connects the island with the mainland. The island is of great interest to the tourist and provides some of the most picturesque scenery in Canada. The coastline is deeply indented with numerous bays, and colorful fishing villages are among the principal attractions. Gaelic and French are spoken in some parts of the island. **Cape Breton Highlands National Park** is situated in the northern part of the island along the rugged Atlantic coastline. It forms part of a tableland that in places extends to the sea in bold headlands, which rise almost sheer from the water. At other points streams running down to the sea have carved deep gorges

Fort Anne National Historic Park

Can. Govt. Trav. Bur.

Evangeline's Monument, Grand Pré Park

Assoc. Screen News, Ltd.

Coast of Cape Breton Island, Nova Scotia

Photo, N.F.B.

that widen out at their lower ends to form broad valleys, or intervales, which are characteristic of the region. Along the western shores the hills rise precipitously to a height of about 1,500 feet. The upper slopes are clad with forest growth, and small amber-colored streams drop down their steep sides. The eastern shores are also rocky but lower in elevation and are indented with numerous sandy coves and bays. With the exception of the plateau, which consists mainly of barren and muskeg areas, the park is covered with a typical Acadian forest. Passing through the park at intervals is the Cabot Trail, one of the outstanding scenic highways on the Atlantic Coast. It gives magnificent views of the shoreline and the valleys. **Louisburg National Historic Park,** about 25 miles from Sydney, has the ruins of a walled city erected by the French during the period from 1720 to 1740. It contains the ruins of massive fortifications erected by the French as a military and naval station for the defense of their possessions in New France. The fortress changed hands between the French and British several times and was captured finally by the British in 1758. This achievement led to the fall of Quebec the following year and resulted in the ultimate transfer of Canada from French to British rule. In 1760 the fortress was demolished on orders from the British government. The museum contains many relics of the area. Covering much of Cape Breton Island is the tidal salt-water lake, **Bras d'Or.** Its shoreline is surrounded by hills and indented with small bays. The lake is about 44 miles long, and one section reaches a width of 20 miles. Two channels give it access to the ocean. The lake is especially popular for yachting. **Sydney,** located on a peninsula in Sydney Harbour, is one of the leading coal-shipping ports in Canada and is an important steel-milling center. It has a fine harbor and in the summer is a popular starting-point for trips to the surrounding regions. One of the oldest Anglican churches in Canada is here. The city has a beautiful park, which is the habitat for swans, ducks, and geese.

Fort Anne National Historic Park. Comprising an area of 31 acres at Annapolis Royal, it occupied an important place in the early history of Canada. Around Port Royal, as it was originally known, centered the long struggle between the French and English for control of Acadia. The fort located on the present site of Fort Anne was built about 1635 several miles east of the original habitation. As the capital of Acadia, Port Royal for the next 100 years experienced an eventful career and changed hands many times before its final capitulation by the French. Its name was changed then from Port Royal to Annapolis Royal in honor of the reigning sovereign of England, Queen Anne.

Grand Pré. An old village made famous by Henry Wadsworth Longfellow's poem *Evangeline.* A building of historic interest is the Church of the Covenanters, built at the end of the 18th century by settlers from New England. The Grand Pré National Historic Park has a replica of the original Acadian church; it is also a museum containing many relics of the Acadian period. Evangeline's Monument is on the grounds.

Halifax. The capital of Nova Scotia is picturesquely situated on a fine sheltered bay. It has one of the best harbors in the world and is ice free the year round. The city was established as a military and naval base because of its high, commanding view over the peninsula. The summit that dominates Halifax is the site of **Halifax Citadel National Historic Park.** Four forts were built here at different periods. The first was part of the wooden palisade around the Halifax settlement. The second was built at the time of the War of American Independence. The third was built in the late 18th century, and the fourth was constructed in the early 19th century. This stone fortress is one of the largest in the world. Halifax Citadel contains three spacious museums relating to Canada's naval and military history and the history of the province. Another attraction in the city is the unique Public Gardens. Many paths and colorful gardens are contained in this 16-acre city park. North of the citadel is the Common. This government property was used for reviews, drill parades, and other military purposes. St. Paul's Church, the oldest Protestant church in Canada, is located in the city. The parliament building, known as Province House, is a good example of Georgian-style architecture in Canada. There are many valuable relics and paintings inside. Dalhousie University, named for its founder, Lord Dalhousie, is here. The original college was established in 1818 and was built on the site of the present city hall. Affiliated with the university is King's College, founded in 1789. Point Pleasant Park, which contains about 200 acres of woodland, is located at the southern end of Halifax Peninsula. The park, technically reserved for defense purposes, is very popular for hiking and riding. Several forts are open to the visitor. Halifax Harbour is a bustling port with many trans-atlantic liners and freighters docking. In winter it is the chief terminal for the trans-atlantic shipping lines. Lying across the mouth of the harbor is MacNab's Island, forming two harbor entrances and protecting the shipping from the sea.

Port Royal National Historic Park. An area of 20½ acres at Lower Granville. Along the shore of Annapolis Basin, a replica of the Port Royal Habitation built by Champlain and DeMonts in 1605 has been erected on the original site. Located on a good harbor, the group of buildings sheltered the first settlers in Canada and formed the first permanent trading settlement in North America north of Spanish settlements on the Gulf of Mexico. The original habitation comprised a group of buildings arranged around a courtyard and fortified at two corners by a cannon platform and palisade. It was destroyed by an invading English force from Virginia in 1613. The restoration has been carried out as faithfully as practicable from plans and descriptions left by Champlain and from other data.

Truro. Centrally located at the head of the Bay of Fundy, the town originally had a large Acadian population. The nearby trout streams and lakes offer recreation for fishermen and tourists. The hunting of grouse, moose, and deer in the area is another attraction. Southeast of the town is Victoria Park, a wooded area noted for its two beautiful waterfalls.

Wedgeport. Site of the International Tuna Cup, this town is famous for its tuna fishing. An offshore stream, about 1 mile wide, is an excellent area for catching blue-fin tuna, starting in early summer. Many world records in tuna fishing have been made here.

Yarmouth. A seaport that was one of the great shipbuilding centers when wooden vessels were popular. It is now a manufacturing town, a seaport, and resort. The town offers swimming, sailing, fishing for trout and salmon, and hunting for wild ducks, bear, and deer. Scenic drives in and around the town provide fine views of the region.

ONTARIO

Not only because Ontario lies close to the greatest population densities of the United States does the province attract numerous visitors, but cool forests, quiet lakes, good roads, and plentiful and excellent accommodations also play their part in making it a key province for tourist travel. It has an impressive number of superhighways, and from north to south its climate and its countryside vary greatly. Northern Ontario is mainly a region of forests, mineral lands, rivers, and lakes. There are millions of acres of forests, abounding in game, rich in timber, and possessing great resources of pulpwood. These forest regions are ideal for camping, fishing, and hunting. World-famous for its mines, Northern Ontario is an important producer of gold and other minerals, although many of its resources in this direction are still largely unexplored. This section also possesses many acres of fine farmland, and already some districts are well farmed. Southern Ontario, that portion of the province south of the Ottawa River and Lake Nipissing, enjoys the natural conditions ideal for varied and intensive agriculture, and attractive and fertile farms predominate. Here are also large and thriving industrial and commercial cities, such as Toronto, Hamilton, Ottawa, Windsor, London, and Kingston.

Algonquin Park. This 2,750-square-mile game preserve, located less than 100 miles west of Ottawa, is open to lovers of outdoor life for camping, fishing, boating, hiking, and nature study. Park naturalists maintain a nature museum, give lectures, show films, and conduct nature hikes. Through the park run nature trails with interesting trees, plants, and animal homes marked and identified.

CORNWALL. Canadian headquarters of the

Canadian Horseshoe Falls (right), Niagara Falls

Can. Natl. Ry.

PLACES OF INTEREST IN CANADA

Grain elevators at Port Arthur, Ontario

The Royal Ontario Museum in Toronto

Ontario's Parliament buildings at Toronto

St. Lawrence Seaway. The city was founded in 1784 by United Empire Loyalists. It now boasts the only lacrosse factory in the world, which stands near the Seaway Bridge connecting Cornwall to New York. It maintains one of the three dams in the 47-mile stretch of the International Rapids section. Bus and boat tours are available for those who wish to see the technological accomplishments more closely. Canada route No. 2 parallels the St. Lawrence River as far as Kingston. Along the way is **Upper Canada Village,** which provides a glimpse of Canadian life of a century ago. The Village is part of Chrysler Farm Battlefield Park, a memorial to the loyalists who settled, fought, and died here. Farther upstream is Prescott, the upper end of the International Rapids section. Here, overlooking the St. Lawrence is **Fort Wellington National Historic Park.** The park covers 8.5 acres with well-preserved fortifications which date from 1812, when they were built to defend the now-peaceful border. A portion of the fort serves as a museum and contains many interesting exhibits.

Fort Malden National Historic Park. This park, covering 5 acres, is situated at Amherstburg, just south of Windsor. Fort Malden was constructed on the banks of the Detroit River between 1797 and 1799 after the surrender of Detroit by British forces in 1796, and for the next 40 years it was one of the principal frontier military posts in Upper Canada. During the War of 1812 Fort Malden played a conspicuous part and was occupied by an invading force from the United States. Evacuated in 1815, it again became an important military post during the border raids of 1837-1838.

Fort William and Port Arthur. Two great grain ports on the northwestern shore of Lake Superior. Perhaps the most impressive sights in these twin cities are the enormous grain elevators along the waterfront, where the great wheat shipments from the prairie provinces are stored while awaiting transfer to lake steamers. From the summit of Mt. McKay, just south of Fort William, there is an excellent view of the cities, their port facilities, and the surrounding countryside. **Kakabeka Falls,** to the west, are a spectacular sight. Both cities offer fine facilities for aquatic sports, excursions, and cruises.

Georgian Bay. The eastern part of Lake Huron, separated from the lake proper by the Bruce Peninsula and Manitoulin Island. The northern coast of Georgian Bay is rocky and high, but on the east the shore, although rocky, is low. The delightful scenery is made even more beautiful by the thousands of islands that dot the bay's surface. A number of these islands have been set aside as **Georgian Bay Islands National Park,** which comprises a total area of slightly more than 5 square miles. Beausoleil Island, the largest

in the park, contains the remains of former Indian settlements. Swimming, boating, fishing, and hiking may be enjoyed on the island. There are well-equipped camping sites, and along the southeastern shore are a number of excellent beaches. Animals found include deer, fox, raccoon, porcupine, skunk, muskrat, mink, beaver, and weasel. Many species of songbirds and birds of brilliant plumage may be observed. Waterfowl are abundant. **Flowerpot Island** lies in a channel connecting Georgian Bay with Lake Huron. The island owes its name to two large rock pillars—sculptured by wave action and erosion from the adjacent limestone cliffs—that stand out boldly on the eastern shore like two immense flowerpots. Small trees and shrubs growing in fissures accentuate the resemblance.

Among the popular vacation resorts on the shores of Georgian Bay are **Wassaga Beach** and the lake port of **Midland,** with its Huronia House museum. The museum contains a splendid collection of pioneer and Indian exhibits.

Hamilton. Lake port and industrial city on the western shore of Lake Ontario. Its excellent location for importing coal, iron ore, and limestone has given rise to its most important industry, the production of steel. It is also the site of McMaster University, which moved here from Toronto in 1930. Located in the center of the city, behind the city hall, is an open-air market, considered the largest in Canada. It features a colorful display of fruits, vegetables, and flowers grown in the district. Hamilton's art gallery has five large galleries that contain some of the finest collections in Canada. Among the points of historical interest is the museum Dundurn Castle, the former home of Sir Allan MacNab. Hamilton's **Rock Gardens** are located at the western entrance to the city. The display of flowers, shrubs, and trees presents an outstanding horticultural attraction. It is part of the **Royal Botanical Gardens,** which extend along the shoreline of Hamilton Bay to McMaster University and cover approximately 1,800 acres. West of the gardens are the beautiful **Webster's Falls.** At the eastern end of the city **Albion Falls,** near the King's Forest, present another popular sight.

Kingston. Historic port city at the northern end of Lake Ontario. Its location at the point where the lake enters the St. Lawrence River made it important not only for military and naval purposes but also commercially. It lies also at the southern end of the **Rideau Canal,** completed in 1832. The canal was the result of the British government's desire during the War of 1812 for a route whereby British gunboats could avoid American gunfire from the U. S. side of the St. Lawrence River. A string of lakes connected by canals and locks, it runs from Kingston on Lake Ontario to Ottawa and the Ottawa River. Of little commercial importance today, the Rideau Canal

The rock gardens at Hamilton, Ontario

Exhibition Park in Toronto

Photo, Peter Smith, Stratford, Ont.

Stage, Stratford Shakespearean Festival

Can. Govt. Trav. Bur.

Georgian Bay Islands National Park, Ontario

for pleasure cruises. The Rideau Lakes offer excellent fishing, and migratory waterfowl are also found. Boating on the lakes is also popular. Deer inhabit the surrounding countryside, which is sparsely settled and heavily forested. Kingston's excellent harbor, considered one of the best on the lake, is well equipped with numerous docks, a large grain elevator, and other port facilities. On a peninsula, Point Frederick, stands the Royal Military College, sometimes called the Sandhurst of Canada. Its attractive grounds and the Memorial Arch are worth visiting. On the other side of Navy Bay, opposite the military college, is historic **Fort Henry.** For many years an army garrison, the fort now contains a fine collection of firearms and other military objects. Guards, dressed in the redcoat uniform of a century ago, parade for the entertainment of visitors. Queen's University, originally established as a Presbyterian college, is in Kingston. Other points of interest in the city include St. George's Anglican Cathedral, St. Mary's Roman Catholic Cathedral, the Court House, and Murney Tower, built in 1846 for defense of the city.

Lake Nipigon. Largest lake in Ontario. It lies just north of Lake Superior, into which it flows via the Nipigon River. Dotted with thousands of islands, it offers magnificent scenery. The lake is especially noted for its excellent fishing. Waterfowl are found in season, and in the surrounding country moose and caribou roam.

Lake of the Woods. Largest of the maze of interconnected lakes that cover southwestern Ontario. Its coastline is extremely irregular, and its waters are dotted with nearly 15,000 islands. The lake is noted especially for its abundance of fish, and in the adjacent pine forests deer and moose are plentiful. **Kenora** is a popular tourist center located on its shores. The southwestern extremity of the lake lies in Minnesota.

Manitoulin Island. The world's largest lake island, it lies in the northern part of Lake Huron. It contains several sizable lakes, and a number of large bays indent its northern coastline. Fishermen and hunters frequent the northern part of the island because of its abundant fish resources and the availability of deer and bear.

Niagara Falls. Tourist center and industrial city, overlooking one of the best known waterfalls in North America. Niagara Falls, N.Y., is located on the other side of the Niagara River. The bulk of the river's waters plunges over the Canadian part of the falls, known as **Horseshoe Falls.** Beautifully illuminated at night, the falls are immensely popular with tourists and are visited particularly by newlyweds. Alongside the Niagara Gorge is **Queen Victoria Park,** with an excellent and varied display of attractive flowers. From the observation tower in **Table Rock House,** in the southern end of the park, an especially good view of Horseshoe Falls may be obtained. In the **Oakes Garden Theatre,** with its ornamental fountains and pools, is an impressive array of rock gardens, terraces, flowerbeds, and lily ponds. Nearby the **Rainbow Bridge** crosses to the United States. On its Canadian side is the Carillon Tower, where bell concerts may be heard. The **Whirlpool Rapids Bridge** also offers an interesting sight. Far below it the swirling waters of the Whirlpool may be watched.

Ottawa. Canada's national capital. It lies on the southern bank of the Ottawa River at its junction with the canalized Rideau River. (See RIDEAU CANAL under Kingston.) The city is dominated by the parliament buildings, which are set on a promontory overlooking the Ottawa River in a park of 35 acres known as Parliament Hill. The **Peace Tower,** constructed of stone with a copper-covered spire, immediately catches the eye. Almost 300 feet high, the tower contains a carillon and is sometimes compared to Giotto's bell-tower in Florence, Italy. Its Memorial Chamber is dedicated to the Canadian war dead. Behind the main Parliament Building stands the library, its flying buttresses and dome presenting a beautiful architectural sight. The National War Memorial, built of Canadian granite, consists of a great archway surmounting a massive pedestal that supports figures representing the various services. It commemorates the Canadians who died in World War I.

Among the many other places of interest in Ottawa is the Roman Catholic University of Ottawa. The National Gallery of Canada houses representative collections of Canadian painting and sculpture as well as European paintings, especially of the British, French,

Italian, and Dutch schools. The National Museum of Canada is a natural-history museum showing extensive collections of Canadian birds, mammals, reptiles, fish, and other animals; it includes mineral and fossil displays and Indian and Eskimo exhibits. Once the home of Sir Wilfrid Laurier, Laurier House was also the residence of William Mackenzie King, both men former prime ministers of Canada. The present official residence of the Canadian prime minister was completed in 1951 and is situated on a beautiful bluff overlooking the Ottawa River. The Royal Canadian Mint, where Canada's coins are made, is located in Ottawa. At the Public Archives the official records of Canada are kept, together with maps, pictures, books, and pamphlets related to Canadian history. The Canadian War Museum contains an interesting collection of war trophies and pictures taken during World Wars I and II. Near the foot of the Rideau Canal locks is the Bytown Museum. It contains one of the oldest complete buildings dating from the days when Ottawa was the little lumber town of Bytown; it also has a valuable collection of items relating to the history of Ottawa. Other places of special interest in Ottawa are the Central Experimental Farm, covering more than 1,000 acres devoted to extensive plant research; the Arboretum, with trees, shrubs, and plants from all vegetation areas of the world; and the Dominion Observatory.

Point Pelee National Park. Recreational area, comprising 6 square miles on Lake Erie, southeast of Windsor. Along the shoreline of the park are beautiful, broad beaches of silvery sand. Other recreational opportunities include camping, hiking, fishing, and aquatic sports in summer and skating on the big ponds in winter. The park is a place of unusual interest because it supports vegetation of a southern type. Its flora, rarely found in northern latitudes, includes the cactus plants, red mulberry, and many other botanical species commonly found in more southern regions. On one of the main routes followed by waterfowl and other birds on their northern and southern migrations, the park is also an important bird sanctuary. There is a remarkably varied forest growth. Besides being a summer and autumn playground for those who come to enjoy its opportunities for outdoor life and recreation, this entire park area offers naturalists, especially ornithologists and botanists, an excellent field for study.

Porcupine Gold Field. One of the principal gold-mining areas in North America. The chief mines are the famous Hollinger, Dome, and McIntyre mines, located near the town of **Timmins,** which is the region's commercial center. The Kirkland Lake gold field is nearby.

Quetico Provincial Park. A wilderness area covering 1,720 square miles of western On-

University College, University of Toronto

Univ. of Toronto

PLACES OF INTEREST IN CANADA

Old Fort Henry, Kingston, Ontario

tario along the Minnesota border. It is a region of numerous lakes set among rugged forested hills and is popular for canoeing. A game preserve, it includes moose and deer among its abundant wildlife.

St. Lawrence Islands National Park. The islands are part of the Thousand Islands, which lie in the great St. Lawrence River between Kingston and Brockville. The islands and the mainland area that form the park are popular recreational and camping spots. There is good fishing in the waters near the park islands. Facilities for swimming, sailing, canoeing, and other aquatic sports, as well as tennis and golf, are provided. Cedar Island, the most westerly of the park units, lies just outside the harbor of Kingston. Stovin Island is situated near Brockton.

Sault Sainte Marie. Important industrial city and tourist center on the northern shore of the St. Marys River. Its history is closely related to that of Sault Sainte Marie, Mich., which lies on the opposite side of the river. Through the famous Soo locks and canals passes the world's greatest marine commercial tonnage. These canals bypass the rapids in the river to allow transportation of the great cargoes of iron ore, grain, and lumber from Lake Superior to Lake Huron. The city is also the gateway to the fishing and hunting resorts of the woods and lakes of the Algoma district.

Stratford. Named after the English birthplace of William Shakespeare. A city of beautiful parkland and ponds, it is known for its Shakespeare Memorial Theatre. Thousands of theater lovers flock here every summer to enjoy its celebrated Shakespearean festival.

Sudbury. Center of one of the greatest nickel-mining areas in the world. Although nickel mining, smelting, and refining dominate the city, it is also important in the pro-

Parliament Building, Ottawa

duction of copper, platinum, and other minerals. Hunters and fishermen visit Sudbury for the wealth of game and fish in the forests, lakes, and streams of the surrounding country.

Toronto. Capital of Ontario and one of Canada's most populous cities. It lies on the northwestern shore of Lake Ontario and is a lake port with excellent harbor facilities. The province's Parliament Buildings, situated in Queen's Park, present an attractive sight. Nearby are the buildings of the University of Toronto, among which are Hart House, University College, and King's College. The open-air Shakespeare Festival, held every summer in the university's Trinity College quadrangle, is a favorite with theater lovers. A few blocks south of the Parliament Buildings stands Osgoode Hall, the seat of Ontario's High Court, and nearby is the city hall with its 300-foot clock tower. Not far from Toronto's waterfront lies the city's financial and commercial district. The Stock Exchange on Bay Street, sometimes called the Wall Street of Canada, is of interest. From the observation tower of the Bank of Commerce, one of the city's remarkable skyscrapers, a splendid view of Toronto and its surrounding countryside may be obtained. Noteworthy churches are the Anglican St. James' Cathedral, with its lofty spire and its stained glass windows, and the Roman Catholic St. Michael's Cathedral. Old Fort York, captured by U. S. troops in 1813, is of historic interest. The city's art gallery contains an outstanding collection of works by Canadian artists as well as many fine European paintings. The Sigmund Samuel Canadiana Gallery houses a magnificent collection of fine paintings of episodes and landscapes important in Canadian history. The Royal Ontario Museum, renowned for its large Chinese collection, also has excellent geological, archeological, and zoological exhibits. Mackenzie House, former home of William Lyon Mackenzie, leader of the 1837 rebellion and first mayor of Toronto, has been restored and is now a national museum containing interesting souvenirs of his life and times. One of Toronto's unusual attractions is the Casa Loma, a huge, fabulous castle with turrets, spires, and other medieval trimmings. Built as a private residence by a Toronto millionaire, it is now operated as a showplace by the Kiwanis Club.

The great Canadian National Exhibition is held annually in Exhibition Park, which is situated along the lake shore. The world's largest yearly exhibition, it has exhibits ranging from agriculture and industry to fashion and sports. It attracts millions of visitors every year. Among the city's many other parks are High Park, also on the lake shore, and Toronto Island Park, south of the harbor and reached by ferry. One of Canada's busiest ports, Toronto has an excellent harbor with well-equipped dock facilities for the loading and unloading of all types of cargo. Its waterfront development includes not only harbor improvements but also the reclamation of land for park and recreational purposes.

Welland Ship Canal. Waterway providing passage for large lake steamers between Lake Ontario and Lake Erie. It runs more or less parallel to the Niagara River, which cannot be used for interlake transportation because of the falls. Of special interest are the giant twin locks at the industrial city of **Thorold.** These locks, part of the series that lift vessels between the two lake levels, are some-

times compared with the Gatun Locks of the Panama Canal.

Windsor. Industrial city opposite Detroit, Mich. It is the center of the Canadian automobile industry and maintains close communication with Detroit, to which it is connected by bridge and tunnel. The Ambassador Bridge is one of the longest suspension bridges in the world. Millions of persons enter Canada from the United States through Windsor every year, and the city is Canada's main point of entry for American visitors. Parks and beaches line the riverside. In Willistead Park are the library and the art gallery.

Woodside National Historic Park. This 11-acre site in Kitchener, established as a national historic park in 1954, contains the large gray brick building that was the boyhood home of William Lyon Mackenzie King, former prime minister of Canada.

PRINCE EDWARD ISLAND

Canada's smallest province is a land of tourist delights. It has a unique red soil that contrasts with the low, rolling, green pastures. There are no great extremes of temperature because of the moderating influence of the sea. In the summer months visitors are attracted to the island by the charm of the rural scenery and by the splendid bathing beaches of the northern coast. These sandy and gently sloping beaches are sheltered by sandbanks, which protect them from the full force of the sea. The storied home of Anne of Green Gables is found in Prince Edward Island National Park. There are many attractions for the tourists, such as swimming, boating, fishing in the small rivers and along the coast, golf, and game-bird hunting. The tree-shaded roads, the charming farmhouses, the green meadows, and the general mildness of the climate make a holiday on the island a most restful and enjoyable one.

Charlottetown. The capital of the province is situated on a long inlet known as Hillsborough Bay, and has an excellent harbor. It is the commercial and communications center for the island. The city is regarded as the birthplace of the Canadian Confederation because the first of the conferences that resulted in the formation of the Dominion of Canada was held here in 1864. The Provincial Building was the setting of this historic conference. Now the most important building in the city, it is the home of the legislative assembly. The official residence of the lieutenant governor is the Government House. Charlottetown is the seat of Prince of Wales College and nearby St. Dunstan's University.

Prince Edward Island National Park. The

Tignish Run, Prince Edward Island

park extends along the northern shore of the island, along the Gulf of St. Lawrence, for a distance of nearly 25 miles. Among its outstanding features are its magnificent beaches. Adjacent to them, sand dunes and sandstone cliffs rise to considerable heights. Across the mouths of several bays, small islands and shoals give protection to the inner waters. The park is composed of three main sections, each of which borders the seashore. The eastern, or Dalvay-Stanhope, section extends from Tracadie Bay to Covehead Harbour and contains the administrative headquarters of the park. The Brackley Beach lies between Covehead Harbour and Rustico Bay. The Cavendish, or Green Gables, section forms the western part and extends along the coast from Rustico Harbour to New London Bay. At Green Gables is the romantic old farmhouse made famous by the novels of the Canadian author Lucy Maud Montgomery.

QUEBEC

Quebec, largest of the Canadian provinces, has been justly called the Cradle of Canada. It was up the broad St. Lawrence River that Jacques Cartier sailed on his epochal voyage of discovery in 1534, and from the resulting French settlements stemmed much of Canada's early history. Today Quebec is the guardian of French-Canadian culture, and in that role it preserves a way of life that is of infinite travel charm. Visitors find unending pleasure in this ancient province, famed for its Old World hospitality, customs, and traditions. Its great cities of Quebec and Montreal have historic, architectural, and economic interest. Except for the region north of the Saguenay River, between Labrador and Hudson Bay, which is largely unexplored, the coastal areas, especially the Gaspé Peninsula, the wooded lakeland regions, and the mountain playgrounds, offer scenic beauty and recreational facilities for the tourist. In the valley of the St. Lawrence, which includes the lowlands extending along the river from the city of Quebec to the western extremity of the province, are situated the chief cities and towns. The mountainous region south of the St. Lawrence includes the Notre Dame Mountains country. To the northeast lies the high, forest-clad region of the Gaspé Peninsula.

Fort Chambly National Historic Park. Situated on the Richelieu River about 20 miles from Montreal, the fort was one of several constructed along the river by the French for the protection of settlers against attack by the Iroquois. The first fort, erected in 1665, served until 1702, when it was burned by the Indians. Replaced on a smaller scale, it was rebuilt of stone in its present proportions in 1710-1711. It changed hands several times during the wars of the 18th century. Abandoned

as a military post about the middle of the 19th century, the site, covering 2½ acres, was acquired by the National Parks Branch in 1921. Since that time considerable restoration work has been carried out. Inside the main entrance a stone museum houses an interesting group of exhibits.

Fort Lennox National Historic Park. Comprising an area of 210 acres on Ile aux Noix in the Richelieu River near the U.S. border, the park includes the well-preserved buildings of one of the largest forts constructed in Canada. The fortifications are the outgrowth of a defense post built by the French in 1759 to resist the advance of the English from the south. Its surrender in 1760 to the English was a prelude to the fall of Montreal and the ultimate transfer of New France to British rule. Garrisoned by British troops from the time of its occupation, Fort Lennox fell to an invading American force in 1775 but was evacuated the following year. The present fortifications were commenced in 1782, with further additions made during the War of 1812. The fort was abandoned as a military post in 1870.

Gaspé Peninsula. This ruggedly beautiful peninsula, which extends into the Gulf of St. Lawrence, has many rivers and lakes in its heavily wooded, mountainous, and uninhabited interior. The population is centered along the coast in picturesque settlements. A 550-mile highway circles the entire peninsula and passes through beautiful countryside enhanced by many old customs and folklore. The people, deeply attached to their religion, preserve those ancient traditions, which are not the least of Gaspé's many attractions. **Gaspesian Provincial Park** includes a mountainous area where the highest mountains in southeastern Canada are found. An impressive view of the surrounding mountains may be had from Mt. Jacques Cartier (4,160 feet) in the Shickshock Mountains, an extension of the Appalachian chain. There are lakes that offer excellent fishing in the park. Percé is a fishing village at the foot of Percé Mountain. An ancient mission is located here. Percé Rock, which has so often been described, painted, and photographed, lies just offshore. Swarming with gulls and cormorants, it is a fascinating tourist attraction. Its height ranges from 154 feet to 290 feet. Its length from one tip to the other is 1,565 feet, and it does not measure more than 300 feet in width. Opposite is **Bonaventure Island,** a bird sanctuary, with picturesque ancient houses.

Isle of Orleans. The old churches and manor houses in this district display the skill of 18th-century French-Canadians. These churches are also repositories of exquisite wood carvings and creations of the goldsmiths and silversmiths who worked in and near Quebec.

The ancient parishes witnessed the earliest days of the colony. Their yellowed registers record births, marriages, and deaths in families that, over 300 years ago, settled on farms and work the same soil to this day. Because it was relatively inaccessible until the bridge was built in 1932, the Isle of Orleans has maintained much of the old 18th-century French-Canadian atmosphere, little changed by modern life. Consequently it is one of Quebec's most charming and interesting showplaces.

Laurentian Mountains. Miles of mountainous area, covered with forests and thousands of glittering streams and lakes, make this a very popular natural playground. The hills range from 1,000 to 2,000 feet and rise to a height of 3,905 feet in Laurentides Park. The area is well equipped and easily accessible for the sports enthusiast and tourist. Fishing, hunting, swimming, and sailing are among the favorite forms of recreation. In the winter the area is excellent for skiing. There are numerous well-developed ski centers. **Laurentides Provincial Park,** with an area of 3,613 square miles, lies in a mountainous area of the Laurentian Plateau. Its many lakes and streams are known for their fine trout fishing. Another park with numerous lakes, some excellent for fishing, is **La Vérendrye Provincial Park.** The park contains an area of 4,747 square miles. The largest body of water in the park is the Cabonga reservoir, part of a hydroelectric power development that covers an area totaling more than 250 square miles. **Montagne Tremblante Provincial Park** is a noted resort area in the Laurentians. The many lakes in this forested, mountainous region offer excellent fishing. This area is especially famous for having some of the finest downhill skiing in eastern North America. The ski facilities and accommodations are excellent.

Montmorency Falls. Not far from the city of Quebec the Montmorency River tumbles 274 feet into the St. Lawrence River to form the spectacular Montmorency Falls. They are among the highest in Canada and are higher than those at Niagara although with considerably less volume.

Montreal. A major seaport and commercial center of Canada, it is the second-largest French-speaking city in the world. Located on Montreal Island in the St. Lawrence River, this cosmopolitan city has many historic relics of the French rule. Dominion Square is an impressive setting in the center of a commercial area. There are various monuments on the square. On one side of the tree-shaded park is the building of the Sun Life Insurance Company of Canada. This huge landmark is one of the largest office buildings in the world. Opposite is the Cathedral of St. James, a

Sainte Anne de Beaupré, Quebec
Que. Prov. Publicity Bur.

Montmorency Falls near Quebec city
Can. Natl. Ry.

Percé, a village on Gaspé Peninsula, Quebec
Can. Natl. Ry.

Can. Pac. Ry. Co.
Montreal harbor on the St. Lawrence River

Can. Natl. Ry.
Winter on Mount Royal in Montreal

Can. Natl. Ry.
Quebec's Citadel (left) from the St. Lawrence

Can. Natl. Ry.
Skiing at St. Sauveur, in the Laurentians

Que. Prov. Publicity Bur.
Ski lodge in the Laurentian Mountains

The port city of Montreal
Can. Natl. Ry.

reproduction of St. Peter's in Rome. One-half the size of the original, it is 333 feet long and 222 feet wide. The striking dome rises 250 feet above the street level and is surmounted by a great gilded cross. The façade of the basilica is impressive, with its 13 large bronze statues of saints, which 13 parishes in the diocese of Montreal presented as a gift. The dignified interior has an altar surmounted by a very ornamental baldachin, as in St. Peter's. In the downtown section is the Place d'Armes. Here is the mother church of Montreal, Notre Dame. It stands on the site of the first church of Montreal. One of the largest churches in North America, its two towers rise to about 215 feet above the Place d'Armes. Because of its double galleries, this vast church can accommodate 12,000 persons. The interior is decorated with wood sculptures and many beautiful paintings. Many of the stained-glass windows depict incidents of old Ville Marie, the settlement founded here in 1642. The museum attached to the church contains paintings, old works of art, sculptures, and ornaments. In the Place d'Armes is the Maisonneuve monument erected in memory of the founder of Montreal. At the foot of its pedestal are figures of prominent early citizens. The old Château de Ramezay was erected in 1705 by Claude de Ramezay, governor of Montreal. It served as the residence of the British governors after the French defeat. At present it is a museum that houses various objects from the French period. Jacques Cartier Square is the site of the provincial Bonsecours market, the oldest and largest in Montreal. It is very picturesque on market day when farmers and merchants sell their produce and wares. Nelson monument, a column commemorating the defeat of the Franco-Spanish fleet at Trafalgar in 1805, is situated in the square. The piers, which are berths for the transatlantic ships, are along one side of the square. The oldest church in Montreal, Notre Dame de Bonsecours, is located next to the market. For more than 300 years this church has served as a sanctuary for sailors. The exterior has been restored, but the interior still has some fine old mosaics. A narrow stairway gives access to a tiny chapel in the tower. Lying midstream in the St. Lawrence River and connected to Montreal by a bridge, is St. Helen's Isle. This 135-acre site is the site of a public park where an old restored French fort is located. Beautiful gardens, immense trees, and an artificial lake are found at La Fontaine Park. A bandstand is the scene of many summer evening concerts. Nearby are the Botanical Gardens. This parkland area contains over 10,000 varieties of plants selected from all parts of the world. Two world-renowned universities are located in Montreal. McGill University is one of the most respected in the scholastic world and is known especially for its medical and engineering schools. Located above the older sections of the city, the buildings and grounds cover several city blocks. This English-speaking university was named after James McGill, who bequeathed his estate and £10,000 for the founding of a college. The center of French culture and learning is the University of Montreal. Founded in 1876 as part of the University of Laval in Quebec city, it is the largest French-speaking university outside France. In 1919 it became an autonomous university. Its present buildings on the slope of Mount Royal were commenced in 1928. Mount Royal, the remains of a lofty volcanic peak, has been transformed into a fine park, which covers an

Can. Natl. Ry.
Gannets on Bonaventure Island, Quebec

area of 480 acres overlooking the city. In one part of the park is a 100-foot-high illuminated cross, which is symbolic of Maisonneuve's religious fervor. The summit gives a fine view of the city stretching out to the broad St. Lawrence River. In the winter the ski trails and toboggan slides are favorites of many sports enthusiasts from all parts of the metropolitan area. Opposite the Mount Royal Park is the famous St. Joseph Shrine. It was founded by Brother André in glorification of the patron saint of Canada, St. Joseph. It is now one of North America's principal religious shrines. The first shrine was a wooden chapel built in 1904. The news of miracles that benefited many sufferers and were attributed to Brother André's intercession soon brought many pilgrims to the chapel. A new chapel was started in 1924. This huge, striking oratory is a monument to St. Joseph and also contains the tomb of Brother André. Nearby is the Wax Museum, which contains over 200 life-size wax figures, including one of Brother André. Many scenes of Canadian history and other events appear in realistic form. As a great seaport and growing commercial center, Montreal owes much to its harbor. It is a great inland port, about 1,000 miles from the ocean, and therefore has no interference from the tides. It is accessible to large ocean liners during the navigation season, when the river is not frozen. Montreal also is one of the world's largest grain-shipping ports.

Quebec, the capital of the province of Quebec. It is a picturesque city with an Old World background, and it abounds with historical buildings. The historic **Plains of Abraham,** situated on a plateau in the southwestern part of the city, were the scene of the battle between British and French troops in September, 1759, that resulted in the capitulation of Quebec and final British control over Canada. The area is now a city park, Parc des Champ de Batailles, or Battlefields Park. Panoramic views of the St. Lawrence River and the distant shore may be obtained from the old observation post. An interesting monument in the park is one of Joan of Arc on horseback. The Provincial Museum contains natural-history exhibits and examples of Canadian art. It also houses the archives of the city, including the surrender papers of 1759. A monument has been erected in honor of James Wolfe, the British general who died in this memorable battle.

Quebec has a combination of the new and the old. The city consists of an upper and lower town. The lower town is at the foot of the cliff. This formed the trading district in the early days and was the first part to be inhabited. It is a crowded area with many narrow streets, as Sous-le-Cap Street, one of

Photos: N.F.B., Can. Natl. Ry.

Notre Dame de Bonsecours, Montreal; Mount Royal's giant cross; Notre Dame Church, Montreal; Château Frontenac, Quebec

the narrowest in America. At one time this was the fashionable district of Quebec. The upper town, built above the cliff, is noted for its quaint little houses, many of them period homes, with little green shutters, red roofs, and tiny windows. This is the section where the first religious, official, and military buildings were erected. The fashionable district of the lower town moved to this area to what is now known as the Latin Quarter. Dominating the city is the internationally known Château Frontenac. This hotel is an impressive sight with its French-style turrets and cupolas and its steeply pitched copper roof. Dufferin Terrace, a wide boardwalk beside the hotel, offers magnificent views of the lower town and the river.

In 1663 the Seminary of Quebec was founded by Bishop François Xavier de Laval-Montmorency to train missionaries for the Indians and men for the priesthood. Some of the old buildings that were destroyed by fire have been replaced by more modern structures. Laval University, which was founded in 1852, had its beginnings in the Seminary of Quebec. This school has a fine museum containing sections for art, natural history, and religious, geological, and ethnological relics. Quebec is filled with historic places of worship and is the headquarters of the Roman Catholic Church in Canada. The oldest church in the city is the Basilica of Notre Dame, the seat of the cardinal archbishop of Quebec. It stands today on the original foundations of 1647, although it was three times rebuilt following disastrous fires. In the crypt are buried the remains of some 900 leading figures in Canada's history. Quebec has been called the Fortified City. The fortifications, the third the city has known, were constructed between 1823 and 1832. They center around the Citadel, a diamond-shaped fortress situated atop 360-foot-high Cape Diamond. It is now the home of Quebec's famed Royal 22d Regiment, which still changes the guard every day in a traditional ceremony, and it is also the summer residence of the governor general of Canada. The enclosing wall circles the old city and gives entrance to it through three remaining gates. The part known as the Ramparts is studded with old cannons that stood watch over the harbor. The Martello Towers form the outer defense of the system. Three of the four original towers remain.

Quebec has a number of important public buildings that enable it to fulfill its function as capital and as a center of French-Canadian culture. The stately Parliament Buildings, dating back to 1878, are architecturally outstanding. The central tower is about 172 feet high and resembles the famed Peace Tower on Parliament Hill at Ottawa. Along the main façade, 16 bronze statues of important soldiers, statesmen, and churchmen face the old wall of Quebec. Here the Legislative As-

sembly and the Legislative Council meet in richly furnished chambers. There are also excellent libraries and vaults containing most of the original archives of New France. The surrounding gardens add to the natural beauty of the site. The Ursuline Convent, founded in 1639, contains the tomb of Montcalm, the French general who died in the Plains of Abraham battle. Also here in the chapel is a votive lamp that has never gone out since it was first lighted in 1717. An interesting building in the lower town is the little church of Notre Dame des Victoires, which dates back to 1688. Parts of the original church remain, although the structure has been extensively restored. Inside are stored such treasures as old battle flags and paintings by Rubens and Vandyke.

Sainte Anne de Beaupré. This famous shrine dates back to 1658 and is known throughout the world as a great place of pilgrimage. According to tradition, some Breton sailors were saved from shipwreck and built a little chapel in honor of their patron saint, Sainte Anne. The first miracle, according to tradition, took place in 1658, and since then pilgrims have flocked to this church. A huge cathedral, which replaced the one destroyed by fire in 1922, dominates the town. Among other attractions are the Commemorative Chapel, the life-size Stations of the Cross, and the "Cyclorama," a circular sacred painting 360 feet in circumference. Sainte Anne de Beaupré is also a popular center of winter sports and offers excellent skiing facilities.

St. Lawrence River. The great water highway of Canada. Measured from its source to its mouth, the St. Lawrence is one of the longest rivers in the world. In its course it expands into the five Great Lakes—Lakes Superior, Michigan, Huron, Erie, and Ontario—which contain about half of the fresh water on the surface of the globe. The commercial importance of the St. Lawrence River and the Great Lakes can hardly be overestimated. However, navigation from the sea to the Great Lakes involves a canal system that enables ships to bypass the rapids in the river. Because of the difference in level of the lakes a system of locks is necessary. With the opening of the St. Lawrence Seaway in 1959, most of the world's ocean-going ships are now able to navigate to the Great Lakes. The seaway project involved deepening existing channels, constructing new ones, and reducing the number of locks. Previously only small ocean vessels specially designed for the Great Lakes trade were able to negotiate this passage.

Sherbrooke. Situated on the St. Francis River at the mouth of the Magog River, this city is the commercial center of the Eastern Townships. Abundant, cheap hydroelectric power has been an aid in the city's economic growth.

The population is predominantly French. Among the most interesting buildings are the cathedral and the nearby archbishop's palace. An illuminated cross 75 feet high is situated on a hill to the south of the city. There are many parks. Especially inviting are the Zoological Gardens, Victoria Park, and Jacques Cartier Park. Winter sports are very popular in and around Sherbrooke. There are open ski slopes in the city, and nearby are also excellent slopes and trails.

Trois Rivières, or **Three Rivers.** This city is a busy port located at the confluence of the St. Lawrence and St. Maurice rivers. It is also a busy commercial center and one of the greatest newsprint producers in the world. The city abounds with old buildings dating from the 17th and 18th centuries, the time of the French regime. Among the principal places of interest are the Recollet Monastery, which was constructed in 1698; the Ursuline Convent, established in 1697; and old homes like the Manor Boucher de Niverville and the Hertel de la Frenière house. Not far from Trois Rivières, at suburban Cap de la Madeleine, is the famous Shrine of the Holy Rosary, one of Canada's leading shrines. The original wooden chapel was built here in 1659. This was replaced in 1720 by a stone building, which today is one of the oldest buildings of its kind in Canada. Trois Rivières is also a very popular winter-sports center. In the surrounding area are excellent trails and open slopes, in addition to a fine ski jump.

SASKATCHEWAN

Canada's granary of the west, Saskatchewan with its tree-lined lakes and many miles of deep forest also provides opportunity for excellent fishing and hunting. The northern part of the province is characterized by count-

Photo, N.F.B.

City Hall, Regina, Saskatchewan

Steamship, docked at Carcross on Lake Bennett, Yukon Territory

less lakes, rivers, and muskegs with numerous outcroppings of rock, worn smooth by erosion. The whole area is covered by forest growth. The southern portion of Saskatchewan, the Great Plains, is, in general, a region of rolling prairie interrupted by ridges and valleys. Here are the province's extensive wheatlands. But, contrary to widespread belief, less than one-third of Saskatchewan consists of prairie. The main rivers are the North and South Saskatchewan, which unite in the central part of the province; the Qu'Appelle; and the Carrot. In the north are many rivers including the Churchill River, and a great number of lakes, including Lake Athabaska and Reindeer Lake.

Fort Battleford National Historic Park. Situated 4 miles south of the city of North Battleford, this park contains some of the buildings that formed part of the original Northwest Mounted Police post established there in 1876. The existing buildings are the commanding officer's residence, the officers' quarters, the sick-horse stable, the guardroom, and the messhall and kitchen. The park area is surrounded by a log stockade, and the buildings house an interesting museum collection pertaining to the Northwest Mounted Police, the Indians, the fur trade, the early settlers, and the general development of the West. The site, comprising 36.7 acres, was established as a national historic park in 1951.

Moose Jaw. Railroad center and industrial city situated in Saskatchewan's wheat-growing region. It has extensive stockyards and flour mills; oil refining is important. Of interest is the city's natatorium, where there is indoor swimming in natural hot mineral water, which is piped to the pool. The Wild Animal Park attracts many visitors. Buffalo, deer, elk, antelope, and mountain sheep, some of the species of wildlife found there, wander freely through the grounds.

Prince Albert National Park. Situated in the central part of Saskatchewan, it covers an area of 1,496 square miles. It is a fine example of the lake and woodland country that lies north of the great agricultural prairies. Hundreds of lakes, varying in size from tiny rock basins to bodies of water 20 miles long, dot the forested landscape. Under normal water conditions these lakes, lined with white sand beaches, form connected waterways and provide excellent opportunities for canoeing and boating. The summer resort of Waskesiu is situated at the eastern end of Lake Waskesiu.

Regina. Capital of Saskatchewan, it is located in the province's rich southern wheat plains. The legislative buildings stand in the beautifully landscaped grounds of a 167-acre park on the shore of the artificial Wascana Lake. In the Provincial Museum of Natural History are displays of zoology, archeology, and paleontology related to Saskatchewan. The Regina

Exhibition, held every summer, attracts many visitors each year. When Regina became the capital of the Northwest Territories in 1883, it was also made headquarters of the Northwest Mounted Police, now called the Royal Canadian Mounted Police. The city has remained an important administrative and training center for the mounted police force, and a tour of its barracks and the museum, where much of the early romantic history of the Mounties is depicted, provides interesting information to visitors.

Saskatoon. Commercial and industrial city built on both banks of the South Saskatchewan River. The giant grain elevator and flour mills indicate the importance of wheat to Saskatoon. The city is the home of the University of Saskatchewan, whose distinctive white limestone buildings are of architectural interest. Among Saskatoon's tourist attractions is the Western Development Museum, in which a unique collection of early farm machinery, antique cars and buggies, and pioneer furnishings are preserved as relics of bygone days. During exhibition time each summer the museum comes to life with full-scale demonstrations of pioneer activities of all kinds. The castle-like Bessborough Hotel is also of interest to visitors.

Radium and uranium mines at Port Radium, Northwest Territories

NORTHWEST TERRITORIES

The Northwest Territories contain the mainland portion of Canada lying north of the 60th parallel of latitude between Hudson Bay on the east and Yukon Territory on the west, together with the islands lying between the mainland of Canada and the North Pole, including those in Hudson Bay, James Bay, and Hudson Strait. For purposes of organization and administration, this vast area, covering more than a third of Canada, is divided into three districts—Mackenzie, Keewatin, and Franklin.

Great Bear Lake. Large lake in the northwestern part of the Northwest Territories. It is notable because pitchblende, source of radium and uranium, was discovered on its eastern shore in 1930. This discovery resulted in establishment of the town of Port Radium at the site.

Great Slave Lake. Another large lake, situated south of Great Bear Lake. From its western end the great Mackenzie River flows northwestward into the Arctic Ocean. Great Slave Lake is important for its commercial fisheries, the principal catch being whitefish and lake trout. On the northern shore of the lake is the gold-mining center, Yellowknife, one of the chief settlements in the Northwest Territories.

YUKON TERRITORY

Comprising the extreme northwestern portion of the mainland of Canada, the Yukon Territory is generally mountainous, although there are many stretches of rolling country with wide flats in the river valleys. Most of the region is drained by the Yukon River and its tributaries into the Bering Sea. Air travel is the chief means of transportation to the northern part of the territory. Through the southern part runs the Alaska Highway, which stretches between Dawson Creek, British Columbia, and Fairbanks, Alaska.

Dawson. Center of the Klondike gold-mining region and former capital of Yukon Territory. The famous Klondike gold rush began after gold was discovered in 1896 on Bonanza Creek near here, and the town of Dawson came into being as a result. During the height of its prosperity the town was much larger than it is today. For more than half a century it was the administrative center of the Yukon Territory.

Mount Logan. Highest mountain peak in Canada. Situated in the St. Elias Mountains near the Alaska border in the southwestern part of the Yukon Territory, Mt. Logan rises to a height of 19,850 feet. Nearby on the Alaska boundary Mt. St. Elias rises to 18,008 feet.

Whitehorse. Capital of Yukon Territory. The principal population center along the Alaska Highway, Whitehorse is connected with Skagway, Alaska by White Pass and Yukon Railway. It is also the head of navigation on the Yukon River. Scenic attractions near the city are Miles Canyon and Whitehorse Rapids, which were navigated by many of the Klondike gold seekers in 1897 and 1898. The Yukon division of the Royal Canadian Mounted Police has its headquarters in Whitehorse.

The town of Whitehorse, Yukon Territory, on the Yukon River

PLACES OF INTEREST IN
MEXICO AND CENTRAL AMERICA

MEXICO

From the majestic mountain ranges of the Sierra Madre to the shores of the Rio Grande, Mexico is a land of startling contrasts. Here is a country rich in Aztec tradition and yet completely in tune with the 20th century. Modern Mexican life places Parisian fashions alongside the simple garb of the peasant, the baseball field next to the bullring, and the cosmopolitan high rise side by side with the baroque church. Mexico could be called a veritable empire, covering 761,530 square miles, an area greater than the size of Sweden, Germany, France, and Spain combined. In shape, Mexico resembles a cornucopia—appropriately enough for a land so rich in natural resources. For over four centuries, Mexico has supplied more than one-third of the world's silver; it has huge deposits of copper and iron ore; and it is the fourth largest petroleum producer in the Western Hemisphere. According to tradition, the great Aztec Empire in Mexico had its beginnings when the Aztecs departed from Aztlán around A.D. 820, and after many centuries arrived at what is today the Valley of Mexico. It is believed that they chose this site because of a prophecy which instructed them to build a capital where they saw an eagle holding a serpent in its claws. Mexico City is now located on this

Mexican Government Tourist Department

The library at the Ciudad Universitaria in Mexico City is famous for the striking murals covering its walls. Many other examples of this colorful art may be found throughout the capital.

Delta Air Lines

Donkeys, still widely used as a means of transportation in Mexico, are a familiar sight in the countryside and in smaller towns.

site. Officially, Mexico is known as "Los Estados Unidos Mexicanos," or, the Mexican United States. Within the country the name Mexico refers to the capital, Mexico City. Mexico is divided into 29 states, two federal territories, and one federal district, each with its own capital and local administration.

Aguascalientes

Located in north central Mexico, Aguascalientes, or "Hot Waters," is noted for its fine climate and the many hot mineral springs which have given it its name. One of Mexico's smallest states, Aguascalientes is a country of vivid colonial charm.

Aguascalientes, the capital, is also called La Ciudad Perforada because of the network of underground tunnels built by unknown, ancient Indian peoples. Like the rest of the state, the capital abounds in mineral springs. The colorful annual festival and the haciendas that breed fighting bulls are two more sight-seeing attractions. The site of the capital was discovered by one of Cortés' men in 1522, and the city was founded in 1575. Industries include cotton mills, pottery factories, and tanneries. The city is also noted for its fine linens. Buildings representing Mexican architecture include the Government Palace and the Church of San Antonio.

Baja California

Known as the "backwoods of Mexico," Baja California is the youngest state of Mexico, occupying the northern half of the peninsula of Lower California. It is a region of deserts and mountains with wildly beautiful scenery. The coastal area provides some of the best deep-sea fishing in the world. It has several colorful border communities.

Ensenada. Built around beautiful blue Todos Santos Bay, this delightful resort town offers excellent facilities for fishing and surfing. The locality's colorful history of pirates who preyed on treasure-laden ships provided inspiration for Robert Louis

Stevenson's *Treasure Island.* Miramar Chapultepec Lookout on a hill behind the city is a fine vantage point for viewing the surrounding area.

Mexicali. Capital of Baja California, it is located across the border from Calexico, California. Symbolizing the friendship between the United States and Mexico, the name Mexicali combines the first two syllables of Mexico and California. It is an agricultural area.

Tijuana is a popular border town opposite Tijuana, California. Points of special interest include numerous souvenir shops, night clubs, jai alai games, and the Agua Caliente race track.

Baja California Sur

Mexico's federal territory of Baja California Sur, located in the southern half of the peninsula of Lower California, remains almost the same as it was centuries ago: a region of mountain-desert wilderness with occasional adobe houses and mission churches. Naturalists and archeologists find the area valuable for the study of marine flora and fauna and Indian relics. In recent years, the entire Baja peninsula has come into some prominence as the "Indianapolis" of off-road racing because of its annual auto race, the "Baja 1000." Starting at Ensenada in upper Baja, the race ends at La Paz, near the southern tip of Baja California Sur.

La Paz. This 18th century town, capital of the territory of Baja California Sur, still retains much of its quiet charm. It has handsome palm-lined boulevards, fine residences, glorious sunsets, and a mild climate the year round. The harbor at La Paz is considered to be one of the best game fishing areas in the world. La Paz, once known as "City of Pearls" because of the rare black pearls found in the gulf nearby, is the most truly Mexican city of the Baja.

Mulegé. The Baja's only genuine oasis, Mulegé is a picturesque little town set amidst palm trees and citrus orchards. It is situated at the mouth of Concepción Bay, regarded as one of the most beautiful in the world, and is another excellent fishing spot in Mexico.

Campeche

Campeche, a state between Tabasco and Yucatán on the Gulf of Mexico, has many rivers, islands, and jungles, and is rich in tropical flora and fauna. One of the chief exports is logwood called *campeche.*

Campeche. Built in 1540, the capital of the state is one of Mexico's oldest cities and the second largest on the Yucatán peninsula. Pirate walls and forts left over from buccaneer days are a picturesque reminder that pirates once found Campeche worth attention. It is a major fishing port, and also produces tortoise-shell combs and Panama hats. Campeche's two museums are of interest; the Archeological Museum contains many objects of the Mayan culture, and the Museo de las Armas is filled with artifacts of the famed conquistadores.

Chiapas

The state of Chiapas, one of the most remote regions in Mexico, is a paradise for archeologist and anthropologist alike. Here, in the uplands, the pursuit of Mayan relics and ruins goes on as relentlessly as does the study of the Indians themselves, who still speak their ancient language and practice their old customs. Chiapas, bordering on Guatemala, is bounded by mountains, jungles, ocean, and rivers. It is exceedingly fertile and grows everything from coffee, rice, and wheat to tropical flowers, including incredibly beautiful orchids. Chiapas is thought to have vast natural resources as yet unexplored.

Tuxtla Gutiérrez. A clean, modern city with an inviting plaza, famous for cheese and fine horses, rich in mahogany and tropical flowers—so goes the description of Tuxtla, capital of the state, on Suchiapa River. Nearby is the Cañón Sumidero, known as the "Aztec Leap." It was here that Aztecs leaped to their death in the rapids below rather than submit to Spanish rule. Tuxtla Gutiérrez has a Museo Regional with fine archeological pieces, and a zoo housing local animals.

Palenque. In the famous Chiapas archeological zone, the mystique of the Mayas is dramatically preserved in the Palenque ruins. The temples include the Temple of the Sun, the Temple of the Laws, and the Temple of the Cross. Largest of the buildings is the Palenque Palace which stands on a pyramid forty feet high. Rich frescoes adorn the walls of these edifices, which are among the most majestic of the ancient Maya civilization.

San Cristóbal de las Casas. High in a shining valley, rimmed by mountains, San Cristóbal de las Casas is called the "jewel" of Mexico. It is an unchanged colonial town where contact with the past is ever present. Indians from many tribes are seen in their colorful native costumes in the picturesque marketplace.

Chihuahua

The largest state in Mexico is the northern border state of Chihuahua, with the massive range of the Sierra Madre Occidental in the west and vast desert basins in the north and east. Chihuahua is also one of the wealthiest states, due to its rich mineral deposits of silver, gold, and copper.

Chihuahua, the capital, is a busy industrial city. However, it is not known for industry alone. The main plaza area rivals Mexico City's uptown area in sophistication and wealth. One of the city's most beautiful architectural attractions is the Palacio de Gobierno, which has the tower where Miguel Hidalgo, the father of Mexican independence, was imprisoned and executed. The house where Pancho Villa lived is now a museum containing mementos of his stormy life. Among the curiosities of Chihuahua are the barefoot Tarahumara Indians who come to town in colonial regional dress. The men of the tribe are famous as endurance runners. Another curiosity is the miniature hairless Chihuahuan dog. A few miles outside Chihuahua are the celebrated Eulalia mine, the great stone aqueduct, and the ruins of the mission of Santa Ana de Chinarras.

Ciudad Juárez. Juárez, Mexico's oldest and largest border city, is connected to El Paso, Texas, by the International Bridge over the Rio Grande. Souvenir shops abound, as does a glittering array of nightclubs and restaurants. The Juárez bullring is the second largest in Mexico. New structures built for the 1968 Olympic Games include the Museum of Art and History and the Convention Hall. Especially notable is the Misión de Nuestra Señora de Guadalupe, with a handsome hand-carved altar.

Coahuila

Located in northeast Mexico, the state of Coahuila is the chief coal-producing area of Mexico. Lumbering and cattle raising are also important activities. A popular point of entry into Mexico is the border town of Piedras Negras, linked to Eagle Pass, Texas, by a long toll bridge.

Saltillo. The old colonial city of Saltillo, the capital of Coahuila, occupies a wide mountain-ringed valley. The State College of Coahuila and the Interamerican University attract many American students in the summer. Some of the finest and most colorful serapes in Mexico can be found in Saltillo's marketplace. The 210-year-old Cathedral on the Plaza de Armas is a fine example of Churrigueresque architecture.

Colima

One of Mexico's smallest states, Colima is situated in the cool highlands of the Sierra Madre Occidental. On the mountain slopes grows some of Mexico's finest coffee.

Colima. The historic capital, Colima, is situated in a tropical river valley below the snow-capped peaks of Nevada and Colima volcanoes. Of interest are the twin-spired Cathedral, the Museo de Antigua with a collection of antique cars, and the El Chanal archeological zone just outside the city.

Manzanillo. A seaport since the days of Cortes and just south of Guadalajara, Manzanillo is one of the finest fishing resorts on the Pacific Ocean. The town is so picturesque it might be the setting for a South Sea novel, yet it is also a busy commercial shipping center. Among the many beaches, Santiago is the most famous. The beautiful walks and drives along La Audiencia promontory offer a spectacular view of the area.

Distrito Federal

Mexico City. One of the most exciting cities on the face of the globe is Mexico City in the Distrito Federal. Mexico City would almost seem a magnificent myth were it not for the fact that everything which has been said about its natural beauty, cosmopolitan sophistication, and archeological splendor is true. Nowhere is

Modern buildings line Paseo de la Reforma in Mexico City. The Mexican capital is an elegant and dynamic metropolis, bubbling with life, as forward-looking as it is steeped in the past.

there to be seen so eloquent a blend of the old and the new. Mexico is futuristic in thinking, with a cultural history almost as old as mankind. It has great glass-and-steel skyscrapers, beautiful boulevards, nightclubs, bullfights, and fiestas, making it an international favorite and one of the most luxurious residential areas in the world; yet nearby, the footsteps of history are traced in majestic volcanic cones and in ancient pyramids with a noble past. Mexico City is the capital and the largest city of Mexico. It is the commercial, industrial, financial, political, and cultural center of the nation. It is the sixth largest city in the Western Hemisphere, the oldest large city in the western world, and the highest major city in the world It might be said of Mexico City that it combines the past, the present, and the future in a panoramic history of man.

Palace of Fine Arts. A city landmark known simply as Bellas Artes, the Palace of Fine Arts is Mexico City's opera house and theater for the performing arts. The artistry presented reflects Mexico's rich cultural heritage. A huge building that also houses a museum, the Palace of Fine Arts was begun in 1900 and completed about thirty years later, at a cost of about fifteen million dollars. During intermission, lights play on the famous Tiffany Glass curtain, revealing luminous sunrise and sunset scenes over Mexico's famed volcanoes, known popularly as Popo and Ixta.

Ballet Folklórico de Mexico. It has been said that between Mexico's traditional folk dances and today's modern style lies a desert, and the oasis is the Ballet Folklórico. The home company of the Folklórico performs several times each week in Mexico City; the popular road company tours the United States and other countries. It offers a modernized version of ancient songs and dances, beautifully costumed and staged. Mexico City is also famed for its strolling musicians known as *mariachis* who entertain everywhere, even in the International Airport.

Guadalupe National Shrine. Built on the site where a poor Indian named Juan Diego is reputed to have seen a vision of the Virgin Mary in 1531, the Basilica of Guadalupe, the most impressive shrine in Mexico, is visited daily by Catholics from all over the world. One special exhibit is Juan Diego's mantle, imprinted with an image of the Virgin.

National Palace. The president of the republic and other public officials have their offices in the imposing Palacio Nacional, which covers an entire city block and occupies the original site of Montezuma's palace. Of special interest are the historical murals by Diego Rivera.

National Cathedral. Mexico City's largest Christian church, and the most famous in Mexico, is the National Cathedral. It is an enormous structure that took almost a century to complete. The cathedral has many notable art and religious treasures.

Alameda Park. This lovely park in downtown Mexico City has a unique history. It was once the site of the pre-Hispanic city of Tenochtitlan; during the Inquisition hundreds of people were strangled or burned here. Today, it is filled with flowers and fountain displays and is one of the most beautiful small parks in the city.

The Floating Gardens. Just outside the village of Xochimilco, near Mexico City, are the famous Floating Gardens. Here, flower-decked boats with strumming troubadours are seen drifting among floating islands. Throughout Mexico City itself, flower markets abound where an armful of fresh flowers can be purchased for a few pesos.

the oldest natural park in the Western Hemisphere, Chapultepec is situated on a hill about 200 feet high. Crowning the hill is famed Chapultepec Castle, one of the most fascinating buildings in the western world. The Castle has a most unusual history: it is believed to have been an Aztec fortress, then a castle for Montezuma II, and finally a palace and summer home for Maximilian and Carlotta. It has since been converted into the National Museum of History, containing many of the rich fur-

Delta Air Lines

Every weekend tourists and natives enjoy rides in flower-decked boats along the canals of the well-known floating gardens at Xochimilco near Mexico City.

The Bullring. The Plaza Mexico is the biggest bullring in the world; it seats fifty thousand spectators and is usually filled during the professional season. Bullfighting is an extremely dramatic spectacle to witness in Mexico, with the fiercest bulls competing against celebrated matadors.

Tepito or Thieves Market. This area is filled with stalls offering goods of every description, from baubles, bangles, and beads to antiques. Such a fantastic array of objects is not to be found anywhere else in Mexico, and bargaining is expected.

Jardines del Pedregal. Mexico City is surrounded by smart suburbs, and the Pedregal is the most luxurious and wealthiest. Pedregal means lava, and some 2,000 years ago, this enormous area was covered by volcanic lava. Today the district is lined with spacious villas and sumptuous gardens built on lava rock.

University City. The National University of Mexico is the oldest university and yet one of the most strikingly futuristic campuses in North America. Founded in 1551, its spectacular new fifty-million-dollar University City was completed in 1954. It is symbolic in concept, combining Indian, Spanish, and modern architecture. The most unique building is the library covered with colored mosaics depicting the history of Mexican culture. The number of stones used is estimated to be in the millions.

Chapultepec Park and Castle. One of the most beautiful parks in the world and

nishings of Carlotta's period. Chapultepec Castle is high above Mexico City and affords a magnificent view of the city and surrounding valley. Also in the Chapultepec Park area is a vast complex of the major museums of Mexico City.

National Museum of Anthropology. Called the world's finest museum, it houses archeological treasures that trace Mexico from its remote origin through the more recent epochs of its ancient life—the Toltec, Mayan, and Aztec. Among the priceless relics is the Calendar Stone weighing 22 tons, probably the most famous single archeological treasure in Mexico. Included also are scale models of ancient temples and examples of age-old handicrafts and art. Built by architect Luis Ramirez Vasquez, the museum is breathtaking in its splendor.

Museum of Modern Art. This is a gleaming new building, in contrast to the ancient dignity of the Museum of Anthropology. It contains the works of contemporary artists, with a permanent collection of paintings by Diego Rivera.

Museum of Natural History. This is another modern building, spectacular in beauty, and similar to the Guggenheim Museum in New York City. A condensed history of Mexico is shown in vivid dioramas.

Diego Rivera Museum. Called the Anahuacalli Museum, it was designed by Rivera before his death in 1957, and is devoted to his works and his extensive pre-Columbian art collection. Nearby is the Frida Kahlo Museum, named for Rivera's wife. It was once their home and studio, and has been left intact. Other museums in Mexico City are the Museum of Ethnography, the Museum of Graphic Arts, and the Museum of the City of Mexico.

Teotihuacán Pyramids. In the archeological zone of San Juan Teotihuacán, covering eight square miles, are the famed Teotihuacán Pyramids. Tremendously impressive, they were built over 1,000 years ago by an unknown civilization. They are Mexico's most dramatic and largest

Delta Air Lines

This detail from the Temple of Quetzalcoatl, built over 1,000 years ago, shows the importance of the serpent in Toltec culture.

archeological ruins. The Pyramid of the Sun dominates the entire zone, rising to a height of 216 feet, and is larger than any pyramid in Egypt. It has 248 steps leading to the top, where the view of the tranquil valley below is extraordinarily beautiful. The 140-foot Pyramid of the Moon stands nearby. At the southern end of the zone is a magnificient monument, the Temple of Quetzalcoatl. The Temple is lined with massive sculpturing, including the heads of carved serpents, which are symbolic of Mexico's heritage. Near the temple is a handsome new museum containing arts, crafts, and industries from the various epochs in the valley's history.

Ixta-Popo Park includes the two snow-capped volcanoes near Mexico City: Popocatepetl, or Smoking Mountain, and Ixtaccihuatl, or White Lady. Ascending the lava-encrusted slopes of Popo is almost like taking a walk on the moon; neighboring Ixta is somewhat easier to climb.

Durango

The mighty Sierra Madre Occidental has played a great part in the wealth and history of the state of Durango. The Spanish conquered and colonized the area in the 16th century because of the rich mineral resources found in the nearby slopes of the Sierra. Today it is a center for silver, gold, iron, and coal mining.

Durango, the capital, is often called the "City of Sunshine" because of its ideal climate. An old city which has preserved much colonial charm, Durango has been used by Hollywood movie companies for "location" shots. Durango is also an important mining center; El Cerro del Mercado, a small mountain of almost solid iron, is said to have one of the world's richest iron deposits. The town's massive twin-towered cathedral is a fine example of the Spanish Renaissance plateresque style of architecture.

Guanajuato

Located in central Mexico, the state of Guanajuato is famous for the immense quantities of silver and gold extracted from its mines. At the time of their greatest production, no other mines in the world could equal them. Guanajuato is also a leading agricultural area.

Celaya. The old city of Celaya is particularly notable as the birthplace of Francisco Eduardo Tresguerras, one of Mexico's greatest architects. His works are found throughout the city. El Carmen Church, with a dome of gold and green glazed tiles, is considered to be his masterpiece.

Guanajuato, the capital, is a romantic colonial city, once the wealthiest mining city in the world. Magnificent statuary, churches, and fountains built with mining money are vestiges of the opulent past. It has pastel-tinted Moorish houses and winding cobblestone streets, such as the famed Callejón del Beso, or Alley of the Kiss. It also has a modern two-mile subway for automobiles. Historical sights include the massive Alhondiga de Granaditas, a granary turned into a fortress and now a museum, famed for its important role in the War of Independence; the Panteon lined with above-ground vaults; and the Church of La Valenciana, which is said to have been mortared with powdered silver and gold mixed with wine. Guanajuato is also famous as the birthplace of Mexico's most celebrated artist, Diego Rivera.

León. Largest city in the state, León is a shoe and leather manufacturing center. It has plazas, ancient churches, and the ornate Palacio Municipal as reminders of a picturesque colonial past. In contrast is the new Expiatory Temple, a modern cathedral under construction since 1915 and noted for exotic altars.

San Miguel De Allende. Preserved for posterity as a national monument, San Miguel is considered to be one of the finest

Mexican National Tourist Council

An eight-foot statue of Coatlicue, the Aztec goddess of the Earth and Death, and mother of the War God, Moon, and Southern stars.

Delta Air Lines

Taxco, in the state of Guerrero, is a colorful historic village of steep, narrow streets, and is known mainly for its countless silversmith workshops. The Mexican government has declared Taxco a national monument, and no modernization is permitted in this picturesque town.

examples of the colonization period. Attesting to its picturesque charm is the fact that it now houses a large colony of American writers and painters. Notable are the Institute Allende and the Academia Hispano-Americano, which attract hundreds of American students every summer. Dominating the main plaza is the imposing San Miguel Church.

Guerrero

The state of Guerrero in southern Mexico is bounded by the Pacific Ocean on the southwest and the Sierra del Sur mountain range to the north. It is primarily an agricultural state, with some mineral deposits of silver and gold. However, Guerrero is famed for its man-made attractions, such as Acapulco, and its native industries, such as the silverwork of Taxco.

Acapulco. An internationally famous playground, Acapulco rivals southern Europe's Riviera as a resort paradise. It has miles of white sandy beaches, great glittering hotels that cap dramatic red cliffs, a beautiful blue bay ringed with sapphire hills, and the most glorious sunsets in the world. And when the sun sets, Acapulco's night life comes alive, running the gamut from supper clubs with continental cuisine to swinging spots with hard rock bands. Points of interest a few miles outside of Acapulco include Revolcadero Beach; an ultramodern airport reached by a superbly scenic drive; Avenida Presidente Alemán, a beautifully landscaped boulevard; Fort San Diego, a photogenic hilltop fortress built over 300 years ago; and La Quebrada where, at dusk, young natives dive by torchlight from great heights into the waves below. About 150 miles northwest of Acapulco is Zihuatenejo, a hideaway resort of historic charm.

Chilpancingo, the capital, was founded in the 18th century. Its colonial ruins include an ancient stone bridge and church. Near the town are ruins with hieroglyphics resembling Egyptian characters and relics thought to belong to the Toltec civilization.

Taxco. Called the "Silver Capital of the World," Taxco is Mexico's most picturesque town. To preserve its historic charm, the government has made Taxco a national monument and no modernization is permitted. It is a medieval town with steep cobblestone streets, fountains, and houses terraced one above the other. Its colorful atmosphere attracts writers and artists from all over the world. Points of interest include the eighteenth century Church of Santa Prisca, with twin pink towers and altars of gold; and the Casa Figueroa, furnished as in colonial days. However, it is silver for which Taxco is famous; native silversmiths still use primitive tools to create great works of art.

Hidalgo

Situated in central Mexico, Hidalgo is a leading state in the production of silver, gold, copper, and iron. Rugged mountain ranges and fertile valleys provide some of the most spectacular scenery in all of Mexico.

Pachuca, the capital, is one of the great mining centers of Mexico. It is a pictur-

National Railway of Mexico

Tula, a town in the state of Hidalgo and only a few hours from Mexico City, is known for its imposing Toltec ruins. This fragment shows the skill and imagination of ancient artists.

Carnegie Institution of Washington

The Temple of the Warriors, also known as the Temple of the Thousand Columns, is one of several Mayan buildings which have been found in Chichén-Itzá, in the state of Yucatán.

esque city situated high in the Sierra Madre Oriental. Nearby are the interesting old mining town of Real del Monte with its cobbled streets, and the mountain resort of Hacienda San Miguel Regla.

Zimapán. Another quaint old mining town, Zimapán is located in a scenic mountainous area. Many mines surround the town and provide a glimpse into the past. The parish church, with its ornate facade, is topped by a huge tower.

Jalisco

If Jalisco were the only state in the republic, its natural scenic splendor is such that Mexico's reputation as one of the

world's most romantic and beautiful areas would still prevail. Located in central west Mexico, Jalisco is a major crop producer and livestock breeder.

Guadalajara. Capital of the state and second largest city in Mexico, Guadalajara has compelling beauty both in terrain and in architectural treasures. It is an exciting, modern metropolis and, with an altitude of one mile, has one of the best climates to be found. Nowhere does the modern mingle with the past so gracefully. A few steps from a luxury hotel, colonial buildings come into view—such is the multifaceted charm of Guadalajara. The people love to be entertained; the city is known as the home of mariachis and the Mexican hat dance. The great cathedral, amidst four beautiful plazas, combines towers and golden domes in awe-inspiring majesty; inside is Murillo's celebrated painting, "Assumption of the Virgin." The Palacio del Gobierno, dating from 1643, is the proud home of murals by José Clemente Orozco. His famed Museum-Workshop nearby contains many of his paintings and home furnishings. The renowned Degollado Theater, Guadalajara's center of music and the performing arts, is classic in style with its vaulted ceiling rising theatrically. The State Museum houses the state library, and exhibits Murillo's paintings of the life of Saint Francis. The ornate facade of the Church of Santa Mónica eloquently expresses plateresque design. Hospicio Cabañas, an orphanage and home for the elderly, has a chapel dome adorned with Orozco's celebrated mural, "The Man of Fire." Environs of Guadalajara offer visual beauty of another type.

Tlaquepaque, a small village just outside Guadalajara, is noted for pottery and for the strolling mariachis who are always ready to perform.

Zapopan, a charming town, is especially famous for its seventeenth century church, the Basilica of Zapopan, with a lovely ten-inch image of the Virgin. During the yearly festival honoring the Virgin of Zapopan, her image is taken by Cadillac automobile to every church in Guadalajara.

Lake Chapala. The largest lake in Mexico, Chapala is a popular resort center and a fisherman's paradise. Villages along the shoreline include Chapala, with the famous Juanacatlan Falls nearby; Ajijic, a mecca for writers and artists; and Jocotepec, famed for beautiful serapes and a colorful fiesta.

Puerto Vallarta. For centuries Puerto Vallarta, though of picture-book loveliness, was an unknown Pacific fishing village. Then, in the 1950's, the faraway charm of this sleepy little town "caught on" and Puerto Vallarta became one of the most popular resort areas in the world. Understandably so, because it has all the ingredients of a popular resort: superb climate, a spectacularly beautiful setting on Banderas Bay, exotically lush tropical foliage, and unexcelled swimming and deep-sea fishing. To the dismay of many visitors to this Eden of the west, Puerto Vallarta has become commercialized with sophisticated restaurants and luxurious hotels. Its fame increased when Hollywood chose Puerto Vallarta as the setting for the filming of *Night of the Iguana.*

Mexico

The state of Mexico nearly encircles the Federal District that includes Mexico City. On the southeastern border of the state rise the snow-capped peaks of famed Popocatepetl and Ixtaccihuatl volcanoes.

Toluca, capital and chief city of the state of Mexico, has an imposing natural setting high in Toluca Valley. Towering above the city is the majestic Nevado de Toluca volcano, with two tiny, deep blue lakes, the Lakes of the Sun and the Moon. The market in Toluca is one of the busiest, biggest, and most interesting in Mexico. On Fridays, natives come to town with

their colorful wares of baskets, pottery, hand-loomed serapes, and embroidery. Other interesting sights are the Museo de Arte Popular, the State Museum, and the churches of El Carmen and Santa Veracruz. Just outside Toluca is the recently discovered Calixtlahuaca Archeological Zone, a group of scattered mounds with relics of a pre-Aztec civilization.

Michoacán

As far as the eye can see, majestic mountains loom over the lovely state of Michoacán, located in central Mexico. It is predominantly an agricultural state, with the advantage of lying in the most favorable region in Mexico.

Morelia, the capital, was named after the patriot priest, José María Morelos y Pavón, hero of Mexico's Revolution for Independence. One of the oldest and best representatives of the Spanish colonial period, Morelia is a living museum. It is a treasure-house of old churches, public buildings, and mansions, including the centuries-old house of Morelos. Other points of interest are the cathedral with handsome twin domes; the huge old aqueduct; the Palacio del Gobierno; the State Museum noted for a fine collection of Tarascan relics; and the ancient college of St. Nicholas, second oldest university in the Americas.

Fantastically shaped green, orange, and white stalactites and stalagmites fill the Grutas de Cacahuamilpa near Cuernavaca.

Lake Patzcuaro, high in the mountains in the state of Michoacán, is one of the world's highest and most beautiful lakes. Local fishermen use unique, graceful butterfly nets on the lake.

Patzcuaro, a proud old city, is the home of the ancient Tarascan Indians. It abounds with buildings that recall the colonial past, including buttressed churches, fountains, and convents La Colegiata, a massive old church, dominates the town. The Museum of Popular Arts and Archeology has a superb collection of Tarascan art. Patzcuaro was selected for a United Nations project established for the improvement of local living standards and the training of teachers. On Friday, the big market day, whole families of Indians come to town with their wares.

Lake Patzcuaro, one of the highest and

most beautiful lakes in the world, is famous for the charming and graceful butterfly nets used by native fishermen to catch the almost transparent white fish.

San José Purúa, a celebrated resort area, has radioactive springs which are said to have therapeutic value.

Uruapan, a picturesque Tarascan town of cobbled streets, red tiled roofs, markets, and plazas, is known for the lacquer work made in local shops.

Morelos

Morelos, located in central Mexico, is the second smallest state in the republic. Pri-

The cathedral in Guadalajara, the capital of the state of Jalisco, is surrounded by beautiful plazas. Murillo's well-known painting "Assumption of the Virgin" is in the cathedral.

marily an agricultural state, it is mountainous and picturesque. Because Morelos is favored by a superb climate, resort areas flourish.

Cuernavaca, the capital, is a rendezvous for an international group of celebrities, including movie stars, diplomats, and jet-set society. It is also a favorite weekend playground for wealthy Mexicans from nearby Mexico City. Cuernavaca has palatial estates, beautiful hotels, and sophisticated restaurants. The city has another side that provides a look backward in time. Cortés Palace, housing murals by Rivera, is one of the oldest buildings in the western world, while the massive Cathedral of Cortés, founded in 1529, is said to be the oldest existing church in the Western Hemisphere. The famed Borda Gardens, once the summer home of Maximilian and Carlotta, were designed after those at Versailles.

Cuautla, a quaint resort town with huge hot spa swimming pools, is a popular retreat. Nearby are mountain villages with thermal springs.

Tepoztlán, one of the least changed villages in Mexico, has been the subject of two important works in anthropology. Natives are so resistant to change that they still speak Aztec. Dominating the area are the archeological ruins of the Pyramid of Tepozteco, an Aztec temple. Tepoztlán also has a famed Gothic convent built by the Dominicans in the 16th century.

Lake Tequesquitengo, a sparkling blue haven rimmed by villas and hotels, is one of Mexico's most popular lakes. Near the lake are many Indian villages and the famed hot springs of Tehuixtla.

Nayarit

A small state in central west Mexico on the Pacific coast, Nayarit has the Sierra Madre Occidental in the west and tropical plains in the north. It produces a variety of agricultural crops, including more than half of Mexico's tobacco.

The statue of Benito Juárez in Mexico City honors the memory of the former Mexican president (1861–72) and political reformer.

San Blas, an unspoiled tropical village, was once a busy seaport. Today it is a secluded resort with endless miles of beaches. The most interesting building is a crumbling Spanish fort.

Tepic, the capital, lives up to the meaning of its name, "hard stone." It is solidly built at the foot of extinct Sanganguay volcano. Two interesting buildings are the cathedral, built in 1750, and the Church of the Holy Cross.

Nuevo León

The state of Nuevo León lies in northeast Mexico within the highest elevations of the Sierra Madre Oriental. Mining provides most of its wealth.

Monterrey is the capital of the state and the third largest city in Mexico (after Mexico City and Guadalajara). Apart from being a modern industrial metropolis, Monterrey has significant landmarks that give an insight into the past and present city. The cathedral on Zaragoza Plaza, dating from 1790, is filled with famous murals and sculptures; El Obispado Palace, now a museum, was once a fortress during Monterrey's colorful history. Also worth seeing are La Purísima Church, ultramodern and famed for its sweeping parabolic lines, with a row of carved impressionistic statues of the Apostles across the facade; Monterrey Institute of Technology, one of Mexico's finest schools; the Casino, where debutante balls and wedding receptions are held; Círculo Mercantil Mutalista, an athletic center, with the best gymnasium facilities in Mexico; Cuahtemoc Brewery, one of the largest breweries in Mexico, famed for some of the finest pilsner beers in the world; and Colón Market, with a thriving business in leatherwork and silver. More interesting sites lie outside the city. Jusasteca Canyon, a dramatic gorge with remarkable rock formations, has walls rising 1,000 feet; García Caves, with beautifully pillared limestone caverns, are said to be among the largest and most outstanding on the American continent; Chipinque Mesa, an area of thrilling views, has a small resort; Horsetail Falls, with three small falls called the "Three Graces," spills a deep 275 feet down a mossy cliff.

Oaxaca

Oaxaca in southeastern Mexico is regarded as one of the most interesting states in the republic. In some areas, it seems as if time has been standing still. Of all the states, Oaxaca has the largest Indian population, including both primitive and progressive tribes. Agriculture is the basis of the economy.

Oaxaca, the capital, is a city of old-world charm. The Church of Santo Domingo, a massive fortresslike building, is baroque in style with one of the most ornate interiors in Mexico; the State Museum has achieved world-wide fame for its array of lapidary art of the Mixtecs and spectacular jewels from nearby Monte Alban. Outside Oaxaca are fascinating historic sites: the famous Tule Tree, said to be the oldest living thing in Mexico and probably in the world; the Mitla Ruins, originally an ancient Zapotec city and believed to have once been a religious center; and Monte Albán, a famous archeological zone, where recent excavations have yielded opulent treasures.

Puebla

The mountainous state of Puebla in central Mexico includes the three highest peaks in Mexico. It is an agricultural, mining, and cattle-raising region.

Puebla, the capital, is a big commercial city where historical edifices abound. It is called the "Rome of America" because of its many churches, some of which are the Cathedral of the Immaculate Conception, the exquisite Rosary Chapel in the Church of Santo Domingo, the Secret Convent of

Santa Monica with 39 rooms formerly entered by hidden passageways, and El Carmen Church and Convent with an exterior of glazed tile. Other landmarks include the Plaza de las Americas with a bubble-domed auditorium; Casa de Alfenique, called the Sugarcake House because of its ornate decorations; and Forts Loreta and Guadalupe, just outside the city, offering a fine view of the area. Puebla is also known for tile and Spanish pottery.

Cholula. A fantastic city of churches, Cholula is said to have 365 of them, one for each day of the year. The most important, El Santuario de Los Remedios, sits on the ruins of an ancient pyramid.

Queretaro

Located in central Mexico, the state of Queretaro is a region of high plateaus and valleys.

Queretaro, the capital, is a prosperous colonial city, one of the oldest in Mexico. Opals and other semiprecious stones from nearby mines have created a thriving industry. Queretaro is important historically for the major role it played in Mexico's fight for independence; nearby is the hill where the emperor Maximilian was captured and executed. Of special architectural interest are the stone aqueduct that is still in use; the Church of San Francisco, renowned for tilework and the parchment books housed in nearby Pío Mariano Museum; and the Fountain of Neptune by Mexico's famous 19th century architect, Tresguerras.

Quintana Roo

The territory of Quintana Roo is the region with the smallest population in Mexico. Covering the eastern half of the Yucatán Peninsula, Quintana Roo is primitively beautiful.

Chetumal, the capital, is a tropical seaport on the Bay of Chetumal. The most prominent building is the "Castle," a pyramid-shaped structure. Chetumal is the main border point of entry into British Honduras. Near the town are the archeological sites of Tulum and Punta Soluman.

San Luis Potosi

Located in north central Mexico, San Luis Potosi is a leading mining state, with its wealth coming from gold and silver.

San Luis Potosi, the capital, is at the geographical center of Mexico. It is a pleasant city with a centuries-old atmosphere. The main plaza and commercial street are paved in tile, for which the city is noted. Other striking examples of tilework are found on the beautiful domes of the Church of Our Lady of Carmen and the Church of San Francisco. The local silver mines are also noteworthy.

Tamazunchale, in the heart of the Huasteca Indian region, is an old town in a tropical setting. It is a favorite haven for ornithologists and entomologists studying the rare birds and butterflies that inhabit the area.

Sinaloa

Located on the Gulf of California and the Pacific coast, the central west state of Sinaloa derives its wealth from rich silver and gold deposits.

Culiacán, the capital, has many strikingly modern buildings, yet it still preserves a languid colonial air. Interesting sights include the imposing cathedral, the plaza or Zócalo, and Rosales Gardens. Nearby are thermal springs and deep-sea fishing.

Mazatlán, built on a peninsula of fanciful rock formations, is a popular fishing and beach resort. El Faro lighthouse, the second highest in the world, is an interesting landmark.

Sonora

Located on the Gulf of California, the state of Sonora is very similar in terrain to its northern neighbor, Arizona. Gold, silver, and other metals are found in this mountainous region.

Hermosillo, the capital, is a prosperous, growing city with chic stores and the largest university in northwest Mexico. The

ultramodern State Museum features a mummified Yecora Man said to be some 11,000 years old. The cathedral, the Palacio Federal, and the Parque Madero are other sights to see.

Alamos, a charming silver-mining town, has been designated as a historical monument. Alamos once flourished as one of Mexico's richest colonial cities; today it has a growing American colony. The Plaza de Armas with the beautiful bell-towered cathedral and the ancient cemetery with above-ground vaults are a few of the interesting sights. The legend persists that Alamos still has an incredibly rich mine yet to be found.

Guaymas, a winter playground in the Bocochibampo Bay area, has become a popular game-fishing resort. Of special interest are the twin-towered Church of San Fernando and the Palacio Municipal.

Nogales is separated from Nogales, Arizona, by a wire fence. It contains colorful markets, department stores, and La Caverna café, formerly an old mine cave and prison from which Gerónimo is said to have escaped.

Ciudad Obregón, a thriving city, is a conglomeration of adobe huts and modern buildings. Outside the town, the Obregón Dam with its planned irrigation system has changed the Yaqui Valley into an area of fertile farmlands.

Tabasco

Located in southeast Mexico on the Gulf of Campeche, the state of Tabasco is predominantly a region of dense forests. Agriculture, once the main occupation, has given way to oil production, which has greatly altered the economy.

Villahermosa, the capital, is noted for two impressive museums. The Museo de Tabasco, housing an excellent collection of Indian artifacts, is the second most important museum in Mexico. Museo de la Venta contains gigantic Olmec stone heads and altars from the great La Venta archeological zone. Near the city is the famous Mayan Palenque ruins (see state of *Chiapas*).

Tamaulipas

Located in central Mexico on the Gulf of Mexico, the state of Tamaulipas is chiefly an agricultural and mining region. Tampico is the major port.

Victoria, the capital, was named for Guadalupe Victoria, Mexico's first president. Noteworthy are the buildings and gardens of Tamaulipas State College, Palacio del Gobierno, Plaza de Armas, and the cathedral.

Tlaxcala

The smallest state in the republic, Tlaxcala in central Mexico is an agricultural region, famed for its fighting bulls. Once the ancient kingdom of Tlaxcala, it was conquered by Cortés and named for his Mexican mistress.

Tlaxcala. Capital of the state, Tlaxcala's chief industry is the weaving of wool. Landmarks include the Church of San Francisco, filled with ancient paintings, and the Shrine of Ocotlán, one of Mexico's most revered shrines.

El Paso Sunland Club

A torero executes the final stroke during a bullfight at Plaza Balderas in Ciudad Juárez. Bullfights are very popular in Mexico; some of the best toreros in recent years have been Mexicans.

Veracruz

The state of Veracruz lies in central Mexico, the most important area in the republic. Situated along the Gulf of Mexico, with the majestic Sierra Madre Oriental at its back door, Veracruz is mainly agricultural. Oil is the principal natural resource.

Jalapa, the picturesque capital, is located in a tropical valley with luxuriant gardens and cobbled streets. Jalapa has little level land and is one of the few cities of the country built without a central plaza.

Córdoba. A charming city in a beautiful setting, Córdoba's most interesting building is the Hotel Zevallos, where the Treaty of Córdoba, establishing Mexican independence, was signed in 1821.

Fortín de las Flores. A popular resort town, it lies in one of the most beautiful floral regions in all Mexico. Gardenias, camellias, orchids, and azaleas grow in profusion.

Yucatán

In southeast Mexico, amidst the ruins of America's greatest civilization, lies the state of Yucatán. It occupies the northwest portion of the Yucatán Peninsula, between Campeche and Quintana Roo. Rich as it is in ruins at Chichén-Itzá and Uxmal, Yucatán also has wealth of a different kind—it is the world's leading producer of henequen, or sisal hemp. While many of the ruins of Yucatán are still an enigmatic puzzle, new archeological discoveries constantly reveal more of Mexico's past.

Mérida is the capital of Yucatán. Regarded as one of Mexico's cleanest cities, Mérida is often called the "White City." It also is said to have more windmills than any other city in the world. The 20,000 windmills are used to pump water from underground reservoirs. Mérida is the world's largest shipping center for sisal hemp, a major source of revenue. Built on the site of a Mayan temple, Mérida has many historical landmarks, including the austere 16th century cathedral, Yucatán's largest church; Casa Montego, the palatial home of Francisco de Montego and the city's oldest house; and the Monumento de La Patria with a sculptured frieze depicting the history of Mexico. Many visitors use Mérida as a base for explorations to the spectacular Mayan ruins located near the city.

Chichén-Itzá. Once a city covering about six square miles, Chichén-Itzá is the largest and most famous of Yucatán's ancient ruins. Evidence indicates it was built in the fourth and fifth centuries, abandoned for several hundred years, and reoccupied in the tenth century. The technological achievements of a once glorious civilization are visible in its remains. Here can be seen a theory of evolution carved in stone over 1,000 years before Darwin, an observatory for daylight study of the stars, and a calendar more accurate than ours today. Among the chief buildings are El Castillo, or the Kukulkán Pyramid, with the famous red jaguar; the ceremonial Ball Court, where rubber ball games originated; and the Temple of the Warriors with its corridor of One Thousand Columns. Some distance away is the famed Sacred Well;

the Nunnery; the Observatory, also called the Caracol; and the Temple of the High Priests. Nearby, too, is Old Chichén, older than its larger counterpart, containing the Temple of the Four Lintels.

Uxmal. Heroic in conception, the ruins at Uxmal are famed for the beauty of their proportion and the intricacy of their flawless filigree carvings. Thirteen temples and palaces stand on pyramids and terraces, including the monumental Prince's Palace.

Kabah. Resembling a fortress, the largest and most fascinating of the reconstructed Kabah ruins is the Palace of Masks, whose entire facade is covered with serpent masks.

Zacatecas

Located in central west Mexico, the state of Zacatecas is a region of semiarid plains and mountains; the western half is dominated by the Sierra Madre Occidental. Zacatecas is second only to Guanajuato in Mexican wealth.

Zacatecas, the capital, is an old mining city with narrow, cobbled streets so steep that some of them become steps. The main point of interest is the cathedral which houses many treasures. A beautiful view of the area can be seen from atop La Bufa Hill, which contains the city's richest silver mine.

British Honduras Inf. and Com. Department

Mahogany logs in British Honduras are trimmed and cut for shipping to sawmills. Timber is the country's major export.

BRITISH HONDURAS

British Honduras, a self-governing colony within the British Commonwealth, is a remote country of Mayan ruins, primitive towns, and virgin land. With an area of 8,867 square miles, it is bordered by Guatemala to the south and west, Mexico to the north and northwest, and the Caribbean Sea to the east. The basically flat terrain is almost completely covered by densely forested jungle. The Maya Mountains, running through the center of the country, descend in the east to swampy coastal lowlands. Between ten and forty

miles offshore is the largest barrier reef in the Western Hemisphere. A line of foaming surf, nearly unbroken for 190 miles, results from the heavy ocean seas breaking against the reef. Inside the reef, the surf flows into languid lagoons studded with numerous coral islands. These sheltered waters with their deep harbors were once hideouts for British pirates harassing the Spanish fleet. Now these islands are tiny retreats for bathers and sportsmen. Both sides of the reef provide some of the best game fishing in the world. Although originally claimed by Spain, British Honduras was colonized by the British who recognized the commercial value of the abundant forests. (Guatemala, in a continuing border dispute, has claimed that it inherited Spanish sovereignty over the area and that British possession is invalid.) Today, the economy is based on wood products such as logwood, mahogany, chicle, cedar, and pine. However, the forests are rapidly being depleted, and the country is putting more emphasis on agriculture. Cultivation of bananas, citrus, and sugar cane is increasing, as are fishing and cattle raising. The population is a mixture of British, Indian, Creole, Carib, and Spanish stocks.

Belmopan, the capital since August, 1970, lies fifty miles inland from the former capital. Although the city is still under construction, most governmental functions have been transferred here.

Belize, the principal seaport and the former capital, is located at the mouth of the Belize River. Once a colonial town of whitewashed wooden houses, Belize was virtually destroyed by a severe hurricane in 1961. Although Belize was rebuilt, the government decided to avoid a similar disaster and moved the seat of administration to Belmopan. Although still a primitive town, Belize has several fine hotels to accommodate tourists. The environs of Belize include dense jungle teeming with wildlife and winding rivers filled with game fish.

Atlun Ha, north of Belize, is noted for the ruins of what was once an impressive Mayan metropolis. Archeological findings in this area include a Mayan chieftain's tomb and a three-tiered temple with wide staircases and ceremonial platforms.

Xunantunich Ruins, near Benque Viego on the Guatemalan border, is another elaborate Mayan ceremonial city. Huge pyramids tower above thirty feet of jungle growth. The tallest of the sixteen uncovered temples features an intricately carved frieze.

The Turneffe Islands, a group of coral cays lying twenty miles east of Belize, is another locale that attracts avid fishermen. Sheltered lagoons, edged by palm trees and white beaches, and mangrove-lined channels abound with numerous species of fish.

Ambergris Island is a tropical paradise lying 500 yards within the barrier reef. Fast developing into one of the Caribbean's major resorts, the island features mile upon mile of sandy beach, shaded by palm trees that reach the shoreline. Bathing and fishing are excellent here. San Pedro is one of the few small villages on Ambergris. Other islands with excellent fishing but limited tourist facilities are Calabash Cay, Laughing Bird Cay, and Wild Cane Cay.

United Fruit Company

A Guatemalan farmer plows a field near the newly restored Mayan temple at Zaculeu. Interest in pre-Columbian cultures is growing as new archeological zones are unearthed.

GUATEMALA

A progressive country that loyally respects its past, Guatemala is a splendid union of three diverse cultures: that of the Maya-Quiché Indians, whose pure-blooded descendants remain bound to ancient customs; the Spanish, of which the colonial influence on art and architecture is still evident; and today's world, with modern techniques which have increased industrialization. A republic covering 42,042 square miles, Guatemala has the largest population of the Central American countries. It is bordered by Mexico on the north and west, the Caribbean Sea on the northeast, Honduras and El Salvador on the east, and the Pacific Ocean on the south. Although the country contains coastal plains and a central plateau, Guatemala's terrain is predominantly mountainous. The major ranges are the Sierra Madre and the Cuchumatanes. A chain of 33 volcanoes, few of which are still active, runs parallel to the Pacific Ocean and accounts for the highest peaks in Central America. The fertile land supports rich harvests of coffee, bananas, cotton, tropical fruits, and the exquisite "Monja Blanca," a white orchid which grows only in Guatemala. The climate is generally delightful.

Guatemala City, the capital, was founded in 1776 to replace Antigua, which had been virtually destroyed by earthquakes. Resting on a high plateau in the shadows of smoldering Pacaya and Fuego volcanoes, Guatemala City pays tribute to the past and present alike. The majestic Cathedral, with five arched naves and 16 altars, houses many art treasures rescued from the damaged churches in Antigua. The Church of Santo Domingo is a popular shrine, for it is here that the patron saint of Guatemala is enthroned. Beautiful Parque Minerva is highlighted by the celebrated relief map of Guatemala, constructed in 1905 by Francisco Vela and Claudio Urritia which covers over one quarter of an acre. The 229-foot Tower of the Reformer honors the centenary of the birth of former President Justo Rufino Barrios. In Aurora Park, the Institute of Anthropology and History exhibits many valuable artifacts of the ancient Mayan civilization. The National Palace, following Spanish Renaissance lines, houses most of the governmental departments. Finished in 1943, it is built of native stone and hardwoods; its interior was decorated by the country's outstanding artists. Three large markets offer a potpourri of wares, from colorful native textiles to foodstuffs to religious items.

Chinautla, a small village on the outskirts of the capital, has retained its Indian heritage. Its famous pottery is hand molded by native women and decorated with traditional designs.

Lake Amatitlán, southwest of Guatemala City, is a scenic resort area overlooked by Pacaya volcano. Landscaped gardens, water-sport facilities, and rambling trails make this a popular vacation retreat.

Antigua, 25 miles west of Guatemala City, was the nation's capital until floods and earthquakes demolished the city and forced the movement of the center of government to its present location. Today Antigua is a living museum of Spanish facades, patios, arcades, and magnificent ruins overrun by semitropical vegetation. The peaks of Agua and Fuego volcanoes overlook the city. Antigua is known as the "city of eternal roses," because here these flowers bloom all year round. The Church of La Merced is one of the few that withstood the earthquakes. Its facade is heavily embellished with holy figures and designs, and the church is filled with magnificent paintings and statues. The city's finest fountain is found in the monastery adjoining La Merced. The Colonial Museum houses a marvelous array of art treasures, paintings, and sculptures that adorned the homes and churches during the Spanish rule. Other landmarks in Antigua include the Church and Convent of Santa Clara; the Church of Our Lady of El Carmen; and the Church of La Compañía de Jesús, formerly a Jesuit convent and now a public market. The Palace of the Captains-General is considered to be one of America's finest examples of Spanish colonial architecture. It was completed in 1764 but was severely damaged in 1773.

Lake Atitlán, a beautiful blue-green body of water, is set in a triangle of cloud-tipped volcanic peaks. The shore is lined by over a dozen isolated Indian villages, several of them named after the apostles. Although in some cases just a few miles apart, each community has retained its individuality in costume, dialect, and special native craft. The colorful markets attract many visitors.

Chichicastenango is a superb representative of the native's traditional life style. This Indian village is noted for the pageantry of its semiweekly market, the most festive in all of Guatemala. Market day is a time of worship for many of the inhabitants who practice a curious blend of pagan ritual and Christian prayer. At the steps of the beautiful Spanish colonial Church of Santo Tomás, the Indians offer incense to their ancestral gods; within the church, they light candles honoring the Christian saints.

Quezaltenango, Guatemala's second largest industrial and trading center, was built over an ancient town. It is named for the quetzal, a rare, brilliantly colored bird of great symbolic importance to the Mayas. Since it dies in captivity, the quetzal represents beauty and liberty to all Guatemalans. Narrow cobblestone streets and shaded plazas contrast sharply with the rest of the modern landscape. The daily market offers a variety of exclusively Indian handicrafts, including beautiful blankets.

Huehuetenango, surrounded by lofty mountains, is the chief trading center for the dozens of villages located in this wildly beautiful northwestern area. The daily market is enlivened by the distinct costumes of natives who come from the mountains as well as from the plateau and the coast. Chief wares include pottery, leather, textiles, and locally famous merino blankets. This remote region is rich in lead, silver, and copper, although these deposits have remained unexploited. Nearby are the partially restored ruins of Zaculeu, an ancient Mayan city. Also in the area is the old town of Chiantla, whose colonial church displays the solid silver statue of the Virgin of Candelaria and is the destination of a great annual pilgrimage.

Esquipulas, on the western boundary with Honduras, is best known for its gleaming white basilica which displays the revered Black Christ. Dating back to the late sixteenth century, the Black Christ was carved by Quirio Cataño from dark orangewood. Reputed to have worked many miracles, the five-foot image has become even darker with age and with the smoke from thousands of candles offered by worshipers.

Flores, on a small island in Lake Petén, is built on the site of the ancient Mayan city of Tayasal and serves as a base for archeological expeditions. It is a major producer of chicle.

Tikal, in the northern highlands, was once the principal city of the ancient Mayan civilization. It is hidden within a tropical rain forest—a jungle so dense that Tikal is accessible only by air. Rediscovered, excavated, and reconstructed after more than 1,000 years of anonymity, this ceremonial city has revealed vestiges of a highly complex culture. Most of the populace lived on surrounding farmlands, while the city itself was inhabited by priests, mathematicians, engineers, artists, and craftsmen. Remnants of this once thriving metropolis include the Grand Plaza, which was the center of elaborate rituals; hundreds of towering stelae, with carved hieroglyphic texts recording dates and events; immense pyramids which were dedicated to principal deities; and huge reservoirs which once held millions of gallons of water. Other excavations have revealed the temple of the Giant Jaguar, primitive ball courts, the main Acrópolis, and lesser pyramids and temples.

United Fruit Company

A Honduran worker stacks bananas for shipment. Bananas thrive in this tropical climate and are a main export of Honduras.

HONDURAS

"Depths" (*honduras* in Spanish) is the name Columbus chose for this land in 1502, after anchoring in the deep offshore waters along the northern coast. He found a country characterized by rugged mountain terrain and inhabited by Indians steeped in the traditions of their Mayan forebears. What has emerged from this background is a culture composed of the ancient, the colonial, and the modern. With an area of 43,227 square miles, Honduras is bordered by Guatemala, El Salvador, Nicaragua, the Caribbean Sea, and the Gulf of Fonseca, off the Pacific Ocean. Two mountain ranges running parallel to the coasts cover three-fourths of the land. Between them lie fertile valleys and forested plateaus. Along the lower eastern Caribbean coast, the terrain is called the "Mosquitia," a vast area of mountains, dense forests, and swamps. Honduras is predominantly agricultural, and the topography determines the commercial output of

the various regions: bananas from the lowlands; cacao from the midlands; coffee, tobacco, and livestock from the highlands; and minerals from the mountains. The climate fluctuates with altitude—the heat and humidity, high at the coasts, decreases toward the mountainous interior. The bulk of the population, mostly of mixed European and Indian stock, is concentrated in the highlands, valleys, and coastal lowlands.

Tegucigalpa, the capital and commercial center of Honduras, is a picturesque city set high in a mountain-rimmed valley. The capital is actually two towns—Tegucigalpa proper and Comayagüela—with the Choluteca River flowing between them. Founded in the sixteenth century, Tegucigalpa has been spared the ravages of earthquakes and hurricanes. The original Spanish colonial buildings, with massive entrances, grilled windows, and balconies, stand flush with narrow cobblestone streets. Interesting landmarks dot the city and its environs. Parque Morazán, in the heart of Tegucigalpa, is dedicated to Honduras' national hero, General Francisco Morazán. Surrounded by lush formal gardens, a statue honors his years spent promoting Central American unity. The magnificent Cathedral of San Miguel is recognized as one of the finest in Central America. The ornate facade is topped by an octagonal cupola and twin towers containing bells brought from Spain. The interior is highlighted by a baptismal font carved from a single piece of rock and an elaborate pulpit of carved and gilded wood. The National Museum features a scale model of the ancient Mayan ruins at Copán. Elsewhere in the museum are found Mayan artifacts and exhibits of the native flora and fauna. Concordia Park, the church of the Virgin of Los Dolors and the adjoining market, and the Presidential Palace are also interesting to the visitor. On the edge of town is the mountain El Picacho; the newest and most luxurious residences in the city are built on its terraced lower slopes. A huge reservoir and the lovely Park of the United Nations crown El Picacho. The Church of the Virgin of Suyapa lies just outside the capital. The destination of many pilgrimages, its shrine contains a tiny wooden figure of the Virgin which is credited with miraculous healing powers.

Choluteca, settled in the sixteenth century, is one of the oldest and most famous Spanish cities on the Pacific coastal plain in Central America. Lying on the wide, fertile flood plain of the Choluteca River, it is the center of a cattle-raising and coffee-growing district. The local sawmill prepares famous Honduras mahogany.

San Juancito, northeast of Tegucigalpa, is the site of the Rosario gold and silver mines. These mines, once worked by Spanish colonists, are still in active production.

Comayagua, the capital of Honduras until 1880, was founded in the early sixteenth century. This city has some of the most authentic examples of Spanish colonial architecture found in the country. Rows of massive, one-storied, whitewashed houses front cobblestone streets. The first Spanish university in Central America was established here in 1632. The Cathedral, Spanish in design with pronounced Indian

Organization of American States

A statue of Francisco Morazán in Tegucigalpa, Honduras, honors the statesman who attempted to unify Central America.

influences, is topped by a clock tower, said to be the first in America. Inside the Cathedral is a glassed crypt containing the mummified bodies of ten bishops, the religious leaders of the diocese from the Spanish conquest through the colonial period.

Lake Yojoa, believed to be an extinct volcanic crater, is one of the most beautiful mountain lakes in all of Central America. The area's lush vegetation, inhabited by duck, puma, jaguar, and bear, attracts many hunters and campers

San Pedro Sula, the second largest city in the republic, is a bustling metropolis of modern residences, wide thoroughfares, and lovely parks. The center of banana and sugar-refining industries, San Pedro Sula is also an important distribution point for the area. Nearby are the ruins of Travesía, an aboriginal city of probable Mayan origins.

La Ceiba, the principal banana port of Honduras, lies in a fertile valley along the Atlantic coast. In the background looms Pico Bonito Mountain, part of the coastal range. This busy city is the headquarters for the Standard Fruit and Steamship Company. As a major distribution center, La Ceiba handles the fruits and hides raised in the northern and northeastern sections of the country.

Puerto Cortés, an important banana port on the Gulf of Honduras, is partially surrounded by Lake Alvarado. This palm-lined body of fresh water is a popular fishing spot.

The Bay Islands form an 80-mile chain running parallel to the northern coast of Honduras. Archeological findings indicate that the islands were once the site of a typical Central American aboriginal civilization. They are historically famous as the place where Columbus first landed in 1502. Roatán, the largest island and capital of the group, is populated mainly by islanders of British ancestry. They are descendants of English settlers who ruled the islands during the days of the buccaneers. These beautiful islands are now a haven for vacationers and archeologists alike.

The Ruins of Copán, near the Guatemalan border, are all that remain of an ancient Mayan capital. Once a ceremonial city covering 15 square miles, Copán was abandoned for unknown reasons. Lying in a valley sheltered by lofty mountains, the ruins are overrun by dense tropical forests. Uncovered artifacts include a ball court encircled by a vast amphitheater, the Hieroglyphic Stairway leading to the Lions' Court, the magnificent Acropolis, and numerous temples, palaces, and carved stelae.

Organization of American States

Izalco volcano erupted regularly until 1967 when it became inactive. Central America still has several other active volcanoes.

Organization of American States

Lush tropical vegetation in Amapulapa Parque in San Salvador provides a striking background for this natural swimming pool.

EL SALVADOR

With an area of 8,236 square miles, El Salvador is the smallest of the republics. It is also the most densely populated. The country has made economic progress by growth of light industry and diversification in agriculture. It is the only republic which does not contact both the Caribbean Sea and the Pacific Ocean. With 14 volcanoes located within its boundaries, El Salvador is the only country in the world where one can see a volcano on every horizon. Nestled on the lower slopes of the Central America cordillera, the terrain is a mixture of rugged mountains, fertile highlands, and gently rolling hills, interspersed with beautiful lakes, inviting beaches, and rocky cliffs. Crops thrive in the upland plains, which are covered with a deep layer of porous soil formed from ash and lava. El Salvador is bordered by Honduras to the north, Nicaragua to the east, the Pacific Ocean to the south, and Guatemala to the west. Primarily an agricultural country, El Salvador bases its economy on coffee and cotton. The majority of the population is of mixed Spanish and Indian stock. The country has a moderate climate with temperatures varying according to the altitude.

San Salvador, the capital of El Salvador, is set in a high valley amid mountains dominated by El Salvador volcano. The modern buildings are purposely low and solid—a precaution against the frequent earthquakes. Beautiful private homes of Spanish style are enhanced by lush formal gardens. Plaza Bolívar, the main square, contains an imposing equestrian statue of General Barrios. Located in the center of town, this plaza is a logical starting place for viewing the city's most important public buildings, including the National University, the Archbishop's Palace, the National Treasury, the Presidential Mansion, and the National Palace. The public market, directly behind the National Palace, is a lively place filled with local products, including woodenware, silverware, and shoes. The National Museum has an interesting collection of jade and pottery relics from the Mayan ruins. The cathedral, built in 1881, is made entirely from wood to cushion it from jolts of earthquakes. Its Spanish Gothic styling is highlighted by beautiful wood carvings. The Church of La Merced is the oldest in San Salvador. Its tower still holds the bell Father Delgado rang in 1811 in his first effort to free his people. Many lovely spots are located in San Salvador's environs. Planes de Renderos is a new residential district on the slopes of San Jacinto Mountain. Its palatial homes and villas are set on park-size estates. The mountain is topped by Balboa Park, which offers magnificent views of the city and valley below. Beyond this park is Panchimalco, an Indian village whose inhabitants still adhere to many of their ancient customs. Its Spanish colonial church houses an outstanding collection of religious art. Lake Ilopango, a favorite resort of San Salvadoreans, lies inside an ancient volcanic crater. The shores of this large lake are dotted by vacation homes, hotels, and old fishing villages.

Santa Tecla, also called Nuevo Salvador, was founded in 1854 after San Salva-

dor had been destroyed by an earthquake. Although the original capital was rebuilt, Santa Tecla has remained important. The city lies in a valley surrounded by flourishing coffee plantations. Its beautiful residences abound with gardens of tropical flowers.

El Salvador Volcano, near Santa Tecla, has been inactive in recent years. The huge crater is about a half mile in width and depth; its steep slopes are sandy and forested. At the bottom is a smaller cone left by the eruption of 1917. The panoramic view from the summit is spectacular.

La Libertad is a major port and the principal ocean resort in El Salvador. Rocky cliffs overlook its beautiful beaches of black volcanic sand.

Cojutepeque has twice been the capital of El Salvador. Its annual fair honoring the feast of St. John attracts thousands of visitors, including Indians who come to sell and trade their native handicrafts. North of Cojutepeque is the town of Ilobasco, best noted for its delightful miniature dolls and clay pottery.

Izalco Volcano, in the western part of El Salvador, had been one of the most active volcanoes in Central America until it suddenly became silent in 1967. It was formerly known as the "lighthouse of the Pacific," for its continuous smoke and flames acted as a guide to ships at sea. Two towns lie at the foot of Izalco—one Indian, the other mixed Spanish and Indian. Although the towns are physically united, each has retained its distinctive native heritage. The best view of Izalco is from Cerro Verde, a national park built on the crest of an extinct volcano above Lake Coatepeque.

Sonsonate, one of the oldest cities in El Salvador, is a fine blend of colonial and contemporary architecture. Its popular Sunday market attracts colorfully dressed Indians who sell a variety of products ranging from live iguanas to liquors to soap. The city's beautiful cathedral is topped by 17 cupolas of various sizes. Just outside the city is the Church of San Antonio whose shrine has drawn visitors since early colonial times.

Acajutla, the republic's most important port on the Pacific Ocean, is an excellent resort area surrounded by tropical vegetation. The stretch of coast between Acajutla and La Libertad is known as the Balsam Coast. The special variety of balsam tree, indigenous to only this area, yields the valuable medicine and perfume base called "balsam of Perú."

Santa Ana, the second largest commercial center of El Salvador, lies in a fertile valley ringed by mountains. This modern metropolis is the coffee capital of the country. There are several public buildings of classic Spanish Gothic design, notably the cathedral and the National Theater. Near Santa Ana is Lake Guija, a haven for the hunter and fisherman. Its islands bear ruins of an ancient city, thought by some archeologists to be the original Tule, the birthplace of the Toltec and Mayan civilizations.

Chalchuapa is an urban center that artfully combines modern structures with colonial buildings. The city and its surrounding area have been inhabited for hundreds of years, and numerous Mayan relics have been found in the area. The ruins of the pre-Spanish city of Pampe, lying outside of Chalchuapa and amid hot lava beds, have yielded pottery, carved stones, and other archeological treasures. An image of the Virgin Mary found here is on display in the National Museum at San Salvador.

Lake Coatepeque, at the foot of Santa Ana volcano, is also called the "Eye of the Sea." Its slightly saline waters have a mineral content comparable to the famous Vichy waters of France. A favorite vacation resort, it is completely hemmed in by forested hills and its shores are lined by beautiful private residences.

San Vicente is a beautiful seventeenth century city that, unlike many other Salvadorean cities, has preserved its early heritage. Structures damaged by the severe 1936 earthquake were rebuilt along their original colonial lines. Landmarks include the Church of the Virgin of El Pilar, and the historic Tempisque tree, under which the city's charter was signed in 1635. The colorful annual fair honoring the Salvadorean saint, Ana Guerra, attracts a variety of visitors traveling by foot, horseback, oxcart, and automobile. San Vicente is also an important commercial center for the surrounding area.

NICARAGUA

Although composed of lowlands, lakes, and volcanoes, Nicaragua's geography has been significant to the development of the country—significant enough for Spain and her European rivals to spend centuries struggling for supremacy of this area. The San Juan River and Lake Nicaragua provide a natural transportation route between the Atlantic and the Pacific oceans; control of this vital waterway gave Europeans access to the riches shipped through Nicaragua from all parts of Central America. Now the largest country in Central America, Nicaragua covers 75,145 square miles. It is bordered by Honduras, Costa Rica, the Caribbean Sea, and the Pacific Ocean. Unlike the highland countries of Honduras, El Salvador, and Costa Rica, the heart of Nicaragua lies in the lowlands. Here is found the heaviest concentration of people, cities, and agricultural and commercial activities. This fertile area is dominated by two large lakes—Nicaragua and Managua—which are connected by the Tipitapa River. Flanking the western shores of these lakes are more than twenty volcanoes which belong to the northern extension of the Andes Mountains. Across the mountain range are the Caribbean lowlands—an area called the Mosquito Coast after the tribe of Indians who inhabit the area. This hot, humid region is covered by dense jungles and is sparsely populated. The climate of Nicaragua is generally humid and tropical and the frequent earthquakes have been extremely destructive. It is predominantly an agricultural country; corn is the chief sustenance crop, and coffee, cotton, and cacao are the principal commercial crops. Mineral resources are relatively undeveloped, although gold, silver, and copper are

Managua, the capital of Nicaragua, lies on the shore of Lake Managua, which has the dubious distinction of being the only lake in the world infested by sharks.

mined. Native handicrafts to tempt the shopper include alligator-skin products, gold and silver filigree jewelry, woven straw goods, hammocks, and carved gourds. The people are mainly of mixed Spanish and Indian ancestry.

Managua, on the southeastern shore of beautiful Lake Managua, is framed by smoking volcanic peaks. One of the newest Central American capitals, Managua was severely damaged by an earthquake and fire in 1931 and by another great fire in 1936. Reconstruction was directed toward a contemporary style of architecture that could better withstand the effects of such natural disasters. The delightful result of this planning is a modern city of low, pastel-tinted buildings with colorful red-tiled roofs. These are in unique contrast to the few Moorish-styled stone residences still remaining from the colonial period. Parque Central, on the lakefront, is a peaceful haven containing beautiful statuary, an illuminated fountain, the Temple of Music bandshell, and lush vegetation, including the amate tree which has been pruned to resemble a giant beehive. Parque Darío contains an elaborate monument honoring Rubén Darío, the world-renowned Nicaraguan modern poet. In El Cauce Park are found the *Huellas de Acahualinca*, footprints preserved in mud of primitive men and animals thought to be fleeing some volcanic eruption. Estimated to be between 2,000 and 5,000 years old, they may be the oldest traces of man yet found in Central America. The large market abounds with local products, from meat to tropical fruits and vegetables to native handicrafts. Other interesting sights in Managua are the National Palace and the Campo de Marte, a military parade ground. More attractions are found outside the city proper. Las Piedrecitas is a charming residential section enhanced by a lovely park. This park is filled with gardens and terraces, and offers a magnificent view of the surrounding area. The Presi-

This pre-Columbian incense burner from the Mangue-Chorotega culture is displayed in the Nindirí Museum in Masaya, Nicaragua.

dential Palace is a Moorish-styled building atop a hill that overlooks Lake Tiscapa, a lovely lake inside the crater of an extinct volcano.

Tipitapa is a modern resort on Lake Managua, outside the capital. The spa, whose waters are extremely hot and sulphurous, has been carefully landscaped to blend with the natural beauty of the spot. The local market is one of the largest and most complete in Nicaragua.

Lake Managua was originally named Xolotlán by the Indians who lived there prior to the Spanish conquest. Its blue waters reflect majestic Momotombo volcano which is at the northwest end of the lake. At the foot of the still active volcano are the ruins of León Viejo, the old colonial capital that was demolished by an earthquake in 1609.

Masaya, at the foot of smoldering Masaya volcano, is the heart of Nicaragua's major tobacco region. A city brightened by many gardens, Masaya is known as the "City of Flowers." It is also noted for its hammock industry and the large assortment of handicrafts made by the Indian population.

Jinotepe, a major coffee center, is especially noted for its church, a miniature replica of the grand cathedral in León. Many of its valuable images were brought from Spain. The annual fair honoring its patron saint draws many visitors.

Lake Nicaragua, the largest lake in Central America, is dotted by hundreds of small volcanic islands. The largest of these islands is Ometepe, crowned by two high volcanic peaks. Ancient idols and carvings have been found on some of the islands. La Isla Zapatera, the cone of an extinct volcano, is overrun with tropical vegetation. Isla de los Muertos is uninhabited and avoided by superstitious natives; the legend is that this island was once forbidden to ordinary men and great temples of the high priests were erected here. Lake Nicaragua is unique in that, although a freshwater lake, it contains some salt-water species of fish—swordfish, shark, and tarpon—that have gradually adapted to an unfavorable environment.

Granada, on Lake Nicaragua, lies a short distance from Mombacho volcano. The first Nicaraguan city colonized by the Spanish, Granada has been the center of commerce and wealth since its founding in 1523. It is the nucleus of an agricultural district rich in coffee, sugar, cotton, and cacao. In colonial times, its strategic location on the transisthmian route between the Atlantic and Pacific oceans made Granada an important inland port for trading with Spain. Today it is a charming, leisurely town, still adhering to the ways of the past. Many buildings from the Spanish conquest remain, and new structures are styled along similar lines. Among the lovely churches are the Cathedral, the Church of La Merced, the Church of San Francisco, the chapel of Maria Auxiliadora, and the colonial church of Jalteva. La Pólvora (Powder Magazine), an ancient fortress, is now used as headquarters for the National Guard.

León, a classic colonial city, was moved to its present location in 1610 after a disastrous earthquake destroyed the original city. It was the provisional capital until Managua became the national capital in 1852. The boyhood home and death place of Rubén Darío, León honors his memory with an impressive tomb in the Cathedral. This splendid church, started in 1746 and finished almost a century later, is the largest in Central America. Other interesting landmarks include the Palacio Episcopal; the Colegio San Ramón; the Instituto Nacional, which is housed in an ancient monastery; and the churches of San Francisco, La Recolección, San Juan de Dios, and La Merced. The parish church in the suburb of Sutiaba, dating from 1560 and one of the oldest in America, is noted for its beautiful Spanish-baroque altars.

Poneloya, near León, is a popular resort on the Pacific Ocean. It is famed for its inviting beaches, colorful sunsets, and the Peña del Tigre (Tiger Rock)—a cave where, according to legend, two lovers once hid and were devoured by a tiger.

San Juan Del Norte, at the mouth of the San Juan River on the Caribbean coast, is historically important as the passageway to Lake Nicaragua. It was used by English, Dutch, and French privateers to launch lucrative attacks on Spanish ships. In the gold rush days of 1849, travelers from New England landed here to board boats going up the San Juan River, en route to the Pacific Ocean and California.

United Fruit Company

Workers at a coffee plantation turn over the beans several times a day to insure even drying. Costa Rica was the first Central American country to produce coffee.

COSTA RICA

The Spanish colonists who settled this land in the 1560's named it Costa Rica, or "Rich Coast," in anticipation of the gold they hoped to find. But the riches of Costa Rica are of other kinds. The actual wealth lies in the fertile soil, which is enriched by volcanic ash deposits; in the terrain, covered by verdant plantations, lush rain forests, broad rivers, and lofty mountains; and in the Spanish people themselves, who proudly claim that there are more teachers than soldiers in Costa Rica. The second smallest Central American republic, Costa Rica covers 19,653 square miles. It is bordered by Nicaragua to the north, the Caribbean Sea to the east, Panama to the south, and the Pacific Ocean to the west. Three great volcanic mountain ranges span Costa Rica—Guanacaste, Central, and Talamanca. The climate and terrain vary with the altitude: the grassy, forested coastal plains are in the hot zone; the fertile Meseta Central, or Central Plateau, is in the temperate zone; and the mountainous highlands are in the cool zone. The

Meseta Central lies in the heart of the nation. Its extremely productive land and delightful climate have made this region the governmental and population center. Costa Rica was the first Central American country to produce coffee, and agriculture is the chief occupation, with coffee and bananas the principal crops. Cattle raising and industry are growing in economic importance. Holidays and holy days are celebrated with colorful fiestas. These occasions are enhanced by the painted oxcarts which have become almost symbolic of the people's zest for living. The intricately decorated oxcarts have wheels made from sixteen wedges of seasoned wood, carefully joined to create resonant music as the wheels turn.

San José, the capital of Costa Rica, is nestled in a high fertile valley of the Meseta Central, surrounded by volcanic mountains and rich coffee plantations. Architecturally a blend of old Spanish and contemporary American, the trend in newer buildings leans toward modern styling. A lovely city of spacious parks and elegant residences, San José is the commercial, political, social, and travel center of the country. Many fascinating landmarks are found within the city and the surrounding area. The National Theater is an elegant Renaissance building with solid marble balconies and staircases, beautiful statues and sculptures, and superb murals. Its dazzling foyer is decorated with mirrors, red velvet, and gold. The National Museum, located in a former fortress, has an extensive collection of preserved native flora and fauna. Also displayed here are Indian relics, Mayalike carvings, and pottery from Costa Rica's early cultures. Central Park, with beautiful walks and lush vegetation, is an attractive setting for the traditional *retreta*, the triweekly promenade of girls who walk arm in arm in one direction around the plaza, while the young men walk in the opposite direction. Merced Park contains an enormous spherical stone, a relic from an ancient aboriginal native civilization. National Park features a magnificent bronze monument dedicated to the five sister republics of Central America, recalling the defeat of William Walker, the Tennessee filibuster who attempted to make himself dictator of Central America in 1856. Paseo Colón, a wide boulevard leading to the airport, is lined with beautiful trees and luxurious residences. The administration building at La Sabana Airport features hand-carved woodwork and wrought-iron grillwork, said to be among the finest examples of Spanish and Moorish design in Central America. Next to the airport is the National Stadium, usually filled to its capacity of 20,000 during the soccer and polo matches.

Alajuela, the second largest city in Costa Rica, lies 14 miles northwest of San José. It is a center for sugar, coffee, gold, and cattle production, and a popular resort. The city is noted for its exquisite flowers, the weekly cattle fair, and the Escuela de Tejidos (Weaving School). Here you will see the statue dedicated to Juan Santamaría, called *Erizo* (Hedgehog), who as a mere drummer boy routed William Walker, the Tennessee filibuster, by setting fire to the building in Nicaragua where Walker was entrenched with his followers. Near Alajuela is Ojo de Agua (Eye of Water), the most popular bathing resort in Costa Rica. A lavish mountain spring where the water flows at the rate of 6,000 gallons a minute, it supplies water to the towns on the Pacific coast. The overflow cascading down also forms a beautiful, crystal-clear pool.

Cartago, the former capital and the oldest Spanish city in Costa Rica, lies 14 miles southeast of San José. Although damaged by earthquakes, Cartago has preserved much of its traditional Spanish architecture. The famous church, Shrine of Our Lady of Angels, houses a statue of *La Negrita*, the patroness of the country and one of the renowned Black Virgins of America. The church was erected over a spring where, according to legend, the Virgin is believed to have presented this five-inch, black stone image of herself to a slave girl. The spring's bubbling waters are said to have miraculous powers. The image, still preserved and much revered, has been stolen several times but has always mysteriously returned. Cartago's Sunday market attracts many local people who, dressed in their best attire, bring their wares of flowers, fruits, coffee, and leather goods.

Orosi, a small village near Cartago, is historically important for its Spanish mission, the first in Costa Rica. Although built 300 years ago by Franciscan monks, the mission and its beautifully carved altars and pillars, fine old paintings, and other religious treasures are remarkably well preserved.

Irazú, north of Cartago, may be reached by a road winding steeply upward through beautiful scenery. On clear days both the Atlantic and the Pacific oceans are visible from Irazú. At the top of Irazú volcano, amidst clouds of vapor and smoke, one can gaze down into the vast, seemingly bottomless chasm filled with molten lava and boiling sulphur. This is one of few active volcanoes that can be viewed so closely.

Heredia, six miles northwest of San José, is the center of the coffee industry. The influence of its colonial Spanish settlers is evident in the church towers rising about red-tiled roofs, the iron grills on windows, and the brilliantly colored gardens set among whitewashed adobe walls.

Poás, west of San José, is an active volcano that contains the world's largest geyser. Its crater, more than a mile across and several hundred feet deep, is one of the largest and most impressive in the world. Its sheer walls drop into a steaming sulphur lake which erupts frequently.

Puerto Limón, on the Caribbean Sea, is built over the site of the old Indian village of Cariarí, where Columbus landed on his fourth and last voyage to America. The bulk of Costa Rica's exports pass through this port. The atmosphere of Puerto Limón is modern, with few reminders of a Spanish colonial past. The people are mostly Jamaican Negroes originally imported to work the banana and cacao plantations on the coastal plain. Interesting landmarks include the Cathedral; the Parque Vargas, with a miniature botanical garden of tropical flowers and palm-lined promenades; the Club Miramar, with a salt-water pool and bathing pavilion; and the United Fruit Company Zone, with trim houses, hospital, community houses, and gardens.

Puntarenas, an important port on the Pacific Ocean, lies on a narrow strip of land that juts three miles into the Gulf of Nicoya. Beautiful beaches and excellent deep-sea fishing as well as preserved ancient Indian sites, attract many vacationers. At the mouth of the harbor is the island of San Lucas, the nation's penal settlement. It has few guards and no high fence, for not many convicts try to escape in the shark-infested waters. Mother-of-pearl, found along this coast, is an important source of revenue.

PANAMA

As the connecting link between North and South America and between the Atlantic and the Pacific oceans, Panama's geographic location has been the most significant element in the country's history. During the Spanish conquest, several Panamanian ports were important distribution centers for treasures from the New World and were under constant attack from privateers, notably Henry Morgan. With the completion of the Panama Canal in 1914, Panama teemed with foreign ships carrying diverse cultural influences as well as diverse cargoes. Covering 29,201 square miles, Panama is bordered by the Caribbean Sea to the north, Colombia to the east, the Pacific Ocean to the south, and Costa Rica to the west. An isthmus running east and west in an S-shaped curve, Panama is divided nearly in half by the Canal Zone. Two main mountain ranges cross the country's entire length; in their shadows lie fertile valleys and plains, heavily forested hills, and dense jungles. The long shorelines are dotted by many lovely islands and deep bays. Most of the people live in and around the larger cities in the coastal regions; the interior is sparsely populated. Panama, with the smallest population of all the Central

Organization of American States

A statue of the legendary Indian chief Urraca stands in the park bearing his name in Panama City, capital of the Republic of Panama.

Braniff International Airways

The Indians who inhabit the San Blas Islands off the coast of Panama still wear their colorful costumes and unique adornments.

American countries, is inhabited by people of Indian, Asian, European, Negro, and mixed stocks. The equable climate is tropical and humid. The land is rich in natural resources, but agriculture is superseded by commercial activities stemming from the canal.

Panama City, the nation's capital, was built in 1673 after Henry Morgan had sacked Old Panama. Strategically located near the Pacific entrance to the Panama Canal, Panama City is the entrepôt for the republic. In addition to the numerous local products, a wide variety of international goods are collected and distributed here. Panama City is a fascinating composite of colonial charm and modern progress, with oriental overtones. It abounds with memorable landmarks. In the heart of the city is the Plaza Catedral, also known as the Plaza de la Independencia. Busts of the republic's founders are displayed here. Las Bóvedas (The Vaults) is a stone sea wall built by the Spanish to fortify the city. Underneath the wall are dungeons where political enemies were imprisoned. The stone sentry tower and the carving of the Virgin on the gateway are also of interest. The Presidential Palace, one of the city's most impressive public buildings, is Panama's "White House." Its most outstanding feature is the Moorish courtyard highlighted by columns studded with mother-of-pearl. Tame egrets wander around the patio. Its Golden Hall, used for state occasions, is decorated with a magnificent fresco of Balboa discovering the Pacific. The Plaza de Francia, in the oldest section of the city, contains a monument honoring France's early attempts to build the Panama Canal. The National Museum has a beautiful collection of pottery, articles of wrought gold, and other artifacts from early Panamanian cultures. The Church of Santo Domingo, now in ruins, is noted for its flat arch. Although a fire destroyed the church in 1737, the arch still stands. This indicated to engineers that Panama is relatively free from earthquakes, which influenced the decision to build the interoceanic canal through Panama rather than through Nicaragua. San José Church is famous for its magnificent altar, a masterpiece of colonial art which originally adorned a church in Old Panama. Carved from solid mahogany and overlaid with pure gold, it was painted to disguise it from Morgan and his pirates. The altar was later moved to its present location. Other interesting landmarks in Panama City include the National Cathedral, the Palace of Justice, the Union Club, the *Colegio La Salle,* and the colorful market.

Old Panama, seven miles from Panama City, was once the capital and the major distribution center for the New World. Although restoration was attempted, it never regained the prominence it had enjoyed before Morgan's attack in 1671. Now it is a city dominated by interesting ruins and dense vegetation. Landmarks include the four-storied square tower of the Cathedral and the King's Bridge, linking the city with the Cruces Trail.

Taboga Island is a vacationer's paradise in the Bay of Panama. Lovely gardens and palm-fringed beaches justify its being called "the isle of flowers." Found on this picturesque spot are the ruins of fortifications built by the Spanish to protect their ships from pirates.

The Canal Zone is a five-mile-wide strip of land on either side of the Panama Canal. A 1903 treaty gave the U.S. jurisdiction over this area for the construction, operation and defense of the canal. About 50 miles long overall, the canal took ten years to complete. Ships crossing this north-south link between the Atlantic and Pacific oceans are raised and lowered by a series of · immense locks. A boat trip through the canal affords the passenger a close-up view of this engineering marvel at work. The equally spectacular scenery along the route includes the Gaillard Cut, where mountains were dynamited to make way for the canal; beautiful Miraflores and Gatún lakes, dotted with numerous islands; lush terrain abounding with tropical flora and fauna; and various Canal Zone towns.

Colón, the Atlantic gateway to the Panama Canal, is the second largest entrepôt in Panama. Ships from all over the world

Portobelo, northeast of Colón, was the colonial period's greatest trading center until it was destroyed by Henry Morgan. Now it is a city of few people and many ruins. Portobelo revives itself for its annual Feast of the Black Christ, patron saint of the city. Many legends persist about the origins of this life-sized wooden statue, which is still reputed to have miraculous powers.

The San Blas Islands form an archipelago of about 365 emerald-green islands, ranging from tiny islets with just a few palm trees to large, densely populated islands. The Cuna Indians who inhabit about 50 of these islands forbid marriage with other races, so their heredity has remained pure. The natives wear traditional costumes colorfully accented with beads, earrings, and nose rings. Extremely independent and unaffected by modern civilization, they govern their own territory and regulate visits from outsiders.

David, Panama's third largest city, is the center of the richest agricultural region of the country. The city is a subtle contrast of colonial and contemporary sights.

Braniff International Airways

The Panama Canal, linking the Pacific and Atlantic oceans since 1914, has become overcrowded. Several sites are under consideration for another route through Central America.

pass through Limón Bay, which is beautifully landscaped by distant foothills of the cordillera, palm-lined beaches, and imposing city skylines. The town of Cristóbal, under the jurisdiction of the United States, adjoins Colón at the docks, which are filled with watercraft ranging from luxury liners to navy transports to dugout Indian canoes. A free port, Colón has many shops filled with items from the U.S., Asia, and Europe. One of the most cosmopolitan cities in the world, Colón also has a fine array of public buildings, churches, and modern hotels. Interesting sights include the new Cathedral, the United States-owned Hotel Washington, and Paseo Centenario with its famed statue of Columbus and an Indian girl.

Modern shops mingle with the traditional public market. The old Church of San José is notable for its separate bell tower, which also served as a defense against Indian attacks. *El Retiro,* a residential suburb, is profuse with lovely gardens. The city is also noted for its excellent saddles and harnesses.

The Chiriquí Highlands, near Costa Rica, is a mountainous region of banana, coffee, and flower plantations. Its variety of natural attractions draws many visitors: excellent hunting and fishing for the sportsman, multipeaked El Volcán for the mountain climber, gold for the prospector, Indian graves with ancient pottery for the archeologist, and many species of orchids for the botanist.

PRESIDENTS
of the UNITED STATES

The president is the chief executive of the United States. His office was originally established in 1789 to overcome the disadvantages of a weak central government. It has since become the most powerful political office in the country.

Under present statutes, an elected president is guaranteed at least one four-year term in office. He may be elected to two full terms and may serve a maximum of ten years if he started during his predecessor's term. Although exempt from all court actions while president, he may be impeached, and removed from office if convicted.

The duties and powers of the president, as delineated in the Constitution, are checked and balanced by the judicial and legislative branches of government. As chief executive he enforces federal legislation and supervises administrative agencies. These responsibilities are actually delegated to department heads, who are chosen by the president and approved by the Senate. The president also appoints judicial officials and foreign diplomats. He participates in the nation's lawmaking process by supporting certain laws and vetoing those laws passed by Congress which he feels would not be in the nation's best interest. As commander in chief of the armed forces, he assigns military commissions and directs the national war defense. He also has the power, subject to Senate approval, to negotiate foreign treaties.

George Washington (1732-1799)
Term 1789-1797, FIRST PRESIDENT

The high courage and strong but disciplined will of George Washington brought endurance and purpose to the cause of American independence. The son of a planter, he was born on the frontier of Virginia. His schooling, inspired by his half-brother Lawrence and by family friends, consisted largely of mathematics and military skills. At sixteen he was earning his own living as a surveyor. At twenty-one he had completed a hazardous mission through the wilderness to the Ohio country. Other important military and civic activities rapidly followed. In 1759 he married Martha Custis and began the extensive development of the Mount Vernon estate. Armed conflict called him in 1775 to the command of the Continental Army. Throughout the long and difficult struggle which followed, Washington held the ragged, unpaid, and hungry soldiers together until final victory came. From a well-deserved retirement he was called to preside at the Constitutional Convention. Unanimously chosen the first President of the United States, unanimously re-elected, he declined a third term. In 1798, Washington was appointed Lieutenant-General of the U.S. armies. He died at Mount Vernon, regarded as a successful general, a fine statesman, and an inspiring leader who became "first in the hearts of his countrymen."

John Adams (1735-1826)
Term 1797-1801, SECOND PRESIDENT

John Adams was one of the most learned of the public men of his day. He had been sent to Harvard College to prepare for the ministry; but upon graduation, he chose the law for his career. In 1764 he married Abigail Smith, a brilliant and capable woman, who, in her own right, became one of the famous characters of American history. Noteworthy success came to John Adams in law and in civic affairs. In the troubled time of 1771 he won a seat in the Massachusetts Assembly. Deep concern about Colonial grievances inspired his leadership against the mother country. No one saw more clearly than he that the logical outcome of resistance would be war and independence. The fervent patriotism of John Adams gave direction to the Continental Congress, certainty to the Declaration of Independence—and resulted in his selection to represent the United States abroad. He negotiated a loan from Holland, participated in making a favorable peace, and served as the first minister to Great Britain. In 1788 John Adams returned from Europe in time to have his ability, distinction, and achievement rewarded with the vice-presidency of the United States, the first man to be so honored. As a candidate of the Federalist party, he defeated Thomas Jefferson in 1796, and became the only man to serve eight years as Vice-President and then to become President.

Thomas Jefferson (1743-1826)
Term 1801-1809, THIRD PRESIDENT

Thomas Jefferson's estimate of his own greatest achievements is indicated by the simple epitaph he asked to be inscribed on his tomb: "Here was buried Thomas Jefferson, Author of the Declaration of American Independence, of the Statute of Virginia for Religious Freedom, and Father of the University of Virginia." Jefferson was born in Albemarle County, Virginia, the son of a frontiersman and of Jane Randolph of the prominent Virginia Randolphs. From his mother and his classical education at the College of William and Mary he acquired the social graces and tastes of quality which gave distinguished charm to his personality; but the wisdom of his philosophy and the practicality of his politics were outgrowths of the frontier democracy of his childhood. Jefferson was probably the most versatile leader of his time. Skilled in horsemanship, music, drawing, mathematics, architecture, writing, education, farm management, law, and diplomacy, he had a genius for using these varied abilities to strengthen his own leadership and to improve the public welfare. It was Jefferson's sense of the need for security and expansion which helped in obtaining approval of the treaty for the purchase of Louisiana, and thus laid the basis for the future greatness of the United States. Jefferson retired at 65 and devoted himself largely to establishing the University of Virginia.

James Madison (1751-1836)
Term 1809-1817, FOURTH PRESIDENT

James Madison was preparing for the ministry, shortly after his graduation from Princeton, when the need for public leadership sought him out to head the Orange County Committee on Public Safety. His father owned a large estate in Orange County, Virginia, although James had been born at Port Conway in King George County some few miles away. The stirring demands of the Revolutionary period and the first years of the new Republic found expression in Madison's constructive skill, drafted to help write the state constitution of Virginia. He was twice elected as member of the state legislature and he was chosen a delegate to the Continental Congress and the Constitutional Convention. In the writing of the federal Constitution, and in the struggle over its ratification, Madison reached the peak of his public achievement. He earned the title, "Father of the Constitution." No man did more to perfect the instrument itself or to obtain its acceptance. Madison did all that he could to prevent the War of 1812. Ironically, his opponents called it, "Mr. Madison's War." Despite his genius at constitution-making, Madison had no genuine liking for the political arena, and welcomed retirement to his beautiful home, "Montpelier," in Orange County. Here he enjoyed his books and farming until his death at the age of eighty-five.

James Monroe (1758-1831)
Term 1817-1825, FIFTH PRESIDENT

James Monroe was the fourth Virginian to become President of the United States. He was born in Westmoreland County, the son of a planter of modest means. His college career at William and Mary was interrupted by his enlistment in the Colonial Army. After the war, Monroe turned to the practice of law and was soon immersed in politics. He represented his native state in the Assembly, in the Continental Congress, and in the United States Senate. President Washington appointed him minister to France; and, on his return, he was elected governor of Virginia. Under President Madison he served as Secretary of State and as Secretary of War. Few men have been better qualified by training and experience for the national presidency to which he was elected by the Democratic-Republican party in 1816. There was no opposition to his re-election four years later. The chief events of Monroe's administration were the pronouncement of the independent position of the Western Hemisphere (later to become famous as the Monroe Doctrine), the Anglo-American peace pledge over the Canadian border, the Florida Purchase from Spain, and the Missouri Compromise. He died in New York City at the age of seventy-three —five years after his retirement from a life of devoted service to his country.

John Quincy Adams (1767-1848)
Term 1825-1829, SIXTH PRESIDENT

John Adams was a great American, but perhaps in both learning and achievement his son, John Quincy Adams, surpassed him. The younger Adams received his early education in Europe. Exceptionally brilliant, he was secretary to the United States minister to Russia at fourteen. Later he was graduated from Harvard, and soon gained admission to the Massachusetts bar. President Washington appointed him minister to Holland; then, in turn, he became minister to Prussia, England, and Russia. Before going to Berlin, he married Louisa Johnson, whose father was the United States Consul in London. In 1814 Adams was one of the commissioners who negotiated the peace with Great Britain at Ghent, bringing to an end the War of 1812. Under President Monroe, Adams became a bold and successful Secretary of State. Adams' ideas prompted the National-Republican party to select him as its nominee in 1824. The election failed to return a majority, and Adams was chosen President by the House of Representatives. Adams sought to improve governmental efficiency and to extend foreign commerce. His concept of public service has been rarely, if ever, surpassed. He was more interested in being right and in the general good than he was in gaining popularity and in extending political patronage.

Andrew Jackson (1767-1845)

Term 1829-1837, SEVENTH PRESIDENT

Already a renowned Indian fighter, General Andrew Jackson emerged a national hero from the amazing victory of American frontiersmen over British regulars at New Orleans in 1815. In 1780, at the age of thirteen, he had fought the British in the Battle of Hanging Rock. An orphan at seventeen, he began the study of law, and was admitted to practice three years later. Within a year he was appointed prosecuting attorney for the western part of North Carolina (now Tennessee). He moved to Nashville, and in 1791 married Rachel Robards. One of the framers of Tennessee's constitution, he became, in quick succession, United States Representative and Senator, and judge of the Supreme Court of Tennessee. Impulsive and headstrong, his flaming energy carried him into quarrels, duels, and political conflicts. The western frontier was seething with reaction against the "aristocratic" leadership of the East; and "Old Hickory" was the ideal border captain to lead the way to the White House, which he reached in 1828. "Jacksonian Democracy" was a political triumph for the "common man." It developed the "spoils system," strengthened the federal government over the states, and ended the United States Bank. Retiring after two terms to his beloved estate, "The Hermitage," near Nashville, he continued to influence his party until his death.

Martin Van Buren (1782-1862)

Term 1837-1841, EIGHTH PRESIDENT

Martin Van Buren was the first president born a citizen of the United States. At the age of fourteen, he began the study of law while serving as office boy to the village lawyer at Kinderhook, New York, his native town. His interest in politics began even earlier, and by the age of eighteen he was an active party worker. Twice he was elected to the New York Senate; in 1821 he entered the United States Senate; for two months in 1829 he was governor of New York, but resigned to enter the Cabinet of President Jackson. Van Buren's vigorous support of Andrew Jackson in 1828 was rewarded with appointment as Secretary of State. Two years later he was chosen Vice-President. His loyalty and his political skill endeared him to President Jackson in such measure that Van Buren was selected to inherit the presidential mantle, which he received in the election of 1836. One of the most significant accomplishments of the period of his presidency was the creation of the independent treasury system. Martin Van Buren wrestled unsuccessfully with the reaction from the extremes of Jacksonian democracy. The Jackson inheritance proved too heavy a burden; and with other difficulties, it combined to prevent Van Buren's re-election. His interest in politics, however, continued for many years.

William Henry Harrison (1773-1841)

Term 1841, NINTH PRESIDENT

The father of William Henry Harrison was a Virginian of prominent social position who served as governor of his state. He lived at Berkeley, in Charles City County, Virginia, where his son, William, was born. Young Harrison attended Hampden-Sidney College, and later studied medicine in Philadelphia; in 1791 he enlisted in the United States Army. He became a staff officer for General Wayne in the campaigns against the Indians of the Northwest Territory. Briefly he served as Secretary of the Northwest Territory and as a delegate from the Territory to the national Congress. From 1801 to 1812 he was governor of Indiana Territory. In this position he won acclaim as an Indian fighter, particularly for his victory at Tippecanoe. In the War of 1812 Harrison became a major-general in full command of the Northwest frontier. After the War of 1812, he served in both houses of the Congress, in the Ohio Senate, and as minister to Colombia. The Whigs persuaded Harrison to be their candidate in 1840 with John Tyler, another Virginian, as his running mate. "Tippecanoe and Tyler too" won an overwhelming victory in the log cabin and hard cider campaign. President Harrison died of pneumonia one month after his inauguration. His grandson, Benjamin Harrison, also became President.

John Tyler (1790-1862)
Term 1841-1845, TENTH PRESIDENT

John Tyler became President by succession, at President Harrison's death, one month after the inauguration. Like Harrison, he was born in Charles City County of Virginia; and his father, like Harrison's, had been governor of Virginia. Young Tyler was graduated from William and Mary College at seventeen. At twenty-one he was a member of the state legislature. Later he represented Virginia in both houses of the Congress, with an intervening term as governor of his state. Consistently John Tyler opposed policies which strengthened the national government at the expense of the states. Although a Democrat, Tyler's forceful opposition to "Jacksonianism" had, in the eyes of the Whigs, made him appear desirable for the vice-presidency. They had not thought of the possibility of dealing with him as the President. Tyler's independent nature was shown in his decision to be President in the fullest sense and not merely a substitute as provided in the Constitution; thereby he set a precedent that has become the rule. His administration was marked by controversies with Congress, and by a trend toward territorial expansion; Texas was annexed shortly before the end of his term. Tyler's first wife died when he was in office; in June, 1844, twenty-one months later, he remarried.

James K. Polk (1795-1849)
Term 1845-1849, ELEVENTH PRESIDENT

An important issue in the campaign of 1844 was westward expansion, and closely bound up with it was the problem of the extension of slavery. Van Buren was the popular Democratic nominee for the presidency until he spoke against annexation. James Knox Polk, little known nationally, had received some mention for the vice-presidency; but it was his support of annexation which brought him the chance to be nominated and to be elected President. His administration became famous for the addition of Texas, California, New Mexico, Utah, Nevada, and the western part of Colorado to the United States; the "Oregon question" was also settled. Polk was born in Mecklenburg County, North Carolina. In 1806 the family moved to Tennessee. After Polk had been graduated from the University of North Carolina in 1818 at the head of his class, he returned to Tennessee and began preparation in the law. Attracted to politics, Polk soon became a member of the state legislature. In 1824 he was elected to the Congress, and in 1835 he became Speaker of the House—the only Speaker ever to reach the presidency. He retired from the Congress in 1839, was for one term governor of Tennessee, and in 1844 emerged as the successful "dark horse" candidate for President. In 1824 he married Sarah Childress.

Zachary Taylor (1784-1850)
Term 1849-1850, TWELFTH PRESIDENT

A few months after his birth in Orange County, Virginia, Zachary Taylor was taken by his parents by ox-cart to the Kentucky frontier. His boyhood was spent in the country near Louisville. An early desire to become a soldier was realized in 1808 when he joined the regular army. In the War of 1812 Taylor served with distinction. His brilliant defense of Fort Benjamin Harrison against a large force of Indians won him much acclaim. Later he led important commands against the Indians in Illinois and in Florida. By 1845 Taylor was a brigadier-general and in command of the troublesome Southwest. Ordered to the Rio Grande, he was attacked by the Mexicans; but he quickly won the battles of Palo Alto and Resaca de la Palma. Later, against heavy odds, he inspired his men to the new victory of Buena Vista. "Old Rough and Ready," as his soldiers admiringly called him, was a popular hero by 1848; and the Whigs chose him for their presidential candidate. An honest soldier, with no political ambitions or obligations, he protested against the "spoils system." It seemed that he might ease the tensions between the North and the South when suddenly, on July 4, 1850, he was stricken with fever and died five days later —a little more than a year and four months after his inauguration.

Millard Fillmore (1800-1874)
Term 1850-1853, THIRTEENTH PRESIDENT

Millard Fillmore came to the presidency by the accident of President Taylor's death. His political life was a familiar pattern. State-wide success as a lawyer and terms in the New York state legislature and the national Congress placed him high in the councils of the Whig party. Fillmore came from a humble farm family of Cayuga County, New York. As a youth he was apprenticed to a clothier, but he rebelled and studied law instead. He worked for eight years as a clerk in a law office. This different apprenticeship prepared him for the New York bar and fitted him to become a partner in a prominent Buffalo firm. Fillmore's political competitors were men of unusual gifts in oratory when debating skill was at its political peak. Perhaps it was the rivalry among such masters as Clay, Calhoun, and Webster which played a part in giving lesser men an inning of recognition. The highly controversial Compromise of 1850 received Fillmore's support, although President Taylor had opposed it. President Fillmore also signed the Fugitive Slave Law, which further fired the controversy. President Fillmore failed to obtain renomination from the waning Whig party and never again held high political office; he spent the remainder of his life at his home in Buffalo, New York, where he was chancellor at the University of Buffalo.

Franklin Pierce (1804-1869)
Term 1853-1857, FOURTEENTH PRESIDENT

When the Whigs nominated General Scott for the presidency in 1852, the Democrats sought a rival candidate, experienced in politics—with military glamour, and with political appeal to both Northern and Southern Democrats. Franklin Pierce qualified as the successful nominee. Pierce was born at Hillsborough, New Hampshire, and was graduated from Bowdoin College, Maine, in the class of 1824, one class ahead of Longfellow and Hawthorne. Pierce studied law, gained admission to the bar in 1827, and two years later was a member of the New Hampshire legislature. In 1833 he was sent to the House of Representatives at Washington, and in 1837 he entered the Senate. When war was declared with Mexico, Pierce volunteered as a private, but was commissioned as a colonel. His political background, pleasing personality, and steady application brought rapid promotion; and he emerged from the war a brigadier-general. The Pierce administration made the Gadsden Purchase from Mexico, opened up Japanese ports to American traders, furthered plans for the first railroad across the continent to the Pacific, and approved the Kansas-Nebraska Bill—an act which brought the question of slavery extension squarely before the people. Franklin Pierce failed to satisfy his own party and was not renominated.

James Buchanan (1791-1868)
Term 1857-1861, FIFTEENTH PRESIDENT

James Buchanan was born in southwestern Pennsylvania near Mercersburg. In his sixteenth year he entered Dickinson College. After his graduation, he studied law and was admitted to the bar at the age of twenty-one. While serving in the War of 1812, he was elected to the Pennsylvania legislature; and thus he began a long life of public service, including membership in both houses of the national Congress. He started his political career as a Federalist, but soon switched to the Democrats. He was President Polk's Secretary of State; and President Pierce made him minister to Great Britain. Three times his name was placed before national nominating conventions as a candidate for the presidency, and in 1856 he was nominated and elected. Slavery and states' rights became flaming questions during his administration. Although he was convinced that slavery was morally wrong, he believed that, under the Constitution, he could not interfere with slavery or prevent secession. Buchanan's administration has been held as inadequate in a time of great crisis. Four Cabinet members resigned, partly in protest against his do-nothing policy. Before a new President could take over the faltering ship of state, South Carolina had seceded, the Confederacy was founded, and war loomed between the North and South.

Abraham Lincoln (1809-1865)

Term 1861-1865, SIXTEENTH PRESIDENT

Whenever men speak of great leaders, the name of Abraham Lincoln is heard. No national leader has come from more humble beginnings, and none has achieved a more revered memory. Born in a log cabin, he was tested and trained by the rough, frontier life of Kentucky and Indiana. He had almost no formal schooling, but he was a devoted student of people and of the books that he could buy or borrow. In 1831 he settled in New Salem, Illinois. In turn, he was storekeeper, postmaster, and surveyor—earning the high regard of his neighbors as "Honest Abe." Already marked for leadership, Lincoln moved to Springfield in 1837 and began the practice of law. He was elected to the state legislature, became successful as a circuit-riding lawyer, and served for one term as Representative in Congress. Lincoln's loyalty to the Union inspired his belief that the nation could not endure "half slave and half free." As the Republican candidate for Senator, he opposed the extension of slavery in the famous debates with Stephen A. Douglas. He lost the election, but he won a national renown which elected him President in 1860. War followed his inauguration. Confusion and disaster endangered the Union cause, but Lincoln's courage and faith surmounted all obstacles. Five days after Lee's surrender, Lincoln was shot by John Wilkes Booth.

Andrew Johnson (1808-1875)

Term 1865-1869, SEVENTEENTH PRESIDENT

At the age of ten Andrew Johnson was apprenticed to a tailor. At that time he could neither read nor write. When he was eighteen, he left his birthplace, Raleigh, North Carolina—settling at Greenville in eastern Tennessee. The following year he married Eliza McCardle, who had a good education, and she began at once to teach her husband reading, writing, and arithmetic. Johnson became interested in politics as a Jacksonian Democrat. In 1830 he was elected mayor of Greenville; then, for several years he was a member of the state legislature; in 1843 he was sent to the House of Representatives at Washington; in 1853 he became governor of Tennessee; and in 1857 he entered the United States Senate where he advocated and secured passage of a homestead bill which President Buchanan vetoed. Although a sincere Southerner, he could not accept secession. He placed his faith and his devotion in the Union. This action separated him from the South and Lincoln appointed him military governor of Tennessee. Two years later he was chosen Vice-President. Lincoln's death thrust Johnson into a situation for which he seemed unfitted, but possibly no more so than were his associates. Politics led to impeachment proceedings; these failed, but Johnson was not renominated. Seven years later he was returned to the Senate.

Ulysses Simpson Grant (1822-1885)

Term 1869-1877, EIGHTEENTH PRESIDENT

Ulysses Simpson Grant was born at Point Pleasant, Clermont County, Ohio. He attended school and worked on his father's farm until, at the age of seventeen, he entered the Military Academy at West Point. Soon after his graduation, Grant took part in every important battle of the Mexican War, except Buena Vista; and he was twice cited for gallantry. In 1854 he resigned his captain's commission, and the next seven years saw Grant a dismal failure at farming, at selling real estate, and at clerking—the latter in his brother's store at Galena, Illinois. When war began in 1861, the Governor of Illinois put Grant to work at drilling recruits. Eight months later he was a major-general with brilliant victories to his credit. The North had found the military leader who could save the Union. The Republican party selected the victorious Grant for its candidate in 1868. Having no interest in politics, he reluctantly accepted the presidential honor which a grateful people awarded him. Grant's administration faced complex problems of reconstruction in the South, serious questions of national finance, and important matters in foreign policy. Despite difficulties, disagreements, and dissatisfactions, the Republicans returned him for a second term. He married Julia T. Dent of St. Louis, Missouri. He died at Mt. McGregor, New York, after a long illness.

Rutherford B. Hayes (1822-1893)
Term 1877-1881, NINETEENTH PRESIDENT

The war record of Rutherford Birchard Hayes, distinctive with brave exploits and topped in 1865 by a major-general's rank, gave him great prestige in his native state of Ohio. The state Republicans persuaded him to become a Congressman; and in 1867 he was elected Governor of Ohio. In 1875 he was chosen Governor for a third term, the first man in Ohio to gain this honor. The resulting acclaim brought to him national recognition and the Republican nomination for the presidency. In the campaign of 1876 he defeated Samuel J. Tilden by one electoral vote in a disputed election. His administration was peaceful and honorable. He fought for an improved civil service; and he opposed political patronage. Rutherford Hayes was unusually well educated. His first schooling was received from his widowed mother in the town of Delaware, Ohio. A kindly uncle sent him to a Connecticut academy and later to Kenyon College. At twenty he was graduated as the valedictorian and the youngest member of his class. He entered the Harvard University Law School, finished the course in two years, and in 1845 began the practice of law in Fremont, Ohio. Hayes married Lucy Ware Webb in 1852. They had seven sons and one daughter. He died at his Spiegel Grove estate in Fremont, Ohio, and was buried in Spiegel Grove State Park.

James Abram Garfield (1831-1881)
Term 1881, TWENTIETH PRESIDENT

Like most of the national leaders James A. Garfield came from sturdy pioneer stock. A Puritan ancestor was one of the founders of Watertown, Massachusetts, in 1630. His father, Abraham Garfield, moved to Ohio 200 years later, settling in Cuyahoga County—where James was born. His father died when James was two. His mother and older brother assured him a good education. Life was hard on the frontier, and James helped to earn his own way by working at various jobs. He taught country school, attended Geauga Seminary, and then worked his way through Williams College, graduating with honors. Returning to Hiram, Ohio, he taught school, preached sermons, made political speeches, studied law, became principal of the Eclectic Institute at Hiram, and was admitted to the bar. When the war between the states broke out, Garfield received a commission and served so well that he attained the rank of major-general. While still in service, he was elected to the Congress as Representative from his Ohio district. In 1880 Republican factions, after much difficulty in selecting candidates, compromised by nominating Garfield for President, with Chester A. Arthur as his running mate. On July 2, a few months after his inauguration, the President was fatally shot by Charles Guiteau.

Chester Alan Arthur (1830-1886)
Term 1881-1885, TWENTY-FIRST PRESIDENT

The choice of Chester A. Arthur in 1880 as nominee for the vice-presidency was the result of a settlement between two Republican factions. Thus, the incident of compromise plus the accident of President Garfield's death brought Arthur to the presidency. As Collector of the Port of New York, Arthur opposed President Hayes' attempt to bring his office, with its many small jobs, under the civil service, and he was removed from office by the President. The solemn obligations of the presidency changed Arthur's attitudes and actions. He served with ability and distinction. His old political associates were surprised as he now supported civil service reform and put the welfare of the country above party ambitions. By these actions he lost the support of his own political group, and he was not renominated. Arthur was born at Fairfield, Vermont, the eldest son of Reverend William Arthur. His school days began at Union Village in Washington County. At the age of eighteen he was graduated from Union College. He taught school while he studied law, became principal of an academy, and in 1853 he was admitted to the New York bar. Professional success came rapidly. During the war between the states, Arthur served as quartermaster-general of the New York State Militia and recruited and prepared troops for the front.

Grover Cleveland (1837-1908)

Terms 1885-1889, 1893-1897, TWENTY-SECOND PRESIDENT AND TWENTY-FOURTH PRESIDENT

Grover Cleveland's birthplace was Caldwell, New Jersey. Later the family moved to Fayetteville, New York, where Grover attended the village school. At sixteen his father's death forced him to earn his own way. He studied law in Buffalo, New York, and was admitted to practice in 1859. Cleveland's political career started with his appointment as assistant district attorney of Erie County, and shortly afterward he was elected sheriff. The citizens of Buffalo were seeking a courageous and honest mayor to end a long period of political corruption. The Democrats nominated Cleveland, and to the surprise of the political bosses he was elected. Cleveland's zeal for good government was rewarded further by his election in 1882 to the New York governorship. In 1884 a national recognition of his merit swept him into the Democratic nomination and the nation's highest office. In 1886 he became the first President to be married in the White House. His bride was Frances Folsom. Cleveland's strength within the party gained him the Democratic renomination in 1888, but the Republicans won the election. The Democrats chose him again in 1892, many independent voters came to his support, and he won easily. His honesty and unwavering courage were ably applied to his office.

Benjamin Harrison (1833-1901)

Term 1889-1893, TWENTY-THIRD PRESIDENT

Benjamin was the second Harrison to become President. His grandfather, William Henry Harrison, was ninth President of the United States, and his great-grandfather, Benjamin Harrison, was a governor of Virginia. His father, John Scott Harrison, was a member of the Congress for four years. Benjamin Harrison was born at North Bend, Ohio, where he attended school until he was fourteen. In 1852 he was graduated from Miami University. The next year he married Miss Caroline Scott, and in 1854 he was admitted to the bar, and settled in Indianapolis, Indiana. When war came, Harrison was active in recruiting the Seventieth Indiana Regiment of Volunteers. He served in the western campaigns; and in 1865 was mustered out a brigadier-general. He was defeated for the governorship of Indiana in 1876. He became United States Senator in 1881, but he was not re-elected to the legislature. The Republicans, searching for a candidate with good political traditions, preferably from the Middle West, found Harrison to be the right man, and he defeated Cleveland in the election of 1888. Benjamin Harrison was the fourth general to become President since 1868. Under Harrison's administration six states were admitted to the Union: South Dakota, North Dakota, Montana, and Washington in 1889; and Idaho and Wyoming in 1890.

William McKinley (1843-1901)

Term 1897-1901, TWENTY-FIFTH PRESIDENT

William McKinley was the third President to be assassinated. Shot by an anarchist, Leon Czolgosz, September 6, 1901, at the Pan-American Exposition, Buffalo, New York, he died eight days later. The McKinley family lived at Niles, Ohio, when William was born. At seventeen he entered Allegheny College at Meadville, Pennsylvania. Later he taught school, then enlisted in the Twenty-third Ohio Volunteers. In four years of war he rose to the rank of major and was cited for gallantry by President Lincoln. On his return from the war, he completed a law course, married Miss Ida Saxton, and settled in Canton, Ohio, to practice his profession. As the prosecuting attorney of Stark County in 1869, he began a long and honorable career in the public service. From 1876 until 1891 he served in the national House of Representatives; then he was twice elected governor of Ohio. McKinley's staunch Republican record, as well as his support of a high tariff and of the gold standard, won popularity for him among the Republicans. He was nominated and elected President in the campaign of 1896. His administration was distinguished by victory in the Spanish-American War, annexation of Hawaii, and acquisition of the Philippines, Puerto Rico, and Guam. In 1900 McKinley was elected to a second term.

Theodore Roosevelt (1858-1919)

Term 1901-1909, TWENTY-SIXTH PRESIDENT

Theodore Roosevelt was born in New York City, where his ancestors, of Dutch origin, had lived since 1644. During his childhood Theodore was afflicted with asthma and near-sightedness. By unusual tenacity of purpose and effort, he overcame his physical handicaps, and at eighteen entered Harvard University, graduating in 1880. In 1882 he turned to politics, and with Republican party aid, he was elected to the New York legislature. Two years later he suddenly lost both his mother and his young wife. His health was not equal to this double tragedy, and he sought the curative qualities of a Dakota ranch. Returning to New York in 1886, he again threw his energy into politics and served as civil service commissioner and police commissioner of New York City. When the Spanish War came, he was the Assistant Secretary of the Navy, a post he resigned to organize the 1st U. S. Cavalry (Roosevelt's Rough Riders). In 1898 he was elected governor of New York; in 1900 popular approval of his attacks upon unfair practices increased his political strength and brought him the vice-presidency; in 1901 McKinley's assassination made him President; and in 1904 he was elected President. His term was noted for "trust busting," vigorous foreign policy, and for the Panama Canal Project. In 1912 he ran for President, but was defeated.

William Howard Taft (1857-1930)

Term 1909-1913, TWENTY-SEVENTH PRESIDENT

Nine years as Chief Justice of the Supreme Court and four years as Chief Executive of the United States made William Howard Taft the only American who has been chief of both judicial and executive branches of the national government. His father, a Superior Court judge, a Secretary of War, and an Attorney-General, set a pattern which his son exceeded. William became a judge of the Superior Court in Cincinnati (his native city), a United States Solicitor-General for President Harrison, and a Secretary of War for President Theodore Roosevelt. Taft was also a Federal Circuit judge and a Professor of Law in Yale University. In 1900 he was appointed Civil Governor of the Philippines and in 1906 took temporary charge of affairs in Cuba. In 1908 he was elected President, but the famous Republican split spelled defeat for him in 1912. Though Taft's administration was a stormy one, he was personally well-liked. He was notably successful as a lawyer, jurist, and public administrator. The postal savings bank and the parcel post system were created in his term; and the Sixteenth and Seventeenth Amendments were passed by the Congress. He was well educated, graduating from Yale University with high honors in 1878 and from the Cincinnati Law School in 1880. In 1886 he married Helen Herron.

Woodrow Wilson (1856-1924)

Term 1913-1921, TWENTY-EIGHTH PRESIDENT

Staunton, Virginia, was the birthplace of Thomas Woodrow Wilson, the eighth Virginian to become President. Young Wilson's early schooling was irregular, but a cultured home formed his character with wisdom and refinement. He was graduated from Princeton in. 1879; and two years later he received a law degree at the University of Virignia. A zest for learning and for teaching led him into further study at Johns Hopkins University. Teaching positions at Bryn Mawr College and at Wesleyan and Princeton Universities followed. In 1902 he was chosen president of Princeton and served until 1910. From 1911 to 1913 he was governor of New Jersey. The Democrats, looking for a candidate of liberal views, selected Wilson as their leader in the 1912 campaign and the Taft-Roosevelt feud insured a Democratic victory. In Wilson's first term important legislation affected banking, trusts, tariff, labor, and income taxation. Wilson's personal strength and his sincere attempts to avert war won his re-election in 1916. Despite Wilson's efforts the inevitable war came, and he was compelled to give leadership for the great task of victory. As a world leader his fourteen points formed a basis for peace, and he insisted upon the acceptance of the League of Nations. which the United States, alone of the great nations, rejected.

Warren Gamaliel Harding (1865-1923)

Term 1921-1923, TWENTY-NINTH PRESIDENT

Warren Harding, the seventh President from Ohio, was born on a farm near the village of Corsica. As a boy he learned the printer's trade in a small shop at Caledonia, Ohio. For a time young Warren attended Ohio Central College, but a newspaper job at Marion lured him away from school and into a lifetime of newspaper work. Failing, by his Republican activities, to please his Democratic employer, Harding gained independence by purchasing the *Marion Star*, an enterprise which became a major success. From 1900 to 1904 he served in the Ohio State Senate, but he was defeated for the governorship in 1910. Ohio sent him to the United States Senate in 1915. The Republicans in 1920 were deadlocked over presidential candidates until some ardent Ohioans, supported by a small bloc of Senators and a few party leaders, manipulated a triumph for Warren Harding. The chief campaign issue was the acceptance of the League of Nations, but those who opposed it, or wished reservations, won out. Harding's distinguished appearance, genial nature, and political experience forecast a normal administration; but instead came such things as the "Teapot Dome" affair and the President's tragic death. Two unworthy Cabinet members were the chief figures in the Teapot Dome oil scandal.

Calvin Coolidge (1872-1933)

Term 1923-1929, THIRTIETH PRESIDENT

The news of Harding's death came to Calvin Coolidge in the little farmhouse at Plymouth, Vermont, where he was born. His father, a local justice, administered the oath of office to the new President by the light of a kerosene lamp. After a boyhood combining farm life with good schooling, Calvin entered Amherst College. He was graduated with honors in 1895. On leaving college, he began to read law in Northampton, Massachusetts, and two years later he was admitted to practice. In 1905 he married Grace A. Goodhue, who was to become one of the best liked of the White House hostesses. Coolidge served Massachusetts in both houses of the legislature and then became governor in 1919. The vigorous words and effective actions which Coolidge as governor applied to the Boston police strike rang favorably throughout the country. He was re-elected governor by a large majority; and he was at once proposed for the presidency, which he was to gain later by way of the vice-presidency. Coolidge brought native forthrightness, sparse utterance, and a thrifty economy to the White House. Drastic reduction of expenditures followed in all departments of the government. With rare political courage he vetoed a soldiers' bonus bill. Elected in his own right, in 1924, Coolidge declined renomination in 1927.

Herbert Clark Hoover (1874-1964)

Term 1929-1933, THIRTY-FIRST PRESIDENT

At nine years of age Herbert Hoover was left an orphan in his native village of West Branch, Iowa. Herbert went to live with his Quaker uncle in Oregon. He worked at various jobs, attended night school, and was admitted to Leland Stanford University, where he studied geology and mining. After several years of hard experience Hoover became chief engineer for a mining company in Australia. Then he was director-general of mines for the Chinese government, and soon thereafter he filled assignments the world over as a mining expert. When World War I began, Hoover was made chairman of the American Relief Commission in Belgium. In 1917 he was appointed Food Administrator for the United States. After the Armistice he became head of the European Economic Council and gave several years to the relief of distressed peoples. In 1921 when Hoover accepted the Secretary of Commerce post, he was probably the most favorably known American throughout the world. The American public continued to think well of him, electing him President in 1928. His term started smoothly, but was soon overwhelmed by world-wide depression and panic. His administration was blamed for the disaster, causing his defeat in 1932. Hoover was one of the most honored of presidents, receiving many honorary degrees in his lifetime.

Franklin Delano Roosevelt (1882-1945)
Term 1933-1945, THIRTY-SECOND PRESIDENT

Franklin D. Roosevelt, a fifth cousin of Theodore Roosevelt, was born at Hyde Park, New York. Privately tutored until fourteen, he prepared for college at Groton Academy. In 1904 he was graduated from Harvard and then attended Columbia University Law School, during which time he married Anna Eleanor Roosevelt. He was already interested in politics, and in 1910 was elected to the state senate on the Democratic ticket. Roosevelt was appointed Assistant Secretary of the Navy in 1913, serving until 1920, resigning to accept the nomination for Vice-President. Shortly after the Democratic defeat, he was stricken with infantile paralysis; but persistent treatment plus heroic courage permitted him to return to political activity. He carried on to be elected governor of New York for two terms, a record which brought him the presidential nomination in the depression year of 1932. New social legislation followed. Roosevelt was renominated and re-elected in 1936; in 1940 (the first third term); and for a fourth term in 1944. Long threatening war broke on December 7, 1941. Roosevelt met with Churchill to discuss global war's demands and later held further conferences with Churchill and Soviet Premier Stalin to outline postwar policies. Roosevelt died suddenly, April 12, 1945.

Harry S Truman (1884-1972)
Term 1945-1953, THIRTY-THIRD PRESIDENT

Harry S Truman was the seventh Vice-President to receive the presidential mantle by the constitutional provision of immediate succession. He accepted the heavy obligations of the presidency with courage and with resolution to successfully complete the plans already made for Allied victory. Before his election to the vice-presidency, Truman was, for ten years, a member of the United States Senate. He won commendation for his work as the chairman of a Senate committee on defense expenditures. Harry Truman spent the early years of his life on a farm near his birthplace, Lamar, Missouri. He combined farming with schooling, including music lessons, and was graduated from the Independence, Missouri, high school. He held jobs as a drugstore clerk, railroad timekeeper, bank clerk, and haberdasher. Entering World War I as a private, he became captain of a battery of field artillery and saw action in the famous battles of St. Mihiel and Meuse-Argonne. Truman, elected president in 1948, had to deal with the problems of postwar recovery, of the "Cold War," and of rearmament and the economic dislocations caused by it. He led opposition to the spread of communism in Europe with the Marshall Plan and in Asia with the signing in 1951 of the Pacific Pact and the Japanese Peace Treaty. He declined to be a candidate in 1952.

Dwight David Eisenhower (1890-1969)
Term 1953-1961, THIRTY-FOURTH PRESIDENT

The second graduate of West Point to become President, Dwight David Eisenhower was born in Denison, Tex. He was graduated from the United States Military Academy in 1915 and the following year married Mamie Geneva Doud. He was a member of Gen. Douglas MacArthur's staff, 1933-39. Having advanced rapidly in rank prior to U.S. entry in World War II he was supreme commander of the Allied forces in the North Africa invasion of 1942. As supreme commander of the Allied Expeditionary Forces, he directed the landing on the Normandy beaches. In December, 1944, he was made General of the Army, the highest military rank. He served as commander of the U.S. Occupation Forces in Germany. After serving as Chief of Staff, 1945-48, he retired from military service to become president of Columbia University. In 1950 he accepted a new post as supreme commander of NATO forces, but soon resigned to become the Republican presidential candidate in 1952. He was elected President the same year. Seeking re-election in 1956, the President campaigned on a platform of continued "Peace and Prosperity," and won a large majority of the popular vote and an overwhelming majority in the electoral college. During his second term, 1961, Eisenhower was the oldest—70 years 3 months—U.S. President in history.

John Fitzgerald Kennedy (1917-1963)
Term 1961-1963, THIRTY-FIFTH PRESIDENT

John Fitzgerald Kennedy, the second-youngest man to become President, was born in Brookline, Mass. He graduated *cum laude* from Harvard in 1940, and the following year enlisted in the U.S. Navy, and served with distinction throughout World War II. Entering politics in 1946 after a brief but highly successful career in journalism, he was elected on the Democratic ticket from the Eleventh District of Massachusetts to the House of Representatives; re-election followed in 1948 and 1950. In 1952, after a vigorous campaign, he was elected senator from Massachusetts, defeating the incumbent Republican, Henry Cabot Lodge, Jr., whom Kennedy was again to oppose and defeat in the 1960 presidential election, in which Lodge was Richard Nixon's Republican vice-presidential running mate. The year 1956 saw the publication of Kennedy's best-selling, Pulitzer prize-winning *Profiles in Courage;* it also saw the youthful Massachusetts senator capture the political limelight by nearly winning the Democratic vice-presidential nomination. In 1958 he was re-elected senator. At the Democratic National Convention in July, 1960, he was the overwhelming choice of the assembled delegates, who gave him the nomination on the first ballot. He was elected President the following November. On November 22, 1963, he was assassinated.

Lyndon Baines Johnson (1908-1973)
Term 1963-1969, THIRTY-SIXTH PRESIDENT

Lyndon Baines Johnson was born near Stonewall, Tex. Supporting himself at Southwest Texas State Teachers College by doing janitorial work, he was graduated with a B.S. in 1930. From 1932 to 1935 he served as secretary to Representative Richard M. Kleberg of Texas. In 1934 he was married to Claudia Alta Taylor. After a year in law school and a year as state director of the National Youth Administration of Texas, he was elected to the U.S. House of Representatives, where he served five terms interrupted only by a tour of duty with the U.S. Navy in World War II. Elected to the U.S. Senate in 1943, he became in 1953 the youngest Senate party leader in U.S. history. As Vice-President in the Kennedy administration, he was an important governmental representative abroad. He also became chairman of the National Aeronautics and Space Council. On Nov. 22, 1963, after President Kennedy's assassination, Johnson was sworn in as President at Dallas, Tex. He was elected President in 1964. During his administration, Congress passed a number of bills that he had requested to support his Great Society program, such as Medicare, antipoverty legislation, civil rights, and aid to education. In foreign affairs, the role of the United States in Vietnam became a subject of controversy. In 1968 he declined to run for re-election.

Richard Milhous Nixon (1913-   )
Term 1969-1974, THIRTY-SEVENTH PRESIDENT

Richard Milhous Nixon, born in Yorba Linda, Calif., received his education in Whittier College and Duke University Law School. After serving in the Navy during World War II he was elected, in 1946, to Congress, where he was catapulted to fame by his handling of the Chambers-Hiss case. In 1950 he moved to the Senate and in 1952 was elected Vice-President. He narrowly lost the 1960 presidential election to Kennedy and returned to California where, in 1962, he was badly defeated in the election for governor. He recovered from the defeat and, in 1968, was elected to the presidency. He was re-elected in 1972 by one of the largest majorities in the nation's history. Nixon's presidency was marked by strong achievements in foreign affairs: détente with Russia and China, termination of U.S. participation in the Vietnam war, truce in the Middle East. But at home his administration collapsed: his Vice-President, Spiro Agnew, resigned in disgrace, and, as the Watergate Scandal unfolded, twenty-eight of his aides were either convicted or indicted for criminal offenses. When, in 1974, further revelations showed his own part in the scandal and impeachment and conviction seemed certain, Nixon became the first President in the history of the United States to resign. His resignation became effective on August 9, and he was succeeded in office by his Vice-President.

Gerald Rudolph Ford (1913-   )
Term 1974-1977, THIRTY-EIGHTH PRESIDENT

Gerald Rudolph Ford was born in Omaha, Neb. and christened Leslie Lynch King. His name was changed two years later when his mother remarried. Ford graduated from the University of Michigan in 1935 and, supporting himself as a football and boxing coach, continued his studies at Yale Law School, from which he was graduated in the top third of his class in 1941. He then practiced law in Grand Rapids, Mich.—with a four-year interruption while he served in the Navy during World War II—until he was elected to the House of Representatives from Michigan's Fifth District in 1948. Shortly before that election he met and married Elizabeth Bloomer. He was returned to Congress in six succeeding elections, never with less than 60 percent of the vote. In 1951 he was assigned to the House Appropriations Committee and in 1965 defeated Charles Halleck for the position of House Minority Leader. He defines his political philosophy as that of "... a conservative in fiscal affairs, a moderate in domestic affairs, and a liberal in foreign policy." At the urging of his wife, he had decided to retire from politics by 1976, but in 1973, upon Spiro Agnew's resignation, he was appointed Vice-President by Richard Nixon, and in 1974, when Nixon himself resigned, Gerald Ford assumed the office of the presidency.

James Earl (Jimmy) Carter, Jr. (1924-   )
Term 1977-1981, THIRTY-NINTH PRESIDENT

Jimmy Carter was born and grew up in Plains, Georgia. He attended Georgia Southwestern College and the Georgia Institute of Technology in 1941 and 1942 and then entered the U.S. Naval Academy in Annapolis, graduating in 1946. Carter remained in the Navy until 1953. During his naval career he worked with Adm. Hyman Rickover whose influence on him was, according to Carter's autobiography, perhaps second only to that of his parents. Carter left the Navy in 1953 as a lieutenant. After his father's death in 1953, Carter entered the family business and became a successful peanut farmer. He had married Rosalynn Smith of Plains in 1947 and they had three sons and one daughter. In Plains, Carter became active in community affairs and local politics. In 1962, he won a seat in the state senate. Carter had a liberal voting record during his two senate terms. In 1966, he ran for governor of Georgia against segregationist Lester Maddox. Carter lost but ran again in 1970, this time winning both the primary and the general election. Carter began to broaden his political base in 1974 when he traveled as Democratic Party national campaign coordinator for the 1974 elections. He gained national notice in 1976 by intense campaigning, won the Democratic nomination, and finally defeated Gerald Ford in a closely fought race.

Ronald Wilson Reagan (1911-   )
Term 1981-   , FORTIETH PRESIDENT

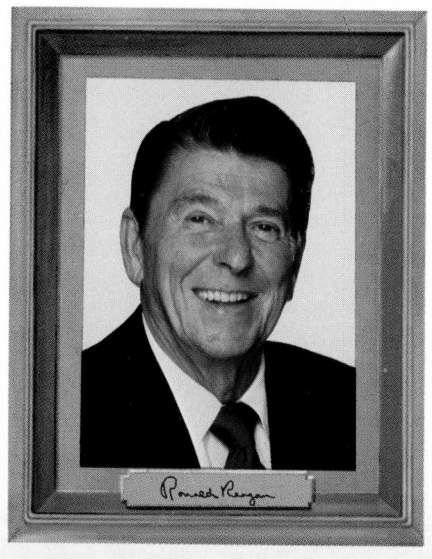

Ronald Wilson Reagan, the only former actor to become President, was born in Tampico, Illinois. He received his education from Eureka College, graduating in 1932, became a radio sports announcer that same year in Davenport, Iowa. In 1937, while covering a sports assignment, he came to the attention of a Warner Brothers agent who gave him a screen test and signed him to a movie contract. Over the next several years he appeared in numerous pictures. His acting career was interrupted during World War II when he served in the Army Air Corps making training films. After the war, while continuing his work in the entertainment industry, he became increasingly involved in politics. Although at first active in many liberal political organizations, he soon became fearful of Communist subversion and moved to the right testifying before the House Un-American Activities Committee in 1947 on Communist influence in the movie industry. After 1965, he devoted full time to politics. In 1966 he campaigned for the governorship of California and beat Democratic incumbent Edmund G. Brown. In 1968 he made an unsuccessful bid for the Republican presidential nomination but was easily reelected Governor in 1970. He tried for the presidential nomination again in 1976 but again was unsuccessful. Finally in 1980, after intense campaigning, he won the nomination and went on to defeat Jimmy Carter, winning a large majority of the popular vote and an overwhelming majority in the electoral college.

NOMINATING CONVENTIONS

Every four years and during the summer preceding the presidential election, each major political party holds a national nominating convention to choose its presidential and vice-presidential candidate. Also adopted at this time are the party platforms and the rules governing the national party organization. The candidates are chosen by delegates who are selected from each state. About two-thirds of the states select their delegations at party conventions, while the remaining one-third select their delegates through primary votes.

National political conventions originated out of necessity and dissatisfaction with the old method of choosing a presidential candidate. Prior to the election of James Monroe in 1816, presidential nominations were made at informal party caucuses. During the Monroe administration, however, organized political parties, as they existed in the past, collapsed. The breakdown was most evident in the hotly contested election of 1824 when four candidates independently sought the office of the presidency. As a result of this election, political leaders came to realize the need for a party system that would enable them to form the alliances necessary to capture the presidency. After the election of Andrew Jackson in 1828, party lines became more defined, and in 1832 opposition parties met for the first time at national party conventions to prepare for the presidential elections. Since then, all candidates elected to the office of the presidency have been chosen from the two major political parties.

Today, political aspirants for their party's nomination may prove their merit by entering primary elections prior to the convention. By successfully campaigning in a given primary election, the perspective nominee may accumulate the necessary delegation commitments to aid in securing his nomination at the convention. These elections also serve to focus national attention on the nominees.

Although current nominating procedures of the two major political parties are similar, some variations exist. For example, in the Republican convention, each delegate is allowed to cast his vote as he chooses, while in the Democratic convention, a modified "unit vote" rule is imposed. Under this method, some states must cast their votes as a unit if instructed to do so by their state conventions, while other states allow their delegates to cast their votes individually if they were elected in the state primary. Another difference concerns the number of votes needed by a candidate to win his party's nomination. The Republicans have always required their candidate to gain a simple majority. This was not true for the Democrats until the 1936 convention. Before then, a candidate needed a two-thirds majority to win the nomination.

Balloting continues in each convention until one presidential nominee has received a simple majority. Although prolonged balloting is unusual, there have been some exceptions. In Democratic conventions 46 ballots were required in 1912, 44 in 1920, and 103 in 1924. The Republicans have been more successful in choosing their candidates on fewer ballots. Delegates often use their ballots for political maneuvering. They may cast their ballots for a candidate who cannot win in order to prevent another from winning, or they may withhold their ballots at first, only to release them later and thus show a candidate gaining strength. Most of the time, however, a given candidate is nominated on the first ballot.

Once the presidential nominee has been selected, delegates cast their ballot for a vice-presidential candidate. This ballot is usually perfunctory, as delegates as a rule unanimously endorse the running mate selected by the presidential nominee. After the vice-president is nominated the task of the convention is complete.

THE ELECTORAL COLLEGE

The electoral method of choosing the president was adopted by the Constitutional Convention on September 7, 1787. Other methods were discussed and debated but eventually rejected because they failed to engender adequate support. One method suggested that Congress choose the president. However, a deadlock resulted over the distribution of congressional voting power; that is, whether it should be by joint ballot or whether each state should have a single vote. The impasse was resolved by the complete rejection of the legislative electoral method. Another method suggested that the president be chosen by the direct vote of the people. This method had been discussed before and twice defeated when brought to a vote. Few delegates felt the nation was sufficiently mature to entrust the choice of a president directly to the people. The method finally accepted after many compromises was the intermediate elector plan. Under this plan the president would be chosen by representative electors from each state. The actual procedure for choosing electors is stated in Article II, Section I of the Constitution:

Each state shall appoint, in such manner as the legislature thereof may direct, a number of electors, equal to the whole number of senators and representatives to which the state may be entitled in the Congress: but no senator or representative, or person holding an office of trust or profit under the United States, shall be appointed an elector.

It was not decided how the state legislatures should select their electors until September 13, 1788 when the Continental Congress directed the states to individually determine the selection of their electors. The actual duties of the electors are redefined in the twelfth amendment to the Constitution which was adopted on September 24, 1804:

The Electors shall meet in their respective states, and vote by ballot for President and Vice-President, one of whom, at least, shall not be an inhabitant of the same state with themselves; they shall name in their ballots the person voted for as President, and in distinct ballots the person voted for as Vice-President, and they shall make distinct lists of all persons voted for as President, and of all persons voted for as Vice-President, and of the number of votes for each, which lists they shall sign and certify, and transmit sealed to the seat of the government of the United States, directed to the President of the Senate;—The President of the Senate shall, in the presence of the Senate and House of Representatives, open all the certificates and the votes shall then be counted;—The person having the greatest number of votes for President, shall be the President, if such number be a majority of the whole number of Electors appointed; and if no person has such majority, then from the persons having the highest numbers not exceeding three on the list of those voted for as President, the House of Representatives shall choose immediately, by ballot, the President. But in choosing the President, the votes shall be taken by states, the representation from each state having one vote; a

quorum for this purpose shall consist of a member or members from two-thirds of the states, and a majority of all the states shall be necessary to a choice. . . . The person having the greatest number of votes as Vice-President, shall be the Vice-President, if such number be a majority of the whole number of Electors appointed, and if no person have a majority, then from the two highest numbers on the list, the Senate shall choose the Vice-President; a quorum for the purpose shall consist of two-thirds of the whole number of Senators, and a majority of the whole number shall be necessary to a choice. But no person constitutionally ineligible to the office of President shall be eligible to that of Vice-President of the United States.

The electoral plan was adopted because it offered something to each faction: the large states received representation of electors according to the size of their population; the small states got equal voting rights in contingent elections if the majority of electors failed to choose a president; those advocating States' rights were acknowledged by allowing the state legislature the right to select electors as they saw fit; and those favoring a direct popular vote got at least an approximation of a direct vote if the electors reflected the popular will.

Today, most states nominate their electors at the individual party conventions. After the popular presidential election, the designated party electors meet when the electoral college convenes and formally vote for the candidate with the greatest popular vote in their respective states. A given state's entire electoral vote goes to the candidate with the greatest popular vote.

The present electoral college consists of 538 votes: 435 correspond to the number of representatives in the House of Representatives; 100 represent the number of senators; and 3 represent the number for the District of Columbia. The votes are apportioned as follows:

Alabama 9	Kentucky 9	North Dakota 3
Alaska 3	Louisiana 10	Ohio 25
Arizona 6	Maine 4	Oklahoma 8
Arkansas 6	Maryland 10	Oregon 6
California 45	Massachusetts 14	Pennsylvania 27
Colorado 7	Michigan 21	Rhode Island 4
Connecticut 8	Minnesota 10	South Carolina ... 8
Delaware 3	Mississipi 7	South Dakota 4
District of Columbia 3	Missouri 12	Tennessee 10
Florida 17	Montana 4	Texas 26
Georgia 12	Nebraska 5	Utah 4
Hawaii 4	Nevada 3	Vermont 3
Idaho 4	New Hampshire .. 4	Virginia 12
Illinois 26	New Jersey 17	Washington 9
Indiana 13	New Mexico 4	West Virginia ... 6
Iowa 8	New York 41	Wisconsin 11
Kansas 7	North Carolina ..13	Wyoming 3

PRESIDENTS OF THE UNITED STATES

Name	Held Office	From State	Born	Died	Brithplace	Party	Vice-President
1. GEORGE WASHINGTON	1789-1797	Va.	1732	1799	Westmoreland Co., Va.	Fed.	JOHN ADAMS
2. JOHN ADAMS	1797-1801	Mass.	1735	1826	Quincy, Mass.	Fed.	THOMAS JEFFERSON
3. THOMAS JEFFERSON	1801-1809	Va.	1743	1826	Shadwell, Va.	Rep.[1]	AARON BURR / GEORGE CLINTON
4. JAMES MADISON	1809-1817	Va.	1751	1836	Port Conway, Va.	Rep.[1]	GEORGE CLINTON
5. JAMES MONROE	1817-1825	Va.	1758	1831	Westmoreland Co., Va.	Rep.[1]	DANIEL D. TOMPKINS
6. JOHN QUINCY ADAMS	1825-1829	Mass.	1767	1848	Quincy, Mass.	Rep.[1]	JOHN C. CALHOUN
7. ANDREW JACKSON	1829-1837	Tenn.	1767	1845	New Lancaster Co., S.C.	Dem.	JOHN C. CALHOUN / MARTIN VAN BUREN
8. MARTIN VAN BUREN	1837-1841	N.Y.	1782	1862	Kinderhook, N.Y.	Dem.	RICHARD M. JOHNSON
9. WILLIAM HENRY HARRISON	1841	Ohio	1773	1841	Berkeley, Va.	Whig	JOHN TYLER
10. JOHN TYLER	1841-1845	Va.	1790	1862	Greenway, Va.	Whig	
11. JAMES KNOX POLK	1845-1849	Tenn.	1795	1849	Mecklenburg Co., N.C.	Dem.	GEORGE M. DALLAS
12. ZACHARY TAYLOR	1849-1850	La.	1784	1850	Orange Co., Va.	Whig	MILLARD FILLMORE
13. MILLARD FILLMORE	1850-1853	N.Y.	1800	1874	Cayuga Co., N.Y.	Whig	
14. FRANKLIN PIERCE	1853-1857	N.H.	1804	1869	Hillsboro, N.H.	Dem.	WILLIAM R. KING
15. JAMES BUCHANAN	1857-1861	Pa.	1791	1868	Mercersburg, Pa.	Dem	JOHN C. BRECKINRIDGE
16. ABRAHAM LINCOLN	1861-1865	Ill.	1809	1865	Hardin Co., Ky.	Rep.[2]	HANNIBAL HAMLIN / ANDREW JOHNSON
17. ANDREW JOHNSON	1865-1869	Tenn.	1808	1875	Raleigh, N.C.	Dem.[2]	
18. ULYSSES SIMPSON GRANT	1869-1877	Ill.	1822	1885	Point Pleasant, Ohio	Rep.	SCHUYLER COLFAX / HENRY WILSON
19. RUTHERFORD BIRCHARD HAYES	1877-1881	Ohio	1822	1893	Delaware, Ohio	Rep.	WILLIAM A. WHEELER
20. JAMES ABRAM GARFIELD	1881	Ohio	1831	1881	Orange, Ohio	Rep.	CHESTER A. ARTHUR
21. CHESTER ALAN ARTHUR	1881-1885	N.Y.	1830	1886	Fairfield, Vt.	Rep.	
22. GROVER CLEVELAND	1885-1889	N.Y.	1837	1908	Caldwell, N.J.	Dem.	THOMAS A. HENDRICKS
23. BENJAMIN HARRISON	1889-1893	Ind.	1833	1901	North Bend, Ohio	Rep.	LEVI P. MORTON
24. GROVER CLEVELAND	1893-1897						ADLAI E. STEVENSON
25. WILLIAM McKINLEY	1897-1901	Ohio	1843	1901	Niles, Ohio	Rep.	GARRET A. HOBART / THEODORE ROOSEVELT
26. THEODORE ROOSEVELT	1901-1909	N.Y.	1858	1919	New York, N.Y.	Rep.	CHARLES W. FAIRBANKS
27. WILLIAM HOWARD TAFT	1909-1913	Ohio	1857	1930	Cincinnati, Ohio	Rep.	JAMES S. SHERMAN
28. WOODROW WILSON	1913-1921	N.J.	1856	1924	Staunton, Va.	Dem.	THOMAS R. MARSHALL
29. WARREN GAMALIEL HARDING	1921-1923	Ohio	1865	1923	Blooming Grove, Ohio	Rep.	CALVIN COOLIDGE
30. CALVIN COOLIDGE	1923-1929	Mass.	1872	1933	Plymouth, Vt.	Rep.	CHARLES G. DAWES
31. HERBERT CLARK HOOVER	1929-1933	Calif.	1874	1964	West Branch, Iowa	Rep.	CHARLES CURTIS
32. FRANKLIN DELANO ROOSEVELT	1933-1945	N.Y.	1882	1945	Hyde Park, N.Y.	Dem.	JOHN N. GARNER / HENRY A. WALLACE / HARRY S TRUMAN
33. HARRY S TRUMAN	1945-1953	Mo.	1884	1972	Lamar, Mo.	Dem.	ALBEN W. BARKLEY
34. DWIGHT DAVID EISENHOWER	1953-1961	N.Y.	1890	1969	Denison, Texas	Rep.	RICHARD M. NIXON
35. JOHN FITZGERALD KENNEDY	1961-1963	Mass.	1917	1963	Brookline, Mass.	Dem.	LYNDON B. JOHNSON
36. LYNDON BAINES JOHNSON	1963-1969	Texas	1908	1973	Johnson City, Texas	Dem.	HUBERT H. HUMPHREY
37. RICHARD MILHOUS NIXON	1969-1974	N.Y.	1913		Yorba Linda, Calif.	Rep.	SPIRO T. AGNEW[3] / GERALD R. FORD
38. GERALD RUDOLPH FORD	1974-1977	Mich.	1913		Omaha, Neb.	Rep.	NELSON ROCKEFELLER
39. JAMES EARL CARTER, JR.	1977-1981	Ga.	1924		Plains, Ga.	Dem.	WALTER F. MONDALE
40. RONALD WILSON REAGAN	1981-	Calif.	1911		Tampico, Ill.	Rep.	GEORGE BUSH

1. Now the Democratic party   2. Candidate of the National Union Party (1864) and elected on that ticket   3. Resigned October 10, 1973

PLACES OF INTEREST IN THE UNITED STATES AND ITS POSSESSIONS

ALABAMA

Cathedral Caverns. These deep, immense caverns, located near Grant, contain numerous brilliantly colored calcite formations. Goliath, the largest stalagmite in the world, 60 feet high and 200 feet wide, is found here. Cathedral Caverns is one of four major caverns in northern and central Alabama. Most cavern areas provide camping and other facilities.

Dadeville. Near this town, Andrew Jackson fought the Battle of Horseshoe

Cathedral Caverns, Inc.

The largest stalagmite in the world, appropriately named Goliath, is located in the Cathedral Caverns in Grant, Alabama.

Bend in 1814 against the Upper Creek Indians that ended the power of the Creek nation. This battle is electronically reproduced in miniature several times each day. Fifteen miles away is the battle site itself in Horseshoe Bend National Military Park.

Huntsville. This is a city of firsts. It was the first permanent English settlement in Alabama, the home of the first state constitution, and the site of the inauguration of the first state governor and the first session of the state legislature. Points of interest are numerous ante-bellum houses, churches, and the space center. Redstone Arsenal in Huntsville is one of the world's major centers for rocket production. In the George C. Marshall Space Flight Center are many exhibits to keep children amused and puzzled, while adults are attracted by informative displays and literature.

Mobile. A seaport town and the location of Alabama's first permanent white settlement, Mobile is noted for its Civil War history. In the surrounding locale are many forts dating from the Civil War or before. Fort Alabama has an excellent museum covering 200 years of Alabama history. Twenty miles south on Dauphin Island in Mobile Bay is Fort Gaines, built in the 1850's on orders from Secretary of War Jefferson Davis. Fort Morgan, star-shaped

and noted for its excellent architecture, is located just across the mouth of the bay; it was the last Confederate fort to fall to the North and bloodstains of an anonymous Confederate soldier are still visible on its granite steps. Many gardens and parks as well as preserved and restored ante-bellum buildings are found in and around Mobile.

Montgomery. Here in the capital, many of the historic state buildings are open to the public. Worth seeing are the Capitol Building, where Jefferson Davis was inaugurated; the first Confederate White House; and the Department of Archives and History, in the capitol complex. Nearby are the Governor's Mansion and Teague House, the Chamber of Commerce building.

Mound State Monument. Situated near Moundville is Mound State Monument, a group of 40 temple mounds built by Indian residents of Alabama 600 years ago. The exhibits in the museum show that these Indians were among the most advanced tribes north of Mexico. The park, which covers 320 acres, is an interesting place to visit, to see the mounds, or to search for broken bits of pottery made before the arrival of white men in America.

Selma. The main attraction in the city is Sturdivant Hall, designed by Thomas Helm Lee, Robert E. Lee's cousin. Sturdivant Hall is one of the South's best neoclassical constructions. It has been expanded into a museum, and is furnished with Persian rugs, English furniture, and cut-crystal chandeliers. One of the most popular dis-

plays is the collection of antique dolls.

Tuscaloosa. This is the home of the University of Alabama. The beautiful campus was set on fire during the Civil War. Only four buildings remained standing, including the only military installation on campus, and they still attract visitors. The Museum of Natural History in Smith Hall with its many informative and

delightful displays is a favorite with visitors. The city also offers many other interesting prewar structures, including the Friedman Library and Friedman Home.

ALASKA

Anchorage. This is the largest city in Alaska, and was once the headquarters of the Willow Creek gold district. South of Anchorage is Mt. Aleskya, a winter sports area. Katmai National Monument on the Alaska Peninsula includes Mt. Katmai, an active volcano, and the Valley of Ten Thousand Smokes. Kenai Peninsula, south of Anchorage, offers excellent hunting and fishing and beautiful scenery.

Fairbanks. Gold mining and lumbering are two of the principal industries of this city. Points of interest include the Ester Creek gold operation and the University of Alaska with its museum. Fairbanks is a departure point for trips on the Chena River and to Chena Hot Springs which can only be reached by air. Good hunting and fishing is available in this area; big game hunting, with a licensed guide, is legal in some seasons.

Juneau. The state capital, Juneau, is the third largest city in Alaska. Popular public attractions are the Mendenhall Glacier, and the Alaska Historical Library and Museum, which contains Eskimo antiquities, Russian documents, and other exhibits. The major industry is gold mining; two principal locations for mining are the Alaska-Juneau gold mine and Gold Creek,

Pacific Northern Airlines

Twin Glacier Lake, southwest of Anchorage, Alaska, is named for the two glaciers—one at the base of each of the twin mountain peaks. About 3 percent of Alaska is glaciated.

located on Mt. Roberts.

Mt. McKinley National Park. Mount McKinley, the highest mountain in the United States, extends 20,320 feet above sea level. Unexplored ice-capped domes rise above mossy vegetation near the glaciers. The park is a wildlife preserve.

Nome. Located on the Seward Peninsula, Nome is the starting point for trips into the upper regions of Alaska. Gold, silver, and other valuable minerals are found and mined here. It is accessible mostly by plane; few good roads are in the area.

ARIZONA

Grand Canyon. This natural masterpiece is, in the words of Teddy Roosevelt, "the one great sight every American should see." Ten million years of river, rain, wind, and frost have dug this mile-deep, 217-mile long, and 4- to 18-mile wide chasm in northern Arizona. At the bottom of the canyon is the raging Colorado River. The Grand Canyon is a spectacular display of rocky mountain peaks and constantly changing colors. The North Rim affords many fine views, notably Bright Angel, Point Imperial, and Cape Royal. On the South Rim there are Mather Point, Maricopa Point, Yavapai Point, and other viewing spots. Bright Angel Trail leads to the

dwellings where Indians lived 700 years ago; and Inscription House, a trading post from early pioneer days. The Monument is only a small part of the Navajo-Hopi reservation which occupies the northeastern corner of Arizona. This is one of 19 reservations in Arizona. Most of the Indians welcome visitors and will guide them through the reservations. The public may also attend many of the Indian ceremonies and festivals. Handicraft products are available in reservation shops and trading posts.

Petrified Forest National Park. This is one of the world's vastest stretches of beautifully colored petrified wood. It includes six individual forests, each with huge logs—some up to 250 feet long—lying on the ground.

Phoenix. The capital and largest city of Arizona, Phoenix has increased its size more than five times since 1950. The warm

Phoenix Chamber of Commerce

Montezuma Castle National Monument, north of Phoenix, is one of Arizona's best-preserved Indian cliff dwellings.

attractions are Boot Hill and an old mine where silver abounds but is unreachable because of flooding by an underground river. There are more than 30 ghost towns in Arizona. In many, among remains of diggings, small pieces of gold and other precious metals are often found. A visit to such places will prove exciting and rewarding, though possibly dangerous. For the adventurous, there are many legendary hidden treasures, including the famous Lost Dutchman Mine.

Tucson. Tucson is a popular winter resort area and a rapidly growing southwestern city. Here the University of Arizona offers theater, speakers, and art shows to the residents of Tucson. Old Tucson, a recreation of a section of the city as it existed in 1860, is interesting to visit. Exhibits relating to the history of the state are on display in two museums: the Arizona State Museum and the Arizona Pioneers Historical Society.

Union Pacific Railroad

Bright Angel Point, on the rim of the Grand Canyon in Arizona, offers an excellent view of this spectacular area. The Grand Canyon was declared a national park in 1919.

canyon floor. Within the Grand Canyon National Park are tourist and camping facilities, some of which are open all year.

Hoover Dam. Built on the Arizona-Nevada state border (1931–36) and spanning the Colorado River, the Hoover Dam produces great amounts of hydroelectric power for the surrounding states, holds water for irrigation, and forms Lake Mead, the largest man-made lake in the United States. Lake Mead provides fine waters for fishing and water sports.

Jerome State Historic Park. A picturesque town, Jerome had active mining operations as recently as 1952; then, operations suddenly ceased and it became a ghost town. Citizens who remembered the boom days formed the Jerome Historical Society and created the attractive ghost town, complete with museums, old buildings, and tours of abandoned mines.

Navajo National Monument. The Monument, near the Utah border, contains three points of particular interest: Betatakin and Keet Seel, which are the ruins of

climate contributed to this rapid growth and is of prime importance to the many retirees who have settled here. Phoenix, however, has something of interest for almost everyone. Spectator and participation sports are in season the year round. Points of interest include Arizona State University, the State Capitol Building and other state buildings, and the Library of Archives. There are also a number of museums, including the Heard Museum and the American Heritage Wax Museum in Scottsdale. In the surrounding area are many parks and gardens.

Tombstone. A boom town of the gold rush days, Tombstone is now a quiet, sedate town. It is probably best known because of the Earp brothers' participation in its development, and the gunfight at the O.K. Corral. This episode is reenacted each year in October during the Helldorado Days. Many of the old buildings are still standing, including the office of Tombstone's newspaper, the *Epitaph*, and the Birdcage Theater. Other popular tourist

ARKANSAS

Arkansas Post State Park. In 1686, the white men who explored this area made it one of the first permanent settlements in the Mississippi Valley. In 1819, after being part of the Louisiana and Missouri territories, the settlement became the capital of the newly created Arkansas Territory. It is now known primarily for its historic ruins.

Hot Springs National Park. This is the oldest national park in the United States. Of its 47 hot mineral springs, 45 are sealed so the waters can be conditioned and supplied to the park's bathhouses. Bathhouse Row in the park offers whirlpool baths and massages. Local physicians registered with the federal government recommend patients for hydrotherapy at the Libbey Memorial Physical Medical Center, also located in the park. Facilities are also available for fishing, boating, golf, horseback riding, and hiking.

Little Rock. This is the state capital and the largest city in Arkansas. The present Capitol Building, containing the State History Museum, was preceded by two others—the State House which is now a

Arkansas Publicity and Parks Commission

Life in the Arkansas Ozark Mountains, the only upland region in the midst of the expanse of the midwestern plains, still retains some of the ruggedness of the pioneer days.

museum, and the Territorial Capitol which has been completely and authentically restored. Little Rock's MacArthur Park, commemorating the birthplace of General Douglas MacArthur, contains museums of natural history and fine arts.

The Ozarks. These mountains extend from the southern part of Missouri to northern Oklahoma and Arkansas. Their highest ranges are in Arkansas. Caves, great forests, clear streams, and lakes make the Ozarks a popular attraction. Bull Shoals Lake and Mammoth Springs are great attractions in northern Arkansas. Eureka Springs, a health resort known for its mineral waters and also for its many limestone caves, is located northeast of Fayetteville, the location of the University of Arkansas.

Petit Jean State Park. The park, located on Petit Jean Mountain, is a good vacation spot and place for outdoor recreation. It offers many natural attractions, including Pioneer Cabin, Cedar Falls, and Bear Cave. Lake Bailey has facilities for fishing and other water sports.

CALIFORNIA

Death Valley. Named in 1849 for pioneers who died there, Death Valley was declared a national monument in 1933. Badwater, in Death Valley, is 282 feet below sea level, and is the lowest point on the North American continent. Only 80 miles west of Death Valley is Mt. Whitney, the highest point in the contiguous United States.

Humbolt Redwoods State Park. The home of the world's largest trees, the redwoods, Humbolt Redwoods State Park is a part of the Redwood Empire that extends from the middle of California north along the coast to southwestern Oregon. Two species of redwood still exist: the coastal and the Sierra redwoods. In Humbolt Bull Grove stands one of the tallest redwoods in the coastal area, 364 feet high. Southeast of

the state park, in the Sierra Nevada range, are two Sierra redwood national parks, Sequoia and Kings Canyon. Some of the trees date back 3,000 years and have a diameter of 35 feet.

Los Angeles. Sometimes described as "nineteen suburbs in search of a city," Los Angeles is one of the most modern cities in the country. Its new central-core development program will include buildings for the arts, as well as beautiful and functional office and municipal buildings. The Olvera Street section with its interesting old shops and restaurants is the home of the original city. One of the city's most famous streets is Wilshire Boulevard; lined with

modern shops, stores, and offices, it leads to residential areas where fine homes and beautiful gardens abound. The University of Southern California and the Los Angeles branch of the University of California are here, with their museums and other facilities for the public. Located on the Pacific Ocean, Los Angeles has innumerable beaches with some of the world's best swimming, sunning, surfing, and fishing. The freeway puts Hollywood, movie capital of the world, a few minutes away. Universal City provides tours of its studios. Near Hollywood is Beverly Hills where many of the stars' homes are located. Farther inland are Pasadena, home of the New Year's Day Rose Parade and Rose Bowl Football Classic, and San Marino with the Huntington Library and Art Gallery. Anaheim is the home of the perennially favorite Disneyland, the land of imagination.

Missions. Some of the 21 missions which the Spanish built during the early colonization of California remain today. These missions were built along the coast between San Diego and Sonoma. One of the best preserved is the San Luis Rey Mission. The San Juan Capistrano mission is where the swallows return with extreme regularity each year.

Monterey. This is a beautiful city on the bay with many old buildings reflecting its Spanish heritage. It was under Spanish and Mexican rule before becoming a part of the United States. Cannery Row, which novelist John Steinbeck made famous, is located here. Carmel, on the Monterey Peninsula, is a quaint town noted for its art galleries and many interesting shops, and is a popular spot with artists and writers as well as with tourists. The drive from Monterey to the Big Sur area is one of the most beautiful in the United States. It passes along the cliffs of the Pacific shoreline, and the ocean can be seen and heard pounding the rocks below. Point Lobos

California Mission Trails Association, Ltd.

San Carlos Borromeo Mission, Carmel, California, was founded by Father Junipero Serra in 1770. The buildings are typical of Spanish-American architectural style.

San Diego Convention and Visitors Bureau

Surf, sand, and mild climate along the Pacific Ocean near San Diego, California, provide outdoor recreation, such as swimming and surfing, throughout the year.

Firefall in which a great log is burnt to embers, then pushed over the rim at Glacier Point, falling to a ledge 1,000 feet below in the valley.

COLORADO

Aspen. Aspen is located on Roaring Fork River just west of the Continental Divide. Although it is known primarily for its wonderful skiing facilities, that is by no means its only attraction. During the summer, Aspen is one of the cultural centers of the West, hosting major music festivals in its new music center. There is also ample opportunity for fishing, hiking, and sightseeing.

Boulder. Boulder is the location of the University of Colorado and is the site of the first schoolhouse in the state. Nearby are Boulder Canyon, Roosevelt National Forest, and Rocky Mountain National Park.

Central City. The first gold mining town to spring up in the Rockies, and once called "the richest square mile on earth," Central City is now a ghost town. Some of the old buildings remain, however, and are open to the public. The old Opera House hosts the July Opera Festival.

Reserve, located in this area, comprises 1,250 acres of land maintained as a wildlife sanctuary.

Sierra Nevadas. The great Sierra Nevada mountain range stretches along the eastern edge of the state and provides an excellent opportunity for sports the year round. Lake Tahoe, within these mountains, has facilities for swimming, boating, and fishing in the summer and skiing in the winter. Squaw Valley, site of the 1960 Winter Olympics, provides some of the best skiing in the world and, in the summer, has facilities for hiking, camping, tennis, and riding. Deep within the mountains is the Mother Lode, a rich vein of gold. Visitors may still pan for gold in these hills.

Sacramento. The capital of California, Sacramento is located in the central valley of the state. The Capitol Building, which can be seen from miles away, is considered by many to be one of the finest such structures in the United States. Points of interest in Sacramento are the Crocker Art Gallery, one of the best in the United States; the restored Sutter's Fort where Captain John Sutter began a settlement in 1839; and in nearby Coloma, Sutter's Sawmill, the site of the first gold discovery in 1848.

San Diego. One of this city's major attractions is Balboa Park which covers 1,400 acres and includes museums, art galleries, arcades, and the famous San Diego Zoo. A major United States naval training center is located here. Old Town, an interesting section of San Diego to visit, is the original site of the city and of the Mission San Diego de Alcala, which is now located outside of the city. Replacing the mission in Old Town is the Sierra Museum. Other points of interest in the San Diego area are Mount Palomar, 55 miles away, site of the world's largest telescope; Point Loma, site of the Cabrillo National Monument; and the Old Spanish Lighthouse, which marks the spot where explor-

ers first set foot in California. Tijuana, south of the nearby border, and Coronado, the year-round vacation resort across San Diego Bay, are also of interest. In nearby Mission Bay is Sea World, a seaquarium with many ocean animals. The whole Mission Bay area is a seaside playground, and is only a small part of the 70 miles of shoreline of San Diego County.

San Francisco. Built on hills, San Francisco is one of the most beautiful cities in the United States. Picturesque cable cars provide an enjoyable ride and a look at the city's many interesting views. Some of the more popular viewing locations are Coit Tower on Telegraph Hill and the Twin Peaks Scenic Drive. Across the Golden Gate, a strait between San Francisco Bay and the Pacific Ocean, is the famous Golden Gate Bridge connecting San Francisco with Marin County; another beautiful bridge is the Bay Bridge across San Francisco Bay, leading to Oakland and to Berkeley, the location of the main campus of the University of California. The most famous sections of the city are Fisherman's Wharf, North Beach, and Chinatown. Other attractions are the Civic Center, Dolores Mission, and Golden Gate Park, which contains the Steinhart Aquarium and DeYoung Museum. A variety of life styles is typical of the city. Night life of every kind can be found in over 2,500 restaurants and numerous clubs and theaters.

Yosemite National Park. This beautiful national park is set in the Sierra Nevada mountains in eastern California. In spring and summer, waterfalls and wildlife provide spectacular views, while in fall and winter, snow blankets the mountains, providing excellent skiing conditions. The park contains 700 miles of trails to explore. The longest drop of waterfall is 2,425 feet from the Upper Fall to the base of the Lower Fall. One of the favorite summertime events staged for tourists is the

Chamber of Commerce, Colorado Springs, Colorado

Snow-capped Pikes Peak and red sandstone rock formations dominate the Garden of the Gods, near Colorado Springs, Colorado.

Colorado Springs. Colorado Springs is a famous resort town built on the Fountain and Monument rivers. Just outside the city is Pikes Peak, whose summit towers 14,110 feet. Points of interest in and around the city are the Garden of the Gods, a natural garden of rock formations; Cave of the Winds, where underground formations are mixed with eerie wind sounds; Manitou Springs; Seven Falls; Cheyenne Canyon; and the Will Rogers Shrine of the Sun Memorial. Colorado Springs is also the home of the United States Air Force Academy; its beautiful campus, set in the mountains, is distinguished by a multispired interfaith chapel. Southwest of Colorado Springs on the Arkansas River is the Royal Gorge, spanned by the world's highest suspension bridge.

Union Pacific Railroad

A rancher distributes feed to cattle grazing near the Rocky Mountains outside of Walden, north central Colorado, one of the highest regions in the United States.

Denver. The state capital is known as the Mile-High City because it is 5,280 feet above sea level. Some attractions include the Colorado Capitol Building with its many pillars and golden dome, and the Museum of Natural History with its interesting and unusual planetarium. Also located here are the University of Denver, the United States Mint, and the Denver Union Stockyards. The nearby mountain parks include Park of the Red Rocks and Lookout Mountain, the site of Buffalo Bill's grave. Estes Park, a beautiful resort center, is northwest of Denver.

Dinosaur National Monument. Large deposits of dinosaur bones and other ancient animal fossils have been discovered here and are being preserved by paleontologists. Other national monuments in Colorado are the Great Sand Dunes, 57 square miles of white sand cradled in the Sangre de Cristo Mountains; and Black Canyon of the Gunnison, another wonder sculptured and painted by nature for thousands of years.

Mesa Verde National Park. About 1,600 years ago, cave-dwelling Indians built the first pueblo villages on this mesa, and many are still perfectly preserved; Cliff Palace is the largest and most famous of these dwellings. On the top of this mesa is the Sun Temple, with an ingeniously placed stone marking the vernal and autumnal equinoxes. There are also hundreds of dwellings in caves beneath the rim of the cliff; however, untutored hiking is prohibited, not only because the cliffs have been dangerously weakened by time, but also because unwary hikers might destroy or damage clues about the ancient inhabitants.

Rocky Mountain National Park. The park straddles the Continental Divide and is a haven for the nature lover. At a height of one and one half miles, forests of pine and fir abound; above the 11,000-foot timberline, grasses and alpine flowers grow. Many species of wildlife are common, including elk, deer, bighorn sheep, and mountain lions. Much of the spectacular natural scenery can be seen from Trail Ridge Road, a beautiful 44-mile long highway, 11 miles of which stretch above the timberline across the park to Grand Lake. There are also 200 trails which penetrate deep into the heartland of Colorado's mountains.

CONNECTICUT

Bridgeport. Birthplace of P. T. Barnum, the circus man, Bridgeport hosts the P. T. Barnum Museum, which contains circus mementos from Barnum's collection, as well as articles once owned by Tom Thumb and Jenny Lind. Other attractions in Bridgeport include Seaside Park and the Museum of Art, Science, and Industry.

Gillette Castle State Park. Designed and built near Hadlyme in 1913 by the actor William Gillette, the castle was originally called the Seventh Sister, for the series of hills on which it is built. There are 24 rooms in the castle, all reflecting Gillette's creativity. After Gillette's death in 1937, the executors of his will secured the status of a state park for the home. Today the 122 acres of his estate are open to visitors who may see the home, or hike, picnic, and explore the grounds, which contain the remains of a three-mile, full-scale railroad.

Hartford. The state capital, Hartford is located in the northern part of Connecticut. Points of interest in Hartford include the Old State House, designed by Charles Bullfinch; the Wadsworth Atheneum, an excellent art museum; and Constitution Plaza, one of the most modern and impressive urban renewal developments in the United States. A main attraction in the western part of Hartford is Nook Farm and the Nook Farm Research Library. Two noted writers' homes, the Mark Twain Memorial and the Harriet Beecher Stowe House, are in this area.

Mystic. Mystic seaport, a re-creation of the 19th-century maritime community, berths many ships, each with a unique and dramatic past; among them are the *Charles W. Morgan*, last of the New England whalers, and the *Joseph Conrad*, a training ship. Visitors may watch shipwrights working as they did a century ago. Many original buildings remain and some are still furnished as they were in the 1840's. Local museums house exhibits of sailing handicraft and equipment.

Newgate. Originally Simsbury copper mine, the buildings at Newgate came to be used, in 1773, as the first state prison in

Connecticut Development Commission

Mystic seaport in Connecticut was an important shipbuilding and whaling center during the 18th and 19th centuries, and has preserved paraphernalia from those days.

Connecticut, an important source of tobacco, is known for its high-quality shade-grown leaf used for cigar wrappers, as seen on this farm in West Suffield.

Connecticut. After 50 years, the prison was abandoned and the buildings are now used as a museum.

New Haven. Points of interest in the city include various types of museums, such as the Winchester Gun Museum with weapons and firearms dating from the 1400's; the New Haven Colony Historical Society, featuring Eli Whitney's original cotton gin; and the Peabody Museum, with an excellent natural history collection. Yale University, the third oldest university in the country, is located here. Its excellent library and the Yale University Art Gallery are among the attractions seen on guided tours. A few miles from New Haven, in Stratford, is the American Shakespeare Festival Theatre, a replica of London's Globe Theatre.

DELAWARE

Dover. Dover was established as the capital of Delaware in 1777. Its historical points of interest include the Governor's House, which before and during the Civil War was a station of the Underground Railroad; the Hall of Records containing the state's public archives; and the John Dickinson Mansion. Dickinson, called the "Penman of the Revolution," wrote many important historical documents even before the Declaration of Independence was penned. Also of interest is the Delaware State Museum, which exhibits various phases of Delaware life. Located on the Dover Green, the Old State House is the second oldest building in the United States; built in 1792, it is still being used and is open to the public.

Lewes. Among the attractions in Lewes are the Zwaanendael Museum, built to commemorate the first Dutch settlement in Delaware and containing exhibits from colonial days, and Memorial Park with cannons from the War of 1812. Lewes Beach is one of many along Delaware Bay.

New Castle. New Castle's many historic homes and buildings give it a colonial atmosphere. Attractions include the Old Court House, the first Statehouse of Delaware; the Amstel House and the Old Dutch House, both of which are now small museums; and the Immanuel Church, built in 1703. West of the city is the Town Common, a farming grant which still yields revenue.

Wilmington. The largest city in Delaware, Wilmington dates back to 1638 when the Dutch settled at Fort Christina. There are many museums in the city. Old Town Hall, in governmental use from 1798 to 1916, was purchased by the Historical Society of Delaware and is now a museum containing exhibits which date back to the Revolutionary War. The Hagley Museum is located in the old DuPont Powder Company yards near Wilmington. Formerly a textile mill, the museum's main building now exhibits water wheels, papermills, tanneries, and the inventions of Oliver Evans. The steps followed in manufacturing gunpowder are demonstrated in another former industrial building. Also located in Wilmington is the Delaware Art Center. Perhaps the most elegant museum in the Wilmington area is the Henry Francis DuPont Winterhur Museum located just outside the city. The museum has over 100 rooms showing domestic America from 1640 to 1840. Ten rooms may be viewed without an appointment; the remaining rooms may be toured by appointment only.

DISTRICT OF COLUMBIA

Washington. Washington, the capital of the United States, is dominated by the White House on Pennsylvania Avenue. Blackened during the burning of Washington in the War of 1812, this official residence of the President was painted white at President Monroe's request. Visitors may now tour its public rooms daily except Sunday and Monday. Two impressive monuments are nearby: the Washington Monument with almost 900 stairs leading to the 500-foot level, providing a breath-taking view of the capital area; and the beautiful Jefferson Memorial across the Tidal Basin with its rounded, domed architecture reminiscent of Jefferson's home, Monticello. Northwest across the Basin is the Lincoln Memorial, a Grecian structure containing Chester French's seated statue of the 16th president. The texts of Lincoln's Gettysburg Address and Second Inaugural Address are inscribed in the granite walls of the shrine. West of the Lincoln Memorial is the Arlington Memorial Bridge leading to Arlington National Cemetery, and eastward is the reflecting pool beneath the Washington Monument. Many of the nation's best-known government buildings border the nearby Mall,

Zwaanendael Museum, in Lewes, Delaware, was built in the Dutch Renaissance style. The museum commemorates the first settlement in Delaware by the Dutch who arrived in 1631.

one of the world's most famous parkways. The Departments of Labor, Agriculture, and the Department of Health, Education and Welfare, as well as the National Archives, the Smithsonian Institution, and the National Gallery of Art are all in this area. The far east end of the Mall is dominated by the Capitol Building on Capitol Hill. Sessions of the Senate and the House of Representatives may be observed from visitors' galleries in the Capitol. Nearby is the Supreme Court Building, and across

National Park Service

The white-domed Thomas Jefferson National Memorial, on the south bank of the Tidal Basin of the Potomac River, is one of the most beautiful buildings in Washington, D.C.

the street is the Library of Congress. Every book copyrighted in the United States is on file here. It also has a replica of the Magna Carta, Lincoln's draft of his Gettysburg Address, and Jefferson's first draft of the Declaration of Independence. The Folger Shakespeare Library, in the Library of Congress, has many works and documents on Shakespeare and a replica of London's Globe Theatre. Across the Potomac River from Washington is the Pentagon, the largest office building in the world, which houses the Department of Defense. Ford's Theater in downtown Washington, where President Abraham Lincoln was shot, has been restored for use and is also a museum of Lincoln memorabilia.

FLORIDA

Everglades National Park. This national park, the third largest in the country, is located at the southern tip of Florida. Once inhabited by the Seminole Indians, it was known only to hunters, explorers, and Indians as recently as 1915, when it became a state park. In 1947, it was named a national park, and today thousands of visitors can view more than 230 species of birds and many other species of wildlife here. Many areas of the Everglades have been developed for tours, trails, and exhibits, while other areas are still as wild as they were centuries ago. There are campgrounds in the park, and

numerous places to stay in the area. A marina is available for people who wish to visit it by boat. Fishing and other water sports are permitted.

Key Largo. Having its land base on Key Largo in the Upper Keys is the John Pennekamp Coral Reef State Park, the first underwater park in America. This colorful park contains many species of coral and other sea life, which can be viewed from glass-bottom boats and explored by skindivers. Numerous water sports can be enjoyed here. The park also offers a marina and camping facilities.

Key West. Key West, the southernmost city in the United States, is situated on the tip of the Florida Keys. The Overseas Highway traverses the entire length of the Keys and makes Key West accessible by car. It is a modern, but picturesque, city with commercial fishing and shrimping, and a large naval base. All of the Florida Keys offer opportunities for fishing, golfing, swimming, and sightseeing.

Miami and Miami Beach. Points of interest in Miami, Florida's largest city, include the Seaquarium, Monkey Jungle, Parrot Jungle, and Serpentarium. Also of interest are Hialeah Park and Race Track, with its flamingoes; streets lined with royal palm trees; the Miami docks; and the University of Miami at Coral Gables. Across Biscayne Bay reached by any of several causeways is the fashionable resort city, Miami Beach, where beautiful ocean-front hotels and motels host vacationers the year round.

Saint Augustine. Founded in 1565, Saint Augustine is the oldest city in the United States; reminders of its long history are everywhere in the city. Some points of interest are the Spanish Treasury, the Zero Milestone at the start of the trail to California, the Castillo de San Marcos, and the Cathedral of St. Augustine. Nearby is the Ponce de Leon Springs, where the Spanish explorer supposedly drank the waters of the Fountain of Youth.

Sarasota. Jungle Gardens, a world-renowned tropical garden, is one of the main attractions of Sarasota; it is also a bird sanctuary, where hundreds of birds can be seen in natural settings. The favorite attraction of Sarasota, however, is the trio of Ringling Museums, left to the state by John Ringling at his death in 1936. One is the Ringling residence, Ca'd'zan, built in the style of a Venetian palace; the interior and exterior are both extravagant and exquisite, costing $1.5 million to build in 1925. The Ringling Museum of the Circus contains relics of the business which made

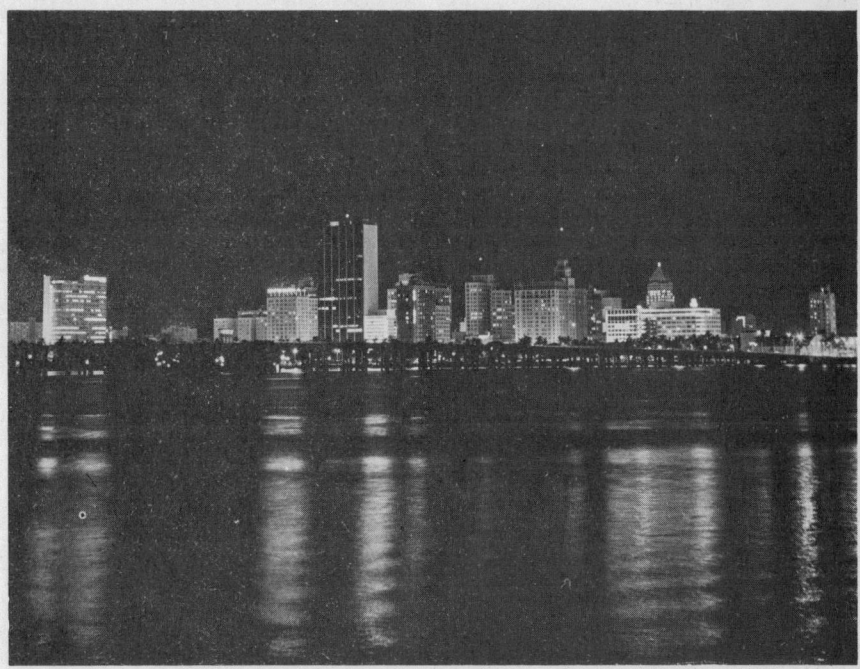

Metro-Miami Department of Publicity and Tourism

Miami, Florida, seen across Biscayne Bay, grew almost overnight from a small village to a famous resort area. It is the southernmost large city in the United States.

Florida News Bureau

Magnificent grazing land and a temperate climate make Florida an ideal state for horse breeding. This thoroughbred horse farm is located in Tallahassee, Florida.

John and his brothers famous. The Ringling Museum of Art contains an important collection of European Baroque art, and the largest U.S. collection of the 17th-century master Peter Paul Rubens. Occasionally loan exhibitions are held in its new wing. The Ringling complex also contains the Asolo Theater, the official state theater of Florida.

Saint Petersburg. Situated on Florida's west coast is Saint Petersburg, the "Sunshine City." Because of its mild weather and daily sunshine, it is an ideal place for outdoor sports, including swimming and deep-sea fishing. Among Saint Petersburg's scenic attractions are the Sunken Gardens, acres of beautiful tropical gardens, birds, and flowers; Tiki Gardens, nearby at Indian Rocks Beach; and natural tropical jungles such as Fort De-Soto Park and Lake Maggiore Park.

Silver Springs. Silver Springs, near Ocala, is one of the world's major freshwater springs, and the largest in Florida. It offers tours of the jungle and of the underwater world, the latter in glass-bottom boats. The International Deer Ranch, with more than 300 tame deer from all over the world, is located near Silver Springs. Nearby are Rainbow Springs and Homosassa Springs.

Tampa. Located on Tampa Bay, this was originally a Spanish trading post and is now an industrial city. Favorite attractions in Tampa are the cigar-making factories, the beer breweries, and the tropical Busch Gardens.

GEORGIA

Atlanta. Atlanta was not settled until 1833, and did not assume the status of a capital until 1868. Points of interest in Atlanta are the State Capitol Building; the campus of Georgia Institute of Technology; and "Wren's Nest," Joel Chandler Harris's

home. There are some 88 parks in the city, including Piedmont, Grant, and Lakewood. Near Atlanta is the huge granite Stone Mountain on which is carved the unfinished Confederate Memorial.

Bell & Stanton, Inc.

The skyline of Atlanta, Georgia, has been rapidly changing since 1960, when a major building boom resulted in the construction of many new major office structures.

Okefenokee Swamp. The swamp covers more than a 600-square-mile area. It is a marshy land covered with flowers and shaded by pine, bay, cypress, and gum trees. Within the area are panthers, deer, bear, and a variety of birds and fish.

Savannah. Savannah was founded in 1733 by James Oglethorpe. Now a modern city and important shipping point, Savannah has one of the oldest histories in the United States. Many colonial buildings

have been carefully preserved. Among the historic points of interest are Johnson Square, where lies the grave of Nathaniel Greene, a Revolutionary War general; Mulberry Grove, General Greene's estate, where Eli Whitney invented the cotton gin; and Trustee Garden Village, on the waterfront, with many renovated houses and shops. Also of interest is the Owens-Thomas House Museum, an excellent historic museum. Savannah's historical past lies in a setting of wide streets, broken regularly by beautifully landscaped squares and parks.

HAWAII

Hawaii. Hawaii is the largest island of the state of Hawaii. Called also "Big Island," and "the Orchid Isle," it is an important orchid-growing center. The island was formed by volcanic mountains, some of which are still active; Mauna Loa erupted as recently as 1955. Among the attractions on the island is Hawaii Volcanoes National Park, the location of active volcanoes such as Kilauea Crater. Other features are the orchid nurseries around Hilo, pineapple canneries, and sugar mills. On the western side of the island is the Kona area with peaceful coves, native villages, and ruins of temples. Parker Ranch, a large cattle ranch, is in this area.

Kauai. This island, called the "Garden Island," was the first one known to western explorers. Captain Cook visited Kauai in 1778, when it was the only island which King Kamehameha had not conquered. It

is the oldest and most eroded island of the group. Kauai receives more than 400 inches of rain annually and is covered with a luxuriant growth. Although there are several good beaches, most of the island is covered by the beautiful mountain Waialeale. Other attractions of the island are Waimea Canyon, Hanalei Valley, the Napali coast of precipices, and the Fern Grotto.

Maui. This is the second largest island

Pan American World Airways

Hawaiians use huge nets to harvest fish, an important source of food for the islands. Many tourists enjoy watching the natives at work and admiring their colorful catch.

of the group. Mt. Haleakala, a large dormant volcano, offers an excellent view of the area. The windward side of Maui is a succession of gorges crossed by a scenic drive. On the leeward side are located Iao Valley, Wailuku Valley, and brightly

Hawaii Visitors Bureau

The Iao Needle rises in the western mountains on Mauri. Mauri is one of the eight principal islands of Hawaii.

colored canyons. Along the coast are the resort areas of Kaanapali, Hana, Napili, and Lahaina.

Molokai. Human population is sparse and there is much wildlife on Molokai. The biggest industry is pineapple growing, which is confined mainly to the western half of the island. The eastern side is mostly fish ponds, and visitors can watch fishing here as it has been done since early times.

Oahu. Although third is size and fifth in height, Oahu is the main island of the chain. Honolulu, the island's largest city,

is the state capital. One of the state buildings, the Iolani Palace, was originally the home of the kings of Hawaii. The University of Hawaii is located in this city. The city's harbor carries much tourist and commercial traffic. Military shipping goes to nearby Pearl Harbor where Battleship Row, the site of sunken and half-sunken ships, is a major attraction and reminder of the Japanese attack in 1941. Other features on Oahu are the Punchbowl Crater where the Pacific War Memorial National Cemetery is located, and Paradise Park,

containing a rain forest, jungle trail, orchid jungle, native bird exhibits, and floral nurseries. Waikiki, east of the city, is a beautiful resort haven. Farther east is Diamond Head, a massive rock formation and famous landmark. Beaches ring the island and provide good surfing and other water sports.

IDAHO

Boise. This city, the largest in Idaho, is the state's capital. The State Capitol Building is an impressive sight, reaching a height of 195 feet at its dome. Reservoir lakes formed by dams such as the Arrowrock Dam offer water recreation in the vicinity of Boise. Bogus Basin is a popular ski area near Boise.

Coeur d'Alene. The city itself is a lumber and mining center, and headquarters for the Coeur d'Alene National Forest. The scenic attraction of the area is Lake Coeur d'Alene. Here hydroplane races held each year add excitement to the normally quiet area.

Craters of the Moon National Monument. Prehistoric lava flows and subterranean explosions formed the craters and crags of this area. Other natural phenomena in southern Idaho which have been created by lava flows and volcanic eruptions are the Thousand Springs near Buhl, Shoshone Falls east of Twin Falls, and Hot Springs Resort with its therapeutic hot mineral springs.

Hell's Canyon. This area, on the western border of Idaho, is also known as the "Grand Canyon of the Snake River." It is the deepest gorge in the country—deeper than the Grand Canyon—5,500 feet deep on the average and 7,900 feet at the deepest point. Four miles across, on the other side of the gorge, is Oregon. In the surrounding area is the Seven Devils Monument Park, a series of peaks which seem

American Forest Products Industries, Inc.

Timber growing is an important industry in Idaho. All of the wood for the buildings and fence posts on this northern Idaho farm was obtained in the nearby forest.

Idaho Department of Commerce and Development and Ernest E. Day, Boise, Idaho

Stanley Lake is one of many blue glacier lakes in the Sawtooth Mountains of Idaho. The spectacular scenery and recreational facilities attract millions of visitors each year.

Sports are popular, and Chicago has professional teams in every major sport. One summer highlight is the College All-Star football game in Soldier Field. A popular spot is Old Town, the part of the city which survived the Great Chicago Fire of 1871, and where small shops and night enter-

Association of Commerce and Industry, Springfield, Illinois

This house in Springfield, Illinois, was the only home Abraham Lincoln ever owned. It is furnished the way it was when he lived in it.

forbidding but, although snow-capped all year, are easily accessible.

Nez Percé National Historical Park. This park in northern Idaho preserves the Indian lore of the Nez Percé Indians. One of the oldest tribes of American Indians, the Nez Percé have lived in the Kamiah Valley since prehistoric times. Important sites in the park are White Bird Battlefield, starting point of the 1877 Nez Percé War; Fort Lapwai, the major military base during the war; and Coyote's Fishnet, an important site in Nez Percé folklore. Lewis and Clark passed through this area on their journey to the Pacific Ocean; some sites in Nez Percé Park commemorate their journey.

Sun Valley. Located in central Idaho is Sun Valley, one of the world's best and most well-known ski resorts. Two mountains are available for skiing: Dollar Mountain with slopes for beginners as well as experts, and Baldy Mountain for more experienced skiers. An unusual summer feature at Sun Valley is the outdoor ice-skating rink.

ILLINOIS

Chicago. This city, the Midwest's largest, is the country's leading rail center. It is also served by water, land, and air routes, making it one of the nation's leading travel, transportation, and industrial cities. O'Hare International Airport serves the area. The southern part of the city is heavily industrialized, with steel and metal products the main industries. The downtown section of the city or "Loop" is a big business section which is bounded roughly by the encircling elevated tracks, from which the area takes its name. Here are many fine stores and office buildings, including the Merchandise Mart, Marshall Field & Co., the Prudential Building, and

the Board of Trade. The new John Hancock Center just to the north of the Loop offers an excellent view of the city from the ninety-sixth floor. Cultural interests are served by a variety of museums, libraries, and societies: the Field Museum of Natural History, the Museum of Science and Industry, the Art Institute, Chicago Historical Society, the Chicago Academy of Sciences, and John Crerar Library. Lincoln Park includes both a zoo and a plant conservatory. The city offers many forms of entertainment including opera, symphony, theater, and ballet. For evening entertainment, there are many night clubs and cabarets.

tainment are the primary attractions. There are many universities in the area: the University of Chicago in the Hyde Park section; Roosevelt University in the Loop; University of Illinois, Circle Campus, west of the Loop; Loyola University; De Paul University; and Northwestern University in Evanston. West of the city is the Brookfield Zoo, one of the country's best, with natural-habitat, barless enclosures.

Springfield. The Springfield area demonstrates why the state is called "Land of Lincoln." Springfield, the capital of Illinois, has the Lincoln Tomb in Oak Ridge Cemetery. In addition, it has the Old State House, which was recently bought by the state and restored to its appearance in

Chicago Convention and Tourism Bureau

Grant Park in Chicago is surrounded by the skyscrapers of the business district. Beaches and harbors along Lake Michigan are among the city's recreation areas.

State of Illinois Tourist Division

Rock formations of great geological interest rise as high as 125 feet above the Illinois River in Starved Rock State Park, near La Salle, in northern Illinois.

the neighboring cities. Many of the steel plants offer tours for visitors. Just east of this area is Indiana Dunes State Park on Lake Michigan.

Indianapolis. This is the state capital and also the largest city in Indiana. In the center of the business district is Monument Circle, containing the Soldiers and Sailors Monument. Other points of interest include the Capitol Building; Indiana University Medical Center for Children, which has James Whitcomb Riley's poems illustrated on stained-glass windows and murals; and James Whitcomb Riley's home. Also of interest are the Scottish Rite Cathedral, a good example of old-world architecture, with its huge pipe organ and carillon; the World War Memorial; the Benjamin Harrison Home; the John Herron Art Institute; and the Children's Museum. An annual attraction is the Memorial Day 500-mile race at the Indianapolis Speedway outside the city. East of Indianapolis is Riley Memorial Park, a memorial to James Whitcomb Riley.

Nancy Hanks Lincoln Memorial. This memorial in southern Indiana marks the site of Nancy Hanks Lincoln's grave. She was the mother of Abraham Lincoln and died when he was nine years old. Here, too, is Lincoln's boyhood home; its fireplace has been reconstructed with the original stones. Nearby is Lincoln State Park and Lincoln Pioneer Village, the latter containing many reconstructed buildings, including Aunt Lepha McKay House, Gentry

Lincoln's time. The Old State House is also a memorial of two other giants of Illinois history, Stephen Douglas and Ulysses S. Grant. Northwest of Springfield is New Salem State Park. The park has facilities for camping, picnicking, and other outdoor activities, but it is best known for the 23 restored buildings from the mid-1800's. North of Springfield is the town of Lincoln, named for Lincoln before his presidency. A replica of the original Postville Courthouse, where he argued many cases as a circuit rider, is here. There are 12 other historic sites in Lincoln, including the Postville Park which Lincoln helped plan. East of Springfield is Decatur, where Lincoln was started on his way to the presidency. Today it is an important industrial center, but there are still many restored and rebuilt houses. North of Decatur is Champaign-Urbana where the main campus of the University of Illinois is located. East of Champaign is the Kickapoo State Park, a depleted strip-mining site that has been converted into a 1,600-acre recreational area.

Starved Rock State Park. The park gets its name from the large rock where white men besieged a group of Indians. Rather than starve, the Indians chose to leap to their deaths. La Salle, the French explorer, built a fort here in 1683 to guard the river. The park is a favorite vacation center in northern Illinois.

INDIANA

Brown County State Park. The beautiful Brown County State Park in south central Indiana is set in a hilly and wooded area. Nearby in Nashville is an art colony.

Evansville. Evansville has many reminders of Ohio River history, and this large old city is a good base for exploring the lush Ohio River Valley. Points of interest here are the Soldiers and Sailors Memorial Coliseum and Mesker Municipal

Park. The Willard Carpenter Homestead is a good example of Georgian architecture.

Gary. This is one of the best known of the Indiana steel cities; most of Indiana's heavy industry is concentrated here and in

Indiana Department of Conservation

Indiana Dunes State Park, on the southern shore of Lake Michigan near Chesterton, Indiana, is a three-mile stretch of white sand dunes and beaches, forests, and marshes.

A barge turns in the basin of a steelworks in Gary, Indiana. Gary is part of a huge industrial complex that includes Hammond, East Chicago, and Whiting.

camping, and recreational facilities. Red Rock Refuge, on the lake, is an Iowa State Conservation Commission water fowl management area. The surrounding communities offer a variety of tourist and social diversions.

Sioux City. This industrial city in northwestern Iowa is a meat-packing center. Among the parks and monuments are Grand View Park, with a natural amphitheater where summer concerts are given; War Eagle Park, dedicated to the great Sioux Indian chief and containing his grave; and Floyd Monument, named after the first U.S. soldier to die west of the Mississippi. Farther down the Missouri River and overlooking Omaha, Nebraska, is Council Bluffs, the great meeting place of the Sioux nation. Museums and parks honoring the Sioux exist throughout the area.

KANSAS

Abilene. During the 1800's, this famous frontier cow town was the northern terminus of the Chisholm Cattle Trail. It is now better known as the home and burial place of Dwight D. Eisenhower, thirty-fourth president of the U.S. The Eisenhower Center, built here in his memory, consists of the Eisenhower Museum, containing a collection of his personal effects; the Eisenhower home, where he grew to manhood; the Eisenhower Library, one of the largest and most complete research centers in the Midwest; and the Meditation Chapel.

Mansion, and Pigeon Creek Baptist Church.

Spring Mill State Park. Located in the southern portion of the state, this park features an old stone grist mill surrounded by a restored pioneer village. Here visitors may see meal ground by water power as it was done in the early 1800's. In addition to the buildings, there are acres of land and miles of trails to explore. There are also stalactite caves and an underground river.

Turkey Run State Park. This park, which is located in the north central portion of the state, is one of the most scenic in Indiana. It is known for its beautiful gorges, deeply carved in sandstone and covered with vegetation. Throughout the acres of forest are trails and campgrounds.

IOWA

Des Moines. The state capital is located on the Des Moines and Raccoon rivers. Points of interest in the city include the gold-domed Capitol Building; other federal and municipal buildings at the Civic Center; the State Historical, Memorial and Art Building, with displays from pioneer and Civil War times; and the campus of Drake University.

Effigy Mound National Monument. The monument is located along the western bank of the Mississippi River at Marquette near the Wisconsin border. The mounds, in the shapes of animals with some as long as 300 feet, were built by the Indians centuries ago. McGregor State Park and Pictured Rocks are nearby.

Fort Dodge. This replica of a government fort contains one of the best museums of Indian and pioneer history in the state. Originally built as a defense against the Sioux Indians, it now includes the museum, a curio shop, and a restored school house. Historically, Fort Dodge figured prominently in the Spirit Lake Massacre relief tragedy. A company of 125 perished here while returning from a vain

attempt to help survivors of the Spirit Lake Massacre. Spirit Lake is now a popular resort area. Within a 25-mile radius are beautiful Lake Okoboji, Dolliver State Park, Indian Mound, and Twin Lakes,

Zebulon Pike Locks at Eagle Point Dam are near Dubuque, Iowa, on the Mississippi River. Dubuque is an important agricultural area and manufacturing center for farm machinery.

which offer boating, fishing, and swimming.

Red Rock Dam. This $80-million project has created the largest body of water in Iowa, Red Rock Lake, which provides both recreational and business opportunities. The dam itself is at the eastern end of the lake; around the shores are picnic,

Dodge City. Dodge City is in the center of the wheat country. Located on the Arkansas River, it made an ideal watering and shipping place for cattlemen. Remnants of the Wild West can still be seen at Boot Hill Cemetery and along a replica of Front Street, the scene of many gun battles in the days of notorious outlaws and

famous lawmen. Dodge City was also the site of Fort Dodge, the base of operations in the Indian Wars. Here, as throughout the state, visitors can see memorials. Other memorial forts in the state are Forts Leavenworth, Scott, Larned, and Riley.

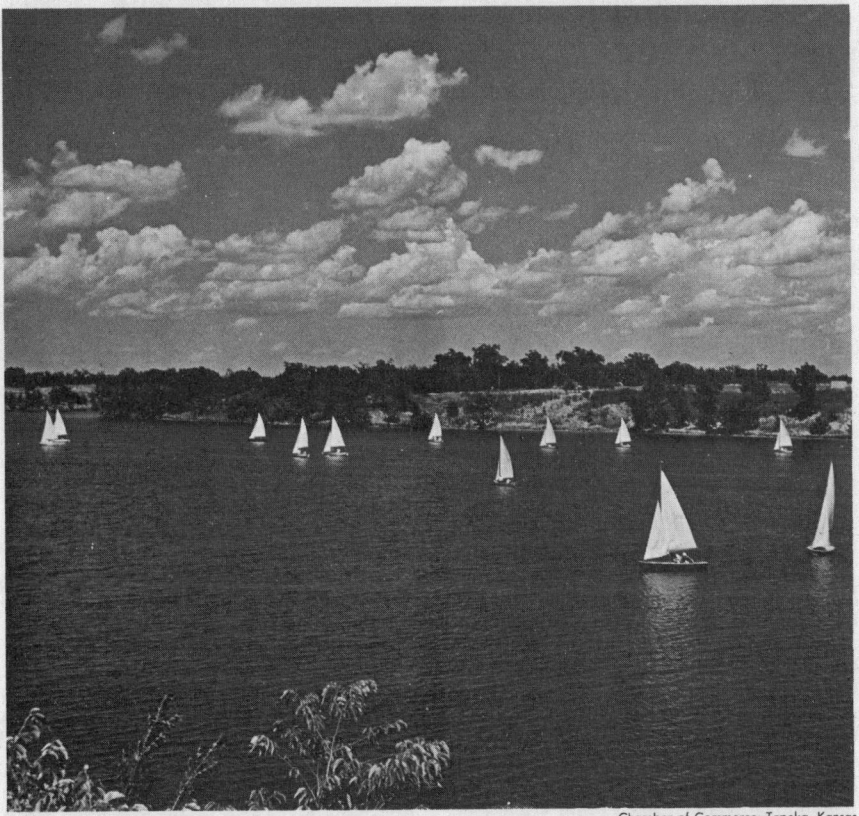

Chamber of Commerce, Topeka, Kansas

Lake Shawnee, a man-made lake which is ideal for fishing, swimming, and boating, is located in a park of 1,165 acres near Topeka, Kansas.

Kansas City. An important meat-packing center, Kansas City is located on the Missouri River, just opposite Kansas City, Missouri. Nearby are Wyandotte County Park and the Shawnee Methodist Mission.

Topeka. Divided by the Kansas River, the capital city has experienced several serious floods. Of interest in Topeka are the Menninger's Foundation, a center for the treatment of mental illnesses; the State Capitol Building with John Stuart Curry's murals of John Brown; Constitution Hall; the Kansas Memorial Building housing the State Historical Society's library and museum; and the Underground Railroad Station of Civil War days.

KENTUCKY

Abraham Lincoln National Historic Park. In this park, located just south of Hodgenville, is the reputed birthplace cabin of Abraham Lincoln. To the northeast, at Springfield, is the Lincoln Homestead, which includes the log house where Nancy Hanks, Lincoln's mother, lived. Nearby in Bardstown is the house where Stephen Foster's song "My Old Kentucky Home" was written.

Frankfort. The State Capitol and Governor's Mansion in Frankfort are structures typical of the Old South. The Old State House still remains, and is the headquarters of the Kentucky Historical Soci-

ety. In the cemetery are the graves of Daniel and Rebecca Boone.

Lexington. In the center of the bluegrass region is Lexington, the second largest city in the state and home of the University of Kentucky. Horse-breeding farms in this area are open to visitors. Man o' War was raised here, and his statue stands at Faraway Farm.

Louisville. The largest and most industrial city in Kentucky is Louisville. Each year it hosts the Kentucky Derby at Churchill Downs, the most prestigious race

Three Lions

Floyd Collins Crystal Cave in Mammoth Cave National Park in central Kentucky contains formations of onyx and crystal.

for three-year-olds in the world. Noted buildings are the J. B. Speed Art Museum, the largest in the state; the Filson Club Library, specializing in state and regional history; and the American Printing House for the Blind, one of the largest of its kind in the world. Other points of interest are Iroquois Park, containing an amphitheater for musical programs; George Rogers Clark's grave; and the Haymarket, formerly a lively trading place for farmers.

Mammoth Cave National Park. This park, located in west central Kentucky, is noted for its extensive caves containing passages, waterfalls, underground rivers, deep pits, two lakes, and stalagmite and stalactite formations. Guided trips, varying in length, are available. Features on the trails include Frozen Niagara, Crystal Lake, Star Chamber, and Mammoth Dome. There are also cruises along the Echo River. Elsewhere in the park facilities are provided for hiking, picnicking, and fishing.

Perryville. Near the town of Perryville in central Kentucky is the Perryville Battlefield State Shrine, site of one of the bloodiest battles of the Civil War (Oct., 1862). Markers and monuments explain the field to visitors, and a museum contains relics and scenes from the battle. A tour of the scarred but standing buildings that survived the war is available.

LOUISIANA

Baton Rouge. The state capital, Baton Rouge has been under ten flags since its founding. Although the modern Capitol Building was built in 1932, the old State Capitol, a castle of Mediterranean Gothic design, remains as a museum. The state's largest center of higher education, Louisiana State University, is here. One of the nation's finest planetariums is housed in the Old Governor's Mansion, one-time home of Huey Long. After the deepening of the Mississippi River channel, Baton Rouge became one of the leading seaports in the country. In the nearby area are the towns of St. Francisville and Clinton, restored examples of the Old South. Also nearby is Audubon State Park which includes the Oakley Plantation, where John James Audubon painted some of the birds of the area.

Lafayette. Located in the parish of Acadia is Lafayette, a city of extremes. Although it is a thriving oil center with over 700 companies, the city abounds with beautiful parks and landscapes. Lafayette is also the home of the University of Southern Louisiana. Common year-round sports within the area are professional golf, bowling, horseracing, tennis, fishing, and hunting. The city's cuisine is authentic Acadian, and the meals are slow and excellent. South of Lafayette, on Bayou Teche, is the city of New Iberia where many ante-bellum buildings are found; the most popular is The Shadows, a museum of the Old South. Further south is Avery Island, home of Bird City and the Jungle Gardens. In nearby St. Martinville is the grave of Emmeline Labiche, Longfellow's "Evangeline."

New Orleans. The annual Mardi Gras carnival is one of the best-known events of

New Orleans life. Also of interest is the New Year's Day Sugar Bowl Football classic following the December Sports Carnival. An all-year attraction is the French Quarter, also called the Vieux Carré; the sights in here can best be seen on a walking tour. On each side of the narrow streets are Spanish and French buildings, many of which have beautiful iron-lacework balconies. Around Jackson Square are the St. Louis Cathedral; the Pontalba Buildings, said to be the first apartments in the United States; the Cabildo, where the Louisiana Purchase was signed; and the Presbytere. There are many restaurants and night clubs providing a cosmopolitan atmosphere and featuring excellent Creole cuisine and Dixieland jazz. In the French Market, food is sold in the open air. Other buildings in the city date from Civil War times. New Orleans in its newer sections is a diversified industrial city yielding hundreds of manufactured products.

Union Pacific Railroad

This lighthouse on West Quoddy Head warns mariners nearing the coast of Lubec, Maine. In the background is Sail Rock, the easternmost point of land in the United States.

New Orleans Tourist Commission

The port of New Orleans, Louisiana, 110 miles from the mouth of the Mississippi River, receives ships from all over the world.

Shreveport. Founded in 1837 as a frontier town on the Red River, Shreveport is now a cultural, industrial, and trade center. It has one of the finest community buildings in the state, the Civic Center. Visitors can see Fort Humbug, named for the fake cannons set there during the Civil War. Shreveport also hosts each fall the Louisiana State Fair. North of the city are the oil towns of Rodessa and Plain Dealing, where visitors may watch the refining process. In Plain Dealing is Dogwood Drive, a hilly scenic drive which provides a pleasant break from the industry of the area. South of Shreveport are Mansfield Battle Park and the Confederate Museum.

MAINE

Acadia National Park. Situated on Mount Desert Island, Acadia National Park is the only national park bordering on the Atlantic Ocean. The entrance is in Bar Harbor, a fashionable resort town. The park offers the rugged charm of the Maine seacoast, with many trails and byways for exploration. There are also several summits for climbers, among them Mount Cadillac, 1,532 feet high.

Augusta. The state capital is located on the Kennebec River, which bisects the city. The Capitol Building was designed in 1829 by Charles Bulfinch, but only the portico remains intact after a 1911 remodeling. A state museum is in the south wing of the building. The James Blaine House is now the governor's mansion. Just down the river is Fort Western, a restored 18th-century fortification.

Brunswick. Brunswick is the home of Bowdoin College, where Henry Wadsworth Longfellow taught. His home, Emmons House, still stands in the city. Here, too, is the house where Harriet Beecher Stowe wrote *Uncle Tom's Cabin*. Brunswick has a professional musical repertory theater.

Portland. The state's largest city, Portland has been a major port since colonial times. One of its famous citizens was the poet Henry Wadsworth Longfellow. A monument has been built in the city square honoring his name. His boyhood home, Wadsworth-Longfellow House, is open to the public. The Museum of the Maine Historical Society and the L.D.M. Sweat Art Museum are other cultural points of interest in the city. Two landmarks are the Portland Observatory, built in 1807, and the Portland Head Light, built in 1791. Along Maine's coast there are historic forts, landmarks, and lighthouses; many of the lighthouses are still in use and have interesting legends.

MARYLAND

Annapolis. Annapolis, the state capital, is the home of the U.S. Naval Academy. A few miles away is the campus of St. John's College, one of the oldest universities in

Maryland Department of Economic Development

The original Star-Spangled Banner flew over Fort McHenry in Baltimore, Maryland, as the British bombarded the fort in the War of 1812. The fort is now a national monument.

the country. In this historic city is the Statehouse; built in 1779, it was the nation's first capitol building. It is still used by the state government, but a part has been reserved and restored to the period of the 1780's when the peace treaty with Great Britain was signed.

Baltimore. Baltimore, a seaport, is important as a shipping, industrial, and cultural center. Cultural highlights of the city include the Johns Hopkins University, the Peale Museum, the Baltimore Museum of Art, the Walters Art Gallery, the Maryland Historical Society, and the Baltimore and Ohio Railroad Museum. Important industrial plants are McCormick Spice Company, Chevrolet, and Bethlehem Steel. "The Star-Spangled Banner," America's national anthem, was written by Francis Scott Key at what is now the Fort McHenry National Monument outside the city.

Frederick. In Frederick is Barbara Fritchie's House, a reconstructed home and museum featuring the relics and belongings of the heroine of Whittier's poem. Nearby is Fort Frederick State Park, a huge stone fort dating back to the French and Indian Wars. Here during the summer, 18th-century military exercises are reenacted. Farther west near Sharpsburg is Antietam National Battlefield, the site of a major Civil War battle (Sept., 1862).

MASSACHUSETTS

Boston. The state capital, Boston is located on the Mystic and St. Charles rivers near the Atlantic seaboard. The city's character varies from the old-world quaintness of crooked and narrow streets to the new-world atmosphere of luxury hotels and motels. Many of the city's historic spots can be seen on a walking tour along Freedom Trail in Old Boston: Boston Common, the Old State House, Paul Revere's House, and the Old North Church are just a few. Also of interest are the Bunker Hill Monument and the U.S.S. *Constitution* in the Boston Navy Yard. The

city's cultural attractions include the Peabody Museum, the Museum of Fine Arts, the Institute of Contemporary Art, and Symphony Hall, which hosts both the Boston Symphony and the Boston Pops orchestras. There are professional teams in all major sports. Deep-sea fishing, swimming, sailing, tennis, and golf are among the major sport activities. The area is famous for seafood and other culinary specialties. Across the St. Charles River in Cambridge is Harvard University, oldest in the country; here, too, are Radcliffe College and Massachusetts Institute of Technology. The homes and graves of poets Longfellow and Lowell are in Boston.

Cape Cod. The arm of Cape Cod curves 65 miles into the Atlantic Ocean. One of the favorite resort spots in New England, Cape Cod boasts over 120 public beaches of all sizes, five of which are within the Cape Cod National Seashore. The water is warmed by the Gulf Stream. The area offers art shows and galleries, antique shops and auctions, and a Summer Theater for pre- and post-Broadway shows. Woods Hole, at the southern end of the cape, is a departure point for the island resorts of Nantucket and Martha's Vineyard, the "Storybook Island." Nantucket is a delightful spot with green fields, golden beaches, and quaint villages. The island was important in the whaling days, and much of the island's decor reveals its whaling history, which is perpetuated in a whaling museum. There are many villages to visit here, each with its own distinctive personality. There are wild grapevines, flowers, and beaches with lively surf. To the northeast are the quiet waters of Martha's Vineyard; Edgartown is a fine resort on this island.

Concord and Lexington. The American Revolution started on a battlefield near these towns when "the shot heard round the world" was fired at the British. The battleground and the old bridge are maintained as historic sites. At Concord are the Old Manse and Wayside, homes of

The 17th-century home of famous patriot Paul Revere is one of many historic sites in Boston, Massachusetts.

author Nathaniel Hawthorne. The Hancock-Clarke House nearby is now a museum. At Orchard House, Louisa May Alcott wrote *Little Women*. Near Concord is Walden Pond, where Henry David Thoreau lived while writing *Walden*. The site retains much of the beauty that existed in Thoreau's day. At Lexington is the Minute Man Monument commemorating the battle of Lexington.

Plymouth. Plymouth Rock, the "cornerstone of the nation," is enshrined here. There is also a reconstructed village showing the life of the Pilgrims. Some 17th-century homes remain, and plaques mark the spot where others stood. A replica of the *Mayflower* is moored at the dock. Visitors can also see the historic Wax Museum. Plymouth offers facilities for various types of outdoor recreation such as sailing, fishing, swimming, and horseback riding.

Salem. Salem, an old seaport town north of Boston, is the home of the Salem Maritime National Historic Site, which includes the Custom House, built in 1819, and the Derby Wharf, which dates back to pre-Revolutionary days. Elsewhere in the city is Witch House, home of Jonathan Corwin, one of the judges in the historic witch trials. Another famous building is the House of Seven Gables, built in 1668 and immortalized by Nathaniel Hawthorne's novel of the same name. Many other structures reflect the days when Salem was an important seaport.

MICHIGAN

Dearborn. Henry Ford's home is located in Dearborn. Greenfield Village, a model of an early American town, includes a collection of historic buildings brought from other parts of the U.S.; among them are the home where Henry Ford was born, the home of Noah Webster, and Edison's Menlo Park Laboratory. The 14-acre Henry Ford Museum displays highlights of America's growth since colonial times, including replicas of historic buildings and early American crafts.

Detroit. The world's largest automobile manufacturing city has many auto assembly plants in and around it. Plants offering tours to visitors include Cadillac, Chrysler, Dodge, Plymouth, Lincoln-Mercury, and

Fishing boats in the harbor at Gloucester, Massachusetts, a charming summer resort and haven for artists on the historic rocky coast of the Cape Ann Peninsula.

Henry Ford Museum

This replica of the brick shed where Henry Ford started to build his first automobile in 1893 can be visited in Greenfield Village, Dearborn, Michigan.

Pontiac. Other attractions in the city are the Institute of the Arts, the Detroit Historical Museum, the Detroit Zoological Park, and Belle Isle, an amusement park on an island in the Detroit River.

Grand Rapids. Grand Rapids is an industrial community as well as a cultural center. The Art Museum, Ryerson Library, Civic Auditorium, Civic Theater, and Grand Valley State College provide a well-rounded cultural program. Furniture-making is the city's major industry, and at the Furniture Museum visitors may watch craftsmen at their work. Other attractions are the General Motors plants and the Vandenberg Center. Just southwest of Grand Rapids, in Holland, is the Dutch Village, a reconstructed village which features crafts, food, dress, and buildings in the style of the old country. There is a wooden shoe factory where visitors may watch blocks of wood being carved into boatlike clogs. The annual tulip festival in Holland is an event which attracts visitors from all over the Midwest.

Isle Royale. Isle Royale, the largest island in Lake Superior, was declared a national park in 1940. One of few primitive areas left in the United States, Isle Royale has no roads and can only be reached by boat or plane. A variety of wildlife, including a moose herd, is found in the island's forested area. The many sheltered harbors and coves are landings for fishermen, hikers, and campers.

Mackinac Island. Ferries from Mackinaw City on the mainland cross the Straits of Mackinac to the island where no automobiles are permitted. The island is a popular summer resort. Major points of interest on the island are the John Jacob Astor Fur Post, Fort Mackinac, and Fort Holmes. Mackinac City is important in its own right as the home of Major Robert Rogers, commander of Fort Mackinac (1765–1768), who unsuccessfully tried to prove the existence of a Northwest Passage. The bridge

over the straits connecting the Upper and Lower peninsulas between Mackinaw City and St. Ignace was opened in 1957. An imposing structure with an overall length of five miles, it gives the motorist easy access to the vacation spots of the entire state. At St. Ignace is Father Marquette's grave.

Sault Ste. Marie. The first permanent white settlement in Michigan was at Sault Ste. Marie on the Canadian border. A major shipping port, the Soo locks and St. Mary's Ship Canal connect Lake Superior with Lake Huron, and thence with the Atlantic Ocean through the St. Lawrence Seaway. Just outside the American city of Sault Ste. Marie is the Shrine of the Missionaries, with its 160-foot sightseeing tower.

MINNESOTA

Bemidji. The city was built on the site of the Indian settlement founded by the

Chippewa chief, Bemidji. It is located at the southern end of Lake Bemidji, one of the reputed 10,000 lakes of Minnesota. Bemidji is also a center of the folklore of Paul Bunyan, hero of Minnesota loggers.

Duluth. Duluth is one of the leading seaports in the world. Ocean-going ships travel up the St. Lawrence Seaway and through the Great Lakes to Duluth, where more than three million tons of cargo are shipped annually, making it second only to New York City in annual tonnage. The city itself rises 800 feet above the lake level on rocky bluffs. Skyline Parkway, a scenic drive, provides an excellent view of the area. Some of the city's attractions are the Aerial Lift Bridge, the ore docks, and the Incline Railway.

Lake Itasca. Here at Lake Itasca, 2,546 miles from New Orleans, are the headwaters of the Mississippi River, only one and one-half feet wide and one foot deep. Lake Itasca, the center of Itasca State Park, offers visitors year-round recreational facilities and accomodations. There is also a museum depicting the history and development of northern Minnesota.

Minneapolis–St. Paul. Minneapolis, the state's largest city, has many beautiful lakes and parks within its limits. Minnehaha Park, situated on the Mississippi River, contains Minnehaha Falls, immortalized in Henry Wadsworth Longfellow's "Song of Hiawatha." Points of interest in Minneapolis include the campus of the University of Minnesota, the Walker Art Center, the Tyrone Guthrie Repertory Theater, and Fort Snelling. Also of interest are the world's largest flour mills, many of which offer tours for visitors. Twin city St. Paul is the state capital and the state's second largest city. There are weekday guided tours of the Capitol Building, a beautiful Italian Renaissance structure. Nearby is the Minnesota State Historical Society with its noteworthy museum displays of Indian and pioneer life. The Alexander Ramsey House, completed in 1872 and home of the first governor of the Minnesota Territory, is an outstanding example of Victorian architecture. Victorian furnishings and personal belongings of the Ramsey family give it added interest. In

Northwest Orient Airlines

Saint Paul, the capital of Minnesota, is located on the Mississippi River and is built on a series of terraces which rise nearly 200 feet above the river valley.

the eastern part of the city is Twenty Nine Mounds Park with six Indian burial sites believed to be 3,000 years old.

Rochester. Visitors and persons seeking medical treatment come from all parts of the world to the famous Mayo Clinic, nearly doubling the city's official population. Because of this, there are many hotels and apartment houses in the area. The Mayo family is highly regarded in Rochester, and one of the city's attractions is Mayowood, home of Dr. Charles H. Mayo. Mayo House, the early home of the family, is located in LeSueur, west of Rochester; of special interest in this small structure is the restored office of Doctor W. W. Mayo, who, with his two sons, founded the Mayo Clinic. The towns of Traverse des Sioux and New Ulm and Fort Ridgely State Memorial Park, all important during the Indian uprisings of the mid-1800's, are within a 30-mile radius of LeSueur.

grimage, all 29 homes are open to the public. Also of interest are Rosalie, General Grant's headquarters when he occupied Natchez; Stanton Hall and Arlington, two beautiful estates; and the Briars, where Jefferson Davis was married. Nearby is a section of the old and scenic Natchez Trace Parkway, a trail that ran from Natchez to Nashville.

Vicksburg. Vicksburg is the site of one of the most strategic battles of the Civil War. Forty-seven days of siege and starvation were needed to break the Confederate defense of this river port. One of the attractions here is the Vicksburg National Military Park with its many monuments and markers. Before seeing the battlefield, visitors usually stop at the headquarters and museum, where an automated lecture and electric diagram explain the progress of the battle. Other points of interest in the city are the Old Courthouse Museum in

MISSOURI

Hannibal. This was the boyhood home of Mark Twain, born Samuel Clemens and one of America's best-known writers. The entire area is dedicated to his memory, and visitors can roam the terrain where Huck Finn and Tom Sawyer had their adventures. The house in which Mark Twain grew up is now a museum. Many spots mentioned in his books can be seen: Becky Thatcher's house, the fence Tom Sawyer whitewashed, and the caves in which Tom Sawyer and Huck Finn were lost. Southwest of Hannibal at Paris, Missouri, are the Mark Twain State Park and the Mark Twain Wildlife Refuge, both offering facilities for camping, picnicking, and fishing. A shrine enclosing the house where Mark Twain was born is located in the park.

Independence. Just south of Kansas City on the Missouri River is Independence, once a famous frontier town. The Santa Fe and the Oregon trails started here, and it was an important terminal of the Overland Stage. Points of interest include the blacksmith shop, where wagons were assembled for the trip west, and the Old Public Spring. Independence is the home of former President Harry S. Truman, and houses the Harry S. Truman Library and Museum. Due south in Lamar is his birthplace.

Kansas City. Although Kansas City is a modern city, an industrial center, and a major market, remnants of the days of the Santa Fe Trail are evident in such memorials as Fort Osage. Swope Park offers golf, tennis, a zoo, and the Starlight Theater. There are also professional football, baseball, and hockey teams. Cultural centers include the William Rockhill Nelson Gallery of Art, Mary Atkins Museum of Fine Arts, and the Kansas City Art Institute and School of Design. One of the city's most inspiring sights is the Liberty Memorial. Built to honor those who served in World War I, it features a Torch of Liberty.

Ozarks. The beautiful Ozark Mountains stretch from the southern end of the Missouri River to Arkansas and Oklahoma.

Vicksburg Chamber of Commerce, Mississippi

The largest sternwheel towboat in the world, the Sprague, docked on the Mississippi River, near Vicksburg, Mississippi, is both a river museum and a showboat.

MISSISSIPPI

Jackson. Here, in the state capital, the Mississippi Ordinance of Secession was passed; years later Jefferson Davis made his last appearance before retiring to his home, Beauvoir, in Biloxi. The city itself was almost completely destroyed by General Sherman's troops during the Civil War. The few remaining buildings have been restored and are open to visitors the year round. Other attractions are the state complex, which includes the State Hall of Fame and the Department of Archives and History, both located in the War Memorial Building. Nearby is the Governor's Mansion; built in 1842, it is the oldest governor's mansion in the United States. Also of interest is the State Historical Museum which has an extensive and interesting collection of artifacts depicting Mississippi's history.

Natchez. Once a river town where steamboat races were the biggest events, Natchez is a city rich in southern tradition and history. The city's main attractions are the ante-bellum mansions and spectacular gardens, many of which are open the year round; in the spring, during the pil-

downtown Vicksburg and the showboat steamer Sprague, the largest sternwheeler ever to ply the Mississippi.

Walker-Missouri Tourism Commission

The Gateway Arch in St. Louis, Missouri, on the western bank of the Mississippi River, was designed by Eero Saarinen to commemorate America's westward expansion.

Turner's Mill, a relic of the past, on the Eleven Points River in the Ozark Mountains near Alton, Missouri, is in a region of hills, plateaus, and deep valleys.

lakes. It is on the sheer precipices that the Rocky Mountain goat may be glimpsed—a favorite sight of the park visitor. The scenic Going-to-the-Sun Highway crosses the park from the eastern side at St. Mary's Lake to the town of West Glacier on the western side. Browning, just east of the park, is the home of the Museum of the Plains Indians.

Great Falls. There are numerous histori-

A national monument in Montana commemorates the battle of Little Bighorn where General Custer's army was defeated in 1876.

Numerous springs, lakes, hardwood forests, and caves make it a noted recreational area. Big Spring and Bennett Springs state parks contain huge natural springs where some of nature's finest caves have been formed. The most popular are Meramec and Missouri caverns, and Bridal and Jacob's caves. Near the middle of the state, in Lake of the Ozarks State Park, is the man-made Lake of the Ozarks, behind the Bagnell Dam on the Osage River; it is an excellent spot for water sports. In the winter there is skiing on the nearby slopes. Lake of the Ozarks State Park, the largest in Missouri, provides many facilities, including an airport for private planes and six organized group camps.

St. Louis. Missouri's largest city and natural port is located on the Mississippi River. The recently remodeled river front is the main attraction for sightseers. The Gateway Arch commemorates the fact that St. Louis was the Gateway to the West; visitors can ride to the top of the arch. The Missouri Botanical (Shaw's) Gardens display over 12,000 species of plant life under the Climatron, the world's first geodesic greenhouse. The Jefferson National Expansion Memorial now preserves the old courthouse and other historical buildings. Also of interest are Forest Park, a cultural center containing the Art Museum; the Jefferson Memorial Building, housing the documents of the Louisiana Purchase and many of Charles Lindbergh's momentos; the Planetarium; Municipal Opera; and the St. Louis Zoological Park. The city has professional football, baseball, and hockey teams; Civic Center Busch Memorial Stadium contains the St. Louis Sports Hall of Fame.

MONTANA

Custer Battlefield National Monument. Because the Little Big Horn River flows through the Crow Reservation, the site of Custer's Last Stand is now, ironically, surrounded by Indian homeland. Con-

flicting reports about the battle may be one reason why many people hunt the battlefield for clues to the true story. Headstones mark the places where men died, and visitors to the museum can see dioramas and exhibits depicting what may have happened here.

Glacier National Park in the Rocky Mountains of Montana is a wilderness of forests and natural wonders. It is one of the largest national parks in the United States.

Glacier National Park. Glacier National Park, established in 1910 and straddling the Continental Divide, is part of the Waterton-Glacier International Peace Park. The park, which is partly in Montana and partly in Alberta, Canada, contains some of the most primitive wilderness in America and abounds in forests, waterfalls, and high peaks. In the park's 1,600 square miles are more than 1,000 miles of trails, over 60 glaciers, and 200

cal sights in the city, many related to the Lewis and Clark Expedition. The Charles M. Russell Studio and his gallery, which contains many of his paintings and sculptures of the American West, are in Great Falls. Also in Great Falls is the smelting

plant of the Anaconda Company where copper and zinc ore from Butte are refined.

Helena. Montana's capital was a gold rush town in the 1800's; the Old Placer Diggings in Dry Gulch, where gold is still washed, will remind visitors of Helena's origin as a mining town. Some of the city's streets wind along the gulches as they did in early days. Points of interest in the city include the State Historical Society and the State Capitol Building, which has paintings of historical figures and events. Southeast of the capital is Livingston, the northern gateway to Yellowstone National Park in Wyoming.

NEBRASKA

Lincoln. Lincoln's 400-foot Capitol Building is visible from miles away. The structure and decorations combine the simplicity of Indian and pioneer cultures with the high ideals of the state. Other points of interest in Lincoln include the State Historical Society Museum, the University of Nebraska and its archaeological museum, the Sheldon Art Gallery, the his-

Union Pacific Railroad

Scotts Bluff, in western Nebraska, was an important landmark for the westward migration along the Oregon Trail. It was declared a national monument in 1919.

toric Kennard House, and Fairview, home of three-time presidential candidate William Jennings Bryan.

Ogallala. Ogallala was Nebraska's cowboy capital one hundred years ago. Now those days are relived on Front Street at the Cowboy Museum, the Crystal Palace Saloon, and the General Store. The dance hall still has shows, and the stagecoach still runs. Fifty miles east is North Platte, home of Buffalo Bill Cody. His ranch, where the famous Wild West show was rehearsed, is now a state historical park. To the north, near the South Dakota border, is Valentine, the center of the beautiful Niobrara area, and nearby is Fort Niobrara National Wildlife Refuge, a division of the Nebraska National Forest with 14 lakes. Here some of the last remaining herds of bison and longhorn cattle can be seen. The museum holds relics of frontier days.

Omaha. The state's largest city is a transportation center with a number of railroad trunk lines and a modern jetport near the river. It was from Omaha that the first transcontinental railroad was built; the Union Pacific has established a museum here in its honor. Omaha also has one of the largest stockyards in the world. The cultural center is the Joslyn Art Mu-

seum, which houses a huge concert hall in addition to the exhibition area. Also in the city are the Mormon Cemetery and monument which honor the Mormons who died near Omaha on their trip westward. Boys Town, the noted community founded in 1917 for homeless boys, is on the western outskirts of the city. South of Omaha are the headquarters for the Strategic Air Command and the Aerospace Museum.

Scotts Bluff. At Gering, Nebraska, is the Scotts Bluff National Monument, once an important landmark for westward travelers on the Oregon Trail. The Pony Express and the first transcontinental telegraph passed through Mitchell Pass, on the Bluff. Also of interest in the area is the Oregon Trail Museum. A few miles east of the monument is Chimney Rock Historical Site, another landmark on the trail. Farther north are Agate Fossil Beds National Monument and Pine Ridge, a division of the National Forest.

NEVADA

Carson City. Carson City is the smallest state capital in the U.S. First a Pony Express station, then a boom town in the gold rush days, it was named for Kit Carson. The Capitol Building, State Library, and Supreme Court Building are the main points of interest in the administrative complex. The old U. S. Mint now houses the State Museum. On the river just east of Carson City are markers at the sites of mills where ore from the Comstock Lode was treated.

Las Vegas. Once a small desert town, Las Vegas has experienced a phenomenal growth, particularly since World War II. It is now the largest city in Nevada, known primarily as a tourist and convention center. Its hotels are among the most luxurious in the world and are especially noted for their opulent night clubs and casinos. Las Vegas is not far from Hoover Dam, completed in 1936, and the recreational area of Lake Mead, where there is ample opportunity for water sports, camping, and fishing.

Reno. Reno, once an important campsite beside the Truckee River on the Donner Pass route to California, is now the region's bustling commercial and shipping center. The county seat of Washoe County is perhaps best known as an early mecca for those seeking quick divorces. Legalized gambling and the surrounding recreational areas have also contributed to Reno's prosperity. The University of Nevada is located here; some of its facilities are open

Union Pacific Railroad

Hoover Dam, in Nevada, harnesses the Colorado River to provide electricity and water for irrigation. It is the highest concrete arch dam in the United States.

to the public. South of the city is a marker on the site of Junction House, the first permanent settlement on the Truckee meadows. The Truckee River leads southward to Lake Tahoe and the Sierra Nevada winter sports area, which includes Squaw Valley, site of the 1960 Winter Olympics, Mt. Rose, and Slide Mountain.

Virginia City. Founded in 1859, this city, located between Reno and Carson City, once produced millions of dollars in gold and silver from the Comstock Lode. During the 1870's it was the most prosperous mining metropolis of the West. Today, it is almost a ghost town. Many of its famous buildings, such as the Crystal Bar, the International Hotel, Piper's Opera House, and the office of the *Territorial Enterprise* where Mark Twain worked as a reporter, are preserved.

NEW HAMPSHIRE

Concord. This city, located on the Merrimack River in the central part of the state, has been the state capital since 1808. The Capitol Building is an impressive white granite structure. Points of interest in Concord include the Statehouse and State Library, Kent House, the New Hampshire Historical Society and Museum, and the granite quarries. A few miles away is Bow, the birthplace of Mary Baker Eddy, founder of the Christian Science religion.

Franconia Notch. A deeply cut pass between two ranges in the White Mountains, Franconia Notch is dominated by a natural formation, the 40-foot granite profile of the Old Man of the Mountain, made famous by Nathaniel Hawthorne's *Great Stone Face*. Also of interest in the area are Echo Lake, the Cannon Mountain Aerial Tramway, and the Flume Gorge, a deep natural chasm in the granite walls. South of the White Mountain National Forest is Lake Winnipesaukee, the largest lake in the state and an excellent resort area.

Hanover. Located near the junction of the White and Connecticut rivers in east-

ern New Hampshire, Hanover is the site of Dartmouth College, chartered in 1769. Of interest on the campus are the Colonial and Georgian buildings and such contrasting modern ones as the Hopkins Center, with its complex of art galleries, two theaters, a concert hall, workshops, and studios. Winter sports are traditional at Dartmouth and the Dartmouth Outing Club, founded in 1910, has helped popularize skiing, ice skating, and other winter sports in America.

Manchester. New Hampshire's largest city, located south of Concord on the Merrimack River, is a leading industrial and agricultural center. Attractions in the city include the Historic Association Building; the home of General John Stark, commander in the American Revolutionary War; Stark Park; the Western Observatory; and the Currier Art Gallery.

Portsmouth. Located on the coast, Portsmouth has been an important port since before the Revolution. The United States Naval Shipyard is located in the harbor. A portion of the downtown area is now being restored in the likeness of Strawberry Banke, the original settlement in Portsmouth. Other places of interest include the Old State House, Pitt Tavern, Fort Constitution, Fort Stark, the John Paul Jones House, and the Wentworth-Coolidge Mansion. A popular recreational area is Hampton Beach, a three and one-half-mile strand on the Atlantic in southern Portsmouth.

and shops. There are five amusement piers and a municipal auditorium; the latter is the site of the annual Miss America Pageant. Atlantic City is the prototype for such popular resort cities as Seaside, Asbury Park, and Wildwood, which stretch along the 127-mile shoreline of New Jersey.

Delaware Water Gap. Bordering Pennsylvania, the water gap is a picturesque break in the Kittatinny Mountains. There are many places to camp, and the water sports on the river make it one of the most popular spots for vacations or overnight visits in the state.

Morristown. An important town during the Revolutionary War, Morristown is rich in historic sites. Ford Mansion, within the city, was the headquarters of General George Washington during the war. The Historical Museum, behind the mansion, contains documents and relics from his stay. A few miles from the city is the Morristown National Historical Park and Jockey Hollow where Revolutionary soldiers camped. Also nearby is Fort Nonsense, built for no other reason than to keep the soldiers occupied.

Newark. Newark is the state's largest and most industrially active city. It has a teeming harbor, and its airport is one of the busiest in the country. There are several breweries in the city offering tours of their plants. Historical attractions in Newark include the Trinity Episcopal Church, the John Plume House, Military Park, and the

Allegheny Airlines

In Atlantic City, New Jersey, beaches are popular vacationlands. New Jersey's Atlantic shoreline has some 50 resort towns between Sandy Hook and Cape May.

C. T. Bodwell, New Hampshire Planning and Development Commission

Old Man of the Mountain, formed by the upper cliffs of the Profile Mountain, overlooks the Franconia Notch, New Hampshire.

NEW JERSEY

Atlantic City. One of the favorite resort and convention cities on the eastern seaboard, Atlantic City accommodates well over 16,000,000 visitors each year. The first boardwalk, a broad wooden walk paralleling the shore, was built here in 1870, and the first rolling chairs made their appearance in 1884. Today's boardwalk, extending for four miles, is lined with hotels

Newark Academy, which was once a troops' barracks in the Revolutionary War.

Princeton. Nassau Hall is the first college building of what is today Princeton University. During the Revolutionary War, it was used as a barracks, first by the British and later by the Continental army. The Battle of Princeton ended in the Hall, and in 1783 it served as the site where the declaration of peace was signed by the Continental Congress. Not far away is the

Princeton Battle Monument. Just outside the city is Morven, original home of Richard Stockton, a signer of the Declaration of Independence; it is now the official residence of the governor of New Jersey. North of the city is Rocky Hill, the site where Washington wrote and delivered his farewell address to the army.

Trenton. On Christmas night, 1776, General Washington and his troops crossed the Delaware River and staged a successful surprise attack on the British forces quartered in Trenton. The battle proved to be a turning point in the war, and the city, which is now the state capital, has commemorated the achievement by building a monument at Washington Crossing. The Trenton Battle Monument marks the spot where Washington placed his artillery.

NEW MEXICO

Albuquerque. Served by land, air, and rail lines, Albuquerque is the commercial center of New Mexico. The city lies on a plain at the foot of the Sandia Mountains, and is a superb scenic and recreational area. Sandia Crest and Sandia Peak Aerial Tramway offer a beautiful view of the surroundings. Old Town, a section of the city, retains part of the original Spanish settlement of 1706. Many of the buildings of the University of New Mexico are of Spanish-Pueblo architecture.

New Mexico Department of Development

Ruins of a prehistoric Pueblo civilization are preserved in Chaco Canyon National Monument in northwest New Mexico.

Carlsbad Caverns. Vast and beautiful limestone caverns are the main feature of this 49,000-acre national park. Rangers of the National Park Service conduct walking tours along the electrically lighted trails leading to such caverns as the Green Lake Room, King's Palace, Queen's Chamber, and the 14-acre Big Room, where the famous Bat Flight occurs nightly. The caverns are located at the foot of the Guadalupe Mountains. Camping facilities are available in the nearby scenic park, and tourists may also enjoy boating or other water sports on the Pecos River.

Four Corners. Named after the area in northwestern New Mexico where four states meet, Four Corners is mostly Indian territory. The area is the home of the Navajos, and farther south, near Gallup, is the Zuni Pueblo, the first village in New Mexico seen by Spanish explorers. In Gallup, a coal-mining region and center for

Allen Green, New York Convention and Visitors Bureau

Skyscrapers in the financial district of Lower Manhattan in New York City create a fantastic skyline for the largest city in the United States.

trade, the Inter-Tribal Indian Ceremonial is held each summer.

Lincoln County. It was during the range war here that William Bonney made his reputation as Billy the Kid. At Lincoln State Monument his exploits are documented, and once each year the town reenacts his final jail escape and death. Not far away is an excellent ski area, near Ruidoso on Sierra Blanca Peak. Ruidoso also has the race track where each summer the All-America Futurity and other races are run. Gran Quivira National Monument, and Abo and the Quarai State Monuments, ruins of the Saline Pueblos and their Spanish missions, are located north of Ruidoso near Cibala National Forest.

Santa Fe. The oldest capital in the United States, Santa Fe has been a capital city under Spanish, Mexican, Confederate, and American flags. It was the end of the Santa Fe Trail and remained the Southwest's supply center for a long time, but now is relatively unindustrialized. The city still reflects the Indian-Spanish architecture and way of life, and the old plaza is still the center of activity. Points of interest in the city include the Palace of the Governors, the San Miguel Church, and the Cathedral of St. Francis of Assisi. Northeast of Sante Fe is Taos, the famous art colony. Once an important Indian and Spanish trading center, Taos began to attract artists and writers around the turn of the century. Activity still centers around the plaza. The shops, galleries, and restaurants in the adjacent narrow streets are an interesting attraction. Numerous small villages in the Sangre de Cristo Mountains are also worth seeing; the area offers not only beautiful scenery, but also camping, hiking, hunting, fishing, and skiing.

NEW YORK

Adirondack Mountains. Located in the northeast corner of the state, this large resort and recreation area is a summer and winter playground. Outdoorsmen are attracted to the trails and campsites of these valleys and mountains, while others enjoy many resort hotels, motels, dude ranches,

and cottages. The region is a land of lakes—Placid, George, and Champlain being the best known. During the summer, there is the lure of water sports, mountaineering, and camping; in winter it is a skiing center. Mt. Marcy, New York's highest mountain, is here. West of Lake Champlain is Ausable Chasm, a magnificent gorge with provisions for tours of the site and a ride through the flume.

Albany. The tulips that blossom each spring in the park across from the Capitol Building are a reminder of the Dutch origin of New York's capital. Guided tours of the Capitol's Senate and Assembly Chambers, Governor's office, and Military Museum are offered. The city's other museums are the Institute of History and Art and the State Museum. Several Revolutionary War buildings are open to the public. Just north of Albany is Saratoga Springs, where a decisive battle was fought during the Revolution. There is a tour route which commemorates the battle, as does the Historical Museum. The city is a popular resort, offering healthful springs and the nation's oldest race track; there is even a museum of horse racing. The New York City Ballet and the Philadelphia Orchestra have their summer homes here. Their performances at the Saratoga Performing Arts Center add a cultural note to the recreational opportunities open to the visitor.

Buffalo. Although Buffalo offers two museums, a fine art gallery, a zoo, theaters, and lake- and rail-shipping facilities, the greatest attraction remains Niagara Falls. There are three falls across the United States-Canada border: American, Bridal Veil, and Horseshoe or Canadian Falls. More than two dozen viewing points are available, some of which take visitors within a few feet of the falls. Many people return at night when giant searchlights are turned upon the falls, changing them into shimmering fantasies of color and sound. The city of Niagara Falls has an aquarium, the Animated Museum of History, the Wax Museum of History, and a zoo. The Niagara Power Project is open to the public and has models, movies, and lectures explaining the $737 million hydroelectric project.

New York City. The largest city in the United States is made up of five separate boroughs: Bronx, Brooklyn, Queens, Richmond (Staten Island), and Manhattan. Most people, however, think of Manhattan when they think of New York City, for it offers an incredible list of interesting places. Gray Line Bus sightseeing tours go to the Empire State Building and the Statue of Liberty, the first points of call for most visitors. At the docks, visitors can see great ships, both cargo and passenger. and on certain days special tours are available. Wall Street, in downtown Manhattan, is the financial center of America. Nearby is the New York Stock Exchange, the nation's largest organized securities market; the Chase Manhattan Bank, one of the world's largest banks; and the Federal Reserve Bank of New York. Farther north is Greenwich Village, a haven for artists, poets, and writers; many shops, restaurants, clubs, and cafes are found around Washington Square where outdoor summer concerts are held. Near midtown is the new Madison Square Garden; the Port Authority Bus Terminal, one of the world's largest bus stations; and the New York Public Library, one of the largest in the U.S. Also in midtown are the Rockefeller Center, Carnegie Hall, and Times Square. On the East River is the United Nations headquarters where tours of the business chambers and galleries are provided. Uptown's favorite attraction is Central Park, with concerts and Shakespearean plays in the summer, a zoo all year, and an outdoor ice-skating rink in the winter. Farther north in Morningside Heights is Columbia University. Nearby, on Riverside Drive overlooking the Hudson, are two famous landmarks, the Riverside Church and Grant's Tomb. The cultural life in New York City is of infinite variety. It includes the Broadway theater district and the off-Broadway theaters centered in the Greenwich Village area. The new Lincoln Center houses, among other cultural facilities, the Philharmonic Hall, the State Theater, and the New Metropolitan Opera House. The most famous art museums are the Metropolitan Museum, the Museum of Modern Art, the Whitney Museum of Art, and the Guggenheim Museum with its spiral building designed by Frank Lloyd Wright. The other boroughs offer other well-known attractions. In Brooklyn are the Brooklyn Botanic Garden; and Coney Island, the amusement playground on the ocean, where the New York Aquarium is located. Linking Brooklyn to Staten Island is the spectacular Verrazano-Narrows Bridge at the entrance to New York Harbor. Bronx has the Bronx Zoo, second largest in America, New York University, and the Hall of Fame. Yankee Stadium is close to the Harlem River. Queens' major attraction is the Flushing Meadow Fair Grounds, site of the 1964–65 World's Fair and the 1939 World Exposition. A few pavilions are still open to visitors. Near the fair grounds is Shea Municipal Stadium, home of the New York Mets and New York Jets, the city's professional baseball and football teams. Aque-

duct Race Track, one of the finest in the country, is also in Queens.

Finger Lakes. Six lakes in west central New York comprise the Finger Lakes region. This is one of the finest resort areas in the state, with beautiful scenery and excellent water facilities. Its lakeside vineyards are renowned for their fine wines and sparkling champagnes and have made the region famous. Also within the region are the state's third and fourth largest cities, Rochester and Syracuse. Rochester is the photo capital of the country. It is the home of the Eastman Company, makers of Kodak cameras, equipment, and supplies. The George Eastman Home, a national landmark, is now a museum of photography and cameras. Also in Rochester are the University of Rochester and the Eastman School of Music. East of Rochester is Syracuse. Chief among its diversified industries are steel, china, and electronic equipment. Syracuse University is located within the city; other cultural institutions include the Syracuse Civic Symphony Orchestra, the Museum of Natural History, and the Lowe Art Center. In the southern part of the Finger Lakes region is Corning, with its large glassmaking industry; exquisite crystal pieces are on display at the Corning Glass Center. Nearby is Watkins Glen, the noted sports car racing center.

Thousand Islands. There are actually over 1,700 islands scattered at random in the St. Lawrence River near the Canadian border. Many are historic sites and have scenic boat tours. All kinds of water sports are available among the islands. Of interest in the area are the Akwesasne Mohawk Indian Village at Hogansburg and the Boldt Castle on Heart Island, a castle which was abandoned in 1902 before being completed. Along the seaway one can visit hydroelectric plants, which are part of the international electric project. The Power Authority building is upstream from Cornwall, Ontario. Visitors can hear lectures

and receive literature explaining the project.

West Point. The United States Military Academy is located at West Point overlooking the Hudson River; it was founded in 1802. Of interest here are Cadet Chapel, restored Fort Putnam, the Academy Museum, Battle Monument, and the Parade Grounds where daily parades may be viewed.

NORTH CAROLINA

Asheville. North Carolina's entranceway to the Great Smokies, Asheville, provides many resort activities as a prelude to those of the great Smoky Mountain National Park on the Tennessee border. Near Asheville is the Biltmore House, built in the style of a French chateau and displaying art objects. There is a good view of Asheville and the plateau on which it is set from the drive along Elk Mountain Scenic Highway. Visitors will also enjoy the Thomas Wolfe Memorial, the author's boyhood residence made famous in his novel, *Look Homeward, Angel*. Great Smoky Mountain National Park located on the Tennessee and North Carolina border has a great variety of plant life and is a popular area during the flowering of the rhododendrons.

Kittyhawk. The Wright Brothers National Memorial is the site of the first powered aircraft flight, which occurred in 1903. The memorial, set between the Kill Devils Hill and Kittyhawk, contains markers, a museum, a reconstructed hangar and shop, and an airport. South of Kittyhawk is the Fort Raleigh National Historical Site. On Roanoke Island is the memorial to the early, ill-fated colony of Sir Walter Raleigh. Both the settlement and earthworks of Fort Raleigh have been restored and are open to the public.

Raleigh. The Capitol Building, located in Raleigh, is a Grecian-Doric structure. Surrounding it are statues of national and

Atlantic Coast Lines

Greenfield Lake Gardens Park in Wilmington, North Carolina, has a six-mile scenic drive around the lake. The park is landscaped with dogwoods, roses, and azaleas.

state heroes. Many of the state buildings are open to the public, including the Hall of History and the State Historical Museum. A few miles away is Durham, home of Duke University. One of the attractions on the campus is the Duke University Chapel. Durham is also known for its tobacco operations, as are other cities in the state, notably Winston-Salem.

NORTH DAKOTA

Badlands. Once considered "bad lands" by early explorers, the Badlands, an area in the southwestern part of the state, has since been recognized for its scenery. The area abounds in gorges, buttes, and other unusual earth formations, shaped in part by the Little Missouri River. The region was a favorite of President Theodore Roosevelt, after whom a national memorial park within the area was named. His home in the Badlands is near the visitor's center in the park. Near Medora is the Chateau de Mores, home of the man who dreamed of being, but failed to become, king of the Dakota meat-packers. His house and memorabilia provide a glimpse into life during the 1800's. Fishing, hunting, and trail riding are also available for visitors.

Bismarck. The state's unusual 19-story Capitol Building, erected to replace the one that burned in 1930, is open to the public. The Capitol complex also contains the Liberty Memorial Building, housing the state library and museum, and many memorial statues. The log cabin from Theodore Roosevelt's Ranch is near Bismarck.

International Peace Garden State Park. One of the few gardens in the world dedicated to peace is a mile-square area north of Dunseith on the border of North Dakota and Manitoba, Canada. It commemorates the lasting peace between Canada and the United States. In addition, it has facilities for many sports and cultural diversions. Visitors may freely cross between the United States and Canada to view the points of interest in the garden.

Smithsonian Institution

The Serpent Mound in Adams County, Ohio, was built by prehistoric Indians and is 1330 feet long. Archaeologists believe it was used for religious purposes.

OHIO

Cincinnati. Located in southern Ohio, Cincinnati is a busy cultural and industrial center. Many of its diverse industries are open to the public; visitors may observe the construction of a grand piano as well as that of a jet engine. Cultural attractions include the Edgecliff and Shubert theaters, the Opera, Playhouse-in-the-Park, and other music and art centers. An educational center as well, the city is the home of five universities including the University of Cincinnati. Other attractions include the fine parks, the zoo, and the many sports stadiums and arenas hosting professional and amateur sports.

Cleveland. The largest city in Ohio, Cleveland is an iron and steel center and an important Lake Erie port. University Circle, an attractive cultural center, is the home of Case Institute of Technology, Western Reserve University, the Cleveland Museum of Art, and Severance Hall, host of the Cleveland Symphony Orchestra. Other attractions include Terminal Tower, Dunham Tavern, the Auto Aviation Museum, and a museum which was once a stagecoach station. Municipal Stadium hosts the Cleveland Indians in the summer, and the Cleveland Browns in the fall. One terminal of the Ohio-Erie Canal is in Cleveland, and many spots along the canal can be visited. At some of these points, boat rides and demonstrations of canal operations are available.

Columbus. The present capital is the third in Ohio's history, the first having been at Chillicothe and the second at Zanesville. Tours of the Statehouse are available each weekday. They cover departmental offices, the House and Senate Chambers, and the Governor's Cabinet Room. The state museum is located on the Ohio State University campus. Other points of interest include the Civic Center; the Park of Roses, one of the world's largest municipal rose gardens; and the Walk-O-Wonders which has replicas of the Seven Wonders of the World.

Toledo. Although Toledo is known primarily as an industrial center, it also offers varied cultural attractions. The Toledo Museum of Art has 35 galleries. There are orchestra and opera associations in the city; Lyrno Productions provides the city with theatrical performances. It also has one of the finest zoological gardens in the country, the Toledo Zoological Park. The Miami-Erie Canal had a terminus here, and remains of it can be seen at many points between Toledo and Cincinnati.

OKLAHOMA

Oklahoma City. The state capital since 1910, Oklahoma City is the largest city in the state. The present Capitol Building, erected in 1917, spans two land tracts donated for its construction. The Capitol faces a mall, around which is the rest of the Capitol complex. Some of the state's

National Park Service

Theodore Roosevelt National Memorial Park in North Dakota includes the Badlands, the Grand Canyon of the Little Missouri River, and petrified forests.

Bob Hawks, Inc.

Tulsa, Oklahoma, was settled by Indians of the Five Civilized Tribes. Since the discovery of oil in the area in 1901, Tulsa has been called the oil capital of the world.

largest oil companies have their headquarters in the city. The Oklahoma Historical Society is next to the proposed site of the International Oil Museum, which is to be built by contributions from the oil industry. Oil derricks are everywhere and oil is a major source of income for the city. Other points of interest in Oklahoma City include the Oklahoma Art Center, the stockyards, and the National Cowboy Hall of Fame and Western Heritage Center.

Platt National Park. The park, located in southern Oklahoma, is noted not only for its plant and animal life, but also for the numerous mineral and fresh-water springs, including bromide waters which flow through its 900 acres of wooded hills. The most beautiful streams in the valley are Travertine Creek and Rock Creek. In addition to this national park, Oklahoma has numerous state parks with excellent recreational facilities and accommodations including spacious resort lodges and free campsites.

Tulsa. Tulsa is the home of many oil companies and is appropriately called "the oil capital of the world." There are many refineries, and some have tours of their facilities. The International Petroleum Exposition is held annually in Tulsa. Cultural attractions in the city include the Gilcrease Institute of American History and Art, the Philbrook Art Center, and the University of Tulsa. Of special interest among the city's 44 parks are Mohawk Park and the Woodward Park where the Municipal Rose Gardens are located.

OREGON

Bonneville Dam. This huge dam, 39 miles east of Portland, cuts across the Columbia River and provides electricity for the area. It also has one of the largest fish hatcheries in the country as well as salmon ladders which migratory fish use to run upstream and spawn. The river is widened and deepened at The Dalles, allowing navigation to that point. At The Dalles there is

the Archaeological Museum containing Indian exhibits. This scenic area can be viewed from sightseeing boats as well as from highways.

Crater Lake. Crater Lake, in Crater Lake National Park, is an unusual, brilliant blue lake in the heart of a once-active volcano. The 2,000-foot deep lake is encircled by multicolored lava walls 500 to 2,000 feet high. The park provides excellent camping, fishing, and boating facilities. A wide assortment of wildlife, especially bird life, can be found in the area.

Mount Hood. Part of the Cascade Range, Mt. Hood is Oregon's highest mountain, rising 11,245 feet above sea level. The mountain is a summer recreational center and a winter ski resort. Timberline Lodge, located near the summit, is easily accessible by road. From this point spectacular views of the Willamette Valley may be had. The mountains of Oregon are excellent recreational areas for the outdoorsman.

Portland. The largest city in Oregon is on the Willamette River near its confluence with the Columbia River. Mount Hood, 45 miles to the east, dominates the horizon. Each June, Portland becomes the Kingdom of Rosaria for ten days during the rose festival. The rest of the year there are other attractions, notably the Portland Zoological Gardens, Hoyt Arboretum, golf courses, and 125 parks. The Scenic Parkway Drive gives an overall view of the valley and the surrounding area, passing many of Portland's points of interest.

Salem. About 40 miles south of Portland on the Willamette River is Salem, the state capital. The Capitol Mall, a complex of five buildings, dominates the city. Salem is also the seat of Willamette University. Farther south on the Willamette River is the University of Oregon at Eugene.

PENNSYLVANIA

Bethlehem. Bethlehem is eastern Pennsylvania's steel center. The Schwab Memorial Library in the Bethlehem Steel Office Building has an exhibit of the history of steelworks. Other points of interest in Bethlehem are the Gemein Haus, the city's oldest structure; the Kemerer Museum; and the Moravian Museum.

Gettysburg. The most famous battle of the Civil War was fought here July 1-3, 1863. Four months later President Lincoln returned to the scene and delivered his Gettysburg Address at the dedication of the National Cemetery commemorating the battle. There are a number of buildings in and near Gettysburg which explain the battle and its surrounding circumstances. The Electric Map in the Gettysburg National Museum uses audio-visual techniques to recreate the battle. The National Civil War Museum contains over 200 life-size wax figures of the Civil War era. Other buildings of interest are the Lincoln Room Museum, Jennie Wade House, General Lee's Headquarters, Fort Defiance Museum and Frontier Town, and the Hall of Presidents. There are bus tours of the battlefield itself, although a walking tour is favored by many. Tour guides highlight the area's most famous spots: Cemetery Hill, Seminary Ridge, the ground over

Portland Chamber of Commerce

Ecola State Park is located north of Cannon Beach on Oregon's 296-mile coast line. Oregon has 221 state parks in addition to Crater Lake National Park.

The Declaration of Independence was adopted on July 4, 1776, in Independence Hall in Philadelphia, Pennsylvania.

which Pickett's Charge was made, and Culp's Hill.

Harrisburg. Capital of Pennsylvania since 1812, Harrisburg is a steelmaking center. Its Capitol Building reflects Renaissance architecture. North of the Capitol is the William Penn Memorial Museum with its planetarium and exhibits of documents, natural history, and the arts. The old homes in Harrisburg include that of John Harris, the city's founder. Twelve miles east is Hershey, "Chocolate Town U.S.A." Other attractions in the area are the zoo, Rose Gardens and Arboretum, and facilities for a variety of sports. The Pennsylvania Dutch Days are celebrated annually in late summer.

Lancaster. South central Pennsylvania is the heart of the Pennsylvania Dutch country. In addition to the Pennsylvania Dutch restaurants, museums, and markets, Lancaster has many historical buildings such as Wheatland, the home of James Buchanan, and the Fulton Opera House, America's oldest operating theater. Also of interest in Lancaster County is the 18th-century restoration of the German protestant monastic settlement at Ephrata. Northeast is Kutztown, which holds an annual Folk Festival in early July. The festival has exhibits and demonstrations of arts and crafts, cookery, and other facets of Pennsylvania Dutch life.

Philadelphia. One of the nation's oldest cities, Philadelphia is second only to Boston in historical significance. Its biggest attraction and one of America's most meaningful shrines is Independence Hall, where the Declaration of Independence and the Constitution were signed and where the Liberty Bell is now preserved. The surrounding area has been designated Independence National Park. Other points of interest are the Betsy Ross House, William Penn House, Benjamin Franklin's grave at Christ Church, and Carpenters' Hall. Outdoor attractions include Fairmount Park with its restored colonial mansions; the zoological gardens; Robin Hood Dell where summer concerts are held; Liberty Bell

Park and trackway; Washington Square; and the port of Philadelphia on the Delaware River. Other points of interest are the new U.S. Mint, the Museum of Art, the Art Alliance, the Academy of Music, the Rodin Museum, the Franklin Institute, and the University of Pennsylvania, founded in 1740.

Pittsburgh. Once one of the country's smokiest cities, Pittsburgh has undergone massive urban renewal programs and is now one of America's most beautiful and progressive cities. The view from Mt. Washington overlooking the city is particularly exciting at night. There are many colleges and universities in the city including the University of Pittsburgh in the "Cathedral of Learning," the world's tallest school building; Carnegie Institute of Technology; and Chatham College; many have facilities open to the public. Fort Pitt Blockhouse, a museum depicting the country's early days, is in Point State Park on the Golden Triangle. All professional sports are represented, and spectators watch their favorite teams in the newly constructed Civic Arena. Highland Park has three zoos—the main zoo, the children's zoo, and an underground zoo.

Pocono Mountains. The Poconos in northeastern Pennsylvania are quickly becoming one of the favorite vacation areas of eastern U.S. Lakes and rivers provide opportunities for water sports while the resort towns provide facilities for other recreational activities. The low mountains are excellent for many outdoor sports, such as hiking and camping in the summer and skiing in the winter. More than a dozen parks and game lands are in the area.

RHODE ISLAND

Newport. Because of its reputation as a resort, Newport's historic importance is often overlooked. There are many historically significant buildings: the Colony House, a national landmark dating from 1739; and the great mansions Chateau-Sur-Mer, The Breakers, and The Elms. The city also contains the oldest synagogue in America, Touro Synagogue. Newport's 100

beaches cover over 400 miles of seashore and are some of the finest in the state. The city also has one of the largest naval bases in the world. Every summer, Newport invites the best jazz and folk music artists to two festivals, the Newport Jazz and the Newport Folk festivals.

Pawtucket. This was the home of Samuel Slater, the English mechanic who built from memory America's first spinning frame. The Old Slater Mill, birthplace of the American textile industry, is now a national landmark and museum with demonstrations of early techniques of the industry. Also of interest is the Daggett House, which features pewter, china, needlework, and other early relics of the Revolutionary War period.

Providence. Founded in 1636 by Roger Williams, Providence has been the state capital since the Revolution. The Old Statehouse is now maintained as a state museum. The new Capitol also contains some relics. Of interest in Providence are the many buildings from Revolutionary times and before, especially the John Brown House, which now houses the State Historical Society; the Providence Athenaeum, one of America's first private libraries; and the new Statehouse with its beautiful marble dome. More relics from the state's history are on display at Brown University, which offers tours of its campus.

SOUTH CAROLINA

Charleston. Although Charleston is now an important seaport, the city's most interesting sites reflect its historical prominence. The most significant site is old Fort Sumter on an island in Charleston Harbor. The Civil War began here as Confederate batteries bombarded the entrenched Union troops. The tiny island has a museum run by historians from the National Park Service who provide lectures and tours. Other attractions include the Boone Hall Plantation, the Old Slave Market Museum, and many beautiful pre-Revolutionary homes.

Columbia. The state capital, Columbia's

The Old Slater Mill in Pawtucket, Rhode Island, has been meticulously preserved. Built by Samuel Slater in 1793, it is the oldest cotton mill in the United States.

South Carolina Development Board

The Magnolia Gardens, near Charleston, South Carolina, are famous for both their native magnolias and azaleas, and for camellias and rare trees imported from Asia.

colorful history is reflected by such sites as the Statehouse; bombarded during the Civil War by General Sherman's troops, the building's scars are now marked by brass stars. Also of interest is President Wilson's boyhood home and articles associated with his life. Two of the city's landmarks are the Robert Mills Historic House and Park and the Boyleston House and Garden; the former is known for its architectural significance, and the latter for its private gardens. The University of South Carolina is one of the six colleges and universities in the area. Twenty miles northeast of Columbia is Camden, the oldest inland city of South Carolina. Camden was burned by the British in 1781, devastated by a fire in the early 1800's, and demolished by Federal troops during the Civil War.

Greenville. Although not really a resort, Greenville has the attractions of one. Professional and college sports abound all year round and there are excellent areas for hunting, fishing, camping, and hiking. Greenville's cultural life is enhanced by the internationally famous art gallery and museum at Bob Jones University. Nearby is Spartanburg, a large and diversified industrial town. It is the seat of Converse College as well as a regional campus of the University of South Carolina. The Spartanburg area was the scene of eleven major battles during the Revolutionary War. Nearby, in the Blue Ridge Mountains, is a popular recreation site.

SOUTH DAKOTA

Badlands National Monument. Barren buttes, pinnacles, and gorges cut by millions of years of erosion form the Badlands of South Dakota, an area in the western part of the state, southeast of Rapid City. The formations change color from pale gold to red and gold as the sun moves across the horizon. There are good roads through the area. Archaeologists have uncovered numerous fossils in the monument, many of which are on display. Rapid City College has a large exhibit of fossils and information on prehistoric inhabitants of the Badlands.

Black Hills. The Black Hills National Forest is best known for its Mount Rush-

more National Memorial. The 465-foot heads of Washington, Jefferson, Lincoln, and Theodore Roosevelt were carved from the mountainside and reflect the sun's rays most of the day. Southwest is the Crazy Horse Monument, an entire mountain being carved by Korczak Ziolkowski; it will hold the riding figure of Crazy Horse, chief of the Sioux. Mt. Rushmore National Memorial borders on Custer State Park, a 60,000-acre area encompassing three lakes and noted not only for its herds of bison, deer, and elk, but also its zoo, museum, and Black Hills Playhouse. To the north is Deadwood, where Wild Bill Hickok was killed. Each night during the summer, the town puts on a show depicting the story of his death. Also commemorated are the July, 1876, gold rush days of Deadwood. Just outside the Black Hills near Spearfish is the scenic Spearfish Canyon. A production of the 700-year-old passion play depicting the last days of Christ is held each year in Spearfish.

Sioux Falls. The largest city in the state is located in southeastern South Dakota on the Big Sioux River. It is a pros-

Chicago and North Western Railway

Each face carved in granite is 60–70 feet high in the Mount Rushmore National Memorial, in the Black Hills of South Dakota.

perous city with beautiful parks and homes and such attractions as the Great Plains Zoo and the Dennis the Menace Park nearby. There are other recreational facilities at the Palisades and Dells of the Sioux River. Farther north, near Madison, is Prairie Village, a replica of a frontier town of the 1890's. Actual buildings and farm machinery of that era have been assembled here through the efforts of the Prairie Historical Society.

TENNESSEE

Chattanooga. Many Civil War battles were fought in the Chattanooga area. Civil War buffs can visit the battle sites of Chickamauga, Chattanooga, Orchard Knob, Lookout Mountain, and Missionary Ridge. There is also the Confederama which re-creates battles with toy soldiers and special effects. From the summit of Lookout Mountain, one gets excellent views of Lake Chickamauga and the Tennessee River. The Lookout Mountain Caverns, among the major caverns in the state, are also a worthwhile attraction.

Chickamauga and Chattanooga National Military Park. This national military park is located in Georgia and Tennessee. It includes the Civil War battlefields of Chickamauga, Orchard Knob, Lookout Mountain, and Missionary Ridge of the Chattanooga Campaign. Established in 1890, the park is maintained by the National Park Service.

Great Smoky Mountains. These scenic mountains in the Blue Ridge section of eastern Tennessee and western North Carolina derive their name from the smoke-like haze covering the many mile-high peaks. Favorite spots in the Great Smoky Mountains National Park are Mt. LeConte, Chimney Tops, Newfound Gap, and Clingman's Dome, Tennessee's highest spot named for Thomas Clingman who first explored the area in the mid-1800's. Hardwood and evergreen forests, rhododendron and mountain laurel shrubs, and many kinds of wildflowers cover the slopes; bears, turkey, and deer abound. Within the park are facilities for horseback riding, swimming, camping, hiking, fishing, and in the winter, skiing.

Knoxville. Once the state capital, Knoxville is now a center for sports, recreation, and education. The city is located on the Tennessee River and thus provides easy access to the vast recreational facilities of the lakes and dams of the Tennessee Valley Authority. A popular tourist attraction is the spring Dogwood Festival. Knoxville is also the home of the University of Tennessee. Other points of interest include the Market Square Mall, the Oak Ridge Atomic Energy Museum, and the Blount Mansion, home of the first governor of the Southwest Territory.

Memphis. Located on the Mississippi River, Memphis is not only Tennessee's largest city, but also its commercial, industrial, and transportation center. It is one of the world's leading hardwood lumber and cotton markets. Each May visitors are attracted to the Cotton Carnival, a festive occasion dedicated to the area's king crop. Also of interest are the modern replicas of steamboats which make short trips to

Tennessee Valley Authority

The Norris Dam on the Clinch River in eastern Tennessee was the first dam to be constructed by the Tennessee Valley Authority. It was completed in 1936.

nearby river spots. The Mississippi River and Lake McKeller provide facilities for numerous water sports. Other attractions are a zoo and the Brooks Memorial Art Gallery located in Overton Park.

Nashville. Although the neoclassical Capitol Building and the statuary are great favorites, they are not the only attractions of the state's second largest city. Artistic and intellectual interests are served by the Parthenon, a full-scale reproduction of the temple in Athens; Cheekwood Botanical Gardens and Fine Arts Center; and many college and university campuses. Among the latter are Vanderbilt and Fisk universities and George Peabody College for Teachers. Nashville is also the Country and Western music capital. At the head of Record Row is the Country Music Hall of Fame. The Grand Ole Opry is located in Nashville, and tours are available of the Opry stars' homes. Nashville is also a historical city where tourists can visit Andrew Jackson's Hermitage, 12 miles from the city; and Fort Nashborough, a reproduction of the stockade which protected the early settlers. Other points of interest are the State Museum; Traveller's Rest, built in 1792 by John Overton, the founder of Memphis; and Belle Meade Mansion, an outstanding example of Greek Revival architecture and site of one of the first thoroughbred horse-breeding farms in the United States.

TEXAS

Austin. Originally settled in 1838 as Waterloo, the capital of the Texas republic, it was renamed Austin in 1839 in honor of Stephen F. Austin, a leader in the colonization of Texas. It became the permanent capital of the state of Texas in 1870. The Capitol complex is dominated by one of the largest capitol buildings in the United States. The architecture is classically southern; the rooms contain antique furniture and items of historical significance. Also located in Austin is the main campus of the University of Texas. Fifty miles west of the city is the LBJ Ranch, home of former president Lyndon B. Johnson.

Big Bend National Park. This national park is located in the great bend of the Rio Grande River on the border of Texas and Mexico. It is full of magnificent mountain and desert scenery and various types of geologic formations. The park contains a variety of indigenous plants and animal life. Also of interest are the trails leading to Juniper Flat, the South Rim, and the Widow; particularly scenic are Bouquillas and Santa Elena canyons. There are also facilities for camping, hiking, and horseback riding.

Corpus Christi. The focal point for most visitors is the marina with its resort facilities and amusements. The city is also an important seaport and cultural center. Offshore is the Padre Island National Seashore, an 80-mile natural shoreline preserve located on Padre Island.

Dallas. Although the city started as one cabin built in 1841 near the present county courthouse lawn, Dallas is now a cultural center known for its symphony halls, theaters, art galleries, and museums. Also of interest are the Hall of State, Southern Methodist University, and the Marsalis Zoo. Another attraction is the Dallas Theater Center, the only theater designed by Frank Lloyd Wright. In addition, the city's excellent climate makes outdoor entertainment a popular activity. The Dallas Cowboys, a professional football team, play in the Cotton Bowl Stadium, and the Spurs, a minor league baseball team, play in Turnpike Stadium. State Fair Park, nearby, is the home of the largest state exposition in the country; it includes an aquarium, Cotton Bowl Stadium, Garden Center, and several museums.

El Paso. One of the oldest towns in west Texas, El Paso is the home of many Spanish missions, some older than the famous California missions. Because it is the largest of the border cities, it is an important trade center. However, the greatest attraction of El Paso is its international atmosphere emphasized by bilingual traffic signs and advertisements. Just across the Rio Grande is Juarez, which adds the flavor of Mexico to the varied life-style of El Paso. Along the border to the southeast are the Quitman, Vieja, and Chinati mountains.

Fort Worth. Although an important livestock center, Fort Worth is also a leading manufacturer of aircraft, boats, mobile homes, and candy. Of interest in the city are the Will Rogers Memorial Museum, the Nobel Planetarium, and Texas Christian University. Culturally, the city is served by the Fort Worth Art Center, the Amon Carter Museum of Western Art, and the Fort Worth Opera and Symphony. Nearby, at Arlington, is Six Flags Over Texas, a family entertainment complex and historical display center.

Houston. Texas' largest city has become one of the finest cultural and resort centers in the South. It is also a major port, having access to the Gulf via the Houston Ship Channel. There are many parks and monuments in the city; among them are Sam Houston National Forest, San Jacinto Battleground State Park, and Hermann Park with its zoo, gardens, and amphitheater. Adjacent to the zoo is a reminder of the city's role in the scientific world, the Texas Medical Center. Twenty miles outside of

Texas Highway Department

The Alamo, in Texas, was the site of the last stand by a group of Texans in their fight for independence from Mexico in 1836.

Houston is the Manned Spacecraft Center of the National Aeronautics and Space Administration. NASA has a museum in the center which is open to the public a few hours each day. Other attractions in Houston include the Museum of Fine Arts and the Contemporary Arts Museum. Rice University is one of Houston's many institutions of higher learning. A popular tourist attraction is the Astrodome, America's largest enclosed stadium, home of the Houston Astros baseball team and the National Football League Houston Oilers. It is also used for boxing matches and other sporting events, and for conventions.

San Antonio. Of all the historical landmarks in the Southwest, San Antonio's Alamo is probably the best known. It was originally the chapel of a mission founded in 1718. In 1836, 187 Americans, using it as a fortress, held Santa Anna's Mexican army at bay for 13 days before being overrun. The Spanish heritage is preserved in La Villita (the little village), the famous San Jose Mission, and the Paseo del Rio (the river walk), an art and recreational center. In contrast to its old-world charm are the modern features of the state's third largest city. Brackenridge Park holds one of the nation's largest zoos and the lovely Chinese Gardens. St. Mary's and Trinity universities lie within the city. Annual rodeos, festivals, and musical performances are popular. Huge military centers are in the area.

UTAH

Bryce Canyon National Park. Bryce Canyon's 14 horseshoe-shaped amphitheaters comprise the 55-square-mile park located in southwestern Utah, 275 miles south of Salt Lake City. Eroded limestone formations of every conceivable shape fill these amphitheaters with imaginary temples and castles. The pinks, reds, and oranges of the pinnacles change with the moving sun. A highway along the rim of the plateau above leads to Rainbow Point; it passes by 12 scenic viewing areas which have trails leading to the canyon floor below. Although the campgrounds and other accommodations are closed for the winter by early October, the major viewing areas

Utah Tourist and Publicity Council

Queen's Castle, in Bryce Canyon National Park in Utah, is one of many erosion-produced rock formations in the area.

and the visitor center are open all year. Campgrounds and rooms can be found nearby.

Salt Lake City. Salt Lake City is a cultural and commercial metropolis located at the foot of the Wasatch Mountains in the Great Salt Lake Valley. Brigham Young founded the city in 1847 for his Mormon followers who were unwelcome in other areas of the country. It became the state capital when Utah was admitted to the Union in 1896. Weekday tours of the Capitol Building include the rotunda, exhibition hall, gold room, and the third floor Senate, House, and Supreme Court Chambers. Nearby are Capitol Hill Park and the Mormon Battalion Monument. A few blocks south is Temple Square and the famous Mormon Temple and Tabernacle. Although the Temple is not open to the public, the Tabernacle is. Built from native timber, the Tabernacle has a fine 11,000-pipe organ which is used for organ and

choir concerts and recitals. The Tabernacle Choir is one of the most respected choral groups in the world. Other attractions in the Temple Square area are the Assembly Hall, the unique Seagull Monument, and the Church Museum. Also nearby are Beehive House, which was Brigham Young's home, Hansen Planetarium, Liberty Park, and the Salt Lake Art Center. A few miles west is the Great Salt Lake, remarkable for its saline content. Once a deep prehistoric lake covering a vast area, it has since receded to form the Great Salt Lake Desert and the Bonneville Salt Flats, an unusually level stretch of terrain famous for world land-speed records.

Zion National Park. The colorful, deep, narrow canyons and rock masses in this area were formed by erosion and faulting patterns which in turn created phenomenal shapes and landscapes. Zion Canyon is an awe-inspiring, vertically walled chasm. Formerly, there was volcanic activity in this area. Zion's 155 miles of trails pass numerous masses of rock formations, many named by the Mormons: Great White Throne, Three Patriarchs, Checkerboard Mesa, and others. The Mount Carmel Highway passes through a mile-long tunnel blasted from solid granite. Large windows cut in the tunnel's sides frame the spectacular views.

VERMONT

Bennington. Three villages make up the Bennington area complex. Old Bennington has a Revolutionary War center, with an obelisk commemorating the war. Nearby is the site where John Stark won the Battle of Bennington. Just south is a monument on the site of the Old Catamount Tavern where Ethan Allen planned to seize Fort Ticonderoga. Bennington Village, a center for both crafts and industry, has a museum of early American artifacts. Bennington College, a pioneer among independent study institutions, is in North Bennington. The town is also the home of Cushman Colonial furniture, whose products are exhibited in the family's stone mansion. Farther north is Manchester and the Southern Vermont Art Center.

Burlington. Vermont's largest city is located on Lake Champlain. Formerly an important lumber port, today it is the cultural center of the area; the University of Vermont, Trinity College, and Champlain College contain numerous museums and host concerts, public lectures, and dramatic performances. Less than 150 miles east of the city in the Green Mountain range is Stowe, a ski resort on the slopes of Mt. Mansfield. Horseback riding, golf, tennis, and hiking are as popular as winter skiing. The Green Mountains, which extend the length of the state, were the home of Ethan Allen and his Green Mountain Boys of the Revolution in New England.

Montpelier. Built on hills, Montpelier is recognized from miles away by the State Capitol's gold dome. The Vermont Historical Society Museum is filled with objects from the settlement days. Within the Supreme Court Building is the State Library. Wood Gallery of Art was established by the Vermont artist Thomas W. Wood. The National Life Insurance Company headquarters overlooks the city and provides free tours, movies, and lectures on Vermont.

VIRGINIA

Arlington–Alexandria. Just across from the nation's capital on the west side of the Potomac River is Arlington National Cemetery; its scores of white crosses mark the graves of men who died in the country's defense. Also in the cemetery are the graves of Robert F. and John F. Kennedy, the Tomb of the Unknown Soldier, and the Custis-Lee Mansion. There are many old buildings in the Alexandria area. The favorite is Mt. Vernon, George Washington's home for many years. Others are Gunston Hall, Woodlawn, and Pohick Church.

Charlottesville. Thomas Jefferson took 35 years building his home near Charlottesville. When he was through, he had created Monticello, one of the nation's greatest architectural achievements. It is ingenious in its gadgetry and beautiful in its design. In the city is one of Jefferson's favorite creations—the University of Virginia. He designed the buildings, and as

Vermont Development Department

Skiing facilities are excellent at Mount Mansfield, the highest peak in the Green Mountains of Vermont. The area contains some of the leading ski resorts in New England.

Virginia Department of Conservation and Development

The view from the Peaks of Otter, a scenic point overlooking the Blue Ridge Parkway near Bedford, Virginia, is unobstructed for almost 100 miles in every direction.

the school's first rector, he set the high standards that are still maintained. In the vicinity are Michie Tavern, where the waltz was introduced to Virginia; and Ash Lawn, home of James Monroe.

Fredericksburg. Fredericksburg was the site of a major Civil War battle in which the city changed hands several times; it was finally retained by the Confederate troops under General Longstreet until the close of the Civil War. This battlefield and that of Chancellorsville are now historic national military parks where Civil War buffs can retrace the battles. Nearby is the house where Stonewall Jackson died, and the law office of James Monroe.

Newport News–Hampton. Newport News, one of the ports on Hampton Roads in southwest Virginia, is the home of the world's largest privately owned shipyard, the Newport News Shipbuilding and Dry Dock Center. It is also the home of America's largest naval installation, the Norfolk Naval Station. The area has many naval and maritime museums including the Mariners Museum and the War Memorial Museum. Just south is the east coast surfing capital, Virginia Beach.

Williamsburg–Jamestown. Located in southeastern Virginia between the James and York rivers is Williamsburg, the most ambitious colonial restoration in America. The reconstruction of the city began in 1927; today 83 original 18th-century structures stand restored, and 48 major colonial buildings have been rebuilt on their original sites. These structures include the Capitol, meeting place of the Virginia Assembly; the Raleigh Tavern, center of pre-Revolutionary political activity; and the Burton Parish Church, one of the oldest Protestant Episcopal churches in America. Williamsburg is also the site of William and Mary College; the school's original building is the oldest college building still in use in the United States. At the west end

of the city are many restored craft shops where the work of 18th-century artisans is demonstrated. Costumed craftsmen explain their work to visitors.

Ten miles south of Williamsburg is the island Jamestown, site of the first permanent English settlement in America. Most of the area is included in the Colonial National Historical Park. The tower from the Jamestown Church and the old cemetery are two of the few remaining relics in Jamestown.

Richmond. Since 1779 Richmond has been the capital of the Commonwealth of Virginia, the Confederacy, and now the state of Virginia. In 1865, during the final evacuation before the oncoming Federal forces, the citizens set fire to their own city; the flames, however, missed some of the most famous structures which are preserved today. One of these is St. John's Church where Patrick Henry delivered his

famous speech which included the lines "Give me liberty or give me death." The White House of the Confederacy, once the home of Jefferson Davis, has a museum of relics from the Civil War. The Capitol Building also hosts a museum and displays the only statue of George Washington made during his lifetime. Throughout the city there are many statues of notables from Virginia and the Confederacy. At Richmond Battlefield Park visitors can relive the maneuvers of Lee and Grant, and McClellan and Jackson during their Civil War battles. Richmond is now one of the most progressive cities in the South; its Museum of Fine Arts pioneered mobile galleries to carry exhibits throughout the state.

Shenandoah Valley. Called "Daughter of the Stars" by the Indians, the valley is one of the most beautiful places in the state. There are specific attractions in the mountains: battlefield parks, McCormick's farm where the reaper was invented, apple blossom festivals, many caverns, and the Virginia Military Institute at Lexington. The real attraction of the area, however, is the scenery. Skyline Drive runs along the ridge of the Blue Ridge Mountains, surrounded by Shenandoah National Park, which has facilities for camping, fishing, hiking, and other outdoor amusements.

WASHINGTON

Grand Coulee Dam. Northwest of Spokane on the Columbia River is the Grand Coulee Dam, the world's largest concrete dam. It has converted a large portion of the river into a reservoir and has helped irrigate acres of farmland as well as provide electrical power for the state.

Mount Rainier National Park. Mt. Rainier is a 14,410-foot high dormant volcano. Its craterlike summit is a favorite goal of climbers. The greatest single-peak glacial system in the United States originates from its summit and slopes. It is an excellent ski area. The peak is snow-covered throughout the year. There are guided tours of the peak and the nearby glaciers and caves.

Olympia. The capital city is at the

Union Pacific Railroad

Mount Rainier, rising 14,410 feet in the Cascade Range southeast of Tacoma, is the highest peak in the state of Washington. The mountain peak is a dormant volcano.

southern end of Puget Sound, gateway to the Olympic Peninsula. The State Legislative building is the center of a large Capitol complex which contains 17 state buildings. On the peninsula is a large recreational area, Olympic National Park. The park in the Olympic Mountains is a wilderness preserve with rain forests, wildlife, and glaciers.

Seattle. Seattle is a seaport and home of the University of Washington. The Seattle Center, near Puget Sound, is a concentration of amusements and cultural facilities, including the Space Needle, Opera House, and Coliseum. A monorail leads to the Center from downtown. Cruises and tours of the docks and the surrounding waterfront are a sightseeing adventure. Along the salt-water strip one may find shops with imports from the Far East as well as restaurants specializing in seafood. The city's aquarium has killer whales and other sea animals. The old section of Seattle, which was destroyed by fire in 1889, has since been rebuilt on higher ground. Many storefronts still exist underground and can be seen on the Underground Tour. Lake Washington borders the city on the east. Along its western shore are lakefront parks with facilities for water sports. Seattle is also a starting point for tours of the surrounding areas of Mt. Rainier, the Cascade Range, Olympic Peninsula, and the San Juan Islands.

WEST VIRGINIA

Charleston. The state capital, located on the Kanawha River and at the mouth of the Elk River, is the state's industrial center. Dominating the city is the Capitol Building, with its 300-foot high dome. Included in the Capitol complex are the state museum, and the Stonewall Jackson and Pioneer monuments. Sunrise, an estate containing two restored mansions, is

ers, Harpers Ferry played an important role in the Civil War. Harpers Ferry National Historic Park, scene of John Brown's raid in 1859, is located here. A monument marks the site where John Brown met final defeat; nearby is the place where he was hanged. The engine house, known as John Brown's Fort, now contains a museum; it is located on the Storer College campus.

Huntington. This city, 30 miles west of Charleston, is the home of one of the state's biggest glassmaking plants. There are six plants which offer tours of their facilities; visitors can watch the art of glass blowing as it has been done for centuries.

WISCONSIN

Madison. Madison is both the state capital and the home of the University of Wisconsin. The State Building, known for its dome which is second in height only to that of the White House, has an observation platform near the top which provides an excellent view of the lakes in the surrounding area. The University of Wisconsin, one of the nation's ten largest, borders on Lake Mendota. Many of its facilities are open to the public. Other points of interest in Madison are the World Shrine of Our Lady of the Green Scapular, the U. S. Forest Products Laboratory, and the Vilas Park zoo. In the vicinity are Cave of the Mounds and the Aztalan Historical-Memorial Park with its stockade and Indian mounds.

Milwaukee and Environs. Milwaukee, strategically located on Lake Michigan, is known to millions as the beer capital of the United States. Some of the country's largest breweries are found here and offer daily tours through their facilities. The city is known for its German cuisine. The Public Museum, the new Public Museum of Science and Industry, the Milwaukee Art

the finest in the country. Fifty-five miles north of Milwaukee is Sheboygan, a shipping center and also noted for the production of bratwurst, spices, and herbs. Southwest of Milwaukee is the popular resort area of Lake Geneva, with its many fine estates and sailboat races. At Williams Bay stands Yerkes Astronomical Observatory, operated by the University of Chicago. Northwest of Milwaukee are the resort areas of Lake Winnebago, Fond du Lac, and Door County.

Northwoods Country. This name is applied to the counties in north-central Wisconsin which border on Michigan's

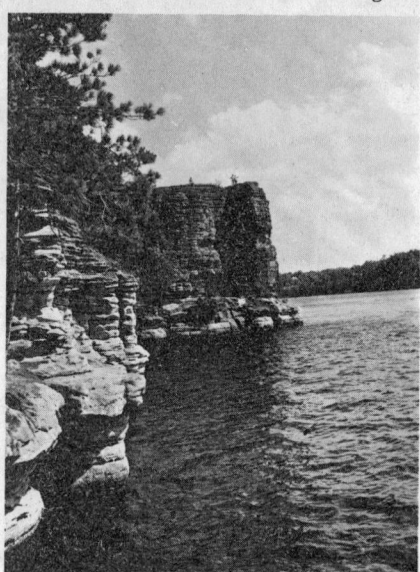
Wisconsin Conservation Department

The Wisconsin Dells is a gorge that was cut into the sandstone when glaciers dammed the Wisconsin River a million years ago.

Upper Peninsula. Rhinelander is the southern gateway to the area which abounds in lakes, streams, and forests. Long a popular region of summer resorts, it has become a year-round recreation center because of improved accessibility. In winter, the sports of skiing and snowmobiling draw many visitors to the area.

Wisconsin Dells. The Dells is an area of beautiful rock and cliff formations along the Wisconsin River. The Upper Dells are best viewed from both land and water; boat rides are available. The Lower Dells can be seen on a one-hour boat ride. Other attractions in the Dells are the Storybook Gardens and the Tommy Bartlett Water Show. Baraboo is 13 miles south. For many years the home of the Ringling Brothers Circus, it now has the Circus World Museum which offers special shows about life in the circus. A few miles farther is Devil's Lake State Park. Glaciers which cut the lake left many unusual geological formations, notably Devil's Doorway, Turk's Head, The Needle, and Ancient Rock.

WYOMING

Cheyenne. Cheyenne, an important trade and transportation center, draws much of its wealth from the cattle industry. The city is world-famous for the rodeos, which are held every July during the Frontier Days celebration. Points of inter-

West Virginia Conservation Commission

The New River winds through Grandview State Park in West Virginia. The state's spectacular scenery and its many mineral springs attract a million visitors each year.

of interest to visitors; one of the mansions is occupied by the Children's Museum and Planetarium.

Harpers Ferry. Situated at the confluence of the Potomac and Shenandoah riv-

Center, and the Allis Art Library enhance Milwaukee's cultural life. Recreational facilities are available at the many fine parks, at the professional sporting events, and at the Milwaukee County Zoo, one of

Union Pacific Railroad

The majestic Teton Peaks tower above the mountain valley of Jackson Hole, formed by the winding Snake River in Grand Teton National Park in northwestern Wyoming.

est are the Capitol Building; Frontier Park; Fort Warren; Holliday Park, where Cheyenne of 100 years ago is recreated; and the State Historical Museum, which contains exhibits of Wyoming frontier history.

Devil's Tower National Monument. Designated by President Theodore Roosevelt in 1906 as the country's first national monument, Devil's Tower is an 865-foot volcanic neck, formed about 50 million years ago. In the surrounding area are the Black Hills National Forest and Keyhole State Park, both of which provide year-round facilities for hunting, camping, boating, and fishing.

Grand Teton National Park. The series of peaks comprising the most impressive part of the Teton range makes up Grand Teton National Park. In earlier days, these beautiful grey-blue, snow-capped peaks were a noted landmark for the Indians. Grand Teton Park, the Snake River, and Jackson Lake are excellent places to fish, boat, ski, and sail. The park is open all year, but the guest ranches, lodges, cabins, and campgrounds are open only during the summer. A point of interest is the Church of the Transfiguration. The surrounding Jackson Hole country is an excellent resort area.

Yellowstone National Park. Yellowstone is the first and largest of the country's national parks. It is the world's greatest geyser area, with about 3,000 geysers and hot springs. Old Faithful Geyser, which erupts every hour, is a major attraction. Others erupting less regularly are Grand Geyser, Grotto, Little Cub, Daisy, and Jewel. The park is rich in wildlife; the bears which roam the park freely provide memorable entertainment. Also of interest are the waterfalls and the Grand Canyon of Yellowstone, both products of the Yellowstone River and easily accessible by roads and trails. Facilities are available for lodging or camping within the park; the surrounding area has many other accommodations.

GUAM

Since the disastrous typhoons of 1962 and 1963, Guam has become a tourist mecca. With 90 percent of the housing and industry destroyed, the government came to regard the beaches and subtropical climate as the major asset of the island and began a program to develop tourism.

Several cultures have intermingled on Guam for many years. Still visible around the island are ruins of the Chamorros, the island's first inhabitants. Agana, the capital, resembles a modern U.S. community. Old Agana was completely destroyed during the reoccupation of the island by American Forces in 1944. The island villages are quite picturesque. Recreational activities on the island include legalized cockfights and other gambling games, fiestas, and a 50-mile trip around the island. Because Guam is duty-free, prices of foreign goods are quite attractive to tourists. Bargains from Japan and Hong Kong are found in most shops and stores in the cities.

Guam is one of the important military bases of the United States in the Pacific; the island's economy is based primarily on employment on military installations. Agriculture is the other important element in the economy.

PUERTO RICO

Puerto Rico's balmy climate, natural beaches, and blue skies make tourism its richest natural resource. Its potential became evident with the building of the Caribe Hilton in 1950. The hotel's success induced other private investors to develop resort facilities on the island. Puerto Rico's hotels have increased their capacity by 3,200 rooms since 1950. Experts estimate that five times that number will be needed by 1980 to accommodate the increasing numbers of visitors. Many hotels have been built in cities around the island: large hotels in San Juan, Dorado, and Fajardo, and smaller ones in Mayaquez and Ponce.

The major cities are resort areas. All are on the seashore and occupy only a small part of the hundreds of miles of ocean front. Some of the areas are highly developed; others are completely deserted. Puerto Rican law has made all beaches public land; the most famous are those near San Juan and Luquillo. The steady, high waves have made surfing one of the most popular sports on the island. The beaches near Mayaquez were chosen as the site of the 1968 world surfing championships. Deep-sea fishing facilities are provided at Mayaquez, San Juan, Fajardo, and Ponce. Inland, there are many freshwater streams and pools which are beautiful but dangerous. Swimming in them is

Delta Air Lines

An old fortress, San Geronimo, in San Juan, Puerto Rico, now stands amid a modern luxury hotel district. San Juan has one of the largest harbors in the West Indies.

not recommended because they are infested with a parasitic blood fluke genus *Schistosoma*, harmful to man. The other main inland attractions are the mountain coffee plantations above Utado and the ruins of the Taino Indian culture.

The main historic sites in Puerto Rico are the Spanish forts which protected the settlers from the Carib Indians first, then the privateers, and then the enemies of Spain in the New World. El Morro and San Christobal are now maintained by rangers from the National Park Service. A smaller fort, San Geronimo, is maintained as a military history museum. Old San Juan is a seven-block-square area enclosed by Spanish walls, offering visitors a glimpse of the colonial life in Puerto Rico. San Germán in the southwest is a well-preserved colonial settlement; its Porta Coeli Museum of religious art is the focus of interest.

The island's 350 years of Spanish rule are most evident in its night life. The most popular attractions are the flamenco dance shows and guitarists, the Latin combos and jazz musicians, and Mexican and Puerto Rican songfests. Some clubs offer a discotheque atmosphere and contemporary shows with rock groups and electric light shows.

The tourist trade annually brings over 200 million dollars to Puerto Rico and directly provides 15,000 jobs for Puerto Ricans; other jobs are created by the construction of future tourist facilities. The economic development program, Operation Bootstrap, inaugurated in the 1940's, has helped the island make great strides in its industrial and agricultural expansion. Extensive urban renewal projects have also bolstered the economy.

VIRGIN ISLANDS OF THE U.S.

Lying in the Caribbean, the Virgin Islands are a subtropical paradise. Numbering over 50 islands or keys in all, those of St. Croix, St. Thomas, and St. John are the largest. The annual average temperature is in the high 70's, the same as Hawaii's. Although the islands lie in the hurricane belt of the Atlantic, modern forecasting techniques have eliminated most of the danger. Their proximity to the United States mainland has made them a popular, easily accessible, winter vacation spot. Many tourists are now recognizing their value as a summer resort, for the differences here between the seasons are very slight. The official language is English, and American money, postage, and other conventions are used.

The greatest attraction of the Virgin Islands are the beaches. There are miles of developed and natural beaches. The best are usually found around the cities, but most bays and inlets which ring the islands also have excellent beaches. Magens Bay on the north side of St. Thomas has one of the ten most beautiful beaches in the world. The sparkling white sands and clear water provide excellent facilities for swimming, sailing, water-skiing, and snorkeling. Game fishing is popular, and charter boats set out daily to the surrounding waters for record-size game fish. Other popular outdoor activities are tennis, baseball, and basketball.

Although St. Croix is flat, St. Thomas and St. John are fairly mountainous. They

Farley Manning Association, Inc.

The harbor at Charlotte Amalie, St. Thomas, U.S. Virgin Islands, with its duty-free bargains and picturesque scenery, is the busiest cruise port in the Carribean Sea.

rise from the same plateau, and their peaks reach up 1,500 feet above sea level, offering an excellent view of the countryside.

There are several cities which are of particular interest. Christiansted on St. Croix dates from the early days of the Danish occupation. Fort Christiansted is now a National Historic Site, a fine example of early Danish military architecture. The Steeple Building which was previously a church, a bakery, a hospital, and a school, is now a museum. Government House was once the seat of the Danish government and the home of the Danish governors. Its Grand Ballroom is furnished with Danish antiques, a gift from Denmark. Other buildings in the Danish style are preserved, and many house shops stock merchandise from all over the world. Fredericksted, a picturesque city on western St. Croix, is best known for the Whim estate a few miles away. The Whim Greathouse is of classic 18th-century design; it houses collections of furniture, china, and other artifacts which date back to its plantation days. Charlotte Amalie on St. Thomas is the territorial capital. The hilltops surrounding St. Thomas harbor and Charlotte Amalie offer spectacular views of the adjacent islands. The harbor, sidewalk cafes, and seaplane rides are other attractions. The main feature on St. John is the Virgin Islands National Park which comprises two-thirds of this island. St. John has no airport and no industry; the beach is its main attraction. Tektite II, the laboratory habitat of aquanauts engaged in an underwater exploration program, is anchored on the bottom of Lameshur Bay, St. John.

Although the Carib Indians and the Spanish were here for many years, only occasional historical structures are found. The most famous is La Fortaleza, a fort built to protect settlers from Carib attacks. Most historical sites are of Danish origin. Annaberg, on St. John, is a good example. A plantation and factory for the production of sugar, molasses, and rum remains almost intact. During the 1700's over 100 plantations and 20 factories were built. However, the abolition of slavery in 1848 precipitated a decline in the plantation industry. Ruins of the Danish plantation system remain on the islands.

Native entertainment offers the most popular night life. Clubs, cafes, and restaurants feature Latin dancing, limbo, calypso singers, and Latin combos. The favorite instrument is the pan, improvised from an oil drum and played with mallets. There are also contemporary music and modern film and stage theaters.

While tourism is an important industry here, it is not as crucial as in some other territories. The main crop of the Virgin Islands is sugar cane. It is slowly becoming less profitable, however, and the flatlands of St. Croix are being used more and more for cattle grazing, which has become the Islands' second leading industry. This uses most of the arable land, so the agriculture industry is decreasing; what little remains is mostly in vegetables and fruits. The biggest use for the sugar cane grown here is in the rum for which the area is famous. A few small businesses have plants here, taking advantage of its duty-free status.

LAW
FOR THE
LAYMAN

A Concise Encyclopedia

Edited by
Hugo Sonnenschein
LL.B., LL.M., J.D.

Edited by
Hugo Sonnenschein, LL.B, LL.M., J.D.

Mr. Sonnenschein is a member of the Illinois and Federal Bars and is a practicing attorney in Chicago. He is past Editor of The Chicago Bar Record *and has taught Labor Law at Lake Forest College. He has contributed articles on law and economics in various legal and commercial journals.*

LAW FOR THE LAYMAN
A Concise Encyclopedia

INTRODUCTION

The law touches almost every aspect of modern life. Every worker has certain legal rights regarding his employment and certain responsibilities he must fulfill. In buying a home, a car, or a toy for a child, each person has certain rights that are guaranteed to him. Whether driving to work, moving to another state, or traveling to a foreign country, the citizen is protected by the law. In order to function effectively in modern society, each citizen needs a basic understanding of his rights and responsibilities before the law.

The laws of the United States of America have a dual foundation. The Constitution provides an outline of the rights guaranteed to every citizen. The common law establishes, in a large measure, the rules and regulations under which we live. The *common law* is a body of law and jurisprudence that was originated, developed, and formulated in England prior to the settlement of North America. It has become the basis of the law in most of the United States. The common law records legal decisions that serve as precedents to be followed in cases of the same general nature.

From this foundation the law is constantly changing, growing to meet the needs of an expanding society. Laws may be changed in two ways: by statute, or by court decision. A legislature may pass new laws, called *statutes,* to deal with modern problems. Workmen's compensation, social security, and antitrust laws were created in this way. Or, where statutes or legal precedents do not offer clear guidelines, the court makes its decision by interpreting the earlier law to fit a new situation.

In cases involving similar facts, of course, the courts are bound by precedents, and the lower courts are bound by decisions of the higher courts. The federal courts in a particular state must follow the decisions of the supreme and appellate courts of that state, except in cases involving the interpretation of the Constitution and laws of the United States or on questions that are purely procedural. The courts in one state are not bound by the decisions of a court in another state. Of course a common law decision may be set aside by statute, or modified when it no longer applies to present conditions.

There are four main classes of courts in each of the states. The first are the courts that have jurisdiction over petty criminal offenses and in which minor suits are brought. Second, there are the courts of general jurisdiction, in which more important suits are brought. Next are the appellate courts, and finally there is the state supreme court, or court of last resort, which reviews decisions of lower courts.

Of course, the judicial system varies widely in the different states. For example, the 1971 Constitution of the State of Illinois provides that "the judicial power is vested in a Supreme Court, an Appellate Court, and Circuit Courts. Circuit Courts ... have original jurisdiction of all judicial matters except where the Supreme Court has original and exclusive jurisdiction ...." The larger counties of the state divide the circuit court into various divisions—chancery, criminal, county, divorce, juvenile, laws and probate—to hear special types of cases. Cities over a certain size have municipal courts with jurisdiction over cases confined to the city.

There are three classes of federal courts. The lowest is called the District Court, taking its name from the fact that the country as a whole is divided into districts, with one court for each district. Next is the Circuit Court of Appeals, to which appeals from the District Court are taken. And finally, there is the United States Supreme Court, in which appeals may be sought from decisions of the courts of appeal, of the supreme courts of the several states and, in certain criminal cases, directly from decisions of the Federal District Courts.

Upon application made in proper form, an appeals court decides whether or not it will review a particular case. A court will review the decision of a lower court only if the application is founded on errors in the former proceedings. For example, the proof of wrongful admission of evidence or of refusal to admit proper evidence in the former trial would be sufficient to obtain a hearing.

Evidence includes all means and ways by which the truth of an alleged fact is established or disproved. *Direct evidence* is the testimony of a witness or of written documents and records that are competent, relevant, and material to issues joined and that, if believed, prove the existence of the fact in issue without any inference. *Circumstantial evidence* is a chain of facts or circumstances, all tending, when connected, to establish a logical inference or conclusion that such a fact does exist.

The difference between civil and criminal law is not always understood. *Criminal law* may be defined as the law dealing with offenses against the people as a whole. The acts that are crimes are clearly defined by statute, and the cases are prosecuted by public officers. *Civil law* covers laws dealing with wrongs against an individual or a group. Wrongful acts may be subject to both criminal and civil actions. If a man steals an automobile, he has committed a crime against the state; at the same time the person robbed may bring civil action against him for the loss. See CRIMINAL LAW; TORTS.

The two terms *law* and *equity* are also frequently misunderstood. The word *law* signifies a rule of action, either written or unwritten. *Equity* looks to the substance rather than to the form. When an act is equitable it may be just, even though it has no foundation in the law. Formerly, separate courts existed to try cases in equity, but the modern tendency is to combine law and equity and to give judges the power to try both law and equity cases. See EQUITABLE REMEDIES; LEGAL REMEDIES.

Law for the Layman includes information on such recent legal developments as job discrimination, consumer protection, and truth in advertising. In addition, it defines and clarifies traditional legal concepts. Unfamiliar legal terms are defined in the text, and a glossary explains some of the more frequently used terms. Entries are cross-referenced to make information easier to find.

Law for the Layman is not intended to provide the reader with enough knowledge to act as his own lawyer—the law is far too complex for that. But the editors have made every effort to explain basic legal ideas concisely and clearly, so that the layman will have a better understanding of his rights and obligations under the law.

LAW FOR THE LAYMAN

Acknowledgment

1. DEFINITION—An *acknowledgment* is a statement sworn in the presence of a proper authority that a certain document is the free and voluntary act of the person making the acknowledgment. All chattel mortgages and all documents relating to or affecting real estate—such as deeds, mortgages, and releases—must be acknowledged.

2. WHO MAY TAKE ACKNOWLEDGMENTS—Notaries public, justices of the peace, masters in chancery, and judges and clerks of courts of record are authorized to take acknowledgments in most cases. The official attaches a *certificate of acknowledgment* to the document.

3. SPECIAL CASES—The laws of some states require the acknowledgment to show, in cases where an instrument is signed by both husband and wife, that the wife signed out of the presence of her husband. Many states also require that an acknowledgment taken before a notary public must show the date his commission expires. See NOTARIES PUBLIC: ACKNOWLEDGMENTS.

4. FORMS—These forms are commonly used for certificates of acknowledgment.

CHATTEL MORTGAGE

STATE OF ILLINOIS,)
KANE COUNTY.　　　)ss.

I, John Richard, a Justice of the Peace in the Town of Dundee, in and for the said County, do hereby certify that this mortgage was duly acknowledged before me by the above named.........................,
the grantor therein named, and entered by me this 17th day of July, 19 .....

　　Witness my hand and seal.
　　(Seal)

　　　　　　　　　　JOHN RICHARD
　　　　　　　　　　Justice of the Peace

RELEASE

STATE OF ILLINOIS,　　　)
COUNTY OF DU PAGE.)ss.

I, John Smith, a Notary Public in and for said County, and in the State aforesaid, do hereby certify that James Y. Scammon, who is personally known to me to be the same person whose name is subscribed to the foregoing instrument, appeared before me this day in person and acknowledged that he signed, sealed, and delivered the said instrument as his free and voluntary act for the uses and purposes therein set forth.

　　Given under my hand and Notarial Seal this 13th day of May, 19 .....
　　(Notarial Seal)

　　　　　　　　　　JOHN SMITH
　　　　　　　　　　Notary Public

MORTGAGES AND DEEDS

STATE OF ILLINOIS,　　　)
COUNTY OF DU PAGE)ss.

I, John Smith, a Notary Public in and for said County in the State aforesaid, do hereby certify that Samuel P. Smith and Sarah E. Smith, his wife, who are personally known to me to be the same persons whose names are subscribed to the foregoing instruments, appeared before me this day in person and acknowledged that they signed, sealed, and delivered said instrument as their free and voluntary act for the uses and purposes therein set forth, including a release and waiver of all rights under and by virtue of the homestead exemption laws of this State.

　　Given under my hand and Notarial Seal this first day of January, A.D. 19.....
　　(Notarial Seal)

　　　　　　　　　　JOHN SMITH
　　　　　　　　　　Notary Public

GENERAL AND SHORT FORM

STATE OF ILLINOIS,)
COUNTY OF COOK.)ss.

　　On the................. day of .... in the year one thousand nine hundred and ....., before me personally came (names of both parties), who are known to me to be the individuals described in, and who executed, the foregoing instrument, and acknowledged that they executed the same.

　　　　　　　　　　(Signature)

Affidavits

1. DEFINITIONS—An *affidavit* is a voluntary statement of fact reduced to writing and sworn to or affirmed before an authorized public officer. An affidavit is not admissible as testimony in a court of law because the maker, or *affiant,* cannot be cross-examined, but a person who makes a false affidavit may be punished for perjury.

2. FORM—The following is a common form, which, with certain modifications, can be made to apply to most cases.

AFFIDAVIT

STATE OF ILLINOIS,)
COUNTY OF COOK.)ss.

　　John Jones being duly sworn on his oath states that he is well acquainted with the handwriting of Daniel Seitz, one of the subscribing witnesses to the deed hereto attached; that affiant has frequently seen him write and knows his signature; that he believes that the name of the said Daniel Seitz, signed in the said deed, is in the handwriting of the said Daniel Seitz, and further affiant says not.

　　　　　　　　　　(Signed)
　　　　　　　　　　JOHN JONES

　　Subscribed and sworn to before me this 28th day of February, A.D. 19 ....
　　(Notarial Seal)

　　　　　　　　　　E. M. SCHWARTZ
　　　　　　　　　　Notary Public

Agency

1. DEFINITIONS—*Agency* is the relationship between two or more persons by which the *agent* represents the *principal* in the transaction of lawful acts or business. Agents are of two kinds, general and special. A *general agent* is authorized to represent the principal in all of his business, or in all business of a particular kind. A *special agent* is authorized to do a specific thing, such as sell a farm, buy a house, or transact some special business for the principal.

2. PRINCIPAL AND AGENT—Any person who is legally able to act for himself may act as principal. This excludes a lunatic, an alien enemy, or any other person incapable of contracting. On the other hand, any person who is of sound mind and understanding may act as an agent. Husband and wife may act for each other except where prevented by the statutes of the particular state. A person unable to contract on his own account, such as a person under age, may sometimes act as an agent. Anyone except a lunatic, imbecile, or

infant of tender years may be an agent. Corporations often act as agents.

3. AUTHORITY, HOW GIVEN—The authority of an agent may be constituted in three ways: by deed under seal, by writing, or merely by word. Express authority is given to an agent by what is called a *power of attorney*. If the authority is to execute a writing under seal and acknowledged, the power of attorney must be likewise under seal and acknowledged. In a few states, however, this rule has been changed by statute. An agent to sell land or to do any other important business where he is required to make contracts or to draw or sign notes, drafts, or checks, should be appointed by a carefully drawn legal document. Agency may be implied from previous dealings and transactions between the parties. If the principal has held a person out as an agent he will be bound by his acts, even though as a matter of fact the agent had no express authority to represent him.

4. AGENT'S RESPONSIBILITY—The agent must obey the instructions of his principal and act in good faith, using all necessary care and skill in conducting agency business. He cannot appoint a substitute or delegate his authority to another without consent of his principal. An agent concealing the identity of his principal is himself responsible and, if acting fraudulently or deceitfully, is himself responsible to third parties. If an agent embezzles his principal's property, it may be reclaimed if it can be identified or distinctly traced. An agent employed to sell property cannot buy it himself; an agent employed to purchase property cannot buy from himself.

5. PRINCIPAL'S LIABILITY—The principal is liable for all acts of his agent within the scope of the agency. Also, the knowledge of the agent relating to the business of the agency is binding upon the principal; therefore, notice to an agent as to matters relating to the agency is notice to the principal. The principal is liable to third persons for the negligence or unskillfulness of the agent acting in the fulfillment of the agency business, although money mistakenly paid by an agent can be recovered by the principal. Any acts or contracts of an agent made beyond the scope of his authority may be ratified by the principal and when so ratified are binding on the latter. The general rule with respect to the liability of a principal for unauthorized acts of his agent is that the principal is liable to third persons for any acts done by the agent for the principal in the course of his duties and within the actual or apparent scope of his agency.

6. REVOCATION OF AUTHORITY—The authority of an agent may be terminated in seven ways: (a) by the express revocation thereof by the principal, (b) by renunciation of such power by the agent, (c) by the death of the principal, (d) by the expiration of the time within which the agent was to perform the acts that were to be done by him, or by his having completed and fully performed the commission and closed the business which he was to transact, (e) by the sale of the subject matter of the agency, (f) by the insanity of either principal or agent, or (g) by the bankruptcy of the principal or the agent. A revocation of authority takes effect, insofar as the agent is concerned, when he receives notice thereof; insofar as the third persons are concerned, when they receive notice of such revocation. Personal notice or its equivalent is required, and is sufficient, to those who have dealt with the agent. Advertising the fact would be sufficient as to all others. Without a sufficient notice of the revocation, a contract made in good faith with the agent after a revocation will bind the principal the same as before. However, incapacity or death of either party terminates the agency even without notice.

7. SPECIAL RULES OF AGENCY—An agent cannot delegate his powers to another without the consent of the principal, unless the act to be done is a minor service, or one requiring no personal ability or skill. Both principal and agent are liable if the persons with whom the agent is transacting business do not know of the agency relationship. An agent can receive no personal profit from a transaction.

8. DEALING THROUGH AN AGENT—Persons dealing with agents who are strangers should be very careful to ascertain that the agent has authority to transact business in hand. In all transactions in regard to real estate, the authority of the agent should be in writing, signed by the owner of the property, in order to be binding upon the owner. In all cases of doubt as to the authority of an agent or as to the extent of his authority, it would be wise to require of the agent a written proof of his agency and the extent of his authority.

9. POWER OF ATTORNEY—Whenever it becomes necessary to delegate to an agent the power to sign notes, checks, or other legal documents, it is advisable to grant such powers in a written document. Such document is usually called a *power of attorney*. It should be signed by the principal and witnessed, and should set forth exactly and explicitly what the attorney or agent has power to do. If the agent is to deal in real estate it is sometimes required by law, and in any event always advisable, that such power of attorney be under seal.

10. FORMS:

POWER OF ATTORNEY, GENERAL FORM

Know all men by these presents, That I, James L. Binton, of Naperville, County of Du Page, and State of Illinois, have made, constituted and appointed, and by these presents do make, constitute and appoint, Chas. A. Lerch true and lawful attorney for me and in my name, place and stead, (here state the purpose for which the power is given), giving and granting unto my said attorney full power and authority to do and perform all and every act and thing whatsoever, requisite and necessary to be done in and about the premises, as fully, to all intents and purposes, as I might or could do if personally present, with all power of substitution and revocation, hereby ratifying and confirming all that my said attorney or his substitute shall lawfully do or cause to be done by virtue thereof.

In witness whereof, I have hereunto set my hand and seal the 2nd day of January, one thousand nine hundred....................

Signed, Sealed and Delivered
    in Presence of

....

JAMES L. BINTON (Seal)

Note: This form should be properly acknowledged before an officer, the same as a deed according to the law of the State.

PROXY OR POWER OF ATTORNEY TO VOTE

Know all men by these presents: That I, David E. Hughes, do hereby constitute and appoint C. A. Brown my true and lawful attorney, for me and in my name, place and stead, to vote as my proxy and representative at the .... meeting of the stockholders of the ...., a corporation, and at any adjournment of said meeting, all of the .... shares of the capital stock of said corporation standing in my name on the books of said corporation, as fully and amply as I could or might do were I personally present; with full power of substitution and revocation.

Witness my hand and seal at Aurora, Illinois, this 26th day of June, A.D. 19 . . . .

E. R. ZEMMER (Seal)

REVOCATION OF POWER OF ATTORNEY

Whereas, I, Sylvester Jones, of Aurora, County of Kane, and State of Illinois, did on the tenth day of June, 19 . . . . ., by my letter or power of attorney appoint John C. Cook of Chicago my true and lawful attorney, for me and in my name to (here state in precise language what he was authorized to do) as by the said power of attorney, reference thereunto being had, will fully appear;

Therefore, know all men by these presents, That I, Sylvester Jones, aforesaid, have revoked and recalled the said power of attorney, and by these presents do revoke and recall all power and authority thereby given to the said John C. Cook.

Given this tenth day of October, 19 . . . .
Signed and sealed in presence
of . . . .

SYLVESTER JONES (Seal)

Antitrust Law

1. DEFINITION—A *trust* is a corporation or conglomerate having monopolistic power within its field of commerce. Various laws have been passed to prevent such combinations from using unfair methods of competition. The federal antitrust laws are the Sherman Act, the Clayton Act, the Federal Trade Commission Act, and the Robinson-Patman Act. The Sherman Act is concerned with agreements in restraint of trade and actual and attempted monopolization of markets. The Clayton and Federal Trade Commission Acts are concerned with anticompetitive exclusive dealing arrangements and mergers and with unfair methods of competition. The Robinson-Patman Act is concerned with discriminatory pricing and promotions in the distribution of goods.

2. HISTORY OF THE SHERMAN ACT—Through various conspiratorial and predatory practices, numerous monopolies had emerged in the United States by 1890 in such diverse industries as whiskey, petroleum, sugar, cotton, oil, and lead. They were called *trusts* because competing companies were typically combined in restraint of trade by transferring controlling stock interests in them to a board of trustees for integrated noncompetitive operation. Soon the "holding company" corporation replaced the trust as the device used.

3. PASSAGE OF THE SHERMAN ACT—To break up these monopolies, combinations, and conspiracies, Congress passed the Sherman Act. Under Section 1 of that act, "Every contract, combination in the form of trust or otherwise, or conspiracy, in restraint of trade or commerce among the several states, or with foreign nations, is declared to be illegal. . . ."

4. THE COURT CONSTRUES THE SHERMAN ACT—In 1911 in the Standard Oil and American Tobacco cases the United States Supreme Court held that against its common law background the Sherman Act must be read to forbid only "contracts or acts" having a "monopolistic tendency," and hence only unreasonable restraints of interstate or foreign commerce; that is, any undue interference with freely competitive markets. Under this "rule of reason" the Court will

consider economic evidence to determine whether a restrictive agreement unduly hampers competition.

5. RESTRAINTS OF TRADE UNREASONABLE PER SE—Beginning with Standard Oil, however, the Court has declared certain forms of conduct to be violations of the statute per se—that is, such restraints are unreasonable as a matter of law "because of their pernicious effect on competition and lack of any redeeming virtue"—and no economic evidence will be received "as to the precise harm they caused or the business excuse for their use." Forming the core of regulations under Section 1, the principal "per se categories" are agreements between competitors to fix prices, to limit production, to divide markets or customers, or to boycott other businessmen.

a. *Price Fixing.* A seller may not agree horizontally with his competitors on the price at which they will sell, or vertically with his customers on their resale prices; whether or not the participants have power to control the market price, or such prices are "reasonable" or yield only a "reasonable profit," or are minimums designed to preserve a product's quality image, or are maximums intended to insure competitive resale price levels or to prevent overcharging.

b. *Production Limitations.* Agreements of suppliers to limit their production affect fundamental supply and demand relationships and are automatically outlawed.

c. *Market Division.* Suppliers are not allowed to divide the market even if necessary to avoid "ruinous competition" among themselves or to compete with the larger national chain stores.

d. *Tying Arrangements.* Tying arrangements condition the sale of one product, the "tying" product, on the purchase of another, the "tied" product, from the same seller. For example, a manufacturer of a popular brand of cold cream might decide to sell that product only to retailers who purchase a certain quota of the manufacturer's lipstick. The cold cream would be the "tying" product, the lipstick the "tied" product. The tying arrangement would permit the manufacturer to boost sales of lipstick even though his competitors might offer a better product. Such arrangements are bad per se "whenever a party has sufficient economic power with respect to the tying product to appreciably restrain free competition in the market for the tied product."

6. REASONABLE RESTRAINTS OF TRADE—Outside of these per se categories the rule of reason will support restraints of trade that serve legitimate business goals and are not seriously anticompetitive. Covenants, reasonable in time and space, forbidding the seller of a business from competing with the buyer, and covenants granting exclusive franchises within a shopping center, are two examples of reasonable restraints.

7. CONSPIRACY OR COMBINATION—So little is needed to support a finding of agreement or conspiracy that competitors should not discuss subjects on which they could not legally agree, for example, setting prices or refusing to deal with third parties, for such a discussion followed by parallel action will support a finding of commitment to a common plan.

8. MONOPOLIZATION—Section 2 of the Sherman Act makes it unlawful to "monopolize, or attempt to monopolize, or combine or conspire with any other person or persons, to monopolize any part of" the interstate or foreign commerce of the United States.

9. HISTORY OF THE CLAYTON ACT—The Clayton Act was passed in 1914 during President Wilson's first term. The statute reflected the general sentiment that the Sherman Act standing alone was inadequate to guarantee free com-

petition, partly because the Sherman Act dealt with accomplished restraints, as distinguished from incipient abuses. Consequently, among other things, the Clayton Act forbids exclusive dealing and certain mergers where the effect may substantially lessen competition or tend to create a monopoly. The Federal Trade Commission may halt incipient restraints through its power to forbid unfair methods of competition in interstate commerce.

10. EXCLUSIVE DEALING—Section 3 of the Clayton Act forbids any interstate supplier to sell commodities on the condition that the buyer will not use or deal in the goods of a firm competing with the seller. This law applies to any case where the exclusive dealing may substantially lessen competition in any line of commerce.

11. MERGERS—Section 7 of the Clayton Act forbids the acquisition of all or any part of the stock or assets of a corporation doing an interstate business "where in any line of commerce in any section of the country, the effect of such acquisition may be substantially to lessen competition or tend to create a monopoly." The statute regulates mergers between competing corporations ("horizontal"), between corporations in a supplier-customer relationship ("vertical"), and all other mergers ("conglomerate") where reasonably probable anticompetitive effects are shown.

12. PRICE DISCRIMINATION—The original price discrimination provisions of the Clayton Act were intended principally to prevent interstate sellers from lowering prices to destroy local competitors while maintaining prices elsewhere. With the advent of retail chains, the statute had proved inadequate to prevent the chains from exacting from sellers discriminatory prices and related concessions through the use of their superior purchasing power. Since they could pay lower prices for their merchandise, retail chains could sell at lower prices and drive smaller retail stores out of the market.

13. ROBINSON-PATMAN ACT—As amended in 1936 by the Robinson-Patman Act, Section 2(a) of the Clayton Act broadens the law to prohibit price discrimination that gives unfair advantage either to the seller, as in the case of a chain store lowering prices in one part of the country to destroy competition there, or to the buyer, as in the case of a chain store demanding price reductions from its supplier, or to the customers of the seller or the buyer.

14. GOVERNMENT ENFORCEMENT OF CIVIL REMEDIES — Violations may be restrained by injunctions and by administrative cease-and-desist orders ranging from a simple prohibition of price fixing to broad orders limiting specific business practices that, in and of themselves, would not have been antitrust violations. A civil penalty of up to $5,000 is provided for each violation of a final cease-and-desist order issued by the FTC, with each day's noncompliance constituting a separate violation.

15. PRIVATE ENFORCEMENT OF CIVIL REMEDIES—Section 4 of the Clayton Act provides that "any person who shall be injured in his business or property by reason of anything forbidden in the antitrust laws shall recover three fold [sic] the damages by him sustained, and the cost of suit, including a reasonable attorney's fee."

Auctioneer

1. DEFINITION—An *auctioneer* is a person employed to sell property to the highest bidder at public sale.

2. AGENT FOR BOTH BUYER AND SELLER—An auctioneer is the exclusive agent of the owner until the auctioneer accepts the purchaser's bid and knocks down the property to him. On accepting the bid the auctioneer becomes the agent of the purchaser also, and thus represents both parties.

3. COMPLETION OF THE SALE—A sale by auction is completed when the auctioneer announces its completion by the fall of the hammer, or in any other customary manner. Until such announcement is made, the auctioneer may withdraw the property from sale unless the sale has been advertised to be without reserve. Any bidder may also withdraw his bid at any time before the fall of the hammer.

4. RESPONSIBILITY OF AUCTIONEER—Authority to sell property does not imply power to sell at auction. Thus a purchaser buying goods from an auctioneer, when he knows the auctioneer has no authority to sell them at auction, acquires no title to the property thus purchased. The seller or owner is not bound by any statements by the auctioneer. An auctioneer must accept the most favorable bid. He cannot refuse to accept legitimate bids, but he is justified in rejecting the bids of insane or drunken persons, minors, trustees of the property, and persons who refuse to comply with the terms of the sale.

5. THINGS AN AUCTIONEER CANNOT DO—An auctioneer is not permitted to delegate his duties to another, except minor or incidental duties. He cannot act contrary to the wishes and instructions of the owners in any matters relating to the details of the sale. He may not permit a bidder to withdraw his bid after its acceptance, without the consent of the owner. He cannot sell the property to himself or employ another to bid for him. He is not permitted to sell at private sale contrary to the owner's instructions.

Automobile

1. THE RIGHT TO USE THE HIGHWAYS—The public has a right to use the public roads to travel and transport property. Drivers of automobiles have an equal right on the highways with other vehicles, but they do not have any greater right. The courts hold that all travelers have equal right to use the highways. Thus, a pedestrian has the same right as the driver of an automobile. The state cannot exclude nonresidents from the public roads or place greater restrictions or burdens on nonresident motorists than those imposed on its own citizens.

2. PARKING—In the absence of any city ordinance or statutory regulation, an automobile may be left at the side of the road with the engine shut off and the brakes set. However, an automobile so left after dark must be properly lighted.

3. LICENSE—The several states issue licenses to the owners of automobiles, motorcycles, and trucks, permitting them to use the public highways. Many cities require a municipal license. Such a license is neither a contract nor a tax, but a *statutory entitlement* that may be revoked only through due process of law. The license does not pass to a purchaser of the vehicle.

4. RENTED VEHICLES—The owner of a rented vehicle is not liable for the negligence of the operator. For example, if A rents his automobile to B for a certain consideration, the law will not hold A responsible for the negligent acts of B even if B is an unskilled driver. On the other hand, if A knew when he rented the car that B was an immature child or a person of low mentality or under the influence of alcohol, the courts would hold him responsible. If the owner lends his car with a chauffeur, he will be held liable for the negligent acts of the chauffeur. In case of damage to the rented car, the renter is liable only if it can be proved that he did not exercise ordinary prudence and care. Should the renter sell the car without the owner's authority, the owner can recover even from an innocent purchaser. The owner of an automobile is entitled to a fair compensation for its use, even if no definite sum is agreed upon, and he can collect a reasonable hire if his automobile is used by another without

his knowledge or consent. Criminal liability also is attached to the unlawful use of another's automobile.

5. THE SPEED OF AUTOMOBILES along a public road is regulated by law. Some state laws prescribe the maximum rates of speed for business districts, residential districts, and country roads. A municipality has the right to modify the speed laws in accordance with local requirements. Courts of most states hold that it is the duty of a driver on a public highway to have his car under control and to operate it at a reasonable rate of speed, having regard to the traffic and other conditions. He must so operate it as to avoid endangering the life or limb of any person or the safety of anyone's property.

6. THE LAWS OF THE ROAD are intended to prevent collisions and accidents.

a. Vehicles approaching each other from opposite directions are required to keep to the right of the road. If, therefore, two automobiles collide in a street that is wide enough for safe passage, the driver on the left side of the road is responsible for the other driver's injury, provided of course that the other was not himself guilty of negligence.

b. Each driver must pass on his right side of the center of the traveled road. This applies even to roads covered with snow, to side roads, and to roads under construction.

c. It is the duty of every driver to exercise reasonable care in avoiding accidents or injuries to others. This rule applies just as strongly when the driver's car is on the right side of the road.

d. At street intersections it is customary to allow the right of way to the vehicle approaching from the right and, in many states and municipalities, this rule has been embodied in the statutes and ordinances.

e. It is the duty of the driver to keep his car under control at all times.

f. If one willfully or negligently drives a car on a street or road at an unlawful speed, thereby killing another, he may be guilty of homicide.

g. The driver of a car may be charged with negligence if, without warning to others, he suddenly changes the course of his vehicle or backs his car.

7. THE FITNESS OF THE DRIVER—The driver of an automobile should be physically and mentally fit. A man who is subject to fainting spells or epileptic attacks has no right to drive a car upon the public highway. The same rule applies to one with defective eyesight, but it has been held that proper eyeglasses may restore the competency of the driver. No person should ever attempt to drive an automobile while intoxicated, thereby endangering the lives of others.

8. THE CHAUFFEUR'S LIABILITY—As a general rule the owner is liable for the acts of his chauffeur, provided the chauffeur is acting within the scope of the owner's business. However, should the chauffeur use the car without the consent or knowledge of the owner, or should he be using it for his own business and without the owner's consent, the owner is not liable for the driver's acts. The same rule applies when the owner's child uses the parent's car without the parent's knowledge or consent. If the car is run with his knowledge by a member of his family, or for the convenience of other members of the family, the parent may be liable for the negligent acts of the driver. Most states require a chauffeur to take out a license.

9. MINORS—The statutes of most states forbid children under a certain age to drive automobiles. The ages vary in different states. Thus the owner of a car who allows a child to operate it may be held responsible for accident or injury resulting from the child's negligence.

10. THE CHAUFFEUR'S RIGHTS—A chauffeur may recover damages from his employer for injury received while operating the car, provided that the employer is in some way responsible for the injury. On the other hand, if his injury was due to a defective part, he could not recover from his employer unless it so happened that the employer knew of the defect and the chauffeur did not. If a chauffeur should be injured while riding in a car driven by the owner, the chauffeur could recover for injuries sustained due to the owner's negligence.

11. THE OWNER'S INJURY—If the owner of a car be injured in any way through the wrongful acts or negligence of his chauffeur, the chauffeur may be held liable.

12. GARAGE KEEPER—A garage keeper is bound to exercise reasonable care with reference to vehicles entrusted to him. The owner of a car is not liable to third parties for the negligence of the garage keeper or his employees in the care and operation of his automobile. If a garage keeper or his employee operates an automobile, the garage keeper is liable for any damage done to the car or to third persons. A public garage, while not considered a public nuisance, is subject to public regulations as to location, odors, noise, and fire hazards. A garage keeper is entitled to a reasonable compensation for storage of a car or for repairs that he has been instructed to make. He is not liable for fire damage to the automobile unless the fire is caused by his own negligence or that of his employees. He is liable for theft if he fails to use reasonable precautions to guard against it See also BAILMENTS.

13. NEW CAR PURCHASE—The law treats a new car much like any other goods—the manufacturer and seller make an implied warranty that the product is safe for its usual uses. See also PRODUCTS LIABILITY.

14. USED AUTOMOBILES—The dealer is required by law to inspect a used automobile and tell the buyer about any flaw that would make it dangerous to operate. However, the seller's responsibility is less than for a new car. The buyer accepts responsibility for any visible defects and, unless otherwise specified in a written contract, he cannot force the dealer to repair mechanical failures. The buyer must beware when purchasing a used automobile.

15. BILL OF SALE—Statutes in most states require that a bill of sale be given, and the purchaser should be careful to see that the statute is complied with. The bill of sale should be drawn in accordance with the laws of the state where the purchase is made.

The following form will answer the purpose in most of the states:

BILL OF SALE

Know all men by these presents, that I (here insert name and address of party selling the car) in the county of ......, state of .... , in consideration of (here insert amount of money to be paid party selling by party buying) dollars this day to me in hand paid, do hereby grant, sell, transfer and deliver unto the said (here insert name of party buying) the following goods and chattels, to wit: (then insert name of automobile, its model, the engine number and the car number, also the type of car, its color, together with any other information that will help to identify it); to have and to hold said goods and chattels to the said (name of purchaser), his executors, administrators and assigns to their use forever.

I hereby covenant with the said grantee that I am the lawful owner of the said goods and chattels; that they are free and clear from all incumbrances; that I have good right to sell the same and that I will warrant and defend the same against the lawful claims and demands of all persons.

In witness whereof, I, the said (name of party selling) hereunto set my hand and seal the . . . . . day of . . . . , 19 . . . .

Signature of party selling . . . . (Seal)

16. THE DRIVER'S RESPONSIBILITIES – The driver of a vehicle involved in a collision has certain responsibilities:

a. Do not drive away without reporting the facts to the police or nearest police station, or without giving your name, address, and license number to the other party involved. Leaving the scene of an accident may constitute a crime punishable by fine or imprisonment.

b. Be sure to get the name and address of the other party or, if he drives away, his license number.

c. Get the names and addresses of all persons who witnessed the accident, or saw the results of it, including all injured persons.

d. Try to visualize just how it happened, remember your own position and that of the other party, both before and after the accident, and note carefully the wheel marks on the road or pavement.

e. Be calm and courteous. Do not admit that you are in the wrong or accuse the other party.

f. Do not make immediate settlement or offer to do so, or incur any expense except for necessary medical relief.

Bailment

1. DEFINITIONS – A *bailment* is a delivery of a thing in trust for some special object or purpose with the understanding, expressed or implied, that the person receiving it shall return it when that purpose has been fulfilled. A *bailor* is one who makes a bailment or delivers goods to a *bailee*. A *bailee* is a person who receives goods of another to hold according to the purpose of delivery.

2. BAILOR AND BAILEE – To create this relationship the property must be delivered to the bailee. Thus if A takes his car to a public garage to remain overnight, the garage owner becomes a bailee for hire. The contract of bailment also exists when a man takes a suit of clothes to a tailor shop to be altered, or when a farmer takes a load of oats to a mill to be ground.

3. THE BAILEE'S RESPONSIBILITY – A bailee can limit his liability by agreement, provided the limitation is not in violation of law or public policy and does not excuse him from negligence or fraud on his part. He becomes the custodian of the goods and is generally required to exert reasonable care against accident or loss resulting from the nature of the goods stored. For example, if a truckload of fruit arrives at a cold-storage plant, the owner is not responsible for any loss due to the condition of the fruit when it arrived. On the other hand, if an employee of the storage company negligently allows the goods to spoil, the owner of the fruit can recover from the storage company.

Suppose your bank grants you the privilege of keeping a strongbox in the bank building without paying the normal charges. The bank, of course, is not bound to exercise as much care as a regular safety deposit company, but it is required to take reasonable precaution, that is, as much care as it uses to protect its own property. Suppose a cashier steals the box. Would the bank be liable to you for the loss? If the bank exercised reasonable care, and if the cashier were a long-trusted employee against whom there was no cause for suspicion, the bank would not be held responsible.

4. THE BAILEE'S DUTY – The bailee is usually a keeper only. However, if he is keeping livestock, he must supply the food necessary to the animals' good condition. Milch cows must be properly milked; and in case of sickness animals must be given proper medical care and attention. In every case the bailee is required to exercise reasonable care for the goods in the bailment.

5. THE BAILOR'S RESPONSIBILITY – The bailor must pay any reasonable charges incurred in the maintenance and preservation of the goods in the bailment. He must also pay for any services rendered pertaining to the purpose of the bailment, such as fees for storing a car or charges for the services of a cleaner or tailor. If the bailor is unwilling or unable to pay such charges the bailee may keep the goods of the bailment as a lien until full payment is made.

Bankruptcy

1. DEFINITION – *Bankruptcy* is a legally declared condition of solvency, that is, of inability to pay one's debts. The property of a bankrupt is divided among his creditors in proportion to their claims, and the bankrupt is absolved of responsibility for past debts. The bankrupt is entitled to certain exemptions; usually he may keep adequate clothing, some furniture, and the tools of his trade. The Bankruptcy Act of 1938, popularly known as the Chandler Act, now contains the law on this subject.

2. EXEMPT CORPORATIONS – Building and loan associations and municipal, railroad, insurance, and banking corporations are exempt from bankruptcy proceedings because other laws govern their insolvency.

3. BANKRUPTS – Bankrupts are of two classes, voluntary and involuntary. *Voluntary bankrupts* are those who are declared bankrupt upon their own petitions. Under the new act, any person or nonexempt corporation owing debts is entitled to the benefits of the act as a voluntary bankrupt. *Involuntary bankrupts* are those who are declared bankrupt on petitions from their creditors. Any nonexempt corporation or any person, except farmers and those earning less than $1,500 a year, owing debts to the amount of $1,000 or over, may be adjudged an involuntary bankrupt.

4. ACTS OF BANKRUPTCY – To have a person declared an involuntary bankrupt his creditors must show that he has committed any of the following acts of bankruptcy:

a. Transferred, concealed, or removed any part of his property with the intent to delay or defraud his creditors.

b. Transferred, while insolvent, any portion of his property to one or more of his creditors with the intent to prefer such creditors over his other creditors.

c. Permitted, while insolvent, any creditor to obtain a lien upon any of his property and not discharged that lien within thirty days.

d. Made a general assignment for the benefit of his creditors, that is, transferred property to his creditors as a group in order to repay his debts.

e. Admitted in writing his inability to pay his debts and his willingness to be adjudged a bankrupt.

5. FILING A VOLUNTARY PETITION – Any eligible person who wishes to declare bankruptcy should file his petition with the clerk of the court in the district where he has had his principal place of business or his domicile for the preceding six months. With the petition he must file (a) a schedule listing the names of his creditors, their residences, the amount due each, and what security each holds, (b) a description of the petitioner's property showing its nature, location, and value, and (c) his claim for any legal exemptions. As soon as these documents are submitted and verified, the petitioner is declared a bankrupt.

6. FILING AN INVOLUNTARY PETITION—If a nonexempt person owing debts to the amount of $1,000 has committed an act of bankruptcy, three or more creditors who have provable claims against such person amounting to $500 or more may file a petition to have him adjudged a bankrupt. If the alleged bankrupt has fewer than twelve creditors, the petition may be filed by one creditor whose claim totals $500 or more. The petition must be duly signed and verified and include the following information and allegations:

a. The name of the alleged bankrupt.

b. That he has had his principal place of business within the judicial district for the preceding six months.

c. That he owes debts to the amount of $1,000 and is not exempt from the laws of bankruptcy.

d. The names and addresses of the petitioning creditors.

e. That they have provable claims against the alleged bankrupt amounting to $500 or more.

f. The nature and amount of petitioners' claims.

g. That within the four months preceding the filing of the petition, the alleged bankrupt committed an act of bankruptcy.

h. A statement as to what acts on his part are alleged to have constituted said act of bankruptcy.

Upon receiving the petition the clerk will issue a subpoena and a copy of the petition to the alleged bankrupt, who has opportunity to file an answer within a certain time. The court may appoint a receiver to take charge of the alleged bankrupt's property if it is necessary to prevent loss. If the alleged bankrupt fails to reply within the time allowed, the court will adjudicate him bankrupt if the petition is in correct form.

7. HEARING IN INVOLUNTARY PROCEEDINGS—If the alleged bankrupt wishes to deny any of the matters set out in the petition, he may do so by filing his sworn answer within the time allowed by law. The matter will then be set down for hearing, and on the day set the petitioners must prove the allegations in their petition or the court will dismiss it. If the allegations are proven, the court will enter the order of adjudication and set a date for the first meeting of the creditors. The bankrupt is then required to file schedules of his creditors, his property, and his exemptions similar to those filed by a voluntary bankrupt.

8. PROCEDURE OUTLINE—After adjudication, the procedure for voluntary and involuntary bankruptcy is the same. The court calls a meeting of the creditors, presided over by a referee. Creditors file proof of their claims and elect a trustee, and the bankrupt is questioned publicly. The trustee takes charge of the estate and calls further meetings as necessary. When his estate has been liquidated and distributed among his creditors, the bankrupt is discharged.

9. STATEMENT OF AFFAIRS—At least five days prior to the first meeting of his creditors, the bankrupt must file a formal statement of his affairs. This information will assist the creditors and the trustee in administering the bankrupt's affairs and in examining the bankrupt.

10. FIRST MEETING OF CREDITORS—The court must schedule the first meeting of the creditors to be held not less than ten nor more than thirty days after adjudication. At that time creditors file proof of their claims against the bankrupt and appoint a trustee to act as their representative in taking charge of the bankrupt's estate and converting his assets to cash. In addition, the creditors may appoint a committee of three or more of their number to consult with and advise the trustee in the administration of the estate. The referee or trustee must examine the bankrupt at this meeting.

11. FUNCTION OF THE REFEREE—The referee is the officer of the court who is in charge of a bankruptcy proceeding. He presides at all meetings of the creditors, holds evidence and records, and furnishes information to interested parties. He must verify and accept each claim before the creditor can vote at meetings; he is empowered to hold hearings and pass judgment on contested issues. He supervises the examination of the bankrupt, but usually delegates the actual questioning to the trustee. He audits the accounts of the trustee and grants final discharge to the bankrupt.

12. RESPONSIBILITY OF THE TRUSTEE—The trustee must liquidate the bankrupt's estate, that is, convert his property into cash, and distribute the proceeds among the creditors. He usually examines the bankrupt publicly in order to determine that the bankrupt has not fraudulently concealed any property or given unlawful preference to any creditor. He must recover any property wrongfully removed from the estate, sell all property for the best price available, and bring necessary legal actions on behalf of the estate. He may make contracts as agent for the estate. He is accountable to the creditors and to the referee.

13. PROOF OF CLAIMS—In order to share in any dividends that may be paid to creditors out of the property of the bankrupt, a creditor must file his claim in court within six months after the first meeting of creditors, prove his claim, and have it allowed by the court. Only claims provable in law or equity are provable in bankruptcy; contingent claims are not provable. The law requires that a written proof of claim signed by the creditor be filed setting forth (a) the claim, (b) the consideration therefor, (c) what securities are held against it, (d) what payments have been made on the debt, and (e) that the claim is justly owing from the bankrupt to the creditor. Any written instrument supporting the claim should be filed with the proof of claim. Properly presented claims are allowed unless objected to by parties in interest or by the court. If objected to, they are set down for hearing before the referee.

14. VOTING AT MEETINGS—Matters submitted to creditors at their meetings are passed upon by vote of a majority in number of all proven creditors who are present, which number must also represent a majority in amount of all proven debts of the bankrupt. Relatives of the bankrupt or, when the bankrupt is a corporation, its stockholders, officers, and directors, are not allowed to vote. Creditors holding claims that are secured or have priority are not entitled to vote on the strength of such claims. Such claims are not counted in computing either the number of creditors or the amount of their claims, except in cases where the amounts of such claims exceed the values of such securities and priorities, and then only for such excess. Claims of $50 or less are not counted in computing the number of creditors voting or present at meetings, but shall be counted in computing the amount.

15. SUBSEQUENT MEETINGS—The trustee may call a meeting of the creditors whenever he deems it necessary. In addition, the law provides that the court shall call a meeting of creditors whenever one-fourth or more in number of those who have proven their claims shall file a written request for a meeting. Whenever the affairs of the bankrupt's estate are ready to be closed, the court orders a final meeting of creditors. A case in which there are no assets may be closed without such final meeting.

16. LEGAL EXEMPTIONS—The kinds of property that cannot be taken from a bankrupt are established by the laws of the various states. Generally, the bankrupt cannot be reduced to destitution, that is, left without adequate clothing and shelter, nor be deprived of the tools of his trade. See EXEMPTIONS.

17. PRIORITY OF CLAIMS—Before distributing any proceeds of the estate among the creditors, the trustee must meet certain obligations. Property and funds held in trust by the bankrupt must be returned to the rightful owners, and certain debts and expenses must be paid in the following priority:

a. Costs incurred in maintaining and administering the estate, such as storage fees, fees for filing petitions, and fees for referee, trustee, and lawyers.

b. Wages due employees of the bankrupt up to $600 per employee.

c. All taxes, whether federal, state, or local.

d. Certain kinds of debts granted priority by state or federal law.

18. DISCHARGE OF THE BANKRUPT—The discharge in bankruptcy is the final ruling of the court releasing the bankrupt from all past debts voidable through bankruptcy. A bankrupt cannot be discharged if he has acted fraudulently to obtain credit while insolvent, if he has attempted to defraud his creditors or to conceal material information during bankruptcy proceedings, or if he has been discharged from bankruptcy during the past six years. A bankrupt corporation may file an application for discharge within six months after its adjudication. A bankrupt individual need not file such application, for his adjudication operates as an application for discharge. After the bankrupt individual has been examined, the court fixes a time for the filing of objections to the bankrupt's discharge and gives notice to all parties in interest. If no objection is filed within the fixed time, the court discharges the bankrupt. A discharge in bankruptcy releases the bankrupt from all of his provable debts except the following:

a. Taxes.

b. Liabilities for obtaining money by false pretenses, for willful and malicious injuries to the person or property of another, for alimony or support of wife or child, for seduction, or for adultery.

c. Debts not scheduled in time for proof and allowance, unless the creditor had notice or actual knowledge of the proceedings in bankruptcy.

d. Liabilities created by the bankrupt's fraud or embezzlement while acting as an officer or in any fiduciary capacity.

e. Wages due to employees of the bankrupt.

f. Debts for moneys deposited with the bankrupt by his employee as security for the faithful performance of the terms of a contract of employment.

19. COMPOSITION—After a bankrupt has filed the schedule of his property and list of his creditors and has been examined in open court or at a meeting of creditors, he may offer terms of *composition*. That is, he offers to make immediate payment of a certain proportion of each general claim provided the creditor will release him from the balance. The bankrupt must still pay the whole amount owing on any priority claims. This is, of course, precisely what happens by operation of law if the bankruptcy proceeding is carried to a conclusion, but a composition is often more desirable because it can be carried out at once, thus dispensing with a good many of the costs of longer proceedings and preserving the estate in cases where the property is of a nature that will deteriorate or accumulate expense during a delay. Then, too, if the composition is confirmed by the court the debtor is spared some of the ignominy of having gone through bankruptcy and received a discharge. Before being filed in court, the composition must have been accepted in writing by a majority in number of all creditors whose claims have been allowed, which number must also represent a majority in amount of such claims. When the application for confirmation of the composition is filed in court, the money necessary to carry the composition into effect, together with that necessary to pay all debts that have priority and to pay the costs of the proceedings that have already taken place, must be deposited in a place designated by the judge. If the judge is then satisfied at a hearing that the composition is for the best interests of the creditors and is offered by the bankrupt in good faith, he will confirm it and dismiss the case after each creditor has received his share of the money set aside by the bankrupt as a consideration for the composition. The confirmation of a composition has the same effect as a discharge in that it releases all debts of the bankrupt that would be released by a discharge in regular form.

Bonds

1. DEFINITIONS—A *bond* is a certificate of obligation, usually an evidence of debt. It is a form of contract that is almost infinite in variety. The parties to the bond are the *obligor* and the *obligee,* the former being the one who makes the promise and the latter the person to whom the promise is made.

2. A SIMPLE BOND is an instrument promising payment of money at a certain time, and generally bears interest at the rate specified in the bond. Nearly all corporate and municipal bonds are of this character and contain no condition except for the payment of the amount of the bond at a certain time and place with a certain specified rate of interest. Frequently interest coupons are attached to the original bond, providing for the payment of the several installments of interest as they come due.

The following is the form commonly in use for such bonds:

UNITED STATES OF AMERICA.

JEFFERSON CITY, STATE OF MISSOURI.

RENEWAL SCHOOL BOND.

INTEREST 6 PER CENT, PAYABLE SEMI-ANNUALLY.

The Board of Education of the City of Jefferson, County of Cole, and State of Missouri, being legally organized under and pursuant to an act of the General Assembly of the State of Missouri entitled "An act to revise and amend the Laws in relation to Public Schools in Cities, Towns and Villages," approved April 26th, 19 . . ., for value received promise to pay to the bearer ten years after the date hereof One Thousand Dollars ($1,000) at the St. Louis National Bank, in the City of St. Louis, Missouri, together with interest thereon at the rate of six per centum per annum from the date hereof, which interest shall be payable semi-annually at said St. Louis National Bank in the City of St. Louis, Missouri, on the surrender of the proper interest coupons hereto attached. This bond shall be redeemable at the pleasure of the said Board of Education of the City of Jefferson at any time after the expiration of five years from the date hereof, and is issued under and pursuant to an act of the General Assembly of the State of Missouri, entitled "An Act to Authorize Boards of Education to Issue Renewal Funding School Bonds," to be sold or exchanged for the purpose of meeting and paying matured or maturing bonded indebtedness of school districts and for levying special tax to pay the bonded indebtedness of school districts, approved April 11th, 19 . . . .

In Testimony Whereof: the said Board of Education has caused this bond to be signed by the President, countersigned by the Secretary, authenticated by the seal of said Board of Education and attested by the Clerk of the County Court of said County of Cole, with the seal of said Court affixed this First day of July, 19 . . . .

JOHN JONES, President
WM. SMITH, Secretary
GEO. SMILEY, Clerk County
Court

3. SURETY BONDS—*Surety bonds* are obligations to pay a certain sum of money on condition that if the bonded person—the *obligor*—faithfully performs his duties, the obligation is void. This type of bond is in common use for a variety of purposes. All state, county, town, and city officers who handle public funds must give bond to assure the honest and proper performance of their official duties.

The following form of a bond of city treasurer can be used with a few slight changes for almost any office:

Know all men by these presents, That we, John Jones, Henry Smith, and Charles Marshall of the City of Naperville, County of Du Page, and State of Illinois, are held and firmly bound unto the City of Naperville in the penal sum of Twenty Thousand Dollars ($20,-000), for the payment of which, well and truly to be made, we bind ourselves, our heirs, executors, and administrators jointly and firmly by these presents.

Witness our hands and seals this 14th day of July, 19 . . . .

The condition of the above obligation is such that whereas the said John Jones has been duly elected to the office of City Treasurer of the City of Naperville; Now if the said John Jones shall faithfully perform all the duties of said office and shall account for and pay over all moneys that may come into his hands as such Treasurer, according to law and the ordinances of said City and the order and direction of the City Council of said City, then this obligation is to be void, otherwise to remain in full force and effect.

JOHN JONES   (Seal)
HENRY SMITH   (Seal)
CHARLES MARSHALL   (Seal)

4. BUSINESS—Officers of corporations are often required to give surety bonds for the faithful performance of their duties. The following form can be used for nearly all such bonds:

Know all men by these presents, That we, James Lord, John Williams, and Charles Smith, are held and firmly bound unto the Naperville Manufacturing Company, a corporation duly organized under the laws of the State of Illinois, in the penal sum of Ten Thousand Dollars ($10,000), good and lawful money of the United States, for the payment of which, well and truly to be made to said corporation or its assigns, we bind ourselves jointly and severally.

Witness our hands and seals this 14th day of July, 19 . . . .

The condition of the above obligation is such that whereas the said James Lord has been elected President of the Naperville Manufacturing Company; Now Therefore, if the said James Lord shall well and truly perform the duties of his said office and shall account for and pay over all moneys that shall come into his hands as such President, and do all required of him by the bylaws of said corporation now in force or

hereafter enacted, and obey all orders given him by the board of directors of said corporation, then this obligation shall be void, otherwise to remain in full force and effect.

JAMES LORD   (Seal)
JOHN WILLIAMS   (Seal)
CHARLES SMITH   (Seal)

5. INDEMNIFYING BONDS—Bonds are also frequently given to indemnify persons who incur liability for another in many other walks of life. The following form may be used:

Know all men by these presents, That William Marsh, Principal, and John Henry, Surety, are held and firmly bound unto John Jones in the penal sum of One Hundred Dollars ($100), lawful money of the United States, for the payment of which, well and truly to be made, we bind ourselves, our heirs, executors, and administrators, jointly, severally and firmly by these presents.

Witness our hands and seals this 1st day of June, A.D. 19 . . . . .

The condition of the above obligation is such that whereas the said John Jones has been surety for the above William Marsh on his note for One Thousand Dollars ($1,000) payable to the order of Charles William, due in one year from the date hereof, with interest at the rate of 6 per cent per annum.

Now, Therefore, if the said William Marsh shall well and truly pay the said note with all interest thereon when the same comes due and shall from time to time and at all times hereafter save, keep harmless and indemnify the said John Jones of and from all actions, suits, costs, charges, damages, and expenses whatsoever, including attorney's fees, which shall or may at any time hereafter happen or come to him for any reason, by reason of his becoming surety on said note, then this obligation is to be void, otherwise to remain in full force and effect.

WILLIAM MARSH   (Seal)
JOHN HENRY   (Seal)

6. EXECUTOR'S BOND—Executors, administrators, guardians, and conservators are required to enter into bonds to be approved by the proper court before they are allowed to enter upon their duties as such. The forms for such bonds, however, vary in the different states.

Broker

1. DEFINITIONS—A *broker* is a middleman or negotiator between parties. He conducts transactions in his specialized field, but he does not have custody of the property. The person who employs a broker is called the *principal*. *Brokerage* is the fee charged by a broker for transacting business.

2. WHY BROKERS ARE EMPLOYED—Brokers are often employed to transact business or to negotiate bargains between different individuals. By specializing in a single line or a limited number of lines of business, they acquire a knowledge and skill that an average merchant does not possess. It is often advantageous for large firms to employ brokers to buy their raw materials. Brokers may also specialize in real estate, insurance, or securities. The business of brokerage is regulated largely by the customs of the particular trade.

3. A BROKER'S LIABILITY—A broker usually has no special property in the goods he sells. If he does not disclose the principal's name he is liable to the same extent as other agents. (See AGENCY: AGENTS' RESPONSIBILITY.) He must serve faithfully and cannot act for both parties in the same transaction without the consent and knowledge of both. Neither can he delegate his powers without the principal's assent. He is bound to obey the express instructions of his principal, and to keep accurate accounts of his transactions.

4. A BROKER'S COMPENSATION—Usually a broker's compensation is a commission or percentage of the value of the thing sold or exchanged. If the amount of the compensation is not fixed, the custom of the trade rules. A broker is entitled to a reasonable compensation for his services.

5. A REAL ESTATE BROKER must act for his principal alone. He is employed to negotiate sales and exchanges of land, and often has such additional duties as renting real estate, collecting rent, and procuring loans. To gain his commission on the sale he must produce a customer who is ready, able, and willing to accept and live up to the terms of the sale. A property owner cannot avoid paying the commission or brokerage by selling the property himself, or at a lower price than he listed with the broker.

6. PAWNBROKERS—The business of a pawnbroker, the rate of interest he may charge, and the sale of pawned goods are usually regulated by law. A license is usually required and the business is always subject to regulation and control. Suppose A takes a watch to a pawnbroker who advances him $20. A, or his assignee, or the purchaser of the pawn ticket, may redeem it within the fixed time, or even beyond that time if the pawnbroker has not exercised his right to sell the watch. A, the pawner, has the right to assign or sell his interest in the watch. If A fails to redeem the watch, the pawnbroker can usually hold him for any deficiency after the watch is sold.

Carriers

1. DEFINITIONS—A *carrier* is a person or company that undertakes, or whose business it is, to carry persons or merchandise for hire. Carriers are of two kinds, private and common. A *private carrier* is one who carries only occasionally, and not as a public business. Such a carrier need not serve all who wish to employ him, but is liable for negligence in transporting the goods he accepts. A *common carrier* is one whose regular business it is to carry goods or passengers from place to place for all persons who elect to employ and pay him.

2. EXAMPLES—A private carrier is usually an individual who, without being engaged in such business as a public employment, carries merchandise from one point to another for a consideration. He is bound to exercise such care of the property as a man of ordinary intelligence would his own property. Common carriers hold themselves out to carry goods or passengers from one place to another, for all persons who offer to employ them. Examples of common carriers are railroad companies, steamship companies, streetcar companies, taxicab companies, truckmen, and express companies.

3. BILL OF LADING—A *bill of lading* is the receipt given by the common carrier to the owner of the goods desiring to have the same shipped, and should contain a description of (a) the quantity, (b) the marks on the merchandise, (c) the names of the shipper or the person sending the goods, the consignee, and the person to whom the goods are shipped, (d) the place of departure and place of discharge of the goods, (e) the price of freight, and (f) the weight of the separate packages and the number of the car in which the same were shipped.

4. RESPONSIBILITY—Common carriers are generally responsible for all loss and damage caused by transportation from whatever cause, except the act of God or of the public enemy, and they are bound to carry all goods that are offered them, provided such goods come within the class of articles they hold themselves out to carry. The carrier is not responsible for losses occurring from natural causes, such as frosts, fermentation, or natural decay of perishable articles, or the necessary and natural wear in the course of transportation, provided the carrier exercises all reasonable care to keep the loss or deterioration as minimal as practical. The carrier is liable for any and all loss occasioned by accidental fire.

5. PERISHABLE GOODS—Carriers are not responsible for loss to fruits that decay in their possession through no fault of theirs or for goods shipped in defective boxes, such as glassware and other easily broken articles that are not properly packed. Goods must be properly packed in order to make the carrier responsible.

6. BAGGAGE—In the transportation of the baggage of passengers the liability of the carrier for loss to the same is the same as in the case of transportation of goods for hire, and in case of loss the carrier must make it good.

7. WHEN LIABILITY BEGINS AND ENDS—The responsibility of the common carrier begins upon the delivery of the goods for immediate transportation. A delivery at the usual place of receiving freight or to the employee of the company in the usual course of business is sufficient. The responsibility of the carrier as such terminates after the arrival of the goods at their destination and sufficient time has elapsed thereafter for the owner to have received them during business hours. After the expiration of such time the responsibility of the carrier is simply that of a warehouseman and he is required only to keep the goods with ordinary care.

8. LIMITATION OF LIABILITY—A carrier can limit his liability by contract, unless forbidden by statute. Thus a statement limiting the amount of a carrier's liability may be put on a bill of lading given as a receipt for a freight or express shipment, or on a receipt for a freight or express shipment, or on a receipt given a passenger for his baggage. Such statement is considered binding by the courts and relieves the carrier of additional liability. The general rule is that a carrier may relieve himself from all liability except for loss or damage caused by his own negligence.

9. THE PASSENGER'S RIGHTS—The law requires common carriers to carry all passengers who pay the required fare and who are in a sufficiently intelligent condition to travel. The carrier must exercise great care in transporting passengers and is liable for injury due to the carrier's negligence. If the passenger was himself negligent and contributed to his own injury, he cannot as a rule hold the carrier liable.

10. EQUAL LIABILITY—Railroad companies and other carriers who allow express companies to carry parcels and packages on their cars or other vehicles are as liable as the common carriers for all damages that occur, without regard to the contract between them and such express company.

11. DIFFERENT LINES—Where goods are accepted for shipment to points beyond the line of the carrier to whom they are first delivered, such carrier is responsible for the delivery of the goods at their destination. The law now provides that under such circumstances the carrier shall be liable for any loss or injury occurring during the shipment, whether on its own line or on that of the connecting carrier.

12. DEMURRAGE is the sum charged by transportation companies for goods not removed from their cars within the time fixed by the rules of the companies. The rules of a large number of railroad companies require that the cars be unloaded within twenty-four hours after the train's arrival at the destination. A fixed rate of demurrage for each twen-

ty-four hours of delay after the expiration of the usual time for unloading is imposed on the persons to whom goods are shipped.

13. THE CARRIER'S RIGHTS—The carrier is entitled to a reasonable compensation for his services, and may demand payment in advance. The shipper is liable for freight, unless the carrier agrees to look exclusively to some other party. After delivery the carrier may recover the amount of freight from the consignee. But freight may be collected only for the goods actually delivered, unless the delivery be prevented by the owner or unless it be agreed that freight shall be payable regardless of losses by the way. The carrier also has a lien on the goods for his freight and advances on such goods, and may refuse to deliver until such charges be paid. This lien has priority over the owner's right of stoppage in transit and the claims of the general creditors of the owner or consignee. A carrier by water also has a lien for salvage and for customs duties advanced on imported goods.

14. COMMUNICATIONS—Telegraph and telephone companies are not common carriers and may therefore establish their own regulations for the transmission of messages. Like common carriers, however, they are required to serve all who apply and offer to pay the charges, and are liable for damages when messages are not sent promptly and accurately. They come within the classification of public service corporations, and are subject to legislative regulation and control as to kind of service to be rendered and rates for such service.

Chattel Mortgage

1. DEFINITIONS—A *chattel mortgage* is an instrument by which the owner conveys conditional title to personal property to secure the payment of a debt or the performance of a contract or other obligation. It is a pledge that the debt will be paid. Any personal property that may be sold may be mortgaged, such as automobiles, livestock, machinery, farm implements, life-insurance policies, corporation stock, and crops. The *mortgagor* is the person who conveys the property. The *mortgagee* is the person to whom the transfer is made.

2. FORM OF MORTGAGE—The usual form of a chattel mortgage is a bill of sale with the *conditional clause* stating the terms of the loan, and that on the mortgagor's failure to pay, the mortgagee may take possession of the property. Any person competent to make a contract, or his agent, may make a chattel mortgage. Partners or joint tenants may mortgage jointly on their individual interests. A corporation may also mortgage its personal property.

Chattel mortgages are usually given to secure notes in the same way in which real estate mortgages are given to secure notes. Greater strictness, however, is required in the acknowledgment, docketing, and recording of chattel mortgages than in the case of real estate mortgages. A chattel mortgage must be acknowledged before a justice of the peace or some other person authorized by law to take acknowledgments.

3. DESCRIBING THE PROPERTY—The property mortgaged must be described clearly enough to enable third persons to identify it, but this is determined largely by the nature of the chattels. "All" articles in a stated place is generally a valid description.

4. FORECLOSURE—When the mortgagor fails to pay his debt, the right of the mortgagee to proceed in taking the property is regulated by law. In most chattel mortgages a clause is included permitting the mortgagee to seize and sell the property should the mortgagor fail to make payment.

5. GENERAL PRINCIPLES—A chattel mortgage remains in effect as between the parties themselves until it is released or becomes barred by what is known as the statute of limitations. However, in order to preserve the mortgage's validity against creditors of the mortgagor and subsequent purchasers of the mortgaged property, it must be refiled or renewed periodically. The periods vary in different states but are generally from one to three years. To sell property covered by a chattel mortgage for a valuable consideration without notifying the purchaser of the existence of the mortgage is a criminal offense. Statutes in a few states provide that notes secured by chattel mortgages must show on their faces that they are secured by chattel mortgages, or they are absolutely void. In other states, chattel mortgages on household goods must be signed by both the mortgagor and his wife. See also MORTGAGE; SECURED TRANSACTIONS.

6. FORMS—The following forms are often used for the various documents relating to chattel mortgages.

CHATTEL MORTGAGE WITH POWER OF SALE

Know all men by these presents, that I, A.B., in consideration of the sum of $........ paid by C.D., have bargained and sold, and by these presents do hereby sell and convey to said C.D., the following goods and chattels, to wit: (describe the articles mortgaged, or refer to them as the goods and chattels mentioned in the schedule hereto annexed), and which are now in my possession.

Whereas, the said A.B. is justly indebted to C.D., in the sum of $............, payable on the ....day of ...., 19....., with interest at six per cent from the ....day of ...., 19....., (upon a promissory note of even date herewith, or for goods sold and delivered).

Now the condition of the above obligation is such that if the said A.B. shall well and truly pay the said C.D. said sum of money and interest when the same shall become due, then this conveyance shall be void, otherwise to remain in full force and effect. It is also agreed that said A.B. may retain possession of the said mortgaged property until said debt becomes due. But if default be made in the payment of said sum or any part thereof, the said C.D. and his assigns are hereby authorized to sell said goods and chattels, or so much thereof as will be necessary to satisfy the amount then due, together with the cost and expenses incurred by reason of said default.

(Signed)   A.B.
In the presence of E.F.

MORTGAGE ON GOODS AND CHATTELS

Know all men by these presents, that A.B., residing at ...., of the first part, for securing the payment of the ...., hereinafter mentioned, and in consideration of the sum of One Dollar ($1), to ..... in hand paid, at or before the execution and delivery of these presents, by C.D., of the second part, the receipt whereof is hereby acknowledged, has (have) granted, bargained, sold, and assigned, and by these presents does (do) grant, bargain, sell, and assign unto the said party (parties) of the second part, all .... now remaining and being ....

To have and to hold, all and singular, the goods and chattels above bargained and sold, or intended so to be, unto the said party (parties) of the second part, ... executors, administrators, and assigns forever. And the said party (parties) of the first part, for .... heirs, executors, and adminis trators, all and singular, the said goods and chattels above bargained and sold unto the said party (parties) of the second part, ... executors, administrators, and assigns, against the said party (parties) of the first part, and against all and every person or persons whomsoever shall and will warrant, and by these presents forever defend.

Upon condition, that if the said party (parties) of the first part shall and does (do) well and truly pay, or cause to be paid, unto the said party (parties) of the second part, ... executors, administrators, or assigns, the sum of ......, then these presents and everything herein contained shall cease and be void. And the said party (parties) of the first part, for .... executors, administrators, and assigns, does (do) covenant and agree to and with the said party (parties) of the second part, ... executors, administrators, and assigns, to make punctual payment of the money hereby secured .... And in case default shall be made in payment of the said sum above mentioned, or in case the said party (parties) of the second part shall sooner choose to demand the said goods and chattels, it shall and may be lawful for, and the said party (parties) of the first part does (do) hereby authorize and empower the said party (parties) of the second part, ... executors, administrators, and assigns, with the aid and assistance of any person or persons, to enter and come into and upon the dwelling house and premises of the said party (parties) of the first part, and in such other place or places as the said goods and chattels are or may be held or placed, and take and carry away the said goods and chattels to sell and dispose of the same for the best price he (they) can obtain, at either public or private sale, and out of the money to retain and pay the said sum above mentioned, with the interest and all expenses and charges thereon, rendering the overplus (if any) unto the said party (parties) of the first part, ... executors, administrators, and assigns. And until default be made in the payment of the aforesaid sum of money, the said party (parties) of the first part to remain and continue in quiet and peaceable possession of the said goods and chattels, and the full and free enjoyment of the same, unless the said party (parties) of the second part, ... executors, administrators, or assigns, shall sooner choose to demand the same; and until such demand be made, the possession of the said party (parties) of the first part shall be deemed the possession of an agent or servant, for the sole benefit and advantage of his principal, the said party (parties) of the second part.

In witness whereof, the said party (parties) of the first part, has (have) hereunto set .... hand(s) and seal(s) this .... day of ...., 19.......

Sealed and delivered in the presence of ......, County of ....ss.:

On this .... day of............, 19........, before me came ...., to me known to be the person(s) described in and who executed the foregoing instrument, and .... acknowledged that he (they) executed the same.

NOTICE OF SALE UNDER CHATTEL MORTGAGE

Notice is hereby given that by virtue of a chattel mortgage, dated on the .... day of ...., 19 ...., and duly filed in the office of the county clerk of .... county, ..., on the ...... day of ...., 19 ....., in book ....., of ....,

on page ...., and executed by A. B. to C. D. to secure the payment of the sum of $ ...., and upon which there is now due the sum of $.............. Default having been made in the payment of said sum, and no suit or other proceeding at law having been instituted to recover said debt or any part thereof, therefore, I will sell the property therein described, viz: (here describe the articles substantially as in the mortgage) at public auction to the highest bidder, for cash, at ...., in the (city, town, or precinct) of ...., in .... county, on the .... day of ...., at one o'clock P.M. of said date.

C.D.
Mortagee

Dated ...., 19 ......

ASSIGNMENT OF MORTGAGE

This instrument, made this ...., day of ...., 19 ....., between ...., of the first part, and ...., of the second part, witnesseth: That the party (parties) of the first part, for a good and valuable consideration, to .... in hand paid by the party (parties) of the second part, has (have) sold, assigned, transferred, and conveyed, and does (do) hereby sell, assign, transfer, and convey to the party (parties) of the second part, a certain mortgage bearing date the .... day of ......, 19 ...., made by ...., recorded in the clerk's office of .... county in book ..... of mortgages, at page ....., on the .... day of ...., 19 ...., at .... o'clock ..... m., together with the bond accompanying said mortgage, and therein referred to, and all sums of money due and to grow due thereon. And the party (parties) of the first part hereby covenant that there is .... due on the said bond and mortgage the sum of ....

In witness whereof, the party (parties) of the first part has (have) hereunto set .... hand(s) and seal(s) the day and year first above written.

Citizenship

1. DEFINITION—A *citizen* is a member of a state or nation who enjoys political rights and is entitled to public protection. Citizenship, therefore, carries with it the duty of allegiance to the government and the right of protection by it.

2. GENERAL PRINCIPLES—A citizen residing in any of the several states owes an allegiance both to the United States and to the state, and may demand protection from each government. A citizen residing in the District of Columbia is a citizen of the United States only. A citizen's ordinary rights are protected by the state government.

All persons born or naturalized in the United States and subject to its jurisdiction or persons born abroad of American parents are citizens of the United States. Formerly a woman took the citizenship of her husband upon marriage. Now marriage does not affect the American citizenship of the wife unless she chooses to renounce it. Neither does naturalization of the husband operate to confer citizenship upon the wife.

3. NATURALIZATION—In order to be naturalized, an alien must follow the forms prescribed by law. His entry into the country must have been lawful, and he must furnish a certificate showing the time, place, and manner of his arrival.

He must declare on oath, before the clerk of an authorized court in the district in which he resides, his intention of becoming a citizen of the United States and of residing here permanently, and he must renounce all allegiance to any foreign power. Not less than two nor more than seven years after he has made such declaration of intention, he must file his petition for admission to citizenship. He must declare on oath in open court that he will support and defend the Constitution of the United States, and he must renounce allegiance to any foreign power. The law also requires that no alien shall be admitted to citizenship unless immediately preceding the date of his petition he has resided continuously within the United States for at least five years, and within the county where he resided when he filed his petition for at least six months. Naturalization of the parent confers citizenship on his minor children if they reside in the United States at the time or subsequently begin to reside here permanently.

4. ALIENS' RIGHTS—Aliens have the right to hold and transfer title to real estate. At common law they are entitled to purchase, own, and sell personal property, to engage in business, and to make contracts or wills. In return they must obey the laws of the land in which they reside.

Contracts

1. DEFINITIONS—A *contract* is a mutual agreement between two or more competent parties for a valuable consideration to do or not to do a particular thing. A *simple contract* may or may not be in writing and requires no seal. A *specialty* is a contract in writing that does require a seal to the signatures. An *executed contract* is completed; an *executory contract* is one still to be executed or completed. An *express contract* is a contract actually made between two or more parties; an *implied contract* is one in which some of the provisions or the entire agreement must be implied from previous agreements, from existing customs, or from the acts of the parties.

2. REQUIREMENTS—A contract must have
a. Two or more competent parties.
b. Legal subject matter.
c. Consideration.
d. Assent of the parties.
There cannot be a contract when any of these are wanting.

3. THE FORM OF THE CONTRACT—In many written contracts the parties are referred to as "party of the first part," or "party of the second part," according to the order in which their names first appear. It does not matter which name is written first. A contract contains certain information in the following order:
a. A written contract begins with a statement of the date, the names of the parties, and their places of residence. Then appears a statement of the consideration, followed by a full statement of all that the first party agrees to do, and all that the second party agrees to do.
b. Next appears a statement of the penalties or forfeitures in case either party does not faithfully and fully perform, or offer to perform, his part of the agreement.
c. The contract ends with the signatures of the parties and their seals and the signatures of witnesses. A seal is simply the mark of a pen around the word "seal," written after the signature, or the word "seal" in parentheses printed or typewritten on the form. Many states no longer require this formality.

4. OTHER FACTORS—Competent lawyers should be employed in the drafting of a contract. Errors in grammar or spelling do not affect the legality of the agreement. If the language should be obscure on certain points, the court will try to determine the intent of the parties when they entered into the agreement, providing the intent can be gathered from the terms of the instrument itself. It is of the utmost importance that the terms of the contract be specifically and explicitly stated.

5. THE VITAL PART OF A CONTRACT: CONSIDERATION—A *consideration* is the thing that induces a party to make a contract. It is the substantial cause or reason inducing the parties to enter into an agreement. A *valuable consideration* is one that is equal to money or may be translated into monetary terms. It is sometimes defined as "money or its equivalent." The law does not require that the consideration should be a good or bad bargain. As long as something is done or suffered by either party, always providing it is not illegal, the consideration is good. The smallest consideration is sufficient to make it legal. The value of the consideration is generally unimportant. All considerations that are immoral are consequently illegal, and contracts based upon them are generally void.

6. THE LAW GOVERNING CONTRACTS—Several basic principles of law apply to all contracts.
a. An intentional alteration in a material part of a contract, made by one party without the consent of the other, discharges the other party from his obligations under the contract.
b. A contract made by a minor is not binding upon him, yet he can hold the other party to all the conditions of the contract.
c. A fraudulent contract may be binding on the party guilty of fraud, although not laying any obligation on the part of the party acting in good faith.
d. A contract for the sale or purchase of personal property over a certain amount—ranging from $30 to $500 in the different states—must be in writing.
e. A contract that cannot be performed within a year must be in writing.
f. If no time of payment is stated in the contract, payment must be made on the delivery of the goods.
g. A contract totally restraining the exercise of a man's trade or profession is void, but one restraining him in any particular place is not void.
h. An offer or proposal that includes the essential parts of a contract becomes a contract as soon as accepted. Generally the acceptance must be at the time of receiving the offer. The offer may be withdrawn at any time before it has been accepted. Offers may be made and accepted within a reasonable time by word of mouth, telephone, telegraph, or mail.
i. A contract required by law to be in writing cannot be changed by verbal agreement.
j. A contract cannot be rescinded except by consent of both parties unless one party has given the other legal grounds to rescind, such as default or fraud.
k. A contract binding in the place where it is made is binding everywhere, but courts of one state will not enforce contracts made in another state where to do so would be in violation of the statutes or public policy of their own state.
l. Each party to an agreement or contract should retain a signed copy.
m. While signatures or contracts written with a pencil are valid in law, it is always safer to write them in ink.

7. UNLAWFUL CONTRACTS—Some kinds of contracts are unlawful or unenforceable by their very nature.
a. A contract to commit a breach of peace.
b. An agreement for immoral purposes.
c. An agreement procured by threats, violence, or fraud.
d. Wagers or bets cannot be collected by law.

e. Interest at rates higher than the maximum rate fixed by law cannot be collected.

f. A contract with an intoxicated person, lunatic, or minor cannot be enforced by the other party.

g. A contract in violation of a statute in the state in which it is made.

h. An agreement to prevent competition on a sale under an execution.

i. An agreement to prohibit the carrying on of a trade throughout the state.

j. Where consent to an agreement is given by mistake and the other party knows of the mistake, such agreement cannot be enforced.

k. The right to vote or hold a public office cannot be sold by contract.

l. A contract without a consideration, such as a promise to make a gift, cannot be enforced.

m. Two or more persons cannot intentionally make a contract to willfully injure a third person.

n. Contracts for concealing felony, for violating public trust, for bribery, or for extortion are prohibited.

o. Useless things, such as agreeing not to go out of the house for a month, cannot become the subject of a contract.

p. A verbal release without payment satisfaction for the debt is not good. Release must be under seal, unless made for some new consideration.

q. If two parts of a contract are in direct conflict with each other, the former part holds good in preference to the latter.

r. Contracts in which there is misrepresentation or concealment of material facts cannot be enforced by the party guilty of such misrepresentation or concealment.

s. If a thing contracted for is not in existence at the time of making the contract, as in a case where parties contract for the purchase and sale of a horse without knowing that the horse is dead at the time, the contract is not valid.

t. If a person agrees to serve as a laborer or clerk, he cannot be compelled to fulfill his agreement; damages, however, can be recovered for a failure to perform.

u. An agreement with a thief to drop a criminal prosecution in consideration of his bringing back the goods and paying all damages is not good and will be no bar to a future prosecution.

v. Guardians, trustees, executors, administrators, or attorneys cannot take advantage of those for whom they act by becoming parties to contracts in which the persons for whom they are acting are interested.

8. QUASI CONTRACTS—A *quasi contract* may be defined as a contract implied in law, or in the nature of a contract. It is a legal obligation resulting from some direct or indirect benefit accruing to one party from the other. Even without any express agreement on the part of the first party, the law compels him to pay. For example

a. One who has reason to believe that payment for goods tendered is expected must not accept them unless he intends to pay for them. If he accepts the goods, he can be compelled to pay for them.

b. A man employed under the promise of good wages or division of profits is entitled to fair treatment, even though such an arrangement is no contract at all.

c. Money paid on an illegal contract, or on one which is void because of nonexistence of the property, may be recovered.

d. If an express company delivers valuable goods to the wrong party, the company can recover from the person who wrongfully accepted them.

e. If, on account of a mistake, a man pays his grocery bill twice for the same period, he can recover.

f. Action to recover can be brought against a man who sells property that is not his own, or that proves to be worthless.

g. Liability is imposed regardless of consent, as distinguished from a contract implied in fact, which is an actual contract, and based on presumed intent or consent. All these questions hinge on the presence or absence of consideration in the agreement.

9. STATUTE OF FRAUDS—In every state there is a statute called the *statute of frauds,* which provides that certain contracts must be in writing to bind the parties. Thus

a. Agreements for the sale of real estate are unenforceable unless they are in writing.

b. A contract for the sale of goods for more than a certain amount, which amount varies in different states, must be in writing, or there must be actual delivery and acceptance of the goods, or part payment must be made for them.

c. A contract must be in writing to charge the defendant upon any special promise to answer for the debt, default, or miscarriage of another person or to charge any executor or administrator upon any special promise to answer any debt or damages out of his own estate.

d. A written contract is necessary to charge any person upon any agreement made upon consideration of marriage, or upon any agreement that cannot be performed within the space of one year from the making thereof.

10. DAMAGES FOR VIOLATION OF CONTRACT—A statute that provides no penalties for the lawbreaker is merely the expression of a wish or the giving of advice. Similarly, a contract must be binding on both parties. This element of mutual obligation is the very essence of a contract. The following are general rules that apply to violations of contracts:

a. Where no actual loss has been sustained by the violation of a contract, the plaintiff is entitled to nominal damages only. For example, A contracts to drill a well for B and to complete same within a specified time or forfeit $1000, said amount being intended not as an assessment of the damages that would probably be actually sustained, but to secure the performance of the contract by the imposition of a penalty. The courts will not compel A to pay the $1000 to B. They will, however, permit B to recover from A such damages as he actually sustained as a result of A's failure to complete the well within the specified time.

b. Expected profits on speculations in real property cannot be recovered in case of a violation of contract.

c. Failure on the part of the seller to convey real estate or deliver personal property according to agreement entitles the plaintiff to recover damages or to sue for specific performance of the contract.

d. In case of loss of goods by a common carrier, the plaintiff is entitled to the value of the goods where they were to be delivered, less the freight on such goods.

e. If a party contracts to employ another for a certain time, at a specified compensation, and discharges him without cause before the expiration of the time, the employee can obtain judgment for the full amount of wages for the entire unexpired balance of the time, provided he is unable to secure employment in the same line of work after making an earnest effort to do so. Should he obtain work at a lower wage he can collect the difference.

f. To prevent lawsuits and disputes the amount of damages for the violation of contracts is sometimes fixed by the parties themselves by inserting in the contract some such provision as the following:

And it is further agreed that the party that shall fail to perform this agreement on his part shall pay to the other the full sum of (here state amount), as liquidated damages.

11. FORM:

GENERAL FORM OF CONTRACT

This agreement, made and entered into this . . . . . . day of . . . ., 19 . . . ., by and between Clarence Ranck of Aurora, County of Kane, State of Illinois, party of the first part, and Charles Vandersall of Columbus, Ohio, party of the second part, witnesseth:

In consideration of (insert consideration), it is agreed between the parties hereto as follows:

Said party of the first part agrees (insert agreement of party of the first part).

Said party of the second part agrees (insert agreement of the party of the second part).

In witness whereof the said parties have hereunto set their hands and seals the day and year first above written.

CLARENCE RANCK   (Seal)
CHARLES VANDERSALL   (Seal)

Copyright

1. DEFINITION—A *copyright* is the exclusive right to reproduce, publish, and sell a literary or artistic work. Under the United States copyright law, a copyright may be granted for the following classes of material:

a. Books, including collections, anthologies, and encyclopedias.
b. Magazines and newspapers.
c. Lectures, sermons, and other addresses for oral delivery.
d. Dramatic and musical-dramatic compositions.
e. Musical compositions.
f. Maps.
g. Works of art, including models and designs.
h. Reproductions of works of art.
i. Scientific or technical drawings or plastic work.
j. Photographs.
k. Prints and pictorial illustrations.
l. Motion-picture photoplays.
m. Other motion pictures.

Copyrights can also be secured on compilations, abridgments, arrangements, and adaptations, whether of non-copyrightable material or, with the permission of the copyright holder, of material that has been copyrighted already. Republished works that include new material are also copyrightable.

2. HOW TO OBTAIN—To secure a copyright on a work that is to be reproduced for sale or public distribution, the work should be published with a copyright notice, which may be in the following form:

Copyright © 1960
by
Jones, Smith, and Company

On maps, photographs, pictures, and other works where it is difficult to place a complete copyright notice, the letter *C* enclosed in a circle, ©, is used; it must be accompanied by a

symbol or mark of the owner of the copyright, and his name must appear elsewhere on the work. After publication of the work, two copies of the best edition, or one copy, in the case of a work by a foreign citizen that was first published in another country, should be sent to the Copyright Office, Washington, D.C., with an application for registration. Books by American authors and proprietors or by alien authors and proprietors domiciled within the United States must be accompanied by an affidavit stating that the typesetting, printing, and binding were done in the United States. Forms for the affidavit and application for registration are supplied by the Copyright Office upon request.

3. FEES—The fee for registration of a published work is $6; payment of this sum also entitles one to a certificate under seal of the Copyright Office. The charge for the renewal of a copyright is $4. Copyrights may be assigned to other persons.

4. HOW TO OBTAIN A COPYRIGHT FOR OTHER ARTICLES—A copyright may also be obtained on certain works not published or reproduced for sale by filing an application for registration; the fee is $6. The application should be accompanied by one manuscript of the work, if it is a lecture, sermon, address, or dramatic or musical composition; by one print, for copyright of a photograph not intended for general circulation; or by a photograph or reproduction in the case of works of art, scientific or technical drawings, or plastic works. To obtain a copyright on a motion picture photoplay not published or for sale, the application for registration must be accompanied by the title, description, and a print from each scene or act. An application for registration of another type of motion picture must be accompanied by the title, description, and two prints from different sections of the picture.

5. DURATION OF COPYRIGHT—A copyright is valid for 28 years and may be renewed for the same length of time, provided application for renewal is made and registered within one year prior to the expiration of the original term of copyright. It cannot be renewed again. If an author is not living, his copyright may be renewed by the widow, the widower, or the children. If none of these are living the executors have the right of renewal, and if there is no will the copyright may be renewed by the next of kin. The person to whom a copyright has been assigned may also renew it at the expiration of the original 28-year period.

6. PRINTS AND LABELS—Copyrights may be taken out on prints and labels for advertising purposes. They first must be published with a notice of copyright. Application for registration would then be filed by the owner or author. These copyrights are also effective for 28 years and may be renewed for a similar period.

7. UNIVERSAL COPYRIGHT—The United States is a party to the Universal Copyright Convention that became effective in September 1955. There are over fifty-five contracting states to this convention.

Under the terms of the agreement each state provides for the protection of the rights of authors and other copyright owners in literary, scientific, and artistic works, including writings, music, drama, cinematographic works, paintings, engravings, and sculpture. Works first published in any member nation will generally get the same protection in other member nations as they afford their own nationals. The copyright symbol © accompanied by the name of the copyright owner and the date of publication is sufficient to obtain protection for the work in any country that is a party to the Universal Copyright Convention.

Foreign works need not fulfill the United States requirement of deposit and registration if they are first published in a country party to the Universal Copyright Convention or if they are written by nationals of any of the contracting states.

8. APPLICATIONS for registration of claims to copyright are filed with the Register of Copyrights, Library of Congress, Washington, D.C. 20025. These application forms as well as information circulars covering the various subjects are furnished free upon request to the Register of Copyrights. Changes to the copyright law, proposed by the Subcommittee on Patents, Trademarks, and Copyrights of the Senate Committee on the Judiciary, may be obtained from the U.S. Government Printing Office.

Corporations

1. DEFINITION—A *corporation* is a group of persons empowered to act as a single individual, and treated by the law as such in many respects.

2. KINDS OF CORPORATIONS—*Business corporations,* engaged in enterprise to earn profit, are the most common. *Public corporations* are agencies of the government. Railroad corporations and other public service corporations, though performing a public service, are nevertheless *private corporations.* Then there are *religious, charitable and beneficial corporations,* usually organized for beneficial purposes, not for profit. *Quasi corporations,* such as school districts, resemble corporations in some ways. They can own and manage real estate, make contracts, sue and be sued like any other corporation. A *close corporation* is one whose capital stock or ownership is confined to one family or distinct group of individuals.

3. FORMATION OF A CORPORATION—The formation of a corporation involves numerous legal questions, and should never be attempted without the services of a competent corporation lawyer. In most states the first step after having a certain amount of stock subscribed and paid for is to file with the secretary of the state a statement giving name, object, amount of capital stock, amount of stock paid for, location of office, and duration of the proposed corporation. The charter is then issued and a meeting of stockholders is called to elect directors. State laws vary, but usually three or more individuals may form a corporation. Corporations created in one state may transact any lawful business in another state, and they can acquire and transfer property as individuals, provided they comply with the law of the state in which they do business and obtain a license to do business there.

4. LIFE OF A CORPORATION—A corporation exists until the expiration of its charter unless it fails or is discontinued for other good reasons. Most charters are now perpetual. The stockholder's rights may pass from one to another by sale or by inheritance.

5. CAPITAL STOCK—Corporations generally have assets composed of money, real estate, buildings, machinery, patents, copyrights, etc. Capital stock is divided into parts called *shares,* and the owners of the shares are called *stockholders* or *shareholders.* By sale of shares the necessary money for the enterprise may be collected from many different sources, and unlike members in a partnership, the individual stockholders are not personally liable for the debts of the corporation. In large measure these facts account for the great popularity of the corporate form of organization. Corporations may increase or decrease the amount of their capital stock, provided the change is made in good faith without intent to defraud. See SECURITIES LAW.

6. WHO MAY SUBSCRIBE FOR STOCK—Anyone capable of making a contract may subscribe for the stock of a corporation. Minors are excluded. Where fictitious subscriptions are used to induce others to buy, the purchaser may refuse to

pay his subscription; he may recover the money already paid, or he may keep the stock and sue for damages. The selling of subscriptions to stock is now very strictly regulated by statute.

7. THE STOCK CERTIFICATE is a written statement of the number and par value of the shares to which the holder is entitled. In other words, it is the evidence of ownership. A stockholder may prove ownership even though a certificate has never been issued him. When the capital stock of a corporation is increased, each shareholder usually has the right to purchase a portion of the new stock before it can be offered for sale to outsiders.

8. PREFERRED STOCK—This kind of stock takes preference over the ordinary or common stock of a corporation. The holders of preferred stock are entitled either to a stated percentage annually out of the net earnings of the corporation before a dividend can be declared on the common stock or to some other preference set out in the certificate. Preference, rather than actual payment, is guaranteed. Holders of preferred stock usually have the right to vote at any stockholders' meeting on the same basis as the holders of common stock. In some states, the law requires that each share of stock have equal voting rights with every other share.

9. COMMON STOCK—The ordinary stock of a corporation is called common stock. The holders are entitled to all the rights incident to their ownership.

10. TRANSFER OF STOCK—This is provided for by statute. Usually the seller must assign the certificate to the transferee, execute a power of attorney, and deliver the certificate to the company for cancellation. The transfer agent then issues a new certificate to the purchaser.

11. SUBSCRIPTION—A subscription for stock is a contract and must be in writing. An agent cannot refuse to receive a subscription from a competent person, nor can he release a subscriber or alter the terms of the contract. The subscriber must inform himself as to his obligations and cannot evade payment unless he can prove fraud.

12. THE SHAREHOLDER'S LIABILITY—As stated previously, a corporation differs from a partnership in that the shareholders in a corporation are liable only for the amount of stock they own, while each member of a partnership is liable for all the debts of the firm. However, in the case of national banks the shareholders are liable for double the amount of their holdings in case the bank fails, if that much more is required to pay the debts. The amount of a stockholder's liability is fixed by statute. A stockholder in any corporation is liable for the full amount of his stock, whether paid in full or not.

13. RECEIVERSHIP—When a corporation fails, a receiver is sometimes appointed by the court to take charge of its affairs. The receiver has the power to convert the property into cash, levy and collect assessments from the shareholders, where authorized by law, and pay dividends to the creditors, as in the case of bankruptcy proceedings (see also BANKRUPTCY). The receiver may be an individual, a group of individuals, or a trust company.

14. MANAGEMENT—The power of a corporation rests in its members or individual stockholders except as restricted or limited by law. Unless the charter or state laws alter the case, policies are determined by a majority vote; usually a shareholder has as many votes as he has shares in the corporation. The right to vote in a stockholders' meeting is determined by the stock record of ownership as of the date of meeting, or as of the date the books are closed prior to the meeting. The bylaws of the corporation generally fix the time for the closing of the books. A stockholder has the right to vote even if no certificate has been issued to him. He may

vote in person or by proxy. An executor or trustee may vote the stock of the estate.

15. MEETINGS—The statutes or the bylaws of a corporation usually prescribe the manner in which meetings are to be called, and the bylaws fix the time and place of meetings. Should the proper officer fail to call a meeting at the required time, the meeting may lawfully be held later, and if he should refuse to issue the proper notice, he may be compelled by mandamus proceedings to do so. Regular meetings are held in the manner set forth by the charter or bylaws, and the object of the meeting need not be stated in the notice. On the other hand, special meetings may be called at any time on proper authority, but the notice must state the object of the meeting and no other business may be there transacted. Any authorized meeting may be adjourned from time to time or from day to day, and the adjournments must be considered as the same meeting. Even if a meeting is illegally called it becomes a valid meeting by ratification of the proper official or by the shareholders. Notice of meeting is sent to whoever has the right to vote the stock.

16. DIRECTORS—Management of a corporation is vested in the directors. Most corporations delegate managerial powers to directors who are elected either by a majority vote of the shareholders or by a cumulative system of voting in states in which such system is used. Their powers are established by statute, charter, or bylaws. As a rule they have general supervision over the business of the corporation. Their authority may be delegated to committees, corporate officials, or individuals. Thus the president, the secretary, the treasurer, and other officers and committees of the corporation are chosen by the board of directors to act in the capacity of agents in administering corporation affairs. A director may not act for the corporation individually, but his unauthorized acts would bind the corporation if subsequently ratified. A director may not act both for the corporation and for himself in the same transaction. Unless otherwise provided, directors are not entitled to compensation for their services.

17. THE DIRECTORS' LIABILITY—The directors of a company are liable to the company and to shareholders and outsiders for negligence, fraud, or for acts committed outside the scope of their authority. These are questions of fact to be determined by the courts. The directors of a corporation are personally liable for its debts if it can be proved that they incurred the obligations knowing that the corporation was insolvent. They have been held personally, jointly, and severally liable as partners for debts of the corporation contracted in a state in which the company was found to have been doing business without having taken out a license.

18. OFFICERS—The officers of a corporation are usually the president, vice-president, secretary, and treasurer chosen by, and often from, the board of directors. The ordinary rules of agency govern their powers and duties.

a. The *president* is the chief executive officer and usually presides at meetings of the board of directors.

b. The *vice-president* takes over the duties of the president when, for any reason, the latter is unable to perform them. Quite frequently there are numerous vice-presidents assigned to different duties.

c. The *secretary* is the keeper of the records and the chief clerk of the corporation. He usually has the custody of the corporate seal.

d. The *treasurer* has charge of the corporation's finances. He is usually under bond for the faithful performance of his duties.

19. DIVIDENDS—A dividend is a payment to the shareholders out of the net profits of the corporation. A dividend may not be paid out of stated capital, but may be paid out of capital surplus. It may be in actual cash, in property, or in additional stock. When stock is selling above par on the exchange, corporations sometimes grant shareholders the right to purchase additional stock at par instead of declaring a cash stock dividend. The law will not permit the payment of dividends out of capital or from borrowed money without the consent of the stockholders, and the directors would be liable for such a fraudulent payment. Furthermore, illegally paid dividends may be recovered for the benefit of creditors. The net profit of a corporation is an asset, and not secure against creditors until the money has been declared as a dividend. When the dividend has been legally declared payable, no action can be brought by creditors to stop its payment. The directors must act in good faith, but they cannot be compelled to pay dividends when they do not deem it advisable to do so. The courts hold that dividends must be general on all stock of the same class, so that each shareholder in that class will receive his just share, and that the dividends shall be paid to the owner as determined by the books of the company.

20. LIABILITIES OF A CORPORATION—Through its agents or servants a corporation can be guilty of slander, libel, false representation, trespass, or negligence, and can be sued accordingly.

21. THE SHAREHOLDER'S RIGHTS—In most states a shareholder has the right to inspect the company's books at any reasonable time for any proper purpose. Furthermore, he may employ an expert accountant to go through the records if he has reason to believe that the affairs of the company are not being handled properly. This right is limited in some states. In Illinois, for instance, the stockholder must either own 5 percent of the stock or have been a shareholder for six months in order to inspect the books.

22. FORMS—These forms relate to voting by proxy in a corporation.

GENERAL PROXY

Know all men by these presents, that I, ..., the undersigned, do hereby constitute and appoint .... my attorney and agent (with power of substitution for me and in my name, place and stead) to vote as my proxy for the election of directors and upon all matters that may be considered at the annual meeting of the stockholders of the .... company, to be held at its office at the city of ...., of the county of ...., state of ...., on the .... day of ...., 19 ...., at ..... o'clock .....M., or any adjournment thereof, according to the number of votes I should be entitled to vote if I were personally present at said meeting, hereby revoking all former proxies by me made and given.

In witness whereof, I have hereunto set my hand and seal this .... day of ...., 19 ....

Witness:

.... (Signature)

REVOCATION OF PROXY

Know all men by these presents, that I, the undersigned, do hereby revoke and annul a certain proxy by me given to .... (or, any and all proxies or powers of attorney heretofore given by me) authorizing and empowering the said .... to represent me and to vote in my name and stead and to act for me in any way whatsoever at any meeting or

meetings of the stockholders of the . . . .
. . . . company.

In witness whereof, I have hereunto set my hand and seal this . . . . day of . . . . . . , 19 . . . .
(Witnessed) (Signed)

Criminal Law and Procedure

1. DEFINITIONS—A *crime* is an act in violation of some existing prohibitory statute and the common morality of the country. An individual cannot compromise a criminal wrong, for crime is a matter for the state to settle. Crimes may be classified as *felonies,* or more serious offenses, and *misdemeanors,* or less serious offenses, but the distinction is largely an arbitrary one.

2. BURDEN OF PROOF—The burden of proof is upon the state. In other words, a person accused of a crime is presumed to be innocent until the contrary is proved. Most states require that the verdict of the jury be unanimous to convict. If any reasonable doubt remains in the minds of the jury after it has heard all the evidence, it is its duty to acquit the defendant. Once acquitted, a prisoner cannot be brought to trial a second time for the same offense in the same jurisdiction.

3. DEFENSES—Two defenses that are often raised are the defense of insanity and that of self-defense. A person who cannot distinguish right from wrong is insane and cannot be held responsible for his acts, but the insanity must be proved. Also, a person may defend his person, family, or property and may use such force as is necessary. If a person can show that the act was committed in self-defense he is guilty of no crime.

4. CONFESSION—A legal confession must be voluntary and free from all compulsion, either physical or mental. Third-degree methods are unlawful, and a confession procured by the use of threats or violence has no standing in court.

5. TRIAL BY JURY—A person accused of a crime is guaranteed the right to a fair and impartial trial by a jury (see JURIES) and the right to be represented by a competent lawyer. The trial must occur in the county where the crime was committed unless a change of venue is granted. The defendant is entitled to a change of venue if it can be proved that on account of prejudice on the part of the judge or jury the accused could not receive a fair trial in the county where the alleged crime was committed.

6. HABEAS CORPUS—A writ of habeas corpus is sometimes issued by the court to prevent people from being unlawfully deprived of their liberty. The prisoner is brought before the court and is released unless cause can be shown for his detention. This is a fundamental right under the Constitution.

7. CRIMINAL PROCEDURE—The first step in criminal procedure in most states is generally the issuing of a warrant by a justice of the peace or other judicial officer. When arrested, the accused is either placed in custody or, if he can furnish a satisfactory bond, released on bail awaiting trial. *Bail* means the sureties who bind themselves to have the accused present in court when required for trial. If the offense is a misdemeanor the case is usually tried and settled before the justice. If it is a felony, the justice holds a preliminary trial, certifying his findings to the grand jury. Acting in an investigating capacity, the grand jury may indict the accused, and the case is tried on its merits in the regular criminal court. If the grand jury fails to indict, the charge may be dropped on account of insufficient evidence.

8. CRIMINAL LAW IN BRIEF—The acts described in the following list are violations of criminal law in most states.

Accessory to the Crime. Any person assisting another to commit a crime or to escape from the scene of the crime is equally guilty with the principal.

Adultery. In many of the states, it is a crime for any married person to live openly with any person of the opposite sex who is not his lawful spouse.

Assault and Battery. A person who threatens or attempts to strike another person is guilty of assault, even though the threat is not followed by actual battery. Assault becomes battery when injury is actually done. The slightest unlawful touching may be battery.

Bigamy. A person having more than one husband or wife at one time is guilty of the crime of bigamy.

Bribery consists in the offering or giving of money or other valuable consideration to a public officer or one performing a public duty, as an inducement for him to commit an unlawful act. The giver and the receiver of the bribe are equally guilty.

Burglary consists in the unlawful breaking into and entering of the building of another with the intent to commit a crime.

Conspiracy. When two or more persons agree to do an unlawful act, the agreement is called a conspiracy, and is in itself a crime.

Contempt of Court. Any attempt to obstruct justice or to injure the dignity of the court is punishable by the action of the court.

Embezzlement is the wrongful appropriation and use of the personal property of another person by one to whom it has been voluntarily turned over for some lawful use.

Extortion is the asking and accepting of unlawful fees by a public officer.

False Pretense. It is a criminal offense to obtain money or other things of value by the false or fraudulent representation of a past or existing fact.

Forgery is the false making, or the material alteration, of a written instrument, contract, or any other legal paper with intent to defraud.

Fornication is illicit sexual intercourse other than adultery, as that between unmarried persons. It is punishable in some states.

Larceny is the unlawful appropriation and use of a person's property. It differs from embezzlement in that the original taking is unlawful.

Malicious Mischief is a crime that consists of the willful and intentional injury of another's property.

Manslaughter is the unlawful killing of a human being without malice or premeditation.

Mayhem is the act of maiming, disfiguring, or cutting away any part of the human body.

Murder is the unlawful taking of a human life with malice and premeditation.

Offenses on the High Seas are tried by the country under whose flag the ship is sailing.

Perjury is the false swearing of a person under oath. A person inducing another to perjure himself is equally guilty.

Rape. It is a felony to have sexual intercourse with a girl or woman without her consent.

Robbery is stealing property from another by force and intimidation. It is a felony punishable by imprisonment in the penitentiary.

Seduction. To have intercourse with a woman of chaste reputation through false promises of marriage is a crime.

Stolen Property. It is a crime to buy, receive, or conceal stolen property with the intent not to return it to the rightful owner. When buying property the buyer should demand proof of ownership.

Treason. It is treason to make war against, or to assist the enemies of, the existing government. Treason is punishable by death. A foreigner, owing no allegiance to the government, cannot be guilty of treason.

Unlawful Assembly. It is a criminal offense for two or more persons to assemble in contemplation of some unlawful act.

Deeds

1. DEFINITIONS—A *deed* is a written document conveying real estate. There are two kinds of deeds in general use: warranty deeds and quitclaim deeds. Any person of legal age, competent to transact business and owning real estate, may convey it by deed. The seller is called the *grantor,* the buyer the *grantee.* See also REAL ESTATE TRANSACTIONS.

2. A WARRANTY DEED is one in which the seller or grantor warrants the title to be good, and agrees to defend the same against all parties. Such a deed usually provides (a) that a seller has a right to convey the real estate, (b) that he is the owner of the land mentioned in the deed, (c) that the land is free and clear from all former and other grants, bargains, sales, liens, taxes, assessments, and encumbrances of any kind, and (d) that the purchaser will have quiet enjoyment of the real estate; that is, that he will not be put out of possession by anyone having superior title. If it afterwards develops that the grantor did not have the right to sell, or if the grantee discovers an encumbrance on the land, or if he has any trouble about the title, the purchaser has a good cause of action against the seller.

3. A QUITCLAIM DEED conveys only what interest the grantor may have in the property. This form of deed is often given by one whose title to the real estate may be defective. A quitclaim deed contains no warranties; the seller conveys only whatever interest he may have.

4. GENERAL PRINCIPLES:

a. Deeds must be written, typewritten, or printed.

b. The names of the parties and places of residence are generally written first.

c. The property must be fully described. The description should be by bounds, or by divisions of United States surveys, or by subdivisions into blocks and lots, as shown on the records in the county recorder's office.

d. The deed must express a consideration, and be signed and sealed by the grantor or grantors. A deed without consideration is void.

e. Numbers should always be written in words followed by figures in parentheses, thus, Two Hundred Dollars ($200).

f. If the grantor is married, both husband and wife should join in the deed, and it should be executed and acknowledged by both.

g. The acknowledgment of a deed can be made only before persons authorized by law to take the same, such as justices of the peace, notaries, masters in chancery, and judges and clerks of the courts.

h. The deed takes effect upon its delivery to the person authorized to receive it, and should be recorded at once.

i. After the signing and acknowledgment of a deed the parties have no right to make the slightest alteration.

j. A person should never purchase real estate without a careful examination of the title by a trusted attorney.

k. Before advancing money or signing a contract for purchase of land or lots, the buyer should always procure an abstract of title or guaranty policy. See REAL ESTATE TRANSACTIONS.

l. A deed in which a mistake has been made can be corrected in all cases of fraud or accident.

m. In investigating the title to real estate, the attorney is bound to make a careful examination of the records and report the facts and his conclusions with respect to the condition of the title, and is liable for any injury resulting from his negligence.

n. A deed is considered recorded as soon as it reaches the recording officer, who generally notes upon it the day, hour, and minute when it was received by him.

o. If the land is a gift and no price is paid for it, it is customary to insert the words "in consideration of one dollar and other good and valuable considerations."

5. FORMS:

WARRANTY DEED

Know all men by these presents, that we . . . . and . . . ., husband and wife, in consideration of the sum of $ . . . . in hand paid, do hereby grant, bargain, sell and convey to . . . ., of . . . . county, ..., the following described real estate situated in the county of . . . ., and state of . . . ., to wit: (describe premises), to have and to hold to his heirs and assigns forever. Together with all of the tenements, hereditaments, and appurtenances thereto belonging. And we hereby covenant with said . . . . that we are lawfully seized of said premises; that they are free from incumbrances; that we have good right and lawful authority to sell the same, and we covenant to warrant and defend the same against the lawful claims of all persons whosoever. And the said . . . . hereby relinquishes her right of dower in said premises.

In witness whereof we have hereunto set our hands and seals this . . . . . . day of . . . ., 19 . . . .

In presence of   . . . .(Seal)

. . . .(Seal)

State of . . . .

. . . . County.

. . . .

. . . .

On this . . . . day of . . . ., 19 . . . ., before me, a notary public in and for said county, personally came the above named . . . . and . . . ., his wife, who are known to me to be the identical persons whose names are affixed to the above deed as grantors, and severally acknowledge the instrument to be their voluntary act and deed.

In witness whereof I have hereunto set my hand the day and year above written.

. . . .

Notary Public

Note: Statutes in many states provide for a short form which may be used in place of the above and has the same effect.

QUITCLAIM DEED

The grantor (here insert name or names of grantor or grantors and place or places of residence), of the city of . . . ., for the consideration of (here insert consideration), convey and quitclaim to (here insert name or names of grantee or grantees) all interest in the following described real estate (here insert description), situated in the county of . . . . in the state of . . . .

Dated this . . . . day of . . . ., A.D. 19 . . . .

. . . . . . (Seal)

Note: Use same form of acknowledgment as that shown for warranty deeds above.

Discrimination in Employment

1. INTRODUCTION—Title VII of the Civil Rights Act of 1964 prohibits employment practices that discriminate because of race, color, religion, sex, or national origin. The law applies to employers who have twenty-five or more employees, to employment agencies, and to labor organizations.

2. UNLAWFUL PRACTICES OF EMPLOYERS—It is an unlawful employment practice for an employer to fail or refuse to hire or to discharge any individual, or otherwise to discriminate against any individual with respect to his compensation, terms, conditions, or privileges of employment, because of such individual's race, color, religion, sex, or national origin.

3. UNLAWFUL PRACTICES OF EMPLOYMENT AGENCIES—It is an unlawful employment practice for an employment agency to fail or refuse to refer for employment, or otherwise to discriminate against any individual, or to classify or refer for employment any individual, on the basis of or because of his race, color, religion, sex, or national origin.

4. UNLAWFUL PRACTICES OF LABOR ORGANIZATIONS—It is an unlawful employment practice for a labor organization to exclude or to expel from its membership, or otherwise discriminate against, any individual because of race, color, religion, sex, or national origin.

5. EMPLOYMENT PRACTICES NOT IN VIOLATION OF THE LAW—The act specifically refers to the following practices as not constituting a violation of the law:

a. Any discrimination based on religion, sex, or national origin where religion, sex, or national origin is a bona fide occupational qualification reasonably necessary to the normal operation of that particular business or enterprise.

b. A policy by a church-supported educational institution to hire only employees who have certain religious beliefs.

c. Any discrimination based on a seniority, merit or incentive system or other like reasons that are not the result of any intention to discriminate because of race, color, religion, sex, or national origin.

Examples of unlawful practices include

a. Certain "male only" job classifications.

b. Wage differences between men and women doing the same work.

c. Not granting maternity leave to pregnant employees.

d. Nonequalization of male and female retirement ages.

e. Separate male and female seniority lists.

f. Allowing men but not women to smoke at their desks.

Dower

1. DEFINITIONS—*Dower* is the provision that the law makes for the support of a widow out of her deceased husband's estate. Unless modified by statute, this interest consists of the use for life of one-third of her husband's land after his death. During the husband's life, the law protects the wife's interest by prohibiting the sale of real estate unless she joins with him in signing the deed. If the property is sold and she does not sign the deed, she still has her dower right in the property. The interest that a husband acquires in the land belonging to his wife after her death is called *curtesy*. In some states the term *curtesy* has been abolished and the word *dower* substituted, so that the latter term applies to the interest of either the husband or the wife in the land of the deceased spouse.

2. GENERAL PRINCIPLES—The dower right is regulated by widely differing statutes in the several states. If the land is subject to a prior lien or to a mortgage that was signed by the wife along with her husband, the wife cannot get possession until the encumbrance has been removed. A woman may release her dower right by signing with her husband a deed for the conveyance of the real estate. A husband can will his wife a certain amount in place of her dower, but the wife can claim the dower instead if she prefers it. The widow is usually entitled to administer the estate of her deceased husband. Dower exists in growing crops and trees, and also in mines and quarries opened during the husband's lifetime. The widow of a partner is entitled to her dower in the partnership land after payment of all debts of the partnership. A legal marriage is necessary to sustain a dower estate. An absolute divorce divests the wife of her dower if the divorce was granted to the husband by reason of the wife's misconduct. Dower is assigned to the widow either by direction of the court or by agreement. Dower may be barred by a marriage settlement or agreement made before marriage.

Drunkenness

1. INTOXICATION—Both the civil and criminal courts are frequently called upon to rule on cases in which one of the parties involved was intoxicated.

2. GENERAL PRINCIPLES—It is the duty of those who deal with an intoxicated person to take his condition into consideration. A sober party must exercise a reasonable degree of care to avoid injury to a drunken individual. A railroad company is also bound to take into account the helpless condition of its passenger, and to exercise reasonable care in keeping him out of danger. Drunkenness is not a legal excuse for the commission of a crime, but sometimes it is evidence of the absence of malice.

3. IN CIVIL CASES the courts have recognized cases in which intoxication was an excuse for repudiating a contract. The mental condition must be taken into consideration, especially where a man has become utterly incompetent or insane as a result of his intemperate habits. As we have seen before, such a man cannot make a contract. If one party is visibly intoxicated, the contract could be declared void on the ground that the other party must have realized his condition. The element of fraud enters if one party deliberately induced the condition of the other. However, if the intoxicated party ratifies the agreement when sober, or fails to repudiate it, he would be legally bound by it.

4. IN CRIMINAL CASES the courts hold that one who voluntarily becomes intoxicated cannot claim his intoxication as an excuse for his criminal acts. Yet in all such cases the facts must show intent to commit the crime before there can be any conviction. This aspect has been brought up in many cases where the defendant was so drunk that he entered the wrong house, or carried off the property of others, or slandered the reputation of another. Voluntary intoxication is a defense only where intent is an element of the crime.

Employer and Employee

1. EXPLANATION—The term *employee* refers to a person who is hired by a contract of service to perform certain duties for another person, called the *employer*.

2. KINDS OF CONTRACTS—There are two types of general employment contracts: (a) contracts to do some particular thing such as to buy and sell stocks or provisions, or collect accounts, and (b) contracts to do whatever the employer may direct. Farm hands, domestic servants, and clerks

belong to this second class. Such contracts are frequently verbal, or even only implied, rather than written.

3. COMPENSATION—If no agreement has been made beforehand, the employee is entitled to the wages usually paid for such service. If the employee leaves because of insufficient food, ill-treatment, or disabling sickness, he is entitled to payment for the time he worked.

4. DUTIES OF EMPLOYEE—The employee is expected to perform faithfully the services for which he contracted for the entire term or period of service. In many cases, as in those of workers employed by the day or hour, this period of service may be very short. Courts frequently hold that if an employee leaves before expiration time, he can claim no pay for the work done. Some judges have held, however, that even in this case the employee is entitled to pay for work done, less what the employer lost by necessity of paying higher wages to the employee's successor, or what he lost by the employee's failing to perform his contract. The employee is bound to take reasonable care of the property in his care, and is liable for any loss or injury to it when due to his negligence.

5. DISCHARGE—An employee may be discharged at the end of his contract without any cause or previous notice. If he is discharged without good cause before the termination of his agreement, however, he is entitled to pay for the whole period, provided he has first made an earnest attempt to secure other employment in the same kind of work. If he gets work at lower wages, he is entitled to the difference. If his pay is equal to, or higher than, the former rate, he cannot collect. If, however, the discharge is on account of incapacity, dishonesty, or misconduct, he is not entitled to any pay for the unexpired period. Frequently a person is hired for a month, or for a year, at the termination of which the work continues. In such cases the law presumes a new contract on the same terms.

6. LIABILITY OF EMPLOYER—An employer's liability is of two kinds: (a) liability for the acts of his employees, and (b) liability for the injury or death of his employees.

7. LIABILITY FOR ACTS OF EMPLOYEE—The employer is liable for the wrongful acts of his employee producing injury to others, provided the acts are done in the course of the ordinary employment. Thus a railroad company is liable to passengers for negligence of conductors and engineers.

8. LIABILITY FOR INJURY OF EMPLOYEES—Workmen's compensation acts have largely provided new remedies to take the place of the employee's right to sue his employer for injuries incurred in the course of his employment. Under these acts liability is generally imposed upon the employer without regard to the question as to whether or not the employer was at fault, and payments are made as insurance rather than as damages.

9. WORKMEN'S COMPENSATION—Any person employed by a contract of service who is under the control of the employer while at work at the machine or other device from which the injury arose is entitled to compensation. Previous physical condition is not considered in determining the amount.

10. WHO IS EXCLUDED—The workmen's compensation acts differ in the several states. The federal act protects persons employed by the United States and workmen engaged in interstate commerce. While it is difficult to give a general rule, the following are excluded from the benefits in most states, and in others the compensation is optional:
a. Minors and apprentices.
b. Farm laborers.
c. Domestic servants.
d. Casual employees.
e. Independent contractors.
f. Public officers.

11. DEPENDENTS—The law also provides that the compensation be paid to dependents in case of death. Payments may be made only to actual dependents or to partial dependents in accordance with the degree of dependency. These include widows, children, stepchildren, illegitimate children, adopted children, or a dependent parent.

12. PAYMENTS—The compensation acts provide for payments to the injured or his dependents in case of partial incapacity, permanent incapacity, or death, in amounts depending on the earning power of the injured at the time of the accident. Maximum and minimum amounts are usually specified.

13. INSURANCE—The compensation laws are rigidly enforced, and to protect themselves employers often take out liability insurance on the life and health of each employee. Then, when an accident occurs, the insurance company assumes all liability and relieves the employer of any claims that might be made under the workmen's compensation law. This method of limiting liability is provided for in the laws of all the states. The cost of such insurance is based on the size of the payroll and the nature of the employment. It ranges from a purely nominal figure for office work to a rather high rate for the more hazardous occupations.

14. VARIATIONS—It is impossible in a brief space to attempt an explanation of the workmen's compensation laws in the different states. In some states deductions are made for contributory negligence; in others, awards are fixed for specific injuries; and in almost every state there can be found numerous variations.

15. SOURCES OF INFORMATION—Copies of the compensation and liability statutes may be secured free of charge by writing to the Secretary of State of the state for which information is desired. He should be addressed at the state capital. Owing to the technical nature of the subject, however, it is always a good plan to ask an insurance adviser to explain the duties and obligations under the law.

16. THE FAIR LABOR STANDARDS ACT—In 1938 Congress enacted the Fair Labor Standards Act, which set a minimum wage and maximum workweek for employees engaged in interstate commerce or in the production of goods for commerce. Because of the broad interpretation by the Supreme Court of the federal government's constitutional power to regulate interstate commerce, this act has a widespread effect on employment.

There are also provisions in the act restricting the employment of children. Children under eighteen years of age may not engage in hazardous occupations. Children under sixteen years may work for their parents in nonmining or nonmanufacturing occupations. Children between the ages of fourteen and sixteen years may work at nonmining and nonmanufacturing occupations after school hours and under conditions that will not affect their health or well-being.

The Fair Labor Standards Act is administered by the Wage and Hour Division of the United States Department of Labor at Washington, D.C. Many of the states have similar legislation affecting employment conditions among employees working in business wholly within the state.

17. THE NATIONAL LABOR RELATIONS ACT AND LABOR-MANAGEMENT RELATIONS ACT—The National Labor Relations Act, known as the Wagner Act, has given employees the legal right to organize and bargain collectively with their employers without interference or coercion by the employers. The National Labor Relations Board enforces the act and may, upon request of the employer or employees, hold an election to determine which union shall act as bargaining agent. The Board may prohibit the employer from using unfair labor practices and may, after proper

hearing, compel the reinstatement of a former employee discharged because of union activities. The act has been amended by the Labor-Management Relations Act known as the Taft-Hartley Act, which has added such things as prohibitions against unfair labor practices by employees. Some states have legislation patterned after these acts.

18. THE NORRIS-LA GUARDIA ACT—Another federal act affecting employer-employee relationships is the Norris-La Guardia Act, which restricts the power of the federal courts to issue injunctions in labor disputes, although these restrictions have been eased somewhat by the Taft-Hartley Act, and prohibits them from enforcing "yellow dog" contracts. A *yellow dog contract* is one by which the employee, as a condition of his employment, agrees to withdraw from, or refrain from joining, a labor organization. Some states have similar laws affecting their own courts.

19. THE SOCIAL SECURITY ACT—The two phases of the Social Security Act that are most important to employer and employee are: (a) that which sets up a permanent system of old-age benefits, and (b) that which promotes the enactment of permanent unemployment insurance systems by the states. The old-age benefit system is administered by the federal government, and to support the plan, employer and employee pay a tax based on the size of the employee's wage, which the employer must remit to the federal treasury. When the employee reaches 65, his monthly benefit payments begin and their amount is calculated with reference to the total tax he has paid over his years of work. These benefit provisions apply to all classes of persons within the act, and should not be confused with old-age pensions to needy persons.

The act attempts to induce the states to enact and administer unemployment insurance systems. The employer must pay a tax on his total payroll into the federal treasury. If the state has an unemployment insurance act that meets the standards set up by Congress, the federal government will grant money to the state to help pay the cost of the insurance. The employer may also deduct up to 90 per cent of the federal tax to pay the state unemployment insurance tax.

Other sections of the Social Security Act provide for federal grants to the states for maternal and child welfare, for public health work, and for aid to the blind, the needy aged, and dependent children. Medicare and Medicaid programs are also administered under the Social Security Act. See MEDICARE.

Equitable Remedies

1. DEFINITION—A *remedy* is the legal means employed to enforce a right or redress an injury. Suppose A has purchased an automobile from B who refused to deliver it. In a court of equity A could compel B to deliver the car; this would be an equitable remedy. In a court of law A could recover damages for the loss he had sustained through B's refusal to deliver the automobile; this would be a legal remedy.

2. THE COMMON REMEDY—Relief in equity is often sought to compel a person to execute a contract that he has made. It quite frequently happens that a seller regrets his action after the contract has been made. The court of equity will compel him to deliver the property, provided that the law gives the purchaser no adequate remedy. When an article has a peculiar sentimental value, when it is of rare value, like an heirloom, or when it is an article that cannot be easily purchased in the open market, the one party can compel the other to fulfill his contract. Ordinarily, the buyer of articles like cattle, lumber, dry goods, or hardware has only the legal remedy to recover damages.

3. CONDITIONS FOR RELIEF BY EQUITY—Equity will enforce agreements or grant relief:
a. When legal remedies or damages would be inadequate.
b. When the seller of a business agrees not to enter into competition with the buyer.
c. When an employee agrees not to disclose the trade secrets of his employer.
d. When a tenant threatens or attempts to injure the real estate of the landlord.
e. When an established patent has been infringed.
f. In many other similar cases.

4. EQUITY WILL NOT ENFORCE AGREEMENTS OR GRANT RELIEF:
a. When the law has an adequate remedy.
b. When the goods contracted for can be readily purchased in the open market.
c. To force a person to perform his contract to render personal services.
d. When the contract in question is one where one party agrees to lend money to the other.
e. When there is a contract to form a partnership.
f. When such agreement would be in restraint of trade, would create a monopoly, or would be illegal for any other reason.

5. INJUNCTIONS—Relief in equity is often brought about by the means of an injunction. An *injunction* is a restraining order issued by a court of equity on petition of the injured party. If the need is great the court will immediately issue a temporary injunction that orders the injuring party to do, or not to do, certain things, and fixes the time for a hearing. At this hearing, which is fixed within a reasonable time, and which is conducted like any ordinary trial, the court decides whether the injunction will be dissolved or whether it will be made permanent. Injunctions came into especial prominence through their use against labor unions during strikes. Injunctions were issued and upheld enjoining the members of labor unions from picketing, or otherwise preventing other workers from taking their places. Legislation has curbed the use of injunctions against labor groups although they are still legal in some cases.

Exemptions

1. DEFINITIONS—*Exemption* is a right granted to debtors, especially bankrupts, that protects the homestead or other property from the claims of creditors. A *homestead* is the abode or dwelling house of a family landowner and includes a specific amount of the adjacent land, varying in the different states. *Exemption laws* protect those who are unable to pay their debts without causing distress to themselves and their families.

2. GENERAL PRINCIPLES—The laws in some states provide that a person can waive his exemption rights in a promissory note or other written contract. The laws of other states provide that exemptions cannot be waived. In nearly all the states an exemption in wages cannot be waived. A legal homestead is generally in one piece, but it may be divided by a road and in some states may consist of several distinct pieces. A homestead is exempt from all debts except taxes, although in some states it is not exempt from pre-existing liens, fines for public offenses, and similar debts. A person who is the head of a family, within the legal meaning of the term, is generally entitled to homestead exemption. This right survives to the husband or the wife in case of death, or to the surviving children until they come of age. In divorce cases the wife ceases to be a member of the family and thus loses her homestead right unless reserved in the decree. Desertion of the husband by the wife does not destroy his

homestead right but does destroy hers. A homestead may be sold or mortgaged regardless of the claims of creditors.

Guaranty

1. DEFINITIONS—A *guaranty* is a written promise that a person will perform some duty or contract, or answer for the payment of some debt, in case of the failure of another person. The person who guarantees the faithfulness of another is called the *guarantor*. The *guarantee* or creditor is the person to whom the pledge is made.

2. GENERAL PRINCIPLES:

a. A guaranty must be in writing.

b. A guaranty, to be binding, must be for a consideration.

c. A guaranty must be accepted in order for it to become a contract, and the guarantor must have notice of its acceptance within a reasonable time.

d. A guarantor, after paying the debt, can become the legally recognized creditor of the person for whom he was guarantor.

3. FORMS:

GUARANTY ON BACK OF A NOTE

Fort Scott, Kansas, Oct. 12, 19.....

For value received, I hereby guarantee the payment of the note.

JAMES GLOVER

GUARANTY FOR PAYMENT OF A BILL

Dayton, Ohio, Aug. 30, 19.....

W. Reinke, Esq.
Dear Sir:

I hereby guarantee the payment of any bill or bills of merchandise Mr. John A. Dahlem may purchase from you, the amount of this guaranty not to exceed Five Hundred Dollars ($500), and to expire at the end of three months from date.

CHAS. ADAMS

GUARANTY OF A DEBT ALREADY INCURRED

St. Louis, Mo., July 10, 19.....

Messrs. H. E. Bechtel & Co., West Salem
Gentlemen:

In consideration of One Dollar ($1) and other good and valuable considerations paid me by yourselves, the receipt of which I hereby acknowledge, I guarantee that the debt of Four Hundred Dollars ($400) now owing to you by Ira J. Ferry shall be paid at maturity.

W. A. PIPER

Infants

1. DEFINITIONS—While the word *infant* in its ordinary usage signifies a child of a tender and helpless age, the word *infant* as used in law refers to a person who has not arrived at his majority as fixed by law. *Majority* is the age at which the disabilities of infancy are removed, and hence a person who has reached his majority is entitled to the management of his own affairs and to the enjoyment of civic rights.

2. NATURE OF INFANCY—The disabilities of infancy are in fact personal privileges conferred on infants by law, and as such they constitute limitations on the legal capacity of infants, not to defeat their rights but to shield and protect them from the acts of their own improvidence as well as from acts of others.

3. TERMINATION OF INFANCY—Under the common law, infants, whether male or female, attain their majority at the age of 21 years, and this rule has generally remained in force throughout the United States, unless changed by statute. As a result of the new equal protection decisions and the Twenty-sixth Amendment to the federal Constitution lowering the minimum voting age to 18, there is a nationwide trend to establish the age of 18 as the termination of infancy for both males and females. The period of incapacity arising from infancy is limited by law, and cannot in any case be enlarged or diminished by evidence.

4. EMANCIPATION—An infant may be emancipated by an act of his parent, or by his marriage, or by his enlistment in the military service. While parental emancipation or emancipation by marriage or by enlistment affects the parent's rights and obligations to the infant, such emancipation does not otherwise remove the incapacity of his infancy or affect the avoidability of his contracts.

5. REAL ESTATE—An infant is capable of taking title to real estate granted to him by a deed.

6. PROGRESSIVE CAPACITY—While a person is an infant in the eyes of the law until he arrives at the age of majority fixed by law, his actual capacity to do acts involving legal consequences and the practical necessity of his doing such acts increases from babyhood to the age of majority, and the law necessarily recognizes such progressive capacity. Thus, subject to certain conditions provided by statute, an infant over a certain age may select his own guardian, or may enter into a valid and binding marriage, or may enlist in the military service.

7. RIGHT TO REPUDIATE COMPROMISE OR SETTLEMENT—If a compromise or settlement of an infant's claim or cause of action is made on his behalf by a third person, such as his parent, he may repudiate such agreement before reaching his majority or within a reasonable time thereafter, unless it is made by a guardian with authority to do so or is otherwise approved by a court.

8. CONTRACTS—The prevailing rule today is that, in the absence of a statute to the contrary, an infant's contracts or conveyances are voidable, with the exception of certain limited classes of contracts or transactions that are valid and binding. This rule is applicable to both executed and executory contracts, although in some cases it is held that the infant is bound by the term of his employment contract to the extent that he has executed it without dissent.

9. TORT LIABILITY—The general rule is that an infant is liable for his own torts in the same manner and to the same extent as an adult, if the tort does not arise out of, or is not connected with, a contract. Infancy is not a shield against tort liability except to the extent that infants are incapable of forming the mental attitudes that are necessary elements of certain torts. Thus, an infant may be held liable for injuries caused by his negligence, and ordinarily infancy cannot be pleaded as a defense in an action for fraud, for assault and battery, or for trespass.

10. NEGLIGENCE—In determining whether an infant is guilty of actionable negligence, the standard of care applicable to him is the standard of a child of similar age and experience. According to some recent cases, however, this rule is not applicable when a minor engages in such adult and potentially dangerous activities as the operation of an automobile or other motor-powered vehicles, and a minor operating such a vehicle or craft is to be held to the same standard of care as an adult. Whether or not a minor has been negligent under a particular set of circumstances is or-

dinarily a question of fact, although infants of very tender years, usually seven or under, may be conclusively presumed incapable of negligence.

Innkeeper

1. DEFINITION—An *innkeeper* is one who keeps a public house for the reception and entertainment of travelers.

2. GAINING ADMISSION TO AN INN OR HOTEL—An innkeeper is required to accommodate all comers with the following exceptions, which vary in different states:

a. He may exclude anyone if he has no accommodations.

b. He may exclude those who do not come at a suitable time or in a proper manner.

c. He must exclude certain persons such as criminals and thieves.

d. He may refuse admission to those he believes would disturb the peace and safety of his guests.

e. He can expel any guest who does disturb the peace and safety of his other guests.

If he refuses to provide reasonable and proper accommodations, he is liable. He need not provide any particular room. If he operates a garage or stable in connection with the inn, he is under the same obligation to receive and care for the automobiles or horses of his guests.

3. THE INNKEEPER'S LIABILITY—The law fixes the liability and responsibility of an innkeeper:

a. An innkeeper is responsible for the loss or damage to a guest's baggage committed to his care unless such loss is caused by an act of God, a public enemy, or neglect or fault of the owner of the baggage.

b. In most states innkeepers are relieved from liability for loss by fire unless the fire is caused by the negligence of the innkeeper or his servants.

c. An innkeeper is liable for goods of a guest if they were stolen by the innkeeper's servants, by another guest, or by an outsider. However, he is not liable if the loss was due to the negligence of the owner.

d. The innkeeper is bound to secure honest and trustworthy employees.

e. If two guests occupy the same room, the innkeeper can be held responsible if a theft is committed by one against the other.

4. LIENS—An innkeeper has a lien on a guest's baggage or other property left in his care, to secure the payment for the accommodations.

5. REGULATIONS—An innkeeper may make regulations for the observance of his guests in order to protect their property. Thus he may limit his liability somewhat by notifying the guests that he is not responsible for the loss of valuable articles unless they are deposited with him. Such regulations will bind the guest if brought to his notice.

6. LODGING AND BOARDING HOUSES—The keepers of lodging or boarding houses do not come under the same head as innkeepers as far as the law is concerned. They are not required to accommodate all who may apply. They are not liable for refusing to accommodate all comers.

Insurance

1. DEFINITIONS—*Insurance* is a contract stating that one party, the *underwriter,* will compensate another party, the *insured,* for any damage to a specific thing caused by a specified danger or for liability incurred under certain circumstances. Insurance contracts are called *policies.* The consideration paid by the insured to the underwriter is called the *premium.* Fire insurance and life insurance are two important basic kinds of insurance.

2. FIRE INSURANCE—*Fire insurance* is indemnity against loss by fire. That is, the underwriter agrees to reimburse the insured for damage caused to the insured property by fire. Thus it provides a means of distributing the cost of damages caused by fire. A fund is supplied by the payment of premiums, from which the insurance company agrees to pay the loss in case of fire. Fire insurance is now generally furnished by large stock companies or by mutual companies.

3. MUTUAL COMPANIES are generally established by statute and provide for the payment of losses by pro rata assessment upon the policyholders, who constitute the stockholders and who manage the affairs of the company. In effect, each member of a mutual company gains protection for his insured property and accepts a small part of the risk of the other members. Some of these mutual companies require a small premium paid in advance, which, unless unusual losses occur, is enough to pay all the losses for the year. Others simply require a small fee to pay for the expense of making the survey and issuing the policy. In case of loss, all mutual companies, however, make an assessment pro rata upon the policyholders to pay the same.

4. STOCK INSURANCE COMPANIES—The insurance business of private corporations is carried on for profit.

5. GENERAL PRINCIPLES—The following general principles apply to property and fire insurance.

a. The property insured, and the terms of the contract, must be clearly defined.

b. If the written part of the policy contradicts the printed sections, the written part will hold.

c. Clerical or typographical errors may usually be corrected when discovered.

d. The insurance on the building covers those things that have become a part of it, but does not include fixtures or surrounding sheds or buildings.

e. Misrepresentation or fraud on the part of the insured renders the insurance policy null and void.

f. If a policyholder secures additional fire insurance on his property without the consent of the insurance company, his former policy becomes void. Most policies today, however, consent to the writing of additional insurance on the property by other companies and in case of loss the liability is prorated.

g. In addition to the actual fire loss, most policies cover damage by water used to put out the fire, damage to goods while being removed to avoid fire, and damage from an explosion caused by fire.

h. An insurance company is not responsible for goods stolen while they are being removed during a fire.

i. An ordinary policy of insurance does not usually insure against lightning, but lightning clauses will be attached to nearly all policies if requested at the time of issue.

j. The insurance company is not relieved from liability by the carelessness of the policyholder, yet the insured is bound to take reasonable care to prevent fire.

k. In a total loss the insurance company is liable for the full value of the property, provided that this value does not exceed the amount of the insurance. In a partial loss the company is liable only for the actual loss.

l. In an *open policy* the amount of the insurer's liability is not fixed until after the loss. In a *valued policy* the maximum liability for a total loss is fixed.

m. In order to calculate the approximate loss on merchandise in case of fire, the value of the following items should be ascertained: (1) the most recent inventory; (2) invoices for goods bought subsequent to that inventory; (3) freight and dray bills on same; (4) credit memoranda for merchandise returned; (5) production department payrolls; and (6) appreciation in value of goods since purchase. These items should be added together and from their sum should be subtracted the sum of the following items: (1) outgoing charges, representing goods sold since the last inventory; (2) depreciation in value of goods since purchase; and (3) salvage, or market value, of goods not destroyed. The remainder gives the approximate value of goods destroyed, for which insurance compensation can be obtained.

6. UNDERWRITERS' ASSOCIATIONS—The stock fire insurance companies all submit complete underwriting and loss figures to the National Board of Underwriters, which, in addition to compiling and publishing such information, supervises common services to the public, such as fire protection, information, and grading. There are also local agents' boards and state associations operating to promote uniformity of service and contract. Fire insurance rates are usually established by rating bureaus, which are administered and paid for by a majority of companies doing business in the state or locality. Rates are usually adhered to by all agents either by common agreement or as directed by state law. Specific rates are published for mercantile houses, warehouses, office buildings, and manufacturing buildings. Rates by classes are used for dwellings, small apartment houses, farms, and similar property.

7. CLASSIFICATION—In order that each person thus protected from loss may contribute the proper amount to this fund, a system of classification has been worked out to establish fair premium rates. This classification is based on the probability of fire. The National Board of Fire Underwriters, having the reports of the various insurance companies, knows the probable number of fires and the value of the property involved. Statistics show that a certain percentage of residences, barns, schools, merchandise, etc., will be burned each year, and that buildings of one type of construction are more likely to burn than those of some other type of construction. Population, water pressure, fire department, building contents, and many other elements are taken into consideration by the rating bureau in determining the rate each person must pay for insurance.

8. REDUCING THE RATE—When you pay your premium, you can judge by the rate you pay what the experience of the insurance companies has been with regard to similar property, with similar conditions. If the rate is high, find out just what factors make it high. Then you may be able to make such changes or take such precautions that your rate will be reduced.

9. WHO HAS AN INSURABLE INTEREST—In order to be indemnified against loss the insured must have an interest in the property or goods insured, both at the time the insurance is issued and at the time of the loss. Thus the following may be insured:
a. A bailee (one who receives goods of another to hold).
b. A consignee (one to whom property is consigned or shipped).
c. A mortgagee (one who holds a mortgage on real or personal property).
d. An assignee (one to whom property is assigned).
e. A warehouseman.
f. An executor or an administrator.
g. A landlord.
h. A tenant.
i. The holder of a lien on property.
j. An agent who has the custody or care of the principal's property.
All these as well as many others have what is called an insurable interest. If all insurable interests in a property are not noted on the policy at the time of loss, the company is not liable to the party having an interest which is not so noted.

10. THE INSURANCE POLICY is a contract between the insurance company and the insured, by which the first party insures the property of the second party against loss by fire. The consideration, or premium, is usually paid when the policy is issued, although it may be charged on account or paid by check or note. The contract becomes binding and valid when the policy is properly executed. Actual delivery of the policy to the insured is not necessary. Thus if a loss occurs after the duly executed policy is in the hands of the insurance company's agent, but before it has been delivered to the insured, the company must pay the loss. A preliminary contract is sometimes made, in which case the risk, that is, the liability of the insurance company, begins immediately upon the signing, even though such contract be dated several days before the policy is actually issued. Most local agents have authority to protect an applicant for insurance against loss for a period of 5 to 30 days preceding acceptance of the risk by the company.

11. CANCELLATION—A fire insurance contract, like any other contract, may be canceled by mutual agreement, but unless otherwise stated in the policy the company cannot cancel the contract without the consent of the policyholder.

12. LIFE INSURANCE—*Life insurance* is a contract whereby the insurer agrees, on the payment of a fixed premium, to pay a certain sum of money to the insured when he reaches a certain age, or to his beneficiaries at his death. Thus it is possible for a man to insure his productive ability for the amount of money it would be worth to him if he were to live for his expected time.

13. APPLICATIONS—Nearly all companies require applications for life insurance to be in writing and accompanied by the report of a medical examination made by the local medical examiner of the company. These applications are forwarded to the home office and, if they pass the head medical examiner, the policy is issued to the insured and the application is made a part of the policy. Any false statement contained therein that is material to the risk will vitiate the policy, and applicants for insurance should be careful to see that all questions are fully and truthfully answered. The moral hazard involved is also carefully considered by the insuring company. Most life insurance policies provide that the insurance shall not be in force until the first premium is paid, and most policies are now incontestable after the payment of a certain number of premiums. By the laws of all states, in case default is made in the payment of a premium after a certain number of full premiums have been paid, the policyholder may have the option to select any one of the following nonforfeiture provisions:
a. Cash surrender value.
b. Reduced paid-up insurance.
c. Term insurance for the full face amount of the policy.

14. GENERAL PRINCIPLES—The following general principles apply to life insurance.
a. Unless forbidden by statute, a life insurance policy may be assigned to one having an insurable interest, or to a person without such an interest, provided that the assignment is made in good faith. An assignment is often made for the benefit of creditors, or as security for the payment of a debt.
b. A contract for insurance does not take effect until it has been approved by the company, and the insured has paid the first premium.
c. A general agent can bind his principal even against the express terms of the policy provided that the insured was not negligent in failing to advise himself concerning the terms.
d. A life insurance contract may be void on account of a mistake in issuing it, on account of violation of statute,

on account of fraud by either party, or if the policy is contrary to public policy.

e. Words or figures written or printed on the margin or on the back of the policy, or on a slip attached to the policy, must be considered as an integral part of the agreement.

f. The payment of premiums to an agent will bind the company, unless the insured has received notice to the contrary.

g. A policy may be canceled by mutual agreement, and the insured is then entitled to the surrender value of the policy or any other nonforfeiture option contained therein.

15. THE POLICY—The usual clauses contained in life insurance policies are these: (a) that the insurance ceases unless the premiums are promptly paid, (b) that the company shall be exempt if, within two years after the issuance of the policy, the insured commits suicide whether sane or insane, or if death shall come by the hands of justice for a violation of law, (c) that agents are not authorized to alter or discharge any part of the contract, (d) that assignments of the policy shall not take effect until notice thereof shall be received by the company at its home office, (e) that after two years the policy will be incontestable except for fraud or nonpayment of premium. All policies also provide for a 30- or 31-day period of grace after the due date for payment of premiums.

16. INSURABLE INTEREST—In order for an insurance policy to be valid the person taking out the policy must have an insurable interest in the subject matter of the insurance, that is, the policyholder must be one who would suffer loss, financial or otherwise, on the happening of the event insured against. However, such a person may name any beneficiary, although companies hesitate to approve applications for life insurance where the named beneficiary has no such interest. The relationship of uncle or aunt and nephew or niece, or that of cousins is generally not sufficient unless other circumstances show an insurable interest.

17. KINDS OF POLICIES—There are many kinds of life insurance policies. Among the more common are the following:

a. *Ordinary Life Policy* in which premiums are paid during life and in which the face value of the policy is payable at death. This is the simplest and lowest-premium form of life insurance.

b. *Limited Payment Plan*—The face value of the policy is payable only at death, and premiums are payable only for a limited period of years, or until death if it occurs within that period.

c. *Endowment Policy*—The insurance company agrees to pay a fixed sum at the end of a fixed term of years, or at death, if it occurs before the expiration of the term, provided a fixed premium is paid during the entire term.

d. *Convertible Term Policy* insures against death for a limited term of years, and may be converted into any other form of insurance, without medical examination, within a stated period.

e. *Income Agreements* may be issued on any of the other plans, with a provision that the face value of the policy is to be paid in monthly installments instead of in a lump sum.

18. AUTOMOBILE INSURANCE—The owner of a car may be held liable for damage done by his vehicle, even when someone else is driving it. And damage done to his automobile and its occupants, either through collision or by some other cause, may be expensive. To protect himself against financial loss related to his automobile, the owner may take out an automobile insurance policy. Automobile insurance is of four kinds: liability, collision, comprehensive, and no-fault.

a. *Liability Insurance* protects the owner, up to the limits stated on the policy, against liability for damage done by his automobile through fault of an authorized operator. Such insurance policies cover property damage done to other cars and expenses for personal injury to occupants of the insured vehicle, to occupants of other cars, and to injured pedestrians. Since the law considers an automobile an inherently dangerous machine, many states require that an automobile owner must have liability insurance in order to register and license his vehicle.

b. *Collision Insurance*—Damage to the insured vehicle and injuries to its occupants are covered by collision insurance. If the operator of an insured vehicle is at fault in an accident, or if the insured vehicle is damaged through fault of an uninsured motorist, collision insurance will cover the owner's loss.

c. *Comprehensive Coverage* insures an automobile against damage not related to traffic accidents. The policy may cover loss by fire, theft, severe weather, vandalism, and falling objects, depending on the terms of the policy. It does not cover damages caused by collision.

d. *No-Fault Insurance*—Many court cases involve disagreements over which driver is at fault in an accident and what damages should be paid to injured parties. These cases may involve much time and great expense. In order to reduce the load on the courts and the cost of liability insurance, some states are instituting forms of *no-fault insurance*. No-fault insurance imposes on the owners of motor vehicles a limited liability, without regard to fault, for personal injuries or death caused by the operation of their motor vehicles. It can be considered a form of strict liability similar to workmen's compensation. See EMPLOYER AND EMPLOYEE: WORKMEN'S COMPENSATION.

19. OTHER FORMS OF INSURANCE:

a. *Accident Insurance* may be secured against all kinds of accidents. Upon payment of small premiums, policies may be had insuring against accident from one day to ten years, for any reasonable amount. The rates generally depend upon the occupation of the insured.

b. *Marine Insurance* is governed largely by the same rules that control fire insurance. This form of insurance may include all casualties resulting from unusual or violent actions of the elements, foundering at sea, grounding, collision, fire, perils of war, rests and restraints, jettison, and any other perils, losses, or misfortunes of the sea.

c. *Fraternal Insurance* is one of the oldest forms of insurance, originating with the ancient secret societies. Originally the societies assumed an obligation to pay sick and death benefits to their members. Today there are numerous societies that issue standard life insurance policies, with a fixed premium rate and a limited amount of insurance payable at death.

d. *Industrial Insurance*—Many large business organizations issue this form of insurance for the benefit of their employees. The amounts are usually small and the weekly or monthly payments are deducted from the wages of the insured.

e. *Other Kinds of Insurance* include employers' liability (see EMPLOYER AND EMPLOYEE: INSURANCE), public liability, tornado, explosion, health, hospital, automobile, burglary, fraud, insolvency, and loss through bad debts. Almost every kind of risk imaginable may be covered by insurance.

20. FORM:

ASSIGNMENT OF POLICY OF INSURANCE

Know all men by these presents, that I, ... of the village of ...., for and in consideration of ...., to me in hand paid by .... of the same place, the receipt whereof is hereby acknowledged, have sold, assigned, transferred, and set over, and by these presents do sell, assign, transfer, and set over, unto the said .... the policy of insurance known as policy No ..... of the .... Insurance Company, and all sum and sums of money, interest, benefit, and advantage whatsoever, now due, or hereafter to arise, or to be had or made by virtue thereof, to have and to hold the same unto the said .... and his assigns forever.

In witness whereof, I have hereto affixed my hand this 20th day of June, 19 ......

(Acknowledgment)   (Name)

International Law

1. DEFINITION—*International law* is the body of rules designed to govern the conduct of nations toward one another. It includes customs and usages that have grown up among nations and have become generally accepted by them as well as the enactments contained in treaties and conventions. International law is intended to do for nations what the domestic law does for individuals.

2. GENERAL PRINCIPLES—There are certain well-established principles of international law, which provide as follows:

a. One nation cannot interfere with the internal affairs of another.

b. Crimes committed on the high seas are under the jurisdiction of the nation under whose flag the ship sails.

c. The property of alien enemies is subject to confiscation.

d. A neutral country must be fair and impartial in its relations with warring nations.

e. It is a violation of international law for a warring nation to fight on, or cross the territory of, a neutral power.

f. It is also a violation of international law to carry the necessary finished goods or materials of warfare to a combatant nation.

g. A fugitive criminal cannot be brought back from another nation unless the terms of the treaty between the two nations so provide.

h. Confiscation is the penalty for attempting to violate a blockade in time of war.

3. TREATIES—Much international law is embodied in treaties. A *treaty* is an agreement between two or more nations to adjust differences or to govern future conduct. Treaties are sometimes made for a limited period of years, but a treaty made by one administration is binding upon the following administration.

4. REPRESENTATIVES—*Ambassadors* are the authorized diplomatic representatives of nations. They are immune from civil or criminal liability, but may be tried for crime by their home governments. A *consul* is a commercial representative sent by one nation to another to aid in the establishment and maintenance of trade relations between the nations, and to look after the interests of the citizens or subjects of his country. He is personally liable for his actions.

5. PASSPORTS—A *passport* is a document granted by the government to a citizen enabling him to travel to other countries. See PASSPORTS.

Juries

1. DEFINITION—A *jury* is a body of laymen selected by lot, or by some other fair and impartial means, to ascertain, under the guidance of a judge, the truth in questions of fact arising in either a civil or criminal proceeding. At common law a jury was composed of 12 persons summoned from the vicinity, duly examined and sworn to try the case on the facts presented by the evidence introduced at the trial.

2. FUNCTION OF JURY—In general terms, the province of the modern-day jury is the determination of questions of fact arising in the trial of the action in which it sits. A *jury trial* is a proceeding in which the jurors are the judges of the facts and the court is the judge of the law. In early times, the jury served as a body of witnesses acting upon their own personal knowledge, but the accepted principle now is that the jury exercises its province upon the evidence introduced at the trial, not upon its own knowledge obtained elsewhere.

3. RIGHT TO A JURY TRIAL— The right to have a trial by jury is a fundamental right in our democratic system. and is recognized as such in the Magna Carta, the Declaration of Independence, the federal Constitution, and the constitutions of the various states. The Federal Rules of Civil Procedure also state that the right of trial by jury as declared by the Seventh Amendment to the Constitution, or as given by a statute of the United States, must be preserved to the parties inviolate. And the United States Code sets forth matters in connection with juries and trial by jury. While the right to a jury trial is guaranteed in the Constitution, the specific rules governing juries are somewhat flexible. A jury may be composed of fewer than twelve members, and a jury need not unanimously agree on a verdict. These matters are left to the discretion of the states.

4. FEDERAL CONSTITUTIONAL PROVISIONS—When the Constitution of the United States was amended to include the Bill of Rights, the people, by virtue of the Seventh Amendment, secured from general encroachment the right to trial by jury in all actions at common law in the federal courts where the value in controversy exceeds $20. This means that if the suit were of the kind which was triable as of right by jury in 1791, when the Seventh Amendment was adopted, it is triable as of right by jury today. Since the legal terminology has changed since the eighteenth century, it is necessary to look at the substance of the particular lawsuit to determine whether it is of the type triable by jury then.

One example that points up the contrast is workmen's compensation. This type of action was unknown in 1791 and no right of jury trial had therefore become attached to it. Thus there is no such right in the federal courts today in such an action.

5. APPLICABILITY TO STATE COURTS —The federal Constitution does not in any place expressly guarantee the right of trial by jury in any state court or in any territories which have not been incorporated into the Union.

6. STATE CONSTITUTIONAL PROVISIONS—The constitutions of the several states generally contain express guaranties of the right to a jury trial. The typical provision is that the right shall be and remain inviolate, or that the right, as heretofore enjoyed, shall remain inviolate. Such provisions apply to both civil and criminal cases. The right is secured, and not granted, by such a provision.

Lease

1. DEFINITIONS—The phrase *landlord and tenant* denotes the relationship that exists by virtue of a contract expressed or implied between two or more persons for the possession or occupancy of lands or tenements either for a

definite period or at will. The landlord or *lessor* is the person who lets the land or premises. The tenant or *lessee* is the one who occupies the land or premises. The *lease* is the contract between the two.

2. LEASES SHOULD BE IN WRITING—Leases that are to remain in force for more than a year or that are not to be performed within a year must be in writing, or they are invalid. Leases for a year or less and that can be performed within a year are valid even if not in writing. To avoid misunderstandings, disputes, and possible litigation it is always best, however, that the lease be in writing and signed by both parties, regardless of the length of the term.

3. LEASES FOR LIFE are those that are terminated by death either of the lessee or of some other person living at the date of the lease. Unless such leases contain covenants to the contrary, the life tenant or the lessee is required to pay all taxes on the premises and keep the same in repair.

4. LEASES FOR YEARS—The lessor, unless it is otherwise expressly provided in the lease, is under obligation to see that his tenant's possession is not disturbed by any title paramount to the landlord's. He is not required to make repairs unless he agrees to do so in the lease, nor is there an implied contract on his part that the premises are fit for the purpose for which they are let. For residential leases, however, most states tend to interpret the lease as an implied covenant of habitability. The landlord must pay all the taxes regularly levied and assessed against said premises and keep the buildings on said premises insured at his own expense if he desires to carry insurance.

5. IMPLIED AGREEMENT BY TENANT—Where there is no agreement to the contrary, the tenant is bound to take possession of the premises, take ordinary care of the same, keep them in a tenantable condition, and make repairs made necessary by his negligence, but he need not make repairs made necessary by ordinary wear and tear or inevitable accident.

If the premises leased be a farm, he is also required to cultivate the same in the manner required of good husbandry. He must not commit waste nor alter buildings or fences, and must surrender up the premises at the end of his term in as good condition as when entered upon originally, ordinary wear and tear excepted. He is not required to pay taxes or keep buildings insured, but must pay the stipulated rent at the time it becomes due by the terms of his lease. If no time is specified in his lease, then the rent is due at the end of the term. He may sublet the premises or assign the lease unless it contains provisions to the contrary.

If he places permanent improvements upon the premises that are so attached to the buildings or land that they cannot be removed without injury to the buildings or land, he has no right to remove the same unless his lease so provides. He may remove trade fixtures, provided they are removed from the premises before the expiration of his lease.

6. COMMON PROVISIONS OF A LEASE—Most leases provide for the yielding up of the possession of the premises at the end of the term without notice, in as good condition as when they were entered upon by the lessee, loss by fire, inevitable accident, and ordinary wear excepted. There is frequently a provision against subletting or assigning the lease, and a clause stating that in case of nonpayment of rent, or failure to perform any of the covenants of the lease, the lessor shall have the right to terminate the lease and recover possession of the premises.

Farm leases usually provide, in addition to the stipulations mentioned above, that the tenant shall keep the fruit and ornamental trees, vines, and shrubbery free from injury by stock, plowing, or otherwise; that the lessee will draw out the manure and spread it on the premises; that no straw shall be sold or removed from the premises during the term or at its termination; that the tenant will keep the buildings and fences in repair, the landlord to furnish necessary material; that the landlord may do fall plowing on the stubble ground after the grain has been removed therefrom, and that he may enter for the purpose of making repairs or viewing the premises. Sometimes the landlord covenants to make all new fences, to furnish water, and to carry out other provisions that may be inserted in the lease.

7. TERMINATION OF LEASE—Under the strict rules of the common law the landlord might terminate the lease for nonpayment of rent, but in order to do so it would have been necessary for him to go upon the premises and make a demand for the exact amount of rent due upon the very day that the rent came due, and a failure to do this waived the right to obtain forfeiture. This strict rule of the common law has been modified in nearly all the states so that it is no longer necessary to make a demand for the rent on the day the rent comes due. Instead of this, most of the states provide that before the landlord shall declare a forfeiture, a written demand for the amount of rent due shall be served upon the tenant, and he be notified that in case he fails to pay the rent within a fixed time, generally five or ten days, the landlord will elect to terminate his lease. In such cases the tenant has until the end of the last day fixed in the notice to pay the rent and prevent the forfeiture. The statutes of the various states also provide that in case of breaches of other agreements contained in the lease, notice of such breaches and intention of the landlord to terminate the lease shall be served upon the tenant.

8. TERMINATION OF TENANCY FROM YEAR TO YEAR AND MONTH TO MONTH—Where a tenant has a lease for a year, and at the end of his term remains in possession of the property without a new agreement, the law construes this to be a leasing from year to year, and such tenancy at common law could be terminated only by either party's giving the other six months' notice prior to the end of any year. In Illinois, this notice has been changed by a statute to sixty days prior to the end of any year, and a shorter time has been fixed in other states. A tenant who has a lease on property for one or more months and who remains on the property after the termination of his lease, is termed a tenant from month to month, and such tenancy can be terminated only by either party giving the other party thirty days' notice. A tenancy from month to month may also be created by agreement. A tenancy at will is one which can be terminated at any time by either party.

9. DEMAND—It is a general rule, subject to few exceptions, that in order to get possession of property where the original occupancy by the tenant was lawful, either a notice to quit or a demand for possession is necessary on the part of the owner before commencing proceedings to get possession.

10. SECURING POSSESSION—When a lease has been terminated either by its term or by notice, and the landlord is entitled to possession, the most common method of recovering possession is to commence an action of forcible entry and detainer against the tenant for the possession of the premises. This may be done by filing a complaint and having a summons issued. If the possession of the tenant was lawful at the time of its beginning, the landlord has no right to dispossess him forcibly, and if he does so it is at his peril. Taking possession by force may subject the landlord to an action for damages. Leases sometimes contain clauses stating that where a forfeiture has taken place the landlord shall have the right to take possession of the premises leased, by force if necessary. Such provisions, however, cannot be enforced and do not justify the landlord in using force. The only legal course for the landlord is to begin an action, obtain a judg-

ment for possession, and have the constable or sheriff put him in legal possession.

11. DISTRESS FOR RENT—An effective method of collecting rent is by *distress warrant*. This is a warrant issued by the landlord to some third person, authorizing and empowering such third person to levy said warrant upon any personal property of the tenant for the satisfaction of the rent. A very important advantage of this remedy is that it enables the landlord to seize the personal property of the tenant without delay. This process is of very ancient origin. As used here the term *personal property* means property other than real estate. The statutes of most of the states provide for this remedy, and the mode of procedure is generally prescribed by the statute. In general, it is the duty of the officer, as soon as the levy is made, to file with a justice of the peace or with the clerk of the court an inventory of the property levied upon, together with a copy of his warrant, and usually a summons is issued.

12. TIME OF LEVY—Under the common law the tenant had all of the day on which the rent came due to make payment, and a distress warrant could not be levied until the day after the rent came due. In some states, however, in case the tenant sells or attempts to dispose of the crop grown upon the premises, thereby endangering the landlord's lien for his rent, a distress warrant may be levied before the rent comes due. The person making the levy should be careful not to levy on more property than is necessary in order to satisfy the rent due; otherwise he may be liable to the tenant for making an excessive levy.

13. LANDLORD'S LIEN—Under the common law the landlord had no lien upon the property of the tenant until a distress warrant was actually levied upon the property of the tenant. Most of the states, however, now provide that the landlord shall have a lien upon all the crops grown upon the leased premises until the rent for the year in which said crop was grown has been paid, and this lien is ahead of all other liens, even though another legal claim may have been levied upon such crops. The landlord's lien is paramount until the rent is satisfied. The usual method of enforcing the lien of the landlord is by distress warrant.

14. COURT DECISIONS REGARDING RENT—The courts have held that
a. Unless the tenant makes a specific agreement relieving himself, he is liable for the rent of the building on the land leased, after the building has burned down, just as if he were still occupying it.
b. When the terms of a lease are in doubt, the courts endeavor to ascertain the intention of the parties from the lease itself and from the circumstances under which it was made.
c. The term of a lease expiring on a specified day continues through the whole of that day.
d. When the tenant continues to occupy the premises without the consent of the landlord after the expiration of the lease, the landlord may treat him either as a trespasser or as a tenant for another term.
e. A lease may be made to take effect at some future date.
f. A lease must clearly define the property, but no special form or wording is necessary.
g. Valid leases may be made by minors, corporations, executors, administrators, or trustees, subject to certain restrictions. However, there is always uncertainty in a contract with a minor.
h. A lease for an unlawful purpose is generally held to be void.
i. As in other contracts, if the printed and the written parts of a lease do not agree, the written part will usually hold.

j. Most states are coming to interpret a lease as an implied covenant of habitability. That is, the lease of a private house is a warranty that it is fit to be lived in or occupied.
k. When a landlord agrees to keep the building in repair and fails to do so, the tenant's remedy is to sue for damages. He may not continue to occupy the premises and refuse to pay rent.
l. When a tenant is evicted he is excused from the payment of rent for any time after his eviction. Any act by the landlord that renders the property unfit for, or impossible of, occupancy is an eviction.
m. If land is rented on shares, the relation of landlord and tenant usually exists even if the rent is to be paid in produce instead of cash.
n. The landlord is liable for injuries caused by defective stairways, open elevator shafts, or other dangerous conditions that exist in the parts of a rented building that are under his control.

15. FORM:

SHORT FORM OF LEASE

This indenture, made this sixth day of April, 19...., between John Parks, as lessor, and J. B. Moulton, as lessee, witnesseth: That the lessor has this day leased to the lessee the premises known as number 142 Archer Street, in the City of Chicago and State of Illinois, to be occupied by the lessee as a residence (or insert any other purpose for which building is leased) only, for and during the term commencing on the first day of May, 19....., and ending on the thirtieth day of April, 19...., upon the terms and conditions hereinafter set forth; and in consideration of said demise and the covenants and agreements hereinafter set forth, it is covenanted and agreed as follows:

FIRST.—The lessee shall pay to the lessor at the office of the lessor as rent for said leased premises for said term the sum of Six Hundred Dollars ($600) payable in advance in equal monthly installments upon the first day of each and every month during the term hereof.

SECOND.—The lessee has examined said premises prior to and as a condition precedent to his acceptance and the execution hereof and is satisfied with the physical condition thereof, and the lessee's taking possession thereof shall be conclusive evidence of the lessee's receipt thereof in good order and repair, except as otherwise specified herein, and the lessee agrees to keep said premises and the appurtenances thereto in a clean, sightly, and healthy condition and in good repair, and to yield back said premises to the lessor upon the termination of this lease, whether such termination shall occur by expiration of the term hereof or in any other manner whatever, in the same condition of cleanliness, sightliness, and repair as at the date of the execution hereof, loss by fire or other casualty, and ordinary wear and tear excepted.

THIRD.—The lessee agrees to pay the water tax charged against said premises when due.

FOURTH.—The lessee agrees to allow the lessor free access to the leased premises for the purpose of examining or exhibiting the same, or making any needful repairs or alterations of said premises which the lessor may see fit to make; also to allow to be placed upon said premises at all times during the term hereof "For Sale" and "To Rent" signs and not to interfere with the same.

FIFTH.—The lessee agrees not to assign this lease, nor sublet said leased premises, or any part thereof, without the written consent of the lessor endorsed hereon.

SIXTH.—In case said leased premises shall be vacated during said term the lessor may take immediate possession thereof for the remainder of the term and in his discretion relet the same and apply the proceeds upon this lease, the lessee to remain liable for the unpaid balance of the rent.

SEVENTH.—The failure of the lessee to perform the foregoing covenants, or any of them, shall constitute a forfeiture of all of the lessee's rights under this lease and the further occupancy by the lessee of said leased premises after such forfeiture shall be deemed and taken as a forcible detainer of such premises by the lessee, and the lessor may, without notice, re-enter and take possession thereof, with or without force, and with or without legal process, evict and dispossess the lessee from and of said leased premises.

EIGHTH.—The foregoing covenants, and the terms and conditions of this lease, shall inure to the benefit of and be binding upon the respective heirs, devisees, personal representatives, successors, and assigns of the parties hereto, except as herein otherwise provided.

Witness the hands and seals of the parties hereto, the day and the year first above written.

JOHN PARKS   (Seal)

. . . .
Lessor

J. B. MOULTON   (Seal)

. . . .
Lessee

Legal Remedies

1. DEFINITION—A *remedy* is a legal means employed to enforce a right or redress an injury. For example, suppose A and B enter into a binding contract for the purchase and sale of land. If A, the seller, refuses to live up to his contract, B can sue A for the damages he sustained through A's refusal to sell the land. This would be a *legal remedy*. If in a court of equity B could compel A to sell him the land, that would be an *equitable remedy*. See EQUITABLE REMEDIES.

2. STEPS NECESSARY TO SECURE A LEGAL REMEDY—When one party to a contract has a legal cause of action against the other, he brings suit as follows:

a. B files a complaint against A, stating the agreement and giving the facts of A's failure to fulfill his contract, and the loss resulting to B from such violation.

b. A is summoned to appear in court to answer the charge and the court is asked to render judgment against A for the damage resulting from A's refusal to fulfill the contract, and for the costs.

c. The case is then tried, and if judgment is rendered against A, the court empowers the sheriff to levy on any property A may have above statutory exemptions, sell it, and turn the proceeds over to B for the damages awarded, returning any surplus to A.

3. VARIOUS KINDS OF ACTIONS—The common-law forms of action have been abolished in most states, but similar actions are allowed by the codes that have supplanted the common-law forms of action. The following is a list of actions, for the most part designated and defined as they were at common law:

a. *Complaint* is the general name used in many states for the pleading used to institute any legal action.

b. *Ejectment* is a form of action to determine the title to land and right of possession.

c. *Habeas Corpus* is an action or writ used to recover a person's liberty from illegal restraint.

d. *Libel* is an action brought to collect damages for any malicious writing tending to injure the business or reputation of the plaintiff. Although malice is an element of libel, malice will be conclusively presumed even if the defamation was an accident.

e. *Mandamus* is an action to compel someone to do some specific thing pertaining to his office or duty.

f. *Quo Warranto* is a writ used to recover an office or a franchise from the person or corporation in possession of it.

g. *Replevin* is a form of action for the recovery of the possession of specific personal property.

h. *Slander* is an action to collect damages for malicious defamation by word of mouth.

i. *Tort* is an action to recover damages for a private or civil wrong or injury arising independent of any contract.

License

1. DEFINITIONS—A *license* is a right or permission granted by competent authority to a person, giving him the right to do something that otherwise he would not have the right to do. The *licensor* is the one who grants the license. The *licensee* is the one to whom the license is issued.

2. KINDS OF LICENSES—Licenses are of almost infinite variety and are issued not only by the federal government, but by states, counties, cities, towns, and villages. They may be issued to manufacturers or dealers in certain articles, such as tobacco or liquor, to proprietors of amusement places, peddlers, transportation companies, chauffeurs, automobile owners, itinerant merchants, and cab drivers. Such licenses are issued under what is known as the police power of the state.

3. ILLEGAL LICENSES—Cities sometimes require the payment of a local license fee by salesmen or canvassers who are taking orders for goods to be shipped from another state at some future time. Such licenses are legitimate in themselves, but the Supreme Court has ruled that when the fees become excessive, this type of license operates as an undue restraint of interstate commerce and is therefore illegal.

4. MARRIAGE LICENSES—All states require a marriage license. The person who performs the ceremony is required by law to note the fact of the marriage on the face of the license, and to return it to the county recorder for record.

Lien

1. A LIEN is a legal claim upon property for the payment of a debt. It is the right to hold possession of property, usually until some claim against the owner has been satisfied.

2. POSSESSION is always necessary to create a lien, except in cases of mortgages and judgments and statutory liens such as mechanics' liens. The lien simply permits the holding of the property in question until the debt is satisfied. The property cannot be sold without the consent of the owner, except by order of the court.

3. LAW—The existence of a lien does not prevent the party entitled to it from collecting the debt or claim by taking it into court.

4. PARTIES ENTITLED TO LIENS —Warehousemen, carpenters, tailors, dyers, millers, printers, etc., or any persons who perform labor or advance money on property or goods of another, usually have a lien on that property or those goods until all charges are paid.

5. HOTEL KEEPERS have a lien on the baggage of the guests whom they have accommodated.

6. COMMON CARRIERS have a lien on goods carried for transportation charges.

7. AGENTS have a lien on goods of their principals for money advanced.

8. REAL PROPERTY—If the debt is on a house, barn or other real property, the creditor may file a lien on the whole property, and have it recorded in the county recorder's office. The claim then partakes of the nature of a mortgage.

9. MECHANIC'S LIEN—Nearly all the states permit liens designed to protect certain classes of individuals, who furnish material and labor for the erection, construction, repair, and improvement of buildings. The method of securing these liens and enforcing them varies so widely in the different states that it is almost impossible to give such a statement as will cover all states. The courts have construed such laws very strictly, and in order to entitle a person to such lien the provisions of the law granting the same must be strictly complied with. Individuals desiring to avail themselves of these statutes should consult a lawyer and have him prepare the necessary papers.

10. FORM OF MECHANIC'S LIEN—The following form is commonly in use in the state of Illinois:

STATE OF ILLINOIS,)
COUNTY OF DU PAGE.) ss.
Julius Warren)
      vs.)   Claim for Lien
Martin Smith)

The Claimant, Julius Warren, of the City of Wheaton, County of Du Page, State of Illinois, hereby files a Claim for Lien against Martin Smith of Du Page County, Illinois, and states:

That on the first day of October, 19 . . . ., said Martin Smith was the owner of the following described land, to wit: Lot two (2) in Block three (3) of the original town of Hinsdale, in the County of Du Page and State of Illinois.

That on the first day of October, 19 . . . ., the Claimant made a contract with said owner to furnish labor and materials for the building to be erected on said land for the sum of Seven Hundred Fifty Dollars ($750), and on the 23rd day of October, 19 . . . ., completed all work required to be done by said contract.

That said owner is entitled to credits on account thereof totaling Two Hundred Fifty Dollars ($250), leaving due, unpaid and owing to the Claimant on account thereof, after allowing all credits, the balance of Five Hundred Dollars ($500), for which, with interest, the Claimant claims a lien on said land and improvements.

JULIUS WARREN

. . . .

STATE OF ILLINOIS,)
COUNTY OF DU PAGE.) ss.
Julius Warren, being first duly sworn, on oath deposes and says, That he is the above named Claimant, that he has read the foregoing Claim for Lien,

knows the contents thereof, and that all the statements therein contained are true.

JULIUS WARREN

. . . .

Subscribed and sworn to before me this 1st day of November, 19 . . . .

GEORGE JOHNSON

. . . .
Notary Public

(Seal)

Marriage

1. MARRIAGE is a civil contract. Marriage licenses are required by all the states, and many restrictions concerning the issuing of such licenses have been made within recent years. Unlike other contracts, marriage cannot be terminated by the consent of both parties.

2. GENERAL PRINCIPLES—The following principles apply to a contract of marriage.

a. There must be a serious agreement or mutual assent of both parties.

b. A marriage may be declared void because of fraud, incompetence of one of the parties, or the fact that one of the parties is underage.

c. The legal age at which marriage can legally be contracted without parental consent varies from state to state. With consent of parents or guardians, the minimum age in several states is 18 for men and 16 for women; in states under common law the ages are 14 and 12 respectively. As a result of the new equal protection decisions and the Twenty-sixth Amendment to the federal Constitution lowering the minimum voting age to 18, there is a nationwide trend to establish the age of 18 as the legal age for both males and females.

d. A marriage is not void simply because it has been improperly performed or licensed, but the officials responsible are liable.

e. At common law a wife is solely responsible for her crimes unless they were committed in her husband's presence, in which case coercion on the part of the husband is presumed. In many states this law has been changed so that the husband is responsible only when he participated in the crime, unless coercion is proved.

f. A married man can sue for the alienation of his wife's affections. In some states the wife has a similar right. Suits for alienation of affections are now prohibited by the laws of a number of states.

g. Either husband or wife may act as the agent for the other party.

h. The husband is not responsible for the debts or wrongs of his wife unless, of course, the debts are necessary for the support of the family.

i. The husband must provide a home, and support and protect his wife and children. His duty to protect his family carries with it all the rights of "self-defense."

j. He must maintain law and order in his household, and may use force in preventing a member of his family from committing a crime.

k. A wife is required to care for the house and family. She cannot be forced to go into business or enter any gainful occupation.

l. The husband must support his wife, and she can pledge his credit for articles necessary to sustain life and maintain her social position.

3. A MARRIAGE CONTRACT—A marriage is a civil contract, and is entered into by the consent of the parties. If a man says to a woman, "Will you marry me?" or words to that effect, and she says "Yes," or words that imply an affirmative answer, it is, by law, an agreement or promise of marriage, and both parties are legally held to carry out in good faith the promise thus made. Mutual promise by a man and a woman to marry at some future day constitutes a valid contract in some states.

4. BREACH OF PROMISE—If either party refuses to carry out the contract, he or she is guilty of breach of promise, and in some states the other party may recover damages. It is not very often that the man sues the woman, though he has an equal right to do so if she fails to make good her promise. In several states, however, suits for breach of promise are now outlawed.

5. NECESSARY PROOF—Generally in case of a lawsuit for breach of promise, there are no direct witnesses, as people usually become engaged without the presence of a third party. The engagement may be implied from the conduct of the party sued.

6. IMPLIED EVIDENCE—In states where suit for breach of promise is recognized, a promise of marriage may be implied from circumstances such as constant visits, presents, open declaration of the parties, and their reception by the parents or friends as an engaged couple without any objections from the party being sued.

7. EXCUSES FOR BREAKING THE PROMISE—A refusal to marry may be justified on the ground of the bad character or conduct of the other party; poor health of either party is sometimes a good excuse, but not generally. If the woman were a widow or a divorcee and concealed this fact from the man, this justifies a refusal on his part to marry.

8. TIME OF MARRIAGE—When a man promises to marry a woman without stating any special time, the law may hold him guilty of breach of promise unless he is ready to fulfill his engagement within a reasonable time; five years was held in one instance to be an unreasonable time.

9. WHEN A PROMISE IS NOT BINDING—If either party is underage, he or she is not bound by promise to marry and the law will excuse the party underage.

10. SEDUCTION—Seduction of a woman under promise of marriage and subsequent refusal on the man's part to marry subjects him to damages in a civil action and often to criminal liability as well.

11. SEPARATION—The law allows agreements between husband and wife in which they agree to live separately. This does not in any way abolish the wife's rights in the husband's estate unless the contract so specifies.

12. DIVORCE—Divorces are of two kinds: (a) absolute divorces, and (b) judicial separation, generally known as separate maintenance. The word *divorce* as now commonly used has the former meaning. In the case of an absolute divorce the marriage is ended and the parties become single. A *judicial separation* is a limited divorce in which the court gives one party the right to live separately from the other. The decree of divorce usually makes provision for the payment of alimony, for the custody and support of any children, and for the settlement of property rights between the parties. The divorce laws of the several states vary, although most states recognize and respect the laws of the other states.

13. AUTHORITY OF WIFE LIVING APART FROM HUSBAND TO BIND HIM—Whether or not the person who supplies a wife with necessaries has knowledge of her husband's provision for her support, the presumption of a wife's authority to pledge her husband's credit is negatived by the fact of their living apart, and the tradesman who supplies her under such circumstances upon the credit of her husband, and without the husband's express sanction or approval, does so at his own peril. In order to charge her husband with the cost of supplies furnished her, the tradesman must show not only that they were of the kind usually regarded as "necessaries," but that in consequence of the inadequacy of the husband's provision, they were actually required for the wife's proper support, commensurate with the husband's means and the wife's station in the community.

14. PROPERTY RIGHTS OF MARRIED WOMEN—Nearly all the states have enacted legislative provisions for the benefit of married women. These laws vary greatly in the different states, and there are frequent changes, but all tend toward the releasing of woman from her former condition of absolute dependence upon her husband. By the old common law a married woman had few rights. She was subject to the authority of her husband, and he could rule over her. This condition has now been changed, however, and the rights of married women are recognized by every court. All property owned by the wife before marriage, or received after marriage and held as her separate property, can be sold and transferred without the consent of her husband except his rights of dower or curtesy in her real estate. If a husband fails to make provision for the support of his wife, the law will compel him to furnish her proper support if he has sufficient means.

Medicare

1. DEFINITION—*Medicare* is a federal program of health insurance for the aged. The Medicare program enacted in 1965 provides a comprehensive medical benefit program administered by the Social Security Administration of the Department of Health, Education and Welfare. The two basic benefits are generally referred to as Hospital Insurance (Part A) and Medical Insurance (Part B), the first providing hospital, extended care and home health benefits and the second providing the services of physicians and ambulance, outpatient hospital and home health services.

2. ELIGIBILITY FOR HOSPITAL INSURANCE BENEFITS—Persons who have attained age 65 and are entitled to monthly insurance benefits under the Social Security system or who are qualified railroad retirement beneficiaries are entitled to benefits under Part A. Disqualification to receive some or all of the retirement benefits by reason of earnings is not a disqualification to receive Part A benefits. Application for these benefits should be made within the three-month period before the person attains age 65.

3. SCOPE OF HOSPITAL INSURANCE BENEFITS—For each benefit (spell of illness), a person is entitled to the following Part A benefits:
a. Up to 90 days in a hospital.
b. Up to 100 days of posthospital care in an extended care facility.
c. Up to 100 visits for posthospital home health services, such as visits by nurses, therapists and health aides, during a one-year period following release from a hospital or extended care facility.

4. BENEFIT PERIODS—A *benefit period* is a period of consecutive days beginning with the first day the individual is furnished inpatient hospital services or extended care services and ending with the close of the first period of 60 consecutive days in which the individual is not an inpatient of a hospital or of an extended care facility. There is no limit to the number of benefit periods that a person may have. Once a person enters a new benefit period he is entitled to a new round of benefits. In addition, each person has a "lifetime reserve" of 60 additional hospital days that can be drawn on

for any days in excess of 90 that he remains in the hospital during any benefit period. These days are used automatically at the first opportunity unless the person specifies that he does not desire to use them.

5. PAYMENTS—During each benefit period Medicare pays for all covered services for the first 60 days except a small initial amount—presently $60—which will increase with the annual rise in hospital costs. For the 61st through 90th day Medicare pays for all covered services except $15 per day. There are special rules for benefits in psychiatric hospitals including a lifetime reserve of 190 hospital benefit days.

6. ELIGIBILITY FOR MEDICAL INSURANCE BENEFITS—Whereas those who qualify for Hospital Insurance under Part A and make application therefor are automatically eligible, the Medical Insurance benefits are available only to persons 65 years of age or over who elect to enroll in the program and who pay the premiums. An individual is eligible to enroll only if he has attained age 65 and (a) is a resident of the United States, either as a citizen or as an alien lawfully admitted for permanent residence who has resided in the United States continuously during the five years immediately preceding the month in which he applies for enrollment for medical insurance, or (b) is entitled to hospital benefits under Part A.

7. SCOPE OF MEDICAL INSURANCE BENEFITS—The services covered by Part B include

a. Medical and surgical services by a doctor of medicine or osteopathy, wherever furnished.

b. Certain medical and surgical services by a doctor of dental medicine or a doctor of dental surgery.

c. Other services ordinarily furnished in a doctor's office.

d. Outpatient hospital benefits, including laboratory, diagnostic, X-ray and radiology services, emergency room, and medical supplies.

e. Outpatient physical therapy services furnished under direct and personal supervision of a doctor or by a qualified hospital, extensive care facility, home health agency or public health agency and under a plan established and periodically reviewed by a doctor.

f. Up to 100 home health visits if all of the following are present: (1) the individual needs part-time skilled nursing care or physical or speech therapy services; (2) the individual is confined to his home; (3) a doctor determines that home health care is needed; (4) a doctor sets up and periodically reviews the plan for home health care; and (5) the home health agency is participating in Medicare.

8. LIMITATIONS—The medical services covered by Part B are subject to the following limitations:

a. For each calendar year, the insured individual pays for the first $50 of reasonable charges. Expenses incurred in the last three months of a year may be credited toward the deductible for that year if the deductible has not been previously met in that year and will also be credited toward the deductible for the following year.

b. After the deductible has been met, Medicare pays 80 percent of the reasonable charges for covered services.

c. "Reasonable charges" are determined by the Medicare carriers, that is, hospitals and other health facilities, in each state and take into account the customary charges for medical and other health services in the community.

9. PREMIUMS—One-half of the premium for Part B benefits is paid by the individual and one-half by the government. The individual portion is paid monthly and, for persons receiving social security or railroad retirement benefits, is deducted from the monthly benefit check. Persons not entitled to retirement benefits but who have enrolled pay their premiums directly to the Social Security Administration. For the person who does not enroll during his initial enrollment period, but enrolls in a subsequent period, the monthly premium is increased by 10 percent of the monthly premium he would pay had he enrolled during his initial period, for each full 12 months in which he could have been, but was not, enrolled.

10. CLAIM PROCEDURE—Claims for payment under Part A are generally made by the hospital or extended care facility. Claims for payment under B are generally made by the physician or other person furnishing the service. Claims are made to the Medicare carrier in the locality where the services are furnished. If the physician does not accept responsibility for filing the claim for Part B benefits, the insured forwards the claim directly to the carrier for payment.

Mortgage

1. DEFINITIONS—A *mortgage* is an instrument in writing designating certain property, either real or personal, to secure the payment of a debt. When the debt is paid the mortgage becomes void and is released. The person who mortgages his property is called the *mortgagor*. The person to whom the mortgage is given is the *mortgagee*. Some states consider the mortgage as a conditional transfer of property, giving the mortgagee legal title until the debt and interest are paid; others regard the mortgagor as the holder of the legal title at all times and the mortgagee as the holder of an enforceable lien on the property.

2. GENERAL PRINCIPLES:

a. A mortgage may be made to cover future advances.

b. As the county records are public and may be examined by anyone, the injured party alone is responsible if he buys, or lends money on, a piece of property without first making certain that there are no encumbrances on it.

c. The law assumes that the mortgage contract covers all the agreements concerning the payment of the debt and the return of the property. The courts, therefore, ignore other agreements made at the same time. Later agreements, however, will hold if based on valid consideration.

d. Several mortgages may be made on the same piece of real estate. The one recorded first has the first lien.

e. A creditor cannot compel payment of the mortgage before it is due. Neither can the debtor compel the creditor to accept the payment before it is due.

f. If after a foreclosure there is any deficit due the mortgagee, the mortgagor is still liable. See CHATTEL MORTGAGE.

g. A trust deed serves the same purpose as a real estate mortgage but conveys the property to a third party as trustee to hold title for the mortgagee, instead of conveying title directly to the mortgagee himself. This deed is very extensively used because it takes the place of a mortgage deed and renders the note negotiable. States frequently have statutory forms for trust deeds, and where such forms exist it is advisable to use them.

3. REQUIREMENTS—All real estate mortgages must be in writing, and under seal unless the seal has been abolished by statute. The instrument must clearly state the amount of the debt and the day on which it falls due. The property must be clearly described. The mortgage must then be acknowledged before the proper public official and properly recorded in the county records. The mortgagor usually gives a bond or note as evidence of the indebtedness, stating on its face that it is secured by a mortgage of the same date.

4. POSSESSION OF THE PROPERTY generally remains with the mortgagor. The mortgagor also receives all rents and profits from the property, and pays all taxes and other expenses.

5. IMPROVEMENTS TO THE PROPERTY—If a mortgagor erects buildings on mortgaged land and the mortgage is foreclosed, the mortgagee in taking possession gets all these additions. If the mortgagee erects buildings and the mortgagor thereafter redeems his land, he gets the buildings without paying for them.

6. ASSIGNMENT—A mortgagee can transfer, sell, or assign his mortgage at any time regardless of the wishes of the mortgagor. On the other hand, if the mortgagor wishes to sell his real estate he must sell subject to the mortgage. In other words, he can do nothing to invalidate the mortgagee's security.

7. INSURANCE—The property may be insured by both parties. In case of loss by fire the holder of the mortgage can collect the insurance that he had on the property. Practically all mortgages now contain provisions requiring the mortgagor to keep the property properly insured. The insurance policy contains a clause showing the name of the mortgagee or trustee and providing for his protection in case of loss by fire; the policy itself is usually held by the mortgagee.

8. FORECLOSURE—A *foreclosure* is a legal proceeding to sell the property mortgaged to satisfy the debt. If the property is sold to satisfy the debt, the mortgagor has a right to purchase it. The following steps are necessary for a foreclosure:

a. Application to a court.
b. A hearing by the court.
c. Referring to a master in chancery or a referee.
d. Advertising the property.
e. Public sale to the highest bidder.
f. Deeding the property to the purchaser.
g. Paying the money due to the mortgagee.
h. Returning any surplus to the mortgagor.

9. REDEMPTION—Formerly, a mortgagor could redeem his land only before or when the debt became due, but further time is now given. This right to redeem is called a *right in equity to redeem,* or an *equity of redemption.* The redemption period varies in different states according to statutes. This right to redeem is considered of so much importance that no party is permitted to lose it even by his own agreement. Even though the mortgagor agrees in the most positive terms to forefeit his equity of redemption, the law disregards such agreement and gives the debtor full time to redeem his property.

10. FORMS:

ASSIGNMENT OF MORTGAGE BY ENDORSEMENT

Know all men by these presents, That I, Henry Betzoid, the within named Mortgagee, for a consideration of Eight Hundred Dollars ($800), hereby sell, assign, transfer, and set over unto E. B. Newman, his heirs and assigns, the within named instrument of mortgage, and all the real estate, with appurtenances therein mentioned and described, and the promissory note, debts, and claims thereby secured, to have and to hold the same forever, subject to the conditions therein contained.

In witness whereof the party of the first part has hereunto set his hand and seal this third day of March, in the year of our Lord nineteen hundred and ....

Sealed and delivered in the presence of
E. E. Hawthorne

(Most states no longer require this attestation.)

HENRY BETZOID (Seal)

RELEASE

Know all men by these presents, That I, James Y. Scammon, of the County of Cook, and State of Illinois, for and in consideration of One Dollar ($1), to me in hand paid, and for other good and valuable considerations, the receipt whereof is hereby confessed, do hereby grant, bargain, remise, convey, release, and quitclaim unto Samuel P. Smith and Sarah E. Smith, of the County of Du Page and State of Illinois, all the right, title, interest, claim, or demand whatsoever I may have acquired in, through or by a certain indenture or mortgage deed, bearing date the first day of January, A.D. 19 ...., and recorded in the recorder's office of Du Page County, Illinois, in book 25 of mortgages, page 100, in and to the premises situated in the ...... of ...., in said county of ....., and in said mortgage deed described as follows, to wit: (description) and which said deed was made to secure two certain promissory notes, bearing even date with said deed, for the sum of Twenty-Five Hundred Dollars ($2,500).

Witness my hand and seal this 28th day of February, A.D. 19 ....

JAMES Y. SCAMMON (Seal)

TRUST DEED

This deed, made this ..... day of ...., 19 ...., between ..... of .... county of .... and state of ...... of the one part, and .... of ...., and ..... of ...., of the other part, witnesseth, that the party of the first part doth grant unto the parties of the second part the following property, to wit:
[Insert description of property]
in trust, to secure to ...... of ....., in the state of ......, the payment of .... dollars in ...... years from this date, with interest at .... percent per annum thereon, according to a promissory note made by the party of the first part to said .... for said sum.

In event that default shall be made in the payment of the above-mentioned sum as it becomes due and payable, then the trustees, or either of them, on being required so to do by ...., his executors, administrators, or assigns, shall sell the property hereby conveyed. And it is covenanted and agreed between the parties aforesaid that in case of a sale the same shall be made after first advertising the time, place, and terms thereof for ..... days in some newspaper published in the said county of ...., and upon the following terms, to wit: for cash as to so much of the proceeds as may be necessary to defray the expenses of executing this trust, the fees for drawing and recording this deed, if then unpaid, and to discharge the amount of money then payable upon said note; and if there be any residue of such purchase money, the same shall be made payable at such time, and be secured in such manner, as ....., his executors, administrators, or assigns, shall prescribe and direct, or in case of his or their failure to give such direction, at such time and in such manner as the trustees, or either of them, shall think fit. The party of the first part covenants to pay all taxes, assessments, dues, and charges upon the said property hereby conveyed so long as he or his heirs or assigns shall hold the same, and hereby waives the benefit of all homestead exemptions as to the debt secured by this deed.

If no default shall be made in the payment of the above-mentioned debt, then, upon the request of the party of the first part, a good and sufficient deed of release shall be executed to him at his own proper costs.

Witness, the hand .... and seal ...... of said Grantor this ..... day of ......, A.D. 19 ......

.............(Seal)

.............(Seal)

Municipal Corporations

1. DEFINITION—A *municipal corporation* is a corporation formed to carry on the work of government in a town or city. Its charter is granted by the state and it possesses only such powers as the state confers upon it, and no others.

2. POWERS—A city government is usually given the power:
a. To make its own laws or ordinances with reference to matters over which its charter gives it jurisdiction.
b. To enforce its laws.
c. To control all matters and things within its corporate boundaries within the limits fixed by its charter.
d. To issue bonds.

3. OFFICERS OF A MUNICIPAL CORPORATION—The mayor is usually the chief executive of a municipality, and the Board of Aldermen its lawmaking body. The titles of these officers vary widely, however, in the different states. Under the commission form of government the above offices are held by a commission of three or five men who have complete charge of the business of city government. The judicial power is usually vested in the police magistrate's court, or in larger cities in the municipal court. These are courts of limited jurisdiction only, however, and their jurisdiction does not supersede or conflict with that of the courts of the county in which they are situated.

4. WRONGFUL ACTS OF OFFICERS—The city is not responsible for damage for injuries to persons or property caused in the execution of a governmental duty. But what is considered a governmental duty is a question that has been the source of much litigation. The city is not liable for false arrest, false imprisonment, or assaults by police officers. If any wrongful act is committed by an officer while acting in his official capacity, he is liable personally.

5. THE CITY'S DUTY—It is the duty of the city government to provide and maintain safe and passable streets and highways, maintain police and fire protection, and provide for the general safety and welfare of its citizens.

6. LIABILITY—If the city fails to maintain safe and passable streets, the city is liable for damages resulting to those rightfully upon the streets, provided the city had notice that the streets were unsafe and impassable, and failed to exercise reasonable care to make the streets safe. It is almost universally held that a city is not liable for loss or injury resulting from failure to maintain proper police and fire protection.

7. POLICE POWER OF CITIES—The police power of a city extends to the city limits and a reasonable distance beyond the city limits in certain instances. The police magistrate,

sometimes called the recorder, sits in a court having jurisdiction equal to that of a justice of the peace. The police magistrate and the police officers are bound to enforce the laws of the city, called *ordinances*. An officer may arrest a person:
a. When a wrongful act is committed in his presence.
b. Upon a valid warrant.
c. Upon *probable cause*.
An officer may not arrest on mere suspicion, but only upon a reasonable ground for belief in guilt by a reasonable, cautious, and prudent police officer judged in the light of his experience and training.

8. SCHOOLS—The schools of a city are usually controlled by a board of education. This board has control and supervision over teachers, students, buildings, and all other matters pertaining to public education.

9. PUBLIC SERVICE CORPORATIONS—Any corporation furnishing the public as a whole a service or commodity is called a *public service corporation*. Its activities are as a rule controlled and supervised by a public service commission having the power to fix prices and regulate many of the activities of the corporations that affect the public.

Negotiable Instruments

1. DEFINITIONS—A *negotiable instrument* is any legal document that may be transferred by endorsement or delivery in such a way as to give the person receiving it the right to bring suit thereon in his own name. The person who promises to pay is called the *maker* or *drawer*, and the one to whom he promises is called the *payee*.

2. KINDS OF NEGOTIABLE INSTRUMENTS—Almost every written contract or agreement to pay money is negotiable, in the sense that the owner can sell it to a third person who can enforce it against the maker. However, in the more strict sense of the word there are three common forms of negotiable paper, namely, checks, notes, and bills of exchange or drafts.

3. FORM OF NEGOTIABLE INSTRUMENTS—The law does not require negotiable instruments to be in any prescribed form. However, certain things are necessary in all checks, notes, or bills of exchange to make them negotiable:
a. The instrument must be in writing.
b. It must be signed by the maker or drawer.
c. It must contain a promise or order to pay.
d. The promise or order must be unconditional.
e. The promise or order must be a promise or order to pay a certain sum in money.
f. The instrument must be payable on demand or at a fixed or determinable time in the future.
g. The instrument must be payable to the order of some person, or to bearer.
h. If the instrument is addressed to a drawee, as would be the case if it were a bill of exchange or draft, the drawee must be named or otherwise indicated in the instrument with reasonable certainty.

4. CONSIDERATION—While it is not always necessary to express any consideration in negotiable paper, it is safer to do so. When an instrument is in the hands of an innocent third party, the law assumes a valuable consideration. The words "for value received" usually appear on promissory notes.

5. PROTEST—A *protest* of a note, check, or draft is a formal statement by a notary public that the paper was presented for payment and was refused. The costs are added to the instrument. See also NOTARIES PUBLIC.

6. NEGOTIABILITY—The words "to bearer," or "to the order of," or words of like effect, render a paper negotiable.

Any person capable of making a contract is capable of making a negotiable instrument. A person who receives a negotiable instrument under the conditions hereinafter mentioned becomes what is known as a "holder in due course," and certain defenses that might have been raised against the original holder cannot be raised against him. He must have taken the instrument under the following conditions:

a. The instrument must be complete and regular on its face.

b. It must not have been overdue, and the holder must not have known it was previously dishonored if such were the fact.

c. He must have taken it in good faith and paid value for it.

d. At the time he took it he must have had no notice of any infirmity in the instrument or defect in the title of the person negotiating it to him.

7. NOTES—A *note* is a simple written promise to pay a certain sum at a certain time to a person named therein. An *individual promissory note* is a note in which one party promises to pay another a certain sum of money at a specified time. A *joint promissory note* is the same as an individual note except that it is signed by two or more parties, all of whom are liable jointly but not severally. In a *joint and several promissory note* two or more parties severally and separately agree to pay a certain sum at a specified time, and each signer is responsible for the whole amount. Statutes in many states provide that all joint obligations shall be held to be joint and several.

8. TRANSFERRING NOTES—The following rules govern the transferring of notes:

a. Instruments payable to bearer may be transferred by delivery, payable to order by endorsement.

b. An *endorser* is a person who writes his name on the back of a note or other instrument.

c. *Endorsement in blank* is an endorsement that does not mention the name of the person in whose favor it is made.

d. The endorser is liable for the payment of a note if the maker fails to meet it and the endorser is properly notified.

e. An endorser who is compelled to pay a note has a claim against the maker and against each endorser whose name appears above his own.

f. An endorser to whose order a note is drawn or endorsed can transfer it without becoming liable for its payment by writing the words "without recourse" over his signature on the back.

9. COLLECTING NOTES—The following rules govern the collection of notes:

a. A note destroyed by mistake or accident can be collected upon proof of loss.

b. Money paid by mistake must be refunded.

c. If no time is specified the note is payable on demand.

d. The *day of maturity* is the day on which a note becomes legally due.

e. In finding the day of maturity, actual days must be counted if the note falls due a specific number of days after the day on which it was drawn, but months are counted when the note falls due a specific number of months after the day on which it was drawn.

f. Negotiable paper to bearer or endorsed in blank, which has been lost or stolen, cannot be collected by the finder or thief, but a holder who innocently receives it in good faith before maturity for value received can hold it against the owner's claims.

g. A note made in one state, payable in another, must be governed by the laws of that state in which it is to be paid.

h. Demand for payment of a note must be made upon the day of maturity and at the place named. If no place is specified, it is payable at the maker's place of business or at his residence. In most of the states, when a note falls due on a Sunday or legal holiday, by statute the maker is given until the following day to pay the same.

i. An extension of the time of a note granted by the holder releases sureties and endorsers, unless consent to such extension has been given by the endorsers or sureties.

j. If the maker refuses to pay a mature note presented to him by a holder in due course, the holder must immediately give notice of default to the endorser in order to hold that endorser liable for the debt.

10. PAYMENT OF NOTES—All the parties who have endorsed a note are liable for the full amount, but only one satisfaction can be recovered. In certain cases notes are unenforceable, especially when held by the original payee. Among such cases are the following:

a. A note given by one who is not of age, unless the minor ratified it after becoming of age.

b. A note made by an intoxicated person.

c. A note not witnessed, given by one who cannot write.

d. A note obtained by duress, by putting the maker in fear of illegal imprisonment, or by threats that would lead an ordinary person to fear injury to his person, his reputation, or his property.

e. A note obtained by fraud.

f. A note given for illegal consideration.

One who receives a note knowing it to have defects has no better right to collect it than the maker had to present it. If a person at the time of taking a note has notice that it is void because of fraud or for any other reason, he cannot collect it.

11. FORMS OF NOTES:

NEGOTIABLE BY ENDORSEMENT

$375.00   Naperville, Ill., Oct. 7, 19 . . . .

For value received, one year after date I promise to pay to the order of J. L. Nichols the sum of Three Hundred and Seventy-Five Dollars with interest at six percent from date until paid.

J. R. PRICE

NEGOTIABLE WITHOUT ENDORSEMENT

$100.00   Cleveland, O., Aug. 1, 19 . . . .

Ninety days after date I promise to pay to bearer, One Hundred Dollars, value received.

E. M. KECK

NOT NEGOTIABLE

$100.00   Chicago, Ill., Dec. 10, 19 . . . .

Sixty days after date I promise to pay Geo. C. Dixon One Hundred Dollars, value received.

EUGENE LANSING

A CORPORATION NOTE

$200.00   Augusta, Me., Mar. 18, 19 ....
   Nine months after date, the Granite Stone Company, a corporation, promises to pay S. A. Chilton, or order, Two Hundred Dollars, with interest at six percent. Value received.
   Attest: I. K. Dawes, Secretary.

                    Granite Stone Company
                    O. R. PHILLIPS, President

Note.—If corporation notes are drawn and signed in the above manner, the officers are not personally liable.

COLLATERAL NOTE

$500.00   Mendota, Tex., Sept. 25, 19 ....
   Sixty days after date, for value received, I promise to pay to the order of T. J. Boyd, the sum of Five Hundred Dollars, with interest at the rate of six percent per annum after date, having deposited United States Bonds of the face value of Six Hundred Dollars ($600), which I authorize the holder of this Note, upon the nonperformance of this promise at maturity, to sell, at public or private sale, without further notice, and to apply proceeds, or as much thereof as may be necessary to the payment of this Note, and all necessary expenses and charges, holding myself responsible for any deficiency.

                    W. W. STRATTON

JUDGMENT NOTE

$2,000.00   Philadelphia, Pa., Jan. 4, 19 ...
   Six months after date, for value received, I promise to pay to the order of J. W. Krasley Two Thousand Dollars, with interest at the rate of 6 percent per annum, after maturity, until paid.
   And to secure the payment of said amount, I hereby authorize any attorney of any court of record to appear for me in such court, in term time or vacation, at any time after maturity, to waive a jury trial and confess judgment, without process, in favor of the holder of the note, for such amount as may appear to be paid thereon, together with costs and five percent attorney's fees, and to waive and release all errors which may intervene on any such proceedings, and consent to immediate execution upon such judgment; hereby ratifying and confirming all my said attorney may do by virtue hereof.

                    GEORGE W. BAIRD

PAYABLE AT BANK

$440.00   Chicago, Ill., Oct. 10, 19 ...
   Two years after date, for value received, I promise to pay T. M. Culver, or order, Four Hundred Forty Dollars at Second National Bank, with interest at six percent per annum.

                    CHARLES HEARN

ON DEMAND

$25.67   Kansas City, Mo., Oct. 12, 19 ...
   On demand I promise to pay to the order of J. T.

Connor, Twenty-Five 67-100 Dollars. Value received, with interest at six percent.

                    A. H. SIMPSON

Note.—This note answers the same purpose as a note written one day after date.

JOINT NOTE

$200.00   Lisle, Ill., Jan. 1, 19 ....
   One year from date, we promise to pay D. F. Shaw, or order, Two Hundred Dollars. Value received. Interest at six percent.

                    J. LEWIS BEAN
                    B. A. WHITE

JOINT AND SEVERAL NOTE

$2,000.00   Ottawa, Ont., Nov. 25, 19 ...
   Ten months after date, we, or either of us, promise to pay Maggie Patterson Two Thousand Dollars, value received. Interest at five percent.

                    J. C. HARDY
                    R. E. WOOD

PRINCIPAL AND SURETY NOTE

$600.00   New York, N.Y., Sept. 21, 19 ....
   For value received, on or before July 27, 19 ...., I promise to pay to the order of John Jackson, Six Hundred Dollars. Interest at five percent.

                    W. J. SHAW, Principal
                    THOS. RODDEN, Surety

Note.—The general form of a principal and surety note is for the principal to properly sign the note and for the surety to endorse it.

A NOTE BY ONE WHO CANNOT WRITE

$49.50   Cleveland, Ohio, Mar. 20, 19 ...
   One year after date, I promise to pay N. Bowker, or order, Forty-Nine 50-100 Dollars, with interest at five percent. Value received.

H. A. STARR, Witness.

                            his
                    JOHN X ROURKE
                            mark

Note.—A note made by a person who cannot write should always be witnessed by a disinterested person.

MY OWN ORDER

$200.00   New Orleans, La., July 20, 19 ...
   For value received, I promise to pay, sixty days after date, to my own order, Two Hundred Dollars, with interest at eight percent.

                    A. S. BARNARD

Note.—A note may be drawn to the maker's own order, with his endorsement in favor of the creditor.

NOTE SECURED BY A MORTGAGE

$1,000.00   Chicago, Ill., April 15, 19 . . .

Six months after date I promise to pay to John Williams One Thousand Dollars with interest at six percent.

This note is secured by a mortgage of even date herewith from Robert Jones to John Williams.

ROBERT JONES

12. CHECKS—A *check* is an order drawn upon a bank, payable on demand. The person who writes the check is the *drawer;* the bank on which the check is drawn is called the *drawee;* the person to whom the check is made payable is called the *payee.*

13. SIGNATURE—A check must be properly signed by the drawer or his duly authorized agent. A signature made on behalf of the drawer by another person is valid if authorized. It should, of course, be written in ink, but a signature made with a pencil or rubber stamp is valid if intended as a signature.

14. PRESENTATION—A check must be presented for payment within a reasonable time after its issue, or the drawer will be discharged from liability thereon to the extent of the loss caused by the delay. It is generally held that one day after the receipt of the check is a reasonable time to present or forward the same for presentation.

15. THE AGREEMENT TO PAY is between the bank and the depositor. For this reason a check, of itself, does not operate as an assignment of any part of the funds to the credit of the drawer with the bank. Consequently, should the bank refuse to pay the check, the holder cannot bring action against the bank, unless or until the bank has accepted or certified the check. On the other hand, if the bank fails to fulfill its contract with the depositor, he has a just cause of action against the bank. Should the bank refuse to honor a customer's check owing to an employee's mistake in bookkeeping, the bank could be held responsible for any loss resulting therefrom.

16. CERTIFYING A CHECK—A certification of a check by the bank is equivalent to an acceptance, and discharges the drawer and all the endorsers preceding the holder who secures the certification. When a check is presented to a bank for this purpose, the bank charges the drawer's account with the amount so that, as far as the drawer and the bank are concerned, the check has actually been paid. Therefore, if a certified check is not presented at the drawer's bank for payment and is returned to the drawer, it should not be destroyed but should be redeposited as cash.

17. STOPPING PAYMENT—The drawer of the check may order the bank to stop payment on a check before it is presented. The bank is required to follow these instructions and is liable for any loss resulting from failure to do so.

18. FORGED CHECKS—The law insists that the banker exercise the greatest care in paying the checks of customers. If the signature has been forged or the amount of the check altered, the bank is liable for any improper payment. The drawer of the check must also use every precaution to prevent alterations. He should write in a way to avoid confusing the banker who is to pay the check. The bank is not responsible for any loss caused by negligence on the part of the drawer in making out the check.

19. VITAL POINTS ON CHECKS—A check is not due until presented. It is negotiable. It has no days of grace. Giving a check is not payment on an indebtedness, unless the check is paid, or unless it is accepted as payment. The death of the drawer of the check before it is presented to the bank renders the check null and void. The amount of the check should always be written out in words as well as in figures.

If a raised check is paid by the bank, the bank can charge the depositor only the amount for which he drew the check, unless the raising of the check was made possible by the carelessness of the drawer. In that case the drawer would be responsible for the loss.

If you write a check for a stranger who needs identification at your bank, have him endorse the check in your presence and under his endorsement write "Endorsement above guaranteed," signing your name. He can then usually cash the check, without further identification, by signing his name again in the presence of the banker.

20. DRAFTS—A *draft* is a written order by one person on another for the payment of a specified sum of money to a designated third person. The one who writes the draft is called the *drawer,* the one on whom it is written, the *drawee,* and the one to whom it is to be paid, the *payee.*

21. KINDS OF DRAFTS—Drafts may be made payable at sight, on demand, at a certain time after date, or after sight. A *sight draft* or *demand draft* is drawn by one person on another and is payable when presented. *Time drafts* are similar to sight drafts, but are payable a certain number of days after presentation. A *bill of exchange* is an unconditional order in writing addressed by one person to another, signed by the person giving it, requiring the person to whom it is addressed to pay on demand or at a fixed or determinable future time a certain sum of money to order or to bearer. The term includes drafts and checks.

22. ACCEPTANCE—Sight and demand drafts are presented for payment only. Time drafts require acceptance by the party against whom they are drawn in order to bind him. The usual method of acceptance is to write across the face of the draft in red ink the word "accepted," followed by the date and the signature of the drawee. Should the person on whom the draft is drawn die before it was accepted, it should be presented to his legal representative for acceptance. When either acceptance or payment is refused, the draft may be protested like any note or check. Drafts are negotiable both before and after acceptance.

23. FORMS OF DRAFTS:

BANK DRAFT

$100.00   State of Illinois, May 10, 19 . . . .

The First National Bank of Naperville. Pay to the order of F. A. Lueben, One Hundred Dollars.

To Union National Bank,   W. L. HETZ, Cashier
   Chicago, Ill.

DEMAND DRAFT

$100.00   Troy Grove, Ill., Aug. 1, 19 . . . .

On demand pay to the order of Frank Myers at the Mendota First National Bank, One Hundred Dollars. Value received.

To Charles Lerch,   A. S. HUDSON
   Mendota, Ill.

SIGHT DRAFT

$500.00   Naperville, Tenn., July 10, 19 . . . .

At sight pay to the order of C. Parman, Five Hundred Dollars, and charge to the account of

To Jessee Lerch,   H. H. ZEMMER
   Meriden, Ill.

TIME DRAFT

$450.30   Ottawa, Fla., July 5, 19 . . . .

Ten days from date pay to J. L. Nichols, or order, Four Hundred Fifty 30-100 Dollars. Value received.

To Alvin Brown,   C. E. LAMALE
   Ottawa, Fla.

24. ENDORSEMENTS—An *endorsement* is a writing on the back of a negotiable instrument for the purpose of transferring the title or ownership from one person to another. The writing may be in pen or pencil upon any part of the instrument or upon a paper attached thereto. It consists ordinarily of the payee's signature and those of other holders, if any.

25. HOW TO ENDORSE—Write across the back of the paper, not lengthwise, near the left end. Always endorse a check or note exactly as your name appears on the face. If the check is payable to F. Black, do not write Frank Black. If your name is misspelled, endorse first as it appears on the face and then write your correct signature underneath. No written explanation is necessary: banks are familiar with this practice. The same rules govern the endorsement of notes, drafts, and other written instruments. A check or other instrument may be endorsed and title thereby transferred many times. Each endorser is liable to those who endorse after him.

26. KINDS OF ENDORSEMENTS—An *endorsement in blank* is made when the payee simply signs his name in the proper place, across the left end of the reverse side, without any statement of conditions. Such a note or check is negotiable without further endorsement. Endorsement in blank is commonly used when a check is deposited or cashed at a bank. It should not be used when there is danger of the check's being lost or stolen.

An *endorsement in full* or special endorsement consists of writing the name of the person to whom, or to whose order, the money is to be paid, followed by the payee's signature. For example: "Pay to F. Black or order, J. Jones"; when endorsed in this form, the check cannot be cashed until F. Black endorses it.

In a *qualified endorsement* the endorser relieves himself of any liability in connection with the instrument, by writing above his signature the words "Without recourse"; thus, "Without recourse, J. Jones."

A *restrictive endorsement* limits the payment of the note, bill, or check. The endorser writes "pay to F. Black only," or "for deposit in the First National Bank," signing his name underneath. A check or other instrument so endorsed cannot be further negotiated by the person or bank receiving it. Restrictive endorsement is a wise precaution when there is danger of a negotiable instrument being lost or stolen after endorsement.

A *conditional endorsement* is one directing payment only upon the performance of a certain condition. The endorser's liability is thereby limited. For example, "Pay to the order of F. Black unless he previously receives the amount from my agent, J. Jones." Neither the original character of the note nor its negotiability is affected by such an endorsement. It may affect, however, the title of the one to whom it is transferred.

Endorsement by an agent is made in the following form: "J. Jones, by H. Smith, his agent." In this manner the agent endorses for his principal.

In a *guaranteed endorsement* one party guarantees payment on a note for another party. He writes above his signature "I hereby guarantee payment of this note," or words to like effect. He is then absolutely liable for the amount due by the terms of the note in case the maker fails to pay. In effect, he becomes a co-maker.

27. IOU—An *IOU* is not a promissory note, and is not negotiable. It is evidence of a debt due by virtue of a previous contract. The following is an example:

Chicago, Ill., June 4, 1940

Mr. A. O. Rogers
IOU Sixty Dollars ($60.00).

W. G. ALLEN

28. DUE BILLS—A *due bill* is not payable to order, nor is it assignable by mere endorsement. It is simply the acknowledgment of a debt, yet it may be transferred. It may be payable in money, in merchandise, or in services.

Due bills do not draw interest unless so specified. Common forms are the following:

$125.00   Chicago, Aug. 14, 19 . . . .
Due Henry Harrington, for value received, One Hundred and Twenty-Five Dollars with interest at six percent.

Q. YINZER

ON DEMAND

$250.00   Naperville, Ill., July 1, 19 . . . . .
Due E. E. Miller, on demand, Two Hundred Fifty Dollars in goods from my store, for value received.

A. T. HANSON

IN MERCHANDISE

$1,000.00   Lincoln, Neb., Nov. 1, 19 . . . .
Due R. William, One Thousand Dollars, payable in wheat at market price, on the first day of January, 19 . . . . . .

CHARLES SCHUERER

29. RECEIPTS—A *receipt* is an acknowledgment in writing that a certain sum of money or a thing has been received by the party giving and signing the same. A complete receipt requires the following statements: (a) that a payment has been received; (b) the date of the payment; (c) the amount of article received; (d) from whom received, and, if for another, on whose behalf payment is made; (e) to what debt or purpose it is to be applied; (f) the signature of the person receiving the property, and, if for another, on whose behalf it was received.

30. GENERAL PRINCIPLES GOVERNING RECEIPTS—When an agent signs a receipt, he should sign his principal's name and then write his name underneath as agent. If payment is made upon account, upon a special debt, or in full, it should be so stated in the receipt. It is not necessary to take a receipt on paying a note, draft, or other instrument endorsed by the payee, because the instrument itself becomes a receipt. If a receipt is obtained through fraud, or given under error or mistake, it is void. If the giving and taking of receipts were more generally practiced in business transactions, less trouble, fewer lawsuits, and the saving of thousands of dollars would result.

31. FORMS OF RECEIPTS:

RECEIPT FOR PAYMENT ON ACCOUNT

$250.00   Naperville, Ill., July 6, 19 . . . .
Received of J. L. Nichols, Two Hundred and Fifty Dollars on account.

J. K. ROHMER

RECEIPT FOR SETTLEMENT OF AN ACCOUNT

$220.14   Joliet, Ill., March 20, 19 . . . .
Received of Thomas Rourke, Two Hundred and Twenty 14-100 Dollars, in full settlement of account to date.

C. S. SELBY

RECEIPT IN FULL OF ALL DEMANDS

$1,000.00   Meriden, Conn., Jan. 14, 19 ....
Received of C. F. Hetche, One Thousand Dollars, in
full of all demands to date.

O. N. OBRIGHT

RECEIPT FOR A PARTICULAR BILL

$400.00   Brooklyn, N. Y., Aug. 1, 19 ....
Received of Morris Cliggitt, Four Hundred Dollars,
in payment for a bill of Merchandise.

R. ZACHMAN

RECEIPT FOR RENT

$40.00   Snyder, Tex., Mar. 20, 19 ....
Received of L. Heininger, Forty Dollars in full for
one month's rent, for month ending April 20, 19 .....,
for resident at 44 Olive Street.

J. LEWIS BEAN

RECEIPT FOR A NOTE

$1,220.00
Received, Buffalo, March 6, 19 ...., from Messrs.
Taylor & Co., their note of this date, at three months,
our favor, for Twelve Hundred and Twenty Dollars;
which, when paid, will be in full of account rendered
to 1st instant.

C. H. OLIVER

RECEIPT FOR SERVICES

$44.00   Lemont, Ill., July 23, 19 ....
Received of Samuel Lynn, Forty-Four Dollars, in
full for services to date.

DANIEL FURBUSH

RECEIPT FOR MONEY ADVANCED ON A CONTRACT

$500.00   Chicago, Ill., May 10, 19 ....
Received of Arthur Kahl the sum of Five Hundred
Dollars, part payment on contract to build for him a
house at No. 1439 Perry St., Chicago.

CARL DIENST

RECEIPT FOR INTEREST DUE ON A MORTGAGE

$75.00   Chicago, August 1, 19 ....
Received of G. A. Caton, Seventy-Five Dollars in full
of six months' interest due this day, on his note to me
dated August 1st, 19 ....., for Twenty-Five Hundred
Dollars ($2,500), secured by mortgage on property at
1430 Maple Street, Chicago.

EDWARD TRONT

Notaries Public

1. DEFINITION—A *notary public* is a state officer whose functions are (a) to attest and certify, by his hand and official seal, various documents, in order to give them authenticity in other jurisdictions, (b) to take acknowledgments of deeds and other conveyances and instruments, and to certify the same, and (c) to perform other official acts, the power to do which is conferred by statutory enactment. As a general rule the functions of a notary are ministerial, not judicial. They are confined to the civil, as distinguished from the criminal, branch of the law.

2. THE OFFICE AND ITS FUNCTIONS—The office of notary public as it exists in the several states today is the outgrowth of various practices traceable to the Roman Empire. Merely a scribe in ancient times, the notary has been granted increasing power and more duties by successive legislative enactments in order to meet the needs of changing conditions and a growing civilization. His commission is granted upon representation of his capacity and integrity. In accepting office the notary contracts the obligation to fill it intelligently and honestly. A notary public is responsible for a number of important functions.

3. PROTESTING BILLS OF EXCHANGE—A notary public is empowered to protest inland and foreign bills of exchange and promissory notes, authenticating their dishonor by the refusal of the drawee or payee to accept or pay them on presentation or when due. The term *protest* as applied to commercial paper means the taking of such steps as are required to charge or fix liability upon one secondarily liable, such as an endorser. As applied to the notarial act, it means a declaration made in writing by a notary public after doing the acts certified, that the bill or note to which it relates was, on the day it became due, presented for payment, and that payment was refused.

4. AUTHENTICATION OF DOCUMENTS—A notary public is empowered to authenticate transfers or conveyances of property, and other documents required by law to be authenticated. To *authenticate* a document means for a notary to certify under his hand and seal of office, together with a notice of the date and, in most states, the expiration date of his commission, such facts as the law requires to give the document operative effect.

5. TAKING DEPOSITIONS—A notary may take depositions under the rules and instructions of the courts when cases are pending. A *deposition* is the testimony of a witness taken down in writing, under oath or affirmation before a notary public, and usually subscribed by the witness, pursuant to special authority granted by a court after notice to the adverse party. It is authenticated by the notary.

6. TAKING ACKNOWLEDGMENTS—A notary public may take acknowledgments of various written instruments. An *acknowledgment* is an oral declaration or admission made by one who has executed a document, made before a notary public or other officer authorized by law to take acknowledgments, to the effect that the execution is his act and deed. The written certificate on the document endorsed by the officer taking the acknowledgment, certifying to the facts of the same, is sometimes referred to as "an acknowledgment," but is more properly called a *certificate of acknowledgment*. It is not part of the execution of a document, but only evidence of execution. The function of a certificate of acknowledgment is twofold—to authorize the document to be given in evidence without further proof of its execution, and to entitle it to be recorded. At least six essential facts must appear in a certificate of acknowledgment: (a) the designation of the officer making the certificate; (b) the name of the person making the acknowledgment, and that he or she personally appeared before the officer; (c) that there was an acknowledgment; (d) that the person who made the acknowledgment was identified as the one who executed the instrument; (e) that such identity was personally known or proved by the officer taking the acknowledgment; and (f) the day and year when the acknowledgment was made.

7. TAKING AFFIDAVITS—A notary public may take affidavits as to the truth of statements made in legal papers for use in proceedings before courts of civil or maritime juris-

diction. An *affidavit* is a voluntary statement, formally reduced to writing and sworn to or affirmed and subscribed before a notary public. See AFFIDAVITS.

8. ADMINISTERING OATHS—A notary may administer oaths and affirmations as to correctness of accounts. An *oath* is an outward pledge, given by the person taking it, that his attestation or promise is made under an immediate sense of his responsibility to God.

9. FORM AND MANNER OF ADMINISTERING OATHS, AFFIDAVITS, AND AFFIRMATIONS—The customary and approved manner of administering an oath or taking an affidavit is to have the person making the same raise his hand and swear by the ever-living God. There should be at least some manifestation that the officer and the person taking the oath understand the nature of their undertaking; a mere mental process is not sufficient. In many states the form and manner of taking an oath are prescribed by law.

Any person who desires may in lieu of an oath or affidavit take and subscribe or assent to an affirmation, which is administered by the officer repeating the words, "You do solemnly, sincerely and truly declare and affirm that," etc., "and so you do affirm." It is not unusual to ask the question, "Do you swear or affirm" rather than to wait for the deponent to express his desire. A strict and solemn compliance with these forms is important. Any person who willfully and falsely swears or affirms to any material matter is guilty of perjury. The average citizen is inclined to attach only such importance and solemnity to these acts as the officer administering them shows. To perform these acts in a perfunctory manner is to deprive them of their intended value, and in some instances to encourage perjury.

FORM OF AFFIDAVIT OR AFFIRMATION

STATE OF PENNSYLVANIA,)
COUNTY OF PHILADELPHIA.) ss.

Allen B. White, being duly sworn (or affirmed), according to law, deposes and says (or in case of affirmation, in lieu of "deposes and says" insert "affirms and declares") that he is the person who executed the foregoing instrument (or if by an officer or agent of a corporation, insert in lieu of "he is the person," etc., the following: "he is the [name of office] of the [name of corporation] above named, that he has authority from it to make this affidavit [or affirmation] in its behalf); and that the facts therein set forth are true to the best of his (add "and its" where made by officer or agent for corporation) knowledge, information and belief.

Sworn (or affirmed) and
subscribed before me this
22nd day of November, A.D. 19 . . . .

ALLEN B. WHITE
C. D. BLACK

(Seal)
    Stamp com. expires.

FORM OF ACKNOWLEDGMENT RECOMMENDED BY AMERICAN BAR ASSOCIATION— BY SINGLE PERSON OR BY HUSBAND AND WIFE

STATE OF ILLINOIS,)
COUNTY OF COOK.) ss.

On this . . . . day of . . . ., 19 . . . . ., before me, the subscriber (here insert title of officer), personally appeared A. B. (and C. B., his wife, if so), to me known to be the person (or persons) described in and who executed the foregoing instrument, and acknowl-

edged that he (she or they) executed the same as his (her or their) free act and deed.
(Seal)

(Signature and title), etc.

Parent and Child

1. ANCIENT AUTHORITY—In past ages the father was by custom considered an absolute monarch of the home. In the Oriental countries of today the same custom still prevails. Modern progress and modern ideas, however, have changed old customs, and the authority of the parent in Western countries has been considerably limited by law.

2. RIGHTS OF PARENTS—The parent has the right of control over his child, and has all reasonable authority to enforce obedience. As long as the parent treats his child properly, no one has a right to interfere with his authority, or take the child away and retain him against the wishes of the parent.

3. A RUNAWAY CHILD—A child has no right to leave home without permission of the parent, and should a child run away he can be brought back by force. If relatives or other parties keep him and refuse to give him up, the parent by legal process can obtain possession of his child, unless it can be shown that the parent is brutal, or is not a fit person, on account of drunkenness or other causes, to take proper care of the child.

4. PUNISHMENT OF CHILDREN—A parent has a right to punish his minor child, provided he is not guilty of cruelty or brutality, which are crimes punishable by severe legal penalties. The parent must be reasonable in his punishment, and in no way injure the health of the child.

5. RIGHTS TO EARNINGS—A parent is entitled to all the earnings of his minor child. If the child should refuse to turn over his earnings to the parent, the employer of the child may be notified, and be compelled to pay the parent only.

6. SPECIAL RIGHTS—The parent may, however, free his child from all obligations to himself and allow the child to collect his own wages for himself. When a parent thus makes public such a declaration, he cannot thereafter collect the child's wages.

7. THE PROPERTY OF THE CHILD—A parent may control the earnings of the child, yet he has no control of the property belonging to the child, acquired by gift, by legacy, or in any other way. If a parent should appropriate his child's property, it would be just as criminal in the eyes of the law as stealing.

8. PARENT'S OBLIGATION TO SUPPORT—Parents are legally held for the support of their minor children. The fact that a child has property does not relieve the parent from the support of his child; he can, however, apply to court and get permission to use part, or all of the income of the property for the child's support.

9. ILLEGITIMATE CHILDREN—It is a parent's duty to support an illegitimate child. Such a child has legally no father, but his *putative father,* as he is called, may be compelled to furnish the child with reasonable support so that it shall not become a burden upon the community. All children born in wedlock are legitimate, unless it is proved that the husband could not possibly be the father. The adultery of the wife cannot affect the legitimacy of the child. It is presumed to be that of the husband. It makes no difference how soon after marriage the child is born. A child born the same day as the marriage, if birth is subsequent to the ceremony, is legitimate unless there is reason for believing that the husband is not the actual father.

10. EFFECT OF ILLEGITIMACY—The only important legal effect of illegitimacy is that the child usually cannot inherit property from his father. He may, of course, take a legacy

given to him by his putative father's will, but if there is no will he generally cannot inherit. An illegitimate child usually inherits from his mother even though there are legitimate children.

11. CHILDREN'S OBLIGATIONS—Where the parents or grandparents are unable to support themselves, in many states the child is legally held for their support and care.

12. CRIMES—A parent cannot be held for crimes committed by his minor child. If a child commits a premeditated crime, he is personally liable.

13. GUARDIAN—If a child has no parents living, a guardian may be appointed. If the child has arrived at a certain age, varying in different states, he may petition the court for the appointment of his own guardian, who will in a legal sense exercise the prerogatives of a parent.

14. CONTRACTS WITH A MINOR—A contract made by a minor is valid if it is for necessities. Just what constitutes a necessity depends on the circumstances and is a matter for the jury to decide. If a minor contracts for other things, the contract is not always void, but may be avoided by the minor. Even though a minor fraudulently represents himself to be of age and makes a contract for goods, the seller cannot recover on the contract. His only remedy is an action of deceit. A minor who has a parent or guardian cannot make a contract even for necessities. But if the minor receives and retains such articles, with the permission of the parent or guardian, the parent or guardian will be deemed to have ratified the contract and will be held personally liable. If the parent or guardian is unwilling to provide the necessities he can be compelled to do so by the courts.

Parliamentary Law

1. NECESSITY FOR PARLIAMENTARY RULES—In every community it is necessary to hold public meetings from time to time. In order to expedite the proceedings of such meetings, as well as to settle matters of dispute, it is necessary that rules of procedure be adopted. In order to be able to take an intelligent interest and to participate in such meetings, it is essential that young and old be informed of the most important points of parliamentary rules.

2. RULES OF PARLIAMENTARY LAW—The following rules and suggestions will be found helpful in conducting public meetings:

a. The chairman selected should be a person of maturity and one held in respect and confidence.

b. Permission to address the meeting must be obtained from the chairman by rising and saying: "Mr. President" or "Mr. Chairman."

c. No speaker should be interrupted unless his remarks are out of order, when he should be called to order by the chair. If the chairman fails to call him to order, any member may do so.

d. The proper way to make a motion is to say: "Mr. Chairman, I move that (here state motion)."

e. When a motion is presented to the meeting and seconded, it should be stated or read by the secretary or chairman.

f. After debate, the motion should be put to the meeting, the chairman announcing the result.

g. A speaker is out of order when he is speaking of matters and things foreign to the issue before the house.

h. Any violation of rules must be recognized and checked by the presiding officer.

i. When a member is called to order by the president, he should take his seat, unless he is permitted to explain.

j. Any ruling of the chairman may be appealed and decided by a vote.

k. It is the privilege of any member to call for the yeas and nays and thus put on record the vote of every member.

l. The chairman is the servant, not the master, of the house. To get rid of an undesirable chairman, the house may refuse to do any business, or may adjourn.

m. A motion to adjourn is always in order and is not debatable.

3. RULES OF ORDER—Common problems of parliamentary order are listed below. Following each item is a group of numbers which refer to the numbered points of order in section 4. Simply look up each of these references to learn what points of order apply to each specific problem.

Forms in which questions may be put	28, 29, 30, 31, 32
Questions of precedence of questions	19, 20, 21, 22, 23, 24, 25, 26, 27
Motion to withdraw a motion	1, 5, 7, 9, 13, 14, 16
To take up a question out of its proper order	1, 5, 7, 9, 12, 14, 16
Motion to take from the table	1, 5, 7, 11, 12, 14, 16
Motion to suspend the rules	3, 5, 8, 10, 13, 14, 16
To substitute in the nature of an amendment	3, 5, 8, 9, 13, 14, 16
Motion to make subject a special order	3, 5, 8, 9, 12, 14, 16
Question whether subject shall be discussed	1, 5, 7, 9, 12, 15, 17
Motion that committee do not rise	1, 5, 7, 10, 13, 14, 16
Motion to refer a question	3, 6, 8, 10, 13, 14, 16
Motion to reconsider an undebatable question	1, 5, 7, 10, 13, 14, 18
Motion to reconsider a debatable question	3, 6, 7, 10, 13, 14, 16
Reading papers	1, 5, 7, 9, 13, 14, 16
Questions of privilege	3, 5, 8, 9, 13, 14, 16
Questions touching priority of business	1, 5, 8, 9, 13, 14, 16
Motion for previous question	1, 5, 7, 9, 13, 14, 16
Motion to postpone indefinitely	3, 6, 7, 9, 13, 14, 16
Motion to postpone to a definite time	4, 5, 8, 9, 13, 14, 16
Motion for the orders of the day	1, 5, 7, 9, 13, 15, 17
Objection to consideration of question	1, 5, 7, 9, 12, 15, 17
Motion to limit debate on question	1, 5, 8, 9, 12, 14, 16
Motion to lay on the table	1, 5, 7, 11, 13, 14, 16
Leave to continue speaking after indecorum	1, 5, 7, 9, 13, 14, 16
Motion to extend limits of debate on question	1, 5, 8, 9, 13, 14, 16
Motion to commit	3, 6, 8, 9, 13, 14, 16
Motion to close debate on question	1, 5, 8, 9, 12, 14, 16
Call to order	1, 5, 7, 9, 13, 15, 17

Motion to appeal from
  Speaker's decision
  generally............... 3, 5, 7, 9, 13, 14, 17
Motion to appeal from
  Speaker's decision
  re indecorum 1, 5, 8, 9, 13, 14, 17
Motion to amend the
  rules.................. 3, 5, 8, 9, 12, 14, 16
Motion to amend an
  amendment 3, 5, 7, 9, 13, 14, 16
Motion to amend......... 3, 5, 8, 9, 13, 14, 16
Motion to determine
  time to which to ad-
  journ.................. 2, 5, 8, 9, 13, 14, 16
Motion to adjourn......... 1, 5, 7, 10, 13, 14, 16

4. POINTS OF ORDER:

1. Question undebatable; sometimes remarks tacitly allowed.
2. Undebatable if another question is before the assembly.
3. Debatable question.
4. Limited debate only on propriety of postponement.
5. Does not allow reference to main question.
6. Opens the main question to debate.
7. Cannot be amended.
8. May be amended.
9. Can be reconsidered.
10. Cannot be reconsidered.
11. An affirmative vote on this question cannotsbe reconsidered.
12. Requires two-thirds vote, unless special rules have been enacted.
13. Simple majority suffices to determine the question.
14. Motion must be seconded.
15. Does not require to be seconded.
16. Not in order when another has the floor.
17. Always in order though another may have the floor.
18. May be moved and entered on the record when another has the floor, but the business then before the assembly may not be put aside. The motion must be made by one who voted with the prevailing side, and on the same day the original vote was taken.
19. Fixing the time to which an adjournment may be made; ranks first.
20. To adjourn without limitation; second.
21. Motion for the Orders of the Day; third.
22. Motion to lay on the table; fourth.
23. Motion for the previous question; fifth.
24. Motion to postpone definitely; sixth.
25. Motion to commit; seventh.
26. Motion to amend; eighth.
27. Motion to postpone indefinitely; ninth.
28. On motion to strike out words ("Shall the words stand as part of the motion?") unless a majority sustains the words they are struck out.
29. On motion for previous question the form to be observed is: "Shall the main question be now put?" This, if carried, ends debate.
30. On an appeal from the chair's decision ("Shall the decision be sustained as the ruling of the house?") the chair is usually sustained.
31. A motion for Orders of the Day is put in the following form: "Will the house now proceed to the Orders of the Day?" This, if carried, supersedes intervening motions.
32. When an objection is raised to considering question ("Shall the question be considered?") objection may be made by any member before debate has commenced, but not subsequently.

Partnership

1. DEFINITION—The Uniform Partnership Act defines a *partnership* as "an association of two or more persons to carry on as coowners a business for profit."

2. KINDS OF PARTNERSHIP—A *general partnership* is one in which the partners agree to enter into a certain business without limitation or condition. There may also be a partnership in a single transaction, such as to buy or sell a single oil lease. An *implied partnership* is one in which one party acts in such a way as to lead outsiders to believe that partnership actually exists. In a *special* or *limited partnership* there may be general partners with unlimited liability and special partners with limited liability.

3. KINDS OF PARTNER—A *general partner* is one who is generally known as a partner and whose liability is not limited. A *secret partner* is one who is not openly declared as a partner. A *silent partner* takes no active part in the business but shares in the profits, losses, and liabilities. A *nominal partner* is held out as a partner without sharing in the profits or losses of the business, although he may be active in it.

4. FORMING A PARTNERSHIP—A partnership is formed by an agreement, usually in writing, though it may be oral. Any persons competent to transact business in their own names may become partners. Partners often have separate fields of endeavor, each doing the work for which he is best fitted. The article of agreement should specify the division of profits and losses and should be very carefully drawn. In the absence of any written agreement the law assumes that the partners share profits and losses equally. A partnership may hold both real and personal property.

5. LIABILITY—Each partner is a general agent and has full authority to act for the partnership. Not only common property, but also all the private property of each partner may be taken to satisfy the debts of the firm. A partner cannot make the firm responsible for his separate or private debts, nor bind the firm by entering into engagements unconnected with, or foreign to, the partnership. The authority of a partner usually extends to the making or endorsing of negotiable paper, and to all transactions fairly connected with the business. A person who, after due care, lends money to one member of a partnership firm for the firm, can hold the firm liable even if the money is fraudulently appropriated by the partner to his own use. An illegal contract made by one partner will not bind the partnership.

6. HOW TO AVOID LIABILITY—In order to avoid individual liability in transacting business, the partners may form a corporation or a limited liability partnership. The latter consists of two or more general partners and also special partners, whose contribution and liability are made known to the public. These special partners are liable only for the amount of capital they advanced.

7. DISSOLUTION—There are numerous ways in which a partnership may be dissolved:
a. Any partner, upon due notice to the others, may withdraw at any time provided no specific date for the dissolution of the partnership is mentioned in the articles of agreement. There is some authority, however, to the effect that the power to withdraw should be exercised in good faith so as not to prejudice the other partners. The retiring partner should notify the public of his retirement in order to relieve himself from future liability.
b. The partnership may be dissolved by mutual consent.
c. The death of one of the partners automatically dissolves the partnership.
d. The taking in of a new partner constitutes a new

partnership. This is usually a matter of reorganization, and the new partnership may or may not assume liabilities of the old firm.

e. The insanity or bankruptcy of one of the partners ends the partnership.

f. A court may dissolve a partnership for any good reason such as incapacity, drunkenness, or fraud.

g. The expiration of the time specified in the articles of partnership acts as a dissolution.

8. LIQUIDATION—In case of failure, the assets of the partnership must be used to pay the debts of the partnership, the assets of the partners to pay their personal debts. If in either case any property remains, the partnership property is applied on the personal debts, and the partners' personal property must go towards the partnership debts. The affairs of the insolvent partnership are usually placed in the hands of one of the partners, subject to control of the court, or turned over to a receiver appointed by the court, either of whom has the right to liquidate the affairs of the partnership.

9. FORMS:

ARTICLES OF COPARTNERSHIP

Articles of agreement, made ....., 19 ....., between ...... and ....

The said parties hereby agree to become copartners, under the firm name of ......, and as such partners to carry on together the business of buying and selling all sorts of dry goods, at ...... street, in the city of ....

The said ...... agrees to contribute Two Thousand Dollars ($2,000) to the capital of said firm; and the said ..... agrees to contribute One Thousand Dollars ($1,000) to the same; the sum of Twenty-Five Hundred Dollars ($2,500) of said capital to be expended in the purchase of a stock in trade.

The said ..... shall have exclusive charge of all the buying for the firm.

All the net profits arising out of the business shall be divided in the following proportions, two-thirds to the said ..... and one-third to the said ....

Each partner shall devote all his time, attention, and efforts to the said business.

Neither partner shall, without the consent of the other in writing, sign any bond, bill or note as surety, or otherwise become obligated as security for any other person.

Witness the hands and seals of the parties hereto, this ... day of ...., A.D. 19 ....

.... (Seal)
.... (Seal)

AGREEMENT TO DISSOLVE PARTNERSHIP

We, the undersigned, do mutually agree that the within mentioned partnership be, and the same is, hereby dissolved, except for the purpose of final liquidation and settlement of the business thereof, and upon such settlement wholly to cease and determine.

Witness our hands and seals this ...... day of ....., nineteen hundred and .....

Signed, Sealed and Delivered
in Presence of

....

....

(Most states do not require this attestation.)

.... (Seal)
.... (Seal)

Passports

1. DEFINITIONS—A *passport* is a warrant of authority to travel, granted by a government to a citizen intending to travel outside the country. Passports are issued by the United States Department of State for the purpose of providing citizens and nationals who are traveling abroad with documentary evidence identifying them as entitled to the protection afforded such persons. Some countries require a *visa*, that is, a stamp of approval, to be affixed to the passport by the consulate of the country to be visited. Other countries do not insist on this formality. Some countries that do not require visas ask visitors making a short stay to fill out tourist cards.

The United States government does not issue passports for travel to Communist-controlled parts of China, Korea, or Vietnam or to Albania or Cuba unless special circumstances prevail that require travel to either Albania or Cuba.

2. APPLICATION—An application for a passport must be executed before a clerk of a federal court or a state court authorized to accept applications, in some post offices in metropolitan areas, or before an agent of the Passport Office, Department of State. Passport agents are located in Boston, Chicago, Honolulu, Los Angeles, Miami, New Orleans, New York, San Francisco, Seattle, and Washington, D.C.

3. OBTAINING A PASSPORT—To obtain a passport, a native-born citizen must submit a birth certificate, baptismal certificate, or a certified copy of the record of baptism. If these are not available, he may submit secondary evidence. No witness is required if proof of identity is sufficient. Otherwise a witness must take oath that he has known the applicant for over two years. A person claiming U.S. citizenship through birth abroad must present a consular report of birth, birth certificate, certificate of citizenship, or evidence of parent's citizenship. A person who claims American citizenship by naturalization must submit with his application a certificate of naturalization. A person who claims citizenship by the naturalization of a parent must submit with his application for passport the naturalization certificate of the parent. Persons traveling because of a contract with the U.S. government must submit letters from their employer stating their position and the purpose of travel. Persons of military draft age may receive passports but should inform their draft boards of their whereabouts. An alien leaving the United States must request passport facilities from his home government. He must have a permit from his local Collector of Internal Revenue. If he wishes to return to the United States, he should request a re-entry permit from the Immigration and Naturalization Service before he departs.

4. PHOTOGRAPHS—Two recently taken photographs (duplicates) of each person named in the application must be submitted. One photograph should be affixed to the application; the other, signed by the applicant, must accompany the application unattached. A group photograph should be used when a wife, or wife and children, are included in one application. Photographs must be full face, on thin paper, with a light background, and not over 3 x 3 inches nor less than 2½ x 2½ inches in size. Photographs printed on photographic paper the back of which is glazed will not adhere to passports and therefore will not be accepted.

5. HEALTH REQUIREMENTS—A valid smallpox vaccination certificate issued within three years must be shown by all persons entering the United States. Valid vaccination certificates are required if a person has left a cholera-infected area within the last five days. Similar certificates are required from persons who left yellow fever-infected areas within six days and who are destined for receptive areas in

the United States. Vaccinations should be recorded on International Certificates of Vaccination. The smallpox and cholera vaccination certificates should be stamped by the local or state health office.

6. FEES—Passport fees are established by Congress. Besides the basic fee, there are nominal handling charges, depending upon the agency executing the passport, and added charges for emergency passport service. A person on official business need not pay the passport fee if he has a sponsoring letter.

7. VALIDITY OF PASSPORTS—Passports are valid for five years, unless limited, and may not be renewed. If a passport is lost, the U.S. Department of State should be notified. If it is lost abroad, the owner should report the loss to the U.S. consul.

8. CITIZENSHIP—A naturalized American citizen who visits his homeland may be subject to military service and other regulations there. The U.S. State Department recommends that such a naturalized citizen get specific information from the consulate of the country of origin before departure.

a. A British citizen who becomes a naturalized American citizen is considered a British citizen by the British government until he makes a formal renunciation of British nationality before the British authorities.

b. A French citizen wishing to become an American citizen is required by French law to have French authorization any time within 15 years of his enrollment in the army unless he has been exempted, has a final discharge, or is over military age, or unless he has fulfilled his military obligations in the U.S. Army during World War I or World War II. An American woman who marries a Frenchman acquires French nationality unless she declines it prior to her marriage.

c. For Israel there are two types of visas: visitor's visas and immigration visas. A visitor's visa is limited to three months and may be renewed. An immigration visa must be obtained by a person who wishes to live in Israel permanently. Such a person must give military service if a male between 18 and 49 inclusive or if a female between 18 and 38 inclusive. Authorization must be obtained from the Ministry of Defense if the person wishes to leave the country before completing military service. Jews who have immigration visas acquire Israeli nationality automatically unless they disavow any intention to the consul of Israel or to the Israeli government.

d. An American citizen who voluntarily joins a foreign army loses his American citizenship unless he has the written consent of the U.S. government to do so.

9. CUSTOMS INFORMATION—Each returning resident of the United States, whether a citizen or not, may bring in merchandise for personal use worth a maximum of $100 free of duty. Members of a family may pool their exemptions if they live in the same household and travel together. The exemption cannot be claimed more often than once in 31 days. Articles purchased abroad and intended to be gifts may be shipped to the United States before or after the return of the U.S. resident. They must be addressed to him or to him in care of some other person and declared in customs. Also, free entry is permitted for bona fide gifts not exceeding $10 in value and sent to persons in the U.S.

Patents

1. DEFINITION—As here used the word *patent* means the granting by the United States to inventors for a limited time the exclusive right to the use, manufacture, and sale of their own inventions. The instrument by which this privilege is confirmed to the inventor is called the *patent* and is issued in the name of the United States of America under the seal of the Patent Office. It is signed by the Secretary of the Interior and countersigned by the Commissioner of Patents.

2. PATENTABLE ITEMS—Any new and useful art, machine, manufacture, or substance may be patented. The patented item may be a completely new invention or discovery, or it may be an "improvement on the art," that is, a new improvement on some existing item. The primary restriction is that the item to be patented must be new; it must not have been sold, used, or known of for any more than a year before patent is applied for. If the discoverer pays all fees and completes the necessary legal proceedings, and if his creation meets the necessary qualifications, he is granted a patent.

3. FOREIGN PATENTS—A person is not debarred from receiving a patent for his invention or discovery by reason of its first having been patented in a foreign country, unless his application for the foreign patent was filed more than twelve months prior to his filing of the application in the United States. In the case of patenting designs, the interval is limited to six months.

4. DURATION OF PATENT—A patent is good for seventeen years, and cannot be extended except by act of Congress. Patents for inventions previously patented in a foreign country must expire at the same time that the foreign patent expires, but in no case shall they be extended more than seventeen years.

5. HOW SECURED—The method of securing patents is by petition, which must be in writing addressed to the Commissioner of Patents. The application must (a) state the name and residence of the petitioner requesting the granting of a patent; (b) designate by title the invention sought to be patented; and (c) contain a reference to the specifications of the invention. It must be signed by the applicant and attested by two witnesses. An alien may obtain a patent on the same terms as a citizen.

6. SPECIFICATIONS—The specifications above referred to are a written description of the invention or discovery, and the manner of making, constructing, composing, and using the same. Specifications are required to be in such full, clear, concise, and exact terms as to enable any person skilled in the art or science to which the invention or discovery appertains to make, construct, compose, and use the same. The inventor or discoverer must point out in particular how his invention or discovery is different from others in the same line. The specifications and claims should be written on but one side of the paper and signed by the applicant. All interlineations and erasures should be avoided.

7. THE OATH—The applicant for a patent must make oath or affirmation that he verily believes himself to be the first and original discoverer of the art, machine, manufacture, composition, other article, or improvement for which he solicits a patent; and that he does not know and does not believe that the same was ever known or used. In addition he should state of what country he is a citizen and where he resides, and whether he is a sole or joint inventor. The oath should be sworn to before a notary public or some other officer authorized to administer oaths.

8. DRAWINGS—The applicant for patent is required also to furnish drawings of his invention whenever the nature of the case admits. Drawings must be signed by the inventor and must be attested by two witnesses; they must show every feature of the invention covered by the claims. When the invention is an improvement on some existing machine, a drawing must exhibit in one or more views the invention itself disconnected from the old structure, and also in another view so much of the old structure as will suffice to show the connection of the invention therewith.

9. MATERIAL—Drawings must be made upon pure white, calendered, smooth, Bristol board of three-sheet thickness. India ink alone must be used. Sheets must be exactly ten by fifteen inches in size. Drawings must be made with pen only, and must be absolutely black. Drawings must be made with the fewest lines possible consistent with clearness. The scale to which a drawing is made must be large enough to show the mechanism without crowding.

10. SIGNATURE of the inventor should be placed at the lower righthand corner of each sheet of drawing and two attesting witnesses should sign at the lower lefthand corner. Drawings should be rolled for transmission to the patent office. The drawings must never be folded.

11. MODEL—A model must be furnished when required by the commissioner.

12. SPECIMENS must be furnished when required by the commissioner.

13. ATTORNEYS—The practice of the Patent Office allows the applicant to retain an attorney, and when the petition is prosecuted by an attorney a power of attorney should be included in the petition. In ordinary cases it is always best to retain some experienced patent attorney to prosecute the application.

14. CAVEATS—Formerly an inventor could file a *caveat* setting forth the object and distinguishing characteristics of his invention and asking protection for his right until he had finished his invention. This operated for one year. This law was repealed in 1910, so that the only way an inventor can secure any form of federal protection on his patent is by applying for letters patent.

15. FEES—The schedule of fees and prices of publications can be had on application to the Commissioner of Patents, Washington, D.C. For any other information concerning patents an inquiry should be addressed to the Commissioner of Patents.

16. PRELIMINARY EXAMINATIONS—An applicant for a patent may often save considerable expense by having a preliminary examination made of the patents allowed by the Patent Office, to determine whether or not the invention has been patented by somebody else. This examination cannot be made by the Commissioner or anyone of his office, but patent attorneys will make the examination for a small fee.

17. ASSIGNMENTS—Patents may be assigned in whole or in part, and the right to manufacture, sell, and use the patent in any county, state, township, or other district may be granted by the holder of the patent. All such assignments or transfers should be in writing, and are void unless recorded in the Patent Office within three months from their date.

18. FOREIGN PATENT POLICIES—Contrasted with most foreign countries the cost of a patent is very low in the United States, and the law is liberal in allowing the inventor to exploit it. The patent will remain protected even though the invention is not manufactured at all. Some European countries will protect patents only as long as the articles are actually manufactured within their own borders, and as long as the taxes are paid. In the United States foreigners can have their inventions patented without manufacturing them here, and without any taxes whatever.

Payment

1. LEGAL TENDER—In all agreements the payment is to be made in cash unless otherwise stipulated. Since 1933 all coins and currencies of the United States, including Federal Reserve notes, are legal tender for all debts. The United States, however, has ordered that gold coins and certificates payable in gold be exchanged at the Treasury for silver and silver certificates. Any provision in an obligation that calls for payment in gold is against public policy; the obligation may be discharged by payment in legal tender.

2. CHECKS—In modern times checks are given and received in payment of debts. Legally, however, a check is not payment until it is cashed. In other words, a check is a conditional payment and if the check is not honored, the creditor can sue on the check. He can also sue any of the endorsers whose names appear on the check. But if the holder of the check does not present it for payment within a reasonable time and the bank on which it is drawn fails, he must suffer the loss caused by the delay.

3. NOTES—A note given in payment for a debt may or may not cancel the debt. If the parties intended the note as actual payment, the creditor cannot sue on the original debt; he must sue to recover on the note itself. This is a question of the facts in the case, to be determined by the court.

4. APPLYING PAYMENT WHEN THERE IS MORE THAN ONE DEBT—If a debtor owes more than one debt to the same creditor, he can apply his payments in any way he sees fit. If he fails to do so, the creditor can make the application, and if neither does so, the law applies the payment first to interest due, and then applies the balance to the oldest debt. A signer on a note may insist that payment be applied first to the debt on which he is surety.

5. RECEIPTS—A receipt for a debt is regarded on its face as evidence of payment. This evidence, however, is not conclusive and can sometimes be contradicted by other evidence. For example, suppose A gave B a receipt for $20 and afterwards discovered that the bill B had given him was a counterfeit. A could introduce evidence to prove fraud and thus invalidate the receipt. A contract embodied in a receipt without consideration is not binding, but if there is a valuable consideration, or if the instrument is under seal, such a contract would be as lawful as any other.

Prescriptive Rights or Easements to Title

1. DEFINITION—A *prescriptive right* is a right acquired by use and time and allowed by law.

2. RIGHT OF WAY—A person may acquire a permanent right of way over another's land by passing over that land to his own land for a period of time fixed by law. This right of way cannot be acquired against a minor or against anyone who is incapable of defending his possessions. A person attempting to establish such a right of way can be stopped by appropriate legal action.

3. WAY OF NECESSITY—Sometimes a person sells a part of his farm that is not located on the road. The law allows the purchaser the right to enter and leave the premises, and such a right is called a *way of necessity*. The buyer must exercise reasonable care in selecting his road to the main road, and this road ultimately becomes part of the title to the property.

4. RESTRICTIONS—The law prescribes restrictions on the use of a right of way or a way of necessity. Thus the purchaser of the farm away from the road could not subdivide the farm and transfer his right of way to others without permission of the real owner of the way. However, more than one person can claim a right of way. A tenant can never acquire a right of way beyond the duration of his lease.

5. BUILDING RIGHTS:
a. The owner of a building has no action against one who cuts off his light, air, or view by erecting a building on adjacent land, unless the right has been expressly acquired. The right to light, air, and unobstructed view may sometimes be acquired by deed or by presumption.

If the owner has acquired such a right, he loses it if he tears down the building and erects a new one.

b. A person has the right to the lateral support of his land. If, for example, a neighbor excavates in an unreasonable manner and a building consequently falls down, the owner has an action against the neighbor and any excavator hired by him.

6. WATER RIGHTS:

a. The water that runs through a person's land may legally be held back for a short time to furnish water power, or it may be used for any other reasonable purpose.

b. Neither a person nor a municipality may dump impurities or sewage into a stream, making the water unfit for use downstream.

c. As a general rule ditches or obstructions may not be dug either to hinder or to hasten the flow of water from one person's land to another in other than the natural way.

d. A riparian owner has the right to cut and sell the ice that forms over the portion of the bed of the stream that he owns, provided he does not interfere with the rights of other owners.

e. A person digging a well cannot be held for cutting off his neighbor's water supply, unless it can be proved that he acted maliciously.

Products Liability

1. DEFINITION—A consumer has a right to products that are reasonably safe. If a product proves to be dangerous, the purchaser may be able to hold the manufacturer or retailer liable for damages. A manufacturer's liability is in general the most extensive created by the law. This liability may be based upon one of four theories: negligence, breach of warranty, strict liability, or misrepresentation.

2. NEGLIGENCE:

a. *Failure to Warn Adequately.* The manufacturer is under a duty to warn of risks with which he is familiar, or with which in the exercise of reasonable care he should have been familiar.

b. *Improper Design.* The manufacturer must so design his product as to make it reasonably safe for its foreseeable uses.

c. *Failure to Test and Inspect Adequately.* The manufacturer is under a duty to turn products out of his production line without unintended defects. There is a breach of this duty where he fails to make reasonable inspections and tests on his product during the course of construction. This includes a duty to make proper tests before the product is first marketed to make sure it will be safe.

3. BREACH OF WARRANTY:

a. *Implied Warranties.* The manufacturer is understood by the marketing of his chattel to make the general implied warranties or promises that his product is both merchantable and reasonably fit for the general uses intended. In the case of food and drugs, this warranty is sometimes called a *warranty of wholesomeness.*

b. *Express Warranty.* If the manufacturer makes an assertion of fact as to the nature, quality, or use of his product, which assertion tends to induce the sale or use of the product, he is exposed by the common law or the sales acts to liability if injury arises proximately from a breach of that warranty or promise.

4. STRICT LIABILITY—*Strict liability* is a new concept, holding the manufacturer liable without fault on his part for injuries arising from the marketing of a product that is defective or unreasonably dangerous.

5. MISREPRESENTATION:

a. *Intentional.* The traditional fraud action in products cases is that against a manufacturer who makes a material misrepresentation of fact that he knows to be false and that he makes with the intent that the injured person rely upon it, if the injured person relies on the misrepresentation to his own injury in ignorance of its falsity. The same liability exists where the statements are made recklessly rather than intentionally.

b. *Negligent.* Here the manufacturer may be liable, in some states, for making the representation carelessly.

c. *Innocent.* New section 402B of the Restatement of Torts, 2d, creates liability for injuries arising out of reliance by a person upon representations that are false even though they are made wholly innocently.

6. RETAILER—The retailer may be liable under any of the four theories listed above, but often his liability is of a narrower scope than that of the manufacturer.

a. *Negligence.* The retailer is under a duty to warn of the dangers in the use of the products of which he is aware.

b. *Breach of Warranty.* As a rule the seller makes the same implied warranties as does the manufacturer. This makes him liable for all defects, even though he was under no duty to discover them and even though they might have been latent. A retailer can make an express warranty about his product just as the manufacturer can, and he frequently does make one orally at the point of sale. Where the only express representation comes from the manufacturer, however, as through national advertisement, and all the retailer does is pass on the product without repetition or addition, it is generally recognized that the retailer has no potential liability for breach of express warranty.

c. *Strict Liability.* Recent cases make it clear that the retailer, like any other supplier, is strictly liable when products are sold in a defective state.

7. SELLERS OF SECONDHAND GOODS—As a rule, the seller of used goods has the same responsibilities of care as the seller of new goods. For example, where a new car dealer has an obligation to inspect, so does a used car dealer. The liability based upon breach of warranty, however, is much less for the secondhand dealer, partly because the buyer's expectations might be less.

8. PURCHASERS—The purchaser is the traditional plaintiff. Actions by purchasers today run back against various parties in the distributive chain, and particularly back to the manufacturer of the product involved. There is no requirement that the plaintiff be in a direct contractual relationship with the defendant.

9. ULTIMATE CONSUMERS—Any consumer can sue for damages, even though he was not the purchaser of the product. The consumer can and does sue anyone in the distributive chain, especially the manufacturer.

10. USERS IN A NONSALE, AMBIGUOUS SALES-SERVICE SITUATION—Often the injured person neither bought the product involved nor got it from someone who had direct dealings with a retailer.

a. *Restaurants.* Almost all courts agree that a restaurant or other place serving food or drink has no defense based on an argument that rather than selling food, it "served" it. If the food is unwholesome, the customer has a breach of warranty action.

b. *Miscellaneous.* Liability has also been held to exist where the product was obtained as a free sample, had been picked out by a prospective purchaser but not yet paid for, or was being tried out by a prospective purchaser.

11. BYSTANDERS—When a defective car goes out of control suddenly, it may injure a pedestrian. The question of the retailer's or manufacturer's liability to the pedestrian is generally analyzed as the liability of the supplier to a "bystander"—someone not in the chain of distribution. Upon reflection it will be seen that any sort of product can injure bystanders, including those products intended for "intimate consumption," such as the hair spray that gets into brother's eye, or the polio vaccine that causes polio in the fetus when the mother takes it for immunization. In negligence actions, there is little hesitation to include the bystander among proper plaintiffs who may sue when injury arises from a defect in a product. The natural limits here would only be those in tort cases generally—zone of the risk and foreseeability of danger.

Professional Men

1. DOCTORS—A *doctor* or *physician* is a person who has (a) been educated in the science of medicine and surgery, (b) been graduated from a medical college, (c) passed the state medical examination, and (d) been licensed by the state to practice his profession.

2. CONFIDENTIAL DISCLOSURES—It frequently happens that a doctor is called upon to give expert testimony in a civil or criminal case. He is not, however, required or permitted to divulge on the witness stand any confidential statement or information obtained in his professional relationship with his patient, except in the following cases:
a. Homicide cases where disclosures relate to homicide.
b. Suits against a doctor for malpractice.
c. Cases in which the patient gives consent for his doctor to testify.
d. Suits against insurance companies.
e. Will contests.
f. Abortion cases.
g. Child abuse cases.

3. LIABILITY—A doctor is not legally liable for the success or failure of his treatment in the absence of an express contract. He is required to exercise the greatest care, diligence, and skill in his work, and can be held criminally liable only for carelessness and gross negligence. The crime of malpractice consists of any injurious or improper treatment.

4. LAWYERS—A *lawyer* is a person who has (a) been educated in the science of law, (b) been graduated from a law school or, in a few states, been apprenticed to an attorney, and (c) passed the state bar examination. Every man is entitled by law to have a lawyer represent him in his trial, but the court will furnish the services of a lawyer only in criminal cases and certain civil cases.

5. CONFIDENTIAL DISCLOSURES—What has already been said about the confidential relationship existing between doctors and patients applies even more strongly to attorneys and their clients. The matters spoken of between them are confidential; no law can force the lawyer to divulge them on the witness stand.

6. LIENS—An attorney has a lien for the payment of his fee on all documents, moneys, and other things coming into his possession.

7. LIABILITY—A lawyer cannot be held liable for the failure of his case unless he did not exercise reasonable care and judgment.

Real Property Transactions

1. DEFINITION—*Real property* is land and anything permanently attached to it. This includes not only buildings and their fixtures, but also plants, minerals beneath the land, and the air space above it.

2. CONTRACTS OF SALE—An agreement to purchase real estate must be in writing and should be signed by both buyer and seller. The writing need not mention the amount to be paid for the land. It should be signed in ink, but is not invalid if signed with a lead pencil or even with a rubber stamp. The entire contract need not be on the same sheet of paper, and it sometimes happens that two or more sheets of paper constitute the contract, as in cases where the agreement to purchase land is completed through correspondence between the two parties. See also CONTRACTS.

3. ORAL AGREEMENTS are not binding in the sale of real property. For example, if a purchaser makes an oral agreement to purchase land and pays part of the purchase price, he cannot compel the seller to give him a deed to the real estate. The purchaser can, however, compel the seller to return the money he has paid down.

4. EXCEPTIONS—There are some exceptions to the rule that oral agreements in real estate transactions are unenforceable. For example, A sells a piece of property to B, receives the purchase price, and without written agreement allows B to take possession of the property. If B makes valuable and lasting improvements on the property, the courts will compel A to give B a deed to the property. Generally, if the acts of the buyer and seller provide strong evidence that a contract exists, or if the buyer has made substantial improvements in the property, the courts will enforce an oral contract.

5. OPTIONS—An *option* is a contract by which the owner of property agrees that the other party shall have the right to purchase the property at a fixed price within a certain time. For example, A agrees to sell a piece of property to B for $10,000 within six months, for which B gives A a valuable consideration. B must either exercise his option and purchase the property before six months pass or forfeit his consideration. All options must be in writing. If no time limit is fixed in the agreement, the option must be exercised within a reasonable time.

6. TRANSFER OF TITLE—In most real estate contracts the seller agrees to furnish the buyer with a good and merchantable title. He also agrees to transfer title to the property by a warranty deed, which warrants the title in him and the buyer against any loss that might be occasioned by defects in the title. A purchaser should always insist that the contract provide that the seller is to furnish and deliver a merchantable title. The contract should also require the seller to furnish evidence that he has good title. This is done by producing either an abstract, guaranty policy, or Torrens certificate showing good title in the seller. See also DEEDS: WARRANTY DEEDS.

7. ABSTRACT OF TITLE—An *abstract* is a statement in substance of what appears in the public records affecting the title to the land in question from the time it was owned by the government down to date. The public records are searched and the matters shown therein. An abstract will show all transfers, mortgages, judgments, tax sales, liens of all kinds, court proceedings, and everything of record affecting the title to the property. These abstracts are prepared by private concerns or individuals known as *abstract companies* or *abstracters*. To determine whether or not the seller's title is good, the purchaser should have the abstract examined by an attorney competent to pass upon the law of real property. This examination by an attorney will reveal the validity or merchantability of the title. The objections to a clear title may be simple or exceedingly complex, and require the services of a competent attorney in that field. Usually the seller pays all of the expenses incidental to

bringing the abstract up to date. The purchaser generally pays the examination fee.

8. TITLE INSURANCE OR GUARANTY POLICY—Under this system the title company issues a policy guaranteeing the holder of the policy against any loss he might sustain by reason of any defect in the title, whether of record or otherwise, existing before or at the time of the issuance of the policy. This system is becoming more popular in cities because of the demand for facilities to expedite real estate transactions and also because of the system's protective features.

9. TORRENS SYSTEM—The *Torrens system* is a system providing for the registration of land titles in such a manner that, when the title is once registered, a certificate of the registrar of titles will show the exact condition of the title. In order to register a title under this system, it is necessary that a court proceeding be had first in which the decree of the court settles and establishes the title. After this has been done, the registrar of titles will issue an official certificate that will show who has title to the land, and what defects, if any, appear in his title. After the title to a particular parcel of property has been so registered, all subsequent transactions affecting the title to that property must be filed with the registrar of titles, and are noted upon the certificate of title. This enables a purchaser to determine the true state of the title by merely examining the certificate of the registrar. The purpose of the system is to simplify the transfer of real estate, and it is now in force in a number of states.

10. FORMS:

CONTRACT FOR SALE OF LAND

This agreement, made and entered into this ...... day of ..... by and between ...., party of the first part, and ...., party of the second part, witnesseth:

1. The said party of the first part, for and in consideration of the sum of $ .... to be paid as hereinafter provided, hereby agrees to sell unto the party of the second part the following described tract of land:

|Description|

2. The said party of the second part hereby agrees to purchase said premises at said consideration of $......., and to pay the same as follows: (set out terms of payment).

3. The said party of the first part, upon receiving the final payment mentioned above, shall execute and deliver to the said party of the second part, or to his assigns, a duly acknowledged Warranty Deed, conveying to him or them the fee simple title to said premises, free and clear from all incumbrance.

In witness whereof the said parties have hereunto set their hands and seals the day and year first above written.

OPTION

For and in consideration of the sum of .... dollars to me in hand paid, the receipt whereof is hereby acknowledged, I hereby grant unto .... an option for ...... days from the .... day of ...., 19 ...., to purchase for the sum of .... dollars, the following described lands situated in the County of .... and State of ....

|Insert description of property|

upon the following terms and conditions: (insert terms of sale), said .... to signify his intention to take or reject the same by due notice in writing within the time above specified, and a failure to serve such notice within the time specified shall terminate this option without further action, time being the essence of this agreement.

In case said notice shall be served in due time, then thirty days shall be given in which to examine abstract or other evidence of title, and close the sale.

Sale and Transfer of Property

1. DEFINITIONS—A *sale* is the exchange of property for a consideration called the *price*, which is either to be paid at once or at some future date. An agreement to sell at a future date is called an *executory sale*. A present sale is called an *executed sale*. A sale may be made either in writing or orally.

The following general principles apply to sales.

a. Sales are based on mutual agreement.

b. Either the thing sold must exist at the time of the sale or there must be reason to believe that it will be in existence and in possession of the seller. For example: if a man sold a horse for $100 and the horse died before the actual time of the sale, the transaction would not be a sale.

c. Grain or other produce not yet sowed or planted can be sold because the seller may reasonably expect a crop. Machinery or other manufactured goods may be sold before they are made and the seller can be held to perform his part of the contract as though the articles actually existed at the time of the sale.

d. The thing sold must be specified and set apart as the property of the buyer in order to complete the sale.

e. When nothing is said as to the time of payment when the sale is made, the law presumes that the property must be paid for before the purchaser can secure possession. If credit is agreed upon, the buyer is entitled to immediate possession.

f. When goods are sold on *sale or return* the title passes to the buyer when he signifies his approval or when he keeps them beyond the time set for their return.

g. When no price is fixed in the agreement, the purchaser must pay a reasonable price.

h. Goods are often sold and shipped subject to bill of lading; that is, payment is not made until the goods are delivered. Thus the seller controls the property until it is paid for, although the title may pass to the buyer.

2. STATUTE OF FRAUDS—The Uniform Commercial Code provides that a contract to sell $500 worth of goods or more cannot be enforced unless the purchaser advances a sum of money to bind the bargain, or unless the contract is in writing. This rule, of course, does not apply when the goods sold are to be manufactured especially for the buyer and would not be readily salable to others.

3. RELIEVING THE BUYER—The buyer's obligation is limited in various ways. For instance, the contract may be voided (a) if the goods purchased have been damaged or destroyed before delivery, or (b) if in the buyer's opinion the goods are not satisfactory.

4. WARRANTIES—When goods are sold there are certain warranties by the seller that may be either expressed or implied. Any statement made by the seller tending to induce the buyer to purchase is an express warranty. In every sale there are implied warranties that the seller has the title to the property, and that the goods will correspond with the description or sample. Any defects that can be seen in property when sold do not relieve the buyer from meeting his contract though he claims that he did not see the defects.

The law does not furnish eyes for the purchaser of property. But defects in property that cannot be seen and of which the seller makes no statement release the buyer from his contract. See also TRUTH IN ADVERTISING; PRODUCTS LIABILITY.

5. THE BULK SALES LAW is a part of the law of many states. It provides that when a stock of goods or merchandise is sold, transferred, or consigned in bulk, the seller's creditors must be notified in writing a certain number of days before the sale is completed. Thus when a merchant sells his merchandise in bulk, the buyer should keep the following considerations in mind: First, he should demand a bill of sale. Second, he should either demand an affidavit from the seller that he has notified the creditors, or secure a sworn list of the creditors and notify them himself. This law applies to corporations, partnerships, and individuals, and any attempt to evade its provisions carries with it a penalty of a fine, a year's imprisonment, or both. If the creditors are not properly notified they can hold the purchaser liable for the debts.

6. STOCK MARKET SPECULATION—Trading in stocks, grains, and cotton, together with the buying and selling of futures, is now largely regulated by statute. A contract of this kind which involves the actual delivery of property is perfectly legal, even if the seller did not own the property at the time the sale was made. However, when no exchange of property is ever contemplated and the parties merely propose to effect a settlement based on the market changes, the contract is not legal.

7. FORMS:

BILL OF SALE

Know all men by these presents, That I, ...
of ...., County ...., in consideration of Six Hundred Dollars ($600) to me in hand paid by .... of the same place, the receipt of which is hereby acknowledged, do hereby grant, sell, assign, transfer, and deliver unto the said ...., his heirs and assigns, the following goods and chattels, to wit:

Four Yearling Heifers, at $50 each $200
30 head of Sheep, at $4 each 120
Five sets of Harness, at $20 each 100
Two Farm Wagons, at $35 each 70
One Corn Planter, at $20 20
Six Plows, at $15 each 90

To have and to hold all of the said goods and chattels to the said ...., his heirs and assigns forever. And I do hereby covenant to and with the said .... that I am the legal owner of said goods and chattels; that they are free and clear from all other and prior sales and incumbrances; that I have good right to sell and convey the same as aforesaid, and that in the peaceable possession of the said .... I will forever warrant and defend the same against the lawful claims and demands of all persons whomsoever.

In witness whereof, I have hereunto set my hand and seal this 29th day of June, A.D. 19 ....

In the presence of

....

....

(Signed) .... (Seal)

Note: In selling or buying automobiles, especially used cars, it is always wise to insert the name of the machine, its model, the engine number, the car number, the type of car, its color, and any other information that will help to identify it.

Secured Transactions

1. DEFINITION—A *secured credit sale* is a sale in which the possession of the goods and the risk of loss pass to the buyer, but the seller retains a security interest in the goods until he has been paid in full. The seller's security interest entitles him to repossess the goods when the buyer fails to make payments as required or when in any other way the buyer commits a breach of the purchase contract. This right of repossession is in addition to the right to sue on the purchase contract for the amount of the purchase price. A security interest for the protection of the seller arises as soon as the seller and buyer agree that the buyer shall have property rights in particular goods and that the seller shall have a security interest in them. It is immaterial whether or not the sales agreement provides for the passage of title to the buyer prior to his payment in full for the goods.

2. SECURITY AGREEMENT—The agreement of the seller and buyer that the seller shall have a security interest in the goods must be evidenced by a written *security agreement*, which is signed by the buyer and which describes the collateral. This description need only reasonably identify the collateral. A description is sufficient when it would enable a third person, aided by inquires made to others, to determine what goods were involved.

3. RIGHTS OF SELLER INDEPENDENT OF DEFAULT—The seller may transfer or assign his interest under the sales contract and under the security agreement to a third person, and the assignee acquires all the rights and interest of the seller. As soon as the security agreement is executed, the secured credit seller of consumer goods has rights that are effective not only against the buyer but also against purchasers of the property from the buyer. From that moment on, the seller's interest is generally effective against third persons and is described as a *perfected security interest*.

4. FILING—In an ordinary sale of consumer goods under a secured transaction, no filing is required in order to perfect the secured seller's interest. Such a seller is protected against purchasers from and creditors of the buyer who may acquire the property thereafter. Although this is the general rule, there are some exceptions:

a. The seller's security interest is not perfected, and filing is required to perfect it, if the goods purchased are to be attached to buildings or land as a fixture or if they consist of farm equipment sold for a purchase price of over $2,500.

b. A security interest in a motor vehicle required to be licensed is not perfected unless the vehicle is licensed with a notation of the security interest made in the title certificate, if such is required by law. If the law does not require this notation on the title, the seller must file his security interest in order to perfect it.

5. RIGHTS OF THE BUYER—The buyer has certain rights of ownership in the collateral. It is not material whether technically he is the owner of the title. Whatever interest he owns he may transfer voluntarily, and his creditors may reach it by the process of the law as fully as though there were no security agreement. Such third persons generally cannot acquire any greater rights than the buyer, and therefore they hold the property subject to the security interest of the seller.

It is common practice for credit sellers to seek to protect themselves by prohibiting the buyer from reselling the property. Such a provision has no effect and does not prevent an effective resale, even though the security agreement expressly makes it a default or breach of the contract to make a resale.

6. BUYER'S RIGHTS AS A DEBTOR —The secured transaction buyer is a debtor to the extent that there is a balance due on the purchase price. In order for the buyer to know just how much he owes and to check with his own records what the seller claims to to be due, the buyer has the right to compel the seller to state what balance is owed and also to specify in what collateral the seller claims a security interest.

7. WAIVER OF DEFENSES—It is common practice for finance companies that have a standing agreement to purchase sales contracts from a credit seller to provide him with forms to be signed by the buyer. These forms generally specify that the buyer waives, as against the assignee of the sales contract and security agreement, any right that he would have against the seller. Both express and implied waivers are valid and bind the buyer if the assignee takes his assignment for value, in good faith, and without notice or knowledge of any claim or defense of the buyer. The validity of any waiver of defense is subject to two limitations:

a. Those defenses that could be raised against the holder in due course of commercial paper cannot be waived.

b. The waiver is not effective if a statute or decision establishes a different rule for buyers of consumer goods.

8. REPOSSESSION—When the buyer under the secured credit sale defaults by failing to pay an installment due, the secured party is entitled to take the collateral or purchased property from the buyer. If he can do so without causing a breach of the peace, the seller may repossess the property without legal proceedings. In any case he may use legal proceedings if he desires.

9. RESALE OF COLLATERAL—The seller who has repossessed the goods may resell them at a private or public sale at any time and place and on any terms. He must, however, act in good faith and in a manner that is commercially reasonable. The seller must give the buyer reasonable advance notice of a resale unless the goods are perishable, or unless they threaten to decline speedily in value, or unless they are of a type customarily sold on a recognized market. The seller's resale destroys all interest of the buyer in the goods.

10. REDEMPTION OF COLLATERAL—If the buyer acts in time, he may redeem or obtain the return to him of the goods by tendering to the secured party the amount that is owed him, including expenses and any legal costs that have been incurred. The right to redeem is destroyed if the seller has made a resale or entered into a binding contract for resale.

11. ACCOUNTING AFTER RESALE—When the secured party, that is, the original seller, makes a resale of repossessed goods, the proceeds of the resale are applied in the following order to pay (a) reasonable costs of repossession, storage, and resale of the goods, (b) the balance due, including interest and any proper additions such as attorney's fees, and (c) subsequent security interests on the property that are discharged by the resale. If any balance remains after the payment of these claims, the buyer is entitled to the surplus. Conversely, if the net proceeds of resale are insufficient to pay the costs and the debt due the seller, the buyer is liable for such deficiency unless it has been otherwise agreed by the parties.

12. RETENTION OF COLLATERAL—If the buyer has paid less than 60 percent of the cash price of the consumer goods, the secured seller may propose in writing that he, the seller, keep the repossessed collateral in payment of the debt. If the buyer does not object to this proposal, the secured party keeps the collateral and the secured obligation is automatically discharged. If the buyer makes written objection to the proposal within 30 days, the secured party must then

proceed to dispose of the collateral by resale or other reasonable manner.

13. SECURED CREDIT SALES OF INVENTORY—In contrast with one who buys personal property for his own use, the buyer may be a merchant or dealer who intends to resell the goods. The goods that such a merchant or dealer buys are classified as *inventory*. Filing of a *financing statement* is required to perfect the creditor's interest in inventory or the proceeds therefrom. An exception is made when a statute, such as a motor vehicle statute, requires the security interest to be noted on the title certificate issued for the property.

14. FINANCING STATEMENT— The financing statement is distinct from the security agreement that was executed by the parties to give rise to the secured transaction. The financing statement must be signed by both the debtor and the secured party; it must give an address of the secured party, from which information concerning the security interest may be obtained, and a mailing address of the debtor; and it must contain a statement indicating the types, or describing the items, of collateral.

15. PROTECTION OF CUSTOMER OF THE BUYER—The customer of the buyer takes the goods free from the secured interest of the secured party. That is, one who buys in the ordinary course of business items of property taken from the original buyer's inventory is free from the secured party's interest, even though that interest was perfected and even though such ultimate customer knew of the secured party's interest.

16. RIGHTS AND REMEDIES AFTER DEFAULT—The rights and remedies of the secured party and the buyer of inventory after a default on the part of the latter are similar to those in the case of a secured credit sale of consumer goods.

Securities Law

1. DEFINITION—Stocks, bonds, and notes are commonly called *securities*, but this term has received an expanded interpretation by the courts. It clearly covers not only stocks, bonds, and notes, but any offering that constitutes an investment, regardless of form. It covers monies paid over as loans, such as bonds, debentures, or promissory notes, as well as purchases of equity or ownership interests.

2. STATE REGULATION OF SECURITIES —Nearly every state has some kind of "blue sky" law, that is, a law designed to regulate and supervise the issuance and selling of securities. Such laws were first written to outlaw the sale of stock in fraudulent corporations whose primary asset was the "blue sky." The laws' main function now is to assure disclosure of all material facts about securities that are offered for sale. Several types of these laws are in effect:

a. *Fraud:* The simplest are laws that simply impose civil or criminal sanctions for any fraud in connection with the sale or issuance of securities.

b. *Registration.* Other laws require that the stock be registered with an appropriate state officer or agency prior to issuance. The registration must contain a complete description of the issuance, and the shares must be sold as so described. The purpose of this type of statute is simply disclosure. There is generally no discretion in the state to deny permission to issue.

c. *Permit.* The most advanced and complex type of blue sky law is the permit or license type, which in effect provides that no stock may be issued until a permit is obtained.

3. FEDERAL REGULATION OF SECURITIES—The Securities Act of 1933 and the Securities Exchange Act of 1934 provide the basic framework for federal regulation of the sale

of securities in interstate commerce. The 1933 act deals with initial issuance of shares, while the 1934 act is aimed principally at sales by underwriters, on stock exchanges, etc. These acts provide for a *registration* system of regulation, the purpose of which is to assure a full disclosure of all pertinent facts to any prospective investor.

4. SECURITIES ACT OF 1933—The 1933 act prohibits the offer or sale of nonexempt securities to the public in interstate commerce unless and until a registration statement has been filed with the Securities and Exchange Commission. The S.E.C. has no power to disapprove or veto a proposed issuance. Its only power is to compel disclosure of all pertinent details. The following types of transactions are expressly exempted from the 1933 act:

a. *Sale by Private Investor.* Any transaction by a person who is the owner of the shares is exempt. Such is deemed a casual sale, not a public offering.

b. *Private Offering.* Sales or issuance by the corporation to a specific, limited number of private subscribers, usually no more than 25, are exempt as long as no resale to the public is contemplated.

c. *Intrastate Transactions.* Where the sale or issuance is entirely intrastate, that is, when the seller and the purchaser are both bona fide residents of the same state and no interstate mail or communications are used to advertise or effect the sale of issue, federal law does not apply.

d. *Small Issues.* Where the total amount of the issue is under $300,000 an abbreviated registration statement is accepted in lieu of the more detailed statement otherwise required.

5. REGISTRATION STATEMENT—The corporation must file with the S.E.C. a statement of all matters pertaining to the proposed issuance. The form required is designed to force disclosure of all factors that may affect the fairness of the issue and the financial status of the corporation. Full details must be provided as to the identity and background of all corporate officers and directors, the compensation they receive, the sales costs, underwriting commission and discounts, and other relevant matters.

6. FRAUD IN THE REGISTRATION STATEMENT—Where the registration statement filed contains a misstatement or omission of material fact, the holder of the securities is entitled to maintain an action for damages, that is, the amount he lost on the investment, against all persons connected with the issuance. In effect, absolute liability is imposed. The holder does not have to prove fraud in the torts sense or show that he relied on the misstatement. The holder need not even prove that the misstatement caused the decline in the value of the securities. The liability for damages extends not only to the corporation, and any underwriter, but to all persons who signed the registration statement, or who were directors or partners of the issuer at the time the registration statement was filed, or who were named therein as prospective directors or partners. If any accountant or other expert certifies portions of the registration statement which are false or misleading, he is liable.

7. FRAUD OTHER THAN IN REGISTRATION STATEMENT —The 1933 act also provides a right of action in favor of the original buyer of a security for an untrue statement or omission of material fact in any transaction connected with the issuance of the security, where the misstatement or omission is either intentional or could have been avoided by exercise of due diligence. Liability here extends to misrepresentations in the offering prospectus or any oral misstatements by the issuer, as well as to any misstatement in the registration statement filed with the S.E.C.

8. SECURITIES EXCHANGE ACT OF 1934—The 1934 act re-

quires registration of any stock that is traded on a national securities exchange, or in any over-the-counter market, if the corporation has total assets exceeding $1,000,000 and a class of equity security held by 500 or more persons. A corporation so qualified must file continuing periodic reports with the S.E.C. as to all of the various matters that may affect the financial status of the corporation and its outstanding securities. The most important provision of the 1934 act in regard to the issuance of securities is Section 10b which provides that it is unlawful "to use or employ ... any manipulative or deceptive device" in connection with the purchase or sale of any security.

9. RULE 10b-5—To execute Sec. 10b, the S.E.C. promulgated Rule 10b-5, which, in effect, makes it unlawful for any person, in connection with the purchase or sale of any security, (a) to employ any device to defraud, (b) to make any untrue statement of a material fact, (c) to omit to state a material fact necessary in order to make the statements made not misleading, or (d) to engage in any act, practice or course of business that would operate as fraud or deceit upon any person. Rule 10b-5 applies to any person; it is not limited to officers, directors, and controlling shareholders of the issuer who are ordinarily considered to be "insiders." Securities of all issuers are covered by the rule; thus, the prescriptions of Rule 10b-5 apply to the securities of small, closely held corporations as well as to the securities of publicly owned corporations.

10. REMEDY—In addition to action taken by the S.E.C. pursuant to Rule 10b-5, whether for injunction against an issuer or relief of allegedly defrauded persons, a private party may also bring a civil suit in the federal courts based upon an alleged violation of the rule. Although neither the 1934 act nor the rule itself specifically affords a civil remedy, the courts have consistently found one. Many courts have construed Rule 10b-5 liberally in favor of investors and, although it is a fraud rule, they have either watered down or discarded some of the elements necessary to prove common-law fraud.

11. SHORT-TERM PROFITS BY INSIDERS—Section 16b of the Securities Exchange Act of 1934 creates a conclusive presumption that any gain from short-term transactions is the result of "inside information." The section provides that any profits made by a director or a ten-percent shareholder as the result of any purchase and sale of a registered security that take place within six months of each other belong to the corporation. The purpose is to discourage persons who have access to special information from taking advantage of their position.

Shipping

1. REGISTRATION—The law requires all ships flying the United States flag to file papers with the collector of customs in the district where the ship's home port is situated. This formality is called *registration* for ships engaged in foreign trade, *enrollment* in the case of large ships engaged in coastwise or internal commerce, and *license* for smaller ships.

2. OWNERSHIP—Vessels may be owned by individuals, partnerships, or corporations, and the ownership may be acquired either by purchase or construction. If several individuals own a ship, they are tenants in common where there is no other relation between the part owners of a vessel than that arising out of joint ownership. Each part owner has his share of the profits and expenses, and no one individual can bind the others except for the necessary maintenance of the ship. When a partnership or corporation owns a vessel, the ordinary rules of corporations and partnerships apply.

3. SALE—The owner of a ship can sell or mortgage his interest at any time, but in order to effect a good title against third parties the contract should be in writing. If a ship is sold while it is at sea, the buyer takes it subject to all contracts made by the master before learning of the sale. In all other cases the buyer is not liable for repairs made or supplies furnished previous to the sale.

4. MARITIME LOANS—In cases of great emergency, for example when a ship is in a foreign port without funds to purchase necessary supplies, a master can secure a maritime loan in which the vessel is put up as security. If the vessel fails to reach home the lender loses his money, but in the event of a safe arrival he has the boat as security and can hold the master personally. Such a contract calls for a high rate of interest but is perfectly legal. The technical name for the contract is *contract of bottomry*.

5. THE MASTER of a vessel is the chief officer. The law gives him authority to bind the owners for necessary repairs or supplies. He must render accurate accounts of his actions and money received, but his first duty is to the passengers and the crew. He has the power to regulate their actions in any manner that is necessary to their safety, comfort, and good order. If on account of illness, insanity, or other reason, the master is unable to perform his duties properly, those duties pass to the lower officers in the order of their rank.

6. THE SEAMEN—Statutes and maritime law generally require the execution of shipping papers between the master and the seamen before starting on a voyage to a foreign country or from one state to another. These articles must specify:
a. The exact nature of the voyage.
b. The destination.
c. The duration.
d. The amount of wages to be paid each seaman.

If shipping articles are not properly executed, or if the master violates the contract, the seaman can leave the ship and recover the highest rate of wages, his expenses home, and damages. On the other hand, a seaman may be discharged for reasons that show him to be unfit for the service or to be trusted in the vessel, such as long-continued disobedience, drunkenness, or incapacity due to his own conduct.

7. COURTS OF ADMIRALTY have jurisdiction over all maritime contracts, torts, injuries, or offenses.

Statutes of Limitation

1. DEFINITION—A *statute of limitation* is a law that specifies the time after which debts or actions are no longer enforceable. All states have such laws providing different periods of time, varying from one to twenty years, within which legal actions must be brought before the courts are closed to them.

2. COMPUTING TIME—Time is computed from the date the debt is incurred or, in accounts, from the date of the last purchase or from the time of the injury complained of. The debt may be renewed by a partial payment of principal or interest, or by a written acknowledgment in a note or paper, with an expressed willingness to pay indicated by the debtor.

Torts or Wrongs

1. DEFINITION—A *tort* is a private or civil wrong or injury arising independent of contract. The proper remedy is an action for damages.

2. TORTS AND CRIMES—There is a distinction between torts and crimes. If a wrongful act violates a private right it is a *tort;* if it violates a public right it is a *crime.* Very frequently the wrongful act is in violation of both private and public rights. In such cases, even if the wrongdoer makes personal restitution or settlement with the person wronged, the state still has the right to punish the wrongdoer for the crime. Suppose A steals $500 from B, who finds it out and succeeds in getting A to return the money. A has still committed a crime against the public and can be punished as the law provides.

3. ASSAULT AND BATTERY—A person who intentionally invades the person of another by physical contact, or puts him in apprehension of an invasion of his person by threat of immediate physical contact, without such person's consent, and not in reasonable defense of person or other interest, and not in the performance of some duty imposed by law, or the exercise of some privilege by reason of the relation of the parties, is liable in damages. A successful assault becomes a battery when the injury is actually done.
a. Every person is entitled by law to liberty, security of life, and security of his property.
b. Mere words do not constitute an assault.
c. The wrong consists not so much in the actual striking of the person as in the manner and spirit of the act.
d. Accidental injury is not a battery.
e. A blow unlawfully aimed at one person but striking another is a battery.
f. Reasonable methods of self-defense may be employed in resisting a battery and in defending either a member of one's family or one's property.

4. DEFAMATION—A *defamation* is a false and malicious imputation of bad character or reputation either by slander or by libel.
a. Every person has a right to his good reputation.
b. Every person is assumed to have a good reputation until the contrary is proved.
c. *Slander* is oral defamation.
d. *Libel* is defamation in writing or printing.

5. SLANDER—In simple words, this tort consists of speaking words in another's hearing that injure a third person's reputation. The United States Supreme Court has classified slanderous words that are objectionable:
a. Words falsely spoken of a person that impute to the party the commission of some criminal offense involving moral turpitude for which the party, if the charge is true, may be indicted and punished.
b. Words falsely spoken of a person that impute that the party is infected with some infectious disease, which, if the charge is true, would exclude the party from society.
c. Defamatory words spoken of a party that impute to the party unfitness to perform the duties of an office or employment for profit, or the want of integrity in the discharge of the duties of such an office or employment.
d. Defamatory words falsely spoken of a party that prejudice such party in his or her profession or trade.
e. Defamatory words falsely spoken of a person that, though not in themselves actionable, occasion the party special damage.

6. LIBEL—It is even more dangerous to defame a person's character in writing. Many words when written or printed are libelous, which if spoken would not be slanderous without proof of special injury.
a. The owners of books and newspapers generally are liable for the publication of libelous matter, even though printed without their knowledge and even against their orders.
b. News dealers are immune from any liability for selling or displaying newspapers or magazines that contain

libelous matter, providing such dealers have no knowledge of the libelous matter.

c. In order to hold the editor or proprietor of the printing plant, the injured party must prove that the libelous matter could be recognized by an intelligent person as libel.

7. DEFENSES AGAINST CHARGES OF DEFAMATION are given below:

a. The truth of the charge is generally a complete defense against an action for damages. Statutes, however, sometimes require that not only must the words be true, but they must also be uttered in good faith.

b. A privileged communication, such as what is said or written in a judicial proceeding or in a legitimate newspaper report thereof, is not held to be libelous matter. This privilege extends to the heads of the executive departments of government. Statements rendered by mercantile agencies and the reports of many semi-public societies are also conditionally privileged.

c. Fair comment is still another defense. The conduct of public men is held to be a proper matter for public discussion, so long as the writer keeps within the bounds of an honest intention to discharge a duty to the public, and does not make the occasion a mere cover for false allegations. The same rule applies to newspaper reports of literary or artistic productions offered to the public.

8. FALSE IMPRISONMENT is a crime, and the person unlawfully imprisoned has the right to a civil action for damages. The defense may be that the officer was clothed with the proper authority and acted upon probable cause. In a case involving parent and child, guardian and ward, or teacher and pupil, it may be shown that the alleged wrongdoer was acting within his duty.

9. MALICIOUS PROSECUTION is another wrong. This is the malicious instituting of suit without probable cause, and both the malice and the lack of probable cause must be proved. A suit to recover for this wrong cannot be started before the alleged malicious prosecution has come to an end. That the accused party acted on the advice of his attorney after a full and fair disclosure of the facts is a good defense against a charge of malicious prosecution.

10. CONSPIRACY—A conspiracy is a combination of two or more persons to accomplish an unlawful end that is injurious to another. Thus members of a trade union may lawfully agree that they will stop work, or that they will not work with certain other laborers, but they commit a wrong as soon as they interfere with the liberty of others. Employers who combine to use unlawful methods to exclude a certain class of workmen are also guilty of a wrong. An agreement among manufacturers that they will all operate as the majority agree may be a conspiracy in restraint of trade.

11. SEARCH AND SEIZURE—It is unlawful to search private premises unless a search warrant has been issued by proper authority. It is a criminal offense to open another's letters, or to retain or pry into them. The federal and state constitutions protect persons against unreasonable searches and seizures.

12. NUISANCES—A nuisance is anything wrongfully done or permitted that injures or annoys another in the enjoyment of his legal rights. Below is a list of some of the nuisances subject to an action in tort:

a. To remove or weaken the lateral support of the adjoining land.

b. To mine or tunnel under another's land without providing suitable support.

c. To extend buildings over another's land.

d. To allow filthy deposits to accumulate on one's property.

e. To deposit refuse in a stream of water.

f. To erect a dam, backing up the water to injure the land of another.

g. To use or care for explosives, loaded weapons, or dangerous machines in a negligent manner.

h. To conduct a place of business or amusement, or engage in any activity, in a way that will materially interfere with the ordinary physical comfort of others.

i. To allow poisonous or offensive materials to remain in a place where they may cause injury to others.

j. To put or allow a heavy article or substance to remain where it is likely to fall and injure persons or property.

k. To erect, operate, and maintain electrical appliances without reasonable care in proportion to their danger.

l. For a state, county, or municipality to allow defects in streets, highways, or sidewalks that result in injury to persons or property.

Trademarks

1. DEFINITION—A trademark is an emblem or symbol to designate the goods of a merchant or manufacturer. The owner of a trademark may have it registered in the U.S. Patent Office and thus acquire the right to keep others from using it.

2. REGISTRATION—The first step of trademark registration is to file or sign an application addressed to the Commissioner of Patents. This application must include

a. The name, domicile, location, and citizenship of applicant.

b. A description of the goods for which trademark is used.

c. The method of affixing trademark.

d. Length of time the trademark has been used.

e. Description of trademark.

f. Drawing and specimens of the trademark.

The next step is the payment of a fee for registration.

3. REGISTER—There are two registers of the U.S. Patent Office on which trademarks may be registered. To be registered on the Principal Register, the trademark must be coined, arbitrary, fanciful, or suggestive; these are usually called technical marks. If the trademark is merely descriptive of goods or their regional origin or is primarily a surname, it is placed on the Supplemental Register.

4. LENGTH OF TIME A TRADEMARK IS PROTECTED—The registration of a trademark remains in force for twenty years. It may be renewed for a period of twenty years if it is still used in trade regulated by the U.S. Congress. The fee for renewal is $25. A trademark may be canceled or surrendered. It is canceled if within one year next preceding the expiration of six years from the date of registration the applicant fails to file an affidavit either affirming that he is using the mark or showing that he has reason for nonuse. Unless the affidavit is filed, the registration is canceled after six years.

5. RESTRICTIONS—The law has placed certain restrictions on the registration of trademarks. For example, it is impossible to register a trademark if

a. It comprises immoral, deceptive, or scandalous matter.

b. It contains matter that may disparage or falsely suggest a connection with persons living or dead.

c. It contains matter that may disparage or falsely suggest a connection with institutions, beliefs, or national symbols.

d. It consists of, or includes, the flag or coat of arms or other insignia of the United States, any state, municipality, or foreign nation.

e. It uses, without his consent, the portrait, signature, or name of a living person, or those of a deceased President of the United States without consent of his widow.

6. REGISTRATION OF OTHER MARKS — The law provides for the registration of service marks, certification marks, and collective marks. A *service mark* is a mark used in the sale or advertising of services to identify the services of one person and distinguish them from the services of others. A *certification mark* is used to certify origin or quality of goods; an example is a union label. A *collective mark* is used by an association, such as a cooperative.

7. ADDITIONAL INFORMATION — A pamphlet, *General Information Concerning Trademarks,* is available from the U.S. Patent Office, Washington, D.C. 20025. It describes the way applications and drawings are to be prepared and gives sample forms for applications. The Official Gazette contains information on trademarks registered, renewed, or published for opposition.

Truth in Advertising

1. DEFINITION — *Advertising* is any public statement, whether written, filmed, or spoken, that is designed to attract public attention. Any assertion made in an advertisement becomes a warranty; it must not mislead the public. In *FTC* v. *Algoma Lumber Co.,* the United States Supreme Court derived from the Federal Trade Commission Act a rule that "the public is entitled to get what it chooses, though the choice may be dictated by caprice or by fashion or perhaps by ignorance." In advertising, nothing less than the most literal truthfulness is tolerated.

2. APPLICATION OF PRINCIPLE — This principle has been interpreted as forbidding a businessman (a) to state falsely that his product ordinarily sells for a higher price but is offered at a bargain, even if the purchaser is in fact receiving his money's worth; (b) to misrepresent to the public that he is in a certain line of business, even though the misstatement bears no relationship to the quality of his product; (c) to merchandise reprocessed products without disclosing that they are "used," even if they are functionally identical with new products; (d) to misappropriate another's trademark; (e) to state falsely that a product has received a testimonial from a respected source; or (f) to state falsely that product claims have been certified by a testing agency.

3. A NEW APPLICATION — The Supreme Court recently added to this list the creation in a television commercial of the false impression that the viewer is seeing a test, experiment, or demonstration of a product's qualities when, because of the undisclosed use of "mockups," the viewer is not seeing an actual test of the product photographed as performed. Even if the product will in fact pass the test and "mockups" are used only because of technical problems of photography, the Supreme Court could see no difference between this practice and the use of false testimonials or testing-agency certification.

4. LITERAL TRUTH SOMETIMES INSUFFICIENT — Advertisements are not intended to be carefully dissected with a dictionary at hand, but rather to produce an overall impression on the ordinary purchaser. An advertiser cannot present one overall impression yet protect himself by presenting a contrary impression in a small and inconspicuous portion of the advertisement. Even though every sentence considered separately is true, the advertisement as a whole may be misleading because factors are omitted or the message is composed in a misleading way. An advertisement that can be read to have two meanings is illegal if one of them is false or misleading.

5. KNOWLEDGE OF FALSITY AND INTENT — Because a basic purpose of the law is consumer protection, the government does not have to prove knowledge of falsity on the part of the advertiser; the businessman acts at his peril. The intent of the advertiser is also entirely immaterial. An advertiser may possess a wholly innocent intent and still violate the law.

Vicious Animals

1. THE OWNER'S RESPONSIBILITY — The owners of vicious animals are responsible for any injuries the animals may cause while running at large. If a dog annoys travelers on a public road by scaring horses or frightening children, the owner is responsible in damages to the injured party. The owner of a vicious bull or stallion is required to exercise the greatest care in protecting the public from injury. If a person on a social or business errand is injured by a savage animal on the premises of the owner, the owner is responsible.

2. TRESPASSERS — These rules do not apply to trespassers who know the dangerous nature of the animal.

3. DOMESTIC ANIMALS — The owner of domestic animals is responsible in case injury results because of his own negligence. On the other hand, if the animals trespass on a neighbor's land, they cannot be injured or killed by the neighbor. The neighbor has a legal remedy, however, and can collect damages.

4. FENCE LAWS — In certain sections of the country there are open lands where cattle and other animals are allowed to graze at will. The owners of cultivated land are there required to provide their own protection against the animals. Most states, however, have stock laws providing that animals must be kept within an enclosure, and if damage results the owner of the animals is responsible.

Wills

1. DEFINITIONS — A *will* or *testament* is generally a written instrument making disposition of a person's property, to take effect after his death. A *testator* is the maker of a will when the same is made by a male person; if a female, the maker is called a *testatrix*. A *codicil* is an addition or alteration of a part of an executed will. A *legacy* is a gift or bequest of money or personal property by will. The person to whom it is given is called a *legatee,* and if the gift consists of the remainder of the property after paying all debts and other legacies, he is called the *residuary legatee.* A person to whom real estate is given is called a *devisee.* An *executor* is a male person named in the will to whom is entrusted the duty of administrating the estate of the testator according to the provisions of the will. If the will names a female person, she is called the *executrix.* An *administrator* is a male person appointed by the court to administer the estate of a deceased person who did not have a will or whose will named as executor a party incompetent or unwilling to act in that capacity. If the party appointed by the court is a female person, she is called the *administratrix.* Some states have abandoned terminology that distinguishes between the sexes, using *administrator* or *testator* for persons of either sex.

2. WHO MAY MAKE A WILL — All persons are competent to make wills except infants, persons of unsound mind, and idiots. In like manner any person who is competent to make a will can appoint his own executor. If the person so appointed is legally competent to transact business, the court will confirm the appointment if he lives within the jurisdiction of the court.

3. KINDS OF WILLS — There are two kinds of wills, written and unwritten. An unwritten will is called *nuncupative.* Such a will might be made by a soldier in active service or a sailor at sea, and depends upon proof of the persons hearing it.

4. REQUIREMENTS:

a. A will should be written.

b. A will should be dated.

c. Testator should sign his name in full, by mark if necessary.

d. A will should be witnessed by two or more disinterested parties, the number of witnesses varying according to statutes.

e. The witnesses need not know the contents of the will. It is generally necessary that the testator acknowledge to them that it is his will, sign it in their presence, and request them to sign as witnesses in his presence and in the presence of each other.

f. The wishes of the testator should be fully and clearly expressed in the will.

g. No exact form of words is necessary to make a will.

h. In writing wills simple language should be used. Statements concerning every provision or condition of the will should be fully and plainly made.

i. A will is valid even if written with a lead pencil.

j. To be effective in matters pertaining to real estate, a will must be executed according to the laws of the state in which the real estate is located. This requirement is generally in regard to the number of witnesses to a will. Care should be exercised to dispose of all the property belonging to the person making a will. In order to accomplish this, a will should have a clause, "all the rest, residue, and remainder of my estate, I give ..." etc., or "all the rest, residue, and remainder of my estate shall be divided into the following parts, 1/3 to ......, 1/6 to ......," etc.

k. Personal property may be conveyed in accordance with the law of the state in which the testator resides.

l. If trust provisions or limited estates are to be provided for in a will, it is best to have the will drawn by a competent lawyer, as these provisions are very technical, and may result in much litigation if not carefully drawn.

m. Generally a person does not need to give his property or any part of it to his children, but mention of the names of all the children is evidence of the testator's competency.

5. CODICILS—The same principles apply to a codicil as to a will. A codicil must be signed in the presence of witnesses.

6. MARRIED WOMEN—A wife is entitled to a certain portion of her husband's property called the dower. If the will does not provide that amount for her, she can have it set aside and claim her dower right.

7. A WILL IS SET ASIDE under the following conditions:

a. When it can be proved that the testator was feeble-minded or lacking in mental capacity.

b. When the testator revokes it before death, in which case it is usually destroyed.

c. When the property devised has been disposed of during the testator's lifetime.

8. GENERAL PRINCIPLES:

a. Any person may be a devisee or a legatee, including married women, minors, or corporations.

b. Testator's property is primarily liable for testator's debts and funeral expenses, which must be paid before any part of the property can be distributed to legatees.

c. A will has no force or effect until after testator's death.

d. The last will annuls all former wills.

e. A will takes effect from the day of the testator's death.

f. All matters pertaining to wills and inheritances are handled by the court having probate jurisdiction.

9. EXECUTORS AND ADMINISTRATORS—An executor is named in a will to execute that will and settle the estate. If the will does not name an executor, or if the named executor will not or cannot act, the probate court, in some states called the surrogate court, in others orphans' court, appoints an administrator with the will annexed. If a person dies without leaving a will, the court appoints an administrator, whose duty is the same as that of an executor except that he, having no will of the deceased, distributes the property as the law directs. The duties of an executor are:

a. To see that the deceased is suitably buried, avoiding unreasonable expense if the estate is insolvent.

b. To offer the will for probate, or proving, and to conform to the laws of his state and rules of the court, the clerk of which will give full instructions.

c. To make and return to the court within required time an inventory of the property. Real estate lying in another state need not be inventoried, for that must be administered upon in the state where it lies; but personal property situated in another state should be inventoried. Any encumbrances upon real estate should be noted and described.

d. To collect the property, pay the debts and dispose of the remainder as the law and will, or either, directs. Generally the debts should be paid as follows: (1) funeral expenses, (2) expenses of last sickness, (3) debts due the United States, (4) debts due the state, and (5) claims of creditors.

e. To render the accounts as directed by the court. The law provides that the widow of the intestate shall be the first entitled to act as administrator; next, the nearest of kin who is competent; next, any creditor who will accept the trust; and lastly, any other suitable person. Executors and administrators are required to take an official oath and also to give bond, usually for double the amount of the estate. Any blanks for probate may usually be secured from the clerk of the court having probate jurisdiction.

10. FORM OF WILL—To be valid, a will must be in writing and signed at the end by the testator in the presence of at least two witnesses or, in some jurisdictions, three witnesses, who must all be present when the testator signs his name to the will. The witnesses must also sign their names as such witnesses in the presence of each other and in the presence of the testator. If the will is written on more than one single sheet, it is a wise precaution for the testator and all of the witnesses to sign their names on each sheet.

WILL FORM

I, ..., residing in ...., in the County of ...., and State of ...., being of sound mind and disposing memory do make, ordain, publish, and declare this to be my Last Will and Testament, hereby revoking all former Wills and Codicils by me made.

[Here insert all bequests and instructions]

Lastly, I make, constitute, and appoint .... to be the executor(trix) of this my Last Will and Testament.

In witness whereof, I have hereunto subscribed my name and affixed my seal the ...... day of ...., in the year of Our Lord, One Thousand Nine Hundred and ....

..............(Seal)

Testator's Signature

This instrument was on the day of the date hereof, signed, published, and declared by the said testator .... to be his (her) Last Will and Testament in the presence of us who at his (her) request have subscribed our names hereto as witnesses, in his (her) presence, and in the presence of each other.

[Witnesses' names and addresses]

abrogate. To repeal or set aside a statute or ruling.

access. The right to enter and leave a tract of land from a public way.

acknowledgment. A sworn statement that a legal document was executed by the person making the acknowledgment. The statement is made before a public official, who attaches a certificate of acknowledgment to the document.

administrator. A person appointed by a probate court to settle the affairs of an individual dying without a will.

ad valorem. Designates an assessment of taxes against property according to value.

affidavit. A voluntary written statement of fact sworn before an authorized public official.

agent. A person authorized to represent another person and conduct business transactions in his name.

amortization. The act or process of extinguishing a debt, usually with equal payments at regular intervals over a specific period of time.

ancillary. Designating or pertaining to a document, proceeding, officer or office, etc., that is subordinate to, or in aid of, another primary or principal one; as, an ancillary attachment, bill or suit presupposes the existence of another principal proceeding.

annuity. A sum of money or its equivalent that constitutes one of a series of periodic payments. Any advance that may be interpreted in terms of money and answers the requirements of regularity may be considered an annuity.

antitrust law. A body of law designed to prevent corporations or conglomerates from developing monopoly power or unlawful combinations.

appraisal. An estimate of quantity, quality or value. The process through which conclusions of property value or property facts are obtained; also commonly the report setting forth such estimate and conclusion.

assessment. A non-recurring charge levied against property to meet some specific purpose portioned either by benefit derived to property or based on value of property. The valuation of property for taxation; also the value so assigned.

assets. Property of all kinds under a single ownership.

auctioneer. A person employed for compensation to sell property to the highest bidder at a public sale.

authenticate. To give authority to a legal document so it may be used as evidence in a court of law. Notaries public and other public officials are empowered to authenticate documents.

avoid. To set aside or make void.

B

bailment. A temporary transfer of personal property for some specific purpose. The property is to be returned after the purpose has been executed.

bankruptcy. The legally declared condition of being unable to pay one's debts.

bill of exchange. An unconditional order in writing from one person to another directing that a certain sum of money be paid to a third person; sometimes called a *draft.*

bill of sale. A legal paper transferring title to personal property from one person to another.

blue sky law. A popular name for a law designed to regulate and supervise the issuance and selling of securities.

bond. 1. A legal instrument binding a person to pay a specific sum of money to another person at a specified time. **2.** A certificate of obligation, usually an evidence of debt.

broker. A person who conducts transactions in his specialized field.

C

capital. Accumulated wealth. A portion of wealth which is set aside for the production of additional wealth; specifically, the funds belonging to the partners or shareholders of a business, invested with the expressed intention of their remaining permanently in the business.

carrier. A person whose business is to transport passengers or merchandise.

certificate of title. A document usually given to the home buyer with the deed stating that title to the property is clear; it is prepared by a title company or an attorney and is based on the abstract of title.

chancery. Equity. A *master in chancery* is an assistant to the judge in a court of equity.

chattel. Any item of movable or immovable property other than real estate.

chattel mortgage. An instrument conveying conditional title to personal property as security for the repayment of a debt or for the performance of some other act.

citizen. An inhabitant of a nation who enjoys political rights.

class action suit. A lawsuit filed on behalf of all people who find themselves in the same factual situation.

clear title. A title which is not encumbered or burdened with defects.

codicil. An addition to or modification of a will. A codicil requires the same formalities as a will.

collateral. Any property designated as security for the payment of a debt or for the execution of a contract.

commercial paper. Negotiable instruments, such as checks, bills of exchange, or bank notes given as unconditional payment in business transactions.

commission. Payment for the performance of specific duties; in real estate, usually payment measured by a percentage of another sum, i.e., as a percentage of the sales price paid for selling a property.

common property. Land or a tract of land considered as the property of the public in which all persons enjoy equal rights; property not owned by individuals or government, but by groups or in formal villages.

complaint. The initial statement made by the plaintiff in a civil case, stating the reasons the plaintiff is entitled to the aid of the court.

compound interest. Interest paid both on the original principal and on interest accrued from the time it fell due.

condemnation. The taking of private property for public use through the exercising of due process of law.

condominium. A form of property ownership providing for individual ownership of a specific apartment together with an undivided interest in the land or other parts of the structure in common with other owners.

consideration. That which a party to a contract gains from the contract; any valuable benefit gained by the signer of a contract. No contract is valid unless it expresses a consideration.

consignee. A person to whom goods are shipped or transferred.

contempt of court. Violation of the rules of a court of law or disruption of its proceedings.

contingent claim. A claim against a person that is conditional on some event that may not happen. Contingent claims are not allowable in bankruptcy proceedings.

contract. A mutual agreement between two or more competent parties who, for a valuable consideration, assent to do or not to do a particular thing.

convey. The act of deeding or transferring title to another.

conveyance. A written legal document transferring title to real property from one person to another.

copyright. The exclusive right to sell, reproduce, or use in any way a literary or artistic work.

corporation. 1. An association of persons created under the law and legally empowered to act as a single person in regard to some common purpose of the members. 2. A group of persons empowered to act as a single individual, and treated as such, in many respects, by the law.

covenant. An agreement written into deeds and other instruments promising performance or nonperformance of certain acts or stipulating certain uses or nonuses of the property.

crime. A wrong which violates a statute and injures or endangers the public.

curtesy. The interest which a husband acquires in land belonging to his wife after her death; sometimes called *dower*.

D

debenture. An instrument, given by a corporation to certain investors, promising to repay their investments with interest, securing the debts with company assets, and giving the investors priority claims.

deed. A written document conveying real estate from one owner to another.

default. Failure to carry out a legally binding promise.

defeasance. A provision or condition in a deed or in a separate instrument which, being performed, renders the instrument void.

demand draft. A draft drawn by one person on another which is payable when presented.

demurrage. The sum charged by transportation companies for goods not removed from their cars within a fixed time.

deposition. The sworn testimony of a witness taken down in writing before a notary public and signed by the witness.

devise. A gift of real property by last will and testament.

devisee. A person given real estate by a will.

discrimination. Any act which denies rights or equal treatment to a person because of race, color, religion, or sex.

docketing. Scheduling a case to be heard before a court of justice.

domicile. The permanent home of a person. Temporary homes are *residences*.

double indemnity. An agreement in a life insurance or accident policy providing for payment of twice the value of the policy in case of accidental death.

dower. The provision the law makes to support a widow out of her deceased spouse's estate.

draft. A written order by one person on another demanding the payment of a specified sum of money to a designated third person.

drunkenness. The state of being so influenced by alcohol that judgment and reflexes are impaired.

E

easement. The right to use or enjoy certain privileges that appertain to the land of another such as the right of way, or the right to receive air and light by reason of an agreement of record with the owner of adjacent property.

ejectment. An action to determine the title to land and right of possession.

emancipation. The release of control by a parent over a minor.

embezzlement. The use of another person's money or property for one's own benefit by a person such as an agent, an executor, or a public official.

eminent domain. The power to appropriate private property for public use. If public welfare is served, the right of eminent domain may be granted by the state to quasi-public or even private bodies such as railroad, water, light and power companies.

encumbrance. Any claim, such as a mortgage or a lien, against a piece of real or personal property.

endorsement. The signature of the owner on the back of a check or other negotiable instrument, by which he transfers the instrument to another person.

equity. 1. Equity of redemption. 2. A body of laws supplementing and overriding the limitations and inflexibility of common law.

equity of redemption. The right of a mortgagor to redeem his property within a certain time after foreclosure.

escheat. Reversion of property to the state by reason of failure of persons legally entitled to hold or lack of heirs.

escrow. A deed or other instrument placed in the hands of a disinterested person (sometimes called the *escrowee*) for delivery upon performance of certain conditions or the happening of certain contingencies.

estate. A right in property. An *estate in land* is the degree, nature or extent of interest which a person has in it.

evidence. Any statement or object presented in court to convince the judge or jury of the truth of an argument.

execution. The completion or fulfillment of anything, such as a contract. An *executed contract* is one whose terms have already been completed.

exemption. A right granted to debtors that protects certain property from the claims of creditors.

F

fee. Remuneration for services. When applied to property, an inheritable estate in land.

fiduciary. The relationship between a person charged with the duty of acting for the benefit of another, as between guardian and ward.

forced sale. The act of selling property under compulsion as to time and place. Usually a sale made by virtue of a court order, ordinarily at public auction.

foreclosure. Taking mortgaged property from an owner who fails to pay the debt secured by the mortgage.

forfeiture. A statement entitling a landlord to terminate a lease and reclaim property if a tenant fails to pay rent.

franchise. A privilege or right conferred by governmental grant or contractually by a business enterprise upon an individual or group of individuals. Usually, an exclusive privilege or right to furnish public services or sell a particular product in a certain community.

G

guaranteed mortgage. A mortgage in which a mortgage company buys the mortgages with its own funds and in turn sells these mortgages to its clients, who receive all of the papers in connection with the mortgage, including the bond, the mortgage and the assignment, together with the company's policy of guarantee. The company guarantees the payment of both principal and interest and assumes the responsibility of complete supervision of the mortgage, for which it receives a fee out of the interest, as it is collected.

guaranty. A written promise by one party to perform some duty or pay some debt if another party should fail to do so.

guaranty policy. Insurance that protects the buyer from loss due to any defect in title to a piece of real property.

H

habeas corpus. A writ ordering a law enforcement officer to bring a certain prisoner into court and show legal reasons to keep him in custody.

heir. One who might inherit or succeed to an interest in lands under the rules of law, applicable where an individual dies without leaving a will.

I

indemnify. To protect from loss or damage, especially by agreeing to reimburse a person for certain kinds of loss.

indemnity. Repayment by an insurer for a loss the insured person has suffered.

indenture. A type of written instrument in which both parties agree to do certain things.

infant. A person too young, in the eyes of the law, to manage his own affairs and enjoy full rights of citizenship; a minor.

injunction. A court order forbidding a person or his associates from doing or continuing to do certain actions.

innkeeper. The proprietor of a public house that receives and entertains travelers.

insolvency. Inability of a person or business to pay his or its debts.

instrument. A formal legal document.

insurance. A contract stating that one person will compensate another for certain specific kinds of losses.

interlocutory decree. An intermediate or temporary ruling of a court, not a final decision of a case.

international law. A body of rules governing the conduct of nations.

intestate. A person who dies without leaving a valid last will and testament.

J

jury. A body of laymen selected impartially to determine the truth in a legal proceeding.

L

lease. A contract for the possession or occupancy of land or buildings.

legacy. A gift left by means of a will to a named person, who is called the *legatee*. The *residuary legatee* is the person named to receive all property not specifically given to someone else.

lessee. One who possesses the right to use or occupy a property under lease agreement.

lessor. One who holds title to and conveys the right to use and occupy a property under lease agreement.

letters patent. The legal document granting a patent to an inventor.

liable. Legally responsible. The law will force a person to pay for damage he is liable for.

license. A permission granted by a competent authority allowing a person to do something that he would otherwise have no right to do.

lien. The right to hold or sell the property of another person as security or for the payment of a debt.

liquidated. 1. Set or determined. A liquidated debt is for a specific amount. **2.** Settled by payment or other means, as a debt.

liquidated damages clause. A statement in a contract setting a monetary penalty for violation of the contract.

litigation. 1. A legal action for the purpose of enforcing a law. **2.** The undertaking of a legal action.

M

mandamus. A command from a court

to a public or private official requiring him to do some act that is his official duty.

material. Important. A material fact influences the decision of the court.

mechanic's lien. A claim against a piece of property to insure payment for labor or materials used in building or repairing the property.

Medicare. A federal program of health insurance for the aged.

monument. A stone or other fixed object used to establish real estate boundaries.

mortgage. An agreement designating certain property as security for the payment of a debt.

motion. 1. In parliamentary law, a formal proposal to be considered by a meeting. **2.** An application to a court for a rule or other order.

municipal corporation. A corporation formed to govern a town or a city.

N

negotiable instrument. Any legal document which may be transferred by endorsement.

notary public. A public official empowered by law to administer oaths and to attest writings for the purpose of establishing their authenticity.

note. An instrument of credit given to attest a debt.

nuncupative will. A will made orally, in the presence of several witnesses, during the testator's last illness.

O

obligation. A conditional bond agreeing to pay a certain sum of money if the signer fails to do a specified thing.

option. An agreement granting the exclusive right during a stated period of time, without creating any obligation to purchase, sell or otherwise direct or contract the use of a property.

ordinance. A regulation passed by a municipal government.

P

parliamentary law. The generally accepted rules of procedure for public meetings or deliberative bodies.

partnership. An association of two or more persons to carry on as coowners of a business for profit.

passport. An official document of identification given to travelers to prove their citizenship.

patent. The exclusive right to manufacture and sell an invention, granted to its inventor for a limited time.

personalty. Property which is movable. All property is either personalty, realty or mixed.

plaintiff. The person who sues another in civil court.

power of attorney. A legal document by one person authorizing another person to act for him in certain specified matters.

power of sale. A clause inserted in a will or deed of trust agreement authorizing the sale or transfer of land in accordance with the terms of the clause.

prescriptive right. A legal right acquired by uninterrupted use of the right over a long period of time.

principal. 1. A sum lent or employed as a fund or investment, as distinguished from its income or profits. **2.** The original amount (as of a loan) of the total due and payable at a certain date. **3.** A party to a transaction, as distinguished from an agent. **4.** Head of a business.

privileged communication. A confidential statement to a trusted person such as a doctor, lawyer, priest, or spouse; these persons are not allowed to reveal that information in court.

products liability. The liability of a manufacturer or seller of a product for any injury to a consumer using the product for its intended purposes.

property. The exclusive right to control an economic good. The recognized attribute that human beings may have in their relation with wealth. A property refers to units capable of being used independently in a single ownership. A property may consist of the rights to a single parcel of land, a house and lot, a complete manufacturing plant or any one of the items assembled together to constitute such a plant. It may also consist of the rights developed and inherent in the attached business of an enterprise or any one of the elements reflected therein, such as the rights to a patent, a trademark, a contract or the proven goodwill of the public.

prorate. To allocate between seller and buyer their proportionate share of an obligation paid or due. For example, a prorate of real property taxes or fire insurance.

prospectus. A description of a company which invites the public to buy the securities of that company.

protest. A formal declaration, signed by a notary public, that a check or other negotiable instrument was presented for payment and that payment was denied.

proxy. A statement by a stockholder of a corporation appointing another person to vote in his place at stockholders' meetings.

putative father. The father of an illegitimate child.

Q

quitclaim deed. A deed transferring whatever interest the seller may have in a piece of real property. See also *warranty deed.*

R

real property. Land or anything permanently attached to it.

receiver. A person appointed by the court to hold and manage property that is involved in a lawsuit.

recording. The entering or recording of a copy of certain legal instruments or documents, as a deed, in a government office provided for this purpose; thus making a public record of the document for the protection of all concerned and giving constructive notice to the public at large.

redeem. To gain full possession of property by paying off a mortgage or other obligation.

redemption. The recovery, by payment of all proper charges, of property which has been lost through foreclosure of a mortgage or other legal process.

release. A legal document by which one party in a dispute transfers its claim to another party.

release clause. A clause relinquishing a right or claim by the person in whom it exists to the person against whom it could be enforced; such as a clause in a mortgage deed reconveying the legal title to the mortgagor upon payment of the mortgage debt.

remise. A formal term meaning to give up.

replevin. A lawsuit to recover goods which have been illegally taken, usually goods taken to secure payment of rent.

S

seal. A formal marking or stamp on a legal document; now rarely used.

secure. To guarantee that a debt will be paid by giving the creditor security, such as a lien or a mortgage. In bankruptcy, a secured claim is backed by some special right to the debtor's property.

secured credit sale. A sale in which the seller has the right to repossess the goods he sold if he is not fully paid.

securities. Any form of investment, including stocks, bonds, and notes.

Also, property set aside to assure the payment of a debt.

security agreement. A contract signed by both buyer and seller stating that the seller has an interest in the goods until they are paid for.

specialty. A contract under seal, legally more binding than a simple contract.

squatter's right. The right to occupancy of land created by virtue of long and undisturbed use but without legal title or arrangement; in the nature of a right at common law.

statute. Any written law created by a legislature.

statute of limitations. A law stating that if a lawsuit is not begun within a specified time after a wrong occurred, the lawsuit becomes invalid.

statutory exemptions. Certain kinds of property that are protected by law from the claims of creditors.

statutory lien. A claim on property not in the creditor's possession, such as a mechanic's lien.

stoppage in transit. A right of the seller to reclaim goods before they are delivered to a purchaser if the goods are not paid for and if the purchaser is insolvent.

sublease. An agreement conveying the right of use and occupancy of a property in which the lessor is the lessee in a prior lease.

sue. To commence legal proceedings.

surety. A person who accepts final responsibility to fulfill another person's obligation if the other person should default.

surrogate court. A court that oversees the administration of wills.

T

tangible property. Property that by its nature is susceptible to the senses. Generally the land, fixed improvement, furnishings, merchandise, cash and other items of working capital used in carrying on an enterprise.

tenancy. A holding, as of land, by any kind of title, occupancy of land, a house or the like under a lease or on payment of rent or tenure.

tenancy in common. A tenancy shared by two or more parties.

tenant. Any person in possession of

real property with the owner's permission.

time draft. A draft that is payable at a specified time after it is presented.

title. Evidence that a person owns a piece of property. A merchantable title is entirely free from other claims of ownership.

tort. A wrong committed against an individual or his property independent of a contract.

trademark. A distinctive, legally registered marking or symbol used by manufacturers to distinguish their products.

trust deed. A type of mortgage given to trustees in order to provide security for a number of creditors.

U

underwriter. 1. In insurance, the person or company that issues an insurance policy. 2. In securities, a person or group that agrees to buy a large amount of a new stock issue.

V

valuable consideration. Something of worth given as part of a contract agreement.

W

waive. To give up a right by free choice.

warrant. 1. To assure a buyer that he will receive valid title to property, or to swear that facts stated in a contract are true. 2. The act of a criminal court authorizing the arrest of a person or the search or seizure of property.

warranty. A statement relating to a sale of goods which assures the buyer that he will receive good quality merchandise.

warranty deed. A deed in which a seller of real estate guarantees that the title to the property is good.

will. A written declaration expressing a person's intention regarding the disposition of his property after his death.

without recourse. A phrase signifying a qualified endorsement—the signer denies liability for the negotiable instrument he endorses.

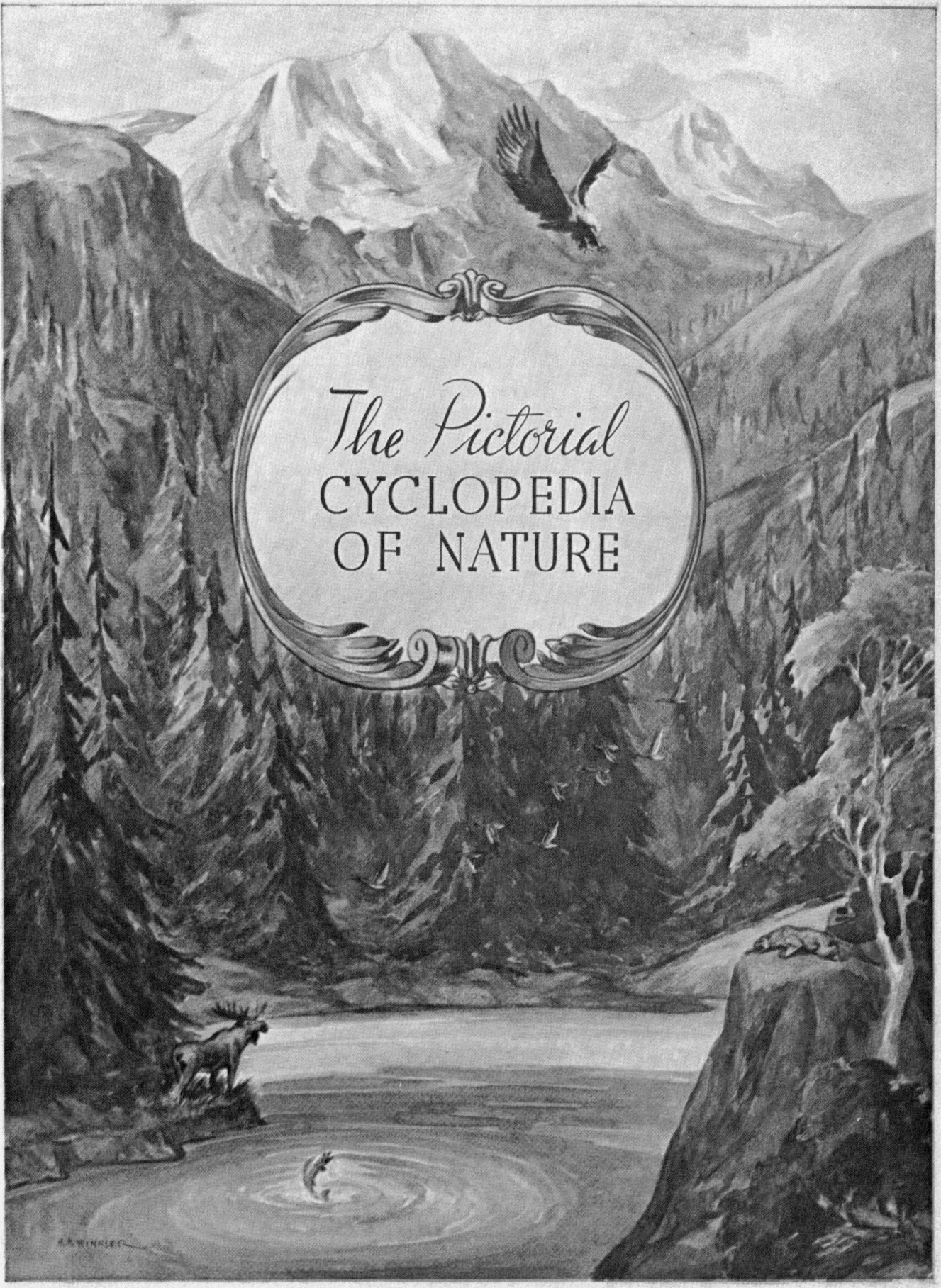

The Pictorial
CYCLOPEDIA
OF NATURE

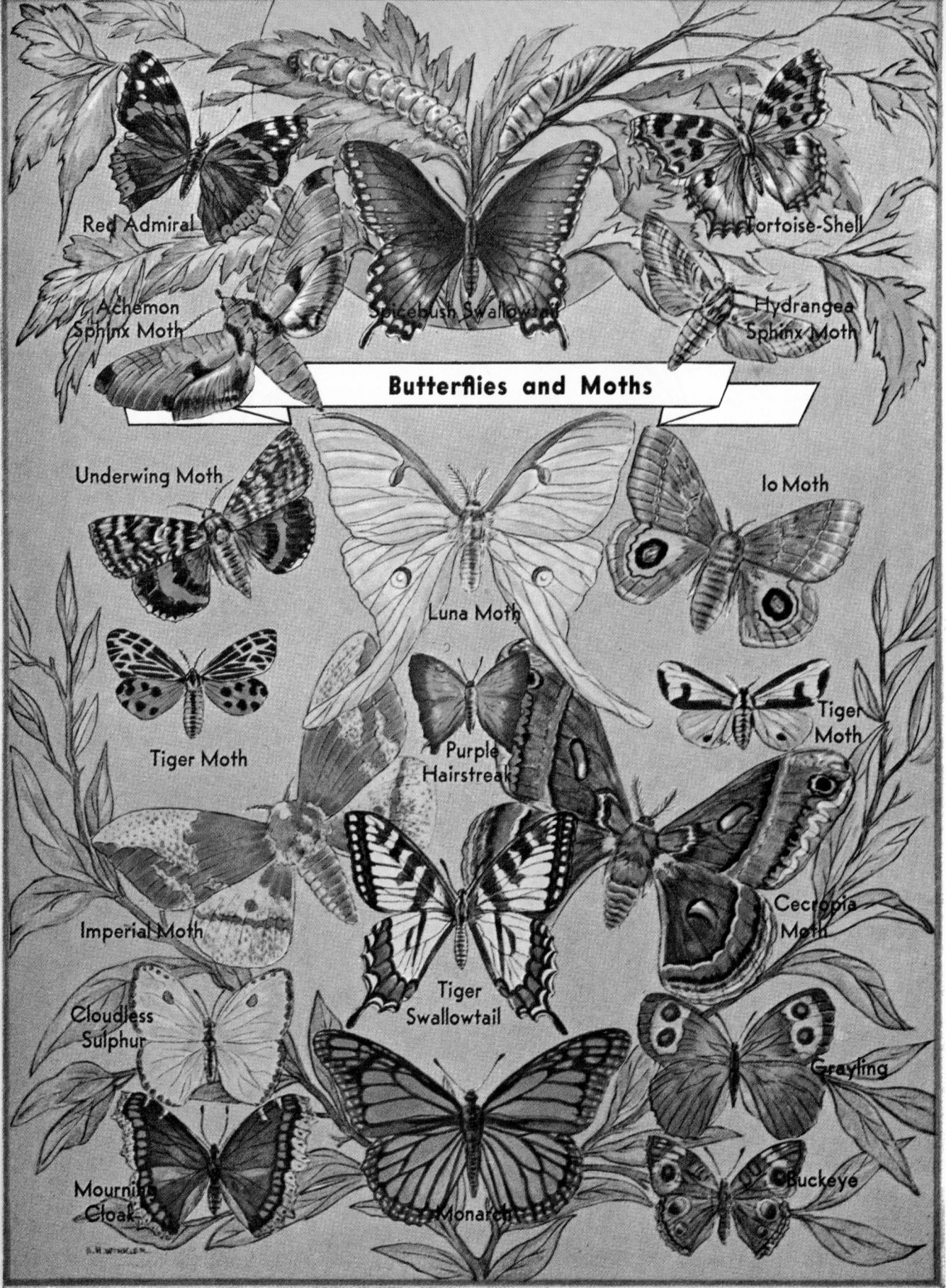

Butterflies and Moths

Red Admiral

Achemon Sphinx Moth

Spicebush Swallowtail

Tortoise-Shell

Hydrangea Sphinx Moth

Underwing Moth

Luna Moth

Io Moth

Tiger Moth

Purple Hairstreak

Tiger Moth

Imperial Moth

Cecropia Moth

Cloudless Sulphur

Tiger Swallowtail

Grayling

Mourning Cloak

Monarch

Buckeye

Wood Duck

Ring-necked Pheasant

Blue-winged Teal

Canvasback

Gadwall

Mallard

Wilson's Snipe

Ruffed Grouse

GAME BIRDS

Quail

AMERICAN

White-fronted Goose

Canada Goose

Valley Quail

Mountain Quail

Wild Turkey

Woodcock

Prairie Chicken

Herring Gull

California Condor

Road Runner

Osprey

Swallow-Tailed Kite

Great Horned Owl

Rough-Legged Hawk

Red-Tailed Hawk

Bald Eagle

CARRION BIRDS AND BIRDS OF PREY

Marsh Hawk

Turkey Buzzard

Raven

Kingfisher

NORTH AMERICAN INSECTS

Cotton Stainer
Calicoback
Eastern Long-horned Beetle
Tiger Beetle
Western Long-horned Beetle
Japanese Beetle
Maple Borer
Squash Bug Ally
Buprestid Beetle
Assassin Bug
Short-horned Grasshopper
Snapping Beetle
Wasp
Wasp
Yellow Jacket
Syrphus Fly
Robber Fly
Cicada
Goldsmith Beetle
Queen
Ground Beetle
Bumblebee
Meloid Beetle
Velvet Ant
Ichneumon Fly
Sawfly
Dragonfly
Stinkbug
Stinkbug
Tumblebug
Tortoise Beetle
Tachina Fly
Squash Ladybird
Figeater

A. H. WINKLER

AMERICAN GAME FISH

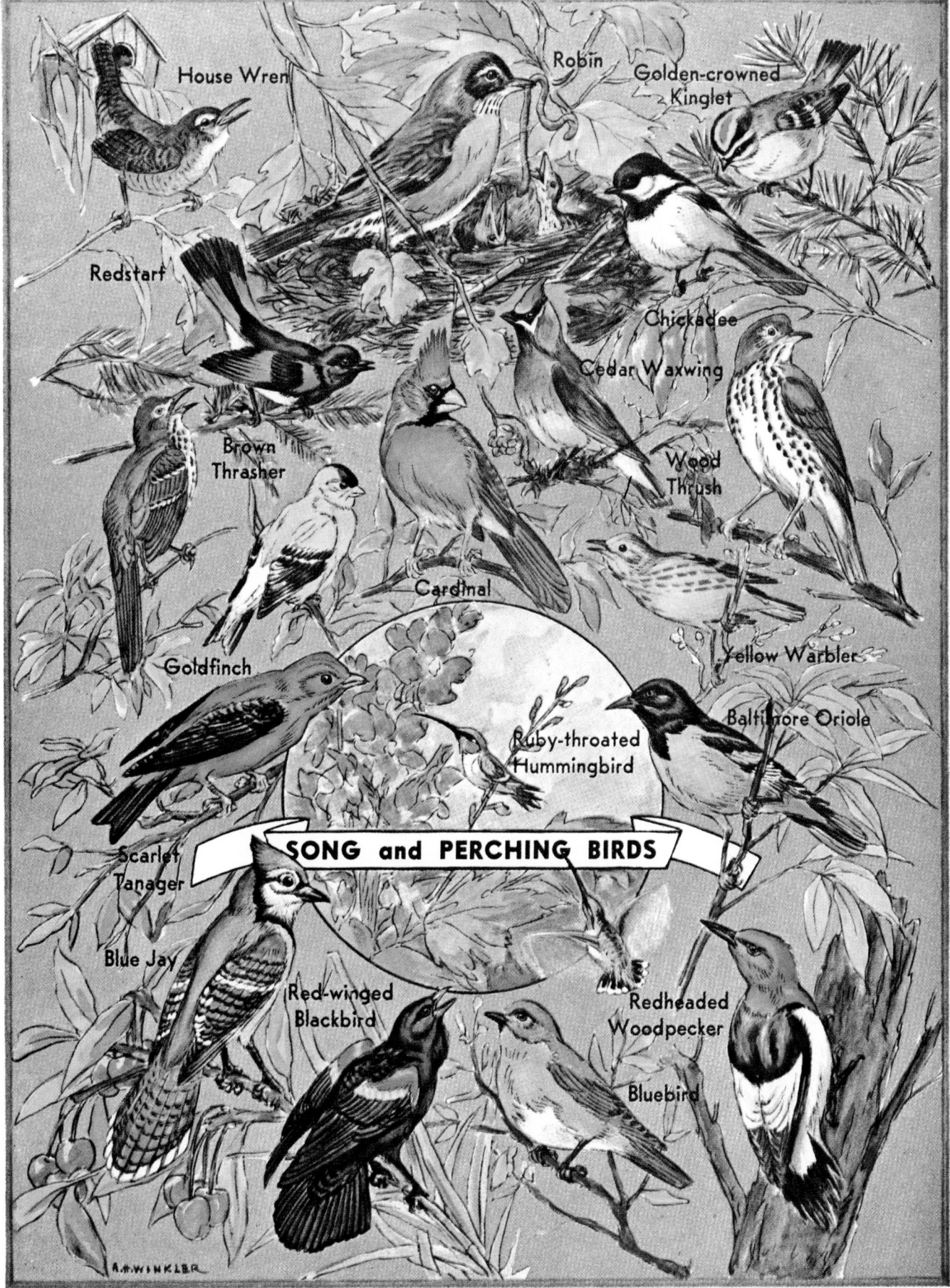

House Wren

Robin

Golden-crowned Kinglet

Redstart

Chickadee

Cedar Waxwing

Brown Thrasher

Wood Thrush

Goldfinch

Cardinal

Yellow Warbler

Scarlet Tanager

Ruby-throated Hummingbird

Baltimore Oriole

SONG and PERCHING BIRDS

Blue Jay

Red-winged Blackbird

Redheaded Woodpecker

Bluebird

A. WINKLER

AMERICAN FUR-BEARING ANIMALS

Rocky Mountain Goat

Virginia Deer

Wapiti

Moose

Coyote

Rocky Mountain Sheep

Lynx

WILD ANIMALS OF NORTH AMERICA

Puma

Pronghorned Antelope

Bison

Grizzly Bear

Timber Wolf

GARDEN FLOWERS

Boletus

Garlic Mushroom

Field Mushroom

Little Wheel Mushroom

Fairy-Ring Mushroom

Gemmed Puffball

Morel

Oyster Mushroom

Glistening Coprinus

Pear-Shaped Puffball

Inky Coprinus

MUSHROOMS WARNING: Many of these edible native mushrooms very closely resemble deadly poisonous varieties.

Equestrian Tricholoma

Orange-Milk Lactar

Skull Puffball

Caesar's Agaric

Early Pholiota

Gypsy Mushroom

Velvet-Stemmed Collybia

FLOWERING TREES AND SHRUBS

Mock Orange

Bridal Wreath

Lilac

Forsythia

Magnolia

Flowering Crab

Flowering Cherry

Rhododendron

Dogwood

Honeysuckle

AMERICAN WILDFLOWERS

Mexican Rose

Beavertail Cactus

Giant Cactus

Candlewood

Soapweed Tree

Organ Pipe Cactus

Barrel Cactus

Barrel Cactus

Grizzly Bear Cactus

Sitting Cactus

Spanish Bayonet

Century Plant

Torch Cactus

Long Mamma

AMERICAN DESERT PLANTS

Silver Cholla

Nipple Cactus

Clock Face Cactus

Devil's Pincushion

Prickly Pear Cactus

Living Rock

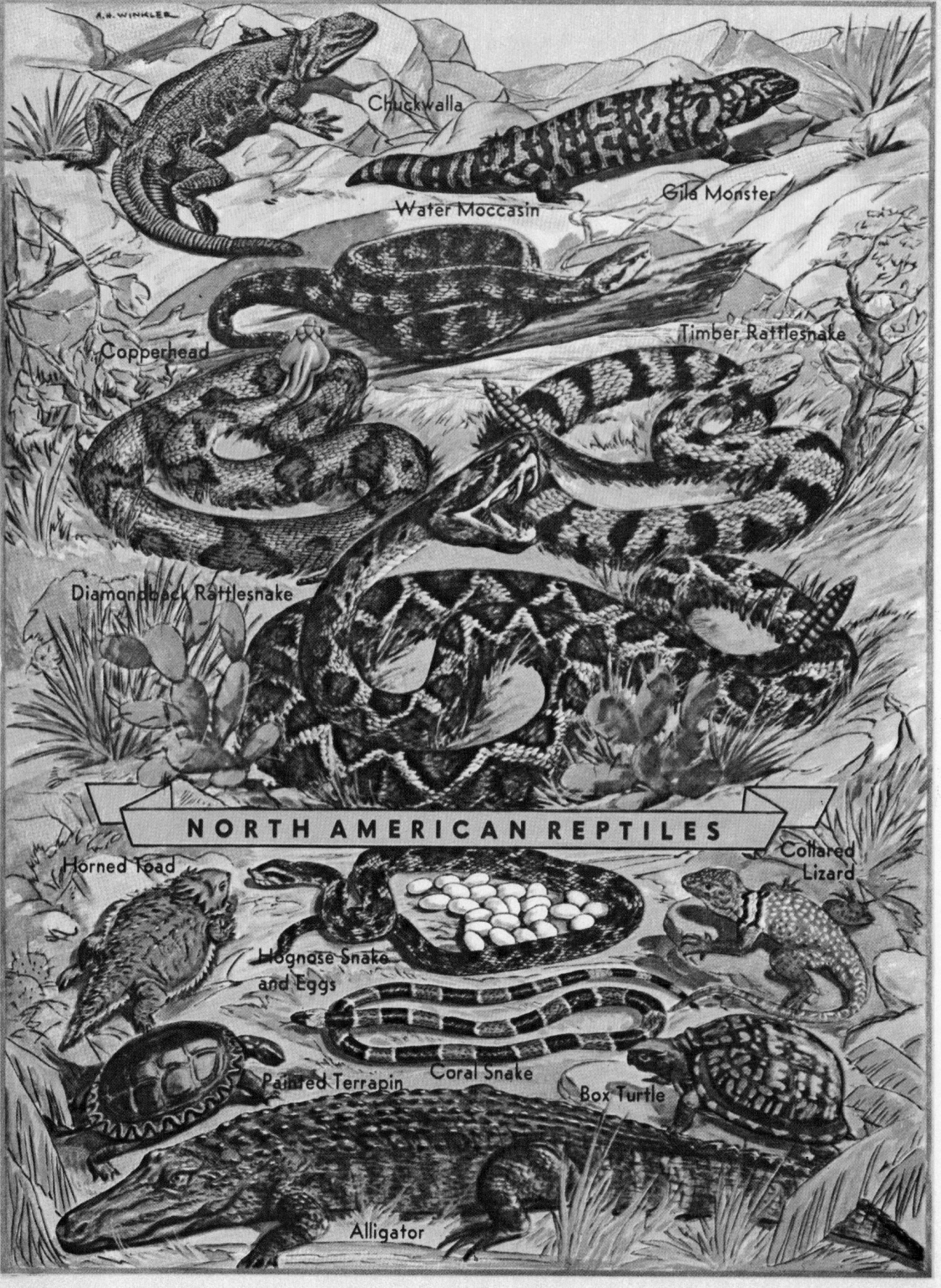

NORTH AMERICAN REPTILES

HOW TO USE
THE METRIC SYSTEM

Contents

ROUGHLY SPEAKING...

A meter is about 39 inches, or about 3 inches longer than a yard.

A kilogram is about 2.2 pounds.

A second is about the time needed to say "one thousand."

An ampere is about enough electric current to power a 100-watt bulb.

A kelvin (like a Celsius degree) is about 2 Fahrenheit degrees.

A candela is not enough light intensity by which to read a book; about 30 candelas are needed.

A radian is a plane angle (like a slice of pie) measuring about a 6th part of a circle.

A steradian is a solid angle (like a cone with a rounded bottom) measuring about a 12th part of a sphere.

THE METRIC LOOK

The changeover to the Metric System in the United States will alter the look of many commonplace things, such as highway markers, rulers, thermometers, gas pumps, and food packages. A few of the more common changes are illustrated here. Dimensions given here are for purposes of illustration only; exact dimensions and relationships are given in the text.

AREA

VOLUME

SPEED

WEIGHT

VOLUME

WEIGHT

TEMPERATURE

LINEAL MEASURE

DISTANCE

INTRODUCTION

A system of measurement is a necessary tool for carrying out commerce, science, and industry in every society. Weights and measures have been used by man since the dawn of civilization and have contributed much to his social progress. The first weights and measures probably arose out of ancient man's desire to obtain a fair exchange of gold and silver for his livestock or grain. The early Egyptian farmers along the Nile River may have wished to know how much land they owned, and then calculated the length and width of their fields by walking these distances and counting so many strides or paces. But whatever the origins of weights and measures, it is certain that the units were randomly chosen. Units of mass, length, and capacity from primitive times to the present have often been as diverse and variable as the livestock, metal, land, or grain they measured.

A survivor of this random system of weights and measures may still be found in the United States today. For example, a mile equals 8 furlongs, a furlong 40 rods, a rod 16½ yards, and so on. In random systems of weights and measures, the mathematical relationship between units is arbitrary, and conversion from one unit to another is often confusing and time-consuming.

In an attempt to overcome this problem, France adopted, in the latter part of the eighteenth century, the metric system of measurement, which allows for easy and accurate conversion of units. Since then, all major nations of the world except the United States and parts of the British Commonwealth have adopted the metric system, and the United States, too, will soon be using the metric system. To understand why the metric system has been accepted as the common language of measurement throughout the world, it is important to understand the history of the metric system and how the system works.

The first man to propose the logical systematization of units of weights and measures was the French mathematician and astronomer, Gabriel Mouton (1618–1694), rector of St. Paul's Church, Lyons. In his book *Observations Concerning the Diameter of the Sun and the Phases of the Moon* (1670), Mouton suggested that a decimal system be used for units of measurement, having as a basis the length of an arc of one minute of a great circle of the earth.

During the next century, the idea of a decimal system of measurements spread and found favor with many scientists. It is a telling point, however, that not until the time of the French Revolution, when a new social order was established, were the majority of Frenchmen willing to discard their traditional weights and measures in favor of the more efficient metric system.

On May 8 1790 the National Assembly of France ordered the French Academy of Sciences to develop a new standard of weights and measures. The chief supporter of this decree was the revolutionary bishop of Autun, Charles Maurice de Talleyrand (1754–1838). The following year, the National Assembly named a commission of twelve reputable scientists to lay plans for the revision of the measurement system. Most of their attention was given to revision of units of mass and length, which were to be derived from some natural measure, such as the dimensions of the earth, and were to be based on the decimal system. The unit of length in the new system, the meter, was to be a ten-millionth part of the quarter-meridian (a hypothetical line from the North Pole to the equator) passing through Paris. The unit of mass, the gram, was defined as the mass of a cubic centimeter of water at maximum density. As can be seen, the hope was to interrelate the units of length, mass, and capacity in order to simplify the various conversions necessary in using a weights-and-measures system.

The quarter-meridian had to be accurately measured. Two astronomers, Jean Delambre (1749–1822) and Pierre Méchain (1744–1804), were assigned the job. From 1792 to 1798 they measured the distance from Barcelona, Spain, to Dunkerque, France, and, with this work as a basis, calculated the remainder of the quarter-meridian. A standard meter and kilogram were then constructed, based on the two astronomers' measurement work, and presented to the legislative body in Paris. Called the *mètre des archives* and the *kilogramme des archives*, these fundamental units of the metric system were established as the legal standards of length and mass by the French National Assembly on December 10, 1799.

Much of the credit for encouraging the use of the metric system throughout Europe belongs to Napoleon (1769–1821), who, as a result of his military conquests, introduced the metric system into several countries. However, Napoleon delayed a complete changeover to the metric system in France by permitting, for political reasons, the old French units to be used again. Finally, in 1840 the French Parliament outlawed all weights and measures except those of the metric system. From that time until today there has been a gradual progression of metric usage throughout the world, fulfilling the hope of the system's founders that common measurement would lead to more efficient commercial transactions and exchanges of scientific information between nations.

Before 1840 Greece, the Netherlands, and much of Italy were using metric measurements. Between 1840 and 1870 most of the countries of Europe and South America embraced the metric system. It was adopted by Spain in 1849, and permitted in England in 1864, in the United States in 1866, and in Germany in 1868. Two years later, at the invitation of the French Government, representatives from the nations of Austria, Colombia, Ecuador, Great Britain, Greece, Italy, Norway, Peru, Portugal, Russia, Spain, Switzerland, Turkey, and the United States convened in Paris to discuss how the metric system might be improved. Halted by the Franco-Prussian War, the conference did not meet again until 1872, when it initiated the machinery to establish an international standardizing bureau of weights and measures.

In 1875 seventeen countries, including the United States, ratified the treaty known as the Metric Convention, creating the International Bureau of Weights and Measures. Each nation agreed to send delegates to a General Conference on Weights and Measures, which would meet every six years to consider improvements in and modifications of metric standards. An International Committee on Weights and Measures, composed of eighteen scientists who were elected by the General Conference, was charged with caring for the bureau's laboratory at Sèvres, near Paris, and with carrying on research to improve the measurements and definitions of metric standards.

From 1799 to 1889 the meter had been defined as the length of the *mètre des archives*, from end to end, as based upon a ten-millionth part of the quarter-meridian passing through Paris. It was thought, however, that less error would result by defining the meter as the length between two lines on a bar, so the International Prototype Meter, a platinum line standard, was approved as the new definition of a meter by the General Conference in 1889. A copy of the International Prototype Meter was then presented to all member nations of the Metric Convention.

As rapid industrialization made the twentieth century the age of technology, more and more nations joined the Metric Convention and adopted the metric system. Aside from a handful of small nations, the Commonwealth of Great Britain and the United States were the only major powers not committed to metric measures by the end of World War II. Meanwhile, the General Conference on Weights and Measures had grown to include almost all the nations of the world, and had made significant improvements in the metric system. In 1960 the General Conference formally added the ampere to the metric system as a unit of electrical current, the candela as a unit of luminous intensity, and the kelvin degree as a unit of temperature. The mole, a unit of amount of substance, was adopted by the General Conference in 1971. With the meter, kilogram, and liter, these units form the *Système International d'Unités*, universally abbreviated "SI." It is called by English-speaking peoples the *International System of Units*. Also significant at the 1960 General Conference was the redefinition of the meter as 1 650 763.73 wavelengths of the orange-red radiation of a krypton-86 atom. This definition allows a standard meter to be reproduced in any properly equipped physics laboratory.

It is ironic that the metric system, which is the most advanced system of measurement created by man, is still not generally employed in the United States, the most technologically developed nation of the world. As early as 1821, John Quincy Adams (1767–1848) had remarked to Congress on the consistency of the metric system. In 1866 the National Academy of Sciences urged its adoption. More than a century elapsed, however, before the matter was again seriously pursued by Congress. In 1968, by order of Congress, the Commerce Department undertook a three-year study to decide whether the United States should adopt the metric system. Released in 1971, the title of the study provided the answer: *A Metric America: A Decision Whose Time Has Come*. In his 1972 State of the Union address, President Richard Nixon urged Congress to pass a bill declaring that it be the national policy to convert to the metric system. The president felt that the metric system would "enhance our competitive position." It appears likely, therefore, that America will soon begin a ten-year conversion to the metric system, like Great Britain, which began such a program in 1965.

When the United States adopts the metric system of measurement, Americans will be faced with learning a new set of terms and working with units both smaller and larger than the familiar units they have used since childhood. A speed limit on a local highway may be 50 miles per hour now, but signs will soon appear warning drivers not to travel faster than the equivalent 80 *kilometers* per hour. By metric standards, a 150-pound person with a height of 5 feet 8 inches will weigh 70 *kilograms* and stand 172 *centimeters* tall. School children, during the lunch hour, will be served ½-*liter* cartons of milk instead of pint cartons. All these little things of life, which most persons seldom think about yet always need to know or use, will be affected by the changeover to the metric system. But this should not be disturbing, for the transition from the inch to the *centimeter*, from the foot to the *meter*, from the pound to the *kilogram*, etc. can be carried out smoothly—with preparation.

One fear that should be put to rest at once is that every man, woman, and child will be asked to immediately stop using the U.S. Customary System of measurements and begin using metric units. Congress has allowed for a ten-year conversion period, during which people will be educated about the metric system through posters, pamphlets, radio, and television. The changeover will proceed gradually, each individual working with metric units only as much as he wants or feels necessary. Government and private industry will set the pace, as new metric standards are fixed for such things as bottles, cartons, and cans. These will be marked, for most of the conversion period, as weighing so many pounds and ounces as well as so many kilograms and grams. Some measuring devices, the ruler and yardstick for example, are already often marked in metric units. Americans will not be asked to give up their scales, yardsticks, measuring tapes, or measuring spoons, and may keep using them throughout the ten-year conversion period until they are accustomed to metric units.

It is clear that the changeover to the metric system will have an enormous effect on the American economy, especially in the field of engineering. Many manufacturing firms will not want to replace expensive, working machinery with metric-designed machinery, and they should not be expected to do so. In fact, one of the good points of the proposed changeover is that private industry will not be forced to adopt metric units; rather, each entity's own readiness for the metric system will determine when and how it converts. In the manufacturing industries the general policy will probably be to begin using metric-designed equipment as the old equipment wears out.

The changeover will be simplified by the fact that many sectors of American society have already adopted the metric system. Film and camera equipment are made according to metric specifications. Long ago, the pharmaceutical industry stopped measuring drugs in drams, grains, and scruples, and is now using grams, milligrams, and milliliters. To service and repair the many foreign cars on American roads, automobile shops now have an array of metric-scaled tools. Almost all swimming pools are constructed according to metric standards, so that swimmers can train for international events. Scientists, of course, have been using the metric system for decades.

The use of metric measurements by Americans will greatly expand this country's overseas trade. Fully 90 percent of the world's population now uses the metric system, and as time passes, foreigners importing from the American market will be more apt to purchase merchandise measured in meters and grams than in feet and pounds.

Compared to the U.S. Customary System, the metric system is beautifully consistent and simple, and the American consumer will in time appreciate this simplicity when shopping for bargains in the supermarket. For example, when a consumer wishes to know whether to buy a 1 pound 3 ounce box of cereal for 89¢ or a 12-ounce box for 59¢, he must convert 1 pound 3 ounces to 19 ounces before he divides the prices of both boxes by their sizes and realizes that the larger box is the better buy. Such a tangle of arithmetic would be simplified by the metric system, since the sizes of the boxes will be given in units related by the power of ten. To find out whether a 600-gram box at 38¢ is a better buy than a 1.2-kilogram box of cereal at 69¢, the same shopper need only consider the 1.2-kilogram box to be a 1200-gram box, and then perform the divisions to realize that the larger box is the better buy.

The foregoing example illustrates the basic principle of the metric system: units are related by multiples and sub-multiples of ten. To show this relationship, Greek prefixes are assigned to the multiples of the base units, while Latin prefixes are assigned to the submultiples. For instance, 10 meters equal a dekameter, 100 meters equal a hectometer, and 1000 meters equal a kilometer. *Deka-* indicates multiplication by 10, *hecto-* by 100, and *kilo-* by 1000. The submultiples of the meter follow the same logical pattern. Ten decimeters equal a meter, as do 100 centimeters and 1000 millimeters. The Latin prefixes *deci*, *centi-*, and *milli-* indicate division by 10, 100, and 1000 respectively. Changing 27.19 inches to feet and inches is an involved mathematical problem in the U.S. Customary System of measurement. But changing 27.19 meters to centimeters requires only moving the decimal point two places to the right.

Considering how much the metric system will enter into the daily lives of Americans, the cost of the changeover for most individuals will be surprisingly low. Necessary items for the most part will include a meter stick, a scale showing weights in kilograms, a scale showing weights in grams, a set of cylinders for measuring liquids in liters and milliliters, a Celsius thermometer, and measuring cups. Two useful aids for the person seriously interested in mastering the metric system are a pocket-sized metric conversion card and a metric con-version handbook. However, rather than working with the old units and then converting them to metric equivalents, a better way to learn the metric system quickly and thoroughly would be to start thinking metric and using metric units.

Man has come a long way since the early Egyptian farmers measured their fields by walking so many paces. The French scientists of the eighteenth century were bold in daring to construct a new system of weights and measures, based on decimal relationships. The U.S. Commerce Department, in its study entitled *A Metric America: A Decision Whose Time Has Come*, states: "Eventually the United States will join the rest of the world in the use of the metric system as the pre-dominant common language of measurement." That prediction is yet to be fulfilled; but the time of the decision is close.

COUNTRIES CURRENTLY USING THE METRIC SYSTEM

Afghanistan	Congo, Republic of	Iceland	Mexico	Spain
Albania	Costa Rica	India	Monaco	Sudan
Algeria	Cuba	Indonesia	Mongolia	Swaziland
Andorra	Czechoslovakia	Iran	Morocco	Sweden
Argentina	Dahomey	Iraq	Netherlands	Switzerland
Austria	Denmark	Israel	Nicaragua	Syria
Bahamas	Dominican Republic	Italy	Niger	Thailand
Bahrain	Ecuador	Ivory Coast	Norway	Togo
Bangladesh	Egypt	Japan	Oman	Tunisia
Belgium	El Salvador	Jordan	Panama	Turkey
Bolivia	Ethiopia	Khmer Republic	Paraguay	Union of Arab
Brazil	Finland	Korea, North	Peru	Emirates
Bulgaria	France	Korea, South	Philippines	United Kingdom
Burundi	Gabon	Kuwait	Poland	Upper Volta
Cameroon	Germany, East	Laos	Portugal	Uruguay
Central African	Germany, West	Lebanon	Qatar	U.S.S.R.
Republic	Greece	Libya	Rhodesia	Venezuela
Chad	Guatemala	Liechtenstein	Rumania	Vietnam, North
Chile	Guinea	Luxembourg	Rwanda	Vietnam, South
China, People's	Guyana	Malagasy Republic	San Marino	Yugoslavia
Republic of	Haiti	Mali	Saudi Arabia	Zaire
China, Republic of	Honduras	Mauritania	Senegal	
Colombia	Hungary	Mauritius	Somali Republic	

COUNTRIES NOT CURRENTLY USING THE METRIC SYSTEM

Australia	Ireland	Malta	South Africa	Western Samoa
Barbados	Jamaica	Nauru	Sri Lanka	Yemen, People's
Botswana	Kenya	Nepal	Tanzania	Republic of
Burma	Lesotho	New Zealand	Tonga	Yemen Arab
Canada	Liberia	Nigeria	Trinidad and	Republic
Cyprus	Malawi	Pakistan	Tobago	Zambia
Gambia	Malaysia	Sierra Leone	Uganda	
Ghana	Maldive Islands	Singapore	United States	

DEFINITIONS OF METRIC UNITS

Originally, metric units were based on prototypes—physical objects which represented the exact quantity of each unit. The prototype meter was a metal bar with two lines etched in it to show the length of a meter, and the prototype kilogram was a metal cylinder whose mass acted as the standard for all kilograms.

As technology advanced, it became apparent that these standards were not precise enough for exact measurement. The prototype meter, even when stored in conditions of stable temperature and humidity,. would still expand and contract measurably. In addition, each country espousing the metric system needed its own prototype meters, so the difficult task of duplicating the original prototype as exactly as possible was undertaken.

The prototype problem was resolved in 1960 by the Eleventh General (International) Conference on Weights and Measures. The conference endeavored to define the meter not only in terms that were utterly precise, but also in such a way that the exact meter length could be duplicated easily anywhere in the world. Because of these criteria, the definition of a meter could not be based on a physical object, so the conference defined it as a specific number of wavelengths of the radiation from the element krypton. Not only is this measure precise enough to satisfy all scientific requirements, but it can also be duplicated in any properly equipped physics laboratory in the world.

Today the krypton-wavelength meter is the basis of all linear measurements in the metric system. The only unit in the metric system still based on a physical object is the kilogram, the prototype of which is located in a subterranean vault under the International Bureau of Weights and Measures in Sèvres, France. This prototype is a platinum-iridium cylinder, about 39 millimeters in diameter. Many copies of this prototype have been made, and each copy is numbered and has a certificate of authentication. The United States possesses two of these prototypes—numbers 4 and 20.

THE SEVEN BASE UNITS

Meter (m): The base unit of length. Equal to 1 650 763.73 wavelengths of the orange-red radiation corresponding to the transition between the levels $2p_{10}$ and $5d_5$ of the krypton-86 atom, taken in a vacuum.

Kilogram (kg): The base unit of mass. Equal to the mass of the International Prototype Kilogram, kept by the International Bureau of Weights and Measures in Sèvres, France.

Second (s): The base unit of time. Equal to the 9 192 631 770 periods of the radiation corresponding to the transition between the two hyperfine levels of the ground state of the cesium-133 atom.

Ampere (A): The base unit of electric current. Equal to the amount of current which, if maintained in two straight parallel conductors of infinite length, of negligible circular cross section, and placed 1 meter apart in vacuum, would produce between these conductors a force equal to 2×10^{-7} newton per meter of length.

Kelvin (K): The base unit of temperature. Equal to the fraction 1/273.16 of the thermodynamic temperature of the triple point of water, and starting at absolute zero ($-273.16°C$) and advancing at increments equal to those used in the Celsius (centrigrade) scale.

Mole (mol): The base unit of amount of substance. Equal to the amount of substance of a system that contains as many elementary entities as there are atoms in 0.012 kilogram of carbon-12.

Candela (cd): The base unit of light intensity. Equal to the intensity of 1/600 000 square meter of a blackbody radiator at the temperature of the solidification of platinum (2045°K) under a pressure of 101 325 newtons per square meter.

THE TWO SUPPLEMENTARY UNITS

Radian (rad): The base unit of the plane angle. Equal to a plane angle with its vertex at the center of a circle that is subtended by an arc equal in length to the radius.

Steradian (sr): The base unit of the solid angle. Equal to a solid angle with its vertex at the center of a sphere that is subtended by an area of the spherical surface equal to that of a square with sides equal in length to the radius.

METRIC PREFIXES

The three most commonly used quantities of the metric system are the meter, the gram, and the liter. Prefixes, based on the power of 10, provide multiples and submultiples when added to these units. For example, *kilometer* means meter times 10^3, or 1000 meters; and *centimeter* means meter times 10^{-2}, or $\frac{1}{100}$ meter. (For an explanation of scientific notation, see "Conversion Factors," page 17.) In the chart below, symbols are listed in parentheses.

Submultiples				Basic Units			Multiples
deci-	(d)	10^{-1}	.1	meter	10	10^1	(da) deka-
centi-	(c)	10^{-2}	.01		100	10^2	(h) hecto-
milli-	(m)	10^{-3}	.001	gram	1 000	10^3	(k) kilo-
micro-	(μ)	10^{-6}	.000 001		1 000 000	10^6	(M) mega-
nano-	(n)	10^{-9}	.000 000 001	liter	1 000 000 000	10^9	(G) giga-
pico-	(p)	10^{-12}	.000 000 000 001		1 000 000 000 000	10^{12}	(T) tera-

PRONUNCIATIONS OF METRIC UNITS AND PREFIXES

ampere /am′pēr/
candela /kan·dē′lə/
centi- /sen′tə/
centimeter /sen′tə·mē″tər/
deci- /des′ə/
deka- /dek′ə/

giga- /jī′gə/
hecto- /hek′tə/
kelvin /kel′vin/
kilo- /kil′ə/
kilogram /kil′ə·gram″/
kilometer /ki·lom′i·tər/

mega- /meg′ə/
meter /mē′tər/
micro- /mī′krə/
milli- /mil′ə/
millimeter /mil′ə·mē″tər/
mole /mōl/

nano- /nā′nə/
pico- /pī′kə/
radian /rā′dē·ən/
second /sek′ənd/
steradian /stə·rā′dē·ən/
tera- /ter′ə/

SOME DERIVED METRIC UNITS

There are seven base units (ampere, candela, kelvin, kilogram, meter, mole, and second) and two supplementary units (radian and steradian) which can be considered to be the fundamental units of the metric system. These units are adequate for most nonscientific measurements, but the metric system has also incorporated many units of specific quantities used in scientific work. These additional units are derived from the base metric units.

Quantity	Unit	Symbol	Derivation
acceleration	meter per second squared	m/s^2	
angular acceleration	radian per second squared	rad/s^2	
angular velocity	radian per second	rad/s	
area	square meter	m^2	
density	kilogram per cubic meter	kg/m^3	
dynamic viscosity	newton-second per square meter	$N \cdot s/m^2$	
electric capacitance	farad	F	$A \cdot s/V$
electric charge	coulomb	C	$A \cdot s$
electric field strength	volt per meter	V/m	
electric resistance	ohm	Ω	V/A
flux of light	lumen	lm	$cd \cdot sr$
force	newton	N	$kg \cdot m/s^2$
frequency	hertz	Hz	s^{-1}
illumination	lux	lx	lm/m^2
inductance	henry	H	$V \cdot s/A$
kinematic viscosity	square meter per second	m^2/s	
luminance	candela per square meter	cd/m^2	
magnetic field strength	ampere per meter	A/m	
magnetic flux	weber	Wb	$V \cdot s$
magnetic flux density	tesla	T	Wb/m^2
magnetomotive force	ampere	A	
power	watt	W	J/s
pressure	newton per square meter	N/m^2	
velocity	meter per second	m/s	
voltage, potential difference, electromotive force	volt	V	W/A
volume	cubic meter	m^3	
work, energy, quantity of heat	joule	J	$N \cdot m$

CAPSULE PRONUNCIATION KEY: *fat, fāte, met, mē, mēre, pin, pīne, not, nōte.* The schwa symbol, ə, respresents the sound of *a* in *ago, e* in *happen, i* in *fossil, o* in *collect,* and *u* in *virus.*

METRIC AND U.S. CUSTOMARY SYMBOLS

Unit	Symbol	Unit	Symbol	Unit	Symbol	Unit	Symbol
acre	a	cup	c	inch	in	pint	pt
ampere	A	decigram	dg	kelvin, degree	°K	pound	lb
barrel	bbl	deciliter	dl	kilogram	kg	quart	qt
bushel	bu	decimeter	dm	kiloliter	kl	radian	rad
candela	cd	dekagram	dag	kilometer	km	second	s
Celsius, degree	°C	dekaliter	dal	liter	l	square centimeter	cm²
centare	ca	dekameter	dam	meter	m	square decimeter	dm²
centigram	cg	dram, avdp	dr avdp	microgram	μg	square dekameter	dam²
centiliter	cl	Fahrenheit, degree	°F	microliter	μl	square foot	ft²
centimeter	cm	fluid ounce	fl oz	micron	μ	square hectometer	hm²
cubic centimeter	cm³	foot	ft	mile	mi	square inch	in²
cubic decimeter	dm³	gallon	gal	milligram	mg	square kilometer	km²
cubic dekameter	dam³	grain	gr	milliliter	ml	square meter	m²
cubic foot	ft³	gram	g	millimeter	mm	square mile	mi²
cubic hectometer	hm³	hectare	ha	minute	min	square millimeter	mm²
cubic inch	in³	hectogram	hg	mole	mol	square yard	yd²
cubic kilometer	km³	hectoliter	hl	ounce	oz	steradian	sr
cubic mile	mi³	hectometer	hm	ounce, avdp	oz avdp	tablespoon	tbsp
cubic millimeter	mm³	hour	hr	ounce, troy	oz tr	teaspoon	tsp
cubic yard	yd³	hundredweight	cwt	peck	pk	yard	yd

COMPARISON OF METRIC UNITS WITH U.S. CUSTOMARY UNITS

Since there is no obvious similarity between the metric system units and the United States Customary System units, it is sometimes confusing, when converting from one system to the other, to decide which units are roughly equivalent. The intrinsic simplicity of the metric system makes this a fairly easy problem to solve.

The metric system reserves one unit for each quantity: length in meters; volume in cubic meters; capacity in liters; weight in grams. Therefore, all quantities can be expressed by using one of these units or a division of one of these units (see list of prefixes on page 11). When compared to the metric system, the quantities in the United States Customary System are illogical and disorganized: length in inches, feet, yards, or miles; area in square inches, square feet, square yards, acres, or square miles; volume in cubic inches, cubic feet, or cubic yards; capacity in fluid ounces, pints, quarts, pecks, bushels, or gallons; weight in grains, ounces, pounds, or tons.

The chart below lists both the most common United States Customary units and the most common metric quantities. A complete list of all metric units is on page 10. Conversion factors for all these units begin on page 17, and an explanation of metric cooking terms is on page 14.

U.S. Customary	Metric Equivalent		Metric	U.S. Equivalent
inch	2.54 cm	length	centimeter	.3937 in
foot	30.48 cm		meter	39.37 in
yard	.9144 m		kilometer	.6214 mi
rod	5.029 m			
mile, statute	1.609 km			
mile, nautical	1.853 km			
dram	1.7718 g	mass	gram	.0353 oz
ounce	28.3495 g		kilogram	2.205 lbs
pound	.4536 kg			
ton	907.1848 kg			
cubic inch	16.39 c³	volume	cubic centimeter	.0621 in³
cubic foot	28.32 l		cubic meter	1.308 yd³
cubic yard	764.6 l			
gallon	3.785 l	liquid capacity	liter	1.057 qts
quart	.9463 l			
pint	.4732 l			
fluid ounce	29.57 c³			
fluid dram	3.69 c³			
pint	.5507 dm³	dry capacity	cubic decimeter	.9079 qt
quart	1.1014 dm³			
peck	8.809 dm³			
bushel	35.238 dm³			
square inch	6.452 cm²	area	square centimeter	.1550 in²
square foot	.0929 m²		square meter	10.76 ft²
square yard	.8361 m²		hectare	2.471 a
acre	.4047 ha			
square mile	259.008 ha			
miles per hour	1.609 km/hr	velocity	kilometers per hour	.6214 mph

TEMPERATURE EQUIVALENTS

The United States Customary System of Measurement employs the Fahrenheit scale in temperature measurement. In this scale, the freezing point of water is 32° and the boiling point of water is 212°. This differs significantly from temperature measurement in the metric system, which uses the Kelvin and Celsius (formerly Centigrade) scales. In both of these metric scales, the graduations are exactly the same, but zero in the Kelvin system is at absolute zero (−273.16°C) while zero in the Celsius scale is at the freezing point of water. The formulas below show how to compute temperature equivalents in all three systems.

COMPARISON OF FAHRENHEIT AND CELSIUS

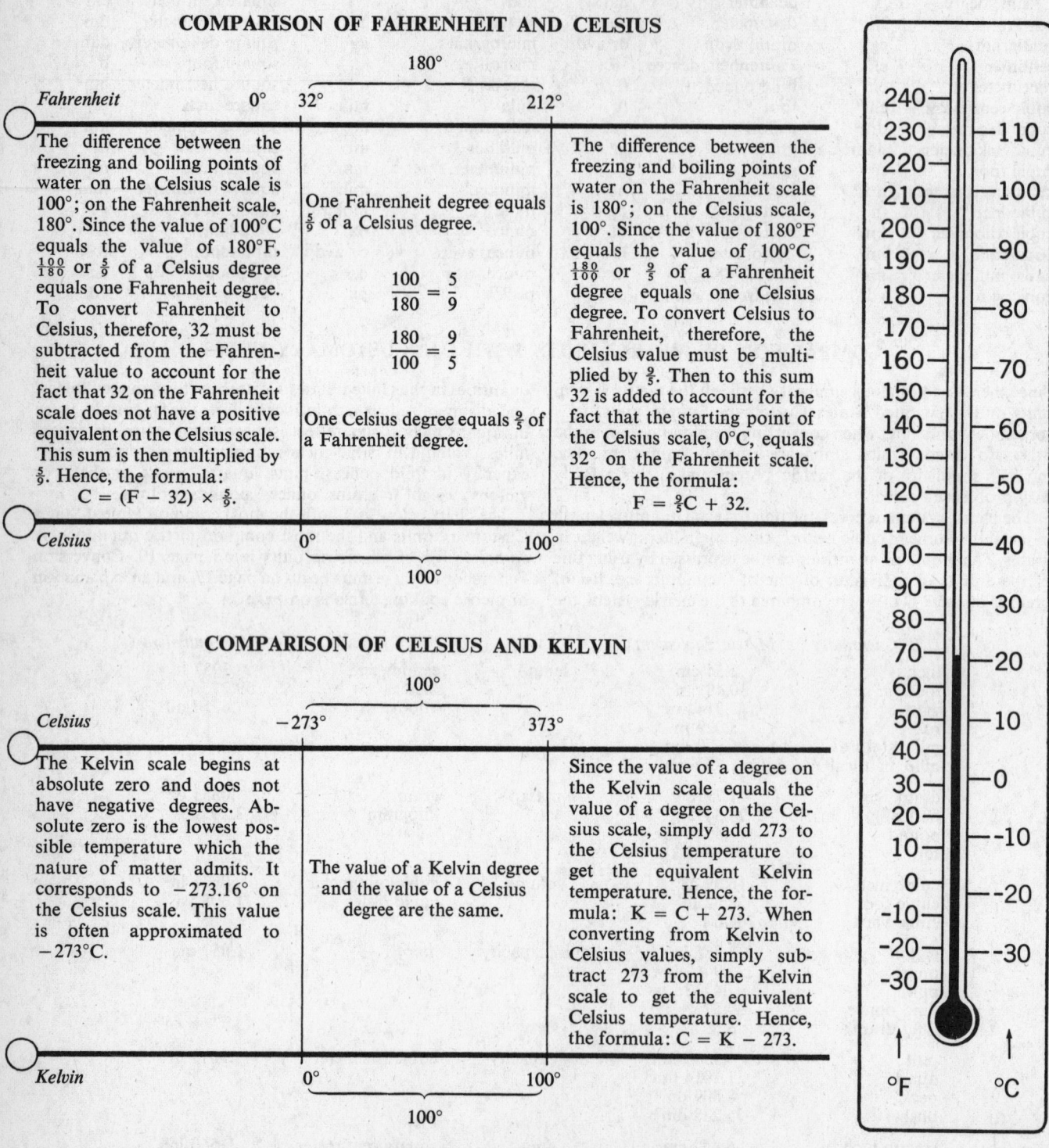

Fahrenheit · 0° · 32° · 180° · 212°

The difference between the freezing and boiling points of water on the Celsius scale is 100°; on the Fahrenheit scale, 180°. Since the value of 100°C equals the value of 180°F, $\frac{100}{180}$ or $\frac{5}{9}$ of a Celsius degree equals one Fahrenheit degree. To convert Fahrenheit to Celsius, therefore, 32 must be subtracted from the Fahrenheit value to account for the fact that 32 on the Fahrenheit scale does not have a positive equivalent on the Celsius scale. This sum is then multiplied by $\frac{5}{9}$. Hence, the formula:
$$C = (F - 32) \times \tfrac{5}{9}.$$

One Fahrenheit degree equals $\frac{5}{9}$ of a Celsius degree.

$$\frac{100}{180} = \frac{5}{9}$$

$$\frac{180}{100} = \frac{9}{5}$$

One Celsius degree equals $\frac{9}{5}$ of a Fahrenheit degree.

The difference between the freezing and boiling points of water on the Fahrenheit scale is 180°; on the Celsius scale, 100°. Since the value of 180°F equals the value of 100°C, $\frac{180}{100}$ or $\frac{9}{5}$ of a Fahrenheit degree equals one Celsius degree. To convert Celsius to Fahrenheit, therefore, the Celsius value must be multiplied by $\frac{9}{5}$. Then to this sum 32 is added to account for the fact that the starting point of the Celsius scale, 0°C, equals 32° on the Fahrenheit scale. Hence, the formula:
$$F = \tfrac{9}{5}C + 32.$$

Celsius · 0° · 100° · 100°

COMPARISON OF CELSIUS AND KELVIN

Celsius · −273° · 100° · 373°

The Kelvin scale begins at absolute zero and does not have negative degrees. Absolute zero is the lowest possible temperature which the nature of matter admits. It corresponds to −273.16° on the Celsius scale. This value is often approximated to −273°C.

The value of a Kelvin degree and the value of a Celsius degree are the same.

Since the value of a degree on the Kelvin scale equals the value of a degree on the Celsius scale, simply add 273 to the Celsius temperature to get the equivalent Kelvin temperature. Hence, the formula: $K = C + 273$. When converting from Kelvin to Celsius values, simply subtract 273 from the Kelvin scale to get the equivalent Celsius temperature. Hence, the formula: $C = K - 273$.

Kelvin · 0° · 100° · 100°

TABLE OF CONVERSION FORMULAS

Fahrenheit to Celsius $C = \frac{5}{9}(F - 32)$ Kelvin to Celsius $C = K - 273$ Celsius to Fahrenheit $F = (\frac{9}{5}C) + 32$

Fahrenheit to Kelvin $K = \frac{5}{9}(F - 32) + 273$ Kelvin to Fahrenheit $F = \frac{9}{5}(K - 273) + 32$ Celsius to Kelvin $K = C + 273$

METRIC QUANTITIES USED IN COOKING

It is thought that when the United States adopts the metric system cooks will be forced to give up many kitchen utensils, such as measuring spoons and cups, pint- and quart-sized jars and pitchers, 9-inch pie and cake pans, and the Fahrenheit cooking thermometer. But the actual changeover to the metric system will be quite simple.

To cook the metric way, all that needs to be purchased for use in the kitchen are a Celsius thermometer, a scale with readings in grams and kilograms, and a cylinder or set of cylinders for measuring in milliliters and liters rather than cups, quarts, and fluid ounces. During the ten-year conversion period, both metric utensils and the more familiar U.S. Customary utensils will be used side by side. New cookbooks will gradually begin using metric measurements, but almost every cookbook will also provide U.S. Customary measurements. As people become accustomed to cooking the metric way they will be in less need of nonmetric measuring utensils, but they may continue to use them. The charts below are designed to help those cooks who wish to continue using U.S. Customary measurements and for those who, in the early stages of the metric conversion period, are still uncertain of metric quantities used in cooking and want to know what the equivalent U.S. Customary measurement is.

United States Cooking Measurements

3 teaspoons	=	1 tablespoon
2 tablespoons	=	1 fluid ounce
8 fluid ounces	=	1 cup
2 cups	=	1 pint
2 pints	=	1 quart
4 quarts	=	1 gallon
2 gallons	=	1 peck
4 pecks	=	1 bushel
16 ounces avdp	=	1 pound avdp
12 inches	=	1 foot

United States Measure	Approximate Metric Measure
teaspoon (tsp)	5 milliliters
tablespoon (tbsp)	15 milliliters
fluid ounce (fl oz)	30 milliliters
cup (c)	.24 liter
pint (pt)	.47 liter
quart (qt)	.95 liter
gallon (gal)	3.80 liters
peck (pk)	8.80 liters
bushel (bu)	35.24 liters
ounce avdp (oz avdp)	28 grams
pound avdp (lb avdp)	.45 kilogram
inch (in)	2.54 centimeters

Teaspoons	Milliliters
1	4.929
2	9.858
3	14.787

Tablespoons	Milliliters
1	14.787
2	29.574

Fluid Ounces	Milliliters	Milliliters	Fluid Ounces
1	29.574	1	.033 81
2	59.148	2	.067 62
3	88.722	3	.101 43
4	118.296	4	.135 24
5	147.87	5	.169 05
6	177.444	6	.202 86
7	207.018	7	.236 67
8	236.592	8	.270 48
9	266.166	9	.304 29
10	295.74	10	.3381
11	325.314		
12	354.888		
13	384.462		
14	414.036		
15	443.61		
16	473.184		

Cups	Liters	Liters	Cups
1	.2366	1	1.0565
2	.4732	2	2.113
3	.7098	3	3.1695
4	.9464	4	4.226
5	1.183	5	5.2825

Pints	Liters	Liters	Pints
1	.4732	1	2.113
2	.9464	2	4.226
3	1.4196	3	6.339
4	1.8928	4	8.452
5	2.366	5	10.565

Quarts	Liters	Liters	Quarts
1	.9463	1	1.057
2	1.8926	2	2.114
3	2.8389	3	3.171
4	3.7852	4	4.228
5	4.7315	1	5.285
6	5.6778	6	6.346
7	6.6241	7	7.399
8	7.5704	8	8.456
9	8.5167	9	9.513
10	9.463	10	10.57

Gallons	Liters		Liters	Gallons
1	3.7854		1	.264 17
2	7.5408		2	.528 34
3	11.3562		3	.792 51
4	15.1416		4	1.056 68
5	18.927		5	1.320 85
6	22.7124		6	1.585 02
7	26.4678		7	1.849 19
8	30.2832		8	2.113 36
9	34.0686		9	2.377 53
10	37.854		10	2.6417

Pecks	Liters
1	8.809 582
2	17.619 164
3	26.428 746
4	35.238 328

Bushels	Liters
1	35.24

Ounces	Grams		Grams	Ounces
1	28.349 527		1	.035 27
2	56.699 054		2	.070 54
3	85.048 581		3	.105 81
4	113.3981		4	.141 08
5	141.747 63		5	.176 35
6	170.097 16		6	.211 62
7	198.446 68		7	.246 89
8	226.7962		8	.282 16
9	255.145 74		9	.317 43
10	283.495 27		10	.3527
11	311.814 79			
12	340.194 32			
13	368.513 84			
14	396.893 36			
15	425.242 89			
16	453.5924			

Pounds	Kilograms		Kilograms	Pounds
1	.4536		1	2.205
2	.9072		2	4.41
3	1.3608		3	6.615
4	1.8144		4	8.82

(Continued from previous column)

Pounds	Kilograms		Kilograms	Pounds
5	2.268		5	11.025
6	2.7216		6	13.23
7	3.1752		7	15.435
8	3.6288		8	17.64
9	4.0824		9	19.845
10	4.536		10	22.05

Pounds	Grams
$\frac{1}{4}$	113.3981
$\frac{1}{2}$	226.7962
$\frac{3}{4}$	340.1943
1	453.5924
2	907.1848
3	1360.7772
4	1814.3696
5	2267.962
6	2721.5544
7	3175.1468
8	3628.7392
9	4082.3316
10	4535.924

Inches	Centimeters		Centimeters	Inches
1	2.54		1	.3937
2	5.08		2	.7874
3	7.62		3	1.1811
4	10.16		4	1.5748
5	12.7		5	1.9685
6	15.24		6	2.3622
7	17.78		7	2.7559
8	20.32		8	3.1496
9	22.86		9	3.5433
10	25.4		10	3.937
11	27.94		20	7.847
12	30.48		30	11.811
18	45.72		40	15.748
24	60.96		50	19.685
30	76.2		60	23.622
36	91.44		70	27.559
			80	31.496
			90	35.433
			100	39.37

OVEN TEMPERATURES

Fahrenheit	Celsius	Fahrenheit	Celsius	Oven Temperature Terms	Fahrenheit	Celsius
200	93	375	191	Very Slow	250–275	121–135
225	107	400	204	Slow	300–325	149–163
250	121	425	218	Moderate	350–375	177–191
275	135	450	232	Hot	400–425	204–218
300	149	475	246	Very Hot	450–475	232–246
325	163	500	260	Extremely Hot (Broil)	500–525	260–274
350	177	525	274			

SPECIAL LOCAL UNITS

For the world traveler and tourist, the special measurements of each nation can often cause awkward problems, especially in those small neighborhood pubs, shops, and restaurants which the tourist so often seeks out to avoid the rush of the city. Even though the metric system has been adopted by all European countries and most other nations of the world people cling to the familiar: Austrians still order a *seidel* of beer, Chinese measure distances by the *li* as well as the kilometer, French-Canadians speak of *pieds* and *pouces*, and Americans will probably eat foot-long hot dogs at fairs and picnics long after the United States adopts the metric system. In short, the traditional units of measurement continue to be used side by side with the metric system.

These traditional units of measurement are often as hard for the tourist to unravel as the metric system is easy to understand. Most English-speaking persons know that sixteen ounces equal a pound and that thirty-six inches equal a yard, but few realize the length of a Greek *pecheus*, the capacity of a Malaysian *chupak*, or the weight of a Polish *funt*. Nor can Greeks, Malaysians, or Poles be expected to know how the English system of measurement works. It is not necessary for the tourist to know all the special local units of each country he visits. Rather, a working knowledge of the basic units he will most likely encounter would prove helpful and convenient. Such is the purpose of the list below: to acquaint the world traveler, tourist, student, or person generally interested in systems of measurement with a few special local units he might one day need to know.

Certain units should be noted. The pound, for example, is common to most European countries, being called a *zollpfund* in Germany, a *pond* in the Netherlands, a *pund* in Norway, a *funt* in Poland, and a *founte* or *funt* in the Soviet Union. The word ultimately derives from the Latin *pondus*, meaning weight. Examples of other measures shared by many countries are the ounce, the *livre*, and the foot. The *catty*, variously called *gin*, *kin*, *kon*, or *kati*, is found in most Far Eastern countries. Some nations, such as Turkey and the Netherlands, have adopted the metric system, but assigned traditional names to the metric units. In the list, each unit is followed by its equivalent in both metric and U.S. Customary units.

Argentina
frasco: 2.38 liters (2.42 quarts)
libra: .46 kilogram (1.01 pounds)
Austria
seidel: .35 liter (.74 pint)
Belgium
aune: 1 meter (39.37 inches)
livre: 1 kilogram (2.21 pounds)
pied: 30 centimeters (11.81 inches)
pot: 1.5 liters (1.58 quarts)
Canada
arpent (Quebec): 58.52 meters (192 feet)
perche (Quebec): 5.85 meters (19.20 feet)
pied (Quebec): 32.48 centimeters (12.79 inches)
China
ch'ih: 35.81 centimeters (14.10 inches)
chin, or catty: .61 kilogram (1⅓ pounds)
li: 536.45 meters (.33 mile)
pu: 1.79 meters (70.47 inches)
t'sun: 3.58 centimeters (1.41 inches)
Denmark
fod: .31 meter (12.20 inches)
pot: .97 liter (1.03 quarts)
Egypt
diraa, or pik: .58 meter (22.83 inches)
keddah: 2.06 liters (2.18 quarts)
oke: 1.25 kilograms (2.75 pounds)
France
aune: 1.19 meters (46.85 inches)
brasse: 1.62 meters (72.78 inches)
livre: .49 kilogram (1.08 pounds)
once: 30.59 grams (1.07 ounces)
pinte: .93 liter (.98 quart)
pouce: 27.07 millimeters (1.07 inches)
Germany
schoppen: .5 liter (.53 quart)
stab: 1 meter (39.37 inches)
zollpfund: .5 kilogram (1.10 pounds)
Great Britain
foot: 30.48 centimeters (1 U.S. foot)
inch: 2.54 centimeters (1 U.S. inch)
mile, statute: 1.61 kilometers (1 U.S. statute mile)
ounce, avdp.: 28.35 grams (1 U.S. ounce, avdp.)

ounce, fluid: 28.42 cubic centimeters (.96 U.S. fluid ounce)
pint, fluid: .57 liter (1.20 U.S. fluid pints)
pound, avdp.: .45 kilogram (1 U.S. pound, avdp.)
quart, fluid: 1.14 liters (1.20 U.S. fluid quarts)
yard: .91 meter (1 U.S. yard)
Greece
mna: 1.5 kilograms (3.31 pounds)
pecheus: .65 meter (25.51 inches)
India
coss: 1.83 kilometers (1.14 miles)
hat'h, or moolum: 45.72 centimeters (18 inches)
seer: .93 kilogram (2.06 pounds)
Italy
denaro: 1 gram (15.43 grains)
dito: 1 centimeter (.39 inch)
libbra: 1 kilogram (2.21 pounds)
Japan
bu, or tsubo: .3 centimeter (.12 inch)
kin: .60 kilogram (1⅓ pounds)
ri: 3.92 kilometers (2.44 miles)
shaku: .30 meter (11.92 inches)
shô: 1.80 liters (1.91 quarts)
Korea
kon, or catty: .61 kilogram (1⅓ pounds)
Malaysia
chupak: 1.14 liters (1.20 quarts)
gantang: 4.55 liters (4.81 quarts)
kati, or gin: .61 kilogram (1⅓ pounds)
Mexico
libra: .46 kilogram (1.01 pounds)
Netherlands
duim: 2.54 centimeters (1 inch)
el: 1 meter (39.37 inches)
kan: 1 liter (1.06 quarts)
pond: .5 kilogram (1.10 pounds)
wichtje: 1 gram (15.43 grains)
Norway
fot: .31 meter (12.35 inches)
pot: .97 liter (1.02 quarts)
pund: .5 kilogram (1.10 pounds)
Poland
funt: .41 kilogram (.89 pound)
kwarta: 1 liter (1.06 quarts)
stopa: .29 meter (11.34 inches)

Portugal
estadio: 258 meters (.15 mile)
libra, or arratel: .46 kilogram (1.01 pounds)
polegada: 27.77 millimeters (1.09 inches)
vara: 1.10 meters (43.31 inches)
South Africa
foot: 31.38 centimeters (12.36 inches)
Spain
libra: .46 kilogram (1.01 pounds)
pie: 28 centimeters (10.97 inches)
pulgada: 23 millimeters (.91 inch)
Sweden
fot: 29.69 centimeters (11.69 inches)
kanne, or kanna: 2.62 liters (2.77 quarts)
pund, or skaal-pund: .43 kilogram (.94 pound)
Switzerland
fusz: 1 meter (39.37 inches)
pfund: .5 kilogram (1.10 pounds)
pot: 1.5 liters (1.58 quarts)
schoppen: .38 liter (.40 quart)
zoll: 3 centimeters (1.18 inches)
Thailand
catty: 1.21 kilograms (2.67 pounds)
thanan, or fanan: 1 liter (1.06 quarts)
Turkey
archin: 1 meter (39.37 inches)
khat: 1 centimeter (.39 inches)
ock: 1 kilogram (2.21 pounds)
Union of Soviet Socialist Republics
duim: 2.54 centimeters (1 inch)
founte, or funt: .41 kilogram (.90 pound)
foute, or fut: 30.48 centimeters (1 foot)
versta, or verst: 1.07 kilometers (.66 mile)
United States
foot: 30.48 centimeters
inch: 2.54 centimeters
mile, statute: 1.61 kilometers
ounce, avdp.: 28.35 grams
ounce, fluid: .03 liter
pint, fluid: .47 liter
pound, avdp.: .45 kilogram
quart, fluid: .94 liter
yard: .91 meter

METRIC CONVERSION FACTORS

All of the conversion factors in this table are given to at least four decimal places and some are given to six decimal places. This will give a degree of accuracy of at least 99 percent in all conversions, which is adequate for all but the most precise mathematical computations.

All measurement units are listed alphabetically on the left-hand side of the following columns. To use the tables, first locate the unit in the left column, then locate the alternate unit in the middle column and multiply the first unit by the factor in the right column. For example, to convert 12 inches to centimeters, find inches in the *To Convert* column and centimeters in the *Into* column. The conversion factor, listed in the *Multiply by* column, is 2.540, so 12 inches equals 30.48 centimeters (12 × 2.540 = 30.48).

Note: Unless otherwise indicated, the units of measure listed below are U.S. Customary units.

Scientific notation is easy to use and easy to understand. Just as 10^2 is 10 × 10 (100) and 10^3 is 10 × 10 × 10 (1000), so also 10^5 is 10 × 10 × 10 × 10 × 10 (100 000), and so on. 10^1 is simply 10, and 10^0 is by definition 1. These multiples of 10 are called *positive exponents*.

Working with submultiples of 10 can be easy, too. 10^{-1} is simply .1, or one tenth. Just as 10^{-2} is .1 × .1 (.01) and 10^{-3} is .1 × .1 × .1 (.001), so also 10^{-5} is .1 × .1 × .1 × .1 × .1 (.00 001), and so on. These submultiples of 10 are called *negative exponents*.

When beginning to work with positive and negative exponents, perhaps the surest way to know what is happening is to count out the decimal places. The chart below illustrates the process for the numbers 2.9 and 8.1.

$2.9 = 2.9 \times 10^0$	When multiplying a number by 10^x, where x is a *positive* number,	$8.1 \times 10^0 = 8.1$
$29.0 = 2.9 \times 10^1$	move the decimal point to the *right* x number of places. For	$8.1 \times 10^{-1} = 0.81$
$290.0 = 2.9 \times 10^2$	example, 2.9×10^2 has the decimal	$8.1 \times 10^{-2} = 0.081$
$2\,900.0 = 2.9 \times 10^3$	point moved 2 places to the right, equaling 290.	$8.1 \times 10^{-3} = 0.008\,1$
$29\,000.0 = 2.9 \times 10^4$	When multiplying a number by 10^x, where x is a *negative* number,	$8.1 \times 10^{-4} = 0.000\,81$
$290\,000.0 = 2.9 \times 10^5$	move the decimal point to the *left* x number of places. For example,	$8.1 \times 10^{-5} = 0.000\,081$
$2\,900\,000.0 = 2.9 \times 10^6$	8.1×10^{-2} has the decimal point moved 2 places to the left, equaling .081.	$8.1 \times 10^{-6} = 0.000\,008\,1$

To Convert	Into	Multiply by
A		
acre	hectare	0.4047
acre	sq meter	4047.0
ampere-hr	coulomb	3600.0
ampere-hr	faraday	0.037 51
angstrom unit	meter	1×10^{-10}
angstrom unit	micron	1×10^{-4}
astronomical unit	km	1.495×10^8
atmosphere	cm of mercury	76.0
atmosphere	dyne/sq cm	1.0133×10^6
atmosphere	kg/sq cm	1.0333
atmosphere	kg/sq meter	10 332.0
B		
bar	dyne/sq cm	1×10^6
bar	kg/sq meter	1.020×10^4
Btu	erg	1.0550×10^{10}
Btu	gram-calorie	252.0
Btu	gram-cm	1.0756×10^7
Btu	horsepower-hr	3.931×10^{-4}
Btu	joule	1054.8
Btu	kg-calorie	0.2520
Btu	kg-meter	107.5
Btu	kilowatt-hr	2.928×10^{-4}
Btu	watt-hr	0.292 99

To Convert	Into	Multiply by
Btu/hr	gram-calorie/sec	0.0700
Btu/hr	horsepower-hr	3.926×10^{-4}
Btu/hr	watt	0.2931
Btu/min	horsepower	0.023 56
Btu/min	kilowatt	0.017 57
Btu/min	watt	17.57
bushel (dry)	cu meter	0.035 24
bushel (dry)	liter	35.24
C		
candle/sq cm	lambert	3.142
centare	sq meter	1.0
centigram	gram	0.01
centiliter	cu inch	0.6103
centiliter	dram	2.705
centiliter	liter	0.01
centiliter	ounce (liq.)	0.3382
centimeter	ell	8.7489×10^{-3}
centimeter	em, pica	2.3624
centimeter	foot	3.281×10^{-2}
centimeter	hand	0.9843
centimeter	inch	0.3937
centimeter	km	1×10^{-5}
centimeter	meter	0.01
centimeter	mil	393.7

To Convert	Into	Multiply by
centimeter	mile	6.214×10^{-6}
centimeter	mm	10.0
centimeter	yard	1.094×10^{-2}
cm of mercury	atmosphere	0.013 16
cm of mercury	foot of water	0.4461
cm of mercury	kg/sq meter	136.0
cm of mercury	pound/sq foot	27.85
cm of mercury	pound/sq inch	0.1934
cm/sec	foot/min	1.1969
cm/sec	foot/sec	0.032 81
cm/sec	km/hr	0.036
cm/sec	knot	0.1943
cm/sec	meter/min	0.6
cm/sec	mile/hr	0.022 37
cm/sec	mile/min	3.728×10^{-4}
cm/sec/sec	foot/sec/sec	0.032 81
cm/sec/sec	km/hr/sec	0.036
cm/sec/sec	meter/sec/sec	0.01
cm/sec/sec	mile/hr/sec	0.022 37
cm-dyne	cm-gram	1.020×10^{-3}
cm-dyne	meter-kg	1.020×10^{-8}
cm-dyne	pound-foot	7.376×10^{-8}
cm-gram	cm-dyne	980.7
cm-gram	meter-kg	1×10^{-5}
cm-gram	pound-foot	7.233×10^{-5}
chain	meter	20.12
circular mil	sq cm	5.067×10^{-6}
circular mil	sq inch	7.854×10^{7}
circular mil	sq mil	0.7854
circumference	radian	6.283
coulomb	ampere-hr	2.7777×10^{-4}
coulomb	faraday	1.036×10^{-5}
coulomb/sq cm	coulomb/sq inch	64.52
coulomb/sq cm	coulomb/sq meter	1×10^{4}
coulomb/sq inch	coulomb/sq cm	0.1550
coulomb/sq inch	coulomb/sq meter	1550.0
coulomb/sq meter	coulomb/sq cm	1×10^{-4}
coulomb/sq meter	coulomb/sq inch	6.452×10^{-4}
cu centimeter	cu foot	3.531×10^{-5}
cu centimeter	cu inch	0.061 02
cu centimeter	cu meter	1×10^{-6}
cu centimeter	cu yard	1.308×10^{-6}
cu centimeter	dram (liq.)	0.2705
cu centimeter	gallon (liq.)	2.642×10^{-4}
cu centimeter	liter	0.001
cu centimeter	minim (liq.)	16.2306
cu centimeter	pint (liq.)	2.113×10^{-3}
cu centimeter	quart (liq.)	1.057×10^{-3}
cu cm/sec	cu foot/min	2.1186×10^{-3}
cu foot	cu cm	28 320.0
cu foot	cu meter	0.028 32
cu foot	liter	28.32
cu foot/min	cu cm/sec	472.0
cu foot/min	liter/sec	0.4720
cu foot/sec	liter/min	1.6989×10^{3}
cu inch	cl	1.6385
cu inch	cu cm	16.39
cu inch	cu meter	1.639×10^{-5}
cu inch	liter	0.016 39
cu meter	bushel (dry)	28.38
cu meter	cu cm	1×10^{6}
cu meter	cu foot	35.31
cu meter	cu inch	61 023.0
cu meter	cu yard	1.308
cu meter	gallon (liq.)	264.2
cu meter	liter	1000.0
cu meter	pint (liq.)	2113.0
cu meter	quart (liq.)	1057.0
cu yard	cu cm	7.646×10^{5}
cu yard	cu meter	0.7646
cu yard	liter	764.6
cu yard/min	liter/sec	12.74

D

To Convert	Into	Multiply by
day	hour	23.9981
day	second	86 400.0
decibel	neper	0.1151
decigram	gram	0.1
deciliter	liter	0.1
decimeter	meter	0.1
degree (angle)	minute	60
degree (angle)	radian	0.017 45
degree (angle)	second	3600.0
degree/sec	radian/sec	0.017 45
degree/sec	rev/min	0.1667
degree/sec	rev/sec	2.778×10^{-3}
dekagram	gram	10.0
dekaliter	liter	10.0
dekameter	meter	10.0
dram	cl	0.3697
dram	gram	1.7718
dram (liq.)	cu cm	3.6967
dyne	gram	1.020×10^{-3}
dyne	joule/cm	1×10^{-7}
dyne	joule/meter	1×10^{-5}
dyne	kg	1.020×10^{-6}
dyne	newton	1×10^{-5}
dyne	pound	2.2481×10^{-6}
dyne	poundal	7.2327×10^{-5}
dyne/cm	erg/sq mm	0.01
dyne/sq cm	atmosphere	9.869×10^{-7}
dyne/sq cm	bar	1×10^{-6}
dyne/sq cm	inch of mercury	2.953×10^{-5}
dyne/sq cm	inch of water	4.015×10^{-4}
dyne/sq cm	ounce/sq inch	2.3207×10^{-4}

E

To Convert	Into	Multiply by
ell	cm	114.30
em, pica	cm	0.4233
erg	Btu	9.480×10^{-11}
erg	dyne-cm	1.0
erg	gram-calorie	0.2389×10^{-7}
erg	gram-cm	1.020×10^{-3}
erg	horsepower-hr	3.725×10^{-14}
erg	joule	1×10^{-7}
erg	kg-calorie	2.389×10^{-11}
erg	kg-meter	1.020×10^{-8}
erg	kilowatt-hr	0.2778×10^{-13}
erg	watt-hr	0.2778×10^{-10}
erg/sec	dyne-cm/sec	1.000
erg/sec	kg-calorie/min	1.433×10^{-9}
erg/sec	kilowatt	1×10^{-10}

To Convert	Into	Multiply by
erg/sec	Planck's quantum	1.5096×10^{26}
erg/sec	watt	9.3458×10^{-3}

F

To Convert	Into	Multiply by
farad	microfarad	1×10^6
faraday	ampere-hr	26.80
faraday	coulomb	9.649×10^4
fathom	meter	1.828 804
foot	cm	30.48
foot	km	3.048×10^{-4}
foot	meter	0.3048
foot	mm	304.8
foot of water	cm of mercury	2.2416
foot of water	kg/sq cm	0.030 48
foot of water	kg/sq meter	304.8
foot/min	cm/sec	0.5080
foot/min	km/hr	0.018 29
foot/min	meter/min	0.3048
foot/min	meter/sec	5.0813×10^{-3}
foot/sec	cm/sec	30.48
foot/sec	km/hr	1.097
foot/sec	meter/min	18.29
foot/sec	meter/sec	0.3048
foot/sec/sec	cm/sec/sec	30.48
foot/sec/sec	km/hr/sec	1.097
foot/sec/sec	meter/sec/sec	0.3048
foot-candle	lumen/sq meter	10.764
foot-pound	gram-calorie	0.3238
foot-pound	kg-calorie	3.24×10^{-4}
foot-pound	kg-meter	0.1383
foot-pound	kilowatt-hr	3.766×10^{-7}
foot-pound/min	kg-calorie/min	3.24×10^{-4}
foot-pound/min	kilowatt	2.260×10^{-5}
foot-pound/sec	kilowatt	1.356×10^{-3}

G

To Convert	Into	Multiply by
gallon	cu cm	3785.0
gallon	cu meter	3.785×10^{-3}
gallon	liter	3.785
gallon/min	liter/sec	0.063 08
gallon/sec	liter/min	227.1178
gauss	line/sq cm	1.0
gauss	weber/sq cm	1×10^{-8}
gauss	weber/sq meter	1×10^{-4}
gill	liter	0.1183
grain	gram	0.064 80
grain	mg	64.7989
grain/gallon	gram/liter	1.7118×10^{-3}
gram	cg	100
gram	dg	10
gram	dag	0.1
gram	dram	0.5644
gram	dyne	980.7
gram	grain	15.43
gram	hg	0.01
gram	joule/cm	9.807×10^{-5}
gram	joule/meter	9.807×10^{-3}
gram	kg	0.001
gram	mg	1000.0
gram	ounce	0.035 27
gram	ounce (troy)	0.032 15

To Convert	Into	Multiply by
gram	pound	2.205×10^{-3}
gram	pound (troy)	2.6792×10^{-3}
gram	poundal	0.070 93
gram/cm	pound/inch	5.600×10^{-3}
gram/cm/sec	poise	1.0
gram/cu cm	kg/cu meter	1000
gram/cu cm	pound/cu foot	62.43
gram/cu cm	pound/cu inch	0.036 13
gram/cu cm	pound/mil-foot	3.405×10^{-7}
gram/liter	grain/gallon	58.417
gram/liter	part/million	1000.0
gram/liter	pound/cu foot	0.062 427
gram/liter	pound/1000 gallons	8.345
gram/sq cm	pound/sq foot	2.0481
gram-calorie	Btu	3.9683×10^{-3}
gram-calorie	erg	4.1868×10^7
gram-calorie	foot-pound	3.0880
gram-calorie	horsepower-hr	1.5596×10^{-6}
gram-calorie	kilowatt-hr	1.1630×10^{-6}
gram-calorie	watt-hr	1.1630×10^{-3}
gram-calorie/sec	Btu/hr	14.286
gram-cm	Btu	9.297×10^{-8}
gram-cm	erg	980.7
gram-cm	joule	9.807×10^{-5}
gram-cm	kg-calorie	2.343×10^{-8}
gram-cm	kg-meter	1×10^{-5}

H

To Convert	Into	Multiply by
hand	cm	10.16
hectare	acre	2.471
hectare	sq foot	1.076×10^5
hectogram	gram	100.0
hectoliter	liter	100.0
hectometer	meter	100.0
hectowatt	watt	100.0
henry	millihenry	1000.0
horsepower	Btu/min	42.44
horsepower	kg-calorie/min	10.68
horsepower	kilowatt	0.7457
horsepower	watt	745.7
horsepower-hr	Btu/hr	2547.0
horsepower-hr	erg	2.6845×10^{13}
horsepower-hr	gram-calorie	641 190.0
horsepower-hr	joule	2.684×10^6
horsepower-hr	kg-calorie	641.1
horsepower-hr	kg-meter	2.737×10^5
horsepower-hr	kilowatt-hr	0.7457
hour	day	4.167×10^{-2}
hour	week	5.952×10^{-3}

I

To Convert	Into	Multiply by
inch	cm	2.540
inch	km	0.254×10^{-4}
inch	meter	2.540×10^{-2}
inch	mm	25.40
inch of mercury	dyne/sq cm	3.3864×10^4
inch of mercury	kg/sq cm	0.034 53
inch of mercury	kg/sq meter	345.3
inch of water	dyne/sq cm	2.4907×10^3
inch of water	kg/sq cm	2.540×10^{-3}

To Convert	Into	Multiply by

J

joule	Btu	9.480×10^{-4}
joule	erg	1×10^{7}
joule	gram-cm	1.0197×10^{4}
joule	horsepower-hr	3.7251×10^{-7}
joule	kg-calorie	2.389×10^{-4}
joule	kg-meter	0.1020
joule	kilowatt-hr	0.2777×10^{-6}
joule	watt-hr	2.778×10^{-4}
joule/cm	dyne	1×10^{7}
joule/cm	gram	1.020×10^{4}
joule/cm	joule/meter	100.0
joule/cm	kg	10.1968
joule/cm	pound	22.48
joule/cm	poundal	723.3
joule/meter	dyne	1×10^{5}
joule/meter	gram	101.968
joule/meter	joule/cm	0.01
joule/meter	kg	0.101 97
joule/meter	poundal	7.2306

K

kilogram	dyne	980 665.0
kilogram	gram	1000.0
kilogram	joule/cm	0.098 07
kilogram	joule/meter	9.807
kilogram	millier	0.001
kilogram	pound	2.205
kilogram	poundal	70.93
kilogram	slug	0.068 54
kilogram	ton (long)	9.842×10^{-4}
kilogram	ton (metric)	0.001
kilogram	ton (short)	1.102×10^{-3}
kg/cu meter	gram/cu cm	0.001
kg/cu meter	pound/cu foot	0.062 43
kg/cu meter	pound/cu inch	3.613×10^{-5}
kg/cu meter	pound/mil-foot	3.405×10^{-10}
kg/meter	pound/foot	0.6720
kg/sq cm	atmosphere	0.9678
kg/sq cm	dyne	980 665.0
kg/sq cm	foot of water	32.81
kg/sq cm	inch of mercury	28.96
kg/sq cm	inch of water	393.7
kg/sq cm	pound/sq foot	2048.0
kg/sq cm	pound/sq inch	14.22
kg/sq meter	atmosphere	9.678×10^{-5}
kg/sq meter	bar	98.07×10^{-6}
kg/sq meter	cm of mercury	7.3529×10^{-3}
kg/sq meter	foot of water	3.281×10^{-3}
kg/sq meter	inch of mercury	2.896×10^{-3}
kg/sq meter	kg/sq mm	1×10^{-6}
kg/sq meter	pound/sq foot	0.2048
kg/sq meter	pound/sq inch	1.422×10^{-3}
kg/sq mm	kg/sq meter	1×10^{6}
kg-calorie	Btu	3.968
kg-calorie	foot-pound	3088.0
kg-calorie	gram-cm	4.268×10^{7}
kg-calorie	horsepower-hr	1.560×10^{-3}
kg-calorie	joule	4186.0
kg-calorie	kg-meter	426.9
kg-calorie	kilojoule	4.186

kg-calorie	kilowatt-hr	1.163×10^{-3}
kg-calorie	watt-hr	1.1621
kg-calorie/min	erg/sec	6.9784×10^{8}
kg-calorie/min	foot-pound/min	3.0864×10^{3}
kg-calorie/min	horsepower	0.093 63
kg-calorie/min	kilowatt	6.9735×10^{-2}
kg-calorie/min	watt	69.7837
kg-meter	Btu	9.294×10^{-3}
kg-meter	erg	9.804×10^{7}
kg-meter	foot-pound	7.233
kg-meter	gram-cm	1×10^{5}
kg-meter	horsepower-hr	3.6536×10^{-6}
kg-meter	joule	9.804
kg-meter	kg-calorie	2.342×10^{-3}
kg-meter	kilowatt-hr	2.723×10^{-6}
kg-meter	watt-hr	2.7233×10^{-3}
kilojoule	kg-calorie	0.2389
kiloline	maxwell	1000.0
kiloliter	liter	1000.0
kilometer	astronomical unit	6.6889×10^{-9}
kilometer	cm	1×10^{5}
kilometer	foot	3281.0
kilometer	inch	3.937×10^{4}
kilometer	light-year	$1.056\ 98 \times 10^{-13}$
kilometer	meter	1000.0
kilometer	mil	393.7
kilometer	mile	0.6214
kilometer	mm	1×10^{6}
kilometer	parsec	3.2425×10^{-14}
kilometer	yard	1094.0
km/hr	cm/sec	27.78
km/hr	foot/min	54.68
km/hr	foot/sec	0.9113
km/hr	knot	0.5396
km/hr	meter/min	16.67
km/hr	meter/sec	0.2777
km/hr	mile/hr	0.6214
km/hr/sec	cm/sec/sec	27.78
km/hr/sec	foot/sec/sec	0.9113
km/hr/sec	meter/sec/sec	0.2778
km/hr/sec	mile/hr/sec	0.6214
km/min	meter/sec	16.6666
km/min	mile/hr	37.2856
km/min	mile/min	0.6215
kilowatt	Btu/min	56.92
kilowatt	erg/sec	1×10^{10}
kilowatt	foot-pound/min	4.426×10^{4}
kilowatt	foot-pound/sec	737.6
kilowatt	horsepower	1.341
kilowatt	kg-calorie/min	14.34
kilowatt	watt	1000.0
kilowatt-hr	Btu	3413.0
kilowatt-hr	erg	3.600×10^{13}
kilowatt-hr	foot-pound	2.655×10^{6}
kilowatt-hr	gram-calorie	859 850.0
kilowatt-hr	horsepower-hr	1.341
kilowatt-hr	joule	3.6×10^{6}
kilowatt-hr	kg-calorie	860.5
kilowatt-hr	kg-meter	3.671×10^{5}
kilowatt-hr	watt-hr	1000
knot	cm/sec	5.1467

To Convert	Into	Multiply by
knot	km/hr	1.8532
knot	meter/min	30.8833

L

To Convert	Into	Multiply by
lambert	candle/sq cm	0.3183
light-year	km	$9.460\ 91 \times 10^{12}$
line/sq cm	gauss	1.0
line/sq inch	weber/sq meter	1.550×10^{-5}
liter	bushel (dry)	0.028 38
liter	cl	100
liter	cu cm	1000.0
liter	cu foot	0.035 31
liter	cu inch	61.02
liter	cu meter	0.001
liter	cu yard	1.308×10^{-3}
liter	dl	10
liter	dal	0.1
liter	gallon (liq.)	0.2642
liter	gill	8.4531
liter	hl	0.01
liter	kl	0.001
liter	ml	1000
liter	ounce (liq.)	33.8181
liter	peck	0.1135
liter	pint (liq.)	2.113
liter	quart (liq.)	1.057
liter/min	cu foot/sec	5.886×10^{-4}
liter/min	gallon/sec	4.403×10^{-3}
liter/sec	foot/min	2.1186
liter/sec	cu yard/min	7.8493×10^{-2}
lumen	watt	0.001 496
lumen/sq foot	lumen/sq meter	10.76
lumen/sq meter	foot-candle	9.2902
lumen/sq meter	lumen/sq foot	9.2937×10^{-2}

M

To Convert	Into	Multiply by
maxwell	kiloline	0.001
maxwell	weber	1×10^{-8}
megaline	maxwell	1×10^{6}
megohm	microhm	1×10^{12}
megohm	ohm	1×10^{6}
meter	angstrom unit	1×10^{10}
meter	cm	100.0
meter	chain	4.9702×10^{-2}
meter	dm	10
meter	dam	0.1
meter	foot	3.281
meter	hm	0.01
meter	inch	39.37
meter	km	0.001
meter	micron	1×10^{6}
meter	mile (nautical)	5.396×10^{-4}
meter	mile (statute)	6.214×10^{-4}
meter	mm	1000.0
meter	millimicron	1×10^{9}
meter	rod	0.1988
meter	yard	1.094
meter/min	cm/sec	1.667
meter/min	foot/min	3.281
meter/min	foot/sec	0.054 68
meter/min	km/hr	0.06

To Convert	Into	Multiply by
meter/min	knot	0.032 38
meter/min	mile/hr	0.037 28
meter/sec	foot/min	196.8
meter/sec	foot/sec	3.281
meter/sec	km/hr	3.6
meter/sec	km/min	0.06
meter/sec	mile/hr	2.237
meter/sec	mile/min	0.037 28
meter/sec/sec	cm/sec/sec	100.0
meter/sec/sec	foot/sec/sec	3.281
meter/sec/sec	km/hr/sec	3.6
meter/sec/sec	mile/hr/sec	2.237
meter-kg	cm-dyne	9.807×10^{7}
meter-kg	cm-gram	1×10^{5}
meter-kg	pound-foot	7.233
microfarad	farad	1×10^{-6}
microgram	gram	1×10^{-6}
microhm	megohm	1×10^{-12}
microhm	ohm	1×10^{-6}
microliter	liter	1×10^{-6}
micron	angstrom unit	1×10^{4}
micron	meter	1×10^{-6}
mil	cm	2.540×10^{-3}
mil	km	2.540×10^{-3}
mil	mm	0.0254
mile (nautical)	km	1.853
mile (nautical)	meter	1853.0
mile (statute)	cm	1.609×10^{5}
mile (statute)	km	1.609
mile (statute)	meter	1609.0
mile/hr	cm/sec	44.70
mile/hr	km/hr	1.609
mile/hr	km/min	0.026 82
mile/hr	meter/min	26.82
mile/hr	meter/sec	0.447 02
mile/hr/sec	cm/sec/sec	44.70
mile/hr/sec	km/hr/sec	1.609
mile/hr/sec	meter/sec/sec	0.4470
mile/min	cm/sec	2682.0
mile/min	km/min	1.609
mile/min	meter/sec	26.824 03
millier	kg	1000.0
milligram	grain	0.015 43
milligram	gram	0.001
mg/liter	part/million	1.0
millihenry	henry	0.001
milliliter	liter	0.001
millimeter	cm	0.1
millimeter	foot	3.281×10^{-3}
millimeter	inch	0.039 37
millimeter	km	1×10^{-6}
millimeter	meter	0.001
millimeter	mil	39.37
millimeter	mile	6.214×10^{-7}
millimeter	yard	1.094×10^{-3}
millimicron	meter	1×10^{-9}
minim	cu cm	0.061 612
minute (angle)	degree	0.016 67
minute (angle)	quadrant	1.852×10^{-4}
minute (angle)	radian	2.909×10^{-4}
minute (angle)	second	60.0

To Convert	Into	Multiply by

N

neper . . . . decibel 8.686
newton . . . . dyne . . . . 1×10^5

O

ohm . . . . megohm . . . . 1×10^{-6}
ohm . . . . microhm . . . . 1×10^6
ounce . . . . gram 28.349 527
ounce . . . . ton (metric) . . . . 2.835×10^{-5}
ounce (liq.) . . . . cl 2.9568
ounce (liq.) . . . . liter 0.029 57
ounce (troy) . . . . gram 31.103 481
ounce/sq inch . . . . . . dyne/sq cm 4309.0

P

parsec . . . . km . . . . 3.084×10^{13}
part/million . . . . gram/liter 0.001
part/million . . . . mg/liter 1.0
peck . . . . liter 8.809 582
pint (liq.) . . . . cu cm 473.2
pint (liq.) . . . . cu meter . . . . 4.732×10^{-4}
pint (liq.) . . . . liter 0.4732
Planck's quantum . . . erg-sec . . . . 6.624×10^{-27}
poise . . . . gram/cm sec 1.00
pound . . . . dyne . . . . 44.4823×10^4
pound . . . . gram 453.5924
pound . . . . joule/cm 0.044 48
pound . . . . joule/meter 4.448
pound . . . . kg 0.4536
pound . . . . ton (metric) . . . . 4.5351×10^{-4}
pound (troy) . . . . . . gram 373.241 77
pound (troy) . . . . . . ton (metric) . . . . 3.7324×10^{-4}
pound/cu foot . . . . . gram/cu cm 0.016 02
pound/cu foot . . . . . gram/liter 16.0187
pound/cu foot . . . . . kg/cu meter 16.02
pound/cu inch . . . . . gram/cu cm 27.68
pound/cu inch . . . . . kg/cu meter . . . . 2.768×10^4
pound/foot . . . . kg/meter 1.488
pound/inch . . . . gram/cm 178.6
pound/mil-foot . . . . . gram/cu cm . . . . 2.306×10^6
pound/mil-foot . . . . . kg/cu meter . . . . 2.9369×10^9
pound/1000 gallons . . gram/liter 0.1198
pound/sq foot . . . . . . cm of mercury . . . . 3.5906×10^{-2}
pound/sq foot . . . . . gram/sq cm 0.4882
pound/sq foot . . . . . kg/sq meter 4.882
pound/sq inch . . . . . cm of mercury 5.1706
pound/sq inch . . . . . kg/sq cm 0.7032
pound/sq inch . . . . . kg/sq meter 703.1
pound-foot . . . . cm-dyne . . . . 1.356×10^7
pound-foot . . . . cm-gram 13 825.0
pound-foot . . . . meter-kg 0.1383
poundal . . . . dyne 13 826.0
poundal . . . . gram 14.10
poundal . . . . joule/cm . . . . 1.383×10^{-3}
poundal . . . . joule/meter 0.1383
poundal . . . . kg 0.014 10

Q

quadrant (angle) . . . . degree 90.0
quadrant (angle) . . . . minute 5400.0
quadrant (angle) . . . . radian 1.571

To Convert	Into	Multiply by

quadrant (angle) . . . . rev 0.25
quadrant (angle) . . . . second . . . . 3.24×10^5
quart (liq.) . . . . cu cm 946.4
quart (liq.) . . . . cu meter . . . . 9.464×10^{-4}
quart (liq.) . . . . liter 0.9463

R

radian . . . . circumference 0.1592
radian . . . . degree 57.30
radian . . . . minute 3438.0
radian . . . . quadrant 0.6366
radian . . . . rev 0.1592
radian . . . . second . . . . 2.063×10^5
radian/sec . . . . degree/sec 57.30
radian/sec . . . . rev/min 9.549
radian/sec . . . . rev/sec 0.1592
radian/sec/sec . . . . . . rev/min/min 573.0
radian/sec/sec . . . . . . rev/min/sec 9.549
radian/sec/sec . . . . . . rev/sec/sec 0.1592
revolution . . . . degree 360.0
revolution . . . . quadrant 4.0
revolution . . . . radian 6.283
rev/min . . . . degree/sec 6.0
rev/min . . . . radian/sec 0.1047
rev/min . . . . rev/sec 0.016 67
rev/min/min . . . . radian/sec/sec . . . . 1.745×10^{-3}
rev/min/min . . . . rev/min/sec 0.016 67
rev/min/min . . . . rev/sec/sec . . . . 2.778×10^{-4}
rev/min/sec . . . . rev/min/min 60
rev/min/sec . . . . rev/sec/sec 0.016 66
rev/sec . . . . degree/sec 360.0
rev/sec . . . . radian/sec 6.283
rev/sec . . . . rev/min 60.0
rev/sec/sec . . . . radian/sec/sec 6.283
rev/sec/sec . . . . rev/min/min 3600.0
rev/sec/sec . . . . rev/min/sec 60.0
rod . . . . meter 5.029

S

second . . . . day . . . . 1.1574×10^{-5}
second (angle) . . . . . . degree . . . . 2.778×10^{-4}
second (angle) . . . . . . minute 0.016 67
second (angle) . . . . . . quadrant . . . . 3.087×10^{-6}
second (angle) . . . . . . radian . . . . 4.848×10^{-6}
slug . . . . kg 14.59
sphere . . . . steradian 12.57
sq centimeter . . . . . . circular mil . . . . 1.973×10^5
sq centimeter . . . . . . sq foot . . . . 1.076×10^{-3}
sq centimeter . . . . . . sq inch 0.1550
sq centimeter . . . . . . sq meter 0.0001
sq centimeter . . . . . . sq mil . . . . 1.5499×10^5
sq centimeter . . . . . . sq mile . . . . 3.861×10^{-11}
sq centimeter . . . . . . sq mm 100.0
sq centimeter . . . . . . sq yard . . . . 1.196×10^{-4}
sq foot . . . . hectare . . . . 9.2937×10^{-6}
sq foot . . . . sq cm 929.0
sq foot . . . . sq meter 0.092 90
sq foot . . . . sq mm . . . . 9.290×10^4
sq inch . . . . sq cm 6.452
sq inch . . . . sq meter . . . . 6.4516×10^{-4}
sq inch . . . . sq mm 645.2

To Convert	Into	Multiply by
sq kilometer	acre	247.1
sq kilometer	sq cm	1×10^{10}
sq kilometer	sq foot	10.76×10^6
sq kilometer	sq inch	1.550×10^9
sq kilometer	sq meter	1×10^6
sq kilometer	sq mile	0.3861
sq kilometer	sq yard	1.196×10^6
sq meter	acre	2.471×10^{-4}
sq meter	centare	1.0
sq meter	sq cm	1×10^4
sq meter	sq foot	10.76
sq meter	sq inch	1550.0
sq meter	sq km	1×10^{-6}
sq meter	sq mile	3.861×10^{-7}
sq meter	sq mm	1×10^6
sq meter	sq yard	1.196
sq mil	sq cm	6.452×10^{-6}
sq mile	sq cm	2.59×10^{10}
sq mile	sq km	2.590
sq mile	sq meter	2.590×10^6
sq millimeter	circular mil	1973.0
sq millimeter	sq cm	0.01
sq millimeter	sq foot	1.076×10^{-5}
sq millimeter	sq inch	1.550×10^{-3}
sq millimeter	sq meter	1×10^{-6}
sq millimeter	sq yard	$1.196\ 03 \times 10^{-6}$
sq yard	sq cm	8361.0
sq yard	sq km	8.3612×10^{-7}
sq yard	sq meter	0.8361
sq yard	sq mm	8.361×10^5
steradian	sphere	0.079 55

T

To Convert	Into	Multiply by
ton (long)	kg	1.016×10^3
ton (metric)	kg	1000.0
ton (metric)	ounce	3.5273×10^4
ton (metric)	pound	2205.0
ton (metric)	ton (short)	1.1016
ton (short)	kg	907.1848
ton (short)	ton (metric)	0.9078

V

To Convert	Into	Multiply by
volt/inch	volt/cm	0.393 70
volt/cm	volt inch	2.54

W

To Convert	Into	Multiply by
watt	Btu/hr	3.4129
watt	Btu/min	0.056 88
watt	erg/sec	107.0
watt	hectowatt	0.01
watt	horsepower	1.341×10^{-3}
watt	kg-calorie/min	0.014 33
watt	kilowatt	0.001
watt	lumen	668.4492
watt-hr	Btu	3.413
watt-hr	erg	3.60×10^{10}
watt-hr	gram-calorie	859.85
watt-hr	joule	3.5997×10^3
watt-hr	kg-calorie	0.8605
watt-hr	kg-meter	367.2
watt-hr	kilowatt-hr	0.001
weber	kiloline	1×10^5
weber	maxwell	1×10^8
weber/sq cm	gauss	1×10^4
weber/sq cm	weber/sq inch	6.4516
weber/sq cm	weber/sq meter	1×10^4
weber/sq inch	weber/sq cm	0.1550
weber/sq inch	weber/sq meter	1.5499×10^3
weber/sq meter	gauss	1×10^4
weber/sq meter	line/sq inch	6.452×10^4
weber/sq meter	weber/sq cm	1×10^{-4}
weber/sq meter	weber/sq inch	6.452×10^{-4}
week	hour	168.010 75

Y

To Convert	Into	Multiply by
yard	cm	91.44
yard	km	9.144×10^{-4}
yard	meter	0.9144
yard	mm	914.4

METRIC AND U.S. CUSTOMARY TABLES

FRACTIONS OF INCH TO MILLIMETERS

in	mm	in	mm	in	mm	in	mm
$\frac{1}{64}$	0.40	$\frac{9}{64}$	3.57	$\frac{17}{64}$	6.75	$\frac{25}{64}$	9.92
$\frac{1}{32}$	0.79	$\frac{5}{32}$	3.97	$\frac{9}{32}$	7.14	$\frac{13}{32}$	10.32
$\frac{3}{64}$	1.19	$\frac{11}{64}$	4.37	$\frac{19}{64}$	7.54	$\frac{27}{64}$	10.72
$\frac{1}{16}$	1.59	$\frac{3}{16}$	4.76	$\frac{5}{16}$	7.94	$\frac{7}{16}$	11.11
$\frac{5}{64}$	1.98	$\frac{13}{64}$	5.16	$\frac{21}{64}$	8.33	$\frac{29}{64}$	11.51
$\frac{3}{32}$	2.38	$\frac{7}{32}$	5.56	$\frac{11}{32}$	8.73	$\frac{15}{32}$	11.91
$\frac{7}{64}$	2.78	$\frac{15}{64}$	5.95	$\frac{23}{64}$	9.13	$\frac{31}{64}$	12.30
$\frac{1}{8}$	3.18	$\frac{1}{4}$	6.35	$\frac{3}{8}$	9.53	$\frac{1}{2}$	12.70

FRACTIONS OF INCH TO MILLIMETERS

in	mm	in	mm	in	mm	in	mm
$\frac{33}{64}$	13.10	$\frac{41}{64}$	16.27	$\frac{49}{64}$	19.45	$\frac{57}{64}$	22.62
$\frac{17}{32}$	13.49	$\frac{21}{32}$	16.67	$\frac{25}{32}$	19.84	$\frac{29}{32}$	23.02
$\frac{35}{64}$	13.89	$\frac{43}{64}$	17.07	$\frac{51}{64}$	20.24	$\frac{59}{64}$	23.42
$\frac{9}{16}$	14.29	$\frac{11}{16}$	17.46	$\frac{13}{16}$	20.64	$\frac{15}{16}$	23.81
$\frac{37}{64}$	14.68	$\frac{45}{64}$	17.86	$\frac{53}{64}$	21.03	$\frac{61}{64}$	24.21
$\frac{19}{32}$	15.08	$\frac{23}{32}$	18.26	$\frac{27}{32}$	21.43	$\frac{31}{32}$	24.61
$\frac{39}{64}$	15.48	$\frac{47}{64}$	18.65	$\frac{55}{64}$	21.83	$\frac{63}{64}$	25.00
$\frac{5}{8}$	15.88	$\frac{3}{4}$	19.05	$\frac{7}{8}$	22.23	1	25.40

Length

INCHES TO CENTIMETERS				CENTIMETERS TO INCHES				FEET TO METERS				METERS TO FEET			
in	*cm*	*in*	*cm*	*cm*	*in*	*cm*	*in*	*ft*	*m*	*ft*	*m*	*m*	*ft*	*m*	*ft*
1	2.54	51	129.54	1	0.39	51	20.08	1	0.31	51	15.55	1	3.28	51	167.32
2	5.08	52	132.08	2	0.79	52	20.47	2	0.61	52	15.85	2	6.56	52	170.60
3	7.62	53	134.62	3	1.18	53	20.87	3	0.91	53	16.15	3	9.84	53	173.89
4	10.16	54	137.16	4	1.58	54	21.26	4	1.22	54	16.46	4	13.12	54	177.17
5	12.70	55	139.70	5	1.97	55	21.65	5	1.52	55	16.76	5	16.40	55	180.45
6	15.24	56	142.24	6	2.36	56	22.05	6	1.83	56	17.07	6	19.69	56	183.73
7	17.78	57	144.78	7	2.76	57	22.44	7	2.13	57	17.37	7	22.97	57	187.01
8	20.32	58	147.32	8	3.15	58	22.84	8	2.44	58	17.68	8	26.25	58	190.29
9	22.86	59	149.86	9	3.54	59	23.23	9	2.74	59	17.98	9	29.53	59	193.57
10	25.40	60	152.40	10	3.94	60	23.62	10	3.05	60	18.29	10	32.81	60	196.85
11	27.94	61	154.94	11	4.33	61	24.02	11	3.35	61	18.59	11	36.09	61	200.13
12	30.48	62	157.48	12	4.72	62	24.41	12	3.66	62	18.90	12	39.37	62	203.41
13	33.02	63	160.02	13	5.12	63	24.80	13	3.96	63	19.20	13	42.65	63	206.69
14	35.56	64	162.56	14	5.51	64	25.20	14	4.27	64	19.51	14	45.93	64	209.97
15	38.10	65	165.10	15	5.91	65	25.59	15	4.57	65	19.81	15	49.21	65	213.26
16	40.64	66	167.64	16	6.30	66	25.98	16	4.88	66	20.12	16	52.49	66	216.54
17	43.18	67	170.18	17	6.69	67	26.38	17	5.18	67	20.42	17	55.77	67	219.82
18	45.72	68	172.72	18	7.09	68	26.77	18	5.49	68	20.73	18	59.06	68	223.10
19	48.26	69	175.26	19	7.48	69	27.17	19	5.79	69	21.03	19	62.34	69	226.38
20	50.80	70	177.80	20	7.87	70	27.56	20	6.10	70	21.34	20	65.62	70	229.66
21	53.34	71	180.34	21	8.27	71	27.95	21	6.40	71	21.64	21	68.90	71	232.94
22	55.88	72	182.88	22	8.66	72	28.35	22	6.71	72	21.95	22	72.18	72	236.22
23	58.42	73	185.42	23	9.06	73	28.74	23	7.01	73	22.25	23	75.46	73	239.50
24	60.96	74	187.96	24	9.45	74	29.13	24	7.32	74	22.56	24	78.40	74	242.78
25	63.50	75	190.50	25	9.84	75	29.53	25	7.62	75	22.86	25	82.02	75	246.06
26	66.04	76	193.04	26	10.24	76	29.92	26	7.93	76	23.17	26	85.30	76	249.34
27	68.58	77	195.58	27	10.63	77	30.32	27	8.23	77	23.47	27	88.58	77	252.63
28	71.12	78	198.12	28	11.02	78	30.71	28	8.53	78	23.77	28	91.86	78	255.91
29	73.66	79	200.66	29	11.42	79	31.10	29	8.84	79	24.08	29	95.14	79	259.19
30	76.20	80	203.20	30	11.81	80	31.50	30	9.14	80	24.38	30	98.43	80	262.47
31	78.74	81	205.74	31	12.21	81	31.89	31	9.45	81	24.69	31	101.71	81	265.75
32	81.28	82	208.28	32	12.60	82	32.28	32	9.75	82	24.99	32	104.99	82	269.03
33	83.82	83	210.82	33	12.99	83	32.68	33	10.06	83	25.30	33	108.27	83	272.31
34	86.36	84	213.36	34	13.39	84	33.07	34	10.36	84	25.60	34	111.55	84	275.59
35	88.90	85	215.90	35	13.78	85	33.47	35	10.67	85	25.91	35	114.83	85	278.87
36	91.44	86	218.44	36	14.17	86	33.86	36	10.97	86	26.21	36	118.11	86	282.15
37	93.98	87	220.98	37	14.57	87	34.25	37	11.28	87	26.52	37	121.39	87	285.43
38	96.52	88	223.52	38	14.96	88	34.65	38	11.58	88	26.82	38	124.67	88	288.71
39	99.06	89	226.06	39	15.35	89	35.04	39	11.89	89	27.13	39	127.95	89	292.00
40	101.60	90	228.60	40	15.75	90	35.43	40	12.19	90	27.43	40	131.23	90	295.28
41	104.14	91	231.14	41	16.14	91	35.83	41	12.50	91	27.74	41	134.51	91	298.56
42	106.68	92	233.68	42	15.54	92	36.22	42	12.80	92	28.04	42	137.79	92	301.84
43	109.22	93	236.22	43	16.93	93	36.61	43	13.11	93	28.35	43	141.08	93	305.12
44	111.76	94	238.76	44	17.32	94	37.01	44	13.41	94	28.65	44	144.36	94	308.40
45	114.30	95	241.30	45	17.72	95	37.40	45	13.72	95	28.96	45	147.64	95	311.68
46	116.84	96	243.84	46	18.11	96	37.80	46	14.02	96	29.26	46	150.92	96	314.96
47	119.38	97	246.38	47	18.50	97	38.19	47	14.33	97	29.57	47	154.20	97	318.24
48	121.92	98	248.92	48	18.90	98	38.58	48	14.63	98	29.87	48	157.48	98	321.52
49	124.46	99	251.46	49	19.29	99	38.98	49	14.94	99	30.17	49	160.76	99	324.80
50	127.00	100	254.00	50	19.69	100	39.37	50	15.24	100	30.48	50	164.04	100	328.08

YARDS TO METERS

yd	m	yd	m
1	0.91	51	46.63
2	1.83	52	47.55
3	2.74	53	48.46
4	3.66	54	49.38
5	4.57	55	50.29
6	5.49	56	51.21
7	6.40	57	52.12
8	7.32	58	53.04
9	8.23	59	53.95
10	9.14	60	54.86
11	10.06	61	55.78
12	10.97	62	56.69
13	11.89	63	57.61
14	12.80	64	58.52
15	13.72	65	59.44
16	14.63	66	60.35
17	15.55	67	61.27
18	16.46	68	62.18
19	17.37	69	63.09
20	18.29	70	64.01
21	19.20	71	64.92
22	20.12	72	65.84
23	21.03	73	66.75
24	21.95	74	67.67
25	22.86	75	68.58
26	23.77	76	69.49
27	24.69	77	70.41
28	25.60	78	71.32
29	26.52	79	72.24
30	27.43	80	73.15
31	28.35	81	74.07
32	29.26	82	74.98
33	30.18	83	75.90
34	31.09	84	76.81
35	32.00	85	77.72
36	32.92	86	78.64
37	33.83	87	79.55
38	34.75	88	80.47
39	35.66	89	81.38
40	36.58	90	82.30
41	37.49	91	83.21
42	38.41	92	84.13
43	39.32	93	85.04
44	40.23	94	85.95
45	41.15	95	86.87
46	42.06	96	87.78
47	42.98	97	88.70
48	43.89	98	89.61
49	44.81	99	90.52
50	45.72	100	91.44

METERS TO YARDS

m	yd	m	yd
1	1.09	51	55.77
2	2.19	52	56.87
3	3.28	53	57.96
4	4.37	54	59.06
5	5.47	55	60.15
6	6.56	56	61.24
7	7.66	57	62.34
8	8.75	58	63.43
9	9.84	59	64.52
10	10.94	60	65.62
11	12.03	61	66.71
12	13.12	62	67.80
13	14.22	63	68.90
14	15.31	64	69.99
15	16.40	65	71.09
16	17.50	66	72.18
17	18.59	67	73.27
18	19.69	68	74.37
19	20.78	69	75.46
20	21.87	70	76.55
21	22.97	71	77.65
22	24.06	72	78.74
23	25.15	73	79.83
24	26.25	74	80.93
25	27.34	75	82.02
26	28.43	76	83.11
27	29.53	77	84.21
28	30.62	78	85.30
29	31.72	79	86.30
30	32.81	80	87.49
31	33.90	81	88.58
32	35.00	82	89.68
33	36.09	83	90.77
34	37.18	84	91.86
35	38.28	85	92.96
36	39.37	86	94.05
37	40.46	87	95.14
38	41.56	88	96.24
39	42.65	89	97.33
40	43.74	90	98.43
41	44.84	91	99.52
42	45.93	92	100.61
43	47.03	93	101.71
44	48.12	94	102.80
45	49.21	95	103.89
46	50.31	96	104.99
47	51.40	97	106.08
48	52.49	98	107.17
49	53.59	99	108.27
50	54.68	100	109.36

MILES TO KILOMETERS

mi	km	mi	km
1	1.61	51	82.08
2	3.22	52	83.69
3	4.83	53	85.30
4	6.44	54	86.91
5	8.05	55	88.51
6	9.66	56	90.12
7	11.27	57	91.73
8	12.88	58	93.34
9	14.48	59	94.95
10	16.09	60	96.56
11	17.70	61	98.17
12	19.31	62	99.78
13	20.92	63	101.39
14	22.53	64	103.00
15	24.14	65	104.61
16	25.75	66	106.22
17	27.36	67	107.83
18	28.97	68	109.44
19	30.58	69	111.05
20	32.19	70	112.65
21	33.80	71	114.26
22	35.41	72	115.87
23	37.02	73	117.48
24	38.62	74	119.09
25	40.23	75	120.70
26	41.84	76	122.31
27	43.45	77	123.92
28	45.06	78	125.53
29	46.67	79	127.14
30	48.28	80	128.75
31	49.89	81	130.36
32	51.50	82	131.97
33	53.11	83	133.58
34	54.72	84	135.19
35	56.33	85	136.79
36	57.94	86	138.40
37	59.55	87	140.01
38	61.16	88	141.62
39	62.76	89	143.23
40	64.37	90	144.84
41	65.98	91	146.45
42	67.59	92	148.06
43	69.20	93	149.67
44	70.81	94	151.28
45	72.42	95	152.89
46	74.03	96	154.50
47	75.64	97	156.11
48	77.25	98	157.72
49	78.86	99	159.33
50	80.47	100	160.93

KILOMETERS TO MILES

km	mi	km	mi
1	0.62	51	31.69
2	1.24	52	32.31
3	1.86	53	32.93
4	2.49	54	33.55
5	3.11	55	34.18
6	3.73	56	34.80
7	4.35	57	35.42
8	4.97	58	36.04
9	5.59	59	36.66
10	6.21	60	37.28
11	6.84	61	37.90
12	7.46	62	38.53
13	8.08	63	39.15
14	8.70	64	39.77
15	9.32	65	40.39
16	9.94	66	41.01
17	10.56	67	41.63
18	11.19	68	42.25
19	11.81	69	42.88
20	12.43	70	43.50
21	13.05	71	44.12
22	13.67	72	44.74
23	14.29	73	45.36
24	14.91	74	45.98
25	15.53	75	46.60
26	16.16	76	47.22
27	16.78	77	47.85
28	17.40	78	48.47
29	18.02	79	49.09
30	18.64	80	49.71
31	19.26	81	50.33
32	19.88	82	50.95
33	20.51	83	51.57
34	21.13	84	52.20
35	21.75	85	52.82
36	22.37	86	53.44
37	22.99	87	54.06
38	23.61	88	54.68
39	24.23	89	55.30
40	24.86	90	55.92
41	25.48	91	56.55
42	26.10	92	57.17
43	26.72	93	57.79
44	27.34	94	58.41
45	27.96	95	59.03
46	28.58	96	59.65
47	29.20	97	60.27
48	29.83	98	60.89
49	30.45	99	61.52
50	31.07	100	62.14

Area

SQUARE INCHES TO SQUARE CENTIMETERS

in²	cm²	in²	cm²
1	6.45	51	329.03
2	12.90	52	335.48
3	19.36	53	341.94
4	25.81	54	348.39
5	32.26	55	354.84
6	38.71	56	361.29
7	45.16	57	367.74
8	51.61	58	374.19
9	58.06	59	380.64
10	64.52	60	387.10
11	70.97	61	393.55
12	77.42	62	400.00
13	83.87	63	406.45
14	90.32	64	412.90
15	96.77	65	419.35
16	103.23	66	425.81
17	109.68	67	432.26
18	116.13	68	438.71
19	122.58	69	445.16
20	129.03	70	451.61
21	135.48	71	458.06
22	141.94	72	464.52
23	148.39	73	470.97
24	154.84	74	477.42
25	161.29	75	483.87
26	167.74	76	490.32
27	174.19	77	496.77
28	180.65	78	503.23
29	187.10	79	509.68
30	193.46	80	516.13
31	200.00	81	522.58
32	206.45	82	529.03
33	212.90	83	535.48
34	219.35	84	541.93
35	225.81	85	548.39
36	232.26	86	554.84
37	238.71	87	561.29
38	245.16	88	567.74
39	251.61	89	574.19
40	258.06	90	580.64
41	264.52	91	587.10
42	270.97	92	593.55
43	277.42	93	600.00
44	283.87	94	606.45
45	290.32	95	612.90
46	296.77	96	619.35
47	303.23	97	625.81
48	309.68	98	632.26
49	316.13	99	638.71
50	322.58	100	645.16

SQUARE CENTIMETERS TO SQUARE INCHES

cm²	in²	cm²	in²
1	0.16	51	7.91
2	0.31	52	8.06
3	0.47	53	8.22
4	0.62	54	8.37
5	0.78	55	8.53
6	0.93	56	8.68
7	1.09	57	8.84
8	1.24	58	8.99
9	1.40	59	9.15
10	1.55	60	9.30
11	1.71	61	9.46
12	1.86	62	9.61
13	2.02	63	9.77
14	2.17	64	9.92
15	2.33	65	10.08
16	2.48	66	10.23
17	2.64	67	10.39
18	2.79	68	10.54
19	2.95	69	10.70
20	3.10	70	10.85
21	3.26	71	11.01
22	3.41	72	11.16
23	3.57	73	11.32
24	3.72	74	11.47
25	3.88	75	11.63
26	4.03	76	11.78
27	4.19	77	11.94
28	4.34	78	12.09
29	4.50	79	12.25
30	4.65	80	12.40
31	4.81	81	12.56
32	4.90	82	12.71
33	5.12	83	12.87
34	5.27	84	13.02
35	5.43	85	13.18
36	5.58	86	13.33
37	5.74	87	13.49
38	5.89	88	13.64
39	6.05	89	13.80
40	6.20	90	13.95
41	6.36	91	14.11
42	6.51	92	14.26
43	6.67	93	14.42
44	6.82	94	14.57
45	6.98	95	14.73
46	7.13	96	14.88
47	7.29	97	15.04
48	7.44	98	15.19
49	7.60	99	15.35
50	7.75	100	15.50

SQUARE FEET TO SQUARE METERS

ft²	m²	ft²	m²
1	0.09	51	4.74
2	0.19	52	4.83
3	0.28	53	4.93
4	0.37	54	5.02
5	0.46	55	5.11
6	0.56	56	5.20
7	0.65	57	5.30
8	0.74	58	5.39
9	0.84	59	5.48
10	0.93	60	5.57
11	1.02	61	5.67
12	1.12	62	5.76
13	1.21	63	5.85
14	1.30	64	5.95
15	1.39	65	6.04
16	1.49	66	6.13
17	1.58	67	6.22
18	1.67	68	6.32
19	1.77	69	6.41
20	1.86	70	6.50
21	1.95	71	6.60
22	2.04	72	6.69
23	2.14	73	6.78
24	2.23	74	6.88
25	2.32	75	6.97
26	2.42	76	7.06
27	2.51	77	7.15
28	2.60	78	7.25
29	2.69	79	7.34
30	2.79	80	7.43
31	2.88	81	7.53
32	2.97	82	7.62
33	3.07	83	7.71
34	3.16	84	7.80
35	3.25	85	7.90
36	3.34	86	7 99
37	3.44	87	8.08
38	3.53	88	8.18
39	3.62	89	8.27
40	3.72	90	8.36
41	3.81	91	8.45
42	3.90	92	8.55
43	4.00	93	8.64
44	4.09	94	8.73
45	4.18	95	8.83
46	4.27	96	8.92
47	4.37	97	9.01
48	4.46	98	9.10
49	4.55	99	9.20
50	4.65	100	9.29

SQUARE METERS TO SQUARE FEET

m²	ft²	m²	ft²
1	10.76	51	548.96
2	21.53	52	559.72
3	32.29	53	570.49
4	43.06	54	581.25
5	53.82	55	592.01
6	64.58	56	602.78
7	75.35	57	613.54
8	86.11	58	624.31
9	96.88	59	635.07
10	107.64	60	645.83
11	118.40	61	656.60
12	129.17	62	667.36
13	139.93	63	678.13
14	150.70	64	688.89
15	161.46	65	699.65
16	172.22	66	710.42
17	182.99	67	721.18
18	193.75	68	731.95
19	204.51	69	742.71
20	215.28	70	753.47
21	226.04	71	764.24
22	236.81	72	775.00
23	247.57	73	785.77
24	258.33	74	796.53
25	269.10	75	807.29
26	279.86	76	818.06
27	290.63	77	828.82
28	301.39	78	839.58
29	312.15	79	850.35
30	322.92	80	861.11
31	333.68	81	871.88
32	344.45	82	882.64
33	355.21	83	893.40
34	365.97	84	904.17
35	376.74	85	914.93
36	387.50	86	925.70
37	398.26	87	936.46
38	409.03	88	947.22
39	419.79	89	957.99
40	430.56	90	968.75
41	441.32	91	979.52
42	452.08	92	990.28
43	462.85	93	1001.04
44	473.61	94	1011.81
45	484.38	95	1022.57
46	495.14	96	1033.33
47	505.90	97	1044.10
48	516.67	98	1054.86
49	527.43	99	1065.63
50	538.20	100	1076.39

SQUARE YARDS TO SQUARE METERS | SQUARE METERS TO SQUARE YARDS | ACRES TO HECTARES | HECTARES TO ACRES

yd²	m²	yd²	m²	m²	yd²	m²	yd²	a	ha	a	ha	ha	a	ha	a
1	0.84	51	42.64	1	1.20	51	61.00	1	0.41	51	20.64	1	2.47	51	126.02
2	1.67	52	43.48	2	2.39	52	62.19	2	0.81	52	21.04	2	4.94	52	128.50
3	2.51	53	44.32	3	3.59	53	63.39	3	1.21	53	21.45	3	7.41	53	130.97
4	3.34	54	45.15	4	4.78	54	64.58	4	1.62	54	21.85	4	9.88	54	133.44
5	4.18	55	45.99	5	5.98	55	65.78	5	2.02	55	22.26	5	12.36	55	135.91
6	5.02	56	46.82	6	7.18	56	66.98	6	2.43	56	22.66	6	14.83	56	138.38
7	5.85	57	47.66	7	8.37	57	68.17	7	2.83	57	23.07	7	17.30	57	140.85
8	6.69	58	48.50	8	9.57	58	69.37	8	3.24	58	23.47	8	19.77	58	143.32
9	7.53	59	49.33	9	10.76	59	70.56	9	3.64	59	23.88	9	22.40	59	145.79
10	8.36	60	50.17	10	11.96	60	71.76	10	4.05	60	24.28	10	24.71	60	148.26
11	9.20	61	51.00	11	13.16	61	72.96	11	4.45	61	24.69	11	27.18	61	150.73
12	10.03	62	51.84	12	14.35	62	74.15	12	4.86	62	25.09	12	29.66	62	153.21
13	10.87	63	52.68	13	15.55	63	75.35	13	5.26	63	25.50	13	32.12	63	155.68
14	11.71	64	53.51	14	16.74	64	76.54	14	5.67	64	25.90	14	34.60	64	158.15
15	12.54	65	54.35	15	17.94	65	77.74	15	6.07	65	26.31	15	37.07	65	160.62
16	13.38	66	55.18	16	19.14	66	78.94	16	6.48	66	26.71	16	39.54	66	163.09
17	14.21	67	56.02	17	20.33	67	80.13	17	6.88	67	27.11	17	42.01	67	165.56
18	15.05	68	56.86	18	21.53	68	81.33	18	7.28	68	27.52	18	44.48	68	168.03
19	15.89	69	57.69	19	22.72	69	82.52	19	7.69	69	27.92	19	46.95	69	170.50
20	16.72	70	58.53	20	23.92	70	83.72	20	8.09	70	28.33	20	49.42	70	172.97
21	17.56	71	59.37	21	25.12	71	84.92	21	8.50	71	28.73	21	51.89	71	175.45
22	18.40	72	60.20	22	26.31	72	86.11	22	8.90	72	29.14	22	54.36	72	177.92
23	19.23	73	61.04	23	27.51	73	87.31	23	9.31	73	29.54	23	56.83	73	180.39
24	20.07	74	61.87	24	28.70	74	88.50	24	9.71	74	29.95	24	59.31	74	182.86
25	20.90	75	62.71	25	29.89	75	89.70	25	10.12	75	30.35	25	61.78	75	185.33
26	21.74	76	63.55	26	31.10	76	90.90	26	10.52	76	30.76	26	64.25	76	187.80
27	22.58	77	64.38	27	32.29	77	92.09	27	10.93	77	31.16	27	66.72	77	190.27
28	23.41	78	65.22	28	33.49	78	93.29	28	11.33	78	31.57	28	69.19	78	192.74
29	24.25	79	66.05	29	34.68	79	94.48	29	11.74	79	31.97	29	71.66	79	195.21
30	25.08	80	66.89	30	35.88	80	95.68	30	12.14	80	32.38	30	74.13	80	197.68
31	25.92	81	67.73	31	37.08	81	96.88	31	12.55	81	32.78	31	76.60	81	200.16
32	26.76	82	68.56	32	38.27	82	98.07	32	12.95	82	33.18	32	79.07	82	202.63
33	27.59	83	69.40	33	39.47	83	99.27	33	13.36	83	33.59	33	81.55	83	205.10
34	28.43	84	70.24	34	40.66	84	100.46	34	13.76	84	33.99	34	84.02	84	207.57
35	29.26	85	71.07	35	41.86	85	101.66	35	14.16	85	34.30	35	86.49	85	210.04
36	30.10	86	71.91	36	43.06	86	102.86	36	14.57	86	34.80	36	88.96	86	212.51
37	30.94	87	72.74	37	44.25	87	104.05	37	14.97	87	35.21	37	91.43	87	214.98
38	31.77	88	73.58	38	45.45	88	105.25	38	15.38	88	35.61	38	93.90	88	217.45
39	32.61	89	74.42	39	46.64	89	106.44	39	15.78	89	36.02	39	96.37	89	219.92
40	33.45	90	75.25	40	47.84	90	107.64	40	16.19	90	36.42	40	98.84	90	222.40
41	34.28	91	76.09	41	49.04	91	108.84	41	16.59	91	36.83	41	101.31	91	224.87
42	35.12	92	76.92	42	50.23	92	110.03	42	17.00	92	37.23	42	103.78	92	227.34
43	35.95	93	77.76	43	51.43	93	111.23	43	17.40	93	37.64	43	106.26	93	229.81
44	36.79	94	78.60	44	52.62	94	112.42	44	17.81	94	38.04	44	108.73	94	232.28
45	37.63	95	79.43	45	53.82	95	113.62	45	18.21	95	38.45	45	111.20	95	234.75
46	38.46	96	80.27	46	55.02	96	114.82	46	18.62	96	38.85	46	113.67	96	237.22
47	39.30	97	81.10	47	56.21	97	116.01	47	19.02	97	39.26	47	116.14	97	239.69
48	40.13	98	81.94	48	57.41	98	117.21	48	19.43	98	39.66	48	118.61	98	242.16
49	40.97	99	82.78	49	58.60	99	118.40	49	19.83	99	40.06	49	121.08	99	244.63
50	41.81	100	83.61	50	59.80	100	119.60	50	20.23	100	40.47	50	123.55	100	247.11

FLUID OUNCES TO MILLILITERS				MILLILITERS TO FLUID OUNCES				CUBIC INCHES TO CUBIC CENTIMETERS				CUBIC CENTIMETERS TO CUBIC INCHES			
fl oz	*ml*	*fl oz*	*ml*	*ml*	*fl oz*	*ml*	*fl oz*	*in³*	*cm³*	*in³*	*cm³*	*cm³*	*in³*	*cm³*	*in³*
1	28.41	51	1449.06	1	0.04	51	1.80	1	16.39	51	835.74	1	0.06	51	3.11
2	56.83	52	1477.48	2	0.07	52	1.83	2	32.77	52	852.13	2	0.12	52	3.17
3	85.24	53	1505.89	3	0.11	53	1.87	3	49.16	53	868.52	3	0.18	53	3.23
4	113.65	54	1534.30	4	0.14	54	1.90	4	65.55	54	884.90	4	0.24	54	3.30
5	142.07	55	1562.72	5	0.18	55	1.94	5	81.94	55	901.29	5	0.31	55	3.36
6	170.48	56	1591.13	6	0.21	56	1.97	6	98.32	56	917.68	6	0.37	56	3.42
7	198.89	57	1619.54	7	0.25	57	2.01	7	114.71	57	934.07	7	0.43	57	3.48
8	227.30	58	1647.95	8	0.28	58	2.04	8	131.10	58	950.45	8	0.49	58	3.54
9	255.72	59	1676.37	9	0.32	59	2.08	9	147.48	59	966.84	9	0.55	59	3.60
10	284.13	60	1704.78	10	0.35	60	2.11	10	163.87	60	983.23	10	0.61	60	3.66
11	312.54	61	1733.19	11	0.39	61	2.15	11	180.26	61	999.61	11	0.67	61	3.72
12	340.96	62	1761.61	12	0.42	62	2.18	12	196.65	62	1016.00	12	0.73	62	3.78
13	369.37	63	1790.02	13	0.46	63	2.22	13	213.03	63	1032.39	13	0.79	63	3.84
14	397.78	64	1818.43	14	0.49	64	2.25	14	229.42	64	1048.77	14	0.85	64	3.91
15	426.20	65	1846.85	15	0.53	65	2.29	15	245.81	65	1065.16	15	0.92	65	3.97
16	454.61	66	1875.26	16	0.56	66	2.32	16	262.19	66	1081.55	16	0.98	66	4.03
17	483.02	67	1903.67	17	0.60	67	2.36	17	278.58	67	1097.94	17	1.04	67	4.09
18	511.43	68	1932.08	18	0.63	68	2.39	18	294.97	68	1114.32	18	1.10	68	4.15
19	539.85	69	1960.50	19	0.67	69	2.43	19	311.36	69	1130.71	19	1.16	69	4.21
20	568.26	70	1988.91	20	0.70	70	2.46	20	327.74	70	1147.10	20	1.22	70	4.27
21	596.67	71	2017.32	21	0.74	71	2.50	21	344.13	71	1163.48	21	1.28	71	4.33
22	625.09	72	2045.74	22	0.77	72	2.53	22	360.52	72	1179.87	22	1.34	72	4.39
23	653.50	73	2074.15	23	0.81	73	2.57	23	376.90	73	1196.26	23	1.40	73	4.46
24	681.91	74	2102.56	24	0.85	74	2.60	24	393.29	74	1212.65	24	1.47	74	4.52
25	710.33	75	2130.98	25	0.88	75	2.64	25	409.68	75	1229.03	25	1.53	75	4.58
26	738.74	76	2159.39	26	0.92	76	2.68	26	426.07	76	1245.42	26	1.59	76	4.64
27	767.15	77	2187.80	27	0.95	77	2.71	27	442.45	77	1261.81	27	1.65	77	4.70
28	795.56	78	2216.21	28	0.99	78	2.75	28	458.84	78	1278.19	28	1.71	78	4.76
29	823.98	79	2244.63	29	1.02	79	2.78	29	475.23	79	1294.58	29	1.77	79	4.82
30	852.39	80	2273.04	30	1.06	80	2.82	30	491.61	80	1310.97	30	1.83	80	4.88
31	880.80	81	2301.45	31	1.09	81	2.85	31	508.00	81	1327.36	31	1.89	81	4.94
32	909.22	82	2329.87	32	1.13	82	2.89	32	524.39	82	1343.74	32	1.95	82	5.00
33	937.63	83	2358.28	33	1.16	83	2.92	33	540.77	83	1360.13	33	2.01	83	5.07
34	966.04	84	2386.69	34	1.20	84	2.96	34	557.16	84	1376.52	34	2.08	84	5.13
35	994.46	85	2415.11	35	1.23	85	2.99	35	573.55	85	1392.90	35	2.14	85	5.19
36	1022.87	86	2433.52	36	1.27	86	3.03	36	589.94	86	1409.29	36	2.20	86	5.25
37	1051.28	87	2471.93	37	1.30	87	3.06	37	606.32	87	1425.68	37	2.26	87	5.31
38	1079.69	88	2500.34	38	1.34	88	3.10	38	622.71	88	1442.07	38	2.32	88	5.37
39	1108.11	89	2528.76	39	1.37	89	3.13	39	639.10	89	1458.45	39	2.38	89	5.43
40	1136.52	90	2557.17	40	1.41	90	3.17	40	655.48	90	1474.84	40	2.44	90	5.49
41	1164.93	91	2585.58	41	1.44	91	3.20	41	671.87	91	1491.23	41	2.50	91	5.55
42	1193.35	92	2614.00	42	1.48	92	3.24	42	688.26	92	1507.61	42	2.56	92	5.61
43	1221.76	93	2642.41	43	1.51	93	3.27	43	704.65	93	1524.00	43	2.62	93	5.68
44	1250.17	94	2670.82	44	1.55	94	3.31	44	721.03	94	1540.39	44	2.69	94	5.74
45	1278.59	95	2699.24	45	1.58	95	3.34	45	737.42	95	1556.77	45	2.75	95	5.80
46	1307.00	96	2727.65	46	1.62	96	3.38	46	753.81	96	1573.16	46	2.81	96	5.86
47	1335.41	97	2756.06	47	1.65	97	3.41	47	770.19	97	1589.55	47	2.87	97	5.92
48	1363.82	98	2784.47	48	1.69	98	3.45	48	786.58	98	1605.94	48	2.93	98	5.98
49	1392.24	99	2812.89	49	1.73	99	3.48	49	802.97	99	1622.32	49	2.99	99	6.04
50	1420.65	100	2841.30	50	1.76	100	3.52	50	819.36	100	1638.71	50	3.05	100	6.10

QUARTS TO LITERS				LITERS TO QUARTS				GALLONS TO LITERS				LITERS TO GALLONS			
qt	l	qt	l	l	qt	l	qt	gal	l	gal	l	l	gal	l	gal
1	0.95	51	48.26	1	1.06	51	53.89	1	3.79	51	193.06	1	0.26	51	13.47
2	1.89	52	49.21	2	2.11	52	54.95	2	7.57	52	196.84	2	0.53	52	13.74
3	2.84	53	50.16	3	3.17	53	56.00	3	11.36	53	200.63	3	0.79	53	14.00
4	3.79	54	51.10	4	4.23	54	57.06	4	15.14	54	204.41	4	1.06	54	14.27
5	4.73	55	52.05	5	5.28	55	58.12	5	18.93	55	208.20	5	1.32	55	14.53
6	5.68	56	53.00	6	6.34	56	59.17	6	22.71	56	211.98	6	1.59	56	14.79
7	6.62	57	53.94	7	7.40	57	60.23	7	26.50	57	215.77	7	1.85	57	15.06
8	7.57	58	54.89	8	8.45	58	61.29	8	30.28	58	219.55	8	2.11	58	15.32
9	8.52	59	55.83	9	9.51	59	62.34	9	34.07	59	223.34	9	2.38	59	15.59
10	9.46	60	56.78	10	10.57	60	63.40	10	37.85	60	227.12	10	2.64	60	15.85
11	10.41	61	57.73	11	11.62	61	64.46	11	41.64	61	230.91	11	2.91	61	16.11
12	11.36	62	58.67	12	12.68	62	65.51	12	45.42	62	234.70	12	3.17	62	16.38
13	12.30	63	59.62	13	13.74	63	66.57	13	49.21	63	238.48	13	3.43	63	16.64
14	13.25	64	60.57	14	14.79	64	67.63	14	53.00	64	242.27	14	3.70	64	16.91
15	14.20	65	61.51	15	15.85	65	68.68	15	56.78	65	246.05	15	3.96	65	17.17
16	15.14	66	62.46	16	16.91	66	69.74	16	60.57	66	249.84	16	4.23	66	17.44
17	16.09	67	63.41	17	17.96	67	70.80	17	64.35	67	253.62	17	4.49	67	17.70
18	17.03	68	64.35	18	19.02	68	71.85	18	68.14	68	257.41	18	4.76	68	17.96
19	17.98	69	65.30	19	20.08	69	72.91	19	71.92	69	261.19	19	5.02	69	18.23
20	18.93	70	66.24	20	21.13	70	73.97	20	75.71	70	264.98	20	5.28	70	18.49
21	19.87	71	67.19	21	22.19	71	75.02	21	79.49	71	268.76	21	5.55	71	18.76
22	20.82	72	68.14	22	23.25	72	76.08	22	83.28	72	272.55	22	5.81	72	19.02
23	21.77	73	69.08	23	24.30	73	77.14	23	87.06	73	276.34	23	6.08	73	19.28
24	22.71	74	70.03	24	25.36	74	78.19	24	90.85	74	280.12	24	6.34	74	19.55
25	23.66	75	70.98	25	26.42	75	79.25	25	94.64	75	283.91	25	6.60	75	19.81
26	24.61	76	71.92	26	27.47	76	80.31	26	98.42	76	287.69	26	6.87	76	20.08
27	25.55	77	72.87	27	28.53	77	81.37	27	102.21	77	291.48	27	7.13	77	20.34
28	26.50	78	73.82	28	29.59	78	82.42	28	105.99	78	295.26	28	7.40	78	20.61
29	27.44	79	74.76	29	30.64	79	83.48	29	109.78	79	299.05	29	7.66	79	20.87
30	28.39	80	75.71	30	31.70	80	84.59	30	113.56	80	302.83	30	7.93	80	21.13
31	29.34	81	76.65	31	32.76	81	85.59	31	117.35	81	306.62	31	8.19	81	21.40
32	30.28	82	77.60	32	33.81	82	86.65	32	121.13	82	310.40	32	8.45	82	21.66
33	31.23	83	78.55	33	34.87	83	87.71	33	124.92	83	314.19	33	8.72	83	21.93
34	32.18	84	79.49	34	35.93	84	88.76	34	128.70	84	317.97	34	8.98	84	22.19
35	33.12	85	80.44	35	36.98	85	89.82	35	132.49	85	321.76	35	9.25	85	22.45
36	34.07	86	81.39	36	38.04	86	90.88	36	136.27	86	325.55	36	9.51	86	22.72
37	35.02	87	82.33	37	39.10	87	91.93	37	140.06	87	329.33	37	9.77	87	22.98
38	35.96	88	83.28	38	40.15	88	92.99	38	143.85	88	333.12	38	10.04	88	23.25
39	36.91	89	84.23	39	41.21	89	94.05	39	147.63	89	336.90	39	10.30	89	23.51
40	37.85	90	85.17	40	42.27	90	95.10	40	151.42	90	340.69	40	10.57	90	23.78
41	38.80	91	86.12	41	43.32	91	96.16	41	155.20	91	344.47	41	10.83	91	24.04
42	39.75	92	87.06	42	44.38	92	97.22	42	158.99	92	348.26	42	11.10	92	24.30
43	40.69	93	88.01	43	45.44	93	98.27	43	162.77	93	352.04	43	11.36	93	24.57
44	41.64	94	88.96	44	46.49	94	99.33	44	166.56	94	355.83	44	11.62	94	24.83
45	42.59	95	89.90	45	47.55	95	100.39	45	170.34	95	359.61	45	11.89	95	25.10
46	43.53	96	90.85	46	48.61	96	101.44	46	174.13	96	363.40	46	12.15	96	25.36
47	44.48	97	91.80	47	49.66	97	102.50	47	177.91	97	367.18	47	12.42	97	25.62
48	45.42	98	92.74	48	50.72	98	103.56	48	181.70	98	370.97	48	12.68	98	25.89
49	46.37	99	93.69	49	51.78	99	104.61	49	185.49	99	374.76	49	12.94	99	26.15
50	47.32	100	94.64	50	52.83	100	105.67	50	189.27	100	378.54	50	13.21	100	26.42

Weight

OUNCES TO GRAMS				GRAMS TO OUNCES				POUNDS TO KILOGRAMS				KILOGRAMS TO POUNDS			
oz	*g*	*oz*	*g*	*g*	*oz*	*g*	*oz*	*lb*	*kg*	*lb*	*kg*	*kg*	*lb*	*kg*	*lb*
1	28.35	51	1445.83	1	0.04	51	1.80	1	0.45	51	23.13	1	2.21	51	112.44
2	56.70	52	1474.18	2	0.07	52	1.83	2	0.91	52	23.59	2	4.41	52	114.64
3	85.05	53	1502.52	3	0.11	53	1.87	3	1.36	53	24.04	3	6.61	53	116.85
4	113.40	54	1530.87	4	0.14	54	1.90	4	1.81	54	24.49	4	8.82	54	119.05
5	141.75	55	1559.22	5	0.18	55	1.94	5	2.27	55	24.95	5	11.02	55	121.25
6	170.10	56	1587.57	6	0.21	56	1.98	6	2.72	56	25.40	6	13.23	56	123.46
7	198.45	57	1615.92	7	0.25	57	2.01	7	3.18	57	25.86	7	15.43	57	125.66
8	226.80	58	1644.27	8	0.28	58	2.05	8	3.63	58	26.31	8	17.64	58	127.87
9	255.15	59	1672.62	9	0.32	59	2.08	9	4.08	59	26.76	9	19.84	59	130.07
10	283.50	60	1700.97	10	0.35	60	2.12	10	4.54	60	27.22	10	22.05	60	132.28
11	311.85	61	1729.32	11	0.39	61	2.15	11	4.99	61	27.67	11	24.25	61	134.48
12	340.19	62	1757.67	12	0.42	62	2.19	12	5.44	62	28.12	12	26.46	62	136.69
13	368.54	63	1786.02	13	0.46	63	2.22	13	5.90	63	28.58	13	28.66	63	138.89
14	396.89	64	1814.37	14	0.49	64	2.26	14	6.35	64	29.03	14	30.87	64	141.10
15	425.24	65	1842.72	15	0.53	65	2.29	15	6.80	65	29.48	15	33.07	65	143.30
16	453.59	66	1871.07	16	0.56	66	2.33	16	7.26	66	29.94	16	35.27	66	145.51
17	481.94	67	1899.42	17	0.60	67	2.36	17	7.71	67	30.39	17	37.48	67	147.71
18	510.29	68	1927.77	18	0.63	68	2.40	18	8.17	68	30.84	18	39.68	68	149.91
19	538.64	69	1956.12	19	0.67	69	2.43	19	8.62	69	31.30	19	41.89	69	152.12
20	566.99	70	1984.47	20	0.71	70	2.47	20	9.07	70	31.75	20	44.09	70	154.32
21	595.34	71	2012.82	21	0.74	71	2.50	21	9.53	71	32.21	21	46.30	71	156.53
22	623.69	72	2041.17	22	0.78	72	2.54	22	9.98	72	32.66	22	48.50	72	158.73
23	652.04	73	2069.52	23	0.81	73	2.58	23	10.43	73	33.11	23	50.71	73	160.94
24	680.39	74	2097.86	24	0.85	74	2.61	24	10.89	74	33.57	24	52.91	74	163.14
25	708.74	75	2126.21	25	0.88	75	2.65	25	11.34	75	34.02	25	55.12	75	165.35
26	737.09	76	2154.56	26	0.92	76	2.68	26	11.79	76	34.47	26	57.32	76	167.55
27	765.44	77	2182.91	27	0.95	77	2.72	27	12.25	77	34.93	27	59.53	77	169.76
28	793.79	78	2211.26	28	0.99	78	2.75	28	12.70	78	35.38	28	61.73	78	171.96
29	822.14	79	2239.61	29	1.02	79	2.79	29	13.15	79	35.83	29	63.93	79	174.17
30	850.49	80	2267.96	30	1.06	80	2.82	30	13.61	80	36.29	30	66.14	80	176.37
31	878.84	81	2296.31	31	1.09	81	2.86	31	14.06	81	36.74	31	68.34	81	178.57
32	907.19	82	2324.66	32	1.13	82	2.89	32	14.52	82	37.20	32	70.55	82	180.78
33	935.53	83	2353.01	33	1.16	83	2.93	33	14.97	83	37.65	33	72.75	83	182.98
34	963.88	84	2381.36	34	1.20	84	2.96	34	15.42	84	38.10	34	74.96	84	185.19
35	992.23	85	2409.71	35	1.23	85	3.00	35	15.88	85	38.56	35	77.16	85	187.39
36	1020.58	86	2438.06	36	1.27	86	3.03	36	16.33	86	39.01	36	79.37	86	189.60
37	1048.93	87	2466.41	37	1.31	87	3.07	37	16.78	87	39.46	37	81.57	87	191.80
38	1077.28	88	2494.76	38	1.34	88	3.10	38	17.24	88	39.92	38	83.78	88	194.01
39	1105.63	89	2523.11	39	1.38	89	3.14	39	17.69	89	40.37	39	85.98	89	196.21
40	1133.98	90	2551.46	40	1.41	90	3.17	40	18.14	90	40.82	40	88.19	90	198.42
41	1162.33	91	2579.81	41	1.45	91	3.21	41	18.60	91	41.28	41	90.39	91	200.62
42	1190.68	92	2608.16	42	1.48	92	3.25	42	19.05	92	41.73	42	92.59	92	202.83
43	1219.03	93	2636.51	43	1.52	93	3.28	43	19.51	93	42.18	43	94.80	93	205.03
44	1247.38	94	2664.86	44	1.55	94	3.32	44	19.96	94	42.64	44	97.00	94	207.24
45	1275.73	95	2693.20	45	1.59	95	3.35	45	20.41	95	43.09	45	99.21	95	209.44
46	1304.08	96	2721.55	46	1.62	96	3.39	46	20.87	96	43.55	46	101.41	96	211.64
47	1332.43	97	2749.90	47	1.66	97	3.42	47	21.32	97	44.00	47	103.62	97	213.85
48	1360.78	98	2778.25	48	1.69	98	3.46	48	21.77	98	44.45	48	105.82	98	216.05
49	1389.13	99	2806.60	49	1.73	99	3.49	49	22.23	99	44.91	49	108.03	99	218.26
50	1417.48	100	2834.95	50	1.76	100	3.53	50	22.68	100	45.36	50	110.23	100	220.46

Temperature

DEGREES FAHRENHEIT TO DEGREES CELSIUS

DEGREES CELSIUS TO DEGREES FAHRENHEIT

°F	°C	°F	°C	°F	°C	°F	°C	°C	°F	°C	°F	°C	°F	°C	°F
−50	−45.6	1	−17.2	51	10.6	101	38.3	−50	−58.0	1	33.8	51	123.8	101	213.8
−49	−45.0	2	−16.7	52	11.1	102	38.9	−49	−56.2	2	35.6	52	125.6	102	215.6
−48	−44.4	3	−16.1	53	11.7	103	39.4	−48	−54.4	3	37.4	53	127.4	103	217.4
−47	−43.9	4	−15.6	54	12.2	104	40.0	−47	−52.6	4	39.2	54	129.2	104	219.2
−46	−43.3	5	−15.0	55	12.8	105	40.6	−46	−50.8	5	41.0	55	131.0	105	221.0
−45	−42.8	6	−14.4	56	13.3	106	41.1	−45	−49.0	6	42.8	56	132.8	106	222.8
−44	−42.2	7	−13.9	57	13.9	107	41.7	−44	−47.2	7	44.6	57	134.6	107	224.6
−43	−41.7	8	−13.3	58	14.4	108	42.2	−43	−45.4	8	46.4	58	136.4	108	226.4
−42	−41.1	9	−12.8	59	15.0	109	42.8	−42	−43.6	9	48.2	59	138.2	109	228.2
−41	−40.6	10	−12.2	60	15.6	110	43.3	−41	−41.8	10	50.0	60	140.0	110	230.0
−40	−40.0	11	−11.7	61	16.1	111	43.9	−40	−40.0	11	51.8	61	141.8	111	231.8
−39	−39.4	12	−11.1	62	16.7	112	44.4	−39	−38.2	12	53.6	62	143.6	112	233.6
−38	−38.9	13	−10.6	63	17.2	113	45.0	−38	−36.4	13	55.4	63	145.5	113	235.4
−37	−38.3	14	−10.0	64	17.8	114	45.6	−37	−34.6	14	57.2	64	147.2	114	237.2
−36	−37.8	15	−9.4	65	18.3	115	46.1	−36	−32.8	15	59.0	65	149.0	115	239.0
−35	−37.2	16	−8.9	66	18.9	116	46.7	−35	−31.0	16	60.8	66	150.8	116	240.8
−34	−36.7	17	−8.3	67	19.4	117	47.2	−34	−29.2	17	62.6	67	152.6	117	242.6
−33	−36.1	18	−7.8	68	20.0	118	47.8	−33	−27.4	18	64.4	68	154.4	118	244.4
−32	−35.6	19	−7.2	69	20.6	119	48.3	−32	−25.6	19	66.2	69	156.2	119	246.2
−31	−35.0	20	−6.7	70	21.1	120	48.9	−31	−23.8	20	68.0	70	158.0	120	248.0
−30	−34.4	21	−6.1	71	21.7	121	49.4	−30	−22.0	21	69.8	71	159.8	121	249.8
−29	−33.9	22	−5.6	72	22.2	122	50.0	−29	−20.2	22	71.6	72	161.6	122	251.6
−28	−33.3	23	−5.0	73	22.8	123	50.6	−28	−18.4	23	73.4	73	163.4	123	253.4
−27	−32.8	24	−4.4	74	23.3	124	51.1	−27	−16.6	24	75.2	74	165.2	124	255.2
−26	−32.2	25	−3.9	75	23.9	125	51.7	−26	−14.8	25	77.0	75	167.0	125	257.0
−25	−31.7	26	−3.3	76	24.4	126	52.2	−25	−13.0	26	78.8	76	168.8	126	258.8
−24	−31.1	27	−2.8	77	25.0	127	52.8	−24	−11.2	27	80.6	77	170.6	127	260.6
−23	−30.6	28	−2.2	78	25.6	128	53.3	−23	−9.4	28	82.4	78	172.4	128	262.4
−22	−30.0	29	−1.7	79	26.1	129	53.9	−22	−7.6	29	84.2	79	174.2	129	264.2
−21	−29.4	30	−1.1	80	26.7	130	54.4	−21	−5.8	30	86.0	80	176.0	130	266.0
−20	−28.9	31	−0.6	81	27.2	131	55.0	−20	−4.0	31	87.8	81	177.8	131	267.8
−19	−28.3	32	0.0	82	27.8	132	55.6	−19	−2.2	32	89.6	82	179.6	132	269.6
−18	−27.8	33	0.6	83	28.3	133	56.1	−18	−0.4	33	91.4	83	181.4	133	271.4
−17	−27.2	34	1.1	84	28.9	134	56.7	−17	1.4	34	93.2	84	183.2	134	273.2
−16	−26.7	35	1.7	85	29.4	135	57.2	−16	3.2	35	95.0	85	185.0	135	275.0
−15	−26.1	36	2.2	86	30.0	136	57.8	−15	5.0	36	96.8	86	186.8	136	276.8
−14	−25.6	37	2.8	87	30.6	137	58.3	−14	6.8	37	98.6	87	188.6	137	278.6
−13	−25.0	38	3.3	88	31.1	138	58.9	−13	8.6	38	100.4	88	190.4	138	280.4
−12	−24.4	39	3.9	89	31.7	139	59.4	−12	10.4	39	102.2	89	192.2	139	282.2
−11	−23.9	40	4.4	90	32.2	140	60.0	−11	12.2	40	104.0	90	194.0	140	284.0
−10	−23.3	41	5.0	91	32.8	141	60.6	−10	14.0	41	105.8	91	195.8	141	285.8
−9	−22.8	42	5.6	92	33.3	142	61.1	−9	15.8	42	107.6	92	197.6	142	287.6
−8	−22.2	43	6.1	93	33.9	143	61.7	−8	17.6	43	109.4	93	199.4	143	289.4
−7	−21.7	44	6.7	94	34.4	144	62.2	−7	19.4	44	111.2	94	201.2	144	291.2
−6	−21.1	45	7.2	95	35.0	145	62.8	−6	21.2	45	113.0	95	203.0	145	293.0
−5	−20.6	46	7.8	96	35.6	146	63.3	−5	23.0	46	114.8	96	204.8	146	294.8
−4	−20.0	47	8.3	97	36.1	147	63.9	−4	24.8	47	116.6	97	206.6	147	296.6
−3	−19.4	48	8.9	98	36.7	148	64.4	−3	26.6	48	118.4	98	208.4	148	298.4
−2	−18.9	49	9.4	99	37.2	149	65.0	−2	28.4	49	120.2	99	210.2	149	300.2
−1	−18.3	50	10.0	100	37.8	150	65.6	−1	30.2	50	122.0	100	212.0	150	302.0
0	−17.8							0	32.0						

SUGGESTED FURTHER READING

Bigourdan, Guillaume. *Le Système Métrique des Poids et Mesures*. Paris: Gauthier-Villars, 1901.

Donovan, Frank. *Prepare Now for a Metric Future*. New York: Weybright and Talley, 1970.

Fischer, Louis A. *History of the Standard Weights and Measures of the United States*, Miscellaneous Publication 64. Washington, D.C.: National Bureau of Standards, 1925.

Guillaume, Charles E. *La creation du Bureau International des Poids et Mesures et son oeuvre*. Paris: Gauthier-Villars, 1927.

Hallock, William and Wade, Herbert T. *Outlines of the Evolution of Weights and Measures and the Metric System*, New York: Macmillan, 1906.

Judson, Lewis V. *Weights and Measures Standards of the United States—Brief History*, Miscellanous Publication 247. Washington, D.C.: National Bureau of Standards, 1963.

Kellaway, F. W. *Metrication in Science and Technology*. Harmondsworth, England: Penguin Books, 1968.

Kendig, Frank. "Coming of the Metric System." *Saturday Review*, December 1972. pp. 40–44.

McNish, A. G. "The International System of Units." *Annual Technical Conference Transactions of the American Society for Quality Control*, 1965.

Mechtly, E. A. *The International System of Units—Physical Constants and Conversion Factors*, NASA SP-7012. Washington, D.C.: U.S. Government Printing Office, 1964.

Moreau, Henri. "The Genesis of the Metric System and the Work of the International Bureau of Weights and Measures." Translated by R. E. Oesper. *Journal of Chemical Education*, Vol. 30 (1953), pp. 3–20.

National Bureau of Standards. *International Metric System of Weights and Measures*, Miscellaneous Publication 135. Washington, D.C., 1932.

National Bureau of Standards. *A Metric America: A Decision Whose Time Has Come*. Washington, D.C., 1971.

National Bureau of Standards. *Report of the Metric Study Task Force*. Washington, D.C., 1961.

National Bureau of Standards. *Units of Weights and Measures: International (Metric) and U.S. Customary*, Miscellaneous Publication 286. Washington, D.C., 1963.

National Council of Teachers of Mathematics. "The Metric System of Weights and Measures." *20th Yearbook of the National Council of Teachers of Mathematics*. New York: Bureau of Publications, Teachers College, Columbia University, 1948.

Owen, W. J. *The History of the English System of Weights and Measures*, Miscellaneous Publication 272. Washington, D.C.: National Bureau of Standards, 1966.

Page, Chester, ed. and Vigoureux, Paul, ed. *The International System of Units (SI)*, Special Publication 330. Washington, D.C.: National Bureau of Standards, 1972.

1001
HELPFUL FAMILY HINTS

1001
HELPFUL FAMILY HINTS

Editor-in-Chief
DONALD D. WOLF

Illustrator
JAMES E. BARRY

Design, Layout
and Production
MARGOT L. WOLF

Adapted from the *Timely Tips Series* copyright © 1980 by
Delair Publishing Company, Inc.

ISBN: 0-8326-2246-X

Contents

**Written by
MARTIN SHARP**

High
Blood
Pressure

Contents

What is Blood Pressure?

Everyone has blood pressure. It is the force of the blood against the walls of the blood vessels—the arteries and veins—in your body. Without blood pressure, the blood could not circulate. How and why the blood circulates and what creates the pressure is explained later.

In all human beings, blood pressure varies from day to day and from moment to moment. It goes up when we are excited, and it goes down when we are at rest or asleep. Changes in blood pressure such as these are normal. It is *not* normal when blood pressure goes up and stays up. This condition is called *high blood pressure,* and it is a definite chronic illness that may have very serious consequences such as stroke, heart failure, and kidney failure.

The plagues of the past, cholera, bubonic plague, and tuberculosis, have been almost wiped out. In modern life, these mass killers of human beings have been replaced by a new kind of plague: high blood pressure. The old-time plagues were contagious diseases that spread from person to person, raging through whole continents and killing millions of people. Today, millions of people have high blood pressure and millions die from its consequences, although high blood pressure, unlike the plagues, is not contagious.

About one out of every five adults has high blood pressure, and one out of every five deaths of persons below the age of 65 is caused by its consequences.

Why High Blood Pressure Is Dangerous

When blood pressure is high, the heart has to pump harder to circulate the blood within the blood vessels, which are resisting its flow. After a period of years the heart muscle tires, and failure of the heart can result. Also, continued high pressure against the walls of arteries can eventually cause them to leak and burst. The damage to the arteries of the heart causes a heart attack; of the kidneys, kidney failure; and of the brain, stroke. Persons with high blood pressure have twice the chance of having a fatal stroke or heart attack as do those with normal blood pressure.

A Silent Killer

High blood pressure is a chronic, lifelong, usually incurable disease which, however, can nearly always be controlled with proper and continuing treatment. Few if any symptoms are noticeable until the blood pressure has been high for a long time, often many years, and has caused damage to major organs of the body such as the heart, brain, or kidneys. The lack of symptoms for so long a time while damage is being done has caused high blood pressure to be called "the silent killer."

People are aware of diseases that produce discomfort or pain. Silent diseases that require preventive action based on knowledge of the disease rather than physical pain do not

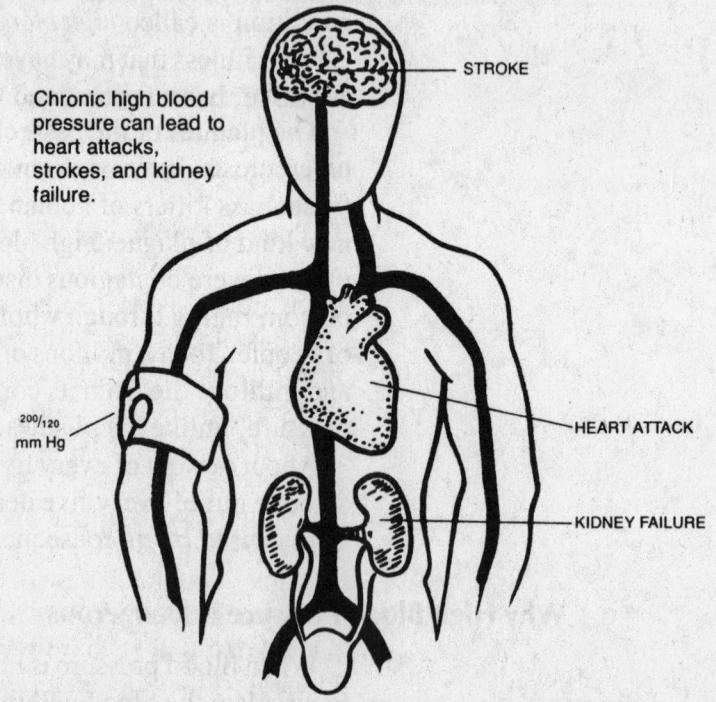

Chronic high blood pressure can lead to heart attacks, strokes, and kidney failure.

STROKE

200/120 mm Hg

HEART ATTACK

KIDNEY FAILURE

attract the average person's attention. Yet if those who have high blood pressure can be made aware of its consequences and be convinced that it can be controlled, a large drop in the number and severity of cases of heart attack, stroke, and kidney disease will follow.

Too many people believe that high blood pressure is only a moderately important disease and are reluctant to accept, or are unaware of, its serious consequences. A patient who goes to a specialist for the treatment of an acute disease or a surgical problem and is told that he or she also has high blood pressure may ignore the warning.

Who Can Tell You If You Have High Blood Pressure?

Since, as we have seen, high blood pressure does not produce dramatic symptoms until it has caused severe damage to vital organs, an untrained person cannot tell if he or she has high blood pressure. The only way to find out is to have your blood pressure measured by a physician or other medically trained professional. Measurement of blood pressure is painless and takes only a few minutes, but it may save your life or prevent years of disablement.

High blood pressure is found in all groups of society, but the incidence is higher in blacks (and more often in black women than in black men), in overweight persons, persons living on an income of less than $5,000 a year, people over 65 years of age, or people who have a family history of high blood pressure. If you belong to one of these groups, have your blood pressure checked regularly. This does not mean, however, that anybody outside these groups should not do the same.

Though high blood pressure is called the silent killer, there are some symptoms that should not be overlooked. Among them are persistent headaches, fatigue, dizziness, and feelings of tension. Also, persons with high blood pressure may experience shortness of breath because of the additional work their hearts must do. The absence of these symptoms is in no way a reason to be careless.

There is much you can do to prevent any of the disastrous consequences of high blood pressure, once you have learned that you have the disease. The first step is to see a doctor, who will give you a schedule of things you must do in order to bring your blood pressure down to normal limits, or at least to a level that will keep it from damaging your heart, brain, or kidneys. What the doctor will ask you to do will be painless and will not require much time or effort: have your blood pressure measured at regular intervals, make the prescribed changes in your diet and living habits, and take medicine exactly as ordered. These simple measures should control your blood pressure and enable you to lead a normal and productive life.

The Cardiovascular System

The blood flows through the heart, arteries, and veins. These and the brain center and nerves that control the beating of the heart are called the *cardiovascular system*.

The heart is a muscle about the size of a fist. It has four chambers, two on each side. The upper chambers are called *auricles* (or *atria*); the lower are *ventricles*. Blood enters the heart through a large *vein* called the *vena cava*, which opens into the right auricle (or atrium). This blood has come to the heart from all parts of the body through a network of veins. From the atrium the blood flows through a one-way valve, composed of muscle, to the right ventricle. The ventricle has thick muscular walls that contract and force the blood out of the heart through large arteries called the *pulmonary arteries*. These arteries conduct the blood to the lungs, where the red blood cells take on oxygen from the air in the lungs. Blood then goes back to the heart through the *pulmonary veins*, entering the left atrium. Again it passes through a valve, flowing down into the left ventricle. As the left ventricle contracts, it pumps blood into a large artery called the *aorta*. This artery carries the blood, via a network of smaller

Blood circulation (schematic).

12

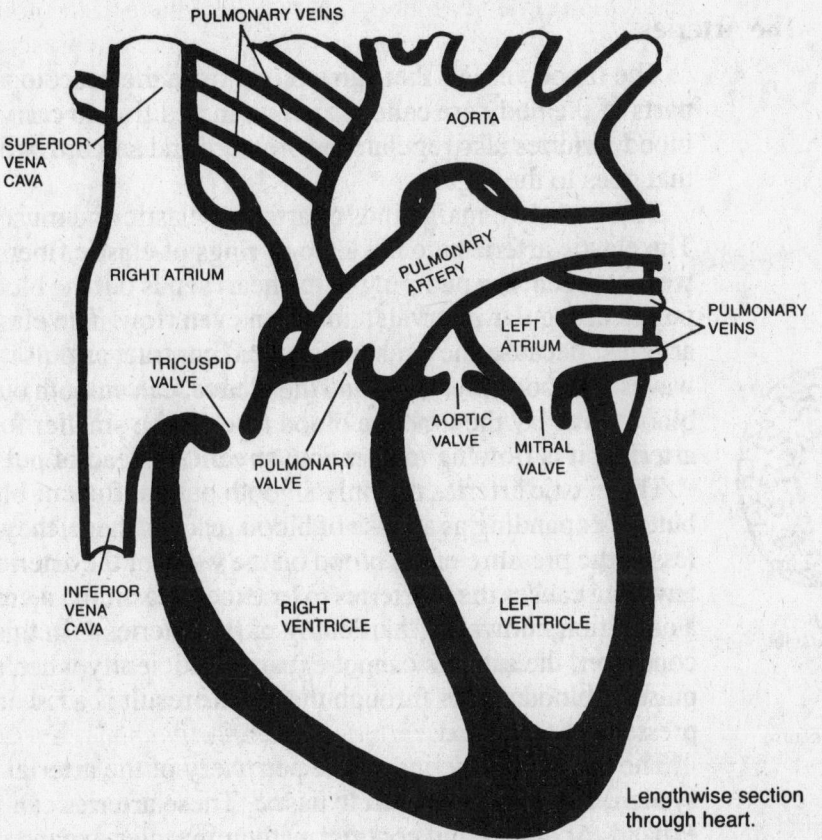

PULMONARY VEINS

AORTA

SUPERIOR
VENA
CAVA

RIGHT ATRIUM

PULMONARY
ARTERY

PULMONARY
VEINS

LEFT
ATRIUM

TRICUSPID
VALVE

AORTIC
VALVE

MITRAL
VALVE

PULMONARY
VALVE

INFERIOR
VENA
CAVA

RIGHT
VENTRICLE

LEFT
VENTRICLE

Lengthwise section
through heart.

arteries, to all parts of the body. The path of the blood in your body, then, is: veins — heart — lungs — heart — arteries — veins, around and around. This continual movement is called the *circulation* of the blood. Each contraction of the ventricles is a heartbeat. A normal heart beats 60 to 90 times each minute when the body is at rest.

Systole and Diastole

When the left ventricle contracts, it pumps a jet of blood into the arteries. The blood flows through the arteries as a wave, or *pulse*. When a doctor or nurse "feels your pulse," it is this wave of blood that he or she feels passing beneath the fingertips held on your wrist. The wave of blood causes a temporary increase in the amount of blood in the part of the artery through which it passes. This increases the pressure of the blood on the walls of the artery. The momentary increase is called *systole*. As we shall see, it is important when measuring blood pressure. After the ventricles contract, they rest for a little less than a second while blood flows into them from the atria. During this resting time, which is called *diastole*, blood pressure is lowest.

13

The Arteries

The blood vessels that carry blood from the heart to all parts of the body are called *arteries*. In addition to carrying blood, arteries also regulate the pressure and amount of blood that goes to the organs.

There are two main kinds of arteries: elastic and muscular. The elastic arteries are made up of rings of elastic fibers. As we have seen, the pumping of the heart sends out the blood in pulses at regular intervals, not as an even flow. The elastic arteries, because they can expand and contract as pulse waves of blood enter them and then leave, can smooth out the blood flow. By the time the blood reaches the smaller arteries, it is flowing in a smooth stream, instead of pulses.

The elastic arteries not only smooth out the flow of blood, but, by expanding as a pulse of blood reaches them, they also lessen the pressure of the blood on the walls of the arteries. If anything causes these arteries to lose their elasticity, it creates a condition known as "hardening of the arteries." In this condition, the arteries cannot expand sufficiently when a pulse of blood passes through them. The result is a rise in the pressure of the blood.

The muscular arteries, at the periphery of the arterial system, have walls of muscle tissue. These arteries can expand (or dilate) and contract as their muscles expand or contract. As they expand or contract, they help the heart to move blood to those parts of the body that need it most at any time.

The smallest muscular arteries are called *arterioles*. They branch into even smaller ones, the *capillary arteries,* which bring oxygen and food to the tissues of all the organs of the body.

If the muscular arteries do not expand and contract in rhythm with the pulses of blood flowing through them, they can offer considerable resistance to the flow of blood. This may raise the pressure of the blood. The resistance of all the arterioles and capillary arteries is called *peripheral arterial resistance* and is an important factor in the level of blood pressure in the arterial system.

By far the most important cause of hardening of the arteries is *atherosclerosis*. In this condition, fatty deposits form on the inner walls of arteries. These deposits may eventually become so thick that they fill the whole artery, completely choking off the flow of blood through it. The fatty deposits cause the artery to lose its suppleness and become "hard."

Section through artery:
A. Fat, longitudinal muscle and elastic fibers.
B. Circular muscle.
C. Elastic membrane.
D. Thin lining (endothelium).

The cause of fatty deposits is an excess of blood fats, which are called *lipids*. The two most dangerous of these substances are cholesterol and triglycerides. Cholesterol is found in many foods, such as fatty meats, sausages, shellfish, egg yolks, and inner organs such as liver and brains. The body converts carbohydrates such as sugar, flour, bread, and bread products into fats called triglycerides.

Once an artery has developed a deposit of blood fat, it is almost impossible to remove it. However, a diet low in cholesterol, triglycerides, and other fats will go a long way toward preventing hardening of the arteries.

The Veins

The blood vessels that carry blood from the tissues back to the heart are the *veins*. Blood begins its return journey to the heart in the capillary veins, which gather carbon dioxide and waste materials from the cells that make up the tissues. The capillaries unite with larger veins, and these in turn unite with still larger ones. Finally, the veins merge into two very large ones, called the *venae cavae*. Blood returning from the head, neck, and arms to the heart passes through the *superior vena cava;* blood returning from the trunk and legs flows through the *inferior vena cava*. Both these large veins carry blood to the right atrium of the heart.

The walls of veins are much thinner than those of arteries, and the pressure in the veins is very low—almost unnoticeable.

CORONARY ARTERIES

CORONARY ARTERIES

The Heart as a Pump

With each heartbeat, the left ventricle sends into the arteries a measurable amount of blood, and the number of heartbeats is easily counted. Thus we can calculate the amount of work the heart does. When the heart is beating at a normal rate, 60 to 80 beats per minute, it pumps 3 to 5 quarts of blood per minute. This amount of blood can increase greatly when one does strenuous work. This remarkable pump works year after year with no time out for repair. It gets its energy from nutrients in the blood—not directly from the blood passing through the atria and ventricles, but rather from its own set of blood vessels. They bring to the heart muscle fuel to furnish energy and oxygen to burn the fuel, and muscle material for repair. They carry away the waste and are essential for the life and activity of the heart. These *coronary arteries* branch out from the base of the aorta just as it leaves the left chamber of the heart and just above the valves that separate the aorta from the ventricle. They and the network of vessels branching from them come down over the top of the heart like a crown (corona). They are the most important blood vessels in the body, and leakage, blockage, or bursting of weakened coronary blood vessels almost surely leads to death.

The Rise and Fall of Blood Pressure

In normal, healthy persons, blood pressure is constantly rising and falling. When you are lying down, especially when asleep, blood pressure is lowest. When you sit up, certain muscles need more blood, and the heart pumps harder and faster to supply this blood. As a result, your blood pressure goes up. When you stand up, more muscles need increased amounts of blood, and blood pressure goes higher. Walking, climbing stairs, running, and other strenuous activities raise the blood pressure even higher. Certain emotions, such as anger, fear, anxiety, or elation, also cause the blood pressure to rise. The rise of blood pressure due to emotions causes more blood to flow to the brain and makes the person more alert and responsive.

In a normal person, when physical exercise is over or strong emotions subside, the blood pressure returns to its normal level. If your heart and blood vessels are in healthy condition, the temporary rise in blood pressure does no harm. It is when pressure remains higher than normal, causing damage to the blood vessels, that a sudden rise in blood pressure can be dangerous and even fatal.

How the Body Regulates Blood Pressure

The body must constantly adjust the pressure and distribution of blood in the arteries to meet the changing demands of the organs for blood. To accomplish this, the body has a *feedback system,* comparable to that of many electrical and electronic devices.

How does this blood-pressure feedback work? The walls of certain large arteries, especially the aorta and the kidney arteries, are lined with cells that are sensitive to pressure. These act as tiny gauges, measuring the pressure of the blood that passes through the arteries. The pressure-sensitive cells are connected by nerves to that part of the brain which controls blood circulation. "Messages" about the level of blood pressure in the arteries are continually passing along the nerves to the brain. The circulation center in the brain collates the bits of information it receives from the arteries. Another part of the nervous system connects the circulation center with the heart and the muscles of the arterial walls. If more blood is needed in any part of the body—for example, in a muscle—a message is sent from the brain to the adrenal gland. This organ then secretes a powerful hormone, *noradrenalin,* into the bloodstream, which causes the arterioles and capillary arteries to contract. It also causes the heart to beat harder. With a more powerful heartbeat pumping blood through narrowed arteries, the pressure must rise.

If the messages from the pressure-sensitive cells tell the brain that the increased blood pressure exceeds the need for it, the circulation center stops the secretion of noradrenalin, the narrowed arteries relax and widen, and the blood pressure soon lowers to normal.

What Is Normal Blood Pressure?

Blood pressure, as we have seen, varies from moment to moment. It also varies with age, often becoming higher as a person grows older. Furthermore, as we have also learned, blood pressure increases at systole, when the left ventricle is pumping blood into the arteries; and pressure lowers at diastole, when the ventricles are filling with blood. Thus, a single measurement is not enough. However, if we measure the pressure both at systole (systolic pressure) and at diastole (diastolic pressure), we get two useful measurements.

Blood pressure measurements are reported in millimeters of mercury, usually abbreviated as "mm Hg." (Hg is the chemical symbol for mercury). The mercury is contained in a narrow glass tube, and the level of the column of mercury rises and falls as blood pressure rises and falls. Thus, a pressure of 120 mm Hg means that the height of the column is 120 millimeters.

Millions of blood pressure measurements have established that a normal range of blood pressure is systolic 160 mm Hg and diastolic 90 mm Hg. These are usually reported as 160/90, and are read as "160 over 90." It is possible to have slightly higher pressures than these and still be healthy, but 160/90 are the standards for comparing pressures.

How Blood Pressure Is Measured

When a physician or nurse measures blood pressure, he or she wraps a cloth-covered rubber cuff around your arm just above the elbow. The cuff is actually a bag from which two rubber tubes project. The free end of one tube is connected to a rubber bulb. The free end of the other tube connects with a glass tube that is partially filled with mercury, or it may connect with a hollow metal container that has a numbered dial and a needle that moves over the numbers. This instrument is called a *sphygmomanometer*.

In a thorough job, your blood pressure is measured three times: when you are lying down, sitting, and standing; but sometimes the last of these is omitted.

To begin the measurement, the doctor or nurse tightens a knob on the rubber bulb. This causes the air that is pumped from the bulb by squeezing it to move through the rubber tube to the cuff. As the cuff fills with air, it presses on the artery that runs to your hand. Eventually, it presses hard enough to stop the flow of blood in the artery. The air entering the cuff also pushes up the column of mercury in the glass tube. Next to the glass tube is a scale of marks, one millimeter apart. The cuff is pumped until the column of mercury rises to a level even higher than it would be in a case of high systolic blood pressure. Then a stethoscope is placed on your arm at the bottom of the cuff and in line with the artery.

Next, the knob on the bulb is loosened to allow air to escape from the cuff. This lessens the pressure in the cuff. As the pressure goes down, the level of the column of mercury in the tube also goes down. When the pressure in the cuff is low enough to let blood flow again in the artery, the doctor begins to hear the pumping of the heart as it moves blood through the artery. At this point, he or she notes the height of the column of mercury. This is the systolic blood pressure—the pressure at the time the heart is pushing blood out of the left ventricle.

As air continues to escape from the cuff, the heart sounds grow louder and then begin to fade away. At the moment when the sounds can no longer be heard, the height of the column of mercury is again noted. This is the diastolic blood pressure—the pressure when the heart is resting and filling with blood.

A person suffering from high blood pressure can measure his or her own blood pressure at home. There are good and quite inexpensive sphygmomanometers on the market today. Most are the type with a numbered dial and needle to indicate millimeters of mercury. Some are electronic and automatically display the pressure in illuminated numbers. You can easily learn to use one of these instruments. It will be useful when the doctor has brought your blood pressure down and your visits to his office are at longer intervals. During these intervals, you yourself can check your blood pressure.

What Causes High Blood Pressure?

There are two main kinds of high blood pressure, or *hypertension*. They are *malignant hypertension* and *benign hypertension*.

The cause of malignant hypertension is not known. It occurs more often in young people than in old. In this disease, the pressure is very high. The patient's vision is usually affected. His or her kidneys function poorly and decline rapidly. He or she may have spells of breathlessness. At one time a patient died within months or at most a year after malignant hypertension was diagnosed. Currently this disease can be controlled successfully, and patients can look forward to useful lives of normal length.

Benign hypertension is certainly a misnomer. In medicine, *benign* means mild or harmless; and a disease that disables and kills as many people as high blood pressure does is not harmless. Still the name persists. Benign hypertension, unlike the malignant form, progresses slowly. For many years it may create no symptoms: no dramatic loss of vision, no breathless spells, no sudden kidney failure. Nevertheless, benign hypertension slowly damages the heart and the arteries, paving the way for heart failure, stroke, and kidney failure.

In more than 90 percent of people who have benign hypertension, no physical cause can be found. This kind of hypertension is called *essential hypertension,* or *primary high blood pressure*. If the small arteries become narrowed and stay that way, blood pressure rises and stays up. Why this happens is still not completely understood.

Experts who have studied essential hypertension report that a tendency toward the condition is often inherited. They believe that inherited high blood pressure does not reveal itself until middle age. The degree of the rise of blood pressure is higher if both parents suffered from the disease. If the tendency toward hypertension is not inherited from either parent, blood pressure will rise very little as a person grows older.

Eating large amounts of salt may cause high blood pressure, but not everybody who eats large amounts of salt

Measuring blood pressure with a sphygmomanometer.

develops the disease. Some investigators believe that persons who inherit the tendency toward high blood pressure are more likely to develop the disease from eating large amounts of salt.

There is evidence that people who live in areas where the water is soft (lacking dissolved calcium and magnesium) are more susceptible to high blood pressure than those who live in areas where the water is hard (containing calcium and magnesium). Another suspected chemical cause is the element cadmium in soft drinking water. Hard water coats water pipes with calcium, thus preventing the dissolving of tiny amounts of cadmium in the water. Cadmium is suspected because persons with hypertension have higher then normal concentrations of cadmium in their kidneys.

A 30-year continuing study of the blood pressure of thousands of the citizens of Framingham, Massachusetts, has led to the conclusion that obesity and overweight greatly increase the risk of developing hypertension. A decrease in blood pressure was observed in persons who lost weight.

As mentioned earlier, strong emotions such as fear and anger cause stress, or tension. Studies have shown that when blood pressure rises because of stress, it usually lowers again when the tension eases. This is usually the case even when the stress lasts for months or a few years. In some persons, however, the pressure does not go down when stress ends.

Some people respond to life situations with more anxiety —stress—than others. The blood pressure of these people is continually being raised as they meet daily situations. Eventually the pressure may remain high. Investigators say that these people have a "hypertensive personality."

In only about 10 percent of high blood pressure cases, a definite cause is known. Infection of the kidneys is one such cause. Another is damage to the adrenal glands that lie atop the kidneys. An obstruction in the artery that carries blood to the kidneys also can cause hypertension. So can a constriction of the aorta, the large artery feeding the heart. When any of these conditions is corrected, the hypertension usually disappears.

Normal artery.

Fatty streaks in artery.

Partial occlusion of artery.

Almost complete occlusion of artery.

Hardening of the Arteries and High Blood Pressure

We frequently hear people talk about "hardening of the arteries" as being a cause of one or another kind of illness. Hardening of the arteries, which physicians call *atherosclerosis,* is a condition in which the arteries become "hard" or less elastic. This happens because the inner walls of an artery become coated with a fatty deposit, which not only hardens the artery's wall but also narrows its diameter. A narrowed artery carries less blood than a healthy one. Also, the fatty deposits create on the artery walls a rough surface that holds back the flow of blood. As a result of these conditions, the heart has to pump harder to move blood through the arteries, so the pressure of the blood rises.

Who Develops High Blood Pressure?

Anyone can have high blood pressure. There are no age limits, and the disease attacks anyone of any race, income, occupation, or place of residence. However, certain groups —in the United States and some other industrialized countries—have a greater risk of developing high blood pressure.

Older people have more high blood pressure than younger ones. Since the outward symptoms of high blood pressure may take a long time to appear, the higher incidence of the disease in older people probably means that many had the disease when younger but did not know it. Not all older persons have high blood pressure, so the disease is not caused simply by growing old.

In the United States, more black people have high blood pressure than whites and people of other races. Since high blood pressure is a silent killer, it is hard to say just how many people in any group have the disease. But a government survey found that only 22 percent of whites, compared with 34 percent of blacks and 25 percent of other minorities, have ever been told that they had high blood pressure.

In blacks, the high blood pressure occurs at an earlier age and is more severe. Also, black women have higher pressure than black men. It cannot be said definitely what is the reason for the racial difference in hypertension, but there is some reason to believe that it is connected with the greater social pressures under which most blacks live. Those with low income and little education usually live under higher tension than those who are better educated and earn more money. As stress can create high blood pressure, the uneducated low-income group are more likely to suffer from the disease.

For the better educated person, the pressure of family and the need to succeed in work are most likely to be felt between the ages of 35 and 49. A government survey pointed to the possibility that the stress of not making a financial success may have an effect on high blood pressure.

Among men, the number of those with hypertension increases with age up to the age of 50 but then levels out. The leveling begins somewhat earlier for blacks than whites.

Among women, the number with high blood pressure increases continuously with age. At each age level, without exception, black women have higher levels of hypertension than do white women. As a group, more women have high blood pressure than do men. Among whites, there is little difference between men and women in the incidence of hypertension in each group up to the age of 65. At that age, the number of women with hypertension increases much faster than the number of men. Among blacks, women have higher levels of hypertension than do men of each age group.

A study of men found that the more active ones were less likely to have high blood pressure than those who worked less. However, this observation is ambiguous, because men who worked less than 40 hours a week had lower blood pressures than those who worked 40 to 50 hours, and those who worked more than 50 hours had the highest pressures.

As mentioned, overweight and high blood pressure often go together; therefore, fat people are more likely to suffer from hypertension than thin ones.

How to Tell Whether You Have High Blood Pressure

When you become sick, your body gives certain tell-tale signals. For example, if you contract measles, you develop a rash all over your body; if you have a cold, you cough and sneeze and may have a sore throat; if you have the flu, you run a fever, may have aches in your joints, and may cough. These signals are called *symptoms*. They tell you clearly that something is wrong with the functioning of your body. A very short time after you contract a disease, you can see or feel its symptoms. But, as we have seen, with high blood pressure, the silent killer, it usually takes years from the time the pressure of the blood begins to rise to the appearance of symptoms.

There are some symptoms that appear early, but since they are also symptoms of other diseases, they may not be recognized as being caused by high blood pressure. These,

COMPLAINT	APPROXIMATE FREQUENCY
Chest pains	26%
Depression, lack of drive	7%
Dizziness	30%
Headaches	23%
Nervousness	35%
Palpitation of the heart	32%

and the frequency with which they appear, are listed in the chart below.

Young people may have trouble sleeping or digesting their food. They may perspire a lot when it is not particularly hot; they may feel fatigued without having worked hard; or they may become excited for no apparent reason. All these complaints can be symptoms of high blood pressure.

Persons above 45 years of age may complain of general malaise. They cannot concentrate on their jobs and so do not perform well; they tire easily; they cannot endure stress as well as they formerly could; their sexual drive declines. These complaints, too, can be symptoms of elevated blood pressure.

Even if high blood pressure does not make itself known through one of the foregoing signs or symptoms, it is still possible for you to have it, and it is advisable to have regular checkups.

If high blood pressure is not treated for some time, it causes damage that may produce tightness and pain radiating to the left shoulder and down the left arm to the hand. These symptoms are very serious. They can indicate a blockage of the flow of blood in the coronary arteries that supply the heart muscle and can be a forewarning of a heart attack.

Repeat attacks of dizziness, lapses of memory, and inability to concentrate are early symptoms of insufficient flow of blood through the arteries of the brain. These symptoms will be followed by fainting, temporary difficulties in speaking, intermittent weakness of the arms or legs or both, and difficulty in walking, which indicate a slight stroke or warnings of one to come.

Shortness of breath after only a little exercise or physical work, frequent urination at night, and a persistent cough may be warnings of heart failure in the near future. Swelling of the ankles, at first only during the day, but later at night, too, and finally swelling of the entire legs are more specific signs of heart failure.

Another sign of the damage caused by high blood pressure is cramps in one leg at a time or, rarely, both at the same time. The cramps may come while the afflicted person is walking and force him to stop and rest. These symptoms result from a lessened flow of blood in the arteries of the pelvis and legs.

Any of the symptoms described above should be reported to your doctor, because he is the only one who can decide definitely whether the cause of the symptom is high blood pressure or some other disease. In any case, the visit to your doctor may save your life.

Suppose You Do Have High Blood Pressure

Once your physician has determined that you have high blood pressure, he or she will seek to find out three basic things: (1) how far the disease has gone and what organs it may have damaged; (2) what is causing it; and (3) what else you may be doing that could worsen the condition.

Your physician will give you a series of examinations that will determine what damage, if any, has taken place in your heart, arteries, kidneys, and possibly your brain.

The doctor will try to find a cause, or perhaps more than one, for your elevated blood pressure. It is simple common sense that unless the cause of the high blood pressure is eliminated, treatment of the condition is impossible. It may turn out that the cause can be entirely eliminated by surgery (a tumor on the adrenal gland) or by medication (infection of the kidneys). If this can be done, the blood pressure will return to normal.

Since a number of people have hypertension for which no clear-cut cause can be found, it is important that the physician look for factors that may be aggravating the disease. Among these, called *risk factors*, are overweight, smoking, stress, diabetes, and a diet high in cholesterol, triglycerides, or salt.

High Blood Pressure, the Pill, and Pregnancy

High blood pressure is a rare side effect of the use of birth control pills. A survey of 600 women in inner-city Washington showed that 7 percent who had no history of elevated blood pressure before taking the pill developed high blood pressure while taking it. But it is not known how many of these women would have developed high blood pressure anyway. This is an important question, because most of the women were black and it is known that blacks—especially black women—have a higher rate of elevated blood pressure than whites.

Treatment Plans

When the doctor has determined what damage high blood pressure has done to a patient, what the cause of the ailment is, and what, if any, risk factors are present, he or she must decide on a plan of treatment. Different findings require different kinds of treatment. High blood pressure caused by a tumor on an adrenal gland requires immediate surgery. If a patient is young, is of a nervous disposition, and is under stress in school or work, and if the blood pressure is much above normal, the doctor may simply monitor the blood pressure at regular intervals. If, when the stressful condition no longer exists, the patient's pressure does not lower, then the doctor may prescribe medication.

If a physician finds that a young black woman has a slight rise in blood pressure, is of nervous disposition, and is under stress in school or work, a different course of treatment is called for. The woman's race provides the high risk that her slightly increased blood pressure will develop into a severe chronic condition. Therefore the physician immediately prescribes medication to lower the pressure.

If a man in his 60's has high blood pressure because of atherosclerosis which raises his systolic pressure to between 170 and 180 and also has a high blood-fat level, the doctor may not prescribe any medication. In this case medicine will not cure the atherosclerosis nor extend the patient's life expectancy, but proper diet will help to keep the atherosclerosis from increasing rapidly.

These three examples show that not all cases of high blood pressure can be treated in the same way. It is important to realize this and to maintain confidence in your doctor, even if a friend or relative, also suffering from hypertension, is treated differently. There is no standard overall treatment that can be used for all who suffer from the disease.

Confidence in the physician and mutual understanding and respect are even more necessary in the treatment of essential hypertension, as the patient must remain under doctor's care for life.

Medication

Many laymen believe that, since high blood pressure may be due to stress, tranquilizers and sedatives should be used to combat it. However, these two types of drugs are not effective.

The cornerstone of most treatment programs is a diuretic agent. This is a type of drug that eliminates excess sodium (usually found in salt) from the body. Some of these (with their trade names in parentheses) are chlorothiazide (Diuril), hydrochlorothiazide (Esidrix, Hydrodiuril, Oretic), benzoflumethiazide (Naturetin), chlorthalidone (Hygrotin), furosemide (Lasix), and methyclothrozide (Enduron). Since all these drugs perform the same function, the doctor will probably prescribe the one with which he is most familiar and to which the patient reacts most favorably.

If the use of a diuretic does not succeed in bringing the blood pressure down to normal, the doctor may add other drugs to his treatment program. Among the more effective drugs that might be added are the ones derived from reserpine, a chemical compound, which itself is derived from a group of plants called *Rauwolfia serpentina*. Some of these and their trade names are alpha methyldopa (Aldomet), propranolol (Inderal), hydralazine (Apresoline), guanethedine (Ismelin), clonodine (Catapres), and prazosin (Minipres). These drugs relax the narrowed arteries, which lowers blood pressure. But the lowering takes place only while the drug is in the bloodstream. Therefore, its use can never be stopped, even after the blood pressure has been lowered. This may mean taking the drug for the rest of the patient's life. These drugs usually are combined with a diuretic in a single pill, so that the number of pills to be taken in a day can be reduced.

If you are taking any of these drugs, your doctor must watch their effects on your blood pressure. Since some persons react to some drugs by developing unwanted symptoms, called *side effects*, the doctor must know about these, too. Some side effects are headache, dizziness, nausea, pains in the joints, drowsiness, fever, and diarrhea. You must continue to visit your doctor often—at least until your blood pressure is brought under control. Then you may visit him or her less often, but this is a decision for the doctor, not the patient, to make.

Since each person is an individual with his or her own life history and reactions to drugs, a doctor may have to try several drugs before the right one is found—the one that lowers the blood pressure and has the fewest side effects.

Living With High Blood Pressure

Take your medicine regularly.

Stick to your diet.

Don't smoke.

Once you learn that you have high blood pressure and your doctor has brought the pressure down to acceptable levels, you must accept the fact that you will have to live with your ailment for the rest of your life. At first this may seem frightening, but you will soon learn that your life can be quite normal—even, in some ways, better than before.

In addition to giving you medicine, your doctor will prescribe a sodium-free diet. Actually, most foods in their natural state contain very little, if any, sodium. Foods that must be avoided usually contain sodium in the form of salt that was added in the commercial preparation of the foods; frankfurters are an example. All in all, you will find that it is quite easy to have tasty meals that are very low in sodium content.

Learn to relax.

Play.

Mix play with work.

Take a vacation every year.

Get enough rest.

Exercise moderately.

The one strict rule in the diet will be that you must not add table salt (sodium chloride) to your food either when cooking or eating it. Fortunately, there is another kind of salt, potassium chloride, that is available in supermarkets and other food stores. This kind of salt is not as salty to the taste but is a good substitute for table salt. Furthermore, you can soon learn how to use spices and herbs to make your food tasty.

We have seen the harmful effect of overweight on blood pressure, so if you are overweight, you will have to go on a reducing diet in addition to the low-sodium one. You definitely should avoid any kind of crash diet, but rather lose weight gradually and sensibly. Your doctor will help you with your reducing problems and might also prescribe a diet low in cholesterol and triglycerides, even if your weight is normal.

Since high blood pressure is a very serious matter, you should set a routine for yourself and stick to it. Your routine should consist of the following:

Take your medicine regularly.

Stick to your diet.

Don't smoke.

Learn to relax and play, and alternate these activities with work. Take at least one vacation a year.

Get enough sleep to feel rested.

Exercise moderately.

See your doctor regularly for checkups.

You may have to change your work habits. You may have to choose between a coveted promotion or income level and continuing to remain alive. Reevaluate your goals and slow down.

Can You Still Use Stimulants?

High blood pressure patients may drink coffee, tea, and cocoa in moderate amounts. However, since the stimulants (caffeine, aminophyllin, and theobromine) in these beverages may cause the drugs the patient is taking to produce undesirable side effects, the doctor may forbid drinking one or another of the beverages. On the other hand, the stimulants may help the patient to overcome the drowsiness that some antihypertensive drugs cause. Again,

Have regular checkups.

27

the doctor must decide whether you can make this use of coffee, tea, or cocoa.

A glass of wine or beer after a day of work is not forbidden a high blood pressure patient. But alcohol can intensify the fatigue produced by some blood pressure drugs. This could be a hazard to the patient who drinks an alcoholic beverage before driving, since it may make him or her too drowsy to drive safely.

Some Final Advice

Don't be frightened or depressed by high blood pressure. It can be treated effectively.

Follow the orders your doctor gives you. Simple measures such as faithfully taking diuretic pills produce good results.

Persons who are taking blood pressure medication should carry in their purse or wallet an identification card that states the type and dosage of the medicines, their most recent blood pressure reading, and the address of their doctor. Your physician can give you one of these ID cards.

Don't run from one doctor to another, looking for a quick and easy miracle drug. Stick to one reliable doctor or one good clinic, and follow the plan of treatment given you.

If your doctor does prescribe drug treatment, be patient; don't stop taking the drugs because they produce annoying side effects. Tell your doctor about these effects.

Give yourself a chance to adjust to the action of a blood pressure drug. It may take weeks to act, but the end results will reward your persistence.

Modern treatment of hypertension may be complicated and may require much time, patience, and understanding by both patient and physician. It is annoying to take pills and experience unpleasant side reactions when you may have felt well before treatment—but remember, you were *not* well; the silent killer was at work. Don't be discouraged if you must continue treatment for the rest of your life. All your effort is less than it would be if you let the complications of high blood pressure set in. Most high blood pressure cases respond to treatment, and most patients whose blood pressure is being successfully treated live long and *normal* lives.

The Drugs You Take

Written by
MARTIN SHARP

Contents

Millions of Dollars for Medicines

Almost everyone in the United States takes drugs of some kind. Even healthy persons have an occasional muscle pain or headache, for which they take aspirin or another painkiller. The prescriptions for medicines written by physicians are counted in the billions every year. American consumers spend about $9 billion each year for medicines.

The science of medicines, pharmacology, has progressed further in the past 30 years than in the previous 30 centuries. Many medicines available today had not even been discovered 40 years ago.

Although a great amount of money is spent on medicines, it does not always buy good health. People sometimes take medicines to wake up, to get to sleep, to relax from everyday tensions, to stimulate or reduce appetite. Health can actually be harmed by continual taking of medicines for these purposes. The misuse or excessive use of medicines is a major drug problem in America.

This does not mean that you should not take medicines when you need them, but you should know when and how to use them. You can protect your health, prevent accidents or illness or even death, and save a lot of money by knowing the best ways to buy and use medicines.

Over-the-Counter and Prescription Drugs

For the consumer, there are two types of medicine: over-the-counter (OTC) and prescription (R$_x$) drugs.

Over-the-counter medicines are also known as patent medicines or home remedies. They include such common drugs as aspirin, laxatives, and antacids. If you use these drugs according to the directions on the label, they are relatively safe. This means that you must not take them oftener or in larger doses than is indicated by the label. You can buy OTC drugs without a prescription in any drugstore and in many supermarkets.

Prescription drugs (which bear the symbol R$_x$) can be ordered or prescribed only by a doctor and can be sold only by a registered pharmacist. R$_x$ drugs are generally more powerful than OTC drugs and are more likely to cause side effects such as rashes, nausea, dizziness, shortness of breath, and others.

When Should You Take Medicines?

You should not always reach for a medicine when you don't feel good. Feeling tired, a little tense during the working day, or perhaps a bit nauseated are parts of everyday living. A little extra sleep and time out for relaxation may cause most of these symptoms to disappear.

Newspaper or magazine advertisements or broadcast commercials may make you think you have a condition that is described. Then you reach for, or go out and buy, the medicine the sponsor is selling. It would be better to wait a while and see if the symptom you think you have does not go away without medication.

Many OTC and R$_x$ medicines relieve pain, nasal stuffiness, or a headache without curing the condition that brought on these, and other, symptoms. A cold remedy may make you feel more comfortable by reducing sniffles and sneezes, but your cold will last as long as if you had taken no medicine at all.

When you take a medicine that relieves unpleasant or painful symptoms, you naturally will want to take it again if the symptoms return. However, you should not do this for very long. If pain, fever, headache, or other symptoms persist, it is important for you to see a doctor about them. They may be the symptoms of a serious disease.

All medicines affect the way your body functions. OTC medicines generally affect you less than R$_x$ medicines because they are less powerful.

A medicine that is safe and effective for most people may cause problems for others who have unpleasant or allergic reactions to certain drugs. Some people get a skin rash if they take even one aspirin.

Many medicines decrease or increase in strength as time passes. This points to the fact that buying the large, economy size of a drug may not be economical if it remains in your medicine cabinet unused for a long time. On the other hand, many R$_x$ drugs are so expensive that it may pay to buy in large quantities. If you must take an R$_x$ drug, ask your doctor or pharmacist how long it will keep its proper strength; then you will know whether or not to buy a large quantity.

Buying OTC Drugs.

Before you buy any OTC drug, ask yourself if you really need it. Do you feel you should buy it because you were persuaded by a TV commercial, a friend who said it helped him or her, or an article in a newspaper or magazine? If you feel tired, should you buy a medicine to relieve the tiredness or should you relax frequently or get more sleep? Or should you see your doctor?

If you feel that you do need an OTC medicine, ask your pharmacist's advice and be sure to read the label. You may change your mind.

On the labels of OTC drugs you will find certain information that federal law requires all manufacturers to give:

• The name of the medicine and the name and address of the manufacturer, packer, or distributor.

• The active ingredients. This information will help you to avoid any allergic reactions or other sensitivities that you may have to certain ingredients. Also, this information can save you money, because many OTC medicines contain exactly the same ingredients and differ from each other only in brand name. Knowing that two medicines are identical should keep you from buying both.

• Directions for safe use. For example, certain drugs cause drowsiness and should not be taken if you are going to drive a car or operate certain kinds of machinery soon after you have taken them. Others should not be taken by people with high blood pressure. The label may warn you not to take the drug for too long or in larger than recommended amounts; for example, "Do not take more than two tablets in four

33

hours or more than six in 24 hours." The label may contain the warning, "If symptoms persist more than 24 hours, see your doctor."

Pharmacists Can Help You

Pharmacists are well-trained professionals who can help their customers to understand how to buy and use drugs. Pharmacists are not allowed to prescribe R_x drugs.

Your pharmacist can explain to you the meaning of terms on labels. He or she may be able to recommend a lower-priced brand of drug than the one you chose.

Don't be afraid to ask a pharmacist for help; your health is at stake, and the pharmacist will be glad to help.

How to Buy Prescription Medicines

When you see your doctor, besides telling him the symptoms that brought you to his office, tell him of any bad experience you have had with taking medicines and of any allergies you may have. This information will enable him or her to avoid giving you a medicine that will cause such side effects.

Don't expect the doctor to prescribe medicine every time you see him; often he won't find it necessary to prescribe any. When a medicine is prescribed for you, make sure you know the answers to these questions before leaving his office:

What is the name of the medicine? Since the names of medicines are not common words, write down the name of the one you are given. You may need to tell another doctor about it later.

When and how often should I take it? If the doctor tells you to take the medicine three times a day, ask whether it should be taken before or after meals. Some drugs taken on an empty stomach may cause you to feel upset; others should be taken only on an empty stomach.

Can the least expensive brand of the medicine be prescribed? Many medicines are very expensive, so you should not be afraid to ask your doctor for the least expensive brand that will be effective. Ask if you can be given a prescription for the generic name of the medicine rather than the brand name. Drugs bought by generic name are usually cheaper. If the doctor will not prescribe a particular medicine by generic name, he probably feels that a brand-name medicine will help you more.

Can the new medicine be taken with others? If you are

34

taking other medicines, you should have told your doctor; if you haven't, tell him before he writes your prescription. This knowledge will help the doctor to prescribe properly.

What reactions, or side effects, can I expect? In some people, certain medicines may cause drowsiness, nausea, vomiting, dizziness, nervousness, or other reactions. These are unfortunate but unavoidable. If the side effects become severe, tell the doctor, who will probably prescribe another medicine.

What precautions should I take? As with OTC drugs, you should be warned not to engage in certain activities soon after taking a dose of certain medicines.

Can the prescription be refilled? If the medicine is to be taken frequently or for a long time, you may need to have the prescription refilled. If so, ask your doctor about this. When you have taken all the medicine prescribed, the doctor may want to reexamine you to see if you still need that medicine or perhaps a different one; or the doctor may allow a limited number of refills.

Must I finish all the medicine that has been prescribed for me? If your symptoms disappear before you finish the medicine the doctor has prescribed, should you stop taking it? Should you continue in order to prevent a recurrence of the illness? Does the doctor want you to check with him after you have taken a certain amount of the prescribed medicine? You should find out the answers to these questions.

If, after leaving the doctor's office, you have more questions or have forgotten some of the answers, don't hesitate to call the doctor.

Choosing a Pharmacy

When you need a medicine immediately—perhaps for a child running a high fever—you will want to go to the pharmacy that is nearest and gives the quickest service. However, when you are using the same medicine for a long time, you may be wise to shop around and compare prices. On the other hand, you may be using a pharmacy that gives you just the kind of service you want, and you may not want to change. An advantage to buying from the same pharmacy over a long period of time is that the pharmacist has a record of the drugs you and your family have been using. This may enable him to spot undesirable combinations of medicines that you and your doctor may not be aware of.

Before you leave a pharmacy with your newly filled

prescription, look at the label on the medicine. It should contain the following:
• the pharmacy's name, address, and phone number
• the prescription number
• the patient's name
• how often and when to take the drug
• how much to take each time
• special instructions (shake well, refrigerate, etc.)
• the doctor's name
• the date the prescription was filled
• the name of the drug (if the doctor says it should be put on the label)

If any of this information is not on the label or if you think any of it is wrong, ask the pharmacist about it. If you are still not sure, call your doctor.

When you have a prescription refilled, write the date on the label. The pharmacist uses the date the prescription was first filled.

Using and Storing Medicines

Directions. With both R_x and OTC drugs, carefully follow the directions about how much to take and when. Continue taking an R_x drug for the entire time the doctor ordered. If you stop taking it too soon, you may prevent the drug from accomplishing what the doctor prescribed it for — and find yourself sick again.

Side effects. As we have seen, some drugs cause unwanted side effects such as rash, nausea, dizziness, or headache. If this happens to you, immediately consult your doctor or pharmacist. The drug may be discontinued, the dosage changed, or another drug may be prescribed.

Combining drugs. Always consult your doctor or pharmacist before you take two medicines together. Failure to do this may result in great harm or even death. If you are taking any medicines at all, don't drink alcohol without first consulting your doctor. Failure to do so may result in death.

Storing drugs. Always look at the labels of both OTC and R_x drugs for special storage instructions. If the label says, "Keep in a cool, dry place," do not store the drug in the medicine cabinet of a warm, steamy bathroom; store it in the refrigerator.

Clean out your medicine cabinet regularly. Throw out old medicines that may have lost or gained strength or have changed chemically. Throw out a medicine when your doctor tells you to stop taking it.

Labels. Keep the label on or in the container. You need it to identify the medicine and to refer to the directions. When you pour liquid medicines, keep the label side on top so that any spilled liquid won't run down the side and blot out the print on the label.

Don't share drugs. Your doctor prescribes an R$_x$ drug for you and you alone. Never give the drug to anyone else or let anyone share it because you think his symptoms are the same as yours. Only a doctor can tell whether the symptoms really are the same. Your guess may do serious harm to the other person.

Look carefully. Many pillboxes, bottles, and drugs look alike. Don't take a drug until you have read the label on the container. Never take medicines in the dark.

When you travel. If you need to take prescription medicines with you on a long trip, be sure to take enough. Carry them in the original labeled containers. Pharmacists may not fill prescriptions written by out-of-state doctors. In an emergency, go to a hospital. If you move to another city, take enough medicine to last until you find another doctor. Also, arrange with your doctor to forward your medical record when you have found a new doctor.

Precautions with children. Medicines cause more accidental poisonings among children under five than any other materials in the household. Toddlers like to crawl and climb and get into things. A bottle of medicine can look as inviting to a child as a bottle of soda pop, a bottle of brightly colored pills as interesting as colored candy. And what toddlers can get their hands on, they put into their mouths. All medicines — as well as any other chemicals used in the home — should be kept on a high shelf out of children's reach, or better still, in a locked cabinet.

But this precaution is not enough. Medicines should not

be left in handbags that are then left on chairs, beds, or other low places that a child can reach. Children love to explore pocketbooks.

If the phone or doorbell rings when you are about to take or have just taken medicine, don't walk away from the medicine leaving it where a child can reach it. It takes only a few seconds for a child to imitate you by taking your medicine. The results can be tragic.

To protect children from poisoning by medicines, the Food and Drug Administration (FDA), under the Poison Prevention Packaging Act, requires that all poisonous substances be enclosed in safety packaging. Such packaging is designed to be especially hard for children to open, but it works only if you make sure that you close the package in the correct manner.

When you give children medicine, don't tell them it is candy or something else they like. They may try to get more of it when they are alone.

You Can Help

If, after buying a medicine, you notice that it does not seem to be the right color or has a different odor, *don't use it*. Return it to the pharmacy. If a medicine packaged by the manufacturer seems to be discolored or otherwise bad, report this fact to the FDA—don't just toss it away. The address of the nearest FDA field office or resident inspection station is in the phone book under U.S. Department of Health, Education, and Welfare; Food and Drug Administration. Or you can write directly to FDA headquarters at 5600 Fishers Lane, Rockville, MD 20852.

Generic Drugs: How Good Are They?

All drugs, whether they are sold under brand names or their generic names, must meet the same FDA standards for safety, purity, strength, and effectiveness. All drug manufacturers, large and small, are subject to FDA inspection and must follow the FDA's current Good Manufacturing Practice Regulations. That is why the FDA sees no significant difference in quality between brand-name and generic drugs.

The generic name is also called the "official" or "nonproprietary" name. A generic name is assigned to a drug when it appears to be of some use in the curing of disease. Generic names are usually contractions of complex chemical names. The new drug also is given a brand name by its developer or manufacturer. This name is generally short, easy to remember, and often devised to suggest the action of the drug.

It is the brand name that is used to advertise the drug to the medical profession. However, the generic name must also appear in advertising and labeling in letters half as big as those of the brand name. Aspirin is the generic name for the leading OTC painkiller; Bayer and St. Joseph's are brand names for two manufacturers' aspirin. Potassium penicillin, G is a generic name for a kind of penicillin. *Pentids*® is the registered name for the same drug as sold by Squibb Laboratories. The drug with the generic name *reserpine* is used for lowering blood pressure. It is marketed under more than 40 brand names.

It is a popular misconception that brand-name drugs are produced only by large, well-known firms, and generic drugs are made by small, almost unknown companies. This is not a fact. Any drug manufacturer, no matter how small, can put a brand name on its product, and many large manufacturers can and do sell the same product under both a brand name and a generic name.

Not only must each drug meet FDA requirements, but so must each drug plant — large or small. All drug manufacturers must register with the FDA; all are subject to periodic inspection; and all must follow FDA Good Manufacturing Practice Regulations that touch on every aspect of making drugs, from plant maintenance to quality control. These regulations apply to all producers and are intended to assure that all drugs meet the same standards of safety, strength, purity, and effectiveness. These requirements were written into the 1962 amendments to the food and drug laws for the very purpose of encouraging physicians to make wider use of generic drugs in order to lower the cost of medical care.

Thus, FDA Commissioner Donald Kennedy could say, "There simply is no evidence to support the notion of serious quality differences between generic and brand-name drugs."

Drug Development

The development of a new drug is a long and complex process that can begin in many places — a drug manufacturer's laboratory, a chemical company, or a research lab at the National Institutes of Health. The development hopefully will culminate in benefits to all sick persons.

By the time a new medicine becomes available to the

public, it has been thoroughly tested in both animals and humans under carefully controlled conditions, and information has been approved for physicians to help them prescribe the drug correctly.

The Food and Drug Administration is responsible for approving the marketing of all new drugs sold in the United States and for monitoring their use after approval.

The first step in the development of a new drug is research into the chemistry or anatomy of a disease, or the discovery that a chemical has possible use as a drug.

The chemical is subjected to screening tests and to testing in animals. This is done to see whether the drug has the desired effects. If it does, additional testing is done to determine what side effects the drug might have, what dosage amounts are poisonous, what the safe dosage range might be for human beings, and whether there is any reason to test the drug on human beings.

Before the new drug can be used in any way on human beings, it is tested on hundreds or thousands of animals. The FDA does not monitor these tests, but if the animal tests are successful or promising in effectiveness against a disease and the drug seems safe enough to use in human beings, the FDA steps in. The drug is then known as an Investigational New Drug (IND). At this point, the sponsor must submit to the FDA the complete composition of the drug, its source, how it is made, and documented results of the animal tests showing clearly the disease-combating qualities of the drug and proving its safety for testing on human beings.

Human testing is divided into three phases. Phase I is directed at determining the chemical actions of a drug, how it is absorbed into the body, how it should be given (by mouth or injection, for example), and the safe dosage range. These tests usually involve fewer than ten patients. The safety record of such research is excellent. The FDA knows of no volunteer patient who has been permanently harmed as a result of Phase I testing. Some, however, have become ill.

In Phase II testing is done on a limited number of human beings to learn if the drug actually does prevent or cure a specific disease. If Phase II shows that the drug may be useful in treating a disease and long-term animal testing has shown no unwarranted harm, the sponsor is allowed to proceed to Phase III.

In Phase III the drug is tested extensively. Again the effectiveness, desirable dosage, and safety are tested—this time on a large number of patients. In this phase the drug is used as it would be if prescribed by a physician. Several hundred or several thousand patients are involved in these tests. If the sponsor is satisfied that all has gone well up to this point, it applies to the FDA for approval to market the drug. This application, called a New Drug Application (NDA), may run into thousands of pages.

The FDA Bureau of Drugs reviews the NDA. The Bureau has six divisions: cardiopulmonary-renal, neuropharmacological, metabolic-endocrine, anti-infective, oncology-radiopharmaceutical, and surgical-dental. Each division is composed of physicians, pharmacists, chemists, and other professionals experienced in evaluating new drugs.

The Bureau of Drugs must determine whether the benefits of the drug when used properly outweigh the risks to the patient. If a drug is used to combat a deadly disease such as cancer, it is reasonable to allow it to be more of a risk to the patient than a drug that is an antacid, with no risk tolerated.

The amount of work involved is huge when several experts must read possibly several thousand pages of an NDA in order to make a decision on the safety and effectiveness of a drug. The result has been long delays in approving some drugs. Modern methods, such as computerized searches of literature on drugs, have helped, but the time needed for thorough investigation before approval is still great. This is another aspect of the risk-benefit equation: how short an investigation can be risked in order to obtain the possible benefits of a new drug.

Although the FDA makes every effort to assure the safety of drugs, the present procedure that leaves the testing in the hands of the sponsors has had some tragic results. In 1962 a firm filed a New Drug Application for a so-called anti-cholesterol drug, which was supposed to destroy cholesterol in the blood and thereby end the risk of hardening of the arteries. The manufacturer, in the Phase III testing, dispensed the drug widely. The result was that some of the test subjects suffered permanent loss of hair, cataracts, and total loss of sight. The FDA—by sheerest accident—found that the manufacturer's records had been falsified. This incident illustrates the risk involved in allowing the sponsor of a drug to do the testing. Yet it would be physically impossible for any government agency to take over such testing or even to closely supervise testing by sponsors.

Mixing Medicines

Although the FDA requires that the manufacturer of a new drug prove its safety and effectiveness, the drug producer is not required by law to carry out tests that involve the use of the new drug along with other drugs. Such testing would be almost impossible, since there is no way of knowing what other medicines a patient might be taking. The only sources of information on drug interaction are the physicians and pharmacists who report harmful interactions to the FDA.

If you are taking one kind of medicine and wish to take an OTC medicine at the same time, read the label or the manufacturer's insert in the package carefully. It may tell you that you should not take the medicine along with certain other drugs. Even better, ask the pharmacist about mixing the drugs; he should be able to tell you whether doing so will be dangerous. If you are taking one or more R_x drugs and want to take an OTC medicine, be sure to consult the physician who prescribed the R_x medicines for you. A mistake in mixing drugs can cause them to become ineffective against the disease for which you are taking them, at best; at worst, it can kill you. The one rule to follow when thinking about mixing medicines is *consult your pharmacist or doctor first*.

Food and Drug Interactions

If you are taking a drug, the food you eat could make it work faster or slower or even prevent it from working at all. Eating certain foods while taking certain drugs can be dangerous, and some drugs can affect the way your body uses food.

Would it occur to you not to swallow a tetracycline capsule with a glass of milk? Or to avoid aged cheese and Chianti wine if you are taking a certain medicine to combat depression. Or to eat more leafy green vegetables if you are on the Pill? Probably not. Yet the effects foods and drugs have on each other can determine whether medicines do their job and whether your body gets the nutrients it needs.

The extent of the interaction between foods and drugs depends on the drug dosage and on the patient's age, size, and medical condition. In general, however, the presence of food in the stomach and intestines can influence a drug's effectiveness by slowing down or speeding up the time it takes the medicine to go through the gastrointestinal tract to the part of the body where it is needed.

Foods contain natural and added chemicals that can react with certain drugs in ways that can make the drugs useless. Some reactions can be dangerous, and some can even cause death.

It is because of these interactions that your doctor tells you to take certain medicines before meals, with meals, or after meals.

There are many ways in which certain medicines can prevent the body from getting full benefit from the foods eaten. Usually the drug interacts with only a single kind of food. Fortunately, most Americans eat a sufficiently well-balanced diet so that a single medicine will not cause malnutrition.

More serious are certain specific reactions. For example, soybeans, rutabagas, brussels sprouts, cabbage, and kale contain substances that inhibit the production of the thyroid hormone, a condition that leads to goiter.

Alcohol does not mix well with a large number of medicines. A good rule of thumb is to avoid alcoholic beverages when taking any kind of OTC or R_x medicine.

What can you do to prevent undesirable food-drug interactions?

• Read the label on an OTC drug to see when it should be taken and if it should not be taken with any particular foods.

• Follow your doctor's orders about when to take a drug and what foods or beverages to avoid while taking it.

• Ask your doctor how the drug he prescribes may interact with your favorite foods, especially if you eat large amounts of them. While taking a prescribed drug, be sure to tell your doctor about any unusual symptoms that follow eating particular foods.

• Eat a nutritionally well-balanced diet, so that any medicine you are taking will not be able to deplete the nutrients or vitamins you need.

Painkillers: Their Uses and Abuses

Americans swallow 19 billion aspirin tablets a year, making aspirin the most widely used OTC drug. Aspirin and other painkillers, however easy they are to obtain, should not be taken lightly. A panel of experts cautioned against the use of any product containing aspirin by people who have an upset stomach—even if the aspirin is intended to relieve a headache that occurs at the same time as the stomach distress. Aspirin can cause bleeding of the stomach walls. For the same reason—the causing of stomach bleeding—the experts warned against the long-term use of aspirin or aspirin-containing products for the treatment of rheumatism or arthritis, except under the supervision of a doctor.

Although aspirin has the possible side effects noted above, it can be reasonably safe if used properly. Therefore aspirin was approved, along with four other aspirinlike drugs and one other drug, as safe and effective if taken as recommended on the package. The other drugs are calcium carbaspirin, choline salicylate, magnesium salicylate, sodium salicylate, and acetaminophen. Read the labels on these drugs. These analgesics (or painkillers) should be labeled "for temporary relief of occasional minor aches, pains, and headache," and should be used only for these purposes. The word "occasional" is important. If pain persists for more than a day or two, the use of painkillers should be discontinued and a doctor should be consulted.

Aspirin and the other salicylates interfere with blood-clotting and if taken in the last three months of pregnancy can prolong the pregnancy and cause bleeding before and after delivery. Chewable aspirin and aspirin-containing gum should not be taken for seven days after a tonsillectomy or oral surgery. Because aspirin and the other salicylates do cause bleeding of the stomach, they obviously should not be taken to relieve the pain of ulcers. Nor should they be taken by persons who are taking prescription drugs for thinning of the blood, diabetes, gout, or arthritis, except under the supervision of a physician.

Fortunately, salicylates have a built-in warning system. Overdosing causes a ringing in the ears. The panel of experts recommended that labels on these drugs caution consumers to stop taking the drugs if ringing in the ears occurs.

Sleep Aids

Counting sheep is a time-worn remedy for sleeplessness, but it is not known to be very effective. Nowadays when sleep avoids you, you take a sleep-aid drug, many of which can be bought as OTC drugs.

A panel of experts reviewing sleep aids for the FDA found that some of the ingredients in the drugs do not do the job, some are dangerous, and others are safe but too low in dosage to be effective. The last named are antihistamines. If the sleep aid you have been using has not been working, look at the label to see if it contains antihistamines (such as propanolamine, phenylephrine, or pheniramine). If it does, discard it and ask your doctor for a sleep aid. If you have a sleep problem that lasts for a long time, you should not try to self-prescribe medicine. Rather consider it an illness and see your doctor.

Sleep aids that contain bromides are considered dangerous by the panel of experts. Large doses of bromides are necessary to produce sleep, and such doses can produce harmful concentrations of bromide. Side effects may include rash, dizziness, irritability, and mental disturbances. For a pregnant woman, the side effects include an increased danger that her child will be born mentally retarded or physically handicapped.

Scopolamine, which is found in some sleep aids, was labeled undesirable by the panel, which found that this drug can cause outbursts of uncontrolled behavior.

Three drugs—aspirin, salicylamide, and acetaminophen—that are found in some sleep aids, were said to have no sleep-inducing properties. Nor do passionflower extract and vitamin B_1 (thiamine), which are supposed to be good for the "nerves" that are supposed to be the cause of sleeplessness.

The panel on sleep aids also reviewed "wake-up" drugs, which are supposed to increase the mental alertness of persons who are lacking sleep. Only one drug—caffeine—was found to be effective, if taken in doses of 100 to 200 milligrams every three to four hours. A cup of strong tea or coffee has about 100 milligrams of caffeine.

Laxatives: What Does "Regular" Mean?

Television commercials tell us that for good health and well-being we should all be "regular." We needn't be troubled with "irregularity," after-meal discomfort, biliousness, or headaches if we take the laxative being advertised.

A panel of experts reporting to the FDA said that "irregularity" as a reason for the use of laxatives is misleading because regularity of bowel movement is not essential to health or well-being. Studies show that having as few as three bowel movements a week can be regular and pose no threat to health.

Commercials and ads claim that laxatives made from certain plant products are best because they are "natural." The panel said, "Any statement that suggests a laxative is somehow 'natural' because of its source is misleading." It "implies that the product or ingredient is a 'natural way' to induce laxation. It is not considered natural to take any laxative."

The panel divided laxatives into four broad categories:

• Bulk-forming laxative: promotes evacuation of the bowel by increasing bulk volume and water content of stools. Ingredients of this type of laxative found safe by the panel are dietary bran, cellulose derivatives, karaya, malt soup extract polycarbophil, and psyllium preparations. (Look at the package to see which ingredients a laxative contains.)

• Stimulant laxative: promotes bowel movement by one or more direct actions on the intestine. Safe ingredients are aloe, bisacodyl, cascara segrada, castor oil, danthron, dehydrocholic acid, phenolphthalein, and senna. Castor oil should be taken infrequently and then only as a one-time single dose.

• Hyperosmotic and saline laxatives: promote bowel movement by attracting water into the stool (hyperosmotic) and increasing the amount of water in the lower intestine (saline). Safe ingredients in hyperosmotic laxatives are glycerine and sorbitol; in saline laxatives, magnesium citrate (citrate of magnesia), magnesium hydroxide (milk of magnesia), magnesium sulfate, and phosphate preparations.

• Lubricant and stool softener laxatives: these lubricate the intestinal tract or penetrate and soften the stool. Safe ingredients are plain mineral oil and emulsified mineral oil (lubricants) and sulfosuccinate preparations (stool softener).

Some laxatives interact with certain medicines. If you are taking some kind of medicine regularly and want to take a laxative, consult your doctor on the effects of the laxative on the medicine.

The whole matter of taking laxatives over any period of time should be taken up with a doctor. First, laxatives can become habit-forming. Second, a doctor may be able to tell you what is the source of the irregularity, or constipation, that causes you to feel the need for continual use of a laxative; then this source may be eliminated.

Tranquilizers: Use, Abuse, and Dependency

Widespread use of tranquilizers to relieve tension and stress has led to a growing problem of dependency on legal drugs, especially among women. A person can become "hooked" on legal tranquilizers just as on narcotics. Women are much more likely than men to have tranquilizers prescribed for them, and surveys show that many women fail to recognize the danger in taking tranquilizers regularly.

The tranquilizer most frequently taken is Valium®, which is generally considered to be safe. No deaths have been attributed to Valium alone, but Valium in combination with other drugs — especially alcohol — can be deadly.

Other commonly used tranquilizers include Miltown® or Equanil®, Librium®, Librax®, Serax®, and Verstran®. Doctors write an estimated 90 million prescriptions annually for these and other chemicals that are intended to calm the nerves.

Job pressure has led businessmen to use tranquilizers as a way of helping them cope. Women are thought to feel the need for tranquilizers because of their changing social roles, feelings of worthlessness, boredom that comes from too much leisure, problems of child-rearing, or the "empty nest" syndrome that appears when the children are grown and leave home.

The FDA does not question the safety and effectiveness of most tranquilizers for short-term use. They do relieve minor tension and have medical uses in alcoholism, epilepsy, and severe muscle spasms. However, overuse can lead to dependency on these drugs. When this happens, the tranquilizer abuser is faced with new problems, usually much greater than the ones for which the drug was originally taken. Stopping the use of tranquilizers can result in true withdrawal symptoms similar to those associated with harder drugs such as barbiturates: delirium, trembling, psychoses, and exaggeration of reflexes.

Because use of tranquilizers can be easily abused, the Drug Enforcement Administration has placed a number of these drugs under the Controlled Substances Act. This means that a prescription for Miltown®, Valium®, Librium®, and other tranquilizers can be good for only six months and can be refilled only five times. Unfortunately, persons wanting tranquilizers visit several physicians, thereby obtaining more than one prescription.

If you believe that you have been taking tranquilizers for too long and are hooked on them, tell your doctor or visit your local mental health center. There are ways to become "unhooked" that are painless and rewarding.

Drugs and Pregnancy

Are you pregnant, or do you think you might be? If the answer is yes to either question, you should know that some drugs taken during pregnancy can harm the mother or her baby. We have become so used to "pill popping," taking medicines for every minor ache, pain, and other ailment, that we don't think about the amount of medicine we are taking. Thus, it is common for women to continue to "pop pills" when they become pregnant just as they did before.

A drug taken by an expectant mother enters her bloodstream and in most instances passes through her unborn child. It was formerly believed that the placenta served as a barrier to protect the child from the effects of drugs taken by the mother. It is now known, however, that most drugs pass through the placenta, enter the unborn child, and then pass back into the mother's bloodstream.

Some drugs are harmless to the unborn child, but others are very harmful. One of the most dramatic and tragic examples of the latter was the terrible consequence of taking the sedative thalidomide by pregnant women in the late 1950's and early 1960's. This supposedly safe sedative was sold without prescription in West Germany and England. Women who took thalidomide gave birth to infants with deformed limbs or no limbs at all.

The use of the hormones estrogen and progestin during the first three or four months of pregnancy can increase the risk of birth defects. Because estrogen and progestin are used in oral contraceptives, a woman who becomes pregnant or who thinks she may have become pregnant although taking oral contraceptives should stop using them immediately and consult her physician. Women who discontinue use of the Pill in the hope of becoming pregnant should wait at least three months before attempting to become pregnant, using some other method of contraception during the waiting period. A child conceived immediately after discontinuance of the Pill has a higher than normal risk of birth defects.

Antibiotics of the tetracycline type should be avoided during pregnancy because they have been shown to cause permanent discoloration of the child's teeth.

Minor tranquilizers such as Valium®, Librium®, Miltown®, and others containing meprobamate or

48

benzodiazepine derivatives, when taken by a mother during early pregnancy, may increase the risk that the baby will be born with a cleft lip or palate.

Aspirin and other drugs containing salicylate should not be taken during the last three months of pregnancy except under a doctor's supervision. Salicylates may prolong pregnancy and labor and may cause excessive bleeding before and after delivery.

One of the most common causes of damage to the unborn child is the use of alcohol, which is actually a powerful drug. The more a pregnant woman drinks, the greater her risk of giving birth to an abnormal baby. Studies show that alcoholic women give birth to an increased number of premature, mentally retarded, or physically deformed infants; and these women have a higher than normal number of stillbirths.

Tars are not ordinarily considered to be drugs, but they are the sources of many drugs. Tar is ingested during smoking, and women who smoke heavily have an increased chance of having a baby of less than normal birth weight.

A pregnant woman, then, should be very careful of what drugs she takes. The only really safe way of finding out what drugs can and cannot be taken during pregnancy is to tell a doctor about all drugs being taken just before pregnancy and during very early pregnancy.

Laetrile: The Fatal Cure

Cancer, as almost everyone knows, is an almost incurable disease except in its very early stages. There are drugs that can destroy or greatly slow the growth of cancers. The drug called Laetrile is *not* one of these drugs. This drug, which has recently been much in the news, was first tried several decades ago by a California physician and his son. Laetrile is made from apricot pits, which contain the poison cyanide. According to the makers of Laetrile, the cyanide can poison cancer cells while doing no harm to other cells of the body.

Laetrile has been carefully investigated by government and private laboratories. No proof of the makers' claim has been found. Several persons who have taken Laetrile in large doses have died of cyanide poisoning. Besides being useless as a cancer cure, Laetrile is very expensive. The drug is supposed to be taken every day. A three-dose vial of Laetrile may cost $50 to $100, thereby providng large profits for the sellers of this useless substance.

Far greater than the risk of being poisoned by Laetrile is

the certainty that untreated cancer will eventually kill the person suffering from it. Since Laetrile does nothing to destroy cancer cells, a person taking it is for all practical purposes going untreated. Except for the fact that rarely some cancers disappear (for an unknown reason), untreated cancer results in death. Taking a useless substance such as Laetrile is the same as letting a cancer go untreated; death will almost surely result.

It is understandable that persons who are in the terminal stages of cancer should be willing to try anything claimed to be a cure. Many such persons try Laetrile in a futile attempt to prolong their lives. These people actually lose little, although they gain nothing. The tragedy of Laetrile is that persons who could be cured of cancer in its early stages or who could have their lives prolonged for years by chemotherapy, surgery, or radiation therapy, take Laetrile and face certain death.

A 35-year-old mother of three children was diagnosed to have very early, treatable cancer of the uterus. Her doctor recommended surgery and radiation treatment. Instead, this woman went to Mexico and spent $3,000 on Laetrile treatments. When she realized that the Laetrile was worthless, she returned to her doctor for the treatment he had prescribed. But by that time, the cancer had spread to her pelvis and rectum. A month later she died.

Drugs and You

Because of the extremely widespread use of drugs in the United States, the chances are that you are now taking one or more drugs, or that you use them occasionally. We hope this book has convinced you that the taking of drugs is a serious matter; that you should get the advice of a doctor before deciding to try to cure an illness by taking OTC drugs; that you should take both OTC and R_x drugs only as recommended on the package or by your doctor; and that when buying drugs, you should consult a pharmacist and shop for the best buys.

Compiled by
DAVID W. DEE

A Fitness Program for Adults

Contents

What Is Fitness?

Fitness means many things to many people. The physician may view fitness as the absence of disease. The body-builder may consider it well-developed muscles, while the young woman may think it's a curvaceous figure. The coach defines fitness as those factors related to success in sports, and the physical educator looks for strength, endurance, flexibility, speed, agility.

In more meaningful personal terms, fitness is a reflection of your ability to work with vigor and pleasure, without undue fatigue, with energy left for enjoying hobbies and recreational activities and for meeting emergencies. It relates to how you look and how you feel — and, because the body is not a compartment separate from the mind, it relates to how you feel mentally as well as physically.

Physical fitness is many-faceted. Basic to it are proper nutrition, adequate rest and relaxation, good health practices, and good medical and dental care.

But these are not enough. An essential element is physical activity — exercise for a body that needs it.

To look your best, to feel your best, and to be able to do your best, you must exercise regularly. That is man's nature, and modern technology can't change it.

When the activity required of you by your job and other duties falls below the level necessary to support good health, you must supplement it with planned activity. Your sense of well-being, your ability to perform and even your survival depend on it.

Regular, vigorous exercise increases muscle strength and endurance. It also improves the functioning of the lungs, heart, and blood vessels; promotes flexibility of the joints; releases mental and physical tensions; and aids in weight control or reduction.

More than half of all lower back pain is due to poor tone and flexibility of the back and abdominal muscles. In many cases, this problem could be prevented or corrected by proper exercise.

In short, exercise can make the difference. The options are mere existence or a full life. The choice is yours.

Exercise and the Heart

An old-fashioned idea—that exercise may be bad for the heart—has been shown to be without scientific foundation. Not only that—it has been proven that appropriate exercise strengthens the heart.

A noted heart specialist recently commented: "The best insurance against heart disease is exercise—lots of it."

Backing up this conviction is a growing body of evidence. It includes findings of lower cholesterol values in active people, faster clearing of fats from the blood after meals, and sharply reduced heart-attack rates.

Additionally, studies indicate that, when a heart attack does occur, the physically active person is more likely to recover. One possible reason: there is evidence that exercise may promote development of supplementary blood vessels that can take over the burden of nourishing the heart muscle when a coronary artery is blocked in a heart attack.

Exercise and Aging

There is strong authoritative support for the concept that regular exercise can help prevent degenerative disease and slow down the physical deterioration that accompanies aging.

The evidence is conclusive: people who consistently engage in proper physical activity have better job performance records, fewer degenerative diseases, and probably a longer life expectancy than the population at large. By delaying the aging process, proper exercise also prolongs your active years.

Exercise and Weight Control

A common misconception is that exercise does not aid in weight control. This is not the case. Fat piles up in most people by only a few calories a day; an excess of only 100 calories a day can produce a 10-pound gain in a year—and the extra calories could be burned up by a 15- to 20-minute daily walk; obese people almost invariably tend to be much less active than those of normal weight; individual weight, moreover, is a factor in energy expenditure. If you are overweight, you burn up more calories in performing exercise than does a person of normal weight.

Weight control is maintained by keeping energy intake (food) and energy output (physical activity) in balance. This is true at all ages for both sexes. When the calories consumed in food equal those used to meet the body's needs, weight will remain about the same. When one eats more than this amount, one will put on fat unless physical activity is increased proportionately.

For years physicians have talked about the varying caloric needs of differing occupations and physical recreations. Yet in their attempts to lose excess fat, weight watchers have often concentrated on counting the calories in their diets and have neglected the role of exercise. For those who are fat, increasing physical activity can be just as important as decreasing food intake.

Weight depends not only on how many calories are taken in during the day, but also on how many are used up in physical activity. The fat person who merely cuts down his intake of food to lose weight will make slow progress, because the number of calories needed to maintain the body is much smaller than most people think.

In fact, lack of exercise has been cited as the most important cause of the "creeping" obesity found in modern mechanized societies. Few occupations now require vigorous physical activity. Although more time is available for recreation, many people fail to fill this gap by choosing leisure time activities that give them exercise. Even among those who do exercise, their activity is often neither vigorous nor sustained.

Recent studies indicate that lack of physical activity is more often the cause of overweight than is overeating. These studies have compared the food intake and activity patterns of obese persons with persons of normal weight. Several age levels — teen-agers, adults, and older persons — have been studied. In each instance, the findings showed that the obese people did not consume any more calories than their normal-weight age mates, but that they were very much less active. The person who has a trim figure and wants to keep it should exercise regularly and eat a balanced, nutritious diet that provides sufficient calories to make up for the energy expended. The thin person who wishes to gain weight should exercise regularly and increase the number of calories consumed until the desired weight is reached. The overweight person should decrease the food intake and step up the amount of physical activity. Since a large proportion of the U.S. population is overweight, the latter group is a matter of concern to those who are interested in the nation's fitness.

If you need to lose weight, do so under the direction of your physician. Don't lose more than two pounds per week without his knowledge and consent. Determine to reduce gradually and consistently. Determine to develop proper eating habits. A change in diet—perhaps a change as slight as taking a little less sugar or none in beverages—may be all that is necessary to bring your weight down and keep it down, especially if coupled with the essential exercise regimen.

Even the Handicapped Should Exercise

Where there is impairment or illness, any and all exercise should be medically prescribed and regulated.

Today, physicians are using exercise as an aid in combatting many chronic problems, including arthritis, asthma, diabetes, and emphysema. A common type of low back pain has been traced to weakened back muscles, and exercise has been used both to produce relief and to help prevent recurrence.

How Long and How Often Should You Exercise

The official position of the American Medical Association is that human beings must exercise regularly to become physically fit. Sufficient rest and sleep, an adequate diet, the absence of excesses, and physical activity are essential to maintaining physical capacity. The amount of exercise needed varies from one person to another, but the AMA recommends 30 to 60 minutes daily as a minimum.

No one can achieve satisfactory levels of strength, endurance, and flexibility by working out once a week. More frequent workouts are required to bring about significant changes, and both experience and scientific studies show that daily exercise produces the best results.

The way in which an exercise is done is just as important as how often it is done. For maximum benefit, physical activity must be vigorous enough to give a tonic effect. In other words, the person must work hard enough to breathe heavily and "break a sweat."

People who are unschooled in human physiology or

unfamiliar with the principles of exercise seldom work hard enough or long enough to improve circulatory and respiratory performance or to strengthen muscles. One reason for this is that many of our more popular and enjoyable participatory sports are not taxing enough for fitness purposes. They make a contribution but should be supplemented by an exercise regimen.

Popular games — tennis, handball, racketball, basketball — are fine for *maintaining* fitness. But no serious fitness enthusiast considers them adequate for training. Most tennis or handball players run to get in shape for competition. Games are not a substitute for real fitness activity. They don't allow you to maintain your heart rate in the training zone. They often include brief periods of extreme exertion. You should be fit before you compete in strenuous sports.

Dynamic good health is the objective of a physical fitness program. Performing exercises halfheartedly or working out briefly and sporadically cannot move you significantly closer to that goal. Hard work on a regular, sustained basis is the answer.

The level of fitness you can reach depends on your age, your body's built-in potential, and previous conditioning. It also depends on your state of mind. When you want to do something and believe you can, it is much easier to do than it would be otherwise.

When you begin your personal exercise program, you should not expect dramatic changes overnight. But, gradually over the next weeks and months, you will begin to notice a new spring in your step, a new ease in carrying out ordinary daily activities. You will find yourself with more energy left at the end of the working day and a new zest for recreation in the evening. Quite likely, you will be sleeping more soundly than you have for many years and waking more refreshed in the morning. In short, you will be on your way to a better and more complete life.

Medical Advice

Before beginning any exercise program, it is advisable to have a medical checkup. If you have not had an examination in the past year, if you are past 30, if you are overweight, or if you have a history of high blood pressure or heart trouble, such an examination may help you to avoid serious consequences.

Chances are your physician will be able to give you an unconditional go-ahead. If not, he may be able to modify the exercises you plan so that they are suited to you.

There are few people who, for medical reasons, should not undertake any exercise program unless and until those reasons have been eliminated.

Only a qualified physician can say for sure if the exercise program outlined in the following pages is advisable for you. Show him this booklet and ask his advice.

Illness or Injuries

If you develop an illness, ask your physician about the advisability of continuing to jog. Any persistent pain or soreness also should be reported.

Blisters: Blisters can be prevented by wearing good, properly fitted shoes. At the first hint of discomfort, cover the area with moleskin or a large bandage. If you do develop a blister, puncture the edge with a sterilized needle to drain the accumulated fluid, treat with an antiseptic, cover with gauze, circle with foam rubber, and go back to work. It's wise to keep the items needed for blister care at hand.

Muscle soreness: Soreness, usually due to exercise after long inactivity, may be caused by microscopic tears in the muscle or connective tissue, or to contractions of muscle fibers. It is almost impossible to avoid soreness when you first begin exercising. Minimize it by exercising modestly, at least at first, and by doing mild stretching exercises when soreness does occur. Massage and warmth also seem to minimize the discomfort of soreness.

Muscle cramps: Cramps are powerful involuntary muscle contractions. Immediate relief comes when the cramped muscle is stretched and massaged. However, that does not remove the underlying cause of the contraction. Salt and potassium are both involved in the chemistry of contraction and relaxation. Cold muscles seem to cramp more readily. It's always wise to warm up before vigorous effort and to replace salt and potassium lost through sweating in hot weather.

Knee problems: A knee injury suffered early in life can affect the ability to exercise. For example, a knee injured playing high school football may lead to signs of arthritis in the late 20's or early 30's. Such degenerative changes often restrict the ability to run, ski, or engage in other vigorous activities. Persons with knee problems should consult a physician for ways to relieve the limitations they impose. Knee problems also can result from improper foot strike, worn shoes, or improper foot support. Repair worn shoes, and if knee problems persist, see a podiatrist.

What the Exercise Program Consists Of

There are three general categories—warm-up exercises, conditioning exercises, and circulatory activities.

The warm-up exercises stretch and limber the muscles and speed up the action of the heart and lungs, thus preparing the body for greater exertion and reducing the possibility of unnecessary strain.

The conditioning exercises are systematically planned to tone up abdominal, back, leg, arm, and other major muscles.

The circulatory activities produce contractions of large muscle groups for relatively longer periods than the conditioning exercises—to stimulate and strengthen the circulatory and respiratory systems.

Among the circulatory activities, you choose one each workout—alternate running and walking, skipping rope, and running in place. All are effective. You can choose running and walking on a pleasant day and one of the others for use indoors when the weather is bad. You can also switch about the variety.

The routines described in this booklet are equally beneficial for men and women.

Each exercise session should consist of warm-up, conditioning exercises, and circulatory activities.

If during the early stages of the program you become overly stiff or sore, and especially if you experience pain in the feet or knees, reduce or stop the walking-jogging part of the program until pain or soreness disappears.

Do not discontinue the warm-up or the conditioning exercises.

If pain or soreness persists for several weeks, check with your physician.

The following exercises are for both men and women (no matter which sex the illustrations show) and should be considered as a starter program for physical fitness.

WARM-UP EXERCISES

Standing Reach
Starting position: Stand erect, feet shoulder-width apart, arms extended over head.
Action: Stretch as high as possible, keeping heels on ground. Hold for 15 to 30 counts.

Flexed-leg Back Stretch
Starting position: Stand erect, feet shoulder-width apart, arms at sides.
Action: Bend trunk forward and down, flexing knees. Stretch gently in attempt to touch fingers to toes or floor. Hold for 15 to 30 counts. Return to starting position.
Repeat 2 to 3 times.

Knee Lift
Starting position: Stand erect, feet comfortably apart, arms at sides.
Action: Raise left knee as high as possible, grasping leg with hands and pulling knee against body while keeping back straight. Hold for a 5 count. Lower to starting position. Repeat with right knee.
Repeat 5 to 8 times with each leg.

Double Knee Pull
Starting position: Lie on back, feet extended, hands at sides.
Action: Pull both legs to chest, lock arms around legs, pull buttocks slightly off ground. Hold for 20 to 40 counts. Return to starting position.
Repeat 7 to 10 times.

Wing Stretch
Starting position: Stand erect, feet comfortably apart, elbows at shoulder height, fists clenched in front of chest.
Action: Thrust elbows backward vigorously without arching back. Return to starting position. Repeat 10 to 15 times.

Quarter Knee Bend
Starting position: Stand erect, feet comfortably apart, hands on hips.
Action: Bend knees to 45°, keeping heels on floor. Return to starting position.
Repeat 15 to 20 times.

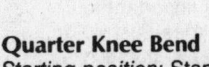

Horizontal Arm Circles
Starting position: Stand erect, feet shoulder-width apart, arms extended sideways at shoulder height, palms up.
Action: Describe small circles backward with hands and arms. Reverse, turn palms down, and do small circles forward.
Repeat 12 to 15 times.

Neck Circles
Starting position: Stand erect, feet shoulder-width apart, arms at sides.
Action: Gently roll head in full circle, first in one direction, then in the other.
Repeat 3 times in each direction.

Body Bender
Starting position: Stand, feet shoulder-width apart, hands behind neck, fingers interlaced.
Action: Bend trunk sideward to left as far as possible, keeping hands behind neck. Return to starting position. Repeat to the right.
Repeat 6 times in each direction.

CONDITIONING EXERCISES

Knee Pushup (Beginner)
Starting position: Lie on floor, face down, legs together, knees bent with feet raised off floor, hands on floor under shoulders, palms down, fingers pointing forward.
Action: Push upper body off floor until arms are fully extended and body is in straight line from head to knees. Return to starting position. Repeat 5 to 10 times.

PUSHUPS

When doing the following exercises it is important to keep the back straight. Start with the knee pushup and continue for several weeks until your stomach muscles are toned up enough to keep your back straight. Then try the intermediate. After mastering this, go on to the advanced.

Pushup (Intermediate)
Starting position: Lie on floor, face down, legs together, feet on floor, hands on floor under shoulders, palms down, fingers pointing forward.
Action: Push body off floor by extending arms so that weight rests on hands and toes, keeping back straight. Lower the body until chest touches floor. Return to starting position. Repeat 10 to 20 times.

CURLUPS

The following exercises are designed to strengthen the abdominal muscles. Select the one for you.

Head and Shoulders Curl (Beginner)
Starting position: Lie on back, legs straight, hands tucked under small of back, palms down.
Action: Tighten abdominal muscles, lift head, and pull shoulders and elbows off floor. Hold this position for 5 counts. Return to starting position. Repeat 10 to 15 times.

Situp, Arms Crossed (Intermediate)
Starting position: Lie on back, arms crossed on chest, hands grasping opposite shoulders, knees bent to right angle, feet flat on floor.
Action: Curl up to sitting position. Curl down to starting position. Repeat 10 to 15 times.

Situp, Fingers Laced (Advanced)
Starting position: Lie on back, fingers laced behind neck, knees bent, feet flat on floor.
Action: Curl up, turn trunk to right, touch left elbow to right knee. Return to starting position. Curl up, turn trunk to left, touch right elbow to left knee. Curl down to starting position. Repeat 15 to 25 times.

Sitting Single Leg Lift
Starting position: Sit erect, hands on side of chair seat for balance, legs extended at angle to floor.
Action: Raise left leg waist-high. Return to starting position. Repeat with right leg. Repeat 10 to 15 times.

Back Leg Swing
Starting position: Stand erect behind chair, feet together, hands on chair for support.
Action: Lift one leg back and up as far as possible. Return to starting position. Repeat with other leg. Repeat 20 times.

Heel Raiser
Starting position: Stand erect, hands on hips, feet together.
Action: Raise body on toes. Return to starting position. Repeat 20 times.

Side-lying Leg Lift
Starting position: Lie on right side, legs extended.
Action: Raise left leg as high as possible. Lower to starting position. Repeat on opposite side. Repeat 10 to 15 times.

Giant Arm Circles
Starting position: Stand erect, feet shoulder-width apart, arms at sides.
Action: Bring arms upward and sideward, crossing overhead, completing a full arc in front of body. Do equal number in each direction. Repeat 10 times.

63

Circulatory Activities

As we have mentioned, the circulatory activities can consist alternately of rope skipping, running in place, and walking-jogging-running.

Rope: Skip or jump rope continuously using any form for 30 seconds and then rest 60 seconds. Repeat 3 times.

Run in place: Raise each foot at least 4″ off floor and jog in place. Count 1 each time left foot touches floor. Do this for 1 to 3 minutes.

Jogging: As jogging has become increasingly popular, we shall treat it in more detail in the following pages, giving not only the starter program (developed by the President's Council on Physical Fitness and Sports) but also an intermediate jog-run program developed for the Forest Service of the U.S. Department of Agriculture. From the same source we provide some suggestions for advanced training.

Jogging Guidelines

HOW TO JOG

Run in an upright position, avoiding the tendency to lean. Keep back as straight as you can and still remain comfortable, and keep head up. Don't look at your feet.

Hold arms slightly away from body, with elbows bent so that forearms are approximately parallel to the ground. Occasionally shaking and relaxing the arms and shoulders will help reduce the tightness that sometimes develops while jogging. Periodically taking several deep breaths and blowing them out completely also will help you to relax.

It is best to land on the heel of the foot and rock forward so that you drive off the ball of the foot for your next step. If this proves difficult, try a more flat-footed style. Jogging only on the balls of the feet, as in sprinting, will produce severe leg soreness.

Keep steps short, letting foot strike the ground beneath the knee instead of reaching to the front. Length of stride should vary with your rate of speed.

Breathe deeply, with mouth open. Do not hold breath.

If for any reason you become unusually tired or uncomfortable, slow down, walk, or stop.

64

WHAT TO WEAR

Select loose, comfortable clothes. Dress for warmth in the winter, for coolness in the summer. "Jogging suits" or "warmups" are not necessary, but they are extremely practical and comfortable, and they can help create a feeling of commitment to jogging.

Do not wear rubberized or plastic clothing. Increased sweating will not produce permanent weight loss, and such clothing can cause body temperature to rise to dangerous levels. It interferes with evaporation of sweat, which is the body's chief temperature control mechanism during exercise. If sweat cannot evaporate, heat stroke or heat exhaustion may result.

Properly fitting shoes with firm soles, good arch supports, and pliable tops are essential. Shoes made especially for distance running or walking are recommended. Ripple or crepe soles are excellent for running on hard surfaces. Beginners should avoid inexpensive, thin-soled sneakers. Wear clean, soft, heavy, well-fitting socks. Beginners may want to wear thin socks under the heavier pair.

WHERE TO JOG

If possible, avoid hard surfaces such as concrete and asphalt for the first few weeks. Running tracks (located at most high schools), grass playing fields, parks, and golf courses are recommended. In inclement weather, jog in church, school, or YMCA gymnasiums; in protected areas around shopping centers; or in your garage or basement. Varying locations and routes will add interest to your program.

WHEN TO JOG

The time of day is not important, although it is best not to jog during the first hour after eating, or during the middle of a hot, humid day. The important thing is to commit yourself to a regular schedule. Some believe that people who jog early in the morning tend to be more faithful than those who run in the evenings. Persons who jog with family members or friends also tend to adhere to their schedules better. However, companionship — not competition — should be your goal when jogging with someone else.

Starter Programs

Take the *walk test* to determine your exercise level.

Walk Test. The object of this test is to determine how many minutes (up to 10) you can walk at a brisk pace, on a level surface, without undue difficulty or discomfort.

If you can't walk for 5 minutes, begin with phase I.

If you can walk more than 5 minutes but less than 10, begin with the third week of phase I.

If you can walk for the full *10 minutes* but are somewhat tired and sore as a result, start with phase II. If you can breeze through the full 10 minutes, you're ready for bigger things. Wait until the next day and take the 10-minute *walk-jog test*.

Walk-Jog Test. In this test you alternately walk 50 steps (left foot strikes ground 25 times) and jog 50 steps for a total of 10 minutes. Walk at the rate of 120 steps a minute (left foot strikes the ground at 1-second intervals). Jog at the rate of 144 steps a minute (left foot strikes ground 18 times every 15 seconds.)

If you can't complete the 10-minute test, begin at the third week of phase II. If you can complete the 10-minute test but are tired and winded as a result, start with the last week of phase II before moving to phase III. If you can perform the 10-minute walk-jog test without difficulty, start with phase III.

Phase 1
WALKING PROGRAM

Week	Activity (every other day at first)
1	Walk at a brisk pace for 5 minutes, or for a shorter time if you become uncomfortably tired. Walk slowly or rest for 3 minutes. Again walk briskly for 5 minutes, or until you become uncomfortably tired.
2	Same as week 1, but increase pace as soon as you can walk 5 minutes without soreness or fatigue.
3	Walk at a brisk pace for 8 minutes, or for a shorter time if you become uncomfortably tired. Walk slowly or rest for 3 minutes. Again walk briskly for 8 minutes, or until you become uncomfortably tired.
4	Same as week 3, but increase pace as soon as you can walk 8 minutes without soreness or fatigue.

When you've completed week 4 of phase 1, begin at week 1 of phase 2.

Phase 2
WALK-JOG PROGRAM

Week	Activity (four times a week)
1	Walk at a brisk pace for 10 minutes, or for a shorter time if you become uncomfortably tired. Walk slowly or rest for 3 minutes. Again, walk briskly for 10 minutes, or until you become uncomfortably tired.
2	Walk at a brisk pace for 15 minutes, or for a shorter time if you become uncomfortably tired. Walk slowly for 3 minutes.
3	Jog 10 seconds (25 yards). Walk 1 minute (100 yards). Do 12 times.
4	Jog 20 seconds (50 yards). Walk 1 minute (100 yards). Do 12 times.

When you've completed week 4 of phase 2, begin at week 1 of phase 3.

Phase 3
JOGGING PROGRAM

Week	Activity (five times a week)
1	Jog 40 seconds (100 yards). Walk 1 minute (100 yards). Do 9 times.
2	Jog 1 minute (150 yards). Walk 1 minute (100 yards). Do 8 times.
3	Jog 2 minutes (300 yards). Walk 1 minute (100 yards). Do 6 times.
4	Jog 4 minutes (600 yards). Walk 1 minute (100 yards). Do 4 times.
5	Jog 6 minutes (900 yards). Walk 1 minute (100 yards). Do 3 times.
6	Jog 8 minutes (1,200 yards). Walk 2 minutes (200 yards). Do 2 times.
7	Jog 10 minutes (1,500 yards). Walk 2 minutes (200 yards). Do 2 times.
8	Jog 12 minutes (1,760 yards). Walk 2 minutes (200 yards). Do 2 times.

Intermediate Program (jog-run)

If you've followed the starter program or are already reasonably active, you're ready for the intermediate program. You're able to jog 1 mile slowly without undue fatigue, rest 2 minutes, and do it again. Your sessions consume about 250 calories.

You're ready to increase both the intensity and the duration of your runs. You'll begin jogging 1 mile in 12 minutes, and when you finish this program you may be able to complete 3 or more miles at a pace approaching 8 minutes a mile. Each week's program includes three phases — the basic workout, longer runs (overdistance), and shorter runs (underdistance). If a week's program seems too easy, move ahead; if it seems too hard, move back a week or two. Remember to make a warm-up and a cool-down part of every exercise session.

Week 1

Basic Workout (Monday, Thursday)

1 mile in 11 minutes; active recovery (walk). Run twice.

Underdistance (Tuesday, Friday)

¼ to ½ mile slowly.

½ mile in 5 minutes 30 seconds. Run twice (recover between repeats).

¼ mile in 2 minutes 45 seconds. Run 4 times (recover between repeats).

Jog ¼ to ½ mile slowly.

Overdistance (Wednesday, Saturday or Sunday)

2 miles slowly. (Use the talk test: Jog at a pace that allows you to converse.)

Week 2

Basic Workout (Monday, Thursday)

1 mile in 10 minutes 30 seconds; active recovery. Run twice.

Underdistance (Tuesday, Friday)

¼ to ½ mile slowly.

½ mile in 5 minutes.

¼ mile in 2 minutes 30 seconds. Run 2 times (recover between repeats).

¼ mile in 2 minutes 45 seconds. Run 2 times (recover between repeats).

220 yards in 1 minute 20 seconds. Run 4 times (recover between repeats).

¼ to ½ mile slowly.

Overdistance (Wednesday, Saturday or Sunday)

2¼ miles slowly.

Week 3

Basic Workout (Monday, Thursday)

1 mile in 10 minutes, active recovery. Run twice.

Underdistance (Tuesday, Friday)

¼ to ½ mile slowly.

½ mile in 4 minutes 45 seconds.

¼ mile in 2 minutes 30 seconds. Run 4 times (recover between repeats).

220 yards in 1 minute 10 seconds. Run 4 times (recover between repeats).

100 yards in 30 seconds. Run 4 times (recover between repeats).

¼ to ½ mile slowly.

Overdistance (Wednesday, Saturday or Sunday)

2½ miles slowly.

●

Week 4

Basic Workout (Monday, Thursday)

1 mile in 9 minutes 30 seconds; active recovery. Run twice.

Underdistance (Tuesday, Friday)

¼ to ½ mile slowly.

½ mile in 4 minutes 45 seconds. Run twice (recover between repeats).

¼ mile in 2 minutes 20 seconds. Run 4 times (recover between repeats).

220 yards in 1 minute. Run 4 times (recover between repeats).

¼ to ½ mile slowly.

Overdistance (Wednesday, Saturday or Sunday)

2¾ miles slowly.

●

Week 5

Basic Workout (Monday, Thursday)

1 mile in 9 minutes; active recovery. Run twice.

Underdistance (Tuesday, Friday)

¼ to ½ mile slowly.

½ mile in 4 minutes 30 seconds.

¼ mile in 2 minutes 20 seconds. Run 4 times (recover between repeats).

220 yards in 60 seconds. Run 4 times (recover between repeats).

100 yards in 27 seconds. Run 4 times (recover between repeats)

¼ to ½ mile slowly.

Overdistance (Wednesday, Saturday or Sunday)

3 miles slowly.

Week 6

Basic Workout (Monday, Thursday)

1½ miles in 13 minutes 30 seconds; active recovery. Run twice.

Underdistance (Tuesday, Friday)

¼ to ½ mile slowly.

½ mile in 4 minutes 30 seconds. Run twice (recover between repeats).

¼ mile in 2 minutes 10 seconds. Run 4 times (recover between repeats).

220 yards in 60 seconds. Run 4 times (recover between repeats).

100 yards in 25 seconds. Run twice (recover between repeats).

¼ to ½ mile slowly.

Overdistance (Wednesday, Saturday or Sunday)

3 miles slowly; *increase pace* last ¼ mile.

●

Week 7

Basic Workout (Monday, Thursday)

1½ miles in 13 minutes; active recovery. Run twice.

Underdistance (Tuesday, Friday)

¼ to ½ mile slowly.

½ mile in 4 minutes 15 seconds. Run twice (recover between repeats).

¼ mile in 2 minutes. Run 4 times (recover between repeats).

220 yards in 55 seconds. Run 4 times (recover between repeats)

¼ to ½ mile slowly.

Overdistance (Wednesday, Saturday or Sunday)

3½ miles slowly; always increase pace near finish.

Week 8

Basic Workout (Monday, Thursday)

1 mile in 8 minutes; active recovery; run 1 mile in 8 minutes 30 seconds; active recovery; repeat (total of 3 miles).

Underdistance (Tuesday, Friday)

¼ to ½ mile slowly.

½ mile in 4 minutes. Run twice (recover between repeats).

¼ mile in 1 minute 50 seconds. Run 4 times (recover between repeats).

220 yards in 55 seconds. Run 4 times (recover between repeats).

100 yards in 23 seconds. Run 4 times (recover between repeats).

¼ to ½ mile slowly.

Overdistance (Wednesday, Saturday or Sunday)

3¾ miles slowly.

Week 9

Basic Workout (Monday, Thursday)

1 mile in 8 minutes. Run 3 times (recover between repeats).

Underdistance (Tuesday, Friday)

¼ to ½ mile slowly.

½ mile in 3 minutes 30 seconds.

¼ mile in 1 minute 45 seconds. Run 4 times (recover between repeats).

220 yards in 50 seconds. Run 4 times (recover between repeats).

100 yards in 20 seconds. Run 4 times (recover between repeats).

50 yards in 10 seconds. Run 4 times (recover between repeats).

¼ to ½ mile slowly.

Overdistance (Wednesday, Saturday or Sunday)

4 miles slowly.

Week 10

Basic Workout (Monday, Thursday)

1½ miles in 12 minutes. Run twice (recover between repeats).

Underdistance (Tuesday, Friday)

¼ to ½ mile slowly.

½ mile in 3 minutes 45 seconds. Run 3 times (recover between repeats).

¼ mile in 1 minute 50 seconds. Run 6 times (recover between repeats).

220 yards in 45 seconds. Run twice (recover between repeats).

¼ to ½ mile slowly.

Overdistance (Wednesday, Saturday or Sunday)

4 miles; increase pace last ½ mile.

•

Week 11

Basic Workout (Monday, Thursday)

1 mile in 7 minutes 30 seconds. Run 3 times (recover between repeats).

Underdistance (Tuesday, Friday)

¼ to ½ mile slowly.

½ mile in 3 minutes 50 seconds. Run 4 times (recover between repeats).

¼ mile in 1 minute 45 seconds. Run 4 times. Recover between repeats).

220 yards in 45 seconds. Run 2 times (recover between repeats).

¼ to ½ mile slowly.

Overdistance (Wednesday, Saturday or Sunday)

Over 4 miles slowly (more than 400 calories per workout).

•

Week 12

Basic Workout

1½ miles in 11 minutes 40 seconds.

You have now achieved the fitness standard that allows you to proceed to the advanced training programs.

Advanced Training

This section is for the well-trained runner. Some suggestions are provided for advanced training, but keep in mind that there is no single way to train. If you enjoy underdistance training, by all means use it. If you find that you prefer overdistance, you'll like the suggestions offered here.

Long, slow distance running seems to be the ideal way to train. It combines the features of overdistance and underdistance with a minimum of discomfort. Simply pick up the pace as you approach the end of a long run, and you'll receive an optimal training stimulus. Moreover, since the speed work is limited to a short span near the end of the run, discomfort is brief.

Consider the following suggestions:

Always warm up before your run.

Use the high fitness heart rate training zone.

Vary the location and distance of the run day by day (long-short; fast-slow; hilly-flat; hard-easy).

Set distance goals:

Phase 1: 20 miles a week

Phase 2: 25 miles a week (ready for 3- to 5-mile road races)

Phase 3: 30 miles a week

Phase 4: 35 miles a week (ready for 5- to 7-mile road
 races)

Phase 5: 40 miles a week

Phase 6: 45 miles a week (ready for 7- to 10-mile road
 races)

Phase 7: More than 50 miles a week (consider longer
 races such as the marathon — 26.2 miles)

Don't be a slave to your goals, and don't increase weekly mileage unless you enjoy it.

Run 6 days a week if you enjoy it; otherwise, try an alternate-day schedule with longer runs.

Try one long run (not over one-third of weekly distance) on Saturday or Sunday.

Try two shorter runs if the long ones seem difficult: 5 + 5 instead of 10.

Keep records if you like — you'll be surprised! Record date, distance, comments. Note resting pulse, body weight. At least annually, check your performance over a measured distance to observe progress (use a local road race or the 1½-mile-run test). Check your fitness score on the step test several times a year.

Don't train with a stopwatch. Wear a wristwatch so you'll know how long you've run.

Increase speed as you approach the finish of a run.

Always cool down after a run.

Compiled by
DAVID W. DEE

First
Aid

Contents

What Is First Aid?

First aid is emergency treatment for illness or injury while waiting for medical help. At one time or another almost everyone is called upon to render first aid. Unless he or she has taken a course on the subject, there is usually confusion and doubt as to what should be done.

Statistics show that in most cases it is better for the person untrained in first aid to do too little than too much. This is particularly true in urban and suburban areas where medical help can easily be obtained. If it is not possible to reach a doctor, police or firemen are better equipped to give first aid than are the uninitiated.

It is advisable for at least one member of the family to take a First Aid course, and it is a necessity for each household to have a good emergency medical manual and a first-aid kit. Consult your local Red Cross for First Aid instructions, and ask your physician to advise you which of the many medical manuals to buy.

This booklet is designed to be used *only* as a quick reference during an emergency. Therefore it contains *only* the basic-life support techniques. Always keep in mind that first aid does *not* replace the doctor but merely attempts to keep the victim alive and in the best condition possible until medical aid arrives.

Telephone operators usually know how to obtain help in the quickest way. Dial O and tell the operator that it's an emergency. Be sure the operator has your right address. But to be prepared, one should have a list of emergency telephone numbers handy.

The First Aid Kit

You can buy a pre-assembled commercial kit, or you can put together your own kit. You should have also one for your car. If you go hiking or camping, special snakebite kits are available. A basic kit should contain:*

First-aid manual • Small box of absorbent cotton • Box of adhesive strip bandages, assorted sizes (such as Band-Aids or Curads) • Rolls of adhesive tape, ½", 1", 2" wide • Rolls of gauze bandage, 1", 2", 3" wide • Box of cotton-tipped swabs

---

*Not included are boric acid, Mercurochrome, tincture of iodine, or pain or discomfort relievers containing either bromides or phenacetin (available over the counter) because some physicians consider them either useless or toxic or both.

• Large triangular bandages • Small boxes of gauze pads, 3x3-inch, 2x4-inch • Sterile eye pads • Wood arm splint • Sturdy cloth 2″ wide and 20″ long for tourniquet • Wood tongue depressors • Tweezers • Bandage scissors (sharp scissors with rounded ends) • Paper cups • Measuring cup • Measuring spoons • Thermometer • Small bottle of 70% alcohol (to be used as a disinfectant) • Ammonia inhalant (in case of fainting) • Tube of antibiotic ointment • Tube of antibiotic eye ointment • Box of salt tablets (in case of heat exhaustion) • Calamine lotion • Hydrogen peroxide • Petroleum jelly • Oil of cloves (in case of minor toothache) • Safety pins • Sharp needles (must be sterilized before removing splinters).

Lifesaving Measures

There are four basic life-threatening conditions in which correct and immediate first-aid procedures are in the true sense a question of life and death.

They are: *impaired breathing, heart failure, severe bleeding,* and *shock.* Seconds count in the recognition and correction of these conditions. Emergency treatment should be given in this order, as necessary: 1. Clear the air passage. 2. Restore breathing and heartbeat. 3. Stop bleeding. 4. Administer treatment for shock.

Do not move an injured person until you have a clear idea of the injury and have applied first aid, unless the victim is exposed to further danger at the accident site. If the injury is serious, if it occurred in an area where the victim can remain safely, and if medical aid is readily obtainable, it is sometimes best not even to attempt to move the person, but to employ such emergency care as is possible at the site until more highly qualified emergency personnel arrive.

Impaired Breathing

The causes of impaired breathing could be: (a) suffocation; (b) electrical shock; (c) gas poisoning; (d) drowning; (e) heart failure.

The symptoms are easily recognizable: The chest or abdomen does not rise and fall; air cannot be felt exiting from the nose or mouth.

Actions to take: If a patient stops breathing you must assist him immediately. The situation will dictate the method to be used. The respiratory failure can be caused by blockage of

Clear the upper airway of the victim.

Tilt his head back.

Breathe forcefully into the victim's mouth.

Listen for the return of air from the patient's lungs.

the air passages by foreign matter such as water (drowning), mud, food particles, etc. In an unconscious patient in the supine position (lying on the back), the tongue may drop back and block the throat. The cardiovascular system may fail to circulate red blood cells, which can be caused by heart failure. Regardless of the cause, however, immediate steps must be taken to clear the airway. When the airway is cleared, if spontaneous breathing does not resume, artificial respiration must be applied immediately. There are two methods of artificial respiration; mouth-to-mouth or mouth-to-nose resuscitation and a manual method. The manual method is not recommended except when the rescuer is unable to perform mouth-to-mouth or mouth-to-nose resuscitation; for example, when massive facial injuries absolutely prevent it. In cases of heart failure, mouth-to-mouth resuscitation in combination with cardiac compressions should be administered. However, the cardiac compressions should be executed only by a person with special training in this method.

ARTIFICIAL RESPIRATION FOR ADULTS
Mouth-to-Mouth (-Nose) Technique

1. Place the patient on his back. If it is necessary to roll the victim over, try to roll him over as a single unit, keeping the back and neck straight to avoid aggravation of any spinal injury.
2. Loosen all tight clothing.
3. Clear the upper airway by running your fingers behind his lower teeth and over the back of his tongue. Remove dentures or foreign material.
4. Turn his head face up. Tilt the head back so that the neck is stretched and the chin is up.
5. Adjust the lower jaw so that it juts out. This position-ing moves the base of the tongue away from the back of the throat, thus clearing or enlarging the air passage to the lungs.
6. Seal the airway opening (either the nose or the mouth) that is not being used. The seal must be secure to keep air from leaking during inflation. Pinch the nostrils shut with your free fingers (if you use mouth-to-mouth resuscitation) or seal the mouth by placing two fingers lengthwise over the patient's lips (if you use mouth-to-nose resuscitation).
7. Take a deep breath. Open your mouth wide and make an airtight seal around the patient's mouth or nose by placing

Kneel at the victim's head, place your hands on the victim's back (left).
Rock forward until your arms are vertical (center).
Rock back grasping the victim's elbows (right).

your mouth over his mouth or nose. Breathe into the victim's mouth or nose until his chest rises.

8. Breathe into the patient a total of four times as quickly as possible. If you feel or hear no air exchange, retilt his head and try again. If you still feel no air exchange, again sweep the mouth of foreign objects and breathe again into the victim. If you still have no air exchange, turn the victim on his side and slap him on the back between the shoulder blades. This should free anything blocking the throat. Again sweep his mouth to remove foreign matter. (If none of the above steps clear the air passage, repeat the blows to the back and retilt the head.)

9. Repeat breathing. Remove mouth each time to allow air to escape. If the exhalation is noisy, elevate his jaw further.

10. This procedure should be repeated twelve times per minute. Use deep breaths. As the victim begins to breathe, maintain head tilt.

Back Pressure Arm Lift Method

If it is impossible because of severe facial injuries to administer mouth-to-mouth or mouth-to-nose resuscitation try the following:

1. Place the victim face down, after first having cleared his mouth. Bend his elbows and place his hands one upon the other at eye level under his head. Turn the victim's head to one side, making sure the chin juts out.

2. Kneel at the victim's head. Place your hand on his back so that palms lie just below an imaginary line between his armpits.

3. Rock forward until your arms are vertical and the weight of your body exerts steady pressure on your hands.

4. Rock back, grasping victim's elbows, and draw victim's arms up toward you until you feel resistance at the shoulders.

5. Lower victim's arms to the ground.

Repeat about twelve times per minute (every 5 seconds). Keep checking to see if the mouth is clear, the airway is open, and the heart is beating. *Note.* In both methods of artificial respiration, continue your efforts until the victim breathes normally or a doctor pronounces him dead, or a more qualified person takes charge, or you are physically unable to continue. If the patient must be moved, continue artificial ventilation.

ARTIFICIAL RESPIRATION FOR CHILDREN AND INFANTS

The method is similar with slight modifications.

1. Clear mouth with finger.

2. Place child on his back.

3. Lift jaw so it juts out as with adults.

4. Place your mouth over both mouth and nose of the child to make an airtight seal.

5. Gently blow puffs of air, about twenty per minute.

Otherwise the procedure is the same with one exception: instead of the slaps between the shoulder blades to remove foreign matter, hold the infant by the ankles upside down and give several sharp pats between the shoulder blades to free the air passage.

Choking

How to help
a choking victim.

The cause: In most cases food particles or bones caught in the windpipe instead of going into the esophagus.

The symptoms: The victim gasps for breath or has violent fits of coughing, quickly turns pale then blue, and cannot talk.

Actions to take: If the victim is still able to cough, don't interfere. It is quite possible that he will cough up the foreign object. If any of the other symptoms occur, open the victim's mouth and grasp the foreign object with your index and middle finger, trying to remove it.

If you can't reach the obstruction with your fingers, use the following method:

1. Stand behind the choking victim, with your arms around

him, thumb side of your fist against his stomach, just above the navel and below the ribcage.

2. Grasp your fist with your other hand and make four quick upward thrusts. This will force air out of the lungs and may expel the obstruction. Repeat this procedure if necessary.

Cardiac Arrest

PRESSURE POINT

Location of pressure point.

The causes: Insufficient oxygen supply to the heart or the brain, blockage of blood vessels of the heart, heart disease, embolism (foreign particles in the bloodstream), or overdose of certain drugs. Respiratory arrest is the most common cause of cardiac arrest. The heart stops within minutes after breathing ceases.

The symptoms: No breathing, no pulse, unconsciousness, dilated pupils of the eyes, limp body, and flaccid skin.

Actions to take:

1. Roll the victim on his back.

2. Loosen all tight clothing.

3. Check the airway and remove any obstruction.

4. Hyperextend the neck and lift the lower jaw for mouth-to-mouth artificial respiration.

5. Give the patient five quick puffs of air by mouth-to-mouth.

*6. Place the heel of your hand on the lower half of the breastbone and press down until the breastbone is depressed about 2 inches. Repeat the compression about 15 times, about once per second. (To determine the pressure point for cardiac compressions, locate the bony tip of the breastbone with your ring finger and place two fingers just above that point.)

Apply cardiac compression only if you are trained in CPR.

7. Return to mouth-to-mouth artificial respiration and give the victim two respirations.

8. Repeat this 15–2 cycle until help arrives or the patient is pronounced dead.

9. If help is available, one person should give the cardiac compressions and the other should give mouth-to-mouth artificial respiration. The ratio with two operators should be five compressions to one artificial respiration. The compressions should not be interrupted, even for

---

*Cardiac compressions should be attempted only if the first aider is well trained in cardiopulmonary resuscitation (CPR).

respirations. When respiration is being applied, the compressions must be stopped only momentarily.

10. The cardiac compressions should equal about 60 per minute, the respirations about 12 per minute.

Severe Bleeding

Acute hemorrhage is a rapid loss of blood from the blood vessels. In the event of an acute severe hemorrhage (loss of at least 2 pints of blood) an emergency is present. If the bleeding is not stopped, the patient will die.

1. Arterial bleeding

The symptoms: Spurting blood, bright red in color.

The blood leaves the heart through the arteries under pressure. If an artery is opened, blood will spurt out forcefully. With each beat of the heart there will be a corresponding spurt of blood. The larger the artery, the more rapid the blood loss.

2. Venous bleeding

The symptoms: Continuous flow of blood, dark red in color.

Blood flowing through the veins is under less pressure than in the arteries. However, a break in a vein will allow blood to flow out of it. The rate of blood loss depends upon the size of the opened vein.

3. Capillary bleeding

BRACHIAL ARTERY

FEMORAL ARTERY

Apply pressure to the pressure point closest to the wound and between the wound and the heart.
Pressure point to control bleeding of an open arm wound (top). Pressure point to control severe bleeding of an open leg wound (left). Pressure points for head wounds (above). From left to right: Wound above level of eye; below eyelevel, above jawbone; bleeding from neck, mouth, or throat.

The symptoms: Blood oozing from a wound.

The blood loss is usually not serious, as the bleeding is limited.

Actions to take: Control of hemorrhage is primarily mechanical and consists of closing off the opened blood vessel.

1. Direct pressure: Cover the wound with the cleanest cloth immediately available or with your bare hand, and apply direct pressure on the wound. Most bleeding can be stopped this way.

2. Digital pressure (in case of arterial bleeding and if direct pressure does not do the trick). Apply your fingers to the appropriate pressure point — a point where the main artery supplying blood to the wound is located (see diagram). The three pressure points in the head and neck should be used only as a last resort if there is a skull fracture and direct pressure cannot be used. If direct pressure can be used, it will stop bleeding on the head in about 95 percent of injuries.

The pressure-point method is not recommended if pressure must be maintained for a long period of time, but it may be useful temporarily until a pressure dressing can be applied.

Use a tourniquet only as a last resort.

3. Elevation: If bleeding from a wound is only venous or capillary, elevation of the wound above the heart may slow the flow of blood. However, elevation is of no value in control of arterial bleeding, and it may aggravate fractures.

4. Tourniquet: Applying a tourniquet to an arm or a leg should be done only as a last resort when all other methods fail. A tourniquet is applied between the wound and the point at which the limb is attached to the body, as close to the wound as possible but never over a wound or fracture. Make sure it is applied tightly enough to stop bleeding completely.

Although the tourniquet will stop the bleeding by compressing all the vessels, it is potentially dangerous, because it deprives the uninjured tissues of blood.

Patients who have tourniquets applied should be clearly identified with a "T" on the forehead. Once applied, a tourniquet should never be loosened or removed except under the supervision of a doctor.

In the case of an improvised tourniquet, the material should be wrapped twice around the extremity and half-knotted. Place a stick or something similar on the half-knot and tie a full knot. Twist the stick to tighten the tourniquet only until the bleeding stops — no more. Secure the stick or level in place with the loose ends of the tourniquet, another strip of cloth, or other improvised material.

Note: A tourniquet can be improvised from a strap, belt, handkerchiefs, necktie, cravat bandage, etc. Never use wire, cord, or anything that will cut into the flesh.

INTERNAL BLEEDING

The symptoms: Cold and clammy skin, weak and rapid pulse, eyes dull and pupils enlarged, nausea and vomiting, pain in the affected area, especially the abdomen and chest.
Actions to be taken:
1. Treat victim for shock (see below).
2. Anticipate that victim may vomit; therefore give nothing by mouth.
3. Keep the patient still to allow maximum flow of blood to vital organs and prevent further internal damage.
4. Get the patient to professional medical help as quickly and safely as possible.

Shock

The causes: Shock is a complex subject, but basically the causes may be: Loss of blood, breathing impairment, heart failure, or burns. The most common cause is hemorrhage, when blood escapes from the vascular system and consequently does not reach the tissues.

Shock can kill; treat as soon as possible, and continue until medical aid is available.
The symptoms: Shallow breathing, rapid and weak pulse,

nausea, collapse, vomiting, shivering, pale and moist skin, mental confusion, drooping eyelids.

Actions to take:

1. Establish and maintain an open airway.
2. Stop the bleeding and insure that the patient is breathing adequately.
3. Place the patient on his back with his head down (by elevating the feet with a pillow or blankets) to improve the flow of blood to the brain. Exceptions: head and chest injuries, heart attack, stroke, sunstroke. If there is no spine injury, the victim may be more comfortable and breathe better in a semireclining position. If in doubt, keep the victim flat.
4. Make sure the patient is comfortable and reassure him. This can help to prevent worsening of the shock.
5. Maintain normal body temperature. Place blankets under and over the victim.
6. Give nothing by mouth, especially stimulants or alcoholic beverages.
7. Always treat for shock in cases of serious injuries, and watch for it in minor ones.

First Aid for Specific Injuries

Burns

Burns are damage to tissue caused by exposure to excessive heat, strong chemicals, or electricity. They are classified by cause, degree, and extent. All classifications should be considered in the treatment and disposition of a burn patient.

HEAT BURNS

First-degree Burns

The symptoms: Reddened skin.

Actions to take:

1. Immerse quickly in cold water or apply ice until pain stops.
2. Apply a dry dressing if necessary.

*Second-degree Burns

The symptoms: Reddened skin, blisters.

Actions to take:

1. Cut away loose clothing.

2. Apply freshly laundered cloth that has been wrung out in ice water.

3. If limb is involved, immerse in cold water (not ice water) for relief of pain.

4. Apply dry, sterile gauze or clean cloth as protective bandage.

5. Do *not* break blisters or remove tissue; do *not* apply ointment, commercial preparations, grease, or other home remedies.

*Third-degree Burns

The symptoms: Skin destroyed, tissues damaged, charring.

Actions to take:

1. Cut away loose clothing (do *not* remove clothing adhering to skin).

2. Cover burns with thick sterile dressing or fresh household linen.

3. If hands are involved keep them above the level of the victim's heart. Keep burned feet or legs elevated.

4. Treat for shock.

5. Arrange transportation to the hospital as quickly as possible.

*CHEMICAL BURNS

The causes: Harsh chemicals or corrosive poisons spilled on the skin.

Actions to take:

1. Remove victim's clothing, because chemical may be retained by it.

2. Remove all chemicals by flooding the affected area with water for at least 20 minutes.

3. Apply a dressing and get medical aid.

Frostbite

The cause: Constriction of vessels by extreme cold prevents circulation of blood in the involved area and the tissue freezes.

The symptoms: The skin at first is red, then pale or waxy white. The injured part has no feeling while it is frozen.

---

*If medical help is not available within an hour and the victim is conscious and not vomiting, give him a weak solution of salt and soda: 1 level teaspoon of salt and ½ level teaspoon of baking soda to 1 quart of water. The water should be lukewarm. Allow the victim to sip a half glass slowly over a period of 15 minutes.

Actions to take:

1. Remove all wet or tight clothing from the frostbitten area.
2. Warm the area. The best method of warming is to place the area in a warm-water bath (102° – 105°F) and make sure the water remains warm. Never thaw the area if the victim has to go back out into the cold, which may cause the affected area to be refrozen.
3. Cover the frostbitten area with a loose, dry dressing.
4. Once the area is thawed, have the victim gently exercise it.

Do not rub, chafe, or manipulate frostbitten parts. *Do not* use hot water bottles or a heat lamp. *Do not* place the victim near a hot stove. *Do not* allow the victim to walk if the feet are affected. *Do not* allow the victim to smoke, because the nicotine in tobacco may further constrict the blood vessels.

Fractures

Fractures, or broken bones, are the result of a strong blow or stress against the body causing one or more bones to crack or break completely. Fractures are either closed (no break in the skin) or open (skin broken). Open fractures are generally more serious, because of the danger of infection. *The symptoms:* Pain at the fracture site, great difficulty in moving the part of the body beyond the fracture, swelling and tenderness of the fracture, possible deformity of the limb, discoloration of the skin, exposed bone and bleeding (in case of broken fracture). Ultimately, X rays will be needed to establish the diagnosis and extent of the fracture. *Actions to take:*

1. Stop external bleeding.
2. Treat for shock, as almost every fracture is accompanied by significant internal bleeding with the danger of developing hemorrhagic shock.
3. Administer analgesic against pain.
4. Splint the broken part.

Splinting:

A. Splints should be long enough to support joints above and below the fracture.
B. Splints should be rigid enough to support the fracture.
C. Improvised splints should be well enough padded to insure even contact and pressure between the limb and the splint and to protect all bony prominences. (An improvised splint may be made of any rigid material that is readily

Dressing and using an improvised splint for an open fracture (left top and bottom). If available, a more rigid material for the splint and more ties are preferable.

A jacket is used as improvised sling.

available, as a padded board, a rolled blanket, tools, newspapers, or magazines.)

When you apply a splint, handle the patient as gently as possible. This work should be done in pairs, one person to immobilize the limb and one to apply the splint:

1. Apply slight traction to the affected limb.

2. A second person (if available) should place the padded splint under, above, or beside the limb.

3. Tie the limb and the splint together with bandaging material so the two are held firmly together. Leave fingers or toes exposed, if they are not involved, so that the circulation can be checked constantly.

Note: Do *not* attempt to reduce or set the broken bone. In general, splint the fractured limb as you find it, checking the pulse beyond the fracture before and after splinting. If the pulse disappears after the splint is applied, it is too tight and must be loosened.

Open Wounds

There are five types of wounds.

• 1. Abrasions: The outer layers of the protective skin are damaged, as when the skin is scraped against a hard surface. Limited bleeding.

If there is nothing available to splint a broken leg, tie the injured leg to the uninjured one with padding between the legs.

Cover the wound with the cleanest cloth available and apply direct pressure.

• 2. Incisions: Tissue is cut by a knife or other sharp object. Bleeding may be heavy.

• 3. Lacerations: Tissue is cut, and the wound displays a jagged, irregular, or blunt tearing. Heavy bleeding is possible, and chance of later infection is present.

• 4. Punctures: Skin layers and tissue are pierced by pointed objects such as nails, pins, splinters, glass fragments. Little bleeding.

• 5. Avulsions: These wounds occur when tissue is forcibly separated or torn from a victim's body; for instance, a torn ear. Heavy rapid bleeding is usually observed.

Actions to take:

1. Stop the bleeding (as previously described).

2. Cover with the cleanest cloth available, preferably a sterile dressing.

3. Provide shock care when wound is bleeding severely.

4. Obtain medical attention.

5. Wash with soap and water wounds that involve surface area with little bleeding.

6. If a puncture wound is caused by wood splinters or glass fragments, they often remain in the skin tissue or tissues just beneath the surface. Such objects usually only irritate the victim, but if they are not removed, they can cause infection. Therefore, sterilize tweezers over a flame or in boiling water, and pull out the foreign matter.

Remove splinter with sterilized tweezers.

If the objects are imbedded just beneath the skin, sterilize the tip of a needle in a flame or in rubbing alcohol, scratch the top layer of the skin, and lift the object out with the top of the needle. If the object is more deeply imbedded, it should be removed by a physician.

Note: If a wound is caused by being impaled by an object, do *not* remove the imbedded object. Cut clothing away from injury site. Stabilize the object with a bulky dressing. If available, put a paper cup over the imbedded object to prevent movement, and apply a bandage. If a large object is imbedded, cut off only enough to permit transportation of victim.

Eye Injuries

The cause: Foreign object blown or rubbed into the eye.
The symptoms: Redness of eye, burning sensation, pain, headache, tearing.
Actions to take:
1. Try to flush out the foreign object with clean water (if available, use an eye cup).
2. If you don't succeed, pull down the lower lid to determine whether or not the object lies on the inner surface of the lid.
3. If so, lift it gently with the corner of a clean handkerchief, a paper tissue, or sterile gauze.
4. If the object is not on the lower lid, check whether it is lodged beneath the upper lid. While the victim looks down, gently grasp the lashes of the upper lid. Pull the upper lid forward and down over the lower lid. The object may be dislodged by the tears.

Roll up upper eyelid over matchstick (left) and remove foreign object with corner of clean handkerchief (right).

5. If this does not help, depress the victim's upper lid with a matchstick placed horizontally on the cartilage and roll the lid by pulling upward on the lashes against the matchstick. If you see the foreign object, remove it with a clean handkerchief or sterile gauze.
6. Flush the eye again with clean water.
7. If the object is still there, you have to suspect that it is imbedded in the eyeball. Cover the eye with a dry protective dressing and consult a doctor.
Note: In all phases, prevent the victim from rubbing the eye.

Nosebleed

The cause: Injury of the nose, including fracture, or disease such as high blood pressure. Very often nosebleeds occur after a cold, exposure to high altitudes, or strenuous activity.

Disregarding fracture and disease as causes, nosebleeds are generally more annoying than dangerous, and they usually stop spontaneously. If, however, nosebleeds occur often within a short period, see a doctor.

Actions to take:

1. Keep the victim quiet.
2. Place him with head bent slightly forward in a sitting position.
3. Apply pressure with your thumb and index finger directly at the site of the bleeding if bleeding occurs from both nostrils, or press the bleeding nostril with your index finger toward the middle.
4. Apply cold compresses to victim's nose and face.
5. If bleeding is not stopped by the preceding measures, insert a small, clean pad of gauze into one or both nostrils. Part of the gauze should extend outside the nostril, so that the pad can be removed later without blowing the nose and reinjuring it. Do not use cotton instead of gauze. If bleeding cannot be stopped, call a physician.

Poisoning

Note: It is important in all cases of poisoning, which might have many more causes than we mention, that you call a physician immediately. If you suspect that drugs are the cause, call your poison center to find out the antidote for the poison. Get the patient to a hospital at once, and take with you the bottle that may have contained the poisonous drug. Only if you cannot get the patient to a hospital or a doctor immediately should you start first aid.

FOOD POISONING

When a person complains of stomach pain, nausea, vomiting, or diarrhea after eating or drinking some questionable substance, you should suspect poisoning. Do not wait for more symptoms to develop. Additional symptoms may include dizziness, drowsiness, slurred speech, lack of coordination, cold clammy skin, thirst, convulsions.

Actions to take:

1. Encourage the patient to drink plenty of water. Filling the stomach with water dilutes the poison.
2. Instruct the patient to stick his finger behind his tongue to trigger the gag reflex. If he is unable to do this, you can do it for him to induce vomiting.
3. When he starts to vomit, make sure his head is between his legs.
4. This process may be repeated once or twice, depending on how much foreign material is flushed out of the stomach. If the contents of the stomach comes out as a clear liquid it is proof that it is free of foreign material.
5. Treat for shock.

Note: This treatment is a first-aid measure if you don't know exactly what poisonous substance the patient has swallowed, and if it was not acid, alkali, or petroleum poisoning.

ACID, ALKALI, AND PETROLEUM POISONING

The symptoms of acid and alkali poisoning: Burns around the mouth, lips, and tongue; burning sensation in the mouth, throat, and stomach; bloody diarrhea.

The symptoms of petroleum poisoning: Burning irritation; coughing; coma.

Actions to take:

1. If the patient is conscious, make him drink as much milk as he can tolerate.
2. Loosen tight clothing.
3. Treat for shock.

Note: Do not induce vomiting.

INHALED POISON

The cause: Auto exhaust, chemical fumes, industrial gases.

The symptoms: Irritated nose, throat, eyes; coughing; shortness of breath, dizziness, unconsciousness.

Actions to take:

1. Remove person from the source of the poison.
2. Loosen tight clothing.
3. Treat for shock.

Insect Bites

The symptoms: Local irritation and pain, moderate swelling and redness, itching and/or burning.

Actions to take:

1. If stinger is left in the wound, withdraw it with tweezers.
2. Apply paste of baking soda and water.
3. Immediate application of ice or ice water to the bite or sting relieves pain.
4. Insect bites may be merely a nuisance, but they may be serious for persons who are allergic to them. Severe reaction may follow. Use a constricting bandage (if the sting is on an extremity) and ice. Get medical help immediately.

Animal Bites

Actions to take:

1. Wash animal bites with soap and water. If possible, use running water.
2. Cover with a sterile gauze pad.
3. If the bite goes through the skin, see a doctor, as a tetanus shot might be necessary.

Note: Try to find out what animal made the wound. Bites by dogs, skunks, cats, bats, and other animals can cause rabies. If the animal is not found and examined for rabies, the patient must undergo rabies treatment, as rabies is a killer. Even bites from healthy animals can cause serious infections. That is why a doctor should be consulted if a bite is bleeding.

Snakebite

Snakebite is unusual, even in snake-infested areas. Generally, a snake will avoid a human unless it is forced to defend itself. If you encounter a snake at close range, do not make any sudden moves. Back away slowly. A snake can strike accurately for a distance equal to about one-half of its length. Both poisonous and nonpoisonous snakes will bite if provoked.

The symptoms of poisonous snakebites: Puncture marks, severe burning, pain and spreading swelling, discoloration, early signs and symptoms of shock, headache, dizziness, blurred vision, respiratory distress.

Actions to take:

1. Immobilize the victim immediately, with the injured part lower than the rest of the body. Any activity will stimulate the spread of the poison.
2. Remove rings, watches, and bracelets.

3. Apply a constricting band above the swelling caused by the bite. It should be tight, but not tight enough to stop arterial circulation.

4. If medical help is more than one-half hour away, make an incision, no more than ⅛ inch deep nor more than ½ inch long, lengthwise through fang marks. Press around cut to make it bleed.

5. Apply suction to the wound with the device found in a snakebite kit. If no kit is available, use your mouth (if you have no open sores in your mouth or on your lips) and spit out the blood. Cutting and suction are of no value unless done immediately. Do not cut if bite is near a major blood vessel.

6. If there are no serious signs or symptoms, treat the symptoms that are present but still call for medical help.

Dressings and Bandages

A *dressing* is a pad that is applied directly over a wound. A prepared dressing is usually made of gauze, but it can be made of any absorbent material. The main purpose of a dressing is to control hemorrhage and protect the wound against further contamination. Almost all external bleeding can be controlled with a correctly applied dressing.

A *bandage* is a piece of material used to cover a dressing, apply additional pressure, or immobilize a part of the body. Bandages may be made of gauze, muslin, or elastic cotton.

SELF-STICKING ADHESIVE BANDAGES

MULTILAYERED STERILE GAUZE COMPRESSES

ADHESIVE TAPE

BANDAGE COMPRESSES

"CRAVAT"

ARM SLING

ROLLER GAUZE

They may be rolled or folded. Elastic bandages are used to reinforce dressings in the control of hemorrhage and to support ankles, knees, wrists, and elbows in case of strain or sprain. Triangular muslin bandages are sometimes used for support but are used mostly as tourniquets. Folded triangular bandages (cravats) are useful in applying improvised splints.

Principles of Bandaging

1. Never tie a tight bandage around the neck; it may cause strangulation.
2. A bandage should be tight enough to prevent slipping, but not so tight as to cut off circulation.
3. Loosen bandages immediately if victim complains of numbness or a tingling sensation.
4. Leave fingers and toes exposed, if not injured, to watch for swelling or changes of color and feel for coldness, which signal interference with circulation.
5. Once a dressing is in place do not remove it. If blood saturates the dressing, put another on top of it.

Written by
MARTIN SHARP

The
Food
You Eat

Contents

"Tell Me What You Eat, and I Will Tell You What You Are"

Nutrition is one of the most important factors in the achievement of good health. Good health does not only mean being free of disease; it also means having a sense of vitality and well-being. Nutrition is important for your physical fitness and your mental alertness. Eating the proper foods will help you to feel better, think better, work better.

"Tell me what you eat, and I will tell you what you are." This is a quotation from Anthelme Brillat-Savarin, a Frenchman known for his witty sayings on the art of dining. His aphorism is true in more ways than one, because one of the main jobs of food is to supply enough energy to support the many functions of the body. Food energy is measured in calories.

Your body is continually replacing many of its parts. The outer layer of the skin is shed and renewed; your nails grow during your entire life; hairs grow, fall out, and new ones grow; all the red blood cells are replaced within weeks, and so is the entire lining of the digestive tract. The food you eat is responsible for your growth from infancy to adulthood and the constant renewal of your body.

If you eat the right foods or **nutrients** in the proper quantities, you will have a very good chance of fighting off diseases and staying healthy.

Nutrients—What They Do and Where They Are Found

Nutrients are divided by food scientists into six classes: carbohydrates, fats, proteins, vitamins, minerals, and water.

It is interesting to know that, if a complete chemical analysis were made of a person whose proper weight, for example, was 150 pounds, 90 pounds would be water; 30 pounds, fat; almost 30 pounds protein, carbohydrate, and the major minerals of the bones (calcium and phosphorus); and a fraction of a pound vitamins and other minerals.

Most foods contain not only the nutrients mentioned, but also materials that cannot be broken down by the body but are needed for bulk, and some minerals that are of no nutritional value. Let's examine the various nutrients:

Carbohydrates

The necessity for carbohydrates in the diet is often underestimated by people who are weight-conscious in the belief that they are too fattening. This, however, is only partially true. The main job of carbohydrates in the diet is to provide energy for the work of the body. They also aid in the manufacture of some of the B vitamins, and they form parts of many compounds in the body.

Carbohydrate is the name of a group of organic substances that are made up of carbon, hydrogen, and oxygen. The name itself indicates the combination: Carbo (carbon), hydrate (water, which is a combination of hydrogen and oxygen).

Plants that contain chlorophyll (the substance that gives them their green color) are the main source of carbohydrates. These plants use energy from the sun to combine carbon dioxide from the air and water from the soil to manufacture carbohydrates. Because carbohydrates are a main source for life, no living creature can exist without eating plants. Even animals that eat only meat get their carbohydrate supply by eating the flesh of animals that live on plants.

Foods supply carbohydrates in three main forms: starches, sugars, and cellulose (fiber). Starches and sugars are the main sources of energy for human beings. Cellulose is among the food materials that cannot be digested; it provides bulk in the diet.

Glucose, commonly called blood sugar, is the form in which starches and sugars are mainly used by body cells to furnish energy for body processes, activity, and growth.

Carbohydrates are economical to produce; growing plants is cheaper than raising animals for food. In the United States and Canada carbohydrates provide 40 to 50 percent of the total food energy. The entire population of the world obtains 70 percent of its energy from carbohydrates, because most peoples cannot afford foods containing large amounts of the other nutrients, proteins and fats.

Good sources of carbohydrates are grains (such as corn, oats, wheat, and rice), products made from grain (such as macaroni, spaghetti, noodles, grits, breads, and breakfast cereals), and potatoes, sweet potatoes, dried beans, and peas.

Carbohydrates can also be obtained from other vegetables and from fruits. In vegetables, the carbohydrates are mainly in the form of starches; in fruits, they are chiefly sugars. Cane and beet sugars, jellies, jams, candy and other sweets, honey, molasses, and syrups are concentrated sources of sugar in our diets.

Sucrose, which is common table sugar, is produced mostly from sugar cane and sugar beets. Table sugar, or refined sugar, is an unusual food in that it is pure carbohydrate. It is a source of calories (measures of heat energy) only; that is, it contains no vitamins, minerals, or any other food substances. For this reason, sugar is sometimes called "empty calories."

Fats

The main sources of fat in foods are butter, margarine, lard, meat fat, animal and vegetable oils, cream, most cheeses, and nuts. There are other foods that have smaller amounts of fat.

Although the main nutritional task of carbohydrates is to provide energy for the body, fats are even more concentrated sources of energy. Weight for weight, fats give twice as much energy — calories — as either carbohydrates or proteins.

There are saturated and unsaturated fats, and the difference between them is important. Large amounts of saturated fats can eventually produce very serious diseases such as high blood pressure and consequent heart attacks.

Fats are composed mainly of fatty acids. Each fatty acid is made up of carbon atoms joined like links in a chain. The carbon chains vary in length, with most edible fats containing 4 to 20 carbon atoms. Each carbon atom has hydrogen atoms attached to it as charms might be attached to the links of a bracelet. When each carbon atom in the chain has attached to it as many hydrogen atoms as it can hold (usually two), the fatty acid is said to be saturated. When a hydrogen atom is missing from two neighboring carbon atoms, a double bond forms between them, and the fatty acid is said to be unsaturated. A fatty acid that contains more than one such double bond is called polyunsaturated.

Probably the most important polyunsaturated fatty acid is linoleic acid. The body cannot manufacture this acid, so it must be obtained from food. A lack of this fatty acid causes the skin to become reddened and irritated and abnormalities of the liver to develop, especially in very young children. Linoleic acid is found in valuable amounts in many plant oils, such as corn, cottonseed, soybean, sesame, safflower, and wheat-germ oils. (The difference between a fat and an oil is that an oil is liquid at ordinary temperatures and fat is solid.) Margarine, salad dressings, mayonnaise, and cooking fats are usually made from one of these oils. Walnuts are high in linoleic acid, but other kinds of nuts are not. Poultry fat and fish fat and oil have more linoleic acid than do other animal fats, which rank fairly low as sources of this acid.

The body changes some fats into compounds called lipids. These can, over a period of years, form fatty deposits on the insides of arteries, causing the condition called hardening of the arteries, which may lead to high blood pressure and possible heart attack. Food scientists believe that polyunsaturated fats are less likely to be turned into lipids and therefore may help to prevent heart attack and high blood pressure.

Another important function of fats in the diet is to carry the fat-soluble vitamins A, D, E, and K.

In cooking, fats add flavor and variety to many foods. Fats also make foods and meals satisfying, because they are digested slowly and delay a feeling of hunger before the next meal.

Proteins

All life requires protein. It is the basic substance of every cell in the body, the chief tissue builder. Proteins are the body builders and maintainers: they help in the development of muscles, and they create a feeling of well-being and fitness. In addition, proteins help to make hemoglobin (the blood protein that carries oxygen to the cells and carries carbon dioxide away from the cells). Proteins make the parts of cells that control the genetic code and therefore all hereditary characteristics in body cells; build the thousands of enzymes, the substances that control the speed of chemical reactions within the body; and make hormones, such as insulin and thyroxin, which regulate chemical processes and growth in the body. Proteins also form antibodies that can prevent diseases caused by foreign proteins (such as bacteria) that enter the body.

Proteins supply energy when the diet does not provide enough carbohydrates and fats.

The chief sources of protein are meat, poultry, fish, milk, eggs, cheese, beans, peas, and nuts.

Breads, cereals, vegetables, and fruits contain relatively smaller amounts of protein.

Proteins are made up of smaller units called amino acids. When foods containing proteins are digested, the proteins are broken down into the amino acids. These are then rearranged to make enzymes, hormones, and other special proteins.

The proteins in foods are usually made up of 18 or more amino acids. The body can make its own supply of more than half of the needed amino acids, but the rest, called essential amino acids, must come ready-made from food.

The amino acid makeup of a food protein determines its nutritive value. Proteins that supply the essential amino acids in about the same proportions as needed by the body are the proteins that are highest in nutritional value. Foods that provide good amounts of these top-ranking proteins are the foods that best meet the body's needs. Generally, these are foods of animal origin—meat, poultry, fish, eggs, and milk.

Proteins from cereal grains, vegetables, and fruits do not provide as broad an assortment of amino acids as do animal proteins, but legumes, especially soybeans, peanuts, and chickpeas, provide proteins almost as good as those from animal tissues.

Combining a small amount of animal protein—eggs, milk, cheese—with cereal, and meat or fish with vegetables will help to provide sufficient protein at a lower cost. Examples of tasty combinations are milk and cereal, macaroni and cheese, beans and peas with corn, beans with rice, and peanut butter with wheat (in bread).

Children urgently need protein for normal growth, and every person needs protein throughout life for maintenance and repair of body tissues.

Vitamins

Vitamins are substances that occur in small amounts in a wide variety of foods and are needed for good health. They take part in the release of energy from foods, promote normal growth of many kinds of tissues, and are essential for the proper functioning of nerves and muscles.

More than a dozen vitamins that are needed for good health have been identified. Ordinarily, you can get all the vitamins you need by eating a well-balanced diet of everyday foods, such as those suggested in the Daily Food Guide given later in this book.

Following is a summary of the most important vitamins, including some of their functions, and a list of foods that are dependable sources.

VITAMIN A

Vitamin A is needed for normal bone growth, and it helps the eyes adjust to dim light. It also promotes healthy, infection-resistant skin and mucous membranes.

Vitamin A is found only in foods of animal origin. Liver is a good source; so are eggs, butter, margarine, whole milk, and cheese made from whole milk.

Dark-green and deep-yellow vegetables and deep-yellow fruits contain a substance called carotene that the body can convert into vitamin A.

VITAMIN D

Vitamin D is important in building strong bones and teeth, because it enables the body to use calcium and phosphorus supplied by food.

Not many foods contain vitamin D naturally. Cod liver oil is a good source but is not likely to be part of a daily diet. Smaller amounts are found in eggs, butter, and liver; and somewhat larger amounts are found in sardines, salmon, tuna, and herring. Since vitamin D is not found in most foods and since it is so important for normal growth of children, synthetic vitamin D is added to almost all the milk sold in the United States and Canada.

Vitamin D is also produced in the human body by the direct action of sunlight on the skin.

VITAMIN C, OR ASCORBIC ACID

Vitamin C helps to form and maintain "cementing materials" that hold body cells together and strengthen the walls of blood vessels. Because of this property, it assists in normal tooth and bone formation and aids in healing wounds.

Citrus fruits—oranges, lemons, grapefruits, and their juices, and fresh strawberries are excellent sources of ascorbic acid. Less important, but still good, sources are tomatoes and tomato juice, broccoli, brussels sprouts, cabbage, cantaloupe, cauliflower, and green peppers. Other sources are some dark-green leafy vegetables —such as collards, kale, mustard greens, spinach, and turnip greens —and watermelon. White and sweet potatoes cooked in their skins provide vitamin C.

When a person is under stress, the body utilizes larger-than-normal amounts of vitamin C. A person in this situation should make sure that he or she gets an extra amount of it.

This vitamin is soluble in water; therefore, foods containing it should not be overcooked, causing all the vitamin C to be dissolved in the cooking water.

THE B VITAMINS

There are a number of B vitamins—thiamin, riboflavin, niacin, pyridoxine, folic acid, cobalamin, and possibly others.

Three of these, thiamin, riboflavin, and niacin, play a central role in the release of energy from food. They also help in maintaining normal appetite, good digestion, healthy skin, and good nerve functioning. Meats are the leading source of the B vitamins, and whole grain bread and enriched white bread and cereals supply small but important amounts. A few foods are outstanding sources: lean pork for thiamin, milk for riboflavin, and organ meats for all three.

A deficiency of thiamin causes the disease known as beriberi, which is practically unknown in the U.S. and Canada. Too little riboflavin causes sore lips, tongue, and mouth and a rough, scaly skin. A deficiency of niacin causes pellagra, the symptoms of which

are inflamed skin, diarrhea, and mental confusion progressing to delirium; untreated, it can be fatal.

Obtaining enough niacin is not a problem if sufficient protein is included in the daily diet, because an essential amino acid—tryptophan—present in protein can be converted into niacin by the body.

Other B vitamins—pyridoxine (B_6), folic acid, and cobalamin (B_{12})—help to prevent anemia (the loss of red blood cells) and to build proteins. Vitamin B_6 and folic acid are widely distributed in foods. The largest amounts of folic acid are found in organ meats and dark-green leafy vegetables. Good sources of vitamin B_6 include most meats, whole-grain cereals, beans, potatoes, and dark-green leafy vegetables. Vitamin B_{12} is found only in foods of animal origin—liver, kidney, muscle meats, fish, eggs, oysters, and milk.

VITAMIN K

Vitamin K is important for its role in the clotting of blood and the proper functioning of the liver. Egg yolks, organ meats, and green leafy vegetables are sources of this vitamin. Some Vitamin K is produced by bacteria that live in the intestinal tract.

VITAMIN E

Vitamin E is known as an antioxidant; it prevents an unwanted chemical reaction — oxidation — from destroying certain nutrients such as polyunsaturated fats. It is stored in muscles and fat deposits and is found in wheat germ, leafy vegetables, legumes, whole grains, liver, milk, butter, and eggs.

The RDA

Food scientists have worked out the amounts of vitamins the body should have each day. This amount is called the **recommended daily allowance,** or **RDA.** If for some reason you cannot eat enough of the foods that provide the needed vitamins, you can supplement them by taking vitamin capsules. For people below the age of 60, such capsules and a reasonably good diet will provide the RDA for all vitamins. Capsules that provide larger doses are not recommended; the body destroys or excretes most vitamins in amounts larger than it can use or store; therefore, buying large-dose capsules is a waste of money. Also, overdoses of some vitamins, such as A and D, can cause serious bodily harm.

For persons over 60 the RDA increases, but the amount of vitamins they should take must be established by consulting a doctor, not by arbitrarily increasing the dose.

Cholesterol

Cholesterol is a fatlike substance made in the body and found in every cell. It is a normal constituent of blood and tissues. A certain amount of cholesterol is necessary for good health, but large amounts are suspected of causing fatty deposits to form on the insides of arteries and, like lipids, causing hardening of the arteries. There is still no certainty about how much cholesterol is necessary and how much is too much. Many factors influence the amount of cholesterol found in blood; one of these is the foods we eat.

Cholesterol is found in foods of animal origin. It is not found in fruits, vegetables, cereal grains, legumes, nuts, or vegetable oils. The greatest amounts of cholesterol are found in organ meats — brain, liver, kidney, heart, sweetbreads, and gizzard. Egg yolk, too, is high in cholesterol.

Minerals

Minerals make up another important food group. They influence a large number of bodily functions and give strength and rigidity to certain body tissues.
• Calcium is the most abundant mineral in the body. Combined with phosphorus, it causes bones and teeth to be hard. Ninety-nine percent of the calcium in the body is found in bones and teeth.

The rest of the calcium is important for the proper functioning of the heart and other muscles as well as the nerves. Calcium also is a factor in the coagulation of blood during bleeding.

Milk and milk products are the main source of calcium. It is also present in certain dark-green leafy vegetables (collards, kale, mustard greens, turnip greens).

• Iodine. Iodine deficiency results in the disease called goiter, a swelling of the thyroid gland. Iodine is found in seafood—fish, clams, oysters, and mussels—and in seaweed. People who live near the seacoast usually get enough iodine because their diet includes seafood. People living inland will get enough iodine if it is a constituent of the soil. Where the soil does not contain iodine, people are at risk of developing goiter. The absence of iodine in the environment can be made up for by eating canned or frozen seafood and using iodized salt, which is ordinary table salt with a little potassium iodide added.

• Iron is needed by the body in relatively small amounts, but these amounts are vital. Iron combines with protein to make hemoglobin, the red substance of blood that carries oxygen from the lungs to body cells and removes the waste product carbon dioxide from the cells. By carrying oxygen to each cell, iron makes it possible for the cells to obtain energy from food.

Only a few foods contain much iron. Liver is a particularly good source (but remember that liver is high in cholesterol). So are heart and kidney, but again these are high in cholesterol. Other sources of iron are lean meats, shellfish, dry beans, dry peas, dark-green vegetables, oats, dried fruit, egg yolk (high in cholesterol), and molasses. Whole-grain breads and cereals contain smaller amounts of iron, but because they are eaten frequently they can be an important source.

Research shows that the diets of young children, preteen- and teenage girls, and women of childbearing age are most likely to have iron deficiencies. It is therefore recommended that they eat enough foods containing this mineral.

• Two other vitally important minerals are phosphorus and magnesium. Like calcium, the body needs them for bones and teeth; they also aid in converting foods into energy.

Good amounts of magnesium are found in nuts, whole-grain products, dry beans, dry peas, and dark-green vegetables.

If your diet contains foods that provide enough protein and calcium, you probably will get enough phosphorus as well.

• There are about 10 other essential minerals, only very small amounts of which are needed for good health. If your diet is balanced between carbohydrates, fats, and proteins you will get sufficient amounts of these minerals.

Fluorine, which is one of the 10 essential minerals not specifically discussed here, and which helps to protect teeth from decay, may be an exception to the above statement, as you will not get it automatically in a balanced diet. During the years when teeth are being formed, drinking water should contain a proper amount of fluorine in the form of natural or added fluoride, which will make teeth more resistant to decay.

Water

Water is essential for life. It ranks next to oxygen in importance. The body's need for water exceeds even its need for food. You can live for days, even weeks, without food, but only for two or three days without water.

About one-half to two-thirds of the body is made up of water. It is the solvent for everything we digest, and it holds nutrients in solution and carries them through the bloodstream. Water is an important part of every cell structure, and it carries away the body's waste products.

Water also regulates body temperature by evaporating through the skin as perspiration.

A healthy body needs a regular and generous intake of water to perform all these tasks. It is provided largely by the fluids we drink, whether water itself or other liquids such as coffee, tea, juices, milk, or soft drinks. Many foods also contain water: celery and lettuce are good examples.

Although water supplies neither energy nor vitamins, it does contain minerals, for instance fluorine, which are helpful for the body.

A Healthful Diet

Now that you understand a little of the what, why, and how of nutrients, let's apply this information to daily eating patterns.

Keep in mind that everyone needs the same nutrients throughout life, but in different amounts. Proportionately greater amounts are needed for the growth of the body than just for its upkeep. Boys and girls need proportionately more energy and nutrients than do men and women. Large people need more than small people. Active persons need more food energy than inactive ones.

Foods vary in the amounts of nutrients they contain. No single food provides all the necessary nutrients. That is why you need a variety of foods each day.

A diet that provides all the nutrients in the amounts needed is called a balanced diet.

A Guide to Good Eating

Nutrition scientists have translated knowledge of the nutritional needs of the average family into an easy-to-use form: the Daily Food Guide. The Guide is divided into four categories according to the similarity in nutrient content of the foods in each. The categories are: the **milk group,** the **meat group,** the **fruit and vegetable group,** and the **bread and cereal group.** Each of the broad groups makes a special contribution toward a nourishing balanced diet.

A Daily Food Guide

Meat Group: Beef • Lamb • Pork • Variety meats such as liver, heart, kidney. Poultry and eggs • Fish and shellfish. **As Alternates:** Dry beans • Dry peas • Lentils • Nuts • Peanuts • Peanut butter.
Amounts Recommended: Choose 2 or more servings every day.
Count as a serving: 2 to 3 ounces of lean cooked meat, poultry, or fish (all without bone) • one egg • ½ cup cooked dry beans, dry peas, or lentils • 2 tablespoons peanut butter may replace ½ serving of meat.
Vegetable Group: All vegetables and fruits. This guide emphasizes those that are valuable as sources of vitamin C and vitamin A.
Good Sources of Vitamin C: Grapefruit or grapefruit juice • Orange or orange juice • Cantaloupe • Guave • Mango • Papaya • Raw strawberries • Broccoli • Brussels sprouts • Green pepper • Sweet red pepper.
Fair Sources of Vitamin C: Honeydew melon • Lemon • Tangerine or tangerine juice • Watermelon • Asparagus • Cabbage • Collards • Garden cress • Kale • Kohlrabi • Mustard greens • Potatoes and sweet potatoes cooked in the jacket • Spinach • Tomatoes or tomato juice • Turnip greens.
Sources of Vitamin A: Dark-green and deep-yellow vegetables and a few fruits: Apricots • Broccoli • Cantaloupe • Carrots • Chard • Collards • Cress • Kale • Mango • Persimmon • Pumpkin • Spinach • Sweet potatoes • Turnip greens • Other dark-green leaves • Winter squash.
Amounts Recommended: Choose 4 or more servings every day, including: 1 serving of a good source of vitamin C or 2 servings of a fair source • 1 serving, at least every other day, of a good source of vitamin A (if the food chosen for vitamin C is also a good source of vitamin A, the additional serving of a vitamin A food may be

omitted) • The remaining 1 to 3 servings may be of any vegetable or fruit, including those that are valuable for vitamin C and for vitamin A. **Count as 1 serving:** ½ cup of vegetable or fruit • 1 medium: apple • banana • orange • potato • half a medium grapefruit • half a medium cantaloupe • juice of 1 lemon.

Milk Group: Milk (fluid whole, evaporated, skim, dry, buttermilk) • Cheese (cottage, cream, Cheddar-type, natural, or process) • Ice cream.

Amounts Recommended: Some milk every day for everyone. Recommended amounts are given in terms of 8-ounce cups of whole fluid milk: Children under 9: 2 to 3 cups • Children 9 to 12: 3 cups or more • Teenagers: 4 cups or more • Adults: 2 cups or more • Pregnant women: 3 cups or more • Nursing mothers: 4 cups or more.

Part or all of the milk may be fluid skim milk, buttermilk, evaporated milk, or dry milk.

Cheese and ice cream may replace part of the milk. The replacement is figured on the basis of calcium content. Common portions of cheese and of ice cream and their equivalents in calcium are: 1-inch cube Cheddar-type cheese = ½ cup milk • ½ cup cottage cheese = ⅓ cup milk • 2 tablespoons cream cheese = 1 tablespoon milk • ½ cup ice cream or ice milk = ⅓ cup milk.

Bread-Cereal Group: All breads and cereals that are whole grain, enriched, or restored (check labels to be sure). Specifically, this group includes: Breads • Cooked cereals • Ready-to-eat cereals • Cornmeal • Crackers • Flour • Grits • Macaroni and spaghetti • Noodles • Rice • Rolled oats • Quick breads and other baked goods if made with whole-grain or enriched flour • Bulgur and parboiled rice and wheat.

Amounts Recommended: Choose 4 servings or more daily. If no cereals are chosen, have an extra serving of breads or baked goods, which will make at least 5 servings from this group daily. **Count as 1 serving:** 1 slice bread • 1 ounce ready-to-eat cereal • ½ to ¾ cup: cooked cereal • cornmeal • grits • macaroni • noodles • rice • spaghetti.

Other Foods: To round out meals and meet energy needs, everyone will use some foods not specified in the four groups. Such foods include: Unenriched, refined bread, cereals, flours • Sugars • Butter • Margarine • Other fats. These often are ingredients in a recipe or are added to other foods during preparation or at the table. Try to include some vegetable oil among the fats used.

How to Use the Daily Food Guide

Homemakers who follow the Guide will find it flexible enough to use in choosing foods for the entire family.

Food choices within the groups are wide enough to allow for a variety of everyday foods. Meals can be planned to include family favorites, foods in season, and foods to fit the family budget.

The size of the servings can be suited to the needs of family members—small servings for children and for those wanting to lose weight; extra larger servings (or seconds) for very active adults, teenagers, those wanting to gain weight, and pregnant and nursing women, who also need more food.

Foods from the Daily Food Guide can easily fit into the family's pattern of eating. Enough milk is suggested for children to have some at each meal, and for adults at two meals. Milk can be served as a beverage, used in cooking, or poured over cereals or fruit. Some of the milk allowance may be used in the form of cheese and ice cream.

A meat or alternate is usually a part of noon and evening meals and may be included in breakfast as well. This more than takes care of the minimum servings suggested from the meat group.

A fruit or juice at breakfast is customary in many families. The additional three or more servings of fruits and vegetables suggested can be divided between the other two meals.

A serving of bread or cereal readily fits into each meal. Cereal includes items such as macaroni, spaghetti, noodles, and rice. Some meals may contain both bread and cereal.

Foods from each group often appear in each meal, but this is not essential. The important thing is that the suggested number of servings from each food group be included sometime during the day.

Many people need and want more food than the minimum servings suggested from the four food groups. To round out meals and satisfy appetites, you can include additional foods from the four groups as well as other foods not listed in the groups.

Meal planning from the Food Guide is more easily said than done. The problem is that many foods we buy are not single foods, and since in some cases we can add nutrients, we cannot identify which food group they fall into. This does not mean that you cannot use the basic four food groups to guide yourself in selecting a good diet, but there are two types of foods that make it difficult. The first are conventional foods that are combinations of several groups. Pizza is a good example. The base of a pizza pie is a cereal product. This is then covered with tomato paste and has cheese, a dairy product, on top; some pizzas also contain meat. The quality of the cheese and meat determines whether it is really a good source of the nutrients expected from those products. But you won't find pizza in any food group in the Guide, so you must try to estimate how much cereal, cheese, and meat are contained in such a complex food.

The second type of foods that make the use of food groupings difficult are the reconstituted foods. For example, soybeans fall into the cereal group, but food processors reconstitute soybeans so that they look like meat. Then they fortify the product so that it provides all the nutrients not only of meat but also of the dairy group. If the consumer puts the soybean product in the cereal group, she or he will miss the fact that soybeans are a good source of protein as well as calcium and vitamin A that are normally found in the dairy group and part of the vegetable group.

Despite these difficulties in identifying the food group for some foods, the complex and reconstituted foods can be good sources of nutrition. Whatever errors you make in judging how much of the basic food groups a certain food contains, you will not do yourself or your family any harm — unless you make these hard-to-judge foods a main part of most of your meals.

Tips on Meal Planning

Keep these points in mind when you plan meals:
• Include a variety of foods each day and from day to day. Introduce a new food from time to time.
• Vary flavors and textures. Contrast strong flavor with mild, sweet with sour. Combine crisp textures with smooth.
• Try to have some meat, poultry, fish, eggs, milk, or cheese at each meal.
• Make a collection of nutritious recipes that you or your family enjoy and serve them often.
• Brighten food with color — a slice of red tomato, a sprig of dark greens, or other garnish.
• Combine different sizes and shapes of food in a meal when possible.

The Bonus of Breakfast

Food starts to work for you early in the day when you eat breakfast. It is a research fact that people who eat a good breakfast are more alert and productive in the morning and more resistant to fatigue through the day than those who skip breakfast.

After the fast of the night, the body needs to be replenished with food to get the energy and other materials—proteins, minerals, and vitamins—required to keep it working efficiently. With today's convenience foods, breakfasts can be prepared in a matter of minutes.

Buying Food

After knowing what you want your family to eat by having consulted the Daily Food Guide, you should shop for that food wisely.

• For economy, select the less expensive foods from each of the four food groups.

• Check special sales in food store advertisements.

• Look at each food critically:
Is it costly compared to other foods that might be served?
Will the family eat and enjoy it?
Is there time to prepare it?

• Learn to estimate accurately the amount of food needed to feed your family. No eating pleasure or nourishment comes from food that is bought and then thrown out.

• Use unit pricing to find the brand and container size of food that costs the least per unit—pound, ounce, or pint. Even if it is a better buy, select a food only if it can be stored properly and conveniently and used without waste.

• Avoid foods that are packed as individual servings. The extra packaging boosts the price. Examples are individual bags of potato chips, ready-to-eat cereals, raisins, and tea.

• Check the date on a perishable food. Be sure you can use all of the food before it spoils.

• Use meat, poultry, and fish sparingly—usually no more than a moderately large serving for each person daily. Use some egg, cheese, dry beans, dry peas, or peanut butter, too. These foods provide protein and most other nutrients that meat, poultry, and fish supply.

• When buying meat, consider the amount of lean meat in the cut, as well as the price per pound. A relatively high-priced cut of meat with little or no waste provides more meat for your money than a low-priced cut with a great deal of bone, gristle, or fat. Chicken and turkey are usually bargains when compared to other meats. One way to find the best buy is to compare the cost of packages of meat, poultry, and fish that will provide enough for a family meal. It may help control costs to set a top limit on the amount to spend for the main meal of the day, or to set an average amount to spend, allowing for some medium- and some low-cost items throughout the week.

• Use nonfat dry milk, which is less expensive than fluid milk, in cooking and as a beverage at least part of the time. Buy fresh milk in a food or dairy store in half- or one-gallon containers. Milk in smaller containers, and milk home-delivered or from special service stores usually costs more.

• When buying vegetables and fruit, take advantage of seasonal abundance. Foods in season are at their peak in quality and often are lower in cost. However, you must judge whether its cost fits into your budget.

• Try low-priced brands. They may be similar in quality to the more expensive ones.

• Use whole-grain and enriched flour, bread, or cereal in some form at every meal to get your money's worth in nutrients. Enriched bread and flour are important for the iron and certain B vitamins that they contribute. In addition to the many nutrients cereals supply, whole grains, especially bran, provide fiber, which is necessary for the normal functioning of the intestinal tract.

• For economy, use cereals prepared at home rather than instant or ready-to-eat ones; for example, whole-grain, rather than precooked, rice. When buying ready-to-eat cereals, select those that are not sugar-coated and those in family-size boxes.

• Consider the cost and the quality of the finished product in deciding whether to buy convenience foods. Some convenience foods are both easy to prepare and inexpensive. Among these are many canned and frozen vegetables, fruits, and juices; instant dehydrated potatoes; canned and dried soups; nonfat dry milk; prepared mixes for making biscuits and cakes; and some ready-to-eat or "quick" cereals.

After groceries are brought home, check them critically. Are your choices economical compared to other choices that might have been made? Did you buy some foods that were not on the list? If so, can these impulse purchases be justified as important for meeting food needs, being real bargains, or providing a worthwhile taste treat?

Food Labels

No matter how shrewd a shopper a person may be, she or he cannot tell what the ingredients of most prepared foods are. For this reason, the federal government requires that food processors provide on the label information as to the contents of their products. Some of this information is required by the Food and Drug Administration; some is included voluntarily by the processor.

Certain information must be on all food labels:

• The name of the product.

• The net weight or net contents in ounces, pints, or quarts. On canned food, the net weight includes the liquid in which the product is packed, such as water in canned vegetables or syrup in canned fruit.

• The name and place of business of the manufacturer, packer, or distributor.

• The ingredient present in the largest amount, by weight, followed in descending order of weight by the other ingredients.

• Any additives used in the product, with the exception of the names of artificial color and flavor where it is sufficient, but necessary, to mention the fact that artificial color or flavor has been used.

The Food and Drug Administration (FDA) has set "standards of identity" for certain foods such as butter, cheese, catsup, mayonnaise, and ice cream. These foods must contain certain ingredients, and the manufacturer is not required to list them on the label.

Nutritional Information

Under FDA regulations, any food to which a nutrient has been added, or any food for which a nutritional claim has been made, must have the nutritional content of its ingredients listed on the label. Many manufacturers give this information on their products voluntarily.

Nutrition labels tell you how many calories and how much protein, carbohydrate, and fat are in a serving of the product, as well as the U.S. Recommended Daily Allowance (RDA) of protein and seven important vitamins and minerals that the product might contain. The listing of 12 of the vitamins and minerals and of cholesterol, fatty acid, and sodium content is optional.

What "Imitation" Means

Some foods are labeled as imitations of other foods. Under FDA regulations, the word "imitation" must be used on the label when the product is not as nutritious as the product it resembles and for which it is a substitute. If a product is similar to an existing one and is just as nutritious, a new name can be given to it instead of calling it "imitation." For example, eggless products that are as nutritious as eggs have been given names such as Eggbeaters and Scramblers.

Common or Usual Name

To prevent deception if a product is packaged or looks like another more nourishing or expensive product, the FDA has ruled that such foods must have a "common or usual" name that gives the consumer accurate information about what is in the package or container. For example, a beverage that looks like orange juice but contains very little orange juice must use a name such as "diluted orange juice drink" or simply "orange drink." It must also state how much of the characterizing ingredient it contains; for example, "orange drink, contains 10 percent orange juice."

Another special labeling requirement concerns packaged food designated as "main dishes" or "dinners" which do not contain the main ingredient or component of a recipe (for example, a product called "chicken casserole" that does not contain chicken). On such foods the label must mention:
• The common name of each ingredient in descending order by weight, for example, "noodles and tomato sauce."
• Identification of the food to be prepared from the package, for example, gravy "for preparation of chicken casserole."

• A statement of ingredients that must be added to complete the recipe, for example, "You must add chicken to complete the recipe."

Grades

Some food products carry a grade on the label, such as "U.S. Grade A." Grades are set by the U.S. Department of Agriculture, based on the quality levels inherent in a product: its taste, texture, and appearance. U.S. Department of Agriculture grades are *not* based on nutritional content. Milk products in most states carry a "Grade A" label based on FDA recommended sanitary standards for the processing of milk, and also certain amounts of vitamins A and D when these vitamins are added to the milk.

Food Fads

There are many foods and food supplements on the market that promise the consumer improvement in health, longer life, the cure of certain diseases, or greater vitality, as well as a host of other health and psychological benefits. These foods and food supplements often are labeled by their makers as "natural" or "organic."

In the first place, a consumer who buys such foods is at the mercy of the seller. For example, an "organic" food or a "natural" food is one that is grown without the use of chemical fertilizers or pesticides. To monitor the growing of any crop from seed to harvest would be very difficult, time-consuming, and prohibitively expensive. So the storekeeper must depend on the honesty of the distributor, who in turn must depend on the honesty of the grower— and the customer depends on the honesty of all three. Even if all three are honest, the consumer, who pays a much higher price for organically grown foods, gains nothing nutritionally. Many tests have found no difference between organically and chemically fertilized foods.

The same lack of benefits applies to "natural" versus synthetic food supplements. Research has shown that there are no benefits in natural nutrients that are not also in synthetic ones, which are usually cheaper. Synthetic vitamin C, for example, is cheaper than vitamin C from rose hips.

Food Additives

Synthetic materials or extracts from plants and minerals are added to many food items by the manufacturer or processor for one or another reason. These materials are called food additives. Food manufacturers contend that consumers expect food to keep well and be nutritious and consistent in taste and appearance. They also contend that consumers expect the food to be processed and ready-to-eat and to be abundantly available at the lowest possible price, all year round, regardless of where the consumer may live. Nevertheless, many concerned persons would prefer to do without the literally thousands of additives food technologists have produced during the years.

The law requires that most additives, such as dough softeners and anti-spoilage agents, be mentioned on food labels.

Besides the agents put intentionally into food by the manufacturer or processor, incidental or indirect additives get into the food during the processing or from the package material.

The Food and Drug Administration has set standards to regulate additives. There are those that are called GRAS substances; the acronym stands for "*G*enerally *R*ecognized *A*s *S*afe." These are additives that have been used for many decades and are recognized as safe by food experts. Then there are "prior sanctioned substances," which were permitted as food additives before 1958, when an important amendment to the Food, Drug, and Cosmetic Act was passed by Congress. These have "squatter's rights" but can be banned if they are shown not to be safe. Color additives used for coloring foods must be given provisional or final approval by the FDA. Last are pesticides used to kill insects, worms, and rodents during growing and storage of food crops, which may enter crops through the roots or leaves or may remain on leaves and skins as a residue. There are strict federal regulations for the use of pesticides. However, the various government agencies are hard pressed to keep up with the testing of the many new ones appearing continually on the market.

The whole matter of pesticides and food additives is a very controversial one, especially with the increasing cancer research and the finding that many additives are cancer-causing agents in test animals.

Food Safety

You have shopped wisely for nutritious and economical foods. You have avoided as many food additives as you can. You still have one more thing to do in order to insure the health of yourself and your family: store the food safely.

Fruits and Vegetables

Fresh fruits and vegetables should be thoroughly washed to remove any pesticide residues and waste-matter droppings from insects, worms, and rodents. After washing, inspect the food carefully to see that there are no rotten, ill-smelling, or moldy spots. If you find any areas that look or smell bad, immediately throw out the affected food unless you can cut out the bad spots. Be sure to cut deeply and widely around them. Don't skimp on this! This safety precaution applies to all kinds of food, but especially to fruits and vegetables.

Fresh fruits should be ripe when stored in the refrigerator. Some unripe fruits may be left at room temperature—preferably in a cool room between 60° and 70°F—to ripen.

Sweet corn keeps best if refrigerated uncovered but still in the husks; use it promptly. Removing tops from carrots, beets, and radishes reduces wilting. Storing potatoes in a cool, dark place prevents greening of the skin and retards sprouting. (Green-skinned and sprouting potatoes contain small amounts of powerful poisons that can make you very sick. Peeling and thoroughly boiling these potatoes will make them edible again.)

Meat, Poultry, Fish

All meat should be promptly refrigerated. So should poultry and fish, immediately upon being brought home from the store. Eggs, too, should be put into the refrigerator immediately, stored large end up.

Butter and margarine should be kept in the refrigerator, as should open containers of lard and other cooking fats, and also cooking and salad oils.

Cured and Smoked Meats, Dried Foods

Ham, frankfurters, bacon, and sausage should be stored in their original containers in the refrigerator. When the containers have been opened, use whole hams within one week, half hams and slices within 3 to 5 days; bacon, franks, and smoked sausages within a week.

Dried foods may ordinarily be kept at room temperature. In hot, humid weather, however, these foods should be refrigerated.

Spoilage

Spoilage, or rotting, is due to the growth of bacteria, molds, or other organisms on food. These organisms cannot grow well—or at all—in cold temperatures. That is why foods are refrigerated or frozen. Broiling, frying, roasting, or baking kill these organisms. However, the cooking processes must be thorough. Simply warming food will not kill harmful organisms; it may make them grow faster. Eating raw or undercooked animal products is risky to your health.

There is one type of bacteria that deserves special mention: *Clostridium botulinum,* which produces a deadly poison. The illness that comes from eating this bacterium is botulism, or ptomaine poisoning.

The cause of botulism is mainly canned food. Contamination with these deadly bacteria results from inadequate sterilization techniques in the preparation of the food. A sign of inadequate sterilization is the presence of gas in the can. Therefore, *never* buy a can of food that is even slightly swollen at the top or bottom.

Another tip: Cook pork products thoroughly, as heat will kill disease-bearing trichina, a parasitic worm that sometimes occurs in pork.

• • •

If you plan menus according to their nutritional values, shop wisely, and keep food safe, you and your family can live healthy lives.

Compiled by
CULINARY ARTS INSTITUTE STAFF

Food and Cooking Tips

Contents

Equipping Your Kitchen

Your choice of equipment often depends upon the amount of cupboard and other storage space available. With a minimum of space one must choose essential items wisely, making sure that a bulky item such as a large saucepot or skillet can serve more than one purpose. The following list should help in making a wise choice of equipment.

For Food Preparation:

- Set of measuring spoons: ¼ teaspoon, ½ teaspoon, 1 teaspoon, 1 tablespoon
- Set (or nest) of measuring cups: ¼ cup, ⅓ cup, ½ cup, 1 cup
- Glass measuring cups for liquids: 1 cup, 2 cups (1 pint), 4 cups (1 quart)
- Mixing bowls: 1 pint, 1 quart, 3 quarts
- Knives: butcher knife, serrated bread knife, slicing knife (with long, thin blade), chopping knife (French), paring knives, grapefruit knife
- Forks: long-handled fork, two-tined fork, two or three small forks, blending fork

- Spoons: three wooden spoons of various sizes and lengths, slotted metal spoon, slotted wooden spoon, two metal tablespoons, three metal teaspoons
- Spatulas: small, medium
- Rubber scrapers: two plate and bowl scrapers (wide), one bottle and jar scraper (narrow)
- Beater: hand rotary type
- Strainers: small, medium
- Colander
- Cookie cutters: assorted sizes and shapes
- Juicer or reamer
- Vegetable parer
- Vegetable brush (stiff)
- Kitchen shears

- Apple corer
- Graters: small hand grater, set of larger graters for fine and coarse grating and shredding
- Cutting board
- Wire cooling racks: two or three
- Pancake turner
- Pastry blender
- Rolling pin (stockinette cover)

- Pastry brush
- Pastry canvas
- Flour sifter
- Flour shaker
- Salt and pepper shakers
- Can opener (wall-type or electric)
- Funnels
- Ladle
- Tongs

For Baking and Top-of-Range Cooking:

- Custard cups: six (6 ounce)
- Muffin (or cupcake) pans: two sets of six (one set 1¾ x 1 inch, one set 2½ x 1¼ inch)
- Casseroles with covers: 1½, 2, and 3 quarts
- Individual casseroles or ramekins: six
- Pie pans: 8 inch, 9 inch
- Cake pan (square): 8 inch, 9 inch
- Cake pans (round): two or three 8 or 9 inch
- Cake pan (tubed): 9 or 10 inch
- Baking pan: 11 x 7 x 1½ inch
- Loaf pan: 9 x 5 x 3 inch

- Open roasting pan: 13 x 9 x 2 inch
- Double boiler: 1½ quarts
- Saucepans with tight fitting covers: 1, 2, and 3 quarts
- Dutch oven: 3 quarts
- Coffee maker: 4 or 6 cups
- Teakettle
- Teapot: 6 cups
- Toaster
- Skillets with tight fitting covers: two (one small 6 or 8 inch, one large deep 10 inch)
- Molds: two or three, including a ring mold

Miscellaneous Items (Handy to Have):

- Corkscrew and bottle opener
- Knife sharpener
- Tea ball
- Thermometers: meat, candy, deep frying, portable oven thermometer (if oven is unreliable)
- Sink strainer
- Steam cooker
- Ice cream scoop
- Juice can opener
- Biscuit and bun warmer
- Jars with screw-top covers (for storing foods in refrigerator and on cupboard shelves)
- Canister set
- Hot pads, tiles, or stands (for hot dishes)

- Food mill
- Garlic press
- Meat grinder
- Timer
- Wooden chopping bowl and chopper
- Potato masher or ricer
- Melon ball cutter
- Pot holders
- Garbage can
- Freezer storage containers and moisture-vaporproof bags
- Refrigerator storage dishes with covers
- Aluminum foil
- Paper baking cups
- Waxed paper
- Paper towels

Nice-to-Have Appliances:

- Coffee maker
- Waffle baker
- Blender

- Electric mixer (table-type or portable)
- Electric skillet

MEASUREMENTS AND EQUIVALENTS

Dash, speck or few grains . . . . .less than ⅛ teaspoon
60 drops . . . . .1 teaspoon
3 teaspoons (½ fluid ounce) . . . . .1 tablespoon
⅛ cup (1 fluid ounce) . . . . .2 tablespoons
¼ cup (2 fluid ounces) . . . . .4 tablespoons
⅓ cup .5 tablespoons plus 1 teaspoon
½ cup (4 fluid ounces) . . . . .8 tablespoons
⅔ cup . . . . .10 tablespoons plus 2 teaspoons
¾ cup (6 fluid ounces) . . . . .12 tablespoons
1 cup (8 fluid ounces) . . . . .16 tablespoons
2 cups (16 fluid ounces) . . . . .1 pint
4 cups (32 fluid ounces) . . . . .1 quart
2 pints . . . . .1 quart
2 quarts . . . . .½ gallon
4 quarts (liquid) . . . . .1 gallon
8 quarts (dry) . . . . .1 peck
4 pecks . . . . .1 bushel
16 ounces (dry measure) . . . . .1 pound

SPECIFIC EQUIVALENTS

Bread:
   1 to 2 slices (soft) . . . . .1 cup crumbs
   1 pound loaf . . . . .10 cups small bread cubes

Butter or margarine:
   1 ounce . . . . .2 tablespoons
   1 stick (4 ounces) . . . . .½ cup

Chocolate, unsweetened:
   1 ounce . . . . .1 square

Cream, heavy (40%):
   1 cup . . . . .2 cups whipped

Eggs:
   4-6 whole . . . . .1 cup
   8-10 whites . . . . .1 cup
   10-14 yolks . . . . .1 cup

Marshmallows:
   16 large . . . . .4 ounces

Sugar:
   granulated, 2¼ cups . . . . .1 pound
   superfine, 2⅓ cups . . . . .1 pound
   brown, about 2¼ cups firmly packed . . . . .1 pound
   granulated brown, about 3⅛ cups . . . . .1 pound
   confectioners', 3½ cups . . . . .1 pound

Syrup:
   corn, about 1½ cups . . . . .1 pound
   maple, about 1½ cups . . . . .1 pound

SOME APPROXIMATE SUBSTITUTIONS

Baking powder: In place of 1 teaspoon baking powder use ¼ teaspoon baking soda plus 1 teaspoon cream of tartar.

Butter: In place of 1 cup butter use ⅞ to 1 cup vegetable shortening or lard plus ½ teaspoon salt.

Chocolate: In place of 1 square use 3–4 tablespoons cocoa plus 1 tablespoon shortening.

Cornstarch: In place of 1 tablespoon cornstarch use 2 tablespoons all-purpose flour.

Cream, light (20%): In place of 1 cup light cream use ⅞ cup milk plus 3 tablespoons butter.

Cream, heavy (40%): In place of 1 cup heavy cream use ¾ cup milk plus ⅓ cup butter.

Flour, cake: In place of 1 cup sifted flour use ⅞ cup all-purpose flour (⅞ cup–1 cup minus 2 tablespoons).

Garlic: In place of 1 clove garlic use ¼ teaspoon garlic powder.

Marshmallows: In place of 10 miniature marshmallows use 1 large marshmallow.

Onion: In place of 1 cup chopped onions use 1 tablespoon instant minced onion or 1 teaspoon onion powder.

COOKING TEMPERATURES

Heat	Fahrenheit	Celsius
Very slow	250–275	121–135
Slow	300–325	149–163
Moderate	350–375	177–191
Hot	400–425	204–218
Very Hot	450–475	232–246
Broil	500–525	260–274

METRIC EQUIVALENTS FOR U.S. COOKING MEASURES

U.S. Measure		Metric Equivalent		U.S. Measure		Metric Equivalent	
¼ teaspoon	=	1.25	milliliters	1 ounce	=	28	grams
½ teaspoon	=	2.5	milliliters	2 ounces	=	56	grams
1 teaspoon	=	5	milliliters	4 ounces	=	113	grams
2 teaspoons	=	10	milliliters	8 ounces	=	226	grams
3 teaspoons	=	15	milliliters	16 ounces	=	452	grams
1 tablespoon	=	15	milliliters	¼ pound	=	.11	kilogram
2 tablespoons	=	30	milliliters	½ pound	=	.23	kilogram
1 fluid ounce	=	30	milliliters	¾ pound	=	.34	kilogram
2 fluid ounces	=	59	milliliters	1 pound	=	.45	kilogram
4 fluid ounces	=	118	milliliters	2 pounds	=	.90	kilogram
8 fluid ounces	=	236	milliliters	4 pounds	=	1.81	kilograms
16 fluid ounces	=	472	milliliters	6 pounds	=	2.72	kilograms
1 cup	=	.24	liter	8 pounds	=	3.62	kilograms
2 cups	=	.47	liter	10 pounds	=	4.54	kilograms

A HANDY METRIC CONVERSION TABLE

To Change	Into	Multiply By	To Change	Into	Multiply By
ounces	grams	28	grams	ounces	.035
pounds	kilograms	.45	kilograms	pounds	2.2
teaspoons	milliliters	5	milliters	teaspoons	.2
tablespoons	milliliters	15	milliters	tablespoons	.067
fluid ounces	milliliters	30	milliliters	fluid ounces	.033
cups	liters	.24	liters	cups	4.2
pints	liters	.47	liters	pints	2.1
quarts	liters	.95	liters	quarts	1.06
gallons	liters	3.8	liters	gallons	.26

What You Should Know About:

Chocolate

The term chocolate refers to **unsweetened chocolate. Sweet chocolate** is chocolate with sugar added. It may also contain cocoa butter and flavorings. It is used for dipping candies and other confections.

Semisweet chocolate is small pieces or 1-ounce squares formed from slightly sweetened chocolate and used for candymaking or baked products, or eaten as a confection. (Also available in the form of bars.)

Cocoa is a powdered chocolate product from which some of the cocoa butter has been removed. The fat content varies from 10% to 22%. **Breakfast cocoa** is a high-fat cocoa which contains at least 22% cocoa fat.

Dutch process cocoa can be either "cocoa" or "breakfast cocoa" which is processed with one or more alkaline materials as permitted under government regulations.

Instant cocoa is a mixture of cocoa, sugar, and an emulsifier. It can be prepared for use by dissolving in hot liquid with no cooking necessary.

Fats and Oils

Butter is fat from sour or sweet cream gathered in a mass, sometimes salted and colored. It contains not less than 80% by weight of milk fat. **Unsalted butter** is butter made from sweet cream. Also called sweet butter. **Whipped butter** is butter into which air has been whipped.

123

Cooking or salad oils include: corn oil, refined from the dried, crushed corn germ; cottonseed oil, refined from the crushed seed of the cotton plant; peanut oil, the oil extracted from peanuts, a by-product of peanut butter; safflower oil, the oil extracted from the seed of the safflower plant, used for cooking purposes and also used commercially for the manufacture of safflower margarine.

Cracklings are the residue from rendered fat of meat.

Hard fats are coconut or palm oils in solid form used mostly in candymaking.

Lard is fat rendered from the fatty tissues of the hog.

Margarine is made by the emulsification of various oils with cultured milk and further processing to produce a consistency similar to that of butter; contains 80% fat; usually colored; may or may not have salt added. Soft-type and whipped margarine are also available.

Olive oil is oil from the flesh of ripe olives. Virgin olive oil is that which is first extracted and is better in flavor and appearance than the oil produced by the second or third pressing. Use olive oil when specified in a recipe.

Poultry fat is a cooking fat made commercially by rendering the leaf fat removed from the body cavities of chickens and turkeys and sometimes from the fat that is skimmed from vats of poultry being cooked for canning.

Shortening is a general term used for cooking fats. May be meat fats or vegetable oils. Or, may be a blend of animal fats; or a blend of vegetable oils; or a blend of animal and vegetable.

Suet is the clear, white fat of beef and mutton.

Flour

The term flour when used in recipes with no other qualifications as to special purpose or preparation (bread, cake, self-rising flour) usually refers to all-purpose or general-purpose flour.

Bread flour is milled from blends of spring and winter hard wheats or from either type alone. It has a fairly high protein content and is slightly granular to the touch. It may be bleached or unbleached and is milled mostly for commercial bakers.

All-purpose flour is a blend of hard or soft wheat flours which are lower in protein content than bread flour, but higher than cake flour. It can usually be used with good results for most home-baked products. Blends are prepared to satisfy the demands of different areas. In the South, for instance, a softer blend is available to make satisfactory quick breads, while in the North a harder blend is marketed for use in making yeast breads and rolls.

Instant-blending flour is an all-purpose flour which some associate with the term "instantized" to indicate that the flour dissolves readily in liquids without forming lumps.

Self-rising flour is flour to which leavening agents and salt have been added in proper proportions for home-baking. The leavening agent most often used, with soda, is calcium phosphate.

Whole-wheat flour (also graham flour) is flour milled so that the natural constituents of the wheat kernel remain unaltered.

Pastry flour is made of either hard or soft wheats, but usually the latter. It is fairly low in protein and finely milled though not as fine as cake flour. It is used chiefly by bakers and biscuit manufacturers.

Cake flour is milled from soft wheats. The protein content is low and the granulation so fine that the flour feels soft and satiny.

Milk and Milk Products

Fresh fluid milk contains not less than 3.25% milk fat and not less than 8.25% milk solids other than fat. **Vitamin D milk** is whole or skim milk in which the vitamin D content has been increased.

Homogenized milk is fresh milk in which the size of the fat globules is reduced so that the cream does not rise to the top.

Evaporated milk is sterilized homogenized milk containing about 60% less water than whole milk. When diluted with an equal amount of water, it is used as fresh whole milk. It is also used, undiluted, as cream.

Sweetened condensed milk is milk from which about half the water has been removed. It contains a large amount of added sugar which acts as a preservative.

Skim milk is milk from which most of the fat has been removed thereby reducing its vitamin A content. Some skim milks are fortified by adding a water-soluble vitamin A and D concentrate.

Buttermilk as sold in retail markets is usually a cultured (fermented) product made of fresh skim milk. (It is also the by-product from churning cream into butter.) The bacterial culture used converts the milk sugar into lactic acid. Cultured buttermilk may also be made from fresh fluid whole milk, concentrated fluid milk, or reconstituted nonfat dry milk.

125

Dry milk (whole) and dry milk (nonfat) are made from fresh whole milk and skim milk respectively. After most of the water has been removed from them they are dried until a fine-textured powder results. The process has no appreciable effect on the nutritive value and when mixed with water these products have the original composition of pasteurized milk.

Yogurt is a cultured product (with a consistency resembling custard) usually made from fresh partially skimmed milk enriched with added milk solids other than fats. Fermentation is accomplished by a mixed bacterial culture.

Half and half is a mixture of milk and cream, usually 10% to 12% fat. **Light cream,** sometimes referred to as table or coffee cream contains 18% to 20% fat. **Heavy (or whipping) cream** contains between 30% and 36% fat.

Dairy sour cream is a cultured product sold commercially and made by adding bacterial cultures to pasteurized and homogenized cream.

Sugars and Syrups

Granulated sugar is a highly refined white sugar composed of almost pure sucrose which is found in large quantities in sugar cane and sugar beets.

Superfine granulated sugar is a specially screened, uniformly fine-grained sugar used in cakes and in mixing drinks.

Confectioners' (powdered) sugar is granulated sugar crushed and screened to desired fineness. A small amount of cornstarch is added to prevent caking. Confectioners' sugar is used in frostings and icings and for dusting doughnuts, pastries, etc.

Brown sugar is unrefined cane sugar which varies in color from very light to very dark. It contains various amounts of molasses, some non-sugars (ash) naturally present in molasses, and moisture.

Granulated brown sugar is a specially processed brown sugar which does not harden and can be poured from the package. To substitute for regular brown sugar, see manufacturer's equivalents table.

Maple sugar is a solid product obtained by evaporating maple sap or maple syrup to the point where crystallization occurs.

Molasses is the liquor remaining after the crystallization of raw sugar from the concentrated sap of the sugar cane. Sometimes a second and third crystallization is made, resulting in two grades of molasses known as "light" and "dark" molasses. When a large proportion of the sugar has been removed, the resulting product has a strong flavor and is called "black strap." It is used for fermentation purposes.

Sorghum (or sorgo) is a syrup somewhat resembling molasses produced from a cane-like grass. It has a mild flavor appealing to many people especially in the Southwest where the grass is grown.

Corn syrup is a product resulting from the partial hydrolysis of cornstarch with coloring and flavoring usually added to the syrup. Light and dark corn syrups are marketed. Many table syrups contain some corn syrup combined with such sweeteners as sorghum, cane syrup, or honey and butterscotch or vanilla for flavoring.

Honey is defined as "the nectar and saccharine exudations of plants gathered, modified, and stored by the honey bee." Honey must contain not more than 25% water. The flavor and color of honey depends upon the source of the nectar. Orange blossoms, clover, buckwheat, and basswood are common sources.

Maple syrup comes from the sap of the maple tree collected in early spring and concentrated to the desired consistency. Pure maple syrup contains not over 35% water.

Sugar syrup is a solution of sugar and water used to sweeten beverages.

Sugar substitutes are non-caloric sweetening agents.

Definitions

Bake: To cook in a container (covered or uncovered) in an oven or oven-type appliance. Usually called roasting when applied to meats.

Barbecue: To roast or broil on a rack over hot coals or on a revolving spit in front of or over heat source.

Baste: To spoon liquid (or use baster) over cooking food to add moisture and flavor.

Beat: To make a mixture smooth by introducing air with a brisk motion that lifts the mixture over and over, or with a rotary motion as with a hand rotary beater or electric mixer.

Blanch: To preheat or precook in boiling water or steam. This process is used to inactivate enzymes and shrink food for canning, freezing, and drying. The blanching process is also used to aid in the removal of skins from nuts.

Blend: To mix two or more ingredients so that each loses its identity.

Boil: To cook in liquid in which bubbles rise continually and break on the surface. Boiling temperature of water at sea level is 212°F.

Braise: To cook slowly in a covered utensil in a small amount of liquid or in steam. (Meat may or may not be browned in small amount of fat before braising.)

Bread: To coat with bread crumbs alone or to coat with bread crumbs, then with diluted slightly beaten egg or evaporated milk, and again with crumbs.

Broil: To cook by direct heat.

Candy: To cook fruit (also citrus fruit peel and ginger) in a heavy syrup until plump and transparent, then drain and dry. Candied product is also known as crystallized fruit, peel, or ginger. Term also applied to vegetables cooked in a syrup or sugar and fat mixture (*i.e.,* candied sweet potatoes or carrots). Candy is synonymous with glaze (*i.e.,* glazed or candied cherries).

Caramelize: To heat dry sugar or foods containing sugar until a brown color and characteristic flavor develop.

Chop: To cut into pieces with a knife or other sharp tool. (Also see *Mince, below*.)

Coddle: To cook slowly just below the boiling point (as applied to eggs and fruit).

Combine: To mix ingredients.

Cream: To mix one or more foods together until soft and creamy. Usually applied to shortening and sugar.

Cube: See *Dice, below*.

Cut in: To distribute solid fat in dry ingredients by chopping with pastry blender or knives until finely divided.

Devil: To mix with hot seasoning as pepper, mustard.

Dice: To cut into small cubes.

Dissolve: To cause a liquid and a dry substance to pass into solution.

Dredge: To coat or sprinkle with flour or other fine substance.

Flake fish (freshly cooked or canned): Gently separating the fish into flakes, using a fork. Remove the bony tissue from crab meat while flaking it. (Bones of salmon are edible and need not be removed.

Fold: To combine by using two motions, one which cuts vertically through the mixture (using a flexible metal or rubber spatula or wire whisk) and the other which turns the mixture over by sliding the implement across the bottom of the mixing bowl.

Fricassee: To cook by braising (usually applied to poultry, rabbit, and veal).

Fry: To cook in fat; called **sauté** or **panfry** when cooking with a small amount of fat; called **deep-fat frying** when cooking in a deep layer of fat.

Glacé: To coat with a thin sugar syrup cooked to the crack stage. When used for pies and certain types of bread the mixture may contain a thickening, but it is not cooked to such a concentrated form as for a glacé; or it may be uncooked.

Grate: To reduce to small particles by rubbing on anything rough and indented. Use a rotary-type grater with hand-operated crank for grating chocolate and nuts, following manufacturer's directions. Grated chocolate and nuts should be fine and light.

Grill: To broil on open grill or griddle.

Grind: To reduce food to particles by cutting, crushing (electric blender may be used), or by forcing through a food chopper.

Knead: To manipulate with a pressing motion plus folding and stretching.

Lard: To insert matchlike strips of fat, called lardoons, into gashes in side of uncooked lean meat by means of a larding needle or skewer; or to place on top of meat.

Marinate: To allow food to stand in liquid (usually a seasoned oil and acid mixture) to impart additional flavor.

Mask: To cover completely; usually applied to the use of mayonnaise or other thick sauce but may refer to forcemeat or jelly.

Mince: To cut or chop into small, fine pieces.

Mix: To combine ingredients in any way that effects a distribution.

Panbroil: To cook uncovered on a hot surface, usually in a skillet.

Parboil: To boil uncooked food until partially cooked. The cooking is usually completed by another method.

Parch: To brown by means of dry heat. Applied to grains.

Pare: To cut off the outside covering. Applied to potatoes, apples, etc.

Pasteurize: To preserve food by heating to a temperature (140° to 180°F) which will destroy certain microorganisms and arrest fermentation. Applied to milk and fruit juices.

Peel: To strip off the outer covering. Applied to oranges, grapefruit, etc.

Poach: To cook in a hot liquid using precautions to retain shape. The temperature used varies with the food.

Purée: To force through a fine sieve or food mill or to blend in an electric blender until a smooth thick mixture is obtained.

Reconstitute: To restore concentrated foods to their normal state, usually by adding water. Applied to such foods as nonfat dry milk or frozen fruit juices.

Reduce liquid: To continue cooking the liquid until the amount is sufficiently decreased, thus concentrating flavor and sometimes thickening the original liquid. Simmer when wine is used; boil rapidly for other liquids.

Render: To remove fat from connective tissue over low heat.

Rice: To force food through ricer, sieve, or food mill.

Roast: To cook by dry heat, usually in an oven.

Scald milk: To heat in top of a double boiler over simmering water or in a heavy saucepan over direct heat just until a thin film appears. The term scald is also used when simmering certain foods in boiling water for a few seconds.

Scallop: To bake food, usually with sauce or other liquid. The top may be covered with crumbs. The food and sauce may be mixed in the baking dish or arranged in alternate layers with or without crumbs.

Score: To make cuts in the surface of meat before roasting, usually making a diamond pattern (example roast ham).

Sear: To brown meat quickly with intense heat.

Shirr: To break eggs into a dish with cream or crumbs and bake in oven.

Sieve: To force through a sieve.

Simmer: To cook in a liquid just below boiling point; bubbles form slowly and break below surface.

Skewer: To pierce or fasten with skewers—as a piece of meat.

Steam: To cook in steam with or without pressure. The steam may be applied directly to food (*i.e.,* pressure cooker).

Steep: To allow a substance to stand in liquid below the boiling point for the purpose of extracting flavor, color, or other qualities.

Sterilize: To destroy microorganisms. For culinary purposes this is usually done at a high temperature with steam, dry heat, or by boiling in a liquid.

Stew: To cook slowly in a small amount of liquid.

Stir: To mix food ingredients with a circular motion in order to blend them.

Truss: To fasten the cavity of stuffed poultry or meat with skewers and/or cord.

Whip: To beat rapidly to produce expansion due to incorporation of air as applied to eggs, gelatin mixtures, and cream.

Helpful Hints for the Cook

Beverages

• To frost glasses rub the edge of each glass with cut surface of lemon, lime, or orange. Or brush rim with citrus juice. Dip the rim of each glass in fine granulated or confectioners' sugar. Place glasses in refrigerator to chill. Carefully pour beverage into glasses without touching frosted edges.

• To make decorative ice cubes fill ice cube tray one third full with water. Place in freezing compartment of refrigerator; remove ice cube tray when water is partially frozen. Place well-drained maraschino cherry, mint sprig, pineapple chunk, orange wedge, berry, or small piece of fruit, and a mint leaf in each cube section. Fill tray with water and freeze.

• To make stronger flavored iced coffee pour coffee over coffee ice cubes. Using ½ measuring cup water per standard measure of coffee, prepare drip coffee or any variation. Pour coffee into ice cube tray and place in freezing compartment of refrigerator. Fill tall glasses to brim with ice cubes. Pour the hot coffee over the ice. Serve with granulated or confectioners' sugar, sugar syrup, cream, or whipped cream sprinkled with ground cinnamon.

Bread

• To butter bread for thin sandwiches, spread end of loaf with softened butter, then cut off a slice as thin as possible. Repeat buttering and slicing.

• To freshen rolls, place them in a heavy paper bag. Twist top of bag and place in a 400°F oven 10 to 15 minutes. (Or wrap securely in aluminum foil.)

• Store bread in a cool dry place. If a loaf is not consumed in several days, keep it fresh by placing in a moisture-vaporproof bag and storing it in the refrigerator. If you bake or purchase more than one loaf at a time, keep one loaf in the refrigerator and wrap the other loaf in freezer wrap and place it in the freezer. If loaf has been sliced before freezing, remove only the number of slices required for a single meal and thaw at room temperature. Baked rolls and biscuits are stored in a similar manner.

Cakes, Cookies, and Pies

• Use fluted paper baking cups when preparing cupcakes. They save greasing of pans and eliminate sticking. They also make pan washing easy.

• When baking an upside-down cake, line cake pan with aluminum foil, folding foil over the edges of pan. After cake is baked, let cool on rack about 5 minutes. Then place serving plate on top of cake, turn cake upside down and remove the pan. Carefully lift off the foil. Cake comes out of pan easily and pan is easy to clean.

• To store cookies, cool thoroughly before placing in cookie jar, canister, or casserole having a cover. Do not store crisp cookies with other types. If they have softened during storage, place them in a 300°F oven for a few minutes to restore crispness.

• To soften cookies, store for several days with a piece of apple or orange.

• To pack cookies for mailing, wrap (separately if possible) in moisture-vaporproof material in sturdy container lined with extra wrapping material. Use crumbled waxed paper, popcorn, or shredded packing material to fill extra space.

• To prevent juice from cooking out of pies into the oven, place a strip of dampened cloth or pastry tape around the edge of the pie or place a tiny funnel or 4-inch stick of uncooked macaroni in the center of the pie.

• To avoid shrinkage of a pastry crust, roll out the pastry, place in a pie pan without stretching, and set aside about 5 minutes before fluting the edge. Or place a second pie pan on the pastry before baking. Remove the second pan after about 10 minutes of baking to allow the pastry shell to brown on the inside.

Eggs and Cheeses

• Whether the color of the egg shell is brown or white makes no difference in the quality or food value of the egg, though in some localities it does influence price. Eggs with brown shells sometimes have yolks of deeper yellow color than those with white shells.

• As soon as possible after purchasing, store eggs in the refrigerator in their own egg container to keep them upright, or store on the egg shelf of the refrigerator door, small ends down. Remove only as many eggs as needed at one time.

• To divide a raw egg, beat well before measuring with a tablespoon.

• To hard-cook egg yolks, use only unbroken yolks and slip

132

them gently into simmering water. Keep below boiling point until yolks are firm. Remove with a slotted spon.
- To slice hard-cooked eggs without breaking the yolk, dip knife into water before slicing.
- When adding whole eggs or egg yolks to a sauce, always stir a little of the hot sauce into the slightly beaten eggs; immediately blend into the remaining hot sauce. Cook 3 to 5 minutes, stirring to keep the mixture cooking evenly.
- For the fullest enjoyment of most cheeses, remove them from the refrigerator at least 1 hour before serving; the interior of Camembert and Brie should be almost runny. Serve Neufchâtel, cottage, and cream cheeses chilled.

Fish

- Fresh fish are best prepared as soon as possible after being caught. When fresh, they have red gills, bright eyes, and bright-colored scales adhering tightly. The flesh is firm and elastic, and practically free from odor. Fresh fish should be packed in ice until purchased; at home, wrap in foil or moisture-vaporproof material and store in the refrigerator.
- Frozen fish is available the year around in market forms such as steaks, fillets, and sticks. It should be solidly frozen and *never refrozen after thawing*.
- Salted fish are prepared either by "dry-salting" or by pickling in a brine. Firm, coarse-fleshed fish such as cod, hake, and haddock are dry-salted by packing in dry salt after cleaning. Fat and oily fish are "salted" in brine, then are frequently smoked. Finnan Haddie is prepared in this way.
- Smoked fish is a delicacy: salmon, whitefish, and haddock are popular varieties. It is usually eaten without further cooking.
- Canned fish is easy to store and convenient to serve. Sardines, tuna, cod, salmon, mackerel, and kippered herring are some of the varieties.
- To make poached fish firm and white, add a little lemon juice to the cooking liquid.
- To remove fish odors from utensils, add 2 tablespoons baking soda to the dishwashing water.
- To store fresh fish, wrap the whole fish or fillets or steaks in moisture-vaporproof material or in waxed paper. Use fish the same day as purchased, if possible. Place in freezer if fish is not to be used in one or two days.

Shellfish

- Live shellfish are those which should be alive when purchased, such as crabs, lobsters, clams, and oysters (except when purchasing cooked lobsters and crabs in the shell).
- Shucked shellfish are those which have been removed from their shells.
- Frozen shellfish available are shrimp, crab, lobster, lobster tails, scallops, and oysters.
- When clams are purchased, the shells should be tightly closed or should close at a touch. They may be opened with a knife or be steamed open.
- If serving boiled lobster whole and cold, rub shell parts with salad oil to improve color. If saving shell parts for Thermidor, brush them with oil.
- Oysters in the shell are sold by the dozen. They must be alive with shells tightly closed; when dead, the shells open automatically and shellfish are no longer edible.
- To open oyster shells wash them thoroughly and rinse in cold water but do not soak. Insert a strong thin knife between shells near the thick end and run it around back of shell until muscle holding shells is cut. Discard flat shell, save liquor from oysters, and remove any small pieces of shell from oysters. Serve oysters on the deep half of the shell.
- Fresh shrimp with heads removed are sold by the pound either fresh or frozen. Shrimp are graded according to the number per pound—jumbo (under 25); large (25 to 30); medium (30 to 42); and small (42 and over). *Cooked shrimp* with shells removed are also sold by the pound; the meat is pink. *Canned shrimp* are available in several sizes of cans and may be used in place of cooked shrimp.

Meats

- All meats processed by packers must pass Federal inspection and be stamped with the Federal inspection stamp. The quality grading is also done by stamping the meat. The purple ink used for both inspection and grading stamps is a harmless vegetable dye which need not be cut away before cooking.
- 1 pound boneless meat (boned meats, ground meats, flank steaks, liver, heart, kidneys, sausages, brains, sweetbreads, and most canned meats) makes 4 servings.
- 1 pound meat with a small amount of bone (round steak, pot roasts, ham slices, rib roasts) makes 3 servings.
- 1 pound meat with a large amount of bone or fat (most

steaks, poultry, shoulder cuts, short ribs, neck, chops, breasts, plate, brisket) makes 2 servings.

• Purchase ground beef that has been *freshly* ground, either regular (contains not more than 25% fat) or lean (contains not more than 12% fat). Or buy a cut of beef such as chuck, round, flank, plate, brisket, shank, or neck meat and have it ground. If the cut is quite lean, have 2 ounces of suet per pound of beef ground with the cut. A coarse grind helps to insure extra-juicy patties.

• Purchase pork that has been *freshly* ground or have pork shoulder meat ground.

• Purchase lamb that has been *freshly* ground or have lamb shoulder meat ground.

• Store ground meat uncovered or lightly covered in refrigerator. Partial drying on the surface of meat increases its keeping quality. Use within two days of purchase.

• Store frozen ground meat in the freezing compartment of the refrigerator or in a freezer, wrapped in freezer wrapping material.

• Always cook pork until well done.

• To keep bacon from curling while broiling or panfrying, snip edges with shears before cooking.

• To make a flavorful gravy from pot roast drippings, add canned consommé (instead of water) to the meat during cooking.

Poultry

• When grading and inspection labels are not present, the consumer may be guided by some of the standards used in official grading. Young birds have smooth, soft, thin skin, little fat, and flexible-tipped breastbones; as the bird ages, the skin coarsens, more fat is deposited along the backbone, and the breastbone becomes more rigid. Grade A quality requires that a bird be well-formed and full-fleshed, with no defects, tears, or bruises in the skin, clean and free from pinfeathers.

• To store fresh poulty or ice-chilled ready-to-cook chicken or turkey, remove from store wrappings. Remove neck and giblets. Wrap bird (whole or cut in pieces) loosely in waxed paper or transparent, moisture-vaporproof material, ends open to let in air. Place in a shallow pan and store in the coldest part of the refrigerator. Use within 48 hours. If poultry is to be frozen, wrap securely in freezer wrap and place immediately in freezer.

• Quick-frozen poultry must be kept frozen until ready to use and once thawed must not be refrozen. In thawing frozen poultry before cooking, follow directions on the label, if available. Or use one of the following methods: *Refrigerator thawing* — Keep in original wrapping and place on a tray in refrigerator from 1 to 3 days. A 4-pound chicken or turkey requires about 1 day while a 20- to 24-pound turkey may take as long as 3 to 3½ days. *Cold-water thawing* — Place bird in its original wrapper in a large pan or in the sink; cover completely with very cold water. Change water frequently so that it will remain cold. An 8- to 12-pound requires 3 to 6 hours; 12- to 20-pound bird 6 to 8 hours; 20- to 24-pound bird 10 to 12 hours. Once it is thawed, refrigerate poultry if not cooking immediately. *Room-temperature thawing* — This method is less satisfactory than other methods. If time permits, refrigerator thawing is the most satisfactory method.

• Cooked poultry, gravy, and stuffing should not be left at room temperature for longer than it takes to finish the meal. Never store bird with stuffing; remove stuffing and store it covered in refrigerator; cover gravy and refrigerate. If only one side of a roast bird has been carved, wrap remainder of bird in waxed paper, aluminum foil, or moisture-vapor-proof material; store in refrigerator. If more than one half of the meat has been used, remove the remaining meat from the bones and wrap tightly before storing. Cooked pieces should be tightly wrapped and refrigerated. Do not keep cooked poultry, however carefully stored, for more than a few days. If keeping leftover turkey or other poultry for more than several days, immediately remove meat from bones, wrap meat in moisture-vapor-proof material, and store in freezer.

Fruits

• To obtain maximum juice from lemons and limes, firmly roll the fruit on a hard surface before squeezing.
• To extract juice from a lemon when only a small amount is needed, puncture fruit with a fork and gently squeeze out desired amount of juice.

• To keep juice in fruit which has been cut, cover exposed part with waxed paper and place fruit, cut side down, on a dish, or fit cut side with a transparent bowl cover.

• To remove pits from cherries, insert a new pen point into penholder, pointed end in, and remove pits with the rounded end of pen point.

• To keep cut fruits from discoloring sprinkle lemon or pineapple juice over them.

• Wash berries before hulling to retain juice.

Vegetables

• To freshen fresh asparagus, stand the stalks upright in icy cold water.

• To remove the skins from carrots easily, cover them with boiling water and let stand for a few minutes until the skin loosens.

• To keep cauliflower white while cooking, use half milk and half water; cook, uncovered, until just tender.

• To make celery curls, cut stalks (about 3 inches long) lengthwise into thin strips to within 1 inch of end. Place in cold water until strips begin to curl.

• To make celery very crisp, let stand in icy cold water to which 1 teaspoon sugar per quart of water has been added.

• To garnish lettuce leaves sprinkle some paprika on waxed paper and dip edges of leaves into it.

• To keep onions from affecting eyes, peel them under running water.

• To prevent odor while cooking onions and cabbage, add 1 tablespoon lemon juice or a wedge of lemon to the cooking water.

• Store less perishable vegetables, such as cabbage, potatoes, dry onions, winter squash, and rutabagas, in a cool, dry, well-ventilated place without beforehand washing. Keep onions separate from other vegetables. Store potatoes in a dark place and not directly on the floor.

• Wash vegetables, such as radishes, lettuce, and other leaf vegetables before storing; drain thoroughly and gently pat dry with a soft clean towel or absorbent paper. Rinse head lettuce under running water, drain, and shake off excess water thoroughly. For long storage do not remove core until lettuce is used. Place vegetables in refrigerator in vegetable drawers or plastic bags, or wrap tightly in waxed paper or moisture-vaporproof material to prevent vegetables from wilting unless refrigerator maintains a high humidity. Do not soak vegetables for any length of time when washing them. If they are wilted, put them in icy water for only a few minutes. Shake off all moisture left from washing, drain thoroughly amd gently pat dry.

• Store peas and lima beans in the pod to keep fresh. Pods may be washed before storage; quickly rinse peas and lima beans after shelling.

Soups

• To avoid curdling of cream of tomato suup, thicken the sieved tomatoes before adding (hot) to the cold milk, stirring constantly.

• The electric blender is the modern way to quick-and-easy blending of everything and anything into savory soups. Remember, when using it, to pour the liquid into container first, usually ½ to 1 cup, then gradually add the other ingredients.

• Cool soups to lukewarm before storing in covered container in the refrigerator; keep several days only. Store in freezer for longer periods.

Preserving

• To remove odors from jars and bottles, pour a solution of water and dry mustard into them and let stand several hours. Or use a dilute chlorine solution and rinse jars in hot water.

• When covering jelly with melted paraffin, pour a thin layer over top; place a strong piece of string on paraffin with end over edge of glass. Pour another layer of paraffin over string. Set aside until paraffin is firm. When jelly is to be used, lift off the paraffin layer by using the string.

• To open glass jars containing fruit easily, set them upside down in hot water for a few minutes.

Written by
CULINARY ARTS INSTITUTE STAFF

How To
Entertain

Contents

Entertaining Is Easy!

The secret of successful entertaining is to enjoy your own parties. Entertaining should be as much fun for the hostess as it is for the guests. If you plan carefully, adapting your plans to the special conditions of your home, everything is bound to run along smoothly with everyone having a wonderful time, including you.

Some people seem to be born with a knack for entertaining. Good food appears at their parties as if by magic, the guests are relaxed and conversation flourishes. You may be sure, however, that none of this just "happens." The food appears because someone has prepared it; the guests are relaxed because their hostess feels no strain; conversation flows because their hostess is on hand to help it along instead of coping with a crisis in the kitchen. And all of this means that she has planned carefully. She has planned a menu that requires a minimum of attention after the guests arrive, planned and arranged the flowers and other accessories, and set out all the little appurtenances of comfort. She probably has planned her guest list, too, inviting only persons who will be congenial. And if she is the completely thoughtful hostess, her menu has been planned with due regard for the food likes and dislikes of her guests.

In planning a company menu it is wise to follow the same principles that guide all menu-making. Avoid repetition of foods in the same meal—if fish is the appetizer do not use it for the main dish. Maintain a balance between firm and soft foods. Do not serve too many starches (rice, potatoes, and bread at the same meal are not good planning) or too much of any other single food stuff. Avoid too many strong flavors—flavors should harmonize or contrast but not compete. Plan meals with an eye to the over-all arrangement, varying the foods in color, texture and flavor. Include something sweet and something tart, something hot and something cold in every meal. Delight guests with an occasional surprise, but try out the new recipe on the family first.

It is a good idea to make notes in a diary about what you served to whom and at which party to avoid serving the same menu to the same guests when you invite them again.

Brunch & Morning Coffee

Brunch, a delightful meal combining both breakfast and lunch, may be served any time before one o'clock in the afternoon. When served early, brunch usually means simple breakfast foods. Served later, the menu may be an expanded and more elaborate breakfast, possibly served buffet style. Or it may more closely resemble a luncheon except for soup and salad which seldom are included in a brunch menu. If dessert is served it is a light fruit in season and/or cookies.

A mid-morning social gathering often called simply "morning coffee" is sometimes used by hostesses as an easy, informal, and friendly means of entertaining a few friends. It is almost certain to be a feminine affair with the menfolks safely out of the house. It is a gracious way to entertain an out-of-town friend when time is limited.

Most informal of all is the impromptu coffee (the *kaffeeklatsch*) to which neighbors drift in and are welcomed by plenty of hot coffee accompanied by coffee cake, sweet rolls, or doughnuts. No specific service is required; a bright sunny kitchen is usually a pleasant place for a gathering of a few neighbors or good friends.

When guests have been invited for a real morning coffee "party," usually about 10 or 11 o'clock, more elaborate preparations are in order.

Coffee, coffee breads, and one or more trays of bite-size relishes of contrasting color and flavor (sweet and sour, bland and savory), may all be arranged on a prettily spread buffet table in living or dining room. The hostess herself will want to pour the coffee for her guests—a hospitable as well as a practical gesture; but a stack of plates on the table, with napkins and teaspoons arranged beside them, will permit each guest to serve herself to whatever she wants of the other foods provided. The "main course" will be bread and a good plan is to allow one big, beautiful coffee cake of the good-without-butter kind, already cut for the convenience of the guests, when the party is small; when the group is larger, a selection of delicious sweet rolls should be added.

The relish tray may hold tangy cheese bits, crisp radish roses or celery curls, ripe or green olives, along with fruits such as small clusters of grapes, whole strawberries washed but with hulls intact for finger eating, pineapple chunks, melon balls, or hulled berries impaled on picks. An attractive fresh fruit relish bowl can be made by cutting into halves and scooping out a chilled honeydew melon or a fresh pineapple with its spiny crown intact, and heaping with balls or chunks cut from the fruit bowl itself and other fruits, all on wooden picks.

Luncheons

All parties are fun, but luncheons are in a class by themselves. They are usually given by women and for women, and so the light and even "fancy" touches which are special fun for the hostess are quite appropriate.

Whether you invite one guest or a dozen, you will summon all the artistry at your command to make the setting of your party beautiful and appropriate. Almost any kind of cloth, table mat, or runner is suitable if it harmonizes with the dishes and other accessories, the flowers, and to some extent with the season.

Table decorations, as at any meal, should be kept low, pretty but unobtrusive. Flowers are always appropriate, and so are attractive arrangements of fruits, foliage, handsome vegetables, vines, shells, quaint or beautiful figurines, and low-growing plants. Since luncheons are mid-day affairs, candles are not suitable. Flatware and crystal are placed as for a dinner party.

Luncheon for a group may be introduced by cocktails and appetizers in the living room. The luncheon menu itself may include two to four courses, the wise hostess planning it according to what she can handle easily and gracefully. The main dish is often a creamed mixture served in croustades, patty shells, or over split baking powder biscuits. It may be accompanied by salad or not. Particularly if salad is omitted, a nice touch is to garnish the plates with spiced fruit such as spiced crab apples or peaches, watermelon pickles or the like, or with crisp bread-and-butter pickles or preserved kumquats. The dessert should be keyed to the rest of the meal: If the main dish is a rich creamed mixture, serve a light dessert—fruit or a fruit mold or sherbet; if a salad bowl is the main course, an elaborate dessert is in order.

The manner of service depends upon your home, your facilities and your guests. Keep it simple and informal, and be your most gracious self.

Teas

A pleasant and flexible way of entertaining friends or acquaintances is the afternoon tea. There is not very much difference between a formal and informal tea, except the difference involved in serving a larger or a smaller number of guests. The usual hour for tea is between four and five, but it may be extended if many of the guests are career women, and may start earlier if a large number is expected.

THE INFORMAL TEA

Invitations to informal teas are usually extended in person, by telephone, or by an informal note, with the time stated. The number invited may vary from five or six to a large number, depending upon the occasion. If a hostess has asked a few friends to drop in for tea, she may serve it in the living room. The tea service should be arranged on an uncovered tray and placed on a low table, spread with a cloth which may

144

barely cover the table or may hang as much as eighteen inches over the sides.

If the hostess has a silver tea service with an alcohol lamp, the tray will contain a kettle of water kept boiling over the flame (which should be lighted only after the tray is safely placed on the table), an empty tea pot, creamer, sugar bowl, a plate of lemon slices with a lemon fork, a tea caddy, and an empty bowl for tea leaves and for dregs poured from the guests' cups before refilling. In this case the hostess makes the tea in the presence of the guests and serves it with or without additional hot water, according to preference, and with or without cream, sugar, or lemon. If the hostess prefers, or if she does not have a tea service with a means of keeping water boiling, the tea may be brewed and strained in the kitchen into a heated tea pot, and boiling water poured into a second heated pot to dilute the strong tea as guests request. In this case water should be kept boiling on the range so the supply may be frequently replenished and always hot.

Cups and saucers with teaspoons laid on the saucers to the right of the cups may be placed on the tea tray if it will hold them all, or some may be on the table beside it. Tea plates (7 to 8 inches in diameter), in a stack, and 12-inch tea napkins are also on the table near the tray. If possible little tables or some other convenient surface should be provided near the chair of each guest to hold plate, cup, and saucer. Many hostesses omit saucers entirely, in which case tea cup and food are both placed on the tea plate.

The food provided may consist only of strips of cinnamon toast, finger sandwiches spread with whipped butter, cucumber or watercress sandwiches, or tiny hot biscuits with jam. Small crisp cookies or thinly sliced fruit cake, mints, and salted nuts may be served too. Only at small intimate teas will hot crumpets or buttered toasted English muffins be offered in the fashion of a hearty English tea. The serving of these, or of jam, requires spreaders. At formal teas or for a larger group, serve only finger foods.

For a large group, or even in a small group if the hostess knows that some guests prefer it, coffee may be offered as well as tea; and in warm weather there may be some who will like the strong, hot tea or coffee poured over cracked ice in tall glasses. On very hot days a bowl of fruit punch with plenty of ice may replace the tea service altogether.

If the group, even at an informal tea, is quite large, the hostess may ask one close friend to pour the tea for her, another to pour the coffee, and perhaps a third to assist by keeping the serving plates replenished with food, so that she herself may be free to greet her guests. Constant replenishing of the serving plates is necessary to keep the arrangement of the tea table attractive.

THE FORMAL TEA

These large teas are seldom given except for a special occasion—perhaps to introduce a visiting celebrity, or for a club meeting or other official event. Invitations (on a correspondence card or on the hostess' visiting card, with "To meet _____" across the top and the date and hour in a lower corner) are issued about two weeks before the event.

A long table is used for a formal tea, with flowers and tall, white, formal candles (which if present should be lighted, but should not be present unless needed). The cloth, of formal damask or lace, usually hangs over the table edge from one-quarter to one-half yard. The tea tray, arranged just as for an informal tea, will be at one end of the table. At the other end will be a coffee or chocolate service, or on a warm day, a bowl of ice fruit punch. Only finger foods should be served. Cucumber and watercress sandwiches are traditional at a formal tea, as are little cakes such as petits fours, thinly sliced fruitcake, mints, and salted nuts.

Tea cups and saucers with teaspoons laid on the saucer at the right of the cup are usually arranged near each beverage service; additional plates for sandwiches and cakes may be stacked (not more than six or eight high) on the table with napkins. The foods and the cups, saucers, plates, and napkins should be replenished as they are used.

Two intimate friends of the hostess, preferably ladies who are acquainted with most of the guests, should be asked to pour the beverages. They may be replaced by two others at the end of an hour, if the tea is large. Their assistance, and that of a third person to replenish the serving plates and remove the guests' cups and plates as they are emptied, will permit the hostess, together with the guest of honor, to receive her guests.

146

Dinners

"Company" dinners are classified according to their formality. Most of the dinners an average hostess will give are informal and the rest are semiformal. The formal dinner is characterized by written or engraved invitations in the third person (also answered in the same manner), by full-evening dress, by a menu written in French (sometimes accompanied by an English translation), and consisting of no fewer than seven courses, but often as many as twelve with six or more wines. Preparation and serving of a seven course formal dinner consisting of appetizer, soup, fish, meat with vegetables, salad, dessert, and fruit (also nuts), followed by coffee or liqueurs in the drawing room, demands skilled help provided by a trained service staff. The style of service used is known as *Russian* or *Continental,* with host and hostess taking no part in it. The average family would find little occasion to use this formal style of service.

For the family with no outside kitchen help the *English* or *family style* of service is more practical. All the food is served at the table by the host and hostess instead of being served from the kitchen in individual servings.

A third type, usually called *"compromise"* service, is also used especially for semiformal meals and is described below.

THE SEMIFORMAL DINNER

This is the most formal meal most homemakers are likely to give. Invitations may be partially engraved, with names, dates, and hours filled in by hand; or they may be extended in an informal letter or by telephone. The time is usually eight or eight-thirty. Men are usually expected to wear dinner jackets, black or, in warm weather, white, rather than business suits; and women usually wear informal evening dress or dinner dresses. The considerate hostess will include a hint of the degree of formality in her invitation.

The dinner itself consists of only four or five courses — soup, fish (usually in the form of a cocktail), meat and vegetables, salad, and dessert, and of these either the fish course or the salad is often omitted. After-dinner coffee is usually served in the living room.

Service of a semiformal dinner is known as "compromise" service and is a combination of English and Russian style, sometimes called American. It is suited to the home with one maid or with a part-time waitress, and means that while the first course, salad, and dessert are served by the maid, the host or the host and hostess participate in serving the main course. The host generally carves the meat and places it on plates, which may be passed by the maid or handed down the table by the guests. The hostess sometimes serves the potatoes and vegetables; or the serving dishes may be offered to the guests by the maid. When there is no man of the house, the carving may be done by a close friend; or the hostess may do all the serving.

THE INFORMAL DINNER

Invitations to the most frequent and most intimate form of dinner may be issued personally, by telephone, or by informal letter. The guests will seldom number more than ten, especially if there is no maid. The guests' dress is dictated by custom; it is perfectly proper for the men to come in business suits and the women to dress accordingly. If the meal is a real "party" on a non-business day, dinner jackets and dinner dresses are quite in order.

The menu may consist of only two or three courses—either soup or fish, meat and vegetables, and dessert; or casserole, salad, and dessert. After-dinner coffee in the living room is still a pleasant custom, but coffee may be served at the table. The "family-style" service may be assisted by a maid, or by a member of the family or a guest, but the hostess will probably do most of the serving. And the hour may be any time from six to eight-thirty.

TABLE SETTING

The hostess's common sense as well as her knowledge of tradition will be called upon in setting the table for dinner. Everything should be correctly planned in an orderly manner.

The first step is to lay the cloth. For a really formal dinner a pure white or pale cream-colored cloth of linen damask is traditional, though a handsome lace cloth may be used. At least 9 inches of overhang should be allowed at each end. For less formal dinners, pastel damask, lace, linen edged with lace, or place mats may be used. A silence cloth or felt is always used under damask or linen.

Next, the dinner plates are placed. These should be spaced equidistant from each other, and one inch from the edge of the table. To allow the guests elbow room, a minimum of twenty inches must be allowed for each place—twenty-five or thirty inches is better.

The flat silver is arranged next. Only pieces actually needed for the food to be served should be put on the table, and these should be arranged in the order in which they will be used, starting from the outside. Forks (except cocktail forks) are placed to the left of the plate; knives, spoons, and cocktail forks to the right. All should be parallel to each other and at right angles to the edge of the table, with the handles an inch from the edge. Butter knives are placed on the butter plates, either parallel or at right angles to the table edge. Dessert forks or spoons are usually brought in with the dessert, though at an informal dinner they may be placed on the table.

The water glass is set at the tip of the dinner knife. Other glasses (for wines) are placed to the right and slightly in front of the water glass. The butter plate occupies the position at the tip of the dinner fork. Folded napkins are placed on the dinner plate if it is empty when the guests come to the table, or at the left of the forks; the folding should display the monogram, if there is one, and the open edges should be parallel with the fork and edge of the table and next to the fork. Individual ashtrays with matches and a few cigarettes should be supplied at each place. Iced water should be poured at the last moment; there should be no ice in the glasses.

Any centerpiece should be low enough to permit conversation across the table. Candles should be tall enough to burn above eye level.

SEATING OF GUESTS

When dinner is announced, at a semiformal dinner, the hostess leads the way in to the dining room, followed by the ladies and then by the gentlemen, with the host. Only at very formal dinners does the host enter first with the lady guest of honor on his arm; then the hostess goes in last with the gentleman guest of honor. The host is always seated at one end of the table with the lady of honor at his right, and the hostess at the opposite end with the gentleman guest of honor at her left. If there is no difference in age, rank, or distinction among the guests, the lady at the host's right and the gentlemen at the hostess' left have the positions of honor. Ladies and gentlemen alternate along the sides of the table, with husbands and wives usually not seated side by side.

A thoughtful hostess will make her seating plan with her guests' interests and tastes in mind, and try to place together those who will find one another interesting and congenial. In a large party, place cards will be helpful, but at a smaller dinner she may indicate to each guest where he or she is to sit.

SERVING PROCEDURE

Whatever the degree of formality, the lady seated at the host's right is always the first to be served. The hostess is never served first, unless she is the only lady present. Nor should the hostess ever be the first to help herself from an untouched serving dish. The classic sequence of serving goes clockwise around the table, starting with the lady guest of honor, but other sequences are also possible and correct; *i.e.*, one course clockwise, the next counter-clockwise, so that a different gentleman is last to be served in each case. When several have been served, guests may begin eating without waiting for the hostess, but the considerate hostess will lay her fork on her plate as a signal if she sees that the guests are waiting for her to begin. She should always be the last to finish.

All plates are placed and all serving dishes offered to guests from the left. The plates are always removed from the right. Ideally, the dishes offered should be held in the waitress's left hand, but in the interest of saving time, she may bring in two dishes at once, or present two dishes on a tray. Water and wine should both be poured from the right, by the waitress's right hand.

Dishes are always removed singly, never "stacked" on the table. When the main course is finished, serving dishes are removed first; then each place is cleared; then the maid takes away the pepper and salt shakers and the breadbasket on a tray, and crumbs the table, using a folded napkin and a clean plate. Dessert plates and silver are then put on the table.

Serving after-dinner coffee in the living room is a practical as well as a pleasant custom. It may be done in three ways, according to the size and character of the group, the formality of the occasion, and the service available. One way is to pour the coffee in the kitchen and have it brought in to the living room on a tray by the maid. Another way is to carry in to the living room a tray containing the silver coffee pot, creamer, sugar bowl, and the cups; the hostess then pours and hands the cups to guests who are nearby, or the host or other member of the family, who will hand them to more distant guests. The hostess may ask each guest for his cream and sugar preference, or they may help themselves. And the third way, perfectly acceptable at informal gatherings, is for the hostess to make the coffee freshly in the presence of the guests, using an electric coffee maker on a tray.

SOME FACTORS IN A SUCCESSFUL DINNER

Formal or informal, any dinner party will be more successful if it has been planned in detail. Whether the hostess expects to have a regular or part-time maid for part of the service or to handle it all herself, writing down the work schedule will help to prevent last-minute confusion. A maid brought in for the occasion will work more smoothly if time can be given to rehearsal beforehand.

Since the food is still the most important part of the dinner party, its quality should be safeguarded. Hot foods must be piping hot when they are brought from the kitchen, and cold foods should be served very cold. Serving platters and dishes for hot meats and vegetables should be warmed and plates for salads and for refrigerator or frozen desserts chilled.

More important than the observance of every rule of etiquette is that the dinner party should be enjoyed by everyone, guests and hostess alike. This happy result is more easily attained if the hostess has invited no more guests than she can comfortably seat and serve, and if her planning has been such that everything goes smoothly without visible effort. A dinner is a challenge for any hostess, and it can be fun too.

THE COCKTAIL HOUR

The hour before dinner is, in many homes, the cocktail hour—a pleasant interlude during which guests may relax from the cares of the day and become better acquainted before they dine.

The appetizers that are served with the cocktails should be

both delicious and attractive. One or two kinds are enough—perhaps a piquant dip served with crisp crackers or potato chips, and a tiny hot appetizer such as cheese balls. Hot appetizers are better served with before-dinner cocktails than at a cocktail party, because the hostess can be reasonably sure they will be eaten before they cool.

As always, when cocktails are served, a nonalcoholic beverage should be provided for guests who prefer it. It may be a well-seasoned tomato juice, a fruit juice or tart fruit punch.

Buffets

Buffet service fits perfectly into the relaxed, informal pattern of contemporary living. If you have limited dining space, or if you are a do-it-yourself hostess, buffet service permits you to entertain with more ease than any other type of service, and just as graciously and pleasantly.

Your buffet table may be set against a wall, or in the center of the room. For only six or eight guests, it is often placed with the long side against a wall; a larger number may need both long sides for sufficient elbow room when serving themselves. Because it presents all the food to the guests at one time and is thus the center of interest, the table should be arranged with care and artistry—and with common sense too, for the buffet table is functional and its arrangement is as important as its beauty.

The table itself should be dressed as attractively as possible, in lace, linen, or pretty place mats. And this is the time for bringing out your beautiful serving trays and plates. Flowers have an important role to play on the buffet table. If the table is against the wall, the flower arrangement may be a background for the foods; if in the center of the room, it will probably be a centerpiece. Since guests will all be standing, there is no need to keep it low. If candles are used for lighting the table, be sure to use plenty of them, placed so they really illuminate.

For the convenience of your guests, plan the arrangement of the table carefully. Confusing traffic plans should be avoided in order to help the serving line progress with ease and speed. Place a stack of large dinner plates at the point where guests are to start—probably at one end of the table. Napkins and silverware should be where they will be picked up last, after the plates are filled. Unless the guests are to eat at small tables, it is customary to serve only foods that can be eaten with a fork, since use of a knife is difficult. Rolls are usually buttered before they are put on the buffet. If you serve a tossed salad, tongs are far more easily handled than the conventional salad fork and spoon, when one hand is occupied by a plate. Since seasoning is so largely a matter of individual preference, individual salt and pepper shakers should be provided on snack tables or other convenient surfaces near the guests' chairs rather than on the buffet. A side table may hold a tray with goblets or glasses and a pitcher of iced water.

When guests have served themselves, partially emptied serving dishes should be refilled and empty ones removed from the buffet. Second servings may be passed by the hostess, or she may ask the guests to return to the buffet to serve themselves. When the first course is eaten, the buffet table is cleared, and dessert and the dishes in which it is to be served are then brought out.

The basic pattern of buffet service is varied in many ways. For the most informal type of service, guests may serve themselves with everything, even pouring their own coffee. At a semiformal buffet party, the hostess or a friend may pour the coffee at one end of the table; sometimes another friend may be asked to serve the main hot dish, if it is a casserole. Ornamental trays large enough to hold the plate and coffee cup, napkin and silverware, and water glass may be provided for the guests; the trays may be held on the guests' laps, or they may be mounted on folding legs; if trays are not provided, snack tables or card tables should be provided to set things on while guests deal with their plates on their laps. Plates and silver used in the first course may be returned by the guests (either to the kitchen, if the party is very informal, or to a table set up near the kitchen), or cleared away by the hostess or the host, or a friend. On some occasions, when space allows, a partial buffet may be preferred. Under this arrangement, guests select their food and seat themselves at smaller tables, such as card tables, where a place is set for each one.

Courses for a buffet meal are usually limited to just two—a main course with salad and rolls, and a dessert. Dishes should be chosen that are easy to serve and that stand up well. Casserole dishes are better than delicate soufflés which need to be served immediately. A chafing dish is a great convenience on a buffet table; heat-retaining casseroles are also an aid in keeping hot food hot. Mixtures should not be too thin and runny, salads not too juicy. Tossed or molded salads are always good; fruit salad mixtures may be served in lettuce cups which can be transferred to plates.

Remember to consider eye appeal of foods as well as their taste appeal. The colors of the foods themselves as well as their arrangement on serving dishes and their garnishings are important, for a buffet meal provides almost the only opportunity for guests to see the whole menu at once. In planning for your party, be sure to estimate quantities generously, for there is something about a buffet which is irresistible to the appetite!

Larger, heartier buffet meals are sometimes served. For one such, a roast turkey may be placed at one end, and a handsomely garnished baked tender ham at the other; both of these may be set out either hot or cold, and sliced or partly sliced beforehand, or else sliced and served by the hostess's helpers. To complete this particular meal, little hot Southern biscuits are delicious, with a big relish tray of carrot sticks, celery curls, olives, cranberry jelly to go with the turkey and spiced crab apples or peaches for the ham, a platter of sliced tomatoes drizzled with French dressing, cauliflower polonaise, and lemon meringue tarts. Sumptuous!

THE COCKTAIL PARTY

The cocktail party is a special kind of buffet party. The purpose of hors d'oeuvres at this party is a little different from the before-dinner cocktail hour, since no other food is ordinarily to be provided. A variety should be served, allowing at least five or six "pieces" for each guest. Hot hors d'oeuvres should not be attempted unless they can be served piping hot. Tiny and attractively garnished canapés are very much in order. One non-alcoholic beverage should be provided.

In keeping with the delicate and fine quality of cocktail glasses, other serving equipment and the service itself will tend to be formal rather than informal. A beautiful tablecloth, flowers, and candles form an attractive background for the hors d'oeuvres trays. Small plates may or may not be provided, but plenty of cocktail napkins should be placed at both ends of the table.

SMÖRGÅSBORD

Best-known of all Scandinavian dining customs is the smörgåsbord—usually the prelude to the feast, but on some occasions the whole feast itself. In Sweden, where the custom is believed to have originated in the festivities of country people, the smörgåsbord is served as a first course. A small number of appetizers, which invariably include herring, are presented buffet-style to guests who relax and nibble, exchange toasts and conversation, and then assemble around the dining table with appetites pleasantly stimulated but unimpaired. In other countries, and especially in America, the character and function of the smörgåsbord have altered and it may comprise the principal part of a meal. A munificent variety of fish, meat, cheese, egg, and vegetable dishes is arranged on a necessarily commodious buffet or table and guests visit it as often as they please. A dessert (by recommendation, simple) and good strong coffee bring the feast to a close.

A time-tried ritual is prescribed for the proper enjoyment of either a small smörgåsbord or the full-scale, panoramic affair. First, and always first if one is to observe the Scandinavian spirit of the occasion, the herring! Then one adventures (with clean plate in hand) through dishes in which fish is combined with other ingredients, then cold meats, the delicious hot dishes, the salads and aspics, and finally, for digestion's sake and to soothe a possibly jaded palate, a bit of cheese.

In Norway, the smörgåsbord is also called *koldt bord*. It usually consists of a few appetizers—fish, meat, and cheese —but on special occasions may be elaborate and bountiful, including roasts of meat and several kinds of fish. Roast beef tenderloin, for example, and loin of pork served with prunes and apple slices; boiled lobster with mayonnaise, whole baked or boiled salmon with sour cream; and a whole cold ham. Include parsley potatoes in the more elaborate type of smörgåsbord. Rum pudding usually rounds out these heroic collations.

A Swedish adaptation of the smörgåsbord is the gracious *supé* – a late supper served after the theater or an evening of dancing. The supé too is governed to some extent by tradition. Hot dishes are always served. They may be croustades with creamed filling, an omelet or soufflé, new potatoes with fresh dill. Breads, especially the fragrant limpa, accompany the dishes. Fish and a relish, such as sliced tomatoes, are included as a matter of course. Amounts served are not lavish. The dishes are kept small, but always garnished with the flair for beauty that characterizes Scandinavian cuisine. Cookies are sometimes included in supé and coffee is always served. To precede a Swedish dinner, a plate of three (it must be three) canapés is placed before each individual. Canapés would not be served with a smörgåsbord.

The American homemaker can make a respectable gesture toward a smörgåsbord with herring, sardines, anchovies or other small canned fish, a platter of ready-to-serve meats and cheese, and a relish or two—all of which may also be included in a much more elaborate buffet.

A word about bread and cheeses: Custom dictates that only the dark breads belong to the smörgåsbord and that knackebrod (hardtack in American parlance) should be among them. Cheese may be Swiss, Danish Bleu, Edam, goat cheese, or bond ost, but it is never proffered in slices. Guests cut it to individual preference.

Dessert Parties

Most feminine of all forms of entertaining is probably the dessert party. There are a dozen excuses for it: a club meeting in the home, an afternoon of bridge, a shower for bride- or baby-to-be, the introduction of a newcomer in the neighborhood to your friends. It's a gay sort of affair, usually given in the afternoon when the men are away, but occasionally late of an evening when they may possibly be persuaded to participate. And it calls for your most special magic to produce a really breath-taking pièce de résistance.

The dessert's the thing—for a dessert party is not and should not be a meal, but merely a gesture of dainty, delectable hospitality. The whole menu served at the dessert party need consist of no more than the dessert itself— eye-appealing, taste tempting, and irresistibly delicious— with, of course, a beverage of distinction. Include salted nuts and mints if you wish.

Service for the dessert party should be of the simplest. You may have your card table or tables spread with dainty cloths and set with silver and napkins when your guests arrive; this permits your guests to finish eating and you to clear the tables before the business or pleasure of the meeting gets under way. Or finish the business first, and then set the tables, so guests may relax over your dessert masterpiece. The dessert itself may either be served and prettily garnished in the kitchen; or if the dessert is particularly beautiful, by all means display the attractively garnished platter before you serve it with a flourish.

Serving Wine with Your Meal

Wine through the years has meant many things to many people around the world. To the average Frenchman or Italian, wine, along with bread, is almost as important as life itself and is a daily requisite at family meals.

Probably due to increased travel to foreign countries where wine is a familiar commodity, large numbers of Americans have been added to the list of wine-lovers. Today the domestic wines grown in California, New York, and Ohio compete strongly with the traditionally more famous but much more expensive imports from France, Italy, and Spain. There is one basic fact, however, which one should keep in mind—that choosing a wine is a matter of personal taste plus a consideration of the money available for purchasing it.

WINE & FOOD CHART

Wine Class	Best-Known Types	Wine and Food Combinations
Appetizer Wines	Sherry Vermouth Flavored wines	Serve at cocktail time, chilled, without food, or with hors d'oeuvres, nuts, cheeses
White Table Wines	Sauterne Chablis Rhine Wine	Serve well chilled with lighter dishes such as chicken, fish, shellfish, omelets, any white meat
Red Table Wines	Burgundy Chianti Claret Rosé "Vino" types	Serve at cool room temperature with hearty dishes such as steaks, chops, roasts, game, cheese dishes, spaghetti (Rosé with all foods)
Dessert Wines	Muscatel Angelica Cream (sweet) Sherry Port Tokay	Serve at dessert, chilled or at cool room temperature, with fruits, cookies, nuts, cheese, fruit cake, pound-cake
Sparkling Wines	Champagne Pink Champagne Sparkling Burgundy Cold Duck	Serve well chilled with any food —appetizers, the main course, or dessert (especially good in party punches)

Wine-serving tips

• Wine-serving etiquette requires that the host be served first for a very practical reason—to sniff or taste the wine to check on its quality before offering it to guests.
• Wine is appreciated most when served with food, so make it easily available by placing it on the dining table.
• If served in its own bottle and if it is a wine that has to be chilled, place it in a wine cooler. If it is a red wine that should be served at room temperature, place it in a wine basket in which the bottle lies on its side. The slanting position of the bottle keeps any sediment in the bottom.
• Covering the bottle with a napkin is unnecessary as many people like to see the label to know what they are drinking. The purpose of the napkin is to keep the bottle, if iced, from

slipping in your hand, also to absorb drops of wine that might fall. If a napkin is used, hold a small one in your left hand while pouring with your right. For an elaborate table setting one might stand the bottle in an antique silver holder designed for serving wine at the table.

• The familiar rule of serving white wine with white meat and red wine with red meat should not be considered a binding one. It often needs modification, and it is the individual who must decide which wine gives him the most enjoyment with certain foods. For instance, there are wine connoisseurs who find the full red wines of Bordeaux perfect with roast chicken or some of the red wines of Burgundy good with roast turkey. A not-too-dry white wine is delightful with roast ham or a vin rosé with roast pork. A rather light red Bordeaux or a Beaujolais is a perfect foil for veal or sweetbreads. A red Bordeaux also goes well with roast leg of lamb and a full-flavored red Burgundy adds to the enjoyment of a good lamb stew.

• Vins rosé are in a class by themselves and are pink in color and rather light-bodied. They are usually considered to be compatible with all types of food, but this, too, is just a generalization.

• There is an old saying that no aged wine should ever be served over 72°F. Today, it is customary to serve red wines at room temperature (meaning 65° to 75°F), dry wines and vins rosé cooled, and sweet wines and champagne cooler still. It is said that no wine should be icy-cold as it deadens the taste. Here again one must add that many wine drinkers find white wines and rosés much more refreshing when thoroughly chilled.

• Wine left in the bottle after a meal may be "held over" as long as it is used within a week and provided the wine, if it had been chilled, remains chilled. If there is no sediment in the bottom of the bottle the wine may be used also for cooking.

• The so-called cooking wines obtainable at the market should be avoided unless their quality is comparable to a good table wine. As wine users know, the alcohol in the wine, also the water, evaporates during the cooking process and all that remains in the food is the flavor. Since that is the reason for adding the wine in the first place one must be sure the flavor is a pleasant one. It should be added here that wine labeled "cooking wine" indicates that salt has been added. Therefore, if this type is used in recipes, it is often necessary to adjust the amount of salt called for in the recipe. Wine with

salt added is unpalatable for drinking, and it is said that the practice developed in restaurants to discourage the employees from drinking wine intended for cooking.
• When serving more than one wine at a meal a dryer wine should precede a sweeter one and a lighter wine come before a heavier one.

Wine Glasses

To play up the beautiful color and the delightful bouquet of good wine to best advantage, use a stemmed glass made of clear crystal, at least 6-ounce capacity and tulip-shaped. A large bowl enables the taster to swirl the wine around in the glass which should not be filled more than half. The tapering of the glass at the top serves as a sort of chimney allowing the wine bouquet to rise up to the nose as one sniffs the wine. Many connoisseurs still prefer to serve wine in the traditional Rhine wine römer. If your budget and storage space are limited, select one wine glass appropriate for most types of wine. Champagne, however, requires a special type of glass. Be sure that wine glasses are always sparkling clean and free of any detergent odors.

Written by
RICHARD EKSMED

Basic Tools

Contents

Toolbox with liftout tray.

Starting Your Tool Collection

All the how-to talent in the world won't help you if you don't have a proper set of tools. Don't make the mistake of going out and investing a small or large fortune in whatever the local hardware store has in stock, but—if you are new to the do-it-yourself game—have on hand a few basic items. You can buy others as the need arises.

When you inhabit a furnished room or an apartment, your tool needs are few. But when you own your own home, you will find that you need a small arsenal of basic tools to take care of the place.

Never bargain-shop for tools. Don't settle for a lesser type or smaller size than you really need. And don't skimp on quality. A penny saved can mean a dollar lost—or worse. Whatever the tool, look for a sturdy body and smooth finish. Metal surfaces should be coated for rust prevention; wood parts should be varnished, waxed, or lacquered for durability and protection against splinters.

Check all moving parts of a tool before purchase to make sure that they work smoothly and easily but are free of any play or wiggle. Look for tools that are permanently marked with the manufacturer's name or symbol as an indication of careful construction and quality materials. Some quality tools even have performance warranties.

Your Most Valuable Tools

What would you pay for the most valuable tools in the world? These tools can help you grip, grasp, push, twist, and help you operate equipment. They can distinguish temperature variations and are sensitive to touch. It is impossible to purchase such tools—they are your hands.

These fabulous tools are subject to injury by being caught in machines, cut by a variety of sharp-edged tools, crushed by whatever objects fall on them. They can be damaged by being burned, fractured, or sprained unless you are always alert.

Protect these most valuable tools, because you cannot replace them.

Hanging tools on perforated hardboard.

Tool Storage

You are going to need a place to keep all those shiny new tools. The kitchen "junk" drawer might be okay to start with, but you'll soon find that the screwdriver is hopelessly entangled with string when you want it most. One of the first things you should do in your new home is to make some sort of plan for tool storage. In the beginning, as long as you have only a few tools, or if you are an apartment dweller, a simple toolbox might do. It will keep your tools in good condition, help to protect them from dust and moisture, and provide a convenient organizer, storage space, and carrying case as well.

A good start toward tool storage is also a piece of perforated cardboard (popularly known as Pegboard, a trade name). When you buy the board get one of the kits that contain hardware for attaching it to the wall as well as the hooks, hangers, and assorted accessories for accommodating various tools. Hang it in the basement or garage. Later on, you'll probably want a workbench, so make sure there is room for one underneath your storage wall.

CERTAIN BASIC SAFETY TIPS

They apply to tool usage, regardless of what the tool may be.

• Never use a tool with a dulled cutting blade or bit or a loose part.
• Use tools only for the work they were intended to do. Never use a screwdriver to pry, chip, or pound; a wood bit to drill masonry or metal; pliers to pound or cut taut wire, or a wrench to hammer.

• Never expose pliers, screwdrivers, or wrenches to extreme heat; they could become weakened and suddenly give way during use.
• Do not try to repair a tool yourself unless you know what you are doing. Either buy a new one or take the crippled tool to an expert.

Your First Toolbox

In this booklet you'll find a great number of tools described and illustrated. Which ones you need depends on how ambitious a do-it-yourselfer you are and what kinds of jobs you plan to do. If you live in an apartment we recommend a toolkit that contains: A claw hammer • Pliers • A Phillips screwdriver and a regular one • A hand drill and bits • An awl • An adjustable wrench • A plane • A utility knife • A nailset • A crosscut saw • A steel tape measure • A level • Assorted screws and nails • Glue • A paintbrush • An assortment of sandpaper grades and a holder • Assorted faucet washers • Liquid drain cleaner • A toilet plunger.

Buying Tools

Does a devoted fisherman buy a cheap rod and reel? Does a dentist buy a bargain-basement drill? Of course not. The same attitude should apply to any tool. A good hammer is precisely tooled, properly weighted, and has maximum strength so that it will drive a nail straight, true, and fast. A cheap hammer will slip off the nail, drive it crookedly, and require more strokes. Often the head is poorly attached so that it might fly off at a crucial moment and possibly even become a lethal missile. It just isn't worth it. The same applies to all tools. So let's remember this principle and shop for:

Hammers

There are many kinds of hammers: ball peen for metalwork, tack for upholstery, mason's for brickwork, mallets with heads of wood, plastic or rubber to drive chisels without marring the surface, sledge hammers to break up cement or blacktop, to name just a few. What most laymen, however, mean by a "hammer" is the common claw,

Ball peen hammer.

Tack hammer.

Sledge hammer.

How to use a
claw hammer correctly.

Rubber mallet.

Claw hammer.

Pulling out nails with
a claw hammer.

or nail, hammer. The claw hammer is the basic hammer for jobs like whacking wood into place, but it is designed primarily for driving in or pulling out nails. The best claw hammer for general use has a 16-ounce head that is firmly attached to a wood handle, either with a solid wedge or glue on top, or both, or forged in a single piece with the handle, which is then covered with rubber, plastic, or leather for a firm grip.

To use a hammer correctly, grip it at or near the end of the handle and swing it from your shoulder. You may miss the nail at first, but keep trying (on scrap wood) until you get the "swing" of it. It's well worth the practice.

Nails and Screws

Box nail.

Finishing nail.

Screws.

Nails come in two shapes: box nails and finishing nails. Box nails have large heads. Use them for rough work when appearance doesn't matter. Finishing nails have very small heads. You can drive them below the surface with a nailset or another nail, and cover them. Use them where appearance is important, as in putting up paneling or building shelves.

Screws are best where holding strength is important. Use them to install towel bars, curtain rods, to repair drawers, or to mount hinges. Where screws work loose, you can refill the holes with matchsticks or wood putty and replace them.

Nailsets

Driving finishing nails
with nailset.

A nailset is used to drive finishing nailheads below the surface of woodwork (paneling, floorboards, etc). After the nailhead disappears below the surface, the hole is filled with putty or cement. Nailsets are made to suit different sizes of nailheads, ranging from $1/32$ inch to $5/32$ inch. The nail is usually driven with a nail hammer up to slightly above the surface to prevent possible marring of the wood with the hammer; then the nailset, which has a tip slightly smaller than the head of the nail, is used.

Screwdrivers

Screwdriver with clip to hold screws.

Making a starter hole with an awl.

Use two hands on screwdriver.

Screwdriver bit in place.

Another familiar tool is the screwdriver, designed to provide good turning leverage for driving and removing screws. It comes in two basic styles. The flat-tip style is for the single slot screws used in walls, woodwork, and furniture. The Phillips fits the cross-slotted screws found on many home appliances. If you don't own at least one of each, you should buy them, keeping the following points in mind.

The most generally useful flat-tip model has a wedge-shaped end about ¼ inch wide and a blade about 6 inches long. A No. 2 Phillips with a 4-inch blade works on most cross-slotted screws. Either style should have a large, fluted handle with a gently rounded butt end for firm, comfortable gripping. If compact storage is desirable, look for a model with a detachable, reversible blade—flat-tipped at one end and Phillips style at the other.

Assorted tip sizes and blade lengths may be a good investment if you use tools often. A flat-tip driver wider than the screw will scar the surrounding surface; a tip too narrow gives poor leverage and may damage the screw slot. Shorter blades are helpful in cramped quarters. Either prepackaged sets or three flat-tipped drivers—4, 6, and 8 inches—plus No. 1 and No. 2 Phillips meet most household needs.

A screwdriver is simple to use once the screw is started. Many novices try to use the screwdriver without starting the hole first. This may sometimes work in soft wood but is virtually impossible in hard wood. Use an awl, a nail, or a tool specifically designed for starting screws. Many old-timers start the screw by banging it in with a hammer, but this often results in damage and hard-to-work screw slots. It is helpful to hold the blade and screw head together in the beginning. This is not always possible, however, and some screwdrivers have metal clips over the blade that hold the screw head to the blade for use in hard-to-reach areas. Firm pressure should be applied against the screw during driving to keep the blade in place. When the wood is very hard, it is wise to predrill the entire hole. Special drill bits are available for this purpose, matching screw sizes. It sometimes helps to use both hands once the screw is started, one turning the handle, and the other held flat against the end of it to apply more pressure.

It is easy to remove screws once you get them loosened. The trouble, again, is getting them started, or "broken." Don't forget

Flat-tip screwdriver.

Phillips screwdriver.

Multipurpose pliers.

Locking pliers.

Water-pump pliers.

that screws are driven in clockwise and removed counterclockwise. If a screw won't budge, give it a quick twist in both directions. For larger stubborn screws, a screwdriver bit in a brace provides extra leverage.

Pliers

Pliers are probably the most misunderstood and misused of all tools. They are used as substitutes for hammers, wrenches, bottle openers, and who knows what else. When properly applied they can perform many holding and gripping operations.

There are numerous types of pliers, most of them used by specialists such as electricians and electronics workers. The kind the homeowner uses most often is the slip-joint pliers. It performs numerous holding tasks — and is often the wrong tool for the job. Pliers are not really designed for tightening and loosening nuts — wrenches are. Yet this is a common household use, and it will do if you don't have the right wrench in your toolbox.

The slip-joint pliers *is* the right tool for grasping, turning, bending, or pulling bolts, wires, broken glass, and sharp or small objects. The term "slip-joint" is applied because the tool has two slots in which the center fastener pin can be located. In one slot, the pliers grip small objects with the forward jaws tight and parallel. When the pin is in the other slot, the concave inner jaws can go around larger objects. Some pliers have cutting jaws just inside the curved portion. These are for cutting wires, small nails, etc.

When shopping for pliers, choose ones that have been drop-forged and have either a polished surface or a bluish-black sheen. The pin should be solidly fastened so that you can't remove it. The outer parallel jaws should have fine grooves or cross-hatching, the inner ones sharp, rugged teeth. Handles should be scored or tooled so that you can grip them firmly.

Specialized pliers for plumbing repairs are water-pump pliers, channel-lock pliers, and locking pliers.

The water-pump pliers are designed for tightening or removing water-pump packing nuts. One jaw is adjustable to several different positions. The inner surface of the jaws consists of a series of deep grooves adapted to grasping cylindrical objects.

Small-nosed pliers.

Lineman's pliers.

Channel-lock pliers.

Slip-joint pliers.

Slip-joint pliers cutting wire.

Slip-joint pliers gripping small object.

Slip-joint pliers gripping large object.

Channel-lock pliers are similar to water-pump pliers, but the jaw-opening adjustment is different. Lands (raised areas) on one jaw fit into grooves on the other. Channel-lock pliers are less likely to slip from the adjustment setting than water-pump pliers, but they are less effective as a wrench and should be used only where it is impossible to fit a wrench.

Locking pliers are very useful when working with small-diameter pipe. They can be clasped on an object and will stay by themselves, leaving your hands free for other work. The jaw opening is adjusted by turning a thumbscrew at the end of one handle.

Specialized pliers for electrical repairs are small-nosed pliers, lineman's pliers, and multipurpose pliers.

Small-nosed pliers (sometimes called needle-nosed pliers) have narrow, tapered jaws to make it easy to bend wire into loops around terminals and to reach into such tight quarters as switch and outlet boxes. The better ones have insulated handles to help protect against shock.

Lineman's pliers are heavy-duty pliers used for firmly gripping cable, connectors, and the like. They also have side jaws that are used for cutting wire.

There are several varieties of multipurpose electrician's pliers. All have as their purpose the combining of as many operations as possible into one tool. The tool usually operates as a pliers, stripper, crimper, and cutter. It may also do other jobs, depending on the model.

169

Handsaws

Saws, too, come in a wide variety of sizes and types. The homeowner should purchase an 8- or 10-point crosscut saw for all-around work. The "8-point" means that there are 8 teeth per inch. "Crosscut" means that the teeth are beveled slightly outward and knife-shaped, designed for cutting across the grain of the wood —the most common type of cut.

A ripsaw has squarish, chisellike teeth, and it cuts with the grain. Most do-it-yourselfers have little need for a ripsaw. If you must do a lot of ripping, a power saw of some kind is preferred.

A hacksaw is used for cutting metals and some plastics. It has a wide U-shaped frame with devices on each end for holding the removable, fine-toothed saw blade. A thumbscrew draws the blade taut.

A coping saw is somewhat similar in design to a hacksaw, except that the blade is much thinner and has larger teeth. A coping saw blade can be turned to various angles for making curving cuts in wood.

Keyhole and compass saws are similar, with the keyhole blade being thinner and finer. Both are used to make curving cuts and small cuts when only one side of the work is accessible, such as in paneling, wallboard, and similar materials that are already nailed up.

The backsaw is made in 10- to 16-inch lengths, usually with 12 or 13 teeth per inch. It is designed for joint-cutting work, for smooth cuts with or across the grain. A longer version of the backsaw with 11 teeth per inch is the miter box saw.

When buying a saw, look for a tempered steel or chrome-nickel blade. Handles should be removable hardwood or high-impact plastic. Better saws have taper-ground blades, and some have a Teflon coating for rust resistance and less binding.

Crosscut saw.

Ripsaw.

Keyhole, compass saw.

Coping saw.

Mitering a molding with a backsaw and a miter box.

Hacksaw.

Brace and bit (left), extension bit (right).

Push drill.

Rotary-crank drill.

Electric power drill.

Hand Drills

To insert long screws or bolts into or through wood or wallboard, you first need to make neat, straight holes for them. Either a rotary cranking or a push-style hand drill can do the job. Each is sold with interchangeable bits for making holes at least ¾ inch deep and up to ¼ inch wide. The handles are hollow for bit storage, and replacement bits are available at most hardware stores.

The rotary-cranking style is easy to control and versatile. By turning a crank you set gears in motion to activate the bit at any speed you want. The drill chuck holds bits of many sizes and types. However, a quality model is nearly a foot long and weighs several pounds; it is bulky to store.

The push drill is generally less than a foot long and under a pound in weight. Forward or downward pressure on the handle activates an inner spiral, or ratchet, that turns the bit. Some have a reverse mechanism that allows a bit to be backed out of a deep hole or one in which it is stuck.

The use of an electric drill makes jobs go faster and easier (but also noisier). However, it's not much good if electricity is not available. In that case, or if you do not yet have an electric drill, a brace and bit can do the same job as a power drill because it provides more leverage than any other hand drill.

Wrenches

There are probably more types of wrenches than of any other tool. There are open-end and box wrenches, some with a combination of each, and some with half-boxes. (A box wrench completely encloses the nut.) There are ratchet wrenches that are turned like a crank, pipe wrenches, chain wrenches, and countless others.

Packing nut socket wrench.

Your first wrench acquisition should be an adjustable wrench. These come in various sizes, but one about 8 inches long, with jaw capacity up to an inch, is a good starter. This wrench has one fixed jaw and another that is moved away from or toward the fixed jaw by means of a knurled knob.

The adjustable open-end wrench is used on square or hexagonal nuts and for working on the interior parts of many types of faucets and valves. If you buy more than one wrench, a 12-inch one is good for most minor plumbing jobs and a 6-inch wrench comes in handy for smaller work.

Place the wrench on the nut so that you pull the handle toward the side with the adjustable jaw. This will prevent the jaw from opening and slipping off the nut. Be sure that the nut is all the way into the throat of the jaws, and that the jaws are adjusted to fit snugly around the nut. Otherwise, you may damage the nut or valve.

A monkey wrench is used for the same purpose and in the same way as the adjustable open-end wrench. Force is applied to the back of the handle — the side of the wrench opposite the jaw opening.

In buying a wrench, look for a drop-forged, alloy steel wrench with a chrome-polished or blue-black sheen. The jaws should be exactly parallel and not loose (check that by wiggling the movable jaw). Some have a locking device that holds the adjustable jaw in a constant position.

Fixed wrenches (open-end and box) are of a specific size and cannot be adjusted. When you buy fixed wrenches, get a quality set of graduated sizes. For working in tight places, special thin open-end wrenches, called closet spud wrenches, are particularly helpful.

Packing nut socket wrenches come in various sizes to fit tub and shower faucet assemblies. Hexagonal in shape and with a hollow core, this type of wrench fits over the faucet stem to remove the valve packing nuts and stem assembly. Since these parts are made of brass, ordinary wrenches should not be used on them. Application of too much pressure will bend or break the fittings, which are very difficult to replace since they are inside the wall. It is far cheaper to buy and use the right wrench for the job than to have to tear apart the wall.

Open-end wrench.

Closet spud wrench.

Box wrench.

Right and wrong way to use an adjustable open-end wrench.

Right and wrong way to use a monkey wrench.

Pipe wrench.

Stillson wrench.

Pipe wrenches are adjustable wrenches designed to grip round surfaces. There are several types: the strap wrench for working with brass, aluminum, soft metal, or plastic pipe, the chain wrench used on large-diameter pipe, such as cast-iron drain pipe, and many others. In a narrower sense, the term "pipe wrench" is used to designate one particular type. This type of wrench has hardened steel jaws that provide excellent bite and grip. It is often called a Stillson wrench, which is only a slight misnomer. The main difference between a pipe wrench and a Stillson wrench is that the latter has a separate housing in which the adjusting nut operates. In both types the movable jaw is pivoted to permit a gripping action on the work. Both are used for working with steel or iron pipe.

Pipe wrenches come in many sizes. For small pipe work, a 6-inch or 8-inch length is best. For pipe in the ½-inch to 1½-inch range, a 12-inch or 14-inch wrench should be used. For pipe up to 2 inches, the wrench should be 18 inches long.

Two wrenches are needed in most applications, unless the work is held in a vise. One is used to hold the pipe, the other turns the fitting. Pipe wrenches work in one direction only, so they are placed on the work in opposing directions.

Utility Knife

Utility knife.

The small, sharp blade of the utility knife held firmly by a sturdy handle can save you time and effort in cutting twine, trimming carpet, tile or wallpaper, and opening cartons. It is specially designed to lessen the chance of cutting accidents during handyman jobs and is an excellent safety investment for your toolbox.

Look for a utility knife with a single-edge, replaceable blade held securely by a screw at the throat of the handle. The handle should be shaped to fit your hand and hollow for the storage of extra blades. Some handles have a push-button to retract the blade or extend it for conveniently cutting different thicknesses.

Putty Knife

A putty knife helps you attain a smooth finish when spreading spackling compound into chipped spots or small holes in walls, applying putty to window frames, or inserting grout between tiles. Those with stiffer blades can also be used for minor scraping of paint, plaster, or adhesive.

The thin, polished blade should have a blunt end and no sharp edges; it should be firmly attached to the handle by two rivets or eyelets. A good style for general use has a blade about 3 inches wide and is about 7 inches long.

Chisels

Putty knife.

A wood chisel consists of a steel blade usually fitted with a wooden or plastic handle. It has a single beveled cutting edge on the end of the blade. According to construction, chisels are divided into two general classes: tang chisels, in which part of the chisel enters the handle, and socket chisels, in which the handle enters into a part

Tang chisel.

Cold chisel.

Socket chisel.

of the chisel. A socket chisel is designed for striking with a wooden mallet (never a steel hammer), whereas a tang chisel is designed for hand use only.

Wood chisels are also divided into types, depending on their weight and thickness, the shape or design of the blade, and the work they are intended to do. For general household use, a ½-inch or ¾-inch paring chisel is probably best. It has a relatively thin blade and is beveled along the sides.

Another type of chisel for exterior work is the cold chisel. This is made of hardened, tempered alloy steel and is used for striking steel, concrete, stone, and other hard materials. A cold chisel is struck with a ball peen or other heavy hammer.

Measuring Tools

Folding rule.

Steel tape.

A 6-foot folding rule is a good all-around measuring device. The readings are large and easily read, and some have red markings every 16 inches (the standard "centering" for framing).

A steel tape that is rigid when extended but flexible enough to retract into a small case is especially convenient if you work without a helper. A 10-foot model with a ½-inch blade is useful for home purposes. The tape is marked in inches and $1/16$-inch intervals and ends in a hook that holds onto objects being measured. The case should prevent the extended tape from turning over and should have measuring marks that can be read as an extension of the tape. Many cases have a friction lock to hold the tape at a desired length.

Try Square

Try square.

The try square consists of two parts at right angles to each other: a thick wood or iron stock and a thin steel blade. Most try squares are made with the blades graduated in inches and fractions of an inch. The blade length varies from 2 to 12 inches. This tool is used for setting or checking lines or surfaces that have to be at right angles to each other.

Levels

The carpenter's level is a tool designed to determine whether a plane or surface is true horizontal or true vertical. It is a simple instrument consisting of a liquid, such as alcohol or chloroform, partially filling a glass vial or tube so that a bubble remains. The vial is mounted in a frame of aluminum, magnesium, or wood. Levels

174

Carpenter's level.

Line level.

Torpedo level.

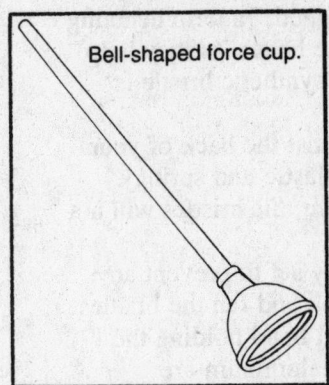
Bell-shaped force cup.

are usually equipped with two or more vials. One vial is built into the frame at right angles to another. The vial is slightly curved, causing the bubble always to seek the highest point in the tube. On the outside of the vial are two sets of gradation lines separated by a space. Leveling is established when the air bubble is centered between the gradation lines.

There are several other types of level. A torpedo level is useful in tight places. It has a top-reading vial so that you can place it on a low or deep surface and tell whether it's level without bending way down to look at it. A line level hooks onto a piece of twine or string and is useful when working with concrete forms, brick, and similar jobs where lines are used.

Force Cup

Ball-shaped force cup.

Aptly called "the plumber's helper," a force cup is the well-known tool of first defense against clogged sink or bathtub drains and overflowing toilets. By providing pressure and suction into stopped-up pipes, it can help you avoid water damage or costly plumber's bills.

Force cups are available with either a bell- or ball-shaped flexible cup screwed onto a wood handle. A ball-shaped style with a 2-foot handle is satisfactory for most households. It has a smaller end opening than the more conventional bell-shaped model for easier insertion in toilet discharge pipes, but it can also be conveniently used on drains.

Planes

Block plane.

The plane is the most extensively used of the hand shaving tools. Most of the lumber handled by anyone working with wood is dressed on all four sides, but when performing jobs such as fitting doors and sash and interior trim work, planes must be used.

Bench and block planes are designed for general purpose smoothing and squaring. Other planes are designed for special types of surface work.

For your basic toolbox buy a block plane, the smallest (about 6 inches long). Its blade is mounted bevel up at a low angle, and it is used for smoothing all plane surfaces on very small work. It can also be used for cross-grain squaring of end-stock. The angle of the blade can be adjusted with the adjustment screw. Make sure before starting to plane that the iron is sharp.

Paintbrushes

Your basic toolbox should contain at least one good brush. If you should, however, decide to paint your house, rooms, or furniture, one brush certainly won't do the job.

Quality is a very important factor in selecting a brush, regardless of the size or style needed for a particular project. A good brush will hold more paint and enable you to apply the paint more smoothly and with less effort.

All good brushes have bristles that are "flagged," a term denoting splits on the bristle end. The more "flags" the better, as they help retain paint. Hog bristle is naturally flagged; synthetic bristle is artifically flagged or split.

Test for "bounce" by brushing bristles against the back of your hand. In a good brush, the bristles will feel elastic and springy. When the brush is gently pressed on any surface, the bristles will not fan out excessively.

Check the setting. Bristles should be solidly set to prevent any chance of fallout during painting. Jar the brush and fan the bristles. Any loose bristles will be apparent. The metal band holding the bristles is called a ferrule. Stainless steel and aluminum are generally used on better-grade brushes for greater resistance to corrosion.

Both the surface area and type of paint determine the size and style of brush to be used. Calcimine brushes with very long, tough, and elastic gray hog bristles are best for applying water-thinned paints to large areas. Enamel and varnish brushes, both flat and chisel-shaped, are best for applying oil-based paints and lacquers. The shape and length of the latter type help secure a smoother flow and prevent lap marks.

The following brush styles and sizes are recommended for most painting projects around the home:
• Flat wall brushes: sizes vary from 3 to 6 inches in width with thicknesses of ¾ to 1½ inches and bristles from 2 to 7 inches long. They are best suited for painting large surfaces such as walls, ceilings, and floors.
• Varnish brushes: sizes range from 1 to 3½ inches in width, with

Flagged bristles.

Wall brushes.

BAD   GOOD
Pressing the brush on a surface to test for bounce.

Fan brush to check for loose bristles.

Flat, chisel-shaped varnish brushes.

Sash, trim, artist's brushes.

176

bristles from 2 to 4½ inches long. They are ideally suited for painting baseboards, window frames, narrow boards, or enameling and varnishing furniture and small panels.

• Round sash and flat trim brushes: sizes range from 1 to 1½ inches in width. Trellises, screens, small pipes, toys, and all small areas are best painted with sash, trim, or even artist's brushes.

In addition to these general styles, most dealers carry special brushes for bronzing, roofing, stippling, and stenciling.

A quality brush is a fine tool and should be properly used and cared for. For example, a wide brush should never be used to paint pipes and similar surfaces. This causes the brush to "fishtail." A brush should never be left standing on its bristles. The weight causes the edge to bend and curl, ruining the fine painting tips.

Always clean a brush while it is still soft after painting. Once it is thoroughly cleaned it should be properly stored. For long-term storage, make sure that the bristles are completely dry, then wrap the brush in foil or heavy paper. Hang by the handle in an out-of-the-way place.

Electric Drill

An electric drill can do so many jobs that it is almost a must in the do-it-yourselfer's toolbox. With it you can make holes in almost any material. By using its accessories and attachments you can sand, polish, grind, buff, stir paint, and drive screws.

Electric drill accessories.
Wire brush disc.
Hole saw.
SAW BLADE
PILOT BIT
Sanding disc.
ARBOR ADAPTER
Grinding wheel.
SLOTTED
PHILLIPS
Screw-driving bit.

Filing burrs from end of a cut pipe.

Files

A toolkit is not complete unless it contains at least one if not an assortment of files. A number of different types of files are in common use, and each type may range in length from 3 to 18 inches.

Files are graded according to the degree of fineness and according to whether they have single- or double-cut teeth. The selection of files calls for matching the file to the job and to the material on which it is used.

C-clamp.

C-Clamp

Named for the shape of its frame, the C-clamp holds work in place or presses two pieces together for gluing. It is handy when you use adhesive to repair furniture or objects made of metal or plastic.

A 6-inch, light-duty type with an extra-deep opening can accommodate fairly large items but adjusts by means of a screw for smaller work. A sliding handle turns the screw to tighten the clamp, and a swivel button prevents the screw end from marring the work surface. For many jobs you will need a pair.

Other Tools

There are literally hundreds of specialized tools that you may use for specific tasks. Buy these as the need arises, as your skills increase, and as you undertake more detailed work around the house — especially if you begin making improvements as well as routine repairs. Power tools will make your work easier and the results better. The ones you will probably buy are: a saber saw, for fast cutting of curved and straight lines in wood and other materials; a circular saw for extensive cutting of straight lines and invaluable for major jobs such as installing wood siding; and an electric sander, for smooth, speedy removal of wood, paint, or anything else removable by regular sandpaper.

Electric sander.

Circular saw.

Saber saw.

Written by
DONALD F. LOW

Interior
Home
Repairs

Contents

Cross section of a faucet.

HANDLE

PACKING NUT

PACKING OR O-RING

SPINDLE

WASHER

VALVE SEAT

Fix-It-Yourself!

No matter how well your house or apartment is built or how well made and expensive the fixtures are, things will go wrong occasionally. "Fix-it-yourself" has become a way of life for a generation of Americans. Some of them derive pleasure from working with tools; for most, however, it has become a necessity because the neighborhood handyman-for-hire either doesn't come or has become prohibitively expensive.

In this booklet is a selection of simple home repairs that can be executed with the most basic tools.

Every effort has been made to insure the accuracy of the information and instructions. However, we are not infallible, and neither are you. We cannot guarantee that there are no human or typographical errors herein, nor can we guarantee that you will not err in following our directions. We only hope that, if this happens, it will not discourage you from trying again.

LEAKY FAUCET

The problem: A leaky faucet wastes water • The dripping water may discolor the sink • The noise of a dripping faucet can cause daytime irritation and nighttime insomnia.

Tools you need to fix it: A screwdriver • An adjustable wrench • Assorted sizes of washers.

Fig. 2

WASHER

Fig. 3

Fig. 1

Fig. 4

The basic steps:

1. Shut off the water supply at the supply stop in the line below the faucet (the valve nearest to the faucet to be repaired). Then turn on the faucet until the water stops running.
2. Loosen packing nut with wrench (fig. 1). Wrap the nut with tape or rags to protect the chrome finish before you start.
3. Remove the faucet stem or spindle (fig. 2). Use the handle to pull out the unit.
4. Remove the screw that holds the washer at bottom of the valve unit (fig. 3).
5. Put in new washer and replace screw (fig. 4).
6. Put valve unit back in faucet and turn the handle to the proper position.
7. Turn on the water at the shut-off valve.

Note: Mixing faucets, used on sinks and bathtubs, are actually two separate units (fig. 5) with the same spout. If leaking occurs, each unit must be repaired separately.

Fig. 5

NOISY FAUCET

If a faucet squeals or chatters when you turn it on or off, take it apart as described above and check whether the washer is tightly screwed to the stem. Replace the washer if it is worn, even if the faucet does not leak.

If the stem of the faucet can be moved up and down, the threads are probably worn and the old stem must be replaced with a new one.

CLOGGED TOILET

The problem: When you flush the toilet, the water level in the bowl rises rather than recedes.

Tools you need to fix it: A plunger • A closet auger • An adjustable wrench.

The basic steps:

1. Place the plunger over the discharge opening in the toilet bowl and work it vigorously up and down. This should clear the stoppage (fig. 1).

2. If this does not help, try the auger, commonly called a snake. (Be careful not to scratch the inside of the toilet bowl.) Work the snake into the trap and crank it in one direction until it becomes tight (fig. 2). Pull it back; often it will bring the obstruction with it. If it doesn't, try again, cranking the snake until it pushes through and clears the stoppage.

3. If this also fails, bail out as much water as possible from the bowl and soak up the rest with rags.

4. Remove the toilet from the floor, using the wrench to loosen the bolts (fig. 3).

5. Put the toilet (upside down) on a piece of paper to the side.

6. Work the obstruction out through the discharge opening.

7. If it has already passed into the waste line and is stuck there, work it out with the snake (fig. 4).

8. Put the toilet back in place.

Fig. 1

Fig. 2

Fig. 3

Fig. 4

Fig. 1

Fig. 2

Fig. 3

FROZEN PIPE

The problem: No water runs through the pipe • Pipes may burst • The joints may be forced open.

Tools you need to fix it: A kettle with boiling water • A piece of burlap or cloth • A blowtorch • Electric heating cable.

The basic steps:
1. Open all faucets in the frozen line.
2. Wrap cloth or burlap around the pipe and pour boiling water over it (fig. 1). Keep on doing so until the water in the line is flowing freely.
3. The use of a blowtorch or propane torch (fig. 2) might be faster, but use it only if the pipe is in an absolutely safe location away from flammable walls or other materials.
4. If you use a torch, don't concentrate on a single spot; rather move it along the pipe toward an open faucet, so that steam generated within the pipe can escape.
5. Use of electric heating cable is the best method of thawing frozen pipes, because the entire length of the pipe is thawed at the same time (fig. 3).

CLOGGED SINK DRAIN

The problem: The sink may overflow.

Tools you need to fix it: Dry or liquid chemical drain cleaner • A plunger or a force pump • An auger • An adjustable wrench.

184

Fig. 1

The basic steps:

1. If the drain is not completely clogged, try running scalding water into it for several minutes.

2. If this doesn't work, use a chemical drain cleaner, following manufacturer's instructions.

3. If this helps, flush the drain for several minutes with hot water.

4. If the chemical doesn't work, remove the strainer from the drain and use the plunger. Make sure there is enough water in the sink to cover the plunger, providing a good seal. Work the plunger up and down until the drain is cleared and the water runs out normally (fig. 1).

5. If you prefer to use a force pump rather than the plunger, place it squarely over the drain, covered with enough water to make a firm seal.

Fig. 2

6. Pump the handle to clear away the obstruction by air pressure (fig. 2).

7. If neither plunger nor force pump does the job, look for the cleanout plug under the sink. Place a pail below it to catch the water. Remove the plug and try to clear away the obstruction (fig. 3).

8. If that doesn't work, or if there is no cleanout plug, loosen the slipnuts with the wrench and remove the trap (fig. 4).

9. If the stoppage is in the trap, remove it. If not, use the drain auger, feeding it into the drain line.

10. Rotate the auger repeatedly until the obstruction is cleared (fig. 5).

11. Reassemble the trap and run scalding water down the drain for several minutes.

Fig. 3

Fig. 4

Fig. 5

Fig. 1

Fig. 2

Note for electrical repairs: When you make a mistake in plumbing repairs, you might get wet, you might flood the basement or even the house, but it's unlikely that you would drown. Making electrical repairs, however, leaves no margin for error. If you mess up here it could result in fire, serious injury, or worse.

Always exercise a healthy respect and never "play around" with electricity.

Never work on an appliance that is plugged in (fig. 1); always disconnect the appliance first (fig. 2).

BLOWN FUSE

Fig. 1

Fig. 2

The problem: A portion of your electrical system is off
• Lamps or appliances do not work.

Materials you need to fix it: A set of fuses of the same amperage that you have in your entrance panel.

The basic steps:
1. Check the entrance panel for a blown fuse.
2. If the copper strip in the center of the fuse is melted apart (fig. 1), the cause is probably overload.
3. If the window of the fuse is darkened, perhaps so much that you can't even see the copper strip, a short circuit is the prime suspect (fig. 2).
4. If it is overload, disconnect some appliances. If it is a short, try to find where it is located.
5. If you have removed the possible source, replace the fuse, but always with one of the same amperage.
Note: It is not impossible that the temporary aberration may

have been caused by a sudden power surge. In this case merely replace the blown fuse or flip the breaker switch if you have a circuit breaker box. If the fuse does not blow again, your troubles are over.

If the entire house is plunged into darkness, either it is a general blackout or something is seriously wrong and the main fuse of the house has blown. If your neighbors *do* have light, you can exclude a general power failure and you had better call an electrician; the trouble that causes a main to blow is nothing for a do-it-yourselfer to fix.

DAMAGED ELECTRIC PLUG OR CORD

Fig. 1

The problem: A lamp or appliance does not work properly • A damaged plug is dangerous • A damaged or loose cord in a plug can cause a short circuit.

Tools you need to fix it: A new plug (if the old one cannot be used anymore) • A screwdriver • A knife or a wire stripper • A needle-nose pliers • A lineman's pliers.

The basic steps if the plug is attached to thin, flexible cord:
1. Cut the cord beyond the break (fig. 1).
2. Bare the wires at the end of the cord and reinstall the plug (fig. 2).
3. If the original plug was a molded one (fig. 3), do not bare the ends of the wires after having cut the cord; replace the original plug with a lever-type snap-on plug (fig. 4).

Note: As an alternative to the snap-on plug, you can use a squeeze-type plug: Slip body over cord (fig. 5), squeeze prongs together (fig. 6), and pull body over prongs (fig. 7).

Fig. 2

Fig. 3

Fig. 4

Fig. 5

Fig. 6

Fig. 7

Fig. 8

Fig. 9

Fig. 10

Fig. 11

The basic steps if the plug is attached to heavy appliance cord:

1. Cut the cord above the molded plug or break in the wire (fig. 8).
2. Separate the wires at the end of the cord, and strip off about ⅝ inch of insulation of each (fig. 9). A wire stripper is the best tool for the job; if you use a knife, be careful not to cut into the wire.
3. Remove the fiber insulating cover from the prongs of the plug if it is not a molded one (fig. 10).
4. Loosen the terminal screws to release the wires, then pull off the plug.
5. Untie the Underwriter's knot, if there is one.
6. Remove the old plug and slip the new one over the cord (fig. 11).
7. Tie an Underwriter's knot: separate about 3 inches of wire. Loop the black wire behind itself and the white wire (fig. 12). Loop the white wire over the end of the black and bring it up through the black loop (fig. 13).
8. Tighten the knot and pull it down snugly into the plug body (fig. 14).
9. Bend loops in the ends of the bared wires with needle-nose pliers (fig. 15).
10. Fit the wires inside the plug and place the loops clockwise around the terminal screws (fig. 16), black to brass, white to chrome.
11. Tighten the screws and replace the fiber insulating cover over the prongs of the plug.

Note: Replacement of a three-prong plug is similar. Follow all steps as above. Instead of the Underwriter's knot, tie the 3 wires together in a tight knot and pull the cord until the knot is

Fig. 12   Fig. 13   Fig. 14

Fig. 15

Fig. 16

snug against the plug. Loop the green wire clockwise around the green or dark-colored screw, the black wire around the brass screw, and the white wire around the chrome screw. Tighten the screws.

BROKEN ELECTRIC BULB

The problem: The base of the broken bulb is stuck in the socket of the lamp.

Tools and materials you need to fix it: A wad of newspaper • Needle-nose pliers • A screwdriver.

The basic steps:
1. Unplug the lamp.
2. Wad up newspaper, press it down firmly on the broken bulb, and turn it counterclockwise until the bulb base is removed (fig. 1).
3. If this does not work because the glass is broken off right down to the base, try turning it out with needle-nose pliers (fig. 2).
4. If it still won't come out, wedge a screwdriver inside the base, pressing it against the sides while turning until the base is removed (fig. 3).

Fig. 1

Fig. 2

Fig. 3

DAMAGED CORD OF A TABLE LAMP

The problem: Lamp does not light or flickers • Damaged cord might cause a short circuit or even a fire.

Tools you need to fix it: A screwdriver • A knife • An open-end wrench.

The basic steps:
1. Unplug the lamp.
2. Remove shade and bulb from the lamp (fig. 1).
3. Pry off felt pad on lamp base carefully with a knife (fig. 2).
4. If the base contains a weight, remove the nut holding it in place and take the weight out (fig. 3).
5. Lift the tube that runs through the lamp body about 6 inches out of the top (fig. 4). Turn the tube counterclockwise or loosen the setscrew (or both, depending on the installation) to remove the tube from the lamp socket.
6. Press in at bottom of the socket's metal outer shell (fig. 5).
7. Lift the outer shell straight up (fig. 6).
8. Loosen the terminal screws and remove the wire (fig. 7).
9. Pull out the old cord at the bottom of the lamp (fig. 8).
10. Thread new cord through the tube.

Fig. 1

Fig. 2

Fig. 3

Fig. 4

PRESS

Fig. 5

Fig. 6

Fig. 7

Fig. 8

190

11. Strip the ends of the wires and attach them to the terminals on the socket, then reassemble (fig. 9).

Fig. 9

DAMAGED LAMP SOCKET

The problem: The lamp switch, incorporated in the socket, is worn and the lamp cannot be turned on or off properly.

Tools you need to fix it: A screwdriver.

The basic steps:
1. Unplug the lamp, remove shade and bulb.
2. Remove the socket as described above and shown in Figures 5, 6, 7.
3. Buy a new socket (take the old one with you to get a replacement of the same type).
4. Remove the outer and the insulated shell from the new socket and loosen the terminal screws.
5. Fit the cord through the new socket cap and install the wires on the screws, looping them around so that, as the screws are tightened, the ends of the wires are tightened around them (fig. 1).
6. Fasten new socket cap on tube (fig. 2).
7. Pull the wire through the lamp bottom until the socket sits firmly in the cap (fig. 3).
8. Place the insulated shell over the socket (fig. 4).
9. Press the bottom into the cap; it should snap securely in place (fig. 5).
10. Reassemble the lamp.

Fig. 1

Fig. 2

Fig. 3

Fig. 4

Fig. 5

191

BROKEN WINDOW

The problem: Loss of heat in winter • Loss of cool air in summer • Rain and snow may ruin draperies and carpets.

Tools and materials you need to fix it: Window glass • A glass cutter • A putty knife • A small wood chisel • Putty or glazing compound • Pliers • A hammer • Glazier's points.

The basic steps:
Work from the outside of the window.
1. Remove broken pieces of glass from the frame, wearing heavy work gloves (fig. 1).
2. Clean out old putty with a small wood chisel (fig. 2). Be careful not to damage the frame.
3. Extract glazier's points with pliers (fig. 3).
4. Mark replacement glass with a sharpened crayon. It should be $1/16$ inch smaller all around than the frame opening.
5. Score the glass with a glass cutter, using a steel straightedge to guide the cut (fig. 4).
6. Lay the glass over the edge of the work table and apply pressure on both sides of the score to break it cleanly (fig. 5).
7. If the piece to be broken off is very narrow, snap it off with the slotted head of the cutting tool (fig. 6).
8. Paint the groove in the frame with linseed oil to prevent drying out and cracking of the body (fig. 7).
9. Apply ⅛ inch thickness of putty all around the frame (fig. 8).
10. Press the glass into place, making sure it lies flat against the shoulders of the frame (fig. 9).
11. Insert glazier's points. Tap them in carefully to avoid breaking the glass. Points should be placed all around the frame every 4 to 6 inches (fig. 10).
12. Roll some more putty into a "rope" about ½ inch thick. Use your fingers to press it against the wood and glass around the frame.
13. Smooth and bevel the putty with the blade of a putty knife (fig. 11). The putty should form a smooth seal around the window.

Note: For metal windows special clips are used instead of glazier's points (fig. 12). If there are metal strips screw them back into place.

Fig. 1

Fig. 2

Fig. 3

Fig. 4

Fig. 5

Fig. 6

Fig. 7

Fig. 8

Fig. 9

Fig. 10

Fig. 11

Fig. 12

Fig. 1

Fig. 2

DAMAGED SCREEN

Fig. 3

Fig. 4

The problem: Insects come through holes in the screen • Small holes tend to become larger • New screens are expensive.

Tools and materials you need to fix it: Heavy-duty scissors • A ruler or a small block of wood with straight edges • Screening or ready-cut screen patches • Waterproof cement.

The basic steps:
1. Trim the hole in the screen to make smooth edges.
2. Cut a rectangular patch of wire screen material ½ inch larger than the hole.
3. Unravel two wires at each side of the patch (fig. 1).
4. Bend the ends of the wires at a right angle on all four sides (fig. 2); use the block of wood or the edge of a ruler to do this.
5. Put the patch over the hole from the outside. Hold it tight against the screen so that the bent wire ends go through the screen (fig. 3).
6. From the inside, bend the ends of the wires toward the center of the hole (fig. 4). You may need someone outside to press against the patch while you do this, to secure the patch firmly.

Note: If the hole in the screen is very small, a drop or two of waterproof cement will do the job (fig. 5); the cement hardens into a film that covers the hole.

Fig. 5

194

Fig. 1 Fig. 2 Fig. 3 Fig. 4

STICKING WINDOW

The problem: You cannot open the window.

Tools and materials you need to fix it: A hammer or a mallet • A hatchet • A screwdriver • A chisel • A paint scraper • A wood block • Lubricating oil.

The basic steps to repair a paint-stuck window:
1. Tap along both sides of the window with a hammer or mallet on a block of wood (fig. 1).
2. If this does not free the window, insert the blade of a paint scraper or a broad, thin chisel between the sash and the stop molding (fig. 2).
3. Tap the blade in with a hammer, then rock the tool back and forth gently to force the sash back from the molding. Repeat this at several points on each side of the sash until the window moves freely again. Never use a screwdriver for this purpose, as it will leave marks in the wood.
4. If all this doesn't help, hammer a hatchet or any broad, hard metal wedge along the bottom of the sash. Pry as you go along (fig. 3). Do this from the outside, to avoid damaging the finish of the window and windowsill.
5. Once the window is free, scrape off any crust of paint at the back face of the stop molding (fig. 4).
6. Sand the molding lightly and touch up the window track.

The basic steps to repair a window that is permanently swollen out of shape:
1. Cut a block of wood that will fit snugly into the channel between the inside and outside window stops above or below the sash.

Fig. 1

2. Give the block several taps with a hammer at both sides of the window (fig. 1).

3. This should free the sash so that it can be raised (or lowered) at least partially. Repeat the procedure at the exposed channels at the bottom or top (fig. 2).

4. Apply a lubricant such as paraffin or candle wax to the channels.

5. If this doesn't help, take out the window (fig. 3).

6. Remove stop molding on a window that has sash cords (fig. 4).

7. Disengage sash cord at both sides (fig. 5).

8. Keep sash cord from slipping past pulley with a nail or a strip of wood (fig. 6).

9. If the pulley is stiff, lubricate it with a few drops of oil (fig. 7).

10. Sand or plane the wood of the sash to make it fit.

11. Reassemble the window.

Note: If a window has tension strips, try first to adjust them by turning their mounting screws (fig. 8). If this doesn't do the trick, remove the tension strips and proceed as in Steps 10 and 11.

Fig. 2

Fig. 3

Fig. 4

Fig. 5

Fig. 6

Fig. 7

Fig. 8

Written by
DONALD F. LOW

Exterior
Home
Repairs

Contents

Emergency arsenal.

Emergency Repairs

When the wind starts to howl and the snow is piling up, the home owner should be prepared and be aware that just about anything might happen. He has to be armed with at least enough emergency tools to have a fighting chance. The emergency tool kit should include a claw hammer, an assortment of nails, a screwdriver, pliers, a knife, a staple gun with a good supply of staples, and at least one flashlight. Also included in the emergency supplies should be a couple of kerosene lanterns, a supply of candles, a loaded calking gun, a can of asphalt cement, a shovel, a couple of large plastic sheets, a roll of masking tape, wire and rope, and several lengths of 1 x 2 or 1 x 3 lumber. It's handy to have rock salt and/or an electric heating cable to attack ice buildup.

BROKEN WINDOW

Fig. 1

The problem: Loss of heat in winter • Loss of cool air in summer • Rain and snow may ruin drapes and carpets • Weather conditions at the moment prevent you from making a permanent repair.

Tools and materials you need: A staple gun • Plastic sheets • Masking tape.

The basic steps for temporary repair:
1. Staple the sheeting around the window frame (fig.1).
2. Double it at the edges for additional strength.
3. Seal the edges with masking tape.

199

ROOF LEAK

Fig. 2

The problem: Rain or snow will seep into the house • It would be foolish to attempt to go on the roof to make repairs when it is wet or covered with ice or snow.

Tools and materials you need: A claw hammer • A piece of wire • Asphalt roofing cement • A piece of wood • Nails.

The basic steps for emergency repairs from the inside:
1. If the leak is not easily visible because water flows along the roofboards or rafters before dripping down, probe with a wire until you find it (fig.2).
2. Coat the leaking area with asphalt roofing cement (fig.3).
3. Cut a 1 x 6 or similar board to fit between the rafters, and toenail it in place beneath the asphalt patch (fig.4).
Note: After the storm subsides it may be possible to make a temporary repair from above provided the leak is close enough to the edge of the roof so that you can reach it from a ladder:
1. Slip a plastic sheet under the course of shingles above the leaking area and staple it to the roof (fig.5).
2. Calk around the edges (fig.6).
3. Nail 1 x 2 strips around the exposed edges. Later, when you make a permanent repair, the nail holes will have to be filled, but this is certainly better than having water pour through the leak.

Fig. 3

Fig. 4

Fig. 5

Fig. 6

200

BURST WATER PIPE

Fig. 7

Fig. 8

The problem: Flooding • Ruining of floors, ceilings, and walls.

Tools and materials you need: A piece of sheet rubber or a section of garden hose • Hose clamps or C-clamps.

The basic steps for temporary repair:
1. Close shutoff valve nearest leak (fig.7). If there is no shutoff nearby, turn off the main intake valve.
2. If the water is still running, because of a worn or damaged valve, wrap a piece of sheet rubber firmly around the leaky section and clamp it tightly; special clamps for this are available in various pipe sizes (fig.8).
3. Instead of sheet rubber you can cut a section of garden hose, slit it, and place it over the leak, holding it in place with a C-clamp.
Note: Permanent repairs should be made as soon as possible.

ICY WALKS

The problem: An invitation to injuries and lawsuits.

Materials you need: Rock salt • Clean sand.

The basic steps:
1. Sprinkle plenty of rock salt on the icy walks. This chemical melter has the disadvantage that it may do some damage to concrete as well as corrosion to cars that are driven over it (small consequences compared to the alternatives).
2. You might also consider keeping a large supply of clean sand and using it to skidproof walks and driveways.

Assuming the Role of "Handyman"

DAMAGED PORCH FLOORBOARDS

The problem: Boards or planks are broken • Boards or planks have holes or are badly splintered.

Tools and materials you need: A framing square • An electric drill or a brace and bit • A wood chisel • A mallet • Aluminum or galvanized flooring or finishing nails • A nailset • Replacement flooring • Wood filler.

Fig. 1

The basic steps: (The damaged section must be cut away over the nearest joists. Be very careful not to mar the surrounding boards).

1. With a framing square, mark off the section of board to be removed at an exact right angle to the boards (fig.1).

2. Drill large, interconnected holes inside the lines on both sides of the damaged section with an electric drill or a brace and bit (fig.2).

3. Break out the damaged portion with a wood chisel by striking along the grain (fig.3).

4. Remove the pieces, being particularly careful not to damage the tongue or groove of the boards on either side.

5. Chisel out the remainder of the board on the outside of the drilled holes, making sure that you cut exactly on the line (fig.4), pull out any remaining nails, and clean away all debris.

6. Put a replacement board along the removed section and mark carefully where the damaged section was, again at an exact right angle, using the framing square (fig.5).

7. Saw along the lines and chisel off the *bottom* of the grooved edge (fig.6) so that the board will slip into the open space. (Leave the top portion of the grooved edge.)

8. Slip the board into place (fig.7).

9. Nail through the top with aluminum or galvanized flooring or finishing nails. Use two nails on each end.

10. Set the nails with a nailset (fig.8) and cover with wood filler.

Fig. 2

Fig. 3

Fig. 4

Fig. 5

Fig. 6

Fig. 7

Fig. 8

Fig. 1

DETERIORATED PORCH RAILING

The problem: Rail and/or baluster has rotted.

Tools you need: A hammer • Nails • Replacement rail and/or baluster.

The basic steps:
1. Knock out the deteriorated pieces with a hammer.
2. Replace rotted rail with a new one, nailing it to the baluster.
3. Replace baluster if you can find a matching piece, or take the old one to a millworking shop and have a new one turned.
4. Without complicated joinery, nail through the rail into the baluster or toenail the baluster to the rail (fig.1).

WORN PORCH STEPS

Fig. 1

Fig. 2

The problem: Treads or risers are loose, sagging, broken, or warped.

Tools and materials you need: A wrecking bar • A hammer • Aluminum or galvanized finishing nails • A nailset • A rasp • Sandpaper • Wood putty.

The basic steps:
1. Pry up worn tread with a wrecking bar (fig.1).
2. Turn it over and nail it in place, bottom side up, with aluminum or galvanized finishing nails (fig.2).
3. Set the nails and fill the holes with wood putty.
4. Duplicate rounded edges with a rasp and sandpaper.

Note: When new treads or risers are needed, take an old one to the lumberyard and try to find a match. Apply wood preservative to new wood before nailing in place.

HEAVED OR SETTLED BRICK
IN BRICK-IN-SAND PATIO

The problem: Uneven surfaces are dangerous.

Tools and materials you need: An old screwdriver • A shovel • A broom • Sand.

Fig. 1 Fig. 2 Fig. 3

Fig. 4 Fig. 5 Fig. 6

The basic steps:

1. Dislodge the first heaved or sunk brick with an old screwdriver (fig.1).

2. Lift out the adjacent bricks by hand.

3. If the brick has settled, lay in some extra sand—any sand will do for this, even beach sand (fig.2)—and tamp it down well.

4. Watering helps to settle the sand and compact it (fig.3).

5. When the bed is satisfactory, reinstall the bricks the same way they were laid before, butted tightly against one another (fig.4).

6. When all have been replaced, spread more sand over the top (fig.5).

7. Work the sand down between the cracks with a stiff-bristled broom (fig.6).

8. Spray the patio with a hose, then sweep in more sand. (It may take three or more similar applications before the brick is again locked into position and no more sand can be worked in.)

HEAVED OR SETTLED BRICK IN MORTARED BRICK PATIOS

(Since mortared brick patios should be set on top of a concrete base slab, heaving or settling of the brick itself should be relatively rare.)

Fig. 7

Fig. 8

Fig. 9

The problem: Uneven surfaces are dangerous.

Tools you need: A brick chisel or a cold chisel • A wrecking bar • A trowel • Mortar.

The basic steps:
1. Chip out mortar (fig.7).
2. Pry up settled brick (fig.8).
3. Lay in enough new mortar to bring the surface level with the rest (fig.9). Standard or common brick is nominally 2¾ inches in depth, counting mortar, with the actual brick size 2¼ inches. But not all brick is alike, so measure what you have. For mortar, it is easiest to purchase premixed mortar from a masonry or building supply dealer.
4. When the brick is heaved, the brick and mortar must be removed and the concrete base chipped off to bring it down to the surrounding level.
5. Then proceed as above.

HEAVED, SETTLED, OR BROKEN STONES IN FLAGSTONE PATIO

(Flagstone patios, whether they are built with random shaped and colored stones or with matched rectangular stones, are constructed the same way as brick patios.)

The problem: Uneven surfaces are dangerous.

Tools you need: A piece of pipe, or a wood dowel, or a steel rod • A pry bar • A trowel • A cold chisel • A mash hammer.

The basic steps:
1. Place a piece of pipe or a wood dowel or a steel rod next to the stone to be removed.
2. Lift the stone with the pry bar just enough to rest a corner on the rod.

3. Shove the stone onto the rod and roll it away so that you can work beneath.

4. If the stone has been broken badly, it must be replaced. The replacement is easier to find with random shaped and colored stones, since they don't have to match their mates in either size or shape. It can be somewhat smaller but not larger.

5. Fill in the surrounding spaces with mortar.

6. If you can't find a matching rectangular stone as a replacement, ask a stone dealer to cut one to your specifications—it is difficult to do this yourself. If you have to cut it yourself, it can be done with a cold chisel and a heavy mash hammer. First score a line on all sides with the chisel, then keep banging at it on one side and then the other until it breaks.

HEAVED SIDEWALK

Fig. 1

The problem: Small cracks in sidewalks are becoming larger • It can cause accidents to you and your family • You are responsible if strangers are hurt.

Tools and materials you need: A sledgehammer or a jackhammer • An ax • A trowel • Wire reinforcing mesh • Vinyl or epoxy patching mix.

The basic steps:

1. If weather conditions prevent a complete repair, it will help to avoid accidents if you create a slope around the heaved portion of walk. Use vinyl or epoxy patching mix to smooth the section as best you can (fig.1). But vow to do a complete repair job in the not-too-distant future.

Fig. 2

2. For permanent repair, break up the old section using a sledgehammer or, if you can rent or borrow one, a jackhammer (fig.2).

3. When the old concrete has been removed, you can determine whether or not tree roots are the cause of the trouble. If so, take an ax and cut off the offending roots

4. If no roots are found, you can assume that Jack Frost did the dirty deed. In that case, it is wise to install wire reinforcing mesh (fig.3) before pouring the new section.

CRACKED BLACKTOP DRIVEWAYS

Fig. 3

The problem: The potholes can damage your car • You can hurt yourself • Water and oil can seep through and attack from underneath.

Fig. 1

Fig. 2

Fig. 3

Fig. 4

Tools and materials you need: A shovel • A metal tamper • Blacktop patch • An applicator for sealer.

The basic steps:

1. Remove the deteriorated sections when blacktop starts to crack and break up.
2. Dig out the area underneath (fig.1).
3. Fill in with the old broken-up blacktop.
4. Tamp down the subgrade thoroughly (fig.2) and fill with gravel or other solid material if the depth is more than 2 inches.
5. Pour in new blacktop patch (available at reasonable cost from most building supply dealers) and smooth over the top with a shovel (fig.3).
6. Tamp down thoroughly again (fig.4). A metal tamper is a necessity. You should be able to rent one.
7. Keep tamping until the patch is smooth and level, then run over it a few times with your car's tires (fig.5). Do this as gently as possible. Your car is merely acting as a roller.
8. Let the patch dry and harden for a few days.

Note: To prevent cracking, a good sealer should be applied every year or two.

Blacktop must not be applied when the temperature is likely to fall below 50° F.

Fig. 5

Fig. 1

Fig. 2

DEFECTIVE MORTAR JOINTS IN BRICK WALLS

Fig. 3

Fig. 4

The problem: Joints may become porous • Bricks may become loose • Air and moisture enter the wall.

Tools and materials you need: A ballpeen or mash hammer • A cold chisel • A pointed trowel • A wire brush • A dowel • Mortar mix.

The basic steps:

1. Chisel out loose or crumbling mortar (fig.1).
2. Clean the joint with a wire brush and wet it thoroughly (fig.2).
3. Mix the mortar, following the directions on the package (you can buy a prepared mortar mix at your hardware or building supply store).
4. Force the mortar into the joint with the trowel (fig.3).
5. Form it with the point of the trowel to match the surrounding mortar joints (fig.4).
6. A concave joint can be formed by using a dowel or a small piece of pipe to finish off the new mortar (fig.5).
7. If the mortar joints of an entire wall become porous, either because of age or of poor original workmanship, apply a clear waterproofing compound, available at masonry and building supply stores, to each joint (fig.6).

Fig. 5

Fig. 6

LOOSE OR BADLY DAMAGED BRICK

The problem: Other bricks may be affected • Air and moisture enter the wall.

Tools and materials you need: A ballpeen or mash hammer • A cold chisel • A pointed trowel • Mortar.

The basic steps:
1. Chisel out the mortar all around the loose or damaged brick (fig.7). Be careful not to damage the surrounding bricks.
2. Take out the loose or damaged brick.
3. Chisel away any remaining mortar in the opening and clean away dust and debris.
4. Wet down the opening.
5. Apply mortar to the sides and back of the opening (fig.8).
6. Dampen the replacement brick.
7. Coat it with mortar and press it into place (fig.9).
8. Finish the mortar joint with a trowel.

Note: In brick veneer walls, the brick is laid against a wood-sheathed wall behind it, attached by small metal clips (fig.10). To allow proper drainage of this cavity, there are usually weep holes along the base of the wall to permit water to run off. Make sure that these holes are not blocked, either by dirt or fallen mortar, and clean them out occasionally with stiff wire or a masonry drill (fig.11).

Fig. 7

Fig. 8

DAMAGED WOOD SIDING

The problem: Boards are loose, warped, or split • Cracks have developed • Air and moisture enter the wall.

Tools and materials you need: A putty knife • A chisel • A claw hammer • Nails • Waterproof glue • Lead-base putty.

Fig. 9

Fig. 10

Fig. 11

Fig. 1

Fig. 2

Fig. 3

Fig. 4

The basic steps:

1. Fill small cracks with lead-base putty.
2. Work putty into the crack with the putty knife (fig.1).
3. If a board has split along the grain, pry up the loose portion of the board and apply waterproof glue along the split (fig.2).
4. Press the split together and drive galvanized nails beneath the board to hold the edges together until the glue is dry (fig.3).
5. Remove the nails and fill the holes with putty.

Note: Loose wood shingles can be secured with galvanized or aluminum serrated nails driven along the edges (fig.4).

LOOSE OR CRACKED ASBESTOS CEMENT SHINGLES

Fig. 5

The problem: Air and moisture seep in, causing more deterioration.

Tools you need: An electric drill • A claw hammer • Nails • A nailset • A chisel • Pliers • A hacksaw.

Fig. 6

The basic steps:

1. Drill pilot holes for the nails when you are repairing a material such as asbestos cement shingles, which are very brittle (fig.5).
2. Countersink nails (fig.6).
3. Fill holes with putty.

Fig. 7

Fig. 8

Fig. 9

Fig. 10

4. Paint over putty.

5. Break off cracked or otherwise damaged shingles piece by piece, striking them with a hammer and chisel (fig. 7); be careful not to damage the surrounding siding.

6. Exposed nails can be pulled out with pliers (fig. 8).

7. Cut the nails of the shingle above with a hacksaw.

8. Another method is to drill the nails through the outside (fig. 9), slip the replacement shingle of the same size into position, and drill pilot holes for nails.

9. Use a nailset to drive the nails home so that the hammer does not damage the new shingle.

10. Some asbestos shingles are attached to boards, usually about 4 feet in length. When one of these is damaged, it is generally advisable to replace the entire panel (fig. 10). This is done in the same way as replacing individual shingles.

CALKING AIR LEAKS AROUND WINDOWS, DOORS, FAUCETS, CHIMNEYS, ETC.

The problem: Big heating and cooling bills • Moisture, dust, and dirt come through cracks • Insects enter the house through them • Water seeps through cracks around the chimney.

Calking gun and cartridge.

Tools and materials you need: A calking gun • A putty knife or other scraping tool • A screwdriver • Calking compound (polyvinyl acetate type, in both rope and bulk form) • Cleaning fluid • A ladder.

The basic steps:

1. Load the calking gun and make a thorough examination of the outside of the house, looking for any area where air could leak in (wherever two different materials or parts of the house meet).

211

Fig. 1

Fig. 2

Fig. 3

Fig. 4

Fig. 5

2. Before applying calking compound, clean the area of paint buildup, dirt, or deteriorated calk, using solvent and a putty knife or other scraping tool (fig.1).

3. For extra long cracks, use calking compound that comes in rope form. Force it into the cracks with the fingers or a screwdriver (fig.2).

4. Draw a good bead of calk with the gun, and make sure the bead overlaps both sides for a tight seal around windows (fig.3), around water faucets that penetrate the outside house surface (fig.4), around the chimney (fig.5), and between the main body of the house and the porch (fig.6).

Note: Estimating the number of cartridges of calking compound needed is difficult, since the number will vary greatly with the size of the cracks to be filled. If possible, it's best to start with a half dozen cartridges and then purchase more as the job continues and you need more.

Calking a house usually requires the use of a ladder. Be sure you use it safely. Carry the calking gun in a sling (fig.7) so that you can use both hands climbing the ladder, and don't try to reach for that extra bit (fig.8). Get down and move the ladder.

Fig. 6

Fig. 7

Fig. 8

212

Fig. 1

CLOGGED OR LEAKING GUTTERS
AND DOWNSPOUTS

Fig. 2

Fig. 3

The problem: Water stands in the gutter • Water overflows or spills over the edge of the gutter • Water leaks from the gutter or downspout and seeps into the earth around the building, causing wet basements, wood decay, peeling paint, and even termite damage.

Tools and materials you need: A pail • A putty knife • A hammer • A screwdriver • Gutter hangers • Galvanized nails • Galvanized screws • Gutter guards • Electric heating cable • A garden hose • Wood preservatives • Exterior paint • Roofing cement • Tarpaper • Asphalt cement.

The basic steps:
1. Inspect and clean gutter and downspouts at least twice a year.
2. Remove all leaves and other debris from the gutter and check for loose joints.
3. Check gutter pitch by pouring a pail of water in the end of the gutter opposite the downspout or leader end (fig.1). Because water seeks its own level, a slight downward pitch to the drainage end of the gutter is necessary.
4. Make note of the areas where water accumulates.
5. To increase the pitch or elevate a sagging length of gutter, install gutter hangers (fig.2). They are available at most hardware stores.
6. If gutter hangers are already in place, check them for tightness; if loose, renail with a galvanized nail or tighten with a galvanized screw.
7. Install gutter guards (fig.3), which will prevent leaves and debris from accumulating.
8. Check the gutter outlet opening where the water flows into the downspout. It should have either a leaf guard or a leaf

Fig. 4

strainer (fig.4); clean debris from the guard or strainer and replace in position.

9. With a good strainer properly installed, downspouts rarely become clogged. Nonetheless, it is a good idea to flush them out once a year with a garden hose (fig.5), thus forcing out small particles that could accumulate and become a clogging problem.

10. All gutters should slant outward (fig.6).

11. Check that the outsides of the gutters are hung lower than the edge of the roof eaves. In winter this allows ice to slide off without taking the gutter along.

12. If this does not prevent snow or ice buildup, install electric heating cables where accumulation is a problem (fig.7).

Note: Wood gutters, rare today, should be treated with wood preservatives and then coated with exterior paint. Lining the inside of these gutters with roofing cement will further prevent decay. Small holes in wood gutters can be patched with pieces of tarpaper and asphalt cement (fig.8).

Fig. 5

Fig. 6

Fig. 7

Fig. 8

Compiled by
CHRISTOPHER SETON

Credit

WHAT YOU SHOULD KNOW ABOUT IT

Contents

Quick Credit Guide

A. Spend wisely • B. Know the cost of credit • C. Before you sign • D. Understand the annual percentage rate.

A. SPEND WISELY

• Wise use of consumer credit begins with wise spending.
• Must you buy now? Can you wait a little and pay more of it in cash?
• Is having something NOW worth the extra cost of credit?
• Does your decision fit into your family's budget and plans?
• Can you meet the new payments, plus all other existing payments?
Will you have money left for emergencies?

B. KNOW THE COST OF CREDIT

• Credit comes from stores, dealers, finance companies, credit unions, and banks.
• Do you know how much you are paying for the use of credit?
• The Truth in Lending law requires that you be told the dollar amount of finance charge — total cost of the credit including interest, service, and carrying charges, plus any charges for required insurance — and the annual percentage rate.

C. BEFORE YOU SIGN

• Read and understand the contract. Don't rush.
• Never sign a contract with spaces left blank.
• Be sure the contract tells:
  • Exactly what you are buying.
  • Purchase price.
  • Down payment and trade-in allowance.
  • Amount borrowed.
  • Total amount due.
  • Interest and service charge in dollars and the annual percentage rate.
• Know to whom you make payments, and when payments are due.
• What if you can't pay on time? Or if you pay ahead?
• What are seller's commitments for maintenance, service, or replacement?
• Be sure you get a copy of the contract to keep.
• How much cash will you actually get?
• How much will you have to repay?
• What are the interest, service, and other charges?
• What is the annual percentage rate?
• What if you miss a payment?
• How does the lender figure the balance due if you refinance?
• If you pay ahead of time is there a penalty? Will you get a refund?

D. UNDERSTAND THE ANNUAL PERCENTAGE RATE

• If you borrow $100 for one year for a finance charge of $6 and at the end of the year repay $106, the annual percentage rate is 6 percent. You have use of the $100 all year.
• If you repay the $100 plus $6 finance charge (total of $106) during the year in equal monthly payments, the annual percentage rate is 11.1 percent. You have use of only about half the $100 for the full year.

• The annual percentage rates for typical charges based on amount borrowed and repaid in 12 equal monthly installments are:

Finance Charge	Annual Percentage Rate
$6 per $100 per year	11.1%
$8 per $100 per year	14.8%
$10 per $100 per year	18.5%
$12 per $100 per year	22.2%

• Some interest rates are quoted on a monthly basis; for example, 1½% per month on the unpaid balance. But remember that this is only for one month. The annual percentage rate would be 12 times the monthly rate, or 18 percent.

• The annual percentage rates for typical monthly rates are:

Rate Per Month	Annual Percentage Rate
¾ of 1%	9%
1%	12%
1¼%	15%
1½%	18%
2%	24%
2½%	30%

• If the monthly percentage rate is based on unpaid balance, you will pay a lower dollar finance charge than if based on the previous month's balance (before any payment is deducted).

• Use only the annual percentage rate when comparing the cost of credit from different lenders and creditors.

What You Should Know About Credit

Credit has many forms: installment buying, revolving accounts, credit cards, charge cards, buying on time. Whatever it is called, credit is an arrangement to receive cash, goods, or services now and pay later. For example, if a lender hands you money, if a store lets you take a washing machine to keep, or if a garage repairs your car and you pay later, you are using credit.

Whether you will pay more by using credit rather than cash depends on how soon you pay. Many stores and bank credit cards allow you to pay within 25 or 30 days without an extra charge. Unless you pay all that you owe, you will be billed for an extra amount of money called a finance charge. The Federal Consumer Credit Protection Act, popularly known as the Truth in Lending law, requires lenders to express interest or carrying charges with the words "finance charge."

When you remember that the bank, store, or garage has to pay its bills such as wages, heat, electricity, and insurance while it is waiting to receive payments from you, you should not be surprised when credit costs you extra money in the form of a finance charge.

Credit can be a help or a hindrance, depending on how you use it. It has helped many families to furnish a home, buy a car, and meet all kinds of financial emergencies. It also has caused many families worry, hardship, and loss.

You are urged to use installment credit by merchants who want to sell their goods and by banks and loan companies that want to lend their money. You are encouraged with promises of "loans on your signature," "no money down," and "very easy payments." You can easily be carried away by such promises. It is wise to learn the facts about installment credit so that you can make sensible decisions about it.

Consumers can obtain installment credit in a number of places. Retail merchants offer credit in the form of deferred payments for goods you take and use while you are paying for them. Banks, credit unions, finance companies, and small loan companies lend money, which you repay in small amounts at a time.

Buying on the Installment Plan

When you buy goods on the installment plan, you pay more than when you buy for cash. When you get an installment loan, you pay back more than you receive. The installment seller or lender adds a charge to cover such costs as investigating to find out if you are a good credit risk; the work of making out the contract, collecting the installments, and keeping the records; and interest on his money while you have the use of it. He may also add the cost of filing fees, insurance to protect him from loss should you die before the debt is paid, and other charges.

Some merchants and lenders charge more for credit than others. Charges for different kinds of loans differ, too. The credit rate is usually higher for small than large loans and for unsecured than for secured loans.

For example, the rate is higher when the lender has only your signature or promise to assure him of getting his money back (this is an "unsecured" loan) than when you put up a car, refrigerator, bonds, or some other security he can take if you do not pay.

How Credit Charges Are Figured

Lenders use different methods of figuring credit charges on installment purchases and loans. There are two common methods. One is to calculate the amount you owe for credit each time you pay an installment. It is figured as a percentage of the debt you owe at that time (the "unpaid balance"), so it gets smaller as the debt decreases.

The lender quotes the charge as a certain percentage of the unpaid balance per month. Notice that this is per month and not per year. If you want to know the rate per year, multiply the monthly rate by 12. Here are some typical monthly rates and corresponding yearly rates:

If the Monthly Rate Is	The Rate Per Year (Annual Percentage Rate)
¾ of 1%	9%
1%	12%
1½%	18%
2%	24%
2½%	30%
3%	36%

Spend wisely.

This method of calculating credit charges is generally used by credit unions and small loan companies. Retail merchants use it for revolving or budget charge accounts.

Another way of figuring credit charges is to calculate the credit charge all at one time, when you get the loan or make the installment purchase. It is figured as a percentage of the total amount you borrow or the price of the item you buy. The charge for the entire loan period is added to the loan by some lenders and subtracted from it by others. Then the total is divided into installments.

The lender may quote the charge as a certain number of dollars per $100 per year — say, $8 or $10 per $100. Take a loan at $8 per $100 as an example. If the lender adds the charge ("add-on" method), you receive $100 and pay back $108. If he subtracts it ("discount" method), you receive $92 and pay back $100.

A credit charge of $8 or $10 per $100 per year on these loans appears to be 8 or 10 percent a year, and the lender sometimes quotes it that way. Actually, however, since you do not have the use of the entire $100 for a whole year, the true annual rate is much higher than that. In fact, it turns out to be about double. (*See Table 1.*)

Usually banks and sales finance companies use either the add-on

Table 1			
THE ANNUAL RATES ON LOANS REPAID IN 12 MONTHLY INSTALLMENTS			
If the Credit Charge per Year Is:	The Quoted Rate per Year Is:	The True Rate per Year Is:	
		For "add-on"	For "discount"
$ 4 per $100	4%	7.4%	7.7%
$ 6 per $100	6%	11.1%	11.8%
$ 8 per $100	8%	14.8%	16.1%
$10 per $100	10%	18.5%	20.5%
$12 per $100	12%	22.2%	25.2%

or the discount method of calculating credit charges when they make loans for buying cars and other consumer durable goods. The retail dealer usually figures your debt by the add-on method when you buy equipment or furniture on time. He is likely to quote you the total credit charge in dollars rather than the credit rate.

You should also be aware that lenders sometimes add more charges on top of the add-on or discount rates they quote. These may include charges for investigation of your credit rating, credit insurance, filing fees, and others. Watch for these extras, for they make the true annual credit rate higher.

You may have to pay very high rates for credit, especially when you compare them with the rate of interest you receive on your savings. Think of this if you have savings you could use instead of credit.

Credit costs may be easier to understand if you see them in dollars rather than percentages. Here is how the dollar cost of a loan on a new car worked out for one buyer—a fairly typical case. He bought a car priced at $5,575, received $1,275 for his old car as a trade-in, and made a cash down payment of $800. He financed the rest of the cost through the dealer (who probably turned it over to a sales finance company), who added $141 to cover insurance for the loan. The buyer agreed to pay 36 monthly installments of $119.

Calculations to find out the dollar cost were:

(1) Price of the car $5,575
(2) Value of trade-in $1,275
(3) Cash down payment . . . . $ 800
(4) Total down payment (2) + (3) $2,075
(5) To be financed on car cost (1) − (4) $3,500
(6) Loan insurance . . . . $ 141
(7)   Total to be financed (5) + (6) $3,641
(8) 36 payments of $119 each $4,284
(9) Dollar cost of credit (8) − (7) . . . . $ 643
(10) Annual percentage rate 11.74%

This buyer paid $643 more for his car than if he had bought it for cash. This is not an unusually large amount to pay for credit on a major purchase like an automobile.

Here is an example of how dollar costs can add up on smaller purchases. Many families equip their homes (or replace household equipment) by buying pieces one by one on the installment plan.

Let's say a family plans to buy a washing machine, a dryer, a refrigerator, an electric range, and a vacuum cleaner. Buying them from a mail-order company, one after the other, the family would pay about $400 more for them on the company's installment purchase plan than by paying cash. The credit price would be about $2,060; the cash price, $1,660. By planning and saving ahead, the family could pay cash and save enough to buy another convenience —perhaps an air conditioner, a TV set, or a piece of furniture.

Table 2 gives the dollar cost of credit charges on a debt of $1,000, at different credit rates. It shows how the cost mounts when you take longer to pay off a debt. Take a loan of $1,000 at an add-on rate of $8 per $100 per year as an example. The credit charge would cost $80 if you repaid the debt in 12 monthly payments, but $240 if you took 36 months to pay it. It would be to your advantage to choose as short a repayment period as you could manage.

Table 2

DOLLAR COST OF CREDIT CHARGES ON A $1,000 LOAN AT DIFFERENT CREDIT RATES, REPAID IN DIFFERENT NUMBERS OF INSTALLMENTS

Credit Rate	Dollar Cost of Credit Charges When Number of Monthly Installments Is:					
	12	18	24	30	36	42
"Add-on" rate (added to beginning amount of debt):						
$ 4 per $100 per year	$ 40	$ 60	$ 80	$100	$120	$140
$ 6 per $100 per year	$ 60	$ 90	$120	$150	$180	$210
$ 8 per $100 per year	$ 80	$120	$160	$200	$240	$280
$10 per $100 per year	$100	$150	$200	$250	$300	$350
$12 per $100 per year	$120	$180	$240	$300	$360	$420
Percent of unpaid balance						
¾ of 1% per month	$ 49	$ 73	$ 96	$120	$145	$169
1% per month	$ 66	$ 98	$130	$162	$196	$230
1½% per month	$100	$149	$198	$249	$301	$355
2% per month	$135	$201	$269	$340	$412	$488
2½% per month	$170	$254	$342	$433	$528	$627

Shopping for Credit

You should shop for credit the way you shop for anything else. It's best to shop at more than one place, and it's best to know what to look for. A typical household with a good credit rating can save enough for an annual vacation by shopping for the money it "rents" in order to buy now and pay later.

Here are some pointers to help you shop for money for installment buying through contracts and through credit cards and other kinds of revolving charge plans.

Compare Costs

Credit can cost you pennies or dollars. It depends on your character, your capital and your capability to repay, the money market, and other economic factors.

Two choices you frequently have are closed-end and revolving transactions. Under the closed-end plans you ordinarily sign a promissory note, if you are borrowing cash, or a retail installment contract, if you are using sales credit. You agree in advance on the specific amount to borrow, the number and size of weekly or monthly payments, and a due date.

On the other hand, the revolving charge plan is open-ended. A top limit is agreed upon, but purchases are added as they are made and finance charges are figured on the unpaid balance each month. A monthly interest rate is quoted—usually 1 or 1½ percent a month, which is a 12 or 18 percent annual rate.

Revolving charges come in many forms. There are credit cards from stores and gasoline and other companies for charging at branches. Bank credit cards (such as Visa and Master Charge) and those issued by "travel and entertainment" groups (Diners Club, Carte Blanche, American Express) allow you to arrange a line of credit and to charge at many participating retailers, or even to borrow cash.

Credit cards are conveniences we've all come to rely on, but they charge some of the highest interest rates around—18 percent annually, or 1½ percent monthly. (If you itemize your tax returns, you can deduct this interest.)

If you keep money in a savings account earning only, for example, 5 percent, why should you pay 18 percent per year for interest on credit card purchases just to avoid touching your savings? Of course, to many people, saving is a matter of discipline, but is it worth the 13 percent you end up paying? Why not buy only what you really can afford—use credit cards to get free use of that money until the bill is due, then pay the bill on time and avoid finance charges.

Banks and some credit unions also offer books of special checks or drafts indicating preapproved loans. As you spend the checks or

To finance $2,000 for 2 Years:

CAR DEALER

ANNUAL PERCENTAGE
RATE 12-25%
Credit might cost $574.*

FINANCE COMPANY

ANNUAL PERCENTAGE
RATE 12-30%
Credit might cost $684.*

CREDIT UNION

ANNUAL PERCENTAGE
RATE 6-12%
Credit might cost $260.*

BANK

ANNUAL PERCENTAGE
RATE 8-15%
Credit might cost $327.*

**SAVINGS & LOAN ASSO-
CIATIONS**

ANNUAL PERCENTAGE
RATE 6-15%
Credit might cost $327.*

LIFE INSURANCE POLICY

ANNUAL PERCENTAGE
RATE 4-6%
Credit might cost $127.*

Finance with the lender
that offers you the lowest
annual percentage
rate (APR).

*Figured on highest rate
shown. These are estimates of
national averages.
Maximum rates vary,
according to state laws.

drafts, interest begins. For occasional credit, many people now have
checking accounts with overdraft privileges, which allow them to
write a check for more than their balance. But overdraft privileges
(usually limited to $700 or so) may cost as much as store credit.
Before signing up for an overdraft account, be sure to find out the
interest rate. Banks may charge anywhere from 10 to 18 percent for
overdrafts. Some banks also charge a fee per transaction in addition
to regular interest rates.

Banks make overdraft advances either for the exact amount or in
multiples. Therefore, if the bank lends only in multiples of $100,
you would have to borrow $100 and pay interest on it even though
you only wanted $10. Some banks charge a monthly fee for
overdraft privileges in addition to interest. Find out whether
deposits to your checking account automatically apply to an

overdraft balance or whether you must specifically repay the overdraft account.

What you pay for credit depends a good deal on whether you use closed-end or revolving charge plans and where you arrange for them. In buying a car, for instance, what you would pay for the use of $2,000 for two years might vary from $127 to $684, which is from a 4 percent (available on some insurance loans) to a 30 percent annual rate, depending on where you financed it and the plan you used.

The kind of security the lender or dealer requires from you also affects the cost. Sometimes the word collateral is used instead of security. Both words mean "something having money value." As a general rule, the more security you can offer, the lower the cost of credit. A cosigner or comaker may lower the cost for you.

You may have other borrowing options. Does your life insurance policy have a loan clause? If you have paid-up insurance, can you risk short-changing your protection? If so, some insurance loans run at a 4 to 6 percent annual rate.

Another option might be borrowing on passbook savings you have at a savings and loan association.

Truth in Lending: Annual Percentage Rate

Annual percentage rate, which is the unit pricing of money, is the key to cutting your cost of credit. It's a relatively new approach made possible by the Truth in Lending law. Here is how you use the annual percentage rate approach in shopping for closed-end credit.

All merchants and lenders are required under the Truth in Lending law to show the unit price for money on all consumer credit contracts. They do this by stating the cost in terms of the annual percentage rate (APR), the cost of buying an item or service on time, expressed as a percentage figured on the unpaid balance.

Just as consumer sense has taught you to shop for the lowest cost per pound on grocery items, economy dictates that you shop for money by looking for the lowest annual percentage rate.

Here's how it works in closed-end credit shopping. Often each lender you approach offers you a different loan amount, for a different time period, with a different sized payment. For his special package, he works out the finance charge. This is the dollar cost including interest and other charges for extending the credit. He converts the finance charge into the annual percentage rate he can offer for his transaction.

You can quickly tell which deal offers you the most credit for the money. It's the one with the lowest annual percentage rate. Meanwhile you compare total dollar cost through the finance charge. Be sure to ask the lender specifically for annual percentage rate. Some lenders might make loan rates sound lower by quoting some other rate.

With regard to revolving charge, you simply look for the lowest annual percentage rate to compare cost. To save the most when using revolving credit, join the one-third of all consumers who pay within the 25 or 30 days allowed without any finance charges. This gives you the convenience at the same cost as paying cash.

The Truth in Lending law does not fix interest rates or other credit charges. Your state may have a law setting a limit on interest rates, which would still apply.

Chances are that if the monthly statements and other materials you receive from companies giving you credit look different now, it doesn't mean they've changed their rates, only their way of showing them to comply with the Truth in Lending law. Your department store bills, for example, should now list both a monthly rate (for example, 1 percent, 1½ percent, or some other number) and the annual percentage rate. This may be 12 percent, 18 percent, or some other percentage, but it will usually be 12 times the monthly rate.

Protection Under Truth in Lending

Pay within the
25 or 30 days allowed
without any
financial charges.

The law also gives a new look to the advertising of credit terms. It says that if a business is going to mention one feature of credit in its advertising, such as the amount of down payment, it must mention all other important terms, such as the number, amount, and period of payments that follow. If an advertisement states "Only $2 down," it must also state, for example, that you will have to pay $10 a week for the next two years. Here again, the intent is to provide you with full information so that you can make informed decisions.

One other important provision of the law is designed for your protection in case you use your home as collateral in a credit transaction. This frequently occurs when you are having a major repair or remodeling job done on your home. Today, when you enter into a credit transaction in which your home is used as collateral, the law gives you three business days to think about it and to cancel the transaction during that period if you wish. The creditor must give you written notice of your right to cancel, and if you decide to cancel the transaction, you have to notify him in writing.

Under this right of cancellation, the contractor cannot start work until the three days are up. You may give up your right to cancel and get the work started without the three-day wait if you notify the creditor in writing that you face a real financial emergency and need the credit immediately to finance repairs necessary to avoid danger to you, your family, or your property.

The right of cancellation does not apply when you sign a first mortgage to finance the purchase of a home.

You may sue for twice
the amount of
the financial charge.

The law, and the regulations issued by the Board of Governors of the Federal Reserve System to carry it out, contain many other detailed provisions. Businessmen extending credit should familiarize themselves with all of these, to make sure they are complying with the law. You as an individual may sue if a businessman fails to make the required disclosures. You may sue for twice the amount of the finance charge—for a minimum of $100, up to a maximum of $1,000—plus court costs and reasonable attorney's fees.

226

If you cannot meet your payments, you may have to give back the merchandise.

Compare Other Terms

There are things to consider other than cost in shopping for closed-end credit. When you buy on credit, you make many promises. If you cannot meet your payments, you may have to give back the merchandise, pay damages, and continue to make the payments you owe. You may even have to forfeit personal belongings right down to your silverware.

Closed-end contracts vary a good deal from one lender to another. Let's say you want to buy a $600 stereo. You've found just the right one. You know that you do not have to finance it through the dealer and that closed-end credit may be less expensive than letting the salesperson charge it on your revolving account or your bank credit card.

You must know the size of payment that you can handle each week or month without risking disaster. Let's say that you have talked to three lenders and found the deal with the lowest annual percentage rate. But the payment was too high, so you have just about decided to borrow on a plan that allows you to pay less each time by stretching out the payments for a longer period. You recognize that credit will cost you more this way, but there is less risk that you will be unable to meet the payments.

Before you sign the contract, it's important to weigh the other risks. This checklist should help you:

• **Down payment:** A larger down payment can help cut the cost of the credit. But beware of borrowing the down payment from a second lender. This means two payments instead of one.

• **Size of Payments:** Are they all the same? Watch out for a larger final payment or "balloon clause." Even if you make all but the balloon payment, you may lose everything.

• **Your home as security:** Is it included? If so, the seller should give you a cancellation form. The Truth in Lending law allows you three days to change your mind and rescind.

• **Repayment in advance:** Is there any refund of the finance charge?

• **Missing a payment:** What happens? Penalty charges? Entire debt due? Immediately?

• **Default:** What if you can't pay and have to default? Collection charges? Storage or court costs? Can you reclaim the item? If it's sold but doesn't cover your debt, must you pay the difference?

• **Faulty work or merchandise:** Is there a time limit for your complaints? To whom should you complain? Your installment contract probably will be sold to another company; will the new creditor stand behind your purchase?

• **Moving the merchandise:** Can you remove it from the state?

• **Insurance:** Is it involved? On the item? On you, to assume full payment of the debt in case of accident, illness, death? Who collects? Can you get cheaper coverage from your own insurance company?

• **Waiving your rights:** Must you sign away other rights? Avoid signing a statement that work has been completed or an item received when it hasn't been.

• **Add-on contract:** Think twice before you add an item to a contract you already have with a store. A missed payment can mean you lose all the items even though you've paid for the first ones.

If there are contract terms you do not want, ask the lender to strike them out. If he agrees, you and he both must initial the modifications on his copy and on yours. It's only the written agreement that counts, not verbal promises.

It's only the written agreement that counts.

If you cannot understand the contract, ask for a blank, unsigned copy. Compare terms other than cost, and discuss it with someone (a friend or a relative) who can help you. Avoid signing any statement or contract that is not completely filled out. Such action allows the lender to fill in amounts and terms that you did not agree to in conversation.

The foregoing checklist is useful primarily for closed-end credit but can be used for revolving plans. Here are more pointers on revolving credit.

• Notice how much you are paying each month. Total all the finance charges from your bills for a typical month. Multiply by 12 for the yearly cost. Is the credit worth it?

• When amounts outstanding become sizable, would you do better to pay them off by arranging a closed-end credit deal? Or by arranging a less expensive revolving plan? Some credit unions offer annual percentage rates lower than 18 percent on their "draft" preapproved loans. Some banks offer less than 18 percent on their check credit plans.

• In considering which system might be less costly, keep in mind these variables among revolving plans: Some require an initial or annual fee. Some do not. Some allow more time than others between date of purchase and due date. And some have a way of figuring the finance charge so that their credit costs you less than others.

Your Credit Rating

If you have a charge account, a mortgage on your home, life insurance, or have applied for a personal loan or even a job, it is almost certain that there is a "file" existing somewhere that shows how you pay your bills, if you have been sued or arrested, if you

228

have filed for bankruptcy. Some of these files include your neighbors' and friends' views of your character, general reputation, or manner of living.

The companies that gather and sell such information to creditors, insurers, employers, and other businesses are called "consumer reporting agencies," and the legal term for the report is a "consumer report."

If, in addition to credit information, the report involves interviews with a third person about your character, reputation, or manner of living, it is referred to as an "investigative consumer report."

The Fair Credit Reporting Act was passed by Congress to protect consumers against the circulation of inaccurate or obsolete information, and to insure that consumer reporting agencies exercise their responsibilities in a manner that is fair and equitable to consumers.

Under this law you can now take steps to protect yourself if you have been denied credit, insurance, or employment, or if you believe you have had difficulties because of a consumer report on you. Here are the steps you can take. You have the right:

1. To be told the name and address of the consumer reporting agency responsible for preparing a consumer report that was used to deny you credit, insurance, or employment or to increase the cost of credit or insurance.

2. To be told by a consumer reporting agency the nature, substance, and sources (except investigative-type sources) of the information (except medical) collected about you.

3. To take anyone of your choice with you when you visit the consumer reporting agency to check on your file.

4. To obtain all information to which you are entitled, free of charge, when you have been denied credit, insurance, or employment within 30 days of your interview. Otherwise, the reporting agency is permitted to charge a reasonable fee for giving you the information.

5. To be told who has received a consumer report on you within the preceding six months, or within the preceding two years if the report was furnished for employment purposes.

6. To have incomplete or incorrect information re-investigated, unless the request is frivolous, and, if the information is found to be inaccurate or cannot be verified, to have such information removed from your file.

7. To have the agency notify those you name (at no cost to you) who have previously received the incorrect or incomplete information that this information has been deleted from your file.

8. To have your version of a dispute placed in the file and included in future consumer reports when a dispute between you and the reporting agency about information in your file cannot be resolved.

9. To request the reporting agency to send your version of the dispute to certain businesses for a reasonable fee.

10. To have a consumer report withheld from anyone who under the law does not have a legitimate business need for the information.

11. To sue a reporting agency for damages if it wilfully or negligently violates the law and, if you are successful, to collect attorney's fees and court costs.

12. Not to have adverse information reported after seven years; one major exception is bankruptcy, which may be reported for 14 years.

13. To be notified by a business that it is seeking information about you that would constitute an investigative consumer report.

14. To request from the business that ordered an investigative report more information about the nature and scope of the investigation.

15. To discover the nature and substance (but not the sources) of the information that was collected for an investigative consumer report.

The Fair Credit Reporting Act does not:

1. Give you the right to request a report on yourself from the consumer reporting agency.

2. Give you the right, when you visit the agency, to receive a copy of or to physically handle your file.

3. Compel anyone to do business with an individual consumer.

4. Apply when you request commercial (as distinguished from consumer) credit or business insurance.

5. Authorize any federal agency to intervene on behalf of an individual consumer.

If you want to know what information a consumer reporting agency has collected about you, either arrange for a personal interview at the agency's office during normal business hours or telephone in advance for an interview.

The consumer reporting agencies in your community can be located by consulting the Yellow Pages of your telephone directory under such headings as "Credit" or "Credit Rating or Reporting Agencies."

If you decide to visit a consumer reporting agency to check on your file, the following checklist may be of help. Did you:

1. Learn the nature and substance of all information in your file?

2. Find out the names of each of the businesses (or other sources) that supplied information on you to the reporting agency?

3. Learn the names of everyone who received reports on you within the past six months (or the last two years if the reports were for employment purposes)?

4. Request the agency to re-investigate and correct or delete information that was found to be inaccurate, incomplete, or obsolete?

5. Follow up to determine the results of the re-investigation?

6. Ask the agency, at no cost to you, to notify those you name who received reports within the past six months (two years if for employment purposes) that certain information was deleted?

Request the agency
to re-investigate.

7. Follow up to make sure that those named by you did in fact receive notices from the consumer reporting agency?

8. Demand that your version of the facts be placed in your file if the re-investigation did not settle the dispute?

9. Request the agency (if you are willing to pay a reasonable fee) to send your statement of the dispute to those you name who received reports containing the disputed information within the past six months (two years if received for employment purposes)?

Should You or Shouldn't You?

You now have information about where you can get installment credit and how much it costs, and your credit rating is such that you will have no trouble getting a loan. The next question is whether you want to get into this sort of thing at all.

If you have in mind some particular item to buy, you might consider such questions as: Could you pay cash for it without using too much of your savings? Is having it now worth the extra cost of buying it "on time"? Can you handle this much debt?

Perhaps you have read the rule of thumb that a family should not commit itself for installment payments amounting to more than 20 percent of its income. The truth is that many families would be unwise to commit as much as 15, 10, or even 5 percent of their income to installment payments. Some, on the other hand, might pay installments amounting to more than 20 percent of their income — for a time, at least — without hardship.

Each family has different financial resources, as well as different needs, wants, goals, future prospects, and management skills. These are the things that will determine how much installment debt they can handle.

Instead of searching for a rule to tell you how much installment debt you can safely assume, take stock of your own financial situation. Have a family budget session to review your spending plan, your accounts, assets, and liabilities.

Considering these questions will help you to make a decision:

• How much do you have left from your income each month now, after you have paid all your living expenses, made the payments on your presents debts, put the planned amount into your savings account, and taken care of other obligations? (It makes sense not to take on another installment payment larger than this amount.)

• Is it always easy to make the payments on your present debt? (If it sometimes means scraping and squeezing or skipping a payment, better think twice before taking on another debt.)

• How much do you have in savings accounts, bonds, or other funds that you can easily draw on? (Unless it is enough to pay living expenses and keep up debt payments for at least a month or so in case of illness or layoff from work, go slow.)

• Will some debt be paid off soon, so you can use the money you now pay on that for installments on a new debt? (A "yes" here may be a go-ahead indicator.)

• Will another installment debt mean you have to postpone or give up some goal you have planned for? (If the answer is "yes," weigh the pros and cons carefully.)

Taking time to think things through like this may save you from the kind of impulse installment buying that gets families into trouble. Every installment payment you promise to make has to fit into the budget somewhere. The time to make sure it does is before you sign on the dotted line.

Mind Made Up?

Once you have made up your mind to buy or borrow on the installment plan, keep the price you pay for credit as low as possible.

First, shop around for a good credit deal. If you are considering credit from a retailer, compare prices on the item you are buying as well as the credit charges. Sometimes merchants who sell on time charge more for the goods they sell.

Also, look into the possibility of getting a loan from a bank or credit union instead. Either way, be sure you are doing business with an established dealer or lending agency — one with a good reputation.

Do not be taken in by the unknown door-to-door salesman who offers to sell on the installment plan. Merchandise sold door-to-door is often overpriced and may be of poor quality. Take two days to think it over. Any honest salesman will be happy to come back. Compare prices of similar merchandise in stores before you buy from a door-to-door salesman. Don't sign any papers promising to pay unless you know the total cost. (High interest, credit insurance, and other service charges may double the price.)

Make as large a down payment as you can without reducing your savings to the danger point.

Finally, make monthly payments as large as your budget will allow. This way, you can pay the debt in the shortest possible time and save dollars.

When you buy things on time or get an installment loan, you have to sign a contract. Be sure you get a copy. Keep it in a safe place so you can refer to it if you need to.

Before you sign the contract:

To avoid credit trouble, estimate first the regular income and obligations you have.

232

- Read and understand everything in it, including the fine print.
- See that there are no blank spaces left when you sign.
- Be sure the contract tells exactly what you are buying: the purchase price, or the amount of cash you will receive from the loan; all the credit charges; the down payment and trade-in allowance, if any; the total amount you have to pay; the amount you have to pay for each installment; the number of installments to be made, and the dates due.
- Find out to whom you are to make the payments.
- Know what will happen if you cannot pay, and if you want to pay ahead.
- Know what the seller's responsibility is for maintenance, service, or replacement of the goods purchased.

Once you have made a credit deal, it's up to you to see that the installments are paid regularly. If you fail to make the payments, the creditor can take the washing machine, car, or whatever it is you owe for. This means you lose the money you have already paid on it. In some states, you can be required to pay more, too, if the creditor cannot sell the washer or the car for as much as you owe.

Your rating as a credit risk depends on how prompt you are in paying your debts. Because you will probably want credit again, it will pay you to keep this rating good.

In Case You Get Into Credit Trouble...

FEDERAL WAGE GARNISHMENT LAW

Basic Provisions: Limits amount of employee earnings that may be withheld for garnishment in any workweek or pay period and protects employee from being fired if pay is garnisheed for only one debt (regardless of number of levies made to collect).

Authority and Enforcement: Title III, Consumer Credit Protection Act; enforced by Wage and Hour compliance officers located across the U.S.

Coverage and Earnings: Law protects everyone receiving personal earnings; i.e., wage, salary, commission, bonus, and income from pension or retirement program. (Tips are generally not considered earnings for purposes of this law.)

Restrictions on Garnishment: Amount of total pay subject to garnishment is based on employee's "disposable earnings," the amount left after legally required withholdings for federal, state, and local taxes and for social security. Deductions such as those for union

233

dues, health and life insurance, and savings bonds are not considered required by law.

In any workweek, garnishment is limited to the lesser of: 1) 25 percent of disposable earnings, or 2) the amount by which disposable earnings for that week exceed 30 times the highest current federal minimum wage. However, employee is protected by garnishment law, even if not covered by minimum wage.

Exceptions: Law does not apply to: 1) court orders for support of any person; 2) court orders in personal bankruptcy cases; or 3) state or federal tax levies. Wage assignments are not generally within the law's scope.

State Laws: When state garnishment laws conflict with federal, the law resulting in smaller garnishment applies.

Further Information: Available from local Wage and Hour offices, listed in most phone directories under U.S. Government, Department of Labor, Employment Standards Administration.

AVOIDING CREDIT PROBLEMS

The best way to avoid credit problems is not to use credit. However, you probably will need to borrow money or to use credit accounts for some expensive items during your life. You can avoid many difficulties with credit by using the following guides:

• Make a list of each monthly payment you have already agreed to make, for example:

rent	$280
washing machine	$ 32

Compare the total of these payments and other living expenses with the take-home paychecks you expect for the same months. Try to allow some income for emergencies and savings.

• Use credit only for the higher-priced purchases you must have now.
• Shop for the lowest finance charges you can get.
• Make your payments only as large as you can meet regularly.

EQUAL CREDIT OPPORTUNITY ACT

The Equal Credit Opportunity Act starts all credit applicants off on the same footing. The law does not guarantee that you will get credit; you must still pass the creditor's tests of creditworthiness. But the creditor must apply these tests fairly, impartially, and without discrimination against you on any of the following grounds: age, sex, marital status, race, color, religion, national origin, because you are on welfare or social security, or because you exercise your rights under federal credit laws. This means that a creditor may not use any of those grounds as an excuse to:

• discourage you from applying for a loan;
• refuse you a loan if you qualify;
• lend you money on terms different from those granted another person with similar income, expenses, credit history, and collateral.

Under the Equal Credit Opportunity Act, you must be notified within 30 days after your application for a loan has been completed whether it has been approved or not. If credit is denied, this notice must be in writing and it must explain the specific reasons for denying credit or tell you of your right to request an application. You have the same rights if an account you have had is closed.

If you think you can prove that a creditor has discriminated against you for any reason prohibited by the Act, you may sue for actual damages plus punitive damages—that is, damages for the fact that the law has been violated—of up to $10,000 if the violation is proved to have been intentional. In a successful suit, the court will award you court costs and a reasonable amount for attorney's fees.

Written by
RICHARD ARLEN

Buying Insurance

Contents

Insurance, Protection Against Risk

"There's no one with endurance like the man who sells insurance." We all know that. But what about those of us who must buy it? Do we have the endurance to persevere through the Clauses, Provisions, Endorsements, Exceptions—all written in legalese jargon that would tax the talents of the cryptographers who broke the Imperial Japanese Code in World War II? Still, we all need a basic understanding of insurance, since it is our first line of defense against many of life's problems and catastrophes.

How would your family react to the emotional and financial impact of a long-term illness? A legal suit brought against you because of inadequate car insurance? The death of the breadwinner of your family?

An insurance policy, whether it be health, car, home, or life, is protection for you and your family against risk. A policy is the document given to you by the insurance company to explain the protection and the conditions under which payments or indemnities (compensations) will be made in event of loss or damage.

Health Insurance

Good health is one of the most valuable things in life, but good health does not remain the same throughout life. By having adequate health insurance, the risk of financial disaster from a long-term illness can be largely reduced.

It is often difficult to sort out the facts and obtain the kind of health insurance you are seeking because health insurance contracts are detailed and difficult to understand. A policy that satisfactorily addresses the following six items will be most likely to provide you with the essentials necessary for a sound health insurance plan:

- What types of expenses are covered by the policy?

Every policy covers certain kinds of expenses, and these expenses will be subject to certain conditions. Hospital indemnity, which is one of the simplest forms of health insurance, will pay only a fixed amount while you are hospitalized. If you receive outpatient treatment, you probably will collect nothing.

- How much will the policy pay?

The glowing ads give the maximum payments possible, but few policyholders receive the top payment. To be certain what the policy does and does not cover, get a copy of the actual policy and read it carefully.

When the ad for a health insurance plan says, "Up to $40,000 extra cash when you're in the hospital" and "Get $200 tax-free each week," stop and do some thinking and figuring. To collect the $40,000 at the benefit rate of $200, you would have to be hospitalized for almost four years!

Excluding maternity, mental and TB cases, only 15 out of 100 people are hospitalized during any one year. The average hospital stay is 5 days. Those with the highest hospitalization rate stay an average of 12 days.

Examine the clauses designed to limit payment. These might include deductibles, co-payment provisions requiring you to pay a portion of the expenses, and the specified amount allotted for various kinds of operations.

Always find out what the limits and restrictions are in any policy. If, for example, you are paying $200 a day for your room, plus drugs, X rays and operating room expenses, and the indemnity policy pays $50 a day, you are going to be left with the remainder of the hospitalization expense.

• Is there a waiting period before the policy goes into effect?

Usually, individual policies (in contrast to group policies) have a clause stating that you can't collect during the first year or two years for an illness that was treated before you enrolled in the plan, or you may not receive benefits even though you didn't know the condition existed at the time.

Be alert for such clauses as "benefit builder" period. Be sure you get the details. In some policies there may be more than one kind of waiting period.

• Is the policy renewable?

If a policy is stated as non-cancellable, the company can't cancel unless the premium payment on the policy lapses. However, the company can refuse to renew the policy. Few companies offer a truly non-cancellable policy.

When reading the ads and policies you will find that the company can cancel, refuse renewal, or raise premiums if it does so for all policyholders of the same "class." What is a "class"? It can mean all people in the same state with the same coverage, or all people in the same age group. Some companies guarantee renewal but maintain the right to raise rates on a class basis.

• Does the coverage supplement Medicare?

Medicare does not cover services such as dental treatment, eyeglasses, medical appliances, and drugs not supplied by a hospital. (See Tables 1 A and B.) If the policy being considered to supplement Medicare concentrates its benefits on hospitalization or on services covered by Medicare, it still isn't going to provide the coverage needed. The policyholder will have to pay for the uncovered costs.

• Is the company licensed in your state?

To some extent, you can protect yourself more adequately and efficiently by insuring with companies licensed by your state. If you have a complaint against a company licensed in your state, the state insurance department can proceed against the company more easily.

When considering a given company, be sure to find out if the company is licensed. Your state insurance department will be able to provide this information.

When starting your health insurance program, begin with basic coverage. No policy will cover all the potential costs.

BASIC HOSPITAL COVERAGE—PART A

TYPE OF SERVICE	TIME LIMIT	PATIENT PAYS	MEDICARE PAYS	QUALIFICATIONS	EXCLUSIONS
HOSPITAL (a) CONFINEMENT Semi-private room and board unless a private room is required for medical reasons. Covers general nursing, drugs, and normal services, including operating & recovery rooms.	First 60 days each benefit period (b).	First $144		*Age 65 and:* (1) Entitled to Social Security (or Railroad Retirement) benefits; or (2) is *not* entitled, a citizen or permanent resident for 5 years, may enroll by paying $63 per month plus 10% to 40% more if you did not sign up when you were first eligible, plus Part B (cost below). *Under 65 when:* (1) Social Security (or Railroad Retirement) disability benefits payable for 24 consecutive months, or (2) any worker (or dependents) with chronic kidney disease who need dialysis, or (3) disabled widow (or disabled widower) between 50 & 65, or (4) children (of retired, disabled or deceased workers) disabled before age 22.	First three pints of blood, private duty nurses, non-covered levels of care, and services covered under Part B.
	Next 30 days continuous hospital confinement.	$36 each day	Balance		
	Lifetime aggregate reserve of 60 additional days.	$72 each day			
SKILLED NURSING FACILITIES (a) following hospital confinement.	First 20 days each benefit period (b).	Nothing	100%	Must require care within 14 days (may be extended to 28 days) after hospital confinement which lasted at least 3 days.	Same as above: unskilled medical care (such as "Old Age Homes" and Custodial Care).
	Next 80 days continuous confinement.	$18 each day	Balance		
HOME HEALTH CARE (a) by visiting nurses, aides, therapists following hospital confinement.	100 visits during the 1 year following hospital confinement.	Nothing	100%	Must require care for same or related causes as hospital stay, within 14 days after hospital stay, plus home confinement.	Full time (private duty) nursing, self-administered drugs, services covered under Part B.
PSYCHIATRIC CONFINEMENT CARE	Same as Hospital Confinement Benefits with a lifetime			maximum limit of 190 days.	

SUPPLEMENTAL MEDICAL COVERAGE—PART B

TYPE OF SERVICE	TIME LIMIT	PATIENT PAYS	MEDICARE PAYS	QUALIFICATIONS	EXCLUSIONS
PHYSICIANS AND SURGEONS services at home, hospital or office.	No Time Limit	First $60 (d) per calendar year, then 20% of reasonable charges.	Balance of reasonable charges (c) (pays *full* reasonable charges for radiology and pathology services while hospital confined).	Voluntary enrollment, costs $8.20 or more a month, depending on date of enrollment, and subject to change each July.	Services covered by Workmen's Compensation, private duty nurse, eye-glasses, routine physicals, dental work, hearing aids, orthopedic shoes, non-skilled nursing care, plastic surgery, charges made by a relative, first 3 pints of blood in a calendar year, vaccinations, self-administered drugs, services in a foreign country.
MEDICAL SERVICES & SUPPLIES diagnostic tests, surgical dressings, casts, splints, braces, artificial limbs and eyes, rental or purchase of medical equipment, ambulance, X-ray therapy, professionally administered drugs, some chiropractic services, non-routine footcare.					
HOSPITAL CARE Outpatient.					
HOME HEALTH CARE visiting nurses, aides, therapists.	100 visits per year (may be in addition to Part A).	First $60 (d)	100%	Home confinement required but prior hospital care not required.	
PSYCHIATRIC OUTPATIENT CARE	Per calendar Year	First $60 (d)	50% of charges	paid up to a maximum of $250	

(a) Hospital or Skilled Nursing Facility or Home Health Care Agency must be qualified and have signed Participation Agreement with U.S. Department of H.E.W.

(b) Each benefit period begins with first day of hospital confinement and ends after having been discharged from a hospital or Skilled Nursing Facility for 60 consecutive days.

(c) Reasonable charges are determined by the Medicare administration in the recipient's area. The charge approved will be either the customary charge, the prevailing charge, or the actual charge, whichever is lowest.

(d) All Part B expenses (i.e. Medical Services & Supplies or Home Health Care or Psychiatric Outpatient Care), including expenses incurred during last 3 months of previous year, can be counted toward the $60 deductible.

This chart is a brief description, further details can be found in Social Security literature. For use by MacArthur Insurance Companies Agents only. Includes changes effective 7-1-78.

TABLE 1

Table 1. If you are over 65 — and in some instances, if you become disabled before you are 65 — Medicare pays a major part of most medical bills, as shown in the Table. You may want to purchase "add-on" insurance from a private company to cover the rest.

Begin with an insurance that pays for a range of major costs —hospitalization and surgery. Then choose a reliable "major medical" policy that is designed to cover the costs of serious illness.

Before buying any insurance, whether it is through a group protection or an individual policy, carefully review the insurance coverage you already have. Remember, group protection usually provides more comprehensive coverage at a lower rate.

If you are nearing 65, it is particularly important to review your existing coverage, because many policies reduce benefits when you qualify for Medicare. If you are interested in learning more about the Medicare program, ask for a free copy of *Your Medicare Handbook* at the Social Security Administration office in your area.

Automobile Insurance

Shopping for automobile insurance can present many problems and leave you very distraught. However, if you know the basic features to look for, you can shop with more confidence and are likely to get more for your money.

Auto insurance can be bought in the form of package coverage, or each section can be purchased separately.

Liability is the core of an auto policy. With liability coverage the insurance company pays for bodily injury and property damage to others when you are legally responsible for an accident.

Claims against you may be settled out of court, but if court action is brought against you, the company will defend you. The protection covers you, resident members of the family, and others who drive with your approval. You and members of your family are also covered when driving another car with the owner's consent.

Liability coverage is listed separately for bodily injury and property damage. The maximum coverage is generally stated in a form such as 10/20/5. This means that the company is liable for up to $10,000 for any one person injured; up to $20,000 for all injuries in the same accident; and up to $5,000 for damage to the other car, fences and private property. You are responsible for damages exceeding these amounts.

Liability coverage pays for other people's injuries—not yours. Medical payments cover you and your passengers' medical fees regardless of who was to blame for the accident. Medical payments coverage is sold in amounts ranging from $1,000 up. The limit is for each person injured, so with a $1,000 plan, four people would collect a total of $4,000.

Uninsured motorist coverage offers protection to you, your spouse, and resident children if you are injured by an uninsured or hit-and-run driver while driving or walking. (See Table 2 at the end of the book.)
• The coverage applies only when the other driver was to blame for the accident.
• Bodily injury payments generally are limited to minimums of state liability regardless of the face value of the basic policy.

Collision insurance pays for damage to your car when you hit another vehicle or an object such as a tree or a telephone pole.

Collision coverage is usually sold in the forms of $50, $100, and $200 deductible. If you hit a tree, do $150 damage to your car, and have a $50 deductible, the company will pay $100.

The larger the amount of the deductible, the lower the premium. In most instances, by buying a $100 deductible collision policy rather than $50 deductible, you can cut about 20 percent of the collision premium.

The company restricts its responsibility to the "actual cash value" of the car. This means that if your car is worth $1,600, that is the most you can expect to collect on a collision claim. No matter how dear to your heart the "old crate" is, the company will not spend $1,800 to repair it. Consider the book value of your car. It is often economically unwise to buy collision coverage for an old car.

Losses caused by fire, wind, theft, vandalism, collision

with animals, explosions, flood, and lightning are covered by the comprehensive coverage feature. Comprehensive provides limited coverage for personal property left in the car. If you have a homeowner's insurance policy (explained later in this booklet), there may be additional coverage. Discuss this with the agent who sold you the homeowner's policy.

Accidental death and dismemberment coverage pays a lump sum for death in a car accident, loss of a limb, blindness, fractures, and dislocations, plus a disability benefit each week. This accidental death coverage often overlaps coverage from liability and other insurance. Therefore, you may be spending premium money for overlapping coverages.

Premium rates vary by locality and state and according to the loss experience of the company. But these factors are heavily weighted according to:
• The purposes for which your car is used: pleasure, business, or farm work. Business receives the highest rate and farm work the lowest.
• Age (teenagers are considered a high risk).
• Marital status (a young married man is considered a better risk than a young bachelor).
• Whether you drive to work, and the distance to work if you do.
• Total mileage. A car driven more than a certain distance in a year is often subject to a higher insurance rate.

Special rating factors can help trim premiums. Some of the examples for you to explore are the following:
• If your son or daughter ranks in the top 20 percent of his or her class, or is on the dean's list, ask the company if it has a good-student discount.
• Encourage your young person to take driver training. Generally, that will qualify him for a driver-training discount.
• If another car is bought for the family, include the car on

your policy. This will entitle you to a multi-car discount on the second car.

• Check with the company about the age at which a young driver passes from the high-premium category to the lower-premium adult category, and remind the company when he reaches this age.

• When buying a car, find out if the car is subject to the "souped-up" car surcharge.

• Check on companies offering the "safe driver" plan. If you have an "accident- or traffic violation-free" driving record, you can realize considerable savings on your auto insurance premiums.

• Remember that there is no best company. Be knowledgeable about the types of coverage available and do some cost comparing among two or three companies.

For many years, our auto insurance system depended largely on the person at fault paying for the damage. The "fault" system has been under criticism as being inequitable and costly in settling claims.

Today, many states have adopted the "no-fault" system, in which injured persons are paid by their own companies up to certain amounts for medical expenses and loss of income, regardless of who is responsible for the accident. In states where the no-fault system has been enacted, a reduction of premium rates has occurred. The U.S. Department of Transportation has recommended that all states adopt a no-fault system. Some Congressmen are urging that the federal government make such a system mandatory throughout the country.

Life Insurance

Life insurance is financial protection for dependents against economic loss as a result of the breadwinner's death. Because of the dependence on cash and credit by today's families, life insurance is a way through which families can gain protection and financial security.

Life insurance is not a savings plan or an investment plan. Neither is it the best method for building an educational fund for children. Life insurance is often sold for such purposes, but there are better ways of obtaining these objectives than through life insurance.

When the breadwinner dies, a family must face many

financial difficulties. The problems usually come in this order:

- Burial expenses and any medical expenses not covered by health insurance.
- Adequate funds to meet the family's living expenses until the spouse and/or the children can make employment arrangements.
- Educational funds for children.

Regardless of the extravagant claims made about some life insurance policies, there are four basic types of life insurance: term, straight life, limited payment life, and endowment.

Term insurance provides simple protection, whereas the other three have a savings feature. But remember that the basic principle is to gain the greatest protection for the family at the lowest cost should the breadwinner die.

Term insurance is a type of life insurance that provides protection only. As the name implies, the policy covers the holder for a term of 1, 5, 10, 20, or some other pre-set number of years. At the end of the term the coverage stops and the policy has no cash value. It is wise to buy a "renewable term" policy. This allows the policy owner to renew the policy for another term without another physical examination.

Term insurance gives the family the greatest amount of protection for a limited period at the least cost. It generally is best to buy term insurance on a reducing coverage basis so that it can be reduced or terminated as dependents become older and no longer require as much protection.

Term insurance can be increased to the maximum protection as each child is born or can be decreased to no insurance on the breadwinner as the children become economically independent. Several term policies rather than one or two large policies can be purchased. This allows the policyholder to increase coverage or to drop policies to best meet his needs. Buying term insurance in this way also allows for convenient distribution of premium dates.

Straight life insurance, also known as ordinary life or whole life insurance, provides for a certain amount of coverage throughout life. It differs from term insurance in that straight life combines a decreasing amount of protection with an increasing amount of savings in the policy. Because of the savings element as well as the protection in the straight life plan, the premium for a certain amount of straight life at a given age is higher than the premium for term insurance.

The premium for straight life remains the same through the length of the policy. In the early years, the policyholder is actually paying more for the cost of protection. The extra portion of the premium is what builds up the savings element of the policy.

In a straight life policy the terms "face value" and "cash surrender value" are often used. The face value is the amount payable at the insured's death. The cash surrender value is the amount of savings that has built up in the policy.

The cash value increases while the policy is in force. The insured may cash the policy in at any time, but this will terminate the policy and the protection stops. If the insured desires, he may borrow the cash value from the company. But when the policy is borrowed from, the coverage is reduced until the loan is repaid.

Limited payment life insurance is comparable to straight life except that the policyholder pays the premiums on the policy in a given number of years. Usually the premiums are for 20 or 30 years, or until the insured reaches age 65.

Premiums for limited payment life insurance at a certain age are higher than premiums for straight life. The reason for the difference is that all the premiums are paid within a given number of years.

After the policy is paid up, it remains in force for the rest of the insured's life, unless he wishes to withdraw the cash value. If the policy's cash value is withdrawn, the coverage stops.

Families that have very high incomes in their early years and whose income may decrease in later years may want to make use of the limited payment life insurance policy. The average family would not possess ample funds and would have difficulty purchasing enough coverage to meet its needs.

The fourth type of life insurance is the endowment policy. Saving is the primary emphasis in an endowment policy, but some protection is also included. The primary purpose is to build up a certain amount of money in a given number of years. Endowment insurance can be purchased on the basis of 10, 15, 20, 25, or 30 years, or mature to cash at a given age. When the endowment policy has reached a point at which the cash savings equal the amount of the face value, the policy matures. (See Table 3 at the end of the book.)

At this point, with the total cash available to the policyholder, the protection portion is zero and the coverage ends.

The premiums are much higher for endowment policies than for other types because of the emphasis placed upon savings.

When purchasing life insurance there are many important considerations other than the four basic types of insurance just discussed. When you and your family are establishing a life insurance program, consider these very important factors:

• Buy the policies that will give the most protection at the least cost.
• Insure the right family members.
• Consider the family's financial needs.
• Buy the insurance from companies that are financially sound and are represented by honest, well-trained agents.

To illustrate the kinds of life insurance needed in particular situations, let's consider some individuals at various stages in the life cycle.

Peter is single and has no dependents. Probably the only life insurance he needs is enough to cover his debts and burial expenses.

Insurance can be purchased at a lower rate during the young years, but by buying while young, Peter will be paying the premiums for a longer period of time. In the end, the amount paid in for premiums is about the same. But he is paying for protection that really isn't necessary.

Suppose that Peter marries Susan, who is a college graduate and is working. Perhaps only enough insurance would be needed to cover their debts and burial expenses.

Later, Susan has quit work and is pregnant with their first

child. They have purchased a home with a small down payment and a 30-year mortgage. The situation regarding life insurance takes on a different aspect. There are dependents who need financial protection. Now the question is not whether they need insurance, but how much?

As the family increases in size, it is essential to add more insurance on the father or the breadwinner to protect the dependents. The time when the children are young and depend upon the family for financial needs is precisely the time when families with modest incomes have difficulty providing enough life insurance on the father to protect the mother and the children.

Families with modest to average incomes should insure the breadwinner or breadwinners first. When considering the amount of insurance for the mother with dependent children, the need for substitute child care should be planned for until the children can care for themselves. The death of a small child would have no effect upon the income of the family. Perhaps a policy to meet funeral expenses would be sufficient for the young child.

Families should consider the other resources available. Social Security benefits are available to most people with dependent children under the age of 18 and to widows when they reach age 62. Also, families should strive toward savings to be used for emergencies and have some stocks or real estate or both that will increase in market value during inflationary times.

As the children become financially independent, the emphasis on family financial security will shift from protection to saving for the retirement years. Every family situation is different, and it is important that each family give adequate thought and study to planning its financial future.

Homeowner's Insurance

We all hear about property losses but relatively few of us, fortunately, have firsthand experience with them. Each loss is unexpected, and many people have the feeling "it won't happen to me."

The value and importance of your property can be quickly demonstrated if you list all your personal belongings, household goods, and the house itself. Then add up how much it would cost for replacements if they were lost or damaged. Generally, you accumulate property over the years and don't realize how much you have, nor how it would be missed if it were gone. Inflation probably has substantially increased replacement costs, and any significant loss would hurt financially.

Many steps can be taken to prevent or reduce loss from fire, wind, theft, and other perils, and some losses that may happen will not be large enough to be serious. For substantial losses, insurance is the best method of protection. By paying a relatively small, set payment to an insurance company, homeowners can protect themselves against the possibility of a large and unpredictable loss.

Property owners can insure themselves in several ways. They can build up their protection by buying insurance for most losses separately, or they can buy a package policy that protects against a dozen or more perils. Even with a package policy, additional insurance for special needs can be purchased by paying an extra premium.

When separate insurance coverages are bought, property owners usually start with a standard fire policy that insures the home and contents against fire and lightning. Then for an additional premium they may get extended coverage to include damage from wind, hail, smoke, explosion, riot, vehicles, and aircraft.

Another policy—for burglary and theft protection—is available. Still another, called liability insurance, will protect against losses from lawsuits for injuries suffered by visitors or damage caused to the property of others.

Buying insurance through separate policies may be the best solution for owners of specialized property or those facing certain definite dangers. Also, in some localities package policies may not be readily available or may provide more costly protection than is needed or wanted. The value of some homes and their contents may be less than the minimum amounts of protection that must be bought in package policies. Separate insurance policies are used more for protection in rural areas than in urban communities.

The federal government has cooperated with the insurance industry in making several types of protection available. Flood insurance, for one, generally has been impossible to obtain because of the potential catastrophic nature of this peril in certain areas. Now it is available at low cost through governmental cooperation in about 1,200 communities where there is danger of flooding. To be eligible for governmental participation, the community must pledge to set certain construction standards and to enforce land-use controls in flood-prone areas.

In some cities and high-crime localities, homeowners have had difficulty in getting fire, theft, and vandalism insurance. To meet such needs, private insurers as a group with government cooperation have developed FAIR (Fair Access to Insurance Requirements) Plans.

Property and liability insurance is generally regulated and supervised by states and not the federal government. The obligation of each state is to make certain that insurance companies do not overcharge or discriminate against customers and that companies remain in sound financial condition so as to be able to pay for losses.

If you feel you have been unfairly denied insurance protection or charged excessive premium rates, you should complain to the state supervisory official, usually called the commissioner of insurance, located in the capital city of your state.

Package policies that protect against losses from a variety of perils have been spreading rapidly over the past two decades. The most familiar package policies are the homeowner's, farmowner's, and renter's policies.

Such policies, as suggested earlier, are not always available, nor are they the best for everybody, but they do have advantages. You usually have only one policy and one premium to worry about, and the wide variety of protection costs less than if the same coverages were purchased in separate policies.

To buy a homeowner's policy you must own and occupy a one- or two-family residence. The policy protects the house and additions to it such as an attached garage. It also insures other structures including toolsheds and detached garages; these latter are called "appurtenant structures" in the policy.

Buildings used for commercial purposes or rented to others (except garages) are not covered.

All household goods and personal property owned or used by the family are protected. Losses to personal belongings and other property are frequently covered whether they occur at home or away. An inventory and photographs of personal property, especially of more valuable items, are helpful in filing a claim in the event of fire, theft, or other loss.

The homeowner's policy specifies some exceptions and conditions under which indemnities for losses may not be paid. For example, pets are not covered, and protection for jewelry and furs is usually limited to $500 or $1,000 unless otherwise specified. Theft of credit cards may be excluded, as well as the loss of boats and trailers when away from the insured premises.

Consult with your insurance agent to avoid any misunderstanding about your coverage. The extra protection you need may be available if you pay an additional premium.

Another coverage included in the homeowner's policy is additional living expense. This pays for the expenses incurred if damage to the house is so severe that it cannot be occupied. It would cover the cost of hotels, motels, and restaurant meals.

There are three types of homeowner insurance policies: basic, broad, and comprehensive.

The basic homeowner's policy usually protects against 11 perils to property: fire and lightning, wind and hail, explosion, riot, aircraft, vehicles, smoke, vandalism, theft, breakage of glass, and loss of property removed from premises endangered by fire or other perils.

The broad homeowner's policy covers seven additional perils: falling objects, weight of ice and snow, collapse of building, sudden and accidental damage to a steam or hot-water heating system or water heater, accidental leakage within a plumbing, heating, or air-conditioning system, freezing of these systems, and accidental injury from artificially generated currents to electrical appliances and wiring (excluding TV and radio tubes).

The comprehensive homeowner's policy covers all perils except earthquake, landslide, floods of various kinds, backing up of sewers, seepage, war, and nuclear radiation.

In buying a homeowner's policy, the property owner decides the amount of coverage he wants on his dwelling. On this basis, the amounts on appurtenant structures, personal property, and additional living expense are automatically determined as 10 percent, 50 percent, and 20 percent, respectively, of the dwelling coverage. For example, if the dwelling is insured for $40,000 the coverage would be $4,000 on appurtenant structures, $20,000 on personal property, and $8,000 for additional living expenses.

A homeowner's policy, besides paying for property losses from such perils as fire and wind, provides liability coverage for family members living in the home. Under the personal liability feature, you are protected against lawsuits from people who believe that you, your family, or your pets are responsible for their injuries or damage to their property. It covers accidents both on and away from the insured property.

For example, if your dog bites a neighbor or a visitor is hurt in a fall and you are sued, the insurance company will pay the legal costs and any damages assessed against you. The minimum personal liability protection offered in a homeowner's policy is $25,000, but larger amounts can be purchased for an additional premium.

Medical payment to others also is a feature of homeowner's insurance. Such payments are made for injuries to other people caused by you, your family, or pets. This coverage is similar to personal liability except that it is designed mainly for minor injuries, and payments may be made regardless of who is at fault. Medical payments to any one person are limited to a specified amount.

A farmowner's package policy that provides basic protection comparable to the homeowner's policy is available to owners of farms in many areas. Any protection needed on the farm service buildings, livestock, and machinery is added to coverages related to the dwelling.

Insurance for the Renter

A tenant's or renter's policy, similar in many respects to a homeowner's policy, is available for those who live in an apartment or rent a home. (In some cases, such a policy may go by the name of a homeowner's policy). It insures contents of a home and personal possessions of the family against most of the same perils and also provides personal liability protection and medical payments to others.

Costs

The cost of property and liability insurance to a homeowner or a renter depends on a variety of factors. The value of your property and the amount of protection you want are, of course, basic. Cost also varies with the number of perils protected against and differences in location and condition of property that may increase or decrease the risks of loss. Homes located far from fire departments or hydrants or those with faulty electrical wiring or heating systems would be relatively costly to insure.

Some insurance companies may charge more than others

for the same protection, but competition and state regulation tend to hold premium rate differences to a minimum.

Developing an insurance program at reasonable cost should begin with an appraisal of the perils faced. Consider the financial consequences of damages or losses. Study the various kinds of available insurance coverages and their costs. Select what matches as closely as possible your needs for protection.

Don't overinsure, as you won't be paid more than the replacement cost of any loss regardless of the insurance you carry. Talk with several reputable insurance agents to find the lowest reasonable premium rates. Repairing hazardous wiring, roofs, and chimney conditions may be worthwhile in terms of lower insurance costs.

Insurance under which the property owner himself bears any losses up to the amount of a deductible will provide savings. Many policies already include a deductible of $50, but insurance with larger deductibles is available at lower rates.

Determining the value of your house or other property is often difficult, especially in times of rapid inflation or deflation. Talking with neighbors and others about the going price of houses like yours can be of some help. Real estate tax assessments are usually a specified percentage of market values and may be a guide.

The insurance agent, too, will have useful information on sales prices and construction costs. In fact, someone from the insurance company will probably inspect the property before the policy is approved to check on values and make sure no fire hazards or other conditions make it uninsurable.

What your insurance pays after a loss is spelled out in the policy, and it may not reach the exaggerated levels that you hear or read about. Most policies state that the company will pay "the actual cash value at the time of loss." This means that only the depreciated value is paid.

For example, if a five-year-old TV set is destroyed by fire, you should not expect to recover its original cost of $500, because it is not worth that much. Nor should you expect your insurance to give you the price of a brand-new storm door to replace an old one that has been broken during a windstorm.

By paying an additional premium, however, you usually can get protection for the replacement cost rather than the depreciated value.

With a homeowner's policy, you can receive full payment (except for deductible amounts) for any damage to the dwelling, up to the amount of the coverage, provided it is insured for at least 80 percent of its value. In periods of rising property values and building costs, it is important to maintain this level of protection.

At the time you buy a homeowner's policy, you probably can get an endorsement that automatically increases the protection every three months or so.

Insurance—and your enduring insurance man—can be your best friend in time of need. Take the time to consider the various types of insurance in terms of your family's needs. Just knowing you are protected in case of trouble will help you to enjoy life more.

TABLE 2	REQUIRED BY STATE LAW		AVAILABLE AT POLICY-HOLDER'S REQUEST
	MAY NOT Be Rejected	MAY Be Rejected	
ALABAMA		X	
ALASKA		X	
ARIZONA	X		
ARKANSAS		X	
CALIFORNIA		X	
COLORADO		X	
CONNECTICUT	X		
DELAWARE		X	
DIST. OF COL.			X
FLORIDA		X	
GEORGIA		X	
HAWAII		X	
IDAHO		X	
ILLINOIS	X		
INDIANA		X	
IOWA		X	
KANSAS		X	
KENTUCKY		X	
LOUISIANA		X	
MAINE	X		
MARYLAND †			X
MASSACHUSETTS	X		
MICHIGAN		X	
MINNESOTA *	X		
MISSISSIPPI		X	
MISSOURI	X		
MONTANA		X	
NEBRASKA		X	
NEVADA		X	
NEW HAMPSHIRE	X		
NEW JERSEY	X		
NEW MEXICO		X	
NEW YORK	X		
NORTH CAROLINA		X	
NORTH DAKOTA	X		
OHIO		X	
OKLAHOMA		X	
OREGON	X		
PENNSYLVANIA	X		
RHODE ISLAND		X	
SOUTH CAROLINA	X		
SOUTH DAKOTA	X		

Table 2 cont.

	REQUIRED BY STATE LAW		AVAILABLE AT POLICY- HOLDER'S REQUEST
	MAY NOT Be Rejected	MAY Be Rejected	
TENNESSEE		X	
TEXAS		X	
UTAH		X	
VERMONT	X		
VIRGINIA	X		
WASHINGTON		X	
WEST VIRGINIA	X		
WISCONSIN	X		
WYOMING		X	

* Uninsured Motorist Coverage may be rejected on commercially rated vehicles.
† Uninsured Motorist Coverage in Maryland applies only to accidents occurring outside the state.

Table 2. Some states require Uninsured Motorists Coverage as part of all automobile liability policies. Other states allow the policyholder to reject this coverage by giving written notice to the insurance company.

Table 3. The spread between premiums for different types of life insurance is greatest for young insurance buyers.

TABLE 3

ANNUAL PREMIUM RATES PER $1,000 OF INSURANCE

AGE OF IN- SURED AT ISSUANCE OF POLICY	ORDINARY LIFE	20-PAYMENT LIFE	20-YEAR ENDOWMENT
PARTICIPATING INSURANCE (ANY DIVIDENDS PAID WILL REDUCE THESE COSTS)			
20	$18.00	$30.00	$49.00
25	21.00	33.00	50.00
30	24.00	36.00	51.00
35	28.00	40.00	52.00
40	33.00	44.00	54.00
45	39.00	50.00	57.00
50	47.00	56.00	62.00
55	58.00	65.00	69.00
60	73.00	78.00	79.00
65	94.00	95.00	96.00

PRONUNCIATION SYMBOLS USED IN THIS DICTIONARY

′ primary accent ″ secondary accent

For definition of *schwa*, see opposite page.

a	fat, band
ā	fate, tame
â	fare, pair
ä	far, father
ạ	fall, ought, orb
a	schwa sound, as in ago
b	bat, abide, bib
c	catch, because, idealistic
ch	chain
d	date, ladder, road
e	met, threat
ē	me, feat
ė	her, fir, urn
e	schwa sound, as in happen
ēr	mere, rear
f	fine, muffin, leaf
g	gold, ingrate, log
h	hang, behold
hw	whig
i	pin, hymn
ī	pine, by
i	schwa sound, as in fossil
j	job, rigid, edge
k	king, lake, clock
l	like, whole, mail
m	make, pamper, palm
n	name, pencil, pan
ng	sing
o	not, squat, yacht
ō	note, boat
ö	move, groove
o	schwa sound, as in gallop
oi	oil
ou	pound, now
p	pea, paper, lamp
r	rust, narrow, latter

Continued on opposite page

Guide word, in a left-hand column, a guide to the first entry word on the page.

sabra

Entry word

sa·bra, sä′bra, sä′brä, *n.* A native of Israel.

sac·cate, sak′it, sak′āt, *a. Biol.* furnished with or having the form of a sac or pouch.

sake, sāk, *n.* [O.E. *sacu,* contention, case or suit at law; Icel. *sök,* L.G. *sake,* G. *sache,* suit, affair, thing; akin to O.E. *sacan,* Icel. *saka,* to contend, accuse, etc.] Purpose; benefit; interest; account, used with *for;* as, *for* his *sake, for* the *sake* of the community.

Variant spelling of entry word

sa·ke, sa·ki, sä′kē, *n.* An alcoholic beverage made in Japan from fermented rice, usu. served hot.

salt·pe·ter, *Brit.* **salt·pe·tre,** sạlt″pē′ter, *n.* [For M.E. *salpetre,* < O.Fr. *salpetre,* Fr. *salpêtre* < M.L. *salpetra,* for *sal petræ,* 'salt of rock' (because found as an incrustation on rocks).] Potassium nitrate, KNO_3. Sodium nitrate, $NaNO_3$, a crystalline compound used as a fertilizer; also *Chile saltpeter.*

Syllabication, indicated by raised center dot

sa·lu·ta·to·ri·an, sa·lö″ta·tõr′ē·an, sa·lö″ta·tạr′ē·an, *n.* In some colleges and high schools in the U.S., the second highest-ranking student in the graduating class who delivers the salutatory oration at commencement.

Pronunciation

sa·lu·ta·to·ry, sa·lö′ta·tõr″ē, sa·lö′ta·tạr″ē, *a.* [L. *salutatorius.*] Pertaining to or of the nature of a salutation; as, a *salutatory* oration.—*n.* pl. **sa·lu·ta·to·ries.** An address of welcome usu. delivered at the beginning of commencement ceremonies.

salv·a·ble, sal′va·bl, *a.* That which may be salved or salvaged; savable.—**sal·va·bil·i·ty,** *n.*—**sal·va·bly,** *adv.*

Foreign pronunciation

sans-cu·lotte, sanz″kü·lot′, *Fr.* sän·ky·lạt′, *n.* pl. **sans-cu·lottes,** *Fr.* sän·ky·lạt′. [Fr., without breeches.] A revolutionary, orig. a derisive term used by aristocrats at the time of the French Revolution of 1789; later, a popular designation for a revolutionary; any radical or revolutionary.—**sans-cu·lot·tic,** sanz″kü·lot′ik, *a.*—**sans-cu·lot·tish,** *a.*—**sans-cu·lot·tism,** *n.*—**sans-cu·lot·tist,** *n.*

Part of speech

San·ta Ger·tru·dis, san′ta ger·trö′dis, *n.* A type of beef cattle in the western U.S., which is a Brahman-Shorthorn crossbreed, valued for its resistance to hot climates.

Etymology

sa·pi·ent, sā′pē·ent, *a.* [L. *sapiens, sapientis,* wise, discreet, pp. of *sapio,* to taste, to know, to be wise; *sapid, insipid, savor, sage,* are of similar origin.] Wise; sage; knowing; discerning, often used ironically. Pertaining to affected wisdom.—**sa·pi·ent·ly,** *adv.*

Inflected form, comparative and superlative

sap·py, sap′ē, *a.*—**sappier, sappiest.** Abounding with sap; juicy; succulent; energetic; young. *Slang,* stupid; sentimental.

Inflected form, irregular plurals

sar·coph·a·gus, sär·kof′a·gus, *n.* pl. **sar·coph·a·gi, sar·coph·a·gus·es,** sär·kof′a·jī″. [Gr. *sarkophagos*; it was orig. the name of a type of stone used for making coffins, and believed to have the property of consuming the dead bodies.] A stone tomb or coffin usu. ornamented and open to view, as a monument.

Inflected form, irregular of verb

sate, sāt, *v.t.*—*sated, sating.* [Perh. < O.E. *saed, satisfied,* satiated, the form having been influenced by *satisfy, satiate.*] To satisfy completely, as the appetite or desire; to glut or satiate.

sat·is·fac·tion, sat″is·fak′shan, *n.* [O.Fr. Fr. *satisfaction,* < L. *satisfactio(n-).*] The act of satisfying, or the state of being satisfied; fulfillment of desires, demands, or needs. Gratification or pleasure occasioned by some fact or circumstance; the cause of such gratification; payment, as for debt; discharge, as of obligations; reparation, as of a wrong or injury; the opportunity of repairing a supposed wrong, as by a duel; release from doubt or conviction; *eccles.* the performance by a penitent of the penal acts enjoined by ecclesiastical authority.—**sat·is·fac·tion·al,** *a.*

Separation of definitions, by period or semicolon

Pronunciation key, a capsule guide

a- fat, fāte, fär, fâre, fạll;   **e-** met, mē,